- The Reader's Catalog is divided by subject matter into 15 broad categories and 208 subcategories. You should be able to find the topic you are looking for by checking the table of contents. If you are looking for a particular author, the subject of a biography, or a major subject heading, you will find it in the index.

- Books that were announced too late for inclusion in the catalog itself will be found in the Late Arrivals section at the back. Of course, any new book, whether listed in the catalog or not, can be ordered either through your bookseller or directly from The Reader's Catalog.

- Each entry is accompanied by a book number, the name of the publisher, the format (hardcover if not otherwise indicated, paperback if marked "pb"), and the price.

- For all inquiries other than orders, please call (212) 333-7900. (No collect calls, please.)

How To Order

- Ask your local bookseller. Or, if you wish to order directly from The Reader's Catalog, you may do so in three ways:
  — By calling 1-800-882-8770 (U.S. customers only).
  — By faxing your order to 212-307-1973.
  — By mailing your order to: The Reader's Catalog, 250 West 57th Street, New York, NY 10107.
  An order form will be found after the index. The minimum order is $15.

- You may order by phone between 8:00 AM and 10:00 PM (Eastern Time) from Monday through Friday. When ordering by phone, please have the following information ready: your name, address, and credit card number (American Express, Visa, Mastercard) and the book number, title, author, price, and quantity of each book you would like to order.

- When faxing your order, please complete the order form which appears at the end of the catalog, adding the appropriate postage and handling charge, and sales tax where applicable. If you do not have an order form, include the necessary information on a separate sheet. It is important that you print legibly and include your phone number. Please sign your order form. Only credit card orders can be accepted by Fax.

- When mailing your order, please complete and sign the order form, or include the necessary information on a separate sheet. When paying by check be sure to include the appropriate postage and handling charge, and sales tax where applicable. If paying by credit card, be sure to give us your credit card number and expiration date.

Shipping

- The postage and handling charges appear on the order form. Please calculate the appropriate amount for your order.

- We prefer to ship UPS. (If you prefer that we not use UPS, please let us know.) Since UPS does not deliver to P.O. boxes, we need a street address or, if you have a rural route number, a complete address and nearest crossroad. If you prefer delivery to your work place, list that address under "Ship To." Please include your daytime phone number so we can call you if a problem arises.

- For Canadian and foreign orders please add 8%. These orders will be shipped by air.

- For only $8.00 extra, we can speed your order to you via Federal Express.

- Prices and availability are subject to change without notice. Both are the domain of the publisher, not of the bookseller or The Reader's Catalog.

Gifts

- You may send books, gift certificates, or The Reader's Catalog itself as gifts by marking the order form where indicated and filling in the recipient's name and address.

- If you would like to receive timely bulletins of forthcoming books, please send us your name, address, and the subjects in which you are interested.

The Reader's Catalog aims to provide access for book buyers to a wide range of titles, many of them hard to find. The Reader's Catalog hopes to stimulate diversity in publishing and bookbuying, enabling publishers to keep their backlist titles in print by bringing a great variety of useful and important books to the attention of the widest possible readership.

The editors of The Reader's Catalog have tried to list a very broad range of titles within each category. However, publishers' inventories are continually changing as titles go out of print and new ones are added. If you are looking for a title that does not appear in The Reader's Catalog, please inquire. The publisher may have re-issued it since the catalog went to press.

THE
READER'S
CATALOG

THE READER'S CATALOG

AN ANNOTATED SELECTION OF
MORE THAN 40,000 OF THE BEST BOOKS
IN PRINT IN 208 CATEGORIES

EDITED BY
GEOFFREY O'BRIEN

WITH
STEPHEN WASSERSTEIN
AND
HELEN MORRIS

JASON EPSTEIN, PUBLISHER

EDITOR Geoffrey O'Brien
EDITORIAL DIRECTOR Stephen Wasserstein
ASSOCIATE EDITOR Helen Morris
SENIOR EDITOR Ellen Livingston
OFFICE ADMINISTRATOR Tracy A. Smith

CONTRIBUTING EDITORS
Mark Caldwell
Peter Cosgrove
Barbara Epstein
Judy Hendra
Joel Honig
Lawrence Klepp
Simon Pleasance
Robert B. Silvers
Bob Tashman
Doron Weber

ART DIRECTOR Beth Tondreau
DESIGNER Derek Ungless
COVER DESIGNER R.D. Scudellari
PICTURE EDITOR Valerie Humes

PRODUCTION CONSULTANT Ellen L. Vanook
PROGRAMMING CONSULTANT Anthony W. Toogood
INDEXERS AEIOU Inc.
ASSOCIATE DESIGNER Laurence Vétu-Kane
ASSOCIATE DESIGNER Nöel Claro
ASSISTANT ART DIRECTOR Gabrielle Hamberg
ASSISTANT ART DIRECTOR Jane Treuhaft

EDITORIAL STAFF
Marguerite Jones
Jacquelin McCarthy
Thomas Nissley
Marpessa Dawn Outlaw
Freya A. Read
Jasjiv Sahney
Sal Terillo
Fronza Woods
Peter Zabelskis

PUBLISHER Jason Epstein
SECRETARY-TREASURER Blynn Garnett

Copyright © 1989 by The Reader's Catalog, Inc.

THE READER'S CATALOG
250 West 57th Street
New York, New York 10107

LIBRARY OF CONGRESS CATALOGING-IN-PUBLICATION DATA
The reader's catalog: an annotated selection of more than 40,000
of the best books in print in 208 categories/edited by Geoffrey
O'Brien with Stephen Wasserstein and Helen Morris.—1st ed.
ISBN 0-924322-00-4
1. Bibliography—Best books. I. O'Brien, Geoffrey, 1948– II.
Wasserstein, Stephen. III. Morris, Helen, 1947–   .
Z1035.R26 1989   89-10578
011′.73—dc20   CIP

Printed in the United States of America

CONTENTS

PART 4

POPULAR READING

PART 5

BOOKS FOR YOUNG READERS

PART 6

ART

PART 7

ARCHITECTURE AND DESIGN

PART 8

PERFORMING ARTS AND MEDIA

PART 9

WORLD HISTORY AND CURRENT AFFAIRS

PART 10

HISTORY OF THE AMERICAS

PART 11

RELIGION AND PHILOSOPHY

PART 12

SOCIAL STUDIES

PART 13

SCIENCE

PART 14

PRACTICAL ADVICE

PART 15

LEISURE

LITERATURE OF EUROPE, AFRICA, AND ASIA

Literature of the Ancient Near East

Utnapishtim said, "There is no permanence. Do we build a house to stand for ever, do we seal a contract to hold for all time? Do brothers divide an inheritance to keep for ever, does the flood-time of rivers endure? It is only the nymph of the dragon-fly who sheds her larva and sees the sun in his glory. From the days of old there is no permanence. The sleeping and the dead, how alike they are, they are like a painted death. What is there between the master and the servant when both have fulfilled their doom? When the Annunaki, the judges, come together, and Mammetun the mother of destinies, together they decree the fates of men. Life and death they allot but the day of death they do not disclose."

N.K. Sandars, translator
THE EPIC OF GILGAMESH
0–14–044100–X Penguin pb $2.95

• Michael D. Coogan, editor
STORIES FROM ANCIENT CANAAN
Four principal works of Ugaritic literature, and Ugaritic influence on Hebrew poetry
0–664–24184–0 Westminster pb $7.95

• John Gardner & John Maier, translators
GILGAMESH
0–394–74089–0 Random House pb $10.95

• Alexander Heidel
THE BABYLONIAN GENESIS
A translation of creation stories from cuneiform tablets
0–226–32399–4 Chicago pb $6.00

THE GILGAMESH EPIC AND OLD TESTAMENT PARALLELS
Literary and religious themes held in common by these two ancient texts
0–226–32398–6 Chicago pb $8.95

• Thorkild Jacobsen
THE HARPS THAT ONCE . . . : Sumerian Poetry in Translation
A generous selection of the poetry preserved in the Sumerian tablets, including a number of works never before translated
0–300–03906–9 Yale $35.00

• Maureen Gallery Kovacs, translator
THE EPIC OF GILGAMESH
0–8047–1711–7 Stanford pb $4.95

• Samuel Noah Kramer
FROM THE POETRY OF SUMER: Creation, Glorification, Adoration
0–520–03703–0 California $29.95

HISTORY BEGINS AT SUMER: Thirty-Nine "Firsts" in Man's Recorded History
Classic introduction to Sumerian literary and religious texts
0–8122–7812–7 Pennsylvania $39.95
0–8122–1276–2 Pennsylvania pb $17.95

IN THE WORLD OF SUMER: An Autobiography
Kramer's autobiography is also the story of the recovery of Sumerian literature
0–8143–2121–6 Wayne State pb $14.95

• Samuel Noah Kramer, editor
MYTHOLOGIES OF THE ANCIENT WORLD
Essays by ten scholars on the mythologies of Egypt, China, Sumer, and other cultures such as Hittite and Canaanite
0–385–09567–8 Doubleday pb $6.95

• Wilfred Lambert
BABYLONIAN WISDOM LITERATURE
0–19–815424–0 Oxford $62.00

• James B. Pritchard, editor
THE ANCIENT NEAR EAST: An Anthology of Texts and Pictures
The most important documents in the literature and history of Egypt, Mesopotamia, and the Levant from the third to the first millennium BC

Volume 1
0–691–03501–6 Princeton $28.50
0–691–00200–2 Princeton pb $8.95

Volume 2
0–691–03549–0 Princeton $30.00
0–691–00209–6 Princeton pb $8.95

• Erica Reiner
YOUR THWARTS IN PIECES, YOUR MOORING ROPE CUT: Poetry from Babylonia and Assyria
Translations and analytical essays which, though sometimes technical, are fascinating for the light they throw on the function of poetry in ancient Near Eastern societies
0–936534–04–4 Michigan pb $10.00

• N.K. Sandars, translator
POEMS OF HEAVEN AND HELL FROM ANCIENT MESOPOTAMIA
0–14–044249–9 Penguin pb $6.95

THE EPIC OF GILGAMESH
The story of Gilgamesh, ruler of Uruk (Biblical Erech) in the mid-3rd millennium BC. "*The Epic of Gilgamesh* dates from the beginnings of civilization in Mesopotamia . . . It is a spiritual adventure, a story of self-realization, the discovery of the meaning of the personality, of a type that would never change down the four-thousand-year-long history of human imagination. Its figures have the cogency of symbols that will never alter. It is modern because it is like a dream of a modern man"—Kenneth Rexroth, *Classics Revisited*
0–14–044100–X Penguin pb $2.95

• Diane Wolkstein & Samuel Noah Kramer
INANNA: Queen of Heaven and Earth
Kramer's translations reworked by a folklorist
0–06–014713–X Harper & Row $16.95

In most periods, with the exception of the Old Babylonian, it is the formal libraries from palace and temple that preserved the mass of literary texts . . . The literary libraries largely consisted of standard texts copied and recopied from one generation to the next. Occasional new texts were added from time to time, but they were few by comparison with the great mass of traditional material. Much of this was not what we today would regard as literature, even if Assyriologists continue to call it such. The largest group of texts consists of omens, collections of observations made over hundreds of years concerned with the stars, the appearance of the liver of a sacrificial sheep, the movements of birds, etc. Other categories of texts were the lexical lists, incantations, prayers, and the well-known epic literature. The late Leo Oppenheim, in a summary of traditional Mesopotamian literature, calculated that the whole of the standard corpus as represented in a library like Ashurbanipal's could have run to as many as fifteen hundred different tablets of between eighty and two hundred lines each; for many texts Ashurbanipal had several copies.

C.B.F. Walker
CUNEIFORM
0–520–06115–2 California pb $7.95

Ancient Egyptian Literature

Ancient Egyptian occupies a special position among the languages of the world. It is not only one of the very oldest recorded languages (probably only Sumerian is older) but it also has a documented history longer by far than that of any other. It was first written down toward the end of the fourth millennium BC and thereafter remained in continuous recorded use down to about the eleventh century AD, a period of over 4,000 years . . . Although it can only be a minute fraction of what was actually produced, the body of written material to have survived in Egyptian is, nevertheless, enormous. It consists, in large part, of religious and funerary texts, but it also includes secular documents of many different types—administrative, business, legal, literary and scientific—as well as private and official biographical and historical inscriptions. This record is our most important single source of evidence on ancient Egyptian society.

W.V. Davies
EGYPTIAN HIEROGLYPHS
0–520–06287–6 California pb $7.95

- Carol Andrews & Raymond Faulkner
THE ANCIENT EGYPTIAN BOOK OF THE DEAD
The most recent edition, with an illuminating introduction
0–02–901470–0 Macmillan $40.00

- E.A. Wallis Budge
THE EGYPTIAN BOOK OF THE DEAD: The Papyrus of Ani in the British Museum
The collection of religious documents for the guidance of the soul in the world after death
0–486–21866–X Dover pb $8.95

- Miriam Lichtheim
ANCIENT EGYPTIAN LITERATURE: A Book of Readings
The most comprehensive collection of Egyptian literature

Volume 1: The Old and the Middle Kingdoms
0–520–02899–6 California pb $10.95

Volume 2: The New Kingdom
0–520–03615–8 California pb $10.95

Volume 3: The Late Period
0–520–04020–1 California pb $10.95

- James M. Robinson
THE NAG HAMMADI LIBRARY
The only comprehensive general survey of the Gnostic texts from this Coptic monastery
0–06–066929–2 Harper & Row $23.50
0–06–066933–0 Harper & Row pb $11.50

- William Kelley Simpson
THE LITERATURE OF ANCIENT EGYPT: An Anthology of Stories, Instructions, and Poetry
0–300–01711–1 Yale pb $11.95

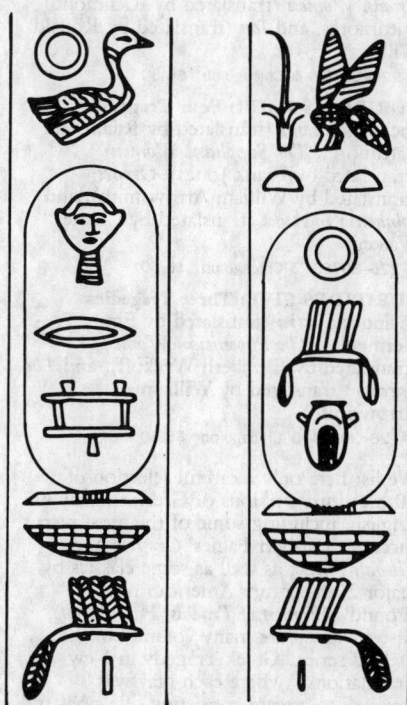

From Egyptian Hieroglyphs *by W.V. Davis (California)*

The All-Lord said, after he had come into being:

"I am he who came into being as Khepri. When I had come into being, being (itself) came into being, and all beings came into being after I came into being. Many were the beings which came forth from my mouth, before heaven came into being, before earth came into being, before the ground and creeping things had been created in this place. I put together (some) of them in Nun as weary ones, before I could find a place in which I might stand. It (seemed) advantageous to me in my heart; I planned with my face; and I made (in concept) every form when I was alone, before I had spat out what was Shu, before I had sputtered out what was Tefnut, and before (any) other had come into being who could act with me."

From the ancient Egyptian text "The Repulsing of the Dragon and the Creation" in

Barbara C. Sproul, editor
PRIMAL MYTHS: Creating the World
0–06–67500–4 Harper & Row pb $11.95

Ancient Greek Literature

THE ARCHAIC PERIOD

Greek literature from the period before the Persian invasion of 480 BC differs in fundamental ways from what follows. The bards at the beginning of the tradition (Homer, Hesiod, Orpheus, and Musaeus) were personae rather than poets, legendary identities that stood for the creators of poetic traditions, rather than individuals with biographies. Their lives were continually re-invented. Even such an undoubtedly historic figure as the Athenian poet-politician Solon is steeped in legend. But whatever their origins, these earliest voices laid the foundation for a tradition that had taken to heart the principle later enunciated by Aristotle that "that which is oldest is likewise most honored."

Homer

- Homer
THE ILIAD OF HOMER
An "Iliad of woes" that does remarkable justice to the somber majesty of the original. Lattimore, an accomplished scholar and a fine poet in his own right, attempts to match the length of the Homeric line and, to some extent, the formulaic nature of the language, rendering the Greek with astonishing immediacy
Translated by Richmond Lattimore
0–226–46940–9 Chicago pb $8.95

THE ILIAD
Translated by Robert Fitzgerald
0–385–05941–8 Doubleday pb $8.95

THE ODYSSEY
Faithfulness to the repetitive use of formulaic phrases helps recapture the cadence of oral poetry
Translated by Richmond Lattimore
0–06–090479–8 Harper & Row pb $5.95

THE ODYSSEY
The work of a poet thoroughly in sympathy with the poet of the original; Fitzgerald's pentameter trips along at a speed perfectly adapted to the twists and turns of the hero's wanderings
Translated by Robert Fitzgerald
0–385–05040–2 Doubleday pb $7.95

THE ODYSSEY
A prose translation that presents the *Odyssey* as a novel
Translated by E.V. Rieu
0–14–044001–1 Penguin pb $2.95

THE ODYSSEY
An elegant translation into an English prose that no one would confuse with American
Translated by Walter Shewring
0–19–281542–3 Oxford pb $2.95

THE HOMERIC HYMNS
Traditionally attributed to Homer, this collection of prologues to epic performances is basic for understanding archaic Greek theology. A vigorous verse translation with helpful notes
Translated by Apostolos N. Athanassakis
0–8018–1791–9 Johns Hopkins $15.00
0–8018–1792–7 Johns Hopkins pb $6.95

Hesiod

As Homer founded the heroic epic tradition, Hesiod, the shepherd of Ascra, wrote the earliest Greek wisdom poetry (*Works and Days*) and theological poetry (*Theogony*). Much "Hesiodic" poetry is lost, but we do have the mannered and lovely *Shield of Herakles*.

- Hesiod
THE WORKS AND DAYS
An excellent verse translation of *Works and Days, Theogony, The Shield of Herakles,* with a useful introduction. This is arguably the greatest accomplishment of Lattimore's career as a translator
Translated by Richmond Lattimore
0–472–43903–0 Michigan $10.95

THEOGONY & WORKS AND DAYS
A verse translation with very generous notes. Remarkable for its use of parallels from modern Greek folklore
Translated by Apostolos N. Athanassakis
0–8018–2998–4 Johns Hopkins $20.00
0–8018–2999–2 Johns Hopkins pb $8.95

THEOGONY & WORKS AND DAYS
This newest translation, with concise and valuable notes, by the greatest living expert on Hesiod, is a peculiar, often fascinating mix of styles and diction. West keeps the promise of his prefatory note: "If I have sometimes made Hesiod sound a little

quaint and stilted, that is not unintentional: he is"
Translated with notes by M.L. West
0–19–251038–X Oxford $36.00
0–19–281788–4 Oxford pb $4.95

HESIOD & THEOGNIS
A solid, credible blank verse translation. The unlovely Theognis is good to have for comparison and contrast
Translated by Dorothea Wender
0–14–044283–9 Penguin pb $4.95

Lyric Poetry

Greek lyric poetry begins in the archaic period and extends into the classical; certain types, notably the epigram, continued to be created into the Byzantine period. Here more than anywhere, the reader is at the mercy of the translator. Fortunately, many scholar-poets and poet-scholars have successfully re-thought and re-created the originals as living poetry.

• Willis Barnstone, translator
SAPPHO AND THE GREEK LYRIC POETS
The most inclusive anthology
Preface by William McCulloh
0–8052–0831–3 Schocken pb $12.95

• Richmond Lattimore, translator
GREEK LYRICS
Contains over 100 poems and fragments in first-class verse translations. Includes the more substantial fragments of Archilochus, Callinus, Semonides, Hipponax, Tyrtaeus, Mimnermus, Solon, Xenophanes, Alcman, Ibycus, Sappho, Alcaeus, Anacreon and Simonides, some fragments of Pindar, and five poems of Bacchylides
0–226–46944–1 Chicago pb $4.95

• Guy Davenport, translator
ARCHILOCHOS, SAPPHO, ALKMAN: Three Lyric Poets of the Seventh Century B.C.
The best contemporary version, by an American poet
Introduction by Guy Davenport
0–520–03823–1 California $30.00
0–520–05223–4 California pb $10.95

> Percussion, salt and honey,
> A quivering in the thighs;
> He shakes me all over again,
> Eros who cannot be thrown,
> Who stalks on all fours
> Like a beast.
>
> Sappho
>
> Guy Davenport, translator
> **ARCHILOCHOS, SAPPHO, ALKMAN**
> 0–520–05223–4 California pb $10.95

• Pindar
THE ODES OF PINDAR
The language of Pindar's victory odes is so dense that a fully satisfactory translation is almost unthinkable. Lattimore's is the best

and most credible—and often touches on the sublime of the original
Translated by Richmond Lattimore
0–226–66845–2 Chicago pb $8.00

THE ODES OF PINDAR
Translated by C.M. Bowra
0–14–044209–X Penguin pb $6.95

Sappho
SAPPHO
Translated by Richard O'Connell
0–685–62621–0 Atlantis pb $6.00

SAPPHO: A New Translation
Translated by Mary Barnard
0–520–01117–1 California pb $5.95

SAPPHO: Poems and Fragments
Translated by Josephine Balmer
0–8216–2000–2 Lyle Stuart pb $6.95

The Greek Anthology

This Byzantine compilation brings together thousands of short poems from the 7th century BC to the High Middle Ages. A complete prose translation takes up five volumes of the Loeb Classical Library, but a substantial number of the jewels can be found in the following selections.

• Peter Jay, editor
THE GREEK ANTHOLOGY
A selection in modern verse translation
0–14–044285–5 Penguin pb $6.95

• Kenneth Rexroth, translator
POEMS FROM THE GREEK ANTHOLOGY
0–472–06063–5 Michigan pb $4.95

THE CLASSICAL PERIOD

The century and a half from the Persian Wars to the death of Alexander the Great in 323 BC stands out as the "classical" period. The process of canonization began quickly. Even before Alexander, the Athenian plays of the 5th century were enjoying revivals. All the surviving tragedies as well as the earliest historical writing belong to that period.

Tragedy

• David Grene & Richmond Lattimore, editors
THE CHICAGO COMPLETE GREEK TRAGEDIES
For countless modern readers the voices of Aeschylus, Sophocles, and Euripides have been heard through the brilliant translations of David Grene, Richmond Lattimore, William Arrowsmith, and other contributors to the University of Chicago *Complete Greek Tragedies*. The series is no longer available as a single unit, but all of its components can be found in the following volumes.

AESCHYLUS ONE: The Oresteia
Includes *The Oresteia*, consisting of *Agamemnon, The Libation Bearers,* and *The Eumenides*
Translated with an introduction by Richmond Lattimore
0–226–30778–6 Chicago pb $6.50

AESCHYLUS TWO: Four Tragedies
Includes *Prometheus Bound* and *Seven Against Thebes* (translated by David Grene), *The Persians,* and *The Suppliant Maidens* (translated by Seth Benardete)
0–226–30779–4 Chicago pb $6.50

SOPHOCLES ONE: Three Tragedies
Includes *Oedipus the King* (translated by David Grene), *Oedipus at Colonus* (translated by Robert Fitzgerald), and *Antigone* (translated by Elizabeth Wycoff)
0–226–30785–9 Chicago pb $6.50

SOPHOCLES TWO: Four Tragedies
Includes *Ajax* (translated by John Moore), *Women of Trachis* (translated by Michael Jameson), *Electra,* and *Philoctetes* (translated by David Grene)
0–226–30786–7 Chicago pb $6.50

EURIPIDES ONE: Four Tragedies
Includes *Alcestis* (translated by Richmond Lattimore), *Medea* (translated by Rex Warner), *Heracleidae* (translated by Ralph Gladstone), and *Hippolytus* (translated by David Grene)
0–226–30780–8 Chicago pb $6.50

EURIPIDES TWO: Four Tragedies
Includes *Cyclops* and *Heracles* (translated by William Arrowsmith), *Iphigenia in Tauris* (translated by Witter Bynner), and *Helen* (translated by Richmond Lattimore)
0–226–30781–6 Chicago pb $6.50

EURIPIDES THREE: Four Tragedies
Includes *Hecuba* and *Andromache* (translated by William Arrowsmith), *The Trojan Women* (translated by Richmond Lattimore), and *Ion* (translated by Ronald Willetts)
0–226–30782–4 Chicago pb $6.50

EURIPIDES FOUR: Four Tragedies
Includes *Rhesus* (translated by Richmond Lattimore), *The Suppliant Women* (translated by Frank Jones), *Orestes* (translated by William Arrowsmith), and *Iphigenia in Aulis* (translated by Charles Walker)
0–226–30783–2 Chicago pb $6.50

EURIPIDES FIVE: Three Tragedies
Includes *Electra* (translated by Emily T. Vermeule), *The Phoenician Women* (translated by Elizabeth Wyckoff), and *The Bacchae* (translated by William Arrowsmith)
0–226–30784–0 Chicago pb $6.50

We list here only a careful selection of 20th-century versions of Greek tragedy in English, including some of the most recent successes (Robert Fagles' *Oresteia* and *Theban Plays*), as well as some classics by major 20th-century American poets (Pound's *Women of Trachis,* H.D.'s *Ion*). Also included are many volumes of the Oxford series "Greek Tragedy in New Translations," where each play was assigned to a team consisting of a poet and a classical scholar. All are remarkable translations, and a few (including *Seven Against Thebes* by Anthony Hecht and Helen Bacon) are works of genius.

The cart of Thespis, from The Theatre: A Concise History *by Phyllis Hartnoll (Thames & Hudson)*

- Aeschylus

THE ORESTEIA
Includes *Agamemnon, The Libation Bearers,* and *The Eumenides.* A verse translation in a more modern idiom than Lattimore's. Highly recommended
Translated by Robert Fagles
0–670–52832–3 Viking $20.00
0–14–044333–9 Penguin pb $3.95

THE ORESTEIA OF AESCHYLUS
Translated by Robert Lowell
0–374–22723–3 Farrar, Straus & Giroux $8.95
0–374–51549–2 Farrar, Straus & Giroux pb $6.95

THE PERSIANS
Translated by Janet Lembke & C. John Herington
0–19–502777–9 Oxford $24.95

SEVEN AGAINST THEBES
Tense, intelligent verse restores to this problematic, static, and intensely verbal play a richness that no other translator has approached
Translated by Anthony Hecht & Helen Bacon
0–19–501732–3 Oxford $19.95

THE SUPPLIANTS
Translated by Janet Lembke
0–19–501933–4 Oxford $19.95

- Sophocles

THE THREE THEBAN PLAYS
Includes *Antigone, Oedipus the King,* and *Oedipus at Colonus.* This highly readable translation has many advantages over the Grene/Fitzgerald/Wyckoff translations in the Chicago series: the plays are arranged in the order in which they were written, and Bernard Knox has contributed introductions and notes about the plays' relationship to the audience that first viewed them in the Theater of Dionysus
Translated by Robert Fagles
0–670–69805–9 Viking $25.00
0–14–044425–4 Penguin pb $2.95

ANTIGONE
Translated by Richard Braun
0–19–501741–2 Oxford $19.95

ELECTRA & OTHER PLAYS
Also includes *Ajax, Women of Trachis,* and *Philoctetes*
Translated by E.F. Watling
0–14–044003–8 Penguin pb $3.50

OEDIPUS THE KING
Translated by Stephen Berg & Diskin Clay
0–19–502325–0 Oxford $19.95

PHILOKTETES
Translated by Gregory McNamee
1–55659–002–4 Copper Canyon pb $8.00

WOMEN OF TRACHIS
Translated by C.K. Williams & Gregory Dickerson
0–19–502050–2 Oxford $19.95

WOMEN OF TRACHIS
Translated by Ezra Pound
0–8112–0948–2 New Directions pb $6.95

- Dana F. Sutton

THE LOST SOPHOCLES
A translation, with discussion, of the fragments of Sophocles' lost plays
0–8191–4031–7 University Press pb $12.00

- Euripides

ALCESTIS & OTHER PLAYS
Also includes *Hippolytus* and *Iphigenia in Tauris*
Translated by Philip Vellacott
0–14–044031–3 Penguin pb $2.95

ALCESTIS
Translated by William Arrowsmith
0–19–501861–3 Oxford $19.95

THE BACCHAE & OTHER PLAYS
Also includes *Ion, The Women of Troy,* and *Helen*
Translated by Philip Vellacott
0–14–044044–5 Penguin pb $3.50

THE CHILDREN OF HERAKLES
Translated by Henry Taylor & Robert Brooks
0–19–502914–3 Oxford $19.95

HELEN
Translated by James Michie & Colin Leach
0–19–502870–8 Oxford $24.95

HIPPOLYTUS
Translated by Robert Bagg
0–19–501740–4 Oxford $19.95

ION
Translated by H.D.
0–933806–24–8 Black Swan $20.00

IPHIGENEIA AT AULIS
Translated by W.S. Merwin & George Dimock, Jr.
0–19–502272–6 Oxford $19.95

IPHIGENEIA IN TAURIS
Translated by Richmond Lattimore
0–19–501736–6 Oxford $19.95

MEDEA & OTHER PLAYS
Includes *Hecuba, Electra,* and *Heracles*
Translated by Philip Vellacott
0–14–044129–8 Penguin pb $2.95

ORESTES & OTHER PLAYS
Also includes *The Children of Heracles, Andromache, The Suppliant Women, The Phoenician Women,* and *Iphigenia in Aulis*
Translated by Philip Vellacott
0–14–044259–6 Penguin pb $6.95

THE PHOENICIAN WOMEN
Translated by Peter Burian & Brian Swann
0–19–502923–2 Oxford $19.95

RHESOS
Translated by Richard Braun
0–19–502049–9 Oxford $19.95

Comedy

Athenian Old and Middle Comedy are known only through the eleven surviving plays of Aristophanes, which date between 425 and 388 BC. Because of its pervasive obscenity, this drama has not been given adequate translation until quite recently.

- Aristophanes

THE COMPLETE PLAYS OF ARISTOPHANES
Includes *The Acharnians, The Birds, The Clouds, Ecclesiazusae, The Frogs, The Knights, Lysistrata, Peace, Plutus, Thesmophoriazusae,* and *The Wasps.* This handy volume has the virtue of completeness but cannot seriously be compared with the Arrowsmith series
Translated by Moses Hadas & others
0–553–21164–1 Bantam pb $3.50

FOUR COMEDIES
Includes *Lysistrata, The Congresswomen,* and *The Frogs.* This and the following volume contain all the translations from the William Arrowsmith edition currently in print. They are far and away the best English translations ever made
Translated by Richmond Lattimore & Douglas Parker
Edited by William Arrowsmith
0–472–06152–6 Michigan pb $9.95

THREE COMEDIES
Includes *The Birds* and *The Clouds* (translated by William Arrowsmith), and *The Wasps* (translated by Douglass Parker)
Edited by William Arrowsmith
0–472–06153–4 Michigan pb $9.95

THE CLOUDS, WOMEN IN POWER & THE KNIGHTS
Translated by K. McLeish
0–521–22900–6 Cambridge $29.95
0–521–29707–9 Cambridge pb $9.95

THE FROGS & OTHER PLAYS
Also includes *The Wasps* and *The Poet and the Women*
Translated by David Barrett
0–14–044152–2 Penguin pb $3.95

THE KNIGHTS, PEACE, THE BIRDS, THE ASSEMBLYWOMEN & WEALTH
Translated by David Barrett & Alan Sommerstein
0–14–044332–0 Penguin pb $3.95

LYSISTRATA & OTHER PLAYS
Also includes *The Acharnians* and *The Clouds*
Translated by Alan Sommerstein
0–14–044287–1 Penguin pb $3.95

History

The classical historians whose work survives substantially intact are Herodotus (who researched the background of the Persian invasions of Greece in 490 and 480 BC),

Thucydides (who explored the war between Athens and Sparta that dominated the latter part of the 5th century), and Xenophon (whose supplement to Thucydides' narratives extends down into the 4th century).

- Herodotus
THE HISTORIES
An attempt to find an English equivalent for Herodotus' deceptively simple style
Translated by David Grene
0–226–32772–8 Chicago pb $7.95

THE HISTORIES
An uncompromising modern prose version
Translated by Aubrey De Selincourt
0–14–044034–8 Penguin pb $5.95

- Thucydides
THE PELOPONNESIAN WAR
Translated by Richard Crawley & revised by T.E. Wick
0–07–554372–9 McGraw-Hill pb $6.95

THE PELOPONNESIAN WAR
Translated by Rex Warner
0–14–044039–9 Penguin pb $5.95

- Xenophon
A HISTORY OF MY TIMES
Translated by Rex Warner
0–14–044175–1 Penguin pb $6.95

THE PERSIAN EXPEDITION
Translated by Rex Warner
0–14–044007–0 Penguin pb $6.95

> But whence each of these gods came into existence, or whether they were for ever, and what kind of shape they had were not known until the day before yesterday, if I may use the expression; for I believe that Homer and Hesiod were four hundred years before my time—and no more than that. It is they who created for the Greeks their theogony; it is they who gave to the gods the special names for their descent from their ancestors and divided among them their honors, their arts, and their shapes.
>
> Herodotus
> **THE HISTORIES**
> Translated by David Grene
> 0–226–32772–8 Chicago pb $7.95

Oratory

Oratory was central to Athenian society. Sophists charged high fees to teach the art of public speaking and successful orators used language to exert influence, whether in the assembly, the law court, or the theater.

- W. Robert Connor, editor
GREEK ORATIONS: Fourth Century BC
0–88133–282–8 Waveland pb $5.95

- A.N. Saunders, translator
GREEK POLITICAL ORATORY
0–14–044223–5 Penguin pb $6.95

Philosophy

Greek thought forged the fundamental concepts that form the root of European philosophical inquiry. The beginnings of Greek philosophy, up to the time of Socrates (who died in 399 BC), reach us only in remarkably accessible fragments.

▶ **See also Western Philosophy**

- G.S. Kirk, J.E. Raven & M. Schofield, editors
THE PRESOCRATIC PHILOSOPHERS
A new, expanded edition of the standard collection
0–521–25444–2 Cambridge $70.00
0–521–27455–9 Cambridge pb $20.95

- Plato
THE COLLECTED DIALOGUES OF PLATO
A one-volume edition with excellent translations by various translators, and an exemplary index
Edited by Edith Hamilton & Huntington Cairns
0–691–09718–6 Princeton $27.50

PLATO'S REPUBLIC
The best overall translation, with just enough notes to make it accessible
Translated by G.M.A. Grube
0–915144–04–2 Hackett $22.50
0–915144–03–4 Hackett pb $4.95

- Aristotle
BASIC WORKS OF ARISTOTLE
Edited by Richard P. McKeon
0–394–41610–4 Random House $27.95

THE COMPLETE WORKS OF ARISTOTLE
The revised Oxford translation in a 2-volume set
Edited by Jonathan Barnes
0–691–09950–2 Princeton $79.00

THE HELLENISTIC AND ROMAN PERIODS

During the 3rd and 2nd centuries BC there was a great burst of literary activity in Alexandria, Alexander's new city on the edge of the Egyptian desert. With the coming of Roman military and economic dominance in the East, Greek wisdom, oratory, and literature spread throughout the Mediterranean world. Divorced from the world that had given it birth, Greek literature became the international standard of clear thought and articulate speech.

Drama

We have only scant examples of Attic New Comedy from the period around 300 BC, all of them by Menander. This drama was imitated by the Roman writers Plautus and Terence and became the foundation of comedy in the West. With Menander, Greek drama turns away from the divine and achieves dignity in human scale.

- Menander
Newly discovered papyri have increased our knowledge of the comic dramatist Menander; we now have two of his plays complete, or nearly so, the *Bad-Tempered Man* and the *Samian Woman*, as well as a substantial fragment of *The Shield*.
PLAYS AND FRAGMENTS
The revised Penguin Menander makes available to a general audience the recently recovered Menander plays and fragments
Translated by Norma Miller
0–14–044501–3 Penguin pb $6.95

THE DYSKOLOS
The only essentially intact play (though others can be credibly restored to near-completeness)
Translated by Caroll Moulton
0–452–00865–4 NAL pb $4.95

THE GIRL FROM SAMOS
The pioneering reconstruction of this beautiful play
Translated by Eric Turner
0–485–12019–4 Humanities pb $17.50

Alexandrian Poetry

In the 3rd century BC, Alexandria saw the birth of a new genre, pastoral poetry, whose belated influence on western European literature from the Middle Ages to the 18th century was to be decisive. Alexandria also saw the extension of earlier genres, such as the epic and the hymn.

- Apollonius Rhodius
THE VOYAGE OF ARGO
This richly ironic epic is the principal bridge from Homer to Virgil
Translated by E.V. Rieu
0–14–044085–2 Penguin pb $5.95

- Callimachus
HYMNS, EPIGRAMS, SELECT FRAGMENTS
Translated by Stanley Lombardo & Diane Rayor
Foreword by D.S. Carne-Ross
0–8018–3280–2 Johns Hopkins $18.50
0–8018–3281–0 Johns Hopkins pb $7.95

- Theocritus
IDYLLS
Translated by Robert Wells
0–85635–711–1 Carcanet $21.50

THE IDYLLS OF THEOCRITUS: A Verse Translation
Translated by Thelma Sargent
0–393–00073–7 Norton pb $4.95

THEOCRITUS: Idylls and Epigrams
Translated by Daryl Hine
0–689–11320–X Atheneum $17.95
0–689–11321–8 Atheneum pb $10.95

GREEK KNOWLEDGE

- Apollodorus
GODS AND HEROES OF THE GREEKS: The "Library" of Apollodorus
When the Greeks started collecting the old stories for their own sake, the results were compilations like this one—pedantic, pedestrian, and systematic. Apollodorus is

the least unreadable of the Greek
mythographers
Translated by Michael Simpson
Illustrated by Leonard Baskin
0–87023–206–1 Massachusetts pb $10.95

● Hippocrates & others
HIPPOCRATIC WRITINGS
A fascinating introduction to Greek
medicine in theory and practice
Translated by J. Chadwick & W.N. Nann
Edited with an introduction by G.E.R. Lloyd
0–14–044451–3 Penguin pb $6.95

● Pausanias
GUIDE TO GREECE
A selection from the 2nd-century BC
description by Pausanias, reorganized
around a geographical pattern more useful
to the tourist than that of the original
Translated by Peter Levi

Volume 1: Central Greece
0–14–044225–1 Penguin pb $7.95

Volume 2: Southern Greece
0–14–044226–X Penguin pb $7.95

● Plutarch
PLUTARCH'S LIVES
The only one-volume translation currently
available—and still quite readable
Translated by John Dryden
0–394–60407–5 Modern Library $15.95

PROSE FICTION, FABLES, AND ROMANCES

● Moses Hadas, translator
THREE GREEK ROMANCES
The best introduction to Greek erotic and
romantic fiction. Includes *Daphnis and
Chloe* by Longus, *An Ephesian Tale* by
Xenophon, and *The Hunters of Euboea*, by
Dio Chrysostom
0–672–60442–6 Bobbs-Merrill pb $6.65

● Aesop
FABLES OF AESOP
Translated by S.A. Handford
0–14–044043–7 Penguin pb $4.95

*The ox and the frog in a 1485 edition of
"The Fables of Aesop," from* An Introduction
to a History of Woodcut *by Arthur M.
Hind (Dover)*

● Longus
DAPHNIS AND CHLOE
0–14–044059–3 Penguin pb $5.95

● Lucian
SELECTED SATIRES OF LUCIAN
Translated and edited by Lionel Casson
0–393–00443–0 Norton pb $10.95

GREEK LITERARY CRITICISM

● T.S. Dorsch, translator
CLASSICAL LITERARY CRITICISM
Includes Aristotle's *Poetics*, Horace's *Ars
Poetica*, and Longinus' *On the Sublime*
0–14–044155–7 Penguin pb $5.95

ANTHOLOGIES

● W.H. Auden, editor
THE PORTABLE GREEK READER
With an illuminating introduction
0–14–015039–0 Penguin pb $6.95

● Michael Grant, editor
GREEK LITERATURE: An Anthology
A collection of excerpts from the whole
range of Greek writing, interesting
primarily for its sampling of translations,
including many now out of print
0–14–044323–1 Penguin pb $6.95

● Constantine A. Trypanis
**THE PENGUIN BOOK OF GREEK
VERSE**
From Homer to Odysseus Elytis, this
collection covers 3000 years of Greek
poetry and presents the original texts with
literal translations
0–14–058595–8 Penguin pb $9.95

CRITICAL STUDIES

The enduring critical engagement with
the classical world is not only stimulated
by the continuous discovery of archaeological material but also reflects new approaches
that derive from modern theory, from modern concern with the histories of minorities,
and from new scholarship in linguistics,
anthropology, and other disciplines.

For example, Homeric studies have been
revolutionized by Milman Parry's attempt to
demonstrate that "Homer" was an illiterate
poet (or poets); Eric Havelock's thesis that
the Greeks did not become truly literate
until well into the 4th century BC has raised
controversial issues about the origin and
nature of extant texts; and, whereas Victorian scholars emphasized the resemblances
between Western democratic man and his
Greek forbears, historians now stress the
difference, the strangeness of many aspects
of the ancient world.

● Charles Rowan Beye
**ANCIENT GREEK LITERATURE AND
SOCIETY**
Vigorous and irreverent—an account that
takes the Greeks off their pedestals and
finds values in them for our time
0–8014–1874–7 Cornell $39.50
0–8014–9444–3 Cornell pb $9.95

● R.R. Bolgar
**THE CLASSICAL HERITAGE AND ITS
BENEFICIARIES**
The essential introduction to the paths by
which Greek and Latin literature reached
the West in the Middle Ages and
Renaissance
0–521–09812–2 Cambridge pb $22.95

● P.E. Easterling & Bernard Knox,
editors
**THE CAMBRIDGE HISTORY OF
CLASSICAL LITERATURE: Greek
Literature**
An ingeniously organized group effort,
offering a coherent and highly credible
survey. Tremendously valuable for
bibliography
0–521–21042–9 Cambridge $95.00

● Moses Hadas
ANCILLA TO CLASSICAL READING
A concise introductory survey by a great
classicist of the last generation
0–231–08517–6 Columbia pb $16.00

HELLENISTIC CULTURE
A sensitive, integrated picture
0–393–00593–3 Norton pb $5.95

● Eric Havelock
PREFACE TO PLATO
Perhaps the most influential discussion of
the oral nature of early Greek literature
0–674–69906–8 Harvard pb $9.95

**THE LITERATE REVOLUTION IN
GREECE AND ITS CULTURAL
CONSEQUENCES**
0–691–00026–3 Princeton pb $13.95

Greek Tragedy

● H.C. Baldry
THE GREEK TRAGIC THEATRE
Includes a lengthy analysis of Greek
dramatic festivals and the mechanics of
theater and performance
0–393–00585–2 Norton pb $6.95

● Simon Goldhill
READING GREEK TRAGEDY
Challenging, fresh readings
0–521–30583–7 Cambridge $42.50
0–521–31579–4 Cambridge pb $13.95

● H.D.F. Kitto
GREEK TRAGEDY: A Literary Study
0–416–68900–0 RC&H pb $14.95

● Bernard Knox
**WORD AND ACTION: Essays on the
Ancient Theater**
Essays and reviews full of rich analyses and
insights
0–8018–3409–0 Johns Hopkins pb $12.95

Nicole Loraux
TRAGIC WAYS OF KILLING A WOMAN
A single class of tragic episodes unexpectedly reveals much about the values of Athenian life
0–674–90225–4 Harvard $17.95

• Charles Segal
INTERPRETING GREEK TRAGEDY: Myth, Poetry, Text
Important essays by an insightful contemporary interpreter
0–8014–9362–5 Cornell pb $12.95

• Oliver Taplin
GREEK TRAGEDY IN ACTION
Concentrates on the *Oresteia* and six other plays, reconstructing staging conventions and acting styles
0–520–03949–1 California pb $9.95

• Jean-Pierre Vernant & Pierre Vidal-Naquet
MYTH AND TRAGEDY IN ANCIENT GREECE
A major contribution from the anthropological wing of contemporary French scholarship
Translated by Janet Lloyd
0–942299–18–3 Zone (2-volume set) $28.95

Comedy

• R.L. Hunter
THE NEW COMEDY OF GREECE AND ROME
New comedy and its Latin adaptations, treated as an integral body
0–521–31652–9 Cambridge pb $14.95

• F.H. Sandbach
THE COMIC THEATRE OF GREECE AND ROME
A broad but concise introduction
0–393–04483–1 Norton $9.95

Lyric Poetry

• Anne Burnett
THREE ARCHAIC POETS: Archilochus, Alcaeus, Sappho
0–674–88820–0 Harvard $27.00

Individual Authors
(alphabetical by subject)

• D.J. Conacher
AESCHYLUS' ORESTEIA: A Literary Commentary
On the model of Conacher's earlier *Prometheus* commentary
0–8020–5716–0 Toronto $35.00

AESCHYLUS' PROMETHEUS BOUND: A Literary Commentary
"Should be extremely profitable to any student of the *Prometheus*, at any level"—C.J. Herington, *Phoenix*
0–8020–6416–7 Toronto pb $8.95

• John Herington
AESCHYLUS
The best available introduction
0–300–03643–4 Yale pb $9.95

• Thomas Rosenmeyer
THE ART OF AESCHYLUS
A rich introductory study
0–520–04608–0 California pb $12.95

• K.J. Dover
ARISTOPHANIC COMEDY
Play-by-play analysis by a major scholar
0–520–02211–4 California pb $11.95

• Rosemary Harriott
ARISTOPHANES: Poet and Dramatist
0–8018–3279–9 Johns Hopkins $22.50

• Ann Michelini
EURIPIDES AND THE TRAGIC TRADITION
0–299–10760–4 Wisconsin $32.98

• Cedric Whitman
EURIPIDES AND THE FULL CIRCLE OF MYTH
"Responsive to the true strategies of Euripides"—*Greece and Rome*
0–674–26920–9 Harvard $12.00

• J.A.S. Evans
HERODOTUS
"A balanced and thoughtful account of Herodotus as a working historian"—*American Journal of Philology*
0–8057–6488–7 G.K. Hall $16.95

Aubrey De Selincourt
THE WORLD OF HERODOTUS
"De Selincourt, like Herodotus, loves the Greeks, but not blindly; he is committed to them, but without falsifying; he can treasure a tradition, and yet question it"—Paul MacKendrick, *Classical World*
0–86547–070–7 North Point pb $12.00

• Robert Lamberton
HESIOD
"Combines the sophistication of cultural anthropology with a refined sense for the mechanics and aesthetics of archaic Greek literature and gives Hesiod a fresh and original reading"—Gregory Nagy, Harvard University
0–300–04068–7 Yale $27.50
0–300–04069–5 Yale pb $9.95

• Mark Edwards
HOMER: Poet of the Iliad
0–8018–3329–9 Johns Hopkins $29.50

• John Finley, Jr.
HOMER'S ODYSSEY
Perhaps the first reading of the *Odyssey* to do justice to the role of Penelope
0–674–40614–1 Harvard $22.00

M.I. Finley
THE WORLD OF ODYSSEUS
The revision of Finley's 1956 book locating the world of the *Odyssey* in the early Dark Age of Greece. A pioneering application of sociological and anthropological insights
0–14–020570–5 Penguin pb $6.95

• Jasper Griffin
HOMER
A concise introduction
0–19–287532–9 Oxford pb $4.95

HOMER ON LIFE AND DEATH
"Restores to Homer the humanity he had steadily lost in recent years to the computer and the microphilologists of formulaic analysis"—*American Journal of Philology*
0–19–814026–6 Oxford pb $16.95

• G.S. Kirk
HOMER AND THE EPIC
A concise, focused account of the relationship of the *Iliad* and the *Odyssey* to oral tradition
0–521–09356–2 Cambridge pb $14.95

• Robert Lamberton
HOMER THE THEOLOGIAN: Neoplatonist Allegorical Reading and the Growth of the Epic Tradition
0–520–06607–3 California pb $12.95

• Albert B. Lord
THE SINGER OF TALES
A classic account of the relationship between Homeric epic poetry and living traditions of oral epic
0–674–80881–9 Harvard pb $10.95

• Martin Mueller
THE ILIAD
A vivid, accessible introduction
0–04–800087–6 Unwin Hyman pb $9.95

• Gregory Nagy
THE BEST OF THE ACHAEANS
Hero cult and epic hero in an Indo-European context. "Learned, clever, and disturbing"—*TLS*
0–8018–2388–9 Johns Hopkins pb $12.00

• Milman Parry
THE MAKING OF HOMERIC VERSE: The Collected Papers of Milman Parry
Parry's demonstration of the structural similarities between Homeric epic and living oral epic was a watershed in Homeric scholarship
Edited by Adam Parry
0–19–520560–X Oxford pb $17.95

• Seth Schein
THE MORTAL HERO: An Introduction to Homer's Iliad
The best recent introduction
0–520–05626–4 California pb $10.95

Scylla from John Flaxman's illustrations for "The Odyssey"

Latin Literature

Latin literature is a strange anomaly: an imitation which has itself been abundantly imitated. From its earliest appearance in the 3rd century BC, the literature of ancient Rome drew on the subject matter, plots, and even specific lines of Greek drama, comedy, and epic. But the Roman authors transformed these models into their own ways of seeing, and western literary traditions owe more to this hybrid than to the Greek sources. The poised satire of Horace rather than the vigorous iambs of Archilochus; the melodrama of Seneca rather than the restraint of the Greek tragedians; Virgil's teleological epic rather than Homer's naturalism: these have been primary influences on the great European poets and dramatists, Shakespeare and Milton among them.

THE EARLY PERIOD

Most of the literature of the older republic has been lost, depriving us of the important dramas and epics of Ennius and others. But the works of two comic playwrights from the late 3rd and early 2nd century BC are treasures of world literature. Plautus, who rose from miller's apprentice to popular dramatist, and Terence, a freed North African slave, added a robust Roman quality to their adaptations of Greek plays while retaining the cleverness of the original models.

- Simone Weil

THE ILIAD, OR THE POEM OF FORCE
Intelligence, insight, and compassion combine to make this brief essay the most moving reading of the *Iliad* in our time
0–87574–091–X Pendle Hill pb $2.50

- Malcolm Willcock

A COMPANION TO THE ILIAD
A commentary based on the Lattimore translation
0–226–89855–5 Chicago pb $8.95

- C.M. Bowra

PINDAR
After a generation, still a useful introduction, especially for those with some knowledge of Greek
0–19–814338–9 Oxford $32.50

- D.S. Carne-Ross

PINDAR
Readings of twelve odes that bring home much of this evasive poet's richness
0–300–03383–4 Yale $27.50
0–300–03393–1 Yale pb $9.95

- Julia Annas

AN INTRODUCTION TO PLATO'S REPUBLIC
A remarkable achievement. The reader is walked through the arguments and the problems raised by this difficult text
0–19–827429–7 Oxford pb $10.95

- D.A. Russell

PLUTARCH
The standard introduction in English
0–7156–1611–0 Longwood pb $12.00

- Judy Grahn

THE HIGHEST APPLE: Sappho and the Lesbian Poetic Tradition
More about recent poets than about Sappho, but more about poetry than is to be found in most studies of Sappho
0–933216–12–2 Spinsters/Aunt Lute pb $6.95

Bernard M. Knox

THE HEROIC TEMPER: Studies in Sophoclean Tragedy
An essential introduction to the craggy, intractable Sophoclean hero
0–520–04957–8 California pb $10.95

- David Halperin

BEFORE PASTORAL: Theocritus and the Ancient Tradition of Bucolic Poetry
Pastoral theory and the originality of Theocritus
0–300–02582–3 Yale $32.00

- Thomas Rosenmeyer

THE GREEN CABINET: Theocritus and the European Pastoral Lyric
"Many brilliant insights"—P.V. Marinelli, *Phoenix*
0–520–02362–5 California pb $10.95

- W. Robert Connor

THUCYDIDES
An insightful evocation of the somber, threatening world-view of the historian whose panoramic presentation of the Peloponnesian War is an indictment not only of the failures of democracy but also of human nature
0–691–10239–2 Princeton pb $14.50

- J.K. Anderson

XENOPHON
Especially valuable for its presentation of the historian's life
0–7156–1610–2 Longwood pb $12.00

- Plautus

THE POT OF GOLD & OTHER PLAYS
Includes *The Brothers Menaechmus, The Prisoner, The Swaggering Soldier,* and *Pseudolus.* Rough farce and exuberant word-play give new life to standardized Greek plots. *The Brothers Menaechmus* is the basis for Shakespeare's *Comedy of Errors,* and the title play influenced Moliere's *L'Avare*
Translated by E.F. Watling
0–14–044149–2 Penguin pb $4.95

THE ROPE & OTHER PLAYS
Includes *The Ghost, The Three-Dollar Day,* and *Amphitryon.* In *The Rope,* low comedy rises to genuine romance, while Jupiter Almighty becomes the humorous butt of *Amphitryon*
Translated by E.F. Watling
0–14–044136–0 Penguin pb $4.95

- Terence

THE COMEDIES
Includes the complete plays: *The Girl from Andros, The Mother-in-Law, The Self-Punisher, The Eunuch, Phormio,* and *The Brother.* More refined and original than the works of his older contemporary Plautus, Terence's plays are among the earliest comedies of manners
Translated by Betty Radice
0–14–044324–X Penguin pb $6.95

THE GOLDEN AGE

Usually taken to refer to the years from the Social War in 70 BC to the end of the reign of Augustus in AD 14, this period encompasses a heterogeneous group of Rome's most brilliant writers. Preeminent among poets in the late republic were the passionate lyricist Catullus and the moody optimist, Lucretius, while the principate triumphant produced the stabilizing synthesis of Virgil's epic and the civilized verse forms of Horace and Ovid.

• Catullus
THE POEMS OF CATULLUS
A sharp-edged and colloquial translation by an English poet of modernist bent
Translated by Peter Whigham
0–14–044180–8 Penguin pb $5.95

ODI ET AMO: The Complete Poetry of Catullus
Translated by Roy Swanson
0–024–18490–X Macmillan pb $7.25

• Cicero
Orator and statesman, lawyer and philosopher, Marcus Tullius Cicero was the consummate Roman, whose intellectual abilities were always at the service of public affairs. He transmitted Greek thought to Rome, and in the Renaissance his oratorical style was a model for the great Italian scholars and writers.

THE NATURE OF THE GODS
An elegant discussion of the popular Greek philosophies of Epicureanism, Stoicism, and the New Academic skepticism
Translated by Horace McGregor
Introduction by J.M. Ross
0–14–044265–0 Penguin pb $6.95

ON THE GOOD LIFE
0–14–044244–8 Penguin pb $5.95

Aubrey Beardsley's 1898 illustration of Catullus' "Ave Atque Vale"

SELECTED LETTERS
Cicero's correspondence gives an intimate portrait of the man and his times
Translated by D.R. Shackleton-Bailey
0–14–044458–0 Penguin pb $5.95

SELECTED POLITICAL SPEECHES
Decisions in the contentious Roman Senate were often based on persuasive speech-making, of which Cicero was a master
Translated by Michael Grant
0–14–044214–6 Penguin pb $5.95

SELECTED WORKS
Includes *Against Verres, Twenty-Three Letters, Second Philippic Against Antony, On Duties,* and *On Old Age.* A wide-ranging selection of speeches, letters, and essays, from Cicero's prosecution of corrupt colonial administrators and his scathing denunciation of Mark Antony, to his placid and witty encomium on old age
Translated by Michael Grant
0–14–044099–2 Penguin pb $5.95

MURDER TRIALS
Speeches demonstrating Cicero's unrivalled abilities as a trial lawyer
Translated by Michael Grant
0–14–044288–X Penguin pb $6.95

• Horace
COMPLETE ODES AND EPODES
The son of a freedman whose poetic talents gained him fame and fortune at the court of Augustus, Horace appears in this collection in all his extraordinary variety
Translated by W.G. Shepherd
Introduction by Betty Radice
0–14–044422–X Penguin pb $5.95

THE ESSENTIAL HORACE: Odes, Epodes, Satires and Epistles
This selection displays Horace's agile wit, matchless grace, and economy of language
Translated by Burton Raffel
0–86547–111–8 North Point $22.50
0–86547–112–6 North Point pb $13.50

• Horace & Persius
THE SATIRES OF HORACE AND PERSIUS
A generation apart, these two social commentators display the contrasting qualities of smooth bonhomie and crabbed erudition
Translated by Niall Rudd
0–14–044279–0 Penguin pb $6.95

• Lucan
THE CIVIL WARS
A new translation of the *Pharsalia,* the chief Roman epic after *The Aeneid*
Translated by P.F. Widdows
0–253–31399–6 Indiana $47.50

• Lucretius
THE WAY THINGS ARE: The De Rerum Natura of Titus Lucretius Carus
An excellent verse translation of the philosophical poem which exults in the freedom from tyrannical gods conferred by Epicurean materialism
Translated by Rolfe Humphries
0–253–20125–X Indiana pb $6.95

ON THE NATURE OF THE UNIVERSE
A straightforward prose version of *De Rerum Natura*
Translated by Ronald Lathan
0–14–044018–6 Penguin pb $4.95

From all this it follows that *death is nothing* and no concern of ours, since our tenure of the mind is mortal. In days of old, we felt no disquiet when the hosts of Carthage poured in to battle on every side—when the whole earth, dizzied by the convulsive shock of war, reeled sickeningly under the high ethereal vault, and between realm and realm the empire of mankind by land and sea trembled in the balance. So, when we shall be no more—when the union of body and spirit that engenders us has been disrupted—to us, who shall then be nothing, nothing by any hazard will happen any more at all. Nothing will have power to stir our senses, not though earth be fused with sea and sea with sky.

Lucretius
ON THE NATURE OF THE UNIVERSE
Translated by Ronald Lathan
0–14–044018–6 Penguin pb $4.95

• Ovid
THE EROTIC POEMS
Ovid's manuals on the art of love have influenced poets and lovers ever since
Translated by Peter Green
0–14–044360–6 Penguin pb $5.95

THE ART OF LOVE
Translated by Rolfe Humphries
0–253–10391–6 Indiana $22.50
0–253–20002–4 Indiana pb $7.95

Pyramus and Thisbe in a 1484 edition of Ovid's "Metamorphoses"

THE METAMORPHOSES
This retelling of the Greek myths, held together by the theme of physical transformation, has provided Western writers with innumerable plots and images
Translated by Rolfe Humphries
0–253–33755–0 Indiana $20.00
0–253–20001–6 Indiana pb $6.95

THE METAMORPHOSES
A superbly fluent verse rendering
Translated by Horace Gregory
0–451–62622–2 NAL pb $4.95

THE METAMORPHOSES
Watts uses heroic couplets to render Ovid's masterpiece. "The best [translation] the reviewer has encountered: faithful to the text in spirit and in letter, it is poetry in its

➤ **FOR OVERSEAS ORDERING INFORMATION, SEE PAGE 1**

own right"—*Classical Philology*. Illustrated with etchings by Picasso
Translated by A.E. Watts
0–86547–019–7 North Point pb $12.50

• **Propertius**
THE POEMS
Lyrics at once sophisticated and sincere, by a friend of Ovid
Translated by W.G. Shepherd
0–14–044464–5 Penguin pb $5.95

THE POEMS OF SEXTUS PROPERTIUS
Translated by J.P. McCulloch
0–520–02774–4 California pb $2.95

• **Tibullus**
POEMS OF TIBULLUS
The gentleness and sensitivity of these poems to Delia contrast with the often harsh attitude toward women of the early empire
Translated by Philip Dunlop
0–14–044266–9 Penguin pb $5.95

• **Virgil**
THE WORKS OF VIRGIL IN ENGLISH (1697)
Dryden's 17th-century versions have not been surpassed for clarity and power
Translated by John Dryden
Edited by William Frost & Vinton Dearing

Volume 5: Eclogues, Georgics, Aeneid I–IV
0–520–02121–5 California $55.00

Volume 6: Aeneid VII–XII
0–520–02122–3 California $55.00

THE AENEID
Virgil's great epic transforms the Homeric tradition into a triumphal statement of the Roman civilizing mission. Fitzgerald's version is up to the high standard established by his Homer translations
Translated by Robert Fitzgerald
0–394–52827–1 Random House $19.95
0–394–72596–4 Random House pb $9.95

THE AENEID OF VIRGIL: A Verse Translation
Translated by Allen Mandelbaum
0–520–04550–5 California pb $12.95
0–553–21041–6 Bantam pb $2.95

THE ECLOGUES
Virgil's earliest work brings an apocalyptic element to the pastoral tradition of Theocritus
Translated with an introduction by Guy Lee
0–14–044419–X Penguin pb $4.95

THE GEORGICS
Gibbon claimed that this poem in praise of rural life was designed to help Augustus' discharged veterans adjust to conditions on the farm
Translated by L.P. Wilkinson
0–521–29323–5 Cambridge pb $17.95
0–14–044414–9 Penguin pb $5.95

THE GEORGICS
Translated by Robert Wells
0–85635–338–8 Carcanet $11.50

THE SILVER AGE

• Lucius Apuleius
THE GOLDEN ASS
Apuleius' supremely entertaining novel combines the theme of spiritual pilgrimage with a rich assortment of erotic and melodramatic elements; the narrator, transformed into an ass, is granted a vision of truth at the mysteries of Isis
Translated by Robert Graves
0–374–50532–2 Farrar, Straus & Giroux pb $7.95

• Juvenal
THE SIXTEEN SATIRES
The most savage of Roman satirists lashes out at the corruption of Antonine Rome
Translated by Peter Green
0–14–044194–8 Penguin pb $5.95

THE SATIRES OF JUVENAL
Translated by Rolfe Humphries
0–253–20020–2 Indiana pb $5.95

• Martial
THE EPIGRAMS
Witty miniatures from the Rome of Domitian, ranging from pathos to burlesque
Translated by James Michie
0–14–044350–9 Penguin pb $6.95

Petronius
THE SATYRICON
A picaresque account of the vices high and low of Nero's Rome, by the arbiter of elegance who turned his enforced suicide into a triumph of Epicurean indifference. Arrowsmith's translation is outstanding
Translated by William Arrowsmith
0–452–00964–2 NAL pb $4.50

THE SATYRICON
Also includes Seneca's *Apocolocyntosis*, in which he mocks the deification of emperors
Translated by J.P. Sullivan
0–14–044489–0 Penguin pb $4.95

• Pliny the Younger
THE LETTERS OF THE YOUNGER PLINY
An autobiography through personal letters shows the best side of the civilized Roman aristocrat
Translated by Betty Radice
0–14–044127–1 Penguin pb $6.95

• Seneca
FOUR TRAGEDIES & OCTAVIA
These unrestrained melodramas were a prime influence on the Elizabethan tragedians
Translated by E.F. Watling
0–14–044174–3 Penguin pb $5.95

LETTERS FROM A STOIC
The courtly skill of Nero's tutor only makes his adherence to the self-denying precepts of Stoicism more interesting
Edited by Robin Campbell
0–14–044210–3 Penguin pb $6.95

STOIC PHILOSOPHY OF SENECA: Essays and Letters
Edited by Moses Hadas
0–393–00459–7 Norton pb $6.95

LATE WRITERS

• St. Augustine
THE CONFESSIONS
Translated by R.S. Pine Coffin
0–14–044114–X Penguin pb $4.95

• Boethius
THE CONSOLATION OF PHILOSOPHY
The Roman adviser to the Gothic king Theodoric wrote this amalgamation of Roman and Christian wisdom while awaiting execution
Translated by V.E. Watts
0–14–044208–1 Penguin pb $4.95

• Harold Isbell, translator
THE LAST POETS OF IMPERIAL ROME
The final act of classical civilization produced, among others, the poet Claudian, whose Latin verse Gibbon held to be as pure as Virgil's
0–14–044246–4 Penguin pb $5.95

ANTHOLOGIES

• Basil Davenport, editor
THE PORTABLE ROMAN READER
0–14–015056–0 Penguin pb $7.95

• Michael Grant, editor
LATIN LITERATURE: An Anthology
An anthology of relatively brief excerpts which offers a rich sampling of all eras of English translation
0–14–044389–4 Penguin pb $6.95

• Frederic Wheelock
LATIN LITERATURE: A Book of Readings
0–06–460080–7 Harper & Row pb $6.95

CRITICAL STUDIES

• E.J. Kenney & W.V. Clausen, editors
THE CAMBRIDGE HISTORY OF CLASSICAL LITERATURE: LATIN LITERATURE

Part 1: The Early Republic
0–521–27375–7 Cambridge pb $16.95

Part 2: The Late Republic
0–521–27374–9 Cambridge pb $14.95

Part 3: The Age of Augustus
0–521–27373–0 Cambridge pb $16.95

Part 4: The Early Principate
0–521–27372–2 Cambridge pb $16.95

Part 5: The Later Principate
0–521–27371–4 Cambridge pb $16.95

• Jasper Griffin
VIRGIL
A compact introduction, from the Past Masters series
0–19–287654–6 Oxford pb $5.95

• Moses Hadas
ANCILLA TO CLASSICAL READING
The classicist unbuttoned shares the literary gossip of antiquity
0–231–08517–6 Columbia pb $16.00

A HISTORY OF LATIN LITERATURE
Hadas' conversational style draws the reader deep into the recesses of the Roman literary world
0–231–01848–7 Columbia $44.00

• Gilbert Highet
THE CLASSICAL TRADITION: Greek and Roman Influences in Western Tradition
0–19–500206–7 Oxford pb $14.95

GORE VIDAL:
Some Favorite Latin Writers

As a child, my serious reading began with *Tales from Livy*, a Victorian version of Titus Livius' history of Rome. *The Satyricon* is one of the great novels of our culture, while *The Golden Ass* is one of the most witty and strange. In all the writers I've listed we are able to see what our world was like before Christianity darkened human relations and made sex either sin or dogged duty. For Roman writers and readers, love, in our sense, was not a subject. Lust and obsession existed, and were often treated as comedy. Women play an important part in Roman literature as they did in real life until religion found woman to be unclean and man fallen, thus replacing the idea of joy in the flesh and in the day with guilt and the vision of a hectic hereafter. No matter how brutal their city world was (Juvenal) nor serene the pastoral (Horace), man here is, simply, man, unshadowed by deity, undamaged by the mad notion of original sin.

Petronius
THE SATYRICON
Translated by William Arrowsmith
0–452–00653–8 NAL pb $2.95

Apuleius
THE GOLDEN ASS
Translated by Robert Graves
0–374–50532–2 FS&G pb $7.95

Suetonius
THE TWELVE CAESARS
Translated by Robert Graves
0–14–044072–0 Penguin pb $4.95

Tacitus
ANNALS OF IMPERIAL ROME
Translated by Michael Grant
0–14–044060–7 Penguin pb $5.95

Horace
THE ESSENTIAL HORACE: Odes, Epodes, Satires & Epistles
Translated by Burton Raffel
0–86547–112–6 North Point pb $13.50

Martial
THE EPIGRAMS
Translated by James Michie
0–14–044350–9 Penguin pb $6.95

Juvenal
THE SIXTEEN SATIRES
Translated by Peter Green
0–14–044194–8 Penguin pb $5.95

• Sara Mack
OVID
A study aimed at the general reader, focusing on the originality of Ovid's narrative techniques
0–300–04295–7 Yale pb $9.95

• R.M. Ogilvie
ROMAN LITERATURE AND SOCIETY
Two histories rolled into one, without academic stuffiness
0–14–022081–X Penguin pb $6.95

• Paul Veyne
ROMAN EROTIC ELEGY: Love, Poetry, and the West
Veyne applies contemporary critical theory to the work of Propertius, Tibullus, Catullus, and Ovid
Translated by David Pellaner
0–226–85432–9 Chicago pb $13.95

• Gordon Williams
THE NATURE OF ROMAN POETRY
Williams emphasizes how the Romans turned the Greek inheritance to their own uses
0–19–872115–3 Oxford pb $15.95

The Loeb Classics

The Loeb Classics is the only existing series of books which gives access to all that is important in Greek and Latin literature in convenient pocket-sized volumes, with an up-to-date text and an English translation on the facing page. Each volume is annotated and is prefaced by a brief biography, and most contain a bibliography. Greek authors are bound in green; Latin, in red.

GREEK LITERATURE

• Achilles Tatius
CLITOPHON & LEUCIPPE
0–674–99050–1 Harvard $14.50

• Aelian
ON THE CHARACTERISTICS OF ANIMALS

Volume 1: Books 1–5
0–674–99491–4 Harvard $14.50

Volume 2: Books 6–11
0–674–99493–0 Harvard $14.50

Volume 3: Books 12–17
0–674–99494–9 Harvard $14.50

• Aenias Tacticus & others
AENIAS TACTICUS, ASLEPIODOTUS, AND ONASANDER
0–674–99172–9 Harvard $14.50

• Aeschines
SPEECHES
0–674–99118–4 Harvard $14.50

• Aeschylus
AESCHYLUS

Volume 1
Includes *Suppliant Maidens, Persians, Prometheus,* and *Seven Against Thebes*
0–674–99160–5 Harvard $14.50

Volume 2
Includes *Agamemnon, Libation Bearers,* and *Eumenides*
0–674–99161–3 Harvard $14.50

• Alciphron, Aelian & Philostratus
LETTERS
0–674–99421–3 Harvard $14.50

• Antiphon & others
MINOR ATTIC ORATORS

Volume 1: Antiphon & Andocides
0–674–99340–3 Harvard $14.50

Volume 2: Lycurgus, Dinarchus, Demades & Hyperides
0–674–99434–5 Harvard $14.50

• Apollodorus
LIBRARY

Volume 1: Books 1–3 (9)
0–674–99135–4 Harvard $14.50

Volume 2: Book 3 (10–16) & Epitome
0–674–99136–2 Harvard $14.50

• Apollonius Rhodius
APOLLONIUS RHODIUS
0–674–99001–3 Harvard $14.50

• Appian
ROMAN HISTORY

Volume 1: Books 1–8, Part 1
0–674–99002–1 Harvard $14.50

Volume 2: Book 8, Parts 2–12
0–674–99004–8 Harvard $14.50

Volume 3: Civil Wars, Books 1–3 (26)
0–674–99005–6 Harvard $14.50

Volume 4: Civil Wars, Book 3 (27–5)
0–674–99006–4 Harvard $14.50

• Aristides
ARISTIDES

Volume 1
Includes *Panathenaic Oration,* and *In Defense of Oratory*
0–674–99505–8 Harvard $14.50

• Aristophanes
ARISTOPHANES

Volume 1
Includes *Archarnians, Knights, Clouds,* and *Wasps*
0–674–99197–4 Harvard $14.50

Volume 2
Includes *Peace, Birds,* and *Frogs*
0–674–99198–2 Harvard $14.50

Volume 3
Includes *Lysistrata, Thesmophoriazusae, Ecclesiazusae,* and *Plutus*
0–674–99199–0 Harvard $14.50

- Aristotle
ARISTOTLE

Volume 1
Includes *Categories, On Interpretation*, and *Prior Analytics*
0–674–99359–4 Harvard $14.50

Volume 2
Includes *Posterior Analytics* and *Topica*
0–674–99430–2 Harvard $14.50

Volume 3
Includes *On Sophistical Refutations, On Coming To-Be and Passing Away*, and *On the Cosmos*
0–674–99441–8 Harvard $14.50

Volume 4: Physics, Books 1–4
0–674–99251–2 Harvard $14.50

Volume 5: Physics, Books 5–8
0–674–99281–4 Harvard $14.50

Volume 6: On the Heavens
0–674–99372–1 Harvard $14.50

Volume 7: Meteorologica
0–674–99436–1 Harvard $14.50

Volume 8
Includes *On the Soul, Parva Naturalia*, and *On Breath*
0–674–99318–7 Harvard $14.50

Volume 9: Historia Animalium, Books 1–3
0–674–99481–7 Harvard $14.50

Volume 10: Historia Animalium, Books 4–6
0–674–99482–5 Harvard $14.50

Volume 11: Historia Animalium, Books 7–9
0–674–99483–3 Harvard $14.50

Volume 12
Includes *Parts of Animals, Movement of Animals*, and *Progression of Animals*
0–674–99357–8 Harvard $14.50

Volume 13: Generation of Animals
0–674–99403–5 Harvard $14.50

Volume 14: Minor Works
Includes *On Colours, On Things Heard, Physiognomics, On Plants, On Marvellous Things Heard, Mechanical Problems, On Indivisible Lines, The Situation and Names of Winds, On Melissus, Xenophanes*, and *Gorgias*
0–674–99338–1 Harvard $14.50

Volume 15: Problems, Books 1–21
0–674–99349–7 Harvard $14.50

Volume 16: Problems, Books 22–38 & Rhetorica ad Alexandrum
0–674–99350–0 Harvard $14.50

Volume 17: Metaphysics, Books 1–9
0–674–99299–7 Harvard $14.50

Volume 18: Metaphysics, Books 10–14, Oeconomica & Magna Moralia
0–674–99317–9 Harvard $14.50

Volume 19: Nicomachean Ethics
0–674–99081–1 Harvard $14.50

Volume 20
Includes *Athenian Constitution, Eudemian Ethics*, and *Virtues and Vices*
0–674–99315–2 Harvard $14.50

Volume 21: Politics
0–674–99291–1 Harvard $14.50

Volume 22: Art of Rhetoric
0–674–99212–1 Harvard $14.50

Volume 23
Includes *Poetics*; Longinus' *On the Sublime*; and Demetrius' *On Style*
0–674–99219–9 Harvard $14.50

- Arrian
ARRIAN

Volume 1: Anabasis of Alexander, Books 1–4
0–674–99260–1 Harvard $14.50

Volume 2: Anabasis of Alexander, Books 5–7 & Indica
0–674–99297–0 Harvard $14.50

- Athenaeus
DEIPNOSOPHISTS

Volume 1: Books 1–3 (106e)
0–674–99224–5 Harvard $14.50

Volume 2: Book 3 (106e)–5
0–674–99229–6 Harvard $14.50

Volume 3: Books 6–7
0–674–99247–4 Harvard $14.50

Volume 4: Books 8–10
0–674–99259–8 Harvard $14.50

Volume 5: Books 11–12
0–674–99302–0 Harvard $14.50

Volume 6: Books 13–14 (653b)
0–674–99361–6 Harvard $14.50

Volume 7: Book 14 (653b)–15
0–674–99380–2 Harvard $14.50

- Babrius & Phaedrus
BABRIUS & PHAEDRUS
0–674–99480–9 Harvard $14.50

- St. Basil
LETTERS

Volume 1: Letters 1–58
0–674–99209–1 Harvard $14.50

Volume 2: Letters 59–185
0–674–99237–7 Harvard $14.50

Volume 3: Letters 186–248
0–674–99268–7 Harvard $14.50

Volume 4: Letters 249–368 & Address to Young Men on Greek Literature
0–674–99298–9 Harvard $14.50

- Callimachus
CALLIMACHUS
Includes *Aetia, Iambi, Hecale, Other Fragments*; and Musaeus' *Hero and Leander*
0–674–99463–9 Harvard $14.50

HYMNS AND EPIGRAMS
Also includes the works of Lycophron and Aratus
0–674–99143–5 Harvard $14.50

- Callinus & others
GREEK ELEGY AND IAMBUS

Volume 1: Elegiac Poets from Callinus to Critias
0–674–99284–9 Harvard $14.50

Volume 2
Includes *Elegiac Poetry of the Fourth Century, Iambic Poets, Anonymous Inscriptions and Fragments*, and *Anacreontea*
0–674–99285–7 Harvard $14.50

- Clement & others
APOSTOLIC FATHERS

Volume 1
Includes *I Clement, II Clement*, Ignatius, Polycarp, *Didache*, and *Barnabas*
0–674–99027–7 Harvard $14.50

Volume 2
Includes *Shepherd of Hermas, Martyrdom of Polycarp* and *Epistle to Diognetus*
0–674–99028–5 Harvard $14.50

- Clement of Alexandria
CLEMENT OF ALEXANDRIA
Includes *Exhortations to the Greeks, Rich Man's Salutation, To the Newly Baptized*
0–674–99103–6 Harvard $14.50

- Demosthenes
DEMOSTHENES

Volume 1
Includes *Olynthiacs 1–3, Philippic 1, On the Peace, Philippic 2, On the Halonnesus, On the Chersonese, Philippics 3 and 4, Philip's Letter, Answer to Philip's Letter, On Organization, On the Navy-Boards, For the Liberty of the Rhodians, For the People of Megalopolis, On the Treaty with Alexander, Against Leptines (1–17 and 20)*
0–674–99263–6 Harvard $14.50

Volume 2: De Corona & De Falsa Legatione (18–19)
0–674–99171–0 Harvard $14.50

Volume 3
Includes *Against Meidias, Against Androtion, Against Aristocrates, Against Timocrates, Against Aristogeiton (1–2, 21–26)*
0–674–99330–6 Harvard $14.50

Volume 4: Private Orations (27–40)
0–674–99351–9 Harvard $14.50

Volume 5: Private Orations (41–49)
0–674–99381–0 Harvard $14.50

Volume 6: Private Orations (50–58) & In Neaeram (59)
0–674–99386–1 Harvard $14.50

Volume 7
Includes *Funeral Speech (60), Erotic Essay (61), Exordia, Letters*, and General Index
0–674–99412–4 Harvard $14.50

- Dio Cassius
ROMAN HISTORY

Volume 1: Fragments of Books 1–11
0–674–99036–6 Harvard $14.50

Volume 2: Fragments of Books 12–35 & Fragments of Uncertain Reference
0–674–99041–2 Harvard $14.50

Volume 3: Books 36–40
0–674–99059–5 Harvard $14.50

Volume 4: Books 41–45
0–674–99073–0 Harvard $14.50

Volume 5: Books 46–50
0–674–99091–9 Harvard $14.50

Volume 6: Books 51–55
0–674–99092–7 Harvard $14.50

Volume 7: Books 56–60
0–674–99193–1 Harvard $14.50

Volume 8: Books 61–70
0–674–99195–8 Harvard $14.50

Volume 9: Books 71–80 & General Index
0–674–99196–6 Harvard $14.50

• Dio Chrysostom
DIO CHRYSOSTOM

Volume 1: Discourses 1–11
0–674–99283–0 Harvard $14.50

Volume 2: Discourses 12–30
0–674–99374–8 Harvard $14.50

Volume 3: Discourses 31–36
0–674–99395–0 Harvard $14.50

Volume 4: Discourses 37–60
0–674–99414–0 Harvard $14.50

Volume 5
Includes *Discourses 61–80, Fragments, Letters, Testimony regarding Dio's life and Writings,* and General Index
0–674–99424–8 Harvard $14.50

• Diodorus Siculus
LIBRARY OF HISTORY

Volume 1: Books 1–2 (34)
0–674–99307–1 Harvard $14.50

Volume 2: Books 2 (35)–4 (58)
0–674–99334–9 Harvard $14.50

Volume 3: Books 4 (59)–8
0–674–99375–6 Harvard $14.50

Volume 4: Books 9–12 (40)
0–674–99413–2 Harvard $14.50

Volume 5: Books 12 (41)–13
0–674–99422–1 Harvard $14.50

Volume 6: Books 14–15 (19)
0–674–99439–6 Harvard $14.50

Volume 7: Books 15 (20)–16 (65)
0–674–99428–0 Harvard $14.50

Volume 8: Books 16 (66)–17
0–674–99464–7 Harvard $14.50

Volume 9: Books 18–19 (65)
0–674–99415–9 Harvard $14.50

Volume 10: Books 19 (66)–20
0–674–99429–9 Harvard $14.50

Volume 11: Fragments of Books 21–32
0–674–99450–7 Harvard $14.50

Volume 12: Fragments of Books 33–40 & General Index
0–674–99465–5 Harvard $14.50

• Diogenes Laertius
LIVES OF EMINENT PHILOSOPHERS

Volume 1: Books 1–5
0–674–99203–2 Harvard $14.50

Volume 2: Books 6–10
0–674–99204–0 Harvard $14.50

• Dionysius of Halicarnassus
ROMAN ANTIQUITIES

Volume 1: Books 1–2
0–674–99352–7 Harvard $14.50

Volume 2: Books 3–4
0–674–99382–9 Harvard $14.50

Volume 3: Books 5–6 (48)
0–674–99394–2 Harvard $14.50

Volume 4: Books 6 (49)–7
0–674–99401–9 Harvard $14.50

Volume 5: Books 8–9 (24)
0–674–99410–8 Harvard $14.50

Volume 6: Books 9 (25)–10
0–674–99416–7 Harvard $14.50

Volume 7: Book 11, Fragments of Books 12–20 & General Index
0–674–99427–2 Harvard $14.50

CRITICAL ESSAYS

Volume 1
0–674–99512–0 Harvard $14.50

Volume 2
0–674–99513–9 Harvard $14.50

• Epictetus
EPICTETUS

Volume 1: Discourses, Books 1–2
0–674–99145–1 Harvard $14.50

Volume 2
Includes *Discourses* (Books 3–4), *Fragments,* and *Encheiridion*
0–674–99240–7 Harvard $14.50

• Euripides
EURIPIDES

Volume 1
Includes *Iphigeneia at Aulis, Rhesus, Hecuba, Daughters of Troy,* and *Helen*
0–674–99010–2 Harvard $14.50

Volume 2
Includes *Electra, Orestes, Iphigeneia in Taurica, Andromache,* and *Cyclops*
0–674–99011–0 Harvard $14.50

Volume 3
Includes *Bacchanals, Madness of Hercules, Children of Hercules, Phoenician Maidens,* and *Suppliants*
0–674–99012–9 Harvard $14.50

Volume 4
Includes *Ion, Hippolytus, Medea,* and *Alcestis*
0–674–99013–7 Harvard $14.50

• Eusebius
ECCLESIASTICAL HISTORY

Volume 1: Books 1–5
0–674–99169–9 Harvard $14.50

Volume 2: Books 6–10
0–674–99293–8 Harvard $14.50

• Galen
ON THE NATURAL FACULTIES
0–674–99078–1 Harvard $14.50

Daphnis and Chloe in a 1930s woodcut by Maillol

• Greek Anthology
GREEK ANTHOLOGY

Volume 1: Books 1–6
0–674–99074–9 Harvard $14.50

Volume 2: Books 7–8
0–674–99075–7 Harvard $14.50

Volume 3: Book 9
0–674–99093–5 Harvard $14.50

Volume 4: Books 10–12
0–674–99094–3 Harvard $14.50

Volume 5: Books 13–16
0–674–99095–1 Harvard $14.50

• Herodian
HERODIAN

Volume 1: Books 1–4
0–674–99500–7 Harvard $14.50

Volume 2: Books 5–8
0–674–99501–5 Harvard $14.50

• Herodotus
HERODOTUS

Volume 1: Books 1–2
0–674–99130–3 Harvard $14.50

Volume 2: Books 3–4
0–674–99131–1 Harvard $14.50

Volume 3: Books 5–7
0–674–99133–8 Harvard $14.50

Volume 4: Books 8–9
0–674–99134–6 Harvard $14.50

• Hesiod & others
HESIOD, HOMERIC HYMNS, FRAGMENTS OF THE EPIC CYCLE, HOMERICA
0–674–99063–3 Harvard $14.50

• Hippocrates
HIPPOCRATES

Volume 1
Includes *Ancient Medicine, Airs, Waters, Places, Epidemics 1–2, Oath, Precepts,* and *Nutriment*
0–674–99162–1 Harvard $14.50

Volume 2
Includes *Prognostic, Regimen in Acute Diseases, Sacred Disease, Art, Breaths, Law, Decorum, Physician* (Chapter 1), and *Dentition*
0–674–99164–8 Harvard $14.50

Volume 3
Includes *On Wounds in the Head, In the Surgery, On Fractures, On Joints,* and *Mochlikon*
0–674–99165–6 Harvard $14.50

Volume 4
Includes *Nature of Man, Regimen in Health, Humours, Aphorisms, Regimen 1–3, Dreams, Heracleitus' On the Universe,* and General Index
0–674–99166–4 Harvard $14.50

HOMER

Iliad, Books 1–12
0–674–99188–5 Harvard $14.50

Iliad, Books 13–24, Index
0–674–99189–3 Harvard $14.50

IF YOU CAN'T FIND IT, LOOK IN THE INDEX

Odyssey, Books 1–12
0-674-99116-8 Harvard $14.50

Odyssey, Books 13–24, Index
0-674-99117-6 Harvard $14.50

• Isaeus
ISAEUS
0-674-99222-9 Harvard $14.50

• Isocrates
ISOCRATES

Volume 1
Includes *To Demonicus, To Nicocles, Nicocles or Cyprians, Panegyricus, To Philip,* and *Archidamus*
0-674-99231-8 Harvard $14.50

Volume 2
Includes *On the Peace, Areopagiticus, Against the Sophists, Antidosis,* and *Panathenaicus*
0-674-99252-0 Harvard $14.50

Volume 3
Includes *Evagoras, Helen, Busiris, Plataicus, Concerning the Team of Horses, Trapeziticus, Against Callimachus, Aegineticus Against Lochites, Against Euthynus, Letters 1–9,* and General Index
0-674-99411-6 Harvard $14.50

• St. John Damascene
BARLAAM AND IOASAPH
0-674-99038-2 Harvard $14.50

• Josephus
JOSEPHUS

Volume 1: Against Apion
0-674-99205-9 Harvard $14.50

Volume 2: Jewish War, Books 1–3
0-674-99223-7 Harvard $14.50

Volume 3: Jewish War, Books 4–6 & Indexes to Volumes 2–3
0-674-99232-6 Harvard $14.50

Volume 4: Antiquities, Books 1–4
0-674-99267-9 Harvard $14.50

Volume 5: Antiquities, Books 5–8
0-674-99310-1 Harvard $14.50

Volume 6: Antiquities, Books 9–11
0-674-99360-8 Harvard $14.50

Volume 7: Antiquities, Books 12–14
0-674-99402-7 Harvard $14.50

Volume 8: Antiquities, Books 15–17
0-674-99451-5 Harvard $14.50

Volume 9: Antiquities, Books 18–20 & General Index
0-674-99477-9 Harvard $14.50

• Julian
JULIAN

Volume 1: Orations 1–4
0-674-99014-5 Harvard $14.50

Volume 2
Includes *Orations 6–8; Letters to Themistius, to the Senate and People of Athens, to a Priest; Caesars,* and *Misopogon*
0-674-99032-3 Harvard $14.50

Volume 3
Includes *Letters 1–73, Letters 74–83 (Apocryphal), Shorter Fragments, Epigrams, Against the Galilaeans,* and *Fragments*
0-674-99173-7 Harvard $14.50

• Libanius
LIBANIUS

Volume 1: Selected Orations
0-674-99496-5 Harvard $14.50

Volume 2: Selected Orations
0-674-99497-3 Harvard $14.50

• Longus
DAPHNIS AND CHLOE
Includes Parthenius' *Love Romances* and *Fragments of the Ninus Romance*
0-674-99076-5 Harvard $14.50

• Lucian
LUCIAN

Volume 1
Includes *Phalaris 1–2, Hippias or Bath, Dionysus, Heracles, Amber or Swans, Fly, Nigrinus, Demonax, Hall, My Native Land, Octogenarians, True Story 1–2, Slander, Consonants at Law,* and *Carousal or Lapiths*
0-674-99015-3 Harvard $14.50

Volume 2
Includes *Downward Journey or Tyrant, Zeus Catechized, Zeus Rants, Dream or Cock, Prometheus, Icaromenippus or Sky-Man, Timon or Misanthrope, Charon or Inspectors, Philosophies for Sale*
0-674-99060-9 Harvard $14.50

Volume 3
Includes *Dead Come to Life or Fisherman, Double Indictment or Trials by Jury, On Sacrifices, Ignorant Book-Collector, Dream or Lucian's Career, Parasite, Lover of Lies, Judgement of the Goddesses,* and *On Salaried Posts in Great Houses*
0-674-99144-3 Harvard $14.50

Volume 4
Includes *Anarchasis or Athletics, Menippus or Descent Into Hades, On Funerals, Professor of Public Speaking, Alexander the False Prophet, Essays in Portraiture, Essays in Portraiture Defended,* and *Goddess of Surrye*
0-674-99179-6 Harvard $14.50

Volume 5
Includes *Passing of Peregrinus, Runaways, Toxaris or Friendship, Dance, Lexiphanes, Eunuch, Astrology, Mistaken Critic, Parliament of the Gods, Tyrannicide,* and *Disowned*
0-674-99333-0 Harvard $14.50

Volume 6
Includes *How to Write History, Dipsads, Saturnalia, Herodotus or Aetion, Zeuxis or Antiochus, Slip of the Tongue in Greeting, Apology for the "Salaried Posts in Great Houses", Harmonides, Conversations with Hesiod, Scythian or Consul, Hermotimus or Concerning the Sects, To One Who Said "You're a Prometheus in Words",* and *Ship or Wishes*
0-674-99474-4 Harvard $14.50

Volume 7
Includes *Dialogues of the Dead, Dialogues of the Sea-Gods, Dialogues of the Gods,* and *Dialogues of the Courtesans*
0-674-99475-2 Harvard $14.50

Volume 8
Includes *Soloecista, Lucius or Ass, Amores, Halycon, Demosthenes, Podagra, Ocypus, Cyniscus, Philopatris, Charidemus,* and *Nero*
0-674-99476-0 Harvard $14.50

• Lysias
LYSIAS
0-674-99269-5 Harvard $14.50

• Manetho
AEGYPTIACA & OTHER WORKS
0-674-99385-3 Harvard $14.50

• Marcus Aurelius
MARCUS AURELIUS
0-674-99064-1 Harvard $14.50

• Menander
MENANDER
0-674-99147-8 Harvard $14.50

• Nonnos
DIONYSIACA

Volume 1: Books 1–15
0-674-99379-9 Harvard $14.50

Volume 2: Books 16–35
0-674-99391-8 Harvard $14.50

Volume 3: Books 36–48
0-674-99393-4 Harvard $14.50

• Oppian & others
OPPIAN, COLLUTHUS, AND TRYPHIODORUS
0-674-99241-5 Harvard $14.50

Papyri

PAPYRI

Volume 1: Non-Literary Papyri: Private Documents
0-674-99294-6 Harvard $14.50

Volume 2: Non-Literary Papyri: Public Documents
0-674-99312-8 Harvard $14.50

Volume 3: Literary Papyri: Poetry
0-674-99397-7 Harvard $14.50

• Pausanias
DESCRIPTION OF GREECE

Volume 1: Books 1–2 (Attica & Corinth)
0-674-99104-4 Harvard $14.50

Volume 2: Books 3–5 (Laconia, Messenia, Elis 1)
0-674-99207-5 Harvard $14.50

Volume 3: Books 6–8 (21) (Elis 2, Achaia, Arcadia)
0-674-99300-4 Harvard $14.50

Volume 4: Books 8 (22)–10 (Arcadia, Boeotia, Phocis & Ozolian Locris)
0-674-99328-4 Harvard $14.50

Volume 5: Maps, Plans, Illustrations & General Index
0-674-99329-2 Harvard $14.50

• Philo
PHILO

Volume 1: On the Creation, Allegorical Interpretation
0-674-99249-0 Harvard $14.50

Volume 2
Includes *On the Cherubim, Sacrifices of Abel and Cain, Worse Attacks the Better, On the Posterity and Exile of Cain,* and *On the Giants*
0-674-99250-4 Harvard $14.50

Volume 3
Includes *On the Unchangeableness of God, On Husbandry, Concerning Noah's Work as a Planter, On Drunkenness,* and *On Sobriety*
0–674–99272–5 Harvard $14.50

Volume 4
Includes *On the Confusion of Tongues, On the Migration of Abraham, Who is the Heir of Divine Things?,* and *On Mating* with the Preliminary Studies
0–674–9928703 Harvard $14.50

Volume 5
Includes *On Flight and Findings, On the Change of Names,* and *On Dreams*
0–674–99303–9 Harvard $14.50

Volume 6
Includes *On Abraham, On Joseph,* and *Moses*
0–674–99319–5 Harvard $14.50

Volume 7
Includes *On the Decalogue,* and *On the Special Laws* (Books 1–3)
0–674–99353–5 Harvard $14.50

Volume 8
Includes *On the Special Laws* (Book 4), *On the Virtues,* and *On Rewards and Punishments*
0–674–99376–4 Harvard $14.50

Volume 9
Includes *Every Good Man is Free, On the Contemplative Life, On the Eternity of the World, Against Flaccus, Apology for the Jews,* and *On Providence*
0–674–99400–0 Harvard $14.50

Volume 10: On the Embassy to Gaius, General Index
0–674–99417–5 Harvard $14.50

Supplement 1: Questions and Answers on Genesis
0–674–99418–3 Harvard $14.50

Supplement 2: Questions and Answers on Exodus
0–674–99442–6 Harvard $14.50

- Philostratus
  PHILOSTRATUS

  Volume 1: Life of Apollonius of Tyana, Books 1–4
  0–674–99018–8 Harvard $14.50

  Volume 2
  Includes *Life of Apollonius of Tyana* (Books 6–8), Apollonius' *Epistles,* and Eusebius' *Treatise*
  0–674–99019–6 Harvard $14.50

  LIVES OF THE SOPHISTS
  Includes Eunapius' *Lives of the Philosophers and Sophists*
  0–674–99149–4 Harvard $14.50

- Philostratus the Elder
  IMAGINES, BOOKS I AND II
  Includes Philostratus the Younger's *Imagines* and Callistratus' *Descriptions*
  0–674–99282–2 Harvard $14.50

- Pindar
  PINDAR
  0–674–99062–5 Harvard $14.50

- Plato
  PLATO

  Volume 1
  Includes *Euthyphro, Apology, Crito, Phaedo,* and *Phaedrus*
  0–674–99040–4 Harvard $14.50

  Volume 2
  Includes *Laches, Protagoras, Meno,* and *Euthydemus*
  0–674–99183–4 Harvard $14.50

  Volume 3
  Includes *Lysis, Symposium,* and *Gorgias*
  0–674–99184–2 Harvard $14.50

  Volume 4
  Includes *Cratylus, Parmenides, Greater Hippias,* and *Lesser Hippias*
  0–674–99185–0 Harvard $14.50

  Volume 5, 1: Republic, Books 1–5
  0–674–99262–8 Harvard $14.50

  Volume 5, 2: Republic, Books 6–10
  0–674–99304–7 Harvard $14.50

  Volume 6: Theaetetus & Sophist
  0–674–99137–0 Harvard $14.50

  Volume 7, 1: Laws, Books 1–6
  0–674–99206–7 Harvard $14.50

  Volume 7, 2: Laws, Books 7–12
  0–674–99211–3 Harvard $14.50

  Volume 8
  Includes *Charmides, Alcibiades I-2, Hipparchus, Lovers, Theages, Minos,* and *Epinomis*
  0–674–99221–0 Harvard $14.50

- Plotinus
  PLOTINUS

  Volume 1: Life of Plotinus & Ennead 1
  0–674–99484–1 Harvard $14.50

  Volume 2: Ennead 2
  0–674–99486–8 Harvard $14.50

  Volume 3: Ennead 3
  0–674–99487–6 Harvard $14.50

  Volume 4: Ennead 4
  0–674–99488–4 Harvard $14.50

  Volume 5: Ennead 5
  0–674–99489–2 Harvard $14.50

  Volume 6: Ennead 6, 1–5
  0–674–99490–6 Harvard $14.50

  Volume 7: Ennead 6, 6–9
  0–674–99515–5 Harvard $14.50

- Plutarch
  MORALIA

  Volume 1
  Includes *Education of Children, How the Young Man Should Study Poetry, On Listening to Lectures, How to Tell a Flatterer from a Friend,* and *How a Man May Become Aware of His Progress in Virtue*
  0–674–99217–2 Harvard $14.50

  Volume 2
  Includes *How to Profit by One's Enemies, On Having Many Friends, Virtue and Vice, Letter of Condolence to Apollonius, Advice About Keeping Well, Advice to Bride and Groom, Dinner of the Seven Wise Men,* and *Superstition*
  0–674–99245–8 Harvard $14.50

An Athenian reading lesson, from The Oxford History of the Classical World *edited by John Boardman and others*

Volume 3
Includes *Sayings of Kings and Commanders, Sayings of Romans, Sayings of Spartans, Ancient Customs of Spartans, Saying of Spartan Women,* and *Bravery of Women*
0–674–99270–9 Harvard $14.50

Volume 4
Includes *Roman Questions, Greek Questions, Greek and Roman Parallel Stories, On the Fortune of the Romans, On the Fortune or the Virtue of Alexander,* and *Were the Athenians More Famous in War or in Wisdom?*
0–674–99336–5 Harvard $14.50

Volume 5
Includes *Isis and Osiris, The E at Delphi, The Oracle at Delphi No Longer Given in Verse,* and *The Obsolescence of Oracles*
0–674–99337–3 Harvard $14.50

Volume 6
Includes *Can Virtue Be Taught?, On Moral Virtue, On the Control of Anger, On Tranquility of Mind, On Brotherly Love, On Affection for Offspring, Whether Vice Be Sufficient to Cause Unhappiness, Whether the Affections of the Soul Are Worse Than Those of the Body, Concerning Talkativeness,* and *On Being a Busy-body*
0–674–99371–3 Harvard $14.50

Volume 7
Includes *On Love of Wealth, On Compliancy, On Envy and Hate, On Praising Oneself Inoffensively, On the Delays of the Divine Vengeance, On Fate, On the Sign of Socrates, On Exile,* and *Consolation to His Wife*
0–674–99446–9 Harvard $14.50

Volume 8: Table-Talk, Books 1–6
0–674–99466–3 Harvard $14.50

Volume 9: Table-Talk, Books 7–9 & Dialogue on Love
0–674–99467–1 Harvard $14.50

Volume 10
Includes *Love Stories, That a Philosopher Ought to Converse Especially with Men in Power, To an Uneducated Ruler, Whether an Old Man Should Engage in Public Affairs, Precepts of Statecraft, On Monarchy, Democracy, and Oligarchy, That We Ought Not Borrow, Lives of the Ten Orators,* and *Summary of a Comparison Between Aristophanes and Menander*
0–674–99354–3 Harvard $14.50

✉ **TO ORDER BOOKS AS GIFTS, SEE PAGE 1**

Volume 11: On the Malice of Herodotus & Causes of Natural Phenomena
0–674–99469–8 Harvard $14.50

Volume 12
Includes *Concerning the Face Which Appears in the Orb of the Moon, On the Principle of Cold, Whether Fire or Water Is More Useful, Whether Land or Sea Animals Are Cleverer, Beasts Are Rational,* and *On the Eating of Flesh*
0–674–99447–7 Harvard $14.50

Volume 13, 1: Platonic Essays
0–674–99470–1 Harvard $14.50

Volume 13, 2: Stoic Essays
0–674–99517–1 Harvard $14.50

Volume 14
Includes *That Epicurus Actually Makes a Pleasant Life Impossible, Reply to Colotes in Defence of the Other Philosophers, Is "Live Unknown" a Wise Precept?,* and *On Music*
0–674–99472–8 Harvard $14.50

Volume 15: Fragments
0–674–99473–6 Harvard $14.50

PARALLEL LIVES

Volume 1
Includes *Theseus and Romulus, Lycurgus and Numa,* and *Solon and Publicola*
0–674–99052–8 Harvard $14.50

Volume 2
Includes *Themistocles and Camillus, Aristides and Cato Major,* and *Cimon and Lucullus*
0–674–99053–6 Harvard $14.50

Volume 3
Includes *Pericles and Fabius Maximus* and *Nicias and Crassus*
0–674–99072–2 Harvard $14.50

Volume 4
Includes *Alcibiades and Coriolanus* and *Lysander and Sulla*
0–674–99089–7 Harvard $14.50

Volume 5
Includes *Agesilaus and Pompey* and *Pelopidas and Marcellus*
0–674–99097–8 Harvard $14.50

Volume 6
Includes *Dion and Brutus* and *Timoleon and Aemilius Paulus*
0–674–99109–5 Harvard $14.50

Volume 7
Includes *Demosthenes and Cicero* and *Alexander and Caesar*
0–674–99110–9 Harvard $14.50

Volume 8
Includes *Sertorious and Eumenes* and *Phocion and Cato the Younger*
0–674–99111–7 Harvard $14.50

Volume 9
Includes *Demetrius and Antony* and *Pyrrhus and Gaius Marius*
0–674–99112–5 Harvard $14.50

Volume 10
Includes *Agis and Cleomenes, Tiberius and Gaius Gracchus,* and *Philopoemen and Flamininus*
0–674–99113–3 Harvard $14.50

Volume 11
Includes *Aratus, Artaxerxes, Galba, Otho,* and General Index
0–674–99114–1 Harvard $14.50

• Polybius
HISTORIES

Volume 1: Books 1–2
0–674–99142–7 Harvard $14.50

Volume 2: Books 3–4
0–674–99152–4 Harvard $14.50

Volume 3: Books 5–8
0–674–99153–2 Harvard $14.50

Volume 4: Books 9–15
0–674–99175–3 Harvard $14.50

Volume 5: Books 16–27
0–674–99176–1 Harvard $14.50

Volume 6: Books 28–39
0–674–99178–8 Harvard $14.50

• Procopius
HISTORY OF THE WARS & SECRET HISTORY

Volume 1: Books 1–2, Persian War
0–674–99054–4 Harvard $14.50

Volume 2: Books 3–4, Vandalic War
0–674–99090–0 Harvard $14.50

Volume 3: Books 5–6 (15), Gothic War
0–674–99119–2 Harvard $14.50

Volume 4: Books 6, (16)–7, 35, Gothic War
0–674–99191–5 Harvard $14.50

Volume 5: Books 7, (36)–8, Gothic War
0–674–99239–3 Harvard $14.50

Volume 6: Anecdota or Secret History
0–674–99320–9 Harvard $14.50

Volume 7: On Buildings & General Index
0–674–99378–0 Harvard $14.50

• Ptolemy
TETRABIBLOS
0–674–99479–5 Harvard $14.50

• Quintus Smyrnaeus
FALL OF TROY
0–674–99022–6 Harvard $14.50

• Sappho & others
GREEK LYRIC

Volume 1: Sappho & Alcaeus
0–674–99157–5 Harvard $14.50

Volume 2: Alcman, Anacreon, Terpander & others
0–674–99158–3 Harvard $14.50

Volume 3
Includes works by Myrtis, Corinna, Lamprocles, Charixena, Dionysius, Lamprus, Pratinas, Diagoras, Cydias, Cedeides, Praxilla, Bacchylides, Sophocles' *Paeans,* Ion of Chios, Melanippides, Euripides, Hieronymus, Cleomenes, Lamynthius, Gnesippus, Leotrophides, Cinesias, Phyrnis, Pronomus, Telestes, Timotheus Licymnius, and Philoxenus (3), Ariphron, Polyidus, Telles, Lysimachus, Aristotle, Hermolochus, Lycophronides, Xenocritus, Xenodamus, Myia, Mynna, Theano, *Anonymous Fragments, Folk-songs,* and *Scolia*
0–674–99159–1 Harvard $14.50

• Sextus Empiricus
SEXTUS EMPIRICUS

Volume 1: Outlines of Pyrrhonism
0–674–99301–2 Harvard $14.50

Volume 2: Against the Logicians
0–674–99321–7 Harvard $14.50

Volume 3: Against the Physicists & Against the Ethicists
0–674–99344–6 Harvard $14.50

Volume 4: Against the Professors
0–674–99420–5 Harvard $14.50

• Sophocles
SOPHOCLES

Volume 1
Includes *Oedipus the King, Oedipus at Colonus,* and *Antigone*
0–674–99023–4 Harvard $14.50

Volume 2
Includes *Ajax, Electra, Trachiniae,* and *Philoctetes*
0–674–99024–2 Harvard $14.50

• Strabo
GEOGRAPHY

Volume 1: Books 1–2
0–674–99055–2 Harvard $14.50

Volume 2: Books 3–5
0–674–99056–0 Harvard $14.50

Volume 3: Books 6–7
0–674–99201–6 Harvard $14.50

Volume 4: Books 8–9
0–674–99201–6 Harvard $14.50

Volume 5: Books 10–12
0–674–99233–4 Harvard $14.50

Volume 6: Books 13–14
0–674–99246–6 Harvard $14.50

Volume 7: Books 15–16
0–674–99266–0 Harvard $14.50

Volume 8: Book 17 & General Index
0–674–99295–4 Harvard $14.50

• Thales & others
GREEK MATHEMATICAL WORKS

Volume 1: From Thales to Euclid
0–674–99369–1 Harvard $14.50

Volume 2: From Aristarchus to Pappus
0–674–99399–3 Harvard $14.50

• Theocritus & others
GREEK BUCOLIC POETS: Theocritus, Bion & Moschus
0–674–99031–5 Harvard $14.50

• Theophrastus
CHARACTERS
Also includes works by Herodes, Cercidas, and the Greek Choliambic Poets
0–674–99248–2 Harvard $14.50

ENQUIRY INTO PLANTS

Volume 1: Books 1–5
0–674–99077–3 Harvard $14.50

Volume 2: Books 6–9
0–674–99088–9 Harvard $14.50

• Thucydides
HISTORY OF THE PELOPONNESIAN WAR

Volume 1: Books 1–2
0–674–99120–0 Harvard $14.50

Volume 2: Books 3–4
0–674–99121–4 Harvard $14.50

Volume 3: Books 5–6
0-674-99122-2 Harvard $14.50

Volume 4: Books 7–8, General Index
0-674-99187-7 Harvard $14.50

● Xenophon
XENOPHON

Volume 1: Hellenica, Books 1–4
0-674-99098-6 Harvard $14.50

Volume 2: Hellenica, Books 5–7
0-674-99099-4 Harvard $14.50

Volume 3: Anabasis, Books 1–7
0-674-99100-1 Harvard $14.50

Volume 4
Includes *Memorabilia, Oeconomicus, Symposium,* and *Apologia*
0-674-99186-9 Harvard $14.50

Volume 5: Cyropaedia, Books 1–4
0-674-99057-9 Harvard $14.50

Volume 6: Cyropaedia, Books 5–8
0-674-99058-7 Harvard $14.50

Volume 7
Includes *Scripta Minora,* and *Constitution of the Athenians*
0-674-99202-4 Harvard $14.50

LATIN LITERATURE

● Apuleius
THE GOLDEN ASS
0-674-99049-8 Harvard $14.50

● Saint Augustine
THE CITY OF GOD

Volume 1: Books 1–3
0-674-99452-3 Harvard $14.50

Volume 2: Books 4–7
0-674-99453-1 Harvard $14.50

Volume 3: Books 8–11
0-674-99455-8 Harvard $14.50

Volume 4: Books 12–15
0-674-99456-6 Harvard $14.50

Volume 5: Books 16–18 (35)
0-674-99457-4 Harvard $14.50

Volume 6: Books 18 (36)–20
0-674-99458-2 Harvard $14.50

Volume 7: Books 21–22, Index
0-674-99459-0 Harvard $14.50

THE CONFESSIONS

Volume 1: Books 1–8
0-674-99029-3 Harvard $14.50

Volume 2: Books 9–13
0-674-99030-7 Harvard $14.50

SELECTED LETTERS
0-674-99264-4 Harvard $14.50

● Ausonius
AUSONIUS

Volume 1: Books 1–17
0-674-99107-9 Harvard $14.50

Volume 2
Includes *Books 18–20,* and Paulinus Pellaeus' *Eucharisticus*
0-674-99127-3 Harvard $14.50

● Bede
HISTORICAL WORKS

Volume 1: Ecclesiastical History, Books 1–3
0-674-99271-7 Harvard $14.50

Volume 2
Includes *Ecclesiastical History* (Books 4–5), *Lives of the Abbots,* and *Letter to Egbert*
0-674-99273-3 Harvard $14.50

● Boethius
BOETHIUS
Includes *Theological Tractates,* and *Consolation of Philosophy*
0-674-99083-8 Harvard $14.50

● Caesar
CAESAR

Volume 1: Gallic War
0-674-990803 Harvard $14.50

Volume 2: Civil Wars
0-674-99013-9 Harvard $14.50

Volume 3: Alexandrian, African and Spanish Wars
0-674-99443-4 Harvard $14.50

● Cato & Varro
ON AGRICULTURE
0-674-99313-6 Harvard $14.50

● Catullus & others
CATULLUS, TIBULLUS & PERVIGLIUM VENERIS
0-674-99007-2 Harvard $14.50

● Celsus
ON MEDICINE

Volume 1: Books 1–4
0-674-99322-5 Harvard $14.50

Volume 2: Books 5–6
0-674-99335-7 Harvard $14.50

Volume 3: Books 7–8
0-674-99370-5 Harvard $14.50

● Cicero
RHETORICAL TREATISES

Volume 1: Rhetorica ad Herennium
0-674-99444-2 Harvard $14.50

Volume 2
Includes *De Inventione, De Optimo Genere Oratorum,* and *Topica*
0-674-99425-6 Harvard $14.50

Volume 3: De Oratore, Books 1–2
0-674-99383-7 Harvard $14.50

Volume 4
Includes *De Oratore, Book III, De Fato, Paradoxa Stoicorum,* and *De Partitione Oratoria*
0-674-99384-5 Harvard $14.50

Volume 5: Brutus, Orator
0-674-99377-2 Harvard $14.50

ORATIONS

Volume 6
Includes *Pro Quinctio, Pro Roscio Amerino, Pro Roscio Comoedo,* and *Three Speeches on the Agrarian Law Against Rullus*
0-674-99265-2 Harvard $14.50

Volume 7: The Verrine Orations 1
Includes *Against Caecilius, Against Verres* (Parts 1–2), Books 1–2
0-674-99243-1 Harvard $14.50

Volume 8: The Verrine Orations 2
Includes *Against Verres* (Part 2), Books 3–4
0-674-99323-3 Harvard $14.50

Volume 9
Includes *Pro Lege Manilia, Pro Caecina, Pro Cluentio,* and *Pro Rabirio Perduellionis Reo*
0-674-99218-0 Harvard $14.50

Volume 10
Includes *In Catilinam* (1–4), *Pro Murena, Pro Sulla,* and *Pro Flacco*
0-674-99358-6 Harvard $14.50

Volume 11
Includes *Pro Archia, Post Reditum in Senatu, Post Reditum ad Quirites, De Domo Sua, De Haruspicum Responsis,* and *Pro Cn. Plancio*
0-674-99174-5 Harvard $14.50

Volume 12: Pro Sestio & In Vatinium
0-674-99341-1 Harvard $14.50

Volume 13
Includes *Pro Caelio, De Provinciis Consularibus,* and *Pro Balbo*
0-674-99492-2 Harvard $14.50

Volume 14
Includes *Pro Milone, In Pisonem, Pro Scauro, Pro Fonteio, Pro Rabirio Postumo, Pro Marcello, Pro Ligario,* and *Pro Rege Deiotaro*
0-674-99278-4 Harvard $14.50

Volume 15: Philippics
0-674-99208-3 Harvard $14.50

PHILOSOPHICAL TREATISES

Volume 16
Includes *De Re Publica,* and *De Legibus*
0-674-99-235-0 Harvard $14.50

Volume 17: De Finibus
0-674-99044-7 Harvard $14.50

Volume 18: Tusculan Disputations
0-674-99156-7 Harvard $14.50

Volume 19
Includes *De Natura Deorum,* and *Academica 1–2*
0-674-99296-2 Harvard $14.50

Volume 20
Includes *De Senectute, De Amicitia,* and *De Divinatione*
0-674-99170-2 Harvard $14.50

Volume 21: De Officiis
0-674-99033-1 Harvard $14.50

LETTERS

Volume 22: Letters to Atticus, Books 1–6
0-674-99008-0 Harvard $14.50

Volume 23: Letters to Atticus, Books 7–11
0-674-990009-9 Harvard $14.50

Volume 24: Letters to Atticus, Books 12–16
0-674-99108-7 Harvard $14.50

Volume 25: Letters to His Friends, Books 1–6
0-674-99225-3 Harvard $14.50

Volume 26: Letters to His Friends, Books 7–12
0-674-99238-5 Harvard $14.50

Volume 27
Includes *Letters to His Friends* (Books 13–16), *Letters to his Brother Quintus,* and *Letters to Brutus*
0-674-99253-9 Harvard $14.50

Volume 28
Includes *Letters to his Brother Quintus,
Letters to Brutus, Handbook of Electioneering,*
and *Letter to Octavian*
0–674–99509–0 Harvard $14.50

- Claudian
CLAUDIAN

Volume 1
Includes *Panegyric on Probinus and
Olybrius, Against Rufinus 1–2, War Against
Gildo, Against Eutropius 1–2, Fescennine
Verses on the Marriage of Honorius,
Epithalamium of Honorius and Maria,
Panegyrics on the Third and Fourth
Consulships of Honorius, Panegyric on the
Consulship of Manlius,* and *On Stilicho's
Consulship 1*
0–674–99150–8 Harvard $14.50

Volume 2
Includes *On Stilicho's Consulship 2–3,
Panegyric on the Sixth Consulship of
Honorius, Gothic War, Shorter Poems,* and
Rape of Proserpina 1–3
0–674–99151–6 Harvard $14.50

- Columella
DE RE RUSTICA

Volume 1: Books 1–4
0–674–99398–5 Harvard $14.50

Volume 2: Books 5–9
0–674–99448–5 Harvard $14.50

Volume 3: Books 10–12
0–674–99449–3 Harvard $14.50

- Ennius & others
REMAINS OF OLD LATIN

Volume 1: Ennius & Caecilius
0–674–99324–1 Harvard $14.50

Volume 2
Includes works by Livius Andronicus,
Naevius, Pacuvius, and Accius
0–674–99347–0 Harvard $14.50

**Volume 3: Lucilius & Laws of the XII
Tables**
0–674–99363–2 Harvard $14.50

Volume 4: Archaic Inscriptions
0–674–99396–9 Harvard $14.50

- Florus & Cornelius Nepos
FLORUS & CORNELIUS NEPOS
0–674–99254–7 Harvard $14.50

- Frontinus
STRATAGEMS & AQUEDUCTS
0–674–99192–3 Harvard $14.50

- Fronto
CORRESPONDENCE

Volume 1
0–674–99124–9 Harvard $14.50

Volume 2
0–674–99125–7 Harvard $14.50

- Gellius
ATTIC NIGHTS

Volume 1: Books 1–5
0–674–99215–6 Harvard $14.50

Volume 2: Books 6–8
0–674–99220–2 Harvard $14.50

Volume 3: Books 14–20
0–674–99234–2 Harvard $14.50

- Horace
ODES & EPODES
0–674–99037–4 Harvard $14.50

SATIRES, EPISTLES & ARS POETICA
0–674–99214–8 Harvard $14.50

- Saint Jerome
SELECT LETTERS
0–674–99288–1 Harvard $14.50

- Juvenal & Persius
JUVENAL & PERSIUS
0–674–99102–8 Harvard $14.50

- Livy
ROMAN HISTORY

Volume 1: Books 1–2
0–674–99126–5 Harvard $14.50

Volume 2: Books 3–4
0–674–99148–6 Harvard $14.50

Volume 3: Books 5–7
0–674–99190–7 Harvard $14.50

Volume 4: Books 8–10
0–674–99210–5 Harvard $14.50

Volume 5: Books 21–22
0–674–99256–3 Harvard $14.50

Volume 6: Books 23–25
0–674–99392–6 Harvard $14.50

Volume 7: Books 26–27
0–674–99404–3 Harvard $14.50

Volume 8: Books 28–30
0–674–99419–1 Harvard $14.50

Volume 9: Books 31–34
0–674–99326–8 Harvard $14.50

Volume 10: Books 35–36
0–674–99326–8 Harvard $14.50

Volume 11: Books 37–39
0–674–99346–2 Harvard $14.50

Volume 12: Books 40–42
0–674–99366–7 Harvard $14.50

Volume 13: Books 43–45
0–674–99435–3 Harvard $14.50

Volume 14: Summaries & Fragments
Also includes writings by Julius Obsequens
and the general index
0–674–99445–0 Harvard $14.50

- Lucan
CIVIL WAR (Pharsalia)
0–674–99242–3 Harvard $14.50

*The Roman navy in a 15th-century Venetian
edition of Livy*

- Lucretius
LUCRETIUS
0–674–99200–8 Harvard $14.50

- Manilius
ASTRONOMICA
0–674–99516–3 Harvard $14.50

- Ammianus Marcellinus
ROMAN HISTORY

Volume 1
0–674–99331–4 Harvard $14.50

Volume 2
0–674–99348–9 Harvard $14.50

Volume 3
0–674–99365–9 Harvard $14.50

- Martial
EPIGRAMS

Volume 1: Books 1–7
0–674–99105–2 Harvard $14.50

Volume 2: Books 7–14
0–674–99106–0 Harvard $14.50

- Publilius Syrus & others
MINOR LATIN POETS
Includes Publilius Syrus, *Elegiae in
Maecenatem,* Grattius, Calpurnius Siculus,
Laus Pisonis, Einsiedeln Eclogues, Aetna,
Florus, Hadrian, Nemesianus, Reposianus,
Tiberianus, *Dicta Catonis, Phoenix,*
Avianus, and Rutilius Namatianus
0–674–99314–4 Harvard $14.50

- Ovid
OVID

Volume 1: Heroides & Amores
0–674–99045–5 Harvard $14.50

Volume 2
Includes *Art of Love, Remedies of Love, De
Medicamine Faciei, Nux, Ibis, Halieuticon,*
and *Consolatio ad Liviam*
0–674–99255–5 Harvard $14.50

Volume 3: Metamorphoses, Books 1–8
0–674–99046–3 Harvard $14.50

Volume 4: Metamorphoses, Books 9–15
0–674–99047–1 Harvard $14.50

Volume 5: Fasti
0–674–99279–2 Harvard $14.50

Volume 6: Tristia & Ex Ponto
0–674–99167–2 Harvard $14.50

- Petronius
SATYRICON
Also includes Seneca's *Apocolocyntosis*
0–674–99016–1 Harvard $14.50

- Plautus
PLAUTUS

Volume 1
Includes *Amphitryon, Comedy of Asses, Pot of
Gold, Two Bacchises,* and *Captives*
0–674–99067–6 Harvard $14.50

Volume 2
Includes *Casina, Casket Comedy, Curculio,
Epidicus,* and *Two Menaechmuses*
0–674–99068–4 Harvard $14.50

Volume 3
Includes *Merchant, Braggart Warrior, Haunted House,* and *Persian*
0–674–99181–8 Harvard $14.50

Volume 4
Includes *Little Carthaginian, Pseudolus,* and *Rope*
0–674–99286–5 Harvard $14.50

• Pliny
NATURAL HISTORY

Volume 1: Books 1 and 2
0–674–99364–0 Harvard $14.50

Volume 2: Books 3–7
0–674–99388–8 Harvard $14.50

Volume 3: Books 8–11
0–674–99389–6 Harvard $14.50

Volume 4: Books 12–16
0–674–99408–6 Harvard $14.50

Volume 5: Books 17–19
0–674–99409–4 Harvard $14.50

Volume 6: Books 20–23
0–674–99431–0 Harvard $14.50

Volume 7: Books 24–27
0–674–99432–9 Harvard $14.50

Volume 8: Books 28–32
0–674–99460–4 Harvard $14.50

Volume 9: Books 33–35
0–674–99433–7 Harvard $14.50

Volume 10: Books 36–37
0–674–99461–2 Harvard $14.50

• Pliny the Younger
LETTERS AND PANEGYRICUS

Volume 1: Books 1–7
0–674–99061–7 Harvard $14.50

Volume 2: Books 7–10 & Panegyricus
0–674–99066–8 Harvard $14.50

• Propertius
PROPERTIUS
0–674–99021–8 Harvard $14.50

• Prudentius
PRUDENTIUS

Volume 1
0–674–99426–4 Harvard $14.50

Volume 2
0–674–99438–8 Harvard $14.50

• Quintilian
QUINTILIAN

Volume 1: Books 1–3
0–674–99138–9 Harvard $14.50

Volume 2: Books 4–6
0–674–99139–7 Harvard $14.50

Volume 3: Books 7–9
0–674–99140–0 Harvard $14.50

Volume 4: Books 10–12
0–674–99141–9 Harvard $14.50

• Quintus Curtius
HISTORY OF ALEXANDER

Volume 1: Books 1–4
0–674–99405–1 Harvard $14.50

Volume 2: Books 6–10
0–674–99407–8 Harvard $14.50

• Sallust
SALLUST
0–674–99128–1 Harvard $14.50

• Scriptores Historiae Augustae
HISTORIA AUGUSTA

Volume 1
Includes works on Hadrian, Aelius, Antoninus Pius, Marcus Aurelius, L. Verus, Avidius Cassius, Commodus, Pertinax, Didius Julianus, Septimius Severus, Pescennius Niger, and Clodius Albinus
0–674–99154–0 Harvard $14.50

Volume 2
Includes works on Caracalla, Geta, Opellius Macrinus, Diadumenianus, Elagabalus, Severus Alexander, Two Maximini, Three Gordians, Maximus, and Balbinus
0–674–99155–9 Harvard $14.50

Volume 3
Includes works on Two Valerians, Two Gallieni, Thirty Pretenders, Deified Claudius, Deified Aurelian, Tacitus, Probus, Firmus, Saturninus, Proculus, and Bonosus, Carus, Carinus, and Numerian
0–674–99290–3 Harvard $14.50

• The Elder Seneca
THE ELDER SENECA

Volume 1: Controversiae, Books 1–6
0–674–99510–4 Harvard $14.50

Volume 2: Controversiae (Books 7–10) & Suasortiae
0–674–99511–2 Harvard $14.50

• Seneca
SENECA

Volume 1: Moral Essays
Includes *De Providentia, De Constantia, De Ira, De Clementia*
0–674–99236–9 Harvard $14.50

Volume 2: Moral Essays
Includes *De Consolatione ad Marciam, De Vita Beata, De Otio, De Tranquilitate Animi, De Brevitate Vitae, De Consolatione ad Polybium, De Consolatione ad Helviam*
0–674–99280–6 Harvard $14.50

Volume 3: Moral Essays
Includes *De Beneficiis* Books 1–7
0–674–99343–8 Harvard $14.50

Volume 4: Epistulae Morales, Letters 1–65
0–674–99084–6 Harvard $14.50

Volume 5: Epistulae Morales, Letters 66–92
0–674–99085–4 Harvard $14.50

Volume 6: Epistulae Morales, Letters 93–124
0–674–99086–2 Harvard $14.50

Volume 7: Naturales Quaestiones (1)
0–674–99495–7 Harvard $14.50

Volume 8: Tragedies
Includes *Hercules Furens, Troades, Medea, Hippolytus or Phaedra,* and *Oedipus*
0–674–99069–2 Harvard $14.50

Volume 9: Tragedies
Includes *Agamemnon, Thyestes, Hercules Oetaeus, Phoenissae, Octavia*
0–674–99087–0 Harvard $14.50

Volume 10: Naturales Quaestiones (2)
0–674–99503–1 Harvard $14.50

• Sidonius
POEMS AND LETTERS

Volume 1: Poems, Letters (Books 1–2)
0–674–99327–6 Harvard $14.50

Volume 2: Letters (Books 3–4)
0–674–99462–0 Harvard $14.50

• Silius Italicus
PUNICA

Volume 1: Books 1–8
0–674–99305–5 Harvard $14.50

Volume 2: Books 9–17
0–674–99306–3 Harvard $14.50

• Statius
STATIUS

Volume 1
Includes *Silvae* (Books 1–4), *Thebaid* Books 1–4
0–674–99226–1 Harvard $14.50

Volume 2
Includes *Thebaid* (Books 5–7), *Achilleid* (Books 1–2)
0–674–99228–8 Harvard $14.50

• Suetonius
SUETONIUS

Volume 1:
Includes *Lives of the Caesars* from Deified Julius to Gaius Caligula
0–674–99035–8 Harvard $14.50

Volume 2:
Includes *Lives of the Caesars* from Deified Claudius to Domitian, *Lives of Illustrious Men, Grammarians and Rhetoricians,* and *Poets*
0–674–99042–0 Harvard $14.50

• Tacitus
TACITUS

Volume 1: Agricola, Germania & Dialogus
0–674–99039–0 Harvard $14.50

Volume 2: Histories 1–3
0–674–99123–0 Harvard $14.50

Volume 3: Histories 4–5, Annals 1–3
0–674–99274–1 Harvard $14.50

Volume 4: Annals 4–6, 11–12
0–674–99345–4 Harvard $14.50

Volume 5: Annals 13–16
0–674–99355–1 Harvard $14.50

• Terence
TERENCE

Volume 1
Includes *Lady of Andros, Self-Tormenter,* and *Eunuch*
0–674–99025–0 Harvard $14.50

Volume 2
Includes *Phormio, Mother-in-Law,* and *Brothers*
0–674–99026–9 Harvard $14.50

• Tertullian
APOLOGY & DE SPECTACULIS
Includes Minucius Felix's *Octavius*
0–674–99276–8 Harvard $14.50

➤ **FOR OVERSEAS ORDERING INFORMATION, SEE PAGE 1**

Theater performance in a 1497 edition of Terence

- Valerius Flaccus
ARGONAUTICA
0–674–99316–0 Harvard $14.50

- Varro
DE LINGUA LATINA
Volume 1: Books 5–7
0–674–99367–5 Harvard $14.50
Volume 2: Books 8–10 & Fragments
0–674–99368–3 Harvard $14.50

- Velleius Paterculus
RES GESTAE DIVI AUGUSTI
0–674–99168–0 Harvard $14.50

- Virgil
VIRGIL
Volume 1
Includes *Eclogues, Georgics* (Books 1–4), and *Aeneid* (Books 1–6)
0–674–99070–6 Harvard $14.50
Volume 2
Includes *Aeneid* (Books 7–12) & *Minor Poems*
0–674–99071–4 Harvard $14.50

- Vitruvius
ON ARCHITECTURE
Volume 1: Books 1–5
0–674–99277–6 Harvard $14.50
Volume 2: Books 6–10
0–674–99309–8 Harvard $14.50

Medieval Literature

In this catalog, writings of the Middle Ages will be found within each of the national literatures. The following list offers for convenience a selective sampling of some of the high points of medieval literature, along with some useful critical studies.

- Abelard & Heloise
LETTERS
0–14–044297 Penguin pb $4.95

- Dante Alighieri
THE DIVINE COMEDY
Translated by Charles S. Singleton
Volume 1: Inferno
0–691–01832–4 Princeton pb $20.50
Volume 2: Purgatorio
0–691–01843–X Princeton pb $18.50
Volume 3: Paradiso
0–691–01844–8 Princeton pb $18.50

- Bede
THE HISTORY OF THE ENGLISH CHURCH AND PEOPLE
0–14–044042–9 Penguin pb $4.95

- Giovanni Boccaccio
THE DECAMERON
Translated by G.H. McWilliam
0–14–044269–3 Penguin pb $6.95

- Geoffrey Chaucer
THE CANTERBURY TALES
Translated by Nevill Coghill
0–14–044022–4 Penguin pb $2.95
TROILUS AND CRISEYDE
Translated by Nevill Coghill
0–14–044239–1 Penguin pb $4.95

- Wolfram von Eschenbach
PARZIVAL
Translated by A.T. Hatto
0–14–044361–4 Penguin pb $6.95

- Jean Froissart
CHRONICLES
Translated by Geoffrey Brereton
0–14–044200–6 Penguin pb $6.95

- Geoffrey of Monmouth
THE HISTORY OF THE KINGS OF BRITAIN
Translated by Lewis Thorpe
0–14–044170–0 Penguin pb $5.95

- Gregory of Tours
THE HISTORY OF THE FRANKS
0–14–044295–2 Penguin pb $7.95

- Guillaume de Lorris & Jean de Meun
THE ROMANCE OF THE ROSE
Translated by Charles Dahlberg
0–87451–267–0 New England pb $16.00

- Thomas Malory
LE MORTE D'ARTHUR
Edited by Janet Cowen
Volume 1
0–14–043043–1 Penguin pb $3.95

Volume 2
0–14–043044–X Penguin pb $3.95

- John Mandeville
THE TRAVELS OF SIR JOHN MANDEVILLE
0–14–044435–1 Penguin pb $5.95

- Joanot Martorell & Marti Joan De Galba
TIRANT LO BLANC
Translated with an introduction by David Rosenthal
0–446–32584–8 Warner pb $4.95

- Christine de Pisan
THE BOOK OF THE CITY OF LADIES
Translated by Earl Richards
0–89255–066–X Persea pb $13.95

- Marco Polo
THE TRAVELS OF MARCO POLO
0–14–044057–7 Penguin pb $4.95

- Gottfried von Strassburg
TRISTAN
Translated by A.T. Hatto
0–14–044098–4 Penguin pb $4.95

- Chrétien de Troyes
YVAIN: The Knight of the Lion
Translated by Burton Raffel
0–300–03838–0 Yale pb $7.95

- François Villon
THE POEMS OF FRANCOIS VILLON
Translated by Galway Kinnell
0–87451–236–0 New England pb $9.95

François Villon in a 1489 edition of his work

Anonymous Works and Anthologies (alphabetical by title)

- Michael Alexander, translator
BEOWULF
0–14–044268–5 Penguin pb $2.25

THE EARLIEST ENGLISH POEMS
0–14–044172–7 Penguin pb $6.95

- Magnus Magnusson & Hermann Palsson, translators
LAXDAELA SAGA
0–14–044218–9 Penguin pb $5.95

- Jeffrey Gantz, translator
THE MABINOGION
0–14–044322–3 Penguin pb $3.95

- R.T. Davies, editor
MEDIEVAL ENGLISH LYRICS: A Critical Anthology
0–571–06571–6 Faber & Faber pb $11.95

- A.T. Hatto, editor
THE NIBELUNGENLIED
0–14–044137–9 Penguin pb $4.95

- Magnus Magnusson & Hermann Palsson, translators
NJAL'S SAGA
0–14–044103–4 Penguin pb $4.95

- W.S. Merwin, translator
THE POEM OF THE CID
0–452–00790–9 NAL pb $7.95

- James B. Ross & Mary M. McLaughlin, editors
THE PORTABLE MEDIEVAL READER
0–14–015046–3 Penguin pb $9.95

- Paul Blackburn, translator
PROENSA: An Anthology of Troubador Poetry
0–520–02985–2 California $35.00

- Patricia Terry, translator
RENARD THE FOX: The Misadventures of an Epic Hero
0–930350–48–0 Northeastern pb $11.95

- David Parlett, translator
SELECTIONS FROM THE CARMINA BURANA: A Verse Translation
0–14–044440–8 Penguin pb $6.95

- Brian Stone, translator
SIR GAWAIN AND THE GREEN KNIGHT
0–14–044092–5 Penguin pb $2.95

- Robert Harrison, translator
THE SONG OF ROLAND
0–451–62623–0 NAL pb $3.95

- Thomas Kinsella, translator
THE TAIN
0–19–281090–1 Oxford pb $9.95

CRITICAL STUDIES

- William Cook & Ronald Herzman
THE MEDIEVAL WORLD VIEW: An Introduction
0–19–503090–7 Oxford pb $9.95

- E.R. Curtius
EUROPEAN LITERATURE AND THE LATIN MIDDLE AGES
Translated by Willard Trask
0–691–01793–X Princeton pb $16.95

- Umberto Eco
ART AND BEAUTY IN THE MIDDLE AGES
0–300–03676–0 Yale $15.00
0–300–04207–8 Yale pb $7.95

- Michael Haren
MEDIEVAL THOUGHT: The Western Intellectual Tradition from Antiquity to the 13th Century
0–312–52816–7 St. Martin's $27.50

- Jacques Le Goff
THE MEDIEVAL IMAGINATION
Translated by Arthur Goldhammer
0–226–47084–9 Chicago $27.50

- C.S. Lewis
ALLEGORY OF LOVE: A Study of Medieval Tradition
0–19–500343–8 Oxford pb $9.95

- James J. Murphy
RHETORIC IN THE MIDDLE AGES: A History of Rhetorical Theory from Saint Augustine to the Renaissance
0–520–04406–1 California pb $12.95

Arthurian Lore

Geoffrey Ashe
THE LANDSCAPE OF KING ARTHUR
Lovely views of landscapes Arthur would have known, with comments by a major Arthurian scholar
0–8050–0711–3 Henry Holt $24.95

Leslie Alcock
ARTHUR'S BRITAIN
0–14–021396–1 Pelican pb $7.95

Richard Cavendish
KING ARTHUR AND THE GRAIL: The Arthurian Legends and Their Meaning
0–8008–4466–1 Taplinger pb $6.95

Norma L. Goodrich
KING ARTHUR
0–06–097182–7 Harper & Row pb $10.95

MERLIN
0–06–097183–5 Harper & Row pb $10.95

Nikolai Tolstoy
THE QUEST FOR MERLIN
0–316–85080–2 Little, Brown pb $9.95

Norris J. Lacy, editor
THE ARTHURIAN ENCYCLOPEDIA
0–87226–164–6 Peter Bedrick pb $16.95

French Literature to 1900

THE MIDDLE AGES

French freed itself from the dominance of Latin to emerge as a literary language in the 11th century. Among the earliest surviving works are the *chansons de geste*—epic paeans to the heroic deeds of knights in Carolingian times, of which the most famous is the early 12th-century *Song of Roland*.

The medieval period also produced a strong current of lyric poetry in French as well as in the Provençal of the troubadours. In addition there evolved a cycle of courtly romances based on Arthurian legend.

Two very different types of "verse tales" flourished: the *fabliau*—ranging in tone from satirical banter to bawdy irreverence— and the *fable* such as *Renard the Fox,* in which animal characters expose the vagaries of feudal society.

- Joseph Bédier
THE ROMANCE OF TRISTAN AND ISEULT
A compelling amalgam of several versions of the Tristan story
0–394–70271–9 Random House pb $2.50

- Marie de France
THE LAIS OF MARIE DE FRANCE
Short narrative poems by a late 12th-century Anglo-Norman poet, based on Celtic tales and often containing supernatural elements. These translations are in prose
Translated by Glyn S. Burgess & Keith Busby
0–14–044476–9 Penguin pb $5.95

- Jean Froissart
CHRONICLES
Froissart's book is a triumph both of literary art and reportorial skill. To read his firsthand accounts of the Hundred Years War, the Black Death, or the court of Richard II is to breathe the air of the 14th century
Translated by Geoffrey Brereton
0–14–044200–6 Penguin pb $6.95

- Guillaume de Lorris & Jean de Meun
THE ROMANCE OF THE ROSE
This immense dream allegory, written over 50 years by two poets, is the culminating work of the medieval courtly tradition. The first half is an idealistic account of a lover's adventures, the second a cynical satire against love and the church
Translated by Charles Dahlberg
0–87451–267–0 New England pb $16.00

- Charles d'Orléans
SELECTED POEMS
The duke of Orléans, a prisoner in England for 25 years following the Battle of Agincourt, later became an exemplar of French poetic practice; he also composed

poetry in English, on which this collection chiefly focuses
Edited by Sally Purcell
0–902145–69–X Carcanet pb $7.50

● Christine de Pisan
THE BOOK OF THE CITY OF LADIES
The author, often called the first French woman of letters, responded in prose and poetry to the prevailing misogyny of her time
Translated by Earl Richards
0–89255–066–X Persea pb $13.95

A MEDIEVAL WOMAN'S MIRROR OF HONOR: The Treasury of the City of Ladies
A companion volume to *The Book of the City of Ladies*
Translated with an introduction by Charity Cannon Willard
0–89255–144–5 Persea $22.50
0–89255–135–6 Persea pb $11.95

● Chrétien de Troyes
PERCEVAL: Or, The Story of the Grail
An accurate translation of Chrétien's greatest work, a highly original treatment of Arthurian legend
Translated by Ruth Cline
0–8203–0812–9 Georgia pb $10.00

YVAIN: The Knight of the Lion
A verse translation that admirably captures the narrative cadences of this Arthurian romance
Translated by Burton Raffel
0–300–03838–0 Yale pb $7.95

● Geoffrey de Villehardouin & Jean de Joinville
CHRONICLES OF THE CRUSADES
These chronicles, among the earliest French literary prose, remain remarkably gripping historical accounts
Translated by Margaret R. Shaw
0–14–044124–7 Penguin pb $5.95

Christine de Pisan in her study, from her book A Medieval Woman's Mirror of Honor *(Braziller)*

● François Villon
THE POEMS OF FRANCOIS VILLON
The felonious career and literary brilliance of this 15th-century rogue and vagabond calls to mind the 20th century's Jean Genet. Villon's highly personal and technically accomplished poetry has always presented a challenge to translators; Kinnell's version is outstanding
Translated by Galway Kinnell
0–87451–236–0 New England pb $9.95

● James Cable, translator
THE DEATH OF KING ARTHUR
0–14–044255–3 Penguin pb $5.95

● Norman Shapiro, translator
FABLES FROM OLD FRENCH: Aesop's Beasts and Bumpkins
Illustrated with 26 woodcuts
Introduction by Howard Needler
0–8195–5074–4 Wesleyan $26.00
0–8195–6143–6 Wesleyan pb $14.95

● Robert Harrison, translator
GALLIC SALT: Eighteen Fabliaux Translated from the Old French
Funny, bawdy tales of peasant life
0–520–02418–4 California $42.00

● Frederick Goldin, editor & translator
LYRICS OF THE TROUBADOURS AND TROUVERES: An Anthology and a History
A generous and finely translated selection of the lyrics of these balladeers, writing respectively in the *langue d'oc* of Provence and the *langue d'oïl* of the North
0–8446–5036–6 Peter Smith $16.00

● Paul Blackburn, translator
PROENSA: An Anthology of Troubador Poetry
Blackburn's superb translations invent a modern American equivalent to the diction and rhythms of the troubadours
0–520–02985–2 California $35.00

● P.M. Matarasso, translator
THE QUEST OF THE HOLY GRAIL
A cycle of journeys in which evil enchantresses lay traps for Christian knights
0–14–044220–0 Penguin pb $4.95

● Patricia Terry, translator
RENARD THE FOX: The Misadventures of an Epic Hero
This cycle of animal fables uses the sly Renard, the powerful wolf Isengrim, and other beasts to depict the classes and character types of medieval France
0–930350–48–0 Northeastern pb $11.95

● Robert Harrison, translator
THE SONG OF ROLAND
A lucid and energetic poetic translation of the great medieval epic, which tells of the death in battle of Charlemagne's commander in the Pyrenees
0–451–62623–0 NAL pb $3.95

THE RENAISSANCE

The 16th century in France was marked by a revival of interest in classical antiquity that created a climate for new ideas and a more humanistically centered world view. This new orientation manifested itself in the urbane and contemplative writings of Montaigne, Rabelais' boisterous celebration of human life, and the works of the seven poets of the Pléiade, led by Ronsard and du Bellay, who were eager to free the French language from pedantic dependence on Italian literary forms.

● Théodore-Agrippa d'Aubigné
HIS LIFE, TO HIS CHILDREN
The remarkable autobiographical work by the great Huguenot poet who died in 1630 includes a gallery of portraits ranging from queens to peasants
Translated with an introduction by John Nothnagle
0–8032–1682–3 Nebraska $20.00

● Joachim du Bellay
THE REGRETS
A sequence of poems lamenting the ruins (real and figurative) of Rome, and satirizing the corruption of the modern city, translated with flair by a contemporary British poet
Translated by C.H. Sisson
0–85635–471–6 Carcanet pb $8.50

● Michel de Montaigne
THE COMPLETE WORKS OF MONTAIGNE: Essays, Travel Journal, Letters
A sturdy and complete edition of the definitive versions
Translated by Donald M. Frame
0–8047–0484–8 Stanford $42.50

THE COMPLETE ESSAYS OF MONTAIGNE
"A perfect translation of Montaigne appears impossible, yet Donald Frame has accomplished this feat"—André Maurois, *NY Times*
Translated by Donald M. Frame
0–8047–0485–6 Stanford $35.00
0–8047–0486–4 Stanford pb $15.95

AN APOLOGY FOR RAYMOND SEBOND
A new translation of Montaigne's eloquent disquisition on human ignorance and the folly of fanaticism
Translated by M. Screech
0–14–044493–9 Penguin pb $5.95

TRAVEL JOURNAL
In 1580 Montaigne began a 17-month journey to Rome by way of Austria and Switzerland, compiling this account along the way
Translated by Donald M. Frame
Foreword by Guy Davenport
0–86547–123–1 North Point pb $11.50

● Marguerite de Navarre
THE HEPTAMERON
These 72 stories, inspired by Boccaccio's *Decameron*, range from the courtly to the ribald
Translated by Paul A. Chilton
0–14–044355–X Penguin pb $7.95

From Gustave Doré's illustrations to François Rabelais

- **François Rabelais**
GARGANTUA AND PANTAGRUEL
Rabelais drew on all levels of society to create his literary carnival. Cohen's translation does not always capture the bravura of the original but offers a faithful and complete rendering of Rabelais' full-bodied masterpiece
Translated by J.M. Cohen
0–14–044047–X Penguin pb $6.95

- **Pierre de Ronsard**
POEMS OF PIERRE DE RONSARD
"Poet royal" and leader of the Pléiade, Ronsard broadened the scope of French poetic genres with sonnets, odes, elegies, and eclogues
Translated by Nicholas Kilmer
0–520–03078–8 California $27.50

THE AGE OF CLASSICISM

The 17th century—*le grand siècle*—established the norms destined to dominate—or oppress—French literature ever after. The animated conflict between champions of creative freedom and advocates of literary dogma was eventually resolved in favor of the formal, elegant aesthetic of classicism.

No external cause or principles however, can account for the period's extraordinary procession of writers: France's three greatest dramatists, Corneille, Racine, and Molière; the first "analytical" novelist in French literature, Mme. de La Fayette; the fabulist, La Fontaine; and the mathematician and philosopher Pascal.

- **Pierre Corneille**
The father of French tragedy, rivaled only by Racine, Corneille exalts man's freedom to fashion his fate in the age-old duel between duty and inclination. Such grandeur and heroism tend to sound bombastic in English, but the translations by John Cairncross work hard to do justice to the exuberant theatricality of these dramas.
THE CID, CINNA & THE THEATRICAL ILLUSION
Two early tragedies (*The Cid* marks the true birth of French classical tragedy) and a comedy
Translated by John Cairncross
0–14–044312–6 Penguin pb $5.95

POLYEUCTUS, THE LIAR & NICOMEDES
Translated by John Cairncross
0–14–044349–5 Penguin pb $4.95

RODOGUNE
An important late work; this edition offers the French text with a facing English translation
Translated by William G. Clubb
0–8032–0501–5 Nebraska $15.50

- **Jean de La Fontaine**
THE COMPLETE FABLES
A bilingual edition; Spector's translation faithfully but somewhat laboriously attempts to duplicate the original rhymes and rhythms
Edited and translated by Norman Spector
0–8101–0759–7 Northwestern $42.95

FIFTY FABLES OF LA FONTAINE
Translated by Norman R. Shapiro
0–252–01513–4 Illinois $29.95

SELECTED FABLES
The charms and hidden depths of La Fontaine, so dependent on quicksilver shifts in tone, are resistant to translation. Michie, however, does well by the challenge
Translated by James Michie
0–14–044376–2 Penguin pb $4.95

- **Madame de La Fayette**
THE PRINCESSE DE CLEVES
This subtle and notably unsentimental work has been called the first French psychological novel, or "novel of character"
Translated by Nancy Mitford
0–14–044337–1 Penguin pb $4.95

- **La Rochefoucauld**
MAXIMS
Penetrating, acerbic aphorisms on the harsh truths of self-love, self-interest, and self-deceit
Translated by Leonard Tancock
0–14–044095–X Penguin pb $4.95

- **Molière**
The master of French high comedy, Molière appealed to many levels of sophistication and was equally skilled at classical verse and rough farce.
THE LEARNED LADIES
Wilbur's translations have made Molière accessible as never before to both readers and audiences
Translated by Richard Wilbur
0–685–81644–3 Dramatists Play Service pb $3.50

THE MISANTHROPE & OTHER PLAYS
Includes *Tartuffe, The Imaginary Invalid, The Doctor in Spite of Himself,* and *The Sicilian*
Translated by John Wood
0–14–044089–5 Penguin pb $3.50

THE MISANTHROPE & TARTUFFE
The cantankerous idealist and the religious hypocrite; invigoratingly translated
Translated by Richard Wilbur
0–15–660517–1 HBJ pb $5.95

THE MISER & OTHER PLAYS
Includes *The Would-Be Gentleman, That Scoundrel Scapin, Don Juan,* and *Love's the Best Doctor*
Translated by John Wood
0–14–044036–4 Penguin pb $3.95

THE SCHOOL FOR WIVES
A brilliant and irreverent comedy, rich in hopeless misunderstandings and indiscreet confidences
Translated by Richard Wilbur
0–15–679501–9 HBJ pb $4.95

TARTUFFE & OTHER PLAYS
Includes *Ridiculous Precieuses, School for Husbands, School for Wives, Critique for the School for Wives, Versailles Impromptu,* and *Don Juan*
Translated by Donald M. Frame
0–451–52011–4 NAL pb $3.50

- **Blaise Pascal**
PENSEES
Translated by A.J. Krailsheimer
0–14–044171–9 Penguin pb $3.95

THE PROVINCIAL LETTERS
A theological debate on Jansenism, revealing Pascal's mastery of polemic
0–14–044196–4 Penguin pb $4.95

- **Jean Racine**
Though Racine presents enormous difficulties of translation, Richard Wilbur and C.H. Sisson have recently had some notable successes.
ANDROMACHE
A new translation of Racine's first major tragedy
Translated by Richard Wilbur
0–15–607510–5 HBJ pb $6.95

ANDROMACHE & OTHER PLAYS
Also includes *Britannicus* and *Bérénice*
Translated by John Cairncross
0–14–044195–6 Penguin pb $4.95

BRITANNICUS, PHAEDRA & ATHALIAH
Translated by C.H. Sisson
0–19–281758–2 Oxford pb $3.95

PHAEDRA
A passionate drama that shocked 17th-century audiences, this profound study of adulterous love and murderous jealousy is based on Euripides' *Hippolytus*
Translated by Richard Wilbur
0–15–171731–1 HBJ $15.95
0–15–675780–X HBJ pb $5.95

PHAEDRA
More Lowell than Racine, but fascinating
Translated by Robert Lowell
0–374–95132–2 Hippocrene $12.00

PHAEDRA & OTHER PLAYS
Also includes *Iphigenia* and *Athaliah*
Translated by John Cairncross
0–14–044122–0 Penguin pb $3.95

IF YOU CAN'T FIND IT, LOOK IN THE INDEX

• Madame de Sévigné
SELECTED LETTERS
Much of our direct knowledge of social and literary life in the age of Louis XIV comes from these witty and perspicacious letters
Translated by Leonard Tancock
0–14–044405–X Penguin pb $6.95

THE ENLIGHTENMENT

The 18th century was stirred by a new spirit of scientific inquiry; and consequently much of 18th-century literature is inherently didactic, veering away from *belles lettres* toward philosophy, and from the orthodoxies of Versailles toward the more liberal, frequently libertine salons of Paris.

▶ See also Early Modern Europe & Political Thought

• Pierre-Augustin de Beaumarchais
THE BARBER OF SEVILLE & THE MARRIAGE OF FIGARO
An adventurer in life as well as art, Beaumarchais is remembered primarily for these two comedies of intrigue, with their bold strokes of social satire
0–14–044133–6 Penguin pb $4.95

From Madame de Sévigné: A Life and Letters *by Frances Mossiker (Knopf)*

• Giacomo Casanova
THE LIFE AND MEMOIRS OF CASANOVA
A one-volume abridgement of the Venetian adventurer's memoirs, originally written in French
Translated by Arthur Machen
Edited by George Gribble
Introduction by Erica Jong
0–306–80208–2 Da Capo pb $13.95

• Nicolas-Sébastien de Chamfort
PRODUCTS OF THE PERFECTED CIVILIZATION
Disenchanted observations on the lofty social circles on which the author—a

champion of the Revolution—somewhat begrudgingly relied
Translated by W.S. Merwin
0–86547–145–2 North Point pb $12.50

• Denis Diderot
Philosopher and critic, novelist and playwright, Diderot was one of the century's most influential figures. As editor of the *Encyclopédie*, he was instrumental in the popularization of science and philosophy.
JACQUES THE FATALIST AND HIS MASTER
This rambling picaresque novel is structured around the highly animated, wide-ranging dialogue between Jacques and his master
Translated by Michael Henry
0–14–044472–6 Penguin pb $4.95

THE NUN
A reluctant nun's sufferings in the cloister form the basis for a virulent condemnation of the hypocrisy of religiosity
Translated by Leonard Tancock
0–14–044300–2 Penguin pb $5.95

RAMEAU'S NEPHEW & D'ALEMBERT'S DREAM
A brilliant satire on corrupt contemporary society, and a dialogue on materialistic philosophy
0–14–044173–5 Penguin pb $6.95

• Joseph Joubert
THE NOTEBOOKS OF JOSEPH JOUBERT: A Selection
Joubert's aphorisms are more profound than witty, and foreshadow many concerns of the 19th and 20th centuries. The translation is excellent
Translated by Paul Auster
0–86547–145–2 North Point pb $12.50

1805
Those thoughts that come to us suddenly and that are not yet ours.

All things that are easy to say have already been perfectly said.

"The art is in hiding art." Yes, in everything that should resemble nature. But isn't there anything that should resemble art and therefore show itself?

To live without a body!

All these young minds the revolution has heated up and brought to flower before their time, before their age.

Joseph Joubert
THE NOTEBOOKS OF JOSEPH JOUBERT: A Selection
Translated by Paul Auster
0–86547–108–8 North Point pb $12.50

• Choderlos de Laclos
LES LIAISONS DANGEREUSES
The famous epistolary novel of systematic seduction has obviously struck a chord, to judge by its many stage and screen adaptations
Translated by P.W. Stone
0–14–044116–6 Penguin pb $5.95

• Pierre Carlet de Marivaux
SEVEN COMEDIES BY MARIVAUX
The largest single collection in English of the plays of this great comic writer, whose characters' witty, often precious banter is known as *marivaudage*
0–8191–4121–6 University Press pb $16.50

UP FROM THE COUNTRY, INFIDELITIES & THE GAME OF LOVE AND CHANCE
Up from the Country is a translation of the novel *Le Paysan Parvenu*. Also included are two of Marivaux's best comedies
Translated by Leonard Tancock
0–14–044303–7 Penguin pb $5.95

• Charles de Montesquieu
THE PERSIAN LETTERS
A satire on French institutions, thinly disguised as the observations of two Persians visiting Paris
Translated by C.J. Betts
0–14–044281–2 Penguin pb $6.95

• Abbé Prévost
MANON LESCAUT
Those who know the heroine only from the operatic versions will be surprised at the unsparing sharpness of the original character
Translated by Donald M. Frame
0–452–00654–6 NAL pb $3.50

• Jean-Jacques Rousseau
This *philosophe* shared with his colleagues a loathing of the Old Regime, yet he also opposed certain of the Enlightenment's principal tenets.
THE CONFESSIONS
The keystone of Rousseau's writings: a self-portrait preserving the author's contradictions and self-doubts
Translated by J.M. Cohen
0–14–044033–X Penguin pb $5.95

EMILE
Rousseau's treatise on education, advocating a return to nature and rural values
Translated by Allan Bloom
0–465–01931–5 Basic Books pb $14.95

LA NOUVELLE HELOISE: Julie, or The New Eloise
A portrayal of idealized conjugal fidelity set against a joyous rustic backdrop
Translated by Judith McDowell
0–271–00602–1 Pennsylvania State pb $14.95

REVERIES OF THE SOLITARY WALKER
Ten meditations on different stages in the philosopher's life
Translated by Peter France
0–14–044363–0 Penguin pb $4.95

• Marquis de Sade
JULIETTE
The alternative title—*Or the Benefits of Vice*—makes clear de Sade's advocacy in this volume written behind bars
Translated by Austryn Wainhouse
0–394–17131–4 Grove pb $14.95

JUSTINE
Includes *Philosophy in the Bedroom, Eugenie De Franval* and other writings. The

alternative title—*Or the Drawbacks of Virtue*—needs no comment
Translated by Richard Seaver & Austryn Wainhouse
Introduction by Jean Paulhan & Maurice Blanchot
0–394–17123–3 Grove pb $12.50

THE 120 DAYS OF SODOM & OTHER WRITINGS
De Sade's most notorious work
Edited by Austryn Wainhouse & Richard Seaver
0–394–17119–5 Grove pb $12.50

• Voltaire
Philosopher, poet, tragedian, and man of letters, Voltaire is the emblematic figure of his age. Unfortunately, only a small selection of his works is represented in English.

CANDIDE
This "philosophical tale" of human calamity is a satirical counterpoint to the bland optimism of Rousseau and Leibniz
Translated by John Butt
0–14–044004–6 Penguin pb $2.25

LETTERS ON ENGLAND
A witty account of English religious tolerance, political freedom, and literary and scientific genius, banned in France because of its subversive implications
Translated by Leonard Tancock
0–14–044386–X Penguin pb $5.95

PHILOSOPHICAL DICTIONARY
Principally a mordant onslaught on religious dogma
Translated by Theodore Besterman
0–14–044257–X Penguin pb $6.95

THE PORTABLE VOLTAIRE
Including *Candide* (Part 1), *Zadig*, *Micromegas*, *The Story of a Good Brahmin*, selections from the *Philosophical Dictionary*, *The English Letters*, *The Lisbon Earthquake*, *Essay on the Manners and Spirit of Nations*, and 35 selected letters
Edited by Ben R. Redman
0–14–015041–2 Penguin pb $7.95

ZADIG & L'INGENU
Two "philosophical tales," the first hitting out at the clergy and Catholic dogma, the second a thinly veiled attack on the powers-that-be
Translated by John Butt
0–14–044126–3 Penguin pb $3.95

THE 19TH CENTURY: Romanticism and Realism

The period following the Napoleonic era saw the novel come into its own as an instrument for registering social upheaval. A radical change in direction was signaled by the extreme subjectivity and rich rhetoric of Romanticism; unfortunately, such leading figures as Chateaubriand remain inaccessible in English translation.

Balzac by Félix Vallotton

• Honoré de Balzac
Balzac's is a literature of vigorous documentation and powerful obsession, moving from dreamlike melodrama to drab photorealism and forming one of the great exceptions to the French tradition of concision and balance. *La Comédie humaine*, with its cast of thousands, written over the best part of a decade, must be viewed as a whole to be fully appreciated.

THE BLACK SHEEP
Two brothers struggle over an inheritance
Translated by Donald Adamson
0–14–044237–5 Penguin pb $5.95

THE CHOUANS
An early, highly Romantic novel of antirevolutionary guerrilla warfare in Brittany
0–14–044260–X Penguin pb $5.95

COUSIN BETTE
The celebrated study of the tumult ensuing from unbridled jealousy and licentiousness
Translated by Marion Crawford
0–14–044160–3 Penguin pb $4.95

COUSIN PONS
A classic portrait of the "poor relation"
Translated by Herbert Hunt
0–14–044205–7 Penguin pb $5.95

EUGENIE GRANDET
The colorful study of a rich miser and the almost improbable goodness of his daughter
Translated by Marion Crawford
0–14–044050–X Penguin pb $4.95

A HARLOT HIGH AND LOW
A swirling, intrigue-ridden panorama of Parisian life, embracing the worlds of high finance and low crime, and dominated by the sinister figure of Vautrin
Translated by Rayner Heppenstall
0–14–044232–4 Penguin pb $5.95

HISTORY OF THE THIRTEEN
These "Scenes of Parisian Life," loosely linked by the activities of a powerful secret society, include *Farragus*, *The Duchess of Langeais*, and *The Girl with the Golden Eyes*
Translated by Herbert Hunt
0–14–044301–0 Penguin pb $5.95

THE LILY OF THE VALLEY
0–88184–482–9 Carroll & Graf pb $9.95

LOST ILLUSIONS
A provincial poet attempts to rise in Parisian high society in this relentlessly detailed account of the French publishing world at its seamiest
Translated by Herbert Hunt
0–14–044251–0 Penguin pb $6.95

> Only a few devotees, people who never walk along in heedless inattention, sip and savour their Paris and are so familiar with its physiognomy that they know its every wart, every spot or blotch on its face. For all others, Paris is still the same monstrous miracle, an astounding assemblage of movements, machines and ideas, the city of a thousand different romances, the world's thinking-box. But, for the devotees, Paris is sad or gay, ugly or beautiful, living or dead; for them Paris is a sentient being; every individual, every bit of a house is a lobe in the cellular tissue of that great harlot whose head, heart and unpredictable behaviour are perfectly familiar to them.
>
> Honoré de Balzac
> **HISTORY OF THE THIRTEEN**
> Translated by Herbert Hunt
> 0–14–044301–0 Penguin pb $5.95

A MURKY BUSINESS
Political intrigue in the Napoleonic era
0–14–044271–5 Penguin pb $4.95

OLD GORIOT
The poignant and Lear-like tale of ungrateful daughters and the thanklessness of parental sacrifice
Translated by Marion Crawford
0–14–044017–8 Penguin pb $3.95

THE RISE AND FALL OF CESAR BIROTTEAU
A scent-merchant falls prey to dreams of wealth and pomp—and the nightmare of debt. "A study in morals, the picture of a world which Balzac knew from top to bottom because he came from it"—André Maurois
Translated by Francis Furey
0–88184–448–9 Carroll & Graf pb $8.95

SELECTED SHORT STORIES
Includes "A Study in Feminine Psychology," "An Incident in the Reign of Terror," "The Atheists' Mass," and nine others
Translated and edited by Sylvia Raphael
0–14–044325–8 Penguin pb $4.95

URSULE MIROUET
A novel demonstrating Balzac's deep involvement in occult lore
Translated by Donald Adamson
0–14–044316–9 Penguin pb $4.95

THE WILD ASS'S SKIN
A Faustian tale of magic and damnation, set against a backdrop of garrets and gambling halls
Translated by Herbert Hunt
0–14–044330–4 Penguin pb $5.95

TO ORDER BOOKS AS GIFTS, SEE PAGE 1

- Benjamin Constant

ADOLPHE
Although his work is classical in style, Constant gave the Romantic age an idealized image of itself in his portrait of the self-doubting, world-weary Adolphe
Translated by Leonard Tancock
0–14–044134–4 Penguin pb $4.95

- François-René de Chateaubriand

ATALA & RENE
These Romanticized novellas of American Indian life (which the author had observed at first hand) give only a small idea of Chateaubriand's talents
Translated by Irving Putter
0–520–00223–7 California pb $8.95

- Alexandre Dumas

This most popular Romantic novelist ran a veritable writing factory, producing some 1,200 works of fiction.

CASTLE EPPSTEIN
Translated by Norma Lorre Goodrich
0–531–15102–6 Watts $19.95

THE COUNT OF MONTE CRISTO
The definitive melodrama of revenge
Illustrated by Mead Schaeffer
0–396–08255–6 Dodd, Mead $13.95

THE THREE MUSKETEERS
Countless movie versions later, Dumas' great adventure novel remains fresh and often startling
0–14–044025–9 Penguin pb $5.95

- Alexandre Dumas fils

LA DAME AUX CAMELIAS
This tale of doomed love is important if only for the material it provided for Verdi and Garbo
Translated by David Coward
0–19–281736–1 Oxford pb $5.95

- Théophile Gautier

MADEMOISELLE DE MAUPIN
A poet's novel, with an ample share of exotic and erotic elements. The sensuous descriptions of physical beauty caused a scandal
Translated with an introduction by Joanna Richardson
0–14–044398–3 Penguin pb $4.95

- Victor Hugo

The grand old man of the Romantic movement embarked at an early age on his prolific literary career, which spanned almost the entire 19th century.

THE DISTANCE, THE SHADOWS
A selection of Hugo's poetry
Translated by Harry Guest
0–85646–068–0 Longwood pb $12.95

LES MISERABLES
Hugo's immense, powerful novel is one of the century's most representative creations; Denny's excellent translation trims a few marginal passages
Translated by Norman Denny
0–14–044430–0 Penguin pb $8.95

LES MISERABLES
A complete translation revised from an 1863 edition
0–451–52157–9 NAL pb $6.95

NINETY-THREE
A novel of the counterrevolutionary Vendée uprising
0–88184–405–5 Carroll & Graf pb $8.95

NOTRE-DAME OF PARIS
The hunchback Quasimodo, the gypsy Esmeralda, and the sinister priest Frollo are set against the minutely drawn tumult of medieval Paris
0–14–044353–3 Penguin pb $5.95

- Jules Michelet

Michelet, the great Romantic historian, used magnificent, unrestrained rhetoric and picturesque narrative in his evocations of the past.

HISTORY OF THE FRENCH REVOLUTION
Michelet's account expresses his fiercely democratic sympathies
Translated by Charles Cocks
Edited with an introduction by Gordon Wright
0–226–52333–0 Chicago pb $14.95

JOAN OF ARC
Translated by Albert Guerard
0–472–06122–4 Michigan pb $6.95

THE PEOPLE
Translated with an introduction by John McKay
0–252–00321–7 Illinois $19.50
0–252–00331–4 Illinois $9.95

SATANISM AND WITCHCRAFT
In effect, a long prose poem on the darker side of the Middle Ages as distilled through a Romantic consciousness
0–8065–0059–X Lyle Stuart pb $5.95

- Henri Murger

LA BOHEME
The 1851 novel on which Puccini based his opera
Translated by Elizabeth W. Hugus
0–87905–335–6 Peregrine Smith pb $10.95

- Charles-Augustin Sainte-Beuve

LITERARY CRITICISM OF SAINTE-BEUVE
Rigorous intellectual discipline sets Sainte-Beuve apart from most of his contemporaries
Edited by Emerson Marks
0–8032–0465–5 Nebraska $16.95

- Jacques-Henri Bernardin de Saint-Pierre

PAUL AND VIRGINIA
0–14–044546–3 Penguin pb $5.95

- George Sand

Sand's reputation is now being reevaluated in light of feminist criticism; and her novels, long unavailable, are again finding many readers.

CONSUELO: A Romance of Vienna
A sentimental account of a gypsy chanteuse who passes through many dangers
0–306–80102–7 Da Capo pb $8.95

THE HAUNTED POOL
Sand's masterpiece, a tale of country life, revealing her love of nature
Translated by Frank Potter
Afterword by Alta
0–915288–26–5 Shameless Hussy pb $5.95

INDIANA
A beautiful Creole flees a sadistic husband
Translated by George Ives
0–915864–57–6 Academy Chicago pb $8.95

THE INTIMATE JOURNAL
Translated by Marie Howe
0–915864–50–9 Academy Chicago pb $6.95

LAVINIA
Translated by George Ives
Afterword by Daniel Skarry
0–915288–28–1 Shameless Hussy pb $2.95

LEONE LEONI
Translated by George Ives
0–915864–61–4 Academy Chicago pb $5.95

LETTRES D'UN VOYAGEUR
An account of Sand's liaison with Musset, including their visit to Italy
Translated by Sacha Rabinovitch
0–14–044411–4 Penguin pb $6.95

LUCREZIA FLORIANI
Translated by Julius Eker
0–89733–143–5 Academy Chicago $16.95

MAUPRAT
A cruel brute is transformed by the power of love
Translated by Stanley Young
0–915864–43–6 Academy Chicago pb $8.95

MY CONVENT LIFE
Translated by Maria McKaye
0–915864–38–X Academy Chicago pb $6.95

- Stendhal

Barely appreciated in his own lifetime, Stendhal evolved a style combining elegant aphorism and realistic psychological description.

THE CHARTERHOUSE OF PARMA
A novel of intrigue at the court of Parma in the early 19th century
Translated by M.R. Shaw
0–14–044061–5 Penguin pb $5.95

Stendhal by Vallotton

THE LIFE OF HENRY BRULARD
A thinly disguised autobiography, posthumously published, that details the author's bitterly unhappy youth
Translated by Jean Stewart
0–226–77251–9 Chicago $12.95

LOVE
An amusingly ironical study of that "malady of the soul" called love
Translated by Gilbert & Suzanne Sale
0–14–044307–X Penguin pb $6.95

ON LOVE
"Love for Stendhal, as for Proust, is nine-tenths imagination, a leap into the feverish secrecy of the mind with a name and a pretty face as a pretext . . . [On Love] is almost always delicate, often brilliant, a book to keep quoting from"—Michael Wood
Translated by C. Scott Moncrieff
0–306–80194–9 Da Capo pb $10.95

MEMOIRS OF A TOURIST
Translated by Allan Seager
Illustrated by Roger Barr
0–8101–0707–4 Northwestern pb $12.95

THE PINK AND THE GREEN
An unfinished novel, published in English for the first time. This edition also includes the story *Mina de Vanghel*
Translated with an afterword by Richard Howard
0–8112–1062–6 New Directions $17.95

SCARLET AND BLACK
An excellent translation of *Le Rouge et le Noir*, Stendhal's most celebrated book, notable for its portrait of the frustrated rebel Julien Sorel and the post-Napoleonic conformity that oppresses him
Translated by Margaret Shaw
0–14–044030–5 Penguin pb $3.95

● Eugène Sue
THE MYSTERIES OF PARIS
Sue's melodramatic novel of the Parisian underworld was enormously popular and influential
0–94662–6308–8 Dedalus pb $9.95

THE LATER 19TH CENTURY: Symbolism, Naturalism, and the Roots of Modernism

With the later 19th century we are on familiar ground. The great writers—Baudelaire, Flaubert, Mallarmé, Rimbaud—are very much a part of our own world; indeed, they played a major part in creating it.

● Charles Baudelaire
Baudelaire's verse technique was classical, but his themes and point of view could not have been less so. He defined the role of the modern poet, even as he railed against the modern age.
SELECTED POEMS
Translated by Geoffrey Wagner
0–394–17831–9 Grove pb $2.95

LES FLEURS DU MAL
This widely praised translation of the complete text won the American Book Award in 1983. Bilingual edition
Translated by Richard Howard
0–87923–425–3 Godine $25.00
0–87923–462–8 Godine pb $15.95

THE FLOWERS OF EVIL
A selection by a variety of translators. Bilingual edition
Edited by Jackson & Marthiel Mathews
0–8112–0006–X New Directions pb $5.95

PARIS SPLEEN
Prose poems of the metropolis
Translated by Louise Varese
0–8112–0007–8 New Directions pb $4.95

TWENTY PROSE POEMS
A bilingual edition
Translated with an introduction by Michael Hamburger
0–87286–216–X City Lights pb $4.95

INTIMATE JOURNALS
Translated by Christopher Isherwood
Introduction by T.S. Eliot
0–87286–146–5 City Lights pb $4.95

LA FANFARLO
Baudelaire's only novella, based on his complicated relationship with his mistress, Jeanne Duval. A bilingual edition
Translated by Greg Boyd
0–88739–003–X Creative Arts pb $6.95

SELECTED WRITINGS ON ART AND ARTISTS
Includes pieces in support of such figures as Courbet, Corot, and Manet before they found acceptance
Translated by P.E. Charvet
0–521–28287–X Cambridge pb $23.95

ART IN PARIS, 1845–1862: Reviews of Salons and Other Exhibitions
Edited by Jonathan Mayne
0–8014–9227–0 Cornell pb $14.95

THE PAINTER OF MODERN LIFE & OTHER ESSAYS
Edited by Jonathan Mayne
0–306–80279–1 Da Capo pb $11.95

BAUDELAIRE AS A LITERARY CRITIC
Translated by Lois Hyslop & Francis Hyslop, Jr.
0–271–73051–X Pennsylvania State $27.50

BAUDELAIRE ON POE: Critical Papers
Baudelaire's intense identification with Poe blossomed in a series of complex essays and brilliant translations
Translated by Lois Hyslop & Francis Hyslop, Jr.
0–271–00317–0 Pennsylvania State $19.75

SELECTED LETTERS OF CHARLES BAUDELAIRE: The Conquest of Solitude
"Unable to excel in virtue, he made himself a legend in vice"—Morris Bishop
Translated and edited by Rosemary Lloyd
0–226–03928–5 Chicago $24.95

● Georges Feydeau
Feydeau's genius for plot construction has given his lively farces remarkable durability.
FEYDEAU, FIRST TO LAST: Eight One-Act Comedies
Translated by Norman Shapiro
0–8014–9271–8 Cornell pb $9.95

FOUR FARCES
Includes *Wooed and Viewed, On the Merry-Go-Wrong, Not by Bed Alone,* and *Going to Pot*
Translated and edited by Norman Shapiro
0–226–24477–6 Chicago pb $9.95

THREE BOULEVARD FARCES
Includes *A Little Hotel on the Side, A Flea in Her Ear,* and *The Lady from Maxim's*
Translated by John Mortimer
0–14–048191–5 Penguin pb $5.95

● Gustave Flaubert
"Flaubert's aloof, melancholic temperament caused some of the bleakness of his vision, as any writer's negations or affirmations owe something to his temperament. Yet the bleakness is also inherent in an Old World skepticism concerning human nature as manifested in society, the only form in which human nature can be known."—F.W. Dupee

BOUVARD AND PECUCHET
A satirical epic, never completed, of two retired clerks who uncomprehendingly traverse the entire realm of 19th-century thought and experience
Translated by A.J. Krailsheimer
0–14–044320–7 Penguin pb $5.95

THE DICTIONARY OF ACCEPTED IDEAS
Flaubert's extraordinary catalog of clichés and banalities was intended as part of the unfinished *Bouvard and Pecuchet,* to which it now forms a sort of addendum
Translated by Jaques Barzun
0–8112–0054–X New Directions pb $5.95

ABELARD. No need to have any notion of his philosophy, nor even to know the titles of his works. Just refer discreetly to his mutilation by Fulbert. The grave of Abelard and Heloise: if someone tells you it is apocryphal, exclaim: "You rob me of my illusions!"

ABSINTHE. Extra-violent poison: one glass and you're dead. Newspapermen drink it as they write their copy. Has killed more soldiers than the Bedouin.

ACCIDENT. Always "regrettable" or "unlucky"—as if a mishap might sometimes be a cause for rejoicing.

ACTRESSES. The ruin of young men of good family. Are fearfully lascivious; engage in "nameless orgies"; run through fortunes; end in the poorhouse. "I beg to differ, sir: some are excellent mothers!"

AFFAIRS (BUSINESS). Come first. A woman must not refer to hers. The most important thing in life. Be-all and end-all.

AIR. Beware of drafts of air. The depths of the air are invariably unlike the surface. If the former are warm, the latter is cold, and vice versa.

Gustave Flaubert
THE DICTIONARY OF ACCEPTED IDEAS
Translated by Jacques Barzun
0–8112–0054–X New Directions pb $5.95

THE FIRST SENTIMENTAL EDUCATION
Translated by Douglas Garman
0–520–01967–9 California $31.00

FLAUBERT IN EGYPT
A compilation of Flaubert's travel notes and letters from his Egyptian journey of 1849–50. "By turns beautiful, rapturous, bawdy, hideous and brutal . . . also from time to time quite funny"—William Styron
Edited and translated by Francis Steegmuller
0–89733–018–8 Academy Chicago pb $6.95

MADAME BOVARY
Flaubert's meticulous, superbly controlled study of the romantic reveries and less-than-romantic adventures of a provincial doctor's wife
Translated by Alan Russell
0–14–044015–1 Penguin pb $2.95

MADAME BOVARY
Steegmuller's is generally acknowledged to be the finest English translation of Flaubert's masterpiece
Translated by Francis Steegmuller
0–394–60460–1 Modern Library $8.95
0–394–32986–4 Random House pb $4.00

NOVEMBER
A short coming-of-age novel
0–88184–334–2 Carroll & Graf pb $7.95

SALAMMBO
Flaubert's penchant for decadent Romanticism emerges in full splendor in this violent and erotic novel of Carthage
Translated by A.J. Krailsheimer
0–14–044328–2 Penguin pb $4.95

THE SENTIMENTAL EDUCATION
"If one rereads it in middle age, one finds that the author's tone no longer seems quite so acrid, that one is listening to a muted symphony of which the varied instrumentation and the pattern, the marked rhythms and the melancholy sonorities, had been hardly perceptible before. There are no hero, no villain, to arouse us, no clowns to entertain us, no scenes to wring our hearts. Yet the effect is deeply moving"—Edmund Wilson
Translated by Robert Baldick
0–14–044141–7 Penguin pb $3.95

THE TEMPTATION OF SAINT ANTHONY
A fluid dramatization of the anchorite's ordeal in the desert; Flaubert displays his pedantic knowledge with great gusto
Translated by Kitty Mrosovsky
0–8014–1239–0 Cornell $29.95
0–14–044410–6 Penguin pb $5.95

THREE TALES
Includes *A Simple Heart, The Legend of Saint Julian Hospitalor* and *Herodias:* three very different examples of Flaubert's skill in narrative
Translated by Robert Baldick
0–14–044106–9 Penguin pb $3.95

THE LETTERS OF GUSTAVE FLAUBERT
Translated and edited by Francis Steegmuller

Volume 1: 1830–1857
0–674–52636–8 Harvard $20.00
0–674–52637–6 Harvard $6.95

Volume 2: 1857–1880
0–674–52640–6 Harvard $20.00

• J.K. Huysmans
AGAINST NATURE
A textbook of decadence (sometimes translated as *Against the Grain*), with a somewhat cheerless aftertaste
Translated by Robert Baldick
0–14–044086–0 Penguin pb $4.95

LA BAS
This largely autobiographical work charts the progress of a young man embracing Catholicism after a skirmish with Satanism
0–946626–19–7 Hippocrene pb $7.95

• Eugène Labiche
A prolific producer of farce and burlesque
THE ITALIAN STRAW HAT
Includes *Spelling Mistakes*
Translated by Frederick Davies
0–87830–543–2 Theatre Arts pb $3.50

A SLAP IN THE FARCE
Includes *A Matter of Wife and Death*
Translated by Norman Shapiro
0–936839–82–1 Theatre Arts pb $5.95

• Jules Laforgue
MORAL TALES
Elaborately composed satirical versions of old stories, including a parody of Flaubert's *Herodias*
Translated by William Jay Smith
0–8112–0943–1 New Directions pb $8.95

THE POEMS OF JULES LAFORGUE
Laforgue's *vers libre,* slangy and sardonic, had great influence on the work of Ezra Pound and T.S. Eliot
Translated by Peter Dale
0–85646–145–8 Longwood $32.00

• Lautréamont
MALDOROR & POEMS
Lautréamont's hallucinatory prose poems were hailed by the Surrealists as precursors of automatic writing
0–14–044342–8 Penguin pb $6.95

• Pierre Loti
MADAM CHRYSANTHEMUM
Loti describes Japanese life in his patented vein of richly colored exoticism
Translated by Laura Ensor
0–7103–0138–3 RC&H pb $14.95

THE MARRIAGE OF LOTI
A romance of the South Pacific
Translated by Clara Bell
0–7103–0231–2 RC&H pb $12.95

• Pierre Loüys
THE SONGS OF BILITIS
In an Ossianic literary hoax, Loüys claimed that these prose poems were translated from a Greek poetess contemporary with Sappho
0–486–25670–7 Dover pb $5.95

• Stéphane Mallarmé
"Hero, prophet, magus, and tragedian, it was fitting that this feminine little man, discreet and not much drawn to women, should die on the brink of our century: he announces it. More and better than Nietzsche, he lived the Death of God; well before Camus, he realized that suicide is the primary question that man must ask himself; his daily battle against chance will be taken up by others, but none will surpass his lucidity. For in essence he asked himself: Can one find, within determinism, a means by which to exit from it?"—Jean-Paul Sartre

Mallarmé by Vallotton

SELECTED POEMS
The abstraction and musicality of Mallarmé's poetry make it border on the untranslatable. This older edition has the French text on facing pages
Translated by C.F. MacIntyre
0–520–00801–4 California pb $6.95

SELECTED POETRY AND PROSE
Relatively literal newer versions, with French text
Edited with an introduction by Mary Ann Caws
0–8112–0822–2 New Directions pb $6.95

A TOMB FOR ANATOLE
Mallarmé's uncompleted work on the death of his son. "Auster's translation is accurate and faithful"—*Choice*
Translated by Paul Auster
0–86547–135–5 North Point pb $13.50

To Leo d'Orfer
27 June 1884
It's a real punch, momentarily blinding, that abrupt demand of yours: "Define Poetry." Bruised, I stutter:
Poetry is the expression, in human language restored to its essential rhythm, of the mysterious meaning of the aspects of existence: in this way it confers authenticity on our time on earth and constitutes the only spiritual task there is.
Farewell, but you owe me an apology.

Stephane Mallarmé
SELECTED LETTERS OF STEPHANE MALLARME
Edited and translated by Rosemary Lloyd
0–226–48841–1 Chicago $27.50

• Guy de Maupassant
BEL-AMI
A journalist fights and inveigles his way to the top of Parisian society
Translated by Douglas Parmee
0–14–044315–0 Penguin pb $5.95

PIERRE AND JEAN
Considered his best novel. A preface sets out Maupassant's concept of the novelist's function and describes the instruction received from his mentor, Flaubert
Translated by Leonard Tancock
0–14–044358–4 Penguin pb $4.95

SELECTED SHORT STORIES
Maupassant's reputation is linked to his
mastery of the *conte*
Translated by Roger Colet
0–14–044243–X Penguin pb $4.95

SELECTED STORIES
Translated by Andrew MacAndrew
Introduction by Edward Sullivan
0–452–00686–4 NAL pb $4.95

A WOMAN'S LIFE
Depicts a woman's lonely life in
Normandy, the author's home ground
Translated by H.N. Sloman
0–14–044161–1 Penguin pb $4.95

● Gérard de Nerval
THE CHIMERAS
A sensitive and painstaking rendering of
the twelve celebrated sonnets, written a
year before Nerval's suicide
Translated by Peter Jay
0–933806–34–5 Black Swan $17.50

JOURNEY TO THE ORIENT
A lively midcentury travelogue
Translated by Norman Glass
0–918825–09–1 Moyer Bell pb $6.95

● Arthur Rimbaud
"No one else has ever had the faith, the
hope, and the lack of charity to attack
poetry the way Rimbaud did. No one else
with so much strength and intelligence has
ever had the innocence to take all of its
most extravagant claims with complete
seriousness. Rimbaud tried to do to and
with poetry what others only pretended
. . . to be able to do. Poetry has never
recovered. To say it has never been the
same since is not slang, but simple fact"—
Kenneth Rexroth

COMPLETE WORKS
"Schmidt has tackled poems, prose and
letters. He has adopted a new and
persuasive chronological arrangement of
the work. And he has nimbly compressed
the life of the poet into engaging prefaces
for each of the eight 'seasons' "—Raymond
Sokolov
Translated by Paul Schmidt
0–06–090490–9 Harper & Row pb $7.95

Rimbaud by Vallotton

**COMPLETE WORKS WITH SELECTED
LETTERS**
Translated by Wallace Fowlie
0–226–71973–1 Chicago pb $10.95

COLLECTED POEMS
Translated by Oliver Bernard
0–14–042064–9 Penguin pb $6.95

ILLUMINATIONS
Rimbaud's prose poems, compressed and
infinitely suggestive, have exerted
extraordinary influence on 20th-century
poetics
0–8112–0184–8 New Directions pb $5.95

A SEASON IN HELL
Also includes the long poem *The Drunken
Boat*
Translated by Louise Varese
0–8112–0185–6 New Directions pb $4.95

**A SEASON IN HELL &
ILLUMINATIONS**
Translated by Enid Peschel
Introduction by Henri Peyre
0–19–501727–7 Oxford $18.95
0–19–501760–9 Oxford pb $8.95

A Poet makes himself a visionary through
a long, boundless, and systematized
disorganization of *all the senses.* All forms
of love, of suffering, of madness; he
searches himself, he exhausts within himself all poisons, and preserves their quin-
tessences. Unspeakable torment, where
he will need the greatest faith, a superhuman strength, where he becomes
among all men the great invalid, the
great criminal, the great accursed—and
the Supreme Scientist! For he attains the
unknown! Because he has cultivated his
soul, already rich, more than anyone! He
attains the unknown, and if, demented,
he finally loses the understanding of his
visions, he will at least have seen them!
So what if he is destroyed in his ecstatic
flight through things unheard of, un-
nameable: other horrible workers will
come; they will begin at the horizons
where the first one has fallen!

Letter to Paul Demeny, May 15, 1871 in

Arthur Rimbaud
COMPLETE WORKS
Translated by Paul Schmidt
0–06–090490–9 Harper & Row pb $7.95

● Marcel Schwob
THE KING IN THE GOLDEN MASK
Steeped in the exotic and the decadent,
Schwob's stories meditate on strange
moments in history. This excellent
collection includes his masterful *The
Children's Crusade*
Translated by Iain White
0–85635–403–1 Carcanet $14.95
0–85635–579–8 Carcanet pb $6.50

● Paul Verlaine
SELECTED POEMS
Bilingual edition
Translated by C.F. MacIntyre
0–520–01298–4 California pb $7.95

CONFESSIONS OF A POET
An account of his early life, including his
encounter and liasion with Rimbaud
Translated by Joanna Richardson
0–88355–875–0 Hyperion $19.75

● Jules Verne
Verne was a varied and profound writer
whose obsession with scientific,
geographical, and political information
combines with a capacity for broad and
potent—and often unconscious—
symbolism.

**AROUND THE WORLD IN EIGHTY
DAYS**
Translated by George Towle
0–553–21145–5 Bantam pb $2.25

THE FUR COUNTRY
Translated by Edward Baxter
0–920053–82–3 Toronto pb $12.95

**A JOURNEY TO THE CENTER OF THE
EARTH**
Verne's first great popular success describes
a geological descent that takes on
dreamlike fascination
0–451–51982–5 NAL pb $2.75

THE MYSTERIOUS ISLAND
Captain Nemo's last stand
0–451–52066–1 NAL pb $2.50

**TWENTY THOUSAND LEAGUES
UNDER THE SEA**
Captain Nemo is a diabolical,
technologized counterpart to the Count of
Monte Cristo; Verne's complex attitude
toward his hero-villain gives the book its
power
0–14–035053–5 Penguin pb $2.25

● Villiers de l'Isle-Adam
CRUEL TALES
Good examples of the horror genre
Edited by A.W. Raitt
Translated by Robert Baldick
0–19–281696–9 Oxford pb $5.95

TOMORROW'S EVE
This curious novel, a semiscientific vision
of the future written by a reactionary's
reactionary, includes Thomas Edison
among its characters
Translated by Robert Adams
0–252–00942–8 Illinois $22.95

● Emile Zola
Zola created in his fiction a huge canvas
upon which he depicts the duel between
traditional and "modern" culture.

**THE ATTACK ON THE MILL & OTHER
STORIES**
Includes *The Way People Die, Dead Men
Tell No Tales, Priests and Sinners,* and
others
Edited by Douglas Parmee
0–19–281695–7 Oxford pb $6.95

THE DEBACLE
A novel of the Franco-Prussian War
Translated by Leonard Tancock
0–14–044280–4 Penguin pb $5.95

THE EARTH
The extremely Naturalistic focus here is on
the grimmer aspects of peasant existence
Translated by Douglas Parmee
0–14–044387–8 Penguin pb $5.95

GERMINAL
Zola's most celebrated work, depicting a
failed strike, is deeply informed by his
sympathies
Translated by Leonard Tancock
0–14–044045–3 Penguin pb $3.95

➤ **FOR OVERSEAS ORDERING INFORMATION, SEE PAGE 1**

Zola by Vallotton

L'ASSOMMOIR
A vivid portrait of working-class life
0–14–044231–6 Penguin pb $5.95

THE MASTERPIECE
The central character was modeled on
Cézanne—for which the painter never
forgave Zola
0–472–06145–3 Michigan pb $8.95

NANA
This tale of a call-girl permits Zola to delve
into the seamy side of Second Empire
society
Translated by George Holden
0–14–044263–4 Penguin pb $5.95

THE SIN OF FATHER MOURET
Priestly temptation and self-betrayal
Translated by Sandy Petrey
0–8032–4902–0 Nebraska $24.50
0–8032–9901–X Nebraska pb $7.50

THERESE RAQUIN
A powerful early Realist novel of relentless
passion, culminating in a lovers' joint
suicide
Translated by Leonard Tancock
0–14–044120–4 Penguin pb $4.95

ANTHOLOGIES

• Morris Bishop
SURVEY OF FRENCH LITERATURE
Volume 1: The Middle Ages to 1800
0–15–584963–8 HBJ $22.95
Volume 2: The 19th and 20th Centuries
0–15–584964–6 HBJ $22.95

• Domna Stanton, editor
**THE DEFIANT MUSE: French Feminist
Poems from the Middle Ages to the Present**
A bilingual anthology
0–935312–52–8 Feminist Press pb $11.95

• Eric Bentley, editor
**THE MISANTHROPE & OTHER
FRENCH CLASSICS**
Includes Racine's *Phaedra*, Corneille's *The
Cid*, and Beaumarchais *Figaro's Marriage*,
in well-chosen translations
0–936839–19–8 Applause pb $7.95

• Stephen S. Stanton, editor
CAMILLE & OTHER PLAYS
Includes Augustin Scribe's *A Peculiar
Position* and *The Glass of Water*, Victorien
Sardou's *A Scrap of Paper*, and *Olympe's
Marriage* by Emile Augier
0–8090–0706–1 Hill & Wang pb $9.95

CRITICAL STUDIES

• Paul Harvey & Janet E. Heseltine,
editors
**THE OXFORD COMPANION TO
FRENCH LITERATURE**
0–19–866104–5 Oxford $49.95

• Joyce M. Reid, editor
**THE CONCISE OXFORD DICTIONARY
OF FRENCH LITERATURE**
0–19–866118–5 Oxford $24.95
0–19–281200–9 Oxford pb $12.95

• Morris Bishop
THE MIDDLE AGES
0–317–40578–0 Houghton Mifflin pb $9.95

• Lynette R. Muir
**LITERATURE AND SOCIETY IN
MEDIEVAL FRANCE: The Mirror and the
Image 1100–1500**
0–312–48748–7 St. Martin's $29.95

• Geoffroy Atkinson & Abraham Keller
**PRELUDE TO THE ENLIGHTENMENT:
French Literature, 1690–1740**
0–295–95082–X Washington $20.00

• James Allen
**POPULAR FRENCH ROMANTICISM:
Authors, Readers, and Books in the 19th
Century**
0–8156–2232–5 Syracuse $20.00

• Henri Peyre
WHAT IS ROMANTICISM?
Translated by Roda Roberts
0–8173–7003–X Alabama $15.50

• Harry Levin
**THE GATES OF HORN: A Study of Five
French Realists**
0–19–500620–8 Oxford $27.50
0–19–500727–1 Oxford pb $12.95

• Victor Brombert
**THE HIDDEN READER: Stendhal,
Balzac, Hugo, Baudelaire, Flaubert**
0–674–39012–1 Harvard $27.50

• Roger L. Williams
**THE HORROR OF LIFE: Charles
Baudelaire, Jules de Goncourt, Gustave
Flaubert, Guy de Maupassant, Alphonse
Daudet**
0–226–89919–5 Chicago pb $12.95

• Anna Balakian
**THE SYMBOLIST MOVEMENT: A
Critical Appraisal**
0–8147–0994–X NYU pb $16.50

Individual Writers
(alphabetical by subject)

• André Maurois
PROMETHEUS: The Life of Balzac
0–88184–023–8 Carroll & Graf pb $11.95

• Roland Barthes
S–Z
A scrupulous literary analysis of *Sarrasine*,
a short story by Balzac
Translated by Richard Miller
0–8090–1377–0 Hill & Wang pb $7.95

• Jean-Paul Sartre
BAUDELAIRE
Translated by Martin Turnell
0–8112–0189–9 New Directions pb $6.95

• Enid Starkie
BAUDELAIRE
1–55778–003–X Paragon pb $12.95

• Martin Turnell
BAUDELAIRE: A Study of His Poetry
0–8112–0212–7 New Directions pb $3.45

• Arthur M. Wilson
DIDEROT
0–19–501506–1 Oxford $45.00

• Jean-Paul Sartre
**THE FAMILY IDIOT: Gustave Flaubert,
1821–1857**
Translated by Carol Cosman
Volume 1:
0–226–73509–5 Chicago $25.00
Volume 2:
0–226–73510–9 Chicago $27.50

• Francis Steegmuller
**FLAUBERT AND MADAME BOVARY: A
Double Portrait**
0–226–77137–7 Chicago pb $5.95

• Barbara Beaumont, editor
**FLAUBERT AND TURGENEV: A
Friendship in Letters—The Complete
Correspondence**
0–393–02206–4 Norton $19.95

• Jonathan Culler
FLAUBERT: The Uses of Uncertainty
0–8014–9305–6 Cornell pb $12.95

• Mario Vargas Llosa
**THE PERPETUAL ORGY: Flaubert and
Madame Bovary**
0–374–23077–3 Farrar, Straus & Giroux $17.95
0–374–52062–3 Farrar, Straus & Giroux pb $8.95

• Henri Peyre
VICTOR HUGO: Philosophy and Poetry
Translated by Roda Roberts
0–8173–0017–1 Alabama $14.00

• David Arkell
**LOOKING FOR LAFORGUE: An
Informal Biography of Jules Laforgue**
0–89255–042–2 Persea $20.00

• Leo Bersani
**THE DEATH OF STEPHANE
MALLARME**
0–521–23863–3 Cambridge $22.95

- Wallace Fowlie
MALLARME
0–226–25881–5 Chicago pb $2.45

- Austin Gill
THE EARLY MALLARME: Parentage, Early Years and Juvenilia
0–19–815726–6 Oxford $39.95

- Jean-Paul Sartre
MALLARME, OR THE POET OF NOTHINGNESS
Translated by Ernest Sturm
0–271–00498–3 Pennsylvania State $22.50

- Roland Barthes
MICHELET
Translated by Richard Howard
0–8090–1535–8 Hill & Wang pb $8.95

- Mikhail Bulgakov
THE LIFE OF MONSIEUR DE MOLIERE
Translated by Mirra Ginsburg
0–8112–0984–9 New Directions $17.95
0–8112–0956–3 New Directions pb $9.95

- Peter Burke
MONTAIGNE
0–19–287522–2 Oxford pb $3.95

- Donald Frame
MONTAIGNE: A Biography
0–86547–143–6 North Point pb $15.00

- Mikhail Bakhtin
RABELAIS AND HIS WORLD
Translated by Helene Iswolsky
Introduction by Michael Holquist
0–253–34830–7 Indiana $29.50
0–253–20341–4 Indiana pb $10.95

- Roland Barthes
ON RACINE
0–933826–56–7 Performing Arts pb $7.95

- Robert G. Cohn
THE POETRY OF RIMBAUD
0–691–06244–7 Princeton $45.00

- Henry Miller
THE TIME OF THE ASSASSINS: A Study of Rimbaud
0–8112–0115–5 New Directions pb $6.95

- Pierre Petitfils
RIMBAUD
Translated by Alan Sheridan
0–8139–1142–7 Virginia $34.95

- Enid Starkie
ARTHUR RIMBAUD
0–8112–0197–X New Directions pb $10.95

- André Maurois
LELIA: The Life of George Sand
Translated by Gerard Hopkins
0–14–004354–3 Penguin pb $5.95

- Frances Mossiker
MADAME DE SEVIGNE: A Life and Letters
0–394–41472–1 Knopf $22.95
0–231–06153–6 Columbia pb $16.00

- Victor Brombert
STENDHAL: Fiction and the Themes of Freedom
0–226–07548–6 Chicago pb $15.00

- Theodore Besterman
VOLTAIRE
0–226–04430–0 Chicago $33.00

- Alan Schom
EMILE ZOLA: A Biography
0–8050–0710–5 Henry Holt $19.95

Modern French Literature

Much modern French writing does not lend itself to convenient categorizing. Indeed, questioning the notion of genre itself is fundamental to much of it; and one finds memoir as fiction, poem as analytical essay, novel as collage.

▶ See also Modern European Drama

POETRY

- Anne-Marie Albiach
MEZZA VOCE
Albiach, who has translated American writers such as Louis Zukofsky and Frank O'Hara, is one of the most striking of contemporary French poets
Translated by Joseph Simas & others
0–942996–11–9 Post-Apollo pb $12.95

- Guillaume Apollinaire
This tirelessly inquisitive intellectual was not only involved with Cubism and Futurism but is also credited with coining the terms "Orphism" and "Surrealism."
ALCOOLS
A bilingual edition. Apollinaire's poetic masterpiece, published in 1913, blends traditional forms and free verse, in poems that range from the quintessentially modernist "Zone" to the songlike simplicity of "Sous le Pont Mirabeau"
Translated with annotations by Anne Hyde Greet
0–520–00029–3 California pb $9.95

CALLIGRAMMES
Shaped compositions that foreshadow the work of the concrete poets. A bilingual edition
Translated by Anne Hyde Greet
0–520–01968–7 California $27.50

SELECTED WRITINGS
Includes poems, criticism, and fiction
Translated by Roger Shattuck
0–8112–0003–5 New Directions pb $9.95

- Yves Bonnefoy
POEMS, 1959–1975
Defining his work, Bonnefoy has written: "Poetry does not interest itself in the shape of the world itself, but in the world that this universe will become"
Translated by Richard Pevear
0–394–73956–6 Random House pb $7.95

WORDS IN STONE: Pierre Ecrite
Translated by Susanna Lang
0–87023–203–7 Massachusetts $11.00

- André Breton
POEMS OF ANDRE BRETON: A Bilingual Anthology
A rich selection of the poetry of the "pope" of the Surrealist movement. A bilingual edition
Translated by Jean-Pierre Cauvin & Mary Ann Caws
0–292–76476–6 Texas $27.50
0–292–76477–4 Texas pb $16.95

- Blaise Cendrars
COMPLETE POSTCARDS FROM THE AMERICAS: Poems of Road and Sea
This precursor of Apollinaire and the Surrealist poets introduced syncopated jazz and African rhythms into his poetry
0–520–02716–7 California $33.00

Aimé Césaire
THE COLLECTED POETRY
Césaire, born in Martinique, was a founder of the *Négritude* movement. "More vividly perhaps than in the work of the Surrealists of France, Césaire's poetry embodies the twin aspirations of political and aesthetic revolution, and in such a way that they are inseparably joined"—Paul Auster
Translated by Clayton Eshleman & Annette Smith
0–520–04347–2 California $35.00
0–520–05320–6 California pb $13.95

- René Char
POEMS OF RENE CHAR
The work of this sometimes elliptical, unwaveringly humanistic poet reflects a profound preoccupation with man in nature
Translated by Jonathan Griffin & Mary Anne Caws
0–691–06297–8 Princeton $34.00

- Michel Deguy
GIVEN GIVING: Selected Poems of Michel Deguy
"Always present in Deguy's work are his wit, his experimentation, his sensuous intellectuality, the seeming urgency of what he has to say about what moves him to write"—Kenneth Koch
Translated by Clayton Eshleman
Introduction by Kenneth Koch
0–520–04728–1 California $28.00
0–520–06458–5 California pb $12.95

- Paul Eluard
SELECTED POEMS
Shifting from Surrealism to an engaged Marxist stance in his work, Eluard is notable above all for his very pure and intense love poetry
Translated by Gilbert Bowen
0–7145–3995–3 Riverrun pb $9.95

LAST LOVE POEMS OF PAUL ELUARD
Translated by Marilyn Kallet
0–8071–0681–X Louisiana State $17.95

- Jean Follain
D'APRES TOUT: Poems by Jean Follain
Follain's work has a concrete sharpness rare in modern French poetry. Characteristically, he takes a real or imagined moment in history and, in a few

lines, enters it completely. A bilingual edition
Translated by Heather McHugh
0–691–06476–8 Princeton $13.00
0–691–01372–1 Princeton pb $5.95

• Jean Genet
TREASURES OF THE NIGHT: Collected Poems of Jean Genet
Translated by Steven Finch
0–917342–76–3 Gay Sunshine pb $6.95

• Yvan Goll
SELECTED POEMS
Goll, a German poet deeply involved with Dada and Surrealism, wrote primarily in French after 1933
Translated by Rainer Schulte & Michael Bullock
0–939378–02–7 Mundus Artium pb $8.00

• Eugene Guillevic
SELECTED POEMS
The stark materiality of Guillevic's poetry is influenced by both his Communist convictions and his Breton origins
Translated by Denise Levertov
0–8112–0283–6 New Directions $5.95

• Emmanuel Hocquard
A DAY IN THE STRAIT
Hocquard is also an influential publisher of contemporary poetry; his own work is steeped in Mediterranean landscapes and historical echoes
Translated by Maryann DeJulio & Jane Staw
0–87376–045–X Red Dust pb $4.95

Edmond Jabès
In 1972 Jacques Derrida wrote: "In the last ten years nothing of interest has been written in France that does not have its precedent somewhere in the texts of Jabès." Since that time the Egyptian Jewish poet, who fled to France because of political persecution during the Nasser regime, has extended his influence to English-language poets. *The Book of Questions* and its successor, *The Book of Dialogue,* are extraordinary probings into the nature of language, Kabbalistic in their openness to multiple layers of meaning. Waldrop's version is one of the great translations of recent years.
THE BOOK OF DIALOGUE
Translated by Rosemarie Waldrop
0–8195–5147–3 Wesleyan $18.95

THE BOOK OF QUESTIONS
A 4-volume set
Translated by Rosemarie Waldrop
0–8195–6108–8 Wesleyan $40.00

Volume 1
0–8195–6043–X Wesleyan pb $10.95

Volume 2: The Book of Yukel & Return to The Book
0–8195–6049–9 Wesleyan pb $9.95

Volume 3: Yael, Elya & Aely
0–8195–6103–7 Wesleyan pb $9.95

Volume 4: El, or The Last Book
0–8195–6107–X Wesleyan pb $9.95

IF THERE WERE ANYWHERE BUT DESERT: The Selected Poems of Edmond Jabès
The earlier, more lyrical work preceding *The Book of Questions*
Translated by Keith Waldrop
0–88268–052–8 Station Hill $16.95

• Philippe Jaccottet
"Jaccottet is one of a group of poets who turned away from the Surrealists' sometimes abstruse experiments with form in favor of a muted lyrical expression born of a quasi-fraternal bonding with the wonder of earth, light, water, sky. This lyricism is steeped in an ambiguous sense of our planet's vulnerability in this nuclear age"—Germaine Brée
SELECTED POEMS
A selection that surveys Jaccottet's whole career, translated by a leading Irish poet
Translated by Derek Mahon
0–916390–31–4 Wake Forest pb $8.95

SEEDTIME
Translated by André Lefevère & Michael Hamburger
0–8112–0637–8 New Directions $3.25

• Francis Jammes
SELECTED POEMS OF FRANCIS JAMMES
The initially bucolic verse of this poet from the Pyrenees veered more toward spiritual questions as he wrestled with Catholicism
Translated by Barry Gifford & Bettina Dickie
0–87421–086–0 Utah State $7.95

• Jean Joubert
BLACK IRIS
Translated by Denise Levertov
1–55659–015–6 Copper Canyon pb $9.00

• Robert Marteau
SALAMANDER: Selected Poems of Robert Marteau
Translated by A. Winters
0–691–01357–8 Princeton pb $6.50

• Henri Michaux
SELECTED WRITINGS OF HENRI MICHAUX
Michaux, who traveled widely in Africa, Asia, and the Americas, was both a painter and a poet; he is noted especially for his exploration of the prose poem
Translated by Richard Ellmann
0–8112–0316–6 New Directions $7.50

• Oscar V. de Lubicz Milosz
THE NOBLE TRAVELLER: The Life and Selected Writings of Oscar V. de Lubicz Milosz
A Lithuanian writer and diplomat who had become a French citizen by the time of his death in 1939, Milosz explores occult themes in much of his poetry
Translated by David Gascoyne, Kenneth Rexroth, Edouard Roditi & others
Introduction by Czeslaw Milosz
0–89281–064–5 Inner Traditions pb $14.95

• Charles Péguy
THE MYSTERY OF THE CHARITY OF JOAN OF ARC
This work illustrates Péguy's almost obsessive veneration for Joan of Arc
Translated by Jeffrey Wainwright
0–85635–690–5 Carcanet pb $9.50

• Benjamin Péret
FROM THE HIDDEN STOREHOUSE: A Selection of Poems
Péret was a poet absolutely committed to Surrealism, as well as to the political ideals for which he fought in the Spanish Civil War
Translated by Keith Hollaman
Introduction by Charles Simic
0–932440–10–X Oberlin $10.95
0–932440–11–8 Oberlin pb $5.95

A MARVELOUS WORLD
Translated by Elizabeth Jackson
0–8071–0664–X LSU $22.50

• Saint-John Perse
Diplomat, traveler, scholar and Nobel laureate, Perse wrote large-scale, metaphysical, fundamentally optimistic poetry celebrating the wonders of the physical world and human resilience.
SELECTED POEMS
Translated with an introduction by Mary Ann Caws
Edited by T.S. Eliot
0–8112–0855–9 New Directions pb $9.95

ANABASIS
A long prose poem describing ancient nomadic wanderings and conquests, written while Perse was serving as a diplomat in China. A bilingual edition
Translated by T.S. Eliot
Preface by Valéry Larbaud
0–15–607406–0 HBJ pb $2.95

BIRDS
A bilingual edition
Translated by Robert Fitzgerald
0–691–09713–5 Princeton $39.50

ELOGES & OTHER POEMS
Poems reflecting Perse's childhood in Guadeloupe
Translated by Louise Varese
0–691–09731–3 Princeton $21.00

EXILE & OTHER POEMS
Written after his expulsion by the Vichy government in 1940, these poems reflect his despair at France's fate
Translated by Denis Devlin
0–691–09740–2 Princeton $21.00

SONG FOR AN EQUINOX
Translated by Richard Howard
0–691–09938–3 Princeton pb $12.50

• Francis Ponge
THE MAKING OF THE PRE
Ponge's dismantling of language in order to get at objects themselves has made him an influential figure for more recent French poets
Translated by Lee Fahnestock
0–8262–0381–7 Missouri pb $14.95

THINGS: Selected Writings of Francis Ponge
Translated by Cid Corman
0–934834–70–9 White Pine pb $7.50

• Jacques Prévert
BLOOD AND FEATHERS: Selected Poems of Jacques Prévert
Prévert's work is marked by a blend of brisk satire and languid sentimentality, couched in an accessible style that has made him one of the most popular modern poets
Translated & edited by Harriet Zinnes
0–8052–4040–3 Schocken $14.95
0–8052–0907–7 Schocken pb $8.95

SELECTIONS FROM PAROLES
Ferlinghetti's translations of Prévert have been popular ever since they appeared in the 1950s
Translated by Lawrence Ferlinghetti
0–87286–042–6 City Lights pb $3.00

● Pierre Reverdy
SELECTED POEMS
"Reverdy's strange landscapes, which combine an intense inwardness with a proliferation of sensual data, bear in them the signs of a continual search for an impossible totality. Almost mystical in effect, his poems are nevertheless anchored in the minutiae of the everyday world"— Paul Auster
Translated by Kenneth Rexroth
0–8112–0373–5 New Directions $6.50
0–8112–0458–8 New Directions pb $2.25

● Philippe Soupault
PM LYING: Selected Poems
Soupault was a prominent Surrealist until he was expelled from the movement for political reasons
Translated by Paulette Schmidt
0–918786–30–4 Lost Roads pb $5.95

● Jules Supervielle
SELECTED WRITINGS
This witty humanist expressed what he called a "pansympathy" with nature, as well as a mindfulness of death
0–8112–0389–1 New Directions $7.50

● Tristan Tzara
PRIMELE POEME: First Poems
A founder of Dada, Tzara was one of the movement's most radically experimental poets
Translated by Michael Impey & Brian Swann
0–89823–084–5 New Rivers pb $2.50

SEVEN DADA MANIFESTOES
Essential texts, published between 1916 and 1920
Translated by Barbara Wright
0–7145–3762–4 Riverrun pb $5.95

● Paul Valéry
SELECTED WRITINGS
A devoted disciple of Mallarmé, Valéry published between 1917 and 1922 some of the most dense and obscure poetry in French—and then largely abandoned verse for discursive prose
0–8112–0213–5 New Directions pb $6.95

Paul Auster, editor
THE RANDOM HOUSE BOOK OF TWENTIETH-CENTURY FRENCH POETRY
A dual-language edition with translations by American and British poets
0–394–52197–8 Random House $25.00
0–394–71748–1 Random House pb $11.95

FICTION

● Alain-Fournier
LE GRAND MEAULNES
This influential novel of innocence and first love, published in 1913, ran counter to the naturalist approach then prevalent
Translated by Frank Davison
0–14–002466–2 Penguin pb $3.95

● Guillaume Apollinaire
LES ONZE MILLE VIERGES
In addition to being a poet and art critic, Apollinaire was a writer of erotic fiction, tempering his violent fantasies with considerable humor
Translated by Nina Rootes
Introduction by Richard N. Coe
0–8008–2384–2 Taplinger $7.95

THE POET ASSASSINATED & OTHER STORIES
The poet's best-known work of fiction, along with fifteen other pieces
Translated by Ron Padgett
0–86547–151–7 North Point pb $12.50

● Louis Aragon
THE ADVENTURES OF TELEMACHUS
A satirical anti-novel, rich in verbal play, based on the didactic 17th-century work by Fénélon. "Essential for the understanding of Aragon, and of his concept of art and of the surrealist undertaking"—Mary Ann Caws
Translated by Renée & Judd Hubert
0–8032–1021–3 Nebraska $18.95

Guillaume Apollinaire fights for France in a drawing by Picasso, from John Willet's Art and Politics in the Weimar Period (Pantheon)

● Georges Bataille
L'ABBE C
Depicts the intense relationship between twin brothers, one an unabashed libertine, the other an improbably devout priest. "Bataille speaks about man's condition, not his nature. Bataille has survived the death of God"—Jean-Paul Sartre
Translated by Philip A. Facey
0–7145–2709–2 Marion Boyars $13.95
0–7145–2848–X Marion Boyars pb $9.95

BLUE OF NOON
In a prewar novel now attracting new attention, Bataille describes a dark journey through the psyche of the 1930s French intelligentsia
Translated by Harry Mathews
0–7145–2850–1 Marion Boyars pb $9.95

STORY OF THE EYE
These fantasies of sexual excesses "indicated the aesthetic possibilities of pornography as an art form"—Susan Sontag
Translated by Joachim Neugroschel
0–87286–209–7 City Lights pb $6.95

● Simone de Beauvoir
THE BLOOD OF OTHERS
An existentialist novel focusing on the autonomous act as a vehicle of personal emancipation
Translated by Roger Senhouse & Yvonne Moyse
0–394–72411–9 Pantheon pb $7.95

THE MANDARINS
A fictionalized group portrait of Sartre and the inner circle of existentialists, and of an American novelist modeled on Nelson Algren
Translated by Leonard Friedman
0–89526–898–1 Regnery pb $9.95

WHEN THINGS OF THE SPIRIT COME FIRST
Translated by Patrick O'Brian
0–394–72235–3 Pantheon pb $6.95

● Georges Bernanos
THE DIARY OF A COUNTRY PRIEST
An austere Catholic drama of spirituality in the face of materialistic values. "A strange and sad, yet beautiful and triumphant story"—NY Times
Translated by Pamela Morris
0–88184–013–0 Carroll & Graf pb $8.95

MOUCHETTE
A 14-year-old girl chooses suicide
Preface by Richard Gilman
Translated by Colin Whitehouse
1–55554–023–6 PAJ pb $5.95

● Maurice Blanchot
Often likened to the work of Kafka and Beckett, Blanchot's writing paints a sharp picture of an absurd world and points forward to the antinovel. His fiction, which has only recently become widely available in English, has begun to exert its influence on American writers.

DEATH SENTENCE
"A transumptive romance of the erotic triangle of death, consciousness and the possible world of narrative"—John Hollander
Translated by Lydia Davis
0–930794–04–4 Station Hill pb $5.95

THE MADNESS OF THE DAY
"A story of madness that consists in seeing the light, vision or visibility, from an experience of blindness"—Jacques Derrida
Translated by Lydia Davis
0–930794–39–7 Station Hill $8.50
0–930794–36–2 Station Hill pb $3.95

THOMAS THE OBSCURE
Translated by Robert Lamberton
0–88268–076–5 Station Hill pb $8.95

VICIOUS CIRCLES
"Illuminates with hallucinatory intensity certain consequences of the hopeless and irresistible human longing to communicate through language"—Harry Mathews
Translated by Paul Auster
0–930794–93–1 Station Hill $14.95
0–930794–92–3 Station Hill pb $7.95

WHEN THE TIME COMES
A semantically demanding work whose style has been described as having a "limpid obscurity"
Translated by Lydia Davis
0–930794–96–6 Station Hill $12.95
0–930794–95–8 Station Hill pb $5.95

• André Breton
NADJA
A Surrealist romance describing the author's relationship with a girl who is not so much a person as a state of mind
Translated by Richard Howard
0–802–150268–7 Grove pb $8.95

• Albert Camus
THE FALL
A late work whose pessimistic view of man caused some surprise after the more positive final note of *The Plague*, written a decade earlier
Translated by Justin O'Brien
0–394–70223–9 Random House pb $4.95

A HAPPY DEATH
An early version of *The Stranger*
Translated by Richard Howard
0–394–71865–8 Random House pb $5.95

THE PLAGUE
An epidemic serves as a telling symbol for the Nazi occupation of France and, by extension, for human existence as a whole. The characters rediscover dignity and meaning through collective endeavor
Translated by Stuart Gilbert
0–394–71258–7 Random House pb $3.50

THE STRANGER
Among the most widely read novels of the century, this study of individual alienation in a bourgeois society is still remarkable for its resonant tone of understatement
Translated by Stuart Gilbert
0–394–70002–3 Random House pb $2.95

THE STRANGER
A new translation that comes close to the directness of Camus' style
Translated by Matthew Ward
0–394–53305–4 Random House $16.95
0–679–72020–0 Random House pb $5.95

• Francis Carco
PERVERSITY
The sinister side of Bohemian life in Montmartre
Translated by Jean Rhys
0–88739–048–X Black Lizard pb $3.95

• Emmanuel Carrère
THE MUSTACHE
"In its wit and strangeness, Emmanuel Carrère's new novel recalls certain works of the Russians . . . especially of Gogol"—Madison Smartt Bell
Translated by Lanie Goodman
0–02–018870–6 Collier pb $7.95

• Louis-Ferdinand Céline
CASTLE TO CASTLE
Translated by Ralph Manheim
0–88184–360–1 Carroll & Graff pb $8.95

DEATH ON THE INSTALLMENT PLAN
A "creative confession" that continues Céline's litany of disgust with his fellow creatures
Translated by Ralph Manheim
0–8112–0017–5 New Directions pb $9.95

GUIGNOL'S BAND
Translated by Bernard Frechtman & Jack T. Nile
0–8112–0018–3 New Directions pb $9.95

JOURNEY TO THE END OF NIGHT
Celine's misanthropic 1932 novel broke radically with French literary traditions in both style and subject matter. "Céline often said that he regarded himself primarily as a stylist . . . He held that the French literary language was stiff and spent with age, that classicism and academicism had emasculated the language of Villon and Rabelais, and that in our age emotion could be captured only in the spoken tongue"—Ralph Manheim
Translated by Ralph Manheim
0–8112–0847–8 New Directions pb $9.95

• Blaise Cendrars
THE ASTONISHED MAN
An adventurous, quasi-autobiographical narrative
Translated by Nina Rootes
0–7206–0677–2 Dufour $14.95

GOLD: The Marvelous History of General John Augustus Sutter
Cendrars' vivid evocation of the Gold Rush of 1849
Translated by Nina Rootes
0–935576–09–6 Michael Kesend pb $8.95

• Jean Cocteau
THE HOLY TERRORS
The perverse loyalties and passions of childhood; also well-known under its French title, *Les Enfants Terribles*
Translated by Rosamond Lehmann
0–8112–0021–3 New Directions pb $6.95

THE IMPOSTOR
Translated by Dorothy Williams
0–7206–4370–8 Dufour $21.00

• Colette
THE BLUE LANTERN
Translated by Roger Senhouse
0–374–11497–8 Farrar, Straus & Giroux $10.00
0–374–51387–2 Farrar, Straus & Giroux pb $2.95

BREAK OF DAY
A reminiscence of the writer's girlhood, and a portrait of her mother
Translated by Enid McLeod
0–374–51221–3 Farrar, Straus & Giroux pb $5.95

CLAUDINE AT SCHOOL
A depiction of schoolgirl life
Translated by Antonia White
0–345–30056–4 Ballantine pb $2.50

CLAUDINE IN PARIS
Translated by Antonia White
0–345–30708–9 Ballantine pb $2.50

THE COLLECTED STORIES OF COLETTE
One hundred stories written between 1908 and 1945. "No other woman seems to have had as much lived experience to draw upon or as much sexual sophistication"—Phyllis Rose, *NY Times*
Edited with an introduction by Robert Phelps
Translated by Matthew Ward & others
0–374–12629–1 FS&G $22.50
0–374–51865–3 FS&G pb $12.95

CREATURES GREAT AND SMALL
Fiction and essays reflecting Colette's deep attachment to animals
Translated by Enid McLeod
0–374–13102–3 Farrar, Straus & Giroux $10.00

GIGI, JULIE DE CARNEILHAN & CHANCE ACQUAINTANCES
Three key works, including the novel around which Vincente Minnelli structured his musical film. *Julie,* based on Colette's last years with her second husband, is a lively study of a clash of wills
Translated by Roger Senhouse & Patrick Fermor
0–374–51317–1 Farrar, Straus & Giroux pb $8.95

MITSOU & MUSIC-HALL SIDELIGHTS
Translated by Raymond Postgate & Anne-Marie Callimachi
0–374–51377–5 Farrar, Straus & Giroux pb $2.95

MY APPRENTICESHIPS
Reminiscences of Colette's literary beginnings
Translated by Helen Beauclerk
0–374–21660–6 Farrar, Straus & Giroux $10.00
0–374–51458–5 Farrar, Straus & Giroux pb $4.95

MY MOTHER'S HOUSE & SIDO
Two autobiographical works dealing with Colette's childhood
Translated by Una V. Troubridge & Enid McLeod
0–374–51218–3 Farrar, Straus & Giroux pb $8.95

THE OTHER ONE
Translated by Elizabeth Tait & Roger Senhouse
0–374–22801–9 Farrar, Straus & Giroux $10.00
0–374–51388–0 Farrar, Straus & Giroux pb $2.95

THE PURE AND THE IMPURE
Translated by Herma Briffault
0–374–50692–2 Farrar, Straus & Giroux pb $6.50

RETREAT FROM LOVE
The first novel in the Claudine series offers bucolic impressions of rural life and "reflections on the heights and depths of Claudine's narcissism"—*New Yorker*
Translated by Margaret Crosland
0–15–676588–8 HBJ pb $5.95

THE SHACKLE
Translated by Antonia White
0–374–26184–9 Farrar, Straus & Giroux $7.95
0–374–51311–2 Farrar, Straus & Giroux pb $3.95

THE TENDER SHOOT & OTHER STORIES
Eleven of Colette's best stories
Translated by Antonia White
0–374–27310–3 Farrar, Straus & Giroux $10.00
0–374–51258–2 Farrar, Straus & Giroux pb $7.95

THE VAGABOND
A portrait of music-hall life
Translated by Enid McLeod
0–374–28233–1 Farrar, Straus & Giroux $8.95

• René Crevel

BABYLON
A "free spirit" turns a defiant face to the various powers, human and otherwise, that conspire against her
Translated by Kay Boyle
0–86547–191–6 North Point $15.50

DIFFICULT DEATH
A novel of homosexuality, rebellion, and suicide, first published in 1926
Translated by David Rattray
Foreword by Salvador Dali
0–86547–246–7 North Point pb $11.95

René Daumal
Works by this erudite and intellectual writer (a Sanskrit scholar and sometime pupil of Gurdjieff) are stamped by the eclecticism of his knowledge and the relentlessness of his search for an "absolute truth."

MOUNT ANALOGUE: A Novel of Symbolically Authentic Non-Euclidean Adventures in Mountain Climbing
Daumal's crew sets sail in the yacht *Impossible,* in quest of the symbolic mountain that represents an impossible truth
Translated by Roger Shattuck
0–87773–381–3 Shambhala pb $5.95

A NIGHT OF SERIOUS DRINKING
This picaresque vision of hell as an all-night drinking bout is "a mysterious account, superbly translated, of what today would be called a trip" —Roger Shattuck
Translated by David Coward & E.A. Lovatt
0–39474–217–6 Shambhala pb $7.95

• Marguerite Duras
Duras, one of the foremost exponents of the *nouveau roman,* describes a world in which banal surfaces are constantly ruffled by an agitated inner world of spontaneous impulse.

FOUR NOVELS
Includes *The Afternoon of Mr. Andesmas, Ten-Thirty on a Summer Night, Moderato Cantabile* and *The Square*
Translated by Richard Seaver & others
0–394–17987–0 Grove pb $9.95

L'AMANTE ANGLAISE
A deaf-mute is brutally murdered; the killer, her cousin, may or may not be mad
Translated by Barbara Bray
0–394–75022–5 Pantheon pb $6.95

BLUE EYES, BLACK HAIR
0–394–56320–4 Pantheon $13.95
0–679–72280–7 Pantheon pb $6.95

DESTROY, SHE SAID
The London *Times* described these "exotic intrigues of a quartet of two women and two men masking a chillingly deceptive form of madness" as "a very extraordinary achievement"
Translated by Barbara Bray
0–394–62326–6 Grove pb $6.95

LITTLE HORSES OF TARQUINIA
While the characters sip drinks and plan trips—one of them to see equine frescos at Tarquinia—a young man is killed by a mine in the Mediterranean hills
Translated by Peter DuBerg
0–7145–0348–7 Riverrun pb $7.95

Marguerite Duras (photo by Roger Viollet-Paris)

THE LOVER
Set in prewar Indochina, this tale of a teenage girl and her wealthy Chinese lover vividly evokes life at the end of the colonial era. Winner of the 1984 Goncourt Prize
Translated by Barbara Bray
0–394–54588–5 Pantheon $11.45
0–06–097040–5 Harper & Row pb $6.95

THE MALADY OF DEATH
Translated by Barbara Bray
0–394–53866–8 Grove $9.95
0–8021–3036–4 Grove pb $5.95

THE RAVISHING OF LOL STEIN
A young woman recreates a past tragedy of abandonment; then she voyeuristically spies on the characters she has called back into play
Translated by Richard Seever
0–394–74304–0 Pantheon pb $6.95

THE SAILOR FROM GIBRALTAR
A beautiful, errant woman searches for a nameless sailor who has aroused in her an insatiable taste for love
Translated by Barbara Bray
0–394–74451–9 Pantheon pb $8.95

THE SEA WALL
A French widow buys land on the coast of Vietnam. Each year the land is inundated by the Pacific, so that she must struggle repeatedly against elemental absurdity
Translated by Herma Briffault
0–06–097053–7 Harper & Row pb $6.95

THE VICE-CONSUL
A tale of desperate passion, set in India with a cast of French diplomats
Translated by Eileen Ellenbogen
0–394–55898–7 Pantheon $10.95
0–394–75026–8 Pantheon pb $6.95

Anatole France
When Anatole France won the Nobel Prize in 1921 he was one of the world's best known writers, but since then his reputation has languished. The brilliance and control of his style and the ferocity of his satire make him overdue for a revival.

THE GODS WILL HAVE BLOOD
A novel of the Terror, in which a young idealist is transformed by slow stages into a merciless Jacobin
Translated by Frederick Davies
0–14–044352–5 Penguin pb $4.95

PENGUIN ISLAND
A parody of French history, culminating in a savagely satirical treatment of the Dreyfus case
Translated by A.W. Evans
0–918172–09–8 Leete's Island pb $6.95

THAIS
Religious fanaticism founders on the shoals of repressed sexuality
Translated by Basia Gulati
0–226–25989–7 Chicago pb $3.95

• Romain Gary

THE LIFE BEFORE US: Madame Rosa
An orphaned Arab boy's devotion to a dying Auschwitz survivor forms the basis for a macabre tale of love, with a supporting cast of pimps, shamans, and transvestites
Translated by Ralph Manheim
0–8112–0961–X New Directions pb $7.95

PROMISE AT DAWN
An autobiographical novel chronicling Gary's childhood in Russia, Poland, and on the French Riviera, and telling above all of his mother's love and support
Translated by John M. Beach
0–8112–1016–2 New Directions pb $10.95

• Jean Genet
Thief, recidivist, homosexual, and poet, Genet is the modern French writer who most thoroughly and compellingly rejects accepted social values, in both his art and his life.

FUNERAL RITES
Genet's grief for his lover, killed during the liberation of Paris, is matched by his perverse attraction to a collaborator
Translated by Bernard Frechtman
0–8021–3087–9 Grove pb $9.95

MIRACLE OF THE ROSE
Portraits of men encountered behind bars merge to become extensions of Genet himself, a rootless figure in total revolt
Translated by Bernard Frechtman
0–8021–3088–7 Grove $10.95

OUR LADY OF THE FLOWERS
Genet's first and perhaps greatest novel, an autobiographical work written in prison
Translated by Bernard Frechtman
Introduction by Jean-Paul Sartre
0–8021–3013–5 Grove pb $8.95

QUERELLE
Taking the Dostoevskian theme of murder as an act of absolute liberation, this book is "a confrontation with the basest of angels . . . sailor, assassin, dealer in opium, homosexual, thief and traitor"—Michael Levenson, *Harper's*
Translated by Anselm Hollo
0–394–62368–1 Grove pb $7.95

THE THIEF'S JOURNAL
The record, worthy of Rimbaud, of a pilgrimage in quest of the deepest imaginable state of evil. "The most

TO ORDER BOOKS AS GIFTS, SEE PAGE 1

beautiful book that Genet has written"—
Jean-Paul Sartre
Translated by Bernard Frechtman
Foreword by Jean-Paul Sartre
0-8021-3014-3 Grove pb $8.95

• André Gide
CORYDON
Dialogues on homosexuality, of which the
author wrote: "*Corydon* remains in my
opinion the most important of my books"
Translated by Richard Howard
0-374-13012-4 Farrar, Straus & Giroux $16.95
0-374-51777-0 Farrar, Straus & Giroux pb $7.95

THE COUNTERFEITERS
A novel whose innovative structure
presents an apparently haphazard series of
events encompassing several generations of
characters—one of whom is a novelist at
work on a book called *The Counterfeiters*
Translated by Dorothy Bussy
0-394-71842-9 Random House pb $6.95

THE IMMORALIST
The famous novella of a man who pursues
every impulse regardless of moral
consequence; his "immorality" resides in
his languid duty to be happy
Translated by Richard Howard
0-394-60500-4 Modern Library $7.95
0-394-70008-2 Random House pb $3.95

LAFCADIO'S ADVENTURES
In this novel of farcical intrigue, Gide's
preoccupation with the unmotivated crime
receives its most thorough treatment
Translated by Dorothy Bussy
0-394-70096-1 Random House pb $4.95

STRAIT IS THE GATE
A probing study of scruple in the figure of
Alissa and her refusal to give in to her
emotions
Translated by Dorothy Bussy
0-394-70027-9 Random House pb $4.95

TWO SYMPHONIES
Includes *Isabelle* and *The Pastoral Symphony*,
two short pre-war romantic novels on the
themes of renunciation and the tragedy of
sacrifice
Translated by Dorothy Bussy
0-394-72454-2 Random House pb $5.95

Jean Giono (photo courtesy of Aline Giono)

Jean Giono
Giono is renowned for his pastoral,
pagan studies of Provençal life. The
existence he paints is hard but
rewardingly simple and contrasts with
his distaste for most of the modern
world.
BLUE BOY
An autobiographical novel of Giono's
childhood in pre-World War I
Provence
Translated by Katherine A. Clarke
0-86547-037-5 North Point pb $9.50

HARVEST
A brief, intensely poetic novel based on
the seasonal rhythms of peasant life
Translated by Henri Fluchere & Geoffrey Myers
0-86547-124-X North Point pb $9.00

THE HORSEMAN ON THE ROOF
A young man journeys through
southern France during the cholera
epidemic of 1838. This repetitive and
relentless chronicle has a cumulative
hypnotic power
Translated by Jonathan Griffin
0-86547-060-X North Point pb $12.50

JOY OF MAN'S DESIRING
"Giono has created his own private
terrestrial domain, a mythical domain
far closer to reality than books of
history or geography . . . It is a land in
which things 'happen' to men as aeons
ago they happened to the gods"—
Henry Miller
Translated by Katherine Allen Clarke
0-86547-015-4 North Point pb $12.50

THE SONG OF THE WORLD
An adventure novel of epic
spaciousness, set in a peasant world
where barely a trace of modernity can
be detected
Translated by Henri Fluchère & Geoffrey Myers
0-86547-038-3 North Point pb $12.50

• Julien Gracq
BALCONY IN THE FOREST
A second-generation surrealist, Gracq
advocates the joys of political
noninvolvement in resolutely anti-Sartrian
fashion
Translated with a preface by Richard Howard
0-231-06643-0 Columbia pb $9.95

THE OPPOSING SHORE
A novel set in a mythical nation that has
been at war for three centuries
Translated by Richard Howard
0-231-05789-X Columbia pb $10.95

• Julien Green
This French-American novelist explores the
theme of anguish issuing from the conflict
between spirit and flesh.
ADRIENNE MESURAT
0-8419-1193-2 Holmes & Meier $29.95

DIARY: 1928-1957
0-88184-119-6 Carroll & Graf pb $9.95

MEMORIES OF EVIL DAYS
Edited by Jean-Pierre J. Piriou
0-8139-0553-2 Virginia $16.95

• Eugène Ionesco
THE HERMIT
A portrait of a petty clerk who is prey to
startling visions, illustrating "Ionesco's
ability to turn reality into phantasmagoria
and nightmare"—*The New Republic*
Translated by Richard Seaver
0-8050-0178-6 Seaver pb $7.95

• Alfred Jarry
SELECTED WORKS OF ALFRED JARRY
A representative collection of "black
humor, wild obscenity, delicate lyricism,
mechanized eroticism, pure love, gay
blasphemy and the calm of the infinite"—
London Observer. Includes *Ubu Cuckolded,
Exploits and Opinions of Doctor Faustroll,
Pataphysican*, and other writings
Edited by Roger Shattuck & Simon W. Taylor
0-394-17604-9 Grove pb $6.95

THE SUPERMALE
A tightly structured fantasy of a machine
that develops an amorous relationship with
its maker
Translated by Ralph Gladstone & Barbara Wright
0-8112-0632-7 New Directions $7.50
0-8112-0633-5 New Directions pb $2.45

• Pierre Klossowski
THE BAPHOMET
A novel involving the souls of the Knights
Templar who, falsely accused of sexual
crimes and blasphemies, were executed in
the 14th century. "The novel . . . takes
place almost entirely outside of time, so
rather than fantastic, it would be more
accurate to term it theological and
metaphysical"—Juan Garcia Ponce
Translated by Sophie Hawkes & Stephen Sartarelli
Foreword by Michel Foucault
0-941419-16-9 Eridanos $24.00
0-941419-17-7 Eridanos pb $15.00

**ROBERTE CE SOIR & THE
REVOCATION OF THE EDICT OF
NANTES**
Two of the three novels forming the
Polish-born writer's major work, *The Laws
of Hospitality*
Translated by Austryn Wainhouse
0-7145-2739-4 Marion Boyars pb $10.95

• Michel Leiris
NIGHTS AS DAY, DAYS AS NIGHT
A diary-like work made up of over a
hundred short dream-pieces. Leiris, active
as a Surrealist in the 1920s, was
subsequently involved in psychology,
linguistics, and anthropology
Translated by Richard Sieburth
Introduction by Roger Shattuck
0-941419-06-1 Eridanos $22.00
0-941419-07-X Eridanos pb $13.00

• André Malraux
MAN'S FATE
Translated by Haakon Chevalier
0-394-70479-7 Random House pb $5.95

MAN'S HOPE
A celebration of libertarian democratic
promise set during the Spanish Civil War
Translated by Stuart Gilbert & Alastair MacDonald
0-394-17093-8 Grove pb $12.50

• François Mauriac
The work of this Nobel laureate is stamped
by Catholicism, although he makes a

consistent separation between religious and sociopolitical life.

THE DESERT OF LOVE
Translated by Gerard Hopkins
0–88184–485–3 Carroll & Graf pb $6.95

THERESE
Mauriac's best-known work is a four-part study of a provincial who attempts to murder her husband and spends the rest of her life living with the consequences
Translated by Gerard Hopkins
0–374–50333–8 Farrar, Straus & Giroux pb $8.95

VIPER'S TANGLE
A family caught up in undercurrents of greed and suspicion
Translated by Gerard Hopkins
0–88184–305–9 Carroll & Graf pb $8.95

THE WOMAN OF THE PHARISEES
A self-righteous Catholic attempts to dominate the lives of those around her
Translated by Gerard Hopkins
0–88184–371–7 Carroll & Graf pb $8.95

● Henry de Montherlant
THE GIRLS
A frank and sardonic portrait of the women who fall in love with a cold and fastidious writer for whom sex is an adjunct to work
0–88184–115–3 Carroll & Graf pb $11.95

● Paul Morand
FANCY GOODS, OPEN ALL NIGHT
An impressionistic picture of European night-life in the 1920s
Translated by Ezra Pound
Preface by Marcel Proust
0–8112–0889–3 New Directions pb $7.50

● Paul Nizan
ADEN & ARABIE
Unflattering depictions of colonial, capitalist Aden in the late 1920s
Translated by Joan Pinkham
Introduction by Jean-Paul Sartre
0–231–06357–1 Columbia pb $7.95

ANTOINE BLOYE
A novel striving toward "socialist realism" by a militant Marxist
Translated by Edmund Stevens
0–85345–309–8 Monthly Review pb $7.00

● Marcel Pagnol
JEAN DE FLORETTE & MANON OF THE SPRINGS: Two Novels
Now a successful two-part film, this tale of legendary vengeance exacted by a mysterious shepherdess is enhanced by Pagnol's keen understanding of the rugged hinterland near Marseilles
Translated by W.E. Van Heyningen
0–86547–311–0 North Point $30.00
0–86547–312–9 North Point pb $14.95

● Georges Perec
LIFE: A User's Manual
A wittily irreverent masterpiece by an energetic member of OuLiPo, the "Workshop of Potential Literature" organized by Raymond Queneau
Translated by David Bellos
0–87923–700–7 Godine $24.95
0–87923–751–1 Godine pb $14.95

W: Or The Memory of Childhood
Translated by David Bellos
0–87923–756–2 Godine $16.95

Georges Perec (photo courtesy of Godine)

● Benjamin Péret
DEATH TO THE PIGS & OTHER WRITINGS
This first authorized collection of the work of the writer most admired by the Surrealists includes the title novel, poetry, critical pieces, and miscellanea such as "The Round-the-World Calendar of Tolerable Inventions"
Translated by Rachel Stella & others
0–8032–3685–9 Nebraska $20.00
0–8032–8721–6 Nebraska pb $8.95

● Robert Pinget
A prolific practitioner of the *nouveau roman*, Pinget has been well served in English by the remarkable translations of Barbara Wright.

THE APOCRYPHA
The story of a shepherd becomes the story of several people, with voices, fragments, and notes from earlier texts linked in a succession of seasons
Translated by Barbara Wright
0–87376–050–6 Red Dust $12.95

BAGA
Translated by John Stevenson
0–7145–0099–2 Riverrun pb $6.95

BETWEEN FANTOINE AND AGAPA
Translated by Barbara Wright
0–87376–040–9 Red Dust $8.95

FABLE
"A love story, or rather the story of a betrayal. The man betrayed doesn't cry out for vengeance, he is prostrated. He tries to turn the tragedy to ridicule"—Robert Pinget in a letter to the translator
Translated by Barbara Wright
0–87376–036–0 Red Dust $6.95
0–7145–3792–6 Riverrun pb $4.95

THE INQUISITORY
The interrogation of a servant opens a window on provincial life, in Pinget's longest and best-known novel
Translated by Donald Watson
0–7145–3911–2 Riverrun pb $11.95

THE LIBERA ME DOMINE
The anatomy of a tragedy that occurred a decade earlier is pieced together through hearsay and a "network of gossip and absurd remarks"—resulting in a powerful uncertainty about everything
Translated by Barbara Wright
0–87376–025–5 Red Dust $10.50
0–7145–0339–8 Riverrun pb $9.95

PASSACAGLIA
A fragmentary, oblique story of a mysterious death, possibly a murder, in a small village
Translated by Barbara Wright
0–87376–033–6 Red Dust $6.95

SOMEONE
A writer's tryst with writing, portrayed as a hateful but almost involuntary occupation
Translated by Barbara Wright
0–87376–043–3 Red Dust $12.95

THAT VOICE
A tale of death and disintegration in a French village
Translated by Barbara Wright
0–87376–041–7 Red Dust $10.95

Marcel Proust
"Supremely sensitive, and with a prodigious memory for recording sensations, he laid his own mind and body open like an intricate musical instrument for experience to play on, studying every note, always searching for a mysterious underlying theme half-perceived from the first. This theme he was to discover was Time."—William Sansom

REMEMBRANCE OF THINGS PAST
A 3-volume set
Translated by C. Scott Moncrieff & Terence Kilmartin
0–394–50643–X Random House $75.00
0–394–71243–9 Random House pb $40.00

Volume 1
Includes *Swann's Way* and *Within a Budding Grove*
0–394–50644–8 Random House $25.00
0–394–71182–3 Random House pb $14.95

Volume 2
Includes *The Guermantes Way* and *Cities of the Plain*
0–394–50645–6 Random House $25.00
0–394–71183–1 Random House pb $12.95

Volume 3
Includes *The Captive, The Fugitive,* and *Time Regained*
0–394–50646–4 Random House $25.00
0–394–71184–X Random House pb $12.95

● Raymond Queneau
THE BARK TREE
Translated by Barbara Wright
0–8112–0167–8 New Directions pb $3.95

THE BLUE FLOWERS
Translated by Barbara Wright
0–8112–0945–8 New Directions pb $8.95

EXERCISES IN STYLE
Queneau's most famous text consists of a single banal incident on a bus, recounted in 99 different styles. Barbara Wright works wonders with material that at first glance might appear untranslatable
Translated by Barbara Wright
0–8112–0789–7 New Directions pb $5.95

THE FLIGHT OF ICARUS
In which the theme is the association between author and characters
Translated by Barbara Wright
0–8112–0482–0 New Directions pb $7.50

PATAPHYSICAL POEMS
An expanded version that includes many new poems
Translated by Teo Savory
0–87775–172–2 Unicorn $25.00
0–87775–173–0 Unicorn pb $9.00

THE SUNDAY OF LIFE
Translated by Barbara Wright
0–8112–0645–9 New Directions $12.00
0–8112–0646–7 New Directions pb $3.95

WE ALWAYS TREAT WOMEN TOO WELL
Translated by Barbara Wright
Introduction by Valerie Caton
0–8112–0793–5 New Directions pb $5.95

ZAZIE IN THE METRO
A country girl's disjointed jaunt to Paris, rendered even zanier by Queneau's use of phonetic transcription as part of his program to introduce a "neo-French" incorporating argot and other jargon
Translated by Barbara Wright
0–7145–3872–8 Riverrun $13.95
0–7145–3923–6 Riverrun pb $7.95

• Raymond Radiguet
Though he died of typhoid fever at 20, this talented protégé of Cocteau produced two powerful and erotic analytical novels.

COUNT D'ORGEL'S BALL
The story of an unusual love triangle
Translated by Annapaolo Cancogni
Foreword by Jean Cocteau
0–941419–31–2 Eridanos $20.00
0–941419–30–4 Eridanos pb $11.00

THE DEVIL IN THE FLESH
A 14-year-old boy is propelled by wartime circumstances into precocious maturity
Translated by A.M. Smith
0–7145–0193–X Marion Boyars pb $7.95

• Alain Robbe-Grillet
"Forerunner of a revolution in the novel"—Claude Mauriac

THE ERASERS
Twenty-four hours in a Flemish town where, for eight days, a murder a day has been committed. One of the most influential *nouveaux romans*
Translated by Richard Howard
0–8021–5086–1 Grove pb $12.95

IN THE LABYRINTH & JEALOUSY
Two of Robbe-Grillet's earliest and best books
Translated by Richard Howard
0–394–17297–3 Grove pb $7.95

LA MAISON DE RENDEZ-VOUS & DJINN
La Maison enigmatically portrays crime, intrigue, and passion in the lower depths of Hong Kong; in *Djinn*, a young man pursuing an androgynous girl is led into a bizarre clandestine world
Translated by Richard Howard, Yvonne Lenard & Walter Wells
0–8021–3017–8 Grove pb $8.95

PROJECT FOR A REVOLUTION IN NEW YORK
A novel whose central character is New York City itself
Translated by Richard Howard
0–394–17768–1 Grove pb $3.95

RECOLLECTIONS OF THE GOLDEN TRIANGLE
A literary thriller mingling fantasy, dream and erotic invention; the reader is challenged to play detective
Translated by J.A. Underwood
0–394–55564–3 Grove $16.95
0–394–62275–8 Grove pb $6.95

SNAPSHOTS
Six short pieces that represent the "new novelist's" most accessible fiction
Translated by Bruce Morrissette
0–8101–0728–7 Northwestern pb $6.95

TOPOLOGY OF A PHANTOM CITY
Translated by J.A. Underwood
0–394–42196–5 Grove $8.95
0–394–17012–1 Grove pb $3.95

THE VOYEUR
Inside the mind of an unsuccessful traveling salesman turned homicidal maniac. But did the crime really occur, and if so, when?
Translated by Richard Howard
0–8021–3165–4 Grove pb $8.95

• Jacques Roubaud
OUR BEAUTIFUL HEROINE
A parodistic detective story by a member of the OuLiPo group
Translated by David Kornacker
0–87951–290–3 Overlook $17.95

Raymond Roussel
Committed as he was to linguistic experimentation in pre-Surrealist days, Roussel had a considerable influence on later writers.

IMPRESSIONS OF AFRICA
A shipwrecked party of white men is detained by a black ruler
Translated by Rayner Heppenstall
0–7145–0289–8 Riverrun pb $9.95

LOCUS SOLUS
A scientist showing visitors around his estate explains his discoveries and inventions. On each item in the collection there hangs a tale
Translated by Rupert C. Cunningham
0–7145–0734–2 Riverrun pb $9.95

Raymond Roussel & Ron Padgett
AMONG THE BLACKS
A clear insight into Roussel's special vision, in a perceptive translation. Also included is an autobiographical essay by Padgett
0–939691–03–5 Avenue B $18.00
0–939691–02–7 Avenue B pb $7.50

• Françoise Sagan
DEAR SARAH BERNHARDT
Translated by Sabine Desiree
0–8050–0845–4 Henry Holt $18.95

A RELUCTANT HERO: A Novel of World War II
Translated by Christine Donougher
0–525–24550–2 Dutton $16.95

SALAD DAYS
Translated by C.J. Reynolds
0–525–24238–4 Dutton $13.95

• Antoine de Saint-Exupéry
FLIGHT TO ARRAS
A pilot's experiences in wartime. "A flight not only of an airplane but of a spirit"— William Rose Benét, *Saturday Review*
Translated by Lewis Galantière
0–15–631880–6 HBJ pb $4.95

THE LITTLE PRINCE
A children's story that has achieved worldwide popularity
Translated by Katherine Woods
Illustrated by Antoine de Saint-Exupéry
0–15–246503–0 HBJ $9.95
0–15–646511–6 HBJ pb $5.95

NIGHT FLIGHT
A spare and riveting tale of adventure, published in 1931
Translated by Stuart Gilbert
0–15–665605–1 HBJ pb $4.95

SOUTHERN MAIL
A novel evoking the early days of aviation in Africa and South America in the 1920s
Translated by Curtis Cate
0–15–683901–6 HBJ pb $2.95

WIND, SAND AND STARS
Saint-Exupéry's forceful expression of man's striving to exceed his limitations led him to be described as "the Joseph Conrad of the air"
0–15–697090–2 HBJ pb $3.95

• Nathalie Sarraute
One of the leading theorists and exponents of the *nouveau roman*, Sarraute stripped her fiction of realistic and didactic elements in order to construct a world out of "sensations."

GOLDEN FRUITS
A novel about a novel
Translated by Maria Jolas
0–7145–0258–8 Riverrun $10.95
0–7145–0259–6 Riverrun pb $4.95

THE PLANETARIUM
Parisian society and its pretensions
Translated by Maria Jolas
0–7145–0444–0 Riverrun pb $4.95

TROPISMS
A collection of shorter pieces built around evanescent sensations that trigger emotional responses
Translated by Maria Jolas
0–8076–0412–7 Braziller pb $4.95

THE USE OF SPEECH
Translated by Barbara Wright
0–8076–0978–1 Braziller $10.95
0–8076–0979–X Braziller pb $5.95

• Jean-Paul Sartre
NAUSEA
Sartre's famous 1938 novel, with its relentless analysis of the consciousness of its protagonist, did much to popularize the concepts of existentialism
Translated by Lloyd Alexander
0–8112–0188–0 New Directions pb $5.95

THE WALL
These five stories, including *Intimacy* and *The Childhood of a Leader,* deal broadly with the dilemma generated by commitment to a chosen course of often political action. Sartre presents many instances of his concept of "bad faith"
Translated by Lloyd Alexander
0–8112–0190–2 New Directions pb $5.95

Jean-Paul Sartre and Simone de Beauvoir

THE AGE OF REASON
The first part of the trilogy *The Roads to Freedom,* which charts the period from Munich to the fall of France in 1940. *The Age of Reason* describes events in 1938, already darkened by the shadow of war
0–394–71838–0 Random House pb $4.95

THE REPRIEVE
Part two depicts the critical eight days before the invasion of Czechoslovakia in 1938
Translated by Eric Sutton
0–394–71839–9 Random House pb $6.95

TROUBLED SLEEP
The final volume describes the fall of France to the Nazis and its repercussions on the lives of a small group of French men and women
Translated by Gerard Hopkins
0–394–71840–2 Random House pb $5.95

● André Schwarz-Bart
THE LAST OF THE JUST
A novel of the Holocaust. "Transcends the definition of fiction. It's part history, part vision, forged into a single echoing, terrifying outcry"—*NY Times*
Translated by Stephen Becker
0–689–70365–1 Atheneum pb $12.95

● Claude Simon
A major proponent of the *nouveau roman,* Simon has experimented with stream of consciousness, working outside of ordinary linear structures. He won the Nobel Prize in 1985.
CONDUCTING BODIES
Translated by Helen Lane
0–71450–332–0 Riverrun pb $4.95

THE FLANDERS ROAD
This widely read novel deals with the capitulation of France in 1940
Translated by Richard Howard
0–7145–3994–5 Riverrun pb $8.95

THE GEORGICS
A major novel that moves through different historical periods
Translated by John Fletcher
0–7145–4089–7 Riverrun $19.95

THE GRASS
Translated by Richard Howard
0–8076–1156–5 Braziller pb $8.95

TRIPTYCH
Translated by Helen Lane
0–7145–3787–X Riverrun pb $8.95

THE WIND
A novel of pedestrian lives caught up in a tide of clashing emotional forces when a wayfarer claims his inheritance, a vineyard
Translated by Richard Howard
0–8076–1155–7 Braziller pb $8.95

● Philippe Sollers
THE PARK
The literary theorist's early novel is rooted in a keen appreciation of the process of writing
Translated by A. Sheridan Smith
0–87376–012–3 Red Dust $4.95
0–87376–013–1 Red Dust pb $2.25

● Philippe Soupault
LAST NIGHTS OF PARIS
A thriller-like hallucination, with the City of Light playing the heroine's role; written by a Surrealist poet
Translated by William Carlos Williams
0–916190–18–8 Full Court Press $8.95

● Michel Tournier
A leading postwar writer, Tournier has a knack for taking familiar stories in totally unexpected directions.
THE FETISHIST
Fourteen stories that probe sexuality and death, art and life, often with a shattering twist
0–452–25755–7 NAL pb $6.95

THE FOUR WISE MEN
A lively update of the nativity story
0–394–72618–9 Random House pb $8.95

FRIDAY
A rich reworking of *Robinson Crusoe*
0–394–72880–7 Pantheon pb $7.95

GILLES AND JEANNE
A novel based on the relationship between Joan of Arc and the child-murderer Gilles de Rais
Translated by Alan Sheridan
0–8021–0021–X Grove $15.95

GOLDEN DROPLET
Translated by Barbara Wright
0–385–23759–6 Doubleday $16.95

THE OGRE
A submissive schoolboy is transformed into an "ogre" who recruits children for a Nazi school. Tournier's second, award-winning novel takes a deep look into the dark heart of fascism
Translated by Barbara Bray
0–394–72407–0 Pantheon pb $9.95

● Monique Wittig
LES GUERILLERES
Translated by David Le Vay
0–8070–6301–0 Beacon pb $7.95

THE LESBIAN BODY
Translated by David Le Vay
Introduction by Margaret Crosland
0–8070–6307–X Beacon pb $7.95

● Marguerite Yourcenar
THE ABYSS
A novel of 16th-century France
Translated by Grace Frick
0–374–10040–3 Farrar, Straus & Giroux $15.00
0–374–51666–9 Farrar, Straus & Giroux pb $12.95

ALEXIS
Set in Austria-Hungary just before the outbreak of the First World War, this early novel takes the form of a lengthy letter of confession
Translated by Walter Kaiser
0–374–51906–4 Farrar, Straus & Giroux $6.95

A COIN IN NINE HANDS
In Rome in 1933, a coin passes through the hands of nine startlingly different people
Translated by Dori Katz
0–374–12522–8 Farrar, Straus & Giroux $11.95
0–374–51953–6 Farrar, Straus & Giroux pb $7.95

COUP DE GRACE
The tale of an unhappy youthful triangle, set in the Baltic in the aftermath of World War I
Translated by Grace Frick
0–374–51631–6 Farrar, Straus & Giroux pb $8.95

FIRES
Nine monologues and narratives based on classical Greek stories, interspersed with personal notations
Translated by Dori Katz
0–374–51748–7 Farrar, Straus & Giroux pb $8.95

MEMOIRS OF HADRIAN
Yourcenar's major work, which presents the fictitious memoirs of the Roman Emperor, earned her a place among the great contemporary French writers
0–374–20728–3 Farrar, Straus & Giroux $17.95
0–394–60505–5 Modern Library $10.95
0–374–50348–6 Farrar, Straus & Giroux pb $10.95

ORIENTAL TALES
Something of a tour of China, Japan, the Balkans, and India, showing "the fabulist

➤ **FOR OVERSEAS ORDERING INFORMATION, SEE PAGE 1**

as mythographer and sage"—Stephen Koch, *NY Times Book Review*
Translated by Alberto Manguel
0–374–22728–4 Farrar, Straus & Giroux $6.98

TWO LIVES AND A DREAM
Three late tales
Translated by Walter Kaiser
0–374–28019–3 Farrar, Straus & Giroux $16.95
0–374–52091–7 Farrar, Straus & Giroux pb $8.95

> Writing is that *play* by which I turn around as well as I can in a narrow place: I am wedged in, I struggle between the hysteria necessary to write and the image-repertoire, which oversees, controls, purifies, banalizes, codifies, corrects, imposes the focus (and the vision) of a social communication. On the one hand I want to be desired and on the other not to be desired: hysterical and obsessional at one and the same time.
>
> Roland Barthes
> **ROLAND BARTHES**
> Translated by Richard Howard
> 0–8090–1385–1 Hill & Wang pb $7.25

ESSAYS: Personal, Literary, and Philosophical

Antonin Artaud by André Masson, from Artaud Anthology (*City Lights*)

Antonin Artaud
ARTAUD ANTHOLOGY
Edited by Jack Hirschman
0–87286–000–0 City Lights pb $7.95

ARTAUD: Four Texts
Translated by Clayton Eshleman
0–915572–57–5 Panjandrum $15.95
0–915572–56–7 Panjandrum pb $6.95

SELECTED WRITINGS OF ARTAUD
Over 600 pages of work in all genres by one of the most influential modern writers. "In Artaud, the artist as seer crystallizes, for the first time, into the figure of the artist as pure victim of his consciousness"—Susan Sontag
Translated by Helen Weaver
Edited with an introduction by Susan Sontag
0–374–26048–6 FS&G $20.00
0–374–51399–6 FS&G pb $9.95

THE THEATER AND ITS DOUBLE
These major statements of dramatic theory, influenced by Balinese and Mexican Indian culture, focus on restoring myth and mystery to the stage
Translated by Mary C. Richards
0–802–15030–6 Grove pb $8.95

• Roland Barthes
A principal exponent of the application of structuralism and semiotics to the study of literature and society, Barthes is widely regarded as a central intellectual figure of our era.

▶ **For a full listing of Barthes' works, see Literary Criticism and Theory**

A BARTHES READER
The topics in this selection of essays range from Gide to Garbo to Buffet to Tacitus to the *Encyclopédie*
Edited by Susan Sontag
0–3745–2144–1 Hill & Wang pb $14.95

• Georges Bataille
EROTISM: Death and Sensuality
A broad sweep of discussion covering prostitution, de Sade, mystical ecstasy, Emily Brontë, cruelty, Lévi-Strauss
Translated by Mary Dalwood
0–87286–190–2 City Lights pb $10.95

LITERATURE AND EVIL
Translated by Alastair Hamilton
0–7145–0346–0 Marion Boyars pb $8.95

THE TEARS OF EROS
Bataille traces the relationship between eroticism and death from prehistoric times to the 20th century
Translated by Peter Connor
0–87286–222–4 City Lights pb $12.95

VISIONS OF EXCESS: Selected Writings, 1927–1939
Essays on fascism, Marxism, de Sade, Nietzsche, Breton, Hegel
Translated by Allan Stoekl
0–8166–1283–8 Minnesota pb $14.95

• Simone de Beauvoir
ADIEUX: A Farewell to Sartre
Beauvoir's last ten years with Sartre, mapped out year by year
Translated by Patrick O'Brian
0–394–72898–X Pantheon pb $8.95

THE ETHICS OF AMBIGUITY
0–8065–0160–X Lyle Stuart pb $5.95

MEMOIRS OF A DUTIFUL DAUGHTER
This autobiographical work is "a record of the emotional and intellectual birth pangs of a fascinating woman"—*Time*
0–06–090351–1 Harper & Row pb $8.95

THE SECOND SEX
The classic work that has profoundly influenced contemporary feminist thought
Translated by H.M. Parshley
0–394–44415–9 Knopf $25.00
0–394–71227–7 Random House pb $5.95

A VERY EASY DEATH
A stark yet warm account of the struggle of the author's mother against terminal illness
Translated by Patrick O'Brian
0–394–72899–8 Pantheon pb $5.95

• Samuel Beckett
PROUST
A guide to "that double-headed monster of damnation and salvation—Time"—Samuel Beckett
0–394–47523–2 Grove $10.00
0–802–15025–X Grove pb $7.95

Maurice Blanchot
THE GAZE OF ORPHEUS & OTHER LITERARY ESSAYS
Blanchot has been a major influence on recent literary criticism. "A profound theoretical investigation of literature and those who make it . . . beautifully translated"—Gilbert Sorrentino, *NY Times*
Translated by Lydia Davis
Edited by P. Adams Sitney
0–930794–38–9 Station Hill pb $9.95

THE SIRENS' SONG: Selected Essays of Maurice Blanchot
Translated by Sacha Rabinovitch
Edited by Gabriel Josipovici
0–253–35255–X Indiana $22.50

THE SPACE OF LITERATURE
Translated by Ann Smock
0–8032–1166–X Nebraska $23.50

THE WRITING OF THE DISASTER
A treatment of the notion that, in Blanchot's words, "disaster belongs to a past that never ceases to impend"
Translated with an introduction by Ann Smock
0–8032–1186–4 Nebraska $19.95
0–8032–6077–6 Nebraska pb $7.95

• André Breton
MAD LOVE
A primary text of Surrealism. "I have wanted to show above all what precautions and what ruses desire takes, in search of its object and evading it"—André Breton
Translated by Mary Ann Caws
0–8032–1200–3 Nebraska $17.50
0–8032–6072–5 Nebraska pb $6.95

MANIFESTOES OF SURREALISM
Translated by Richard Seaver & Helen R. Lane
0–472–06182–8 Michigan pb $10.95

WHAT IS SURREALISM?: Selected Writings
Edited by Franklin Rosemont
0–913460–60–5 Anchor Foundation pb $18.95

• Michel Butor
THE SPIRIT OF MEDITERRANEAN PLACES
Translated by Lydia Davis
0–910395–17–9 Marlboro pb $9.00

● Albert Camus

LYRICAL AND CRITICAL ESSAYS
Sartre, Gide, Melville, and Faulkner are among those discussed
0-394-70852-0 Random House pb $4.95

THE MYTH OF SISYPHUS & OTHER ESSAYS
In the famous title essay, Camus "analyzes a contemporary malady: the recognition of the absurdity of human life"—Justin O'Brien
0-394-70075-9 Random House pb $4.95

NOTEBOOKS: 1935–1942
0-15-667400-9 HBJ pb $3.95

THE REBEL
"The logbook of the intellectual's pilgrimage to paradise on earth, the biography of that European rebellion which was born with the French Revolution"—Manes Sperber, *NY Times*
0-394-44232-6 Knopf $13.50

RESISTANCE, REBELLION AND DEATH
Twenty-three essays on capital punishment, the Hungarian uprising, Spanish fascism, Nazism, the French Resistance, and underlying it all, the writer's commitment to the service of truth and freedom
0-394-71966-2 Random House pb $4.95

● Aimé Césaire

DISCOURSE ON COLONIALISM
Translated by Joan Pinkham
0-85345-226-6 Monthly Review pb $6.00

● Jean Cocteau

BEAUTY AND THE BEAST: Diary of a Film
Introduction by George Amberg
0-486-22776-6 Dover pb $5.95

OPIUM: The Diary of a Cure
Translated by Margaret Crosland & Sinclair Road
0-394-17737-1 Grove pb $6.95

PAST TENSE: The Cocteau Diaries
A memorable tour of modern French culture
Translated by Richard Howard
Introduction by Ned Rorem

Volume 1
0-15-171289-1 HBJ $19.95
0-15-671360-8 HBJ pb $7.95

Volume 2
0-15-171291-3 HBJ $24.95

● René Daumal

RASA, OR KNOWLEDGE OF THE SELF
Writings on Indian culture, by the poet and scholar of Sanskrit
Translated by Louise Landes Levi
0-8112-0825-7 New Directions pb $5.95

● Marguerite Duras

THE WAR: A Memoir
Paris during the Nazi occupation and the first month of liberation
Translated by Barbara Bray
0-394-75039-X Pantheon pb $6.95

● Michel Foucault

THE FOUCAULT READER
Edited by Paul Rabinow
0-394-71340-0 Pantheon pb $9.95

● André Gide

AMYNTAS: North African Journals
An excursion through the cultures of Tunis and Algiers
Translated by Richard Howard
0-88001-165-3 Ecco $17.00
0-88001-166-1 Ecco pb $7.50

THE JOURNALS OF ANDRE GIDE
"The central pier upon which the imposing edifice of his work is built"—Louise Bogan, *The Nation*
Translated with an introduction by Justin O'Brien

Volume 1
0-8101-0764-3 Northwestern pb $14.95

Volume 2
0-8101-0765-1 Northwestern pb $14.95

RETURN FROM THE U.S.S.R. & AFTERTHOUGHTS ON MY RETURN
Translated by Richard Howard & Susan Sontag
0-374-24950-4 Farrar, Straus & Giroux $15.95

TRAVELS IN THE CONGO
0-14-009555-1 Penguin pb $7.95

● Eugène Ionesco

NOTES AND COUNTERNOTES
Translated by Donald Watson
0-7145-0044-5 Riverrun pb $9.95

PRESENT PAST, PAST PRESENT
Translated by Helen R. Lane
0-394-17783-5 Grove pb $1.95

● Julia Kristeva

A KRISTEVA READER
Edited by Toril Moi
0-231-06324-5 Columbia $32.00
0-231-06325-3 Columbia pb $14.50

● Michel Leiris

BRISEES: Broken Branches
"Back in 1949, Maurice Saillet and I conceived the plan of collecting in a single volume a number of texts I had written that were not strictly literary . . . Now, I can say in any case I have the material, not for a 'pure collection,' but for a fairly complete picture of what has preoccupied me, in very different fields, since the distant period at which I hoped that a certain way of pulverizing words would allow me to grasp the last word in all things" —from the Author's Note
Translated by Lydia Davis
0-86547-375-7 North Point $21.95

MANHOOD: A Journey from Childhood into the Fierce Order of Virility
Leiris is one of the most original modern practitioners of the traditional French genre of self-analysis
Translated by Richard Howard
0-86547-173-8 North Point pb $8.00

● Claude Lévi-Strauss

TRISTES TROPIQUES
From a purely literary point of view, the anthropologist's most compelling work
Translated by John & Doreen Weightman
0-689-70122-5 Atheneum pb $14.95
0-671-45850-7 Washington Square pb $4.95

● André Malraux

THE VOICES OF SILENCE
Meditations on the meaning of art
Translated by Stuart Gilbert
0-691-09941-3 Princeton $64.00
0-691-01821-9 Princeton pb $17.50

In November 1929, after various disappointments and disasters dating back to the spring before (consistently abortive attempts at love; scandalous drunkenness; almost bloody bites inflicted on my hands by a woman with whom I had once been in love; all-night debauchery after which, having been unable to achieve my purpose with a little American Negro dancer, I appeared at a friend's house around five in the morning and asked to borrow his razor with the—more or less sham—intention of castrating myself, a request my friend evaded by informing me that all he had was an electric razor), I realized that disease played a part in every one of these manifestations, and I decided to undertake psychoanalytic treatment.
Michel Leiris
MANHOOD
0-86547-173-8 North Point pb $8.00

● Henri Michaux

A BARBARIAN IN ASIA
Impressions of the Far East, in a classic translation
Translated by Sylvia Beach
0-8112-0991-1 New Directions pb $7.95

● Marcel Pagnol

MY FATHER'S GLORY AND MY MOTHER'S CASTLE: Marcel Pagnol's Memories of Childhood
Translated by Rita Barisse
0-86547-257-2 North Point pb $9.95

● Marcel Proust

ON READING RUSKIN
0-300-03513-6 Yale $22.50

● Alain Robbe-Grillet

FOR A NEW NOVEL: Essays on Fiction
Translated by Richard Howard
0-394-17107-1 Grove pb $2.25

GHOSTS IN THE MIRROR
Robbe-Grillet recounts his childhood in the first volume of his memoirs
Translated by Jo Levy
0-8021-1036-3 Grove $16.95

● Antoine de Saint-Exupéry

WARTIME WRITINGS, 1939–1944
0-15-194680-9 HBJ $1.98

● Nathalie Sarraute

CHILDHOOD
A critically acclaimed memoir. "A merciless coaxing of memory into images and then into refractions of images"—Jane Kramer, *New Yorker*
Translated by Barbara Wright
0-8076-1116-6 Braziller pb $8.95

● Jean-Paul Sartre

ANTI-SEMITE AND JEW
A provocative analysis of the anti-Semitic personality
0-8052-3004-1 Schocken pb $6.95

BAUDELAIRE
Sartre's study of Baudelaire is not quite like anyone else's, but he comes to life vividly
Translated by Martin Turnell
0–8112–0189–9 New Directions pb $6.95

THE FAMILY IDIOT: Gustave Flaubert, 1821–1857
Sartre's last monumental work, an exhaustive and unfinished study of the evolution of Flaubert's consciousness
Translated by Carol Cosman

Volume 1
0–226–73509–5 Chicago $25.00

Volume 2
0–226–73510–9 Chicago $27.50

LITERARY ESSAYS
0–8065–0647–4 Lyle Stuart pb $2.25

LITERATURE AND EXISTENTIALISM
The classic literary manifesto addressing the basic dilemma: Why write, and for whom?
0–8065–0105–7 Lyle Stuart pb $4.95

MALLARME, OR THE POET OF NOTHINGNESS
Translated by Ernest Sturm
0–271–00498–3 Pennsylvania State $22.50

POLITICS AND LITERATURE
Discusses relations between politics and literature, the intellectual and the revolution, and myth and reality in theatre, with essays and interviews on language and its uses
0–7145–0823–3 Riverrun $12.95

SAINT GENET
A massive philosophical and psychoanalytic study of the writer who for Sartre embodied Existential Man
0–394–71583–7 Pantheon $8.95

THOUGHTFUL PASSIONS: Jean-Paul Sartre's Intimate Letters to Simone de Beauvoir, 1926–1939
Translated by Matthew Ward and Irene Ilton
0–02–606830–3 Macmillan $22.95

THE WAR DIARIES OF JEAN-PAUL SARTRE: November 1939–March 1940
"The most human portrait of Sartre the man, while prefiguring almost all his later work"—*Nation*
0–394–53813–7 Pantheon $17.95

THE WORDS
An autobiography in which Sartre describes his earliest encounters with language
Translated by Bernard Frechtman
0–394–74709–7 Random House pb $5.95

• Michel Serres
THE PARASITE
Translated by Lawrence R. Schehr
0–8018–2456–7 Johns Hopkins pb $6.98

• Philippe Sollers
WRITING AND THE EXPERIENCE OF LIMITS
Translated by Phillip Barnard
Edited by David Hayman
0–231–05292–8 Columbia $26.50

• Paul Valéry
THE COLLECTED WORKS OF PAUL VALERY
Edited by Jackson Matthews

Volume 4: Dialogues
0–691–09840–9 Princeton $24.00

Volume 7: Art of Poetry
Translated by Denise Folliot
0–691–09838–7 Princeton $40.50
0–691–01868–5 Princeton pb $11.50

Volume 9: Masters and Friends
Translated by Martin Turnell
Introduction by J. Frank
0–691–09843–3 Princeton $37.00

Volume 10: History and Politics
0–691–09841–7 Princeton $40.50

Volume 12: Degas, Manet, Morisot
Translated by David Paul
0–691–09839–5 Princeton $22.00

Volume 15: Moi
Translated by Marthiel & Jackson Mathews
0–691–09936–7 Princeton $39.50

SELECTED WRITINGS
0–8112–0213–5 New Directions pb $6.95

• Simone Weil
FORMATIVE WRITINGS, 1929–1941
Translated by Dorothy McFarland
0–87023–632–6 Massachusetts pb $12.95

THE ILIAD OR THE POEM OF FORCE
0–87574–091–X Pendle Hill pb $2.50

LECTURES ON PHILOSOPHY
Translated by H. Price
0–521–29333–2 Cambridge pb $12.95

THE NOTEBOOKS
Translated by Simone Wills

Volume 1
0–7100–8522–2 RC&H pb $20.00

Volume 2
0–7100–8523–0 RC&H pb $20.00

OPPRESSION AND LIBERTY
Translated by Arthur Wills & John Petrie
0–87023–251–7 Massachusetts pb $9.95

TWO MORAL ESSAYS: Human Personality & On Human Obligations
0–686–79299–8 Pendle Hill pb $2.50

WAITING FOR GOD
0–06–090295–7 Harper & Row pb $6.95

• Marguerite Yourcenar
THE DARK BRAIN OF PIRANESI: And Other Essays
Seven critical studies ranging from Agrippa d'Aubigne and the *Historia Augusta* to Mann and Cavafy
Translated by Richard Howard
0–374–17709–0 Farrar, Straus & Giroux $16.95
0–374–51919–6 Farrar, Straus & Giroux pb $8.95

MISHIMA: A Vision of the Void
A literary study of the Japanese novelist
Translated by Alberto Manguel
9–998–19823–2 Farrar, Straus & Giroux pb $6.98

THAT MIGHTY SCULPTOR, TIME
A posthumous collection of essays on Tantrism, Albrecht Dürer, Andalusia, Christian feasts, and the Sanskrit erotic poem *Gita Govinda,* among other subjects
Translated by Walter Kaiser & the author
0–374–27358–8 Farrar, Straus & Giroux $18.95

WITH OPEN EYES: Conversations with Matthieu Galey
Translated by Arthur Goldhammer
0–8070–6354–1 Beacon $19.95
0–8070–6355–X Beacon pb $10.95

However much I huddle up, roll myself into a ball, hide my head under my blankets, fear, a fear such as I never remember having known since, creeps up on me, insinuates itself . . . That's where it comes from . . . I don't even need to look, I can sense it in everything there . . . it gives that light its greenish tinge . . . it is fear, that avenue of pointed, rigid, sombre trees with livid trunks, that procession of ghosts attired in long white robes advancing in a lugubrious file towards the grey flagstones . . . it flickers in the flames of the tall pallid candles they are carrying . . . it spreads all around, fills my room . . . I would like to escape, but I haven't the courage to cross the space impregnated with it that separates my bed from the door.

Nathalie Sarraute
CHILDHOOD
Translated by Barbara Wright
0–8076–1116–6 Braziller pb $8.95

CRITICAL STUDIES

• Raymond Aron
THE OPIUM OF THE INTELLECTUALS
0–8191–4566–1 University Press $15.25

• Anna Balakian
SURREALISM: The Road to the Absolute
0–226–03560–3 Chicago pb $12.50

THE SYMBOLIST MOVEMENT: A Critical Appraisal
0–8147–0994–X NYU pb $16.50

• Germaine Brée
TWENTIETH CENTURY FRENCH LITERATURE
0–226–07196–0 Chicago pb $11.95

• Mary Ann Caws
THE INNER THEATRE OF RECENT FRENCH POETRY: Cendrars, Tzara, Péret, Artaud, Bonnefoy
0–691–06212–9 Princeton $28.00

• Wallace Fowlie
DIONYSUS IN PARIS: A Guide to Contemporary French Theatre
0–8446–0096–2 Peter Smith $11.25

A READING OF PROUST
0–226–25885–8 Chicago $18.00

• Wilbur M. Frohock & others
IMAGE AND THEME: Studies in Modern French Fiction
Includes Georges Bernanos, André Malraux, Nathalie Sarraute, André Gide, and Roger Martin du Gard
Edited by Susan Keane
0–674–44395–0 Harvard pb $4.50

• J.H. Matthews
SURREALIST POETRY IN FRANCE
0–8156–2144–2 Syracuse $24.95

• Vivian Mercier
THE NEW NOVEL: From Queneau to Pinget
0–374–50983–2 Farrar Straus & Giroux pb $2.95

- Warren Motte, editor
OULIPO: A Primer of Potential Literature
0–8032–8131–5 Nebraska pb $9.95

- Lois Oppenheim, editor
THREE DECADES OF THE FRENCH NEW NOVEL
0–252–01158–9 Illinois $28.95

- Marjorie Perloff
THE POETICS OF INDETERMINACY: Rimbaud to Cage
0–691–06462–8 Princeton $31.00

- Melinda Porter
THROUGH PARISIAN EYES: Reflections on Contemporary French Arts and Culture
0–19–504104–6 Oxford $18.95

- Roger Shattuck
THE BANQUET YEARS: The Origins of the Avant-Garde in France, 1885 to World War I
0–394–70415–0 Random House pb $8.95

PROUST'S BINOCULARS: A Study of Memory, Time and Recognition in *A la Recherche du temps perdu*
0–691–01403–5 Princeton pb $9.50

- Mary Ann Witt
EXISTENTIAL PRISONS: Captivity in Mid-20th Century French Literature
0–8223–0631–X Duke $28.75

Individual Authors (alphabetical by subject)

- Bettine Knapp
ANTONIN ARTAUD: Man of Vision
0–8040–0809–4 Ohio pb $9.95

- Martin Esslin
ANTONIN ARTAUD
0–14–004368–3 Penguin pb $5.95

- Lisa Appignanesi
SIMONE DE BEAUVOIR
0–14–008737–0 Penguin pb $4.95

- Margaret Crosland
SIMONE DE BEAUVOIR
0–317–67520–6 Crown $19.95

- Claude Francis & Fernande Gontier
SIMONE DE BEAUVOIR: A Life—A Love Story
0–312–00189–4 St. Martin's $25.00
0–312–02324–3 St. Martin's pb $12.95

- Anna Balakian
ANDRE BRETON: Magus of Surrealism
0–19–501298–4 Hawkshead $20.00

- David Sprintzen
CAMUS: A Critical Examination
0–87722–544–3 Temple $34.95

- Merlin Thomas
LOUIS-FERDINAND CELINE
0–8112–0754–4 New Directions $16.50

- Francis Steegmuller
COCTEAU: A Biography
0–87923–606–X Godine pb $15.95

- Geneviève Dormann
COLETTE: A Passion for Life
0–89659–583–8 Abbeville $39.95

- Keith Beaumont
ALFRED JARRY: A Critical and Biographical Study
0–312–01712–X St. Martin's $35.00

- George Painter
MARCEL PROUST: A Biography
Volume 1
0–394–72561–1 Random House pb $4.95
Volume 2
0–394–72562–X Random House pb $4.95

- William Sansom
PROUST
0–500–26020–6 Thames & Hudson pb $9.95

- Roger Shattuck
MARCEL PROUST
0–691–06513–6 Princeton $25.50

- Annie Cohen-Solal
SARTRE: A Life
Translated by Anna Cancongi
0–394–75662–2 Pantheon $11.95

- Ronald Hayman
SARTRE: A Life
0–671–45442–0 Simon & Schuster $22.95

Spanish Literature

THE MIDDLE AGES

- Rita Hamilton & Janet Perry, translators
THE POEM OF THE CID
The Spanish national epic of the Christian Reconquest, in a prose translation with the original Spanish text on facing pages
0–14–044446–7 Penguin pb $5.95

- W.S. Merwin, translator
THE POEM OF THE CID
A verse translation by a leading American poet
0–452–00790–9 NAL pb $7.95

- Juan Ruiz, Archpriest of Hita
THE BOOK OF GOOD LOVE
A prose translation of *El Libro de Buen Amor*, a long medieval poem comparable to Chaucer's work in its humor and erudition
Translated by Rigo Mignani & Mario Cesare
0–87395–048–8 Medieval & Renaissance $49.50

THE BOOK OF TRUE LOVE (EL LIBRO DE BUEN AMOR): A Bilingual Edition
"Well-executed, readable, and informative. The volume has an assured place among translations of the Spanish masterpiece"—*Hispanic American Historical Review*
Original text edited by Anthony Zahareas
Translated by Saralyn Daly
0–271–00545–9 Pennsylvania pb $14.95

- Fernando de Rojas
THE CELESTINA: A 15th-Century Spanish Novel in Dialogue
A long play of emotional intrigue which, although it is written in dialogue form, is often considered the first great Spanish realist novel
Translated by Lesley Byrd Simpson
0–520–01177–5 California pb $7.95

LA CELESTINA
A 17th-century translation of Rojas' masterpiece, adapted for modern performance by Eric Bentley
Translated by James Mabbe
0–936839–01–5 Applause pb $5.95

- W.S. Merwin, editor & translator
FROM THE SPANISH MORNING
Includes a selection of early Spanish ballads, the first published picaresque novel *Lazarillo de Tormes*, and the play *Eufemia*
0–689–11502–4 Atheneum pb $10.95

THE GOLDEN AGE

- Pedro Calderón de la Barca
"Calderón owes his great place in literature to his being the last heir in the direct line of the inheritance of the Middle Ages. Though he was trained by the Jesuits, and though his plays are full of classical allusions, and the subjects are often borrowed from heathen mythology or Roman history, he was in no sense a child of the Renaissance. His Latin quotations and his allusions to pagan mythology are like Ionic cornices or Corinthian pilasters placed upon the front of a building of the thirteenth century . . . Only in Spain was such a treatment possible in the middle of the seventeenth century."—Norman Maccoll
FOUR COMEDIES BY PEDRO CALDERON DE LA BARCA
Includes *From Bad to Worse, The Secret Spoken Aloud, The Worst Is Not Always Certain*, and *The Advantages and Disadvantages of a Name*. "If some of the poetic quality of the plays is inevitably lost in translation, Calderón's mastery of stagecraft is everywhere apparent. He is as expert as Feydeau in developing dramatic complications from initial situations. One of Calderón's contemporaries praised him for having given to drama the logical form of the syllogism"—Kenneth Muir
Translated by Kenneth Muir
0–8131–1409–8 Kentucky $26.00

THREE COMEDIES BY PEDRO CALDERON DE LA BARCA
Includes *A House with Two Doors is Difficult to Guard, Mornings of April and May*, and *No Trifling with Love*. These versions of Calderón are outstanding for their wit and clarity
Translated by Kenneth Muir & Ann MacKenzie
0–8131–0166–2 Kentucky pb $9.00

BEWARE OF STILL WATERS
A lesser-known Calderón comedy, in a bilingual edition
Translated by David Gitlitz
0–939980–08–8 Trinity pb $12.00

• **Miguel de Cervantes**

"Many people, not all of them Spanish, are on record as believing that *Don Quixote* is the greatest prose fiction ever produced in the Western world . . . It epitomizes the spiritual world of European man at mid-career as *The Odyssey* and *The Iliad* do at his beginnings and as *The Brothers Karamazov* does in his decline. It is so vast, so ecumenical, that it serves only inadequately as the epic of Spain—a role better played by the more national *Poem of the Cid*. *Don Quixote* represents only a part of Spain, but a part that is far greater than the whole."—Kenneth Rexroth in *Classics Revisited*

DON QUIXOTE
Translated by Walter Starkie
0-451-51821-7 NAL pb $4.95

DON QUIXOTE
Translated by J.M. Cohen
0-14-044010-0 Penguin pb $5.95

DON QUIXOTE
Translated with an introduction by Samuel Putnam
0-394-60438-5 Modern Library $11.95

DON QUIXOTE
Translated by Tobias Smollett
Introduction by Carlos Fuentes
0-374-51943-9 FS&G pb $10.95

Don Quichotte by Gustave Doré

EXEMPLARY STORIES
Cervantes' tales of pirates, gypsies, passion, and romance, with their realistic depictions of life in Toledo and Madrid, are supreme examples of his later fiction
Translated by C.A. Jones
0-14-044248-0 Penguin pb $5.95

• **Luis de Góngora**
POLYPHEMUS AND GALATEA: A Study in the Interpretation of a Baroque Poem
An elaborate mythological poem by Spain's master of Baroque verse
Translated by Gilbert Cunningham
Commentary by Alexander Parker
0-292-72421-7 Texas $14.95

• **St. John of the Cross**
The poems of St. John of the Cross run to fewer than a thousand lines, yet their compressed fervor and lyricism establish him as one of the great mystical poets in any language. His prose works, taking the form of commentary on the poems, are major treatises on mystical theology.

THE COLLECTED WORKS OF ST. JOHN OF THE CROSS
Translated by Kieran Kavanaugh & Otilio Rodriguez
0-9600876-7-2 Carmelite Studies pb $8.95

THE POEMS OF ST. JOHN OF THE CROSS
Translated with an introduction by Willis Barnstone
0-8112-0449-9 New Directions pb $5.95

THE POEMS OF ST. JOHN OF THE CROSS
Translated by John Frederick Nims
0-226-40108-1 Chicago $15.50
0-226-40110-3 Chicago pb $4.50

THE DARK NIGHT OF THE SOUL
A prose elaboration on the significance of one of St. John's greatest poems
Translated by Benedict Zimmerman
0-385-02930-6 Doubleday pb $5.95

The spring that brims and ripples oh I know
    in dark of night.

Waters that flow forever and a day
through a lost country—oh I know
    the way
    in dark of night.

Its origin no knowing, for there's
    none.
But well I know, from here all sources
    run
    in dark of night.

No other thing has such delight to
    give.
Here earth and the wide heavens
    drink to live
    in dark of night.

From *Song of the Soul*

St. John of the Cross
THE POEMS OF ST. JOHN OF THE CROSS
Translated by John Frederick Nims
0-226-40110-3 Chicago pb $4.50

• **Lope de Vega**
LA DOROTEA
A unique mix of forms and genres: an autobiographical novel in the form of a multi-act play interspersed with poems, depicting the progress of a courtship in moods ranging from coarse farce to romantic tragedy
Translated by Alan Trueblood & Edwin Honig
0-674-50590-5 Harvard $31.50

THE DUCHESS OF AMALFI'S STEWARD
Edited and translated by Cynthia Rodriguez-Badendyck
0-919473-53-9 Humanities pb $9.95

THE KNIGHT OF OLMEDO (EL CABALLERO DE OLMEDO)
A bilingual edition of one of Lope's great dramas of honor
Translated by Willard King
0-8032-0500-7 Nebraska $17.95

• **St. Teresa of Avila**
THE LIFE OF SAINT TERESA OF AVILA BY HERSELF
The autobiography of the great Carmelite mystic
Translated by J.M. Cohen
0-14-044073-9 Penguin pb $6.95

• **Michael Alpert, translator**
TWO SPANISH PICARESQUE NOVELS
Includes *Lazarillo de Tormes* and Francisco de Quevedo's *The Swindler* (*El Buscón*)
0-14-044211-1 Penguin pb $5.95

• **Eric Bentley, editor**
LIFE IS A DREAM & OTHER SPANISH CLASSICS
Includes, in addition to the title play by Calderón, Lope de Vega's *Fuente Ovejuna* and Tirso de Molina's *The Trickster of Seville*. Campbell's verse translations are infused with energy; they are also eminently actable
Translated by Roy Campbell
0-87910-244-6 Applause pb $8.95

19TH-CENTURY FICTION

• **Leopoldo Alas**
LA REGENTA
This realistic novel of provincial society is now acknowledged as a masterpiece
Translated by John Rutherford
0-8203-0700-9 Georgia $20.00
0-14-044346-0 Penguin pb $14.95

The city of heroes was having a nap. The south wind, warm and languid, was coaxing grey-white clouds through the sky and breaking them up as they drifted along. The streets of the city were silent, except for the rasping whispers of whirls of dust, rags, straw and paper on their way from gutter to gutter, pavement to pavement, street corner to street corner, now hovering, now chasing after one another, like butterflies which the air envelops in its invisible folds, draws together, and pulls apart. This miscellany of left-overs, remnants of refuse, would come together like throngs of gutter urchins, stay still for a moment as if half asleep, and then jump up and scatter in alarm, scaling walls as far as the loose panes of street lamps or the posters daubed up at street corners; and a feather might reach a third floor, and a grain of sand be stuck for days, or for years, in a shop window, embedded in lead.

Leopoldo Alas
LA REGENTA
Translated by John Rutherford
0-14-044346-0 Penguin pb $14.95

• **Benito Perez Galdós**
FORTUNATA AND JACINTA: Two Stories of Married Women
Galdós' masterpiece is a panoramic view of 19th-century Spanish life
Translated by Agnes Gullon
0-8203-0783-1 Georgia $25.00
0-14-043305-8 Penguin pb $10.95

OUR FRIEND MANSO
A poignant tale about a gentle, self-deceived soul
Translated by Robert Russell
0–231–06404–7 Columbia $22.50

TORQUEMADA
An aggressive usurer seeks respectability at any cost in this fascinating psychological study
Translated by Frances López-Morillas
0–231–06228–1 Columbia $30.00

THE GOLDEN FOUNTAIN CAFE
This has been called Spain's first modern novel; the action centers on mid-century political strife
Translated by Walter Rubin
0–935480–36–6 Latin American Lit $17.95

THE SHADOW
A doctor lives a fantastic "second life" which ends in disillusionment
Translated by Karen Austin
0–8214–0553–5 Ohio $10.95

THE GENERATION OF 1898

• Antonio Machado
SELECTED POEMS
A large-scale survey of the work of one of the greatest Spanish poets; the translations are excellent
Translated with an introduction by Alan Trueblood
0–674–04065–1 Harvard $27.00
0–674–04066–X Harvard pb $14.95

SELECTED POEMS OF ANTONIO MACHADO
Translated by Betty Craige
0–8071–0456–6 LSU $20.00

CANCIONES
Translated by Robert Bly
0–915124–46–7 Coffee House pb $4.00

THE LANDSCAPE OF SORIA
Poetry about the melancholy yet beautiful Castilian countryside
Translated by Dennis Maloney
0–934834–57–1 White Pine pb $4.00

• José Ortega y Gasset
THE REVOLT OF THE MASSES
Ortega's renowned study of the forces society brings to bear on the individual
Translated by Anthony Kerrigan
Foreword by Saul Bellow
0–268–01609–7 Notre Dame $20.00

Miguel de Unamuno
FICCIONES: Four Stories and a Play
Translated by Anthony Kerrigan
0–691–01874–X Princeton pb $8.95

NOVELA-NIVOLA
A novel recipe for writing a novel
Translated by Anthony Kerrigan
Foreword by Jean Cassou
0–691–01875–8 Princeton pb $10.50

OUR LORD DON QUIXOTE
"Unamuno transfigures the despised and comic person of Don Quixote. This symbol of his land's wrongheaded action becomes for Unamuno the god of a new Order, the prophet of a new national revelation"—Waldo Frank
Translated by Anthony Kerrigan
0–691–01807–3 Princeton pb $12.95

THREE EXEMPLARY NOVELS
Includes *The Marquis of Lumbria*, *Nothing Less Than a Man*, and *Two Mothers*. Unamuno described these novellas as "glimpses of the deep mystery of man's soul and conscience"
Translated by Angel Flores
0–394–62366–5 Grove pb $7.95

THE TRAGIC SENSE OF LIFE IN MEN AND NATIONS
Unamuno the philosopher engages in a highly personal debate between faith and reason
Edited by Anthony Kerrigan
0–691–01820–0 Princeton pb $13.95

FROM REPUBLICANISM TO THE SPANISH CIVIL WAR

• Rafael Alberti
THE OTHER SHORE: 100 Poems by Rafael Alberti
Surrealist poetry with a strong political vision
Translated by Jose Elgorriaga & Martin Paul
0–916426–05–X Kosmos $20.00
0–916426–06–8 Kosmos pb $7.95

THE LOST GROVE: The Autobiography of a Spanish Poet in Exile
Translated by Gabriel Berns
0–520–04265–4 California pb $8.95

• Vicente Aleixandre
A LONGING FOR THE LIGHT: Selected Poems of Vicente Aleixandre
Often associated with Surrealism in the '20s and '30s, Aleixandre won the Nobel Prize for Literature in 1977
Translated by Stephen Kessler & others
Edited by Lewis Hyde
0–914742–89–2 Copper Canyon pb $10.00

• Luis Cernuda
SELECTED POEMS OF LUIS CERNUDA
Cernuda's poetry is delicate, sometimes surrealist, always intensely personal
Translated by Reginald Gibbons
0–520–20984–4 California $29.95

• Federico García Lorca
THE CRICKET SINGS
Poems and songs for children
Translated by Will Kirkland
Illustrated by Maria Horvath
0–8112–0734–X New Directions pb $4.95

DEEP SONG & OTHER PROSE
The poet states his identification with the traditional Andalusian *cante jondo*
Edited by Christopher Maurer
0–8112–0768–4 New Directions pb $4.95

FIVE PLAYS: Comedies and Tragicomedies
Includes *The Shoemaker's Prodigious Wife*, *Don Perlimplin*, *Dona Rosita the Spinster*, *Billy-Club Puppets*, *The Butterfly's Evil Spell*. Slapstick, a poet-cockroach, puppets and farce are used to censure social injustice and hypocrisy
Translated by Richard O'Connell & James Graham-Lujan
Introduction by Francisco Garcia Lorca
0–8112–0090–6 New Directions pb $7.95

POEM OF THE DEEP SONG
Sad poems of death and loss based on folk ballads of Andalusia, but with a surprisingly playful tone
Translated by Carlos Bauer
0–87286–205–4 City Lights pb $6.95

THE POET IN NEW YORK
One of the most influential poetic sequences of the 20th century, in a new translation
Translated by Greg Simon
Edited by Christopher Maurer
0–374–23539–2 Farrar, Straus & Giroux $25.00
0–374–52083–6 Farrar, Straus & Giroux pb $9.95

THE PUBLIC & PLAY WITHOUT A TITLE: Two Posthumous Plays
In *The Public*, Lorca addresses the issue of homosexuality
Translated with an introduction by Carlos Bauer
0–8112–0881–8 New Directions pb $5.25

SELECTED LETTERS
Edited and translated by David Gershator
0–8112–0873–7 New Directions pb $6.95

Silly Song

Mama,
I wish I were silver.

Son,
You'd be very cold.

Mama,
I wish I were water.

Son,
You'd be very cold.

Mama,
Embroider me on your pillow.

That, yes!
Right away!

Translated by Harriet de Onis

Federico García Lorca
SELECTED POEMS
0–8112–0091–4 New Directions pb $4.95

SELECTED POEMS
A bilingual edition that presents the work of a variety of translators and offers a good sampling of Lorca's many stylistic approaches
Edited by Donald Allen
0–8112–0091–4 New Directions pb $4.95

THREE TRAGEDIES
Includes *Blood Wedding*, *Yerma*, and *The House of Bernarda Alba*. Lorca's best-known trilogy portrays Andalusian peasants torn by sexual passions and the conflicts between tradition and modern life
Translated by Richard O'Connell & James Graham-Lujan
0–8112–0092–2 New Directions pb $6.95

• Jorge Guillén
AFFIRMATION: A Bilingual Anthology 1919–1966
Guillén can be described as a modern Spanish secular mystic who calls upon man to create order out of an absurd existence
Translated by Julian Palley
0–8061–0764–2 Oklahoma $14.95

✉ TO ORDER BOOKS AS GIFTS, SEE PAGE 1

GUILLEN ON GUILLEN: The Poetry and the Poet
A bilingual edition. "A superb introduction to Guillén's work for any reader of poetry"—*World Literature Today*
Translated by Reginald Gibbons & Anthony Geist
0–691–01356–X Princeton pb $9.95

Juan Ramón Jiménez
GOD DESIRED AND DESIRING
A bilingual edition of Jiménez's poems of spiritual crisis
Translated by Antonio De Nicholas
0–913729–23–X Paragon pb $9.95

INVISIBLE REALITY
A bilingual edition of the mature poetry of the 1956 Nobel Prize winner, discovered and published posthumously
Translated by Antonio De Nicolas
Introduction by Louis Simpson
0–913729–34–5 Paragon $18.95

PLATERO AND I
Prose poems about a companionable donkey
Translated by Antonio De Nicolas
0–913729–06–X Paragon pb $9.95

TIME AND SPACE: A Poetic Autobiography
Edited and translated by Antonio de Nicolas
0–913279–71–X Paragon $18.95

• Ramón Pérez de Ayala
BELARMINO AND APOLONIO
This truly Spanish but universal novel, published in 1921, centers on a dialogue between two philosophical shoemakers
Translated by Murray Baumgarten & Gabriel Berns
0–520–04958–6 California pb $7.95

• Pedro Salinas
MY VOICE BECAUSE OF YOU
Salinas is best known for these poems of love and desire
Translated by Willis Barnstone
Preface by Jorge Guillén
0–87395–285–5 SUNY $19.50

TO LIVE IN PRONOUNS: Selected Love Poems
Translated by Edith Helman & Norma Farber
0–393–04389–4 Norton $12.50

THE FRANCO ERA AND AFTER

• J.J. Armas Marcelo
SHIPS AFIRE
A fanciful novel of the Conquistadors. "A novel that is historical, but also one that is full of sharp, Buñuel-esque humor"—Mario Vargas Llosa
0–380–89741–5 Avon pb $7.95

• Fernando Arrabal
THE COMPASS STONE
Bizarre crimes narrated in a surprising memoir
Translated by Andrew Hurey
0–8021–0002–3 Grove $16.95

THE TOWER STRUCK BY LIGHTNING
Tarot cards and a "world war" game of chess in a characteristically surrealist, madcap tale
Translated by Anthony Kerrigan
0–670–81346–X Viking $16.95

• Francisco Ayala
DEATH AS A WAY OF LIFE
An imaginary Latin American nation undergoes the terrors of dictatorship
0–8052–4042–X Schocken $18.95

USURPERS
Seven short stories about power and corruption, set in the Spanish Golden Age but reflecting events of the Civil War
0–8052–3970–7 Schocken $15.95

• Juan Benet
RETURN TO REGION
In this challenging novel, the mythical Region represents all that is paradoxical and mysterious about Spain
Translated by Gregory Rabassa
0–231–05456–4 Columbia $24.00
0–231–05457–2 Columbia pb $9.95

• Juan Luis Cebrián
RED DOLL
A tale of political intrigue and passion in the post-Franco democratic government
Translated by Philip Silver
1–55584–145–7 Weidenfeld & Nicolson $15.95

• Camilo José Cela
THE HIVE
Banned in Spain upon publication in 1951, this influential novel depicts the suffering postwar nation in a cinematic narrative style often imitated during the Franco years
Introduction by Arturo Barea
0–88001–004–5 Ecco pb $6.95

JOURNEY TO THE ALCARRIA
A traveler escaping the city's tumult discovers a surprising inner resilience among the rural poor
Translated by Frances M. López-Morillas
0–299–03250–7 Wisconsin $21.50

• Gabriel Celaya
THE POETRY OF GABRIEL CELAYA
A bilingual edition of the works of an important modern poet concerned with social questions
Translated by Betty Jean Craige
0–8387–5062–1 Bucknell $24.50

Miguel Delibes
FIVE HOURS WITH MARIO
In a tour de force monologue, a middle-aged, middle class woman reflects on her existence as she contemplates her husband's corpse
Translated by Frances López-Morillas
0–231–06828–X Columbia $25.00

THE HEDGE
"Delibes' evocation of totalitarianism is brilliantly convincing and the translation never misses a beat"—*Publishers Weekly*
Translated by Frances López-Morillas
0–231–05460–2 Columbia $25.00

• Jesús Fernandez Santos
EXTRAMUROS
Two nuns are determined to rescue their convent from ruin during the Inquisition
Translated by Helen Lane
0–231–05552–8 Columbia $22.00

• Juan Goytisolo
THE COUNTRYSIDE OF NIJAR
Also includes *La Chanca*. Two documentary novels of travels to Andalusia
Translated by Luigi Luccarelli
0–934184–19–4 Alembic $16.00
0–934184–20–8 Alembic pb $9.00

FORBIDDEN TERRITORY: Memoirs, 1931–1956
"A moving and sympathetic story of how one courageous victim of the Franco regime fought his way out of a cultural and intellectual wasteland, educated himself, and went on to inflict a brilliant revenge on the social system which so insulted and humiliated him"—*TLS*
Translated by Peter Bush
0–86547–337–4 North Point $18.95

LANDSCAPES AFTER THE BATTLE
A collection of journalistic musings on life and society from a European vantage point
Translated by Helen Lane
0–8050–0393–2 Seaver Books $17.95

SPACE IN MOTION
Translated by Helen Lane
0–930829–03–4 Lumen pb $8.95

• Carmen Martín Gaite
THE BACK ROOM
An evocative portrait of the lives of women in Spain
Translated by Helen Lane
0–231–05458–0 Columbia $22.00

• Eduardo Mendoza
THE CITY OF MARVELS
This novel of power and ambition in 19th-century Barcelona was a recent Spanish bestseller
Translated by Bernard Molloy
0–15–118040–7 HBJ $19.95

CATALAN LITERATURE

The literary traditions of Catalonia have produced masterpieces in both the medieval and the modern era. This body of work is only beginning to make its appearance in English translation.

Medieval

• Ramon Llull
SELECTED WORKS OF RAMON LLULL (1232–1316)
Theologian, philosopher, novelist and martyr, Ramon Llull is one of Catalonia's major medieval writers. A two-volume set
Translated & edited by Anthony Bonner
0–691–07288–4 Princeton $160.00

BLANQUERNA
A late 13th-century novel. "[Llull's] fictional works contain such startling and imaginative conceptions that they have become an imperishable part of early Spanish literature. Chief of these books is *Blanquerna*, a kind of Catholic *Pilgrim's Progress*"—Martin Gardner
Translated with an introduction by E.A. Peers
0–87952–376–7 Hippocrene pb $14.95

- Joanot Martorell & Marti Joan De Galba
  TIRANT LO BLANC
  A classic of medieval chivalric literature in a splendid translation by David Rosenthal
  Translated with an introduction by David Rosenthal
  0–446–32584–8 Warner pb $4.95

- David J. Viera
  MEDIEVAL CATALAN LITERATURE: Prose and Drama
  Selections from the literature with critical commentaries
  0–8057–8235–8 G.K. Hall $24.95

Modern

While Catalan letters flourished during the late 19th and early 20th centuries, the language as a literary idiom was suppressed throughout the Franco regime. In recent years, it has once again been at the forefront of innovation in peninsular literature.

Salvadore Espriú
LA PELL DE BRAU
The foremost among the Catalan postwar poets, Espriú in this work views Spanish life through images from Jewish history
Translated by Burton Raffel
0–910395–28–4 Marlboro $9.00

- J.V. Foix
  WHEN I SLEEP, THEN I SEE CLEARLY: Selected Poems
  The selection spans the entire career of Catalonia's major avant-garde poet, who won Spain's 1985 National Prize for Literature
  Translated by David Rosenthal
  0–89255–130–5 Persea pb $12.95

- Joan Perucho
  NATURAL HISTORY
  "This first book by a major contemporary Catalan author to be translated into English is an elegant combination of genres: a bildungsroman in the guise of a vampire tale embedded in a historical novel"—*Booklist*
  Translated by David Rosenthal
  0–394–57058–8 Knopf $17.95

- Merce Rodoreda
  MY CHRISTINA & OTHER STORIES
  Translated by David Rosenthal
  0–915308–64–9 Graywolf $16.00
  0–915308–65–7 Graywolf pb $7.00
  THE TIME OF THE DOVES
  This major work of modern Catalan fiction presents a powerful narration of a woman's life in post-war Barcelona
  Translated by David Rosenthal
  0–915308–75–4 Graywolf pb $7.50

- Kathleen McNerney, editor
  ON OUR OWN BEHALF: Women's Tales From Catalonia
  0–8032–3122–9 Nebraska $24.95

ANTHOLOGIES

- Linton Barrett, editor
  FIVE CENTURIES OF SPANISH LITERATURE: From the Cid Through the Golden Age
  0–06–040499–X Harper & Row pb $19.95

- Richard Chandler & Kessel Schwartz, editors
  NEW ANTHOLOGY OF SPANISH LITERATURE
  Volume 1
  0–8071–0344–6 LSU $30.00
  Volume 2
  0–8071–0345–4 LSU $40.00

- J.M. Cohen, editor
  THE PENGUIN BOOK OF SPANISH VERSE
  The Spanish texts, with literal prose translations on facing pages
  0–14–058570–2 Penguin pb $8.95

- John Crow, editor
  AN ANTHOLOGY OF SPANISH POETRY: From the Beginnings to the Present Day
  Includes both Spanish and Spanish-American poets
  0–8071–0482–5 LSU $27.50

STUDIES OF SPANISH LITERATURE

General

- Richard Chandler & Kessel Schwartz
  NEW HISTORY OF SPANISH LITERATURE
  0–8071–0343–8 LSU $40.00

- Guillermo Díaz-Plaja
  A HISTORY OF SPANISH LITERATURE
  Translated by Hugh A. Harter
  0–8147–1750–0 NYU $35.00

- Paul Ilie
  LITERATURE AND INNER EXILE: Authoritarian Spain, 1939–1975
  0–8010–2424–9 Johns Hopkins $22.00

- C.B. Morris
  A GENERATION OF SPANISH POETS, 1920–1936
  0–521–29481–9 Cambridge pb $14.95

- Marshall Schneider & Irwin Stern, editors
  MODERN SPANISH AND PORTUGUESE LITERATURES
  Selections from criticism on 65 Spanish, Catalan, and Galician writers of the 20th century
  0–8044–3280–5 Continuum $75.00

- James Stamm
  A SHORT HISTORY OF SPANISH LITERATURE
  0–8147–7792–9 NYU pb $17.50

- Philip Ward, editor
  THE OXFORD COMPANION TO SPANISH LITERATURE
  0–19–866114–2 Oxford $49.95

- Howard Young
  VICTORIOUS EXPRESSION: A Study of Four Contemporary Spanish Poets, Unamuno, Machado, Jiménez and Lorca
  0–299–03144–6 Wisconsin pb $9.50

- Henryk Ziomek
  A HISTORY OF SPANISH GOLDEN AGE DRAMA
  0–8131–0158–1 Kentucky pb $10.00

Individual Spanish Authors (alphabetical by subject)

- Edwin Honig
  CALDERON AND THE SEIZURES OF HONOR
  0–674–09075–6 Harvard $18.50

- Robert Ter Horst
  CALDERON: The Secular Plays
  0–8131–1440–3 Kentucky $24.00

- William Byron
  CERVANTES: A Biography
  1–55778–006–4 Paragon pb $12.95

- Vladimir Nabokov
  LECTURES ON DON QUIXOTE
  0–15–649540–6 HBJ pb $7.95

- P.E. Russell
  CERVANTES
  0–19–287570–1 Oxford $14.95
  0–19–287569–8 Oxford pb $4.95

- Rupert C. Allen
  PSYCHE AND SYMBOL IN THE THEATER OF FEDERICO GARCIA LORCA: Perlimplin, Yerma, Blood Wedding
  0–292–76418–9 Texas pb $14.50

Federico García Lorca (photo by Francisco García Lorca, courtesy of New Directions)

- **Francisco García Lorca**
IN THE GREEN MORNING: Memories of Federico
Lorca remembered by his brother
Translated by Christopher Maurer
0–8112–0970–9 New Directions pb $12.95

- **Donald R. Larson**
THE HONOR PLAYS OF LOPE DE VEGA
0–674–40628–1 Harvard $18.95

- **Martin Nozick**
MIGUEL DE UNAMUNO: The Agony of Belief
0–691–01366–7 Princeton pb $11.50

Portuguese Literature

Although Portugal has produced major writers who have garnered fame within Europe, little attention has been paid to them in the United States and few translations exist. Writers such as Camões, Eça de Queiroz, and Fernando Pessoa deserve to be more widely known and appreciated.

MEDIEVAL AND RENAISSANCE

Portugal took form as a nation during the long period of the Christian reconquest of the Iberian peninsula, and became totally unified by the end of the 13th century, although Castilian threats to the new country's independence continued throughout the 14th century. In the age of exploration, Portugal acquired a far-flung empire, which by the mid-16th century included parts of Africa, Asia, and the Americas. Lisbon was Europe's emporium.

- **Fernão Lopes**
THE ENGLISH IN PORTUGAL
Selections from this important medieval historian's vivid chronicles of court intrigues during the reigns of Dom Fernando and Dom Joao I
Translated with an introduction by D.W. Lomax & R.J. Oakley
0–85668–431–8 Aris & Phillips $37.50
0–85668–342–6 Aris & Phillips pb $16.50

- **T.F. Earle**
THE MUSE REBORN: The Poetry of Antonio Ferreira
Selections from and an analysis of the works of a great poet who defended the use of the Portuguese language at a time when Castilian was the fashionable peninsular idiom
0–1981587–56–4 Oxford $60.00

Luis de Camões
THE LUSIADS
Portugal's national poem, an extraordinary epic blending the voyages of Vasco da Gama with elements from classical mythology. Atkinson's straightforward prose version emphasizes Camões' masterful gifts as a storyteller
Translated by William Atkinson
0–14–044026–7 Penguin pb $6.95

THE LUSIADS
Translated with an introduction by Leonard Bacon
0–87535–128–X Hispanic Society pb $4.50

THE 19TH CENTURY

The cost to Portugal of the glorious empire was centuries of decadence. The Napoleonic invasions and liberal revolutions of the early 19th century and the independence of Brazil in 1822 gave rise to a new understanding of the nation's identity—and a preoccupation with the nation's very existence.

- **Viscount Almeida Garrett**
TRAVELS IN MY HOMELAND
In the style of Sterne's *Tristram Shandy*, Garrett takes us on a psychological "voyage" through rural Portugal during the era of the liberal revolutions
Translated with an introduction by John M. Parker
0–7206–0663–2 Dufour $22.50

- **Eça de Queiroz**
LETTERS FROM ENGLAND
Portugal's major realist novelist views English life from his diplomatic post
Translated by Ann Stevens
0–8214–0080–0 Ohio pb $12.00

THE MAIAS
Eça's masterpiece: the tale of a traditional noble family which has fallen on hard times
0–460–01433–1 Everyman pb $9.95

THE 20TH CENTURY

The 40-year dictatorship of Antonio de Oliveira Salazar kept Portugal an undeveloped, inward-looking nation. African liberation movements, which began in the early 1960s, eventually led to the downfall of the regime in 1974 and the subsequent loss of the colonial empire. A new democratic government is gradually healing old wounds and participating in European affairs through membership in the European Economic Community.

- **Eugenio de Andrade**
THE INHABITED HEART: The Selected Poems of Eugenio de Andrade
A bilingual edition of poems by a leading contemporary poet
Translated by Alexis Levitin
Introduction by Pilar Gómez Bedate
0–912288–24–8 Perivale pb $7.95

- **Sophia de Mello Breyner**
MARINE ROSE
A selection of poems written between 1944 and 1982
Translated by Ruth Fainlight
0–933806–37–X Black Swan $20.00

- **José Cardoso Pires**
BALLAD OF DOGS' BEACH
In a powerful mystery novel based on a real event, Portugal's most important 20th-century novelist analyzes the fear that gripped the nation during the Salazar regime
Translated by Mary Fitton
0–8253–0416–4 Beaufort $15.95

Fernando Pessoa
POEMS OF FERNANDO PESSOA
One of the greatest and least-known of modern poets, Pessoa created a series of personalities—heteronyms—for himself, each with its own style and vision
Translated by Susan Brown & Edwin Honig
0–88001–091–6 Ecco $19.95
0–88001–123–8 Ecco pb $10.00

THE KEEPER OF SHEEP
The poems of Alberto Caeiro, perhaps the most compelling of Pessoa's heteronyms
Translated by Susan Brown & Edwin Honig
Introduction by Edwin Honig
0–935296–61–1 Sheep Meadow pb $9.50

THE SURPRISE OF BEING
Poems that Pessoa published under his own name; many are characteristically reflexive considerations on the art of poetry
Translated by James Greene & Clara de Mafra Azevedo
0–946162–24–7 Dufour pb $9.95

ALWAYS ASTONISHED: Selected Prose
Essays, fiction, letters, and journals by the great modernist poet
Edited and translated by Edwin Honig
0–87286–228–3 City Lights pb $8.95

- **José Rodrigues Migueis**
STEERAGE & TEN OTHER STORIES
Compassionate, witty tales of immigrants and the unfortunate by a Portuguese writer self-exiled in New York
Edited with a foreword by George Monteiro
0–943722–06–3 Gavea-Brown pb $6.00

- **Bernardo Santareno**
THE PROMISE
A drama that attacks the repression and censorship of the Salazar regime
Translated by Nelson Vieira
0–943722–04–7 Gavea-Brown pb $4.00

- **Jose Saramago**
BALTASAR AND BLIMUNDA
"Saramago has produced a novel that is deeply imbedded in the history of his land yet moves in mystical realms. It is a romance and an adventure, a rumination on royalty and religion in 18th-century Portugal and a bitterly ironic comment on

the use of power"—Irving Howe, *NY Times*
0–15–110555–3 HBJ $17.95
0–345–35676–4 Ballantine pb $4.95

• **Jorge de Sena**
BY THE RIVERS OF BABYLON & OTHER STORIES
A collection of stories written between 1946 and 1964, many involving historical figures
Edited by Daphne Patai
0–8135–1388–X Rutgers $19.95

IN CRETE WITH THE MINOTAUR & OTHER POEMS
A bilingual edition of Sena's remarkable poetry
0–943722–004 Gavea-Brown pb $6.00

CRITICAL STUDIES

• **Alfred Hower & Richard Preto-Rodas, editors**
EMPIRE IN TRANSITION: The Portuguese World at the Time of Camões
Essays on many aspects of Portuguese, Brazilian, African and European culture
0–8130–0790–9 Florida pb $25.00

• **Henry Hart**
LUIS DE CAMOENS AND THE EPIC OF THE LUSIADS
0–8061–0522–4 Oklahoma $21.50

• **George Monteiro, editor**
THE MAN WHO NEVER WAS: Essays on Fernando Pessoa
0–943722–07–1 Gavea-Brown $17.50
0–943722–08–X Gavea-Brown pb $7.50

• **Marshall Schneider & Irwin Stern, editors**
MODERN SPANISH AND PORTUGUESE LITERATURES: A Library of Literary Criticism
Selections from critical works about 80 20th-century writers of the Iberian Peninsula
0–8044–3280–5 Continuum $75.00

• **Ronald Sousa**
THE REDISCOVERERS: Major Writers in the Portuguese Literature of National Regeneration
Essays on Camões, Eça de Queiroz, Pessoa and others
0–271–00300–6 Pennsylvania State $22.50

Italian Literature

THE MIDDLE AGES

The troubador-inspired love lyrics of the so-called Sicilian school of the 13th century represent the first literature to be written in Italian rather than Latin. But it was the Florentine Dante who properly forged a new national literary language at the beginning of the 14th century by electing to write in his native Tuscan dialect. In refining and strengthening the vernacular, the great Italian writers of the 14th century—Dante, Cavalcanti, Petrarch, Boccaccio—established one of the great European literatures.

• **Dante Gabriel Rossetti**
THE EARLY ITALIAN POETS
A classic 19th-century translation of work by Dante, Cavalcanti, and their contemporaries
Edited by Sally Purcell
0–520–04468–1 California $22.50

• **Dante**
"If we start from his predecessors, Dante's language is a well-nigh incomprehensible miracle. There were great poets among them. But compared with theirs, his style is so immeasurably richer in directness, vigor, and subtlety, he knows and uses such an immeasurably greater stock of forms, he expresses the most varied phenomena and subjects with such immeasurably superior assurance and firmness, that we come to the conclusion that this man used his language to discover the world anew."—Erich Auerbach in *Mimesis*

THE PORTABLE DANTE
This anthology features Lawrence Binyon's outstanding translation of *The Divine Comedy*, of which Ezra Pound wrote: "Binyon sheds more light on Dante than any translation I have ever seen. Almost more than any translation sheds on *any* original." Also included are Dante Gabriel Rossetti's version of *The New Life* and a selection of prose writings
Edited by Paolo Milano
0–14–015032–3 Penguin pb $8.95

THE DIVINE COMEDY
John Ciardi's eminently readable translation, loose at times but full of narrative drive, was admired by Archibald MacLeish and John Crowe Ransom
Translated by John Ciardi
0–393–04472–6 Norton $29.95

THE DIVINE COMEDY OF DANTE ALIGHIERI
"A Dante with clarity, eloquence, terror, and profoundly moving depths"—Robert Fagles. The artwork and typography of this edition have also received much praise
Translated by Allen Mandelbaum
Illustrated by Barry Moser

Volume 1: Inferno
0–520–02712–4 California $37.50
Volume 2: Purgatorio
0–520–04516–5 California $37.50
Volume 3: Paradiso
0–520–04517–3 California $37.50

THE DIVINE COMEDY
An inexpensive paperback edition of the Mandelbaum translation, without the artwork
Translated by Allen Mandelbaum

Volume 1: Inferno
0–553–21339–3 Bantam pb $2.95

The circle of the lustful in Dante's "Inferno," from William Blake, Printmaker *by Robert N. Essick (Princeton)*

➤ **FOR OVERSEAS ORDERING INFORMATION, SEE PAGE 1**

Volume 2: Purgatorio
0–553–21344–X Bantam pb $3.95

Volume 3: Paradiso
0–553–21204–4 Bantam pb $4.95

THE DIVINE COMEDY
Mark Musa's iambic version is clear and musical
Translated by Mark Musa

Volume 1: Inferno
0–14–044441–6 Penguin pb $3.50

Volume 2: Purgatory
0–14–044442–4 Penguin pb $3.95

Volume 3: Paradise
0–14–044443–2 Penguin pb $3.95

THE DIVINE COMEDY
A definitive prose version with facing Italian text and extensive commentary. "What a triumphant joy it is to see the honest light of literality take over again, after ages of meretricious paraphrase"—Vladimir Nabokov
Translated by Charles Singleton

Volume 1: Inferno
0–691–01832–4 Princeton pb $20.50

Volume 2: Purgatorio
0–691–01843–X Princeton pb $22.50

Volume 3: Paradiso
0–691–01844–8 Princeton pb $18.50

DANTE'S RIME
Translated by Patrick Diehl
0–691–06409–1 Princeton $34.00
0–691–01361–6 Princeton pb $9.50

LA VITA NUOVA
A spiritual autobiography, interspersed with poems, in which Dante—writing some years after his beloved's death—charts his devotion to Beatrice Portinari
Translated by Barbara Reynolds
0–14–044216–2 Penguin pb $4.95

LITERATURE IN THE VERNACULAR
A pioneer study of linguistics and style, arguing for the use of common language and the blending of different dialects to create a national literature
Translated by Sally Purcell
0–85635–274–8 Carcanet pb $5.95

• Petrarch
"Petrarch's example aroused in poets all over Europe the hope of achieving classic expressiveness in the mother tongue. The deepest tributes to Petrarch's influence are in poets great enough to make his lessons their own, poets like Ariosto, Michelangelo, Ronsard, Garcilaso de la Vega, Gongora, Camões, Sidney, Donne. He stood for a new sensibility that could combine aristocratic reserve and elegance, wit, allusiveness, Virgilian evocativeness and emotional depth, symbolic complexity—in classically balanced, perfected form."—Robert Durling in *Petrarch's Lyric Poems*

PETRARCH'S LYRIC POEMS: The Rime Sparse & Other Lyrics
A complete prose translation of Petrarch's major collection of more than 350 lyrics, with Italian text
Edited & translated by Robert M. Durling
0–674–66345–4 Harvard $35.00
0–674–66348–9 Harvard pb $11.95

SELECTIONS FROM THE CANZONIERE & OTHER WORKS
A fluently translated selection of love lyrics which Petrarch titled *Rerum vulgarium fragmenta*—"short pieces in the vernacular," and which became a standard model for love poetry; also includes an interesting autobiographical fragment addressed to Laura, the poet's Beatrice
Edited & translated by Mark Musa
0–19–281707–8 Oxford pb $3.95

SONGS AND SONNETS FROM LAURA'S LIFETIME
Controversial translations recasting Petrarch in a modernist idiom
Translated by Nicholas Kilmer
0–86547–028–6 North Point pb $7.50

In my younger days I struggled constantly with an overwhelming but pure love-affair—my only one, and I would have struggled with it longer had not premature death, bitter but salutary for me, extinguished the cooling flames. I certainly wish I could say that I have always been entirely free from desires of the flesh, but I would be lying if I did. I can, however, surely say this: that, while I was being carried away by the ardour of my youth and by my temperament, I always detested such sins from the depths of my soul. When I was nearing the age of forty, and my vigour and passions were still strong, I renounced abruptly not only those bad habits, but even the very recollection of them—as if I had never looked at a woman. This I consider to be among my greatest blessings, and I thank God, who freed me while I was still sound and vigorous from that vile slavery which I always found hateful. But let us turn to other matters now.

from "Letter to Posterity"

Petrarch
SELECTIONS FROM THE CANZONIERE & OTHER WORKS
Edited & translated by Mark Musa
0–19–281707–8 Oxford pb $3.95

• Giovanni Boccaccio
Boccaccio's *Decameron*—a series of 100 tales told by ten Florentines during the plague of 1348 at the rate of one each over ten days—became the first classic of European prose fiction, a book that has been said to herald the passage of western civilization out of the Middle Ages. It has proved an enduring sourcebook into which other writers and artists have been dipping for centuries.

THE DECAMERON
Translated by G.H. McWilliam
0–14–044269–3 Penguin pb $6.95

THE DECAMERON
Edited by Mark Musa & Peter Bondanella
0–393–04458–0 Norton $15.95
0–393–09132–5 Norton pb $8.95

AMOROSA VISIONE
A dream-vision cast as a love allegory in verse
Translated by Robert Hollander & others
0–87451–347–2 New England (bilingual) $30.00

THE CORBACCIO
A misogynistic satire, influential in its day
Translated by Anthony Cassell
0–252–00479–5 Illinois $19.95

THE RENAISSANCE

Humanism

"A belief in the value of classical learning as the molder of a citizen's character, a conviction that great moral value could be derived from a study of its philosophy, became as deeply embedded in the Florentine tradition as it did in nineteenth-century England. And when the Medici founded and encouraged a Platonic academy and patronized handsomely the great philosophers—Ficino, Pico, and the rest—they were no innovators, and the purpose of their patronage was widely understood. It would strengthen an attitude to human life that was thought to be singularly Florentine."—J.H. Plumb, *The Italian Renaissance*

• Leon Battista Alberti
Better known for his theory and practice of architecture, Alberti also authored dialogues, love poetry and literary treatises.
THE ALBERTIS OF FLORENCE: Leon Battista Alberti's Della Famigilia
A classic Renaissance treatise on education
Translated by Guido Guarino
0–8387–7736–8 Bucknell $30.00

• Baldesar Castiglione
THE BOOK OF THE COURTIER
The full art of courtly conduct
Translated by George Bull
0–14–044192–1 Penguin pb $4.95

• Marsilio Ficino
COMMENTARY ON PLATO'S SYMPOSIUM ON LOVE
Ficino, a Christian Platonist who led the humanist revival, championed the idea that philosophy and religion were in harmony. Humankind, in his view, was entrusted with the "bonding" of the universe
0–88214–601–7 Spring pb $18.50

• Niccolò Machiavelli
THE PORTABLE MACHIAVELLI
Contains *The Prince, The Mandrake,* excerpts from *The Discourses,* and other writings
Edited by Mark Musa & Peter Bondanella
0–14–015092–7 Penguin pb $8.95

• Giovanni Pico della Mirandola
ON THE DIGNITY OF MAN
For Pico della Mirandola, man is the divine masterpiece. In his own day his original syntheses laid him open to the charge of heresy. This edition also includes *On Being and Unity* and *Heptaplus*
0–672–60483–3 Bobbs-Merrill pb $7.95

● Angelo Poliziano
THE STANZE OF ANGELO POLIZIANO
A picturesque celebration of a courtly
jousting tournament and the landscape in
which it took place
Edited by David Quint
0–87023–145–6 Massachusetts $11.00

Artists

● Michelangelo Buonarotti
LIFE, LETTERS AND POETRY
An anthology of sonnets and other
writings, with a contemporary biography
Edited by George Bull
0–19–281603–9 Oxford pb $6.95

● Benvenuto Cellini
**THE AUTOBIOGRAPHY OF
BENVENUTO CELLINI**
Revealing, sometimes scurrilous memoirs
Translated by George Bull
0–14–044049–6 Penguin pb $5.95

● Leonardo da Vinci
**THE NOTEBOOKS OF LEONARDO DA
VINCI**
A one-volume selection from Leonardo's
voluminous journals
Edited by Irma Richter
0–19–281538–5 Oxford pb $4.95

● Giorgio Vasari
LIVES OF THE ARTISTS
Perhaps the most entertaining work of art
history ever written. This generous
selection includes an appendix correcting
some of Vasari's attributions and
biographical data
Translated by George Bull
Volume 1
0–14–04450–05 Penguin pb $5.95
Volume 2
0–14–044460–2 Penguin pb $5.95

Epic Poets of the Renaissance

● Ludovico Ariosto
"The *Furioso* is a book unique in its kind,
and can be—or should I say, must be?—
read without reference to any other book
either before or after it. It is a world of its
own that one can travel the length and
breadth of, going in, coming out again,
and losing oneself in it."—Italo Calvino
ORLANDO FURIOSO
Alive with self-mockery and mockery of its
audience, this famous work, depicting a
world sparkling with chivalry, magic and
romance, greatly influenced Elizabethan
and 17th-century English writers. Barbara
Reynolds' skilful translation employs
rhymed octaves
Translated by Barbara Reynolds
Volume 1
0–14–044311–8 Penguin pb $10.95
Volume 2
0–14–044310–X Penguin pb $14.95
ORLANDO FURIOSO
A straightforward prose version
Translated by Guido Waldman
0–19–281636–5 Oxford pb $13.95

Commedia dell'arte figures, from The
Theatre: A Concise History *by Phyllis
Hartnoll (Thames & Hudson)*

● Matteo Mario Boiardo
ORLANDO INNAMORATO
The classic tale of Charlemagne's knight,
Orlando
Translated by Charles Ross
0–520–05978–6 California $80.00

● Torquato Tasso
A great poet of the Italian High
Renaissance and one of its most tragic
figures, Tasso was also a distinguished
critic.
**TASSO'S DIALOGUES: A Selection, with
the Discourse of the Art of the Dialogue**
The subjects covered include philosophy,
morality, literature and aesthetics
Translated by Carnes Lord & Dain Trafton
0–520–04464–9 California (bilingual) $20.50
0–520–04985–3 California (bilingual) pb $7.95
TASSO'S JERUSALEM DELIVERED
A prose translation of the heroic epic of
the recapture of the Holy City from the
Saracens in the First Crusade
Translated by Ralph Nash
0–8143–1830–4 Wayne State pb $16.00

The Tradition of Italian Theater

● Carlo Goldoni
THE LIAR
Translated by Frederick Davies
0–87830–531–9 Theatre Arts pb $3.50
THE SERVANT OF TWO MASTERS
Translated by Frederick Davies
0–87830–537–8 Theatre Arts pb $3.50

● Niccolò Machiavelli
THE COMEDIES OF MACHIAVELLI
A bilingual edition including *The Woman
from Andros, The Mandrake,* and *Clizia.*
Machiavelli's talents were not limited to
history and political theory. His trenchant
Mandragola (*The Mandrake*) is considered
by many to be the greatest Italian play
Translated by David Sices & James Atkinson
0–87451–329–4 New England $27.50

● Pietro Metastasio
THREE MELODRAMAS
Includes *Dido Abandoned, Demetrius,* and
The Olympiad. Metastasio was the chief
literary architect of *opera seria,* and his
librettos were set to music by Mozart,
Gluck, Handel, and Scarlatti
Translated by Joseph Fucilla
0–8131–1400–4 Kentucky $15.00

● Eric Bentley, editor
**THE SERVANT OF TWO MASTERS &
OTHER ITALIAN CLASSICS**
The title play by Goldoni plus Gozzi's *The
King Stag,* Machiavelli's *The Mandrake,*
and Beolco's *Ruzzante Returns from the
Wars*
0–936839–20–1 Applause pb $7.95

● Bruce Penman, editor & translator
**FIVE ITALIAN RENAISSANCE
COMEDIES**
Includes Machiavelli's *Mandragola,*
Ariosto's *Lena,* Aretino's *The Stablemaster,*
Gl'intronati's *The Deceived,* and Guarini's
The Faithful Shepherd
0–14–044338–X Penguin pb $5.95

THE 19TH CENTURY

The 19th century witnessed a decisive
literary rebirth, even though its major
figures are still insufficiently known and
some (Foscolo, Carducci, Pascoli) are barely
represented in English. The stylistic distance
covered in a single century can be measured
by the differences between the disenchanted
classicism of Leopardi at its outset, the epic
historical pageantry of Manzoni at midcentury, and finally the Sicilian *verismo*—
realism—of Verga, signaling a breakthrough
of regional elements and harsh economic
realities. Curiously enough it is Leopardi,
with his clear-eyed contemplation of nothingness, who strikes the most modern note.

● Giuseppe Giocchinio Belli
THE SONNETS OF GIUSEPPE BELLI
A scholarly and comprehensive version
Translated by Miller Williams
0–8071–0762–X LSU $20.00

● Giacomo Leopardi
A LEOPARDI READER
A solid, comprehensive introduction to the
poetry and prose of Italy's greatest 19th-
century lyric poet and philosopher who
saw a pressing need for human brotherhood to counter the brutality of life and
nature
Edited by Ottavio Casale
0–252–00824–3 Illinois $24.95
0–252–00892–8 Illinois pb $9.95
THE MORAL ESSAYS
Leopardi's masterpiece, a book which
creates its own genre: in tones at once
lyrical and bitterly lucid, he invents a
mythology of the death of mythology, a
hymn of non-belief
Translated by Patrick Creagh
0–231–05707–5 Columbia pb $14.00

OPERETTE MORALI: ESSAYS AND DIALOGUES
A bilingual edition of Leopardi's moral essays
Translated by Giovanni del Cecchetti
0–520–04928–4 California pb $10.95

PENSIERI
A selection of Leopardi's maxims, sharply translated
Translated by W.S. Di Piero
0–19–503496–1 Oxford (bilingual) pb $6.95

The time will come when this universe and nature herself will be no more. And just as of very great human kingdoms and empires of their marvelous exploits, which were so very famous in other ages, there remains no sign of fame whatsoever; so too of the entire world, and of the infinite vicissitudes and calamities of all created things, no single trace will remain; but a naked silence and a most profound quiet will fill the immensity of space. Thus, this stupendous and frightening mystery of universal existence, before it can be declared or understood, will vanish and be lost.

from "The Song of the Great Wild Rooster"

Giacomo Leopardi
OPERETTE MORALI: ESSAYS AND DIALOGUES
Translated by Giovanni Cecchetti
0–520–04928–4 California pb $10.95

Alessandro Manzoni
THE BETROTHED
A national institution in Italy, Manzoni's masterwork contains much penetrating political realism along with its captivating narrative of two lovers struggling against war, famine, plague, and feudal abuses. Bruce Penman's translation is exceptionally good. "*The Betrothed* gives us a vision of history as a constant confrontation with catastrophe"—Italo Calvino
Translated by Bruce Penman
0–14–044274–X Penguin pb $7.95

• Giovanni Verga
The late 19th-century novelist, whose *verismo* (realism) often earns him comparisons with Flaubert and Zola, starkly depicts the oppressive impoverishment of the Sicilian peasant class.

THE HOUSE BY THE MEDLAR TREE
Verga's masterpiece describes the tragic futility of the life of fisherfolk
Translated by Raymond Rosenthal
0–520–04850–4 California pb $10.95

MASTRO DON GESUALDO
A study of an arriviste whose social and material success ends in emotional bankruptcy and isolation
Translated by Raymond Rosenthal
0–520–05077–0 California pb $10.95

SHORT SICILIAN NOVELS
Translated by D.H. Lawrence
0–946626–04–9 Hippocrene pb $4.95

THE SHE-WOLF AND OTHER STORIES
Includes *Cavalleria Rusticana*
Translated by Giovanni Cecchetti
0–520–04789–3 California pb $10.95

THE 20TH CENTURY

Fiction

American readers became keenly aware of Italian fiction in the postwar period when they began to encounter translations of writers such as Elio Vittorini, Mario Soldati, Curzio Malaparte, and above all Alberto Moravia. The so-called neorealist style of these novelists—deeply influenced by both Verga's *verismo* and American naturalism—developed within the constraints of Fascist censorship, and reached its full flowering in the war's aftermath.

The realist tendency has remained evident in the work of Natalia Ginzburg, Giorgio Bassani, Elsa Morante, and (in his own idiosyncratic fashion) Pier Paolo Pasolini. On the other hand, a distinctive vein of fantastic fiction has been explored by Dino Buzzati, Tommaso Landolfi, and Italo Calvino. The popularity of Calvino's work in America has been such that a great many other Italian writers are now being translated, making it possible to encounter the younger, often more experimental voices of Andrea de Carlo, Ferdinando Camon, Antonio Tabucchi, and others.

• Anna Banti
ARTEMISIA
A fictional portrayal, first published in 1947, of the intriguing 17th-century Neapolitan portraitist Artemisia Gentileschi, by a woman writer who earned her success well before the feminist era
Translated with an afterword by Shirley D'Ardia Caracciolo
0–8032–1203–8 Nebraska $21.00

• Giorgio Bassani
A rigorous stylist, Bassani focuses on the world of his native Ferrara and its Jewish community during the Nazi persecution.
THE HERON
The killing of a heron triggers a variety of reactions in a Jewish survivor of Mussolini's Italy
Translated by William Weaver
0–15–640085–5 HBJ pb $5.95

• Stefano Benni
TERRA!
Comic science fiction by a political journalist and humorist
Translated by Annapaoloa Cancogni
0–394–74064–5 Pantheon pb $6.95

• Gesualdo Bufalino
THE PLAGUE-SOWER
A powerful novel of a sanitarium in postwar Italy, written over a period of 30

years and published to great acclaim in 1981
Translated by Stephen Sartarelli
Introduction by Leonardo Sciascia
0–941419–12–6 Eridanos $22.00
0–941419–13–4 Eridanos pb $13.00

• Aldo Busi
SEMINAR ON YOUTH
The life and survival of a young male prostitute living in Milan and Paris
Translated by Stuart Hood
0–374–26088–5 Farrar, Straus & Giroux $17.95

• Dino Buzzati
Buzzati was a prolific writer of allegorical and surrealistic fiction.
A LOVE AFFAIR
"A rollicking, lyric, and delightful account of a respectable middle-aged man's devotion to a vulgar, lying, and unfaithful young trollop"—*New Yorker*
Translated by Joseph Green
0–85635–586–0 Carcanet $16.95

RESTLESS NIGHTS
Twenty-three tales of the fantastic
Translated with an introduction by Lawrence Venuti
0–86547–100–2 North Point pb $12.00

THE SIREN
Includes the novella *Barnabo of the Mountain*. "Some dozen stories sharing that blend of surrealist fantasy, quiet humor, satire, and inventiveness one associates with Kafka, Borges, Lem and Calvino"—*Washington Post*
Translated by Lawrence Venuti
0–86547–159–2 North Point pb $10.50

THE TARTAR STEPPE
Soldiers at a remote outpost spend their lifetime waiting for an enemy to appear
Translated by Stuart Hood
0–85635–576–3 North Point pb $7.50

• Italo Calvino
"Calvino does what very few writers can do: he describes imaginary worlds with the most extraordinary precision and beauty."—Gore Vidal

Italo Calvino (photo by Jerry Bauer)

THE BARON IN THE TREES
In this widely admired book, an aristocratic rebel defies parental authority and takes to an arboreal life. From his perch he watches the Age of Voltaire unfold
Translated by Archibald Colquhoun
0–15–610680–9 HBJ pb $5.95

THE CASTLE OF CROSSED DESTINIES
A series of short, fantastic narratives inspired by 15th-century tarot cards and their archetypal images
Translated by William Weaver
0–15–615455–2 HBJ pb $5.95

COSMICOMICS
Fantasies on the evolution of the universe
Translated by William Weaver
0–15–622600–6 HBJ pb $3.95

DIFFICULT LOVES
The intricate inner worlds of ordinary people. "A certain lovable nuttiness makes this collection well worth reading"—Margaret Atwood, *NY Times*
Translated by William Weaver & others
0–15–626055–7 HBJ pb $5.95

IF ON A WINTER'S NIGHT A TRAVELER
Ten different novels interwoven into one. Each chapter begins a new book, a new plot, and a different writing style
Translated by William Weaver
0–15–643961–1 HBJ pb $5.95

INVISIBLE CITIES
Conversations between Marco Polo and Kublai Khan evoke an open-ended series of imaginary cities
Translated by William Weaver
0–15–645380–0 HBJ pb $3.95

MARCOVALDO: The Seasons in the City
Twenty short stories, in settings ranging from the poverty of a northern industrial city in the 1950s to the illusory economic boom of the 1960s
Translated by William Weaver
0–15–657204–4 HBJ pb $3.95

THE NONEXISTENT KNIGHT & THE CLOVEN VISCOUNT
Two novellas: a parody of medieval knighthood and "a dark-hued Gothic gem" (*NY Times*) about a nobleman bisected into his good and evil halves
Translated by Archibald Colquhoun
0–15–665975–1 HBJ pb $5.95

THE PATH TO THE NEST OF SPIDERS
The hero of Calvino's first, neo-realistic novel is a cobbler's apprentice turned partisan who makes common cause with his fellow outcasts
0–670542–69–5 Norton pb $6.95

t-ZERO
Evolutionary and space-time tales blending higher mathematics with higher comedy and poetic imagination
Translated by William Weaver
0–15–692400–5 HBJ pb $3.95

THE WATCHER AND OTHER STORIES
Contains *Smog* and *The Argentine Ant*
Translated by William Weaver & Archibald Colquhon
0–15–694952–0 HBJ pb $3.95

• Ferdinando Camon
"A writer of such importance that one does not know where or with whom to place him in the literature of our time."—Philippe Guilhon, *Le Monde des livres*

THE FIFTH ESTATE
The chronicle of a post-war childhood in a peasant community near Padua
Translated by John Shepley
0–910395–29–2 Marlboro $16.95

LIFE EVERLASTING
A novel of the Resistance, of which the author has said: "On the part of the peasantry that Resistance was a visceral, furious and chaotic reaction against the violence of the invaders . . . They knew nothing about communism or capitalism. They had no ideas at all about creating a new Italy for after the war"
Translated by John Shepley
0–910395–31–4 Marlboro $17.95

MEMORIAL
In writing of the death of his mother Camon also confronts another kind of death: the end of peasant civilization
Translated by David Calicchio
0–910395–07–1 Marlboro pb $7.50

• Grazia Deledda
Deledda, winner of the Nobel Prize in 1926, wrote intense character studies rooted in Sardinian life, of which D.H. Lawrence remarked: "What she does do is create the passionate complex of a primitive populace."

LA MADRE (The Woman and the Priest)
A study of a cleric's spontaneous passion "which only the blind instinct of mother obedience, the child passion, can overcome" (D.H. Lawrence)
0–946626–20–0 Hippocrene pb $7.95

• Umberto Eco
THE NAME OF THE ROSE
The surprise bestseller of the 1980s: a medieval version of Agatha Christie, densely interlarded with contemporary semiotic and political references
Translated by William Weaver
0–15–144647–4 HBJ $24.95
0–446–34410–9 Warner pb $4.95

• Carlo Emilio Gadda
ACQUAINTED WITH GRIEF
A "potpourri of linguistic flights, puns, literary allusions, phonetic tricks and endlessly proliferating verbosity"—*Library Journal*
Translated by William Weaver
0–8076–1115–8 Braziller pb $8.95

THAT AWFUL MESS ON VIA MERULANA
Another stylistically innovative work. "Bawdy, obscene, punning, enormously learned. Gadda explodes language"—*Newsweek*
Translated by William Weaver
Introduction by Italo Calvino
0–8076–1093–3 Braziller pb $8.95

• Natalia Ginzburg
"A brilliant eccentric; she is almost certainly Italy's best woman writer today."—*TLS*
ALL OUR YESTERDAYS
Translated by Angus Davidson
0–8050–0005–4 Carcanet pb $8.95

THE CITY AND THE HOUSE
Translated by Dick Davis
0–8050–0392–4 Seaver $16.95

FAMIGLIA
Two early novellas which deal with the decay of the family through "hypocrisy, resignation and unhappiness"
Translated by Beryl Stockman
0–8050–0856–X Henry Holt $15.95

THE LITTLE VIRTUES
Translated by Dick Davis
0–8050–0077–1 Seaver $13.95

• Giuseppe Tomasi di Lampedusa
THE LEOPARD
The decline of the Sicilian aristocracy, traced in a classic novel that is both an indictment and a lament
Translated by Archibald Colquhoun
0–394–43291–6 Pantheon $13.95
0–394–75668–1 Pantheon $7.95

• Tommaso Landolfi
AN AUTUMN STORY
One of the great love stories of modern Italian literature
Translated by Joachim Neugroschel
0–941419–27–4 Eridanos $20.00
0–941419–26–6 Eridanos pb $11.00

GOGOL'S WIFE & OTHER STORIES
Landolfi, a master of the fantastic tale and a major influence on Italo Calvino, has been compared with Kafka, Joyce, Borges, and Poe
0–8112–0080–9 New Directions pb $8.95

WORDS IN COMMOTION & OTHER STORIES
Twenty-four stories grouped under such headings as Fantastic, Obsessive, and Horrific
Translated by Kathrine Jason
Introduction by Italo Calvino
0–14–009477–6 Penguin pb $7.95

• Primo Levi
IF NOT NOW, WHEN?
A novel of Jewish resistance to the Nazis
Translated by William Weaver
Introduction by Irving Howe
0–671–49336–1 Summit $15.95
0–14–008492–4 Penguin pb $6.95

THE MONKEY'S WRENCH
Often quirky tales of the joys and passions of work, as told by a construction worker
0–671–62214–5 Summit $15.95
0–14–010357–0 Penguin pb $6.95

• Curzio Malaparte
In these novels of World War II and its aftermath Malaparte shows the demoralization of Italy in the face of foreign invaders: Germans in *Kaputt*, Americans in *The Skin*
KAPUTT
Translated by Cesare Foligno
0–910395–00–4 Marlboro $16.95
0–910395–01–2 Marlboro $9.50

THE SKIN
This sequel to *Kaputt* depicts the Italy of 1943–45 against a canvas of "vast landscapes and seething cities as full of extravagant detail as a crowd sequence directed by Griffith"—*Observer*
Translated by David Moore
0–910395–37–3 Marlboro pb $12.95

  IF YOU CAN'T FIND IT, LOOK IN THE INDEX

• Giuliana Morandini

BLOODSTAINS

The impact of Nazi occupation on an Italian village, seen through the eyes of an adolescent girl

Translated by Blossom S. Kirschenbaum
0–317–65076–9 New Rivers pb $8.95

• Elsa Morante

HISTORY: A Novel

World War II in sometimes agonizing close-up, as experienced by a single luckless family

Translated by William Weaver
0–394–49802–X Knopf $15.45
0–394–72496–8 Vintage pb $10.95

• Alberto Moravia

Moravia's neorealist portrayal of Roman life on all social levels is grounded in a ruthless perception of social alienation and the power of sex and money.

EROTIC TALES

Translated by Tim Parks
0–374–14868–6 Farrar, Straus & Giroux $15.95

1934

Translated by William Weaver
0–374–22254–1 Farrar, Straus & Giroux $14.50

TIME OF DESECRATION

Translated by Angus Davidson
0–374–27781–8 Farrar, Straus & Giroux $12.95

• Marta Morazzoni

GIRL IN A TURBAN

Five densely detailed stories set in a variety of places and historical periods. "We are made to feel the weight of the flesh, the world, and above all, the passing or pressure of the time . . . A very impressive debut"—*TLS*

Translated by Patrick Creagh
0–394–56115–5 Knopf $16.95

• Guido Morselli

DIVERTIMENTO 1889

Morselli committed suicide at 62 before any of his prolific output had been published. This belle epoque fable about King Umberto I's efforts to evade his public duties has been compared to Nabokov

Translated by Hugh Shankland
0–525–24553–7 Dutton $15.95

• Anna Maria Ortese

THE IGUANA

A fantasy novel, published in the late 1960s, concerning an uncharted island off the coast of Portugal. "A satiric fable dense with echoes of Shakespeare's *Tempest* and Kafka's *Metamorphosis*"—*NY Times*

Translated by Henry Martin
0–914232–95–9 McPherson pb $9.00

• Goffredo Parise

SOLITUDES

Short stories by a young Italian writer

Translated by Isabel Quigly
Introduction by Natalia Ginzburg
0–394–72994–3 Random House pb $7.95

• Pier Paolo Pasolini

Susan Sontag described Pasolini, who was murdered in 1975, as "indisputably the most remarkable figure to have emerged in Italian arts and letters since the Second World War." In addition to his fiction his prolific output includes poetry, essays, and screenplays.

THE RAGAZZI

Translated by Emile Capouya
0–85635–691–3 Carcanet pb $8.50

ROMAN NIGHTS & OTHER STORIES

"Several of the stories are so strong, so raw in their homoeroticism, that one is dumbfounded to discover that the earliest was written more than 30 years ago"— Peter Brunette, *NY Times*

Translated by John Shepley
0–910395–20–9 Marlboro pb $9.00

A VIOLENT LIFE

"Not since Hubert Selby's *Last Exit to Brooklyn* have I read a work so muscular and sublimely ugly"—Anne Rice, *NY Times*

Translated by William Weaver
0–85635–591–7 Carcanet pb $8.50

• Cesare Pavese

THE DEVIL IN THE HILLS

An elegant novel of youth set in Pavese's native Piedmont

0–7206–2795–8 Dufour $15.95

THE HOUSE ON THE HILL

A group of friends caught up in the last days of World War II

0–7206–4286–8 Dufour $19.95

STORIES

These tales reflect the often unhappy experiences of Pavese's own life: his inadequacy with woman, his political exile, and his musings on suicide

Translated by A.E. Murch
0–88001–124–6 Ecco pb $12.95

• Luigi Pirandello

Awarded the Nobel Prize in 1934, Pirandello was a prolific writer of fiction before he embarked on his career as a dramatist.

THE LATE MATTIA PASCAL

Pirandello's best novel, published in 1904, tells of a small-town librarian who is erroneously declared dead and tries to make a new life for himself. "For the moment (and God knows how much it pains me), I have died already twice, but the first time was a mistake, and the second . . . well, you may read for yourself"

Translated by William Weaver
0–9414–19–08–8 Eridanos $23.00
0–9414–19–09–6 Eridanos pb $14.00

TALES OF MADNESS

Translated by Giovanni Bussino
0–937832–26–X Dante University $14.50

TALES OF SUICIDE

Translated by Giovanni Bussino
0–937832–31–6 Dante University $11.95

▶ **For Pirandello's plays see Modern European Drama**

• Umberto Saba

ERNESTO

A novel of a young man's homosexual awakening, written by an outstanding lyric poet

Translated by Mark Thompson
0–85635–559–3 Carcanet $15.95

• Alberto Savinio

CHILDHOOD OF NIVASIO DOLCEMARE

An autobiographical novel set in Athens at the turn of the century. Savinio was the brother of the painter Giorgio de Chirico

Translated by Richard Pevear
Introduction by Dore Ashton
0–9414–19–04–5 Eridanos $21.00
0–9414–19–05–3 Eridanos pb $12.00

LIVES OF THE GODS

Translated by James Brook & Susan Etlinger
Preface by Edouard Roditi
1–55554–031–7 Farrar, Straus & Giroux $18.95
1–55554–044–9 Farrar, Straus & Giroux pb $8.95

• Leonardo Sciascia

Sciascia frequently employs the techniques and motifs of detective fiction to illuminate, in unpredictable ways, the social landscape of Italy. "Sciascia . . . invents for us a world quite as real as any that Dreiser ever dealt with, rendered in a style that is, line by line, as jolting as an exposed electrical wire."—Gore Vidal

THE COUNCIL OF EGYPT

Political and literary intrigue in 18th-century Sicily

Translated by Adrienne Foulke
0–85635–740–5 Carcanet $18.95

DAY OF THE OWL & EQUAL DANGER

Two mysteries that confront the Mafia code of *omerta*

Afterword by Frank Kermode
0–87923–516–0 Godine pb $8.95

THE MORO AFFAIR & THE MYSTERY OF MAJORANA

"Ponders Moro's ordeal with human concern, but also with welcome clarity and objectivity"—William Weaver

Translated by Sacha Rabinovitch
0–85635–700–6 Carcanet $16.95

ONE WAY OR ANOTHER

An odd sort of murder mystery, foreshadowing recent Italian political scandals

Translated by Sacha Rabinovitch
0–85635–664–6 Carcanet $16.95
0–85635–781–2 Carcanet pb $8.50

SICILIAN UNCLES: Four Novellas

"The acerbity and gloom at the heart of *Sicilian Uncles* give these four episodes . . . the consistency of a sustained historical essay"—*Observer*

Translated by N.S. Thompson
0–85635–555–0 Carcanet $15.95
0–85635–782–0 Carcanet pb $6.95

THE WINE-DARK SEA: Thirteen Stories

"The well-translated collection is an ideal introduction for anyone who hasn't yet come across one of the major writers of the age"—*TLS*

Translated by Avril Bardoni
0–85635–556–9 Carcanet $14.95
0–85635–783–9 Carcanet pb $6.95

• Ignazio Silone

Silone's literary reputation has faded somewhat but his novels remain primary documents of anti-Fascism.

BREAD AND WINE

Translated by Harvey Ferguson
0–451–51757–1 Signet pb $2.95

FONTAMARA
Translated by Eric Mosbacher
Introduction by Irving Howe
0–452–00743–7 Signet pb $4.50

● Italo Svevo
THE CONFESSIONS OF ZENO
An experimental novel exploring an old man's consciousness. It was a favorite of James Joyce
0–394–70063–5 Random House pb $5.95
0–679–72234–3 Vintage pb $8.95

FURTHER CONFESSIONS OF ZENO
Includes a variety of posthumously published fragments
Translated by Ben Johnson & P.N. Furbank
0–520–01753–6 California pb $7.95

● Antonio Tabucchi
Of the short stories which make up the collections below, Tabucchi has written: "Misunderstandings, uncertainties, belated understandings, useless remorse, treacherous memories, stupid and irredeemable mistakes, all these irresistibly fascinate me."

LETTER FROM CASABLANCA
Translated by Janice Thresher
0–8112–0985–7 New Directions $17.95
0–8112–0986–5 New Directions pb $7.95

LITTLE MISUNDERSTANDINGS OF NO IMPORTANCE
Translated by Frances Frenaye
0–8112–1029–4 New Directions $16.95

● Elio Vittorini
Influenced by Hemingway and other American novelists, Vittorini was a leading practioner of literary neorealism.

MEN AND NOT MEN
This tale of the Resistance in Milan at the end of World War II is "an unsparing analysis of the moral ambiguities inherent in political violence"—*LA Times*
Translated by Sarah Henry
0–910395–13–6 Marlboro $16.95

WOMEN OF MESSINA
Translated by Frances Frenaye & Frances Keene
0–8112–0496–0 New Directions $9.50
0–8112–0497–9 New Directions pb $3.75

Poetry

Modern Italian poetry has known its share of contending schools, ranging from the crepuscularism of the 1880s (which in response to earlier bombast sought a more restrained approach) to the futurism associated with Marinetti and the hermeticism explored by Giuseppe Ungaretti. Ungaretti has been perhaps the most influential Italian poet of this century, although unfortunately his work is currently hard to come by in English. His influence can be traced in the work of Quasimodo, Luzi, Sereni, Sinisgalli, and Erba, all of whom share a certain elusive, almost aristocratic privacy of expression. The other great figures of the era are Eugenio Montale—who won the Nobel Prize in 1975 and whose work represents, among other things, a profound meditation on Italy's experience under Fascism—and the short-lived Cesare Pavese, in whose poems realism achieves the mysteriousness of a dream.

Recent years have witnessed an extravagant variety of stylistic modes. Out of the welter of the "Roman School," the "neo-avant-garde," and other groupings, a few major voices have emerged: Sandro Penna, the experimentalist Antonio Porta, the more traditional Andrea Zanzotta, and the filmmaker and novelist Pier Paolo Pasolini, whose poetry, written in his native Friulano dialect, is considered by many his most important work.

Vigil
A whole night through
flung down beside me
a comrade
slaughtered
his mouth
grimacing
turned to the full moon
his stiffened
hands
penetrating
into my silence
I wrote
letters full of love

Never have I
clung so
close to life

Giuseppe Ungaretti
Translated by Charles Tomlinson in
William Jay Smith & Dana Gioia,
editors
POEMS FROM ITALY
0–89823–060–8 New Rivers pb $12.00

● Dino Campana
ORPHIC SONGS
Campana spent much of his life in mental hospitals, and this passionately imagistic collection, written in 1913, is his only book
Translated by Charles Wright
0–932440–16–9 Oberlin $11.50
0–932440–17–7 Oberlin pb $6.50

● Guido Gozzano
THE COLLOQUIES & SELECTED LETTERS
Described as reluctantly in love with his bourgeois world, this influential "crepuscular" poet "made his debut in a quite casual way, with his hands in his pockets"—Eugenio Montale
Translated with an introduction by J.G. Nichols
0–85635–628–X Carcanet pb $12.50

● Primo Levi
THE COLLECTED POEMS
Levi's poetry engages the same themes of Holocaust and survival as his prose work
Translated by Ruth Feldman & Brian Swann
0–571–15256–2 Faber & Faber pb $8.95

● Mario Luzi
IN THE DARK BODY OF METAMORPHOSIS & OTHER POEMS
A religious poet somewhat in the tradition of Ungaretti
Translated by I.L. Salomon
0–393–04391–6 Norton $6.95
0–393–04403–3 Norton pb $2.50

● Eugenio Montale
"Montale speaks to us of a spinning world driven by a wind of destruction, with no solid ground to stand on . . . It is the world of the First and Second World Wars, and perhaps even of the Third."—Italo Calvino

SELECTED POEMS
Sixty-nine poems, rendered by 16 poet-translators, from the author's first three books; a bilingual edition
Edited by Glauco Cambon
0–8112–0325–5 New Directions $7.50

IT DEPENDS: A Poet's Notebook
A bilingual edition of Montale's last collection, published at age 82
Translated by G. Singh
0–8112–0774–9 New Directions pb $4.95

NEW POEMS
Written after the death of the poet's wife, this collection includes witty and ironical pieces which clearly display his acute critical intelligence
Translated by G. Singh
Essay by F.R. Leavis
0–8112–0598–3 New Directions $7.95
0–8112–0599–1 New Directions pb $2.95

THE OCCASIONS
Montale's second book, published in 1939, contains many of his greatest poems, including "Dora Markus" and the "Motets"
Translated by William Arrowsmith
0–393–02316–8 Norton (bilingual) $15.95
0–393–30324–1 Norton (bilingual) pb $9.95

THE STORM AND OTHER THINGS
Published in 1956 and often considered Montale's masterpiece. "One of the truly distinguished renderings of modern Italian poetry. Arrowsmith is an authentically *poetic* translator surpassed by none of our contemporaries"—Harold Bloom
Translated by William Arrowsmith
0–393–01996–9 Norton (bilingual) $14.95
0–393–30249–0 Norton (bilingual) pb $6.95

● Pier Paolo Pasolini
SELECTED POEMS
Translated by Norman MacAfee & Luciano Martinengo
0–7145–3889–2 Riverrun pb $12.95

ROMAN POEMS
The "infernal" aspect of modern Italian life as witnessed by a poet passionately involved in his country's political upheaval
Translated by Lawrence Ferlinghetti & Francesca Valente
0–87286–187–2 City Lights pb $5.95

● Cesare Pavese
HARD LABOR
Described by its author as "a book that might have saved a generation," this work of prophetic originality, first published in 1936, benefits from Arrowsmith's remarkable translation. "This book in English provides one of those strange occasions when the genius of a great man . . . proves its own miracle by rising from the dead in the genius of his translator"—James Wright
Translated by William Arrowsmith
0–88001–100–9 Ecco pb $9.50

◗ TO ORDER BOOKS AS GIFTS, SEE PAGE 1

• Sandro Penna

THIS STRANGE JOY: Selected Poems of Sandro Penna
Poems dealing largely with homosexual love
Translated by W.S. Di Piero
0–8142–0328–0 Ohio State $15.00

• Lucio Piccolo

THE COLLECTED POEMS OF LUCIO PICCOLO
A Sicilian nobleman, Piccolo was a cousin of Giuseppe di Lampedusa, author of *The Leopard*
Translated by Ruth Feldman & Brian Swann
0–691–06227–7 Princeton $23.50

• Antonio Porta

KISSES FROM ANOTHER DREAM
Bittersweet, defiant lyrics from a leading figure of the Gruppo 63 movement that was committed to politically subversive and formally innovative poetry
Translated by Anthony Molino
0–87286–206–2 City Lights pb $5.95

• Salvatore Quasimodo

THE COMPLETE POEMS OF SALVATORE QUASIMODO
Quasimodo won the Nobel Prize for Literature in 1959
Translated by Jack Bevan
0–8052–0757–0 Schocken pb $8.95

• Rocco Scotellaro

A village mayor at 23, imprisoned for embezzlement, released thanks to the interventions of Carlo Levi and Alberto Moravia, and dead in 1953 at age 30, Scotellaro has received wide-spread posthumous recognition as a poet who speaks for the peasant culture of Southern Italy.

THE DAWN IS ALWAYS NEW: Poetry of Rocco Scotellaro
Translated by Ruth Feldman & Brian Swann
0–691–01370–5 Princeton pb $8.50

• Diego Valeri

MY NAME ON THE WIND: Selected Poems
Translated by Michael Palma
0–691–01462–0 Princeton pb $12.95

• Andrea Zanzotto

SELECTED POETRY OF ANDREA ZANZOTTO
Radical linguistic experimentation combined with multiple layers of literary reference
Translated by Ruth Feldman & Brian Swann
0–691–01323–3 Princeton pb $10.50

Anthologies of Modern Italian Poetry

• Lawrence R. Smith, editor

THE NEW ITALIAN POETRY: 1945 to the Present
Twenty-one realist, hermetic, and avant-garde poets, with an account of each school's development. A bilingual edition
0–520–03859–2 California $37.50
0–520–04411–8 California pb $12.95

• Adriano Spatolo & Paul Vangelisti, editors

ITALIAN POETRY, 1960–1980: From Neo to Post Avant-Garde
The cutting edge of poetic experimentation
0–686–45586–X Invisible City $15.00
0–88031–060–X Invisible City pb $7.50

Essays, Memoirs, and Other Prose

• Benedetto Croce

AESTHETIC: A Science of Expression and General Linguistics
A classic treatise on the theory of art and the origins of language, published in 1909
Translated by Douglas Ainslie
0–87923–255–2 Godine pb $10.95

• Natalia Ginzburg

FAMILY SAYINGS
A collection of autobiographical essays spanning the Fascist era and the war years in Turin
0–8050–0152–2 Seaver pb $7.95

• Carlo Levi

CHRIST STOPPED AT EBOLI
A memoir of the author's internal exile under Mussolini in the impoverished Basilicata region
Translated by Frances Frenaye
0–374–50316–8 Farrar, Straus & Giroux pb $8.95

• Primo Levi

THE DROWNED AND THE SAVED
Translated by Raymond Rosenthal
0–671–63280–9 Summit $17.95
0–679–72186–X Vintage pb $8.95

MOMENTS OF REPRIEVE
Translated by Ruth Feldman
0–671–60535–6 Summit $14.95
0–14–009370–2 Penguin pb $5.95

THE PERIODIC TABLE
"The best introduction to the psychological world of one of the most important and gifted writers of our time"—*Newsweek*
Translated by Raymond Rosenthal
0–8052–0811–9 Schocken pb $7.95

SURVIVAL IN AUSCHWITZ: The Nazi Assault on Humanity & THE REAWAKENING
0–671–60541–0 Summit $19.95

• Eugenio Montale

THE BUTTERFLY OF DINARD
Translated by G. Singh
0–8131–1252–4 Kentucky $16.00

THE SECOND LIFE OF ART: Selected Essays
Edited by Jonathan Galassi
0–912946–84–9 Ecco $17.50
0–912946–85–7 Ecco pb $9.50

• Pier Paolo Pasolini

LUTHERAN LETTERS
Late essays, whose tone can be gauged from this excerpt: "All middle-class persons are, in fact, fascist, always, everywhere"
Translated by Stuart Hood
0–85635–410–4 Carcanet $18.50

• Luigi Pirandello

ON HUMOR
Edited by Antonio Illiano & Daniel Testa
0–8078–7058–7 North Carolina $15.00

Luigi Pirandello

• Alberto Savinio

SPEAKING TO CLIO
A contemplative travel journal concerning Etruscan burial places and the Abruzzi highlands
Translated by John Shepley
0–910395–22–5 Marlboro $14.95
0–910395–23–3 Marlboro pb $9.00

Up to the moment of this writing, and notwithstanding the horror of Hiroshima and Nagasaki, the shame of the Gulags, the useless and bloody Vietnam War, the Cambodian self-genocide, the *desaparecidos* of Argentina, the many atrocious and stupid wars we have seen since, the Nazi concentration camp system still remains a *unicum,* both in its extent and its quality. At no other place or time has one seen a phenomenon so unexpected and so complex: never have so many human lives been extinguished in so short a time, and with so lucid a combination of technological ingenuity, fanaticism, and cruelty.

Primo Levi
THE DROWNED AND THE SAVED
Translated by Raymond Rosenthal
0–671–63280–9 Summit $17.95
0–679–72186–X Vintage pb $8.95

ANTHOLOGIES

• Beverly Allen & others, editors

THE DEFIANT MUSE: Italian Feminist Poems to the Present
A bilingual anthology
0–935312–55–2 Feminist pb $11.95

• Herman W. Haller, editor
THE HIDDEN ITALY: A Bilingual Edition of Italian Dialect Poetry
Poetry in ten dialects, from the Middle Ages to the present, reflecting a new broadening of linguistic tolerance
0–8143–1802–9 Wayne State $39.95

• William Jay Smith & Dana Gioia, editors
POEMS FROM ITALY
This sampling ranges from St. Francis of Assisi to Pier Paolo Pasolini; the translators include Chaucer, Wordsworth, James Merrill, and Seamus Heaney. "One gains from this book a sharpened sense of the continuities and changes of Italian poetry, and of its powerful, sustained influence on poetic performance in English"—Richard Wilbur
0–89823–061–6 New Rivers $25.00
0–89823–060–8 New Rivers pb $12.00

CRITICAL STUDIES

• Giano Paolo Biasin
LITERARY DISEASES: Theme and Metaphor in the Italian Novel
0–292–74614–8 Texas $12.50

• Gregory Lucente
BEAUTIFUL FABLES: Self-Consciousness in Italian Narrative from Manzoni to Calvino
0–8018–3331–0 Johns Hopkins $32.50

• Ernest H. Wilkins
A HISTORY OF ITALIAN LITERATURE
A readable and authoritative overview
0–674–39701–0 Harvard $32.00

Individual Authors
(alphabetical by subject)

• Vittore Branca
BOCCACCIO: The Man and His Works
0–8147–1055–7 NYU pb $15.00

• Frances Yates
GIORDANO BRUNO AND THE HERMETIC TRADITION
A pioneering, sympathetic study of Renaissance uses of ancient magical traditions
0–226–95003–4 Chicago pb $17.00

Erich Auerbach
DANTE: Poet of the Secular World
0–226–03205–1 Chicago pb $13.95

Joan Ferrante
THE POLITICAL VISION OF THE DIVINE COMEDY
An exploration of political issues and ideas relating the poem to the turbulence of Dante's Florence
0–691–06603–5 Princeton $39.00

Giuseppe Mazzotta
DANTE, POET OF THE DESERT: History and Allegory in The Divine Comedy
Special emphasis on Dante's source materials
0–691–10233–3 Princeton pb $16.50

Charles Singleton
AN ESSAY ON THE VITA NUOVA
An erudite commentary on Dante's early masterwork
0–8018–2004–9 Johns Hopkins pb $6.00

JOURNEY TO BEATRICE
An acclaimed study by a preeminent Dante scholar
0–8018–2005–7 Johns Hopkins pb $9.95

• Glauco Cambon
UGO FOSCOLO: Poet of Exile
0–691–06424–5 Princeton $29.00

MICHELANGELO'S POETRY: Fury of Form
0–691–06648–5 Princeton $31.50

EUGENIO MONTALE'S POETRY: A Dream in Reason's Presence
0–691–06520–9 Princeton $28.00

• Davide Lajolo
AN ABSURD VICE: A Biography of Cesare Pavese
0–8112–0850–8 New Directions $18.50
0–8112–0851–6 New Directions pb $9.50

• Eric Bentley
THE PIRANDELLO COMMENTARIES
0–8101–0722–8 Northwestern pb $9.95

• Anne Paolucci
PIRANDELLO'S THEATRE: The Recovery of The Modern Stage for Dramatic Art
0–8093–0594–1 Southern Illinois pb $6.95

• Brian Moloney
ITALO SVEVO
0–85224–248–4 Columbia $18.00

Dutch Literature

• A. Alberts
THE ISLANDS
Translated by Hans Koning
0–87023–385–8 Massachusetts $15.00

• J. Bernlef
OUT OF MIND
A gripping novel about the onset of senility
Translated by Adrienne Dixon
0–87923–734–1 Godine $16.95

• Gerbrand A. Bredero
THE SPANISH BRABANTER: A 17th-Century Dutch Social Satire in Five Acts
Translated by H. David Brumble III
0–86698–018–0 Medieval & Renaissance $15.00

• Jeroen Brouwers
SUNKEN RED
A 1981 novel of a man's relationship with his mother and their imprisonment in a Japanese prisoner of war camp
Translated by Adrienne Dixon
0–941533–19–0 New Amsterdam $15.95

• Louis Couperus
THE HIDDEN FORCE
Translated by Alexander T. DeMattos
0–87023–465–X Massachusetts $24.00

• Maria Dermont
THE TEN THOUSAND THINGS
A novel of Indonesia under Dutch rule
0–394–72443–7 Random House pb $7.95

• Marcellus Emants
A POSTHUMOUS CONFESSION
Introduction by J. M. Coetzee
0–7043–0023–0 Salem House pb $8.95

• Maarten Hart
BEARERS OF BAD TIDINGS: A Story of Father and Son
0–8052–8176–2 Schocken $13.95

• Etty Hillesum
AN INTERRUPTED LIFE: The Diaries of Etty Hillesum, 1941–1943
Translated by Arnold Pomerans
0–394–53217–1 Pantheon $13.95

LETTERS FROM WESTERBORK
Translated by Arnold Pomerans
0–394–55350–0 Pantheon $14.95

• Direk Ayelt Kooiman
A LAMB TO SLAUGHTER
Translated by Adrienne Dixon
0–670–80376–6 Viking $16.95
0–88184–207–9 Carroll & Graf pb $8.95

Harry Mulisch
THE ASSAULT
The sole young survivor of a family slaughtered in a Nazi vendetta massacre confronts the reasons for the incident many years later, despite his efforts to steer clear of the whole affair
Translated by Claire White
0–394–74420–9 Pantheon pb $6.95

LAST CALL
Mulisch's most recent novel, set in present-day Amsterdam, uses the theatrical stage to explore one of his favorite themes: the link between illusion and reality
Translated by Adrienne Dixon
0–670–82549–2 Viking $19.95

TWO WOMEN
Translated by Els Early
0–7145–3810–8 Riverrun $11.95

WHAT POETRY IS
Edited by Stanley H. Barkan
Translated by Claire Nicolas White
0–89304–808–9 Cross-Cultural pb $3.50

● Multatuli
MAX HAVELAAR: Or, The Coffee Auctions of the Dutch Trading Company
A fierce literary onslaught directed at the Dutch colonial masters in the East Indies, by Holland's major 19th-century novelist
Translated by Roy Edwards
Introduction by D. H. Lawrence
0–87023–359–9 Massachusetts $25.00
0–87023–360–2 Massachusetts pb $12.95

● Cees Nooteboom
IN THE DUTCH MOUNTAINS
Translated by Adrienne Dixon
0–8071–1425–1 LSU $14.95

PHILIP AND THE OTHERS
In this first, surrealistic novel, a young man pursues his identity on a hitch-hiking odyssey of self-discovery, but ends up alone
Translated by Adrienne Dixon
0–8071–1376–X LSU $14.95

RITUALS
Translated by Adrienne Dixon
0–8071–1081–7 LSU $14.95

A SONG OF TRUTH AND SEMBLANCE
Translated by Adrienne Dixon
0–8071–1176–7 LSU $11.95

Bert Schierbeek
CROSS ROADS
"For outsiders like me, who have sometimes managed a glimpse of contemporary Dutch poetry, Schierbeek has long appeared as the dominant figure, energetic and graceful over forty years or more. This poem-novel goes beyond anything we've seen, to place him among the masters of an art that breaks distinctions between genres"— Jerome Rothenberg
Translated by Charles McGeehan
0–942668–11–1 Katydid pb $14.95

● Stijn Streuvels
THE FLAXFIELD
1–55713–050–7 Sun & Moon pb $11.95

● Paul Van Ostaijen
FEASTS OF FEAR AND AGONY
An example of the Flemish poet's experimental, expressionist writing, originally published in 1921
Translated by Hidde Van Ameyden van Duym
0–8112–0600–9 New Directions $5.95
0–8112–0601–7 New Directions pb $1.95

● Jan Wolkers
TURKISH DELIGHT
A semi-autobiographical saga of marital turbulence which became the subject of a successful film
Translated by Greta Kilburn
0–7145–2787–4 Marion Boyars pb $7.50

● E. M. Beekman, editor & translator
FUGITIVE DREAMS: An Anthology of Dutch Colonial Literature
0–87023–575–3 Massachusetts $35.00

Peter Glassgold, editor
LIVING SPACE: Poems of the Dutch Fifties
Includes work by Schierbeek, Elburg, Kouwenaar, Lucebert, Polet, Campert, and Claus
Introduction by Peter Glassgold
0–8112–0747–1 New Directions pb $3.95

City Lights
NINE DUTCH POETS
Includes work by Lucebert, Remco Campert, Bert Schierbeek, Simon Vinkenoog, J. Bernles, Jules Deelder, Judith Herzberg, Karel Appel, and Hans Plomp
Foreword by Lawrence Ferlinghetti
0–87286–135–X City Lights pb $3.50

German Literature

MEDIEVAL AND BAROQUE LITERATURE

Germanic peoples are recorded as a distinct tribal presence in the first century, and by the 9th century Old High German was established as the earliest written form of their language. However, no continuous literary tradition emerges until the late 12th century, with the work of the medieval poets Hartmann von Aue, Wolfram von Eschenbach, and Gottfried von Strassburg.

● Francis G. Gentry, editor
GERMAN MEDIEVAL TALES
Includes *The Unfortunate Lord Henry, Reinhart the Fox, The Tale of Doctor Johannes Faustus,* and others
0–8264–0273–9 Continuum pb $10.95

● A.T. Hatto, editor
THE NIBELUNGENLIED
Often regarded as a national epic (though based on the Norse Edda tales), this anonymous 13th-century poem has been read both as a celebration of military heroism and as an urbane critique of an anachronistic warrior's code
0–14–044137–9 Penguin pb $4.95

● Hartmann von Aue
EREC
This long poem from the late 12th century introduced Arthurian romance into German literature
Translated by J.W. Thomas
0–8032–4408–8 Nebraska $13.95

GREGORIUS, THE GOOD SINNER
A poetic version of the legend of the sinner who became pope; Thomas Mann used it as the basis for *The Holy Sinner*
Translated by Sheema Buehne
0–8044–6245–3 Ungar pb $5.95

Wolfram von Eschenbach
PARZIVAL
This long and complex narrative variation on the Grail legend is the crowning masterpiece of medieval German literature
Translated by A.T. Hatto
0–14–044361–4 Penguin pb $6.95

WILLEHALM
An unfinished epic account of the 8th-century Moorish invasion opposed by William of Toulouse
Translated by Marion Gibbs & Sidney Johnson
0–14–044399–1 Penguin pb $4.95

● Gottfried von Strassburg
TRISTAN
Strassburg's version of the Tristan and Isolde story imparts a mystical dimension to the concept of courtly love
Translated by A.T. Hatto
0–14–044098–4 Penguin pb $4.95

● Heinrich von dem Türlin
THE CROWN: A Tale of Sir Gawein and King Arthur's Court
The first English translation of the early 13th-century masterpiece of Arthurian lore
Translated with an introduction by J.W. Thomas
0–8032–4419–3 Nebraska $25.00

● Paul Oppenheimer, translator
A PLEASANT VINTAGE OF TILL EULENSPIEGEL
The peasant prankster Till personifies the popular humor that gives a sense of daily life in the late Middle Ages
0–8195–4043–9 Wesleyan $20.00

● Reinhard Becker, translator
GERMAN HUMANISM AND REFORMATION
Includes writings by von Tepl, Erasmus, Luther, Müntzer, and Brant
0–8264–0261–5 Continuum pb $10.95

● Hans Jakob von Grimmelshausen
Grimmelshausen's grotesque realism is the primary literary testimony of the Thirty Years' War—and the human folly implicit in it—by an errant soldier of fortune.
ADVENTURES OF A SIMPLETON
Influenced by the Spanish picaresque novel, the saga of Simplicius takes its hero through wars, marriages, and travels that culminate on an uncharted South Atlantic island
Translated by Walter Wallich
0–8044–6229–1 Ungar pb $7.50

THE RUNAGATE COURAGE
The rapacious, sexually adventurous heroine was the basis for Brecht's *Mother Courage*
Translated by Robert Hillier & John Osborne
Preface by Eric Bentley
0–8032–0061–7 Nebraska $17.95

ENLIGHTENMENT, STURM UND DRANG, AND CLASSICISM

Emerging a century after the devastation of the Thirty Years' War, the German Enlightenment was committed to rationalism, tolerance, and human progress. That ostensible serenity, however, gave way during the 1770s to a radical protest of the sentiments: this was the *Sturm und Drang* (Storm and Stress) literary movement, which embraces the plays of Lenz and the early works of Goethe (especially *The Sorrows of Young Werther*) and Schiller.

Led by Goethe and Schiller, German classicism was largely an attempt to achieve through art what the French Revolution had failed to achieve through bloodshed.

• Johann Wolfgang von Goethe

"From a translation of *Faust,* any reader can see that Goethe must have been extraordinarily intelligent, but he will probably get the impression that he was too intellectual, too lacking in passion, because no translation can give a proper idea of Goethe's amazing command of every style of poetry, from the coarse to the witty to the lyrical to the sublime."—W.H. Auden in the introduction to *Italian Journey*

Nonetheless, translators keep trying. Of the many versions of his *Faust,* the following are perhaps the most successful:

FAUST
A complete translation of both parts
Translated by Walter Arndt
Edited by Cyrus Hamlin
0–393–09208–9 Norton pb $11.95

FAUST: Part 1
A nimble version in the original meters
Translated by David Luke
0–19–251040–1 Oxford $32.00
0–19–281666–7 Oxford pb $3.95

Mephistopheles and Marguerite from Delacroix's illustration of Goethe's "Faust," from The Oxford Companion to Art *edited by Harold Osborne*

FAUST: Parts 1 and 2
The second part is abridged
Translated by Louis MacNiece
0–19–500410–8 Oxford pb $8.95

THE AUTOBIOGRAPHY OF JOHANN WOLFGANG VON GOETHE
A multivolume account of Goethe's early life and intellectual influences, published under the title *Dichtung und Wahrheit* (Poetry and Truth)

Volume 1
0–226–30057–9 Chicago pb $15.00

Volume 2
0–226–30058–7 Chicago pb $15.00

CONVERSATIONS WITH ECKERMANN
Goethe's table talk, dutifully recorded by an ardent disciple
Translated by John Oxenford
0–86547–148–7 North Point pb $16.50

EGMONT
A great political tragedy based on an incident in the 16th-century Dutch rebellion against Spanish rule
Translated by Willard Trask
0–8120–0060–9 Barron's pb $4.95

ELECTIVE AFFINITIES
A novel that attempts a scientific analysis of two couples and their interlocking passions
0–14–044242–1 Penguin pb $6.95

ITALIAN JOURNEY: 1786–1788
"*Italian Journey* is not only a description of places, persons and things, but also a psychological document of the first importance dealing with a life crisis which, in various degrees of intensity, we all experience somewhere between the ages of thirty-five and forty-five"—W.H. Auden
Translated by W.H. Auden & Elizabeth Mayer
0–86547–076–6 North Point pb $16.50

ROMAN ELEGIES & OTHER POEMS
Along with the complete *Roman Elegies,* contains excerpts from the *Venetian Epigrams* and the *West-Eastern Divan,* a lyrical cycle inspired by Persian poetry
Translated by Michael Hamburger
0–933806–18–3 Black Swan $20.00

SELECTED VERSE
German texts with literal prose translations
Translated by David Luke
0–14–042074–6 Penguin pb $6.95

THE SORROWS OF YOUNG WERTHER
This self-dramatizing epistolary novel of a young man's fatal love for a married woman became one of the most influential statements of European Romanticism
Translated by Louise Bogan, Elizabeth Mayer & W.H. Auden
0–394–71958–1 Random House pb $3.95

TALES FOR TRANSFORMATION
Contains "Fairy Tale," "The New Melusine," and other stories tinged with alchemical imagery
Translated by Scott Thompson
0–87286–211–9 City Lights pb $6.95

WILHELM MEISTER
This seminal *Bildungsroman* was an instrumental link in the tradition that embraces Dickens, Joyce, and Mann
Translated by H.M. Waidson

Volume 1: The Years of Apprenticeship, Books 1–3
0–7145–3675–X Riverrun pb $7.95

Volume 2: The Years of Apprenticeship, Books 4–6
0–7145–3699–7 Riverrun $11.95

Volume 3: The Years of Apprenticeship, Books 7–8
0–7145–3702–0 Riverrun $11.95
0–7145–3928–7 Riverrun pb $7.95

Volume 4: The Years of Travel, Book 1
0–7145–3827–2 Riverrun $11.95

Volume 5: The Years of Travel, Book 2
0–7145–3838–8 Riverrun $11.95
0–7145–3932–5 Riverrun pb $7.95

Volume 6: The Years of Travel, Book 3
0–7145–3934–1 Riverrun pb $7.95

The Suhrkamp Goethe

The German publisher Suhrkamp is currently issuing a twelve-volume edition of Goethe's major writings, in new translations into modern English, and including a number of works never before translated.

SELECTED POEMS
Translators include Michael Hamburger, Christopher Middleton, and David Luke
Translated by Michael Hamburger & others
Edited by Christopher Middleton
3–518–03053–1 Suhrkamp $32.00

FAUST I & II
"Atkins's lively translation will most certainly assume a place of importance among the numerous English versions currently available"—*Choice*
Translated & edited by Stuart Atkins
3–518–03055–8 Suhrkamp $32.00

ESSAYS ON ART AND LITERATURE
"This third volume of the Goethe edition responsibly and fully responds to our questions in an age of theoretical reflections"—Peter Demetz
3–518–03058–2 Suhrkamp $32.00

FROM MY LIFE: Poetry and Truth & Campaign in France 1792/Siege of Mainz
Goethe's autobiography, along with a military chronicle not translated since the 19th century
Translated by Robert Heitner & Thomas Saine
Edited by Thomas Saine & Jeffrey Sammons
3–518–02967–3 Suhrkamp (2-volume set) $69.00

VERSE PLAYS AND EPIC
Includes the plays *Iphigenia in Tauris, Torquato Tasso, The Natural Daughter,* and *Pandora* (the latter two appearing in English for the first time) and the epic poem *Hermann and Dorothea*
Translated by Michael Hamburger & others
Edited by Cyrus Hamlin & others
3–518–02965–7 Suhrkamp $32.50

THE SORROWS OF YOUNG WERTHER, ELECTIVE AFFINITIES & NOVELLA
Three of Goethe's major works
Translated by Victor Lange & Judith Ryan
Edited by David Wellbery
3–518–02966–5 Suhrkamp $32.50

➤ **FOR OVERSEAS ORDERING INFORMATION, SEE PAGE 1**

SCIENTIFIC STUDIES
Writings on anatomy, botany, physics, chemistry, zoology, meteorology, and geology
Translated & edited by Douglas Miller
3-518-02969-X Suhrkamp $34.50

EARLY VERSE DRAMA AND PROSE PLAYS
Includes *Goetz von Berlichingen, Egmont, Clavigo, Stella, Brother and Sister, Prometheus, Jery and Betty,* and *Proserpina*
Translated by Robert Browning & others
Edited by Cyrus Hamlin & Frank Ryder
0-317-69899-0 Suhrkamp $29.50

WILHELM MEISTER'S APPRENTICESHIP
Translated by Eric Blackall & Victor Lange
Edited by Victor Lange
3-518-02963-0 Suhrkamp $32.50

WILHELM MEISTER'S JOURNEYMAN YEARS & CONVERSATIONS OF GERMAN REFUGEES
The final volume of *Wilhelm Meister* and the earlier *Conversations,* a cycle of novellas reflecting the events of the French Revolution
Translated by Krishna Winston & Jan van Heurck
Edited by Jane K. Brown
3-518-03059-0 Suhrkamp $32.50

ITALIAN JOURNEY
Goethe's two-year sojourn in Italy was the wellspring of his subsequent writing
Translated by Robert Heitner
Edited by Thomas Saine & Jeffrey Sammons
3-518-02968-1 Suhrkamp $32.50

● Friedrich Hölderlin
Hölderlin—who immersed himself in Greek classicism and translated Sophocles and Pindar—set the stage for German Romanticism and is now widely regarded as the precursor of poetic modernism.
SELECTED VERSE
Translated by Michael Hamburger
0-85646-147-4 Longwood $22.95
0-85646-148-2 Longwood pb $9.95

HYMNS AND FRAGMENTS
The prophetic late work brilliantly translated and introduced
Translated by Richard Sieburth
0-691-01412-4 Princeton pb $9.95

● Friedrich Hölderlin & Eduard Mörike
SELECTED POEMS OF FRIEDRICH HOLDERLIN AND EDUARD MORIKE
In addition to a generous and ably translated selection from Hölderlin, this volume offers a thorough presentation of Eduard Mörike, a lyricist of the succeeding generation
Translated by Christopher Middleton
0-226-34934-9 Chicago pb $3.75

● Heinrich von Kleist
Before his suicide at 34 in 1811, Kleist had written a series of novellas and tales, plays (of which the greatest was *Prince Frederick of Homburg*), essays, and letters—expressing, with unwavering formal control, themes of emotional devastation.
FIVE PLAYS
A new and excellent translation of Kleist's major dramatic works, *Amphitryon, The Broken Jug, Penthesilea, The Prince of*

Homburg, and *The Tragedy of Robert Guiscard*
Translated by Martin Greenberg
0-300-04238-8 Yale $29.95

PLAYS
Includes the one-act *The Broken Pitcher,* the blank-verse comedy *Amphitryon,* the Amazon tragedy *Penthesilea,* and Kleist's masterpiece *Prince Frederick of Homburg*
Edited by Walter Hinderer
Foreword by E.L. Doctorow
0-8264-0263-1 Continuum pb $10.95

PRINCE FRIEDRICH OF HOMBURG
Translated by Diana Peters
0-8112-0694-7 New Directions pb $6.95

THE MARQUISE OF O— & OTHER STORIES
Includes *Michael Kohlhaas, The Earthquake in Chile,* and *The Foundling*
Translated by David Luke & Nigel Reeves
0-14-044359-2 Penguin pb $4.95

● J.M. Lenz
THE TUTOR & THE SOLDIERS
A didactic comedy of manners and a technically innovative tragedy that influenced Büchner
Translated by William Yuill
0-226-47211-6 Chicago pb $1.95

● Gotthold Lessing
This influential figure of the German Enlightenment suffered censorship for his freethinking theological views.
LAOCOON: An Essay on the Limits of Painting and Poetry
Translated by Edward McCormick
0-8018-3139-3 Johns Hopkins pb $9.95

MINNA VON BARNHELM
A comedy set during the Seven Years' War
Translated with an introduction by Kenneth Northcott
0-226-47341-4 Chicago $10.00

NATHAN THE WISE
Lessing's parable of religious tolerance
Translated by Bayard Morgan
0-8044-6401-4 Ungar pb $6.95

● Friedrich Schiller
Poet and philosopher, dramatist and historian, Schiller is notable above all for his lofty verse tragedies on themes of individual liberty and human dignity.
PLAYS: I
Includes *Intrigue and Love,* an antidespotic domestic tragedy, and *Don Carlos,* a drama of incestuous love and political sacrifice
0-8264-0275-5 Continuum pb $10.95

MARY STUART
Perhaps his finest tragedy, in a 19th-century translation considerably streamlined by Bentley
Translated by Eric Bentley & Joseph Mellish
0-936839-00-7 Applause pb $5.95

THE ROBBERS & WALLENSTEIN
The Robbers, an early work, was a popular Romantic melodrama; *Wallenstein,* a trilogy of the Thirty Years' War, was Schiller's most ambitious dramatic epic
Translated by F.J. Lamport
0-14-044368-1 Penguin pb $6.95

WILHELM TELL
Schiller uses the Tell legend to epitomize the struggle for freedom
Translated by William Mainland
0-226-73801-9 Chicago pb $8.95

ON THE NAIVE AND SENTIMENTAL IN LITERATURE
A discourse on poetic realism (the "naive") and poetic idealism (the "sentimental", perhaps better translated as "reflective")
Translated by Helen Watanabe-O'Kelly
0-85635-331-0 Carcanet pb $8.50

THE 19TH CENTURY: Romanticism

Dismissed by Goethe on occasion as a "disease," German Romanticism nonetheless shared classicism's yearning for the "purity" of ancient Greek culture. German Romanticism derived much of its momentum from the thinking of Kant and Fichte and influenced every aspect of culture and art.

● Jacob & Wilhelm Grimm
The Grimms' collection of 210 fairytales is one of the great monuments of Romantic scholarship.
SELECTED TALES
Translated by David Luke
0-14-044401-7 Penguin pb $4.95

THE COMPLETE GRIMM'S FAIRY TALES
Illustrated by Josef Scharl
0-394-49415-6 Pantheon $17.50
0-394-70930-6 Pantheon pb $11.95

● E.T.A. Hoffmann
A major Romantic author, Hoffmann is now famous chiefly for his weird and often comic tales.
TALES OF E.T.A. HOFFMANN
Edited by Leonard Kent & others
0-226-34789-3 Chicago pb $10.95

THE TALES OF HOFFMANN
0-14-044392-4 Penguin pb $4.95

● Novalis
HYMNS TO THE NIGHT
Six hymns inspired by the death of his fiancée
Translated by Dick Higgins
0-914232-90-8 McPherson pb $5.95

● Friedrich Schlegel
DIALOGUE ON POETRY & LITERARY APHORISMS
The *Dialogue* is a critique in which Schlegel stresses the subjective aspects of literature
Translated by Ernst Behler & Roman Struc
0-271-73136-2 Pennsylvania $18.50

Anthologies

Folktales were a primary influence on the Romantics, in whose hands the novella became the quintessential 19th-century German genre.

● Frank Ryder & Robert Browning, editors
ROMANTIC NOVELLAS
Four works by Kleist and two by Jean Paul
0-8264-0295-X Continuum pb $10.95

- Ronald Taylor, editor
SIX GERMAN ROMANTIC TALES
Contains work by Heinrich von Kleist,
Ludwig Tieck, and E.T.A. Hoffmann
0–946162–17–4 Dufour pb $10.95

- Leslie Willson, editor
GERMAN ROMANTIC CRITICISM
Includes writings by Schleiermacher, Jean
Paul, Novalis, Schlegel, Hölderlin, Kleist,
and Grimm
0–8264–0262–3 Continuum pb $10.95

LATE ROMANTICISM

- Georg Büchner
A political radical who died of typhoid at
24 in 1837, Büchner almost single-
handedly set the agenda for the modern
German theater.
COMPLETE PLAYS AND PROSE
Contains the three major plays: *Danton's
Death, Leonce and Lena,* and *Woyzeck,* and
the story *Lenz*
Translated by Carl Mueller
0–8090–0727–4 Hill & Wang pb $7.95

**DANTON'S DEATH, LEONCE AND
LENA & WOYZECK**
0–19–281827–9 Oxford pb $5.95

- Heinrich Heine
Heine's work evolves from exquisitely
crafted lyricism to an equally exquisite
irony. He was also a great satirist and
polemicist.
SELECTED VERSE
German text with literal prose translations
0–14–042098–3 Penguin pb $7.95

**THE COMPLETE POEMS OF
HEINRICH HEINE: A Modern
English Version**
Heine's poetry takes many tones:
grimly pessimistic, brightly ironical,
witty, and even prophetic. This edition,
running to over a thousand pages,
makes the full range of his work
available in modern English for the first
time
Translated by Hal Draper
3–518–03048–5 Suhrkamp $29.95
3–518–03062–0 Suhrkamp pb $19.95

POETRY AND PROSE
Includes 47 poems in German and English,
The Harz Journey (ridiculing academe),
Ideas—Book Le Grand, and *Germany: A
Winter's Tale,* a mordant critique of social
conditions in Germany
Edited by Jost Hermand & Robert Holub
0–8264–0265–8 Continuum pb $10.95

**JEWISH STORIES AND HEBREW
MELODIES**
Translated by Frederick Ewen & Hal Draper
Illustrated by Max Liebermann
0–910129–62–2 Schocken pb $9.95

**THE ROMANTIC SCHOOL & OTHER
ESSAYS**
Edited by Volkmar Sander
0–8264–0291–7 Continuum pb $10.95

A 19th-century German bibliophile by Carl Spitzweg, from The Delights of Reading *by Otto
Bettmann (Godine)*

- Richard Wagner
TRISTAN AND ISOLDE
Translated by Andrew Porter
0–7145–3849–3 Riverrun pb $4.95

THE RING OF THE NIBELUNG
Translated by Andrew Porter
0–393–00867–3 Norton pb $8.95

THE 19TH CENTURY:
Realist Fiction

No 19th-century German novelist commands the stature of a Balzac or a
Tolstoy; indeed, Thomas Mann once remarked that Wagner's operas represented
the German corollary to the great realist
novels of France and Russia. Nevertheless,
many late 19th-century writers did investigate contemporary social and moral problems. Foremost among them were Theodor
Fontane, whose *Before the Storm* and *Effi
Briest* scrutinize Prussian society and the
emerging metropolis in Berlin, and the Swiss
writer Gottfried Keller.

- Theodor Fontane
BEFORE THE STORM
A slender plot is offset by a Brueghelian
procession of characters
Edited by R.J. Hollingdale
0–19–281649–7 Oxford pb $6.95

EFFI BRIEST
In this richly delineated portrait of stuffy
provincial life, Effi is something of a
German counterpart to Emma Bovary
Translated by Douglas Parmee
0–14–044190–5 Penguin pb $5.95

SHORT NOVELS & OTHER WRITINGS
Includes *A Man of Honor, Jenny Treibel* and
The Eighteenth of March
Edited by Peter Demetz
Foreword by Peter Gay
0–8264–0260–7 Continuum pb $10.95

- Gottfried Keller
GREEN HENRY
The Swiss storyteller and master of the
novella offers a good example of poetic
realism in this autobiographical work
Translated by A.M. Holt
0–7145–0265–0 Riverrun pb $14.95

STORIES
Ten village tales in novella form including *A Village Romeo and Juliet* and *The Banner of the Upright Seven*
Edited by Frank Ryder
Foreword by Max Frisch
0–8264–0266–6 Continuum pb $10.95

HUMOR

The Lion
A leaf of a calendar on the wall
displays a lion, grand and tall.

He views you regal and serene
the whole of April seventeen.

Reminding you, lest you forget,
that he is not extinct as yet.

Christian Morgenstern
THE GALLOWS SONGS
Translated by Max Knight
0–520–00884–7 California pb $8.95

• Wilhelm Busch & others
GERMAN SATIRICAL WRITINGS
Busch's ironic illustrated poems can be seen as precursors of the comic strip. This collection also contains work by Christian Morgenstern, Kurt Tucholsky, and Erich Kästner
Translated by Wilhelm Lotze & Volkmar Sander
0–8264–0285–2 Continuum pb $10.95

• Christian Morgenstern
THE GALLOWS SONGS: Christian Morgenstern's Galgenlieder
Morgenstern cultivated a highly original brand of nonsense poetry with serious undertones. "An amazingly good job of rewording Morgenstern's puns, idioms, neologisms, making the English lines dance to the metrics of the German"—Babette Deutsch
Translated with an introduction by Max Knight
0–520–00883–9 California $15.95
0–520–00884–7 California pb $8.95

MODERN GERMAN LITERATURE: To 1945

The apparent linguistic unity of German literature encompasses a variety of cultural, geographic, and political fragmentations. In the first half of the 20th century, for example, a number of distinct literary cultures can be discerned, among them *fin-de-siècle* Vienna (Schnitzler, Kraus, Musil, Canetti), the German-speaking minority of Prague (Kafka, Rilke), and Berlin between the wars (Brecht, Benn, Döblin).

▶ **For drama of this period, see Modern European Drama**

Poetry

• Gottfried Benn
Benn ranks as the great German Expressionist poet. Something of his tone can be gauged from the titles of his collections: *Morgue, Rubble, Narcosis,* and *Split.*

I saw the ego, the look in its eyes. I dilated its pupil, looked far into it, looked far out of it; the gaze from such eyes is almost expressionless, more like scenting, scenting danger, an age-old danger. From disasters that were latent, disasters that antedated the word, come dreadful memories of the race, hybrid, beast-shaped, sphinx-pouched features of the primal face. I recalled the dicta of certain profoundly experienced men, that evil would come of their telling all they knew. I thought of the strange adages, that one should give up searching for the ultimate words that need only be spoken to un-hinge heaven and earth. I sniffed in masks, I rattled in runes, I dove into demons with sleep-craving brutality, with mythical instincts, in the anteverbal, instinctual threat of prehistoric neura; I began to grasp, I saw the vision: monism in rhythms, mass in intoxications, compulsion and repression, Ananke of the I.
from *Primal Vision* (1931)

Gottfried Benn
PRIMAL VISION
Edited by E.B. Ashton
0–8112–0008–6 New Directions pb $8.95

PRIMAL VISION: Selected Writings of Gottfried Benn
An anthology of poetry and critical prose
Edited by E.B. Ashton
0–8112–0008–6 New Directions pb $8.95

PROSE, ESSAYS, POEMS
Edited by Richard Becker & Wolkmar Sander
Foreword by John Simon
0–8264–0313–1 Continuum pb $10.95

• Bertolt Brecht
POEMS, 1913–1956
This selection of some 500 poems "shows convincingly that his oeuvre is one of the major poetic achievements of the present century" (Stephen Spender)
Edited by John Willett & Ralph Manheim
0–416–00081–9 RC&H $29.95
0–416–00091–6 RC&H pb $14.95

• Else Lasker-Schüler
Lasker-Schüler, an eccentric and visionary Jewish poet closely associated with the Expressionist movement who used much Oriental imagery in her work, settled in Palestine in the late 1930s.
HEBREW BALLADS & OTHER POEMS
Translated by A. Durchslag & J. Litman-Demeestere
0–8276–0179–4 JPS $10.95

YOUR DIAMOND DREAMS CUT OPEN MY ARTERIES
Translated by Robert Newton
0–8078–8100–7 North Carolina $22.50

• Rainer Maria Rilke
"Rilke's special gift as a poet is that he does not seem to speak from the middle of life, that he is always calling us away from it. His poems have the feeling of being written from a great depth in himself. What makes them so seductive is that they also speak to the reader so intimately. They seem whispered or crooned into our inmost ear, insinuating us toward the same depth in ourselves. The effect can be hypnotic . . ."—Robert Hass in the introduction to *The Selected Poetry of Rainer Maria Rilke*

SELECTED POETRY OF RAINER MARIA RILKE
Mitchell's bilingual edition is by far the best selection currently available. It spans the whole of Rilke's career and includes along with much else the complete *Duino Elegies*
Edited and translated by Stephen Mitchell
Introduction by Robert Hass
0–394–52434–9 Random House $25.00
0–679–72201–7 Random House pb $10.95

BETWEEN ROOTS: Selected Poems
Translated by Rika Lesser
0–691–06668–X Princeton $21.00
0–691–01429–9 Princeton pb $9.95

THE COMPLETE FRENCH POEMS OF RAINER MARIA RILKE
Translated by A. Poulin, Jr.
Foreword by W.D. Snodgrass
0–915308–83–5 Graywolf pb $10.00

THE DUINO ELEGIES
Young adopts a stanzaic format of triplets modelled on William Carlos Williams. A bilingual edition
Translated by David Young
0–393–04482–3 Norton $8.95
0–393–04501–3 Norton pb $7.95

THE DUINO ELEGIES & THE SONNETS TO ORPHEUS
A bilingual edition. "Now, because of Mr. Poulin's translations, I experience the *Elegies* almost as English. He gives Rilke the crisp speed of English, and yet seems to remain very close to the original meaning"—Robert Lowell
Translated by A.B. Poulin, Jr.
0–395–25058–7 Houghton Mifflin pb $10.95

NEW POEMS [1907]
This bilingual volume, together with its companion *New Poems: The Other Part,* offers the first complete English translation of what many consider Rilke's most radically original work. The *New Poems* attempt to find a linguistic equivalent to the objective and tactile qualities Rilke discovered in the work of Rodin and Cézanne: "Somehow I too must come to make things; not plastic, but written things—*realities* that emerge from handwork. Somehow I too must discover the smallest basic element, the cell of my art, the tangible immaterial means of representation for everything."
Translated by Edward Snow
0–86547–175–4 North Point $16.50

NEW POEMS [1908]: The Other Part
Translated by Edward Snow
0–86547–271–8 North Point $17.50

POEMS, 1912–1926
A bilingual edition emphasizing work that other translators have largely neglected
Translated by Michael Hamburger
0–933806–17–5 Black Swan $17.50

POEMS FROM THE BOOK OF HOURS
An early work, rendered in Rilke's rhyme scheme
Translated with an introduction by Babette Deutsch
0–8112–0595–9 New Directions pb $4.95

THE SONNETS TO ORPHEUS
Another superior translation by Mitchell, filling out the *Selected Poetry* listed above. Bilingual edition
Translated by Stephen Mitchell
0–671–61773–7 Simon & Schuster pb $7.95

SONNETS TO ORPHEUS
A bilingual edition. "An artful and sensitive translation of this most elusive of Rilke's poetry"—Stanley Plumly
Translated by David Young
0–8195–5159–7 Wesleyan $18.50
0–8195–6165–7 Wesleyan pb $9.95

THE LAY OF THE LOVE AND DEATH OF CORNET CHRISTOPH
This early novella, suffused with idealized militarism, was one of Rilke's most popular works during his lifetime
Translated by Stephen Mitchell
0–915308–77–0 Graywolf pb $7.50

LETTERS TO A YOUNG POET
A passionate exposition of the poetic vocation, addressed to a correspondent Rilke had never met
Translated by Stephen Mitchell
0–394–74104–8 Random House pb $6.95

LETTERS ON CEZANNE
Translated by Joel Agee
0–88064–022–7 Fromm $14.95

THE NOTEBOOKS OF MALTE LAURIDS BRIGGE
"Each reading of this timeless modern classic stirs the imagination with a new remembrance of its richness, originality of design and purity of language"—Elizabeth Hardwick
Translated by Stephen Mitchell
Introduction by William Gass
0–394–71657–4 Random House pb $6.95

WHERE SILENCE REIGNS: Selected Prose
0–8112–0703–X New Directions pb $8.95

LETTERS OF RAINER MARIA RILKE, 1892–1910
Translated by Jane Bannard Greene & Herter Horton
0–393–00476–7 Norton pb $8.95

LETTERS OF RAINER MARIA RILKE, 1910–1926
0–393–00477–5 Norton pb $10.95

WARTIME LETTERS OF RAINER MARIA RILKE, 1914–1921
Translated by M.D.H. Norton
0–393–00160–1 Norton pb $6.45

Buddha in Glory

Center of all centers, core of cores,
almond, that closes in and sweetens,—
this entire world out to all the stars
is your fruit-flesh: we greet you.

Look, you feel how nothing any
    longer
clings to you; your husk is in infinity,
and there the strong juice stands and
    presses.
And from outside a radiance assists it,

for high above, your suns in full
    splendor
have wheeled blazingly around.
Yet already there's begun inside you
what lasts beyond the suns.

Rainer Maria Rilke
NEW POEMS [1908]: The Other Part
Translated by Edward Snow
0–86547–271–8 North Point $17.50

• Georg Trakl
GEORG TRAKL: A Profile
An excellent selection from the imagistic work of the great Austrian poet who committed suicide in a military hospital in 1914
Edited by Frank Graziano
0–937406–28–7 Longman $16.00

SELECTED POEMS
0–918825–94–6 Moyer Bell pb $9.95

SONG OF THE WEST: Selected Poems
A selection of 47 of Trakl's best poems, written between 1912 and 1914
Translated by Robert Firmage
0–86547–352–8 North Point $19.95
0–86547–353–6 North Point pb $9.95

Fiction and Other Prose

Walter Benjamin
This incisive critic and cultural historian, who strove to balance the conflicting influences of Marxism and Jewish theology, committed suicide rather than fall into the hands of the Gestapo.

ILLUMINATIONS
A brilliant selection including "The Task of the Translator," "Unpacking My Library," "Some Reflections on Kafka," and the enormously influential "The Work of Art in the Age of Mechanical Reproduction"
Introduction by Hannah Arendt
0–8052–0241–2 Schocken pb $8.95

MOSCOW DIARY
Translated by Richard Sieburth
Edited by Gary Smith
Foreword by Gershom Scholem
0–674–58743–X Harvard $25.00
0–674–58744–8 Harvard pb $8.95

REFLECTIONS: Essays, Aphorisms, Autobiographical Writings
Translated by Edmund Jephcott
Edited by Peter Demetz
0–8052–0802–X Schocken pb $10.95

• Hermann Broch
THE DEATH OF VIRGIL
Close to despair over the impotence of art and about to burn his *Aeneid*, Virgil receives a deathbed illumination. This highly experimental book owes much to Broch's own close encounter with death following the Anschluss
Translated by Jean Untermeyer
0–86547–115–0 North Point pb $15.50

THE GUILTLESS
A study of "shared guilt" showing how European apathy nurtured the growth of fascism
Translated by Ralph Manheim
0–86547–305–6 North Point pb $13.00

THE SLEEPWALKERS: A Trilogy
A philosophical novel on the deterioration of moral values culminating in Nazism
Translated by Edwin & Willa Muir
0–86547–200–9 North Point pb $15.50

THE SPELL
A reconstruction from various unpublished drafts of Broch's novelistic attempt to analyze Hitler's appeal
Translated by H.F. Broch de Rotherman
0–374–26761–8 Farrar, Straus & Giroux $22.50
0–86547–359–5 North Point pb $14.50

THE UNKNOWN QUANTITY
Broch's second novel, published in 1933, is another meditation on decaying values
Translated by Willa and Edwin Muir
0–910395–36–5 Marlboro pb $10.95

• Elias Canetti
The theme underlying the work of this 1981 Nobel Laureate—who was born in Bulgaria, emigrated to Manchester, and came to rest in German-speaking Europe— is the relationship of the intellectual to the mass, and the relevance of this to fascism.

THE TONGUE SET FREE: Remembrance of a European Childhood
The first installment of Canetti's multivolume memoirs
Translated by Joachim Neugroschel
0–374–51802–5 FS&G pb $9.95

THE TORCH IN MY EAR
The second volume of the memoirs
Translated by Joachim Neugroschel
0–374–27847–4 FS&G $16.50
0–374–51804–1 FS&G pb $9.95

THE PLAY OF THE EYES
The third volume of Canetti's memoirs, set in Vienna in the 1930s, describes his relations with Broch, Musil, Berg, and Alma Mahler
Translated by Ralph Manheim
0–374–23434–5 FS&G $17.95
0–374–52075–5 FS&G pb $9.95

AUTO-DA-FE
A scholarly recluse marries and is destroyed by his brutish housekeeper
Translated by D. V. Wedgewood
0–374–51879–3 Farrar, Straus & Giroux pb $12.95

THE CONSCIENCE OF WORDS
Essays on Confucius, Tolstoy, Kafka, Hitler, and others
Translated by Joachim Neugroschel
0–374–51881–5 Farrar, Straus & Giroux pb $8.95

CROWDS AND POWER
A monumental study of crowd psychology, ranging from the Bushmen and the Pueblo Indians to Christianity and industrial societies
Translated by Carol Stewart
0–374–51820–3 Farrar, Straus & Giroux pb $10.95

EARWITNESS: Fifty Characters
An alternative kind of fiction, consisting of fifty isolated portraits of human types, each an exemplar of a certain type of conduct, from "Tablecloth Lunatic" to "Beauty-Newt"
Translated by Joachim Neugroschel
0–374–51892–0 Farrar, Straus & Giroux pb $6.95

THE HUMAN PROVINCE
A diary spanning the years from 1942 to 1972
Translated by Joachim Neugroschel
0–374–51890–4 Farrar, Straus & Giroux pb $9.95

🐛 **IF YOU CAN'T FIND IT, LOOK IN THE INDEX**

THE SECRET HEART OF THE CLOCK
Collected "notations" present reflections on death and aging
Translated by Joel Agee
0–374–25694–2 Farrar, Straus & Giroux $17.95

THE VOICES OF MARRAKESH: A Record of a Visit
Less a travel book than a record of Canetti's "mental voyage"
Translated by J. A. Underwood
0–374–51823–8 Farrar, Straus & Giroux pb $6.95

● **Alfred Döblin**
"I am greatly indebted to Alfred Döblin . . . He will unsettle you; he will trouble your dreams; you will have difficulty swallowing him; you will find him unsavory; he is indigestible, gristly. He changes his readers. The self-complacent are hereby cautioned against Döblin"— Günter Grass

BERLIN ALEXANDERPLATZ: The Story of Franz Biberkopf
This experimental modernist collage of 1920s Berlin, Joycean in its treatment of time and place, was the source of Fassbinder's cinematic marathon
Translated by Eugene Jolas
0–8044–6121–X Ungar pb $11.95

A PEOPLE BETRAYED: November 1918, A German Revolution
Part One of Döblin's magnum opus. "A panoramic vision of disaster and betrayal that blends realism and fantasy to stunning effect"—Ernst Pawel
Translated by John E. Woods
0–88064–007–3 Fromm $19.95
0–88064–008–1 Fromm pb $10.95

KARL AND ROSA: November 1918, A German Revolution
The second half of Döblin's revolutionary epic pursues the careers of the revolution's leaders, Karl Liebknecht and Rosa Luxemburg
Translated by John Woods
0–88064–011–1 Fromm pb $10.95

TALES OF A LONG NIGHT
Post-World War II England, seen through the lives of an English family coming to terms with the aftermath
Translated by Rita & Robert Kimber
0–88064–016–2 Fromm $18.95
0–88064–017–0 Fromm pb $12.95

● **Hermann Hesse**
Hesse's absorption in Eastern religion and Jungian psychology and his criticism of European bourgeois values made him a great favorite with several generations of young readers.

MAGISTER LUDI: The Glass Bead Game
A study of how the quest for freedom necessarily conflicts with tradition
0–553–26237–8 Bantam pb $4.95

NARCISSUS AND GOLDMUND
Hesse's protagonists express a polarity between artistic revolt and the continuity of social structures
Translated by Ursule Molinaro
0–374–50684–1 Farrar, Straus & Giroux pb $8.95

THE JOURNEY TO THE EAST
An allegorical pilgrimage toward enlightenment
Translated by Hilda Rosner
0–374–50036–3 Farrar, Straus & Giroux pb $6.95

Franz Kafka, from The Delights of Reading *by Otto Bettmann* (Godine)

SIDDHARTHA
The famous novel of spiritual growth
Translated by Hilda Rosner
0–8112–0068–X New Directions pb $3.95

STEPPENWOLF
A surrealist narrative recounted by an artist-outsider who eventually comes to believe that misfits may find harmony with each other
0–553–25533–9 Bantam pb $3.95

● **Ernst Jünger**
THE PARIS DIARIES 1941–1944
An eminent man of letters writes during his service as a German intelligence officer in occupied Paris
Translated by Michael Hulse
0–374–22988–0 Farrar, Straus & Giroux $25.00

THE GLASS BEES
A classic of modern utopian literature, first published in 1957
Translated by Louise Bogan & Elizabeth Mayer
0–374–52173–5 Farrar, Straus & Giroux pb $6.95

● **Franz Kafka**
"Had one to name the author who comes nearest to bearing the same kind of relation to our age as Dante, Shakespeare, and Goethe bore to theirs, Kafka is the first one would think of."—W. H. Auden

THE COMPLETE STORIES
Edited by Nahum Glatzer
0–8052–0873–9 Schocken pb $11.95

SELECTED SHORT STORIES OF FRANZ KAFKA
Translated by Edwin & Willa Muir
Introduction by Philip Rahv
0–394–60422–9 Modern Library $9.95

AMERIKA
A comic masterpiece about a young immigrant's attempt to find a niche in an incomprehensible country
Translated by Edwin Muir
0–8052–3002–5 Schocken $9.50
0–8052–0417–2 Schocken pb $6.95

THE CASTLE
Allegory of a man's hopeless attempt to "reach the Castle" and have his identity acknowledged by its inhabitants
Translated by Willa Muir & others
Commentary by Thomas Mann
0–394–41862–X Knopf $12.95
0–805–20872–0 Schocken pb $8.95

THE TRIAL
"We are taken to the limits of human thought. Indeed, everything in this work is, in the true sense, essential. It states the problem of the absurd in its entirety"— Albert Camus
0–394–44955–X Knopf $16.95
0–8052–0848–8 Schocken pb $5.95

LETTERS TO FELICE
"It is all here—the indecisiveness, the fearfulness, coldness of feeling, detailed description of lovelessness, a helplessness so vast that only exact description makes it believable"—Elias Canetti
Translated by James Stern & Elisabeth Duckworth
Edited by Erich Heller & Juergen Born
0–8052–3500–0 Schocken $17.50
0–8052–0851–8 Schocken pb $13.95

LETTER TO HIS FATHER: Brief an den Vater
0–8052–0426–1 Schocken pb $6.95

LETTERS TO MILENA
The first complete edition
0–8052–4070–5 Schocken $22.95
0–8052–0885–2 Schocken pb $11.95

DIARIES OF FRANZ KAFKA
Edited by Max Brod

Volume 1: 1910–1913
Translated by Joseph Kresh
0–8052–0424–5 Schocken pb $8.95

Volume 2: 1914–1923
Translated by Martin Greenberg
0–8052–0425–3 Schocken pb $8.95

Karl Kraus
This Austrian critic has been described as "probably the greatest satirist of the 20th century" (*Christian Science Monitor*).

HALF-TRUTHS AND ONE-AND-A-HALF TRUTHS: Selected Aphorisms
Translated with an introduction by Harry Zohn
0–85635–580–1 Carcanet pb $8.50

IN THESE GREAT TIMES: A Karl Kraus Reader
A selection of prose satires (including "The Good Conduct Medal," "Promotional Trips to Hell," and "Psychoanalysis"), poems, and excerpts from *The Last Days of Mankind*
Translated by Joseph Fabry & others
Edited by Harry Zohn
0–85635–516–X Carcanet $14.95

THE LAST DAYS OF MANKIND: A Tragedy in Five Acts
Kraus's masterpiece presents an apocalyptic picture of a corrupt Europe
Translated by Alexander Gode & Sue Wright
Edited by Frederick Ungar
0–8044–6366–2 Ungar pb $12.95

NO COMPROMISE: Selected Writings of Karl Kraus
Translated by Sheema Buehne
Edited by Frederick Ungar
0–8044–6373–5 Ungar pb $9.95

Karl Kraus, from Oscar Kokoschka *by Richard Calvocoressi (Guggenheim Museum)*

● **Alexander Lernet-Holenia**
BARON BAGGE & COUNT LUNA
Two novellas by an acclaimed Austrian stylist
Translated by Richard & Clara Winston
0–941419–20–7 Eridanos $23.00
0–941419–21–5 Eridanos pb $14.00

THE RESURRECTION OF MALTRAVERS
Translated by Joachim Neugroschel
0–941419–22–3 Eridanos $23.00
0–941419–23–1 Eridanos pb $14.00

● **Heinrich Mann**
YOUNG HENRY OF NAVARRE
The first installment of a two-volume historical epic dealing with the career of Henry IV
Translated by Eric Sutton
0–87951–981–1 Overlook $25.00
0–87951–206–7 Overlook pb $14.95

HENRY, KING OF FRANCE
Henry's story continued. "Fictional history in the grand manner"—*New Republic*
0–87951–999–1 Overlook $25.00
0–87951–224–5 Overlook pb $15.95

● **Thomas Mann**
Heinrich's younger brother, the foremost German novelist of the 20th century, was awarded the Nobel Prize in 1929 for what many consider his masterpiece, *The Magic Mountain.*

THE BLACK SWAN
An unflattering portrait of an American woman
Translated by Willard Trask
0–394–41708–9 Knopf $11.50

BUDDENBROOKS
The partly autobiographical account of the decline of a patrician family
Translated by H. T. Lowe-Porter
0–394–41801–8 Knopf $15.00
0–394–72637–5 Random House pb $5.95

CONFESSIONS OF FELIX KRULL, CONFIDENCE MAN
Mann's last novel presents its picaresque hero in a tone of serene cynicism
Translated by Denver Lindley
0–394–42012–8 Knopf $15.95
0–394–70496–7 Random House pb $5.95

DEATH IN VENICE & SEVEN OTHER STORIES
Includes *Tonio Kröger, Tristan, Disorder and Early Sorrow, Mario and the Magician, Felix Krull, The Blood of the Walsungs,* and *A Man and His Dog*
Translated by H. T. Lowe-Porter
0–679–72206–8 Random House pb $7.95

DOCTOR FAUSTUS: The Life of the German Composer, Adrian Leverkuhn, As Told by a Friend
A great composer makes a pact with the devil to achieve release from sterility and decadence; Mann's story is filled with echoes of the Hitler era
0–394–71297–8 Random House pb $6.95

THE HOLY SINNER
Mann's rendering of the "birth of the blessed Pope Gregory," modeled on Hartmann von Aue's *Gregorius*
Translated by H. T. Lowe-Porter
0–394–71741–4 Random House pb $7.95

JOSEPH AND HIS BROTHERS
In the Joseph tetralogy Mann explores a more optimistic mode
0–394–43132–4 Knopf $50.00

THE MAGIC MOUNTAIN
This large-scale novel set in a sanatorium charts the ills of Western civilization, while offering hope for the future
Translated by H. T. Lowe-Porter
0–394–43458–7 Knopf $30.00
0–394–70497–5 Random House pb $7.95

ROYAL HIGHNESS
A subtly ironic celebration of Mann's own marriage, the groom a German princeling, the bride an American heiress
Translated by A. Cecil Curtis
0–394–71739–2 Random House pb $7.95

THE TRANSPOSED HEADS
"At once the quintessence and the *reductio ad absurdum* of all love triangles"—Lionel Trilling
0–394–70086–4 Random House pb $3.95

STORIES OF THREE DECADES
Translated by H. T. Lowe-Porter
0–394–44734–4 Knopf $17.95
0–394–60483–0 Modern Library $9.95

● **Robert Musil**
FIVE WOMEN
Five short stories representing "elaborate attempts to use fiction for its true purposes, the discovery and regeneration of the human world" (Frank Kermode)
Translated by Eithne Wilkins & Ernst Kaiser
0–87923–603–5 Godine pb $8.95

THE MAN WITHOUT QUALITIES
0–399–50152–5 Putnam pb $7.95

THE POSTHUMOUS PAPERS OF A LIVING WRITER
Translated by Peter Wortsman
0–941419–00–2 Eridanos $21.00
0–941419–01–0 Eridanos pb $12.00

SELECTED WRITINGS
Contains *Young Törless* (Musil's harsh study of sadism among military cadets),

four stories, and *Posthumous Papers and Other Prose*
Translated by Eithne Wilkins & others
0–8264–0304–2 Continuum pb $10.95

● **Erich Maria Remarque**
ALL QUIET ON THE WESTERN FRONT
Incinerated by the Nazis in 1933, this famous war novel depicts the horror of the front "on a quiet day" with deliberately brutal realism
Translated by A. W. Wheen
0–316–73992–8 Little, Brown $16.95
0–449–21394–3 Fawcett pb $3.95

● **Joseph Roth**
CONFESSION OF A MURDERER: Told in One Night
A tale of collaboration, deception, and exile. "Worthy to sit beside Conrad's and Dostoevsky's excursions into the twisted world of secret agents"—*Times* (London)
0–87951–989–4 Overlook $22.50
0–87951–287–3 Overlook pb $9.95

THE EMPEROR'S TOMB
Translated by John Hoare
0–87951–270–9 Overlook pb $9.95

FLIGHT WITHOUT END
"An important chronicle of the disintegration of early twentieth-century Europe"—*NY Times*
Translated by David Le Vay
0–87951–057–9 Overlook $22.50
0–87951–279–2 Overlook pb $8.95

HOTEL SAVOY
Translated by John Hoare
0–87951–211–3 Overlook $16.95

THE RADETZKY MARCH
Roth's best novel surveys the waning of the Hapsburg Empire
Translated by Eva Tucker
0–87951–198–2 Overlook $22.50
0–87951–189–3 Overlook pb $9.95

● **Robert Walser**
SELECTED STORIES
Tiny masterpieces of comedy, fantasy, and obsession by a long-neglected Swiss author who later succumbed to schizophrenia
Translated by Christopher Middleton
Foreword by Susan Sontag
0–374–25901–1 Farrar, Straus & Giroux $16.50
0–374–52054–2 Farrar, Straus & Giroux pb $8.95

A Little Fable
"Alas," said the mouse, "the world is growing smaller every day. At the beginning it was so big that I was afraid, I kept running and running, and I was glad when at last I saw walls far away to the right and left, but these long walls have narrowed so quickly that I am in the last chamber already, and there in the corner stands the trap that I must run into." "You only need to change your direction," said the cat, and ate it up.

Translated by Willa & Edwin Muir

Franz Kafka
THE COMPLETE STORIES
0–8052–0873–9 Schocken pb $11.95

• **Arnold Zweig**
THE CASE OF SERGEANT GRISCHA
A World War I story of desertion and
military principle
0–14–007057–5 Penguin pb $7.95

POSTWAR LITERATURE

In a short story by Heinrich Böll, a
wounded young soldier in the final days of
World War II is carried into a makeshift
hospital. Gradually he comes to recognize
his surroundings as the high school he had
recently been forced to leave. From his
stretcher he catches a glimpse of his own
handwriting on the blackboard—just as the
surgeon begins to amputate his limbs. This
might be a symbol of the modern German
writer, whose literary traditions were dis-
membered by the Nazis and who is now
forced to confront the consequences of war
and the Holocaust.

▶ For ease of reference, postwar Austrian,
German, and Swiss writers are grouped
together here in alphabetical order

• **Ingeborg Bachmann**
Bachmann, who died at 47 in 1973, has
been claimed as a major influence by Peter
Handke and Christa Wolf.
MALINA
Bachmann's only novel is a complex study
of postwar consciousness and sexual
conflict
0–8419–1192–4 Holmes & Meier $29.95

THE THIRTIETH YEAR
Bachmann's first collection of stories
0–8419–1068–5 Holmes & Meier $19.95

THREE PATHS TO THE LAKE
Translated by Mary Fran Gilbert
0–8419–1070–7 Holmes & Meier $24.50

• **Jurek Becker**
SLEEPLESS DAYS
Becker, a concentration camp survivor, left
East Germany in 1977 after this book was
rejected for publication
0–15–682765–4 HBJ pb $5.95

• **Thomas Bernhard**
CONCRETE
In this macabre tale of failure, a
musicologist strives for ten years to
produce the perfect opening sentence. "A
book of mysterious, dark beauty"—John
Rechy, *LA Times*
Translated by David McLintock
0–226–04398–3 Chicago pb $5.95

GARGOYLES
A doctor's rounds take him through a
panorama of human suffering, ending with
a schizophrenic "whose uninterrupted
monologue for a hundred pages is a
virtuoso verbal performance"—A.C. Foote,
Book World
Translated by Richard & Clara Winston
0–226–04399–1 Chicago pb $9.95

GATHERING EVIDENCE: A Memoir
Translated by David McLintock
0–394–54707–1 Knopf $19.95

THE LIME WORKS
A nameless insurance salesman recounts
the life and crime of a tormented recluse
Translated by Sophia Wilkins
0–226–04397–5 Chicago pb $7.95

WOODCUTTERS
Translated by David McLintock
0–394–55152–4 Knopf $15.95
0–226–04396–7 Chicago pb $10.95

• **Horst Bienek**
SELECTED POEMS, 1958–1988
Bienek spent four years as a political
prisoner in the Urals in the 1950s before
being granted amnesty and settling in West
Germany
0–87775–206–0 Unicorn (bilingual) $20.00
0–87775–207–9 Unicorn (bilingual) pb $10.00

• **Johannes Bobrowski**
Bobrowski, an outstanding East German
poet, explored throughout his work a
visionary geography typified by the title
Shadow Lands.
LEVIN'S MILL
Translated by Janet Cropper
0–7145–0020–8 Marion Boyars $18.95

SHADOW LANDS
Translated by Ruth & Matthew Mead
0–85646–117–2 Longwood $18.95

• **Heinrich Böll**
Awarded the Nobel Prize in 1972, Böll
was an outspoken critic of modern society
who focused on institutional structures
that demand mindless conformity.
ADAM & THE TRAIN
Two war novels based on Böll's
experiences as a draftee in the German
army
Translated by Leila Vennewitz
0–07–006409–1 McGraw-Hill pb $7.95

AND NEVER SAID A WORD
Translated by Leila Vennewitz
0–07–006421–0 McGraw-Hill pb $5.95

BILLIARDS AT HALF-PAST NINE
This highly compressed account of several
generations of a modern German family is
generally regarded as Böll's masterpiece.
"His mocking humor is consistently
directed against militarism and
totalitarianism"—*NY Times*
0–07–006401–6 McGraw-Hill pb $6.95

THE CASUALTY
Translated by Leila Vennewitz
0–374–11967–8 Farrar, Straus & Giroux $16.95
0–393–30599–6 Norton pb $7.95

CHILDREN ARE CIVILIANS TOO
Stories written in the aftermath of World
War II
Translated by Leila Vennewitz
0–07–006430–X McGraw-Hill pb $5.95

THE CLOWN
The life of a professional clown, during
and after the Hitler era
Translated by Leila Vennewitz
0–07–006420–2 McGraw-Hill pb $6.95

**THE LOST HONOR OF KATHARINA
BLUM**
An innocent woman, driven to murder, is
destroyed by slanderous journalism
Translated by Leila Vennewitz
0–07–006429–6 McGraw-Hill pb $6.95

A SOLDIER'S LEGACY
Translated by Leila Vennewitz
0–394–53603–7 Knopf $11.95
0–14–008320–0 Penguin pb $6.95

THE STORIES OF HEINRICH BOLL
These 63 stories and novellas, embracing
the previous collections, mount a dogged
assault on the hypocrisies of modern
Germany
Translated by Leila Vennewitz
0–394–51405–X Knopf $25.00
0–07–006422–9 McGraw-Hill pb $9.95

WHAT'S TO BECOME OF THE BOY
A memoir of childhood in the Third Reich
Translated by Leila Vennewitz
0–394–53016–0 Knopf $11.95
0–14–008321–9 Penguin pb $5.95

• **Paul Celan**
POEMS OF PAUL CELAN
Celan, a concentration camp survivor for
whom German remained in some ways the
speech of The Other, pushes against the
limits of language in his disturbing and
influential poems. This is the most
extensive collection available, in a bilingual
edition
Translated with an introduction by Michael Hamburger
0–89255–140–2 Persea $24.95

LAST POEMS
"I don't know of any humanly more
important work than these late poems of
Celan. They represent nothing less than
the recovery of a language from its
destruction by fire"—Michael Palmer
Translated by Katherine Washburn & Margret Guillemin
0–86547–223–8 North Point $20.00

• **Heimito von Döderer**
THE WATERFALLS OF SLUNJ
Translated by Ernst Kaiser & Eithne Wilkins
0–941419–11–8 Eridanos pb $15.00

• **Friedrich Dürrenmatt**
**THE ASSIGNMENT: Or, On Observing
the Observer of the Observers**
"Misanthropically funny . . . Dark and
devious"—*Chicago Tribune*
0–679–72233–5 Vintage pb $6.95

*Paul Celan (photo courtesy of Persea/
Braziller)*

THE EXECUTION OF JUSTICE
A Swiss politician kills a man in broad daylight
Translated by John Wood
0–394–57802–3 Random House $17.95

THE JUDGE AND HIS HANGMAN & THE QUARRY
Brief, sharp, philosophical detective novels
Afterword by George Stade
0–87923–437–7 Godine pb $7.95

• Günter Eich
VALUABLE NAIL: The Selected Poems of Günter Eich
Good examples of the terse lyrical expression of this Austrian "apostle of brevity"
Translated by David Walker & others
0–932440–08–8 Oberlin $9.95
0–932440–09–6 Oberlin pb $4.95

• Max Frisch
BLUEBEARD
A doctor acquitted of murder relives the events leading to his trial and stands trial all over again in his own mind
Translated by Geoffrey Skelton
0–15–613198–6 HBJ pb $3.95

HOMO FABER
What it means to be human in the age of technology
Translated by Michael Bullock
0–15–642135–6 HBJ pb $4.95

I'M NOT STILLER
A tragicomic absurdist novel of lost identity
0–394–70219–0 Random House pb $3.95

MAN IN THE HOLOCENE
Many consider this short novella to be the Swiss writer's masterpiece
Translated by Geoffrey Skelton
0–15–656952–3 HBJ pb $4.95

MONTAUK
A frank autobiographical account of a relationship at the age of 64
Translated by Geoffrey Skelton
0–15–661990–3 HBJ pb $4.95

SKETCHBOOK: 1946–1949
Scenes and portraits of postwar Europe
Translated by Geoffrey Skelton
0–15–682746–8 HBJ pb $8.95

SKETCHBOOK: 1966–1971
Translated by Geoffrey Skelton
0–15–682747–6 HBJ pb $8.95

• Günter Grass
This most prominent contemporary German writer is widely regarded as the conscience of the postwar generation.
THE FLOUNDER
Novel, fairytale, diary, political commentary, and an account of women's contribution to history
Translated by Ralph Manheim
0–15–631935–4 HBJ pb $11.95

HEADBIRTHS: Or, The Germans Are Dying Out
A satirical discussion of the problems facing the industrialized world: energy, nuclear war, Third World poverty
0–449–20057–4 Fawcett pb $2.95

IN THE EGG & OTHER POEMS
Translated by Michael Hamburger & Christopher Middleton
0–15–672239–9 HBJ pb $5.95

LOCAL ANAESTHETIC
A fragmented portrait of modern Germany
0–15–652940–8 HBJ pb $9.95

THE MEETING AT TELGTE
The most potent minds of 17th-century Germany convene in somewhat disorderly fashion to ponder cosmic paradoxes
Translated by Ralph Manheim
0–15–158588–1 HBJ $9.95
0–449–24504–7 Fawcett pb $3.50

THE RAT
Translated by Ralph Manheim
0–15–175920–0 HBJ $17.95

THE TIN DRUM
Grass's exuberant prose epic, narrated by a dwarf drummer, presents a kaleidoscopic vision of the war years and the postwar period
Translated by Ralph Manheim
0–394–74560–4 Random House pb $7.95

• Peter Handke
"The best writer, altogether, in his language."—John Updike
ACROSS
Translated by Ralph Manheim
0–374–10054–3 Farrar, Straus & Giroux $14.95
0–02–051540–5 Macmillan pb $6.95

THE AFTERNOON OF A WRITER
Fear besets a writer and sends him on an afternoon odyssey
Translated by Ralph Manheim
0–374–10207–4 Farrar, Straus & Giroux $14.95

A MOMENT OF TRUE FEELING
Translated by Ralph Manheim
0–374–17291–9 Farrar, Straus & Giroux $7.95

REPETITION
A search for a missing brother turns into an investigation of language
Translated by Ralph Manheim
0–374–24934–2 Farrar, Straus & Giroux $18.95

SLOW HOMECOMING
0–374–26635–2 Farrar, Straus & Giroux $16.95
0–02–051530–8 Macmillan pb $8.95

THREE X HANDKE
Includes *The Goalie's Anxiety at the Penalty Kick, Short Letter, Long Farewell,* and *A Sorrow Beyond Dreams*
0–02–020761–1 Macmillan pb $8.95

THE WEIGHT OF THE WORLD
Translated by Ralph Manheim
0–374–28745–7 Farrar, Straus & Giroux $16.95

• Uwe Johnson
SPECULATIONS ABOUT JAKOB
An experimental novel dealing with the problematic co-existence of the two Germanies
Translated by Ursule Molinaro
0–15–684719–1 HBJ pb $4.95

ANNIVERSARIES II
A sequel to *Speculations about Jakob,* in which Germany is surveyed from the United States. The East German author again uses an innovative montage technique
Translated by Leila Vennewitz & Walter Arndt
0–15–107562–X HBJ $29.95

• Siegfried Lenz
THE GERMAN LESSON
A juvenile delinquent writes down his life, describing the clash of father against son

and duty against loyalty in wartime Germany
Translated by Ernst Kaiser & Eithne Wilkins
0–8112–0982–2 New Directions pb $10.95

THE HERITAGE
Translated by Krishna Winston
0–8090–1512–9 Hill & Wang pb $8.95

• Jakov Lind
SOUL OF WOOD
A collection of darkly comic stories exploring the atrocities and distortions of wartime
Translated by Ralph Manheim
0–8090–1526–9 Farrar, Straus & Giroux pb $6.95

• Ulrich Plenzdorf
THE NEW SUFFERINGS OF YOUNG W.
A contemporary East German variant on Goethe's novel of youthful despair
Translated by Kenneth P. Wilcox
0–8044–6656–4 Ungar pb $5.95

• Arno Schmidt
Schmidt, who died in 1979, has been compared to Joyce, Queneau, and Beckett.
SCENES FROM THE LIFE OF A FAUN
Small-town life in provincial Germany before and during World War II, transcribed in lively experimental fashion
Translated by John E. Woods
0–7145–2763–7 Marion Boyars pb $8.95

THE EGGHEAD REPUBLIC: A Short Novel from the Horse Latitudes
A science fiction parable set in 2008 in the International Republic of Artists and Scientists—a jet-propelled island where the world's geniuses have been installed to preserve world culture
Translated by Michael Horovitz
Edited by Ernst Krawehl
0–7145–2592–8 Marion Boyars pb $7.95

• Peter Schneider
THE WALL JUMPER
"Peter Schneider's description of the Berlin Wall from both sides—as well as the Wall within our own heads—is the ultimate depiction of this structure"—Werner Herzog
Translated by Leigh Hafrey
0–394–72882–3 Pantheon pb $7.95

• Martin Walser
BREAKERS
Translated by Leila Vennewitz
0–8050–0415–7 Henry Holt $18.95

NO MAN'S LAND
A tale of political intrigue and espionage in divided Germany
Translated by Leila Vennewitz
0–8050–0667–2 Henry Holt $17.95

RUNAWAY HORSE
A couple's staid holiday turns sinister with the arrival of an old schoolmate
0–8050–0359–2 Henry Holt pb $6.95

THE SWAN VILLA
A realtor becomes obsessed with his pursuit of the ultimate deal
Translated by Leila Vennewitz
0–03–059372–7 Henry Holt $14.95
0–8050–0358–4 Henry Holt pb $7.95

• Christa Wolf
ACCIDENT: A Day's News
How an accident, in this instance the

nuclear disaster at Chernobyl, affects a
writer's daily routine
Translated by Heike Schwarzbauer & Rick Takvorian
0–374–10046–2 Farrar, Straus & Giroux $15.95

CASSANDRA: A Novel and Four Essays
A retelling of the Trojan War from
Cassandra's perspective
Translated by Jan Van Heurck
0–374–11956–2 Farrar, Straus & Giroux $17.95
0–374–51904–8 Farrar, Straus & Giroux pb $8.95

NO PLACE ON EARTH
Translated by Jan Van Heurck
0–374–22298–3 Farrar, Straus & Giroux $11.95
0–374–51775–4 Farrar, Straus & Giroux pb $6.95

PATTERNS OF CHILDHOOD
Complex account of growing up in Nazi
Germany; originally titled *A Model
Childhood* in the hardcover edition
Translated by Ursule Molinaro & Hedwig Rappolt
0–374–21170–1 Farrar, Straus & Giroux $17.50
0–374–51844–0 Farrar, Straus & Giroux pb $9.95

THE QUEST FOR CHRISTA T.
Translated by Christopher Middleton
0–374–51534–4 Farrar, Straus & Giroux pb $8.95

ANTHOLOGIES

• Robert Browning, editor
GERMAN POETRY: 1750–1900
0–8264–0283–6 Continuum pb $10.95

• Leonard Forster, editor
**THE PENGUIN BOOK OF GERMAN
VERSE**
German texts with literal prose translations
0–14–058546–X Penguin pb $6.95

• Margaret Herzfeld-Sander, editor
ESSAYS ON GERMAN THEATER
Includes essays by Lessing, Schiller,
Büchner, Wagner, Nietzsche, Brecht,
Lukacs, and Dürrenmatt
0–8264–0297–6 Continuum pb $10.50

• Frank Ryder & Robert Browning,
editors
GERMAN LITERARY FAIRY TALES
Includes work by Goethe, Tieck,
Wackenroder, Novalis, Hoffmann,
Eichendorff, Brentano, Hauff, Mörike,
Storm, Hofmannsthal, and Kafka
0–8264–0277–1 Continuum pb $10.95

• Harry Steinhauser, editor & translator
TWELVE GERMAN NOVELLAS
0–520–03504–6 California $32.00
0–520–03002–8 California pb $11.95

CRITICAL STUDIES

• Russell Berman
**THE RISE OF THE MODERN GERMAN
NOVEL: Crisis and Charisma**
0–674–77250–4 Harvard $29.50

• Robert Browning
**GERMAN BAROQUE POETRY:
1618–1723**
0–271–01146–7 Pennsylvania State $24.50

**GERMAN POETRY IN THE AGE OF
THE ENLIGHTENMENT: From Brockes
to Klopstock**
0–271–00541–6 Pennsylvania State $24.50

• Henry and Mary Garland
**THE OXFORD COMPANION TO
GERMAN LITERATURE**
0–19–866139–8 Oxford $49.95

• Ronald D. Gray
**GERMAN POETRY: A Guide to Free
Appreciation**
0–521–29000–7 Cambridge pb $11.95

• Michael Hamburger
**AFTER THE SECOND FLOOD: Essays on
German Post-War Literature**
0–312–00087–1 St. Martin's $29.95
0–312–00088–X St. Martin's pb $12.95

**A PROLIFERATION OF PROPHETS:
Essays on German Writers from Nietzsche
to Brecht**
0–312–65117–1 St. Martin's $22.50

• Henry Hatfield
**CLASHING MYTHS IN GERMAN
LITERATURE: From Heine to Rilke**
0–674–13375–7 Harvard $17.50

• Anthony Heilbut
**EXILED IN PARADISE: German Refugee
Artists and Intellectuals from the 1930s to
the Present**
0–8070–5411–9 Beacon pb $13.95

• Carl Schorske
**FIN-DE-SIECLE VIENNA: Politics and
Culture**
0–394–50596–4 Knopf $29.95
0–394–74478–0 Vintage $12.95

• John Willett
**THE THEATRE OF THE WEIMAR
REPUBLIC**
0–8419–0759–5 Holmes & Meier $79.50

**ART AND POLITICS IN THE WEIMAR
PERIOD: The New Sobriety, 1917–1933**
0–394–73991–4 Pantheon pb $14.95

Studies of Individual Authors
(alphabetical by subject)

• Gershom Scholem
**WALTER BENJAMIN: The Story of a
Friendship**
Translated by Harry Zohn
0–8276–0197–2 JPS $13.95

• Eric Bentley
THE BRECHT COMMENTARIES
0–394–62373–8 Grove pb $9.95

• Martin Esslin
**BRECHT: A Choice of Evils—A Critical
Study of the Man, His Work, and His
Opinions**
0–413–54750–7 Methuen pb $10.05

• Ronald Hayman
BRECHT: A Biography
0–19–520434–4 Oxford $29.95

• M. B. Benn
**THE DRAMA OF REVOLT: A Critical
Study of Georg Büchner**
0–521–29415–0 Cambridge pb $15.95

• Ronald Gray
GOETHE: A Critical Introduction
0–521–09404–6 Cambridge pb $16.95

• Georg Lukács
GOETHE AND HIS AGE
Translated by Robert Anchor
0–391–01983–X Humanities pb $19.95

• John Ellis
**ONE FAIRY STORY TOO MANY: The
Brothers Grimm and Their Tales**
0–226–20547–9 Chicago pb $6.95

• Max Brod
FRANZ KAFKA: A Biography
0–8052–0047–9 Schocken pb $7.50

• Elias Canetti
**KAFKA'S OTHER TRIAL: The Letters to
Felice**
Translated by Christopher Middleton
0–8052–3553–1 Schocken $11.95

• Erich Heller
FRANZ KAFKA
0–691–01384–5 Princeton pb $9.95

• Ernst Pawel
**THE NIGHTMARE OF REASON: A Life
of Franz Kafka**
0–374–22236–3 Farrar, Straus & Giroux $25.50
0–394–72948–X Random House pb $7.95

• Robert Helbling
**HEINRICH VON KLEIST: The Major
Works**
0–8112–0563–0 New Directions $13.95
0–8112–0564–9 New Directions pb $3.95

• Joachim Maass
KLEIST: A Biography
Translated by Ralph Manheim
0–374–18162–4 Farrar, Straus & Giroux $22.50
0–374–51848–3 Farrar, Straus & Giroux pb $10.95

• Erich Heller
THOMAS MANN: The Ironic German
0–89526–906–6 Regnery pb $5.95

• Donald Prater
**A RINGING GLASS: The Life of Rainer
Maria Rilke**
0–19–815755–X Oxford $29.95

Thomas Mann in 1900 (photo from the Thomas Mann Archive, Zurich)

Scandinavian Literature

OLD NORSE AND ICELANDIC LITERATURE

• **Lee M. Hollander, translator**
THE POETIC EDDA
Compiled in Iceland in the 12th or 13th century, the *Poetic Edda* is the principal compendium of Norse mythology. Hollander's translation endeavors to capture the rhythms and texture of the original language
0–292–76499–5 Texas pb $12.95

• **Magnus Magnusson & Hermann Palsson, translators**
LAXDAELA SAGA
A complex family saga in which the central issue is a love triangle
0–14–044218–9 Penguin pb $5.95

NJAL'S SAGA
This much-praised translation gives new life to the greatest of the Icelandic sagas. "*Njal's Saga* is one of the most complex and dramatic novels ever written. It teems with characters: each sharply, however briefly, drawn; all presented in the most dramatic contexts. The narrative is carried by dialogue and by action of maximum concreteness"—Kenneth Rexroth
0–14–044103–4 Penguin pb $4.95

THE VINLAND SAGAS: The Norse Discovery of America
0–14–044154–9 Penguin pb $5.95

• **Hermann Palsson & Paul Edwards, translators**
EGIL'S SAGA
0–14–044321–5 Penguin pb $5.95

EYRBYGGJA SAGA
0–14–044530–7 Penguin pb $5.95

GONGU-HROLF'S SAGA
0–8020–2392–4 Toronto $16.50

THE ORKNEYINGA SAGA
0–14–044383–5 Penguin pb $5.95

SEVEN VIKING ROMANCES
0–14–044474–2 Penguin pb $5.95

• **Snorri Sturluson**
KING HARALD'S SAGA: Harald Hardradi of Norway
Translated by Magnus Magnusson & Hermann Palsson
0–14–044183–2 Penguin pb $4.95

THE PROSE EDDA OF SNORRI STURLUSON: Tales from Norse Mythology
Originally penned as a manual in skaldic (courtly) poetry, *The Prose Edda* saved from extinction many mythological tales
Translated by Jean Young
0–520–01232–1 California pb $7.95

DANISH LITERATURE

• **Hans Christian Andersen**
EIGHTY FAIRY TALES
The 19th-century Danish master of the fairytale interweaves fantasy and folklore over a ground note of pessimism
Translated by R.P. Keigwin
0–394–52523–X Pantheon $14.45
0–394–71055–X Pantheon pb $11.95

TALES & STORIES
Translated by Patricia Conroy & Sven Rossell
Illustrated by Vilhelm Pedersen & Lorenz Frolich
0–295–95769–7 Washington $22.50
0–295–95936–3 Washington pb $14.95

• **Isak Dinesen**
Somewhat paradoxically, Denmark's best-known 20th-century author lived in Africa and wrote her major works in English.
BABETTE'S FEAST & OTHER ANECDOTES OF DESTINY
Edited by Martha Levin
0–394–75929–X Random House pb $4.95

CARNIVAL: Entertainments & Posthumous Tales
0–226–15304–5 Chicago pb $10.95

EHRENGARD
Published posthumously, this story involves the interference of fate in a vision of existence where the leading players are life and art
0–394–71431–8 Random House pb $1.95

LETTERS FROM AFRICA, 1914–1931
Covering the entire period when Dinesen owned a coffee plantation in British colonial Kenya
Edited by Frans Lasson
Translated by Anne Born
0–226–15309–6 Chicago $25.00

OUT OF AFRICA & SHADOWS ON THE GRASS
The author's highly personal evocation of the continent that was her adopted home breathes with the deeply felt spirit of the land
0–394–74211–7 Random House pb $4.95

OUT OF AFRICA
0–517–56509–9 Crown $24.95
0–394–60498–9 Modern Library $8.95

SEVEN GOTHIC TALES
This collection of highly-colored, sometimes melodramatic stories was an international bestseller in the 1940s
Introduction by Dorothy Canfield
0–394–60496–2 Modern Library $6.95

WINTER'S TALES
0–394–70205–0 Random House pb $4.95

• **Tove Ditlevsen**
EARLY SPRING
Translated by Tiina Nunnally
0–931188–29–6 Seal Press $16.95
0–931188–28–8 Seal Press pb $8.95

• **Martin Anderson Nexö**
DITTE
This important novelist is best known for his proletarian themes, leavening his Marxist approach with tender humor. The *Ditte* trilogy includes *Girl Alive, Daughter of Man,* and *Toward the Stars*
0–8446–1325–8 Peter Smith $16.50

PELLE THE CONQUEROR
Volume 1: Childhood
The basis for the successful movie
Edited by Frank Hugus & Steve Murray
0–94024–40–0 Fjord pb $9.95

• **Klaus Rifbjerg**
ANNA, I, ANNA
A diplomat's wife flees her plush surroundings to roam Europe with a hippie
Translated by Alexander Taylor
0–915306–30–1 Talman pb $9.95

SELECTED POEMS
Translated by Nadia Chistensen & Alexander Taylor
0–915306–48–4 Talman pb $4.50

WITNESS TO THE FUTURE
Translated by Steve Murray
0–940242–18–4 Fjord pb $8.95

• **Villy Sørensen**
THE DOWNFALL OF THE GODS
A re-writing of the mythology of the ancient Nordic world, highlighting the Norse deities and their foibles to reflect current moral crises
Translated by Paula Hostrup-Jessen
0–8032–4201–8 Nebraska $14.95

TUTELARY TALES
A collection of twelve short stories by a leading Scandinavian writer
0–8032–4185–2 Nebraska $21.00

FINNISH LITERATURE

• **Elias Lönnrot**
KALEVALA: The Land of the Heroes
The Finnish national epic, compiled in the 19th century from folk materials still current at the time, centers around three semi-divine brothers who live in Kaleva, a mythical land of plenty and happiness
Edited by Michael Branch
Translated by W.F. Kirby
0–485–12048–8 Humanities pb $14.95

THE KALEVALA: Or Poems of the Kaleva District
Regarded as a more scholarly and readable edition than the "rather antiquated language" (Kenneth Rexroth) of the Kirby translation
Translated by Francis P. Magoun, Jr.
0–674–50000–8 Harvard $25.00
0–674–50010–5 Harvard pb $10.95

• **Pentti Saarikoski**
POEMS 1958–1980
Translated by Anselm Hollo
0–915124–76–9 Toothpaste pb $10.00

• **Frans Emil Sillanpää**
PEOPLE IN THE SUMMER NIGHT: An Epic Suite
This novel by a Nobel laureate delves deeply into the texture of Finnish rural life
Translated by Alan Blair
0–299–03901–3 Wisconsin $15.95

➤ **FOR OVERSEAS ORDERING INFORMATION, SEE PAGE 1**

ICELANDIC LITERATURE

- Gunnar Gunnarsson
BLACK CLIFFS
A novel revolving around themes of
isolation and faith
Translated by Cecil Wood
0–299–04471–8 Wisconsin $17.50

- Halldor Laxness
THE ATOM STATION
A satirical account by this Nobel laureate
of the decline of Icelandic culture,
represented by the admission of US bases
to the country
0–933256–30–2 Permanent $16.95
0–933256–31–0 Permanent pb $8.95

NORWEGIAN LITERATURE

▶ For Ibsen's plays see Modern European Drama

- Knut Hamsun
GROWTH OF THE SOIL
A family struggles for survival in the
Norwegian wilderness
0–394–71781–3 Random House pb $6.95

HUNGER
Hamsun's masterpiece, published in 1890,
focuses with remarkable intensity on a few
days in the life of a young man at the end
of his economic and psychological
resources
Translated by Robert Bly
Introduction by Isaac Bashevis Singer
0–374–50520–9 Farrar, Straus & Giroux pb $7.95

MYSTERIES
An investigation of the mysterious forces
at work in the human psyche
0–88184–031–9 Carroll & Graf pb $8.95

**PAN: From Lieutenant Thomas Glahn's
Papers**
Translated by James W. McFarlane
0–374–50016–9 Farrar, Straus & Giroux pb $8.70

WAYFARERS
Translated by James W. McFarlane
0–374–51592–1 Farrar, Straus & Giroux pb $10.95

THE WOMEN AT THE PUMP
Translated by Oliver & Gunnvor Stallybrass
0–374–29280–9 Farrar, Straus & Giroux $10.95
0–374–51503–4 Farrar, Straus & Giroux pb $4.95

- Torborg Nedreaas
MUSIC FROM A BLUE WELL
"A compelling book wherein adult
problems, decisions, actions are refracted
through the lens of a child"—Marion
Faber, Swarthmore
Translated by Bibbi Lee
0–8032–3315–9 Nebraska $21.00

NOTHING GROWS BY MOONLIGHT
"This glowing, elegantly translated novel
has already earned a wide audience in
Europe and a rising reputation for its
author"—*Publishers Weekly*
Translated by Bibbi Lee
0–8032–3313–2 Nebraska $15.95

- O.E. Rölvaag
THE BOAT OF LONGING
A stark portrait of the hardships of the
immigrant experience by this Norwegian-
American who himself immigrated to the
US in 1896
Translated by Nora O. Solum
0–87351–184–0 Minnesota Historical pb $8.95

GIANTS IN THE EARTH
A translation of the first two novels in
the tetralogy depicting the family of
Per Hansa
0–06–083047–6 Harper & Row pb $4.95

**PEDER VICTORIOUS: A Tale of the
Pioneers Twenty Years Later**
The third title in the Per Hansa
sequence
Translated by Nora Solum & the author
0–8032–8906–5 Nebraska pb $7.50

THEIR FATHERS' GOD
The final installment in the Per Hansa
tetralogy
Translated by Trygve Ager
0–8032–8911–1 Nebraska pb $7.95

THE THIRD LIFE OF PER SMEVIK
The novelist's first, sharply
autobiographical work
Translated by Ella Tweet & Solweig Zempel
0–06–097076–6 Harper & Row pb $6.95

- Cora Sandel
ALBERTA AND FREEDOM
First title of the Alberta trilogy which
unhurriedly charts the growing pains and
pleasures of a provincial Norwegian girl
who comes of age in Paris
Translated by Elizabeth Rokkan
Introduction by Linda Hunt
0–8214–0758–9 Ohio $15.95
0–8214–0759–7 Ohio pb $7.95

ALBERTA AND JACOB
Translated by Elizabeth Rokkan
Introduction by Linda Hunt
0–8214–0756–2 Ohio $15.95
0–8214–0757–0 Ohio pb $7.95

ALBERTA ALONE
Translated by Elizabeth Rokkan
Introduction by Linda Hunt
0–8214–0760–0 Ohio $15.95
0–8214–0761–9 Ohio pb $7.95

KRANE'S CAFE: An Interior with Figures
Translated by Elizabeth Rokkan
0–8214–0796–1 Ohio $18.00

THE LEECH
Translated by Elizabeth Rokkan
0–8214–0837–2 Ohio $17.95
0–8214–0838–0 Ohio pb $7.95

SELECTED SHORT STORIES
Translated with an introduction by Barbara Wilson
0–931188–30–X Consortium pb $8.95

THE SILKEN THREAD
Translated by Elizabeth Rokkan
0–8214–0864–X Ohio $17.95
0–8214–0865–8 Ohio pb $8.95

- Sigrid Undset
KRISTIN LAVRANSDATTER
A trilogy set in medieval Norway, tracing
the protagonist's evolution from girlhood
to maturity against a vividly detailed
historical backdrop
0–394–43262–2 Knopf (1-volume edition) $34.50

Volume 1: The Bridal Wreath
0–394–75299–6 Random House pb $6.95

Volume 2: The Mistress of Husaby
0–394–75293–7 Random House pb $6.95

Volume 3: The Cross
0–394–75291–0 Random House pb $6.95

THE MASTER OF HESTVIKEN
The Nobel laureate's other literary
masterpiece and monument to medieval
Scandinavian history. It was written after
her conversion to Catholicism—a bold step
in Lutheran Norway—and clearly shows
her greater preoccupation with matters
religious
0–452–26034–5 NAL pb $14.95

- Tarjei Vesaas
**SELECTED POEMS: 100 Poems
Translated from the Norwegian with 8
Poems in the Original Nynorsk**
A collection of 100 poems, with the
original Norwegian text provided for eight
of them. Vesaas' poetry is full of stark
landscapes, to which he imparts moods
ranging from domestic warmth to violent
anxiety
0–907954–12–X Allardyce & Barnett pb $15.00

BIRDS
Translated by Trobjorn Stoverud & Michael Barnes
0–7206–0701–9 Dufour $19.95

LAND OF HIDDEN FIRES
Translated by Fritz Konig & Jerry Crisp
0–8143–1496–1 Wayne State (bilingual) $14.95

SWEDISH LITERATURE

- Gunnar Ekelöf
GUIDE TO THE UNDERWORLD
Ekelöf is widely considered the most
distinguished modern Swedish poet
Translated by Rika Lesser
0–87023–306–8 Massachusetts $10.00

A MOLNA ELEGY
Translated by Muriel Rukeyser & Leif Sjöberg
0–87775–153–6 Unicorn pb $7.00

Lars Gustafsson
THE DEATH OF A BEEKEEPER
Translated by Janet K. Swaffer & Guntram H.
Weber
0–8112–0809–5 New Directions $12.95
0–8112–0810–9 New Directions pb $5.95

SELECTED POEMS
Investigations into the essence of
knowledge and the nature of human
relationships
Translated with an introduction by Robin Fulton
Illustrated by Arthur Trees
0–912284–27–7 New Rivers $5.00
0–912284–28–5 New Rivers pb $2.50

SIGISMUND
A novel in which various historical
periods intermingle
Translated by John Weinstock
0–8112–0924–5 New Directions pb $7.70

**THE STILLNESS OF THE WORLD
BEFORE BACH: New Selected Poems**
Translated by Christopher Middleton
0–8112–1058–8 New Directions pb $9.70

STORIES OF HAPPY PEOPLE
Translated by Yvonne L. Sandstroem & John
Weinstock
0–8112–0978–4 New Directions pb $7.70

THE TENNIS PLAYERS
Translated by Yvonne L. Sandstroem
0–8112–0862–1 New Directions pb $6.00

• Lennart Hagerfors
THE WHALES IN LAKE TANGANYIKA
A fictional treatment of Stanley's 1871 quest for Livingstone
Translated by Anselm Hollo
0–8021–1095–9 Grove $15.95

• P.C. Jersild
CHILDREN'S ISLAND
"A satiric novel that reflects . . . deep social commitment . . . 10-year-old Reine decides to miss summer camp so he can stay in Stockholm by himself and devote his last summer before the confusion of adolescence to solving life's major problems"—*Library Journal*
Translated by Joan Tate
0–8032–7567–6 Nebraska pb $11.50

• Eyvind Johnson
DREAMS OF ROSES AND FIRE
Johnson won the Nobel Prize for Literature in 1974
Edited by Erik J. Friis
0–88254–897–2 Hippocrene $14.95

• Pär Lagerkvist
Lagerkvist's spare symbolic words earned him the Nobel Prize in 1951.
BARABBAS
Lagerkvist explores the fate of Barabbas after his liberation
Translated by Alain Blair
0–394–70134–8 Random House pb $3.95
THE DWARF
Translated by Alexandra Dick
0–8090–1303–7 Hill & Wang pb $8.95
THE SIBYL
Translated by Naomi Walford
0–394–70240–9 Random House pb $3.95

1897 photo (courtesy of the Strindberg Museum, Stockholm) from Strindberg: A Biography *by Michael Meyer (Random House)*

• August Strindberg
BY THE OPEN SEA
A naturalistic novel about the destruction of a divided personality
Translated by Mary Sandbach
0–14–044488–2 Penguin pb $5.95
INFERNO & FROM AN OCCULT DIARY
Inferno is Strindberg's extraordinary

account of a spiritual crisis he underwent in Paris in the 1890s
Translated by Mary Sandbach
0–14–044364–9 Penguin pb $6.95
THE ROOFING CEREMONY & THE SILVER LAKE
The Roofing Ceremony, a novella first published in 1906, concerns a man's experiences as he approaches death. "Strindberg's most experimental, most modern work of fiction"—Eric O. Johannesson, *The Novels of August Strindberg*
Translated by David Mel Paul & Margareta Paul
0–8032–4171–2 Nebraska $14.95

▶ **For Strindberg's plays see Modern European Drama**

• Tomas Tranströmer
COLLECTED POEMS
1–85224–023–7 Dufour pb $14.95
SELECTED POEMS
The translators include Robin Fulton, Robert Bly, May Swenson, and Samuel Charters
Edited by Robert Hass
0–88001–105–X Norton $17.50
TRUTH BARRIERS: Poems by Tomas Tranströmer
Translated by Robert Bly
0–87156–235–9 Random House $9.95
0–87156–239–1 Random House pb $5.95
WINDOWS AND STONES: Selected Poems
Translated by May Swenson & Leif Sjoberg
0–8229–3241–5 Pittsburgh $15.95

CRITICAL STUDIES

Sven Rossel
A HISTORY OF SCANDINAVIAN LITERATURE: 1870–1980
Translated by Anne Ulmer
0–8166–0906–3 Minnesota $27.50

• Robert Ferguson
ENIGMA: The Life of Knut Hamsun
0–374–14846–S Farrar, Straus & Giroux $30.00
0–374–52093–3 Farrar, Straus & Giroux pb $14.95

• Michael Meyer
IBSEN
A definitive critical biography by the preeminent Ibsen translator
0–14–058003–4 Penguin pb $9.95

• David Thomas
HENRIK IBSEN
0–394–53862–5 Grove $19.50
0–394–62157–3 Grove pb $9.95

• Michael Meyer
STRINDBERG: A Biography
0–394–50442–9 Random House $24.45
0–19–281995–X Oxford pb $14.95

• Margery Morgan
AUGUST STRINDBERG
0–394–54716–0 Grove $27.50
0–394–62065–8 Grove pb $11.95

Eastern European Literature

ALBANIAN LITERATURE

• Ismail Kadare
CHRONICLE IN STONE
A city in World War II, as filtered through a child's imagination. "A thoroughly enchanting novel—sophisticated and accomplished in its poetic prose and narrative deftness, yet drawing resonance from its roots in one of Europe's most primitive societies"—John Updike
0–941533–00–X New Amsterdam $17.95
0–941533–50–6 New Amsterdam pb $10.95
DORUNTINE
A novel of medieval Albania. "The great modern Albanian writer, Ismail Kadare . . . has given us a masterpiece . . . an age-old legend transformed into a splendid fable"—Alain Bosquet
Translated by Jon Rothschild
0–941533–20–4 New Amsterdam $15.95

BULGARIAN LITERATURE

• Nikolai Haitor
WILD TALES
Sixteen stories of village life and its occasional violence
Translated by Michael Holman
0–7206–0543–1 Dufour $24.00

CZECH LITERATURE

• Karel Capek
Capek was a major playwright, novelist, and essayist, the leading Czech writer of the post-World War I period.
THE ABSOLUTE AT LARGE
An early satirical romance in which the "Absolute" is liberated like a gas and runs amok among the populace
Introduction by William Harkins
0–88355–104–7 Hyperion $12.00
0–88355–133–0 Hyperion pb $3.50
THE GARDENER'S YEAR
Humorous pieces on the joys and frustrations of gardening, with delightful illustrations by the author's brother Josef
0–299–10020–0 Wisconsin $12.95
0–299–10024–3 Wisconsin pb $7.95
WAR WITH THE NEWTS
An intelligent species of newt threatens humanity with extinction, in Capek's most successful work of science fiction, filled with inventive satirical digressions
0–8101–0663–9 Northwestern pb $9.95

• Jirí Grusa
THE QUESTIONNAIRE: Or, Prayer for a Town and a Friend
A picaresque, grotesque, and slightly ribald chronicle of the author's native town
Translated by Peter Kussi
0–374–24010–8 Farrar, Straus & Giroux $15.95
0–394–72212–4 Random House pb $7.95

• Bohumil Harabal
I SERVED THE KING OF ENGLAND
A playful tale of a waiter turned millionaire
0–15–145745–X HBJ $17.95

Jaroslav Hasek
THE GOOD SOLDIER SVEJK AND HIS FORTUNES IN THE WORLD WAR
A major satirical epic about the archetypal little man caught up in the horror and idiocy of war. An important influence on writers like Bertolt Brecht and Joseph Heller
Translated by Cecil Parrott
Illustrated by Josef Lada
0–14–003568–0 Penguin pb $6.95

• Václav Havel
LETTERS TO OLGA: June 1979 to September 1982
Havel's letters to his wife during three years of imprisonment on charges of subversion
Translated by Paul Wilson
0–394–54795–0 Knopf $24.50

• Vladimir Holan
MIRRORING: Selected Poems of Vladimir Holan
Holan is perhaps the most powerful of modern Czech poets; this translation effectively conveys the varied aspects of his prolific output and includes excerpts from the long poem *A Night with Hamlet*
Translated by C. G. Hanzlicek & Dana Habova
0–8195–5129–5 Wesleyan $17.00
0–8195–6119–3 Wesleyan pb $8.95

• Miroslav Holub
THE FLY
Holub's experimental poetry reflects his background and concerns as a renowned immunologist. "Miroslav Holub is one of the half dozen most important poets writing anywhere"—Ted Hughes
Translated by Ewald Osers & others
1–85224–018–0 Dufour $13.00

INTERFERON: or, On Theater
"One of the sanest voices of our time"—A. Alvarez
0–932440–12–6 Oberlin $10.95
0–932440–13–4 Oberlin pb $5.95

In the Microscope
Here too are dreaming landscapes,
lunar, derelict.
Here too are the masses,
tillers of the soil.
And cells, fighters
who lay down their lives
for a song.

Here too are cemeteries,
fame and snow.
And I hear murmuring,
the revolt of immense estates.

Miroslav Holub
THE FLY
Translated by Ian Milner
1–85224–018–0 Dufour $13.00

• Eva Kanturkova
MY COMPANIONS IN THE BLEAK HOUSE
Reminiscences of the author's years in a political prison, and the women she met there
0–87951–289–X Overlook $19.95

• Ivan Klima
MY FIRST LOVES
First US publication of four short pieces banned in Czechoslovakia, like the rest of Klima's work
0–393–30601–1 Norton pb $7.95

MY MERRY MORNINGS
A series of stories about Prague. "That rare genre of a funny—sometimes hilariously funny—surface with a sad and serious iceberg below"—Joseph Skvorecký
0–930523–05–9 Readers International pb $7.95

• Milan Kundera
THE ART OF THE NOVEL
Kundera develops his conception of the European novel and looks closely at such writers as Broch, Kafka, Cervantes, and Flaubert
Translated by Linda Asher & David Bellos
0–8021–0011–2 Grove $17.95

THE BOOK OF LAUGHTER AND FORGETTING
An experimental mixture of history, philosophy, journalism, and fiction; it led to the revocation of Kundera's Czech citizenship in 1979. "A work of social realism and protest coexists with a brittleness, an angelic mockery that, amid such melancholy remembrance and shrewd psychology, makes *us*, the respectful Western readers, uncomfortable"—John Updike
Introduction by Philip Roth
0–394–50896–3 Knopf $17.50
0–14–009693–0 Penguin pb $6.95

Milan Kundera (photo by A. Manheimer, courtesy of Grove Press)

THE FAREWELL PARTY
Life in a small Czech resort town
Introduction by Elizabeth Pochoda
0–14–009694–9 Penguin pb $6.95

THE JOKE
Kundera's first novel concerns a student's innocent joke and the hard price he pays for it in Stalinist Czechoslovakia
Translated by Michael Heim
0–06–014987–6 Harper & Row $14.50
0–14–009692–2 Penguin pb $6.95

LAUGHABLE LOVES
Early stories about love and sex
Translated by Suzanne Rappaport
Introduction by Philip Roth
0–14–009691–4 Penguin pb $6.95

LIFE IS ELSEWHERE
A novel about a young poet who collaborates with the Stalinist regime and brings about his own downfall
0–14–006470–2 Penguin pb $6.95

THE UNBEARABLE LIGHTNESS OF BEING
A novel about two lovers in Prague in 1968; some of the same characters from *The Book of Laughter and Forgetting* reappear. "Kundera has raised the novel of ideas to a new level of dream-like lyricism and emotional intensity"—*Newsweek*
Translated by Michael Heim
0–06–015258–3 Harper & Row $18.50
0–06–091465–3 Harper & Row pb $8.95

• Arnost Lustig
INDECENT DREAMS
Three stories emerging from World War II and the Holocaust. "I know of very few stories that express so vividly the madness of the stream-of-consciousness of people living on the brink of death"—Joseph Skvorecký
0–8101–0772–3 Northwestern $22.95

• Vladimir Paral
CATAPULT
A lurching train catapults a young engineer into the arms of another woman and opens up a rush of new experiences
Translated by William Harkins
0–945774–04–4 Catbird $15.95

• Jaroslav Seifert
THE SELECTED POETRY OF JAROSLAV SEIFERT
A good selection from various periods of the Nobel Prize winner's work
Translated by Ewald Osers & George Gibian
0–02–609150–X Macmillan $17.95
0–02–070760–6 Macmillan pb $9.95

• Josef Skvorecký
DVORAK IN LOVE
A biographical novel about the Czech composer's life in the US in the 1890s
0–393–30548–1 Norton pb $7.95

THE ENGINEER OF HUMAN SOULS: An Entertainment on the Old Themes of Life, Women, Fate, Dreams, the Working Class, Secret Agents, Love and Death
The author's most ambitious novel to date covers a wide canvas, ranging from life in Czechoslovakia under the Nazis to the subsequent life of Czech emigrés in Canada
Translated by Paul Wilson
0–394–50500–X Knopf $17.50
0–671–55682–7 Washington Square pb $9.95

MISS SILVER'S PAST
A largely comic novel featuring hilarious anecdotes about Czech publishing and censorship under communism
Introduction by Graham Greene
0–88001–074–6 Norton pb $7.25

THE MOURNFUL DEMEANOUR OF LIEUTENANT BORUVKA: Detective Tales
The Czech translator of Hemingway, Faulkner and Dashiell Hammett tries his own hand in the detective genre
Translated by Rosemary Kavan & others
0–393–02470–9 Norton $15.50

SINS FOR FATHER KNOX
A collection of Skvorecký's detective tales, with Lieutenant Boruvka as the investigator. The stories are attributed to a certain Father Knox, faintly echoing Chesterton's Father Brown
Translated by Paul Wilson
0–393–02512–8 Norton $17.50

THE SWELL SEASON
The first part of the war trilogy, concerning the young musician Danny's life under Nazi occupation
Translated by Paul Wilson
0–88001–090–8 Norton pb $8.25

THE BASS SAXOPHONE
Two novellas: Skvorecký's young hero plays illegal jazz under the Nazis. This is the second volume of the World War II trilogy
0–671–55681–9 Washington Square pb $5.95

THE COWARDS
In the third volume of the war trilogy, Skvorecký's young hero emerges to confront the invading Russians
Translated by Jeanne Nemcova
0–912946–75–X Ecco pb $8.95

• Ludvik Vaculik
A CUP OF COFFEE WITH MY INTERROGATOR
By the Czech political novelist and author of the manifesto which may have helped precipitate the Soviet invasion. "Vaculik is the night watchman at a temporarily shut-down enterprise whose product is the national soul"—*LA Times*
Translated by George Theiner
0–930523–34–2 Readers International $14.95
0–930523–35–0 Readers International pb $7.95

• Jirí Weil
LIFE WITH A STAR
A novel based on Weil's experience escaping and hiding from the Nazis
Translated by R. Klima
Preface by Philip Roth
0–374–18737–1 Farrar, Straus & Giroux $18.95

ESTONIAN LITERATURE

• Jaan Kaplinski
THE SAME SEA IN US ALL
The first book of poems to appear in English by the gifted Estonian poet. "He is re-thinking Europe, revisioning history, in these poems of our times . . . Poems of

gentle politics and love that sometimes scare you"—Gary Snyder
Translated by Sam Hamill
Introduction by Gary Snyder
0–932576–30–3 Breitenbush pb $8.95

THE WANDERING BORDER
Translated by Riina Tamm, Sam Hamill & the author
1–556–59010–5 Copper Canyon pb $9.00

HUNGARIAN LITERATURE

• Milan Fust
THE STORY OF MY WIFE
The finest novel from the influential Hungarian poet, novelist and aesthetic theorist
Translated by Ivan Sanders
1–55554–018–X PAJ $18.95
0–679–72217–3 Vintage pb $8.95

• Attila József
PERCHED ON NOTHING'S BRANCH
Perhaps the greatest Hungarian poet of the 20th century, József took the proletarian material of his life and fashioned it into a clear, powerful and revolutionary new language
Translated by Peter Hargitai
0–940821–00–1 Apalachee $7.95

• Laszlo Nemeth
GUILT
A novel about the class guilt of a wealthy intellectual, by one of the giants of Hungarian literature and the translator of Tolstoy's *Anna Karenina*
Translated by Gyula Gulyas
0–7206–3845–3 Dufour $17.95

• Miklós Radnóti
UNDER GEMINI: The Selected Poems of Miklós Radnóti with a Prose Memoir
From the major Hungarian poet of the war years, a man obsessed in his work by the inevitability of violent death, which he himself met in 1944
Translated by Jascha Kessler & others
0–8214–0763–5 Ohio $18.00
0–8214–0764–3 Ohio pb $9.95

• Dezso Tandori
BIRDS AND OTHER RELATIONS: Selected Poetry of Dezso Tandori
Translated by Bruce Berlind
0–691–01433–7 Princeton pb $9.50

• Sándor Weöres
ETERNAL MOMENT: Selected Poems
0–89823–101–9 New Rivers pb $8.50

• Sándor Weöres & Fernec Juhasz
SELECTED POEMS
Combines the verse of two of Hungary's leading poets: Juhasz, a bricklayer's son, considered by many to be the heir to Attila József; and Weöres, the son of landowners, a versatile, innovative talent
Translated by Davis Wevill & Edward Morgan
0–8446–0290–6 Peter Smith $12.00

• Jascha Keller, editor
THE FACE OF CREATION: Contemporary Hungarian Poetry
"Evident throughout is a high level of craftsmanship, even as a diverse range of poetic voices are presented: the elegiac

Sandor Csoori, the sarcastic Laszlo Kalnoky, the surrealistic Anna Kiss and the violent Laszlo Nagy"—*Publishers Weekly*
0–918273–20–X Coffee House pb $11.95

• Albert Tezla, editor
OCEAN AT THE WINDOW: Hungarian Prose and Poetry Since 1945
0–8166–0992–6 Minnesota $25.00

POLISH LITERATURE

• Janusz Anderman
THE EDGE OF THE WORLD
"An urgent dispatch to the outer world . . . An outcry, an expose, brimming with talent and frustrated passion"—*NY Times*
Translated by Nina Taylor
0–930523–50–4 Readers International pb $7.95

POLAND UNDER BLACK LIGHT
A collection of short stories depicting Polish life after the imposition of martial law
Translated by Nina Taylor & Andrew Short
0–930523–13–X Readers International $12.50
0–930523–14–8 Readers International pb $6.95

• Tadeusz Borowski
THIS WAY FOR THE GAS, LADIES AND GENTLEMEN
Writings of a legendary Polish writer, who began writing in Nazi-occupied Warsaw, spent two years in Auschwitz, and committed suicide at age 29 in 1951
0–14–004114–1 Penguin pb $6.95

• Kazimierz Brandys
PARIS, NEW YORK, 1982–1984: A Memoir
Memoirs of life in the West since the author went into exile from Poland in 1981 in his seventies
0–394–544492–7 Random House $17.95

• Janusz Glowacki
GIVE US THIS DAY
An account of the August 1980 strike at the Lenin shipyard in Gdansk, to which Glowacki applies a sharp sense of the grotesque
Translated by Konrad Brodzinski
0–312–32741–2 St. Martin's $10.95

• Witold Gombrowicz
Several generations of Polish writers have seen Gombrowicz as their master. "Gombrowicz's provocative writing was a rebellion against all values in literature, against the accepted rules in social life, and the conventional attitudes toward national tradition. But under the mask of grotesque and sarcastic humor Gombrowicz poses the most important questions about the freedom of man."—*Columbia Dictionary of Modern European Literature*
THREE NOVELS
Includes *Ferdydurke, Pornografia,* and *Cosmos. Ferdydurke,* his first and most popular work, centers on an immature 30-year-old man and the forces which keep him in a regressive state
Translated by Eric Mosbacher & Alastair Hamilton
0–394–17067–9 Grove pb $8.95

DIARY: Volume 1
"It is an autobiography and at the same time an autobiographical novel, a discussion of literary and philosophical problems, and a commentary on cultural and social life, his own works, points of view, doubts and obsessions"—Samuel Fiszman
Translated by Lillian Vallee
Introduction by Wojciech Karpinski
0–8101–0715–5 Northwestern pb $12.95

DIARY: Volume 2
Charts the exile's life in Argentina
Translated by Lillian Vallee
0–8101–0717–1 Northwestern pb $12.95

A KIND OF TESTAMENT
Translated by Alisdair Hamilton
0–7145–0916–7 Scribners pb $8.95

POSSESSED: Or The Secret of Myslotch
Translated by J. A. Underwood
0–7145–2738–6 Scribners pb $10.95

- **Zbigniew Herbert**
Herbert is widely regarded as the greatest Polish poet who actually lives in Poland; his background in philosophy, law, and art history gives his work an intellectual tone which has led to comparisons with T. S. Eliot.

SELECTED POEMS
Translated by Czeslaw Milosz & Peter Scott
Introduction by A. Alvarez
0–88001–099–1 Norton pb $7.25

REPORT FROM THE BESIEGED CITY
Translated by John Carpenter & Bogdana Carpenter
0–88001–071–1 Ecco $12.00
0–88001–094–0 Ecco pb $8.25

Ryszard Kapuscinski
A practitioner of the "new journalism" whose writings are often interpreted allegorically.

ANOTHER DAY OF LIFE
The civil war in Angola
Translated by William Brand & Katarzyna Mrozkowska-Brand
0–15–107563–8 HBJ $14.95
0–14–010658–8 Penguin pb $6.95

THE EMPEROR: Downfall of an Autocrat
The last days of Haile Selassie, told through the voices of those who served him
Translated by William R. Brand & Katarzyna Mroczkowska-Brand
0–394–72376–7 Random House pb $7.95

SHAH OF SHAHS
The coming of the Iranian Revolution
Translated by William R. Brand & Katarzyna Mroczkowska-Brand
0–15–181483–X HBJ $12.95
0–394–74074–2 Random House pb $7.95

- **Tadeusz Konwicki**
A DREAMBOOK FOR OUR TIME
Introduction by Leszak Kolakowski
0–14–004115–X Penguin pb $6.95

MOONRISE, MOONSET
Translated by Richard Lourie
0–374–21241–4 Farrar, Straus & Giroux $19.50

THE POLISH COMPLEX
Introduction by Joanna R. Clark
0–374–23548–1 Farrar, Straus & Giroux $12.95
0–14–006590–3 Penguin pb $6.95

- **Stanislaw Lem**
The prolific Lem is an internationally renowned writer of science fiction with a strong philosophical dimension.

CHAIN OF CHANCE
"Written in 1975, as an Eastern European's speculation upon some possible short-term extensions of such Western topical developments as terrorism, space exploration, and chemical pollution"—John Updike
0–15–616500–7 HBJ pb $2.95

THE CYBERIAD: Fables for the Cybernetic Age
Translated by Michael Kandel
0–15–623550–1 HBJ pb $4.95

FIASCO
A saga of warfare in space
Translated by Michael Kandel
0–15–130640–0 HBJ $17.95
0–15–630630–1 HBJ pb $6.95

HOSPITAL OF THE TRANSFIGURATION
A novel set in a mental hospital in 1939 Poland
Translated by William Brand
0–19–142186–2 HBJ $17.95

THE INVESTIGATION
A metaphysical variation on the traditional whodunit
Translated by Adele Milch
0–15–645158–1 HBJ pb $4.95

MEMOIRS FOUND IN A BATHTUB
The destruction of all paper leads to the downfall of a worldwide bureaucracy
Translated by Michael Kandel & Christine Rose
0–15–658585–5 HBJ pb $4.95

SOLARIS
Haunting science-fiction novel about a living planet
0–15–683750–1 HBJ pb $4.95

- **Adam Michnik**
LETTERS FROM PRISON & OTHER ESSAYS
One of the most prominent Polish dissidents and a former advisor to Solidarity, Michnik is also a distinguished philosopher and essayist
0–520–05371–0 California $30.00

- **Czeslaw Milosz**
Probably the best known contemporary Polish writer, Milosz began his literary career before World War II; he left Poland in 1951 and subsequently settled in the United States. He won the Nobel Prize in 1980.

SELECTED POEMS
0–912946–76–8 Norton pb $8.95

THE BELLS IN WINTER
Translated by Lillian Vallee
0–912946–56–3 Norton $15.50

THE CAPTIVE MIND
An analysis of the influence of Stalinist dogma on creativity
0–374–95733–9 Hippocrene $18.50
0–394–74724–0 Random House pb $6.95

EMPEROR OF THE EARTH: Modes of Eccentric Vision
0–520–04503–3 California pb $9.95

THE ISSA VALLEY
A Wordsworthian novel about childhood
Translated by Louis Iribarne
0–374–17798–8 Farrar, Straus & Giroux $14.95
0–374–51695–2 Farrar, Straus & Giroux pb $9.95

THE LAND OF ULRO
Translated by Louis Iribarne
0–374–18323–6 Farrar, Straus & Giroux $17.50
0–374–51937–4 Farrar, Straus & Giroux pb $9.95

NATIVE REALM: A Search for Self-Definition
Translated by Catherine Leach
0–520–04474–6 California pb $9.95

THE SEPARATE NOTEBOOKS
Translated by Robert Hass & others
0–88001–116–5 Norton $12.25

THE SEIZURE OF POWER
A political novel which won the Prix Littéraire Européen
Translated by Celina Wieniewska
0–374–51697–9 Farrar, Straus & Giroux $6.95

UNATTAINABLE EARTH
0–88001–098–3 Norton $17.50

THE WITNESS OF POETRY
The Charles Eliot Norton lectures
0–674–95382–7 Harvard $9.95
0–674–95383–5 Harvard pb $4.95

VISIONS FROM SAN FRANCISCO BAY
A collection of essays comparing Europe and America
Translated by Richard Lourie
0–374–25788–4 Farrar, Straus & Giroux $14.95
0–374–51763–0 Farrar, Straus & Giroux pb $9.95

- **Slawomir Mrozek**
THE ELEPHANT
An early collection of short stories which established his reputation
0–394–62053–4 Grove pb $6.95

Bruno Schulz
Schulz made his name with only two books before he was murdered by a German army officer in 1942. "Bruno Schulz was one of the great *writers*, one of the great transmogrifiers of the world into words."—John Updike

SANATORIUM UNDER THE SIGN OF THE HOURGLASS
Introduction by John Updike
0–14–005272–0 Penguin pb $6.95

THE STREET OF CROCODILES
Introduction by Jerzy Ficowski
0–14–004227–X Penguin pb $5.95

- **Anna Swir**
HAPPY AS A DOG'S TAIL
Swir's poetry, with its affirmation of women's physicality and sexuality, is often compared to the work of American feminists
Translated by Czeslaw Milosz & Leonard Nathan
0–15–138465–7 HBJ $15.95

- **Wislawa Szymborska**
SOUNDS, FEELINGS, THOUGHTS: 70 Poems
Translated by Magnus J. Krynski & Robert A. Maguire
0–691–01380–2 Princeton pb $10.95

● Teresa Toranska
THEM: Stalin's Polish Puppets
A collection of interviews with five high
officials of Stalinist Poland which was the
great bestseller of Poland's underground
press
Translated by Agnieszka Kolakowska
0–06–015657–0 Harper & Row $22.50
0–06–091493–9 Harper & Row pb $9.95

● Aleksander Wat
**MY CENTURY: The Odyssey of a Polish
Intellectual**
Translated by Richard Lourie
Introduction by Czeslaw Milosz
0–520–04425–8 California $35.00
WITH THE SKIN
A selection of poems
Translated by Czeslaw Milosz & Leonard Nathan
0–88001–183–1 Ecco $17.95

● Stanislaw Ignacy Witkiewicz
**THE BEELZEBUB SONATA: Plays, Essays
and Documents**
Probably the most colorful figure of the
modern Polish artistic scene, Witkiewicz
was a painter, photographer, writer, and
philosopher
Edited by Daniel Gerould
Translated by Jadwiga Kosicka
0–933826–09–5 Farrar, Straus & Giroux pb $6.95
SELECTED WRITINGS
Includes excerpts from novels,
correspondence, essays, his chronicle of
drug experiments, as well as his play *The
New Deliverance*
Translated by Daniel Gerould
1–55554–015–5 Farrar, Straus & Giroux $29.95
1–55554–016–3 Farrar, Straus & Giroux pb $11.95

● Adam Zagajewski
TREMOR: Selected Poems
Translated by Renata Gorczynski
Introduction by Czeslaw Milosz
0–374–27873–3 Farrar, Straus & Giroux $12.95
0–374–52027–5 Farrar, Straus & Giroux pb $8.95

● Adam Czeriawski, editor & translator
THE BURNING FOREST
A personal selection of modern Polish
poetry
1–85224–009–1 Dufour $16.95

● Helena Goscilo, editor
**RUSSIAN AND POLISH WOMEN'S
FICTION**
Translated by Helena Goscilo
0–87049–472–4 Tennessee pb $17.95

● Milne Holton & Paul Vangelisti,
editors
**THE NEW POLISH POETRY: A Bilingual
Collection**
0–8229–5292–0 Pittsburgh pb $9.95

● Czeslaw Milosz, editor
**POSTWAR POLISH POETRY: An
Anthology**
0–520–04476–2 California pb $8.95

ROMANIAN LITERATURE

● Tudor Arghezi
**SELECTED POEMS OF TUDOR
ARGHEZI**
Born in the 19th century and first
published at 16, Arghezi wrote poems,
novels and essays until his death in 1967,
gradually creating a rich poetic voice and a
new Romanian literary language
Translated by Michael Impey & Brian Swann
0–691–01328–4 Princeton pb $8.50

● Mircea Eliade
Born in Bucharest, educated in Calcutta,
and a professor at the Sorbonne before
settling at the University of Chicago,
Eliade was considered the foremost
authority on religion in the world. He was
also an original writer of fiction and short
stories, blending philosophy, mythology,
fantasy, and personal narrative.
THE FORBIDDEN FOREST
Translated by Mac Ricketts & Mary Stevenson
0–268–00943–0 Notre Dame $25.00
**THE OLD MAN AND THE
BUREAUCRATS**
Translated by Mary Stevenson
0–268–01497–3 Notre Dame $10.95
0–226–20410–3 Chicago pb $7.95
**TALES OF THE SACRED AND THE
SUPERNATURAL**
0–664–24391–6 Westminster pb $7.95
TWO STRANGE TALES
Translated by William Coates
0–87773–386–4 Random House pb $6.95
**YOUTH WITHOUT YOUTH & OTHER
NOVELLAS**
Translated by Mac Linscott Ricketts
Edited by Matei Calinescu
0–8142–0457–0 Ohio State $18.95

● Liviu Rebreanu
ION
In his major, landmark novel Rebreanu
tells the story of a ruthless peasant
thwarted by his own ambition in pre-
World War I Transylvania
0–7206–4650–2 Dufour $16.95
UPRISING
The tale of a Romanian peasant revolt
0–7206–9382–9 Dufour $16.95

● Mihail Sadoveaunu
EVENING TALES
Stories about ordinary folk which
illuminate the Romanian national spirit
Translated by E. Farcia & L. Marinescu
0–8057–5172–6 Irvington $26.00
THE MUD-HUT DWELLERS
Perhaps the finest Romanian prose stylist,
Sadoveanu here evokes 19th century
peasant life with a deep feeling for the
bond between man and nature
0–8057–5195–5 Irvington $22.00
TALES OF WAR
An early historical novel about the 1877
War of Independence against the Ottoman
Empire
0–8057–5208–0 Irvington $27.00

YUGOSLAVIAN LITERATURE

● Ivo Andrić
THE BRIDGE ON THE DRINA
The most famous work from the only
Yugoslav writer to win the Nobel Prize,
this teeming chronicle spans centuries of
life in a fictionalized Bosnia
Translated by Lovett Edwards
0–226–02045–2 Chicago pb $8.95

● Dobrica Cosic
THIS LAND, THIS TIME
An ambitious series of novels linked by a
grand vision of Serbia, a small nation of
peasants which prevailed against three
empires in World War I
Translated by Muriel Heppell
0–15–690026–2 HBJ pb (4-volume set) $29.95
Volume 1: Into the Battle
0–15–644991–9 HBJ $8.95
Volume 2: Reach to Eternity
0–15–676012–6 HBJ pb $7.95
Volume 3: South to Destiny
0–15–683913–X HBJ pb $7.95
Volume 4: Time of Death
0–15–690445–4 HBJ $7.95

● Milovan Djilas
LAND WITHOUT JUSTICE
0–15–648117–0 HBJ pb $8.95
MONTENEGRO
Translated by Kenneth Johnstone
0–15–162102–0 HBJ pb $9.95
RISE AND FALL
Translated by John Loud
0–15–177572–9 HBJ $24.95
0–15–676708–2 HBJ pb $8.95
WARTIME
0–15–694712–9 HBJ pb $7.95

● Danilo Kis
SANDGLASS
Translated by Ammiel & Klara Alcalay
0–374–25386–2 Farrar, Straus & Giroux $18.50

Milorad Pavic
**DICTIONARY OF THE KHAZARS: A
Lexicon Novel in 100,000 Words**
This first novel by the distinguished
Yugoslav poet comes in two versions,
male and female, which differ by 15
crucial lines. "Pavic is a 20th century
Scheherazade spinning a series of
interconnected folk tales, drawing on a
vast source of literary references,
eventually metamorphosing his
narrative into a murder mystery"—
Publishers Weekly
Translated by Christina Pribicevic-Zoric

Female Version
0–394–57236–X Knopf $19.95

Male Version
0–394–57183–5 Knopf $19.95

● Vasko Popa
COLLECTED POEMS: 1943–1976
Translated by Anne Pennington
Introduction by Ted Hughes
0–89255–034–1 Braziller pb $7.95

TO ORDER BOOKS AS GIFTS, SEE PAGE 1

HOMAGE TO THE LAME WOLF: Selected Poems
From the Serbian poet who led the modernist rebellion in the 1950s
Translated by Charles Simic
0-932440-22-3 Oberlin pb $9.00

- **Vasko Popa, editor**
THE GOLDEN APPLE
Translated by Anne Pennington & Andrew Harvey
0-85646-057-5 Longwood $10.95

- **Aleksandar Tisma**
THE USE OF MAN
Friends and relatives in a small Yugoslav town go in drastically different directions during World War II
Translated by Bernard Johnson
0-15-193203-4 HBJ $19.95

CRITICAL STUDIES

- **Antun Barac**
A HISTORY OF YUGOSLAV LITERATURE
0-930042-49-2 Michigan $15.00

- **Dmitrij Cizevskij**
COMPARATIVE HISTORY OF SLAVIC LITERATURES
Translated by Richard Porter & Martin Rice
0-8265-1159-7 Vanderbilt $12.95

- **Lóránt Czigány**
THE OXFORD HISTORY OF HUNGARIAN LITERATURE: From Earliest Times to the Present
0-19-815781-9 Oxford $79.00

- **Adam Gillon & Ludwik Krzyzanowski, editors**
INTRODUCTION TO MODERN POLISH LITERATURE
0-88254-516-7 Hippocrene pb $12.95

- **Tibor Klaniczay & H. H. Remak, editors**
A HISTORY OF HUNGARIAN LITERATURE
0-8044-3132-9 Harper & Row $60.00

- **Czeslaw Milosz**
THE HISTORY OF POLISH LITERATURE
0-520-04477-0 California pb $11.95

Individual Writers

- **Norman J. Girardot & Mac L. Ricketts, editors**
IMAGINATION AND MEANING: The Scholarly and Literary Worlds of Mircea Eliade
0-8164-2371-7 Harper & Row pb $11.95

- **Stanislaw Baranczak**
A FUGITIVE FROM UTOPIA: The Poetry of Zbigniew Herbert
The author is himself an outstanding younger Polish poet
0-674-32685-7 Harvard $22.50

- **Ewa Czarnecka & Aleksander Fiut**
CONVERSATIONS WITH CZESLAW MILOSZ
Translated by Richard Lourie
0-15-122591-5 HBJ $27.95

- **Donald Davie**
CZESLAW MILOSZ AND THE INSUFFICIENCY OF LYRIC
0-87049-483-X Tennessee pb $8.50

Russian Literature

BEFORE THE 20TH CENTURY

Although Russian literature dates from the Christianization of the Kievan Rus in 988, the earliest texts (mostly chronicles, hagiographies, and other quasi-historical writings) are of interest primarily to specialists. By the end of the 18th century, however, an independent tradition of secular literature had evolved, following the importation and assimilation of a variety of Western genres. It was the life and work of the great poet Alexander Pushkin, born in 1799, that marked Russia's entrance into the community of world literature. Following his death in 1837 a spectacular blossoming of fiction occurred, with Lermontov, Gogol, Dostoevsky, Turgenev, Tolstoy, and Chekhov producing the body of work that made Russian literature internationally respected and influential.

- **Sergei Aksakov**
The following works form an extensive historical trilogy, based loosely on Aksakov's own childhood on the Russian Steppe. When they appeared in the late 1850s, Aksakov was recognized as the most influential Russian writer of his day, not overshadowed until the rise of Tolstoy and Dostoevsky. Although little known in the West, these masterful portraits of country life remain central to the Russian realist tradition.

YEARS OF CHILDHOOD
Translated by J. D. Duff
0-19-281574-1 Oxford pb $7.95

A RUSSIAN SCHOOLBOY
Translated by J. D. Duff
0-19-281575-X Oxford pb $8.95

A RUSSIAN GENTLEMAN
Edited by Edward Crankshaw
0-19-281573-3 Oxford pb $8.95

- **Anton Chekhov**
"One must have Chekhov . . . He is not only a great writer, but even rarer, a liberating one."—Susan Sontag

▶ **For Chekhov's plays see Modern European Drama**

THE DUEL & OTHER STORIES
Also includes *My Wife, Murder, The Black Monk, Terror, The Two Volodyas*
Translated by Ronald Wilks
0-14-044415-7 Penguin pb $4.95

THE FIANCEE & OTHER STORIES
Chekhov's shorter short stories, including *On Official Business, Rothschild's Fiddle, Peasant Women, Three Years, The Bet,* and others
Translated by Ronald Wilks
0-14-044470-X Penguin pb $4.95

THE KISS & OTHER STORIES
In the same volume are *Peasant, The Bishop, The Russian Master, Man in a Case, Gooseberries, Concerning Love, A Case History, In the Gully,* and *Anna Around the Neck*
0-14-044336-3 Penguin pb $3.95

LADY WITH LAPDOG & OTHER STORIES
Chekhov's most celebrated short story, as well as *The Grasshopper, Ward 6, Ariadne, The House with an Attic, Ionych,* and *The Darling*
Translated by David Magarshack
0-14-044143-3 Penguin pb $3.95

THE PARTY & OTHER STORIES
Includes *A Woman's Kingdom, My Life: A Provincial Story, An Unpleasant Business* and *A Nervous Breakdown*
Translated by Ronald Wilks
0-14-044452-1 Penguin pb $3.95

THE SELECTED LETTERS OF ANTON CHEKHOV
Chekhov's funny, intense, compassionate letters show him to be a supreme realist in life as well as in literature
Translated by Sidonie K. Lederer
Edited by Lillian Hellman
0-374-51838-6 Farrar, Straus & Giroux pb $7.95

ANTON CHEKHOV'S LIFE AND THOUGHT: Selected Letters and Commentary
Translated by Simon Karlinsky & Michael Heim
0-520-02684-5 California pb $8.95

THE TALES OF CHEKHOV
A uniform set of Chekhov's short fiction, in 13 volumes, along with the two companion volumes *The Notebook of Anton Chekhov* and *The Unknown Chekhov.* "Our gratitude to The Ecco Press for its publication of *The Tales of Chekhov* series can never be too great"—Eudora Welty
Translated by Constance Garnett

Volume 1: The Darling & Other Stories
0-88001-038-X Ecco pb $9.50

Volume 2: The Duel & Other Stories
0-88001-039-8 Ecco pb $9.50

Volume 3: The Lady With the Dog & Other Stories
0-88001-050-9 Ecco pb $9.50

Volume 4: The Party & Other Stories
0-88001-051-7 Ecco pb $9.50

Volume 5: The Wife & Other Stories
0-88001-052-5 Ecco pb $8.50

Volume 6: The Witch & Other Stories
0-88001-053-3 Ecco pb $8.50

Volume 7: The Bishop & Other Stories
0-88001-054-1 Ecco pb $8.50

Volume 8: The Chorus Girl & Other Stories
0-88001-055-X Ecco pb $8.50

LITERATURE OF EUROPE, AFRICA, AND ASIA

Volume 9: The Schoolmistress & Other Stories
0–88001–056–8 Ecco pb $8.50

Volume 10: The Horse-Stealers & Other Stories
0–88001–057–6 Ecco pb $8.50

Volume 11: The Schoolmaster & Other Stories
0–88001–058–4 Ecco pb $9.50

Volume 12: The Cook's Wedding & Other Stories
0–88001–059–2 Ecco pb $9.50

Volume 13: Love & Other Stories
0–88001–060–6 Ecco pb $9.50

She fed her dog on the best caviare.

Our self-esteem and conceit are European, but our culture and actions are Asiatic.

A black dog—he looks as if he were wearing goloshes.

A Russian's only hope—to win two hundred thousand rubles in a lottery.

She is wicked, but taught her children good.

Every one has something to hide.

Anton Chekhov
THE NOTEBOOK OF ANTON CHEKHOV
0–88001–145–9 Ecco pb $8.50

THE NOTEBOOK OF ANTON CHEKHOV
A look at Chekhov's thoughts and sketches for his work
0–88001–145–9 Ecco pb $8.50

THE UNKNOWN CHEKHOV
Translated by Avrahm Yarmolinsky
0–88001–142–4 Ecco pb $9.50

• **Nikolai Chernyshevsky**
WHAT IS TO BE DONE?
This novel of love and sacrifice by one of the Old Regime's most famous radical critics is a primary text of Russian feminism and socialism
Translated & edited by K. Feuer
0–87501–017–2 Ardis pb $6.95

• **Fyodor Dostoevsky**
THE ADOLESCENT
A powerful study of the psychology of avarice, also translated as *A Raw Youth*
Translated by Andrew MacAndrew
0–393–00995–5 Norton pb $12.95

THE BROTHERS KARAMAZOV
Dostoevsky's crowning achievement, planned as the first volume of a never written trilogy. "I'd die happy if I could finish this final novel, for I would have expressed myself completely"—Dostoevsky
Translated by David Magarshack
0–14–044416–5 Penguin pb $5.95

THE BROTHERS KARAMAZOV
The most influential translation
Translated by Constance Garnett
0–394–60415–6 Modern Library $12.95

CRIME AND PUNISHMENT
"*Crime and Punishment* has upon most readers an impact as immediate and obvious and full as the news of murder next door; one *almost* participates in the crime, and the trivial details become obsessively important"—R. P. Blackmur
Translated by Constance Garnett
0–394–60450–4 Modern Library $8.95

CRIME AND PUNISHMENT
In a new translation
Translated by Jessie Coulson
0–19–281549–0 Oxford pb $3.95

THE DEVILS
In this novel of nihilism, conspiracy, madness, and suicide (also known as *The Possessed*), Dostoevsky fully anticipated the political paranoia of the 20th century
Translated by David Magarshack
0–14–044035–6 Penguin pb $6.95

THE DOUBLE
Golyadkin and his "double," one of Dostoevsky's first studies in split personality
Translated by Evelyn Harden
0–88233–757–2 Ardis pb $6.50

THE GAMBLER
Dostoevsky's own mania for gambling was the basis for this vivid psychological portrait
Translated by Andrew MacAndrew
0–393–00044–3 Norton pb $5.95

THE GAMBLER, BOBOK & A NASTY STORY
Three of Dostoevsky's best-known short works
Translated by Jessie Coulson
0–14–044179–4 Penguin pb $3.95

GREAT SHORT WORKS OF FYODOR DOSTOEVSKY
Includes *The Double, White Nights, Notes From Underground, The Dream of a Ridiculous Man,* and others
Translated by George Bird
Edited by Ronald Hingley
0–06–083081–6 Harper & Row pb $5.95

THE HOUSE OF THE DEAD
The fictional transposition of Dostoevsky's experiences as a prisoner in Siberia
Translated by David McDuff
0–14–044456–4 Penguin pb $3.95

THE IDIOT
Translated by Henry & Olga Carlyle
0–451–52094–7 NAL pb $3.95

Dostoyevsky by Vallotton

THE IDIOT
Translated by David Magarshack
0–14–044054–2 Penguin pb $5.95

NETOCHKA NEZVANOVA
Unfinished owing to the author's arrest in 1849, *Netochka Nezvanova* exhibits Dostoevsky's early penchant for irrationality and caprice, this time in the memoir of a girl brought up among aristocrats and struggling musicians
Translated by Jane Kentish
0–14–044455–6 Penguin pb $3.95

NOTES FROM UNDERGROUND & THE DOUBLE
"Still, I firmly believe that not only too much consciousness, but any sort of consciousness is a disease. I insist upon that"—The Underground Man
Translated by Jessie Coulson
0–14–044252–9 Penguin pb $2.95

POOR FOLK
Dostoevsky's debut, *Poor Folk* caused a sensation when it came out in 1846, eliciting high praise from Russia's radical critics for its depiction of the downtrodden and destitute
Translated by Robert Dessaix
0–686–78410–3 Ardis pb $4.50

THE POSSESSED
The standard translation for many years
Translated by Constance Garnett
Edited by Avram Yarmolinsky
0–394–60441–5 Modern Library $7.95

THE VILLAGE OF STEPANCHIKOVO AND ITS INHABITANTS
Translated by Ignat Avsey
0–8014–2051–2 Cornell $24.95
0–8014–9457–5 Cornell pb $6.95

COMPLETE LETTERS

Volume 1
Edited by David Lowe and Ronald Meyer
0–88233–897–8 Ardis $35.00

• **Nikolai Gogol**
THE COMPLETE TALES OF NIKOLAI GOGOL
Edited by Leonard Kent

Volume 1
Contains *Evenings on a Farm Near Dikanka* (1 & 2) and *Arabesques*
0–226–30068–4 Chicago pb $10.95

Volume 2
Contains *Mirgorod and Other Tales, The Nose, The Coach, The Portrait,* and *The Overcoat*
0–226–30069–2 Chicago pb $10.95

DEAD SOULS
Arguably the most enigmatic of the Russian classics, *Dead Souls* relates the errant quest of its hero for dead serfs, which he buys up as collateral for a mortgage on the estate he hopes someday to own
Translated by Andrew MacAndrew
0–451–52308–3 NAL pb $3.95

THE DIARY OF A MADMAN & OTHER STORIES
Gogol's best short works in an excellent translation. Includes *The Nose, The Overcoat, Taras Bulba,* and others
Translated by Andrew MacAndrew
0–451–52014–9 NAL pb $2.95

DIARY OF A MADMAN
The fictional memoir of a self-styled king of Spain—a psychologist's case study in literary form
Translated by Ronald Wilks
0–14–044273–1 Penguin pb $2.95

THE GOVERNMENT INSPECTOR
A comedy of sycophancy and delusion, this play was a success when it came out in 1836—but for all the wrong reasons in its author's estimation
Translated by Adrian Mitchell
0–413–58470–4 RC&H pb $6.95

INSPECTOR & OTHER PLAYS
Also includes Gogol's brilliant comedies *Marriage* and *Gamblers* and a dramatization of *Diary of a Madman*
Translated with an introduction by Eric Bentley
0–936839–12–0 Applause pb $8.95

THE OVERCOAT & OTHER TALES OF GOOD AND EVIL
"When, as in his immortal *The Overcoat*, he really let himself go . . . Gogol became the greatest artist that Russia has yet produced"—Vladimir Nabokov
Translated by David Magarshack
0–393–00304–3 Norton pb $4.95

• Ivan Goncharov
THE FRIGATE PALLADA
This travel book, based on Goncharov's experience as secretary to an admiral, presents a humorous view of the Orient through the eyes of a less than willing traveler
Translated by Klaus Goetze
0–312–00599–7 St. Martin's $35.00

OBLOMOV
Goncharov's masterpiece is an extended portrait of an obsessively indolent landowner
Translated by David Magarshack
0–14–044040–2 Penguin pb $4.95

• Alexander Herzen
CHILDHOOD, YOUTH AND EXILE: My Past Thoughts
This brilliant synthesis of personal memoir and social criticism is an essential text
Translated by J. D. Duff
Introduction by Isaiah Berlin
0–19–281505–9 Oxford pb $6.95

ENDS AND BEGINNINGS
Translated by Constance Garnett
Edited by Aileen Kelly
0–19–281604–7 Oxford pb $7.95

WHO IS TO BLAME?
Herzen's novel of social convention and its stultifying effects on three characters caught in a love triangle
Translated by Michael Katz
0–8014–9286–6 Cornell pb $9.95

• Mikhail Lermontov
A HERO OF OUR TIME
Lermontov's greatest prose work is a masterful examination of the superfluous man of the 1830s: Byronic, alienated, egotistical and self-absorbed
Translated by Paul Foote
0–14–044176–X Penguin pb $4.95

Nikolai Leskov
THE ENCHANTED WANDERER: Selected Tales
The title story traces the wild adventures of a runaway serf and his ultimate sanctuary in a monastery. Also includes *Lady Macbeth, The Left-Handed Craftsman, The Sentry,* and *The White Eagle*
Translated by David Magarshack
0–374–52057–7 FS&G pb $9.95

FIVE TALES
Includes *Chasing Out the Devil, A Spiteful Fellow, A Shameless Rascal, The Robber,* and *An Iron Will*
Translated by Michael Shotton
0–946162–12–3 Dufour $19.95
0–946162–13–1 Dufour pb $10.95

LADY MACBETH OF THE MTSENSK DISTRICT & OTHER STORIES
The title story was the basis for the libretto of Shostakovich's opera
Translated by David McDuff
0–14–044491–2 Penguin pb $7.95

• Alexander Ostrovsky
THE STORM
Ostrovsky's most noted play, on which Janáček's opera *Katya Kubanova* was based
0–88233–551–0 Ardis pb $5.00

WITHOUT A DOWRY & OTHER PLAYS
Also includes *A Profitable Position, Ardent Heart,* and *Talents and Admirers.* Considered classics in Russia, these plays remain almost unknown in the West
Translated & edited by Norman Henley
0–88233–933–8 Ardis $32.50

• A. F. Pisemsky
NINA, THE COMIC ACTOR & AN OLD FRIEND
Overshadowed during his lifetime by the works of Dostoevsky and Tolstoy, Pisemsky's stories provide a vivid, often satirical view of provincial life and social inequality
Translated by Maya Jenkins
0–88233–986–9 Ardis $17.50

• Alexander Pushkin
THE CAPTAIN'S DAUGHTER & OTHER STORIES
Contains also *The Tales of Belkin, The Queen of Spades, Kirdjali,* and *The Negro of Peter the Great*
0–394–70714–1 Random House pb $4.95

COLLECTED POETRY
An excellent translation of Pushkin's finest poems
Translated by Walter Arndt
0–88233–826–9 Ardis pb $9.50

THE COMPLETE PROSE TALES OF PUSHKIN
Includes *The Tales of Belkin, Queen of Spades, The Captain's Daughter,* and others
0–393–00465–1 Norton pb $10.95

EPIGRAMS AND SATIRICAL VERSE
Translated by Cynthia A. Whittaker
0–88233–886–2 Ardis $15.00

EUGENE ONEGIN
Pushkin's masterpiece, a novel in verse about rejected love
Translated by Walter Arndt
0–525–47591–5 Dutton pb $8.95

EUGENE ONEGIN: A Novel in Verse
With annotations and commentary by Vladimir Nabokov; for the serious student of Pushkin
Translated by Vladimir Nabokov
0–691–09744–5 Princeton (4-vol set) $125.00
0–691–01837–5 Princeton pb (2-vol set) $26.95

EUGENE ONEGIN
This deftly rendered version, employing Pushkin's original rhyme scheme and meter, is preferred by many readers
Translated by Charles Johnston
0–14–044394–0 Penguin pb $4.95

THE HISTORY OF PUGACHEV
A meticulous explication of the social forces leading to the Pugachev Rebellion of 1773–74
Translated by Earl Sampson
0–88233–625–8 Ardis $17.95

MOZART AND SALIERI: The Little Tragedies
Four studies of human weakness: *The Covetous Knight, Mozart and Salieri, The Stone Guest, A Feast During the Plague*
Translated by Antony Wood
0–8023–1282–9 Dufour pb $8.95

THE QUEEN OF SPADES & OTHER STORIES
Also includes *The Negro of Peter the Great, Dubrowsky* and *The Captain's Daughter*
Translated by Rosemary Edmonds
0–14–044119–0 Penguin pb $4.95

THE LETTERS OF ALEXANDER PUSHKIN
Translated by J. Thomas Shaw
0–299–04644–3 Wisconsin pb $18.50

SECRET JOURNAL: 1836–1837
A chronicle of Pushkin's troubled last years
0–916201–03–1 MIP pb $18.00

• M. E. Saltykov-Shchedrin
THE GOLOVLEVS
The best-known novel of this fierce satirist traces the disintegration of a family through hypocrisy, greed, and alcoholism
Translated & edited by K. P. Foote
0–19–281616–0 Oxford pb $4.95

THE HISTORY OF A TOWN: Or, The Chronicle of Foolov
A grotesque parody of Russian government in a provincial town
Translated by Susan Brownsberger
0–88233–610–X Ardis $25.00

THE POMPADOURS
A satire of the provincial bureaucrats who governed the countryside like little czars
Translated with an introduction by David Magarshack
0–88233–743–2 Ardis $24.00

• Leo Tolstoy
ANNA KARENINA
"We are not to take *Anna Karenina* as a work of art; we are to take it as a piece of life. A piece of life as it is"—Matthew Arnold
Translated by Louise & Aylmer Maude
0–19–281510–5 Oxford pb $4.95

ANNA KARENINA
The standard translation for many years
Translated by Constance Garnett
0–394–60448–2 Modern Library $12.95

ANNA KARENINA
Translated by Rosemary Edmonds
0–14–044041–0 Penguin pb $4.95

CHILDHOOD, BOYHOOD, YOUTH
This trilogy (an intended fourth volume was never written) set the standard for the psychological memoir in 19th-century Russian fiction
Translated by Rosemary Edmonds
0–14–044139–5 Penguin pb $4.95

A CONFESSION & OTHER RELIGIOUS WRITINGS
Key texts in the author's spiritual development, essential for understanding Tolstoy's moral and ethical concerns
Introduction by Jane Kentish
0–14–044473–4 Penguin pb $6.95

THE COSSACKS & THE RAID
These two works from Tolstoy's early period explore the themes of individuality and social identity that he later expanded in his greatest works
0–14–044109–3 Penguin pb $2.95

THE FORGED COUPON
Published posthumously, *The Forged Coupon* explores the ethical consequences of minor misdeeds
Translated by David Patterson
0–393–01912–8 Norton $12.95
0–393–30300–4 Norton pb $4.95

GREAT SHORT WORKS OF LEO TOLSTOY
Includes *The Cossacks, Family Happiness, The Death of Ivan Ilych, The Devil, The Kreutzer Sonata,* and others
Introduction by John Bayley
0–06–083071–9 Harper & Row pb $5.95

THE KREUTZER SONATA & OTHER STORIES
Includes *The Devil, The Forged Coupon,* and *After the Ball*
Translated by David McDuff
0–14–044469–6 Penguin pb $4.95

MASTER AND MAN & OTHER STORIES
Also includes *Father Sergius* and *Hadji Murat*
Translated by Paul Foote
0–14–044331–2 Penguin pb $3.95

THE RAID & OTHER STORIES
Tolstoy collaborated with Aylmer and Louise Maude on this translation
Edited by Aylmer & Louise Maude
Introduction by P. N. Furbank
0–19–281584–9 Oxford pb $3.95

RESURRECTION
Tolstoy's last long novel was written to raise money for the Dukhobors, a Christian sect he admired. Considered inferior to his other works, it remains an interesting source for Tolstoy's views of society
Translated by Rosemary Edmonds
0–14–044184–0 Penguin pb $4.95

THE SEBASTOPOL SKETCHES
Translated by David McDuff
0–14–044468–8 Penguin pb $4.95

TOLSTOY'S DIARIES
An obsessive diarist, Tolstoy developed many themes and characters of his novels in his personal journals, here presented in two volumes
Translated & edited by R. F. Christian
0–684–18512–1 Scribners $60.00

WAR AND PEACE
Considered by many the greatest novel ever written
Translated by Ann Dunnigan
0–451–52116–1 NAL pb $5.95

WAR AND PEACE
Translated by Rosemary Edmonds
0–14–044417–3 Penguin pb $8.95

WAR AND PEACE
An excellent translation by a friend of Tolstoy's, with notes and useful critical essays
Translated by Aylmer Maude
0–393–09672–6 Norton $16.95

WAR AND PEACE
Long the standard translation
Translated by Constance Garnett
0–394–60475–X Modern Library $13.95

• **Ivan Turgenev**
DIARY OF A SUPERFLUOUS MAN
Early exposure of the superfluous type in Russian society, later embodied in Goncharov's idle hero, Oblomov
Translated by David Patterson
0–393–30306–3 Norton pb $4.95

FATHERS AND SONS
Turgenev's classic exposition of the generation gap of the 1860s, with his brilliant portrait of the would-be nihilist Evgeny Bazarov. A key work in Russian intellectual history
Translated by Rosemary Edmonds
0–14–044147–6 Penguin pb $2.95

FIRST LOVE
A subtle and lyrical story of love and its betrayal from a boy's perspective
Translated by Isaiah Berlin
Introduction by V. S. Pritchett
0–14–044335–5 Penguin pb $4.95

HOME OF THE GENTRY
A middle-aged landowner returns to Russia after a long residence in Western Europe to find and then lose the love of a young girl
Translated by Richard Freeborn
0–14–044224–3 Penguin pb $4.95

A MONTH IN THE COUNTRY
Turgenev's one memorable play. An outsider upsets the status quo of a country family—a persistent motif in Turgenev's novels
Translated by Isaiah Berlin
0–14–044436–X Penguin pb $4.95

ON THE EVE
Translated by Gilbert Gardiner
0–14–044009–7 Penguin pb $4.95

RUDIN
Turgenev's first full-length novel, depicting an ineffectual hero whose death on the barricades of Paris is emblematic of the failures of Russia's radical intelligentsia
Translated by Richard Freeborn
0–14–044304–5 Penguin pb $5.95

SKETCHES FROM A HUNTER'S ALBUM
Early stories that may have hastened the emancipation of the serfs in 1861
Translated by Richard Freeborn
0–14–044186–7 Penguin pb $4.95

SPRING TORRENTS
Written during the Franco-Prussian War, this short novel—unlike most of Turgenev's other work—does not specifically concern Russia and her political problems but focuses instead on the international crisis of midcentury Europe
Translated by Leonard Shapiro
0–14–044369–X Penguin pb $5.95

THE EARLY 20TH CENTURY

Poetry

• **Anna Akhmatova**
POEMS
Akhmatova was the great proponent of acmeism, a movement focused on precision and emotional clarity
Translated by Lyn Coffin
0–393–01567–X Norton $15.50
0–393–30014–5 Norton pb $7.95

SELECTED POEMS
A sound translation
Translated by Robin Kendall & Carl Proffer
Edited by Walter Arndt
0–88233–180–9 Ardis pb $5.95

SELECTED POEMS
Translated by D.M. Thomas
0–14–058558–3 Penguin pb $7.95

• **Alexander Blok**
THE TWELVE & OTHER POEMS
Blok's masterpiece of the revolution, *The Twelve* is a complex and vivid interweaving of religious, political, and moral problems
Translated by Anselm Hollo
0–917788–04–4 Gnomon pb $4.00

How can we free ourselves from being dominated by people from the past who still retain a shadow of power in the world of space, without soiling ourselves by coming into contact with their lives (we can use the soap of word-creation), and leave them to drown in the destiny they have earned for themselves, that of malicious termites? We are fated to fight with *rhythm and time* for our right to be free from the filthy habits of people from past centuries, and to win that right.
Velimir Khlebnikov
THE KING OF TIME: Poems, Fictions, Visions of the Future
Translated by Paul Schmidt
Edited by Charlotte Douglas
0–674–50515–8 Harvard $20.00

• **Velimir Khlebnikov**
THE KING OF TIME: Poems, Fictions, Visions of the Future
An excellent collection of works by one of Russia's Futurist poets
Translated by Paul Schmidt
Edited by Charlotte Douglas
0–674–50515–8 Harvard $20.00

➤ FOR OVERSEAS ORDERING INFORMATION, SEE PAGE 1

1923 edition of V.V. Mayakovsky's poetry by El Lissitsky, from Treasures from the New York Public Library *(New York Public Library)*

● Osip Mandelstam

"In Mandelstam Russian poetry at last has a poet of a stature comparable to Pushkin's—a claim that even the most fanatical admirers of Blok, Mayakovsky or Pasternak would not dream of making."—Simon Karlinsky

POEMS OF OSIP MANDELSTAM
Selections from *Stone, Tristia,* and other collections of the 1920s and 1930s
Translated by Clarence Brown & W. S. Merwin
0–689–11425–7 Atheneum pb $9.95

STONE
A collection from 1913
Translated by Robert Tracy
0–691–06444–X Princeton $26.50

TRISTIA
Poems published in 1922, also known *The Second Book*
Translated by Bruce McClelland
0–88268–041–2 Station Hill $13.95

● Vladimir Mayakovsky

THE BEDBUG & SELECTED POETRY
A bilingual edition, with an informative introduction
Translated by Max Hayward & George Reavey
Edited by Patricia Blake
0–253–20189–6 Indiana pb $7.95

● Boris Pasternak

MY SISTER-LIFE
A cycle of poems that won Pasternak wide acclaim, this celebration of life was written in the aftermath of war and revolution
Translated with an introduction by Mark Rudman
0–88233–785–8 Ardis pb $7.50

SELECTED POEMS
Translated by Jon Stallworthy & Peter France
0–393–01819–9 Norton $15.00
0–14–042245–5 Penguin pb $7.95

● Marina Tsvetayeva

SELECTED POEMS
"There has been no more passionate voice in 20th century Russian poetry"—Joseph Brodsky
Translated with an introduction by Elaine Feinstein
0–525–48283–0 Dutton pb $12.95

Fiction and Other Prose

● Leonid Andreyev

SELECTED STORIES
Madness, necrophilia, brutality, and death, registered with feverish realism
Edited by M. H. Shotton
0–900186–10–0 Basil Blackwell pb $9.95

VISIONS: Stories and Photographs
A vivid self-portrait of a writer little read in the West
Edited by Olga Andreyev Carlisle
0–15–193900–4 HBJ $21.95

● Issac Babel

BENYA KRIK, THE GANGSTER & OTHER STORIES
Stories featuring Babel's most memorable character, Benya Krik, the Jewish gangster of Odessa
Edited by Avraham Yarmolinsky
0–8052–0244–7 Schocken pb $4.95

COLLECTED STORIES
Some of Babel's best stories, including the *Red Cavalry* series and *Tales of Odessa.* Terse and violent, they present an ironic and stylized view of the Russian Civil War
Translated & edited by Walter Morison
Introduction by Lionel Trilling
0–452–00798–4 NAL pb $8.95

YOU MUST KNOW EVERYTHING
Includes previously untranslated stories and journalistic pieces
Translated by Max Hayward
Edited with an introduction by Nathalie Babel
0–374–51580–8 Farrar, Straus & Giroux pb $6.95

Andrei Bely

THE DRAMATIC SYMPHONY & THE FORMS OF ART
Written between 1899 and 1908, these movements in a prose "symphony" anticipate Bely's later development of rhythmical, poetic prose in his masterwork, *Petersburg*
Translated by Roger Keys, Angela Keys & John Elsworth
0–394–55550–3 Grove $16.95

PETERSBURG
The first definitive edition of what Nabokov considered one of the four greatest novels of the 20th century
Translated by Robert A. Maguire & John E. Malmstad
0–253–20219–1 Indiana pb $10.95

THE SILVER DOVE
"The novel is written in splendid, sustainedly beautiful prose"—D. S. Mirsky
Translated with an introduction by George Reavey
Preface by Harrison Salisbury
0–394–17859–9 Grove pb $4.95

● Mikhail Bulgakov

HEART OF A DOG
An unusual transplant has surprising results
Translated by Mirra Ginsburg
0–802–15059–4 Grove pb $6.95

THE MASTER AND MARGARITA
Translated by Mirra Ginsburg
0–8021–3011–9 Grove Press pb $6.95
0–452–00757–7 NAL pb $4.95

THE WHITE GUARD
Bulgakov's favorite work deals with the successive occupations of Kiev during the Russian Civil War
0–89733–246–6 Academy Chicago pb $8.95

● Ivan Bunin

IN A FAR DISTANT LAND
Bunin's stories are best known for their evocative visual imagery and shifting moods
Translated by Robert Bowie
0–938920–27–8 Hermitage pb $8.50

LONG AGO: Selected Stories
Tales by Russia's first Nobel laureate in literature
Translated by David Richards & Sophie Lund
0–946162–11–5 Dufour pb $10.95

● F. V. Gladkov

CEMENT
The acknowledged prototype for all subsequent "production" novels—a Soviet classic
Translated by A. S. Arthur & C. Ashleigh
0–8044–6178–3 Ungar pb $9.95

● Maxim Gorky

DECADENCE
Also known under the title *The Artamonov Business,* this story traces the dissolution of a middle-class family
Translated by Veronica Dewey
0–8032–7012–7 Nebraska pb $8.95

MOTHER
Gorky's revolutionary novel of 1906 remains one of the most frequently cited works in the Soviet canon
Translated by Isadore Schneider
0–8065–0890–6 Lyle Stuart pb $8.95

This account of Gorky's tumultuous and often difficult life contains some of his most vivid writing.

MY CHILDHOOD
Translated by Ronald Wilks
0–14–044178–6 Penguin pb $4.95

MY APPRENTICESHIP
Translated by Ronald Wilks
0–14–044291–X Penguin pb $6.95

MY UNIVERSITIES
Translated by Ronald Wilks
0–14–044302–9 Penguin pb $5.95

● V. I. Ivanov & M. O. Gershenzon

CORRESPONDENCE ACROSS A ROOM
Translated by Lisa Sergio
0–910395–11–X Marlboro pb $7.25

● Velemir Khlebnikov

LETTERS AND THEORETICAL WRITINGS
Russian Futurism explained
Translated by Paul Schmidt
Edited by Charlotte Douglas
0–674–14045–1 Harvard $35.00

● Mikhail Kuzmin

SELECTED PROSE AND POETRY
Kuzmin was a devoted aesthete whose treatment of erotic and homosexual themes is relatively unusual in the Russian tradition
Edited by Michael Green
0–88233–417–4 Ardis $22.50

Nadezhda Mandelstam
HOPE AGAINST HOPE
The unsparing memoirs of Osip Mandelstam's wife, ranging from her husband's arrest and exile to Soviet Union literary life
Translated by Max Heyward
0–689–70530–1 Atheneum pb $10.95

Osip Mandelstam
SELECTED ESSAYS
Includes his famous work *The Noise of Time* and other essays
Translated by Sidney Monas
0–292–76006–X Texas $17.50

● Vladimir Nabokov
Nabokov wrote his first nine novels in Russian, the last being *The Gift*, written in the late 1930s; thereafter he turned exclusively to English as his medium of expression.

▶ For Nabokov's other novels, see Modern American Fiction

THE ENCHANTER
0–399–13211–2 Putnam $16.95

GLORY
Written in 1932 but not published in English until 40 years later, *Glory* is perhaps Nabokov's most romantic novel
0–07–045727–1 McGraw-Hill pb $4.95

INVITATION TO A BEHEADING
0–399–50115–0 Putnam pb $8.95

KING, QUEEN, KNAVE
A young German, seduced by his aunt, fails in his plot to kill the uncle for his money
0–07–045722–0 McGraw-Hill pb $7.95

LAUGHTER IN THE DARK
0–8112–0708–0 New Directions pb $8.95

A RUSSIAN BEAUTY & OTHER STORIES
Translated by Dmitri Nabokov & Simon Karlinsky
0–07–045711–5 McGraw-Hill pb $7.95

Osip Mandelstam (photo courtesy of Knopf)

● Yury Olesha
ENVY
An overnight sensation in 1927, *Envy* deals with the opposition of the old and the new in a Soviet setting and anticipates Koestler's treatment of mechanized social organization in *Darkness at Noon*
Translated by Thomas Berczynski
0–88233–091–8 Ardis pb $4.95

NO DAY WITHOUT A LINE
A compilation of Olesha's later writing, forming something of an autobiography
0–88233–211–2 Ardis $17.50

● Boris Pasternak
DOCTOR ZHIVAGO
Pasternak's lyrical novel of the Russian Revolution and Civil War won him the Nobel Prize in 1958, but he relinquished the award under government pressure
0–394–42223–6 Pantheon $17.45
0–345–34100–7 Ballantine pb $4.95

I REMEMBER: Sketch for an Autobiography
Translated by David Magarshack
0–674–43950–3 Harvard pb $4.95

SAFE CONDUCT
This account of Scriabin, Mayakovsky, Rilke, and others presents Pasternak's views on poetic creation and the artistic personality
Introduction by Babette Deutsch
0–8112–0135–X New Directions pb $6.25

ZHENIA'S CHILDHOOD
Pasternak's intricate and nearly plotless account of a young girl's development is reminiscent of Rilke's *Diary of Malte Laurids Brigge* in its psychological incisiveness
0–8052–8128–2 Schocken $13.95
0–8052–8129–0 Schocken pb $5.95

The Whites went away with the artillery fire, all scattered through the forest in fear of the white plague, only the Red Army, in tattered greatcoats, in tiny groups—and in their thousands—pushed and pushed ahead. A long time after the Whites, in the machine and assembly shop in the wind, a man hung from a crane, chained by the sides, and in the mines the water came up to the throat, and blue corpses floated by. The March wind roared with snowstorms and ate the snow, out of the March snow, in the gullies around the factory and in the forest around—out of the snow, eaten by the wind—human arms, legs, backs jutted—eaten no longer by the wind, but by dogs and wolves. In the March wind—orphanly in essence—the machine-guns rattled, and like an old man swatting flies on the wall with a swatter, the cannons oohed . . .

Boris Pilnyak
THE NAKED YEAR
Translated by Alexander Tulloch
0–88233–077–2 Ardis $25.00
0–88233–076–4 Ardis pb $5.95

● Boris Pilnyak
THE NAKED YEAR
Pilnyak's first novel, a fragmentary, impressionistic account of the Russian

Civil War, made him one of the dominant figures in early Soviet literature
Translated by Alexander Tulloch
0–88233–077–2 Ardis $25.00
0–88233–076–4 Ardis pb $5.95

● Alexei Remizov
SELECTED PROSE
Long unpublished in the Soviet Union, Remizov influenced such better known writers as Zamyatin and Pilnyak, yet he remains largely (and undeservedly) unknown in the West as well
Edited by Sona Aronian
0–88233–508–1 Ardis $25.00

● Mikhail Sholokhov
AND QUIET FLOWS THE DON
The greatest work of the Nobel laureate
Translated by H. C. Stevens
0–394–70330–8 Random House pb $9.95

● Fyodor Sologub
THE CREATED LEGEND
Sologub's symbolist trilogy on the power of imagination
Translated by John Cournos
0–86527–232–8 Howard Fertig $13.50

THE PETTY DEMON
A provincial schoolteacher's paranoid visions enliven his otherwise dull surroundings
Translated by Sam Cioran
0–88233–808–0 Ardis pb $7.95

● Yevgeny Zamyatin
THE DRAGON: Fifteen Stories
Onetime Bolshevik and subsequent critic of the Soviet regime, Zamyatin wrote in an elliptical, ironic style
Translated by Mirra Ginsburg
0–226–97868–0 Chicago pb $9.95

A SOVIET HERETIC: Essays by Yevgeny Zamyatin
Incisive criticism of early Soviet literature and society
Translated & edited by Mirra Ginsburg
0–226–97866–4 Chicago pb $4.95

WE
The inspiration for Orwell's *1984* presents a futuristic dystopia with wit and black humor
Translated by Mirra Ginsburg
0–380–63313–2 Avon pb $3.95

● Mikhail Zoshchenko
A MAN IS NOT A FLEA: A Collection of Stories
Sharp satires of early Soviet life and other banalities
Translated by Serge Shishkoff
0–87501–023–7 Ardis $20.00

NERVOUS PEOPLE & OTHER SATIRES
Contains the short novels *What the Nightingale Sang, The Lilacs Are Blooming, Michael Sinyagin,* as well as the short stories *Nervous People* and *The Bathhouse*
Translated by Hugh McLean & Maria Gordon
Edited by Hugh McLean
0–253–20192–6 Indiana pb $12.50

SCENES FROM THE BATHHOUSE & OTHER STORIES OF COMMUNIST RUSSIA
Translated by Sidney Monas
0–472–06070–8 Michigan pb $8.95

YOUTH RESTORED
An aging professor proves that youth can be restored by making off with his neighbor's wife
Translated by Joel Stern
0–88233–629–0 Ardis $20.00

RECENT SOVIET WRITERS

Following Stalin's death in 1953 Russian literature experienced a series of alternating periods of relative freedom and repression. The "thaw," lasting until the early 1960s, witnessed such frank depictions of the Stalinist past as Solzhenitsyn's *One Day in the Life of Ivan Denisovich* and Ehrenburg's *The Thaw*. But with the trial of Andrei Sinyavsky and Yuly Daniel in 1966 an era of exile and repression of dissident writers began in earnest; the resulting despair or disillusionment among much of the intelligentsia was evidenced in the work of Aksyonov and Voinovich. With the rise of glasnost, Russian literature may have embarked on a new era.

● Chingiz Aitmatov
THE DAY LASTS MORE THAN A HUNDRED YEARS
A native of Soviet Kirghizia, Aitmatov is widely acclaimed in the Soviet Union. His persistent theme is the clash of Soviet and local culture
Translated by John French
0–253–11595–7 Indiana $25.00
0–253–20482–8 Indiana pb $12.50

THE PLACE OF THE SKULL
Aitmatov's most recent novel shows the influence of glasnost in its depictions of an Orthodox believer, the Soviet drug scene, and environmental problems
Translated by Natasha Ward
0–8021–1000–2 Grove $18.95

● Vassily Aksyonov
THE BURN
An insider's view of the Moscow intelligentsia during the 1960s and early 1970s
Translated by Michael Glenny
0–394–52492–6 Random House $18.95

IN SEARCH OF MELANCHOLY BABY
Aksyonov's humorous observations of America, where he has lived since 1980
Translated by Michael Heim & Antonina Bouis
0–394–54364–5 Random House $15.95

THE ISLAND OF CRIMEA
A response to the disillusionment following the euphoric 1960s
Translated by Michael Heim
0–394–72765–7 Random House pb $8.95

QUEST FOR AN ISLAND
A collection of Aksyonov's stories and plays, including *Destruction of Pompeii, Looking for Climatic Asylum, The Hollow Herring, Quest for an Island, The Four Temperaments,* and *The Heron*
1–55554–020–1 PAJ $17.95

SAY CHEESE
0–394–54363–7 Random House $19.95

SURPLUSSED BARRELWARE
An anthology, containing work written between 1968 and 1979, including the two novellas *Surplussed Barrelware* and *Rendevous*
Translated & edited by Joel Wilkinson & Slava Yastremski
0–88233–904–4 Ardis $23.50
0–88233–905–2 Ardis pb $5.95

● Vasily Aksyonov & others, editors
METROPOL: A Literary Almanac
The celebrated 1979 *samizdat* collection of work by Aksyonov, Akhmadulina, Vysotsky, Voznesensky, Iskander, Bitov, and many others
Foreword by Kevin Klose
0–393–01438–X Norton $24.95

● Yuz Aleshkovsky
THE HAND
A Soviet security policeman confronts his personal enemy, as well as his own quest for vengeance and its possible consequences
Translated by Susan Brownsberger
0–374–16770–2 Farrar, Straus & Giroux $19.95

● Joseph Brodsky
A PART OF SPEECH
Containing his poems written in exile from 1972 to 1976, *A Part of Speech* was largely responsible for Brodsky's winning of the Nobel Prize for literature in 1986. The translators include Anthony Hecht, Howard Moss, and Richard Wilbur
0–374–22987–2 Farrar, Straus & Giroux $15.95
0–374–51633–2 Farrar, Straus & Giroux pb $7.70

TO URANIA
Brodsky's most recent collection of poems
0–374–17252–2 Farrar, Straus & Giroux $14.95

LESS THAN ONE: Selected Essays
The poet explains himself in subtle and elegant essays on childhood, poetry, criticism, Dante, and tyranny
0–374–18503–4 Farrar, Straus & Giroux $29.95
0–374–52055–0 Farrar, Straus & Giroux pb $12.95

● Vasily Grossman
LIFE AND FATE
First published posthumously in France, *Life and Fate* is a vast memoir of the tumultuous century in novel form
0–06–015365–2 Harper & Row $22.50
0–06–091384–3 Harper & Row pb $10.95

● Fazil Iskander
THE GOATIBEX CONSTELLATION
A comic attack on the Khrushchev bureaucracy and Lysenko's bogus school of agrobiology
Translated by H. Burlingame
0–88233–072–1 Ardis pb $3.95

RABBITS AND BOA CONSTRICTORS
A zoological allegory set in Africa
Translated by Ronald Peterson
0–88233–558–8 Ardis $19.50

● Edward Limonov
IT'S ME, EDDIE
A picaresque adventure set in New York, by a recent émigré
0–8021–3007–0 Grove pb $7.95

Anatoly Rybakov
CHILDREN OF THE ARBAT
A major event in the post-Brezhnev era, this novel signaled the beginning of greater freedom in the arts under Gorbachev
0–316–76372–1 Little, Brown $19.95
0–440–20353–8 Dell pb $4.95

● Varlam Shalamov
KOLYMA TALES
"I respectfully confess that he, not I, was to touch those depths of bestiality and despair toward which life in the camps dragged us all"—Aleksandr Solzhenitsyn
Translated by John Glad
0–393–00077–X Norton pb $5.95

GRAPHITE
The sequel to *Kolyma Tales*
Translated by John Glad
0–393–01476–2 Norton $14.95

● Andrei Sinyavsky (Abram Tertz)
FANTASTIC STORIES
A collection of stories steeped in the tradition of Gogol, reflecting Sinyavsky's advocacy of a "phantasmagoric art, with hypotheses instead of purpose"
Translated by Max Hayward & others
0–8101–0727–9 Northwestern pb $12.95

THE TRIAL BEGINS
Essential for understanding modern Soviet policy in the arts. Includes *On Socialist Realism*
Translated by Max Hayward & George Denis
Introduction by Czeslaw Milosz
0–520–04677–3 California pb $10.95

A VOICE FROM THE CHORUS
Excerpts, often cryptic, from Sinyavsky's prison letters to his wife
0–374–28500–4 Farrar, Straus & Giroux $10.00

● Sasha Sokolov
ASTROPHOBIA
The fantastic and parodistic memoirs of a 21st-century Soviet leader, written by the son of an intelligence officer
Translated by Michael Heim
0–8021–1087–8 Grove $18.95

● Aleksandr Solzhenitsyn
AUGUST, 1914
Conceived as the first part of a series of historical novels exploring the meaning of the Bolshevik Revolution
Translated by Harry T. Willetts
0–374–10683–5 Farrar, Straus & Giroux $40.00
0–374–51999–4 Farrar, Straus & Giroux pb $19.95

THE CANCER WARD
Death and moral responsibility, examined in the setting of a provincial hospital
Translated by Nicholas Bethell & David Burg
0–394–60499–7 Modern Library $10.95

THE GULAG ARCHIPELAGO
A monumental exposé of the Stalinist period, based on the author's experience in forced labor camps and in exile. Unsurpassed in its detail and passion
Translated by Thomas Whitney & Harry Willetts
0–06–015474–8 Harper & Row $25.00

LENIN IN ZURICH
This fictional chronicle of Lenin's sojourn in Switzerland before the revolution

---

☞ **FOR ALL OTHER INQUIRIES, PLEASE CALL (212) 333-7900**

portrays the man in exile, from the dual perspective of his public and private life
Translated by Harry Willetts
0–374–18501–8 Farrar, Straus & Giroux $8.95

ONE DAY IN THE LIFE OF IVAN DENISOVICH
Personally sanctioned by Khrushchev for publication in 1963, this grim work made Solzhenitsyn famous overnight
Translated by Ralph Parker
0–525–17088–X Dutton pb $5.95

PRUSSIAN NIGHTS
Solzhenitsyn's long poem, in a bilingual edition
Translated by Robert Conquest
0–374–23845–6 Farrar, Straus & Giroux $8.95
0–374–51391–0 Farrar, Straus & Giroux pb $2.95

WE NEVER MAKE MISTAKES
Translated by Paul W. Blackstock
0–393–00598–4 Norton pb $6.95

• Vladimir Sorokin
THE QUEUE
A comic account of days and nights spent waiting on line in Moscow
Translated with an introduction by Sally Laird
0–930523–45–8 Readers International pb $8.95

Arkady & Boris Strugatsky
Three science-fiction novels by the extremely popular Strugatsky brothers, whose work often includes a degree of social criticism

ALIENS, TRAVELERS AND OTHER STRANGERS
0–02–615230–4 Macmillan $19.95

ESCAPE ATTEMPT
Translated by Roger DeGaris
0–02–615250–9 Macmillan $14.95

THE TIME WANDERERS
Translated by Antonina W. Bouis
0–931933–31–5 Richardson & Steirman $16.95

• Tatyana Tolstaya
ON THE GOLDEN PORCH
Translated by Antonina W. Bouis
0–394–57798–1 Knopf $17.95

• Aleksei N. Tolstoy
AELITA, OR THE DEATH OF MARS
A sci-fi classic about the Soviets landing on Mars
0–88233–788–2 Ardis $15.00
0–88233–789–0 Ardis pb $5.95

• Yuri Trifonov
ANOTHER LIFE & THE HOUSE ON THE EMBANKMENT
Trifonov was one of the few Soviet authors who managed to strike a satisfactory compromise between literary integrity and political "correctness." In these two novels he examines the alienation and amorality of recent Soviet life
Translated by Michael Glenny
Introduction by John Updike
0–671–24266–0 Simon & Schuster $16.95
0–671–60603–4 Simon & Schuster pb $8.95

THE LONG GOODBYE: A Trilogy
Translated by Helen Burlingame & Ellendea Proffer
0–88233–281–3 Ardis pb $7.95

THE OLD MAN
Trifonov's last work, critical of the Soviet malaise of the 1970s
Translated by Jacqueline Edwards & Mitchell Schneider
0–671–25283–6 Simon & Schuster $16.95

• Vladimir Voinovich
THE ANTI-SOVIET SOVIET UNION
A collection of satirical short stories
Translated by Richard Lourie
0–15–107840–8 HBJ $19.95

IN PLAIN RUSSIAN
An amusing collection of essays and fiction
Translated by Richard Lourie
0–374–17580–2 Farrar, Straus & Giroux $11.95

THE IVANKIAD
On the difficulties of getting an apartment in Moscow
Translated by David Lapeza
0–374–51398–8 Farrar, Straus & Giroux pb $7.95

THE LIFE AND EXTRAORDINARY ADVENTURES OF PRIVATE IVAN CHONKIN
A hilarious Soviet version of *The Good Soldier Schweik*
Translated by Richard Lourie
0–374–51752–5 Farrar, Straus & Giroux pb $8.95

MOSCOW 2042
An immensely enjoyable story of a flight into the future, destination Moscow
Translated by Richard Lourie
0–15–162444–5 HBJ $16.95

PRETENDER TO THE THRONE: The Further Adventures of Private Ivan Chonkin
Translated by Richard Lourie
0–374–23715–8 Farrar, Straus & Giroux $17.95

• Andrei Voznesensky
AN ARROW IN THE WALL: Selected Poetry & Prose
Denounced by Khrushchev as a "bourgeois formalist," Voznesensky has skirted the borders of official tolerance
Edited by William Jay Smith & F. D. Reeve
0–8050–0100–X Henry Holt $22.95
0–8050–0784–9 Henry Holt pb $10.95

• Yevgeny Yevtushenko
ALMOST AT THE END
Poetry and prose on censorship, freedom, and the East-West divide
Translated by Anonina Bouis & Albert Todd
Foreword by Harrison Salisbury
0–8050–0148–4 Henry Holt $15.95
0–8050–0785–7 Henry Holt pb $8.95

THE FACE BEHIND THE FACE
"Readers will be mistaken if they imagine that the hero of this book is called Yevgeny Yevtushenko. I myself am, of course, that hero, but it has never been enough for me to be merely myself"— Yevgeny Yevtushenko
Translated by Arthur Boyars & Simon Franklin
0–7145–2616–9 Marion Boyars $12.00

INVISIBLE THREADS
Translated by D. M. Thomas
0–02–632980–8 Macmillan pb $2.98

THE POETRY OF YEVGENY YEVTUSHENKO
0–7145–0482–3 Marion Boyars pb $15.00

ANTHOLOGIES

• Clarence Brown, editor
THE PORTABLE TWENTIETH CENTURY RUSSIAN READER
0–670–80531–9 Penguin pb $8.95

• Nicholas Luker, editor
AN ANTHOLOGY OF SOCIALIST REALISM
0–87501–037–7 Ardis pb $14.95

• Carl Proffer, editor
AN ANTHOLOGY OF CONTEMPORARY RUSSIAN PROSE
0–88233–597–9 Ardis pb $11.95

• Carl & Ellendea Proffer, editors
THE TWENTIES: An Anthology
A representative collection from an interesting and creative epoch
0–88233–821–8 Ardis pb $18.00

• Christine Rydel, editor and translator
THE ARDIS ANTHOLOGY OF RUSSIAN ROMANTICISM
Poetry, prose, and verse narratives from the Golden Age of 19th-century Russian poetry
Afterword by John Mersereau Jr.
0–88233–741–6 Ardis $42.50

Fiction

• Vytas Dukas, editor and translator
TWELVE CONTEMPORARY RUSSIAN STORIES
0–8386–1491–4 Fairleigh Dickinson $16.50

• Helena Goscilo & Byron Lindsey, editors
GLASNOST: The New Soviet Prose
Important works by 19 writers
0–87501–070–9 Ardis $27.95

Poetry

• Dimitri Obolensky, editor
THE HERITAGE OF RUSSIAN VERSE
A collection of some of the finest Russian poetry that includes such ancient monuments as *The Tale of Igor's Campaign* as well as a wide selection of modern verse. A dual-language edition, with commentary
0–253–32736–9 Indiana pb $14.50

• Joseph Brodsky & Alan Myers, editors
AN AGE AGO: A Selection of 19th-Century Russian Poetry
0–374–10442–5 Farrar, Straus & Giroux $19.95
0–374–52084–4 Farrar, Straus & Giroux pb $9.95

• John Glad & Daniel Weissbort, editors
RUSSIAN POETRY: The Modern Period
0–87745–084–6 Iowa pb $12.50

• George Reavey, editor and translator
THE NEW RUSSIAN POETS
0–7145–2715–7 Scribners pb $9.95

IF YOU CAN'T FIND IT, LOOK IN THE INDEX

Drama

- Joshua Cooper, translator
  FOUR RUSSIAN PLAYS
  Four 19th-century classics, including *The Infant* by Fonvizin, *Chatsky* by Griboyedov, *The Inspector* by Gogol, and *Thunder* by Ostrovsky
  0–14–044258–8 Penguin pb $5.95

- F. D. Reeve, editor and translator
  NINETEENTH-CENTURY RUSSIAN PLAYS
  0–393–00683–2 Norton pb $10.95

CRITICAL STUDIES

- Isaiah Berlin
  RUSSIAN THINKERS
  Essays on Herzen, Tolstoy, Belinsky, Turgenev, and others
  0–14022–260–X Penguin pb $7.95

- Katerina Clark
  THE SOVIET NOVEL: History as Ritual
  0–226–10767–1 Chicago pb $11.95

- Robert A. Maguire
  VIRGIN SOIL: Soviet Literature in the 1920s
  0–8014–9447–8 Cornell $12.95

- Dmitry S. Mirsky
  A HISTORY OF RUSSIAN LITERATURE FROM ITS BEGINNINGS
  0–394–70720–6 Random House pb $4.95

- Marc Slonim
  SOVIET RUSSIAN LITERATURE: Writers and Problems, 1917–1977
  0–19–502152–5 Oxford pb $10.95

- Victor Terras
  HANDBOOK OF RUSSIAN LITERATURE
  0–300–03155–6 Yale $45.00

Individual Writers

- V. S. Pritchett
  CHEKHOV: A Spirit Set Free
  0–394–54650–4 Random House $17.95

- Laurence Senelick
  ANTON CHEKHOV
  0–394–54717–9 Grove $27.50
  0–394–62066–6 Grove $11.95

- Ernest Simmons
  CHEKHOV: A Biography
  0–226–75805–2 Chicago pb $3.95

- Peter Conradi
  FYODOR DOSTOEVSKY
  0–312–02053–8 St. Martin's $24.95

- Joseph Frank
  DOSTOEVSKY: The Stir of Liberation
  0–691–01452–3 Princeton pb $9.95
  DOSTOEVSKY: The Years of Ordeal, 1850–1859
  0–691–06576–4 Princeton $29.50
  0–691–01422–1 Princeton pb $9.95

- Konstantin Mochulsky
  DOSTOEVSKY: His Life and Work
  0–691–01299–7 Princeton $16.95

- Jane Grayson & Faith Wigzell, editors
  NIKOLAI GOGOL
  0–312–01696–4 St. Martin's $29.95

- Robert Maguire
  GOGOL FROM THE 20TH CENTURY: Eleven Essays
  0–691–01326–8 Princeton pb $15.95

- Vladimir Nabokov
  NIKOLAI GOGOL
  0–8112–0120–1 New Directions pb $6.95

- Dan Levin
  STORMY PETREL: The Life and Work of Maxim Gorky
  0–8052–0788–0 Schocken pb $11.95

- Boris Eikhenbaum
  LERMONTOV: An Essay in Literary Historical Evaluation
  Translated by Roy Parrott
  0–686–70084–8 Ardis $20.00
  0–88233–705–X Ardis pb $6.50

- Edward Brown
  MAYAKOVSKY: A Poet in the Revolution
  1–055778–002–1 Paragon pb $9.95

- Andrew Field
  VN: The Life and Art of Vladimir Nabokov
  0–517–56113–1 Crown $19.95

- Henry Gifford
  PASTERNAK: A Critical Study
  0–521–28677–8 Cambridge pb $17.95

- Guy de Mallac
  BORIS PASTERNAK: His Life and Art
  0–8061–1660–9 Oklahoma $28.95

- Ernest Simmons
  PUSHKIN
  0–8446–0259–0 Peter Smith $11.25

- Michael Scammell
  SOLZHENITSYN: A Biography
  0–393–01802–4 Norton $29.95
  0–393–30378–0 Norton pb $14.95

- John Bayley
  TOLSTOY AND THE NOVEL
  0226–03960–9 Chicago pb $13.95

- Isaiah Berlin
  THE HEDGEHOG AND THE FOX
  An essay on Tolstoy's theory of history
  0–671–60601–8 Simon & Schuster pb $4.95

- Martine de Courcel
  TOLSTOY: The Ultimate Reconciliation
  A new and insightful account
  0–684–18569–5 Scribners $27.50

- Richard F. Gustafson
  LEO TOLSTOY: Resident and Stranger
  0–691–06674–4 Princeton $29.50

- George Steiner
  TOLSTOY OR DOSTOEVSKY
  0–226–77226–8 Chicago pb $12.95

Tolstoy reading by candlelight, sketched by his friend Ilya Repin, from The Delights of Reading *by Otto Bettmann (Godine)*

- A. N. Wilson
  TOLSTOY: A Biography
  0–393–02585–3 Norton $25.00

- Leonard Shapiro
  TURGENEV: His Life and Times
  0–674–91297–7 Harvard $9.95

- V. S. Pritchett
  THE GENTLE BARBARIAN: The Life and Work of Turgenev
  0–88001–120–3 Ecco pb $9.50

Modern Greek Literature

POETRY

C.P. Cavafy
COLLECTED POEMS
"Cavafy combined a unique voice and a unique sensibility. He is for me not only the great poet of the Levant, but of all culture in decline—which makes him universal in this century"—John Fowles
Translated by Edmund Keeley & Philip Sherrard
Edited by George Savidis
0–691–01320–9 Princeton pb $8.95

COMPLETE POEMS OF CAVAFY
Sixty-three poems have been added to the 1963 edition, helping to complete Cavafy's body of work. The poems frankly and naturally treat what W.H. Auden calls "love, art, politics in the original Greek sense"
Translated by Rae Dalven
Introduction by W.H. Auden
0–15–619820–7 HBJ pb $6.95

• Odysseas Elytis
THE AXION ESTI
The title of this symphonic poem is Greek for "worthy it is." The complex structure is divided into three main parts: Genesis, The Passions, and Gloria
Translated by Edmund Keeley & George Savidis
Foreword by Samuel Hazo
0–8229–5318–8 Pittsburgh pb $6.95

THE LITTLE MARINER
Elytis' major work since winning the Nobel Prize in 1979. "A poetry of luminosity and resonance, clarity of soul, and deep transformative power"—Carolyn Forché
Translated by Olga Broumas
1–55659–014–8 Copper Canyon pb $9.00

WHAT I LOVE: Selected Poems of Odysseus Elytis 1939–1978
Translated by Olga Broumas
0–914742–95–7 Copper Canyon $15.00
0–914742–91–4 Copper Canyon pb $9.00

• Nikos Kazantzakis
THE ODYSSEY: A Modern Sequel
This epic poem by the leading modern Greek novelist begins where Homer's *Odyssey* ends
Translated by Kimon Friar
0–671–20247–2 Simon & Schuster pb $12.95

• Kostis Palamas
TWELVE WORDS OF THE GYPSY
An epic poem embodying the struggle between the ideal and the real in the character of an ancient gypsy
Translated with an introduction by Frederic Will
0–8032–0141–9 Nebraska $18.95

• Yannis Ritsos
EXILE AND RETURN
"This collection contains powerful selections from eight volumes of poetry . . . In a surreal landscape, outer and inner terrains merge, showing how the consciousness of a 'country in exile' affects the individual psyche"—*Bloomsbury Review*
Translated by Edmund Keeley
0–88001–017–7 Ecco $17.50
0–88001–018–5 Ecco pb $8.50

RITSOS IN PARENTHESES
These poems, selected from Ritsos' lesser known work, span a 30-year poetic journey and encompass three volumes: *Parentheses* (1946–47), *Parentheses* (1950–61), and *The Distant* (1975)
Translated by Edmund Keeley
0–691–06397–4 Princeton $25.50
0–691–01358–6 Princeton pb $8.50

SUBTERRANEAN HORSES
Translated by Minas Savvas
Introduction by Vassilis Vassilikos
0–8214–0579–9 Ohio $12.95
0–8214–0580–2 Ohio pb $6.95

George Seferis
COLLECTED POEMS 1924–1955
This bilingual collection supplements and revises the earlier 1967 and 1969 editions. The complete "Notes for a Week" as well as other poems previously unpublished in English appear for the first time
Translated by Edmund Keeley & Philip Sherrard
0–691–06471–7 Princeton $48.50
0–691–01373–X Princeton pb $12.95

POEMS
"I believe Seferis to be one of the three or four most important living European poets . . . His is a poetry which lends itself to English translation, and the versions by Rex Warner which I have seen give us an excellent idea of the original"—C. Day Lewis
Translated by Rex Warner
0–87923–281–1 Godine pb $5.95

POET'S JOURNAL: Days of 1945–1951
Translated by Athan Angnostopoulos
Introduction by Walter Kaiser
0–674–68041–3 Harvard pb $5.95

THREE SECRET POEMS
Seferis stopped writing for eleven years, during which time he served in various diplomatic functions. Following that hiatus he wrote these poems, showing a new and more personal approach to language and style
Translated by Walter Kaiser
0–674–89055–8 Harvard pb $5.95

• Angelos Sikelianos
SELECTED POEMS
Translated in metrics equivalent to the original, this book is the first broad selection of Sikelianos' work in English. The poet employs a multitude of voices and forms to suggest unseen planes of being impinging on visible reality
Translated by Edmund Keeley & Philip Sherrard
0–691–06405–9 Princeton $21.00
0–691–01362–4 Princeton pb $7.50

PROSE

• Nikos Kazantzakis
THE FRATRICIDES
This epic novel follows the struggle of a monk who finds himself caught in the fratricidal turmoil of the Greek Civil War
0–671–27221–7 Simon & Schuster pb $7.95

FREEDOM OR DEATH
0–671–49260–8 Simon & Schuster pb $8.95

THE GREEK PASSION
A Greek village enacts a passion play, with unexpected consequences
0–671–21216–8 Simon & Schuster pb $9.95

JAPAN-CHINA: A Journal of Two Voyages to the Far East
A diary of Asian explorations before and after World War II brings the culture, history, and literature of these two countries into vivid perspective
Translated by George C. Pappageotes
Epilogue by Helen Kazantzakis
0–916870–40–5 Creative Arts pb $9.95

JOURNEYING: Travels in Italy, Egypt, Sinai, Jerusalem, and Cyprus
A posthumously published account of travels made in 1926–27 describes meetings with Mussolini and Cavafy
Translated by Themi & Theodora Vasils
0–916870–67–7 Creative Arts pb $7.95

THE LAST TEMPTATION OF CHRIST
A fictional reinterpretation of the story of the Gospels explores the human component of Christ's being
Translated by P.A. Bien
0–671–21170–6 Simon & Schuster pb $9.95

REPORT TO GRECO
0–671–22027–6 Simon & Schuster pb $10.75

SAINT FRANCIS
A recreation of the life of Saint Francis of Assisi
0–671–21247–8 Simon & Schuster pb $9.95

ZORBA THE GREEK
An English writer's life is transformed by his encounter with a Greek laborer
Translated by Carl Wildman
0–671–21132–3 Simon & Schuster pb $7.95

ANTHOLOGIES AND CRITICAL STUDIES

• Helen Kazantzakis
NIKOS KAZANTZAKIS: A Biography
A must for readers of Kazantzakis, powerfully evocative of his life and work. Included are previously unpublished letters
0–916870–62–6 Creative Arts pb $12.95

• Edmund Keely & Philip Sherrard
VOICES OF MODERN GREECE
Translations of poems by Sikelianos, Seferis, Cavafy, and Elytis. The poems were selected according to how well they translated into English and how representative they were of each particular poet's work
0–691–01382–9 Princeton pb $8.95

• Linos Politis
A HISTORY OF MODERN GREEK LITERATURE
Spans Greek literature from the 11th century epic *Digenis Akritas,* through the Renaissance poets, to such modern writers as Kostis Palamas, Nikos Kazantzakis, and George Seferis. The differences between ancient and modern Greek literature and language are also discussed
0–19–815721–5 Oxford $36.00

• Constantine A. Trypanis, editor
THE PENGUIN BOOK OF GREEK VERSE
From Homer to Elytis, this collection covers 3000 years of Greek poetry. The original Greek texts are accompanied by literal prose translations
0–14–058595–8 Penguin pb $9.95

Modern European Drama

▶ For critical works on major dramatists see the relevant national literatures

IBSEN

"An intellectual pioneer can never gather a majority about him . . . The majority, the masses, the mob, will never catch him up; he can never rally them behind him. I myself feel a similarly unrelenting compulsion to keep pressing forward. A crowd now

TO ORDER BOOKS AS GIFTS, SEE PAGE 1

stands where I stood when I wrote my earlier books. But I myself am there no longer. I am somewhere else—far ahead of them—or so I hope. At present I am struggling with the draft of a new play in four acts. As time passes, various odd ideas settle in one's head, and one must find some outlet for them."—Henrik Ibsen, from a letter to Georg Brandes, June 12, 1883

Ibsen by Vallotton

• **Henrik Ibsen**

COMPLETE MAJOR PROSE PLAYS OF IBSEN
Twelve prose plays in chronological order with introductions and stage histories of productions for each. Fjelde's translations are admirably clear and accurate. "Only by grasping and comprehending my entire production as a continuous and coherent whole will the reader be able to receive the precise impression I sought to convey in the individual parts . . . I therefore appeal to the reader that he not put any play aside, and not skip anything, but that he absorb the plays . . . in the order in which I wrote them"—Henrik Ibsen
Translated by Rolf Fjelde
0–452–25797–2 NAL pb $14.95

THE PLAYS OF IBSEN
"Meyer's translations of Ibsen are a major fact in one's general sense of post-war drama. Their vital pace, their unforced insistence on the poetic center of Ibsen's genius, have beaten academic versions from the field"—George Steiner
Translated by Michael Meyer

Volume 1
Includes *A Doll's House, Emperor and Galilean, John Gabriel Borkman,* and *When We Dead Awaken*
0–671–60764–2 Washington Square pb $4.95

Volume 2
Includes *Hedda Gabler, The Pretenders, Brand,* and *The Pillars of Society*
0–671–60765–0 Washington Square pb $4.95

Volume 3
Includes *Ghosts, The Wild Duck, The Master Builder,* and *An Enemy of the People*
0–671–60766–9 Washington Square pb $4.95

Volume 4
Includes *Peer Gynt, Rosmersholm, The Lady from the Sea,* and *Little Eyolf*
0–671–60767–7 Washington Square pb $4.95

BRAND: A Version for the Stage
An adaptation of Ibsen's dramatic poem, by a distinguished English poet
Adapted by Geoffrey Hill
Introduction by Inga-Stica Ewbank
0–8166–1005–3 Minnesota pb $6.95

AN ENEMY OF THE PEOPLE
Translated by Arthur Miller
0–14–048140–0 Penguin pb $2.95

PEER GYNT
Ibsen's last verse play, based on motifs from Norwegian folklore, follows the light-hearted Peer who escapes conflict by avoiding self-knowledge
Translated by Peter Watts
0–14–044167–0 Penguin pb $3.95

FROM IBSEN'S WORKSHOP: Notes, Scenarios, and Drafts of the Modern Plays
Translated by A.G. Chater
Edited by William Archer
Foreword by John Guare
0–306–80090–X Da Capo pb $7.95

STRINDBERG

"It was reading his [Strindberg's] plays when I first started to write, back in the winter of 1913–14, that, above all else, first gave me the vision of what modern drama could be, and first inspired me with the urge to write for the theatre myself. If there is anything of lasting worth in my work, it is due to that original impulse from him, which has continued as my inspiration down all the years since then."—Eugene O'Neill in his 1936 Nobel Prize acceptance speech

• **August Strindberg**

FIVE PLAYS
Translated into fresh colloquial English, these plays continue Strindberg's tradition of "poetry spoken." Included are his most frequently performed works: *The Father, Miss Julie, A Dream Play, The Dance of Death,* and *The Ghost Sonata*
Translated by Harry Carlson
0–520–04698–6 California pb $11.95
0–451–51862–4 NAL pb $4.95

SELECTED PLAYS
Containing *Master Olof, The Father, Miss Julie, Creditors, The Stronger, Playing with Fire, To Damascus, Crime and Crime, The Dance with Death, A Dream Play, The Ghost Sonata* and *The Pelican.* "Our leading Strindberg critic and biographer has given us some splendid translations of Strindberg's most playable works. His unerring theatrical sense makes these volumes invaluable for both scholars and practitioners"—Robert Brustein
Translated by Evert Sprinchorn
0–8166–1506–3 Minnesota $39.50

APOLOGIA & TWO FOLK PLAYS
Also includes the folk plays *The Crownbride* and *Swanwhite*
Translated by Walter Johnson
0–295–95760–3 Washington $25.00

THE CHAMBER PLAYS
Includes *The Ghost Sonata, The Pelican, Burned House,* and *Storm Weather.* "These Chamber Plays occupy roughly the same place in Strindberg's oeuvre as do the last quartets in Beethoven's"—Evert Sprinchorn
Translated by Evert Sprinchorn & others
0–8166–1031–2 Minnesota pb $7.95

THE DANCE OF DEATH
Strindberg's masterpiece of domestic conflict has profoundly influenced the course of modern drama, from German Expressionism to *Who's Afraid of Virginia Woolf?*
Translated by Arvid Paulson
0–393–04437–8 Norton $7.95
0–393–00820–7 Norton pb $5.95

DRAMAS OF TESTIMONY
Includes *The Dance of Death I & II, Advent, Easter,* and *There Are Crimes and Crimes*
Translated by Walter Johnson
0–295–95433–7 Washington $20.00

A DREAM PLAY & FOUR CHAMBER PLAYS
Includes the Chamber Plays *Storm Weather, The House That Burned, The Ghost Sonata,* and *The Pelican*
Translated by Walter Johnson
0–393–00791–X Norton pb $8.95

PLAYS FROM THE CYNICAL LIFE
Includes the early one-acters *Debit and Credit, Facing Death, The First Warning, Mother Love, Pariah, Playing with Fire* and *Simoon*
Translated by Walter Johnson
0–295–95980–0 Washington $25.00

PLAYS OF CONFESSION AND THERAPY: To Damascus I, II & III
The plays *To Damascus* dramatically chart Strindberg's conversion from atheism to a "Strindbergian" brand of Christianity
Translated by Walter Johnson
0–295–95567–8 Washington $25.00

PRE-INFERNO PLAYS
Includes *The Father, Lady Julie, Creditors, The Stronger* and *The Bond.* The term "inferno" refers to a disastrous period in Strindberg's emotional life in the 1890s
Translated with an introduction by Walter Johnson
0–393–00834–7 Norton pb $7.95

QUEEN CHRISTINA, CHARLES XII & GUSTAV III
These historical plays were planned as part of an uncompleted cycle on the Swedish monarchs
Translated by Walter Johnson
0–295–73899–5 Washington $16.50

CHEKHOV

"In Chekhov's plays, as in his stories, however bewildering the reflections may be, the reflecting surface is cool, shadowless, perfectly clear. It neither judges nor analyzes nor comments, yet the things that show in it will serve as well as anything in literature as the images of truth."—Wallace Stegner

THE MAJOR PLAYS
Includes *Ivanov, The Sea Gull, Uncle Vanya, The Three Sisters,* and *The Cherry Orchard*
Translated by Ann Dunnigan
Afterword by Robert Brustein
0–451–52270–2 NAL pb $3.50

THE BRUTE & OTHER FARCES: Seven Short Plays
Containing *Apologia, The Harmfulness of Tobacco, Swansong, A Marriage Proposal, Summer in the Country, A Wedding* and *The Celebration*
Translated by Theodore Hoffman
Edited by Eric Bentley
0–317–65845–X Applause $19.95
0–317–65846–8 Applause pb $5.95

THE CHERRY ORCHARD
"Nobody in the play gives a damn about the cherry orchard . . . The play is a series of scenes about sexuality, and, particularly, frustrated sexuality"—David Mamet
Translated by David Mamet
0–8021–0007–4 Grove $17.95
0–394–62172–7 Grove pb $7.95

THE CHERRY ORCHARD
Translated by Michael Frayn
0–413–39340–2 RC&H pb $8.95

THE SEA GULL
After the disastrous opening of this play in 1898 Chekhov vowed to give up playwriting. Two years and two plays later, *The Sea Gull* was revived by Konstantin Stanislavsky and enjoyed a critical success
Translated by Oliver Murphy
0–8283–1454–3 Branden pb $3.00

THE THREE SISTERS
"Full of those little liberties and intimacies of ordinary speech which override grammar and syntax and betray moods of ordinary people and impulses of the heart"—John Barber, *Daily Telegraph*
Translated by Michael Frayn
0–413–52450–7 RC&H pb $7.95

UNCLE VANYA
Translated by Michael Frayn
0–413–15950–7 RC&H pb $8.95

WILD HONEY
This play, sometimes known as *Platonov,* was discovered in 1920
Translated by Michael Frayn
0–451–52109–9 NAL pb $3.50

EARLY 20TH CENTURY

● Bertolt Brecht
COLLECTED PLAYS: Volume 1
Includes *Baal, Drums in the Night, In the Jungle of Cities, Edward the Second,* and five one-act plays
Edited by Ralph Manheim & John Willet
0–394–71670–1 Random House pb $6.95

BAAL, A MAN'S A MAN & THE ELEPHANT CALF
Of *Baal* Eric Bentley writes: "For better or worse, a new era in dramatic art dates from this play." The three plays included here represent early Brecht, drawing on techniques taken from music hall and film
Translated by Eric Bentley & Martin Esslin
0–8021–3159–X Grove pb $8.95

Bertolt Brecht's "Three Penny Opera" designed by Caspar Neher (sketch by Mordecai Gorelik)

THE CAUCASIAN CHALK CIRCLE
One of Brecht's most effective plays, based on an ancient Chinese parable
Translated by Eric Bentley & Maja Apelman
0–394–62372–X Grove pb $5.95

EDWARD THE SECOND: A Chronicle Play
Brecht's revision of Christopher Marlowe's classic history play stresses its homosexual elements
Translated with an introduction by Eric Bentley
0–394–17111–X Grove pb $1.95

GALILEO
A critical treatment of Galileo's struggle with the church and his eventual recantation
Translated by Charles Laughton
Edited with an introduction by Eric Bentley
0–8021–3059–3 Grove pb $5.95

THE GOOD WOMAN OF SETZUAN
An eloquent play on the near impossibility of virtue in a rapacious society
Translated with an introduction by Eric Bentley
0–394–17109–8 Grove pb $4.50

HAPPY END
This musical play, "adapted" from a non-existent story by a non-existent Dorothy Lane, anticipates *Guys and Dolls* with its plot involving evangelists and gangsters
Translated by Michael Feingold
0–413–51020–4 Methuen pb $3.00

THE JEWISH WIFE & OTHER SHORT PLAYS
Includes excerpts from *The Private Life of the Master Race* as well as *The Elephant Calf, The Measures Taken, The Exception and the Rule,* and *Salzburg Dance of Death*
Translated with a foreword by Eric Bentley
0–394–17100–4 Grove pb $4.95

JUNGLE OF CITIES & OTHER PLAYS
Jungle of Cities portrays a strange psycho-physical battle between two men in a mythicized world of Chicago gangsters. Also included are *Drums in the Night,* a relatively realistic drama of the Spartacist Revolt, and *Roundheads and Peakheads,* an epic satire of Nazism based on Shakespeare's *Measure for Measure*
Translated by Anselm Hollo, Frank Jones & others
0–394–17428–3 Grove pb $9.95

THE MOTHER
This drama of a working class mother drawn into the Bolshevik revolution, based on Gorky's novel, is Brecht's closest approach to the ideals of Socialist Realism
Translated with an introduction by Lee Baxandall
0–8021–3160–3 Grove pb $8.95

MOTHER COURAGE AND HER CHILDREN
As the owner of a canteen during the Thirty Years' War, Mother Courage tries to make the war serve her own ends
Translated and adapted by Eric Bentley
0–8021–3082–8 Grove pb $4.50

SAINT JOAN OF THE STOCKYARDS
Translated by Frank Jones
0–253–17671–9 Indiana $15.00
0–253–20127–6 Indiana pb $3.95

THE THREEPENNY OPERA
This best-known of Brecht's works, based on John Gay's *The Beggar's Opera,* broke box office records during its original run in Berlin in the 1930s, and became a long-running Off-Broadway success of the 1950s
Translated by Desmond Vesey
Lyrics translated by Eric Bentley
Introduction by Lotte Lenya
0–8021–5039–X Grove pb $4.95

BRECHT ON THEATRE
Selected writings on epic theater and the alienation effect and how these concepts apply to Brecht's own work
Translated by John Willett
0–8090–0542–5 Hill & Wang pb $8.95

● Mikhail Bulgakov
FLIGHT & BLISS
Translated by Mirra Ginsburg
0–8112–0941–5 New Directions pb $9.95

● Elias Canetti
COMEDY OF VANITY & LIFE TERMS
Comedy of Vanity, a satire on mass movements, constructs a world where all mirrors, photographs, and films are taken away. In *Life Terms,* all people are assigned a specific number of years to live and value is determined solely by age
Translated by Gitta Honegger
0–933826–30–3 PAJ $18.95
0–933826–31–1 PAJ pb $7.95

THE WEDDING
Written in 1932, this social allegory is based around an apartment which collapses in the midst of a wild celebration
Translated by Gitta Honegger
1–55554–008–2 PAJ pb $5.95

● Karel Capek
THE MAKROPOULOS SECRET
An entertaining dramatic debate on the question of whether eternal life would benefit or hurt the human race
Edited by Randal Burrell
0–8283–1447–0 Branden pb $3.00

R.U.R. & THE INSECT PLAY
Capek's science-fiction play *R.U.R.* introduced the word "robot"; *The Insect Play,* written in collaboration with his brother Josef, is an entomological allegory much influenced by Maeterlinck's nature writings
0–19–281010–3 Oxford pb $6.95

● Jean Cocteau
THE INFERNAL MACHINE & OTHER PLAYS
The title play recreates the Oedipus myth, while *Bacchus, Orpheus,* and *Knights of the Round Table* transform other familiar stories. Also includes the short play *The*

Eiffel Tower Wedding Party and the text for the Stravinsky opera *Oedipus Rex*
0–8112–0022–1 New Directions pb $10.95

● Jean Giraudoux
FOUR PLAYS
Includes *Ondine, The Enchanted, The Madwoman of Chaillot,* and *The Apollo of Bellac*
Adapted with an introduction by Maurice Valency
0–8090–0712–6 Hill & Wang pb $8.95

● Maxim Gorky
THE LOWER DEPTHS & OTHER PLAYS
Contains *Enemies* and *The Zykovs*
Translated by Alexander Bakshy & Paul S. Nathan
0–300–00100–2 Yale pb $7.95

● Gerhart Hauptmann
THREE PLAYS
The socially aware dramas of this Nobel Laureate influenced many writers including Eugene O'Neill. This volume includes *The Weavers, Hannele,* and *The Beaver*
Translated by Horst Frenz & Miles Waggoner
0–8044–6254–2 Ungar pb $8.95

● Alfred Jarry
SELECTED WORKS OF ALFRED JARRY
Includes *The Ubu Cycle,* a portfolio of illustrations, writings on the theater, poems, essays, and fiction. "Jarry possessed black humor, wild obscenity, delicate lyricism, mechanized eroticism, pure love, gay blasphemy, and the calm of the infinite"—*The Observer*
0–394–17604–9 Grove pb $6.95

UBU ROI
In its handwritten presentation, and with accompanying drawings by Bonnard and Jarry, this volume captures the ferociously irreverent tone of Jarry's play
Translated by Barbara Wright
0–8112–0072–8 New Directions pb $6.95

● Georg Kaiser
PLAYS
The principal works of the leading German Expressionist playwright
Translated by B.J. Kenworthy & others
Edited by J.M. Ritchie

Volume 1
Includes *From Morning to Midnight, The Burghers of Calais,* and the trilogy consisting of *The Coral, Gas One* and *Gas Two*
0–7145–0242–1 Riverrun pb $8.95

Volume 2
Includes *The Flight From Venice, One Day in October, The Raft of the Medusa, David and Goliath,* and *The President*
0–7145–3899–X Riverrun pb $6.95

Karl Kraus
THE LAST DAYS OF MANKIND: A Tragedy in Five Acts
An abridged version of Kraus's brilliant 800-page satiric drama which greatly influenced Brecht and Ionesco among others
Translated by Alexander Gode & Sue Wright
Edited by Frederick Ungar
0–8044–6366–2 Ungar pb $12.95

● Federico García Lorca
FIVE PLAYS: Comedies and Tragicomedies
Includes *The Shoemaker's Prodigious Wife, Don Perlimplin, Dona Rosita the Spinster, Billy-Club Puppets, The Butterfly's Evil Spell.* These comedies range from poetic puppet-farce to highly realistic tragi-comedy
Translated by Richard O'Connell & James Graham-Lujan
Introduction by Francisco Garcia Lorca
0–8112–0090–6 New Directions pb $7.95

THREE TRAGEDIES
Includes Lorca's three major poetic plays: *Blood Wedding, Yerma,* and *The House of Bernarda Alba*
Translated by Richard L. O'Connell & James Graham-Lujan
0–8112–0092–2 New Directions pb $6.95

THE PUBLIC & PLAY WITHOUT A TITLE: Two Posthumous Plays
These plays draw on varied traditions that include surrealism, folk theatre, symbolist poetry, and black humor
Translated with an introduction by Carlos Bauer
0–8112–0881–8 New Directions pb $5.25

● Vladimir Mayakovsky
THE BEDBUG & SELECTED POETRY
The Bedbug is a satirical verse play by the experimental Soviet poet
Translated by Max Hayward & George Reavey
0–253–20189–6 Indiana pb $7.95

● Robert Musil
THE ENTHUSIASTS
This comedy by the author of *The Man Without Qualities* depicts the philosophical and ethical dilemma of an old world threatened by a new, morally free, and scientifically skeptical one
Translated by Andrea Simon
0–933826–47–8 PAJ pb $5.95

● Luigi Pirandello
One of the greatest and most influential modern playwrights, Pirandello summarized his work in these terms: "When someone lives, he lives and does not watch himself. Well, arrange things so that he does watch himself in the act of living, a prey to his passions, by placing a mirror before him; either he will be astonished and dismayed by his own appearance and turn his eyes away so as not to see himself, or he will spit at his image in disgust, or will angrily thrust out his fist to smash it . . . In short, there will be some manifestation of pain. This manifestation of pain is my theater."
PLAYS
The plays included in these volumes make apparent why Pirandello was such an influence on the post-war absurdist school

Volume 1:
Includes *Right You Are, Lazarus,* and *The Man with the Flower in His Mouth*
0–7145–4110–9 Riverrun pb $10.95

Volume 2:
Includes *Six Characters In Search of An Author, All for the Best, The Pleasure of Honesty,* and *Naked*
0–7145–3984–8 Riverrun pb $11.95

NAKED MASKS: Five Plays
Includes *It Is So If You Think So, Henry IV, Six Characters In Search of An Author, Each in His Own Way,* and *Liola*
Edited by Eric Bentley
0–525–48319–5 Dutton pb $7.95

SICILIAN COMEDIES
Includes *Caps and Bells* and *Man, Beast and Virtue*
0–933826–51–6 PAJ pb $6.95

● Arthur Schnitzler
PLAYS AND STORIES
Includes *Flirtations, La Ronde, Countess Mitzi or The Family Reunion, Casanova's Homecoming,* and *Lieutenant Gustl*
0–8264–0271–2 Continuum pb $10.95

ANATOL
Translated by Frank Marcus
0–413–49880–8 Methuen pb $6.95

LA RONDE
Schnitzler's erotic masterpiece, set in turn-of-the-century Vienna, depicts ten characters linked in a sexual chain
Translated by Sue Davies
Edited by John Barton
0–14–048171–0 Penguin pb $3.95

Carl Sternheim
PLAYS
Includes *The Bloomers, The Snob, Paul Schippel, 1913,* and *The Fossil.* Sternheim, an important forerunner of the Expressionists, was the definitive satirist of the German bourgeoisie
0–7145–0027–5 Riverrun pb $6.95

● Odon von Horvath
ODON VON HORVATH
Includes *Kasmir & Karoline, Faith, Hope and Charity, Figaro Gets A Divorce,* and *Judgement Day.* Martin Esslin has called Horvath "the most important, next to Brecht, of the dramatists who wrote in German in this century"
Translated by Martin Esslin
1–55554–003–1 Performing Arts pb $3.98

● Frank Wedekind
THE LULU PLAYS & OTHER SEX TRAGEDIES
Includes *Earth Spirit, Pandora's Box, Death and Devil,* and *Castle Wetterstein*
Translated by Stephen Spender
0–7145–0868–3 Riverrun pb $7.95

SPRING AWAKENING
"Edward Bond seems the right translator for Wedekind in that his laconic style exactly suits the original's innovatory one-sentence line"—*Guardian*
Translated by Edward Bond
0–413–47620–0 Methuen pb $8.95

SPRING AWAKENING
Wedekind's masterpiece, written in a mixture of harsh colloquialisms and lyrical speech, was a radically realistic treatment of adolescent sexual anguish
Translated by Tom Osborn
0–7145–0634–6 Riverrun pb $4.95

POSTWAR EUROPEAN DRAMA

• **Jean Anouilh**
FIVE PLAYS
Containing *Antigone, Eurydice, The Ermine, The Rehearsal,* and *Romeo and Jeanette*
0–8090–0710–X Hill & Wang pb $8.95

BECKET
"Anouilh's essential theme—the portrayal of a life that ends by championing the honor of God, no matter what the cost—has nobility and exaltation"—*NY Times*
0–698–10031–X Putnam pb $6.95

THE LARK
A retelling of the story of Joan of Arc
Translated by Christopher Fry
0–19–500393–4 Oxford $10.95

• **Wolfgang Bauer**
CHANGE & OTHER PLAYS
Bauer, who came to prominence in the 1960s, is noted for his iconoclasm
Introduction by Martin Esslin
0–8090–3403–4 Hill & Wang $10.00
0–8090–0750–9 Hill & Wang pb $00.00

• **Samuel Beckett**
THE COLLECTED SHORTER PLAYS
Includes *Krapp's Last Tape*, mimes, radio and television plays, the screenplay for *Film*, and much more
0–394–53850–1 Grove $19.95
0–8021–5055–1 Grove pb $12.95

CASCANDO & OTHER SHORT DRAMATIC PIECES
Also includes *Words and Music, Eh Joe, Play, Come and Go,* and *Film (Original Version)*
0–394–47496–1 Grove $10.00

COMPANY
A voice from out of the darkness describes important moments in a life from birth to death
0–394–51394–0 Grove $8.95
0–394–17928–5 Grove pb $3.95

ENDGAME & ACT WITHOUT WORDS
0–394–47500–3 Grove $10.00
0–8021–5024–1 Grove pb $4.95

Samuel Beckett (photo by Jerry Bauer)

ENDS AND ODDS: Dramatic Pieces
Eight pieces, including *Footfalls, That Time,* and *Not I,* which A. Alvarez described by saying that it "focuses in one final, unanswerable image all Beckett's lifelong obsessions"
0–8021–5046–2 Grove pb $8.95

HAPPY DAYS
The horror of mutual dependency is personified in the relations between Winnie—buried in a mound of dirt—and the frustratingly silent Willie
0–8021–3076–3 Grove pb $5.95

KRAPP'S LAST TAPE & OTHER DRAMATIC PIECES
Also includes *All That Fall, Acts Without Words I & II,* and the radio play *Embers*
0–394–17223–X Grove pb $7.95

OHIO IMPROMPTU, CATASTROPHE, & WHAT WHERE
0–394–53851–X Grove $12.95
0–394–62061–5 Grove pb $4.95

ROCKABY & OTHER WORKS
0–394–51953–1 Grove $12.50
0–394–17924–2 Grove pb $3.95

WAITING FOR GODOT
0–394–47529–1 Grove $10.00
0–8021–3034–8 Grove pb $4.95

• **Joseph Brodsky**
MARBLES: A Play in Three Acts
Two prisoners discuss freedom, reality and illusion, and literature and politics
Translated by Alan Myers & the author
0–374–20288–5 Farrar, Straus & Giroux $17.95
0–374–52116–6 Farrar, Straus & Giroux pb $7.95

• **Albert Camus**
CALIGULA & THREE OTHER PLAYS
Also includes *The Misunderstanding, State of Siege,* and *The Just Assassins*
Translated by Stuart Gilbert
0–394–70207–7 Random House pb $4.50

• **Jean-Claude Carrière**
THE MAHABARATA
"The immediate impact produced amazement and pleasure; the long term effect is the imprint of images of tenderness, triumph and death that lodge in the memory forever"—*Times* (London)
0–06–039072–7 Harper & Row $18.95
0–06–039079–4 Harper & Row pb $8.95

• **Aimé Césaire**
A TEMPEST
A variation on Shakespeare by the great poet from Martinique
Translated by Richard Miller
0–913745–15–4 Ubu Repertory pb $6.25

• **Friedrich Dürrenmatt**
PLAYS, FICTION & ESSAYS
Includes *Romulus the Great, The Visit, The Judge and His Hangman, Problems of the Theater,* and *A Monster Lecture on Justice and Law*
Edited by Volkmar Sander
Foreword by Martin Esslin
0–8264–0267–4 Continuum pb $10.95

THE PHYSICISTS
Dürrenmatt uses the metaphor of three nuclear scientists in an insane asylum to explore the nuclear predicament
Translated by James Kirkup
0–8021–5088–8 Grove pb $6.95

THE VISIT
A millionairess visits the small town of Guellen and offers to pull it out of bankruptcy on one condition: that they kill someone for her
Translated by Paul Bowles
0–8021–3066–6 Grove pb $6.95

• **Rainer Werner Fassbinder**
PLAYS
Six controversial examples of the late filmmaker's "antitheater": *The Bitter Tears of Petra von Kant, Katzelmacher, Bremen Freedom, Garbage, The City and Death, Pre-Paradise Sorry Now,* and *Blood on the Cat's Neck*
Translated by Denis Calandra
0–933826–81–8 Performing Arts $21.95
0–933826–82–6 Performing Arts pb $8.95

• **Eduardo de Filippo**
SATURDAY, SUNDAY, MONDAY
"Shows a touching understanding not of Italians merely, but of the comic, complex predicaments of family life everywhere"—*Daily Telegraph*
Translated by Keith Waterhouse & Willis Hall
0–435–23201–0 Heinemann pb $6.50

• **Dario Fo**
ARCHANGELS DON'T PLAY PINBALL
A three-act musical farce about how a small-time criminal is accidentally registered as a dog, by Italy's leading political satirist
Translated by R.C. McAvoy & A.M. Giugni
0–413–15630–3 Methuen $8.95

• **Max Frisch**
THE FIREBUGS
A German couple entertain two arsonists in the hope that their hospitality will save their house and themselves
Translated by Michael Bullock
0–8090–1248–0 Hill & Wang pb $6.95

Jean Genet
THE BALCONY
The Balcony is a brothel where the customers enact their fantasies of power and self-abasement. "A theatrical experience as startling as anything since Ibsen"—Kenneth Tynan
Translated by Bernard Frechtman
0–8021–5034–9 Grove pb $7.95

THE BLACKS: A Clown Show
Translated by Bernard Frechtman
0–8021–15028–4 Grove pb $8.95

THE MAIDS & DEATHWATCH
Two astonishing one-act plays: the first an ultimate presentation of role-playing and exchange of identities, the second a portrayal of prisoners awaiting execution
Translated by Bernard Frechtman
Introduction by Jean-Paul Sartre
0–394–17390–2 Grove pb $8.95

➤ **FOR OVERSEAS ORDERING INFORMATION, SEE PAGE 1**

THE SCREENS
Genet's last play is set during the Algerian War and its 17 scenes are populated by over 50 characters; the world of the dead is differentiated from the world of the living by the manipulation of screens
Translated by Bernard Frechtman
0–394–62381–9 Grove pb $7.95

• Vladimir Gubaryev
SARCOPHAGUS: A Tragedy
Gubaryev was the first journalist to cover the disaster at Chernobyl. His play attempts to go beyond journalism in expressing the implications of nuclear devastation
Translated by Michael Glenny
0–394–75590–1 Random House pb $6.95

• Peter Handke
KASPAR & OTHER PLAYS
The story of an autistic adolescent whose identity is manipulated according to how the "prompters" direct his use of language. Also includes two landmarks of antitheatre: *Offending the Audience* and *Self Accusation*
Translated by Michael Roloff
0–374–50824–0 Farrar, Straus & Giroux pb $6.95

• Vaclav Havel
LARGO DESOLATO
A philosopher and human rights activist in a totalitarian state is persecuted for one paragraph in his book and charged with "disturbing the intellectual peace"
0–394–55554–6 Grove $15.95
0–394–62265–0 Grove pb $6.95

THE MEMORANDUM
In Havel's satiric comedy, an artificial language is created to mask the foibles of the bureaucracy
Translated by Vera Blackwell
Introduction by Tom Stoppard
0–394–17653–7 Grove pb $5.95

TEMPTATION
Translated by Marie Winn
0–8021–3100–X Grove pb $7.95

• Rolf Hochhuth
THE DEPUTY
Hochhuth's 1963 play stirred enormous controversy with its attempt to place much of the blame for Nazi genocide on Pope Pius XII's failure to denounce Hitler and his policies
Translated by Richard & Clara Winston
Preface by Albert Schweitzer
0–394–17125–X Grove pb $7.95

• Eugene Ionesco
FOUR PLAYS
Includes *The Bald Soprano, The Lesson, The Chairs,* and *Jack, or The Submission.* "The language, made up of cliches and ready-made phrases, which is our daily speech . . . once it is spoken by actors and exposed on the stage, finds its focus, and acquires the force of revelation"—*France Observateur*
Translated by Donald M. Allen
0–8021–3079–8 Grove pb $7.95

THREE PLAYS
Includes *Amedée, The New Tenant,* and *Victims of Duty.* "In his greatest plays— *Amedée* and *Victims of Duty*—Ionesco has

written works of the same solidity, fullness and permanence as his predecessors in the dramatic revolution that began with Ibsen and is still going on"—Richard Gilman
Translated by Donald Watson
0–8021–3101–8 Grove pb $8.95

EXIT THE KING, THE KILLER, & MACBETT
Translated by Donald Watson
0–394–62199–9 Grove pb $9.95

HUNGER AND THIRST & OTHER PLAYS
Also includes *The Picture, Anger,* and *Salutations*
Translated by Donald Watson
0–394–17316–3 Grove pb $3.95

KILLING GAME
A happy village where everyone speaks in cliches is shattered by the arrival of a mysterious monk and the outbreak of plague
Translated by Helen Bishop
0–394–17822–X Grove pb $2.95

MAN WITH BAGS
Translated by Israel Horowitz
0–394–17021–0 Grove pb $3.95

RHINOCEROS & OTHER PLAYS
Ionesco's satire on conformism was one of his most successful plays. Also includes *The Leader* and *The Future Is in Eggs*
Translated by Derek Prouse
0–8021–3098–4 Grove pb $7.95

• Milan Kundera
JACQUES AND HIS MASTER
Kundera's stage adaptation of Diderot's 18th-century philosophical novel
Translated by Michael H. Heim
0–06–091222–7 Harper & Row pb $7.95

• Slawomir Mrozek
TANGO
Translated by Ralph Manheim & Teresa Dzieduszycka
0–394–17264–7 Grove pb $3.95

THREE PLAYS
Includes *Striptease, Tango,* and *Vatzlav*
Translated by Lola Gruenthal & others
0–394–17933–1 Grove pb $12.50

• Heiner Müller
HAMLETMACHINE & OTHER TEXTS FOR THE STAGE
Also *Quartet, Correction, The Task, Despoiled Shore,* and *Gundling's Life*
0–933826–45–1 PAJ pb $18.95

• Nathalie Sarraute
COLLECTED PLAYS
These plays bring Sarraute's *nouveau roman* style to the stage. Includes *It Is There, It's Beautiful, Izzum, The Life,* and *Silence*
Translated by Maria Jolas & Barbara Wright
0–8076–0940–4 George Braziller pb $5.95

• Jean-Paul Sartre
NO EXIT & THREE OTHER PLAYS
Also includes *Dirty Hands, The Respectful Prostitute,* and *The Flies*
0–394–70016–3 Random House pb $3.95

• Ramón del Valle-Inclán
SAVAGE ACTS: Three Plays
Valle-Inclán's prewar plays prefigure the absurdists
Edited by Robert Lima
1–55554–046–5 PAJ $19.95
1–55554–047–3 PAJ pb $11.95

BARBARIC COMEDIES
Translated by Asa Zatz
0–941419–32–9 Eridanos $25.00
0–941419–32–0 Eridanos pb $16.00

• Peter Weiss
THE PERSECUTION AND ASSASSINATION OF JEAN-PAUL MARAT AS PERFORMED BY THE INMATES OF THE ASYLUM OF CHARENTON UNDER THE DIRECTION OF THE MARQUIS DE SADE
The problem of revolution, the gap between the masses and their leaders, and the question of modern-day sanity are among the themes touched upon in this touchstone of 1960s dramatic radicalism, usually referred to as *Marat/Sade*
English version by Geoffrey Skelton
Verse adaptation by Adrian Mitchell
0–689–70568–9 Atheneum pb $5.95

ANTHOLOGIES

Marketa Goetz-Stankiewicz, editor
DRAMACONTEMPORARY: Czechoslovakia
Includes Milan Kundera's *Jacques and His Master,* Vaclav Havel's *Protest,* Pavel Kohout's *Fire in the Basement,* Ivan Klima's *Games,* Pavel Landovsky's *Detour,* and Milan Uhde's *The Blue Angel*
0–933826–75–3 PAJ pb $9.95

• Daniel Gerould, editor
DOUBLES, DEMONS AND DREAMERS
Fifteen Symbolist plays written between 1890 and 1918, including work by Strindberg, Andreyev, Tagore, Hoffmansthal, Blok, and others
0–933826–77–X PAJ pb $9.95

• Mel Gordon, editor
DADA PERFORMANCE
An important collection of hard-to-find texts by Hugo Ball, Kurt Schwitters, Tristan Tzara, and others
1–55554–010–4 PAJ pb $7.95

EXPRESSIONIST TEXTS
Includes Oskar Kokoschka's *Sphinx and Strawman,* August Stramm's *Sancta Susanna,* Gottfried Benn's *Ithaka,* Georg Kaiser's *From Morn to Midnight,* Ernst Toller's *Transfiguration,* Walter Hasenclever's *The Son,* and Lothar Schreyer's *Crucifixion*
1–55554–013–9 PAJ pb $8.95

• Michael Glenny, editor
THE GOLDEN AGE OF SOVIET THEATRE
Includes *The Bedbug* by Vladimir Mayakovsky, *Marya* by Isaac Babel, and *The Dragon* by Yevgeny Schwartz
0–14–048143–5 Penguin pb $6.95

• Michael Green, translator
THE RUSSIAN SYMBOLIST THEATRE: An Anthology of Plays and Critical Texts
0–88233–798–X Ardis pb $13.95

- Marion Holt, editor
DRAMACONTEMPORARY: Spain
Includes Jaime Salom's *The Cock's Short Flight,* Antonio Buero-Vallejo's *The Foundation,* Francisco Nieva's *Coronada and the Bull,* and José Martin Recuerda's *The Inmates of the Convent of Saint Mary Egyptian*
0–933826–85–0 PAJ pb $9.95

- Michael Kirby & Victoria Nes Kirby, editors
FUTURIST PERFORMANCE
An anthology of theatrical texts and manifestoes by Marinetti, Balla, Boccioni, and others
55554–009–0 PAJ pb $10.95

- Walter Sokel, editor
ANTHOLOGY OF GERMAN EXPRESSIONIST DRAMA
Includes plays by Oskar Kokoschka, Reinhard Sorge, Carl Sternheim, Walter Hasenclever, Georg Kaiser, Yvon Goll, Rolf Lauckner and Bertolt Brecht. Also included are four essays by writers of the period
0–8014–9296–3 Cornell pb $8.95

- Phillipa Wehle, editor
DRAMACONTEMPORARY: France
Includes Marguerite Duras' *Vera Baxter,* Nathalie Sarraute's *Over Nothing At All,* Michel Vinaver's *Chamber Theatre,* Enzo Cormann's *Exiles,* and Gildas Bourdet's *The Gas Station.* With an introduction that sets the plays in their historical and political context
0–933826–94–X PAJ pb $9.95

Modern Hebrew Literature

The classical age of Hebrew literature, commonly known as the biblical period, began 3200 years ago; biblical poems like "The Song of Deborah" and "The Song of the Sea"—which schoolchildren in Israel can still understand—were first set down in the 11th century BCE.

Hebrew ceased to be a spoken language around the 6th century BCE and was used primarily for religious and legal purposes. By the Middle Ages it was known as "the sacred tongue" and was proscribed for colloquial use. Beginning in the 10th century, however, Spain, Provence, and then Italy witnessed a unique flowering of secular Hebrew poetry and philosophy. This Spanish-Arabic period, or "Hebrew Golden Age," was largely a Sephardic phenomenon, confined to the southern Mediterranean, and was already waning by the 15th century. Unfortunately, this work is not widely available in good English translations.

THE 18TH AND 19TH CENTURIES

Modern Hebrew literature, which began to emerge during the late 18th and 19th centuries, mirrored and in some sense shaped the emergence of the Jews from the ghetto into the modern age.

The early proponents of the *Haskalah,* or Enlightenment, embarked on a mission to use literature to educate and transform the Jewish masses. They chose Hebrew as a means of creating a Jewish culture that might take its place with the cultures of other peoples: Yiddish was a "low jargon" associated with the ghetto, while German was considered too "foreign."

In the later 19th century, some Hebrew writers attacked the early, idealistic enlightenment and called for a more realistic literature, which would reflect the true character of the Jewish people and lead to economic and social reform. At the same time, the violent pogroms of 1881–82 shattered any remaining faith in reformism and impelled the first wave of Jews to leave for Palestine.

- Moses Luzzato
Moses Luzzato (known in Hebrew as Moshe Chaim) was an 18th-century Italian-born Hebrew poet and mystic. He is often called the "father of modern Hebrew literature."
DAAT TEVNOTH: The Knowing Heart
Arguing that "man's chief study is reflection upon the Divinity, along with the mysteries of his creations," Luzzato makes an eloquent case for understanding through the heart, not just the intellect
0–87306–345–7 Philipp Feldheim $12.95

GENERAL PRINCIPLES OF KABBALAH
Luzzato was a kabbalist who believed that behind everything there lies a motivating force; nature simply revealed to him the greater glory of God
0–943688–07–8 Kabbalah $15.95
0–943688–31–0 Kabbalah pb $11.95

THE PATH OF THE JUST
Luzzato's most influential book points to the renascent humanism in Hebrew creativity
0–87306–114–4 Philipp Feldheim $12.95

- Moses Mendelssohn
It was with Mendelssohn—"the second Moses"—that the real movement towards the Enlightenment and the outside world began in the early 19th-century. He became accepted as a symbol of the new type of Jew.
JERUSALEM: Or On Religious Power and Judaism
Mendelssohn attempts to reconcile Jewish tradition with the philosophical rationalism of his age
0–87451–263–8 New England $20.00
0–89451–264–6 New England pb $10.00

PHAEDON: Or the Death of Socrates
An investigation into the immortality of the soul
0–405–05282–0 Ayer $22.00

- Hayyim Nachman Bialik
The greatest Hebrew poet since the medieval period, Bialik introduced a flexible style and a personal, individual tone. His poetry provides a profound record of the spiritual crisis of modernity for Jews from a traditional world.
AND IT CAME TO PASS
A collection of legends and stories—ancient, medieval, modern—about King David and King Solomon
0–88482–887–5 Hebrew $6.95

KNIGHT OF ONIONS AND KNIGHT OF GARLIC
A brief, comic elaboration of an eastern European anecdote; illustrated with woodcuts
0–88482–734–8 Hebrew $4.95

SHIROT BIALIK: A New and Annotated Translation of Chaim Nachman Bialik's *Epic Poems*
Includes *In the City of Slaughter* and *On the Slaughter,* the poems that earned Bialik the title of "national poet"
Edited by Stephen L. Jacobs
0–933771–03–7 Alpha $22.95

- Ahad Ha-am
Ahad Ha-am ("One of the Nation") is the pseudonym of Asher Ginzberg, the father of the modern Hebrew essay, a brilliant stylist and cultural Zionist.
SELECTED ESSAYS OF AHAD HA-AM
Edited by Leon Simon
0–318–14661–4 JPS pb $8.95

THE PIONEER PERIOD

After the First World War, Palestine became the base for Hebrew writers. An indigenous literature had been developing since the first migration of the 1880s, but with the third emigration in 1920–24, a younger, more radical literary generation came to the fore.

These were mostly socialist-minded pioneers who had come to build a new society. They challenged Bialik and the old classicism, and were influenced by Russian revolutionary poets and French symbolists.

- S.Y. Agnon
The first and only Hebrew writer to win the Nobel Prize for literature, Agnon used the resources of midrashic, hasidic, and folk literature, to create a unique prose style. Edmund Wilson called him "a man of unquestionable genius."
DAYS OF AWE: A Treasury of Tradition, Legends and Learned Commentaries Concerning Rosh Hashanah, Yom Kippur and the Days Between
0–8052–0100–9 Schocken pb $9.95

A GUEST FOR THE NIGHT
A tragic tale of an anonymous "I" who returns to a ruined town after World War I and finds it in a spiritual shambles
Translated by Misha Louvish
0–8052–3091–2 Random House pb $10.00

IN THE HEART OF THE SEAS: A Story of a Journey to the Land of Israel
A charming novella about pious Jews emigrating to Palestine in the early 19th century
Translated by I.M. Lask
Illustrated by T. Herzl Rome
0–8052–0647–7 Schocken pb $6.95

A SIMPLE STORY
The not-so-simple story of Hershl, who loves the socially inferior Blume but marries the unloved Minna
Translated by Hillel Halkin
0–8052–3999–5 Schocken $14.95
0–8052–0820–8 Schocken pb $8.95

TWENTY-ONE STORIES
Includes *Agunot,* Agnon's first story set in Palestine
Edited by Nahum N. Glatzer
0–8052–0313–3 Schocken pb $8.95

TWO TALES: Betrothed & Edo and Enam
Betrothed is an idyllic story about a marine biologist in pre-1914 Palestine who is caught unawares by love. *Edo and Enam* is a darker tale about restlessness and the urge to escape by traveling
Translated by Walter Lever
0–8052–0814–3 Schocken pb $6.95

SHIRA
Agnon's final novel, published posthumously, involves the adulterous affair in Jerusalem of the 1930s of a middle-aged professor with the enigmatic woman he calls "Shira" (which also means "poetry")
Translated by Zeva Shapiro
0–8052–4043–8 Schocken $24.95

• **David Vogel**
MARRIED LIFE
The story of a penniless Jewish writer trapped in a masochistic marriage with an unfaithful, anti-Semitic Baroness, Vogel's novel is a dark mirror of Vienna in the 1920s
Translated by Dalya Bilu
0–8021–1129–7 Grove $18.95

ISRAELI LITERATURE

Since the establishment of the state of Israel, there have been two main movements in Hebrew literature. The *Palmach,* or '48 generation, writers were the first for whom Hebrew was a natural—rather than a literary—language. They subscribed to the collectivist pioneering ideology of their day and wrote social novels in which the individual was defined by his relations to the community.

In the late 1950s and early 1960s, Hebrew writers began to express their disillusionment with the collectivist ideology and turned to more introspective, alienated characters. The Eichmann trial in 1961 was a national event, opening up the Holocaust as a subject for public debate and private imaginings.

If there is a third "movement" today, it may be characterized by a return to social and psychological realism; the marginal character has moved back to the center of Israeli life in keeping with the society as a whole, which has lost some of its old certainties and self-confidence and become more alienated itself.

Fiction

• **Yehudah Amichai**
NOT OF THIS TIME, NOT OF THIS PLACE
An experimental novel about the split consciousness of a contemporary Israeli, haunted by the Holocaust and the past, lured by love and the present
Translated by Shlomo Katz
0–85303–180–0 Biblio Distribution $15.00

THE WORLD IS A ROOM & OTHER STORIES
An original collection of short stories more reliant on metaphor than on plot
0–8276–0234–0 JPS $13.95

• **Aharon Appelfeld**
Deported to a concentration camp at the age of eight, Appelfeld escaped and wandered the forests for several years, until he reached Palestine in 1946. His short stories and novels dwell on the Holocaust, although it is never mentioned by name or depicted directly.

THE AGE OF WONDERS
A Jewish intellectual and his family cling to their Austrian homeland during the Final Solution—as recorded through the "innocent" eyes of a child who returns years later
Translated by Dalya Bilu
0–671–45858–2 Washington Square pb $3.95

BADENHEIM, 1939
"This fable-like novel is an eerie controlled experiment in silence that makes its readers supply the horrors it never mentions"—Bill Buford, *Time Out*
Translated by Dalya Bilu
0–87923–342–7 Godine $12.95
0–671–43592–2 Washington Square pb $3.50

FOR EVERY SIN
A Holocaust survivor attempts to walk across Europe
1–55584–318–2 Weidenfeld & Nicolson $15.95

THE IMMORTAL BARTFUSS
Translated by Jeffrey M. Green
1–55584–152–X Weidenfeld & Nicholson $15.95

THE RETREAT
A miniature *Magic Mountain,* in which Jewishness is treated as a disease and the patients have all been sent to "the retreat" in the hopes of a cure
Translated by Dalya Bilu
0–14–007660–3 Penguin pb $5.95

TO THE LAND OF THE CATTAILS
A Jewish woman and her half-gentile son travel eastward across Europe on the brink of the Holocaust
Translated by Jeffrey M. Green
1–55584–007–8 Weidenfeld & Nicolson $14.95
0–06–097115–0 Harper & Row pb $6.95

TZILI: The Story of a Life
A feeble-minded Jewish girl is abandoned by her family and forced to fend for herself on the eve of the Holocaust
Translated by Dalya Bilu
0–525–24187–6 Dutton $12.95
0–14–007058–3 Penguin pb $5.95

David Grossman
SEE UNDER: LOVE
Hailed in Israel as the first novel to deal with the Holocaust from the standpoint of the children of the survivors
Translated by Betsy Rosenberg
0–374–25731–0 FS&G $19.45

THE YELLOW WIND
A nonfictional account of relations between Arab and Jew in Israel's occupied territories
Translated by Haim Watzman
0–374–29345–7 FS&G $17.95
0–385–29736–X FS&G pb $8.95

• **Shulamit Hareven**
THE MIRACLE HATER
"An entirely credible story of the Exodus as it might have been told by a hard and dusty but keen-eyed, wise veteran of that till-now unthinkable pilgrimage"—Reynolds Price
Translated by Hillel Halkin
0–86547–329–3 North Point pb $8.95

• **Yoram Kaniuk**
CONFESSIONS OF A GOOD ARAB
The personal and political predicament of a part-Jewish, part-Arab man caught in a tragic conflict. "Of the novelists I have discovered in translation . . . the three for whom I have the greatest admiration are Gabriel García Marquez, Peter Handke and Yoram Kaniuk"—Susan Sontag
Translated by Dalya Bilyu
0–8076–1210–3 Braziller $17.50

HIS DAUGHTER
A major best-seller in Israel
Translated by Seymour Simckes
0–8076–1215–4 Braziller $17.50

• **Joshua Kenaz**
AFTER THE HOLIDAYS
Translated by Dalya Bilu
0–15–103959–3 HBJ $16.95

• **Aharon Megged**
ASAHEL
Translated by Robert Whitehill & Susan C. Lilly
0–8008–0410–4 Taplinger $11.95

THE SHORT LIFE
A dissatisfied writer/academic composes a novel in her head but can never decide on the opening sentence
Translated by Miriam Arad
0–8008–7180–4 Taplinger $10.95

• **Sammi Michael**
REFUGE
A wartime tale of conflicting loyalties—both sexual and political—involving a communist Iraqi couple in Israel and the Arab comrade to whom the wife gives refuge
0–8276–0308–8 JPS $19.95

Amos Oz

Oz was the first contemporary Israeli writer to earn an international reputation. The kibbutz as an emblem of Israeli society—with its morals and ideals as well as the secret passions and seething hatreds—has informed much of his fiction. As a Zionist on the Israeli moderate left, he has become a leading spokesman for reconciliation with the Arabs.

BLACK BOX
A happily married woman obsessively attached to her former husband writes to him about her troubles with their adolescent son
0–15–112888–X HBJ $19.95
0–679–72185–1 Random House pb $8.95

ELSEWHERE, PERHAPS
Life in the kibbutz and its web of complex relationships
Translated by Nicholas De Lange
0–15–628475–8 HBJ pb $6.95

A PERFECT PEACE
A novel about attempted flight from the constricting pressures of life in Israel and, finally, a kind of reconciliation
Translated by Hillel Halkin
0–15–171696–X HBJ $16.95
0–14–008885–7 Penguin pb $6.95

SOUMCHI
A children's story about a young boy in modern-day Jerusalem who trades away one possession after another only to discover something much more wonderful
Translated by Penelope Farmer
Illustrated by William Papas
0–06–024621–9 Harper & Row $8.95

UNTO DEATH
Two short novels: one about a murderous French count on a crusade to the Holy Land, and the other the testimony of an elderly lecturer on Russian Jewry
0–15–693170–2 HBJ pb $3.95

Amos Oz (photo by Jerry Bauer)

• Yaakov Shabtai

PAST CONTINUOUS
One of the outstanding achievements in Israeli fiction, an epochal stream-of-consciousness novel about three intellectual, bohemian Tel Aviv friends
Translated by Dalya Bilu
0–8276–0239–1 JPS $16.95

PAST PERFECT
The posthumously published sequel to *Past Continuous*
Translated by Dalya Bilu
0–670–81308–7 Viking $18.95

• Nathan Shaham

THE OTHER SIDE OF THE WALL: Three Novellas
"Vivid refractions of Israeli society as experienced through the prism of the kibbutz"—*Judaic Book News*
Translated by Leonard Gold
0–8276–0223–5 JPS $13.95

• David Shahar

Known in France as the Israeli Proust, Shahar has won major awards in Israel, including the Agnon and Bialik prizes.

SUMMER IN THE STREET OF THE PROPHETS & A VOYAGE TO UR OF THE CHALDEES
The first two novels in the six-volume cycle *The Palace of Shattered Vessels*, a work of complex structure and texture about life in Jerusalem in the 1930s
Translated by Dalya Bilu
1–55584–068–X Weidenfeld & Nicolson $22.50

• Moshe Shamir

One of Israel's most important and popular novelists, Shamir started out as a characteristic writer of the Palmach generation and later turned to historical epics based on the biblical past.

THE HITTITE MUST DIE
Translated by Margaret Benaya
0–85222–231–9 Hebrew pb $5.95

KING OF FLESH AND BLOOD
Shamir's popular, historical novel about the political folly of the ambitious King Alexander Yannai
0–85222–220–3 Hebrew $5.95

• Anton Shammas

ARABESQUES
Shammas is a young "Israeli Palestinian" who grew up in an Arab village in Galilee. His choice of Hebrew and his mastery of the language are part of an attempt to create a new "identity card" for himself and his fellow Palestinians
0–06–015744–5 Harper & Row $16.95
0–06–091583–8 Harper & Row pb $8.95

• A.B. Yehoshua

Like Amos Oz, Yehoshua explores the ambivance of the Israeli attitude towards the Arab conflict. He began by writing surreal, parable-like stories under the influence of Agnon and Kafka but has lately moved to more realistic, psychological novels.

FIVE SEASONS
The story of Molkho, a middle-aged man set into an ambivalent, erotic freedom by the death of his long-ailing wife
0–385–233130–X Doubleday $19.95

A LATE DIVORCE
A brilliant psychological novel about nine days in the lives of the Kaminka family, narrated through a series of interior monologues
0–525–48399–3 Dutton pb $10.00

THE LOVER
The Yom Kippur War and its aftermath, structured around a husband's obsessive search for his wife's lover; an instant bestseller in Israel
0–525–48400–0 Dutton pb $10.95

POETRY

Early Israeli poets were all connected in some way with revolutionary Zionist ideology. Led by Yehudah Amichai, a "New Wave" in poetry in the 1950s helped introduce a more natural, colloquial idiom, often employing slang and conversational language.

Yehudah Amichai

Amichai was born in Germany but emigrated to Israel at the age of 12 in 1936. His main contribution has been in poetry, although he has written some important fiction. Amichai's insistence on the personal life of the dislocated citizen-soldier, who wants to love but must go instead to war, heralded the rebellion against the generation of '48.

THE SELECTED POETRY OF YEHUDAH AMICHAI
The best introduction and overview of Amichai's work; choice poems from 1955 to 1985
Translated by Stephen Mitchell & Chana Bloch
0–06–055001–5 Harper & Row $22.95

AMEN
Translated by the author & Ted Hughes
0–915943–22–0 Milkweed pb $7.95

GREAT TRANQUILITY: Questions and Answers
Translated by Glenda Abramson & Tudor Parfitt
0–06–091085–2 Harper & Row pb $7.95

LOVE POEMS
Selected from six previous collections
Translated by Glenda Abramson & Tudor Parfitt
0–06–014848–9 Harper & Row $12.00

SONGS OF JERUSALEM AND MYSELF
Jerusalem has been Amichai's home for 50 years, and no one knows it more intimately
Introduction by Ted Hughes
0–06–010097–4 Harper & Row $6.95
0–06–010101–6 Harper & Row pb $2.95

TRAVELS
Amichai's longest, most ambitious work is a series of 56 poems conceived as both poetic autobiography and fiction
Translated by Ruth Nevo
0–935296–62–X Sheep Meadow $13.95
0–935296–63–8 Sheep Meadow pb $9.95

IF YOU CAN'T FIND IT, LOOK IN THE INDEX

• **T. Carmi**

AT THE STONE OF LOSSES
Carmi, the pseudonym of Carmi Charny,
was born in New York City and emigrated
to Palestine in 1947 in time to fight in the
War of Independence. He was one of the
earliest new poets to draw upon American
and French modernist techniques
Translated by Grace Schulman
0–520–05106–8 California $20.00
0–520–05107–6 California pb $9.95

• **Amir Gilboa**

LIGHT OF LOST SUNS
Gilboa's family perished in the Holocaust,
and he fought in the Israeli War for
Independence. War has permeated all his
work; the sacrifice of Isaac is a recurrent
motif
Translated by Shirley Kaufman
0–89255–037–6 Persea $10.00

• **Abba Kovner**

As the partisan leader of the Vilna ghetto
and later a high-ranking commander of the
resistance, Kovner was transformed by the
Holocaust. His poetry deals in a highly
personal way with themes of national
struggle and anti-Nazi resistance.
**MY LITTLE SISTER & SELECTED
POEMS**
In the award-winning title poem, an ironic
travesty on a world without love or pity, a
brother narrates a few episodes in the life
of his "little sister" who was shielded from
the Nazis in a convent
Translated with preface by Shirley Kaufman
0–932440–20–7 Oberlin $13.50
0–932440–21–5 Oberlin pb $7.95

• **Dan Pagis**

POINTS OF DEPARTURE
The Holocaust and the various strategies
and displacements necessary to survive it
are central to the daring poetry of this
Romanian-born writer, himself a
Holocaust survivor
Translated by Stephen Mitchel
0–8276–0200–6 JPS $12.95
0–8276–0201–4 JPS pb $8.95

**VARIABLE DIRECTIONS: The Selected
Poetry of Dan Pagis**
Translated by Stephen Mitchell
0–86547–383–8 North Point $19.95
0–86547–384–6 North Point pb $9.95

Testimony

No no: they definitely were
human beings: uniforms, boots.
How to explain? They were created
in the image.

I was a shade.
A different creator made me.

And he in mercy left nothing of me
    that would die.
And I fled to him, floated up
    weightless, blue,
forgiving—I would even say:
    apologizing—
smoke to omnipotent smoke
that has no face or image.

Dan Pagis
POINTS OF DEPARTURE
Translated by Stephen Mitchell
0–8276–0200–6 JPS $12.95
0–8276–0201–4 JPS pb $8.95

• **Gabriel Preil**

**SUNSET POSSIBILITIES & OTHER
POEMS**
"Romantic, yet fancifully and nakedly
down-to-earth, dreamy as well as
diagnostic"—*NY Times*
Translated by Robert Friend
0–8276–0240–5 JPS $12.95
0–8276–0241–3 JPS pb $8.95

• **Dalia Ravikovitch**

A DRESS OF FIRE
One of the country's leading "New Wave"
poets, Ravikovitch employs ungrammatical
language and unfinished sentences with a
stylized slang to produce a new syntax.
Desolation and loss are her subjects: what
happens "when people break" is her
preoccupation
Translated by Chana Bloch
0–8180–1545–4 Sheep Meadow $7.95
0–8180–1546–2 Sheep Meadow pb $3.95

• **Avoth Yeshurun**

**THE SYRIAN-AFRICAN RIFT & OTHER
POEMS**
One of the most striking statements of the
"spiritual earthquake" that Israel
experienced in the 1970s
Translated by Howard Schimmel
0–8276–0181–6 JPS $11.95
0–8276–0182–4 JPS pb $7.95

• **Natan Zach**

**THE STATIC ELEMENT: Selected Poems
of Natan Zach**
Zach has been known since the 1950s as
the leading spokesman of the modernist
movement in Hebrew poetry. His work is
marked by a guarded, astringent wit
Translated by Natan Zach & Shulamit Yasny-Starkman
0–689–11318–8 Atheneum $12.95
0–689–11319–6 Atheneum pb $7.95

ANTHOLOGIES

• **Robert Alter, editor**

MODERN HEBREW LITERATURE
Excellent, scholarly introductions and
selections from Seforim, Peretz, Bialik,
Brenner, Barash, Agnon, Amichai, Oz, and
Yehoshua
0–87441–235–8 Behrman pb $10.95

• **Warren Bargad & Stanley F. Chyet,
translators**

**ISRAELI POETRY: A Contemporary
Anthology**
0–253–33140–4 Indiana $29.95
0–253–20356–2 Indiana pb $12.50

• **Stanley Burnshaw & others, editors**

THE MODERN HEBREW POEM ITSELF
0–674–57925–9 Harvard pb $14.95

• **T. Carmi, editor**

**THE PENGUIN BOOK OF HEBREW
VERSE**
An outstanding anthology, from biblical
verse to the modern poets
0–14–042197–1 Penguin pb $13.95

• **Myra Glazer, editor**

**BURNING AIR AND A CLEAR MIND:
Contemporary Israeli Women Poets**
Selections from 18 women poets
Illustrated by Shirley Faktor
0–8214–0572–1 Ohio $17.95
0–8214–0617–5 Ohio pb $8.95

• **Herbert S. Joseph, editor**

**MODERN ISRAELI DRAMA: An
Anthology**
0–8386–3104–5 Fairleigh Dickinson $30.00

• **Alan Lelchuk & Gerson Shaked,
editors**

**EIGHT GREAT HEBREW SHORT
STORIES**
A superb, informed selection. Includes
works by Gnessin, Brenner, Shami, Agnon,
Fogel, Oz, Knaz, and Yehoshua
0–452–00605–8 NAL pb $9.95

• **Curt Leviant**

**MASTERPIECES OF HEBREW
LITERATURE: A Treasury of 2000 Years
of Jewish Creativity**
0–87068–079–X Ktav pb $14.95

• **Robert Mezey, editor**

POEMS FROM THE HEBREW
Illustrated by Moishe Smith
0–690–63685–7 Harper & Row $12.70

• **Howard Schwartz & Anthony
Rudolf, editors**

**VOICES WITHIN THE ARK: The
Modern Jewish Poets**
0–380–76109–2 Avon pb $15.95

• **Leon I. Yudkin & Brian Chayette,
editors**

**MODERN HEBREW LITERATURE IN
ENGLISH TRANSLATION**
0–910129–80–0 Markus Wiener pb $14.50

HISTORY AND CRITICISM

• **Glenda Abramson**

MODERN HEBREW DRAMA
0–312–53988–6 Saint Martin's $29.95

• **Robert Alter**

**THE INVENTION OF HEBREW PROSE:
Modern Fiction and The Language of
Realism**
Focuses mainly on Mendele, Gnessin, and
Fogel in discussing how Hebrew writers
created a literary idiom before Hebrew was
revived as a spoken language
0–295–96622–X Washington $15.00

• **Nehama Aschkenasy**

**EVE'S JOURNEY: Feminine Images in
Hebraic Literary Tradition**
0–8122–8033–4 Pennsylvania $31.95

• **Risa Domb**

**THE ARAB IN HEBREW PROSE,
1911–1948**
How Hebrew writers have portrayed the
Arab
0–85303–203–3 Biblio $27.50

- Nathaniel Kravitz
THREE THOUSAND YEARS OF HEBREW LITERATURE: From the Earliest Times Through the 20th Century
0–8040–0505–2 Ohio $20.00

- Eisig Silberschlag
FROM RENAISSANCE TO RENAISSANCE: Hebrew Literature 1492–1967
0–87068–184–2 Ktav $25.00

- Reuben Wallenrod
THE LITERATURE OF MODERN ISRAEL
0–374–98198–1 Hippocrene $20.00

- Leon I. Yudkin
ESCAPE INTO SIEGE: A Survey of Israeli Literature Today
Israeli prose and poetry from the 1940s to the 1970s
0–19–710016–3 Oxford $18.50

Individual Writers

- David Aberbach
AT THE HANDLES OF THE LOCK
The first full-length psychological study of S.Y. Agnon, highlighting his obsession with the love triangle
0–19–710040–6 Oxford $34.50

- Arnold J. Band
NOSTALGIA AND NIGHTMARE: A Study in the Fiction of S.Y. Agnon
A pioneering study and still the basic reference work
0–520–00076–5 California $42.50

- David Aberbach
BIALIK
A good introduction, contrasting the public figure and the inner man
1–870015–05–3 Weidenfeld & Nicolson $15.95

- Jacques Kornberg, editor
AT THE CROSSROADS: Essays on Ahad Ha-am
0–87395–738–5 SUNY $34.50
0–87395–739–3 SUNY pb $10.95

- Arthur Hertzberg, editor
MENDELSSOHN
Part of the "Jewish Thinkers" series, with special attention to Mendelssohn as the founder of Reform, or liberal, Judaism
0–8021–1131–9 Grove $15.95

Yiddish Language and Literature

Yiddish developed among Jews in the Rhine region between the 10th and 12th centuries as a spoken vernacular adapted mainly from Middle High German and transliterated into Hebrew characters. Over the years, this "fusion language" assimilated words and expressions from many European and Near Eastern languages, yet it always managed to preserve its distinctive identity. While Hebrew remained the language of the Jewish religion, Yiddish became its vernacular counterpart.

Though early Yiddish produced many works of interest, it was not until the rise of Hasidism and the Jewish Enlightenment of the 18th and early 19th centuries that a renaissance in Yiddish literature began. Hasidic leaders and poets such as Baal Shem Tov and Rabbi Nachman of Breslov helped legitimize the literary use of Yiddish and set new standards with their inspired handling of folk material and their unique art of traditional storytelling.

The 19th and early 20th centuries were the "golden age" of Yiddish literature, followed by a period of experimentation. But all this intense, creative activity was brutally snuffed out by Nazism and Stalinism which eliminated over half of all Yiddish-speaking Jews. At its height before 1939 Yiddish was spoken by more than 11 million people; today there are no more than two to three million speakers and the language is slowly dying out. Yet the past decade has seen a renewed interest in the language and the literature.

EARLY YIDDISH

- Jacob ben Isaac Ashkenazi of Janow
TZ'ENAH UR'ENAH
These endearingly popular biblical paraphrases and wise sayings from contemporary sages, first published in 1622, were compiled by a serious scholar and itinerant preacher
Translated by Miriam S. Zakon

Volume 1: Bereishis with Haftoros
Focuses on the stories and lessons of the book of Genesis
0–89906–925–8 Mesorah $15.95
0–89906–926–6 Mesorah pb $11.95

Volume 2: Sh'mos-Vayikra with Haftoros
Follows the Bible from Exodus through Leviticus
0–89906–927–4 Mesorah $15.95
0–89906–928–2 Mesorah pb $11.95

Volume 3: Bamidbar-Devarim with Haftoros
Covers the books of Numbers and Deuteronomy
0–89906–929–0 Mesorah $15.95
0–89906–930–4 Mesorah pb $11.95

- Gluckel of Hameln
THE MEMOIRS OF GLUCKEL OF HAMELN
A Hamburg businesswoman at the turn of the 17th century offers a rare glimpse into Jewish life of the period
Translated by Marvin Lowenthal
0–8052–0572–1 Schocken pb $8.95

- Nachman of Breslov
RABBI NACHMAN'S STORIES
These moralistic and symbolic tales by the grandson of the founder of Hasidism influenced Yiddish writing and were widely publicized by Martin Buber
Translated by Aryeh Kaplan
0–930213–02–5 Breslov Research $14.95

THE GOLDEN AGE

By the late 19th and early 20th centuries, Yiddish entered its classical phase, producing three writers of genius: Mendel Mokher Seforim (the pen name of S.Y. Abramovitsch); I.L. Peretz; and Sholom Aleichem (the pen name of S. Rabinowitz). Drawing from both traditional and modern sources, these pioneers fused the vitality of folk and Hasidic tales with the literary sophistication of the Russian novel.

- Sholom Aleichem
FROM THE FAIR: The Autobiography of Sholom Aleichem
The work that introduced the fictionalized autobiography into Yiddish fiction takes us from Aleichem's childhood to his first love and earliest attempts at writing
Translated by Curt Leviant
0–14–008830–X Penguin pb $7.95

HOLIDAY TALES OF SHOLOM ALEICHEM
"Seven stories, two available for the first time in English, capture the essence of the Jewish holidays of Passover, Purim, Chanukah and Sukkot"—*Judaica Book News*
Translated by Aliza Shevrin
Illustrated by Thomas DiGrazia
0–689–71034–8 Macmillan pb $4.95

THE NIGHTINGALE, OR THE SAGA OF YOSELE SOLOVEY THE CANTOR
Translated by Aliza Shevrin
0–399–13098–5 Putnam $16.95
0–452–25933–9 NAL pb $8.95

TEVYE THE DAIRYMAN & THE RAILROAD STORIES
The tales of Tevye and his daughters were the basis of *Fiddler on the Roof* but, according to the translator, they are "more reckless, giddy, wildly funny and wrenchingly painful—and far less sentimental"
Translated by Hillel Halkin
Edited by Ruth R. Wisse
0–8052–4026–8 Schocken $19.95

- I.L. Peretz
SELECTED STORIES
Peretz, who initially looked down on Yiddish as "jargon," became one of its great innovative stylists. His folklike yet sophisticated tales introduced a terse, fast-

paced prose that helped bring Yiddish out of the shtetl and into the modern world
Edited by Irving Howe & Eliezer Greenberg
0–8052–0496–2 Schocken pb $6.95

● **Mendele Mokher Seforim**
TRAVELS AND ADVENTURES OF BENJAMIN THE THIRD
A satiric picture of the unrealistic, narrow, day-dreaming life of the ghetto with its Don Quixote-like Benjamin setting off in search of the legendary Ten Tribes, by the writer known as "the grandfather of Yiddish literature"
0–8052–0176–9 Schocken pb $5.75

THE 20TH CENTURY

In the 20th century, Yiddish literature underwent a rapid series of experiments and movements. In America, Yiddish was introduced by the "sweatshop" or labor poets like Morris Rosenfeld, champion of the immigrant working masses. Abraham Cahan turned his Yiddish *Jewish Daily Forward* into the largest foreign-language daily newspaper in America. A talented group of Yiddish poets known as "Di Yunge" flourished in New York around the First World War, linking Yiddish to the mainstream of European modernism.

● **S. Ansky**
THE DYBBUK
Ansky's highly-wrought symbolic drama about the primacy of spirit over force in Judaism is based on the folk belief in possessed souls
Translated by S. Morris Engel
0–89526–904–X Regnery pb $5.95

● **Sholem Asch**
THE APOSTLE
Part of Asch's epic and controversial New Testament trilogy—along with *Mary* and *The Nazarene*—in which he sought a religious reconciliation between Judaism and Christianity
0–88184–167–6 Carroll & Graf pb $2.98

MARY
0–88184–141–2 Carroll & Graf pb $10.95

THE NAZARENE
0–88184–048–3 Carroll & Graf pb $10.95

EAST RIVER
A sweeping saga of immigrants in turn-of-the-century New York
0–88184–280–X Carroll & Graf pb $4.50

THE MOTHER
0–910129–76–2 Markus, Wiener pb $8.95

THREE CITIES
St. Petersburg, Warsaw, and Moscow; Jewish life in pre- and post-revolutionary Russia
0–88184–009–2 Carroll & Graf pb $10.50

● **David Bergelson**
WHEN ALL IS SAID AND DONE
Among the leading figures of 20th-century Yiddish literature, Bergelson depicts the decay of the Jewish bourgeoisie in pre-revolutionary Russia. In 1952 he was shot on Stalin's orders along with 23 other notable Soviet Jews
Translated by Bernard Martin
0–8214–0392–3 Ohio pb $10.00

● **Meir Blinkin**
STORIES BY MEIR BLINKIN
Blinkin died at 36, a promising member of the "Di Yunge" (The Young) literary group, which rebelled against the social emphasis of the older generation and insisted on a more personal, inward-looking art. These stories are of the shtetl and the Lower East Side of New York
Translated by Max Rosenfeld
Introduction by Ruth R. Wisse
0–87395–818–7 SUNY $10.95

● **Chaim Grade**
THE AGUNAH
The story of a young woman of Vilna whose husband has not returned from World War I and her effort to be legally married again
Translated by Curt Leviant
0–932232–00–0 Menorah pb $3.95

Illustration from Yiddish Folktales *edited by Beatrice Silverman Weinrich (Pantheon)*

MY MOTHER'S SABBATH DAYS: A Memoir
Believing that the Nazis were interested only in able-bodied men, Grade fled to the Soviet Union and left his wife and mother behind; when he returned, he found them dead and his hometown destroyed
Translated by Channa K. Goldstein & Inna H. Grade
0–8052–0839–9 Schocken pb $9.95

RABBIS AND WIVES
Three novellas—*The Rebbetzin, Laybe-layzar's Courtyard* and *The Oath*—that explore marital relationships against the background of Lithuanian Jewish life between the wars
Translated by Harold Rabinowitz & Inna H. Grade
0–394–50979–X Knopf $15.45
0–8052–0840–2 Schocken pb $8.95

THE YESHIVA
A two-volume set. "The first page of *The Yeshiva* states that Tsemakh Atlas, a yeshiva scholar and rabbi, doubts the existence of God and the divinity of the Torah, thus announcing a theme never before attempted in Yiddish literature"— Curt Leviant
Translated by Curt Leviant
0–932232–05–1 Menorah pb $11.95

● **Moyshe-Leyb Halpern**
IN NEW YORK: A Selection
A leading member of the modernist "Di Yunge," Halpern established a new kind of verse narrative, combining folk and didactic elements with American poetry, particularly that of Whitman
Translated by Kathryn Hellerstein
0–8276–0209–X JPS $14.95
0–8276–0210–3 JPS pb $9.95

● **Samuel Lewin**
BETWEEN TWO ABYSSES
The first novel of a trilogy set in a Polish shtetl between the wars covers the collapse of the old way of life and the resulting scramble for survival, the generational struggle, and the moral and political issues that dominated the Jewish community
Translated by Joseph Leftwich
0–8453–4795–0 Cornwall $12.95

DARK MOUNTAINS AND BLUE VALLEYS
Part 2 of the trilogy
Translated by Joseph Leftwich
0–8453–4804–3 Cornwall $12.95

SHINING THROUGH THE CLOUDS
Part 3 of the trilogy
Translated by Joseph Leftwich
0–8453–4805–1 Cornwall $12.95

● **Israel Rabon**
THE STREET
A surrealistic novel about a Jewish soldier who returns to Lodz at the end of World War I and joins the ranks of the unemployed transients
Translated by Leonard Wolf
0–8052–3981–2 Schocken pb $14.95

I.J. Singer
The brother of I.B. Singer, Israel Joshua Singer is himself an important literary figure, the author of massive social novels about Jewish life in Eastern Europe as well as numerous short stories and plays.

THE BROTHERS ASHKENAZI
0–88184–192–7 Carroll & Graf pb $9.95

THE FAMILY CARNOVSKY
A tragic chronicle of three generations of assimilated Jewish families in Nazi Germany
0–8052–0859–3 Schocken pb $11.95

OF A WORLD THAT IS NO MORE
Reminiscences from his childhood
0–571–14685–6 Faber & Faber pb $7.95

YOSHE KALB
Yoshe Kalb ("The Sinners") reworks a popular folk legend about a sensitive young man who marries the daughter of a powerful rabbi and is thrust into the dark world of corrupt Hasidic dynasties
0–8052–0860–7 Schocken pb $8.95

ISAAC BASHEVIS SINGER

"In the years I have been writing I have heard many discouraging words about my themes and languages. I was told that Jewishness and Yiddishness were dying, the short story was out of vogue and about to disappear from the literary market. Some critics decided that the art of telling stories with a beginning, middle and end—as Aristotle demanded—was archaic, a primitive form of fiction. I heard similar degrading opinions about the value of folklore in the literature of our times. I was living in a civilization which despised the old and worshipped the young. But somehow I never took these dire threats seriously. I belong to an old tribe and I know that literature thrives best on ancient faith, timeless hopes and illusions."—I.B. Singer

THE COLLECTED STORIES OF ISAAC BASHEVIS SINGER
Forty-seven of his finest. A cornucopia of invention
0–374–12631–3 Farrar, Straus & Giroux $19.95
0–374–51788–6 Farrar, Straus & Giroux pb $12.95

A CROWN OF FEATHERS
A book of short stories. "A natural storyteller who moves at his own pace, confident of his powers, fertile in invention, able to hold the reader as long as he wishes"—NY Times
0–374–13217–8 Farrar, Straus & Giroux $12.95
0–374–51624–3 Farrar, Straus & Giroux pb $7.95

THE DEATH OF METHUSELAH & OTHER STORIES
0–452–26215–1 NAL pb $8.95

ENEMIES, A LOVE STORY
This farcical comedy of Herman Broder and his three wives is also a subtle exploration of refugees from the Holocaust
0–374–51522–0 Farrar, Straus & Giroux pb $8.95

A FRIEND OF KAFKA & OTHER STORIES
0–374–15880–0 Farrar, Straus & Giroux $12.95

GIMPEL THE FOOL & OTHER STORIES
Translated by Saul Bellow & others
0–374–50052–5 Farrar, Straus & Giroux pb $8.95

THE IMAGE & OTHER STORIES
0–374–52079–8 Farrar, Straus & Giroux $8.95

IN MY FATHER'S COURT
A beautiful, evocative memoir of growing up in Warsaw as the son of a famous rabbi
0–449–24074–6 Fawcett pb $2.50

AN ISAAC BASHEVIS SINGER READER
0–374–17747–3 Farrar, Straus & Giroux $17.95

LOVE AND EXILE: A Memoir
Includes A Little Boy in Search of God, A Young Man in Search of Love, and Lost in America, three parts of Singer's spiritual autobiography that take him from his childhood in Poland to his mid-30s in America
0–374–51992–7 Farrar, Straus & Giroux pb $9.95

THE MAGICIAN OF LUBLIN
"Tales about Yasha Mazur, who makes his living on the circuses and theatres of nineteenth-century Poland. He can skate on high wire, eat fire . . . and above all, charm any woman"—Time
0–449–21479–6 Fawcett pb $3.50

THE MANOR & THE ESTATE
"The Manor begins with the Polish uprising against the Czar in 1863 and The Estate ends in the last years of the nineteenth century—an epoch when humanism undertook to practice what it had preached for generations"—I.B. Singer
0–374–52080–1 FS&G pb $12.95

THE FAMILY MOSKAT
Life in the Warsaw ghetto from the beginning of the century to Hitler; the third of a trilogy beginning with The Manor and The Estate
0–374–50392–3 FS&G pb $12.95
0–449–24066–9 Fawcett pb $2.95

OLD LOVE & OTHER STORIES
0–374–22581–8 Farrar, Straus & Giroux $10.95
0–449–24343–5 Fawcett pb $2.50

PASSIONS
0–374–22993–7 Farrar, Straus & Giroux $8.95

THE PENITENT
A refugee from Nazism becomes a rich, philandering businessman in America before seeking—and finding—salvation in the ancient faith of his fathers
0–449–20612–2 Fawcett pb $2.95

SATAN IN GORAY
A multilayered historical tale of religious hysteria in a Polish shtetl in the mid-17th century, based on the false Messianism of Shabbtai Zevi
Translated by Jacob Sloan
0–374–25404–4 Farrar, Straus & Giroux $8.95

THE SEANCE & OTHER STORIES
0–374–50832–1 Farrar, Straus & Giroux pb $6.95

SHORT FRIDAY & OTHER STORIES
0–374–26300–0 Farrar, Straus & Giroux $10.95

SHOSHA
A novel about a writer caught in Poland on the eve of the war and his lingering attachment to his childhood sweetheart, who has never grown up
0–374–26336–1 Farrar, Straus & Giroux $8.95
0–449–20808–7 Fawcett pb $3.50

THE SLAVE
Jacob of Josefov, a learned son of rich parents, is waylaid by robbers and sold as a slave
Translated by Cecil Hemley
0–374–50680–9 Farrar, Straus & Giroux $7.95

THE SPINOZA OF MARKET STREET & OTHER STORIES
Translated by Elaine Gottleib
0–374–26776–6 Farrar, Straus & Giroux $8.95
0–374–50256–0 Farrar, Straus & Giroux pb $4.95

● **Isaac Bashevis Singer & Richard Burgin**
CONVERSATIONS WITH ISAAC BASHEVIS SINGER
Singer displays his usual candor and outspokenness
0–374–51994–3 Farrar, Straus & Giroux $6.95

Children's Books

Lovers of Singer will enjoy his children's books—illustrated by such outstanding artists as Uri Shulevitz and Maurice Sendak—because they combine the same fluent storytelling with the same curious humanity.

Children are as puzzled by passing time as grown-ups. What happens to a day once it is gone? Where are all our yesterdays with their joys and sorrows? Literature helps us to remember the past with its many moods. To the storyteller, yesterday is still here as are the years and the decades gone by . . . I dedicate this book to the many children who had no chance to grow up because of stupid wars and cruel persecutions which devastated cities and destroyed innocent families. I hope that when the readers of these stories become men and women they will love not only their own children but all good children everywhere.

Isaac Bashevis Singer
ZLATEH THE GOAT & OTHER STORIES
Translated by Elizabeth Shub
0–06–440147–2 Harper & Row pb $4.95

● **Isaac Bashevis Singer**
ALONE IN THE WILD FOREST
Translated by Elizabeth Shub
Illustrated by Margot Zemach
0–374–30238–3 Farrar, Straus & Giroux $8.95

A DAY OF PLEASURE: Stories of a Boy Growing up in Warsaw
Photographs by Roman Vishniac
0–374–41696–6 Farrar, Straus & Giroux pb $3.95

ELIJAH THE SLAVE
The Hebrew legend—possibly the most significant for Yiddish writers—retold with transparent simplicity
Illustrated by Antonio Frasconi
0–374–32084–5 Farrar, Straus & Giroux $14.95
0–374–42047–5 Farrar, Straus & Giroux pb $4.95

THE FOOLS OF CHELM AND THEIR HISTORY
Translated by Elizabeth Shub
Illustrated by Uri Shulevitz
0–374–32444–1 Farrar, Straus & Giroux $11.95

THE GOLEM
Illustrated by Uri Shulevitz
0–374–32741–6 Farrar, Straus & Giroux pb $4.98

MAZEL AND SHLIMAZEL OR THE MILK OF A LIONESS
Illustrated by Margot Zemach
0–374–34884–7 Farrar, Straus & Giroux $11.95

NAFTALI THE STORYTELLER AND HIS HORSE, SUS
Illustrated by Margot Zemach
0–374–45487–6 Farrar, Straus & Giroux pb $3.50

THE POWER OF LIGHT: Eight Stories for Hanukkah
Illustrated by Irene Lieblich
0–374–36099–5 Farrar, Straus & Giroux $13.95

REACHES OF HEAVEN: A Story of the Baal Shem Tov
0–374–24733–1 Farrar, Straus & Giroux $15.00
0–374–51648–0 Farrar, Straus & Giroux pb $8.95

STORIES FOR CHILDREN
0–374–37266–7 Farrar, Straus & Giroux $16.95
0–374–46489–8 Farrar, Straus & Giroux pb $7.95

A TALE OF THREE WISHES
Illustrated by Irene Lieblich
0–374–37370–1 Farrar, Straus & Giroux $11.95

WHEN SHLEMIEL WENT TO WARSAW & OTHER STORIES
Translated by Elizabeth Shub
Illustrated by Margot Zemach
0–374–38316–2 Farrar, Straus & Giroux $10.95
0–374–48365–5 Farrar, Straus & Giroux pb $3.45

WHY NOAH CHOSE THE DOVE
Translated by Elizabeth Shub
Illustrated by Eric Carle
0–374–38420–7 Farrar, Straus & Giroux $13.95
0–374–48382–5 Farrar, Straus & Giroux pb $3.95

ZLATEH THE GOAT & OTHER STORIES
Translated by Elizabeth Shub
Illustrated by Maurice Sendak
0–06–440147–2 Harper & Row pb $4.95

THE LANGUAGE

These books range from the scholarly to the frolicsome, but all have a similar purpose: to preserve this much-loved language and to convey its salty, racy, flavor and the culture for which it speaks.

• Nathan Ausubel, editor
A TREASURY OF JEWISH FOLKLORE
A compendium of stories, traditions, legends, humor, wisdom, and folk songs
0–517–50293–3 Crown $14.95

A TREASURY OF JEWISH HUMOR
0–87131–546–7 M. Evans pb $14.95

• Lillian M. Feinsilver
THE TASTE OF YIDDISH
Basic terms and unique insights into the Jewish cultural experience
0–498–02515–2 Oaktree pb $14.95

• John Geipel
MAME LOSHN: The Making of Yiddish
A popular little book on the "mother tongue" for nonspecialists
0–904526–73–9 Riverrun pb $9.00

• Emmanuel Goldsmith
MODERN YIDDISH CULTURE: The Story of the Yiddish Language Movement
Edited by Malcolm J. Robinson
0–933503–95–4 Shapolsky pb $10.95

• Fred Kogos
DICTIONARY OF YIDDISH SLANG
A bilingual dictionary of "popular and familiar, odd and peppery, words, sayings, proverbs, colloquialisms, maxims, curses, maledictions, taboos, vulgarisms and obscenities"
0–8065–0347–5 Lyle Stuart pb $5.95

INSTANT YIDDISH
0–8065–0114–6 Lyle Stuart pb $3.95

1,001 YIDDISH PROVERBS
Brief, pungent and illustrated. "In it can be described the longings and strivings, the trials and tribulations, the joys and griefs of the Jewish people"—Fred Kogos
0–8065–0455–2 Lyle Stuart pb $3.95

Illustration from Yiddish Folktales *edited by Beatrice Silverman Weinrich (Pantheon)*

• Shirley Kumove, editor
WORDS LIKE ARROWS: A Treasury of Yiddish Folk Sayings
Aphorisms, maxims, and proverbs arranged by subject, in both Yiddish and English
Illustrated by Frank Newfeld
0–446–38193–4 Warner pb $9.95

Leo Rosten
HOORAY FOR YIDDISH
0–671–43026–2 Simon & Schuster pb $7.95

THE JOYS OF YIDDISH
"A cheerful lexicon of Yiddish words which have become part of the English language, plus English words and phrases which have been transformed into Yinglish; the whole garnished with stories, jokes, parables, revered quotations from the Talmud and a glittering gallery of writers, rabbis, sages, wits, with impulsive side trips into the faith, folklore, genius and history of the Jews—from their servitude in Babylon to their magnitude in Beverly Hills"—Leo Rosten
0–671–47349–2 Washington Square pb $4.95

• Ruth Rubin
VOICES OF A PEOPLE: The Story of Yiddish Folksong
From the 16th century on, with music for certain songs
0–8276–0121–2 JPS pb $8.95

• Ruth Rubin, editor
A TREASURY OF JEWISH FOLKSONG
Illustrated by T. Herzl Rome
0–8052–0528–4 Schocken $12.50

• Max Weinreich
HISTORY OF THE YIDDISH LANGUAGE
The monumental life work of the ranking historian of Yiddish, a cardinal contribution to comparative linguistics and Jewish cultural history
Translated by Shlomo Noble & Joshua A. Fishman
0–226–88604–2 Chicago (2-volume set) $60.00

• Uriel Weinreich
COLLEGE YIDDISH: An Introduction to the Yiddish Language and to Jewish Life and Culture
Intended for a one-year college course or for learning on one's own. "Strange as it seems, a rational, practical textbook of Yiddish happens to be a pioneering work"—Roman Jakobson
Introduction by Roman Jakobson
0–914512–04–8 Yivo Institute $15.00

• Uriel Weinreich, editor
THE FIELD OF YIDDISH: Studies in Yiddish Language, Folklore, and Literature
A scholarly collection of essays for the specialist, a milestone in launching serious study of Yiddish following the Holocaust
0–936368–02–0 Lexik House $12.50

• Uriel Weinreich & Beatrice Weinreich
SAY IT IN YIDDISH
0–486–20815–X Dover pb $2.95

ANTHOLOGIES

• Sarah Betsky, editor & translator
ONIONS AND CUCUMBERS AND PLUMS: 46 Yiddish Poems in English
With Yiddish and English on facing pages
0–8143–1080–X Wayne State $12.50

• Jehiel B. Cooperman, editor
AMERICA IN YIDDISH POETRY: An Anthology
Translated by Sarah C. Cooperman
0–682–46879–7 Exposition $10.00

• Moses Gaster, translator
MA'ASEH BOOK: Book of Jewish Tales and Legends
Talmudic and midrashic tales from early Yiddish literature
0–8276–0189–1 JPS pb $10.95

• Jacob Glatstein
ANTHOLOGY OF HOLOCAUST LITERATURE
A wide-ranging selection on the Holocaust, by those who experienced it
0–689–70343–0 Atheneum pb $8.95

• Benjamin & Barbara Harshav
AMERICAN YIDDISH POETRY: A Bilingual Anthology
0–520–04842–3 California $55.00

Irving Howe, Ruth R. Wisse &
Khone Shmeruk, editors
THE PENGUIN BOOK OF MODERN YIDDISH VERSE
Superb selection with an informed introduction consisting of letters between Irving Howe and Ruth Wisse—possibly the two most important scholars and critics associated with Yiddish literature today
0–14–009472–5 Penguin pb $14.95

• Irving Howe & Eliezer Greenberg, editors
ASHES OUT OF HOPE: Fiction by Soviet-Yiddish Writers
Includes "Joseph Schur," "The Hole Through Which Life Slips," and "Civil War" by David Bergelson; "Zelmenyaner" by M. Kulbak; and "Under a Fence" by Der Nister
0–8052–0605–1 Schocken pb $4.95

A TREASURY OF YIDDISH POETRY
A pioneering work that brought the best poets in Yiddish to the attention of English-language readers; with a wonderfully illuminating introduction
0–8052–0546–2 Schocken pb $10.95

A TREASURY OF YIDDISH STORIES
An excellent collection from the 19th and 20th centuries
Illustrated by Ben Shahn
0–8052–0400–8 Schocken pb $13.95

YIDDISH STORIES OLD AND NEW
0–8234–0246–0 Holiday House pb $5.95

• Joseph Landis, editor & translator
THREE GREAT JEWISH PLAYS
Ansky's *The Dybbuk*, Asch's *God of Vengeance*, and Leivick's *The Golem*
0–936839–04–X Applause pb $8.95

• Joseph Leftwich
GREAT YIDDISH WRITERS OF THE TWENTIETH CENTURY
0–87668–952–7 Jason Aronson $40.00

• Joseph Leftwich, editor
AN ANTHOLOGY OF MODERN YIDDISH LITERATURE
Includes 42 Yiddish writers, with biographical notes, glossary, and bibliography
90–2793–496–7 Mouton de Gruyter $18.00

• David Lifson, translator
EPIC AND FOLK PLAYS FROM THE YIDDISH THEATRE
Includes *Favorfn Vinkl* by Hirshbein, *Hirsh Lekert* by Leivick, *Yankel Boyla* by L. Kobrin, and *Recruits* by Aksenfeld
0–8386–1082–X Fairleigh Dickinson $25.00

• Isaac Metzkerf, editor
A BINTEL BRIEF
A "bundle of letters" from the pages of the *Daily Forward,* New York's legendary Yiddish-language newspaper, offering indelible glimpses of immigrant life
0–87441–345–1 Behrman House pb $6.95

Joachim Neugroschel, editor & translator
GREAT WORKS OF JEWISH FANTASY
0–87951–242–3 Overlook pb $15.95

• Howard Schwartz & Anthony Rudolf, editors
VOICES WITHIN THE ARK
Selections from Jewish poets around the globe
0–380–76109–2 Avon pb $15.95

• Beatrice Silverman Weinreich, editor
YIDDISH FOLKTALES
A collection of nearly 200 tales
0–394–54618–0 Pantheon $21.95

• Ruth Whitman
AN ANTHOLOGY OF MODERN YIDDISH POETRY
Introduction by Robert Szulkin
Preface by Isaac Bashevis Singer
0–686–29291–X Workmen's Circle pb $4.95

• Ruth R. Wisse, editor
A SHTETL & OTHER YIDDISH NOVELLAS
Includes *At the Depot* by Bergelson, *Romance of a Horsethief* by Opatoshu, *Behind a Mask* by Ansky, and *Of Bygone Days* by Sforim
0–8143–1848–7 Wayne State $17.50
0–8143–1849–5 Wayne State pb $9.95

HISTORY AND CRITICISM

• Ruth Adler
WOMEN OF THE SHTETL: Through the Eye of I.L. Peretz
0–8386–2336–0 Fairleigh Dickinson $17.50

• Sol Gittleman
FROM SHTETL TO SUBURBIA: The Family in Jewish Literary Imagination
0–8070–6364–9 Beacon $12.95

SHOLOM ALEICHEM: A Non-Critical Introduction
90–2792–606–9 Mouton de Gruyter pb $21.95

• Judith Goldberg
LAUGHTER THROUGH TEARS: The Yiddish Cinema
A retrospective examination of some of the 130 Yiddish films made between 1910 and 1941
0–8386–3074–X Fairleigh Dickinson $22.50

• Janet Hadda
PASSIONATE WOMEN, PASSIVE MEN: Suicide in Yiddish Literature
A provocative work of literary criticism, with some debt to psychoanalysis but an altogether original approach
0–88706–597–X SUNY pb $12.95

• Sol Liptzin
A HISTORY OF YIDDISH LITERATURE
A survey of Yiddish literature from its medieval origins to 1970
0–8246–0307–9 Jonathan David pb $12.95

• Sanford Pinsker
SCHLEMIEL AS METAPHOR: Studies in the Yiddish and American Jewish Novel
Includes a look at the work of Seforim, Sholom Aleichem, and I.B. Singer
0–8093–0480–5 Southern Illinois $6.95

• Maurice Samuel
THE WORLD OF SHOLOM ALEICHEM
An evocative, almost picaresque recreation
0–689–70709–6 Atheneum pb $9.95

• Nahma Sandrow
VAGABOND STARS: A World History of Yiddish Theater
0–87910–060–5 Limelight pb $13.95

• Meyer Waxman
A HISTORY OF JEWISH LITERATURE
From biblical times to the 20th century, with generous portions on Yiddish literature; in six volumes
0–8453–8640–9 Cornwall $50.00

• Shimon Wincelberg & Anita Wincelberg, editors
THE SAMURAI OF VISHOGROD: The Notebooks of Jacob Marateck
Translated by Anita Wincelberg
0–8276–0074–7 JPS pb $5.95

• Ruth R. Wisse
A LITTLE LOVE IN BIG MANHATTAN: Two Yiddish Poets
A double biography of two opposing personalities, Mani Leib and Moishe Leib Halpern, two of the most prominent figures of the "Di Yunge" group
0–674–53659–2 Harvard $25.00

African Literature

Africa has a long tradition—or, more precisely, many distinct traditions—of epics, praise songs, riddles, and proverbs, in some cases committed to memory and recited by generations of carefully trained bard/historians known as *griots*. The written literature is, however, mostly a 20th-century phenomenon. This literature is influenced by both western literature and Africa's own oral tradition.

African writers are not yet widely read in the United States, but they are taken very seriously in their own countries. Almost all of the major writers—Soyinka, Achebe, Ngugi, Laye, to name a few—have been banned or jailed for extended periods in their homelands.

WEST AFRICA

• Chinua Achebe
The Nigerian novelist Chinua Achebe, a fine stylist and an astute social critic, is one of the best-known African writers in the West and his novels are often assigned in university courses. He casts a cold eye on

➤ **FOR OVERSEAS ORDERING INFORMATION, SEE PAGE 1**

the British colonial administration, post-Independence corruption, and the ravages of civil war.

ANTHILLS OF THE SAVANNAH
Achebe's first book in almost 20 years deals with three friends who have come to play major roles in the fictional African nation of Nangan: one as the country's corrupt president, another as a troubled statesman, and the third as an opposition journalist. A riveting portrayal of an educated elite losing touch with the common people
0–385–01664–6 Doubleday $16.95

THINGS FALL APART
Achebe's most famous novel, the first in a trilogy, brilliantly portrays the impact of colonialism on a traditional Nigerian village at the turn of the century. Its hero, Obi Okonkwo, epitomizes both the nobility and the rigidity of the traditional culture
0–8392–5006–1 Astor-Honor pb $7.95
0–435–90001–3 Heinemann pb $4.00

ARROW OF GOD
The second book in the trilogy examines life under colonialism in the early years of the 20th century. The protagonist is a head priest who scores a series of psychological victories over the British administration but is eventually defeated
0–385–01480–5 Doubleday pb $7.95

NO LONGER AT EASE
The trilogy concludes with this fine novel about how a high-ranking and respected villager's western education ends up separating him from his tribal culture
0–8392–1077–9 Astor-Honor $12.95
0–8392–5008–8 Astor-Honor pb $7.95

BEWARE SOUL BROTHER
0–435–90120–6 Heinemann pb $6.50

CHIKE AND THE RIVER
.0–521–04003–5 Cambridge $2.95

GIRLS AT WAR & OTHER STORIES
Tales from the Biafran war and the period of disintegration that followed
0–449–30046–3 Fawcett pb $2.95

● Ama A. Aidoo
OUR SISTER KILL JOY
A play about the difficulties experienced by an American woman who marries into a Ghanaian family
0–88357–064–5 NOK $9.95
0–88357–065–3 NOK pb $4.95

SUNSET IN BIAFRA
An eloquent depiction of the havoc wrought by the Nigerian war with Biafra
0–435–90140–0 Heinemann pb $6.50

● Ayi K. Armah
Ghana's greatest novelist, Armah combines a tremendous versatility of language with deep-rooted social concerns. Although Armah has written few books, his impact on African letters has been considerable.

THE BEAUTYFUL ONES ARE NOT YET BORN
A remarkable portrait of corruption in post-Independence Ghana and of the

disillusionment of the idealistic "been-tos." The graphic description of physical corruption merges with a powerful and detailed portrait of the morally bankrupt officialdom
0–435–90043–9 Heinemann pb $6.50

TWO THOUSAND SEASONS
Based on myth, legend, and praise songs, this unusual book narrates Africa's history through African eyes
0–88378–046–1 Third World pb $8.95

● Mongo Beti
The Cameroonian writer Mongo Beti (a pseudonym for Alexandre Biyidi) is known for his lively and scathingly funny attacks on quasi-westernized Africans and on the role of the church in Africa.

MISSION TO KALA
Jean-Marie Medza goes to the distant country town of Kala to rescue his aunt and incidentally teach the ignorant villagers about the joys of civilization, with hilarious results
0–435–90013–7 Heinemann pb $6.50

THE POOR CHRIST OF BOMBA
The weakness of the Christian mission in Africa is revealed by the actions of a well-intentioned but confused black acolyte, an obtuse Reverend Father Superior, and a salacious cook who takes advantage of the general chaos
0–435–90088–9 Heinemann pb $7.00

● John P. Clark
CASUALTIES: Poems, 1966–1968
Clark is a leading Nigerian playwright and poet whose work has been performed in England by Soyinka's troupe, Masks. His poems are concise, powerful, and imagistic
0–8419–0096–5 Holmes & Meier $14.50

● William Conton
THE AFRICAN
This influential Sierra Leonean novel explores prejudice, presenting a solution in the utopian form of a United States of Africa based on Christian ethics and African nobility of soul
0–435–90012–9 Heinemann pb $6.00

● Bernard Dadié
The best known writer from Côte d'Ivoire (and his country's Director of Cultural Affairs), Dadié wrote about the daily life of the common people.

CLIMBIE
An autobiographical novel about a young Ivorian's growing awareness of the evils of colonialism
Translated by Karen Chapman
0–8419–0080–9 Holmes & Meier $14.50

● Birago Diop
TALES OF AMADOU KOUMBA
A retelling of traditional Senegalese stories told to the author by the griot Amadou Koumba. Widely popular and critically well-received in France, several of the tales were made into plays
0–582–78587–1 Longman pb $8.95

● M.S. Dipoko
BECAUSE OF WOMEN
Dipoko writes frankly about love and the unfortunate destinies of lovers who swim against society's tide. In this novel, a man is torn between two women who love him—a traditional African pregnant with his child and a seductive modern woman
0–435–90057–9 Heinemann pb $6.50

● Cyprian Ekwensi
This Nigerian writer is one of the most popular and prolific of African novelists. His work has been praised for its insights into the problems faced by rural Africans when circumstances force them into the towns and for his vibrant descriptions of town life.

JAGUA NANA
The most acclaimed of Ekwensi's novels tells the story of Jagua Nana, a socially ambitious prostitute who has taken her name from the automobile, the Jaguar
0–435–90678–X Heinemann pb $7.50

LOKOTOWN & OTHER STORIES
Vibrant stories of life in the seething, dirty, dangerous, but always exciting town
0–435–90019–6 Heinemann pb $6.50

● Buchi Emecheta
THE RAPE OF SHAVI
Foreigners who fall from the sky into the mythic and idyllic kingdom of Shavi prove to be the downfall of the local citizens who come to their rescue
0–8076–1118–2 Braziller pb $6.95

SECOND-CLASS CITIZEN
A Nigerian woman's search for independence. "One of the most informative books about contemporary African life that I have read"—Alice Walker
0–8076–1066–6 Braziller pb $6.95

Buchi Emecheta (photo by Valerie Wilmer, courtesy of Braziller)

● Olaudah Equiano

EQUIANO'S TRAVELS: His Autobiography

The classic narrative of a West African who was brought as a slave boy to England and educated there. First published in London in 1745, Equiano's narrative proved so popular it went into 17 consecutive printings

Edited by Paul Edwards
0–435–90010–2 Heinemann pb $8.00

● Nuruddin Farah

MAPS

A Somali boy orphaned in the war with Ethiopia is brought up by a disreputable Ethiopian woman. "A true and rich work of art"—Salman Rushdie
0–394–75548–0 Pantheon pb $7.95

● Sheikh Hamidou Kane

AMBIGUOUS ADVENTURE

Kane seeks to capture the somber beauty of the Koran in this exquisitely written novel about a young man's Islamic education, his subsequent estrangement from both Islamic and western thought, and his fear of mortality
0–435–90119–2 Heinemann pb $7.50

● Camara Laye

One of the most influential francophone African writers, the Guinean novelist Laye created a highly personal vision of Africa, reflecting an organic world view that gives equal weight to African deities, nature, and the thoughts and observations of humankind.

ENFANT NOIR

This lyrical tale beautifully depicts the hero's youth in a traditional Senegalese village and his eventual confrontation with colonial culture. The descriptions of the hero's father's goldsmithing craft are particularly moving
0–521–05357–9 Cambridge pb $6.50

THE RADIANCE OF THE KING

A fantasy in which a Frenchman in Africa is sold into slavery
0–679–72200–9 Vintage pb $9.95

● René Maran

BATOUALA

Originally published in 1921, *Batouala* was the first of many novels by Africans to criticize the colonial regimes, in this case, the French in what is now the Central African Republic. "You smell the smells of the village, you eat its food, you see the white man as the black man sees him, and after you have lived in the village, you die there . . . When you read it, you have been Batoula, and that means that it is a great novel"—Ernest Hemingway
0–435–90135–4 Heinemann pb $7.50

An Epic of Mali

The life of the legendary 13th-century Malian ruler Sundiata (or Son-Jara) became the basis for an oral epic which professional bards (*griots*) have kept alive to the present day.

John Johnson & Fa-Digi Sisoko

THE EPIC OF SON-JARA: A West African Tradition

A careful transcription and translation of a recitation by the Malian griot Fa-Digi Sisoko, along with a detailed essay on the nature of epic in Africa
0–253–31951–X Indiana $35.00

D.T. Niane

SUNDIATA: An Epic of Old Mali

Niane's retelling of the Sundiata story focused new attention on traditional African literature when it appeared in 1960
0–582–64024–5 Humanities pb $6.50

● Nkem Nwankwo

DANDA

Danda is a happy-go-lucky antihero who ignores traditional Ibo virtues of thrift and ambition, but nevertheless rises to become chief of his village
0–435–90067–6 Heinemann pb $6.50

● Flora Nwapa

A major woman writer, Nwapa frequently uses Nigerian myths to create essentially modern stories.

EFURU

A distinguished woman who cannot fit into village life and who loses two husbands and her child, is nevertheless respected by the people around her
0–435–90026–9 Heinemann pb $6.50

IDU

A woman mourns her husband's death so deeply that she finally decides to seek him in the land of ghosts
0–435–90056–0 Heinemann pb $6.50

NEVER AGAIN
978–124–015–6 Three Continents pb $7.00

ONE IS ENOUGH
978–2272–00–0 Three Continents pb $7.00

WIVES AT WAR & OTHER STORIES
978–2272–00–0 Three Continents pb $7.00

● Gabriel Okara

One of the finest African poets, Okara subtly works the rhythms of the Ijaw language into his artful English.

THE FISHERMAN'S INVOCATION
0–435–90183–4 Heinemann pb $7.00

● Christopher Okigbo

LABYRINTHS WITH PATH OF THUNDER

The posthumously collected works of one of Nigeria's leading poets whose career was tragically cut short during the Biafran war
0–8419–0045–0 Holmes & Meier $12.50
0–8419–0016–7 Holmes & Meier pb $7.50

Sembène Ousmane

A great Senegalese writer and Africa's best known filmmaker, Ousmane delineates social themes while creating memorable, lovingly detailed characters.

GOD'S BITS OF WOOD

A novel about a bitter railroad strike in 1947. Although the colonial

---

administration eventually defeats the strikers, it is clear that their life force will triumph in the end. A beautifully drawn, fully realized portrayal of the African people

Translated by Francis Price
0–435–90063–3 Heinemann pb $7.50

XALA

When a corrupt businessman becomes afflicted with impotence (*xala*) he seeks refuge in superstition and folk remedies. A wickedly funny book with a powerful social message

Translated by Clive Wake
0–88208–068–7 Lawrence Hill pb $6.95

● Ferdinand Oyono

HOUSEBOY

A portrait of a houseboy who gradually loses his naive faith in the benevolence of his masters. A witty expose of the deceptions of colonialism

Translated by John Reed
0–435–90029–3 Heinemann pb $6.50

THE OLD MAN AND THE MEDAL

Old Meka is awarded a medal for years of devoted service to the colonial government; all he has given up in return are his lands and his heritage. Oyono creates a first-class satire out of the reactions of the villagers, the colonial official who presents the medal, and the old man himself

Translated by John Reed
0–435–90039–0 Heinemann pb $6.50

ROAD TO EUROPE

Translated by Richard Bjornson
0–89410–590–6 Three Continents $24.00

● Léopold S. Senghor

One of the founders of the *négritude* school of poetry, Senghor eventually became president of Senegal.

SELECTED POEMS

Edited by F.A. Irele
0–521–21339–8 Cambridge $27.95
0–521–29111–9 Cambridge pb $9.95

NOCTURNES
0–435–90071–4 Heinemann pb $6.50

● Wole Soyinka

Winner of the Nobel Prize for Literature in 1986, Soyinka's work is complex and wide-ranging. His plays are a sophisticated blend of African dance rhythms, Yoruba mythology, and oral storytelling combined with western imagery. Many of these plays have been performed by Soyinka's own company, Masks. Soyinka was jailed by the Nigerian government for 27 months for his criticism of their policies, and his experiences are chillingly narrated in *The Man Died*.

AKE: The Years of Childhood

An extraordinarily vivid recreation of a happy middle-class, quintessentially African childhood. "I know of few better illustrations of Baudelaire's statement about the child: 'For him, everything is new; he is always exhilarated' "—*New Society*

0–394–52807–7 Random House $14.95
0–394–72219–1 Random House pb $8.95

☎ **TO ORDER ANY BOOK IN THIS CATALOG, ASK YOUR BOOKSELLER OR CALL 1-800-882-8770**

Wole Soyinka (photo by Rex Collings Ltd., courtesy of Random House)

THE BACCHAE OF EURIPIDES: A Communion Rite
0–393–00789–8 Norton pb $5.95

COLLECTED PLAYS

Volume 1
0–19–281136–3 Oxford pb $8.95

Volume 2
0–19–281164–9 Oxford pb $8.95

DANCE OF THE FORESTS
Possibly Soyinka's most difficult play, it tells the story of a Council member who calls upon the spirits of the dead, expecting to hear tales of the glorious past. Instead, he calls forth two unknown, ordinary shades who criticize the empire that destroyed their lives
0–19–911082–4 Oxford pb $6.95

IDANRE & OTHER POEMS
The title work is a long poem based on the fierce and terrible god Ogun's role in the Yoruba myth of creation
0–8090–5725–5 Hill & Wang $16.95
0–8090–1352–5 Hill & Wang pb $7.95

THE INTERPRETERS
Soyinka's first novel is a complex account of the disintegration of a group of intellectuals in search of their identity
0–8419–0121–X Holmes & Meier $29.50
0–435–90076–5 Heinemann pb $7.00

ISARA
0–394–54077–8 Random House $16.95

KONGI'S HARVEST
A corrupt politician and his effect on those around him
0–19–911085–9 Oxford pb $6.95

THE LION AND THE JEWEL
A farce about a schoolteacher and a wily, older chieftain who are in love with the same woman
0–19–911083–2 Oxford pb $5.95

MADMEN AND SPECIALISTS
Written after Soyinka's incarceration, this play takes a more serious political stance than his earlier work
0–8090–6708–0 Hill & Wang pb $16.95

MANDELA'S EARTH & OTHER POEMS
Soyinka's first book since winning the Nobel Prize
0–394–57021–9 Random House $13.95

ROAD
One of Soyinka's most powerful plays, combining realism and symbolism. The characters are *egungun,* masks, who can become possessed by spirits or who hover between worlds
0–19–911084–0 Oxford pb $5.95

A SHUTTLE IN THE CRYPT
Recent poems
0–8090–8667–0 Hill & Wang $14.95
0–8090–1364–9 Hill & Wang pb $7.95

• **Amos Tutuola**
Combining non-standard pidgin English, oral narrative techniques, and his own deliberately naive forms of expression, Tutuola, a Nigerian, has created a delightfully idiosyncratic version of the English language for his wildly imaginative adventure stories based on African myth.

FEATHER WOMAN OF THE JUNGLE
"A *Pilgrim's Progress* of the devil-world"— *Manchester Guardian*
0–87286–215–1 City Lights pb $6.95

MY LIFE IN THE BUSH OF GHOSTS
A young boy is left to fend for himself amid supernatural terrors. "A fantastic and evocative trip through the dream-jungles of the unconscious"—*Saturday Review*
0–8021–3105–0 Grove pb $9.95

THE PALM-WINE DRINKARD
The most famous of Tutuola's novels tells the story of a "drinkard's" adventures when he visits the land of the dead to try to attain the return of his favorite palm wine tapster who died falling out of a tree
0–8021–5048–9 Grove pb $5.95

PAUPER, BRAWLER AND SLANDERER
0–571–14714–3 Faber & Faber $15.95
0–571–14765–8 Faber & Faber pb $6.95

SIMBI AND THE SATYR OF THE DARK JUNGLE
A wealthy and beautiful woman sets out to experience poverty
0–87286–214–3 City Lights pb $6.95

THE WILD HUNTER IN THE BUSH OF THE GHOSTS
0–89410–452–7 Three Continents $20.00
0–89410–453–5 Three Continents pb $10.00

THE WITCH-HERBALIST OF THE REMOTE TOWN
0–571–11704–X Faber & Faber pb $7.95

• **Donald Wright, editor**
ORAL TRADITION FROM THE GAMBIA: Family Elders
0–89680–084–9 Ohio pb $15.00

EAST AFRICA

• **Taban Lo Liyong**
A Ugandan poet who recast Iwo tales into free verse, Liyong was influenced by P'Bitek but has created a style that is very much his own.

ANOTHER NIGGER DEAD
0–435–90116–8 Heinemann pb $6.50

EATING CHIEFS
Liyong's best-known work, blending traditional tales and folkloric elements
0–435–90074–9 Heinemann pb $5.50

FRANTZ FANON'S UNEVEN RIBS WITH POEMS MORE & MORE
0–435–90090–0 Heinemann pb $6.50

• **Beryl Markham**
THE SPLENDID OUTCAST: Beryl Markham's African Stories
0–86547–301–3 North Point $14.95

WEST WITH THE NIGHT
0–86547–304–8 North Point $19.95
0–86547–118–5 North Point pb $12.50

• **V.Y. Mudimbe**
BEFORE THE BIRTH OF THE MOON
A novel by an award-winning poet and novelist born in Zaire, now a resident professor in North Carolina
0–671–67566–4 Simon & Schuster $17.95
0–671–66840–4 Simon & Schuster pb $7.95

• **Meja Mwangi**
GOING DOWN RIVER ROAD
The powerful and gritty story of a Kenyan day laborer's drinking, womanizing, friendships, and troubles at work
0–435–90176–1 Heinemann pb $6.50

• **Wa Thiong'O Ngugi**
The finest Kenyan novelist, Ngugi has had a powerful impact on all African literature. His novels have a broad historical and political sweep, ranging from the struggle against colonialism to the new ravages committed by an African elite. Imprisoned by the Kenyan government for 18 months, he currently lives in exile in London.

THE BLACK HERMIT
A young man with a European education is unwilling to give up his English girlfriend and fulfill his tribal responsibilities
0–435–90051–X Heinemann pb $5.50

DETAINED: A Writer's Prison Diary
Ngugi's description of his incarceration
0–435–90240–7 Heinemann pb $7.50

DEVIL ON THE CROSS
This novel was written in Gikuyu while Ngugi was imprisoned
Translated by the author
0–435–90844–8 Heinemann pb $7.50

A GRAIN OF WHEAT
Ngugi's best known work tells the stories of four characters looking back with regret on their failure to act in accordance with ideals during Kenya's "Emergency." A powerful vision of salvation through suffering
0–435–90836–7 Heinemann pb $6.00

I WILL MARRY WHEN I WANT
The play that triggered Ngugi's jailing by the Kenyan authorities
0–435–90246–6 Heinemann pb $6.50

PETALS OF BLOOD
A portrayal of the corrupting power of the new African elite who work with the colonials from whom they wrested power
0–525–48235–0 Dutton pb $10.95

THE RIVER BETWEEN
Ngugi has called this novel an attempt to remove the Christian doctrine from its western dress and incorporate it into African mythology
0–435–90017–X Heinemann pb $6.50

THE TRIAL OF DEDAN KIMATHI
A play about the corrupting of the ideas that led to Kenya's struggle for independence
0–435–90191–5 Heinemann pb $6.50

☞ **FOR ALL OTHER INQUIRIES, PLEASE CALL (212) 333-7900**

WEEP NOT CHILD
A young boy's hard-won education is abandoned as he witnesses the brutality of British home rule and decides to join the Mau Mau struggle
0–435–90860–8 Heinemann pb $6.00

• Okot P'Bitek
P'Bitek was an influential Ugandan poet who used Acoli legends and oral storytelling techniques in his work to create a style that was extraordinarily lyrical and uniquely African.

THE HARE AND THE HORNBILL
0–435–90193–1 Heinemann pb $6.50

HORN OF MY LOVE
0–435–90147–8 Heinemann pb $7.00

SONG OF LAWINO AND SONG OF OCOL
These most famous of his works are complementary narrative poems that take the form of a song by a traditional African woman saddened that her husband has become westernized, and her husband's response
Introduction by G.A. Heron
0–435–90266–0 Heinemann pb $7.50

• Tchicaya u Tam'si
A major voice from Zaire and an important figure in the *négritude* movement, Tam'si has had his work translated into many different languages.

THE MADMAN AND THE MEDUSA
Translated by Sonja Haussmann Smith & William Jay Smith
0–8139–1205–9 Virginia $9.95

SELECTED POEMS
0–435–90072–2 Heinemann pb $6.50

• Sony Labou Tansi
THE ANTIPEOPLE
A Zairean novel
Translated by J.A. Underwood
0–7145–2845–5 Marion Boyars $18.95

CENTRAL AND SOUTHERN AFRICA

Olive Schreiner's *The Story of an African Farm,* published in 1883, set the stage for all subsequent South African literature. The novel takes a clear-sighted look at racial inequality, the role of religion in an unjust society, and the difficulties faced by an individual who does not fit in with the country's rigidly conservative social mores. These themes form the dynamic of what is the largest body of literature from any one African country.

The issue of race permeates every aspect of South African daily life and, consequently, is present in every story, novel, and poem—whether or not the writer chooses to make this the central focus. Even such simple acts as buying a loaf of bread differ according to whether the protagonist is classified by the South African government as white, black, coloured, or Asian.

• Peter Abrahams
PATH OF THUNDER
A tragic love affair between a coloured man and a white woman and their eventual defeat and destruction by the pressures of a racist society
0–911860–43–6 Chatham $8.95

MINE BOY
The difficulties faced by a rural African who seeks work in the city. One of the first novels to take the reader behind the scenes in the daily life of an African laborer
0–435–90006–4 Heinemann pb $6.50

TELL FREEDOM
The autobiography of a prominent coloured writer who describes being caught between black and white culture and fitting into neither
0–571–11777–5 Faber & Faber pb $6.95

• Breyten Breytenbach
Breytenbach was a leading figure in "Die Sestigers," the Afrikaans-speaking writers who criticized the policies of the Afrikaner nationalists in their own language. Scion of a powerful family, Breytenbach was a thorn in the government's side, and when he returned to South Africa clandestinely he was arrested and sentenced to seven years in prison.

ENDPAPERS: Political Essay
Essays on life and politics
0–374–14829–5 Farrar, Straus & Giroux $16.95
0–07–007677–4 McGraw-Hill pb $8.95

IN AFRICA EVEN THE FLIES ARE HAPPY
Selected poems
Translated by the author & Denis Hirson
0–7145–3696–2 Riverrun $11.95
0–7145–3871–X Riverrun pb $7.95

MEMORY OF SNOW AND DUST
0–374–20766–6 Farrar, Straus & Giroux $22.95

THE TRUE CONFESSIONS OF AN ALBINO TERRORIST
A masterpiece of prison memoir that earned Breytenbach the sobriquet "South Africa's Solzhenitsyn"
0–07–007674–X McGraw-Hill pb $5.95

• André Brink
Another important member of "Die Sestigers," Brink writes in both English and Afrikaans and has continued to be an outspoken critic of apartheid and censorship.

AMBASSADOR
The new South African ambassador to France, caught up in an illicit love affair, finds that he must question both his own ambitions and the system that he has served so well
0–671–61934–9 Summit pb $7.95

A DRY WHITE SEASON
A man's life is destroyed when he tries to find out why his gardener disappeared after being arrested
0–14–006890–2 Penguin pb $6.95

AN INSTANT IN THE WIND
Using a 19th-century diary as the starting point Brink explores the relationship between a coloured servant and a Swedish woman when they are forced to rely upon each other for survival
0–14–008014–7 Penguin pb $6.95

RUMORS OF RAIN
A wealthy, intelligent, but unscrupulous Afrikaner reviews his life in a series of memos written to himself and unwittingly demonstrates the illusions that sustain him
0–14–006891–0 Penguin pb $6.95

WRITING IN A STATE OF SIEGE
Essays against censorship
0–671–47751–X Summit $15.95
0–671–62289–7 Summit pb $8.95

• Dennis Brutus
Possibly South Africa's most influential black poet, Brutus was instrumental in having the country banned from the Olympic Games. He was a political prisoner on Robben Island for many years, and his poems express the brutality of the prison and of the constant, oppressive presence of the regime's police. Today, Brutus lives and teaches in the United States.

SALUTES AND CENSURES
0–86543–011–X Africa World $19.95
0–86543–012–8 Africa World pb $9.95

A SIMPLE LUST
Poems of jail and exile
0–435–90115–X Heinemann pb $7.50

STUBBORN HOPE: Poems
0–894–10429–2 Three Continents $14.00
0–89410–430–6 Three Continents pb $7.00

• Roy Campbell & Peter Alexander, editors
THE SELECTED POEMS OF ROY CAMPBELL
Campbell was a principal figure in the Natal Renaissance of the late 1920s; his wide range of work is sometimes satirical, sometimes lyrical
0–19–211946–X Oxford $24.95

• Frank Chipasula
O EARTH, WAIT FOR ME
Poems by the exiled Malawian poet and recipient of the Soche Annual Peace Prize
0–86975–258–8 Ohio pb $9.95

• J.M. Coetzee
Increasingly recognized as one of South Africa's finest writers, Coetzee is a brilliant and experimental stylist, and his profound and chilling vision (in the words of Nadine Gordimer) "goes to the nerve center of being. What he finds there is more than most people will ever know about themselves."

FOE
Robinson Crusoe's story as told by his abandoned lover provides new insights into imperialism. "A small miracle of a book . . . of marvelous intricacy and almost overwhelming power"—Russell Banks, *Washington Post*
0–670–81398–2 Viking $15.95
0–14–009623–X Penguin pb $6.95

IN THE HEART OF THE COUNTRY
A woman's journal describes an individual in retreat from sexual and moral imperialism
0–14–006228–9 Penguin pb $5.95

LIFE AND TIMES OF MICHAEL K
Winner of the 1983 Booker McConnell Prize, this powerful Kafkaesque novel

IF YOU CAN'T FIND IT, LOOK IN THE INDEX

portrays a desolate South Africa after the outbreak of civil war
0–14–007448–1 Penguin pb $5.95

WAITING FOR THE BARBARIANS
A magistrate in the outer territories comes to identify with the tortured victims of the government he serves
0–14–006110–X Penguin pb $5.95

• Jeni Couzyn
LIFE BY DROWNING: Selected Poems
Poems by a young Afrikaner
0–88784–098–1 Toronto pb $8.95

• H.I.E. Dhlomo
COLLECTED WORKS
Heroic plays about Dingane, Cetewayo, and Shaka by one of the first Zulu writers. Includes the long autobiographical poem "Valley of a Thousand Hills"
Edited by Tim Couzens & Nick Visser
0–86975–271–5 Ohio pb $25.95

• Modikwe Dikobe
THE MARABI DANCE
The first inside picture of African daily life depicts the chaos of the slums outside Johannesburg and the dilemma of a woman caught between two worlds
0–435–90124–9 Heinemann pb $6.50

• Tony Eprile
TEMPORARY SOJOURNER & OTHER SOUTH AFRICAN STORIES
"Tony Eprile is writing in the realist tradition of Nadine Gordimer, carefully rendering the lives of South Africans at home and abroad . . . Subtly conceived and achieved"—Madison Smartt Bell
0–671–68205–9 Simon & Schuster $16.95
0–671–64596–X Simon & Schuster pb $7.95

• Ahmed Essop
HAJJI MUSA AND THE HINDU FIRE-WALKER
Stories and a novella about the Asians of South Africa. "The vivid aromatic world of Johannesburg's Indian community . . . adds a new world to those already represented in South African fiction"—Lionel Abrahams
0–930523–52–0 Readers International pb $8.95

• Lynn Freed
HOME GROUND
An artistic Jewish family viewed through the eyes of a young girl who doesn't quite fit in
0–671–61965–9 Summit $16.95
0–14–008948–9 Penguin pb $7.95

• Athol Fugard
A world-renowned playwright, Fugard continues to live and work in South Africa with members of his own theater company, some of whom have occasionally had to register as his servants in order to be allowed to travel with the troupe. Fugard's plays explore the limits of the human condition—people pushed to the breaking point.
BOESMAN AND LENA & OTHER PLAYS
Also includes *The Blood Knot, People Are Living Here,* and *Hello and Goodbye*
0–19–281242–4 Oxford pb $9.95

DIMETOS & TWO EARLY PLAYS
0–19–281210–6 Oxford pb $5.95

A LESSON FROM ALOES
A visit from a black friend brings to the surface the tensions of a white couple. The wife is still traumatized by a police raid years before, and the question remains: Who betrayed their friends in the movement? A disturbing work about the fear and distrust created by a police state
0–19–281307–2 Oxford pb $6.95

MASTER HAROLD AND THE BOYS
When young Harold returns to his mother's hotel and visits his old friends he finds that things are not the same
0–394–52874–3 Knopf $11.95

NOTEBOOKS: 1960–1977
Fugard's diaries provide an insight into his creative process. Many entries offer poignant descriptions of South African daily life
0–394–53755–6 Knopf $14.95

THE ROAD TO MECCA
An independent and eccentric woman artist refuses well-intentioned attempts to put her in an old-age home
0–930452–78–X Theatre Communications $14.95
0–930452–79–8 Theatre Communications pb $6.95

STATEMENTS: Three Plays
Includes *Statements After an Arrest Under the Immorality Act, The Island,* and *Sizwe Bansi Is Dead*
0–19–281170–3 Oxford pb $4.95

TSOTSI
A novel about a vicious black gangster in the townships who finds himself saddled with taking care of an abandoned baby and learns tenderness in the process
0–14–006272–6 Penguin pb $4.95

• Arthur N. Fula
THE GOLDEN MAGNET
Fula is one of the few black South Africans to write in Afrikaans. He describes life in the townships and the confusion experienced by rural blacks when they first come to the city
Translated by Carrol Lasker
0–89410–291–5 Three Continents $17.00

• Nadine Gordimer
"Nadine Gordimer is one of the world's finest writers," wrote Joyce Carol Oates in the *New York Times Book Review,* expressing a widely held opinion about the woman who has dominated the South African literary scene for the past 30 years. The evolution of Gordimer's work reflects her growing political involvement: while the earliest stories deal predominantly with the lives of liberal whites and their oblique relationship with blacks, the later work looks towards the future, anticipating a post-revolutionary period.
BURGER'S DAUGHTER
A woman seeks an identity beyond that of being the daughter of a famous activist who died in prison
0–14–005593–2 Penguin pb $6.95

Nadine Gordimer (photo by Fay Godwin, courtesy of Knopf)

THE CONSERVATIONIST
A convincing portrait of an Afrikaner industrialist, a man at once ambitious, cynical, sensual, and sharply observant
0–670–23883–X Viking $12.95
0–14–004716–6 Penguin pb $6.95

THE ESSENTIAL GESTURE: Writing, Politics and Places
Essays on the South African situation
0–394–57397–8 Random House $19.95

A GUEST OF HONOUR
A liberal white tries to come to terms with the increasing divisions in the black African country whose independence he fought for
0–14–003696–2 Penguin Books pb $6.95

JULY'S PEOPLE
A household servant rescues the white family he works for when the city becomes a battleground
0–14–006140–1 Penguin pb $5.95

THE LATE BOURGEOIS WORLD
After her ex-husband betrays the revolutionary movement and then commits suicide, a woman faces active involvement in a perilous mission for a black activist
0–14–005614–9 Penguin pb $5.95

SELECTED STORIES
"A magnificent collection, worthy of all homage"—Graham Greene
0–14–006737–X Penguin pb $6.95

SIX FEET OF COUNTRY
The title story recounts the difficulties of a liberal white farmer who helps his servant to get her brother buried
0–14–006559–8 Penguin pb $5.95

SOLDIER'S EMBRACE
Stories about South Africans at home and in neighboring black Africa. "Like the great nineteenth century novelists, she unites vast scope with minute attention to the ordinary"—*Washington Post*
0–14–005925–3 Penguin pb $6.95

SOMETHING OUT THERE
A collection of short stories
0–14–007711–1 Penguin pb $5.95

A SPORT OF NATURE
A white woman falls in love with a black revolutionary who becomes the first black president of South Africa
0–394–54802–7 Knopf $18.95
0–14–008470–3 Penguin pb $7.95

A WORLD OF STRANGERS
0–14–001704–6 Penguin pb $7.95

• Ernst Havermann
BLOODSONG & OTHER STORIES OF SOUTH AFRICA
Stories of a childhood in Zululand and of contemporary South Africa
0–395–43296–0 Houghton Mifflin $13.95

• Bessie Head
Although Head was South African by birth, most of her work is set in neighboring Botswana where she lived until her death in 1986. Among her favorite themes were the adaptation of villages to change, and individuals to prejudice.
A BEWITCHED CROSSROAD
0–913729–54–X Paragon $21.95

THE COLLECTOR OF TREASURES
Beautifully drawn stories about women in Botswana and township life in South Africa
0–435–90182–6 Heinemann pb $7.00

A QUESTION OF POWER
Written from the viewpoint of a coloured woman exiled to Botswana while undergoing a nervous breakdown, this is a compelling psychological study of African life
0–435–90720–4 Heinemann pb $7.00

SEROWE: Village of the Rain-Wind
A panoramic view of daily life in a Botswanan village
Introduction by Ronald Blythe
0–435–90220–2 Heinemann pb $8.00

• Denis Hirson
THE HOUSE NEXT DOOR TO AFRICA
An experimental work about childhood in South Africa
0–85635–720–0 Carcanet $14.95

• Luis Bernardo Honwana
WE KILLED MANGY-DOG & OTHER STORIES
After the boys in a small village in Mozambique stone a stray dog to death they confront the brutal conditions of their own lives
0–435–90060–9 Heinemann pb $6.50

• Christopher Hope
WHITE BOY RUNNING
A noted satirist makes a return visit to his hometowns of Balfour and Johannesburg: conversations, memories, and a whites-only election provide a revealing mosaic of the country's past and future
0–374–28925–5 Farrar, Straus & Giroux $17.95

BLACK SWAN
A retarded black boy is introduced to *Swan Lake* by a young Swiss nun. South African

society's indifference is exemplified by the subsequent treatment he receives
0–06–015846–8 Harper & Row $10.95

THE HOTTENTOT ROOM
Exiled South Africans dream of returning in triumph to their country
0–374–17284–6 Farrar, Straus & Giroux $16.95

KRUGER'S ALP
The search for a mythical mountain of gold
0–14–007731–6 Penguin pb $6.95

A SEPARATE DEVELOPMENT
A white Catholic teenager realizes that he is dark enough to be considered "coloured" under South Africa's rigid system of racial classification
0–684–17308–5 Scribners $10.95
0–684–17835–4 Scribners pb $4.95

• Noni Jabavu
THE OCHRE PEOPLE
An autobiographical novel about the Xhosa people, their customs, and their relationship with other tribes and with whites, written by the daughter of a famous Xhosa politician and journalist
0–86975–142–5 Ohio pb $11.95

• Dan Jacobson
TIME AND TIME AGAIN: Autobiographies
Autobiographical descriptions of growing up Jewish in a diamond-mining town in South Africa
0–87113–027–0 Atlantic Monthly $15.95

• A.C. Jordan
WRATH OF THE ANCESTORS
Retellings of Zulu myths
0–89410–331–8 Three Continents pb $9.00

• Elsa Joubert
POPPIE NONGENA: A Novel of South Africa
The unhappy story of a coloured woman with bushman ancestors
Foreword by Alan Paton
0–393–02242–0 Norton $15.95
0–8050–0230–8 Henry Holt pb $8.95

• Daniel P. Kunene
FROM THE PIT OF HELL
Stories of people facing difficult choices: a man must decide whether to join a strike, a boy whether to cross a swollen stream
0–86975–272–3 Ohio pb $9.95

• Mazisi Kunene
EMPEROR SHAKA THE GREAT
Kunene is the best-known interpreter of traditional Zulu poems and stories. Here, he has set the epic of the great Zulu conqueror into English
0–435–90211–3 Heinemann pb $10.00

ZULU POEMS
0–8419–0061–2 Holmes & Meier $12.50

• Ellen Kuzwayo
CALL ME WOMAN
Preface by Nadine Gordimer
0–933216–19–X Spinsters pb $8.50

• Alex La Guma
WALK IN THE NIGHT & OTHER STORIES
Apartheid meticulously exposed by one of South Africa's finest writers
0–8101–0139–4 Northwestern pb $8.95

• Hugh Lewin
BANDIET: Seven Years in a South African Prison
Lewin was jailed for politically motivated sabotage; this is the story of the dehumanizing conditions under which he lived as a "bandiet" or prisoner
0–435–90251–2 Heinemann pb $7.00

• Dambudzo Marechera
THE HOUSE OF HUNGER
Stories about poverty and violence in contemporary Zimbabwe
0–435–90207–5 Heinemann pb $7.00

• Don Mattera
GONE WITH THE TWILIGHT: A Story of Sophiatown
Sophiatown was a stronghold of the African National Congress until 1962 when it was erased by bulldozers. "Here is a black South African whose zestful affirmation of life defies oppression from the depths of a generous soul"—Nadine Gordimer
0–86232–747–4 Zed pb $9.95

Thomas Mofolo
CHAKA: An Historical Romance
Written in Sotho in 1925, this breakthrough novel uses the techniques of the oral tradition to create a complex psychological portrait of the great chief who founded the Zulu nation
Translated by F.H. Dutton
0–19–724172–7 Oxford $26.00

• Naboth Mokgatle
THE AUTOBIOGRAPHY OF AN UNKNOWN SOUTH AFRICAN
0–520–02903–8 California pb $8.95

• Es'kia Mphahlele
Mphahlele's insightful fiction and criticism have made him one of the most important African literary figures. He has rendered the joys and horrors of growing up black in South Africa in two extraordinary autobiographies.
AFRIKA MY MUSIC: An Autobiography, 1957–1983
Describes a period of exile and homelessness
0–86975–237–5 Ohio pb $13.95

CHIRUNDU
A novel about black South African expatriates in an independent African country
0–88208–122–5 Lawrence Hill pb $7.95

DOWN SECOND AVENUE: Growing Up in a South African Ghetto
A brilliant autobiographical novel. "Mphahlele's writing is like the taste of blood on the tongue"—Gerald Moore, *Seven African Writers*
0–571–09716–2 Faber & Faber pb $6.95

✉ TO ORDER BOOKS AS GIFTS, SEE PAGE 1

• Percy Mtwa, Mbongeni Ngema &
Barney Simon
WOZA ALBERT!
When Jesus arrives in South Africa, he is
welcomed by the government until he
reveals why he chose to come. This play
was a popular hit on Broadway
0–413–53000–0 RC&H pb $5.95

• Nat Nakasa
**THE WORLD OF NAT NAKASA: Selected
Writings of the Late Nat Nakasa**
Writing by the celebrated journalist and
founder of the influential *Classic Magazine*
Edited by Essop Patel
0–86975–050–X Ohio pb $12.95

• Njabulo S. Ndebele
FOOLS & OTHER STORIES
Vivid tales of contemporary township and
village life
0–930523–20–2 Readers International pb $8.95

• Lewis Nkosi
MATING BIRDS
The major work by a well-known black
intellectual and essayist. "Confronts boldly
and imaginatively the strange interplay of
bondage, desire, and torture inherent in
interracial sexual relationships within the
South African prison house of
apartheid"—Henry Louis Gates, Jr., *NY
Times*
0–06–097085–5 Harper & Row pb $5.95

• Jeff Opland
**XHOSA ORAL POETRY: Aspects of a
Black South African Tradition**
0–521–24113–8 Cambridge $52.50

• Essop Patel, editor
**THE WORLD OF CAN THEMBA:
Selected Writings**
0–86975–145–X Ohio pb $12.95

• Alan Paton
Often considered the greatest South
African writer, Paton was unflagging in his
efforts to encourage racial harmony based
on Christian ideas of brotherly love and
the dignity of man. This pious vision has
been criticized by other African writers as
unrealistic, but few would deny his
courage.
AH, BUT YOUR LAND IS BEAUTIFUL
A novel depicting the courageous self-
sacrifice of those who fight apartheid and
the triumph of human dignity over
oppression
0–684–17830–3 Scribners pb $6.95

CRY, THE BELOVED COUNTRY
Paton's famous 1948 novel traces a Zulu
minister's journey into Johannesburg's
underworld in search of his son. A
passionate exposure of apartheid, the book
has sold more than 17 million copies
0–020–53210–5 Macmillan pb $14.95

JOURNEY CONTINUED
An autobiography of Paton's later years
0–684–18946–1 Scribners $22.50

TOO LATE THE PHALAROPE
A lyrically written novel that conveys the
full tragedy of the Immorality Act, the law
forbidding sex between races
0–684–18500–8 Scribners pb $4.50

**TOWARDS THE MOUNTAIN: An
Autobiography**
0–684–18892–9 Scribners pb $9.95

• Solomon T. Plaatje
MHUDI
An inspirational figure in the history of
black South African literature, Plaatje was
a Boer war correspondent, a journalist
critical of the pass laws restricting black
movement, and the first Secretary General
of the African National Congress. This
novel looks back a century to the war
between the Boers and the Zulu chief
Mzilikazi, interspersing traditional praise
songs throughout the narrative
0–909078–01–7 Three Continents $14.00

• William Plomer
TURBOTT WOLFE
Years ahead of its time when published in
1928, this important novel attacks the
taboo on interracial love. "There is no
native question," says one of the
characters: "It is an answer"
0–15–691490–5 HBJ pb $8.95

• Mewa Ramgobin
WAITING TO LIVE
"To get to know Ramgobin's characters is
to understand—through people so real one
can feel their warm breath and hear their
voices—how the will to freedom has
germinated in South Africa and become
invincible"—Nadine Gordimer
0–394–74432–2 Aventura pb $8.95

• Norman Rush
WHITES
Rush's sensitive stories show the
bewilderment of American expatriates
faced with the mysteries of Botswanan
culture. "I found these stories wonderfully
well written. Their wry humor and
compassion bring to life middle-class
Americans trying to lead a normal life in
the back of beyond"—J.M. Coetzee
0–394–54471–4 Knopf $14.45
0–02–023841–X Macmillan pb $6.95

Olive Schreiner
THE STORY OF AN AFRICAN FARM
Nadine Gordimer has described this
early feminist novel as the book to
which all other South African work has
to measure up
Introduction by Doris Lessing
0–517–56803–9 Crown $24.95
0–14–043184–5 Penguin pb $4.95

DREAM LIFE AND REAL LIFE
0–915864–32–0 Academy Chicago $10.95
0–915864–31–2 Academy Chicago pb $3.95

FROM MAN TO MAN
0–915864–47–9 Academy Chicago pb $6.95

• Sipho Sepamla
A RIDE ON THE WHIRLWIND
A novel about the maelstrom that was the
Soweto Uprising, by an important young
black poet
0–435–90268–7 Heinemann pb $7.50

• Mongane Serote
TO EVERY BIRTH ITS BLOOD
0–435–90263–6 Heinemann pb $7.50

• Carolyn Slaughter
DREAMS OF THE KALAHARI
A novel about a headstrong young
woman's childhood in the Kalahari,
journey to England, and return to
Botswana
0–684–18765–5 Scribners $19.95
0–671–65905–7 Simon & Schuster pb $6.95

THE INNOCENTS
Oppressed by her mother, troubled by her
friendships with her mother's black
companion and with a young black man,
the protagonist seeks to find out about her
parents
0–671–65906–5 Simon & Schuster pb $6.95

• Pauline Smith
THE LITTLE KAROO
Quiet, touching stories about life in the
Karoo, South Africa's equivalent of the
Midwest, written in the 1920s
0–86961–130–5 Brookfield $18.00

• Can Themba
THE WILL TO DIE
Poignant stories of township life by a
brilliant journalist and writer who died
tragically young
0–435–90104–4 Heinemann pb $6.50

• Laurens Van der Post
A widely traveled writer who states that he
has walked over more of Africa than
anyone else alive, Van der Post spent many
years among the bushmen and writes
feelingly of their myths and legends.
THE HEART OF THE HUNTER
A beautifully written if somewhat
romanticized version of bushman myths
and stories
0–15–640003–0 HBJ pb $5.95

A MANTIS CAROL
A Christmas story based on bushman
legend
0–933280–21–1 Island pb $11.95

A STORY LIKE THE WIND
The history of a liberal white family and
their relationships with the Africans and
the land.
0–15–685261–6 HBJ pb $9.95

A FAR-OFF PLACE
In the sequel to *A Story Like the Wind*, a
young white boy and girl, accompanied by
their bushman friend, flee war by crossing
a thousand miles of desert. "The author
creates an enchanted world to go with his
enchanted hero. The Africa through which
his characters move is vivid and
palpable"—*NY Times*
0–15–630198–9 HBJ pb $7.95

A WALK WITH A WHITE BUSHMAN
0–688–07264–X Morrow $18.95

• Zöe Wicomb
YOU CAN'T GET LOST IN CAPETOWN
Stories of a rural childhood, of exile and
return, by a young coloured woman. "Zöe
Wicomb has mined pure gold from that
place—seductive, brilliant, and precious,
her talent glitters. An extraordinary
writer"—Toni Morrison
0–394–75309–2 Pantheon pb $6.95

Zöe Wicomb (photo courtesy of Pantheon)

• Uanhenga Xitu
THE WORLD OF "MESTRE" TAMODA: Angolan Stories
Written while its author was imprisoned by the colonial authorities, these stories are "outrageously funny . . . the stuff of which modern African comedy is made: equal parts African oral narrative tradition and philosophy, garnished with European manners"—*NY Times*
Translated by Annella McDermott
0–930523–42–3 Readers International $16.95
0–930523–43–1 Readers International pb $8.95

• Rose Zwi
ANOTHER YEAR IN AFRICA
A novel about Jewish immigrants in the 1930s
0–86975–316–9 Ohio pb $14.95

ANTHOLOGIES AND CRITICAL STUDIES

• Roger D. Abrahams, editor
AFRICAN FOLKTALES: Traditional Stories of the Black World
0–394–72117–9 Pantheon pb $11.95

• Chinua Achebe & C.L. Innes, editors
AFRICAN SHORT STORIES
Includes selections by Gordimer, Ngugi, Kenyatta, Marechera, and Head
0–435–90270–9 Heinemann pb $7.00

• Chidi Amuta
THE THEORY OF AFRICAN LITERATURE: Implications for Practical Criticism
0–86232–546–3 Zed $49.95
0–86232–547–1 Zed pb $15.95

• Ulli Beier
THE ORIGIN OF LIFE AND DEATH
0–435–90023–4 Heinemann pb $5.50

YORUBA MYTHS
0–521–22995–2 Cambridge $15.95
0–521–22865–4 Cambridge pb $6.95

• Ulli Beier & Gerald Moore, editors
THE PENGUIN BOOK OF MODERN AFRICAN POETRY
0–14–058573–7 Penguin pb $6.95

• Brenda Berrian
BIBLIOGRAPHY OF AFRICAN WOMEN WRITERS AND JOURNALISTS
Preface by Flora Nwapa
0–89410–227–3 Three Continents pb $14.00

• John Biggers
ANANSE: The Web of Life in Africa
Illustrated by John Biggers
Foreword by Barbara Jordan
0–292–70345–7 Texas pb $12.50

• Chinweizu, editor
VOICES FROM 20TH CENTURY AFRICA: Griots and Town Criers
0–571–14929–4 Faber & Faber $24.95
0–571–14930–8 Faber & Faber pb $12.95

• Bernard B. Dadié
THE BLACK CLOTH: A Collection of African Folk Tales
Translated by Karen C. Hatch
Foreword by Es'kia Mphahlele
0–87023–557–5 Massachusetts pb $9.95

• Romanus N. Egudu
CALABASH OF WISDOM & OTHER IGBO STORIES
0–88357–005–X NOK $12.95
0–88357–004–1 NOK pb $4.95

FOUR MODERN WEST AFRICAN POETS
0–88357–027–0 NOK $14.95
0–88357–028–9 NOK pb $5.95

MODERN AFRICAN POETRY AND THE AFRICAN PREDICAMENT
0–06–491916–1 Barnes & Noble $27.50

• Romanus Egudu & Donatus Nwoga
IGBO TRADITIONAL VERSE
0–435–90129–X Heinemann pb $7.50

• Gwyneth Henderson & Cosmo Pieterse, editors
NINE AFRICAN PLAYS FOR RADIO
0–435–90127–3 Heinemann pb $7.00

• Paul Irwin
LIPTAKO SPEAKS: History from Oral Tradition in Africa
0–691–05309–X Princeton $28.00

• Janheinz Jahn
MUNTU: An Outline of the New African Culture
Translated by Marjorie Green
0–394–17238–8 Grove pb $5.95

• Ellen Conroy Kennedy
THE NEGRITUDE POETS: An Anthology of Translations from the French
0–938410–72–5 Thunder's Mouth pb $10.95

• G.D. Killam
AN INTRODUCTION TO THE WRITINGS OF NGUGI
0–435–91669–6 Heinemann pb $12.50

THE NOVELS OF CHINUA ACHEBE
0–8419–0024–8 Holmes & Meier pb $9.95

• G.D. Killam, editor
THE WRITING OF EAST AND CENTRAL AFRICA
0–435–91671–8 Heinemann pb $17.50

• Joseph Miller, editor
THE AFRICAN PAST SPEAKS: Essays on Oral Tradition and History
0–208–01784–4 Shoe String $32.50

• Es'kia Mphahlele
MODERN AFRICAN STORIES
Edited by Ellis A. Komey
0–571–11217–X Faber & Faber pb $5.95

• Wa Thiong'O Ngugi
DECOLONISING THE MIND: The Politics of Language in African Literature
0–435–08016–4 Heinemann pb $10.00

• Lee Nichols
AFRICAN WRITERS AT THE MICROPHONE
Preface by Es'kia Mphahlele
0–89410–164–1 Three Continents $20.00
0–89410–165–X Three Continents pb $10.00

• Oyekan Owomoyela
AFRICAN LITERATURES: An Introduction
0–918456–18–5 African Studies $12.00

• Cosmo Pieterse, editor
TEN ONE-ACT PLAYS
0–435–90034–X Heinemann pb $7.50

• Cosmo Pieterse & Dennis Duerden, editors
AFRICAN WRITERS TALKING
0–8419–0118–X Holmes & Meier $35.00
0–8419–0119–8 Holmes & Meier pb $19.50

• Cosmo Pieterse & Donald Munro, editors
PROTEST AND CONFLICT IN AFRICAN LITERATURE
0–8419–0005–1 Holmes & Meier pb $12.50

• Paul Radin, editor
AFRICAN FOLKTALES
0–8052–0732–5 Schocken pb $11.95

• Wole Soyinka, editor
POEMS OF BLACK AFRICA
0–8090–7747–7 Hill & Wang $12.95

Central and Southern Africa

• André Brink & J.M. Coetzee, editors
A LAND APART: A South African Reader
0–14–010004–0 Penguin pb $7.95

• Frank Chipasula, editor
WHEN MY BROTHERS COME HOME: Poems from Central and Southern Africa
Provides an introduction to the work of otherwise unavailable poets from Mozambique, Zimbabwe, Angola, and Malawi, and includes selections by better known South African poets. "These poems are more than documents and accounts of historical struggle, they are pistol shots in the middle of a concert, sometimes full of rage and anger, with the hope of getting our full attention"—Michael S. Harper
0–8195–5092–2 Wesleyan $35.00
0–8195–6089–8 Wesleyan pb` $14.95

• J.M. Coetzee
WHITE WRITING: On the Culture of Letters in South Africa.
Seven essays on Olive Schreiner, Alan Paton, and others. "I have two concerns in this book: with certain of the ideas, the great intellectual schemas, through which South Africa has been thought by Europe; and with the land itself, South Africa as landscape and landed property"—from the author's introduction
0–300–03974–3 Yale $19.95

• Tim Couzens & Essop Patel, editor
THE RETURN OF THE AMASI BIRD: Black South African Poetry, 1891–1981
0–86975–195–6 Ohio pb $12.95

• Barry Feinberg, editor
POETS TO THE PEOPLE: South African Freedom Poems
0–317–36672–6 Africa Fund pb $4.50

• Judith Gleason
THIS AFRICA: Novels by West Africans in English and French
0–8101–0103–3 Northwestern $22.95

• Stephen Gray
SOUTHERN AFRICAN LITERATURE: An Introduction
0–06–492530–7 Barnes & Noble $28.50

• Stephen Gray, editor
THE PENGUIN BOOK OF SOUTHERN AFRICAN STORIES
0–14–007239–X Penguin pb $6.95

• A.C. Jordan, editor
TALES FROM SOUTHERN AFRICA
Illustrated by Feni Dumile
0–520–01911–3 California $30.00
0–520–03638–7 California pb $3.95

• Bernth Lindfors, editor
CONTEMPORARY BLACK SOUTH AFRICAN LITERATURE: A Symposium
0–89410–454–3 Three Continents $24.00
0–89410–455–1 Three Continents pb $14.00

• Solomon M. Mutswairo
ZIMBABWE: Prose and Poetry
0–914478–82–6 Three Continents $18.00
0–914478–83–4 Three Continents pb $7.00

• Duma Ndlovu, editor
WOZA AFRIKA!: A Collection of South African Plays
Also includes Nongema's *Asinamali!*
Introduction by Wole Soyinka
0–8076–1169–7 Braziller $16.95
0–8076–1170–0 Braziller pb $8.95

• Piniel Viriri Shava
A PEOPLE'S VOICE: Black South African Writing in the 20th Century
An exploration of fiction, poetry, township theater, and autobiography from World War I to now, via the Soweto uprising
0–86232–687–7 Zed pb $15.95

• Dennis Walder
ATHOL FUGARD
0–394–62230–8 Grove pb $7.95

Arabic Literature

Arabic is a particularly difficult language to translate into English, not just because its grammatical concepts are fundamentally different, but also because of the cultural gulf that exists between Arabic and European culture. Few of the classic works of Arabic literature are available in English, but a glimpse of this great canon can be obtained in the titles listed below.

▶ See also Islam

CLASSICAL LITERATURE

• Shah Amin
ASSEMBLIES OF AL-HARIRI
0–900860–86–3 Human Knowledge $16.95

• Esin Atil
KALILA WA DIMNA: Fables from a 14th-Century Arabic Manuscript
0–87474–216–1 Smithsonian $22.50
0–87474–215–3 Smithsonian pb $11.95

J.C. Mardrus & Powys Mathers, translators
THE BOOK OF THE THOUSAND NIGHTS AND ONE NIGHT
The only complete English translation now in print, in a four-volume set. This great cycle of stories, full of ribaldry, humor, and suspense, is the masterpiece of vernacular Arabic, and until the 19th century was not considered part of the classical canon of Arabic literature
0–7102–0869–3 Methuen pb $29.95

• N.J. Dawood, translator
TALES FROM THE THOUSAND AND ONE NIGHTS
0–14–044289–8 Penguin pb $5.95

Anthologies

• Ghazi Algosaibi, translator
LYRICS FROM ARABIA
A bilingual collection of classical poetry, including pre-Islamic work
0–89410–379–2 Three Continents $15.00
0–89410–380–6 Three Continents pb $8.00

• James Kritzeck, editor
ANTHOLOGY OF ISLAMIC LITERATURE: From the Rise of Islam to Modern Times
The best introduction to classical Arabic, Persian, and Turkish literature. From the poetry of pre-Islamic Arabia to the popular dramas of the Ottoman era
0–452–00783–6 NAL pb $12.95

• Omar Pound, editor
ARABIC AND PERSIAN POEMS IN ENGLISH
A fine translation of selected lyrics by Ezra Pound's son
0–89410–466–7 Three Continents $22.00
0–915032–40–6 Natl Poetry Foundation pb $8.95

• Michael Sells, translator
DESERT TRACINGS: Six Classic Arabian Odes by 'Alqama, Shánfara, Labíd, 'Antara, Al-A'sha, Dhu al-Rúmma
0–8195–1158–7 Wesleyan pb $10.95

• Charles G. Tuetey, translator
CLASSICAL ARABIC POETRY: 160 Poems from Imrulkais to Ma'arri
0–7103–0110–3 Methuen $36.00

MODERN LITERATURE

• Jalal al-e Ahmad
BY THE PEN
Translated by M.R. Ghanoonparvar
0–292–70770–3 Texas pb $8.95

• Halim Barakat
DAYS OF DUST
A novel about the Six Day War, viewed from an Arab perspective
Translated by Trevor Le Gassick
0–89410–359–8 Three Continents $18.00

• Mohamed Choukri
FOR BREAD ALONE
Translated by Paul Bowles
0–87286–196–1 City Lights pb $6.95

• Driss Chraibi
THE MOTHER OF SPRING
A Moroccan novel exploring the world of the Berbers in pre-Islamic times
Translated by Hugh Harter
0–89410–402–0 Three Continents $18.00
BIRTH AT DAWN
A sequel to *The Mother of Spring,* concerning the arrival of Islam in the Maghreb
Translated by Sheena Chraibi
0–89410–577–9 Three Continents pb $8.00

• Mahmoud Darwish
THE MUSIC OF HUMAN FLESH
An important contemporary Palestinian writer and poet. One of his poems (not in this book), published in an Israeli newspaper in spring 1988, was the anthem of the uprising in the Occupied Territories
Translated by Denys Johnson-Davies
0–89410–203–6 Three Continents pb $7.00

• Fathy Ghanem
THE MAN WHO LOST HIS SHADOW
Translated by Desmond Stewart
0–89410–206–0 Three Continents $14.00
0–89410–207–9 Three Continents pb $8.00

• Emile Habiby
THE SECRET LIFE OF SAEED, THE ILL-FATED PESSOPTIMIST
A satirical novel by an Arab member of the Israeli Knesset. "The genuine prose masterpiece to derive from the Palestinian quandary"—*TLS*
Introduction by Salma Jayyusi
0–86232–402–5 Humanities pb $6.95

• Tawfiq al-Hakim

PLAYS, PREFACES AND POSTSCRIPTS OF TAWFIQ AL-HAKIM
Edited and translated by William Hutchins

Volume 1: Theater of the Mind
Includes *The Wisdom of Solomon, King Oedipus, Shahrazad, Princess Sunshine,* and *Angels' Prayer*
0–89410–134–X Three Continents pb $12.00

Volume 2: Theater of Society
Includes *Between War and Peace, Tender Hands, Food for the Millions, Poet on the Moon,* and *Voyage to Tomorrow*
0–89410–280–X Three Continents pb $25.00

• Khalil Hawi

NAKED IN EXILE: Khalil Hawi's "The Threshing Floors of Hunger"
The major work by a poet who committed suicide in 1982 during the Israeli invasion of Lebanon
Translated by Adnan Haydar & Michael Beard
0–89410–366–0 Three Continents $22.00
0–89410–367–9 Three Continents pb $12.00

• Taha Hussein

AN EGYPTIAN CHILDHOOD
Egypt's leading man of letters. This is the first volume of his autobiography, one of the great works of modern Arabic literature
Introduction by Pierre Cachia
0–89410–211–7 Three Continents pb $7.00

• Yusuf Idris

THE CHEAPEST NIGHTS: Short Stories
Translated by Wadida Wassef
0–89410–041–6 Three Continents pb $7.00

• Jabra I. Jabra

THE SHIP
Translated by Adnan Haydar & Roger Allen
0–89410–329–6 Three Continents pb $10.00

• Ghassan Kanafani

MEN IN THE SUN
Men in the Sun is an allegorical novella about the Palestinian condition. Kanafani, a leading cultural commissar of the Palestinian nationalist movement, was killed in a car bomb explosion
Translated by Hilary Kilpatrick
0–89410–022–X Three Continents pb $5.00

• Elias Khoury

LITTLE MOUNTAIN
Translated by Maia Tabet
Foreword by Edward Said
0–8166–1770–8 Minnesota pb $9.95

• Naguib Mahfouz
The only Arabic writer to be awarded the Nobel Prize, which he won in 1988, Mahfouz published his own first novel in 1939. His renown as the leading figure in contemporary Arabic letters was established with the publication of his *Cairene Trilogy* in 1956.

AUTUMN QUAIL
977–424–107–X Columbia pb $8.50

THE BEGGAR
Translated by Kristin Henry
977–424–135–5 Columbia pb $8.95

THE BEGINNING AND THE END
Translated by Ramses Awad
977–424–112–6 Columbia pb $10.50

Naguib Mahfouz (drawing by Max Karl Winkler, courtesy of Three Continents)

CHILDREN OF GEBELAWI
An allegorical novel in which Biblical events take place in a Cairo alleyway
Translated by Philip Stewart
0–89410–213–3 Three Continents pb $10.00

FOUNTAIN AND TOMB
A complex, cinematic novel about a child's initiation into the life of modern Cairo
Translated by James Kenneson
0–89410–580–9 Three Continents $18.00
0–89410–581–7 Three Continents pb $8.00

MIDAQ ALLEY
The best-known work by the Nobel Prize winner focuses on a young girl growing up in a poor Cairo neighborhood
0–89410–281–8 Three Continents pb $9.00

MIRAMAR
A hotel in Alexandria provides the setting for one of Mahfouz's best works
Translated by Fatma Moussa-Mahmoud
Introduction by John Fowles
0–89410–462–4 Three Continents pb $8.00

THE SEARCH
977–424–160–6 Columbia pb $10.50

THE THIEF AND THE DOGS
Translated by M.M. Badawi & Trevor Le Gassick
977–424–034–0 Columbia pb $6.95

WEDDING SONG
Translated by Olive Kennedy
977–424–018–9 Columbia pb $8.50

• Sabri Moussa

SEEDS OF CORRUPTION
0–395–28541–0 Houghton Mifflin $7.95

• Mohammed Mrabet

THE BOY WHO SET THE FIRE
Seventeen tales by the Moghrebi storyteller. "Part folklore, part magic, part braggadocio, these sometimes autobiographical, sometimes traditional tales are filled with Mediterranean light, crazy kif wisdom and vivid characters"— Andrei Codrescu
Translated by Paul Bowles
0–87286–230–5 City Lights pb $6.95

THE LEMON
A 12-year-old Moroccan boy runs away from his home in the Rif mountains to Tangier
Translated by Paul Bowles
0–87286–164–3 City Lights pb $6.95

LOVE WITH A FEW HAIRS
"A view of the world where love is a commodity and perfunctory, where the gulfs between humans are not only vast but are also taken for granted as permanent"—*NY Times*
Translated by Paul Bowles
0–87286–192–9 City Lights pb $6.95

M'HASHISH
Translated by Paul Bowles
0–87286–034–5 City Lights pb $3.95

• Abdelrahman Munif

CITIES OF SALT
The impact of American oil workers on an impoverished Persian Gulf community in the 1930s. "It opens up new vistas to the imagination"—Graham Greene
Translated by Peter Theroux
0–394–75526–X Random House pb $10.95

• Nawal el Saadawi

MEMOIRS OF A WOMAN DOCTOR
A novel of a young Egyptian woman in rebellion against social constraints
0–87286–223–2 City Lights pb $6.95

TWO WOMEN IN ONE
A young Egyptian woman's sexual and political awakening
Translated by Osman Nusairi & Jana Gough
0–931188–41–5 Seal Press $14.95
0–931188–40–7 Seal Press pb $7.95

WOMAN AT POINT ZERO
Translated by Sherif Hetata
0–86232–517–X Humanities $13.95
0–86232–110–7 Humanities pb $7.95

• Tayeb Salih

SEASON OF MIGRATION TO THE NORTH
The story of a talented Sudanese whose life goes to waste in the chasm between East and West
Translated by Denys Johnson-Davies
0–89410–199–4 Three Continents $7.00

• Hanan al-Shaykh

THE STORY OF ZAHRA
A 1980 novel of Beirut. "A haunting and chilling study of the fatal fascination of violence"—*The Observer*
0–930523–21–0 Readers International $16.95

Anthologies

• M.M. Badawi, editor

AN ANTHOLOGY OF MODERN ARABIC VERSE
0–19–920032–7 Oxford pb $8.95

• Ben Bennani, editor

BREAD, HASHISH AND MOON: Four Modern Arab Poets
Selected poems of Nizar Qabbani, Badr Shakir al-Sayyab, Adunis, and Mahmud Darwish
0–87775–135–8 Unicorn pb $6.00

• Kamal Boullata, translator & editor

WOMEN OF THE FERTILE CRESCENT: An Anthology of Arab Women's Poems
0–914478–42–7 Three Continents pb $10.00

- Abdel Elmessiri, editor
THE PALESTINIAN WEDDING: A Bilingual Anthology of Contemporary Palestinian Resistance Poetry
Translated by Abdel Elmessiri
Illustrated by Kamal Boullata
0–89410–095–5 Three Continents $20.00
0–89410–096–3 Three Continents pb $10.00

- Salma K. Jayyusi, editor
MODERN ARABIC POETRY: An Anthology
0–231–05272–3 Columbia $45.00

- Denys Johnson-Davies, editor
MODERN ARABIC SHORT STORIES
0–914478–99–0 Three Continents $10.00
0–914478–75–3 Three Continents pb $8.00

- Mahmoud Manzaloui, editor
ARABIC SHORT STORIES: 1945–1965
977–424–121–5 Columbia pb $17.50

ARABIC WRITING TODAY: The Drama
977–424–093–6 Columbia pb $20.00

- Abdullah al-Udhari, editor
MODERN POETRY OF THE ARAB WORLD
0–14–058515–X Penguin pb $5.95

BACKGROUND STUDIES

- A.F. Beeston & others, editors
ARABIC LITERATURE TO THE END OF THE UMAYYAD PERIOD
0–521–24015–8 Cambridge $80.00

- M.H. Bakalla
ARABIC CULTURE: Through Its Language and Literature
0–7103–0027–1 Methuen pb $11.95

- Krishna Chaitanya
A HISTORY OF ARABIC LITERATURE
0–8364–1045–9 South Asia $18.00

- Lila abu-Lughod
VEILED SENTIMENTS: Honor and Poetry in a Bedouin Society
0–520–05483–0 California $37.50

- Reynold A. Nicholson
LITERARY HISTORY OF THE ARABS
0–521–09572–7 Cambridge pb $29.95

- Fran Ringold & Roger Allen, editors
ARABIC LITERATURE: Then and Now
0–942374–07–X Arts Humanities Tulsa pb $5.50

- Annemarie Schimmel
AS THROUGH A VEIL: Mystical Poetry in Islam
A sensitive study, with many examples, by an outstanding scholar of Islamic culture and mystical traditions
0–231–05247–2 Columbia pb $15.00

- Saad Abdullah Sowayan
NABATI POETRY: The Oral Poetry of Arabia
0–520–04882–2 California $35.00

- Michael J. Zwettler
THE ORAL TRADITION OF CLASSICAL ARABIC POETRY: Its Character and Implications
0–8142–0273–X Ohio State $35.00

Persian Literature

Iran has often been called the France of the premodern Middle East—the source and standard-bearer of what people from Constantinople to Delhi considered high culture. But little of its enormous literary output has been translated for Western readers. Having escaped occupation by an imperial power, Iran never had a large number of foreign scholars, civil servants, and missionaries exploring its literature. While it is true that the image of Persia has been a powerful one in the West since the time of the Achmaenid dynasty, the job of making the best of the Persian tradition available to Europeans remains largely uncompleted. As a result the list that follows is necessarily partial and unrepresentative.

CLASSICAL LITERATURE

- Ferdowsi
THE EPIC OF THE KINGS: Shah-Nama
A prose rendering of episodes from the national epic of the Persian people
0–7102–0538–4 RC&H pb $12.95

Farid al-Din Attar
THE CONFERENCE OF THE BIRDS
A stunning English rendering of a classic mystical allegory
Translated by Afkham Darbandi & Dick Davis
0–14–044434–3 Penguin pb $6.95

MUSLIM SAINTS AND MYSTICS: Episodes from the Tadhkirat Al-Auliya (Memorial of the Saints)
The biographical dictionary of saints was a common form of literature in the Islamic world, and this work is considered the finest example of the genre
Translated by A.J. Arberry
0–7100–0169–X RC&H pb $13.95

- Hafiz
FIFTY POEMS OF HAFIZ
Although the selection is fairly small, this is the best introduction to the greatest Persian lyric poet
Edited and translated by A.J. Arberry
0–521–04039–6 Cambridge $49.50

HAFEZ: Dance of Life
Translations of Hafez's poetry accompanied by beautiful illuminations by the Iranian artist Hossein Zenderoudi
Translated by Michael Boylan & Wilberforce Clarke
Edited by M. Batmanglij
0–934211–04–3 Mage $29.95
0–934211–13–2 Mage pb $16.95

- Jami
FITZGERALD'S SALAMAN AND ABSAL
This fascinating volume compares three translations, two by Edward Fitzgerald and one by A.J. Arberry, of the 15th-century narrative poem by Jami
Edited by A.J. Arberry
0–521–05011–1 Cambridge $37.50

- Omar Khayyam
THE RUBAIYAT OF OMAR KHAYYAM
After the King James Bible, Fitzgerald's rather free version of Omar's quatrains is perhaps the most familiar translation in the English language
Translated by Edward Fitzgerald
Illustrated by Willy Pogany
0–245–54234–5 Beaufort pb $8.95

THE RUBA'IYAT OF OMAR KHAYYAM
A new and more accurate translation, with an illuminating introduction
Translated by John Heath-Stubbs & Peter Avery
0–14–044384–3 Penguin pb $3.95

- Sadi
THE ROSE GARDEN
This work is the greatest example of the Persian genre that mixed prose and poetry for the purposes of edification and entertainment. In various translations it has had a continuous influence on literature in Europe
Translated by Edward Eastwick
0–900860–65–0 Ins/Human Knowledge $16.95

- George Morrison, editor
VIS AND RAMIN
Translated by George Morrison
0–231–03408–3 Columbia $35.00

- Jalal al-Din Rumi
MYSTICAL POEMS OF RUMI
The prolific orientalist's translation of two hundred of Rumi's shorter poems
Translated by A.J. Arberry
0–226–73151–0 Chicago pb $7.95

"In Rumi's poetry there is always the mystery of the pronouns. Who is this *you* he addresses? . . . Pronouns dissolve within the pressure of Rumi's recognition of his true identity. The essential power of Rumi's poetry is ecstasy, an ecstasy melting the confinement of the ego into a larger, elastic, cross-pollinating dance of Selves."—Coleman Barks & John Moyne

OPEN SECRET: Versions of Rumi
Translated by Coleman Barks & John Moyne
0–939660–06–7 Threshold pb $7.00

THESE BRANCHING MOMENTS: Forty Odes
Translated by Coleman Barks & John Moyne
0–914278–50–9 Copper Beech pb $6.95

UNSEEN RAIN: Quatrains of Rumi
Translated by Coleman Barks & John Moyne
0–939660–17–2 Threshold $14.00
0–939660–16–4 Threshold pb $8.00

- Sa'd Ud Din Mahmud Shabistari
THE SECRET ROSE GARDEN
A central work in the history of Sufism
Edited by Florence Lederer
0–933999–26–7 Phanes pb $5.95

Anthologies

• **Omar Pound, editor**
ARABIC AND PERSIAN POEMS IN ENGLISH
Free and very convincing translations from a dozen poets
0–89410–466–7 Three Continents $22.00
0–915032–40–6 National Poetry pb $8.95

• **Peter Lamborn Wilson & Nasrollah Pourjavady, editors**
THE DRUNKEN UNIVERSE: An Anthology of Persian Sufi Poetry
0–933999–65–8 Phanes pb $8.95

MODERN PERSIAN LITERATURE

• **Parvin E'tesami**
DIVANE PARVIN E'TESAMI
Parvin was an important woman poet of the first half of the century in whom the transition from classical to modern concerns is clearly represented
Edited by Heshmat Moayyad
0–939214–38–5 Mazda pb $14.95

• **Forugh Farrokhzad**
ANOTHER BIRTH
The most famous volume of poems by Iran's greatest woman poet
Translated by Hasan Javadi & Susan Sallee
0–89410–361–X Three Continents pb $10.00

A REBIRTH: Poems
Translated by David C. Martin
0–939214–30–X Mazda pb $9.95

• **Dilip Hiro**
THREE PLAYS
Includes *To Anchor a Cloud, Apply, No Reply,* and *A Clean Break*
0–946013–01–2 Three Continents pb $10.00

• **Minoo Southgate, editor & translator**
MODERN PERSIAN SHORT STORIES
Excellent translations with a short but useful introduction
0–89410–032–7 Three Continents $20.00
0–89410–033–5 Three Continents pb $9.00

HISTORIES AND CRITICAL STUDIES

• **Edward Granville Browne**
LITERARY HISTORY OF PERSIA
More than sixty years after their completion, these four volumes remain the standard reference work and contain many passages of translation

Volume 1: From the Earliest Times Until Firdawsi
0–521–04344–1 Cambridge $75.00

Volume 2: From Firdawsi to Sa'di
0–521–04345–X Cambridge $75.00

Volume 3: The Tartar Dominion (1265–1502)
0–521–04346–8 Cambridge $80.00

Volume 4: Modern Times (1500–1924)
0–521–04347–6 Cambridge $75.00

Watercolor from Timur and the Princely Vision: Persian Art and Culture in the Fifteenth Century *by Thomas W. Lentz and Glenn D. Lowry (Smithsonian)*

• **Ehsan Yarshater, editor**
PERSIAN LITERATURE
Twenty-one essays by noted scholars, with a great deal of material on the modern period
0–88706–263–6 SUNY $54.50
0–88706–264–4 SUNY pb $19.50

• **Annemarie Schimmel**
AS THROUGH A VEIL: Mystical Poetry in Islam
Schimmel brilliantly discusses religious aspects of both Arabic and Persian poetry
0–231–05247–2 Columbia pb $15.00

Literatures of India

Readers educated in the secular literary traditions of the West tend to experience bewilderment when confronted with the writing of the Indian subcontinent. Literature in India has historically been bound to religious life, and literary artifacts are only imperfectly understood if one forgets that they serve as aids to worship and piety. Secular traditions—such as the court poetry of the Guptas and the Mughals—have developed, but even they acquiesce in crucial ways to the religious institutions that surround them.

Included in this section are a large number of modern works written in English, and most of the available translations of modern literature in the vernaculars.

SANSKRIT LITERATURE

The Vedas and the Great Epics

• **Wendy O'Flaherty, editor**
THE RIG VEDA
The standard contemporary English version of one of the world's oldest religious texts, containing a beautiful version of the Vedic hymn to creation, the earliest extant lyric poem
0–14–044402–5 Penguin pb $6.95

• **William Buck, translator**
THE MAHABHARATA
A highly readable abridgement of the massive epic poem that defines the Indian identity
Illustrated by Shirley Trieste
0–520–04393–6 California pb $11.95

J.A.B. van Buitenen, translator
THE MAHABHARATA
Although left incomplete by Professor Van Buitenen at his death, this translation provides the most direct experience of the epic an English reader can have. Includes *The Book of the Beginning, The Book of the Assembly Hall,* and *The Book of the Forest*
0–226–84649–0 Chicago (set) $42.00

• **Jean-Claude Carrière**
THE MAHABHARATA
The script of the landmark Peter Brook production. A marvel of condensation and dramatic storytelling
Translated by Peter Brook
0–06–039072–7 Harper & Row $18.95
0–06–039079–4 Harper & Row pb $8.95

- **R.K. Narayan**
GODS, DEMONS AND OTHERS
Stories based on the Mahabharata
0–553–21240–0 Bantam pb $3.50

- **William Buck, translator**
THE RAMAYANA
A prose condensation of the epic
0–520–04394–4 California pb $11.95

- **Robert P. Goldman & Sheldon Pollock, translators**
THE RAMAYANA OF VALMIKI: An Epic of Ancient India
The complete poem in a new and definitive translation
Volume 1
0–691–06561–6 Princeton $55.50
Volume 2
0–691–06654–X Princeton $60.00

- **R.K. Narayan**
THE RAMAYANA
A fluent retelling of the story by India's foremost contemporary writer
0–14–004428–0 Penguin pb $4.95

- **Barbara Stoler Miller, translator**
THE BHAGAVAD-GITA: Krishna's Counsel in Time of War
A new and very precise translation. Unlike Zaehner's work, which reflects the subtle influence of its translator's Roman Catholicism, this version maintains a rigorous neutrality with respect to interpretation
0–231–06468–3 Columbia $21.50

- **Robert C. Zaehner, translator & editor**
THE BHAGAVAD-GITA
India's most sacred text, translated by a distinguished student of comparative religion
0–19–501666–1 Oxford pb $12.95

From The Mahabharata *retold by William Buck, illustrated by Shirley Triest (California)*

Tales

- **Roy C. Amore & Larry D. Shinn**
LUSTFUL MAIDENS AND ASCETIC KINGS: Buddhist and Hindu Stories of Life
Anecdotes from the Buddhist and Hindu folk traditions
Illustrated by Sharon Wallace
0–19–502838–4 Oxford $29.95
0–19–502839–2 Oxford pb $6.95

- **Arthur W. Ryder, translator**
THE PANCHATANTRA
The stories the West knows as Aesop's fables, in their original form
0–226–73249–5 Chicago pb $15.00

- **J.A.B. van Buitenen, translator**
TALES OF ANCIENT INDIA
A very entertaining sampling of the enormous body of ancient Indian narratives
0–226–84647–4 Chicago pb $11.95

- **Heinrich Zimmer**
THE KING AND THE CORPSE: Tales of the Soul's Conquest of Evil
Traditional tales rendered by one of the greatest Indologists of the century
Edited by Joseph Campbell
0–691–01776–X Princeton pb $10.95

Poetry and Drama

- **Jayadeva**
LOVE SONG OF THE DARK LORD: Jayadeva's Gitagovinda
A sensual and highly influential medieval devotional poem, in a beautiful translation. "Miller's volume is an essential contribution to Indian study and to poetry in translation in general. She has given us the Indian equivalent of the *Song of Songs* without the usual sentimentality"—David Shapiro, *Parabola*
Translated by Barbara Stoler Miller
0–231–04028–8 Columba $24.00
0–231–04029–6 Columba pb $13.00

Kalidasa
THE ORIGIN OF THE YOUNG GOD: Kalidasa's Kumarasambhava
An epic of sacred eroticism, superbly translated. "This remarkable translation of a previously inaccessible text holds its active authority as poetry throughout, never relaxing into simply prosaic patterns nor the all too usual paraphrase. Hank Heifetz has managed a compelling unity of resources, which I consider an exceptional literary accomplishment"—Robert Creeley
Translated by Hank Heifetz
0–520–05304–4 California $30.00

THE THEATER OF MEMORY: Three Plays of Kalidasa
These translations succeed in giving the reader a sense of why Kalidasa holds a position in Sanskrit literature comparable to that of Shakespeare in English
Translated by Barbara Stoler Miller & others
0–231–05838–1 Columbia $35.00
0–231–05839–X Columbia pb $17.50

THE TRANSPORT OF LOVE: The Meghaduta of Kalidasa
Kalidasa's famous narrative poem, noted for its beautiful descriptions of the Indian landscape
Translated by Leonard Nathan
0–520–03031–1 California $18.00
0–520–03271–3 California pb $6.95

- **Vidyakara**
AN ANTHOLOGY OF SANSKRIT COURT POETRY: Vidyakara's Subhasitaratnakosa
Highly refined and delicate translations by the dean of 20th century American Sanskrit scholars
Translated by Daniel H. Ingalls
0–674–03950–5 Harvard $40.00

SANSKRIT POETRY FROM VIDYAKARA'S TREASURY
A selection from Ingalls' complete translation of Vidyakara's *Treasury;* the best introduction to classical Indian poetry
Translated by Daniel H. Ingalls
0–674–78855–9 Harvard $22.00
0–674–78865–6 Harvard pb $7.95

- **John Brough, translator**
POEMS FROM THE SANSKRIT
0–14–044198–0 Penguin pb $6.95

- **P. Lal, editor**
GREAT SANSKRIT PLAYS IN MODERN TRANSLATION
A handy anthology of Sanskrit plays, here made available to the Western reader
0–8112–0079–5 New Directions pb $8.95

- **W.S. Merwin & J.M. Masson, translators**
THE PEACOCK'S EGG: Love Poems from Ancient India
The distinguished American poet's versions of erotic Sanskrit poetry
0–86547–059–6 North Point pb $10.50

- **Barbara Stoler Miller, translator**
THE HERMIT AND THE LOVE-THIEF: Sanskrit Poems of Bhartrihari and Bilhana
Lyric poems from the devotional tradition
0–231–04644–8 Columbia $27.50
0–231–04645–6 Columbia pb $13.00

- **J.A.B. van Buitenen, translator**
TWO PLAYS OF ANCIENT INDIA
Includes *The Little Clay Cart* and *The Minister's Seal*. These two works from the golden era of Sanskrit drama provide a vivid picture of life in the court
0–231–03046–0 Columbia $39.50

PALI LITERATURE

- **Margaret Cone & Richard Gombrich, editors**
THE PERFECT GENEROSITY OF PRINCE VESSANTARA: A Buddhist Epic
This version of the birth of the Buddha is one of the few translations from the vast Buddhist literature of Sri Lanka
0–19–826530–1 Oxford $42.00

SOUTH INDIAN LITERATURE

Ilango Adigal
SHILAPPADIKARAM: The Ankle Bracelet
A 3rd-century Tamil verse epic especially valued for its detailed information on the arts of its era
Translated by Alain Daniélou
0–8112–0246–1 New Directions pb $6.50

Merchant-Prince Shattan
MANIMEKHALAI: The Dancer with the Magic Bowl
A 4th-century Tamil verse epic which portrays that age through the story of a dancer who dedicates her life to charity
Translated by Alain Daniélou
0–8112–1098–7 New Directions pb $11.95

• **G.L. Hart III**
POETS OF THE TAMIL ANTHOLOGIES
0–691–06406–7 Princeton $23.50

• **Nammalvar**
HYMNS FOR THE DROWNING: Poems for Vishnu by Nammalvar
Devotional poems by one of the most renowned Tamil poet-saints. The translator has been awarded a MacArthur Fellowship for his work in South Indian literatures
Translated by A.K. Ramanujan
0–691–06492–X Princeton $25.00

• **Satyajit Ray**
PHATIK CHAND
Translated by Lila Ray
0–86578–230–X Ind-U S pb $8.00

THE UNICORN EXPEDITION & OTHER FANTASTIC TALES OF INDIA
0–525–24544–8 Dutton $16.95

• **Rabindranath Tagore**
SELECTED POEMS
Edited by William Radice
0–14–007985–8 Penguin pb $6.95

A TAGORE READER
A representative sample from all the work of the Nobel laureate
Edited by Amiya Chakravarty
0–8070–5971–4 Beacon pb $14.95

FIREFLIES
Illustrated by Boris Artzybasheff
0–02–089640–9 Macmillan pb $9.95

GITANJALI: Collection of Prose Translations Made by the Author from the Original Bengali
Tagore's beautiful English translations of his own poems, with an introduction by W.B. Yeats
Introduction by W.B. Yeats
0–02–089630–1 Macmillan pb $5.95

• **Edward C. Dimock, editor**
THIEF OF LOVE: Bengali Tales from Court and Village
Funny and instructive stories drawn from Bengali folklore
Translated by Edward C. Dimock
0–226–15236–7 Chicago pb $3.95

• **Edward C. Dimock & Denise Levertov, translators**
IN PRAISE OF KRISHNA: Songs from the Bengali
The ecstatic nature of Bengali devotion is well captured by this volume, a collaboration between a scholar and a leading American poet
Illustrated by Anju Chaudhuri
0–226–15231–6 Chicago pb $6.95

• **A.K. Ramanujan, translator**
POEMS OF LOVE AND WAR: From the Eight Anthologies and the Ten Songs of Classical Tamil
Dramatic poems from the secular Tamil tradition
0–231–05107–7 Columbia pb $16.00

SPEAKING OF SIVA
Devotional poems originally composed in the South Indian language Kannada, and emanating from the *bhakti* movement of spiritual protest which originated in the 10th century. This is arguably the single best set of translations from an Indian language into English
0–14–044270–7 Penguin pb $5.95

• **Gene Roghair, translator**
THE EPIC OF PALNADU: A Study and Translation of Palnati Virula Katha, a Telegu Oral Tradition from Andhra Pradesh, India
0–19–815456–9 Oxford $56.00

> Does it matter how long
> a rock soaks in the water:
> will it ever grow soft?
>
> Does it matter how long
> I've spent in worship,
> when the heart is fickle?
>
> Futile as a ghost
> I stand guard over hidden gold,
>
> O lord of the meeting rivers.
>
> A.K. Ramnujan, translator
> **SPEAKING OF SIVA**   0–14–044270–7 Penguin pb $5.95

HINDI, URDU AND PERSIAN LITERATURE

• **Ahmed Ali, editor & translator**
THE GOLDEN TRADITION: An Anthology of Urdu Poetry
0–231–03687–6 Columbia $35.00
0–231–03688–4 Columbia pb $15.00

• **Kenneth E. Bryant**
POEMS TO THE CHILD-GOD: Structures and Strategies in the Poetry of Sur Das
Translations and a study of the poems of Sur Das, the greatest of the sectarian medieval poets
0–520–03540–2 California $37.50

• **Faiz Ahmed Faiz**
THE TRUE SUBJECT: Selected Poems of Faiz Ahmed Faiz
Superb translations of the greatest Urdu poet of the 20th century
Translated by Naomi Lazard
0–691–06704–X Princeton $27.00
0–691–01438–8 Princeton pb $10.00

• **Asadullah Ghalib**
GHALIB: Life and Letters, Volume 1
Mirza Ghalib, the last and greatest of the classical Urdu poets, was equally renowned for his prose, extensive translations of which are included in this autobiographical volume
Edited by Ralph Russell & Khurshidul Islam
0–674–35435–4 Harvard $29.50

• **John S. Hawley**
SUR DAS: Poet, Singer, Saint
A study with translations, from the perspective of a student of religions
0–295–96102–3 Washington $25.00

• **Mahmood Jamal, editor**
THE PENGUIN BOOK OF MODERN URDU POETRY
A selection of the major Urdu poets of India and Pakistan
Translated by Mahmood Jamal
0–14–058512–5 Penguin pb $6.95

Kabir
THE BIJAK OF KABIR
Lucid, precise, and faithful translations which also have a great deal of poetic merit. "Kabir has the unusual distinction of being claimed by both Muslims and Hindus as a great teacher ... His teasing verses, authentic and ascribed, were and still are sung all over the vast subcontinent, forming an integral part of its rich oral tradition"—*Booklist*
Translated by Linda Hess & Shukdev Singh
Commentary by Linda Hess
0–86547–114–2 North Point pb $12.50

SONGS OF KABIR
Tagore's highly personal translations are based on Bengali versions of Kabir's poems
Translated by Rabindranath Tagore
0–87728–695–7 Weiser pb $7.95

THE KABIR BOOK: Forty-Four of the Ecstatic Poems of Kabir
Robert Bly's versions, based on Tagore's English text, bear the stamp of his distinctive poetic sensibility
Translated by Robert Bly
0–8070–6379–7 Beacon pb $6.95

• **Gordon Roadarmel, translator & editor**
A DEATH IN DELHI: Modern Hindi Short Stories
A selection of the excellent short fiction produced in Hindi in this century
0–520–02220–3 California $27.50

• **Ralph Russell & Khurshidul Islam**
THREE MUGHAL POETS: Mir, Sauda, Mir Hasan
An acknowledged classic, this book provides an illuminating introduction to

 IF YOU CAN'T FIND IT, LOOK IN THE INDEX

the first great period of classical Urdu poetry
Introduction by Annemarie Schimmel
0–674–88980–0 Harvard $21.00

• Nirmal Verma
THE WORLD ELSEWHERE
Stories by a leading Hindi writer
0–930523–46–6 Readers International $16.95

INDIAN LITERATURE IN ENGLISH

• Mulk Raj Anand & S. Balu Rao
PANORAMA: An Anthology of Modern Indian Short Stories
81–207–0611–0 Sterling $27.50

• Mulk Raj Anand
Along with R.K. Narayan, Anand is one of India's best known novelists. His most successful novels like *Untouchable* and *The Sword and the Sickle* often reveal his strong commitment to socialist values.
ACROSS THE BLACK WATERS
0–86578–081–1 Ind-US pb $5.95
APOLOGY FOR HEROISM
0–86578–074–9 Ind-US pb $3.60
THE BARBER'S TRADE UNION & OTHER STORIES
0–86578–145–1 Ind-US pb $3.00
THE BIG HEART
0–86578–086–2 Ind-US $19.95
0–86578–144–3 Ind-US pb $3.95
CONFESSION OF A LOVER
0–86578–073–0 Ind-US pb $5.75
MORNING FACE
0–86578–062–5 Ind-US pb $5.75
SEVEN SUMMERS
0–88253–124–7 Ind-US pb $3.00
THE SWORD AND THE SICKLE
0–86578–242–3 Ind-US $15.00
UNTOUCHABLE
0–86578–068–4 Ind-US pb $5.00
THE VILLAGE
0–86578–090–0 Ind-US pb $3.00

• Anita Desai
BAUMGARTNER'S BOMBAY
The compelling story of a German Jew who flees the Holocaust and finds refuge in India
0394–57229–7 Knopf $18.95
CLEAR LIGHT OF DAY
"A wonderful novel about silence and music, about the partition of a family as well as a nation"—*NY Times*
0–14–008670–6 Penguin pb $6.95
CRY THE PEACOCK
0–86578–083–8 Ind-US pb $4.50
FIRE ON THE MOUNTAIN
0–8364–1455–1 South Asia $7.50
GAMES AT TWILIGHT
Set in Bombay and other cities, these short stories are peopled with intensely individual characters
0–14–005348–4 Penguin pb $5.95

IN CUSTODY
A lecturer in a small northern town is unexpectedly asked to interview India's greatest living poet. "She tells a touching and moral story supremely well"—*Guardian*
0–14–007752–9 Penguin pb $4.95
VOICES IN THE CITY
0–88253–250–2 Ind-US pb $5.95
WHERE SHALL WE GO THIS SUMMER?
0–86578–125–7 Ind-US pb $4.50

• G.V. Desani
ALL ABOUT H. HATTERR
This brilliant novel, highly praised by T.S. Eliot when it was first published, is one of the neglected treasures of 20th-century literature
0–914232–79–7 McPherson $20.00
0–914232–78–9 McPherson pb $10.00

• Ruth Prawer Jhabvala
HEAT AND DUST
The best-known work of the expatriate writer Ruth Prawer Jhabvala, this novel was awarded the Booker Prize in 1975
0–671–64657–5 Simon & Schuster pb $6.95
THE HOUSEHOLDER
A young teacher in New Delhi has just become a householder and is finding his responsibilities perplexing. "The detail of Prem's daily round, school and domestic, is beautifully done"—*New Statesman*
0–393–00851–7 Norton pb $6.95
HOW I BECAME A HOLY MOTHER & OTHER SHORT STORIES
0–06–012198–X Harper & Row $9.95
0–06–080474–2 Harper & Row pb $2.50
IN SEARCH OF LOVE AND BEAUTY
0–14–006921–6 Penguin pb $5.95
OUT OF INDIA: Selected Stories
Disturbing stories of Indian dislocation
0–688–06382–9 Morrow $16.95
0–671–64221–9 Simon & Schuster pb $7.95
THREE CONTINENTS
Long Island, to London, and then to India, this novel follows the footsteps of the young twins Harriet and Michael Wishwell
0–688–07184–8 Morrow $18.95
TRAVELERS
0–671–64378–9 Simon & Schuster pb $6.95

• Gita Mehta
RAJ
0–671–43248–6 Simon & Schuster $19.50

• Ved Mehta
At the age of 15 Ved Mehta left India to go to the Arkansas School for the Blind. Much of his work is autobiographical, capturing his sightless life in a remarkably vivid and original light.
DADDYJI
0–395–30562–7 Norton pb $8.95
THE FLY AND THE FLY-BOTTLE
Illustrated by Saul Steinberg
0–231–05619–2 Columbia pb $14.50
THE LEDGE BETWEEN THE STREAMS
0–393–01828–8 Norton $17.50
0–393–30244–X Norton pb $9.95

MAMAJI
"Not just an interesting biography but, I think, a work of art"—John Gardner
0–393–30536–8 Norton pb $8.95
SOUND-SHADOWS OF THE NEW WORLD
"As a record of self-reliance and tenacity *Sound-Shadows* is extraordinarily moving; but as an account of one boy's ambition, it is equally remarkable"—Peter Ackroyd
0–393–02225–0 Norton $17.95
0–393–30437–X Norton pb $8.95
VEDI
"His objective world is intensely remote from ours, but his inner world . . . is as close as art can make it. His is obviously a singular life . . . I urge you to catch up with it"—Clark Blaise, *NY Times*
0–19–503005–2 Oxford $18.95
0–393–30417–5 Norton pb $7.95

• Bharati Mukherjee
Writing on the immigrant experience with wit and sensitivity, Mukherjee delineates a class of imperfectly assimilated Indians who never quite manage to break ties with their homeland.
DARKNESS
"Bharati Mukherjee's stories of contemporary Indian immigrants painfully recreating their lives and selves on this continent are astounding and simply brilliant"—Lynne Sharon Schwartz
0–14–007930–0 Penguin pb $6.95
JASMINE
0–8021–1032–0 Grove $17.95
THE MIDDLEMEN & OTHER STORIES
0–8021–1031–2 Grove $15.95
THE TIGER'S DAUGHTER
0–14–009301–X Penguin pb $6.95
WIFE
0–14–009300–1 Penguin pb $6.95

• R.K. Narayan
Many of Narayan's novels center around a sleepy South Indian town of his own creation. Maldugi's inhabitants—civil servants, merchants, artisans—are excellent fodder for rich social satire. Narayan's prose, simple but elegant, describes an unchanging India reluctantly being dragged into the 20th century.
AN ASTROLOGER'S DAY & OTHER STORIES
0–88253–105–0 Ind-US $4.95
THE BACHELOR OF ARTS
A youth is caught between his Western education and the traditional values of the Hindu Orthodoxy
Introduction by Graham Greene
0–226–56832–6 Chicago $13.00
0–226–56833–4 Chicago pb $7.95
THE DARK ROOM
0–226–56836–9 Chicago $15.00
0–226–56837–7 Chicago pb $4.50
THE EMERALD ROUTE
0–86578–075–7 Ind-US pb $4.95
THE ENGLISH TEACHER
0–226–56835–0 Chicago pb $9.95
THE FINANCIAL EXPERT
0–226–56840–7 X Chicago $15.00
0–226–56841–5 X Chicago pb $8.95

GRATEFUL TO LIFE AND DEATH
0-87013-005-6 Michigan State pb $5.50

THE GUIDE
A peasant mistakes Raju, one of India's most corrupt tourist guides, for a holy man. "The best of R.K. Narayan's enchanting novels"—*New Yorker*
0-14-005453-7 Penguin pb $5.95

MALGUDI DAYS
A collection of short stories
0-670-45178-9 Viking $6.95
0-14-006910-0 Penguin pb $6.95

THE MAN-EATER OF MALGUDI
A zealous taxidermist upsets the local citizens when he proposes to shoot and stuff the town's sacred elephant
0-14-006257-2 Penguin pb $4.95

MR. SAMPATH: The Printer of Malgudi
0-226-56838-5 Chicago $15.00
0-226-56839-3 Chicago pb $4.50

MY DATELESS DIARY
0-86578-118-4 Ind-US pb $3.25

THE PAINTER OF SIGNS
In the city of Malgudi, Raman considers giving up sign-painting when he meets Daisy of the Family Planning Center
0-14-006259-9 Penguin pb $5.95

THE PRINTER OF MALGUDI
0-87013-025-0 Michigan State pb $6.00

THE RELUCTANT GURU
0-88253-729-6 Ind-US pb $2.50

SWAMI AND FRIENDS
0-226-56829-6 Chicago $13.00
0-226-56831-8 Chicago pb $6.95

TALKATIVE MAN
Bizarre happenings at Malgudi are heralded by the arrival of a stranger on the Delhi train. "His lean, matter-of-fact prose has lost none of its chuckling sparkle mixed with melancholy"—*Spectator*
0-670-81341-9 Viking $15.95
0-14-010134-9 Penguin pb $5.95

A TIGER FOR MALGUDI
0-14-006911-9 Penguin pb $5.95

UNDER THE BANYAN TREE & OTHER STORIES
0-670-80452-5 Viking $16.95
0-14-008012-0 Penguin pb $6.95

THE VENDOR OF SWEETS
Jagan's patience begins to fray when his son descends on the sleepy town of Malgudi full of modern notions
0-14-006258-0 Penguin pb $5.95

WAITING FOR THE MAHATMA
0-226-56826-1 Chicago $15.00
0-226-56828-8 Chicago pb $4.50

• Raja Rao
KANTHAPURA
The story of the impact of Gandhi's ideas on a village on the tea-growing Malabar coast
0-8112-0168-6 New Directions pb $8.95

THE SERPENT AND THE ROPE
A modern Indian recovers the values of his culture. "A truly contemporary work—one by which an age can measure itself, its values"—Lawrence Durrell
0-87951-220-2 Overlook $22.50
0-87951-243-1 Overlook pb $9.95

• Salman Rushdie
GRIMUS
A combination of fantasy, story-telling, and folklore, Rushdie's first novel is ambitious and strikingly confident
0-87951-093-5 Overlook $22.50
0-87951-138-9 Overlook pb $9.95

MIDNIGHT'S CHILDREN
A prodigiously inclusive piece of fiction about India's first 31 years of Independence. Winner of the Booker Prize
0-394-51470-X Knopf $14.45
0-380-58099-3 Avon pb $5.95

THE SATANIC VERSES
"What is being expressed is a discomfort with plural identity . . . We are increasingly becoming a world of migrants, made up of bits and fragments from here, there. We are here. And we have never really left anywhere we have been"—Salman Rushdie
0-670-82537-9 Viking $19.95

SHAME
A phantasmagoric variation on the history of Pakistan
0-394-53408-5 Knopf $13.95
0-394-72665-0 Random House pb $9.95
0-679-72204-1 Vintage pb $9.95

• Nayantara Sahgal
MISTAKEN IDENTITY
"Many levels of meaning are unfolded—not least the questionable role of the Rajas; through it all, Sahgal sustains the note of suspense while cleverly suggesting the contrast between cultural synthesis and the divide-and-rule of recent, fractured times"—*TLS*
0-8112-1093-6 New Directions $16.95

PLANS FOR DEPARTURE
0-393-02221-8 Norton $14.95

RICH LIKE US
0-393-02309-5 Norton $14.95

• I. Allan Sealy
THE TROTTER-NAMA
0-394-56364-6 Knopf $19.95

• Khushwant Singh
TRAIN TO PAKISTAN
A masterpiece dealing with the partition of the subcontinent into India and Pakistan
0-8021-5023-3 Grove pb $5.95

CRITICAL STUDIES

• Stuart M. Blackburn & others, editors
ORAL EPICS IN INDIA
Essays on the oral tradition with synopses of 14 works
0-520-06324-4 California $35.00

• J.L. Brockington
RIGHTEOUS RAMA: The Evolution of an Epic
An engrossing study of the smaller of the two Indian epic poems
0-19-561710-X Oxford $36.00

• Edward C. Dimock
THE LITERATURES OF INDIA: An Introduction
The standard all-purpose survey, excellent both as a critical introduction and as a reference work
0-226-15233-2 Chicago pb $6.95

• Richard Lannoy
THE SPEAKING TREE: A Study of Indian Culture and Society
A highly praised work of cultural criticism
0-19-501469-3 Oxford $32.50
0-19-519754-2 Oxford pb $12.95

• Sitakant Mahapatra
THE AWAKENED WIND: Oral Poetry of the Indian Tribes
0-7069-2153-4 Advent $32.50

• Meenakshi Mukherjee
REALISM AND REALITY: The Novel and Society in India
A discussion of the uses to which the novel, an imported art form, has been put in modern India
0-19-561648-0 Oxford $23.95

• David Rubin
AFTER THE RAJ: British Novels of India since 1947
A discussion of current fictional attitudes to India. The sections on Paul Scott and Ruth Prawer Jhabvala are particularly illuminating
0-87451-383-9 New England $20.00

• Muhammad Sadig
A HISTORY OF URDU LITERATURE
An opinionated, highly personal, but enormously erudite work on the classical Urdu Indian tradition
0-19-561558-1 Oxford $45.00

• Lee Siegel
FIRES OF LOVE, WATERS OF PEACE
An excellent introduction to the themes and archetypes of Indian civilization
0-8248-0828-2 Hawaii $12.50

• Rashna Singh
THE IMPERISHABLE EMPIRE: A Study of British Fiction on India
A reliable guide to a subject that extends well beyond Forster and Kipling
0-89410-342-3 Three Continents $25.00
0-317-60758-8 Three Continents pb $12.00

Classical Chinese Literature

China has one of the world's oldest continuous literary traditions, going back more than 3000 years. Poetry and historical writing have traditionally been its most esteemed genres. The Chinese poetic voice has made use of certain recurrent themes: the beauty of nature, political and social strife, the joys of wine and friendship, the grief of separation and war. Written predominantly by scholar-officials educated in the classics and the intricacies of the literary langugage, Chinese poetry has also been composed by Buddhist monks, emperors, and dancing girls.

Drama and fiction, which originated with traveling performers, developed comparatively late and was created by storytellers writing in both the literary and vernacular languages. Chinese drama developed a variety of forms, from dramatic romances and detective stories to the stylized Peking opera. The works of the professional storytellers grew in sophistication, culminating in novels of great complexity and length, such as *The Dream of the Red Chamber* (or *The Story of the Stone*), first published in 1792.

Chinese names and titles (except for some modern works) are given in Wade-Giles romanization; Chinese proper names appear in the Chinese manner, surname first.

GENERAL ANTHOLOGIES

• Cyril Birch, editor
ANTHOLOGY OF CHINESE LITERATURE
An excellent introduction encompassing poetry, prose, and drama, with brief prefaces placing the selections in their historical context. The translations have been chosen with care, and many were commissioned especially for this collection. "It is a remarkable Chinese banquet indeed—drinking poems and didactic biographies, cynical love stories and operatic plays, philosophical letters and lyrical religious tracts—it is all a delight"—*New Yorker*

Volume 1: From Early Times to the 14th Century
0–802–15038–1 Grove pb $17.50

Volume 2: From the 14th Century to the Present
0–802–15090–X Grove pb $14.50

• H.C. Chang, editor
CHINESE LITERATURE

Volume 1: Popular Fiction and Drama
Includes short stories, chapters of novels, and scenes from plays. Excellent translations and introductory information
0–231–05367–3 Columbia pb $22.00

Volume 2: Nature Poetry
A slender volume that offers much information and insight
0–231–04288–4 Columbia pb $18.00

Volume 3: Tales of the Supernatural
0–231–05794–6 Columbia pb $25.00

• William T. De Bary, editor
SOURCES OF CHINESE TRADITION
This invaluable survey of Chinese intellectual history is a collection of translated sources with introductions

Volume 1
0–231–08602–4 Columbia pb $17.00

Volume 2
0–231–08603–2 Columbia pb $14.50

POETRY

Poetry has generally been regarded as the glory of the Chinese literary tradition, and certain characteristics make it particularly accessible to non-Chinese readers. The intensely concrete and visual qualities of classical poetry have had wide appeal for 20th-century poets and translators, whose versions have greatly influenced modern poetry in the West.

Chinese poetry is primarily lyrical rather than narrative or dramatic. It generally avoids abstraction and seeks to be concise and suggestive rather than expansive and descriptive.

Burton Watson, translator & editor
THE COLUMBIA BOOK OF CHINESE POETRY: From Early Times to the 13th Century
A comprehensive anthology by a preeminent scholar and translator
0–231–05682–6 Columbia $29.00
0–231–05683–4 Columbia pb $14.50

Jonathan Chaves, translator & editor
THE COLUMBIA BOOK OF LATER CHINESE POETRY: Yüan, Ming, and Ch'ing Dynasties (1279–1911)
A companion to the Watson anthology by an excellent translator who has championed the lesser-known later periods of Chinese poetry
0–231–06148–X Columbia $30.00
0–231–06149–8 Columbia pb $17.50

• Anne Birrell, translator & editor
NEW SONGS FROM A JADE TERRACE: An Anthology of Early Chinese Love Poetry
0–14–044487–4 Penguin pb $6.95

• C.H. Kwock & Vincent McHugh, translators
OLD FRIEND FROM FAR AWAY: 150 Chinese Poems from the Great Dynasties
Experimental translations that attempt to capture the elliptical effects of the Chinese originals. The 50 poets include Wang Wei, Li Po, and Tu Fu
0–86547–018–9 North Point pb $7.50

• David Lattimore, translator
THE HARMONY OF THE WORLD: Chinese Poems
A small volume with an interesting essay on translation
0–914278–31–2 Copper Beech pb $4.50

• Wu-Chi Liu & Irving Yucheng Lo, editors
SUNFLOWER SPLENDOR
The largest and best single-volume anthology in English, containing some 1000 poems. It includes introductions, biographies of the poets, and bibliographies
0–385–09716–6 Doubleday pb $8.95

• Kenneth Rexroth, translator
ONE HUNDRED POEMS FROM THE CHINESE
Rexroth's translations are loose but they are memorable American poetry in themselves
0–8112–0180–5 New Directions pb $5.95

ONE HUNDRED MORE POEMS FROM THE CHINESE: Love and the Turning Year
0–8112–0179–1 New Directions pb $5.95

• Kenneth Rexroth & Ling Chun, translators
WOMEN POETS OF CHINA
Focuses on a neglected area; the translations are not always reliable
0–8112–0821–4 New Directions pb $5.95

• Lucien Stryk & Takashi Ikemoto, editors & translators
THE PENGUIN BOOK OF ZEN POETRY
Includes both Chinese and Japanese poets
0–14–058599–0 Penguin pb $6.95

• Arthur Waley, translator
CHINESE POEMS
Waley's superb translations played a crucial role in introducing both Chinese and Japanese literature to western readers
0–04–895021–1 Allen & Unwin pb $8.95

Early Chinese Poetry

Several poetic genres were practiced in the Han dynasty (202 BC–AD 220). *Fu,* or rhyme-prose, is characterized by long descriptive poetic passages occasionally interspersed with prose, and was used especially to describe palaces, cities, and imperial hunts. *Shih,* or lyrical poetry, developed the major formal characteristics found in later poetry.

Arthur Waley, translator
THE BOOK OF SONGS
The *Book of Songs,* compiled in the 7th century BC, is the oldest collection of Chinese poetry and one of the Five Classics. It includes folk songs, court songs, and sacrificial songs. Its simple style (4-character meter) and sincere emotional expressiveness greatly influenced later poetry
0–802–13021–6 Grove pb $9.95

Ezra Pound, translator
SHIH-CHING: The Classic Anthology Defined by Confucius
This version of *The Book of Songs* is not exactly a translation, but it is a classic in its own right, written in a vein of untrammeled lyricism rare in Pound's later work
0–674–13397–8 Harvard pb $4.95

• David Hawkes, translator
THE SONGS OF THE SOUTH: An Ancient Chinese Anthology of Poems
The second collection of Chinese poetry, very different from *The Book of Songs.* There is much controversy on the attribution of poems to the statesman Ch'ü Yüan. The ostensibly autobiographical poem, *Li Sao* (On Encountering Sorrow), is at once a political allegory and a quasi-shamanistic account of a spiritual quest, laden with exotic imagery and impassioned language
0–14–044375–4 Penguin pb $5.95

• Hsi K'ang
HSI K'ANG AND HIS POETICAL ESSAY ON THE LUTE
The work of a 3rd-century poet, one of the unconventional Seven Sages of the Bamboo Grove. An annotated translation with historical and literary background
Translated by Robert Van Gulik
0–8048–0868–6 Tuttle $15.00

• Tzu Yeh
A GOLD ORCHID: Love Poems of Tzu Yeh
Poems of the Han-Sui periods, written in the voice of a wineshop or entertainment girl. This free translation captures the spirit of the original. An attractive book, including reproductions of Chinese paintings
Translated by Lenore Mayhew & William McNaughton
0–8048–0211–4 Tuttle $9.50

• Yü Hsin
THE LAMENT FOR THE SOUTH: Yü Hsin's Ai Chiang Nan Fu
Yü Hsin was a preeminent Six Dynasties (220–581) literary figure whose work describes his elegant life and the events of the time
Translated by William Graham
0–521–22713–5 Cambridge $39.50

• Burton Watson
CHINESE RHYME-PROSE: Poems in the Fu Form from the Han and Six Dynasties Period
A superb introduction, accessible and a pleasure to read, offering many translations

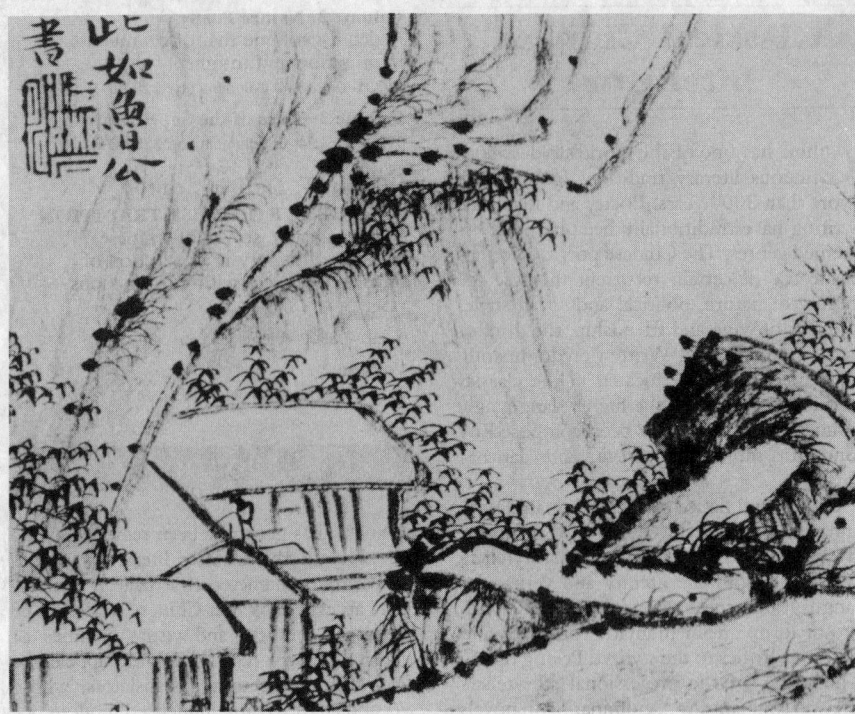
Detail of landscape from Tao-chi's "1700 Peking Album"

of this most expansive of Chinese poetic forms
0–231–03553–5 Columbia $27.00

T'ang Dynasty

Of the T'ang era, traditionally regarded as the most glorious period of Chinese poetry, Cyril Birch has written: "A renaissance was ushered in whose equation with the Italian would not be too misleading. Even the old rites of artificiality were turned to good account in the supreme artistry now sought and attained by the poets."

Poetry presents the thing in order to convey the feeling. It should be precise about the thing and reticent about the feeling, for as soon as the mind responds and connects with the thing the feeling shows in the words; this is how poetry enters deeply into us. If the poet presents directly feelings which overwhelm him, and keeps nothing back to linger as an aftertaste, he stirs us superficially; he cannot start the hands and feet involuntarily waving and tapping in time, far less strengthen morality and refine culture, set heaven and earth in motion and call up the spirits!

Wei T'ai (11th century), quoted in

A.C. Graham
POEMS OF THE LATE T'ANG
0–14–044157–3 Penguin pb $4.95

• Han Shan
COLD MOUNTAIN: 100 Poems by the T'ang Poet Han Shan
Nothing is known of the Buddhist recluse Han Shan beyond what we can learn from these vivid poems of spiritual pilgrimage
Translated by Burton Watson
0–231–03450–4 Columbia pb $10.00

THE COLLECTED SONGS OF COLD MOUNTAIN
Translated by Red Pine
0–914742–69–8 Copper Canyon $20.00

• Li Ho
GODDESSES, GHOSTS, AND DEMONS: The Collected Poems of Li Ho
The work of a tragic-romantic poet, filled with rich and eccentric imagery, translated in full for the first time
Translated by J.D. Frodsham
0–86547–084–7 North Point pb $21.00

• Li Po
THE POETRY AND CAREER OF LI PO
A biography with a selection from Li Po's prolific output. Waley's translations are up to his usual high standard
Translated by Arthur Waley
0–04–895012–2 Allen & Unwin $13.50

• Li Po & Tu Fu
LI PO & TU FU
An introduction to China's two most celebrated poets. Li Po is admired for his simple direct style and spontaneous compositions on nature. Of Tu Fu, Burton Watson has written: "Tu Fu's originality is evident not only in the way he handled poetic form, but in his wide choice of subject matter . . . [He] worked to broaden the definition of poetry by demonstrating

that no subject, if properly handled, need by unpoetic"
Translated by Arthur Cooper
0–14–044272–3 Penguin pb $5.95

BRIGHT MOON, PERCHING BIRD
Poetry of Li Po and Tu Fu in a bilingual edition, with calligraphy by Mo Ji-yu
Translated by J.P. Seaton & James Cryer
0–8195–2143–4 Wesleyan $35.00
0–8195–1144–7 Wesleyan pb $14.95

• James J. Liu
THE POETRY OF LI SHANG-YIN: Ninth-Century Baroque Chinese Poet
A biographical and critical study with many translations. Li Shang-yin's dense and lushly evocative poetry conceals a multitude of hidden meanings, which Liu explicates in fascinating detail
0–226–48690–7 Chicago $18.00

• Ts'ao T'ang
MIRAGES IN THE SEA OF TIME: The Taoist Poetry of Ts'ao T'ang
Translated by Edward H. Schafer
0–520–05429–6 California $27.50

• Tu Fu
THE SELECTED POEMS OF TU FU
"Written largely in poverty and at a time of great political upheaval, Tu Fu's work shows above all its author's persistent humility and humanity"—*American Poetry Review*
Translated by David Hinton
0–8112–1100–2 New Directions pb $10.95

FACING THE SNOW
Translated by Sam Hamill
0–934834–24–5 White Pine pb $10.00

• Wang Wei
POEMS OF WANG WEI
China's great landscape poet "gives the impression of viewing the landscape with perfect Buddhist passivity, not seeking to see anything at all, but merely allowing whatever may lie within the scope of vision to register upon his mind"—Burton Watson
Translated by G.W. Robinson
0–14–044296–0 Penguin pb $4.95

• François Cheng
CHINESE POETIC WRITING: With an Anthology of T'ang Poetry
0–253–31358–9 Indiana $25.00
0–253–20284–1 Indiana pb $12.95

Delicate grasses, faint wind on the bank;
stark mast, a lone night boat;
stars hang down, over broad fields sweeping;
the moon boils up, on the great river flowing.
Fame—how can my writings win me that?
Office—age and sickness have brought it to an end.
Fluttering, fluttering—where is my likeness?
Sky and earth and one sandy gull.

Tu Fu in Burton Watson
CHINESE LYRICISM: Shih Poetry from the 2nd to 12th Century
0–231–03465–2 Columbia pb $14.50

• A.C. Graham, translator
POEMS OF THE LATE T'ANG
Graham's fine translations of some of the major figures—including Tu Fu, Wang Wei, Li Ho, and Li Shang-yin—offer the best introduction to the subject
0–14–044157–3 Penguin pb $4.95

Sung Dynasty

The tenth century saw the full development of a new verse form, the *tz'u*, lyrics written to pre-established musical melodies. Often concerned with love and separation, these lyrics are characterized by delicacy of sentiment, sensuous imagery, and elegant diction.

• Fan Ch'eng-ta
FIVE SEASONS OF A GOLDEN YEAR: A Chinese Pastoral
A series of 60 poems depicting the seasons; with original Chinese text
Translated by Gerald Bullett
0–295–95834–0 Washington $14.50

• Li Ching-chao
THE COMPLETE POEMS
Considered China's most accomplished woman poet. Poetically exciting although not always trustworthy translations
Translated by Kenneth Rexroth & Ling Chung
0–8112–0745–5 New Directions pb $4.95

• Lu Yu
THE WILD OLD MAN: Poems of Lu Yu
Translated by David Gordon
0–86547–150–9 North Point pb $13.50

• Yang Wan-li
HEAVEN MY BLANKET, EARTH MY PILLOW
One of the great Sung poets, he wrote about nature, animals and plants—including such subjects as horse-flies
Translated by Jonathan Chaves
0–8348–0102–7 Weatherhill $7.95
0–8348–0103–5 Weatherhill pb $4.95

• Lois Fusek, translator
AMONG THE FLOWERS: A Translation of the 10th-Century Anthology of Tz'u Lyrics, the Hua-Chien Chi
A major Five Dynasties anthology gracefully and accurately translated
0–231–04986–2 Columbia $37.50
0–231–04987–0 Columbia $14.00

• Sam Hamill, translator
THE LOTUS LOVERS: Poems and Songs by Tzu Yeh and Li Ch'ing Chao
New translations of two of China's leading women poets
0–918273–09–9 Coffee House $11.95

Yüan, Ming, and Ch'ing Dynasties

• Yüan Hung-Tao
PILGRIM OF THE CLOUDS: Poems and Essays from Ming China by Yüan Hung-Tao and His Brothers
Yüan and his brothers were leaders of the individualistic school that flourished in the Ming
Translated by Jonathan Chaves
0–8348–0134–5 Weatherhill pb $6.95

• J.I. Crump
SONGS FROM XANADU: Studies in Mongol Dynasty Song-Poetry (San'ch'ü)
The Yüan dynasty (1260–1368), the period of Mongol rule in China, saw the emergence of a new form of lyric, the *san-ch'ü*, which explored new colloquial areas of language and developed new narrative and descriptive techniques
0–89264–047–2 Michigan pb $10.00

I often see strange people in the cities and regret that I know nothing about their lives. And I regret that of the strange people holed up in the forests and mountains, probably only one out of ten appears in the cities! As for the strange people recorded in the official records and unofficial books, surely they represent no more than one-tenth of those who do appear in the cities. Since these are people with no ambition to become known, and since they associate only with butchers, wine merchants, shop owners, wandering monks and beggars, how many worthy scholar-officials even get to know about them and hand down their stories? In the past, I have heard of a woman known as the Cap-wearing Immortal, and a Taoist of the Single Gourd, both living in Feng-chou. Recently, several people in the Wu-han area have been acting quite strange, and one of them seems to know a thing or two about the Tao. Yes, it appears that this is what is meant by the old saying: "Though he possesses the powers of a dragon, he remains hidden."

Yüan Hung-tao
PILGRIM OF THE CLOUDS
Translated by Jonathan Chaves
0–8348–0134–5 Weatherhill pb $6.95

• Irving Yucheng Lo & William Schultz, editors
WAITING FOR THE UNICORN: Poems and Lyrics of China's Last Dynasty, 1644–1911
Poems of the Ch'ing; Lo co-edited *Sunflower Splendor*
0–253–36321–7 Indiana $27.50

• Jerome Seaton, translator
WINE OF ENDLESS LIFE: Taoist Drinking Songs
0–934834–59–8 White Pine pb $6.00

• Arthur Waley
YUAN MEI: 18th-Century Chinese Poet
A vivid picture of a celebrated Ch'ing man of letters. In the course of the text Waley translates some 100 poems, prose works, and letters
0–8047–0718–9 Stanford $22.50

DRAMA

Chinese drama blends music, dance, song, and speech. Its first great age was the Yüan dynasty, often considered the peak of the tradition, although many individual masterpieces were written later. Chinese drama is stylized and self-consciously theatrical; its texts consist largely of arias, many of them fine poetry in their own right. The longer dramatic works that flourished in the Ming Dynasty, such as *Peach Blossom Fan* and *The Peony Pavilion,* are notable for their elaborate narrative structure.

Kao Ming
THE LUTE
A 14th-century play on the dilemma of filial piety. The translation and introduction are excellent
Translated by Jean Mulligan
0–231–04760–6 Columbia $37.50
0–231–04761–4 Columbia pb $14.00

Kung Shang-jen
THE PEACH BLOSSOM FAN
A famous story of love and political strife by an important Ch'ing playwright. Read in this superb translation, it is as absorbing as a novel
Translated by S.H. Chen, Harold Acton & Cyril Birch
0–520–02928–3 California $33.00
0–520–03201–2 California pb $6.95

T'ang Hsien-tsu
THE PEONY PAVILION
A well-known play by the most talented Ming playwright. The story concerns the heroine's return to earth after her death
Translated by Cyril Birch
0–253–35723–3 Indiana $25.00

- **J.I. Crump, editor**
CHINESE AND JAPANESE MUSIC-DRAMAS
0–89264–019–7 Michigan pb $6.00

- **William Dolby, translator**
EIGHT CHINESE PLAYS: From the 13th Century to the Present
0–231–04488–7 Columbia $21.00

- **George Hayden, translator**
CRIME AND PUNISHMENT IN MEDIEVAL CHINESE DRAMA: Three Judge Pao Plays of the Yüan and Ming Dynasties
Crime and punishment was an important theme in Chinese drama. These have fascinating plots and are written in bawdy language
0–674–17608–1 Harvard $20.00

- **Liu Jung-Er, editor**
SIX YUAN PLAYS
0–14–044262–6 Penguin pb $6.95

- **Colin Mackerras, editor**
CHINESE THEATER: From Its Origins to the Present Day
A recommended history
0–8248–0813–4 Hawaii $19.95

- **A.C. Scott, editor**
TRADITIONAL CHINESE PLAYS
Scott's translations include detailed descriptions of staging and actor's gestures
Volume 1
Includes *Ssu Lang Visits His Mother* and *The Butterfly Dream*
0–299–04134–4 Wisconsin pb $10.25

Volume 2
Includes *Longing for Worldly Pleasures* and *Fifteen Strings of Cash*
0–299–05374–1 Wisconsin pb $10.25

Volume 3
Includes *Picking Up The Jade Bracelet* and *A Girl Setting Out for Trial*
0–299–06630–4 Wisconsin pb $20.00

FICTION

Short Stories

The earliest colloquial works of fiction were the orally transmitted tales. By the Sung dynasty (960–1279) professional storytellers had become so well-established that they had their own union. By the Ming dynasty, the tales of the marvelous were a popular genre. The more polished later stories of Feng Meng-lung and the great Chinese novels derive from these heroic fantastic tales told in the marketplace.

- **Feng Meng-lung**
STORIES FROM A MING COLLECTION
Richly entertaining stories ranging over all the basic genres
Translated by Cyril Birch
0–802–15031–4 Grove pb $9.95

- **Karl S. Kao, editor**
CLASSICAL CHINESE TALES OF THE SUPERNATURAL AND THE FANTASTIC: Selections from the 3rd to the 10th Century
0–253–31375–9 Indiana $27.50

- **Moss Roberts, editor**
CHINESE FAIRY TALES AND FANTASIES
0–394–73994–9 Pantheon pb $9.95

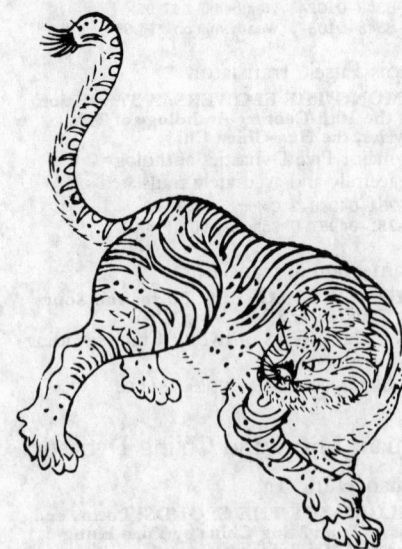

From *Chinese Fairy Tales and Fantasies translated and edited by Moss Roberts (Pantheon)*

Novels (arranged chronologically)

- **Lo Kuan-chung**
THE ROMANCE OF THE THREE KINGDOMS
A saga of battles, intrigue, and bravery compiled in the 14th century and based on historical records. It is set at the fall of the Han dynasty, an age famous for its heroes and villains
Translated by C.H. Brewitt-Taylor
0–8048–0726–4 Tuttle (2-volume set) $37.50

- **Shih Nai-an**
WATER MARGIN
This famous novel, also known as *Outlaws of the Marsh,* recounts in episodic form the adventures of a band of virtuous outlaws living in the marshes who rebel against corrupt officials. It was reportedly Mao's favorite book. This translation leaves much to be desired in terms of English prose, but the narrative vigor of the original still comes through
Translated by J.H. Jackson
0–917056–02–7 Cheng & Tsui $15.95

- **Wu Ch'eng-en**
JOURNEY TO THE WEST
A mixture of allegory, satire, and comedy, this 16th-century work tells of the travels to India of the Buddhist monk Tripitaka and his companions Monkey, Pigsy, and Sandy. "Tripitaka stands for the ordinary man, blundering anxiously through the difficulties of life"—Arthur Waley
Translated by Anthony Yu

Volume 1
0–226–97145–7 Chicago $37.50

Volume 2
0–226–97146–5 Chicago $37.50
0–226–97151–1 Chicago pb $14.95

Volume 3
0–226–97147–3 Chicago $37.50
0–226–97153–8 Chicago pb $14.95

Volume 4
0–226–97148–1 Chicago $37.50
0–226–97154–6 Chicago pb $14.95

MONKEY
A superb partial translation
Translated by Arthur Waley
0–802–13086–0 Grove pb $10.95

- **Wu Ching-tzu**
THE SCHOLARS
A Confucian satire of the 18th century, innovative in its use of strongly drawn characters as models for society
Translated by Yang Hsien-Yi & Gladys Yang
0–917056–64–7 Cheng & Tsui $15.95

Ts'ao Hsüeh-ch'in
THE STORY OF THE STONE
China's greatest novel, also known as *The Dream of the Red Chamber,* tells of the decline and disintegration of a rich, aristocratic family. It mixes sophisticated psychological analysis, a dense and robustly realistic description of social structures, and a layer of religious speculation. The Hawkes-Minford translation is itself a superbly

 ➤ **FOR OVERSEAS ORDERING INFORMATION, SEE PAGE 1**

modulated piece of English writing. A 5-volume set
Translated by David Hawkes & John Minford
0–253–19266–8 Indiana (set) $92.00

Volume 1: The Golden Days
0–253–19261–7 Indiana $25.00
0–14–044293–6 Penguin pb $8.95

Volume 2: The Crab-Flower Club
0–253–19262–5 Indiana $25.00
0–14–044326–6 Penguin pb $8.95

Volume 3: The Warning Voice
0–253–19263–3 Indiana $35.00
0–14–044370–3 Penguin pb $8.95

Volume 4: The Debt of Tears
0–253–19264–1 Indiana $30.00
0–14–044371–1 Penguin pb $8.95

Volume 5: The Dreamer Wakes
0–253–19265–X Indiana $35.00
0–14–044372–X Penguin pb $8.95

- Robert Van Gulik, translator
CELEBRATED CASES OF JUDGE DEE
An early Chinese crime novel, recounting the criminal cases of a T'ang judge. Van Gulik used it as the starting point for his own series of detective novels based on the same character
0–486–23337–5 Dover pb $4.95

- Li Ju-chen
FLOWERS IN THE MIRROR
Translated by Lin Tai-yi
0–520–00747–6 California $33.00

Other Prose

- Shen Fu
SIX RECORDS OF A FLOATING LIFE
A moving autobiographical account of the author's marriage
Translated by Leonard Pratt
0–14–044429–7 Penguin pb $3.95

- Shih S. Liu, translator
CHINESE CLASSICAL PROSE: The Eight Masters of the T'ang-Sung Period
Essays in the classical or literary language, as distinct from colloquial of the great fiction masterpieces
0–295–95662–3 Washington $24.95

CLASSICAL LITERARY CRITICISM

Literary criticism is an extensive and sophisticated tradition in China, but few critical works have been translated into English.

- James J. Liu
CHINESE THEORIES OF LITERATURE
The interpretation and evaluation of traditional Chinese theories of literature, mostly poetry
0–226–48693–1 Chicago pb $4.95

- Adele A. Rickett, editor
CHINESE APPROACHES TO LITERATURE FROM CONFUCIUS TO LIANG CHI-CHAO
There is no general history of Chinese literary criticism in English, but this volume indicates the scope of the tradition
0–691–06343–5 Princeton $34.00

CRITICAL STUDIES OF CLASSICAL CHINESE LITERATURE

General Studies and Reference Works

- Robert E. Hegel & Richard C. Hessney, editors
EXPRESSIONS OF SELF IN CHINESE LITERATURE
0–231–05828–4 Columbia $40.00
0–231–05829–2 Columbia pb $17.50

- William H. Nienhauser, Jr. & others, editors
THE INDIANA COMPANION TO TRADITIONAL CHINESE LITERATURE
A monumental volume, this reference work is indispensable for knowledgeable readers
0–253–32983–3 Indiana $75.00

- Stephen Owen
REMEMBRANCES: The Experience of the Past in Classical Chinese Literature
0–674–76015–8 Harvard $18.50

- Laurence A. Schneider
A MADMAN OF CH'U: The Chinese Myth of Loyalty and Dissent
0–520–03685–9 California $32.50

- Burton Watson
EARLY CHINESE LITERATURE
An excellent guide
0–231–02579–3 Columbia $35.00
0–231–08671–7 Columbia pb $12.50

General Studies of Poetry

- Hans H. Frankel
THE FLOWERING PLUM AND THE PALACE LADY: Interpretations of Chinese Poetry
Poems grouped by themes and styles, plus an extensive bibliography
0–300–01889–4 Yale $32.00
0–300–02242–5 Yale pb $11.95

- Peter H. Lee
CELEBRATION OF CONTINUITY
Chinese poetry compared to Japanese and Korean, with emphasis on images and themes. A mine of information and insight
0–674–10457–9 Harvard $19.50

- James Y. Liu
THE ART OF CHINESE POETRY
The best general introduction to Chinese poetry
0–226–48685–0 Chicago pb $11.00

- Pauline Yu
THE READING OF IMAGERY IN THE CHINESE POETIC TRADITION
0–691–06682–5 Princeton $29.50

Early Chinese Poetry

- Chang Kang-i Sun
SIX DYNASTIES POETRY
0–691–06669–8 Princeton $30.00

- Lin Shuen-fu & Stephen Owen
THE VITALITY OF THE LYRIC VOICE: Shih Poetry from the Late Han to the T'ang
0–691–03134–7 Princeton $50.00

T'ang Poetry

- Stephen Owen
THE GREAT AGE OF CHINESE POETRY: The High T'ang
Excellent studies and new translations by the Yale scholar
0–300–02367–7 Yale $50.00

- Edward H. Schaefer
Schaefer's studies on various aspects of T'ang cultural life, including many examples of poetry, are accurate and a delight to read.
THE GOLDEN PEACHES OF SAMARKAND: A Study of T'ang Exotics
0–520–05462–8 California pb $12.95
PACING THE VOID: T'ang Approaches to the Stars
0–520–03344–2 California $49.50
THE VERMILION BIRD: T'ang Images of the South
0–520–05463–6 California pb $12.95

- Burton Watson
CHINESE LYRICISM: Shih Poetry from the Second to Twelfth Century
Watson traces the critical and historical development of *shih*, the main form of Chinese poetry, with some 200 poems as examples. The text and translations are both outstanding
0–231–03465–2 Columbia pb $14.50

- Eliot Weinberger & Octavio Paz
NINETEEN WAYS OF LOOKING AT WANG WEI
A provocative essay on the ways various Western translators have approached one brief Chinese poem
0–918825–14–8 Moyer Bell pb $5.95

Sung Poetry

- Chang Kang-I Sun
THE EVOLUTION OF CHINESE TZ'U POETRY: From Late T'ang to Northern Sung
A careful analysis of the *tz'u* tradition, interspersed with skillful translations
0–691–06425–3 Princeton $27.50

- Kojiro Yoshikawa
INTRODUCTION TO SUNG POETRY
An important and useful book by a Japanese scholar
Translated by Burton Watson
0–674–46250–5 Harvard pb $12.50

- Lin Shuen-Fu
THE TRANSFORMATION OF A CHINESE LYRICAL TRADITION: Chiang K'uei and Southern Sung Tz'u Poetry
0-691-06351-6 Princeton $29.50

Drama

- J.I. Crump
CHINESE THEATER IN THE DAYS OF KUBLAI KHAN
An excellent study of Yüan drama
0-8165-0656-6 Arizona pb $14.95

- Shih Chung-wen
THE GOLDEN AGE OF CHINESE DRAMA: Yüan Tsa-chü
0-691-06270-6 Princeton $37.00

- Richard E. Strassberg
THE WORLD OF KUNG SHANG-JEN: A Man of Letters in Early Ch'ing China
An account of the author of *The Peach Blossom Fan*
Introduction by Cyril Birch
0-231-05530-7 Columbia $37.50

Fiction

- John L. Bishop
THE COLLOQUIAL SHORT STORY IN CHINA: A Study of the San-Yen Collections
Three anthologies of vernacular short stories by Feng Meng-lung: detective, love, ghosts, and history themes
0-674-14200-4 Harvard pb $4.50

- Robert E. Hegel
THE NOVEL IN SEVENTEENTH-CENTURY CHINA
0-231-04928-5 Columbia $32.00

- C.T. Hsia
THE CLASSIC CHINESE NOVEL: A Critical Introduction
An excellent introduction that discusses the six most important Chinese novels from both western and Chinese viewpoints
0-253-17483-X Indiana $17.50
0-253-20258-2 Indiana pb $7.95

- Andrew H. Plaks
ARCHETYPE AND ALLEGORY IN THE DREAM OF THE RED CHAMBER
0-691-06293-5 Princeton $31.00

THE FOUR MASTERWORKS OF THE MING NOVEL: Ssu ta ch'i-shu
0-691-06708-2 Princeton $62.50

Modern Chinese Literature

By the 20th century, exposure to western culture had introduced many new themes to Chinese literature. Spoken plays (without music) were written, and the novels of the 1930s showed great sophistication. The colloquial written style replaced the traditional literary language, and literature reached large audiences.

The most drastic change in Chinese literature came about as a result of the May 4th Movement in 1919. Acceptance of the vernacular language had several consequences: a dramatic increase in literacy and a new adventurousness on the part of an intellectual class liberated from historical precedent.

POETRY

- Dominic Cheung, translator & editor
THE ISLE FULL OF NOISES: Modern Chinese Poetry from Taiwan
0-231-06402-0 Columbia $27.50

- Hsu Kai-Yu, translator & editor
TWENTIETH CENTURY CHINESE POETRY: An Anthology
The best introduction to the subject; includes a discussion of modern versus traditional poetry and the influence of western poetry
0-8014-9105-3 Cornell pb $14.95

- Angela J. Palandri, translator
MODERN VERSE FROM TAIWAN
The most informative and insightful volume of poetry from Taiwan
0-520-02061-8 California $31.00

DRAMA

- Edward M. Gunn, editor
TWENTIETH-CENTURY CHINESE DRAMA: An Anthology
0-253-36109-5 Indiana $27.50
0-253-20310-4 Indiana pb $15.00

- Ts'ao Yü
THE WILDERNESS
A play of revenge by the most accomplished modern Chinese playwright; includes a good introduction to Ts'ao's work and synopses of his other plays
Translated by Christopher C. Rand & Joseph S.M. Lau
0-253-17297-7 Indiana $12.50

FICTION

- W.J. Jenner, editor
MODERN CHINESE STORIES
Stories of social protest, revolution, and peasant life by such well-known writers as Lao She, Lü Hsün, and Mao Tun
0-19-519788-7 Oxford pb $8.95

- Joseph S. Lau, editor
THE UNBROKEN CHAIN: An Anthology of Taiwan Fiction Since 1926
0-253-36162-1 Indiana $25.00

Fiction 1917–1949

- Hsiao Hung
MARKET STREET: A Chinese Woman in Harbin
Hsiao Hung is known for her vivid accounts of rural poverty and oppression
Translated by Howard Goldblatt
0-295-96266-6 Washington $14.95

- Lao She
RICKSHAW
A bitter tale of social struggle; Lao She's most popular novel was an American best-seller in the 1940s
Translated by Jean M. James
0-8248-0616-6 Hawaii $12.00
0-8248-0655-7 Hawaii pb $5.95

- Lü Hsün
SELECTED STORIES OF LU HSUN
Considered one of the great modern Chinese writers, Lü Hsün is best known for his short stories and essays
Translated by Yang Hsien-yi & Gladys Yang
0-393-00848-7 Norton pb $7.95

- Mao Tun
MIDNIGHT
A panoramic view of the social, political, and economic events of the 1930s, focusing on a Shanghai industrialist and his family: intrigue, romance, strikes, and political uprisings
0-88727-099-9 Cheng & Tsui $12.95

SPRING SILKWORMS & OTHER STORIES
The poignant story of an old peasant and his family
Translated by Sidney Shapiro
0-917056-90-6 Cheng & Tsui $9.95

- Pa Chin
THE FAMILY
A popular novel dealing with family struggles
0-917056-40-X Cheng & Tsui pb $7.95

FROM 1949 TO THE PRESENT

Communist Literature since 1949

Chinese Communist literature has been characterized by party control, socialist realism, the influence of folk literature, and the overwhelming view that literature should serve the people and the revolution. However, since 1980 there has been a loosening of control, producing an increasing body of experimental works.

- Can Xue
DIALOGUES IN PARADISE
A collection of stories set in this young woman writer's nightmarish dream world
Translated with an introduction by Ron Janssen
0-8101-0830-5 Northwestern $16.95
0-8101-0831-3 Northwestern pb $8.95

- Nieh Hua-ling
LITERATURE OF THE HUNDRED FLOWERS
Selected literary works and political essays from the One Hundred Flower Campaign of 1956–57
0–231–05264–2 Columbia (set) $96.00
Volume 1: Criticism and Polemics
0–231–05074–7 Columbia $39.00
Volume 2: Poetry and Fiction
0–231–05076–3 Columbia $61.00

- Ding Ling
I MYSELF AM A WOMAN: Selected Readings of Ding Ling
Translated by Tani Barlow
0–8070–6736–9 Beacon $24.95

- Wang Anyi
LAPSE OF TIME
Six stories and a novella by a leading woman writer from Shanghai
0–8351–2032–5 China Books pb $8.95

- Yang Jiang
SIX CHAPTERS FROM MY LIFE "DOWNUNDER"
A harsh depiction of re-education during the Cultural Revolution, modeled on the classic *Six Chapters from a Floating Life*
Translated by Howard Goldblatt
0–295–96146–5 Washington $10.95

Zhang Xian-Liang
HALF OF MAN IS WOMAN
When first published in China in 1985, this account of a labor camp during the Cultural Revolution stirred up much controversy because of its sexual frankness
Translated by Martha Avery
0–393–02586–1 Norton $17.95

- Michael S. Duke, editor
CONTEMPORARY CHINESE LITERATURE
An anthology of post-Mao fiction and poetry
0–87332–339–4 Sharpe $35.00
0–87332–340–8 Sharpe pb $14.95

- Hsu Kai-yu & Wang Ting, editors
LITERATURE OF THE PEOPLE'S REPUBLIC OF CHINA
An anthology of film scripts, dialogues, stories, opera and poetry—from 1949 through the 1970s
0–253–16015–4 Indiana $37.50
0–253–20257–4 Indiana pb $10.95

- Zhu Hong, translator & editor
THE CHINESE WESTERN: Short Fiction from Today's China
New realistic prose about China's outlying regions. "What's interesting about these exciting Chinese westerns is the way the folk tales, myths, and traditions have remained a part of the story of the political life of all China: the Great Leap Forward, the Cultural Revolution, the end of the Gang of Four happen in the wastes of the Gobi, in the icy western mountains"—Grace Paley
0–345–35140–1 Ballantine pb $5.95

Literature in Taiwan since 1949

Ch'en Jo-hsi
THE EXECUTION OF MAYOR YIN & OTHER STORIES FROM THE GREAT PROLETARIAN CULTURAL REVOLUTION
These stories by a woman now living in Canada depict disillusion among peasants, students, and party members
Translated by Nancy Ing & Howard Goldblatt
0–253–12475–1 Indiana $25.00
0–253–20231–0 Indiana pb $8.95

- Huang Ch'un-ming
THE DROWNING OF AN OLD CAT & OTHER STORIES
Translated by Howard Goldblatt
0–253–20253–1 Indiana pb $9.95

- Li Ang
THE BUTCHER'S WIFE
A brutal novel of a peasant's oppression by her husband. Some Taiwanese critics were shocked by the frankness of its sexual descriptions
Translated by Howard Goldblatt & Ellen Yeung
0–86547–253–X North Point $14.95

- Pai Hsien-yung
WANDERING IN THE GARDEN, WAKING FROM A DREAM: Tales of Taipei Characters
Pai Hsien-yung's stories about exiled Chinese in Taiwan are outstanding works of Taiwanese fiction
Translated by George Kao & others
0–253–19981–6 Indiana $25.00
0–253–20276–0 Indiana pb $8.95

- Joseph S. Lau & Timothy A. Ross, editors
CHINESE STORIES FROM TAIWAN, 1960–1970
The best anthology in English features works of the second-generation writers, less nostalgic than their predecessors, focusing on city life and the conflicts between western and Chinese values
0–231–04007–5 Columbia $37.00

- Yip Wai-lim, translator
MODERN CHINESE POETRY: 20 Poets from the Republic of China, 1955–1965
0–87745–004–8 Iowa $17.50

CRITICAL STUDIES OF MODERN CHINESE LITERATURE

- Merle Goldman
LITERARY DISSENT IN COMMUNIST CHINA
Profiles the major revolutionary writers and discusses their conflict with the Communist party
0–674–53625–8 Harvard $24.50

- Merle Goldman, editor
MODERN CHINESE LITERATURE IN THE MAY FOURTH ERA
This important collection of essays is especially useful as so many English

translations of the great works of this period are now out of print
0–674–57910–0 Harvard $29.50
0–674–57911–9 Harvard pb $10.95

- Hsia Tsi-An
GATE OF DARKNESS: Studies on the Leftist Literary Movement in China
A vivid picture of cultural life in the 1920s and 1930s, critical of the left-wing writers
0–295–78554–3 Washington $15.00
0–295–95142–7 Washington pb $7.95

Poetry

- Julia C. Lin
MODERN CHINESE POETRY: An Introduction
0–295–95145–1 Washington $15.00
0–295–95281–4 Washington pb $6.95

Drama

- Colin Mackerras
THE CHINESE THEATRE IN MODERN TIMES: From 1840 to the Present Day
0–87023–196–0 Massachusetts $20.00

- James R. Pusey
WU HAN: Attacking the Present Through the Past
After his Peking opera *Hai Jui Dismissed from Office* was condemned during the Cultural Revolution, the playwright Wu Han committed suicide
0–674–96275–3 Harvard pb $11.00

Fiction

- Edward M. Gunn
UNWELCOME MUSE: Chinese Literature in Shanghai and Peking, 1937–1945
A study of Chinese literature in Japanese-controlled areas, including Ch'ien Chung-shu and Chang Ai-ling, whose works in English have gone out of print
0–231–04730–4 Columbia $29.50

- George Kao, editor
TWO WRITERS AND THE CULTURAL REVOLUTION: Lao She and Chen Jo-hsi
Translations and essays about Lao She and Chen Jo-hsi, two important writers deeply affected by the Cultural Revolution
0–295–95747–6 Washington $25.00

- William A. Lyell, Jr.
LU HSUN'S VISION OF REALITY
Detailed study for the general reader
0–520–02940–2 California $40.00

- Ranbir Vohra
LAO SHE AND THE CHINESE REVOLUTION
A discussion of Lao She's major novels, placed in their social context
0–674–51075–5 Harvard $20.00

Chinese Literature since 1949

- Jeannette L. Faurot, editor
CHINESE FICTION FROM TAIWAN: Critical Perspectives
A collection of papers
0–253–12409–3 Indiana $20.00

- **Jeffrey C. Kinkley, editor**
  AFTER MAO: Chinese Literature and
  Society, 1978–1981
  0–674–00885–5 Harvard pb $14.00

- **Perry Link**
  ROSES AND THORNS: The Second
  Blooming of the Hundred Flowers in
  Chinese Fiction, 1979–1980
  0–520–04979–9 California $35.00
  0–520–04980–2 California pb $10.95

- **Bonnie S. McDougall, editor**
  POPULAR CHINESE LITERATURE
  AND PERFORMING ARTS IN THE
  PEOPLE'S REPUBLIC OF CHINA,
  1949–1979
  0–520–04852–0 California $45.00

Japanese Literature

Japanese literature dates from AD 712, when the *Kojiki* (*Record of Ancient Matters*), a semi-mythological account of the nation's history, was compiled. Since then Japanese writers have created a rich and increasingly varied tradition of poems, stories, diaries, novels, and dramas. By comparison with other non-western literatures, a large proportion of this work is available in English.

When Japan ended its isolation in the 19th century, a small band of western scholars began to explore the byways of Japanese literature. Their perspective was often limited, however, by preconceptions and insufficient knowledge. Since World War II Japanese studies in English have taken a more systematic turn, largely under the influence of Donald Keene, who remains the outstanding historian and popularizer in the field. Increasingly, translators seem more willing to take Japanese writers on their own terms rather than attempting to fit them into western aesthetic schemes.

GENERAL ANTHOLOGIES

- **Donald Keene**
  TRAVELERS OF A HUNDRED AGES:
  The Japanese as Revealed Through 1000
  Years of Diaries
  0–8050–0751–2 Henry Holt $29.95

- **Donald Keene, editor**
  ANTHOLOGY OF JAPANESE
  LITERATURE: From the Earliest Era to
  Mid-19th Century
  When this collection first appeared in 1955, it opened up to English-language readers the full range and beauty of Japanese writing; three decades later it remains reliable and endlessly readable
  0–8021–5058–6 Grove pb $13.95

Imaginary portrait of Hitomaro by Genkyu, from Tales of Japan (*New York Public Library*)

MODERN JAPANESE LITERATURE:
From 1868 to the Present Day
A follow-up to the previous title, published in 1957; excellent as far as it goes
0–394–17254–X Grove pb $12.95

- **Burton Watson, translator & editor**
  JAPANESE LITERATURE IN CHINESE:
  Poetry and Prose in Chinese by Japanese
  Writers
  Just as Europeans used to write in Latin, Japanese until the 19th century routinely wrote in Chinese (or bastardized Chinese at any rate), and some compositions were far more than mere curiosities

  Volume 1: The Early Period
  0–231–03986–7 Columbia $21.00

  Volume 2: The Later Period
  0–231–04146–2 Columbia $24.00

- **Ryusaku Tsunoda & William Theodore De Bary, editors**
  SOURCES OF JAPANESE TRADITION
  Key religious, philosophical, political, and literary writings

  Volume 1
  0–231–08604–0 Columbia pb $17.00

  Volume 2
  0–231–08605–9 Columbia pb $16.00

Poetry

- **Geoffrey Bownas & Anthony Thwaite, translators & editors**
  THE PENGUIN BOOK OF JAPANESE
  VERSE
  0–14–058527–3 Penguin pb $5.95

- **Steven Carter**
  WAITING FOR THE WIND: 36 Poets of
  Japan's Late Medieval Age
  0–231–06854–9 Columbia $32.50

- **Hiroaki Sato & Burton Watson, translators & editors**
  FROM THE COUNTRY OF EIGHT
  ISLANDS: An Anthology of Japanese
  Poetry
  By far the most generous collection of Japanese poetry in English, with special attention paid to hitherto unfamiliar genres
  Introduction by Thomas Rimer
  0–295–95798–0 Washington $25.00
  0–231–06395–4 Columbia pb $15.00

  I've grown so wretched,
  I'd break this sad body
  off from its roots,
  drift away like a floating weed
  if the current were to beckon

  The beauty of the flowers faded—
  no one cared—
  and I watched myself
  grow old in the world
  as the long rains were falling

  Those who were here are gone,
  and the gone grow in number—
  in this world I sorrow,
  wondering how long
  I myself can go on sighing

  Three tanka by Ono no Komachi
  (mid-9th century)
  Translated by Burton Watson

  Hiroaki Sato & Burton Watson,
  translators & editors
  FROM THE COUNTRY OF EIGHT
  ISLANDS: An Anthology of Japanese
  Poetry
  0–231–06395–4 Columbia pb $15.00

THE ANCIENT PERIOD
(To AD 794)

- **Donald Philippi, translator**
  SONGS OF GODS, SONGS OF
  HUMANS: The Epic Tradition of the Ainu
  There was a literature of Japan before that of the Japanese. Although the Ainu now live only on the northern island of Hokkaido, they are likely to have dwelled earlier in much of Japan. Philippi's translation of 33 of their sacred narratives represents an incomparable linguistic and literary feat
  Foreword by Gary Snyder
  0–86547–063–4 North Point pb $16.75

  KOJIKI
  Philippi, a brilliant scholar and translator, casts fresh light on this somewhat forbidding work, with its blend of mythology and archaic dynastic politics
  0–86008–320–9 Tokyo $29.50

- **The Nippon Gakujutsu Committee**
  THE MANYOSHU
  The earliest and greatest assemblage of classical poetry, most of it written in the enduring 31-syllable tanka form. This selection, produced in the 1930s by a committee of Japanese scholars assisted by the English poet Ralph Hodgson, holds up remarkably well
  Foreword by Donald Keene
  0–231–08620–2 Columbia pb $17.50

• Ian Hideo Levy, translator
THE TEN THOUSAND LEAVES: A Translation of Man'yōshū, Volume 1
When completed, Levy's will be the first complete translation of *The Man'yōshū*. "Levy's new translation of *The Man'yōshū* makes available to us, on our own terms, as it were, one of the glories of Japanese poetry. His work is . . . so lacking in anything approaching affectation on the one hand or pedantry on the other that we will find the translation definitive"—Donald Richie
0–691–06452–0 Princeton $37.00
0–691–00029–8 Princeton pb $12.95

THE HEIAN PERIOD (794–1185)

The court society of the Heian period was virtually a world unto itself, producing masterpieces which continue to dominate Japanese literature: Lady Murasaki's *Tale of Genji*, the *Pillow Book* of Sei Shonagon, and the classical tanka of the imperial anthologies. Much of this literature was written by women, practicing a native style which counteracted the formal influence of Chinese.

Poetry

• Robert H. Brower & Earl Miner
JAPANESE COURT POETRY
A pioneering attempt to understand Japanese court poetry from a Japanese viewpoint; contains many translations
0–8047–0536–4 Stanford $35.00

• Earl Miner
AN INTRODUCTION TO JAPANESE COURT POETRY
A condensed version of *Japanese Court Poetry*
0–8047–0636–0 Stanford pb $6.95

• Laurel R. Rodd & Mary C. Henkenius, translators
KOKINSHU
The *Kokinshū* (or *Kokin Wakashū*), compiled in 905, was the first of 21 "imperial anthologies" of Japanese poetry which appeared over the next five centuries
0–691–06593–4 Princeton $42.00

• Helen C. McCullough, translator
KOKIN WAKASHU: The First Imperial Anthology of Japanese Poetry
Another complete translation; this edition also includes *Tosa Nikki* (the earliest of Japanese diaries, written by the anthology's editor, Ki no Tsurayuki) and the smaller collection *Shinsen Waka*
0–8047–1258–1 Stanford $49.50

• Kenneth Rexroth, translator
ONE HUNDRED POEMS FROM THE JAPANESE
Relatively free translations by a great American lyric poet, drawn mostly from the repertoire of classical tanka
0–8112–0181–3 New Directions pb $5.95

ONE HUNDRED MORE POEMS FROM THE JAPANESE
A sequel to Rexroth's earlier very popular collection
0–8112–0619–X New Directions pb $6.95

Tales, Diaries, and Essays

• Helen C. McCullough, translator
THE TALES OF ISE: Lyrical Episodes from 10th-Century Japan
An early collection of brief tales, mostly about love, interwoven with poems; attributed to the poet Ariwara no Narihara
0–8047–0653–0 Stanford $25.00

• Mildred Tahara, translator
TALES OF YAMATO: A 10th-Century Poem-Tale
0–8248–0617–4 Hawaii $15.00

• Murasaki Shikibu
THE TALE OF GENJI
"The great masterpiece of Japanese literature . . . The translation by Arthur Waley is a marvelous recreation of the original, capturing its beauty and its unique evocative power"—Donald Keene
Translated by Arthur Waley
0–394–60405–9 Modern Library $13.95

THE TALE OF GENJI
Seidensticker's recent translation has been praised for its meticulous accuracy
Translated by Edward G. Seidensticker
0–394–73530–7 Random House pb $17.95

• Izumi Shikibu
THE IZUMI SHIKIBU DIARY: A Romance of the Heian Court
Translated by Edwin Cranston
0–674–46985–2 Harvard $22.50

Lady Murasaki writing "The Tale of Genji"

• Ono no Komachi & Izumi Shikibu
THE INK DARK MOON: Love Poems by Ono no Komachi and Izumi Shikibu
New versions of the work of two great poets of the Heian period
Translated by Jane Hirshfield & Mariko Aratani
0–684–18971–2 Scribners $14.95

• Sei Shōnagon
THE PILLOW BOOK OF SEI SHONAGON
An inside view of Heian court life and amusements. "One of the most delightful works of Japanese literature. The author, a near contemporary of Murasaki Shikibu, was a woman of remarkable talent and wit, and her book is perhaps the closest approach to high comedy in Japanese literature"—Donald Keene
Translated by Ivan Morris
0–14–044236–7 Penguin pb $6.95

> *16. Things That Make One's Heart Beat Faster*
>
> Sparrows feeding their young. To pass a place where babies are playing. To sleep in a room where some fine incense has been burnt. To notice that one's elegant Chinese mirror has become a little cloudy. To see a gentleman stop his carriage before one's gate and instruct his attendants to announce his arrival. To wash one's hair, make one's toilet, and put on scented robes; even if not a soul sees one, these preparations still produce an inner pleasure.
>
> It is night and one is expecting a visitor. Suddenly one is startled by the sound of rain-drops, which the wind blows against the shutters.
>
> *29. Elegant Things*
>
> A white coat worn over a violet waistcoat.
>
> Duck eggs.
>
> Shaved ice mixed with liana syrup and put in a new silver bowl.
>
> A rosary of rock crystal.
>
> Wistaria blossoms. Plum blossoms covered with snow.
>
> A pretty child eating strawberries.
>
> Sei Shōnagon
> **THE PILLOW BOOK OF SEI SHONAGON**
> Translated by Ivan Morris
> 0–14–044236–7 Penguin pb $6.95

• Edward G. Seidensticker, translator
THE GOSSAMER YEARS: The Diary of a Noblewoman of Heian Japan
An account of the restricted life of a 10th-century aristocrat, predating *The Tale of Genji*
0–8048–1123–7 Tuttle pb $5.95

• Helen C. McCullough, translator
OKAGAMI (THE GREAT MIRROR): Fujiwara Michinaga (966–1027) and His Times
A fictionalized historical chronicle of the Heian period
0–691–06419–9 Princeton $39.00

- Royall Tyler
JAPANESE TALES
The most extensive Japanese folk tale collection available
0–394–52190–0 Pantheon $19.95
0–394–75656–8 Pantheon pb $12.95

THE MIDDLE PERIOD (1200–1600)

This era is notable for three literary developments: the linked poetry called renga, in which two or more persons strung together units of 17 and 14 syllables; the war tales attesting to the new dominance of the military class; and the Nō (or Noh) drama which combined poetic texts with music and dance.

Poetry

- Lady Daibu
THE POETIC MEMOIRS OF LADY DAIBU
Translated by Phillip T. Harries
0–8047–1077–5 Stanford $25.00

- Fujiwara no Teika
FUJIWARA TEIKA'S "SUPERIOR POEMS OF OUR TIME": A 13th-Century Poetic Treatise and Sequence
Teika was both the greatest poet of his time and an influential anthologist
Translated by Robert Brower & Earl Miner
0–8047–0171–7 Stanford $15.00

- Fujiwara no Sadaie
THE LITTLE TREASURY OF ONE HUNDRED PEOPLE, ONE POEM EACH
This small collection became the most widely known of poetic anthologies, and even provided the basis for a popular card game
Translated by Tom Galt
0–691–01392–6 Princeton pb $8.50

- Saigyō
MIRROR FOR THE MOON
Saigyō, a Buddhist priest, wrote some of the most remarkable meditative poems in the Japanese tradition
Translated by William LaFleur
Foreword by Gary Snyder
0–8112–0698–X New Directions pb $10.95

- Musō Soseki
SUN AT MIDNIGHT: Poems and Sermons by Musō Soseki
Soseki was a great Zen teacher of the 13th century
Translated by W.S. Merwin & Soiku Shigematsu
0–86547–382–X North Point pb $11.95

Earl Miner
JAPANESE LINKED POETRY
A detailed description of the renga form, with translations of six sequences—two of them "orthodox," four "humorous" (with the poet Bashō a participant in three of the latter)
0–691–01368–3 Princeton pb $14.95

Steven Carter
THREE POETS AT YUYAMA
A full translation of one of the most famous sequences of linked poetry
0–912966–61–0 California pb $12.00

Hiroaki Sato
ONE HUNDRED FROGS: From Renga to Haiku to English
The history of linked poetry and its evolution into haiku
0–8348–0176–0 Weatherhill pb $14.95

- Lucien Stryk & Takashi Ikemoto, translators & editors
THE PENGUIN BOOK OF ZEN POETRY
Contains Zen poems of both Chinese and Japanese origin
0–14–058599–0 Penguin pb $6.95

Prose

- Lady Nijo
THE CONFESSIONS OF LADY NIJO
Translated by Karen Brazell
0–8047–0929–7 Stanford $29.50
0–8047–0930–0 Stanford pb $9.50

- Yoshida Kenkō
ESSAYS IN IDLENESS: The Tsurezuregusa of Kenkō
Humorous and philosophical reflections of a poet and official who became a Buddhist monk
Translated by Donald Keene
0–231–08308–4 Columbia pb $13.50

- Hiroshi Kitagawa & Bruce Tsuchida, translators
THE TALE OF THE HEIKE
The most celebrated of the military tales chronicles the clash between the doomed Taira clan and the ascendant Minamotos in the late 12th century; the tone alternates splendidly between the violent and the meditative
Foreword by Edward G. Seidensticker

Volume 1
0–86008–188–5 Tokyo pb $22.50

Volume 2
0–86008–189–3 Tokyo pb $17.50

- Thomas Cogan, translator
THE TALE OF THE SOGA BROTHERS
The most famous vendetta in early Japanese history
0–86008–411–6 Tokyo $39.50

- Helen C. McCullough, translator
THE TAIHEIKI: A Chronicle of Medieval Japan
Excerpts from a long military tale describing the civil strife in the early 14th century; its characters include Kusunoki Masashige, a genius of guerrilla warfare who became a nationalist icon in pre-World War II Japan
0–8048–1322–1 Tuttle pb $12.95

YOSHITSUNE: A 15th-Century Japanese Chronicle
The life of Minamoto no Yoshitsune, a brilliant, tragic military leader in the war between the Taira and Minamoto clans
0–8047–0270–5 Stanford $22.50

Drama: Nō and Kyōgen

- Zeami Motokiyo
ON THE ART OF THE NO DRAMA: The Major Treatises of Zeami
Zeami was Nō's greatest playwright and subtlest theoretician; his elucidation of the term yūgen (mysterious elegance) is crucial to Japanese aesthetics
Translated by J. Thomas Rimer & Yamazaki Masakazu
0–691–06582–9 Princeton $43.00
0–691–10154–X Princeton pb $16.95

- Ezra Pound
THE CLASSIC NOH THEATRE OF JAPAN
Pound, who knew no Japanese, worked from Fenollosa's notes to create these influential early versions
Notes by Ernest Fenollosa
Introduction by W.B. Yeats
0–8112–0152–X New Directions pb $6.95

From Twenty Plays of the Nō Theatre *edited by Donald Keene (Columbia)*

- Arthur Waley
THE NO PLAYS OF JAPAN
Waley's Nō translations may have been surpassed on the level of scholarship, but their poetic force is undiminished. Nineteen plays are translated in full, and 16 others summarized with excerpts
0–8048–1198–9 Tuttle pb $7.25
0–394–17206–X Grove pb $9.95

- Donald Keene, editor
TWENTY PLAYS OF THE NO THEATRE
A superb anthology that greatly enlarges our knowledge of the literature of Nō
Translated by Royall Tyler & others
0–231–03455–5 Columbia pb $18.00

- Shio Sakanishi, translator
JAPANESE FOLK PLAYS: The Ink Smeared Lady & Other Kyōgen
Kyōgen are farcical interludes which alleviate the solemnity of a Nō performance
0–8048–0297–1 Tuttle pb $4.95

THE EDO PERIOD (1600–1850)

The literature created during Japan's isolation from the outside world is dominated by three writers and three genres: Matsuo Bashō and the 17-syllable haiku form; Ihara Saikaku and the fiction reflecting the concerns of the city-dwelling merchant class; and Chikamatsu Monzaemon and the plays written for the puppet theater (and later, in many cases, adapted for the Kabuki).

Two Versions of Bashō

Days and months are travellers of eternity. So are the years that pass by. Those who steer a boat across the sea, or drive a horse over the earth till they succumb to the weight of years, spend every minute of their lives travelling. There are a great number of ancients, too, who died on the road. I myself have been tempted for a long time by the cloud-moving wind—filled with a strong desire to travel.

THE NARROW ROAD TO THE DEEP NORTH & OTHER TRAVEL SKETCHES
Translated by Nobuyuki Yuasa
0–14–044185–9 Penguin pb $5.95

Moon & sun are passing figures of countless generations, and years coming or going wanderers too. Drifting life away on a boat or meeting age leading a horse by the mouth, each day is a journey and the journey itself home. Amongst those of old were many that perished upon the journey. So—when was it—I, drawn like blown cloud, couldnt stop dreaming of roaming, roving the coast up and down . . .

BACK ROADS TO FAR TOWNS: Bashō's Travel Journal
Translated by Cid Corman & Kamaike Susumy
0–934834–65–2 White Pine pb $10.00

Poetry

• **Harold G. Henderson**
AN INTRODUCTION TO HAIKU: An Anthology of Poems and Poets from Bashō to Shiki
For many years this has remained the standard introduction to haiku
0–385–09376–4 Doubleday pb $4.95

• **Kenneth Yasuda**
THE JAPANESE HAIKU: Its Essential Nature, History and Possibilities in English, with Examples
0–8048–1096–6 Tuttle pb $6.95

• **Earl Miner & Odagiri Hiroko, translators**
THE MONKEY'S STRAW RAINCOAT & OTHER POETRY OF THE BASHO SCHOOL
Haiku originated as the opening stanza of a renga (linked poetry) sequence; Bashō participated as a renga master in the collective sequences translated here
0–691–06460–1 Princeton $42.00

• **Lenore Mayhew, translator**
MONKEY'S RAINCOAT: Linked Poetry of the Bashō School with Haiku Selections
Another sampling of the linked poetry written by Bashō and his students
0–8048–1500–3 Tuttle $8.95

• **Matsuo Bashō**
THE NARROW ROAD TO THE DEEP NORTH & OTHER TRAVEL SKETCHES
Bashō's travel writings mingle prose and poetry to create a startlingly telegraphic record of his experiences
Translated by Nobuyuki Yuasa
0–14–044185–9 Penguin pb $5.95

BACK ROADS TO FAR TOWNS: Bashō's Travel Journal
Corman, an American poet who has lived for many years in Japan, hews as closely as possible to Bashō's syntax, creating an eloquent if at times cryptic effect
Translated by Cid Corman & Kameike Susumu
0–934834–65–2 White Pine pb $10.00

ON LOVE AND BARLEY: Haiku of Bashō
Stryk emphasizes the influence of Zen on Bashō's writing
Translated by Lucien Stryk
0–8248–1012–0 Hawaii $12.00
0–14–044459–9 Penguin pb $3.95

• **Kobayashi Issa**
THE YEAR OF MY LIFE: A Translation of Issa's Oraga Haru
Issa is perhaps the most humanly appealing of the great haiku poets. This autobiographical work blends poetry and prose
Translated by Nobuyuki Yuasa
0–520–02328–5 California $25.00

• **Ryōkan**
ONE ROBE, ONE BOWL: The Zen Poetry of Ryōkan
A Zen monk who was also a great tanka poet
Translated by John Stevens
0–8348–0126–4 Weatherhill pb $11.95

THE ZEN POEMS OF RYOKAN
Translated by Nobuyuki Yuasa
0–691–06466–0 Princeton $26.50

• **Yoel Hoffman, translator & editor**
JAPANESE DEATH POEMS: Written by Zen Monks and Haiku Poets on the Verge of Death
A large collection of traditional *jisei*, verses written at the point or in anticipation of death, with commentary by the translator
0–8048–1505–4 Tuttle $17.50

Prose

• **Ihara Saikaku**
Saikaku's tales of love and money reflect the same "floating world" depicted in the prints and paintings of Utamaro and Kiyonaga.

FIVE WOMEN WHO LOVED LOVE
Translated by William Theodore De Bary
0–8048–0184–3 Tuttle pb $6.50

THE LIFE OF AN AMOROUS WOMAN & OTHER WRITINGS
The best introduction to Saikaku's prolific writings
Translated & edited by Ivan Morris
0–8112–0187–2 New Directions pb $9.95

THE LIFE OF AN AMOROUS MAN
Translated by Hamada Kengi
0–8048–0381–1 Tuttle pb $6.95

• **Howard Hibbett**
THE FLOATING WORLD IN JAPANESE FICTION
A survey of the pleasures of the merchant class, with lengthy excerpts from Saikaku and his contemporary Kiseki
0–8048–1154–7 Tuttle pb $6.50

• **Jippensha Ikku**
SHANK'S MARE
A broadly humorous picaresque novel which was immensely popular in 18th-century Japan
0–8048–0524–5 Tuttle pb $8.25

• **Ueda Akinari**
TALES OF THE SPRING RAIN
Supernatural tales which provided the basis for Mizoguchi's film *Ugetsu*
Translated by Barry Jackman
0–86008–251–2 Tokyo $15.00

Genroku fashion required a very large wardrobe. At a picnic to look at flowers, for instance, a lady would not only dress as elegantly as possible, and see that her attendants did so, in their way; but she would also have servants bring along a carpet, a wind curtain to be hung between the trees, a set of lacquer boxes for food, cosmetics, and other supplies, and a few extra gowns so that she need not spend a whole afternoon in the same costume. The spare kimono, which were no less luxurious, would be draped casually over the curtain, or in place of it, presumably to help screen her from public view as she sat admiring some especially pretty blossoms.

Howard Hibbett
THE FLOATING WORLD IN JAPANESE FICTION
0–8048–1154–7 Tuttle pb $6.50

Drama: Kabuki and Bunraku

• **Chikamatsu Monzaemon**
MAJOR PLAYS OF CHIKAMATSU
Keene's Chikamatsu translations are a monument of scholarship and skill, revealing the poetic splendor and realistic shadings of these merchant-class tragedies
Translated by Donald Keene
0–231–02490–8 Columbia $37.50

• **Kawatake Mokuami**
THE LOVE OF IZAYOI AND SEISHIN
A representative 19th-century play involving murder and attempted suicide
Translated by Frank T. Motofuji
0–8048–0387–0 Tuttle pb $5.75

• **Takeda Izumo II & others**
CHUSHINGURA: The Treasury of Loyal Retainers, a Puppet Play
A complete translation of the original puppet version of the 47 ronin story, Japan's ever-popular drama of loyalty and revenge
Translated by Donald Keene
0–231–03531–4 Columbia pb $12.50

Poetry

As Japan absorbed western culture in the 19th century, sweeping changes took place. Among literary genres, poetry underwent the most remarkable transformation because the earlier formal and stylistic constraints on it had been the greatest. Poets such as Hagiwara, Miyazawa, and Takamura invented new kinds of poetry—open in length and free in structure—without precedent in the Japanese tradition.

• A.R. Davis, editor
MODERN JAPANESE POETRY
Translated by James Kirkup
0–7022–1148–6 Queensland $16.50

• Ooka Makoto & Thomas Fitzsimmons, editors
A PLAY OF MIRRORS: Eight Major Poets of Modern Japan
0–942668–08–1 Hawaii pb $19.95

• Hagiwara Sakutarō
FACE AT THE BOTTOM OF THE WORLD & OTHER POEMS
Hagiwara Sakutarō is a crucial, rather morbid presence in modern Japanese poetry; the translation fails to do justice to his formal originality
Translated by Graeme Wilson
0–8048–0176–2 Tuttle $4.00

• Ishikawa Takuboku
ROMAJI DIARY & SAD TOYS
This tanka poet who died in 1912 is still widely read
Translated by Sanford Goldstein & Shinoda Seishi
0–8048–1494–5 Tuttle pb $8.95

• Kusano Shimpei
ASKING MYSELF/ANSWERING MYSELF
The secret life of frogs and other matters, in poems full of fantasy and humor
Translated by Cid Corman & Kamaike Susumu
0–8112–0887–7 New Directions pb $5.95

• Miyazawa Kenji
A FUTURE OF ICE: Poems and Stories of a Japanese Buddhist
Miyazawa, who died in 1933, blended religious and scientific imagery with close observation of rural poverty in northern Japan; many consider him the greatest modern Japanese poet
Translated with an introduction by Hiroaki Sato
0–86547–373–0 North Point pb $14.95

• Amy Heinrich
FRAGMENTS OF RAINBOWS: The Life and Poetry of Saitō Mokichi, 1882–1953
The biography of a poet-psychologist, including translations of 219 tanka
0–231–05428–9 Columbia $27.00

• Nanao Sakaki
BREAK THE MIRROR
Sakaki, who has spent much time in America, writes in both Japanese and English
Introduction by Gary Snyder
0–86547–298–X North Point pb $9.95

• Shiraishi Kazuko
SEASONS OF SACRED LUST
An outstanding contemporary woman poet, in some ways comparable to America's Beats
Edited with an introduction by Kenneth Rexroth
0–8112–0687–4 New Directions pb $4.95

• Takahashi Mutsuo
A BUNCH OF KEYS: Selected Poems
Intense homoerotic poetry by a leading 20th-century writer
Translated by Hiroaki Sato
0–89594–144–9 Crossing pb $8.95

• Takamura Kōtarō
CHIEKO'S SKY
Takamura helped forge the modern vernacular poetic style; the poems about his wife Chieko, who succumbed to insanity, are enduringly popular. Chieko's paintings illustrate this edition
Translated by Soichi Furuta
0–87011–313–5 Kodansha $15.55

• Tamura Ryūichi
DEAD LANGUAGES: Selected Poems, 1946–1984
A postwar poet who has been compared to T.S. Eliot
Translated by Christopher Drake
0–295–96359–X Washington pb $14.95

• Taneda Santōka
MOUNTAIN TASTING: Zen Haiku
Free-form haiku by a mendicant Zen monk, translated with feeling and precision
Translated by John Stevens
0–8348–0151–5 Weatherhill pb $7.95

• Tanikawa Shuntarō
THE SELECTED POEMS
One of the most popular and prolific of contemporary poets
Translated & edited by Harold Wright
0–86547–133–9 North Point pb $12.50

• Yosano Akiko
TANGLED HAIR: Selected Tanka from Midaregami
First published in 1901, these frank, romantic poems marked a radical break with traditional tanka
Translated by Sanford Goldstein & Shinoda Seishi
Edited by Florence Sakade & Lora Sharnoff
0–8048–1522–4 Tuttle pb $6.95

• Yoshimasu Gozo
A THOUSAND STEPS . . . AND MORE: Selected Poems and Prose, 1964–1984
Yoshimasu's poetry, with its undertones of shamanistic invocation, is among the most powerfully original of recent years
Translated by Richard Arno & others
Edited by Thomas Fitzsimmons
0–942668–10–3 Katydid pb $14.95

• Yoshioka Minoru & Iijima Koichi
CELEBRATION IN DARKNESS & STRANGERS' SKY
A one-volume presentation of two leading contemporary poets
Translated by Tadayoshi Onuma
Edited by Thomas Fitzsimmons
0–942668–07–3 Katydid pb $10.95

Fiction and Other Prose

• Abe Kobo
THE ARK SAKURA
"A large, ambitious work about the lives of outcasts in modern Japan and such troubling themes as ecological destruction, old age, violence and nuclear war"—Edmund White, *NY Times*
Translated by Juliet Winters Carpenter
0–394–55836–7 Knopf $18.95
0–679–72161–4 Random House pb $8.95
THE RUINED MAP
Translated by E. Dale Saunders
0–399–50470–2 Putnam pb $8.95
THE SECRET RENDEZVOUS
Translated by Juliet Winters Carpenter
0–399–50501–6 Putnam pb $4.95
THE WOMAN IN THE DUNES
0–394–71814–3 Random House pb $4.95

• Akutagawa Ryūnosuke
RASHOMON & OTHER STORIES
Some of Akutagawa's greatest short works, including *In a Grove* (source of Kurosawa's *Rashomon*) and *Kesa and Morita* (on which *Gate of Hell* was based)
Translated by Kojima Takashi
0–8048–1457–0 Tuttle pb $4.25
HELL SCREEN, COGWHEELS, & A FOOL'S LIFE
Three essential works in one volume. *A Fool's Life*, the telegraphic novella in which Akutagawa anticipates his own suicide, is swift and unforgettable
Translated by Takashi Kojima, Cid Corman, & Will Petersen
0–941419–02–9 Eridanos $21.00
0–941419–03–7 Eridanos pb $12.00

• Ariyoshi Sawako
THE TWILIGHT YEARS
Translated by Mildred Tahara
0–87011–677–0 Kodansha $16.95
0–87011–852–8 Kodansha pb $5.95
THE RIVER KI
Translated by Mildred Tahara
0–87011–385–2 Kodansha $14.95
0–87011–514–6 Kodansha pb $5.95
THE DOCTOR'S WIFE
Translated by Wakako Hironaka & Ann S. Kostant
0–87011–337–2 Kodansha $12.95
0–87011–465–4 Kodansha pb $5.95

• Dazai Osamu
THE SETTING SUN
Dazai was the classic exponent of postwar alienation
Translated by Donald Keene
0–8112–0032–9 New Directions pb $6.95
NO LONGER HUMAN
Translated with an introduction by Donald Keene
0–8112–0481–2 New Directions pb $6.95
RETURN TO TSUGARU: Travels of a Purple Tramp
Translated by James Westerhoven
0–87011–841–2 Kodansha pb $5.95

• **Enchi Fumiko**
THE WAITING YEARS
Chronicle of an upper-class family in the years following the Meiji Restoration of 1868
Translated by John Bester
0–87011–424–7 Kodansha pb $5.95

• **Endo Shusaku**
THE SAMURAI
Brilliant historical novel of four samurai who leave 17th-century Japan to explore the western world
Translated by Van C. Gessel
0–06–859852–1 Kodansha $12.95
0–394–72726–6 Random House pb $7.95

SCANDAL
A famous writer confronts the darker side of his nature
Translated by Van C. Gessel
0–396–09320–5 Dodd Mead $18.95

SILENCE
Christian martyrs under the Tokugawa shogunate
Translated by William Johnston
0–8008–7186–3 Taplinger pb $6.95

THE SEA AND POISON
Translated by Michael Gallagher
0–8008–7021–2 Taplinger $8.95
0–8008–7022–0 Taplinger pb $5.95

VOLCANO
Translated by Richard A. Schucher
0–8008–8032–3 Taplinger $8.95
0–8008–8033–1 Taplinger pb $5.95

• **Ibuse Masuji**
BLACK RAIN
The bombing of Hiroshima and its aftermath
Translated by John Bester
0–87011–364–X Kodansha pb $6.95

SALAMANDER & OTHER STORIES
Translated by John Bester
0–87011–458–1 Kodansha pb $4.95

• **Inoue Yasushi**
CHRONICLE OF MY MOTHER
An autobiographical account of the mental deterioration of his aging mother, and its impact on her family
Translated by Jean Moy
0–87011–533–2 Kodansha $14.95
0–87011–737–8 Kodansha pb $4.95

THE ROOF TILES OF TEMPYO
A historical novel set in ancient China
Translated by James T. Araki
0–86008–307–1 Tokyo pb $12.50

LOU-LAN & OTHER STORIES
Translated by James T. Araki & Edward G. Seidensticker
0–87011–389–5 Kodansha $9.95
0–87011–472–7 Kodansha pb $5.95

THE HUNTING GUN
Translated by Yokoo Sadamichi & Sanford Goldstein
0–8048–0257–2 Tuttle pb $3.95

THE COUNTERFEITER & OTHER STORIES
Translated by Leon Picon
0–8048–0126–6 Tuttle pb $4.95

WIND AND WAVES
A novel of the Mongols in 13th-century Korea as they prepare their invasion of Japan
Translated by James T. Araki
0–8248–1178–X Hawaii $20.00

• **Kaiko Takeshi**
DARKNESS IN SUMMER
The alienation of modern Japanese living outside Japan
Translated by Cecilia Segawa Seigle
0–8048–1375–2 Tuttle pb $5.95

INTO A BLACK SUN
"At last the sights, sounds and smells of wartime Vietnam have been rendered by a master. Writing from the point of view of a neutral Japanese journalist, Takeshi Kaiko filters his tale through an idiosyncratic but deeply compassionate sensibility"—Edmund White
Translated by Cecilia Segawa Seigle
0–87011–428–X Kodansha $14.95
0–87011–609–6 Kodansha pb $5.95

• **Kawabata Yasunari**
BEAUTY AND SADNESS
Kawabata is the only Japanese writer to have won the Nobel Prize.
Translated by Howard Hibbet
0–399–50529–6 Putnam pb $9.95

THE HOUSE OF THE SLEEPING BEAUTIES & OTHER STORIES
"*The House of the Sleeping Beauties* is most certainly an esoteric masterpiece . . . While in the grip of this story, the reader sweats and grows dizzy, and knows with the greatest immediacy the terror of lust urged on by the approach of death"—Mishima Yukio
Translated by Edward G. Seidensticker
Introduction by Mishima Yukio
0–87011–426–3 Kodansha pb $4.95

THE LAKE
"Readers who have inferred from previously translated novels that everything in Kawabata is delicate and understated will be surprised and perhaps even shocked at the brutal sensuality of some of the scenes"—Donald Keene
Translated by Reiko Tsukimura
0–87011–365–8 Kodansha pb $5.95

THE MASTER OF GO
Austere even by Kawabata's standards, this early novel has the abstract fascination of a game of go
Translated by Edward G. Seidensticker
0–399–50528–8 Putnam pb $7.95

THE OLD CAPITAL
Two generations of traditional artists confront the disorienting changes of postwar Japan
Translated by J. Martin Holman
0–86547–278–5 North Point $15.95

PALM-OF-THE-HAND STORIES
Short short stories written over a period of 50 years. Kawabata's penchant for intense compression reaches its peak here
Translated by Lane Dunlop & J. Martin Holman
0–86547–325–0 North Point $19.95

SNOW COUNTRY
Kawabata's single most famous work
Translated by Edward G. Seidensticker
0–399–50525–3 Putnam pb $6.95

THE SOUND OF THE MOUNTAIN
A long sustained fictional meditation on old age
Translated by Edward G. Seidensticker
0–399–50527–X Putnam pb $8.95

A THOUSAND CRANES
Translated by Edward G. Seidensticker
0–399–50526–1 Putnam pb $7.95

• **Kita Morio**
THE HOUSE OF NIRE
The comic 20th-century saga of the Nire family, eccentric owners of the Nire Mental Hospital. "Savagely funny . . . One of the most important novels of the postwar period"—Mishima Yukio
Translated by Dennis Keene
0–87011–592–8 Kodansha $17.95

THE FALL OF THE HOUSE OF NIRE
Translated by Dennis Keene
0–87011–663–0 Kodansha $16.95

• **Matsumoto Seichō**
POINTS AND LINES
The most famous of Japanese crime novels
0–87011–456–5 Kodansha pb $4.95

• **Mishima Yukio**
AFTER THE BANQUET
One of Mishima's least flashy and most sympathetic novels; its realistic portrait of a politician earned the author a libel suit
Translated by Donald Keene
0–399–50486–9 Putnam pb $8.95

CONFESSIONS OF A MASK
The autobiographical novel which established Mishima's reputation
Translated by Meredith Weatherby
0–8112–0118–X New Directions pb $6.95

FORBIDDEN COLORS
Homosexuality and revenge in Japan's literary world
Translated by Alfred Marks
0–399–50490–7 Putnam pb $8.95

THE SAILOR WHO FELL FROM GRACE WITH THE SEA
Translated by John Nathan
0–399–50489–3 Putnam pb $6.95

THE SEA OF FERTILITY
This tetralogy, Mishima's final work (he mailed the last volume to his publisher on the day of his violent death), constructs an elaborate plot spanning decades of Japanese history and involving reincarnation and confusion of identity

SPRING SNOW
0–394–44239–3 Knopf $13.95
0–671–54062–9 Washington Square pb $4.95

RUNAWAY HORSES
0–394–46618–7 Knopf $13.45

THE TEMPLE OF DAWN
0–394–46614–4 Knopf $13.95
0–671–54063–7 Washington Square pb $4.95

THE DECAY OF THE ANGEL
0–671–55391–7 Washington Square pb $5.95

THE SOUND OF WAVES
A lyrical early novel of young love
Translated by Meredith Weatherby
0–399–50487–7 Putnam pb $6.95

THE TEMPLE OF THE GOLDEN PAVILION
One of Mishima's masterpieces: based on the true story of an acolyte monk who burned down a famous Zen temple
Translated by Ivan Morris
0–399–50488–5 Putnam pb $7.95

THIRST FOR LOVE
Translated by Alfred Marks
0–399–50494–X Putnam pb $7.95

THE WAY OF THE SAMURAI
A commentary on the samurai treatise
Hagakure, reflecting Mishima's obsession
with the warrior code of bushido
0–399–50907–0 Putnam pb $7.95

• Miyazawa Kenji
WINDS FROM AFAR
A selection of children's stories by one of
Japan's most important modern poets
Translated by John Bester
0–87011–171–X Kodansha $15.50

• Mori Ogai
SAIKI KOI & OTHER STORIES
A collection of historical fiction focused on
samurai vendettas
Translated & edited by David Dilworth & J. Thomas
Rimer
0–8248–045406 Hawaii $14.95

VITA SEXUALIS
Banned when it appeared in 1909, this
novel pioneered new levels of sexual
frankness
Translated by Ninomiya Kazuji & Sanford Goldstein
0–8048–1048–6 Tuttle pb $4.95

THE WILD GEESE
A famous and melancholy novel of
frustrated love
Translated by Ochiai Kingo & Sanford Goldstein
0–8048–1070–2 Tuttle pb $5.25

• Nagai Kafu
GEISHA IN RIVALRY
Love and intrigue in the Shinbashi
Licensed Quarter; first published in 1918
Translated by Kurt Meissner
0–8048–0204–1 Tuttle pb $5.75

• Natsume Sōseki
AND THEN
Second in the trilogy also including
Sanshiro and *The Gate*
Translated by Norma Moore Field
0–8071–0387–X LSU $25.00

BOTCHAN
A young man's rebellion against the
system. "Sōseki's lightest and funniest
work"—Donald Keene
Translated by Alan Turney
0–87011–367–4 Kodansha pb $5.95

I AM A CAT
A famous satirical novel: the life of a
Japanese professor of English, seen
through a cat's eyes
Translated by Shibata Katsue & others
0–399–50609–8 Putnam pb $8.95

KOKORO
The best introduction to Sōseki's writings
Translated by Edwin McClellan
0–89526–951–1 Regnery pb $8.95

SANSHIRO
First in a trilogy including *And Then* and
The Gate
Translated by Jay Rubin
0–399–50613–6 Putnam pb $5.95

THE WAYFARER
Translated by Beongcheon Yu
0–8143–1318–3 Wayne State $25.00
0–399–50612–8 Putnam pb $6.95

• Oe Kenzaburo
A PERSONAL MATTER
Wrenching postwar novel centering around
the birth of a retarded son
Translated by John Nathan
0–394–17141–1 Grove pb $6.95

THE SILENT CRY
Translated by John Bester
0–87011–232–5 Kodansha $14.95
0–87011–466–2 Kodansha pb $6.95

**TEACH US TO OUTGROW OUR
MADNESS**
Translated with an introduction by John Nathan
0–394–17002–4 Grove pb $9.95

• Ooka Shohei
FIRES ON THE PLAIN
A Japanese soldier in the Philippines
during World War II
Translated by Ivan Morris
0–8048–1379–5 Tuttle pb $6.50

• Osaragi Jirō
HOMECOMING
A popular novel about the end of the war
Translated by Brewster Horwitz
0–8048–1381–7 Tuttle pb $5.00

• Shiga Naoya
A DARK NIGHT'S PASSING
Translated by Edwin McClellan
0–87011–362–3 Kodansha pb $8.95

THE PAPER DOOR & OTHER STORIES
Seventeen stories demonstrating the range
of an author who has been called "the god
of the Japanese short story"
Translated by Lane Dunlop
0–86547–260–2 North Point $14.95

• Shimazaki Tōson
BEFORE THE DAWN
A monumental novel dealing with the
turbulence before and after Japan's
opening to the West
Translated by William Naff
0–8248–0914–9 Hawaii $30.00

THE BROKEN COMMANDMENT
Breakthrough novel about the sufferings of
the outcaste class
Translated with an introduction by Kenneth Strong
0–86008–191–5 Tokyo pb $12.50

THE FAMILY
Translated by Cecilia Segawa Seigle
0–86008–254–7 Tokyo pb $17.50

• Tanizaki Junichirō
CHILDHOOD YEARS
0–87011–863–3 Kodansha $17.95

DIARY OF A MAD OLD MAN
Tanizaki's final, grotesquely humorous
examination of sexuality in the face of
imminent death
Translated by Howard Hibbett
0–399–50524–5 Putnam pb $4.95

IN PRAISE OF SHADOWS
A brief, brilliant, and characteristically
perverse essay on Japanese aesthetics
Translated by Thomas Harper & Edward G.
Seidensticker
0–918172–02–0 Leete's Island pb $3.95

THE KEY
Translated by Howard Hibbett
0–399–50522–9 Putnam pb $8.95

Tanizaki Junichirō (photo courtesy of Knopf)

THE MAKIOKA SISTERS
A long, meticulously detailed account of
the decline of a genteel merchant family in
prewar Osaka
Translated by Edward G. Seidensticker
0–399–50520–2 Putnam pb $11.95

NAOMI
A novel from the 1920s: a Japanese man
becomes obsessed with a foreign-looking
woman. "Tanizaki writes with an
unabashed sensuality rare in the often
hectic, guilt-ridden annals of
modernism"—John Updike, *New Yorker*
Translated by Anthony Chambers
0–394–53663–0 Knopf $15.95
0–399–51286–1 Putnam pb $8.95

**THE SECRET HISTORY OF THE LORD
OF MUSASHI & ARROWROOT: Two
Novellas**
"These fictions, subversive and self-
referential, join the already dazzling canon
of Tanizaki's work in English . . . I believe
they are masterpieces"—Richard Howard,
Nation
Translated by Anthony Chambers
0–399–50860–0 Putnam pb $5.95

SEVEN JAPANESE TALES
Contains some of Tanizaki's most
impressive writings, including *A Portrait of
Shunkin* and *The Bridge of Dreams*
Translated by Howard Hibbett
0–399–50523–7 Putnam pb $9.95

SOME PREFER NETTLES
Western sophistication in conflict with
Japanese tradition: a brief, razor-sharp
novel written in the 1920s
Translated by Edward G. Seidensticker
0–399–50521–0 Putnam pb $8.95

• Yoshida Mitsuru
REQUIEM FOR BATTLESHIP YAMATO
A modern war tale by a survivor of the
sinking of the "unsinkable" battleship
Yamato in 1945
Translated by Richard Minear
0–295–96216–X Washington $16.95

➤ **FOR OVERSEAS ORDERING INFORMATION, SEE PAGE 1**

- Yoshikawa Eiji
MUSASHI: An Epic Novel of the Samurai Era
A sample of popular fiction: an immensely long and complicated chronicle of a celebrated swordsman
Translated by Charles Terry
0–06–859851–3 Kodansha $22.95

Fiction Anthologies

- Phyllis Birnbaum, translator & editor
RABBITS, CRABS, ETC.: Stories by Japanese Women
0–8248–0777–4 Hawaii $15.00
0–8248–0817–7 Hawaii pb $7.95

- Lane Dunlop, translator & editor
A LATE CHRYSANTHEMUM: 21 Stories from the Japanese
0–86547–229–7 North Point $16.50

- Van C. Gessel & Tomone Matsumoto, editors
THE SHOWA ANTHOLOGY: Modern Japanese Short Stories
Volume 1: 1929–1961
0–87011–739–4 Kodansha $18.95
Volume 2: 1961–1983
0–87011–747–5 Kodansha $18.95

- Noriko Lippit & Kyoko Selden, editors
JAPANESE WOMEN WRITERS
0–87332–193–6 M.E. Sharpe $35.00
0–87332–223–1 M.E. Sharpe pb $15.95

- Oe Kenzaburo, editor
THE CRAZY IRIS & OTHER STORIES OF THE ATOMIC AFTERMATH
Translated by Ivan Morris & others
Introduction by Oe Kenzaburo
0–394–54944–9 Grove $22.50
0–394–62075–5 Grove pb $6.95

- Yukiko Tanaka, editor
TO LIVE AND TO WRITE: Selections by Japanese Women Writers, 1913–1938
Stories and essays by early feminists
Translated by Yukiko Tanaka & others
0–931188–44–X Seal $16.95
0–931188–43–1 Seal pb $9.95

Drama

- Abe Kobo
THE MAN WHO TURNED INTO A STICK: Three Related Plays
Translated by Donald Keene
0–86008–147–8 Tokyo $14.50

- Endo Shusaku
THE GOLDEN COUNTRY: A Play About Martyrs in Japan
Endo, a Japanese Christian, returns to the subject matter of his novel *Silence*
Translated by Francis Mathy
0–8048–0213–0 Tuttle pb $5.25

- Mishima Yukio
FIVE MODERN NO PLAYS
Translated by Donald Keene
0–8048–1380–9 Tuttle pb $9.25

- Ted Takaya, translator
MODERN JAPANESE DRAMA: An Anthology
0–231–04684–7 Columbia $37.00
0–231–04685–5 Columbia pb $18.00

- J. Thomas Rimer, editor
MASK AND SWORD: Two Plays for the Contemporary Japanese Theater
0–231–04932–3 Columbia $29.50

CRITICAL STUDIES AND HISTORIES

- Donald Keene
JAPANESE LITERATURE: An Introduction for Western Readers
Still the most concise survey of the periods and genres of Japanese literature
0–394–17200–0 Grove pb $2.25

These three volumes—encyclopedic in range and often felicitous in style—will eventually be supplemented by a fourth covering the earliest period.
WORLD WITHIN WALLS: Japanese Literature of the Pre-Modern Era, 1600–1867
0–394–17074–1 Grove pb $9.50

DAWN TO THE WEST: Japanese Literature in the Modern Era
Volume 1: Fiction
0–03–062814–8 Henry Holt $60.00
0–8050–0607–9 Henry Holt pb $29.95
Volume 2: Poetry, Drama, Criticism
0–03–062816–4 Henry Holt $40.00
0–8050–0608–7 Henry Holt pb $19.95

THE PLEASURES OF JAPANESE LITERATURE
In his newest book Keene once again sets out the basics of Japanese literary culture for the general reader
0–231–06736–4 Columbia $19.00

SOME JAPANESE PORTRAITS
Lively essays on 21 writers, covering a span of five centuries
0–87011–298–8 Kodansha $15.50
0–87011–575–8 Kodansha pb $5.95

- Kato Shuichi
A HISTORY OF JAPANESE LITERATURE
Volume 1: The First Thousand Years
Translated by David Chibbett
0–87011–491–3 Kodansha pb $6.25
Volume 2: The Years of Isolation
Translated by Don Sanderson
0–87011–568–5 $35.00 Kodansha
Volume 3: The Modern Years
A comprehensive history by a leading critic
Translated by Don Sanderson
0–87011–569–3 Kodansha $35.00

- Konishi Jin'ichi
A HISTORY OF JAPANESE LITERATURE
Volume 1: The Archaic and Ancient Ages
The first in another multi-volume chronicle
Translated by Aileen Gatten
Edited by Earl Miner
0–691–10146–9 Princeton $19.95

- J. Thomas Rimer
PILGRIMAGES: Aspects of Japanese Literature and Culture
Eight essays on modern Japanese fine arts, fiction, drama, and poetry, showing links with older traditions
0–8248–1148–8 Hawaii $17.00

A READER'S GUIDE TO JAPANESE LITERATURE
The former Chief of the Asian Division of the Library of Congress explores fifty of the greatest Japanese literary works
0–87011–896–X Kodansha pb $14.95

Poetry

- Makoto Ueda
MATSUO BASHO
A biography of the great haiku poet
0–87011–553–7 Kodansha pb $6.50

- Robert Aitken
A ZEN WAVE: Bashō's Haiku and Zen
An American Zen master's commentaries on a selection of Bashō's haiku. "Illuminates the angles and corners of lone-ness and community, plainness and beauty, in the homey, homeless way of Zen"—Gary Snyder
Foreword by W.S. Merwin
0–8348–0137–X Weatherhill pb $9.95

- Janine Beichman
MASAOKA SHIKI
A biography of the man who radicalized haiku in the early 20th century
0–87011–753–X Kodansha pb $5.95

Drama

- Don Kenny
ON STAGE IN JAPAN: Kabuki, Bunraku, Noh, Gagaku
A theatergoer's guide
4–07–972045–9 Tuttle pb $9.95

- Komparu Kunio
THE NOH THEATER: Principles and Perspectives
An absolutely thorough, sometimes quite technical description of the many elements involved in a Nō performance
0–8348–1529–X Weatherhill $32.50

- James R. Brandon and others
STUDIES IN KABUKI: Its Acting, Music, and Historical Context
0–8248–0452–X Hawaii pb $9.00

- Earle Ernst
THE KABUKI THEATRE
The social niche occupied by Kabuki performers entailed ramifications as fascinating as the plot of a Kabuki play. This is only one of the aspects that Ernst touches on in this rich account
0–8248–0319–1 Hawaii pb $5.95

- Gunji Masakatsu
KABUKI
An authoritative book featuring hundreds of photos of famous scenes, stock characters, special effects, backstage

---

maneuvers, makeup traditions, and classic performances
Introduction by Donald Keene
0–87011–732–7 Kodansha $55.00

• Kawatake Toshio, editor
KABUKI: An All-Color Exposition of the Kabuki Theater in Japanese Art and Design
An oversized picture book of Kabuki in performance
Photographs by Iwata Akira
0–87701–366–7 Chronicle pb $25.00

• Aubrey S. & Giovanna M. Halford
KABUKI HANDBOOK: A Guide to Understanding and Appreciation
A viewer's guide, with summaries of favorite plays, explanatory notes, and illustrations
0–8048–0332–3 Tuttle pb $8.75

• Barbara C. Adachi
BACKSTAGE AT BUNRAKU: A Behind-the-Scenes Look at Japan's Puppet Theatre
Members of the Osaka Bunraku Troupe reveal secrets of puppet theatre; many photographs and stage diagrams
Photographs by Joel Sackett
0–8348–0199–X Weatherhill pb $25.00

• A.C. Scott
THE PUPPET THEATRE OF JAPAN
An introduction to Bunraku, with summaries of ten popular plays
0–8048–1116–4 Tuttle pb $5.50

• James T. Araki
THE BALLAD-DRAMA OF MEDIEVAL JAPAN
A little-known form derived from medieval military tales; contains synopses of 50 plays and complete texts of two
0–8048–1279–9 Tuttle pb $4.25

The Tale of Genji

Ivan Morris
THE WORLD OF THE SHINING PRINCE
Morris, a great translator, was also a subtle and original interpreter of Japanese culture. This book is indispensable for readers of *The Tale of Genji*
0–14–055083–6 Penguin pb $7.95

Edward G. Seidensticker
GENJI DAYS
A diary Seidensticker kept while at work on his translation of *The Tale of Genji*, interspersing the events of his own life with reflections on Heian-period Japan
0–87011–296–1 Kodansha $15.50
0–87011–640–1 Kodansha pb $5.25

Modern Fiction

• Masao Miyoshi
ACCOMPLICES OF SILENCE: The Modern Japanese Novel
An absorbing study of Kawabata, Dazai, Mishima, and other modern writers
0–520–04609–9 California $35.00

• J. Thomas Rimer
MODERN JAPANESE FICTION AND ITS TRADITIONS: An Introduction
The influence of classical traditions on modern writing
0–691–10225–2 Princeton pb $14.95

• Makoto Ueda
MODERN JAPANESE WRITERS AND THE NATURE OF LITERATURE
0–8047–0904–1 Stanford $32.50

• Robert L. Danly
IN THE SHADE OF SPRING LEAVES: The Life and Writings of Higuchi Ichiyō, A Woman of Letters in Meiji Japan
0–300–02981–0 Yale pb $13.95

• Marguerite Yourcenar
MISHIMA: A Vision of the Void
A literary analysis of Mishima's work by the great French writer
Translated by Alberto Manguel
0–374–52061–5 Farrar, Straus & Giroux pb $7.95

• Henry Scott Stokes
THE LIFE AND DEATH OF YUKIO MISHIMA
Stokes, an excellent journalist, was a friend of Mishima
0–374–51703–7 Farrar, Straus & Giroux pb $8.95

• Edwin McClellan
WOMAN IN THE CRESTED KIMONO: The Life of Shibue Io and Her Family Drawn from Mori Ogai's Shibue Chusai
An independent woman of the Meiji era, as portrayed by an early modern novelist
0–300–03484–9 Yale $18.95

• Edward G. Seidensticker
KAFU THE SCRIBBLER: The Life and Writings of Nagai Kafū, 1879–1959
The curious career of the chronicler of geisha life
0–8047–0267–5 Stanford $37.50

• Doi Takeo
THE PSYCHOLOGICAL WORLD OF NATSUME SOSEKI
A noted Japanese psychiatrist studies the most significant of early modern Japanese novelists
Introduction by William J. Tyler
0–674–72116–0 Harvard $20.00

Haiku in English

Of all Japanese literary forms, the 17-syllable haiku has had the greatest worldwide influence, and has been adopted by many poets writing in English and other languages.

William J. Higginson
THE HAIKU HANDBOOK
A meticulous and comprehensive guide to haiku in Japanese and other languages
0–07–028786–4 McGraw-Hill pb $8.95

Cor Van den Heuvel, editor
THE HAIKU ANTHOLOGY: Haiku and Senryu in English
A representative gathering of contemporary English-language haiku poets
0–671–62837–2 Simon & Schuster pb $9.95

Other Asian Literatures

INDONESIAN LITERATURE

• Kratini Raden Adjeng
LETTERS OF A JAVANESE PRINCESS
Letters of a young noblewoman, now beloved as an early advocate of feminist and nationalist ideas
Translated by Agnes L. Symmers
0–8191–4758–3 University Press pb $10.25

• Harry Aveling, translator & editor
CONTEMPORARY INDONESIAN POETRY
0–7022–0932–5 Queensland pb $10.95

• Burton Raffel
THE DEVELOPMENT OF MODERN INDONESIAN POETRY
0–87395–024–0 SUNY $44.50

• Burton Raffel, editor
ANTHOLOGY OF MODERN INDONESIAN POETRY
0–87395–031–3 SUNY pb $14.95

• Philip Ward
INDONESIAN TRADITIONAL POETRY
0–902675–49–4 Oleander $13.50

KOREAN LITERATURE

• Chong-un Kim, editor
POSTWAR KOREAN SHORT STORIES: An Anthology
0–8248–0833–9 Hawaii $18.00

• Chongwha Chung, editor
KOREAN CLASSICAL LITERATURE: An Anthology
0–7103–0279–7 RC&H $22.50
LOVE IN MID-WINTER NIGHT: Korean Sijo Poetry
0–7103–0104–9 RC&H $24.95

• Hwang Sun-won
MASKS & OTHER STORIES
Outstanding late stories by a leading figure of modern Korean literature
Edited with an introduction by J. Martin Holman
0–930523–58–X Readers International pb $9.95

- In-sob Zong
FOLK TALES FROM KOREA
"These 99 examples are as various as they are enjoyable, some fantastic, some ironic, others with morality as their aim. All are presented in clear and comfortable English"—*TLS*
0–930878–15–9 Tuttle $18.95

A GUIDE TO KOREAN LITERATURE
0–930878–29–9 Tuttle $22.00

- Peter H. Lee
SONGS OF FLYING DRAGONS: A Critical Reading
0–674–82075–4 Harvard $22.50

- Peter H. Lee, editor
ANTHOLOGY OF KOREAN LITERATURE: From Early Times to the 19th Century
0–8248–0756–1 Hawaii pb $12.00

FLOWERS OF FIRE: 20th-Century Korean Stories
0–8248–1036–8 Hawaii pb $13.50

THE SILENCE OF LOVE: 20th-Century Korean Poetry
0–8248–0711–1 Hawaii pb $17.95
0–8248–0732–4 Hawaii pb $8.95

- Peter H. Lee, translator
LIVES OF EMINENT KOREAN MONKS: The Haedong Kosung Chon
0–674–53662–2 Harvard pb $7.00

- David R. McCann, editor
BLACK CRANE: An Anthology of Korean Literature
Volume 1
0–939657–14–7 Cornell pb $5.00
Volume 2
0–939657–24–4 Cornell pb $5.00

- Myung-Ho Sym
THE MAKING OF MODERN KOREAN POETRY: Foreign Influences and Native Creativity
0–8248–0935–1 Hawaii $18.00

- So Chongju
SELECTED POEMS
Translated by David McCann
0–231–06794–1 Columbia $30.00

- Yun Heung-gil
THE HOUSE OF TWILIGHT
A collection of stories by an iconoclastic chronicler of today's Korea
Edited with an introduction by J. Martin Holman
0–930523–60–1 Readers International pb $9.95

MONGOLIAN LITERATURE

- Francis Woodman Cleaves, translator & editor
THE SECRET HISTORY OF THE MONGOLS
0–674–79670–5 Harvard $22.50

- Paul Kahn
THE SECRET HISTORY OF THE MONGOLS: An Adaptation
Kahn takes Cleaves' translation as his point of departure to create this poetically charged retelling. "Using modern English and a prose form that is in keeping with the original, Paul Kahn has made this grand epic accessible to non-academic readers"—*Middle East Journal*
0–86547–138–X North Point pb $14.00

PHILIPPINE LITERATURE

- Nick Joaquin
THE WOMAN WHO HAD TWO NAVELS
0–686–18676–1 Cellar Book Shop pb $7.50

- F. Sionil José
MY BROTHER, MY EXECUTIONER
A novel dealing with the Huk rebellion
0–686–26426–6 Cellar Book Shop pb $8.75

THE PRETENDERS
The Philippine elite and its temptation to deny its own ethnic identity
0–686–09504–9 Cellar Book Shop pb $6.50

TREE
The still feudalistic life of the sugar lands
0–686–27005–3 Cellar Book Shop pb $6.00

- Linda Ty-Casper
AWAITING TRESPASS
Ty-Casper has been publishing her realistic novels of contemporary Philippine life and politics since the early 1960s. "This deeply moving book is full of good people, good talk, and a wisdom regarding the inner life"—*Kirkus Reviews*
0–930523–12–1 Readers International pb $7.95

WINGS OF STONE
A novel set against the chaotic backdrop of the Marcos regime in its final years
0–930523–27–X Readers International pb $8.95

SOUTHEAST ASIAN LITERATURE

- John Balaban, translator & editor
CA DAO VIETNAM: Bilingual Anthology of Vietnamese Folk Poetry
0–87775–128–5 Unicorn $15.00
0–87775–129–3 Unicorn pb $6.00

- Sanh Huynh
THE HERITAGE OF VIETNAMESE POETRY: An Anthology
0–300–02264–6 Yale $35.00

- Jan Knappert
MALAY MYTHS AND LEGENDS
0–686–72738–X Heinemann pb $8.50

- Burton Raffel, translator
FROM THE VIETNAMESE: Ten Centuries of Poetry
0–8079–0053–2 October House pb $4.25

- Edwin Thumboo, editor
SEVEN POETS OF SINGAPORE AND MALAYSIA
0–8214–0484–9 Ohio $18.00

TURKISH LITERATURE

- Melih Anday
RAIN ONE STEP AWAY
Poems by a modern Turkish writer who has excelled in many genres
Translated by Talat Halman & Brian Swann
0–910350–00–0 Charioteer $7.50

- Fazil Huznu Daglarca
THE BIRD AND I
A chapbook of poetry by a prolific and highly esteemed contemporary writer
Translated by Talat Halman
0–89304–803–8 Cross Cultural pb $2.00

- Nazim Hikmet
Hikmet, who wrote in many genres and suffered long periods of imprisonment for his political views, is the major figure of modern Turkish literature, and a poet of world stature.
THE EPIC OF SHEIK BEDREDDIN & OTHER POEMS
Translated by Randy Blasing & Mutlu Konuk
0–89255–024–4 Persea pb $5.95

HUMAN LANDSCAPES
Translated by Randy Blasing & Mutlu Konuk
0–89255–068–6 Persea pb $9.95

MOSCOW SYMPHONY & OTHER POEMS
Translated by Taner Baybars
0–8040–0217–7 Ohio pb $6.95

RUBAIYAT
Translated by Randy Blasing & Mutlu Konuk
0–914278–48–7 Copper Beech pb $4.95

SELECTED POEMS
Translated by Randy Blasing & Mutlu Konuk
0–89255–101–1 Persea pb $9.95

- Yashar Kemal
MEMED, MY HAWK
Translated by Edouard Roditi
0–394–71016–9 Pantheon pb $6.95

SEAGULL
Translated by Thilda Kemal
0–394–51856–X Pantheon pb $11.95

- Aziz Nesin
ISTANBUL BOY
An autobiographical volume by a satirist who often came into conflict with the government, subtitled "That's How It Was But Not How It's Going To Be"
Translated by Joseph S. Jacobson
0–292–73810–2 Texas $11.95

- Orhan Veli
I, ORHAN VELI
Humorous and sensual poems by a writer who introduced everyday language into Turkish poetry
Translated by Murat Nemet-Nejat
0–914610–64–3 Hanging Loose pb $8.00

- Talat S. Halman, editor
CONTEMPORARY TURKISH LITERATURE: Fiction and Poetry
0–8386–1360–8 Fairleigh Dickinson $39.50

• Geoffrey Lewis, translator
THE BOOK OF DEDE KORKUT
Twelve traditional stories set in the heroic
age of the Oghuz Turks
0–14–044298–7 Penguin pb $6.95

Australian Literature

The Australian Aboriginal oral tradition,
with its myths of ancestral "dreamtime,"
endured uninterrupted until the intrusion of
European settlers in the late 18th century.
Gradually an émigré literature began to
record often astonished impressions of the
exoticism of Australia (designed chiefly for
European consumption). Convict themes
frequently played a large part, as in the work
of Marcus Clarke. By the end of the 19th
century a new literature imbued with political nationalism gave rise to more positive
images of Australian life, typified by the
notion of "outback individualism." This
genre of local writing, often colored by
social realism, persisted between the wars.

In the postwar period a less parochial,
more introspective tone becomes evident,
along with a broadening of subject matter
and the tempering of pride and self-confidence with self-criticism. The Australian historical experience—with its imagery of
isolation, exile, and escape—remains important but often in a more symbolic fashion.
Most of the works listed below are relatively
recent, an indication of the continuing vitality and expansion of Australian writing.

• Glenda Adams
DANCING ON CORAL
0–670–81242–0 Viking $16.95
0–14–009343–5 Penguin pb $7.95

• Jessica Anderson
THE ONLY DAUGHTER
A family becomes entangled in a question
of inheritance in this "comedy of class and
manners"—*Ms*
0–14–006333–1 Penguin pb $6.95

AN ORDINARY LUNACY
0–14–009707–4 Penguin pb $6.95

**STORIES FROM THE WARM ZONE &
SYDNEY STORIES**
0–670–81626–4 Penguin $15.95

TIRRA LIRRA BY THE RIVER
An old woman recalls her past. "A wry,
romantic story that should make
Anderson's American reputation"—
Washington Post
0–14–006945–3 Penguin pb $6.95

• Thea Astley
THE ACOLYTE
A penetrating study of the damage
wrought by obsessive egotism
0–7022–1540–6 Queensland pb $10.95

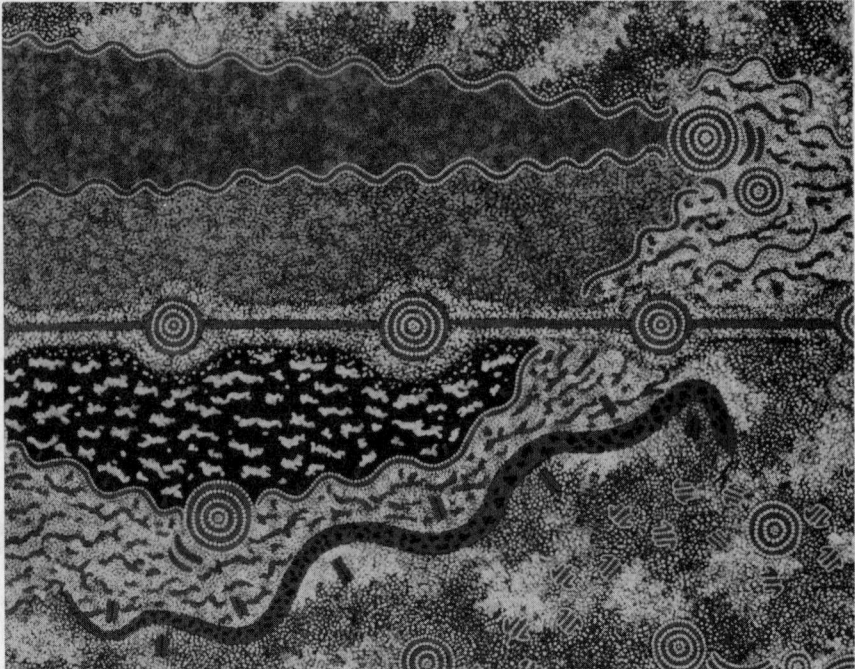

From Dreamings: The Art of Aboriginal Australia *by Peter Sutton* (Braziller)

BEACHMASTERS
A desire for self-rule among island natives
leads to a "polite revolution"
0–14–010946–3 Penguin pb $6.95

A DESCANT FOR GOSSIPS
A vivid portrait of a small-minded small
town
0–7022–1843–X Queensland pb $8.95

GIRL WITH A MONKEY
A young schoolteacher's flight from a
stifling town and a stifling relationship
with an older man
0–14–009881–X Penguin pb $5.95

IT'S RAINING IN MANGO
0–399–13302–X Putnam $17.95
0–14–011403–3 Penguin pb $6.95

AN ITEM FROM THE LATE NEWS
A quest for safety from nuclear holocaust
leads to a remote spot in the outback
where the final clash—and flash—is
unexpected. "An appalling and scathing
vision of life in rural Australia"—
Australian Book Review
0–14–006948–8 Penguin pb $5.95

THE WELL-DRESSED EXPLORER
The adventures of a clever rake
0–14–009882–8 Penguin pb $6.95

• Murray Bail
**THE DROVER'S WIFE & OTHER
STORIES**
A collection of short stories, often satirical,
surreal, and bush-inspired
0–571–13860–8 Faber & Faber pb $6.95

HOMESICKNESS
The comic transworld pilgrimage of
members of an Australian package tour
0–571–13840–3 Faber & Faber pb $8.95

• Marjorie Barnard
**THE PERSIMMON TREE & OTHER
STORIES**
Stories that often explore the complicated
bonds among women
0–14–016148–1 Penguin pb $6.95

• Barbara Baynton
THE PORTABLE BARBARA BAYNTON
Best known for her 19th-century
publication *Bush Studies,* Baynton depicts
the bush as a malevolent force—and a
theater for fear and loneliness
Edited by Sally Krimmer & Alan Lawson
0–7022–1377–2 Queensland $32.50
0–7022–1469–8 Queensland pb $12.00

• Martin Boyd
THE CARDBOARD CROWN
A turn-of-the-century, upper-middle-class
family never feels completely at home
either in Australia or England
0–14–006904–6 Penguin pb $4.95

A DIFFICULT YOUNG MAN
A study in ambition and the forces that
trigger a young man's mutiny. "A subtle
and beautifully observed social comedy"—
TLS
0–14–006906–2 Penguin pb $4.95

THE PICNIC
Australians in England try to be a little
more English than the natives and do not
altogether succeed
0–14–007955–6 Penguin pb $5.95

• John Bryson
EVIL ANGELS
An account of the famous murder trial, in
which a woman was accused of slaying her
own child
0–671–63163–2 Summit $18.95
0–553–27207–1 Bantam pb $4.95

● Ada Cambridge
THE THREE MISS KINGS
A heartfelt late-19th-century evocation of Australia and a sardonic portrait of its *nouveaux riches*
0–14–016164–3 Penguin pb $6.95

● Peter Carey
Carey is an important young novelist, often described as a Borgesian fabulist whose tone ranges from macabre to realistic.
BLISS
The momentary "deaths" of a salesman interrupt the 39-year hell of his life and lead him on to some very unusual happenings
0–06–014959–0 Harper & Row $13.95
0–06–091355–X Harper & Row pb $7.95

ILLYWHACKER
The portrait of an endearing 139-year-old con man in the world of "wool, wheat and athletes." "A big, garrulous, funny novel, touching, farcical and passionately bad-tempered"—*NY Times*
0–06–015425–X Harper & Row $18.95
0–06–091331–2 Harper & Row pb $9.95

OSCAR AND LUCINDA
Set in 1864 aboard a ship, Carey's most recent novel links a gambling seminarian with an Australian heiress
0–06–015908–1 Harper & Row $18.95
0–06–091592–7 Harper & Row pb $8.95

● Robert Carter
THE PLEASURE WITHIN
Unusual short stories from an award-winning writer
0–689–11998–4 Macmillan $15.95

THE SUGAR FACTORY
"Carter balances grief, pain, violence and humor with such deft control that we laugh aloud one moment and churn with terror the next"—*Chicago Tribune*
0–689–11926–7 Atheneum $14.95

● Nancy Cato
ALL THE RIVERS RUN
Formerly a journalist, Cato reworked this version of her best-known work—a trilogy written in the 1950s—twenty years later
0–451–12535–5 NAL pb $3.95

> Marcus Clarke
> **HIS NATURAL LIFE**
> The most famous 19th-century Australian novel is a long, sometimes melodramatic story of the injustices of convict life; also known as *For the Term of His Natural Life*
> Edited by Stephen Murray-Smith
> 0–14–043051–2 Penguin pb $7.95

● Eleanor Dark
LANTANA LANE
Stories and essays by a major figure in the Australian feminist movement published some 15 years after her early death at the end of World War II
Introduction by Helen Garner
0–14–016132–5 Penguin pb $6.95

THE LITTLE COMPANY
This novel grapples with issues of pacifism in wartime
0–14–016150–3 Penguin pb $6.95

● Robert Drewe
THE BODYSURFERS
A collection of short stories set for the most part at the sea's edge
0–571–13389–4 Faber & Faber pb $6.95

● A.B. Facey
A FORTUNATE LIFE
An autodidact's autobiographical "microcosm of the earlier life of Australia" tells of boyhood hardship, Gallipoli, and beyond
0–670–80307–3 Viking $30.00

● Miles Franklin
Miles Franklin was the pseudonym of Stella Franklin, who escaped from the humble origins of her squatter family to become a journalist and early feminist.
BRING THE MONKEY
0–7022–1817–0 Queensland $15.95
0–7022–1809–X Queensland pb $8.95

> **MY BRILLIANT CAREER**
> Rightly regarded as a classic, this 1901 *Bildungsroman* traces the evolution of a bright country girl struggling against prejudice in the late-19th-century outback
> 0–671–45915–5 Washington Square pb $3.95
>
> **THE END OF MY CAREER**
> The hard-hitting sequel to *My Brilliant Career*
> 0–671–49937–8 Washington Square pb $3.95

ON DEARBORN STREET
In which a spirited lady-executive in Chicago is not inclined to wedlock
0–7022–1954–1 Queensland pb $8.95

SOME EVERYDAY FOLK AND DAWN
A stark picture of small town life
0–14–016131–7 Penguin pb $6.95

● Joseph Furphy
THE PORTABLE JOSEPH FURPHY
Alias "Tom Collins," the self-styled "half bushman, half bookworm" achieved renown with a single volume, *Such Is Life*, a vivid turn-of-the-century picture of what he calls "offensively Australian" country life
Edited by John Barnes
0–7022–1611–9 Queensland $32.50
0–7022–1612–7 Queensland pb $12.95

● Helen Garner
THE CHILDREN'S BACH
0–14–008371–5 Penguin pb $4.95

POSTCARDS FROM SURFERS
0–14–008462–2 Penguin pb $4.95

● Kate Grenville
BEARDED LADIES
Selected stories that have earned Grenville comparison with Hemingway
0–7022–1715–8 Queensland $15.00
0–7022–1716–6 Queensland pb $8.95

DREAMHOUSE
0–670–81040–1 Viking $14.95

LILIAN'S STORY
A daughter escapes from her well-to-do family and her old-fashioned despotic father
0–14–008547–5 Penguin pb $6.95

● Rodney Hall
Hall is known for both his poetry and his fiction.
CAPTIVITY CAPTIVE
A novel exploring the repercussions of a multiple murder committed decades earlier. "Stands at once as an absorbing detective story and as a Faulknerian parable about innocence and guilt, passion and betrayal"—*NY Times*
0–317–59265–3 Farrar, Straus & Giroux $15.95
0–671–67575–3 Farrar, Straus & Giroux pb $9.95

THE MOST BEAUTIFUL WORLD:
Fictions and Sermons
0–7022–1587–2 Queensland $13.50

A PLACE AMONG PEOPLE
0–7022–0963–5 Queensland pb $7.95

SELECTED POEMS
0–7022–0994–5 Queensland $17.50

● Barbara Hanrahan
Hanrahan's work shows a pervasive concern with the choices women confront.
DOVE
A generational study of the relationship between a mother and daughter
0–7022–1880–4 Queensland $17.50
0–7022–1890–1 Queensland pb $7.95

THE FRANGIPANI GARDEN
Respectable Adelaide society—and its dark secrets—in the 1920s
0–7022–1562–7 Queensland $19.25
0–7022–1563–5 Queensland pb $7.95

THE PEACH GROVES
The setting switches between Adelaide and New Zealand in the 1880s
0–7022–1458–2 Queensland $17.50
0–7022–1459–0 Queensland pb $6.00

WHERE THE QUEENS ALL STRAYED
0–7022–1305–5 Queensland pb $7.95

● Shirley Hazzard
THE BAY OF NOON
Uprooting and early loss are replaced by a complex web of intertwined relationships, with Naples as the backdrop
0–14–010450–X Penguin pb $6.95

CLIFFS OF FALL
Short stories set in Italy, the United States, and Switzerland
0–515–08574–X Jove pb $3.50

THE EVENING OF THE HOLIDAY
An encounter in Italy develops into an overwhelming, doomed love
0–14–010451–8 Penguin pb $6.95

PEOPLE IN GLASS HOUSES
A tale of faction and strife in an organization dedicated to improving and promoting the "cause of humanity." Places the author "on a high ground between Katherine Mansfield and Evelyn Waugh"—*NY Times*
0–515–08626–6 Jove pb $3.50

• Dorothy Hewett
BOBBIN UP
A novel based on the factory experiences of a card-carrying Communist and radical—Hewett herself
0–14–016175–9 Penguin pb $6.95

• David Ireland
Ireland is an experimental novelist whose often caustic social commentary is lightened by his absurdist sense of humor.
ARCHIMEDES AND THE SEAGULL
0–14–008090–2 Penguin pb $6.95

• Clive James
James is a lively, irreverent critic, as iconoclastic about his adopted home (England) and its more voguish enclaves as he is about his birthplace.
FALLING TOWARDS ENGLAND: Unreliable Memoirs II
An autobiographical account of James's arrival, early adventures and first impressions of England
0–393–02360–5 Norton $15.95

FLYING VISITS: Postcards from the Observer
0–393–02294–3 Norton $14.95

• Elizabeth Jolley
FOXYBABY
"This is prose, thought, and art of the highest elegance and quality"—*LA Times*
0–14–008380–4 Penguin pb $5.95

MISS PEABODY'S INHERITANCE
"Jolley's humor is infectious and sparked with surprises"—*People*
0–14–007743–X Penguin pb $6.95

MR. SCOBIE'S RIDDLE
0–14–007490–2 Penguin pb $6.95

MY FATHER'S MOON
A novel of London during the Blitz
0–06–016062–4 Harper & Row $15.95

THE NEWSPAPER OF CLAREMONT STREET
An office cleaning lady turns out to be an unexpected source of wisdom
0–14–008582–3 Penguin pb $6.95

PALOMINO
The love of two women, one decades older than the other. "The hypnotic style and emotional richness make it clear that Jolley is very much . . . a voice that can pierce right to the heart of emotion"—*San Francisco Chronicle*
0–89255–136–4 Persea pb $8.95

STORIES
0–670–82113–6 Viking $17.95

THE SUGAR MOTHER
0–06–015940–5 Harper & Row $16.95

THE WELL
Vast farmlands provide the backdrop for an unusual relationship between two women, a spinster and an orphan, whose world is suddenly intruded upon by a stranger
0–14–008901–2 Penguin pb $6.95

WOMAN IN A LAMPSHADE
0–14–008418–5 Penguin pb $6.95

• Rod Jones
JULIA PARADISE
A novel set in Shanghai in 1927. "A tour de force . . . Cousin to *The White Hotel* and *The Alexandria Quartet*"—*Newsweek*
0–14–010077–6 Penguin pb $6.95

• Thomas Keneally
BRINGS LARKS AND HEROES
An Irish soldier's experiences in a penal colony, written during the Australian involvement in the Vietnam war
0–14–010929–3 Penguin pb $6.95

THE CHANT OF JIMMY BLACKSMITH
Racism in 19th-century Australia leads to rebellion and murder
0–14–006973–9 Penguin pb $6.95

CONFEDERATES
A stirring tale set in the United States in 1862 and culminating in the battle of Antietam. "The best Civil War novel since *The Killer Angels*"—*Library Journal*
0–06–091446–7 Harper & Row pb $7.95

A DUTIFUL DAUGHTER
0–14–003391–2 Penguin pb $6.95

A FAMILY MADNESS
"A disturbing look at obsessions and their impact on the human spirit"—*Toronto Globe and Mail*
0–671–61175–5 Simon & Schuster $17.95
0–14–009796–1 Penguin pb $6.95

GOSSIP FROM THE FOREST
A recreation of the making of the armistice that ended World War I
0–15–636469–7 HBJ pb $6.95

THE PLAYMAKER
To mark the King's birthday in 1789, an officer stages a play with a group of convicts who in time cast a weird spell over their director. "A world so rich and strange that we experience it as if in a dream"—*Chicago Tribune*
0–671–49343–4 Simon & Schuster $18.95
0–06–097189–4 Harper & Row pb $8.95

SCHINDLER'S LIST
The story of a Catholic director of a Nazi factory—and prison camp—who saved many Jewish lives, reconstructed from the testimony of those who came to be known as *Schindlerjuden*
0–14–006784–1 Penguin pb $6.95

A SEASON IN PURGATORY
In the struggle against the Nazis in Yugoslavia two lovers—a British doctor and an impassioned partisan—also struggle to retain their humanity
0–15–679850–6 HBJ pb $6.95

THE SURVIVOR
The survivor of a polar expedition confronts doubt and guilt when the body of the dead leader is exhumed 40 years later
0–14–003217–7 Penguin pb $5.95

THREE CHEERS FOR THE PARACLETE
A priest teaching at a seminary comes under close scrutiny
0–14–003099–9 Penguin pb $5.95

VICTIM OF THE AURORA
Murder adds spice to a 1910 expedition to the South Pole. "Edwardian innocence and stuffiness crashing against the Antarctic void"—*Washington Post*
0–15–693534–1 HBJ pb $6.95

• C.J. Koch
THE DOUBLEMAN
A probing study of a Catholic childhood
0–07–035221–6 McGraw-Hill $15.95
0–380–70310–6 Avon pb $4.50

• Henry Lawson
THE PENGUIN HENRY LAWSON
Master of the short story, "poet of the people," folk writer and balladeer, Lawson was accorded a state funeral on his death in 1922
Edited with an introduction by John Barnes
0–14–009215–3 Penguin pb $6.95

• Colleen McCullough
A CREED FOR THE THIRD MILLENNIUM
0–380–70134–0 Avon pb $4.95

AN INDECENT OBSESSION
A psychiatric hospital is the setting for an admixture of romance, violence, and paranoia
0–06–014920–5 Harper & Row $14.45

THE LADIES OF MISSALONGHI
0–06–015739–9 Harper & Row $12.95
0–380–70458–7 Avon pb $3.95

THE THORN BIRDS
0–06–012956–5 Harper & Row $19.95
0–380–56390–8 Avon pb $6.95

TIM
A feeble-minded but Adonis-like laborer strikes up a relationship with a plain spinster
0–06–012891–7 Harper & Row $15.95
0–446–31047–6 Warner pb $3.50

• David Malouf
CHILD'S PLAY: The Bread of Time to Come
A terrorist sets a trap to assassinate a famous author, and finds himself ensnared by the writer's plot
0–8076–1032–1 Braziller $10.95

FIRST THINGS LAST
0–7022–1564–3 Queensland $15.00
0–7022–1565–1 Queensland pb $9.50

HARLAND'S HALF ACRE
"The most satisfying and accurate look into the mind of a painter since Virginia Woolf's portrayal of Lily Briscoe in *To the Lighthouse*"—*Village Voice*
0–394–53919–2 Knopf $13.45
0–671–60019–2 Washington Square pb $5.95

AN IMAGINARY LIFE
Reinvents the last years of Ovid in exile and explores the poet's relationship with a wolf-child
0–8076–1114–X Braziller pb $6.95

• Olga Masters
AMY'S CHILDREN
A mother's tale of abandonment and renewal in wartime Sydney
0–393–02574–8 Norton $16.95

• Frank Moorhouse
ROOM SERVICE
An intellectual radical surveys areas of Australian society
0–14–010198–5 Penguin pb $5.95

TO ORDER BOOKS AS GIFTS, SEE PAGE 1

• Sally Morgan

MY PLACE
An exploration of the author's Aboriginal roots. "Sally Morgan's extraordinary work is about a quest for the past of one person and one family, an individual past which turns out to be a communal past, which is, in turn, the history of a people"—Janette Turner Hospital, *NY Times*
0–8050–0911–6 Seaver $19.95

Les A. Murray

Murray is the pre-eminent figure among contemporary Australian poets, a writer of great range and verbal inventiveness.

THE DAYLIGHT MOON & OTHER POEMS
"It would be as myopic to regard Mr. Murray as an Australian poet as to call Yeats an Irishman. He is, quite simply, the one by whom the language lives"— Joseph Brodsky
0–89255–125–9 Persea $17.95
0–89255–138–0 Persea pb $9.95

THE VERNACULAR REPUBLIC
"One of the greatest poets, in my opinion, in the English-speaking world. What he gives is enormous and quite beyond price"—Thomas Keneally
0–89255–064–3 Persea $16.95
0–89255–063–5 Persea pb $8.95

• Hal Porter

BAIRNSDALE: Portrait of an Australian Country Town
Edited by Tony Barker
0–909134–03–0 Australia International $24.95

THE EXTRA
0–7022–2052–3 Queensland pb $10.95

THE PAPER CHASE
0–7022–1504–X Queensland pb $12.95

• Peter Porter

COLLECTED POEMS
0–19–211965–6 Oxford pb $7.95

THE AUTOMATIC ORACLE
0–19–282088–5 Oxford pb $8.95

FAST FORWARD
0–19–211967–2 Oxford pb $7.95

• Thomas Shapcott

Shapcott is an important anti-establishment poet who came to prominence in the 1960s.

TRAVEL DICE
0–7022–2077–9 Queensland pb $8.95

WELCOME!
0–7022–1922–3 Queensland $15.95

• Nevil Shute

ON THE BEACH
A suspenseful apocalyptic novel in which Australia becomes the last haven in a world devastated by nuclear holocaust
0–434–69919–5 David & Charles $23.95
0–345–31148–5 Ballantine pb $2.95

A TOWN LIKE ALICE
A classic story of survival concerning a Japanese death march through Malaya during the Second World War
0–345–35374–9 Ballantine pb $3.95

Christina Stead (photo courtesy of Henry Holt)

• Christina Stead

Rebecca West described Stead as "one of the few people really original since the war." Her powerfully realistic novels, set in Australia, England, and the United States, reflect her involvement with feminist and left-wing issues.

HOUSE OF ALL NATIONS
A scathing picture of the world of high finance
0–380–01259–6 Avon pb $2.45

I'M DYING LAUGHING
0–8050–0462–9 Henry Holt $19.95

LETTY FOX: Her Luck
Stead observes the ways of a young woman of easy virtue
0–15–650885–0 HBJ $5.95

LITTLE HOTEL
A cross-section of human life under the roof of a Swiss hotel
0–380–48389–0 Avon pb $2.50

THE MAN WHO LOVED CHILDREN
Stead's most famous book, a masterpiece of modern fiction, is a chilling novel of family life filled with loathing, manipulation, and madness
Introduction by Randall Jarrell
0–03–057642–3 Henry Holt pb $11.95

MISS HERBERT: The Suburban Wife
A portrait of a woman's dual character
0–15–660762–X HBJ pb $5.95

AN OCEAN OF STORY: The Uncollected Stories of Christina Stead
"Brims over with her curiosity about other people's lives and her compulsion to record what happened to them"—*NY Times*
Edited with an afterword by R.G. Geering
0–670–80996–9 Viking $19.95
0–14–010021–0 Penguin pb $7.95

• Randolph Stow

THE GIRL GREEN AS ELDERFLOWER
A love story set in England in the 1960s
0–8008–3269–8 Taplinger pb $5.95

THE MERRY-GO-ROUND IN THE SEA
0–8008–5195–1 Taplinger $14.95

THE SUBURBS OF HELL
0–8008–7487–0 Taplinger $13.95

TO THE ISLANDS
The journey of a dying missionary who manages to transcend his white heritage
0–8008–7739–X Taplinger $9.95

TOURMALINE
0–8008–7797–7 Taplinger $10.95

THE VISITANTS
0–8008–8017–X Taplinger pb $7.95

• Patrick White

THE AUNT'S STORY
The journey of an independent lady from rugged Australia to crazy pre-war Europe and on to the United States
0–14–004145–1 Penguin pb $6.95

THE BURNT ONES
Eleven short stories
0–14–002776–9 Penguin pb $6.95

THE EYE OF THE STORM
A callous woman on her deathbed elicits varying waves of love and hate from those gathered around her
0–670–30374–7 Viking $13.95
0–14–003963–5 Penguin pb $7.95

FLAWS IN THE GLASS: A Self-Portrait
0–14–006293–9 Penguin pb $6.95

A FRINGE OF LEAVES
White's version of a classic Australian adventure story, involving shipwreck, escaped convicts, and Aborigines
0–14–004409–4 Penguin pb $6.95

THE LIVING AND THE DEAD
0–14–002623–1 Penguin pb $6.95

MEMOIRS OF MANY IN ONE
A nine-lived heroine—among her roles, that of a suburban shoplifter—asks Mr. White to edit her journal. "An irreverent and moving literary *trompe l'oeil*"—David Leavitt
0–670–81320–6 Viking $15.95

RIDERS IN THE CHARIOT
0–14–002185–X Penguin pb $6.95

THE SOLID MANDALA
An explorer's encounter with a virgin land and a young orphan is an examination of "the Australian dilemma, the human condition of life down under"—*Library Journal*
0–670–65632–1 Viking $12.95
0–14–002975–3 Penguin pb $6.95

THE TREE OF MAN
0–14–001657–0 Penguin pb $6.95

THE TWYBORN AFFAIR
0–14–005544–4 Penguin pb $6.95

THE VIVISECTOR
Incapable of love, a painter assiduously dissects the weaknesses of others
0–670–74739–4 Viking $13.95
0–14–003693–8 Penguin pb $6.95

VOSS
White's masterpiece, centered around a brutal journey across 19th-century

---

Australia, formulates a defining myth of the Australian experience
0–670–74807–2 Viking $13.95
0–14–001438–1 Penguin pb $7.95

- **B. Wongar**
"B. Wongar" is the pseudonym of a Yugoslavian anthropologist who writes with a profound understanding of Aboriginal culture.
BABARU
0–252–00995–9 Illinois $11.95
BILMA
0–8142–0370–1 Ohio State $12.50
GABO DJARA
0–396–08861–9 Dodd, Mead $15.95
KARAN: A Novel of the Australian Hinterland
0–396–08722–1 Dodd, Mead $16.95
WALG: A Novel of Australia
Foreword by Simone De Beauvoir
0–396–08189–4 Dodd, Mead $14.95

- **Judith Wright**
THE CRY FOR THE DEAD
0–19–554296–7 Oxford $32.50

ANTHOLOGIES

- **Don Anderson, editor**
TRANSGRESSIONS: Australian Writing Now
0–14–008393–6 Penguin pb $5.95

- **Murray Bail, editor**
THE FABER BOOK OF CONTEMPORARY AUSTRALIAN SHORT STORIES
0–571–14763–1 Faber & Faber $25.00
0–571–15083–7 Faber & Faber pb $9.95

- **Ronald M. Berndt**
LOVE SONGS OF ARNHEM LAND
0–226–04389–4 Chicago $22.50

- **Leon Cantrell, editor**
THE 1980s: Stories, Verses & Essays
Includes pieces by Henry Lawson and Christopher Brennan
0–7022–1038–2 Queensland pb $12.95

- **Brian Elliott, editor**
THE JINDYWOROBAKS
Selections from the nationalist poetry movement of the 1930s
0–7022–1297–0 Queensland pb $12.95

- **Kevin Gilbert, editor**
INSIDE BLACK AUSTRALIA: An Anthology of Aboriginal Poetry
Forty contemporary Aboriginal poets
0–14–011126–3 Penguin pb $7.95

- **Laurie Hergenhan, editor**
THE AUSTRALIAN SHORT STORY: An Anthology from the 1890s to the 1980s
0–7022–1787–5 Queensland pb $10.50

- **Leonie Kramer & Adrian Mitchell, editors**
THE OXFORD ANTHOLOGY OF AUSTRALIAN LITERATURE
0–19–554476–5 Oxford $29.95

- **James McAuley, editor**
A MAP OF AUSTRALIAN VERSE: The Twentieth Century
0–19–550474–7 Oxford pb $24.95

- **Roger McDonald, editor**
FIRST PAPERBACK POETS ANTHOLOGY
0–7022–0916–3 Queensland $19.95

- **Thomas Shapcott, editor**
CONSOLIDATION: The Second Poets Anthology
0–7022–1676–3 Queensland $18.00
0–7022–1677–1 Queensland pb $9.50
CONTEMPORARY AMERICAN AND AUSTRALIAN POETRY
0–7022–1201–6 Queensland $19.95
0–7022–1211–3 Queensland pb $12.95

ELISABETH WYNHAUSEN: Some Favorite Works of Australian Literature

Elizabeth Wynhausen is the New York correspondent for *The Age* (Melbourne).

Thea Astley
IT'S RAINING IN MANGO
0–399–13302–X Putnam $17.95
0–14–011403–3 Penguin pb $6.95

John Bryson
EVIL ANGELS
0–553–27207–1 Bantam pb $4.50

Peter Carey
ILLYWHACKER
0–06–015425–X Harper & Row $18.95
0–06–091331–2 Harper & Row pb $9.95

Albert Facey
A FORTUNATE LIFE
0–670–80307–3 Viking $30.00

Helen Garner
THE CHILDREN'S BACH
0–14–008371–5 Penguin pb $4.95

Thomas Keneally
SCHINDLER'S LIST
0–14–006784–1 Penguin pb $6.95

Sally Morgan
MY PLACE
0–8050–0911–6 Seaver $19.95

Les Murray
THE VERNACULAR REPUBLIC
0–89255–063–5 Persea pb $8.95

Christina Stead
THE MAN WHO LOVED CHILDREN
0–03–057642–3 Henry Holt pb $11.95

Patrick White
FLAWS IN THE GLASS: A Self-Portrait
0–14–006293–9 Penguin pb $6.95

New Zealand Literature

- **Sylvia Ashton-Warner**
I PASSED THIS WAY
0–394–42612–6 Knopf $15.95
TEACHER
0–671–61768–0 Simon & Schuster pb $7.95

- **James K. Baxter**
HORSE
0–19–558140–7 Oxford pb $8.95

- **Charles Brasch**
COLLECTED POEMS
Edited by Alan Roddick
0–19–558105–9 Oxford $34.95
INDIRECTIONS
0–19–558050–8 Oxford $39.95

- **Dan Davin**
THE SALAMANDER AND THE FIRE
Stories mainly from the last war with additional postwar pieces by one of New Zealand's prominent writers of fiction
0–19–558147–4 Oxford pb $8.95

- **Marilyn Duckworth**
A GAP IN THE SPECTRUM
0–19–558143–1 Oxford pb $9.95
THE MATCHBOX HOUSE
An unhappy wife retreats into fantasy
0–19–558171–7 Oxford pb $9.95

- **Janet Frame**
FACES IN THE WATER
Ostensibly about the insane, the semi-autobiographical *"Faces in the Water* is especially brilliant in its descriptions of what happens inside the patient's mind" (*Time*)
0–8076–0957–9 Braziller pb $5.95
LIVING IN THE MANIOTOTO
The tale of a ventriloquist, "full of wordplays, cameo portraits and deliberate mystery"—*Publishers Weekly*
0–8076–0926–9 Braziller $8.95
0–8076–0958–7 Braziller pb $4.95
OWLS DO CRY
Possibly her best work, this first part of a trilogy (continued in *Faces in the Water*) introduces us to an impoverished, though literate New Zealand family
0–8076–0956–0 Braziller pb $5.95
THE POCKET MIRROR: Poems
0–8076–0408–9 Braziller pb $4.95
SCENTED GARDENS FOR THE BLIND
0–8076–0985–4 Braziller pb $4.95
A STATE OF SIEGE
0–8076–0986–2 Braziller pb $4.95

TO THE ISLAND
The first part of Frame's autobiography. "My life had been for many years in the power of words. I was driven now by a constant search and need for what was, after all, only a word—imagination"
0–8076–1042–9 Braziller $10.95

AN ANGEL AT MY TABLE
The second volume of Frame's autobiography
0–8076–1090–9 Braziller $12.95

THE ENVOY FROM MIRROR CITY
Perhaps the most involving of her three-part autobiography, this volume describes her drab neighborhood in postwar London, Soho poets, travels to Ibiza, and her return to somewhat posher London quarters
0–8076–1124–7 Braziller $14.95

• Maurice Gee
COLLECTED STORIES
Deftly brushed pictures of New Zealand life
0–14–008804–0 Penguin pb $6.95

• Patricia Grace
Of Maori descent, Grace's persistent theme is the status of the Maori—and Maori culture—in white New Zealand society.
THE DREAM SLEEPERS & OTHER STORIES
Tales of Maoris in a society where the prevalent values are alien to them
0–582–70620–3 Three Continents pb $7.00

THE DREAMERS & OTHER STORIES
0–317–58078–7 Penguin pb $4.95

ELECTRIC CITY & OTHER STORIES
Thirteen stories of "conflict, misunderstanding—and sunlight"
0–14–010151–9 Penguin pb $5.95

MUTUWHENUA: The Moon Sleeps
0–14–008945–4 Penguin pb $4.95

POTIKI
0–14–008803–2 Penguin pb $5.95

WAIARIKI & OTHER STORIES
0–14–008947–0 Penguin pb $3.95

• Noel H. Hilliard
Hilliard is an active commentator on the condition of the Maori in modern urban surroundings.
MAORI GIRL
0–86863–671–1 International $9.95

Keri Hulme
THE BONE PEOPLE
The prize-winning tale of a strange trio—an artist-cum-anchorite, her boy lover, and the boy's foster father—"reminding us of things in heaven and earth we too often forget or provincially ignore"—*Houston Post*
0–14–008922–5 Penguin pb $7.95

THE SILENCES BETWEEN: Moeraki Conversations
Poems by the Maori novelist
0–19–648007–8 Oxford pb $6.95

TE KAIHAU: The Windeater
0–8076–1168–9 Braziller $15.95

• Robin Hyde
Robin Hyde was the pseudonym of Iris Wilkinson, an anguished and peripatetic writer who took her own life on the eve of World War II.

SELECTED POEMS
Edited by Linda Wevers
0–19–558114–8 Oxford $14.95

• Witi Ihimaera
THE NEW NET GOES FISHING: Short Stories
0–86863–682–7 International pb $4.95

POUNAMU, POUNAMU: Short Stories
0–86863–675–4 International pb $4.95

TANGI
0–89955–372–9 International pb $4.95

WHANAU
0–89955–373–7 International $6.50

Katherine Mansfield
Nowadays considered among the preeminent practitioners of the modern short story, Mansfield's art has been likened to that of Chekhov.
THE COLLECTED LETTERS OF KATHERINE MANSFIELD, 1888–1917

Volume 1
Edited by Vincent O'Sullivan & Margaret Scott
0–19–812613–1 Oxford $27.50

THE CRITICAL WRITINGS OF KATHERINE MANSFIELD
Includes material from letters, diaries, and reviews
Edited with an introduction by Clare Hanson
0–312–17514–0 St. Martin's $29.95

THE JOURNAL OF KATHERINE MANSFIELD
0–88001–023–1 Ecco pb $6.95

THE SHORT STORIES OF KATHERINE MANSFIELD
0–88001–025–8 Ecco pb $15.70

SHORT STORIES OF KATHERINE MANSFIELD
0–394–44532–5 Knopf $22.50

STORIES
Twenty-seven thoughtfully selected tales. "Katherine Mansfield was not a rebel, she was an innovator . . . simply, she passed beyond the English tradition of prose narrative"—Elizabeth Bowen
Edited by Elizabeth Bowen
0–394–70036–8 Random House pb $4.95

• Ronald H. Morrieson
PREDICAMENT
Preface by Maurice Shadbolt
0–14–008841–5 Penguin pb $4.95

• Frank Sargeson
Held by many to be the foremost novelist from New Zealand and certainly one of the most satirical, his work unfortunately has not been widely available in the United States.
CONVERSATION IN A TRAIN & OTHER CRITICAL WRITING
Edited by Kevin Cunningham
0–19–648023–X Oxford pb $24.95

MEMOIRS OF A PEON
A comic, picaresque look at the New Zealand working class
0–89955–369–9 International pb $4.95

• Maurice Shadbolt
SEASON OF THE JEW
0–393–02431–8 Norton $16.95

A TOUCH OF CLAY
A reclusive potter collides with both New Zealand's past and his own neighbors
0–19–558173–3 Oxford pb $9.95

• Ian Wedde
DRIVING IN THE STORM: Selected Poems
0–19–558167–9 Oxford pb $9.95

SYMMES HOLE
0–14–008840–7 Penguin pb $7.95

ANTHOLOGIES

• Fleur Adcock, editor
THE OXFORD BOOK OF CONTEMPORARY NEW ZEALAND POETRY
0–19–558092–3 Oxford pb $17.95

• MacDonald P. Jackson & Vincent O'Sullivan, editors
THE OXFORD BOOK OF NEW ZEALAND WRITING SINCE 1945
0–19–558097–4 Oxford pb $45.00

• Vincent O'Sullivan, editor
AN ANTHOLOGY OF TWENTIETH CENTURY NEW ZEALAND POETRY
0–19–558163–6 Oxford pb $22.95

• Ian Wedde & Harvey McQueen, editors
THE PENGUIN BOOK OF NEW ZEALAND VERSE
0–14–042333–8 Penguin pb $9.95

• Lydia Wevers, editor
YELLOW PENCILS: Contemporary Poetry by New Zealand Women
0–19–558178–4 Oxford pb $13.95

Literary Criticism

LITERARY ESSAYISTS

• Robert Alter
THE PLEASURES OF READING IN AN IDEOLOGICAL AGE
0–671–62783–X Simon & Schuster $18.95

• Jorge Luis Borges
SEVEN NIGHTS
Seven lectures on *The Divine Comedy*, nightmares, *The One Thousand and One Nights*, Buddhism, poetry, blindness, and the Kabbalah
Translated by Eliot Weinberger
Introduction by Alastair Reid
0–8112–0905–9 New Directions pb $6.95

• Kenneth Burke

LANGUAGE AS SYMBOLIC ACTION: Essays on Life, Literature, and Method
An "attempt" (in Burke's words) "to define and track down the implications of the term 'symbolic action' and how the marvels of language and literature look when considered from that point of view"
0–520–00192–3 California pb $12.95

THE PHILOSOPHY OF LITERARY FORM
A brilliant selection of his work from the 1930s in the field of poetic theory
0–520–02483–4 California pb $11.95

A RHETORIC OF MOTIVES
Burke as the philosopher of language and human conduct, with an analysis of persuasion and identification and what lies behind them
0–520–01546–0 California pb $10.95

• Leon Edel

WRITING LIVES: Principia Biographica
"Edel has brilliantly provided for the art of biography a much-needed statement of first principles"—Louis Auchincloss
0–393–30382–9 Norton pb $6.95

• Northrop Frye

"No doubt the most distinguished literary theorist writing in English today."—*NY Review of Books*
ANATOMY OF CRITICISM
A synoptic view of the scope, theory, principles, and techniques of literary criticism
0–691–06004–5 Princeton $40.50
0–691–01298–9 Princeton pb $9.95

FABLES OF IDENTITY: Studies in Poetic Mythology
0–15–629730–2 HBJ pb $8.95

THE SECULAR SCRIPTURE: A Study of the Structure of Romance
How the simplest stories work and rework archetypal themes. "*The Secular Scripture* is in fact the most sophisticated study of popular culture, considered on a world scale, that we have yet had"—*Washington Post*
0–674–79675–6 Harvard $16.00
0–674–79676–4 Harvard pb $7.95

SPIRITUS MUNDI: Essays on Literature, Myth, and Society
0–253–35432–3 Indiana $20.00
0–253–20289–2 Indiana pb $7.95

• Irving Howe

POLITICS AND THE NOVEL
0–452–00844–1 NAL pb $9.95

• Randall Jarrell

KIPLING, AUDEN AND CO.: Essays and Reviews, 1935–1964
0–374–18153–5 Farrar Straus & Giroux $17.95
0–374–51668–5 Farrar Straus & Giroux pb $9.95

• Hugh Kenner

A COLDER EYE: The Modern Irish Writers
0–394–42225–2 Knopf $16.95
0–14–006760–4 Penguin pb $12.95

THE COUNTERFEITERS: An Historical Comedy
Illustrated by Guy Davenport
0–8018–2981–X Johns Hopkins $22.50
0–8018–2983–6 Johns Hopkins pb $7.95

MAZES: 64 Essays
0–86547–341–2 North Point $22.95

THE MECHANIC MUSE
How such inventions as the linotype and the subway altered the literary imaginations of Eliot, Pound, Joyce, and Beckett
0–19–504142–9 Oxford $15.95
0–19–505423–7 Oxford pb $7.95

THE POUND ERA
Kenner's major work is also a study of the many aspects of modernism on which Pound's career impinged
0–520–01860–5 California $37.50
0–520–02427–3 California pb $14.95

A SINKING ISLAND: The Modern English Writers
A pungent, lively and thoughtful literary tour
0–394–54254–1 Knopf $22.95

THE STOIC COMEDIANS: Flaubert, Joyce and Beckett
0–520–02584–9 California $5.95

Founded on faith in the possibility of insight—the Joycean epiphany, the Poundian image that can flash in an instant of time; on faith, too, that technology need not consign the arts to irrelevance, the Modernist enterprise evolved its verbal technologies, its poem- and novel-machines of intricate interacting discrete pieces. The technology on which it drew for tacit analogies is largely obsolescent now: as much so as, say, Dante's Earth-centered cosmos. The Dublin trams are long gone, and the linotype machine; the typewriter is going; Bloom's watch with hands will some day need a footnote. Already students need the explanation that when a telephone whirs and a man says "Twentyeight. No. Twenty. Double four, yes" [7.385] he has cranked the magneto and is now requesting a number. That world survives now, like Dante's world, in art. Its assumptions survive in the structures of its art: complex artifacts we even sometimes take apart for maintenance.

Hugh Kenner
THE MECHANIC MUSE
0–19–504142–9 Oxford $15.95
0–19–505423–7 Oxford pb $7.95

• Frank Kermode

THE ART OF TELLING: Essays on Fiction
0–674–04828–8 Harvard $16.00
0–674–04829–6 Harvard pb $6.95

THE CLASSIC: Literary Images of Permanence and Change
0–674–13398–6 Harvard pb $6.95

ROMANTIC IMAGE
A redefinition of the romantic tradition, especially in its relation to English poetry and criticism
0–7448–0037–4 RC&H pb $7.95

THE SENSE OF AN ENDING: Studies in the Theory of Fiction
The relationship of fiction to age-old conceptions of chaos and crisis. "An impressively learned, eloquent and brilliant

defense of a non-schismatic use of human time"—Leo Bersani, *NY Times*
0–19–500770–0 Oxford pb $8.95

• Vladimir Nabokov

LECTURES ON LITERATURE: British, French and German Writers
0–15–649589–9 HBJ pb $9.95

• Mario Praz

THE FLAMING HEART: Essays on Crashaw, Machiavelli, and Other Studies from Chaucer to T.S. Eliot
0–393–00669–7 Norton pb $3.95

ROMANTIC AGONY
0–19–281061–8 Oxford pb $12.95

• Jean-Paul Sartre

LITERARY ESSAYS
Essays on Faulkner, Camus, Dos Passos, and Kafka
0–8065–0647–4 Lyle Stuart pb $2.25

• Susan Sontag

A SUSAN SONTAG READER
An interview, three short stories, an excerpt from "On Photography," two novels, and a selection of essays including "Notes on Camp," "On Style," "The Pornographic Imagination," and "Fascinating Fascism"
Introduction by Elizabeth Hardwick
0–394–71569–1 Random House pb $9.95

AGAINST INTERPRETATION
Selections from her early writings about the arts and contemporary culture, including "Notes on Camp" and "The Imagination of Disaster"
0–374–52040–2 Farrar, Straus & Giroux pb $7.95

AIDS AND ITS METAPHORS
0–374–10257–0 Farrar, Straus & Giroux $14.95

ILLNESS AS METAPHOR
0–317–67507–9 Farrar, Straus & Giroux pb $5.95

ON PHOTOGRAPHY
0–374–52113–1 Farrar, Straus & Giroux pb $7.95

1836 Paris bookworm by Cham, from The Delights of Reading *by Otto Bettmann (Godine)*

STYLES OF RADICAL WILL
Extends her investigations to film, literature, politics, and pornography
0–374–51364–3 Farrar, Straus & Giroux pb $7.95

● George Steiner
AFTER BABEL: Aspects of Language and Translation
"Great erudition brought to bear on linguistics . . . celebrates the beauty and mystery of the subject"—*NY Times*
0–19–502048–0 Oxford pb $10.95

GEORGE STEINER: A Reader
A rich sampling of Steiner's ideas
0–19–520458–1 Oxford $25.00
0–19–505068–1 Oxford pb $9.95

IN BLUEBEARD'S CASTLE: Some Notes Toward the Redefinition of Culture
0–300–01710–3 Yale pb $8.95

LANGUAGE AND SILENCE: Essays on Language, Literature and the Inhuman
Essays (as Steiner describes them) "about language and politics, language and the future of literature, about the pressures on language of totalitarian lies and cultural decay, about language and other modes of meaning (music, translation, mathematics), about language and silence"
0–689–70226–4 Atheneum pb $9.95

● Lionel Trilling
BEYOND CULTURE
0–15–111987–2 HBJ $10.95
0–15–611891–2 HBJ pb $4.95

THE LAST DECADE: Essays and Reviews, 1965–1975
Edited by Diana Trilling
0–15–148421–X HBJ $9.95
0–15–648892–2 HBJ pb $7.95

THE OPPOSING SELF
This 1955 collection includes essays on *Little Dorrit, Anna Karenina, The Bostonians, Bouvard and Péchuchet,* and *Mansfield Park*
0–15–170068–0 HBJ $10.95
0–15–670065–4 HBJ pb $3.95

SINCERITY AND AUTHENTICITY
How sincerity—being true to oneself—came to occupy a place of supreme importance in the moral life and how it was replaced by the more strenuous ideal of authenticity. Ranges over the whole of Western literature
0–15–182645–5 HBJ $12.95

Edmund Wilson
AXEL'S CASTLE: A Study in the Imaginative Literature of 1870–1930
0–393–30194–X Norton pb $7.95

PATRIOTIC GORE: Studies in the Literature of the American Civil War
Foreword by C. Vann Woodward
0–930350–61–8 Northeastern pb $13.50

THE SHORES OF LIGHT: A Literary Chronicle of the 1920s and 1930s
0–930350–68–5 Northeastern pb $13.50

TO THE FINLAND STATION
0–374–51045–8 FS&G pb $11.95

THE TRIPLE THINKERS & THE WOUND AND THE BOW: A Combined Volume
0–930350–67–7 Northeastern pb $11.95

THE MODERNIST REVOLUTION

● T.S. Eliot
SELECTED PROSE OF T.S. ELIOT
Edited by Frank Kermode
0–15–180702–7 HBJ $10.95
0–15–680654–1 HBJ pb $9.95

THE SACRED WOOD
Includes Eliot's famous essay on *Hamlet*
0–416–67610–3 RC&H pb $12.95

THE USE OF POETRY AND THE USE OF CRITICISM
0–674–93150–5 Harvard pb $4.95

● Ezra Pound
ABC OF READING
The "Ezuversity" at work, laying down how and what to read, from Sappho to Laforgue
0–8112–0151–1 New Directions pb $6.95

GUIDE TO KULCHUR
0–8112–0156–2 New Directions pb $7.95

LITERARY ESSAYS
0–8112–0157–0 New Directions pb $12.95

SELECTED PROSE, 1909–1965
Essays carefully selected to show the evolution of Pound's aesthetic
Edited by William Cookson
0–8112–0574–6 New Directions pb $12.95

● Marcel Proust
MARCEL PROUST ON ART AND LITERATURE
0–88184–114–5 Carroll & Graf pb $8.95

● Gertrude Stein
HOW TO WRITE
0–486–23144–5 Dover pb $5.95

LECTURES IN AMERICA
0–8070–6353–3 Beacon pb $10.95

● Paul Valéry
THE ART OF POETRY
"These essays should come into the hands of everyone interested not only in the now almost mythical figure of Valéry but in the evolving situation of poetry and poetic theory in our time"—*New Yorker*
Translated by Denise Folliot
Edited by Mathews Jackson
0–691–01868–5 Princeton pb $11.50

● William Carlos Williams
IN THE AMERICAN GRAIN
Meditations on American history and its myths, including chapters on Cotton Mather, Daniel Boone, Abraham Lincoln, and the conquest of Mexico
0–8112–0230–5 New Directions pb $6.95

● Virginia Woolf
THE COLLECTED ESSAYS OF VIRGINIA WOOLF: 1904–1912
A brilliant selection covering her early years as a literary journalist
Edited by Andrew McNeillie

Volume 1
0–15–129055–5 HBJ $19.95

Volume 2
0–15–129056–8 HBJ $22.95

THE NEW CRITICISM

Under the influence of modernism, criticism became professionalized as an academic discipline. The so-called New Criticism of the 1940s and '50s, which helped establish modernist literature in academe, has been seen both as modernism's apotheosis and as its betrayal.

● R.P. Blackmur
SELECTED ESSAYS OF R.P. BLACKMUR
Complex discussions of Emily Dickinson, Hart Crane, Henry James, Thomas Mann, and others
Edited by Denis Donoghue
0–88001–083–5 Norton pb $17.50

● Cleanth Brooks
THE WELL WROUGHT URN: Studies in the Structure of Poetry
Detailed commentaries on ten British poets from Elizabethan times to the 20th century, including Donne, Shakespeare, Milton, Pope, Wordsworth, Keats, and Yeats
0–15–695705–1 HBJ pb $8.95

● William Empson
SEVEN TYPES OF AMBIGUITY
Revised twice since 1930, this remains one of the most widely read and quoted works of literary analysis
0–8112–0037–X New Directions pb $7.95

SOME VERSIONS OF PASTORAL
"Unquestionably one of the keenest, most independent and most imaginative books of criticism"—Kenneth Burke
0–8112–0038–8 New Directions pb $8.95

● John Crowe Ransom
SELECTED ESSAYS OF JOHN CROWE RANSOM
From the leading exponent of New Criticism
Edited by Thomas D. Young & John Hindle
0–8071–1130–9 LSU $32.50

● I.A. Richards
PRINCIPLES OF LITERARY CRITICISM
0–15–674592–5 HBJ pb $7.95

● William K. Wimsatt
THE VERBAL ICON: Studies in the Meaning of Poetry
Combines theoretical vigor with precise case studies
0–8131–0111–5 Kentucky pb $8.00

● Yvor Winters
IN DEFENSE OF REASON
Includes *Primitivism and Decadence, Maule's Curse,* and *The Anatomy of Nonsense*
Edited with a preface by Kenneth Fields
0–8040–0151–0 Ohio pb $17.95

CONTEMPORARY WRITERS ON WRITING

Though critics profess to unravel the workings of a writer's mind, authors themselves frequently offer quite a different view of the creative process.

• **Malcolm Cowley & George Plimpton,** editors
WRITERS AT WORK: The Paris Review Interviews

First Series
Featuring: E.M. Forster, Joyce Carey, Dorothy Parker, James Thurber, Thornton Wilder, William Faulkner, Frank O'Connor, Robert Penn Warren, Alberto Moravia, Angus Wilson, William Styron, Truman Capote, Françoise Sagan
0–14–004540–6 Penguin pb $9.95

Second Series
Featuring: Ezra Pound, Ernest Hemingway, Aldous Huxley, Robert Frost, T.S. Eliot, Robert Lowell, Henry Miller, Lawrence Durrell, Marianne Moore, S.J. Perelman, Boris Pasternak, Mary McCarthy, Katherine Anne Porter, Ralph Ellison
0–14–004541–4 Penguin pb $9.95

Third Series
Featuring: Jean Cocteau, Blaise Cendrars, Arthur Miller, Allen Ginsberg, Norman Mailer, William Carlos Williams, Saul Bellow, Evelyn Waugh, Louis-Ferdinand Céline, William Burroughs, Harold Pinter, Lillian Hellman, Edward Albee, James Jones
0–14–004542–2 Penguin pb $9.95

Fourth Series
Featuring: Conrad Aiken, Robert Graves, John Dos Passos, Vladimir Nabokov, John Steinbeck, Christopher Isherwood, W.H. Auden, Eudora Welty, John Berryman, Anthony Burgess, Jack Kerouac, Anne Sexton, John Updike
0–14–004543–0 Penguin pb $9.95

Fifth Series
Featuring: Kingsley Amis, John Cheever, James Dickey, Joan Didion, William Gass, Henry Green, Joseph Heller, Jerzy Kosinski, Archibald Macleish, Pablo Neruda, Joyce Carol Oates, Isaac Bashevis Singer, Irving Shaw, Gore Vidal, P.G. Wodehouse
0–14–005818–4 Penguin pb $9.95

Sixth Series
Featuring: Rebecca West, Stephen Spender, Tennessee Williams, Elizabeth Bishop, Bernard Malamud, William Goyen, Kurt Vonnegut Jr., Nadine Gordimer, James Merrill, Gabriel García Márquez, Carlos Fuentes, John Gardner
0–14–007736–7 Penguin pb $9.95

Seventh Series
Featuring: Malcolm Cowley, Arthur Koestler, Eugène Ionesco, Elizabeth Hardwick, May Sarton, Philip Larkin, John Ashbery, Milan Kundera, John Barth, Philip Roth, Raymond Carver
Introduction by John Updike
0–14–008500–9 Penguin pb $7.95

Eighth Series
Featuring: Joseph Brodsky, Eli Wiesel, James Laughlin, Robert Fitzgerald, Anita Brookner, Leon Edel, Robert Stone, John Hersey, John Irving, Cynthia Ozick, E.B. White, Derek Walcott, E.L. Doctorow
0–14–010761–4 Penguin pb $8.95

THE BIBLE

• **Robert Alter**
THE ART OF BIBLICAL NARRATIVE
The Bible from a literary point of view, with a penetrating analysis by a major Hebrew scholar and critic
0–465–00424–5 Harper & Row $14.95
0–465–00427–X Harper & Row pb $9.95

• **Robert Alter & Frank Kermode**
THE LITERARY GUIDE TO THE BIBLE
"A veritable thesaurus of literary and human evaluation of the Scriptures, both absorbing and authoritative"—Amos N. Wilder, Harvard University
0–674–87530–3 Harvard $29.95

• **Richard Elliott Friedman**
WHO WROTE THE BIBLE?
A distinguished Biblical scholar and linguist combines his knowledge of the ancient world with recent archaeological evidence and new methods of literary analysis to solve the puzzle of Biblical authorship
0–671–63161–6 Simon & Schuster $18.95

• **Northrop Frye**
THE GREAT CODE: The Bible in Literature
"May be one of the most provocative books ever written about the Bible. No one has ever stated so broadly the literary debt we owe it"—*Cleveland Plain Dealer*
0–15–636480–8 HBJ pb $5.95

• **David Rosenberg,** editor
CONGREGATION: Contemporary Writers Read the Jewish Bible
The continuing relevance of the Bible to the life and work of contemporary writers, including Isaac Bashevis Singer, Mordecai Richler, and Cynthia Ozick
0–15–146350–6 HBJ $29.95

POETRY

• **David Daiches**
GOD AND THE POETS
0–19–812862–2 Oxford pb $16.95

• **Angus Fletcher**
ALLEGORY: The Theory of a Symbolic Mode
"An encyclopaedic storehouse of theory . . . which no one in my generation is likely to surpass"—Harold Bloom
0–8014–9238–6 Cornell $12.95

• **John Hollander**
RHYME'S REASON: A Guide to English Verse
0–300–02735–4 Yale $19.00
0–300–02740–0 Yale pb $6.95

• **Czeslaw Milosz**
THE WITNESS OF POETRY
0–674–95382–7 Harvard $9.95
0–674–95383–5 Harvard pb $4.95

• **Octavio Paz**
CHILDREN OF THE MIRE: Modern Poetry from Romanticism to the Avant-Garde
The underlying myths of modern poetry, explored by the great Mexican poet in brilliant aphoristic style
0–674–11626–7 Harvard pb $5.95

David Perkins
A HISTORY OF MODERN POETRY
A judicious and well-informed survey, gracefully written

Volume 1: From the 1890s to the High Modernist Mode
0–674–39941–2 Harvard $32.00
0–674–39945–5 Harvard pb $12.95

Volume 2: Modernism and After
0–674–39946–3 Harvard $25.00

• **Marjorie Perloff**
THE DANCE OF THE INTELLECT: Studies in the Poetry of the Pound Tradition
Ten essays addressing the problem of structure, mode, and genre in postmodernist and contemporary poetry
0–521–30498–9 Cambridge $24.95
0–521–34756–4 Cambridge pb $12.95

THE FUTURIST MOVEMENT: Avant-Garde, Avant Guerre, and the Language of Rapture
0–226–65731–0 Chicago $24.95

THE POETICS OF INDETERMINACY: Rimbaud to Cage
0–691–06462–8 Princeton $31.00

• **Christopher Ricks**
THE FORCE OF POETRY
"Exactly the kind of critic every poet dreams of finding"—W.H. Auden
0–19–282046–X Oxford pb $12.95

• **M.L. Rosenthal**
POETRY AND THE COMMON LIFE
Explores the sources of poetry in our daily lives and reintroduces those elements of poetry which speak of our daily preoccupations
0–89255–118–6 Persea pb $8.95
0–8052–0738–4 Schocken pb $6.95

• **M.L. Rosenthal & Sally M. Gall**
THE MODERN POETIC SEQUENCE: The Genius of Modern Poetry
"The most useful critical book in years"—Hugh Kenner
0–19–503170–9 Oxford $39.95
0–19–503734–0 Oxford pb $11.95

• **Andrew Ross**
THE FAILURE OF MODERNISM
0–231–06330–X Columbia $27.00

• **Helen Vendler**
THE MUSIC OF WHAT HAPPENS: Poems, Poets, Critics
Recent essays by one of the best-known American critics
0–674–59152–6 Harvard $29.50

• Andrew Welsh
ROOTS OF LYRIC: Primitive Poetry and Modern Poetics
0–691–06345–1 Princeton $34.50

Translation

• Edwin Honig
THE POET'S OTHER VOICE: Conversations on Translating Poetry
0–87023–477–3 Massachusetts pb $11.95

• Barbara Reynolds & William Radice, editors
THE TRANSLATOR'S ART: Essays in Honor of Betty Radice
Dedicated to the late editor of Penguin Classics
0–14–009226–9 Penguin pb $8.95

NARRATIVE

• Erich Auerbach
MIMESIS: The Representation of Reality in Western Literature
This legendary work has lost none of its power. "There is no other work in contemporary literary criticism, known to me, that is comparable . . . in scope, in analytical and historical richness; it is actually a history of European literature from the *Odyssey* to *Ulysses* and shows a quiet mastery of all the literatures of the West"—Alfred Kazin
Translated by Willard R. Trask
0–691–06078–9 Princeton $41.00
0–691–01269–5 Princeton pb $9.95

> Abraham, Jacob, or even Moses produces a more concrete, direct, and historical impression than the figures of the Homeric world—not because they are better described in terms of sense (the contrary is the case) but because the confused, contradictory multiplicity of events, the psychological and factual cross-purposes, which true history reveals, have not disappeared in the representation but still remain clearly perceptible.
>
> Erich Auerbach
> **MIMESIS**
> 0–691–06078–9 Princeton $41.00
> 0–691–01269–5 Princeton pb $9.95

• Wayne C. Booth
THE RHETORIC OF FICTION
0–226–06558–8 Chicago pb $12.95

• Peter Brooks
READING FOR THE PLOT
Plots and plotting, and our desire and need for them
0–394–50597–2 Random House $17.95

• Lennard J. Davis
RESISTING NOVELS: Ideology and Fiction
How fiction works subliminally to resist change and to detach the reader from the world of lived experience
0–416–37820–X RC&H $37.50
0–416–37830–7 RC&H pb $12.95

• Georg Lukács
THEORY OF THE NOVEL
An early (1920) and important work
Translated by Anna Bostock
0–262–62027–8 MIT pb $7.95

• Tony Tanner
ADULTERY IN THE NOVEL: Contract and Transgression
0–8018–2471–0 Johns Hopkins pb $12.95

• Tzvetan Todorov
THE POETICS OF PROSE
Translated by Richard Howard
0–8014–0857–1 Cornell $32.50
0–8014–9165–7 Cornell pb $9.95

Popular Fiction

Tony Bennett & Janet Woollacott
BOND AND BEYOND: The Political Career of a Popular Hero
0–416–01351–1 RC&H $27.50
0–416–01361–9 RC&H pb $11.95

Michael Denning
COVER STORIES: Narrative and Ideology in the British Spy Thriller
Mixing cultural history with narrative analysis, Denning unravels the politics of popular fiction and illuminates the continuing fascination with spies
0–7100–9642–9 RC&H pb $10.95

MECHANIC ACCENTS: Dime Novels and Working-Class Culture in America
The first detailed study of the dime novel—the most widely read literature of the 19th century
0–86091–889–0 RC&H pb $13.95

Janice A. Radway
READING THE ROMANCE: Women, Patriarchy, and Popular Literature
0–8078–1590–X North Carolina $25.00
0–8078–4125–0 North Carolina pb $8.95

SUSAN SONTAG: Ten Neglected Novels

Charlotte Bronte
VILLETTE
0–14–043118–7 Penguin pb $5.95

George Meredith
THE EGOIST
0–14–043034–2 Penguin pb $6.95

Machado de Assis
EPITAPH FOR A SMALL WINNER

Alfred Döblin
BERLIN ALEXANDERPLATZ: The Story of Franz Biberkopf
0–8044–6121–X Ungar pb $11.95

Witold Gombrowicz
FERDYDURKE
0–14–008576–9 Penguin pb $7.95

Knut Hamsun
HUNGER
0–374–50520–9 FS&G pb $7.95

Venedikt Erofeev
MOSCOW TO THE END OF THE LINE
Out of print

Randall Jarrell
PICTURES FROM AN INSTITUTION: A Comedy
0–226–39374–7 Chicago pb $7.95

Italo Calvino
INVISIBLE CITIES
0–15–645380–0 HBJ pb $3.95

Jiri Grusa
THE QUESTIONNAIRE
0–394–72212–4 Random House pb $7.95

Woodcut by Gustave Doré showing critics at work, from The Delights of Reading *by Otto Bettmann* (Godine)

Literary Theory

SEMIOTICS AND STRUCTURALISM

Narrative became central to literary theory in the 1960s. Since then, semiotics (the study of sign systems) and anthropology (the study of culture in the broadest sense) have been enlisted, along with other disciplines, to offer a global perspective on literature that makes much traditional criticism seem narrow in scope.

Overviews

• Jonathan Culler
ON DECONSTRUCTION: Theory and Criticism after Structuralism
Deconstruction as the principal source of energy and innovation in contemporary criticism
0–8014–1322–2 Cornell $29.95
0–8014–9201–7 Cornell pb $8.95

THE PURSUIT OF SIGNS: Semiotics, Literature, Deconstruction
0–8014–1417–2 Cornell $27.50
0–8014–9224–6 Cornell pb $8.95

STRUCTURALIST POETICS: Structuralism, Linguistics and the Study of Literature
A good introduction to the field
0–8014–9155–X Cornell pb $9.95

• Fredric Jameson
THE PRISON-HOUSE OF LANGUAGE: A Critical Account of Structuralism and Russian Formalism
0–691–01316–0 Princeton pb $9.95

• Edith Kurzweil
THE AGE OF STRUCTURALISM: Lévi-Strauss to Foucault
0–231–04920–X Columbia $32.00
0–231–04921–8 Columbia pb $14.00

• Christopher Norris
DECONSTRUCTION: Theory and Practice
0–416–32060–0 RC&H $25.00
0–416–32070–8 RC&H pb $13.95

An 1840s Parisian gentleman in the grip of the latest novel, from The Delights of Reading *by Otto Bettmann (Godine)*

Major Texts

• Marshall Blonsky, editor
ON SIGNS
A witty and elegant anthology that offers a good sampling of diverse tendencies
0–8018–3007–9 Johns Hopkins pb $14.95

• Umberto Eco
A THEORY OF SEMIOTICS
The author of *The Name of the Rose* is a leading figure in the field of semiotics. "In many respects it constitutes the greatest contribution to this field since the pioneering work of C.S. Peirce and Charles Morris"—Robert Scholes, *Journal of Aesthetics and Art Criticism*
0–253–35955–4 Indiana $25.00
0–253–20217–5 Indiana pb $10.95

• Julia Kristeva
"Julia Kristeva changes the places of things: she always destroys the *latest preconception,* the one we thought we could be comforted by, the one of which we could be proud; what she displaces is the illusion that it has all been said already"— Roland Barthes
A KRISTEVA READER
Edited by Toril Moi
0–231–06324–5 Columbia $32.00
0–231–06325–3 Columbia pb $14.50

DESIRE IN LANGUAGE: A Semiotic Approach to Literature and Art
0–231–04806–8 Columbia $30.00
0–231–04806–8 Columbia pb $15.00

THE REVOLUTION IN POETIC LANGUAGE
Translated by Margaret Waller
0–231–05642–7 Columbia $35.00

• Claude Lévi-Strauss
STRUCTURAL ANTHROPOLOGY
"A useful 'sampler' that gives a reader the full range of Lévi-Strauss's interests"—*NY Times*

Volume 1
0–465–09516–X Harper & Row pb $13.95

Volume 2
0–226–47491–7 Chicago pb $14.00

THE SAVAGE MIND
0–226–47484–4 Chicago pb $10.95

• Michael Riffaterre
SEMIOTICS OF POETRY
Looking at 19th- and 20th-century poetry, Riffaterre maintains that poetic discourse represents nothing but itself
0–253–35165–0 Indiana $25.00
0–253–20332–5 Indiana pb $10.95

The Russian Formalists and the Prague School

• Mikhail Bakhtin
THE DIALOGIC IMAGINATION: Four Essays
Examines the difficulty of arriving at a generic definition of the novel
Translated by Caryl Emerson
Edited by Michael Holquist
0–292–71534–X Texas pb $12.95

PROBLEMS OF DOSTOEVSKY'S POETICS
Translated and edited by Caryl Emerson
0–8166–1228–5 Minnesota $14.95

RABELAIS AND HIS WORLD
Discusses the world of carnival in Rabelais as symbolic of popular culture and the destruction of authority—and links this with the age of revolution in Russia
Translated by Helene Iswolsky
0–253–34830–7 Indiana $29.50
0–253–20341–4 Indiana pb $10.95

SPEECH GENRES AND OTHER LATE ESSAYS
Essays on Dostoevsky, Rabelais, Saussure, and the theory of the novel
Translated by Vern W. McGee
Edited by Caryl Emerson & Michael Holquist
0–292–72046–7 Texas $25.00
0–292–77560–1 Texas pb $10.95

• Mikhail Bakhtin & P.N. Medvedev
THE FORMAL METHOD IN LITERARY SCHOLARSHIP: A Critical Introduction to Sociological Poetics
A critique of formalism, first published in 1928
Translated by Albert J. Wehrle
0–674–30921–9 Harvard pb $9.95

• Victor Erlich
RUSSIAN FORMALISM: History-Doctrine
0–300–02635–8 Yale pb $12.95

• Roman Jakobson
VERBAL ART, VERBAL SIGN, VERBAL TIME
Essays on the structuralist approach to linguistics and literature by the Russian formalist
0–8166–1358–3 Minnesota $29.50
0–8166–1361–3 Minnesota pb $13.95

• Daniel P. Lucid, editor
SOVIET SEMIOTICS: An Anthology
0–8018–1980–6 Johns Hopkins $28.50

• V. Propp
MORPHOLOGY OF THE FOLKTALE
Translated by Laurence Scott
0–292–78376–0 Texas pb $7.95

• Peter Steiner, editor
THE PRAGUE SCHOOL: Selected Writings, 1929–1946
0–292–78043–5 Texas $27.50

Roland Barthes

"Roland Barthes must be counted the most characteristic and important French intellectual of the structuralist generation that gained worldwide attention starting in the 1960s."—Peter Brooks

• Roland Barthes
A BARTHES READER
An excellent introduction to Barthes' thinking as applied to such diverse topics as Gide, Garbo, striptease, photography, and the Eiffel Tower
Edited by Susan Sontag
0–374–52144–1 Farrar, Straus & Giroux pb $14.95

CAMERA LUCIDA: Reflections on Photography
Translated by Richard Howard
0–374–52134–4 Farrar, Straus & Giroux pb $6.95

🐛 IF YOU CAN'T FIND IT, LOOK IN THE INDEX

THE EIFFEL TOWER & OTHER MYTHOLOGIES
Barthes at his most accessible ranges from Billy Graham to Racine to African grammar
Translated by Richard Howard
0–8090–4115–4 Farrar, Straus & Giroux $9.95
0–8090–1391–6 Farrar, Straus & Giroux pb $5.25

ELEMENTS OF SEMIOLOGY
A fairly technical analysis of writing's relation to a general science of signs
Translated by Annette Lavers & Colin Smith
0–374–52146–8 Farrar, Straus & Giroux pb $5.95

THE EMPIRE OF SIGNS
The semiotics of Japan, from simple food to sumptuous gift wrapping. "Paradise indeed for the great student of signs"—Edmund White
Translated by Richard Howard
0–8090–4222–3 Hill & Wang $13.50
0–8090–1502–1 Farrar, Straus & Giroux pb $6.95

THE FASHION SYSTEM
Translated by Matthew Ward & Richard Howard
0–8090–1503–X Farrar, Straus & Giroux pb $7.95

THE GRAIN OF THE VOICE
A collection of interviews
Translated by Linda Coverdale
0–8090–5088–9 Hill & Wang $24.95
0–8090–1521–8 Farrar, Straus & Giroux pb $9.95

IMAGE-MUSIC-TEXT
Translated by Stephen Heath
0–374–52136–0 Farrar, Straus & Giroux pb $9.95

A LOVER'S DISCOURSE: Fragments
"Barthes surprises us by making love, in its most absurd and sentimental forms, an object of interest"—Jonathan Culler
Translated by Richard Howard
0–8090–6689–0 Hill & Wang $10.00
0–8090–1388–6 Farrar, Straus & Giroux pb $8.95

MICHELET
Recovers the "structure of an existence" of France's great 19th-century romantic historian
Translated by Richard Howard
0–8090–6926–1 Hill & Wang $18.95
0–8090–1535–8 Farrar, Straus & Giroux pb $8.95

MYTHOLOGIES
"Each of the little essays in this book wrenches a definition out of a common but unconstructed object, making the object speak its hidden, but ever-so-present, reservoir of manufactured sense"—Edward Said
Translated by Annette Lavers
0–374–52150–6 Farrar, Straus & Giroux pb $5.95

ON RACINE
A personal view of theater arranged in three long essays exploring space, erotics, and human relations in Racine's plays
0–933826–56–7 PAJ pb $7.95

THE PLEASURE OF THE TEXT
Barthes' brilliant effort to define an erotics of reading
Translated by Richard Miller
0–8090–1380–0 Hill & Wang pb $6.95

ROLAND BARTHES
Barthes' exercise in self-analysis
Translated by Richard Howard
0–8090–1385–1 Farrar, Straus & Giroux pb $7.25

THE RUSTLE OF LANGUAGE
Forty-five essays on literature and teaching, from Brecht to Proust and Jakobson to Kristeva
Translated by Richard Howard
0–8090–8344–2 Hill & Wang $25.00
0–8090–1527–7 Farrar, Straus & Giroux pb $9.95

SADE-FOURIER-LOYOLA
Translated by Richard Miller
0–8090–8380–9 Farrar, Straus & Giroux pb $8.95

THE SEMIOTIC CHALLENGE
"A grave, poker-faced parody of conventional scholarship whose serene, fastidious tones barely conceal the most impudently subversive of intents"—Terry Eagleton, *TLS*
Translated by Richard Howard
0–8090–8529–1 Farrar, Straus & Giroux $30.00

S/Z
One of Barthes' most influential books: a sentence-by-sentence analysis of a story by Balzac
Translated by Richard Miller
0–8090–1377–0 Hill & Wang pb $8.95

WRITING DEGREE ZERO
"The book that began Barthes' career as the most provocative critic to emerge in France since the war"—Michael Woods, *NY Review of Books*
Translated by Annette Lavers & Colin Smith
Preface by Susan Sontag
0–374–52139–5 Farrar, Straus & Giroux pb $8.95

> The text you write must prove to me *that it desires me*. This proof exists: it is writing. Writing is: the science of the various blisses of language, its Kama Sutra (this science has but one treatise: writing itself).
>
> Roland Barthes
> **THE PLEASURE OF THE TEXT**
> Translated by Richard Miller
> 0–8090–1380–0 Hill & Wang pb $6.95

POSTSTRUCTURALISM

Those who accept the distinction between structuralism and poststructuralism credit the latter with calling into question the former's pretense to scientific objectivity. By the same token, they credit poststructuralism with extending the "everything is narrative" idea to other discourses, as well as inward to criticism itself.

The Yale Critics

The so-called Yale critics—although no longer unified or all at Yale—are deconstructionism's most brilliant advocates.

• Harold Bloom

AGON: Towards a Theory of Revisionism
"Readers . . . will be unsettled by Bloom's deliberately provocative sentences on anxiety, knowledge, evasion, negation, rhetoric"—Helen Vendler
0–19–502945–3 Oxford $27.95
0–19–503354–X Oxford pb $8.95

THE ANXIETY OF INFLUENCE: A Theory of Poetry
How strong poets make history by "misreading" one another so as to clear imaginative space for themselves—and how they wrestle with their precursors and with their anxieties of indebtedness
0–19–501896–6 Oxford pb $8.95

THE BREAKING OF THE VESSELS
0–226–06043–8 Chicago $10.00
0–226–06044–6 Chicago $4.95

FIGURES OF CAPABLE IMAGINATION
0–8264–0103–1 Harper & Row $14.95

A MAP OF MISREADING
0–19–502809–0 Oxford pb $8.95

RUIN THE SACRED TRUTHS: Poetry and Belief from the Bible to the Present
0–674–78027–2 Harvard $20.00

> All literary tradition has been necessarily elitist, in every period, if only because the Scene of Instruction always depends upon a primal choosing and a being chosen, which is what "elite" means. Teaching, as Plato knew, is necessarily a branch of erotics, in the wide sense of desiring what we have not got, of redressing our poverty, of compounding without our fantasies. No teacher, however impartial he or she attempts to be, can avoid choosing among students, or being chosen by them, for this is the very nature of teaching. Literary teaching is precisely like literature itself; no strong writer can choose his precursors until first he is chosen by them, and no strong student can fail to be chosen by his teachers. Strong students, like strong writers, will find the sustenance they must have. And strong students, like strong writers, will rise in the most unexpected places and times, to wrestle with the internalized violence pressed upon them by their teachers and precursors.
>
> Harold Bloom
> **A MAP OF MISREADING**
> 0–19–502809–0 Oxford pb $8.95

• Harold Bloom & others

DECONSTRUCTION AND CRITICISM
The "manifesto" of one of the most pervasive movements in contemporary letters, written by Harold Bloom, Paul De Man, Jacques Derrida, Geoffrey Hartman, and J. Hillis Miller
0–8264–0010–8 Harper & Row pb $11.95

• Paul De Man

ALLEGORIES OF READING: Figural Language in Rousseau, Nietzsche, Rilke, Proust
Examines the unreliability of language and argues that all writing concerns itself with its own activity
0–300–02845–8 Yale pb $12.95

BLINDNESS AND INSIGHT: Essays in the Rhetoric of Contemporary Criticism
Questions the problematic nature of reading itself
Introduction by Wlad Godzich
0–8166–1134–3 Minnesota $29.50
0–8166–1135–1 Minnesota pb $13.95

Paul De Man
WARTIME JOURNALISM, 1940–42
Facsimile reprints of all De Man's articles for the pro-Nazi Brussels *Le Soir:* music and literary reviews, newspaper interviews, and pieces on cultural politics
Edited by Werner Hamacher & others
0–8032–1684–X Nebraska $35.00
0–8032–6576–X Nebraska pb $15.95

Werner Hamacher & others, editors
RESPONSES: On Paul De Man's Wartime Journalism
Contributors include Yves Bonnefoy, Jacques Derrida, and Barbara Johnson
0–8032–2352–8 Nebraska $25.00
0–8032–7243–X Nebraska pb $12.95

● Jacques Derrida
GLAS
Translated by John P. Leavey Jr. & Richard Rand
0–8032–1667–X Nebraska $50.00

MARGINS OF PHILOSOPHY
Dismantles the philosophic tradition of Plato, Kant, Hegel, and Nietzsche, among others
Translated by Alan Bass
0–226–14326–0 Chicago pb $12.95

OF GRAMMATOLOGY
Translated by Gayatri C. Spivak
0–8018–1879–6 Johns Hopkins pb $9.95

THE POST CARD: From Socrates to Freud and Beyond
A systematic deconstruction of Western metaphysics
Translated by Alan Bass
0–226–14322–8 Chicago pb $18.95

WRITING AND DIFFERENCE
Translated by Alan Bass
0–226–14329–5 Chicago pb $12.00

● Geoffrey H. Hartman
CRITICISM IN THE WILDERNESS: The Study of Literature Today
0–300–02085–6 Yale $33.00
0–300–02839–3 Yale pb $10.95

EASY PIECES
"Delightful flippant 'communications' from one of today's best critics"—*Publisher's Weekly*
0–231–06018–1 Columbia $27.50
0–231–06019–X Columbia pb $14.50

SAVING THE TEXT: Literature, Derrida, Philosophy
0–8018–2452–4 Johns Hopkins $24.50
0–8018–2453–2 Johns Hopkins pb $6.95

● Barbara Johnson
THE CRITICAL DIFFERENCE: Essays in the Contemporary Rhetoric of Reading
0–8018–2728–0 Johns Hopkins pb $7.95

● J. Hillis Miller
THE ETHICS OF READING: Kant, De Man, Eliot, Trollope, James and Benjamin
Explores the question of the ethical dimension in the act of reading
0–231–06334–2 Columbia $21.50

Michel Foucault

Foucault's emphasis on history and politics takes him well beyond the limits of literary studies, and has produced great excitement among younger critics.

● Michel Foucault
THE FOUCAULT READER
Presents many aspects of Foucault's investigation of the nature of power in society
Edited by Paul Rabinow
0–394–52904–9 Pantheon $19.50
0–394–71340–0 Pantheon pb $9.95

THE ARCHAEOLOGY OF KNOWLEDGE
0–394–71106–8 Pantheon $8.50
0–06–131901–5 Harper & Row pb $4.95

THE BIRTH OF THE CLINIC: An Archeology of Medical Perception
"It continues his brilliant history, not of ideas as such, but of the structures of perception"—*NY Times*
0–394–71097–5 Pantheon pb $6.95

DEATH AND THE LABYRINTH: The World of Raymond Roussel
An analysis of avant-garde writing and postmodernism in relation to the author of *Locus Solus* and *Impressions of Africa*
Translated by Charles Ruas
Introduction by John Ashbery
0–520–05990–5 California pb $9.95

DISCIPLINE AND PUNISH: The Birth of the Prison
Translated by Alan Sheridan
0–394–72767–3 Random House pb $8.95

THE HISTORY OF SEXUALITY
Translated by Robert Hurley

Volume 1: An Introduction
0–394–41775–5 Pantheon $8.95
0–394–74026–2 Pantheon pb $4.95

Volume 2: The Use of Pleasure
0–394–54349–1 Pantheon $17.95

Volume 3: The Care of the Self
0–394–54814–0 Pantheon $18.95

LANGUAGE, COUNTER-MEMORY, PRACTICE: Selected Essays and Interviews
Translated by Sherry Simon
Edited by Donald F. Bouchard
0–8014–0979–9 Cornell $29.95
0–8014–9204–1 Cornell pb $9.95

MADNESS AND CIVILIZATION: A History of Insanity in the Age of Reason
0–679–72110–X Random House pb $7.95

THE ORDER OF THINGS: An Archaeology of the Human Sciences
0–394–71935–2 Random House pb $5.95

Critics attack a book, from The Delights of Reading *by Otto Bettmann (Godine)*

POWER/KNOWLEDGE: Selected Interviews & Other Writings, 1972–1977
Investigations of prisons, schools, factories, and other social institutions that control our bodies and minds
0–394–73954–X Pantheon pb $8.95

THIS IS NOT A PIPE: Illustrations and Letters by René Magritte
Explores the nuances and ambiguities of Magritte's visual critique of language
Translated by James Harkness
Illustrated by René Magritte
0–520–04232–8 California $22.00
0–520–04916–0 California pb $7.95

● Jonathan Arac
CRITICAL GENEALOGIES: Historical Situations for Postmodern Literary Studies
A remarkable application of Foucault's theories
0–231–06254–0 Columbia $32.50

● Paul Bove
INTELLECTUALS IN POWER: A Genealogy of Critical Humanism
A brilliant extension of Foucault
0–231–06010–6 Columbia $29.00

● David Hoy, editor
FOUCAULT: A Critical Reader
Major criticisms of Foucault by other writers
0–631–14042–5 Basil Blackwell pb $14.95

Other French Theorists

The resurgence of French thought has brought to the fore some previously neglected writers who in many ways prefigured current preoccupations.

Concurrently, some younger figures continue to challenge the assumptions of their immediate predecessors.

● Maurice Blanchot
THE GAZE OF ORPHEUS & OTHER LITERARY ESSAYS
"Exemplary for its clearly translated and well-chosen excerpts from Blanchot's many influential books"—Geoffrey Hartman
Translated by Lydia Davis
Edited with an afterword by P. Adams Sitney
Preface by Geoffrey Hartman
0–930794–38–9 Talman pb $9.95

THE SIRENS' SONG: Selected Essays of Maurice Blanchot
Translated by Sacha Rabinovitch
Edited by Gabriel Josipovici
0–253–35255–X Indiana $22.50

THE WRITING OF THE DISASTER
Reflections on writing as the response to disaster by one of France's most powerful literary intellects
Translated by Ann Smock
0–8032–6077–6 Nebraska pb $7.95

● Georges Bataille
EROTISM: Death and Sensuality
Translated by Mary Dalwood
0–87286–190–2 City Lights pb $10.95

INNER EXPERIENCE
Translated with an introduction by Leslie A. Boldt
0–88706–634–8 SUNY $29.50
0–88706–635–6 SUNY pb $9.95

▣ **TO ORDER BOOKS AS GIFTS, SEE PAGE 1**

LITERATURE AND EVIL
The French novelist and critic explores the value of evil as expressed in the work of Sade, Emily Brontë, Genet, and others
Translated by Alastair Hamilton
0–7145–0345–2 Marion Boyars $15.00
0–7145–0346–0 Marion Boyars pb $8.95

VISIONS OF EXCESS: Selected Writings, 1927–1939
Translated by Allan Stoekl
0–8166–1280–3 Minnesota $29.50
0–8166–1283–8 Minnesota pb $14.95

• Jean Baudrillard
SELECTED WRITINGS
Translated by Jacques Mourrain
Edited by Mark Poster
0–8047–1480–0 Stanford pb $10.95

FOR A CRITIQUE OF THE POLITICAL ECONOMY OF THE SIGN
Translated by Charles Levin
0–914386–23–9 Telos Press $16.00
0–914386–24–7 Telos Press pb $6.50

THE MIRROR OF PRODUCTION
Translated by Mark Poster
0–914386–06–9 Telos Press pb $5.50

• Denis Hollier, editor
THE COLLEGE OF SOCIOLOGY
Founded by Georges Bataille, Roger Caillois, and Michel Leiris, the prewar "College of Sociology" examined contemporary society with an emphasis on the formation of close-knit communities—brotherhoods, orders, secret societies, churches, and armies. A valuable glimpse of the 1930s as well as of some of the forerunners of poststructuralism
0–8166–1592–6 Minnesota pb $19.95

• Jean-François Lyotard & Jean-Loup Thebaud
JUST GAMING
Translated by Wlad Godzich
Afterword by Samuel Weber
0–8166–1281–1 Minnesota $19.50
0–8166–1277–3 Minnesota pb $9.95

READER-RESPONSE CRITICISM

As theory has shaken the authority of the author and the text, it has often relocated meaning in the reader's own interpretive activities. But this approach serves less to anchor meaning than to open up new ways for it to drift—as the diversity of reader-response theories testifies.

• Umberto Eco
THE ROLE OF THE READER: Explorations in the Semiotics of Texts
Addresses musical composition, contemporary art, and aesthetic manipulations of language
0–253–20318–X Indiana pb $10.95

• Stanley Fish
IS THERE A TEXT IN THIS CLASS?: The Authority of Interpretive Communities
"It is a great . . . pleasure these days to find a critic willing to discuss language, literature, reading, writing, and the community of readers on the understanding that the reader plays a real part in the production of his experience"—Denis Donoghue
0–674–46726–4 Harvard pb $9.95

• Robert C. Holub
RECEPTION THEORY: A Critical Introduction
0–416–33580–2 RC&H $25.00
0–416–33590–X RC&H pb $10.95

• Roman Ingarden
THE LITERARY WORK OF ART
Translated by George G. Grabowicz
0–8101–0537–3 Northwestern pb $14.95

• Wolfgang Iser
THE ACT OF READING: A Theory of Aesthetic Response
An important work that analyzes the relation between reader and text
0–8018–2371–4 Johns Hopkins pb $8.95

THE IMPLIED READER: Patterns of Communication in Prose Fiction from Bunyan to Beckett
"When the present flurry of works on the theory of narrative fiction comes to an end . . . this seems likely to be one of the survivors"—Frank Kermode
0–8018–2150–9 Johns Hopkins pb $9.95

• Hans Robert Jauss
AESTHETIC EXPERIENCE AND LITERARY HERMENEUTICS
Translated by Michael Shaw
Introduction by Wlad Godzich
0–8166–1006–1 Minnesota pb $13.95

TOWARDS AN AESTHETIC OF RECEPTION
Translated by Timothy Bahti
Introduction by Paul De Man
0–8166–1034–7 Minnesota $22.50
0–8166–1037–1 Minnesota pb $11.95

• Walter J. Ong
INTERFACES OF THE WORD: Studies in the Evolution of Consciousness and Culture
0–8014–9240–8 Cornell pb $13.95

ORALITY AND LITERACY: The Technologizing of the World
The intellectual, literary and social effects of writing
0–416–71380–7 RC&H pb $12.95

THE PRESENCE OF THE WORD: Some Prolegomena for Cultural and Religious History
Discusses the relationship between modes of thought and communication technologies
0–8166–1043–6 Minnesota $12.95

• Jane P. Tompkins, editor
READER-RESPONSE CRITICISM: From Formalism to Post-Structuralism
0–8018–2401–X Johns Hopkins pb $9.95

PSYCHOANALYTIC CRITICISM

Psychoanalytic criticism has come a long way from decoding texts into phallic symbols and traumatized childhoods. Diagnosis of the author has been displaced by examination of the reader and self-examination of the critic. Under the influence of feminism and the French psychoanalyst Jacques Lacan, critics today take Freud's writings as an object of, rather than a guide to, analysis.

• Rudolf Arnheim
BAUDELAIRE AND FREUD
0–520–03402–3 California $23.00

THE FREUDIAN BODY: Psychoanalysis and Art
0–231–06218–4 Columbia $17.50

• Leo Bersani
A FUTURE FOR ASTYNAX
0–231–05938–8 Columbia $35.00
0–231–05939–6 Columbia pb $15.00

• Bruno Bettelheim
THE USES OF ENCHANTMENT: The Meaning and Importance of Fairy Tales
0–394–49771–6 Knopf $21.95
0–394–72265–5 Random House pb $6.95

• Robert C. Davis, editor
LACAN AND NARRATION: The Psychoanalytic Difference in Narrative Theory
0–8018–2414–1 Johns Hopkins pb $12.95

• Gilles Deleuze & Felix Guattari
ANTI-OEDIPUS
0–670–12941–0 Viking $16.95

• Shoshana Felman
THE LITERARY SPEECH ACT
Translated by Catherine Porter
0–8014–1458–X Cornell $22.50

WRITING AND MADNESS: Literature, Philosophy, Psychoanalysis
Translated by Martha N. Evans & Brian Massumi
0–8014–1285–4 Cornell $27.50
0–8014–9394–3 Cornell pb $9.95

• Geoffrey Hartman, editor
PSYCHOANALYSIS AND THE QUESTION OF THE TEXT
0–8018–3160–1 Johns Hopkins pb $7.95

• Jacques Lacan
ECRITS: A Selection
Translated by Alan Sheridan
0–393–01129–1 Norton $19.95
0–393–30047–1 Norton pb $10.95

TELEVISION
The texts of a series of French television appearances
Translated by Denis Hollier & others
0–393–02496–2 Norton $19.95

• Steven Marcus
FREUD AND THE CULTURE OF PSYCHOANALYSIS: Studies in the Transition from Victorian Humanism to Modernity
A close reading of Freud's theoretical and clinical texts
0–04–800018–3 Allen & Unwin $34.95
0–393–30410–8 Norton pb $7.95

CULTURAL CRITICISM: Marxists and Others

Like psychoanalysis, Marxism has been carried along on the wave of European theory and significantly transformed in the process. Current "post-Marxist" thinking co-exists uneasily with poststructuralism and with earlier versions of cultural critique.

The Frankfurt School

The most powerful influence on American Marxist criticism has been the Frankfurt school, a group of German-Jewish expatriates whose diagnosis inverted the privileging of economic base over cultural superstructure. For the Frankfurt school, culture and aesthetics have become central Marxist concerns.

- Theodor W. Adorno
AESTHETIC THEORY
0–7100–9204–0 RC&H $49.95
0–7102–0990–8 RC&H pb $16.95

MINIMA MORALIA
A trenchant criticism of contemporary arts and culture
0–8446–6135–X Peter Smith pb $15.50

PRISMS
Translated by Samuel & Shierry Weber
0–262–51025–1 MIT pb $7.95

- Walter Benjamin
ILLUMINATIONS
Benjamin was the foremost writer to emerge from the Frankfurt school; he has been called the finest critic of the 20th century. Whether talking about Baudelaire, photography, storytelling, or unpacking a library, Benjamin always touches a nerve
Introduction by Hannah Arendt
0–8052–0241–2 Schocken pb $8.95

REFLECTIONS: Essays, Aphorisms, Autobiographical Writings
"There has been no more original, no more serious critic and leader in our time"—George Steiner
Edited by Peter Demetz
Translated by Edmund Jephcott
0–8052–0802–X Schocken pb $10.95

Illustration from Didbin's "Bibliomania," reproduced in The Delights of Reading *by Otto Bettmann (Godine)*

- Martin Jay
THE DIALECTICAL IMAGINATION: A History of the Frankfurt School and the Institute of Social Research, 1923–1950
The best overall account
0–316–45830–9 Little, Brown pb $11.95

- Herbert Marcuse
THE AESTHETIC DIMENSION: Toward a Critique of Marxist Aesthetics
0–8070–1519–9 Harper & Row pb $9.95

The New York Intellectuals

In America the fusing of Marxism and modernism was attempted by the so-called New York intellectuals, chief among whom were Irving Howe and Lionel Trilling. (Howe's and Trilling's works are listed under Literary Criticism.)

Alexander Bloom
PRODIGAL SONS: The New York Intellectuals and Their World
0–19–505177–7 Oxford $11.95

Mark Krupnick
LIONEL TRILLING AND THE FATE OF CULTURAL CRITICISM IN AMERICA
0–8101–0713–9 Northwestern pb $11.95

Alan M. Wald
THE NEW YORK INTELLECTUALS: The Rise and Decline of the Anti-Stalinist Left from the 1930s to the 1980s
"Wald's grasp of the ideological twists and turns of his protagonists is first-rate . . . His story has an epic sweep"—*Village Voice*
0–8078–4169–2 North Carolina pb $12.95

Recent Marxist Criticism

- Terry Eagleton
MARXISM AND LITERARY CRITICISM
0–520–03243–8 California pb $8.95

- Fredric Jameson
MARXISM AND FORM: 20th-Century Dialectical Theories of Literature
0–691–01311–X Princeton pb $10.50

THE POLITICAL UNCONSCIOUS: Narrative As A Socially Symbolic Act
0–8014–9222–X Cornell pb $9.95

- Frank Lentricchia
ARIEL AND THE POLICE: Michel Foucault, William James, Wallace Stevens
0–299–11540–2 Wisconsin $22.95

CRITICISM AND SOCIAL CHANGE
0–226–47199–3 Chicago $15.00
0–226–47200–0 Chicago pb $10.95

- Edward W. Said
THE WORLD, THE TEXT, AND THE CRITIC
"The book issues from a remarkable sharp intelligence, forcing us to face questions and possiblities that literary theorists on the whole prefer not even to raise"—*New Republic*
0–674–96187–0 Harvard pb $8.95

- Raymond Williams
THE COUNTRY AND THE CITY
"A critical history of English literature from a stimulatingly original point of view"—*Nation*
0–19–519810–7 Oxford pb $9.95

KEYWORDS: A Vocabulary of Culture and Society
Focuses on the sociology of language, showing how it reflects the political bent and values of society
0–19–520469–7 Oxford pb $9.95

MARXISM AND LITERATURE
Analyzes Marxist theory of literature from Marx to Lukacs, Althusser, and Goldman
0–19–876061–2 Oxford pb $6.95

LITERATURE AND ETHNICITY

- Houston A. Baker, Jr.
BLUES, IDEOLOGY, AND AFRO-AMERICAN LITERATURE: A Vernacular Theory
0–226–03536–0 Chicago $22.00
0–226–03538–7 Chicago pb $8.95

- Bonnie J. Barthold
BLACK TIME: Fiction of Africa, the Caribbean, and the United States
0–300–02573–4 Yale $25.00

- Barbara Christian
BLACK FEMINIST CRITICISM: Perspectives on Black Women Writers
0–08–031956–4 Pergamon $36.00
0–08–031955–6 Pergamon pb $16.00

- Henry L. Gates, Jr.
FIGURES IN BLACK: Words, Signs and the Racial Self
0–19–503564–X Oxford $29.95

THE SIGNIFYING MONKEY: A Theory of Afro-American Literary Criticism
0–19–503463–5 Oxford $29.95

- Henry L. Gates, Jr., editor
BLACK LITERATURE AND LITERARY THEORY
0–416–37230–9 RC&H $29.95
0–416–37240–6 RC&H pb $13.95

RACE, WRITING, AND DIFFERENCE
Investigates "race" as a meaningful category in the study of literature, with contributions from Derrida, Edward Said, Barbara Johnson and others
0–226–28435–2 Chicago $15.95

- Marie Harris & Kathleen Aguero, editors
A GIFT OF TONGUES: Critical Challenges in Contemporary American Poetry
Essays on marginalized groups in American writing, studying the works of Chicano, Native American, Appalachian, black, gay, and prison writers
0–8203–0953–2 Georgia pb $15.00

- Peter Hulme
COLONIAL ENCOUNTERS: Europe and the Native
0–416–41860–0 RC&H $29.95

- **C.L.R. James**
  THE FUTURE IN THE PRESENT:
  Selected Writings of C.L.R. James
  0–88208–125–X Lawrence Hill pb $6.95

- **Arnold Krupat & Brian Swan, editors**
  RECOVERING THE WORD: Essays on
  Native American Literature
  0–317–44756–4 California pb $14.95

- **Kenneth Lincoln**
  NATIVE AMERICAN RENAISSANCE
  0–520–05457–1 California pb $10.95

- **Jerome & Diane Rothenberg**
  SYMPOSIUM OF THE WHOLE: A Range
  of Discourse Toward an Ethnopoetics
  0–520–04530–0 California $29.95
  0–520–04531–9 California pb $15.95

- **Marta E. Sanchez**
  CONTEMPORARY CHICANO POETRY:
  A Critical Approach to an Emerging
  Literature
  0–520–05888–7 California pb $11.95

FEMINIST CRITICISM

Salvaging neglected writing by women, revising accepted views of the classics, and rethinking the meaning of literature and interpretation have made feminist criticism among the most exciting branches of literary studies today.

- **Nina Auerbach**
  COMMUNITIES OF WOMEN: An Idea in
  Fiction
  "Auerbach's beautiful book seems to restructure its ideals on that . . . philosophical tradition which saw friendship between members of the same sex as more of a cornerstone of human happiness"—*NY Times*
  0–674–15169–0 Harvard pb $8.95

  ROMANTIC IMPRISONMENT: Women
  and Other Glorified Outcasts
  0–231–06004–1 Columbia $30.00
  0–231–06005–X Columbia pb $14.50

- **Paula Bennett**
  MY LIFE A LOADED GUN: Female
  Creativity and Feminist Poetics
  0–8070–6308–8 Harper & Row $21.95

- **Mary V. Dearborn**
  POCAHONTAS'S DAUGHTERS: Gender
  and Ethnicity in American Culture
  Ethnic and female literature as an essential part of the American identity
  0–19–505182–3 Oxford pb $11.95

- **Rachel Blau DuPlessis**
  WRITING BEYOND THE ENDING:
  Narrative Strategies of Twentieth Century
  Women Writers
  0–253–36705–0 Indiana $27.50
  0–253–20345–7 Indiana pb $12.95

- **Mary Eagleton**
  FEMINIST LITERARY THEORY: A
  Reader
  0–631–14805–1 Basil Blackwell pb $14.95

- **Judith Fryer**
  THE FACES OF EVE: Women in the
  Nineteenth Century American Novel
  0–19–502025–1 Oxford $22.50
  0–19–502431–1 Oxford pb $5.95

- **Sandra M. Gilbert & Susan Gubar**
  THE MADWOMAN IN THE ATTIC: A
  Study of Women and the Literary
  Imagination in the Nineteenth Century
  "Like gnostic heretics who claim to have found the secret code that unlocks the mysteries in old texts, the authors force us to take a new look at the grandes dames of English literature, and the result is that they will never seem quite the same again"—Le Anne Schreiber, *NY Times*
  0–300–02596–3 Yale pb $19.95

  NO MAN'S LAND: The Place of the
  Woman Writer in the 20th Century

  Volume 1: The War of the Words
  0–300–04005–9 Yale $22.95

  Volume 2: Sexchanges
  0–300–04005–9 Yale $29.95

- **Sandra M. Gilbert & Susan Gubar,**
  editors
  SHAKESPEARE'S SISTERS: Feminist
  Essays on Women Poets
  0–253–11258–3 Indiana $25.00
  0–253–20263–9 Indiana pb $12.95

- **Carolyn G. Heilbrun**
  REINVENTING WOMANHOOD
  "Ranks with de Beauvoir's *The Second Sex* as a landmark work"—Claudia Dreifus
  0–393–00997–1 Norton pb $8.95

- **Margaret Homans**
  WOMEN WRITERS AND POETIC
  IDENTITY: Dorothy Wordsworth, Emily
  Brontë and Emily Dickinson
  0–691–06440–7 Princeton $29.50
  0–691–10218–X Princeton pb $13.50

- **Toril Moi**
  SEXUAL-TEXTUAL POLITICS
  Weighs the strengths and limitations of the Anglo-American and the French strands in feminist criticism
  0–416–35360–6 RC&H $25.00
  0–416–35370–3 RC&H pb $13.95

- **Adrienne Rich**
  BLOOD, BREAD AND POETRY: Selected
  Prose, 1979–1985
  Essays on feminism, heterosexism, and racism from a major American poet
  0–393–02376–1 Norton $15.95
  0–393–30397–7 Norton pb $7.95

  ON LIES, SECRETS AND SILENCE:
  Selected Prose, 1966–1978
  "An indispensable historical document of the women's movement"—Mary Daly
  0–393–01233–6 Norton $15.95
  0–393–00942–4 Norton pb $6.95

- **Elaine Showalter, editor**
  THE NEW FEMINIST CRITICISM:
  Essays on Women, Literature, and Theory
  0–394–53913–3 Random House $22.95
  0–394–72647–2 Random House pb $14.95

French Feminism

Hélène Cixous & Catherine Clement
THE NEWLY BORN WOMAN
Translated by Betsy Wing
0–8166–1465–2 Minnesota $25.00
0–8166–1466–0 Minnesota pb $12.95

Jane Gallop
THE DAUGHTER'S SEDUCTION:
Feminism and Psychoanalysis
Examines the relation between contemporary feminism and Lacan's psychoanalytic theories
0–8014–9235–1 Cornell pb $9.95

Luce Irigaray
SPECULUM OF THE OTHER
WOMAN
Posits that masculine ideology is implicit in psychoanalytic theory and in western discourse in general
Translated by Gillian C. Gill
0–8014–9330–7 Cornell pb $16.95

THIS SEX WHICH IS NOT ONE
Reconsiders the question of female sexuality in a variety of contexts
Translated by Catherine Porter & Carolyn Burke
0–8014–1546–2 Cornell $29.95
0–8014–9331–5 Cornell pb $12.95

Elaine Marks & Isabelle De Courtivron, editors
NEW FRENCH FEMINISMS: An
Anthology
0–8052–0681–7 Random House pb $9.95

Juliet Mitchell
PSYCHOANALYSIS AND FEMINISM
"Anyone who thinks Freud's work has been conclusively revised, updated or overthrown will have to contend for a long time to come with this withering rejoinder"—*NY Review of Books*
0–394–71442–3 Random House pb $6.95

Juliet Mitchell & Jacqueline Rose, editors
FEMININE SEXUALITY: Jacques
Lacan and the Ecole Freudienne
0–393–01633–1 Norton $19.50
0–393–30211–3 Norton pb $9.95

THE DEBATE ON PORNOGRAPHY

- **Hannah Alderfer & others**
  CAUGHT LOOKING: Feminism,
  Pornography and Censorship
  Essays from a feminist perspective that take issue with the anti-pornography movement, with explicit illustrations
  0–9617884–0–2 Caught Looking pb $10.00

- **Varda Burstyn, editor**
  WOMEN AGAINST CENSORSHIP
  0–88894–455–1 Salem House pb $8.95

- **Angela Carter**
  THE SADEIAN WOMAN AND THE
  IDEOLOGY OF PORNOGRAPHY
  0–394–75893–5 Random House pb $7.95

- Murray S. Davis
  SMUT: Erotic Reality, Obscene Ideology
  0–226–13792–9 Chicago pb $10.95

- Edward Donnerstein, Daniel Linz &
  Steven Penrod
  THE QUESTION OF PORNOGRAPHY:
  Research Findings and Policy Implications
  0–02–907521–1 Free Press $24.95

- Susan Griffin
  PORNOGRAPHY AND SILENCE:
  Culture's Revolt Against Nature
  0–06–090915–3 Harper & Row pb $7.95

- Susan Gubar & Joan Hoff-Wilson,
  editors
  FOR ADULT USERS ONLY: The
  Dilemma of Violent Pornography
  0–253–32365–7 Indiana $39.95
  0–253–20508–5 Indiana pb $14.95

- Walter Kendrick
  THE SECRET MUSEUM: Pornography in
  Modern Culture
  0–670–81363–X Viking $18.95
  0–14–010947–1 Penguin pb $7.95

- Steven Marcus
  THE OTHER VICTORIANS: A Study of
  Sexuality and Pornography in Mid-19th
  Century England
  0–393–30236–9 Norton pb $7.95

- Simon Watney
  POLICING DESIRE: Pornography, AIDS,
  and the Media
  0–8166–1643–4 Minnesota $35.00
  0–8166–1644–2 Minnesota pb $14.95

GENERAL HISTORIES AND ANTHOLOGIES

- Meyer H. Abrams
  THE MIRROR AND THE LAMP:
  Romantic Theory and the Critical Tradition
  0–19–501471–5 Oxford pb $10.95

- Hazard Adams
  CRITICAL THEORY SINCE PLATO
  0–15–516142–3 HBJ $39.95

- Hazard Adams & Leroy Searle,
  editors
  CRITICAL THEORY SINCE 1965
  0–8130–0844–1 Florida pb $32.95

- Chris Baldick
  THE SOCIAL MISSION OF ENGLISH
  CRITICISM, 1848–1932
  0–19–812979–3 Oxford pb $18.95

- Walter J. Bate
  CRITICISM: The Major Texts
  0–15–516148–2 HBJ $37.50

- Terry Eagleton
  LITERARY THEORY: An Introduction
  Witty and comprehensive
  0–8166–1241–2 Minnesota pb $12.95

*Paul Verlaine's years as an English school-
teacher, drawn by Max Beerbohm*

- Gerald Graff
  PROFESSING LITERATURE: An
  Institutional History
  Wide-ranging and provocative
  0–226–30603–8 Chicago $24.95

- Frank Lentricchia
  AFTER THE NEW CRITICISM
  An inviting overview
  0–226–47198–5 Chicago pb $13.00

- René Wellek
  A HISTORY OF MODERN CRITICISM,
  1750–1950
  A definitive if daunting work of
  scholarship
  0–300–03378–8 Yale (4-volume set) $30.00

  Volume 1: The Later Eighteenth Century
  0–521–28295–0 Cambridge pb $18.95

  Volume 2: The Romantic Age
  0–521–28296–9 Cambridge pb $18.95

  Volume 3: The Age of Transition
  0–521–27074–X Cambridge pb $20.95

  Volume 4: The Later Nineteenth Century
  0–521–27075–8 Cambridge pb $22.95

  Volume 5: English Criticism, 1900–1950
  0–300–03378–8 Yale $30.00
  0–300–04202–7 Yale pb $14.95

  Volume 6: American Criticism, 1900–1950
  0–300–03486–5 Yale $30.00
  0–300–04203–3 Yale pb $14.95

- William K. Wimsatt & Cleanth
  Brooks
  LITERARY CRITICISM: A Short History
  The standard account, and still the best, of
  criticism from the Greeks to Yeats and
  Eliot

  Volume 1
  0–226–90175–0 Chicago pb $15.00

  Volume 2
  0–226–90176–9 Chicago pb $15.00

World Literature: Surveys and Anthologies

Elsewhere in *The Reader's Catalog*, literary works have been classified according to an essentially geographical scheme, with three main sections: Literature of Europe, Africa, and Asia; Literature of the British Isles; and Literature of the Americas.

Under the present heading we have grouped together those general works which do not fit easily into that scheme.

GENERAL ANTHOLOGIES AND STUDIES

- Malcolm Bradbury
  THE MODERN WORLD: Ten Great
  Writers
  Commentaries on Dostoevsky, Ibsen,
  Conrad, Mann, Proust, Joyce, Eliot,
  Pirandello, Woolf, and Kafka
  0–670–82443–7 Viking $18.95

- W. Theodore de Bary & Ainslie
  Embree, editors
  A GUIDE TO ORIENTAL CLASSICS
  0–231–06674–0 Columbia $32.50
  0–231–06675–9 Columbia pb $18.00

- Bill Henderson, editor
  THE PUSHCART PRIZE X: Best of the
  Small Presses
  0–14–008008–2 Penguin pb $9.95

  THE PUSHCART PRIZE XI: Best of the
  Small Presses
  0–14–009469–5 Penguin pb $9.95

  THE PUSHCART PRIZE XII: Best of the
  Small Presses
  0–14–009470–9 Penguin pb $9.95

- William Hornstein & others, editors
  THE READER'S COMPANION TO
  WORLD LITERATURE
  0–451–62441–6 NAL pb $5.95

- Robert Motherwell, editor
  THE DADA PAINTERS AND POETS: An
  Anthology
  Foreword by Jack D. Flam
  0–674–18500–5 Harvard pb $19.95

- James B. Ross & Mary M.
  McLaughlin, editors
  THE PORTABLE MEDIEVAL READER
  0–14–015046–3 Penguin pb $9.95

  THE PORTABLE RENAISSANCE
  READER
  0–14–015061–7 Penguin pb $8.95

- Martin Seymour-Smith
  THE NEW GUIDE TO MODERN
  WORLD LITERATURE
  0–87226–000–3 Peter Bedrick $60.00

➤ **FOR OVERSEAS ORDERING INFORMATION, SEE PAGE 1**

Dante in Oxford: "Your name and college?"
by Max Beerbohm

Oral Traditions

Jerome Rothenberg, editor
TECHNICIANS OF THE SACRED: A Range of Poetries from Africa, America, Asia, Europe, and Oceania
An influential anthology in which contemporary poets translate or rework oral poetry from around the world
0–520–04900–4 California $47.50
0–520–04912–8 California pb $15.95

Jerome & Diane Rothenberg, editors
SYMPOSIUM OF THE WHOLE: A Range of Discourse Toward an Ethnopoetics
0–520–04530–0 California $27.50
0–520–04531–9 California pb $14.95

POETRY ANTHOLOGIES

• Fleur Adcock, editor
THE FABER BOOK OF TWENTIETH CENTURY WOMEN'S POETRY
0–571–13693–1 Faber & Faber pb $7.95

• Robert Bly, editor
NEWS OF THE UNIVERSE: Poems of Twofold Consciousness
0–87156–199–9 Sierra Club pb $8.95

• Keith Bosley, editor
THE POETRY OF ASIA: Five Millenniums of Verse from 33 Languages
0–8348–0139–6 Weatherhill $17.50

• Stanley Burnshaw, editor
THE POEM ITSELF
An anthology of poems in the original French, German, Italian, Spanish, Portuguese, and Russian, with detailed commentaries
0–671–67808–6 Simon & Schuster pb $10.95

• Carol Cosman & others, editors
THE PENGUIN BOOK OF WOMAN POETS
0–14–058533–8 Penguin pb $7.95

• Richard Ellmann & Robert O'Clair, editors
MODERN POEMS: An Introduction to Poetry
0–393–09187–2 Norton pb $16.95

• Clayton Eshleman, editor
CONDUCTORS OF THE PIT
A selection of five modern poets including Rimbaud, Artaud, Vallejo, Césaire, and Holan
1–55778–126–5 Paragon pb $12.95

• Geoffrey Grigson, editor
THE FABER BOOK OF LOVE POEMS
0–571–13118–2 Faber & Faber pb $7.95

THE FABER BOOK OF NONSENSE VERSE
0–571–11356–7 Faber & Faber pb $12.95

THE FABER BOOK OF REFLECTIVE VERSE
0–571–13300–2 Faber & Faber pb $8.95

• Seamus Heaney & Ted Hughes, editors
THE RATTLE BAG: An Anthology of Poetry
An excellent anthology ostensibly aimed at younger readers
0–571–11976–X Faber & Faber pb $10.95

• W.S. Merwin
SELECTED TRANSLATIONS: 1968–1978
0–689–10903–2 Atheneum pb $6.95

SELECTED TRANSLATIONS: 1948–1968
0–689–10194–5 Atheneum pb $5.95

• George E. Murphy, Jr., editor
THE POET'S CHOICE: One Hundred American Poets' Favorite Poems
0–937504–00–9 Tendril pb $5.95

• Iona & Peter Opie, editors
THE OXFORD BOOK OF NARRATIVE VERSE
0–19–214131–7 Oxford $25.00
0–19–282243–8 Oxford pb $9.95

• Tom Paulin, editor
THE FABER BOOK OF POLITICAL VERSE
0–571–13667–2 Faber & Faber pb $14.95

• Robert Richman, editor
THE DIRECTION OF POETRY: An Anthology of Rhymed and Metered Verse Written in the English Language Since 1975
0–395–48355–7 Houghton Mifflin pb $12.95

• Michael Roberts, editor
THE FABER BOOK OF MODERN VERSE
0–571–18017–5 Faber & Faber pb $7.95

• Jon Stallworthy, editor
THE OXFORD BOOK OF WAR POETRY
0–19–214125–2 Oxford $24.95

• Charles Tomlinson, editor
THE OXFORD BOOK OF VERSE IN ENGLISH TRANSLATION
0–19–281426–5 Oxford pb $12.95

FICTION ANTHOLOGIES

• Rosemary Creswell, editor
HOME AND AWAY: Travel Stories
0–14–008075–9 Penguin pb $6.95

• Daniel Halpern, editor
THE ART OF THE TALE: An International Anthology of Short Stories, 1945–1985
0–670–80592–0 Viking $24.95
0–14–007949–1 Penguin pb $10.95

• V.S. Pritchett, editor
THE OXFORD BOOK OF SHORT STORIES
0–19–214116–3 Oxford $29.95
0–19–282113–X Oxford pb $11.95

LITERATURE
OF THE
BRITISH ISLES

The Anglo-Saxon Period

The Anglo-Saxon (or Old English) period extends from the dawn of English literary culture in the 5th century AD through the Norman Conquest in the 11th century. Though many of its seminal texts, like *Beowulf*, are at least nominally Christian, both the poetry and prose of this period reflect an older and darker culture, by turns fatalistic, brutal, and elegiac. Stark and often strange, these works are the bedrock of English literature, and their influence on later writing, though often hidden, is pervasive.

• Michael Alexander, translator
BEOWULF
Beowulf is the great native English epic, overlaid with Christian elements but imbued with the brooding pessimism of the pagan culture behind it. Alexander has made a powerful attempt to approximate the textures of the Anglo-Saxon verse
0–14–044268–5 Penguin pb $2.25

• Howell D. Chickering, Jr., translator
BEOWULF: A Dual Language Edition
The Anglo-Saxon text with Chickering's excellent translation on facing pages
0–385–06213–3 Doubleday pb $10.95

Gliding through the shadows
came the walker in the night; the
    warriors slept
whose task was to hold the horned
    building,
all except one. It was well-known to
    men
that the demon could not drag them
    to the shades
without God's willing it; yet the one
    man kept
unblinking watch. He awaited, heart
    swelling
with anger against his foe, the ordeal
    of battle.
Down off the moorlands' misting fells
    came
Grendel stalking; God's brand was on
    him.
The spoiler meant to snatch away
from the high hall some of human
    race.

Michael Alexander, translator
BEOWULF
0–14–044268–5 Penguin pb $2.25

• Michael Alexander, translator
THE EARLIEST ENGLISH POEMS
Another of Michael Alexander's outstanding fusions of Modernist poetics and Anglo-Saxon tonalities
0–14–044172–7 Penguin pb $6.95

• Kevin Crossley-Holland, editor & translator
THE ANGLO-SAXON WORLD: An Anthology
A compact collection of documents and poems, including a complete translation of *Beowulf*
0–19–281632–2 Oxford pb $6.95

• Burton Raffel, translator
POEMS FROM THE OLD ENGLISH
Introduction by R. Creed
0–8032–5154–8 Nebraska pb $3.95

Medieval Literature

POETRY

Though much of medieval poetry is uncomplicated lyricism, the major poets—such as Chaucer, Gower, and the anonymous author of *Sir Gawain and the Green Knight*—are remarkable for their sophistication and their skeptical (though tolerant) rendering of human frailties. By the 14th century London and the English court had both a discriminating audience for poetry and a wide selection of targets for social analysis and satire.

Chaucer

"Chaucer has given us something of every variety of medieval story. The romances are represented by the *Knight's Tale,* and the *Squire's Tale,* while their decadence is satirized in the *Tale of Sir Thopas.* Medieval delight in lives of saints and of miracle working is satisfied by such stories as those of the Prioress, the Second Nun, and the Monk. The tales of the Man of Law or of the Clerk, of Melibeus or of the Franklin, dealt with various attitudes to life full of interest to Chaucer's audience. Again, the *Wife of Bath's Tale* delighted them with a story of 'faerye,' and the *Nun's Priest's Tale* and the *Pardoner's Tale* amused while they instructed. And besides these Chaucer gave, in good measure, that body of 'churl's tales' which bring us so close to 'l'homme moyen

The Wife of Bath, circa 1484, from An Introduction to a History of the Woodcut *by Arthur M. Hind (Dover)*

sensuel.' In the tales of the Miller, Reeve, Shipman, Summoner, Merchant or Friar the brilliance of the telling makes us condone the coarse nature of the tale."—H.S. Bennett, *Chaucer and the Fifteenth Century*

• Geoffrey Chaucer
THE CANTERBURY TALES
The most enduringly popular translation; an idiomatic but accurate rendering
Translated by Nevill Coghill
0–14–044022–4 Penguin pb $2.95

TROILUS AND CRISEYDE
An incomparable, novelistic love story, at once romantic and sardonic
Translated by Nevill Coghill
0–14–044239–1 Penguin pb $4.95

LOVE VISIONS
Modern English versions of *The Book of the Duchess, The Parliament of Birds, The Legend of Good Women,* and *The House of Fame*
Translated by Brian Stone
0–14–044408–4 Penguin pb $6.95

THE RIVERSIDE CHAUCER
Chaucer is not difficult to read in the original. The impeccably edited *Riverside Chaucer* has full and convenient annotations which make the Middle English text highly accessible
Edited by Larry D. Benson
0–395–29031–7 Houghton Mifflin $53.50

Other Medieval Poets

• William Dunbar
THE POEMS OF WILLIAM DUNBAR
"Dunbar is professional through and through; the accomplished master of one tradition that goes back to *Beowulf* and of another that goes back to the Troubadours . . . When you are in the mood for it, his poetry has a sweep and volume of sound and an assured virility which (while the mood lasts) makes most other poets seem a little faint and tentative and half-hearted"—C.S. Lewis
Edited by James Kinsley
0–19–811888–0 Oxford $95.00

• John Gower
CONFESSIO AMANTIS
A debate on the nature of love, supplemented by a vast collection of romantic tales in polished verse, by Chaucer's sometime friend and most accomplished rival
Edited by Russell A. Peck
0–8020–6438–8 Toronto pb $12.95

SELECTED POETRY
Edited by Carole Weinberg
0–85635–415–5 Carcanet pb $7.50

• Robert Henryson
THE MORAL FABLES OF AESOP
Henryson's recastings of Aesop are realistic and elegant; at his best he is fully worthy of comparison with Chaucer. This edition has a modern English translation on the facing page
Edited by George D. Gopen
0–268–01361–6 Notre Dame $22.95
0–268–01362–4 Notre Dame pb $9.95

THE POEMS OF ROBERT HENRYSON
"Critical studies will henceforth be able to utilize the wealth of information that Fox provides on the literal meaning of the poems. The strength of the new edition, and it is great, lies in its clarification of Henryson's text"—*Speculum*
Edited by Denton Fox
0–19–812324–8 Oxford pb $19.95

THE TESTAMENT OF CRESSEID & OTHER POEMS
Henryson deeply influenced the work of Hugh MacDiarmid and other modern Scottish poets
Edited by Hugh MacDiarmid
0–14–044507–2 Penguin pb $4.95

- Thomas Hoccleve
SELECTED POEMS
Hoccleve's poetry has an autobiographical dimension unusual among medieval writers
Edited by Bernard O'Donoghue
0–85635–321–3 Carcanet pb $7.50

- William Langland
PIERS PLOWMAN
The "B" text of the poem, generally regarded as the most authoritative, with notes and glossary
Edited by Jack A. Bennett
0–19–871090–9 Oxford pb $12.95

PIERS THE PLOUGHMAN
A modern prose rendering of the most sweeping (and ambiguous) of medieval moral allegories; the masterpiece of the so-called "alliterative" tradition
Translated by J.F. Goodridge
0–14–044087–9 Penguin pb $4.95

- John Gardner, editor
THE ALLITERATIVE MORTE ARTHUR, THE OWL AND THE NIGHTINGALE & FIVE OTHER MIDDLE ENGLISH POEMS
0–8093–0648–4 Southern Illinois pb $13.95

- J.A. Burrow, editor
SIR GAWAIN AND THE GREEN KNIGHT
The original text of a linguistically difficult but endlessly fascinating poem, a deft and entertaining yet serious allegory of love, pleasure, and responsibility
0–14–042295–1 Penguin pb $5.95

- Brian Stone, translator
SIR GAWAIN AND THE GREEN KNIGHT
A modern English verse translation
0–14–044092–5 Penguin pb $2.95

KING ARTHUR'S DEATH: The Alliterative Morte Arthure & The Stanzaic Le Morte Arthur
New translations of two great medieval poems
0–14–044445–9 Penguin pb $5.95

THE OWL AND THE NIGHTINGALE, CLEANNESS & ST. ERKENWALD
Three important Middle English poems
0–14–044245–6 Penguin pb $6.95

- Marie Boroff, translator
PEARL: A New Verse Translation
Perhaps the most tantalizingly mysterious and moving of medieval English religious allegories
0–393–04456–4 Norton $7.95
0–393–09144–9 Norton pb $3.95

Anthologies

- J.A.W. Bennett & G.V. Smithers, editors
EARLY MIDDLE ENGLISH VERSE AND PROSE
A large-scale collection spanning all the genres and styles of the period
0–19–871101–8 Oxford pb $26.00

- R.T. Davies, editor
MEDIEVAL ENGLISH LYRICS: A Critical Anthology
A rich sampling of the early English tradition
0–571–06571–6 Faber & Faber pb $11.95

- Douglas Gray, editor
THE OXFORD BOOK OF LATE MEDIEVAL VERSE AND PROSE
0–19–812452–X Oxford $29.95

- Robert D. Stevick, editor
ONE HUNDRED MIDDLE ENGLISH LYRICS
A standard college text and a useful introduction to the medieval lyric in all its variety
0–02–417290–1 Macmillan $10.50

- Brian Stone, editor & translator
MEDIEVAL ENGLISH VERSE
Translations into modern English
0–14–044144–1 Penguin pb $5.95

DRAMA

Of all medieval genres, drama is perhaps the most accessible. The English mystery plays performed during religious festivals are exhilarating blends of piety, awe, storytelling vigor, and high spirits that sometimes border on the scatalogical. Because drama was a folk genre, even the more sophisticated morality plays—for all their elaborate allegorical underpinnings—share the immediacy of the mysteries.

- David Bevington, editor
MEDIEVAL DRAMA
The most comprehensive generally available anthology
0–395–13915–5 Houghton Mifflin $40.95

- A.C. Cawley, editor
EVERYMAN & MEDIEVAL MIRACLE PLAYS
0–460–10381–4 Biblio $12.95

- John Gassner, editor
MEDIEVAL AND TUDOR DRAMA
A selection of English mystery and miracle plays, *Everyman,* Tudor interludes and comedies, and some interesting source materials
0–936839–84–8 Applause Theatre pb $8.95

- Peter Happe, editor
ENGLISH MYSTERY PLAYS
A generous selection indicating the range of subject matter of the mysteries
0–14–043093–8 Penguin pb $7.95

FOUR MORALITY PLAYS
Includes *The Castle of Perseverance,* John Skelton's *Magnyfycence,* John Bale's *King Johan,* and David Lindsay's *Ane Satire of the Thrie Estaitis*
0–14–043119–5 Penguin pb $7.95

- Martial Rose, editor
THE WAKEFIELD MYSTERY PLAYS
A complete cycle, including examples of raucous comedy and genuine folk piety
0–393–00483–X Norton pb $10.95

- William Tydeman, editor
FOUR TUDOR COMEDIES
Includes *Jacke Jugeler, Ralph Roister Doister, Gammer Gurton's Needle,* and *Mother Dombie*
0–14–043202–7 Penguin pb $6.95

PROSE

Malory's *Morte d'Arthur* is the great monument of late Middle English prose, a digest of Arthurian material as well as a compendium of late medieval attitudes toward ethics, chivalry, and even romantic love. Among shorter prose works, the most memorable are contemplative treatises like the anonymous *Cloud of Unknowing* and Julian of Norwich's *Revelations of Divine Love.* They bear witness to an enduring tradition of medieval spirituality, an intensely private, often mystical sensibility that did not always tamely accept the yoke of the medieval church.

- Thomas Malory
KING ARTHUR AND HIS KNIGHTS
Selected tales of Arthur and his court, with a thorough introduction and supplementary critical material
0–19–501905–9 Oxford pb $8.95

LE MORTE D'ARTHUR
The complete text of Malory's monumental compilation of Arthurian legend, one of the most influential books in English
Edited by Janet Cowen

Volume 1
0–14–043043–1 Penguin pb $3.95
Volume 2
0–14–043044–X Penguin pb $3.95

WORKS
The standard scholarly edition, first published in 1947
Edited by Eugene Vinaver
0–19–254163–3 Oxford pb $24.95
0–19–281217–3 Oxford pb $13.95

Medieval Mysticism

Walter Hilton
THE LADDER OF PERFECTION
Hilton remains the most accessible of the 14th-century mystics; this book of advice to a female hermit is his best-known work
0–14–044511–0 Penguin pb $6.95

Julian of Norwich
REVELATIONS OF DIVINE LOVE
Perhaps the best-known of medieval mystical meditations. It includes the phrase made famous by T.S. Eliot's *Four Quartets*: "All shall be well and all shall be well and all manner of thing shall be well"
Translated by Clifton Wolters
0–14–044177–8 Penguin pb $4.95

Richard Rolle
THE FIRE OF LOVE
Rolle is among the most fervently rapturous of the medieval English mystics
Translated by Clifton Wolters
0–14–044256–1 Penguin pb $4.95

Clifton Wolters, translator
THE CLOUD OF UNKNOWING & OTHER WORKS
Many consider *The Cloud of Unknowing* the greatest product of the 14th-century mystical tradition
0–14–044385–1 Penguin pb $3.95

Other Prose Works

● Richard Barber, editor
THE PASTONS: The Letters of a Family in the Wars of the Roses
A fascinating, uniquely detailed portrait of daily life in England during the 15th century
0–14–057002–0 Penguin pb $6.95

● Norman Davis, editor
THE PASTON LETTERS: A Selection
0–19–281615–2 Oxford pb $6.95

● Margery Kempe
THE BOOK OF MARGERY KEMPE
A religious work with a fascinating autobiographical dimension, including an unforgettable account of Kempe's trial for heresy
Translated by Barry Windeatt
0–14–043251–5 Penguin pb $6.95

The 16th Century

The rather uncertain productions characteristic of the first decades give only occasional promise of the imaginative explosion that was to take place during the reign of Elizabeth. Voracious in its interests, bountifully (at times carelessly) exuberant in its expression, Elizabethan lyric poetry is by turns delicately sensuous, ribald, anguished. Drama, though it was yet to attain the self-confident mastery of Shakespeare, gave evidence in Marlowe and Kyd of a new inventiveness and energy.

POETRY

With the generation of Spenser and his contemporaries in the 1570s a new and more avowedly gorgeous poetic vernacular emerged, sensuous and musical. Nowhere is it better illustrated than in the period's acknowledged masterpiece, Spenser's *The Faerie Queene*.

● Thomas Campion
THE WORKS OF THOMAS CAMPION
The complete poetry of one of the most musical poets in the language; also includes Campion's theoretical writings on the art of poetry
Edited by Walter R. Davis
0–393–00439–2 Norton pb $2.95

THE ESSENTIAL CAMPION
A well-chosen selection. "Campion was not rediscovered until the late nineteenth century. Since then, it's been difficult to imagine the history of poetry without him. Whoever dreams of a poem where language begins to resemble music, thinks of him"—Charles Simic
Edited by Charles Simic
0–88001–172–6 Ecco pb $5.75

THE SELECTED SONGS OF THOMAS CAMPION
A selection of Campion's poems accompanied by his original musical settings
Edited by W.H. Auden
Introduction by John Hollander
0–87923–091–6 Godine pb $10.00

● Henry Howard, Earl of Surrey
SELECTED POEMS
Surrey virtually invented the mellifluous iambic line that became the standard of later English poetry. His verse is remarkable for its urbanity; his love poems to Geraldine made her into the near-proverbial lady-love of the 16th century
Edited by Dennis Keene
0–85635–552–6 Carcanet pb $7.50

● Ben Jonson
THE COMPLETE POEMS
Jonson's genius as a playwright has sometimes obscured his greatness as a poet; he is by turns acerbic, sensual, musical, political, and passionate
Edited by George Parfitt
0–14–042277–3 Penguin pb $10.95

THE OXFORD AUTHORS: BEN JONSON
Includes *Volpone*, *The Alchemist*, the complete poems, aphorisms, and William Drummond's remarkable account of his conversations with Jonson
Edited by Ian Donaldson
0–19–254178–1 Oxford $38.00
0–19–281339–0 Oxford pb $11.95

● Christopher Marlowe
THE COMPLETE POEMS & TRANSLATIONS
Though less well known than Shakespeare's *Venus and Adonis*, Marlowe's *Hero and Leander* is one of the high points of English erotic poetry, poised elegantly between the sensuous and the comic, with overtones of dark melancholy. This edition also includes Marlowe's deft versions of Ovid's love poems
Edited by Stephen Orgel
0–14–042267–6 Penguin pb $6.95

He dissuaded me from poetry, for that she had beggared him, when he might have been a rich lawyer, physician, or merchant . . .
In his merry humour he was wont to name himself The Poet . . .
He is a great lover and praiser of himself, a contemner and scorner of others, given rather to lose a friend than a jest, jealous of every word and action of those about him (especially after drink, which is one of the elements in which he liveth), a dissembler of ill parts which reign in him, a bragger of some good that he wanteth, thinketh nothing well but what either he himself or some of his friends and countrymen hath said or done . . .
Oppressed with fantasy, which hath ever mastered his reason, a general disease in many poets.

William Drummond on Ben Jonson in

Ian Donaldson, editor
THE OXFORD AUTHORS: BEN JONSON
0–19–281339–0 Oxford pb $11.95

● Walter Ralegh
SELECTED WRITINGS
"Spend a few unsettling but profitable hours with Sir Walter Ralegh, and you'll learn something about despair: modern gloom seems frivolous, almost amateur, by comparison"—Mark Caldwell, *Village Voice*
Edited by Gerald Hammond
0–85635–440–6 Carcanet $21.00

● Philip Sidney
THE POEMS OF SIR PHILIP SIDNEY
The standard edition, and a monument of modern textual scholarship
Edited by William A. Ringler, Jr.
0–19–811834–1 Oxford $74.00

SELECTED WRITINGS
Edited by Richard Dutton
0–85635–625–5 Carcanet pb $7.50

● John Skelton
THE COMPLETE ENGLISH POEMS
Skelton, who died in 1529, is one of the great eccentrics of English poetry, remarkable for the improvisational wordplay and untrammeled rhyme of such poems as "Philip Sparrow" and "The Tunnyng of Elynour Rummyng"
Edited by John Scattergood
0–300–02971–3 Yale pb $12.95

SELECTED POEMS
Edited by Gerald Hammond
0–85635–308–6 Carcanet pb $7.50

● Edmund Spenser
EDMUND SPENSER'S POETRY
Includes a generous selection of the shorter poems, and excerpts from *The Faerie Queene*
Edited by Richard S. Sylvester & Hugh MacLean
0–393–95138–3 Norton pb $14.95

THE FAERIE QUEENE
A readable edition of the quintessential English Renaissance poem, with convenient notes
Edited by Thomas P. Roche & C.P. O'Donnell
0–14–042207–2 Penguin pb $12.95

THE SHORTER POEMS OF EDMUND SPENSER
Edited by William A. Oram & others
0–300–04244–2 Yale $55.00
0–300–04245–0 Yale pb $9.95

• Thomas Wyatt
THE COMPLETE POEMS
Wyatt wrote some of the greatest and most complex lyrics in English, including "They Flee from Me that Sometime Did Me Seek" and "Awake, My Lute"
Edited by R.A. Rebholz
0–300–02688–9 Yale pb $11.95
0–14–042227–7 Penguin pb $7.95

THE ESSENTIAL WYATT
Edited by W.S. Merwin
0–88001–180–7 Ecco pb $6.00

Anthologies

• Norman Ault, editor
ELIZABETHAN LYRICS
A pleasant collection of lyrics, arranged chronologically
0–571–13929–9 Faber & Faber pb $16.95

• Gerald Bullett, editor
SILVER POETS OF THE SIXTEENTH CENTURY
Includes the work of Wyatt, Surrey, Ralegh, and John Davies' long philosophical poems *Orchestra* and *Nosce Teipsum*
0–460–00985–0 Biblio $14.95
0–460–11985–0 Biblio pb $4.50

• E.K. Chambers, editor
THE OXFORD BOOK OF SIXTEENTH CENTURY VERSE
A solid collection including much work that is otherwise difficult to find
0–19–812126–1 Oxford $49.95

• William B. Hunter, Jr., editor
THE ENGLISH SPENSERIANS
An unusual and typographically elegant anthology that includes work by Phineas and Giles Fletcher, Michael Drayton, George Wither, and Henry More
0–87480–110–9 Utah $29.95

• Edward Lucie-Smith, editor
ELIZABETHAN VERSE
Well-chosen selections, but sometimes tantalizingly too brief
0–14–042083–5 Penguin pb $6.95

• Hugh MacDonald, editor
ENGLANDS HELICON
Perhaps the most typical, certainly one of the most delightful, of the poetical miscellanies—the collections of short lyrics by various hands that were a staple of Elizabethan literary taste
0–674–25551–8 Harvard pb $8.95

• Hyder E. Rollins, editor
A HANDFUL OF PLEASANT DELIGHTS
0–486–21382–X Dover pb $3.50

Robin Hood, from A Social History of England: From the Romans to Mrs. Thatcher *by Asa Briggs (Penguin)*

PHOENIX NEST (1593)
0–674–66610–0 Harvard $16.50

TOTTEL'S MISCELLANY (1557–1587)
A 2-volume set
0–674–89610–6 Harvard $50.00

• Richard S. Sylvester, editor
ENGLISH SIXTEENTH CENTURY VERSE: An Anthology
0–393–30206–7 Norton pb $12.95

PROSE

The achievement of 16th-century prose writers is considerable, although less familiar to modern readers then that of their 17th-century successors. Richard Hooker's *Laws of Ecclesiastical Polity* is a magisterial paean to high Elizabethan values, an eloquent plea for the virtues and the beauties of civilization. And in Sir Philip Sidney's *Arcadia* the reader can discern an early precursor of the novel.

• Muriel S. Byrne & Bridget Boland, editors
THE LISLE LETTERS: An Abridgment
A collection of early 16th-century letters written to and from Arthur Plantagenet, Viscount Lisle, offering a revealing mirror of life at the beginning of the Renaissance
0–226–08810–3 Chicago $12.95

• Thomas Dekker
THE WONDERFUL YEAR, THE GULL'S HORN-BOOK, PENNY WISE, POUND FOOLISH, ENGLISH VILLAINIES DISCOVERED BY LANTERN AND CANDLELIGHT & SELECTED WRITINGS
No writer illustrates better than Dekker the hearty vigor of Elizabethan and Jacobean popular taste. These pamphlets present an incomparably vivid picture of daily life in London at the turn of the 17th century, from fashion to street crime to the grisly visitations of the Black Plague
Edited by Eric D. Pendry
0–674–88486–8 Harvard $25.00

• Richard Hakluyt
VOYAGES AND DISCOVERIES
The most complete firsthand record of England's voyages (and occasional piracies) in the northern and western seas during the great age of exploration. This selection includes such powerful narratives as Walter Ralegh's "Discoverie of Guiana," the story of the shipwrecked sailor Miles Phillips, and dramatic narratives of Martin Frobisher's Arctic voyages
Edited by Jack Beeching
0–14–043073–3 Penguin pb $5.95

• Richard Hooker
OF THE LAWS OF ECCLESIASTICAL POLITY

Volume 1: Preface and Books 1–5
Edited by W. Speed Hill
0–674–63205–2 Harvard $90.00

Volume 2: Books 6–8
Edited by P.G. Stanwood
0–674–63210–9 Harvard $75.00

• Hugh Latimer
SELECTED SERMONS OF HUGH LATIMER
A collection of sermons especially striking for Latimer's homely but telling similes
Edited by Allan Chester
0–918016–43–6 Folger $16.00

• Thomas More
THE APOLOGY
More's famous defense of his conduct in relation to Henry VIII and the English church
Edited by J.B. Trapp
0–300–02067–8 Yale $65.00

A DIALOGUE OF COMFORT AGAINST TRIBULATION
A strong and moving treatise on coping with adversity
0–300–01609–3 Yale $77.00

THE HISTORY OF KING RICHARD III & SELECTIONS FROM THE ENGLISH AND LATIN POEMS
The *History of King Richard III* popularized and helped to perpetuate the view of Richard as a deformed, inhuman monster that became a fixture of Tudor propaganda and the basis of Shakespeare's dramatic portrait
0–300–01840–1 Yale $27.50

UTOPIA
The ancestor of all later ideal commonwealths, and a subtle expression both of More's idealism and his penchant for satire
Edited & translated by Robert M. Adams
0–393–04397–5 Norton $12.95
0–393–09256–9 Norton pb $5.95

• Thomas Nashe
THE UNFORTUNATE TRAVELLER & OTHER WORKS
Nashe's inexhaustible imagination—hilarious, surrealistic, and at times deeply unsettling—foreshadows (and sometimes outdoes) Dickens
Edited by J.B. Steane
0–14–043067–9 Penguin pb $5.95

- Paul Salzman, editor
AN ANTHOLOGY OF ELIZABETHAN PROSE FICTION
0–19–281744–2 Oxford pb $8.95

- Philip Sidney
ARCADIA
Sidney's greatly expanded version of his pastoral novel
Edited by Maurice Evans
0–14–043111–X Penguin pb $7.95

THE COUNTESS OF PEMBROKE'S ARCADIA (THE OLD ARCADIA)
The original version of Sidney's epic romantic fiction, much simpler and more classical in plot structure than his more-often-read reworking
Edited by Katherine Duncan-Jones
0–19–281690–X Oxford pb $7.95

> When they were landed they fiercely assaulted our men with their bows and arrows, who wounded three of them with our arrows: and perceiving themselves thus hurt, they desperately leapt off the rocks into the sea, and drowned themselves. Two women not being so apt to escape as the men were, the one for her age, and the other being encumbered with a young child, we took. The old wretch, whom divers of our sailors supposed to be either a devil, or a witch, had her buskins plucked off to see if she were cloven-footed, and for her ugly hue and deformity we let her go: the young woman and the child we brought away. We named the place where they were slain, Bloody Point.
>
> The second voyage of Martin Frobisher to Baffin Island, in
>
> Richard Hakluyt
> **VOYAGES AND DISCOVERIES**
> 0–14–043073–3 Penguin pb $5.95

DRAMA

By the late 1580s, London's stages had become famous throughout Europe, and the drama that flourished there during the years before Shakespeare had immense imaginative vitality. At its best, as in Kyd's *Spanish Tragedy* and Marlowe's *Tamburlaine* and *Dr. Faustus*, it could be a powerful combination of ravishing poetry and overpowering dramatic action.

- Thomas Dekker
THE SHOEMAKER'S HOLIDAY
A drama with an engaging tradesman as its hero, and aimed expertly at an audience of common Londoners; perhaps the most winning of the Elizabethan popular comedies
Edited by D.J. Palmer
0–393–90005–3 Norton pb $4.95

- Thomas Dekker, John Ford & William Rowley
JAMES THE FOURTH
Edited by J.A. Lavin
0–393–90012–6 Norton pb $2.95

THE WITCH OF EDMONTON
0–413–53260–7 Methuen pb $3.95

- Ben Jonson
BEN JONSON'S PLAYS AND MASQUES
Includes *Volpone, Epicoene, The Alchemist, The Sad Shepherd*, four masques, and a selection of critical essays
Edited by Robert M. Adams
0–393–09035–3 Norton pb $9.95

THE COMPLETE MASQUES
The masques contain some of Jonson's most magnificent verse, and introduce the modern reader to an extravagant theatrical form long since vanished from the stage
Edited by Stephen Orgel
0–300–01181–4 Yale $55.00

FIVE PLAYS
Includes *Every Man in His Humour, Sejanus, Volpone, The Alchemist,* and *Bartholomew Fair*
Edited with an introduction by G.A. Wilkes
0–19–281782–5 Oxford pb $6.95

THREE PLAYS
Includes *Volpone, The Alchemist,* and the riotous London comedy *Bartholomew Fair*
0–14–043013–X Penguin pb $4.95

THE ALCHEMIST
An intricate and explosive satirical comedy that makes bravura use of alchemical terms and other contemporary jargon
Edited by Douglas Brown
0–393–90014–0 Norton pb $4.95

EVERY MAN IN HIS HUMOUR
A pathbreaking comedy that exemplifies Jonson's theory of character
Edited by Martin Seymour-Smith
0–393–90015–0 Norton pb $4.95

VOLPONE
Unquestionably the greatest satiric play in English. "The characters are named after creatures that feed on carrion; thus Jonson drives home Dante's point—the worship of money is life-denying"—Kenneth Rexroth
Edited by Alvin B. Kernan
Preface by Richard B. Young
0–300–00139–8 Yale pb $8.95

- Thomas Kyd
THE SPANISH TRAGEDY
A searing drama of revenge, and the play most often credited (or blamed) for the potent doses of dramatic violence so frequent in Elizabethan and Jacobean plays
Edited by J.R. Mulryne
0–393–90017–7 Norton pb $2.95

- Christopher Marlowe
THE COMPLETE PLAYS
Contains *Dr. Faustus, Tamburlaine the Great, The Jew of Malta, Edward II, Dido Queen of Carthage,* and *The Massacre at Paris*
Edited by Stephen J. Orgel
0–14–043037–7 Penguin pb $6.95

Anthologies

- Bernard Beckerman, editor
FIVE PLAYS OF THE ENGLISH RENAISSANCE
Includes *Dr. Faustus, Volpone, The Duchess of Malfi, Women Beware Women,* and *'Tis Pity She's a Whore*
0–452–00881–6 NAL pb $6.95

Shakespeare

No writer's work has been as universally appreciated or as variously (and often contentiously) interpreted as Shakespeare's, and virtually every opinion expressed has also been authoritatively, sometimes violently, confuted. If Shakespeare's plays elude easy characterization, it may be precisely because they were written at an unsettled time, by a writer whose genius turned ambiguity to advantage. Teasing, mysterious, and endlessly fascinating, they hold an undiminished interest for the contemporary reader.

- William Shakespeare
THE COMPLETE PELICAN SHAKESPEARE
An attractive, durable one-volume edition of the Pelican Shakespeare text
Edited by Alfred Harbage
0–14–071449–9 Penguin pb $29.95

THE COMPLETE WORKS
A new edition that proposes a novel chronological order, revised stage directions, two separate versions of *King Lear,* and the complete text of *The Two Noble Kinsmen*
Edited by Stanley Wells & others
0–19–821926–2 Oxford $45.00

WILLIAM SHAKESPEARE: The Complete Works
Compact edition
Edited by Stanley Wells & Others
0-19-811747-7 Oxford $24.95

THE COMPLETE WORKS OF WILLIAM SHAKESPEARE
An edition for the general reader, popular for many years because of its readable type and striking woodcut illustrations; the text is that of the Cambridge edition
Edited by William Aldis Wright
Illustrated by Rockwell Kent
0–385–00049–9 Doubleday pb $22.95

THE NORTON FACSIMILE: The First Folio of Shakespeare
A photographic reproduction of the earliest authoritative collection of Shakespeare's plays, first published in 1623
Edited by Charlton Hinman
0–393–09843–5 Norton $100.00

THE RIVERSIDE SHAKESPEARE
Includes the complete plays and poetry, thoroughly annotated and fully introduced. There are also valuable textual notes, a wealth of illustrative material, a chronology, a list of Shakespeare's sources, and more. The best one-volume edition
Edited by G. Blakemore Evans & others
0–395–04402–2 Houghton Mifflin $42.50

Single-Play Editions

Of the many editions in print, we have selected three. The Signet Shakespeare (published by NAL) is an economical choice for the beginning student, with clear notes particularly well tailored to American readers. The New Penguin Shakespeare, also inexpensive and accessible to the nonspecialist, offers somewhat more elaborate commen-

✉ **TO ORDER BOOKS AS GIFTS, SEE PAGE 1**

tary and a pleasing typographical style. The Oxford Shakespeare, still in progress, provides a level of textual sophistication more likely to appeal to the specialist, and incorporates sometimes controversial innovations in the establishment of a definitive text.

ALL'S WELL THAT ENDS WELL
0-451-51944-2 NAL pb $2.95

ALL'S WELL THAT ENDS WELL
0-14-070720-4 Penguin pb $3.75

ANTONY AND CLEOPATRA
0-451-5195-6 NAL pb $2.95

ANTONY AND CLEOPATRA
0-14-070731-X Penguin pb $3.75

ANTONY AND CLEOPATRA
Edited by Ralph E.C. Houghton
0-19-831929-0 Oxford pb $5.95

AS YOU LIKE IT
Edited by Albert Gilman
0-451-52131-5 NAL pb $2.50

AS YOU LIKE IT
0-14-070714-X Penguin pb $3.75

THE COMEDY OF ERRORS
0-451-52163-3 NAL pb $2.95

THE COMEDY OF ERRORS
0-14-070725-5 Penguin pb $3.75

THE COMPLETE NON-DRAMATIC POETRY
Edited by William Burto
0-451-52039-4 NAL pb $4.95

CORIOLANUS
0-451-52296-6 NAL pb $3.50

CORIOLANUS
0-14-070703-4 Penguin pb $3.75

CYMBELINE
0-14-071428-6 Penguin pb $3.95

HAMLET
Edited by Edward Hubler
0-451-52128-5 NAL pb $2.75

HAMLET
0-14-070734-4 Penguin pb $3.75

HAMLET
Edited by G.R. Hibbard
0-19-812910-6 Oxford $34.00

HENRY IV, PART 1
Edited by Maynard Mack
0-451-52130-7 NAL pb $2.50

HENRY IV, PART 1
0-14-070718-2 Penguin pb $3.75

HENRY IV, PART 1
Edited by David Bevington
0-19-812915-7 Oxford $24.95

HENRY IV, PART 2
Edited by Norman N. Holland
0-451-52253-2 NAL pb $2.95

HENRY IV, PART 2
0-14-070728-X Penguin pb $3.75

HENRY V
Edited by John Russell Brown
0-451-52162-5 NAL pb $3.50

HENRY V
0-14-070708-5 Penguin pb $3.75

HENRY V
Edited by Gary Taylor
0-19-281438-9 Oxford pb $6.95

HENRY VI, PART 1
0-14-070735-2 Penguin pb $3.75

HENRY VI, PART 2
0-14-070736-0 Penguin pb $3.75

HENRY VI, PART 3
0-14-070737-9 Penguin pb $3.75

HENRY VI, PARTS 1, 2 & 3
0-451-52037-8 NAL pb $4.95

HENRY VIII
0-14-070722-0 Penguin pb $3.75

JULIUS CAESAR
Edited by William & Barbara Rosen
0-4512-52124-2 NAL pb $1.95

JULIUS CAESAR
Edited by Arthur Humphreys
0-19-281445-1 Oxford pb $6.95

JULIUS CAESAR
0-14-070704-2 Penguin pb $3.75

KING JOHN & HENRY VIII
0-451-52038-6 NAL pb $4.95

KING JOHN
Edited by A.R. Braunmuller
0-19-812930-0 Oxford $36.00

KING JOHN
0-14-070727-1 Penguin pb $3.75

KING LEAR
Edited by Russell Fraser
0-451-52282-6 NAL pb $2.75

KING LEAR
0-14-070724-7 Penguin pb $3.75

LOVE'S LABOR'S LOST
Edited by John Arthos
0-451-52267-2 NAL pb $3.50

LOVE'S LABOR'S LOST
0-14-070738-7 Penguin pb $3.75

MACBETH
Edited by Sylvan Barnet
0-451-52135-8 NAL pb $2.75

MACBETH
0-14-070705-0 Penguin pb $3.75

MEASURE FOR MEASURE
0-451-52259-1 NAL pb $2.95

MEASURE FOR MEASURE
0-14-070715-8 Penguin pb $3.75

THE MERCHANT OF VENICE
Edited by Kenneth Myrick
0-451-52133-1 NAL pb $2.25

THE MERCHANT OF VENICE
0-14-070706-9 Penguin pb $3.75

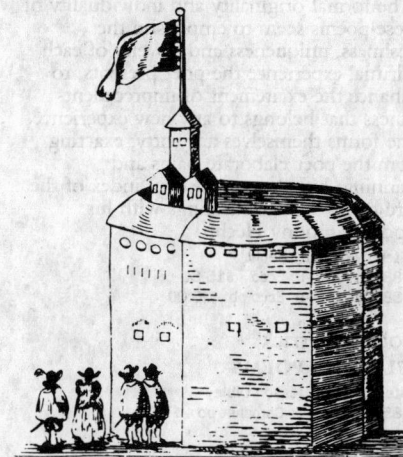

The Globe Theater

THE MERRY WIVES OF WINDSOR
0-14-070726-3 Penguin pb $3.75

A MIDSUMMER NIGHT'S DREAM
Edited by Wolfgang Clemen
0-451-52137-4 NAL pb $2.75

A MIDSUMMER NIGHT'S DREAM
0-14-070702-6 Penguin pb $3.75

MUCH ADO ABOUT NOTHING
Edited by David L. Stevenson
0-451-52159-5 NAL pb $2.95

MUCH ADO ABOUT NOTHING
0-14-070709-3 Penguin pb $3.75

THE NARRATIVE POEMS
0-14-071437-5 Penguin pb $3.95

OTHELLO
Edited by Alvin Kernan
0-451-52132-3 NAL pb $3.50

OTHELLO
0-14-070707-7 Penguin pb $3.75

PERICLES
0-14-070729-8 Penguin pb $3.75

PERICLES, CYMBELINE & THE TWO NOBLE KINSMEN
0-451-52042-4 NAL pb $4.95

THE RAPE OF LUCRECE
0-14-070723-9 Penguin pb $3.75

RICHARD II
0-451-52217-6 NAL pb $2.75

RICHARD II
0-14-070719-0 Penguin pb $3.75

RICHARD III
Edited by Mark Eccles
0-451-51936-1 NAL pb $2.75

RICHARD III
0-14-070712-3 Penguin pb $3.75

ROMEO AND JULIET
Edited by J.A. Bryant, Jr.
0-451-52136-6 NAL pb $2.75

ROMEO AND JULIET
0-14-070701-8 Penguin pb $3.75

THE SONNETS & A LOVER'S COMPLAINT
0-14-070732-8 Penguin pb $5.95

THE TAMING OF THE SHREW
Edited by Robert B. Heilman
0-451-52126-9 NAL pb $2.50

THE TAMING OF THE SHREW
Edited by H.J. Oliver
0-19-281440-0 Oxford pb $6.95

THE TAMING OF THE SHREW
0-14-070710-7 Penguin pb $3.75

THE TEMPEST
Edited by Robert Langbaum
0-451-52125-0 NAL pb $2.25

THE TEMPEST
0-14-070713-1 Penguin pb $3.75

THREE COMEDIES
Includes *Love's Labor's Lost, The Two Gentlemen of Verona,* and *The Merry Wives of Windsor*
Edited by John Arthos, Bertrand Evans & William Green
0-451-52026-2 NAL pb $4.95

TIMON OF ATHENS
0-14-070721-2 Penguin pb $3.75

TITUS ANDRONICUS & TIMON OF ATHENS
Edited by Maurice Charney & Sylvan Barnet
0-451-52034-3 NAL pb $3.95

TITUS ANDRONICUS
Edited by Eugene M. Waith
0–19–812902–5 Oxford $22.00
0–19–281442–7 Oxford pb $7.95

TROILUS AND CRESSIDA
0–451–51946–9 NAL pb $2.75

TROILUS AND CRESSIDA
Edited by Kenneth Muir
0–19–281439–7 Oxford pb $6.95

TROILUS AND CRESSIDA
Edited by R.A. Foakes
0–14–070741–7 Penguin pb $3.75

TWELFTH NIGHT
0–451–52129–3 NAL pb $2.75

TWELFTH NIGHT
0–14–070711–5 Penguin pb $3.75

THE TWO GENTLEMEN OF VERONA
0–14–070717–4 Penguin pb $3.75

THE TWO NOBLE KINSMEN
Edited by Eugene M. Waith
0–19–812939–4 Oxford $39.95

THE TWO NOBLE KINSMEN
0–14–070730–1 Penguin pb $3.75

THE WINTER'S TALE
Edited by Frank Kermode
0–451–52260–5 NAL pb $2.95

THE WINTER'S TALE
0–14–070716–6 Penguin pb $3.75

The Early 17th Century

With the turn of the 17th century, the great Elizabethan consensus began to break down, and a new spirit of doubt and pessimism became evident. Seventeenth-century literature reflects the uneasiness as well as the exhilaration of its times, from the restless, supercharged imagination of John Donne to the meditative inwardness of Thomas Browne and George Herbert.

POETRY

Donne's name and style tend to dominate discussions of 17th-century poetry. Indeed, the "metaphysical" style that he pioneered, with its startling imagery and exhilarating pursuit of wit, remained widely influential throughout his own century as well. Yet the era produced other kinds of poetry as well: religious and meditative, light and deftly entertaining, even cheerfully obscene. As England slid toward civil war, writers often turned inward. Seventeenth-century poetry is a study in surprise, rich in personal and sometimes idiosyncratic voices.

● Richard Crashaw
THE COMPLETE POETRY
Religious poetry was no novelty in the 17th century, but Crashaw's Catholicism transformed him into a highly original writer, whose verse remains remarkable for the rhapsodic, baroque voluptuousness with which it renders religious experience
Edited by George W. Williams
0–393–00728–6 Norton pb $5.95

● Samuel Daniel
POEMS & A DEFENCE OF RYME
Daniel was the sober humanist of the late 16th century, calm, deliberate, philosophical, a serious and sometimes anguished student of the human condition
Edited by Arthur C. Sprague
0–226–13609–4 Chicago pb $2.95

● John Donne
THE COMPLETE ENGLISH POEMS
A useful inexpensive edition, with reliable texts and succinct notes
Edited by A.J. Smith
0–14–042209–9 Penguin pb $8.95

JOHN DONNE'S POETRY
An annotated text with critical essays
Edited by Arthur L. Clements
0–393–09642–4 Norton pb $7.95

● Michael Drayton
SELECTED POEMS
Drayton was the most urbane of Elizabethan poets; contemporary readers will find his combination of sardonic humor and light sensuousness surprisingly modern
Edited by Vivien Thomas
0–85635–225–X Carcanet pb $7.50

POLY-OLBION: A Chronologic Description of Great Britain
An enormously long, but in its day enormously influential, poetic tour of England, and still of interest to the lover of local legends and folklore
0–8337–0921–6 Franklin $78.50

● George Herbert
THE ENGLISH POEMS OF GEORGE HERBERT
Though he is often labeled as a Metaphysical poet, the intense, tortured, yet finally serene tenor of Herbert's religious poetry places him in a class by himself. One of the most accomplished lyric poets of any century
Edited by C.A. Patrides
0–460–11040–3 Biblio pb $5.00

THE ESSENTIAL HERBERT
"The formal originality and individuality of these poems seem to emphasize the freshness, uniqueness and novelty of each spiritual experience the poet presents, to enhance the excitement of unprecedentedness that belongs to any new experience. The forms themselves are witty, exacting from the poet elaborate pains and planning; but they are also an index of the care he takes in his dealings with his God"—Anthony Hecht
Edited by Anthony Hecht
0–88001–158–0 Ecco $15.50
0–88001–159–9 Ecco pb $6.00

● Robert Herrick
SELECTED POEMS
Edited by David Jesson-Dibley
0–85635–320–5 Carcanet pb $7.50

● Richard Lovelace
SELECTED POEMS
Edited by Gerald Hammond
0–85635–673–5 Carcanet pb $9.50

● Thomas Traherne
SELECTED WRITINGS
Traherne's poetry was not discovered until the 20th century; he now stands as one of England's most remarkable poets of religious ecstasy
Edited by Dick Davis
0–85635–231–4 Carcanet pb $7.50

● Henry Vaughan
THE COMPLETE POEMS
One of the great religious lyricists of the 17th century; his mystical view of nature influenced Wordsworth
Edited by Alan Rudrum
0–300–02680–3 Yale $47.00
0–300–02687–0 Yale pb $3.00

THE COMPLETE POETRY
Edited by French Fogle
0–393–00438–4 Norton pb $8.95

SELECTED POEMS
Edited by Robert Shaw
0–85635–139–3 Carcanet pb $7.50

● John Wilmot, Earl of Rochester
THE POEMS OF JOHN WILMOT, EARL OF ROCHESTER
The unexpurgated Rochester, and a delightful shock even to those jaded by 20th-century sexual permissiveness
Edited by Keith Walker
0–631–15497–3 Blackwell $14.95

Anthologies

● Helen Gardner, editor
THE METAPHYSICAL POETS
Intelligent selections from Donne, Herbert, Vaughan, Traherne, Cowley, and others
0–14–042038–X Penguin pb $6.95

● Germaine Greer, editor
KISSING THE ROD: An Anthology of 17th-Century Women's Verse
0–374–52164–6 Farrar, Straus & Giroux pb $13.95

● Herbert J. Grierson, editor
METAPHYSICAL LYRICS AND POEMS OF THE SEVENTEENTH CENTURY: Donne to Butler
0–19–881102–0 Oxford pb $9.95

● Herbert J. Grierson & Geoffrey Bullough, editors
THE OXFORD BOOK OF SEVENTEENTH CENTURY VERSE
0–19–812125–3 Oxford $49.95

● R.G. Howarth, editor
MINOR POETS OF THE SEVENTEENTH CENTURY
Includes the works of Carew, Suckling, Lovelace, and Lord Herbert of Cherbury
0–460–00873–0 Biblio $14.95

● Louis L. Martz, editor
ENGLISH SEVENTEENTH-CENTURY VERSE
0–393–00675–1 Norton pb $12.95

- **A.C. Partridge**, editor
  THE TRIBE OF BEN: Pre-Augustan Classical Verse in English
  0–87249–159–5 South Carolina pb $5.95

- **Alexander M. Witherspoon & Frank J. Warnke**
  SEVENTEENTH-CENTURY PROSE AND POETRY
  0–15–580237–2 HBJ $37.50

DRAMA

- **Francis Beaumont**
  THE KNIGHT OF THE BURNING PESTLE
  A delightful and sophisticated comedy in which a London grocer and his wife take over a play in progress, remolding it to their alternately sentimental and bloodthirsty taste
  Edited by John Doebler
  0–8032–0250–4 Nebraska $14.95

- **Francis Beaumont & John Fletcher**
  THE MAID'S TRAGEDY
  A romantic tragedy typifying the popular taste of the early 17th century
  Edited by Howard B. Norland
  0–8032–5253–6 Nebraska pb $6.95
  PHILASTER
  A romantic comedy popular in its time
  Edited by Dora J. Ashe
  0–8032–0291–1 Nebraska $16.95

- **George Chapman**
  THE PLAYS OF GEORGE CHAPMAN: The Comedies
  Edited by Alan Holaday
  0–252–78423–5 Illinois $39.95
  BUSSY D'AMBOIS
  A difficult, impressive political tragedy
  Edited by Robert J. Lordi
  0–8032–5257–9 Nebraska pb $4.25

Edmund Kean in "A New Way to Pay Old Debts," from The Oxford Illustrated History of English Literature *edited by Pat Rogers*

- **John Ford**
  THE SELECTED PLAYS
  Includes *The Broken Heart, 'Tis Pity She's a Whore,* and *Perkin Warbeck*
  Edited by C. Gibson
  0–521–29545–9 Cambridge pb $20.95
  THREE PLAYS
  Includes *'Tis Pity She's a Whore, The Broken Heart,* and *Perkin Warbeck*
  0–14–043059–8 Penguin pb $5.95

- **John Marston**
  SELECTED PLAYS
  Edited by M. Jackson & M. Neill
  0–521–29247–6 Cambridge pb $19.95

- **Philip Massinger**
  A NEW WAY TO PAY OLD DEBTS
  Long one of the most popular English plays, notable for its characterization of the grasping Sir Giles Overreach
  0–413–53310–7 Methuen pb $4.95

Thomas Middleton
FIVE PLAYS
Middleton's work, encompassing realistic comedy and hard-edged melodrama, has risen in critical estimation in recent years. This edition includes *A Trick to Catch the Old One, The Revenger's Tragedy* (often attributed to Cyril Tourner), *A Chaste Maid in Cheapside, Women Beware Women,* and *The Changeling*
Edited by Bryan Loughrey & Neil Taylor
0–14–043219–1 Penguin pb $6.95

- **Thomas Middleton & Thomas Dekker**
  THE ROARING GIRL
  An exhilarating comedy whose protofeminist heroine has had much appeal for recent readers
  Edited by A.H. Gomme
  0–393–90024–X Norton pb $3.95

- **Thomas Middleton & William Rowley**
  THE CHANGELING
  Edited by N.W. Bawcutt
  0–7190–1610–X St. Martin's pb $5.00

- **Cyril Tourneur**
  THE REVENGER'S TRAGEDY
  The most splendidly horrific of Jacobean revenge plays; its conceits include a fatal kiss administered to a skull with poisoned lips
  Edited by R.A. Foakes
  0–4131–6610–4 St. Martin's pb $8.95
  THE ATHEIST'S TRAGEDY
  Edited by Brian Morris & Roma Gill
  0–393–90030–4 Norton pb $2.95

- **John Webster**
  THREE PLAYS
  After Shakespeare, perhaps the most powerful of Jacobean tragedians. Includes *The Duchess of Malfi, The White Devil,* and *The Devil's Law Case*
  Edited by D.C. Gunby
  0–14–043081–4 Penguin pb $6.95

Anthologies

- **Gamini Salgado**, editor
  FOUR JACOBEAN CITY COMEDIES
  Includes Marston's *The Dutch Courtesan,* Middleton's *A Mad World, My Masters,* Jonson's *The Devil Is an Ass,* and Massinger's *A New Way to Pay Old Debts*
  0–14–043101–2 Penguin pb $6.95
  THREE JACOBEAN TRAGEDIES
  Includes Tourneur's *The Revenger's Tragedy,* Webster's *The White Devil,* and Middleton and Rowley's *The Changeling*
  0–14–043006–7 Penguin pb $5.95

- **A.H. Gomme**, editor
  JACOBEAN TRAGEDIES
  0–19–281059–6 Oxford pb $10.95

PROSE

- **Francis Bacon**
  THE ESSAYS
  Bacon, a cardinal figure in the history of philosophy, is also a formidable, if restrained, stylist, master of a forceful yet elliptical prose
  Edited by John Pitcher
  0–14–043216–7 Penguin pb $5.95
  THE ADVANCEMENT OF LEARNING
  Edited by G.W. Kitchin
  Introduction by Arthur Johnston
  0–460–10719–4 Biblio $17.00
  0–460–11719–X Biblio $3.50
  THE NEW ORGANON & RELATED WRITINGS
  Edited by Fulton H. Anderson
  0–672–60289–X Bobbs-Merrill pb $9.95

- **Thomas Browne**
  THE MAJOR WORKS
  0–14–043109–8 Penguin pb $7.95
  SELECTED WRITINGS
  Edited by Geoffrey Keynes
  0–226–07636–9 Chicago pb $3.25

- **John Bunyan**
  GRACE ABOUNDING TO THE CHIEF OF SINNERS
  Bunyan's spiritual autobiography; an epic of ceaselessly tested faith
  Edited by W.R. Owens
  0–14–043280–9 Penguin pb $5.95
  THE PILGRIM'S PROGRESS
  After the Bible the most-read book in the history of English literature
  Edited by Roger Sharrock
  0–14–043004–0 Penguin pb $2.95

- **John Donne**
  DEVOTIONS UPON EMERGENT OCCASIONS
  Edited by Anthony Raspa
  0–19–504174–7 Oxford $28.00
  0–19–504173–9 Oxford $12.95
  SELECTED PROSE
  Edited with an introduction by Neil Rhodes
  0–14–043239–6 Penguin $7.95
  SERMONS ON THE PSALMS AND GOSPELS: With a Selection of Prayers & Meditations
  Edited with an introduction by Evelyn M. Simpson
  0–520–00340–3 California pb $8.95

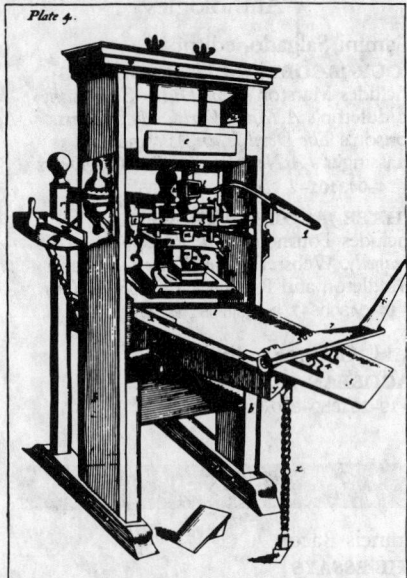

Late 17th–century printing press, from Prints and People: A Social History of Printed Pictures *by A. Hyatt Mayor (Princeton)*

• **Thomas Traherne**
CENTURIES
Meditations on divine benevolence
Edited by H.M. Margoliouth
0–8192–1397–7 Morehouse pb $8.95

• **Izaak Walton**
THE COMPLEAT ANGLER
Walton's treatise on fishing is one of the most treasured books in English
0–14–059007–2 Penguin pb $4.95

THE COMPLEAT ANGLER
This edition also includes Charles Cotton's additions to Walton's original text
Edited by John Buxton
0–19–281511–3 Oxford pb $5.95

The Restoration and the 18th Century

In the period following the restoration of Charles II, the neoclassical strain pioneered nearly 60 years before by Ben Jonson acquired new polish with Dryden, Pope, Prior, and Gay. Judicious, economically expressed wit became the lingua franca of poetry and the intellectual coin of a newly vigorous urban culture.

POETRY

• **Robert Burns**
A CHOICE OF BURNS'S POEMS AND SONGS
Among the most beloved poets in English, a master of both broad sentiment and low comedy
0–571–06835–9 Faber & Faber pb $6.95

POEMS AND SONGS
Edited by James Kinsley
0–19–281114–2 Oxford pb $13.95

SELECTED POEMS
Edited by Kotewall Beattie
0–14–058535–4 Penguin pb $5.95

• **Thomas Chatterton**
SELECTED POEMS
Chatterton remains one of the most bizarre figures in English literary history. His forged pseudomedieval poems reflect a precocious talent cut short at the age of 18
Edited by Grevel Lindop
0–85635–694–8 Carcanet pb $7.50

• **William Collins**
THE WORKS OF WILLIAM COLLINS
Collins is an underestimated poet; his best work, like the "Ode to Evening," combines the finish of high Augustan poetry with the intense feeling for nature typical of the Romantics
Edited by Richard Wendorf & Charles Ryskamp
0–19–812749–9 Oxford $75.00

• **Charles Cotton**
SELECTED POEMS
A friend of Walton and Lovelace, Cotton celebrated his native Staffordshire landscapes
Edited by Ken Robinson
0–85635–413–9 Carcanet pb $7.50

• **William Cowper**
THE POEMS OF WILLIAM COWPER, Volume 1: 1748–1782
Cowper is surely, and undeservedly, the least-read major poet in English
Edited by John D. Baird & Charles Ryskamp
0–19–811875–9 Oxford $85.00

SELECTED POEMS
Edited by Nick Rhodes
0–85635–414–7 Carcanet pb $7.50

• **George Crabbe**
SELECTED POEMS
Crabbe was both an accomplished formalist, skilled in his use of heroic couplets, and a realistic chronicler of life along the Suffolk coast
Edited by Jem Poster
0–85635–621–2 Carcanet pb $7.50

• **John Dryden**
"Dryden's performances were always hasty, either excited by some external occasion, or extorted by domestic necessity; he composed without consideration, and published without correction. What his mind could supply at call, or gather in one excursion, was all that he sought, and all that he gave. The dilatory caution of Pope enabled him to condense his sentiments, to multiply his images, and to accumulate all that study might produce, or chance might supply. If the flights of Dryden therefore are higher, Pope continues longer on the wing. If of Dryden's fire the blaze is the brighter, of Pope's the heat is more regular and constant. Dryden often surpasses expectation, and Pope never falls below it. Dryden is read with frequent astonishment, and Pope with perpetual delight."—Samuel Johnson, *Lives of the Poets* (1781)

THE OXFORD AUTHORS: DRYDEN
Includes, along with much else, the complete *Fables Ancient and Modern, Religio Laici,* and a generous selection from the translations
Edited by Keith Walker
0–19–254192–7 Oxford $39.95
0–19–281402–8 Oxford pb $14.95

POEMS
Edited by Douglas Grant
0–14–058503–6 Penguin pb $5.95

SELECTED POETRY AND PROSE
0–394–30063–7 Random House pb $5.95

• **Anne Finch, Countess of Winchilsea**
SELECTED POEMS
A poet of minor lyric gifts, nonetheless significant in the emergence of women in literature
Edited by Denys Thompson
0–85635–624–7 Carcanet pb $7.50

• **John Gay**
POETRY AND PROSE
A 2-volume set
Edited by Charles E. Beckwith & Vinton A. Dearing
0–19–811897–X Oxford $74.00

SELECTED POEMS
Edited by Marcus Walsh
0–85635–280–2 Carcanet pb $7.50

• **Thomas Gray**
POEMS, LETTERS & ESSAYS
0–460–00628–2 Euman $14.95

SELECTED POEMS
Gray's reputation rests largely on the familiar "Elegy in a Country Churchyard," obscuring the satirical wit and originality of poems like "On the Death of a Favorite Cat"
Edited by John Heath-Stubbs
0–85635–317–5 Carcanet pb $7.50

• **Thomas Gray & William Collins**
GRAY AND COLLINS: Poetical Works
Edited by Roger Lonsdale
0–19–281169–X Oxford pb $13.50

• **Samuel Johnson**
THE COMPLETE ENGLISH POEMS
Though better known for his prose, as a poet Johnson was one of the most accomplished English moralists, as evident in his masterpiece, "The Vanity of Human Wishes"
Edited by J.D. Fleeman
0–300–02826–1 Yale pb $9.95

• **Andrew Marvell**
THE COMPLETE POEMS
The last of the great Metaphysical poets, author of some of the greatest and most complex lyrics in English
Edited by Elizabeth S. Donno
0–14–042213–7 Penguin pb $6.95

• **John Milton**
"Milton . . . always labours and almost always succeeds. He strives hard to say the finest things in the world, and he does say them. He adorns and dignifies his subject to the utmost: he surrounds it with every possible association of beauty or grandeur, whether moral, intellectual, or physical. He refines on his descriptions of beauty; loading sweets on sweets, till the sense

➤ FOR OVERSEAS ORDERING INFORMATION, SEE PAGE 1

aches at them; and raises his images of terror to a gigantic elevation."—William Hazlitt, *Lectures on the English Poets* (1818)

COMPLETE POETRY OF JOHN MILTON
A well-edited and typographically attractive edition
Edited by John T. Shawcross
0–385–02351–0 Doubleday pb $9.95

THE COMPLETE POEMS & MAJOR PROSE
The best and most comprehensive one-volume edition, with useful if occasionally pedantic notes
Edited by Merritt Y. Hughes
0–02–358290–1 Macmillan pb $38.00

PARADISE LOST
Edited by Scott Elledge
0–393–09230–5 Norton pb $8.95

PARADISE LOST
Edited by William G. Madsen
0–394–30997–9 Random House pb $5.00

THE PORTABLE MILTON
Edited by Douglas Bush
0–14–015044–7 Penguin pb $7.95

• Alexander Pope
"Of his intellectual character, the constituent and fundamental principle was good sense, a prompt and intuitive perception of consonance and propriety. He saw immediately, of his own conceptions, what was to be chosen, and what to be rejected; and, in the works of others, what was to be shunned, and what was to be copied. But good sense alone is a sedate and quiescent quality, which manages its possessions well, but does not increase them; it collects few materials for its own operations, and preserves safety, but never gains supremacy. Pope had likewise genius: a mind active, ambitious, and adventurous, always investigating, always aspiring; in its widest searches still longing to go forward, in its highest flights still wishing to be higher."—Samuel Johnson, *Lives of the Poets* (1781)

Cover design by Aubrey Beardsley for Pope's "The Rape of the Lock"

THE POEMS OF ALEXANDER POPE
A one-volume edition of the famous Twickenham text, with selected annotations
Edited by John Butt
0–300–00340–4 Yale $50.00
0–300–00030–8 Yale pb $16.95

POETICAL WORKS
Edited by Hubert Davis
0–19–254155–2 Oxford $35.00
0–19–281246–7 Oxford pb $14.95

POEMS AND PROSE
Edited by Douglas Grant
0–14–058508–7 Penguin pb $4.95

• Christopher Smart
THE POETICAL WORKS OF CHRISTOPHER SMART
Jubilate Agno, written in a madhouse and imitative of Hebrew verse forms, is an extraordinarily original outpouring of ecstatic poetry. Smart's wild musicality is also apparent in the earlier "A Song to David"

Volume 1: Jubilate Agno
Edited by Karina Williamson
0–19–811869–4 Oxford $49.95

Volume 2: Religious Poetry, 1763–1771
Edited by Karina Williamson & Marcus Walsh
0–19–812767–7 Oxford $72.00

SELECTED POEMS
Edited by Marcus Walsh
0–85635–307–8 Carcanet pb $7.50

• Jonathan Swift
THE COMPLETE POEMS
Swift's genius as a prose writer has overshadowed his poetic accomplishments. He wrote some of the greatest and most savage (and occasionally scatological) satirical verse in the language
Edited by Pat Rogers
0–300–02966–7 Yale $45.00
0–14–042261–7 Penguin pb $14.95

POETICAL WORKS
Edited by Herbert Davis
0–19–254161–7 Oxford $37.50

James Thomson
THE SEASONS & THE CASTLE OF INDOLENCE
Thomson's evocations of landscape and seasonal change were unrivaled in the 18th century, and strongly influenced the Lake Poets of the 19th century
Edited by James Sambrook
0–19–871070–4 Oxford pb $10.95

• Edward Young
SELECTED POEMS
Perhaps the best-known figure in the Graveyard school, remarkable for his searching melancholic meditations
Edited by Brian Hepworth
0–85635–140–7 Carcanet pb $7.50

NIGHT THOUGHTS, OR THE COMPLAINT AND THE CONSOLATION
Blake's engravings serve as a tribute to a poet who deeply influenced him
Illustrations by William Blake
0–486–20219–4 Dover pb $6.00

Anthologies
• Dennis Davison, editor
THE PENGUIN BOOK OF EIGHTEENTH CENTURY ENGLISH VERSE
0–14–042169–6 Penguin pb $6.95

• Roger Lonsdale, editor
THE NEW OXFORD BOOK OF EIGHTEENTH CENTURY VERSE
0–19–214122–8 Oxford $29.95

DRAMA

Restoration and 18th-century plays seem divided by more than a mere century from the brutal world of late Elizabethan and Jacobean tragedy. Comedy was the chosen mode for Congreve, Wycherley, and Sheridan, and though heroic tragedy survived (notably in Dryden's *All for Love*), it was overshadowed by a keenly observed world of rakes, fools, jealous husbands, lecherous dowagers, and wayward ladies' maids. With Sheridan, the satire grew less bitter, but the unblinking observation of folly no less acute.

• Aphra Behn
THE LUCKY CHANCE
0–413–57120–3 RC&H pb $6.95

THE ROVER
Edited by Frederick M. Link
0–8032–5350–8 Nebraska pb $4.50

• William Congreve
THE COMEDIES OF WILLIAM CONGREVE
Includes *The Old Bachelor, The Double Dealer, Love for Love*, and *The Way of the World*
Edited by Eric S. Rump
0–14–043231–0 Penguin pb $6.95

LOVE FOR LOVE
Edited by Emmett L. Avery
0–8032–5353–2 Nebraska pb $3.95

THE WAY OF THE WORLD
One of the great English comedies, relentless and unsparing
Edited by Brian Gibbons
0–393–90004–5 Norton pb $5.95

• John Dryden
ALL FOR LOVE
Antony and Cleopatra in a surprisingly romantic treatment from the great neoclassicist
Edited by Nicholas J. Andrew
0–393–90006–1 Norton pb $4.95

AURENG-ZEBE
Edited by Frederick M. Link
0–8032–5376–1 Nebraska pb $4.95

MARRIAGE A LA MODE
Edited by Mark S. Auburn
0–8032–6556–5 Nebraska pb $4.95

• George Etherege
THE PLAYS OF SIR GEORGE ETHEREGE
Edited by Michael Cordner
0–521–28879–7 Cambridge pb $16.95

THE MAN OF MODE
Edited by W.B. Carnochan
0-8032-5356-7 Nebraska pb $4.50

● George Farquhar
THE BEAUX' STRATAGEM
Edited by Charles N. Fifer
0-8032-5384-2 Nebraska pb $2.75

THE RECRUITING OFFICER
Edited by Michael Shugrue
0-8032-5357-5 Nebraska pb $3.25

● Henry Fielding
THE AUTHOR'S FARCE
Edited by Charles B. Woods
0-8032-5358-3 Nebraska pb $4.50

THE GRUB-STREET OPERA
Edited by Edgar V. Roberts
0-8032-5359-1 Nebraska pb $4.25

● Oliver Goldsmith
SHE STOOPS TO CONQUER
One of the gentlest and most enduringly popular comedies of the English stage
Edited by J.A. Lavin
0-393-90046-0 Norton pb $6.95

● George Lillo
FATAL CURIOSITY
Edited by William H. McBurney
0-8032-0364-0 Nebraska $8.95
0-8032-5364-8 Nebraska pb $2.95

THE LONDON MERCHANT
A bourgeois tragedy of a London clerk gone wrong
Edited by William H. McBurney
0-8032-5365-6 Nebraska pb $3.95

● Thomas Otway
THE ORPHAN
Edited by Aline M. Taylor
0-8032-0383-7 Nebraska $12.50

VENICE PRESERVED
Otway was the last heir to the poetic splendor of Jacobean drama
Edited by Malcolm Kelsall
0-8032-0366-7 Nebraska $11.95

● Richard Brinsley Sheridan
SHERIDAN'S PLAYS
Sheridan represents a more genial—and genteel—version of Restoration satire. Includes *The School for Scandal, The Rivals, The Critic, A Trip to Scarborough, The Duenna,* and *St. Patrick's Day*
Edited by Cecil Price
0-19-254169-2 Oxford $29.95
0-19-281158-4 Oxford pb $9.95

THE RIVALS
Edited by J. Lavin
0-393-90044-4 Norton pb $6.95

THE SCHOOL FOR SCANDAL
Edited by C.J. Price
0-19-911008-5 Oxford pb $6.95

● John Vanbrugh
FOUR COMEDIES
Includes *The Relapse, The Provoked Wife, The Confederacy,* and *A Journey to London*
Edited with an introduction by Michael Cordner
0-14-043276-0 Penguin pb $7.95

● William Wycherley
THE PLAYS OF WILLIAM WYCHERLEY
Wycherley, the roughest of the great Restoration dramatists, raises sexual disgust to an art form. Includes *The Country Wife, The Plain Dealer, Love in a Wood,* and *The Gentleman Dancing Master*
Edited by P. Holland
0-521-23250-3 Cambridge $59.50
0-521-29880-6 Cambridge pb $17.95

THE COUNTRY WIFE
Edited by Thomas H. Fujimura
0-8032-5371-0 Nebraska pb $3.50

THE PLAIN DEALER
An adaptation of Molière's *The Misanthrope*
Edited by James L. Smith
0-393-90042-8 Norton pb $7.95

Anthologies

● Brice Harris, editor
RESTORATION PLAYS
Includes Villiers' *The Rehearsal,* Wycherley's *The Country Wife,* Etherege's *The Man of Mode,* Otway's *Venice Preserved,* Vanbrugh's *The Relapse,* Congreve's *The Way of the World,* and Farquhar's *The Beaux' Stratagem*
0-07-553658-7 McGraw-Hill pb $6.95

● Gamini Salgado, editor
THREE RESTORATION COMEDIES
Includes Wycherley's *The Country Wife,* Congreve's *Love for Love,* and Etherege's *The Man of Mode*
0-14-043027-X Penguin pb $5.95

FICTION

The informality and frequent eccentricity of the 18th-century novel make it a constant source of surprise and delight—from the moral analysis of Richardson's *Clarissa* to the picaresque verve of Fielding and Smollett and the Gothic fiction of Beckford, Walpole, and Radcliffe.

● William Beckford
VATHEK
Among the most delightfully perverse books in English, a Gothic romance in Arabian dress
Edited by Roger Lonsdale
0-19-281645-4 Oxford pb $5.95

● Aphra Behn
Behn, a highly successful playwright and novelist, was England's first professional woman of letters.
LOVE LETTERS BETWEEN A NOBLEMAN AND HIS SISTER
Introduction by Maureen Duffy
0-14-016160-0 Penguin pb $7.95

OROONOKO: Or, the Royal Slave
A Rousseauan evocation of the Noble Savage, and a condemnation of the slave trade
0-393-00702-2 Norton pb $4.95

Fanny Burney
CAMILLA
Edited by Edward A. Bloom & Lillian D. Bloom
0-19-281662-4 Oxford pb $8.95

CECILIA
Edited by Peter Sabor
0-19-281742-6 Oxford pb $7.95

EVELINA
An entertaining epistolary novel that combines humor and satire with strong moralism
Edited by Edward A. Bloom
0-19-281596-2 Oxford pb $6.95

● John Cleland
FANNY HILL: Or, Memoirs of a Woman of Pleasure
Cleland's use of elaborate and elegant figurative language to describe explicit sexual episodes sets his book apart from most erotic literature
Edited by Peter Wagner
0-14-043249-3 Penguin pb $2.95

● Daniel Defoe
COLONEL JACK: The History and Remarkable Life of the Truly Honorable Colonel Jacque, Commonly Called Colonel Jack
Edited by Samuel H. Monk
0-19-281076-6 Oxford pb $4.95

A JOURNAL OF THE PLAGUE YEAR
A classic early text in the literature of disease; a harrowing blend of fiction and fact
Edited by Anthony Burgess
0-14-043015-6 Penguin pb $4.95

MOLL FLANDERS
"It is most popularly thought of as a tale of thievery and prostitution, of crime, punishment and worldly success: a lively account of an attractive, independent and wicked woman who eventually makes good—both morally and economically. In fact *Moll Flanders* is throughout as much about financial investment as about theft, as much about marriage as about prostitution"—Juliet Mitchell
Edited by Juliet Mitchell
0-14-043107-1 Penguin pb $2.95

ROBINSON CRUSOE
"*Robinson Crusoe* falls most naturally into place, not with other novels, but with the great myths of Western civilization, with *Faust, Don Juan,* and *Don Quixote*"—Ian Watt
0-14-035072-1 Penguin pb $2.25

ROXANA
Edited by David Blewett
0-14-043149-7 Penguin pb $4.95

● Henry Fielding
AMELIA
An uncharacteristically sentimental novel about a virtuous wife, modeled on the author's spouse
Edited by David Blewett
0-14-043229-9 Penguin pb $5.95

THE JACOBITE'S JOURNAL & RELATED WRITINGS
In addition to his work as novelist and

playwright, Fielding was a prolific journalist
Edited by William Coley
0-8195-4072-2 Wesleyan $35.00

JONATHAN WILD
The law and the criminal underworld intermingle in this story of a doomed rake
Edited by David Nokes
0-14-043151-9 Penguin pb $5.95

JOSEPH ANDREWS
Fielding's first full-fledged novel features the great comic creations Lady Booby and Mrs. Slipslop
Edited by R.F. Brissenden
0-14-043114-4 Penguin pb $3.95

JOSEPH ANDREWS, SHAMELA & RELATED WRITINGS
Shamela (a takeoff on Richardson's *Pamela*) is perhaps the most skillful extended parody in English
Edited by Homer Goldberg
0-393-95555-9 Norton pb $8.95

TOM JONES, A FOUNDLING
Fielding's masterpiece, in a splendidly designed scholarly edition
Edited by Fredson Bowers
Introduction by Martin C. Battestin
0-8195-6048-0 Wesleyan pb $12.95

TOM JONES
Edited by Reg Mutter
0-14-043009-1 Penguin pb $3.95

• Sarah Fielding
DAVID SIMPLE
A "Moral Romance" by the sister of Henry Fielding
0-19-281766-3 Oxford pb $7.95

• William Godwin
CALEB WILLIAMS
Godwin's novel of vengeance and remorse reflects his radical political ideas; it also played a crucial role in the evolution of the detective novel
0-14-043256-6 Penguin pb $6.95

• Oliver Goldsmith
THE VICAR OF WAKEFIELD
0-14-043159-4 Penguin pb $2.50

• Elizabeth Inchbald
A SIMPLE STORY
"Daring in theme, elegant in style, *A Simple Story* is one of the most remarkable novels of the late eighteenth century . . . Inchbald's concise, ironic narrative style anticipates Austen, while the passionate heroine she creates to disrupt the world of social comedy looks further forward, to the work of the Brontës"—Jane Spencer
Edited by J.M.S. Tompkins
Introduction by Jane Spencer
0-19-281849-X Oxford pb $7.95

• Samuel Johnson
THE HISTORY OF RASSELAS, PRINCE OF ABISSINIA
Johnson's characters, searching for a "choice of life," encounter only the endless vanity of human pretensions
Edited by D.J. Enright
0-14-043108-X Penguin pb $3.95

• Charlotte Lennox
THE FEMALE QUIXOTE
"Dr. Johnson, Samuel Richardson and Henry Fielding all thought she merited the label 'genius,' with Henry Fielding rating her *Female Quixote* as surpassing Cervantes' work"—Dale Spender
Introduction by Sandra Shulman
0-86358-080-7 RC&H pb $7.95

Matthew Lewis
THE MONK
Murder, rape, torture, the Inquisition, and a diabolical pact are some of the ingredients of Lewis' archetypal Gothic novel, which shocked his contemporaries
Edited by Howard Anderson
0-19-281524-5 Oxford pb $4.95

• Henry Mackenzie
THE MAN OF FEELING
An example of the "Novel of Sentiment"
Edited by Brian Vickers
0-19-281776-0 Oxford pb $5.95

• Ann Radcliffe
Radcliffe, the most talented of the Gothic novelists, was remarkable for her ability to transform the creaky melodramatics of her plots through the expressive use of landscape and supernaturally charged imagery.
THE ITALIAN
Edited by Frederick Garber
0-19-281572-5 Oxford pb $6.95

THE MYSTERIES OF UDOLPHO
Edited by Bonamy Dobrée
0-19-281502-4 Oxford pb $5.95

THE ROMANCE OF THE FOREST
Edited with an introduction by Chloe Chard
0-19-281712-4 Oxford pb $6.95

• Samuel Richardson
CLARISSA: Or the History of a Young Lady
A complete text of Richardson's immensely long epistolary novel of threatened but ultimately triumphant virtue
Edited by Angus Ross
0-14-043215-9 Penguin pb $15.95

PAMELA: Or Virtue Rewarded
A shorter, earlier novel prefiguring *Clarissa's* moral drama
Edited by Peter Sabor
Introduction by Margaret Doody
0-14-043140-3 Penguin pb $5.95

SIR CHARLES GRANDISON
A long novel portraying a moral paragon of virtue who became a prototype for later 18th-century sentimental heroes
Edited with an introduction by Jocelyn Harris
0-19-281745-0 Oxford pb $13.95

• Tobias Smollett
Smollett's picaresque novels are rougher and more episodic than Fielding's; they are also closer to the ugly realities of 18th-century urban squalor.
THE ADVENTURES OF PEREGRINE PICKLE
A satirical Grand Tour of Europe
Edited by James L. Clifford
0-19-281663-2 Oxford pb $8.95

THE ADVENTURES OF RODERICK RANDOM
This masterpiece contains one of the earliest descriptions of English naval life
Edited by Paul-Gabriel Bouce
0-19-255370-4 Oxford $45.00
0-19-281261-0 Oxford pb $6.95

THE EXPEDITION OF HUMPHREY CLINKER
The inimitable dyspepsia of Matthew Bramble, reflecting Smollett's own temperament, meets its match in the maddening provocations supplied by his sister Tabitha
Edited by Angus Ross
0-14-043021-0 Penguin pb $4.95

THE LIFE AND ADVENTURES OF SIR LAUNCELOT GREAVES
A lesser-known Smollett novel modeled on *Don Quixote*
0-14-043306-6 Penguin pb $6.95

• Laurence Sterne
THE LIFE AND OPINIONS OF TRISTRAM SHANDY, GENTLEMAN
The first antinovel: an uproarious attack on the conventions of fiction and a celebration of unbridled eccentricity
Edited by Ian C. Ross
0-19-818524-3 Oxford $57.00

THE LIFE AND OPINIONS OF TRISTRAM SHANDY, GENTLEMAN
Edited by Graham Petrie
0-14-043019-9 Penguin pb $4.95

• Horace Walpole
THE CASTLE OF OTRANTO
Historically important as the first Gothic novel
Edited by W.S. Lewis & Joseph W. Reed, Jr.
0-19-281606-3 Oxford pb $3.95

• Mary Wollstonecraft
MARY & THE WRONGS OF WOMAN
Edited by Gary Kelly
0-19-281527-X Oxford pb $3.95

PROSE

• Joseph Addison & Richard Steele
SELECTIONS FROM THE TATLER AND THE SPECTATOR
Addison and Steele pioneered the informal journalistic essay
0-14-043298-1 Penguin pb $7.95

John Aubrey
AUBREY'S BRIEF LIVES
Aubrey is one of the great gossips of literary history; if his accounts of writers and other public figures from Sidney and Jonson to Hobbes and Hooker are not always accurate, they are unfailingly entertaining
Edited by Oliver L. Dick
0-14-043079-2 Penguin pb $7.95

• James Boswell
LIFE OF JOHNSON
In this monumental work Boswell invented the modern art of biography, and supplied posterity with a gold mine of anecdotal

---

☞ **FOR ALL OTHER INQUIRIES, PLEASE CALL (212) 333-7900**

information about the 18th century's leading man of letters
Edited by R.W. Chapman & J.E. Fleeman
Introduction by Pat Rogers
0–19–281537–7 Oxford pb $13.95

BOSWELL: The English Experiment, 1785–1789
Edited by Irma S. Lustig & Frederick A. Pottle
0–07–039116–5 McGraw-Hill $24.95

BOSWELL'S LONDON JOURNEY
0–07–006603–5 McGraw-Hill pb $8.95

● Edmund Burke
REFLECTIONS ON THE REVOLUTION IN FRANCE
A classic of political writing first published in 1790
0–14–043204–3 Penguin pb $5.95

● Lord Chesterfield
LETTERS TO HIS SON AND OTHERS
Worldly wisdom from a statesman and friend of Pope
Introduction by R.K. Root
0–460–11823–4 Biblio pb $5.95

● Colley Cibber
AN APOLOGY FOR THE LIFE OF COLLEY CIBBER
The butt of Pope's merciless satire in *The Dunciad* responds with a vivid account of a life in the roistering world of the 18th-century theater
0–460–00668–1 Biblio $14.95

● Daniel Defoe
A TOUR THROUGH THE WHOLE ISLAND OF GREAT BRITAIN
0–14–043066–0 Penguin pb $7.95

● John Dryden
SELECTED CRITICISM
Dryden pioneered a natural, colloquial style, unobtrusive yet forceful, artful but transparent, that became the model for Addison, Steele, and Edmund Burke
Edited by James Kinsley & G.A. Parfitt
0–19–871051–8 Oxford pb $8.95

● John Evelyn
THE DIARY OF JOHN EVELYN
Evelyn's diary focuses on the public formalities of his period, and also supplies portraits of some of its leading figures
Edited by John Bowle
0–19–281529–6 Oxford pb $7.95

Edward Gibbon
Eighteenth-century prose style reached its apogee in the limpid ironies of the narration that Gibbon composed out of his vast researches into the fall of Rome. "The style is as smooth as a Flemish picture and the muscles are concealed and only for natural uses, not exaggerated like Michelangelo's to show the painter's skill in anatomy."— Horace Walpole
THE DECLINE AND FALL OF THE ROMAN EMPIRE
Bury's scholarly edition, reprinted here as a 7-volume set, is still unsurpassed. His footnotes and appendixes are a compendium of classical knowledge in themselves
Edited by J.B. Bury
0–404–02820–9 AMS $300.00

THE DECLINE AND FALL OF THE ROMAN EMPIRE
Edited by Dero A. Saunders & Charles A. Robinson, Jr.

Volume 1
0–394–60401–6 Modern Library $12.95

Volume 2
0–394–60402–4 Modern Library $12.95

Volume 3
0–394–60403–2 Modern Library $12.95

THE DECLINE AND FALL OF THE ROMAN EMPIRE
A one-volume abridgment
0–14–043189–6 Penguin pb $6.95

MEMOIRS OF MY LIFE
"Intelligent, entertaining, dignified and often amusing . . . One of the minor masterpieces of its century"—E.M. Forster
Edited by Betty Radice
0–14–043217–5 Penguin pb $4.95

● Richard Gough
THE HISTORY OF MYDDLE
"The most remarkable local history ever written . . . No contemporary writer has provided such memorable details about the qualities and foibles of his neighbours. Gough pulled no punches, and by the time he had finished his History he had written a pungent commentary upon all, or nearly all, the fellow members of his rural community"—David Hey
Edited with an introduction by David Hey
0–14–043314–7 Penguin pb $6.95

● Samuel Johnson
THE OXFORD AUTHORS: SAMUEL JOHNSON
A generous and well-chosen selection illustrating the enormous range of Johnson's output
Edited by Donald Greene
0–19–281340–4 Oxford pb $11.95

SELECTED WRITINGS
Edited by Patrick Cruttwell
0–14–043033–4 Penguin pb $7.95

JOHNSON ON JOHNSON: A Selection of the Personal and Autobiographical Writings of Samuel Johnson (1709–1782)
Edited by John Wain
0–460–01003–4 Biblio pb $6.95

THE JOURNEY TO THE WESTERN ISLANDS OF SCOTLAND
Johnson's piece of travel writing is the occasion of an unlikely outpouring of sympathy
Introduction by J.D. Fleeman
0–19–812766–9 Oxford $65.00

THE LETTERS OF SAMUEL JOHNSON WITH MRS. THRALE'S GENUINE LETTERS TO HIM
Edited by R.W. Chapman

Volume 1
0–19–818536–7 Oxford $34.50

Volume 2
0–19–818537–5 Oxford $34.50

Volume 3
0–19–818538–3 Oxford $34.50

LIVES OF THE POETS: A Selection
One of the most influential single texts in the history of English literary criticism
Edited by J.P. Hardy
0–19–871052–6 Oxford pb $9.95

Dr. Johnson, *from* The Delights of Reading *by Otto Bettmann (Godine)*

LIVES OF THE ENGLISH POETS
0–460–00770–X Biblio $12.95
0–460–01770–5 Biblio pb $7.95

The Yale Edition of the Works of Samuel Johnson

DIARIES, PRAYERS & ANNALS
Edited by E.L. McAdam, Jr.
0–300–00733–7 Yale $55.00

THE IDLER & THE ADVENTURER
Edited by W.J. Bate
0–300–00294–7 Yale $54.00

JOHNSON ON SHAKESPEARE
A 2-volume set
Edited by Arthur Sherbo
Introduction by Bertrand Bronson
0–300–00605–5 Yale $95.00

JOURNEY TO THE WESTERN ISLANDS OF SCOTLAND
Edited by Mary Lascelles
0–300–01251–9 Yale $40.00

POLITICAL WRITINGS
Edited by Donald J. Greene
0–300–01593–3 Yale $52.00

THE RAMBLER
A 3-volume set
Edited by W.J. Bate
0–300–01157–1 Yale $100.00

SELECTED ESSAYS FROM THE RAMBLER, ADVENTURER & IDLER
Edited by W.J. Bate
0–300–00364–1 Yale $50.00
0–300–00016–2 Yale pb $10.95

SELECTIONS FROM JOHNSON ON SHAKESPEARE
0–300–03707–4 Yale $42.50
0–300–03708–2 Yale pb $13.95

SERMONS
Edited by Jean H. Hagstrum and James Gray
0–300–02104–6 Yale $42.00

A VOYAGE TO ABYSSINIA
Edited by Joel J. Gold
0–300–03003–7 Yale $50.00

● Samuel Johnson & James Boswell
A JOURNEY TO THE WESTERN ISLANDS OF SCOTLAND & THE JOURNAL OF A TOUR TO THE HEBRIDES
Johnson's account of the Hebrides paired with Boswell's; the latter focuses more on Johnson himself than on their surroundings
Edited by Peter Levi
0–14–043221–3 Penguin pb $6.95

IF YOU CAN'T FIND IT, LOOK IN THE INDEX

• Charles Kerby-Miller, editor
THE MEMOIRS OF THE EXTRAORDINARY LIFE, WORKS AND DISCOVERIES OF MARTINUS SCRIBLERUS
A satire of educational and artistic practices, produced by a club whose members included Pope, Swift, Gay, and Arbuthnot
0–19–520648–7 Oxford pb $9.95

• Mary Wortley Montagu
THE COMPLETE LETTERS OF LADY MARY WORTLEY MONTAGU
Edited by Robert Halsband

Volume 1: 1708–1720
0–19–811446–X Oxford $55.00

Volume 2: 1721–1751
0–19–811455–9 Oxford $55.00

THE SELECTED LETTERS OF LADY MARY WORTLEY MONTAGU
Edited by Robert Halsband
0–14–057026–8 Penguin pb $6.95

• Dorothy Osborne
LETTERS TO SIR WILLIAM TEMPLE
A classic of ingenuous eloquence, including a loving evocation of the details of daily life
0–14–043265–5 Penguin pb $7.95

• Samuel Pepys
THE DIARY OF SAMUEL PEPYS
The only complete and unexpurgated edition of Pepys's incomparable diary. Perhaps no other human being has ever recorded his own life in such compulsively honest detail
Edited by Robert Latham & William Matthews

Volume 1: 1660
0–520–01575–4 California $35.00

Volume 2: 1661
0–520–01576–2 California $35.00

Volume 3: 1662
0–520–01577–0 California $35.00

Volume 4: 1663
0–520–01857–5 California $35.00

Volume 5: 1664
0–520–01858–3 California $35.00

Volume 6: 1665
0–520–01859–1 California $35.00

Volume 7: 1666
0–520–02094–4 California $35.00

Volume 8: 1667
0–520–02095–2 California $35.00

Volume 9: 1668–1669
0–520–02096–0 California $35.00

THE SHORTER PEPYS
A useful and conveniently annotated one-volume selection from the complete California edition
Edited by Robert Latham
0–520–03426–0 California $37.50

• Tobias Smollett
TRAVELS THROUGH FRANCE AND ITALY
A classic of travel literature which emphasizes the author's own discomforts and dissatisfactions; on the basis of this

book, Sterne satirized Smollett as "Smelfungus"
Edited by Frank Felsenstein
0–19–281569–5 Oxford pb $7.95

• Laurence Sterne
A SENTIMENTAL JOURNEY, THE JOURNAL TO ELIZA & A POLITICAL ROMANCE
This edition includes several of Sterne's lesser-known works
0–19–281685–3 Oxford pb $3.95

A SENTIMENTAL JOURNEY THROUGH FRANCE AND ITALY
A travel book whose open structure captures the spontaneity and unpredictability of travel
Edited by Graham Petrie
Introduction by A. Alvarez
0–14–043026–1 Penguin pb $3.95

• Jonathan Swift
"The true greatness of Swift as a prose stylist lies in the taut, nervous energy of his sentences; he was a man whose every word was alive with the instincts of attack and defense. Very often the severe conformist values for which he stood are deeply concealed behind the complacent masks of his bland and superficial narrators, but they give edge and bite to his writing . . . Swift was not really a black humorist in our modern sense; most of his jokes were *against* despair, not expressions of despair."—Robert M. Adams, *The Land and Literature of England*
THE OXFORD AUTHORS: JONATHAN SWIFT
Includes *The Battle of the Books, A Tale of a Tub,* excerpts from the *Journal to Stella,* and a large selection of poems, letters, pamphlets, and other writings
Edited by Angus Ross & David Woolley
0–19–254176–5 Oxford $29.95
0–19–281337–4 Oxford pb $11.95

Is that tobacco at the top of the paper, or what? I don't remember I slobbered. Lord, I dreamed of Stella, &c. so confusedly last night, and that we saw Dean Bolton and Sterne go into a shop; and she bid me call them to her, and they proved to be two parsons I know not; and I walked without till she was shifting, and such stuff, mixed with much melancholy and uneasiness, and things not as they should be, and I know not how; and it is now an ugly gloomy morning—
from *Journal to Stella* in
Jonathan Swift
THE OXFORD AUTHORS: JONATHAN SWIFT
Edited by Angus Ross & David Woolley
0–19–281337–4 Oxford pb $11.95

THE PORTABLE SWIFT
Edited by Carl Van Doren
0–14–015037–4 Penguin pb $8.95

GULLIVER'S TRAVELS
Illustrated by Warren Chappell
Introduction by Jacques Barzun
0–19–519978–2 Oxford $19.95

GULLIVER'S TRAVELS
0–14–006507–5 Penguin pb $2.50

JOURNAL TO STELLA
0–86299–111–0 Academy Chicago pb $6.95

SATIRES & PERSONAL WRITINGS
Edited by W.A. Eddy
0–19–254147–1 Oxford $35.00

A TALE OF A TUB & RELATED PIECES
Edited by Angus Ross & David Woolley
0–19–281689–6 Oxford pb $2.95

The Basil Blackwell Edition of Jonathan Swift

The Blackwell edition is a definitive scholarly presentation of Swift's work including much unfamiliar material. The series is edited by Herbert Davis, L. Landa, and others.
THE DRAPIER'S LETTERS & OTHER WORKS, 1724–25
0–631–00270–7 Blackwell $60.00

THE EXAMINER & OTHER PIECES
0–631–00200–6 Blackwell $60.00

HISTORY OF THE FOUR LAST YEARS OF THE QUEEN
0–631–00240–5 Blackwell $60.00

IRISH TRACTS, 1720–1723 & SERMONS
0–631–00260–X Blackwell $60.00

IRISH TRACTS, 1728–1733
0–631–00290–1 Blackwell $60.00

POLITICAL TRACTS, 1711–1713
0–631–00230–8 Blackwell $60.00

POLITICAL TRACTS, 1713–1719
0–631–00250–2 Blackwell $60.00

A PROPOSAL FOR CORRECTING THE ENGLISH TONGUE, POLITE CONVERSATIONS, ETC.
0–631–00210–3 Blackwell $60.00

• Horace Walpole
HORACE WALPOLE'S MISCELLANY 1786–1795
Edited by Lars Troide
0–300–02105–4 Yale $31.50

• Gilbert White
THE NATURAL HISTORY OF SELBORNE
An unsentimental and yet constantly moving description of the rhythms of life in a remote English parish
0–14–043112–8 Penguin pb $6.95

The 19th Century

THE ROMANTIC MOVEMENT

• Thomas Lovell Beddoes
SELECTED POEMS
Beddoes' morbid lyricism—extreme even by the standards of the Romantic movement—was profoundly influenced by Jacobean writers such as Webster and Tourneur
Edited by Judith Higgens
0–85635–192–X Carcanet pb $7.50

- **William Blake**

THE COMPLETE POETRY AND PROSE
The standard scholarly edition of Blake's writings; the typography is clumsy, but the texts are authoritative
Edited by David V. Erdman
0–385–15213–2 Doubleday pb $17.95

THE COMPLETE POEMS
Another up-to-date scholarly edition, in a convenient format
Edited by Alicia Ostriker
0–14–042215–3 Penguin pb $12.95

THE ESSENTIAL BLAKE
A selection emphasizing the lyric aspect of Blake's work
Edited by Stanley Kunitz
0–88001–138–6 Ecco $12.50
0–88001–139–4 Ecco pb $5.00

THE OXFORD AUTHORS: BLAKE
An annotated and modernized selection, including most of Blake's poetry and prose works; the prophetic poems *Milton* and *Jerusalem* are presented in full
Edited by Michael Mason
0–19–282001–X Oxford pb $15.95

AMERICA, A PROPHECY & EUROPE, A PROPHECY
Facsimile editions of two of Blake's major prophetic poems
0–486–24548–9 Dover pb $6.95

THE BOOK OF URIZEN
A facsimile of what is perhaps the most strikingly designed—and accessible—of Blake's shorter prophetic poems
0–87024–065–X Miami pb $5.95

THE MARRIAGE OF HEAVEN AND HELL
A facsimile of Blake's most concise exposition of his symbolic system, including some of his most celebrated aphorisms ("Energy is Eternal Delight")
Introduction and commentary by Geoffrey Keynes
0–19–281167–3 Oxford pb $10.95

SONGS OF INNOCENCE AND EXPERIENCE
Blake's popular early poems are presented here in a facsimile edition
Introduction by Geoffrey Keynes
0–19–281089–8 Oxford pb $10.95

> **To the Accuser who is The God of This World**
>
> Truly, My Satan, thou art but a Dunce,
> And dost not know the Garment from the Man.
> Every Harlot was a Virgin once,
> Nor can'st thou ever change Kate into Nan.
> Tho' thou art Worship'd by the Names Divine
> Of Jesus & Jehovah, thou art still
> The Son of Morn in weary Night's decline,
> The lost Traveller's Dream under the Hill.
>
> William Blake in
> **ENGLISH ROMANTIC VERSE**
> Edited by David Wright
> 0–14–042102–5 Penguin pb $6.95

- **Emily Brontë**

THE COMPLETE POEMS
"Her poems need to be read not merely for their passing felicities of melody . . . but for the profoundly original conceptions that propel them, hidden at times in the most deceptively simple forms. Hers is the poetry of a refusal to mediate between her vision and the world, a refusal to modify or compromise or translate into more accessible terms"—*Village Voice*
Edited by C.W. Hatfield
0–231–01222–5 Columbia $30.00

- **The Brontës**

SELECTED BRONTE POEMS
A well-chosen selection from the works of Emily, Charlotte, Anne, and their brother Branwell
Edited by Edward Chitham & Tom Winnifrith
0–631–14565–6 Blackwell pb $12.95

- **Lord Byron**

THE OXFORD AUTHORS: LORD BYRON
Edited by Jerome McGann
0–19–254184–6 Oxford $45.00
0–19–281349–8 Oxford pb $13.95

DON JUAN
Byron's masterpiece, alternately hilarious, indignant, savage, and tender; yet uniformly readable. "What had been Byron's defect as a serious poet, his lack of reverence for words, was a virtue for the comic poet. Serious poetry requires that the poet treat words as if they were persons, but comic poetry demands that he treat them as things and few, if any, English poets have rivaled Byron's ability to put words through the hoops"—W.H. Auden
Edited by T.G. Steffan & others
0–300–02678–1 Yale $33.00
0–14–042216–1 Penguin pb $8.95

THE ESSENTIAL BYRON
Edited by Paul Muldoon
0–88001–181–5 Ecco pb $6.00

POEMS
A compact selection from the Penguin Poets series
0–14–058507–9 Penguin pb $6.95

POETICAL WORKS
Edited by Frederick Page & John Jump
0–19–281068–5 Oxford pb $13.95

BYRON'S LETTERS AND JOURNALS
This definitive edition clearly establishes Byron as one of the great prose writers of the 19th century
Edited by Leslie A. Marchand

Volume 1: In My Hot Youth: 1798–1810
0–674–08940–5 Harvard $17.50

Volume 2: Famous in My Time: 1810–1812
0–674–08941–3 Harvard $17.50

Volume 3: Alas! The Love of Women: 1813–1814
0–674–08942–1 Harvard $17.50

Volume 4: Wedlock's the Devil: 1814–1815
0–674–08944–8 Harvard $18.50

Volume 5: So Late into the Night: 1816–1817
0–674–08945–6 Harvard $17.50

Volume 6: The Flesh is Frail: 1818–1819
0–674–08946–4 Harvard $17.50

Volume 7: Between Two Worlds: 1820
0–674–08947–2 Harvard $17.50

Volume 8: Born for Opposition: 1821
0–674–08948–0 Harvard $19.50

Volume 9: In the Wind's Eye: 1821–1822
0–674–08949–9 Harvard $17.50

Volume 10: A Heart for Every Fate: 1822–1823
0–674–08952–9 Harvard $17.50

Volume 11: For Freedom's Battle: 1824
0–674–08953–7 Harvard $17.50

Volume 12: The Trouble of An Index
0–674–08954–5 Harvard $17.50

SELECTED LETTERS AND JOURNALS
Edited by Leslie A. Marchand
0–674–53912–5 Harvard pb $7.95

SELECTED PROSE
For many modern readers, Byron's letters and journals are as enthralling as his poetry. For all his Romantic posturing, he was a satirist of admirable sharpness but unfailing good humor
Edited by Peter Gunn
0–14–057007–1 Penguin pb $7.95

- **John Clare**

THE OXFORD AUTHORS: JOHN CLARE
Clare, who enjoyed brief celebrity as a "peasant poet" before succumbing to madness, is increasingly admired not so much for the Romantic coloring of his verse as for the meticulous natural observation at its core. This edition is the best available introduction to the full range of Clare's writing. "Although born in the Age of Enlightenment, Clare speaks in the tones of a more archaic culture. Much of the daily life he knew as a child would not have been out of place in a medieval Book of Hours . . . In the scurryings of Clare's birds and beasts we hear the cadences of the last medieval poet"—*Village Voice*
Edited by Eric Robinson & David Powell
0–19–281395–1 Oxford pb $10.95

THE PARISH
A satirical poem of village life, showing the harsher side of Clare's talents
Edited by Eric Robinson
Notes by David Powell
0–14–043242–6 Penguin pb $6.95

THE SHEPHERD'S CALENDAR
The complete text of a long poem describing the cycles of rural life
Edited by Eric Robinson & Geoffrey Summerfield
0–19–211249–X Oxford $21.00
0–19–281142–8 Oxford pb $9.95

AUTOBIOGRAPHICAL WRITINGS
Includes the famous "Journey Out of Essex," Clare's harrowing account of his escape from the madhouse
Edited by Eric Robinson
0–19–211774–2 Oxford $16.95
0–19–281923–2 Oxford pb $7.95

JOHN CLARE'S BIRDS
Edited by Eric Robinson & Richard Fitter
0–19–212977–5 Oxford $16.50

THE NATURAL HISTORY PROSE WRITINGS OF JOHN CLARE
Edited by Margaret Grainger
0–19–818517–0 Oxford $74.00

TO ORDER BOOKS AS GIFTS, SEE PAGE 1

There is nothing but poetry about the existance of childhood real simple soul moving poetry the laughter and joy of poetry and not its philosophy and there is nothing of poetry about manhood but the reflection and the remembrance of what has been nothing more Thus it is that our play prolonging moon on spring evenings shed a richer lustre than the midday sun that surrounds us now in manhood for its poetical sunshine hath left us it is the same identical sun and we have learned to know that—for in boyhood every new day brought a new sun we knew no better and we was happy in our ignorance.

John Clare in
THE OXFORD AUTHORS: JOHN CLARE
Edited by Eric Robinson & David Powell
0–19–281395–1 Oxford pb $8.95

• Samuel Taylor Coleridge
POEMS
The format is rather crabbed, but this is the fullest readily available edition of Coleridge's verse
Edited by E.H. Coleridge
0–19–254120–X Oxford $35.00
0–19–281051–0 Oxford pb $13.95

THE OXFORD AUTHORS: SAMUEL TAYLOR COLERIDGE
Contains a generous selection of poetry and the complete *Biographia Literaria*
Edited by H.J. Jackson
0–19–254189–7 Oxford $38.00
0–19–281383–8 Oxford pb $11.95

POEMS AND PROSE
Selected by Kathleen Raine
0–14–058501–X Penguin pb $4.95

THE PORTABLE COLERIDGE
Edited by I.A. Richards
0–14–015048–X Penguin pb $7.95

BIOGRAPHIA LITERARIA
A scholarly, well-designed edition of Coleridge's critical masterpiece
0–691–01861–8 Princeton pb $19.95

SELECTED LETTERS OF SAMUEL TAYLOR COLERIDGE
Edited by H.J. Jackson
0–19–282140–7 Oxford pb $11.95

• Thomas De Quincey
CONFESSIONS OF AN ENGLISH OPIUM EATER
De Quincey's narration of his long-term addiction combines florid Romantic style with unexpected moments of psychological realism
Edited by Alethea Hayter
0–14–043061–X Penguin pb $4.95

RECOLLECTIONS OF THE LAKES AND THE LAKE POETS
A fascinating and revealing memoir whose candid portraits of Wordsworth and Coleridge are tinged with resentment
0–14–043056–3 Penguin pb $6.95

• William Hazlitt
LIBER AMORIS: Or, The New Pygmalion
A painful account of Hazlitt's obsessive and unrequited love for a young girl
Edited by Gerald Lahey
0–8147–5000–1 NYU pb $3.00

SELECTED WRITINGS
Hazlitt is perhaps the most underestimated major critic in English
0–14–043050–4 Penguin pb $7.95

• John Keats
COMPLETE POEMS
Edited by John Barnard
0–14–042210–2 Penguin pb $7.95

COMPLETE POEMS
The definitive scholarly edition
Edited by Jack Stillinger
0–674–15431–2 Harvard pb $9.95

THE ESSENTIAL KEATS
Edited by Philip Levine
0–88001–134–3 Ecco $14.50
0–88001–135–1 Ecco pb $6.00

POEMS
Selected by J.E. Morpurgo
0–14–058500–1 Penguin pb $3.95

LETTERS OF JOHN KEATS
"In the history of literature the letters of John Keats are unique . . . Because of the letters it is impossible to think of Keats only as a poet—inevitably we think of him as something more interesting than a poet, we think of him as a man, and as a certain kind of a man, a hero"—Lionel Trilling
Edited by Robert Giddings
0–19–281081–2 Oxford pb $10.95

• John Keats & Percy Bysshe Shelley
COMPLETE POETICAL WORKS
0–394–60466–0 Modern Library pb $13.95

• Charles Lamb
Lamb was long the most beloved of English essayists; he remains the most approachable of the great Romantic prose stylists.

THE PORTABLE CHARLES LAMB
Edited by John M. Brown
0–14–015043–9 Penguin pb $7.95

SELECTED PROSE
Edited by Adam Phillips
0–14–043238–8 Penguin pb $6.95

ELIA AND LAST ESSAYS OF ELIA
0–19–281764–7 Oxford pb $8.95

• Charles Lamb & Mary Lamb
TALES FROM SHAKESPEARE
0–451–52065–3 NAL pb $2.95

• Walter Savage Landor
SELECTED POEMS AND PROSE
Landor is today better known for his "imaginary conversations" in prose than for his poetry, but he is nonetheless an occasionally gifted lyricist
Edited by Keith Hanley
0–85635–272–1 Carcanet $14.50

• Walter Scott
COMPLETE POETICAL WORKS
Scott's poems display the same narrative and lyrical powers as his novels. Includes the long poems *The Lady of the Lake* and *Marmion*
0–395–07493–2 Houghton Mifflin pb $12.50

SELECTED POEMS
Edited by Thomas Crawford
0–19–871059–3 Oxford pb $9.95

• Percy Bysshe Shelley
POETICAL WORKS
This is the standard scholarly edition of a poet whose reputation has shifted dramatically in the 20th century
Edited by Thomas Hutchinson & G.M. Matthews
0–19–281070–7 Oxford pb $12.95

A CHOICE OF SHELLEY'S VERSE
Edited by Stephen Spender
0–571–08790–6 Faber & Faber pb $6.95

POEMS
Selected by Isabel Quigly
0–14–058504–4 Penguin pb $4.95

• Edward J. Trelawny
RECORDS OF SHELLEY, BYRON, AND THE AUTHOR
An anecdotal memoir by a hanger-on of the great Romantics
Edited by David Wright
0–14–043088–1 Penguin pb $5.95

• Dorothy & William Wordsworth
HOME AT GRASMERE
Extracts from Dorothy Wordsworth's journal are juxtaposed with the poems William was writing on the days described, to telling effect
Edited by Clark Colette
0–14–043136–5 Penguin pb $6.95

• Dorothy Wordsworth
THE GRASMERE JOURNAL
In recent years the singularity of Dorothy Wordsworth's talent has generated new interest
Edited by Jonathan Wordsworth
0–8050–0630–3 Henry Holt $24.95

JOURNALS OF DOROTHY WORDSWORTH
Edited by Mary Moorman
0–19–281103–7 Oxford pb $9.95

LETTERS OF DOROTHY WORDSWORTH
Edited by Alan G. Hill
0–19–281318–8 Oxford pb $5.95

"Wordsworth in the Lake District at Cross-Purposes" by Max Beerbohm

- William Wordsworth

THE OXFORD AUTHORS: WILLIAM WORDSWORTH
An abundant selection of poetry, including the complete 1805 text of *The Prelude*
Edited by Stephen Gill
0–19–254175–7 Oxford $29.95
0–19–281333–1 Oxford pb $13.95

POEMS
A splendidly edited and designed edition containing all of Wordsworth's poetry except *The Prelude*
Edited by John Hayden

Volume 1
0–300–02751–6 Yale $57.00

Volume 2
0–300–02752–4 Yale $55.00

THE PRELUDE: A Parallel Text
The 1805 and 1850 texts are printed on facing pages
Edited by J.C. Maxwell
0–300–02753–2 Yale $40.00
0–14–042214–5 Penguin pb $8.95

THE PRELUDE, OR, GROWTH OF A POET'S MIND
The 1805 text, in a revised version of Selincourt's classic edition
Edited with an introduction by Ernest de Selincourt
0–19–281074–X Oxford pb $8.95

THE LETTERS OF WILLIAM WORDSWORTH: A New Selection
Edited by Alan G. Hill
0–19–818529–4 Oxford $34.95
0–19–281372–2 Oxford pb $7.95

SELECTED PROSE WRITINGS
Edited by John O. Hayden
0–14–043292–2 Penguin pb $7.95

GUIDE TO THE LAKES
Edited by Ernest de Selincourt
0–19–281219–X Oxford pb $6.95

- William Wordsworth & Samuel Taylor Coleridge

LYRICAL BALLADS, 1798
The book that launched the Romantic movement in England
Edited by W.J. Owen
0–19–911006–9 Oxford pb $6.95

When we were in the woods beyond Gowbarrow Park we saw a few daffodils close to the water-side. We fancied that the lake had floated the seeds ashore, and that the little colony had so sprung up. But as we went along there were more and yet more; and at last, under the boughs of the trees, we saw that there was a long belt of them along the shore, about the breadth of a country turnpike road. I never saw daffodils so beautiful. They grew among the mossy stones about and about them; some rested their heads upon these stones as on a pillow for weariness; and the rest tossed and reeled and danced, and seemed as if they verily laughed with the wind, that blew upon them over the lake; they looked so gay, ever glancing, ever changing.

Dorothy Wordsworth's Journal, April 15, 1802, in

Dorothy & William Wordsworth
HOME AT GRASMERE
0–14–043136–5 Penguin pb $6.95

LATER 19TH-CENTURY POETRY

- Matthew Arnold

THE OXFORD AUTHORS: MATTHEW ARNOLD
This excellent selection shows the many sides of Arnold's accomplishment, both as poet and critic
Edited by Miriam Allott & Robert H. Sugar
0–19–254187–0 Oxford $38.00
0–19–281376–3 Oxford pb $13.95

POEMS
Arnold's poetic voice, ruminative and alienated, epitomizes the Victorian sensibility
Selected by Kenneth Allott
0–14–058509–5 Penguin pb $4.95

- Robert Bridges

A CHOICE OF BRIDGES' VERSE
Bridges was popular in his lifetime, and uniquely survived the transition from Victorian to modern
Edited by David Cecil
0–571–13845–4 Faber & Faber $14.95
0–571–13844–6 Faber & Faber pb $7.95

- Elizabeth Barrett Browning

SELECTED POEMS
"In all her poetry from 1844 feminist themes are strong . . . She wanted, above all, to 'tell the truth' and to tell it in particular for women"—Margaret Forster
Edited by Margaret Forster
0–8018–3754–5 Johns Hopkins pb $9.95

AURORA LEIGH
A "novel in verse" about the life of a woman writer. "One of the longest poems in the world, and there is not a dead line in it"—Algernon Swinburne
0–915864–85–1 Academy Chicago pb $7.95

SONNETS FROM THE PORTUGUESE & OTHER LOVE POEMS
0–385–01463–5 Doubleday pb $10.95

- Robert Browning

POEMS
Browning's energy and vast intellectual interests make him perhaps the most engaging, occasionally even shocking, of the major Victorian poets. This excellent two-volume edition includes all of his poems except *The Ring and the Book*
Edited by John Pettigrew

Volume 1
0–300–02675–7 Yale $57.00
0–14–042259–5 Penguin pb $14.95

Volume 2
0–300–02676–5 Yale $57.00
0–14–042260–9 Penguin pb $14.95

SELECTED VERSE
Edited by W.E. Williams
0–14–058537–0 Penguin pb $6.95

THE RING AND THE BOOK
A long narrative poem told from a series of different viewpoints, reconstructing the events surrounding a 17th-century Italian murder case
Edited by Richard D. Altick
0–300–02677–3 Yale $45.00
0–14–042294–3 Penguin pb $8.95

- Lewis Carroll

HUMOROUS VERSE OF LEWIS CARROLL
0–486–20654–8 Dover pb $6.50

- G.K. Chesterton

COLLECTED POEMS
0–396–07896–6 Dodd, Mead pb $5.95

- Arthur Hugh Clough

SELECTED POEMS
Edited by Shirley Chew
0–85635–622–0 Carcanet pb $9.50

THE BOTHIE OF TOBER-NA-VUOLICH
The 1848 text of Clough's poem in hexameters about a student outing in Scotland
Edited by Patrick Scott
0–7022–1153–2 Queensland $14.95
0–7022–1163–X Queensland pb $10.95

- Samuel Ferguson

POEMS
Ferguson was an important contributor to the revival of Irish culture and nationalism in the 19th century; his narrative poems are based on Gaelic legend and history
Introduction by Padraic Colum
0–900372–67–2 Irish Book Center pb $3.50

- Edward Fitzgerald

THE RUBAIYAT OF OMAR KHAYYAM
The classic statement of hedonism that influenced a generation; the sardonic music of Fitzgerald's verse remains impressive
Illustrated by Edmund Dulac
0–385–00146–0 Doubleday $10.95

- W.S. Gilbert

THE BAB BALLADS
Masterpieces of humorous verse
Edited by James Ellis
0–674–05800–3 Harvard $27.00
0–674–05801–1 Harvard pb $9.95

- Thomas Hardy

THE COMPLETE POEMS
Edited with an introduction by James Gibson
0–02–069600–0 Macmillan pb $14.95

SELECTED POEMS
Edited by John Crowe Ransom
0–02–070490–9 Macmillan pb $10.95

- Gerard Manley Hopkins

THE OXFORD AUTHORS: GERARD MANLEY HOPKINS
"He wrote religious lyrics that are thoroughly of the nineteenth century and yet are unsurpassed by anything written in the great ages of religion"—Robert Lowell
Edited by Catherine Phillips
0–317–52878–5 Oxford $29.95
0–19–254190–0 Oxford pb $12.95

POEMS AND PROSE OF HOPKINS
Edited by W.H. Gardner
0–14–042015–0 Penguin pb $5.95

- A.E. Housman

COLLECTED POEMS OF A.E. HOUSMAN
Housman's chief work, the nostalgic neoclassical *A Shropshire Lad*, is filled with homoerotic feeling
0–03–085490–3 Henry Holt pb $7.95

☞ **TO ORDER NEW BOOKS NOT YET LISTED, ASK YOUR BOOKSELLER OR CALL 1-800-882-8770**

- Rudyard Kipling

Kipling's verse is more varied, subtle, and politically sophisticated than is generally imagined.

A CHOICE OF KIPLING'S VERSE
Edited by T.S. Eliot
0–571–114703–8 Faber & Faber pb $10.95

COMPLETE VERSE
0–385–26088–1 Doubleday $24.95
0–385–26089–X Doubleday pb $12.95

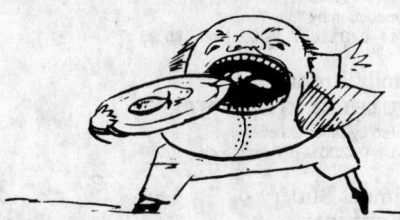

"There was an old man of the South, who had an immoderate mouth..."—Edward Lear

---

Edward Lear
THE COMPLETE NONSENSE OF EDWARD LEAR
Includes "The Pobble Who Has No Toes," "The Dong with the Luminous Nose," and Lear's other great comic creations
0–486–20167–8 Dover pb $5.95

EDWARD LEAR'S NONSENSE OMNIBUS
Introduction by E. Strachey
0–14–008776–1 Penguin pb $6.95

- George Meredith
SELECTED POEMS
Contains selections from the moving sonnet sequence *Modern Love,* which tells the story of a disintegrating marriage
Edited by Keith Hanley
0–85635–416–3 Carcanet pb $9.50

- Alice C. Meynell
POEMS
Edited by Frederick Page
0–88355–704–5 Hyperion $18.50

- Christina Rossetti
A CHOICE OF CHRISTINA ROSSETTI'S VERSE
Rossetti's odd metrical patterns and hidden refinement have recently stimulated new interest in her work
Edited by Elizabeth Jennings
0–571–09018–4 Faber & Faber pb $6.95

GOBLIN MARKET
Superficially a children's fairy story, *Goblin Market* can be read as a psychologically astute allegory of female sexuality
Illustrated by George Gershinowitz
0–87923–488–1 Godine pb $2.98

SELECTED POEMS
Edited with an introduction by C.H. Sisson
0–85635–533–X Carcanet pb $7.50

- Robert Louis Stevenson
A CHILD'S GARDEN OF VERSES
An attractive edition of poetry that has retained undiminished appeal for the young
Illustrated by Tasha Tudor
0–528–82401–5 Macmillan $12.95
0–528–80073–6 Macmillan pb $8.00

- Charles Algernon Swinburne
SELECTED POEMS
The great master of English metrics and a lyricist of exceptional morbidity
Edited by L.M. Findley
0–85635–137–7 Carcanet $12.50
0–85635–728–6 Carcanet pb $8.50

- Alfred Tennyson
THE POEMS OF TENNYSON
A new 3-volume edition that has been hailed for its scholarship
Edited by Christopher Ricks
0–520–06012–1 California $225.00

POEMS
Selected by W.E. Williams
0–14–058502–8 Penguin pb $3.95

POETICAL WORKS
Introduction by Robert Stange
0–395–18014–7 Houghton Mifflin $24.50

TENNYSON: A Selected Edition
Edited by Christopher Ricks
0–520–06588–3 California $48.50

SELECTED POEMS
Edited by Michael Millgate
0–19–911056–5 Oxford pb $7.95

IDYLLS OF THE KING
The perennially popular poetic retelling of the Arthurian legends
Edited by J.M. Gray
0–300–03059–2 Yale $32.50
0–14–042253–6 Penguin pb $6.95

IDYLLS OF THE KING & A SELECTION OF POEMS
Foreword by G. Baker
0–451–52258–3 NAL pb $3.95

IN MEMORIAM
Tennyson's masterful account of the cycles of grief and spiritual doubt occasioned by the death of a close friend
Edited by Robert H. Ross
0–393–09379–4 Norton pb $9.95

- Francis Thompson
THE HOUND OF HEAVEN
A classic of fervent although reluctant Catholic spirituality
0–8192–1205–9 Morehouse-Barlow pb $1.50

Anthologies

- W.H. Auden & Norman Holmes Pearson, editors
ROMANTIC POETS: Blake to Poe
An outstanding collection, the only part of the multivolume *Portable Poets of the English Language* currently in print
0–14–015–052–8 Penguin pb $8.95

- Harold Bloom & Lionel Trilling, editors
ROMANTIC POETRY AND PROSE
0–19–501615–7 Oxford pb $19.95

- George MacBeth, editor
VICTORIAN VERSE
An idiosyncratic and carefully conceived anthology that sheds light on a great many obscure figures and on relatively obscure poems by major poets. "It is the great and crucial merit of this volume that it changes one's attitude to contemporary poetry, as well as to that of the period it sets out to cover"—Edward Lucie-Smith
0–14–042110–6 Penguin pb $6.95

Christopher Ricks, editor
THE NEW OXFORD BOOK OF VICTORIAN VERSE
"Succeeds triumphantly . . . Almost everywhere you turn . . . you are likely to be struck by the scope of Victorian poetry, by its humour, musicality and most of all its frank appeal to the feelings and emotional power"—John Gross, *The Observer*
0–19–214154–6 Oxford $30.00

- David Wright, editor
ENGLISH ROMANTIC POETRY
Traces the movement from its 18th-century roots (Thomson, Collins, Cowper) through its major figures, finding room also for such less familiar poets as Elliot, Darley, and Mangan
0–14–042102–5 Penguin pb $6.95

19TH-CENTURY DRAMA

By comparison with the Elizabethan and Restoration periods, the theater of Victoria's age has left us a short roster of plays that are still viable. Aside from the comedies of Wilde and the early plays of Shaw (which will be found under Modern English and Irish Drama) the century's chief theatrical legacy was the ever popular work of Gilbert and Sullivan.

- W.S. Gilbert
THE COMPLETE PLAYS OF GILBERT AND SULLIVAN
0–393–00828–2 Norton pb $12.95

PLAYS
Edited by George Rowell
0–521–23589–8 Cambridge $39.50
0–521–28056–7 Cambridge pb $13.95

- Henry Arthur Jones
PLAYS
Jones helped to rescue the English theater of his day from trivial melodrama. This volume includes *The Silver King, The Case of Rebellious Susan,* and *The Liars*
Edited by Russell Jackson
0–521–29936–5 Cambridge pb $15.95

- Arthur Wing Pinero
Pinero was a master of the craft of playwriting who best represents 19th-century English dramatic taste.

DANDY DICK
A highly amusing farce that has been revived with great success
0–435–20711–3 Heinemann pb $6.00

PLAYS
Includes *The Schoolmistress, The Second Mrs. Tanqueray, Trelawny of the Wells,* and *The Thunderbolt*
0–521–28440–6 Cambridge pb $17.95

Anthologies

- Gerald B. Kauvar & Gerald C. Sorensen, editors
NINETEENTH CENTURY ENGLISH VERSE DRAMA
0–8386–7631–6 Fairleigh Dickinson $28.50

- George Rowell, editor
NINETEENTH CENTURY PLAYS
0–19–281104–5 Oxford pb $10.95

19TH-CENTURY FICTION

- Jane Austen
THE OXFORD ILLUSTRATED JANE AUSTEN
All of Austen's major and minor novels as a 6-volume set, with 19th-century illustrations and R.W. Chapman's notes
Edited by R.W. Chapman
0–19–254707–0 Oxford $60.00

THE PENGUIN COMPLETE NOVELS OF JANE AUSTEN
0–14–009002–9 Penguin pb $11.95

EMMA
"In *Emma* the heroine is made to stand at bay to our adverse judgment through virtually the whole novel, but we are never permitted to close in for the kill—some unnamed quality in the girl, some trait of vivacity or will, erects itself into a moral principle, or at least a vital principle, and frustrates our moral blood-lust"—Lionel Trilling
Edited by Ronald Blythe
0–14–043010–5 Penguin pb $2.50

LADY SUSAN, THE WATSONS & SANDITON
Three fragmentary novels unpublished in Austen's lifetime but fascinating to enthusiasts of her work
Edited by Margaret Drabble
0–14–043102–0 Penguin pb $4.50

MANSFIELD PARK
Fanny Price is Austen's most difficult protagonist, and *Mansfield Park* her darkest—but to some readers her finest—novel
Edited by Tony Tanner
0–14–043016–4 Penguin pb $3.50

NORTHANGER ABBEY
A genial parody of Gothic melodrama
Edited by Anne Ehrenpries
0–14–043074–1 Penguin pb $2.50

PERSUASION
In Austen's last completed novel she explores emotion (including problems of conscience) without her characteristic skeptical edge
Edited by D.W. Harding
0–14–043005–9 Penguin pb $2.95

PRIDE AND PREJUDICE
In Elizabeth Bennet and Fitzwilliam Darcy, Austen draws a masterful portrait of love as the play of intelligence and good sense
Edited by Tony Tanner
0–14–043072–5 Penguin pb $1.95

SENSE AND SENSIBILITY
In this, her first mature novel, Austen contrasts the personalities of the sisters Elinor and Marianne Dashwood
Edited by Tony Tanner
0–14–043047–4 Penguin pb $2.95

Jane Austen & Charlotte Brontë
THE JUVENILIA OF JANE AUSTEN AND CHARLOTTE BRONTE
"These juvenilia are, of course, sometimes crude and sometimes childish. But they also serve to demonstrate their authors' originality and freedom of spirit, their delight in the very process of creation, their changing attitudes towards character and style . . . Both sets of juvenilia provide us with an extraordinary opportunity to watch the growth and coalescence of the creative consciousness"—Frances Beer
Edited by Frances Beer
0–14–043267–1 Penguin pb $5.95

- George Borrow
THE ROMANY RYE
A first-hand account of English Gypsy life
0–19–281406–0 Oxford pb $8.95

- Mary Elizabeth Braddon
LADY AUDLEY'S SECRET
An ancestor of the modern detective novel, and still fascinating; an evil adventuress, a spectacular fire, murder, and a grisly denouement
Edited by David Skilton
0–19–281741–8 Oxford pb $6.95

- Anne Brontë
AGNES GREY
A modest portrait of the life of a 19th-century governess
Introduction by Anne Smith
0–14–043210–8 Penguin pb $4.95

THE TENANT OF WILDFELL HALL
A Byronic hero and a passionate denunciation of the ravages of drink
Edited by G.D. Hargreaves
Introduction by Winifred Gerin
0–14–043137–3 Penguin pb $4.95

- Charlotte Brontë
JANE EYRE
"One and all are full of praise of this great, unknown genius, which suddenly appeared amongst us. Conjecture as to the authorship ran about like wild-fire. People in London . . . were astonished and delighted to find that a fresh sensation, a new pleasure, was in reserve for them in the uprising of an author, capable of depicting with accurate and Titanic power the strong, self-reliant, racy, and individual characters which were not, after all, extinct species, but lingered still in existence in the North"—Elizabeth Gaskell
Edited by Q.D. Leavis
0–14–043011–3 Penguin pb $2.25

THE PROFESSOR
A novel whose materials were later reworked into the more ambitious *Villette*
0–14–043311–2 Penguin pb $4.95

SHIRLEY
A novel of industrialism and labor strife in the Yorkshire mills; Brontë's realism will surprise some readers of *Jane Eyre*
Edited by Andrew & Judith Hook
0–14–043095–4 Penguin pb $4.95

VILLETTE
By many accounts Charlotte Brontë's best novel; a low-keyed and remarkably subtle study of frustrated passion in a Belgian boarding school
Introduction by Tony Tanner
0–14–043118–7 Penguin pb $5.95

- Emily Brontë
WUTHERING HEIGHTS
Edited by David Daiches
0–14–043001–6 Penguin pb $2.50

- Samuel Butler
EREWHON
A curious satire on Darwinism, industrialism, and other matters, set in an alternate world
0–14–043057–1 Penguin pb $3.95

THE WAY OF ALL FLESH
Perhaps the most harrowing account of father-fixation and Victorian religiosity ever recorded
Edited by James Cochrane
Introduction by Richard Hoggart
0–14–043012–1 Penguin pb $5.95

- Wilkie Collins
ARMADALE
Collins' most memorable villainess, Lydia Gwilt, dominates this baroque melodrama involving a pair of long-separated twins and culminating in an experimental madhouse
0–486–23429–0 Dover pb $9.95

BLIND LOVE
A neglected novel from Collins' late period
0–486–25189–6 Dover pb $6.95

THE DEAD SECRET
An early novel of suspense involving a harrowing search for a lost document
0–486–23775–3 Dover pb $6.95

THE HAUNTED HOTEL
A late novella memorable for one of Collins' edgiest adventuresses
0–486–24333–8 Dover pb $3.00

HIDE AND SEEK
Introduction by Norman Donaldson
0–486–24211–0 Dover pb $5.95

LITTLE NOVELS
0–486–23506–8 Dover pb $5.95

THE MOONSTONE
A tale of theft, drugs, an apparently cursed Indian gem, enriched by Collins' knack for Dickensian caricature
0–14–043014–8 Penguin pb $3.95

NO NAME
Often considered Collins' best novel, a protofeminist tale of prim Victorian maidens cast on the mercy of cruel and opportunistic strangers
Edited by Virginia Blain
0–19–281648–9 Oxford pb $7.95

➤ **FOR OVERSEAS ORDERING INFORMATION, SEE PAGE 1**

A ROGUE'S LIFE
A comic, picaresque short novel
0–86299–183–8 Academy Chicago pb $4.95

TALES OF TERROR AND THE SUPERNATURAL
Edited with an introduction by Herbert Van Thal
0–486–20307–7 Dover pb $6.50

THE WOMAN IN WHITE
Collins' beautifully engineered plot touches on madness, bigamy, and stolen inheritances
Edited by Julian Symons
0–14–043096–2 Penguin pb $3.95

● Marie Corelli

A ROMANCE OF TWO WORLDS
Corelli was a widely popular novelist of the occult whose work has gained a recent underground following (Henry Miller was a fan)
0–910122–03–2 Amherst pb $5.95

● Charles Dickens

"Chesterton asserted that time would show that Dickens was not merely one of the Victorians, but incomparably the greatest English writer of his time; and Shaw coupled his name with that of Shakespeare. It is the conviction of the present writer that both these judgments were justified. Dickens—though he cannot of course pretend to the rank where Shakespeare has few companions—was nevertheless the greatest dramatic writer that the English had had since Shakespeare, and he created the largest and most varied world"—Edmund Wilson in *The Wound and the Bow*

AMERICAN NOTES FOR GENERAL CIRCULATION
Dickens' disgruntled, and often very amusing, account of his first American tour
Edited by John Whitley
0–14–043077–6 Penguin pb $5.95

BARNABY RUDGE
The anti-Catholic Gordon riots of 1780 provide the turbulent backdrop for one of Dickens' most neglected novels
0–14–043090–3 Penguin pb $5.95

BLEAK HOUSE
One of Dickens' greatest works, centered on the interminable lawsuit of *Jarndyce* v. *Jarndyce*
Introduction by J. Hillis Miller
0–14–043063–6 Penguin pb $4.95

THE CHRISTMAS BOOKS
Edited by Michael Slater

Volume 1
Includes *A Christmas Carol* and *The Chimes*
0–14–043068–7 Penguin pb $4.95

Volume 2
Includes *The Cricket on the Hearth, The Battle of Life,* and *The Haunted Man and the Ghost's Bargain*
0–14–043069–5 Penguin pb $3.95

A CHRISTMAS CAROL
0–14–007120–2 Penguin pb $3.95

DAVID COPPERFIELD
Dickens' favorite among his books, full of echoes of his own traumatic childhood and containing many of his best-known creations: Barkis, Micawber, Peggotty, Steerforth, Uriah Heep
Edited by Trevor Blount
0–14–043008–3 Penguin pb $3.95

> Fog everywhere. Fog up the river, where it flows among green aits and meadows; fog down the river, where it rolls defiled among the tiers of shipping and the waterside pollutions of a great (and dirty) city. Fog on the Essex marshes, fog on the Kentish heights. Fog creeping into the cabooses of collier-brigs; fog lying out on the yards and hovering in the rigging of great ships; fog drooping on the gunwales of barges and small boats. Fog in the eyes and throats of ancient Greenwich pensioners, wheezing by the firesides of their wards; fog in the stem and bowl of the afternoon pipe of the wrathful skipper, down in his close cabin; fog cruelly pinching the toes and fingers of his shivering little 'prentice boy on deck. Chance people on the bridges peeping over the parapets into a nether sky of fog, with fog all round them, as if they were up in a balloon and hanging in the misty clouds.
>
> Charles Dickens
> **BLEAK HOUSE**
> 0–14–043063–6 Penguin pb $4.95

A DECEMBER VISION & OTHER THOUGHTFUL WRITINGS
Edited by Neil Phillip & Victor Nueburg
0–8264–0392–1 Continuum $18.95

DOMBEY AND SON
A somber dramatization of the corrupting influence of money, and—in Florence and Paul Dombey—the transfiguring power of innocence
0–14–043048–2 Penguin pb $5.95

GREAT EXPECTATIONS
This late masterpiece is, perhaps, Dickens' most penetrating treatment of adolescence
Edited by Angus Calder
0–14–043003–2 Penguin pb $2.95

HARD TIMES
An unusually spare novel of protest against the harshness of utilitarianism and industrialism, as espoused by the humorless schoolmaster Gradgrind and the fraudulent capitalist Bounderby
Edited by David Craig
0–14–043042–3 Penguin pb $2.25

LITTLE DORRIT
"The whole book is much gloomier than *Bleak House,* where the fog is external to the characters and represents something removable, the obfuscatory elements of the past. The murk of *Little Dorrit* permeates the souls of the people . . . The fable is here presented from the point of view of imprisoning states of mind as much as from that of oppressive institutions"—Edmund Wilson
Edited by John Holloway
0–14–043025–3 Penguin pb $5.95

MARTIN CHUZZLEWIT
Dickens' "American" novel, today one of his less popular books but nonetheless containing such unforgettable figures as Mr. Pecksniff, Sairey Gamp, and Poll Sweedlepipes
Edited by P.N. Furbank
0–14–043031–8 Penguin pb $6.95

THE MYSTERY OF EDWIN DROOD
Dickens' last novel, a melodrama of murder and opium addiction that even in

its tantalizingly unfinished state ranks as one of his most original novels
Introduction by Angus Wilson
0–14–009258–7 Penguin pb $3.95

NICHOLAS NICKLEBY
A grim exposé of maltreated schoolboys under the tutelage of the brutal Wackford Squeers and a wonderful evocation of Vincent Crummles' traveling players are the highlights of this homage to the picaresque novel
Edited by Michael Slater
0–14–043113–6 Penguin pb $4.95

THE OLD CURIOSITY SHOP
The epitome of Dickens' sentimental strain, featuring the tragic Little Nell and a host of characters, including Mr. Quilp, Dick Swiveller, and Miss Wackles
Edited by Angus Easson
0–14–043075–X Penguin pb $5.95

OLIVER TWIST
The novel in which Dickens broke decisively with the good cheer of *The Pickwick Papers,* producing a violent melodrama of child abuse and the criminal underworld
Edited by Angus Wilson
0–14–043017–2 Penguin pb $3.50

OUR MUTUAL FRIEND
Dickens' last completed work is perhaps his darkest vision of urban decay and corruption, centering on a garbage heap in which various characters scavenge for hidden treasure
Edited by Stephen Gill
0–14–043060–1 Penguin pb $4.95

THE PICKWICK PAPERS
Dickens' first great comic triumph immediately became part of English literary mythology
Edited by Robert L. Patten
0–14–043078–4 Penguin pb $4.95

SELECTED SHORT FICTION
A gathering of supernatural tales, impressionistic sketches, and dramatic monologues
Edited by Deborah Thomas
0–14–043103–9 Penguin pb $4.95

SIKES AND NANCY & OTHER PUBLIC READINGS
These are Dickens' adaptations of episodes from his novels, which he read to fantastic acclaim in his latter years; the nervous exhaustion induced by these readings probably shortened his life
Edited by Philip Collins
0–19–281617–9 Oxford pb $6.95

A TALE OF TWO CITIES
The famous historical novel of the French Revolution, inspired by Carlyle
Edited by George Woodcock
0–14–043054–7 Penguin pb $2.25

THE NEW OXFORD ILLUSTRATED DICKENS
A moderately priced presentation of Dickens' work as a 21-volume set, with evocative period illustrations by Phiz, George Cruikshank, and others
0–19–254522–1 Oxford $185.00

Volume 1: The Old Curiosity Shop
0–19–254506–X Oxford $9.95

Volume 2: Our Mutual Friend
0–19–254510–8 Oxford $9.95

Volume 3: The Personal History of David Copperfield
0–19–254502–7 Oxford $9.95

Volume 4: The Posthumous Papers of the Pickwick Club
0–19–254501–9 Oxford $9.95

Volume 5: Sketches By Boz: Illustrative of Every-Day Life and Every-Day People
0–19–254518–3 Oxford $9.95

Volume 6: A Tale of Two Cities
0–19–254504–3 Oxford $9.95

Volume 7: The Uncommercial Traveller & Reprinted Pieces
0–19–254521–3 Oxford $9.95

Volume 8: The Adventures of Oliver Twist
Introduction by Humphry House
0–19–254505–1 Oxford $9.95

Volume 9: American Notes & Pictures from Italy
Introduction by Sacheverell Sitwell
0–19–254519–1 Oxford $9.95

Volume 10: Barnaby Rudge: A Tale of the Riots of 'Eighty
0–19–254513–2 Oxford $9.95

Volume 11: Bleak House
Introduction by Osbert Sitwell
0–19–254503–5 Oxford $9.95

Volume 12: Christmas Books
Introduction by Eleanor Farjeon
0–19–254514–0 Oxford $9.95

Volume 13: Christmas Stories
0–19–254517–5 Oxford $9.95

Volume 14: Dealings with the Firm of Dombey and Son, Wholesale, Retail, and for Exploration
Introduction by H.W. Garrod
0–19–254507–8 Oxford $9.95

Volume 15: Great Expectations
0–19–254511–6 Oxford $9.95

Volume 16: Hard Times for These Times
Introduction by Dingle Foot
0–19–254515–9 Oxford $9.95

Volume 17: The Life and Adventures of Martin Chuzzlewit
Introduction by Geoffrey Russell
0–19–254509–4 Oxford $9.95

Volume 18: The Life and Adventures of Nicholas Nickleby
Introduction by Dame Sybil Thorndike
0–19–254508–6 Oxford $9.95

Volume 19: Little Dorrit
0–19–254512–4 Oxford $8.95

Volume 20: Master Humphrey's Clock & A Child's History of England
0–19–254520–5 Oxford $9.95

Volume 21: The Mystery of Edwin Drood
Introduction by S.C. Roberts
0–19–254516–7 Oxford $9.95

● Benjamin Disraeli
CONINGSBY
The Tory creed forms the basis for one of the most memorable Victorian political novels
Edited by Thom Braun
0–14–043192–6 Penguin pb $5.95

SYBIL
A fresco of social conditions in the 1840s, with a memorable evocation of the Chartist movement
Introduction by R.A. Butler
0–14–043134–9 Penguin pb $6.95

● George Douglas
THE HOUSE WITH GREEN SHUTTERS
A tale of greed and ambition set in a Scottish village
Edited by Dorothy Parker
0–14–043218–3 Penguin pb $5.95

● George Du Maurier
TRILBY
The famous tale of the poor artist's model who becomes a singing star under the influence of the sinister Svengali
0–460–01863–9 Biblio pb $3.95

● Maria Edgeworth
THE ABSENTEE
This comic novel about absentee landownership in Ireland was first published in 1812
Edited with an introduction by W.J. McCormack & Kim Walker
0–19–281682–9 Oxford pb $8.95

BELINDA
Introduction by Eva Figes
0–86358–074–2 RC&H pb $7.95

CASTLE RACKRENT
A rich and boisterous anecdotal picture of the decayed Irish gentry of the 18th century; a pioneering historical novel, first published in 1800
Edited by George Watson
0–19–281539–3 Oxford pb $3.95

HELEN
Edgeworth's last novel, an exploration of the moral consequences of untruthfulness
Introduction by Dale Spender
0–86358–104–8 RC&H pb $8.95

PATRONAGE
0–86358–106–4 RC&H pb $10.95

● George Eliot
ADAM BEDE
An unflinching depiction of English village life and of the consequences of seduction
Introduction by Stephen Gill
0–14–043121–7 Penguin pb $4.95

DANIEL DERONDA
One of Eliot's masterpieces; Gwendolen Harleth is perhaps her most intriguing heroine
Edited with an introduction by Barbara Hardy
0–14–043020–2 Penguin pb $4.95

FELIX HOLT, THE RADICAL
George Eliot's most political novel; the crowd scenes are masterful
Edited by Peter Coveney
0–14–043084–9 Penguin pb $6.95

THE LIFTED VEIL
0–14–016116–3 Penguin pb $5.95

MIDDLEMARCH
One of the greatest Victorian novels; a magisterial and multilayered recreation of English life
Edited with an introduction by W.J. Harvey
0–14–043002–4 Penguin pb $4.95

THE MILL ON THE FLOSS
An almost nightmarish evocation of a spirited woman's childhood and its destructive consequences
Edited by Gordon S. Haight
0–19–281567–9 Oxford pb $3.95

ROMOLA
Although somewhat mannered, this novel convincingly recreates Renaissance Florence
Edited by Andrew Sanders
0–14–043139–X Penguin pb $5.95

SCENES FROM CLERICAL LIFE
The unpromising title belies three engaging, realistic tales dealing with such themes as alcoholism and romance among the aged
Edited by David Lodge
0–14–043087–3 Penguin pb $4.95

SILAS MARNER
Eliot's most familiar tale, and a high point of 19th-century pastoral fiction
0–14–043030–X Penguin pb $2.95

● John Galt
ANNALS OF THE PARISH
A satirical novel contrasting the trivialities of Scottish parish life with great events in the outside world
Introduction by James Kinsley
0–19–281735–3 Oxford pb $3.95

THE ENTAIL
Edited by Ian A. Gordon
0–19–281694–2 Oxford pb $7.95

THE PROVOST
Edited by Ian A. Gordon
0–19–281629–2 Oxford pb $5.95

● Elizabeth Gaskell
COUSIN PHILLIS & OTHER TALES
Edited by Angus Easson
0–19–281554–7 Oxford pb $3.95

CRANFORD
A charming tale of English village life
Edited by Elizabeth Watson
0–19–281531–8 Oxford pb $2.95

THE MANCHESTER MARRIAGE
0–86299–247–8 Academy Chicago pb $6.95

MARY BARTON
A vivid picture of life in working-class Victorian Manchester
Edited by Stephen Gill
0–14–043053–9 Penguin pb $5.95

MY LADY LUDLOW
0–86299–248–6 Academy Chicago pb $5.95

NORTH AND SOUTH
The story revolves around a contrast between England's bucolic South and the grim industrial conditions of the North
Edited by Dorothy Collin
Introduction by Martin Dodsworth
0–14–043055–5 Penguin pb $5.95

RUTH
Edited by Alan Shelston
0–19–281669–1 Oxford pb $4.95

SYLVIA'S LOVERS
Edited by Andrew Sanders
0–19–281571–7 Oxford pb $7.95

WIVES AND DAUGHTERS
Edited by Frank G. Smith
Introduction by Laurence Lerner
0–14–043046–6 Penguin pb $5.95

● George Gissing
After a long period of neglect, George Gissing's powerfully realistic, relentlessly pessimistic novels have been rediscovered.
EVE'S RANSOM
0–486–24016–9 Dover pb $3.95

IN THE YEAR OF JUBILEE
A satirical look at the middle classes
0–701–20734–5 Dover pb $8.95

NEW GRUB STREET
A brilliant and complex novel about
literary failure
Edited by Bernard Bergonzi
0–14–043032–6 Penguin pb $6.95

THE ODD WOMEN
A unusually subtle view of London society
that has stirred much recent interest among
feminist critics
Introduction by Elaine Showalter
0–452–00748–8 NAL pb $4.95

THE PRIVATE PAPERS OF HENRY RYECROFT
0–19–281749–3 Oxford pb $6.95

SLEEPING FIRES
0–8032–7011–9 Nebraska pb $4.95

H. Rider Haggard

AYESHA: The Return of She
The immortal She-Who-Must-Be-
Obeyed surfaces again in Tibet
0–486–23649–8 Dover pb $4.95

KING SOLOMON'S MINES
The archetypal British imperialist
adventure story, and perhaps Haggard's
most entertaining book
0–14–035014–4 Penguin pb $2.25

SHE, KING SOLOMON'S MINES & ALLAN QUATERMAIN
A convenient volume including the
mesmerizing *She,* a story of
reincarnation and immortality that was
one of Carl Jung's favorite books
0–486–20643–2 Dover pb $7.95

• **Thomas Hardy**

A CHANGED MAN
A collection of twelve tales of fate
originally published in magazines. Hardy
called them "minor novels"
0–86299–149–8 Academy Chicago pb $6.95

DESPERATE REMEDIES
A strongly plotted suspense novel,
enriched by Hardy's eye for the detail of
English rural life
Introduction by J.C. Beatty
0–312–19494–3 St. Martin's pb $3.95

THE DISTRACTED PREACHER & OTHER TALES
0–14–043124–1 Penguin pb $5.95

FAR FROM THE MADDING CROWD
Perhaps Hardy's most affecting and
explosive mixture of tragedy and comedy;
the troubled love affair of the hero, Gabriel
Oak, is the focus for a melodrama of
seduction and desertion, set against the
eternal cycles of the country year
Edited by Ronald Blythe
0–14–043126–8 Penguin pb $2.95

THE HAND OF ETHELBERTA
The tale of an opportunistic yet ultimately
loyal adventuress, who begins humbly and
ends as the wife of a rakish aristocrat
0–312–35736–2 St. Martin's pb $2.95

JUDE THE OBSCURE
Hardy's bleakest and greatest novel of fate
0–14–043131–4 Penguin pb $2.95

"Mr. Thomas Hardy Composing a Lyric" by Max Beerbohm

A LAODICEAN
A minor novel about the dying aristocracy,
giving way to the onslaught of a new
generation of self-made men
Introduction by Barbara Hardy
0–312–46936–5 St. Martin's pb $3.95

LIFE'S LITTLE IRONIES
A collection of short stories, some grimly
fatalistic, others broadly comic
0–86299–069–6 Academy Chicago pb $4.95

THE MAYOR OF CASTERBRIDGE
One of Hardy's masterpieces, and perhaps
his most purely tragic novel
0–14–043125–X Penguin pb $2.95

A PAIR OF BLUE EYES
A love triangle set in Cornwall, in which
the heroine's innocence ironically leads to
tragedy
Edited by Roger Ebbatson
0–14–043266–3 Penguin pb $4.95

THE RETURN OF THE NATIVE
Egdon Heath is one of Hardy's most
striking pieces of landscape painting,
providing a brooding backdrop for the
story of Clym Yeobright and Eustacia Vye
0–14–043122–5 Penguin pb $2.95

TESS OF THE D'URBERVILLES
A harrowing novel of seduction and
abandonment. Tess is Hardy's most
memorable heroine
Edited by A. Alvarez & David Skilton
0–14–043135–7 Penguin pb $2.95

THE TRUMPET-MAJOR
A suspenseful but ultimately happy love
story, set during the reign of George III,
and a welcome relief from Hardy's habitual
fatalism
0–14–043142–X Penguin pb $4.95

UNDER THE GREENWOOD TREE
The first of Hardy's Wessex novels is a
largely comic peasant love story
0–14–043123–3 Penguin pb $3.95

THE WELL-BELOVED
An artist pursues his ideal woman through
three generations
Introduction by J. Hillis Miller
0–312–86172–9 St. Martin's pb $3.95

WESSEX TALES
Six stories, including "The Three
Strangers," "The Withered Arm,"
"Interlopers at the Knap," "Fellow
Townsmen," and "The Distracted
Preacher"
Introduction by F.B. Pinion
0–312–86276–8 St. Martin's pb $3.95

THE WOODLANDERS
A tale of destructive passions, set in
Dorsetshire
Edited by Dale Kramer
0–19–281600–4 Oxford pb $4.95

• **James Hogg**

THE PRIVATE MEMOIRS AND CONFESSIONS OF A JUSTIFIED SINNER
First published in 1824, this morbidly
exact portrait of a self-righteous religious
fanatic and his diabolical alter ego is
surprisingly modern in its depiction of
alienation and split personality
Edited by John Wain
0–14–043198–5 Penguin pb $6.95

• **Anthony Hope**

THE PRISONER OF ZENDA
The famous romance of look-alike cousins
who switch identities in the intrigue-ridden
kingdom of Ruritania
0–14–035032–2 Penguin pb $2.25

RUPERT OF HENTZAU
A sequel to *The Prisoner of Zenda*
0–14–035033–0 Penguin pb $2.25

• **W.H. Hudson**

GREEN MANSIONS
The tragic romance of Rima the bird-girl
in the jungles of Venezuela
Introduction by N.R. Teitel
0–486–25993–5 Dover pb $7.95

• **Thomas Hughes**

TOM BROWN'S SCHOOLDAYS
The classic English public school story
0–14–035022–5 Penguin pb $2.25

• **Richard Jefferies**

AFTER LONDON: Wild England
A prophetic novel of industrial decay and
rural resurgence
Introduction by John Fowles
0–19–281266–1 Oxford pb $3.95

• **Jerome K. Jerome**

THREE MEN IN A BOAT
A popular comic novel about a trio of
young men idling on the Thames
0–14–001213–3 Penguin pb $4.95

THREE MEN ON THE BUMMEL
A sequel to *Three Men in a Boat*
0–14–006392–7 Penguin pb $3.95

• **Charles Kingsley**

ALTON LOCKE, TAILOR AND POET: An Autobiography
A fictional exposition of Kingsley's
doctrine of Christian socialism
Edited by Elizabeth A. Cripps
0–19–281633–0 Oxford pb $6.95

THE WATER BABIES
A favorite children's book of the Victorian era
0–14–035035–7 Penguin pb $2.25

> The dense wet heat that hung over the face of land, like a blanket, prevented all hope of sleep in the first instance. The cicalas helped the heat, and the yelling jackals the cicalas. It was impossible to sit still in the dark, empty, echoing house and watch the punkah beat the dead air. So, at ten o'clock of the night, I set my walking-stick on end in the middle of the garden, and waited to see how it would fall. It pointed directly down the moonlit road that leads to the City of Dreadful Night.
>
> from "The City of Dreadful Night" in
> Rudyard Kipling
> **LIFE'S HANDICAP**
> Edited with an introduction by A.O.J. Cockshut
> 0–19–281671–3 Oxford pb $5.95

• **Rudyard Kipling**
CAPTAINS COURAGEOUS
0–451–51751–2 NAL pb $1.95

THE DAY'S WORK
Twelve stories from the 1890s, written at the height of Kipling's powers and demonstrating the range of his subject matter. Includes "The Bridge-Builders," "The Tomb of His Ancestors," ".007," "The Brushwood Boy," and others
Edited by Thomas Pinney
0–19–281714–0 Oxford pb $5.95

THE JUNGLE BOOKS
The saga of the lost boy Mowgli and his animal brothers, and other tales
Edited with an introduction by P.N. Furbank
0–14–043282–5 Penguin pb $2.95

JUST SO STORIES
Animal fables that retain their magic
Edited with an introduction by Peter Levi
0–14–043302–3 Penguin pb $2.95

KIM
Espionage in northern India provides the pretext for Kipling's most richly detailed Asian panorama
Edited with an introduction by Edward Said
0–14–035076–4 Penguin pb $2.25

LIFE'S HANDICAP
Contains some of Kipling's best stories of India, including "The Incarnation of Krishna Mulvaney," "The Courting of Dinah Shadd," "Without Benefit of Clergy," "The Mark of the Beast," and "Moti Guj—Mutineer"
Edited with an introduction by A.O.J. Cockshut
0–19–281671–3 Oxford pb $5.95

THE LIGHT THAT FAILED
0–88184–277–X Carroll & Graf pb $4.50

THE MAN WHO WOULD BE KING & OTHER STORIES
A good selection containing many of Kipling's most famous stories
Edited by Louis L. Cornell
0–19–281674–8 Oxford pb $6.95

PLAIN TALES FROM THE HILLS
The early tales that made Kipling famous
Edited by H.R. Woudhuysen
Introduction by David Trotter
0–14–043287–6 Penguin pb $5.95

Rudyard Kipling by Max Beerbohm

PUCK OF POOK'S HILL
A fantasy journey through English history
Edited by Sarah H. Wintle
0–14–043284–1 Penguin pb $3.95

REWARDS AND FAIRIES
A sequel to *Puck of Pook's Hill*
Edited by Roger Lewis
0–14–043315–5 Penguin pb $3.95

TRAFFICS AND DISCOVERIES
Edited by Sarah Wintle
0–14–043286–8 Penguin pb $5.95

> Joseph Sheridan Le Fanu
> "He took great pleasure in ghost stories, and was fascinated by hints of the supernatural . . . He was a writer of remarkable power in creating suspense, at his best a master of plot, and the creator of some of the most satisfying villains in Victorian literature."—Julian Symons
> **BEST GHOST STORIES**
> Includes "Carmilla" (one of the best—and most erotic—of vampire stories) and the brief shocker "Green Tea," among others
> Edited by E.F. Bleiler
> 0–486–20415–4 Dover pb $7.95
>
> **GHOST STORIES & MYSTERIES**
> Edited with an introduction by E.F. Bleiler
> 0–486–20715–3 Dover pb $6.95
>
> **GUY DEVERELL**
> 0–486–24618–3 Dover pb $6.95
>
> **THE ROSE AND THE KEY**
> 0–486–24377–X Dover pb $6.95
>
> **UNCLE SILAS**
> A terrifying novel of a young girl in the hands of a ruthless and greedy relative
> Edited by W.J. McCormack
> 0–19–281541–5 Oxford pb $7.95
>
> **WYLDER'S HAND**
> 0–486–23570–X Dover pb $7.95

• **George MacDonald**
AT THE BACK OF THE NORTH WIND
Part children's story, part religious meditation, with indelible descriptions of nature
0–14–035030–6 Penguin pb $2.25

LILITH
0–85031–626–X Schocken pb $6.95

PHANTASTES
0–8052–0722–8 Schocken pb $5.95

• **Arthur Machen**
THE HILL OF DREAMS
A young man is caught up in his own dreams, with baleful consequences
0–486–24994–8 Dover pb $5.95

• **Charles Maturin**
MELMOTH THE WANDERER
A Gothic novel of diabolical wanderings that reads in parts like a fever dream
Edited by Alethea Hayter
0–14–043110–1 Penguin pb $7.95

• **George Meredith**
THE ADVENTURES OF HARRY RICHMOND
Edited by L.T. Hergenhan
0–8032–0712–3 Nebraska $29.95

BEAUCHAMP'S CAREER
0–19–281751–5 Oxford pb $8.95

THE EGOIST
Probably Meredith's masterpiece, featuring the inimitably vacuous Willoughby Patterne, of whom the most complimentary thing that can be said is "he has a leg"
Edited by George Woodstock
0–452–00820–4 Penguin pb $5.95

THE ORDEAL OF RICHARD FEVEREL
A frequently nightmarish tale of the relations between a son and a domineering father
Edited by John Halperin
0–19–281637–3 Oxford pb $8.95

• **George Moore**
ESTHER WATERS
This story of the wretched life of a servant girl seduced and abandoned is a landmark of English naturalism
Edited by David Skilton
0–19–281578–4 Oxford pb $7.95

• **Arthur Morrison**
A CHILD OF THE JAGO
Slum life in the streets of East London; first published in 1896
0–85115–203–1 Academy Chicago pb $8.95

THE HOLE IN THE WALL
Another of Morrison's explorations of the lives of London's poorest
0–85115–205–8 Academy Chicago pb $8.95

TALES OF MEAN STREETS
0–85115–221–X Academy Chicago pb $6.95

• **Margaret Oliphant**
A BELEAGUERED CITY & OTHER STORIES
The title novella is a haunting supernatural story about the dead coming to life
Edited by Merryn Williams
0–19–281835–X Oxford pb $7.95

THE DOCTOR'S FAMILY & OTHER STORIES
Edited with an introduction by Merryn Williams
0–19–281733–7 Oxford pb $4.95

THE PERPETUAL CURATE
Introduction by Penelope Fitzgerald
0–14–016161–9 Penguin pb $7.95

THE RECTOR & THE DOCTOR'S FAMILY
Edited with an introduction by Merryn Williams
0–14–281733–7 Penguin pb $6.95

SALEM CHAPEL
Introduction by Penelope Fitzgerald
0–14–016152–X Penguin pb $6.95

• Baroness Orczy
THE SCARLET PIMPERNEL
The stirring adventures of an English aristocrat during the French Revolution
0–451–52315–6 NAL pb $3.95

• Walter Pater
MARIUS THE EPICUREAN
An elaborately written philosophical novel of ancient Rome which incorporates a retelling of Apuleius' story of Cupid and Psyche
Edited by Michael Levey
0–14–043236–1 Penguin pb $5.95

• Thomas Love Peacock
HEADLONG HALL & GRYLL GRANGE
Peacock's first and last novels
Edited by Michael Baron & Michael Slater
0–19–281693–4 Oxford pb $5.95

NIGHTMARE ABBEY & CROTCHET CASTLE
Unique, good-natured satirical novels in dialogue form, featuring a cast of memorably eccentric characters, some of them modeled on famous acquaintances like Shelley and Byron
0–14–043045–8 Penguin pb $4.95

• Walter Scott
THE HEART OF MIDLOTHIAN
The tragic story of Effie Deans is the center of this most widely praised of Scott's novels, remarkable for its portrait of humble Scottish life in the 18th century
Edited by Clare Lamot
0–19–281583–0 Oxford pb $10.95

IVANHOE
The famous novel of England under Norman rule
Edited by A.N. Wilson
0–14–043143–8 Penguin pb $4.95

OLD MORTALITY
A novel concerning the Covenanters' rebellion of 1685
Edited by Angus Calder
0–14–043098–9 Penguin pb $5.95

REDGAUNTLET
A novel of Jacobite conspiracy that includes the famous "Wandering Willie's Tale"
Edited by Kathryn Sutherland
0–19–281668–3 Oxford pb $6.95

THE TALISMAN
A highly colored novel of the Crusades, with Richard the Lion-Hearted and Saladin playing major roles
0–460–01144–8 Biblio pb $4.50

THE TWO DROVERS & OTHER STORIES
0–19–281718–3 Oxford pb $6.95

WAVERLY
The novel that initiated Scott's long series of historical romances
0–14–043071–7 Penguin pb $5.95

• Percy Bysshe Shelley
ZASTROZZI & ST. IRVYNE
Early, rather primitive Gothic novellas written when the poet was in his teens
Edited with an introduction by Stephen Behrendt
0–19–281724–8 Oxford pb $3.95

Mary Shelley
FRANKENSTEIN
Those who know the story only from the film versions will be amazed by the depth and sophistication of the original
Edited by Maurice Hindle
0–14–043237–X Penguin pb $1.95

THE LAST MAN
A plague depopulates the earth
Edited by Hugh J. Luke, Jr.
0–8032–5182–3 Nebraska pb $5.95

• Robert Louis Stevenson
THE BLACK ARROW: A Tale of the Two Roses
Vigorous adventure tale of medieval England
Illustrated by N.C. Wyeth
0–684–18877–5 Macmillan $22.95

DR. JEKYLL AND MR. HYDE
One of the most controlled and powerful of Stevenson's works
Edited by Jenn Calder
0–14–043117–9 Penguin pb $2.95

KIDNAPPED & CATRIONA
The famous novel of youthful adventure and its sequel (sometimes known as *David Balfour*)
Edited by Emma Letley
0–19–281726–4 Oxford pb $5.95

THE MASTER OF BALLANTRAE
Stevenson's most complex novel experiments with point of view and chronology to tell an already fractured story of conflict between two brothers
Edited by Emma Letly
0–19–281635–7 Oxford pb $6.95

THE NEW ARABIAN NIGHTS
Includes "The Suicide Club" and other fantasy stories. "There is no Oriental coloring here; the cycle unfolds in the alleys, drawing rooms, and hidden courtyards of Paris and London . . . The labyrinthine coilings of the narrative make it clear why Stevenson was Borges's favorite writer"—*Village Voice*
0–87773–382–1 Shambhala pb $6.95

TREASURE ISLAND
The novel that revolutionized popular fiction by inventing a more realistic style of adventure story
Edited by Emma Letley
0–19–281681–0 Oxford pb $2.25

WEIR OF HERMISTON & OTHER STORIES
Many consider *Weir of Hermiston*, unfinished at the author's death, to be Stevenson's finest work
Edited by Paul Binding
0–14–043138–1 Penguin pb $4.95

• Bram Stoker
THE BRAM STOKER BEDSIDE COMPANION
Ten stories by the author of *Dracula*
Edited by Charles Osborne
0–8008–0964–5 Taplinger pb $4.95

DRACULA
The definitive literary incarnation of the undead
Edited by A.N. Wilson
0–19–281598–9 Oxford pb $2.95

• Robert Smith Surtees
MR. FACEY ROMFORD'S HOUNDS
A comedy of the fox-hunting gentry, published in 1865
Edited by Jeremy Lewis
0–19–281657–8 Oxford pb $5.95

MR. SPONGE'S SPORTING TOUR
Illustrated by John Leech
Introduction by Joyce Cary
0–19–281521–0 Oxford pb $7.95

• William Makepeace Thackeray
THE BOOK OF SNOBS
Edited by J. Sutherland
0–312–09011–0 St. Martin's $25.00

THE HISTORY OF HENRY ESMOND
A historical novel of the early 18th century
Edited by John Sutherland
0–14–043049–0 Penguin pb $5.95

THE HISTORY OF PENDENNIS
A novel of London life, much influenced by Fielding and containing many autobiographical elements
Edited by Donald Hawes
Introduction by J.M. Stewart
0–14–043076–8 Penguin pb $5.95

THE MEMOIRS OF BARRY LYNDON
The life of an Irish adventurer, source of the Stanley Kubrick film
Edited by Andrew Sanders
0–19–281667–5 Oxford pb $7.95

VANITY FAIR
By far the most popular of Thackeray's novels: Becky Sharp remains one of the great comic creations of the 19th century
Edited by J.M. Stewart
0–14–043035–0 Penguin pb $4.95

• Anthony Trollope
COLLECTED SHORT STORIES
0–486–25484–4 Dover pb $7.95

THE COMPLETE SHORT STORIES
Edited by Betty J. Breyer

Volume 1: The Christmas Stories
0–912646–56–X Texas Christian $17.50

Volume 2: Editors and Writers
0–912646–57–8 Texas Christian $17.50

Volume 3: Tourists and Colonials
0–912646–62–4 Texas Christian $17.50

Volume 4: Courtship and Marriage
0–912646–75–6 Texas Christian $17.50

Volume 5: Various Stories
0–912646–79–9 Texas Christian $17.50

Drawing by Thackeray of a somnolent reader, from The Delights of Reading *by Otto Bettmann (Godine)*

THE BARSETSHIRE NOVELS
In the Barsetshire series Trollope invented a wholly fictional yet beautifully complete west-country county. "I had it all in my mind," he wrote, "its roads and railroads, its towns and parishes, its members of Parliament, and the different hunts which rode over it."

THE WARDEN
Edited by Robin Gilmour
0–14–043214–0 Penguin pb $3.95

BARCHESTER TOWERS
Edited by James R. Kincaid
Illustrated by Edward Ardizzone
0–19–281507–5 Oxford pb $4.95

DOCTOR THORNE
Edited by David Skilton
0–19–281508–3 Oxford pb $7.95

FRAMLEY PARSONAGE
Edited with an introduction by David Skilton & Peter Miles
0–14–043213–2 Penguin pb $5.95

THE SMALL HOUSE AT ALLINGTON
Edited by James Kincaid
0–19–281552–0 Oxford pb $7.95

THE LAST CHRONICLE OF BARSET
Edited by Peter Fairclough
0–14–043024–5 Penguin pb $6.95

THE AMERICAN SENATOR
An American politician visits, and is comically puzzled by English social and political mores
Edited with an introduction by John Halperin
0–19–281739–6 Oxford pb $6.95

AYALA'S ANGEL
A young girl must choose among three suitors, each with his own disadvantages
Edited with an introduction by Julian Thompson-Furnival
0–19–281747–7 Oxford pb $7.95

THE BELTON ESTATE
Edited with an introduction by John Halperin
0–19–281725–6 Oxford pb $7.95

THE BERTRAMS
0–486–25119–5 Dover pb $8.95

CASTLE RICHMOND
0–486–24760–0 Dover pb $7.95

THE CLAVERINGS
A novel of conflicting choices in love, often accounted one of Trollope's best
Edited with an introduction by David Skilton
0–19–281727–2 Oxford pb $7.95

COUSIN HENRY
Edited by Julian Thompson
0–19–281784–1 Oxford pb $6.95

DR. WORTLE'S SCHOOL
Scandal and blackmail, combined with one of Trollope's most revealing self-portraits
Edited by John Halperin
0–19–281673–X Oxford pb $5.95

HARRY HEATHCOTE OF GANGOIL
A novella of Australian bush life, with a hero more complex than he at first appears
0–486–25317–1 Dover pb $3.95

HE KNEW HE WAS RIGHT
A novel of obsessive jealousy and the disintegration of a marriage
Edited by John Sutherland
0–19–281692–6 Oxford pb $8.95

IS HE POPENJOY?
Edited with an introduction by John Sutherland
0–19–281716–7 Oxford pb $7.95

THE KELLYS AND THE O'KELLYS
An early novel of Irish life
Edited by W.J. McCormack
Introduction by William Trevor
0–19–281577–6 Oxford pb $7.95

KEPT IN THE DARK
0–486–23609–9 Dover pb $2.95

LADY ANNA
0–486–24669–8 Dover pb $6.95

MARION FAY
Edited by R.H. Super
0–932282–18–0 Caledonia pb $15.95

MISS MACKENZIE
0–486–25201–9 Dover pb $7.95

MISTER SCARBOROUGH'S FAMILY
A late, surprisingly sardonic work
0–486–25782–7 Dover pb $8.95

ORLEY FARM
An intricate plot revolving around a complex law case and troubled family relations. Lady Mason is among Trollope's most successful female characters
Edited by David Skilton
0–19–281713–2 Oxford pb $7.95

RACHEL RAY
0–486–23930–6 Dover pb $6.95

RALPH THE HEIR
0–486–23642–0 Dover pb $6.50

SIR HARRY HOTSPUR OF HUMBLETHWAITE
0–486–24953–0 Dover pb $5.95

THE THREE CLERKS
A novel of civil-service life
0–486–24099–1 Dover pb $8.95

THE VICAR OF BULLHAMPTON
A heroic clergyman attempts to clear an innocent man charged with murder
Edited by David Skilton
0–19–282163–6 Oxford pb $8.95

THE WAY WE LIVE NOW
One of Trollope's darkest novels: a panoramic fictional overview of English life, rural and urban, high and low, with a plot that moves easily from business and politics to romance
Edited by John Sutherland
0–19–281576–8 Oxford pb $9.95

The Palliser Novels
Popularized by a BBC television adaptation, the Palliser novels are Trollope's hardheaded essay in the interplay between politics and personal ambition.

CAN YOU FORGIVE HER?
Edited by Stephen Wall
0–14–043086–5 Penguin pb $6.95

PHINEAS FINN
Edited by Jacques Berthoud
0–19–281587–3 Oxford pb $6.95

THE EUSTACE DIAMONDS
Edited by Stephen Gill & John Sutherland
0–14–043041–5 Penguin pb $6.95

PHINEAS REDUX
Edited by John C. Whale
0–19–281589–X Oxford pb $6.95

THE PRIME MINISTER
Edited by Jennifer Uglow & John McCormick
0–19–281590–3 Oxford pb $6.95

THE DUKE'S CHILDREN
Edited by Hermione Lee
0–19–281586–5 Oxford pb $6.95

• Mrs. Humphrey Ward
HELBECK OF BANNISDALE
A drama of religious conflict
Edited by Brian Worthington
0–14–043194–2 Penguin pb $6.95

MARCELLA
0–14–016103–1 Penguin pb $1.95

ROBERT ELSMERE
A celebrated novel of religious thought in the wake of the Oxford Movement
Edited by Clyde De L. Ryals
0–8032–5210–2 Nebraska pb $6.95

• Oscar Wilde
THE COMPLETE SHORTER FICTION OF OSCAR WILDE
Edited by Isobel M. Murray
0–19–281500–8 Oxford pb $3.95

LORD ARTHUR SAVILE'S CRIME & OTHER STORIES
Also includes "The Canterville Ghost" and such morbid children's stories as "The Happy Prince" and "The Birthday of the Infanta"
0–14–001021–1 Penguin pb $3.95

THE PICTURE OF DORIAN GRAY
Edited by Peter Ackroyd
0–14–043187–X Penguin pb $2.95

• Mrs. Henry Wood
EAST LYNNE
First published in 1861, this intense melodrama of illicit passion and motherly love became one of the most popular stories of the 19th century
Edited by Sally Mitchell
0–8135–1042–2 Rutgers pb $11.00

Lewis Carroll

THE COMPLETE WORKS OF LEWIS CARROLL
Illustrated by John Tenniel
Introduction by Alexander Woollcott
0–394–60485–7 Modern Library $15.95
0–394–71661–2 Random House pb $9.95

ALICE'S ADVENTURES IN WONDERLAND
Illustrated by John Tenniel
0–14–035038–1 Penguin pb $2.25

ALICE'S ADVENTURES IN WONDERLAND & THROUGH THE LOOKING-GLASS
Edited by Roger L. Green
Illustrated by John Tenniel
0–19–281620–9 Oxford pb $2.25

THE ANNOTATED ALICE: Alice's Adventures in Wonderland & Through the Looking Glass
Edited by Martin Gardner
Illustrated by John Tenniel
0–452–00931–6 NAL pb $8.95

THE HUNTING OF THE SNARK
Edited by R. Eugene Jackson & David Ellis
0–88680–273–3 I.E. Clark pb $3.00

PILLOW PROBLEMS & A TANGLED TALE
0–486–20493–6 Dover pb $4.95

Multitudes of packages had arrived, by land and water, from London, and Liverpool, and Chester, and Manchester, and Birmingham, and various parts of the mountains: books, wine, cheese, globes, mathematical instruments, turkeys, telescopes, hams, tongues, microscopes, quadrants, sextants, fiddles, flutes, tea, sugar, electrical machines, figs, spices, air-pumps, soda-water, chemical apparatus, eggs, French-horns, drawing books, palettes, oils, and colours, bottled ale and porter, scenery for a private theatre, pickles and fish-sauce, patent lamps and chandeliers, barrels of oysters, sofas, chairs, tables, carpets, beds, looking-glasses, pictures, fruits and confections, nuts, oranges, lemons, packages of salt salmon, and jars of Portugal grapes.

from Headlong Hall in

Thomas Love Peacock

HEADLONG HALL & GRYLL GRANGE
Edited by Michael Baron & Michael Slater
0–19–281693–4 Oxford pb $5.95

19TH-CENTURY PROSE

The ambitious mid-19th-century pundits—Carlyle, Mill, Arnold, Ruskin, and Pater—have aptly been called "Victorian Sages," writers who included everything within their purview. They were literary critics, moralists, sociologists, economists, whose interests ranged from the culture of the urban factory to the craftsmanship of the Gothic cathedral.

Unlike modern cultural critics, they were unhampered by the restraints of academic specialization; seeing human culture as ultimately seamless, they felt a responsibility to confront it as a whole rather than in fragments.

• Matthew Arnold

CULTURE AND ANARCHY
An attack on the narrow-minded cultural provincialism that Arnold labeled "philistine"
0–521–09103–9 Cambridge pb $11.95

LITERATURE AND DOGMA
Edited by James Livingston
0–8044–6011–6 Ungar pb $3.45

SELECTED PROSE
Edited by P.J. Keating
0–14–043058–X Penguin pb $7.95

• Jane Austen

SELECTED LETTERS, 1796–1817
Edited by R.W. Chapman
Introduction by Marilyn Butler
0–19–281485–0 Oxford pb $7.95

• Hilaire Belloc

THE FOUR MEN: A Farrago
"*The Four Men* is one of Belloc's most beautiful books, a hymn to stability by one of the most restless beings who ever crashed about the surface of the Earth"—A.N. Wilson
Introduction by A.N. Wilson
0–19–281434–6 Oxford pb $6.95

THE PATH TO ROME
An account of Belloc's journey from France to Rome on foot. In later years he wrote, "I hate writing. I wouldn't have written a word if I could have helped it. I only wrote for money. *The Path to Rome* is the only book I ever wrote for love"
0–14–009530–6 Penguin pb $6.95

• George Borrow

THE BIBLE IN SPAIN
The title is misleading. This is a vivid, although partly fictional travel book by a lively and eccentric observer
0–7126–1039–1 David & Charles pb $15.95

• Thomas Carlyle

SELECTED WRITINGS
In the highly rhetorical prose of such works as *Chartism* and *The French Revolution* (excerpted here), Carlyle established himself as a kind of official moral opposition to his era. The excitement and power of his finest work exerted a profound influence on writers as diverse as Mill and Emerson, Dickens and George Eliot, Thackeray and Whitman
Edited by A. Shelston
0–14–043065–2 Penguin pb $6.95

A CARLYLE READER
Edited by G.B. Tennyson
0–521–27873–2 Cambridge pb $10.95

ON HEROES, HERO-WORSHIP AND THE HEROIC IN HISTORY
First delivered as a series of lectures in 1840, included here are essays on Dante, Rousseau, Cromwell, and Napoleon
Edited by Carl Niemeyer
0–8032–5030–4 Nebraska pb $6.95

PAST AND PRESENT
The best example of Carlyle's contemporary social criticism
Edited by Richard D. Altick
0–8147–0562–6 NYU pb $15.00

SARTOR RESARTUS
Carlyle's spiritual autobiography, written in a powerful metaphorical style
Edited by Peter Sabor & Kerry McSweeney
0–19–281757–4 Oxford pb $7.95

Charles M. Doughty

TRAVELS IN ARABIA DESERTA
Doughty's wanderings in Arabia are recorded in a unique and self-invented prose style rich in archaisms and poetic figures
Introduction by T.E. Lawrence

Volume 1
0–486–23825–3 Dover pb $14.95

Volume 2
0–486–23826–1 Dover pb $14.95

PASSAGES FROM ARABIA DESERTA
A convenient abridgment of Doughty's enormous work
Edited by Edward Garnett
0–14–009508–X Penguin pb $7.95

George Eliot

• George Eliot

SELECTIONS FROM GEORGE ELIOT'S LETTERS
Eliot stood at the center of high Victorian literary culture, into which her letters offer fascinating insight
Edited by Gordon S. Haight
0–300–03326–5 Yale $35.00

• Elizabeth Gaskell

THE LIFE OF CHARLOTTE BRONTE
A classic biography by a close friend of the novelist
Edited by Alan Shelston
0–14–043099–7 Penguin pb $5.95

• Gerard Manley Hopkins

SELECTED PROSE
Edited by Gerald Roberts
0–19–281272–6 Oxford pb $10.95

- John Stuart Mill

THE AUTOBIOGRAPHY
One of the most penetrating accounts of
depression and recovery ever written
0–395–05120–7 Houghton Mifflin pb $6.95

- William Morris

**THE IDEAL BOOK: Essays and Lectures
on the Arts of the Book**
Edited by William S. Peterson
0–520–05625–6 California pb $15.95

**NEWS FROM NOWHERE & SELECTED
WRITINGS AND DESIGN**
Morris, a key figure in the revival of
interest in medieval culture and traditional
crafts, was also the author of utopian
fiction and heroic poetry
Edited by Asa Briggs
0–14–043115–2 Penguin pb $5.95

- John Henry Newman

APOLOGIA PRO VITA SUA
A humane and intellectually incisive
testament to Newman's fervent yet
independent-minded Catholic faith
Edited by David DeLaura
0–393–09766–8 Norton pb $12.95

**AN ESSAY IN AID OF A GRAMMAR OF
ASSENT**
Introduction by Nicholas Lash
0–268–01000–5 Notre Dame pb $10.95

THE IDEA OF A UNIVERSITY
Edited by Martin J. Svaglic
0–268–01150–8 Notre Dame pb $10.95

LOSS AND GAIN
A fictionalized retelling of Newman's
conversion to Catholicism
Edited with an introduction by Alan G. Hill
0–19–281687–X Oxford pb $5.95

**A PACKET OF LETTERS: A Selection
from the Correspondence of John Henry
Newman**
Edited by Joyce Suggs
0–19–826442–9 Oxford $21.95

- Walter Pater

APPRECIATIONS
0–8101–0747–3 Northwestern pb $11.95

THE RENAISSANCE
A touchstone of aestheticism
Edited by Adam Philips
0–19–281737–X Oxford pb $4.95

**THE RENAISSANCE: Studies in Art and
Poetry**
A scholarly edition
Edited by Donald H. Hill
0–520–03664–6 California pb $11.95

- John Ruskin

"He was one of those rare men who think
with their hearts, and so he thought and
said not only what he himself had seen and
felt, but what everyone will think and say
in the future."—Leo Tolstoy

ART CRITICISM
Ruskin endowed criticism with a moral
fervor, demanding of art that it speak
eloquently to the human condition
Edited by R.L. Herbert
0–8446–0694–4 Peter Smith $13.25

THE ELEMENTS OF DRAWING
Introduction by Lawrence Campbell
0–486–22730–8 Dover pb $4.50

**THE KING OF THE GOLDEN RIVER
OR THE BLACK BROTHER**
A fairy tale that achieved great popularity
Illustrated by Richard Doyle
0–486–20066–3 Dover pb $2.25

MODERN PAINTERS
An abridged edition of Ruskin's landmark
work of art criticism
Edited by David Berrie
0–394–56846–X Knopf $45.00

**THE SEVEN LAMPS OF
ARCHITECTURE**
0–374–50188–2 Farrar, Straus & Giroux pb $8.95

THE STONES OF VENICE
Ruskin's most accessible exposition of his
principles
Edited by J.G. Links
0–306–80244–0 Da Capo pb $9.95

**UNTO THIS LAST & OTHER
WRITINGS**
Also includes *The King of the Golden River*
and excerpts from *The Stones of Venice,
Sesame and Lilies,* and *Fors Clavigera*
Edited by Clive Wilmer
0–14–043211–6 Penguin pb $6.95

- Robert Louis Stevenson

IN THE SOUTH SEAS
Firsthand impressions of the Marquesas
and the Paumotus and Gilbert Islands
0–7103–0140–5 RC&H pb $12.95

TRAVELS IN HAWAII
Edited with an introduction by A. Grove Day
0–8248–0257–8 Hawaii $10.50

- John Addington Symonds

SELECTED WRITINGS
Edited by R.V. Holdsworth
0–85635–059–1 Carcanet pb $7.50

**THE MEMOIRS OF JOHN ADDINGTON
SYMONDS: The Secret Homosexual Life of
a Leading Nineteenth-Century Man of
Letters**
Edited by Phyllis Grosskurth
0–394–54085–9 Random House $19.95
0–226–78783–4 Chicago pb $11.95

- Anthony Trollope

AUTOBIOGRAPHY
Edited by P.D. Edwards
0–19–281509–1 Oxford pb $5.95

- Oscar Wilde

**THE OXFORD AUTHORS: OSCAR
WILDE**
A large-scale collection that includes *The
Picture of Dorian Gray, Lady Windermere's
Fan, The Importance of Being Earnest, The
Critic as Artist, The Ballad of Reading Gaol,*
as well as other, less familiar works
Edited by Isobel Murray
0–19–281978–X Oxford pb $16.95

THE PORTABLE OSCAR WILDE
Edited by Stanley Weintraub
0–14–015093–5 Penguin pb $7.95

**SELECTED LETTERS OF OSCAR
WILDE**
Edited by Rupert Hart-Davis
0–19–281218–1 Oxford pb $9.95

**THE ARTIST AS CRITIC: Critical
Writings of Oscar Wilde**
Edited by Richard Ellmann
0–226–89764–8 Chicago pb $12.50

DE PROFUNDIS & OTHER WRITINGS
Wilde's famous and anguished letter to
Alfred Douglas, written from prison
0–14–043089–X Penguin pb $4.95

20th-Century
British and Irish
Fiction

THE EARLY 20TH CENTURY

- Maurice Baring

C
A nostalgic novel of life before the First
World War. "There is through everything
he does a streak of real originality"—J.B.
Priestley
0–19–281942–9 Oxford pb $8.95

H.E. Bates

**ELEPHANT'S NEST IN A RHUBARB
TREE & OTHER STORIES**
0–8112–1088–X New Directions pb $9.95

LOVE FOR LYDIA
Source of the recent public-television
series
0–14–001165–X Penguin pb $4.95

**A MONTH BY THE LAKE & OTHER
STORIES**
"Nearly perfect stories . . . He is as
adept at the seductive rise and fall of
his narrative voice as he is cunning
with naturalistic dialogue. Comparisons
to Joyce, Chekhov, and Mansfield are
inevitable"—*Publishers Weekly*
Introduction by Anthony Burgess
0–8112–1036–7 New Directions pb $8.95

MY UNCLE SILAS
"Bates understood the power of the
short story form perfectly, and these
pieces must not be missed by anyone
who favors short fictions"—*Booklist*
Introduction by V.S. Pritchett
0–915308–63–0 Graywolf pb $7.00

**A PARTY FOR THE GIRLS: Six
Stories**
Six long stories. "He achieved such
sovereignty of what literary land he
inherited that he deserves the homage
of our uncomplicated enjoyment"—
Anthony Burgess
0–8112–1051–0 New Directions pb $10.95

- Samuel Beckett

DISJECTA
The first publication of these miscellaneous
criticisms, reviews, and selected letters
sheds new light on Beckett's work
Edited by Ruby Cohn
0–394–62489–0 Grove pb $5.95

FIRST LOVE & OTHER SHORTS
The two outcasts of *First Love* succeed in
making a mockery of the title
0–394–17850–5 Grove pb $7.95

FIZZLES
A sequence of extremely brief prose works
0–394–17917–X Grove pb $1.95

HOW IT IS
"What *is* the story? Well, it is spoken by a nameless man face down in mud, and apart from him its principal character is called Pim. Three sections describe how it was before, with and after this Pim, who is therefore a measure of time and history"— Frank Kermode
0–8021–5066–7 Grove pb $10.95

ILL SEEN ILL SAID
0–394–17953–6 Grove pb $4.95

THE LOST ONES
A compressed and very powerful late work. "*The Lost Ones* imagines the death of imagination, the end of life on the planet"—Christopher Ricks
0–394–17786–X Grove pb $8.95

MALONE DIES
A cosmic tramp's interior monologue as he resists (or welcomes?) eternal silence; the central panel of the triptych that also includes *Molloy* and *The Unnamable*
0–394–17028–8 Grove pb $5.95

MERCIER AND CAMIER
An early work of fiction
0–394–17835–1 Grove pb $6.95

MOLLOY
The first novel of Beckett's trilogy is, for all its austerity, one of the richest of his fictions
Translated by Samuel Beckett & Patrick Bowles
0–394–17027–X Grove pb $10.95

MORE PRICKS THAN KICKS
A collection of stories that first appeared in 1934
0–394–17789–4 Grove pb $7.95

MURPHY
Beckett's first novel, published in 1938
0–394–17210–8 Grove pb $8.95

STORIES AND TEXTS FOR NOTHING
"This art often casts a cold eye of contempt over that which is the supreme mark of humanity: curiosity about the world and about the undiscovered possibilities of human life. Saint Beckett records with supreme skill the solipsist visions of the pillar and the desert, instead of preaching to the birds"—Matthew Hodgart, *NY Review of Books*
0–8021–5062–4 Grove pb $8.95

THREE NOVELS
Includes *Molloy, Malone Dies,* and *The Unnamable.* "Beckett relentlessly reduces his characters from pitiful creatures with few possessions—a hat, a pot, a stub of pencil—to voices, who have only the inner torments of their past life to sustain their present existence, doomed to repeat themselves until finally even the voice, their last vestige of humanity, is stilled"— Deirdre Bair, *NY Times*
0–394–17299–X Grove pb $7.95

THE UNNAMABLE
"You must say words, as long as there are any, until they find me, until they say me . . ."
0–394–17030–X Grove pb $3.95

WATT
A richly—and darkly—comic early novel. "An appalling perception of the degrees

and fine shades of human misery seems to fill Mr. Beckett with horror and compassion. On the other hand his Irish wit and realism tell him that there is nothing people cannot eventually get used to"—Cyril Connelly
0–394–17216–7 Grove pb $10.95

WORSTWARD HO!
"Focuses to a pinpoint one of the great sensibilities in modern world literature"— *Washington Post*
0–394–53230–9 Grove pb $8.95

• **Sybille Bedford**
A LEGACY
"A book of entirely delicious quality. Two families, vastly dissimilar, the one Jewish inartistic millionaires, the other slightly decadent Catholic aristocrats, become joined in marriage. Everything is new, cool, witty, elegant, and some scenes are uproariously funny"—Evelyn Waugh
0–912946–26–1 Ecco pb $8.50

• **Max Beerbohm**
THE ILLUSTRATED ZULEIKA DOBSON
An elegant pastiche of the highly proper decadence of the British Empire
Introduction by N. John Hall
0–300–03389–3 Yale $22.50

SEVEN MEN AND TWO OTHERS
These fantasies from the Cafe Royal include the story of Enoch Soames, a minor poet, who learns on a trip to the future that he is remembered only as Beerbohm's fictional character, and A.V. Laider, a liar of cosmic proportions
0–19–281512–1 Oxford pb $4.95

ZULEIKA DOBSON
Inspired whimsy in which unrequited love for the devastating Zuleika causes the entire Oxford student body to commit suicide
0–14–006713–2 Penguin pb $6.95

• **Arnold Bennett**
ANNA OF THE FIVE TOWNS
Anna's choice between love with a bankrupt or marriage to a bore is sketched against the provincial background of Britain's pottery industry
Introduction by Frank Swinnerton
0–14–000033–X Penguin pb $6.95

THE CARD
0–14–003826–4 Penguin pb $5.95

CLAYHANGER
Gladstone's Home Rule bills and Victoria's Jubilee lend a lively sense of period to the childhood and adolescence of Edwin Clayhanger
0–14–000997–3 Penguin pb $5.95

THE GRIM SMILE OF THE FIVE TOWNS
Short stories set in the potteries district
0–14–000519–6 Penguin pb $4.95

THE OLD WIVES' TALE
The contrasting life-stories of two sisters— a stay-at-home and a wanderer—form the basis for Bennett's best novel
Edited by John Wain
0–14–043163–2 Penguin pb $5.95

RICEYMAN STEPS
A book dealer and his marriage provide the basis for a strong realistic novel
0–89733–093–5 Academy Chicago pb $8.95

E.F. Benson
MAKE WAY FOR LUCIA
A one-volume edition of the complete Lucia cycle, one of the peaks of modern comic writing. Includes *Queen Lucia, Miss Mapp, Mapp and Lucia, Lucia in London, Trouble for Lucia,* and *The Worshipful Lucia.* "The most enchantingly malicious works written by the hand of man"—Gilbert Seldes
Introduction by Nancy Mitford
0–06–015678–3 Harper & Row $29.95
0–06–091508–0 Harper & Row pb $15.95

QUEEN LUCIA
Introduction by Nancy Mitford
0–06–091372–X Harper & Row pb $6.95

MISS MAPP
0–06–091374–6 Harper & Row pb $5.95

MAPP AND LUCIA
Source of the wickedly funny PBS series
Introduction by Nancy Mitford
0–06–091328–2 Harper & Row pb $6.95

LUCIA IN LONDON
0–06–091373–8 Harper & Row pb $5.95

TROUBLE FOR LUCIA
0–06–091376–2 Harper & Row pb $5.95

THE WORSHIPFUL LUCIA
Introduction by Nancy Mitford
0–06–091375–4 Harper & Row pb $5.95

• **Elizabeth Bowen**
"She is what happened after Bloomsbury . . . the link that connects Virginia Woolf with Iris Murdoch and Muriel Spark."— Victoria Glendinning

THE COLLECTED STORIES OF ELIZABETH BOWEN
"To see anew these bright stars set among their own constellations . . . is to experience in its full force that concentration of imaginative power which was hers"—Eudora Welty
Introduction by Angus Wilson
0–394–51666–4 Knopf $20.00
0–88001–224–2 Ecco pb $13.95

THE DEATH OF THE HEART
Sensitive observation of the adolescence of the orphaned Portia, whose caretakers' indifference propels her into an affair with a cad
0–14–008543–2 Penguin pb $6.95

EVA TROUT
0–14–008542–4 Penguin pb $6.95

FRIENDS AND RELATIONS
0–14–000398–3 Penguin pb $5.95

THE HEAT OF THE DAY
A wartime love affair turns tragic when one of the lovers is revealed as a spy
0–14–088539–1 Penguin pb $6.95

THE HOTEL
0–14–000449–1 Penguin pb $5.95

THE HOUSE IN PARIS
An illegimate boy's agonizing search for his real mother
0–14–000535–8 Penguin pb $6.95

THE LAST SEPTEMBER
0–14–000372–X Penguin pb $5.95

THE LITTLE GIRLS
"We might conceivably be reminded of Wallace Stevens's poetry with its pure crystalline exterior and its metaphysical interior"—Allen E. Austen
0–14–005785–4 Penguin pb $6.95

TO THE NORTH
0–14–000534–X Penguin pb $6.95

A WORLD OF LOVE
0–14–008541–6 Penguin pb $5.95

• **Joyce Cary**
EXCEPT THE LORD
The second volume in the Chester Nimmo trilogy, which begins with *Prisoner of Grace*
0–8112–0965–2 New Directions pb $7.95

HERSELF SURPRISED
A picaresque tale of the femme moyenne sensuelle, Sarah Munday, told in her own words with verve and vivacity
0–7145–0270–7 Riverrun pb $4.95

THE HORSE'S MOUTH
The Blake-quoting old reprobate Gulley Jimson struggles for his art against the wiles of his discarded mistress and his skinflint patron
0–06–080046–1 Harper & Row pb $4.95

A HOUSE OF CHILDREN
An evocation of the Ireland of Cary's childhood. "The organization—the progress of children toward maturity by means of sudden epiphanies—is remarkable. The characters, based on Cary's cousins and aunts and the author himself, are charming. The language is intoxication"—Edwin Christian
0–8112–1008–1 New Directions pb $8.95

MISTER JOHNSON
0–8112–1030–8 New Directions pb $9.95

NOT HONOUR MORE
The third volume of the Nimmo trilogy consists of the less than contrite confession of the messianic reformer's assassin
0–8112–0966–0 New Directions pb $7.95

PRISONER OF GRACE
The first volume of a trilogy presents the career of Chester Nimmo, a mixture of radical politician and religious charlatan, through the eyes of his wife
0–8112–0964–4 New Directions pb $7.95

• **Claud Cockburn**
BEAT THE DEVIL
The novel of intrigue on which John Huston's famous movie was based
0–7012–0582–2 Hogarth pb $5.95

• **Ivy Compton-Burnett**
"Her work is an arras of embroidered concealments beneath which the sharp cat's claws flash out and are withdrawn, behind which the bitter quarrels of the soul are conducted 'tiffishly.' "—Pamela Hansford Johnson

BROTHERS AND SISTERS
0–8052–8213–0 Schocken pb $5.95

DARKNESS AND DAY
0–575–03477–7 David & Charles $22.95

DAUGHTERS AND SONS
0–575–01796–1 David & Charles $17.95
0–8052–8214–9 Schocken pb $5.95

ELDERS AND BETTERS
0–575–02371–6 David & Charles $18.95
0–8052–8211–4 Schocken pb $5.95

A FAMILY AND A FORTUNE
0–575–02579–4 David & Charles $17.95
0–14–001713–5 Penguin pb $6.95

A FATHER AND HIS FATE
An emotionally manipulative father's attempt to seize his nephew's fiancée against the wishes of his three daughters is frustrated by the return of his wife
0–19–281853–8 Oxford pb $5.95

A GOD AND HIS GIFTS
The pretensions of a male genius are cruelly exposed as his wife and sons become aware that his sexual rapacity indiscriminately devours every woman in the family
0–14–006125–8 Penguin pb $5.95

A HERITAGE AND ITS HISTORY
0–575–02723–1 David & Charles $16.95

A HOUSE AND ITS HEAD
0–575–01579–9 David & Charles $20.95
0–14–001317–2 Penguin pb $6.95

THE LAST AND THE FIRST
0–575–00614–5 David & Charles $18.95

MANSERVANT AND MAIDSERVANT
Introduction by Penelope Lively
0–575–02706–1 David & Charles $18.95
0–19–281380–3 Oxford pb $5.95

MEN AND WIVES
0–575–01581–0 David & Charles $22.95
0–8052–8215–7 Schocken pb $5.95

THE MIGHTY AND THEIR FALL
0–575–02704–5 David & Charles $19.95

MORE WOMEN THAN MEN
0–8052–8210–6 Schocken pb $5.95

PARENTS AND CHILDREN
0–575–01578–0 David & Charles $19.95
0–14–003090–5 Penguin pb $6.95

PASTORS AND MASTERS
0–575–02705–3 David & Charles $15.95
0–8052–8212–2 Schocken pb $5.95

THE PRESENT AND THE PAST
It is Cassius Clare, not his second wife, Flavia, who must beware when her divorced predecessor, Catherine, decides to reenter their life
0–575–01416–4 David & Charles $16.95
0–14–003347–5 Penguin pb $6.95

TWO WORLDS AND THEIR WAYS
0–575–02610–3 David & Charles $18.95

• **Joseph Conrad**
ALMAYER'S FOLLY
Conrad's first novel traces the downfall of a young Dutchman at a remote trading outpost in Borneo
0–14–000036–4 Penguin pb $4.95

CHANCE
The romantic tale of Flora de Barral was Conrad's first great popular success
0–19–281709–4 Oxford pb $4.50

HEART OF DARKNESS
The horrors perpetrated in the name of civilization by the 19th-century rush to colonize attain symbolic power in the narrative of an innocent young ship's officer
0–14–043168–3 Penguin pb $1.95

Joseph Conrad

LORD JIM
His romantic self-image shattered by momentary cowardice, Jim spends his life seeking to recoup his lost honor through an act of heroism
0–19–281625–X Oxford pb $1.95
0–14–043169–1 Penguin pb $1.95

THE NIGGER OF THE "NARCISSUS"
0–19–281623–3 Oxford pb $3.95

THE NIGGER OF THE "NARCISSUS," TYPHOON & OTHER STORIES
0–14–002061–6 Penguin pb $3.95

NOSTROMO
A hero of the people breaks under the conflicting demands of a South American revolution that preserves the silver-producing province for an Anglo-American consortium
0–19–281624–1 Oxford pb $3.95
0–14–043171–3 Penguin pb $3.95

AN OUTCAST OF THE ISLANDS
A tale of self-destruction in the tropics, in the lush and clotted style of Conrad's early novels
0–14–004054–4 Penguin pb $3.95

THE SECRET AGENT
Idealistic anarchists in London destroy their own association by an act of terrorism
0–14–043228–0 Penguin pb $2.50

THE SHADOW LINE
0–19–281686–1 Oxford pb $3.95

TALES OF UNREST
Early stories, including "The Lagoon," in the lush prose typical of Conrad's first period
0–14–003885–X Penguin pb $3.95

TYPHOON & OTHER STORIES
Typhoon's central character, Captain MacWhirr, "is not," Conrad wrote, "an acquaintance of a few hours, or a few weeks, or a few months. He is the product of twenty years of life. My own life"
Introduction by Cedric Watts
0–19–281711–6 Oxford pb $2.95

UNDER WESTERN EYES
The psychological self-destruction of Razumov among prerevolutionary Russian exiles in Geneva
0–14–043243–4 Penguin pb $4.95

YOUTH & THE END OF THE TETHER
0–14–004055–2 Penguin pb $3.95

➤ **FOR OVERSEAS ORDERING INFORMATION, SEE PAGE 1**

● E.M. Delafield
DIARY OF A PROVINCIAL LADY
A popular novel of country life in the
1930s. "What makes it so endearing is the
ambivalence of the tart and rueful narrator
. . . Thoroughly delightful"—*Christian
Science Monitor*
Introduction by Mary Borden
0–89733–053–6 Academy Chicago pb $8.95

● Walter de la Mare
**BEST STORIES OF WALTER DE LA
MARE**
0–571–13076–3 Faber & Faber pb $9.95

MEMOIRS OF A MIDGET
A dark, grotesque, and yet strangely
convincing life-story of a mysteriously
disappearing heroine
Introduction by Angela Carter
0–19–281344–7 Oxford pb $6.95

● Norman Douglas
SOUTH WIND
A colonial bishop is contaminated by the
frivolity of artistic, witty, and eccentric
British expatriates on Capri
0–14–008202–6 Penguin pb $6.95
0–486–24361–3 Dover pb $5.95

● Daphne du Maurier
REBECCA
The famous Gothic novel of an aristocrat's
ingenuous second wife struggling against
the malevolent influence of her dead
predecessor
0–385–04380–5 Doubleday $15.95

THE SCAPEGOAT
A melodrama of exchanged identities
0–88184–409–8 Carroll & Graf pb $4.50

Ronald Firbank
FIVE NOVELS
Includes *Valmouth, Artificial Princess,
The Flower Beneath the Foot, Prancing
Nigger,* and *The Eccentricities of
Cardinal Pirelli.* Plots constantly on the
verge of expiring breathe the purest
spirit of persiflage in these late blooms
of imperial decadence
0–8112–0799–4 New Directions pb $8.95

THREE MORE NOVELS
Includes *Vainglory, Inclinations,* and
Caprice
Introduction by Ernest Jones
0–8112–0975–X New Directions pb $9.95

● Penelope Fitzgerald
INNOCENCE
0–8050–0373–8 Henry Holt $16.95

OFFSHORE
Richly eccentric characters in a houseboat
community in Battersea Reach during the
1960s
0–8050–0561–7 Henry Holt $15.95

● Ford Madox Ford
"There is no novelist of this century more
likely to live than Ford Madox Ford . . . In
an age of increasing carelessness among
good writers, Ford was an artist. No one
in our century except Henry James has
been more attentive to the craft of
letters."—Graham Greene

A CALL
A novel of sophisticated London life
0–88001–072–X Ecco pb $8.50

THE FIFTH QUEEN
A trilogy about the life of Catherine
Howard, the fifth of Henry VIII's six
wives
0–88001–101–7 Ecco pb $12.95

THE FORD MADOX FORD READER
A large and well-stocked collection that
demonstrates the many aspects of Ford's
talent, as evidenced in stories, excerpts
from novels, essays, and poems
Introduction by Graham Greene
0–88001–122–X Ecco pb $13.50

THE GOOD SOLDIER
A tragic quartet of cross-purposes and
ambiguous motivations; a meticulously
told and ultimately horrifying tale, which
many consider Ford's masterpiece
0–394–71386–9 Random House pb $4.95

LADIES WHOSE BRIGHT EYES
The English riposte to Twain's *A
Connecticut Yankee at King Arthur's Court*
0–88001–088–6 Ecco pb $9.50

NO ENEMY
The aftereffects of World War I on a single
personality
0–88001–062–2 Ecco pb $8.50

PARADE'S END
The complete Tietjens tetralogy, consisting
of *Some Do Not, No More Parades, A Man
Could Stand Up,* and *Last Post.* The
misadventures of a public-school Candide
during World War I expose the hypocrisy
and corruption of military and civilian
alike, and provide an elegy for a lost era
0–394–43972–4 Knopf $18.95
0–394–74108–0 Random House pb $9.95

THE RASH ACT
"*The Rash Act* ought to be bought and
read by all interested in the novel as an art
form . . . The action takes place in the
French South which Ford loved, but man
no longer sustains the tradition of myth
and history which that region once
represented"—Anthony Burgess
Introduction by C.H. Sisson
0–85635–399–X Carcanet $14.95
0–85635–529–1 Carcanet pb $8.50

● E.M. Forster
**THE CELESTIAL OMNIBUS & OTHER
STORIES**
A blind alley is the departure point for a
tour of heaven conducted by Sir Thomas
Browne; a lonely soul breaks out of the
automated world of the future and once
again sees the stars
0–394–72176–4 Random House pb $3.95

COLLECTED TALES OF E.M. FORSTER
"What binds all these stories together . . .
is the myth of the Gay Noble Savage"—
Stanton & Crichfield
0–394–41978–2 Knopf $19.95

**THE ETERNAL MOMENT & OTHER
STORIES**
0–15–629125–8 HBJ pb $4.95

HOWARDS END
Forster contrasts the inner lives of the half-
German Schlegels and the robust English
Wilcoxes
0–553–21208–7 Bantam pb $3.95

**THE LIFE TO COME & OTHER
STORIES**
Introduction by Oliver Stallybrass
0–393–30442–6 Norton pb $5.95

THE LONGEST JOURNEY
The contrast of the lives of two half-
brothers elevates a crude zest for life over
public-school stuffiness
0–394–70040–6 Random House pb $4.95

MAURICE
In this posthumous publication, Forster
draws on his own experiences as a
homosexual in an unforgiving society
0–393–00026–5 Norton pb $4.95

A PASSAGE TO INDIA
The social chasm between ruled and ruler
in British India contributes to bitterly
ironic misunderstandings when an attempt
is made to bridge the gap
0–15–171141–0 HBJ $11.95
0–15–671142–7 HBJ pb $5.95

PHAROS AND PHARILLON
0–916870–28–6 Creative Arts pb $4.95

A ROOM WITH A VIEW
Lucy Honeychurch is torn between a
vibrant railway clerk and a desiccated
intellectual
0–553–21323–7 Bantam pb $3.95

WHERE ANGELS FEAR TO TREAD
British priggishness in conflict with Italian
ardor over the offspring of a misalliance
between two families
0–8419–5803–3 Holmes & Meier $29.50

● John Galsworthy
THE FORSYTE SAGA
The fortunes of an English family from
1886 to the 1920s pivot on the contrast
between Soames, the man of property, and
his artistic cousin Jolyon. Originally
published separately as *The Man of
Property, In Chancery,* and *To Let*
0–684–17653–X Scribners pb $15.95

A MODERN COMEDY
A continuation of the Forsyte saga,
encompassing *The White Monkey, The
Silver Spoon,* and *Swan Song*
0–02–542370–3 Macmillan $50.00

● Rumer Godden
THE DARK HORSE
0–670–25664–1 Viking $11.95

AN EPISODE OF SPARROWS
0–670–29734–8 Viking $7.95

● Robert Graves
I, CLAUDIUS
The pedantic ugly duckling of the imperial
family survives mad rulers and political
purges to inherit the Roman Empire
0–394–60811–9 Modern Library $8.95
0–394–72536–0 Random House pb $5.95

CLAUDIUS THE GOD
A bumbling nonentity proves his ability to
govern Rome before succumbing to the
poisoned mushrooms of his power-mad
wife
0–394–60812–7 Modern Library $8.95
0–394–72537–9 Random House pb $4.95

COLLECTED SHORT STORIES
0–14–002881–1 Penguin pb $6.95

COUNT BELISARIUS
The military genius of Justinian's empire recovers Italy and Africa from Vandals and Goths, but at Theodora's demand submits to his wife's infidelities
0–374–51739–8 Farrar, Straus & Giroux pb $12.95

HERCULES, MY SHIPMATE
Graves recreates the search for the Golden Fleece
0–374–51677–4 Farrar, Straus & Giroux pb $9.95

HOMER'S DAUGHTER
A novel rooted in Graves's theories on the authorship of *The Odyssey*. "Here," he wrote, "is the story of a high-spirited and religious-minded Sicilian girl who saves her father's throne from usurpation, herself from a distasteful marriage and her two younger brothers from butchery by boldly making things happen, instead of sitting still and hoping for the best"
0–89733–059–5 Academy Chicago pb $8.95

KING JESUS
A characteristically unorthodox treatment
0–374–18114–4 Farrar, Straus & Giroux $20.00
0–374–51664–2 Farrar, Straus & Giroux pb $6.95

SERGEANT LAMB'S AMERICA
A novel of the American Revolution from the English point of view
0–89733–213–X Academy Chicago pb $7.95

THEY HANGED MY SAINTLY BILLY
A Victorian fresco, based on a murder trial of the era
0–89733–029–3 Academy Chicago pb $6.95

WATCH THE NORTH WIND RISE
A magical utopia situated in the future
0–374–51679–0 Farrar, Straus & Giroux pb $9.95

• Henry Green
Green's terse, elliptical, and utterly serious comedies are among the most original creations of modern British fiction. Unfortunately, several of his best books—notably *Loving* and *Party Going*—are (we trust momentarily) out of print.

BACK
The aftermath of World War II as experienced by a returning veteran
0–8112–0798–6 New Directions pb $7.95

CONCLUDING
In a state dystopia of the future, two girls escape from a soulless institution to seek out other free spirits
Foreword by Eudora Welty
0–226–30611–9 Chicago pb $7.95

NOTHING, DOTING & BLINDNESS
An omnibus of three novels
0–14–005664–5 Penguin pb $6.95

• Graham Greene
COLLECTED STORIES
0–670–22911–3 Viking $16.95
0–14–008070–8 Penguin pb $7.95

BRIGHTON ROCK
In this precursor of *A Clockwork Orange*, an alienated teenage gang leader at a holiday resort waits for his enemies to catch up with him
0–14–000442–4 Penguin pb $3.95

A BURNT-OUT CASE
A celebrity and philanderer ends up working at an African leper colony
0–14–001894–8 Penguin pb $3.95

THE CAPTAIN AND THE ENEMY
Greene's most recent novel
0–670–82405–4 Viking $17.95
0–14–012418–7 Penguin pb $7.95

THE COMEDIANS
A tense drama of foreigners caught up in the violence of Papa Doc Duvalier's Haiti
0–14–002766–1 Penguin pb $4.95

THE CONFIDENTIAL AGENT
An anti-Fascist emissary in London encounters a nightmare world of betrayal and murder
0–14–001895–6 Penguin pb $3.95

DR. FISCHER OF GENEVA, OR THE BOMB PARTY
0–670–27522–0 Viking $20.00

THE END OF THE AFFAIR
An adulterous affair ends tragically in one of Greene's best novels, which hinges ultimately on Catholic doctrine
0–14–004696–8 Penguin pb $5.95

ENGLAND MADE ME
"The fragments of reality are wonderfully magnified through the glass of a strange powerful imagination"—Julian Symons
0–14–003146–4 Penguin pb $4.95

A GUN FOR SALE
A suspense novel about a hit man, also known as *This Gun for Hire*
0–670–70172–6 Viking $16.95
0–14–001896–4 Penguin pb $3.95

THE HEART OF THE MATTER
Scobie, a West African police commissioner during the war, allows compassion for his wife and his mistress to overcome his sense of duty. Many find this Greene's most powerful book
0–14–001789–1 Penguin pb $4.95

THE HONORARY CONSUL
A British derelict in Argentina tries to maintain tone throughout terrorist activity
0–670–37872–0 Viking $20.95

THE HUMAN FACTOR
An ironic novel of espionage. "The most near-perfect novel in English of the last ten years and his own best"—Don Coles
0–670–38625–1 Viking $20.95

IT'S A BATTLEFIELD
0–14–000257–X Penguin pb $4.95

LOSER TAKES ALL
0–14–003277–0 Penguin pb $3.95

THE MAN WITHIN
0–14–003283–5 Penguin pb $3.95

MAY WE BORROW YOUR HUSBAND? & Other Comedies of the Sexual Life
0–14–003030–1 Penguin pb $3.95

THE MINISTRY OF FEAR
A thriller about a network of Nazi spies in wartime London
0–14–001897–2 Penguin pb $4.95

OUR MAN IN HAVANA
An ironic touch alleviates the tragic consequences of a vacuum salesman's unwitting involvement in spy games between great powers
0–14–001790–9 Penguin pb $4.95

STAMBOUL TRAIN
Greene's first successful novel, a thriller published in 1932; also known as *Orient Express*
0–14–001898–0 Penguin pb $3.95

THE THIRD MAN & LOSER TAKES ALL
0–670–70084–3 Viking $20.95

THE THIRD MAN & THE FALLEN IDOL
The sources for two outstanding British films of the late '40s
0–14–003278–9 Penguin pb $3.95

TWENTY-ONE STORIES
0–14–003093–X Penguin pb $3.95

THE POWER AND THE GLORY
An alcoholic priest in poverty-stricken Mexico struggles to vindicate the kingdom of heaven within and without
0–670–56979–8 Viking $16.95
0–14–001791–7 Penguin pb $3.95

THE QUIET AMERICAN
A prescient novel of Vietnam, published in 1955: A cynical British opium addict's resentment against American inheritors of French colonialism leads to betrayal and murder
0–14–001792–5 Penguin pb $4.95

TRAVELS WITH MY AUNT
0–14–003221–5 Penguin pb $4.95

• Radclyffe Hall
ADAM'S BREED
0–14–016124–4 Penguin pb $6.95

THE WELL OF LONELINESS
The classic novel of lesbianism provoked a storm of opposition when published in 1928
0–380–54247–1 Avon pb $5.95

• Patrick Hamilton
THE SLAVES OF SOLITUDE
Introduction by Claud Cockburn
0–19–281359–5 Oxford pb $5.95

• L.P. Hartley
THE COMPLETE SHORT STORIES OF L.P. HARTLEY
"Matches the obsessive images of evil and horror with the observation of the endless capriciousness of life, and horror with the most sophisticated humour"—John Athos
0–8253–0353–2 Beaufort $24.95

• Winifred Holtby
THE LAND OF GREEN GINGER
A young woman outgrows her illusions
0–915864–25–8 Academy Chicago pb $5.95

• Aldous Huxley
AFTER MANY A SUMMER DIES THE SWAN
Huxley's entry in the Britisher-in-Hollywood genre stages an intellectual firework display against the backdrop of a hilarious burlesque of Hearst's San Simeon
0–06–091063–1 Harper & Row pb $5.95

BRAVE NEW WORLD
The most famous dystopia of them all satirizes a rationalist paradise where genetic and social control breeds out creativity and passion, and breeds in hygienic promiscuity
0–06–012037–1 Harper & Row $12.95
0–06–083095–6 Harper & Row pb $4.95

BRAVE NEW WORLD & BRAVE NEW WORLD REVISITED
0–06–090101–2 Harper & Row pb $8.95

EYELESS IN GAZA
0–88184–460–8 Carroll & Graf pb $9.95

ISLAND
A late novel of a utopian society founded on the benefits of a mystical drug
0–06–083101–4 Harper & Row pb $3.95

POINT COUNTER POINT
A brilliant novel containing thinly disguised portraits of some of Huxley's contemporaries
0–06–012105–X Harper & Row $12.95
0–06–083048–4 Harper & Row pb $4.95

• Christopher Isherwood

ALL THE CONSPIRATORS
0–8112–0725–0 New Directions pb $7.95

THE BERLIN STORIES
Includes *Goodbye to Berlin* and *The Last of Mr. Norris*. Portrays more sensitively than its musical offshoot, *Cabaret*, the erosion and decadence of the last years of the Weimar Republic
0–8112–0070–1 New Directions pb $7.95

DOWN THERE ON A VISIT
"It belongs with Rousseau's *Confessions* and Gide's *Journal* and it has about it the authentic ring of a small offbeat classic"—William Peden, *Saturday Review*
0–374–52052–6 Farrar, Straus & Giroux pb $8.95

A MEETING BY THE RIVER
0–374–52076–3 Farrar, Straus & Giroux pb $6.95

THE MEMORIAL: Portrait of a Family
0–374–52067–4 Farrar, Straus & Giroux pb $7.95

PRATER VIOLET
The tragic aura of events from the Reichstag fire to the Anschluss darkens this satire about a Viennese producer's frothy movie project
0–374–52053–4 Farrar, Straus & Giroux pb $5.95

A SINGLE MAN
The Britisher-in-Hollywood genre receives a twist in this novel of a day in the life of an older man who has just lost his male lover
0–374–52038–0 Farrar, Straus & Giroux pb $6.95

THE WORLD IN THE EVENING
0–374–52088–7 Farrar, Straus & Giroux pb $8.95

James Joyce
DUBLINERS
Joyce described these stories as chapters in the moral history of Dublin. "In calling his original jottings 'epiphanies,' Joyce underscored the ironic contrast between the manifestation that dazzled the Magi and the apparitions that manifest themselves on the streets of Dublin; he also suggested that those pathetic and sordid glimpses . . . offer a kind of revelation"—Harry Levin
0–14–015505–8 Penguin $9.95
0–394–60464–4 Modern Library $6.95
0–14–004222–9 Penguin pb $4.95

GIACOMO JOYCE
Edited by Richard Ellmann
0–571–13164–6 Faber & Faber pb $4.95

FINNEGANS WAKE
"It is a strange book, a compound of fable, symphony, and nightmare—a monstrous enigma beckoning

---

imperiously from the shadowy pits of sleep"—Joseph Campbell & Henry Morton Robinson
0–670–31538–9 Viking $30.00
0–14–006286–6 Penguin pb $8.95

A PORTRAIT OF THE ARTIST AS A YOUNG MAN
In writing the story of the growth of a human soul and of an artist, Joyce sought to portray the past as what he called a "fluid succession of presents." "The first page, which looks like a long passage of baby talk, is an elaborate construct that relates the development of the senses to the development of the arts"—Frank O'Connor
Edited by Richard Ellmann
0–14–004221–0 Penguin pb $3.95

THE PORTABLE JAMES JOYCE
A useful collection that includes the lyrics and verse satires as well as selections from the major works
Introduction by Harry Levin
0–14–015030–7 Penguin pb $8.95

STEPHEN HERO
A discarded early version of *A Portrait of the Artist*, couched in the realistic manner of the late 19th century
Introduction by Theodore Spencer
0–8112–0074–4 New Directions pb $7.95

ULYSSES
"On nothing is *Ulysses* more insistent than on the fact that there is no Bloom there, no Stephen there, no Molly there, no Dublin there, simply language. To say this is by no means to surrender to the artificer's whimsical virtuosity. We and he are co-creators; characters and city have their existence in our minds"—Hugh Kenner
0–394–60486–5 Modern Library $15.95

ULYSSES: The Corrected Text
This new text, claiming to correct many errors that crept into previous editions, has provoked a storm of controversy
Introduction by Richard Ellmann
0–394–55373–X Random House $24.45
0–394–74312–1 Random House pb $15.95

James Joyce by Wyndham Lewis, from The Oxford Illustrated History of English Literature

---

• Molly Keane (M.J. Farrell)

DEVOTED LADIES
0–14–016101–5 Penguin pb $6.95

FULL HOUSE
Introduction by Caroline Blackwood
0–14–016154–6 Penguin pb $6.95

GOOD BEHAVIOUR
"A dark, subtle, savagely amusing study of the decline of a well-born Irish family after the First World War"—Anne Tyler, *NY Times*
0–394–51818–7 Knopf $10.95
0–525–48224–5 Dutton pb $8.95

RISING TIDE
0–14–016100–7 Penguin pb $7.95

TIME AFTER TIME
"Thoroughly well-organized traditional study of intrigue, malice, and roguery . . . It is spirited, without tears . . . No Celtic twilight here!"—V.S. Pritchett, *NY Review of Books*
0–394–53280–5 Knopf $13.45
0–525–48159–1 Dutton pb $8.95

• Arthur Koestler

DARKNESS AT NOON
The complicated dance of idealism and falsehood in the thoughts of an imprisoned former commissar who is required to distort his own lifework for the good of the regime
0–02–565200–1 Macmillan $27.50
0–553–26595–4 Bantam pb $4.50

• D.H. Lawrence
The intemperate, tubercular coal miner's son looked like a satyr, at times filled his writing with crazed messianism, was accused by Bertrand Russell and others of espousing fascism, and—by loosening the sexual clamp on the English novel of the 1910s, '20s, and '30s—excited the imaginations of several generations of readers. Among the editions listed below, the Cambridge series presents new texts incorporating recent research.

THE COMPLETE SHORT STORIES OF D.H. LAWRENCE

Volume 1
0–14–004382–9 Penguin pb $4.95

Volume 2
0–14–004255–5 Penguin pb $4.95

Volume 3
0–14–004383–7 Penguin pb $4.95

AARON'S ROD
"If *Aaron's Rod* can be said to have a theme it is the gratification of [Lawrence's] always frustrated longing for power . . . We have a dilution of what he called his philosophy, but chiefly we have the satirical Lawrence, not at his best, but almost at the level of spiteful gossip"—Richard Aldington
0–14–000755–5 Penguin pb $5.95

THE BOY IN THE BUSH
0–14–001935–9 Penguin pb $6.95

KANGAROO
Lawrence's brilliant evocation of the strange life forms of the Antipodes overwhelms the somewhat dubious political intentions of his novel
0–14–009892–5 Penguin pb $5.95

LADY CHATTERLEY'S LOVER
The gamekeeper and the lady celebrate the triumph of sexual love in Lawrence's most programmatic novel
0–451–52247–8 NAL pb $2.95

THE LOST GIRL
0–14–000752–0 Penguin pb $5.95

LOVE AMONG THE HAYSTACKS & OTHER STORIES
0–521–26836–2 Cambridge $59.50
0–521–33674–0 Cambridge pb $19.95

MR. NOON
Not discovered until 1972, *Mr. Noon* is a semiautobiographical sequel to *Sons and Lovers* in which a young schoolmaster's love affair causes him to break with provincial life. "For anyone interested in the derivation and interpretation of Lawrence's sexual doctrine, it is mandatory reading"—Diana Trilling
0–521–25251–2 Cambridge $24.95
0–670–80818–0 Viking $22.50
0–521–27247–5 Cambridge pb $12.95
0–14–008341–3 Penguin pb $7.95

THE PLUMED SERPENT
The mythic undertones of Aztec Mexico revitalize the tired blood of western tourists. "For sheer magnificence of writing, Lawrence has surpassed himself"—Katherine Anne Porter
0–521–22262–1 Cambridge $79.50
0–521–29422–3 Cambridge pb $24.95

THE PRUSSIAN OFFICER & OTHER STORIES
Rebellious spontaneity against the rigidity of domination in a love/hate clash between a martinet and his valet
0–670–58053–8 Viking $18.95
0–521–28985–8 Cambridge pb $19.95

THE RAINBOW
The Brangwen sisters, Ursula and Gudrun, free themselves from the deeply rooted traditions of their Midlands family
0–14–043155–1 Penguin pb $4.95

SONS AND LOVERS
The talents of a sensitive young man are liberated from a coal-mining background by an intelligent but dominating mother
0–14–004217–2 Penguin pb $4.95

ST. MAWR & OTHER STORIES
0–521–29425–8 Cambridge pb $19.95

THE TRESPASSER
0–670–72991–4 Viking $20.00

THE VIRGIN AND THE GIPSY
0–394–72666–9 Random House pb $5.95

THE WHITE PEACOCK
0–670–76358–6 Viking $22.50

WOMEN IN LOVE
Love for the Brangwen sisters breaks Gerald Crich, the masterful man of affairs, but enhances the life of the artist Rupert Birkin
0–14–004260–1 Penguin pb $3.95

• Rosamond Lehmann
THE ECHOING GROVE
An exploration of the relationship between a married woman and her sister, who becomes her husband's lover
0–15–627487–6 HBJ pb $5.95

• C.S. Lewis
THE SPACE TRILOGY
0–02–022360–9 Macmillan pb (boxed set) $11.95

Volume 1: Out of the Silent Planet
Ransom struggles against interplanetary rationalist science to keep the cosmos safe for Christian fundamentalism
0–02–086910–X Macmillan pb $3.95

Volume 2: Perelandra
A replay of the Adam and Eve story on Venus has a happy ending when the serpent, a scientist from earth, is thwarted by a theologically minded philologist
0–02–086950–9 Macmillan pb $3.95

Volume 3: That Hideous Strength
The ancient powers of Arthurian Britain triumph over satanic rationalism and restore Miltonic marriage ethics
0–02–086960–6 Macmillan pb $4.50

TILL WE HAVE FACES
Transposes into Tolkienlike fantasy the Greek myth of Cupid and Psyche while retaining its allegorical force
0–15–690436–5 HBJ pb $5.95

• Wyndham Lewis
Publisher, novelist, painter, and ferocious critic, Lewis was described by Ezra Pound as "the only English writer who can be compared to Dostoievski." His work, much of it long out of print, has been revived in recent years.

THE APES OF GOD
"No satire in English is more comprehensive and unrelenting than that in *The Apes of God*. The reader looks in vain for a character who embodies the positive values against which the rest are measured"—Paul Edwards
Afterword by Paul Edwards
0–87685–512–5 Black Sparrow pb $15.00

THE COMPLETE WILD BODY
Lewis' major collection of short fiction
Edited by Bernard Lafourcade
0–87685–551–6 Black Sparrow pb $12.50

> **THE HUMAN AGE**
> An elaborate satirical fantasy, only three of whose four projected volumes were completed
> **THE CHILDERMASS**
> 0–7145–0163–8 Riverrun pb $5.95
> **MALIGN FIESTA**
> 0–7145–0355–X Riverrun pb $5.95
> **MONSTRE GAI**
> 0–7145–0386–X Riverrun pb $5.95

THE REVENGE FOR LOVE
A savage novel, ranging in setting from London cocktail parties to the front lines of the Spanish Civil War, which dissects the uses of political ideology. First published in 1937, this is one of Lewis' most accessible works
0–89526–908–2 Regnery pb $5.95

SELF-CONDEMNED
A bitter, revealing novel that reflects the personal failures of Lewis' later life
Afterword by Rowland Smith
0–87685–575–3 Black Sparrow pb $12.50

SNOOTY BARONET
Edited by Bernard Lafourcade
0–87685–599–0 Black Sparrow pb $12.50

THE VULGAR STREAK
One of the more entertaining and formally conventional of Lewis' novels
Afterword by Paul Edwards
0–87685–628–8 Black Sparrow pb $12.50

• Malcolm Lowry
HEAR US O LORD FROM HEAVEN THY DWELLING PLACE
0–88184–281–8 Carroll & Graf pb $9.95

ULTRAMARINE
A semiautobiographical first novel that describes the adventures of a young man with a guitar who runs away to sea
0–88184–258–3 Carroll & Graf pb $7.95

UNDER THE VOLCANO
Lowry's masterpiece renders the last day in the life of an alcoholic Englishman in Mexico with linguistic splendor that transfigures its essentially self-pitying subject matter
0–06–015367–9 Harper & Row $15.95
0–452–25595–3 NAL pb $6.95

• W. Somerset Maugham
THE COLLECTED SHORT STORIES
Maugham's talent flourished best in the short story; a number of his tales have virtually become part of 20th-century mythology

Volume 1
Thirty stories set in Europe and the Pacific, including the famous "Rain"
0–14–001871–9 Penguin pb $4.95

Volume 2
Includes "The Alien Corn" and "The Vessel of Wrath"
0–14–001872–7 Penguin pb $4.95

Volume 3
Contains the espionage stories originally published as *Ashenden*
0–14–001873–5 Penguin pb $4.95

Volume 4
Thirty stories written before World War II, and set in various outposts of the British Empire
0–14–001874–3 Penguin pb $4.95

CAKES AND ALE
One of Maugham's most entertaining novels, a satirical *roman à clef* about the literary life
0–14–000651–6 Penguin pb $4.95

CHRISTMAS HOLIDAY
0–14–002646–0 Penguin pb $5.95

LIZA OF LAMBETH
An early naturalistic novel of Cockney poverty
0–14–002643–6 Penguin pb $5.95

THE MAGICIAN
A melodramatic tale based on the career of the sinister magus Aleister Crowley
0–14–002668–1 Penguin pb $4.95

THE MERRY-GO-ROUND
0–14–003373–4 Penguin pb $5.95

THE MOON AND SIXPENCE
Paul Gauguin was the basis for the character of Charles Strickland, who gives up his family and his job in the city to paint in Tahiti
0–14–000468–X Penguin pb $4.95

MRS. CRADDOCK
0–14–002645–2 Penguin pb $4.95

THE NARROW CORNER
0–14–001859–X Penguin pb $4.95

OF HUMAN BONDAGE
Semiautobiographical novel follows the crippled Philip Carey from his lonely childhood in Blackstable through medical school. The fascinating, cruel waitress Mildred was immortalized on film by Bette Davis
0–14–001861–1 Penguin pb $5.95

THE PAINTED VEIL
A doctor's attempt to punish his wife's infidelity during a cholera epidemic in British Burma has an ironic outcome
0–14–000872–1 Penguin pb $4.95

THE RAZOR'S EDGE
Larry Darrell's training at a Tibetan ashram gives him a unique perspective on the struggle for fun and status in Paris and Chicago in the 1920s
0–14–001860–3 Penguin pb $4.95

UP AT THE VILLA
A brief and ultimately violent novella of sexual passion
0–14–002670–3 Penguin pb $4.95

● Nancy Mitford
CHRISTMAS PUDDING
0–88184–342–3 Carroll & Graf pb $3.95

HIGHLAND FLING
0–88184–390–3 Carroll & Graf pb $3.95

Flann O'Brien
AT SWIM-TWO-BIRDS
A phantasmagoria of a comic novel, first published in 1939, in which multiple plots intrude on each other with maddening unpredictability, and language runs wild on every page
0–452–25913–4 NAL pb $8.95

THE POOR MOUTH: A Bad Story About the Hard Life
Some Irish readers had trouble forgiving O'Brien for this savagely parodistic novel, originally written in Gaelic, which depicts traditional Irish peasant life in less than idyllic terms
Translated by Patrick Power
Illustrated by Ralph Steadman
0–394–17849–1 Seaver pb $4.95

THE THIRD POLICEMAN
O'Brien depicts—with wild humor masking ultimate horror—a circular Hell inhabited largely by semi-human bicycles
0–452–25912–6 NAL pb $7.95

● Frank O'Connor
COLLECTED STORIES
0–394–51602–8 Knopf $20.00
0–394–71048–7 Random House pb $10.95

● Sean O'Faolain
THE COLLECTED STORIES OF SEAN O'FAOLAIN
0–316–63294–5 Little, Brown $29.95

BIRD ALONE
Introduction by Benedict Kiely
0–19–281906–2 Oxford pb $5.95

● Liam O'Flaherty
FAMINE
A chronicle of the Great Hunger of the 1840s
Afterword by Thomas Flanagan
0–87923–412–1 Godine $18.95
0–87923–434–2 Godine pb $9.95

THE INFORMER
A drunkard is destroyed by his own guilt after betraying an IRA leader to the authorities
0–15–644356–2 HBJ pb $4.95

THE WILDERNESS
Foreword by A.A. Kelly
0–396–09130–X Dodd, Mead $16.95

● George Orwell
ANIMAL FARM
A farmyard parable of revolution in which the new regime comes to look much like the old
0–15–107252–3 HBJ $12.95
0–452–25428–0 NAL pb $4.95

BURMESE DAYS
An early novel based on Orwell's experiences in the colonial service
0–15–114975–5 HBJ $8.95
0–15–614850–1 HBJ pb $4.95

A CLERGYMAN'S DAUGHTER
A mysterious relocation into London's lower depths transforms the quiet life and orthodox views of a proper young lady
0–15–618065–0 HBJ pb $8.95

COMING UP FOR AIR
An insurance salesman breaks out of his daily routine to revisit his native village
0–15–619625–5 HBJ pb $6.95

KEEP THE ASPIDISTRA FLYING
0–15–646899–9 HBJ pb $6.95

1984
The most famous dystopian novel ever written
0–452–25426–4 NAL pb $5.95

● Anthony Powell

A DANCE TO THE MUSIC OF TIME

Volume 1: First Movement
Includes *A Question of Upbringing, A Buyer's Market, The Acceptance World.* "The most sophisticated chronicle of modern life we have"—C. David Benson, *New Republic*
0–316–71535–2 Little, Brown $24.95

Volume 2: Second Movement
Includes *At Lady Molly's, Casanova's Chinese Restaurant, The Kindly Ones*
0–316–71536–0 Little, Brown $24.95

Volume 3: Third Movement
Includes *The Valley of Bones, The Soldier's Art, The Military Philosophers*
0–316–71546–8 Little, Brown $24.95

Volume 4: Fourth Movement
Include *Books Do Furnish a Room, Temporary Kings, Hearing Secret Harmonies*
0–316–71548–4 Little, Brown $24.95

A QUESTION OF UPBRINGING
The transition of Nick Jenkins, the youthful narrator, from Eton to London introduces such central characters as

Widmerpool, Stringham, and the unbowed Uncle Giles
0–445–20010–3 Warner pb $3.95

A BUYER'S MARKET
Stringham and Mr. Deacon bring a flavor of the demi-monde to Nick's unavailing attendance on London debutantes
0–445–20021–9 Warner pb $3.95

THE ACCEPTANCE WORLD
The reappearance of Peter Templer and his sister Jean jolts Nick out of his routine among the literary lights of the capital
0–445–20032–4 Warner pb $3.95

AT LADY MOLLY'S
A madly eccentric cast of dispossessed aristocrats and upward-bound parvenus attend the seedy salon of Lady Molly in the 1930s
0–445–20055–3 Warner pb $3.95

CASANOVA'S CHINESE RESTAURANT
Nick marries into the Tolland family and recognizes old friends amid the hubbub of the Abdication and the Spanish Civil War
0–445–20070–7 Warner pb $3.95

THE KINDLY ONES
Retrospective to scenes from Nick's childhood, and the egregiousness of Widmerpool in the days after Munich
0–445–20111–8 Warner pb $3.95

THE VALLEY OF BONES
Nick's wartime service begins in backwater posts in Ireland and Wales among an assortment of military oddballs
0–445–20144–4 Warner pb $3.95

THE SOLDIER'S ART
Back in London during the Blitz, Nick acridly observes Major Widmerpool jockeying against Hogbourne-Jones for precedence
0–445–20126–6 Warner pb $3.95

BOOKS DO FURNISH A ROOM
0–445–20135–5 Warner pb $4.50

THE MILITARY PHILOSOPHERS
0–445–20133–9 Warner pb $4.50

TEMPORARY KINGS
Nick's literary talents gain recognition while the now-enobled Widmerpool contends with his wife's numerous lovers
0–445–20145–2 Warner pb $4.50

HEARING SECRET HARMONIES
Britain in the '60s daunts all the Old Guard except Widmerpool, who attaches himself to the counterculture hero Scorpio Murtlock
0–445–20146–0 Warner pb $4.50

John Cowper Powys
A GLASTONBURY ROMANCE
A monumental novel first published in 1932, set in the modern era but drawing on the supernatural legends associated with Glastonbury
0–87951–282–2 Overlook $24.95

MAIDEN CASTLE
0–912568–01–1 Colgate $14.00

RODMOOR
0–912568–05–4 Colgate $14.00

THREE FANTASIES
Afterword by Glen Cavaliero
0–85635–693–X Carcanet pb $7.50

• J.B. Priestley

ANGEL PAVEMENT
A bittersweet 1930 novel concerning the effects of venture capitalism on the employees and families of a small London fine arts dealer
0–226–68210–2 Chicago pb $8.95

BRIGHT DAY
0–226–68211–0 Chicago pb $7.95

THE GOOD COMPANIONS
Edwardian propriety goes unsullied in this picaresque tale of the jolly adventures of a theatrical company in the provinces
0–226–68223–4 Chicago pb $9.95

• V.S. Pritchett

COLLECTED STORIES
"Pritchett remains one of the few writers who can discern in the distances between the pieces of furniture a story as dramatic as a divorce"—*Boston Globe*
0–394–52417–9 Random House $20.00

MORE COLLECTED STORIES
0–394–53128–0 Random House $17.95

MR. BELUNCLE
A fond but lucid eye for the idiosyncrasies of British dissenters informs this tale of an adherent of the Parkinsonian sect
0–19–281960–7 Oxford pb $6.95

CAMBERWELL BEAUTY & OTHER STORIES
0–394–49222–6 Random House $9.95

DEAD MAN LEADING
Introduction by Paul Theroux
0–19–281469–9 Oxford pb $6.95

ON THE EDGE OF THE CLIFF & OTHER STORIES
0–394–50485–2 Random House $11.95
0–394–74047–5 Random House pb $3.95

• Herbert Read

THE GREEN CHILD
Introduction by Kenneth Rexroth
0–8112–0172–4 New Directions pb $5.95

• Mary Renault

THE BULL FROM THE SEA
A retelling of the story of Theseus, Hippolyta, and the Amazons
0–394–71504–7 Random House pb $4.95

THE CHARIOTEER
A young man who discovers his homosexuality when convalescing after Dunkirk must choose between a heroic naval officer or a conscientious objector
0–394–71480–6 Pantheon pb $4.95

FIRE FROM HEAVEN
0–394–42492–1 Pantheon $15.95
0–394–72291–4 Random House pb $5.95

THE FRIENDLY YOUNG LADIES
0–394–73369–X Pantheon pb $6.95

FUNERAL GAMES
0–394–52068–8 Pantheon $14.00

THE KING MUST DIE
Recreating the story of Theseus and the labyrinth of Crete, Renault effectively transmutes archaic history
0–394–43195–2 Pantheon $15.95
0–394–75104–3 Random House pb $6.95

THE LAST OF THE WINE
0–394–71653–1 Random House pb $4.95

THE MASK OF APOLLO
0–394–75105–1 Random House pb $6.95

THE PERSIAN BOY
Alexander the Great through the eyes of his young catamite of Persian noble birth
0–394–48191–7 Pantheon $15.95
0–394–75101–9 Random House pb $6.95

THE PRAISE SINGER
0–394–50273–6 Pantheon $12.95
0–394–75102–7 Random House pb $6.95

• Jean Rhys

John Updike has described Jean Rhys's fiction as "amazing in its resolute economy of style and in its illusionless portrait of a drifting heroine, a portrait . . . stunningly honest and severe."

> **THE COMPLETE NOVELS**
> Includes *After Leaving Mr. Mackenzie, Voyage in the Dark, Quartet, Good Morning, Midnight,* and *Wide Sargasso Sea*
> Photographs by Brassaï
> Introduction by Diana Athill
> 0–393–02226–9 Norton $25.00
>
> **THE COLLECTED SHORT STORIES**
> 0–393–02375–3 Norton $19.95

GOOD MORNING, MIDNIGHT
Rhys searingly depicts the vulnerability of a young woman adrift in Paris and at the mercy of a predatory male
0–393–30394–2 Norton pb $6.95

VOYAGE IN THE DARK
0–393–00083–4 Norton pb $3.95

WIDE SARGASSO SEA
Derived from *Jane Eyre*, this *tour de force* about the adolescence and marriage of Rochester's first wife turns the tropical landscape of the West Indies into an image for her tormented soul
0–393–00056–7 Norton pb $3.95

• Dorothy Richardson

THE QUEST OF SIMON RICHARDSON
0–575–03853–5 David & Charles $24.95

> **Frederick Rolfe (Baron Corvo)**
> **THE DESIRE AND PURSUIT OF THE WHOLE: A Romance of Modern Venice**
> Introduction by W.H. Auden
> 0–306–80258–9 Da Capo pb $9.95

• Vita Sackville-West

FAMILY HISTORY
Introduction by Victoria Glendinning
0–14–016156–2 Penguin pb $6.95

NO SIGNPOSTS IN THE SEA
0–14–016107–4 Penguin pb $6.95

• Saki

"The Edwardian era, in spite of its political idiocies and a sinister sense of foreboding which, to intelligent observers, underlay the latter part of it, must have been, socially at least, very charming. It is this evanescent charm that Saki so effortlessly evoked."—Noel Coward

THE BEST OF SAKI
Witty and malign gems idealize (or satirize) the Edwardian dandies who were to die in the trenches
Edited with an introduction by Graham Greene
0–14–004484–1 Penguin pb $6.95

THE CHRONICLES OF CLOVIS
The scourge of the country-house set: no bridge game, no hunting party, no children's game, is safe from Clovis' clever pranks
Introduction by Auberon Waugh
0–14–008355–3 Penguin pb $4.95

THE SHORT STORIES OF SAKI
Introduction by Christopher Morley
0–394–60428–8 Modern Library $10.95

THE STORY-TELLER
Thirteen stories about children getting revenge on their elders
Illustrated by Jeanne Titherington
0–87923–646–9 Godine pb $9.95

THE UNBEARABLE BASSINGTON
The blasé tone of the short stories is maintained and improved upon in Saki's only novel
Introduction by Joan Aiken
0–19–281371–4 Oxford pb $5.95

> **Siegfried Sassoon**
> **COMPLETE MEMOIRS OF GEORGE SHERSTON**
> Sassoon traces the career of the author's fictional alter ego from his privileged early manhood through his protest against the militaristic folly of the conduct of the Great War
> 0–571–06146–X Faber & Faber $18.95
> 0–571–09913–0 Faber & Faber pb $11.95
>
> **MEMOIRS OF A FOX-HUNTING MAN**
> The first volume of Sherston's memoirs recounts with nostalgia the pre-war world of the sportsman and cricketer
> 0–571–06454–X Faber & Faber pb $6.95
>
> **MEMOIRS OF AN INFANTRY OFFICER**
> The second volume of the Sherston memoirs describes a young subaltern who makes a quixotic protest against the horror of the trenches
> 0–571–06410–8 Faber & Faber pb $6.95
>
> **SHERSTON'S PROGRESS**
> Sherston returns to the war from his enforced hospitalization following his antimilitarist protest
> 0–571–13033–X Faber & Faber pb $6.95

• C.P. Snow

STRANGERS AND BROTHERS
A semi-autobiographical series of novels about Lewis Eliot's progress from a poor home to a position of importance as assistant to the secretary of war

Volume 1
0–684–18374–9 Scribners $14.95

Volume 2
0–684–18375–7 Scribners $14.95

Volume 3
0–684–18376–5 Scribners $14.95

TO ORDER BOOKS AS GIFTS, SEE PAGE 1

TIME OF HOPE
From a modest background, Lewis Eliot struggles to establish himself in professional life and free himself from an unhappy affair
0–684–15315–7 Scribners $20.00

HOMECOMINGS
After one lover's suicide, Lewis Eliot almost destroys his own happiness and that of the woman he loves before he discovers his real feelings
0–684–15133–2 Scribners $17.50

THE AFFAIR
Conflict in Cambridge over the dismissal of a physicist for possible Communist affiliations is resolved by a cynical compromise
0–684–15317–3 Scribners $20.00

A COAT OF VARNISH
0–684–16949–5 Scribners pb $7.95

IN THEIR WISDOM
0–02–025400–8 Macmillan pb $9.95

THE LIGHT AND THE DARK
Roy Calvert's search for meaning among the political ideologies of the 1930s reveals the spiritual emptiness of a generation
0–684–14841–2 Scribners $20.00

THE MASTERS
Inside look at Senior Common Room politics over the election of a new master of a Cambridge college
0–684–14744–0 Scribners $20.00
0–684–71897–9 Scribners pb $9.95

THE REALISTS
0–02–025410–5 Macmillan pb $9.95

James Stephens
THE CROCK OF GOLD
A lilting, sentimental novel that takes a fantasy journey into the heart of Irish folklore
0–02–025520–9 Macmillan pb $8.95

• Rex Warner
THE AERODROME
Warner, a great classical scholar, published this dark political fantasy in 1941
Introduction by Anthony Burgess
0–19–281336–6 Oxford pb $7.95

• Sylvia Townsend Warner
FOUR IN HAND: A Quartet of Novels
Introduction by William Maxwell
0–393–02356–7 Norton $25.00

LOLLY WILLOWES
"The witty, eerie, tender but firm life history of a middle-class Englishwoman who politely declines to make the expected connection with the opposite sex and becomes a witch instead"—John Updike
Introduction by Anita Miller
0–915864–92–4 Academy Chicago $14.95
0–915864–91–6 Academy Chicago pb $7.95

SUMMER WILL SHOW
0–14–016176–7 Penguin pb $6.95

• Evelyn Waugh
BLACK MISCHIEF
Satire and Grand Guignol whimsy in postcolonial Africa as a band of British colonists flees revolution
0–316–92613–2 Little, Brown $15.95
0–316–92609–4 Little, Brown pb $7.95

BRIDESHEAD REVISITED
Roman Catholic aristocrats succumb to age and alcohol, but bequeath their spirit to the middle-class narrator
0–316–92627–2 Little, Brown $15.95
0–316–92634–5 Little, Brown pb $7.95

CHARLES RYDER'S SCHOOLDAYS & OTHER STORIES
The title story tells more about the protagonist of *Brideshead Revisited*
0–316–92638–8 Little, Brown $15.95
0–316–92639–6 Little, Brown pb $7.95

A HANDFUL OF DUST
"Waugh treats society as a wonderland in which he plays the part of a rude, libellous, yet domestic Alice"—V.S. Pritchett
0–316–92614–0 Little, Brown $15.95
0–316–92605–1 Little, Brown pb $7.95

THE LOVED ONE
This classic Britisher-in-Hollywood novel inters the burlesque fantasia of L.A. funeral customs with mordant wit
0–316–92618–3 Little, Brown $13.95
0–316–92608–6 Little, Brown pb $6.95

SWORD OF HONOUR TRILOGY
"Through the ranks of Waugh's army move some of the phoniest, most brazen picaroons in English literature, and in its infinite, inefficient reaches lurk the grotesques, fossils, and fantasts of all good burlesque"—Steven Marcus

MEN AT ARMS
0–316–92629–9 Little, Brown $15.95
0–316–92628–0 Little, Brown pb $7.95

OFFICERS AND GENTLEMEN
0–316–92631–0 Little, Brown $15.95
0–316–92630–2 Little, Brown pb $7.95

THE END OF THE BATTLE
0–316–92621–3 Little, Brown $15.95
0–316–92620–5 Little, Brown pb $7.95

PUT OUT MORE FLAGS
An acerbic description of the Bright Young Things at war includes vignettes of Auden and Isherwood
0–316–92615–9 Little, Brown $15.95
0–316–92612–4 Little, Brown pb $7.95

SCOOP
An error that assigns an eccentric bird-watcher to cover an African revolution provides the basis for this satire of the newspaper business
0–316–92617–5 Little, Brown $15.95
0–316–92610–8 Little, Brown pb $7.95

VILE BODIES
The amusing effects of an American revivalist carnival on the habitués of the society pages in the London papers. "Derisive, staccato, slightly cockeyed, and somehow heartbreaking . . . The defiant hilarity of a dance on a sinking ship"—Alexander Woolcott
0–316–92616–7 Little, Brown $15.95
0–316–92611–6 Little, Brown pb $7.95

Mary Webb
GONE TO EARTH
The spirits of a violated earth struggle against the triumphant aggressors in

this tale of a half-wild Gypsy girl and her pet fox cub
0–7156–1339–1 Macmillan pb $4.95

PRECIOUS BANE
Introduction by Erika Duncan
0–268–01541–4 Notre Dame $14.95
0–268–01538–4 Notre Dame pb $8.95

• H.G. Wells
THE COMPLETE SHORT STORIES OF H.G. WELLS
0–317–64891–8 St. Martin's $19.95

SELECTED SHORT STORIES
0–14–008247–6 Penguin pb $4.95

HISTORY OF MISTER POLLY
Sick of the routine of modern existence, a shopkeeper burns down his shop and finds fulfillment in returning to an older way of life
Edited by Gordon N. Ray
0–395–05149–5 Houghton Mifflin pb $5.95

KIPPS
Artie Kipps struggles to survive in a more rarefied society when sudden wealth lifts him above his station in the world
Introduction by Benny Green
0–19–281477–X Oxford pb $6.95

LOVE AND MR. LEWISHAM
Introduction by Benny Green
0–19–281398–6 Oxford pb $5.95

▶ For other fiction by H.G. Wells, see Science Fiction

• Rebecca West
COUSIN ROSAMUND
Afterword by Victoria Glendinning
0–670–81150–5 Viking $16.95
0–14–010130–6 Penguin pb $6.95

THE FOUNTAIN OVERFLOWS
"It is as full of characters . . . as a pudding of plums; full of incident, full of family delights, full of parties and partings, strange bits of London, the lobby of the House of Commons, a classic murder with portraits of the murderer, the murderee and a couple of innocent bystanders, bill collectors, kitchen fires, good food, and a considerable quota of ghosts"—Elizabeth Janeway
0–14–007322–1 Penguin pb $7.95

Rebecca West

SUNFLOWER
A posthumously published early novel. "This unfinished novel, written in the mid 1920s, is a study in frustration—for its readers, in that the problems it poses remain unresolved, and for Sunflower and her creator in that it is about the unsatisfied physical desire of a woman for a man, unusual for the period and unusual for Rebecca West"—Victoria Glendinning
Afterword by Victoria Glendinning
0–670–81386–9 Viking $18.95
0–14–009497–0 Penguin pb $7.95

THIS REAL NIGHT
A sequel to *The Fountain Overflows,* posthumously published. "Shows no falling off in intensity or purpose—rather the reverse. It is full of vitality and contains some of her best writing and some extraordinary scenes and set-pieces"—Victoria Glendinning
0–14–008684–6 Penguin pb $6.95

● T.H. White
THE ONCE AND FUTURE KING
This retelling of King Arthur was the basis for *Camelot,* and contains fascinating information about living in the Middle Ages
0–441–62740–4 Ace pb $4.95

● Virginia Woolf
"Virginia Woolf stands as the chief figure of modernism in England and must be included with Joyce and Proust in the realization of experiments that have completely broken with tradition."—*NY Times*

THE COMPLETE SHORTER FICTION OF VIRGINIA WOOLF
A gathering of nearly 50 stories
Edited by Susan Dick
0–15–118983–8 HBJ $16.95

BETWEEN THE ACTS
Woolf's last novel moves between eras while describing a pageant on a country estate
0–15–611870–X HBJ pb $5.95

A HAUNTED HOUSE & OTHER SHORT STORIES
Foreword by Leonard Woolf
0–15–639401–4 HBJ pb $4.95

JACOB'S ROOM
An elegiac early novel about a young man who becomes a casualty of the First World War
0–15–645742–3 HBJ pb $6.95

MRS. DALLOWAY
A 1925 landmark of modernist fiction that follows an MP's wife on an outing, tracing the shifting consciousness of herself and others, including a shell-shocked veteran whose destiny briefly intersects with hers
0–15–662863–5 HBJ pb $5.95

MRS. DALLOWAY'S PARTY: A Short Story Sequence
Seven stories related to *Mrs. Dalloway*
Introduction by Stella McNichol
0–15–662900–3 HBJ pb $4.95

NIGHT AND DAY
A novel of London artists and political activists, published in 1919
0–15–665600–0 HBJ pb $8.95

ORLANDO: A Biography
A historical fantasy following a single hero/heroine through sexual metamorphoses from Elizabethan times to the present
0–15–670160–X HBJ pb $7.95

THE PARGITERS: The Novel-Essay Portion of The Years
A restoration of Woolf's originally projected form for the first section of *The Years*
0–15–671380–2 HBJ pb $4.95

TO THE LIGHTHOUSE
"One of few books which are filled with goodness and genuine love but also, in its feminine way, with irony, amorphous sadness, and doubt of life"—Eric Auerbach
0–15–690738–0 HBJ pb $5.95

THE VIRGINIA WOOLF READER
An abundant selection from Woolf's fiction and nonfiction
Edited by Mitchell A. Leaska
0–15–193782–6 HBJ $22.95
0–15–693590–2 HBJ pb $10.95

THE VOYAGE OUT
Woolf's first novel is less experimental in form, but emotionally powerful
0–15–693625–9 HBJ pb $7.95

THE WAVES
Woolf interweaves six interior voices in one of her most complex works. "In each soliloquy in this pattern of soliloquies we ourselves are at the centre. We are Bernard, we are Susan, but with this difference: that we have borrowed, for a moment, the lamp of genius, and by its light may read the secrets of our private universe"—Gerald Bullett
0–15–694960–1 HBJ pb $5.95

THE YEARS
A generational novel spanning half a century, from 1880 to the 1930s
0–15–699701–0 HBJ pb $9.95

THE MIDDLE GENERATION

● Richard Adams
THE GIRL IN A SWING
0–394–51049–6 Knopf $11.95
0–451–13467–2 NAL pb $4.50

MAIA
0–451–14035–4 NAL pb $4.95

SHARDIK
An exciting animal allegory of a huge bear that becomes Messiah to a remote imperial outpost
0–380–00516–6 Avon pb $4.95

TRAVELLER
0–394–57055–3 Knopf $18.95

THE UNBROKEN WEB
0–345–30368–7 Ballantine pb $3.95

WATERSHIP DOWN
The quest of a band of Berkshire rabbits for a new home has allegorical overtones but treats the conditions of wildlife with astonishing fidelity. "His true achievement lies in the altogether enchanting civilization he has created"—Peter S. Prescott
0–02–700030–3 Macmillan $24.95
0–380–00293–0 Avon pb $4.95

● Kingsley Amis
THE GREEN MAN
A philandering innkeeper struggles with his addictions and a chthonic presence in his pub
0–89733–220–2 Academy Chicago pb $4.95

JAKE'S THING
In quest of a renewed libido, Oxford don Jake Richardson embarks on a merry chase through an astonishing variety of sex therapies
0–14–005096–5 Penguin pb $5.95

LUCKY JIM
Amis's widely hailed first novel about an Angry Young Man at a provincial university in England
0–14–001648–1 Penguin pb $4.95

THE OLD DEVILS
A mischievous look at middle-class, middle-aged Welshpersons. "The old robust tradition of British comedy, from Fielding and Smollett, continues in our own vernacular"—V.S. Pritchett
0–671–63704–5 Summit $18.95
0–06–097146–0 Harper & Row pb $7.95

STANLEY AND THE WOMEN
A novel whose sexual attitudes stirred controversy
0–671–60317–5 Summit $14.95
0–06–097145–2 Harper & Row pb $6.95

● Beryl Bainbridge
"Short, laconic and rich in black comedy, her novels deal with the lives of characters at once deeply ordinary and highly eccentric, in a world where violence and the absurd lurk beneath the daily routine of urban domesticity."—*Oxford Companion to English Literature*

MUM AND MR. ARMITAGE
"Savage irony, supernatural adventures, gothica, misunderstandings, each story is a gem"—*Publishers Weekly*
0–07–003261–0 McGraw-Hill $15.95
0–07–003264–5 McGraw-Hill pb $7.95

SWEET WILLIAM
0–8076–0816–5 Braziller $7.95

WATSON'S APOLOGY
The inner causes of a Victorian case of wife-murder, sensitively traced through a combination of novelistic techniques and official documents
0–07–003255–6 McGraw-Hill pb $4.95

A WEEKEND WITH CLAUDE
A country sojourn with an art dealer, interrupted by the mysterious wounding of a female guest, leads to some tense reevaluations among friends
0–8076–1031–3 Braziller $10.95

● J.G. Ballard
THE DAY OF CREATION
0–02–041514–1 Macmillan pb $7.95

EMPIRE OF THE SUN
Ballard's autobiographical novel about his capture and imprisonment by the Japanese following the fall of Shanghai became the basis for Steven Spielberg's movie
0–671–64877–2 Pocket Books pb $4.50

▶ **For other J.G. Ballard titles see Science Fiction**

John Berger
G
This sharply focused chronicle of a child of post-Garibaldian Italy won the Booker Prize in 1972
0–394–73967–1 Pantheon pb $10.95

PIG EARTH
Stories, essays, and poems about French peasant life dramatize the struggle between the sons of the soil and heartless bureaucrats; the initial volume of the projected trilogy *Into Their Labors*
0–394–75739–4 Pantheon pb $7.95

ONCE IN EUROPA
The second volume of the trilogy *Into Their Labors,* Berger's indelibly original evocation of rural France as the site of a battle between archaic patterns and new technologies
0–394–53992–3 Pantheon $14.95
0–394–75164–7 Pantheon pb $7.95

● Caroline Blackwood
CORRIGAN
An unlikely romance
0–14–007732–4 Penguin pb $6.95

THE STEPDAUGHTER
In these imaginary confessional letters, a woman struggles with her hatred for a clumsy stepdaughter abandoned to her care by her faithless husband
0–14–006923–2 Penguin pb $5.95

● Malcolm Bradbury
CUTS
A send-up of the television industry and the state of England under Thatcher's ax
Illustrated by Tom Phillips
0–06–015845–X Harper & Row $10.95

EATING PEOPLE IS WRONG
A spirited satire of British and Commonwealth university types
0–89733–189–3 Academy Chicago pb $4.95

MY STRANGE QUEST FOR MENSONGE
Bradbury's hero tries to live deconstructively in this jibe at "theory" and structuralist intellectualizing
0–14–010706–1 Penguin pb $6.95

RATES OF EXCHANGE
A barbed account of an English academic in Eastern Europe
0–14–007631–X Penguin pb $1.95

● Melvyn Bragg
HIRED MAN
The saga of the rural Tallentine family, from a well-known television personality who began his career as a serious social novelist
0–436–06705–6 David & Charles $15.95

THE MAID OF BUTTERMERE
A love story set against the Cumbrian lakes
0–399–13225–2 Putnam $19.95

● Anita Brookner
"These are novels for a disciplined sensibility—not the excesses of the groaning board but the light sufficiency of the luncheon table."—Frances Taliaferro

THE DEBUT
0–394–72856–4 Random House pb $5.95

FAMILY AND FRIENDS
0–671–62575–6 Washington Square pb $6.95

A FRIEND FROM ENGLAND
0–394–56387–5 Pantheon $15.95

HOTEL DU LAC
Edith Hope, recovering in a quiet Swiss hotel from an affair with a younger married man, has her pain revived by the attentions of a guest
0–394–54215–0 Pantheon $13.95
0–525–48204–0 Dutton pb $6.95

LOOK AT ME
After her mother's death, a woman tends a collection of medical prints while casting around for an escape from her depressing self-absorption
0–394–52944–8 Pantheon $11.95
0–525–48156–7 Dutton pb $7.95

THE MISALLIANCE
0–394–55340–3 Pantheon $14.95
0–06–097134–7 Harper & Row pb $6.95

PROVIDENCE
0–394–52945–6 Pantheon $13.95
0–525–48157–5 Dutton pb $7.95

● Anthony Burgess
A CLOCKWORK ORANGE
An original, futuristic vision of authoritarian society and teenage gangs on the loose. "Much more than a linguistic *tour de force*. It is also the most devastating piece of satire since Zamiatin's *We*"—Geoffrey Aggeler
0–393–02439–3 Norton $14.95
0–393–30553–8 Norton pb $7.95

THE DOCTOR IS SICK
A philologist in the throes of a dissolving marriage embarks on a burlesque quest through the seamy side of '50s London
0–393–00959–2 Norton pb $3.95

INSIDE MR. ENDERBY
The first of the Enderby novels which tells the story of a flatulent middle-aged writer able to write only in the lavatory, whose life after marriage becomes a series of incredible adventures.
0–07–008973–6 McGraw-Hill $12.95
0–07–008970–1 McGraw-Hill pb $5.95

ENDERBY OUTSIDE
The second of the Enderby books
0–07–008974–4 McGraw-Hill $12.95
0–07–008971–X McGraw-Hill pb $5.95

THE CLOCKWORK TESTAMENT
The third and final part of the Enderby trilogy
0–07–008975–2 McGraw-Hill $12.95
0–07–008972–8 McGraw-Hill pb $5.95

ENDERBY'S DARK LADY: Or, No End to Enderby
A coda to the Enderby trilogy
0–07–008976–0 McGraw-Hill pb $4.95

THE END OF THE WORLD NEWS: An Entertainment
0–14–006746–9 Penguin pb $6.95

THE EVE OF SAINT VENUS
This "commedia dell Aldwych" captures some of the vivacity of British farce while satirizing the "literary" drama of Eliot and Fry
0–393–00915–7 Norton pb $1.95

HONEY FOR THE BEARS
0–393–00905–X Norton pb $5.95

THE KINGDOM OF THE WICKED
0–671–62527–6 Washington Square pb $4.95

THE LONG DAY WANES: A Malayan Trilogy
Victor Crabbe, the hero of Burgess' first published novel, is a comic, victimized colonial administrator caught up in the decay of empire in Malaya during the Second World War
0–393–00864–9 Norton pb $4.95

NOTHING LIKE THE SUN
Shakespeare's lusty and turbulent affair with the Dark Lady of the sonnets, rendered in a lusty, turbulent pastiche of Elizabethan prose
0–393–00795–2 Norton pb $6.95

THE PIANOPLAYERS
0–87795–832–7 Arbor House $16.95
0–671–63792–4 Washington Square pb $4.95

THE RIGHT TO AN ANSWER
0–393–00887–8 Norton pb $3.95

TREMOR OF INTENT
"Using the spy as missile-era folk-hero, he creates a gleaming novel of ideas—troubling ideas about the survival value of ideology, the disease of our appetites, our malevolent innocence as we perpetrate incredible atrocities and feel no guilt"—*NY Times*
0–393–00416–3 Norton pb $6.95

THE WANTING SEED
A witty vision of an overpopulated futuristic state whose ideology oscillates between pessimistic Augustinianism and optimistic Pelagianism
0–393–00808–8 Norton pb $7.95

● Leonora Carrington
THE HOUSE OF FEAR: Notes from Down Below
Introduction by Marina Warner
0–525–24648–7 Dutton $17.95

● Isabel Colegate
DECEITS OF TIME
0–670–82405–4 Viking $17.95

A GLIMPSE OF SION'S GLORY & OTHER STORIES
0–1400–8374–X Viking $14.95

THE ORLANDO TRILOGY
The "Cliveden set" of the '30s provides the background for the parliamentary career of a man modeled on Oedipus
0–14–006546–6 Penguin pb $8.95

THE SHOOTING PARTY
Adultery and competitiveness among the Edwardian upper classes; a novel that recalls Jean Renoir's *Rules of the Game*
0–380–59543–5 Avon pb $3.50

STATUES IN A GARDEN
0–380–60368–3 Avon pb $2.95

THREE NOVELS
Includes *The Blackmailer, A Man of Power*, and *The Great Occasion*
0–670–52409–3 Viking $25.00
0–14–006975–5 Viking pb $9.95

• Barbara Comyns
THE JUNIPER TREE
0–312–44858–9 St. Martin's $12.95

SISTERS BY A RIVER
Introduction by Ursula Holden
0–14–016167–8 Penguin pb $6.95

THE SKIN CHAIRS
Introduction by Ursula Holden
0–14–016138–4 Penguin pb $5.95

WHO WAS CHANGED AND WHO WAS DEAD
0–14–016158–9 Penguin pb $5.95

• Noel Coward
THE COLLECTED STORIES OF NOEL COWARD
0–525–24207–4 Dutton $20.00
0–525–48210–5 Dutton pb $11.95

A WITHERED NOSEGAY: Three Cod Pieces
"Once again Mr. Coward exerts his glittering talent—terribly, terribly amusing"—Quentin Crisp
0–88184–316–4 Carroll & Graf pb $8.95

POMP AND CIRCUMSTANCE
Coward's only novel, first published in 1960
0–525–48019–6 Dutton pb $5.95

• Roald Dahl
THE BEST OF ROALD DAHL
Dahl, a master of the bizarre, creates terrifying effects by combining the mundane with the grotesque
0–394–72549–2 Random House pb $9.95

KISS, KISS
0–394–43202–9 Knopf $19.95

ROALD DAHL'S TALES OF THE UNEXPECTED
0–394–74081–5 Random House pb $5.95

• Lawrence Durrell
THE ALEXANDRIA QUARTET
Includes *Justine, Balthazar, Mountolive*, and *Clea*. "People are always saying—inaccurately—that something or another is like a dream, but Durrell's Alexandria *is* actually like the landscape of a dream. A hot, dry city, surrounded by desert, raked by winds and by contradictions. A relentless yet voluptuous city, beautiful and squalid, overcivilized and primitive"—Anatole Broyard, *NY Times*
0–525–48242–3 Dutton pb (boxed set) $24.95

CONSTANCE: Or, Solitary Practices
0–670–23909–7 Viking $15.95
0–14–007026–5 Penguin pb $6.95

THE DARK LABYRINTH
0–14–005025–6 Penguin pb $4.95

LIVIA: Or, Buried Alive
0–670–43447–7 Viking $12.95
0–14–007101–6 Penguin pb $6.95

MONSIEUR
0–670–48678–7 Viking $12.95
0–14–007102–4 Penguin pb $6.95

NUNQUAM
A sequel to *Tunc*
0–525–16969–5 Dutton $7.95
0–14–005189–9 Penguin pb $5.95

QUINX: Or, The Ripper's Tale
0–670–80658–7 Viking $15.95
0–14–008059–7 Penguin pb $5.95

TUNC
0–14–005184–8 Penguin pb $5.95

G.B. Edwards
THE BOOK OF EBENEZER LE PAGE
Edwards' only novel, written in old age and published posthumously, chronicles an isolated life on the island of Guernsey. "Like Proust, Edwards can make us feel the passage of time as a tragic force. Like Proust, he has a surprise for us that can only be convincingly revealed in the fullness of time. For this is a novel you must read every word of, or miss the deeply human meaning altogether"—Guy Davenport, *NY Times*
Introduction by John Fowles
0–394–51651–6 Knopf $13.95

• J.G. Farrell
THE SIEGE OF KRISHNAPUR
"This novel of the Sepoy mutiny of 1857 begins as a comedy of Victorian conventions and imperial pride and accelerates into a terrific narrative of action"—Walter Clemons, *Newsweek*
0–88184–195–1 Carroll & Graf pb $4.95

SINGAPORE GRIP
0–88184–124–2 Carroll & Graf pb $4.95

TROUBLES
In the decaying Majestic Hotel in Dublin, the disintegrating remnants of the Anglo-Irish ascendancy slowly live out their last days
0–88184–269–9 Carroll & Graf pb $4.95

• Eva Figes
LIGHT
A day in the life of Claude Monet. "Monet . . . is the novella's center, its focus of consciousness. He moves like a demigod through the human world, not precisely a tyrant but fully in control of his household and his art . . . Its prose is unhurried, richly descriptive, rarely ornamental or excessive—indeed, a kind of Impressionism in words"—Joyce Carol Oates, *NY Times*
0–345–31898–6 Ballantine pb $2.95

THE SEVEN AGES
0–394–55540–6 Pantheon Books $14.45
0–345–35199–1 Ballantine pb $3.95

WAKING
"Eva Figes has chosen to examine the life of a woman by revealing her thoughts in the quiet time between sleeping and waking, at different stages of her life. . . . The atmosphere of silence; the relationship of a woman to her body, tender and wondering in youth, bitter in age; one's sense of the changing, darkening seasons of life—these are beautifully evoked"—D.M. Thomas, *NY Times*
0–394–72227–2 Pantheon pb $4.95

• John Fowles
THE ARISTOS
"An attempt to present the author's views on the role of man in the contemporary world in a collection of aphorisms"—Walter Allen
0–452–26044–2 NAL pb $5.95

THE COLLECTOR
A disturbing psychological portrait of a young man driven to kidnap the young woman he loves
0–316–29096–3 Little, Brown $17.95
0–440–31335–X Dell pb $4.50

DANIEL MARTIN
A successful novelist looks back from Hollywood at his childhood in Devon and his schooldays at Oxford, in a quest that parallels the theme of the novel he is writing
0–451–12210–0 NAL pb $4.50

THE EBONY TOWER
This collection of stories ranges from a study of the subtle eroticism of a French master-painter's old age to the vivid retelling of a medieval "lay"
0–316–29093–9 Little, Brown $19.95
0–451–15691–9 NAL pb $4.50

THE FRENCH LIEUTENANT'S WOMAN
Ostensibly a Victorian romance, this novel's own narrative ploys are analogs of the male desire to rationalize and manipulate the enigma of woman
0–316–29099–8 Little, Brown $24.95
0–451–13598–9 NAL pb $3.95

A MAGGOT
An unusual historical novel, with Fowles's characteristic blend of the magical and the erotic
0–316–28994–9 Little, Brown $19.95
0–451–14476–7 NAL pb $4.50

THE MAGUS
A popular novel set on a Greek island, in which a local magician leads a young Englishman to self-knowledge through a series of fantastic adventures
0–440–35162–6 Dell pb $5.95

MANTISSA
One of Fowles's more experimental works, with an emphasis on erotic and mythic elements
0–316–28980–9 Little, Brown $16.95
0–452–25429–9 NAL pb $6.95

• Penelope Gilliatt
SUNDAY BLOODY SUNDAY
A middle-aged doctor and his ex-wife struggle with their attraction to an uncommitted young artist
0–396–08492–3 Dodd, Mead $16.95
0–396–08539–3 Dodd, Mead pb $8.95

• William Golding
THE BRASS BUTTERFLY
"His novels . . . with the perspicuity of realistic narrative art and the universality of myth, illuminate the human condition in the world today"—Nobel Prize citation
0–571–09073–7 Faber & Faber pb $4.95

CLOSE QUARTERS
A sequel to *Rites of Passage,* on the transition from youth to manhood
0–374–12510–4 Farrar, Straus & Giroux $16.95

 ➤ **FOR OVERSEAS ORDERING INFORMATION, SEE PAGE 1**

THE INHERITORS
The brutal conquest of the Neanderthals by Homo sapiens. "*The Inheritors* captures with marvelous ability a wholly realistic sense of the Neanderthal world as well as reenacting on the wider level the confrontation between Innocence and Experience"—William Boyd, *London Magazine*
0–671–53139–5 Washington Square pb $3.95

LORD OF THE FLIES
Golding's best-known book: schoolboys marooned on a desert island revert to primitive savagery and superstition
0–698–10219–3 Putnam $18.95
0–399–50148–7 Putnam pb $3.95

THE PAPER MEN
An English novelist declining into drink and self-pity turns the tables on a young American academician who aspires to become his biographer. A satire on the literary establishment, published the year after Golding's Nobel Prize
0–15–670800–0 HBJ pb $5.95

PINCHER MARTIN
The survivor of a torpedoed destroyer summons up his internal resources as he clings to a bare mid-Atlantic rock
0–15–671833–2 HBJ pb $4.95

RITES OF PASSAGE
The journal of a voyage to the Antipodes during the Napoleonic era, with vivid descriptions of shipboard life
0–374–25086–3 Farrar, Straus & Giroux $14.95

Alasdair Gray
THE FALL OF KELVIN WALKER
0–8076–1144–1 Braziller $14.95

JANINE 1982
"Every stylistic excess and moral defect which critics conspired to ignore in the author's first books is to be found here in concentrated form"—the author
0–14–007110–5 Penguin pb $6.95

LANARK: A Life in Four Books
"The saga of a city where reality is about as reliable as a Salvador Dali watch"—Brian Aldiss
0–8076–1108–5 Braziller $20.00
0–8076–1162–X Braziller pb $9.95

● Brion Gysin
THE LAST MUSEUM
"Who was Brion Gysin? The only authentic heir to Hassan-i-Sabbah, the Old Man of the Mountains"—William S. Burroughs. This novel by a mentor of the Beats is a Tibetan Book of the Deliberate Derangement of the Senses
Introduction by William S. Burroughs
0–394–55555–4 Grove $17.95
0–394–62263–4 Grove pb $2.98

THE PROCESS
0–87951–277–6 Overlook $18.95

● Aidan Higgins
BALCONY OF EUROPE
Semiautobiographical story of an adulterous love affair among artistic expatriates in Spain. "The underwater love-scene is the literary equivalent of Esther

Self-portrait by Alisdair Gray

Williams in its virtuosity"—John Montague
0–7145–0103–4 Riverrun pb $8.95

BORNHOLM NIGHT FERRY
0–8052–8219–X Schocken $13.95

LANGRISHE GO DOWN
Pre-war tale of a young German who brings cruelty and passion to one of the daughters of a remote, decaying Irish country house
0–7145–0329–0 Riverrun pb $6.95

SCENES FROM A RECEDING PAST
A novel of childhood set in Ireland, in which Higgins captures the protagonist's evolving consciousness through corresponding stylistic changes
0–7145–3556–7 Riverrun pb $9.95

● Anna Kavan
Kavan's fragmented, sometimes surrealistic fiction, stemming from a troubled life, has won her a cult following
ICE
0–393–30256–3 Norton pb $5.95

JULIA AND THE BAZOOKA & OTHER STORIES
0–393–30284–9 Norton pb $5.95

SLEEP HAS HIS HOUSE
0–87951–143–5 Overlook $25.00

● Benedict Kiely
A LETTER TO PEACHTREE
0–87923–727–9 Godine $17.95

NOTHING HAPPENS IN CARMINCROSS
An Irishman returns to his birthplace to celebrate his niece's wedding in this widely acclaimed novel
0–87923–585–3 Godine $16.95
0–87923–725–2 Godine pb $8.95

PROXOPERA
A novella involving the IRA and "the Troubles"
0–87923–651–5 Godine $12.95

THE STATE OF IRELAND: A Novella and Seventeen Stories
"He is, quite simply, the finest writer out of Ireland today"—*Publishers Weekly*
Introduction by Thomas Flanagan
0–87923–320–6 Godine $16.95

● Philip Larkin
A GIRL IN WINTER
"He wrote these books like poems. Fastidiousness is everywhere and flamboyance non-existent; the touch is unfaltering"—Clive James
0–87951–2172 Overlook pb $8.95

JILL
A scholarship boy at Oxford fantasizes about a sister/lover as a defense against his arrogant playboy roommate
0–87951–038–2 Overlook $22.50
0–87951–961–4 Overlook pb $7.95

● Doris Lessing
AFRICAN STORIES
Tales deriving from the Rhodesia in which Lessing grew up
0–671–42809–8 Simon & Schuster pb $13.95

BRIEFING FOR A DESCENT INTO HELL
A nightmare in the form of a medical report, exploring themes of individual and collective breakdown and violence
0–394–74662–7 Random House pb $4.95

CHILDREN OF VIOLENCE
This multivolume work, written over a period of 17 years, follows Martha Quest in her search for identity through the competing social and political forces of the decades from the '30s to the '60s

Volume 1: Martha Quest
Martha roams the veldt of her African home defiantly toting Havelock Ellis on sexuality, warily conscious of the adult society she is about to enter
0–452–26124–4 NAL pb $8.95

Volume 2: A Proper Marriage
Martha suffers the pains of a conventional marriage and awakens to political consciousness
0–452–25789–1 NAL pb $7.95

Volume 3: A Ripple from the Storm
A liberated Martha, remarried to a Communist Party member, finds that ideals can be turned to jargon and personal advantage
0–452–25632–1 NAL pb $6.95

Volume 4: Landlocked
The scene changes to England as Martha's activism wanes
0–452–25775–1 NAL pb $3.95

Volume 5: The Four-Gated City
A brilliant conclusion to the *Children of Violence* series, exploring the corruptions of postwar London
0–452–26114–7 NAL pb $12.95

THE FIFTH CHILD
A powerful novel of horror within the family
0–394–57105–3 Knopf $16.95

Doris Lessing (photo by Peter Lessing, courtesy of Knopf)

THE GOLDEN NOTEBOOK
"Her most important work has left its mark upon the ideas and feelings of a whole generation of women"—Elizabeth Hardwick
0–671–28770–2 Simon & Schuster $24.95
0–553–26210–6 Bantam pb $5.95

THE GOOD TERRORIST
0–394–74629–5 Random House pb $5.95

THE GRASS IS SINGING
Lessing's first novel, set in Africa, concerns a white farmer's wife and her relationship with an African servant
0–452–26119–8 NAL pb $9.95

THE HABIT OF LOVING
Early stories, first published in 1957
0–452–25704–2 NAL pb $8.95

A MAN AND TWO WOMEN
Sketches and three longer pieces
0–671–54190–0 Simon & Schuster pb $9.95

CANOPUS IN ARGUS: ARCHIVES
In this cycle of futuristic allegories—a radical break in style and subject matter from Lessing's earlier work—the powerful and benign Canopus receives reports from agents throughout the universe. Each of these illuminates some aspect of our current political or emotional problems

SHIKASTA
"A dissection of the political illusions of our own terrestrial twentieth century and a parable about how language is debased when used as a political instrument"—*NY Times Book Review*
0–394–50732–0 Knopf $13.95

RE: COLONIZED PLANET 5-SHIKASTA
A century of increasingly advanced warfare on the earthlike planet Shikasta culminates, through greed and political obsessions, in a near-fatal conflict
0–394–74977–4 Random House pb $6.95

THE MARRIAGES BETWEEN ZONES THREE, FOUR, AND FIVE
0–394–50914–5 Knopf $13.45
0–394–74978–2 Random House pb $7.95

THE SIRIAN EXPERIMENTS
0–394–51231–6 Knopf $13.45
0–394–75195–7 Random House pb $7.95

THE MAKING OF THE REPRESENTATIVE FOR PLANET EIGHT
0–394–51906–X Knopf $13.95
0–6797–2015–4 Random House pb $6.95

DOCUMENTS RELATING TO THE SENTIMENTAL AGENTS IN THE VOLYEN EMPIRE
0–394–52968–5 Knopf $12.45
0–394–72386–4 Random House pb $4.95

THE MEMOIRS OF A SURVIVOR
Visions of a grim and anarchic near future
0–394–75759–9 Random House pb $6.95

STORIES
0–394–50009–1 Knopf $17.50
0–394–74249–4 Random House pb $11.95

THE SUMMER BEFORE THE DARK
0–394–71095–9 Random House pb $5.95

• **David Lodge**
THE BRITISH MUSEUM IS FALLING DOWN
0–436–25530–8 David & Charles $25.95

CHANGING PLACES
0–14–004656–9 Penguin pb $4.95

SMALL WORLD
A clever *roman à clef* exposing highjinks on the international academic conference circuit
0–446–34143–6 Warner pb $4.50

• **John McGahern**
HIGH GROUND
Short stories set mainly in rural Ireland
0–670–81181–5 Viking $15.95

THE PORNOGRAPHER
A blackly humorous tale, set in a seedy Dublin milieu, of a down-at-heels writer whose life cannot compare with his fantasies
0–14–006489–3 Penguin pb $6.95

• **Colin MacInnes**
ABSOLUTE BEGINNERS
An ebullient glimpse into the colorful underworld of immigrant London, where West Indian and South African pimps and dealers play an upbeat game of cops and robbers against stuffy British detectives
0–525–48189–3 Dutton pb $7.95

MR. LOVE AND JUSTICE
A follow-up to *Absolute Beginners*
0–525–48207–5 Dutton pb $7.95

• **Olivia Manning**
THE BALKAN TRILOGY
The ironical and fastidious eye of a British diplomat's wife registers both the personal and the political during the shattering events of World War II in Greece and the Balkans. Includes *Great Fortune, Spoilt Clay,* and *Friends and Heroes*
0–14–010996–X Penguin pb $9.95

THE LEVANT TRILOGY
Manning's second trilogy follows a young wartime couple moving from Romania to Greece to Egypt, just ahead of the German army. Includes *The Danger Tree, The Battle Lost and Won,* and *The Sum of Things*
0–14–010995–1 Penguin pb $8.95

• **John Mortimer**
PARADISE POSTPONED
0–670–80094–5 Viking $17.95
0–14–009864–X Penguin pb $6.95

SUMMER'S LEASE
0–670–81984–0 Viking $19.95

• **Iris Murdoch**
Murdoch's novels are carefully plotted works whose layers of intricacy reflect the author's philosophical training. They are kept buoyantly afloat by the lucid, ironic language of her upper-middle-class characters. "What an incorrigible, irresistible conjurer-up this woman is! . . . Let it be asked now: what other living novelist in the language is the peer of Iris Murdoch at inventing characters and moving them *fascinatingly*, at least as long as the book is in our hands?"—John Updike

ACASTOS
0–14–008696–X Penguin pb $5.95

AN ACCIDENTAL MAN
A study in survival at the expense of others
0–14–003611–3 Penguin pb $7.95

THE BELL
The inhabitants of a monastery find themselves trapped between a desire for a higher order and an inability to lead normal lives
0–14–001688–0 Penguin pb $6.95

THE BLACK PRINCE
A kind of psychological whodunit involving an older man's love for a young woman and a murder
0–14–003934–1 Penguin pb $7.95

THE BOOK AND THE BROTHERHOOD
A student reunion reveals a shift from radical energy to languor, and awakens sleeping passions
0–670–81912–3 Viking $19.95

BRUNO'S DREAM
The grotesque efforts of a dying old man to establish his first bonds of love and affection with the world
0–14–003176–6 Penguin pb $4.95

FAIRLY HONOURABLE DEFEAT
A Machiavellian intruder into a conventional group of people forces them to reconsider their lives by destroying their complacency
0–14–003332–7 Penguin pb $4.95

THE FLIGHT FROM THE ENCHANTER
0–14–001770–4 Penguin pb $4.95

THE GOOD APPRENTICE
0–14–009815–1 Penguin pb $7.95

HENRY AND CATO
A priest and an art historian meet again, years after their boyhood friendship
0–14–004569–4 Penguin pb $6.95

THE ITALIAN GIRL
A servant girl achieves power over an unhappy family
0–14–002559–6 Penguin pb $4.95

THE NICE AND THE GOOD
"Sweeps up black magic, science fiction, thriller and half-a-dozen kinds of novel into the wittiest sort of concoction"—*NY Times*
0–14–003034–4 Penguin pb $6.95

NUNS AND SOLDIERS
"She has perfected her technique and pulled off the big one: a book that unwinds with all the sinuous inevitability of a contortionist to rise into the higher spheres of myth"—*Atlantic Monthly*
0–14–006143–6 Penguin pb $6.95

THE PHILOSOPHER'S PUPIL
A renowned philosopher goes home to an English spa. "The author does what old-fashioned novelists did when they could; she makes us gods, observing, weighing, rebuking, forgiving, and happy with our omniscience . . . It is one of the most difficult and rewarding things a novelist can do for us"—Robertson Davies, *Washington Post*
0–14–007614–X Penguin pb $7.95

THE RED AND THE GREEN
A novel set in Dublin in 1916, the year of the Easter Rising
0–14–002756–4 Penguin pb $6.95

THE SACRED AND PROFANE LOVE MACHINE
A man must choose between wife and mistress. "*The Sacred and Profane Love Machine* reads like a breeze, a whirlwind of deepening surprise, a provocation to the intellect and an invitation to the heart"—John Updike
0–14–004111–7 Penguin pb $5.95

SANDCASTLE
A middle-aged married man's passion for a much younger artist transfixes him with guilt
0–14–001474–8 Penguin pb $6.95

THE SEA, THE SEA
This study of a theater director's obsessive passion for a childhood sweetheart won the Booker Prize
0–670–62651–1 Viking $12.95
0–14–005199–6 Penguin pb $7.95

A SEVERED HEAD
A satirical portrait of the variously adulterous and incestuous liaisons of a Bloomsbury-like social set
0–14–002003–9 Penguin pb $4.95

THE TIME OF THE ANGELS
A wasteland rectory beset by evil
0–14–002848–X Penguin pb $6.95

UNDER THE NET
Murdoch's first novel describes a writer's search for a place to live in London, and much more
0–14–001445–4 Penguin pb $6.95

THE UNICORN
0–14–002476–X Penguin pb $6.95

AN UNOFFICIAL ROSE
0–14–002154–X Penguin pb $4.95

A WORD CHILD
Hilary Brede, nursing guilt and disappointment in a dull civil service job, discovers that a man he hurt and betrayed has become his superior
0–14–008153–4 Penguin pb $6.95

• **Robert Nye**
TALES I TOLD MY MOTHER
Rabelaisian and poetic variations on the theme of literary biography turns Chatterton, the Rossettis, and others into something rich and strange
0–7145–2741–6 Marion Boyars pb $7.95

• **Edna O'Brien**
THE COUNTRY GIRLS TRILOGY & EPILOGUE
A saga of escape from girlhood, countryside, and convent to the big city. Includes *Country Girls*, *The Lonely Girl*, and *Girls in Their Married Bliss*. "Despite feminist efforts on behalf of their kind, Miss O'Brien's sex-dazzled heroines continue to race like lemmings towards unhappiness"—Julia O'Faolain
0–374–13027–2 Farrar, Straus & Giroux $18.95
0–452–25926–6 NAL pb $9.95

A FANATIC HEART: Selected Stories of Edna O'Brien
A recent choice of her best stories, with four new ones
Foreword by Philip Roth
0–374–15342–6 Farrar, Straus & Giroux $17.95
0–452–26116–3 NAL pb $9.95

THE HIGH ROAD
0–374–29273–6 Farrar, Straus & Giroux $18.95

NIGHT
Erotic memories of Irishwoman recalling her awakening to maturity in the odyssey from rural Ireland to London
0–374–22198–7 Farrar, Straus & Giroux $15.95
0–374–52051–8 Farrar, Straus & Giroux pb $4.95

• **Joe Orton**
HEAD TO TOE
"To him nothing was sacred, but the fury of his attack, its peculiar combination of joy and horror, was not without a broader spiritual motive. Orton wanted to shock the society but also to reform it"—John Lahr
0–312–00718–3 St. Martin's $13.95

Mervyn Peake
THE GORMENGHAST TRILOGY
A moody and compelling fantasy about the struggles of the young heir of an ancient castle: first to preserve its moribund rituals from evil within, and then to escape them
Introduction by Anthony Burgess
0–87951–974–6 Overlook $25.00

Volume 1: TITUS GROAN
0–87951–143–5 Overlook $25.00

Volume 2: GORMENGHAST
0–87951–144–3 Overlook $25.00

Volume 3: TITUS ALONE
0–87951–145–1 Overlook $25.00

• **Dennis Potter**
BLACKEYES
A novel by the celebrated television writer
0–679–72047–2 Random House pb $6.95

• **Barbara Pym**
"In her novels the reader is always on the verge of smiling. Amusement is constantly foiling more pretentious emotion, but emotion is there all the same."—Philip Larkin, *TLS*

AN ACADEMIC QUESTION
0–525–24441–7 Dutton $15.95
0–452–25996–7 NAL pb $7.95

CIVIL TO STRANGERS & OTHER WRITINGS
Edited by Hazel Holt
0–525–24593–6 Dutton $18.95

CRAMPTON HODNET
0–452–25816–2 NAL pb $7.95

EXCELLENT WOMEN
Mildred Lathburn, a clergyman's daughter, observes with a penetrating but sympathetic eye the Napiers' marriage, and yearns discreetly for Everard Bone
0–525–10116–0 Dutton $13.95
0–525–48377–2 Dutton pb $7.95

A FEW GREEN LEAVES
A comic account of village life, published posthumously
0–06–097032–4 Harper & Row pb $6.95

A GLASS OF BLESSINGS
"The layers of this world are onion-thin: she takes them apart gently, with no malice, not even a mild contempt. Insights are light and oblique but flashingly brilliant"—Henrietta Buckmaster, *CSM*
0–06–097074–X Harper & Row pb $6.95

JANE AND PRUDENCE
Comic complications as Jane, the vicar's wife, plays matchmaker for her young protégée escaping a dull London routine
0–06–097101–0 Harper & Row pb $6.95

LESS THAN ANGELS
A gentle satire on the loves and lives of a group of anthropologists
0–06–097117–7 Harper & Row pb $6.95

NO FOND RETURN OF LOVE
0–06–097043–X Harper & Row pb $6.95

QUARTET IN AUTUMN
Retired from the office, Marcia becomes lonelier and more eccentric, but Letty tries to reach out to the world around her. "*Quartet in Autumn* is a marvel of fictional harmonics, a beautifully calm and rounded passage in and out of four isolated individuals as they feebly, fitfully grope toward an ideal solidarity"—John Updike
0–06–097031–6 Harper & Row pb $6.95

SOME TAME GAZELLE
0–06–097042–1 Harper & Row pb $7.95

THE SWEET DOVE DIED
The aging and fastidious Leonora finds that her play for her suitor's nephew brings her into collision with the passionate Phoebe and the sinister American Ned
0–525–21318–X Dutton $13.95
0–06–080511–0 Harper & Row pb $6.95

AN UNSUITABLE ATTACHMENT
0–06–097055–3 Harper & Row pb $6.95

• **Frederic Raphael**
OXBRIDGE BLUES
0–938626–28–0 Arkansas pb $8.95

THINK OF ENGLAND
0–684–18972–0 Scribners $15.95

- **Simon Raven**

Simon Raven is a scathing chronicler of the upper echelons of postwar English society.

FIELDING GRAY
0–8253–0310–9 Beaufort $13.95

THE OLD SCHOOL
0–241–11929–4 David & Charles $34.95

THE RICH PAY LATE
0–8253–0415–6 Beaufort $15.95

THE SABRE SQUADRON
0–317–46031–5 Beaufort $15.95

SOUND THE RETREAT
0–8253–0343–5 Beaufort $14.95

- **Paul Scott**

THE BENDER
An acid comedy of the conflict between George Spruce's aspirations to gentility and the limitations of his income
0–88184–231–1 Carroll & Graf pb $3.95

THE BIRDS OF PARADISE
The scion of an Anglo-Indian family recalls life's vicissitudes—from adviser to nabobs to Japanese POW
0–88184–232–X Carroll & Graf pb $4.50

THE CORRIDA AT SAN FELIU
0–88184–274–5 Carroll & Graf pb $3.95

THE CHINESE LOVE PAVILION
Brent of military intelligence and the guerrilla leader Saxby play a homicidal game in the Malayan jungle
0–88184–190–0 Carroll & Graf pb $4.50

A MALE CHILD
0–88184–323–7 Carroll & Graf pb $3.95

THE MARK OF THE WARRIOR
A contest of wills between the introspective and inept C.O. of a British army unit and an efficient subordinate
0–88184–189–7 Carroll & Graf pb $3.95

THE RAJ QUARTET
A boldly brushed picture of British colonials in India during and just after World War II, as independence approaches. A massive one-volume edition (nearly 2000 pages long) including *The Jewel in the Crown*, *The Towers of Silence*, *The Day of the Scorpion*, and *The Division of the Spoils*
0–688–04212–0 William Morrow $27.50

- **Tom Sharpe**

BLOTT ON THE LANDSCAPE
An alliance of wife and gardener prevents a pernicious peer from grabbing her inheritance and running a motorway through one of England's beauty spots
0–436–45803–9 David & Charles $25.95

THE GREAT PURSUIT
0–436–45806–3 David & Charles $22.95
0–06–014011–9 Harper & Row pb $9.95

INDECENT EXPOSURE
"Banning cricket tours may be one way of civilizing South Africa, but Tom Sharpe's remorseless mockery is a lot more fun"—Stanley Reynolds, *Punch*
0–87113–142–0 Atlantic Monthly pb $6.95

RIOTOUS ASSEMBLY
Slapstick but ultimately serious farce about police power and racism in South Africa
0–436–45800–4 David & Charles $25.95
0–87113–143–9 Atlantic Monthly pb $6.95

THE THROWBACK
0–394–72439–9 Random House pb $5.95

VINTAGE STUFF
0–394–72417–8 Random House pb $3.95

WILT
0–436–45804–7 David & Charles $25.95
0–394–72418–6 Random House pb $3.95

THE WILT ALTERNATIVE
"An old-fashioned English silliness is let loose like some belligerent eccentric in a wheel-chair"—Peter Kemp
0–436–45808–X David & Charles $24.95
0–394–72621–9 Random House pb $3.95

WILT ON HIGH: Being the Further Misadventures of One Henry Wilt
0–394–74321–0 Random House pb $4.95

- **Alan Sillitoe**

THE LONELINESS OF THE LONG-DISTANCE RUNNER
A juvenile delinquent at reform school deliberately sacrifices the goodwill of the authorities when he realizes the dehumanizing effect of "finding his niche"
0–394–43389–0 Knopf $10.95
0–451–14835–5 NAL pb $2.95

SATURDAY NIGHT AND SUNDAY MORNING
Sillitoe's first novel introduced the prototype of the Angry Young Man, in a chronicle of petty victories and defeats in the north of England
0–394–44377–2 Knopf $16.95
0–451–13590–3 NAL pb $3.50

- **Muriel Spark**

THE ABBESS OF CREWE
A Watergate-inspired satire about politics, ecclesiastical and otherwise
0–399–50952–6 Putnam pb $6.95

THE BALLAD OF PECKHAM RYE
A bizarre story of the London underworld
0–399–50650–0 Putnam pb $5.95

THE DRIVER'S SEAT
A woman is possessed by a death wish
0–399–50928–3 Putnam pb $6.95

Muriel Spark

A FAR CRY FROM KENSINGTON
A war widow's reflections on the postwar era
0–395–47694–1 Houghton Mifflin $17.95

MEMENTO MORI
A macabre study of the lives of a set of octogenarians victimized by a mysterious phone caller who tells them to "remember death"
0–399–50665–9 Putnam pb $8.95

THE PRIME OF MISS JEAN BRODIE
An Edinburgh schoolmistress who tries to dispel provincial ideas is betrayed by a student
0–452–26179–1 NAL pb $6.95

ROBINSON
An allegorical variation on Defoe, this time complicated by a female presence
0–380–01388–6 Avon pb $2.50

THE STORIES OF MURIEL SPARK
0–525–24330–5 Dutton $18.95
0–452–25880–4 NAL pb $7.95

- **Tom Stoppard**

LORD MALQUIST AND MR. MOON
0–571–11529–2 Faber & Faber pb $5.95

- **Elizabeth Taylor**

THE BLUSH
Short stories about ordinary middle-class life. "Mrs. Taylor's mastery is such that she can express her characters' feelings about one another through their exasperation with one another's children and chows"—Brigid Brophy, *Collected Views and Reviews*
Introduction by Paul Bailey
0–14–016157–0 Penguin pb $6.95

THE DEVASTATING BOYS
In the title story, the stodgy lives of an Oxford couple undergo pleasurable and painful changes when they invite two immigrant boys from London's East End to stay with them
0–14–016106–6 Penguin pb $6.95

A GAME OF HIDE AND SEEK
0–14–016137–6 Penguin pb $6.95

PALLADIAN
0–14–016113–9 Penguin pb $6.95

A VIEW OF THE HARBOUR
Love and passion at a drab seaside spa
Introduction by Robert Liddell
0–14–016165–1 Penguin pb $6.95

THE WEDDING GROUP
The foolish but pretty wife of a weak man becomes subordinated to his domineering mother
0–14–016114–7 Penguin pb $6.95

- **D.M. Thomas**

ARARAT
0–670–13009–5 Viking $13.50
0–671–47435–9 Washington Square pb $3.50

THE FLUTE PLAYER
"A fantasy based sometimes loosely, sometimes very directly, on the lives and works of Mandelstam, Pasternak, Akhmatova, and Tsvetaeva, and above all on the survival of poetry, love, and humanity in an imaginary city that has a strong resemblance to Leningrad"—Alex de Jonge
0–525–10727–4 Dutton $8.95
0–671–50885–7 Washington Square pb $3.95

SPHINX
0–670–81415–6 Viking $17.95
0–671–64158–1 Washington Square pb $4.95

SUMMIT
0–670–81921–2 Viking $15.95

SWALLOW
0–671–60607–7 Washington Square pb $4.50

THE WHITE HOTEL
"The diagnosis of an epoch through the experience of an individual. The opening sentences are so authoritative and imaginatively daring that I quickly came to the conclusion that I had found that mythical book that would explain us to ourselves"—Leslie Epstein
0–671–661–485 Washington Square pb $4.95

● Dylan Thomas

ADVENTURES IN THE SKIN TRADE & OTHER STORIES
The semiautobiographical title piece was never completed, but contains the quintessence of Thomas' humor
0–8112–0202–X New Directions pb $5.95

A CHILD'S CHRISTMAS IN WALES
An evocation of childhood that has long been one of Thomas' most popular works. This 1980 edition was chosen as one of the year's ten best illustrated books by *The New York Times* and *Time*
Illustrated by Edward Ardizzone
0–87923–339–7 Godine $11.95
0–87923–529–2 Godine pb $6.95

THE COLLECTED STORIES
Introduction by Leslie Norris
0–8112–0918–0 New Directions $16.95
0–8112–0998–9 New Directions pb $10.95

PORTRAIT OF THE ARTIST AS A YOUNG DOG
The amusing and whimsical adventures of a provincial young man's first days in London
0–8112–0207–0 New Directions pb $5.95

QUITE EARLY ONE MORNING
A collection of short stories
0–8112–0208–9 New Directions pb $5.95

REBECCA'S DAUGHTERS
A 19th-century adventure about the midnight raids of Welsh saboteurs against villainous landlords
Illustrated by Fritz Eichenberg
0–8112–0852–4 New Directions $8.50
0–8112–0884–2 New Directions pb $5.95

● E.P. Thompson

THE SYKAOS PAPERS
Allegorical science fiction by the celebrated historian. "A wonderful, moving, and hilarious answer to *E.T.*"—Ariel Dorfman
0–394–56828–1 Pantheon $19.95

● William Trevor

ANGELS AT THE RITZ & OTHER STORIES
"He gives us the joy of admiring how very unplaceable people really are: eternally shifting, unfolding new surfaces and capable of endless surprises"—Anne Tyler, *NY Times*
0–670–12594–6 Viking $10.95

BEYOND THE PALE & OTHER STORIES
0–670–16115–2 Viking $12.95

CHILDREN OF DYNMOUTH
Mocking, malicious, fatherless Timothy Gedge brings trouble to everyone he meets in a seaside town
0–670–21665–8 Viking $11.95

ELIZABETH ALONE
0–670–29189–7 Viking $11.95

FOOLS OF FORTUNE
The love between an Irish and an English cousin is frustrated by civil violence
0–14–006982–8 Penguin pb $6.95

MRS. ECKDORF IN O'NEILL'S HOTEL
A German photographer, who intends to expose the drunks and fantastics of a gritty Dublin hotel, falls prey herself to the prevailing Celtic madness
0–14–006014–6 Penguin pb $6.95

THE NEWS FROM IRELAND & OTHER STORIES
"I don't know who now has most right to claim Mr. Trevor, England or Ireland, nor do I much care, since it is clear to me that his excellence comes from a happy marriage of central values in both traditions"—John Fowles
0–670–81069–X Viking $16.95
0–14–008857–1 Penguin pb $6.95

NIGHTS AT THE ALEXANDRIA
A recent novella
Illustrated by Paul Hogarth
0–06–015848–4 Harper & Row $10.95

OTHER PEOPLE'S WORLDS
0–14–005767–6 Penguin pb $6.95

THE SILENCE IN THE GARDEN
The latest of Trevor's stories about the last scions of an Anglo-Irish house facing up to the ghost of the distant and not-so-distant past
0–670–82404–6 Viking $17.95

THE STORIES OF WILLIAM TREVOR
0–14–006092–8 Penguin pb $8.95

● Alexander Trocchi

CAIN'S BOOK
A lean and unsentimental novel of adultery, murder, and addiction in Trocchi's native Scotland
Introduction by Richard W. Seaver
0–394–17403–8 Grove pb $3.50

YOUNG ADAM
Trocchi, who died in 1984, was a leading figure of the English literary underground of the '50s and '60s
0–7145–3925–2 Riverrun pb $12.95

● Fay Weldon

DOWN AMONG THE WOMEN
"Her major subject is the experience of women. But she is not tedious about the rich texture of everyday female existence. She most often selects the telling and the funny, the absurd and the horrifying"—Agate Nesaule Krouse
0–89733–116–8 Academy Chicago pb $7.95

THE FAT WOMAN'S JOKE
When Alan and Esther Sussman decide to go on a diet, a marriage based on food consumption begins to decompose
0–89733–236–9 Academy Chicago pb $6.95

FEMALE FRIENDS
Three friends survive the various catastrophes of their private lives
0–89733–290–3 Academy Chicago pb $7.95

Fay Weldon (photo by Jerry Bauer, courtesy of Pantheon)

THE HEARTS AND LIVES OF MEN
0–317–66204–X Viking $18.95
0–440–20322–8 Dell pb $4.95

LEADER OF THE BAND
0–670–82440–2 Viking $18.95

THE LIFE AND LOVES OF A SHE-DEVIL
The humble Ruth reveals her true nature, ousts her husband's mistress, turns him into a doormat, and has plastic surgery that makes her irresistible to men
0–394–53920–6 Pantheon $13.95
0–345–32375–0 Ballantine pb $4.50

POLARIS & OTHER STORIES
0–14–009747–3 Penguin pb $6.95

REMEMBER ME
The ghost of a divorced woman haunts her husband's new wife until she behaves better to her stepdaughter
0–345–32976–7 Ballantine pb $3.50

THE RULES OF LIFE
0–06–015759–3 Harper & Row $10.95

THE SHRAPNEL ACADEMY
0–670–81482–2 Viking $15.95
0–14–009746–5 Penguin pb $6.95

● Angus Wilson
"Who would choose to live in a novel by Angus Wilson? . . . Since 1949 . . . he has been animating a vast, disturbing tableau of English society. It is a portrait of the kind of hell which vulnerable private people create when they attempt to live with each other"—Jonathan Raban, *New Review*

AS IF BY MAGIC
The lively journeying of a breeder of "magic" rice and his nubile goddaughter
0–14–004062–5 Penguin pb $3.95

HEMLOCK AND AFTER
The tribulations of an aging writer
0–586–04903–7 Academy Chicago pb $5.95

LATE CALL
A retired manager is forced to live with her widowed son in a chillingly described New Town
0–586–04895–2 Academy Chicago pb $5.95

THE MIDDLE AGE OF MRS. ELIOT
After the assassination of her husband, an elegant woman frees herself from genteel seclusion and begins a more vibrant life
0–14–001502–7 Penguin pb $6.95

NO LAUGHING MATTER
This traditional generational novel follows the fortunes of an eccentric and privileged

British family from 1912 to the present. "Wilson is masterly on clothes and colours; superb on dialogue, good on anything that concerns art and politics and class"— *Evening Standard*
0–586–04897–9 Academy Chicago pb $5.95

THE OLD MEN AT THE ZOO
A parable that turns on the adaptation of animal management to the political dangers of a future Britain
0–586–04902–9 Academy Chicago pb $5.95

THE WRONG SET
A collection of short stories. "Unfailingly witty, sharp, observant and amusing"— Margaret Drabble
0–586–04905–3 Academy Chicago pb $5.95

YOUNGER WRITERS

• Peter Ackroyd
CHATTERTON
A fictional exploration of the strange career of the short-lived 18th-century poet
0–8021–0041–4 Grove $17.95

THE LAST TESTAMENT OF OSCAR WILDE
A fictional recreation of Wilde's last years in Paris
0–06–015187–0 Harper & Row $12.45

HAWKSMOOR
The spirit of a sinister 18th-century architect haunts an investigation of satanic murders in modern London
0–06–015503–5 Harper & Row $16.95
0–06–091390–8 Harper & Row pb $7.95

• Martin Amis
DEAD BABIES
A futuristic satire. "Rather as I hope for society that this is no true prophecy, I hope for Martin Amis that the nightmare of this vision will rapidly become part of his past. In the meanwhile, it is a remarkable fantasy"—Elaine Feinstein, *New Statesman*
0–517–56866–7 Crown pb $8.95

EINSTEIN'S MONSTERS
Five pieces dealing with nuclear madness
0–517–56520–X Crown $12.95

MONEY: A Suicide Note
A fresco of contemporary greed. "A highly original and often dazzling piece of work"—John Gross, *NY Times*
0–14–008891–1 Penguin pb $6.95

THE RACHEL PAPERS
A first novel about youthful naughtiness
0–517–56777–6 Crown pb $7.95

SUCCESS
0–517–56649–4 Crown $15.95

• Julian Barnes
BEFORE SHE MET ME
A middle-aged academic becomes obsessed with his beautiful second wife's premarital affairs
0–07–003747–7 McGraw-Hill pb $4.95

FLAUBERT'S PARROT
A charming and digressive entertainment— erudite, ironical, and amusing—that hinges on a biographer's obsession with Flaubert.

"A most brilliant and impressive book"— James Fenton
0–07–003748–5 McGraw-Hill pb $4.95

METROLAND
The sophisticated attitudes of two schoolboys prevent them from coming to terms with their feelings. "Its crisp one-liners, cultural jokes and lyrical *aperçus* are organized with the tension of poetry"— Angela Carter
0–07–003746–9 McGraw-Hill pb $4.95

STARING AT THE SUN
Barnes traces the course of a woman's life and the philosophical issues she encounters
0–394–55821–9 Knopf $15.95
0–06–097148–7 Harper & Row pb $7.95

• William Boyd
A GOOD MAN IN AFRICA
The comic misadventures of a bumbling but decent British diplomat in West Africa. "A sweaty tropical setting in which dead bodies rapidly become unapproachable and live ones, even if lusted for, have a certain grotesquerie"—Alan Hollinghurst
0–14–005887–7 Penguin pb $4.95

AN ICE-CREAM WAR: A Tale of the Empire
German and British settlers in West Africa wage an absurd counterpart to WWI in Europe
0–14–006571–7 Penguin pb $4.95

THE NEW CONFESSIONS
A Scottish moviemaker sets about filming Rousseau. "Turn-of-the-century Edinburgh, the 1914–18 trenches, 1920s Berlin, inter- and postwar Los Angeles are reconstructed with a density of detail that is marvelously pleasurable. Boyd has written funny novels and clever novels. *The New Confessions* one can confidently call a great novel"—John Sutherland, *Listener*
0–688–07761–7 William Morrow $19.95
0–14–010699–5 Penguin pb $8.95

ON THE YANKEE STATION
A collection of short stories
0–14–006087–1 Penguin pb $4.95

STARS AND BARS
A mild-mannered Brit encounters a not-so-mild New York City
0–688–02599–4 William Morrow $16.95
0–14–008889–X Penguin pb $6.95

• J.L. Carr
A MONTH IN THE COUNTRY
0–89733–124–9 Academy Chicago pb $6.95

Angela Carter
THE BLOODY CHAMBER
A collection of stories that retell the great Western fairy tales with vivid imagination and flawless style
0–14–005404–9 Penguin pb $5.95

FIREWORKS: Nine Profane Pieces
"The real world—principally here her experience of Japan—is reshaped subjectively so that real cities, real situations, blossom strangely. They are the result of her preoccupation with the imagery of the unconscious"—Victoria Glendinning, *New Statesman*
0–06–014852–7 Harper & Row $10.95
0–14–010588–3 Penguin pb $5.95

THE INFERNAL DESIRE MACHINES OF DOCTOR HOFFMAN
Metaphysical fantasy of a magic land where Desiderio, detailed by the logical Minister of Determination to destroy the wizard of dreams, falls in love with the latter's beautiful daughter
0–14–005651–3 Penguin pb $6.95

NIGHTS AT THE CIRCUS
Fevvers and Lizzie are performers of almost magical skills in this 19th-century circus fantasy spanning every country in Europe. "A couple of sexual revolutionaries taking over the male illusion game"—Valerie Cunningham, *Observer*
0–14–007703–0 Penguin pb $6.95

SAINTS AND STRANGERS
0–670–81139–4 Viking $13.95
0–14–008973–X Penguin pb $5.95

• Bruce Chatwin
ON THE BLACK HILL
A novel about a rural Welsh community
0–670–52492–1 Viking $14.75
0–14–006896–1 Penguin pb $7.95

THE SONGLINES
This fascinating picture of the interraction of Aborigine and Anglo cultures in Australia is also a philosophical meditation on the human potential of "nomadism"
0–670–80605–6 Viking $18.95
0–14–009429–6 Penguin pb $7.95

UTZ
Chatwin's final novel
0–670–82497–6 Viking $16.95

THE VICEROY OF OUIDAH
The colorful life of a Spanish slave merchant in Africa and his impact on the culture and customs of the local peoples
0–671–41253–1 Summit $11.95
0–686–36917–3 Summit pb $4.95

• Margaret Drabble
THE GARRICK YEAR
The character of the dedicated mother, Emma, draws on Drabble's own experiences of marriage to an actor
0–452–25590–2 NAL pb $6.95

THE ICE AGE
0–452–26046–9 NAL pb $7.95

JERUSALEM THE GOLDEN
A woman attempts to escape her puritanical upbringing through an affair with the elegant son of a worldly London family
0–452–25935–5 NAL pb $8.95

THE MILLSTONE
A young woman working on a dissertation decides to keep the baby conceived in a casual love affair
0–452–26126–0 NAL pb $7.95

THE RADIANT WAY
0–394–56143–0 Knopf $18.95

A SUMMER BIRD-CAGE
"Warm, humorous, gently intelligent, she possesses the Jamesian talent for discerning possibilities of adventure as well as the Jamesian position of observer"—Joyce Carol Oates
0–452–26050–7 NAL pb $8.95

✉ **TO ORDER BOOKS AS GIFTS, SEE PAGE 1**

THE WATERFALL
0–452–25825–1 NAL pb $6.95

• Terry Eagleton
SAINTS AND SCHOLARS
An unlikely cast, including Wittgenstein and Leopold Bloom, struggle with social and philosophical issues amid the beautiful desolation of Connemara
0–86091–180–2 RC&H $14.95

• Zoe Fairbairns
CLOSING
In Fairbairns' fiction an undogmatic feminism combines with whimsical imagination
0–525–24642–8 Dutton $19.95

• Penelope Farmer
CHARLOTTE SOMETIMES
0–440–41261–7 Dell pb $4.95

EMMA IN WINTER
0–440–42308–2 Dell pb $2.95

EVE: Her Story
0–916515–25–7 Mercury House $15.95

THE SUMMER BIRDS
0–440–47737–9 Dell pb $2.50

• Ronald Frame
SANDMOUTH
A realistic and disturbing portrait of a '50s seaside resort
0–394–56357–3 Knopf $19.95

• George Macdonald Fraser
The Flashman novels are a rollicking series of historical adventures set in the 19th century.
FLASHMAN
In the first novel of the series, the drunken bully deservedly expelled from Harrow in *Tom Brown's Schooldays* begins a sidesplitting career of unparalleled success in Victorian England
0–452–25961–4 NAL pb $7.95

FLASH FOR FREEDOM!
0–452–25677–1 NAL pb $6.95

FLASHMAN AND THE DRAGON
0–394–55357–8 Knopf $16.95
0–452–26191–0 NAL pb $8.95

FLASHMAN AND THE REDSKINS
0–394–52852–2 Knopf $14.95
0–452–26066–3 NAL pb $8.95

FLASHMAN AT THE CHARGE
0–452–25957–6 NAL pb $7.95

FLASHMAN'S LADY
0–452–26080–9 NAL pb $8.95

• Carlo Gebler
THE ELEVENTH SUMMER
Middle-aged Paul Weisman recalls his adolescence during a fateful summer in Ireland shortly after his mother's suicide
0–525–24331–3 Dutton $13.95

WORK AND PLAY
0–312–01847–9 St. Martin's $12.95

• Maggie Gee
THE BURNING BOOK
0–312–10862–1 St. Martin's $13.95

DYING, IN OTHER WORDS
Gee's first novel involves a mysterious death at Oxford
0–7108–0030–4 Faber & Faber $13.95
0–571–12527–1 Faber & Faber pb $7.95

• Andrew Harvey
ONE LAST MIRROR
0–395–36975–4 Houghton Mifflin $15.95

THE WEB
0–395–42921–8 Houghton Mifflin $16.95

• Alan Hollinghurst
THE SWIMMING-POOL LIBRARY
"Beautifully welds the standard conventions of fiction to a tale of modern transgressions. It tells of impurities with shimmering elegance, and of complexities with camp-fired wit"—Catharine R. Stimpson
0–394–57025–1 Random House $16.95
0–679–72256–4 David McKay pb $8.95

• Ian McEwan
A CHILD IN TIME
0–395–42912–9 Houghton Mifflin $16.95

THE CEMENT GARDEN
Disturbing and laconic tale of four London children who conceal their mother's death to avoid appropriation by the state apparatus
0–14–011282–0 Penguin pb $6.95

• Bernard MacLaverty
THE GREAT PROFUNDO & OTHER STORIES
0–80211048–7 Longwood $15.95

A TIME TO DANCE & OTHER STORIES
0–8076–1135–2 Braziller $5.95

Timothy Mo
AN INSULAR POSSESSION
Nineteenth-century Hong Kong is the setting for a story of two young Americans trying to prevent British importation of opium to China
0–394–55430–2 Random House $19.95

THE MONKEY KING
A clash of family values between a modern young man and his in-laws' Chinese traditions
0–688–06189–3 William Morrow $16.95
0–571–12966–8 Faber & Faber pb $8.95

SOUR SWEET
The world of Chinese immigrants in London during the 1960s includes the gang warfare of the triads as well as closely observed domestic life
0–394–73680–X Random House pb $8.95

• Piers Paul Read
THE FREE FRENCHMAN
A dramatic novel about the French Resistance
0–394–55887–1 Random House $19.95
0–8041–0253–8 Ballantine pb $4.95

• Salman Rushdie
GRIMUS
0–87951–138–9 Overlook pb $10.95

MIDNIGHT'S CHILDREN
A fantastic epic of Indian independence and its aftermath. "Dense with passion, intelligence, excitement, and every vocal and literary effect conceivable"—Margo Jefferson, *Village Voice*
0–394–51470–X Knopf $14.95
0–380–58099–3 Avon pb $5.95

THE SATANIC VERSES
"What is being expressed is a discomfort with plural identity . . . We are increasingly becoming a world of migrants, made up of bits and fragments from here, there. We are here. And we have never really left anywhere we have been"—Salman Rushdie
0–670–82537–9 Viking $19.95

SHAME
Of this novel, the author has said, "One of my central ideas during the writing of *Shame*, though it is stated nowhere in the book, is that what you have in Pakistan is a tragedy on a very large scale. But the protagonists are not tragic actors. It's as if you had *Macbeth* and you cast a group of second-rate vaudeville clowns in it, and you have clowns trying to speak those great lines"
0–394–53408–5 Knopf $13.95
0–394–72665–0 Random House pb $9.95

Graham Swift
LEARNING TO SWIM & OTHER STORIES
0–671–61834–2 Washington Square pb $6.95

OUT OF THIS WORLD
"This is a powerful and exciting book that raises uncomfortable political questions . . . It deals with estrangement in families, and the estrangement of our generation, which sees life through a camera lens"—Philip Howard, *Times* (London)
0–671–65827–1 Poseidon $16.95

SHUTTLECOCK
0–671–54612–0 Washington Square pb $7.95

THE SWEET-SHOP OWNER
0–671–54611–2 Washington Square pb $7.95

WATERLAND
A novel that earned Swift acclaim as one of the most promising younger English writers
0–671–49863–0 Poseidon $15.95
0–317–56956–2 Washington Square pb $6.95

• Jeanette Winterson
THE PASSION
"We can't help recalling Gabriel García Márquez. Magical touches dance like highlights over the fairy-tale about passion, gentility, madness and androgynous ecstasy"—Edmund White
0–87113–183–8 Little, Brown $16.95

20th-Century British and Irish Poetry

BRITISH POETS

Modern British poetry has been heavily influenced by external events and trends. The First World War, the ideological struggles of the 1930s, the decline of the British Empire, and the postwar economic austerity form the historical backdrop. In purely literary terms, the native tradition found itself more open to foreign influences—to international modernism and the new poetics of American verse—than at any time in four centuries. As a result, the 20th century has been a time of movements and countermovements (the New Apocalypse, the Movement, the Liverpool Poets, the Martians), of poets judged as much by their politics as by their poetry, and of a general lack of consensus. Many of the greatest figures (David Jones, Hugh MacDiarmid, D.H. Lawrence, Basil Bunting) worked in isolation from the literary establishments of London, Oxford, and Cambridge, and this splendid individualism persists in many latter-day practitioners.

• Dannie Abse
COLLECTED POEMS
A leading Welsh poet of the postwar years, who is also a practicing physician
0–8229–5276–9 Pittsburgh pb $9.95

• John Agard
MANGOES AND BULLETS: New and Selected Poems
Politically charged poetry by a leading black writer
0–7453–0028–6 Longwood pb $6.75

• John Ash
THE BRANCHING STAIRS
"This may be the most auspicious debut of its kind since Auden's"—Carolyn Kizer, *NY Times*
0–85635–501–1 Carcanet pb $7.50

DISBELIEF
"Ash's poetry is . . . resonant with gorgeous imagery. It seems both familiar and strange, noble and funny, romantic and level-headed"—John Ashbery
0–85635–695–6 Carcanet pb $9.95

W.H. Auden
COLLECTED POEMS
0–394–40895–0 Random House $29.95

COLLECTED SHORTER POEMS
0–394–40333–9 Random House $22.50

THE ENGLISH AUDEN: Poems, Essays, and Dramatic Writings, 1927–1959
Edited by Edward Mendelson
0–571–11502–0 Faber & Faber pb $15.00

SELECTED POEMS OF W.H. AUDEN
Edited by Edward Mendelson
0–394–72506–9 Random House pb $8.95

EPISTLE TO A GODSON & OTHER POEMS
0–394–48203–4 Random House $10.95

• George Barker
COLLECTED POEMS
Barker is a frequently autobiographical poet who was for a time associated with the romantically tinged New Apocalypse movement of the 1940s
Edited by Robert Fraser
0–571–13972–8 Faber & Faber $45.00

• James Berry
CHAIN OF DAYS
Poetry that draws on the cultures of the Old World and the New, and on the relationship between the colonizers and the colonized
0–19–211964–8 Oxford pb $8.95

• John Betjeman
A NIP IN THE AIR
Betjeman, who was appointed Poet Laureate in 1972, was one of the most widely read postwar poets
0–393–04423–8 Norton pb $2.50

• Edmund Blunden
SELECTED POEMS
Blunden wrote memorable poetry of the First World War and survived to flourish as a poet of landscape and a distinguished scholar
Edited by Robyn Marsack
0–85635–425–2 Carcanet pb $8.50

• Rupert Brooke
THE POETICAL WORKS OF RUPERT BROOKE
0–571–04704–1 Faber & Faber pb $6.95

Basil Bunting (courtesy of Moyer Bell, Ltd.)

Basil Bunting
COLLECTED POEMS
A close associate of Ezra Pound, Bunting did not become widely known until he published his magnificent autobiographical poem "Briggflatts" in the 1960s. "Bunting compresses immensities of experience into clipped, tightly stitched lines. The miniature epic 'Briggflatts' is only 22 pages long, but in the mind it expands to infinitely greater length . . . The poet makes himself an instrument of the world, constructs a summing-up of earthly elements, a catalogue of smells and colors, the distillation of a life into essential—and often microscopic—perceptions"—*Village Voice*
Introduction by Jonathan Williams
0–918825–27–X Moyer Bell $22.50
0–918825–16–4 Moyer Bell pb $12.95

• Charles Causley
COLLECTED POEMS 1951–1975
0–87923–168–8 Godine pb $7.95

• Wendy Cope
MAKING COCOA FOR KINGSLEY AMIS
A witty collection that has proven immensely popular
0–571–13747–4 Faber & Faber pb $9.95

• Adam Cornford
ANIMATIONS
0–87286–208–9 City Lights pb $5.95

• Donald Davie
COLLECTED POEMS: 1970–1983
Davie, also a distinguished literary critic, was a leading figure in The Movement, the anti-Romantic group of the 1950s
0–268–00745–4 Notre Dame $16.95

SELECTED POEMS
0–85635–595–X Carcanet pb $7.50

• Walter de la Mare
COLLECTED POEMS
A poet of often striking effects, whose work is tinged with the supernatural and the perverse
0–571–11382–6 Faber & Faber pb $15.95

SELECTED POEMS
0–571–10401–0 Faber & Faber pb $6.95

• Keith Douglas
THE COMPLETE POEMS
"The *Complete Poems* of Keith Douglas . . . confirms that when Douglas was killed in Normandy, three days after D-day, at the age of 24, we lost the finest poet to come out of the Second World War"—Robert Nye
0–19–281964–X Oxford pb $11.95

• Maureen Duffy
COLLECTED POEMS
0–241–11667–8 David & Charles pb $14.95

• Douglas Dunn
SELECTED POEMS: 1964–1983
0–571–14620–1 Faber & Faber pb $7.95

• Lawrence Durrell
THE IKONS & OTHER POEMS
Poems imbued with the spirit of the Greek islands
0–933806–01–9 Black Swan $15.00

• William Empson
COLLECTED POEMS
Empson's intricate, difficult poetry reflects the concerns of his criticism
0–15–618839–2 HBJ pb $4.95

• D.J. Enright
COLLECTED POEMS, 1987
"Often he seems to be quite simply the funniest writer alive. But his humour is tempered by his very large compassion, which is always directed to living particulars"—John W. Aldridge, *NY Times*
0–19–282061–3 Oxford pb $12.95

• Gavin Ewart
SELECTED POEMS 1933–1987
A survey of the work of England's best-known comic poet. "The most remarkable phenomenon of the English poetic scene during the last ten years has been the advent, or perhaps I should say the irruption, of Gavin Ewart"—Philip Larkin
0–8112–1055–3 New Directions pb $8.95

THE COMPLETE LITTLE ONES
0–09–167311–9 David & Charles pb $15.95

Roy Fisher
POEMS, 1955–1987
Fisher has a jazz pianist's ear and the chiseled line of a modernist poet. His collected poems reveal him as one of the most powerful English poets of recent decades. "Fisher's work has always been an original mixture of real experiment and physical observation"—*Observer*
0–19–282230–6 Oxford pb $13.95

A FURNACE
A sustained, unerringly musical meditation on the ruined landscape of Britain's industrial north
0–19–281958–5 Oxford pb $7.95

• Roy Fuller
COLLECTED POEMS
"Has all the qualities—formal control, rationality, social awareness—that the Movement poets were demanding in the fifties . . . He is a calm, sad, intelligent moralist and a very good poet"—*Guardian*
0–8023–1046–X Dufour $14.95

• David Gascoyne
COLLECTED POEMS
Gascoyne was a precocious writer who initiated a Surrealist strain in modern English poetry
0–19–211801–3 Oxford pb $12.95

• W.S. Graham
SELECTED POEMS
0–912946–74–1 Ecco pb $6.95

• Robert Graves
COLLECTED POEMS, 1975
0–19–505143–2 Oxford $27.50

• Geoffrey Grigson
PERSEPHONE'S FLOWERS & OTHER POEMS
Grigson, a poet, critic, and scholar of distinction, was a native of Cornwall, which figures significantly in his writing
0–436–18807–4 David & Charles pb $16.95

• Thom Gunn
SELECTED POEMS, 1955–1975
A gathering of the work of an outstanding poet long resident in the United States. "With their undemonstrative virtuosity, their slightly corrupt openness, their atmosphere of unfathomable secrets and their intimacy, so like that of a reticent friend who has something crucial to confess, these poems strike a chord at once insinuatingly familiar and infinitely alien"—M.L. Rosenthal, *NY Times*
0–374–25865–1 Farrar, Straus & Giroux $12.95
0–374–51595–6 Farrar, Straus & Giroux pb $5.95

JACK STRAW'S CASTLE & OTHER POEMS
0–374–17851–8 Farrar, Straus & Giroux $8.95
0–374–51417–8 Farrar, Straus & Giroux pb $3.95

MOLY & MY SAD CAPTAINS
A combined edition of two of Gunn's earlier volumes
0–374–21190–6 Farrar, Straus & Giroux $7.50
0–374–51072–5 Farrar, Straus & Giroux pb $4.95

THE PASSAGES OF JOY
"The poet does a very fine job of interpreting closed realms, whether the realm is a religious painting, animals, a rock star, a transvestite, or a sluggish young cousin. Toward all these 'foreign powers,' the poet conducts himself with generosity"—Mary Kinzie, *American Poetry Review*
0–374–22990–2 Farrar, Straus & Giroux $10.95
0–374–51796–7 Farrar, Straus & Giroux pb $6.95

• Ivor Gurney
COLLECTED POEMS OF IVOR GURNEY
A composer as well as a poet, Gurney was wounded in World War I and spent much of the rest of his life in a mental hospital
Edited by P.J. Kavanagh
0–19–211963–X Oxford pb $7.95

Tony Harrison
SELECTED POEMS
Harrison is a poet and translator whose realistic vision and technical skill have attracted much attention in recent years
0–394–56126–0 Random House $15.45

THE MYSTERIES
0–571–13790–3 Faber & Faber pb $10.95

• Adrian Henri
COLLECTED POEMS, 1967–1985
Henri became well known in the 1960s as one of the pop-influenced Liverpool Poets
0–8052–8267–X Schocken pb $9.95

• Geoffrey Hill
COLLECTED POEMS
Includes the acclaimed sequences *For the Unfallen, King Log, Mercian Hymns,* and *Tenebrae*
0–19–520499–9 Oxford $22.95

THE MYSTERY OF THE CHARITY OF CHARLES PEGUY
A meditation on the work and political career of the French poet
0–19–503515–1 Oxford pb $7.95

• Ted Hughes
"Ted Hughes seems to me quite simply the best living English poet . . . Ted Hughes is not the only poet whose books are events in my life, but there are none whose works I anticipate with greater excitement and few who give me more consistent pleasure."—Dave Smith

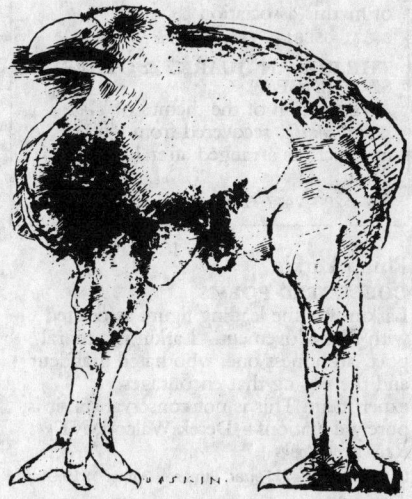

Cover illustration by Leonard Baskin for Ted Hughes' "Crow," from The Oxford Illustrated History of English Literature

NEW SELECTED POEMS
0–06–090925–0 Harper & Row pb $9.95

CROW: From the Life and Songs of the Crow
First published in 1970, this was the first of Hughes's long series of violent, myth-making poetic sequences
0–06–011989–6 Harper & Row $9.50
0–06–090905–6 Harper & Row pb $6.95

FLOWERS AND INSECTS: Some Birds and a Pair of Spiders
Illustrated by Leonard Baskin
0–394–55738–7 Knopf $14.95

THE HAWK IN THE RAIN
0–571–08614–4 Faber & Faber pb $4.95

LUPERCAL
0–571–09246–2 Faber & Faber pb $6.95

RIVER
0–06–015298–2 Harper & Row $12.95
0–06–091137–9 Harper & Row pb $6.95

WODWO
0–571–09714–6 Faber & Faber pb $6.95

• Elizabeth Jennings
COLLECTED POEMS
A poet whose work often deals intimately with her own troubled life
0–85635–721–9 Carcanet pb $10.50

SELECTED POEMS
0–85635–282–9 Carcanet pb $8.00

David Jones
THE ANATHEMATA
A difficult and extraordinarily beautiful orchestration of paleolithic, Christian, and ancient British themes; W.H. Auden called it "very probably the finest long poem written in English in this century"
0–571–10127–5 Faber & Faber pb $9.95

IN PARENTHESIS
This 1937 masterpiece, written in a combination of verse and prose, is a palimpsest in which Jones's World War I combat experiences merge with layers of mythic association
0–571–05661–X Faber & Faber pb $9.95

THE ROMAN QUARRY & OTHER SEQUENCES
An extension of the themes of *The Anathemata*, recovered from manuscripts arranged after Jones's death
0–935296–24–7 Sheep Meadow pb $14.95

• Philip Larkin
COLLECTED POEMS
Larkin was the leading figure associated with The Movement. "Larkin is a moral poet, an honest one, who hated grandeur and the posing that encourages experiment. This is not conservatism, it is, purely devotion"—Derek Walcott, *NY Review of Books*
0–374–12623–2 Farrar, Straus & Giroux $19.95

HIGH WINDOWS
"The total impression of *High Windows* is of despair made beautiful. Real despair and real beauty, with not a trace of posturing"—Clive James, *Encounter*
0–374–51212–4 Farrar, Straus & Giroux pb $7.95

THE NORTH SHIP
0–571–10503–3 Faber & Faber pb $6.95

THE WHITSUN WEDDINGS
0–571–09710–3 Faber & Faber pb $5.95

• D.H. Lawrence
THE COMPLETE POEMS OF D.H. LAWRENCE
A work of scholarship which provides for the first time a fair estimate of Lawrence's stature as one of the major poets of the century
Edited by Vivian De Sola Pinto & F. Warren Roberts
0–14–042220–X Penguin pb $17.95

• Laurie Lee
SELECTED POEMS
Lee's writing often evokes the natural world of the Cotswolds
0–233–97503–9 David & Charles pb $10.95

• Peter Levi
COLLECTED POEMS, 1955–1975
A classical translator and a former priest, Levi weaves a variety of cultural strands into his work
0–85646–135–0 Longwood pb $12.95

• Wyndham Lewis
COLLECTED POEMS AND PLAYS
Reveals a less familiar side of the vorticist painter and novelist
Introduction by C.H. Sisson
0–89255–054–6 Persea pb $7.95

• Christopher Logue
WAR MUSIC: An Account of Books 16 to 19 of Homer's Iliad
A transmutation of Homer into contemporary language. "Logue's miniature epic is a remarkable achievement, and one that justifies its title. The war it portrays is real, and harsh, and horrible; but the music is real, too"—John Gross, *NY Times*
0–374–52089–5 Farrar, Straus & Giroux pb $7.95

• George MacBeth
THE LONG DARKNESS
0–689–11461–3 Atheneum pb $7.95

POEMS OF LOVE AND DEATH
0–689–11064–2 Atheneum pb $5.95

• Hugh MacDiarmid
THE COMPLETE POEMS
MacDiarmid began by reinventing the Scottish language and ended up writing long verse discourses on science and politics. "Once he got beyond his early lyrics, MacDiarmid was no longer interested in just the sliver of moonlight on the ocean, but in the tidal pull, the contours of the shoreline, the position and philosophical prejudices of the observer, the chemical components of the brine, and the profusion of sea life below the water's surface . . . He dilates syntax, finds spacious unforeseen cavities within clauses, slows down the rhythm of the poem until each syllable seems enormous"—*Village Voice*

Volume 1
0–14–007913–0 Penguin pb $15.95

Volume 2
0–14–007914–9 Penguin pb $15.95

• Louis MacNeice
SELECTED POEMS
As an associate of Auden and Spender, MacNeice was very much in the forefront of the politically conscious poets of the 1930s
Edited by W.H. Auden
0–571–06089–7 Faber & Faber pb $5.95

• E.A. Markham
HUMAN RITES: Selected Poems, 1970–1982
0–85646–113–X Longwood pb $9.95

Charlotte Mew
COLLECTED POEMS AND PROSE
Mew, who committed suicide in 1928, has found an increasing number of appreciative readers
Edited by Val Warner
0–85635–260–8 Carcanet $21.00

• Christopher Middleton
TWO HORSE WAGON GOING BY
"Middleton is easily the most intelligent and serious of our innovators, a poet with a disconcerting knack of making it new in almost every poem"—*New Statesman*
0–85635–661–1 Carcanet pb $8.50

• Adrian Mitchell
ON THE BEACH AT CAMBRIDGE
A recent collection by a poet much associated with the avant-garde of the 1960s
0–8052–8187–8 Schocken pb $5.95

• Andrew Motion
THE PLEASURE STEAMERS
Motion made a splash in recent years as a leader of the so-called "Martian" school
0–85635–247–0 Carcanet pb $5.95

• Edwin Muir
SELECTED POEMS
A sampling of the work of a Scottish poet deeply influenced by psychoanalysis and German literature
0–571–06342–X Faber & Faber pb $4.95

• Douglas Oliver
KIND: Collected Poems
0–907954–05–7 Small Press pb $12.00

• Wilfred Owen
COLLECTED POEMS
Owen's trench poems are now indelibly part of our conception of the First World War
Edited by C. Day Lewis
0–8112–0132–5 New Directions pb $5.95

• Tom Pickard
CUSTOM AND EXILE
A Northumbrian poet who has emerged as an outstanding and experimental lyricist
0–85031–657–X Schocken pb $6.95

F.T. Prince
COLLECTED POEMS
"Undervalued at home and abroad, F.T. Prince ranks with Auden and Spender as one of the major English poets of his generation"—John Ashbery
0–8180–1548–9 Sheep Meadow pb $4.95

• Kathleen Raine
THE PRESENCE: Poems 1984–87
Raine, a Blake scholar, writes a poetry grounded in mystical awareness and a powerful sense of the forces of nature
0–89281–082–3 Inner Traditions pb $11.95

SELECTED POEMS
0–89281–083–1 Inner Traditions pb $12.95

• Peter Redgrove
THE MAN NAMED EAST & OTHER NEW POEMS
Redgrove's employment of imagery—a fluid network of natural and imaginary symbols proliferating with breathtaking energy—marks him as one of the most powerful contemporary English poets
0–7102–0014–5 Methuen pb $9.95

• Siegfried Sassoon
COLLECTED POEMS, 1908–1956
Sassoon is especially notable for his unsparingly harsh poems of the First World War
0–571–13262–6 Faber & Faber pb $9.95

SELECTED POEMS
0–571–08540–7 Faber & Faber pb $6.95

➤ FOR OVERSEAS ORDERING INFORMATION, SEE PAGE 1

THE WAR POEMS OF SIEGFRIED SASSOON
Edited by Rupert Hart-Davis
0–571–13010–0 Faber & Faber $13.95
0–571–13010–0 Faber & Faber pb $6.95

• Penelope Shuttle
Shuttle's sensually vibrant poetry has attracted a growing number of readers.
ADVENTURES WITH MY HORSE
0–19–282218–7 Oxford pb $9.00

THE ORCHARD UPSTAIRS
0–19–211938–9 Oxford pb $11.95

WAILING MONKEY EMBRACING A TREE
0–7145–0939–6 Scribners $9.95

• Jon Silkin
POEMS NEW AND SELECTED
Silkin, who founded the influential poetry magazine *Stand*, often juxtaposes exact natural description with historical elements
0–8195–2030–6 Wesleyan $17.00

THE LITTLE TIME-KEEPER
Poems ranging geographically and historically through the Hebrides, Australia, and the Third Reich
0–393–04492–0 Norton pb $2.95

• C.H. Sisson
COLLECTED POEMS: 1943–1983
The lifework of an often caustic formalist. "I think he is worth a place on the short shelf reserved for the finest twentieth-century poets, with Eliot and Rilke and MacDiarmid"—Robert Nye, *Scotsman*
0–85635–498–8 Carcanet $21.00

Stevie Smith
COLLECTED POEMS
"Stevie Smith was an artist of the utmost sophistication . . . calculating her linguistic effects with such precision that they sound as innocently commanding as a baby's cry in the night"—Clive James, *New Yorker*
Edited by James MacGibbon
0–8112–0882–6 New Directions pb $15.95

NEW SELECTED POEMS
A new chronological selection containing 165 poems and many drawings
0–8112–1068–5 New Directions pb $7.95

ME AGAIN: Uncollected Writings of Stevie Smith
Edited with an introduction by Jack Barbera and William McBrien
Preface by James MacGibbon
0–374–20494–2 FS&G $15.95

• Stephen Spender
COLLECTED POEMS: 1928–1985
"One of the important poets of the meaninglessness of war, and of the baseness of feeling it engenders, even in civilians"—Helen Vendler
0–394–54601–6 Random House $19.95
0–19–505210–2 Oxford pb $12.95

• Jon Stallworthy
THE ANZAC SONATA: New and Selected Poems
0–393–02449–0 Norton $15.95

• D.M. Thomas
SELECTED POEMS
0–14–042306–0 Penguin pb $8.95

• Dylan Thomas
THE COLLECTED POEMS: 1934–1954
Thomas' surreal lyricism decisively marked postwar poetry, while his reckless career made him the pre-eminent icon of the self-destroying poet
0–8112–0205–4 New Directions pb $7.95

THE POEMS OF DYLAN THOMAS
This collection adds 102 poems to those already gathered in the *Collected Poems*
Edited by Daniel Jones
0–8112–0398–0 New Directions $14.00

UNDER MILK WOOD: A Play for Voices
The famous radio play of Welsh village life
0–8112–0209–7 New Directions pb $4.95

• R.S. Thomas
POEMS OF R.S. THOMAS
A deeply religious poet whose work is imbued with the spirit of the Welsh countryside
0–938626–47–7 Arkansas pb $9.95

• Charles Tomlinson
COLLECTED POEMS
Tomlinson is a lucid and strongly visual poet whose formal concerns reflect his involvement with such American poets as Williams, Zukofsky, and Oppen
0–19–282072–9 Oxford pb $14.95

• Gael Turnbull
A GATHERING OF POEMS, 1950–1980
Turnbull, a practicing physician, has suffered inexplicable neglect during his long career as a poet of immense vitality and originality
0–85646–088–5 Longwood pb $9.95

• Vernon Watkins
SELECTED POEMS
One of the leading Welsh poets of his generation, Watkins was a close friend of Dylan Thomas
0–8112–0214–3 New Directions pb $2.25

• Peter Whigham
THINGS COMMON, PROPERLY: Selected Poems, 1942–1982
Whigham (praised by William Carlos Williams as "the most delightful translator of Catullus") lived in Italy and California; this collection reflects his wide sense of poetic tradition, and includes translations of Sappho and Ronsard, among others
0–933806–21–3 Black Swan $20.00

IRISH POETS

• Samuel Beckett
COLLECTED POEMS IN ENGLISH AND FRENCH
0–394–17013–X Grove pb $8.95

• Austin Clarke
THE SELECTED POEMS
Overshadowed by his contemporaries Joyce and Yeats, Clarke was nonetheless a highly significant figure in the Irish Renaissance
Edited by Thomas Kinsella
0–916390–03–9 Wake Forest pb $7.95

• Eamonn Grennan
WHAT LIGHT THERE IS & OTHER POEMS
0–86547–371–4 North Point pb $10.95

• Seamus Heaney
POEMS: 1965–1975
A comprehensive gathering of one of the most widely praised poets now writing, including work from *Death of a Naturalist, Door into the Dark, Wintering Out,* and *North*
0–374–23496–5 Farrar, Straus & Giroux $12.95
0–374–51652–9 Farrar, Straus & Giroux pb $7.25

DEATH OF A NATURALIST
0–571–09024–9 Faber & Faber pb $5.95

FIELD WORK
"A superb book, the most eloquent and far-reaching book he has written, a perennial poetry offered at a time when many of us have despaired of seeing such a thing"—Denis Donoghue
0–374–15482–1 Farrar, Straus & Giroux $10.95
0–374–51620–0 Farrar, Straus & Giroux pb $5.95

THE HAW LANTERN
"Heaney is keyed and pitched unlike any significant poet now at work in the language, anywhere"—Harold Bloom
0–374–16837–7 Farrar, Straus & Giroux $12.95

NORTH
0–571–10813–X Faber & Faber pb $5.95

STATION ISLAND
"As fine a long poem as we've had in fifty years"—Hugh Kenner
0–374–26978–5 Farrar, Straus & Giroux $11.95
0–374–51935–8 Farrar, Straus & Giroux pb $6.95

SWEENEY ASTRAY
Heaney's rendering of the ancient Irish poem
0–374–27221–2 Farrar, Straus & Giroux $13.95
0–374–51894–7 Farrar, Straus & Giroux pb $7.95

• James Joyce
COLLECTED POEMS
0–14–058593–1 Penguin pb $6.95

• Patrick Kavanagh
THE COLLECTED POEMS
Includes the long poem "The Great Hunger," a bleakly powerful depiction of Irish peasant life
0–393–00694–8 Norton pb $7.95

• Thomas Kinsella
PEPPERCANISTER POEMS: 1972–1978
"Among the true poets, not only of Ireland but among all who write in English in our day"—M.L. Rosenthal
0–916390–12–8 Wake Forest pb $7.95

• Maedbh McGuckian
ON BALLYCASTLE BEACH
The third book by a younger poet who lives in Belfast. "The cumulative effect . . . is to give the sense of a highly wrought and expanding imaginative world which can give symbolic expression to intimate physical experience"—*New Statesman*
0–916390–30–6 Wake Forest pb $6.95

• Derek Mahon
POEMS: 1962–1978
Includes most of the poems from the collections *Night Crossing, Lives,* and *The Snow Party*
0–19–211897–8 Oxford pb $9.95

THE HUNT BY NIGHT
Mary Kinzie in *American Poetry Review* has written of Mahon's "multiple gift of cultivation, verbal sophistication, rhetorical daring, high descriptive subtlety and accuracy, and public conscience"
0–916390–17–9 Wake Forest pb $4.95

• John Montague
"In Mr. Montague's fine, firm poems . . . loving force is always made real by being felt as threatened by the angers of Ireland and of this Irishman."—Christopher Ricks, *NY Times*
SELECTED POEMS
0–916390–15–2 Wake Forest pb $7.95

THE DEAD KINGDOM
0–916390–20–9 Wake Forest pb $6.50

• Paul Muldoon
SELECTED POEMS, 1968–1986
Gathered from six previous volumes. "Muldoon seems to me unusually gifted, endowed with an individual sense of rhythm, a natural and copious vocabulary, a technical accomplishment and intellectual boldness that mark him as the most promising poet to appear in Ireland for years"—Seamus Heaney
0–88001–154–8 Ecco $16.50

• Tom Paulin
LIBERTY TREE
0–571–13025–9 Faber & Faber pb $7.95

W.B. Yeats by John Singer Sargent, from The Oxford Illustrated History of English Literature

William Butler Yeats
THE COLLECTED POEMS: A New Edition
0–02–055650–0 Macmillan $14.95

THE POEMS OF W.B. YEATS
"Early and late he has the simple, indispensable gift of enchanting the ear . . . Though he plunged deep into arcane studies, his themes are most clearly the general ones of life and death, love and hate, man's condition, and history's meanings . . . He grew at last into the boldest, most vigorous voice of this century"—M.L. Rosenthal
Edited by Richard J. Finneran
0–02–632940–9 Macmillan $24.95

SELECTED POEMS & THREE PLAYS
Edited by M.L. Rosenthal
0–02–071560–9 Macmillan pb $10.95

COLLECTED PLAYS
Yeats's verse plays were deeply influenced by Irish myth and Japanese Nō theater
0–02–632630–2 Macmillan $17.95

ANTHOLOGIES

• James Berry, editor
NEWS FOR BABYLON
Black poets of contemporary England
0–7011–2797–X Salem House pb $8.95

• Anthony Bradley, editor
CONTEMPORARY IRISH POETRY
0–520–05874–7 California pb $12.95

• Philip Larkin, editor
THE OXFORD BOOK OF TWENTIETH-CENTURY ENGLISH VERSE
0–19–812137–7 Oxford $35.00

• Paul Muldoon, editor
THE FABER BOOK OF CONTEMPORARY IRISH POETRY
0–571–13761–X Faber & Faber pb $13.95

• Frank Ormsby, editor
THE LONG EMBRACE: 20th Century Irish Love Poems
2–904394–32–X Faber & Faber pb $10.95

• Jon Silkin, editor
THE PENGUIN BOOK OF FIRST WORLD WAR POETRY
A superb collection that includes generous selections from Isaac Rosenberg, Wilfred Owen, Herbert Read, Siegfried Sassoon, Edmund Blunden, Edward Thomas, Ivor Gurney, and other English poets, as well as a sampling of work by such European writers as Heym, Trakl, Goll, Ungaretti, and Blok
0–14–008032–5 Penguin pb $5.95

20th-Century British and Irish Drama

THE EARLY 20TH CENTURY

• John Galsworthy
FIVE PLAYS
Includes *Strife, Justice, The Eldest Son, The Skin Game,* and *Loyalties.* Galsworthy established himself as the preeminent dramatist of class conflict. "He was born a peacemaker who, for that very reason, elected to be a war correspondent; and, at its not infrequent best, his dispassionate passion makes us feel the terror, the pity and the waste of the fray"—Benedict Nightingale
Introduction by Benedict Nightingale
0–413–54290–4 RC&H pb $5.95

TEN BEST PLAYS
Includes *The Silver Box, Strife, Justice, The Skin Game, Loyalties, Windows, Old English, Escape, The Roof,* and *Joy*
0–7156–0797–9 Longwood $40.50

• Lady Gregory
COLLECTED PLAYS OF LADY GREGORY
Lady Augusta Gregory was a pioneer of Irish theater, collaborating with Yeats and championing the work of Synge and O'Casey. Her own plays include the famous one-acters *The Rising of the Moon, The Workhouse Ward,* and *Spreading the News*
Edited by Ann Saddlemyer

Volume 1: Comedies
0–86140–016–X Dufour pb $7.95

Volume 2: Tragedies and Tragic Comedies
0–86140–017–8 Dufour pb $9.95

Volume 3: Wonder and Supernatural Plays
0–86140–018–6 Dufour pb $12.95

Volume 4: Collaborations, Adaptations, and Translations
0–86140–019–4 Dufour pb $10.95

• George Bernard Shaw
"It was clear from the start that Bernard Shaw was a man of ideas. Later it turned out that he was a fabulous entertainer. But few have granted that the two Shaws were one . . . The shock of that long career in the theater has still not been absorbed. Shaw has not yet been seen in perspective."—Eric Bentley
BERNARD SHAW'S PLAYS
Includes *Major Barbara, Heartbreak House, Saint Joan,* and *Too True to Be Good*
Edited by Warren S. Smith
0–393–09942–3 Norton pb $9.95

FOUR PLAYS
Four of Shaw's best-known works, including *Mrs. Warren's Profession, Arms and the Man, Candida,* and *Man and Superman*
Foreword by Eric Bentley
0–451–52200–1 NAL pb $4.95

Caricature of Bernard Shaw as a demonic Russian king, from The Oxford Illustrated History of English Literature

THREE PLAYS
Includes *Major Barbara, Caesar and Cleopatra,* and *The Doctor's Dilemma*
Foreword by Sylvan Barnet
0–451–51903–5 NAL pb $4.95

THE PORTABLE BERNARD SHAW
Includes *The Devil's Disciple, Pygmalion, In the Beginning, Heartbreak House, Shakes Versus Shav,* the "Don Juan in Hell" scene from *Man and Superman, The Adventures of the Black Girl in Her Search for God,* letters, articles, reviews, and speeches
Edited by Stanley Weintraub
0–14–015090–0 Penguin pb $7.95

ANDROCLES AND THE LION
The fable of the lion and the thorn provides the opportunity for an unidealized depiction of martyrs
0–14–048010–2 Penguin pb $3.95

THE APPLE CART
0–14–048008–0 Penguin pb $4.95

ARMS AND THE MAN
A satire on the romantic glorification of war
0–14–048102–8 Penguin pb $2.95

BACK TO METHUSELAH
Shaw's longest play is a pageant of human evolution, past and future
0–14–045014–9 Penguin pb $5.95

CAESAR AND CLEOPATRA
The legendary couple dramatized with an eye to contemporary parallels
0–14–048100–1 Penguin pb $3.95

CANDIDA
A triangle in which a woman is caught between cleric husband and poet suitor
0–14–048103–6 Penguin pb $3.95

THE DEVIL'S DISCIPLE
A comedy of the American Revolution
0–14–048101–X Penguin pb $3.50

THE DOCTOR'S DILEMMA
0–14–045027–0 Penguin pb $3.50

GETTING MARRIED
A classically constructed play about the institution of marriage. Also includes *Press Cuttings,* whose text was compiled from

daily papers during the Women's War of 1909
0–14–048205–9 Penguin pb $5.95

HEARTBREAK HOUSE
"Shaw confronts, for the first time in his imaginative writing, the small extent of his faith in man. What lies beneath the play's surface is despair. It is thus in intention, radically different from almost all the rest of his work"—J.M. Stewart
0–14–05017–3 Penguin pb $3.95

MAJOR BARBARA
A complex debate on morality, pitting a munitions manufacturer against an officer in the Salvation Army
0–14–045018–1 Penguin pb $3.50

MAN AND SUPERMAN
Don Juan versus the Life Force
0–14–045019–X Penguin pb $3.95

THE MILLIONAIRESS
0–14–048009–9 Penguin pb $3.95

PLAYS POLITICAL
Includes *The Apple Cart, On the Rocks,* and *Geneva*
0–14–048204–0 Penguin pb $5.95

PLAYS UNPLEASANT
Includes *Widowers' House, The Philanderer,* and *Mrs. Warren's Profession*
0–14–048012–9 Penguin pb $3.95

PYGMALION
One of Shaw's most popular plays, later adapted into *My Fair Lady*
0–14–045022–X Penguin pb $2.95

SAINT JOAN
Premiered in 1923, *Saint Joan* was a tremendous international success and is often considered one of Shaw's greatest works
0–14–048005–6 Penguin pb $2.95

SELECTED ONE-ACT PLAYS
Includes *The Shewing Up of Blanco Posnet, How He Lied to Her Husband, O'Flaherty V.C., The Inca of Jerusalem, Anna Janska, Village Wooing, Overruled, The Dark Lady of the Sonnets, Great Catherine, Augustus Does His Bit,* and *The Six of Calais.* With prefaces by Shaw
0–14–048123–0 Penguin pb $4.95

THE SHEWING-UP OF BLANCO POSNET & FANNY'S FIRST PLAY
0–14–045025–4 Penguin pb $5.95

• John Millington Synge
COMPLETE PLAYS OF JOHN MILLINGTON SYNGE
All of these plays were produced at the Abbey Theatre, which Synge founded with Lady Gregory and W.B. Yeats. The predominant style of the Abbey Theatre was split between the Yeats's mythic poeticism and Gregory's domestic realism. Synge fused the two into powerful and often extremely controversial drama. Includes *The Playboy of the Western World, Riders to the Sea, In the Shadow of the Glen, The Well of the Saints, The Tinker's Wedding,* and *Deirdre of the Sorrows*
0–394–70178–X Random House pb $3.95

THE COLLECTED WORKS OF JOHN MILLINGTON SYNGE

Volume 1: The Poems
Edited by Robin Skelton
0–8132–0562–X Catholic University pb $5.95

Volume 2: The Prose
Edited by Alan Price
0–8132–0564–6 Catholic University pb $10.95

Volume 3: The Plays (Book 1)
Includes *Riders to the Sea, The Shadow of the Glen, The Well of the Saints,* and the previously unpublished *When the Moon Has Set*
Edited by Ann Saddlemyer
0–8132–0566–2 Catholic University pb $10.95

Volume 4: The Plays (Book 2)
Includes *The Tinker's Wedding, The Playboy of the Western World,* and *Deirdre of the Sorrows*
Edited by Ann Saddlemyer
0–8132–0568–9 Catholic University pb $10.95

THE PLAYBOY OF THE WESTERN WORLD
Synge was accused of insulting the Irish national character in this play about a man who becomes a town hero after boasting how he murdered his own father. Also includes *Riders to the Sea*
0–06–463226–1 Harper & Row pb $5.95

• Oscar Wilde
THE PLAYS OF OSCAR WILDE
Includes *Salome, The Importance of Being Ernest, Lady Windemere's Fan, An Ideal Husband,* and *A Woman of No Importance.* "A work of art is useless as a flower is useless. A flower blossoms for its own joy. We gain a moment of joy by looking at it"—Oscar Wilde
Introduction by John Lahr
0–394–75788–2 Random House pb $9.95

Oscar Wilde by Aubrey Beardsley

THE PORTABLE OSCAR WILDE
Includes *The Picture of Dorian Gray, De Profundis, Salome, The Importance of Being Earnest,* selections from three comedies, letters, reviews, poems, "Phrases and Philosophies for the Young," and "The Critic as Artist"
Edited by Stanley Weintraub
0–14–015093–5 Penguin pb $7.95

SELECTED PLAYS
Includes *The Importance of Being Ernest, An Ideal Husband, Lady Windermere's Fan, A Woman of No Importance,* and *Salome*
0–14–048209–1 Penguin pb $2.95

THREE PLAYS
Includes *Lady Windermere's Fan, An Ideal Husband,* and the three-act version of *The Importance of Being Earnest,* with excerpts from the original four-act version
Introduction by T.R. Henn
0–413–48530–7 RC&H pb $4.95

THE IMPORTANCE OF BEING EARNEST
"It is exquisitely trivial, a delicate bubble of fancy, and it has its philosophy . . . that we should treat all the trivial things of life seriously, and all the serious things of life with sincere and studied triviality"—Oscar Wilde
Introduction by Adeline Hartcup
0–413–31000–0 RC&H pb $6.95

LADY WINDERMERE'S FAN
Edited by Ian Small
0–393–90048–7 Norton pb $5.95

SALOME
"Few English plays have such a peculiar history. Written in French in 1893, it was in full rehearsal by Madame Bernhardt at the Palace Theatre when it was prohibited by the Censor. Oscar Wilde immediately announced his intention of changing his nationality, a characteristic jest, which was only taken seriously, oddly enough, in Ireland. The interference of the Censor has seldom been more popular or more heartily endorsed by English critics"—from "Note on Salome" by Robert Ross
Illustrated by Aubrey Beardsley
0–8283–1466–7 Branden pb $25.00

• William Butler Yeats
COLLECTED PLAYS
Twenty-six plays by the man whom T.S. Eliot called "the greatest poet of our time—certainly the greatest in his language, and so far as I can judge, in any language"
0–02–632630–2 Macmillan $17.95

ELEVEN PLAYS OF WILLIAM BUTLER YEATS
Of his verse plays, Yeats wrote, "I wanted all my poetry to be spoken on a stage or sung." Includes *On Baile's Strand, Deirdre, The Player Queen, Resurrection, Words Upon the Window Pane, A Full Moon in March, Herne's Egg, Cathleen Ni Houlihan, The Only Jealousy of Emer, Purgatory,* and *The Death of Cuchulain*
Edited by A. Norman Jeffares
0–02–012970–X Macmillan pb $5.95

THE 1920s, '30s, AND '40s

• Agatha Christie
THE MOUSETRAP & OTHER PLAYS
In addition to the title work—the longest-running play in history—includes *Ten Little Indians, Appointment with Death, The Hollow, Witness for the Prosecution, Towards Zero, Verdict,* and *Go Back for Murder*
0–396–07631–9 Dodd, Mead $12.95
0–553–27298–5 Bantam pb $5.50

• Noel Coward
PLAYS
Terence Rattigan described the prolific and enormously popular Coward as "simply a phenomenon, and one which is unlikely to occur ever again in theatre history." Of his own dramatic ambitions Coward wrote, "I am not particularly interested in reforming the human race. Indeed, if I did there would be nothing to write about"

Volume 1
Includes *Hay Fever, The Vortex, Fallen Angels,* and *Easy Virtue*
Introduction by Raymond Mander & Joe Mitchenson
0–394–17940–4 Grove pb $9.95

Volume 2
Includes *Private Lives, Bitter-Sweet, The Marquise,* and *Post-Mortem*
0–394–17941–2 Grove pb $9.95

Volume 3
Includes *Design for Living, Cavalcade, Conversation Piece,* and three short plays from the revue *Tonight at 8:30, Hands Across the Sea, Still Life,* and *Fumed Oak*
0–394–17942–0 Grove pb $9.95

Volume 4
Includes *Blithe Spirit, Present Laughter, This Happy Breed, Ways and Means, The Astonished Heart,* and *Red Peppers* (from *Tonight at 8:30*)
0–394–17943–9 Grove pb $9.95

Volume 5
Includes *Relative Values, Look After Lulu!, Waiting in the Wings,* and *Suite in Three Keys* (comprising "A Song at Twilight," "Shadows of the Evening," and "Come into the Garden")
0–394–62456–4 Grove pb $9.95

THREE PLAYS
Includes *Blithe Spirit, Hay Fever,* and *Private Lives*
0–394–17535–2 Grove pb $7.95

Noël Coward by Max Beerbohm

THE LYRICS OF NOEL COWARD
"Mad Dogs and Englishmen," "Don't Put Your Daughter on the Stage, Mrs. Worthington," and other songs
0–87951–197–4 Overlook $25.00
0–87951–187–7 Overlook pb $10.95

• T.S. Eliot
THE COMPLETE POEMS AND PLAYS, 1909–1950
In addition to Eliot's poetry, includes *Murder in the Cathedral, The Family Reunion,* and *The Cocktail Party*
0–15–121185–X HBJ $19.95

CATS
The book of the musical, based on *Old Possum's Book of Practical Cats*
0–15–615582–6 HBJ pb $14.95

THE COCKTAIL PARTY
"By using very little imagery, by his language which is so idiomatic that one accepts his rhythm as that of ordinary speech with an insistent beat pulsing through it . . . Eliot really does portray real-seeming characters. He cuts down his poetic effects to a minimum, and then finally rewards us with most beautiful poetry"—Stephen Spender
0–15–618289–0 HBJ pb $4.95

THE CONFIDENTIAL CLERK
0–15–622015–6 HBJ pb $6.95

THE FAMILY REUNION
"Mr. Eliot has re-created a Greek tragedy in an English country house . . . the crowding ideas behind the rhythmic power of verse soon raise to great drama"—*Catholic World*
0–15–630157–1 HBJ pb $6.95

MURDER IN THE CATHEDRAL
0–15–663277–2 HBJ pb $3.95

• Christopher Fry
SELECTED PLAYS
Includes *The Boy with a Cart, A Sleep of Prisoners, The Lady's Not for Burning, A Phoenix Too Frequent,* and *Curtmantle*
0–19–281873–2 Oxford pb $10.95

THE DARK IS LIGHT ENOUGH
A verse play set during the Hungarian revolution
0–19–500155–9 Oxford $9.95

THE LADY'S NOT FOR BURNING & A PHOENIX TOO FREQUENT
Fry's two most successful attempts at modern verse drama. Also includes the essay "An Experience of Critics"
0–19–519916–2 Oxford pb $6.95

VENUS OBSERVED
Originally commissioned by Laurence Olivier. "A breath-taking verbal dance"—*NY Times*
0–19–500395–0 Oxford $9.95

YARD OF SUN
A dark comedy that combines a medieval horse race with post-World War II Italy
0–19–501245–3 Oxford $9.95

• D.H. Lawrence
THREE PLAYS
Includes *A Collier's Friday Night, The Daughter-in-Law,* and *The Widowing of Mrs. Holroyd*
0–14–048086–2 Penguin pb $5.95

- Sean O'Casey

SEVEN PLAYS
Includes *The Shadow of a Gunman, Juno and the Paycock, The Plough and the Stars, The Silver Tassie, Red Roses for Me, Cock-a-Doodle Dandy,* and *The Bishop's Bonfire*
Edited by Ronald Ayling
0–312–71323–1 St. Martin's $32.50

THREE PLAYS
Three of the major works of O'Casey's early realist phase: *Juno and the Paycock, The Shadow of a Gunman,* and *The Plough and the Stars*
0–312–80290–0 St. Martin's pb $4.95

- Terence Rattigan

PLAYS
Rattigan's superb craftsmanship is amply displayed in these plays from the '30s and '40s: *French Without Tears, The Winslow Boy, The Browning Version,* and *Harlequinade.* "One of the most reliable entertainers in the English theatre"—John Russell Taylor
Introduction by Anthony Curtis
0–394–17743–6 Grove pb $5.95

- Dylan Thomas

UNDER MILK WOOD
A radio play written for the BBC. "It was lyrical, impassioned and funny, an *Our Town* given universality: by comparison with anything broadcast for a very long time, it exploded on the air like a bomb—but a life-giving bomb"—*New Statesman & Nation*
0–8112–0209–7 New Directions pb $4.95

THE 1950s AND '60s

- John Arden

"Arden is a genuine original, and far more important than the differences between his plays and those of his contemporaries is the internal consistency which makes them a logical, coherent progression, all first, foremost, and unmistakably the product of one exceptional mind."—John Russell Taylor

PLAYS
Includes *Armstrong's Last Goodnight, Serjeant Musgrave's Dance,* and *The Workhouse Donkey*
0–394–17061–X Grove pb $4.95

PEARL
"The time is the late 1630s, the political and religious climate is deeply troubled, the moment could be right for something extraordinary to happen which will change the course of history"—Gillian Reynolds, *Daily Telegraph*
0–413–40100–6 RC&H pb $6.95

- John Arden & Margaretta D'Arcy

THE BUSINESS OF GOOD GOVERNMENT: A Christmas Play
One of several collaborations between Arden and his actress wife, this 1960 nativity play was originally produced at a Somerset church as an experiment in community theater
0–413–53460–X RC&H pb $4.95

THE HERO RISES UP
A history play based on the rise and fall of Admiral Nelson
0–416–13960–4 RC&H pb $6.95

VANDALEUR'S FOLLY: An Anglo-Irish Melodrama
"Vandaleur was an Irish landowner in the 1830s who turned his estate into an agriculture cooperative. His folly was to lose it again as a gambling debt. It is an ideal subject for Margaretta D'Arcy and John Arden"—Jeremy Treglown, *Times* (London)
0–413–48540–4 RC&H pb $5.95

Brendan Behan

THE COMPLETE PLAYS
Includes *The Hostage, The Quare Fellow, Richard's Cork Leg,* and *Three One Act Plays for Radio.* "It seems to be Ireland's function, every twenty years or so, to provide a playwright who will kick English drama from the past into the present. Brendan Behan may well fill the place vacated by Sean O'Casey"—Kenneth Tynan
Introduction by Alan Simpson
0–8021–3070–4 Grove pb $9.95

- Robert Bolt

A MAN FOR ALL SEASONS
Sir Thomas More against Henry VIII. "An extraordinarily lucid play about an extraordinarily difficult subject: the authority of the individual conscience"—Walter Kerr
0–394–40623–0 Random House $10.95
0–394–70321–9 Random House pb $2.95

- Edward Bond

THE BUNDLE
"I've tried to demystify the use of moral argument so that we can't be morally blackmailed anymore. In order to change society structurally, you may find yourself doing what is, in quotes, wrong"—Edward Bond
0–413–39360–7 RC&H pb $6.95

EARLY MORNING
A play populated by such figures as Florence Nightingale, Queen Victoria, and Benjamin Disraeli
0–7145–0206–5 Riverrun $9.95
0–7145–0207–3 Riverrun pb $4.95

THE FOOL & WE COME TO THE RIVER
Based on the life of the 19th-century poet John Clare. Also included is the libretto from the opera *We Come to the River*
0–413–34770–2 RC&H pb $8.95

THE NARROW ROAD TO THE DEEP NORTH
The rise and fall of a dictator seen through the eyes of the Japanese poet Bashō
0–413–30840–5 RC&H pb $6.95

SAVED
The scene in which a baby is stoned to death caused the play to be banned. Laurence Olivier commented that the violence of this one scene blinded critics to "the rare qualities shown in the rest of the play, which from time to time achieves astonishing heights of dramatic prowess"
0–413–31360–3 RC&H pb $6.95

- Shelagh Delaney

A TASTE OF HONEY
Written when Delaney was 17, this realistic drama about the life of a working-class girl made a tremendous impact when produced in 1958
0–394–17480–1 Grove pb $6.95

- Ann Jellicoe

THE KNACK & THE SPORT OF MY MAD MOTHER
A youthful comedy from the early '60s and a more experimental play by the same author
0–571–13470–X Faber & Faber pb $9.95

- David Mercer

AFTER HAGGERTY
While trying to escape his own past, a man is forced to confront the past of his new apartment's previous occupants
0–413–39860–9 RC&H pb $7.95

NO LIMITS TO LOVE
"The play says a great deal about what people have become through the great social and economic disintegration of the '70s"—David Mercer
0–413–48260–X RC&H pb $6.95

- Peter Nichols

JOE EGG
"A remarkable play about . . . living with a child born so hopelessly crippled as to be, as the father in it says brutally, 'a human parsnip.' For all that, it has to be described as a comedy, one of the funniest and most touching I've seen"—Ronald Bryden, *Observer*
0–394–17484–4 Grove pb $9.95

THE NATIONAL HEALTH
"A portrait of six male inmates in a hospital ward. It also amounts to a study of organization versus the individual, and to a microcosm of our society"—Irving Wardle, *Times* (London)
0–394–17836–X Grove pb $3.95

PASSION PLAY
About marriage and how to function within it
0–413–47800–9 RC&H pb $6.95

A PIECE OF MY MIND
"A witheringly funny play about middle-aged failure"—John Peter, *Times* (London)
0–413–17360–7 RC&H pb $9.95

PLAYS: One
Includes *Forget-Me-Not, Hearts and Flowers, Neither Up Nor Down, Chez Nous, The Common, Privates on Parade* plus an unperformed sketch for *Oh! Calcutta!*
0–413–42330–1 RC&H pb $8.95

POPPY
Pantomime and spectacle are essential elements in a play based on the 19th-century Opium Wars
0–413–49490–X RC&H pb $6.95

PRIVATES ON PARADE
Chronicles the adventures of an army entertainment troupe around 1950. "The play is continuously funny"—*Times* (London)
0–571–11142–4 Faber & Faber pb $6.95

Joe Orton
THE COMPLETE PLAYS
Includes every radio, television, and stage play that Orton wrote during his brief career: *Entertaining Mr. Sloane, Loot, What the Butler Saw, The Ruffian on the Stair, The Erpingham Camp, Funeral Games,* and *The Good and Faithful Servant*
Introduction by John Lahr
0–8021–3039–9 Grove pb $10.95

• John Osborne
THE ENTERTAINER
A searing portrait of a small-time music hall performer
0–14–048178–8 Penguin pb $5.95

LOOK BACK IN ANGER
"Presents post-war youth as it really is. It is a minor miracle"—Kenneth Tynan, *Observer*
0–14–048175–3 Penguin pb $4.95

LUTHER
0–451–14474–0 NAL pb $3.95

A PATRIOT FOR ME & A SENSE OF DETACHMENT
In the first play, a homosexual officer in the Austro-Hungarian army is blackmailed into becoming a spy
0–571–13041–0 Faber & Faber pb $7.95

• Harold Pinter
"There are two silences. One when no word is spoken. The other when perhaps a torrent of language is employed. This speech is speaking a language locked beneath it. That is its continual reference. The speech we hear is an indication of what we don't hear."—Harold Pinter
COMPLETE WORKS

Volume 1:
Includes *The Birthday, The Black and White, The Dumb Waiter, The Examination, A Night Out, The Room,* and *A Slight Ache*
0–394–17019–9 Grove pb $8.95

Volume 2:
Includes *The Caretaker, The Collection, The Dwarfs, Five Revue Sketches, The Lover,* and *Night School*
0–394–17020–2 Grove pb $6.95

Volume 3:
Includes *The Basement, Landscape, Silence, Six Revue Sketches, Tea Party* (A Play), and *Tea Party* (A Short Story)
0–8021–5049–7 Grove pb $9.95

Volume 4:
Includes *Old Times, No Man's Land, Betrayal, Monologue,* and *Family Voices*
0–8021–5050–0 Grove pb $9.95

BETRAYAL
A drama of adultery in which time runs backwards
0–8021–3080–1 Grove pb $7.95

THE BIRTHDAY PARTY
Two classic early plays
0–394–17232–9 Grove pb $6.95

THE CARETAKER
Pinter's most celebrated work. Also includes *The Dumb Waiter*
0–8021–5087–X Grove pb $7.95

THE HOMECOMING
A man returns with his wife to his cloistered, male-dominated family
0–394–17251–5 Grove pb $5.95

THE HOTHOUSE
A black comedy built around a suspicious death in a government-run mental institution
0–394–17675–8 Grove pb $4.95

MOUNTAIN LANGUAGE
A recent play about political oppression and torture
0–8021–3168–9 Grove pb $6.95

NO MAN'S LAND
"A masterly summation of all the themes that have long obsessed Pinter"—Michael Billington, *Arts Guardian*
0–394–17885–8 Grove pb $7.95

OLD TIMES
A couple are reunited with an old friend after an absence of twenty years. The ensuing conversation threatens the present with intimations of an unknown and disturbing past
0–8021–5029–2 Grove pb $7.50

ONE FOR THE ROAD
"*One For the Road* is an expression of a series of events where we are looking at people who have been tortured or will be tortured. It's brutally real: my earlier plays were perhaps metaphors for states of affairs in various respects. This is not a metaphor about anything—it's just a brutal series of facts"—Harold Pinter
0–394–62363–0 Grove pb $7.95

OTHER PLACES: Three Plays
Includes *A Kind of Alaska, Victoria Station,* and *Family Voices*
0–394–53131–0 Grove $15.00
0–394–62449–1 Grove pb $6.95

• N.F. Simpson
ONE WAY PENDULUM
A successful absurdist play first performed in 1959. "Mr. Simpson is ceaselessly, mortally, relentlessly funny"—Kenneth Tynan
0–571–06087–0 Faber & Faber pb $7.95

• Arnold Wesker
THE MERCHANT
A variant on *The Merchant of Venice* that examines anti-Semitism in 16th-century Venice, by a preeminent socially conscious playwright who emerged in the 1950s
0–413–51620–2 RC&H pb $3.95

• John Whiting
THE DEVILS
A history play based on Aldous Huxley's account of diabolical possession among 17th-century Ursuline nuns
0–435–22943–5 Heinemann pb $5.50

MARCHING SONG
0–87830–078–3 Theatre Arts pb $1.00

• Alan Ayckbourn
A CHORUS OF DISAPPROVAL
A tough-minded comedy centering on an amateur production of *The Beggar's Opera*
0–571–13917–5 Faber & Faber pb $8.95

CONFUSIONS
Five interlocking one-act plays
0–413–53270–4 RC&H pb $5.95

HENCEFORWARD
"A fable not of social observation but of personal obsession: in particular, that of artistic self-hatred . . . In telling this essentially one-character story, Ayckbourn succeeds yet again in discovering achingly funny means of expressing extreme distress"—*Times* (London)
0–571–15185–X Faber & Faber pb $7.95

THE NORMAN CONQUESTS
Includes *Table Manners, Living Together,* and *Round and Round the Garden.* Three full-length plays that take place simultaneously in three different parts of the same house: an extraordinary technical accomplishment
0–394–17082–2 Grove pb $6.95

A SMALL FAMILY BUSINESS
Ayckbourn's first play
0–571–14970–7 Faber & Faber pb $6.95

THREE PLAYS
Includes *Absurd Person Singular, Absent Friends,* and *Bedroom Farce*
0–394–17083–0 Grove pb $6.95

WOMAN IN MIND
A wife's "vitality is directed into an active fantasy life, peopling the play with an idealized family, invisible to others, which positively mirrors the negative gaps in her own reality"—*Guardian*
0–571–14520–5 Faber & Faber pb $7.95

• Howard Barker
STRIPWELL & CLAW
Stripwell's characters include a judge, his son, a drug dealer, his lover, and a go-go dancer. "The social, psychological, sexual and political are interwoven with an unnerving dexterity"—John Ford, *Plays and Players*
0–7145–3572–9 Riverrun pb $4.50

TWO PLAYS FOR THE RIGHT
Includes *The Loud Boys' Life* and *Birth on a Hard Shoulder*
0–7145–3896–5 Riverrun $7.95

• Alan Bennett
ENJOY
A family in Northern England finds it hard to break free from its own past
0–571–11734–1 Faber & Faber pb $6.95

THE OLD COUNTRY
0–571–11242–0 Faber & Faber pb $5.95

• Howard Brenton
PLAYS: One
Includes *Christie in Love, Magnificence, The Churchill Play, Weapons of Happiness, Epsom Downs,* and *Sore Throats*
0–413–40430–7 RC&H pb $9.95

BLOODY POETRY
An artist in conflict with middle-class English society
0–413–58350–3 RC&H pb $7.95

THE CHURCHILL PLAY
"One of the few matters on which it is still generally assumed that there is a consensus of opinion is that in May 1940, England found a man who could and did save her. The haunting and alarming suggestion made in Mr. Brenton's powerful play . . . is that the man England found was the wrong man"—Harold Hobson, *Sunday Times* (London)
0–413–33390–6 RC&H pb $7.95

EPSOM DOWNS
"Brenton's portrait of Derby Day is . . . an exuberant documentary about a secular English festival"—Michael Billington, *Guardian*
0–413–38930–8 RC&H pb $6.95

THE ROMANS IN BRITAIN
"The first part concerns the period before the Roman conquest, the brief and unimportant second raid by Julius Caesar in 54 BC; while the second part oscillates between a date a century after the departure of the Romans (515 AD) and the present day. The play therefore turns out to be about imperialism in a rather special sense"—*TLS*
0–413–48670–2 RC&H pb $8.95

● Caryl Churchill
"A playwright of genuine audacity and assurance, able to use her considerable wit and intelligence in ways at once unusual, resonant and dramatically riveting."—Benedict Nightingale, *New Statesman*
PLAYS: One
Includes *Owners, Traps, Vinegar Tom, Light Shining in Buckinghamshire,* and *Cloud Nine*
0–413–56670–6 RC&H pb $5.95

CLOUD NINE
"Miss Churchill has found a theatrical method that is easily as dizzying as her theme. Not only does she examine a cornucopia of sexual permutations—from heterosexual adultery right up to bisexual incest—but she does so with a wild array of dramatic styles and tricks"—Frank Rich, *NY Times*
0–416–00951–4 RC&H pb $4.25

FEN
"It scrutinizes the lives of . . . people trapped by a life that is as dour, sombre and flat as the land they inhabit"—*City Limits*
0–413–52990–8 RC&H pb $4.95

SERIOUS MONEY
A comedy in rhymed verse about high finance
0–413–16660–0 RC&H pb $8.95

SOFTCOPS
"There is a constant attempt by governments to depoliticise illegal acts, to make criminals a separate class from the rest of society so that subversion will not be general, and part of this process is the invention of the detective and the criminal,

the cop and the robber"—from the Author's Note
0–413–54910–0 RC&H pb $4.95

TOP GIRLS
"In this bold and original play, Caryl Churchill . . . forces brilliant women of history into the context of their less brilliant sisters' timeless struggle against poverty and oppression"—*City Limits*
0–413–55480–5 RC&H pb $7.95

● Michael Frayn
PLAYS: One
Includes *Alphabetical Order, Donkey's Years, Clouds, Make and Break,* and *Noises Off*
0–317–39293–X RC&H pb $6.95

BALMORAL
This farce takes place in 1937 in a hypothetical Britain that has become a Soviet republic. The play centers around the occupants of the "State Home for Writers"
0–413–17180–9 RC&H pb $8.95

BENEFACTORS
"On the ground floor, it is about a master-builder . . . who wants to erect tower-blocks for town-planners rather than homes for people. But, on the upper-storey, it is a philosophical comedy about good and evil, life and death, liberal tolerance and destructive faith"—Michael Billington, *Guardian*
0–413–54160–6 RC&H pb $7.95

NOISES OFF
Frayn's tremendously popular farce about a theatrical touring company
0–413–50670–3 RC&H pb $8.95

● Brian Friel
SELECTED PLAYS OF BRIAN FRIEL
Introduction by Seamus Deane
0–8132–0627–8 Catholic University pb $9.95

THE COMMUNICATION CORD
A farce about a peasant cottage transformed into a yuppie weekend retreat
0–571–13092–5 Faber & Faber pb $7.95

THE FAITH HEALER
0–571–11473–3 Faber & Faber pb $6.95

● Pam Gems
THREE PLAYS
Includes *Piaf, Camille,* and *Loving Women*
0–14–048203–2 Penguin pb $6.95

● Simon Gray
PLAYS: One
Contains five of Gray's best-known plays: *Butley, Otherwise Educated, The Rear Column, Quartermaine's Terms,* and *The Common Pursuit*
0–413–40420–X RC&H pb $8.95

BUTLEY
"The stark, unsentimental approach to the homosexual relationships, the cynical send-up of academic life, the skeptical view of the teacher-pupil associations are all stunningly illuminated by continuous explosions of sardonic needling, feline, vituperative, and civilized lines"—Milton Shulman, *Evening Standard*
0–413–34060–0 RC&H pb $7.95

THE COMMON PURSUIT
The lives of six friends, from college days to middle age
0–413–55990–4 RC&H pb $6.95

OTHERWISE ENGAGED & OTHER PLAYS
"There's a lot of crackling dialog in this minuet about the stricken upperclass English, much of it darkly comic and bitter"—*Variety*
0–413–34430–4 RC&H pb $7.95

QUARTERMAINE'S TERMS
A comedy about a teacher of English as a second language
0–413–52830–8 RC&H pb $6.95

THE REAR COLUMN & OTHER PLAYS
Includes *The Rear Column,* based on an incident in the Congo in 1887; *Molly,* based on the Alma Rottenberg murder case in the 1930s, and *Man in a Sidecar,* charting the breakdown of a marriage and the bystander who is drawn into it
0–413–39170–1 RC&H pb $5.95

● Trevor Griffiths
COMEDIANS
"The subject of Trevor Griffith's serious and funny play is laughter. . . . How and why it is engineered, what dark secrets within us trigger mirthful responses to shaped remarks about sex, ethnic groups and physical disabilities"—Michael Coveney, *Financial Times*
0–571–04986–9 Faber & Faber pb $5.95

OI FOR ENGLAND
0–571–11977–8 Faber & Faber pb $7.95

THE PARTY
This play takes place in 1968 and contains a British discussion of the possibilities of socialism and the Paris student riots
0–571–10647–1 Faber & Faber pb $6.95

● Christopher Hampton
LES LIAISONS DANGEREUSES
An adaptation of the 1782 Laclos novel about the decadence of the French aristocracy
0–571–13724–5 Faber & Faber pb $7.95

THE PHILANTHROPIST: A Bourgeois Comedy
A soon-to-be-married bachelor gives a tumultous dinner party
0–571–13488–2 Faber & Faber pb $8.95

SAVAGES
"A play that delicately, with cumulative power, transcribes Mr. Hampton's sorrow and indignation at the gradual extinction

Illustration from Landscapes and Voices *by Franz Masereel (Schocken)*

---

of the Brazilian Indians, and his reluctant but inexorable disillusionment with freedom fighters and liberal champions of good causes"—Howard Hobson, *Sunday Times* (London)
0–571–10348–0 Faber & Faber pb $6.95

TOTAL ECLIPSE
Deals with the relationship between Arthur Rimbaud and Paul Verlaine
0–571–18048–5 Faber & Faber pb $6.95

• David Hare
THE ASIAN PLAYS
Includes *Fanshen*, *Saigon*, and *A Map of the World*
0–571–13990–6 Faber & Faber pb $9.95

THE HISTORY PLAYS
Includes *Plenty*, *Knuckle*, and *Licking Hitler*
0–571–13132–8 Faber & Faber pb $10.95

PLENTY
In scenes spanning twenty years, the heroine rejects the loss of ideals she perceives in the postwar world
0–452–25956–8 NAL pb $7.95

WETHERBY
0–571–13489–0 Faber & Faber pb $8.95

• Ronald Harwood
THE DRESSER
An examination of the relationship between a celebrated actor-manager and his dresser
0–394–17936–6 Grove pb $5.95

Michael Hastings
TOM AND VIV
A study of T.S. Eliot's tumultuous marriage, and of how his wife and her nervous breakdown create a presence in his poetry
0–14–007594–1 Penguin pb $4.95

• Barrie Keefe
SUS
"Two detectives keenly await the Tory landslide while interrogating a black suspect—not for the 'sus' charge which he so cheerily expects, but for the brutal murder of his heavily pregnant wife"—*Time Out*
0–413–46870–4 RC&H pb $4.95

• Hugh Leonard
DA
0–689–70580–8 Atheneum pb $4.95

• Louise Page
GOLDEN GIRLS
"A topically Olympic account of women training for the 100 meters relay . . . It's really about the impossibility of running clean or free in a world where sexism and racism and sponsorship and drugs have already taken their toll on a sporting ethic"—*Punch*
0–413–57960–3 Heinemann pb $6.95

REAL ESTATE
0–413–57950–6 Heinemann pb $7.95

• Steven Poliakoff
BREAKING THE SILENCE
An autobiographical play about the war's effects on a Russian family
0–413–41020–X Heinemann pb $4.95

THE SUMMER PARTY
The stars of an outdoor music festival receive a surprise visit from the police
0–41347600–6 Heinemann pb $4.95

• Bernard Pomerance
THE ELEPHANT MAN
0–8021–3041–0 Grove pb $5.95

• Anthony Shaffer
MURDERER
An obsession with murder, and its consequences
0–7145–2545–6 Marion Boyars pb $6.95

SLEUTH
A successful display of theatrical sleight-of-hand
0–7145–0763–6 Marion Boyars pb $7.95

• Peter Shaffer
AMADEUS
The rise and fall of Mozart through the eyes (and psyche) of his rival Salieri
0–06–014032–1 Harper & Row pb $11.95
0–451–12893–1 NAL pb $3.50

EQUUS
A psychiatrist analyzes a boy who has blinded six horses
0–14–048185–0 Penguin pb $3.95

YONADAB
0–06–039061–1 Harper & Row pb $7.95

• Tom Stoppard
DALLIANCE & UNDISCOVERED COUNTRY
Dalliance is set in 1890s Vienna
0–571–14739–9 Faber & Faber pb $7.95

THE DOG IT WAS THAT DIED & OTHER PLAYS
The title play, as well as *The Dissolution of Dominic Boot* and *'M' is for Moon Among Other Things*, were written for radio. Also included are four comedies for television: *Teeth*, *Another Moon Called Earth*, *A Separate Peace*, and *Neutral Ground*
0–571–13183–2 Faber & Faber pb $5.95

EVERY GOOD BOY DESERVES FAVOR & PROFESSIONAL FOUL
0–394–50157–8 Grove pb $8.95

JUMPERS
"The New Radical Liberal Party has made the ex-Minister of Agriculture Archbishop of Canterbury, British astronauts are scrapping with each other on the moon, and spritely academics steal about London by night indulging in murderous gymnastics"—Michael Billington, *Guardian*
0–394–17866–1 Grove pb $6.95

ON THE RAZZLE
A comedy with affinities to Thorton Wilder's *The Matchmaker*
0–571–11835–6 Faber & Faber pb $4.95

THE REAL INSPECTOR HOUND & AFTER MAGRITTE
0–394–17313–9 Grove pb $7.95

THE REAL THING
"An intelligent play about love"—*Guardian*
0–571–11983–2 Faber & Faber pb $5.95

ROSENCRANTZ AND GUILDENSTERN ARE DEAD
Hamlet viewed from an oblique angle; the play that made Stoppard's reputation
0–8021–3033–X Grove pb $5.50

ROUGH CROSSING
Adapted from a Ferenc Molnár farce
0–571–13595–1 Faber & Faber pb $5.95

TRAVESTIES
"Tom Stoppard is not the first man to have noticed that Lenin, James Joyce, and the Dadaist Tristan Tzara were all living in Zurich during the Great War . . . From this obscure footnote to *Ulysses* Stoppard has spun out a fantastically elaborate web to snare his three giants in the same play"—Irving Wandle, *Times* (London)
0–394–17884–X Grove pb $4.95

• C.P. Taylor
AND A NIGHTINGALE SANG
"Refreshingly different in its portrait of a working-class family in Newcastle-upon-Tyne in World War II"—*Daily Express*
0–413–46860–7 RC&H pb $6.95

GOOD
"An original and intelligent play . . . that tries to work out how decent, liberal, humane men came to be swept up by the Nazi juggernaut"—Michael Billington, *Guardian*
0–413–52130–3 RC&H pb $7.95

ANTHOLOGIES

• Roger Cornish & Violet Ketels, editors
LANDMARKS OF MODERN BRITISH DRAMA: The Plays of the '60s
"Angry Young Men" was a label pegged to many of the playwrights represented here. Included are John Arden's *Serjeant Musgrave's Dance*, Harold Pinter's *The Caretaker*, John Osborne's *A Patriot for Me*, Joe Orton's *Loot*, Arnold Wesker's *Roots*, Edward Bond's *Saved*, and Peter Barnes's *The Ruling Class*
0–413–59080–1 Methuen $29.95
0–413–57260–9 Methuen pb $8.95

LANDMARKS OF MODERN BRITISH DRAMA: The Plays of the '70s
Includes Howard Brenton's *Weapons of Happiness*, Alan Ayckbourn's *Just Between Ourselves*, Tom Stoppard's *Every Good Boy Deserves Favour*, Peter Shaffer's *Amadeus*, Simon Gray's *Quartermaine's Terms*, Peter Nichols' *Passion Play*, and Caryl Churchill's *Top Girls*
0–413–59090–9 Methuen $29.95
0–413–57270–6 Methuen pb $8.95

20th-Century British Essays and Other Prose

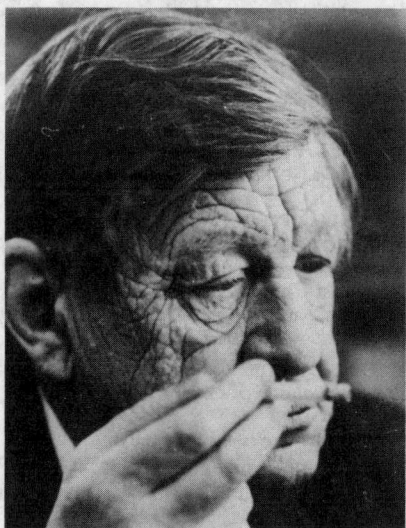

W.H. Auden (photo by Jill Krementz, courtesy of Random House)

W.H. Auden

THE ENCHAFED FLOOD
A study in the Romantic sensibility, exploring at length the images encountered in a single passage by Wordsworth
0–8139–0827–2 Virginia $15.00
0–8139–0820–5 Virginia $7.50

FOREWORDS AND AFTERWORDS
Brief occasional essays on a range of subjects illustrating Auden's extraordinarily eclectic interests
0–394–48359–6 Random House $19.95

• John Berger
A celebrated Marxist art critic, John Berger is also a novelist, screenwriter, and painter.

ABOUT LOOKING
Essays across ten years, most of which first appeared in *New Society*, focusing on the search for meaning within and behind what is looked at. Includes discussions of Millet, Courbet, Turner, Magritte, and Francis Bacon
0–394–51124–7 Pantheon $10.95
0–394–73907–8 Pantheon pb $6.95

AND OUR FACES, MY HEART, BRIEF AS PHOTOS
A short, poetic essay that uses Berger's own experience—"What draws me to love?"—as a springboard for larger investigations, from Van Gogh to 20th-century homelessness
0–394–72427–5 Pantheon pb $5.95

ART AND REVOLUTION: Ernst Neizvestny and the Role of the Artist in the USSR
A provocative study of a Russian sculptor whose work Berger knows only through photographs. The author has written: "By

taking and considering in depth a particular example, it throws light on the character of Russian art, the situation of the visual artist today in the USSR, the meaning of politically revolutionary art and some of the future consequences of revolutionary consciousness"
0–394–41562–0 Pantheon pb $8.95

PERMANENT RED: Essays in Seeing
0–906495–07–5 Writers & Readers $12.95
0–904613–92–5 Writers & Readers pb $6.95

THE SENSE OF SIGHT
A wide-ranging collection of essays spanning three decades. Includes the classic "Moment of Cubism"
0–394–74206–0 Pantheon pb $8.95

THE SUCCESS AND FAILURE OF PICASSO
A companion to *Art and Revolution* examining the individual artist under capitalism. This critical reassessment of Picasso sees him as a "primitive" who burst upon civilization and conquered it—and who paid the price for his conquest in terms of exile, isolation, and loneliness
0–679–72272–6 Pantheon pb $8.95

WAYS OF SEEING
An essay on the ideological and technological conditioning of our ways of seeing both art and the world, based on the acclaimed BBC series
0–14–021631–6 Penguin pb $5.95

• John Berger & Jean Mohr
A FORTUNATE MAN
0–394–73999–X Pantheon pb $6.95

• John Berger, Jean Mohr & Nicolas Philibert
ANOTHER WAY OF TELLING
An experimental combination of stories, theory, portrait, confession, and 150 photographs that seeks "another way of telling" the life of a peasant woman
0–394–51294–4 Pantheon $17.50
0–394–73998–1 Pantheon pb $13.95

• Anthony Burgess
LITTLE WILSON AND BIG GOD: The Autobiography
The first installment of a projected two-volume autobiography. "A delight to read"—Robertson Davies
1–55584–100–7 Weidenfeld & Nicolson $22.50

99 NOVELS: The Best in English Since 1939
An opinionated, informed list that includes Ian Fleming's *Goldfinger* and excludes Nabokov's *Lolita*—as well as any books by Cheever, Capote, Vonnegut, and le Carré
0–671–52407–0 Summit $10.95
0–671–55485–9 Summit pb $4.95

RE JOYCE
Arguing that "the appearance of difficulty is part of Joyce's big joke," Burgess provides a readable, accessible guide. "Mr. Burgess has written a brilliant and humane study of the most brilliant and humane of twentieth-century humanists"—Philip Toynbee, *Observer*
0–393–00445–7 Norton pb $7.95

Mary Butts
THE CRYSTAL CABINET: My Childhood at Salterns
An autobiographical work by one of the more mysterious figures of the modernist period, originally published in an edited version following her death in 1937; this edition presents the full text for the first time. "Mary Butts is one of twentieth-century literature's best-kept secrets. How wonderful to have one of her books back in print for the first time since her death half a century ago"—John Ashbery
Preface by Camilla Bagg
0–8070–7038–6 Beacon $19.95

• G.K. Chesterton
"He is as much a political writer as George Orwell. Politics, in the narrow, as well as the widest, sense, informs and inspires his writing, which is why he remained all his life a journalist, to the despair of those who recognized the enormous scale of his gifts. But that is what Chesterton wanted to be, a 'jolly journalist' . . . because he thought his message important, and from Fleet Street it could reach the people who needed it most, and who perhaps had the best chance of understanding it."—P.J. Kavanagh

DAYLIGHT AND NIGHTMARE
0–396–08889–9 Dodd, Mead $14.95

THE EVERLASTING MAN
0–385–07198–1 Doubleday pb $4.50

ORTHODOXY
0–385–01536–4 Doubleday pb $4.50

SAINT FRANCIS OF ASSISI
0–385–02900–4 Doubleday pb $4.95

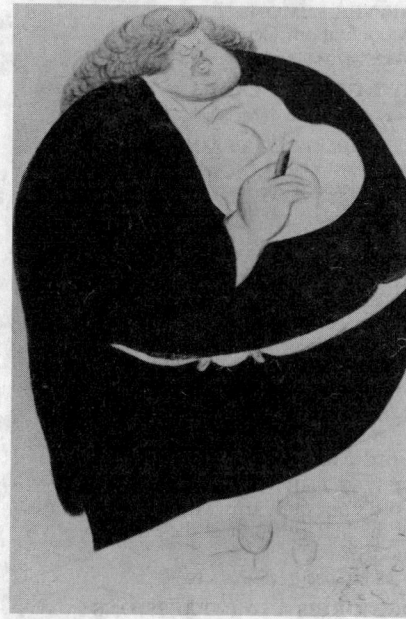

G.K. Chesterton by Max Beerbohm

Cyril Connolly
ENEMIES OF PROMISE
Essays on the writer in modern society, and the forces that conspire to bring him down
0–89255–078–3 Persea pb $6.95

THE EVENING COLONNADE
A collection of later literary essays. "Remember that the object of the critic is to revenge himself on the creator"—Cyril Connolly
0–15–629060–X HBJ pb $9.95

THE UNQUIET GRAVE
A series of meditative essays originally published in 1944 under the pseudonym Palinurus
0–89255–058–9 Persea pb $9.95

• **Joseph Conrad**
THE COLLECTED LETTERS
Edited by Frederick Karl and Laurence Davies

Volume 1: 1861–1897
0–521–24216–9 Cambridge $44.50

Volume 2: 1898–1902
0–521–25748–4 Cambridge $44.50

Volume 3: 1903–1907
0–521–32387–8 Cambridge $49.50

THE MIRROR OF THE SEA
A memoir of Conrad's life as a sailor: "I have attempted here," he wrote, "to lay bare with the unreserve of a last hour's confession the terms of my relation to the sea"
0–910395–34–9 Marlboro pb $8.95

A PERSONAL RECORD
0–910395–46–2 Marlboro pb $8.95

• **Lawrence Durrell**
BITTER LEMONS
A book about Cyprus
0–525–47044–1 Dutton pb $8.95

THE GREEK ISLANDS
0–14–005661–0 Penguin pb $14.95

THE SPIRIT OF PLACE: Letters and Essays on Travel
Edited by Alan G. Thomas
0–918172–17–9 Leete's Island pb $8.95

• **James Fenton**
ALL THE WRONG PLACES: Adrift in the Politics of the Pacific Rim
Fenton, one of the most acclaimed English poets of his generation, writes about the fall of Saigon, the upheaval in the Philippines, and other events
0–87113–204–4 Atlantic Monthly pb $7.95

• **Ford Madox Ford**
IT WAS THE NIGHTINGALE
Ford's not quite trustworthy reminiscences of the literary world of the early modernists
0–88001–034–7 Ecco pb $9.50

MEMORIES AND IMPRESSIONS
Ford's subjects include D.H. Lawrence and Henry James
0–88001–087–8 Ecco pb $9.50

PROVENCE
Ford's deep emotional ties to southern France are beautifully expressed in this memoir
Illustrated by Biala
0–912946–63–6 Ecco pb $8.50

RETURN TO YESTERDAY
0–87140–563–6 Liveright $12.95
0–87140–271–8 Liveright pb $7.95

• **E.M. Forster**
ABINGER HARVEST
0–15–602610–4 HBJ pb $6.95

ALEXANDRIA: A History and Guide
0–19–504066–X Oxford pb $9.95

ASPECTS OF THE NOVEL
A classic discussion of the techniques and structure of fiction, with a focus on craft
0–15–609180–1 HBJ pb $4.95

A COMMONPLACE BOOK
Edited by Philip Gardner
0–8047–1280–8 Stanford $39.50
0–8047–1422–3 Stanford pb $12.95

THE HILL OF DEVI
Life in India as private secretary to the Maharajah of Dewas
0–15–640265–3 HBJ pb $4.95

SELECTED LETTERS OF E.M. FORSTER
Edited by Mary Lago and P.N. Furbank

Volume 1: 1879–1920
0–674–79825–2 Harvard $20.00

Volume 2: 1921–1970
0–674–79827–9 Harvard $29.95

TWO CHEERS FOR DEMOCRACY
0–15–692025–5 HBJ pb $9.95

• **William Golding**
AN EGYPTIAN JOURNAL
0–571–12547–6 Faber & Faber pb $9.95

A MOVING TARGET
"200 pages of intelligence, wit, originality, sculpted prose"—John Rechy
0–374–51850–5 Farrar, Straus & Giroux pb $7.95

Edmund Gosse
FATHER AND SON
Gosse's moving account of his upbringing and his conflicts with his father's allegiance to a narrow religious sect: "This book is the record of a struggle between two temperaments, two consciences, and almost two epochs. It ended, as was inevitable, in disruption. Of the two human beings here described, one was born to fly backward, the other could not help being carried forward . . . But, at least, it is some comfort to the survivor that neither, to the very last hour, ceased to respect the other, or to regard him with a sad indulgence"—from the first chapter
0–86299–094–7 Academy Chicago pb $4.95

• **Robert Graves**
GOODBYE TO ALL THAT
Graves's "bitter leave-taking of England" at 33, in a classic autobiography (first

published in 1929) about coming of age in the trenches of World War I
0–385–09330–6 Doubleday pb $6.95

IN BROKEN IMAGES: Selected Correspondence of Robert Graves
0–918825–82–2 Moyer Bell pb $6.95

THE WHITE GODDESS: A Historical Grammar of Poetic Myth
Graves's celebrated and widely contested theory of poetic inspiration
0–374–50493–8 Farrar, Straus & Giroux pb $9.95

• **Robert Graves & Alan Hodge**
THE LONG WEEKEND: A Social History of Great Britain, 1918–1939
0–393–00217–9 Norton pb $10.95

• **Graham Greene**
COLLECTED ESSAYS
Over 80 miscellaneous pieces, divided into "The Lost Childhood", "Novels and Novelists", and "Some Characters"
0–14–003159–6 Penguin pb $7.95

A SORT OF LIFE
The first volume of Greene's ongoing autobiography
0–671–45198–7 Washington Square pb $2.95

WAYS OF ESCAPE
The second installment of the autobiography
0–671–43820–4 Washington Square pb $3.95

GETTING TO KNOW THE GENERAL: The Story of an Involvement
A memoir of Greene's friendship with General Omar Torrijos Herrera of Panama, from 1976 to his mysterious death in a plane crash in 1981
0–671–54160–9 Simon & Schuster $14.95

IN SEARCH OF A CHARACTER
Two journals of two trips Greene made to Africa—which resulted in two novels, *The Heart of the Matter* and *A Burnt-Out Case*
0–14–002822–6 Penguin pb $4.95

JOURNEY WITHOUT MAPS
A record of Greene's first trip outside Europe, into the heart of Liberia
0–14–003280–0 Penguin pb $5.95

• **Thom Gunn**
THE OCCASIONS OF POETRY: Essays in Criticism and Autobiography
Fifteen essays, including writings on Hardy, Pound, Williams, Eliot, and James Merrill
0–86547–207–6 North Point pb $11.50

• **Seamus Heaney**
PREOCCUPATIONS: Selected Prose 1968–1978
Heaney discusses, among others, Wordsworth, Keats, Hopkins, Yeats, Kavanagh, and Robert Lowell
0–374–51650–2 Farrar, Straus & Giroux pb $7.95

• **Geoffrey Hill**
THE LORDS OF LIMIT: Essay on Literature and Ideas
Essays by a leading poet of the postwar period
0–19–503517–8 Oxford pb $8.95

• **Aldous Huxley**
BEYOND THE MEXIQUE BAY
0–586–08481–9 Academy Chicago pb $5.95

➤ **FOR OVERSEAS ORDERING INFORMATION, SEE PAGE 1**

BRAVE NEW WORLD REVISITED
An explicit, as opposed to the fictionalized, warning about freedom and its enemies and how we must fight to protect ourselves
0–06–080023–2 Harper & Row pb $4.95

THE DOORS OF PERCEPTION & HEAVEN AND HELL
Huxley's exploration of mescaline and LSD paved the way for much of the hallucinogenic experimentation that followed
0–06–090007–5 Harper & Row pb $6.95

GREY EMINENCE
A biography of Father Joseph, Cardinal Richelieu's principal associate and collaborator, becomes, in Huxley's hands, a bold look at the antecedents of modern war and terror. "A brilliant study of politics, morals, mysticism"—*TLS*
0–88184–168–4 Carroll & Graf pb $4.95

MOKSHA: Writings on Psychedelics and the Visionary Experience (1931–1963)
Edited by Michael Horowitz & Cynthia Palmer
0–87477–208–7 Tarcher pb $7.95

THE PERENNIAL PHILOSOPHY
A collection of aphorisms and brief extracts relating to mystical experience. "It is both an anthology and an interpretation of the supreme mystics, East and West . . . This is the first time that anybody has adequately covered the field and showed an equal familiarity with all fields. It is a magnificent achievement"—Rufus Jones
0–06–090191–8 Harper & Row pb $8.95

Christopher Isherwood
CHRISTOPHER AND HIS KIND
A partial autobiography covering the years from his first visit to Germany in 1929 to his move to the United States ten years later includes vignettes of Auden and Forster
0–374–52036–4 FS&G pb $8.95

MY GURU AND HIS DISCIPLE
"A sweetly modest and honest portrait of Isherwood's spiritual instructor, Swami Prabhavananda, the Hindu priest who guided Isherwood for some thirty years. It is also a book about the often amusing and sometimes painful counterpoint between worldliness and holiness in Isherwood's own life"—Edmund White
0–374–21702–5 FS&G $12.95
0–374–52087–9 FS&G pb $8.95

• David Jones
EPOCH AND ARTIST
Essays by the great Welsh poet and painter, author of *In Parenthesis* and *The Anathemata*
0–571–10152–6 Faber & Faber pb $6.95

• James Joyce
JAMES JOYCE'S LETTERS TO SYLVIA BEACH, 1921–1940
Edited by Melissa Banta & Oscar A. Silverman
0–253–32334–7 Indiana $25.00

• Arthur Koestler
ARROW IN THE BLUE
0–02–565020–3 Macmillan $14.95

THE CASE OF THE MIDWIFE TOAD
0–394–71823–2 Random House pb $3.50

JANUS: A Summing Up
On the "evolution, creativity and pathology of the human mind" and the position of man in a post-Hiroshima world. "A splendid overview of some of the most remarkable developments in recent intellectual history"—*LA Times*
0–394–72886–6 Random House pb $4.95

• Philip Larkin
REQUIRED WRITING: Miscellaneous Pieces 1955–1982
Writings on topics that include jazz, crime fiction, and Emily Dickinson
0–374–24948–2 Farrar, Straus & Giroux $17.95
0–374–51840–8 Farrar, Straus & Giroux pb $9.95

• D.H. Lawrence
APOCALYPSE: Definitive Text
"It protests against the dehumanizing of men and women by Christianity . . . and it protests against their dehumanization by science, which has taken the gods out of heaven and the heart out of man"—Richard Aldington
0–14–003856–6 Penguin pb $4.95

APOCALYPSE & OTHER WRITINGS ON REVELATION
Edited by Mara Kalnins
0–521–22407–1 Cambridge $34.50

D.H. LAWRENCE AND ITALY
A collection of three of his most evocative books on Italy: *Twilight in Italy, Sea and Sardinia,* and the posthumously published *Etruscan Places*
0–14–009520–9 Penguin pb $7.95

FANTASIA OF THE UNCONSCIOUS & PSYCHOANALYSIS AND THE UNCONSCIOUS
Two unbridled essays that seek to redefine the unconscious as "only another word for life"
0–14–003303–3 Penguin pb $6.95

PHOENIX: The Posthumous Papers of D.H. Lawrence
Unpublished essays, sketches, and critical studies from 1912 to 1930, including a book-length appraisal of Thomas Hardy, a major influence
Edited by Edward D. McDonald
0–14–004375–6 Penguin pb $15.95

PHOENIX TWO
Uncollected, unpublished, and other prose works. Includes "Reflections on the Death of a Porcupine," "Assorted Articles," and "A Propos of *Lady Chatterly's Lover*." "The flotsam and jetsam of the greatest literary genius of the transition from pre-war to post-war England"—*NY Times*
Edited by Warren Roberts & Harry T. Moore
0–14–004231–8 Penguin pb $11.95

REFLECTIONS ON THE DEATH OF A PORCUPINE & OTHER ESSAYS
Edited by Michael Herbert
0–521–35847–7 Cambridge pb $24.95

SELECTED LETTERS
Lawrence's letters are full of the same vital engagement with the world that marks his fiction
0–14–000759–8 Penguin pb $5.95

STUDIES IN CLASSIC AMERICAN LITERATURE
Lawrence's pioneering studies of Cooper, Poe, Hawthorne, Melville, Dana, and Whitman have had an indelible effect on the way American literature is read
0–14–003300–9 Penguin pb $5.95

• T.E. Lawrence
REVOLT IN THE DESERT
An abridged (by over half) version of *The Seven Pillars of Wisdom*. "It may be said of him that he suffered in his own person the neurotic ills of an entire generation"—Christopher Isherwood
0–7126–1281–5 David & Charles pb $13.95

SEVEN PILLARS OF WISDOM
"The revolt in Arabia against the Turks, as it appeared to an Englishman who took part. Round this tentpole of a military chronicle T.E. has hung an unexampled fabric of portraits, descriptions, philosophies, emotions, adventures, dreams"—E.M. Forster
0–14–001696–1 Penguin pb $7.95

• Doris Lessing
PRISONS WE CHOOSE TO LIVE INSIDE
Five lectures on the art of thinking for oneself
0–06–039074–3 Harper & Row $14.95
0–06–039077–8 Harper & Row pb $6.95

• C.S. Lewis
A GRIEF OBSERVED
Lewis' effort to console himself after the death of his wife—and to defend against his loss of belief in God. "The author has done something I believed impossible—assuaged his own grief by conveying it"—Anne Freemantle
0–553–27486–4 Bantam pb $3.95

THE LETTERS OF C.S. LEWIS
Edited by W.H. Lewis
0–15–650870–2 HBJ pb $5.95

MERE CHRISTIANITY
One of Lewis' most popular books, originally broadcast as informal radio "talks" and later published as three separate books
0–02–570590–3 Macmillan $12.95
0–02–086940–1 Macmillan pb $5.95

ON STORIES & OTHER ESSAYS ON LITERATURE
"If wit and wisdom, style and scholarship, are requisites to passage through the pearly gates, then Mr. Lewis will be among the angels"—*New Yorker*
0–15–668788–7 HBJ pb $4.95

THE PROBLEM OF PAIN
"A theologian for everyman"—Anthony Burgess
0–02–086850–2 Macmillan pb $4.50

THE SCREWTAPE LETTERS
A classic satiric work consisting of a series of letters from Screwtape, an elderly devil, advising his nephew Wormwood, an apprentice devil, how to corrupt his earthly "patient"
Introduction by Richard Gilman
0–553–26369–2 Bantam pb $3.50
0–451–62610–9 NAL pb $2.95

THE SEEING EYE & OTHER SELECTED ESSAYS
Selected essays from *Christian Reflections*. "Lewis is the ideal persuader for the half-convinced, the man who would like to be a Christian but finds his intellect getting in the way"—Anthony Burgess, *NY Times Book Review*
0–345–32866–3 Ballantine pb $3.50

SURPRISED BY JOY: The Shape of My Early Life
Lewis' spiritual journey from Christianity to atheism and back again to Christianity. "Anyone approaching this book as a study in the psychology of conversion will find the greatest interest in the dual paths—intellectual and intuitive—which converged at last"—*Saturday Review*
0–15–687011–8 HBJ pb $5.95

• Wyndham Lewis
BLASTING AND BOMBARDIERING
0–7145–0130–1 Riverrun pb $8.95

THE CALIPH'S DESIGN
An essay in art criticism
Afterword by Paul Edwards
0–87685–665–2 Black Sparrow $20.00
0–87685–664–4 Black Sparrow pb $9.50

JOURNEY INTO BARBARY
A voyage to Morocco
Edited by C.J. Fox
0–87685–519–2 Black Sparrow $20.00
0–87685–518–4 Black Sparrow pb $12.50

MEN WITHOUT ART
"*Men Without Art* is Wyndham Lewis' defense of his second calling, literature. It is also his liveliest and most accessible book of literary criticism. For its sustained analyses of individual major figures alone—the essays on Hemingway, Faulkner, Virginia Woolf, and (above all) T.S. Eliot—it deserves a permanent place in the criticism of modern literature"—Seamus Cooney
Edited by Seamus Cooney
0–87685–687–3 Black Sparrow $20.00
0–87685–686–5 Black Sparrow pb $12.50

POUND/LEWIS: The Letters of Ezra Pound and Wyndham Lewis
Edited by Timothy Materer
0–8112–0932–6 New Directions $37.50

ROTTING HILL
Edited by Paul Edwards
0–87685–647–4 Black Sparrow $20.00
0–87685–646–6 Black Sparrow pb $12.50

RUDE ASSIGNMENT
Edited by Toby Foshay
0–87685–604–0 Black Sparrow $20.00
0–87685–603–2 Black Sparrow pb $12.50

• W. Somerset Maugham
THE MERRY-GO-ROUND
0–14–003373–4 Penguin pb $5.95

THE SUMMING UP
"In this book I am going to sort out my thoughts on a number of subjects that have chiefly interested me during the course of my life"—W. Somerset Maugham
0–14–001852–2 Penguin pb $4.95

A WRITER'S NOTEBOOK
Selections from the journals he kept from 1912 to 1949 that show Maugham's

evolution as his literary professionalism takes over
0–14–002644–4 Penguin pb $5.95

• Nancy Mitford
NOBLESSE OBLIGE: An Enquiry into the Identifiable Characteristics of the English Aristocracy
Includes Mitford's famous distinction between "U" and "non-U"
Illustrated by Osbert Lancaster
0–689–70704–5 Atheneum pb $6.95

A TALENT TO ANNOY: Essays, Articles and Reviews, 1929–1968
Edited by Charlotte Mosley
0–8253–0429–6 Beaufort $16.95

VOLTAIRE IN LOVE
0–525–48190–7 Dutton pb $9.95

• Malcolm Muggeridge
CONFESSIONS OF A TWENTIETH CENTURY PILGRIM
0–06–066037–6 Harper & Row $14.95

SOMETHING BEAUTIFUL FOR GOD
0–8027–2474–4 Walker pb $8.95

A THIRD TESTAMENT
0–345–30516–7 Ballantine pb $2.95

• Flann O'Brien
THE BEST OF MYLES
A hilarious collection of O'Brien's columns from *The Irish Times*
0–14–006366–8 Penguin pb $7.95

• Sean O'Casey
AUTOBIOGRAPHIES ONE
The first volumes of the playwright's much-praised series of autobiographies, beginning with *I Knock at the Door* and his childhood education on the streets of Dublin
0–88184–033–5 Carroll & Graf $21.95
0–88184–049–1 Carroll & Graf pb $10.95

AUTOBIOGRAPHIES TWO
The final volumes, ending with *Sunset and Evening*
0–88184–035–1 Carroll & Graf $21.95
0–88184–075–0 Carroll & Graf pb $10.95

• Joe Orton
THE ORTON DIARIES
Edited by John Lahr
0–06–015743–7 Harper & Row $19.95

• George Orwell
A COLLECTION OF ESSAYS
Includes such classics as "Such, Such Were the Joys," "Shooting an Elephant," "Politics and the English Language," and "Why I Write"
0–15–618600–4 HBJ pb $4.95

DICKENS, DALI AND OTHERS
0–15–626053–0 HBJ pb $4.95

DOWN AND OUT IN PARIS AND LONDON
Orwell's first published work, a worm's-eye-view of life as a kitchen hand in Paris and a tramp in London, peppered with some hard-earned insights on poverty
0–15–626224–X HBJ pb $4.95

HOMAGE TO CATALONIA
Orwell's indignant telling of his experiences in the Spanish Civil War, and

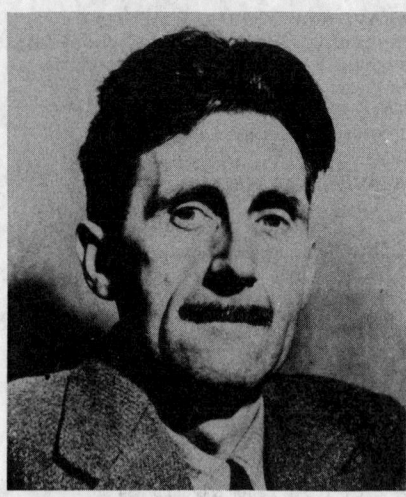
George Orwell

of the betrayal of anarchist partisans by Stalinists
0–15–642117–8 HBJ pb $4.95

THE ROAD TO WIGAN PIER
A powerful account of unemployment and proletarian life in the north of England
Foreword by Victor Gollancz
0–15–676750–3 HBJ pb $4.95

SHOOTING AN ELEPHANT
The unsurpassed title essay is at once a gripping adventure story and a withering indictment of British imperialism
0–15–182043–0 HBJ $12.95

THE UNKNOWN ORWELL
Little-known writings, including radio scripts written for the BBC in the '40s
0–586–08178–X Academy Chicago pb $6.95

COLLECTED ESSAYS, JOURNALISM & LETTERS
"These books are among the most valuable literary productions of the decade. Open them anywhere and you touch a man very close to your best self, that self that exists for most of us only in wistful imaginings"—Richard Schickel, *Chicago Sun-Times*
Edited by Sonia Orwell & Ian Angus

Volume 1: An Age Like This, 1920–1940
0–15–118546–8 HBJ $17.95

Volume 2: My Country Right or Left, 1940–1943
0–15–118547–6 HBJ $15.95

Volume 3: As I Please, 1943–1945
0–15–118548–4 HBJ $15.95

Volume 4: In Front of Your Nose, 1945–1950
0–15–118549–2 HBJ $17.95

• V.S. Pritchett
A MAN OF LETTERS: Selected Essays
0–394–54982–1 Random House $19.95

THE MYTH MAKERS
Essays on European and Latin American writers
0–394–50472–0 Random House $11.95
0–394–74682–1 Random House pb $4.95

- Peter Quennell
THE PURSUIT OF HAPPINESS
0-316-72895-0 Little, Brown $17.95

- Kathleen Raine
THE INNER JOURNEY OF THE POET
With a naturalistic, Scottish-inspired "sense of the sacred"
0-8076-1039-9 Braziller $20.00

- Herbert Read
THE MEANING OF ART
A popular introduction to understanding and appreciating art, with an illustrated historical survey
0-571-09658-1 Faber & Faber pb $6.95

- Bertrand Russell
BASIC WRITINGS OF BERTRAND RUSSELL
An authorized and representative selection of 81 essays and self-contained excerpts from a half-century of Bertrand Russell's work as a philosopher, psychologist, historian, analyst of international relations, essayist, short-story writer, and autobiographer. "I should wish to thank the editors once again for having brought together in one volume so just an epitome of my perhaps unduly multifarious writings"—Bertrand Russell
Edited by Robert E. Egner & Lester E. Dennon
0-671-20154-9 Simon & Schuster pb $15.95

MYSTICISM AND LOGIC & OTHER ESSAYS
0-389-20135-9 Barnes & Noble pb $8.95

PHILOSOPHICAL ESSAYS
0-671-50583-1 Simon & Schuster pb $5.95

UNPOPULAR ESSAYS
"Mr. Russell has written a set of sermons which make their point by refusing to sermonise, a series of adventures in moral philosophy which are serenely irreverent of much that is called moral or goes under the name of philosophy. Mr. Russell pursues his theme with that combination of grace, lucidity and high spirits which is almost unique with him"—Charles Frankel, Columbia University
0-671-20253-7 Simon & Schuster pb $9.95

WHY I AM NOT A CHRISTIAN & OTHER ESSAYS ON RELIGION AND RELATED SUBJECTS
Essays collected between 1899–1954, all centering on one deeply held conviction: "I am as firmly convinced that religions do harm as I am that they are untrue"—Bertrand Russell
0-671-20323-1 Simon & Schuster pb $8.95

- Vita Sackville-West
THE LETTERS OF VITA SACKVILLE-WEST TO VIRGINIA WOOLF
Edited by Louise Desalve & Mitchell A. Leaska
0-688-06271-7 Morrow pb $8.95

- George Bernard Shaw
COLLECTED LETTERS, 1874–1950
"This collection reinforces the already established judgment that Shaw was one of the world's great letter-writers"—Saturday Review
Edited by Dan H. Laurence
Volume 1: 1874–1897
0-670-80543-2 Viking $45.00

Volume 2: 1898–1910
0-670-80544-0 Viking $45.00

Volume 3: 1911–1925
0-670-80545-9 Viking $45.00

Volume 4: 1925–1950
0-670-82109-8 Viking $45.00

COLLECTED MUSIC CRITICISM OF BERNARD SHAW
Includes London Music in 1888–1889 as Heard by Corno di Bassetto and Music in London 1890–1894. A 4-volume set
0-8443-0063-2 Vienna House $75.00

THE INTELLIGENT WOMAN'S GUIDE TO SOCIALISM, CAPITALISM, SOVIETISM AND FASCISM
0-14-020001-0 Penguin pb $6.95

MAJOR CRITICAL ESSAYS
Includes The Quintessence of Ibsenism, The Perfect Wagnerite, and The Sanity of Art
Introduction by Michael Holroyd
0-14-043261-2 Penguin pb $6.95

- Osbert Sitwell
BEFORE THE BOMBARDMENT
Introduction by Victoria Glendinning
0-19-281903-8 Oxford pb $6.95

ESCAPE WITH ME!: An Oriental Sketchbook
The stops on Sitwell's 1933 tour of the East included Peking and the ruins of Angkor
0-19-583736-3 Oxford pb $8.95

- Stephen Spender
JOURNALS: 1939–1983
0-394-54602-4 Random House $19.45
0-19-505209-9 Oxford pb $12.95

LETTERS TO CHRISTOPHER: Stephen Spender's Letters to Christopher Isherwood, 1929–1939
Includes The Line of the Branch
Edited by Lee Bartlett
0-87685-469-2 Black Sparrow pb $8.50

- Lytton Strachey
BIOGRAPHICAL ESSAYS
Thirty-five essays, whose subjects include Frederick the Great, Voltaire, Gibbon, and Rousseau
0-15-612616-8 HBJ pb $6.95

EMINENT VICTORIANS
Quietly devastating thumbnail biographies of four quintessential high Victorians (Cardinal Manning, Dr. Arnold, Florence Nightingale, and General Gordon)
Introduction by Michael Holroyd
0-15-628697-1 HBJ pb $6.95

LITERARY ESSAYS
The subjects include Rabelais, Racine, Pope, and Blake
0-15-652781-2 HBJ pb $5.95

THE SHORTER STRACHEY: Selected Essays of Lytton Strachey
Edited by Michael Holroyd & Paul Levy
Illustrated by Dora Carrington & Henry Lamb
0-19-212211-8 Oxford $22.50

- Dylan Thomas
SELECTED LETTERS
"We are enchanted. We are charmed. It takes some time to realize that what we are being charmed into is a nightmare—the history of a wildly gifted and brilliant child, not only stumbling and bumbling his way to the grave, but digging it for himself in the process"—Howard Moss
Edited by Constantine Fitzgibbon
0-8112-0399-9 New Directions $10.00

- Kenneth Tynan
THE SOUND OF TWO HANDS CLAPPING
0-306-80164-7 Da Capo pb $7.95

- Evelyn Waugh
THE LETTERS OF EVELYN WAUGH
Edited by Mark Amory
0-14-004595-3 Penguin pb $9.95

A LITTLE LEARNING
0-316-92645-0 Little, Brown pb $7.95

A LITTLE ORDER: A Selection from His Journalism
0-316-92633-7 Little, Brown $13.45

A TOURIST IN AFRICA
0-316-92650-7 Little, Brown pb $7.95

- Rebecca West
BLACK LAMB AND GREY FALCON
This epic of Yugoslavia—written in 1941 and blending travel, history, and memoir—is usually considered West's masterpiece
0-14-006355-2 Penguin pb $14.95

FAMILY MEMORIES: An Autobiographical Journey
0-670-81384-2 Viking $19.95

THE NEW MEANING OF TREASON
0-14-007379-5 Penguin pb $7.95

- Raymond Williams
Williams was one of the most influential cultural critics of our day.
THE COUNTRY AND THE CITY
0-19-519810-7 Oxford pb $9.95

CULTURE AND REVOLUTION
0-86091-943-9 RC&H pb $14.95

KEYWORDS: A Vocabulary of Culture and Society
0-19-520469-7 Oxford pb $9.95

MARXISM AND LITERATURE
0-19-876061-2 Oxford pb $6.95

- Colin Wilson
THE ESSENTIAL COLIN WILSON
0-89087-472-7 Celestial Arts pb $8.95

THE OUTSIDER
A work of popular philosophy, heavily influenced by Existentialism, which established Wilson's reputation when it appeared in 1956
0-87477-206-0 Jeremy Tarcher pb $8.95

- Virginia Woolf
THE VIRGINIA WOOLF READER
Edited by Mitchell A. Leaska
0-15-193782-6 HBJ $22.95
0-15-693590-2 HBJ pb $10.95

BOOKS AND PORTRAITS
0-15-613560-4 HBJ pb $4.95

THE CAPTAIN'S DEATH BED & OTHER ESSAYS
Includes essays on Ruskin, Goldsmith, Turgenev, and Conrad. "Perhaps the greatest gift which Woolf possessed was the gift of stimulation. Everything that she touches shines with a fresh iridescence"—Harold Nicholson, Observer
0-15-615395-5 HBJ pb $7.95

Virginia Woolf

THE DEATH OF THE MOTH & OTHER ESSAYS
"There is warmth and wit in her writing and at moments, as in the shorter papers on Shelley and Coleridge, a rare wondering tenderness towards great men of whom she could not quite approve"—*Saturday Review*
0–15–625234–1 HBJ pb $4.95

THE DIARY OF VIRGINIA WOOLF
Although only recently published in its complete form, Woolf's journal has already taken its place as one of the great English literary diaries, an unrivaled record of the growth of a writer's mind, and a crystalline portrait of the society of high modern English culture
Edited by Anne O. Bell

Volume 1: 1915–1919
0–15–626036–0 HBJ pb $8.95

Volume 2: 1920–1924
0–15–626037–9 HBJ pb $7.95

Volume 3: 1925–1930
0–15–626038–7 HBJ pb $10.95

Volume 4: 1931–1935
0–15–626039–5 HBJ pb $7.95

Volume 5: 1936–1941
0–15–626040–9 HBJ pb $8.95

FLUSH: A Biography
In this highly original exercise in point of view, Woolf undertakes to write the biography of Elizabeth Barrett Browning's cocker spaniel
0–15–631952–7 HBJ pb $4.95

THE LETTERS OF VIRGINIA WOOLF
Edited by Nigel Nicholson & Joanne Trautmann

Volume 1: 1888–1912
0–15–650881–8 HBJ pb $12.95

Volume 2: 1912–1922
0–15–650882–6 HBJ pb $5.95

Volume 3: 1923–1928
0–15–650883–4 HBJ pb $5.95

Volume 4: 1929–1931
0–15–650884–2 HBJ pb $8.95

Volume 5: 1932–1935
0–15–650886–9 HBJ pb $9.95

Volume 6: 1936–1941
0–15–650887–7 HBJ pb $9.95

A ROOM OF ONE'S OWN
"Future historians will place Mrs. Woolf's little book beside Mary Wollstonecraft's *A Vindication of the Rights of Women* and John Stuart Mill's *The Subjection of Women*. It does for the intellectual and spiritual liberation of women what these works did for their political emancipation. But *A Room of One's Own* outshines them both in genius"—*Spectator*
0–15–678732–6 HBJ pb $4.95

THE SECOND COMMON READER
On English literature, with a special interest in women writers. "As nearly perfect as Heaven grants it to a critic to be"—*NY Times*
0–15–619808–8 HBJ pb $7.95

THREE GUINEAS
0–15–690177–3 HBJ pb $5.95

WOMEN AND WRITING
Edited by Michele Barrett
0–15–693658–5 HBJ pb $5.95

A WRITER'S DIARY: Being Extracts from the Diary of Virginia Woolf
"I have never read any book that conveyed more truthfully what a writer's life was like"—W.H. Auden
Edited by Leonard Woolf
0–15–698380–X HBJ pb $6.95

• William Butler Yeats
A VISION
Yeats's explanation of his mystical system
0–02–055600–4 Macmillan pb $10.95

Celtic Literature

The British Isles are home to literary traditions independent of, but often influential upon, English. The Celtic languages dominated Britain for centuries before the ascendancy of English, and (with some exceptions) they continue not only to exist but also to support thriving and highly distinctive literatures.

In the early Middle Ages, Ireland had perhaps the most accomplished and sophisticated literature in Europe, with a rich tradition of lyric poetry and highly developed narratives, at once heroic and sardonic, like the stories in the *Tain*. By the 9th century Welsh literature had produced the epic *Gododdin,* several complete cycles of bardic poetry, the wealth of narrative material that would form the basis of the King Arthur stories, and the beginnings of the collection of prose tales later famous as the *Mabinogion.* Welsh, Irish, and Scottish Gaelic all boast important contemporary writers, who continue to work in these languages.

• Jeffrey Gantz, translator
EARLY IRISH MYTHS AND SAGAS
0–14–044397–5 Penguin pb $4.95

THE MABINOGION
The classic collection of medieval Welsh tales, ranging from very early and rather primitive stories to elaborate Arthurian romances
0–14–044322–3 Penguin pb $3.95

• Gerald of Wales
THE JOURNEY THROUGH WALES & THE DESCRIPTION OF WALES
Also known as Giraldus Cambrensis, Gerald compiled his topography in the late 12th century
0–14–044339–8 Penguin pb $6.95

THE HISTORY AND TOPOGRAPHY OF IRELAND
Realism and fantasy alternate in this none too flattering early description of Ireland
0–14–044423–8 Penguin pb $5.95

• David H. Greene, editor
AN ANTHOLOGY OF IRISH LITERATURE
0–8147–2954–1 NYU (2-volume set) $22.50

• Seamus Heaney, translator
SWEENEY ASTRAY
"It takes a superb poet to capture, in translation from the Irish, the full range of pain and beauty in Sweeney's poetry. Seamus Heaney has produced an exhilarating version of this most unusual story poem"—Brendan Kennelly, *NY Times*
0–374–27221–2 Farrar Straus Giroux $13.95
0–374–51894–7 Farrar Straus Giroux pb $7.95

• Kenneth Jackson, translator
A CELTIC MISCELLANY
0–14–044247–2 Penguin pb $5.95

• Gwyn Jones, editor
THE OXFORD BOOK OF WELSH VERSE IN ENGLISH
0–19–211858–7 Oxford $22.50

• Brendan Kennelly, editor
THE PENGUIN BOOK OF IRISH VERSE
Includes translations from Gaelic and English-language writing
0–14–058526–5 Penguin pb $6.95

• Thomas Kinsella, translator
THE TAIN
An elegantly designed edition of the early Irish heroic tales, in a translation by a leading contemporary poet
0–19–281090–1 Oxford pb $9.95

• Thomas Kinsella, editor & translator
THE NEW OXFORD BOOK OF IRISH VERSE
0–19–211868–4 Oxford $21.95

• John MacQueen & Tom Scott, editors
THE OXFORD BOOK OF SCOTTISH VERSE
0–19–812131–8 Oxford $35.00

• Brian Merriman
THE MIDNIGHT COURT
0–85342–658–9 Irish Books Media pb $17.95

• John Montague, editor
THE BOOK OF IRISH VERSE: An Anthology of Irish Poetry from the Sixth Century to the Present
0–02–070190–X Macmillan pb $9.95

- Frank O'Connor, translator
  THE WILD BIRD'S NEST: Poems from the Irish
  0–7165–1374–9 Biblio $15.00

- Sean O'Tuama, editor
  AN DUANAIRE /AN IRISH ANTHOLOGY, 1600–1900: Poems of the Dispossessed
  A bilingual anthology, with translations by an outstanding contemporary Irish poet, presenting the poetry of "the troubled centuries from the collapse of the old Gaelic order to the emergence of English as the dominant vernacular"
  Translated by Thomas Kinsella
  0–937702–02–1 Irish Books Media pb $11.95

- Alywn & Brinley Rees
  CELTIC HERITAGE: Ancient Tradition in Ireland and Wales
  "What the Grimm brothers are to fairy tales and philology, the Rees brothers are to Celtic culture"—*Seattle Post Intelligencer*
  0–500–27039–2 Thames & Hudson pb $10.95

Anthologies and Studies

GENERAL ANTHOLOGIES

- M.H. Abrams & others
  THE NORTON ANTHOLOGY OF ENGLISH LITERATURE
  Volume 1
  0–393–95476–5 Norton pb $22.95
  Volume 2
  0–393–95478–1 Norton pb $22.95

- Frank Kermode & John Hollander, editors
  THE OXFORD ANTHOLOGY OF ENGLISH LITERATURE
  Volume 1: The Middle Ages Through the Eighteenth Century
  0–19–501657–2 Oxford pb $21.95
  Volume 2: 1800 to the Present
  0–19–501658–0 Oxford pb $21.95

Poetry

- Kingsley Amis, editor
  THE NEW OXFORD BOOK OF LIGHT VERSE
  0–19–211862–5 Oxford $25.00

- W.H. Auden, editor
  THE OXFORD BOOK OF LIGHT VERSE
  0–19–881331–7 Oxford pb $8.95

- John Barrell & John Bull, editors
  THE PENGUIN BOOK OF ENGLISH PASTORAL VERSE
  0–14–042178–5 Penguin pb $7.95

- Donald Davie, editor
  THE NEW OXFORD BOOK OF CHRISTIAN VERSE
  0–19–213426–4 Oxford $27.50

- Helen Gardner, editor
  THE NEW OXFORD BOOK OF ENGLISH VERSE
  0–19–812136–9 Oxford $35.00

- Geoffrey Grigson, editor
  THE OXFORD BOOK OF SATIRICAL VERSE
  0–19–281425–7 Oxford pb $12.95

- G.B. Harrison, editor
  A BOOK OF ENGLISH POETRY
  0–14–058579–6 Penguin pb $5.95

- Frank Kermode, editor
  ENGLISH PASTORAL POETRY: From the Beginnings to Marvell
  0–393–00612–3 Norton pb $3.95

- James Kinsley, editor
  THE OXFORD BOOK OF BALLADS
  0–19–281330–7 Oxford pb $12.95

- Francis T. Palgrave & John Press, editors
  THE GOLDEN TREASURY OF THE BEST SONGS AND LYRICAL POEMS IN THE ENGLISH LANGUAGE: From Shakespeare to Larkin
  0–19–282035–4 Oxford pb $8.95

Drama

- Sylvan Barnet, editor
  THE GENIUS OF THE EARLY ENGLISH THEATRE
  Includes *Abraham and Isaac, The Second Shepherd's Play, Everyman, Doctor Faustus, Macbeth, Volpone,* and *Samson Agonistes*
  0–451–62443–2 NAL pb $4.95

- Janet M. Morrell, editor
  FOUR ENGLISH COMEDIES
  Includes *Volpone, The Way of the World, She Stoops to Conquer,* and *The School for Scandal*
  0–14–043158–6 Penguin pb $4.95

Fiction

- Malcolm Bradbury, editor
  THE PENGUIN BOOK OF MODERN BRITISH SHORT STORIES
  0–670–81926–3 Viking $18.95
  0–14–006306–4 Penguin pb $7.95

- T.S. Dorsch, editor
  CHARMED LIVES: Classic English Short Stories
  0–19–282150–4 Oxford pb $7.95

- Christopher Isherwood, editor
  GREAT ENGLISH SHORT STORIES
  0–440–33084–X Dell pb $4.95

- Frederick A. Karl, editor
  THE SIGNET BOOK OF BRITISH SHORT STORIES
  0–451–51948–5 NAL pb $4.95

- V.S. Pritchett, editor
  THE OXFORD BOOK OF SHORT STORIES
  0–19–214116–3 Oxford $29.95

- William Trevor, editor
  THE OXFORD BOOK OF IRISH SHORT STORIES
  0–19–214180–5 Oxford $24.95

GENERAL HISTORIES AND STUDIES

- Robert M. Adams
  THE LAND AND LITERATURE OF ENGLAND: A Historical Account
  0–393–01704–4 Norton $29.95
  0–393–30343–8 Norton pb $14.95

- Denis Donoghue
  WE IRISH: Essays on Irish Literature and Society
  0–394–55451–5 Knopf $18.95
  0–520–06425–9 California pb $10.95

- Margaret Drabble
  A WRITER'S BRITAIN: Landscape in Literature
  Photographs by Jorge Lewinski
  0–394–50819–X Knopf $22.50
  0–500–27340–5 Thames & Hudson pb $15.95

- Margaret Drabble, editor
  THE OXFORD COMPANION TO ENGLISH LITERATURE
  0–19–866130–4 Oxford $45.00

- Dorothy Eagle & Hilary Carnell, editors
  THE OXFORD LITERARY GUIDE TO THE BRITISH ISLES
  0–19–869123–8 Oxford $24.95
  0–19–285098–9 Oxford pb $9.95

Boris Ford, editor
THE NEW PELICAN GUIDE TO ENGLISH LITERATURE: A Guide for Readers
0–14–022530–7 Penguin pb $7.95

MEDIEVAL LITERATURE: Chaucer and the Alliterative Tradition
0–14–022264–2 Penguin pb $6.95

MEDIEVAL LITERATURE: The European Inheritance
0–14–022272–3 Penguin pb $6.95

THE AGE OF SHAKESPEARE
0–14–022265–0 Penguin pb $7.95

FROM DONNE TO MARVELL
0–14–022266–9 Penguin pb $6.95

FROM DRYDEN TO JOHNSON
0–14–022267–7 Penguin pb $6.95

FROM BLAKE TO BYRON
0–14–022268–5 Penguin pb $6.95

FROM DICKENS TO HARDY
0–14–022269–3 Penguin pb $6.95

FROM JAMES TO ELIOT
0–14–022270–7 Penguin pb $6.95

THE PRESENT
0–14–022271–5 Penguin pb $7.95

• Ian Ousby, editor
THE CAMBRIDGE GUIDE TO LITERATURE IN ENGLISH
0–521–26751–X Cambridge $39.50

• Pat Rogers, editor
THE OXFORD ILLUSTRATED HISTORY OF ENGLISH LITERATURE
0–19–812816–9 Oxford $30.00

• George Sampson
THE CONCISE CAMBRIDGE HISTORY OF ENGLISH LITERATURE
0–521–09581–6 Cambridge pb $24.95

• James Sutherland, editor
THE OXFORD BOOK OF LITERARY ANECDOTES
0–19–812139–3 Oxford $29.95

Poetry

• Joan Bennett
FIVE METAPHYSICAL POETS: Donne, Herbert, Vaughan, Crashaw, Marvell
0–521–09238–8 Cambridge pb $9.95

• Douglas Bush
MYTHOLOGY AND THE ROMANTIC TRADITION IN ENGLISH POETRY
0–674–59825–3 Harvard $30.00

• Louis Martz
THE PARADISE WITHIN: Studies in Vaughan, Traherne, and Milton
0–300–00164–9 Yale pb $10.95

• Christopher Ricks
THE FORCE OF POETRY
0–19–811722–1 Oxford $36.00
0–19–282046–X Oxford pb $12.95

Drama

• Marie Axton & R. Williams, editors
ENGLISH DRAMA
0–521–21588–9 Cambridge $32.00

• Philip Edwards
THRESHOLD OF A NATION: A Study in English and Irish Drama
0–521–27695–0 Cambridge pb $14.95

Emblematic frontispiece to Thomas Vaughan's "Silex Scintillans," from The Oxford Illustrated History of English Literature

• Christopher Ricks, editor
ENGLISH DRAMA TO 1710
A volume in the New History of Literature series
0–87226–127–1 Peter Bedrick $38.00

• Gamini Salgado
ENGLISH DRAMA: A Critical Introduction
0–312–25429–6 St. Martin's $27.50

Fiction

• Mary Eagleton & David Pierce
ATTITUDES TO CLASS IN THE ENGLISH NOVEL: From Walter Scott to David Storey
0–500–51002–4 Thames & Hudson $17.95

• Avrom Fleishman
THE ENGLISH HISTORICAL NOVEL: Walter Scott to Virginia Woolf
0–8018–1433–2 Johns Hopkins pb $9.95

• Ford Madox Ford
THE ENGLISH NOVEL
0–85635–480–5 Carcanet pb $8.50

• E.M. Forster
ASPECTS OF THE NOVEL
0–15–609180–1 HBJ pb $4.95

• David Skilton
DEFOE TO THE VICTORIANS: Two Centuries of the English Novel
0–14–022599–4 Penguin pb $7.95

SPECIALIZED STUDIES

Anglo-Saxon and Medieval

• Michael Alexander, editor
OLD ENGLISH LITERATURE
0–8052–3862–X Schocken $28.50

• W.F. Bolton, editor
THE MIDDLE AGES
A volume in the New History of Literature series
0–87226–125–5 Peter Bedrick $38.00

• Stephen Coote
ENGLISH LITERATURE OF THE MIDDLE AGES
0–14–022790–3 Penguin pb $7.95

• C.S. Lewis
STUDIES IN MEDIEVAL AND RENAISSANCE LITERATURE
0–521–29701–X Cambridge pb $11.95

• A.C. Spearing
MEDIEVAL TO RENAISSANCE IN ENGLISH POETRY
0–521–31533–6 Cambridge pb $15.95

From the Elizabethan Age to the Commonwealth

• Muriel C. Bradbrook
THE RISE OF THE COMMON PLAYER
0–521–29527–0 Cambridge pb $12.95

• Julia Briggs
THIS STAGE PLAY WORLD: English Literature and Its Background, 1580–1625
0–19–289134–0 Oxford pb $9.95

• C.S. Lewis
ENGLISH LITERATURE IN THE SIXTEENTH CENTURY
0–19–812204–7 Oxford $49.95

• Christopher Ricks, editor
ENGLISH PROSE AND POETRY: 1540–1674
A volume in the New History of Literature series
0–87226–126–3 Peter Bedrick $38.00

• E.M. Tillyard
THE ELIZABETHAN WORLD PICTURE
0–394–70162–3 Random House pb $4.50

• Basil Willey
THE SEVENTEENTH CENTURY BACKGROUND: Studies in the Thought of the Age in Relation to Poetry and Religion
0–231–01395–7 Columbia $34.00

The Restoration and the 18th Century

• Derek Brewer & A. Norman Jeffares, editors
ENGLISH GOTHIC LITERATURE
0–8052–3861–1 Schocken $28.50

• Leopold Damrosch, editor
MODERN ESSAYS ON EIGHTEENTH-CENTURY LITERATURE
0–19–504923–3 Oxford $34.00
0–19–504924–1 Oxford pb $12.95

• Roger Lonsdale, editor
DRYDEN TO JOHNSON
A volume in the New History of Literature series
0–87226–128–X Peter Bedrick $38.00

The 19th Century

• M.H. Abrams
THE CORRESPONDENT BREEZE: Essays on English Romanticism
0–393–01837–7 Norton $22.50
0–393–30340–3 Norton pb $9.95

• Harold Bloom
THE VISIONARY COMPANY: A Reading of English Romantic Poetry
0–8014–9117–7 Cornell pb $14.95

• C. Maurice Bowra
THE ROMANTIC IMAGINATION
0–19–281006–5 Oxford pb $9.95

• Julia P. Brown
A READER'S GUIDE TO THE NINETEENTH-CENTURY ENGLISH NOVEL
0–02–517370–7 Macmillan $15.95
0–02–079560–2 Macmillan pb $7.95

✉ **TO ORDER BOOKS AS GIFTS, SEE PAGE 1**

Painting by Edward Sorel showing, left to right, J.M. Synge, Oliver St. John Gogarty, Lady Gregory, Samuel Beckett, Sean O'Casey, W.B. Yeats, and James Joyce, from A Colder Eye: The Modern Irish Writers *by Hugh Kenner (Knopf)*

• Arthur Pollard, editor
THE VICTORIANS
A volume in the New History of Literature series
0–87226–130–1 Peter Bedrick $38.00

The 20th Century

• Valentine Cunningham, editor
THE SPANISH FRONT: Writers on the Civil War
0–19–282006–0 Oxford pb $8.95

• Richard Ellman
FOUR DUBLINERS: Wilde, Yeats, Joyce and Beckett
0–8076–1185–9 Braziller $12.95
0–8076–1208–1 Braziller pb $6.95

Robert Hewison
UNDER SIEGE: Literary Life in London, 1939–1945
0–19–519993–6 Oxford $21.95

IN ANGER: British Culture in the Cold War, 1945–1960
0–19–520238–4 Oxford $24.95

• Samuel Hynes
THE AUDEN GENERATION: Literature and Politics in England in the 1930s
0–691–01395–0 Princeton pb $11.50

• Hugh Kenner
A COLDER EYE: The Modern Irish Writers
0–394–42225–2 Knopf $16.95

A SINKING ISLAND: The Modern English Writers
0–394–54254–1 Knopf $22.95

• William Pritchard
SEEING THROUGH EVERYTHING: English Literature Between the Wars
0–19–519951–0 Oxford $18.95

• S.P. Rosenbaum, editor
THE BLOOMSBURY GROUP: A Collection of Memoirs, Commentary and Criticism
0–8020–6268–7 Toronto pb $19.95

• John I. Stewart
EIGHT MODERN WRITERS
Studies of Hardy, James, Shaw, Conrad, Kipling, Yeats, Joyce, and Lawrence
0–19–881300–7 Oxford pb $5.95

Poetry

• Calvin Bedient
EIGHT CONTEMPORARY POETS
Focuses on eight major figures of recent decades: Charles Tomlinson, Donald Davie, R.S. Thomas, Stevie Smith, Thomas Kinsella, Ted Hughes, Philip Larkin, and W.S. Graham
0–19–519825–5 Oxford pb $3.95

• Martin Booth
BRITISH POETRY 1964–1984: Driving Through the Barricades
0–7100–9606–2 RC&H $32.50

• John Hollander, editor
MODERN POETRY: Essays in Criticism
0–19–500757–3 Oxford pb $10.95

• John Lehmann
THE ENGLISH POETS OF THE FIRST WORLD WAR
0–500–01256–3 Thames & Hudson $19.95

• Lucy McDiarmid
SAVING CIVILIZATION: Yeats, Eliot, and Auden Between the Wars
0–521–26930–X Cambridge pb $10.95

David Perkins
A HISTORY OF MODERN POETRY: From the 1880s to the High Modernist Mode
0–674–39941–2 Harvard $32.00
0–674–39945–5 Harvard pb $12.95

A HISTORY OF MODERN POETRY: Modernism and After
0–674–39946–3 Harvard $25.00

• John Wain
PROFESSING POETRY
0–14–004933–9 Penguin pb $3.95

STUDIES OF INDIVIDUAL AUTHORS

Medieval and Renaissance

• Anthony Quinton
FRANCIS BACON
0–19–287524–8 Oxford pb $4.95

• H.S. Bennett
CHAUCER AND THE FIFTEENTH CENTURY
0–19–812201–2 Oxford $42.50

• John C. Gardner
THE LIFE AND TIMES OF CHAUCER
0–394–49317–6 Knopf $22.50
0–394–72500–X Random House pb $9.95

• Donald R. Howard
CHAUCER: His Life, His Works, His World
0–525–24400–X Dutton $29.95
0–394–90341–9 Fawcett pb $12.95

• D.W. Robertson, Jr.
PREFACE TO CHAUCER: Studies in Medieval Perspective
0–691–01294–6 Princeton pb $22.50

• Amy M. Charles
A LIFE OF GEORGE HERBERT
0–8014–1014–2 Cornell $29.95

• Claude J. Summers & Ted-Larry Pebworth, editors
TOO RICH TO CLOTHE THE SUNNE: Essays on George Herbert
0–8229–3421–3 Pittsburgh $24.95

• Anne Barton
BEN JONSON, DRAMATIST
0–521–27748–5 Cambridge pb $19.95

• David Riggs
BEN JONSON: A Life
0–674–06625–1 Harvard $35.00

• Judith Weil
CHRISTOPHER MARLOWE
0–521–21554–4 Cambridge $39.50

• Anthony Kenny
THOMAS MORE
0–19–287573–6 Oxford pb $4.95

• Andrew Sinclair
SIR WALTER RALEIGH AND THE AGE OF DISCOVERY
0–14–007245–4 Penguin pb $7.95

• Angus Fletcher
THE PROPHETIC MOMENT: An Essay on Spenser
0–226–25332–5 Chicago $20.00

• C.S. Lewis
SPENSER'S IMAGES OF LIFE
0–521–29284–0 Cambridge pb $9.95

Shakespeare

• Muriel C. Bradbrook
THE LIVING MONUMENT: Shakespeare and the Theatre of His Time
0–521–21255–3 Cambridge $44.50

• A.C. Bradley
SHAKESPEAREAN TRAGEDY: Lectures on Hamlet, Othello, King Lear, Macbeth
Introduction by John R. Brown
0–312–71427–0 St. Martin's $32.50

• John Drakakis, editor
ALTERNATIVE SHAKESPEARES
0–416–36850–6 RC&H $29.95
0–416–36860–3 RC&H pb $9.95

• Terry Eagleton
WILLIAM SHAKESPEARE
0–631–14553–2 Blackwell $14.95
0–631–14554–0 Blackwell pb $9.95

• Philip Edwards
SHAKESPEARE: A Writer's Progress
0–19–219184–5 Oxford $29.95
0–19–289166–9 Oxford pb $11.95

• Una Ellis-Fermor
SHAKESPEARE'S DRAMA
Edited by Kenneth Muir
0–416–74090–1 Methuen pb $29.95

• Russell Fraser
YOUNG SHAKESPEARE
0–231–06764–X Columbia $29.00

Cover art for Reinventing Shakespeare: A Cultural History, 1642–1986 *by Gary Taylor (Weidenfeld & Nicolson)*

• Northrop Frye
A NATURAL PERSPECTIVE: The Development of Shakespearean Comedy and Romance
0–8446–6318–2 Peter Smith $15.25
0–15–665414–8 HBJ pb $4.95

NORTHROP FRYE ON SHAKESPEARE
Edited by Robert Sandler
0–300–03711–2 Yale $25.00
0–300–04208–6 Yale pb $7.95

• Robert Giroux
THE BOOK KNOWN AS Q: A Consideration of Shakespeare's Sonnets
0–689–11260–2 Atheneum $17.95

• Harley Granville-Barker
PREFACES TO SHAKESPEARE

Volume 1:
Hamlet, King Lear, The Merchant of Venice, Antony and Cleopatra, Cymbeline
0–691–01350–0 Princeton pb $16.95

Volume 2:
Othello, Coriolanus, Julius Caesar, Romeo and Juliet, Love's Labors Lost
0–691–01351–9 Princeton pb $12.95

• Stephen Greenblatt
SHAKESPEAREAN NEGOTIATIONS: The Circulation of Social Energy in Renaissance England
0–520–06159–4 California $20.00

• Germaine Greer
SHAKESPEARE
0–19–287539–6 Oxford $16.95
0–19–287538–8 Oxford pb $4.95

• F.E. Halliday
SHAKESPEARE
0–500–26021–4 Thames & Hudson pb $9.95

• Alfred Harbage
SHAKESPEARE'S AUDIENCE
0–8446–2203–6 Peter Smith $20.00

• Graham Holderness, editor
THE SHAKESPEAREAN MYTH
0–7190–1488–3 St. Martin's $39.95

• Samuel Johnson
SELECTIONS FROM JOHNSON ON SHAKESPEARE
0–300–03707–4 Yale $42.50
0–300–03708–2 Yale pb $13.95

• G. Wilson Knight
SHAKESPEARIAN DIMENSIONS
0–389–20458–7 Barnes & Noble $28.50

THE CROWN OF LIFE: Essays in Interpretation of Shakespeare's Final Plays
0–416–68770–9 Methuen pb $14.95

THE IMPERIAL THEME: Further Interpretations of Shakespeare's Tragedies Including the Roman Play
0–416–68740–7 Methuen pb $13.95

THE WHEEL OF FIRE: Interpretations of Shakespearean Tragedy
0–416–67620–0 Methuen pb $13.95

• Jan Kott
THE BOTTOM TRANSLATION: Marlowe and Shakespeare and the Carnival Tradition
Translated by Daniela Miedzyrzecka & Lillian Vallee
0–8101–0737–6 Northwestern $32.95
0–8101–0738–4 Northwestern pb $14.95

SHAKESPEARE OUR CONTEMPORARY
Introduction by Martin Esslin
0–393–00736–7 Norton pb $9.95

• Clifford Leech
SHAKESPEARE—THE TRAGEDIES: A Collection of Critical Essays
0–226–47018–0 Chicago pb $15.00

• Harry Levin
THE QUESTION OF HAMLET
0–19–500808–1 Oxford pb $5.95

SHAKESPEARE AND THE REVOLUTION OF THE TIMES: Perspectives and Commentaries
0–19–501982–2 Oxford $25.00
0–19–502362–5 Oxford pb $9.95

• Kenneth Muir
SHAKESPEARE: Contrasts and Controversies
0–8061–1940–3 Oklahoma $19.95

• Kenneth Muir, editor
INTERPRETATIONS OF SHAKESPEARE
0–19–812952–1 Oxford pb $18.95

• Samuel Schoenbaum
WILLIAM SHAKESPEARE: A Compact Documentary Life
0–19–502211–4 Oxford $22.50
0–19–505161–0 Oxford pb $13.95

SHAKESPEARE: The Globe and the World
0–19–502646–2 Oxford pb $9.95

SHAKESPEARE'S LIVES
0–19–501243–7 Oxford $39.95

• Marvin Spevack, editor
THE HARVARD CONCORDANCE TO SHAKESPEARE
0–674–37475–4 Harvard $75.00

• Caroline Spurgeon
SHAKESPEARE'S IMAGERY
0–521–09258–2 Cambridge pb $16.95

• Gary Taylor
REINVENTING SHAKESPEARE: A Cultural History, 1642–1986
1–55584–078–7 Weidenfeld & Nicolson $29.95

The Restoration and the 18th Century

• Frank Brady
JAMES BOSWELL: The Later Years, 1769–1795
0–07–050558–6 McGraw-Hill $24.95

• Frederick A. Pottle
JAMES BOSWELL: The Earlier Years, 1740–1769
0–07–050578–0 McGraw-Hill $24.95

• Louise J. Kaplan
THE FAMILY ROMANCE OF THE IMPOSTER-POET THOMAS CHATTERTON
0–689–11896–1 Atheneum $24.95

• John R. Moore
DANIEL DEFOE: Citizen of the Modern World
0–226–53577–0 Chicago $20.00

- Pat Rogers
  DEFOE
  0–7102–0595–3 RC&H pb $24.00

- George McFadden
  DRYDEN THE PUBLIC WRITER, 1660–1685
  0–691–06350–8 Princeton $29.00

- James A. Winn
  JOHN DRYDEN AND HIS WORLD
  0–300–02994–2 Yale $29.95

- Walter Jackson Bate
  SAMUEL JOHNSON
  0–15–679259–1 HBJ pb $10.95

  THE ACHIEVEMENT OF SAMUEL JOHNSON
  0–226–03895–5 Chicago pb $4.95

- James L. Clifford
  DICTIONARY JOHNSON
  0–07–011379–3 McGraw-Hill pb $6.95

  YOUNG SAM JOHNSON
  0–07–011381–5 McGraw-Hill pb $6.95

- Paul Fussell
  SAMUEL JOHNSON AND THE LIFE OF WRITING
  0–393–30258–X Norton pb $6.95

- R. Wilcher
  ANDREW MARVELL
  0–521–27722–1 Cambridge pb $11.95

- David Daiches
  MILTON
  0–393–00347–7 Norton pb $4.95

- Christopher Ricks
  MILTON'S GRAND STYLE
  0–19–812090–7 Oxford pb $12.95

- A.N. Wilson
  THE LIFE OF JOHN MILTON
  0–19–211776–9 Oxford $22.95
  0–19–281473–7 Oxford pb $11.95

- Maynard Mack
  ALEXANDER POPE: A Life
  0–393–02208–0 Norton $25.95
  0–393–30529–5 Norton pb $14.95

- Jocelyn Harris
  SAMUEL RICHARDSON
  0–521–30501–2 Cambridge $39.50
  0–521–31542–5 Cambridge pb $11.95

- Arthur H. Cash
  LAURENCE STERNE: The Early and Middle Years
  0–416–82210–X RC&H $85.00

  LAURENCE STERNE: The Later Years
  0–416–32930–6 RC&H $60.00

- Denis Donoghue
  JONATHAN SWIFT
  0–521–07564–5 Cambridge $49.50

- Irvin Ehrenpreis
  SWIFT: The Man, His Works, and the Age

  Volume 1: Mr. Swift and His Contemporaries
  0–674–85830–1 Harvard $27.00

  Volume 2: Dr. Swift
  0–317–85832–8 Harvard $37.00

  Volume 3: Dean Swift
  0–674–85835–2 Harvard $40.00

- David Nokes
  JONATHAN SWIFT, A HYPOCRITE REVERSED: A Critical Biography
  0–19–812834–7 Oxford $35.00

The 19th Century

- Park Honan
  MATTHEW ARNOLD: A Life
  0–07–029697–9 McGraw-Hill $19.95
  0–674–55465–5 Harvard pb $10.95

- Lionel Trilling
  MATTHEW ARNOLD
  0–15–657734–8 HBJ pb $6.95

- David Cecil
  A PORTRAIT OF JANE AUSTEN
  0–8090–1392–4 Hill & Wang pb $9.95

- John Halperin
  THE LIFE OF JANE AUSTEN
  0–8018–3410–4 Johns Hopkins pb $10.95

- Marghanita Laski
  JANE AUSTEN
  0–500–26015–X Thames & Hudson pb $9.95

- Tony Tanner
  JANE AUSTEN
  0–674–47174–1 Harvard pb $8.95

- Foster S. Damon
  A BLAKE DICTIONARY: Ideas and Symbols of William Blake
  Foreword by Morris Eaves
  0–87451–436–3 New England pb $18.00

- David V. Erdman
  BLAKE: Prophet Against Empire
  0–691–01329–2 Princeton pb $17.95

- Northrop Frye
  FEARFUL SYMMETRY: A Study of William Blake
  0–691–01291–1 Princeton pb $14.95

- Kathleen Raine
  WILLIAM BLAKE
  0–500–20107–2 Thames & Hudson pb $11.95

- Phyllis Bentley
  THE BRONTES
  0–500–26016–8 Thames & Hudson pb $9.95

- Rebecca Fraser
  THE BRONTES
  0-517-56438-6 Crown $25.00

- Elizabeth Gaskell
  THE LIFE OF CHARLOTTE BRONTE
  0–14–043099–7 Penguin pb $5.95

- John Maynard
  CHARLOTTE BRONTE AND SEXUALITY
  0–521–26181–3 Cambridge $34.50
  0–521–33587–6 Cambridge pb $14.95

- Edward Chitham
  A LIFE OF EMILY BRONTE
  0–631–14751–9 Blackwell $24.95

- Winifred Gerin
  EMILY BRONTE
  0–19–281251–3 Oxford pb $9.95

- Leslie A. Marchand
  BYRON: A Portrait
  0–226–50436–0 Chicago pb $7.95

- Jerome McGann
  BYRON
  0–19–281349–8 Oxford pb $13.95

- Frederic Raphael
  BYRON
  0–500–01278–4 Thames & Hudson $18.95

- Fred Kaplan
  THOMAS CARLYLE: A Biography
  0–8014–1508–X Cornell $39.95

- A.L. Le Quesne
  CARLYLE
  0–19–287563–9 Oxford $16.95

- Walter Jackson Bate
  COLERIDGE
  0–674–13680–2 Harvard pb $11.95

- Richard Holmes
  COLERIDGE
  0–19–287591–4 Oxford $4.95

- Basil Willey
  SAMUEL TAYLOR COLERIDGE
  0–393–00696–4 Norton pb $2.95

- Peter Ackroyd
  DICKENS' LONDON: An Imaginative Vision
  0–7472–0028–9 David & Charles $24.95

- Michael Allen
  CHARLES DICKENS' CHILDHOOD
  0–312–01275–6 St. Martin's $29.95

- Edgar Johnson
  CHARLES DICKENS: His Tragedy and Triumph
  0–14–058027–1 Penguin pb $8.95

- Fred Kaplan
  DICKENS: A Biography
  0–688–04341–0 William Morrow $24.95

- Norman MacKenzie & Jeanne MacKenzie
  DICKENS: A Life
  0–19–211741–6 Oxford $35.00

- George Bernard Shaw
  SHAW ON DICKENS
  Edited by Dan Laurence & Martin Quinn
  0–8044–2494–2 Ungar $15.95

- Rosemary Ashton
  GEORGE ELIOT
  0–19–287627–9 Oxford $14.95
  0–19–287626–0 Oxford pb $4.95

● Gillian Beer
GEORGE ELIOT
0–253–30100–9 Indiana $27.50
0–253–25450–7 Indiana pb $7.95

● Gordon S. Haight
GEORGE ELIOT
0–14–058025–5 Penguin pb $10.95

● R.T. Jones
GEORGE ELIOT
0–521–09613–8 Cambridge pb $8.95

● Marghanita Laski
GEORGE ELIOT
0–500–26023–0 Thames & Hudson pb $9.95

● Jennifer Uglow
GEORGE ELIOT
0–394–75359–3 Pantheon pb $9.95

● L.J. Butler
THOMAS HARDY
0–521–21743–1 Cambridge $32.50
0–521–29271–9 Cambridge pb $11.95

● Irving Howe
THOMAS HARDY
0–02–052010–7 Macmillan pb $6.95

● Michael Millgate
THOMAS HARDY: A Biography
0–19–281472–9 Oxford pb $13.95

● Kenyon Critics
GERARD MANLEY HOPKINS
0–8112–0479–0 New Directions pb $2.45

● John Barnard
JOHN KEATS
0–521–31806–8 Cambridge pb $11.95

● Walter Jackson Bate
JOHN KEATS
0–674–47825–8 Harvard pb $14.95

● Robin Mayhead
JOHN KEATS
0–521–05706–X Cambridge $27.95

● Helen Vendler
THE ODES OF JOHN KEATS
0–674–63075–0 Harvard $20.00

● Kingsley Amis
RUDYARD KIPLING
0–500–26019–2 Thames & Hudson pb $9.95

● Angus Wilson
THE STRANGE RIDE OF RUDYARD KIPLING
0–14–005122–8 Penguin pb $6.95

● Peter Stansky
WILLIAM MORRIS
0–19–287571–X Oxford pb $4.95

● Owen Chadwick
NEWMAN
0–19–287567–1 Oxford pb $4.95

● Brian W. Martin
JOHN HENRY NEWMAN: His Life and Work
0–19–520387–9 Oxford $35.00

● Tim Hilton
JOHN RUSKIN: The Early Years, 1819–1859
0–300–03298–6 Yale $25.00

● George Landow
RUSKIN
0–19–287603–1 Oxford pb $4.95

● Marcel Proust
ON READING RUSKIN
0–300–03513–6 Yale $22.50

● Robin Mayhead
WALTER SCOTT
0–521–09781–9 Cambridge pb $9.95

● Jenni Calder
ROBERT LOUIS STEVENSON: A Life Study
0–19–520210–4 Oxford $27.50

● Donald Thomas
SWINBURNE: The Poet of His World
0–19–520136–1 Oxford $22.95

● F.B. Pinion
A TENNYSON COMPANION: Life and Works
0–312–79107–0 St. Martin's $27.50

● Alan Sinfield
ALFRED TENNYSON
0–631–13583–9 Blackwell pb $9.95

● Winifred G. Gerould & James T. Gerould
A GUIDE TO TROLLOPE: An Index to Characters and Places, and Digests of the Plots, in All of Trollope's Work
0–691–01441–8 Princeton pb $12.95

● Walter Kendrick
THE NOVEL MACHINE: The Theory and Fiction of Anthony Trollope
0–8018–2301–3 Johns Hopkins $17.50

● Richard Ellmann
OSCAR WILDE
0–394–55484–1 Knopf $24.95

● Vyvyan Holland
OSCAR WILDE
0–500–26031–1 Thames & Hudson pb $9.95

● H. Montgomery Hyde
OSCAR WILDE
0–306–80147–7 Da Capo pb $11.95

● Edouard Roditi
OSCAR WILDE
0–8112–0995–4 New Directions pb $10.95

● Robert Gittings & Jo Manton
DOROTHY WORDSWORTH
0–19–282048–6 Oxford pb $9.95

● Geoffrey H. Durrant
WILLIAM WORDSWORTH
0–521–07608–0 Cambridge $32.50
0–521–09584–0 Cambridge pb $10.95

● Jonathan Wordsworth
WILLIAM WORDSWORTH: The Borders of Vision
0–19–812831–2 Oxford pb $24.95

The 20th Century

● Edward Callan
AUDEN: A Carnival of Intellect
0–19–503168–7 Oxford $27.95

● Howard Griffin
CONVERSATIONS WITH AUDEN
0–912516–56–9 Grey Fox pb $5.95

● Edward Mendelson
EARLY AUDEN
0–670–28712–1 Viking $20.00
0–674–21986–4 Harvard pb $9.95

● A.L. Rowse
THE POET AUDEN: A Personal Memoir
Edited by Bill Strachan
1–55584–198–8 Weidenfeld & Nicolson $14.95

● Ian Watson
CONVERSATIONS WITH AYCKBOURN
0–571–15192–2 Faber & Faber pb $10.95

● J.G. Riewald, editor
THE SURPRISE OF EXCELLENCE: Modern Essays on Max Beerbohm
0–208–01443–8 Shoe String $27.50

● Patricia Craig
ELIZABETH BOWEN
0–14–008710–9 Penguin pb $4.95

● Dennis Hall
JOYCE CARY: A Reappraisal
0–312–44516–4 St. Martin's $20.00

● Joseph Conrad
JOSEPH CONRAD ON FICTION
Edited by Walter F. Wright
0–8032–0452–3 Nebraska $21.50
0–8032–5452–0 Nebraska pb $5.95

● Ford Madox Ford
JOSEPH CONRAD
0–88001–176–9 Ecco pb $9.95

● William Cookson & Peter Dale, editors
FORD MADOX FORD
0–933806–52–3 Black Swan pb $17.50

● Arthur Mizener
THE SADDEST STORY: A Biography of Ford Madox Ford
0–88184–187–0 Carroll & Graf pb $12.95

● Ezra Pound & Ford Madox Ford
POUND-FORD: The Story of a Literary Friendship
Edited by Brita L. Seyersted
0–8112–0833–8 New Directions $22.95

● Francis King
E.M. FORSTER
0–500–26029–X Thames & Hudson pb $9.95

➤ **FOR OVERSEAS ORDERING INFORMATION, SEE PAGE 1**

- Richard P. Graves
  ROBERT GRAVES: The Assault Heroic,
  1895–1926
  0–670–81326–5 Viking $24.95

- Martin Seymour-Smith
  ROBERT GRAVES: His Life and Work
  0–913729–18–3 Paragon pb $10.95

- Sybille Bedford
  ALDOUS HUXLEY
  0–88184–145–5 Carroll & Graf pb $14.95

Aldous Huxley

- John Lehmann
  CHRISTOPHER ISHERWOOD: A
  Personal Memoir
  0–8050–0435–1 Henry Holt $16.95

- Chester G. Anderson
  JAMES JOYCE
  0–500–26018–4 Thames & Hudson pb $9.95

- Anthony Burgess
  JOYSPRICK: An Introduction to the
  Language of James Joyce
  0–15–646561–2 HBJ pb $3.95

  RE JOYCE
  0–393–00445–7 Norton pb $7.95

- Joseph Campbell &
  Henry Morton Robinson
  A SKELETON KEY TO FINNEGANS
  WAKE
  0–14–004663–1 Penguin pb $8.95

- Richard Ellmann
  JAMES JOYCE
  0–19–503381–7 Oxford pb $18.95

- Gisele Freund
  THREE DAYS WITH JOYCE
  A photographic record
  Preface by Richard Ellmann
  0–89255–142–9 Persea pb $9.95

- Hugh Kenner
  DUBLIN'S JOYCE
  0–231–06632–5 Columbia $35.00
  0–231–06633–3 Columbia pb $15.00

JOYCE'S VOICES
0–520–03206–3 California $17.00
0–520–03935–1 California pb $9.95

- Arthur Power
  CONVERSATIONS WITH JAMES JOYCE
  Edited by Clive Hart
  0–226–67720–6 Chicago pb $4.95

- Iain Hamilton
  KOESTLER: A Biography
  0–02–547660–2 Macmillan $19.95

- F.R. Leavis
  D.H. LAWRENCE: Novelist
  0–226–46971–9 Chicago pb $6.95

- Harry T. Moore & Warren Roberts
  D.H. LAWRENCE
  0–500–26030–3 Thames & Hudson pb $9.95

- Anaïs Nin
  D.H. LAWRENCE: An Unprofessional
  Study
  Introduction by H.T. Moore
  0–8040–0067–0 Ohio pb $4.95

- Keith M. Sagar
  THE LIFE OF D.H. LAWRENCE
  0–394–50953–6 Pantheon $17.95

- Jane Farrington
  WYNDHAM LEWIS
  Foreword by Timothy Clifford
  Introduction by Sir John Rothenstein
  0–85331–434–9 Humanities pb $25.00

- Fredric Jameson
  FABLES OF AGGRESSION: Wyndham
  Lewis, The Modernist as Fascist
  0–520–03792–8 California $27.50
  0–520–04398–7 California pb $5.95

- Douglas Day
  MALCOLM LOWRY: A Biography
  0–19–503523–2 Oxford pb $9.95

- Ted Morgan
  MAUGHAM: A Biography
  0–671–50581–5 Simon & Schuster pb $12.95

- John Lahr
  PRICK UP YOUR EARS: The Biography
  of Joe Orton
  0–87910–057–5 Limelight pb $10.95
  0–394–75305–4 Random House pb $4.95

- David L. Kubal
  OUTSIDE THE WHALE: George Orwell's
  Art and Politics
  0–268–00514–1 Notre Dame pb $6.95

- Peter Stansky & William Abrahams
  ORWELL: The Transformation
  0–586–08375–8 Academy Chicago pb $6.95

- Jon Stallworthy
  WILFRED OWEN
  0–19–211719–X Oxford $29.95

- Carole Angier
  JEAN RHYS
  0–670–80626–9 Viking $13.95
  0–14–008001–5 Penguin pb $4.95

- Nigel Nicolson
  PORTRAIT OF A MARRIAGE
  A memoir about the author's parents, Vita
  Sackville-West and Harold Nicolson
  0–689–70597–2 Macmillan pb $10.95

- Eric Bentley
  BERNARD SHAW: A Reconsideration
  0–87910–037–0 Limelight pb $7.95

- Michael Holroyd
  BERNARD SHAW
  Volume 1: The Search for Love, 1856–1898
  0–394–52577–9 Random House $24.95

- Francis Spalding
  STEVIE SMITH: A Biography
  0–393–02672–8 Norton $19.95

- John Malcolm Brinnin
  DYLAN THOMAS IN AMERICA
  1–55778–161–3 Paragon pb $12.95

- Caitlin Thomas & George Tremlett
  CAITLIN: Life with Dylan Thomas
  0–8050–0769–5 Henry Holt pb $8.95

- Martin Stannard
  EVELYN WAUGH: The Early Years,
  1903–1939
  0–393–02450–4 Norton $24.95

- Victoria Glendinning
  REBECCA WEST
  0–394–53935–4 Knopf $19.95

- Fay Weldon
  REBECCA WEST
  0–670–80627–7 Viking $13.95

- Quentin Bell
  VIRGINIA WOOLF: A Biography
  0–15–693580–5 HBJ pb $9.95

- Lyndall Gordon
  VIRGINIA WOOLF: A Writer's Life
  0–393–01891–1 Norton $17.95
  0–393–30342–X Norton pb $8.95

- Phyllis Rose
  WOMAN OF LETTERS: A Life of Virginia
  Woolf
  0–19–502370–6 Oxford $22.50
  0–15–698190–4 HBJ pb $8.95

- Richard Ellmann
  THE IDENTITY OF YEATS
  0–19–500712–3 Oxford pb $9.95

  YEATS: The Man and the Masks
  0–393–00859–2 Norton pb $9.95

- Ian Fletcher
  W.B. YEATS AND HIS
  CONTEMPORARIES
  0–312–85306–8 St. Martin's $27.50

- David Lynch
  YEATS: The Poetics of the Self
  0–226–49812–3 Chicago pb $7.50

- Kathleen Raine
  YEATS THE INITIATE: Essays on Certain
  Themes in the Work of William Butler
  Yeats
  0–8076–1073–9 Braziller $30.00

PART 3

LITERATURE OF THE AMERICAS

Native American Literatures

"At the heart of the American Indian oral tradition is a deep and unconditional belief in the efficacy of language. Words are intrinsically powerful. They are magical. By means of words one can bring about physical change in the universe. By means of words one can quiet a raging weather, bring forth the harvest, ward off evil, rid the body of sickness and pain, subdue an enemy, capture the heart of a lover, live in the proper way, and venture beyond death. Indeed there is nothing more powerful . . . To be careless in the presence of words, on the inside of language, is to violate a fundamental morality."—N. Scott Momaday in *The Columbia Literary History of the United States*, edited by Emory Elliott

▶ See also Native American Cultures & Mythology and Folklore

TRADITIONAL LITERATURE: Poetry, Stories, Oratory

• Paula Gunn Allen
SPIDER WOMAN'S GRANDDAUGHTERS: Traditional Tales and Contemporary Writing by Native American Women
0–8070–8100–0 Beacon $19.95

• John Bierhorst, editor
FOUR MASTERWORKS OF AMERICAN INDIAN LITERATURE
Includes *Quetzalcoatl* (the only complete English translation of the Classical Nahuatl myths of Quetzalcoatl), *The Ritual of Condolence, Cuceb,* and *The Night Chant*
0–8165–0886–0 Arizona pb $10.95

IN THE TRAIL OF THE WIND: American Indian Poems and Ritual Orations
0–374–33640–7 Farrar, Straus & Giroux pb $6.95

THE RED SWAN: Myths and Tales of the American Indians
"Bierhorst's brilliant selection of myths and tales—each representative, significant and interesting in itself—is designed to present a comprehensive view of the world"—*Kirkus Reviews*
0–374–51393–7 Farrar, Straus & Giroux pb $11.95

THE SACRED PATH: Spells, Prayers, and Power Songs of the American Indians
0–688–02647–8 Morrow pb $7.95

• Gordon Brotherston
IMAGE OF THE NEW WORLD: The American Continent Portrayed in Native Texts
A rich gathering of native materials from both North and South America
0–500–01206–7 Thames & Hudson $19.95
0–500–27232–8 Thames & Hudson pb $10.95

• Ella E. Clark
INDIAN LEGENDS FROM THE NORTHERN ROCKIES
Gathered from the traditions of twelve tribes, including the Nez Perces, the Kalispels, the Arapahoes, and the Blackfeet
0–8061–0701–4 Oklahoma $18.95

INDIAN LEGENDS OF THE PACIFIC NORTHWEST
A compendium of over a hundred tales. "The vast amount of research the author has put into preparing this collection is obvious but never intrusive. The book remains . . . thoroughly readable"—*Indian Times*
0–520–00243–1 California pb $10.95

• A. Grove Day
THE SKY CLEARS: Poetry of the American Indians
An older anthology, sometimes dated but full of interesting materials
0–8032–5047–9 Nebraska pb $3.95

• Jaime De Angulo
INDIAN TALES
A classic collection of Indian folklore that won praise from Marianne Moore and William Carlos Williams
0–8090–0049–0 Farrar, Straus & Giroux pb $7.95

• D.M. Dowling, editor
THE SONS OF THE WIND: The Sacred Stories of the Lakota
0–930407–00–8 Kampmann pb $8.95

• Jamake Highwater
ANPAO: An American Indian Odyssey
0–06–090762–2 Harper & Row pb $8.95

NATIVE LAND: Sagas of the Indian Americas
0–316–36087–2 Little, Brown $24.95

• Karl Kroeber, editor
TRADITIONAL LITERATURES OF THE AMERICAN INDIAN: Texts and Interpretations
0–8032–7753–9 Nebraska pb $5.95

• Howard Norman, translator
WHERE THE CHILL CAME FROM: Cree Windigo Tales and Journeys
Thirty-one Cree Indian tales from Canada about the Windigo, a spirit being who has wandered Cree territory since ancient times. Howard Norman's translations, and the background material that accompanies them, are outstanding
0–86547–047–2 North Point $17.50
0–86547–048–0 North Point pb $9.00

• Paul Radin
THE TRICKSTER: A Study in American Indian Mythology
A psychological interpretation of an enduring figure in Native American mythology; contains much oral material
Commentaries by Karl Kerenyi & C.G. Jung
Introduction by Stanley Diamond
0–8052–0351–6 Random House pb $8.95

• Jarold Ramsey, editor
COYOTE WAS GOING THERE: Indian Literature of the Oregon Country
0–295–95731–X Washington pb $12.95

READING THE FIRE: Essays in the Traditional Indian Literatures of the Far West
0–8032–3864–9 Nebraska $21.95

• Jerome Rothenberg, editor
SHAKING THE PUMPKIN: Traditional Poetry of the Indian North Americas
Both a collection of American Indian poetry and a reflection of its influence on contemporary poets, as ethnological material is reworked by writers such as Rothenberg, Armand Schwerner, Anselm Hollo, W.S. Merwin, and others. "Jerome Rothenberg is an exception to the general misuse of Native America . . . an example of the kind of borrowing that is possible: one that allows the dignity of giver and taker to remain not only undisturbed, but celebrated, illuminated, made clear"—Paula Gunn Allen
0–912383–10–0 Van Der Marck pb $14.95

> *Magic Words (after Nalungiaq)*
> In the very earliest time,
> when both people and animals lived
>   on earth,
> a person could become an animal if he
>   wanted to
> and an animal could become a human
>   being.
> Sometimes they were people
> and sometimes animals
> and there was no difference.
> All spoke the same language.
> That was the time when words were
>   like magic.
> The human mind had mysterious
>   powers.
> A word spoken by chance
> might have strange consequences.
> It would suddenly come alive
> and what people wanted to happen
>   would happen—
> all you had to do was say it.
> Nobody could explain this:
> That's the way it was.
>
> English version by Edward Field, from
> Knud Rasmussen
>
> Jerome Rothenberg, editor
> **SHAKING THE PUMPKIN**
> 0–912383–10–0 Van Der Marck pb $14.95

• Gary Snyder
HE WHO HUNTED BIRDS IN HIS FATHER'S VILLAGE: The Dimensions of a Haida Myth
An early dissertation by Snyder, in which many elements of his later thought are already present
Preface by Nathaniel Tarn
0–912516–38–0 Grey Fox pb $5.95

• Brian Swann, editor
SMOOTHING THE GROUND: Essays on the Native American Oral Literature
0–520–04902–0 California $37.50
0–520–04913–6 California pb $11.95

• Dennis Tedlock, translator
FINDING THE CENTER: Narrative Poetry of the Zuni Indians
Tedlock brilliantly captures the effect of traditional oral recitation through a range of poetic and typographic devices
0–8032–4401–0 Nebraska $25.95
0–8032–9400–X Nebraska pb $7.95

• Frederick W. Turner 3rd, editor
THE PORTABLE NORTH AMERICAN INDIAN READER
0–14–015077–3 Penguin pb $8.95

• W.C. Vanderwerth, editor
INDIAN ORATORY: A Collection of Famous Speeches by Noted Indian Chieftains
A comprehensive anthology ranging from the 18th to the 20th century
Foreword by William R. Carmack
0–8061–1575–0 Oklahoma pb $10.95

• Alan R. Velie
AMERICAN INDIAN LITERATURE: An Anthology
Includes tales, songs, memoirs, oratory, poetry, and fiction by traditional and contemporary authors
0–8061–1523–8 Oklahoma pb $11.95

• Gerald Vizenor
EARTHDIVERS: Tribal Narratives on Mixed Descent
0–8166–1048–7 Minnesota pb $14.95

THE PEOPLE NAMED THE CHIPPEWA: Narrative Histories
0–8166–1306–0 Minnesota pb $12.95

• Gerald Vizenor, editor
NARRATIVE CHANCE: Postmodern Discourse on Native American Literatures
0–8263–1117–2 New Mexico $29.95

TOUCHWOOD: A Collection of Ojibway Prose
0–89823–091–8 New Rivers pb $9.95

• Paul G. Zolbrod
DINE BAHANE: The Navajo Creation Story
"A brilliant rendering of a folk epic into a fascinating and highly literate work of art"—*NY Times*
0–8263–0833–3 New Mexico pb $14.95

Mexico, Central and South America

• John Bierhorst
BLACK RAINBOW: Legends of the Incas and Myths of Ancient Peru
0–374–30829–2 Farrar, Straus & Giroux pb $9.95

CANTARES MEXICANOS: Songs of the Aztecs
The principal source of Aztec poetry in a complete English-Nahuatl edition
0–8047–1182–8 Stanford $55.00

• Marc de Civrieux
WATUNNA: An Orinoco Creation Cycle
One of the most complete mythic records available from a South American indigenous group, in this case the Yekuana Indians of Venezuela. Guss's translation maintains a high level of intensity
Translated and edited by David Guss
0–86547–003–0 North Point pb $12.50

Mayan emblem glyphs from Classic monuments, from The Maya *by Michael Coe (Thames & Hudson)*

There was Kahuna, the Sky Place. The Kahuhana lived there, just like now. They're good, wise people. And they were in the beginning too. They never died. There was no sickness, no evil, no war. The whole world was Sky. No one worked. No one looked for food. Food was always there, ready.

There were no animals, no demons, no clouds, no winds. There was just light. In the highest sky was Wanadi, just like now. He gave his light to the people, to the Kahuhana. He lit everything down to the very bottom, down to None, the Earth. Because of that light, the people were always happy. They had life. They couldn't die. There was no separation between Sky and Earth. Sky had no door like it does now. There was no night, like now. Wanadi is like a sun that never sets. It was always day. The Earth was like a part of the sky.

Marc de Civrieux
WATUNNA: An Onnoco Creation Cycle
Translated & edited by David Guss
0–86547–003–0 North Point pb $12.50

• Alvaro Estrada
MARIA SABINA: Her Life and Chants
Biography and shamanic chants of the famous Mazatec wise woman
0–915520–32–X Hippocrene pb $8.95

• Larry Evers & Felipe S. Molina
YAQUI DEER SONGS/MASO BWIKAM
Lore of the Yaqui Deer Dance
0–8165–0991–3 Arizona $29.95
0–8165–0995–6 Arizona pb $15.95

• Miguel Léon-Portilla
PRE-COLUMBIAN LITERATURES OF MEXICO
Early colonial Aztec and Maya song texts, myths, orations, and chronicles, examined for literary values
0–8061–1974–8 Oklahoma pb $7.95

• Christopher Sawyer-Lauçanno
THE DESTRUCTION OF THE JAGUAR: Poems from the Books of the Chilam Balam
Poetic adaptations from the ancient Mayan sacred text
0–87286–210–0 City Lights pb $6.95

Dennis Tedlock, translator
POPOL VUH: The Definitive Edition of the Mayan Book of the Dawn of Life and the Glories of Gods and Kings
Newest translation of the Quiche Maya classic; combines anthropological and literary values
0–671–45241–X Simon & Schuster $19.95
0–671–61771–0 Simon & Schuster pb $10.95

AUTOBIOGRAPHICAL ACCOUNTS

• Charles A. Eastman
FROM THE DEEP WOODS TO CIVILIZATION: Chapters in the Autobiography of an Indian
One of the best-known Indians of his time, Eastman witnessed the Wounded Knee massacre and devoted his life to helping Indians come to terms with the white world
0–8032–5873–9 Nebraska pb $7.95

THE SOUL OF THE INDIAN: An Interpretation
In this 1911 book Eastman set out "to paint the religious life of the typical American Indian as it was before he knew the white man"
0–8032–6701–0 Nebraska pb $5.95

• Charles Hamilton, editor
CRY OF THE THUNDERBIRD: The American Indian's Own Story
The voices gathered here include those of Black Elk, Tecumseh, Sitting Bull, and Geronimo. With paintings by George Catlin and sketches by American Indian artists
0–8061–1292–1 Oklahoma pb $9.95

• Adolf & Beverly Hungry Wolf
SHADOWS OF THE BUFFALO: A Family Odyssey among the Indians
0–688–05937–6 Morrow pb $6.95

• Arnold Krupat
FOR THOSE WHO COME AFTER: A Study of Native American Autobiography
0–520–05307–9 California $25.00

• T.C. McLuhan
TOUCH THE EARTH: A Self Portrait of Indian Existence
0–671–22275–9 Simon & Schuster pb $9.95

• Rosalio Moises & others
A YAQUI LIFE: The Personal Chronicle of a Yaqui Indian
"The nightmare world of witchcraft and dream-dependence is one of the major fascinations of this strange and moving book"—*Southern California Quarterly*
0–8032–0944–4 Nebraska $23.95
0–8032–5857–7 Nebraska pb $5.95

• N. Scott Momaday
THE NAMES: A Memoir
0–8165–1046–6 Arizona pb $9.95

• Polingaysi Qoyawayma (Elizabeth Q. White)
NO TURNING BACK: A Hopi Indian Woman's Struggle to Live in Two Worlds
A Hopi woman and her career as an educator
As told to Vada F. Carlson
0–8263–0439–7 New Mexico pb $8.95

• Paul Radin, editor
CRASHING THUNDER: The Autobiography of an American Indian
After many years of living among the Winnebago, Radin was able to elicit this autobiographical narrative
0–8032–3867–3 Nebraska $21.00
0–8032–8910–3 Nebraska pb $6.95

• Nancy O. Lurie, editor
MOUNTAIN WOLF WOMAN, SISTER OF CRASHING THUNDER: The Autobiography of a Winnebago Indian
Foreword by Ruth Underhill
0–472–06109–7 Michigan pb $7.95

• Luther Standing Bear
LAND OF THE SPOTTED EAGLE
Growing up among the Teton Sioux
0–8032–5890–9 Nebraska pb $6.95

MY PEOPLE THE SIOUX
"The account he gives us of his people . . . is one of the most engaging and veracious we have ever had"—*Van Wyck Brooks*
0–8032–0874–X Nebraska $23.95
0–8032–5793–7 Nebraska pb $6.95

• Brian Swann & Arnold Krupat, editors
I TELL YOU NOW: Autobiographical Essays by Native American Writers
0–8032–2714–0 Nebraska $21.00

Canadian Literature

• Margaret Atwood
BLUEBEARD'S EGG & OTHER STORIES
"These tales expand in the mind until they become novels. The characters . . . take on lives of their own; they take over yours"— Susan Schaeffer
0–395–40424–X Houghton Mifflin $16.95
0–449–21417–6 Fawcett pb $4.95

CAT'S EYE
In Atwood's most recent novel, a successful artist relives painful episodes from her Toronto childhood
0–385–26007–5 Doubleday $18.95

THE CIRCLE GAME
0–88784–070–1 Toronto pb $4.95

DANCING GIRLS & OTHER STORIES
Fourteen stories
0–553–34115–4 Bantam pb $6.95

THE HANDMAID'S TALE
Atwood's most widely read book to date depicts a future society founded on the oppression of women
0–395–40425–8 Houghton Mifflin $16.95
0–449–21260–2 Fawcett pb $4.95

JOURNALS OF SUSANNA MOODIE: Poems
0–19–540169–7 Oxford pb $6.95

LADY ORACLE
A writer fakes her own death to escape the success of a bestseller
0–449–21376–5 Fawcett pb $4.95

LIFE BEFORE MAN
Both parties to a slowly decaying marriage take lovers
0–449–21377–3 Holt, Rinehart & Winston pb $4.95

POWER POLITICS
0–88784–020–5 Toronto pb $4.95

SECOND WORDS: Selected Critical Prose
0–8070–6359–2 Beacon pb $9.95

SELECTED POEMS, 1965–1975
0–395–40422–3 Houghton Mifflin pb $9.95

SELECTED POEMS II: Poems Selected and New, 1976–1986
0–395–40423–1 Houghton Mifflin $16.95
0–395–45406–9 Houghton Mifflin pb $9.95

SURFACING
A woman's weekend excursion in quest of her father is enlivened by the complexities of a foursome
0–449–21375–7 Fawcett pb $4.50

• Robertson Davies
HIGH SPIRITS
Eighteen ghost stories, committed to paper exactly as originally told out loud
0–14–006505–9 Penguin pb $5.95

THE LYRE OF ORPHEUS
0–670–82416–X Viking $19.95

Robertson Davies (photo by Jerry Bauer, courtesy of Viking)

THE MIRROR OF NATURE
0–8020–6536–8 Toronto pb $6.95

ONE HALF OF ROBERTSON DAVIES
Stories, essays, lectures, and more, on writing and writers
0–14–004967–3 Penguin pb $5.95

THE PAPERS OF SAMUEL MARCHBANKS
0–670–81145–9 Viking $22.50

THE REBEL ANGELS
0–670–59063–0 Viking $13.95
0–14–006271–8 Penguin pb $4.95

THE SALTERTON TRILOGY
Includes *Tempest Tost, Leaven of Malice,* and *A Mixture of Frailties*
0–14–008446–0 Penguin pb $9.95

WHAT'S BRED IN THE BONE
Portrait of an art expert with a stash of secrets. "Literary sleuthwork at its most inspired"—*Newsweek*
0–14–009711–2 Penguin pb $6.95

THE DEPTFORD TRILOGY
The same tale is told from three separate vantage points. This compendium volume is made up of the three titles listed below
0–14–006500–8 Penguin pb $10.95

FIFTH BUSINESS
A rational man discovers that wonders are simply an aspect of reality
0–14–004387–X Penguin pb $4.95

THE MANTICORE
The manticore has the head of a man, the body of a lion, and the tail of a scorpion
0–14–004388–8 Penguin pb $4.95

WORLD OF WONDERS
The tale of a master magician. "Among contemporary novelists only Graham Greene has trod this ground and gleaned it so successfully"—*New Republic*
0–14–004389–6 Penguin pb $4.95

• Christopher Dewdney
THE IMMACULATE PERCEPTION
Dewdney is sometimes associated with the American "Language" poets
0–88784–151–1 Toronto pb $9.95

• Timothy Findley
DINNER ALONG THE AMAZON
Twelve short stories
0–14–007304–3 Penguin pb $6.95

NOT WANTED ON THE VOYAGE
This revised version of the Great Flood has been called a mixture of "*Tobacco Road, Monty Python, Mutiny on the Bounty* and *Charlotte's Web*"—*NY Times*
0–440–36499–X Dell pb $4.95

THE TELLING OF LIES
A staid hotel is turned into a condominium complex. A magnate is found dead. Who killed him becomes less crucial than why
0–440–55001–7 Dell pb $7.95

- Mavis Gallant
HOME TRUTHS
Sixteen stories about Canadians—children, lovers, exiles—at home and abroad
0–394–53198–1 Random House $17.95
0–440–33659–7 Dell pb $4.50

OVERHEAD IN A BALLOON: Twelve Stories of Paris
0–394–54511–7 Random House $16.95
0–393–30546–5 Norton pb $7.95

PARIS NOTEBOOKS: Essays and Reviews
0–394–56201–1 Random House $17.95

THE PEGNITZ JUNCTION
Europeans trying to piece their lives back together in the aftermath of the war
0–915308–60–6 Graywolf $6.00

- Daryl Hine
DAYLIGHT SAVING
0–689–10880–X Atheneum pb $6.95

MINUTES
0–689–10120–1 Atheneum pb $2.50

RESIDENT ALIEN
0–689–10651–3 Atheneum pb $6.95

SELECTED POEMS
0–689–11117–7 Atheneum $11.95
0–689–11118–5 Atheneum pb $6.95

- Ann Ireland
A CERTAIN MR. TAKAHASHI
0–8149–0918–3 Vanguard $14.95

- Joy Kogawa
OBASAN
0–87923–429–6 Godine $14.95
0–87923–491–1 Godine pb $9.95

- Margaret Laurence
THE DIVINERS
0–7704–2176–8 Bantam pb $4.95

THE STONE ANGEL
A disturbing study of senility set against the breadth of the Canadian prairie
0–7704–2177–6 Bantam pb $4.50

- Irving Layton
The Romanian-born Layton is one of Canada's most prolific and intellectually adventurous poets.
THE GUCCI BAG
0–88962–245–0 Riverrun pb $7.95

LOVE POEMS OF IRVING LAYTON
0–3176–0709–X Riverrun pb $7.95

THE SELECTED POEMS OF IRVING LAYTON
Introduction by Hugh Kenner
0–8112–0641–6 New Directions $8.50
0–8112–0642–4 New Directions pb $2.25

- Steve MacAffery
NORTH OF INTENTION
Contemporary literary essays by a leading Canadian experimental poet
0–937804–23–1 Segue pb $12.95

- W.O. Mitchell
SINCE DAISY CREEK
A later work by a writer greatly influenced by the world of the prairie
0–8253–0303–6 Beaufort $16.95

- L.M. Montgomery
ANNE OF GREEN GABLES
0–451–52112–9 NAL pb $2.50

- Susanna Moodie
ROUGHING IT IN THE BUSH
An autobiographical work, published in 1852, which describes the life of early pioneers in the Canadian hinterland
Introduction by Margaret Atwood
0–8070–7023–8 Beacon pb $10.95

- Brian Moore
BLACK ROBE
0–449–20947–4 Fawcett pb $3.50

CATHOLICS
Set on an Irish island, this tells the tale of a liberal papal envoy and a tradition-bound abbot. "Probably the best book of a writer whom I very much admire"—Graham Greene
0–525–48206–7 Dutton pb $6.95

COLD HEAVEN
0–449–20602–5 Fawcett pb $2.95

THE COLOR OF BLOOD
A "moral thriller" in which a senior cleric keeps a fragile peace between a totalitarian regime and the fundamentalist wing of his church
0–525–24539–1 Dutton $16.95

THE GREAT VICTORIAN COLLECTION
0–525–48178–8 Dutton pb $7.95

I AM MARY DUNNE
0–525–48179–6 Dutton pb $7.95

THE LONELY PASSION OF JUDITH HEARNE
The Irish-Canadian's first novel. "A penetrating, comic, tragic tale of a plain woman . . . It is a novel that occasionally sings with the lilt of the Irish greats"—San Francisco Chronicle
0–316–57966–1 Little, Brown pb $6.95

THE TEMPTATION OF EILEEN HUGHES
0–374–27285–9 Farrar, Straus & Giroux $11.95

- Raul Morin
AMONG THE VALIANT
0–87505–116–2 Borden $7.95

- Alice Munro
A gifted short story writer and novelist who tends to focus her realistic, minutely rendered tales on the lives of women in small rural towns.
THE BEGGAR MAID
With her ten "stories of Flo and Rose" she "manages to reproduce the vibrant practice of life while scrutinizing the workings of her own narrative art"—NY Times
0–14–006011–1 Penguin pb $6.95

DANCE OF THE HAPPY SHADES & OTHER STORIES
0–14–006681–0 Penguin pb $6.95

LIVES OF GIRLS AND WOMEN
0–452–25975–4 NAL pb $7.95
0–451–14733–2 NAL pb $3.95

THE MOONS OF JUPITER
Eleven stories on love, aging, and relationships
0–394–52952–9 Knopf $13.95
0–14–006547–4 Penguin pb $6.95

THE PROGRESS OF LOVE
0–394–55272–5 Knopf $16.95
0–14–009879–8 Penguin pb $6.95

SOMETHING I'VE BEEN MEANING TO TELL YOU
Thirteen stories
0–452–26021–3 NAL pb $7.95

- B.P. Nichol
TRANSPLATING TRANSLATING APOLLINAIRE
0–87924–031–8 Membrane pb $6.00

- Michael Ondaatje
THE COLLECTED WORKS OF BILLY THE KID
A composite of eyewitness accounts, tall tales, facts, and photographic documents vividly construct the world of Billy the Kid
0–14–007280–2 Penguin pb $6.95

COMING THROUGH SLAUGHTER
0–393–08765–4 Norton $9.95
0–14–007281–0 Penguin pb $6.95

IN THE SKIN OF A LION
A country lad plunges into the world of immigrant workers in Toronto
0–394–56363–8 Knopf $16.95

RUNNING IN THE FAMILY
A fictional memoir of Ondaatje's family's "carefree but doomed" life in Sri Lanka
0–393–01637–4 Norton $12.95
0–14–006966–6 Penguin pb $6.95

SECULAR LOVE
0–393–01991–8 Norton $14.95
0–393–30247–4 Norton pb $6.95

THERE'S A TRICK WITH A KNIFE I'M LEARNING TO DO: Poems 1962–1978
0–393–01191–7 Norton $12.95

- Mordecai Richler
A popular Montreal Jewish writer notable for his ability to elicit sympathy for unsympathetic characters.
HOME SWEET HOME: My Canadian Album
0–394–53756–4 Knopf $16.95

JOSHUA THEN AND NOW
0–394–49351–6 Knopf $11.95
0–7704–2035–4 Bantam pb $4.95

- Sinclair Ross
AS FOR ME AND MY HOUSE
This classic prairie novel about an artist turned priest gives a stark picture of rural desolation
Introduction by David Stouck
0–8032–8900–6 Nebraska pb $6.95

- Peter Dale Scott
COMING TO JAKARTA: A Poem About Terror
A long poem based on the 1965 massacre in Indonesia
0–8112–1095–2 New Directions pb $7.95

- Sarah Sheard
ALMOST JAPANESE
0–684–18805–8 Scribners $14.95
0–684–18806–6 Scribners pb $6.95

- Elizabeth Spencer
JACK OF DIAMONDS & OTHER STORIES
0–670–82261–2 Viking $15.95

THE LIGHT IN THE PIAZZA
0–14–008712–5 Penguin pb $6.95

MARILEE
0–87805–141–4 Mississippi pb $3.95

THE SALT LINE
0–14–007665–4 Penguin pb $6.95

STORIES OF ELIZABETH SPENCER
Foreword by Eudora Welty
0–14–006436–2 Penguin pb $7.95

QUEBECOIS (FRENCH-CANADIAN) LITERATURE

Quebec's literary production since the 1960s has the vitality and daring of a revolutionary literature. Rooted in the North American continent, it also has powerful ties to France, resulting in unique tensions and a unique literary situation. This distinctive minority literature is notable for its political humor and satire and its lively linguistic play on the mixture of French, English, and Joual (the Quebec language).

- **Hubert Aquin**
THE ANTIPHONARY
Translated by Alan Brown
0–88784–426–X Toronto pb $9.95

- **Yves Beauchemin**
THE ALLEY CAT
Translated by Sheila Fischman
0–8050–0795–4 Henry Holt pb $8.95

- **Marie-Claire Blais**
THE DAY IS DARK & THREE TRAVELERS
0–14–007911–4 Penguin pb $6.95

DEAF TO THE CITY
0–87951–276–8 Overlook $16.95

A SEASON IN THE LIFE OF EMMANUEL
A grim saga of nastiness graduating to cruelty among the 16 offspring of a French-Canadian farming family, both at home and out in the world
Translated by Derek Coltman
Introduction by Edmund Wilson
0–374–51616–2 Farrar, Straus & Giroux pb $5.95

ST. LAWRENCE BLUES
Translated by Ralph Mannheim
0–374–25350–1 Farrar, Straus & Giroux pb $7.95

- **Louis Caron**
THE DRAFT DODGER
Translated by David Toby
0–88784–085 Toronto pb $9.95

- **Roche Carrier**
FLORALIE, WHERE ARE YOU?
Translated by Sheila Fischman
0–88784–317–4 Toronto pb $6.95

THE GARDEN OF DELIGHTS
Translated by Sheila Fischman
0–88784–066–3 Toronto pb $8.95

HEARTBREAKS ALONG THE ROAD
Translated by Sheila Fischman
0–88784–146–2 Toronto pb $19.95

THE HOCKEY SWEATER & OTHER STORIES
Translated by Sheila Fischman
0–88784–310–7 Toronto pb $7.95

IS THIS THE SUN, PHILIBERT?
Translated by Sheila Fischman
0–88784–321–2 Toronto pb $6.95

LADY WITH CHAINS
Translated by Sheila Fischman
0–88784–139–2 Toronto pb $9.95

LA GUERRE, YES SIR!
Translated by Sheila Fischman
0–88784–310–7 Toronto pb $6.95

NO COUNTRY WITHOUT GRANDFATHERS
Translated by Sheila Fischman
0–88784–090–6 Toronto pb $8.95

THEY WON'T DEMOLISH ME!
Translated by Sheila Fischman
0–88784–328–X Toronto pb $7.95

- **Jacques Ferron**
SELECTED TALES
Translated by Betty Bednarski
0–88784–140–6 Toronto pb $9.95

- **Jacques Godbout**
AN AMERICAN STORY
Translated by Yves Saint-Pierre
0–8166–1709–0 Minnesota $19.95
0–8166–1710–4 Minnesota pb $8.95

Anne Hébert (photo by Ulf Anderson, copyright Editions du Seuil)

- **Anne Hébert**
SELECTED POEMS
The selection includes several previously uncollected and untranslated poems by Canada's most important French poet of the 20th century. "There is a persistent grandeur in Anne Hébert's writing that is startling . . . Both the tradition and iconoclasm in the work of this French poet of North America invite us to listen to something beyond our own conventions"—W.S. Merwin
Translated by A. Poulin, Jr.
0–918526–57–4 BOA pb $10.00

- **Gaston Miron**
THE MARCH TO LOVE: Selected Poems
Translated by Douglas Jones & others
0–8214–0877–1 Ohio $19.95
0–8214–0878–X Ohio pb $10.95

- **Jacques Poulin**
SPRING TIDES
Translated by Sheila Fischman
0–88784–149–X Toronto pb $9.95

THE JIMMY TRILOGY
Translated by Sheila Fischman
Introduction by Roche Carrier
0–88784–074–4 Toronto pb $8.95

ANTHOLOGIES

- **Margaret Atwood, editor**
THE NEW OXFORD BOOK OF CANADIAN VERSE IN ENGLISH
0–19–540396–7 Oxford $25.00

- **Margaret Atwood & Robert Weaver, editors**
THE OXFORD BOOK OF CANADIAN SHORT STORIES IN ENGLISH
0–19–540565–X Oxford $21.95
0–19–540597–8 Oxford pb $12.95

- **Matt Cohen & Wayne Grady, editors**
INTIMATE STRANGERS: New Stories from Quebec
0–14–0097958–0 Penguin pb $6.95

- **Richard Teleky & Marie-Claire Blais, editors**
THE OXFORD BOOK OF FRENCH-CANADIAN SHORT STORIES
0–19–540298–7 Oxford pb $12.95

CRITICAL STUDIES

- **André G. Bourassa**
SURREALISM AND QUEBEC LITERATURE: History of a Cultural Revolution
The winner of the Prix France-Canada on the role of Québecois poets and artists in the revolt against technology and instrumental reason
0–8020–6528–7 Toronto $20.00

- **J. Madison Davis, editor**
CONVERSATIONS WITH ROBERTSON DAVIES
0–87805–383–2 Mississippi $27.95
0–87805–384–0 Mississippi pb $14.95

- **Carl F. Klinck, editor**
LITERARY HISTORY OF CANADA: Canadian Literature in English

Volume 1: From the Beginning to 1920
0–8020–6276–8 Toronto pb $13.95

Volume 2: From 1920–1960
0–8020–6277–6 Toronto pb $13.95

Volume 3: From 1960 to 1974
0–8020–6278–4 Toronto pb $13.95

- **B.W. Powe**
A CLIMATE CHARGED: Essays on Canadian Writers
0–88962–258–2 Kampmann pb $9.95

- **George Woodcock**
THE WORLD OF CANADIAN WRITING: Critiques and Recollections
Insights into Canadian literary circles by a longtime member
0–295–95721–2 Washington $20.00

✉ TO ORDER BOOKS AS GIFTS, SEE PAGE 1

American Literature to 1900

THE EARLY COLONIAL PERIOD

• William Bradford
OF PLYMOUTH PLANTATION: 1620–1647
In his history of the Pilgrim settlement, Plymouth's governor aspired to "a plain style, with singular regard unto the simple truth in all things"
Edited by Samuel Eliot Morison
0–394–43895–7 Knopf $22.50

OF PLYMOUTH PLANTATION: 1620–1647
Edited by Francis Murphy
0–394–32602–4 Random House pb $9.50

• Anne Bradstreet
THE WORKS OF ANNE BRADSTREET
The first important American poet published her major collection, *The Tenth Muse Lately Sprung Up in America*, in 1650
Edited by Jeannie Hensley
Foreword by Adrienne Rich
0–674–95999–X Harvard pb $8.95

• Cotton Mather
MAGNALIA CHRISTI AMERICANA: Or the Ecclesiastical History of New England
Mather wrote of his theological chronicle, which touches on many aspects of early New England history: "I write the wonders of the Christian religion, flying from the depravations of Europe, to the American strand"
Edited by Kenneth B. Murdock
0–674–54155–3 Harvard $40.00

• John Smith
CAPTAIN JOHN SMITH: A Select Edition of His Writings
A rich collection of writings, arranged thematically, focusing on the founding of Jamestown and on Smith's relations with the Indians
Edited by Karen Ordahl Kupperman
0–8078–1778–3 Chapel Hill $32.50

• Edward Taylor
POETICAL WORKS OF EDWARD TAYLOR
Taylor's meditative writings are very much in the tradition of Metaphysical poets such as Herbert and Vaughan
Edited by Thomas H. Johnson
0–691–01275–X Princeton pb $12.50

Anthologies

• Alan Heimert & Andrew Delbanco, editors
THE PURITANS IN AMERICA: A Narrative Anthology
0–674–74065–3 Harvard $27.00
0–674–74066–1 Harvard pb $9.95

• Harrison T. Meserole, editor
AMERICAN POETRY OF THE SEVENTEENTH CENTURY
The works of Bradstreet, Taylor, Wigglesworth, and others, presented in a well-designed scholarly edition
0–271–00419–3 Penn State $29.75
0–271–00418–5 Penn State pb $16.95

• Perry Miller, editor
THE AMERICAN PURITANS: Their Prose and Poetry
Miller did more than anyone in this century to create new interest in America's Puritan inheritance
0–231–05419–X Columbia pb $15.00

• Perry Miller & Thomas H. Johnson, editors
THE PURITANS: A Sourcebook of Their Writings
The classic, comprehensive anthology
Volume 1
0–06–131093–X Harper & Row pb $9.95
Volume 2
0–06–131094–8 Harper & Row pb $8.95

THE EIGHTEENTH CENTURY

• William Bartram
TRAVELS
A naturalist in 18th-century Florida: one of the most extraordinary American prose works, a blend of the scientific, the fantastic, and the lyrical
Introduction by James Dickey
0–14–017008–1 Penguin pb $7.95

> The verges and islets of the lagoon were elegantly embellished with flowering plants and shrubs; the laughing coots with wings half spread were tripping over the little coves, and hiding themselves in the tufts of grass; young broods of the painted summer teal, skimming the still surface of the waters, and following the watchful parent unconscious of danger, were frequently surprised by the voracious trout; and he, in turn, as often by the subtle greedy alligator. Behold him rushing forth from the flags and reeds. His enormous body swells. His plaited tail brandished high, floats upon the lake. The waters like a cataract descend from his opening jaws. Clouds of smoke issue from his dilated nostrils. The earth trembles with his thunder.
>
> William Bartram
> **TRAVELS**
> 0–14–017008–1 Penguin pb $7.95

• Charles Brockden Brown
As an American novelist, Brown could not be more prototypical, with his blending of Gothic plots and indigenous landscapes, scientific rationalism and superstitious dread.
WIELAND
Hypnotism and religious obsession propel a tale of murder and suicide•in Pennsylvania
0–385–03100–9 Doubleday pb $5.95

WIELAND & MEMOIRS OF CARWIN
Edited by Sydney J. Kraus
0–87338–160–2 Kent State $35.00

EDGAR HUNTLY: Memoirs of a Sleep Walker
A typically circuitous narrative of trance and violence, set against a wilderness background
Edited by Norman Grabo
0–14–039062–6 Penguin pb $6.95

ORMOND, OR THE SECRET WITNESS
Sexual conflict incites murder and attempted rape
0–87338–277–3 Kent State $35.00

ARTHUR MERVYN, OR MEMOIRS OF THE YEAR 1793
A novel revolving around Philadelphia's yellow fever epidemic of 1793
0–87338–241–2 Kent State $35.00

• J. Hector St. John de Crevecoeur
LETTERS FROM AN AMERICAN FARMER & SKETCHES OF EIGHTEENTH-CENTURY AMERICA
"Franklin is the real *practical* prototype of the American. Crevecoeur is the emotional. To the European, the American is first and foremost a dollar-fiend. We tend to forget the emotional heritage of Hector St. John de Crevecoeur"—D.H. Lawrence
Edited by Albert E. Stone
0–14–039006–5 Penguin pb $5.95

• Jonathan Edwards
FREEDOM OF THE WILL
The major expression of Edwards' Calvinist doctrine, first published in 1754
Edited by Arnold S. Kaufman & William K. Frankena
0–8290–1264–8 Irvington pb $14.95

SELECTED WRITINGS OF JONATHAN EDWARDS
Edited by Harold P. Simonson
0–8044–6132–5 Ungar pb $7.95

• Benjamin Franklin
THE AUTOBIOGRAPHY OF BENJAMIN FRANKLIN
Edited by Kenneth Silverman
0–14–039052–9 Penguin pb $3.50

WRITINGS
This collection displays Franklin's talents and personality as never before, including generous samplings from his work as a journalist. Contains *Silence Dogood, Poor Richard's Almanac, Political Satires, Pamphlets, Letters and Bagatelles, Journalism,* and *The Autobiography*
Edited by J.A. Leo Lemay
0–940450–29–1 Library of America $30.00

• Thomas Jefferson
WRITINGS
A comprehensive gathering of Jefferson's remarkably varied writings, including *Autobiography, A Summary View of the Rights of British America, Public Papers, Miscellany,* and a large selection of letters. The letters in particular create a three-dimensional and often surprising portrait
Edited by Merrill D. Peterson
0–940450–16–X Library of America $30.00

• **Thomas Paine**
COMMON SENSE
Paine's call to revolution sold over 100,000 copies in a three-month period in 1776
0–14–039016–2 Penguin pb $2.95

THE RIGHTS OF MAN
A defense of the French Revolution against the attacks of Edmund Burke
0–14–039015–4 Penguin pb $2.95

THE THOMAS PAINE READER
Includes *Common Sense* and excerpts from *The Rights of Man, The American Crisis* and *The Age of Reason*
Edited by Michael Foot & Isaac Kramnick
0–14–044496–3 Penguin pb $7.95

• **Susanna Rowson**
CHARLOTTE TEMPLE
One of the most enduringly popular novels of early America, published in 1791. The author's declared intention was to "be of service to some who are so unfortunate as to have neither friends to advise or understanding to direct them through the various and unexpected evils that attend a young and unprotected woman in her first entrance into life"
Introduction by Cathy Davidson
0–19–504238–7 Oxford pb $7.95

• **John Woolman**
THE JOURNAL OF JOHN WOOLMAN
A spiritual classic of Quakerism
Introduction by Frederick B. Tolles
0–8065–0294–0 Lyle Stuart pb $7.95

THE NINETEENTH CENTURY: To the Civil War

• **William W. Brown**
CLOTEL; OR, THE PRESIDENT'S DAUGHTER
This story of a mulatto born to Jefferson's housekeeper was issued in the U.S. without references to the President as *Clotelle: A Tale of the Southern States* in 1864
Introduction by William Edward Farison
0–8216–0180–6 Lyle Stuart pb $7.95

• **James Fenimore Cooper**
"James Fenimore Cooper, once the most familiar of American writers, has by now become very nearly the strangest. He is an ancestor just remote enough to be impenetrable, the voice of an origin to which we no longer feel intimately linked. Only a generation separates him from Melville, but that generation marks a great divide: in our perspective Melville seems the first of the moderns, and Cooper the last of the ancients . . . The glades and rapids and rocky barricades of *The Last of the Mohicans* and *The Deerslayer* have served American literature as an internalized theme park, a terrain whose every cranny became absorbed into the collective unconscious."—Geoffrey O'Brien, *Village Voice*

THE LEATHERSTOCKING TALES
The Library of America edition presents Cooper's Natty Bumppo saga in order of original publication
Edited by Blake Nevius

Volume 1
The Pioneers, The Last of the Mohicans, The Prairie
0–940450–208 Library of America $27.50

Volume 2
The Pathfinder, The Deerslayer
0–940450–216 Library of America $27.50

THE DEERSLAYER
The earliest adventures of Natty Bumppo, in what was actually the last of the *Leatherstocking Tales* to be written
Introduction by Donald Pease
0–14–039061–8 Penguin pb $3.95

THE LAST OF THE MOHICANS
Upstate New York in the throes of the French and Indian War
Edited by Richard Slotkin
0–14–039024–3 Penguin pb $3.95

THE PATHFINDER
The third installment of *The Leatherstocking Tales* is devoted largely to maritime exploits on Lake Ontario
0–14–039071–5 Penguin pb $4.95

THE PIONEERS
Natty in discontented old age, a victim of progress in the rapidly developing frontier settlements
0–14–039007–3 Penguin pb $4.95

THE PRAIRIE
The last days of Natty, who is caught up in a conflict among the Sioux, the Pawnees, and a band of outlaw emigrants
Introduction by Blake Nevius
0–14–039026–X Penguin pb $3.95

THE BRAVO
A novel of political corruption in Renaissance Venice; one of the sharpest and most controlled of Cooper's works. "The manner in which the aristocrats themselves are corrupted by their fear of each other—the subtle inter-relation and inter-propagation among such vices as avarice, desire for power, and fear—offers a moral portrait worthy of Hawthorne"—Yvor Winters
0–8084–0065–7 New College $15.95
0–8084–0066–5 New College pb $9.95

THE OAK OPENINGS
Representative late Cooper, with the themes of wilderness becoming infused with religious allegory
Introductions by Don Byrd, John Morgan & Will Baker
0–938190–33–4 North Atlantic $40.00

The SUNY Cooper

The State University of New York's scholarly edition of Cooper is in the process of shedding new light on a voluminous and today largely unread body of work.

THE DEERSLAYER
Edited by Lance Schachterle
0–87395–790–3 SUNY pb $18.95

THE LAST OF THE MOHICANS
Edited by James A. Sappenfield & E.N. Feltskog
Introduction by James F. Beard
0–87395–470–X SUNY pb $18.95

THE PATHFINDER: Or the Inland Sea
Introduction by Richard D. Rust
0–87395–477–7 SUNY pb $18.95

THE PIONEERS
Edited by James F. Beard
0–87395–423–8 SUNY pb $18.95

THE PILOT
Edited by Kay S. House
0–87395–791–1 SUNY pb $18.95

LIONEL LINCOLN, OR THE LEAGUER OF BOSTON
0–87395–671–0 SUNY pb $16.95

WYANDOTTE
Edited by Thomas Philbrick & Marianne Philbrick
0–87395–469–6 SUNY pb $18.95

• **Richard Henry Dana, Jr.**
TWO YEARS BEFORE THE MAST
"It is the story of a man pitted in conflict against the sea, the vast, almost omnipotent element . . . He comes out victorious, but not till the sea has tortured his living, integral body, and made him pay something for his triumph in consciousness . . . Dana's small book is a very great book"—D.H. Lawrence, *Studies in Classic American Literature*
Edited by Thomas Philbrick
0–14–039008–1 Penguin pb $4.95

Emily Dickinson (photo courtesy Harvard University Press)

Emily Dickinson
THE COMPLETE POEMS OF EMILY DICKINSON
Edited by Thomas H. Johnson
0–316–18414–4 Little, Brown $25.00
0–316–18413–6 Little, Brown pb $11.95

FINAL HARVEST: Emily Dickinson's Poems
A selection from Johnson's edition of the complete poems
Edited by Thomas H. Johnson
0–316–18416–0 Little, Brown $17.95
0–316–18415–2 Little, Brown pb $7.95

☞ **TO ORDER NEW BOOKS NOT YET LISTED, ASK YOUR BOOKSELLER OR CALL 1-800-882-8770**

THE MANUSCRIPT BOOKS OF EMILY DICKINSON: A Facsimile Edition
Given the contentiousness which still surrounds the proper way to edit Dickinson's poetry, the serious student will want to look at her original manuscripts. A two-volume set
Edited by Ralph W. Franklin
0-674-54828-0 Harvard $125.00

SELECTED LETTERS
Dickinson's poetry has to some extent overshadowed the range, inventiveness, and intensity of her letters
Edited by Thomas H. Johnson
0-674-25070-2 Harvard pb $9.95

• Frederick Douglass
NARRATIVE OF THE LIFE OF FREDERICK DOUGLASS, AN AMERICAN SLAVE
First published in 1845, this became the most famous of all slave narratives
Edited by Houston A. Baker, Jr.
0-14-039012-X Penguin pb $3.95

FREDERICK DOUGLASS: The Narrative and Selected Writings
Introduction by Michael Meyer
0-394-32981-3 Modern Library pb $6.95

• Ralph Waldo Emerson
"There was a strange charm in Emerson's eyes, which I felt then and always, something like that I saw in Lincoln's, but shyer, but sweeter and less sad. His smile was the very sweetest I have ever beheld ... It was his great fortune to have been mostly misunderstood, and to have reached the dense intelligence of his fellow-men after a whole lifetime of perfectly simple and lucid appeal, and his countenance expressed the patience and forbearance of a wise man content to bide his time."—William Dean Howells
ESSAYS AND LECTURES
Includes *Nature, Essays: First Series, Essays: Second Series, Representative Men, English Traits, The Conduct of Life,* addresses, lectures, and uncollected prose
Edited by Joel Porte
0-940450-15-1 Library of America $27.50

THE PORTABLE EMERSON
Edited by Carl Bode and Malcolm Cowley
0-14-015094-3 Penguin pb $7.95

THE SELECTED WRITINGS OF RALPH WALDO EMERSON
Edited by Brooks Atkinson
0-394-60418-0 Modern Library $12.95

SELECTED ESSAYS
Edited by Larzer Ziff
0-14-039013-8 Penguin pb $3.95

EMERSON IN HIS JOURNALS
Edited by Joel Porte
0-674-24861-9 Harvard $29.50

• Margaret Fuller
ESSAYS IN AMERICAN LIFE AND LETTERS
Writings by one of the major figures of the Transcendentalist circle
0-8084-0416-4 New College pb $11.95

WOMAN IN THE NINETEENTH CENTURY
The first major work of American feminism, published in 1845
0-393-00615-8 Norton pb $7.95

• Nathaniel Hawthorne
"For spite of all the Indian-summer sunlight on the hither side of Hawthorne's soul, the other side—like the dark half of the physical sphere—is shrouded in a blackness, ten times black ... Whether there really lurks in him, perhaps unknown to himself, a touch of Puritanic gloom,—this, I cannot altogether tell. Certain it is, however, that this great power of blackness in him derives its force from its appeals to that Calvinistic sense of Innate Depravity and Original Sin, from whose visitations, in some shape or other, no deeply thinking mind is always and wholly free."—Herman Melville reviewing Hawthorne's *Mosses from an Old Manse* in 1850
TALES AND SKETCHES
The most complete collection of Hawthorne's short fiction ever assembled
Edited by Roy Harvey Pearce
0-940450-03-8 Library of America $27.50

NOVELS
Includes *Fanshawe, The Scarlet Letter, The House of the Seven Gables, The Blithedale Romance,* and *The Marble Faun*
Edited by Millicent Bell
0-940450-08-9 Library of America $27.50

THE BLITHEDALE ROMANCE
"*The Blithedale Romance,* long considered the least of his four mature romances, is yet the most actual, the most nervously alive, in its first-person voice and in its overwarm, perversely shunned heroine ... The novel in its smallest details conveys Hawthorne's instinctive tenet that matter and spirit are inevitably at war"—John Updike
Introduction by Annette Kolodny
0-14-039028-6 Penguin pb $4.95

THE HOUSE OF THE SEVEN GABLES
Edited by Milton R. Stern
0-14-039005-7 Penguin pb $2.95

THE MARBLE FAUN
The most neglected of Hawthorne's major novels is a dark allegory of art and innocence set in Rome
0-452-00903-0 NAL pb $3.95

THE SCARLET LETTER
"It is beautiful, admirable, extraordinary; it has in the highest degree that merit which I have spoken of as the mark of Hawthorne's best things—an indefinable purity and lightness of conception ... One can often return to it; it supports familiarity and has the inexhaustible charm and mystery of great works of art"—Henry James
Illustrated by Barry Moser
0-15-179568-1 HBJ $22.95

THE SCARLET LETTER
0-14-039019-7 Penguin pb $2.25

AMERICAN NOTEBOOKS
Edited by Claude M. Simpson
0-8142-0159-8 Ohio State $45.00

THE FRENCH AND ITALIAN NOTEBOOKS
Edited by Thomas Woodson
0-8142-0256-X Ohio State $45.00

• Washington Irving
HISTORY, TALES AND SKETCHES
Includes *Letters of Jonathan Oldstyle, Gent., Salmagundi, A History of New York,* and *The Sketch Book*
Edited by James W. Tuttleton
0-940450-14-3 Library of America $27.50

THE ADVENTURES OF CAPTAIN BONNEVILLE, U.S.A.: In the Rocky Mountains and the Far West
Edited by Edgeley W. Todd
0-8061-2015-0 Oklahoma pb $12.95

THE ALHAMBRA
An exploration of Moorish legend and history
Edited by Felix O. Darley
0-912882-48-4 Sleepy Hollow $23.95

ASTORIA: Or, Anecdotes of an Enterprise Beyond the Rocky Mountains
The story of John Jacob Astor and his fur-trading empire
Edited by Richard D. Rust
0-8032-7450-5 Nebraska pb $9.95

THE SKETCH BOOK OF GEOFFREY CRAYON, GENT.
The mythic power of "Rip Van Winkle" and "The Legend of Sleepy Hollow" transcend the genial context of this collection of stories and essays
0-14-039032-4 Penguin pb $5.95

A TOUR ON THE PRAIRIES
Irving's rather sedate encounter with the wilderness makes for an interesting study in American sensibility
Introduction by John F. McDermott
0-8061-1958-6 Oklahoma pb $5.95

• Henry Wadsworth Longfellow
EVANGELINE & SELECTED TALES AND POEMS
Edited by Horace Gregory
0-451-52003-3 NAL pb $3.95

SELECTED POEMS
Edited by Lawrence Buell
0-14-039064-2 Penguin pb $4.95

• Herman Melville
TYPEE, OMOO, MARDI
Edited by G. Thomas Tanselle
0-940450-00-3 Library of America $27.50

REDBURN, WHITE-JACKET, MOBY-DICK
Edited by G. Thomas Tanselle
0-940450-09-7 Library of America $27.50

PIERRE, ISRAEL POTTER, THE CONFIDENCE MAN, TALES, BILLY BUDD
Edited by Hayford Harrison
0-940450-24-0 Library of America $27.50

BILLY BUDD & OTHER STORIES
0-14-039053-7 Penguin pb $3.95

MOBY-DICK
"It is a book that is at once primitive, fatalistic, and merciless, like the very oldest books, and yet peculiarly personal, like so many 20th-century novels, in its significant emphasis on the subjective individual consciousness"—Alfred Kazin
Illustrated by Rockwell Kent
0-394-60804-6 Modern Library $14.95

Herman Melville (Houghton Library, Harvard University, courtesy The Library of America)

MOBY-DICK, OR THE WHALE
A beautifully hand-set and illustrated edition first published by Arion Press
Notes by James D. Hart
Designed by Andrew Hoyem
Illustrations by Barry Moser
0–520–04354–5 California $25.00
0–520–04548–3 California pb $9.95

MOBY DICK
Edited by Harold Beaver
0–14–043082–2 Penguin pb $3.95

PIERRE, OR THE AMBIGUITIES
Melville's follow-up to *Moby-Dick* led some critics to charge him with insanity, and some modern readers have been hardly more kind. *Pierre* is the darkest and most disjointed book imaginable, written in a vein of nightmarish splendor; in many ways it prophesies the course of American literature in the 20th century
0–451–51897–7 NAL pb $4.95

REDBURN
Edited by Harold Beaver
0–14–043105–5 Penguin pb $4.95

TYPEE
Melville's first book, based on his experiences among cannibals in the Marquesas, became a bestseller in 1846
Edited by George Woodcock
0–14–043070–9 Penguin pb $3.95

COLLECTED POEMS
Includes all of Melville's poetry except for the epic *Clarel*
Edited by Howard P. Vincent
0–87532–007–4 Hendricks House $12.50

THE ESSENTIAL MELVILLE
A selection of the poetry, including excerpts from *Clarel*. "Melville's poetry belongs to that second half of his life after he had rounded his Horn and was trying to beat north to a latitude where peace might, at last, be possible . . . Melville had touched bottom, and he was now seeking a belief by which life could be considered and his own life rebuilt; and his poetry, in one dimension, may be read as a record of that search"—Robert Penn Warren
Edited by Robert Penn Warren
0–88001–141–6 Ecco pb $5.00

CLAREL
Clarel, an immensely long poem about a young man's loss of faith while on a tour of the Holy Land, is not, to put it mildly, an easy read; but Melville's crankiest work also contains many hidden beauties and surprises
Edited by Walter E. Bezanson
0–87532–011–2 Hendricks House $16.00

The Northwestern Melville

The Northwestern Melville series, intended as the definitive scholarly edition, is still in progress under the editorship of Harrison Hayford and others.

THE CONFIDENCE MAN: His Masquerade
0–8101–0325–7 Northwestern $32.95
0–8101–0324–9 Northwestern pb $13.95

ISRAEL POTTER
0–8101–0552–7 Northwestern $36.95
0–8101–0553–5 Northwestern pb $12.95

MARDI
0–8101–0015–0 Northwestern $42.95
0–8101–0014–2 Northwestern pb $17.95

MOBY-DICK: OR, THE WHALE
0–8101–0269–2 Northwestern $21.95

OMOO
0–8101–0162–9 Northwestern $36.95
0–8101–0160–2 Northwestern pb $12.95

THE PIAZZA TALES & OTHER PROSE PIECES: 1839–1860
0–8101–0550–0 Northwestern $36.95
0–8101–0551–9 Northwestern pb $13.95

PIERRE
0–8101–0266–8 Northwestern $36.95
0–8101–0267–6 Northwestern pb $13.95

REDBURN
0–8101–0013–4 Northwestern $36.95
0–8101–0016–9 Northwestern pb $12.95

TYPEE
0–8101–0161–0 Northwestern $39.95
0–8101–0159–9 Northwestern pb $12.95

WHITE-JACKET
0–8101–0257–9 Northwestern $36.95
0–8101–0258–7 Northwestern pb $12.95

• Francis Parkman
FRANCE AND ENGLAND IN NORTH AMERICA
Whatever its value as history, Parkman's chronicle of the French and English struggle for North America is an authentic American epic in which landscape and climate play as great a role as human personality
Edited by David Levin

Volume 1
Includes *Pioneers of France in the New World, The Jesuits in North America, La Salle and the Discovery of the Great West,* and *The Old Regime in Canada*
0–940450–10–0 Library of America $30.00

Volume 2
Includes *Count Frontenac and New France Under Louis XIV, Montcalm and Wolfe,* and *A Half-Century of Conflict*
0–940450–11–9 Library of America $30.00

THE OREGON TRAIL
A vivid account of Parkman's journey to Wyoming, published in 1849
Edited by David Levin
0–14–039042–1 Penguin pb $4.95

• Edgar Allan Poe
"The evident and most prominent aim of Mr. Poe is originality, either of idea, or the combination of ideas. He appears to think it a crime to write unless he has something novel to write about, or some novel way of writing about an old thing. He rejects every word not having a tendency to develop the effect . . . And he evidently holds whatever tends to the furtherance of the effect, to be legitimate material."— Edgar Allan Poe reviewing his own work anonymously (1845)

POETRY AND TALES
Edited by Patrick F. Quinn
0–940450–18–6 Library of America $27.50

ESSAYS AND REVIEWS
This collection shows Poe as a tireless critic and journalist, deeply involved in trying to influence the direction of American literature
Edited by G.R. Thompson
0–940450–19–4 Library of America $27.50

COMPLETE STORIES AND POEMS OF EDGAR ALLAN POE
"All of Poe's fiction, and the poems as well, can be seen as one coherent piece— the work of one of the greatest ironists of world literature"—G.R. Thompson
0–385–07407–7 Doubleday $16.95

THE PORTABLE POE
An intelligently edited anthology presenting the many sides of Poe's work
Edited by Phillip V. Stern
0–14–015012–9 Penguin pb $7.95

THE UNKNOWN POE
Edited by Raymond Foye
0–87286–110–4 City Lights pb $5.95

THE NARRATIVE OF ARTHUR GORDON PYM OF NANTUCKET
Poe's only novel-length work moves from the realism of a purported sea-log to a dizzying vista of emptiness
Edited by Harold Beaver
0–14–043097–0 Penguin pb $4.95

THE SCIENCE FICTION OF EDGAR ALLAN POE
Edited by Harold Beaver
0–14–043106–3 Penguin pb $4.95

• Harriet Beecher Stowe
THREE NOVELS
Includes *Uncle Tom's Cabin, The Minister's Wooing,* and *Oldtown Folks*
Edited by Kathryn K. Sklar
0–940450–01–1 Library of America $27.50

PINK AND WHITE TYRANNY: A Society Novel
A little-known work showing another side of Stowe's talent
0–452–26177–5 NAL pb $7.95

UNCLE TOM'S CABIN: Or, Life Among the Lowly
Stowe's masterpiece has a scope rare in 19th-century American literature
Edited by Ann Douglas
0–14–039003–0 Penguin pb $3.95

➤ FOR OVERSEAS ORDERING INFORMATION, SEE PAGE 1

• **Henry David Thoreau**

"In reading Henry Thoreau's Journal, I am very sensible of the vigor of his constitution. That oaken strength which I noted whenever he walked or worked or surveyed wood lots, the same unhesitating hand with which a field-laborer accosts a piece of work which I should shun as a waste of strength, Henry shows in his literary task ... In reading him, I find the same thought, the same spirit that is in me, but he takes a step beyond, & illustrates by excellent images that which I should have conveyed in a sleepy generality. 'Tis as if I went into a gymnasium, & saw youths leap, climb, & swing with a force unapproachable—though their feats are only continuations of my initial grapplings & jumps."—Ralph Waldo Emerson in his journal, June 1863

A WEEK ON THE CONCORD AND MERRIMACK RIVERS, WALDEN, THE MAINE WOODS, CAPE COD
Edited by Robert F. Sayre
0–940450–27–5 Library of America $27.50

CAPE COD
Introduction by Paul Theroux
0–14–017002–2 Penguin pb $6.95

THE ILLUSTRATED A WEEK ON THE CONCORD AND MERRIMACK RIVERS
Edited by Carl F. Hode & others
0–691–06573–X Princeton $32.50
0–691–01430–2 Princeton pb $10.50

THE MAINE WOODS
"*The Maine Woods* is very much a book of the body and its limitations, a book that stays close to the ground with an ample stock of mud and rock and rainwater. In this context Thoreau is more aware of his dependence than his liberty"—*NY Review of Books*
Introduction by Richard H. Fleck
0–06–091404–1 Harper & Row pb $8.95

WALDEN & OTHER WRITINGS
Edited with an introduction by Brooks Atkinson
0–394–60421–0 Modern Library $8.95

WALDEN & CIVIL DISOBEDIENCE
Introduction by Michael Meyer
0–14–039044–8 Penguin pb $2.95

• **Susan Bogert Warner**
THE WIDE, WIDE WORLD
A popular novel of an orphan's moral education, first published in 1850
0–935312–66–8 Feminist pb $11.95

• **Walt Whitman**
"I am not blind to the worth of the wonderful gift of *Leaves of Grass*. I find it the most extraordinary piece of wit & wisdom that America has yet contributed. I am very happy in reading it, as great power makes us happy ... I give you joy of your free & brave thought. I have great joy in it. I find incomparable things said incomparably well, as they must be. I find the courage of treatment, which so delights us, & which large perception only can inspire. I greet you at the beginning of a great career, which yet must have had a long foreground somewhere, for such a start."—Ralph Waldo Emerson in a letter to Walt Whitman, July 21, 1855

Walt Whitman (photo courtesy The National Archives)

COMPLETE POETRY & SELECTED PROSE
Edited by Justin Kaplan
0–940450–02–X Library of America $27.50

THE COMPLETE POEMS
Edited by Francis Murphy
0–14–042222–6 Penguin pb $8.95

LEAVES OF GRASS
The first edition, leaner and in many ways quite different from subsequent revisions. "In the first edition everything belongs together and everything helps to exhibit Whitman at his best, Whitman at his freshest in vision and boldest in language, Whitman transformed by a new experience, so that he wanders among familiar objects and finds that each of them has become a miracle"—Malcolm Cowley
Edited by Malcolm Cowley
0–14–042199–8 Penguin pb $2.95

THE ESSENTIAL WHITMAN
Edited by Galway Kinnell
0–88001–137–8 Ecco pb $6.00

• **Harriet E. Wilson**
OUR NIG: Sketches from the Life of a Free Black
A lost 1855 novel rediscovered. What begins very much in the romantic style of the time leaps into an autobiographical recollection of a free black woman's servitude to an indifferent white family in Massachusetts
Edited by Henry L. Gates
0–394–71558–6 Random House pb $8.95

THE SCHOMBURG LIBRARY OF 19TH-CENTURY BLACK WOMEN WRITERS

"The voices of these black women provide a stunning new collective portrait of the Afro-American rise from slavery to freedom ... [The] project will dramatically change the landscape of Afro-American literature and American cultural history."—Eric J. Sundquist, *NY Times*

• **Henry Louis Gates, Jr., general editor**
THE SCHOMBURG LIBRARY OF 19TH-CENTURY BLACK AMERICAN WRITERS
0–19–505267–6 Oxford (30-volume set) $595.00

• **Octavia V. Albert**
THE HOUSE OF BONDAGE OR CHARLOTTE BROOKS AND OTHER SLAVES
Introduction by Frances Foster
0–19–505263–3 Oxford $17.95

• **Hallie Q. Brown**
HOMESPUN HEROINES AND OTHER WOMEN OF DISTINCTION
Introduction by Randall Burkett
0–19–505237–4 Oxford $19.95

• **Anna Julia Cooper**
A VOICE FROM THE SOUTH
Introduction by Mary H. Washington
0–19–505246–3 Oxford $19.95

• **Alice Dunbar-Nelson**
THE WORKS OF ALICE DUNBAR-NELSON
Edited by Gloria T. Hull

Volume 1
0–19–505250–1 Oxford $22.50
Volume 2
0–19–505251–X Oxford $22.50
Volume 3
0–19–505252–8 Oxford $22.50

• **Charlotte Forten Grimké**
THE JOURNALS OF CHARLOTTE FORTEN GRIMKE
Edited by Brenda Stevenson
0–19–505238–2 Oxford $29.95

• **Frances E.W. Harper**
COMPLETE POEMS OF FRANCES E. W. HARPER
Introduction by Maryemma Graham
0–19–505244–7 Oxford $24.95

IOLA LEROY, OR SHADOWS UPLIFTED
Introduction by Frances Foster
0–19–505240–4 Oxford $19.95

• **Pauline E. Hopkins**
CONTENDING FORCES: A Romance Illustrative of Negro Life in the North and South
Introduction by Richard Yarborough
0–19–505258–7 Oxford $22.50

THE MAGAZINE NOVELS OF PAULINE HOPKINS
Includes *Hagar's Daughter* and *Of One Blood*
Introduction by Hazel V. Carby
0–19–505248–X Oxford $29.95

• **Sue Houchins, editor**
SPIRITUAL NARRATIVES
Includes writing by Jarena Lee, Zilipha Elaw, Virginia Broughton, Sara Mix, Julia Foote, Maria Stewart, and Rebecca Stewart
0–19–505266–8 Oxford $22.50

• **Harriet Jacobs**
INCIDENTS IN THE LIFE OF A SLAVE GIRL
Introduction by Valerie Smith
0–19–505243–9 Oxford $19.95

• Amelia A.E. Johnson
CLARENCE AND CORRINE: Or God's Way
Introduction by Hortense Spillers
0–19–505264–1 Oxford $18.95

THE HAZELEY FAMILY
Introduction by Barbara Christian
0–19–505257–9 Oxford $17.95

• Emma Dunham Kelley
MEGDA
Introduction by Molly Hite
0–19–505245–5 Oxford $22.50

• Emma Dunham Kelley-Hawkins
FOUR GIRLS AT COTTAGE CITY
Introduction by Deborah McDowell
0–19–505242–0 Oxford $24.95

• C.W. Larison
SILVIA DUBOIS: A Biografy of the Slav Who Whipt Her Mistres and Gand Her Fredom
Introduction by Jared C. Lobdell
0–19–505239–0 Oxford $19.95

• N.F. Mossell
THE WORK OF THE AFRO-AMERICAN WOMAN
Introduction by Joanne Braxton
0–19–505265–X Oxford $17.95

• Louisa Picquet & others
COLLECTED BLACK WOMEN'S NARRATIVES
Includes works by Louisa Picquet, Nancy Prince, Bethany Vaney, and Susie K. Taylor
Introduction by Anthony Bartholome
0–19–505260–9 Oxford $19.95

• Ann Plato
ESSAYS
Introduction by Kenny J. Williams
0–19–505247–1 Oxford $16.95

• Mary Prince & others
SIX WOMEN'S SLAVE NARRATIVES, 1831–1909
Includes writings by Mary Prince, Mattie Jackson, Elizabeth Delaney, Lucy Delaney, and Kate Drumgoold
Introduction by William Andrews
0–19–505262–5 Oxford $22.50

• Mary Seacole
WONDERFUL ADVENTURES OF MRS. SEACOLE IN MANY LANDS
Edited by William Andrews
0–19–505249–8 Oxford $16.95

• Joan Rita Sherman, editor
COLLECTED BLACK WOMEN'S POETRY
A four-volume set

Volume 1
0–19–505253–6 Oxford $24.95

Volume 2
0–19–505254–4 Oxford $24.95

Volume 3
0–19–505255–2 Oxford $22.50

Volume 4
0–19–505256–0 Oxford $22.50

• Amanda Berry Smith
AN AUTOBIOGRAPHY: The Story of the Lord's Dealings with Mrs. Amanda Smith the Colored Evangelist
Introduction by Jualynne Dodson
0–19–505261–7 Oxford $22.50

• Phillis Wheatley
COLLECTED WORKS OF PHILLIS WHEATLEY
Edited by John Shields
0–19–505241–2 Oxford $22.50

AMERICAN WOMEN WRITERS

This Rutgers University Press series is dedicated to bringing back into print "the most significant, influential, and popular American women writers from the 1820s to the 1920s." Joyce Carol Oates has described the series as "an ambitious, exciting, and highly valuable contribution to the reclamation of American women's lost literature."

• Louisa May Alcott
ALTERNATIVE ALCOTT
Includes the "sensation story" *Behind a Mask, Transcendental Wild Oats,* and other works revealing unfamiliar aspects of the author of *Little Women*
0–8135–1727–7 Rutgers pb $10.00

• Mary Austin
STORIES FROM THE COUNTRY OF LOST BORDERS
Includes *The Land of Little Rain* (1903) and *Lost Borders* (1909), both set in the California desert
Edited by Marjorie Pryse
0–8135–1218–2 Rutgers pb $10.00

• Alice Cary
CLOVERNOOK SKETCHES & OTHER STORIES
Cary, born in 1820 in a small Ohio town, was an early exponent of regional realism
Edited by Judith Fetterly
0–8135–1251–4 Rutgers pb $10.00

• Lydia Maria Child
HOBOMOK & OTHER WRITINGS ON INDIANS
Hobomok, published in 1824, was an early and sympathetic treatment of Indian themes
Edited by Carolyn L. Karcher
0–8135–1164–X Rutgers pb $9.95

• Rose Terry Cooke
HOW CELIA CHANGED HER MIND & SELECTED STORIES
Eleven stories covering Cooke's career from the 1850s to the 1890s, alternating between grim rural realism and playful humor
Edited by Elizabeth Ammons
0–8135–1166–6 Rutgers pb $9.95

• Maria Cummins
THE LAMPLIGHTER
An enormously popular moralistic romance first published in 1854
Edited by Nina Baym
0–8135–1333–2 Rutgers pb $15.00

• Fanny Fern
RUTH HALL & OTHER WRITING
Fern was the first woman newspaper columnist in America; *Ruth Hall* (1855) reflects a spirit of practical feminism
Edited by Joyce W. Warren
0–8135–1168–2 Rutgers pb $9.95

• Nella Larsen
QUICKSAND & PASSING
Novels of the black middle class, written in the 1920s. "*Quicksand* and *Passing* are novels that I will never forget. They open up a whole world of experience that seemed to me, when I first read them years ago, absolutely absorbing, fascinating, and indispensable. They do that still"—Alice Walker
Edited by Deborah E. McDowell
0–8135–1170–4 Rutgers pb $7.95

• Catharine Maria Sedgwick
HOPE LESLIE
A popular 1827 novel of Puritans and Indians
Edited by Mary Kelley
0–8135–1222–0 Rutgers pb $10.00

• E.D.E.N. Southworth
THE HIDDEN HAND
A popular 19th-century novel of comic intrigue
Edited by Joanne Dobson
0–8135–1296–4 Rutgers pb $15.00

Harriet Beecher Stowe (photo courtesy Sophia Smith Collection, Smith College)

• Harriet Beecher Stowe
OLDTOWN FOLKS
A detailed portrait of New England village life in the post-revolutionary period
Edited by Dorothy Berkson
0–8135–1220–4 Rutgers pb $12.00

THE NINETEENTH CENTURY: After The Civil War

• Henry Adams
WRITINGS
Contains *The Education of Henry Adams,*

Mont Saint-Michel and Chartres, and the novels *Democracy* and *Esther*
Edited by Ernest Samuels & Jayne N. Samuels
0–940450–12–7 Library of America $27.50

THE EDUCATION OF HENRY ADAMS
A classic autobiography with an ironic analysis of the culture which formed this scion of a distinguished American family
Edited by Ernest Samuels
0–395–08352–4 Houghton Mifflin pb $9.95

HISTORY OF THE UNITED STATES DURING THE ADMINISTRATIONS OF JEFFERSON AND MADISON
"All things considered, I suspect that it is the greatest historical work in English, with the probable exception of *The Decline and Fall of the Roman Empire* . . . The history is penetrated with precise intelligence in all its parts: it is in this quality, I think, that it surpasses any historical masterpiece with which I am acquainted"—Yvor Winters
Edited by Earl N. Harbert

Volume 1
0–940450–34–8 Library of America $27.50

Volume 2
0–940450–35–6 Library of America $27.50

MONT SAINT-MICHEL AND CHARTRES
A study of the medieval imagination through the religion, art and architecture of the 12th century. "From beginning to end, it reads as from a man in the fresh morning of life, with a frolic power unusual to historic literature"—William James
Introduction by Raymond Carney
0–14–039054–5 Penguin pb $6.95

• **Louisa May Alcott**
THE ALTERNATIVE ALCOTT
Behind a Mask, Transcendental Wild Oats, and other unfamiliar works
Edited by Elaine Showalter
0–8135–1271–9 Rutgers $32.00
0–8135–1727–7 Rutgers pb $10.00

LITTLE WOMEN
The enduringly popular saga of the March sisters—Meg, Jo, Amy and Beth—in Civil War New England. "There was one book in which I believed I had caught a glimpse of my future self: *Little Women* by Louisa May Alcott . . . I identified myself passionately with Jo, the intellectual"—Simone de Beauvoir
Introduction by Elaine Showalter
0–14–039069–3 Penguin pb $5.95

JO'S BOYS
Afterword by Madelain Stern
0–451–52089–0 NAL pb $2.25

LITTLE MEN
0–451–52275–3 NAL pb $3.50

GOOD WIVES
0–14–035009–8 Penguin pb $2.25

A MODERN MEPHISTOPHELES
A *Dorian Gray*-ish melodrama of corruption and sexual entrapment, originally published under a pseudonym
0–553–21266–4 Bantam pb $3.50

• **Horatio Alger, Jr.**
RAGGED DICK & STRUGGLING UPWARD
Alger's optimistic tales of self-betterment sold in the tens of millions of copies
Edited by Carl Bode
0–14–039033–2 Penguin pb $4.95

• **P.T. Barnum**
STRUGGLES AND TRIUMPHS
The memoirs of the archetypal showman
Edited by Carl Bode
0–14–039004–9 Penguin pb $6.95

• **Edward Bellamy**
LOOKING BACKWARD
A century later, Bellamy's mechanistic utopia looks more nightmarish than ever
Edited by Cecelia Tichi
0–14–039018–9 Penguin pb $3.95

• **Ambrose Bierce**
COLLECTED WRITINGS OF AMBROSE BIERCE
Introduction by Clifton Fadiman
0–8065–0180–4 Lyle Stuart pb $11.95

THE DEVIL'S DICTIONARY
A compendium of sardonic aphorisms, originally titled *The Cynic's Word Book*
0–486–20487–1 Dover pb $2.95

GHOST AND HORROR STORIES OF AMBROSE BIERCE
Edited by E.F. Bleiler
0–486–20767–6 Dover pb $3.95

IN THE MIDST OF LIFE
Introduction by Clifton Fadiman
0–8065–0551–6 Lyle Stuart pb $2.95

THE SARDONIC HUMOR OF AMBROSE BIERCE
Edited by George Barkin
0–486–20768–4 Dover pb $4.50

• **George Washington Cable**
THE GRANDISSIMES
A drama of social distinctions in Louisiana, by a sometimes controversial chronicler of Creole life
0–14–043322–8 Penguin pb $5.95

• **Charles W. Chesnutt**
Chesnutt's gifts as a short story writer broke the color line around the turn of the century, but his editors waited twelve years before revealing his racial identity.

THE CONJURE WOMAN
Dialect stories of slavery days, published in 1899
Introduction by Robert Farnsworth
0–472–06156–9 Michigan pb $3.95

THE MARROW OF TRADITION
A novel of Reconstruction
0–472–06147–X Michigan pb $9.95

THE WIFE OF HIS YOUTH & OTHER STORIES
Introduction by E.S. Miers
0–472–06134–8 Michigan pb $9.95

THE SHORT FICTION OF CHARLES W. CHESNUTT
"The collection evinces Chesnutt's incisive humor, his narrative skill, his evocative characterizations, and his essential artistry"—*Choice*
0–88258–012–4 Howard $15.00
0–88258–092–2 Howard pb $7.95

• **Kate Chopin**
THE AWAKENING & SELECTED STORIES
The Awakening, a story about a woman who rebels against her bourgeois husband and falls in love with a younger man, created a scandal when it was first published in 1899
Introduction by Sandra Gilbert
0–14–039022–7 Penguin pb $3.95

A KATE CHOPIN MISCELLANY
Edited by Per Seyersted & Emily Toth
0–317–38876–2 NW Louisiana pb $12.95

Stephen Crane (photo courtesy Newark Public Library)

• **Stephen Crane**
PROSE AND POETRY
A comprehensive collection of Crane's writing: novels, stories, journalism, poems
Edited by J.C. Levenson
0–940450–17–8 Library of America $27.50

MAGGIE: A Girl of the Streets & Other Short Fiction
Introduction by Jayne Anne Phillips
0–553–21198–6 Bantam pb $2.50

THE RED BADGE OF COURAGE: An Episode of the American Civil War
"Crane was a brilliant impressionist and has strong affinities with the Impressionist painters . . . He is aware of the ironical disparity between what imagination and tradition suggest and what in fact is seen"—V.S. Pritchett
Introduction by Pascal Covici
0–14–039021–9 Penguin pb $2.95

THE COMPLETE POEMS OF STEPHEN CRANE
Edited with an introduction by Joseph Katz
0–8014–9130–4 Cornell pb $8.95

• **Paul Laurence Dunbar**
Dunbar, who died in 1906, preferred the poetry he wrote in standard English, and only at the insistence of his editors continued to turn out volumes of the dialect poetry that brought him fame. Nevertheless, among the black poets working in dialect around the turn of the century, Dunbar best evoked the voices and attitudes of real people.

THE COMPLETE POEMS OF PAUL LAURENCE DUNBAR
0–396–07895–8 Dodd, Mead pb $6.95

LYRICS OF LOWLY LIFE
Introduction by William Dean Howells
0–8065–0922–8 Lyle Stuart pb $4.95

Harold Frederic
THE DAMNATION OF THERON WARE
This novel of a minister's loss of faith, subtly disturbing and subversively funny, remains a neglected masterpiece of American writing
0–14–039025–1 Penguin pb $6.95

● Hamlin Garland
MAIN-TRAVELLED ROADS
Realistic stories of the Midwest, by a writer who later became a spokesman for Populism
0–451–52271–0 NAL pb $4.95

A SON OF THE MIDDLE BORDER
An autobiography by the Wisconsin writer
Introduction by Donald Pizer
0–8032–7000–3 Nebraska pb $6.95

● Frances E.W. Harper
IOLA LEROY
A sentimental novel interesting for the depiction of blacks in post-Civil War fiction
Introduction by Hazel Carby
0–8070–6317–7 Beacon pb $8.95

● Joel Chandler Harris
UNCLE REMUS: His Songs and His Sayings
Edited by Robert Hemenway
0–14–039014–6 Penguin pb $5.95

● Bret Harte
THE OUTCASTS OF POKER FLAT
In stories like "The Luck of Roaring Camp" and "Tennessee's Partner" Harte helped mythologize the Gold Rush era
0–451–52344–6 NAL pb $4.50

● William Dean Howells
NOVELS: 1875–1886
Includes *A Foregone Conclusion, A Modern Instance, Indian Summer,* and *The Rise of Silas Lapham*
Edited by Edwin Cady
0–940450–04–6 Library of America $27.50

NOVELS: 1886–1888
Includes *The Minister's Charge, April Hopes,* and *Annie Kilburn*
0–940450–51–8 Library of America $35.00

A HAZARD OF NEW FORTUNES
A drama of capital versus militant labor
Afterword by Benjamin DeMott
0–452–00768–2 NAL pb $4.95

THE LANDLORD AT LION'S HEAD
The evolution of a mountain resort hotel serves as the pretext for a low-keyed but penetrating character study
0–486–24455–5 Dover pb $7.95

A MODERN INSTANCE
"Nothing could be more telling than Howells' description of the religious mood of the '70s and '80s, the movement from the last vestiges of faith to a genteel plausibility, the displacement of doctrine and moral strenuousness by a concern with

'social adjustment' and the amelioration of boredom"—Lionel Trilling
Introduction by Edwin Cady
0–14–039027–8 Penguin pb $6.95

THE RISE OF SILAS LAPHAM
Howell's most famous novel, published in 1885, offers a subtle portrait of a self-made businessman
Introduction by Kermit Vanderbilt
0–14–039030–8 Penguin pb $4.95

● Alice James
THE DIARY OF ALICE JAMES
The sister of Henry and William, long afflicted by physical and psychological problems, kept this acute record of her thoughts in the last two years of her life
Edited by Leon Edel
0–14–039011–1 Penguin pb $5.95

● Henry James
"There is, I think, no more nutritive or suggestive truth . . . than that of the perfect dependence of the 'moral' sense of a work of art on the amount of felt life concerned in producing it. The question comes back thus, obviously, to the kind and degree of the artist's prime sensibility, which is the soil out of which his subject springs. The quality and capacity of that soil, its ability to 'grow' with due freshness and straightness any vision of life, represents, strongly or weakly, the projected morality. That element is but another name for the more or less close connexion of the subject with some mark made on the intelligence, with some sincere experience."—from the preface to the New York Edition of *The Portrait of a Lady*

NOVELS: 1871–1880
Includes *Watch and Ward, Roderick Hudson, The American, The Europeans,* and *Confidence*
Edited by William T. Stafford
0–940450–13–5 Library of America $27.50

NOVELS: 1881–1886
Includes *Washington Square, The Portrait of a Lady,* and *The Bostonians*
Edited by William T. Stafford
0–940450–30–5 Library of America $27.50

NOVELS: 1886–1890
Includes *The Princess Casamassima, The Reverberator,* and *The Tragic Muse*
0–940450–56–9 Library of America $35.00

THE AMBASSADORS
James's classic "center of consciousness" novel, in which all the events are filtered through the mind of Lambert Strether as he struggles with his mission to bring back Chad Newsome from the lures of Paris
Edited by Harry Levin
0–14–043233–7 Penguin pb $3.95

THE AMERICAN
James's earliest foray into the international theme, introducing Christopher Newman, a wealthy, innocent American in Paris
Edited by William Spengemann
0–14–039009–X Penguin pb $3.95

THE ASPERN PAPERS & THE TURN OF THE SCREW
Two of James's most concise and dramatically compelling novellas
Edited by Anthony Curtis
0–14–043224–8 Penguin pb $2.95

Henry James (photo by Katherine McClellan, courtesy Sophia Smith Collection, Smith College)

THE AWKWARD AGE
"In no earlier novel had James called British society so to account. *The Awkward Age* records his complete disenchantment"—Leon Edel
Edited by Ronald Blythe
0–19–281654–3 Penguin pb $4.95

THE BOSTONIANS
"As a representation of the American actuality, *The Bostonians* is in every way remarkable, the more so because it is so original . . . Manners have changed since James wrote, but not the peculiar tenuity of the fabric of American social life"— Lionel Trilling
Edited by R.D. Gooder
0–19–281639–X Oxford pb $2.95

DAISY MILLER
Edited by Geoffrey Moore
0–14–043262–0 Penguin pb $2.50

THE EUROPEANS
A pair of impoverished Continental sophisticates attempt to take advantage of American opportunities
Edited by Tony Tanner
0–14–043232–9 Penguin pb $2.50

THE GOLDEN BOWL
A tragic drama of adultery and betrayal filtered through James's late prose at its most elaborate
Edited by Gore Vidal
0–14–043235–3 Penguin pb $3.95

THE PORTRAIT OF A LADY
"No other American and few Europeans can match the superb feminine creations of the chief American master of the art of fiction"—Oscar Cargill
Edited by Geoffrey Moore
0–14–043223–X Penguin pb $3.95

THE PRINCESS CASAMASSIMA
"*The Princess Casamassima,* with its opening in the prison and its revolutionary exiles in London, deals with issues and social contrasts of a kind that James had never before attempted"—Edmund Wilson
Edited by Derek Brewer
0–14–043254–X Penguin pb $6.95

RODERICK HUDSON
Edited by Geoffrey Moore
0–14–043264–7 Penguin pb $5.95

THE SPOILS OF POYNTON
A novel centered on the valuable
contents of an English country house
0–14–001922–7 Penguin pb $3.95

THE TRAGIC MUSE
0–14–004606–2 Penguin pb $6.95

WASHINGTON SQUARE
A plain heiress-to-be is courted by a
fortune hunter
Edited by Brian Lee
0–14–043226–4 Penguin pb $2.50

WHAT MAISIE KNEW
"If it were not for Henry James's art—his
subtlety, his grace, his handy
euphemisms—this very modern story
about aimless lives and messy marriages
would be practically untellable . . . It is
most of all a novel about a small unselfish
girl and the ways in which she is
passionately victimized by adults"—Paul
Theroux
Edited by Paul Theroux
0–14–043248–5 Penguin pb $3.95

THE WINGS OF THE DOVE
A novel of intrigue, guilt, and retribution,
often considered the masterpiece of James's
late period
Edited by John Bayley
0–14–043263–9 Penguin pb $3.95

**GREAT SHORT WORKS OF HENRY
JAMES**
Includes *Washington Square, Daisy Miller,
The Aspern Papers, The Pupil, The Turn of
the Screw,* and *The Beast in the Jungle*
Introduction by Alan Flower
0–06–083040–9 Harper & Row pb $5.95

**THE GREAT SHORT NOVELS OF
HENRY JAMES**
Includes *The Turn of the Screw, Daisy
Miller, The Aspern Papers, The Beast in the
Jungle, An International Episode, Lady
Barberina,* and others
Edited with introduction by Philip Rahv
0–88184–247–8 Carroll & Graf pb $12.95

**EIGHT TALES FROM THE MAJOR
PHASE**
Includes *The Altar of the Dead, The Figure
in the Carpet, Brooksmith, The Great Good
Place,* and others
Introduction by Morton Dauween Zabel
0–393–00286–1 Norton pb $9.95

STORIES OF THE SUPERNATURAL
Edited by Leon Edel
0–8008–3829–7 Taplinger pb $9.95

**THE FIGURE IN THE CARPET &
OTHER STORIES**
Also includes *The Author of Beltraffio, The
Lesson of the Master, The Middle Years, The
Death of the Lion,* and others
Edited by Frank Kermode
0–14–043255–8 Penguin pb $5.95

**AN INTERNATIONAL EPISODE &
OTHER STORIES**
Also includes *The Pension Beaurepas* and
Lady Barberina
Edited by S. Gorley Putt
0–14–043227–2 Penguin $4.95

IN THE CAGE & OTHER STORIES
0–14–003500–1 Penguin $4.95

THE AMERICAN SCENE
"The criticism of the national life shows an
incisiveness, a comprehensiveness, a
sureness in knowing his way about, a grasp
of political and economic factors, that one
might not have expected of Henry James

returning to Big Business America"—
Edmund Wilson
Edited by Leon Edel
0–253–20110–1 Indiana pb $8.95

**THE ART OF THE NOVEL: Critical
Prefaces**
These detailed accounts of how James
wrote his major works served as prefaces to
the New York edition of 1907–09
Foreword by R.W.B. Lewis
Introduction by R.P. Blackmur
0–930350–60–X Northeastern pb $12.95

AUTOBIOGRAPHY
0–691–06584–5 Princeton $52.00
0–691–01408–6 Princeton pb $13.50

**THE COMPLETE NOTEBOOKS OF
HENRY JAMES**
Edited by Leon Edel and H. Powers Lyall
0–19–503782–0 Oxford $32.95

CRITICISM

**Volume 1: Essays on Literature, American
Writers, English Writers**
Edited by Leon Edel & Mark Wilson
0–940450–22–4 Library of America $27.50

**Volume 2: French Writers, Other European
Writers, and The Prefaces to the New York
Edition**
0–940450–23–2 Library of America $27.50

ENGLISH HOURS
Introduction by Leon Edel
0–19–281321–8 Oxford pb $8.95

ITALIAN HOURS
0–88001–147–5 Ecco pb $10.50

A LITTLE TOUR IN FRANCE
0–374–18956–0 Farrar, Straus & Giroux $18.95
0–374–51807–6 Farrar, Straus & Giroux pb $9.95

THE NOTEBOOKS OF HENRY JAMES
Edited by F.O. Matthiessen & Kenneth B. Murdock
0–226–51104–9 Chicago pb $10.95

SELECTED LETTERS
Edited by Leon Edel & F.W. Dupee
0–674–38793–7 Harvard $29.95

• William James
WRITINGS: 1902–1910
Includes *The Varieties of Religious
Experience, Pragmatism, A Pluralistic
Universe, The Meaning of Truth, Some
Problems of Philosophy,* and *Essays*
Edited by Bruce Kuklick
0–940450–38–0 Library of America $27.50

• Sarah Orne Jewett
A COUNTRY DOCTOR
Introduction by Joy G. Boyum & Ann Shapiro
0–452–00805–0 NAL pb $4.95

**THE COUNTRY OF THE POINTED
FIRS & OTHER STORIES**
"If I were to name the three American
books which have the possibility of a long,
long life, I would say at once *The Scarlet
Letter, Huckleberry Finn,* and *The Country
of the Pointed Firs* . . . The latter book
seems to me fairly to shine with the
reflection of its long, joyous future"—Willa
Cather
Introduction by Marjorie Pryse
0–393–00048–6 Norton pb $7.95

• Frank Norris
NOVELS AND ESSAYS
Includes *Vandover and the Brute,
McTeague, The Octopus,* and *Essays*
Edited by Donald Pizer
0–940450–40–2 Library of America $27.50

McTEAGUE: A Story of San Francisco
A pioneering naturalistic study of greed
and moral decay, taking its hapless
protagonist from San Francisco's Polk
Street to the wastes of Death Valley
Edited by Kevin Starr
0–14–039017–0 Penguin pb $5.95

THE OCTOPUS
"*The Octopus* has been described,
justifiably, as the most ambitious novel up
to its time since *Moby Dick:* ambitious in
terms of its mighty social and
philosophical themes—the clash of frontier
and monopoly, the impersonal forces
represented by technology and corporate
structures, the problem of social justice,
and the reconciling power of nature"—
Kevin Starr
Introduction by Kevin Starr
0–14–039040–5 Penguin pb $5.95

VANDOVER AND THE BRUTE
0–8032–8350–4 Nebraska pb $6.50

• Maria W. Stewart
**MARIA W. STEWART, AMERICA'S
FIRST BLACK WOMAN POLITICAL
WRITER: Essays and Speeches**
Edited by Marilyn Richardson
0–253–20446–1 Indiana pb $8.95

• Mark Twain
**THE INNOCENTS ABROAD &
ROUGHING IT**
Edited by Guy Cardwell
0–940450–25–9 Library of America $27.50

MISSISSIPPI WRITINGS
Includes *The Adventures of Tom Sawyer, Life
on the Mississippi, Adventures of Huckleberry
Finn,* and *Pudd'nhead Wilson*
Edited by Guy Cardwell
0–940450–07–0 Library of America $27.50

**THE COMPLETE SHORT STORIES OF
MARK TWAIN**
Edited by Charles Neider
0–553–21195–1 Bantam pb $4.50

**THE ADVENTURES OF
HUCKLEBERRY FINN**
"Repeated readings of the book only
confirm and deepen one's admiration of
the consistency and perfect adaptation of
the writing. This is a style which at the
period, whether in America or in England,
was an innovation, a new discovery in the
English language"—T.S. Eliot
0–14–039046–4 Penguin pb $1.95

THE ADVENTURES OF TOM SAWYER
0–14–039048–0 Penguin pb $1.95

**A CONNECTICUT YANKEE IN KING
ARTHUR'S COURT**
The famous fantasy of a factory foreman
who wakes up in Medieval England
0–14–043064–4 Penguin pb $2.95

THE GILDED AGE: A Tale of To-Day
This satirical novel was written in
collaboration with Charles Dudley Warner
0–486–25545–X Dover pb $10.95

THE INNOCENTS ABROAD
A comical tour of Europe, Egypt, and the
Holy Land
0–451–51753–9 NAL pb $3.95

LETTERS FROM THE EARTH
Edited by Bernard De Voto
0–06–080331–2 Harper & Row pb $4.95

Mark Twain (courtesy The Mark Twain Memorial)

LIFE ON THE MISSISSIPPI
Introduction by James M. Cox
0–14–039050–2 Penguin pb $4.95

THE MYSTERIOUS STRANGER & OTHER STORIES
0–451–52069–6 NAL pb $2.95

A PEN WARMED UP IN HELL: Mark Twain in Protest
Edited with introduction by Frederick Anderson
0–317–02692–5 Harper & Row pb $6.95

THE PRINCE AND THE PAUPER
Twin boys exchange identities in Tudor England
0–14–035017–9 Penguin pb $2.25

PUDD'NHEAD WILSON
A curious blend of detective novel and racial melodrama
Edited by Malcolm Bradbury
0–14–043040–7 Penguin pb $2.50

ROUGHING IT
Twain out west, with satirical sidelights on Mormons, outlaws, and others
Edited by Hamlin Hill
0–14–039010–3 Penguin pb $4.95

The Mark Twain Library
"The Mark Twain Library offers . . . new and accurate texts . . . sparingly annotated, and integrated once again with the illustrations Mark Twain considered essential to his books."—Robert H. Hirst, General Editor, The Mark Twain Project

THE ADVENTURES OF HUCKLEBERRY FINN
This meticulous edition includes a glossary of slang and all the original 1885 illustrations
Edited by Walter Blair & Victor Fischer
Illustrated by Edward Windsor Kemble
0–520–05337–0 California $25.00
0–520–05520–9 California pb $8.95

THE ADVENTURES OF TOM SAWYER
Edited by John C. Gerber & Paul Baender
Illustrated by True Williams
0–520–04558–0 California $22.50
0–520–04559–9 California pb $7.95

A CONNECTICUT YANKEE IN KING ARTHUR'S COURT
"To my mind the illustrations are better than the book—which is a good deal for me to say, I reckon"—Mark Twain
Edited by Bernard L. Stein
Illustrated by Daniel Carter Beard
0–520–05089–4 California $25.00
0–520–05109–2 California pb $9.95

THE DEVIL'S RACETRACK: Mark Twain's Great Dark Writings
Selections from *Which Was the Dream?* and *Fables of Man*
Edited with an introduction by John S. Tuckey
0–520–03780–4 California $25.00
0–520–03893–2 California pb $12.95

NUMBER FORTY-FOUR: The Mysterious Stranger
The only authentic version of Twain's pessimistic fantasy
Edited by William M. Gibson & John S. Tuckey
0–520–04544–0 California $25.00
0–520–04545–9 California pb $7.95

THE PRINCE AND THE PAUPER
Foreword and notes by Victor Fischer & Michael B. Frank
0–520–05108–4 California pb $7.95

ROUGHING IT
0–520–02018–9 California $35.00
0–520–02478–8 California pb $9.95

TOM SAWYER ABROAD & TOM SAWYER, DETECTIVE
Introduction and notes by John C. Gerber
0–520–04560–2 California $22.50
0–520–04561–0 California pb $7.95

20th-Century American Fiction

"This thing is an essentially American thing this sense of a space of time and what is to be done within this space of time not in any way excepting in the way that it is inevitable that there is this space of time and anybody who is an American feels what is inside this space of time and so well they do what they do within this space of time, and so ultimately it is a thing contained within . . . Think of anything, of cowboys, of movies, of detective stories, of anybody who goes anywhere or stays at home and is an American and you will realize that it is something strictly American to conceive a space that is filled with moving, a space of time that is always filled with moving."—Gertrude Stein in "The Gradual Making of *The Making of Americans*"

The works of any given writer are grouped together. That means, for example, that under The 1940s and '50s are found the more recent works of writers who first came to prominence in those decades.

FROM THE TURN OF THE CENTURY TO WORLD WAR II

• **Edward Anderson**
HUNGRY MEN
The boxcars and soup kitchens of the Depression, transcribed with deadpan precision
0–14–007374–4 Penguin pb $5.95

• **Sherwood Anderson**
DEATH IN THE WOODS & OTHER STORIES
"One of the very best and finest writers in the English language today"—F. Scott Fitzgerald
0–87140–140–1 Norton pb $7.95

THE PORTABLE SHERWOOD ANDERSON
"Sherwood Anderson was the father of all my works—and those of Hemingway, Fitzgerald, etc. We were influenced by him. He showed us the way"—William Faulkner
0–14–015076–5 Penguin pb $8.95

THE TELLER'S TALES: Short Stories
"Sherwood Anderson had a sweetness, and sweetness is rare"—Gertrude Stein
Edited by Frank Gado
0–912756–08–X Union College pb $4.95

WINESBURG, OHIO
Life in a small midwestern town at the beginning of the 20th century. "The only storyteller of his generation who left a mark on the style and vision of the generation that followed . . . Hemingway, Faulkner, Wolfe, Steinbeck, Caldwell, Saroyan, and Henry Miller . . . Each owes an unmistakable debt to Anderson"—Malcolm Cowley
Introduction by Malcolm Cowley
0–14–039059–6 Penguin pb $3.95

Djuna Barnes
NIGHTWOOD
"What I would leave the reader prepared to find is the great achievement of a style, the beauty of phrasing, the brilliance of wit and characterization, and a quality of horror and doom very nearly related to that of Elizabethan tragedy"—T.S. Eliot
Introduction by T.S. Eliot
0–8112–0005–1 New Directions pb $6.25

SELECTED WORKS OF DJUNA BARNES
0–374–25936–4 FS&G $12.95

SMOKE & OTHER EARLY STORIES
"Fourteen stories, startlingly strange, cranky even, but also as raw and exciting as swigs of poteen"—Valentine Cunningham, *TLS*
Edited by Douglas Messerli
0–940650–17–7 Sun & Moon $12.95
1–557–13014–0 Sun & Moon pb $9.95

• **Kay Boyle**
DEATH OF A MAN
The relationship between a pro-Nazi doctor and a young American woman, set in the Tyrolean Alps in the mid-30s
0–8112–1089–8 New Directions pb $10.95

LIFE BEING THE BEST & OTHER STORIES
Introduction by Sandra W. Spanier
0–8112–1052–9 New Directions $18.95
0–8112–1053–7 New Directions pb $8.95

MY NEXT BRIDE
Introduction by Doris Grumbach
0–14–016147–3 Penguin pb $6.95

THREE SHORT NOVELS
Introduction by Margaret Atwood
0–14–006109–6 Penguin pb $6.95

YEAR BEFORE LAST
A writer's life on the French Riviera, as seen by the innovative Modernist
Introduction by Doris Grumbach
0–14–016146–5 Penguin pb $6.95

• **Pearl S. Buck**
THE GOOD EARTH
0–671–50437–1 Pocket pb $3.95

• **James Branch Cabell**
THE CREAM OF THE JEST
Edited by Joseph M. Flora
0–8084–0396–6 New College pb $6.95

JURGEN: A Comedy of Justice
0–486–23507–6 Dover pb $5.95

• **Abraham Cahan**
YEKL AND THE IMPORTED BRIDEGROOM & OTHER STORIES OF THE NEW YORK GHETTO
0–486–22427–9 Dover pb $4.95

THE RISE OF DAVID LEVINSKY
0–06–131912–0 Harper & Row pb $8.50

• **James M. Cain**
THE POSTMAN ALWAYS RINGS TWICE
0–679–72325–0 Random House pb $6.95

DOUBLE INDEMNITY
0–679–72322–6 Random House pb $6.95

THREE BY CAIN
Includes *Serenade, Love's Lovely Counterfeit,* and *The Butterfly*
0–679–72323–4 Random House pb $9.95

MILDRED PIERCE
0–679–72321–8 Random House pb $6.95

• **Erskine Caldwell**
THE BLACK AND WHITE STORIES OF ERSKINE CALDWELL
Edited by Ray McIver
0–931948–63–0 Peachtree $12.95

GOD'S LITTLE ACRE
0–451–51996–5 NAL pb $2.95

TOBACCO ROAD
Once-shocking saga of the shiftless and earthy Lester family. "A master illusionist who can create, as Hemingway did, an impression of absolute reality"—*Time*
0–451–15258–1 NAL pb $3.50

• **Willa Cather**
EARLY NOVELS AND STORIES
Includes *The Troll Garden, O Pioneers!, The Song of the Lark, My Antonia,* and *One of Ours*
Edited by Sharon O'Brien
0–940450–39–9 Library of America $27.50

ALEXANDER'S BRIDGE
Introduction by Sharon O'Brien
0–452–00875–1 NAL pb $4.95

Willa Cather (photo by Edward Steichen)

DEATH COMES FOR THE ARCHBISHOP
A novel of 19th-century mission life in New Mexico
0–394–42154–X Knopf $19.95
0–394–60503–9 Random House pb $9.95

A LOST LADY
0–394–48558–0 Random House $14.95
0–394–71705–8 Random House pb $3.95

LUCY GAYHEART
0–394–71756–2 Random House pb $4.95

MY ANTONIA
This portrait of a pioneer woman is generally considered to be Cather's greatest work. "No romantic novel ever written in America, by man or woman, is one half so beautiful as *My Antonia*"—H.L. Mencken
0–395–07514–9 Houghton Mifflin $18.95
0–395–08356–7 Houghton Mifflin pb $5.95

MY MORTAL ENEMY
0–394–70200–X Random House pb $3.95

O PIONEERS!
The classic novel of pioneer life on the Nebraska prairie, first published in 1913
Introduction by Blanche H. Gelfant
0–14–039070–7 Penguin pb $4.95

OBSCURE DESTINIES
Three novellas of the midwest
0–394–71179–3 Random House pb $5.95

THE OLD BEAUTY AND OTHERS
0–394–72122–5 Random House pb $5.95

ONE OF OURS
0–394–71252–8 Random House pb $5.95

THE PROFESSOR'S HOUSE
0–394–71913–1 Random House pb $4.95

SAPPHIRA AND THE SLAVE GIRL
0–394–71434–2 Random House pb $6.95

SHADOWS ON THE ROCK
A chronicle of 17th-century Quebec
0–394–71680–9 Random House pb $6.95

THE SONG OF THE LARK
A young woman artist attempts to escape from the restrictions of life in a small Colorado town
0–395–34530–8 Houghton Mifflin pb $8.95

THE TROLL GARDEN
This collection of short stories was Cather's first published book of fiction
Afterword by Katherine Anne Porter
0–452–00714–3 NAL pb $3.95

WILLA CATHER'S COLLECTED SHORT FICTION, 1892–1912
Edited by Virginia Faulkner
Introduction by M.R. Bennett
0–8032–0770–0 Nebraska $29.95

YOUTH AND THE BRIGHT MEDUSA
0–394–71684–1 Random House pb $4.95

● e.e. cummings
THE ENORMOUS ROOM
Edited by George J. Firmage
Introduction by Richard S. Kennedy
0–394–60427–X Modern Library $5.95

● H.D. (Hilda Doolittle)
BID ME TO LIVE
"H.D.'s wit, sense of rhythm, and control of language prove the inadequacy of the imagist label that is so often applied to this writer"—*Library Journal*
0–933806–19–1 Black Swan $20.00

HEDYLUS
0–933806–00–0 Black Swan $17.50

HERMIONE
An autobiographical self-portrait. "In writing *Hermione* H.D. committed a daring act, the harbinger of her daringly unconventional life and a lifetime of unconventional works"—*Arizona Quarterly*
Introduction by Perdita Schaffner
0–8112–0817–6 New Directions pb $9.95

NIGHTS
Introduction by Perdita Schaffner
0–8112–0979–2 New Directions pb $19.95

John Dos Passos
U.S.A.
Dos Passos' masterful trilogy, published between 1930 and 1936, uses a wide variety of techniques to create a panorama of America in the early 20th century.

THE 42ND PARALLEL
"What Dos Passos created with *The 42nd Parallel* was in fact another American invention . . . the greatest possible homage to art as a new kind of 'practicality' in getting down the facts of human existence in our century"— Alfred Kazin
0–451–52045–9 NAL pb $4.50

1919
"Dos Passos reports all his characters' utterances to us in the style of a statement to the Press. Their words are thereby cut off from thought, and become pure utterances . . . Dos Passos' man is a hybrid creature, an interior-exterior being. We go on living with him and within him, with his vacillating, individual consciousness, when suddenly it wavers, weakens, and is diluted in the collective consciousness . . . I regard Dos Passos as the greatest writer of our time"—Jean-Paul Sartre
0–451–51508–0 NAL pb $3.50

THE BIG MONEY
"A furious and somber poem, written in a mood of revulsion even more powerful than that which T.S. Eliot expressed in *The Waste Land*"— Malcolm Cowley
Introduction by Alfred Kazin
0–451–51981–7 NAL pb $4.95

MANHATTAN TRANSFER
A novel of New York City in the '20s, in many ways a preparation for the larger scale of *U.S.A.* "It may be the foundation for a whole new school of novel-writing"—Sinclair Lewis
0–395–08375–3 Houghton Mifflin pb $7.95

THREE SOLDIERS
A realistic novel of World War I, published in 1921
0–88184–413–6 Carroll & Graf pb $9.95

● Theodore Dreiser
SISTER CARRIE, JENNIE GERHARDT & TWELVE MEN
Dreiser's first two great novels, along with the non-fiction sketches *Twelve Men*
Edited by Richard Lehan
0–940450–41–0 Library of America $27.50

AN AMERICAN TRAGEDY
Dreiser's masterpiece is a realistic look at the dark side of the American Dream
0–451–52204–4 NAL pb $4.95

THE FINANCIER
The first and best of the Frank Cowperwood trilogy is the closest thing to an epic of American business life
0–451–51719–9 NAL pb $3.95

THE "GENIUS"
An autobiographical novel of an artist's development
0–452–00753–4 NAL pb $5.95

JENNIE GERHARDT
Foreword by Helen Yglesias
0–8052–0692–2 Schocken pb $8.95

SISTER CARRIE
Dreiser's novel of a "fallen woman" was a literary scandal when first published in 1900
0–14–039002–2 Penguin pb $4.95

THE TITAN
The second volume of the Cowperwood trilogy
0–452–00756–9 NAL pb $4.95

● John Fante
Fante began publishing his largely autobiographical novels in the late '30s; they are currently enjoying a rediscovery
ASK THE DUST
0–87685–443–9 Black Sparrow pb $8.00

THE BROTHERHOOD OF THE GRAPE
0–87685–726–8 Black Sparrow pb $10.00

DREAMS FROM BUNKER HILL
0–87685–528–1 Black Sparrow pb $9.00

FULL OF LIFE
0–87685–718–7 Black Sparrow pb $9.00

NINETEEN THIRTY-THREE WAS A BAD YEAR
0–87685–655–5 Black Sparrow pb $8.50

THE ROAD TO LOS ANGELES
0–87685–649–0 Black Sparrow pb $10.00

WAIT UNTIL SPRING, BANDINI
0–87685–554–0 Black Sparrow pb $12.00

WEST OF ROME
0–87685–677–6 Black Sparrow pb $10.00

THE WINE OF YOUTH: Selected Stories of John Fante
0–87685–582–6 Black Sparrow pb $12.50

● James T. Farrell
SAM HOLMAN
0–87975–202–5 Prometheus $20.95

● William Faulkner
"Faulkner at his best—even sometimes at his worst—has a power, a richness of life, an intensity to be found in no other American writer of our time."—Malcolm Cowley
ABSALOM, ABSALOM!
Quentin Compson (from *The Sound and the Fury*) tells the story of the rise and fall of the Sutpen Family
Edited by Noel Polk
0–394–55634–8 Random House $18.95
0–394–74775–5 Random House pb $4.95

AS I LAY DYING
The Bundrens—a backwoods family—trek into Jefferson (the seat of Faulkner's mythical Yoknapatawpha County) to bury their mother
Edited by Noel Polk
0–394–41581–7 Random House $13.95
0–394–74745–3 Random House pb $3.95

THE COLLECTED STORIES
Includes 42 short stories
0–394–41967–7 Random House $22.95
0–394–72257–4 Random House pb $14.95

COUNTRY LAWYER & OTHER STORIES FOR THE SCREEN
Edited by Louis D. Brodsky & Robert W. Hamblin
0–87805–308–5 Mississippi $12.95

A FABLE
A Second Coming parable set in World War I, *A Fable* was awarded the Pulitzer Prize upon its publication in 1954
0–394–42400–X Random House $15.95

FLAGS IN THE DUST
Published in a much shorter version as *Sartoris* in 1929, *Flags in the Dust* is the first of the Yoknapatawpha novels, tracing the history of the Sartoris clan from antebellum days through World War I
Edited by Douglas Day
0–394–46591–1 Random House $13.95
0–394–71239–0 Random House pb $5.95

GO DOWN, MOSES
A collection of stories, including the great novella *The Bear*
0–394–42646–0 Random House $17.95
0–394–71884–4 Random House pb $5.95

THE HAMLET
The first novel in the trilogy which includes *The Town* and *The Mansion*. *The Hamlet* chronicles the inexorable rise of the Snopes family
0–394–42759–0 Random House $16.95
0–394–70139–9 Random House pb $4.95

INTRUDER IN THE DUST
A black teenager, a white teenager, and a 70-year-old spinster clear a black man unjustly accused of murder
0–394–43074–3 Random House $13.95

KNIGHT'S GAMBIT
"Six masterly whodunits"—*NY Times*
0–394–43208–8 Random House $10.00
0–394–72729–0 Random House pb $4.95

☞ **TO ORDER NEW BOOKS NOT YET LISTED, ASK YOUR BOOKSELLER OR CALL 1-800-882-8770**

LIGHT IN AUGUST
Joe Christmas, a drifter of ambiguous race, plays out the doom of the South, while Lena Groves, serene and pregnant, seeks the father of her child
Edited by Noel Polk
0–394–43335–1 Random House $16.95
0–394–74743–7 Random House pb $4.95

THE MANSION
A tale of vengeance, the final volume in the Snopes trilogy
0–394–70282–4 Random House pb $5.95

MOSQUITOES
Faulkner's second novel is an uncharacteristic satire set in New Orleans
0–671–55731–9 Washington Square pb $4.95

NEW ORLEANS SKETCHES
These early stories were written while Faulkner was working for a New Orleans newspaper
Edited by Carvel Collier
0–394–43818–3 Random House $13.95

NOVELS 1930–1935
Includes *As I Lay Dying, Sanctuary, Light in August,* and *Pylon*
Edited by Joseph Blotner & Noel Polk
0–940450–26–7 Library of America $27.50

THE PORTABLE FAULKNER
This anthology, which weaves together stories and novel excerpts to create a portrait of Yoknapatawpha County, played a decisive role in rehabilitating Faulkner's reputation in the '40s
Edited by Malcolm Cowley
0–14–015018–8 Penguin pb $8.95

PYLON
Edited by Noel Polk
0–394–44156–7 Random House $13.95
0–394–74741–0 Random House pb $4.95

THE REIVERS
Faulkner's last novel (a Pulitzer Prize winner in 1962) is a picaresque story about a car, a racehorse, and a prostitute
0–394–44229–6 Random House $17.95
0–394–70339–1 Random House pb $4.95

REQUIEM FOR A NUN
In this sequel to *Sanctuary*, written partially in dramatic form, Temple Drake finds painful redemption. "Among the most successful of Faulkner's many experiments in narrative form"—Malcolm Cowley
0–394–71412–1 Random House pb $5.95

SANCTUARY
Temple Drake, a college girl, is kidnapped, raped, and systematically degraded by Popeye, a cold-blooded killer
Edited by Noel Polk
0–394–74744–5 Random House pb $4.95

SELECTED SHORT STORIES OF WILLIAM FAULKNER
0–394–60456–3 Modern Library $8.95

SOLDIERS' PAY
Faulkner's first novel is the story of a wounded World War I vet's homecoming
0–671–55730–0 Washington Square pb $4.95

THE SOUND AND THE FURY
The fall of the Compson family, a story of suicide and incestuous desire told by three family members (including the retarded Benjy) and finally in a third-person account which focuses on the black servants
Edited by Noel Polk
0–394–53241–4 Random House $17.95
0–394–74774–7 Random House pb $5.95

William Faulkner (photo courtesy Jack Cofield Studio)

THREE FAMOUS SHORT NOVELS
Includes *Spotted Horses, Old Man,* and *The Bear*
0–394–70149–6 Random House pb $3.95

THE TOWN
The second volume of the Snopes trilogy traces the rise of Flem Snopes, who through treachery and trickery becomes Jefferson's leading citizen
0–394–42452–2 Random House $13.95
0–394–70184–4 Random House pb $6.95

THE UNCOLLECTED STORIES OF WILLIAM FAULKNER
Forty-five stories
Edited by Joseph Blotner
0–394–74656–2 Random House pb $7.95

THE UNVANQUISHED
An episodic novel of the Civil War
0–394–70351–0 Random House pb $4.95

THE WILD PALMS
Two interwoven stories set during a flood on the Mississippi
0–394–60513–6 Random House pb $8.95

• F. Scott Fitzgerald
AFTERNOON OF AN AUTHOR
Contains 14 uncollected stories and six uncollected essays
Introduction by Arthur Mizener
0–684–16469–8 Scribners $22.50
0–02–019860–4 Macmillan pb $4.95

BABYLON REVISITED & OTHER STORIES
Ten stories from Fitzgerald's most creative period, the years between 1920 and 1937
0–020–19980–5 Macmillan pb $5.95

THE BASIL AND JOSEPHINE STORIES
Edited by John Kuehl & Jackson R. Bryer
0–684–13398–9 Scribners $20.00
0–684–14693–2 Scribners pb $8.95

THE BEAUTIFUL AND THE DAMNED
An underrated and often overlooked early novel: a young man and woman are undermined by greed and destroyed by their own excesses
0–684–15153–7 Scribners $35.00
0–020–19970–8 Macmillan pb $5.95

THE CRACK-UP
A selection of later writings which becomes an autobiographical account of

Fitzgerald's decline: "Sometimes I don't know whether I'm real or whether I'm a character in one of my own novels"
Edited by Edmund Wilson
0–8112–0051–5 New Directions pb $8.95

THE FITZGERALD READER
Edited by Arthur Mizener
0–02–381830–1 Macmillan $20.50

FLAPPERS AND PHILOSOPHERS
Introduction by Arthur Mizener
0–02–065290–9 Macmillan pb $4.95

THE GREAT GATSBY
One of the great American works of this century. "There is a moment in any real author's career when he suddenly becomes capable of doing his best work. He has found a fable that expresses his central truth and everything falls into place around it, so that his whole experience of life is available for use in his fiction. Something like that happened to Fitzgerald when he invented the story of Jimmy Gatz, otherwise known as Jay Gatsby, and it explains the amazing richness and scope of a very short novel"—Malcolm Cowley
0–684–16498–1 Scribners $25.00
0–02–019960–0 Scribners pb $4.95

THE LAST TYCOON
The unfinished last novel in which Fitzgerald drew upon his own Hollywood experiences to tell the story of a brilliant film producer, allegedly modeled on Irving Thalberg
0–684–15311–4 Scribners $25.00
0–02–019950–3 Scribners pb $4.50

THE PAT HOBBY STORIES
Stories of a struggling Hollywood scriptwriter. "[Fitzgerald's] last word from his last home, for much of what he felt about Hollywood and about himself permeated these stories"—Arnold Gingrich
Introduction by Arnold Gingrich
0–684–16477–9 Scribners $17.50

SIX TALES OF THE JAZZ AGE & OTHER STORIES
Nine stories, including "The Jelly-Bean," "The Camel's Back," and "Gretchen's Forty Winks"
0–684–71762–X Scribners pb $8.95

STORIES OF F. SCOTT FITZGERALD
Twenty-eight stories, including "Babylon Revisited" and "The Diamond as Big as the Ritz"
0–684–15366–1 Scribners $35.00
0–020–19940–6 Macmillan pb $6.95

TENDER IS THE NIGHT
The gradual decline of psychiatrist Dick Diver mirrors Fitzgerald's own destiny
0–684–71763–8 Scribners $9.95

THIS SIDE OF PARADISE
Fitzgerald's first novel painted an influential picture of young collegians of the '20s
0–684–17468–5 Scribners pb $4.95

• Daniel Fuchs
SUMMER IN WILLIAMSBURG
0–88184–006–8 Carroll & Graf pb $8.95

• Inez Hayes Gillmore
ANGEL ISLAND
A feminist fantasy first published in 1914
0–452–26200–3 NAL pb $8.95

• **Ellen Glasgow**
BARREN GROUND
A woman's struggle to define herself in rural Virginia. "Glasgow's was a wit raised to the dignity of a style, a wit that peered through her affection for the life she described and summed up her exasperation with it"—Alfred Kazin, *On Native Ground*
0–15–610685–X HBJ pb $8.95

THE SHELTERED LIFE
0–15–681690–3 HBJ pb $8.95

VEIN OF IRON
0–15–693476–0 HBJ pb $7.95

• **Michael Gold**
JEWS WITHOUT MONEY
A 1935 novel about New York's Lower East Side
0–88184–026–2 Carroll & Graf pb $7.95

• **Caroline Gordon**
Gordon is noted as a penetrating observer of the social values of her native Kentucky.
ALECK MAURY, SPORTSMAN
0–8093–0988–2 Southern Illinois pb $6.95

THE COLLECTED STORIES
Introduction by Robert Penn Warren
0–374–12630–5 Farrar, Straus & Giroux $17.95

• **Ernest Hemingway**
ACROSS THE RIVER AND INTO THE TREES
The love between an American colonel and an Italian countess during World War II
0–02–051920–6 Macmillan pb $5.95

THE COMPLETE SHORT STORIES OF ERNEST HEMINGWAY: The Finca Vigia Edition
0–684–18668–3 Scribners $29.95

A FAREWELL TO ARMS
A love story set on the Italian front of World War I
0–684–10236–6 Scribners $14.95
0–02–051900–1 Macmillan pb $4.95

THE FIFTH COLUMN & FOUR STORIES OF THE SPANISH CIVIL WAR
0–684–15815–9 Scribners $15.00
0–684–12723–7 Scribners pb $7.95

FOR WHOM THE BELL TOLLS
A young American in an antifascist unit during the Spanish Civil War
0–684–10239–0 Scribners $17.95
0–02–051850–1 Macmillan pb $5.95

THE GARDEN OF EDEN
A posthumously published novel dealing with the erotic games of an American writer and his wife on the Côte d'Azur of the 1920s
0–684–18693–4 Scribners $18.95
0–684–18871–6 Macmillan pb $8.95

IN OUR TIME
Short stories and vignettes, first published in 1925, that introduced readers to Nick Adams
0–684–16480–9 Scribners $25.00
0–02–051810–2 Macmillan pb $3.95

ISLANDS IN THE STREAM
0–684–16499–X Scribners $30.00
0–684–14642–8 Scribners pb $12.95

THE NICK ADAMS STORIES
0–684–16940–1 Scribners pb $9.95

MEN WITHOUT WOMEN
This 1927 collection includes some of Hemingway's most celebrated stories, among them "Fifty Grand," "The Undefeated," and "The Killers"
0–684–71803–0 Scribners pb $7.95

THE OLD MAN AND THE SEA
An old Cuban fisherman and his battle with a giant marlin
0–684–18227–0 Scribners $16.95
0–02–051910–9 Macmillan pb $3.95

SHORT STORIES OF ERNEST HEMINGWAY
Forty-nine stories, including "The Snows of Kilimanjaro" and "Soldier's Home"
0–684–15155–3 Scribners $32.50
0–02–051860–9 Macmillan pb $7.95

THE SNOWS OF KILIMANJARO & OTHER STORIES
0–02–051830–7 Macmillan pb $3.95

THE SUN ALSO RISES
The classic portrait of the expatriate generation first appeared in 1926
0–684–10250–1 Scribners $18.95
0–02–051870–6 Macmillan pb $4.95

TO HAVE AND HAVE NOT
The story of Harry Morgan, who runs contraband between Key West and Cuba
0–02–051880–3 Macmillan pb $4.95

THE TORRENTS OF SPRING
Hemingway's first novel, a parody of Sherwood Anderson
0–020550750–8 Macmillan $30.00

WINNER TAKE NOTHING
Includes "A Clean, Well-Lighted Place," "The Gambler, the Nun, and the Radio," and 12 other stories; first published in 1933
0–02–051820–X Macmillan pb $5.95

• **Josephine Herbst**
THE EXECUTIONER WAITS
"For sustained passion its excellence is unsurpassed"—William Carlos Williams
0–446–32869–3 Warner pb $3.95

PITY IS NOT ENOUGH
0–446–32867–7 Warner pb $3.95

ROPE OF GOLD
Afterword by Elinor Langer
0–446–32871–5 Warner pb $4.50

• **Langston Hughes**
THE LANGSTON HUGHES READER
0–8076–0057–1 George Braziller $17.50

NOT WITHOUT LAUGHTER
A novel of small town Kansas life
0–02–052200–2 Macmillan pb $5.95

SOMETHING IN COMMON & OTHER STORIES
0–8090–0057–1 Hill & Wang pb $7.95

THE WAYS OF WHITE FOLKS
0–394–71304–4 Random House pb $4.95

Zora Neale Hurston
Hurston's anthropological research, her elegant use of folk themes, and her treatment of the complex relations between black men and women provided a foundation for the black feminist writing of the 1980s.

I LOVE MYSELF WHEN I AM LAUGHING . . . AND THEN AGAIN WHEN I AM LOOKING MEAN AND IMPRESSIVE: A Zora Neale Hurston Reader
"One of the greatest writers of our time"—Toni Morrison
Edited by Alice Walker
Introduction by Mary H. Washington
0–912670–66–5 Feminist Press pb $9.95

MOSES: Man of the Mountain
The Old Testament Moses and the Moses of black myth are combined in a reworking of Exodus. "One of Hurston's most fascinating books, clearly her most ambitious"—Kenneth Kinnamon
Introduction by Blyden Jackson
0–252–01122–8 Illinois pb $8.95

SPUNK: The Selected Stories of Zora Neale Hurston
Foreword by Bob Callahan
0–913666–79–3 Turtle Island pb $9.95

THEIR EYES WERE WATCHING GOD
"A celebration of black culture, of love between equals, of a woman's self-discovery"—Susan Blake
0–252–00686–0 Illinois pb $6.95

• **Owen Johnson**
THE LAWRENCEVILLE STORIES
0–671–64248–0 Simon & Schuster pb $6.95

• **Ring Lardner**
THE BEST SHORT STORIES OF RING LARDNER
0–684–14743–2 Scribners $25.00
0–684–18363–3 Scribners pb $4.95

HAIRCUT & OTHER STORIES
Introduction by Wilfrid Sheed
0–394–72610–3 Random House pb $6.95

THE RING LARDNER READER
Edited by Maxwell Geismar
0–684–15365–3 Scribners $40.00

YOU KNOW ME AL: A Busher's Letters
The classic baseball novel. "With the surest touch, the sharpest insight, he lets Jack Keefe the baseball player cut his own outline, fill in his own depths, until the figure of the foolish, boastful, innocent athlete lives before us"—Virginia Woolf
Introduction by Wilfrid Sheed
0–394–72634–0 Random House pb $7.95

• **Nella Larsen**
QUICKSAND & PASSING
Edited by Deborah McDowell
0–8135–1170–4 Rutgers pb $7.95

• **Margery Latimer**
THE GUARDIAN ANGEL & OTHER STORIES
0–935312–13–7 CUNY pb $8.95

• **Sinclair Lewis**
ARROWSMITH
The maturing of an idealistic young doctor
0–451–52225–7 NAL pb $4.95

BABBITT
"It is signed in every line with the unique personality of the writer. It is saturated with America's vitality"—Rebecca West
0–15–110421–2 HBJ $14.95
0–451–52242–7 NAL pb $4.95

 ➤ **FOR OVERSEAS ORDERING INFORMATION, SEE PAGE 1**

DODSWORTH
A wealthy American businessman confronts European society
0-451-52177-3 NAL pb $4.95

ELMER GANTRY
The life of a fundamentalist preacher traveling the revival meeting circuit
0-451-52251-6 NAL pb $4.50

IT CAN'T HAPPEN HERE
A fascist dictator gains control of the United States
0-451-15936-5 NAL pb $4.50

MAIN STREET
A young woman moves with her husband to a narrow-minded midwestern town. "A remarkable diary of the middle-class mind in America"—Maxwell Geismar
0-15-155547-8 HBJ $14.95
0-451-52147-1 NAL pb $4.50

• Jack London
NOVELS AND SOCIAL WRITINGS
Includes *The People of the Abyss, The Road, The Iron Heel, John Barleycorn, Martin Eden,* and other works
Edited by Donald Pizer
0-940450-06-2 Library of America $27.50

NOVELS AND STORIES
Includes *The Call of the Wild, White Fang, The Sea Wolf,* and a large selection of stories
Edited by Donald Pizer
0-940450-05-4 Library of America $27.50

THE ASSASSINATION BUREAU, LTD.
0-14-004688-7 Penguin pb $3.95

BEFORE ADAM
0-932458-09-2 Star Rover pb $5.95

THE CALL OF THE WILD, WHITE FANG & OTHER STORIES
Edited by Andrew Sinclair
Introduction by James Dickey
0-14-039001-4 Penguin pb $3.95

THE IRON HEEL
A prophecy of 20th-century totalitarianism, sketched with the starkness of a violent comic book
Introduction by H. Bruce Franklin
0-88208-118-7 Lawrence Hill pb $7.95

MARTIN EDEN
Introduction by Andrew Sinclair
0-14-039036-7 Penguin pb $4.95

Jack London (photo courtesy The Trust of Irving Shepard)

MUTINY ON THE ELSINORE
0-935180-40-0 Mutual Honolulu pb $4.95

THE PEOPLE OF THE ABYSS
A first-hand report on the lower depths of London life
Introduction by Jack Lindsey
0-88208-079-2 Lawrence Hill pb $5.95

THE SEA WOLF
A sailor is captured by a seal-hunting ship, captained by the legendary and brutal Sea Wolf
0-553-21225-7 Bantam pb $1.95

THE STAR ROVER
A novel of reincarnation
0-904526-10-0 Riverrun pb $5.95

TO BUILD A FIRE & OTHER STORIES
0-553-21335-0 Bantam pb $4.50

YOUNG WOLF: The Early Adventure Stories of Jack London
Edited with introduction by Howard Lachtman
0-88496-210-5 Capra pb $8.95

• Claude McKay
BANANA BOTTOM
A Jamaican woman ignores the guidance of her white foster parents in order to search for her true self
0-15-610650-7 HBJ pb $7.95

BANJO
An international novel of black identity, set in 1920s Marseilles
0-15-610675-2 HBJ pb $6.95

HOME TO HARLEM
Two black men struggle against the prejudice of America in the early years of the 20th century. "Here is realism, stark, awful but somehow beautiful. McKay has left no stone unturned, no detail unmentioned in this telling of things as they are"—*NY Herald Tribune*
Foreword by Wayne F. Cooper
1-55553-023-0 Northeastern $30.00
1-55553-024-9 Northeastern $10.95

LONG WAY FROM HOME
0-15-653145-3 HBJ pb $5.95

• John P. Marquand
H.M. PULHAM, ESQ.
0-89733-231-8 Academy Chicago pb $9.95

THE LATE GEORGE APLEY: A Novel in the Form of a Memoir
0-316-54652-6 Little, Brown $15.95

POINT OF NO RETURN
An apparently successful banker re-evaluates his life after returning to his hometown in Massachusetts
0-89733-174-5 Academy Chicago pb $11.95

WICKFORD POINT
0-89733-317-9 Academy Chicago pb $11.95

• Henry Miller
BIG SUR AND THE ORANGES OF HIERONYMUS BOSCH
0-8112-0107-4 New Directions pb $9.95

BLACK SPRING
"What wonderful scenes of realism there are in *Black Spring;* what a marvelously vivid prose style used to describe them— what a great novelist, in the traditional sense, Henry Miller can be"—Maxwell Geismar
0-394-17471-2 Grove pb $4.95

NEXUS
The third volume of *The Rosy Crucifixion*
0-394-62369-X Grove pb $7.95

QUIET DAYS IN CLICHY
0-8021-3016-X Grove pb $6.95

PLEXUS
The second volume of *The Rosy Crucifixion*
0-394-62370-3 Grove pb $9.95

SEXUS
The first volume of the late autobiographical trilogy *The Rosy Crucifixion*
0-394-62371-1 Grove pb $9.95

THE SMILE AT THE FOOT OF THE LADDER
0-8112-0556-8 New Directions pb $3.95

TROPIC OF CANCER
"Miller is at his best in *Tropic of Cancer.* There is an eager vitality and exuberance to the writing which is exhilarating"— William H. Gass
Introduction by Karl Shapiro
0-394-62375-4 Grove pb $7.95

TROPIC OF CAPRICORN
The companion of *Tropic of Cancer.* "Miller has once and for all blasted the very foundation of human hypocrisy—moral, social, and political"—*Nation*
0-394-62379-7 Grove pb $7.95

• Margaret Mitchell
GONE WITH THE WIND
"A remarkable book, a spectacular book, a book that will not be forgotten"—*Chicago Tribune*
0-02-585390-2 Macmillan $17.95
0-380-00109-8 Avon pb $5.95

• Charles Nordhoff & James Norman Hall
MUTINY ON THE BOUNTY
0-316-61168-9 Little, Brown pb $8.95

• John O'Hara
AND OTHER STORIES
0-394-41534-5 Random House $14.95

APPOINTMENT IN SAMARRA
The first and best of O'Hara's novels
0-394-71192-0 Random House pb $4.95

COLLECTED STORIES
0-394-54083-2 Random House $19.50
0-394-74311-3 Vintage pb $9.95

THE EWINGS
0-394-47404-X Random House $14.95

FROM THE TERRACE
O'Hara's attempt at an epic of American life in the first half of the century. "A tremendous story about love, money, and war"—*NY Times*
0-88184-105-6 Carroll & Graf pb $5.95

HOPE OF HEAVEN
A short, sharp novel of Hollywood in the '30s
0-88184-149-8 Carroll & Graf pb $3.95

THE INSTRUMENT
0-394-43093-X Random House $14.95

THE LOCKWOOD CONCERN
The story of an American dynasty
0-88184-217-6 Carroll & Graf pb $4.95

MY TURN
0-394-43735-7 Random House $14.95

THE O'HARA GENERATION
0-394-43126-X Random House $14.95

OURSELVES TO KNOW
0-394-43959-7 Random House $14.95

A RAGE TO LIVE
0-88184-216-8 Carroll & Graf pb $4.95

SELECTED SHORT STORIES OF JOHN O'HARA
Edited by Lionel Trilling
0-394-60494-6 Modern Library $6.95

SERMONS AND SODA WATER
Three novellas. "No one has captured the relevant tones and shapes of American life with greater fidelity"—George Steiner
0-394-44480-9 Random House $12.95
0-88184-271-0 Carroll & Graf pb $4.95

TEN NORTH FREDERICK
0-394-44814-6 Random House $14.95
0-88184-173-0 Carroll & Graf pb $4.50

THE TIME ELEMENT & OTHER STORIES
0-394-48211-5 Random House $14.95

• Kenneth Patchen
THE JOURNAL OF ALBION MOONLIGHT
An allegorical novel inspired by an anonymous pre-Shakespearean lyric. "Albion Moonlight is the most naked figure of a man I have encountered in all literature"—Henry Miller
0-8112-0144-9 New Directions pb $6.95

• Katherine Anne Porter
THE COLLECTED STORIES OF KATHERINE ANNE PORTER
0-15-618876-7 HBJ pb $8.95

THE OLD ORDER
A selection of stories from *Flowering Judas, Pale Horse, Pale Rider,* and *The Leaning Tower*
0-15-668519-1 HBJ pb $4.95

PALE HORSE, PALE RIDER
0-15-170750-2 HBJ $15.95

SHIP OF FOOLS
0-316-71390-2 Little, Brown pb $7.95

• Frederic Prokosch
THE ASIATICS
An American hitchhiking across Asia. "Prokosch has invented what might be called the geographical novel; in which he mingles sensuality with irony, lucidity with mystery"—Albert Camus
Edited by Carl Van Doren
0-374-51767-3 Farrar, Straus & Giroux pb $8.25

THE SEVEN WHO FLED
0-374-26128-8 Farrar, Straus & Giroux $22.00

• Marjorie Kinnan Rawlings
CROSS CREEK
An autobiographic novel set in the Florida Everglades
Illustrated by Edward Shenton
0-02-023820-7 Macmillan pb $4.95

THE YEARLING
The enduringly popular novel of a boy and his pet deer; winner of the 1938 Pulitzer Prize
0-02-044931-3 Macmillan pb $4.95

• Laura Riding
A TROJAN ENDING
Afterword by Laura Riding Jackson
0-85635-524-0 Carcanet $18.50

Henry Roth
CALL IT SLEEP
An immigrant youth's coming of age. "One of the few genuinely distinguished novels written by a 20th-century American"—*NY Times*
0-380-01002-X Avon pb $4.95

SHIFTING LANDSCAPE
A collection of later pieces which come to grips with Roth's long silence after writing *Call It Sleep*
0-8276-0292-8 JPS $19.95

• Damon Runyon
ROMANCE IN THE ROARING FORTIES
0-688-06148-6 Morrow pb $9.95

• William Saroyan
CHANCE MEETINGS
0-393-00969-6 Norton pb $3.50

THE HUMAN COMEDY
Homer Macauley, a young telegraph messenger, and his family during World War II
0-15-142299-0 HBJ $10.95
0-440-33933-2 Dell pb $3.50

MADNESS IN THE FAMILY
Edited by Leo Hamalian
0-8112-1064-2 New Directions $16.95

MY NAME IS ARAM
0-15-163827-6 HBJ $8.95

MY NAME IS SAROYAN: A Collection
"Natural felicity of touch . . . instinctive sense of form"—Edmund Wilson
Edited by James H. Tashijian
0-15-662333-1 HBJ pb $8.95

THE NEW SAROYAN READER: A Connoisseur's Anthology of the Writings of William Saroyan
Edited by Brian Darwent
0-916870-80-4 Creative Arts $17.95
0-916870-81-2 Creative Arts pb $11.50

• Upton Sinclair
THE JUNGLE
The classic muckraking novel that exposed corrupt conditions in the Chicago meatpacking industry
Introduction by Morris Dickstein
0-553-21245-1 Bantam pb $2.25

• Gertrude Stein
THE AUTOBIOGRAPHY OF ALICE B. TOKLAS
"Largely to amuse herself, [Gertrude Stein] wrote *The Autobiography of Alice B. Toklas* in 1932 . . . The book is full of the most lucid and shapely anecdotes, told in a purer and more closely fitting prose . . . than even Gide or Hemingway have ever commanded"—Donald Sutherland
0-394-70133-X Random House pb $3.95

BLOOD ON THE DINING-ROOM FLOOR: A Murder Mystery
Edited with an afterword by John Gill
0-916870-50-2 Creative Arts $12.95

FERNHURST, Q.E.D., & OTHER EARLY WRITINGS
0-87140-082-0 Liveright pb $9.95

HOW TO WRITE
Introduction by Patricia Meyerowitz
0-486-23144-5 Dover pb $5.95

IDA
One of the most accessible and entrancing of Stein's fictions
0-394-71797-X Random House pb $4.95

LECTURES IN AMERICA
0-8070-6352-5 Beacon $23.00
0-8070-6353-3 Beacon pb $10.95

THE MAKING OF AMERICANS
Stein's most famous work appeared in 1925
0-87110-099-1 Ultramarine pb $6.95

MRS. REYNOLDS
An allegorical parable of World War II, with the title character interacting with surrogates for Adolf Hitler and Josef Stalin
1-55713-016-7 Sun & Moon pb $11.95

OPERAS AND PLAYS
0-88268-039-0 Station Hill $29.95

PARIS, FRANCE
0-87140-231-9 Liveright pb $6.95

PICASSO
0-486-24715-5 Dover pb $3.95

PICASSO: The Complete Writings
0-8070-6657-5 Beacon pb $7.95

SELECTED WRITINGS OF GERTRUDE STEIN
0-394-71710-4 Random House pb $8.95

THREE LIVES
Portraits of three very different women. "Stein's most important and influential early work . . . A remarkable book for its time"—James Mellow
0-451-51905-1 NAL pb $3.95

USEFUL KNOWLEDGE
0-88268-075-7 Station Hill $19.95

Gertrude Stein (photo courtesy Yale University)

THE WORLD IS ROUND
A children's book
Illustrated by Clement Hurd
Designed by Andrew Hoyem
0–86547–326–9 North Point $19.95

THE YALE GERTRUDE STEIN
Introduction by Richard Kostelanetz
0–300–02574–2 Yale $50.00
0–300–02609–9 Yale pb $10.95

• John Steinbeck
BURNING BRIGHT: A Play in Story Form
0–14–004999–1 Penguin pb $4.95

CANNERY ROW
0–670–20281–9 Viking $16.95

CUP OF GOLD
Steinbeck's first novel, based on the career of the pirate Henry Morgan
0–14–004234–2 Penguin pb $4.95

EAST OF EDEN
Biblical parallels weigh heavily on this saga of a Salinas Valley rancher and his troubled family
0–670–28738–5 Viking $24.95
0–14–004997–5 Penguin pb $4.95

THE GRAPES OF WRATH
The epic story of the Joads, a family of Oklahoma farmers who flee from their farm to California during the dustbowl years of the 1930s. "*The Grapes of Wrath* is the greatest American novel I have ever read"—Dorothy Parker
0–670–34791–4 Viking $25.00
0–14–004239–3 Penguin pb $4.95

IN DUBIOUS BATTLE
A novel of labor strife, considered Steinbeck's best book by some
0–14–004888–X Penguin pb $4.95

THE LONG VALLEY
Thirteen short stories, including "The Red Pony" and "The Chrysanthemums"
0–14–008038–4 Penguin pb $3.95

THE MOON IS DOWN
A novel set during the German invasion of Norway during World War II
0–14–006222–X Penguin pb $3.95

OF MICE AND MEN & CANNERY ROW
Two novelettes. "Steinbeck makes his country live and his people live as part of it"—*New Republic*
0–14–004891–X Penguin pb $3.95

THE PASTURES OF HEAVEN
Early stories of a California farming valley, first collected in 1932
0–14–004998–3 Penguin pb $3.95

THE PEARL & THE RED PONY
Two of Steinbeck's best-loved works, including his early story of a boy and a sorrel colt
0–14–004232–6 Penguin pb $3.95

SHORT NOVELS OF JOHN STEINBECK
Includes *Tortilla Flat, Of Mice and Men, The Red Pony, The Moon Is Down, Cannery Row,* and *The Pearl*
Introduction by Joseph Henry Jackson
0–670–64138–3 Viking $16.95

THE SHORT REIGN OF PIPPIN IV
0–14–004290–3 Penguin pb $4.95

SWEET THURSDAY
0–14–004889–8 Penguin pb $3.95

TO A GOD UNKNOWN
0–14–004233–4 Penguin pb $4.95

TORTILLA FLAT
0–670–72109–3 Viking $16.95
0–14–004240–7 Penguin pb $3.95

THE WAYWARD BUS
0–14–005001–9 Penguin pb $4.95

THE WINTER OF OUR DISCONTENT
Steinbeck's last major work appeared in 1961
0–14–006221–1 Penguin pb $4.95

• Wallace Thurman
THE BLACKER THE BERRY
A satirical novel from the Harlem Renaissance
0–02–054750–1 Macmillan pb $5.95

• Jean Toomer
CANE
Black life in Georgia during the early years of the 20th century. "No earlier volume of poetry or fiction or both had come close to expressing the ethos of the Negro in the Southern setting as *Cane* did. Even in today's ghettos astute readers are finding that its insights have anticipated and often exceeded their own"—Arna Bontemps
Edited by Darwin T. Turner
0–393–95600–8 Norton pb $6.95

THE WAYWARD AND THE SEEKING: A Collection of Writings by Jean Toomer
Edited by Darwin T. Turner
0–88258–014–0 Howard $14.95
0–88258–028–0 Howard pb $7.95

• B. Traven
Traven, himself a character as mysterious as any in his books, wrote chiefly of Mexico and of the inexorability of class conflict.
THE CARETTA
0–8052–8180–0 Schocken pb $5.95

THE COTTON-PICKERS
0–8052–8164–9 Schocken pb $5.95

THE DEATH SHIP
0–88208–033–4 Lawrence Hill pb $9.95

GOVERNMENT
0–8052–8165–7 Schocken pb $5.95

MARCH TO THE MONTERIA
0–8052–8166–5 Schocken pb $5.95

THE TREASURE OF THE SIERRA MADRE
0–374–52149–2 Farrar, Straus & Giroux pb $8.95

THE WHITE ROSE
0–88208–176–4 Lawrence Hill pb $8.95

• Carl Van Vechten
THE TATTOOED COUNTESS: A Romantic Novel with a Happy Ending
0–87745–186–9 Iowa pb $9.95

• Nathanael West
"Putting down a book by West, a reader is not sure whether he has been presented with a nightmare endowed with the conviction of actuality or with actuality distorted into the semblance of a nightmare; but in either case, he has the sense that he has been presented with a view of a world in which, incredibly, he lives."—Leslie Fiedler

THE DREAM LIFE OF BALSO SNELL & A COOL MILLION
0–374–50292–7 Farrar, Straus & Giroux pb $5.95

MISS LONELYHEARTS & THE DAY OF THE LOCUST
0–8112–0215–1 New Directions pb $5.95

• Edith Wharton
The first woman to win the Pulitzer Prize, Edith Wharton was an immensely popular writer in her day. She depicts the life of the American upper class—a class into which she was born—with irony and satire, exposing its lack of compassion and its stifling of human happiness.

NOVELS
Includes *The House of Mirth, The Reef, The Custom of the Country,* and *The Age of Innocence*
Edited by R.W.B. Lewis
0–940450–31–3 Library of America $27.50

THE AGE OF INNOCENCE
In the highest circle of New York society, a man falls in love with the wrong woman. Winner of the Pulitzer Prize in 1920
0–02–059890–4 Scribners pb $4.95

THE CUSTOM OF THE COUNTRY
One of Wharton's most memorable characters, Undine Spragg, and her ruthless pursuit of social success in old New York and fashionable Paris
0–684–71926–6 Scribners pb $12.95

ETHAN FROME
A simple tale about a poor New England farmer and his ill-fated bid for love
0–684–18906–2 Scribners pb $6.95

GHOST STORIES OF EDITH WHARTON
Eleven supernatural tales. "Flawlessly eerie"—*Ms.*
0–684–18382–X Scribners pb $9.95

THE HOUSE OF MIRTH
Often considered her masterpiece, this is the tragic story of Lily Bart, born into New York society and the victim of its rigid code
Introduction by Cynthia Griffin Wolff
0–14–039037–5 Penguin pb $4.95

HUDSON RIVER BRACKETED
A satirical look at literary life in the 1920s
0–684–18493–1 Scribners pb $10.95

MADAME DE TREYMES & THREE NOVELLAS
A brilliant novella about the life of Americans in French society during the Belle Epoque
Introduction by Susan Mary Alsop
0–02–055420–6 Macmillan pb $4.95

THE MOTHER'S RECOMPENSE
The bitter story of a woman who abandons her husband and child to live with the man she loves
Preface by Louis Auchincloss
0–684–18737–X Scribners pb $8.95

THE REEF
Two Americans abandon society but find they are unable to live by their own rules
Introduction by Louis Auchincloss
0–02–055410–9 Macmillan pb $3.95

ROMAN FEVER & OTHER STORIES
0–02–059880–7 Macmillan pb $4.95

Edith Wharton (photo courtesy Gessford, New York)

SUMMER
Summer in the Berkshires, with passionate, young Charity Royal forced to marry her dour guardian to save her honor
Introduction by Cynthia Griffin Wolff
0–06–080507–2 Harper & Row pb $4.95

● Thornton Wilder
THE BRIDGE OF SAN LUIS REY
Wilder's most famous novel ponders the significance of a random disaster
0–06–014631–1 Harper & Row $12.95
0–06–091341–X Harper & Row pb $5.95

THE CABALA
Pagan gods linger on in modern Rome
0–88184–295–8 Carroll & Graf pb $3.95

THE EIGHTH DAY
Murder in a small Illinois mining town in 1902
0–06–014628–1 Harper & Row $11.95
0–88184–339–3 Carroll & Graf pb $4.95

THE IDES OF MARCH
A fictional look at Julius Caesar. "An absolutely brilliant technical tour de force"—*Yale Review*
0–06–091403–3 Harper & Row pb $7.95

THEOPHILUS NORTH
Life among the wealthy and their servants in the Newport, Rhode Island of the 1920s. "An extremely entertaining array of American life in a bygone era"—*The New Yorker*
0–06–014636–2 Harper & Row $11.95
0–88184–382–2 Carroll & Graf pb $4.95

● William Carlos Williams
THE DOCTOR STORIES
Stories reflecting Williams' career as an obstetrician
Edited by Robert Coles
0–8112–0926–1 New Directions pb $4.95

THE FARMERS' DAUGHTERS: Collected Short Stories
"An American original . . . He stole time to create the most substantial one-man body of literature in our history. When he

died at 79, he had no peer as the total American writer"—Webster Scott, *Life*
Introduction by Van Wyck Brooks
0–8112–0228–3 New Directions pb $8.95

IMAGINATIONS
Radically inventive mixtures of prose and poetry, including *Kora in Hell, The Great American Novel, Spring and All,* and *The Descent of Winter*
Edited by Webster Schott
0–8112–0229–1 New Directions pb $9.95

THE STECHER TRILOGY
A series of realistic novels based on the family history of Williams' wife Flossie, consisting of *White Mule, In the Money,* and *The Build-Up*

WHITE MULE
0–8112–0238–0 New Directions pb $9.95

IN THE MONEY
0–8112–0231–3 New Directions pb $7.95

THE BUILD-UP
0–8112–0227–5 New Directions pb $9.95

A VOYAGE TO PAGANY
A fictional reworking of Williams' trip to Europe
0–8112–0237–2 New Directions pb $8.25

● Owen Wister
THE VIRGINIAN
The original cowboy novel
Introduction by Max Westbrook
0–451–52325–3 NAL pb $4.50

● Thomas Wolfe
THE COMPLETE SHORT STORIES OF THOMAS WOLFE
Edited by Francis E. Skipp
Foreward by James Dickey
0–684–18743–4 Scribners $22.50
0–02–040891–9 Macmillan pb $12.95

FROM DEATH TO MORNING
Fourteen short stories, including "Only the Dead Know Brooklyn" and "The Web of Earth"
0–684–71940–1 Scribners pb $9.95

LOOK HOMEWARD, ANGEL
Wolfe's best known novel tells of a boy's coming of age in North Carolina
0–684–17616–5 Scribners pb $8.95

OF TIME AND THE RIVER
Eugene Gant, the hero of *Look Homeward, Angel,* leaves rural North Carolina for England and France
0–684–16649–6 Scribners pb $19.95

THE SHORT NOVELS OF THOMAS WOLFE
"What he gives is the feel, taste, smell, the very heartbeat of American life as no other modern writer has done"—*Atlanta Journal*
0–684–14554–5 Scribners $17.50

THE WEB AND THE ROCK
0–06–091320–7 Harper & Row pb $10.95

YOU CAN'T GO HOME AGAIN
Wolfe's last novel
0–06–080314–2 Harper & Row pb $5.95

NORMAN MAILER: Ten Favorite American Novels

With the exception of *The Adventures of Huckleberry Finn,* which I reread recently, the other books were devoured in my freshman year at Harvard, and gave me the desire, which has never gone completely away, to be a writer, to be an American writer. They're all selections from the mainstream of American novels, not a surprise on the list, which separates me, I suspect, from my colleagues. But it's an honest list, even if it doesn't bring a deserving writer out of obscurity. Freshman year at Harvard is luminous because of these books.

John Dos Passos
U.S.A.

Mark Twain
THE ADVENTURES OF HUCKLEBERRY FINN

James T. Farrell
STUDS LONIGAN
Out of print

Thomas Wolfe
LOOK HOMEWARD, ANGEL

John Steinbeck
THE GRAPES OF WRATH

F. Scott Fitzgerald
THE GREAT GATSBY

Ernest Hemingway
THE SUN ALSO RISES

John O'Hara
APPOINTMENT IN SAMARRA

James M. Cain
THE POSTMAN ALWAYS RINGS TWICE

Herman Melville
MOBY DICK

• Richard Wright
AMERICAN HUNGER
Afterword by Michel Fabre
0–06–014768–7 Harper & Row $13.95
0–06–090991–9 Harper & Row pb $7.95

EIGHT MEN
"Each story centers on a black man involved cruelly with his surroundings, beaten down by them; each central figure is in one way or another misunderstood by the world he knows; a few misunderstand and misinterpret that world. Altogether the eight men of these stories have in common a desperate . . . heroism"—*NY Times*
Introduction by David Bradley
0–938410–39–3 Thunder's Mouth pb $10.95

THE LONG DREAM
0–06–080869–1 Harper & Row pb $5.95

NATIVE SON
This novel about a young black man who commits murder during a moment of panic in 1930s Chicago created a sensation when it appeared in 1940. It was an immediate best-seller and profoundly influenced an entire generation
0–06–014762–8 Harper & Row $18.95
0–06–080855–1 Harper & Row pb $4.95

THE OUTSIDER
0–06–080022–4 Harper & Row pb $4.95

UNCLE TOM'S CHILDREN
Five stories on violence in the South
0–06–080055–0 Harper & Row pb $3.95

THE 1940s AND '50s

• James Agee
A DEATH IN THE FAMILY
A moving account of the aftermath of death, Agee's only novel is narrated by each of the bereaved family's members in turn
0–553–27011–7 Bantam pb $4.50

Nelson Algren
"Algren can hit with both hands and move around and he will kill you if you are not awfully careful."—Ernest Hemingway
THE NEON WILDERNESS
A collection of short stories originally published in 1947
Introduction by Studs Terkel
Afterword by Terry Southern
0–86316–122–7 Kampmann pb $6.95

NEVER COME MORNING
Introduction by Kurt Vonnegut, Jr.
0–941423–00–X 4 Walls 8 Windows pb $7.95

SOMEBODY IN BOOTS
Algren's first novel, a 1935 chronicle of hobo wanderings and petty crime
0–938410–40–7 Thunder's Mouth pb $8.95

• Harriet Arnow
THE DOLLMAKER
0–380–00947–1 Avon pb $4.95

• Louis Auchincloss
"Auchincloss's genius as a writer and chronicler of upper-class New York is to render even the pettiest of these American aristocrats as recognizably human figures."—*Chicago Tribune*

THE BOOK CLASS
A novel about a women's reading group in Manhattan
0–395–36138–9 Houghton Mifflin $14.95

THE CAT AND THE KING
A historical novel of the French court
0–395–30225–0 Houghton Mifflin $10.95

THE DARK LADY
0–395–25402–7 Houghton Mifflin $8.95

DIARY OF A YUPPIE
In this recent novel, Auchincloss presents an updated picture of Wall Street ethics
0–395–41649–3 Houghton Mifflin $16.95

EXIT LADY MASHAM
0–395–34388–7 Houghton Mifflin $13.95

FELLOW PASSENGERS: A Novel in Portraits
His most recent novel
0–395–49853–8 Houghton Mifflin $17.95

THE GREAT WORLD AND TIMOTHY COLT
0–07–002445–6 McGraw-Hill pb $4.95

HONORABLE MEN
0–07–002434–0 McGraw-Hill pb $4.95

THE HOUSE OF THE PROPHET
The life of a distinguished man, from World War I to Vietnam. "The most accomplished book he has written to date"—*NY Times*
0–395–29084–8 Houghton Mifflin $10.95
0–395–30520–9 Houghton Mifflin pb $3.95

NARCISSA & OTHER FABLES
0–395–33114–5 Houghton Mifflin $13.95

PORTRAIT IN BROWNSTONE
0–07–002441–3 McGraw-Hill pb $4.95

THE RECTOR OF JUSTIN
Auchincloss' most widely acclaimed book is a sharply defined moral portrait of a prep school headmaster
0–940595–09–5 Hill & Wang $9.95

SKINNY ISLAND: More Tales of Manhattan
0–395–43295–2 Houghton Mifflin $17.95

WATCHFIRES
0–395–31546–8 Houghton Mifflin $13.95

• James Baldwin
ANOTHER COUNTRY
0–440–30200–5 Dell pb $4.95

GIOVANNI'S ROOM
A man torn between homosexual love and the love of a woman; set in Paris
0–440–32881–0 Dell pb $4.95

GOING TO MEET THE MAN
A collection of stories
0–440–32931–0 Dell pb $4.95

GO TELL IT ON THE MOUNTAIN
Baldwin's first novel tells the story of two generations of a black American family
0–440–33007–6 Dell pb $4.95

IF BEALE STREET COULD TALK
A black artist is unjustly imprisoned in New York City's notorious Tombs. "A moving, painful story, so vividly human and so obviously based on reality, that it strikes us as timeless"—Joyce Carol Oates
0–451–13789–2 NAL pb $3.95

• Saul Bellow
THE ADVENTURES OF AUGIE MARCH
The life story of a Jewish Huck Finn, from the slums of Chicago to the glitzy capitals of the Continent
0–14–007272–1 Penguin pb $6.95

DANGLING MAN
In Bellow's first novel, a young man is left dangling when the army snarls his induction in red tape
0–8149–0024–0 Vanguard $15.95

THE DEAN'S DECEMBER
"*The Dean's December* is renewed testament to a grand career, our greatest since Faulkner's and Frost's . . . At an age when most writers are hopelessly repeating themselves, Bellow is still finding good new things to do"—*Chicago Sun-Times*
0–06–014849–7 Harper & Row $14.95
0–671–60254–3 Washington Square pb $4.50

HENDERSON THE RAIN KING
Henderson tries to flee modern chaos in African jungles
0–670–36655–2 Viking $12.95
0–14–007269–1 Penguin pb $5.95

HERZOG
Moses Herzog deals with his personal crisis by writing erudite, compulsively readable letters to the living and the dead
0–14–007270–5 Penguin pb $6.95

HIM WITH HIS FOOT IN HIS MOUTH & OTHER STORIES
Four stories ranging from the slums of French Canada to the halls of academe
0–671–55247–3 Pocket pb $4.50

HUMBOLDT'S GIFT
A gifted, troubled writer (modeled on Delmore Schwartz) is torn apart by the conflicting demands of artistic purity and commercial success
0–14–007271–3 Penguin pb $7.95

MORE DIE OF HEARTBREAK
A Russian literature enthusiast comes back from Paris to be with his famous uncle. "Marks a return to the comic exuberance of his most enjoyable fiction . . . Bellow's comedy is cunningly planned: we rollick, then we pause to think"—Walter Clemons, *Newsweek*
0–688–06935–5 Morrow $17.95

MOSBY'S MEMOIRS & OTHER STORIES
A variety of stories, led off by Bellow's classic portrayal of a disaffected Jewish intellectual
0–14–007318–3 Penguin pb $5.95

MR. SAMMLER'S PLANET
An elderly but vivacious man casts a skeptical eye on Manhattan in the radical '60s
0–14–007317–5 Penguin pb $6.95

SEIZE THE DAY
A powerful novella in which a bewildered young New York man is defeated by an implacable father, estranged wife, and beguiling charlatan in one vertiginous day
0–670–63176–0 Viking $7.95
0–14–007285–3 Penguin pb $4.95

A THEFT
0–14–011969–8 Penguin pb $6.95

Jane Bowles

MY SISTER'S HAND IN MINE: An Expanded Edition of the Collected Works of Jane Bowles
One novel, one play, and six short stories; all are remarkable
Introduction by Truman Capote
0–88001–188–2 Ecco pb $14.95

TWO SERIOUS LADIES
The only novel by the woman considered by Tennessee Williams to be the most underrated writer in American literature
0–525–48324–1 Dutton pb $8.95

• **Paul Bowles**

COLLECTED STORIES OF PAUL BOWLES
"A master of suggesting anxiety . . . Bowles has glimpsed what lies back of our sheltering sky . . . an endless flux of stars so like those atoms which make us see that in our apprehension of this terrible infinity, we experience not only horror but likeness"—Gore Vidal
Introduction by Gore Vidal
0–87685–396–3 Black Sparrow pb $12.50

THE DELICATE PREY
Seventeen stories. "One of the most profound, beautifully wrought, and haunting collections in our literature"—Tobias Wolff
0–912946–01–6 Ecco pb $8.95

A HUNDRED CAMELS IN THE COURTYARD
Four stories of contemporary Moroccan life, all dealing with kif-smokers
0–87286–002–7 City Lights pb $5.95

LET IT COME DOWN
A mild-mannered American who goes to Morocco to find himself finds more than he bargained for
0–87685–479–X Black Sparrow pb $12.50

Paul Bowles from An Invisible Spectator *by Christopher Sawyer-Lauçanno (Weidenfeld & Nicolson)*

MIDNIGHT MASS
A collection of recent stories, some with considerably more humor than is generally attributed to Bowles
0–87685–476–5 Black Sparrow pb $7.50

POINTS IN TIME
The points in time are moments in the history of Morocco, imagined with precision and brevity
0–88001–044–4 Ecco $12.50

THE SHELTERING SKY
Americans coming apart in the Sahara: Bowles' first and best novel
0–912946–43–1 Ecco pb $8.95

THE SPIDER'S HOUSE
This account of revolution in Fez in the 1950s is Bowles' most elaborate fiction
0–87685–545–1 Black Sparrow pb $10.00

UNWELCOME WORDS
Seven recent, frequently experimental stories
0–939180–44–8 Tombouctou pb $7.00

UP ABOVE THE WORLD
An American couple descends into drugs and violent death, courtesy of a charming South American psychopath
0–88001–008–8 Ecco pb $7.95

• **William S. Burroughs**
"The only American novelist living today who may conceivably be possessed by genius."—Norman Mailer

CITIES OF THE RED NIGHT
"Burroughs may be our only writer whose socio-political apocalyptica transcends both paranoia and triviality; his imagination is superb, his ear savagely satiric"—*Kirkus Reviews*
0–03–058998–3 Henry Holt $50.00
0–03–061521–6 Henry Holt pb $7.25

EXTERMINATOR!
"Burroughs is the greatest satirical writer since Jonathan Swift"—Jack Kerouac
0–14–005003–5 Penguin pb $5.95

INTERZONE
A collection of hitherto unpublished early writings, some from the same period as *Naked Lunch*
Edited by James Grauerholz
0–670–81347–8 Viking $17.95

JUNKY
This laconic memoir, Burroughs' first book, was first published as a lurid paperback in 1953
0–14–004351–9 Penguin pb $6.95

NAKED LUNCH
"An absolutely devastating ridicule of all that is false, primitive, and vicious in current American life"—Terry Southern
0–394–53884–6 Grove $17.95
0–8021–3093–3 Grove pb $6.95

THE PLACE OF DEAD ROADS
A surreal version of a 19th-century Western. "Bosch-like visions, extraordinarily precise vivid visualizations . . . Outrageous ideas like mind bombs"—Allen Ginsberg
0–03–003684–4 Henry Holt pb $7.95

QUEER
An early work of autobiography, recently published for the first time
0–14–008389–8 Penguin pb $5.95

THE SOFT MACHINE, NOVA EXPRESS & THE WILD BOYS
Three quintessential examples of Burroughs' "cut-up" mode
0–8021–3084–1 Grove pb $8.95

THE TICKET THAT EXPLODED
A prophetic vision of a world in which technology has gone haywire. "His Swiftian vision of a processed, pre-packaged life, a kind of electro-chemical totalitarianism, often evokes the black laughter of hilarious horror"—*Playboy*
0–394–62364–9 Grove pb $6.95

THE WESTERN LANDS
"In Mr. Burroughs' hands, writing reverts to acts of magic, as though he were making some enormous infernal encyclopedia of all the black impulses and acts that, once made, would shut the fiends away forever"—*NY Times*
0–670–81352–4 Viking $18.95

• **Truman Capote**

ANSWERED PRAYERS: The Unfinished Novel
Much discussed but never completed, Capote's last work stands as a bitter portrait of the beau monde on New York's Upper East Side
0–394–55645–3 Random House $16.95

BREAKFAST AT TIFFANY'S
The novella about Holly Golightly, the backwoods girl on the fast track in Manhattan
0–394–41770–4 Random House $13.95
0–451–15644–7 NAL pb $3.50

A CAPOTE READER
0–394–55647–X Random House $25.00

THE DOGS BARK: Private Places and Public People
0–394–48751–6 Random House $10.95
0–452–25909–6 NAL pb $9.95

THE GRASS HARP, A TREE OF NIGHT & OTHER SHORT STORIES
A novella and a group of stories that catch Capote in his early, elegiac, beautifully nostalgic mood
0–451–14092–3 NAL pb $3.50

MUSIC FOR CHAMELEONS: New Writing
A collection of stories, interviews, and sketches, including the famous true-crime grotesque, "Handcarved Coffins"
0–452–25463–9 NAL pb $6.95

OTHER VOICES, OTHER ROOMS
Capote's first novel, the story of a sensitive boy growing up in the American south
0–394–43949–X Random House $15.95
0–451–14463–5 NAL pb $4.50

SELECTED WRITINGS OF TRUMAN CAPOTE
0–394–44467–1 Random House $16.95

THREE BY TRUMAN CAPOTE
0–394–54513–3 Random House $12.95

• **John Cheever**

BULLET PARK
"Cheever's deepest, most challenging book"—John Leonard, *NY Times*
0–394–41819–0 Knopf $13.95
0–345–28590–5 Ballantine pb $2.95

TO ORDER BOOKS AS GIFTS, SEE PAGE 1

FALCONER
A college professor is sentenced to prison for killing his brother
0–345–33145–1 Ballantine pb $3.50

OH WHAT A PARADISE IT SEEMS
"Cheever is the celebrant of the grand poetry of life . . . The paradisiacal elixir . . . is served up sparkling"—John Updike, *New Yorker*
0–345–33832–4 Ballantine pb $2.95

THE STORIES OF JOHN CHEEVER
"Some of the most wonderful stories any American has written"—*Boston Globe*
0–394–50087–3 Knopf $20.00
0–345–33567–8 Ballantine pb $5.95

THE WAPSHOT CHRONICLE & THE WAPSHOT SCANDAL
"John Cheever's prose is always a pleasure to read, because it is both graceful and governed"—*Chicago Tribune*
0–06–010741–3 Harper & Row $15.60

THE WAPSHOT CHRONICLE
A comic-elegiac account of an eccentric New England family
0–06–080295–2 Harper & Row pb $2.25

THE WAPSHOT SCANDAL
A sequel to *The Wapshot Chronicle*. "John Cheever is one of the most urbane moralists of our time; he is also one of our most entertaining story tellers"—*NY Times*
0–345–34323–9 Ballantine pb $4.50

- Walter Van Tilburg Clark
THE OX-BOW INCIDENT
The famous novel of a lynching
0–541–52239–7 NAL $3.50

THE TRACK OF THE CAT
A mountain lion preys on an isolated ranchhouse
0–8032–6307–4 Nebraska pb $5.95

- James Gould Cozzens
BY LOVE POSSESSED
This account of two days in a man's life was a best-seller in 1960
0–15–115113–X HBJ $8.50

GUARD OF HONOR
The Pulitzer Prize novel of 1949 is a long and painstaking account of an incident at a wartime army base
0–15–637609–1 HBJ pb $8.95

THE JUST AND THE UNJUST
A murder trial in a small town
0–15–646578–7 HBJ pb $6.95

THE LAST ADAM
A physician's neglect of his patient leads to an outbreak of typhoid fever in a Connecticut town
0–88184–210–9 Carroll & Graf pb $4.95

- Peter De Vries
THE BLOOD OF THE LAMB
0–316–18173–0 Little, Brown $14.95

FOREVER PANTING
0–14–006188–6 Penguin pb $5.95

THE GLORY OF THE HUMMINGBIRD
A TV quiz show changes the life of a small-town youth
0–316–18199–4 Little, Brown $14.95

I HEAR AMERICA SWINGING
A comic novel of the sexual revolution, published in 1976
0–316–18200–1 Little, Brown $7.95

INTO YOUR TENT I'LL CREEP
0–316–18198–6 Little, Brown $14.95

PECKHAM'S MARBLES
0–399–13188–4 Putnam $17.95
0–07–016650–1 McGraw-Hill pb $4.95

SAUCE FOR THE GOOSE
0–14–006281–5 Penguin pb $4.95

SLOUCHING TOWARDS KALAMAZOO
0–316–18172–2 Little, Brown $13.95
0–14–007070–2 Penguin pb $6.95

- Ralph Ellison
INVISIBLE MAN
Set in the immediate post-Depression era, Ellison's landmark novel is an unforgettable account of a black man's journey from south to north, from immaturity to terrible experience
0–697–72313–7 Random House pb $6.95

- Howard Fast
APRIL MORNING
Coming of age during the American Revolution
0–517–50681–5 Crown $8.95
0–553–27322–1 Bantam pb $3.95

CITIZEN TOM PAINE
A fictionalized biography of the great radical
0–8021–3064–X Grove pb $9.95

- M.F.K. Fisher
NOT NOW, BUT NOW
Fisher's only novel charts a woman's devastating effect on those around her
0–86547–072–3 North Point pb $9.25

- Shelby Foote
FOLLOW ME DOWN
0–394–40875–6 Random House $10.95

LOVE IN A DRY SEASON
0–394–40877–2 Random House $10.00

SEPTEMBER, SEPTEMBER
0–394–40721–0 Random House $10.95

SHILOH
A realistic, close-up treatment of the Civil War battle
0–394–40873–X Random House $11.95

Ralph Ellison (photo copyright Bern Schwartz)

William Gaddis (photo courtesy Knopf)

- William Gaddis
CARPENTER'S GOTHIC
0–670–69793–1 Viking $16.95
0–14–008993–4 Penguin pb $6.95

JR
Told entirely in dialogue, *JR* is the 726-page chronicle of an 11-year-old entrepreneur operating on a mythical scale. "Behind the wild comedy, the frantic pace, the precise satire, the rigorous art, there is the somber mood of something that for want of a better word we might just as well call tragedy"—*NY Times*
0–14–008039–2 Penguin pb $12.95

THE RECOGNITIONS
First published in 1955, Gaddis' long, complex novel of the varieties of forgery has been acclaimed by many as a masterpiece of American modern fiction
0–14–007768–5 Penguin pb $12.95

- Herbert Gold
DREAMING
1–55611–071–5 Fine $17.95

THE MAN WHO WAS NOT WITH IT
A man's journey south to Florida brings him in contact with a strange world of night clubs and carnivals
0–912697–69–5 Algonquin pb $10.95

- Paul Goodman
THE BREAK-UP OF OUR CAMP: Stories, 1932–1935
Edited by Taylor Stoehr
0–87685–329–7 Black Sparrow pb $8.50

A CEREMONIAL: Stories, 1936–1940
Edited by Taylor Stoehr
0–87685–353–X Black Sparrow pb $8.50

THE FACTS OF LIFE: Stories, 1940–1949
Edited by Taylor Stoehr
0–87685–356–4 Black Sparrow pb $8.50

THE GALLEY TO MYTILENE: Stories, 1949–1960
Edited by Taylor Stoehr
0–87685–359–9 Black Sparrow pb $8.50

PARENTS' DAY
Preface by Taylor Stoehr
0–87685–634–2 Black Sparrow pb $12.50

• William Goyen

HAD I A HUNDRED MOUTHS: New and Selected Stories, 1947–1983
Nineteen stories set mostly in East Texas
Introduction by Joyce Carol Oates
0–89255–110–0 Persea pb $9.95

THE HOUSE OF BREATH
A young boy grows up in a small Texas town
0–89255–109–7 Persea pb $9.95

IN A FARTHER COUNTRY
0–7206–4450–X Dufour $17.95

• Shirley Ann Grau

THE HOUSE ON COLISEUM STREET
A novel of a young girl's life in New Orleans
0–380–89939–6 Avon pb $3.95

THE KEEPERS OF THE HOUSE
This portrait of a southern family won the Pulitzer Prize in 1964
0–380–70047–6 Avon pb $4.50

NINE WOMEN
0–394–54845–0 Knopf $15.95
0–380–70107–3 Avon pb $5.95

• A.B. Guthrie, Jr.

THE BIG SKY
One of the most famous Westerns ever written, a novel of early exploration on the Missouri
Introduction by Wallace Stegner
0–395–08393–1 Houghton Mifflin pb $9.95
0–553–26683–7 Bantam pb $4.50

Elizabeth Hardwick

THE GHOSTLY LOVER
A Kentucky family
0–912946–95–4 Ecco $12.95

THE SIMPLE TRUTH
The effects of a murder trial
0–912946–98–9 Ecco $12.95

• Mark Harris

BANG THE DRUM SLOWLY
A dying baseball player
0–8032–7221–9 Nebraska pb $6.50

IT LOOKED LIKE FOR EVER
More about the baseball player Henry W. Wiggen
0–07–026721–9 McGraw-Hill pb $6.95

SOMETHING ABOUT A SOLDIER
0–8032–7226–X Nebraska pb $6.50

THE SOUTHPAW
"By far the best 'serious' baseball novel published"—San Francisco Chronicle
0–8032–7220–0 Nebraska pb $7.95

A TICKET FOR A SEAMSTITCH
Completes the baseball tetralogy begun by The Southpaw, Bang the Drum Slowly, and It Looked Like For Ever
0–8032–7224–3 Nebraska pb $5.95

• John Hawkes

Hawkes defines his writing in these terms: "I began to write fiction on the assumption that the true enemies of the novel were plot, character, setting, and theme, and having once abandoned these familiar ways of thinking about fiction, totality of vision or structure was really all that remained . . . I'm trying to hold in balance poetic and novelistic methods in order to make the novel a more valid and pleasurable experience."

ADVENTURES IN THE ALASKAN SKIN TRADE
The proprietess of an Alaskan whorehouse dreams of her long-lost father
0–14–009283–8 Penguin pb $6.95

THE BEETLE LEG
"John Hawkes is the Cellini of contemporary fiction, a demonic artificer of words"—NY Times
0–8112–0062–0 New Directions pb $5.70

THE BLOOD ORANGES
A comic variation on Ford Madox Ford's The Good Soldier. "Outrageous situations and unforgettable scenes refracted through a lens of rhetoric as beautiful as anything I know of in contemporary fiction"—John Barth
0–8112–0061–2 New Directions pb $7.95

THE CANNIBAL
Introduction by Albert Guerard
0–8112–0063–9 New Directions pb $7.95

HUMORS OF BLOOD AND SKIN: A John Hawkes Reader
"One has a wide choice of what to admire in the work of John Hawkes"—Donald Barthelme
Introduction by William Gass
0–8112–0907–5 New Directions pb $12.95

THE LIME TWIG
"You suffer The Lime Twig like a dream. It seems to be something that is happening to you, that you want to escape from but can't"—Flannery O'Connor
Introduction by Leslie A. Fiedler
0–8112–0065–5 New Directions pb $5.95

LUNAR LANDSCAPES
Includes The Owl and The Goose and the Grave
0–8112–0290–9 New Directions pb $6.95

THE OWL
Introduction by Robert Scholes
0–8112–0665–3 New Directions pb $3.95

SECOND SKIN
0–8112–0067–1 New Directions pb $6.95

VIRGINIE: Her Two Lives
"Hawkes' serene, inviolable prose is so precise, luminous and evocative as to make this novel seem dreamed rather than read"—Angela Carter
0–88184–054–8 Carroll & Graf pb $7.95

WHISTLEJACKET
1–55584–049–3 Weidenfeld & Nicolson $17.95
0–02–043591–6 Macmillan pb $7.95

• John Hersey

A BELL FOR ADANO
American GIs in an Italian town liberated from the Nazis
0–394–75695–9 Random House pb $6.95

THE CALL
0–394–54331–9 Knopf $19.45
0–14–008695–1 Penguin pb $8.95

THE CHILD BUYER
0–394–41910–3 Knopf $11.95

THE WALL
The famous novel of life in the Warsaw ghetto during World War II
0–394–45092–2 Knopf $24.50
0–394–75696–7 Random pb $9.95

• Chester Himes

Best known for his Harlem detective series which was the basis of such films as Cotton Comes to Harlem, Himes began writing while serving a prison term for jewel theft in the 1940s.

BLIND MAN WITH A PISTOL
A late entry in Himes's series about the Harlem detectives Grave Digger and Coffin Ed; this one experiments with an unusually fragmented narrative
0–85031–731–2 Schocken $15.95
0–85031–732–0 Schocken pb $6.95

A CASE OF RAPE
Introduction by Calvin Hernton
0–88258–143–0 Howard $12.95

COTTON COMES TO HARLEM
0–8052–8205–X Schocken $13.95
0–394–75999–0 Schocken pb $5.95

THE CRAZY KILL
0–8052–8206–8 Schocken $13.95
0–8052–8217–3 Schocken pb $5.95

THE HEAT'S ON
0–8052–8251–0 Schocken $13.95
0–394–75997–4 Schocken pb $5.95

IF HE HOLLERS LET HIM GO
A young black encounters endemic racism at a California munitions plant during World War II. Himes's angry first novel still comes across as a tough and risky piece of work
Introduction by Graham Hodges
0–938410–32–6 Thunder's Mouth pb $9.95

LONELY CRUSADE
A novel whose unflattering portrayals of white leftists provoked controversy in the late '40s
Introduction by Graham Hodges
0–938410–37–7 Thunder's Mouth pb $10.95

A RAGE IN HARLEM
The first adventure of the Harlem detectives Coffin Ed Johnson and Grave Digger Jones
0–8052–8239–4 Schocken $13.95
0–8052–8240–8 Schocken pb $5.95

THE REAL COOL KILLERS
0–8052–8237–8 Schocken $13.95
0–679–72039–1 Schocken pb $5.95

THE THIRD GENERATION
0–938410–73–3 Thunder's Mouth pb $11.95

• John Clellon Holmes

GET HOME FREE
"Hope in the afternoon, the last gaudy night, the bleak understanding dawn, a drizzly vision of America in this, an existentialist volume, Holmes's best book"—Jack Kerouac
0–938410–53–9 Thunder's Mouth pb $8.95

GO
The original novel of the Beat Generation
Introduction by James Atlas
0–938410–60–1 Thunder's Mouth pb $9.95

THE HORN
A novel of the jazz world, first published in 1958. "Strongly reflects the history of jazz and many of its people are studies of jazz personalities (The Horn himself seems three parts Coleman Hawkins and one part Lester Young)"—NY Times
Foreword by Archie Shepp
0–938410–50–4 Thunder's Mouth $19.95
0–938410–51–2 Thunder's Mouth pb $9.95

• Charles Jackson
THE LOST WEEKEND
The famous novel of alcoholism has a few
surprises even for those familiar with Billy
Wilder's movie version
0–88184–020–3 Carroll & Graf pb $7.95

• Shirley Jackson
THE HAUNTING OF HILL HOUSE
An influential, disarmingly subtle novel
about a lonely young woman driven to the
brink of madness and beyond by a sinister,
possibly haunted old mansion
0–14–007108–3 Penguin pb $5.95

THE LOTTERY
A well-crafted collection of stories that
includes the universally read title story
about a curious small-town ritual
0–374–51681–2 Farrar, Straus & Giroux pb $8.95

THE SUNDIAL
Informed that the world will be destroyed
and they alone are spared, the eccentric
Halloran family wait in their mansion for
the comic and surprising end
0–14–008317–0 Penguin pb $5.95

• James Jones
FROM HERE TO ETERNITY
A naval base in Hawaii in the days
preceding Pearl Harbor
0–385–28312–1 Delacorte $19.95
0–440–32770–9 Dell pb $5.95

THIN RED LINE
0–684–15555–9 Scribners $30.00

• Jack Kerouac
"Jack Kerouac, new Buddha of American
prose, who spit forth intelligence . . .
creating a spontaneous bop prosody and
original classic literature."—Allen Ginsberg
BIG SUR
0–07–034206–7 McGraw-Hill pb $7.95

THE DHARMA BUMS
A novel of the Beat scene featuring thinly
disguised portraits of Allen Ginsberg, Gary
Snyder, Kenneth Rexroth, and others
0–14–004252–0 Penguin pb $6.95

Jack Kerouac, from Memory Babe: A Criti-
cal Biography of Jack Kerouac *by Gerald
Nicosia (Grove)*

DOCTOR SAX
Autobiographical novel of a French-
Canadian growing up in Lowell,
Massachusetts, haunted by the ghosts and
demons of a fantasy world
0–8021–3049–6 Grove pb $7.95

LONESOME TRAVELER
More life on the road. "There is nothing
nobler than to put up with a few
inconveniences like snakes and dust for the
sake of absolute freedom"—Jack Kerouac
0–8021–3074–7 Grove pb $6.95

ON THE ROAD
Kerouac's most famous novel
0–451–15263–8 NAL pb $3.95

SATORI IN PARIS & PIC
Two short, late works
0–8021–3061–5 Grove pb $7.95

THE SUBTERRANEANS
A love story set in San Francisco, and one
of Kerouac's most popular books
Introduction by Gerald Nicosia
0–8021–5040–3 Grove pb $4.95

THE TOWN AND THE CITY
Kerouac's first novel
0–15–690790–9 HBJ pb $8.95

TRISTESSA
A strung-out Mexican prostitute
0–07–034205–9 McGraw-Hill pb $5.95

VISIONS OF CODY
In part, a memoir of Kerouac's companion
on the road Neal Cassady
Introduction by Allen Ginsberg
0–07–034202–4 McGraw-Hill pb $12.95

VISIONS OF GERARD
The early childhood of Ti Jean Duluoz,
Kerouac's alter ego, as reflected in the
short life of his brother Gerard
0–07–034204–0 McGraw-Hill pb $6.95

• Andrew Lytle
THE VELVET HORN
Afterword by George Core
0–918769–03–5 University of the South pb $10.95

• Mary McCarthy
BIRDS OF AMERICA
An American undergraduate in Paris in
the '60s
0–15–112770–0 HBJ $11.95

A CHARMED LIFE
A New England artists' colony of the '50s
0–15–116907–1 HBJ $15.95

CANNIBALS AND MISSIONARIES
A 1979 novel of terrorists and hostages
0–15–115387–6 HBJ $10.95
0–380–50690–4 Avon pb $2.75

CAST A COLD EYE
Seven short stories
0–15–115941–6 HBJ $12.95

THE COMPANY SHE KEEPS
McCarthy's first novel
0–15–620085–6 HBJ pb $5.95

THE GROUP
Eight Vassar girls of the class of 1933
0–15–137280–2 HBJ $8.50
0–380–52134–2 Avon pb $4.95

• Carson McCullers
**THE BALLAD OF THE SAD CAFE &
OTHER STORIES**
Seven short stories, including the title story
of a tall woman's love for a midget. "I
have found in her work such intensity and
nobility of spirit as we have not had in our
prose-writing since Herman Melville"—
Tennessee Williams
0–553–27254–3 Bantam pb $3.50

THE HEART IS A LONELY HUNTER
Published when she was only 23,
McCullers' first novel catapulted her to
literary prominence
0–395–07978–0 Houghton Mifflin $16.95
0–553–26963–1 Bantam pb $3.95

THE MEMBER OF THE WEDDING
A troubled, perceptive twelve-year-old girl
awaits her brother's wedding
0–8112–0093–0 New Directions pb $5.95

• Norman Mailer
ADVERTISEMENTS FOR MYSELF
A maddening, at times frighteningly acute
dissection of Mailer by Mailer in the form
of excerpts from, and criticisms of, all of
his early works
0–399–50538–5 Putnam pb $6.95

AN AMERICAN DREAM
The middle-aged Rojack murders his
heiress wife in an act of madness
0–8050–0349–5 Henry Holt pb $8.95

ANCIENT EVENINGS
A portrait of Ramses II and ancient Egypt.
"There is . . . power in Mailer's fantasy . . .
and there is a relevance to current reality in
America that actually surpasses that of
Mailer's largest previous achievement"—
NY Review of Books
0–316–54410–8 Little, Brown $19.95
0–446–32109–5 Warner pb $4.95

BARBARY SHORE
A metaphorical New York tenement
houses the obsessed and dispossessed
0–88184–445–4 Carroll & Graf pb $9.95

THE DEER PARK
A realistic, undervalued novel about a
young writer's coming of age amid the
license of a 1950s film colony
0–399–50531–8 Putnam pb $8.95

THE EXECUTIONER'S SONG
Really two books: the first about the
brutal life and death of convicted killer
Gary Gilmore, the second about the
media's no less savage fight for the story
rights. "Not since *The Grapes of Wrath* has
there been an American book that so
discovered the voices in our culture"—
Philadelphia Inquirer
0–316–54417–5 Little, Brown $25.00

THE NAKED AND THE DEAD
Mailer's first novel, a naturalistic account
of a small fighting troop living and dying
on a Pacific island in World War II
0–8050–0522–6 Henry Holt $18.95
0–8050–0521–8 Henry Holt pb $8.95

**SHORT FICTION OF NORMAN
MAILER**
0–523–48009–1 Pinnacle pb $3.50

TOUGH GUYS DON'T DANCE
A thriller set on the East Coast, about a
man who cannot remember whether or not
he killed a girl
0–345–32321–1 Ballantine pb $3.95

WHY ARE WE IN VIETNAM?
In a manic, amphetamine-like style, a young Texan d.j. relates the comic misadventures of a hunting trip with his father in Alaska; Mailer's funniest book
0-03-059977-6 Henry Holt pb $6.25

● Bernard Malamud
THE ASSISTANT
The effect of a young man on an aging grocery store owner and his family
0-374-50484-9 Farrar, Straus & Giroux pb $6.95

THE FIXER
An ordinary man is accused of "ritual murder" in Czarist Russia
0-671-66428-X Pocket pb $4.50

GOD'S GRACE
A prophetic novel examining humanity's dreams and failures. "Both somber and sometimes very funny . . . Malamud may have created his most lasting work"—*Wall Street Journal*
0-374-16466-5 Farrar, Straus & Giroux $13.50
0-380-64519-X Avon pb $3.95

IDIOTS FIRST
A gathering of stories first published in 1963
0-374-17420-2 Farrar, Straus & Giroux $10.95
0-374-52010-0 Farrar, Straus & Giroux pb $8.95

THE MAGIC BARREL
A short story collection which won the National Book Award in 1958
0-374-19576-5 Farrar, Straus & Giroux $14.95

THE NATURAL
Malamud's first novel, about baseball player Roy Hobbs
0-374-21960-5 Farrar, Straus & Giroux $13.95
0-374-50200-5 Farrar, Straus & Giroux pb $8.95

A NEW LIFE
S. Levin, a 30-year-old man, moves to the Pacific Northwest from New York. "Malamud has, among other gifts, a compassionate irony, and Levin's final desperation . . . is that rare fictional achievement, true tragi-farce"—*Newsweek*
0-374-22128-6 Farrar, Straus & Giroux $15.00

REMBRANDT'S HAT
"Malamud magically transposes brief, finite units of experience into the most imaginative and readable art"—Joyce Carol Oates
0-374-24909-1 Farrar, Straus & Giroux $11.95
0-374-52034-8 Farrar, Straus & Giroux pb $8.95

THE STORIES OF BERNARD MALAMUD
0-452-25911-8 NAL pb $8.95

● William Maxwell
ANCESTORS: A Family History
Maxwell traces the history of his family, beginning in Ohio in 1818
0-87923-574-8 Godine pb $9.95

THE CHATEAU
Americans in France after World War II
0-87923-600-0 Godine pb $10.95

THE FOLDED LEAF
Two boys growing up in Chicago
0-87923-351-6 Godine pb $10.95

OVER BY THE RIVER & OTHER STORIES
Twelve short stories. "These stories seem to tell themselves, with each precisely observed detail or snatch of talk tapped home like a design on tinware"—*NY Times*
0-87923-541-1 Godine pb $10.95

SO LONG, SEE YOU TOMORROW
"A tale of inarticulate passion among innocent, middle-aged farming people . . . Maxwell's accomplishment is to present a fascinating tragedy enacted by sincere, gentle, reluctant participants—and to give his account the same integrity that marks their deeds"—*Washington Post*
0-394-50835-1 Knopf $7.95
0-345-29194-8 Ballantine pb $2.95

THEY CAME LIKE SWALLOWS
A portrait of a death in a family. "Here is a rare book . . . an exquisite picture of a mother as seen through the eyes of her two children and her husband"—Lewis Gannett, *NY Herald Tribune*
0-87923-677-9 Godine pb $9.95

TIME WILL DARKEN IT
Small-town Illinois in 1912
0-87923-448-2 Godine pb $10.95

● Arthur Miller
COLLECTED STORIES, 1948–1986
"Miller's stories are carefully ordered to underscore the continuity of his interests—his humanism, his running dispute with American values, his inquiry into personal responsibility"—*Newsweek*
0-06-015639-2 Harper & Row $17.95

THE MISFITS & OTHER STORIES
Nine short stories. "In the intensity of its vision, the force of its prose, in its ability to startle, to delight, to amuse, to catch wonder by surprise, the book is a masterpiece"—*Choice*
0-684-18779-5 Scribners pb $5.95

● Wright Morris
CEREMONY IN LONE TREE
"Wright Morris is one of our best novelists. . . . The elements of symbolic theme which appear throughout this story are all employed with brilliance and economy to pull together various scattered events"—John Hollander
0-8032-5782-2 Nebraska pb $6.95

THE FIELD OF VISION
Americans in Mexico: winner of the 1956 National Book Award
0-8032-5789-9 Nebraska pb $9.95

FIRE SERMON
A drama of old age giving way to youth
0-8032-8104-8 Nebraska pb $3.50

THE FORK RIVER SPACE PROJECT
Space workers on the lookout for UFOs over Kansas
0-8032-8112-9 Nebraska pb $5.95

THE HOME PLACE
An early work combining photographs and text. "As near to a new fiction form as you could get"—*San Francisco Chronicle*
0-8032-5139-4 Nebraska pb $7.95

A LIFE
A sequel to *Fire Sermon*
0-8032-8106-4 Nebraska pb $3.95

LOVE AMONG THE CANNIBALS
0-8032-5842-9 Nebraska pb $8.95

MAN AND BOY
0-8032-5787-2 Nebraska pb $4.25

THE MAN WHO WAS THERE
0-8032-5813-5 Nebraska pb $4.95

ONE DAY
A novel set on the day of JFK's assassination
0-8032-5841-0 Nebraska pb $7.95

PLAINS SONG
0-06-013047-4 Harper & Row $12.95
0-14-005778-1 Penguin pb $6.95

WHAT A WAY TO GO
0-8032-5862-3 Nebraska pb $5.95

THE WORKS OF LOVE
0-8032-5767-8 Nebraska pb $6.95

● Vladimir Nabokov
ADA OR ARDOR: A Family Chronicle
Nabokov's longest and perhaps most brilliant novel fuses his two worlds, Russia and America
0-07-045723-9 McGraw-Hill pb $12.95

BEND SINISTER
0-07-045710-7 McGraw-Hill pb $8.95

DESPAIR
0-679-72343-9 Vintage pb $7.95

GLORY
A young Russian exile is devoured by his fatherland
0-07-045733-6 McGraw-Hill $6.95
0-07-045727-1 McGraw-Hill pb $4.95

INVITATION TO A BEHEADING
0-399-50115-0 Putnam pb $8.95

KING, QUEEN, KNAVE
0-07-045722-0 McGraw-Hill $7.95

LAUGHTER IN THE DARK
"There is probably no more frangible encounter in the whole human gambit than the one between a sensitive, fiftyish man and a cretinous girl one-third his age, and in this short, swift, acrid novel originally published in 1938, the author of *Lolita* gives it as pitiless a treatment as it has ever had on paper"—*NY Sunday Tribune*
0-8112-0708-0 New Directions pb $8.95

Vladimir Nabokov (photo by Maclean Dameron, courtesy Alfred Appel, Jr.)

➤ **FOR OVERSEAS ORDERING INFORMATION, SEE PAGE 1**

LOLITA
The modern classic about Humbert Humbert's passion for a twelve-year-old "nymphet"
0–679–72316–1 Random House pb $7.95

THE ANNOTATED LOLITA
A useful road map into the novel's erudite references
Edited by Alfred Appel, Jr.
0–07–045730–1 McGraw-Hill pb $12.95

LOOK AT THE HARLEQUINS
A novel about a novelist not dissimilar to the author
0–07–045738–7 McGraw-Hill $8.95

NABOKOV'S DOZEN
A tart baker's dozen of short stories that dispatch Pushkin and word games with equal ease
0–385–19117–0 Doubleday pb $6.95

PALE FIRE
A novel, in the form of footnotes to a poem, whose formal inventiveness is matched only by its alternately comic and tragic brilliance
0–679–72342–0 Vintage pb $8.95

THE REAL LIFE OF SEBASTIAN KNIGHT
The first of Nabokov's pseudo-biographies, about an author comically less gifted than his biographer
0–8112–0644–0 New Directions pb $7.95

TRANSPARENT THINGS
A 1972 novella about marriage and murder
0–07–045734–4 McGraw-Hill $9.95

▶ **For Nabokov's Russian works, see Russian Literature**

● **Anaïs Nin**
CITIES OF THE INTERIOR
A five-volume novel-cycle including *Ladders to Fire, Children of the Albatross, The Four-Chambered Heart, A Spy in the House of Love,* and *Seduction of the Minotaur*
0–8040–0665–2 Ohio $19.95
0–8040–0666–0 Ohio pb $12.95

COLLAGES
"Though written as a series of fugue studies, *Collages* spills over into a new and curious thematic relationship with the reality of American character and life"— Marguerite Young
Illustrated by Jean Varda
0–8040–0045–X Ohio pb $3.95

DELTA OF VENUS: Erotica
Seventeen erotic stories written by Nin in the 1940s
0–15–625277–5 HBJ pb $5.95

HOUSE OF INCEST
A prose poem
0–8040–0148–0 Ohio pb $4.50

LITTLE BIRDS: Erotica
More erotic stories
0–15–652798–7 HBJ pb $4.95
0–553–7371–X2 Bantam pb $4.50

WINTER OF ARTIFICE
A collection of novelettes. "Finely-wrought musical writing shot through with clear insights into the inner world of human beings"—Lawrence Durrell
0–8040–0322–X Ohio pb $5.95

● **Edwin O'Connor**
THE LAST HURRAH
The decline of an Irish-American political boss
0–316–62659–7 Little, Brown pb $8.95

● **Flannery O'Connor**
COLLECTED WORKS
Includes *Wise Blood, A Good Man Is Hard to Find, The Violent Bear It Away, Everything That Rises Must Converge,* along with letters, essays, and uncollected stories
Edited by Sally Fitzgerald
0–940450–37–2 Library of America $30.00

THE COMPLETE STORIES
"She was not just the best 'woman writer' of this time and place; she expressed something secret about America, called 'the South,' with that transcendent gift for expressing the real spirit of a culture that is conveyed by those writers . . . who become nothing but what they see"—Alfred Kazin
0–374–12752–2 Farrar, Straus & Giroux $29.95
0–374–51536–0 Farrar, Straus & Giroux pb $9.95

EVERYTHING THAT RISES MUST CONVERGE
Nine short stories
Introduction by Robert Fitzgerald
0–374–50464–4 Farrar, Straus & Giroux pb $7.95

A GOOD MAN IS HARD TO FIND
Ten stories of the south
0–15–636465–4 HBJ pb $4.95

THE VIOLENT BEAR IT AWAY
A boy tries to escape his tragic legacy in this novel of the interplay of cosmic and human forces
0–374–50524–1 Farrar, Straus & Giroux pb $8.95

WISE BLOOD
The grotesque fate of itinerant preacher Hazel Motes
0–374–50584–5 Farrar, Straus & Giroux pb $6.95

● **Ann Petry**
THE NARROWS
A novel of black life in a New England town
Introduction by Nellie McKay
0–8070–8303–8 Beacon pb $10.95

THE STREET
A realistic novel of Harlem, first published in 1946
0–8070–6357–6 Beacon pb $8.95

● **Ayn Rand**
ATLAS SHRUGGED
"Who is John Galt?"
0–394–41576–0 Random House $29.95
0–451–15748–6 NAL pb $5.95

THE FOUNTAINHEAD
The meteoric rise of a callous young architect (modeled on Frank Lloyd Wright) to the peaks of power; influential in its day
0–451–15823–7 NAL pb $5.95

WE THE LIVING
An anti-Communist novel published in 1936
0–394–45124–4 Random House $19.95
0–451–15860–1 NAL pb $4.95

● **J.D. Salinger**
THE CATCHER IN THE RYE
Probably the most famous novel of adolescence
0–316–76953–3 Little, Brown $16.95
0–553–25025–6 Bantam pb $2.95

FRANNY AND ZOOEY
Two long stories about the eccentric Glass family
0–316–76954–1 Little, Brown $16.95
0–553–26973–9 Bantam pb $3.50

NINE STORIES
0–316–76956–8 Little, Brown $15.95
0–553–26360–9 Bantam pb $3.50

RAISE HIGH THE ROOF BEAM, CARPENTERS & SEYMOUR: AN INTRODUCTION
More on the Glass family
0–316–76957–6 Little, Brown $15.95
0–553–26255–6 Bantam pb $3.95

● **May Sarton**
ANGER
0–393–01643–9 Norton $12.95
0–393–30316–0 Norton pb $4.95

AS WE ARE NOW
The old age of a schoolteacher
0–393–08372–1 Norton $10.95
0–393–30049–8 Norton pb $3.95

THE BRIDGE OF YEARS
Belgium between the wars
0–393–30239–3 Norton pb $4.95

CRUCIAL CONVERSATIONS
The end of a marriage, filtered through the talk of those affected
0–393–00986–6 Norton pb $3.95

FAITHFUL ARE THE WOUNDS
0–393–30266–0 Norton pb $4.95

THE FUR PERSON
0–393–08841–3 Norton $10.95
0–393–30131–1 Norton pb $4.95

A GRAIN OF MUSTARD SEED
0–393–04344–4 Norton pb $4.95

JOANNA AND ULYSSES
0–393–30414–0 Norton pb $5.95

KINDS OF LOVE
0–393–00968–8 Norton pb $4.95

THE MAGNIFICENT SPINSTER
0–393–02220–X Norton $16.95

MISS PICKTHORN AND MISTER HARE
0–393–08541–4 Norton $14.95

MRS. STEVENS HEARS THE MERMAIDS SINGING
Introduction by Carolyn G. Heilbrun
0–393–00762–6 Norton pb $4.95

A RECKONING
A woman dying of cancer reassesses her relationship with the important women in her life
0–393–08828–6 Norton $11.95
0–393–00075–3 Norton pb $3.95

SHADOW OF A MAN
The death of his mother enables a 26-year-old man to see the world clearly and with a new maturity
0–393–30030–7 Norton pb $4.95

THE SMALL ROOM
A women's college in New England
0–393–00832–0 Norton pb $4.95

• Budd Schulberg
THE DISENCHANTED
A fictional interpretation of the life of F. Scott Fitzgerald
Introduction by Anthony Burgess
1–55611–027–8 Fine pb $8.95

• Delmore Schwartz
THE EGO IS ALWAYS AT THE WHEEL: Bagatelles
"Delmore Schwartz understood the world's inviolate sadness . . . Tacit in all he wrote was Kafka's parable of 'Infinite hope, but not for us' "—James Atlas
Edited by Robert Phillips
0–8112–1028–6 New Directions pb $8.95

IN DREAMS BEGIN RESPONSIBILITIES
Eight short stories examining the world of New York intellectuals in the 1930s and 1940s
Edited by James Atlas
Foreword by Irving Howe
0–8112–0680–7 New Directions pb $7.95

Irwin Shaw
BEGGARMAN, THIEF
0–440–10701–6 Dell pb $4.95

BREAD UPON THE WATERS
0–440–10844–6 Dell pb $4.95

EVENING IN BYZANTIUM
0–440–13150–2 Dell pb $4.95

RICH MAN, POOR MAN
0–440–17424–4 Dell pb $4.95

SHORT STORIES: Five Decades
Shaw's stories are generally considered his finest work
0–440–34075–6 Dell pb $6.95

THE TROUBLED AIR
A novel of the blacklisting era
0–440–18608–0 Dell pb $4.95

THE YOUNG LIONS
World War II seen from both sides of the battlefield
0–394–60809–7 Modern Library $7.95

• Terry Southern
THE MAGIC CHRISTIAN
Southern's most coherent satire recounts Guy Grand's savage practical jokes directed against the rest of humanity
0–14–007109–1 Penguin pb $5.95

• Terry Southern & Mason Hoffenberg
CANDY
A pornographic comedy that helped break publishing barriers in the '60s
0–14–007027–3 Penguin pb $5.95

• Jean Stafford
BOSTON ADVENTURE
An impoverished ten-year-old girl dreams of escaping from her roots and entering the glittering world of Boston's Beacon Hill
0–15–613611–2 HBJ pb $7.95

THE CATHERINE WHEEL
"Sharpness of dramatic focus and . . . economy of style"—Joyce Carol Oates, *The NY Times*
0–912946–87–3 Ecco pb $7.95

THE COLLECTED STORIES
"This collection will undoubtedly become a textbook for many students of short fiction. Jean Stafford can teach almost anything one could want to know about swiftly and deftly developing characters, balancing them in delicate counterpoint or wrenching conflict, and probing their thoughts and emotions"—*Newsweek*
0–374–12632–1 Farrar, Straus & Giroux $17.50

• Wallace Stegner
ALL THE LITTLE LIVE THINGS
A novel drawing in part on the hippie culture of the late '60s
0–8032–9109–4 Nebraska pb $7.50

ANGLE OF REPOSE
A novel based on the life of the 19th-century Western writer Mary Hallock Foote
0–449–23796–6 Fawcett pb $3.50

THE BIG ROCK CANDY MOUNTAIN
0–8032–9144–2 Nebraska pb $11.95

CROSSING TO SAFETY
0–394–56200–3 Random House $18.95

RECAPITULATION
A diplomat goes home to the West
0–8032–9165–5 Nebraska pb $7.95

SECOND GROWTH
The inner conflicts of life in a New Hampshire village
0–8032–9157–4 Nebraska pb $6.95

THE SPECTATOR BIRD
This follow-up to *All the Little Live Things* won the National Book Award in 1976
0–8032–9107–8 Nebraska pb $5.95

WOLF WILLOW
"By combining history, fiction, and his own memories . . . Wallace Stegner has summarized the frontier story and interpreted it as only one who was a part of it could do"—*NY Times*
0–8032–9108–6 Nebraska pb $7.95

• William Styron
THE CONFESSIONS OF NAT TURNER
The famous historical novel of a slave rebellion
0–394–42099–3 Random House $24.95
0–553–26916–X Bantam pb $4.95

LIE DOWN IN DARKNESS
Styron's first novel tells of a troubled Virginia family
0–394–50659–6 Random House $24.95
0–452–25705–0 NAL pb $7.95

THE LONG MARCH
A brutal novella of marines in training
0–394–43387–4 Random House $10.95

SOPHIE'S CHOICE
The terrible secret of a 1940s immigrant to New York
0–394–46109–6 Random House $29.95
0–553–27749–9 Bantam pb $5.50

• Peter Taylor
Taylor is noted for his nuanced portraits of privileged Southerners.
THE COLLECTED STORIES OF PETER TAYLOR
0–14–008361–8 Penguin pb $9.95

IN THE MIRO DISTRICT & OTHER STORIES
0–88184–005–X Carroll & Graf pb $7.95

THE OLD FOREST & OTHER STORIES
0–345–32778–0 Ballantine pb $4.95

A SUMMONS TO MEMPHIS
0–394–41062–9 Knopf $15.95
0–345–34660–2 Ballantine pb $4.95

A WOMAN OF MEANS
0–380–70099–9 Avon pb $3.95

• Lionel Trilling
THE MIDDLE OF THE JOURNEY
A '50s tangle of political loyalties
0–15–159547–X HBJ $14.95

OF THIS TIME, OF THAT PLACE & OTHER STORIES
Five short stories
0–15–668062–9 HBJ pb $3.95

• Gore Vidal
BURR
One of the best of Vidal's historical novels, about the man who shot Alexander Hamilton
0–394–48024–4 Random House $19.45
0–345–33921–5 Ballantine pb $4.95

THE CITY AND THE PILLAR
A landmark novel, one of the first to deal openly with homosexuality
0–345–33271–7 Ballantine pb $4.95

CREATION
A cavalcade of the ancient world
0–394–50015–6 Random House $15.95
0–345–34020–5 Ballantine pb $4.95

DARK GREEN, BRIGHT RED
An early novel about revolution in Central America
0–345–33457–4 Ballantine pb $4.95

DULUTH
Vidal's own favorite among his books, *Duluth* is an Orwellian tragedy set in a grotesque version of a typical American town
0–345–31220–1 Ballantine pb $3.95

1876
The closest and most corrupt presidential election in American history figures prominently in this realistic historical novel
0–394–49750–3 Random House $19.95
0–345–34626–2 Ballantine pb $4.95

EMPIRE
An epic of America in the Gilded Age. "In writing about how the US became an empire, Vidal gives us a rich and dazzling novel filled with more of the social observations, behavioral insights, political arguments, and personal quirks that have made him our most public of writers"—Webster Schott, *Cleveland Plain Dealer*
0–345–35472–9 Ballantine pb $4.95

THE JUDGEMENT OF PARIS
Americans in postwar Europe
0–345–33458–2 Ballantine pb $4.95

JULIAN
The author's first and funniest historical novel takes the form of a fictional journal of a very catty 4th-century Roman Emperor
0–345–32908–2 Ballantine pb $4.95

KALKI
0–394–42053–5 Random House $14.95

LINCOLN
"The portrait is reasoned, judicious, straightforward and utterly convincing"—Joyce Carol Oates, *NY Times*
0–345–31221–X Ballantine pb $4.95

MESSIAH
The creation of a cult of conformity. "Turns the Christian mythology and its attendant rituals inside out to create a religion based on death"—P. Schuyler Miller
0–345–33917–7 Ballantine pb $4.95

MYRA BRECKINRIDGE & MYRON
The famous comedy of sex and Hollywood, with its delightful sequel
0–394–55376–4 Random House $19.45
0–394–75444–1 Random House pb $8.95

A SEARCH FOR THE KING
A poetic novel on the troubador Blondel. "A chaste, spare, intelligent, and essentially pictorial style, which frequently achieves a vividness equal to that of the best imagist poets"—*Chicago Tribune*
0–345–33272–5 Ballantine pb $4.95

A THIRSTY EVIL: Seven Short Stories
0–917342–84–4 Gay Sunshine Press pb $7.95

TWO SISTERS
0–345–33117–6 Ballantine pb $4.95

WASHINGTON, D.C.
Set in the late Depression, this skillful historical novel traces the parallel lives of a senator and a newspaper publisher joined by a startling marriage between the former's protégé and the latter's daughter
0–345–34236–4 Ballantine pb $4.95

WILLIWAW
This first novel, written when the author was only 19, deals with an American transport crew hit by an Arctic squall in World War II
0–345–33233–4 Ballantine pb $4.95

- **Robert Penn Warren**
ALL THE KING'S MEN
The saga of Willie Stark's political rise and fall
0–394–40502–1 Random House $13.95
0–15–604762–4 HBJ pb $6.95

A PLACE TO COME TO
A 1977 novel about the life of a scholar
0–394–41064–5 Random House $12.95

A ROBERT PENN WARREN READER
0–394–55896–0 Random House $22.50

- **Eudora Welty**
THE COLLECTED STORIES OF EUDORA WELTY
0–15–118994–3 HBJ $22.95
0–15–618921–6 HBJ pb $10.95

THE BRIDE OF THE INNISFALLEN & OTHER STORIES
0–15–614075–6 HBJ pb $4.95

A CURTAIN OF GREEN & OTHER STORIES
Welty's first collection of short stories. "Miss Welty's short stories are deceptively simple. They are concerned with ordinary people, but what happens to them and the manner of the telling are far from ordinary"—*New Yorker*
0–15–623492–0 HBJ pb $6.95

Eudora Welty (photo by Jill Krementz, courtesy of Random House)

DELTA WEDDING
A southern family on a Mississippi plantation in 1923. "Presents the essence of the deep South and does it with infinite finesse"—*Christian Science Monitor*
0–15–625280–5 HBJ pb $5.95

THE GOLDEN APPLES
"I doubt that a better book about the South—one that more completely gets the feel of the particular texture of Southern life, and its special tone and pattern—has ever been written"—*New Yorker*
0–15–636090–X HBJ pb $5.95

LOSING BATTLES
A Mississippi family in the '30s
0–394–43421–8 Random House $13.95
0–394–72668–5 Random House pb $5.95

THE OPTIMIST'S DAUGHTER
Winner of the 1972 Pulitzer Prize
0–394–48017–1 Random House $13.45
0–394–72667–7 Random House pb $3.95

THE PONDER HEART
A wealthy man is accused of murdering his 17-year-old bride in a small southern town
0–15–672915–6 HBJ pb $5.95

THE ROBBER BRIDEGROOM
"A modern fairy tale, where irony and humor, outright nonsense, deep wisdom, and surrealistic extravaganzas become a poetic unity through the power of pure, exquisite style"—*NY Times*
0–15–178318–7 HBJ $19.95
0–15–676807–0 HBJ pb $4.95

SELECTED STORIES
Introduction by Katherine Anne Porter
0–394–60445–8 Modern Library $8.95

THIRTEEN STORIES
Edited by Ruth M. Vande Kieft
0–15–689969–8 HBJ pb $5.95

THE WIDE NET & OTHER STORIES
Eight stories
0–15–696610–7 HBJ pb $6.95

- **Tennessee Williams**
COLLECTED STORIES
"These stories are the true memoir of Tennessee Williams. Whatever happened to him, real or imagined, is here"—Gore Vidal
Introduction by Gore Vidal
0–8112–0952–0 New Directions $19.95
0–345–33587–2 Ballantine pb $5.95

THE ROMAN SPRING OF MRS. STONE
An older American actress and her obsession with a gigolo in Rome. "The Roman Spring is actually Mrs. Stone's Autumn. A sharp, witty, and moving novel"—*Chicago Tribune*
0–345–32690–3 Ballantine pb $3.50

EIGHT MORTAL LADIES POSSESSED
Six short stories
0–8112–0531–2 New Directions pb $1.95

HARD CANDY
Williams' second collection of short stories
0–8112–0221–6 New Directions pb $6.95

ONE ARM & OTHER STORIES
Williams' first collection of short fiction
0–8112–0223–2 New Directions pb $6.95

SINCE 1960

● Edward Abbey
"What entertains many and exasperates others is Abbey's unique prose voice. Alternately misanthropic and sentimental, enraged and hilarious, it is the voice of a full-blooded man airing his passions."—Peter Carlson

BEYOND THE WALL
0–03–069301–2 Henry Holt pb $7.95

THE BRAVE COWBOY
0–8263–0448–6 New Mexico pb $9.95

DOWN THE RIVER
0–525–48408–6 Dutton pb $9.95

FIRE ON THE MOUNTAIN
0–8263–0457–5 New Mexico pb $9.95

THE FOOL'S PROGRESS
0–8050–0921–3 Henry Holt $19.95

THE MONKEY WRENCH GANG
A band of ecologically-minded saboteurs wages war on Western land developers
0–380–00741–X Avon pb $4.95

Walter Abish (photo by Kenneth Feldman, courtesy of New Directions)

● Walter Abish
ALPHABETICAL AFRICA
Chapter by chapter, Abish lets in one letter of the alphabet; then, one at a time, he takes them all away. From this premise arises a mysteriously absorbing narrative of African adventures
0–8112–0533–9 New Directions pb $5.95

HOW GERMAN IS IT
A Germany of the mind, reconstructed with brilliance and perverse humor
0–8112–0776–5 New Directions pb $7.95

IN THE FUTURE PERFECT
Seven short stories, all examining the nature of language
0–8112–0660–2 New Directions pb $5.95

MINDS MEET
Twelve short stories posing the question, "Can fiction explore itself?"
0–8112–0557–6 New Directions $9.50

● Kathy Acker
BLOOD AND GUTS IN HIGH SCHOOL
"A post-modern Colette with echoes of Cleland's *Fanny Hill*"—William Burroughs
0–8021–3075–5 Grove Press pb $8.95

DON QUIXOTE
Don Quixote as a woman on a visionary quest
0–394–62085–2 Grove pb $8.95

EMPIRE OF THE SENSELESS
0–8021–1079–7 Grove $17.95

GREAT EXPECTATIONS
"*Great Expectations* is Kathy Acker's most ambitious, most exciting, and masterful novel to date. Its influence will be long and strongly felt. The novel is as revolutionary in form as it is in content"—Steve Abbott, *Poetry Flash*
0–394–53497–2 Grove $14.95
0–8021–3155–7 Grove pb $7.95

LITERAL MADNESS
Includes *My Death, My Life By Pier Paolo Pasolini, Kathy Goes to Haiti*, and *Florida*
0–8021–0001–5 Grove $19.95
0–8021–3156–5 Grove pb $8.95

● Alice Adams
BEAUTIFUL GIRL
Sixteen stories about American women from the 1930s to the 1960s, written over a 20-year span
0–449–21412–5 Fawcett pb $3.95

FAMILIES AND SURVIVORS
A young southern woman escapes to the California suburbs and discovers adultery, divorce, and other complications of married life
0–14–007375–2 Penguin pb $6.95

LISTENING TO BILLIE
The songs of Billie Holiday serve as a metaphor for the transitions in a New York woman's life
0–14–007376–0 Penguin pb $6.95

RICH REWARDS
A woman flees New York City for San Francisco in the mid-1970s
0–394–51101–8 Knopf $9.95
0–14–005918–0 Penguin pb $6.95

RETURN TRIPS
0–394–53633–9 Knopf $14.50
0–449–20953–9 Fawcett pb $3.95

SECOND CHANCES
0–394–56824–9 Knopf $18.95

SUPERIOR WOMEN
Radcliffe, from the 1940s to the 1980s
0–449–20746–3 Fawcett pb $3.95

TO SEE YOU AGAIN
0–14–006483–4 Penguin pb $6.95

● Renata Adler
PITCH DARK
0–394–50374–0 Knopf $12.95
0–06–097144–4 Harper & Row pb $6.95

SPEEDBOAT
A New York journalist takes stock of her life. Winner of the 1976 Ernest Hemingway Award for best first novel
0–06–097143–6 Harper & Row pb $7.95

● Lisa Alther
KINFLICKS
Funny and explicit account of a woman growing up
0–451–15685–4 NAL pb $4.95

ORIGINAL SINS
0–394–51685–0 Knopf $13.95
0–451–15517–3 NAL pb $4.95

OTHER WOMEN
A woman and her therapist
0–451–13894–5 NAL pb $4.95

● Max Apple
FREE AGENTS
0–06–091140–9 Harper & Row pb $5.95

THE ORANGING OF AMERICA & OTHER STORIES
A collection of ten short stories. "A fantasist of the first rank . . . He is an original"—*Washington Post*
0–14–010310–4 Penguin pb $5.95

THE PROPHETEERS
0–06–096158–9 Harper & Row pb $7.95

ZIP
A nice Jewish boy manages a middleweight Puerto Rican boxer and becomes enmeshed in a scheme that involves Howard Cosell, Jane Fonda, and J. Edgar Hoover
0–446–34179–7 Warner pb $3.50

● Raymond Andrews
APPALACHEE RED
The Deep South from the end of World War I to the beginning of the 1960s
0–8203–0961–3 Georgia pb $9.95

● James Atlas
THE GREAT PRETENDER
"A thoroughly enjoyable chronicle of the intellectual and sexual adventures of a young man 'coming of age,' told with humor and nostalgia"—*Chicago Tribune*
0–689–11800–7 Atheneum $15.95
0–14–009718–X Penguin pb $6.95

● Paul Auster
IN THE COUNTRY OF LAST THINGS
A postapocalyptic quest set against a backdrop of urban deprivation
0–670–81445–8 Viking $15.95

IF YOU CAN'T FIND IT, LOOK IN THE INDEX

THE NEW YORK TRILOGY
Three novels—*City of Glass, Ghosts,* and
The Locked Room—in which Auster reinvents the detective story as a kind of
philosophical endgame

CITY OF GLASS
0–940650–52–5 Sun & Moon $13.95
0–14–009731–7 Penguin pb $5.95

GHOSTS
0–940650–70–3 Sun & Moon $12.95
0–14–009735–X Penguin pb $5.95

THE LOCKED ROOM
0–317–54163–3 Sun & Moon $13.95
0–14–009736–8 Penguin pb $5.95

MOON PALACE
0–670–82509–3 Viking $18.95

• Sheila Ballantyne
IMAGINARY CRIMES
0–14–006540–7 Penguin pb $7.95

LIFE ON EARTH
0–671–60547–X Simon & Schuster $16.95

NORMA JEAN THE TERMITE QUEEN
Matrimony and motherhood vie with the
desire to do creative work
0–14–006551–2 Penguin pb $7.95

• Toni Cade Bambara
GORILLA, MY LOVE
A first collection of short stories
0–394–75049–7 Random House pb $4.95

THE SALT EATERS
A "tribal epic" about southern blacks who
seek out the healing properties of salt
0–394–75050–0 Random House pb $5.95

THE SEA BIRDS ARE STILL ALIVE
Short stories
0–394–71176–9 Random House pb $6.95

• Russell Banks
THE BOOK OF JAMAICA
0–345–33074–9 Ballantine pb $3.95

CONTINENTAL DRIFT
A blue-collar worker leaves New
Hampshire at Christmas time to find the
American nightmare in Florida
0–345–33021–8 Ballantine pb $4.50

FAMILY LIFE
A man's family becomes his mythical
kingdom
0–345–34693–9 Ballantine pb $3.50

HAMILTON STARK
A portrait of a pipefitter living in a New
England town. "A description of the
depths of isolation and despair that
unrelenting passion can bring"—*Chicago
Daily Herald*
0–345–33075–7 Ballantine pb $3.95

THE NEW WORLD STORIES
0–252–00722–0 Illinois pb $8.95

**THE RELATION OF MY
IMPRISONMENT**
0–940650–25–8 Sun & Moon $12.95
0–345–33076–5 Ballantine pb $3.95

SEARCHING FOR SURVIVORS
0–914590–06–5 Fiction Collective pb $12.95

SUCCESS STORIES
Twelve characters who seek success
through wealth, love, or power
0–06–015567–1 Harper & Row $15.95
0–345–34235–6 Ballantine pb $3.95

TRAILERPARK
The lives of a trailer park's inhabitants
change when one of them wins a lottery
0–345–33077–3 Ballantine pb $3.95

• Bill Barich
HARD TO BE GOOD
A collection of seven short stories. "Bill
Barich is a true voice of the New West"—
Harold Brodkey
0–374–16812–1 Farrar, Straus & Giroux $15.95
0–06–097177–0 Harper & Row pb $6.95

• Linda Barry
THE GOOD TIMES ARE KILLING ME
0–941104–22–2 Real Comet pb $16.95

• John Barth
CHIMERA
0–449–21113–4 Fawcett pb $4.50

**GILES GOAT BOY: The Revised New
Syllabus**
The college campus as a satirical
microcosm of the contemporary world
0–385–24086–4 Doubleday pb $9.95

**THE FLOATING OPERA & THE END
OF THE ROAD**
In the former, Barth's first novel, a man
reviews his life as he ponders suicide; the
latter involves a parody of a love triangle.
Both are unmistakably from the hand that
gave us "The Literature of Exhaustion" as
a coda for high modernism
0–385–24089–9 Doubleday pb $8.95

LOST IN THE FUNHOUSE
A collection of 14 pieces thematically
linked by their self-conscious, playful
concern with the act of writing and
reading
0–385–24087–2 Doubleday pb $7.95

THE SOT-WEED FACTOR
Ribald, picaresque take-off of an 18th-
century figure. "The book is a joke book,
an endless series of gags . . . But the
biggest joke of all is that Barth seems to
have written something closer to the Great
American Novel than any other book of
the last decades"—Leslie Fiedler
0–385–24088–0 Doubleday pb $9.95

THE TIDEWATER TALES
0–399–13247–3 Putnam $21.95

• Donald Barthelme
COME BACK, DR. CALIGARI
"Outrageous imagination, fine black
humor, a genius for absurd juxtaposition,
an eye for the madness of life in America
today, and for the emptiness, loneliness,
and violence that lie behind its comedy of
strangers always briefly meeting"—*Nation*
0–316–08254–6 Little, Brown pb $7.95

THE DEAD FATHER
A macabre tale of 19 children dragging the
body of their father across a city to his
death
0–14–008667–6 Penguin pb $6.95

FORTY STORIES
0–399–13299–6 Putnam $17.95
0–14–011245–6 Penguin pb $7.95

GREAT DAYS
0–374–16628–5 Farrar, Straus & Giroux pb $7.95

**OVERNIGHT TO MANY DISTANT
CITIES**
0–14–007580–1 Penguin pb $6.95

SIXTY STORIES
0–525–48453–1 Dutton pb $11.95

SNOW WHITE
His first novel, a contemporary fairy tale
0–689–70331–7 Macmillan pb $6.95

• Frederick Barthelme
CHROMA
"Consumer passions don't seem painted on
in these stories but rather create a texture
and a spooky land for modern fairy
tales"—*NY Times*
0–14–010753–3 Viking pb $6.95

MOON DELUXE
"I admire his peculiar grasp of the slant
side of human relationships. *Moon Deluxe*
is something else entirely—superbly
written and very funny"—Raymond Carver
0–14–007130–X Penguin pb $6.95

SECOND MARRIAGE
0–14–008274–3 Penguin pb $6.95

TRACER
"Frederick Barthelme is doing for the '80s
what Raymond Chandler did for the '30s.
He does for the 7-Eleven what Edward
Hopper did for the all-night diner—*Tracer*
crackles with dry wit"—*Baltimore Sun*
0–14–008969–1 Penguin pb $4.95

TWO AGAINST ONE
A 15-year marriage laid bare and examined
in the light of a new triangle
1–55584–214–3 Weidenfeld & Nicolson $17.95

• Jonathan Baumbach
CHEZ CHARLOTTE & EMILY
0–914590–56–1 Fiction Collective $12.95
0–914590–57–X Fiction Collective pb $6.95

MY FATHER MORE OR LESS
0–914590–66–9 Fiction Collective $12.95
0–914590–67–7 Fiction Collective pb $6.95

**THE LIFE AND TIMES OF MAJOR
FICTION**
0–932511–08–2 Fiction Collective $15.95

• Richard Bausch
SPIRITS & OTHER STORIES
Nine short stories. "Bausch combines a
poet's sense of rhythm with a philosophic
quest for truth, but he is first of all a most
original storyteller"—*LA Times*
0–671–63875–0 Simon & Schuster $15.95

• Ann Beattie
THE BURNING HOUSE
Sixteen stories of interpersonal relations by
one of the leading "minimalists"
0–345–35182–7 Ballantine pb $3.95

CHILLY SCENES OF WINTER
Beattie's first novel, a portrait of
disenchanted '70s youth
0–446–31343–2 Warner pb $3.95

DISTORTIONS
"Nineteen stories as arresting as Diane
Arbus photographs"—*Chicago Sun-Times*
0–446–31338–6 Warner pb $3.95

FALLING IN PLACE
The misfortunes of a suburban Connecticut family. "What . . . *The Heart Is a Lonely Hunter* was to the early forties and . . . *The Catcher in the Rye* was to the fifties"—*Vogue*
0–446–31112–X Warner pb $3.50

LOVE ALWAYS
"The semi-beautiful people of late 20th-century media-fringe America"—Margaret Atwood
0–394–74418–7 Random House pb $5.95

SECRETS AND SURPRISES
Fifteen stories
0–446–31381–5 Warner pb $3.95

WHERE YOU'LL FIND ME & OTHER STORIES
Sixteen stories from the 1980s
0–02–016560–9 Macmillan pb $7.95

● Madison Smartt Bell
A SOLDIER'S JOY
0–89919–836–8 Ticknor & Fields $19.95

STRAIGHT CUT
"Bell is, quite simply, a virtuoso novelist. Imagine Graham Greene melding his 'entertainments' with his sober efforts and you'll have some idea of *Straight Cut*"—*Philadelphia Inquirer*
0–14–010471–2 Penguin pb $3.95

WAITING FOR THE END OF THE WORLD
0–14–009330–3 Penguin pb $6.95

THE WASHINGTON SQUARE ENSEMBLE
The denizens of New York's Washington Square Park in a portrait of that city's seedy underworld
0–14–007025–7 Penguin pb $6.95

THE YEAR OF SILENCE
0–89919–490–7 Ticknor & Fields $16.95

ZERO db & OTHER STORIES
Eleven short stories. "Contemporary literature is receiving a welcome healthy impetus from the presence of Madison Smartt Bell; and *Zero db*, this impressive book of short fiction, will likely stand as one of his best achievements"—*Washington Post*
0–89919–489–3 Ticknor & Fields $15.95

● Thomas Berger
BEING INVISIBLE
An ordinary man discovers that he has the power to become invisible
0–316–09158–8 Little, Brown $16.95

THE HOUSEGUEST
0–316–09163–4 Little, Brown $16.95

LITTLE BIG MAN
An 111-year-old man who has seen the worlds of both the white man and the Cheyenne Indian. "The sort of book that many a writer writes in his sleep but hasn't the courage to wake up and put down on paper"—Henry Miller
0–440–34976–1 Dell pb $5.95

NEIGHBORS
0–385–28745–3 Doubleday pb $5.95

NOWHERE
0–385–29464–6 Dell pb $8.95

WHO IS TEDDY VILLANOVA?
An elaborate variation on the hard-boiled detective genre
0–385–29149–3 Doubleday pb $3.95

● Gina Berriault
THE DESCENT
A 1960 vision of the nuclear arms race
0–86547–220–3 North Point pb $7.95

THE INFINITE PASSION OF EXPECTATION: 25 Stories
"There is not a story among them that is less than elegant, less than perfectly observed, perfectly resolved fiction"—*NY Times*
0–86547–082–0 North Point pb $12.50

THE LIGHTS OF EARTH
"Its central character is a woman, Ilona Lewis, who confronts loss of earthly love. But Ilona's experience is far more complex than losing a man because he has become a celebrity. Berriault expands her theme through minor characters until it involves the hearts of all of us seeking the lights of earth, the soul's blessing in its long, dark night"—André Dubus, *America*
0–86547–141–X North Point $12.50

THE SON & CONFERENCE OF VICTIMS
Two novels that examine the nature of love
0–86547–198–3 North Point pb $13.50

● Wendell Berry
NATHAN COULTER
The first in Berry's series of novels set in Port William, Kentucky
0–86547–184–3 North Point pb $8.50

A PLACE ON EARTH
0–86547–044–8 North Point pb $15.00

REMEMBERING
Berry's first novel in 14 years takes place in a single day in Port William
0–86547–330–7 North Point $14.95

THE WILD BIRDS: Six Stories of the Port William Membership
0–86547–216–5 North Point $13.95

● David Bottoms
ANY COLD JORDAN
"His first novel recalls Thomas McGuane's *92 in the Shade* and James Dickey's *Deliverance*"—*Ft. Lauderdale News-Sentinel*
0–934601–12–7 Peachtree $14.95

● T. Coraghessan Boyle
BUDDING PROSPECTS
0–14–008151–8 Penguin pb $6.95

DESCENT OF MAN
Seventeen "wild and absurd stories that give new dimension to black humor"—*Publisher's Weekly*
0–14–009286–2 Penguin pb $6.95

GREASY LAKE & OTHER STORIES
"Satirical fables of contemporary life, so funny and acutely observed that they might have been written by Evelyn Waugh as sketches for the old 'Saturday Night Live' "—*NY Times*
0–14–007781–2 Penguin pb $6.95

IF THE RIVER WAS WHISKEY
Boyle's most recent collection of short stories
0–670–81480–6 Viking $19.95

T. Coraghessan Boyle (photo by Pablo Campos, courtesy of Viking)

WATER MUSIC
0–14–006550–4 Penguin pb $7.95

WORLD'S END
A man's search for his lost father spans many centuries of Hudson Valley history to reveal hidden family secrets. Winner of the PEN/Faulkner Award for American fiction
0–670–81489–X Viking $19.95

● Richard Brautigan
TROUT FISHING IN AMERICA, THE PILL VERSUS THE SPRING HILL MINE DISASTER & IN WATERMELON SUGAR
0–395–500076–1 Houghton-Mifflin pb $8.95

● Harold Brodkey
FIRST LOVE AND OTHER SORROWS
"A clever, eager, perceptive series of sketches underlying the various manners of youthful American love"—*New Statesman*
0–679–72075–8 Random House pb $7.95

STORIES IN AN ALMOST CLASSICAL MODE
A collection of all his major stories. "For years, a small clutch of writers and critics not ordinarily given to breathtaking adoration has compared Brodkey to Freud, Wordsworth, and Whitman"—*Washington Post*
0–394–50699–5 Knopf $24.95

● Rita Mae Brown
BINGO
0–553–05306–X Bantam $18.95

RUBYFRUIT JUNGLE
A witty autobiographical novel of a young lesbian's coming of age
0–553–23813–2 Bantam pb $3.95

SIX OF ONE
Two sisters raise hell in the American South
0–553–23768–3 Bantam pb $3.95

■ TO ORDER BOOKS AS GIFTS, SEE PAGE 1

SOUTHERN DISCOMFORT
Interactions in early 20th-century
Montgomery, Alabama, involving gay
women, one macho man, and cocaine
0–553–27446–5 Bantam pb $4.50

STARTING FROM SCRATCH
0–553–05246–2 Bantam $16.95

SUDDEN DEATH
Lesbian love on the professional tennis
circuit
0–553–26930–5 Bantam pb $4.50

• Rosellen Brown
CIVIL WARS
A white family living in a black
neighborhood in mid-'60s Mississippi
0–394–53478–6 Knopf $16.95
0–14–007783–9 Penguin pb $6.95

TENDER MERCIES
A happy marriage is shattered when a man
accidentally paralyzes his wife in a boating
accident
0–14–008579–3 Penguin pb $6.95

• Charles Bukowski
"A professional disturber of the peace . . .
Laureate of the Los Angeles
netherworld"—*Newsweek*
FACTOTUM
0–87685–264–9 Black Sparrow $20.00
0–87685–263–0 Black Sparrow pb $9.00

HAM ON RYE
0–87685–558–3 Black Sparrow $20.00
0–87685–557–5 Black Sparrow pb $12.50

HOLLYWOOD
0–87685–764–0 Black Sparrow $20.00
0–87685–763–2 Black Sparrow pb $11.00

**THE MOST BEAUTIFUL WOMAN IN
TOWN**
0–87286–156–2 City Lights pb $7.95

NOTES OF A DIRTY OLD MAN
"Bukowski writes like a latter-day Céline, a
wise fool talking straight from the gut
about the futility and beauty of life"—
Publisher's Weekly
0–87286–074–4 City Lights pb $7.95

POST OFFICE
0–87685–086–7 Black Sparrow $7.00

TALES OF ORDINARY MADNESS
Thirty-four autobiographical short stories
0–87286–155–4 City Lights pb $7.95

WOMEN
"I was fifty years old and hadn't been to
bed with a woman for four years"—from
Women
0–87685–391–2 Black Sparrow $20.00
0–87685–390–4 Black Sparrow pb $12.50

• Olive Burns
A COLD SASSY TREE
"One of the best portraits of small-town
Southern life ever written"—Pat Conroy
0–89919–309–9 Ticknor & Fields $16.95
0–440–51442–8 Dell pb $8.95

• Frederick Busch
MANUAL LABOR
0–8112–0535–5 New Directions $8.50
0–8112–0536–3 New Directions pb $3.95

ROUNDS
0–374–25258–0 Farrar, Straus & Giroux $9.95
0–345–29253–7 Ballantine pb $2.95

SOMETIMES I LIVE IN THE COUNTRY
A 13-year-old boy is disoriented when his
parents divorce, and he moves from his
native Brooklyn to upstate New York. "A
powerful and disturbing novel about the
constant menace that hides in all arenas of
the American Dream"—*San Francisco
Chronicle*
0–87923–622–1 Godine $15.95
0–452–25932–0 NAL pb $7.95

TAKE THIS MAN
0–374–27246–8 Farrar, Straus & Giroux $11.95
0–345–30548–5 Ballantine pb $2.95

**TOO LATE AMERICAN BOYHOOD
BLUES**
0–452–25757–3 NAL pb $6.95

• Octavia E. Butler
ADULTHOOD RITES
0–446–51422–5 Warner $16.95

DAWN
0–445–20516–4 Warner pb $3.95

KINDRED
Introduction by Robert Crossley
0–8070–8305–4 Beacon pb $8.95

WILD SEED
0–671–43066–1 Pocket pb $2.75

• Hortense Calisher
AGE
1–55584–132–5 Weidenfeld & Nicolson $14.95

FALSE ENTRY
Calisher's first novel is written as the
journal of a man ruled by his own
pretenses
1–55584–196–1 Weidenfeld & Nicholson $9.95

KISSING COUSINS
1–55584–194–5 Weidenfeld & Nicolson $14.95

THE NEW YORKERS
A generational novel hinging on a long-
buried family secret
1–55584–195–3 Weidenfeld & Nicholson $9.95

• Peter Cameron
ONE WAY OR ANOTHER
0–06–091421–1 Harper & Row pb $5.95

• Ethan Canin
EMPEROR OF THE AIR: Stories
0–06–097208–4 Harper & Row pb $7.95

• Jay Cantor
KRAZY KAT
"An X-rated sort of sequel to the comic
strip . . . sprightly, delightful, insightful"—
NY Times
0–02–042081–1 Macmillan pb $7.95

• Philip Caputo
DEL CORSO'S GALLERY
0–03–058277–6 Henry Holt $15.95

HORN OF AFRICA
0–03–042136–5 Henry Holt $12.95
0–440–33675–9 Dell pb $4.95

INDIAN COUNTRY
Eleven years after the war, a Vietnam vet
confronts the hostile territory of his
experiences in Michigan's Indian
wilderness. "Terrifying, heartbreaking, and
dead-true"—Tim O'Brien
0–553–05187–3 Bantam $18.95
0–553–27029–X Bantam pb $4.95

A RUMOR OF WAR
0–345–33122–2 Ballantine pb $3.95

• Don Carpenter
THE CLASS OF '49
"A thoughtful examination, wonderfully
written, of a group of high school seniors
coming of age in Oregon"—*Esquire*
0–86547–213–0 North Point $14.50

A COUPLE OF COMEDIANS
The world of comedy teams in Las Vegas
and Hollywood. "The best novel I've ever
read about contemporary show biz"—
Norman Mailer
0–86547–303–X North Point pb $9.25

THE DISPOSSESSED
"A beautifully crafted novel of struggle
rooted in nature"—*Booklist*
0–86547–221–1 North Point $15.95

HARD RAIN FALLING
0–345–33903–7 Ballantine pb $3.95

• Raymond Carver
CATHEDRAL
"A dozen stories that overflow with the
danger, excitement, mystery and possibility
of life . . . Carver is a writer of astonishing
compassion and honesty"—Jonathan
Yardley, *Washington Post*
0–394–52884–0 Knopf $13.95
0–394–71281–1 Random House pb $4.95

FIRES
Selected essays, poems, and stories written
between 1968 and 1983
0–394–72299–X Random House pb $5.95

ULTRAMARINE
0–394–55379–9 Random House $14.95
0–394–75535–9 Random House pb $6.95

**WHAT WE TALK ABOUT WHEN WE
TALK ABOUT LOVE**
Seventeen spare stories from the '70s.
"Real as discount stores, time clocks, the
franchises in small towns, bad marriages"—
Stanley Elkin
0–394–51684–2 Knopf $9.95
0–394–75080–2 Random House pb $4.95

**WHERE I'M CALLING FROM: New and
Selected Stories**
0–87113–216–8 Atlantic Monthly $19.95

*Raymond Carver (photo by Marion Ettlinger,
courtesy of Random House)*

- **Michael Chabon**
  THE MYSTERIES OF PITTSBURGH
  0–06–097212–2 Harper & Row pb $7.95

- **Susan Chace**
  INTIMACY
  0–394–57030–8 Random House $14.95

- **Joan Chase**
  DURING THE REIGN OF THE QUEEN OF PERSIA
  "A Norman Rockwell painting gone bad, the underside of the idyllic hometown, main street, down-on-the-farm dream of Middle America"—Margaret Atwood
  0–06–015136–6 Harper & Row $13.95
  0–345–31525–1 Ballantine pb $3.50

  THE ENEMY WOLVES
  A poetic novel about American family life, seen through the eyes of two young sisters
  0–374–15003–6 Farrar, Straus & Giroux $18.95

- **Carolyn Chute**
  THE BEANS OF EGYPT, MAINE
  0–446–30010–1 Warner pb $3.50

  LETOURNEAU'S USED AUTO PARTS
  0–89919–500–8 Ticknor & Fields $16.50
  0–06–097225–4 Harper & Row pb $7.95

- **Andrei Codrescu**
  MONSIEUR TESTE IN AMERICA & OTHER INCIDENCES OF REALISM
  0–918273–32–3 Coffee House Press pb $9.95

- **Christopher Coe**
  I LOOK DIVINE
  "A fascinating account of the relationship between two brothers"—Village Voice
  0–89919–530–X Ticknor & Fields $12.95
  0–394–75995–8 Random House pb $5.95

- **Linda Collins**
  GOING TO SEE THE LEAVES
  0–670–80881–4 Viking $15.95
  0–14–009920–4 Penguin pb $6.95

- **Cyrus Colter**
  THE AMORALISTS & OTHER TALES
  Short stories set in Chicago during the 1960s
  0–938410–65–2 Thunder's Mouth pb $9.95

  THE BEACH UMBRELLA
  "When I came upon his tales, I suddenly found myself having a lovely time. He was telling all sorts of magical things about life I'd never known"—Kurt Vonnegut
  Preface by Vance Bourjaily
  0–87745–005–6 Iowa $16.00
  0–8040–0555–9 Ohio pb $4.95

  A CHOCOLATE SOLDIER
  "Cyrus Colter tackles epic themes as though they were wild horses—and he tames them. . . . A knockout!"—Studs Terkel
  0–938410–42–3 Thunder's Mouth $18.95
  0–938410–49–0 Thunder's Mouth pb $9.95

  THE HIPPODROME
  A Chicago man decapitates his wife and is discovered by two women who blackmail him into performing in a homosexual circus
  0–8040–0625–3 Ohio $10.95

  NIGHT STUDIES
  0–8040–0827–2 Ohio $19.95

THE RIVERS OF EROS
0–8040–0563–X Ohio $10.95

- **Laurie Colwin**
  ANOTHER MARVELOUS THING
  Eight connected stories on love, marriage, and birth
  0–14–009854–2 Penguin pb $5.95

  FAMILY HAPPINESS
  "A novel of a woman torn between her sense of family obligation and a wildly fulfilling love affair"—NY Times
  0–449–20275–5 Fawcett pb $3.50

  HAPPY ALL THE TIME
  0–14–007687–5 Penguin pb $6.95

  THE LONE PILGRIM
  "Laurie Colwin's witty, graceful stories convey both leisurely walks and sudden, unexpected springs . . . She is a remarkably cheerful messenger"—Paul Gray, Time
  0–394–51453–X Knopf $9.95
  0–671–43489–6 Washington Square pb $3.95

  PASSION AND AFFECT
  "She gives the impression that she has single-handedly revitalized the short story"—Robert Kirsch, LA Times
  0–14–007415–5 Penguin pb $5.95

  SHINE ON, BRIGHT AND DANGEROUS OBJECT
  0–14–007414–7 Penguin pb $5.95

- **Richard Condon**
  PRIZZI'S FAMILY
  The prequel to Prizzi's Honor
  0–515–09106–5 Berkley pb $4.50

  PRIZZI'S GLORY
  0–525–24689–4 Dutton $17.95

  PRIZZI'S HONOR
  Complex story of a romance between two Mafia killers
  0–425–09507–X Berkley pb $3.95

- **Evan S. Connell**
  THE CONNOISSEUR
  The slowly developing obsessions of a novice art collector
  0–86547–245–9 North Point pb $8.95

  THE DIARY OF A RAPIST
  An obscure civil servant escapes from his dreary life through an obsession with a beautiful socialite
  0–86547–308–0 North Point pb $8.95

Evan S. Connell (photo by Thomas Victor, courtesy of North Point)

MRS. BRIDGE
A brilliantly detailed and subtle portrait of a 1930s Midwestern matron. "Funny, sad, touching and beautifully written, these sly yet sympathetic unfrockings of Kansas City's upper-bourgeoisie between the Depression and World War II seem even more readable and timely than when first published"—San Francisco Chronicle
0–86547–056–1 North Point pb $9.95

MR. BRIDGE
The companion volume to Mrs. Bridge
0–86547–054–5 North Point pb $9.95

SAINT AUGUSTINE'S PIGEON: Selected Stories
Sixteen stories spanning Connell's career
0–86547–014–6 North Point pb $10.00

- **Robert Coover**
  GERALD'S PARTY
  "Brilliant, erotic, aesthetic . . . Round the corpse . . . Gerald's party goes on—a chatter of voices, names, faces, feces, overhead gags, endless storytelling, and a mounting curve of desire"—Washington Post
  0–671–60655–7 Simon & Schuster $17.95
  0–452–25878–2 NAL pb $7.95

  A NIGHT AT THE MOVIES: Or You Must Remember This
  Short pieces satirizing movies, movie stars, and movie conventions
  0–671–61796–6 Simon & Schuster $16.95

  THE ORIGIN OF THE BRUNISTS
  0–393–30600–3 Norton pb $10.95

  PRICKSONGS AND DESCANTS
  "The fictions in Robert Coover's remarkable new volume are solitaires— sparkling, sharply drawn, and brightly painted"—NY Times
  0–452–26031–0 NAL pb $7.95

  SPANKING THE MAID
  A formalist variation on some traditional erotic motifs
  0–394–17971–4 Grove pb $4.95

  THE UNIVERSAL BASEBALL ASSOCIATION, J. HENRY WAUGH, PROP.
  Baseball as a metaphor for American life
  0–452–26030–2 NAL pb $7.95

  WHATEVER HAPPENED TO GLOOMY GUS OF THE CHICAGO BEARS?
  0–02–042781–6 Macmillan pb $7.95

- **Stanley Crawford**
  SOME INSTRUCTIONS TO MY WIFE
  A Swiftian satire on marriage manuals
  0–916583–15–5 Dalkey Archive pb $4.50

- **Harry Crews**
  ALL WE NEED OF HELL
  A bodybuilder's life is falling apart. "Lusty and ribald as if Chaucer had set 'The Miller's Tale' in Gainesville, Florida"— Boston Globe
  0–06–015680–5 Harper & Row $14.95
  0–06–091460–2 Harper & Row pb $6.95

  CAR
  Man eats car
  0–688–02145–X Morrow pb $4.95

  A FEAST OF SNAKES
  The annual rattlesnake hunt brings a cast of eccentrics to Mystic, Georgia. "He

begins where James Dickey left off"—
Norman Mailer
0–689–70715–0 Atheneum pb $6.95

FLORIDA FRENZY
0–8130–0726–7 Florida pb $10.00

THE GOSPEL SINGER
A dirt-poor farm boy comes home to
Enigma, Georgia, as a prosperous gospel
singer. "A story of flesh eating flesh and
going hungry"—Andrew Lytle
0–06–097151–7 Harper & Row pb $7.95

THE KNOCKOUT ARTIST
0–06–015893–X Harper & Row $17.95

• John Crowley
AEGYPT
0–553–05194–6 Bantam $17.95
0–553–34592–3 Bantam pb $8.95

• James Crumley
DANCING BEAR
The return of the coked-up hero of *The
Last Good Kiss*
0–394–72576–X Random House pb $5.95

THE LAST GOOD KISS
The wanderings of a Montana private eye
become a low-budget epic of roadside
America
0–394–75989–3 Random House pb $6.95

ONE TO COUNT CADENCE
A novel of Vietnam
0–394–73559–5 Random House pb $5.95

• Guy Davenport
THE JULES VERNE STEAM BALLOON
"Guy Davenport mixes historical fact, a
philosophical imagination, and an almost
hallucinatory prose style to create short
stories that are at once marvelous,
frustrating, and original"—*Virginia
Quarterly Review*
0–86547–295–5 North Point $21.95
0–86547–296–3 North Point pb $11.95

**APPLES AND PEARS & OTHER
STORIES**
Three stories and the long title piece,
which the *San Francisco Chronicle* described
as "one long wet dream of the perfect
sexual family where the child is admitted
to the parents' games, all experience is life-
affirming, and the fun never stops"
Illustrated by the author
0–86547–162–2 North Point $20.00

TATLIN
0–8018–2800–7 Johns Hopkins pb $8.95

ECLOGUES: Eight Stories
Stories derived from Plutarch, Montaigne,
the Acts of the Apostles, and other sources
Illustrated by Roy Behrens
0–86547–029–4 North Point $20.00
0–86547–030–8 North Point pb $11.00

DA VINCI'S BICYCLE: Ten Stories
0–8018–2220–3 Johns Hopkins pb $7.95

• George Davis
COMING HOME
A novel about the damaging psychological
effects of service in Vietnam; Davis is one
of the surprisingly small number of black
writers who have dealt with the subject of
blacks in the armed forces
0–88258–118–X Howard pb $6.95

• Lydia Davis
BREAK IT DOWN
Spare stories employing a wide variety of
linguistic strategies
0–374–52098–4 Farrar, Straus & Giroux pb $6.95

• Don DeLillo
END ZONE
Football and nuclear war. "Like Groucho
Marx on a faked end run"—*Bookworld*
0–14–008568–8 Penguin pb $6.95

GREAT JONES STREET
A rock musician in New York's East
Village. "Finally, a novel that understands
rock and roll"—*Village Voice*
0–394–71718–X Random House pb $7.95

LIBRA
A fictional look at Oswald, Ruby, and the
Kennedy assassination
0–670–82317–1 Viking $19.95

THE NAMES
An American in Europe becomes involved
in international terrorism and intrigue.
"The high-tech, jet-set variation of the
American expatriates in *The Sun Also
Rises*"—Steve Erickson, *LA Reader*
0–394–52814–X Knopf $13.95
0–394–71564–0 Random House pb $6.95

PLAYERS
Unsettling truths behind the attractive
facade of an ideal modern couple
0–394–72382–1 Random House pb $5.95

RATNER'S STAR
Astronomers trapped in an eerie sci-fi
prison/wonderland
0–394–74495–0 Random House pb $8.95

RUNNING DOG
"The best Vietnam novel to appear so
far"—*Houston Post*
0–394–74121–8 Random House pb $7.95

WHITE NOISE
A dark comedy set at a liberal arts college
in middle America. "One of DeLillo's
funniest novels . . . eerie, brilliant, and
touching"—*NY Times*
0–670–80373–1 Viking $16.95
0–14–007702–2 Penguin pb $7.95

• George Dennison
LUISA DOMIC
A refugee from Chilean terror comes to a
home in rural Maine. "*Luisa Domic* has
brought me the particular complicated
shudder of basic political experience in our
years, the utter poignancy of utter horror,
more directly, more sharply, more
completely, than any other book I have
read, no matter what kind"—Hayden
Carruth
0–06–091385–1 Harper & Row pb $6.95

SHAWNO
0–8052–3917–0 Schocken $10.95

**A TALE OF PIERROT & OTHER
STORIES**
Seven short stories written over the past
25 years. "These strong and intelligent
stories are achingly real, unforgettable"—
Hilma Wolitzer
0–06–055079–1 Harper & Row $17.95
0–06–096169–4 Harper & Row pb $8.95

• Pete Dexter
DEADWOOD
0–14–009910–7 Penguin pb $4.95

GOD'S POCKET
0–446–32811–1 Warner pb $3.95

PARIS TROUT
Winner of the National Book Award for
1988
0–394–56370–0 Random House $17.95

• James Dickey
ALNILAM
An elaborate, myth-ridden novel about
flight
0–385–06549–3 Doubleday $19.95

DELIVERANCE
Four suburban businessmen confront their
own primitive impulses while canoeing
down a southern river. "A breathtaking
adventure that is also an acute comment
on America"—*New Yorker*
0–440–31868–8 Dell pb $3.95

• Charles Dickinson
CROWS
0–449–21019–7 Fawcett pb $4.50

WALTZ IN MARATHON
A moneylender in a Michigan small town
finds his orderly life changing after he falls
in love with an attractive attorney
0–452–25593–7 NAL pb $6.95

WITH OR WITHOUT
Eleven short stories. "We come away from
this collection sobered but enlightened . . .
forced to look again, to discover at some
deeper level what we thought we had
already known"—*NY Times*
0–394–55492–2 Knopf $15.95

• Joan Didion
A BOOK OF COMMON PRAYER
"A completely knowing and sophisticated
grasp of realities and all unrealities in our
time and place, together with a lyrical
treatment of them, strikes me as being the
ultimate achievement of a contemporary
novelist. Joan Didion has somehow
accomplished this in *A Book of Common
Prayer*"—Tennessee Williams
0–671–63808–4 Pocket pb $4.50

DEMOCRACY
"The devastating personal and public
consequences of the loss of history are
Didion's theme . . . *Democracy* is absorbing,
immensely intelligent, and witty"—*NY
Review of Books*
0–671–54633–3 Pocket pb $3.95

PLAY IT AS IT LAYS
"A painful and exact novel about a young
Hollywood actress and model whose
balance is upset by a traumatic abortion,
an impending divorce from her film-maker
husband, and the hopeless future of her
retarded daughter . . . Didion is at her
best—her honesty, intelligence, and skill
are wonders to behold"—*Newsweek*
0–671–49590–9 Pocket pb $3.95

RUN RIVER
0–671–60315–9 Washington Square pb $3.95

• Stephen Dixon
GARBAGE
0–943433–00–2 Cane Hill pb $8.95

MOVIES: Seventeen Stories
"Stephen Dixon's stories . . . mirror the tight shadow world of the ordinary city dweller trying desperately to define himself"—*NY Times*
0–86547–129–0 North Point $11.50

THE PLAY & OTHER STORIES
0–918273–45–5 Coffee House pb $9.95

● Stephen Dobyns
THE TWO DEATHS OF SENORA PUCCINI
0–14–010567–0 Penguin pb $7.95

● E.L. Doctorow
BILLY BATHGATE
A young man's dealings with Dutch Schultz and others in '30s New York. "Billy Bathgate is the kind of book you find yourself finishing at three in the morning after promising at midnight that you'll stop after one more page. One scene glides into the next, and yet each is so complete in itself, so fully and precisely observed, that it seems to be encapsulated in a tiny glass paperweight"—Anne Tyler, *NY Times*
0–394–52529–9 Random House $19.95

THE BOOK OF DANIEL
A fictional reconstruction of the Rosenberg case and its consequences
0–394–46271–8 Random House $14.95
0–394–60501–2 Modern Library $8.95

LOON LAKE
0–449–21603–9 Fawcett pb $4.95

E.L. Doctorow (photo copyright Barbara Walz, courtesy of Random House)

RAGTIME
The celebrated collage of turn-of-the-century America, with guest appearances by J.P. Morgan, Evelyn Nesbitt, and other iconic figures
0–394–46901–1 Random House $12.95
0–553–25736–6 Bantam pb $4.95

WELCOME TO HARD TIMES
A bitter little western; Doctorow's first novel
0–394–73107–7 Random House pb $8.95

WORLD'S FAIR
"You get lost in *World's Fair* as if it were an exotic adventure. You devour it with the avidity usually provoked by a suspense thriller"—Christopher Lehmann-Haupt, *NY Times*
0–449–21237–8 Fawcett pb $4.95

● Jim Dodge
FUP
0–933944–04–7 City Miner pb $4.95

NOT FADE AWAY
0–87113–144–7 Atlantic Monthly pb $6.95

● Harriet Doerr
STONES FOR IBARRA
An American couple move to a Mexican village to reopen an abandoned copper mine.
0–670–19203–1 Viking $16.95
0–14–011218–9 Penguin pb $6.95

● Ivan Doig
DANCING AT THE RASCAL FAIR
A chronicle of two immigrants from Scotland who make their way to the American West during the first three decades of the 20th century
0–689–11764–7 Atheneum $18.95

ENGLISH CREEK
0–689–11478–8 Atheneum $15.95
0–14–008442–8 Penguin pb $6.95

THE SEA RUNNERS
0–14–006780–9 Penguin pb $6.95

● J.P. Donleavy
ARE YOU LISTENING RABBI LOW?
0–87113–237–0 Atlantic Monthly $18.95

THE BEASTLY BEATITUDES OF BALTHAZAR B
A young man at prep school in England. "The prep school passages are wonderful, followed by one of the most perfect love affairs in modern literature. This romp of a novel is lush and lovely, bawdy and sad"—*NY Times*
0–87113–225–7 Atlantic Monthly pb $7.95

A FAIRY TALE OF NEW YORK
0–910278–15–6 Boulevard $12.95
0–87113–264–8 Atlantic Monthly pb $7.95

THE GINGER MAN
0–87113–199–4 Atlantic Monthly pb $7.95

A SINGULAR MAN
0–87113–265–6 Atlantic Monthly pb $7.95

● Michael Dorris
A YELLOW RAFT IN BLUE WATER
Three generations of Native American women tell different versions of their family's story
0–8050–0045–3 Henry Holt $16.95

● Rita Dove
FIFTH SUNDAY
0–912759–06–2 Virginia pb $6.00

● Coleman Dowell
THE HOUSES OF CHILDREN
1–55584–043–4 Weidenfeld & Nicolson $15.95

MRS. OCTOBER WAS HERE
0–8112–0519–3 New Directions pb $3.75

ONE OF THE CHILDREN IS CRYING
Dowell's first novel is the story of a prominent southern family coming together for the funeral of their father. "Coleman Dowell sees the world with childhood's raw intensity. His vision of the sinister horrors of family life has the sting of truth"—Maurice Sendak
1–55584–044–2 Weidenfeld & Nicolson pb $7.95

TOO MUCH FLESH AND JABEZ
A story-within-a-story, in which a spinster schoolteacher writes a fantasy about a former student. "A meticulously and subtly composed tour de force of the imagination"—Gilbert Sorrentino
0–916583–21–X Dalkey Archive pb $8.00

WHITE ON BLACK ON WHITE
0–88150–000–3 Countryman $14.95

● Rosalyn Drexler
BAD GUY
1–55554–038–4 PAJ pb $7.95

● André Dubus
ADULTERY AND OTHER CHOICES
0–87923–213–7 Godine $13.95
0–87923–284–6 Godine pb $8.95

FINDING A GIRL IN AMERICA
"Dubus is in top form in this new collection of ten stories and a novella as he continues to introduce us to ourselves, to see into the private worlds of everyday people as they live, dream and act, taking soundings that are deep and true"—*Publisher's Weekly*
0–87923–311–7 Godine $13.95
0–87923–393–1 Godine pb $8.95

THE LAST WORTHLESS EVENING: Four Novellas and Two Short Stories
0–87923–642–6 Godine $15.95
0–517–56625–7 Crown pb $8.95

THE LIEUTENANT
0–9614285–2–X Green Street pb $7.95

NEW TRADITIONS
0–9614285–3–8 Green Street pb $11.95

SELECTED STORIES OF ANDRE DUBUS
"Life goes on, and life's gallant, battered ongoingness, with its complicated fuelling by sex, religion, and liquor, constitutes his sturdy central subject"—John Updike
0–87923–736–8 Godine $19.95

SEPARATE FLIGHTS
0–87923–123–8 Godine pb $8.95

THE TIMES ARE NEVER SO BAD
A novella and eight short stories. "For the lyricism and directness of his language, the richness and precision of his observations, he is among the best short-story writers in America"—Judith Levine, *Village Voice*
0–87923–459–8 Godine $12.95
0–87923–641–8 Godine pb $8.95

➤ **FOR OVERSEAS ORDERING INFORMATION, SEE PAGE 1**

VOICES FROM THE MOON
A day in the life of a twelve-year-old boy from a troubled family
0–517–55846–7 Crown pb $6.95

WE DON'T LIVE HERE ANYMORE
Four novellas. "André Dubus's mastery of his material and therefore of his readers is total . . . Dubus is a writer with real might"—*Washington Post*
0–517–55362–7 Crown pb $7.95

● Bruce Duffy
THE WORLD AS I FOUND IT
A fictional reconstruction of the interrelationships of Ludwig Wittgenstein, Bertrand Russell, and G.E. Moore
0–89919–808–2 Ticknor & Fields pb $8.95

● Henry Dumas
GOODBYE, SWEETWATER: New and Selected Stories
"A cult has grown up around Henry Dumas—a very deserved cult. . . . He was brilliant. He was magnetic, and he was an incredible artist"—Toni Morrison
Edited with a foreword by Eugene B. Redmond
0–938410–58–X Thunder's Mouth pb $9.95

● Katherine Dunn
GEEK LOVE
Tenderness and terror in the lives of a carnival family
0–394–57826–0 Random House $16.95

● John Gregory Dunne
DUTCH SHEA, JR.
0–671–46170–2 Pocket pb $3.95

THE RED, WHITE, AND BLUE
Two decades of American life, from the 1960s to the '80s, through the eyes of a Kennedy-like superfamily. "A slice of America on a plate"—Anne Tyler
0–671–46380–2 Simon & Schuster $18.95

TRUE CONFESSIONS
"Priests, pimps, aging prostitutes, washed-up fighters, cops, midgets, seedy lawyers"—*Baltimore Sun*
0–671–65874–3 Pocket pb $4.50

● William Eastlake
THE BRONC PEOPLE
0–8263–0379–X New Mexico pb $8.95

GO IN BEAUTY
0–8263–0538–5 New Mexico pb $8.95

PORTRAIT OF AN ARTIST WITH TWENTY-SIX HORSES
0–8263–0558–X New Mexico pb $6.95

● Junius Edwards
IF WE MUST DIE
First published in 1963, Edwards' novel is the account of a young black veteran attempting to register to vote
0–88258–117–1 Howard pb $6.95

● Deborah Eisenberg
TRANSACTIONS IN A FOREIGN CURRENCY
Seven short stories. "Deborah Eisenberg has found words for sensations and emotions I have never seen described before"—John Updike
0–14–009855–0 Penguin pb $6.95

● Jill Eisenstadt
FROM ROCKAWAY
0–394–75761–0 Random House pb $6.95

● Stanley Elkin
THE LIVING END
"Nothing less than an exposé of heaven and hell and Minneapolis-St. Paul. From a holdup of a liquor store in the Twin Cities, the novel pursues the lives and afterlives of the victims and the perpetrators of the crime . . . A big book for Stanley Elkin, and a fine and daring novel for our literature"—John Irving, *NY Times*
0–525–48158–3 Dutton pb $7.95

THE RABBI OF LUD
0–684–18902–X Scribners $17.95

THE SIX-YEAR-OLD-MAN
0–917453–16–6 Bamberger $18.00
0–917453–15–8 Bamberger pb $10.00

● Bret Easton Ellis
LESS THAN ZERO
Wealthy young airheads on the prowl in L.A.
0–14–008894–6 Penguin pb $6.95

THE RULES OF ATTRACTION
Alienated California youth at college in New England
0–671–62234–X Simon & Schuster $17.95
0–14–011228–6 Penguin pb $6.95

● Trey Ellis
PLATITUDES
0–394–75439–5 Random House pb $6.95

● Nora Ephron
HEARTBURN
0–671–62483–0 Pocket pb $3.95

● Louise Erdrich
THE BEET QUEEN
A brother and sister arrive in North Dakota by boxcar and stay for 40 years
0–8050–0058–5 Henry Holt $16.95
0–553–26807–4 Bantam pb $4.50

LOVE MEDICINE
"A remarkable first novel . . . conveying unflinchingly the funkiness, humor, and great unspoken sadness of the Indian reservations"—Peter Matthiessen
0–03–070611–4 Henry Holt pb $13.95
0–553–26808–2 Bantam pb $4.50

TRACKS
North Dakota Chippewas fight for survival in the early 20th century
0–8050–0895–0 Henry Holt $18.95

● Margaret Erhart
UNUSUAL COMPANY
0–525–24567–7 Dutton $17.95
0–452–26144–9 NAL pb $7.95

● Steve Erickson
TOURS OF THE BLACK CLOCK
0–671–64921–3 Pocket $18.95

DAYS BETWEEN STATIONS
0–394–74685–6 Random House pb $6.95

RUBICON BEACH
0–671–60458–9 Simon & Schuster $15.95
0–394–75513–8 Random House pb $6.95

Louise Erdrich (photo by Michael Dorris, courtesy of Henry Holt)

● Frederick Exley
A FAN'S NOTES
The drinking life, the New York Giants, and the beauty of women, distilled through an elegiac prose style. "No one should have had Exley's life, and no one who has read it can ever forget it"—James Dickey
0–679–72076–6 Random House pb $7.95

LAST NOTES FROM HOME
0–394–40519–6 Random House $18.95

PAGES FROM A COLD ISLAND
0–394–75977–X Random House pb $6.95

● Ross Feld
ONLY SHORTER
A love affair between two people who meet in a cancer clinic
0–86547–061–8 North Point $15.00

SHAPES MISTAKEN
A comedy of errors
0–86547–367–6 Farrar, Straus & Giroux $18.95

● Roberto Fernández
RAINING BACKWARDS
A satirical look at the Cuban community in Miami
0–934770–79–4 Arte Público pb $8.50

● Rudolph Fisher
THE CITY OF REFUGE: The Collected Stories of Rudolph Fisher
Edited by John McCluskey, Jr.
0–8262–0630–1 Missouri $25.00

● Fannie Flagg
FRIED GREEN TOMATOES AT THE WHISTLE STOP CAFE
0–394–56152–X Random House $17.95
0–07–021257–0 McGraw-Hill pb $5.95

● Patty L. Floyd
THE SILVER DESOTO
0–933031–03–3 Council Oak $14.95
0–671–66939–7 Pocket pb $5.95

● Thomas Flanagan
THE TENANTS OF TIME
A much-praised historical novel of Ireland
0–525–24606–1 Dutton $19.95

THE YEAR OF THE FRENCH
In 1798 French troops aid an Irish
rebellion against the British. "The only
great historical novel in English"—*St. Louis
Post-Dispatch*
0–03–044591–4 Henry Holt $12.95
0–671–66974–5 Pocket pb $5.95

● Richard Ford
A PIECE OF MY HEART
Ford's first novel tells of two men in flight
to an uncharted island in the Mississippi
0–394–72914–5 Random House pb $5.95

ROCK SPRINGS
0–394–75700–9 Random House pb $6.95

THE SPORTSWRITER
0–394–74325–3 Random House pb $6.95

THE ULTIMATE GOOD LUCK
A Vietnam vet mixes with soldiers, drug
dealers, tourists, and Indians in Oaxaca.
"So hardboiled and tough it might have
been written on the back of a
trenchcoat"—Stanley Elkin
0–394–75089–6 Random House pb $5.95

● Leon Forrest
"How admirable the manner in which the
great themes of life and literature are
revealed in the black-white, white-black
Americanness of his characters as
dramatized in the cathedral-high and
cloaca-low limits of his imaginative
ranging."—Ralph Ellison
THE BLOODWORTH ORPHANS
A mythical tale about the descendants of a
Mississippi slave owner; the second of
Forrest's novels
0–9614644–3–7 Another Chicago Press pb $8.95

**THERE IS A TREE MORE ANCIENT
THAN EDEN**
The first part of the Forrest County
trilogy. An adolescent copes with the death
of his mother and some 200 years of
American history in this harrowing dreamlike narrative
0–9614644–5–3 Another Chicago Press pb $8.95

TWO WINGS TO VEIL MY FACE
In the Forrest County trilogy's final
installment, a young man learns the secrets
of his own family's past
0–9614644–4–5 Another Chicago Press pb $8.95

● Paula Fox
DESPERATE CHARACTERS
Afterword by Irving Howe
0–87923–309–5 Godine pb $8.95

A SERVANT'S TALE
A Caribbean woman chooses to work as a
maid for wealthy families
0–14–008386–3 Penguin pb $6.95

THE WIDOW'S CHILDREN
A dinner party goes sour. "A work of
marvelous design and subtle
synchronization"—*Kirkus Reviews*
0–525–23377–6 Dutton pb $9.95

● Jonathan Franzen
THE TWENTY-SEVENTH CITY
An imaginative novel set in St. Louis,
where the newly appointed chief of police,
a woman from Bombay, becomes involved
in a political conspiracy
0–374–27972–1 Farrar, Straus & Giroux $19.95

● Marilyn French
THE BLEEDING HEART
Middle-aged adultery in England
0–345–28896–3 Ballantine pb $3.50

HER MOTHER'S DAUGHTER
0–671–63051–2 Summit $21.95

THE WOMEN'S ROOM
A woman's journey to self-knowledge after
her divorce
0–345–35361–7 Ballantine pb $5.95

● Bruce Jay Friedman
ABOUT HARRY TOWNS
0–87113–263–X Atlantic Monthly pb $7.95

**LET'S HEAR IT FOR A BEAUTIFUL
GUY**
A collection of short fiction
0–88184–138–2 Carroll & Graf pb $3.95

THE LONELY GUY
A parody of self-help books
0–07–022438–2 McGraw-Hill pb $4.95

A MOTHER'S KISSES
A comic variation on the stereotype of the
Jewish mother
0–917657–39–X Donald I. Fine pb $8.95

STERN
0–87113–262–1 Atlantic Monthly pb $7.95

TOKYO WOES
0–14–008705–2 Penguin pb $5.95

● Ernest J. Gaines
**THE AUTOBIOGRAPHY OF MISS JANE
PITTMAN**
The life of a black woman born a slave
0–553–26357–9 Bantam pb $3.50

BLOODLINE
Five stories. "[Gaines] may just be the best
black writer in America. He is so good, in
fact, that he makes the category seem
meaningless, though one of his principal
subjects has been slavery—past and
present"—*Time*
0–393–00798–7 Norton pb $7.95

CATHERINE CARMIER
A novel of Louisiana plantation country
0–86547–022–7 North Point pb $9.95

A GATHERING OF OLD MEN
Murder on a Louisiana sugar cane
plantation in the late 1970s. "The best-
written novel on Southern race relations in
over a decade"—*Village Voice*
0–394–51468–8 Knopf $17.95
0–394–72591–3 Random House pb $4.95

IN MY FATHER'S HOUSE
A minister and civil rights leader in a rural
black community in the South. "A
powerful, deeply probing novel . . . The

Rev. Mr. Martin emerges as a complex,
memorable character"—*NY Times*
0–394–47938–6 Knopf $13.95
0–393–30124–9 Norton pb $6.95

OF LOVE AND DUST
0–393–00914–9 Norton pb $8.95

● Mary Gaitskill
BAD BEHAVIOR
0–679–72327–7 Vintage pb $7.95

● Tess Gallagher
THE LOVER OF HORSES
0–06–015627–9 Harper & Row $16.95
0–06–091435–1 Harper & Row pb $6.95

● Kenneth Gangemi
THE INTERCEPTOR PILOT
The scenario for an imaginary Cold War
adventure
0–7145–2765–3 Marion Boyars pb $7.95

OLT
"The style, the focus on one main
character, and the cool listing of
experiences tend to remind one of
Meursault in *The Stranger*"—*Library
Journal*
0–7145–0660–5 Marion Boyars pb $5.95

● Guy Garcia
SKIN DEEP
A first novel by a talented Hispanic
journalist, the suspense-filled story of a
California Chicano who returns to Los
Angeles after a stint in a large Manhattan
law firm
0–374–26573–9 Farrar, Straus & Giroux $16.95

● John Gardner
**THE ART OF LIVING & OTHER
STORIES**
Ten stories encompassing "just about all of
Gardner's themes: love and vengeance,
fantasy, fear, madness, even occasional
tenderness"—*Boston Globe*
0–394–51674–5 Knopf $12.95
0–345–30371–7 Ballantine pb $3.50

FREDDY'S BOOK
0–394–50920–X Knopf $10.00
0–345–29544–7 Ballantine pb $2.95

GRENDEL
The epic of Beowulf retold from the
monster's viewpoint
0–394–47143–1 Knopf $15.95
0–394–74056–4 Random House pb $4.95

MICKELSSON'S GHOSTS
A philosophy professor goes off the deep
end, and sets about restoring an old farm
house, only to find it's haunted. Gardner's
last novel
0–394–50468–2 Knopf $16.95
0–394–72938–2 Random House pb $6.95

NICKEL MOUNTAIN
0–394–74393–8 Random House pb $6.95

OCTOBER LIGHT
An elderly brother and sister in conflict in
Vermont
0–345–29298–7 Ballantine pb $3.50

THE RESURRECTION
A San Francisco professor develops
leukemia and goes home to upstate New
York to die
0–394–73250–2 Random House pb $5.95

☎ **TO ORDER ANY BOOK IN THIS CATALOG, ASK YOUR BOOKSELLER OR CALL 1-800-882-8770**

STILLNESS AND SHADOWS
Two posthumously published works: one deals with a troubled marriage, the other, unfinished, with an alcoholic detective
0–394–54402–1 Knopf $18.95

THE SUNLIGHT DIALOGUES
0–345–30492–6 Ballantine pb $4.95

THE WRECKAGE OF AGATHON
0–525–48180–X Dutton pb $8.95

● Leonard Gardner
FAT CITY
The world of small-time boxers. "A beautiful story of losers and their banal lives, of the futility that most men, sooner or later, feel creeping up on them . . . From weakness, Gardner has drawn strength, and from dullness, beauty"— Peter S. Prescott, *Life*
0–394–74316–4 Random House pb $6.95

● Martin Gardner
THE FLIGHT OF PETER FROMM
The well-known mathematician tackles a man's crisis in faith. "A beautifully illuminating metaphysical novel"—*NY Times*
0–379–52187–5 Farrar, Straus & Giroux pb $7.95

● William Gass
IN THE HEART OF THE HEART OF THE COUNTRY & OTHER STORIES
However cerebral in conception, Gass's virtuoso metafictions are naturalistic in their power, vividness, and grim humor
0–87923–374–5 Godine pb $8.95

● Barry Gifford
LANDSCAPE WITH TRAVELER: The Pillow Book of Francis Reeves
0–03–060604–7 Henry Holt pb $6.75

PORT TROPIQUE
A dreamlike recasting of *film noir* against the background of a corrupt waterfront
0–88739–012–9 Black Lizard pb $3.95

● Ellen Gilchrist
THE ANNA PAPERS
0–316–31316–5 Little, Brown $16.95

THE ANNUNCIATION
0–316–31302–5 Little, Brown $14.95
0–316–31308–4 Little, Brown pb $7.95

Ellen Gilchrist (photo by Jerry Bauer, courtesy of Little, Brown)

DRUNK WITH LOVE
Short stories. "Her stories are perceptive, her manner is both stylish and idiomatic— a rare and potent combination"—*TLS*
0–316–31311–4 Little, Brown $15.95
0–316–31314–9 Little, Brown pb $7.95

FALLING THROUGH SPACE: The Journals of Ellen Gilchrist
0–316–31315–7 Little, Brown $15.95

IN THE LAND OF DREAMY DREAMS
Stories. "Ellen Gilchrist is terrific"— Norman Mailer
0–316–31304–1 Little, Brown $14.95
0–316–31306–8 Little, Brown pb $7.95

VICTORY OVER JAPAN: A Book of Stories
0–316–31303–3 Little, Brown $15.95
0–316–31307–6 Little, Brown pb $7.95

● Gary Glickman
YEARS FROM NOW
0–394–55513–9 Knopf $16.95
0–452–26142–2 NAL pb $7.95

● Thomas Glynn
TEMPORARY SANITY
0–914590–29–4 Fiction Collective pb $5.95

WATCHING THE BODY BURN
0–394–57176–2 Knopf $18.95

● Gail Godwin
DREAM CHILDREN
Fifteen stories of women's madness
0–380–62406–0 Avon pb $4.50

THE FINISHING SCHOOL
A young girl forms a disturbing friendship with an older woman
0–380–69869–2 Avon pb $4.50

GLASS PEOPLE
0–14–008222–0 Penguin pb $6.95

A MOTHER AND TWO DAUGHTERS
"A superb novel in the Southern tradition of Flannery O'Connor and Eudora Welty"—*Minneapolis Tribune*
0–670–49021–0 Viking $16.95
0–380–61598–3 Avon pb $4.95

MR. BEDFORD AND THE MUSES
A novella and six short stories about a young American woman living with a London family
09–998–21054–2 Avon pb $4.95

THE ODD WOMAN
Attending her grandmother's funeral, a single woman confronts death, feminism, and sex
0–14–008221–2 Penguin pb $7.95

THE PERFECTIONISTS
"A kinky erotic masterpiece"—Kurt Vonnegut, Jr.
0–14–008388–X Penguin pb $6.95

A SOUTHERN FAMILY
0–688–06530–9 Morrow $18.95

VIOLET CLAY
A struggling young artist in New York searches for identity
0–14–008220–4 Penguin pb $6.95

● Donald Goines
Goines's violent novels of street life and ghetto crime have remained steadily in print since his murder in the 1970s.

BLACK GANGSTER
0–87067–263–0 Holloway House pb $2.50

BLACK GIRL LOST
0–87067–042–5 Holloway House pb $2.25

DADDY COOL
0–87067–041–7 Holloway House pb $2.25

DOPEFIEND
0–87067–044–1 Holloway House pb $2.25

ELDORADO RED
0–87067–067–0 Holloway House pb $2.25

INNER CITY HOODLUM
0–87067–033–6 Holloway House pb $2.25

STREET PLAYERS
0–87067–034–4 Holloway House pb $2.25

WHITE MAN'S JUSTICE, BLACK MAN'S GRIEF
0–87067–027–1 Holloway House pb $2.25

WHORESON
0–87067–046–8 Holloway House pb $2.25

● Rebecca Goldstein
THE LATE SUMMER PASSION OF A WOMAN OF MIND
A middle-aged émigré professor at an American university; her life past and present
0–374–18406–2 Farrar, Straus & Giroux $18.95

THE MIND-BODY PROBLEM
"Intelligent and perceptive, bawdy and witty—an articulate writer of great talent" —*LA Times*
0–440–35651–2 Dell pb $4.95

● Genaro González
RAINBOW'S END
Three generations of a Mexican-American family residing in the Lower Rio Grande Valley of Texas
0–934770–81–6 Arte Público pb $8.50

● Mary Gordon
THE COMPANY OF WOMEN
A sheltered, religious girl goes to Columbia in the 1960s
0–394–50508–5 Random House $12.95
0–345–32972–4 Ballantine pb $4.95

FINAL PAYMENTS
A woman comes to terms with her father's death
0–345–32973–2 Ballantine pb $3.95

MEN AND ANGELS
Mother and children at the mercy of a born-again babysitter
0–345–32925–2 Ballantine pb $4.50

TEMPORARY SHELTER
Twenty short stories. "Pitched in a more passionate tone than her novels, these stories have an intensity we have not always expected of the author"—*Newsday*
0–394–55520–1 Random House $16.95

● Lois Gould
FINAL ANALYSIS
0–374–52107–7 Farrar, Straus & Giroux pb $6.95

LA PRESIDENTA
0–374–52180–8 Farrar, Straus & Giroux pb $7.95

NECESSARY OBJECTS
"The four sisters in *Necessary Objects* are heiresses of a Fifth Avenue department-store chain, and Ms. Gould has drawn unmercifully on her background in

newspapers and magazine work to make these particular mannequins breathe fire"—*NY Times*
0–374–52108–5 Farrar, Straus & Giroux pb $6.95

A SEA-CHANGE
A beautiful woman moves to a remote island
0–374–52085–2 Farrar, Straus & Giroux pb $6.95

SUCH GOOD FRIENDS
"Lois Gould's first novel is uncommonly good: adroitly built, witty, illuminating . . ."—*Chicago Sun Times*
0–374–52086–0 Farrar, Straus & Giroux pb $6.95

● Sam Greenlee
THE SPOOK WHO SAT BY THE DOOR
An eerie tale of a black man infiltrating a CIA-type organization
0–8052–8225–4 Schocken pb $5.95

● Todd Grimson
WITHIN NORMAL LIMITS
An emergency room doctor in an emotional crisis. "The world of *Within Normal Limits* is at the same time bleak and exciting, a world of medical and moral emergency that desensitizes even as it relentlessly ups the emotional ante"—Richard Russo
0–394–74617–1 Random House pb $5.95

● William Hamilton
THE LAP OF LUXURY
A witty satire of the rich from the *New Yorker* cartoonist
0–87113–246–X Atlantic Monthly $17.95

● Barry Hannah
"A writer of violent honesty and power in the creative southern tradition"—Alfred Kazin
BOOMERANG
His most recent fiction is an autobiographical tour of the South
0–898–48882–6 Houghton Mifflin $15.95

CAPTAIN MAXIMUS
0–394–54458–7 Knopf $11.95
0–14–008811–3 Penguin pb $5.95

GERONIMO REX
0–14–010514–X Penguin pb $7.95

HEY JACK!
0–525–24558–8 Dutton $15.95

RAY
0–14–010515–8 Penguin pb $5.95

THE TENNIS HANDSOME
0–394–52876–X Knopf $11.95
0–684–18811–2 Scribners pb $4.95

● Joseph Hansen
BOHANON'S BOOK
0–88150–103–4 Countryman $16.95

JOB'S YEAR
0–03–061689–1 Henry Holt $14.95
0–452–26117–1 NAL pb $8.95

A SMILE IN HIS LIFETIME
0–452–25675–5 NAL pb $6.95

● Jim Harrison
DALVA
0–525–24624–X Dutton $18.95
0–671–67817–5 Washington Square pb $7.95

FARMER
0–440–55017–3 Dell pb $7.95

A GOOD DAY TO DIE
0–440–55021–1 Dell pb $7.95

LEGENDS OF THE FALL
0–440–55015–7 Dell pb $8.95

SUNDOG
0–671–67640–7 Washington Square pb $6.95

● Shirley Hazzard
THE BAY OF NOON
A woman becomes involved with a writer, a filmmaker, and a marine biologist
0–14–010450–X Penguin pb $6.95

CLIFFS OF FALL
0–515–08574–X Jove pb $3.50

THE EVENING OF THE HOLIDAY
An Englishwoman finds love on an Italian holiday
0–14–010451–8 Penguin pb $6.95

PEOPLE IN GLASS HOUSES
0–515–08626–6 Jove pb $3.50

● Nathan C. Heard
THE HOUSE OF SLAMMERS
0–02–549760–X Macmillan $14.95

● Larry Heinemann
CLOSE QUARTERS
0–14–008578–5 Penguin pb $6.95

PACO'S STORY
The sole survivor of a massacre in Vietnam returns to the States. Winner of the National Book Award. "Heinemann is slowly gaining a reputation as the grunt's novelist of the Vietnam War. His is the storytelling of life and death between the laager and the tree line, a life of dirt, fear, dope, alcohol, brutality, curses, and evil"—*Washington Post*
0–374–22847–7 Farrar, Straus & Giroux $15.95

● Joseph Heller
CATCH-22
The celebrated novel of World War II. "One of the most bitterly funny books in the language"—*New Republic*
0–440–11120–X Dell pb $4.95

GOD KNOWS
An extended stand-up monologue by David, King of the Jews
9–999–47547–7 Dell pb $4.95

GOOD AS GOLD
The travails of a Jewish intellectual, at home and in Washington
0–671–82388–4 Pocket pb $2.95

PICTURE THIS
Rembrandt's Aristotle contemplating the bust of Homer is the starting point for this freewheeling historical fantasy, which includes among its characters Plato, Hitler, and Cleopatra
0–399–13355–0 Knopf $19.95

SOMETHING HAPPENED
"Splendid, suspenseful, hypnotic, seductive . . . As clear and as hard-edged as a cut diamond"—*NY Times*
0–394–46568–7 Knopf $16.50
0–440–18133–X Dell pb $5.95

● Mark Helprin
ELLIS ISLAND & OTHER STORIES
A novella and ten stories. "A celebration of the transforming power of the imagination"—*Washington Post*
0–440–32204–9 Dell pb $4.50

WINTER'S TALE
A long and intricate exercise in adventurous fantasia
0–15–197203–6 HBJ $14.95
0–671–62118–1 Pocket pb $4.95

● Rolando Hinojosa
CLAROS VARONES DE BELKEN/FAIR GENTLEMEN OF BELKEN COUNTY
"Hinojosa offers an epic survey of life in the Rio Grande Valley . . . a world filled with the everyday sights, sounds, smells, words, ironies, and sympathies that constitute a unique side of the Texas universe"—*Texas Observer*
0–916950–65–4 Bilingual Review $12.00

DEAR RAFE
A bitter-comic story told in epistolary form
0–934770–38–7 Arte Público pb $7.50

KLAIL CITY
0–934770–54–9 Arte Público pb $8.00

THIS MIGRANT EARTH
A montage of stories of migrant workers
0–934770–55–7 Arte Público pb $8.00

● Edward Hoagland
SEVEN RIVERS WEST
Three men and an Indian woman head west in the 1880s. "Hoagland has captured the restless adventuresomeness of our frontiersmen, and the riot of nature in its unspoiled glory"—John Irving, *NY Times*
0–671–60753–7 Summit $18.95
0–14–010276–0 Penguin pb $6.95

● Russell Hoban
RIDDLEY WALKER
0–671–52694–4 Washington Square pb $6.95
0–671–60777–4 Pocket pb $2.95

● Janet Hobhouse
DANCING IN THE DARK
Young professionals at large on Manhattan's Upper West Side
0–394–72588–3 Random House pb $5.95

NOVEMBER
A middle-aged man flees New York City for London after being deserted by his wife
0–394–74665–1 Random House pb $6.95

● Andrew Holleran
DANCER FROM THE DANCE
An evocation of gay life in the 1970s
0–452–26129–5 NAL pb $8.95

● Paul Hoover
SAIGON, ILLINOIS
0–394–75849–8 Random House pb $6.95

● Pauline E. Hopkins
CONTENDING FORCES
Afterword by Gwendolyn Brooks
0–8093–0874–6 Southern Illinois pb $9.95

● James Houston
GIG
0–88739–061–7 Creative Arts pb $8.95

● Maureen Howard
BEFORE MY TIME
0–14–005503–7 Penguin pb $6.95

BRIDGEPORT BUS
0–14–005566–5 Penguin pb $5.95

EXPENSIVE HABITS
A novelist and screenwriter reviews her life, from McCarthy to Watergate
0–671–50625–0 Summit $17.95
0–14–010124–1 Penguin pb $6.95

FACTS OF LIFE
0–14–005500–2 Penguin pb $6.95

GRACE ABOUNDING
A young widow and her daughter enter a world of death, sensuality, betrayal, and eventual fulfillment
0–14–006887–2 Penguin pb $6.95

NOT A WORD ABOUT NIGHTINGALES
A gentleman scholar leaves his New England family to seek the good life in Italy
0–14–005596–7 Penguin pb $5.95

● Josephine Humphreys
DREAMS OF SLEEP
0–14–007787–1 Penguin pb $6.95

RICH IN LOVE
0–14–010283–3 Penguin pb $7.95

● William Humphreys
HOME FROM THE HILL
0–385–29733–5 Dell pb $9.95

THE ORDWAYS
0–385–29734–3 Dell pb $9.95

● Kristin Hunter
GOD BLESS THE CHILD
The life and tragic early death of a black woman
Introduction by Phil Petrie
0–88258–154–6 Howard pb $7.95

LOU IN THE LIMELIGHT
0–684–16880–4 Macmillan $12.95

● John Irving
THE CIDER HOUSE RULES
"The characters . . . break all the rules, and yet they remain noble and free-spirited. Victims of tragedy, violence, and injustice, their lives seem more interesting and full of thought-provoking dilemmas than the lives of many real people"—*Houston Post*
0–688–03036–X Morrow $18.95
0–553–25800–1 Bantam pb $4.95

THE HOTEL NEW HAMPSHIRE
"Some of the most unforgettable characters in recent fiction . . . lively good fun"—*Newsday*
0–671–63752–5 Pocket pb $4.95

THE 158-POUND MARRIAGE
0–671–46811–1 Pocket pb $3.95

A PRAYER FOR OWEN MEANY
0–688–07708–0 Morrow $19.95

SETTING FREE THE BEARS
0–671–46534–1 Pocket pb $3.95

THE WATER METHOD MAN
0–671–46812–X Pocket pb $3.95

THE WORLD ACCORDING TO GARP
Tragicomic account of an eccentric family
0–671–52369–4 Pocket pb $4.95

● Harold Jaffe
BEASTS
Ten short works modeled on the medieval bestiary. "At times surreal, at times overtly political, these stories force us to reexamine our most basic human instincts"—Rochelle Ratner
0–915306–58–1 Curbstone $17.50
0–915306–52–2 Curbstone $9.00

DOS INDIOS
0–938410–10–5 Thunder's Mouth pb $8.95

● Tama Janowitz
A CANNIBAL IN MANHATTAN
A cannibal from a South Sea island descends on the New York art scene
0–671–66598–7 Washington Square pb $7.95

SLAVES OF NEW YORK
Interrelated stories dealing with the artists and poseurs of downtown Manhattan
0–671–63678–2 Washington Square pb $6.95

● Len Jenkin
NEW JERUSALEM
0–940650–43–6 Sun & Moon pb $10.95

● Charles Johnson
FAITH AND THE GOOD THING
0–689–70720–7 Atheneum pb $9.95

OXHERDING TALE
A sharp, comic fantasy of the antebellum South
0–253–16607–1 Indiana $10.95
0–394–62123–9 Grove pb $6.95

● Denis Johnson
ANGELS
"I have not been so impressed by a first novel in years"—John le Carré
0–345–31820–X Ballantine pb $3.50

FISKADORO
"The sort of book Herman Melville might have written had he lived today and studied such disparate works as the Bible, 'The Waste Land,' *Fahrenheit 451,* and *Dog Soldiers,* screened *Star Wars* and *Apocalypse Now* several times, dropped a lot of acid, and listened to hours of Jimi Hendrix and the Rolling Stones"—*NY Times*
0–394–74367–9 Random House pb $6.95

THE STARS AT NOON
A young American woman in Nicaragua in 1984
0–394–53840–4 Knopf $15.95
0–394–75427–1 Random House pb $5.95

● Diane Johnson
PERSIAN NIGHTS
"Johnson's brilliant novel about privileged Americans caught in Iran just before the recent revolution is as exotic . . . as one of Scheherezade's original *Arabian Nights'* tales"—Alison Lurie
0–394–55804–9 Knopf $17.95

THE SHADOW KNOWS
0–449–21560–1 Fawcett pb $3.95

● Joyce Johnson
THE NIGHT CAFE
A love story set in Greenwich Village in the 1960s
0–525–24741–6 Dutton $17.95

● Gayl Jones
CORREGIDORA
0–8070–6315–0 Beacon pb $7.95

EVA'S MAN
0–8070–6319–3 Beacon pb $7.95

THE HERMIT-WOMAN
0–916418–43–X Lotus pb $4.00

SONG FOR ANNINHO
0–916418–26–X Lotus pb $4.50

● Nettie Jones
FISH TALES
0–394–53294–5 Random House $13.95

● Erica Jong
FANNY
0–451–15890–3 NAL pb $4.95

FEAR OF FLYING
Frank and funny account of a young woman's sexual exploits
0–03–010731–8 Henry Holt $12.95
0–451–15851–2 NAL pb $4.95

HOW TO SAVE YOUR OWN LIFE
"A combination of eroticism and wit . . . with a rock-hard base of intelligence in her writing"—*Booklist*
0–451–15948–9 NAL pb $4.95

PARACHUTES AND KISSES
0–451–13877–5 NAL pb $4.95

SERENISSIMA
A Hollywood actress goes to the Venice Film Festival and falls in love with Shakespeare
0–395–42922–6 Houghton Mifflin $17.95
0–440–20104–7 Dell pb $4.95

● Ward Just
THE AMERICAN AMBASSADOR
0–395–42694–4 Houghton Mifflin $17.50

JACK GANCE
A young man's career through the ranks of Chicago politics to the national scene in Washington. A masterful portrayal of American political life
0–395–49337–4 Houghton Mifflin $17.95

STRINGER
0–915308–61–4 Graywolf pb $6.00

● Steve Katz
FLORRY OF WASHINGTON HEIGHTS
A half-Irish, half-Jewish boy growing up in pre-World War II upper Manhattan
0–940650–83–5 Sun & Moon $15.95
0–940650–84–3 Sun & Moon pb $10.95

WIER AND POUCE
"A linguistic tour de force"—*Village Voice*
0–940650–33–9 Sun & Moon $17.95
0–940650–47–9 Sun & Moon pb $10.95

● Janet Kauffman
COLLABORATORS
A woman's relationship with her mother alters when the mother suffers a stroke. "A moving evocation of the real love between mother and daughter, and the burden it places on both of them"—*Cleveland Plain Dealer*
0–394–55080–3 Knopf $13.95
0–14–009342–7 Penguin pb $5.95

PLACES IN THE WORLD A WOMAN COULD WALK
0–14–007664–6 Penguin pb $5.95

- Joe Keenan
BLUE HEAVEN
0–14–010764–9 Penguin pb $7.95

- William Melvin Kelley
DANCERS ON THE SHORE
A collection of 16 short stories
0–88258–114–7 Howard pb $6.95

- Robert Kelly
THE SCORPIONS
0–88268–018–8 Station Hill pb $7.95

A TRANSPARENT TREE: Fictions
Eleven short works. "Astonishing mix of
intellect, romanticism, and daring
imagination"—Robert Coover
0–914232–68–1 McPherson $20.00
0–914232–70–3 McPherson $10.00

- William Kennedy
THE ALBANY CYCLE
A one-volume edition of *Legs, Billy Phelan's
Greatest Game,* and *Ironweed*
0–14–095284–5 Penguin pb $21.95

BILLY PHELAN'S GREATEST GAME
0–14–006340–4 Penguin pb $6.95

THE INK TRUCK
0–14–007674–3 Penguin pb $6.95

IRONWEED
A former baseball player down and out in
Albany, 20 years after the accidental killing
of his son
0–670–40176–5 Viking $16.95
0–14–007020–6 Penguin pb $6.95

LEGS
The life and times of Prohibition-era
gangster Legs Diamond
0–14–006484–2 Penguin pb $6.95

QUINN'S BOOK
0–670–80437–1 Viking $18.95
0–14–007737–5 Penguin pb $8.95

- Susan Kenney
GRAVES IN ACADEME
0–14–009386–9 Penguin pb $3.50

IN ANOTHER COUNTRY
0–14–007407–4 Penguin pb $5.95

SAILING
0–670–81229–3 Viking $18.95
0–14–009333–8 Penguin pb $7.95

- Ken Kesey
**ONE FLEW OVER THE CUCKOO'S
NEST**
0–14–015509–0 Penguin pb $8.95

SOMETIMES A GREAT NOTION
0–14–004529–5 Penguin pb $7.95

- John Oliver Killens
An important figure in the Black Arts
Movement of the 1960s, Killens was a
close friend of Martin Luther King and
other civil rights activists.
YOUNGBLOOD
A generational novel from 1954
Foreword by Addison Gayle
0–8203–0602–9 Georgia pb $8.95

AND THEN WE HEARD THUNDER
Racism in the military during World
War II
Introduction by Mel Watkins
0–88258–115–5 Howard pb $7.95

'SIPPI
A black man's coming of age in Mississippi
in 1954, when the Supreme Court struck
down the "separate but equal" doctrine
0–938410–55–5 Thunder's Mouth pb $9.95

- Jamaica Kincaid
ANNIE JOHN
0–374–10521–9 Farrar, Straus & Giroux $18.95
0–452–26016–7 NAL pb $6.95

AT THE BOTTOM OF THE RIVER
0–374–10660–6 Farrar, Straus & Giroux $9.95
0–394–73683–4 Random House pb $5.95

- Maxine Hong Kingston
TRIPMASTER MONKEY: His Fake Book
The adventures of a Chinese-American in
San Francisco in the 1960s
0–394–56831–1 Knopf $19.95

- John Knowles
PEACE BREAKS OUT
0–553–27574–7 Bantam pb $3.95

THE PRIVATE LIFE OF AXIE REED
0–525–24403–4 Dutton $15.95

A SEPARATE PEACE
A boy's coming of age at a New England
boarding school
0–02–564840–3 Macmillan $20.00
0–553–25052–3 Bantam pb $2.95

A STOLEN PAST
A man returns to Yale 30 years after his
graduation and recalls his past there
0–345–31590–1 Ballantine pb $3.50

- Jerzy Kosinski
BEING THERE
0–553–27930–0 Bantam pb $4.50

**THE HERMIT OF SIXTY-NINTH
STREET: The Working Papers of Norbert
Kosky**
0–8050–0611–7 Henry Holt $19.95

THE PAINTED BIRD
A nightmarish vision of Eastern Europe
during World War II
0–394–60433–4 Modern Library $6.95
0–553–26520–2 Bantam pb $4.50

STEPS
A sequence of surreal episodes, with an
emphasis on sadomasochistic situations
0–394–60209–9 Modern Library $7.95
0–394–75716–5 Random House pb $5.95

- William Kotzwinkle
THE EXILE
A Hollywood film star discovers a parallel
universe in which he is a black marketeer
in World War II Berlin
0–525–24526–X Dutton $17.95

THE FAN MAN
0–525–48307–1 Dutton pb $7.95

HEARTS OF WOOD: Timeless Tales
Illustrated by Joe Servello
0–87923–648–5 Godine $12.95

JEWEL OF THE MOON
Short stories
0–399–13113–2 Putnam $14.95

THE MIDNIGHT EXAMINER
His latest novel, set in the insane world of
tabloid newspapers
0–395–49859–7 Houghton Mifflin $17.95

- Kathryn Kramer
**A HANDBOOK FOR VISITORS FROM
OUTER SPACE**
0–394–72989–7 Random House pb $5.95

- David Leavitt
EQUAL AFFECTIONS
1–55584–202–X Weidenfeld & Nicolson $18.95

FAMILY DANCING
An acclaimed first collection of stories. "An
astonishing collection . . . tender, funny,
eloquent, and wise . . . Regardless of age,
few writers so effortlessly achieve the sense
of maturity and earned compassion so
evident in these pages"—*NY Times*
0–394–53872–2 Knopf $13.95
0–446–32845–6 Warner pb $3.95

THE LOST LANGUAGE OF CRANES
0–394–53873–0 Knopf $17.50
0–553–34465–X Bantam pb $8.95

- Harper Lee
TO KILL A MOCKINGBIRD
A vivid autobiographical account of
growing up in the South
0–397–00151–7 Harper & Row $18.95
0–446–31049–2 Warner pb $3.50

- Brad Leithauser
EQUAL DISTANCE
Young Americans in Japan
0–452–25818–9 NAL pb $6.95

HENCE
0–394–57311–0 Knopf $18.95

- Craig Lesley
RIVER SONG
A Nez Perce drifter and former rodeo
rider, and his father, search for their
personal and tribal heritage in Lesley's
second novel, set in Oregon
0–395–43083–6 Houghton Mifflin $18.95

- Ellen Lesser
THE OTHER WOMAN
0–671–66985–0 Washington Square pb $6.95

- Gordon Lish
PERU
A middle-aged man is haunted by an act of
violence he committed as a child
0–525–24375–5 Dutton $15.95
0–684–18764–7 Scribners pb $8.95

- Ron Loewinsohn
WHERE ALL THE LADDERS START
0–87113–151–X Atlantic Monthly $17.95

- Phillip Lopate
THE RUG MERCHANT
0–670–81434–2 Viking $16.95
0–14–009676–0 Penguin pb $6.95

- Alison Lurie
FOREIGN AFFAIRS
Two Americans abroad, two love affairs;
winner of the 1984 Pulitzer Prize
0–394–54076–X Random House $15.95
0–380–89887–X Avon pb $4.50

          TO ORDER BOOKS AS GIFTS, SEE PAGE 1

Alison Lurie (photo by Jill Krementz, courtesy of Random House)

IMAGINARY FRIENDS
Two sociologists captivated by a teenage psychic
0–380–70073–5 Avon pb $4.50

NOWHERE CITY
A man and his wife are divided by, among other things, their contrasting attitudes toward Los Angeles
0–380–70070–0 Avon pb $4.50

REAL PEOPLE
A New England art colony
0–380–70069–7 Avon pb $3.95

THE TRUTH ABOUT LORIN JONES
0–316–53720–9 Little, Brown $18.95

THE WAR BETWEEN THE TATES
The breakup of a faculty marriage
0–394–46201–7 Random House $16.95

- **Cormac McCarthy**
BLOOD MERIDIAN: Or The Evening Redness in the West
The American West as continuous massacre: a stunningly visualized novel whose prose represents an original blend of dime novel and Old Testament
0–88001–092–4 Ecco pb $9.50

CHILD OF GOD
A ballad-like piece of Southern Gothic, charting the hideous doings of a crazed loner
0–88001–065–7 Ecco pb $7.50

THE ORCHARD KEEPER
0–88001–009–6 Ecco pb $8.50

OUTER DARK
0–88001–064–9 Ecco pb $7.50

SUTTREE
0–394–74145–5 Random House pb $6.95

- **Stephen McCauley**
THE OBJECT OF MY AFFECTION
0–671–61840–7 Simon & Schuster $17.95
0–671–64994–9 Washington Square pb $6.95

- **Kristin McCloy**
VELOCITY
0–394–57022–7 Random House $16.50

- **John A. McCluskey, Jr.**
MR. AMERICA'S LAST SEASON BLUES
0–8071–1120–1 Louisiana $18.95

- **Alice McDermott**
A BIGAMIST'S DAUGHTER
A vanity-press editor helps an author to finish a novel about a bigamist, and in the process learns about her own father
0–06–097142–8 Harper & Row pb $7.95

THAT NIGHT
Young love violently and irrevocably interrupted on Long Island. "Possesses the ability to make us remember our own youth"—*NY Times*
0–374–27361–8 Farrar, Straus & Giroux $14.95
0–06–097141–X Harper & Row pb $6.95

- **Joseph McElroy**
McElroy's novels, complex and hybrid in form, explore late 20th-century crises of survival and personal power.
THE LETTER LEFT TO ME
0–394–57196–7 Knopf $16.95

LOOKOUT CARTRIDGE
0–88184–147–1 Carroll & Graf pb $9.95

PLUS
0–88184–289–3 Carroll & Graf pb $8.95

A SMUGGLER'S BIBLE
0–88184–146–3 Carroll & Graf pb $9.50

WOMEN AND MEN
0–394–50344–9 Knopf $27.50

- **Thomas McGuane**
THE BUSHWHACKED PIANO
0–394–72642–1 Random House pb $5.95

NINETY-TWO IN THE SHADE
A drug addict returns to Key West and becomes involved in rivalry with a skiff guide
0–14–009907–7 Penguin pb $5.95

NOBODY'S ANGEL
An army man returns to Montana. "A thinking man's Western"—*LA Times*
0–394–74738–0 Random House pb $6.95
0–345–33087–0 Ballantine pb $3.50

PANAMA
A fading, coked-up rock star goes to Key West seeking lost love
0–374–22942–2 Farrar, Straus & Giroux $7.95
0–14–009908–5 Penguin pb $5.95

SOMETHING TO BE DESIRED
"Nobody writes so well about the incongruities of modern western America"—*Chicago Tribune*
0–394–73156–5 Random House pb $4.95

THE SPORTING CLUB
A mock duel escalates into bizarre and shocking violence
0–374–26796–0 Farrar, Straus & Giroux $8.95
0–14–009909–3 Penguin pb $5.95

TO SKIN A CAT
0–525–24460–3 Dutton $16.95
0–394–75521–9 Random House pb $5.95

- **Jay McInerney**
BRIGHT LIGHTS, BIG CITY
An aspiring writer high on cocaine in the club scene of lower Manhattan
0–394–75688–6 Random House pb $3.95

RANSOM
An American karate student in Japan
0–394–74118–8 Random House pb $5.95

THE STORY OF MY LIFE
0–87113–238–9 Atlantic Monthly $16.95

- **Terry McMillan**
DISAPPEARING ACTS
The touching and often funny story of an educated black woman who falls in love with a construction worker
0–670–82461–5 Viking $17.95

MAMA
A tough, feisty heroine who'll do anything to keep her family together
0–671–64932–9 Washington Square pb $5.95

- **Larry McMurtry**
ALL MY FRIENDS ARE GOING TO BE STRANGERS
0–671–68103–6 Simon & Schuster pb $7.95

ANYTHING FOR BILLY
0–671–64268–5 Simon & Schuster $18.95

CADILLAC JACK
A rodeo cowboy turned antique scout travels in his Cadillac between Texas and Washington, D.C.
0–671–63720–7 Simon & Schuster pb $6.95

THE DESERT ROSE
A Las Vegas showgirl and her daughter
0–671–63721–5 Simon & Schuster pb $6.95

HORSEMAN, PASS BY
0–89096–241–3 Texas A&M $13.95
0–14–004691–7 Penguin pb $6.95

THE LAST PICTURE SHOW
Life in a small Texas town during the 1950s
0–14–005183–X Penguin pb $5.95

LEAVING CHEYENNE
0–89096–242–1 Texas A&M $15.95
0–14–005221–6 Penguin pb $6.95

LONESOME DOVE
An epic of the Old West, full of humor and action, and long enough to get lost in for a reasonable spell
0–671–50420–7 Simon & Schuster $19.95
0–671–62461–X Pocket Books pb $5.95

MOVING ON
Life in the American West in the 1960s
0–671–63320–1 Simon & Schuster pb $8.95

SOMEBODY'S DARLING
A woman director in Hollywood and the men in her life
0–317–56596–6 Simon & Schuster pb $6.95

TERMS OF ENDEARMENT
The bittersweet relationship between a mother and her daughter
0–671–68208–3 Simon & Schuster pb $8.95
0–451–15817–2 NAL pb $4.50

Larry McMurtry (photo by Lee Marmon, courtesy of Simon & Schuster)

TEXASVILLE
0-671-62533-0 Simon & Schuster $18.95

- **Donald Mackey**
A DIFFERENT DRUMMER
0-9613091-0-5 Donnell $12.95

- **Nathaniel Mackey**
BEDOUIN HORNBOOK
Mackey's notion of fiction embraces poetry, philosophical essay, music criticism, and journal entry; one of the most strikingly original books of the 1980s
0-912759-07-0 Callaloo pb $10.00

- **Norman Maclean**
A RIVER RUNS THROUGH IT & OTHER STORIES
0-226-50055-1 Chicago $15.00
0-226-50057-8 Chicago pb $7.95

- **Clarence Major**
Poet, painter, teacher, lexicographer, and novelist, Major has been on the cutting edge of black fiction for 20 years. The Fiction Collective, a cooperative publishing house, was started by Major and a handful of colleagues in the early 1970s.
EMERGENCY EXIT
0-914590-58-8 Fiction Collective $12.95
0-914590-59-6 Fiction Collective pb $6.95

MY AMPUTATIONS
0-914590-96-0 Fiction Collective $15.95

PAINTED TURTLE: WOMAN WITH GUITAR
"Interspersing the mythic tales that for centuries explained the world to her Zuni ancestors with the realities of modern Indian existence, folksinger Painted Turtle struggles for balance in her life"—*Publishers Weekly*
1-55713-002-7 Sun & Moon $14.95

REFLEX AND BONE STRUCTURE
0-914590-17-0 Fiction Collective pb $6.95

- **Paule Marshall**
BROWN GIRL, BROWNSTONES
Afterword by Mary H. Washington
0-912670-96-7 Feminist Press pb $8.95

THE CHOSEN PLACE, THE TIMELESS PEOPLE
American anthropologists become entangled with inhabitants of a Caribbean island much like Grenada. "A style remarkable for its courage, color, and its natural control"—*New Yorker*
0-394-72633-2 Random House pb $6.95

PRAISESONG FOR THE WIDOW
0-525-48303-9 Dutton pb $7.95

REENA & OTHER STORIES
0-935312-24-2 Feminist Press pb $8.95

SOUL CLAP HANDS AND SING
Four stories of middle age and despair ranging in location from Brooklyn to Barbados to Brazil
Introduction by Phil Petrie
0-88258-155-4 Howard pb $7.95

- **David Martin**
THE BEGINNING OF SORROWS
1-55584-063-9 Weidenfeld & Nicolson $16.95

FINAL HARBOR
0-88184-215-X Carroll & Graf pb $4.95

- **Max Martínez**
SCHOOLLAND
The life of a Mexican-American family in rural Texas during the year of a great drought in the 1950s
0-934770-87-5 Arte Público pb $8.50

- **Bobbie Anne Mason**
IN COUNTRY
A girl comes to terms with her father's death in Vietnam two decades earlier
0-06-015469-1 Harper & Row $15.95
0-06-091350-9 Harper & Row pb $6.95

LOVE LIFE
Short stories
0-06-016042-X Harper & Row $16.95

SHILOH & OTHER STORIES
Sixteen stories set in Kentucky. "A stunning debut"—Raymond Carver
0-06-015062-9 Harper & Row $12.95
0-06-091330-4 Harper & Row pb $7.95

- **Harry Mathews**
CIGARETTES
1-55584-092-2 Weidenfeld & Nicolson $17.95
0-02-013971-3 Macmillan pb $8.95

COUNTRY COOKING & OTHER STORIES
0-930900-82-0 Burning Deck pb $4.00

THE SINKING OF THE ODRADEK STADIUM
0-06-012841-0 Harper & Row $5.95

TLOOTH
0-85635-765-0 Carcanet pb $8.50

TWENTY LINES A DAY
0-916583-27-9 Dalkey Archive $20.00

- **Armistead Maupin**
BABY CAKES: Continuing Tales of the City
0-06-091099-2 Harper & Row pb $8.95

FURTHER TALES OF THE CITY
0-06-090916-1 Harper & Row pb $9.95

MORE TALES OF THE CITY
0-06-090726-6 Harper & Row pb $9.95

SIGNIFICANT OTHERS
0-06-055086-4 Harper & Row $19.95
0-06-096126-0 Harper & Row pb $9.95

TALES OF THE CITY
0-06-090654-5 Harper & Row pb $10.95

- **Lee Maynard**
CRUM
0-671-64842-X Washington Square pb $6.95

- **Louise Meriwether**
DADDY WAS A NUMBERS RUNNER
0-935312-57-9 Feminist Press pb $8.95

- **Leonard Michaels**
GOING PLACES
0-374-51711-8 Farrar, Straus & Giroux pb $6.95

I WOULD HAVE SAVED THEM IF I COULD
0-374-51713-4 Farrar, Straus & Giroux pb $6.95

THE MEN'S CLUB
0-374-20782-8 Farrar, Straus & Giroux $10.95
0-380-58131-0 Avon pb $2.95

- **Sue Miller**
THE GOOD MOTHER
A woman torn between maternity and sexuality. "Goes straight to the dark heart of . . . modern sexual morality"—Russell Banks
0-06-015551-5 Harper & Row $17.95
0-440-12938-9 Dell pb $4.95

INVENTING THE ABBOTTS & OTHER STORIES
"Report from a frontier . . . The battlefields are the kitchen and the bedroom"—*NY Times*
0-06-015755-0 Harper & Row $15.95

- **Steven Millhauser**
IN THE PENNY ARCADE
Short stories. "A collection whose very existence is a cause for celebration"—David Leavitt, *Esquire*
0-394-54660-1 Knopf $14.95
0-317-55999-0 Pocket Books pb $5.95

PORTRAIT OF AN AMERICAN ROMANTIC
"An adolescent *Picture of Dorian Gray* . . . A brilliant, perverse eulogy for American boyhood"—*Boston Globe*
0-317-56560-5 Washington Square pb $6.95

- **Susan Minot**
LUST & OTHER STORIES
0-395-48888-5 Houghton Mifflin $17.95

MONKEYS
"The seven children of a sorrowing alcoholic father and a blithe but most unoblivious mother are the viewpoint of a tale that has the compass of one of the great nineteenth-century novels"—Penelope Gilliatt
0-525-24342-9 Dutton $15.95
0-671-63188-8 Washington Square pb $5.95

- **N. Scott Momaday**
HOUSE MADE OF DAWN
The conflicts of contemporary Native American culture
0-06-080421-1 Harper & Row pb $4.95

- **Susanna Moore**
MY OLD SWEETHEART
0-315-32516-1 Houghton Mifflin $12.95
0-14-006783-3 Penguin pb $6.95

THE WHITENESS OF BONES
0-385-26079-2 Doubleday $17.95

- **Alejandro Morales**
THE BRICK PEOPLE
"Eloquently fuses the fantastic and the factual as he traces the growth of early California from 1892 to the late 1940s"—*Publisher's Weekly*
0-934770-91-3 Arte Público pb $9.50

DEATH OF AN ANGLO
An idealistic young doctor's attempts to improve the lives of Chicano residents in a Texas town
0-916950-83-2 Bilingual pb $12.00

- **Mary M. Morris**
VANISHED
0-670-82216-7 Viking $16.95

☞ **TO ORDER NEW BOOKS NOT YET LISTED, ASK YOUR BOOKSELLER OR CALL 1-800-882-8770**

Toni Morrison (photo by Helen Marcus)

• Toni Morrison

"The ordinary spars with the extraordinary in Morrison's books. What would be a classically tragic sensibility, with its implacable move toward crises and the extremes of pity and horror, is altered and illuminated by a thousand smaller, natural occurrences and circumstances."—Margo Jefferson, *Ms.*

BELOVED
"A work that brings to the darkest corners of American experience the wisdom, and the courage, to know them as they are"—*NY Review of Books*
0–394–53597–9 Knopf $18.95
0–452–26136–8 NAL pb $8.95

THE BLUEST EYE
"The novel becomes poetry . . . But *The Bluest Eye* is also history, sociology, folklore, nightmare, and music"—*NY Times*
0–671–53146–8 Washington Square pb $3.95

SONG OF SOLOMON
An allegorical novel blending the themes of family and conflict and the quest for the past
0–394–49784–8 Knopf $18.95
0–452–26011–6 NAL pb $7.95

SULA
Two women, whose lives take sharply divergent paths, reaffirm the bonds of friendship. "A howl of love and rage, playful and funny as well as hard and bitter"—*NY Times*
0–394–48044–9 Knopf $18.95
0–452–26010–8 NAL pb $6.95

TAR BABY
0–394–42329–1 Knopf $19.95
0–451–12224–0 NAL pb $4.50

• Bradford Morrow

COME SUNDAY
0–02–023001–X Macmillan pb $10.95

• Elias Miguel Muñoz

CRAZY LOVE
An experimental novel reflecting the mosaic of Cuban-American culture
0–934770–83–2 Arte Público pb $8.50

• Gloria Naylor

LINDEN HILLS
Life in an upper-class black community
0–89919–357–9 Ticknor & Fields $16.95
0–14–008829–6 Penguin pb $7.95

MAMA DAY
0–89919–716–7 Ticknor & Fields $17.95
0–679–72181–9 Random House pb $8.95

THE WOMEN OF BREWSTER PLACE
"The most refreshing voice in the black idiom since readers first discovered Toni Morrison"—Claude Brown
0–14–006690–X Penguin pb $6.95

• John Nichols

AMERICAN BLOOD
A Vietnam vet returns to America. "The film *Platoon* is like *Babes in Toyland* after the almost unspeakable horrors that fill the war days of Michael P. Smith, the narrator of *American Blood*"—*Pittsburgh Post Gazette*
0–8050–0374–6 Henry Holt $17.95

A GHOST IN THE MUSIC
0–393–30471–X Norton pb $7.95

THE STERILE CUCKOO
0–393–30472–8 Norton pb $7.95

THE WIZARD OF LONELINESS
A young boy is sent to his father's family in Vermont during World War II
0–393–30569–4 Norton pb $4.95

THE MAGIC JOURNEY
0–345–31049–7 Ballantine pb $4.95

THE MILAGRO BEANFIELD WAR
0–345–00630–5 Ballantine pb $4.95

THE NIRVANA BLUES
0–03–059256–9 Henry Holt $14.95
0–345–30465–9 Ballantine pb $4.95

• Hugh Nissenson

MY OWN GROUND
The spiritual and sexual awakening of a 15-year-old immigrant on New York's Lower East Side
0–06–097075–8 Harper & Row pb $6.95

THE ELEPHANT AND MY JEWISH PROBLEM: Short Stories and Journals, 1957–1987
0–06–015985–5 Harper & Row $18.95

THE TREE OF LIFE
A meditative reconstruction of early America, in the form of a settler's diary; Johnny Appleseed figures prominently in a somewhat sinister role
0–06–015143–9 Harper & Row $15.95
0–06–091362–2 Harper & Row pb $6.95

• Kem Nunn

TAPPING THE SOURCE
Surfers, bikers, druggies, and spiritual seekers populate this panoramic California thriller
0–440–20078–4 Dell pb $4.95

UNASSIGNED TERRITORY
A refugee from a fundamentalist sect gets lost in the Mojave desert
0–385–29536–7 Delacorte $16.95
0–440–50009–5 Dell pb $7.95

• Joyce Carol Oates

ANGEL OF LIGHT
A brother and sister avenge the death of their father, a descendant of John Brown
0–446–30189–2 Warner pb $3.95

THE ASSASSINS
0–8149–0767–9 Vanguard $17.95
0–449–23000–7 Fawcett pb $3.50

THE ASSIGNATION
0–88001–200–5 Ecco $16.95

BELLEFLEUR
Six generations of an aristocratic Adirondack family
0–525–48347–0 Dutton pb $9.95

A BLOODSMOOR ROMANCE
A Gothic novel, reflecting Oates's continuing obsession with popular fiction of the past
0–446–30825–0 Warner pb $3.95

BY THE NORTH GATE
0–8149–0174–3 Vanguard $17.95

CHILDWOLD
A middle-aged man becomes obsessed with a destitute 14-year-old girl
0–8149–0777–6 Vanguard $17.95
0–449–23450–9 Fawcett pb $2.95

CYBELE
A 40-year-old man is involved in a series of grotesque extramarital affairs
0–87685–425–0 Black Sparrow $20.00
0–525–48254–7 Dutton pb $7.95

DO WITH ME WHAT YOU WILL
0–449–20386–7 Fawcett pb $3.95

EXPENSIVE PEOPLE
0–449–20012–4 Fawcett pb $2.95

THE GODDESS AND OTHER WOMEN
0–8149–0745–8 Vanguard $17.95

LAST DAYS: Stories
0–525–24248–1 Dutton $15.95
0–525–48205–9 Dutton pb $7.95

MARYA: A Life
An intellectual, from childhood to her mid-30s
0–525–24374–7 Dutton $16.95

MYSTERIES OF WINTERTHURN
A pastiche of 19th-century detective fiction
0–425–08022–6 Berkley Group pb $4.50

NIGHT-SIDE
0–449–24206–4 Fawcett pb $2.50

RAVEN'S WING
Eighteen stories depict the violence and passion behind everyday life
0–525–24446–8 Dutton $17.95
0–525–48333–0 Dutton pb $8.95

THE SEDUCTION & OTHER STORIES
0–87685–229–0 Black Sparrow $14.00
0–449–24284–6 Fawcett pb $2.75

A SENTIMENTAL EDUCATION: Stories
"These six stories, one of novella length, display the prismatic Oates talent to advantage—subtle characterizations, convincing dialogue, penetrating interior monologues, and, of course, the violent epiphanies that have become her hallmark"—*John Barkham Review*
0–525–48021–8 Dutton pb $4.95

SOLSTICE
0–525–24293–7 Dutton $15.95
0–425–09204–6 Berkley pb $3.95

SON OF THE MORNING
An evangelist succumbs to pride
0–8149–0800–4 Vanguard $17.95
0–449–24073–8 Fawcett pb $2.75

THE TRIUMPH OF THE SPIDER MONKEY
0–87685–291–6 Black Sparrow $14.00
0–87685–290–8 Black Sparrow pb $5.00

THEM
The breakthrough novel that introduced Oates's characteristic themes of violence, passion, and madness underlying American family life. Winner of the 1969 National Book Award
0–449–20692–0 Fawcett pb $4.95

UNHOLY LOVES
0–8149–0813–6 Vanguard $17.95
0–449–24457–1 Fawcett pb $2.95

UPON THE SWEEPING FLOOD
0–8149–0172–7 Vanguard $17.95

YOU MUST REMEMBER THIS
0–525–24545–6 Dutton $19.95
0–06–097169–X Harper & Row pb $8.95

● Tim O'Brien
GOING AFTER CACCIATO
0–440–32966–5 Dell pb $4.95

IF I DIE IN A COMBAT ZONE
0–440–34311–9 Dell pb $4.50

THE NUCLEAR AGE
0–440–55974–X Dell pb $7.95

● Robert Olmstead
RIVER DOGS
Violence, murder, and an enigmatic woman in rural Maine. "Olmstead's New England is far from the quaint white churches of the Updike set"—*New York*
0–394–74684–8 Random House pb $6.95

● Tillie Olsen
TELL ME A RIDDLE
Four short pieces. "Explores the deep pain and real promise of fundamental American experience in a style of incomparable verbal richness and beauty"—Julian Moynihan
0–440–38573–3 Dell pb $3.95

● Toby Olson
THE LIFE OF JESUS: An Apocryphal Novel
A Catholic boyhood, interspersed with garishly lit Biblical fantasies
0–8112–0613–0 New Directions $8.50
0–8112–0614–9 New Directions pb $3.95

SEAVIEW
0–8112–0829–X New Directions pb $6.95

UTAH
0–671–63814–9 Simon & Schuster $17.95

THE WOMAN WHO ESCAPED FROM SHAME
A salesman in Mexico discovers miniature horses being trained to appear in pornographic films. "Imagination rules, creates things not seen before"—John Edgar Wideman
0–394–54715–2 Random House $16.95
0–02–023231–4 Macmillan pb $7.95

● Simon J. Ortiz
FIGHTIN': New & Collected Stories
"Simon Ortiz's registration of dead end drifter and workingman voices, whether white or Indian, from the pueblo or from Kerr McGee's mines, has a way of picking the quiet epiphanies out of the junk and struggle of hard times"—*San Francisco Examiner*
0–938410–15–6 Thunder's Mouth $14.95
0–938410–14–8 Thunder's Mouth pb $6.95

● Cynthia Ozick
BLOODSHED & THREE NOVELLAS
0–525–48065–X Dutton pb $6.95

LEVITATION: Five Fictions
0–394–51413–0 Knopf $11.50
0–525–48442–6 Dutton pb $7.95

THE CANNIBAL GALAXY
0–394–52943–X Knopf $11.95
0–525–48133–8 Dutton pb $7.95

THE MESSIAH OF STOCKHOLM
0–394–54701–2 Knopf $15.95

THE PAGAN RABBI & OTHER STORIES
0–525–48401–9 Dutton pb $8.95

TRUST
0–525–48066–8 Dutton pb $11.95

● Grace Paley
ENORMOUS CHANGES AT THE LAST MINUTE
0–374–51524–7 Farrar, Straus & Giroux pb $6.95

LATER THE SAME DAY
Seventeen short stories written over the past ten years. "Technically, Grace Paley's work makes the novel as a form seem virtually redundant. Each one of her stories has more abundant inner life than most other people's novels"—Angela Carter, *London Review of Books*
0–374–18409–7 Farrar, Straus & Giroux $13.95
0–14–008641–2 Penguin pb $5.95

THE LITTLE DISTURBANCES OF MAN
Paley's first collection of short fiction. "A wonderful writer and troublemaker. We are fortunate to have her in our country"—Donald Barthelme
0–14–007557–7 Penguin pb $5.95

● Breece D'J Pancake
THE STORIES OF BREECE D'J PANCAKE
"An exceptional voice; gritty, mordant, invested with the texture of stroked reality; urgent and haunting"—Margaret Atwood
0–316–69012–0 Little, Brown $15.95
0–03–070623–8 Henry Holt pb $6.95

● Walker Percy
LANCELOT
A modern "knight" surveys the landscapes of contemporary America. "A funny and scarifying jeremiad on the modern age"—*Time*
0–380–01861–6 Avon pb $4.50

THE LAST GENTLEMAN
0–374–50916–6 Farrar, Straus & Giroux pb $9.25
0–380–37796–9 Avon pb $4.50

LOVE IN THE RUINS: The Adventures of a Bad Catholic at a Time Near the End of the World
0–374–19302–9 Farrar, Straus & Giroux $15.95
0–804–10378–X Ivy pb $4.95

THE MOVIEGOER
In this first novel, which won the National Book Award, a New Orleans stockbroker finds the meaning for his life during Mardi Gras week
0–394–43703–9 Knopf $14.95

THE SECOND COMING
Will Barrett, from *The Last Gentleman*, returns 25 years later
0–671–60104–0 Pocket Books pb $4.95

THE THANATOS SYNDROME
A paroled psychiatrist finds that a bizarre increase in sexual behavior is due to unauthorized additives in the water supply
0–374–27354–5 Farrar, Straus & Giroux $17.95

● Richard Perry
MONTGOMERY'S CHILDREN
0–452–25674–7 NAL pb $6.95

● Betty Pesetsky
CONFESSIONS OF A BAD GIRL & OTHER STORIES
0–689–12021–4 Atheneum $17.95

● Jayne Ann Phillips
BLACK TICKETS
A collection of short stories
0–440–55022–X Dell pb $8.95

FAST LANES
0–525–24515–4 Dutton $15.95
0–671–64014–3 Washington Square pb $5.95

MACHINE DREAMS
An ordinary American family from the Depression to Vietnam. "One of the great books of this decade"—Robert Stone
0–317–53290–1 Pocket Books pb $3.95

● Marge Piercy
BRAIDED LIVES
Growing up in 1950s Detroit
0–449–21300–5 Fawcett pb $4.95

DANCE THE EAGLE TO SLEEP
0–449–44540–2 Fawcett pb $3.95

FLY AWAY HOME
A successful author reconstructs her life after a devastating divorce
0–449–20691–2 Fawcett pb $4.95

GOING DOWN FAST
A university's effect upon a depressed inner city neighborhood
0–449–24480–6 Fawcett pb $4.50

GONE TO SOLDIERS
World War II, as experienced by ten people overseas and on the home front. "Piercy is the political novelist of our time"—Marilyn French
0–671–63421–6 Summit $19.95
0–449–21557–1 Fawcett pb $4.95

THE HIGH COST OF LIVING
A woman becomes involved in a romantic triangle with a virgin and a homosexual hustler
0–449–44539–9 Fawcett pb $4.50

SMALL CHANGES
0–449–21083–9 Fawcett pb $3.95

VIDA
A fugitive from the '60s is still on the run ten years later
0–449–20850–8 Fawcett pb $4.50

WOMAN ON THE EDGE OF TIME
A Chicano woman in New York City is committed to a mental hospital
0–449–21082–0 Fawcett pb $3.95

➤ **FOR OVERSEAS ORDERING INFORMATION, SEE PAGE 1**

• David Plante

THE CATHOLIC
0–452–25928–2 NAL pb $7.95

THE COUNTRY
0–689–11189–4 Atheneum $9.95

THE FOREIGNER
A young American in Europe in 1959.
"What is unforgettable about *The Foreigner*
is its recording of a voice . . . haunted by
Hemingway, by Pinter, by Beckett, even,
but a voice with a melancholy timbre all its
own"—*Boston Globe*
0–689–11491–5 Atheneum $12.95
0–525–48209–1 Dutton pb $8.95

**THE FRANCOEUR NOVELS: The Family,
The Country, The Woods**
"[In this] series of novels dealing with the
Francoeurs, a working-class family of
French Canadians settled in Providence,
Rhode Island, Plante manages to surround
almost every object and every
inconsequential event with a kind of
luminescent space, like a halo"—Robert
Towers, *NY Review of Books*
0–525–48067–6 Dutton pb $10.95

THE NATIVE
0–689–11951–8 Atheneum $13.95

THE WOODS
0–689–11289–0 Atheneum $8.95

• Sylvia Plath

THE BELL JAR
Autobiographical account of a young
woman's mental breakdown. "Its most
notable quality is an astonishing
immediacy, like a series of snapshots taken
at high noon"—*Time*
0–06–013356–2 Harper & Row $16.95
0–553–27835–5 Bantam pb $4.95

• Carlene Hatcher Polite

THE FLAGELLANTS
A lyrical novel about a modern day love
affair gone sour
Introduction by Claudia Tate
0–8070–6321–5 Beacon pb $7.95

• Chaim Potok

THE BOOK OF LIGHTS
0–394–52031–9 Knopf $14.95
0–449–24569–1 Fawcett pb $4.95

THE CHOSEN
A young man caught between the lure of
modernity and his orthodox Jewish
upbringing
0–449–20962–8 Fawcett pb $3.50

DAVITA'S HARP
0–394–54290–8 Knopf $16.95
0–449–20775–7 Fawcett pb $4.50

IN THE BEGINNING
0–394–49960–3 Knopf $13.95
0–449–20911–3 Fawcett pb $4.50

MY NAME IS ASHER LEV
0–394–46137–1 Knopf $18.95
0–449–20714–5 Fawcett pb $3.95

THE PROMISE
0–449–20910–5 Fawcett pb $4.95

WANDERINGS
0–449–21582–2 Fawcett pb $4.95

• Richard Powers

PRISONER'S DILEMMA
0–688–07350–6 Morrow $19.95

Chaim Potok (photo by Jill Krementz, courtesy of Knopf)

**THREE FARMERS ON THEIR WAY TO
A DANCE**
0–688–04201–5 Morrow $17.95
0–317–56921–X McGraw-Hill pb $4.95

• Reynolds Price

KATE VAIDEN
A middle-aged woman's search for a son
she abandoned when she was 17
0–689–11787–6 Atheneum $16.95
0–345–34358–1 Ballantine pb $4.95

LOVE AND WORK
"A short, beautifully written novel about a
young teacher and writer, which . . .
represents, I think, one of the most
interesting explanations of the nature and
relationship of art and love ever written"—
Louis D. Rubin, Jr., *Washington Post*
0–345–34995–4 Ballantine pb $3.50

MUSTIAN: Two Novels and a Story
A collection of Price's stories about the
Mustians of the North Carolina
tobacco country. Includes *A Long and
Happy Life, A Generous Man,* and the
story "A Chain of Love"
0–689–11377–3 Atheneum $14.95
0–345–34521–5 Ballantine pb $4.95

A LONG AND HAPPY LIFE
0–689–11947–X Atheneum $14.95

GOOD HEARTS
A continuation of the earlier Mustian
novels
0–689–11973–9 Atheneum $18.95

THE SURFACE OF EARTH
0–345–34994–6 Ballantine pb $4.95

• Richard Price

BLOOD BROTHERS
0–14–008345–6 Penguin pb $6.95

THE BREAKS
The first college graduate in his working-
class family faces the world after
graduation
0–14–007037–0 Penguin pb $6.95

LADIES' MAN
0–14–008346–4 Penguin pb $6.95

• Francine Prose

BIGFOOT DREAMS
A comic look at the life of a reporter for a
sleazy tabloid
0–14–009837–2 Penguin pb $6.95

**WOMEN AND CHILDREN FIRST &
OTHER STORIES**
0–394–56573–8 Pantheon $16.95

• James Purdy

CABOT WRIGHT BEGINS
"Mr. Purdy is a superb writer, using all the
fires of the heart and the crystalline powers
of the brain"—*TLS*
0–88184–196–X Carroll & Graf pb $4.50

THE CANDLES OF YOUR EYES: Stories
1–55584–066–3 Weidenfeld & Nicolson $14.95

IN A SHALLOW GRAVE
"A modern Book of Revelation, filled with
prophecies, visions, and demonic
landscapes"—Jerome Charyn
0–87286–234–8 City Lights pb $6.95

MALCOLM
An innocent young man and his effect
upon those he encounters. "The most
prodigiously funny book to streak across
these heavy-hanging times"—Dorothy
Parker
1–55584–084–1 Weidenfeld & Nicolson pb $7.95

THE NEPHEW
"I am convinced that in the future [Purdy]
will be known as one of the greatest
writers produced in America during the
past hundred years"—Edith Sitwell
1–55584–085–X Weidenfeld & Nicolson pb $7.95

ON GLORY'S COURSE
0–14–007629–8 Penguin pb $6.95

**63: DREAM PALACE & OTHER
STORIES**
"Style as fluid and natural as a man
thinking to himself in the dark, yet
controlled, coherent, with an innate sense
of form, and great powers of
concentration"—Katherine Anne Porter
Introduction by Edward Albee
0–14–005732–3 Penguin pb $4.95

• Thomas Pynchon

THE CRYING OF LOT 49
0–06–091307–X Harper & Row pb $6.95

GRAVITY'S RAINBOW
A highly complex, allusive metaphysical
quest, considered by many critics one of
the great postwar novels
0–14–010661–8 Penguin pb $10.95

SLOW LEARNER: Early Stories
0–316–72442–4 Little, Brown $14.95
0–316–72443–2 Little, Brown pb $7.95

V
The surreal tale of Benny Profane and his
search for the unknown woman V. "May
well stand as one of the very best works of
the century"—*Atlantic Review*
0–06–091308–8 Harper & Row pb $8.95

• John Rechy

BODIES AND SOULS
Los Angeles and the denizens of its fringe
societies
0–88184–003–3 Carroll & Graf $17.95
0–88184–004–1 Carroll & Graf pb $8.95

⇨ **TO ORDER ANY BOOK IN THIS CATALOG, ASK YOUR BOOKSELLER OR CALL 1-800-882-8770**

CITY OF NIGHT
The life of a hustler in the American sexual underworld
0–8021–3083–6 Grove pb $7.95

THE FOURTH ANGEL
"Rechy shows great comic and tragic talent. He is a truly gifted novelist"—Christopher Isherwood
0–394–62469–6 Seaver pb $6.95

MARILYN'S DAUGHTER
A woman suspects that she is the illegitimate daughter of Marilyn Monroe and Robert Kennedy
0–88184–272–9 Carroll & Graf $18.95

NUMBERS
Another exploration of America's sexual underground
0–394–62171–9 Grove pb $8.95

RUSHES
0–394–17883–1 Grove pb $7.95

● Ishmael Reed
Reed's novels are fantastic blends of folklore and contemporary politics. "A prolific writer who . . . works in more than one medium. His novels . . . have already consolidated his reputation as one of those black writers who refuse to be categorized according to the relevance of his theme."—George Lamming, *NY Times*

THE FREE-LANCE PALLBEARERS
Reed's first novel
0–689–70732–0 Atheneum pb $7.95

THE LAST DAYS OF LOUISIANA RED
0–689–70731–2 Atheneum pb $8.95

MUMBO JUMBO
"A novel about writing itself—not only in the figurative sense of the postmodern, self-reflexive text but also in a literal sense"—Henry Louis Gates, Jr.
0–689–70730–4 Atheneum pb $9.95

RECKLESS EYEBALLING
0–312–66580–6 St. Martin's $12.95
0–689–70728–2 Atheneum pb $7.95

Ishmael Reed (photo copyright Michael Simon)

THE TERRIBLE THREES
0–689–11893–7 Atheneum $16.95

THE TERRIBLE TWOS
An elderly gent named St. Nicholas and a dwarf named Black Peter wreak havoc in the Oval Office and on Wall Street
0–689–70727–4 Atheneum pb $8.95

YELLOW BACK RADIO BROKE DOWN
0–689–70813–0 Atheneum pb $8.95

● Tomás Rivera
Y NO SE LO TRAGO LA TIERRA/AND THE EARTH DID NOT DEVOUR HIM
Winner of the first national Chicano literature award in 1970. Stories told in English and Spanish, as witnessed through the eyes of a young boy, the child of migrant farm workers
0–934770–72–7 Arte Público pb $8.50

● Tom Robbins
ANOTHER ROADSIDE ATTRACTION
0–345–35201–7 Ballantine pb $4.50

EVEN COWGIRLS GET THE BLUES
0–553–26611–X Bantam pb $4.95

JITTERBUG PERFUME
0–553–26844–9 Bantam pb $4.95

STILL LIFE WITH WOODPECKER
0–553–25851–6 Bantam pb $4.50

● Marilynne Robinson
HOUSEKEEPING
"A first novel that one reads as slowly as poetry—and for the same reason: the language is so precise, so distilled, so beautiful that one doesn't want to miss any pleasure it might yield up to patience"–*NY Times*
0–553–26238–6 Bantam pb $3.95

● Barbara Rogan
CAFE NEVO
0–689–11840–6 Atheneum $19.95
0–452–26141–4 NAL pb $7.95

● Joel Rose
KILL THE POOR
0–87113–260–5 Atlantic Monthly pb $8.95

● Judith Rossner
ATTACHMENTS
0–671–52786–X Pocket pb $3.95

AUGUST
A woman's relationship with her therapist
0–446–32256–3 Warner pb $4.50

EMMELINE
A young girl in Massachusetts during the early years of the 19th century
0–671–52785–1 Pocket pb $3.95

LOOKING FOR MR. GOODBAR
A young schoolteacher flirts with danger while cruising New York's singles bars
0–671–66205–8 Pocket pb $4.50

TO THE PRECIPICE
0–446–34274–2 Warner pb $4.95

● Philip Roth
THE BREAST
A man wakes up to discover that he has become a woman's breast
0–14–007679–4 Penguin pb $4.95

THE COUNTERLIFE
0–374–13026–4 Farrar, Straus & Giroux $18.95
0–14–009769–4 Penguin pb $4.95

THE FACTS: A Novelist's Autobiography
0–374–15212–8 Farrar, Straus & Giroux $17.95

GOODBYE, COLUMBUS & FIVE SHORT STORIES
The title story, Roth's first success, concerns a love affair between a poor boy from Newark and a rich girl from Radcliffe. Winner of the National Book Award for fiction
0–394–60470–9 Modern Library $8.95

THE GREAT AMERICAN NOVEL
0–14–007678–6 Penguin pb $5.95

LETTING GO
Four young people attempt to come to terms with life in the 1950s. "One of Roth's maturest achievements . . . Among the masterpieces of postwar American literature"—James Atlas
0–449–20728–5 Fawcett pb $4.95

MY LIFE AS A MAN
0–14–007680–8 Penguin pb $5.95

A PHILIP ROTH READER
Introduction by Martin Green
0–374–23170–2 Farrar, Straus & Giroux $17.50
0–374–51604–9 Farrar, Straus & Giroux pb $9.95

PORTNOY'S COMPLAINT
"No one has written so amusingly and yet so crassly about sex since Henry Miller"—*Time*
0–394–44198–2 Random House $15.00
0–449–20291–7 Fawcett pb $4.95

THE PROFESSOR OF DESIRE
0–14–007677–8 Penguin pb $6.95

WHEN SHE WAS GOOD
0–394–45187–2 Random House $10.95
0–14–007676–X Penguin pb $5.95

ZUCKERMAN BOUND: A Trilogy & Epilogue
Includes the entire Zuckerman trilogy (*The Ghost Writer, Zuckerman Unbound,* and *The Anatomy Lesson*), as well as *Epilogue: The Prague Orgy*
0–374–51899–8 FS&G pb $9.95

THE GHOST WRITER
The first novel in the Zuckerman trilogy, in which a young writer thinks that he has met and fallen in love with Anne Frank. "A sensitive, deeply moving, exquisitely crafted portrait of the artist as a young man"—*Chicago Tribune*
0–374–16189–5 FS&G $8.95
0–449–20009–4 Fawcett pb $3.95

ZUCKERMAN UNBOUND
The second novel in the Zuckerman trilogy. "Nathan Zuckerman now struggles with the wealth, fame, intrusions, and estrangements bestowed upon him by the enormous success of his fourth novel . . . The comic diatribes seem almost engraved . . . and the polarities between id and superego, Jew and goy, artistic honesty and human decency are as beautifully played upon as the melodies in a Bach fugue"—*New Yorker*
0–374–29945–5 FS&G $10.95
0–449–21090–1 Fawcett pb $5.95

THE ANATOMY LESSON
The final book in Roth's Zuckerman trilogy. "One finds in Zuckerman's self-doubt, guilt, and quest for meaning the angst of much of 20th century humanity. *The Anatomy Lesson* is vintage Roth . . . His wildest, funniest—and darkest—novel yet"—*Publisher's Weekly*
0–449–20614–9 Fawcett pb $3.95

PHILIP ROTH
Some Favorite Books

Nadine Gordimer
JULY'S PEOPLE

Danilo Kis
A TOMB FOR BORIS DAVIDOVICH

Edna O'Brien
A FANATIC HEART

Nelson Aldrich
OLD MONEY

Robert Caro
THE PATH TO POWER: The Years of Lyndon Johnson

Primo Levi
SURVIVAL IN AUSCHWITZ

Primo Levi
THE REAWAKENING

Primo Levi
THE DROWNED AND THE SAVED

Neil Postman
AMUSING OURSELVES TO DEATH

Judith Thurman
ISAK DINESEN: The Life of a Storyteller

• Richard Russo
MOHAWK
The poor of a small upstate New York town. "Offers a reader the authority of a documentary—yet the novel is full of comic invention"—John Irving
0–394–74409–8 Random House pb $6.95

THE RISK POOL
0–394–56527–4 Random House $19.95

• Jim Sagel
TUNOMAS HONEY
Stories about youth in northern New Mexico
Translated by the author
0–916950–40–9 Bilingual Review pb $10.00

• James Salter
DUSK & OTHER STORIES
"His is to ordinary prose what haiku is to cocktail chatter, what yoga is to mud wrestling"—*Providence Journal*
0–86547–277–7 North Point $14.95
0–86547–389–7 North Point pb $7.95

LIGHT YEARS
0–86547–064–2 North Point pb $12.50

SOLO FACES
"Contrasts a devotion to mountain climbing with the earthbound tugs of love and ordinary life . . . A beautifully composed book that will remind readers of Camus and Saint-Exupéry. It exemplifies the purity it describes"—Michael Dirda, *Washington Post*
0–86547–321–8 North Point pb $8.95

A SPORT AND A PASTIME
0–86547–210–6 North Point pb $7.50

• Glenn Savan
WHITE PALACE
0–553–34419–6 Bantam pb $7.95

• John Sayles
PRIDE OF THE BIMBOS
A softball team travels the sideshow circuits of the Deep South
0–684–18872–4 Scribners pb $8.95

UNION DUES
"A realistic novel about how life is in the working class and around its fringes . . . can be read with great enjoyment just for its actions and descriptions—for the feel of streets and buildings and human associations, the authentic ring of its dialogue in accents that range from West Virginia to South Boston"—*Washington Post*
0–316–77234–8 Little, Brown pb $7.95

• Susan Fromberg Schaeffer
BUFFALO AFTERNOON
The Vietnam War's impact on one man's life
0–394–57178–9 Knopf $27.50

THE INJURED PARTY
0–312–41798–5 St. Martins $16.95
0–312–90624–2 St. Martins pb $3.95

THE MADNESS OF A SEDUCED WOMAN
0–525–24165–5 Dutton $16.95
0–553–24112–5 Bantam pb $3.95

• Lynne Sharon Schwartz
ACQUAINTED WITH THE NIGHT & OTHER SHORT STORIES
0–06–091297–9 Harper & Row pb $7.95

DISTURBANCES IN THE FIELD
0–06–015202–8 Harper & Row $15.95
0–553–34377–7 Bantam pb $8.95

THE MELTING POT & OTHER SUBVERSIVE STORIES
"Urgent reports direct from the frontiers of urban life"—Alix Kates Shulman
0–06–015814–X Harper & Row $16.95

ROUGH STRIFE
0–06–091282–0 Harper & Row pb $7.95

• Hubert Selby, Jr.
THE DEMON
0–7145–2598–7 Marion Boyars $19.95

LAST EXIT TO BROOKLYN
These interrelated and realistic stories of life in the New York borough created a sensation when they were first published in 1964
0–8021–3137–9 Grove pb $8.95

Hubert Selby, Jr. (courtesy of Grove)

REQUIEM FOR A DREAM
0–938410–57–1 Thunder's Mouth $20.00
0–938410–56–3 Thunder's Mouth pb $9.95

THE ROOM
0–7145–0888–8 Marion Boyars $19.95

SONG OF THE SILENT SNOW & OTHER STORIES
Fifteen short stories. "Stories told with astonishing directness and energy [by an] occasionally brilliant and always fascinating writer of uncommon talent and integrity"—*Philadelphia Inquirer*
0–8021–3008–9 Grove pb $6.95

• Mary Lee Settle
THE BEULAH QUINTET
A cycle of five novels
0–684–18975–5 Scribners pb $49.95

CELEBRATION
"Settle is such a thoughtful, generous narrator that this story of a slightly star-crossed quartet of loving friends wins us easily. In an era that honors novels for their fragility and self-consciousness, Settle has chosen another route: the great read"—*Newsweek*
0–374–12005–6 Farrar, Straus & Giroux $17.95

THE CLAM SHELL
A young girl at a southern woman's college is sexually assaulted. "Mary Lee Settle has a grand passion for what she's doing . . . and the instinct of the novelist for panorama"—E.L. Doctorow
0–684–18755–8 Scribners pb $6.95

THE LOVE EATERS
Settle's first novel is a story of a small-town theatrical troupe
0–684–18714–0 Scribners pb $6.95

O BEULAH LAND
0–684–18846–5 Scribners pb $8.95
0–345–32490–0 Ballantine pb $4.95

PRISONS
0–684–18845–7 Scribners pb $8.95
0–345–29312–6 Ballantine pb $3.50

• Fatima Shaik
THE MAYOR OF NEW ORLEANS: Just Talking Jazz
Three novellas that capture the ambience of southern Louisiana
0–88739–071–4 Creative Arts pb $9.95

• Ntozake Shange
BETSEY BROWN
0–312–07727–0 St. Martin's $12.95
0–312–07728–9 St. Martin's pb $6.95

SASSAFRAS, CYPRESS, AND INDIGO
Three sisters growing up in the South
0-312-69972-7 St. Martin's pb $8.95

• David Shields
DEAD LANGUAGES
"Beautifully written, poignant and wise"—Chaim Potok
0-394-57388-9 Knopf $18.95

• Ann Allen Shockley
LOVING HER
0-930044-97-5 Naiad pb $7.95

THE BLACK AND WHITE OF IT
0-930044-96-7 Naiad pb $7.95

• Alix Kates Shulman
IN EVERY WOMAN'S LIFE
The friendship of three women in the 1980s
0-394-55724-7 Knopf $17.95

ON THE STROLL
0-89733-243-1 Academy Chicago pb $8.95

• Joan Silber
IN THE CITY
A woman in the Greenwich Village of 1925. "A look back on an earlier time . . . capturing the feel of its time and place with the immediacy of felt experience"—*Christian Science Monitor*
0-670-81479-2 Viking $16.95
0-14-009742-2 Penguin pb $6.95

• Leslie M. Silko
CEREMONY
0-14-008683-8 Penguin pb $5.95

STORYTELLER
0-865-79004-3 Henry Holt $17.95

• Mona Simpson
ANYWHERE BUT HERE
"There have been many novels about mothers and daughters . . . but Simpson has found a very special, achingly real, yet often funny way of portraying such a relationship that speaks directly to our times"—*Cleveland Plain Dealer*
0-394-55283-0 Knopf $18.95
0-394-75559-6 Random House pb $6.95

• Lee Smith
BLACK MOUNTAIN BREAKDOWN
A girl from Appalachia leaves home for college. "The most evocative book I have read in a long time . . . funny, tragic, and haunting"—Mary Lee Settle
0-345-33849-9 Ballantine pb $4.50

CAKEWALK
0-345-33950-9 Ballantine pb $3.95

FAIR AND TENDER LADIES
0-399-13382-8 Putnam $17.95

FAMILY LINEN
"A childhood memory relived through hypnosis, a funeral that brings about a family reunion, and the excavation of a swimming pool on the site of an old well uncover a family secret in this darkly humorous novel"—*Christian Science Monitor*
0-345-33642-9 Ballantine pb $4.50

FANCY STRUT
Sesquicentennial Week in an Alabama town. "A Southland full of visionaries and dreamers whose illusions tell us enough about reality to drive us to laughter and tears"—*LA Herald Examiner*
0-345-34025-6 Ballantine pb $4.50

ORAL HISTORY
"A novel as dark, winding, complicated as the hill country itself"—*Village Voice*
0-345-31607-X Ballantine pb $3.95

• Roberta Smoodin
WHITE HORSE CAFE
An aspiring actress/waitress in Los Angeles. "Smoodin's temperament and zest . . . make words and ideas snap, crackle, and pop"—*NY Times*
0-14-009838-0 Penguin pb $6.95

PRESTO!
0-689-11273-4 Atheneum $13.95

• Susan Sontag
THE BENEFACTOR
Sontag's first novel. "A major writer, I especially admired how she can make a real story out of dreams and thoughts"—Hannah Arendt
0-374-52056-9 Farrar, Straus & Giroux pb $7.95

DEATH KIT
A young man attempts to "perceive the inventory of the world"
0-374-52042-9 Farrar, Straus & Giroux pb $7.95

I, ETCETERA
Eight short stories
0-317-67512-5 Farrar, Straus & Giroux pb $7.95

• Gilbert Sorrentino
BLUE PASTORAL
0-86547-095-2 North Point $18.00

CRYSTAL VISION
A fugue of neighborhood voices weaving stories within stories at bar, drugstore, and street corner
0-86547-041-3 North Point $17.50

IMAGINATIVE QUALITIES OF ACTUAL THINGS
The New York literary world of the 1950s
0-394-47108-3 Pantheon $14.00

MULLIGAN STEW
0-394-62361-4 Grove pb $9.95

ODD NUMBER
An elaborately structured literary game. "Whether read as literary gossip, an intellectual maze, or a sublime example of high-modern style, Sorrentino's little puzzler of a novel won't disappoint his fans"—*Booklist*
0-86547-212-2 North Point $16.50

ROSE THEATRE
0-916583-23-6 Dalkey Archive $20.00

THE SKY CHANGES
A road novel from the early 1960s
0-86547-243-2 North Point pb $12.50

• Ellease Southerland
LET THE LION EAT STRAW
An affecting novel of a black woman's emotional trials and endurance in Brooklyn between the world wars
0-451-14675-1 NAL pb $3.50

• Scott Spencer
ENDLESS LOVE
The obsessions of adolescent love
0-394-50605-7 Knopf $19.95
0-380-50823-0 Avon pb $4.50

LAST NIGHT AT THE BRAIN THIEVES BALL
0-345-34589-4 Ballantine pb $3.50

PRESERVATION HALL
0-345-34478-2 Ballantine pb $3.95

WAKING THE DEAD
A young attorney running for Congress is haunted by memories of a past lover
0-394-54356-4 Knopf $17.95
0-345-34073-6 Ballantine pb $4.95

• Johnny Stanton
MANGLED HANDS
A Burroughs-like collage of Jesuit missionaries and fantastic shape-changing Indians in an imaginary Canadian wilderness
0-940650-48-7 Sun & Moon pb $10.95

• Richard Stern
THE CHALEUR NETWORK
0-933256-18-3 Second Chance $16.95
0-933256-19-1 Second Chance pb $8.95

GOLK
0-226-77319-1 Chicago pb $9.95

THE INVENTION OF THE REAL
0-8203-0589-8 Georgia $18.00

NOBLE ROT: Stories 1949–1988
0-8021-1056-8 Grove $19.95

THE POSITION OF THE BODY
0-8101-0731-7 Northwestern pb $12.95

• Robert Stone
CHILDREN OF LIGHT
Love, drugs, and alcohol on the Mexican set of a major motion picture
0-345-34086-8 Ballantine pb $4.95

DOG SOLDIERS
Drug runners, Vietnam vets, and backwoods cultists in a violent panorama of late-'60s America
0-14-009835-6 Penguin pb $7.95

A FLAG FOR SUNRISE
"Gringos against Latins, Latins against Indians, Marxists against Christians, spies against innocents, women against men . . . all struggling in an oily whirlpool of betrayal"—*Chicago Sun-Times*
0-345-34249-6 Ballantine pb $4.95

A HALL OF MIRRORS
"A surrealistic vision of a New Orleans rife with political paranoia"—*Newsweek*
0-14-009834-8 Penguin pb $7.95

• Ronald Sukenick
BLOWN AWAY
"The reader who is interested in the future of fiction in this country should have a look at the writings of Sukenick"—*San Francisco Bay Guardian*
0-940650-63-0 Sun & Moon $16.95
0-940650-64-9 Sun & Moon pb $10.95

THE ENDLESS SHORT STORY
0-914590-94-4 Fiction Collective $13.95
0-914590-95-2 Fiction Collective pb $6.95

IF YOU CAN'T FIND IT, LOOK IN THE INDEX

98.6
"The very best sort of experimental writing by one of the best writers of it"—*NY Times*
0-914590-09-X Fiction Collective pb $6.95

• Harvey Swados
NIGHTS IN GARDEN BROOKLYN
0-670-80974-8 Viking $19.95

• Walter Tevis
THE COLOR OF MONEY
A sequel to *The Hustler*
0-446-34419-2 Warner pb $3.95

THE HUSTLER
The world of poolroom hustlers
0-446-34438-9 Warner pb $3.95

• Catherine Texier
LOVE ME TENDER
"A welcome antidote to the more trendy and less gutsy and heartfelt accounts of New York City downtown life"—Kathy Acker
0-14-010016-4 Penguin pb $6.95

• Alexander Theroux
AN ADULTERY
0-671-63589-1 Simon & Schuster $18.95
0-02-008821-3 Macmillan pb $8.95

• Paul Theroux
THE BLACK HOUSE
"*The Black House* remains a suspenseful and often unnerving study of the irrational and instinctive forces in human nature . . . exceedingly well done"—*Houston Post*
0-671-49823-1 Washington Square pb $3.95

THE CONSUL'S FILE
0-671-49825-8 Washington Square pb $3.50

THE FAMILY ARSENAL
"Old-fashioned entertainment in the mode perfected by Graham Greene"—*Time*
0-395-24400-5 Houghton Mifflin $8.95
0-671-49824-X Washington Square pb $4.95

FONG AND THE INDIANS
0-395-25501-5 Houghton Mifflin $9.95

GIRLS AT PLAY
Three women teachers in the bush of East Africa
0-671-49821-5 Washington Square pb $3.95

HALF MOON STREET
Two novellas. " 'Doctor Slaughter' and 'Doctor Demarr,' the novellas that comprise *Half Moon Street,* are unrelated but well-paired, functioning as anima and animus, female and male versions of the title characters' double lives"—*Newsday*
0-671-60289-6 Washington Square pb $5.95

JUNGLE LOVERS
0-395-12107-8 Houghton Mifflin $9.95

THE LONDON EMBASSY
0-395-33107-2 Houghton Mifflin $13.95
0-671-49805-3 Washington Square pb $3.95

THE MOSQUITO COAST
A man's attempt to escape from contemporary civilization
0-380-61945-8 Avon pb $4.50

MY SECRET HISTORY
Theroux's latest novel deals with a middle-aged writer, his career, travels, and love life
0-399-13424-7 Putnam $21.95

O-ZONE
America in the 21st century, a world of aliens, nuclear waste, and mutants
0-399-13186-8 Putnam $19.95
0-8041-0151-5 Ballantine pb $4.95

PICTURE PALACE
0-395-26475-8 Houghton Mifflin $9.95
0-317-56920-1 Pocket pb $4.95

SAINT JACK
An American pimp in Singapore
0-671-49822-3 Washington Square pb $3.95

SINNING WITH ANNIE
0-395-25502-3 Houghton Mifflin $9.95

WORLD'S END & OTHER STORIES
Fourteen short stories. "These stories . . . reinforce Theroux's reputation as a brilliant writer"—*Philadelphia Inquirer*
0-671-49762-6 Washington Square pb $3.95

• Michael M. Thomas
Thomas' novels are financial thrillers which take place in the boardrooms of Wall Street, in museums, in fine Parisian restaurants, literary salons, and the dark alleys of modern life.
GREEN MONDAY
0-449-24400-8 Fawcett pb $3.50

HARD MONEY
0-670-53110-3 Viking $17.95

THE ROPESPINNER CONSPIRACY
0-446-51290-7 Warner $18.95
0-446-34676-4 Warner pb $4.95

• Lawrence Thornton
IMAGINING ARGENTINA
0-385-24027-9 Doubleday $16.95
0-553-34579-6 Bantam pb $7.95

• Lynne Tillman
HAUNTED HOUSES
"Tillman has written down the details of what it is to be female now so simply that the space around these precise details, a space which is almost the void, transforms the account into a film noir"—Kathy Acker
0-671-63719-3 Pocket $16.95
0-671-63011-3 Pocket pb $7.95

• John Kennedy Toole
A CONFEDERACY OF DUNCES
An obese, fractious, fastidious mama's boy cohabits with the denizens of New Orleans' lower depths
Foreword by Walker Percy
0-8071-0657-7 LSU $16.95
0-8021-3020-8 Grove pb $9.95

THE NEON BIBLE
0-8021-1108-4 Grove $15.95

• Susan Trott
DON'T TELL LAURA
0-06-097105-3 Harper & Row pb $6.95

THE HOUSEWIFE AND THE ASSASSIN
A Marin County housewife, after discovering jogging and taking a lover, comes up against a mysterious assassin. "A fresh new Bay Area voice"—Cyra McFadden
0-06-097118-5 Harper & Row pb $6.95

INCOGNITO
0-06-097106-1 Harper & Row pb $6.95

PURSUED BY THE CROOKED MAN
0-06-015853-0 Harper & Row $16.95

SIGHTINGS
"*Sightings* is a mystery, a muddle, an emotional house of mirrors, and it has one of the most satisfying ends of any book you'll read this year"—Martin Cruz Smith
0-671-63804-1 Simon & Schuster $16.95
0-06-097158-4 Harper & Row pb $6.95

WHEN YOUR LOVER LEAVES
0-06-097107-X Harper & Row pb $6.95

• Frederic Tuten
TALLIEN: A Brief Romance
A novel mixing the life of a character from the French Revolution with the narrator's own experiences. "Tuten provides an intelligent, taut, and entertaining change from conventional novels"—John Updike
0-374-27249-2 Farrar, Straus & Giroux $16.95

• Anne Tyler
THE ACCIDENTAL TOURIST
A travel writer hates travel and change. "Tyler is not merely good, she is wickedly good"—John Updike
0-394-54689-X Knopf $16.95
0-425-11423-6 Berkley pb $4.95

BREATHING LESSONS
0-394-57234-3 Knopf $18.50

CELESTIAL NAVIGATION
A painter refuses to leave his rooftop studio fortress
0-425-09840-0 Berkley pb $3.95

THE CLOCK WINDER
0-425-09902-4 Berkley pb $3.95

DINNER AT THE HOMESICK RESTAURANT
"Stunning psychological portrait of a family estranged from itself"—*Saturday Review*
0-394-52381-4 Knopf $19.95
0-425-09868-0 Berkley pb $4.50

EARTHLY POSSESSIONS
A wife leaving her husband is taken hostage by a bank robber
0-425-10167-3 Berkley pb $3.95

IF MORNING EVER COMES
A law student returns to a home overpopulated with women
0-425-09883-4 Berkley pb $3.95

MORGAN'S PASSING
An unconventional hardware store proprietor crashes into middle age
0-394-50958-7 Knopf $13.95
0-425-09872-9 Berkley pb $3.95

SEARCHING FOR CALEB
Family saga spanning a century. "As hauntingly nostalgic as a glimpse into the lighted windows of a home in which you once lived"—*Detroit Free Press*
0-425-09876-1 Berkley pb $3.95

A SLIPPING DOWN LIFE
0-425-10362-5 Berkley pb $3.95

THE TIN CAN TREE
A family loses a young daughter
0-425-09903-2 Berkley pb $3.95

• Sabine Ulibarri
THE CONDOR & OTHER STORIES/EL CONDOR Y OTROS CUENTOS
Stories about Mexican-Americans in an evolving political and economic environment in modern-day New Mexico
0-934770-92-1 Arte Público $8.50

MI ABUELA FUMABA PUROS/MY GRANDMOTHER SMOKED CIGARS
0–88412–105–4 Quinto Sol pb $6.00

PRIMEROS ENCUENTROS/FIRST ENCOUNTERS
Stories about the interaction of Anglos and Hispanos
0–916950–27–1 Bilingual Review pb $7.00

• David Updike
OUT ON THE MARSH
0–87923–728–7 Godine $16.95

• John Updike
BECH: A Book
Bech, the famous writer and Updike's alter ego, reflects upon his life
0–449–20277–1 Fawcett pb $2.95

BECH IS BACK
0–394–41638–4 Knopf $13.95
0–394–74509–4 Random House pb $5.95

THE CENTAUR
0–394–41881–6 Knopf $22.50

THE COUP
Inventive tale of an imaginary African nation. "A black comedy . . . with moments of satirical brilliance"—*Wall Street Journal*
0–449–24259–5 Fawcett pb $4.50

COUPLES
Marriage and adultery in the suburbs
0–394–42066–7 Knopf $22.95
0–449–20797–8 Fawcett pb $4.50

MARRY ME: A Romance
0–449–20361–1 Fawcett pb $3.95

A MONTH OF SUNDAYS
The Reverend Tom Marshfield and his indiscreet behavior with the women in his parish
0–394–49551–9 Knopf $16.95
0–449–20795–1 Fawcett pb $3.50

John Updike (photo by Mary Updike, courtesy of Knopf)

MUSEUMS AND WOMEN & OTHER STORIES
Twenty-nine short stories
0–394–48173–9 Knopf $15.00
0–394–74762–3 Random House pb $8.95

THE MUSIC SCHOOL
0–394–43727–6 Knopf $13.95
0–394–74510–8 Random House pb $6.95

OF THE FARM
0–394–43898–1 Knopf $10.95
0–449–21451–6 Fawcett pb $3.95

PIGEON FEATHERS & OTHER STORIES
0–394–44056–0 Knopf $19.95
0–449–21132–0 Fawcett pb $3.95

THE POORHOUSE FAIR
"A first novel of rare precision and real merit"—*Newsweek*
0–394–41050–5 Knopf $13.95

PROBLEMS & OTHER STORIES
0–394–50705–3 Knopf $14.95
0–449–21103–7 Fawcett pb $4.50

RABBIT RUN
Part one in Updike's continuing saga of a Pennsylvania used-car dealer
0–394–44206–7 Knopf $18.95
0–449–20506–1 Fawcett pb $4.95

RABBIT REDUX
Part two in the Rabbit series. "An anatomy of human life"—*Newsday*
0–394–47273–X Knopf $19.95
0–449–20934–2 Fawcett pb $4.95

RABBIT IS RICH
Rabbit at midlife, circa 1979
0–394–52087–4 Knopf $22.00
0–449–24548–9 Fawcett pb $4.95

ROGER'S VERSION
Theological speculation and erotic intrigue in Boston
0–449–21288–2 Fawcett pb $4.95

S
A witty epistolary novel in which an affluent New England woman leaves her husband for a guru
0–394–56835–4 Knopf $17.95

THE SAME DOOR
0–394–44361–6 Knopf $11.95
0–394–74763–1 Random House pb $4.95

TOO FAR TO GO
"That a marriage ends is less than ideal; but all things end under heaven, and if temporality is held to be invalidating, then nothing real succeeds. The moral of these stories is that all blessings are mixed"— John Updike
0–449–20016–7 Fawcett pb $2.75

TRUST ME
Twenty-two stories
0–394–55833–2 Knopf $17.95

THE WITCHES OF EASTWICK
Three contemporary New England witches
0–449–20647–5 Fawcett pb $4.50

• Jane Vandenburg
FAILURE TO ZIGZAG
A hilarious and touching first novel set in California in the 1960s, the story of a teenage girl and her schizophrenic ventriloquist mother
0–86547–356–0 North Point $16.95

• Henry Van Dyke
LADIES OF THE RACHMANINOFF EYES
Introduction by Phil Petrie
0–88258–150–3 Howard pb $7.95

• Ed Vega
MENDOZA'S DREAMS
"Despite Vega's clowning—gritty tales of El Barrio life: reality beginning in dreams"—*Kirkus Reviews*
0–934770–56–5 Arte Público pb $8.50

William T. Vollman (photo by Jerry Bauer, courtesy of Atheneum)

• William T. Vollman
YOU BRIGHT AND RISEN ANGELS: A Cartoon
0–689–11852–X Atheneum $22.95

• Kurt Vonnegut, Jr.
BLUEBEARD
0–385–29590–1 Delacorte $17.95

BREAKFAST OF CHAMPIONS
"Vonnegut is the most distinctive voice in current American fiction"—*Time*
0–440–13148–0 Dell pb $4.95

CAT'S CRADLE
A mixture of satire and fantasy that is "far more meaningful than the melodramatic tripe most critics seem to consider serious"—Terry Southern
0–440–11149–8 Dell pb $4.95

DEADEYE DICK
"A moving fable of passive resistance. Vonnegut, sweet cynic and ugly duckling, continues to write gentle swan songs for our uncivil society"—*Playboy*
0–440–11765–8 Dell pb $3.95

GALAPAGOS
9–998–31532–8 Dell pb $4.95

GOD BLESS YOU, MR. ROSEWATER
"A hilariously wacky comedy. Its chief target is inherited wealth, but as in his

TO ORDER BOOKS AS GIFTS, SEE PAGE 1

earlier books, Vonnegut takes pot shots at many varieties of folly"—*Saturday Review*
0–440–12929–X Dell pb $4.95

JAILBIRD
Jailbird is an angry man's piercing look at America in the 1970s"—*People*
0–440–15473–1 Dell pb $4.95

MOTHER NIGHT
A satirical look at a former American Nazi
0–440–15853–2 Dell pb $4.95

PALM SUNDAY
0–440–36906–1 Dell pb $4.95

PLAYER PIANO
A man runs away from a comfortable life in middle America
0–440–17037–0 Dell pb $4.95

THE SIRENS OF TITAN
The richest man in America takes a beautiful woman to outer space
0–440–17948–3 Dell pb $4.95

SLAPSTICK: Or, Lonesome No More!
"Vonnegut's ongoing puppet show! . . . A saucy spaghetti of ideas . . . goes down like ice cream . . . The fabulous is reborn"—John Updike, *New Yorker*
0–385–28944–8 Delacorte $13.95
0–440–18009–0 Dell pb $4.95

SLAUGHTERHOUSE FIVE: Or, The Children's Crusade
A former American prisoner of war relives the bombing of Dresden
0–385–28940–5 Dell pb $9.95

WAMPETERS, FOMA AND GRANFALLOONS
0–440–18533–5 Dell pb $4.95

WELCOME TO THE MONKEY HOUSE
Twenty-five short works. "This volume gives everybody a chance to put Kurt Vonnegut, Jr. together"—*St. Louis Globe-Democrat*
0–385–29127–2 Dell pb $9.95

• Rosmarie Waldrop
THE HANKY OF PIPPIN'S DAUGHTER
"A novel rare for its evocation of the early experience of its protagonist, who grows up in the Germany of Hitler's era, and of the unique womanhood she gradually creates for herself after the Second World War and far beyond her native Germany"—John Hawkes
0–88268–038–2 Station Hill $14.95

• Alice Walker
THE COLOR PURPLE
Epistolary novel of a black woman's life; winner of the Pulitzer Prize and the American Book Award in 1982
0–15–119153–0 HBJ $12.95
0–671–52602–2 Washington Square pb $7.95

IN LOVE AND TROUBLE: Stories of Black Women
Thirteen short pieces
0–15–644450–X HBJ pb $3.95

LIVING BY THE WORD: Collected Writings
"One of the most important, grieving, graceful, and honest writers ever to come into print . . . She can teach you to care and she can make you laugh, if you got any soul left . . . Alice seems calm and

gentle and small. But this is a powerful, big, even a wild book"—June Jordan
0–15–152900–0 HBJ $15.95

MERIDIAN
"A classic novel of both feminism and the Civil Rights Movement"—*Ms.*
0–15–159265–9 HBJ $14.95
0–671–47256–9 Washington Square pb $3.95

THE TEMPLE OF MY FAMILIAR
A romance of the last 500,000 years
0–15–188533–8 HBJ $19.95

THE THIRD LIFE OF GRANGE COPELAND
A tenant farmer's life. "Almost no one has tried to tell us about the early lives, the *inner* lives, of black people . . . Alice Walker is a storyteller"—Robert Coles, *New Yorker*
0–671–66142–6 Washington Square pb $3.95

YOU CAN'T KEEP A GOOD WOMAN DOWN
Fourteen short stories. "A major American writer, a cause for gratitude, delight, and celebration"—Tillie Olsen
0–15–699778–9 HBJ pb $4.95

• David Foster Wallace
THE BROOM OF THE SYSTEM
A switchboard operator in the Cleveland, Ohio of 1990. "He often writes like a loquacious angel"—Richard Elman
0–14–009868–2 Penguin pb $7.95

GIRL WITH CURIOUS HAIR
0–14–010969–2 Penguin pb $8.95

• Joseph Wambaugh
THE BLACK MARBLE
A crime novel involving dogs and dog owners
0–440–10644–3 Dell pb $4.95

THE BLUE KNIGHT
0–440–10607–9 Dell pb $4.95

THE CHOIRBOYS
"As if *Catch-22* had been written by Popeye Doyle"—*NY Times*
0–440–11188–9 Dell pb $4.95

THE DELTA STAR
The think-tank world of Nobel Prize chemistry intersects with the sleazy underworld of a murdered streetwalker
0–553–27386–8 Bantam pb $4.95

THE GLITTER DOME
Four sets of police partners amid the glamor and grime of Hollywood
0–553–27529–4 Bantam pb $4.95

LINES AND SHADOWS
"Ten San Diego police officers assigned to patrol the cactus-filled, snake-infested canyons along the Mexican border"—*Kirkus Reviews*
0–553–27148–2 Bantam pb $4.95

THE NEW CENTURIONS
Three new cops on the Los Angeles beat
0–440–16417–6 Dell pb $4.95

THE SECRETS OF HARRY BRIGHT
A detective investigates the murder of a Palm Springs teenager and the meaning of his own son's death
0–553–27430–9 Bantam pb $4.95

• Theodore Weesner
THE CAR THIEF
The love between a boy and his alcoholic father. "A remarkable, gripping first novel . . . Incredibly sympathetic and revealing in its portrayal of a kind of life, and a kind of human personality, that are totally foreign to most of us"—Joyce Carol Oates, *Chicago Tribune*
0–394–74097–1 Random House pb $6.95

THE TRUE DETECTIVE
0–671–40024–X Summit $17.95

• James Welch
THE DEATH OF JIM LONEY
0–14–010291–4 Penguin pb $5.95

FOOLS CROW
The white man's effect upon the Blackfoot Indians in 1870s Montana. "A major contribution to Native American literature"—Wallace Stegner
0–670–81121–1 Viking $18.95
0–14–008937–3 Penguin pb $7.95

WINTER IN THE BLOOD
0–14–008644–7 Penguin pb $5.95

• William Wharton
BIRDY
A troubled youth retreats into a world of birds
0–394–42569–3 Knopf $18.95
0–380–47282–1 Avon pb $4.50

DAD
0–394–51097–6 Knopf $14.95
0–380–58594–4 Avon pb $4.95

A MIDNIGHT CLEAR
0–345–31291–0 Ballantine pb $3.95

PRIDE
A ten-year-old working-class boy growing up in South Philadelphia in the years just prior to World War II
0–394–53636–3 Knopf $16.95
0–440–37118–X Dell pb $4.95

SCUMBLER
0–88184–135–8 Carroll & Graf pb $3.95

TIDINGS
0–8050–0532–3 Henry Holt $17.95

• Edmund White
THE BEAUTIFUL ROOM IS EMPTY
"White is unquestionably the foremost American gay novelist"—*Newsweek*
0–394–56444–8 Knopf $17.95

A BOY'S OWN STORY
A young gay man struggles against his own homosexuality. "This novel about seduction and maturity, about America and about 'homosexual fate,' is a large and happy accomplishment"—Susan Sontag
0–452–26123–6 NAL pb $7.95

CARACOLE
"As a writer, White possesses the rare combination of a poetic sense of language and an ironic sense of humor"—*Newsweek*
0–452–25881–2 NAL pb $7.95

FORGETTING ELENA
White's first book was cited by Vladimir Nabokov as the American novel he most admired
0–14–005983–0 Penguin pb $5.95

NOCTURNES FOR THE KING OF NAPLES
"A Baroque invention of quite startling brilliance and intensity"—Gore Vidal
0–14–005330–1 Penguin pb $6.95

• Edmund White & Adam Mars-Jones
THE DARKER PROOF: Stories from a Crisis
Includes three stories by White, all dealing with AIDS
0–452–26070–1 NAL pb $7.95

• George Whitmore
NEBRASKA
0–671–67234–7 Washington Square pb $6.95

• John Edgar Wideman
DAMBALLAH
0–8052–8174–6 Schocken $13.95

A GLANCE AWAY
A confrontation between a black ex-addict and an alcoholic homosexual
0–03–005602–0 Henry Holt pb $6.95

HIDING PLACE
0–8052–8175–4 Schocken $13.95

HURRY HOME
A black lawyer searches for his roots in Africa
0–03–005242–4 Henry Holt pb $6.95

THE LYNCHERS
Four black men plot to kidnap and lynch a white policeman
0–8050–0118–2 Henry Holt pb $7.95

REUBEN
0–8050–0375–4 Henry Holt $16.95

SENT FOR YOU YESTERDAY
"Hypnotic and deeply lyrical"—*NY Times*
0–8052–8188–6 Schocken $13.95
0–679–72029–4 Random House pb $6.95

• Marianne Wiggins
HERSELF IN LOVE
0–670–81552–7 Viking $16.95

JOHN DOLLAR
Wiggins' most recent novel centers on a group of girls stranded on a desert island
0–06–016070–5 Harper & Row $17.95

SEPARATE CHECKS
0–06–097207–6 Harper & Row pb $7.95

• James Wilcox
MODERN BAPTISTS
0–14–007113–X Penguin pb $5.95

• John A. Williams
THE BERHAMA ACCOUNT
0–88282–009–5 New Horizon $16.95

CAPTAIN BLACKMAN
A black soldier in Vietnam drifts in and out of coma, hallucinating about past and present
0–938410–68–7 Thunder's Mouth pb $10.95

!CLICK SONG
"The 'private and public' vicissitudes of a black novelist trying to establish himself as a writer of distinction are chronicled in this revealing tale of the New York cultural scene from World War II to the present—told with directness of language and feeling"—*NY Times*
Introduction by Ishmael Reed
0–938410–43–1 Thunder's Mouth pb $10.95

JACOB'S LADDER
A political thriller, set in a tiny African country in the late 1960s
0–938410–41–5 Thunder's Mouth $13.95
0–938410–76–8 Thunder's Mouth pb $9.95

THE MAN WHO CRIED I AM
In Amsterdam in the spring of 1964, a black American writer is dying of cancer
0–938410–24–5 Thunder's Mouth pb $10.95

SISSIE
0–938410–66–0 Thunder's Mouth pb $9.95

• Joy Williams
BREAKING AND ENTERING
The travails of a pair of Florida drifters. "Funny, awful, and gruesomely Floridian"—Thomas McGuane
0–394–75773–4 Random House pb $6.95

STATE OF GRACE
A woman's romance is overshadowed by death. "She catches, better than anyone writing today, the ominous vision at the corner of the eye, and makes it inevitable"—Mary Lee Settle
0–684–18645–4 Scribners pb $6.95

TAKING CARE
0–394–52157–9 Random House $12.50

• Leigh Alison Wilson
FROM THE BOTTOM UP
Winner of the Flannery O'Connor Award
0–8203–0647–9 Georgia $13.95
0–14–007071–0 Penguin pb $5.95

WIND
Short stories
0–688–08111–8 Morrow $17.95

• Tom Wolfe
THE BONFIRE OF THE VANITIES
A panorama of New York City in the 1980s
0–374–11534–6 Farrar, Straus & Giroux $19.95
0–553–27597–6 Bantam pb $5.95

• Tobias Wolff
BACK IN THE WORLD
"A captivating, brilliant writer, one of the best we've got"—Annie Dillard
0–395–35416–1 Houghton Mifflin $15.95
0–553–34325–4 Bantam pb $7.95

THE BARRACKS THIEF & SELECTED STORIES
A novella and six short stories. "I have not read a book of stories in years that has given me such a shock of amazement and recognition—and such pleasure"—Raymond Carver
0–553–34675–X Bantam pb $7.95

IN THE GARDEN OF THE NORTH AMERICAN MARTYRS
0–912946–82–2 Ecco $14.95
0–912946–83–0 Ecco pb $9.50

• Hilma Wolitzer
HEARTS
0–374–16870–9 Farrar, Straus & Giroux $10.95

IN THE PALOMAR ARMS
0–374–17656–6 Farrar, Straus & Giroux $14.95

SILVER
0–374–26422–8 Farrar, Straus & Giroux $18.95

• Meg Wolitzer
THIS IS YOUR LIFE
0–517–56929–9 Crown $17.95

• Douglas Woolf
ON US
0–87685–284–3 Black Sparrow pb $5.00

THE TIMING CHAIN
The cross-country odyssey of a writer on the rebound from a soured love affair
0–939180–36–7 Tombouctou pb $7.00

WALL TO WALL
"If you want to re-experience America as it might have been seen by a Smollett, a Sterne, a Fielding, or in places a Cervantes, don't miss [*Wall to Wall*]"—Robert R. Kirsch, *LA Times*
Afterword by Edward Dorn
0–916583–06–6 Dalkey Archive $20.00
0–916583–07–4 Dalkey Archive pb $4.50

• Sarah Elizabeth Wright
THIS CHILD'S GONNA LIVE
Afterword by John O. Killens
0–935312–67–6 Feminist Press pb $9.95

• Richard Yates
COLD SPRING HARBOR
Two families in a pre-World War II Long Island town. "Richard Yates is one of America's least famous great writers"—*Esquire*
0–385–29596–0 Delacorte pb $8.95

LIARS IN LOVE
Seven short stories
0–385–28552–3 Dell $9.95

REVOLUTIONARY ROAD
"Richard Yates is among the very truest of American writers. Each of his novels and each story unfalteringly traces our destinies and rescues us from the lost. He sees eye-to-eye with every one of us"—Gina Berriault
0–679–72191–6 Random House pb $8.95

YOUNG HEARTS CRYING
A man struggles with the conflict between his ideals and his ambitions
0–385–29441–7 Doubleday pb $8.95

• Al Young
SEDUCTION BY LIGHT
0–440–55003–3 Delta pb $7.95

SITTING PRETTY
As the character Sit tells it, his life in and around San Francisco is based on this simple philosophy: "Play all the possibilities and stagger your bets"
0–88739–017–X Creative Arts pb $8.95

SHORT STORY COLLECTIONS

• Mark Helprin, editor
THE BEST AMERICAN SHORT STORIES: 1988
0–395–44256–7 Houghton Mifflin pb $8.95

• Langston Hughes, editor
THE BEST SHORT STORIES BY BLACK WRITERS
0–316–38031–8 Little, Brown pb $9.95

• Charles Jurrist, editor
SHADOWS OF LOVE: American Gay Fiction
1–55583–136–2 Alyson pb $8.95

• Ethan Mordden, editor
I'VE A FEELING WE'RE NOT IN KANSAS ANYMORE: Tales from Gay Manhattan
0–452–25929–0 NAL pb $7.95

• Gloria Norris, editor
NEW AMERICAN SHORT STORIES (2): The Writers Select Their Own Favorites
0–452–26217–8 NAL pb $9.95

• Shannon Ravenel, editor
NEW STORIES FROM THE SOUTH: The Year's Best, 1988
0–912697–93–8 Chapel Hill pb $8.95

• Joel Rose & Catherine Texier, editors
BETWEEN C AND D: New Writing from the Lower East Side Fiction Magazine
0–14–010570–0 Penguin pb $7.95

• Robert Shapiro & James Thomas, editors
SUDDEN FICTION: American Short-Short Stories
0–87905–265–1 Peregrine Smith pb $10.95

TONI MORRISON: Books for Fiction Writers

Beginning fiction writers ought to find the following 13 books helpful in a number of ways.

Flannery O'Connor
THE COMPLETE STORIES

William Faulkner
THE SOUND AND THE FURY

Jean Toomer
CANE

Italo Svevo
THE CONFESSIONS OF ZENO

George Meredith
THE EGOIST

Eudora Welty
ONE WRITER'S BEGINNINGS

Marilynne Robinson
HOUSEKEEPING

Louise Erdrich
LOVE MEDICINE

Franz Kafka
THE METAMORPHOSIS

Toni Cade Bambara
THE SEA BIRDS ARE STILL ALIVE

James Dickey
DELIVERANCE

Marguerite Duras
THE VICE-CONSUL

James Wilcox
MODERN BAPTISTS

• Debra Spark, editor
20 UNDER 30: Best Stories by America's New Young Writers
0–684–18640–3 Scribners pb $8.95

• James Thomas, editor
THE BEST OF THE WEST: New Short Stories from the Wide Side of the Missouri
0–87905–332–1 Peregrine Smith pb $9.95

• David Wheeler, editor
NO, BUT I SAW THE MOVIE: The Best Short Stories Ever Made into Film
0–14–011090–9 Penguin pb $9.95

20th-Century American Poetry

THE MODERNIST GENERATION

"The first thing that strikes a reader about the best American poets is how utterly unlike each other they are. Where else in the world, for example, could one find seven poets of approximately the same generation so different as Ezra Pound, W.C. Williams, Vachel Lindsay, Marianne Moore, Wallace Stevens, E.E. Cummings and Laura Riding?"—W.H. Auden

The first section lists poets born before 1900. The following section, The Second Generation, encompasses those born roughly between 1900 and 1920. These chronological restrictions do not apply to the lists of Objectivists and New American Poets, and there are other exceptions as well; some poets whose publishing activity has mostly been in recent years will be found in the later listings.

• Conrad Aiken
COLLECTED POEMS, 1916–1970
"Aiken became aware of the broken nature of his world in a singularly brutal way: at the age of eleven he found his parents dead; his mother shot by his father, who then committed suicide . . . From that terrifying moment Aiken would search for 'an equivalent to it all, in terms of his own life, or work' . . . His reality was more chaotic, his ego more fragile, his need to grow in consciousness more acute than almost any other modern writer's"—Arthur Waterman, *Critique*
0–19–501258–5 Oxford $35.00

• Louise Bogan
THE BLUE ESTUARIES: Poems, 1923–1968
"No poet has been more adamant than she in demanding the uncluttered line and the precise image . . . *Blue Estuaries* is a cold, comforting book"—William Heyen, *Prairie Schooner*
0–912946–37–7 Ecco pb $8.50

• Hart Crane
THE COMPLETE POEMS, SELECTED LETTERS & PROSE
Includes *The Bridge, White Buildings,* and Crane's other poetry. "Essentially Crane . . . was using rhyme and meter and fantastic images to convey the emotional states that were induced in him by alcohol, jazz, machinery, laughter, intellectual stimulation, the shape and sound of words and the madness of New York in the late Coolidge era"—Malcolm Cowley
Edited by Brom Weber
0–385–01531–3 Doubleday pb $6.95

• e.e. cummings
COMPLETE POEMS, 1913–1962
"His rhetoric was as skillful, approached as nearly to the limit of every last possibility, as the acts of the circus performers or burlesque comedians he felt an admiring kinship for"—Randall Jarrell
0–15–121060–8 HBJ $27.95
0–15–621062–2 HBJ pb $17.95

H.D. (Hilda Doolittle)
COLLECTED POEMS, 1912–1944
A landmark collection of the main body of H.D.'s work, including much poetry never before published
Edited with an introduction by Louis Martz
0–8112–0876–1 New Directions $35.00
0–8112–0971–7 New Directions pb $15.95

SELECTED POEMS
Edited with an introduction by Louis Martz
0–8112–1066–9 New Directions pb $8.95

HELEN IN EGYPT
A book-length poem playing out an alternate ending to the myth of Troy
Introduction by Horace Gregory
0–8112–0544–4 New Directions pb $7.95

HERMETIC DEFINITION
H.D.'s final poems, including sequences dedicated to Ezra Pound and St.-John Perse
Introduction by Norman Holmes Pearson
0–8112–0453–7 New Directions pb $6.95

HIPPOLYTUS TEMPORIZES
An adaptation of Euripides
0–933806–23–X Black Swan $20.00

ION
Another version of Euripides
0–933806–24–8 Black Swan $20.00

TRILOGY
Includes *The Walls Do Not Fall, Tribute to the Angels,* and *The Flowering of the Rod.* This sequence of visionary poems informed by science, Christian lore, and the World War II bombing of London is usually considered H.D.'s masterpiece
Introduction by Norman Holmes Pearson
0–8112–0491–X New Directions pb $7.95

• T.S. Eliot
COLLECTED POEMS, 1909–1962
"Any perspective which misses the abrupt discontinuities in Eliot's work has missed too much, for such discontinuities are the life of the poems. It is not simply that Eliot is a 'poet of fragments,' as Spender says, or that he sees the world as broken in pieces. Eliot specializes in putting fragments together in such a way that we

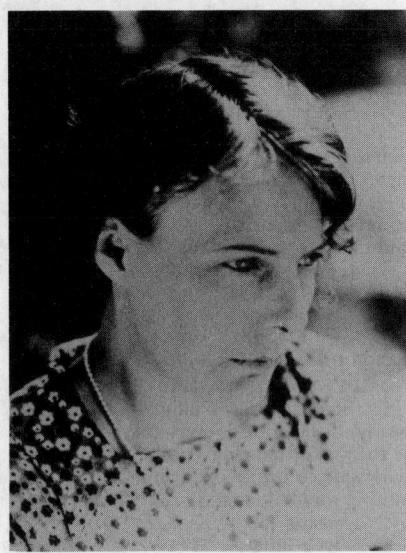

H.D. (photo courtesy The Beinecke Rare Book and Manuscript Library, Yale University; and New Directions)

see the wholeness that we lack"—Michael Wood, *NY Review of Books*
0–15–118978–1 HBJ $14.95

SELECTED POEMS
0–15–680647–9 HBJ pb $4.95

THE COMPLETE POEMS AND PLAYS, 1909–1950
0–15–121185–X HBJ $19.95

• Robert Frost
THE POETRY OF ROBERT FROST
"Frost, along with Stevens and Eliot, seems to me the greatest of the American poets of this century. Frost's virtues are extraordinary. No other living poet has written so well about the actions of ordinary men; his wonderful dramatic monologues or dramatic scenes come out of a knowledge of people that few poets have had, and they are written in a verse that uses, sometimes with absolute mastery, the rhythms of actual speech"— Randall Jarrell
Edited by Edward C. Lathem
0–805–00502–1 Henry Holt $24.95
0–03–049126–6 Henry Holt pb $9.95

NORTH OF BOSTON
A reprinting of Frost's 1914 collection
0–396–07440–5 Dodd, Mead $8.95
0–396–08270–X Dodd, Mead pb $5.95

• Marsden Hartley
THE COLLECTED POEMS OF MARSDEN HARTLEY, 1904–1943
Hartley's poems offer an interesting footnote to his career as a painter, and indicate the close connections between poetry and painting in the Modernist epoch
Edited by Gail R. Scott
0–87685–681–4 Black Sparrow $20.00
0–87685–680–6 Black Sparrow pb $12.50

• Robinson Jeffers
Jeffers' Californian landscapes and ecological pessimism continue to fascinate many poets.

THE COLLECTED POETRY: 1928–1938
Edited by Tim Hunt
0–8047–1723–0 Stanford $60.00

DEAR JUDAS
Introduction by Robert J. Brophy
0–87140–113–4 Liveright pb $7.95

THE DOUBLE AXE
Introduction by William Hotchkiss & William Everson
950–87140–114–2 Liveright pb $7.95

ROCK AND HAWK: A Selection of Shorter Poems
A recent collection designed to create a reassessment of Jeffers' work
Edited by Robert Hass
0–394–55769–7 Random House $19.95

SELECTED POETRY
0–394–40442–4 Random House $24.95

THE WOMEN AT POINT SUR & OTHER POEMS
0–87140–115–0 Liveright pb $7.95

• James Weldon Johnson
GOD'S TROMBONES
Diplomat, cultural observer, songwriter, lawyer, and novelist, Johnson was the most important figure in the transition from 19th-century gentility to the spirit of militant racial awareness
0–14–042217–X Penguin pb $4.95

• Vachel Lindsay
COLLECTED POEMS
0–02–572530–0 Macmillan $19.95

Mina Loy
THE LAST LUNAR BAEDEKER: The Poems of Mina Loy
Loy was a stellar presence on the Modernist scene, but her work remained largely unknown until reassembled for this outstanding volume
0–912330–46–5 Jargon Society $25.00

• Claude McKay
SELECTED POEMS OF CLAUDE MCKAY
In addition to his novels, McKay wrote poems of protest and black consciousness in traditional forms; he is best known for the militant sonnet "If We Must Die"
0–15–680649–5 HBJ pb $3.95

• Archibald MacLeish
NEW AND COLLECTED POEMS: 1917–1984
"His lyrics . . . unite the Romantic styles of the nineteenth century with the modern ones of his youth . . . His poetry is full of things seen, heard, touched, tasted, and smelled with pleasure"—David Perkins
Preface by Richard McAdoo
0–395–39569–0 Houghton Mifflin pb $14.95

• Edgar Lee Masters
SPOON RIVER ANTHOLOGY
This edition of Masters' solitary masterpiece of midwestern portraiture contains some additional poems
0–02–581730–2 Macmillan $14.95

• Edna St. Vincent Millay
COLLECTED LYRICS
Introduction by Norma Millay
0–06–090863–7 Harper & Row pb $7.95

COLLECTED POEMS
0–06–012935–2 Harper & Row $19.95
0–06–090889–0 Harper & Row pb $14.95

COLLECTED SONNETS
0–06–055102–X Harper & Row $15.95
0–06–091091–7 Harper & Row pb $6.95

• Marianne Moore
THE COMPLETE POEMS OF MARIANNE MOORE
"With Miss Moore a word is a word most when it is separated out by science, treated with acid to remove the smudges, washed, dried and placed right sideup on a clean surface . . . In Miss Moore's work the purely stated idea has an edge exactly like a fruit or a tree or a serpent"—William Carlos Williams
0–14–058601–6 Penguin pb $8.95

• Ezra Pound
THE CANTOS, 1–117
Pound's great unfinished, unfinishable "poem containing history." "The poem is vigorous, bold, and packed with personality and diverse life . . . The sweep of the poem in time and geographical space brings into it an extraordinary diversity of settings, manners, and ways of speaking"—David Perkins
0–8112–0350–6 New Directions $23.95

THE CLASSIC ANTHOLOGY DEFINED BY CONFUCIUS
Pound's version of the *Shih-ching* gave him the opportunity for some of his most purely musical writing
0–674–13397–8 Harvard pb $4.95

THE COLLECTED EARLY POEMS OF EZRA POUND
Includes the full text of *A Lume Spento, A Quinzaine for This Yule,* the 1909 *Personae, Canzon,* and other early work
Edited by Michael King
Introduction by Louis Martz
0–8112–0843–5 New Directions pb $11.95

Marianne Moore (photo courtesy Princeton University)

➤ **FOR OVERSEAS ORDERING INFORMATION, SEE PAGE 1**

ELEKTRA
Edited and annotated by Richard Reid
0–691–06778–3 Princeton $19.95

PERSONAE
The essential gathering of Pound's work prior to *The Cantos*, including *Cathay, Homage to Sextus Propertius,* and *Hugh Selwyn Mauberly*
0–8112–0355–7 New Directions $16.95

SELECTED CANTOS
Pound made the selection, intended to touch on all the major motifs of his life work
0–8112–0160–0 New Directions pb $5.95

SELECTED POEMS
0–8112–0162–7 New Directions pb $5.95

TRANSLATIONS
Pound's verse translations—from Chinese, Anglo-Saxon, Provençal, Japanese, Latin, and many other languages—imparted a new sense of context to American poetry
Introduction by Hugh Kenner
0–8112–0164–3 New Directions pb $10.00

WOMEN OF TRACHIS
An idiosyncratic version of Sophocles
0–8112–0948–2 New Directions pb $6.95

• **John Crowe Ransom**
SELECTED POEMS
"The style in itself fascinates . . . There is the unusual structural clarity, the rightness of tone and rhythm, the brisk and effective ingenuity, the rhetorical fireworks of exposition, description, and dialogue; but even more: the sticking to concrete human subjects—the hardest; and a balanced temperament"—Robert Lowell
0–670–3216–3 Ecco pb $4.95

• **Edward Arlington Robinson**
SELECTED POEMS OF EDWARD ARLINGTON ROBINSON
"Though his mind was not rich in a sensuous way, it was both powerful and hesitant, as though suspended between strong magnets . . . From this balance, this desperately poised uncertainty, emanates a compassion both very personal and cosmic—a compassion that one might well see as a substitute for the compassion that God failed to supply"—James Dickey
Edited by Morton Dauween Zabel
Introduction by James Dickey
0–02–070530–1 Macmillan pb $9.95

• **Carl Sandburg**
THE COMPLETE POEMS OF CARL SANDBURG
"A marvelous prosody, a perfect ear for the beautiful potentials of common speech, something he learned from folk song, but mostly he learned from just listening"—Kenneth Rexroth
0–15–120773–9 HBJ $27.95

HARVEST POEMS, 1910–1960
Introduction by Mark Van Doren
0–15–639125–2 HBJ pb $4.95

Gertrude Stein
Stein is a writer who makes the distinction between "prose" and "poetry" meaningless; what cannot be questioned is the depth of her continuing influence on modern

American poets. A longer selection of her works will be found under Modern American Fiction.
SELECTED WRITINGS OF GERTRUDE STEIN
0–394–71710–4 Random House pb $8.95

OPERAS AND PLAYS
0–88268–039–0 Station Hill $29.95

THE YALE GERTRUDE STEIN
A selection from the voluminous riches of Yale's Gertrude Stein series
Introduction by Richard Kostelanetz
0–300–02574–2 Yale $50.00
0–300–02609–9 Yale pb $10.95

• **Wallace Stevens**
THE COLLECTED POEMS
The 1954 gathering of Stevens' work, from *Harmonium* to *The Auroras of Autumn*
0–394–40330–4 Knopf $25.00

OPUS POSTHUMOUS: Poems, Plays, Prose
An enlarged, revised, and corrected edition of the companion volume to *The Collected Poems*
0–394–57792–2 Knopf $30.00

THE PALM AT THE END OF THE MIND: Selected Poems and a Play
"Here is the indispensable presentation of a central American poet, the best and most representative of our time"—Harold Bloom
Edited by Holly Stevens
0–394–71768–6 Random House pb $4.95

• **Sara Teasdale**
MIRROR OF THE HEART
0–02–616870–7 Macmillan $15.95

• **Jean Toomer**
CANE
Fictional sketches interspersed with poetry; a landmark of African-American writing
0–393–95600–8 Norton pb $6.95

COLLECTED POEMS, 1919–1976
Edited by Allen Tate
0–8071–1533–9 LSU pb $9.95

• **John Wheelwright**
COLLECTED POEMS
Edited by Alvin H. Rosenfeld
Introduction by Austin Warren
0–8112–0849–0 New Directions pb $10.00

• **William Carlos Williams**
THE COLLECTED POEMS OF WILLIAM CARLOS WILLIAMS
This new edition of Williams' poetry contains much work previously uncollected or unpublished. "The greatness of a poet is not to be measured by the scale but by the intensity and perfection of his works. Also by his vivacity. Williams is the author of the most *vivid* poems of modern American poetry"—Octavio Paz
Volume 1: 1909–1939
Edited by A. Walton Litz & Christopher MacGowan
0–8112–0999–7 New Directions $35.00
Volume 2: 1939–1963
Edited by Christopher MacGowan
0–8112–1063–4 New Directions $37.00

IMAGINATIONS
Contains some of Williams' greatest and most innovative writings, fusing poetry and prose in a variety of unpredictable ways: *Kora in Hell, Spring and All, The Descent of Winter, The Great American Novel,* and others
Edited by Webster Schott
0–8112–0229–1 New Directions pb $9.95

PATERSON
All five books of Williams' long poem of New Jersey
0–8112–0233–X New Directions pb $7.95

PICTURES FROM BRUEGHEL: Collected Poems, 1950–1962
In addition to the title work, contains the late collections *The Desert Music* and *Journey to Love*
0–8112–0234–8 New Directions pb $5.95

SELECTED POEMS
"Although Williams has sometimes been labeled a Buddhist or Taoist, he's more like a Shintoist: the rocks vibrate, waterfalls are animate, the visible universe harbors deposits of magical energy. The ordinary is *not* ordinary; it's violent, explosive, outrageous"—*Village Voice*
Edited by Charles Tomlinson
0–1928–2563–1 New Directions pb $10.95

• **Elinor Wylie**
LAST POEMS OF ELINOR WYLIE
0–89733–011–0 Academy Chicago pb $5.95

THE SECOND GENERATION

• **John Berryman**
COLLECTED POEMS, 1937–1971
Edited with an introduction by Charles Thornbury
0–374–12619–4 Farrar, Straus & Giroux $25.00

THE DREAM SONGS
Gathers together *77 Dream Songs* and *His Toy, His Dream, His Rest.* "Berryman is touting no theories, promoting no programme for Kulchur or society. The *Dream Songs* are, instead, the fragmentary inner biography, the perceptions by which he lives, of a character called Henry . . . Berryman is deliberately a mannerist who, out of his fraught nerviness, has made an original and remarkably flexible style"—A. Alvarez
0–374–14397–8 Farrar, Straus & Giroux $17.50
0–374–51670–7 Farrar, Straus & Giroux pb $10.95

Elizabeth Bishop
THE COMPLETE POEMS, 1927–1979
"From the moment Miss Bishop appeared on the scene it was apparent to everybody that she was a poet of strange, even mysterious, but undeniable and great gifts"—John Ashbery
0–374–51817–3 FS&G pb $8.95

• **Paul Bowles**
NEXT TO NOTHING: Collected Poems 1926–1977
0–87685–505–2 Black Sparrow pb $14.00

Elizabeth Bishop (photo by J.L. Castel, courtesy of Farrar, Straus & Giroux)

• Gwendolyn Brooks

BLACKS
A comprehensive gathering of Brooks's poetry
0–944191–00–2 David Company pb $15.00

SELECTED POEMS
0–06–010535–6 Harper & Row $11.95
0–06–010536–4 Harper & Row pb $6.95

THE WORLD OF GWENDOLYN BROOKS
0–06–010538–0 Harper & Row $15.75

• Sterling A. Brown

THE COLLECTED POEMS OF STERLING A. BROWN
"Sterling's poems reveal how in the struggle to exist the historic stands alongside the everyday . . . None of the characters in his ballads is treated sentimentally because his first duty was not to his sympathies but to the poem"—Darryl Pinckney
Edited by Michael S. Harper
0–06–010517–8 Harper & Row $14.95
0–06–091016–X Harper & Row pb $7.50

• J.V. Cunningham

COLLECTED POEMS AND EPIGRAMS
"J.V. Cunningham is looking at the modern world from the standpoint of traditional modes of writing, and principally from those of the eighteenth century . . . As a compressor, as a coupleteer, as a fastidious and mordant wit, a man who makes interesting dwellings of the neat cells of the couplet and the quatrain, he is hard to beat"—James Dickey
0–8040–0517–6 Ohio pb $9.95

• Richard Eberhart

COLLECTED POEMS, 1930–1986
"Visionary intensity that throws caution to the winds in order to seize the given insight"—Ralph J. Mills Jr., *Parnassus*
0–19–504055–4 Oxford $29.95

THE LONG REACH: New and Uncollected Poems, 1948–1984
0–8112–0886–9 New Directions pb $8.95

MAINE POEMS
0–19–505526–8 Oxford pb $11.95

• William Everson

THE RESIDUAL YEARS
Introduction by Kenneth Rexroth
0–8112–0273–9 New Directions pb $3.95

THE VERITABLE YEARS: 1949–1966
0–87685–378–5 Black Sparrow pb $8.50

• Robert Francis

COLLECTED POEMS, 1936–1976
A compendium of a poet often compared to Robert Frost
0–87023–510–9 Massachusetts pb $11.95

• Robert Hayden

COLLECTED POEMS
Hayden's "Runagate Runagate," about Harriet Tubman and the Underground Railroad, is one of the most haunting of modern American poems. "[He] has always been a symbolist poet struggling with historical fact, his rigorous portraits of people and places providing the synaptic leap into the interior landscape of the soul"—Michael S. Harper
Edited by Frederick Glaysher
0–393–40649–0 Liveright $14.95
0–87140–138–X Liveright pb $6.95

• Langston Hughes
Hughes was the most important poet to come out of the Harlem Renaissance. He invented his own stanza forms or used blank verse to transcribe urban folk life, the mood of jazz and blues; he is probably the most widely read of all black poets, and by the time of his death in 1967 was known even by the man on the street as the poet laureate of the Negro people.

Langston Hughes

THE LANGSTON HUGHES READER
0–8076–0057–1 Braziller $17.50

THE PANTHER AND THE LASH
A sampling of Hughes's political poems
0–394–40419–X Knopf pb $9.95

SELECTED POEMS OF LANGSTON HUGHES
"In Hughes's poetry, the oral tradition is perhaps strongest in those poems modeled on black music—the jazz and blues poems . . . The blues spirit in fact pervades Hughes's work in all genres"—Onwuchekwa Jemie
0–394–71910–7 Random House pb $5.95

• David Ignatow
"Ignatow talks about a reality few poets perceive, the world where books will *not* help to mitigate the pain . . . There is an honesty, a wholeness of vision, and a simple humanity in the work."—Diane Wakoski

NEW AND COLLECTED POEMS, 1970–1985
0–8195–5169–4 Wesleyan $35.00
0–8195–6174–6 Wesleyan pb $14.95

POEMS, 1934–1969
0–8195–6059–6 Wesleyan pb $12.95

SELECTED POEMS
Edited by Robert Bly
0–8195–6039–1 Wesleyan pb $9.95

• Randall Jarrell

THE COMPLETE POEMS
"Randall Jarrell had his own peculiar and important excellence as a poet . . . His gifts, both by nature and by a lifetime of hard dedication and growth, were wit, pathos, and brilliance of intelligence"—Robert Lowell
0–374–12716–6 Farrar, Straus & Giroux $25.00
0–374–51305–8 Farrar, Straus & Giroux pb $12.95

• Weldon Kees

THE COLLECTED POEMS OF WELDON KEES
All the poetry of a multitalented writer and artist who disappeared in San Francisco in 1955
Edited by Donald Justice
0–8032–0864–2 Nebraska $17.95

• Stanley Kunitz

THE POEMS OF STANLEY KUNITZ, 1928–1978
0–316–50711–3 Atlantic Monthly $19.95
0–316–50710–5 Atlantic Monthly pb $12.95

NEXT-TO-LAST THINGS: New Poems and Essays
0–87113–120–X Atlantic Monthly pb $8.95

THE WELLFLEET WHALE & COMPANION POEMS
0–935296–36–0 Sheep Meadow pb $6.95

• Robert Lowell

SELECTED POEMS
0–374–51400–3 Farrar, Straus & Giroux pb $10.95

DAY BY DAY
Lowell's last book won the National Book Critics Circle prize in 1977
0–374–13525–8 Farrar, Straus & Giroux $12.95
0–374–51471–2 Farrar, Straus & Giroux pb $5.95

FOR LIZZIE AND HARRIET
0–374–15729–4 Farrar, Straus & Giroux $6.95
0–374–51291–4 Farrar, Straus & Giroux pb $2.95

LIFE STUDIES & FOR THE UNION DEAD
Two of Lowell's most influential books. "There is no other poet writing at the moment who can match the dense visual accuracy of Lowell's best work . . . By an

immensely subtle process of reverberation, his images seem to seek each other out, not to be wise so much as to be confirmed in tragedy"—Ian Hamilton
0–374–50628–0 Farrar, Straus & Giroux pb $6.95

LORD WEARY'S CASTLE & THE MILLS OF THE KAVANAUGHS
0–15–653500–9 HBJ pb $3.95

NEAR THE OCEAN
0–374–50968–9 Farrar, Straus & Giroux pb $1.95

Thomas McGrath
SELECTED POEMS, 1938–1988
"Thomas McGrath has been writing remarkable poems of every size and form for nearly fifty years . . . His diction, with its vast word stock and multitude of language layers, is demotic to the core yet spiced with learned terms in Whitman's manner, a voice as richly American as any in our literature"—Terrence Des Pres
Edited by Sam Hamill
1-55659–011–3 Copper Canyon $15.00
1-55659–012–1 Copper Canyon pb $10.00

LETTER TO AN IMAGINARY FRIEND: Parts 1 & 2
0–8040–0186–3 Ohio pb $9.95

LETTER TO AN IMAGINARY FRIEND: Parts 3 & 4
"Not since Pound's *Cantos* has any poet drawn upon such varied sources to make a personal and political statement"—*Library Journal*
0–914742–86–8 Copper Canyon pb $9.00

• William Meredith
PARTIAL ACCOUNTS: New and Selected Poems
"Deeply healing and profoundly humane, a modern *Guide for the Perplexed*, a large-hearted and large-spirited collection of a lifetime's worth of poems"—Edward Hirsch
0–394–75191–4 Knopf pb $10.95

• Thomas Merton
THE COLLECTED POEMS OF THOMAS MERTON
"From his formal early poems to his late experiments in Surrealism, the voice remains vital and believable. It is seldom too religious, too metaphysical, too much the social critic; it is a combination of all of these, a large voice emerging to embody a large country"—Robert McDowell, *Hudson Review*
0–8112–0769–2 New Directions pb $22.95

• Josephine Miles
COLLECTED POEMS, 1930–1983
0–252–01017–5 Illinois $17.50

• Howard Nemerov
THE COLLECTED POEMS
"He is at equal ease in the modes of epigram, comic poem, meditation, and narrative, yet his work in each is now clearly related to his work in all the rest. His style has great range"—Thom Gunn
0–226–57259–5 Chicago $16.95

• Kenneth Patchen
COLLECTED POEMS
0–8112–0140–6 New Directions pb $11.50

SELECTED POEMS
0–8112–0146–5 New Directions pb $5.95

WHAT SHALL WE DO WITHOUT US?: The Voice and Vision of Kenneth Patchen
Examples of Patchen's "poem-paintings"
Introduction by James Laughlin
0–87156–843–8 Sierra Club $25.00
0–87156–818–7 Sierra Club pb $12.95

Kenneth Rexroth (photo by Margo Moore, courtesy of New Directions)

• Kenneth Rexroth
SELECTED POEMS
Philosophical, lyrical, erotic, and economical in its means, Rexroth's poetry is a varied and impressive body of work
Edited by Bradford Morrow
0–8112–0917–2 New Directions pb $7.95

COLLECTED LONGER POEMS
0–8112–0368–9 New Directions $6.50

COLLECTED SHORTER POEMS
0–8112–0178–3 New Directions $8.95

THE MORNING STAR
0–8112–0739–0 New Directions $9.00

NEW POEMS
0–8112–0551–7 New Directions pb $3.95

Laura (Riding) Jackson
THE POEMS OF LAURA RIDING
"Laura Riding is the greatest lost poet in American literature. W.H. Auden once called her the only living philosophical poet . . . The discoveries of Laura Riding's subtle ear escape analysis"—Kenneth Rexroth
0–89255–087–2 Persea pb $12.95

• Theodore Roethke
THE COLLECTED POEMS
"His youthful experience around his father's greenhouse in Michigan provided just the vivid, squirmingly uncomfortable,

and concrete focus his poetry needed to channel and concentrate this emotional tumult. The equally exuberant and disgusted earthiness of these poems, their violent rapport with plants and the slimy sublife of slugs and other such creatures, is unique"—M.L. Rosenthal
0–385–08601–6 Doubleday pb $9.95

• May Sarton
COLLECTED POEMS, 1930–1973
"She attains a delicate simplicity as quickeningly direct as it is deeply given, and does so with the courteous serenity, the clear, caring, intelligent and human calm of the queen of a small, well-ordered country"—James Dickey
0–393–04386–X Norton $19.95

• Delmore Schwartz
SELECTED POEMS: Summer Knowledge
"What renders his work so valuable . . . is Schwartz's profound historical consciousness . . . He relied on literature to explicate existence, much in the manner of a Talmudic scholar poring over some obscure text"—James Atlas
0–8112–0191–0 New Directions pb $6.95

LATE AND LOST POEMS: Revised Edition
Includes 17 recently discovered poems in addition to the contents of the first edition
0–8112–1096–0 New Directions pb $9.95

• Allen Tate
COLLECTED POEMS, 1919–1976
0–8071–1533–9 LSU pb $9.95

• M.B. Tolson
A GALLERY OF HARLEM PORTRAITS
This early work—an approach to the later *Harlem Gallery*—is all that is readily available at present of Tolson's work
Introduction by Robert Farnsworth
0–8262–0276–4 Missouri $20.00

• Robert Penn Warren
NEW AND SELECTED POEMS, 1923–1985
0–394–54380–7 Random House $19.95
0–394–73848–9 Random House pb $13.95

BEING HERE: Poetry, 1977–1980
0–394–51304–5 Random House $10.95
0–394–73935–3 Random House pb $4.95

BROTHER TO DRAGONS
A narrative poem based on an early American murder case. "A brutal, perverse melodrama that makes the flesh crawl . . . Warren has written his best book, a big book"—Robert Lowell
0–394–40312–6 Random House $10.95

NOW AND THEN: Poems, 1976–1978
0–394–50164–0 Random House $11.95
0–394–73515–3 Random House pb $5.95

• Theodore Weiss
FROM PRINCETON ONE AUTUMN AFTERNOON
0–02–071020–8 Macmillan pb $16.95

A SLOW FUSE: New Poems
0–02–071040–2 Macmillan pb $8.95

• Richard Wilbur
NEW AND COLLECTED POEMS
0–15–165206–6 HBJ $27.95

☞ **FOR ALL OTHER INQUIRIES, PLEASE CALL (212) 333-7900**

WALKING TO SLEEP: New Poems and Translations
"Beneath the polished surface of his poems there lies the keenest sensitivity to the disbelief that haunts us, the monstrous deeds of our century"—Ralph J. Mills, Jr.
0–15–694185–6 HBJ pb $4.95

• Yvor Winters
COLLECTED POEMS OF YVOR WINTERS
An idiosyncratic conservative, Winters tried single-handedly to reverse American poetry's modernist course
Introduction by Donald Davie
0–8040–0799–3 Ohio $16.95

The Objectivists

Active since the 1930s (or, in the case of Charles Reznikoff, since around 1918) but not widely discovered until the '60s, the Objectivist poets deeply influenced many younger writers.

Lorine Niedecker
FROM THIS CONDENSERY: The Complete Poems of Lorine Niedecker
"No one is so subtle with so few words"—Basil Bunting
Edited by Robert Bertholf
0–912330–57–0 Jargon Society $30.00

THE GRANITE PAIL
"Savory, laconic, superbly crafted poems"—Jonathan Williams
Edited by Cid Corman
0–86547–215–7 North Point pb $11.00

George Oppen
COLLECTED POEMS
Contains the full texts of *Discrete Series, The Materials, This In Which, Of Being Numerous,* and *Seascape: Needle's Eye,* along with some late poems not elsewhere collected
0–8112–0615–7 New Directions pb $9.95

PRIMITIVE
Oppen's last published book
0–87685–414–5 Black Sparrow pb $3.00

Carl Rakosi
THE COLLECTED POEMS
Early and late, Rakosi has been a mercurial poet offering abundant pleasures of sound, sight, and intellect
0–915032–35–X National Poetry $35.00
0–915032–36–8 National Poetry pb $15.95

Charles Reznikoff
THE COMPLETE POEMS
"No other poet, it strikes me, with perhaps the exception of Williams, has more thoroughly refused the artifices of style and chosen to let words have 'their daylight meanings,' to speak first of all, humanely and communicatively"—Michael Heller
Edited by Seamus Cooney

Volume 1: Poems 1918–1936
0–87685–262–2 Black Sparrow $17.50

Volume 2: Poems 1937–1975
0–87685–301–7 Black Sparrow $17.50

TESTIMONY: The United States, 1885–1915
Incidents of American life reconstructed from old legal records
Edited by Seamus Cooney

Volume 1
0–87685–322–X Black Sparrow $20.00
0–87685–321–1 Black Sparrow pb $7.50

Volume 2
0–87685–333–5 Black Sparrow $14.00
0–87685–332–7 Black Sparrow pb $7.50

HOLOCAUST
Workings from war crimes testimony
0–87685–232–0 Black Sparrow $14.00

Louis Zukofsky
A
The difficult, often extraordinarily musical book-length poem to which Zukofsky devoted most of his creative energies. "Delighting in quirks and quibbles he had an extraordinary capacity for seeing different aspects of a whole as one. He would, for example, modelling a movement of his poem on Bach's chaconne and englishing a verse of Mallarmé's, change one letter to bring a word into line not only with subatomic physics but with a concept of medieval Jewish philosophy"—Kenneth Cox, *Agenda*
0–520–03223–3 California $20.95
0–520–04095–3 California pb $10.95

ALL: The Collected Short Poems, 1956–1964
"These poems are absolute clarification, crystal cabinets full of air and angels"—Kenneth Rexroth
0–393–04266–9 Norton pb $4.50

THE NEW AMERICAN POETRY

Donald Allen's *The New American Poetry*—published in 1960 and out of print at present—was a decisive event in American writing. It grouped together a variety of poets who had functioned under such rubrics as the Beats, the Black Mountain poets, the San Francisco Renaissance, and in the process revealed a new openness in structure, diction, and subject matter. Things have never been quite the same since.

• Helen Adam
GHOSTS AND GRINNING SHADOWS
0–914610–10–4 Hanging Loose pb $6.00

• John Ashbery
Ashbery's adoption by the critical establishment seems to have surprised even himself. He continues to work in the same absolutely individual voice whose echoes are everywhere in contemporary American poetry.
SELECTED POEMS
0–14–058553–2 Penguin pb $9.95

APRIL GALLEONS
0–670–81958–1 Viking $15.95
0–14–058603–2 Penguin pb $7.95

AS WE KNOW
0–14–058591–5 Penguin pb $8.95

THE DOUBLE DREAM OF SPRING
0–912946–30–X Ecco $12.95
0–912946–27–X Ecco pb $6.95

HOUSEBOAT DAYS
0–14–042202–1 Penguin pb $4.95

RIVERS AND MOUNTAINS
Contains the splendid long poems "Clepsydra" and "The Skaters"
0–912946–38–5 Ecco pb $4.95

SELF-PORTRAIT IN A CONVEX MIRROR
"*Self-Portrait* is a laboratory in which past and present, yesterday and today, cross-fertilize each other. The alternating rhythm of withdrawal and arrival, the pendulum swing between past and present, is the mode of life that graphs the underlying blueprint of this poem's wave-like grand sweep"—Laurence Lieberman
0–14–042201–3 Penguin pb $5.95

SHADOW TRAIN
Fifty lyrics of identical length
0–14–042288–9 Penguin pb $5.95

SOME TREES
0–670–65650–X Ecco pb $4.95

THE TENNIS COURT OATH
Ashbery's most radical and controversial book
0–8195–1013–0 Wesleyan pb $8.95

THREE POEMS
Three long meditations in prose that have proven deeply influential. "Against Ashbery's, the work of most other poets seems dismally contingent. Somehow it is just the even weight he allows each thing, the possibility of blending 'in a union too subtle to cause any comment,' that accounts for its stature. This is a vision as simple to understand as it is impossible to learn"—John Koethe, *Parnassus*
0–14–058585–0 Penguin pb $7.95

A WAVE
0–670–75176–6 Viking $15.95
0–14–042343–5 Penguin pb $7.95

Paul Blackburn
THE COLLECTED POEMS OF PAUL BLACKBURN
"His poetry is joyous, gloomy, frisky, reflective and vulnerable to a sense of the living world that he never tried to master, but to inhabit as a kind of sad old citizen, a belonger filled with longing"—Clayton Eshleman
Edited by Edith Jarolim
Foreword by M.L. Rosenthal
0–89255–086–4 Persea $37.50

PROENSA: An Anthology of Troubador Poetry
These brilliant, tensile translations of Troubador poetry contain some of Blackburn's finest work
Edited by George Economou
0–520–02985–2 California $35.00

SELECTED POEMS
Edited with an introduction by Edith Jarolim
Foreword by M.L. Rosenthal
0–89255–123–2 Persea pb $14.95

🍎 IF YOU CAN'T FIND IT, LOOK IN THE INDEX

• Gregory Corso

"Corso is a great word-slinger, first naked sign of a poet, a scientific master of mad mouthfuls of language."—Allen Ginsberg

ELEGIAC FEELINGS AMERICAN
0–8112–0026–4 New Directions pb $3.95

THE HAPPY BIRTHDAY OF DEATH
0–8112–0027–2 New Directions pb $6.95

LONG LIVE MAN
0–8112–0025–6 New Directions pb $7.95

• Robert Creeley

THE COLLECTED POEMS, 1945–1975
"From the first clear grounded 1940s insight snapshots of *For Love* through his recent decade experiments with syllable by syllable intelligence, Robert Creeley has created a noble life body of poetry that extrends the work of his predecessors Pound, Williams, Zukofsky, and Olson"—Allen Ginsberg
0–520–04243–3 California $35.00
0–520–04244–1 California pb $12.95

LATER
0–8112–0736–6 New Directions pb $5.95

MIRRORS
0–8112–0877–X New Directions pb $6.95

• Diane Di Prima

SELECTED POEMS, 1956–1976
0–913028–48–7 North Atlantic $40.00

Robert Duncan

BENDING THE BOW
Initiates the long poem *Passages,* on which Duncan continued to work for the rest of his life
0–8112–0033–7 New Directions pb $4.95

GROUND WORK: Before the War
Later poems, including variations on Dante, Rumi, and various 17th-century poets
0–8112–0896–6 New Directions pb $10.95

GROUND WORK II: In The Dark
Duncan's final work
0–8112–1042–1 New Directions pb $9.95

THE OPENING OF THE FIELD
First published in 1960, this remarkable collection begins the "Structure of Rime" sequence, and contains such major works as "A Poem Beginning with a Line by Pindar" and "Often I Am Permitted to Return to a Meadow"
0–8112–0480–4 New Directions pb $4.95

ROOTS AND BRANCHES
"Robert Duncan is of that most rare order of poets for whom the work is not an occasional exercise, nor a demonstration of metrical abilities, nor any other term of partial commitment, however interesting. This book is the eleventh of a sequence, of a life, in fact, which can only be admitted or experienced in that totality"—Robert Creeley
0–8112–0034–5 New Directions pb $4.95

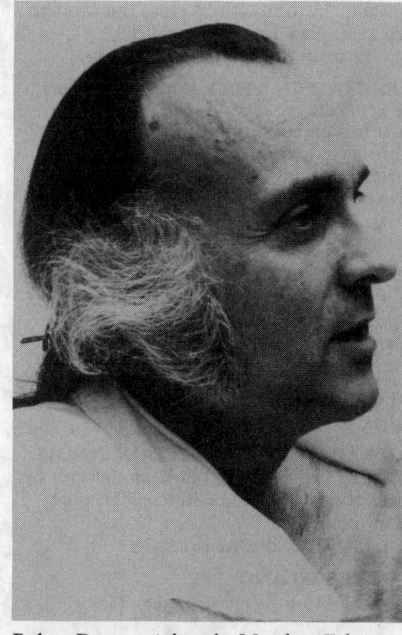

Robert Duncan (photo by Matthew Foley, courtesy of New Directions)

• Larry Eigner

THINGS STIRRING TOGETHER OR FAR AWAY
"It is a full, complete world, even if, for most of the poems, the world extends no farther than his front porch . . . Living on his porch—he is a spastic, forced to spend most of his days in a wheel chair—he has learned to see and hear with a sensitive, untiring coherence"—Samuel Charters
0–87685–187–1 Black Sparrow pb $5.00

WATERS; PLACES; A TIME
Edited by Robert Grenier
0–87685–497–8 Black Sparrow pb $7.50

• Lawrence Ferlinghetti

A CONEY ISLAND OF THE MIND
0–8112–0041–8 New Directions pb $4.95

ENDLESS LIFE: The Selected Poems
0–8112–0797–8 New Directions pb $7.95

• Allen Ginsberg

COLLECTED POEMS 1947–1980
The full texts of *Howl, Kaddish, Reality Sandwiches, Planet News, The Fall of America, Mind Breaths,* and much else
0–06–015341–5 Harper & Row $27.00
0–06–091494–7 Harper & Row pb $15.95

WHITE SHROUD: Poems, 1980–1985
0–06–015714–3 Harper & Row $14.95
0–06–091429–7 Harper & Row pb $8.95

• Bob Kaufman

THE ANCIENT RAIN: Poems, 1956–1978
Edited by Raymond Foye
0–8112–0801–X New Directions pb $4.95

SOLITUDES CROWDED WITH LONELINESS
0–8112–0076–0 New Directions pb $4.95

• Jack Kerouac

MEXICO CITY BLUES (242 Choruses)
0–8021–3060–7 Grove pb $10.95

• Kenneth Koch

ON THE EDGE
50–14–058555–9 Penguin pb $8.95

SEASONS ON EARTH
Includes the fanciful and inventive long poems *Ko, or A Season on Earth* and *The Duplications*
0–14–058576–1 Penguin pb $12.95

• Denise Levertov

COLLECTED EARLIER POEMS, 1940–1960
0–8112–0718–8 New Directions pb $5.95

POEMS, 1960–1967
Includes *The Jacob's Ladder, O Taste and See,* and *The Sorrow Dance*
0–8112–0859–1 New Directions pb $7.95

POEMS, 1968–1972
Includes *Relearning the Alphabet, To Stay Alive,* and *Footprints*
0–8112–1005–7 New Directions pb $9.95

BREATHING THE WATER
0–8112–1027–8 New Directions pb $6.95

THE FREEING OF THE DUST
0–8112–0582–7 New Directions pb $5.95

LIFE IN THE FOREST
0–8112–0693–9 New Directions pb $7.95

OBLIQUE PRAYERS: New Poems with 14 Translations
0–8112–0908–3 New Directions pb $6.95

• Michael McClure

HYMNS TO ST. GERYON & DARK BROWN
Dating from the 1950's, these are two of the strongest of McClure's books
0–912516–33–X Grey Fox pb $5.95

SELECTED POEMS
0–8112–0951–2 New Directions pb $7.95

Frank O'Hara

SELECTED POEMS
Few styles have been more widely imitated than O'Hara's conversational lyricism, open to every passing influence in the inner and outer worlds
Edited by Donald Allen
0–394–71973–5 Random House pb $8.95

POEMS RETRIEVED
Edited by Donald Allen
0–912516–19–4 Grey Fox pb $5.00

• Charles Olson

THE COLLECTED POEMS
Nearly all of Olson's poetry aside from *The Maximus Poems,* including much work never before published
Edited by George Butterick
0–520–05764–3 California $45.00

THE MAXIMUS POEMS
"Olson's spiritual barometers and seismographs give readings that we have to live with for awhile before they begin to render up sense. His view of mankind reaches into the backward abysm. Geologically the world is in the Pleistocene still, the age that evolved the horse, elephant, and cow more or less as we know them. And man. And the arrangements of the continents as they now are . . . The severing of the continents

---

Frank O'Hara

is itself a comprehensive symbol of disintegration, of man's migratory fate, of the tragic restlessness of history"—Guy Davenport
Edited by George Butterick
0–520–04015–5 California $45.00
0–520–05595–0 California pb $27.50

A NATION OF NOTHING BUT POETRY: Supplementary Poems
Work not included in the *Collected Poems*
0–87685–750–0 Black Sparrow pb $12.50

SELECTED WRITINGS
Includes a sampling of Olson's poetry and some of his best-known essays, including "Projective Verse" and "Human Universe"
Edited by Robert Creeley
0–8112–0128–7 New Directions pb $6.75

• Joel Oppenheimer
NEW SPACES: Poems, 1975–1983
0–87685–640–7 Black Sparrow pb $8.50

• James Schuyler
SELECTED POEMS
"One of the most original poets in America . . . He shares with Elizabeth Bishop . . . the knack of making the lyric dramatic"—Howard Moss
0–374–25878–3 Farrar, Straus & Giroux $25.00
0–374–52166–2 Farrar, Straus & Giroux pb $9.95

FREELY ESPOUSING
0–915342–28–6 SUN pb $7.00

THE MORNING OF THE POEM
"The title poem . . . is the amplest in the book, moving freely over the great geodesic dome of consciousness . . . What suppleness of style and limpidity of vision Schuyler displays in this poem; and what vulnerability"—Alfred Corn
0–374–21308–9 Farrar, Straus & Giroux $10.95
0–374–51622–7 Farrar, Straus & Giroux pb $7.95

SELECTED POEMS
0–374–52166–2 Farrar, Straus & Giroux pb $9.95

• Gary Snyder
AXE HANDLES
0–86547–119–3 North Point $12.50
0–86547–120–7 North Point pb $7.50

THE BACK COUNTRY
In many ways the finest and most representative of Snyder's books; also

contains his translations from the modern Japanese poet Kenji Miyazawa
0–8112–0194–5 New Directions pb $5.95

LEFT OUT IN THE RAIN: New Poems, 1947–1986
A revealing collection of outtakes and uncollected work that adds up to an informal graph of Snyder's evolution as a writer
0–86547–267–X North Point $15.95
0–86547–268–8 North Point pb $9.95

MYTHS & TEXTS
A stunning poem cycle interweaving Buddhist and Native American elements with Snyder's own experience as a logger
0–8112–0686–6 New Directions pb $5.95

REGARDING WAVE
0–8112–0196–1 New Directions pb $5.95

RIPRAP & COLD MOUNTAIN POEMS
Snyder's brilliant first book, along with his translations from the Chinese Zen poet Han Shan
0–912516–47–X Grey Fox pb $3.95

TURTLE ISLAND
0–8112–0546–0 New Directions pb $4.95

• Gilbert Sorrentino
SELECTED POEMS, 1958–1980
0–87685–501–X Black Sparrow pb $8.50

Jack Spicer
THE COLLECTED BOOKS OF JACK SPICER
A poet-linguist who died prematurely in 1965, Spicer exercised a subterranean influence on American poetry for many years before his "serial poems" were finally gathered together. This extraordinary volume contains *After Lorca, Billy the Kid, The Heads of the Town On Up to the Aether, A Book of Music, Language, A Book of Magazine Verse,* and all the other late work
Edited by Robin Blaser
0–87685–241–X Black Sparrow pb $12.50

• Lew Welch
RING OF BONE: Collected Poems, 1950–1971
Edited by Donald Allen
0–912516–03–8 Grey Fox pb $6.00

• Philip Whalen
DECOMPRESSIONS: Selected Poems
0–912516–26–7 Grey Fox pb $3.50

SCENES OF LIFE AT THE CAPITAL
A book-length meditative poem; the capital in question is Kyoto
0–912516–00–3 Grey Fox pb $2.50

• John Wieners
SELECTED POEMS, 1958–1984
A thorough presentation of Wieners' work, beginning with the legendary *Hotel Wentley Poems.* "He presents emotion on the spot—despair, nostalgia, bliss of love, dissatisfaction, flesh pressing on flesh"—Allen Ginsberg
Edited by Raymond Foye
Foreword by Allen Ginsberg
0–87685–661–X Black Sparrow pb $12.50

CULTURAL AFFAIRS IN BOSTON: Poetry and Prose, 1956–1985
0–87685–738–1 Black Sparrow pb $9.00

• Jonathan Williams
GET HOT OR GET OUT: A Selection of Poems, 1957–1981
0–8108–1495–1 Scarecrow $13.50

THE 1960s

The '60s were a remarkably rich period for poetry: noisy, varied, and charged with urgency. The political ferment of the period prompted an art directly participating in its time, steeped in its raw data rather than commenting remotely on it. Among the era's diverse manifestations were the insistence on cultural autonomy in the Black Arts Movement and in resurgent Native American cultures; the receptiveness to nonwestern influences typified by writers like Jerome Rothenberg, Nathaniel Tarn, and Clayton Eshleman; and the profusion of found, concrete, improvised, or chance-generated poetries—from Jackson MacLow's computer matrices to James Merrill's Ouija board.

• A.R. Ammons
COLLECTED POEMS, 1951–1971
"Of the poets of my generation, Ammons seems to me the likeliest to attain a central position in our imaginative history . . . His centrality stems from his comprehensiveness, for he offers a heterocosm, an alternate world to the nature he uneasily meets"—Harold Bloom
0–393–04241–3 Norton $17.50

SELECTED LONGER POEMS
0–393–01297–2 Norton $14.95
0–393–00962–9 Norton pb $4.95

LAKE EFFECT COUNTRY
0–393–01702–8 Norton $15.50
0–393–30104–4 Norton pb $5.95

WORLDLY HOPES
0–393–01518–1 Norton $12.95
0–393–00081–8 Norton pb $5.95

• Maya Angelou
JUST GIVE ME A COOL DRINK OF WATER 'FORE I DIIIE
0–394–47142–3 Random House $12.95

OH PRAY MY WINGS ARE GONNA FIT ME WELL
0–394–49951–4 Random House $11.95

• David Antin
SELECTED POEMS: 1963–1973
Includes work from the early collections *Definitions, Autobiography, Code of Flag Behavior,* and others
1–55713–058–2 Sun & Moon pb $12.95

TALKING AT THE BOUNDARIES
Improvised "talk poems"
0–8112–0560–6 New Directions pb $3.95

• James Baldwin
JIMMY'S BLUES: Selected Poems
0–312–44247–5 St. Martin's $11.95

TO ORDER BOOKS AS GIFTS, SEE PAGE 1

• Amiri Baraka (LeRoi Jones)
REGGAE OR NOT!
A recent work by the poet who was the dominant personality of the Black Arts Movement
0–936556–04–8 Contact pb $3.00

• Marvin Bell
NEW AND SELECTED POEMS
0–689–11919–4 Atheneum $21.00
0–689–11920–8 Atheneum pb $12.95

Ted Berrigan
SO GOING AROUND CITIES: New and Selected Poems, 1958–1979
0–912652–62–4 Blue Wind $24.95

• Wendell Berry
THE COLLECTED POEMS, 1957–1982
0–86547–189–4 North Point $16.50
0–86547–197–5 North Point pb $8.50

• Robert Bly
SELECTED POEMS
"Robert Bly has, in his time, changed American poetry: opened up new directions it might move in, inspired some poets to explore those directions, others to react strongly against such prospects. His role, stature, and style seem to me equivalent to that of Ezra Pound in the early decades of this century"—Gregory Orr
0–06–015334–2 Harper & Row $18.95

THE LIGHT AROUND THE BODY
0–06–090786–X Harper & Row pb $5.95

LOVING A WOMAN IN TWO WORLDS
0–06–097083–9 Harper & Row pb $6.95

THE MAN IN THE BLACK COAT TURNS
0–06–097186–X Harper & Row pb $6.95

SLEEPERS JOINING HANDS
0–06–090785–1 Harper & Row pb $5.95

• Philip Booth
RELATIONS: Selected Poems, 1950–1985
0–14–058560–5 Penguin pb $12.95

• William Bronk
LIFE SUPPORTS: New and Collected Poems
"Bronk's is a poetry of the epistemological limit, a message formulated by a border guard on the outer reaches of our shared assumptions . . . There is implied a distrust of the usual devices of ornament or analogy, of metaphor, of anything which might remove the reader from the exacting and naked process of realization"—Michael Heller, *NY Times*
0–86547–040–5 North Point pb $10.50

MANIFEST; AND FURTHERMORE
0–86547–285–8 North Point pb $7.95

• Charles Bukowski
BURNING IN WATER, DROWNING IN FLAME
0–87685–191–X Black Sparrow pb $9.50

THE DAYS RUN AWAY LIKE WILD HORSES OVER THE HILLS
0–87685–005–0 Black Sparrow pb $7.00

LOVE IS A DOG FROM HELL: Poems, 1974–1977
0–87685–362–9 Black Sparrow pb $10.00

MOCKINGBIRD WISH ME LUCK
0–87685–138–3 Black Sparrow pb $7.00

PLAY THE PIANO DRUNK LIKE A PERCUSSION INSTRUMENT UNTIL THE FINGERS BEGIN TO BLEED A BIT
0–87685–437–4 Black Sparrow pb $7.00

THE ROOMINGHOUSE MADRIGALS: Early Selected Poems, 1946–1966
0–87685–732–2 Black Sparrow pb $12.50

YOU GET SO ALONE AT TIMES THAT IT JUST MAKES SENSE
0–87685–683–0 Black Sparrow pb $12.50

• Hayden Carruth
THE SELECTED POETRY OF HAYDEN CARRUTH
Introduction by Galway Kinnell
0–02–069310–9 Macmillan pb $10.95

ASPHALT GEORGICS
0–8112–0938–5 New Directions pb $6.95

• Siv Cedering
LETTERS FROM THE FLOATING WORLD: New and Selected Poems
0–8229–3499–X Pittsburgh $17.95
0–8229–5363–3 Pittsburgh pb $9.95

• Lucille Clifton
GOOD WOMAN: Poems and a Memoir 1969–1980
0–918526–58–2 BOA $25.00
0–918526–59–0 BOA pb $12.00

NEXT: New Poems
0–918526–60–4 BOA $18.00
0–918526–61–2 BOA pb $9.00

TWO-HEADED WOMAN
0–87023–310–6 Massachusetts pb $5.95

Cid Corman
AEGIS: Selected Poems, 1979–1980
"As for the poems, most are brief, somewhat oriental in movement, yet still close to the grain of American speech . . . musical, wonderfully subtle"—Hayden Carruth
0–930794–58–3 Station Hill pb $5.95

AND THE WORD
0–918273–34–X Coffee House pb $8.95

• Jayne Cortez
COAGULATIONS: New and Selected Poems
0–938410–20–2 Thunder's Mouth pb $6.95

• Victor Hernandez Cruz
A poet whose work is informed by intense musicality and the possibilities of Spanish-English bilingualism
BY LINGUAL WHOLES
0–917672–19–4 Momo's pb $5.95

RHYTHM, CONTENT AND FLAVOR: New and Selected Poems
0–934770–93–X Arte Público pb $8.00

• James Dickey
"These are poems of darkness, darkness and a specialized light. Practically everything in them happens at night, by moonlight, starlight, firelight; or else in

other conditions that will make ordinary daytime perception impossible."—Howard Nemerov
BUCKDANCER'S CHOICE
0–8195–1028–9 Wesleyan pb $8.95

THE CENTRAL MOTION: Poems, 1968–1979
0–8195–5091–4 Wesleyan $18.50
0–8195–6088–X Wesleyan pb $12.95

THE EARLY MOTION: Drowning with Others & Helmets
0–8195–6070–7 Wesleyan pb $8.95

• Rose Drachler
THE COLLECTED POEMS OF ROSE DRACHLER
Edited by Jacob Drachler & Rochelle Ratner
Preface by Jerome Rothenberg
0–915066–50–5 Assembling pb $10.00

• Alan Dugan
NEW AND COLLECTED POEMS, 1961–1983
0–88001–085–1 Ecco pb $9.50

• Russell Edson
THE REASON WHY THE CLOSET-MAN IS NEVER SAD
0–8195–2084–5 Wesleyan $17.00
0–8195–1084–X Wesleyan pb $9.95

THE WOUNDED BREAKFAST
0–8195–5113–9 Wesleyan $17.00
0–8195–6105–3 Wesleyan pb $8.95

• Theodore Enslin
SYNTHESIS
0–913028–36–3 North Atlantic pb $6.00

• Clayton Eshleman
FRACTURE
0–87685–580–X Black Sparrow $14.00
0–87685–579–6 Black Sparrow pb $7.50

THE NAME-ENCANYONED RIVER: Selected Poems, 1960–1985
"As a result of his literal and imaginative explorations of the painted and gouged caves, Eshleman has constructed a myth, perhaps the first compelling post-Darwinian myth; that the Paleolithic represents the 'crisis' of the human 'separating out' of the animal, the original birth and the original fall of man"—Eliot Weinberger
Introduction by Eliot Weinberger
0–87685–652–0 Black Sparrow pb $12.50

WHAT SHE MEANS
0–87685–346–7 Black Sparrow pb $6.00

• Dave Etter
ALLIANCE, ILLINOIS
A book-length sequence of midwestern portraits
0–933180–43–8 Spoon River $14.95
0–933180–65–9 Spoon River pb $8.95

• Irving Feldman
NEW AND SELECTED POEMS
0–14–042269–2 Penguin pb $7.95

• Edward Field
VARIETY PHOTOPLAYS
Includes many poems influenced by movies, comics, and other aspects of pop culture
0–917554–02–7 Maelstrom pb $4.00

• Donald Finkel
SELECTED SHORTER POEMS
0–689–11855–4 Atheneum $21.00
0–689–11856–2 Atheneum pb $12.95

• Nikki Giovanni
"Talent is light, but mature talent is a beacon and Nikki Giovanni has . . . joined that small band of talented people who try to show us all the way to go home."—*LA Times*
BLACK FEELING, BLACK TALK
0–910296–07–3 Broadside pb $3.00

BLACK FEELING, BLACK TALK, BLACK JUDGEMENT
0–688–25294–X Morrow pb $5.95

COTTON CANDY ON A RAINY DAY
0–688–08365–X Morrow pb $6.95

MY HOUSE
0–688–05021–2 Morrow pb $5.95

SPIN A SOFT BLACK SONG
0–374–46469–3 Farrar, Straus & Giroux pb $3.50

THOSE WHO RIDE THE NIGHT WINDS
0–688–01906–4 Morrow $9.95
0–688–02653–2 Morrow pb $5.95

• Ramon Guthrie
MAXIMUM SECURITY WARD & OTHER POEMS
"Guthrie belongs to that tragically small company of poets who have done superb work in their seventies or beyond—poets with the power, and courage, to distill in their art their intimate experience of the trials and glories of old age"—M.L. Rosenthal
Edited by Sally M. Gall
Foreword by M.L. Rosenthal
0–89255–080–5 Persea pb $9.95

John Haines
NEWS FROM THE GLACIER: Selected Poems, 1960–1980
"Comforting in the actual, wintry scenes that dominate the pages is something to be cherished and carried along—a human endurance, a sturdiness in confronting what is out there"—William Stafford
0–8195–5064–7 Wesleyan $18.50
0–8195–6072–3 Wesleyan pb $9.95

• Donald Hall
THE HAPPY MAN
0–394–55478–7 Random House $12.95
0–394–74612–0 Random House pb $8.95

THE ONE DAY: A Poem in Three Parts
0–89919–816–3 Ticknor & Fields pb $8.95

• Anthony Hecht
MILLIONS OF STRANGE SHADOWS
0–689–11116–9 Atheneum pb $4.95

THE VENETIAN VESPERS
0–689–11015–4 Atheneum $10.00

• David Henderson
DE MAYOR OF HARLEM
0–938190–39–3 North Atlantic pb $6.95

THE LOW EAST
"Henderson *is* something else. He captures and re-creates moods which in turn fertilize fields of seeing in the mind and soul. And few poets have recaptured the R&B '50s and '60s the way he has"—*Richmond News Leader*
0–913028–73–8 North Atlantic $15.00
0–913028–72–X North Atlantic pb $4.95

• Dick Higgins
POEMS PLAIN AND FANCY
0–88268–022–6 Station Hill pb $7.95

• Daryl Hine
SELECTED POEMS
0–689–11118–5 Atheneum pb $6.95

• John Hollander
HARP LAKE
Hollander's most recent collection
0–394–72051–2 Knopf pb $8.95

NIGHT MIRROR
0–689–10429–4 Atheneum pb $5.95

POWERS OF THIRTEEN
0–689–11371–4 Atheneum $13.95
0–689–11372–2 Atheneum pb $6.95

SPECTRAL EMANATIONS: New and Selected Poems
David Perkins has described the title sequence as "a long work of complex imaginative symbolism and prophecy"
0–689–10878–8 Atheneum pb $7.95

• Anselm Hollo
SOJOURNER MICROCOSMS: New and Selected Poems, 1959–1977
0–912652–38–1 Blue Wind pb $12.95

• Richard Howard
NO TRAVELLER
0–679–72302–1 Knopf pb $9.95

TWO-PART INVENTIONS
A series of long dramatic dialogues. "Richard Howard's verse is elegant and cultured, tasteful and erudite. A man of learning and a connoisseur, he brings to his poetry a mind trained in the rigors of French poetics and an ear attuned to the rhythms of Ronsard as well as those of Browning"—Robert K. Martin, *Parnassus*
0–689–10619–X Atheneum pb $4.95

UNTITLED SUBJECTS
0–689–10136–8 Atheneum pb $6.95

• Richard Hugo
MAKING CERTAIN IT GOES ON: The Collected Poems of Richard Hugo
0–393–01784–2 Norton $24.95

• Kenneth Irby
OREXIS
0–930794–17–6 Station Hill pb $4.50

Ronald Johnson
ARK: The Foundations, 1–33
0–86547–012–X North Point pb $6.00

THE BOOK OF THE GREEN MAN
An American poet's journey through England, in the spirit of John Clare and Samuel Palmer
0–393–04290–1 Norton pb $6.00

• June Jordan
LIVING ROOM
0–938410–26–1 Thunder's Mouth pb $8.95

PASSION: New Poems, 1977 to 1980
0–8070–3219–0 Beacon pb $8.95

• Donald Justice
SELECTED POEMS
0–689–11016–2 Atheneum $10.95
0–689–11020–0 Atheneum pb $7.95

THE SUNSET MAKER
0–689–11904–6 Atheneum pb $8.95

• Robert Kelly
THE ALCHEMIST TO MERCURY
A selection surveying Kelly's prolific career
0–686–69476–7 North Atlantic pb $7.95

KILL THE MESSENGER
0–87685–432–3 Black Sparrow pb $8.50

THE LOOM
0–87685–233–9 Black Sparrow pb $8.50

THE MILL OF PARTICULARS
0–87685–172–3 Black Sparrow pb $5.00

NOT THIS ISLAND MUSIC
0–87685–692–X Black Sparrow pb $9.00

• X.J. Kennedy
CROSS TIES: Selected Poems
0–8203–0738–6 Georgia pb $9.95

• Galway Kinnell
SELECTED POEMS
0–395–32046–1 Houghton Mifflin pb $7.95

THE AVENUE BEARING THE INITIAL OF CHRIST INTO THE NEW WORLD: Poems, 1946–1964
0–395–18628–5 Houghton Mifflin pb $9.95

BODY RAGS
0–395–07856–3 Houghton Mifflin pb $8.95

THE BOOK OF NIGHTMARES
"Throughout his poetry there flows the awareness that growth involves a kind of dying . . . The attention burns through level after level, each vision catching up sparks and flashes from other sightings"—Charles Molesworth, *Western Humanities Review*
0–395–12098–5 Houghton Mifflin pb $8.95

THE PAST
0–395–39386–8 Houghton Mifflin pb $5.95

Carolyn Kizer
CARRYING OVER: Versions of Poems from Old and New China, Pakistan, Macedonian Yugoslavia and Mauritius, with Two Poems from the Yiddish
As a translator, Kizer is best known for her versions of Tu Fu, but this volume also introduces work by little-known poets such as Bogomil Gjuzel, Faiz Ahmed Faiz, and Shu Ting
1–55659–017–2 Copper Canyon pb $9.00

MERMAIDS IN THE BASEMENT: Poems for Women
"Collected new poems by a woman who was writing about women's concerns long before the movement began . . . Much of the pilgrimage of these poems moves from reiteration of griefs to the good grace of letting go"—*NY Times*
0–914742–80–9 Copper Canyon $14.00
0–914742–81–7 Copper Canyon pb $7.00

THE NEARNESS OF YOU
0–914742–96–5 Copper Canyon $15.00
0–914742–97–3 Copper Canyon pb $9.00

YIN: New Poems
0–918526–44–2 BOA $12.95
0–918526–45–0 BOA pb $9.00

Carolyn Kizer (photo courtesy of Copper Canyon)

● Etheridge Knight
THE ESSENTIAL ETHERIDGE KNIGHT
0–8229–5378–1 Pittsburgh pb $9.95

● Bill Knott
POEMS: 1963–1988
0–8229–5416–8 Pittsburgh pb $9.95

● Maxine Kumin
OUR GROUND TIME HERE WILL BE BRIEF
"Kumin has for twenty years explored the pastoral tragi-comedy of what she calls 'the continuum,' describing the daily acts of a family and farm life nested among animal and plant lives. For Kumin there is no hierarchy: humans, animals, and plants uncannily resemble each other"—Alicia Ostriker
0–670–53108–1 Penguin pb $16.95

● Tato Laviera
AmeRícan
"Laviera has two goals in mind . . . to pay homage to his city's ethnic diversity and to forge an 'AmeRícan' identity out of mainland and island traditions"—*Hispania*
0–934770–31–X Arte Público pb $7.00

ENCLAVE
0–934770–11–5 Arte Público pb $5.00

LA CARRETA MADE A U-TURN
0–934770–01–8 Arte Público pb $5.00

MAINSTREAM ETHICS
Laviera's poetry explores the geographic and linguistic imperatives of Hispanics in the United States
0–934770–90–5 Arte Público pb $5.00

● Don L. Lee
WE WALK THE WAY OF THE NEW WORLD
0–910296–26–X Broadside pb $6.00

● Philip Levine
"I really think he is extraordinary, a visionary of our dense, troubled, mysterious time. The grittiest and most brutal of his poems is, to me, an experience I would not hesitate to call ineffable."—Joyce Carol Oates
THE NAMES OF THE LOST
0–689–10748–X Atheneum pb $4.95

NOT THIS PIG
0–8195–1038–6 Wesleyan pb $8.95

SELECTED POEMS
0–689–11456–7 Atheneum $18.95
0–689–11457–5 Atheneum pb $9.95

SWEET WILL
0–689–11586–5 Atheneum pb $5.95

A WALK WITH TOM JEFFERSON
0–394–75859–5 Knopf pb $8.95

● John Logan
ONLY THE DREAMER CAN CHANGE THE DREAM: Selected Poems
0–912946–77–6 Ecco $14.95
0–912946–78–4 Ecco pb $7.95

● Audre Lorde
THE BLACK UNICORN
0–393–04508–0 Norton $9.95
0–393–04516–1 Norton pb $8.95

OUR DEAD BEHIND US
0–393–02329–X Norton $14.95
0–393–30327–6 Norton pb $6.95

ZAMI: A New Spelling of My Name
0–89594–123–6 Crossing $23.95
0–89594–122–8 Crossing pb $8.95

Jackson MacLow
BLOOMSDAY
Photographs by Richard Gumerre
0–88268–008–0 Station Hill pb $5.95

PIECES O' SIX: Poems in Prose
1–55713–060–4 Sun & Moon pb $10.95

REPRESENTATIVE WORKS, 1938–1985
"MacLow's Thoreau: he gives exact attention. No added flavor; just it . . . Musician, he introduced poetry to orchestra without syntax"—John Cage
0–937804–19–3 Segue $18.95
0–937804–18–5 Segue pb $12.95

● Harry Mathews
ARMENIAN PAPERS: Poems, 1954–1984
0–691–01440–X Princeton pb $9.50

● David Meltzer
THE NAME: Selected Poetry, 1973–1983
0–87685–491–9 Black Sparrow pb $8.50

● James Merrill
THE CHANGING LIGHT AT SANDOVER
Merrill's major work takes both its matter and its manner from Ouija board communications, and incorporates the separately published "The Book of Ephraim" (from *Divine Comedies*), *Mirabell,* and *Scripts for the Pageant*
0–689–11282–3 Atheneum $25.00
0–689–11283–1 Atheneum pb $14.95

DIVINE COMEDIES
0–689–10703–X Atheneum $11.95
0–689–10830–3 Atheneum pb $8.95

THE FIRE SCREEN
0–689–10185–6 Atheneum pb $6.95

FROM THE FIRST NINE: Poems, 1946–1976
0–689–11280–7 Atheneum $20.00
0–689–11281–5 Atheneum pb $12.95

THE INNER ROOM
Merrill's most recent collection, including a sequence about Japan
0–394–72049–0 Knopf pb $8.95

LATE SETTINGS
0–689–11572–5 Atheneum $12.95
0–689–11579–2 Atheneum pb $6.95

NIGHTS AND DAYS
0–689–10187–2 Atheneum pb $5.95

SCRIPTS FOR THE PAGEANT
0–689–11065–0 Atheneum pb $8.95

● W.S. Merwin
SELECTED POEMS
0–689–11970–4 Atheneum $22.95
0–689–70736–3 Atheneum pb $12.95

ASIAN FIGURES
Workings from Asian poems and proverbs
0–689–10557–6 Atheneum pb $7.95

THE CARRIER OF LADDERS
0–689–10343–3 Atheneum pb $7.95

THE COMPASS FLOWER
0–689–10768–4 Atheneum pb $5.95

FINDING THE ISLANDS
A collection of haiku-like 3-line poems
0–86547–089–8 North Point pb $6.00

THE LICE
Many would consider this collection, first published in 1967, as Merwin's finest. Its spare lyricism is filled with apocalyptic hints of extinction
0–689–10190–2 Atheneum pb $6.95

THE MINER'S PALE CHILDREN: A Book of Prose
0–689–10356–5 Atheneum pb $6.95

OPENING THE HAND
0–689–11381–1 Atheneum pb $6.95

THE RAIN IN THE TREES
0–394–57039–1 Knopf $16.95
0–394–75858–7 Knopf pb $8.95

SELECTED TRANSLATIONS, 1948–1968
0–689–10194–5 Atheneum pb $5.95

SELECTED TRANSLATIONS, 1968–1978
0–689–10903–2 Atheneum pb $6.95

WRITINGS TO AN UNFINISHED ACCOMPANIMENT
"A prophecy builds: Merwin foresees the total desertion, or secession, of the spirit from our inner life space . . . Merwin translates the international politics of grasping into a personal, spiritual condition which can be satisfied by nothing short of the dream of total acquisitiveness"—Laurence Lieberman, *Yale Review*
0–689–10556–8 Atheneum pb $5.95

• Howard Moss
NEW SELECTED POEMS
0–689–11571–7 Atheneum $20.00
0–689–11578–4 Atheneum pb $10.95

• Larry Neal
HOODOO HOLLERIN' BEBOP GHOSTS
Neal, who died in 1981, wrote of his work: "I've tried to select poems for this volume in which the polemic and poetic merge into an organic, personal statement"
0–88258–011–6 Howard pb $8.95

• Toby Olson
WE ARE THE FIRE: A Selection of Poems
0–8112–0914–8 New Directions pb $7.50

• Simon J. Ortiz
FROM SAND CREEK
"A pained poet sees the My Lai massacre as a reflection of what happened to his own people . . . Truly moving"—*St. Louis Globe-Democrat*
0–938410–00–8 Thunder's Mouth pb $4.95

A GOOD JOURNEY
0–8165–0883–6 Arizona pb $8.95

• Alicia Ostriker
A WOMAN UNDER THE SURFACE: Poems and Prose Poems
0–691–01390–X Princeton pb $6.50

• Marge Piercy
AVAILABLE LIGHT
0–394–56474–X Knopf $16.95
0–394–75691–6 Knopf pb $8.95

CIRCLES ON THE WATER: Selected Poems
0–394–70779–6 Knopf pb $12.95

• Miguel Piñero
LA BODEGA SOLD DREAMS
The only collection of poetry by the author of the acclaimed play *Short Eyes*. "Mixes ghetto invective and a feverish sentimentality, machismo swagger, and its reverse, a soft quality that is inadmissible to life except in art and has no proper name"—*Village Voice*
0–934770–02–6 Arte Público pb $5.00

• Sylvia Plath
COLLECTED POEMS
"She went to the extreme, far edge of the bearable and, in the end, slipped over. That is a risk in handling such touchy, violent material. Yet she turned it, too, to advantage; the courage it took to gamble in this way is reflected in the curious sense of creative optimism, of possibilities in the teeth of the impossible, that stirs in her poems like a moving bass"—A. Alvarez
Introduction by Ted Hughes
0–06–013369–4 Harper & Row $17.95
0–06–090900–5 Harper & Row pb $11.95

• Dudley Randall
A LITANY OF FRIENDS: New and Selected Poems
0–916418–33–2 Lotus $10.00
0–916418–50–2 Lotus pb $6.00

• Ishmael Reed
NEW AND COLLECTED POEMS
0–689–12003–6 Macmillan $22.95

CAB CALLOWAY STANDS IN FOR THE MOON
0–917453–06–9 Bamberger pb $7.00

A SECRETARY TO THE SPIRITS
0–88357–057–2 NOK $11.95
0–88357–058–0 NOK pb $4.95

• Adrienne Rich
DIVING INTO THE WRECK: Poems 1971–72
"With 'Diving into the Wreck,' Rich completes her re-vision of woman as monster. It becomes a source of poetic/political identity extracted from the wreckage of self and society under patriarchal rule. The old dispensation is displaced and a new 'book of myths' can be written"—Terrence Des Pres
0–393–04370–3 Norton $10.95
0–393–04384–3 Norton pb $5.95

THE DREAM OF A COMMON LANGUAGE: Poems 1974–1977
0–393–04502–1 Norton $12.95
0–393–04510–2 Norton pb $5.95

THE FACT OF A DOORFRAME: Poems Selected and New, 1950–1984
0–393–01905–5 Norton $18.95
0–393–30204–0 Norton pb $9.95

TIME'S POWER: Poems 1985–1988
0–393–02677–9 Norton $15.95
0–393–30575–9 Norton pb $7.95

A WILD PATIENCE HAS TAKEN ME THIS FAR: Poems, 1978–1981
0–393–01494–0 Norton $12.95
0–393–00072–9 Norton pb $6.95

Adrienne Rich (photo by Myriam Diaz-Diocaretz, courtesy of Norton)

Jerome Rothenberg
POEMS FOR THE GAME OF SILENCE, 1960–1970
0–8112–0590–8 New Directions pb $3.95

POLAND, 1931
0–8112–0541–X New Directions $7.50
0–8112–0542–8 New Directions pb $3.25

NEW SELECTED POEMS, 1970–1985
0–8112–0996–2 New Directions $23.50
0–8112–0997–0 New Directions pb $8.95

THAT DADA STRAIN
0–8112–0860–5 New Directions pb $7.25

VIENNA BLOOD & OTHER POEMS
0–8112–0759–5 New Directions pb $4.95

• Luis Omar Salinas
THE SADNESS OF DAYS: Selected and New Poems
0–934770–58–1 Arte Público pb $8.00

• Sonia Sanchez
HOMEGIRLS AND HANDGRENADES
Sanchez was one of the outstanding black poets to emerge in the 1960s
0–938410–23–7 Thunder's Mouth pb $8.95

UNDER A SOPRANO SKY
0–86543–052–7 Africa World Press $16.95
0–86543–053–5 Africa World Press pb $6.95

• Ed Sanders
THIRSTING FOR PEACE IN A RAGING CENTURY: Poems, 1961–1985
"Restores Ed Sanders to his rightful place at the forefront of the poetry of his time, and reminds us that spending one's days in active pursuit of the betterment of all life on the planet isn't necessarily antithetical to the creation of first-rate writing"—*San Francisco Chronicle*
0–918273–24–2 Coffee House pb $9.95

• Armand Schwerner
SOUNDS OF THE RIVER NARANJANA
Includes *The Tablets,* Schwerner's ongoing series reflecting the formal influence of cuneiform fragments
0–930794–60–5 Station Hill pb $6.95

• Anne Sexton
COMPLETE POEMS, 1981
0–395–29475–4 Houghton Mifflin $29.95
0–395–32935–3 Houghton Mifflin pb $14.95

• Harvey Shapiro
"Shapiro is *the* American urban poet."—Cynthia Ozick
BATTLE REPORT
0–8195–1032–7 Wesleyan pb $8.95

THE LIGHT HOLDS
0–8195–6096–0 Wesleyan pb $8.95

NATIONAL COLD STORAGE COMPANY: New and Selected Poems
0–8195–2152–3 Wesleyan $20.00
0–8195–1153–6 Wesleyan pb $12.95

THIS WORLD
0–8195–1057–2 Wesleyan pb $8.95

• Louis Simpson
AT THE END OF THE OPEN ROAD
0–8195–1020–3 Wesleyan pb $8.95

➢ **FOR OVERSEAS ORDERING INFORMATION, SEE PAGE 1**

PEOPLE LIVE HERE: Selected Poems 1948–1983
"Simpson's work is unbuttoned, genial, the kind of particularly American poetry that approaches a reader with an easy confidence in a shared language and an ironic civilization of attitude"—Julian Symons
0-918526-43-4 BOA pb $12.00

● **W.D. Snodgrass**
SELECTED POEMS, 1957–1987
0-939149-04-4 Soho $19.95

HEART'S NEEDLE
0-394-72220-5 Knopf pb $6.95

● **Nathaniel Tarn**
THE HOUSE OF LEAVES
0-87685-259-2 Black Sparrow pb $4.00

LYRICS FOR THE BRIDE OF GOD
0-8112-0566-5 New Directions pb $3.75

SEEING AMERICA FIRST
0-918273-53-6 Coffee House pb $9.95

● **Mona Van Duyn**
LETTERS FROM A FATHER & OTHER POEMS
0-689-11287-4 Atheneum pb $6.95

● **Tino Villanueva**
SHAKING OFF THE DARK
A collection by one of the foremost poets of the Chicano Renaissance
0-934770-23-9 Arte Público pb $7.00

● **Diane Wakoski**
CAP OF DARKNESS
0-87685-454-4 Black Sparrow $14.00

THE COLLECTED GREED, Parts 1–13
0-87685-462-5 Black Sparrow pb $10.00

EMERALD ICE: Selected Poems
0-87685-744-6 Black Sparrow pb $12.50

THE RINGS OF SATURN
0-87685-674-1 Black Sparrow pb $9.00

● **Anne Waldman**
SKIN MEAT BONES
0-918273-15-3 Coffee House pb $8.95

James Wright
COLLECTED POEMS
"His poems are shorter, quieter, gentler than Roethke's; they usually present the poet in a specific midwestern locale, contemplating a landscape which seems wholly alien until a sudden gesture or change in perspective momentarily unites poet and nature, self and other, in a muted epiphany"—Marjorie Perloff, *Washington Post*
0-8195-4031-5 Wesleyan $18.00
0-8195-6022-7 Wesleyan pb $9.95

THE BRANCH WILL NOT BREAK
0-8195-1018-1 Wesleyan pb $8.95

SAINT JUDAS
0-8195-1110-2 Wesleyan pb $8.95

THIS JOURNEY
0-394-52365-2 Random House $10.00
0-394-70825-3 Random House pb $5.95

CONTEMPORARIES

● **Ai**
CRUELTY & KILLING FLOOR
"So totally does Ai identify with what she sees that all her poems become, successfully, the voices of men, 40-year-old whores, mad hitchhiker killers, starving tenant farmers, child-beaters, even corpse haulers"—Alice Walker
0-938410-38-5 Thunder's Mouth pb $9.95

SIN
0-395-37908-3 Houghton Mifflin pb $5.95

● **Miguel Algarín**
BODY BEE CALLING FROM THE 21ST CENTURY
An odyssey into the bionic 21st century
0-934770-17-4 Arte Público pb $5.00

TIME'S NOW/YA ES TIEMPO
Poetic travels from the most recondite corners of the soul through the streets of New York and to other battlefields—this time Central America
0-934770-33-6 Arte Público pb $7.00

● **Paula Gunn Allen**
SHADOW COUNTRY
0-935626-26-3 California pb $7.50

● **Lynne Alvarez**
THE DREAMING MAN
"A book . . . [which] must be read as the measure of a new and daring sensibility arisen in the midst of our culture"—David Ignatow
0-943862-15-9 Waterfront pb $6.50

● **Michael Anania**
THE SKY AT ASHLAND
Fluent poems of landscape and color
0-918825-32-6 Moyer Bell pb $7.95

● **Bruce Andrews**
GIVE EM ENOUGH ROPE
0-940650-73-8 Sun & Moon pb $10.95

● **Antler**
FACTORY
0-87286-122-8 City Lights pb $5.00

● **James Applewhite**
RIVER WRITING: An Eno Journal
"Applewhite has found his true subject as a poet, and has developed a stance and style wholly adequate to the philosophical and spiritual reach of his poignant concerns"—Harold Bloom
0-691-01442-6 Princeton pb $8.95

● **Rae Armantrout**
PRECEDENCE
Small, deft constructions by one of the most original of the "language" poets
0-930901-24-X Burning Deck pb $5.00

● **Paul Auster**
DISAPPEARANCES: Selected Poems
Includes the collections *Wall Writing, White Spaces, Facing the Music,* and others, by the author of *The New York Trilogy*
0-87951-328-4 Overlook pb $16.95
0-87951-341-1 Overlook pb $9.95

● **Jimmy Santiago Baca**
MARTIN & MEDITATIONS ON THE SOUTH VALLEY
Two long narrative poems of New Mexico. "He is far from being a naive realist; what makes his writing so exciting to me is the way in which it manifests both an intense lyricism and that transformative vision which perceives the mythic and archetypal significance of life-events"—Denise Levertov
Introduction by Denise Levertov
0-8112-1032-4 New Directions pb $7.95

● **Gerald Barrax**
AN AUDIENCE OF ONE
0-8203-0500-6 Georgia $9.95
0-8203-0502-2 Georgia pb $5.95

THE DEATHS OF ANIMALS AND LESSER GODS
0-912759-02-X Virginia pb $6.00

● **Charles Bernstein**
THE SOPHIST
The most comprehensive collection to date by the co-editor of $L=A=N=G=U=A=G=E$. "Yes, Bernstein is an elegant poet, and his work suggests to me that it is precisely a tradition of elegance which we can see evolving as we pass from Zukofsky to Creeley to, now Bernstein"—Burton Hatlen, *Sagetrieb*
0-940650-78-9 Sun & Moon $16.95
0-940650-79-7 Sun & Moon pb $11.95

● **Karen Brodine**
ILLEGAL ASSEMBLY
0-914610-17-1 Hanging Loose pb $6.00

● **David Bromige**
DESIRE: Selected Poems 1963–1987
0-87685-723-3 Black Sparrow pb $10.00

● **Olga Broumas**
PASTORAL JAZZ
"A lot of people these days write about love and nature, but none do it with Broumas's luminous language"—Susan Mernit
0-914742-70-1 Copper Canyon pb $7.00

Don Byrd
THE GREAT DIMESTORE CENTENNIAL
An ambitious book-length poem mixing together everything from Wittgenstein to Bud Powell
0-88268-024-2 Station Hill pb $7.95

● **Jim Carroll**
LIVING AT THE MOVIES
0-14-042290-0 Penguin pb $6.95

● **Ana Castillo**
WOMEN ARE NOT ROSES
0-934770-28-X Arte Público pb $5.00

● **Joseph Ceravolo**
TRANSMIGRATION SOLO
0-915124-21-1 Toothpaste pb $4.00

- Nicholas Christopher
DESPERATE CHARACTERS: A Novella in Verse & Other Poems
0–14–012116–1 Penguin pb $8.95

ON TOUR WITH RITA
0–394–74998–7 Knopf pb $6.95

- Amy Clampitt
ARCHAIC FIGURE
Of this new collection, the author has written: "The experience of attachment to another person or persons is a recurring theme in these poems, particularly those on George Eliot, Margaret Fuller and Dorothy Wordsworth; and the same theme is continued, sometimes metaphorically, sometimes explicitly, in the final section . . . As before, there are evocations of Maine and other places, including Greece, England, Venice, and my native Midwest"
0–394–55919–3 Knopf $15.95
0–394–75090–X Knopf pb $8.95

THE KINGFISHER
"How to describe the delights of these poems? If Gerard Hopkins and Marianne Moore, those two uniquenesses, had married each other they might have borne Amy Clampitt, who brings to one in truly marvelous abundance, through metaphor, adjective and narrative, the burnished details of the world"—Mona Van Duyn
0–394–52840–9 Knopf $15.95
0–394–71251–X Knopf pb $11.95

WHAT THE LIGHT WAS LIKE
0–394–54318–1 Knopf $14.95
0–394–72937–4 Knopf pb $8.95

- Judith Ortiz Cofer
TERMS OF SURVIVAL
0–934770–73–5 Arte Público pb $7.00

- Wanda Coleman
IMAGOES
0–87685–509–5 Black Sparrow pb $7.50

Clark Coolidge
AT EGYPT
0–935724–35–4 Figures pb $7.50

THE CRYSTAL TEXT
"Coolidge's writing encroaches on the impossible language of dreams . . . He practices an ultimate naturalism, an endless home movie of raw thought"—Village Voice
0–935724–20–6 Figures pb $10.00

MESH
About sex, sort of. Vivid new lyrics by a prolific and inventive writer
0–932597–05–X In Camera pb $4.95

MINE: The One that Enters the Stories
0–935724–14–1 Figures pb $5.00

SOLUTION PASSAGE: Poems 1978–1981
Word-noise as lyric statement, from a young master who makes the concrete abstract and vice versa
0–940650–55–X Sun & Moon $18.95
0–940650–54–1 Sun & Moon pb $11.95

- William Corbett
COLLECTED POEMS, 1968–1984
0–915032–46–5 National Poetry Fdn pb $15.95

- Alfred Corn
A CALL IN THE MIDST OF THE CROWD
0–14–042257–9 Penguin pb $7.95

THE VARIOUS LIGHT
0–14–042284–6 Penguin pb $7.95

THE WEST DOOR
0–670–81956–5 Viking $17.95
0–14–058604–0 Penguin pb $8.95

- Beverly Dahlen
A READING (1–7)
"Her writing abandons the notion of a focal point and deliberately spins off in all directions . . . In a sense you cannot read it, because it has already usurped that function: you can only read with it, as if reading over something you just wrote"—Village Voice
0–917672–23–2 Momo's pb $12.50

- Thulani Davis
PLAYING THE CHANGES
0–8195–1120–X Wesleyan $17.00
0–8195–2119–1 Wesleyan pb $8.95

- W.S. Di Piero
EARLY LIGHT
0–87480–189–3 Utah pb $7.95

- Tom Disch
YES, LET'S: New and Selected Poems
0–8018–3851–7 Johns Hopkins pb $8.95

- Melvin Dixon
CHANGE OF TERRITORY
0–912759–04–6 Virginia pb $5.00

- Stephen Dobyns
THE BALTHUS POEMS
0–689–11279–3 Atheneum pb $6.95

CEMETERY NIGHTS
0–670–81484–9 Viking $18.95
0–14–058584–2 Penguin pb $9.95

- Joseph Donahue
BEFORE CREATION
"The legions of the living shake hands with legions of the dead. The voices of their greetings, messages, and personal ads resonate through these works"—John Yau
0–9622390–1–1 Central Park pb $5.00

- Rita Dove
MUSEUM
0–915604–78–7 Carnegie-Mellon $14.95
0–915604–79–5 Carnegie-Mellon pb $6.95

- Lynne Dreyer
THE WHITE MUSEUM
0–937804–21–5 Segue pb $6.00

- Norman Dubie
SELECTED AND NEW POEMS
0–393–01817–2 Norton $14.95
0–393–30140–0 Norton pb $5.95

- Henry Dumas
KNEES OF A NATURAL MAN
0–938410–75–X Thunder's Mouth $19.95
0–938410–74–1 Thunder's Mouth pb $9.95

- Rachel Blau DuPlessis
TABULA ROSA
Poetry that is both steeped in lyrical tradition and deeply critical of its implications
0–937013–19–6 Potes & Poets pb $8.50

- Barbara Einzig
LIFE MOVES OUTSIDE
0–930901–42–8 Burning Deck pb $7.00

- Louise Erdrich
JACKLIGHT
0–03–068682–2 Henry Holt pb $6.95

- Martin Espada
THE IMMIGRANT ICEBOY'S BOLERO
0–943862–33–7 Waterfront pb $4.00

- Mari Evans
NIGHTSTAR: 1973–1978
0–934934–07–X California pb $5.25

- Carolyn Forché
THE COUNTRY BETWEEN US
Poems dealing, among other things, with Forché's observations of political struggle in El Salvador
0–06–090926–9 Harper & Row pb $7.95

- Kathleen Fraser
NOTES PRECEDING TRUST
0–932499–24–4 Lapis pb $9.95

- Tess Gallagher
WILLINGLY
0–915308–46–0 Graywolf pb $6.00

- Amy Gerstler
THE TRUE BRIDE
0–932499–04–X Lapis pb $9.50

- Barry Gifford
GHOSTS NO HORSE CAN CARRY: Collected Poems, 1967–1987
0–88739–064–1 Creative Arts pb $12.95

- Sandra Gilbert
BLOOD PRESSURE
0–393–02609–4 Norton $15.95

IN THE FOURTH WORLD
Foreword by Richard Eberhart
0–8173–8527–4 Alabama pb $8.50

- Dana Gioia
DAILY HOROSCOPE
0–915308–80–0 Graywolf pb $8.00

Louise Gluck
THE HOUSE ON MARSHLAND
"The most profound source of elation in reading a new species of poet is the surprise in every line as a new voice and a new sensibility declares itself . . . A very peculiar power, and a new style, commanding in its indifference to current modes"—Helen Vendler
0–912946–19–9 Ecco pb $7.95

👁 **TO ORDER ANY BOOK IN THIS CATALOG, ASK YOUR BOOKSELLER OR CALL 1-800-882-8770**

DESCENDING FIGURE
"Her poetry is rock-bottom hard and final yet marked by a sentience next to clairvoyance, and subtle surprise, and strong beauty"—Calvin Bedient
0–912946–71–7 Ecco $9.95
0–912946–72–5 Ecco pb $5.95

THE TRIUMPH OF ACHILLES
0–88001–081–9 Ecco $13.50
0–88001–082–7 Ecco pb $7.50

● John Godfrey
MIDNIGHT ON YOUR LEFT
0–935724–31–1 Figures pb $6.00

● David Graham
MAGIC SHOWS
0–914946–58–7 Cleveland State pb $6.00

● Jorie Graham
THE END OF BEAUTY
"Graham, if we compare her with her Romantic predecessors, is nearest to Shelley in her creation of clouds of thought, accumulating and breaking open in a shower of consequences"—Helen Vendler
0–88001–130–0 Ecco pb $7.50

EROSION
0–691–01405–1 Princeton pb $7.95

● Judy Grahn
THE WORK OF A COMMON WOMAN: Collected Poetry, 1964–1977
0–89594–155–4 Crossing pb $7.95

● Robert Grenier
A DAY AT THE BEACH
0–937804–14–2 Segue pb $6.00

● Allen Grossman
OF THE GREAT HOUSE: A Book of Poems
0–8112–0835–4 New Directions pb $6.95

● Barbara Guest
FAIR REALISM
"Barbara Guest confirms that she is one of our finest poets . . . Her images seem to feed from her hand like birds, and then take wing again"—James Schuyler
1–55713–048–5 Sun & Moon pb $9.95

● Marilyn Hacker
ASSUMPTIONS
"I don't see how anyone who knows versification can help but admire and relish her abilities"—Hayden Carruth
0–394–72826–2 Knopf pb $8.95

● Rachel Hadas
PASS IT ON
0–691–01454–X Princeton pb $9.95

A SON FROM SLEEP
0–8195–1140–4 Wesleyan pb $8.95

● Jessica Hagedorn
PET FOOD AND TROPICAL APPARITIONS
0–917672–14–3 Momo's Press pb $5.95

● Daniel Halpern
TANGO
0–670–81544–6 Viking $17.95
0–14–058588–5 Penguin pb $10.95

● Joy Harjo
SHE HAD SOME HORSES
A poem cycle by a leading Native American poet. "Harjo's second major book of poetry rides an intense passion for survival through dangerous roads in America, in her own heart, in an Indian dream vision that can wrench and heal"—*Ms.*
0–938410–06–7 Thunder's Mouth pb $6.95

● Michael S. Harper
DEAR JOHN, DEAR COLTRANE
0–252–01193–7 Illinois pb $8.95

HEALING SONG FOR THE INNER EAR
0–252–01128–7 Illinois $11.95
0–252–01099–X Illinois pb $8.95

HISTORY IS YOUR OWN HEARTBEAT
0–252–00144–3 Illinois $11.95

IMAGES OF KIN: New and Selected Poems
0–252–00607–0 Illinois pb $9.95

NIGHTMARE BEGINS RESPONSIBILITY
0–252–00466–3 Illinois $12.95
0–252–00226–1 Illinois pb $8.95

SONG: I Want a Witness
0–8229–3254–7 Pittsburgh $15.95
0–8229–5231–9 Pittsburgh pb $6.95

● Robert Hass
PRAISE
0–912946–62–8 Ecco pb $8.95

● Vicki Hearne
IN THE ABSENCE OF HORSES
0–691–01409–4 Princeton pb $8.50

● Lyn Hejinian
MY LIFE
1–55713–006–X Sun & Moon $12.95
1–55713–024–8 Sun & Moon pb $8.95

WRITING IS AN AID TO MEMORY
0–685–99357–4 Figures pb $4.00

● Michael Heller
IN THE BUILDED PLACE
0–918273–58–7 Coffee House pb $8.95

KNOWLEDGE
0–915342–30–8 SUN pb $4.00

● Lance Henson
SELECTED POEMS: 1970–1983
0–912678–62–3 Greenfield Review pb $5.00

● Calvin Hernton
MEDICINE MAN
0–918408–05–9 Reed & Cannon pb $4.95

● Edward Hirsch
WILD GRATITUDE
0–394–74153–6 Knopf pb $9.95

● Linda Hogan
SAVINGS
0–918273–41–2 Coffee House pb $7.95

SEEING THROUGH THE SUN
Winner of an American Book Award from the Before Columbus Foundation
0–87023–472–2 Massachusetts pb $7.95

Garrett Kaoru Hongo
THE RIVER OF HEAVEN
Winner of the 1987 Lamont Poetry Prize
0–394–75785–8 Knopf pb $8.95

YELLOW LIGHT
0–8195–1104–8 Wesleyan pb $8.95

● Fanny Howe
THE LIVES OF A SPIRIT
The author describes herself as having written in "a State of waiting-for-God which passive is yet alert, where everything matters, and there is no escape"
0–940650–95–9 Sun & Moon $10.95

● Susan Howe
ARTICULATION OF SOUND FORMS IN TIME
The most recent work by a writer at once hypnotic and keenly attuned to historical circumstance
0–942433–11–4 Awede pb $8.00

THE EUROPE OF TRUSTS
Collects in one volume *The Liberties, Pythagorean Silence,* and *The Defenestration of Prague*
1–55713–008–6 Sun & Moon $13.95
1–55713–009–4 Sun & Moon pb $9.95

● Frances Jaffer
ALTERNATE ENDINGS
0–933539–00–2 HOW(ever) pb $6.00

● Denis Johnson
THE VEIL
Poetry by the author of *Fiskadoro* and *The Stars at Noon*
0–394–54127–8 Knopf $15.95
0–394–74343–1 Knopf pb $8.95

● Richard Kenney
THE EVOLUTION OF THE FLIGHTLESS BIRD
0–300–03152–1 Yale pb $7.95

● Maurice Kenny
BETWEEN TWO RIVERS: Selected Poems
0–934834–73–3 White Pine pb $10.00

BLACK ROBE
"A Mohawk who has lived for decades in New York City, [Kenny] still speaks of the Akwesasne Reservation along the St. Lawrence River as home . . . One of his most important works is a book-length cycle of poems called *Black Robe* . . . It tells the story of Isaac Jogues, the Jesuit missionary among the Mohawks, from an Iroquois point of view"—Joseph Bruchac
0–918517–05–2 Chauncy pb $10.95

● Faye Kicknosway
WHO SHALL KNOW THEM?
Kicknosway explores the imagined lives of the subjects in Walker Evans' Depression-era photographs
0–670–80515–7 Viking $15.95
0–14–042345–1 Penguin pb $7.95

● **August Kleinzahler**
STORM OVER HACKENSACK
"The poems make amazing sounds, weird and keen, for a dance joining other senses. Not a breath wasted, not a note in excess, Kleinzahler has converted Apollo's lyre into something like a cross between a Jew's harp and a catapult"—Christopher Middleton
0–918825–06–7 Moyer Bell $14.95
0–918825–08–3 Moyer Bell pb $7.95

EARTHQUAKE WEATHER
0–918825–97–0 Moyer Bell $16.95
0–918825–98–9 Moyer Bell pb $8.95

● **John Koethe**
THE LATE WISCONSIN SPRING
0–691–01414–0 Princeton pb $6.95

● **Ann Lauterbach**
BEFORE RECOLLECTION
0–691–06698–1 Princeton $15.00
0–691–01437–X Princeton pb $8.50

● **Brad Leithauser**
CATS OF THE TEMPLE
Leithauser draws on his experiences of Japanese life in many of these poems
0–394–54806–X Knopf $14.45
0–394–74152–8 Knopf pb $7.95

HUNDREDS OF FIREFLIES
"The observations glisten, the feelings ring true. These poems by a young, unostentatious craftsman are made to something very like perfection"—James Merrill
0–394–51949–3 Knopf $11.00
0–394–74896–4 Knopf pb $9.95

● **Larry Levis**
WINTER STARS
0–8229–3511–2 Pittsburgh $15.95
0–8229–5368–4 Pittsburgh pb $6.95

● **Sandra McPherson**
PATRON HAPPINESS
0–88001–021–5 Ecco $12.95
0–88001–022–3 Ecco pb $6.50

Nathaniel Mackey
BEDOUIN HORNBOOK
Prose letters from the musician N. to the Angel of Dust; a book encompassing all genres and belonging to none
0–912759–07–0 Virginia pb $10.00

ERODING WITNESS
"These poems are about prophecy and initiation; the uncompromising narratives that sing but *don't explain* are the sounds of a mythmaker-griot in the midst of ceremonial talk"—Michael S. Harper
0–252–01230–5 Illinois pb $8.95

● **Phillip Mahony**
CATCHING BODIES
Harshly realistic poems by a Brooklyn police officer
1–938190–55–5 North Atlantic pb $7.95

Nathaniel Mackey (photo courtesy University of Illinois Press)

● **Clarence Major**
SURFACES WITH MASKS
"Feeling is my foreground. Subject matter is my middle distance. I look for geometrical dramas in pictures and I try to create them in my poems"—C. Major
0–918273–43–9 Coffee House pb $8.95

● **William Matthews**
SLEEK FOR THE LONG FLIGHT
0–317–61749–4 White Pine pb $8.00

● **Ralph J. Mills, Jr.**
EACH BRANCH
Spare, Williams-like observations of the physical world
0–933180–89–6 Spoon River $11.95
0–933180–90–X Spoon River pb $4.95

● **Paul Monette**
LOVE ALONE: Eighteen Elegies for Rog
"This is real poetry of real love, real death in real life, as it is being experienced by the generation of gay men caught in the war called AIDS"—Judy Grahn
0–312–02602–1 St. Martin's pb $7.95

● **Pat Mora**
BORDERS
"These are arduous expeditions . . . for both writer and reader. . . . You don't plant your flag without earning the right"—*El Paso Times*
0–934770–57–3 Arte Público pb $5.00

CHANTS
0–934770–24–7 Arte Público pb $7.00

● **Hilda Morley**
CLOUDLESS AT FIRST
A new collection by a poet remarkable, among other things, for her flowing visual sense
0–918825–71–7 Moyer Bell $22.50
0–918825–72–5 Moyer Bell pb $12.95

TO HOLD IN MY HAND: Selected Poems, 1955–1983
"Her touchstone for finding her way in the world is the recognition of common feeling, and she describes that recognition as a biological phenomenon . . . We don't often find this much of a human life within a single volume of poetry"—*Village Voice*
Foreword by Stanley Kunitz
0–935296–46–8 Sheep Meadow $13.95
0–935296–49–2 Sheep Meadow pb $8.95

● **Eileen Myles**
BREAD AND WATER
0–937815–02–0 Hanuman pb $4.00

● **Duane Niatum**
DIGGING OUT THE ROOTS
0–06–451155–3 Harper & Row pb $2.50

● **Alice Notley**
AT NIGHT THE STATES
0–916328–18–X Yellow pb $6.95

● **Geoffrey O'Brien**
A BOOK OF MAPS
0–87376–061–1 Red Dust pb $4.00

● **Michael O'Brien**
BLUE SPRINGS
0–915342–06–5 SUN pb $6.00

● **Sharon Olds**
THE DEAD AND THE LIVING
"Sharon Olds is enormously self-aware; her poetry is remarkable for its candor, its eroticism, and its power to move"—David Leavitt, *Village Voice*
0–394–53048–9 Knopf $14.95
0–394–71563–2 Knopf pb $9.95

THE GOLD CELL
0–394–55699–2 Knopf $14.95
0–394–74770–4 Knopf pb $9.95

● **Mary Oliver**
AMERICAN PRIMITIVE
0–316–65002–1 Little, Brown $14.95
0–316–65004–8 Little, Brown pb $6.95

● **Brenda Marie Osbey**
CEREMONY FOR MINNECONJOUX
0–912759–03–8 Virginia pb $5.00

● **Maureen Owen**
HEARTS IN SPACE
0–686–73477–7 Kulchur pb $7.00

● **Michael Palmer**
Palmer practices a spare, abstract lyricism at once musically gratifying and philosophically questioning.
FIRST FIGURE
0–86547–174–6 North Point pb $8.50

NOTES FOR ECHO LAKE
0–86547–024–3 North Point pb $8.50

SUN
0–86547–345–5 North Point pb $9.95

● **Linda Pastan**
A FRACTION OF DARKNESS
0–393–02212–9 Norton $12.95
0–393–30251–2 Norton pb $6.95

🍎 **IF YOU CAN'T FIND IT, LOOK IN THE INDEX**

• Bob Perelman
THE FIRST WORLD
"*The First World* examines our historical (hysterical) moment with the liberated coherence of a Brecht or Rabelais. Perelman's demolition of inscribed cultural myths represents a celebratory reawakening of language to its larger consequences"— Michael Palmer
0–935724–22–2 Figures pb $5.00

• Robert Peters
THE GIFT TO BE SIMPLE: A Garland for Mother Ann Lee
0–87140–103–7 Liveright pb $4.95

• Richard Pevear
NIGHT TALK & OTHER POEMS
0–691–01342–X Princeton pb $8.50

• Pedro Pietri
One of the foremost artists of the Nuyorican School, Pietri is a startling and hilarious performer of his own poetry.
MISSING OUT OF ACTION
0–943862–32–9 Waterfront pb $7.95

PUERTO RICAN OBITUARY
Includes "Suicide Note from a Cockroach in a Low Income Housing Project"
0–85345–330–6 Monthly Review pb $6.50

TRAFFIC VIOLATIONS
A collection of 80 poems, including the elegy "I Hate Trees"
0–943862–06–X Waterfront pb $7.95

Robert Pinsky
AN EXPLANATION OF AMERICA
0–691–06407–5 Princeton $15.00
0–691–01360–8 Princeton pb $6.50

HISTORY OF MY HEART
"The economics of desire, what is given or taken, what is lost, what gets stored and what spent, is Pinsky's thematic center in all his books—that is why he is such a profound traditionalist"— Charles Molesworth, *The Hollins Critic*
0–88001–048–7 Ecco pb $7.50

• Sterling Plumpp
THE MOJO HANDS CALL, I MUST GO
By the author of *Black Rituals;* winner of the 1983 Carl Sandburg Award
0–938410–04–0 Thunder's Mouth pb $5.95

• Jed Rasula
TABULA RASULA
0–930794–62–1 Station Hill pb $5.50

• Leo Romero
CELSO
"Celso is Everyman, his roles ranging from shabby Christ figure to buffoon, drunkard, and ladies' man, alternately unkempt, lascivious, pathetic, witty-cruel, curious, and outrageous"—*Literary Arts*
0–934770–36–0 Arte Público pb $7.00

• William Pitt Root
REASONS FOR GOING IT ON FOOT
0–689–11138–X Atheneum $11.95
0–689–11164–9 Atheneum pb $6.95

• Wendy Rose
THE HALFBREED CHRONICLES & OTHER POEMS
0–931122–39–2 West End pb $4.95

• Mark Rudman
BY CONTRARIES & OTHER POEMS
0–915032–93–7 National Poetry Fdn pb $12.95

• Hiroaki Sato
THAT FIRST TIME: Six Renga on Love & Other Poems
A traditional Japanese form adapted to contemporary life
0–932662–68–4 St. Andrew's $14.00

• Leslie Scalapino
CONSIDERING HOW EXAGGERATED MUSIC IS
0–86547–066–9 North Point pb $10.50

THAT THEY WERE AT THE BEACH
"She proves the absolute master of a uniquely compact perception and an intelligence that can track a plurality of relationships in very few words indeed"— Robert Creeley
0–86547–211–4 North Point pb $9.50

WAY
"A major poet, and somebody worth watching very closely through long passages and infinitely subtle variations"— Andrei Codrescu
0–86547–320–X North Point pb $12.00

• Gjertrud Schnackenberg
THE LAMPLIT ANSWER
"Schnackenberg has a control of line, of pace, and of tone that is rare in her generation"—John Hollander
0–374–18293–0 Farrar, Straus & Giroux $12.95
0–374–51978–1 Farrar, Straus & Giroux pb $6.95

PORTRAITS AND ELEGIES
0–374–51981–1 Farrar, Straus & Giroux pb $6.95

• Barry Schwabsky
FATE: Seen in the Dark
0–930901–34–7 Burning Deck pb $4.00

Leslie Scalapino (photo copyright Thomas Victor, courtesy North Point)

• Hugh Seidman
COLLECTING EVIDENCE
0–317–60988–2 Unmuzzled Ox pb $15.00

Vikram Seth
THE GOLDEN GATE
A deftly executed verse novel about contemporary Californians taking its inspiration from Byron and Pushkin
0–394–54974–0 Random House $17.95
0–394–75063–2 Random House pb $5.95

• Ntozake Shange
A DAUGHTER'S GEOGRAPHY
0–312–18341–0 St. Martin's pb $4.95

RIDIN' THE MOON IN TEXAS: Word Paintings
0–312–88929–1 St. Martin's $16.95

SEE NO EVIL
0–917672–21–6 Momo's pb $5.95

• David Shapiro
TO AN IDEA: A Book of Poems
0–87951–255–5 Overlook pb $8.95

• James Sherry
POPULAR FICTION
0–937804–15–0 Segue pb $6.00

• Aaron Shurin
THE GRACES
0–87704–060–5 Four Seasons pb $4.95

• Leslie Silko
STORYTELLER
Poetry and fiction intermingled, from an important Native American writer
0–394–51589–7 Seaver $17.95
0–394–17795–9 Seaver pb $11.95

• Ron Silliman
THE AGE OF HUTS
0–937804–22–3 Segue pb $10.00

PARADISE
A section from Silliman's long ongoing work *The Alphabet*
0–930901–32–0 Burning Deck pb $7.00

• Charles Simic
SELECTED POEMS, 1963–1983
0–8076–1129–8 Braziller $14.95
0–8076–1130–1 Braziller pb $8.95

AUSTERITIES
0–8076–1044–5 Braziller pb $4.95

RETURN TO A PLACE LIT BY A GLASS OF MILK
0–8076–0733–9 Braziller pb $4.95

WEATHER FORECAST FOR UTOPIA AND VICINITY: Poems, 1967–1982
0–930794–83–4 Station Hill pb $4.95

• Maurya Simon
THE ENCHANTED ROOM
"An extraordinary first book of poetry . . . Almost every single poem is successful per se, includes at times fresh and surprising metaphors, and conveys a quiet, subtle, and crystal-clear view of the world"— Miroslav Holub
0–914742–98–1 Copper Canyon pb $9.00

- Dave Smith
THE ROUNDHOUSE VOICES: Selected and New Poems
0–06–015473–X Harper & Row $16.95

Gustaf Sobin
THE EARTH AS AIR
"Sobin's world . . . is basic, stripped, often sun-drenched, sometimes arid—and mysterious"—Charles Tomlinson
0–8112–0893–1 New Directions pb $7.95

VOYAGING PORTRAITS
Visionary poetry by an American poet long resident in southern France. "The physicality which Sobin brings to poetry is not that of inert chunks of words on a page, but of organic matter in motion"—*Village Voice*
0–8112–1061–8 New Directions pb $9.95

- Cathy Song
FRAMELESS WINDOWS, SQUARES OF LIGHT
0–393–30592–9 Norton pb $7.95

- Gary Soto
One of the most celebrated of contemporary Chicano poets
BLACK HAIR
0–8229–3498–1 Pittsburgh $16.95
0–8229–5362–5 Pittsburgh pb $6.95

SMALL FACES
0–934770–49–2 Arte Público pb $8.00

- Timothy Steele
SAPPHICS AGAINST ANGER & OTHER POEMS
0–394–74287–7 Random House pb $7.95

- Charles Stein
HORSE SACRIFICE
0–930794–30–3 Station Hill pb $3.95

- David St. John
THE ORANGE PIANO
0–89807–135–6 Illuminati pb $5.95

- Patricia Storace
HEREDITY
0–8070–6801–2 Beacon pb $7.95

- Robert Sund
ISH RIVER
"Travels the woods, mountains, farms, and towns of Washington's north country . . . Small events in accurately etched settings come alive for the reader"—*Hudson Review*
0–86547–102–9 North Point pb $7.50

- James Tate
RECKONER
0–8195–6159–2 Wesleyan pb $8.95

- Lorenzo Thomas
THE BATHERS
0–918408–18–0 Reed & Cannon pb $5.95

- Richard Tillinghast
OUR FLAG WAS STILL THERE
0–8195–5106–6 Wesleyan pb $16.00
0–8195–6099–5 Wesleyan pb $8.95

- Tony Towle
AUTOBIOGRAPHY & OTHER POEMS
0–915342–18–9 SUN pb $5.00

- Quincy Troupe
SNAKE-BACK SOLOS
0–918408–11–3 Reed & Cannon pb $5.95

- Frederick Turner
THE NEW WORLD
"*The New World* may be the first straight-forward heroic epic since Tennyson that really works. Turner's stroke of genius was to place the story in the future and tell it in a science-fiction mode. Suddenly all the epic formulas become not only permissible again but credible"—Dana Gioia
0–691–06641–8 Princeton $29.00
0–691–01420–5 Princeton pb $9.95

GENESIS: An Epic Poem
A 10,000-line narrative poem about the exploration of Mars. "A prodigious work"—Brian Aldiss
0–933071–26–4 Saybrook pb $9.95

- Evangelina Vigil-Piñón
THE COMPUTER IS DOWN
"Takes on a sophisticated sheen, at once celebrating the glittery image of the late 20th century American city and taking a hard look at the human realities upon which the image rests"—*San Antonio Light*
0–934770–32–8 Arte Público pb $7.00

THIRTY AN' SEEN A LOT
The first book of poems by this San Antonio native
0–934770–13–1 Arte Público pb $5.00

- Keith Waldrop
THE SPACE OF HALF AN HOUR
0–930901–20–7 Burning Deck pb $4.00

- Rosmarie Waldrop
THE REPRODUCTION OF PROFILES
Prose poems derived from Wittgenstein: "I used Wittgenstein's phrases in an unsystematic way, sometimes quoting, sometimes letting them spark what they would, sometimes substituting different nouns within a phrase"
0–8112–1045–6 New Directions pb $9.95

STREETS ENOUGH TO WELCOME SNOW
0–88268–034–X Station Hill pb $5.95

- Alice Walker
GOOD NIGHT, WILLIE LEE, I'LL SEE YOU IN THE MORNING; REVOLUTIONARY PETUNIAS AND OTHER POEMS & ONCE
A boxed set of Walker's three earlier collections of poetry
0–15–694102–3 HBJ pb $12.95

- Barrett Watten
PROGRESS
0–937804–16–9 Segue pb $7.50

- Michael S. Weaver
WATER SONG
0–912759–05–4 Virginia pb $5.00

- Marjorie Welish
HANDWRITTEN
0–915342–33–2 SUN pb $5.00

- Roberta Hill Whiteman
STAR QUILT
0–930100–17–4 Holy Cow pb $6.95

C.K. Williams
POEMS, 1963–1983
0–374–23516–3 FS&G $19.95

FLESH AND BLOOD
0–374–15636–0 FS&G $14.95
0–374–52090–9 FS&G pb $8.95

- Alan Williamson
THE MUSE OF DISTANCE
0–394–75577–4 Knopf pb $8.95

PRESENCE
0–394–71259–5 Knopf pb $6.95

- Baron Wormser
ATOMS AND SOUL MUSIC
0–671–16714–8 Simon & Schuster $12.95
0–671–16710–5 Simon & Schuster pb $7.95

- Charles Wright
CHINA TRACE
0–8195–1088–2 Wesleyan pb $8.95

BLOODLINES
0–8195–1077–7 Wesleyan pb $8.95

THE OTHER SIDE OF THE RIVER
0–394–72367–8 Random House pb $6.95

THE SOUTHERN CROSS
0–394–74888–3 Random House pb $5.95

- Jay Wright
SELECTED POEMS
Of his work, this southwestern poet has said: "A young man, hearing me read some of my poems, said that I seemed to be trying to weave together a lot of different things. My answer was that they are already woven, I'm just trying to uncover the weave"
Edited by R.B. Stepto
0–691–06687–6 Princeton $26.50
0–691–01435–3 Princeton pb $10.50

THE DOUBLE INVENTION OF KOMO
0–292–71526–9 Texas pb $6.95

DIMENSIONS OF HISTORY
0–87711–063–8 Story Line pb $6.50

EXPLICATIONS/INTERPRETATIONS
0–912759–01–1 Virginia pb $9.00

SOOTHSAYERS AND OMENS
0–913282–10–3 Seven Woods pb $4.25

- Al Young
THE BLUES DON'T CHANGE: New and Selected Poems
0–8071–0979–7 Louisiana pb $7.95

HEAVEN: Collected Poems 1958–1988
0–88739–069–2 Creative Arts pb $16.95

- Geoffrey Young
ROCKS AND DEALS
0–935724–27–3 Figures pb $4.00

- Peter Zabelskis
LOOP: 50 Ideas for Pictures
"The fifty pieces are remarkable condensations . . . Beguilingly short and addictive"—Herbert Blau
0–9616193–1–7 Slate pb $4.95

TO ORDER BOOKS AS GIFTS, SEE PAGE 1

ANTHOLOGIES

A poetry anthology should function as a road map: not a substitute for journeying, but a guide to the available destinations. There is at present no one book that adequately describes modern American poetry; nor is that surprising, given the diversity of its practitioners and audiences, and the gradual splintering of whatever center might once have existed. Each of the books below presents a chunk, large or small, of the overall situation.

- **Arnold Adoff, editor**
  THE POETRY OF BLACK AMERICA: Anthology of the Twentieth Century
  A broad survey covering all the most familiar figures
  Introduction by Gwendolyn Brooks
  0–06–020089–8 Harper & Row $24.95

- **Donald Allen & George F. Butterick, editors**
  THE POSTMODERNS: The New American Poetry
  An updated version of Allen's influential (and now sadly out of print) *The New American Poetry;* the new book adds some important figures, but in some ways muddies the effect of the original
  0–8021–15035–7 Grove pb $13.95

- **John Ashbery, editor**
  THE BEST AMERICAN POETRY: 1988
  An interestingly varied assortment: Nicholas Christopher, Clark Coolidge, Eileen Myles, Richard Wilbur, Robert Creeley, Leslie Scalapino, Jorie Graham, and 68 others
  Introduction by David Lehman
  0–02–044181–9 Macmillan pb $9.95

- **Arna Bontemps, editor**
  AMERICAN NEGRO POETRY
  An update of the 1963 edition
  0–374–521433–X Hill & Wang pb $7.95

- **Joseph Bruchac, editor**
  SONGS FROM THIS EARTH ON TURTLE'S BACK: An Anthology of Poetry by American Indian Writers
  0–912678–58–5 Greenfield Review pb $9.95

- **Janine Canan, editor**
  SHE RISES LIKE THE SUN: Invocations of the Goddess by Contemporary American Women Poets
  Includes work by Diane Di Prima, Joy Harjo, Maya Angelou, Denise Levertov, Anne Waldman, and others
  0–89594–352–2 Crossing pb $8.95

- **Hayden Carruth, editor**
  THE VOICE THAT IS GREAT WITHIN US
  Although dated, this remains the most reliable general anthology on the market; unfortunately, poets are represented only by brief selections, making the book more tantalizing than satisfying
  0–553–26263–7 Bantam pb $5.95

- **Nicholas Christopher, editor**
  UNDER 35: The New Generation of American Poets
  0–385–26035–0 Doubleday pb $9.95

- **Andrei Codrescu, editor**
  UP LATE: American Poetry Since 1970
  An informal assortment of some of the younger practitioners of the '70s and '80s. "This anthology does provide an earnestly comprehensive vita for the alternative poetry scene since 1970. Every tribe and its mutations are charted"—*Village Voice*
  0–941423–03–4 4 Walls 8 Windows $23.95
  0–941423–04–2 4 Walls 8 Windows pb $12.95

- **Richard Ellmann, editor**
  THE NEW OXFORD BOOK OF AMERICAN VERSE
  Gives much space to the moderns, but by sticking to the mainstream misses many aspects
  0–19–502058–8 Oxford $35.00

- **Peter Glassgold, editor & translator**
  HWAET!: A Little Old English Anthology of American Modernist Poetry
  Glassgold renders William Carlos Williams, Marianne Moore, and others into Anglo-Saxon in this enormously entertaining book
  0–940650–42–8 Sun & Moon pb $6.95

- **Donald Hall, editor**
  CONTEMPORARY AMERICAN POETRY
  An older book providing a brief but useful guide to some major tendencies of the postwar scene
  0–14–058618–0 Penguin pb $6.95

- **Daniel Halpern, editor**
  THE AMERICAN POETRY ANTHOLOGY
  0–380–00399–6 Avon pb $9.95

- **William Heyen, editor**
  THE GENERATION OF 2000: Contemporary American Poets
  0–86538–043–0 Ontario Review pb $14.95

- **James Weldon Johnson, editor**
  THE BOOK OF AMERICAN NEGRO POETRY
  First published in 1922, this volume includes critical and biographical notes by the author of *The Autobiography of an Ex-Colored Man*
  0–15–613539–6 HBJ pb $8.95

- **Woodie King, editor**
  THE FORERUNNERS: Black Poets in America
  Focuses on the middle generation between the Harlem Renaissance and the 1960s
  0–88258–015–9 Howard $8.95
  0–88258–093–0 Howard pb $6.95

- **Douglas Messerli, editor**
  LANGUAGE POETRIES: An Anthology
  "The most decisive exploration of poetry's resources and premises since the 1950s"— Robert Creeley
  0–8112–1006–5 New Directions $21.95
  0–8112–1007–3 New Directions pb $9.95

- **Duane Niatum, editor**
  HARPER'S ANTHOLOGY OF TWENTIETH CENTURY NATIVE AMERICAN POETRY
  0–06–250665–X Harper & Row $24.95
  0–06–250666–8 Harper & Row pb $15.95

- **Dudley Randall, editor**
  THE BLACK POETS
  A new anthology that spans the early folk idioms through the present
  0–553–27563–1 Bantam pb $5.95

- **Jerome Rothenberg, editor**
  SHAKING THE PUMPKIN: Traditional Poetry of the Indian North Americas
  "Workings" of Native American poetries by Rothenberg and others
  Preface by Jerome Rothenberg
  0–912383–10–0 Alfred Van der Marck pb $14.95

  TECHNICIANS OF THE SACRED: A Range of Poetries from Africa, America, Asia, Europe and Oceania
  A revised edition of the profoundly influential anthology that focused attention on ethnopoetics
  0–520–04912–8 California pb $16.95

- **Ron Silliman, editor**
  IN THE AMERICAN TREE
  A comprehensive gathering of such "language-centered" poets as Lyn Hejinian, Rae Armantrout, and Bruce Andrews; includes a selection of theoretical statements
  0–915032–34–1 National Poetry Fdn pb $18.95

- **Erlene Stetson, editor**
  BLACK SISTER: Poetry by Black American Women, 1746–1980
  The best of the classics, as well as new voices. Includes Phyllis Wheatley, Anne Spencer, Gayle Jones, Ntozake Shange, and Colleen J. McElroy
  0–253–20268–X Indiana University pb $9.95

Jerome Rothenberg (photo by Diane Rothenberg, courtesy New Directions)

- **Mark Strand, editor**
  CONTEMPORARY AMERICAN POETS
  Another collection from the vantage point
  of the '70s, although its range is narrower
  than its title would indicate
  0–451–62488–2 NAL pb $4.95

- **Helen Vendler, editor**
  **THE HARVARD BOOK OF
  CONTEMPORARY AMERICAN POETRY**
  A rather quirky selection of Vendler's
  favorite poets
  0–674–37340–5 Harvard. $20.00

20th-Century
American Drama

THE 1920s, '30s, AND '40s

- **Lillian Hellman**
  THE COLLECTED PLAYS
  Includes *The Children's Hour, Days to
  Come, The Little Foxes, Watch on the Rhine,
  The Searching Wind, Another Part of the
  Forest, Montserrat, The Autumn Garden,
  The Lark, Candide, Toys in the Attic,* and
  My Mother, My Father and Me
  0–316–35519–4 Little, Brown $25.00

  SIX PLAYS BY LILLIAN HELLMAN
  Includes *The Children's Hour, Days to
  Come, The Little Foxes, Watch on the Rhine,
  Another Part of the Forest,* and *The Autumn
  Garden*
  0–394–74112–9 Random House pb $9.95

- **Langston Hughes**
  FIVE PLAYS BY LANGSTON HUGHES
  Includes *Mulatto, Soul Gone Home, Little
  Ham, Simply Heaven,* and *Tambourines to
  Glory*
  Edited by Webster Smalley
  0–253–32230–8 Indiana $20.00
  0–253–20121–7 Indiana pb $8.95

- **George S. Kaufman & Moss Hart**
  THREE PLAYS
  Includes *Once in a Lifetime, You Can't
  Take It With You,* and *The Man Who
  Came to Dinner,* with two essays by the
  authors
  0–802–15064–0 Grove pb $10.95

- **George S. Kaufman & others**
  **GEORGE S. KAUFMAN AND HIS
  COLLABORATORS: Three Plays**
  Includes *June Moon* (written with Ring
  Lardner), *Bravo!* (inspired by Edna
  Ferber), and *The Late George Apley*
  (adapted from the John P. Marquand
  novel)
  0–933826–65–6 Farrar, Straus & Giroux $19.95
  0–933826–66–4 PAJ pb $3.98

- **Arthur Miller**
  "The suddenness of the '29 crash and the
  chaos that followed offered a pure instance
  of the impotence of individualist solutions
  to so vast a crisis. As a society we learned
  all over again that mass social organization

does not necessarily weaken moral fiber
but may set the stage for great displays of
heroism and self-sacrifice and endurance."
—Arthur Miller
  AFTER THE FALL
  A semi-autobiographical play touching on
  Miller's marriage to Marilyn Monroe
  0–14–048162–1 Penguin pb $3.95

  THE CRUCIBLE: Text and Criticism
  The Salem witch-hunt trials as a parable of
  McCarthyism
  Edited by Gerald Weales
  0–14–015507–4 Penguin pb $9.95

  DANGER: MEMORY!
  Includes *I Can't Remember Anything* and
  Clara
  0–394–56102–3 Grove $14.95
  0–394–62353–3 Grove pb $5.95

  DEATH OF A SALESMAN
  A major American play, winner of the
  Pulitzer Prize and wide international
  acclaim
  0–14–048134–6 Penguin pb $3.95

  THE PORTABLE ARTHUR MILLER
  Includes *Death of a Salesman, The Crucible,
  Incident at Vichy, The Price, The Misfits,*
  two short stories, and selections from *In
  Russia*
  Edited by Harold Clurman
  0–14–015071–4 Penguin pb $7.95

  THE PRICE
  Two brothers reunite after the death of
  their parents
  0–14–048194–X Penguin pb $3.95

  A VIEW FROM THE BRIDGE
  The clash of different "laws" concerning
  two Italian longshoremen illegally in the
  United States
  0–14048135–4 Penguin pb $3.95

Clifford Odets
SIX PLAYS OF CLIFFORD ODETS
Includes *Waiting for Lefty, Awake and
Sing, Golden Boy, Rocket to the Moon,
Till the Day I Die,* and *Paradise Lost*
Introduction by Harold Clurman
0–8021–5060–8 Grove pb $10.95

- **Eugene O'Neill**
  "To me the tragic alone has that significant
  beauty which is truth. It is the meaning of
  life—and the hope. The noblest is eternally
  the most tragic. The people who succeed
  and who do not push on to a greater
  failure are the spiritual middle classes.
  Their stopping at success is the proof of
  their compromising insignificance. How
  petty their dreams must have been."—
  Eugene O'Neill
  COMPLETE PLAYS
  The first complete edition, issued on the
  100th anniversary of O'Neill's birth

  Volume 1
  Includes *Anna Christie, Beyond the Horizon,
  The Emperor Jones,* and O'Neill's early one-
  act plays
  0–940450–48–8 Library of America $35.00

  Volume 2
  Includes *Diff'rent, The First Man, The
  Hairy Ape, The Fountain, Welded, All God's
  Chillun Got Wings, Desire Under the Elms,
  Marco Millions, The Great God Brown,*

*Eugene O'Neill (photo copyright Nickolas
Muray)*

*Lazarus Laughed, Strange Interlude,
Dynamo,* and *Mourning Becomes Electra*
0–940450–49–6 Library of America $35.00

Volume 3
Includes *Ah, Wilderness!, Days Without
End, A Touch of the Poet, More Stately
Mansions, The Iceman Cometh, Long Day's
Journey Into Night, Hughie, A Moon for the
Misbegotten,* and the short story *Tomorrow*
0–940450–50–X Library of America $35.00

NINE PLAYS OF EUGENE O'NEILL
Includes *The Emperor Jones, The Hairy Ape,
Desire Under the Elms, Marco Millions, The
Great God Brown, All God's Chillun Got
Wings, Lazarus Laughed, Strange Interlude,*
and *Mourning Becomes Electra*
0–394–60416–4 Random House $13.95

THE LATER PLAYS
"The view of America projected by
O'Neill's last historical plays is not
redeemed by any saving possibilities. The
dramas form a bitter, uncompromising
indictment of the failure of vision in a land
of hope"—Travis Bogard. Includes *Ah,
Wilderness!, A Touch of the Poet, Hughie,*
and *A Moon for the Misbegotten*
Edited by Travis Bogard
0–394–30991–X Random House pb $5.95

SEVEN PLAYS OF THE SEA
This volume of one-acts includes *The Long
Voyage Home, Moon of the Caribbees, Bound
East for Cardiff, In the Zone, The Rope, Ile,*
and *Where the Cross Is Made*
0–394–71856–9 Random House pb $5.95

**SIX SHORT PLAYS OF EUGENE
O'NEILL**
Includes *The Dreamy Kid, Before Breakfast,
Diff'rent, Welded, Straw,* and *Gold*
0–394–70276–X Random House pb $4.95

THREE PLAYS OF EUGENE O'NEILL
Includes *Desire Under the Elms, Strange
Interlude,* and *Mourning Becomes Electra*
0–394–70165–8 Random House pb $5.95

☞ **TO ORDER NEW BOOKS NOT YET LISTED, ASK YOUR BOOKSELLER OR CALL 1-800-882-8770**

THE UNFINISHED PLAYS: Notes For The Visit
Includes three never-completed plays: *The Visit of Malatesta, The Last Conquest,* and *Blind Alley Guy*
Introduction by Virginia Floyd
0-8044-2674-0 Harper & Row $24.95

THE EMPEROR JONES, ANNA CHRISTIE, THE HAIRY APE
"In each play the central character is one of the insulted and injured: one a Negro, another a stoker, the third a prostitute. But whereas for most of us the plight of such people immediately evokes the social forces that have insulted and injured them, for O'Neill the social insult and injury are not so much facts in themselves as symbols of man's cosmic situation"—Lionel Trilling
0-394-71855-0 Random House pb $4.95

HUGHIE
The only script that remains from a series of eight one-act monologue plays that O'Neill wrote between 1940 and 1941
0-300-02881-4 Yale pb $5.95

THE ICEMAN COMETH
A group of down-and-outers in a bar are forced to confront their flight from reality
0-394-70018-X Random House pb $5.95

LONG DAY'S JOURNEY INTO NIGHT
O'Neill's final, autobiographical masterpiece
0-300-00176-2 Yale pb $5.95

A MOON FOR THE MISBEGOTTEN
0-394-71236-6 Random House pb $2.95

MORE STATELY MANSIONS
This play tracing a family from colonial times to the present is one of an unfinished nine-play cycle called *A Tale of Possessors Self-Dispossessed*
Edited by Donald Gallup
0-300-00177-0 Yale pb $9.95

- **Elmer Rice**
THREE PLAYS
Rice's "impressionistic dramas" were deeply influential in their use of new techniques such as the flashback. Includes *The Adding Machine, Street Scene,* and *Dream Girl*
0-8090-0735-5 Farrar, Straus & Giroux pb $6.95

- **John Van Druten**
I REMEMBER MAMA
A popular play of the 1940s, adapted from Kathryn Forbes's book *Mama's Bank Account*
0-15-176661-4 HBJ $10.95

- **Thornton Wilder**
"I am not an innovator but a rediscoverer of forgotten goods and I hope a remover of obtrusive bric-a-brac. And as I look at the work of my contemporaries I seem to feel that I am an exception in one thing—I give (don't I) the impression of having enormously enjoyed it."—Thornton Wilder
OUR TOWN
When it opened on Broadway in 1938, *Our Town* met with mixed response. Over the next decades this play about "belonging" was to become the most popular American dramatic work of the century
0-06-080779-2 Harper & Row pb $4.95

THREE PLAYS
"The theater has lagged behind the other arts in finding the 'new ways' to express how men and women think and feel in our time. I am not one of the new dramatists we are looking for. I wish I were. I hope I have played a part in preparing the way for them." Includes *Our Town, The Skin of Our Teeth,* and *The Matchmaker*
0-06-091293-6 Harper & Row pb $9.95

- **Tennessee Williams**
"All my life I have been haunted by the obsession that to desire a thing or to love a thing intensely is to place yourself in a vulnerable position, to be a possible, if not a probable, loser of what you most want."—Tennessee Williams
THE THEATRE OF TENNESSEE WILLIAMS

Volume 1
Includes *Battle of Angels, A Streetcar Named Desire,* and *The Glass Menagerie*
0-8112-0417-0 New Directions $21.95

Volume 2
Includes *The Eccentricities of a Nightingale, Summer and Smoke, The Rose Tattoo,* and *Camino Real*
0-8112-0418-9 New Directions $19.95

Volume 3
Includes *Cat on a Hot Tin Roof, Orpheus Descending,* and *Suddenly, Last Summer*
0-8112-0419-7 New Directions $21.95

Volume 4
Includes *Sweet Bird of Youth, Period of Adjustment,* and *Night of the Iguana*
0-8112-0422-7 New Directions $19.95

Volume 5
Includes *The Milk Train Doesn't Stop Here Anymore, Kingdom of the Earth, Small Craft Warnings,* and *The Two-Character Play*
0-8112-0593-2 New Directions $18.00

Volume 6
Includes *Twenty-Seven Wagons Full of Cotton* and other short plays
0-8112-0794-3 New Directions $19.95

Volume 7
Includes *In the Bar of a Tokyo Hotel* and other plays
0-8112-0795-1 New Directions $19.95

DRAGON COUNTRY: Eight Plays
"Dragon Country, the country of pain, is an uninhabitable country which is inhabited"—Tennessee Williams. Includes *In the Bar of a Tokyo Hotel, Mutilated, Gnädiges Fräulein, I Rise in Flames, Cried the Phoenix, I Can't Imagine Tomorrow, Confessional, Frosted Glass Coffin,* and *A Perfect Analysis Given by a Parrot*
0-8112-0219-4 New Directions pb $7.95

FOUR PLAYS
Includes *Summer and Smoke, Orpheus Descending, Suddenly, Last Summer,* and *Period of Adjustment*
0-451-52015-7 NAL pb $4.95

THREE BY TENNESSEE WILLIAMS
Includes *Sweet Bird of Youth, The Rose Tattoo,* and *Night of the Iguana*
0-451-52149-8 NAL pb $4.95

CAMINO REAL
0-8112-0218-6 New Directions pb $6.95

CAT ON A HOT TIN ROOF
0-451-15869-5 NAL pb $3.95

CLOTHES FOR A SUMMER HOTEL
A "ghost play" in which Scott and Zelda Fitzgerald inhabit one psyche
0-8112-0871-0 New Directions pb $4.95

THE GLASS MENAGERIE
His first major success, a powerful semi-autobiographical play that explores the fragility of private dreamworlds
0-8112-0220-8 New Directions pb $3.95

A LOVELY SUNDAY FOR CREVE COEUR
0-8112-0757-9 New Directions pb $5.95

THE RED DEVIL BATTERY SIGN
A surreal Dallas is the setting for this late hallucinatory play
0-8112-1047-2 New Directions pb $6.95

SMALL CRAFT WARNINGS
"Mark Place," a bar on the California coast, and the people who gather there
0-8112-0461-8 New Directions pb $5.95

A STREETCAR NAMED DESIRE
Williams' most famous play has become part of American mythology
0-8112-0765-X New Directions pb $4.95

SWEET BIRD OF YOUTH
A faded movie star and her gigolo, a once-promising young man who pays the price for abandoning his home-town sweetheart
0-8112-0596-7 New Directions pb $5.95

TWENTY-SEVEN WAGONS FULL OF COTTON
Fourteen one-act plays
0-8112-0225-9 New Directions pb $6.95

THE TWO-CHARACTER PLAY
Reality and illusion mix when two actors—a brother and a sister—are abandoned by their troupe in an unidentifiable location
0-8112-0729-3 New Directions pb $5.95

VIEUX CARRE
An examination of various inhabitants of a rooming house, through a series of shifting memory scenes
0-8112-0728-5 New Directions pb $5.95

Tennessee Williams (photo by Bruce Paulson, courtesy of New Directions)

THE 1950s AND '60s

• **Edward Albee**
Albee began his career with brilliant absurdist one-act plays and made his Broadway debut with *Who's Afraid of Virginia Woolf?*, a dissection of marital relationships that stands as a major American play. Calling himself a "demonic social critic," Albee has stated that "the role of the writer is to be, axiomatically, against any society he happens to be living in."

THE AMERICAN DREAM & THE ZOO STORY
In *The Zoo Story*, Albee's first play, a disaffected young man contrives to have himself killed by a stranger in Central Park. In *The American Dream*, conformist parents destroy their son because he fails to live up to their expectations
0–451–15380–4 NAL pb $3.95

COUNTING THE WAYS & LISTENING
A vaudeville sketch and a radio play adapted to the stage
0–689–10785–4 Macmillan pb $7.95

THE MAN WHO HAD THREE ARMS
0–689–11451–6 Macmillan $12.95

THE SANDBOX & THE DEATH OF BESSIE SMITH
Two short plays commissioned for the Festival of Two Worlds in Italy
0–452–26083–3 NAL pb $6.95

THE PLAYS

Volume 2
Includes *Tiny Alice, A Delicate Balance, Box*, and *Quotations from Chairman Mao Tse-tung*
0–689–70614–6 Atheneum pb $12.95

Volume 3
Includes *Seascape, Counting the Ways, Listening*, and *All Over*
0–689–70615–4 Macmillan pb $9.95

Volume 4
Includes *Everything in the Garden* (from the play by Giles Cooper), *Malcolm* (from the novel by James Purdy), and *The Ballad of the Sad Cafe* (from the novella by Carson McCullers)
0–689–70616–2 Macmillan $10.95

WHO'S AFRAID OF VIRGINIA WOOLF?
0–451–14079–6 NAL pb $3.95

• **Woody Allen**
THE FLOATING LIGHT BULB
0–394–52415–2 Random House $10.50

PLAY IT AGAIN, SAM
0–394–40663–X Random House $10.00

• **James Baldwin**
BLUES FOR MISTER CHARLIE
A play based on the Emmett Till case
0–440–30637–X Dell pb $4.95

• **Amiri Baraka**
Baraka, formerly known as LeRoi Jones, was an important voice in the 1960s, with his incendiary work calling for radical social change.
DUTCHMAN & THE SLAVE
Dutchman, a parable of murderous white rule, is about a black man on a subway and the white woman who provokes and finally kills him
0–688–21084–8 Morrow pb $5.95

THE SIDNEY POET HEROICAL
A play in 29 scenes
0–918408–12–1 Reed & Cannon pb $5.95

• **Jules Feiffer**
LITTLE MURDERS
0–14–048118–4 Penguin pb $4.95

• **Maria Irene Fornes**
PLAYS
Includes *Mud, The Danube, Sarita*, and *The Conduct of Life*
0–933826–83–4 Farrar, Straus & Giroux pb $8.95

PROMENADE & OTHER PLAYS
Includes *The Successful Life of Three, Tango Palace, Dr. Kheal, A Vietnamese Wedding*, and *Promenade*
1–55554–014–7 Farrar, Straus & Giroux pb $8.95

• **Bruce J. Friedman**
A MOTHER'S KISSES
Introduction by Stanley Kauffman
0–917657–39–X Donald Fine pb $8.95

• **Jack Gelber**
THE CONNECTION
Junkies wait for their connection, in a play first performed with live jazz accompaniment in 1959
0–394–17222–1 Grove pb $3.95

• **William Gibson**
THE MIRACLE WORKER
The story of Helen Keller and her teacher, Annie Sullivan
0–553–24778–6 Bantam pb $2.95

• **Lorraine Hansberry**
A RAISIN IN THE SUN & THE SIGN IN SIDNEY BRUSTEIN'S WINDOW
Foreword by Robert Nemiroff
0–452–25942–8 NAL pb $8.95

A RAISIN IN THE SUN
This drama of a black family moving into a white neighborhood brought Hansberry overnight fame and success. "Never before in the history of the American Theater had so much of the truth of Black people's lives been seen on the stage"—James Baldwin
0–451–15540–8 NAL pb $3.50

THE COLLECTED LAST PLAYS
Edited by Robert Nemiroff
0–452–25414–0 NAL $8.95

William Inge
FOUR PLAYS
A popular midwestern playwright of the 1950s, Inge wrote psychological dramas about average people coping with the stresses of life. Includes *Bus Stop, Come Back, Little Sheba, The Dark at the Top of the Stairs*, and *Picnic*
0–394–17075–X Grove pb $9.95

• **Arthur Kopit**
"Like the absurdists before him, he chooses to depict a horrific world where logic holds no sway."—Gautam Dasgupta

THE DAY THE WHORES CAME OUT TO PLAY TENNIS & OTHER PLAYS
Includes *Chamber Music, The Questioning of Nick, Sing to Me Through Open Windows, The Hero*, and *The Conquest of Everest*
0–8090–0736–3 Hill & Wang pb $5.95

THE END OF THE WORLD: With a Symposium to Follow
"This play is the most accessible synthesis we've had of Nukespeak, and Kopit at the end has the courage to express his own view of the evil that may break through the circles of logic to unleash a nuclear apocalypse"—Jack Kroll, *Newsweek*
0–8090–1247–2 Hill & Wang pb $6.95

INDIANS
Buffalo Bill in the morally tenuous position between the American Indians and the US government
0–8090–1218–9 Hill & Wang pb $5.95

OH DAD, POOR DAD, MAMMA'S HUNG YOU IN THE CLOSET AND I'M FEELIN' SO SAD
His first play, an absurdist parody about an overprotective mother
0–8090–1202–2 Hill & Wang pb $7.95

WINGS
An aviatrix battles her way back from a stroke
0–8090–1239–1 Hill & Wang pb $8.95

• **Jerome Lawrence & Robert E. Lee**
INHERIT THE WIND
The Scopes "monkey trial" of 1925
0–553–26915–1 Bantam pb $2.95

THE NIGHT THOREAU SPENT IN JAIL
A portrait of Thoreau as conscientious objector
0–553–23417–X Bantam pb $2.95

• **Carson McCullers**
THE MEMBER OF THE WEDDING
The loneliness of a dreamy, oversensitive Georgia girl
0–8112–0093–0 Norton pb $5.95

• **Neil Simon**
One of America's most popular playwrights, Simon has weathered both commercial success and critical disdain. Of his own work, Simon has written: "When I was good, I was very, very good . . . and when I was bad, we folded."

THE COLLECTED PLAYS OF NEIL SIMON

Volume 1
Includes *Come Blow Your Horn, Barefoot in the Park, The Odd Couple, Plaza Suite, The Star-Spangled Girl, Promises, Promises*, and *The Last of the Red Hot Lovers*
0–452–25870–7 NAL pb $12.95

Volume 2
Includes *Little Me, The Gingerbread Lady, The Prisoner of Second Avenue, The Sunshine Boys, The Good Doctor, God's Favorite, California Suite*, and *Chapter Two*
0–394–50770–3 Random House $29.95
0–452–25871–5 NAL pb $12.95

➤ **FOR OVERSEAS ORDERING INFORMATION, SEE PAGE 1**

BRIGHTON BEACH MEMOIRS
Eugene as a teenager, the first of Simon's autobiographical trilogy
0–394–53739–4 Random House $11.95
0–451–14765–0 NAL pb $3.95

BILOXI BLUES
In basic training in 1943, Eugene vows to become a writer, to lose his virginity, and to stay alive
0–394–55139–7 Random House $11.95
0–452–25939–8 NAL pb $5.95

BROADWAY BOUND
The conclusion of the trilogy: two brothers form a comedy team and watch their family and home life disintegrate
0–394–56395–6 Random House $11.95

CHAPTER TWO
0–394–50293–0 Random House $11.95

I OUGHT TO BE IN PICTURES
0–394–51774–1 Random House $9.95

THE ODD COUPLE
0–394–40649–4 Random House $10.95

PLAZA SUITE
0–394–40667–2 Random House $9.95

THE PRISONER OF SECOND AVENUE
0–394–48259–X Random House $9.95

THEY'RE PLAYING OUR SONG
0–394–51069–0 Random House $9.95

● **Megan Terry**
HIGH ENERGY MUSICALS FROM THE OMAHA MAGIC THEATRE
0–88145–013–8 Broadway Play pb $4.00

MOLLIE BAILEY'S TRAVELING FAMILY CIRCUS FEATURING SCENES FROM THE LIFE OF MOTHER JONES
0–88145–010–3 Broadway Play pb $4.00

● **Megan Terry & Rochelle L. Holt**
TWO BY TERRY PLUS ONE: An Anthology of Plays by Women
Includes *Pro Game* and *The Pioneer* by Terry Megan and Rochelle L. Holt's *Walking Into the Dawn: A Celebration*
0–88680–218–0 I.E. Clark pb $3.95

THE 1970s AND '80s

● **Iván Acosta**
EL SUPER
A Cuban family living in exile in New York
0–89729–271–5 Ediciones Universal pb $6.00

● **Frank Chin**
THE CHICKENCOOP CHINAMAN & THE YEAR OF THE DRAGON: Two Plays
0–295–95833–2 Washington pb $9.95

● **Christopher Durang**
LAUGHING WILD & BABY WITH THE BATHWATER
0–8021–3130–1 Grove pb $7.95

THE MARRIAGE OF BETTE AND BOO
0–394–56071–X Grove $16.95
0–394–62347–9 Grove pb $7.95

● **Harvey Fierstein**
SAFE SEX
0–689–11953–4 Atheneum $15.95

TORCH SONG TRILOGY
0–394–53428–X Random House $12.95
0–451–15130–5 NAL pb $3.95

● **Horton Foote**
COURTSHIP, VALENTINE'S DAY, 1918: Three Plays from The Orphans' Home Cycle
Introduction by Reynolds Price
0–394–62344–4 Grove pb $8.95

ROOTS IN A PARCHED GROUND, CONVICTS, LILLY DALE, THE WIDOW CLAIRE: Four Plays from The Orphans' Home Cycle
0–8021–3081–X Grove pb $10.95

● **Richard Foreman**
REVERBERATION MACHINES: The Later Plays and Essays
0–88268–000–5 Station Hill pb $10.95

● **Charles Fuller**
A SOLDIER'S PLAY
0–374–52148–4 Farrar, Straus & Giroux pb $6.95

● **Herb Gardner**
I'M NOT RAPPAPORT
0–8021–3044–5 Grove pb $7.95

A THOUSAND CLOWNS
0–14–048202–4 Penguin pb $5.95

● **John Guare**
THE HOUSE OF BLUE LEAVES & TWO OTHER PLAYS
0–452–25940–1 NAL pb $7.95

● **A.R. Gurney**
FOUR PLAYS
Includes *Scenes from an American Life, Children, The Middle Ages,* and *The Dining Room*
0–380–89498–X Avon pb $4.95

● **William Hoffman**
AS IS
0–394–74286–9 Random House pb $3.95

● **David Henry Hwang**
M. BUTTERFLY
0–452–26230–5 NAL pb $7.95

● **Albert Innaurato**
BEST PLAYS OF ALBERT INNAURATO
Includes *Coming of Age in Soho, Gemini,* and *The Transformation of Benno Blimpie*
0–914017–14–4 Gay Presses pb $7.95

● **Len Jenkin**
DARK RIDE & OTHER PLAYS
Includes an adaptation of Kafka's *A Country Doctor, My Uncle Sam, American Notes,* and *Limbo Tales.* "If *American Notes* were a painting, it might resemble Edward Hopper's Mobil station done over a canvas of melting wax"—*NY Times*
Preface by Joseph Papp
1–55713–073–6 Sun & Moon pb $12.95

● **Larry Kramer**
THE NORMAL HEART
The first play to dramatize the AIDS crisis
0–452–25798–0 NAL pb $6.95

● **David Mamet**
"Mamet deserves recognition for his careful, gorgeous, loving sense of language.

He has the most acute ear for dialogue of any American writer since J.D. Salinger."—*Village Voice*

AMERICAN BUFFALO
0–8021–5057–8 Grove pb $6.95

EDMOND
0–394–62445–9 Grove pb $6.95

GLENGARRY GLENN ROSS
0–8021–3091–7 Grove pb $7.95

GOLDBERG STREET: Short Plays and Monologues
0–394–62006–2 Grove pb $7.95

LAKEBOAT
0–394–17925–0 Grove pb $4.95

A LIFE IN THE THEATRE
0–8021–5067–5 Grove pb $9.95

REUNION & DARK PONY: Two Plays
0–394–17459–3 Grove pb $8.95

SEXUAL PERVERSITY IN CHICAGO & THE DUCK VARIATIONS
0–8021–5011–X Grove pb $7.95

THE SHAWL & PRAIRIE DU CHIEN: Two Plays
0–394–62089–5 Grove pb $6.95

SPEED-THE-PLOW
0–8021–3046–1 Grove pb $6.95

THREE CHILDREN'S PLAYS
Includes *The Poet and the Rent, The Frog Prince,* and *The Revenge of the Space Pandas or Binky Rudich and the Two-Speed Clock*
0–394–55302–0 Grove $18.95
0–394–62167–0 Grove pb $8.95

THREE PLAYS
Includes *The Woods, Lakeboat,* and *Edmond*
0–394–62362–2 Grove pb $9.95

● **Mark Medoff**
CHILDREN OF A LESSER GOD
0–87905–272–4 Gibbs Smith pb $5.95

● **Carlos Morton**
THE MANY DEATHS OF DANNY ROSALES & OTHER PLAYS
Includes *El Jardín, Los Dorados,* and *Rancho Hollywood*
0–934770–16–6 Arte Público pb $10.00

● **Marsha Norman**
FOUR PLAYS
Includes *Getting Out, Third and Oak, The Holdup,* and *Traveller in the Dark*
0–930452–84–4 Theatre Comm $10.95

'NIGHT, MOTHER
0–8090–1246–4 Hill & Wang pb $6.95

● **Robert Patrick**
MERCY DROP & OTHER PLAYS
0–930762–03–7 Calamus pb $5.00

● **Miguel Piñero**
OUTRAGEOUS ONE-ACT PLAYS
0–934770–68–9 Arte Público pb $8.50

SHORT EYES
"An authentic, powerful theatrical piece that tells you more about the anti-universe of prison life than any play outside the work of Jean Genet"—*Newsweek*
0–8090–1232–4 Hill & Wang pb $7.00

⇨ **TO ORDER ANY BOOK IN THIS CATALOG, ASK YOUR BOOKSELLER OR CALL 1-800-882-8770**

Production still of "I was Sitting on My Patio" by Robert Wilson, from American Alternative Theater *by Theodore Shank (St. Martin's)*

THE SUN ALWAYS SHINES FOR THE COOL, MIDNIGHT MOON AT THE GREASY SPOON & EULOGY FOR A SMALL TIME THIEF
0–934770–25–5 Arte Público pb $10.00

● David Rabe
THE BASIC TRAINING OF PAVLO HUMMEL
0–14–048137–0 Penguin pb $6.95

GOOSE & TOM-TOM
0–394–62351–7 Grove pb $7.95

HURLYBURLY
0–394–62011–9 Grove pb $5.95

IN THE BOOM BOOM ROOM
0–394–62205–7 Grove pb $8.95

STREAMERS
0–394–73314–2 Knopf $10.95

Ntozake Shange
FOR COLORED GIRLS WHO HAVE CONSIDERED SUICIDE/WHEN THE RAINBOW IS ENUF
This "choreopoem"—the most talked-about black play of the 1970s—was a radical departure from the standard depiction of black women as either tragic heroines or forebearing mothers.
0–02–024891–1 Macmillan pb $5.95
0–553–26212–2 Bantam pb $3.50

THREE PLAYS
Includes *Spell #7, A Photograph: Lovers in Motion,* and *Boogie Woogie Landscapes*
0–14–0481702 Penguin pb $5.95

● Wallace Shawn
AUNT DAN AND LEMON
0–394–54946–5 Grove $15.95
0–394–62077–1 Grove pb $6.95

MARIE AND BRUCE
0–8021–3018–6 Grove pb $5.95

● Sam Shepard
"It's a real thing, double nature. I think we're split in a much more devastating way than psychology can ever reveal."—Sam Shepard
CHICAGO & OTHER PLAYS
0–317–65849–2 Applause $19.95
0–317–65850–6 Applause pb $9.95

FOOL FOR LOVE & THE SAD LAMENT OF PECOS BILL ON THE EVE OF KILLING HIS WIFE
0–87286–150–3 City Lights pb $5.95

FOOL FOR LOVE & OTHER PLAYS
Also includes *Angel City, Geography of a Horse Dreamer, Action, Cowboy Mouth, Melodrama Play, Seduced,* and *Suicide in B Flat*
0–553–34590–7 Bantam pb $8.95

A LIE OF THE MIND
0–453–00530–6 NAL $14.95
0–452–25869–3 NAL pb $6.95

SEVEN PLAYS
Includes *Buried Child, Curse of the Starving Class, The Tooth of Crime, La Turista, Tongues, Savage Love,* and *True West*
0–553–34611–3 Bantam pb $8.95

THE UNSEEN HAND & OTHER PLAYS
Includes *Chicago, Icarus's Mother, Red Cross, Fourteen Hundred Thousand, Melodrama Play*
0–87910–205–5 Applause pb $9.95

● Michael Weller
FIVE PLAYS
Includes *Loose Ends, Moonchildren, Fishing, At Home (Split, Part 1)* and *Abroad (Split, Part 2)*
0–452–26120–1 NAL pb $9.95

GHOST OF FIRE
0–8021–3010–0 Grove pb $7.95

● August Wilson
FENCES
0–452–25842–1 NAL pb $6.95

JOE TURNER'S COME AND GONE
0–452–26009–4 NAL pb $6.95

MA RAINEY'S BLACK BOTTOM
0–452–26113–9 NAL pb $7.95

● Lanford Wilson
"From his earliest plays to his latest, Lanford Wilson has been firmly committed to the free expression of the individual spirit, no matter how nonconformist or even prodigal that spirit may seem to be."—Mel Gussow
BURN THIS
0–8090–1253–7 Hill & Wang pb $8.95

THE FIFTH OF JULY
0–8090–1240–5 Hill & Wang pb $6.95

THE HOT L BALTIMORE
0–8090–1230–8 Hill & Wang pb $5.95

THE MOUND BUILDERS
0–8090–1235–9 Hill & Wang pb $7.95

THE RIMERS OF ELDRITCH & OTHER PLAYS
Includes *The Rimers of Eldritch, This is the Rill Days Speaking, Wandering, Ahead,* and *The Madness of Lady Bright*
0–8090–1214–6 Hill & Wang pb $6.95

SERENADING LOUIE
0–8090–1249–9 Hill & Wang pb $6.95

TALLEY AND SON
0–8090–1251–9 Hill & Wang pb $7.95

TALLEY'S FOLLY
0–8090–1242–1 Hill & Wang pb $5.95

● George C. Wolfe
THE COLORED MUSEUM
"A bold new voice that is bound to shake up blacks and whites with separate-but-equal impartiality. True satire, fiercely funny"—Jack Kroll, *Newsweek*
0–8021–3048–8 Grove pb $7.95

● Paul Zindel
THE EFFECT OF GAMMA RAYS ON MAN-IN-THE-MOON MARIGOLDS
0–553–28028–7 Bantam pb $3.50

PERFORMANCE ART

● Eric Bogosian
DRINKING IN AMERICA
0–394–75067–5 Random House pb $5.95

● Spalding Gray
SEX AND DEATH TO AGE 14
0–394–74257–5 Random House pb $6.95

SWIMMING TO CAMBODIA
0–930452–50–X Theatre Communications pb $7.95

● Jane Wagner
THE SEARCH FOR SIGNS OF INTELLIGENT LIFE IN THE UNIVERSE
The script of the Broadway show starring Lily Tomlin
Afterword by Marilyn French
0–06–015673–2 Harper & Row $15.95
0–06–091449–1 Harper & Row pb $7.95

THE MUSICAL THEATER

• Leonard Bernstein, Stephen Sondheim & Arthur Laurents
WEST SIDE STORY
0–394–40788–1 Random House $13.95

• Oscar Hammerstein
LYRICS BY OSCAR HAMMERSTEIN II
Edited Stephen Sondheim
0–88188–379–4 Hal Leonard $14.95

SONGS OF OSCAR HAMMERSTEIN II
0–02–871020–7 Schirmer $16.95
0–02–871010–X Macmillan pb $9.95

THE SOUND OF MUSIC
0–394–40724–5 Random House $12.95

• Lorenz Hart
THE COMPLETE LYRICS OF LORENZ HART
Edited by Dorothy Hart & Robert Kimball
0–394–54680–6 Knopf $40.00

• Alan Jay Lerner
A HYMN TO HIM: The Lyrics of Alan Jay Lerner
Edited by Benny Green
Illustrated by Al Hirschfeld
0–87910–109–1 Limelight $20.00

• Alan Jay Lerner & Frederick Loewe
CAMELOT
0–394–40521–8 Random House $10.95

• Cole Porter
THE COMPLETE LYRICS OF COLE PORTER
Edited by Robert Kimball
Foreword by John Updike
0–394–53214–7 Random House $30.00

• George Bernard Shaw, Alan Jay Lerner & Frederick Loewe
PYGMALION & MY FAIR LADY
0–451–51926–4 NAL pb $2.95

• Stephen Sondheim, Burt Shevelove & Larry Gelbart
A FUNNY THING HAPPENED ON THE WAY TO THE FORUM & THE FROGS
0–396–08599–7 Dodd, Mead pb $10.95

• Stephen Sondheim & James Lapine
SUNDAY IN THE PARK WITH GEORGE
0–396–08600–4 Dodd, Mead $16.95

• Stephen Sondheim, Hugh Wheeler & Christopher Bond
SWEENEY TODD: The Demon Barber of Fleet Street
0–396–07776–5 Dodd, Mead $12.95
0–396–08598–9 Dodd, Mead pb $6.95

ANTHOLOGIES

Kenneth MacGowan, editor
FAMOUS AMERICAN PLAYS OF THE 1920s
Includes Eugene O'Neill's *Moon of the Caribbees, What Price Glory* by Maxwell Anderson and Lawrence Stallings,

Sidney Howard's *They Knew What They Wanted, Porgy* by Du Bose and Dorothy Heyward, Elmer Rice's *Street Scene,* and Philip Barry's *Holiday*
0–440–32466–1 Dell pb $6.95

Harold Clurman, editor
FAMOUS AMERICAN PLAYS OF THE 1930s
Includes Clifford Odets' *Awake and Sing,* S.N. Behrman's *End of Summer,* Robert F. Sherwood's *Idiot's Delight,* John Steinbeck's *Of Mice and Men,* and William Saroyan's *The Time of Your Life*
0–440–32478–5 Dell pb $6.95

Henry Hewes, editor
FAMOUS AMERICAN PLAYS OF THE 1940s
Includes Thornton Wilder's *The Skin of Our Teeth, All My Sons* by Arthur Miller, Carson McCullers' *The Member of the Wedding,* Maxwell Anderson's *Lost in the Stars,* and *Home of the Brave* by Arthur Laurents
0–440–32490–4 Dell pb $6.95

Lee Strasberg, editor
FAMOUS AMERICAN PLAYS OF THE 1950s
Includes Tennessee Williams' *Camino Real,* Lillian Hellman's *Autumn Garden,* Robert Anderson's *Tea and Sympathy,* Edward Albee's *The Zoo Story,* and Michael Gazzo's *A Hatful of Rain*
0–440–32491–2 Dell pb $6.95

Harold Clurman, editor
FAMOUS AMERICAN PLAYS OF THE 1960s
Includes Robert Lowell's *Benito Cereno,* William Alfred's *Hogan's Goat,* Joseph Heller's *We Bombed in New Haven,* Israel Horowitz's *The Indian Wants the Bronx,* and Mark Crowley's *The Boys in the Band*
0–440–32609–5 Dell pb $6.95

Ted Hoffman, editor
FAMOUS AMERICAN PLAYS OF THE 1970s
Includes David Rabe's *The Basic Training of Pavlo Hummel,* Michael Weller's *Moonchildren,* Ed Bullins' *The Taking of Miss Janie,* Bernard Slade's *Same Time Next Year,* and Sam Shepard's *Buried Child*
0–440–32537–4 Dell pb $6.95

Robert Marx, editor
FAMOUS AMERICAN PLAYS OF THE 1980s
Includes August Wilson's *Fences,* Sam Shepard's *Fool for Love,* James Lapine and Steven Sondheim's *Sunday in the Park with George,* Wallace Shawn's *Aunt Dan and Lemon,* and Jules Feiffer's *Grownups*
0–440–20150–0 Dell pb $6.95

• Bennett Cerf, editor
FOUR CONTEMPORARY AMERICAN PLAYS
Includes Paddy Chayevsky's *The Tenth Man,* Lorraine Hansberry's *A Raisin in the*

Sun, Lillian Hellman's *Toys in the Attic,* and Saul Levitt's *Andersonville Trail*
0–394–70203–4 Random House pb $4.95

• Allan G. Halline, editor
SIX MODERN AMERICAN PLAYS
Includes Eugene O'Neill's *The Emperor Jones,* Maxwell Anderson's *Winterset,* George S. Kaufman and Moss Hart's *The Man Who Came to Dinner,* Lillian Hellman's *Little Foxes,* and *Mister Roberts* by Joshua Logan and Thomas Heggen
0–394–30985–5 Random House pb $7.95

• Paul Carter Harrison, editor
TOTEM VOICES: Eight Plays from the Black World Repertory
Includes Charles Fuller's *Zooman and the Sign,* Ntozake Shange's *For Colored Girls Who Have Considered Suicide When the Rainbow is Enuf,* Derek Walcott's *Ti Jean and His Brothers,* and Wole Soyinka's *The Strange Breed*
0–8021–3126–3 Grove pb $15.95

• Woodie King & Ron Milner, editors
BLACK DRAMA ANTHOLOGY
Includes *Junebug Graduates Tonight* by Archie Shepp, Lonnie Elder's *Charades on East Fourth Street,* Elaine Jackson's *Toe Jam,* and *The Corner* by Ed Bullins, as well as selections by Amiri Baraka and others
0–42–00902–2 NAL pb $6.95

• James Leverett, editor
NEW PLAYS USA
Includes, among other plays, Jon Robin Baitz's *The Film Society* and George C. Wolfe's *The Colored Museum*
0–930452–80–1 Theatre Comm $24.95
0–930452–81–X Theatre Comm pb $12.95

• Bonnie Marranca, editor
THE THEATRE OF IMAGES
Includes Robert Wilson's *A Letter for Queen Victoria* and Lee Breuer's *The Red Horse Animation*
0–910482–89–6 Drama Book pb $10.00

• Bonnie Marranca & Gantum Dasgupta, editors
THEATRE OF THE RIDICULOUS
Includes Kenneth Bernard's *The Magic Show of Dr. Ma-gico* and Charles Ludlam's *Stage Blood.* "What is the Ridiculous? . . . An anarchic undermining of political, sexual, psychological and cultural categories, frequently in dramatic structures that parody classical literary forms or re-function American popular entertainments"—Bonnie Marranca
0–933826–02–8 PAJ $12.95

• Joseph E. Mersand, editor
THREE COMEDIES OF AMERICAN FAMILY LIFE
Includes Lindsay Howard and Russell Crouse's *Life with Father,* John Van Druten's *I Remember Mama,* and *You Can't Take It With You* by George S. Kaufman and Moss Hart
0–671–66430–1 Pocket Books pb $4.50

• M. Elizabeth Osborn, editor

COMING TO TERMS: American Plays and the Vietnam War
Includes Emily Mann's *Still Life* and Amlin Gray's *How I Got That Story*. "The most accurate, most profound memory of Vietnam lies in the arts . . . The playwright becomes more important than the historian"—James Reston, Jr.
Introduction by James Reston, Jr.
0–930452–44–5 Theatre Comm pb $12.95

ON NEW GROUND: Contemporary Hispanic-American Plays
Playwrights represented include María Irene Fornes, José Rivera, Lynne Alvarez, Milcha Sanchez-Scott, John Jesurun, and Eduardo Machado
0–930452–682–1 Theatre Comm pb $13.00

• Performance Arts Journal

WORDPLAYS: New American Drama

Volume 1
Includes Maria Irene Fornes's *Fefu and Her Friends*, Ronald Tavel's *Boy on the Straight-Back Chair*, Jean-Claude van Itallie's *Naropa*, William Hauptman's *Domino Courts*, Richard Nelson's *Vienna Notes*, and John Wellman's *Starluster*
0–933826–11–7 PAJ pb $7.95

Volume 2
Includes Rochelle Owens' *Chucky's Hunch*, Wallace Shawn's *A Thought in Three Parts*, Harry Kondoleon's *The Brides*, John O'Keefe's *All Night Long*, and Len Jenkin's *Dark Ride*
0–933826–43–5 PAJ pb $6.95

Volume 3
Includes Lee Breuer's *Haji*, Adrienne Kennedy's *A Movie Star Has to Star in Black and White*, Murray Mednick's *Taxes*, Eric Overmyer's *Native Speech*, Jane Martin's *Rodeo* and *Clear Glass Marbles*, and Richard Lees's *Right of Way*
0–933826–60–5 PAJ pb $7.95

Volume 4
Includes Thomas Babe's *Kid Champion*, Charles L. Mee, Jr.'s *The Investigation into the Murder in El Salvador*, Philip Bosakowski's *Chopin in Space*, Jeffrey Jones's *Night Coil*, and JoAnne Akalaitis' *Dressed Like an Egg*
0–933826–72–9 PAJ pb $8.95

Volume 5
Includes James Lapine and Stephen Sondheim's *Sunday in the Park with George*, Kathy Acker's *The Birth of the Poet*, Des McAnuff's *The Death of von Richthofen as Witnessed from Earth*, James Strah's *North Atlantic*, and John Jesurun's *Deep Sleep*
0–55554–007–4 PAJ pb $10.95

• Don Shewey, editor

OUT FRONT: Contemporary Gay and Lesbian Plays
Plays by Robert Chesley, Holly Hughes, Harry Kondoleon, Kathleen Tolan, and others serve what Shewey describes as "the primitive function of affirming the existence of a mistreated minority, confirming its convictions, and acting as a corrective to neglect or abuse by the culture-at-large"
0–8021–3025–9 Grove $14.95

• Mac Wellman, editor

THEATRE OF WONDERS: Six Contemporary American Plays
Includes selections from Len Jenkin, Jeffrey Jones, Des McAnuff, Elizabeth Wray, and Mac Wellman
0–940650–39–8 Sun & Moon pb $10.95

• Margaret B. Wilkerson, editor

NINE PLAYS BY BLACK WOMEN
Includes *The Tapestry* by Alexis DeVeaux, Lorraine Hansberry's *Toussaint: Excerpt from Act I of a Work in Progress*, Alice Childress' *Wedding Band*, and *Paper Dolls* by Elaine Jackson
0–451–623506–4 NAL pb $4.95

20th-Century American Essays and Journalism

• Truman Capote

A CAPOTE READER
A varied sampling of Capote's work, including short stories, travel sketches, reportage, and the novellas *The Grass Harp* and *Breakfast at Tiffany's*. "When God hands you a gift, he also hands you a whip"—Truman Capote
0–394–55647–X Random House $25.00

Evan S. Connell

A LONG DESIRE
A series of historical essays on the human quest for adventure and some of the strange forms it takes. "Quite simply, a great book . . . Combining a poet's vision and the narrative sweep of a born storyteller with painstaking historical research"—*LA Times*
0–86547–334–X North Point pb $8.95

THE WHITE LANTERN
Connell delves into the lore of archaeology, exploration, and anthropology and serves up his findings with his usual narrative flair
0–86547–364–1 North Point pb $9.95

• Francine Du Plessix Gray

ADAM AND EVE AND THE CITY
A collection of her most important nonfiction work, including major pieces on Klaus Barbie, Hawaii, and women writers. "These essays enlarge, enrich and sensitize culture"—Cynthia Ozick
0–671–64497–1 Simon & Schuster $19.95

• Richard Gilman

DECADENCE: The Strange Life of an Epithet
0–374–51553–0 Farrar, Straus & Giroux pb $4.95

• Donald Hall

KICKING THE LEAVES
0–06–090647–2 Harper & Row pb $7.95

TO KEEP MOVING: Essays 1959–1969
0–934888–02–7 Hobart & Smith pb $5.95

• Jonathan Lieberson

VARIETIES: Essays
"The depth of his learning and the excellence of his style make him the most brilliant young intellectual of his generation"—Elizabeth Hardwick
1–55584–059–0 Weidenfeld & Nicolson $19.95

• Dwight MacDonald

AGAINST THE AMERICAN GRAIN: Essays on the Effects of Mass Culture
Critical essays on politics, literature, film, and popular writing—including the famous "Masscult and Midcult"—from a writer who believes that "a people which loses contact with its past becomes culturally psychotic"
Introduction by John Simon
0–306–80205–8 Da Capo pb $9.95

DISCRIMINATIONS: Essays and Afterthoughts
His last collection, with essays on Hemingway, the Constitution, Vietnam, and Hannah Arendt. "He had that rare gift of always speaking out of his own voice"—Norman Mailer
Introduction by Norman Mailer
0–306–80252–X Da Capo pb $11.95

• John McPhee

THE JOHN MCPHEE READER
An impressive gathering comprised of selections from the first twelve books published by "the most versatile journalist in America" (Edward Hoagland)
Edited by William L. Howarth
0–374–17992–1 Farrar, Straus & Giroux $17.50
0–374–51719–3 Farrar, Straus & Giroux pb $9.95

THE DELTOID PUMPKIN SEED
A lively account about the deltoid-shaped Aeron, a modern hybrid of airship and airplane, and the strange cast of characters who tried to get it off the ground
0–374–13781–1 Farrar, Straus & Giroux $14.95
0–374–51635–9 Farrar, Straus & Giroux pb $8.95

ENCOUNTERS WITH THE ARCHDRUID: Narratives About a Conservationist and Three Natural Enemies
Classic encounters in the wilderness between David Brower ("the most militant conservationist in the world") and a mineral engineer, a real estate developer, and a dam builder
0–374–14822–8 Farrar, Straus & Giroux $16.95
0–374–51431–3 Farrar, Straus & Giroux pb $7.95

PIECES OF THE FRAME
McPhee's second collection of essays. "One has the sense always with McPhee of a man at a pitch of pleasure in his work, a natural at it, finding out on behalf of the rest of us how some portion of the world works"—Edward Hoagland
0–374–23281–4 Farrar, Straus & Giroux $14.95
0–374–51498–4 Farrar, Straus & Giroux pb $9.95

TABLE OF CONTENTS
A collection of eight essays written between 1981 and 1984, including "Heirs of General Practice" and "North of the C.P. Line"
0–374–27241–7 Farrar, Straus & Giroux $15.95
0–374–52008–9 Farrar, Straus & Giroux pb $7.95

• Norman Mailer

ADVERTISEMENTS FOR MYSELF
A seminal collection of short stories, excerpts from novels, columns on literature and politics and other incidental writings,

all linked by Mailer's brash introductory "advertisements" claiming a major role for himself as Norman Mailer, the public personage. Includes "The White Negro" and "The Time of Her Time"
0–399–50538–5 Putnam pb $6.95

H.L. Mencken (photo by Alfred A. Knopf, courtesy of Knopf)

• H.L. Mencken
AN AMERICAN SCENE: A Reader
0–394–75214–7 Random House pb $10.95

A CARNIVAL OF BUNCOMBE: Writings On Politics
Edited by Malcolm Moos
0–226–51977–5 Chicago pb $12.95

A CHOICE OF DAYS
0–394–50795–9 Knopf $12.95
0–394–74760–7 Random House pb $7.95

A MENCKEN CHRESTOMATHY
0–394–75209–0 Random House pb $14.95

PREJUDICES: A Selection
Taken from six volumes of collected essays through 1927, from the legendary journalist, editor, lexicographer, and pundit
Edited by James T. Farrell
0–394–70058–9 Random House pb $4.95

VINTAGE MENCKEN
A fine distillation
Edited by Alistair Cooke
0–394–70025–2 Random House pb $5.95

• Henry Miller
THE HENRY MILLER READER
Arranged by themes—"Places," "Stories," "Literary Essays," "Portraits," and "The Man Himself"—this selection from numerous books across many years reveals the underlying unity of the "single, endless autobiography" that is Miller's life work
Edited by Lawrence Durrell
0–8112–0111–2 New Directions pb $9.95

THE COSMOLOGICAL EYE
The first book by Miller that an American publisher dared to print, this is a quintessential collection of stories, essays, and musings
0–8112–0110–4 New Directions pb $9.25

THE HAMLET LETTERS
0–88496–269–5 Capra pb $8.95

REMEMBER TO REMEMBER
0–8112–0113–9 New Directions pb $10.00

STAND STILL LIKE THE HUMMINGBIRD
Stories and essays including "Money and How It Gets That Way," "The Angel is My Watermark," and "First Love"
0–8112–0322–0 New Directions pb $6.95

THE WISDOM OF THE HEART
Writings "from the heart" including "Reflections on Writing," "Balzac and His Double," "The Alcoholic Veteran with the Washboard Cranium," and "Creative Death"
0–8112–0116–3 New Directions pb $9.95

• Calvin Trillin
UNCIVIL LIBERTIES
0–14–010255–8 Penguin pb $7.95

WITH ALL DISRESPECT: More Uncivil Liberties
0–89919–353–6 Ticknor & Fields $14.95
0–14–008819–9 Penguin pb $6.95

Gore Vidal
AT HOME
His most recent collection, literary and political essays centering on America
0–394–57020–0 Random House $18.95

HOMAGE TO DANIEL SHAYS: Collected Essays, 1952–1972
0–394–71950–6 Random House pb $4.95

MATTERS OF FACT AND OF FICTION: Essays, 1973–1976
0–394–41128–5 Random House $14.95
0–394–72516–6 Random House pb $5.95

THE SECOND AMERICAN REVOLUTION
0–394–52265–6 Random House $15.00
0–394–71379–6 Random House pb $5.95

• E.B. White
ESSAYS OF E.B. WHITE
A classic culled from 50 years, by a superb craftsman and master of English prose
0–06–014576–5 Harper & Row $14.95
0–06–090662–6 Harper & Row pb $8.95

LETTERS OF E.B. WHITE
"This is his biggest book . . . and, as he says, his most naked . . . This collection, addressed to many people, will speak to many more"—John Updike
Edited by Dorothy L. Guth
0–06–091517–X Harper & Row pb $14.95

ONE MAN'S MEAT
A collection of White's essays for *Harper's,* written from his saltwater farm in Maine
0–06–091081–X Harper & Row pb $9.95

MEMOIRS AND JOURNALS

• Michael J. Arlen
PASSAGE TO ARARAT & EXILES
Passage to Ararat is an account of the author's trip to Mt. Ararat in search of his Armenian roots; *Exiles* is a touching memoir of his parents
0–14–006311–0 Penguin pb $8.95

• Paul Auster
THE INVENTION OF SOLITUDE
A meditation on fatherhood, prompted by his father's death and then moving to

thoughts of his own son. "Combines the subjects of time, language, and family into a beautifully moving and intelligent mosaic"—Charles Baxter
0–14–010628–6 Penguin pb $6.95

• Russell Baker
GROWING UP
Baker's Pulitzer Prize-winning reminiscences of his childhood
0–452–26132–5 NAL $7.95
0–451–15508–4 NAL pb $4.50

THE GOOD TIMES
The second installment of Baker's memoirs, covering his early years as a reporter
0–688–06170–2 Morrow $19.95

• Wendell Berry
THE HIDDEN WOUND
An autobiographical meditation on racism and its effect on American society: "If the white man has inflicted the wound of racism upon black men, the cost has been that he would receive the mirror image of that wound himself"
0–86547–358–7 North Point pb $9.95

• Edward Dahlberg
BECAUSE I WAS FLESH
A memoir of the author's childhood, with a powerful portrait of his mother
0–8112–0263–1 New Directions pb $6.95

• H.D.
THE GIFT
0–8112–0854–0 New Directions pb $5.95

END TO TORMENT: A Memoir of Ezra Pound
0–8112–0720–X New Directions pb $4.95

TRIBUTE TO FREUD
0–8112–0897–4 New Directions pb $7.95

• John Gregory Dunne
HARP
0–671–67236–3 Simon & Schuster $18.95

• M.F.K. Fisher
AMONG FRIENDS
An evocative account of an Episcopalian childhood in a Quaker town
0–86547–116–9 North Point pb $10.95

• Brendan Gill
HERE AT THE NEW YORKER
A memoir of the magazine's best years
0–88184–350–4 Carroll & Graf pb $12.95

• Richard Gilman
FAITH, SEX, MYSTERY: A Memoir
A conversion and its aftermath
0–14–010587–5 Penguin pb $7.95

• Donald Hall
STRING TOO SHORT TO BE SAVED: Recollections of Summers on a New England Farm
With an album of family snapshots and an added essay about returning 25 years later to spend the rest of his life on the farm
0–87923–282–X Godine pb $8.95

● Lillian Hellman
PENTIMENTO: A Book of Portraits
Scenes from Hellman's early life, with each vignette revolving around one central person in her life. Includes "Julia," the basis for the film
0–451–15442–8 NAL pb $4.50

SCOUNDREL TIME
A subjective, highly controversial account of the McCarthy era
0–316–35515–1 Little, Brown $15.95

AN UNFINISHED WOMAN
Reminiscences about her career in the theater, various stage personalities, her childhood in New Orleans, and the long relationship with Dashiell Hammett
0–316–35518–6 Little, Brown $13.95

● Ernest Hemingway
A MOVEABLE FEAST
Memoirs of Fitzgerald, Stein, and others
0–02–051960–5 Macmillan pb $4.95

● Langston Hughes
THE BIG SEA
The first volume of his autobiography. "*The Big Sea* is a valuable segment in the history of Afro-American literature"—Ralph Ellison
Introduction by Amiri Baraka
0–938410–33–4 Thunder's Mouth pb $10.95

I WONDER AS I WANDER: An Autobiographical Journey
"*I Wonder as I Wander* is actually Hughes's personal history intertwined with personal narratives of his travels—a sort of vagabondia"—*Saturday Review*
0–374–94031–2 Hill & Wang $27.50

● Zora Neale Hurston
DUST TRACKS ON A ROAD
Her rise from childhood poverty in the South to literary prominence. Restores several chapters that were originally cut or altered
Introduction by Larry Neal
Foreword by Robert E. Hemenway
0–252–01047–7 Illinois pb $8.95

● Alfred Kazin
STARTING OUT IN THE THIRTIES
0–8014–9562–8 Cornell pb $6.95

A WALKER IN THE CITY
A lyrical memoir that uses New York as both literal setting and metaphor. "I was aware of being claimed by an extraordinary work of art"—Carson McCullers
0–15–694176–7 HBJ pb $6.95

● Maxine Hong Kingston
THE WOMAN WARRIOR: Memoirs of a Girlhood Among Ghosts
A Chinese-American born in California describes her upbringing in a laundry amid the talk-stories of her mother, Brave Orchid. Winner of the National Book Critics Circle Award
0–394–40067–4 Knopf $15.95
0–394–72392–9 Random House pb $3.95

Maxine Hong Kingston (photo by Floyd K. Takeuchi, courtesy of Knopf)

CHINA MEN
A follow-up into the minds of Chinese men in America. "It captures the emotional truth of the Chinese-American experience far better than any conventional history or biography ever could"—*Newsday*
0–394–42463–8 Knopf $13.95
0–345–34407–3 Ballantine pb $3.95

Phillip Lopate
AGAINST JOIE DE VIVRE: Personal Essays
0–671–67679–2 Simon & Schuster $18.95

BACHELORHOOD: Tales of the Metropolis
0–671–67681–4 Simon & Schuster pb $8.95

BEING WITH CHILDREN
0–671–67680–6 Simon & Schuster pb $8.95

● Mary McCarthy
HOW I GREW
Our "foremost liberal woman of letters" recalls her life between the ages of 13 and 21—from high school in Seattle to college at Vassar
0–15–142193–5 HBJ $16.95

MEMORIES OF A CATHOLIC GIRLHOOD
After an idyllic childhood, McCarthy was orphaned at six, then brought up by relatives of varied religious backgrounds
0–15–658650–9 HBJ pb $7.95

● Hilary Masters
LAST STANDS: Notes from Memory
A moving portrait of the author's father, the poet Edgar Lee Masters
0–87923–443–1 Godine $14.95

● Peter Matthiessen
NINE-HEADED DRAGON RIVER: Zen Journals 1969–1982
0–87773–401–1 Shambhala pb $12.50

● Arthur Miller
TIMEBENDS: A Life
0–8021–0015–5 Grove $25.00
0–06–097178–9 Harper & Row pb $10.95

● Henry Miller
BIG SUR AND THE ORANGES OF HIERONYMUS BOSCH
Miller's life on the famous stretch of California coast, a portrait of the place and many of the extraordinary people he knew there
0–8112–0107–4 New Directions pb $9.95

THE HAMLET LETTERS
0–88496–269–5 Capra pb $8.95

● Henry Miller & Anaïs Nin
A LITERATE PASSION: Letters of Anaïs Nin and Henry Miller, 1932–1953
0–15–152729–6 HBJ $19.95

● Raymond Mungo
TOTAL LOSS FARM: A Year in the Life
Guerrilla journalism in the 1960s
0–914842–16–1 Madrona pb $5.95

● Vladimir Nabokov
SPEAK MEMORY: An Autobiography Revisited
"The finest autobiography written in our time"—*New Republic*
0–399–50220–3 Putnam pb $8.95

● Anaïs Nin
Nin's diaries, a remarkable lifelong undertaking, offer a unique record of self-discovery by a modern woman and writer who moved freely in the cosmopolitan world of art and society. "An extraordinary book . . . its egoism is redeemed and raised to a high standard of art by an extremely subtle sensibility, expressed in a prose style of astonishing beauty."—Herbert Read
THE EARLY DIARIES OF ANAÏS NIN

Volume 1: 1914–1920
0–15–65238–6 HBJ pb $7.50

Volume 2: 1920–1923
0–15–62724–8 HBJ pb $7.95

Volume 3: 1923–1927
0–15–62725–0 HBJ pb $10.95

Volume 4: 1927–1931
0–15–62725–1 HBJ pb $12.95

THE DIARIES OF ANAÏS NIN

Volume 1: 1931–1934
0–15–62602–5 HBJ pb $9.95

Volume 2: 1934–1939
0–15–62602–6 HBJ pb $9.95

Volume 3: 1939–1944
0–15–62602–7 HBJ pb $9.95

Volume 4: 1944–1947
0–15–62602–8 HBJ pb $2.75

Volume 5: 1947–1955
0–15–62603–0 HBJ pb $2.95

Volume 6: 1955–1956
0–15–62603–2 HBJ pb $10.95

Volume 7: 1966–1974
0–15–62603–5 HBJ pb $9.95

HENRY AND JUNE: From the Unexpurgated Diary of Anaïs Nin
0–15–140003–2 HBJ $14.95

◆ **TO ORDER BOOKS AS GIFTS, SEE PAGE 1**

● Geoffrey O'Brien
DREAM TIME: Chapters from the Sixties
"A wonderfully evocative and original contemplation of the Sixties"—Elizabeth Hardwick
0–670–81844–5 Viking $15.95
0–14–010362–7 Penguin pb $7.95

● Reynolds Price
CLEAR PICTURES: First Loves, First Guides
"Evoking the sights and textures of a small-town North Carolina boyhood in the 1930s and '40s, Price's memoir is remarkable for its Proustian recall"—*Publishers Weekly*
0–689–12075–3 Macmillan $19.95

● Kenneth Rexroth
AN AUTOBIOGRAPHICAL NOVEL
Rexroth's account of the first 21 years of his life encompasses a wide spectrum of radical and bohemian experience in the early 20th century
0–915520–15–X Ross-Erikson pb $8.95

● Waverley Root
THE PARIS EDITION: 1927–1934
An autobiographical account of Root's years as Paris correspondent for the *Chicago Tribune*. "224 pages of Parisian charm, newspaper and literary gossip, heroes, fools, brave fliers, drunks, prostitutes, and eccentric millionaires"—*Philadelphia Inquirer*
0–86547–388–9 North Point pb $9.95

● Philip Roth
THE FACTS: A Novelist's Autobiography
0–374–15212–8 Farrar, Straus & Giroux $18.95

● May Sarton
AT SEVENTY: A Journal
Chronicles the year that began on May 3, 1982, her 70th birthday, and the experience of being alive at her home in Maine
0–393–30434–5 Norton pb $7.95

JOURNAL OF A SOLITUDE
"On the surface it is a quiet book, but if you will read it carefully you will be aware of violent needs and a valiant warrior who has battled every inch of the way to a share of serenity"—*Cleveland Plain Dealer*
0–393–00853–3 Norton pb $3.95

RECOVERING: A Journal
"Sarton has fashioned her journals, 'sonatas' as she calls them, into a distinctive form: relaxed yet shapely, a silky weave of reflection, sensuous observation and record of her daily rounds, with the reader made companion to her inmost thoughts"—*Publishers Weekly*
0–393–01402–9 Norton $14.95
0–393–30339–X Norton pb $5.95

Kate Simon
BRONX PRIMITIVE: Portraits in a Childhood
"A classic story of growing up and a poignant evocation of the immigrant experience—written by a master of descriptive prose"—*Newsday*
0–06–091067–4 Harper & Row pb $7.95

A WIDER WORLD: Portraits in an Adolescence
A sequel to *Bronx Primitive* about opening up to the world in Depression era New York
0–06–015526–4 Harper & Row $14.95
0–06–091379–7 Harper & Row pb $6.95

● Gary Snyder
PASSAGE THROUGH INDIA
A travel journal
0–912516–79–8 Grey Fox $12.95
0–912516–80–1 Grey Fox pb $6.95

● Gary Soto
LIVING UP THE STREET
Coming of age in a Chicano world
0–89407–064–9 Strawberry Hill pb $8.00

● John Updike
SELF-CONSCIOUSNESS
"Raw material of an autobiography": Six essays on childhood, psoriasis, writing, the Vietnam War, and other subjects
0–394–57222–X Knopf $18.50

● Eudora Welty
ONE WRITER'S BEGINNINGS
"Miss Welty presents her life as if it were one of her stories, so that the book is something more than a brief autobiography"—*NY Times*
0–674–63925–1 Harvard $10.00

● Edith Wharton
A BACKWARD GLANCE
0–684–15983–X Scribners $27.50
0–684–18381–1 Scribners pb $12.95

● Edmund Wilson
UPSTATE
0–374–28189–0 Farrar, Straus & Giroux $10.95

● Tobias Wolff
THIS BOY'S LIFE: A Memoir
0–87113–248–6 Atlantic Monthly $18.95

● Lawrence Wright
IN THE NEW WORLD: Growing Up with America, 1960–1984
0–394–54282–7 Knopf $18.95
0–394–75964–8 Random House pb $6.95

● Al Young
BODIES AND SOUL: Musical Memoirs
Musical memories of Duke Ellington, Hank Williams, Nat Cole, and Ray Charles
0–916870–39–1 Creative Arts pb $6.95

KINDS OF BLUE: Musical Memoirs
A companion volume to *Bodies and Soul*
0–916870–82–0 Creative Arts pb $7.95

THINGS AIN'T WHAT THEY USED TO BE: Musical Memoirs
From the tango to the bossa nova, Young recaptures the past through the power of music
0–88739–024–2 Creative Arts pb $8.95

REPORTING

▶ See also Journalism

● James Agee & Walker Evans
LET US NOW PRAISE FAMOUS MEN
The 1941 classic about cotton-farming tenantry among white sharecroppers, told through Agee's poetic prose and Evans' stark photographs
0–395–48901–6 Houghton Mifflin $24.95
0–395–48897–4 Houghton Mifflin pb $12.95

● James Agee
JAMES AGEE: Selected Journalism
Edited by Paul Ashdown
0–87049–466–X Tennessee $17.95

● T.D. Allman
MIAMI: City of the Future
"An exuberant portrait of the city of the '80s"—*NY Times*
0–87113–227–3 Atlantic Monthly pb $5.95

● Djuna Barnes
INTERVIEWS
Edited by Alyce Barry
Foreword by Douglas Messerli
0–940650–36–3 Sun & Moon $16.95
0–940650–37–1 Sun & Moon pb $10.95

● Paul Bowles
WITHOUT STOPPING
An idiosyncratic, strangely detached autobiography
0–88001–061–4 Ecco pb $9.50

● Jimmy Breslin
THE WORLD ACCORDING TO BRESLIN
Edited by William Brink & Michael J. O'Neill
0–07–007649–9 McGraw-Hill pb $4.95

● Edna Buchanan
THE CORPSE HAD A FAMILIAR FACE: Covering Miami, America's Hottest Beat
From the legendary *Miami Herald* crime reporter—one of the first women ever to cover the police beat—who has seen "over five thousand corpses"
0–394–55794–8 Random House $17.95

● Truman Capote
IN COLD BLOOD
The original "nonfiction novel," first published in 1966, chronicling the murder of a Kansas family by two drifters
0–394–43023–9 Random House $24.95
0–451–15446–0 NAL pb $4.95

● Marcelle Clements
THE DOG IS US & OTHER OBSERVATIONS
0–14–008445–2 Viking pb $7.95

● Joan Didion
MIAMI
0–671–64664–8 Simon & Schuster $17.95
0–671–66820–X Pocket pb $7.95

SALVADOR
"Didion has that rare gift, the ability to take in the essence of a country through her pores"—Robert E. White, former ambassador to El Salvador
0–671–66880–3 Washington Square pb $6.95

SLOUCHING TOWARDS BETHLEHEM
A collection from the mid-'60s, with the now classic title essay on Haight-Ashbury. "What most captivates the reader is discovering how her brittle sensibilities respond to events. Miss Didion suffers constantly, but compellingly and magically"—*Time*
0–671–66737–8 Washington Square pb $4.95

THE WHITE ALBUM
Includes the title essay plus "California Republic," "Women," "Sojourns," and "On the Morning After the Sixties"
0–671–60103–2 Washington Square pb $3.95

• Nora Ephron
CRAZY SALAD PLUS NINE
0–671–50715–X Pocket Books pb $3.95

• Martha Gelhorn
POINT OF NO RETURN
0–452–26223–2 NAL pb $8.95

• Ernest Hemingway
THE GREEN HILLS OF AFRICA
Hemingway on safari
0–02–051930–3 Macmillan pb $5.95

• John McPhee
THE HEADMASTER: Frank L. Boyden of Deerfield
0–374–16860–1 Farrar, Straus & Giroux $12.95
0–374–51496–8 Farrar, Straus & Giroux pb $7.95

LA PLACE DE LA CONCORDE SUISSE
"McPhee, in showing us as many aspects of the Swiss Army as their famous knife has blades, has produced one of his best books"—*Wall Street Journal*
0–374–18241–8 Farrar, Straus & Giroux $12.95
0–374–51932–3 Farrar, Straus & Giroux pb $6.95

• Dale Maharidge & Michael Williamson
AND THEIR CHILDREN AFTER THEM
A follow-up to *Let Us Now Praise Famous Men* in which the authors go to Alabama to interview and photograph the descendants of Agee and Evans' original subjects
0–394–57766–3 Random House $22.95

• Norman Mailer
THE ARMIES OF THE NIGHT
Mailer's splendid account of the 1967 anti-war march on the Pentagon. "History and personality confront each other with a new sense of liberation"—*New Republic*
0–451–14070–2 NAL pb $4.95

THE EXECUTIONER'S SONG
Pulitzer Prize-winning account of Gary Gilmore, a convicted murderer who was executed in 1977
0–316–54417–5 Little, Brown $25.00

MIAMI AND THE SIEGE OF CHICAGO
Introduction by Tom Wicker
0–917657–85–3 Donald Fine pb $7.95

OF A FIRE ON THE MOON
Inspired account of Apollo 11. "A 20th-century American epic—a Moby Dick of space"—*New York*
0–394–62019–4 Grove pb $3.95

THE PRISONER OF SEX
After the breakup of his fourth marriage, surrounded by his five children, Mailer's

performing self takes on the issue of women's liberation
Introduction by Pete Hamill
0–917657–59–4 Donald Fine pb $8.95

• Henry Miller
THE AIR-CONDITIONED NIGHTMARE
America in the '40s, seen with a deeply unsympathetic eye
0–8112–0106–6 New Directions pb $9.95

• William Least Heat Moon
BLUE HIGHWAYS: A Journey into America
0–316–35395–7 Little, Brown $18.95
0–449–21109–6 Fawcett pb $4.95

• David Rieff
GOING TO MIAMI: Exiles, Tourists and Refugees in the New America
"A shrewd, inquisitive guide to one of the world's oldest and most intensely knit exile communities . . . Read before heading south"—Robert Hughes
0–316–74477–8 Little, Brown $16.95
0–14–011091–7 Penguin pb $7.95

• Susan Sheehan
IS THERE NO PLACE ON EARTH FOR ME?
Winner of the Pulitzer Prize for nonfiction, Sheehan's intense, close-up chronicle of a young woman's struggle with schizophrenia is also a penetrating study of mental health care
Foreword by Robert M. Coles
0–395–31871–8 Houghton Mifflin $14.95
0–394–71378–8 Random House pb $8.95

KATE QUINTON'S DAYS
0–451–62423–8 NAL pb $3.95

A MISSING PLANE
Three experts from different fields team up to unravel the mystery of an aircraft and its 22 passengers who were lost over New Guinea 38 years earlier
0–399–13183–3 Putnam $18.95
0–425–10553–9 Berkley pb $3.50

• Barbara Probst Solomon
HORSE-TRADING AND ECSTASY
Essays and interviews covering a wide territory, and culminating in a report on the war crimes trial of Klaus Barbie
0–86547–348–X North Point $16.95

• Gay Talese
FAME AND OBSCURITY
0–440–32492–0 Dell pb $4.95

HONOR THY FATHER
Saga of the Bonano crime family and the Banana War
0–440–33468–3 Dell pb $4.95

THE KINGDOM AND THE POWER
A report on the inner workings of the *New York Times*
0–440–38497–4 Dell pb $5.95

THY NEIGHBOR'S WIFE
A first-hand, front-line report on American sexuality
0–440–38497–4 Dell pb $5.95

• Hunter S. Thompson
THE CURSE OF LONO
0–553–34523–0 Bantam pb $13.95

FEAR AND LOATHING IN LAS VEGAS
"The best book on the Dope Decade"—*NY Times*
Illustrated by Ralph Steadman
0–446–31393–9 Warner pb $3.95

FEAR AND LOATHING ON THE CAMPAIGN TRAIL '72
"The best account yet published of what it feels like to be out there in the middle of the American political process"—*NY Times*
0–446–31364–5 Warner pb $4.95

THE GREAT SHARK HUNT
A collection of pieces written across two decades from America's quintessential outlaw journalist, the "Duke of Gonzo"
0–446–31440–4 Warner pb $5.95

HELL'S ANGELS
"For all its uninhibited and sardonic humor, Thompson's book is a thoughtful piece of work"—*New Yorker*
0–345–33148–6 Ballantine pb $4.95

• Calvin Trillin
KILLINGS
A collection of true homicide stories. "What makes *Killings* literature is the way he pictures the lives that were interrupted by the murders. Even the most ordinary life makes a terrible noise . . . when it's broken off"—*NY Times*
0–14–007977–7 Penguin pb $6.95

• Edmund White
STATES OF DESIRE: Travels in Gay America
0–525–48223–7 Dutton pb $8.95

• Tom Wolfe
THE ELECTRIC KOOL-AID ACID TEST
"*The Electric Kool-Aid Acid Test* is not only the best book on the hippies. It is the essential book"—*NY Times*
0–374–14704–3 Farrar, Straus & Giroux $22.50
0–374–52071–2 Farrar, Straus & Giroux pb $8.95

FROM BAUHAUS TO OUR HOUSE
An offbeat, iconoclastic essay on the modernist movement in architecture and the pernicious influence of the Bauhaus
0–374–15892–4 Farrar, Straus & Giroux $10.95
0–671–66656–8 Washington Square pb $5.95

IN OUR TIME
Illustrated by Tom Wolfe
0–374–17576–4 Farrar, Straus & Giroux $12.95

THE KANDY KOLORED TANGERINE-FLAKE STREAMLINE BABY
His literary debut, a look at the early '60s and various exotic forms of status seeking, including profiles of Phil Spector and Baby Jane Holzer
0–374–18064–4 Farrar, Straus & Giroux $19.95
0–374–50468–7 Farrar, Straus & Giroux pb $7.95

MAUVE GLOVES AND MADMEN, CLUTTER AND VINE
Stories, essays, and sketches on the mood of the '70s, including "The Me Decade and the Third Great Awakening"
0–374–20424–1 Farrar, Straus & Giroux $18.95
0–374–52092–5 Farrar, Straus & Giroux pb $6.95

THE PAINTED WORD
Wolfe takes on the pretensions of the art world
0–374–22878–7 Farrar, Straus & Giroux $12.95
0–553–27556–9 Bantam pb $4.95

THE PUMP HOUSE GANG
An early collection of essays; the title piece concerns a California surfing elite
0–374–23864–2 Farrar, Straus & Giroux $18.95
0–374–52070–4 Farrar, Straus & Giroux pb $7.95

THE PURPLE DECADES: A Reader
Includes "The Last American Hero," "The Pump House Gang," "The Me Decade and the Third Great Awakening," plus selections from *Radical Chic, The Right Stuff, The Electric Kool-Aid Acid Test,* and *From Bauhaus to Our House*
0–374–23927–4 Farrar, Straus & Giroux $17.50
0–425–06266–X Berkley pb $7.95

RADICAL CHIC & MAU-MAUING THE FLAK CATCHERS
Two essays about political stances and social styles in a status-conscious world. Includes the famous account of Leonard Bernstein's party for the Black Panthers
0–374–24600–9 Farrar, Straus & Giroux $16.95
0–374–52072–0 Farrar, Straus & Giroux pb $5.95

THE RIGHT STUFF
The full, irreverent story of the first Americans in space
0–374–25033–2 Farrar, Straus & Giroux $15.95
0–553–25596–7 Bantam pb $4.50

HISTORY, POLITICS, AND SOCIETY

• **James Baldwin**
EVIDENCE OF THINGS NOT SEEN
A report on the investigation into the Atlanta child murders
0–8050–0138–7 Henry Holt pb $4.95

THE FIRE NEXT TIME
Prophetic warnings in the form of a "Letter to My Nephew on the 100th-Anniversary of the Emancipation"
0–440–32542–0 Dell pb $4.95

NOTES OF A NATIVE SON
His first nonfiction book, essays on life in Harlem, the protest novel, movies, and Americans abroad. "A straight-from-the-shoulder writer, writing about the troubled problems of this troubled earth, with an illuminating intensity that should influence for the better all who ponder on the things books say"—Langston Hughes
0–8070–6431–9 Beacon pb $8.95

THE PRICE OF THE TICKET: Collected Nonfiction, 1948–1985
Includes the full text of "The Fire Next Time," "No Name in the Street," and "The Devil Finds Work," plus many selections
0–312–64306–3 St. Martin's $29.95

• **William F. Buckley, Jr.**
RIGHT REASON
Draws on columns and articles written between 1978 and 1985 by the man who "has been the acknowledged champion of American conservatism for three decades" (Richard Brookhiser)
0–316–11444–8 Little, Brown pb $10.95

• **Evan S. Connell**
SON OF THE MORNING STAR: Custer and the Little Bighorn
"An unconventional, highly evocative retelling of the celebrated military disaster . . . One of the Ten Best of 1984"—*Time*
0–06–097161–4 Harper & Row pb $9.95

• **Paul Fussell**
THE BOY SCOUT HANDBOOK & OTHER OBSERVATIONS
0–19–503102–4 Oxford $22.95
0–19–503579–8 Oxford pb $8.95

CLASS: A Guide Through the American Status System
"Fussell identifies the class significance of not only clothes and houses but cars, food, language, vacations, reading habits and much more . . . Frighteningly acute"—Alison Lurie
0–671–44991–5 Summit $13.95

THE GREAT WAR AND MODERN MEMORY
On the shattering of innocence in 1914–18 and the end of our concept that any war can be heroic. "An original and brilliant piece of cultural history and one of the most deeply moving books I have read in a long time"—Lionel Trilling
0–19–502171–1 Oxford pb $9.95

THANK GOD FOR THE ATOM BOMB & OTHER ESSAYS
0–671–63866–1 Summit $17.95

WARTIME
0–19–503797–9 Oxford $18.95

Jane Jacobs
THE DEATH AND LIFE OF GREAT AMERICAN CITIES
An attack on the principles and aims that have shaped modern orthodox city planning and rebuilding. "This is one of the most remarkable books ever written about the city"—William Whyte
0–394–70241–7 Random House pb $6.95

THE ECONOMY OF CITIES
"This book is radiant with ideas about what makes cities rich or poor, how cities grow, and how city growth affects national economies"—*New Yorker*
0–394–70584–X Random House pb $5.95

• **William Kennedy**
O ALBANY!: An Urban Tapestry
"Kennedy celebrates his hometown in the rich and energetic prose that also distinguishes his fiction"—*Washington Post*
0–14–007416–3 Penguin pb $11.95

• **Jane Kramer**
EUROPEANS
Introduction by William Shawn
0–374–14939–9 Farrar, Straus & Giroux $22.95

• **A.J. Liebling**
THE PRESS
Introduction by Alexander Cockburn
0–394–74849–2 Pantheon pb $6.95

• **Peter Matthiessen**
INDIAN COUNTRY
0–670–39787–3 Viking $17.95

• **Lewis Mumford**
"Lewis Mumford has always been a master connector—connecting the separate domains of philosophy, architecture, anthropology, and literature to one another and to the human domain in general. His knowledge of life on this planet and his concern for its safety are beautifully blended."—Norman Cousins

THE BROWN DECADES: A Study of the Arts in America, 1865–1895
0–486–20200–3 Dover pb $3.95

THE CITY IN HISTORY: Its Origins, Its Transformations and Its Prospects
A monumental work on the origins and nature of the city that traces its historical development from Egypt to the modern world and then offers a new order in urban development. "More than urban history: it is moral philosophy of a high order and tragic poetry"—*NY Times*
0–15–618035–9 HBJ pb $12.95

THE CONDUCT OF LIFE
0–15–621600–0 HBJ pb $7.95

THE CULTURE OF CITIES
0–15–623301–0 HBJ pb $9.95

FROM THE GROUND UP: Observations on Contemporary Architecture, Housing, Highway Building, and Civic Design
0–15–634019–4 HBJ pb $3.50

THE LEWIS MUMFORD READER
"Rereading Lewis Mumford's most important essays makes it obvious why he remains, and perhaps always will be, a major figure in American architectural, planning, and social thought"—Herbert J. Gans
Edited by Donald L. Miller
0–394–74630–9 Pantheon pb $14.95

THE MYTH OF THE MACHINE
Volume 1: Technics and Human Development
0–15–662341–2 HBJ pb $5.95

Volume 2: The Pentagon of Power
0–15–671610–0 HBJ pb $7.95

STICKS AND STONES
0–486–20202–X Dover pb $3.95

• **Norman Podhoretz**
THE BLOODY CROSSROADS: Where Literature and Politics Meet
0–671–61891–1 Simon & Schuster $16.95
0–671–63314–7 Simon & Schuster pb $8.95

• **Marilynne Robinson**
MOTHER COUNTRY
A passionate condemnation of the British government's management of Sellafield, a plutonium waste plant on the Cumbrian coast
0–374–21361–5 Farrar, Straus & Giroux $16.95

• **Robert Scheer**
THINKING TUNA FISH, TALKING DEATH: Essays on the Pornography of Power
0–8050–9316–2 Hill & Wang $19.95

• **Page Smith**
DISSENTING OPINIONS: The Selected Essays of Page Smith
0–86547–154–1 North Point $15.50

• **Gary Snyder**
EARTH HOUSE HOLD
Essays on poetry and ecology and their interconnections
0–8112–0195–3 New Directions pb $6.95

THE OLD WAYS: Six Essays
0–87286–091–4 City Lights pb $4.50

THE REAL WORK: Interviews and Talks
Edited by Scott McLean
0–8112–0761–7 New Directions pb $5.95

• Tom Wicker
UNTO THIS HOUR
0–425–07583–4 Berkley pb $4.95

• George F. Will
THE MORNING AFTER: American Successes and Excesses, 1981–1986
A collection linked thematically by "the nagging sense of the vast inertia in the life of a great nation"
0–02–934430–1 Free Press $19.95

STATECRAFT AS SOULCRAFT: What Government Does
"His central thesis, that American society is rooted (to its detriment) in economic self-interestedness and laissez-faire individualism is an indictment of contemporary conservatism and liberalism"—*Denver Post*
0–671–42734–2 Simon & Schuster pb $7.95

THE PURSUIT OF VIRTUE AND OTHER TORY NOTIONS
0–671–45712–8 Simon & Schuster pb $10.95

• Edmund Wilson
TO THE FINLAND STATION
The roots of modern radicalism, from Fourier and Saint-Simon to Marx and Lenin. "A work of the historical imagination at its most creative . . . puts us in touch with the revolutionary dreams and visions of our past"—*NY Times*
0–374–51045–8 Farrar, Straus & Giroux pb $12.95

LITERATURE

▶ See also Literary Criticism, Literary Theory, and the separate sections devoted to national literatures

• Charles Bernstein
CONTENT'S DREAM: Essays, 1975–1984
Reflections on contemporary poetry, art, and philosophy by a leading "Language" poet
0–940650–56–8 Sun & Moon pb $11.95

• Wendell Berry
STANDING BY WORDS: Essays
0–86547–122–3 North Point pb $10.95

• Elizabeth Bishop
THE COLLECTED PROSE
Edited by Robert Giroux
0–374–12628–3 Farrar, Straus & Giroux $17.50
0–374–51855–6 Farrar, Straus & Giroux pb $8.95

• Kay Boyle
WORDS THAT MUST SOMEHOW BE SAID: Selected Essays, 1927–1981
0–86547–188–6 North Point pb $8.95

• Kay Boyle & Robert McAlmon
BEING GENIUSES TOGETHER: 1920–1930
A dual account of Paris in the '20s
0–86547–149–5 North Point pb $13.50

• William Bronk
VECTORS AND SMOOTHABLE CURVES: Collected Essays of William Bronk
Essays largely on pre-Columbian cultures and 19th-century American writers, by an important contemporary poet
0–86547–126–6 North Point pb $12.50

• Robert Coles
THAT RED WHEELBARROW: Selected Literary Essays
0–87745–208–3 Iowa $24.95

• Edward Dahlberg
THE SORROWS OF PRIAPUS
Illustrated by Ben Shahn
0–7145–0670–2 Marion Boyars pb $10.95

CAN THESE BONES LIVE?
Original and eccentric essays on American literature
Introduction by Herbert Read
0–8112–0264–X New Directions pb $6.50

Guy Davenport
EVERY FORCE EVOLVES A FORM: 20 Essays
Krazy Kat, Pergolesi, Joseph Cornell, and the Civil War diary of Mary Chesnut are among the topics addressed
0–86547–247–5 North Point $16.95

THE GEOGRAPHY OF THE IMAGINATION: 40 Essays
Essays on Whitman, Wittgenstein, Wallace Stevens, and much else, by a brilliant stylist
0–86547–001–4 North Point pb $13.95

• F.W. Dupee
THE KING OF CATS & OTHER REMARKS ON WRITERS AND WRITING
Foreword by Mary McCarthy
0–226–17286–4 Chicago $28.00
0–226–17287–2 Chicago pb $12.50

• Ralph Ellison
SHADOW AND ACT
0–394–71716–3 Random House pb $6.95

• William Gass
FICTION AND THE FIGURES OF LIFE
0–87923–254–4 Godine pb $7.95

ON BEING BLUE: A Philosophical Inquiry
0–87923–183–1 Godine $12.95
0–87923–237–4 Godine pb $6.95

THE WORLD WITHIN THE WORD
0–87923–298–6 Godine pb $8.95

• Elizabeth Hardwick
A VIEW OF MY OWN: Essays on Literature and Society
0–912946–91–1 Ecco pb $6.95

• Mary McCarthy
IDEAS AND THE NOVEL
0–15–143682–7 HBJ pb $7.95

THE STONES OF FLORENCE
0–15–185079–8 HBJ $49.95
0–15–685081–8 HBJ pb $19.95

THE WRITING ON THE WALL & OTHER LITERARY ESSAYS
0–15–698390–7 HBJ pb $4.95

• Oscar Mandel
THE BOOK OF ELABORATIONS
0–8112–1023–5 New Directions pb $12.95

• William Maxwell
THE OUTERMOST DREAM: Essays and Reviews
0–394–57443–5 Knopf $19.95

• James Merrill
RECITATIVE: Prose
Edited by J.D. McClatchy
0–86547–255–6 North Point pb $12.50

• Henry Miller
THE BOOKS IN MY LIFE
0–8112–0108–2 New Directions pb $7.95

HENRY MILLER ON WRITING
Edited by Thomas H. Moore
0–8112–0112–0 New Directions pb $6.25

THE TIME OF THE ASSASSINS: A Study of Rimbaud
"In Rimbaud I see myself as a mirror"—Henry Miller
0–8112–0115–5 New Directions pb $6.95

• Larry Neal
VISIONS OF A LIBERATED FUTURE
A posthumous collection of poetry and essays
0–938410–78–4 Thunder's Mouth $19.95
0–938410–77–6 Thunder's Mouth pb $10.95

• Cynthia Ozick
ART AND ARDOR
"These 23 essays, on subjects ranging from Edith Wharton to John Updike to Gershom Scholem, with stops in between for mulling over what art should be doing and what Jewishness is, are a pleasure to read for their vividness of thought and language"—*Nation*
0–394–53082–9 Knopf $16.95
0–525–48117–6 Dutton pb $8.95

• Walker Percy
THE MESSAGE IN THE BOTTLE
Philosophical reflections on language
0–374–20856–5 Farrar, Straus & Giroux $16.50
0–374–51338–4 Farrar, Straus & Giroux pb $9.95

• Carl Rakosi
THE COLLECTED PROSE
Rakosi's aphorisms have the same balance and wit as his poetry
0–915032–21–X National Poetry Fdn pb $12.95

• Ishmael Reed
WRITIN' IS FIGHTIN': 37 Years of Boxing on Paper
0–689–11975–5 Atheneum $18.95

• Kenneth Rexroth
ASSAYS
0–915520–66–4 Ross-Erikson pb $3.95

CLASSICS REVISITED
Brief and lively essays on 60 literary classics, from *The Iliad* and *The Mahabharata* to the *Goncourt Journals* and *Huckleberry Finn*. "The talk is expansive, linking the archaic and the immediate . . . The books he loved he saw as emanations of living feeling, lines of communication miraculously kept open"—*Village Voice*
Afterword by Bradford Morrow
0–8112–0988–1 New Directions pb $10.95

➤ **FOR OVERSEAS ORDERING INFORMATION, SEE PAGE 1**

MORE CLASSICS REVISITED
The subjects include St. Thomas Aquinas, Ssu-ma Ch'ien's *Records of the Grand Historian of China*, and *Robinson Crusoe*
Edited by Bradford Morrow
0–8112–1083–9 New Directions pb $10.95

WORLD OUTSIDE THE WINDOW: The Selected Essays of Kenneth Rexroth
Twenty-seven essays written over 40 years by an extraordinarily versatile talent. "To define strangeness with no strain is the peculiar province of art; and it is as a master of this great art that Kenneth Rexroth defines and defends our earth for us"—*NY Times*
Edited by Bradford Morrow
0–8112–1025–1 New Directions pb $12.95

● Adrienne Rich
ON LIES, SECRETS AND SILENCE: Selected Prose, 1966–1978
0–393–01233–6 Norton $15.95
0–393–00942–4 Norton pb $6.95

● Philip Roth
READING MYSELF AND OTHERS
0–14–007681–6 Penguin pb $6.95

● Duncan Smith
THE AGE OF OIL
A psychoanalytic and linguistic critique of American pop culture. A fresh, witty comment on the pervasiveness of cars and oil in our society, and other topics
0–9616193–5–X Slate pb $5.95

● Gilbert Sorrentino
SOMETHING SAID: Essays
0–86547–177–0 North Point pb $15.50

● Eliot Weinberger
WORKS ON PAPER
Highly original takes on everything from tigers to nuclear war
0–8112–1001–4 New Directions pb $9.95

● Jonathan Williams
THE MAGPIE'S BAGPIPE
An entertaining catalog of Williams' pleasures, from hiking the English countryside to savoring the poetry of Lorine Niedecker
0–86547–093–6 North Point pb $12.50

● William Carlos Williams
SELECTED ESSAYS
0–8112–0235–6 New Directions pb $6.95

IN THE AMERICAN GRAIN
Brilliantly varied evocations of American history
Introduction by Horace Gregory
0–8112–0230–5 New Directions pb $6.95

● Edmund Wilson
AXEL'S CASTLE: A Study in the Imaginative Literature of 1870–1930
"Edmund Wilson was the first American critic to show that a single impulse persisted through eighty years of quarreling doctrines and self-devouring schools. In *Axel's Castle* he suggested that the name Symbolism was broad enough to cover this whole literary movement. His book was extraordinarily illuminating. Nobody before him had written a better

Edmund Wilson (photo by James A. Sugar, courtesy of Farrar, Straus & Giroux)

exposition of Yeats, Joyce, Proust"—Malcolm Cowley
0–393–30194–X Norton pb $7.95

THE FIFTIES: From Notebooks and Diaries of the Period
"Contains some fine, brief intellectual portraiture—of Cyril Connolly, T.S. Eliot, Isaiah Berlin, André Malraux, W.H. Auden—of the sort one hopes for from the journals of literary men"—*NY Times*
Edited with an introduction by Leon Edel
0–374–15486–4 Farrar, Straus & Giroux $25.00
0–317–65390–3 Farrar, Straus & Giroux pb $12.95

THE FORTIES: From Notebooks and Diaries of the Period
Edited by Leon Edel
0–374–15762–6 Farrar, Straus & Giroux $17.95
0–374–51835–1 Farrar, Straus & Giroux pb $9.25

LETTERS ON LITERATURE AND POLITICS: 1912–1972
Edited by Elena Wilson
0–374–18508–5 Farrar, Straus & Giroux $20.00

O CANADA: An American's Notes on Canadian Culture
0–374–98650–9 Hippocrene $18.00

PATRIOTIC GORE: Studies in the Literature of the American Civil War
An immense and erudite collection of essays whose subjects include Harriet Beecher Stowe, Ulysses S. Grant, William T. Sherman, Mary Chesnut, George Washington Cable, and many lesser-known figures. "The richest and most many-sided book ever produced about the Civil War"—Conor Cruise O'Brien
Foreword by C. Vann Woodward
0–19–500666–6 Oxford $35.00
0–930350–61–8 Northeastern pb $14.95

THE PORTABLE EDMUND WILSON
Edited by Lewis M. Dabney
0–14–015098–6 Penguin pb $7.95

THE SHORES OF LIGHT: A Literary Chronicle of the 1920s and 1930s
Essays on F. Scott Fitzgerald, Edna St. Vincent Millay, Sherwood Anderson, and Gertrude Stein in "a general history of the culture of a recklessly unspecialized era, when minds and imaginations were exploring in all directions" (Edmund Wilson)
Introduction by Daniel Aaron
0–930350–68–5 Northeastern pb $14.95

THE THIRTIES: From Notebooks and Diaries of the Period
Edited by Leon Edel
0–374–27572–6 Farrar, Straus & Giroux $17.50
0–671–43193–5 Washington Square pb $6.95

THE TRIPLE THINKERS & THE WOUND AND THE BOW: A Combined Volume
Two of Wilson's most important collections, including studies of Pushkin, Flaubert, Ben Jonson, Dickens, Casanova, Edith Wharton, and Sophocles
Foreword by Frank Kermode
0–930350–67–7 Northeastern pb $12.95

THE TWENTIES: From Notebooks and Diaries of the Period
Edited with introduction by Leon Edel
0–374–27963–2 Farrar, Straus & Giroux $15.00

ANTHOLOGIES

● Elizabeth Hardwick & Robert Atwan, editors
THE BEST AMERICAN ESSAYS: 1986
0–317–53357–6 Houghton Mifflin $15.95
0–317–53358–4 Houghton Mifflin pb $8.95

● Gay Talese & Robert Atwan, editors
THE BEST AMERICAN ESSAYS: 1987
0–89919–468–0 Ticknor & Fields $16.95
0–89919–533–4 Ticknor & Fields pb $8.95

● Annie Dillard & Robert Atwan, editors
THE BEST AMERICAN ESSAYS: 1988
0–89919–729–9 Ticknor & Fields $17.95
0–89919–730–2 Ticknor & Fields pb $8.95

● Maureen Howard, editor
THE PENGUIN BOOK OF CONTEMPORARY AMERICAN ESSAYS
0–14–006618–7 Penguin pb $7.95

● Robert Pack & Jay Parini, editors
THE BREAD LOAF ANTHOLOGY OF CONTEMPORARY AMERICAN ESSAYS
0–87451–475–4 New England pb $12.95

● Ben Sonnenberg, editor
PERFORMANCE AND REALITY: Essays from Grand Street
0–8135–1409–6 Rutgers pb $14.95

American Literature: Anthologies and Critical Studies

ANTHOLOGIES

• Nina Baym, editor
THE NORTON ANTHOLOGY OF AMERICAN LITERATURE
Volume 1
0–393–95377–7 Norton pb $22.95
Volume 2
0–393–95383–1 Norton pb $22.95

• Richard Ellmann, editor
THE NEW OXFORD BOOK OF AMERICAN VERSE
0–19–502058–8 Oxford $35.00

• Donald McQuade, editor
THE HARPER AMERICAN LITERATURE
Volume 1
0–06–044367–7 Harper & Row pb $24.50
Volume 2
0–06–044368–5 Harper & Row pb $23.95

• F.O. Matthiessen, editor
THE OXFORD BOOK OF AMERICAN VERSE
0–19–500049–8 Oxford $45.00

Specialized Anthologies

• Daniel J. Casey & Robert E. Rhodes, editors
MODERN IRISH-AMERICAN FICTION: A Reader
Short stories and novel excerpts from Peter Dunne, William Kennedy, Mary Gordon, and others
0–8156–2462–X Syracuse $34.95
0–8156–0234–0 Syracuse pb $14.95

• Jeffery Chan & others, editors
AIIIEEEEE!: An Anthology of Asian-American Writers
0–88258–051–5 Howard pb $6.95

• Rayna Green, editor
THAT'S WHAT SHE SAID: Contemporary Poetry and Fiction by Native American Women
0–253–20338–4 Indiana pb $12.50

• William Harmon, editor
THE OXFORD BOOK OF AMERICAN LIGHT VERSE
0–19–502509–1 Oxford $29.95

• Asunción Horno-Delgado & others, editors
BREAKING BOUNDARIES: Latina Writing and Critical Reading
0–87023–635–0 Massachusetts $40.00

• Nicolás Kanellos, editor
A DECADE OF HISPANIC LITERATURE: An Anniversary Anthology
0–934770–18–2 Arte Público pb $12.00

• Kenneth S. Lynn, editor
COMIC TRADITION IN AMERICA: An Anthology of American Humor
0–393–00447–3 Norton pb $11.95

• Ann A. Schockley, editor
AFRO-AMERICAN WOMEN WRITERS, 1746–1933: An Anthology and Critical Guide
0–8161–8823–8 G.K. Hall $40.00

GENERAL STUDIES AND REFERENCE

• Sacvan Bercovitch, editor
RECONSTRUCTING AMERICAN LITERARY HISTORY
0–674–75086–1 Harvard pb $9.95

• Richard Chase
THE AMERICAN NOVEL AND ITS TRADITION
0–8018–2303–X Johns Hopkins pb $9.95

• Emory Elliott, editor
THE COLUMBIA LITERARY HISTORY OF THE UNITED STATES
0–231–05812–8 Columbia $59.95

• James A. Emanuel & Theodore L. Gross, editors
DARK SYMPHONY: Negro Literature in America
0–02–909540–9 Free Press pb $21.95

• Donald Hall, editor
THE OXFORD BOOK OF AMERICAN LITERARY ANECDOTES
0–19–502938–0 Oxford $24.95
0–19–503388–4 Oxford pb $8.95

• James D. Hart, editor
THE CONCISE OXFORD COMPANION TO AMERICAN LITERATURE
0–19–503074–5 Oxford $49.95
0–19–503982–3 Oxford pb $24.95

• Myra Jehlen
AMERICAN INCARNATION
0–674–02426–5 Harvard $22.50

• Alfred Kazin
AN AMERICAN PROCESSION
0–394–50378–3 Knopf $18.95
A WRITER'S AMERICA: Landscape in Literature
0–394–57142–8 Knopf $24.95

• Annette Kolodny
THE LAY OF THE LAND: Metaphor As Experience and History in American Life and Letters
0–8078–4118–8 North Carolina pb $8.95

• D.H. Lawrence
STUDIES IN CLASSIC AMERICAN LITERATURE
0–14–003300–9 Penguin pb $6.95

• Ronald E. Martin
AMERICAN LITERATURE AND THE UNIVERSE OF FORCE
0–8223–0579–8 Duke pb $14.95

• Wendy Martin
AN AMERICAN TRIPTYCH: Anne Bradstreet, Emily Dickinson and Adrienne Rich
0–8078–4112–9 North Carolina pb $8.95

• Leo Marx
THE MACHINE IN THE GARDEN: Technology and the Pastoral Ideal in America
0–19–500738–7 Oxford pb $9.95
THE PILOT AND THE PASSENGER: Essays on Literature, Technology and Culture in the United States
0–19–504875–X Oxford $29.95

• Perry Miller
THE LIFE OF THE MIND IN AMERICA: From the Revolution to the Civil War
0–15–651990–9 HBJ pb $7.95

• Richard Poirier
A WORLD ELSEWHERE: The Place of Style in American Literature
0–299–09934–2 Wisconsin pb $9.95
THE RENEWAL OF LITERATURE: Emersonian Reflections
0–394–50140–3 Random House $19.95
0–300–04086–5 Yale pb $9.95

• Carolyn Porter
SEEING AND BEING: The Plight of the Participant-Observer in Emerson, James, Adams and Faulkner
0–8195–5054–X Wesleyan $27.50

• Douglas Robinson
AMERICAN APOCALYPSES: The Image of the End of the World in American Literature
0–8018–2528–8 Johns Hopkins $32.50

• Carl & Paula Shirley
UNDERSTANDING CHICANO LITERATURE
0–87249–576–0 South Carolina pb $10.95

• Richard S. Slotkin
REGENERATION THROUGH VIOLENCE: The Mythology of the American Frontier, 1600–1860
0–8195–6034–0 Wesleyan pb $14.95
THE FATAL ENVIRONMENT: The Myth of the Frontier in the Age of Industrialization, 1800–1890
0–689–11410–9 Atheneum $37.50
0–8195–6183–5 Wesleyan pb $14.95

• Valerie Smith
SELF-DISCOVERY AND AUTHORITY IN AFRO-AMERICAN NARRATIVE
0–674–80087–7 Harvard $22.50

• Werner Sollors
BEYOND ETHNICITY: Consent and Descent in American Culture
0–19–503694–8 Oxford $27.95
0–19–505193–9 Oxford pb $12.95

• Robert Stepto
FROM BEHIND THE VEIL: A Study of Afro-American Narrative
0–252–00752–2 Illinois $20.50

- Helen Vendler, editor
  VOICES AND VISIONS: The Poet in America
  0–394–53520–0 Random House $29.95

- Hyatt H. Waggoner
  AMERICAN VISIONARY POETRY
  0–8071–1051–5 LSU $22.50

  AMERICAN POETS: From the Puritans to the Present
  0–8071–1163–5 LSU pb $14.95

- Bryan J. Wolf
  ROMANTIC RE-VISION: Culture and Consciousness in Nineteenth Century American Painting and Literature
  0–226–90502–0 Chicago pb $15.95

GENERAL STUDIES: To 1900

Early American Literature

- Sacvan Bercovitch, editor
  TYPOLOGY AND EARLY AMERICAN LITERATURE
  0–87023–096–4 Massachusetts $20.00

- Jane D. Eberwein
  EARLY AMERICAN POETRY: Bradstreet, Taylor, Dwight, Freneau and Bryant
  0–299–07444–7 Wisconsin $14.50

- Emory Elliott
  REVOLUTIONARY WRITERS: Literature and Authority in the New Republic, 1725–1810
  0–19–503995–5 Oxford pb $9.95

- Everett Emerson, editor
  AMERICAN LITERATURE, 1764–1789: The Revolutionary Years
  0–299–07270–3 Wisconsin $32.50

  MAJOR WRITERS OF EARLY AMERICAN LITERATURE: Introductions to Nine Major Writers
  0–299–06194–9 Wisconsin $12.50

- Wayne Franklin
  DISCOVERERS, EXPLORERS, SETTLERS: The Diligent Writers of Early America
  0–226–26071–2 Chicago $15.00

- Moses Coit Tyler
  HISTORY OF AMERICAN LITERATURE, 1607–1783
  Tyler pioneered the systematic study of American literature; his *History* first appeared in 1878
  Edited by Archie H. Jones
  0–226–82021–1 Chicago pb $3.50

The Puritans

Sacvan Bercovitch
THE AMERICAN JEREMIAD
0–299–07354–8 Wisconsin pb $11.75

THE PURITAN ORIGINS OF THE AMERICAN SELF
0–300–02117–8 Yale pb $10.95

Patricia Caldwell
THE PURITAN CONVERSION NARRATIVE: The Beginnings of American Expression
0–521–31147–0 Cambridge pb $14.95

Emory Elliott
POWER AND THE PULPIT IN PURITAN NEW ENGLAND
0–691–07206–X Princeton $30.00

Perry Miller
THE NEW ENGLAND MIND: From Colony to Province
0–674–61306–6 Harvard pb $10.95

Peter White, editor
PURITAN POETS AND POETICS: Seventeenth-Century American Poetry in Theory and Practice
Foreword by Harrison T. Meserole
0–271–00413–4 Pennsylvania State $29.75

The 19th Century

- Nina Baym
  WOMAN'S FICTION: A Guide to Novels By and About Women in America, 1820–1870
  0–8014–9184–3 Cornell pb $12.95

- Warner Berthoff
  THE FERMENT OF REALISM: American Literature, 1884–1919
  0–521–28435–X Cambridge pb $15.95

- Van Wyck Brooks
  THE FLOWERING OF NEW ENGLAND, 1815–1865
  0–395–30522–5 Houghton Mifflin pb $7.95

  NEW ENGLAND: Indian Summer, 1865–1950
  0–226–07578–8 Chicago pb $14.95

- Lawrence Buell
  LITERARY TRANSCENDENTALISM: Style and Vision in the American Renaissance
  0–8014–9152–5 Cornell $12.95

  NEW ENGLAND LITERARY CULTURE: From the Revolution to the Renaissance
  0–521–30206–4 Cambridge $37.50

- Ann Douglas
  THE FEMINIZATION OF AMERICAN CULTURE
  0–385–24241–7 Doubleday pb $10.95

- Irving Howe
  THE AMERICAN NEWNESS: Culture and Politics in the Age of Emerson
  0–674–02640–3 Harvard $12.50

- John T. Irwin
  AMERICAN HIEROGLYPHICS: The Symbol of the Egyptian Hieroglyphics in the American Renaissance
  0–8018–2908–9 Johns Hopkins pb $12.95

- Jackson Lears
  NO PLACE OF GRACE: Antimodernism and the Transformation of American Culture, 1880–1920
  0–394–71116–5 Pantheon pb $8.95

Nathaniel Hawthorne (courtesy The Essex Institute)

- Harry Levin
  THE POWER OF BLACKNESS: Hawthorne, Poe, Melville
  0–8214–0581–0 Ohio pb $6.95

- F.O. Matthiessen
  AMERICAN RENAISSANCE: Art and Expression in the Age of Emerson and Whitman
  0–19–500759–X Oxford pb $18.95

- Donald Pizer
  REALISM AND NATURALISM IN NINETEENTH-CENTURY AMERICAN LITERATURE
  0–8093–1125–9 Southern Illinois $17.95

- David S. Reynolds
  BENEATH THE AMERICAN RENAISSANCE: The Subversive Imagination in the Age of Emerson and Melville
  0–394–54448–X Knopf $35.00

- Joan R. Sherman
  INVISIBLE POETS: Afro-Americans of the 19th Century
  0–252–06061–X Illinois pb $9.95

- John L. Thomas
  ALTERNATIVE AMERICA: Henry George, Edward Bellamy, Henry Demarest Lloyd and the Adversary Tradition
  0–674–01676–9 Harvard $27.00

- Alan Trachenberg
  THE INCORPORATION OF AMERICA: Culture and Society in the Gilded Age
  0–8090–0145–4 Hill & Wang pb $6.95

- Edmund Wilson
  PATRIOTIC GORE: Studies in the Literature of the American Civil War
  Foreword by C. Vann Woodward
  0–930350–61–8 Northeastern pb $14.95

- Larzer Ziff
  THE AMERICAN 1890s: Life and Times of a Lost Generation
  0–8032–9900–1 Nebraska pb $6.95

GENERAL STUDIES: The 20th Century

- Daniel Aaron
  WRITERS ON THE LEFT
  0–19–519970–7 Oxford pb $9.95

- Houston A. Baker, Jr.
  BLUES, IDEOLOGY, AND AFRO-AMERICAN LITERATURE: A Vernacular Theory
  0–226–03538–7 Chicago pb $8.95

  THE JOURNEY BACK: Issues in Black Literature and Criticism
  0–226–03535–2 Chicago pb $7.50

  MODERNISM AND THE HARLEM RENAISSANCE
  0–226–03524–7 Chicago $19.95

  SINGERS OF DAYBREAK: Studies in Black American Literature
  0–88258–025–6 Howard pb $6.95

- Shari Benstock
  WOMEN OF THE LEFT BANK: Paris, 1900–1940
  0–292–79029–5 Texas $26.95
  0–292–79040–6 Texas pb $12.95

- Werner Berthoff
  A LITERATURE WITHOUT QUALITIES: American Writing Since 1945
  0–520–03696–4 California $27.50

- Kay Boyle & Robert McAlmon
  BEING GENIUSES TOGETHER: 1920–1930
  0–86547–149–5 North Point pb $13.50

- Cleanth Brooks
  THE HIDDEN GOD: Studies in Hemingway, Faulkner, Yeats, Eliot and Warren
  0–300–00327–7 Yale $30.00

Malcolm Cowley
THE DREAM OF THE GOLDEN MOUNTAINS: Remembering the 1930s
0–14–005919–9 Penguin pb $8.95

EXILE'S RETURN: A Literary Odyssey of the 1920s
0–14–004392–6 Penguin pb $8.95

A SECOND FLOWERING: Works and Days of the Lost Generation
0–14–005498–7 Penguin pb $7.95

- Arthur P. Davis
  FROM THE DARK TOWER: Afro-American Writers, 1900–1960
  0–88258–004–3 Howard $14.95
  0–88258–058–2 Howard pb $7.95

- Ursula B. Davis
  PARIS WITHOUT REGRET: James Baldwin, Chester Himes, Kenny Clarke, and Donald Byrd
  0–87745–147–8 Iowa $14.95

- Mari Evans, editor
  BLACK WOMEN WRITERS, 1950–1980: A Critical Evaluation
  Introduction by Stephen Henderson
  0–385–17125–0 Doubleday pb $12.95

- Hugh Ford
  PUBLISHED IN PARIS: A Literary Chronicle of Paris in the 1920s and 1930s
  Foreword by Janet Flanner
  0–02–032550–9 Macmillan pb $14.95

- Henry Louis Gates, Jr.
  FIGURES IN BLACK: Words, Signs, and the Racial Self
  0–19–503564–X Oxford pb $29.95

  THE SIGNIFYING MONKEY: A Theory of Afro-American Literary Criticism
  0–19–503463–5 Oxford $29.95

- Henry Louis Gates, Jr., editor
  BLACK LITERATURE AND LITERARY THEORY
  0–416–37240–6 RC&H pb $13.95

  RACE, WRITING, AND DIFFERENCE
  0–226–28435–2 Chicago pb $15.95

- Norman Harris
  CONNECTING TIMES: The '60s in Afro-American Fiction
  0–87805–335–2 Mississippi $27.50

- Charles Johnson
  BEING AND RACE: Black Writing Since 1970
  0–253–31165–9 Indiana $15.95

- Alfred Kazin
  BRIGHT BOOK OF LIFE: Novelists and Storytellers from Hemingway to Mailer
  0–268–00664–4 Notre Dame pb $9.95

  ON NATIVE GROUNDS: An Interpretation of Modern American Prose Literature
  0–15–668751–8 HBJ pb $9.95

- Bruce Kellner, editor
  THE HARLEM RENAISSANCE: A Historical Dictionary for the Era
  0–416–01671–5 Methuen pb $16.95

- Elaine Kim
  ASIAN-AMERICAN LITERATURE: An Introduction to the Writings and Their Social Context
  0–87722–352–1 Temple pb $16.95

- Richard H. King
  SOUTHERN RENAISSANCE: The Cultural Awakening of the American South, 1930–1955
  0–19–502664–0 Oxford $22.50

- Kenneth Lincoln
  NATIVE AMERICAN RENAISSANCE
  0–520–05457–1 California pb $10.95

- Larry McCaffery, editor
  ALIVE AND WRITING: Interviews with American Authors of the 1980s
  0–252–06011–3 Illinois pb $9.95

- David Madden
  TOUGH GUY WRITERS OF THE THIRTIES
  0–8093–0912–2 Southern Illinois pb $9.95

- Ladell Payne
  BLACK NOVELISTS AND THE SOUTHERN LITERARY TRADITION
  0–8203–0536–7 Georgia $11.00

- Monty N. Penkower
  THE FEDERAL WRITERS' PROJECT: A Study in Government Patronage of the Arts
  0–252–00610–0 Illinois pb $17.50

- Donald Pizer
  TWENTIETH-CENTURY AMERICAN LITERARY NATURALISM: An Interpretation
  0–8093–1027–9 Southern Illinois $17.95

- Sigmund Ro
  RAGE AND CELEBRATION: Essays on Contemporary Afro-American Writing
  0–391–03094–9 Humanities $12.50

- Roger Rosenblatt
  BLACK FICTION
  0–674–07622–2 Harvard pb $6.95

- Ted Solotaroff
  THE RED HOT VACUUM
  0–87923–292–7 Godine pb $7.50

- John Tytell
  NAKED ANGELS: The Lives and Literature of the Beat Generation
  0–394–62179–4 Grove pb $8.95

- John Hall Wheelock, editor
  EDITOR TO AUTHOR: The Letters of Maxwell E. Perkins
  0–684–18840–6 Scribners pb $9.95

Poetry

- Houston A. Baker, Jr.
  AFRO-AMERICAN POETICS: Revisions of Harlem and the Black Aesthetic
  0–299–11500–3 Wisconsin $19.95

- Bruce-Novoa
  CHICANO POETRY: A Response to Chaos
  0–292–71092–5 Tennessee pb $9.00

- Frederick Feirstein, editor
  EXPANSIVE POETRY: Essays on the New Narrative and the New Formalism
  0–934257–27–2 Story Line pb $15.95

- Robert Hass
  TWENTIETH CENTURY PLEASURES: Prose on Poetry
  0–88001–045–2 Ecco $17.95
  0–88001–046–0 Ecco pb $9.50

- Michael Heller
  CONVICTION'S NET OF BRANCHES: Essays on the Objectivist Poets and Poetry
  0–8093–1188–7 Southern Illinois pb $9.95

- David Kalstone
  BECOMING A POET: Elizabeth Bishop, with Marianne Moore and Robert Lowell
  Edited with a preface by Robert Hemenway
  Afterword by James Merrill
  0–374–10960–5 Farrar, Straus & Giroux $22.50

  FIVE TEMPERAMENTS: Elizabeth Bishop, Robert Lowell, James Merrill, Adrienne Rich, John Ashbery
  0–19–502260–2 Oxford $22.50

 IF YOU CAN'T FIND IT, LOOK IN THE INDEX

- Diane W. Middlebrook & Marilyn Yalom, editor
COMING TO LIGHT: American Women Poets in the Twentieth Century
0–472–10066–1 Michigan $25.00
0–472–08061–X Michigan pb $12.95

- Alicia Suskin Ostriker
STEALING THE LANGUAGE: The Emergence of Women's Poetry in America
0–8070–6303–7 Beacon pb $10.95

- David Perkins
A HISTORY OF MODERN POETRY: From the 1890s to the High Modernist Mode
0–674–39941–2 Harvard $32.00
0–674–39945–5 Harvard pb $14.00

A HISTORY OF MODERN POETRY: Modernism and After
Useful two-volume history of modern American and English poetic tendencies
0–674–39946–3 Harvard $25.00

- Marjorie Perloff
THE DANCE OF THE INTELLECT: Studies in the Poetry of the Pound Tradition
0–521–34756–4 Cambridge pb $12.95

THE POETICS OF INDETERMINACY: Rimbaud to Cage
0–8101–0661–2 Northwestern pb $14.95

- Robert Pinsky
THE SITUATION OF POETRY: Contemporary Poetry and Its Traditions
0–691–01352–7 Princeton pb $10.95

- J. Saunders Redding
TO MAKE A POET BLACK
Introduction by Henry L. Gates, Jr.
0–8014–9438–9 Cornell pb $6.95

- Helen Vendler
THE MUSIC OF WHAT HAPPENS: Poems, Poets, Critics
0–674–59152–6 Harvard $29.50

PART OF NATURE, PART OF US: Modern American Poets
0–674–65475–7 Harvard $21.00
0–674–65476–5 Harvard pb $8.95

- Stephen Vincent & Ellen Zweig, editors
THE POETRY READING: A Contemporary Compendium on Language and Performance
0–917672–10–0 Momo's pb $9.95

- Robert Von Hallberg
AMERICAN POETRY AND CULTURE: 1945–1980
0–674–03011–7 Harvard $24.50

Poets on Poetry

- Donald M. Allen & Warren Tallman, editors
THE POETICS OF THE NEW AMERICAN POETRY
0–394–17801–7 Grove pb $14.95

- Bruce Andrews & Charles Bernstein, editors
THE L=A=N=G=U=A=G=E BOOK
A gathering of writings from the magazine
L=A=N=G=U=A=G=E
0–8093–1106–2 Southern Illinois pb $14.95

- Robert Bly
TALKING ALL MORNING
0–472–15760–4 Michigan pb $8.95

- Robert Creeley
THE COLLECTED PROSE OF ROBERT CREELEY
0–520–06151–9 California pb $12.95

- James Dickey
BABEL TO BYZANTIUM
0–912946–86–5 Ecco pb $7.95

- Robert Duncan
FICTIVE CERTAINTIES
0–8112–0949–0 New Directions pb $9.95

T.S. Eliot (photo by Kay Bell Reynal, courtesy The National Portrait Gallery)

- T.S. Eliot
SELECTED ESSAYS
0–15–180387–0 HBJ $19.95

THE SACRED WOOD
0–416–67610–3 RC&H pb $13.95

- John Haines
LIVING OFF THE COUNTRY: Essays on Poetry and Place
0–472–06333–2 Michigan pb $8.95

- Robert Hayden
THE COLLECTED PROSE
Edited by Frederick Glaysher
0–472–06351–0 Michigan pb $8.95

- Anthony Hecht
OBBLIGATI: Essays in Criticism
0–689–11570–9 Atheneum $18.95

- Richard Howard
ALONE WITH AMERICA
0–689–11000–6 Atheneum $25.00
0–689–70594–8 Atheneum pb $12.95

- Randall Jarrell
POETRY AND THE AGE
0–912946–70–9 Ecco pb $8.50

- Galway Kinnell
WALKING DOWN THE STAIRS
0–472–52530–1 Michigan pb $8.95

- Maxine Kumin
TO MAKE A PRAIRIE: Essays on Poets, Poetry, and Country Living
0–472–06306–5 Michigan pb $8.95

- David Lehman, editor
ECSTATIC OCCASIONS, EXPEDIENT FORMS: 65 Leading Contemporary Poets Select and Comment on Their Poems
0–02–069840–2 Macmillan pb $10.95

- Denise Levertov
THE POET IN THE WORLD
0–8112–0493–6 New Directions pb $8.95

- Robert Lowell
COLLECTED PROSE
0–374–12625–9 Farrar, Straus & Giroux $25.00

- Michael McClure
SCRATCHING THE BEAT SURFACE
0–86547–073–1 North Point $17.50

- Marianne Moore
THE COMPLETE PROSE OF MARIANNE MOORE
Edited by Patricia C. Willis
0–14–009436–9 Penguin pb $10.95

- Alicia Ostriker
WRITING LIKE A WOMAN
0–472–06347–2 Michigan pb $8.95

- Ezra Pound
ABC OF READING
0–8112–0151–1 New Directions pb $6.95

GUIDE TO KULCHUR
0–8112–0156–2 New Directions pb $7.95

LITERARY ESSAYS
Edited by T.S. Eliot
0–8112–0157–0 New Directions pb $12.95

SELECTED PROSE, 1909–1965
Edited by William Cookson
0–8112–0574–6 New Directions pb $12.95

PAVANNES AND DIVAGATIONS
0–8112–0575–4 New Directions pb $9.95

Ezra Pound

• Theodore Roethke
**STRAW FOR THE FIRE: From the
Notebooks, 1943–63**
Edited by David Wagoner
0–295–95753–0 Washington pb $8.95

• Jerome Rothenberg
PRE-FACES & OTHER WRITINGS
0–8112–0785–4 New Directions $14.95
0–8112–0786–2 New Directions pb $6.95

• Jerome & Diane Rothenberg
**SYMPOSIUM OF THE WHOLE: A Range
of Discourse Toward an Ethnopoetics**
0–520–04530–0 California $29.95
0–520–04531–9 California pb $15.95

• Ron Silliman
THE NEW SENTENCE
0–937804–20–7 Segue pb $12.95

• William Stafford
WRITING THE AUSTRALIAN CRAWL
0–472–87300–8 Michigan pb $8.95

• Diane Wakoski
TOWARDS A NEW POETRY
0–472–06307–3 Michigan pb $8.95

• Richard Wilbur
RESPONSES: Prose Pieces, 1948–1976
0–15–676550–0 HBJ pb $3.95

• Louis Zukofsky
**PREPOSITIONS: The Collected Critical
Essays of Louis Zukofsky**
Foreword by Hugh Kenner
0–520–04361–8 California pb $9.95

Drama

• Ruby Cohn
NEW AMERICAN DRAMATISTS
0–394–17962–5 Grove pb $7.95

• Errol Hill, editor
**THE THEATRE OF BLACK
AMERICANS**
0–936839–27–9 Applause pb $12.95

• Nicolás Kanellos
**HISPANIC THEATRE IN THE UNITED
STATES**
0–934770–44–1 Arte Público pb $8.00

**MEXICAN AMERICAN THEATER:
Legacy and Reality**
0–935480–22–6 Latin American pb $10.00

• Theodore Shank
AMERICAN ALTERNATIVE THEATRE
0–312–02126–7 St. Martin's pb $14.95

Dramatists on Drama

• Arthur Miller
**THE THEATER ESSAYS OF ARTHUR
MILLER**
Edited by Robert A. Martin
0–14–004903–7 Penguin pb $9.95

• Clifford Odets
**THE TIME IS RIPE: The 1940 Journal of
Clifford Odets**
0–8021–1034–7 Grove $22.50

• Thornton Wilder
**THE JOURNALS OF THORNTON
WILDER, 1939–1961**
Edited by Donald Gallup
0–300–0405407 Yale pb $13.95

• David Savran, editor
**IN THEIR OWN WORDS: Contemporary
American Playwrights**
0–930452–70–4 Theatre Comm pb $12.95

• Kathleen Betsko & Rachel Koenig
**INTERVIEWS WITH CONTEMPORARY
WOMEN PLAYWRIGHTS**
0–688–07033–7 Morrow pb $12.95

STUDIES OF INDIVIDUAL AUTHORS
(alphabetical by subject)

To 1900

• R.P. Blackmur
HENRY ADAMS
Introduction by Denis Donoghue
0–15–139997–2 HBJ $19.95
0–306–80219–8 Da Capo pb $10.95

• William Dusinberre
HENRY ADAMS: The Myth of Failure
0–8139–0833–7 Virginia $22.50

• Louisa May Alcott
**THE JOURNALS OF LOUISA MAY
ALCOTT**
Edited by Joel Myerson & Daniel Shealy
0–316–59362–1 Little, Brown $24.95

• Sarah Elbert
**A HUNGER FOR HOME: Louisa May
Alcott's Place in American Culture**
0–8135–1199–2 Rutgers pb $12.00

• Norman S. Grabo
**THE COINCIDENTAL ART OF
CHARLES BROCKDEN BROWN**
0–8078–1474–1 North Carolina $22.00

• Per Seyersted
KATE CHOPIN: A Critical Biography
0–8071–0678–X LSU pb $8.95

• Wayne Franklin
**THE NEW WORLD OF JAMES
FENIMORE COOPER**
0–226–26080–1 Chicago pb $17.00

• Daniel H. Peck
**A WORLD BY ITSELF: The Pastoral
Moment in Cooper's Fiction**
0–300–02027–9 Yale $25.00

• John Berryman
STEPHEN CRANE: A Critical Biography
0–374–51732–0 Farrar, Straus & Giroux pb $9.25

• Gay Wilson Allen & Roger Asselineau
**ST. JOHN DE CREVECOEUR: The Life
of an American Farmer**
0–670–81345–1 Viking $19.95

• Sharon Cameron
**LYRIC TIME: Dickinson and the Limits of
Genre**
0–8018–2116–9 Johns Hopkins pb $12.95

• Jane D. Eberwein
DICKINSON: Strategies of Limitation
0–87023–549–4 Massachusetts pb $11.95

• Susan Howe
MY EMILY DICKINSON
0–938190–52–0 North Atlantic pb $9.95

• Thomas H. Johnson
**EMILY DICKINSON: An Interpretive
Biography**
0–689–70113–6 Atheneum pb $9.95

• Suzanne Juhasz, editor
**FEMINIST CRITICS READ EMILY
DICKINSON**
0–253–32170–0 Indiana $17.50

• Vivian R. Pollak
DICKINSON: The Anxiety of Gender
0–8014–9370–6 Cornell pb $8.95

• Cynthia Griffin Wolff
EMILY DICKINSON
0–394–54418–8 Knopf $25.00

• Perry Miller
JONATHAN EDWARDS
0–87023–328–9 Massachusetts $11.95

• Gay Wilson Allen
WALDO EMERSON: A Biography
0–670–74866–8 Viking $25.00

• Joel Porte
EMERSON: Prospect and Retrospect
0–674–24915–1 Harvard $18.50
0–674–24917–8 Harvard pb $5.95

**REPRESENTATIVE MAN: Ralph Waldo
Emerson in His Time**
0–231–06740–2 Columbia $45.00

*Ralph Waldo Emerson (courtesy The Emerson
National Memorial Association)*

TO ORDER BOOKS AS GIFTS, SEE PAGE 1

- David Robinson
  APOSTLE OF CULTURE: Emerson As Preacher and Lecturer
  0-8122-7824-0 Pennsylvania $22.95

- R.A. Yoder
  EMERSON AND THE ORPHIC POET IN AMERICA
  0-520-03317-5 California $27.50

- Margaret V. Allen
  THE ACHIEVEMENT OF MARGARET FULLER
  0-271-00215-8 Pennsylvania State $24.95

- Paula Blanchard
  MARGARET FULLER: From Transcendentalism to Revolution
  Introduction by Carolyn Heilbrun
  0-201-10458-X Addison-Wesley pb $12.95

- Edgar A. Dryden
  NATHANIEL HAWTHORNE: The Poetics of Enchantment
  0-8014-1028-2 Cornell $19.95

- Philip Young
  HAWTHORNE'S SECRET: An Un-Told Tale
  Literary detective work disclosing the mysteries of Nathaniel Hawthorne's past
  0-87923-515-2 Godine $15.95

- William McMurray
  THE LITERARY REALISM OF WILLIAM DEAN HOWELLS
  0-8093-0237-3 Southern Illinois pb $6.95

- Elizabeth S. Prioleau
  THE CIRCLE OF EROS: Sexuality in the Work of William Dean Howells
  0-8223-0492-9 Duke $28.95

- Elizabeth Allen
  A WOMAN'S PLACE IN THE NOVELS OF HENRY JAMES
  0-312-88653-5 St. Martin's $25.00

- R.P. Blackmur
  STUDIES IN HENRY JAMES
  Edited by Veronica A. Makowsky
  0-8112-0864-8 New Directions pb $9.25

- Peter Brooks
  THE MELODRAMATIC IMAGINATION: Balzac, Henry James, Melodrama, and the Mode of Excess
  0-231-06007-6 Columbia pb $14.50

- Leon Edel
  HENRY JAMES: A Life
  0-06-015459-4 Harper & Row $24.95
  0-06-091432-7 Harper & Row pb $12.95

- Simon Nowell-Smith, editor
  THE LEGEND OF THE MASTER: Henry James as Others Saw Him
  0-19-281921-6 Oxford pb $10.95

- Miranda Seymour
  A RING OF CONSPIRATORS: Henry James and His Literary Circle, 1895–1915
  0-395-51173-9 Houghton Mifflin $19.95

- Edgar A. Dryden
  MELVILLE'S THEMATICS OF FORM: The Great Art of Telling the Truth
  0-8018-2619-5 Johns Hopkins pb $9.95

- Charles Olson
  CALL ME ISHMAEL
  A study of Melville and the writing of *Moby Dick*
  0-87286-036-1 City Lights pb $5.95

- Michael P. Rogin
  SUBVERSIVE GENEALOGY: The Politics and Art of Herman Melville
  0-520-05178-5 California pb $11.95

- Howard P. Vincent
  THE TRYING-OUT OF MOBY DICK
  0-87338-247-1 Kent State pb $8.50

- Charles Baudelaire
  FATAL DESTINIES: The Edgar Allen Poe Essays
  Translated by Joan F. Mele
  0-916696-17-0 Cross Country pb $4.95

  BAUDELAIRE ON POE: Critical Papers
  Edited by Lois & F.E. Hyslop
  0-271-00317-0 Pennsylvania State $20.00

- J. Gerald Kennedy
  POE, DEATH, AND THE LIFE OF WRITING
  0-300-03773-2 Yale $22.50

- Eric Sundquist, editor
  NEW ESSAYS ON UNCLE TOM'S CABIN
  0-521-30203-X Cambridge $19.95
  0-521-31786-X Cambridge pb $7.95

- Karl Keller
  THE EXAMPLE OF EDWARD TAYLOR
  0-87023-174-X Massachusetts $22.50

Edgar Allan Poe (courtesy The American Antiquarian Society)

- Sharon Cameron
  WRITING NATURE: Henry Thoreau's Journal
  0-19-503570-4 Oxford $22.50

- Stanley Cavell
  THE SENSES OF WALDEN: An Expanded Edition
  0-86547-031-6 North Point pb $15.00

- Richard Lebeaux
  THOREAU'S SEASONS
  0-87023-401-3 Massachusetts $28.50

- Robert D. Richardson, Jr.
  HENRY THOREAU: A Life of the Mind
  0-520-06346-5 California pb $10.95

- Louis J. Budd
  OUR MARK TWAIN: The Making of a Public Personality
  0-8122-1204-5 Pennsylvania $16.95

- James M. Cox
  MARK TWAIN: The Fate of Humor
  0-691-01327-6 Princeton pb $13.95

- Bernard De Voto
  MARK TWAIN'S AMERICA: An Essay in the Correction of Ideas
  0-89301-108-8 Idaho pb $10.95

- Justin Kaplan
  MR. CLEMENS AND MARK TWAIN
  0-671-47071-X Simon & Schuster pb $12.95

- Gay Wilson Allen
  THE NEW WALT WHITMAN HANDBOOK
  0-8147-0585-5 NYU pb $20.00

  THE SOLITARY SINGER: A Critical Biography of Walt Whitman
  0-226-01435-5 Chicago pb $15.95

- Justin Kaplan
  WALT WHITMAN: A Life
  0-671-62257-9 Simon & Schuster pb $12.95

- James E. Miller, Jr.
  THE AMERICAN QUEST FOR A SUPREME FICTION: Whitman's Legacy in the Personal Epic
  0-226-52612-7 Chicago pb $9.95

- Paul Zweig
  WALT WHITMAN: The Making of the Poet
  0-317-20657-5 Basic Books pb $8.95

The 20th Century

- Laurence Bergreen
  JAMES AGEE: A Biography
  0-14-008064-3 Penguin pb $8.95

- Edward Albee
  CONVERSATIONS WITH EDWARD ALBEE
  Edited by Philip C. Kolin
  0-87805-342-5 Mississippi pb $15.95

- Irving Howe
  SHERWOOD ANDERSON
  0-8047-0237-3 Stanford pb $9.95

• Kim Townsend
SHERWOOD ANDERSON: A Biography
0–395–36533–3 Houghton Mifflin $22.95

• James Baldwin
CONVERSATIONS WITH JAMES BALDWIN
Edited by Fred L. Standley & Louis H. Pratt
0–87805–389–1 Mississippi pb $14.95

• Quincy Troupe, editor
JAMES BALDWIN: The Legacy
0–671–67650–4 Simon & Schuster $21.95
0–671–67651–2 Simon & Schuster pb $10.95

• Andrew Field
DJUNA: The Formidable Miss Barnes
0–292–71546–3 Texas pb $8.95

• Daniel Fuchs
SAUL BELLOW: Vision and Revision
0–8223–0420–1 Duke pb $13.95

• Millicent Dillon
A LITTLE ORIGINAL SIN: The Life and Work of Jane Bowles
0–03–058317–9 Henry Holt $18.95
0–03–062027–9 Henry Holt pb $9.95

• Richard F. Patteson
A WORLD OUTSIDE: The Fiction of Paul Bowles
0–292–79035–X Texas pb $7.95

• Christopher Sawyer-Lauçanno
AN INVISIBLE SPECTATOR: A Biography of Paul Bowles
1–55584–116–3 Weidenfeld & Nicolson $24.95

• William S. Burroughs
THE JOB: Interviews by Daniel Odier
0–394–17870–X Grove pb $4.95

• Robin Lydenberg
WORD CULTURES: Radical Theory and Practice in William S. Burroughs' Fiction
0–252–01413–8 Illinois $24.95

• Ted Morgan
LITERARY OUTLAW: The Life and Times of William S. Burroughs
0–8050–0901–9 Henry Holt $27.50

• Roy Hoopes
CAIN: The Biography of James M. Cain
0–8093–1361–8 Southern Illinois pb $16.95

• Erskine Caldwell
CONVERSATIONS WITH ERSKINE CALDWELL
Edited by Edwin T. Arnold
0–87805–344–1 Mississippi pb $15.95

WITH ALL MY MIGHT: An Autobiography
0–934601–11–9 Peachtree $19.95

• John Malcolm Brinnin
TRUMAN CAPOTE: Dear Heart, Old Buddy
0–385–29621–5 Delta pb $9.95

• Truman Capote
CONVERSATIONS WITH TRUMAN CAPOTE
Edited by M.T. Inge
0–87805–275–5 Mississippi pb $14.95

• Gerald Clarke
CAPOTE: A Biography
0–671–22811–0 Simon & Schuster $22.95

• E.K. Brown & Leon Edel
WILLA CATHER: A Critical Biography
0–8032–6084–9 Nebraska pb $9.95

• Sharon O'Brien
WILLA CATHER: The Emerging Voice
0–19–504132–1 Oxford $29.95
0–449–90283–8 Fawcett pb $12.95

• Phyllis C. Robinson
WILLA: The Life of Willa Cather
0–03–071931–3 Henry Holt pb $8.95

• James Woodress
WILLA CATHER: Her Life and Art
0–8032–4719–2 Nebraska $22.95

• Frank MacShane, editor
SELECTED LETTERS OF RAYMOND CHANDLER
0–231–05080–1 Columbia $29.50
0–385–29531–6 Dell pb $11.95

• John Cheever
CONVERSATIONS WITH JOHN CHEEVER
Edited by Scott Donaldson
0–87805–331–X Mississippi $25.95
0–87805–332–8 Mississippi pb $14.95

• Susan Cheever
HOME BEFORE DARK
0–671–60370–1 Pocket pb $4.50

• Scott Donaldson
JOHN CHEEVER: A Biography
0–394–54921–X Random House $22.50

• Warner Berthoff
HART CRANE: A Re-Introduction
0–8166–1700–7 Minnesota $30.00
0–8166–1701–5 Minnesota pb $14.95

• Herbert Leibowitz
HART CRANE: An Introduction to the Poetry
0–231–08670–9 Columbia pb $13.00

• George J. Becker
JOHN DOS PASSOS
0–8044–2034–3 Ungar $16.95

• Richard D. Lehan
THEODORE DREISER: His World and His Novels
0–8093–0663–8 Southern Illinois pb $6.95

• Richard Lingeman
THEODORE DREISER: Volume 1, At the Gates of the City, 1871–1907
0–399–13147–7 Putnam $22.95

• Thomas P. Riggio, editor
THE DREISER-MENCKEN LETTERS: The Correspondence of Theodore Dreiser and H.L. Mencken, 1907–1945

Volume 1
0–8122–8008–3 Pennsylvania $35.95

Volume 2
0–8122–8043–1 Pennsylvania $39.95

Theodore Dreiser (courtesy University of Pennsylvania)

• Robert J. Bertholf & Ian W. Reid, editors
ROBERT DUNCAN: Scales of the Marvelous
0–8112–0735–8 New Directions pb $5.95

• Calvin Bedient
HE DO THE POLICE IN DIFFERENT VOICES: The Waste Land and Its Protagonist
0–226–04141–7 Chicago pb $12.95

• Ronald Bush
T.S. ELIOT: A Study in Character and Style
0–19–503376–0 Oxford $29.95

• Helen Gardner
THE ART OF T.S. ELIOT
0–571–08527–X Faber & Faber pb $6.95

• Joseph Blotner, editor
SELECTED LETTERS OF WILLIAM FAULKNER
0–394–72505–0 Random House pb $4.95

• Joseph Blotner
FAULKNER: A Biography, Volume 1
0–394–50413–5 Random House $35.00

• Cleanth Brooks
WILLIAM FAULKNER: First Encounters
0–300–03399–0 Yale pb $9.95

• Malcolm Cowley
THE FAULKNER-COWLEY FILE: Letters & Memories, 1944–1962
0–14–004684–4 Penguin pb $3.95

• Irving Howe
WILLIAM FAULKNER: A Critical Study
0–226–35484–9 Chicago pb $8.00

• Frederick R. Karl
WILLIAM FAULKNER: American Writer
1–555–84088–4 Weidenfeld & Nicolson $35.00

- David Minter
  WILLIAM FAULKNER: His Life and Work
  0-8018-2463-X Johns Hopkins pb $9.95

- Stephen Oates
  WILLIAM FAULKNER: The Man and the Artist
  0-06-091501-3 Harper & Row pb $9.95

- Carolyn W. Sylvander
  JESSIE REDMON FAUSET: Black American Writer
  0-87875-196-3 Whitston $18.50

- Matthew Bruccoli
  SOME SORT OF EPIC GRANDEUR: The Life of F. Scott Fitzgerald
  0-15-683803-6 HBJ pb $12.95

- F. Scott Fitzgerald
  THE LETTERS OF F. SCOTT FITZGERALD
  0-684-16476-0 Scribners $40.00

- James R. Mellow
  INVENTED LIVES: The Marriage of F. Scott and Zelda Fitzgerald
  0-395-34412-3 Houghton Mifflin $22.50

- Andrew Turnbull
  F. SCOTT FITZGERALD: A Biography
  0-02-040621-5 Macmillan pb $10.95

- Nancy Milford
  ZELDA
  Biography of Zelda Fitzgerald
  0-06-091069-0 Harper & Row pb $8.95

- Philip L. Gerber
  ROBERT FROST
  0-8057-7348-7 G.K. Hall $16.95

- Richard Poirier
  ROBERT FROST: The Work of Knowing
  0-19-502615-2 Oxford pb $8.95

- William H. Pritchard
  FROST: A Literary Life Reconsidered
  0-19-503730-8 Oxford pb $8.95

- Barry Miles
  ALLEN GINSBERG
  0-671-50713-3 Simon & Schuster $24.95

- Nikki Giovanni
  GEMINI: An Extended Autobiographical Statement on My First 25 Years of Being a Black Poet
  0-14-004264-4 Penguin pb $4.95

- Diane Johnson
  DASHIELL HAMMETT: A Life
  0-449-90223-4 Fawcett pb $8.95

- Julian Symons
  DASHIELL HAMMETT
  0-15-123950-9 HBJ $24.95
  0-15-623956-6 HBJ pb $12.95

- Lorraine Hansberry
  TO BE YOUNG, GIFTED AND BLACK
  Introduction by James Baldwin
  0-451-13228-9 NAL pb $3.50

- Rachel Blau DuPlessis
  H.D.: The Career of That Struggle
  0-253-32702-4 Indiana $27.50
  0-253-20400-3 Indiana pb $8.95

- Susan S. Friedman
  PSYCHE REBORN: The Emergence of H.D.
  0-253-20449-6 Indiana pb $9.95

- Peter Feibleman
  LILLY: Reminiscences of Lillian Hellman
  0-688-06188-5 Morrow pb $19.95

- Carl Rollyson
  LILLIAN HELLMAN: Her Legend and Her Legacy
  0-312-00049-9 St. Martin's $24.95

- William Wright
  LILLIAN HELLMAN: The Image, The Woman
  0-345-34740-4 Ballantine pb $4.95

- Carlos Baker
  ERNEST HEMINGWAY: A Life Story
  0-02-001690-5 Macmillan pb $12.95

- Denis Brian
  THE TRUE GEN: An Intimate Portrait of Hemingway by Those Who Knew Him
  0-8021-0006-6 Grove $19.95

- Norberto Fuentes
  HEMINGWAY IN CUBA
  0-8184-0356-X Lyle Stuart $22.50

- Peter Griffin
  ALONG WITH YOUTH: Hemingway, the Early Years
  Foreword by Jack Hemingway
  0-19-503680-8 Oxford $19.95
  0-19-505066-5 Oxford pb $8.95

- Gregory H. Hemingway
  PAPA: A Personal Memoir
  Preface by Norman Mailer
  1-55778-068-4 Paragon pb $8.95

- A.E. Hotchner
  PAPA HEMINGWAY: The Ecstasy and Sorrow
  0-688-02042-9 Morrow pb $8.95

- Kenneth S. Lynn
  HEMINGWAY
  0-317-58864-8 Simon & Schuster $24.95
  0-449-90308-7 Fawcett pb $14.95

- Jeffrey Meyers
  HEMINGWAY: A Biography
  0-06-091364-9 Harper & Row pb $9.95

- Michael Reynolds
  THE YOUNG HEMINGWAY
  0-631-14787-X Blackwell $12.95

- Arnold Rampersad
  THE LIFE OF LANGSTON HUGHES
  Volume 1: I, Too, Sing America, 1902–1941
  0-19-504011-2 Oxford $27.50
  0-19-505426-1 Oxford pb $9.95
  Volume 2: I Dream a World, 1941–1967
  0-19-504519-X Oxford $24.95

- Robert E. Hemenway
  ZORA NEALE HURSTON: A Literary Biography
  Foreword by Alice Walker
  0-252-00652-6 Illinois $24.95
  0-252-00807-3 Illinois pb $10.95

- Ralph F. Voss
  A LIFE OF WILLIAM INGE: The Strains of Triumph
  0-7006-0384-0 Kansas $27.50

- Judy Oppenheimer
  PRIVATE DEMONS: The Life of Shirley Jackson
  0-399-13356-9 Putnam $19.95

- Adrienne Kennedy
  PEOPLE WHO LED TO MY PLAYS
  0-394-55660-7 Knopf $17.95

- Ann Charters
  KEROUAC: A Biography
  0-312-00617-9 St. Martin's pb $10.95

- Barry Gifford & Lawrence Lee
  JACK'S BOOK: An Oral Biography of Jack Kerouac
  0-3120-1567-4 St. Martin's pb $9.95

- Joyce Johnson
  MINOR CHARACTERS
  A memoir of Jack Kerouac
  0-671-49681-6 Washington Square pb $3.95

- D. McNally
  DESOLATE ANGEL: Jack Kerouac, the Beat Generation and America
  0-07-045670-4 McGraw-Hill pb $6.95

- Gerald Nicosia
  MEMORY BABE: A Critical Biography of Jack Kerouac
  0-394-52270-2 Grove $22.50
  0-14-058016-6 Penguin pb $9.95

- Jonathan Yardley
  RING: A Biography of Ring Lardner
  0-689-70681-2 Atheneum pb $13.95

- Sheldon N. Grebstein
  SINCLAIR LEWIS
  0-8057-0448-5 G.K. Hall $16.95
  0-8084-0278-1 New College pb $10.95

- Ian Hamilton
  ROBERT LOWELL: A Biography
  0-394-71646-9 Random House pb $8.95

- Philip Hobsbaum
  A READER'S GUIDE TO ROBERT LOWELL
  0-500-15020-6 Thames & Hudson pb $10.95

- Mark Rudman
  ROBERT LOWELL: An Introduction to the Poetry
  0-231-04672-3 Columbia $25.00

- Carol Gelderman
  MARY McCARTHY: A Life
  0-312-00565-2 St. Martin's $24.95

Robert Lowell

- Virginia S. Carr
THE LONELY HUNTER: A Biography of Carson McCullers
0–88184–123–4 Carroll & Graf pb $12.95

- Wayne F. Cooper
CLAUDE McKAY, REBEL SOJOURNER IN THE HARLEM RENAISSANCE: A Biography
0–8071–1310–7 LSU $29.95

- Norman Mailer
CONVERSATIONS WITH NORMAN MAILER
Edited by J. Michael Lennon
0–87805–352–2 Mississippi pb $15.95

- Joseph Wenke
MAILER'S AMERICA
0–87451–393–6 New England $30.00

- Leslie & Joyce Field, editors
BERNARD MALAMUD AND HIS CRITICS
0–8147–2552–X Columbia $40.00

- Arthur Miller
TIMEBENDS: A Life
0–8021–0015–5 Grove $24.95

- Neil Carson
ARTHUR MILLER
0–394–17966–8 Grove pb $6.95

- Lawrence Durrell & Henry Miller
THE DURRELL-MILLER LETTERS, 1935–1980
Edited by Ian S. MacNiven
0–8112–1043–X New Directions $26.95

- Henry Miller
FROM YOUR CAPRICORN FRIEND: Henry Miller and Stroker, 1978–1980
Introduction by Irving Stettner
0–8112–0891–5 New Directions pb $6.25

- Henry Miller & Anaïs Nin
A LITERATE PASSION: Letters of Anaïs Nin and Henry Miller, 1932–1953
0–15–152729–6 HBJ $19.95

- Henry Miller & Brenda Venus
DEAR, DEAR BRENDA: The Love Letters of Henry Miller to Brenda Venus
Edited by Gerald S. Sindell
Preface by Lawrence Durrell
0–8050–0356–8 Henry Holt pb $7.95

- Robert Coles
FLANNERY O'CONNOR'S SOUTH
0–8071–0655–0 LSU $25.00

- Flannery O'Connor
CONVERSATIONS WITH FLANNERY O'CONNOR
Edited by Rosemary M. Magee
0–87805–265–8 Mississippi pb $10.95

THE HABIT OF BEING: Letters of Flannery O'Connor
Edited by Sally Fitzgerald
0–374–16769–9 Farrar, Straus & Giroux $29.50
0–394–74259–1 Random House pb $10.95

- Marjorie Perloff
FRANK O'HARA: Poet Among Painters
0–292–72429–2 Texas pb $7.95

- Don Byrd
CHARLES OLSON'S MAXIMUS
0–252–00779–4 Illinois $15.00

- Sherman Paul
OLSON'S PUSH: Origin, Black Mountain, and Recent American Poetry
0–8071–0461–2 LSU $25.00

- Charles Stein
THE SECRET OF THE BLACK CHRYSANTHEMUM
A study of Charles Olson
0–88268–017–X Station Hill $27.50

- Travis Bogard
CONTOUR IN TIME: The Plays of Eugene O'Neill
0–19–504548–3 Oxford pb $12.95

- Virginia Floyd
THE PLAYS OF EUGENE O'NEILL: A New Assessment
0–8044–6153–8 Ungar pb $15.95

- Arthur & Barbara Gelb
O'NEILL
0–06–090761–4 Harper & Row pb $15.95

- Eugene O'Neill
SELECTED LETTERS OF EUGENE O'NEILL
Edited by Travis Bogard & Jackson Bryer
0–300–04374–0 Yale $35.00

- Louis Sheaffer
O'NEILL, SON AND PLAYWRIGHT
1–55778–185–0 Paragon pb $16.95

- Ronald H. Wainscott
STAGING O'NEILL: The Experimental Years, 1920–1934
0–300–04152–7 Yale $40.00

- Mary Oppen
MEANING A LIFE
A memoir of her life with poet George Oppen
0–87685–375–0 Black Sparrow pb $14.00

- Edward Butscher, editor
SYLVIA PLATH: The Woman and the Work
0–396–08732–9 Dodd, Mead pb $9.95

- Ted Hughes & Frances McCullough, editors
THE JOURNALS OF SYLVIA PLATH
0–345–35168–1 Ballantine pb $4.95

- Linda W. Wagner-Martin
SYLVIA PLATH: A Biography
0–671–60404–X Simon & Schuster $18.95

- Katherine Anne Porter
CONVERSATIONS WITH KATHERINE ANNE PORTER
Edited by Joan Givner
0–87805–267–4 Mississippi pb $12.95

- Humphrey Carpenter
A SERIOUS CHARACTER: The Life of Ezra Pound
0–395–41678–7 Houghton Mifflin $40.00

- Hugh Kenner
THE POUND ERA
0–520–01860–5 California $37.50
0–520–02427–3 California pb $14.95

- James Laughlin
POUND AS WUZ: Essays and Lectures on Ezra Pound
1–55597–098–2 Graywolf pb $9.50

- Noel Stock
THE LIFE OF EZRA POUND: An Expanded Edition
0–86547–075–8 North Point pb $15.00

- John Tytell
EZRA POUND: The Solitary Volcano
0–385–19694–6 Doubleday pb $19.95

- Tony Tanner
THOMAS PYNCHON
0–416–31670–0 RC&H pb $7.95

- Gordon E. Bigelow
FRONTIER EDEN: The Literary Career of Marjorie Kinnan Rawlings
0–8130–0672–4 Florida pb $10.00

- Milton Hindus, editor
CHARLES REZNIKOFF: Man and Poet
0–915032–60–0 National Poetry Fdn pb $15.95

- Philip Roth
READING MYSELF AND OTHERS
0–14–007681–6 Penguin pb $6.95

- Ian Hamilton
J.D. SALINGER: A Writing Life
0–394–53468–9 Random House $17.95

- Lawrence Lee & Barry Gifford
SAROYAN: A Biography
0–913729–96–5 Paragon pb $9.95

- Marita Simpson & Martha Wheelock, editors
  MAY SARTON: A Self-Portrait
  0–393–30535–X Norton pb $7.95

- James Atlas
  DELMORE SCHWARTZ: The Life of an American Poet
  0–15–625272–4 HBJ pb $10.95

- Delmore Schwartz
  LETTERS OF DELMORE SCHWARTZ
  Edited by Robert Phillips
  Foreword by Karl Shapiro
  0–86538–048–1 Ontario Review pb $14.95

- Charles Molesworth
  GARY SNYDER'S VISION: Poetry and the Real Work
  0–8262–0414–7 Missouri pb $8.95

- Richard Bridgman
  GERTRUDE STEIN IN PIECES
  0–19–501280–1 Oxford $29.95

- John Malcolm Brinnin
  THE THIRD ROSE: Gertrude Stein and Her World
  Introduction by John Ashbery
  0–201–05880–4 Addison-Wesley pb $14.95

- Marianne DeKoven
  A DIFFERENT LANGUAGE: Gertrude Stein's Experimental Writing
  0–299–09210–0 Wisconsin $23.95

- Jayne L. Walker
  THE MAKING OF A MODERNIST: Gertrude Stein from Three Lives to Tender Buttons
  0–87023–323–8 Massachusetts $17.50

- Jackson J. Benson
  THE TRUE ADVENTURES OF JOHN STEINBECK, WRITER: A Biography
  0–670–16685–5 Viking $35.00

- Milton J. Bates
  WALLACE STEVENS: A Mythology of Self
  0–520–05871–2 California pb $10.95

Wallace Stevens in Hartford, Connecticut, 1938 (photo copyright Alfred A. Knopf)

- Harold Bloom
  WALLACE STEVENS: The Poems of Our Climate
  0–8014–9185–1 Cornell pb $15.95

- Peter Brazeau
  PARTS OF A WORLD: Wallace Stevens Remembered
  0–86547–190–8 North Point pb $12.50

- Joan Richardson
  WALLACE STEVENS: The Early Years, 1879–1923
  0–688–05401–3 Morrow $21.95
  WALLACE STEVENS: The Later Years, 1925–1955
  0–688–06860–X Morrow $27.95

- Helen Vendler
  ON EXTENDED WINGS: Wallace Stevens' Longer Poems
  0–674–63436–5 Harvard pb $7.95

- William Styron
  CONVERSATIONS WITH WILLIAM STYRON
  Edited by James L. West
  0–87805–261–5 Mississippi pb $12.95

- William Drake
  SARA TEASDALE: Woman and Poet
  0–87049–595–X Tennessee pb $14.95

- Cynthia E. Kerman & Richard Eldridge
  THE LIVES OF JEAN TOOMER: A Hunger for Wholeness
  0–8071–1354–9 LSU $29.95

- Nellie Y. McKay
  JEAN TOOMER, ARTIST: A Study of His Literary Life and Work, 1894–1936
  0–8078–1583–7 North Carolina $25.00

- Ernst Schurer & Philip Jenkins, editors
  B. TRAVEN: Life and Work
  0–271–00382–0 Pennsylvania State $22.50

- Peggy W. Prenshaw, editor
  CONVERSATIONS WITH EUDORA WELTY
  0–671–54167–6 Washington Square pb $4.95

- Jay Martin
  NATHANAEL WEST: The Art of His Life
  0–88184–030–0 Carroll & Graf pb $8.95

- R.W.B. Lewis
  EDITH WHARTON: A Biography
  0–06–012603–5 Harper & Row $18.50
  0–06–090554–9 Harper & Row pb $9.95

- R.W.B. & Nancy Lewis, editors
  THE LETTERS OF EDITH WHARTON
  0–684–18585–7 Scribners $29.95

- Edith Wharton
  A BACKWARD GLANCE
  0–684–18381–1 Scribners pb $12.95

- Cynthia Griffin Wolff
  A FEAST OF WORDS: The Triumph of Edith Wharton
  0–19–502434–6 Oxford pb $7.95

- Gilbert Harrison
  THE ENTHUSIAST: A Life of Thornton Wilder
  0–88064–053–7 Fromm pb $12.95

- Thornton Wilder
  THE JOURNALS OF THORNTON WILDER
  Edited by Donald Gallup
  0–300–04054–7 Yale pb $13.95

- Dotson Rader
  TENNESSEE: Cry of the Heart
  0–452–25801–4 NAL pb $8.95

- Donald Spoto
  THE KINDNESS OF STRANGERS: The Life of Tennessee Williams
  0–345–32618–0 Ballantine pb $4.95

- Tennessee Williams
  WHERE I LIVE: Selected Essays
  Edited by Bob Woods and Christine R. Day
  0–8112–0706–4 New Directions pb $6.95
  CONVERSATIONS WITH TENNESSEE WILLIAMS
  Edited by Albert J. Devlin
  0–87805–263–1 Mississippi pb $14.95

- James E.B. Breslin
  WILLIAM CARLOS WILLIAMS: An American Artist
  0–226–07407–2 Chicago pb $9.95

- Paul Mariani
  WILLIAM CARLOS WILLIAMS: A New World Naked
  0–07–040362–7 McGraw-Hill $24.95
  0–07–040363–5 McGraw-Hill pb $12.95

- Henry M. Sayre
  THE VISUAL TEXT OF WILLIAM CARLOS WILLIAMS
  0–252–01059–0 Illinois $15.95

- William Carlos Williams
  THE AUTOBIOGRAPHY OF WILLIAM CARLOS WILLIAMS
  0–8112–0226–7 New Directions pb $10.95
  I WANTED TO WRITE A POEM
  Edited by Edith Heal
  0–8112–0707–2 New Directions pb $4.95
  SELECTED LETTERS OF WILLIAM CARLOS WILLIAMS
  Edited by John C. Thirlwall
  0–8112–0934–2 New Directions pb $9.95

- David H. Donald
  LOOK HOMEWARD: A Life of Thomas Wolfe
  0–449–90286–2 Fawcett pb $12.95

- Addison Gayle
  RICHARD WRIGHT: Ordeal of a Native Son
  0–8446–6000–0 Peter Smith $14.50

- Margaret Walker
  RICHARD WRIGHT, DAEMONIC GENIUS: A Portrait of the Man, A Critical Look at His Work
  0–446–71001–6 Warner $22.00

Caribbean Literature

▶ The literature of Cuba and Puerto Rico will be found under Latin American Literature

Antigua

● Jamaica Kincaid

Kincaid, an Antiguan writer now based in the US, uses a rich imagery of recollection to evoke coming of age in the Caribbean.

ANNIE JOHN
0–374–10521–9 Farrar, Straus & Giroux $18.95
0–452–26016–7 NAL pb $6.95

AT THE BOTTOM OF THE RIVER
0–394–73683–4 Random House pb $5.95

A SMALL PLACE
0–374–26638–7 Farrar, Straus & Giroux $13.95

Barbados

● Edward L. Brathwaite

A prominent Barbadian academic, historian, critic, and highly accomplished poet, Brathwaite has been a leader in experimental poetry and the use of indigenous speech patterns in Caribbean verse.

THE ARRIVANTS
A trilogy addressing the central themes of Caribbean history, consisting of *Rights of Passage, Masks,* and *Islands*
0–19–911103–0 Oxford pb $8.95

MOTHER POEM
0–19–211859–5 Oxford pb $10.95

SUN POEM
0–19–211945–1 Oxford pb $11.95

X-SELF
0–19–281987–9 Oxford pb $9.95

● Geoffrey Drayton

CHRISTOPHER
A white child's increasing involvement with the black world around him
0–435–98235–4 Heinemann pb $6.00

● George Lamming

THE EMIGRANTS
Of the disappointment and suffering that awaited hopeful West Indian immigrants in 1950s Britain
0–8052–8036–7 Schocken pb $6.95

IN THE CASTLE OF MY SKIN
This major West Indian work of the 1950s focuses on the pains of adolescence
0–8052–0750–3 Schocken pb $9.95

NATIVES OF MY PERSON
The tale of a 17th-century voyage of discovery to the Caribbean leads to discussion of freedom, imperialism, and love
0–85031–695–2 Schocken $17.95
0–85031–696–0 Schocken pb $8.95

OF AGE AND INNOCENCE
An interracial friendship among youths during the pre-independence years of a fictitious Caribbean nation
0–8052–8094–4 Schocken pb $7.95

THE PLEASURES OF EXILE
Collected essays and shorter pieces
0–8052–8193–2 Schocken $14.95
0–8052–8194–0 Schocken pb $6.95

SEASON OF ADVENTURE
A woman's quest for her Caribbean identity
0–8052–8012–X Schocken $14.95

Dominica

● Phyllis S. Allfrey

THE ORCHID HOUSE
The one published novel by the political activist, about a white family whose powers are waning
Introduction by Elaine Campbell
0–89410–433–0 Three Continents $20.00
0–89410–434–9 Three Continents pb $10.00

French Guiana (Guyane)

● Bertène Juminer

THE BASTARDS
The difficulties of reassimilation for a medical student studying in France
Translated with an introduction by Keith Q. Warner
0–8139–1204–0 Virginia pb $9.95

Grenada

● Merle Collins

ANGEL
A young woman's coming of age as she joins her country's move toward political autonomy
0–93118864–4 Seal Press pb $8.95

Guyana

● Joan Cambridge

CLARISE CUMBERBATCH WANT TO GO HOME
0–89919–403–6 Ticknor & Fields $15.95

● Wilson Harris

Using landscape as an aspect of his characters' consciousness, Harris deviates from the descriptive realism typical of much Caribbean fiction.

THE ANGEL AT THE GATE
0–571–11929–8 Faber & Faber $15.95

CARNIVAL
0–571–13449–1 Faber & Faber $19.95

DA SILVA'S CULTIVATED WILDERNESS & GENESIS OF THE CLOWNS
The first of these novellas concerns a Brazilian-born painter living in London; in the second, a surveyor charts the rivers of upper Guyana
0–571–10819–9 Faber & Faber pb $9.95

THE EYE OF THE SCARECROW
0–571–10557–2 Faber & Faber pb $3.95

THE GUYANA QUARTET
Harris's masterpiece, consisting of *Palace of the Peacock, The Far Journey of Oudin, The Whole Armor,* and *The Secret Ladder,* paints a comprehensive picture of contemporary Guyana through "a sacramental union of man and landscape" (John Hearne)
0–571–13451–3 Faber & Faber pb $11.95

THE INFINITE REHEARSAL
0–571–14885–9 Faber & Faber $13.95

PALACE OF THE PEACOCK
The first volume of *The Guyana Quartet,* written with the "staggering ebullience of language we begin to recognize in West Indian writers"—*The Times* (London)
0–571–08930–5 Faber & Faber pb $6.95

● Roy Heath

OREALLA
0–85031–528–X Schocken $14.95

THE REASONABLE ADVENTURER
0–8229–5071–5 Pittsburgh pb $8.95

● Edgar Mittelholzer

CORENTYNE THUNDER
0–435–98593–0 Heinemann pb $6.50

● Denis Williams

OTHER LEOPARDS
An abortive quest for origins set in Sudan, which represents for the author "the *alter ego* of ancestral times that I was sure quietly slumbered behind the cultured mask"
0–435–98590–6 Heinemann pb $7.00

Haiti

● Dany Laferrière

HOW TO MAKE LOVE TO A NEGRO
Translated by David Homel
0–88910–305–4 Coach House pb $10.95

● Paul Laraque

CAMOURADE
Poems spanning 40 years. "Laraque's poems . . . fuse with the more intimately personal works to create a single body of revolutionary hope, the foundation of his every word"—Jack Hirschman
Translated by Rosemary Manno
0–915306–71–9 Curbstone pb $9.95

● Jacques Roumain

MASTERS OF THE DEW
Born into an aristocratic family and a founder of the Haitian Communist party, Roumain is often considered Haiti's most important writer
0–435–98745–3 Heinemann pb $6.50

● Joseph Zobel

BLACK SHACK ALLEY
Translated by Keith Q. Warner
0–914478–68–0 Three Continents pb $8.00

Jamaica

● Peter Abrahams

Abrahams, a former broadcaster and news analyst, emigrated to Jamaica in 1955 from South Africa. His novels are concerned with relations between the races, and the political and social development of his adopted country.

HARD RAIN
0–525–24581–2 Dutton $18.95

THIS ISLAND NOW
0–571–13439–4 Faber & Faber pb $6.95

TELL FREEDOM
"An autobiographical statement . . . where colors and races collide and clash, where

social circumstances are fat with poverty and suffering"—Wilfred Cartey
0–571–11777–5 Faber & Faber pb $4.95

TONGUES OF FIRE
0–671–46419–1 Pocket pb $3.95

THE VIEW FROM COYABA
0–571–13288–X Faber & Faber $23.95
0–571–13289–8 Faber & Faber pb $6.95

● Vernon F. Anderson
SUDDEN GLORY
A tale centered around Mayan excavations in Guatemala
0–435–98808–5 Heinemann pb $8.50

● Michelle Cliff
ABENG: A Novel
0–89594–139–2 Crossing Press pb $8.95

THE LAND OF LOOK BEHIND: Prose and Poetry
0–932379–09–5 Firebrand $14.95
0–932379–08–7 Firebrand pb $6.95

NO TELEPHONE TO HEAVEN
In the period leading up to independence, a woman emigrates and wanders about Europe and North America
0–525–24508–1 Dutton $17.95
0–317–67299–1 Random House pb $6.95

● H.G. DeLisser
JANE'S CAREER
A novel of pre-independence Jamaica
0–435–98540–X Heinemann pb $7.00

● John Hearne
THE SURE SALVATION
0–571–13452–1 Faber & Faber pb $6.95

VOICES UNDER THE WINDOW
"A tight, short, explosive book, remarkably polished" (*Spectator*) about a white islander orator who feels he doesn't really count as white
0–571–09985–8 Faber & Faber pb $5.95

● Roger Mais
BLACK LIGHTNING
Mais, deeply involved in the nationalist movement of the 1930s, was, along with V.S. Reid, Sam Selvon, and George Lamming, one of the founders of modern Caribbean literature
Introduction by Jean D'Costa
0–435–98584–1 Heinemann pb $6.50

BROTHER MAN
The book about the birth of the Rastafarian movement that established Mais's early reputation as a social realist. "His best work because it brings together in one minor classic all of the author's varied talents"—Edward Brathwaite
0–435–98585–X Heinemann pb $6.50

THE HILLS WERE JOYFUL TOGETHER
Under the bittersweet title from Psalm 98 he reveals the dire wretchedness of the slum class in Kingston
0–435–98586–8 Heinemann pb $7.00

● V.S. Reid
THE LEOPARD
The struggle of the Kenyan people during the Mau Mau era. "What the author has done is to give his story the quality of near

myth to make the horror understandable"—*Time*
Introduction by Mervyn Morris
0–435–98660–0 Heinemann pb $6.00

● Michael Smith
IT A COME
Dub poems combining folklore, biblical allusion, and international news items
Preface by Linton Kwesi Johnson
0–87286–217–8 City Lights pb $4.95

● Michael Thelwell
DUTIES, PLEASURES, AND CONFLICTS: Essays in Struggle
Introduction by James Baldwin
0–87023–523–0 Massachusetts pb $10.95

THE HARDER THEY COME
An adaptation of the famous film that goes far beyond the usual "novelization," expanding the film's themes and characterizations
0–802–13138–7 Grove pb $10.95

Martinique

● Aimé Césaire
A prolific poet, critic, and playwright, Césaire has made a great impact on Afro-American and Caribbean letters as the cofounder of the "négritude" movement, aimed at destroying racial stereotypes.
THE COLLECTED POETRY
Translated by Clayton Eshleman & Annette Smith
0–520–04347–2 California $35.00
0–520–05320–6 California pb $13.95

LOST BODY
Translated with an introduction by Clayton Eshelman
Illustrated by Pablo Picasso
0–8076–1148–4 Braziller $14.95

A TEMPEST
A variation on Shakespeare's *Tempest*
Translated by Richard Miller
0–912745–15–4 Ubu Repertory pb $6.25

St. Kitts and Nevis

● Caryl Phillips
Based in Britain, Phillips is a leading and dynamic voice among the latest generation of Caribbean novelists and playwrights.
THE EUROPEAN TRIBE
0–374–14935–6 Farrar, Straus & Giroux $15.95

THE FINAL PASSAGE
The story of a young woman adrift in despair, set against the upheaval of Caribbean emigration and its impact on British society
0–571–13438–6 Faber & Faber pb $8.95

PLAYING AWAY
The screenplay of the novel *The Final Passage*. Includes 20 black-and-white photos
0–571–14583–3 Faber & Faber pb $7.95

A STATE OF INDEPENDENCE
A homecoming to the Caribbean after a 20-year absence creates a sharp sense of dislocation
0–374–26976–9 Farrar, Straus & Giroux $13.95
0–02–015080–6 Macmillan pb $6.95

St. Lucia

● Garth St. Omer
THE LIGHTS ON THE HILL
0–435–98964–2 Heinemann pb $6.50

● Derek Walcott
Unlike many Caribbean writers of his generation, Walcott resisted for a long time the lure of emigration, preferring to help establish a strong Caribbean literary culture from within as both poet and dramatist. As such he is described as "a 20th century man with an Elizabethan sense of language" (G.E. Murray, *Chicago Tribune*).
ANOTHER LIFE
Introduction by Robert Hamner
0–89410–279–6 Three Continents pb $7.50

THE ARKANSAS TESTAMENT
In his eighth collection of poetry the two parts "Here" and "Elsewhere" reflect the problem of allegiance implicit in his recent move to the US
0–374–10582–0 Farrar, Straus & Giroux $14.95
0–374–52099–2 Farrar, Straus & Giroux pb $8.95

COLLECTED POEMS 1948–1984
0–374–12626–7 Farrar, Straus & Giroux $25.00
0–374–52025–9 Farrar, Straus & Giroux pb $13.95

THE FORTUNATE TRAVELLER
Recent poems published in 1982 describe the crisis of traveling from one underdeveloped place to another. "Walcott has sought to cross-fertilize the stately English we recognize with Caribbean dialect"—Mary Jo Salter, *New Republic*
0–374–15765–0 Farrar, Straus & Giroux $11.95
0–374–51744–4 Farrar, Straus & Giroux pb $8.95

MIDSUMMER
A one-summer's-worth 54-poem sequence written in Trinidad by "the outsider, the poet of the periphery, but it may be time to center the compass at his position and draw the circle again"—Sven Birkerts, *New Republic*
0–374–51863–7 Farrar, Straus & Giroux $7.95

OMEROS
0–374–22591–5 Farrar, Straus & Giroux $14.95

REMEMBRANCE & PANTOMIME
Two plays
0–374–24912–1 Farrar, Straus & Giroux $15.95
0–374–51569–7 Farrar, Straus & Giroux pb $7.95

THE JOKER OF SEVILLE & O BABYLON!: 2 Plays
0–374–17998–0 Farrar, Straus & Giroux $15.00

THE STAR-APPLE KINGDOM
A good example of his later cycle of poetry dating from the mid 1970s. In this book he meditates again on the "ancient war between obsession and responsibility"—Robert Mazzocco, *NY Review of Books*
0–374–51532–8 Farrar, Straus & Giroux pb $7.95

THREE PLAYS
Includes *The Last Carnival, Beef, No Chicken*, and *A Branch of the Blue Nile*
0–374–28618–3 Farrar, Straus & Giroux $22.50
0–374–51883–1 Farrar, Straus & Giroux pb $9.95

Trinidad and Tobago

● Michael Anthony
ALL THAT GLITTERS: The Caribbean
0–435–98034–3 Heinemann pb $6.50

CRICKET IN THE ROAD
0–435–98032–7 Heinemann pb $6.00

THE GAMES WERE COMING
The thrills and spills of a cycle race, and the importance of the finish for three characters in particular; Anthony's first novel
0–435–98033–5 Heinemann pb $6.00

GREEN DAYS BY THE RIVER
0–435–98030–0 Heinemann pb $5.50

THE YEAR IN SAN FERNANDO
A classic novel of boyhood, in which a young servant gets a glimpse of grown-ups and their sometimes sordid doings
0–435–98031–9 Heinemann pb $6.00

• Neil Bissoondath
A CASUAL BRUTALITY
A man caught in the web of political disintegration
0–517–57202–8 Clarkson Potter $18.95

DIGGING UP THE MOUNTAINS
Fourteen stories concerned mainly with migration between the West Indies and North America. "Humorous and sad, observant and intuitive, it imparts a very vivid sense of place and how it shapes the lives of the people who live there"—Susan Hill
0–14–008935–7 Penguin pb $6.95

• Ralph de Boissière
DeBoissière was an early member of the literary circle that surrounded C.L.R. James and Alfred Mendes in 1920s Trinidad.
RUM & COCA-COLA
0–8052–8195–9 Schocken $16.95

• Merle Hodge
CRICK CRACK MONKEY
0–435–98401–2 Heinemann pb $6.50

• C.L.R. James
Historian, political theorist, and tireless opponent of imperialism, James introduced social realism into Caribbean writing with *Minty Alley* (1936).

C.L.R. James (photo copyright Val Wilmer/ Format)

AT THE RENDEZVOUS OF VICTORY
0–88208–192–6 Lawrence Hill $17.95
0–88208–191–8 Lawrence Hill pb $8.95

BEYOND A BOUNDARY
This study of cricket and colonialism is a modern classic
Introduction by Robert Lipsyte
0–394–72283–3 Pantheon pb $8.95

THE BLACK JACOBINS: Toussaint L'Ouverture and the San Domingo Revolution
James's most famous book, an influential interpretation of the Haitian revolution of the 1790s
0–394–70242–5 Pantheon pb $6.95

CRICKET
0–8052–8264–5 Schocken $19.95

EVERY COOK CAN GOVERN & WHAT IS HAPPENING EVERY DAY: 1985 Conversations
Edited by Jan Hillegas
0–9616362–0–3 New Mississippi pb $2.00

THE FUTURE IN THE PRESENT: Selected Writings of C.L.R. James
0–88208–125–X Lawrence Hill pb $6.95

MARINERS, RENEGADES AND CASTAWAYS
0–8052–8189–4 Schocken $14.95
0–8052–8190–8 Schocken pb $5.95

NOTES ON DIALECTICS
0–88208–127–6 Lawrence Hill pb $7.95

SPHERES OF EXISTENCE
0–88208–128–4 Lawrence Hill pb $7.95

• Errol John
MOON ON A RAINBOW SHAWL
A domestic drama
0–5771–05403–X Faber & Faber pb $5.95

• Ismith Khan
JUMBIE BIRD
A novel about the plight of Indian immigrants lured to work on Trinidad sugar plantations
0–8392–1055–8 Astor-Honor pb $8.95

• Earl Lovelace
JESTINA'S CALYPSO & OTHER PLAYS
0–435–98751–8 Heinemann pb $6.50

THE SCHOOLMASTER
An idyllic village, untouched by big city vices, is tarnished by the arrival of an avaricious schoolmaster
Introduction by Kenneth Ramchand
0–435–98550–7 Heinemann pb $6.00

THE WINE OF ASTONISHMENT
Written in "richly demotic Caribbean patois (it) charts the struggles of a so-called 'Spiritual Baptist' sent to find toleration and freedom from persecution"—*London Sunday Times*
0–394–72795–9 Random House pb $6.95

• Shiva Naipaul
BEYOND THE DRAGON'S MOUTH: Stories and Pieces
0–670–80392–8 Viking $17.95

THE CHIP-CHIP GATHERERS
0–14–003956–2 Penguin pb $6.95

FIREFLIES
The first novel of V.S. Naipaul's younger brother deals with the decline of Hindu culture in the Caribbean
0–14–003150–2 Penguin pb $6.95

JOURNEY TO NOWHERE: A New World Tragedy
A report on the Jonestown catastrophe
0–14–006189–4 Penguin pb $6.95

LOVE AND DEATH IN A HOT COUNTRY
0–670–44211–9 Viking $14.95
0–14–007663–8 Penguin pb $6.95

NORTH OF SOUTH: An African Journey
A sardonic travelogue charting Naipaul's progress through Kenya, Tanzania, and Zambia
0–14–004894–4 Penguin pb $7.95

AN UNFINISHED JOURNEY
Introduction by Douglas Stuart
0–670–81368–0 Viking $15.95
0–14–010925–0 Penguin pb $6.95

• V.S. Naipaul
A foremost novelist, essayist, and frequently controversial socio-political critic, born of Indian parents in Trinidad, but a British resident since the 1950s.
AMONG THE BELIEVERS: An Islamic Journey
A commentary conducted through Iran, Pakistan, Malaysia, and Indonesia to the "Islamic Winter" of the final chapter
0–394–50969–2 Knopf $15.00
0–394–71195–5 Random House pb $8.95

AN AREA OF DARKNESS
Harsh observation of the subcontinent that met with little Indian popularity in the late 1960s
0–394–74673–2 Random House pb $5.95

A BEND IN THE RIVER
A powerful later work, set in a fictional African state, about the damage inflicted by the West on the Third World
0–679–72202–5 Random House pb $5.95

THE ENIGMA OF ARRIVAL
Recent autobiographical portrait of an author getting on in years in the West Country. "An elegant memoir, a subtly incisive self-reckoning"—*Washington Post*
0–394–50971–4 Knopf $17.45
0–394–75760–2 Random House pb $6.95

FINDING THE CENTER: Two Narratives
Includes *Prologue to an Autobiography* and *The Crocodiles of Yamoussoukro*, a contemporary journey into Africa
0–394–53777–7 Knopf $13.95
0–394–74090–4 Random House pb $4.95

GUERRILLAS
Three would-be revolutionaries in search of a cause.
0–394–49898–4 Knopf $13.95
0–394–74492–6 Random House pb $5.95

A HOUSE FOR MR BISWAS
A large novel in which a mild man's struggle for ownership of his own home represents a higher striving toward individual autonomy
0–394–53400–X Knopf $17.95
0–394–72050–4 Random House pb $5.95

IN A FREE STATE
0–394–72205–1 Random House pb $4.95

INDIA: A Wounded Civilization
Naipaul's scathing critique of India, written more than a decade after *An Area of Darkness*
0–394–72463–1 Random House pb $4.95

THE LOSS OF EL DORADO
A fascinating exploration of the early history of Trinidad
0–394–72124–1 Random House pb $5.95

THE MIDDLE PASSAGE
A satirical version of Caribbean life
0–394–74674–0 Random House pb $4.95

MIGUEL STREET
Naipaul's first novel portrays both the vibrancy and the limitations of a small Trinidadian community
0–394–72065–2 Random House pb $5.95

THE MIMIC MEN
Post-independence politicking in the Third World: an intellectual assumes power, is toppled, and finds time for reappraisal as a recluse in London
0–394–73232–4 Random House pb $5.95

MR. STONE & THE KNIGHTS COMPANION
His only novel set entirely in England betrays a hearty ambivalence about the English, even after being in residence there for more than a decade
0–394–73226–X Random House pb $4.95

THE MYSTIC MASSEUR
A fictitious biography of a masseur who connives his way to political power
0–394–72073–3 Random House pb $4.95

THE OVERCROWDED BARRACOON
Essays on topics ranging from India and the Caribbean to Steinbeck and Soustelle
0–394–72207–8 Random House pb $6.95

THE RETURN OF EVA PERON
Also includes the journalistic piece *The Killings in Trinidad*
0–394–50968–4 Knopf $13.95
0–394–74675–9 Random House pb $4.95

THE SUFFRAGE OF ELVIRA
A comedy about rural council elections in Trinidad, animated by much hustling and bargaining
0–394–73216–2 Random House pb $4.95

A TURN IN THE SOUTH
A recent work relating Naipaul's impressions of the American South
0–394–56477–4 Knopf $18.95

- Sam Selvon

THE HOUSING LARK
A jovial tale of Caribbean immigrant life in London, narrated wholly in Trinidadian dialect
0–89410–602–3 Three Continents $14.00
0–317–60777–4 Three Continents pb $7.00

MOSES ASCENDING
A less merry account of the Caribbean experience in Britain, written a decade after *The Housing Lark*
Introduction by Mervyn Morris
0–435–98750–X Heinemann pb $6.50

TURN AGAIN TIGER
Examines the process of "Creolization" as it affects an Indian couple
0–435–98780–1 Heinemann pb $6.00

ANTHOLOGIES AND STUDIES

- Roger D. Abrahams

THE MAN OF WORDS IN THE WEST INDIES: Performance and the Emergence of Creole Culture
0–8018–2839–2 Johns Hopkins pb $12.95

- Paula Barnett, editor

THE PENGUIN BOOK OF CARIBBEAN VERSE IN ENGLISH
A comprehensive anthology including selections from the dub poets
0–14–058511–7 Penguin pb $8.95

- Lloyd Brown

WEST INDIAN POETRY
Traces the development of both oral and written poetic traditions, focusing on the work of Claude McKay, Derek Walcott, and Edward Brathwaite, as well as the calypsonian Sparrow, and storyteller Louise Bennett
0–435–91830–3 Heinemann pb $16.50

- O.R. Dathorne

DARK ANCESTOR: The Literature of the Black Man in the Caribbean
0–8071–0757–3 LSU $32.50

- Carole B. Davis & Elaine Fido

OUT OF THE KUMBLA: Womanist Perspectives on Caribbean Literature
0–86543–042–X Africa World $35.00
0–86543–043–8 Africa World pb $11.95

- Jean D'Costa & Barbara Lalla

VOICES IN EXILE: A Collection of Archaic Jamaican Texts of the 18th and 19th Centuries
0–8173–0382–0 Alabama $24.50

- Edmundo Desnoes, Luis Rafael Sanchez & Guillermo Cabrera Infante

LITERATURES IN TRANSITION: The Many Voices of the Caribbean
0–935318–10–0 Ed Hispanamerica pb $13.00

- Ellen Conroy Kennedy

THE NEGRITUDE POETS: An Anthology of Translations from the French
Foreword by Maya Angelou
0–938410–72–5 Thunder's Mouth pb $10.95

- Bruce King

WEST INDIAN LITERATURE
0–0208–01814–X Shoe String $23.00

- Sandra P. Pacquet

THE NOVELS OF GEORGE LAMMING
0–435–91831–1 Heinemann pb $13.50

- Kenneth Ramchand

THE WEST INDIAN NOVEL AND ITS BACKGROUND
Sam Selvon, Wilson Harris, and V.S. Naipaul are among the novelists discussed
0–435–98665–1 Heinemann $17.50

- Amon S. Saakana

THE COLONIAL LEGACY IN CARIBBEAN LITERATURE
0–86543–059–4 Africa World $24.95
0–86543–060–8 Africa World pb $7.95

- Patrick Taylor

THE NARRATIVE OF LIBERATION
Perspectives on Afro-Caribbean literature, popular culture, and politics
0–8014–2193–4 Cornell $29.95

- Keith Warner

KAISO!: The Trinidad Calypso
A study of calypso as oral literature; includes a comprehensive discography
0–89410–025–4 Three Continents $24.00
0–89410–026–2 Three Continents pb $12.00

Latin American Literature

"We must not forget that Spanish America has a very old literature, it has a great tradition I will just outline briefly. It starts in the Spanish language with the writing of Columbus and Amerigo Vespucci about the New World. But in the countries of Indian ancestry, such as Mexico and Central America, there was already a great deal of literature. So what we have is the full flowering of a tradition which doesn't culminate with the so-called Boom. It is not the writing of one generation; it includes writers as old as Borges, who died in his late eighties, or as young as Vargas Llosa, who is hardly in his fifties. So, it is not a generation but more a movement in which many strands of our tradition come together and transform the quality and the nature of narrative fiction in Latin America."—Carlos Fuentes in *Interviews With Latin American Writers* by Marie-Lise Gazarian Gautier (Dalkey Archive)

FICTION

Argentina

- José Bianco

SHADOW PLAY & THE RATS: Two Novellas
Human and family relationships among the dead and the living
0–935480–11–0 Latin American pb $9.50

- Adolfo Bioy Casares

ASLEEP IN THE SUN
Translated by Suzanne Jill Levine
0–89255–030–9 Persea pb $8.95

DIARY OF THE WAR OF THE PIG
A 1969 novel that is in some ways eerily prophetic of Argentina's "dirty war" of the following decade. "The intentional simplicity of the plot forces us to focus on the terrifying mysteries of mass psychology that can produce violence as a cure for boredom, cowardly rationalizations by the intelligentsia, and guilt-ridden contributions to their own destruction by the victims of persecution"—*Library Journal*
Translated by Gregory Woodruff & Donald A. Yates
0–525–48423–X Dutton pb $7.95

Adolfo Bioy Casares (photo courtesy of E.P. Dutton)

THE DREAM OF HEROES
"The circularity of time, the fragile borders between realism and fantasy, and a kind of Kafkaesque fatalism are obsessions Bioy shares with Borges but Bioy—more lyrical, less epic than Borges—always returns to the compelling illusion of love"—Suzanne Jill Levine
Translated by Diana Thorold
0–525–24687–8 Dutton $17.95

THE INVENTION OF MOREL & OTHER STORIES
The title novella, a cunning parable about illusion, is among Bioy Casares' best-known works
Translated by Norman Thomas de Giovanni
0–292–73840–4 Texas pb $9.95

A PLAN FOR ESCAPE
A dreamlike novel of a penal colony. "This short novel, firmly rooted in the Borges tradition, reminiscent of H.G. Wells, and thoroughly weird by conventional standards, is an exceptionally ambitious, intellectual mystery woven with horror and science fiction"—*Village Voice*
Translated by Suzanne Jill Levine
1–55597–107–5 Graywolf pb $7.50

● Jorge Luis Borges & Adolfo Bioy Casares
SIX PROBLEMS FOR DON ISIDRO PARODI
An imprisoned detective involved in satiric, philosophical tales of Buenos Aires
0–525–48035–8 Dutton pb $4.95

● Jorge Luis Borges
THE ALEPH & OTHER STORIES: 1933–1969
Some of Borges' most famous tales of fantasy, reality, and Argentine machismo
Translated by Norman Thomas di Giovanni
0–525–48444–2 Dutton pb $9.95

BORGES: A Reader
A selection of 100 poems, stories, and essays
Edited by Emir Rodriguez Monegal & Alastair Reid
0–525–48326–8 Dutton pb $11.95

DREAMTIGERS
Poems, parables, stories, sketches, and aphorisms
Translated by Mildred Boyer & Harold Morland
Introduction by Miguel Enguidanos
0–292–73217–1 Texas $14.95
0–292–71549–8 Texas pb $6.95

EVARISTO CARRIEGO
A pseudobiography of a minor Argentine poet's relationship with Buenos Aires and his influence on Borges
Translated by Norman Thomas di Giovanni
0–525–24164–7 Dutton $16.95

FICCIONES
A collection containing many of Borges' most famous stories, including *The Circular Labyrinth* and *Pierre Menard, Author of Don Quixote*
Edited by Anthony Kerrigan
0–8021–3030–5 Grove pb $6.95

LABYRINTHS: Selected Short Stories & Other Writings
Edited by Donald A. Yates & James E. Irby
Introduction by André Maurois
0–8112–0012–4 New Directions pb $7.95

OTHER INQUISITIONS: 1937–1952
Translated by Ruth L. Simms
0–292–76002–7 Texas pb $9.95

A PERSONAL ANTHOLOGY
An introductory volume compiled by the author
Edited by Anthony Kerrigan
0–8021–3077–1 Grove pb $8.95

● Humberto Constantini
THE GODS, THE LITTLE GUYS AND THE POLICE
A novel of Argentine life during the "dirty war" of the mid-1970s
Translated by Toby Talbot
0–380–69839–0 Avon pb $3.95

THE LONG NIGHT OF FRANCISCO SANCTIS
0–452–28889–8 NAL pb $6.95

● Julio Cortázar
ALL FIRES THE FIRE
Eight stories in Cortázar's best fantastic vein
Translated by Suzanne Jill Levine
0–394–75358–5 Pantheon pb $7.95

BLOW UP & OTHER STORIES
Cortázar wrote some of the most original fantastic tales of this century, including *Axolotl, The Night Face Up,* and the title story, on which Antonioni's famous film is loosely based
Translated by Paul Blackburn
0–394–72881–5 Pantheon pb $6.95

A CERTAIN LUCAS
Translated by Gregory Rabassa
0–394–50723–1 Knopf $12.95

A CHANGE OF LIGHT & OTHER STORIES
Translated by Gregory Rabassa
0–394–50721–5 Knopf $11.95

HOPSCOTCH
Cortázar's most famous novel, set in Paris and Buenos Aires, is an exhilarating intellectual game that can be read either in linear fashion or by "hopscotching" according to the author's elaborate instructions
0–394–75284–8 Pantheon pb $8.95

62: A Model Kit
"An ironic, sentimental journey through a city plan drawn up by the Marx brothers with an assist from Bela Lugosi!"—Carlos Fuentes
Translated by Gregory Rabassa
0–380–01497–1 Avon pb $3.50

WE LOVE GLENDA SO MUCH & OTHER TALES
Translated by Gregory Rabassa
0–394–72297–3 Random House pb $11.95

THE WINNERS
What the winners of the title have won is a voyage on a cruise ship from Buenos Aires to an unknown destination, but the prize turns out to have horrifying implications
Translated by Elaine Kerrigan
0–394–72301–5 Pantheon pb $8.95

● Tomas Eloy Martinez
THE PERON NOVEL
Translated by Asa Zatz
0–394–55838–3 Pantheon $19.95
0–679–72279–3 Pantheon pb $8.95

● Ezequiel Martinez Estrada
HOLY SATURDAY AND OTHER STORIES
An important social critic's stories about small-town life, urban alienation, and bureaucracy
Translated by Leland H. Chambers
0–935480–30–7 Latin American pb $12.95

● Silvina Ocampo
LEOPOLDINA'S DREAM
Short stories. "I don't know of another writer who better captures the magic inside everyday rituals, the forbidden or hidden face that our mirrors don't show us"—Italo Calvino
Translated by Daniel Balderston
0–14–010011–3 Penguin pb $6.95

● Manuel Puig
BETRAYED BY RITA HAYWORTH
Growing up in Argentina in the 1930s and '40s under the influences of Hollywood kitsch and local gossip
Translated by Suzanne Jill Levine
0–525–48285–7 Dutton pb $7.95

BLOOD OF REQUITED LOVE
A love affair of adolescence that perhaps never occurred as described
Translated by Jan L. Grayson
0–394–72440–2 Random House pb $7.95

THE BUENOS AIRES AFFAIR: A Detective Novel
The young boy of *Betrayed by Rita Hayworth* as an adult confronting sexual and social dilemmas
Translated by Suzanne Jill Levine
0–394–74474–8 Random House pb $5.95

ETERNAL CURSE ON THE READER OF THESE PAGES
0–394–71384–2 Random House pb $4.95

HEARTBREAK TANGO: A Serial
Two love triangles involving the adolescent of *Betrayed by Rita Hayworth*
Translated by Suzanne Jill Levine
0–525–48288–1 Dutton pb $7.95

KISS OF THE SPIDER WOMAN
Translated by Thomas Colchie
0–394–74475–6 Vintage pb $5.95

PUBIS ANGELICAL
Translated by Elena Brunet
0–394–74664–3 Random House pb $6.95

• Ernesto Sábato
ON HEROES AND TOMBS
A literary sonata of four parts and four
characters trapped in tragic fates by one of
Argentina's most acclaimed novelists
Translated by Helen R. Lane
0–345–34928–8 Ballantine pb $5.95

THE TUNNEL
Loneliness leads to murder
Translated by Margaret Sayers Peden
0–345–35192–4 Ballantine pb $4.95

• Mario Szichman
AT 8:25 EVITA BECAME IMMORTAL
A Jewish family's difficult assimilation into
Argentine life
Translated by Roberto Picciotto
0–910061–12–2 Ediciones del Norte pb $9.50

• Luisa Valenzuela
HE WHO SEARCHES
"Luisa Valenzuela is the heiress of Latin
American fiction. She wears an opulent,
baroque crown, but her feet are naked"—
Carlos Fuentes
Translated by Helen Lane
0–916583–20–1 Dalkey Archive pb $8.00

THE LIZARD'S TAIL
A tale about power, politics, and magic, or
how Isabel Peron's minister of social
welfare, López Rega, ruled Argentina
through sorcery
Translated by Gregory Rabassa
0–374–18994–3 Farrar, Straus & Giroux $16.50

OTHER WEAPONS
Translated by Deborah Bonner
0–910061–22–X Ediciones del Norte pb $10.00

**STRANGE THINGS HAPPEN HERE: 26
Short Stories & a Novel**
0–15–185782–2 HBJ pb $9.95

Luisa Valenzuela (photo by Jerry Bauer, courtesy of North Point)

Bolivia

• Arturo Von Vacano
BITING SILENCE
Dedicated "to liberty, although it may last
15 minutes"
Translated by Alfred MacAdam
0–380–75060–0 Avon pb $6.95

Brazil

• Jorge Amado
**DONA FLOR AND HER TWO
HUSBANDS**
"Reading *Doña Flor and Her Two Husbands*
is like having a tropical jungle of scented
flowers in blazing colors explode in your
face"—*Cincinnati Enquirer*
0–380–01796–2 Avon pb $4.95

GABRIELA, CLOVE AND CINNAMON
Perhaps the finest example of Amado's
comic, sensuous fiction
Translated by James L. Taylor & William L. Grossman
0–380–75470–3 Avon pb $7.95

HOME IS THE SAILOR
The misadventures of a magnificent
sailor—or a magnificent liar
Translated by Harriet De Onis
0–380–75474–6 Avon pb $7.95

JUBIABA
An early novel of social consciousness-
raising in Bahia
Translated by Margaret A. Neves
0–380–88567–0 Avon pb $4.50

**PEN, SWORD, CAMISOLE: A Fable to
Kindle a Hope**
The specter of Nazism shows its face in the
Brazilian Academy of Letters during World
War II
Translated by Helen R. Lane
0–380–89831–4 Avon pb $3.95

SEA OF DEATH
A sea story of brave men and their
passionate women
Translated by Gregory Rabassa
0–380–88559–X Avon pb $4.50

SHOWDOWN
The biographical tale of an "ambushed"
city in Amado's native cacao region
Translated by Gregory Rabassa
0–553–05174–1 Bantam $18.95
0–553–34666–0 Bantam pb $8.95

**TEREZA BATISTA HOME FROM THE
WARS**
Translated by Barbara Shelby
0–380–01752–0 Avon pb $4.95

TIETA
A hometown girl returns from the evil
metropolis to rescue her people from big
time factories and pollution
Translated by Barbara Shelby Merello
0–380–50815–X Avon pb $4.95

TOWER OF GLASS
Five interrelated tales of oppression in
Brazil during the 1970s
Translated by Ellen Watson
0–380–89607–9 Avon pb $3.95

**THE TWO DEATHS OF QUINCAS
WATERYELL**
A middle-class Bahian takes to drink and is
rewarded with at least two deaths
Translated by Barbara Shelby
0–380–75476–2 Avon pb $5.95

• Joaquim Maria Machado de Assis
COUNSELOR AYRES' MEMORIAL
An old diplomat narrates this love story set
on the eve of the abolition of slavery in
1888
Translated by Helen Caldwell
0–520–02227–0 California $22.00
0–520–04775–3 California pb $8.95

**THE DEVIL'S CHURCH & OTHER
STORIES**
Translated by Jack Schmitt & Lorie Ishimatsu
0–292–71542–0 Texas pb $7.95

EPITAPH OF A SMALL WINNER
From beyond the grave, Braz Cubes
casts a disenchanted eye over his life; a
dry masterpiece of comedy
0–374–52192–1 FS&G $7.95

HELENA
A romantic tale of a proud and mysterious
woman
Translated by Helen Caldwell
0–520–04812–1 California $22.50
0–520–06025–3 California pb $8.95

IAIA GARCIA
Translated by Albert I. Bagby, Jr.
0–8131–1353–9 Kentucky $18.00

PHILOSOPHER OR DOG?
A simple philosophy clashes with the
speculative business world in this excellent
novel of late 19th-century Brazilian life
Translated by Clotilde Wilson
0–380–58982–6 Avon pb $3.95

• Adolpho Caminha
**BOM CRIOULO: The Black Man and the
Cabin Boy**
Latin America's first novel of homosexual
relations
Translated by E.A. Lacey
0–917342–89–5 Gay Sunshine $20.00
0–917342–88–7 Gay Sunshine pb $7.95

• Rubem Fonseca
HIGH ART
American detective fiction of the 1930s is
the inspiration for this surprising narrative
of violence in contemporary Brazil
Translated by Ellen Watson
0–88184–343–1 Carroll & Graf pb $7.95

• Ledo Ivo
**SNAKE'S NEST OR A TALE BADLY
TOLD**
A dissertation on totalitarianism of the
1940s reflects the military repression of the
1970s
Translated by Kern Krapohl
0–8112–0806–0 New Directions $12.95
0–8112–0807–9 New Directions pb $5.95

• Clarice Lispector
THE APPLE IN THE DARK
Translated by Gregory Rabassa
0–292–70392–9 Texas pb $10.95

**AN APPRENTICESHIP OR THE BOOK
OF DELIGHTS**
Translated by Richard A. Mazzara & Lorri A. Parris
0–292–79030–9 Texas $16.95
0–292–79031–7 Texas pb $7.95

FAMILY TIES
Marvelous short tales
Translated by Giovanni Pontiero
0–292–72448–9 Texas pb $7.95

THE HOUR OF THE STAR
A woman from the northeast adrift in the
big city
Translated by Giovanni Pontiero
0–85635–626–3 Carcanet $15.95
0–85635–775–8 Carcanet pb $5.95

THE PASSION ACCORDING TO G.H.
Translated by Ronald W. Sousa
0–8166–1711–2 Minnesota $19.95
0–8166–1712–0 Minnesota pb $8.95

SOULSTORM: Stories
Twenty-nine stories. "Explores feminist
issues on one level, class issues on another
level, and the metaphysical issues of death
and love on its most ambiguous level"—
Baltimore Sun
0–8112–1091–X New Directions pb $10.95

• Lya Luft
THE ISLAND OF THE DEAD
The intricate anguish of family life in a
novel set in southern Brazil
Translated by Carmen Chaves-McClendon &
Betty Jean Craige
0–8203–0836–6 Georgia $13.95

• Rachel de Queiroz
DORA, DORALINA
A woman's gradual achievement of
independence and dignity in modern Brazil
Translated by Dorothy Loos
0–380–84822–8 Avon pb $4.50

THE THREE MARIAS
Woman's lot in traditional Brazil of the
1920s leads to demoralization and
desperation
Translated by Fred P. Ellison
0–292–78079–6 Texas pb $7.95

• Graciliano Ramos
BARREN LIVES
The northeast's periodic drought reduces
its victims to an animal existence
Translated by Ralph E. Dimmick
0–292–73172–8 Texas $12.95
0–292–70133–0 Texas pb $7.95

• Marcos Rey
MEMORIES OF A GIGOLO
A romp through São Paulo's bordellos and
boardrooms
Translated by Clifford E. Landers
0–380–75000–7 Avon pb $7.95

• Darcy Ribeiro
MAIRA
One of Latin America's most important
anthropologists recounts the plight of
Indians confronted by western culture
Translated by E.A. Goodland & Thomas Colchie
0–394–72214–0 Random House pb $7.95

• Moacyr Scliar
THE BALLAD OF THE FALSE MESSIAH
The title story of this collection concerns
Russian Jews arriving in Brazil at the turn
of the century
Translated by Eloah F. Giacomelli
0–345–34904–0 Ballantine pb $4.95

CARNIVAL OF THE ANIMALS
Short short stories about animals and
humans
Translated by Eloah F. Giacomelli
0–345–32853–1 Ballantine pb $4.95

CENTAUR IN THE GARDEN
A Jewish centaur living in southern Brazil
is caught up in frustrating bourgeois
pursuits
Translated by Margaret A. Neves
0–345–35194–0 Ballantine pb $3.95

THE GODS OF RAQUEL
Translated by Eloah F. Giacomelli
0–345–35357–9 Ballantine pb $3.50

THE ONE-MAN ARMY
Mayer Ginsberg's narration of his rise to
become the famous Captain Birobidjan
Translated by Eloah F. Giacomelli
0–345–32858–2 Ballantine pb $5.95

**THE STRANGE NATION OF RAFAEL
MENDES**
Rafael Mendes meets his ancestors on one
catastrophic day
Translated by Eloah F. Giacomelli
0–517–56776–8 Crown $19.95

• Márcio Souza
EMPEROR OF THE AMAZON
The bizarre conquest of the territory of
Acre in a black comedy of colonialism
Translated by Thomas Colchie
0–380–76240–4 Avon pb $2.95

MAD MARIA
A Brazilian railroad in the Amazon runs
from nowhere to nowhere
Translated by Thomas Colchie
0–380–89871–3 Avon pb $4.95

**THE ORDER OF THE DAY: An
Unidentified Flying Opus**
Translated by Thomas Colchie
0–380–89765–2 Avon pb $4.50

• Lygia Fagundes Telles
TIGRELA & OTHER STORIES
Brazilian life during the political repression
of the 1970s
Translated by Margaret A. Neves
0–380–89627–3 Avon pb $3.95

Chile

• Fernando Alegría
THE CHILEAN SPRING
"A brilliant fictionalized account of the
1973 coup"—*San Francisco Review of Books*
Translated by Stephen Fredman
0–935480–00–5 Latin American pb $7.95

THE FUNHOUSE
A surrealistic vision of North American
society during the Vietnam War
0–934770–52–2 Arte Público pb $8.00

• Isabel Allende
CURFEW
Translated by Alfred MacAdam
1–55584–166–X Weidenfeld & Nicolson $18.95

EVA LUNA
Translated by Margaret Sayers Peden
0–394–57273–4 Knopf $18.95

THE HOUSE OF THE SPIRITS
Esteban Trueba's tale of political life from
a distinctly feminist perspective
Translated by Magda Bogin
0–553–27391–4 Bantam pb $4.95

OF LOVE AND SHADOWS
"Allende skillfully evokes both the terrors
of daily life under military rule and the

Isabel Allende (photo copyright Irmeli Jung)

subtler forms of resistance in the hidden
corners"—*NY Times*
Translated by Margaret S. Peden
0–394–54962–7 Knopf $17.95
0–553–27360–4 Bantam pb $4.50

• Maria Luisa Bombal
NEW ISLANDS & OTHER STORIES
Translated by Richard & Lucia Cunningham
0–8014–9538–5 Cornell pb $6.95

• José Donoso
A HOUSE IN THE COUNTRY
A symbolic tale of extravagance and
cannibalism in late 19th-century Latin
America
Translated by David Pritchard with Suzanne Jill Levine
0–394–50949–8 Knopf $16.95
0–394–73657–5 Random House pb $8.95

THE OBSCENE BIRD OF NIGHT
A penetrating view of the decay of modern
social institutions
Translated by Hardie St. Martin & Leonard Mades
0–87923–191–2 Godine pb $10.95

• Ariel Dorfman
**THE LAST SONG OF MANUEL
SENDERO**
0–670–80214–X Viking $18.95
0–14–008896–2 Penguin pb $7.95

WIDOWS
"The first time an author has immersed
himself in the other part of the tragedy of
the missing people: the women left alive
who don't cry anymore, don't dream
anymore, and go on year after year looking
for someone who is already only a dead
body to love and care for"—Jacobo
Timerman
Translated by Stephen Kessler
0–394–71108–4 Random House pb $6.95

• Antonio Skármeta
BURNING PATIENCE
A novel about Pablo Neruda, his postman,
and the power of poetry
Translated by Katherine Silver
0–317–58518–5 Pantheon $10.95
0–317–58519–3 Pantheon pb $6.95

I DREAMT THE SNOW WAS BURNING
Middle-class life in the 1950s
Translated by Malcolm Coad
0–930523–06–7 Readers International $14.95
0–930523–07–5 Readers International pb $7.95

- Mercedes Valdivieso
BREAKTHROUGH
This book, which appeared in Spanish in 1961, is regarded as the first feminist novel of Latin America
Translated by Graciela Daichman
0–935480–33–1 Latin American pb $12.00

- Fernando Alegría, editor
CHILEAN WRITERS IN EXILE
Includes short novels by Alfonso G. Dagnino, Ariel Dorfman, Anibal Quijada, Leandro Urbing, and others
0–89594–060–4 Crossing Press pb $8.95

Colombia

- Gabriel García Márquez
THE AUTUMN OF THE PATRIARCH
A thematically complex novel on the national roots of a "generic" Latin American dictator and his suffering people
Translated by Gregory Rabassa
0–06–011419–3 Harper & Row $13.95
0–380–01774–1 Avon pb $4.50

CHRONICLE OF A DEATH FORETOLD
A prophetic tale of familial duty, honor, and murder
Translated by Gregory Rabassa
0–345–31002–0 Ballantine pb $4.95

COLLECTED STORIES
Translated by Gregory Rabassa & J.S. Bernstein
0–06–015364–4 Harper & Row $16.95
0–06–091306–1 Harper & Row pb $8.95

IN EVIL HOUR
Mysterious messages shake up the power structure in a Colombian village
Translated by Gregory Rabassa
0–06–011414–2 Harper & Row $11.95
0–380–52167–9 Avon pb $3.95

Gabriel García Márquez (photo copyright Eva Rubenstein)

INNOCENT ERENDIRA & OTHER STORIES
Several early stories and a visit to the almost fairy-tale world of Eréndira
Translated by Gregory Rabassa
0–06–011416–9 Harper & Row $11.95
0–06–090701–0 Harper & Row pb $6.95

LEAF STORM & OTHER STORIES
Translated by Gregory Rabassa
0–06–012779–1 Harper & Row $11.50
0–06–090699–5 Harper & Row pb $6.95

LOVE IN THE TIME OF CHOLERA
A novel about love, old age, race, and social life in a 19th-century Colombian small town
Translated by Edith Grossman
0–394–56161–9 Knopf $18.95
0–14–011990–6 Penguin pb $8.95

NO ONE WRITES TO THE COLONEL & OTHER SHORT STORIES
Translated by J.S. Bernstein
0–06–011417–7 Harper & Row $10.50
0–06–090700–2 Harper & Row pb $7.95

ONE HUNDRED YEARS OF SOLITUDE
"The Colombian town of Macondo is Latin America in microcosm: local autonomy yielding to state authority; anticlericalism; party politics; the coming of the United Fruit Company; aborted revolutions; the rape of innocence by history. And the Buendias (inventors, artisans, soldiers, lovers, mystics) seem doomed to ride a biological tragi-cycle in circles from solitude to magic to poetry to science to politics to violence back again to solitude"—John Leonard, *NY Times*
Translated by Gregory Rabassa
0–06–011418–5 Harper & Row $25.00
0–380–01503–X Avon pb $4.95

Cuba

- Reinaldo Arenas
FAREWELL TO THE SEA
Personal obsessions and material problems in revolutionary Cuba
Translated by Andrew Hurley
0–14–006636–5 Penguin pb $7.95

GRAVEYARD OF THE ANGELS
Translated by A. MacAdam
0–380–75075–9 Avon pb $3.95

THE ILL-FATED PEREGRINATIONS OF FRAY SERVANDO
A quixotic black comedy in which a Mexican priest turns revolutionary
Translated by Andrew Hurley
0–380–75074–0 Avon pb $7.95

OLD ROSA: A Novel in Two Stories
Translated by Ann Tashi Slater & Andrew Hurley
0–8021–1092–4 Grove $15.95

SINGING FROM THE WELL
A child's life in the countryside of revolutionary Cuba
0–670–80805–9 Viking $16.95
0–14–009444–X Penguin pb $7.95

- Guillermo Cabrera Infante
THREE TRAPPED TIGERS
A madcap linguistic romp through late 1950s Havana nightlife
Translated by Donald Gardner & Suzanne Jill Levine
0–380–69964–8 Avon pb $5.95

- Alejo Carpentier
REASONS OF STATE
Translated by Frances Patridge
0–904613–52–6 Writers & Readers pb $4.95

- José Lezama Lima
PARADISO
This subtle, verbally intricate novel of family life, first published in 1966, has been widely viewed as a masterpiece
Translated by Gregory Rabassa
0–292–76507–X Texas pb $10.95

- Heberto Padilla
HEROES ARE GRAZING IN MY GARDEN
A somewhat autobiographical novel of disillusionment with the Cuban Revolution, in which the only hero is language
Translated by Andrew Hurley
0–374–16982–9 Farrar, Straus & Giroux $16.95

SELF-PORTRAIT OF THE OTHER: A Memoir
Translated by Alexander Coleman
0–374–26086–9 Farrar, Straus & Giroux $18.95

- Virgilio Piñera
COLD TALES
Stories by an influential writer whose homosexuality brought him into conflict with the Castro regime
Translated by Mark Schaffer
Introduction by Guillermo Cabrera Infante
0–941419–18–5 Eridanos $24.00
0–941419–19–3 Eridanos pb $15.00

- Severo Sarduy
MAITREYA
A journey toward revelation
Translated by Suzanne Jill Levine
0–910061–31–9 Ediciones del Norte pb $9.50

Ecuador

- Jorge Icaza
THE VILLAGERS (HUASIPUNGO)
A brutal confrontation of Indians and whites in one of the most moving novels of Latin American literature
Translated by Bernard M. Dulsey
0–8093–0653–0 Southern Illinois pb $9.50

El Salvador

- Claribel Alegría
LUISA IN REALITYLAND
Translated by Darwin J. Flakoll
0–915306–70–0 Curbstone $17.95
0–915306–69–7 Curbstone pb $9.95

- Manlio Argueta
CUZCATALAN
Popular folklore provides the backdrop for this novel tracing a family's history from the 1930s to the early '80s
Translated by Clark Hansen
0–394–74253–2 Random House pb $8.95

ONE DAY OF LIFE
"Does what virtually no other volume or newspaper story has even begun to do. It renders the Salvadoran peasant visible"— *New Republic*
Translated by Clark Hansen
0–394–72216–7 Random House pb $7.95

Guatemala

- Rodrigo Rey-Rosa
THE BEGGAR'S KNIFE
Stories from a young Guatemalan writer
Translated by Paul Bowles
0–87286–164–3 City Lights pb $5.95

Mexico

• **Homero Aridjis**
PERSEPHONE
The myth of Persephone, with its poetic
and erotic overtones, transposed to Mexico
Translated by Betty Ferber
0–394–74175–7 Random House pb $8.95

• **Juan J. Arreola**
**CONFABULARIO & OTHER
INVENTIONS**
Translated by George D. Schade
0–292–73196–5 Texas $14.95
0–292–71030–5 Texas pb $7.95

THE FAIR
A satire about life in the author's
hometown
Translated by John Upton
0–292–72417–9 Texas $12.95

• **Mariano Azuela**
**THREE NOVELS BY MARIANO
AZUELA**
*The Trials of a Respectable Family, The
Underdogs,* and *The Firefly*
Translated by Frances K. Hendricks & Beatrice Berler
0–911536–78–7 Trinity $15.00

**TWO NOVELS OF MEXICO: The Flies &
The Bosses**
Satiric and somber novelettes of the
Mexican Revolution
Translated by Lesley Byrd Simpson
0–520–00053–6 California pb $8.95

THE UNDERDOGS
Azuela's classic work
Translated by E. Munguia
Foreword by Harriet de Onis
0–451–52255–9 NAL pb $3.95

• **Nellie Campobello**
CARTUCHO/MY MOTHER'S HAND
The Mexican Revolution, from a child's
perspective
Translated by Doris Meyer & Irene Matthews
Introduction by Elena Poniatowska
0–292–71111–5 Viking pb $7.95

• **Carlos Fuentes**
BURNT WATER
Life in modern-day Mexico City
Translated by Margaret S. Peden
0–374–51988–9 Farrar, Straus & Giroux pb $7.95

A CHANGE OF SKIN
Fuentes' most sweeping novel—a search
for individual truth on a journey from
Mexico City to Vera Cruz
Translated by Sam Hileman
0–374–51427–5 Farrar, Straus & Giroux pb $9.95

THE DEATH OF ARTEMIO CRUZ
A peasant rises to power and importance
Translated by Sam Hileman
0–374–50540–3 Farrar, Straus & Giroux pb $8.95

DISTANT RELATIONS
Translated by Margaret S. Peden
0–374–14082–0 Farrar, Straus & Giroux $11.95
0–374–51813–0 Farrar, Straus & Giroux pb $8.95

THE GOOD CONSCIENCE
A semibiographical novel of a youth
coming to terms with his society
Translated by Sam Hileman
0–374–50736–8 Farrar, Straus & Giroux pb $7.95

**HOLY PLACE & BIRTHDAY: Two
Novellas**
Translated by Suzanne Jill Levine & Margaret S. Peden
0–317–53488–2 Farrar, Straus & Giroux pb $9.95

THE HYDRA HEAD
A third world spy thriller: Mexico, the
Middle East, and oil
Translated by Margaret S. Peden
0–374–51563–8 Farrar, Straus & Giroux $9.95

THE OLD GRINGO
An American writer (modeled on Ambrose
Bierce) disappears in Mexico during the
Mexican Revolution
Translated by Margaret S. Peden
0–374–22578–8 Farrar, Straus & Giroux $14.95
0–06–097063–4 Harper & Row pb $7.95

TERRA NOSTRA
A fictional panorama of Spanish and Latin
American history. "*Terra Nostra* implies
taking the whole universe, which is all my
past . . . I am trying to capture that
cultural past, that richness of the
civilization through a multitude of voices,
a multitude of eyes"—Carlos Fuentes
Translated by Margaret S. Peden
Afterword by Milan Kundera
0–374–27327–8 Farrar, Straus & Giroux $20.50
0–374–51414–3 Farrar, Straus & Giroux pb $14.95

WHERE THE AIR IS CLEAR
A fast paced exposé of the foibles and
decadence of the Mexican upper classes
Translated by Sam Hileman
0–374–50919–0 Farrar, Straus & Giroux pb $9.95

• **Sergio Galindo**
LA COMPARSA: A Mexican Masquerade
Translated by John & Carolyn Brushwood
0–935480–17–X Latin American pb $11.50

• **Elena Garro**
**RECOLLECTIONS OF THINGS TO
COME**
A dissection of Mexican small-town life in
the 1920s
Translated by Ruth L. Simms
0–292–77032–4 Texas pb $10.95

• **Jorge Ibarguengoitia**
THE LIGHTNING OF AUGUST
A Mexican general recounts life at the
beginning of the Revolution
Translated by Irene del Corral
0–380–89617–6 Avon pb $3.95

TWO CRIMES
A fast-paced tale of repression, radical
politics, women, and murder in Mexico
City and the provinces
Translated by Asa Zatz
0–380–89616–8 Avon pb $3.95

• **Gregorio López y Fuentes**
EL INDIO
Mexican Indian life on the eve of the
Revolution
Translated by Anita Brenner
0–8044–6429–4 Ungar pb $9.95

• **José Emilio Pacheco**
**BATTLES IN THE DESERT & OTHER
STORIES**
Translated by Katherine Silver
0–8112–1020–0 New Directions pb $8.95

• **Juan García Ponce**
ENCOUNTERS
Three short stories and a novella
Translated by Helen Lane
Introduction by Octavio Paz
0–941419–25–8 Rizzoli $19.00
0–941419–24–X Rizzoli pb $10.00

• **Juan Rulfo**
**THE BURNING PLAIN & OTHER
STORIES**
Fifteen stories about guilt, poverty, and
despair
Translated by George D. Schade
Illustrated by Kermit Oliver
0–292–73685–1 Texas $12.95
0–292–70132–2 Texas pb $7.95

PEDRO PARAMO: A Novel of Mexico
The moving story of the murder of a
small-town tyrant
Translated by Lysander Kemp
0–8021–3119–0 Grove pb $3.95

• **Gustavo Sainz**
THE PRINCESS OF THE IRON PALACE
Life in the fast lane leads a young woman
to disillusionment and spiritual emptiness
Translated by Andrew Hurley
0–394–56066–3 Grove $17.95

• **Augustín Yáñez**
THE EDGE OF THE STORM
Religious oppression and Indian traditions
in a small town just prior to the
Revolution
Translated by Ethel Brinton
0–292–70131–4 Texas pb $9.95

THE LEAN LANDS
The confrontation between traditional life
and industrialization results in tragedy in
rural Mexico of the 1920s
Translated by Ethel Brinton
0–292–78384–1 Texas $14.50

Paraguay

• **Augusto Roa Bastos**
I, THE SUPREME
The rambling, fragmented story of a
paranoid 19th-century dictator
Translated by Helen Lane
0–394–53535–9 Knopf $18.95
0–394–75264–3 Random House pb $10.95

SON OF MAN
Internal warfare in Paraguay between the
years 1912 and 1932. "Because the author
does not lie about his ravaged land,
because the violence is relentless and death
apparently unending, the slow creation of
hope is all the more powerful"—Ariel
Dorfman
Translated by Rachel Caffyn
Foreword by Ariel Dorfman
0–85345–733–6 Monthly Review pb $7.50

Peru

• **Ciro Alegría**
BROAD AND ALIEN IS THE WORLD
A panoramic view of Indian civilization
and life in Peru set against a struggle for
land
0–85036–171–0 Longwood $17.00

• **José M. Arguedas**
DEEP RIVERS
Translated by Frances H. Barraclough
0–292–71533–1 Texas pb $9.95

YAWAR FIESTA
Social relations and influences between
mestizo Indians and the upper classes of

FOR OVERSEAS ORDERING INFORMATION, SEE PAGE 1

the Peruvian highlands of the 1920s and 1930s
0–292–79601–3 Texas $19.95
0–292–79602–1 Texas pb $8.95

• Isaac Goldemberg
THE FRAGMENTED LIFE OF DON JACOBO LERNER
Translated by Robert Picciotto
0–89255–003–1 Persea pb $8.95

• César Vallejo
TUNGSTEN
A denunciation of the brutal treatment of Andean mine workers, written in an uncharacteristic vein of social realism by Peru's great modern poet
Translated by Robert Mesey
0–8156–0226–X Syracuse $19.95

• Mario Vargas Llosa
AUNT JULIA AND THE SCRIPTWRITER
Reality and fantasy: can a real marriage be more than a soap opera?
Translated by Helen R. Lane
0–374–10691–6 Farrar, Straus & Giroux $17.50
0–380–70046–8 Avon pb $9.95

CONVERSATION IN THE CATHEDRAL
Two men from different social classes discuss Peruvian life, violence, and social decay in a bar called the Cathedral
Translated by Gregory Rabassa
0–06–014502–1 Harper & Row $22.95

THE GREEN HOUSE
Translated by Gregory Rabassa
0–374–51888–2 Farrar, Straus & Giroux pb $12.95

THE REAL LIFE OF ALEJANDRO MAYTA
A dissection of Peruvian violence, based on the assassination of a revolutionary figure
Translated by Alfred MacAdam
0–394–74776–3 Random House pb $6.95

THE TIME OF THE HERO
A military academy rife with corruption becomes a microcosm of Peruvian society's outdated social system
Translated by Lysander Kemp
0–374–52021–6 Farrar, Straus & Giroux pb $9.95

THE WAR OF THE END OF THE WORLD
The suppression of a peasant revolt in late 19th-century Brazil
Translated by Helen R. Lane
0–380–69987–7 Avon pb $9.95

WHO KILLED PALOMINO MOLERO?
Police investigate a murder in a nation dominated by corruption
Translated by Alfred MacAdam
0–374–28978–6 Farrar, Straus & Giroux $14.95
0–02–022570–9 Macmillan pb $6.95

Puerto Rico

• Enrique A. Laguerre
BENEVOLENT MASTERS
A Puerto Rican dignitary's ascent to power
0–943862–10–8 Waterfront pb $8.95

THE LABYRINTH
Based on the career of the Dominican dictator Trujillo. "The inner story of Trujillo has been chiseled into baroque sculpture . . . A medieval Passion Play dressed up for the 20th Century"—*New Republic*
Translated by William Rose
0–943862–12–4 Waterfront pb $8.95

• René Marques
THE LOOK
Puerto Rican youth involved with politics, drugs, the island's independence, and Chile during the Allende years
Translated by Charles Pilditch
0–918454–29–8 Senda Nueva pb $11.95

• Luis Rafael Sanchez
MACHO CAMACHO'S BEAT
The realities of daily life in San Juan
Translated by Gregory Rabassa
0–380–58008–X Avon pb $3.50

• Pedro J. Soto
SPIKS
The struggle over assimilation versus acculturation among Nuyoricans (Puerto Ricans born or raised in New York City)
Translated with an introduction by Victoria Ortiz
0–85345–331–4 Monthly Review pb $6.00

• Emilio Diaz Valcarcel
SCHEMES IN THE MONTH OF MARCH
"A brilliant comic novel about exile, the writer as outcast, the Puerto Rican as pariah, and the different languages of banishment he speaks"—*Washington Post*
Translated by Nancy Sebastiani
0–916950–05–0 Bilingual Review pb $13.00

Uruguay

• Antonio Larreta
THE LAST PORTRAIT OF THE DUCHESS OF ALBA
A fictitious memoir of the duchess' affairs in Spanish society
Translated by Pamela Carmell
0–917561–42–2 Adler & Adler $17.95

• Carlos Martinez Moreno
EL INFIERNO
The rise and fall of the Tupamaro guerrillas, and the repression and dictatorship that followed
0–930523–48–2 Readers International pb $8.95

• Horacio Quiroga
THE DECAPITATED CHICKEN & OTHER STORIES
Tales of horror, madness, and death. "Full of psychological shocks and eerie effects"—*New Yorker*
Translated by Margaret S. Peden
Introduction by George D. Schade
0–292–71541–2 Texas pb $6.95

THE EXILES & OTHER STORIES
Thirteen of the best stories by a writer who has been compared to Poe and Kipling
Translated by J. David Danielson
0–292–72050–5 Texas $17.95
0–292–72051–3 Texas pb $8.95

• Cristina Peri Rossi
THE SHIP OF FOOLS
"Her great gift is the ability to project onto the high plains of the imagination the historical present in all its tragic reality"—Julio Cortázar
Translated by Psiche Hughes
0–930523–54–7 Readers International pb $9.95

Venezuela

• Romulo Gallegos
CANAIMA
A 1935 novel of a rough and adventurous life in the Guianan jungles
Translated by Jaime Tello
Introduction by Efrain Subero
0–8061–9928–8 Oklahoma $19.95

POETRY

Argentina

• José Hernandez
THE GAUCHO MARTIN FIERRO
Civilization versus barbarism in this epic of 19th-century Argentine life
Translated by Frank G. Carrino
0–87395–284–7 SUNY pb $7.95

• Roberto Juarroz
VERTICAL POETRY
"Each of Roberto Juarroz's poems is a surprising verbal crystallization: language reduced to a drop of light. A great poet of absolute instants"—Octavio Paz
Translated by W.S. Merwin
0–86547–307–2 North Point pb $10.95

Brazil

• Carlos Drummond de Andrade
THE MINUS SIGN
A collection of verse interpretations of 54 poems by Brazil's greatest poet
Edited and translated by Virginia de Araujo
0–933806–03–5 Black Swan $17.50

TRAVELLING IN THE FAMILY
A wide-ranging collection
Translated by Mark Strand & Gregory Rabassa
Edited by Thomas Colchie & Elizabeth Bishop
0–394–52478–0 Random House $19.95

• Mario de Andrade
HALLUCINATED CITY
This outcry against the unrestrained urbanization of São Paulo in the 1920s is a masterpiece of Brazilian modernism
Translated by Jack E. Tomlins
0–8265–1113–9 Vanderbilt pb $7.95

• Basilio da Gama
THE URUGUAY: A Historical Romance of South America
An epic narration of the 18th-century Seven Missions Wars, which pitted the Spanish and Portuguese against the Jesuits and their Indian flock
Translated by Sir Richard F. Burton
Edited by Frederick G.H. Garcia & Edward Stanton
0–520–04524–6 California $35.00

Elizabeth Bishop & Emanuel Brasil, editors
AN ANTHOLOGY OF TWENTIETH-CENTURY BRAZILIAN POETRY
Selection of poems by members of the modernist generation
Translated by Paul Blackburn & others
0–8195–6023–5 Wesleyan pb $12.95

Emanuel Brasil & William Jay Smith, editors
BRAZILIAN POETRY 1950–1980
Selected works by six recent poets revealing the broad directions of contemporary Brazilian poetry
0–8195–5075–2 Wesleyan $25.00
0–8195–6083–9 Wesleyan pb $12.95

Chile

• Marjorie Agosín
BRUJAS Y ALGO MAS/WITCHES AND SOMETHING MORE
Translated by Colan Franzen
0–935480–16–1 Latin American pb $11.00

• Ariel Dorfman
LAST WALTZ IN SANTIAGO & OTHER POEMS OF EXILE AND DISAPPEARANCE
Translated by Edith Grossman with the author
0–670–82022–9 Viking $17.95

• Oscar Hahn
THE ART OF DYING
0–935480–32–3 Latin American pb $10.00

• Vicente Huidobro
ALTAZOR
A long poem published in 1931. "*Altazor's* space voyage becomes a voyage into language . . . Its words begin to mimic and devour each other; sounds and meanings break away and fuse again in new combinations; waves of punning go on for pages"—*Village Voice*
Translated by Eliot Weinberger
1–55597–106–7 Graywolf pb $8.50

THE SELECTED POETRY OF VICENTE HUIDOBRO
A sample of Huidobro's intensely personal and autobiographical poetry revealing his continual experimentation with language and the poetic tradition
Translated by Eliot Weinberger, Michael Palmer & others
Edited by David M. Guss
0–8112–0805–2 New Directions pb $6.95

• Pablo Neruda
ART OF BIRDS
Translated by Jack Schmitt
0–292–70371–6 Texas $19.95
0–292–70410–0 Texas pb $9.95

THE CAPTAIN'S VERSES
Poetry chronicling a love affair united by dedication to political and social struggle
Translated with an introduction by Donald D. Walsh
0–8112–0457–X New Directions pb $5.95

EXTRAVAGARIA
Translated by Alastair Reid
0–374–15126–1 Farrar, Straus & Giroux pb $8.95

FIVE DECADES: Poems 1925–1970
Translated and edited by Ben Belitt
0–8021–3035–6 Grove pb $14.50

Vicente Huidobro (photo by Hans Arp, courtesy of Graywolf Press)

FULLY EMPOWERED
Translated by Alastair Reid
0–374–15944–0 Farrar, Straus & Giroux $12.95
0–374–51351–1 Farrar, Straus & Giroux pb $8.95

THE HEIGHTS OF MACCHU PICCHU
This meditation on the Inca ruin, a section from Neruda's epic of the Americas *Canto General*, is one of his most sustained and powerful works
Translated by Nathaniel Tarn
0–374–50648–5 Farrar, Straus & Giroux $7.95

INCITEMENT TO NIXONICIDE AND PRAISE FOR THE CHILEAN REVOLUTION
The poet's attack on the causes of the destruction of the government of Salvador Allende
Translated by Steve Kowit
0–686–68219–X Quixote pb $6.00

NEW DECADE: Poems 1958–1967
Translated by Ben Belitt & Alastair Reid
0–394–17275–2 Grove pb $5.95

NEW POEMS: 1968–1970
Edited with an introduction by Ben Belitt
0–394–17793–2 Grove pb $8.95

ONE HUNDRED LOVE SONNETS/CIEN SONETOS DE AMOR
Translated by Stephen Tapscott
0–292–76029–9 Texas $22.50
0–292–76028–0 Texas pb $9.95

RESIDENCE ON EARTH & OTHER POEMS
Neruda's early surrealist poetry, which for many represents his highest achievement
Translated with an introduction by Donald D. Walsh
0–8112–0467–7 New Directions pb $8.95

SELECTED POEMS
Translated with an introduction by Ben Belitt
0–394–17243–4 Grove pb $8.95

A SEPARATE ROSE
A posthumously published collection; the poet in total communion with nature
Translated by William O'Daly
0–914742–88–4 Copper Canyon pb $8.00

STILL ANOTHER DAY
Translated by William O'Daly
0–914742–77–9 Copper Canyon pb $9.00

THE STONES OF CHILE
Translated by Dennis Maloney
0–934834–01–6 White Pine pb $9.50

STONES OF THE SKY
Translated by James Nolan
1–55659–007–5 Copper Canyon pb $9.00

TWENTY LOVE POEMS AND A SONG OF DESPAIR
Poems viewing the stages of love, from infatuation to final parting; an early and popular collection
Translated by W.S. Merwin
0–14–058590–7 Penguin pb $4.95

WINTER GARDEN
Another posthumously published collection
Translated by William O'Daly
0–914742–93–0 Copper Canyon pb $8.00

• Nicanor Parra
ANTIPOEMS: New and Selected
Parra works consciously against the lyrical and rhetorical traditions of Spanish-language poetry, creating a purposely flat and deadpan style
Translated by Miller Williams and others
Edited by David Unger
0–8112–0960–1 New Directions pb $8.95

EMERGENCY POEMS
Translated and edited by Miller Williams
0–8112–0340–9 New Directions pb $8.75

SERMONS AND HOMILIES OF THE CHRIST OF ELQUI
Translated by Sandra Reyes
Foreword by Miller Williams
0–8262–0451–1 Missouri $13.50

• Raul Zurita
ANTEPARADISE: A Bilingual Edition
"The only meaning of art, its only purpose . . . is to make life more humanly livable. In brief, we should keep on proposing Paradise even if the evidence at hand might indicate that such a pursuit is folly"—Raul Zurita
Translated by Jack Schmitt
0–520–05434–2 California $27.50
0–520–05926–3 California pb $11.95

PURGATORIO, 1970–1977
"Zurita's quest for redemption results in a sustained sequence of great power and beauty on the Atacama desert, a spiritual exercise that recalls the experience of fellow poet and countryman Pablo Neruda at Machu Picchu"—*Choice*
Translated by Jeremy Jacobson
0–935480–21–8 Latin American pb $11.95

POEMS OF CHILE: A Bilingual Anthology, 1965–1985
Translated by Steven F. White
0–87775–180–3 Unicorn pb $12.95

Cuba

• Nicolás Guillén
THE GREAT ZOO & OTHER POEMS
A fantasy tour of a Cuban zoo in which humans are seen through animal eyes
Translated and edited by Robert Marquez
0–85345–287–3 Monthly Review pb $8.00

MAN-MAKING WORDS: Selected Poems of Nicolás Guillén
Edited by Robert Marquez & David McMurray
0–87023–101–4 Massachusetts $17.50
0–87023–102–2 Massachusetts pb $8.95

LEGACIES: Selected Poems
Translated by Alastair Reid & Andrew Hurley
0–374–18472–0 Farrar, Straus & Giroux $15.95
0–374–51736–3 Farrar, Straus & Giroux pb $9.95

El Salvador

• Claribel Alegría
FLOWERS FROM THE VOLCANO
Memories of torture and death in El Salvador
Translated by Carolyn Forché
0–8229–3469–8 Pittsburgh $15.95
0–8229–5344–7 Pittsburgh pb $6.95

• Roque Dalton
CLANDESTINE POEMS/POEMAS CLANDESTINOS
A bilingual edition
Translated by Jack Hirschman
Edited by Barbara Paschke & Eric Weaver
0–942638–07–7 New Americas pb $7.00

POEMS
Popular poetry in support of revolution
Translated by Richard Schaaf
0–915306–43–3 Curbstone pb $7.50

• Hugo Lindo
WAYS OF RAIN/MANERAS DE LLOVER
"A song of praise to his tropical homeland. Although inspired by the *Popul Vuh*, Lindo's cosmogony of 28 cantos transcends its locale to become a song to human perseverance generally"—*Choice*
0–935480–24–2 Latin American $14.95

• Gabriela Yanes & others, editors
MIRRORS OF WAR: Literature and Revolution in El Salvador
A collection of prose and poetry of the revolutionary movement in El Salvador
Translated by Keith Ellis
0–85345–687–9 Monthly Review pb $7.95

Guatemala

• Otto R. Castillo
LET'S GO
Works by a Guatemalan guerrilla poet who died under torture
Translated by Margaret Randall
0–915306–44–1 Curbstone pb $7.50

Mexico

• Homero Aridjis
EXALTATION OF LIGHT
Lyricism verges on crystalline abstraction in this effective translation
Translated by Eliot Weinberger
0–918526–28–0 BOA $12.00
0–918526–29–9 BOA pb $6.95

Rosario Castellanos
MEDITATION ON THE THRESHOLD
One of Mexico's most important 20th-century poets and an exponent of feminism
Translated by Julian Palley
0–91695–080–8 Bilingual Review pb $10.00

SELECTED POEMS OF ROSARIO CASTELLANOS
"The image that best represents Castellanos' poetry is her 'heart of thorns and stars' . . . in which two images are united: the Christian heart of the god become man, and the Nahuatl heart, the Cactus abounding in spiny red fruits, the human hearts sacrificed to renew the cycle of life"—Cecilia Vicuña
Translated by Magda Bogin
1–55597–112–1 Graywolf pb $9.50

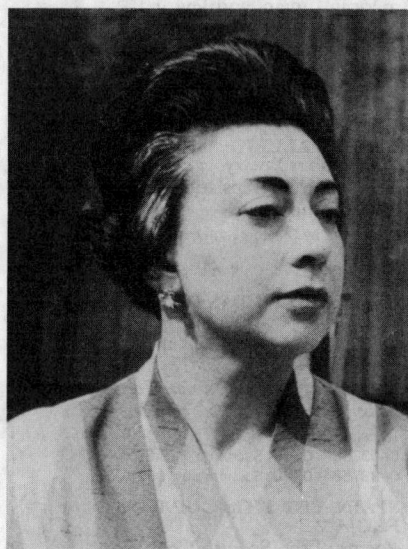

Rosario Castellanos (photo by Lola Alvarez Bravo, courtesy of Graywolf Press)

• Isabel Fraire
POEMS IN THE LAP OF DEATH
A bilingual edition
Translated by Thomas Hoeksema
0–935480–04–4 Latin American pb $8.50

• José Gorostiza
DEATH WITHOUT END
Translated by Laura Villaseñor
0–87959–057–2 Texas pb $10.00

• Marco Antonio Montes de Oca
TWENTY-ONE POEMS
"A talented poet of inner experience whose verse is rich in metaphor and devoid of social commentary"—*Choice*
Translated by Laura Villaseñor
Prologue by Octavio Paz
0–935480–09–9 Latin American pb $9.00

• José Emilio Pacheco
DON'T ASK ME HOW THE TIME GOES BY: Poems
Born in 1939, Pacheco has been among the most prolific and influential of young Mexican poets
Translated by Alastair Reid
0–231–04285–X Columbia pb $13.00

SELECTED POEMS
"The poetry of José Emilio Pacheco is not inscribed in the world of nature, but in culture, and within that in shadow in the midst of it. Each poem by Pacheco is a homage to the No; for José Emilio time is

the agent of universal destruction, and history—the passage of ruins"—Octavio Paz
Edited by George McWhirter
Translated by Thomas Hoeksema & others
0–8112–1022–7 New Directions pb $11.95

SIGNALS FROM THE FLAMES
"Winner of Mexico's national prizes, José Emilio Pacheco appears to be headed for international prominence"—*Choice*
Edited by Yvette E. Miller
Translated by Thomas Hoeksema
0–935480–03–X Latin American pb $8.50

So where does the greater guilt lie
for a passion that should not be:
with the man who pleads out of baseness
or the woman debased by his plea?

Or which is more to be blamed—
though both will have cause for chagrin:
the woman who sins for money
or the man who pays money to sin?

Sor Juana Inés de la Cruz
A SOR JUANA ANTHOLOGY
Translated by Alan S. Trueblood
0–674–82120–3 Harvard $29.50

• Sor Juana Inés de la Cruz
A SOR JUANA ANTHOLOGY
New translations of work by the 17th-century nun who was the first great poet of Latin America, including her baroque masterpiece *First Dream*. "Of all the major poets of the Americas, Sor Juana Inés de la Cruz has until recently been the most neglected . . . [Alan S.] Trueblood has now managed, in the case of Sor Juana's poems, without being unfaithful to them, to create texts in English which have a poetic value of their own"—Octavio Paz
Translated by Alan S. Trueblood
Foreword by Octavio Paz
0–674–82120–3 Harvard $29.50

SOR JUANA INES DE LA CRUZ: Poems
A bilingual anthology
Translated by Margaret Sayers Peden
0–91695–060–3 Bilingual Review pb $9.00

A WOMAN OF GENIUS/LA RESPUESTA A SOR FILOTEA: The Intellectual Autobiography of Sor Juana Inés de la Cruz
Sor Juana's bold response to the church authorities about woman's role in life
Translated with an introduction by Margaret Sayers Peden
0–915998–15–7 Lime Rock pb $6.95

• Octavio Paz
Mexico's great modern poet has explored the same themes over many decades, fusing autobiography and metaphysical speculation, eroticism and politics, vibrant imagery and formal experimentation.
THE COLLECTED POEMS, 1957–1987
A bilingual edition
Translated by Eliot Weinberger & others
Edited by Eliot Weinberger
0–8112–1037–5 New Directions $37.50

CONFIGURATIONS
Translated by Muriel Rukeyser & others
0–8112–0150–3 New Directions pb $5.95

A DRAFT OF SHADOWS & OTHER POEMS
The title poem is a long autobiographical meditation
Translated by Eliot Weinberger
0–8112–0738–2 New Directions pb $6.95

EAGLE OR SUN?
Prose poems
Translated by Eliot Weinberger
0–8112–0623–8 New Directions pb $5.95

EARLY POEMS, 1935–1955
Translated with a preface by Muriel Rukeyser
0–8112–0478–2 New Directions pb $6.95

SELECTED POEMS OF OCTAVIO PAZ
Edited by Eliot Weinberger
Translated by Eliot Weinberger & others
0–8112–0899–0 New Directions pb $6.95

A TREE WITHIN
A recent long poem
Translated by Eliot Weinberger
0–8112–1071–5 New Directions pb $8.95

● Octavio Paz, editor
MEXICAN POETRY: An Anthology
Translated by Samuel Beckett
0–394–62086–0 Grove pb $9.95

● Manuel Ponce
SOME OF MY POEMS
Views of life, death, and God
Translated by Maria Luisa Rodriguez-Lee
0–935480–28–5 Latin American pb $11.50

Nicaragua

● Ernesto Cardenal
APOCALYPSE & OTHER POEMS
Protest poetry by the committed revolutionary priest turned politician
0–8112–0662–9 New Directions pb $5.95

FROM NICARAGUA, WITH LOVE: Poems 1979–1986
Cardenal's most recent poetry
Translated by Jonathan Cohen
0–87286–201–1 City Lights pb $5.95

THE GOSPEL IN SOLENTINAME
Translated by Donald D. Walsh

Volume 1
0–88344–176–4 Orbis pb $11.95

Volume 2
0–88344–175–6 Orbis pb $11.95

Volume 3
0–88344–174–8 Orbis pb $11.95

Volume 4
0–88344–173–X Orbis pb $11.95

WITH WALKER IN NICARAGUA & OTHER EARLY POEMS
Poetry about the United States' past invasions of Nicaragua
Translated by Jonathan Cohen
0–8195–5123–6 Wesleyan $17.00
0–8195–6118–5 Wesleyan pb $9.95

ZERO HOUR & OTHER DOCUMENTARY POEMS
Poetry of the struggle that "debunks, corroborates and mediates" reality, including the post-revolutionary work *Lights*
Translated by Paul W. Borgeson & others
Edited by Donald D. Walsh
0–8112–0767–6 New Directions pb $6.95

● Rubén Dário
SELECTED POETRY
Poems by the founding father of modernism in Spanish and Spanish-American literature
Translated by Lysander Kemp
Prologue by Octavio Paz
0–292–77615–2 Texas pb $6.95

Peru

● Isaac Goldemberg
JUST PASSING THROUGH (HOMBRE DE PASO)
Bilingual poetry on being Latin American, American Indian, and Jewish
Translated by David Unger
0–910061–07–6 Ediciones del Norte pb $7.00

César Vallejo
CESAR VALLEJO: The Complete Posthumous Poetry
The definitive translation of a great 20th-century poet
Translated by Clayton Eshleman and José R. Barcia
0–520–04099–6 California pb $12.95

SELECTED POEMS OF CESAR VALLEJO
Selections from his four most important collections: *The Black Messengers, Trilce, Human Poems,* and *Spain, Take This Cup From Me*
Translated by H.R. Hays
0–937584–01–0 Sachem $13.50
0–937584–02–9 Sachem pb $6.95

SPAIN, LET THIS CUP PASS FROM ME
Poems of the Spanish Civil War
Translated by Alvaro Cardona-Hine
0–88031–049–9 Invisible City pb $5.00

DRAMA

● George W. Woodyard & others, translators
DRAMACONTEMPORARY: Latin America
Includes Carlos Fuentes' *Orchids in the Moonlight,* Mario Vargas Llosa's *Kathie and the Hippopotamus,* Antonio Skármeta's *Burning Patience,* and Manuel Puig's *The Kiss of the Spider Woman*
0–55554–004–X Performing Arts $22.95
1–55554–005–8 Performing Arts pb $9.95

● Manuel Puig
UNDER A MANTLE OF STARS
A heavy dramatic mixture of politics and fantasy with a dash of eroticism
Translated by Ronald Christ
0–930829–00–X Lumen pb $6.95

● Severo Sarduy
FOR VOICE
Sarduy is noted for the brilliance of his linguistic play
Translated by Philip Barnard
Edited by Yvette E. Miller
0–935480–20–X Latin American pb $12.95

● Rodolfo Usigli
TWO PLAYS: Crown of Light & One of These Days
An "antihistorical comedy" and a "nonpolitical fantasy" by a leading Mexican playwright
Translated by Thomas Bledsoe
0–8093–0494–5 Southern Illinois pb $9.95

● Egon Wolff
PAPER FLOWERS: A Play in Six Scenes
Translated by Margaret S. Peden
0–8262–0187–3 Missouri pb $5.95

CRITICISM, MEMOIRS, AND OTHER PROSE

Argentina

● Jorge Luis Borges
SEVEN NIGHTS
Seven lectures on art, literature, and the human condition
Translated by Eliot Weinberger
Introduction by Alastair Reid
0–8112–0905–9 New Directions pb $6.95

Julio Cortázar (photo copyright Anne de Brunhoff)

● Julio Cortázar
AROUND THE DAY IN EIGHTY WORLDS
A kaleidoscopic tour of Cortázar's imagination, including reflections on murder, jazz, and surrealism
Translated by Thomas Christensen
0–86547–203–3 North Point $22.50

● Eduardo Mallea
HISTORY OF AN ARGENTINE PASSION
An essay on the two Argentinas: Buenos Aires and the interior, where the author believed the nation's future lay
Translated by Myron I. Lichtblau
Edited by Yvette E. Miller
0–935480–10–2 Latin American pb $13.95

🐛 IF YOU CAN'T FIND IT, LOOK IN THE INDEX

Brazil

- Elizabeth Bishop, translator
THE DIARY OF "HELENA MORLEY"
A girl's memoir of growing up in Brazil in the 1890s
0–670–27219–1 Ecco pb $6.95

- Euclydes da Cunha
REBELLION IN THE BACKLANDS
The tragic story of the Canudos uprising of the late 1890s
Translated by Samuel Putnam
0–226–12444–4 Chicago pb $12.95

- Clarice Lispector
THE FOREIGN LEGION
Lispector's views of literature and her own working methods
Translated by Giovanni Pontiero
0–85635–627–1 Carcanet $20.00
0–85635–680–8 Carcanet pb $8.50

Chile

- José Donoso
THE BOOM IN SPANISH-AMERICAN LITERATURE: A Personal History
0–231–04165–9 Columbia pb $13.50

- Ariel Dorfman
THE EMPIRE'S OLD CLOTHES: What the Lone Ranger, Babar, and Other Innocent Heroes Do to Our Minds
Translated by Clark Hansen
0–394–71486–5 Pantheon pb $8.95

- Ariel Dorfman & Armand Mattelart
HOW TO READ DONALD DUCK
Imperialism, subtext, and the American comic strip
0–88477–023–0 International General pb $9.95

- Pablo Neruda
ISLA NEGRA: A Notebook
The author's view of the direction his poetry has taken
Translated by Alastair Reid
0–374–17759–7 Farrar, Straus & Giroux $18.95
0–374–51734–7 Farrar, Straus & Giroux pb $12.95
MEMOIRS
Translated by Hardie St. Martin
0–14–004661–5 Penguin pb $7.95
PASSIONS AND IMPRESSIONS
A collection of Neruda's prose works, including his Nobel Award acceptance speech
Translated by Margaret S. Peden
0–374–22994–5 Farrar, Straus & Giroux $25.00
0–374–51811–4 Farrar, Straus & Giroux pb $10.95

Colombia

- Gabriel García Márquez
CLANDESTINE IN CHILE: The Adventures of Miguel Littín
Littín, a Chilean exile, secretly returned to Chile to film; García Márquez narrates his experience
Translated by Asa Zatz
0–8050–0322–3 Henry Holt $13.95
THE STORY OF A SHIPWRECKED SAILOR
"Who drifted on a life raft for ten days without food or water, was proclaimed a national hero, kissed by beauty queens, made rich through publicity, and then spurned by the government and forgotten for all time"
Translated by Randolph Hogan
0–394–75403–4 Random House pb $4.95

Cuba

- Guillermo Cabrera Infante
HOLY SMOKE
A homage to the joys of smoking. "A whirling, free-associating history of the cigar . . . The book has all the lure of the lovingly, wittingly detailed obsession"— *London Times*
0–06–015432–2 Harper & Row $16.95
0–571–14594–9 Faber & Faber pb $8.95
INFANTE'S INFERNO
Translated by Suzanne Jill Levine
0–06–015256–7 Harper & Row $18.95
0–380–69965–6 Avon pb $4.95
VIEW OF DAWN IN THE TROPICS
A stylized recapitulation of Cuban history
Translated by Suzanne Jill Levine
0–916870–37–5 Creative Arts pb $6.95

- Roberto Fernández Retamar
CALIBAN & OTHER ESSAYS
Translated by Edward Baker
0–8166–1743–0 Minnesota pb $14.95

- Severo Sarduy
WRITTEN ON A BODY
Translated by Carol Maier
0–930829–04–2 Lumen pb $8.95

El Salvador

- Roque Dalton
POETRY AND MILITANCY IN LATIN AMERICA
Translated by Arlene & James Scully
0–915–30626–3 Curbstone pb $4.00

Mexico

- Carlos Fuentes
DON QUIXOTE, OR THE CRITIQUE OF READING
0–86728–015–8 Texas pb $2.00
MYSELF WITH OTHERS: Selected Essays
Fuentes on his writing, Cervantes, García Márquez, Buñuel's films, and Borges
0–374–21750–5 Farrar, Straus & Giroux $19.95

- Martin L. Guzman
THE EAGLE AND THE SERPENT
The national polarities reflected in the Mexican Revolution
Translated by Harriet de Onis
0–8446–0668–5 Peter Smith $11.25

- Octavio Paz
ALTERNATING CURRENT
0–8050–0188–3 Henry Holt $14.95
0–8050–0175–1 Henry Holt pb $7.95
THE BOW AND THE LYRE
A panoramic analysis of poetry and its place in history, with references ranging from Homer and Lope de Vega to Rimbaud and Neruda
Translated by Ruth L. Simms
0–292–70764–9 Texas pb $10.95

CHILDREN OF THE MIRE: Modern Poetry from Romanticism to the Avant-Garde
A brilliant series of lectures on modern poetry and its discontents
0–674–11626–7 Harvard pb $5.95
CONVERGENCES: Essays on Art and Literature
Translated by Helen Lane
0–15–122585–0 HBJ $19.95
THE LABYRINTH OF SOLITUDE: Life and Thought in Mexico
Paz's famous essay on the Mexican character
Translated by Lysander Kemp
0–394–52830–1 Grove $19.50
0–394–17992–7 Grove pb $10.95
MARCEL DUCHAMP
Translated by Rachel Phillips & Donald Gardner
0–394–17848–3 Seaver pb $6.95
THE MONKEY GRAMMARIAN
Essays prompted in part by Paz's residence in India
Translated by Helen R. Lane
0–394–51807–1 Seaver $14.95
0–394–17809–2 Seaver pb $7.95
ON POETS AND OTHERS
Translated by Michael Schmidt
0–8050–0003–8 Henry Holt $18.95
ONE EARTH, FOUR OR FIVE WORLDS: Reflections on Contemporary History
Translated by Helen Lane
0–15–169394–3 HBJ $14.95
0–15–668746–1 HBJ pb $5.95
RUFINO TAMAYO: Myth and Magic
Translated by Rachel Phillips
Preface by Henry Berg
0–89207–019–6 Guggenheim pb $12.95

SOR JUANA: Or, the Traps of Faith
"Octavio Paz's book on Sor Juana displays an extraordinary sweep of imagination and intelligence, and it is many things: a biography, a critical study, a re-creation of an era, a meditation on Mexican history, a dialogue of poet with poet, a reflection on the role of the intellectual in the modern world—the world on whose threshold Sor Juana lived and died, and which she often seems to predict"— Michael Wood, *NY Review of Books*
Translated by Margaret Sayers Peden
0–674–82120–3 Harvard $29.50

Nicaragua

- Ernesto Cardenal
IN CUBA
Translated by Donald D. Walsh
0–8112–0538–X New Directions pb $9.95

Peru

- José C. Mariategui
SEVEN INTERPRETIVE ESSAYS ON PERUVIAN REALITY
Translated by Marjory Urquidi
0–292–77611–X Texas pb $9.95

- César Vallejo
AUTOPSY ON SURREALISM
Translated by Richard Schaaf
Edited by James Scully
0–915306–32–8 Curbstone pb $4.00

THE MAYAKOVSKY CASE
Translated by Richard Schaaf
Edited by James Scully
0–915306–31–X Curbstone pb $4.00

● Mario Vargas Llosa
THE PERPETUAL ORGY: Flaubert and Madame Bovary
Flaubert's revolution in literature and his influence on Vargas Llosa
Translated by Helen Lane
0–374–52062–3 Farrar, Straus & Giroux pb $8.95

ANTHOLOGIES

● Mary Crow, editor
WOMAN WHO HAS SPROUTED WINGS: Poems by Contemporary Latin American Poets
0–935480–35–8 Latin American pb $13.95

● Claudio Freoxas, editor
AFRO-CUBAN POETRY
A bilingual critical study, with a selection of poems by José Sanchez Boudy
0–89729–192–1 Ediciones Universal pb $5.00

● Enrique R. Lamadrid, editor
EN BREVE: Minimalism in Mexican Poetry, 1900–1985
Translated by E.A. Mares
0–940510–17–0 Tooth of Time pb $6.00

● Alberto Manguel, editor
OTHER FIRES: Short Fiction by Latin American Women
0–517–55870–X Clarkson Potter pb $9.95

● Emir R. Monegal, editor
THE BORZOI ANTHOLOGY OF LATIN AMERICAN LITERATURE
Volume 1
0–394–73301–0 Knopf pb $14.95
Volume 2
0–394–73366–5 Knopf pb $14.95

● Barbara Paschke & David Volpendesta, editors
CLAMOR OF INNOCENCE: Stories from Central America
Includes works by Manlio Argueta, Miguel Angel Asturias, Ernesto Cardenal, Carmen Naranjo, and others. "These stories have the ring of truth, the sound of having been lived in the heart of the beast"—Lawrence Ferlinghetti
0–87286–227–5 City Lights pb $8.95

Critical Studies

● Rolena Adorno
GUAMAN POMA: Writing and Resistance in Colonial Peru
0–292–72741–0 Texas pb $8.95

● J. Ann Duncan
VOICES, VISIONS, AND A NEW REALITY: Mexican Fiction Since 1970
0–8229–3815–4 Pittsburgh $26.95

● Roberto González Echevarría
THE VOICE OF THE MASTERS: Writing and Authority in Modern Latin American Literature
A study of Cabrera Infante, Cortázar, Fuentes, García Márquez, and others
0–292–78716–2 Texas $20.00

● Marie-Lise Gazarian Gautier
INTERVIEWS WITH LATIN AMERICAN WRITERS
Includes conversations with Isabel Allende, Carlos Fuentes, Manuel Puig, Luisa Valenzuela, and others
0–916583–32–5 Dalkey Archive $19.95

● John King, editor
ON MODERN LATIN AMERICAN FICTION
0–8090–6973–3 Hill & Wang $17.95
0–374–52178–6 Farrar, Straus & Giroux pb $8.95

● Christopher T. Leland
THE LAST HAPPY MEN: The Generation of 1922, Fiction, and the Argentine Reality
0–8156–2376–3 Syracuse $29.95

● Marvin A. Lewis
TREADING THE EBONY PATH: Ideology and Violence in Contemporary Afro-Colombian Prose Fiction
0–8262–0638–7 Missouri $19.00

PART 4

POPULAR READING

Crime Fiction

"Who cares who killed Roger Ackroyd?" Literary critic Edmund Wilson emphatically answered "not I" in his notorious 1943 *New Yorker* essay, dismissing nearly all crime fiction as unreadable rubbish. Yet millions of readers continue to care who committed *The Murder of Roger Ackroyd;* Agatha Christie's classic 1926 puzzler remains one of publishing's all-time, worldwide best-sellers. Moreover, in the decades since Wilson and Christie's heyday, the pure "whodunit" has become just one element in a flourishing literature of overlapping traditions, provocative hybrids, and subtle variations: detective stories, thrillers, spy novels, hard-boiled crime fiction, romantic suspense, studies in psychopathology. The lines between genres have blurred, and the readership—caring not only whodunit but how and why and what it all means—has expanded.

THE RISE OF THE MYSTERY

From Cain and Abel and Oedipus onward, crime stories of one sort or another turn up in all literary traditions. But the origins of our own brand of crime fiction can be traced to the "sensational literature" of the early 1800s, when modern notions of law and order (and the urban police as an organized force) were taking shape in Europe and America. From Poe to Conan Doyle, the rise of the mystery was essentially the rise of the detective-hero: enforcer of social good and brilliant solver (through logic, science, and perseverance) of baffling puzzles.

Pioneers and Landmarks

• Wilkie Collins
THE MOONSTONE
Collins' tale of a stolen gem, told from multiple viewpoints, remains among the most complex and satisfying of mysteries
0–14–043014–8 Penguin pb $3.95

THE WOMAN IN WHITE
A great novel that is also a landmark in romantic suspense
0–14–043096–2 Penguin pb $3.95

• Charles Dickens
THE MYSTERY OF EDWIN DROOD
No clear detective or certain culprit—but a fascinating swarm of plots, villainies, and enigmas
Introduction by Angus Wilson
0–14–009258–7 Penguin pb $3.95

• William Godwin
CALEB WILLIAMS
Godwin's 1794 forerunner is part murder mystery, part hunted-man adventure—with an underlying skepticism about the rule of

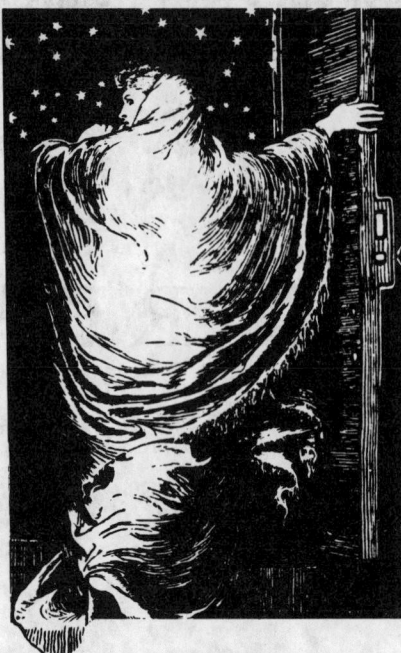

Poster for the 1871 stage production of "The Woman in White" by Wilkie Collins, from The Encyclopedia of Mystery and Detection *edited by Chris Steinbrunner and Otto Penzler (HBJ)*

law that foreshadows everyone from Hammett to Highsmith
Edited by Maurice Hindle
0–14–043256–6 Penguin pb $6.95

• Anna Katherine Green
THE LEAVENWORTH CASE
The first detective novel by a woman (1878), with a sprightly working-class police detective and a shooting in a library
0–486–23865–2 Dover pb $5.00

• Graham Greene & Hugh Greene, editors
VICTORIAN VILLAINIES
Three little-known early thrillers
0–14–006850–3 Penguin pb $7.95

• Joseph Sheridan LeFanu
UNCLE SILAS
A neglected 1864 masterpiece that slowly reveals the truth about a key character—and prefigures stylish Gothics like *Rebecca*
0–19–281541–5 Oxford pb $7.95

WYLDER'S HAND
No detective—but a mysterious disappearance, two vivid villains, and a superior puzzle
0–486–23570–X Dover pb $7.95

• Edgar Allan Poe
THE COMPLETE TALES AND POEMS
"The Murders in the Rue Morgue," "The Mystery of Marie Roget," "The Purloined Letter": these and other classic tales introduced the concept of *ratiocination*—detection through deduction—and the prototype for aristocratic amateur sleuths: the all-seeing C. Auguste Dupin
0–394–71678–7 Random House pb $10.95

Sherlock Holmes

Sherlock Holmes of 221B Baker Street was begotten from the ratiocination of Poe's Dupin, the logic and legwork of Emile Gaboriau's Lecoq, the inscrutability of Wilkie Collins' Sergeant Cuff. Yet Holmes transcended all that had gone before, with the wry textures and fine quirks of his personality, the demonstrable genius of his moment-by-moment deductions, and his evolving relationships with stubborn policeman Lestrade, arch-villain Moriarty, and—above all—the loyal, and plucky, and mildly confused Dr. Watson.

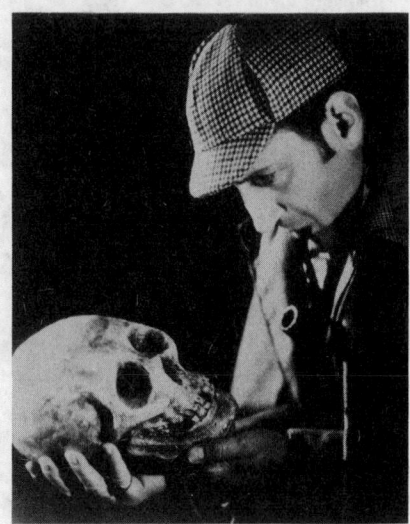

Basil Rathbone as Sherlock Holmes in the 1939 movie (photo: Movie Star News)

• Arthur Conan Doyle
THE COMPLETE SHERLOCK HOLMES
0–385–00689–6 Doubleday pb $19.95

SHERLOCK HOLMES: The Complete Novels and Stories
Introduction by Loren Estleman

Volume 1
0–553–21241–9 Bantam pb $4.95

Volume 2
0–553–21242–7 Bantam pb $4.95

THE HOUND OF THE BASKERVILLES
The beautifully designed Arion Press edition is illustrated with 53 atmospheric moorland photographs
Photographs by Michael Kenna
0–86547–263–7 North Point $17.50

THE ILLUSTRATED SHERLOCK HOLMES
Features the original illustrations from the stories' first magazine appearances
Illustrated by Sidney Paget & others
0–517–55660–X Crown pb $6.95

Crime Fiction After Conan Doyle

Between 1890 and 1920, Holmes's immense popularity inspired an outpouring of similar mystery tales from writers such as R. Austin Freeman and A.E.W. Mason. The Holmesian supersleuths were complemented by heroic criminals like Raffles and Arsène Lupin.

• **E.C. Bentley**
TRENT'S LAST CASE
In its day, this was among the most famous of detective stories, urbane and elaborate
0–06–080440–8 Harper & Row pb $3.50

• **G.K. Chesterton**
THE PENGUIN COMPLETE FATHER BROWN
The metaphysical sleuthings of an intuitive priest. "Pungent, paradoxical, and romantic"—Julian Symons
0–14–009766–X Penguin pb $9.95

THE INNOCENCE OF FATHER BROWN
0–14–008257–3 Penguin pb $4.95

THE MAN WHO WAS THURSDAY
A whimsical morality play with no fewer than six detectives
0–486–25121–7 Dover pb $3.95

R. Austin Freeman
Freeman's solidly built mysteries center on the scientific detection of Dr. Thorndyke, physician and criminologist.
THE BEST DR. THORNDYKE DETECTIVE STORIES
Includes a number of the "inverted tales" that Freeman pioneered, in which the reader knows whodunit from the start
0–486–20388–3 Dover pb $4.95

THE EYE OF OSIRIS
0–88184–268–0 Carroll & Graf pb $3.95

THE RED THUMB MARK
0–88184–240–0 Carroll & Graf pb $3.95

THE STONEWARE MONKEY
0–486–25471–2 Dover pb $5.95

acques Futrelle
BEST THINKING MACHINE DETECTIVE STORIES
Absurd but ingenious: the amusing deductions of a truculent genius-professor
0–486–20537–1 Dover pb $4.50

• **E.W. Hornung**
RAFFLES, THE AMATEUR CRACKSMAN: The Complete Stories of E.W. Hornung
The gentleman is a thief, a master of disguise—and a hero
Introduction by George Orwell
0–918172–20–9 Leete's Island pb $8.95

• **Maurice Leblanc**
THE EXTRAORDINARY ADVENTURES OF ARSENE LUPIN, GENTLEMAN-BURGLAR
The French have a longstanding tradition of the criminal as hero, in which the nimble, gallant rogue Lupin figures importantly
0–486–23508–4 Dover pb $3.95

• **Marie Belloc Lowndes**
THE LODGER
Could the man upstairs be a Jack-the-Ripper-like killer? Genteel shivers and chills from 1913
0–89733–299–7 Academy Chicago pb $4.95

• **A.E.W. Mason**
The first true police detective since Gaboriau: Hanaud of the Sûreté—whose adventures are brightened by mordant humor and wry psychology.
AT THE VILLA ROSE
0–88184–111–0 Carroll & Graf pb $3.50

THE HOUSE OF THE ARROW
0–88184–066–1 Carroll & Graf pb $3.50

• **Arthur Morrison**
BEST MARTIN HEWITT DETECTIVE STORIES
Among the best of the Conan Doyle imitators, Morrison created a more drably realistic aura
0–486–23324–3 Dover pb $4.95

• **Baroness Orczy**
THE OLD MAN IN THE CORNER
A nameless old fellow in a London teashop intuits solutions to unsolved police cases in these twelve stories
0–486–23972–1 Dover pb $4.50

• **Melville Davisson Post**
THE METHODS OF UNCLE ABNER
An early American detective
0–915230–03–8 Rue Morgue pb $6.95

• **Mary Roberts Rinehart**
THE CIRCULAR STAIRCASE
Noises in the night, ghostly lurking, and a feisty spinster-heroine: a 1908 prototype for gothic suspense
0–88184–106–4 Carroll & Graf pb $3.50

Pure Escape: Some Vintage Thrillers

Marcel Allain & Pierre Souvestre
FANTOMAS
Introduction by John Ashbery
0–345–34421–9 Ballantine pb $3.95

Walter Gibson
THE SHADOW AND THE GOLDEN MASTER
0–89296–073–6 Mysterious $15.95

Gaston Leroux
THE PHANTOM OF THE OPERA
0–451–52173–0 NAL pb $3.95

Sax Rohmer
FU MANCHU
0–8065–0899–X Lyle Stuart pb $6.95

Edgar Wallace
THE FOUR JUST MEN
0–486–24642–6 Dover pb $3.50

THE GOLDEN AGE

England

Despite the popularity of Holmes and his followers, the traditional English detective story didn't really hit its stride as a popular form until after World War I. During the 1920s and '30s—the so-called "Golden Age"—mystery novels, produced in great quantities by a new generation of specialists, became the "light reading" of choice. The figure of the Great Detective was filled out with charm and humor, sometimes even emerging as a credible hero. The who, how, and why of the murder puzzles became (in Agatha Christie's work especially) unnervingly elaborate and clever. In some ways, this perfection of the form was a triumph of tunnel vision: escapist, elitist, rarely concerned with social issues. At its best and on its own genteel terms, the English Golden Age mystery represents a high point in the history of popular reading.

• **Margery Allingham**
MORE WORK FOR THE UNDERTAKER
Allingham at her most baroque and Dickensian
0–89190–180–9 Amereon $15.95

SWEET DANGER
0–14–008779–6 Penguin pb $5.95

THE TIGER IN THE SMOKE
A homicidal escaped prisoner at loose in foggy postwar London. "One of the peaks of crime fiction"—H.R.F. Keating
0–89190–198–1 Amereon $16.95

• **Nicholas Blake**
END OF CHAPTER
0–06–080397–5 Harper & Row pb $3.95

THE SMILER WITH THE KNIFE
0–06–080457–2 Harper & Row pb $3.95

• **Ernest Bramah**
THE BEST MAX CARRADOS DETECTIVE STORIES
Wise, witty Max is blind—but a convincing 1920s sleuth who uses his sharp ear, keen nose, and quick mind in Holmes-like feats of deduction
0–486–20064–7 Dover pb $4.95

• **Leo Bruce**
CASE FOR THREE DETECTIVES
This locked-room mystery features down-to-earth Sgt. Beef—but it's also a send-up of Sayers' Wimsey, Christie's Poirot, and Chesterton's Father Brown
0–89733–033–1 Academy Chicago pb $4.95

• **Agatha Christie**
THE ABC MURDERS
A classic Poirot showing Christie's mastery of crime novel as pure puzzle
0–396–08698–5 Dodd, Mead $12.95
0–671–60063–X Pocket Books pb $3.50

AND THEN THERE WERE NONE
A one-of-a-kind, detectiveless landmark (also known as *Ten Little Indians*): ten strangers stranded in an island manse, being murdered one after another
0–396–08572–5 Dodd, Mead $12.95

THE BODY IN THE LIBRARY
A classic Jane Marple novel
0–396–08699–3 Dodd, Mead $12.95
0–671–60255–1 Pocket Books pb $3.50

CARDS ON THE TABLE
0–396–09010–9 Dodd, Mead $14.95
0–425–09317–4 Berkley pb $2.95

CROOKED HOUSE
0–671–54321–0 Pocket pb $3.50

CURTAIN
Hercule's downbeat, ironic adieu
0–671–54717–8 Pocket Books pb $3.95

ENDLESS NIGHT
A late Christie novel quite different in
structure and tone from her other work,
but very effective
0–671–60427–9 Pocket pb $3.50

EVIL UNDER THE SUN
Filmed with Peter Ustinov as Poirot and
also starring Maggie Smith
0–671–60174–1 Pocket pb $3.50

THE HOLLOW
Christie at her most novelistic: Poirot's
"little grey cells" share the stage with tense
close-ups of character and motive
0–425–06784–X Berkley pb $3.50

THE MIRROR CRACK'D
Basis of the movie starring Elizabeth
Taylor, Rock Hudson, and with Angela
Lansbury as Miss Marple
0–671–55701–7 Pocket pb $3.50

MRS. McGINTY'S DEAD
0–671–83440–1 Pocket pb $3.50

MURDER AT THE VICARAGE
Miss Jane Marple at her best—in a gently
comic, ultimately somber study of evil
forces at work in picturesque English-
village surroundings
0–396–08804–X Dodd, Mead $12.95
0–425–09453–7 Berkley pb $3.50

THE MURDER OF ROGER ACKROYD
The 1926 Hercule Poirot mystery that
made Christie famous remains as fresh,
readable, and shrewdly shocking as ever
0–396–08574–1 Dodd, Mead $12.95
0–671–62019–3 Pocket Books pb $3.50

MURDER ON THE ORIENT EXPRESS
0–396–08575–X Dodd, Mead $12.95
0–671–52368–6 Pocket Books pb $3.50

THE MYSTERIOUS AFFAIR AT STYLES
0–553–26587–3 Bantam pb $3.50

THE PALE HORSE
Supernatural elements come into play in
one of Christie's more somber thrillers
0–671–54207–9 Pocket pb $3.50

PERIL AT END HOUSE
0–671–61120–8 Pocket pb $3.50

Agatha Christie

TEN LITTLE INDIANS
0–671–55222–8 Pocket pb $3.50

TOWARDS ZERO
Countdown to inevitable murder at a
family gathering: no Poirot, no Marple,
but sturdy Superintendent Battle copes
admirably
0–396–08872–4 Dodd, Mead $14.95

WHAT MRS. McGILLICUDDY SAW
0–671–55645–2 Pocket pb $3.50

**THE WITNESS FOR THE
PROSECUTION**
The title story was the basis for Christie's
enormously successful play, later filmed
twice
0–425–06809–9 Berkley pb $3.50

• Edmund Crispin
THE MOVING TOYSHIP
This comical cultivated adventure of
Oxford don Gervase Fen is a bit bizarre
and more than a bit rococo
0–14–001315–6 Penguin pb $3.95

• Freeman Wills Crofts
**INSPECTOR FRENCH'S GREATEST
CASE**
French—the prototypical "plodder"
sleuth—at his modest, believable, thorough
best
0–88184–266–4 Carroll & Graf pb $3.50

THE CASK
Dogged policework by Inspector Burnley
over in France circa 1912—with an
unbreakable alibi, fine detail, and special
interest for Berlioz fans
0–486–23457–6 Dover pb $5.95
0–88184–236–2 Carroll & Graf $3.50

Cyril Hare
Hare's amusingly observant
explorations of murder in fascinating
settings frequently hinge on esoteric
points of law.
AN ENGLISH MURDER
0–06–080455–6 Harper & Row pb $3.50
SUICIDE EXCEPTED
0–06–080636–2 Harper & Row pb $2.95

• Georgette Heyer
Heyer, known for her Regency romances,
was also a quintessential Golden Age
writer.
BEHOLD HERE'S POISON
Scotland Yard's Inspector Hannasyde stalks
a diabolically clever murderer
0–425–10354–4 Berkley pb $3.50

THE UNFINISHED CLUE
0–03–003297–0 Henry Holt pb $3.95

THE DAFFODIL AFFAIR
0–14–002202–3 Penguin pb $3.95

• Michael Innes
The "finest of the Farceurs" (Julian
Symons), the most erudite and allusive of a
donnish breed: sleuthing in utterly civilized
surroundings (country houses, elegant
academe) by Sir John Appleby.
HAMLET, REVENGE!
0–396–08801–5 Dodd, Mead $15.95

ONE MAN SHOW
Later Innes (1952) at his best—with stolen
paintings, a missing girl, dukes, art critics,
and chases
0–8240–4994–2 Garland $19.00

SEVEN SUSPECTS
A classic whodunit, Innes' first novel
0–14–006886–4 Penguin pb $3.95

• Philip MacDonald
THE RASP
0–486–23864–4 Dover pb $4.50

WARRANT FOR X
A complex and melodramatic challenge to
the deductive skills of Colonel Anthony
Gethryn, a gentleman detective in the E.C.
Bentley tradition
0–394–71660–4 Random House pb $3.95

• Ngaio Marsh
Part satire, part charm, part mystery; the
low-key investigations of upper-class cop
Roderick Alleyn—in theatrical milieux, in
picturesque villages, and sometimes in
tandem with artist-wife Troy.
ARTISTS IN CRIME
0–515–07534–5 Berkley pb $3.50

CLUTCH OF CONSTABLES
0–515–08775–0 Berkley pb $3.50

DEATH IN ECSTASY
0–515–08592–8 Berkley pb $3.50

ENTER A MURDERER
0–515–07447–0 Berkley pb $2.95

FINAL CURTAIN
0–515–08757–2 Berkley pb $3.50

NIGHT AT THE VULCAN
0–515–07507–8 Berkley pb $2.95

SPINSTERS IN JEOPARDY
0–515–08718–1 Berkley pb $3.50

TIED UP IN TINSEL
0–515–07443–8 Berkley pb $3.50

VINTAGE MURDER
0–515–08084–5 Berkley pb $3.50

• J.C. Masterman
AN OXFORD TRAGEDY
A prototype of the Oxbridge campus
mystery—featuring genuine atmosphere
and a curious sleuth: Austrian law
professor Ernst Brendel
0–486–24165–3 Dover pb $3.95

• A.A. Milne
THE RED HOUSE MYSTERY
A 1922 lark, the ultimate mix of mayhem
and jollity
0–440–17376–0 Dell pb $3.50

• Eden Phillpotts
THE RED REDMAYNES
A classic detective novel about the
systematic extermination of a set of siblings
0–486–24255–2 Dover pb $5.95

• Dorothy L. Sayers
"Dorothy L. Sayers made two great
contributions to the art of crime writing.
She moved the conventional detective
story, the pure puzzle, forward towards
being a book in which a whole social
milieu could be examined and chronicled
with characters much more than cardboard

 IF YOU CAN'T FIND IT, LOOK IN THE INDEX

cut-outs. And she created Lord Peter Wimsey."—H.R.F. Keating

CLOUDS OF WITNESS
0-06-055035-X Harper & Row $17.95
0-06-080835-7 Harper & Row pb $4.50

THE FIVE RED HERRINGS
0-06-080830-6 Harper & Row pb $4.50

GAUDY NIGHT
Fear and suspicion at a women's college
0-06-055022-8 Harper & Row $17.95
0-06-080907-8 Harper & Row pb $4.50

HANGMAN'S HOLIDAY
0-06-055033-3 Harper & Row $17.95
0-06-080837-3 Harper & Row pb $4.50

HAVE HIS CARCASE
0-06-055023-6 Harper & Row $17.95
0-06-080909-4 Harper & Row pb $4.50

LORD PETER
A collection of Lord Peter Wimsey short stories
0-06-055039-2 Harper & Row $17.95

MURDER MUST ADVERTISE
Sayers at her most brightly satirical, as Wimsey sleuths in and about a London ad agency circa 1933
0-06-055024-4 Harper & Row $17.95
0-06-080825-X Harper & Row pb $3.95

THE NINE TAILORS
0-06-080908-6 Harper & Row pb $4.50

STRONG POISON
When Lord Peter first meets Harriet Vane, she is under accusation of murder
0-06-055025-2 Harper & Row $17.95
0-06-080908-6 Harper & Row pb $4.50

UNNATURAL DEATH
0-06-055032-5 Harper & Row $17.95

THE UNPLEASANTNESS AT THE BELLONA CLUB: A Lord Peter Wimsey Mystery
0-06-055026-0 Harper & Row $17.95

WHOSE BODY?
0-06-055036-8 Harper & Row $17.95
0-06-080829-2 Harper & Row pb $4.50

- **Dorothy L. Sayers & Robert Eustace**
THE DOCUMENTS IN THE CASE
Coauthored with physician-scientist Robert Eustace, this Wimseyless mystery is a haunting epistolary novel about a poisoning: philosophical, yet lean and taut
0-06-055034-1 Harper & Row $17.95
0-06-080836-5 Harper & Row pb $4.50

- **Josephine Tey**
BRAT FARRAR
0-02-008822-1 Macmillan pb $3.95

THE DAUGHTER OF TIME
Was Richard III a murderer? A contemporary sleuth tackles the case—and the nature of historical "truth"—from his sickbed
0-02-054550-9 Macmillan pb $3.95

THE FRANCHISE AFFAIR
False accusations of kidnapping destroy a respectable family: a powerful blend of courtroom drama, suspense, and psychology
0-02-008823-X Macmillan pb $3.95

THE MAN IN THE QUEUE
0-02-008824-8 Macmillan pb $3.95

MISS PYM DISPOSES
0-02-054540-1 Macmillan pb $3.95

A SHILLING FOR CANDLES
A body on the beach leads to a call for Scotland Yard—and for Inspector Alan Grant, Tey's gentle, empathetic hero (here at his Scottish best)
0-02-054540-1 Macmillan pb $3.95

THE SINGING SANDS
0-02-008825-6 Macmillan pb $3.95

- **Arthur W. Upfield**
Mayhem in Australia's sheep-station country—investigated by Napoleon ("Bony") Bonaparte of the Queensland Police, a sleuth of mixed aboriginal and European descent.

THE SANDS OF WINDEE
0-684-18502-4 Scribners pb $4.95

VENOM HOUSE
0-02-025901-8 Macmillan pb $4.50

WINDS OF EVIL
0-02-025910-7 Macmillan pb $3.95

- **Patricia Wentworth**
On a par with Miss Marple is Wentworth's governess turned private investigator, Miss Maud Silver.

THE CLOCK STRIKES TWELVE
0-446-34905-4 Warner pb $3.50

THE FINGERPRINT
0-446-34859-7 Warner pb $3.95

THE IVORY DAGGER
0-553-25128-7 Bantam pb $2.95

THE WATERSPLASH
0-446-34448-6 Warner pb $3.50

America

In America, the classic detective story peaked in the mid-1920s with the advent of S.S. Van Dine's phenomenally popular mysteries featuring Philo Vance, the posh British amateur-sleuth with a snobbish New York City veneer. But the best of those who followed—Ellery Queen and Rex Stout above all—were thoroughly American in idiom and approach: more casual, more Twain-laconic than Oxford-droll in humor, more democratic in outlook. And many of those writing in the 1930s were of course influenced by the hardboiled revolution in crime fiction spearheaded by Dashiell Hammett.

- **Earl Derr Biggers**
THE HOUSE WITHOUT A KEY
The 1925 debut of Honolulu police-detective Charlie Chan—and more shrewdly humorous than the old Chan movies would suggest
0-445-40219-9 Mysterious pb $3.95

- **Anthony Boucher**
THE CASE OF THE BAKER STREET IRREGULARS
Murder strikes during a Hollywood filming of Sherlock Holmes. Fine, fair-play puzzlement from the great crime-critic
Introduction by Otto Penzler
0-88184-199-4 Carroll & Graf pb $3.95

- **John Dickson Carr**
Macabre, delightfully improbable sleuthings, mostly conducted by bibulous Dr. Gideon Fell.

THE ARABIAN NIGHTS MURDER
0-02-018600-2 Macmillan pb $3.50

BELOW SUSPICION
0-317-52725-8 International Polygonics pb $4.95

THE BURNING COURT
0-930330-27-7 International Polygonics pb $4.95

THE CASE OF THE CONSTANT SUICIDES
0-02-018860-9 Macmillan pb $3.50

THE DEVIL IN VELVET
0-88184-328-8 Carroll & Graf pb $3.95

FIRE, BURN!
0-88184-336-9 Carroll & Graf pb $3.50

THE HOUSE AT SATAN'S ELBOW
0-930330-61-7 International Polygonics pb $4.95

IT WALKS BY NIGHT
0-8217-1931-9 Zebra pb $3.50

THE MAD HATTER MYSTERY
0-02-018820-X Macmillan pb $3.50

POISON IN JEST
0-02-018400-X Macmillan pb $3.50

THE PROBLEM OF THE GREEN CAPSULE
0-317-52726-6 International Polygonics pb $4.95

THE THREE COFFINS
Generally regarded as the most ingenious of all locked-room mysteries
0-930330-39-0 International Polygonics pb $4.95

TO WAKE THE DEAD
0-02-018750-5 Macmillan pb $3.50

- **Lillian de la Torre**
DR. SAM JOHNSON, DETECTOR
Historical crime stories, with Dr. Johnson as sleuth, Boswell as Watson
0-930330-08-0 International Polygonics pb $6.95

- **Carter Dickson**
The more openly comic side of John Dickson Carr, featuring Sir Henry Merrivale, solver of impossible mysteries
CURSE OF THE BRONZE LAMP
0-88184-101-3 Carroll & Graf pb $3.50

HE WOULDN'T KILL PATIENCE
0-930330-86-2 International Polygonics pb $4.95

THE JUDAS WINDOW
0-930330-62-5 International Polygonics pb $4.95

THE PUNCH AND JUDY MURDERS
0-930330-85-4 International Polygonics pb $4.95

- **Erle Stanley Gardner**
These titles are early, superior Perry Mason—with taut courtroom drama and authentic, science-oriented detection.
THE CASE OF THE BORROWED BRUNETTE
0-345-34374-3 Ballantine pb $2.95

THE CASE OF THE CALENDAR GIRL
0-345-34375-1 Ballantine pb $3.50

THE CASE OF THE CAUTIOUS COQUETTE
0-345-35202-5 Ballantine pb $3.50

THE CASE OF THE PERJURED PARROT
0-345-34685-8 Ballantine pb $2.95

THE CASE OF THE STUTTERING BISHOP
0–345–35680–2 Ballantine pb $3.50

- **Elliot Paul**
  THE MYSTERIOUS MICKEY FINN
  Part parody (of Philo Vance), part traditional detective story: the Rabelaisian adventures of sleuth/bon-vivant Homer Evans
  0–486–24751–1 Dover pb $5.95

- **Ellery Queen**
  The early Ellery Queen books were incomparable exercises in rational deduction—textured with intelligence, zest, and charm. The later works blend the same meticulous plotting with a darker, deeper grasp of psychology and American mores, as evidenced in small-town tensions, apocalyptic urban terror, and religious cults.
  THE AMERICAN GUN MYSTERY
  0–345–32133–2 Ballantine pb $2.50

  AND ON THE EIGHTH DAY
  0–345–31742–4 Ballantine pb $1.95

  THE FINISHING STROKE
  0–88184–398–9 Carroll & Graf pb $3.95

  THE TRAGEDY OF X
  Fetching backgrounds (New York circa 1932), a nasty murder method, and a dandy sleuth: retired Shakespearean actor Drury Lane. The series continues with the tragedies of "Y" and "Z" and *Drury Lane's Last Case*.
  0–930330–43–9 Polygonics pb $4.95

  THE TRAGEDY OF Y
  0–930330–53–6 Polygonics pb $4.95

  THE TRAGEDY OF Z
  0–930330–58–7 Polygonics pb $4.95

  DRURY LANE'S LAST CASE
  0–930330–70–6 Polygonics pb $4.95

- **Rex Stout**
  Nero Wolfe of 35th Street is fat, brilliant, crabby, a connoisseur of beer and orchids—a sedentary legend. But his breezy, slangy assistant Archie Goodwin is, as Howard Haycraft put it, "the one example in history . . . of a Watson who steals the play from his Holmes, and a first-rate Holmes to boot."
  DEATH OF A DOXY
  0–553–27606–9 Bantam pb $3.50

  DEATH TIMES THREE
  0–553–27828–2 Bantam pb $3.95

  FER-DE-LANCE
  0–553–24918–5 Bantam pb $2.95

  TOO MANY COOKS
  0–553–27290–X Bantam pb $3.50

- **Phoebe Atwood Taylor**
  THE CAPE COD MYSTERY
  New England atmosphere and Yankee shrewdness, in the homespun company of "the Codfish Sherlock": taciturn Asey Mayo of Welfleet, Mass.
  0–88150–046–1 Countryman pb $4.95

- **Darwin L. Teilhet**
  THE TALKING SPARROW MURDERS
  Murder in 1934 Germany: "Well worth reading both for its picture of the time and place and as an unusual blend of spy story and mystery"—Julian Symons
  0–930330–29–3 International Polygonics pb $4.95

- **S.S. Van Dine**
  The most popular American mystery novels of the mid-'20s—starring suave, erudite Philo Vance, the much-parodied prototype of the amateur New York City detective.
  THE BENSON MURDER CASE
  0–684–17976–8 Scribners pb $3.95

  THE BISHOP MURDER CASE
  0–684–17976–8 Scribners pb $3.95

  THE CANARY MURDER CASE
  0–684–16404–3 Scribners pb $2.25

  THE DRAGON MURDER CASE
  0–684–18380–3 Macmillan pb $3.95

  THE GREENE MURDER CASE
  0–684–16734–4 Macmillan pb $3.95

THE HARD-BOILED DETECTIVE

By the time that Ogden Nash wrote: "Philo Vance needs a kick in the pance" in the 1930s, S.S. Van Dine and the elegant world of the traditional detective story had already received a firm and decisive kick: the rise of the American "pulp" adventure magazines, with their contemporary slang, racy and violent exploits, rapid pacing, and heroes more notable for toughness than for "little grey cells." The best of the pulps, *Black Mask*, featured the melodramatic yet seedily realistic investigations of professional private detectives. And the best of these "hard-boiled" adventures were written by Dashiell Hammett, a former Pinkerton operative who became—in the words of Ross Macdonald—"the first American writer to use the detective-story for the purposes of a major novelist." In Hammett and his finest successors, this view of a corrupt society is mirrored in street-wise, darkly poetic language.

- **Fredric Brown**
  CARNIVAL OF CRIME: The Best Mystery Stories of Fredric Brown
  Edited with an introduction by Francis M. Nevins
  0–8093–1192–5 Southern Illinois $22.95

  THE FABULOUS CLIPJOINT
  Coming-of-age in gloriously sleazy Chicago: young Ed Hunter in search of his father's killer
  0–87923–597–7 Godine pb $7.95

  THE FAR CRY
  Features one of the best twist endings ever
  0–88739–045–5 Black Lizard pb $3.95

  HIS NAME WAS DEATH
  0–88739–044–7 Black Lizard pb $3.95

  THE SCREAMING MIMI
  A peculiar statue plays a crucial role in this typically inventive Brown thriller
  0–88184–449–7 Carroll & Graf pb $3.50

- **Paul Cain**
  FAST ONE
  The fierce Los Angeles underworld in transition from Prohibition to Repeal. The lean, blunt exploits of a ruthless yet ethical hoodlum-hero
  0–88739–078–1 Black Lizard pb $3.95

  SEVEN SLAYERS
  Pulp stories don't get much more swift and stripped-down than these
  0–88739–077–3 Black Lizard pb $3.95

- **Raymond Chandler**
  THE BIG SLEEP
  The prototypical Southern California mystery—corrupt wealth, secret vices, family scandal—and the debut of Philip Marlowe
  0–394–75828–5 Random House pb $5.95

  FAREWELL, MY LOVELY
  Chandler's second Marlowe novel is in many ways the best of the series
  0–394–75827–7 Random House pb $5.95

  THE HIGH WINDOW
  Nasty rich folk vs. nasty poor folk—in a bitterly tragicomic tale involving mind manipulation and rare coins
  0–394–75826–9 Random House pb $5.95

  THE LADY IN THE LAKE
  Betrayed husband, missing wife—and Marlowe, impeded by a few vicious cops, on the maze-like trail
  0–394–75825–0 Random House pb $5.95

  THE LITTLE SISTER
  A rising movie star, her blackmailing brother, agents, prostitutes, and studio heads. Marlowe sardonically takes on the interlocking levels of Hollywood society
  0–394–75767–X Random House pb $5.95

Raymond Chandler (photo by Alfred Knopf, courtesy of Knopf)

TO ORDER BOOKS AS GIFTS, SEE PAGE 1

THE LONG GOODBYE
Why did Terry Lennox—drunken war hero, victim of Nazism, apparent wife-killer—commit suicide? Chandler's most ambitious blend of genre sleuthing and serious fiction
0–394–75768–8 Random House pb $5.95

PICKUP ON NOON STREET
Pre-Marlowe pulp stories
0–343–33211–3 Ballantine pb $2.95

PLAYBACK
0–394–75766–1 Random House pb $5.95

THE SIMPLE ART OF MURDER
The best of Chandler's pulp stories—plus his notorious attack on Britain's "Golden Age" eminences
0–394–75765–3 Random House pb $6.95

TROUBLE IS MY BUSINESS
0–394–75764–5 Random House pb $8.95

• Carroll John Daly
Daly, a *Black Mask* regular, was in his day one of the most popular of the hardboiled writers, although today his work has a primarily nostalgic appeal.
THE ADVENTURES OF RACE WILLIAMS
0–89296–959–8 Mysterious pb $9.95

THE ADVENTURES OF SATAN HALL
0–89296–939–3 Mysterious pb $8.95

MURDER FROM THE EAST: A Race Williams Story
Edited by Tony Sparafucile
0–930330–01–3 International Polygonics pb $4.95

• Dashiell Hammett
THE BIG KNOCKOVER
Nine standout stories, most featuring the Continental Op
0–679–72259–9 Random House pb $8.95

THE CONTINENTAL OP
Introducing the nameless Continental Op, fat, brutish, and living by the code of the Continental Detective Agency, in *Black Mask* stories that are landmarks in the history of hardboiled style
0–679–72258–0 Random House pb $7.95

THE DAIN CURSE
Stolen diamonds, sexual obsessions, religious cults, as the Continental Op encounters the accursed Dain clan of San Francisco
0–679–72260–2 Random House pb $6.95

THE GLASS KEY
A corrosive study of big-city corruption—with a politico's loyal (yet ambivalent) henchman as sleuth
0–394–71773–2 Random House pb $4.95

THE MALTESE FALCON
The definitive hard-boiled private-eye novel
0–394–71772–4 Random House pb $2.95

THE MALTESE FALCON
This edition of Hammett's masterpiece was designed by Andrew Hoyem, and is illustrated with contemporary and vintage photographs of the book's San Francisco settings
0–86547–156–8 North Point $20.00
0–86547–157–6 North Point pb $9.95

RED HARVEST
Warring gangs and crooked cops in Montana's "Poisonville"—a rotten town

that needs a clean-up visit from the Op. Total violence, raw poetry
0–394–71828–3 Random House pb $3.95

THE THIN MAN
A missing inventor and a murdered secretary, investigated in an urbane wash of booze and wise-cracks, by ex-gumshoe Nick Charles and his wife Nora
0–394–71774–0 Random House pb $2.95

WOMAN IN THE DARK
A novella recently republished for the first time in decades
0–679–72265–3 Random House pb $6.95

• Jonathan Latimer
THE LADY IN THE MORGUE
Farcical hardboiled goings-on, heavily laced with alcohol
0–930330–79–X International Polygonics pb $4.95

SOLOMON'S VINEYARD
Sex, violence, and a warped religious cult; written in the '40s but only now printed in unexpurgated form
0–930330–91–9 International Polygonics pb $4.95

• Ross Macdonald
The bleak, past-haunted investigations of Lew Archer take him through a corrupted southern California full of confused adolescents, hints of incest, family secrets.
ARCHER IN JEOPARDY
A set containing three of the best Archers: *The Doomsters, The Zebra-Striped Hearse,* and *The Instant Enemy*
0–394–50804–1 Knopf $24.95

BLACK MONEY
0–553–27219–5 Bantam pb $3.95

THE BLUE HAMMER
0–553–27548–8 Bantam pb $3.95

THE DROWNING POOL
0–553–27133–4 Bantam pb $3.95

THE IVORY GRIN
0–553–27352–3 Bantam pb $3.95

SLEEPING BEAUTY
0–553–27101–6 Bantam pb $3.50

THE ZEBRA-STRIPED HEARSE
0–553–27362–0 Bantam pb $3.95

• Mickey Spillane
Mike Hammer: the hard-boiled sleuth as right-wing avenger, sadistic dame-killer, and Everyman's fantasy. Unintentionally disturbing, undeniably vital.
I, THE JURY
0–451–13543–1 NAL pb $3.50

KISS ME DEADLY
0–451–13602–0 NAL pb $2.95

VENGEANCE IS MINE
0–451–14687–5 NAL pb $2.95

THE RISE OF THE MODERN CRIME NOVEL

America

The hard-boiled style and outlook—lean, raw, darkly skeptical—helped foster a new focus on crime from the viewpoint of criminals and victims, with the detective either

on the sidelines or entirely absent. The major players were instead gangsters, psychopaths, or semi-innocent bystanders, driven to violence by greed, lust, or fateful circumstance. 1930s crime novelists like James M. Cain and Horace McCoy most often placed their antiheroes in a nightmarish socio-economic landscape. By the late 1940s, with the ascent of Patricia Highsmith, Margaret Millar, and Jim Thompson, the traumas were more likely to be Freudian—or existential.

• John Franklin Bardin
Intense explorations—in crime-novel form—of lives lived in hallucinatory half-worlds.
THE DEADLY PERCHERON
0–14–010733–9 Penguin pb $5.95

DEVIL TAKE THE BLUE TAIL FLY
A 1948 study in dual personality, seen strictly from the inside
0–14–010734–7 Penguin pb $5.95

• W.R. Burnett
HIGH SIERRA
Gangster on the lam as folk hero: source of the classic Raoul Walsh movie
0–88184–282–6 Carroll & Graf pb $3.50

LITTLE CAESAR
Knowledgeable gangster melodrama from 1929
0–88184–235–4 Carroll & Graf pb $3.50

• James M. Cain
DOUBLE INDEMNITY
Adultery, greed, and the perfect insurance policy: the ultimate in simmering cynicism
0–679–72322–6 Random House pb $6.95

MILDRED PIERCE
Not a crime novel, but stamped with Cain's deadpan, antiheroic realism
0–679–72321–8 Random House pb $6.95

THE POSTMAN ALWAYS RINGS TWICE
The stark death row confession of an ordinary guy who became a killer—thanks to the lustful magnetism of a luncheonette owner's frustrated wife
0–679–72325–0 Random House pb $6.95

THREE BY CAIN
Includes *Serenade, The Butterfly,* and *Love's Lovely Counterfeit. Serenade*—with its mix of Mexico, opera, homosexuality, and murder—is perhaps Cain's best book
0–679–72323–4 Random House pb $9.95

• Helen Eustis
THE HORIZONTAL MAN
Murder in academia, with psychosis and thwarted sexuality abounding. "Stands the hair up vertical. Genuinely scary"—Eudora Welty
0–14–000718–0 Penguin pb $3.95

• Steve Fisher
I WAKE UP SCREAMING
0–88739–085–4 Black Lizard pb $4.95

• David Goodis
Pure *noir:* downbeat evocations of an urban underworld where nobody wins.
CASSIDY'S GIRL
0–88739–027–7 Black Lizard pb $3.95

BLACK FRIDAY
0–88739–028–5 Black Lizard pb $3.95

THE BURGLAR
0–88739–131–1 Black Lizard pb $4.95

NIGHTFALL
0–88739–029–3 Black Lizard pb $3.95

SHOOT THE PIANO PLAYER
0–88739–030–7 Black Lizard pb $3.95

● Richard Hallas
YOU PLAY THE BLACK AND THE RED COMES UP
Introduction by David Feinberg
0–88739–006–4 Black Lizard pb $3.95

● W.L. Heath
VIOLENT SATURDAY
A sleepy southern town is ripped apart by a bank robbery
0–916870–93–6 Black Lizard pb $3.95

Patricia Highsmith
"The most important crime novelist at present in practice."—Julian Symons
A DOG'S RANSOM
0–14–003944–9 Penguin pb $3.95

FOUND IN THE STREET
0–87113–208–7 Atlantic Monthly pb $16.95

A GAME FOR THE LIVING
0–87113–210–9 Atlantic Monthly pb $7.95

THE MYSTERIOUS MR. RIPLEY
Liar, psychopath, killer—and hero. Three creepy, funny novels featuring Tom Ripley, cosmopolitan seeker of the good life—and the embodiment of the criminal as free spirit
0–14–007196–2 Penguin pb $10.95

STRANGERS ON A TRAIN
"We murder for each other, see? I kill your wife and you kill my father!" The stunning debut of "the poet of apprehension" (Graham Greene)
0–14–003796–9 Penguin pb $3.95

A SUSPENSION OF MERCY
0–14–003470–6 Penguin pb $3.95

THIS SWEET SICKNESS
Romantic obsession goes over the edge: a stunning psychological portrait, perhaps Highsmith's masterpiece
0–14–003469–2 Penguin pb $4.95

THOSE WHO WALK AWAY
A violent encounter by a Venetian canal is the starting point for a strange war of nerves
0–87113–259–1 Atlantic Monthly pb $7.95

THE TREMOR OF FORGERY
The uneasy, ambiguous wanderings of an American novelist in Tunisia—who may or may not have accidentally murdered someone
0–87113–258–3 Atlantic Monthly pb $7.95

THE TWO FACES OF JANUARY
0–87113–209–5 Atlantic Monthly pb $7.95

● Margaret Millar
AN AIR THAT KILLS
0–930330–23–4 International Polygonics pb $4.95

BEAST IN VIEW
A madwoman's phone calls spread terror. "Simultaneously a whodunit game and a deep and compassionate study of the dark places of the human psyche"—H.R.F. Keating
0–930330–07–2 International Polygonics pb $4.95

THE LISTENING WALLS
0–930330–52–8 International Polygonics pb $4.95

A STRANGER IN MY GRAVE
How does a living person's name come to appear on a tombstone? And whose body is really buried there?
0–930330–06–4 International Polygonics pb $4.95

● Joel Townsley Rogers
THE RED RIGHT HAND
Teetering on the edge of madness, Dr. Harry Riddle struggles to make sense of the grim funhouse he has stumbled into: a cleverly executed nightmare novel
0–88184–008–4 Carroll & Graf pb $3.50

● Jim Thompson
AFTER DARK, MY SWEET
An alcoholic, a schizophrenic, and a bunko artist plan a kidnapping
0–88739–005–6 Black Lizard pb $3.95

FIREWORKS: The Lost Writings of Jim Thompson
Stories, true crime reporting, and a novella
1–55611–067–7 Donald Fine $18.95

THE GETAWAY
A charming psychopath on the run
0–916870–75–8 Black Lizard pb $3.95

THE GRIFTERS
A con-man caught up in spiraling violence
0–916870–90–1 Black Lizard pb $3.95

A HELL OF A WOMAN
Thompson takes us inside his hero's mind as it begins to split apart
0–916870–77–4 Black Lizard pb $3.95

THE KILLER INSIDE ME
Often unnerving, occasionally hilarious: under the corny, folksy facade of a Texas sheriff seethes a homicidal psychopath
0–688–03922–7 Morrow pb $3.50

Jim Thompson (photo courtesy of Sharon Thompson Reed)

NOTHING MORE THAN MURDER
Adultery and murder among small-time movie exhibitors
0–916870–91–X Black Lizard pb $3.95

POP. 1280
"The great merit of the novels of Jim Thompson is that they are completely without good taste, and of them perhaps *Pop. 1280* has the least good taste of all"—H.R.F. Keating
0–916870–76–6 Black Lizard pb $3.95

SAVAGE NIGHT
A pint-sized hit man comes to a grotesquely violent end
0–916870–97–9 Black Lizard pb $3.95

A SWELL-LOOKING BABE
Behind the scenes at a seedy hotel
0–916870–96–0 Black Lizard pb $3.95

WILD TOWN
Murder and madness in Texas oil country
0–916870–95–2 Black Lizard pb $3.95

● Lionel White
THE KILLING
A racetrack heist goes sour; basis for the 1956 Stanley Kubrick film
0–88739–086–2 Black Lizard pb $4.95

● Harry Whittington
Whittington exemplifies the pure storytelling that flourished at such paperback houses as Gold Medal and Lion in the 1950s.
FIRES THAT DESTROY
0–88739–034–X Black Lizard pb $4.95

A TICKET TO HELL
0–88739–033–1 Black Lizard pb $3.95

WEB OF MURDER
0–88739–032–3 Black Lizard pb $3.95

Charles Willeford
THE BURNT ORANGE HERESY
A critic is prepared to go to murderous lengths to secure his position in the art world
0–88739–025–0 Black Lizard pb $3.95

COCKFIGHTER
0–88739–026–9 Black Lizard pb $3.95

HIGH PRIEST OF CALIFORNIA & WILD WIVES
Two bizarre paperback novels originally published in the '50s, highlighting the originality of Willeford's point of view even in the crassest of contexts
0–940642–11–5 Re Search pb $9.95

PICK-UP
Fifties-style alienation relentlessly explored, with a surprise ending
0–88739–046–3 Black Lizard pb $3.95

● Cornell Woolrich
THE BRIDE WORE BLACK
A vengeful, alluring widow commits a series of colorful murders—obsessively stalked through the years by a tough-guy detective
0–345–30487–X Ballantine pb $2.25

PHANTOM LADY
A stockbroker wrongly convicted of his estranged wife's murder—and desperately

searching for the nameless femme fatale who can clear him
0–345–30652–X Ballantine pb $2.50

NIGHT HAS A THOUSAND EYES
Can a paranormal prophecy of death at midnight three weeks hence be thwarted by mere mortals? The Woolrich world of fate and doom at its most nightmarish
0–345–30667–8 Ballantine pb $2.50

England

British writers were also drawn to the unsettling notion of a killer as a curious sort of hero, but their tone tended to be sly and droll rather than grim or fiercely poetic. Murder as black comedy—which would become a popular element in postwar fiction on both sides of the Atlantic—had its first flowering in the British crime-novel of the 1930s.

• Daphne Du Maurier
REBECCA
A haunted widower's new marriage, shadowed by the memory of his charismatic first wife . . . and how she died. Romantic suspense at its classiest
0–385–04380–5 Doubleday $15.95

• Roy Fuller
SECOND CURTAIN
From an Oxford poetry professor: the brooding, timid involvements in crime and punishment of George Carner—a marginal literary type up against malevolent Big Business
0–89733–197–4 Academy Chicago pb $4.95

• Graham Greene
THIS GUN FOR HIRE
Paid assassin—an underprivileged English youth—as pitiable hero: hunted by a police inspector, but viewed compassionately by the inspector's fiancée
0–670–70172–6 Viking $16.95

• Edward Grierson
REPUTATION FOR A SONG
An ironic account of a country solicitor, a family skeleton, a shrewish wife—leading up to a most unjust trial
0–14–008241–7 Penguin pb $5.95

• Richard Hull
THE MURDER OF MY AUNT
Repeated attempts at homicide by an effete, despicable antihero
0–930330–02–1 International Polygonics pb $4.95

• Raymond Postgate
VERDICT OF TWELVE
A woman stands trial for her nephew's murder, but the jurors, and their hidden motives, take center stage
0–89733–198–2 Academy Chicago pb $4.95

Continental Europe

In Europe, the crime novel offered writers a vehicle for dramatizing social tensions, questions of class and politics—and especially after World War II, philosophical nightmares involving guilt, justice, and responsibility.

• Friedrich Dürrenmatt
THE JUDGE AND HIS HANGMAN & THE QUARRY
An old and ailing police inspector uses non-legal means to trap a master-criminal and, later, a concentration-camp monster—in two ironic tales of justice at any cost
0–87923–437–7 Godine pb $7.95

• Georges Simenon
Some of Simenon's most powerful works are those that do *not* feature Inspector Maigret.
THE BLUE ROOM
0–15–613267–2 HBJ pb $2.95
THE CAT
0–15–615549–4 HBJ pb $2.95
THE RULES OF THE GAME
0–15–169475–3 HBJ $18.95
THE VENICE TRAIN
0–15–693523–6 HBJ pb $3.95

THE POLICE PROCEDURAL

Policemen have been an important part of crime fiction since *The Moonstone*. But not until the late 1940s did American and British mystery writers begin to take serious interest in the authentic evocation of nuts-and-bolts policework. The early "procedurals" owed something to the hard-boiled school, something to crime journalism and radio's *Dragnet*, and something to Simenon's purposely drab Maigret novels.

Chester Himes
The highly unofficial doings of two New York cops—Grave Digger Jones and Coffin Ed Johnson—offer "an exhilarating black comic comment on the activities of all other policemen" (Julian Symons).
BLIND MAN WITH A PISTOL
0–85031–732–0 Schocken pb $6.95
COTTON COMES TO HARLEM
0–8052–8205–X Schocken $13.95
0–394–75999–0 Schocken pb $5.95
THE CRAZY KILL
0–8052–8217–3 Schocken pb $5.95
THE HEAT'S ON
0–8052–8252–1 Schocken pb $5.95
A RAGE IN HARLEM
Originally published as *For Love of Imabelle;* first in the Gravedigger and Coffin Ed series
0–8052–8240–8 Schocken pb $5.95
THE REAL COOL KILLERS
0–8052–8238–6 Schocken pb $5.95

• Ed McBain
An imaginary city—very much like New York. A multiethnic team of detectives, juggling caseloads and unsettled personal lives. Welcome to the gritty world of the 87th Precinct, where "the most consistently skillful writer of police novels" (Julian Symons) keeps low-key humor, authentic dialogue, and grim suspense in perfect balance.
HAIL, HAIL, THE GANG'S ALL HERE
0–451–15609–9 NAL pb $3.50
THE HECKLER
0–451–13901–1 NAL pb $2.95
JIGSAW
0–451–15480–0 NAL pb $3.50
KILLER'S PAYOFF
0–451–15081–3 NAL pb $3.50
LIKE LOVE
0–451–13903–8 NAL pb $2.95
THE MUGGER
0–380–70081–6 Avon pb $3.50
THE PUSHER
0–451–15080–5 NAL pb $3.50
SADIE WHEN SHE DIED
0–451–15366–9 NAL pb $3.50

• William P. McGivern
ROGUE COP
Will compromised Philadelphia cop Mike Carmody finally stand up to the mob? Moral dilemmas and pulp-worthy action
0–425–10342–0 Berkley pb $2.95
THE BIG HEAT
The basis for Fritz Lang's *film noir* classic
0–425–10112–6 Berkley pb $2.95

• Georges Simenon
The Maigret series offers police procedure of a very idiosyncratic, very French sort: the patient stares and oblique interrogations of Inspector Maigret, alive to every nuance in people, places, and weather.
MAIGRET AFRAID
0–15–155560–5 HBJ $13.95
0–15–655142–X HBJ pb $3.95
MAIGRET AND THE MILLIONAIRES
0–15–655150–0 HBJ pb $3.95
MAIGRET AND THE YELLOW DOG
0–15–655157–8 HBJ pb $3.95
MAIGRET GOES TO SCHOOL
0–15–655156–X HBJ pb $3.95
MAIGRET'S MEMOIRS
0–15–155148–0 HBJ $13.95
MAIGRET'S MISTAKE
0–15–655155–1 HBJ pb $3.95

• Roy Vickers
THE DEPARTMENT OF DEAD ENDS
Fourteen short stories in a unique, near-documentary style. First the crime—as a sociological event. Then the Scotland Yard solution, often coming years later
0–486–23669–2 Dover pb $4.50

CRIME FICTION TODAY

"We are all murderers, we are all spies, we are all criminals." So writes Nicolas Freeling, creator of Dutch police inspector Piet Van der Valk, in describing the pervasive skepticism and ambivalence of crime fiction in the '60s and after. The influence of the genre's radicals—Hammett, Cain, Simenon, and their followers—has been dramatic, profound, virtually universal.

Few suspense novels in any category still offer the Great Detective's comforting scenario: clear good triumphing over alien evil, restoring the untainted status quo. Today's detective most likely doubts himself or his client or both. The heroes of police fiction mistrust their partners, their captains, the commissioner. Spies fear their masters as much as their enemies. Nearly everyone is suspicious of the System.

Hardboiled Detectives

• Lawrence Block
THE CUTTING EDGE
Scudder investigates the death of a fellow member of Alcoholics Anonymous in Hell's Kitchen
0–688–09069–9 Morrow $17.95

EIGHT MILLION WAYS TO DIE
An alcoholic ex-cop, "hustling for a buck" in New York City's grimiest precinct
0–515–08090–X Berkley pb $3.50

• James Crumley
DANCING BEAR
0–394–72576–X Random House pb $6.95

THE LAST GOOD KISS
The detective novel as alcoholic odyssey into the American heartland, violent and richly humorous by turns
0–394–75989–3 Random House pb $6.95

A 1936 issue of "Black Mask," from The Encyclopedia of Mystery and Detection *edited by Chris Steinbrunner and Otto Penzler* (HBJ)

THE WRONG CASE
0–394–73558–7 Random House pb $5.95

• Thomas B. Dewey
A SAD SONG SINGING
Chicago, the '60s, the hootenanny craze. "One of the ten best private-eye novels ever written"—Bill Pronzini
0–88184–067–X Carroll & Graf pb $3.50

• Loren D. Estleman
SUGARTOWN
A wry, dour, Chandleresque PI in Detroit
0–317–43030–0 Fawcett pb $3.50

• Joe Gores
DEAD SKIP
Tracing debtors and repossessing cars in San Francisco
0–345–29206–5 Ballantine pb $2.25

• Sue Grafton
A convincing and funny female private eye in Southern California.
A IS FOR ALIBI
0–553–26563–6 Bantam pb $3.50

B IS FOR BURGLAR
0–553–26061–8 Bantam pb $3.50

C IS FOR CORPSE
0–553–26468–0 Bantam pb $3.95

• Stephen Greenleaf
GRAVE ERROR
Family scandal, with a San Francisco lawyer-turned-shamus
0–345–30188–9 Ballantine pb $2.50

• Parnell Hall
DETECTIVE
The comic Manhattan maneuvers of a part-time ambulance chaser and would-be sleuth
1–55611–026–X Donald Fine $17.95

Joseph Hansen
Low-key, serious, laconically eloquent: the California cases of gay insurance-investigator Dave Brandstetter.
DEATH CLAIMS
0–03–057484–6 Henry Holt pb $3.95

FADEOUT
0–03–057486–2 Henry Holt pb $3.95

THE MAN EVERYBODY WAS AFRAID OF
0–03–059894–X Henry Holt pb $3.95

SKINFLICK
0–03–057641–5 Henry Holt pb $3.95

TROUBLEMAKER
0–03–057487–0 Henry Holt pb $3.95

• Jack Livingston
A PIECE OF THE SILENCE
The auspicious debut of deaf New York shamus Joe Binney
0–312–61065–3 St. Martin's $13.95

• Arthur Lyons
Nasty, glitzy doings in southern California—as exposed by ex-reporter Jake Asch, the only genuinely hard-boiled Jewish PI.

CASTLES BURNING
0–03–047621–6 Henry Holt pb $8.95

THREE WITH A BULLET
0–03–008539–X Henry Holt pb $3.95

• John D. MacDonald
In the best pulp tradition, with a running commentary on modern American business mores: the adventures of Florida's Travis McGee, private avenger and salvage expert.
DARKER THAN AMBER
0–397–00642–X J.B. Lippincott $9.50
0–449–12752–4 Fawcett pb $3.95

THE DEEP BLUE GOODBYE
0–449–12673–0 Fawcett pb $3.95

DRESS HER IN INDIGO
0–397–00697–7 Harper & Row $9.50
0–449–12984–5 Fawcett pb $3.95

THE LONELY SILVER RAIN
0–449–12509–2 Fawcett pb $4.50

ONE FEARFUL YELLOW EYE
0–449–13292–7 Fawcett pb $3.95

PALE GRAY FOR GUILT
0–397–00792–2 Lippincott $9.50
0–449–13331–1 Fawcett pb $3.95

• William Murray
TIP ON A DEAD CRAB
The horse player as private-eye—with Runyonesque racetrack atmosphere
0–14–007662–X Penguin pb $3.95

• Sara Paretsky
INDEMNITY ONLY
Specializing in white-collar crime but no stranger to violence: Chicago's V.I. (Vicky) Warshawski
9–998–40891–1 Ballantine pb $3.95

Robert B. Parker
Spenser, Boston's enlightened macho man, engages in confrontational sleuthing, hip repartee, and solemn musings on relationships.
GOD SAVE THE CHILD
0–440–12899–4 Dell pb $4.50

THE GODWULF MANUSCRIPT
0–440–12961–3 Dell pb $4.50

LOOKING FOR RACHEL WALLACE
0–440–15316–6 Dell pb $4.50

PROMISED LAND
0–440–17197–0 Dell pb $3.95

• Bill Pronzini
BLOWBACK
San Francisco's "Nameless Detective": middle-aged, overweight, and a collector of the pulp magazines that are Pronzini's inspiration
0–88150–034–8 Countryman pb $4.95

• Roger L. Simon
THE BIG FIX
A Berkeley student radical of the '60s becomes a dope-smoking, slapstick private eye in the '70s
0–44€ 30043–8 Warner pb $3.50

➤ **FOR OVERSEAS ORDERING INFORMATION, SEE PAGE 1**

• Jonathan Valin
THE LIME PIT
Cincinnati sleuthing, gritty and somber
0–380–55442–9 Avon pb $3.50

Traditional Mysteries, English-Style

The heyday of the gentleman sleuth and the "Great Detective" is long gone. The work of P.D. James, Ruth Rendell, or Peter Dickinson is open to new worlds of psychological depth and social detail; the days of pure escapism are over. But "Golden Age" values—richness of language, intricacies of plot, atmospheric charm, and droll humor—remain very much in evidence.

• Marian Babson
An American who lives in England, "Babson writes mysteries with distinctive atmosphere, sympathetic characters, and stylish verve."—*Booklist*
THE TWELVE DEATHS OF CHRISTMAS
0–8027–5426–0 Walker $10.95
0–440–19183–1 Dell pb $3.25

DEATH IN FASHION
0–8027–5647–6 Walker $14.95
0–553–26469–9 Bantam pb $2.95

• Robert Barnard
The most consistently witty and cheerfully misanthropic British mystery talent of the 1980s.
DEATH BY SHEER TORTURE
0–684–17437–5 Scribners $10.95
9–995–17179–1 Dell pb $3.50

DEATH OF A PERFECT MOTHER
0–440–12030–6 Dell pb $3.50

A LITTLE LOCAL MURDER
0–684–17882–6 Scribners $11.95
0–440–14882–0 Dell pb $3.50

• Simon Brett
The sleuthing adventures of seedy, cynical, mostly unsuccessful actor Charles Paris.
MURDER UNPROMPTED
0–684–17659–9 Scribners $10.95

The Shadow, from The Encyclopedia of Mystery and Detection *edited by Chris Steinbrunner and Otto Penzler (HBJ)*

SO MUCH BLOOD
0–440–18069–4 Dell pb $3.50

• Sarah Caudwell
THUS WAS ADONIS MURDERED
In the droll, rococo Edmund Crispin mold: an epistolary tale of London barristers and death in Venice
0–14–006310–2 Penguin pb $3.95

• Colin Dexter
SERVICE OF ALL THE DEAD
The setting is Oxfordshire; the detective is sardonic, boozy Inspector Morse, a rough-edged intellectual
0–553–27239–X Bantam pb $3.95

• Dick Francis
The stoic heroes are jockeys, horse owners, trainers. The action is visceral. The storytelling is lean, crafty, briskly sentimental.
BLOOD SPORT
0–449–21262–9 Fawcett pb $4.50

FORFEIT
0–449–21272–6 Fawcett pb $4.50

NERVE
0–449–21266–1 Fawcett pb $4.50

ODDS AGAINST
0–449–21269–6 Fawcett pb $4.50

WHIP HAND
0–449–21274–2 Fawcett pb $4.50

• Antonia Fraser
An acclaimed biographer, Lady Antonia has achieved popular success with her mysteries featuring fictional British TV personality Jemima Shore.
JEMIMA SHORE'S FIRST CASE & OTHER STORIES
0–393–02453–9 Norton $14.95

YOUR ROYAL HOSTAGE
0–317–67150–2 Atheneum $15.95

• Michael Gilbert
SMALLBONE DECEASED
Comic mayhem on the premises of a London solicitor
0–14–011077–1 Penguin pb $3.95

THE KILLING OF KATIE STEELSTOCK
In a more serious vein: the murder of a TV personality, during a visit to her rural hometown
0–06–011494–0 Harper & Row $11.50
0–14–005838–9 Penguin pb $3.95

• Martha Grimes
With mysteries named after British pubs and featuring Inspector Jury of Scotland Yard, "Martha Grimes . . . is winning the hearts of readers who long to return to the golden age of the dagger beneath the tea cozy and the butler lurking at the drawing-room door."—*San Francisco Chronicle*
THE FIVE BELLS AND BLADEBONE
0–316–32889–8 Little, Brown $15.95
0–440–20133–0 Dell pb $4.50

I AM THE ONLY RUNNING FOOTMAN
0–316–32887–1 Little, Brown $15.95
0–440–13924–4 Dell pb $4.50

THE DIRTY DUCK
0–316–32883–9 Little, Brown $14.95
0–440–12050–0 Dell pb $4.50

• S.T. Haymon
STATELY HOMICIDE
Tangled relationships, sexual frankness, a sense of history: reminiscent of the later Dorothy L. Sayers
0–445–20161–4 Warner pb $3.50

• P.D. James
These are dense, implacably serious whodunits from a "writer who is not going to shirk anything" (H.R.F. Keating).
AN UNSUITABLE JOB FOR A WOMAN
Amateur sleuthing at Oxford. "Superb, with clear echoes of both Dorothy Sayers and Charles Dickens"—Robin Winks
0–446–34832–5 Warner pb $3.95

THE BLACK TOWER
0–446–34824–4 Warner pb $3.95

DEATH OF AN EXPERT WITNESS
0–446–31472–2 Warner pb $4.95

SHROUD FOR A NIGHTINGALE
0–446–31303–3 Warner pb $4.95

THE SKULL BENEATH THE SKIN
0–446–35372–8 Warner pb $4.95

A TASTE FOR DEATH
James's most ambitious book—and one of her best
0–446–32352–7 Warner pb $4.95

• H.R.F. Keating
THE PERFECT MURDER
The novella that introduced hapless, soulful, intuitive Inspector Ghote of Bombay
0–89733–078–1 Academy Chicago pb $4.95

• Peter Lovesey
THE FALSE INSPECTOR DEW
Crossing the Atlantic on a 1921 ocean liner: a tour-de-force historical recreation with a dazzle of tricky plot twists
0–394–71338–9 Pantheon pb $2.95

• Patricia Moyes
WHO IS SIMON WARWICK?
Who, that is, should inherit a dead millionaire's estate? Old-fashioned sleuthing with a few very modern wrinkles
0–03–059783–8 Henry Holt pb $3.95

• Ellis Peters
Mystery meets sinewy costume drama: the detections of a Benedictine monk and herbalist in 12th-century Shrewsbury.
DEAD MAN'S RANSOM
0–449–20819–2 Fawcett pb $2.95

MONK'S HOOD
0–449–20699–8 Fawcett pb $2.95

THE RAVEN IN THE FOREGATE
0–449–21225–4 Fawcett pb $3.95

• Sheila Radley
Those who can't get enough of Ruth Rendell's Inspector Wexford novels will welcome Radley's Inspector Quantrill series. "One of the best new talents in the field."—*New Republic*
DEATH IN THE MORNING
0–684–18582–2 Scribners $13.95
0–553–26857–0 Bantam pb $3.50

FATE WORSE THAN DEATH
"A case saturated in rural atmosphere, rich in ironies that enter the soul"—*Sunday Times*(London)
0–553–26538–5 Bantam pb $3.50

THE CHIEF INSPECTOR'S DAUGHTER
0–553–26942–9 Bantam pb $3.50

WHO SAW HIM DIE?
0–684–18883–X Scribners $14.95
0–553–27607–7 Bantam pb $3.50

• Ruth Rendell
Unflappable Inspector Wexford uncovers dark secrets behind bland middle-class exteriors.
THE BEST MAN TO DIE
0–345–34503–4 Ballantine pb $3.50

DEATH NOTES
0–345–34198–8 Ballantine pb $3.50

A GUILTY THING SURPRISED
0–345–33830–8 Ballantine pb $3.50

SINS OF THE FATHERS
0–345–34253–4 Ballantine pb $3.50

• Julian Symons
THE BLACKHEATH POISONINGS: A Victorian Murder Mystery
0–14–005171–6 Penguin pb $3.95

A THREE-PIPE PROBLEM
A whodunit infused with this influential author's sardonic, radical skepticism
0–14–010903–X Penguin pb $4.95

Traditional Mysteries, American-Style

• George Baxt
A QUEER KIND OF DEATH
Eccentric, satiric, nearly surreal: murder in New York's underground gay/black subculture, circa 1966
0–317–52720–7 International Polygonics pb $4.95

From Grand Guignol *by Mel Gordon (Amok Press)*

• K.K. Beck
Beck's period mysteries set in the Roaring Twenties abound in sparkle and wit.
DEATH IN A DECK CHAIR
0–8027–5601–8 Walker $12.95
0–8041–0118–3 Ivy pb $2.95

MURDER IN A MUMMY CASE
0–8027–5655–7 Walker $15.95
0–8041–0117–5 Ballantine pb $2.95

THE BODY IN THE VOLVO
0–8027–5685–9 Walker $16.95

• Rick Boyer
BILLINGSGATE SHOAL
Edgar-winning detection and action at sea, featuring a Massachusetts oral surgeon in midlife crisis
0–395–32041–0 Houghton Mifflin $11.95
0–446–32739–5 Warner pb $3.50

• Lilian Jackson Braun
Reporter Jim Qwilleran solves crimes with the aid of his Siamese cats, Koko and Yum Yum.
THE CAT WHO ATE DANISH MODERN
0–515–08712–2 Berkley pb $3.50

THE CAT WHO PLAYED BRAHMS
0–515–09050–6 Berkley pb $3.50

• David Carkeet
DOUBLE NEGATIVE
Lethal academic satire—set at an institute for language research in Wabash, Indiana
0–14–006070–7 Penguin pb $3.95

• Amanda Cross
These campus mysteries are for those who care about Auden, Freud, sex roles, and cultivated conversation.
IN THE LAST ANALYSIS
0–380–54510–1 Avon pb $2.95

POETIC JUSTICE
0–380–44222–1 Avon pb $2.95

• Stephen Dobyns
SARATOGA HEADHUNTER
A jockey is beheaded, and engaging soft-boiled sleuth Charlie Bradshaw investigates
0–14–007772–3 Penguin pb $3.50

• Kinky Friedman
A CASE OF LONE STAR
Street-smart Texas-born country singer Friedman makes himself and his friends leading characters in a series of hilarious New York City-based mysteries
0–688–06410–8 Morrow $14.95
0–425–11185–7 Berkley pb $3.50

• Mickey Friedman
HURRICANE SEASON
Swampy doings in 1950s Florida, looked into by the local sheriff's intrepid mother-in-law
0–345–31548–0 Ballantine pb $2.50

• Susan Isaacs
COMPROMISING POSITIONS
Who killed the lecherous Long Island periodontist? A suburban housewife turns sleuth
0–515–09302–5 Jove pb $4.50

• Jonathan Kellerman
WHEN THE BOUGH BREAKS
Grim findings by a California child-psychologist
0–689–11519–9 Atheneum $15.95
0–451–15874–1 NAL pb $4.95

• Harry Kemelman
The sociology of Jewish-American religious life in the suburbs, as mirrored in the subdued detection of Rabbi David Small.
FRIDAY THE RABBI SLEPT LATE
0–449–21180–0 Fawcett pb $3.95

SOMEDAY THE RABBI WILL LEAVE
0–449–20945–8 Fawcett pb $3.50

• Jane Langton
EMILY DICKINSON IS DEAD
Murder at Amherst, with literary motives and Yankee charm
0–14–007771–5 Penguin pb $3.95

• Emma Lathen
The genteel sleuthings of Wall Street banker John Putnam Thatcher offer—along with vivid characters, dry humor, and expert plotting—shrewd close-ups of the business world.
ACCOUNTING FOR MURDER
0–671–64550–1 Pocket pb $3.50

PICK UP STICKS
0–671–50997–7 Pocket pb $2.95

• Gregory McDonald
The breakneck inquiries of a fearless reporter and shameless liar—delivered in bursts of incomparably witty dialogue.
CONFESS, FLETCH
0–380–00814–9 Avon pb $3.95

FLETCH
0–380–00645–6 Avon pb $3.95

• Barbara Michaels
The reigning queen of romantic suspense and in 1986 named Grandmaster in the first Anthony awards, Michaels also writes bestselling mysteries as Elizabeth Peters.
BE BURIED IN THE RAIN
"A new Barbara Michaels always means a day when I quit work early and stay up late; I can't put it down"—Marion Zimmer Bradley
0–689–11618–7 Atheneum $13.95
0–425–09634–3 Berkley pb $3.95

SEARCH THE SHADOWS
0–689–11906–2 Atheneum $17.95
0–425–11183–0 Berkley pb $4.50

SHATTERED SILK
"Superior Michaels! Like the antique gowns its heroine collects, *Shattered Silk* glitters"—*Kirkus Reviews*
0–689–11620–9 Atheneum $15.95
0–425–10476–1 Berkley pb $3.95

SMOKE AND MIRRORS
0–671–67037–9 Simon & Schuster $18.95

• Elizabeth Peters
Peters' spunky, outspoken heroines—Victorian Egyptologist Amelia Peabody and the contemporary art historian Vicki Bliss and librarian Jacqueline Kirby—are especially popular with women readers.

DEVIL-MAY-CARE
0–812–50789–4 Tor pb $4.50

LION IN THE VALLEY
"To our knowledge, Jane Austen never attempted a mystery novel. If she had, it might have been something not unlike the fiction Elizabeth Peters serves up"—*Cleveland Plain Dealer*
0–812–50764–9 Tor pb $3.95

NIGHT OF FOUR HUNDRED RABBITS
0–812–50773–8 Tor pb $4.50

THE DEEDS OF THE DISTURBER
0–689–11907–0 Atheneum $16.95
0–446–35333–7 Warner pb $3.95

THE SEVENTH SINNER
0–445–40225–3 Mysterious pb $3.95

TROJAN GOLD
0–689–11621–7 Atheneum $15.95
0–8125–0758–4 Tor pb $3.95

• Richard D. Rosen
STRIKE THREE, YOU'RE DEAD
Baseball and murder: the ultimate American mix
0–8027–5587–9 Walker $12.95
0–451–14233–0 NAL pb $2.95

• William G. Tapply
THE DUTCH BLUE ERROR
Reluctant sleuthing by a lawyer to Boston's rich
0–345–32341–6 Ballantine pb $2.95

• Gene Thompson
A CUP OF DEATH
"Leading the bloodhounds is a 60-year-old, peppy, philosophical homespun lawyer from San Francisco . . . Gene Thompson has created a very impressive new investigator in Dade Cooley"—*NY Times*
0–394–56140–6 Random House $16.95

MURDER MYSTERY
0–345–32446–3 Ballantine pb $2.95

Crimes and Capers

Nowadays lawbreakers of all kinds can be heroes; many of them, unlike Rico in *Little Caesar*, are even allowed to get away with murder. And while some treatments of outlaw activity reach for pathos or tragedy, more often it is irreverent comedy—light (Donald Westlake), dark (Richard Condon), and darker (Elmore Leonard)—that energizes these sharp-edged excursions into a world of matter-of-fact crime.

• Lawrence Block
THE BURGLAR WHO LIKED TO QUOTE KIPLING
Burglar as likable, light-hearted hero in peril
0–671–61831–8 Pocket pb $3.50

• Richard Condon
PRIZZI'S HONOR
Hit man loves hit woman: a deglamorized black comedy
0–425–09507–X Berkley pb $3.95

• James Ellroy
Starkly realistic, often disturbingly violent evocations of America in the 1940s and '50s
THE BIG NOWHERE
0–89296–283–6 Mysterious $17.50

THE BLACK DAHLIA
0–445–40525–2 Mysterious pb $4.95

• Jonathan Gash
THE VATICAN RIP
A raffish antique dealer out to steal a Chippendale table in Rome
0–14–006431–1 Penguin pb $3.95

• George V. Higgins
THE FRIENDS OF EDDIE COYLE
The world of low-level Boston criminals, recorded with documentary precision
0–345–28635–9 Ballantine pb $2.95

KENNEDY FOR THE DEFENSE
0–345–32612–1 Ballantine pb $2.95

Elmore Leonard (photo by Joan Leonard, courtesy of Morrow)

• Elmore Leonard
Leonard's heroes encompass a wide social spectrum: they have included cops, robbers, ex-cons, photographers, and even a stigmatic candidate for sainthood (*Touch*). Leonard has a remarkable ear for street talk and a gift for ferocious pacing. Asked to explain his books' appeal, he is said to have replied: "I leave out the parts that people skip."
CITY PRIMEVAL: High Noon in Detroit
0–380–56952–3 Avon pb $3.95

52 PICK-UP
An adulterous husband gets more than he bargained for when his mistress is murdered by blackmailing thugs
0–380–65490–3 Avon pb $3.95

FREAKY DEAKY
0–87795–975–7 Morrow $18.95
0–446–35039–7 Warner pb $5.95

GLITZ
0–446–32920–7 Warner pb $4.95

GOLD COAST
0–553–26267–X Bantam pb $3.50

KILLSHOT
1–557–10019–5 Morrow $18.95

LA BRAVA
A shake-down artist versus a former Secret Service agent at a seedy Miami hotel
0–380–69237–6 Avon pb $3.95

MR. MAJESTYK
A melon farmer fights it out with labor racketeers
0–445–40228–8 Mysterious pb $3.95

SPLIT IMAGES
Features one of Leonard's most memorably schizoid bad guys
0–380–63107–5 Avon pb $3.95

STICK
The hapless hero of *Swag* is released from prison only to find himself knee-deep in Miami corruption: one of Leonard's best
0–380–67652–4 Avon pb $3.95

SWAG
Armed robbery for fun and profit
0–440–18424–X Dell pb $3.95

THE SWITCH
Lovable thugs kidnap a rich man's wife
0–553–27665–4 Bantam pb $3.95

TOUCH
0–380–70386–6 Avon pb $4.50

UNKNOWN MAN NO. 89
0–380–67041–0 Avon pb $3.95

• Thomas Perry
THE BUTCHER'S BOY
Hit-man on a killing spree, chased by a female Treasury agent
0–441–08955–0 Berkley pb $3.95

METZGER'S DOG
Blackmailing the CIA, in a revenge/caper comedy
0–441–52867–8 Berkley pb $3.50

• Mario Puzo
THE GODFATHER
The Mafia, romantic-epic style
0–399–10342–2 Putnam $24.95
0–451–15736–2 NAL pb $4.95

• **Richard Stark**

Stark (a pseudonym for Donald Westlake) recounts the grisly exploits of professional thief Parker, an antihero in trouble with the mob.

THE MAN WITH THE GETAWAY FACE
0–8052–8200–9 Schocken $13.95

SLAYGROUND
0–8052–8181–9 Schocken $13.95

• **Donald Westlake**
THE HOT ROCK
Wayward heists by the bumbling Dortmunder gang
0–445–40608–9 Mysterious pb $3.95

The Police Procedural: USA

In the 1960s and '70s, the American cop novel got rougher, deeper, and much more popular. While some writers continued to see policemen as reassuring authority figures, others—like Joseph Wambaugh and Charles Willeford—gave us burnouts, flakes, alcoholics, and sadists, as well as cops with more manageable problems.

• **Rex Burns**
GROUND MONEY
0–14–008515–7 Penguin pb $3.95

• **K.C. Constantine**
Low-key, atmospheric policework in a western-Pennsylvania coal-mining town.
A FIX LIKE THIS
0–87923–718–X Godine pb $3.95

THE MAN WHO LIKED TO LOOK AT HIMSELF
0–87923–663–9 Godine pb $3.95

THE ROCKSBURG RAIL MURDERS
0–87923–662–0 Godine pb $3.95

• **Robert Daley**
YEAR OF THE DRAGON
Don't be put off by the bad movie version. This is a strong, disturbing tale of NYPD corruption—by a former deputy commissioner
0–451–15207–7 NAL pb $4.95

• **John Gregory Dunne**
TRUE CONFESSIONS
Inspired by the real life "Black Dahlia" murder in 1940s Los Angeles: a cop's gloomy inquiries—some of which lead to his brother, a priest
0–671–65874–3 Pocket pb $4.50

• **Bill Granger**
THE EL MURDERS
Scathing treatment of police mores in Chicago
0–8050–0378–9 Henry Holt $16.95

• **Thomas Harris**
RED DRAGON
The most chilling treatment yet of a police manhunt for a psychopathic serial killer
0–553–27522–4 Bantam pb $4.95

THE SILENCE OF LAMBS
The search for yet another serial killer, told with flair
0–312–91543–8 St. Martin's pb $5.95

• **Tony Hillerman**
Haunting, lyrical investigation by Navajo reservation policemen—with plots that turn on questions of cultural identity and tribal beliefs.
PEOPLE OF DARKNESS
0–06–080950–7 Harper & Row pb $3.95

SKINWALKERS
0–06–080950–7 Harper & Row pb $3.95

TALKING GOD
0–06–016118–3 Harper & Row $17.95

• **Lillian O'Donnell**
LADYKILLER
Sergeant Norah Mulcahaney: the most convincing series policewoman
0–317–37993–3 Fawcett pb $2.95

• **Lawrence Sanders**
THE FIRST DEADLY SIN
The Big Daddy of the cops-versus-psycho genre
0–425–10427–3 Berkley pb $4.95

• **Dorothy Uhnak**
THE INVESTIGATION
Based on a true case of a mother charged with child-killing: wrenching suspense, with a "real acknowledgment of the appalling things men and women can do" (H.R.F. Keating)
0–671–46987–8 Pocket pb $3.95

• **Joseph Wambaugh**
Cops at their weary best and garish worst: boozy, randy, miserable, defeated, and valiant.
THE BLACK MARBLE
0–440–10644–3 Dell pb $4.95

THE BLUE KNIGHT
0–440–10607–9 Dell pb $4.95

THE CHOIRBOYS
0–440–11188–9 Dell pb $4.95

THE GLITTER DOME
0–553–27259–4 Bantam pb $4.95

• **Donald Westlake**
LEVINE
A Brooklyn cop with a heart condition—in six stark, tender short stories
0–8125–1054–2 Tor pb $2.95

• **Charles Willeford**
The darkly comic tribulations of Miami cop Hoke Mosley—as he deals with psychos, drug dealers, the housing shortage, his ex-wife, his teenage daughters, and midlife crisis.
MIAMI BLUES
0–345–32016–6 Ballantine pb $2.95

NEW HOPE FOR THE DEAD
0–345–33839–1 Ballantine pb $3.50

SIDESWIPE
0–345–34947–4 Ballantine pb $3.95

THE WAY WE DIE NOW
0–345–35332–3 Ballantine pb $3.95

• **Stuart Woods**
CHIEFS
Three generations of police chiefs in a small Georgia town, all after the same sex-driven killer
9–998–34859–5 Avon pb $4.95

The Police Procedural: International

From class conflict in Glasgow (*Laidlaw*) to South Africa's apartheid (James McClure), from contemporary Japan to Victorian England and ancient China, background becomes foreground in much of the best police fiction from Europe, Asia, and Africa.

• **Nicolas Freeling**
Inspector Van der Valk—the Maigret of Amsterdam—offers social commentary as well as detection. "[Freeling] has moved almost continuously toward the creation of character studies which are also crime stories."—Julian Symons
BECAUSE OF THE CATS
0–14–002282–1 Penguin pb $3.95

THE KING OF THE RAINY COUNTRY
0–14–002853–6 Penguin pb $3.95

LOVE IN AMSTERDAM
0–14–002281–3 Penguin pb $3.95

• **Bartholomew Gill**
McGARR AND THE METHOD OF DESCARTES
Dublin-based police work, with the IRA and other political pressures always shadowing the proceedings
0–14–008405–3 Penguin pb $3.95

> **Reginald Hill**
> A riotously mismatched cop team—fat bigot Dalziel, university-type Pascoe—in grimly realistic Yorkshire sleuthing.
> **AN ADVANCEMENT OF LEARNING**
> 0–451–14656–5 NAL pb $2.95
>
> **AN APRIL SHROUD**
> 0–451–14783–9 NAL pb $3.50
>
> **DEADHEADS**
> 0–451–13559–8 NAL pb $3.50

• **Peter Lovesey**
A CASE OF SPIRITS
Scotland Yard detection in the 1880s, lovingly recreated
0–14–004333–0 Penguin pb $3.95

• **James McClure**
Close-ups of life in 1970s South Africa—framed by the investigations of an Afrikaaner and his Zulu sergeant.
THE STEAM PIG
0–394–71021–5 Pantheon pb $2.95

THE SUNDAY HANGMAN
0–394–72992–7 Pantheon pb $2.95

• **William McIlvanney**
LAIDLAW
"I have seldom been so seized by a style, or so taken by a character as I was by the angry and passionate Glasgow detective, Laidlaw"—Ross Macdonald
0–394–73338–X Pantheon pb $2.95

IF YOU CAN'T FIND IT, LOOK IN THE INDEX

- James Melville

A SORT OF SAMURAI
Frequently surprising glimpses of
contemporary Japanese culture, in the
sturdy company of Supt. Tetsuo Otani
0–449–20821–4 Fawcett pb $2.95

- Maj Sjöwall & Per Wahlöö

Provocative police work in Stockholm—
from the husband/wife team whose
declared intent is "to use the crime novel
as a scalpel cutting open the belly of an
ideologically pauperized and morally
debatable so-called welfare state of the
bourgeois type."

THE ABOMINABLE MAN
0–394–74273–7 Random House pb $3.95

**THE FIRE ENGINE THAT
DISAPPEARED**
0–394–72340–6 Random House pb $4.95

THE LAUGHING POLICEMAN
0–394–72341–4 Random House pb $3.95

THE MAN WHO WENT UP IN SMOKE
0–394–71778–3 Random House pb $3.95

ROSEANNA
0–394–71779–1 Random House pb $3.95

- Martin Cruz Smith

GORKY PARK
The best of several attempts to write a
Moscow police procedural
0–394–51748–2 Random House $13.95
0–345–29834–9 Ballantine pb $3.95

- Trevanian

THE MAIN
A broken-down cop in a tough section of
Montreal
9–999–47735–6 Berkley pb $4.95

- Janwillem Van De Wetering

A wise old police chief, a gruff middle-
aged detective, a young sergeant into Zen
and music: quirky legwork in Amsterdam.

HARD RAIN
0–345–33964–9 Ballantine pb $3.95

THE MAINE MASSACRE
0–345–34496–0 Ballantine pb $3.95

THE STREETBIRD
0–671–47521–5 Pocket pb $3.50

- Robert Van Gulik

Shrewd tales involving Chinese
administration and criminal law, as
dispensed by Judge Dee, a magistrate of
the 7th-century T'ang dynasty.

THE CHINESE BELL MURDERS
0–226–84862–0 Chicago pb $4.95

THE CHINESE NAIL MURDERS
0–226–84863–9 Chicago pb $4.95

**THE HAUNTED MONASTERY & THE
CHINESE MAZE MURDERS**
0–486–23502–5 Dover pb $5.95

Psychological Suspense

"The violence that lives behind the bland
faces most of us present to the world": that,
in Julian Symons' words, continues to be the
primary theme of psychological crime fiction. The personalities of both villains and
victims are subjected to intense, often ironic
scrutiny, and society's presumptions about
guilt and innocence, right and wrong, are
frequently challenged.

- Mary Higgins Clark

Clark's fast-paced suspense dramas have
made her one of the highest-paid mystery
writers in the world.

A STRANGER IS WATCHING
0–440–18127–5 Dell pb $4.95

THE CRADLE WILL FALL
0–440–11545–0 Dell pb $4.95

WHERE ARE THE CHILDREN?
Inspired by the notorious Alice Crimmins
child-murder case
0–440–19593–4 Dell pb $4.95

- Anna Clarke

LETTER FROM THE DEAD
0–55773–147–0 Charter pb $2.95

DESIRE TO KILL
A senior citizen develops a new hobby—
murder
0–557–73118–7 Charter pb $2.95

Peter Dickinson

HINDSIGHT
A biographer tracking down an elusive
memory discovers the evidence of a
long-buried crime
0–394–72603–0 Pantheon pb $3.95

KING AND JOKER
A brilliantly elaborate, ultimately
disturbing puzzle involving an alternate
British Royal Family
0–394–71600–0 Pantheon pb $2.95

TEFUGA
0–394–75181–7 Pantheon pb $4.95

- Stanley Ellin

VERY OLD MONEY
Psychosocial gothic suspense—with a smart
but poor young couple playing butler and
maid to a rich, strange Manhattan family
0–449–20915–6 Fawcett pb $3.50

- Celia Fremlin

THE HOURS BEFORE DAWN
The domestic terrors of a new mother.
"[Fremlin's] great gift is to see horror in
the ordinary"—William Weaver
0–89733–101–X Academy Chicago pb $4.95

- Sebastien Japrisot

**THE LADY IN THE CAR WITH
GLASSES AND A GUN**
A simple journey becomes a labyrinthine
nightmare of mystification
Translated by Helen Weaver
0–14–005361–1 Penguin pb $3.95

- John D. MacDonald

Many fans feel that MacDonald was even
more convincing in his many non-Travis
McGee books.

BARRIER ISLAND
MacDonald's last book is an absorbing
intrigue involving Florida real estate
swindles
0–449–13179–3 Fawcett pb $4.50

THE CROSSROADS
0–449–12871–7 Fawcett pb $2.95

THE DAMNED
Trouble at a Mexican river crossing brings
out the best and worst in a mixed
assortment of travelers
0–449–12887–3 Fawcett pb $2.95

THE EXECUTIONERS
A decent Florida lawyer terrorized by a
rapist-psychopath
0–449–14059–8 Fawcett pb $2.50

A FLASH OF GREEN
An ambitious novel involving the dark side
of land development
0–449–12692–7 Fawcett pb $3.50

THE PRICE OF MURDER
0–449–13045–2 Fawcett pb $2.95

SLAM THE BIG DOOR
MacDonald's own favorite among his
novels
0–89296–190–2 Mysterious $16.95
0–449–13275–7 Fawcett pb $3.95

- Patrick McGinley

BOGMAIL
Black comedy in a wild Donegal setting: a
pub owner commits justifiable homicide—
and finds himself a blackmail victim
0–14–006195–9 Penguin pb $4.95

- Ruth Rendell

THE FACE OF TRESPASS
"From the author who is cherished by
suspense connoisseurs . . . here is one of
the best psychological mysteries of the
season"—*Chicago Tribune Book World*
0–553–25976–8 Bantam pb $3.50

FROM DOON WITH DEATH
0–345–34817–6 Ballantine pb $3.95

LIVE FLESH
0–345–00727–1 Ballantine pb $3.95

MASTER OF THE MOOR
The horrifying secret behind a series of
killings
0–345–34147–3 Ballantine pb $3.95

THE VEILED ONE
0–394–57206–8 Pantheon $17.95

- Julian Symons

THE PLOT AGAINST ROGER RIDER
Crime fiction deepened by satire and
serious philosophical grappling with
morality and madness
0–14–003949–X Penguin pb $3.95

THE PLAYERS AND THE GAME
A grim novel based on the Moors Murders
in northern England
0–14–003808–6 Penguin pb $3.95

- Scott Turow

PRESUMED INNOCENT
This courtroom thriller was an enormous
popular success
0–446–35098–2 Warner pb $4.95

- Barbara Vine

A DARK-ADAPTED EYE
"It's no secret that Barbara Vine is the
distinguished crime writer Ruth Rendell
and in *A Dark-Adapted Eye* we have Ms.
Rendell at the height of her powers . . .

---

combines excitement and psychological subtlety"—P.D. James
0–553–05143–1 Bantam $14.95
0–553–26498–2 Bantam pb $3.95

A FATAL INVERSION
0–553–05215–3 Bantam $14.95
0–553–27249–7 Bantam pb $3.95

ABOUT CRIME FICTION

• John C. Carr
THE CRAFT OF CRIME: Conversations with Crime Writers
Interviews with Rendell, Lathen, McClure, Parker, and others
0–395–33121–8 Houghton Mifflin pb $8.95

• Howard Haycraft
MURDER FOR PLEASURE: The Life and Times of the Detective Story
Shrewd summing up, as of the early 1940s, from the dean of American mystery-watchers. Limited in scope (no thrillers), but still persuasive and flavorsome
0–88184–071–8 Carroll & Graf pb $10.95

• Howard Haycraft, editor
THE ART OF THE MYSTERY STORY
The definitive collection of critical essays, circa 1946—from Edmund Wilson's "Who Cares Who Killed Roger Ackroyd?" to more positive reflections by Sayers, Queen, Anthony Boucher, James Sandoe, and others
0–88184–056–4 Carroll & Graf pb $9.95

• H.R.F. Keating
CRIME AND MYSTERY: The 100 Best Books
The choices range from obvious to idiosyncratic to perverse. The mini-essays of appreciation meander. Nonetheless: charming enthusiasms
0–88184–345–8 Carroll & Graf $15.95

• Victoria Nichols & Susan Thompson
SILK STALKINGS: When Women Write of Murder
A survey of women authors in the crime field, with commentary on nearly 600 characters and over 3000 titles
0–88739–096–X Black Lizard pb $16.95

• Bill Pronzini
GUN IN CHEEK
Hilarious excerpts from some of the worst crime and spy fiction ever written, lovingly presented
0–89296–900–8 Mysterious pb $8.95

SON OF GUN IN CHEEK
0–89296–952–0 Mysterious pb $9.95

• Bill Pronzini & Marcia Muller
ONE THOUSAND AND ONE MIDNIGHTS: The Aficionado's Guide to Mystery and Detective Fiction
Generous, eclectic, with special attention to the hard-boiled school and paperback originals. Despite overdetailed plot summaries and some mediocre entries, a valuable compilation
0–87795–622–7 Arbor House $39.95

• Maureen T. Reddy
SISTERS IN CRIME: Feminism and the Crime Novel
0–8264–0407–3 Ungar $17.95

• Chris Steinbrunner & Otto Penzler, editors
THE ENCYCLOPEDIA OF MYSTERY AND DETECTION
A trove of information on all aspects, with many illustrations
0–15–628787–0 HBJ pb $13.95

• Julian Symons
BLOODY MURDER: From the Detective Story to the Crime Novel
0–670–80096–1 Viking $14.95
0–14–007263–2 Penguin pb $6.95

• Robin Winks
MODUS OPERANDI: An Excursion into Detective Fiction
Serious, witty musings on the genre's themes and patterns
0–87923–406–7 Godine $14.95

• Robin Winks, editor
DETECTIVE FICTION: A Collection of Critical Essays
From W.H. Auden and lesser lights: the more literary, academic kind of crime-fiction essays. Plus a welcome listing of Winks's own favorite mysteries
0–88150–108–5 Countryman pb $10.95

• Dilys Winn
MURDER INK: Revived, Revised, Still Unrepentant
A lighthearted miscellany of essays, lists, interviews, puzzles, quizzes, and aficionado trivia
0–89480–777–3 Workman pb $9.95

Individual Writers

• Eric Ambler
HERE LIES: An Autobiography
0–374–16974–8 Farrar, Straus & Giroux $16.95
0–89296–940–7 Mysterious pb $8.95

• Janet A. Smith
JOHN BUCHAN: A Biography
0–19–281866–X Oxford pb $8.95

• Frank MacShane, editor
SELECTED LETTERS OF RAYMOND CHANDLER
0–231–05080–1 Columbia $29.50
0–385–29531–6 Dell pb $11.95

• Robert Barnard
A TALENT TO DECEIVE: An Appreciation of Agatha Christie
0–396–07827–3 Dodd, Mead $10.00

• Julian Symons
CONAN DOYLE: Portrait of an Artist
0–89296–247–X Mysterious $15.95

• Michael Hardwick
THE COMPLETE GUIDE TO SHERLOCK HOLMES
0–312–00580–6 St. Martin's $16.95

• Julian Symons
DASHIELL HAMMETT
More critical essay than biography
0–15–123950–9 HBJ $24.95
0–15–623956–6 HBJ pb $12.95

• Diane Johnson
DASHIELL HAMMETT: A Life
0–449–90223–4 Fawcett pb $8.95

• Ross Macdonald
INWARD JOURNEY
Edited by Ralph B. Sipper
0–89296–902–4 Mysterious pb $8.95

• Georges Simenon
INTIMATE MEMOIRS
0–15–144892–2 HBJ $22.95

• J.I.M. Stewart
MYSELF AND MICHAEL INNES
Stewart recounts his double life as Oxford scholar and crime novelist under the pseudonym Michael Innes
0–393–02593–4 Norton $17.95

• Charles Willeford
I WAS LOOKING FOR A STREET
Willeford's boyhood in the Depression. "Pure writing, never pretentious or forced, never melodramatic, but honest storytelling of the highest order"—Elmore Leonard
0–88150–112–3 Countryman $14.95

Dashiell Hammett (photo by Azarnick, courtesy of Knopf)

TO ORDER BOOKS AS GIFTS, SEE PAGE 1

Spy Fiction

THE EARLY SPY NOVEL

James Fenimore Cooper's *The Spy* (1821)—which followed a double agent through the Revolutionary War—is generally acknowledged to be the first espionage novel. Nearly a century later, Joseph Conrad's *The Secret Agent* (1907) and *Under Western Eyes* (1911) explored the tormented souls of double-crossed, double-crossing agents. But while these writers foreshadow the serious and ambivalent nature of mid-20th-century espionage fiction, the spy novel as popular genre begins, somewhat ignominiously, with turn-of-the-century thriller writers such as William Le Queux whose fiercely patriotic, stylistically crude novels set the genre's tone for decades.

- **John Buchan**
FOUR ADVENTURES OF RICHARD HANNAY
Including *The 39 Steps, Greenmantle, Mr. Standfast,* and *The Three Hostages*. Clear-cut enemies (usually German), high romanticism, and a patriotic hero in scenic, adventurous action
0–87923–655–8 Godine $19.95

- **Erskine Childers**
THE RIDDLE OF THE SANDS
"Not only a good spy story but also one of the finest tales about small sailing-craft ever written"—Eric Ambler
Introduction by Geoffrey Household
0–14–000905–1 Penguin pb $4.95

- **E. Phillips Oppenheim**
THE GREAT IMPERSONATION
An aristocrat in disgrace redeems himself by one-upping German spies in East Africa
0–486–23607–2 Dover pb $4.50

- **"Sapper"**
BULLDOG DRUMMOND
Xenophobic adventure stories representing the genre's noisiest excesses
0–88184–453–5 Carroll & Graf pb $3.50

THE MODERN SPY NOVEL

The cheery complacency of the pre-1930s thriller—like that of the cozy Golden Age whodunit—was profoundly challenged between the wars by darker, more skeptical attitudes. The absolute rightness of British and American national interests could no longer be assumed. The enemy—once so clearly identifiable—became a shifting, fuzzy target, and agents were revealed to have divided loyalties, ambivalent politics, and a perhaps healthy streak of every-man-for-himself ruthlessness.

- **Eric Ambler**
"Ambler was fascinated by European cities, and his hunts take place against convincing backgrounds in Istanbul, Sofia, Belgrade, Milan. He was interested also in the problems of frontiers and passports, so that the difficulty of moving from one country to another plays a large part in the stories. And he showed from the beginning a high skill, which became mastery, in the construction of plot."—Julian Symons
BACKGROUND TO DANGER
0–425–06420–4 Berkley pb $2.95
EPITAPH FOR A SPY
A young teacher—once Hungarian, once Yugoslav, now stateless—becomes entangled in espionage in a Europe (circa 1937) where Communism often looks better than social democracy
0–425–06564–2 Berkley pb $2.95
THE INTERCOM CONSPIRACY
0–374–51968–4 Farrar, Straus & Giroux pb $3.95
JOURNEY INTO FEAR
An apolitical Englishman finds himself marked for assassination in 1930s Europe. His efforts to outmaneuver his shadowy pursuers make this one of Ambler's most suspenseful early novels
0–425–06391–7 Berkley pb $2.95
THE LIGHT OF DAY
Late, supremely cynical Ambler: the harrowing ordeal of a seedy con man in Turkey, forced to smuggle weapons and spy for the local police
0–425–07455–2 Berkley pb $2.95
PASSAGE OF ARMS
0–425–07137–5 Berkley pb $2.95
THE SCHIRMER INHERITANCE
0–425–07302–5 Berkley pb $2.95

- **Agatha Christie**
N OR M?
Light-hearted espionage with Tommy and Tuppence Beresford
0–425–09845–1 Berkley pb $2.95

- **Manning Coles**
TOAST TO TOMORROW
Tommy Hambledon, language expert and British agent, undercover in World War I Germany: part old-style derring-do, part understated realism
0–918172–15–2 Leete's Island pb $5.95

Ian Fleming
Throwback patriotism, newfangled technology, plus brand-name luxuries and kinky dollops of sex and torture. The early best of James Bond, the pure 007, is "cunningly constructed and beautifully upholstered" (Michael Gilbert).
CASINO ROYALE
0–425–08162–1 Berkley pb $3.50
DOCTOR NO
0–425–08986–X Berkley pb $3.50
FROM RUSSIA WITH LOVE
0–425–08620–8 Berkley pb $3.50
LIVE AND LET DIE
0–425–08759–X Berkley pb $3.50

Sean Connery as James Bond in Ian Fleming's "Doctor No" (photo: Movie Star News)

- **Graham Greene**
THE CONFIDENTIAL AGENT
With the Spanish Civil War as background: the predicament of the agent with scruples, not trusted by his own party—both hero and villain, hunter and hunted
0–14–001895–6 Penguin pb $3.95
THE MINISTRY OF FEAR
Why does everyone want the cake that poor Arthur Rowe wins at a village fair in World War II England? A mesmerizing blend of black-comic menace with ironic musings on guilt and madness
0–14–001897–2 Penguin pb $4.95
OUR MAN IN HAVANA
A British vacuum-cleaner salesman is recruited as a spy and is not at all happy about it. Cold-War-era espionage in all its wiry absurdity
0–14–001790–9 Penguin pb $4.95

- **Geoffrey Household**
ROGUE MALE
A British sportsman sets out to assassinate Europe's foulest tyrant (circa 1939) and ends up as target and fugitive: the quintessential hunted-man adventure
0–14–000695–8 Penguin pb $3.95

- **Helen MacInnes**
ABOVE SUSPICION
Perilous honeymoon: an Oxford professor and his bride are enlisted to track down a missing agent in pre-World War II Germany
0–449–20858–3 Fawcett pb $4.50
THE DOUBLE IMAGE
0–449–20860–5 Fawcett pb $3.50
RIDE A PALE HORSE
0–449–20726–9 Fawcett pb $3.95

THE SALZBURG CONNECTION
0–449–20895–8 Fawcett pb $3.95

- **W. Somerset Maugham**
**COLLECTED SHORT STORIES:
Volume 3**
Originally published as *Ashenden: The British Agent,* this collection contains the first starkly contemporary spy stories: downbeat, less than heroic, derived from Maugham's own experience in the Secret Service. "After the easy, absurd assumptions made by Buchan, Sapper, and Oppenheim, the Ashenden stories have the reality of a cold bath"—Julian Symons
0–14–001873–5 Penguin pb $4.95

CONTEMPORARY SPY FICTION

Loyalty to one's country—which may be in the wrong hands—is no longer a given in espionage fiction. Loyalty to oneself or one's friend or some higher principle might be a worthier priority. This is the central dilemma of the contemporary spy novel, especially as exemplified by the work of John le Carré, the genre's chief practitioner.

- **William F. Buckley, Jr.**
Whimsical 1950s spying in Europe—with a CIA hero and a cheerfully right-wing view of Cold War history
HIGH JINKS
0–440–13957–0 Dell pb $4.50

MONGOOSE, R.I.P.
0–440–20231–0 Dell pb $4.50

STAINED GLASS
0–380–54791–0 Avon pb $3.95

- **Len Deighton**
FUNERAL IN BERLIN
The Angry Young Man of British espionage fiction, with working-class heroes, scathing humor, and elliptical stylishness
0–425–07402–1 Berkley pb $3.50

THE IPCRESS FILE
0–345–33576–7 Ballantine pb $3.95

SPY STORY
0–345–31569–3 Ballantine pb $3.95

SS-GB
0–345–31809–9 Ballantine pb $3.95

GAME, SET, MATCH
The complete trilogy, including *Berlin Game, Mexico Set,* and *London Match*
0–394–57235–1 Knopf $15.95

BERLIN GAME
0–345–31498–0 Ballantine pb $4.50

MEXICO SET
0–345–31499–9 Ballantine pb $4.50

LONDON MATCH
0–345–33268–7 Ballantine pb $4.50

- **Ken Follett**
EYE OF THE NEEDLE
A Nazi agent at large in World War II England
0–451–15524–6 NAL pb $4.95

- **Frederick Forsyth**
THE DAY OF THE JACKAL
Forsyth's first novel, about a plot to kill De Gaulle, remains in many ways his most compelling
0–553–26630–6 Bantam pb $4.95

THE DEVIL'S ALTERNATIVE
0–553–26490–7 Bantam pb $4.95

THE DOGS OF WAR
The inner workings of an African coup engineered by an English magnate
0–553–26846–5 Bantam pb $4.95

THE FOURTH PROTOCOL
A lethal Soviet agent on the loose in England. Documentary-style espionage in convincing detail
0–553–25113–9 Bantam pb $4.95

THE NEGOTIATOR
0–553–05361–2 Bantam $19.95

THE ODESSA FILE
A journalist on the trail of Nazi war criminals
0–553–27198–9 Bantam pb $4.95

- **Brian Freemantle**
THE BLIND RUN
The droll ultimate in cynical spy fiction: a British agent forever at the mercy of his double-crossing commanders
0–553–26503–2 Bantam pb $3.95

CHARLIE M
0–345–30611–2 Ballantine pb $2.50

- **Brian Garfield**
HOPSCOTCH
0–449–22747–2 Fawcett pb $2.50

- **Adam Hall**
THE QUILLER MEMORANDUM
0–515–08503–0 Berkley pb $3.50

- **John le Carré**
CALL FOR THE DEAD
The first appearance of le Carré's classic reluctant spy George Smiley
0–940595–03–6 Hill $9.95

THE HONOURABLE SCHOOLBOY
The scene shifts to Hong Kong as Smiley continues to trace the elusive trail of KGB spymaster Karla
0–553–27437–6 Bantam pb $4.95

THE LITTLE DRUMMER GIRL
By manipulating a left-leaning British actress, Israeli intelligence attempts to penetrate a Palestinian cell
0–394–53015–2 Knopf $15.95
0–553–26757–4 Bantam pb $4.95

THE LOOKING-GLASS WAR
0–553–23693–8 Bantam pb $3.95

A MURDER OF QUALITY
Le Carré veers from espionage toward the tradition of the whodunit as Smiley becomes involved in a murder at an exclusive school
0–940595–04–4 Hill $9.95
0–553–26443–5 Bantam pb $3.95

A PERFECT SPY
Grandly pessimistic, nobly structured, thickly textured: the grim business of spying in the nuclear age
0–553–26456–7 Bantam pb $4.95

THE RUSSIA HOUSE
0–394–57789–2 Knopf $19.95

SMILEY'S PEOPLE
Smiley comes face to face with Karla, his old KGB enemy
0–553–26487–7 Bantam pb $4.95

THE SPY WHO CAME IN FROM THE COLD
The novel that established le Carré as the most original of modern espionage writers
0–553–26442–7 Bantam pb $4.95

TINKER, TAILOR, SOLDIER, SPY
The best of the Smiley books is a complex study of betrayal in the heart of British intelligence
0–553–26778–7 Bantam pb $4.95

- **Robert Littell**
THE SISTERS
0–553–25831–1 Bantam pb $3.95

- **Robert Ludlum**
Ludlum's immensely popular novels are non-stop exercises in global paranoia at its most unfettered.
THE AQUITAINE PROGRESSION
0–553–26256–4 Bantam pb $5.95

THE BOURNE SUPREMACY
0–553–26322–6 Bantam pb $5.95

THE CHANCELLOR MANUSCRIPT
0–553–26094–4 Bantam pb $5.95

THE HOLCROFT COVENANT
0–553–26019–7 Bantam pb $4.95

THE ICARUS AGENDA
0–394–54397–1 Random House $19.95

THE MATARESE CIRCLE
0–553–25899–0 Bantam pb $5.95

THE OSTERMAN WEEKEND
0–553–26430–3 Bantam pb $5.95

THE PARSIFAL MOSAIC
0–553–25270–4 Bantam pb $4.95

THE RHINEMANN EXCHANGE
0–440–15079–5 Dell pb $4.95

THE SCARLATTI INHERITANCE
0–553–25856–7 Bantam pb $4.95

- **Gavin Lyall**
THE CONDUCT OF MAJOR MAXIM
Tough-minded adventure and espionage. "Like most British thriller writers who first published in the 1950s and 1960s," says Lyall, "I was heavily influenced by Hammett and Chandler"
0–14–009417–2 Penguin pb $3.50

THE CROCUS LIST
0–14–009616–7 Penguin pb $3.50

UNCLE TARGET
0–670–82228–0 Viking $16.95

- **Charles McCarry**
McCarry's Jamesian tales of the CIA have been compared to the work of le Carré.
THE BETTER ANGELS
0–449–24495–4 Fawcett pb $2.95

☞ **TO ORDER NEW BOOKS NOT YET LISTED, ASK YOUR BOOKSELLER OR CALL 1-800-882-8770**

THE LAST SUPPER
0–451–15124–0 NAL pb $3.95

THE SECRET LOVERS
0–451–13243–2 NAL pb $3.95

THE TEARS OF AUTUMN
Another angle on the Kennedy
assassination
0–451–13128–2 NAL pb $3.95

• Anthony Price
FOR THE GOOD OF THE STATE
0–445–40701–8 Mysterious pb $4.95

THE LABYRINTH MAKERS
0–445–40242–3 Mysterious pb $3.95

• Ross Thomas
Thomas' novels transcend the boundaries
of spy fiction with their odd blending of
farce, adventure, and all varieties of
domestic and international intrigue. For
sheer ingenuity of plotting, he is
unmatched.
BRIARPATCH
0–14–010581–6 Penguin pb $3.95

CHINAMAN'S CHANCE
0–445–40725–5 Mysterious pb $4.50

THE COLD WAR SWAP
Comically horrific tangles involving
reluctant or expendable spies and semi-
innocent bystanders; the novel that
introduced the McCorkle and Padillo
partnership
0–06–080834–9 Harper & Row pb $3.50

THE EIGHTH DWARF
0–445–40754–9 Mysterious pb $3.95

MISSIONARY STEW
0–14–010582–4 Penguin pb $3.95

THE MORDIDA MAN
0–425–11098–2 Berkley pb $3.95

OUT ON THE RIM
0–445–40693–3 Mysterious pb $4.95

• Trevanian
THE EIGER SANCTION
Wicked satire, nasty violence, and fine
climbing action: a CIA assassin's tricky
mission
0–345–31737–8 Ballantine pb $3.95

ABOUT SPY FICTION

• John Atkins
THE BRITISH SPY NOVEL
0–7145–4056–0 Riverrun pb $12.95

• Michael Denning
**COVER STORIES: Narrative and Ideology
in the British Spy Thriller**
0–7100–9642–9 RC&H pb $11.95

• Anthony Masters
LITERARY AGENTS: The Novelist as Spy
The real life espionage experiences of such
spy novelists as W. Somerset Maugham,
Graham Greene, John le Carré, and Len
Deighton
0–631–14979–1 Blackwell $19.95

True Crime

People have always been fascinated by
real-life stories of murder and other
crimes. Like mystery novels, books on true
crimes let the reader vicariously enter a
world of danger and intrigue made more
unsettling by the fact that these crimes are
often committed in the familiar landscapes
of everyday life.

CLASSIC CRIMINAL CASES

• Tom Callen
CRIPPEN: The Mild Murderer
The seemingly mild-mannered Dr. Crippen
was accused of dismembering his wife in
the London of 1910
0–14–010942–0 Penguin pb $6.95

• Jonathan Goodman
THE CRIPPEN FILE
News clippings and other memorabilia on
the Crippen case
0–8052–8244–0 Schocken pb $8.95

• P.D. James & T.A. Critchley
THE MAUL AND THE PEAR TREE
The story of the Ratcliffe Highway
murders, a series of crimes that shocked
London in the early 19th century
0–89296–152–X Mysterious $17.95
0–445–40562–7 Mysterious pb $3.95

• Stephen Knight
JACK THE RIPPER: The Final Solution
Knight theorizes that the Ripper killings
were the culmination of a top level coverup by the English government
0–89733–209–1 Academy Chicago pb $7.95

• Victoria Lincoln
**A PRIVATE DISGRACE: Lizzie Borden by
Daylight**
A look at the notorious 19th-century case
of a young woman accused of the ax
murder of her parents
0–930330–35–8 International Polygonics pb $5.95

• Joyce G. Williams & others
**LIZZIE BORDEN: A Case Book of Family
and Crime in the 1890s**
The Borden case continues to yield a
variety of conflicting interpretations
0–89917–302–0 TIS pb $9.95

MODERN CRIMINAL CASES

• David Abrahamsen
CONFESSIONS OF SON OF SAM
The story of David Berkowitz, who
terrorized New York as the "Son of Sam"
with a series of killings in the 1970s
0–231–05760–1 Columbia $22.50

• Shana Alexander
NUTCRACKER
The story of Frances Schreuder, the New
York balletomane whose manipulations

*Lizzie Borden at the time of the Borden mur-
ders (photo courtesy of the Fall River Historical Society)*

brought about the murder of her father by
her own son
0–440–16512–1 Dell pb $3.95

**VERY MUCH A LADY: The Untold Story
of Jean Harris & Dr. Herman Tarnower**
A sympathetic account of Jean Harris, the
prim schoolmistress imprisoned for killing
her lover, a prominent physician and
author
0–440–19270–6 Dell pb $4.95

• Susan Crain Bakos
APPOINTMENT FOR MURDER
The story of a respectable St. Louis dentist
who murdered seven people over a 20-year
period
0–399–13341–0 Putnam $18.95

• John Bryson
EVIL ANGELS
A fascinating account of the most
sensational criminal case in recent
Australian history: a woman accused of
killing her baby while vacationing at a
backwoods campground. The case inspired
the film *A Cry in the Dark,* starring Meryl
Streep
0–553–27207–1 Bantam pb $4.95

• Vincent Bugliosi & Curt Gentry
HELTER SKELTER
A harrowing account of the Manson
family's 1969 murder spree
0–553–27829–0 Bantam pb $4.95

• Vincent Bugliosi & Ken Hurwitz
TILL DEATH US DO PART
A story of murder with a backdrop of
singles bars and casual sex, written by
Charles Manson's prosecutor
0–553–27223–3 Bantam pb $4.95

• Truman Capote
IN COLD BLOOD
The now-classic "nonfiction novel" dealing
with the murder of a well-to-do

midwestern family and the subsequent trial of the murderers
0–394–43023–9 Random House $24.95
0–451–15446–0 NAL pb $4.95

• Teresa Carpenter
MISSING BEAUTY: A Story of Murder and Obsession
A fascinating account of a distinguished professor's obsession with a prostitute
0–393–02569–1 Norton $18.95

• Jonathan Coleman
AT MOTHER'S REQUEST
Another account of how New York socialite Frances Schreuder masterminded the murder of her father, one of the richest men in Utah, by her own son
0–671–61106–2 Pocket pb $4.50

• Joyce Eggington
FROM CRADLE TO GRAVE: The Short Lives and Strange Deaths of Marybeth Tinning's Nine Children
The chilling story of the mysterious deaths of Tinning's nine children, undetected until she was arrested for the murder of her ninth and last child
0–688–07566–5 Morrow $19.95

• Jim Fisher
THE LINDBERGH CASE
A new look at the Lindbergh kidnapping, the first book to include recently released evidence from the archives of the New Jersey state police
0–8135–1233–6 Rutgers $22.95

• James Fox
WHITE MISCHIEF: The Murder of Lord Erroll
Murder amid a set of decadent upper-class Englishmen in 1940s Kenya
0–394–75687–8 Random House pb $4.95

• Robert Seitz Frey & Nancy Thompson-Frey
THE SILENT AND THE DAMNED: The Murder of Mary Phagan and the Lynching of Leo Frank
The story of Leo Frank, who, after being falsely accused of murdering 13-year-old Mary Phagan, became the only Jew ever lynched in the United States
0–8191–6491–7 Madison $15.95

• Jonathan Goodman
THE SLAYING OF JOSEPH BOWNE ELWELL
A famous 1920 murder case analyzed and reconstructed in an attempt to find a solution
0–312–01513–5 St. Martin's $15.95

• Jean Harris
STRANGER IN TWO WORLDS
The convicted murderess tells her own story
0–8217–2112–7 Zebra pb $4.50

THEY ALWAYS CALL US LADIES: Stories from Prison
0–684–18963–1 Scribners $18.95

• John Hubner & Lindsey Gruson
MONKEY ON A STICK: The True Story of the Hare Krishna Murders
How an international religious cult turned to drug-running and violence
0–15–162086–5 HBJ $19.95

• Clifford Irving
DADDY'S GIRL: The Campbell Murder Case
The 1982 murders of a prominent Houston couple, a crime that culminated in "the most psychologically complex murder trial in Texas history"
0–671–61458–4 Summit $19.95

• Elizabeth Kendall
THE PHANTOM PRINCE: My Life with Ted Bundy
Life with the deceptively charming serial killer eventually executed in January 1989
0–914842–70–6 Madrona $10.95

• Sidney D. Kirkpatrick
A CAST OF KILLERS
Unearthing the story behind the murder of film director William Desmond Taylor in silent-era Hollywood
0–14–010086–5 Penguin pb $4.95

• Dena Kleiman
A DEADLY SILENCE: The Ordeal of Cheryl Pearson: A Case of Incest and Murder
0–87113–244–3 Atlantic Monthly $19.95

• Elliott Leyton
COMPULSIVE KILLERS: The Story of Modern Multiple Murder
A psychological study of multiple murderers
0–8147–5023–0 NYU $24.95

• John D. MacDonald
NO DEADLY DRUG
The murder trial of Dr. Carl Coppolino
0–449–12809–1 Fawcett pb $4.95

• Joe McGinnis
BLIND FAITH
How a New Jersey businessman plotted to murder his wife. "A harrowing portrait of the American dream misunderstood to the point of perversion"—*Washington Post*
0–399–13352–6 Putnam $21.95

FATAL VISION
The story of Dr. Jeffrey MacDonald, the former Green Beret accused of killing his pregnant wife and two children, a crime he still denies committing
0–451–14422–8 NAL pb $4.50

• Patrick Marcham
TRAIL OF HAVOC: In the Steps of Lord Lucan
The story of the English lord who disappeared under suspicion of attempting to murder his wife in London in the 1970s
0–670–81391–5 Viking $17.95

• Michael Mewshaw
MONEY TO BURN
The murder trial of Steven Benson, accused of killing his mother, millionaire tobacco heiress Margaret Benson, and her adopted son Scott
1–55817–060–X Pinnacle pb $4.50

• William Norris
THE MAN WHO FELL FROM THE SKY
An attempt to unravel the mystery behind the 1928 murder of tycoon Alfred Loewenstein
0–451–82187–4 Penguin pb $4.50

• Mary Phagan
THE MURDER OF LITTLE MARY PHAGAN
Another investigation of the Mary Phagan case, by a descendant of the victim's family
0–88282–039–7 New Horizon $18.95

• Natalie Robins & Steven M.L. Aronson
SAVAGE GRACE
"The true and harrowing story of an Upper East Side New York family, whose cultivation of taste, pursuit of social distinction, and fashionable expatriatism led its members to drugs, to apparent incest, to murder, and to suicide"—E.L. Doctorow
0–440–17576–3 Dell pb $4.95

• Thomas Thompson
SERPENTINE
The riveting account of a naive Canadian girl's involvement with a sociopathic international con man, and her subsequent life of crime and murder
0–440–17611–5 Dell pb $3.50

• Joseph Wambaugh
ECHOES IN THE DARKNESS
A reconstruction of the 1979 murder of a Pennsylvania schoolteacher, a bizarre crime involving other faculty members at the slain woman's high school
0–688–06889–8 Morrow $18.95
0–553–26932–1 Bantam pb $4.95

ORGANIZED CRIME

• Ralph Blumenthal
LAST DAYS OF THE SICILIANS: The New FBI at War with the Mafia
Recent attempts to crack down on the mob
0–8129–1594–1 Times Books $18.95

• Paul Eddy & others
THE COCAINE WARS
Investigation of the multibillion dollar cocaine cartel
0–393–02579–9 Norton $18.95

• Antoinette Giancana & Thomas C. Renner
MAFIA PRINCESS: Growing Up in Sam Giancana's Family
Memoirs by the daughter of a mob honcho
0–380–69849–8 Avon pb $4.50

• Guy Gugliotta & Jeff Leen
KINGS OF COCAINE
The story of Colombia's Medellín cocaine cartel, based on a *Miami Herald* series
0–671–64957–4 Simon & Schuster $18.95

➤ **FOR OVERSEAS ORDERING INFORMATION, SEE PAGE 1**

- Jenna W. Joselit
OUR GANG: Jewish Crime and the New York Jewish Community, 1900–1940
0–253–20314–7 Indiana pb $9.95

- Norman Lewis
HONOURED SOCIETY: The Sicilian Mafia Observed
The Sicilian roots of the Mafia
0–907871–80–1 Hippocrene pb $9.95

- James Mills
THE UNDERGROUND EMPIRE: Where Crime and Governments Embrace
The international drug-smuggling network and its links with national governments
0–440–19206–4 Dell pb $5.95

- Gene Mustain & Jerry Capeci
MOB STAR: The Story of John Gotti
Biography of the self-confessed crime king, the only Mafia boss to survive the recent Federal crackdown
0–531–15073–9 Franklin Watts $18.95

- Gerard O'Neill & Dick Lehr
THE UNDERBOSS: The Rise and Fall of a Mafia Family
How the FBI brought down the Angiulo crime family of Boston
0–312–02619–6 St. Martin's $17.95

- Nicholas Pileggi
WISEGUY: The Rise and Fall of a Mobster
0–671–63392–9 Pocket pb $4.50

- Joseph D. Pistone & Richard Woodley
DONNIE BRASCO: An FBI Agent Undercover in the Mafia
Eyewitness account of how the Mafia works, written by the most successful infiltrator of the mob in law enforcement history
0–453–00557–8 NAL $18.95

- Peter Reuter
DISORGANIZED CRIME: Illegal Markets and the Mafia
A study of the mob's penetration of such illegal activities as drug smuggling and pornography
0–262–68048–3 MIT pb $8.95

- Carl Sifakis
THE MAFIA ENCYCLOPEDIA
More than 400 entries covering everything known about the Mafia
0–8160–1856–1 Facts On File pb $17.95

- Gay Talese
HONOR THY FATHER
Acclaimed portrayal of the Bonanno Mafia dynasty
0–440–33468–3 Dell pb $4.95

THE POLICE

- Robert Daley
PRINCE OF THE CITY
The story of the New York City special investigations unit policeman who exposed corruption within his own department
0–425–09789–7 Berkley pb $3.95

- Marilyn Greene
FINDER: The True Story of a Private Investigator
A glimpse into the life of a contemporary private eye
0–517–56490–4 Crown $18.95

- George Rush
CONFESSIONS OF AN EX-SECRET SERVICE AGENT: The Marty Venker Story
1–55611–054–5 Donald I. Fine $17.95

- Bryna Taubman
LADY COP: True Stories of Policewomen in America's Toughest City
0–446–34684–5 Warner pb $3.95

- H. Richard Uviller
TEMPERED ZEAL: A Columbia Law Professor's Year on the Street with the New York City Police
An academic spends his sabbatical on the streets with members of the New York City Police Department
0–8092–4607–4 Contemporary $19.95

- Joseph Wambaugh
THE ONION FIELD
A gripping account of the aftermath of a cop killing
0–440–17350–7 Dell pb $4.95

GENERAL REFERENCE

- Daniel Cohen
THE ENCYCLOPEDIA OF UNSOLVED CRIMES
An exhaustive collection of famous unsolved mysteries
0–396–08944–5 Dodd, Mead $17.95

- Richard Glyn Jones, editor
THE MAMMOTH BOOK OF TRUE CRIME
Famous mystery writers examine unsolved crimes
0–88184–411–X Carroll & Graf pb $8.95

UNSOLVED!: Classic True Murder Cases
A collection of many of the most famous unsolved murders
0–87226–205–7 Peter Bedrick pb $7.95

- Phil & Karen McArdle
FATAL FASCINATION: Where Fact Meets Fiction in Police Work
A humorous contrast between the realities of police work and the treatment of police in fiction
0–395–46789–6 Houghton Mifflin pb $8.95

- John Mortimer, editor
FAMOUS TRIALS
Some of England's most engrossing murder trials, selected from the Penguin Famous Trials series
0–88029–080–3 Hippocrene $16.95
0–14–006924–0 Penguin pb $7.95

- Carl Sifakis
THE ENCYCLOPEDIA OF AMERICAN CRIME
Comprehensive listings on crime in the United States throughout its history
0–87196–620–4 Facts On File $49.95
0–87196–763–4 Facts On File pb $19.95

Espionage

▶ See also US Politics and Foreign Policy & The Second World War

OVERVIEWS

- Henry S. Becket
THE DICTIONARY OF ESPIONAGE: Spookspeak into English
A definition of over 2000 words used by covert organizations around the world
0–440–11955–3 Dell pb $3.95

- Philip Knightley
THE SECOND OLDEST PROFESSION: Spies and Spying in the 20th Century
A history and critique of modern espionage, in which such famous spies as Mata Hari and Kim Philby are examined
0–393–02386–9 Norton $19.95

- Ernest Volkman & Blaine Baggett
SECRET INTELLIGENCE: Espionage in a Democratic Society
A popular history of espionage
0–385–24590–4 Doubleday $19.95

ESPIONAGE TALES

- Patrick Beesly
VERY SPECIAL INTELLIGENCE
0–345–29798–9 Ballantine pb $2.95

- G. Brook-Sheperd
THE STORM PETRELS
0–345–30125–0 Ballantine pb $2.95

- Peter Calvacorlessi
TOP SECRET ULTRA
The story of Ultra, the greatest achievement in modern intelligence history, which enabled the British Secret Service to read wireless signals within the German High Command
0–345–30069–6 Ballantine pb $2.95

- Richard Deacon
KEMPEI TAI: A History of the Japanese Secret Service
A look at one of the world's most renowned security organizations, about which little has been written
0–8253–0131–9 Beaufort $14.95

- Stanley E. Hilton
HITLER'S SECRET WAR IN SOUTH AMERICA
German covert activity in South America during World War II
0–8071–0751–4 LSU $30.00

• H. Montgomery Hyde
THE ATOM BOMB SPIES
A study of the wave of espionage that
arose after the detonation of the first
atomic bomb
0–345–30028–9 Ballantine pb $2.95

• David C. Martin
A WILDERNESS OF MIRRORS
0–345–29636–2 Ballantine pb $2.95

• Lauran Paine
SILICON SPIES
0–312–00183–5 St. Martin's $14.95

• Vladimir Sakharov & Umberto Tosi
HIGH TREASON
0–345–29698–2 Ballantine pb $2.95

• Andrew Sinclair
**THE RED AND THE BLUE: A Study in
Treason and Intelligence**
0–316–79237–3 Little, Brown $17.95

• Stewart Steven
THE SPYMASTERS OF ISRAEL
An account of both the successes and
blunders of the Israeli intelligence network
0–345–29910–8 Ballantine pb $2.95

• Victor Suvurov
**INSIDE THE AQUARIUM: The Making
of a Top Soviet Spy**
A look at "the Aquarium" where the
Soviet Union trains its spies, written by
one of the Aquarium's graduates
0–425–09474–X Berkley pb $3.95

The KGB

▶ See also Russian and Soviet Studies

• John Barron
KGB
An exposé of the Soviet intelligence
network
0–553–23894–9 Bantam pb $5.50

• Brian Freemantle
KGB
Foreign espionage activities and
intelligence operations of the Russian
security police
0–03–071059–6 Henry Holt pb $6.95

• Jay Tuck
**HIGH-TECH ESPIONAGE: How the
KGB Smuggles NATO's Strategic Secrets to
Moscow**
0–312–37237–X St. Martin's $14.95

A Gallery of Spies

• Aline, Countess Romanones
**THE SPY WORE RED: My Adventures as
an Undercover Agent in World War II**
Memoirs of an American model who, in
1943, infiltrated the upper levels of
Spanish society in order to uncover links
with the Nazis
0–394–55665–8 Random House $18.95
1–55773–034–2 Berkley pb $4.95

• James Barros
**NO SENSE OF EVIL: The Espionage Case
of E. Herbert Norman**
A reconstruction of the Norman case using
previously suppressed information
0–8041–0183–3 Ballantine pb $3.95

• Wolf Blitzer
**TERRITORY OF LIES: The Exclusive
Story of Jonathan J. Pollard**
An account of how Pollard spied on the
U.S. for Israel, and how he was caught
0–06–015972–3 Harper & Row $22.50

• Howard Blum
**I PLEDGE ALLEGIANCE: The True Story
of an American Spy Family**
A fully documented study of the Walker
spy ring as well as a look at the Walker
family itself
0–317–63133–0 Simon & Schuster $17.95

• Anthony C. Brown
**C: The Rise and Fall of Sir Stewart Graham
Menzies, Spymaster to Winston Churchill**
A life of the wartime leader of British
intelligence, later undone by the Philby
scandals of the 1950s
0–317–62139–4 Macmillan $25.00

• Michael Kettle
**SIDNEY REILLY: The True Story of the
World's Greatest Spy**
The career of the British Secret Service's
most renowned spy, who disappeared in
Russia in 1925 under mysterious
circumstances
0–312–72338–5 St. Martin's $12.95

• Peter Maas
MANHUNT
The search for the renegade CIA agent
Edwin P. Wilson who supplied arms to
Libya
0–515–09014–X Berkley pb $3.95

• Anthony Masters
**THE MAN WHO WAS M: The Life of
Maxwell Knight**
The story of the British radio and
television naturalist, also a World War II
counterintelligence officer and the model
for Ian Fleming's "M"
0–631–13392–5 Blackwell $29.95

• Gordon W. Prange & D.M. Goldstein
**TARGET TOKYO: The Story of the Sorge
Spy Ring**
A look at Soviet spy Richard Sorge who
was tried and hanged by the Japanese in
1941
0–07–050678–7 McGraw-Hill pb $4.95

• Bernard Wasserstein
**THE SECRET LIVES OF TREBITSCH
LINCOLN**
0–300–04076–8 Yale $27.50

• David Wise
**THE SPY WHO GOT AWAY: The Inside
Story of Edward Lee Howard**
How and why a CIA agent defected to
Moscow
0–394–56281–X Random House $18.95

Blunt, Philby, Burgess, and Maclean

• Robert Cecil
**A DIVIDED LIFE: A Biography of Donald
Maclean**
0–688–08119–3 Morrow $18.95

• Philip Knightley
**THE MASTER SPY: The Story of Kim
Philby**
Based on an interview granted by Philby a
month before his death in May 1988
0–394–57890–2 Knopf $19.95

• Bruce Page & others
THE PHILBY CONSPIRACY
Story of the upper-class English radicals
who were recruited as Soviet agents
0–345–29726–1 Ballantine pb $3.95

• Barrie Penrose & Simon Freeman
**CONSPIRACY OF SILENCE: The Secret
Life of Anthony Blunt**
0–374–12885–5 Farrar, Straus & Giroux $22.95
0–679–72044–8 Random House pb $10.95

The Spycatcher Affair

• Chapman Pincher
THE SPYCATCHER AFFAIR
0–312–02290–5 St. Martin's $19.95

• Malcolm Turnbull
**THE SPYCATCHER TRIAL: The Scandal
Behind the #1 Best Seller**
A firsthand account by the lawyer who
won Peter Wright's case against the British
government's attempted suppression of
Spycatcher
0–88162–422–5 Salem House $18.95

• Peter Wright
**SPYCATCHER: The Candid
Autobiography of a Senior Intelligence
Officer**
The British government sought
unsuccessfully to suppress these memoirs
of a key figure in British intelligence
0–670–82055–5 Viking $19.95
0–440–20132–2 Dell pb $4.95

Science Fiction and Fantasy

Although Mary Shelley's *Frankenstein* was published in 1818, science fiction's full-scale development has occurred largely within a lifetime; indeed, some of the pioneers of the field remain active within it. But if science fiction's history has been brief, it has also been remarkably varied. In part this is because science fiction, like a volatile chemical, combines readily with other genres. Mysteries, detective stories, romances, adventures, experimental writing: the genre encompasses all of these. Science fiction has also become more complex and demanding as it has evolved. The technological and sociological concepts on which so much SF is based have grown increasingly complex, and SF writers these days tend to be more sophisticated stylists. The best of the current lot is a far cry from the simple-minded space operas of the pulp magazines.

A word on series, with which science fiction and fantasy are riddled. There are series built around charismatic characters and series devoted to worlds and futures in which any number of plots can be set. There has been a tendency toward ever-lengthier works, with an increasing number of trilogies and tetralogies that are really single works published in multiple volumes. In the lists below, these various multiplicities have been handled on a case-by-case basis. Generally, if the initial volume is complete in itself, sequels are noted without being specifically named.

EARLY SCIENCE FICTION

• Edwin A. Abbott
FLATLAND
A two-dimensional world
0–06–463573–2 Harper & Row pb $5.95

• Edgar Rice Burroughs
PELLUCIDAR NOVELS
Contains the first three installments of Burroughs' underground adventure series: *At the Earth's Core, Pellucidar,* and *Tanar of Pellucidar.* Burroughs' works retain a period charm, with their hairbreadth escapes on every other page
0–486–21051–0 Dover pb $5.95

A PRINCESS OF MARS
The first of a series of classic adventures on the red planet of Barsoom
0–345–33138–9 Ballantine pb $2.95

Karel Capek
WAR WITH THE NEWTS
An ecological fantasy with powerful political overtones, by the Czech author of *R.U.R.*
Introduction by Ivan Klima
0–8101–0663–9 Northwestern pb $9.95

• Arthur Conan Doyle
THE BEST SCIENCE FICTION OF ARTHUR CONAN DOYLE
Edited by Charles G. Waugh & Martin H. Greenberg
0–8093–1046–5 Southern Illinois $16.95

• William Hope Hodgson
THE HOUSE ON THE BORDERLAND
0–88184–018–1 Carroll & Graf pb $3.50

THE NIGHT LAND
An extraordinary and lengthy novel combining mysticism and adventure in a bizarre vision of the future
0–89968–179–4 Lightyear $12.95

• C.S. Lewis
Lewis' space trilogy, with its peculiar mix of theology and science, is unique in science fiction.
OUT OF THE SILENT PLANET
0–02–086910–X Macmillan pb $4.95

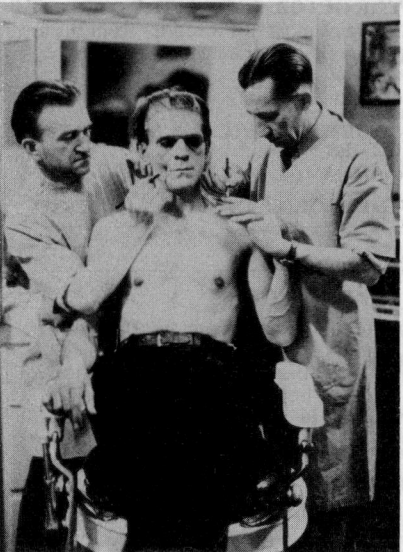

Boris Karloff being made up for "Frankenstein," from The Genius of the System *by Thomas Schatz (Pantheon/photo: The Museum of Modern Art)*

PERELANDRA
0–02–086950–9 Macmillan pb $3.95

THAT HIDEOUS STRENGTH
0–02–086960–6 Macmillan pb $4.50

• Mary Wollstonecraft Shelley
FRANKENSTEIN
The first major work of true science fiction, published in 1818
Edited by Maurice Hindle
0–14–043237–X Penguin pb $1.95

THE LAST MAN
An odd, variegated account of a worldwide plague
0–8032–5182–3 Nebraska pb $5.95

• Olaf Stapledon
LAST AND FIRST MEN & STAR MAKER
A staggering "future history" of mankind through the next two billion years and 18 species
0–486–21962–3 Dover pb $6.95

• Robert Louis Stevenson
DR. JEKYLL AND MR. HYDE & WEIR OF HERMISTON
Stevenson's great fantasy on the moral aspects of scientific progress. Also included is *Weir of Hermiston,* his final, unfinished novel of Scotland
0–19–281740–X Oxford pb $3.95

• Jules Verne
Verne's work is of enduring interest, more for its poetic fantasy and powerful symbolic subtexts than for the mechanical details of his predictions.
AROUND THE WORLD IN 80 DAYS
0–553–21145–5 Bantam pb $2.25

A JOURNEY TO THE CENTER OF THE EARTH
0–451–52343–1 NAL pb $3.50

THE MYSTERIOUS ISLAND
Nemo as *deus ex machina* in a drama of castaways
Edited by Isaac Asimov
0–451–52066–1 NAL pb $2.50

TWENTY THOUSAND LEAGUES UNDER THE SEA
Notable for the powerful archetypal figure of Captain Nemo
0–451–51849–7 NAL pb $2.50

H.G. Wells
SEVEN SCIENCE FICTION NOVELS OF H.G. WELLS
A comprehensive edition of Wells's greatest speculative works. Includes *The First Men in the Moon, The Island of Dr. Moreau, The War of the Worlds, The Invisible Man, The Time Machine, The Food of the Gods,* and *In the Days of the Comet*
0–486–20264–X Dover pb $15.00

THREE PROPHETIC SCIENCE-FICTION NOVELS OF H.G. WELLS
Includes *When the Sleeper Wakes, A Story of the Days to Come,* and *The Time Machine*
0–486–20605–X Dover pb $5.95

BEST SCIENCE FICTION STORIES
0–486–21531–8 Dover pb $4.95

THE DOOR IN THE WALL & OTHER STORIES
A facsimile of the 1911 edition, illustrated by beautiful Coburn photographs
0–87923–326–5 Godine $12.95
0–87923–327–3 Godine pb $6.95

THE INVISIBLE MAN
0–553–21353–9 Bantam pb $2.95

THE TIME MACHINE & THE INVISIBLE MAN
0–451–52238–9 NAL pb $3.95

THE WAR OF THE WORLDS
Afterword by Isaac Asimov
0–451–52276–1 NAL pb $2.50

THE GOLDEN AGE

The period around 1950 was the so-called Golden Age, when the genre was still mostly confined to magazines but was beginning to outgrow the mad scientists and bug-eyed monsters of the pulps. The editor John W. Campbell attracted a stable of brilliant young writers to his magazine *Astounding,* and for the first time the action-adventure and cosmic space operas of American SF were combined with the intelligent extrapolation typical of English writers like Wells and Stapledon. The primary idea, however, was to create worlds and futures founded on a broader base than speculative inventions.

• Poul Anderson
BRAIN WAVE
The intelligence of mankind and other mammals increases suddenly
0–345–32521–4 Ballantine pb $2.50

H.G. Wells, from Miguel Covarrubias Caricatures *by Beverly Cox and Denna Anderson* (Smithsonian)

• Isaac Asimov
THE END OF ETERNITY
Contact and trade between different eras of history
0–345–33655–0 Ballantine pb $3.50

FOUNDATION
The first installment of Asimov's five-part epic of a galactic empire
0–345–33627–5 Ballantine pb $3.95

FOUNDATION AND EMPIRE
0–345–33628–3 Ballantine pb $3.95

SECOND FOUNDATION
0–345–33629–1 Ballantine pb $3.95

FOUNDATION'S EDGE
0–345–30898–0 Ballantine pb $4.95

FOUNDATION AND EARTH
0–345–33996–7 Ballantine pb $4.95

PRELUDE TO FOUNDATION
A "prequel" to the Foundation cycle
0–553–27839–8 Bantam pb $4.95

• Alfred Bester
THE STARS MY DESTINATION
A stunning precursor to much modern SF
0–531–15050–X Franklin Watts $15.95

• Leigh Brackett
THE LONG TOMORROW
Postwar America dominated by fundamentalist survivors
0–345–32926–0 Ballantine pb $2.95

• Ray Bradbury
Bradbury's early novels and stories were key works in the evolution of science fiction.
FAHRENHEIT 451
A future where all books are outlawed
0–345–34296–8 Ballantine pb $3.95

THE ILLUSTRATED MAN
0–553–25483–9 Bantam pb $3.50

THE MARTIAN CHRONICLES
0–553–27822–3 Bantam pb $3.95

THE OCTOBER COUNTRY
Contains most of the stories from his first, very good, very rare collection, *Dark Carnival*
0–345–32448–X Ballantine pb $2.95

SOMETHING WICKED THIS WAY COMES
0–394–53041–1 Knopf $18.95

THE STORIES OF RAY BRADBURY
0–394–51335–5 Knopf $25.00

Arthur C. Clarke
There is no greater master of fiction based on highly complex scientific theories than Clarke. The theoretical basis of his stories is always clear but never gets in the way of his plots.
CHILDHOOD'S END
Clarke's most famous future apart from *2001*, and another next step for man
0–345–34795–1 Ballantine pb $3.95

THE CITY AND THE STARS
A complex and fascinating novel of an advanced telepathic civilization
0–451–14822–3 NAL pb $3.50

THE FOUNTAINS OF PARADISE
0–345–25356–6 Ballantine pb $2.50

RENDEZVOUS WITH RAMA
A guided tour of a gigantic alien ship on a flythrough of our system
0–345–00663–1 Ballantine pb $3.50

THE SONGS OF DISTANT EARTH
A gentle portrait of a human colony on a distant world
0–345–32240–1 Ballantine pb $4.95

2001: A Space Odyssey
0–451–15580–7 NAL pb $3.95

2010: Odyssey Two
0–345–30306–7 Ballantine pb $4.95

2061: Odyssey Three
0–345–35879–1 Ballantine pb $4.95

• L. Sprague De Camp
ROGUE QUEEN
A humanoid matriarchal culture akin to that of bees
0–312–94396–2 Bluejay pb $7.95

• Gordon R. Dickson
DORSAI
0–441–16025–5 Berkley pb $3.50

• Robert A. Heinlein
CITIZEN OF THE GALAXY
Published as a juvenile, but among his best
0–345–32098–0 Ballantine pb $2.50

GLORY ROAD
An amusing sci-fi takeoff on epic fantasy
0–441–29401–4 Berkley pb $3.95

THE GREEN HILLS OF EARTH
0–671–65608–2 Pocket pb $3.50

THE MOON IS A HARSH MISTRESS
Revolt in a lunar colony
0–441–53699–0 Berkley pb $4.95

STRANGER IN A STRANGE LAND
This novel of an alien culture given to "grokking" became a hippie favorite of the 1960s
0–441–79034–8 Berkley pb $4.95

• Henry Kuttner
THE STARTLING WORLDS OF HENRY KUTTNER
Three short novels from the magazine *Startling Stories*
0–445–20328–5 Warner pb $3.95

• Walter M. Miller, Jr.
A CANTICLE FOR LEIBOWITZ
Hugo winner: a widely read dystopia of a postnuclear world
0–553–27381–7 Bantam pb $4.50

• C.L. Moore
DOOMSDAY MORNING
Future America dominated by the communications industry
0–445–20462–1 Warner pb $3.50

• H. Beam Piper
SPACE VIKING
An interstellar Viking culture. Piper often applied to the future the notion of history repeating itself
0–441–77784–8 Berkley pb $2.95

• Eric F. Russell
SINISTER BARRIER
Contemporary humanity is really the property of aliens
0–345–32760–8 Ballantine pb $2.95

• James Schmitz
THE WITCHES OF KARRES
0–441–89450–X Berkley pb $2.95

• Clifford Simak
ALL FLESH IS GRASS
Simak specializes in creating future societies deriving from present-day social trends
0–380–39933–4 Avon pb $3.50

SPECIAL DELIVERANCE
A whacko novel about temporal refugees
0–345–29140–9 Ballantine pb $2.95

WAY STATION
0–345–33246–6 Ballantine pb $2.95

• Cordwainer Smith
THE INSTRUMENTALITY OF MANKIND
Introduction by Frederik Pohl
0–345–32301–7 Ballantine pb $2.95

NORSTRILIA
0–345–32300–9 Ballantine pb $2.95

QUEST OF THE THREE WORLDS
0–345–32931–7 Ballantine pb $2.95

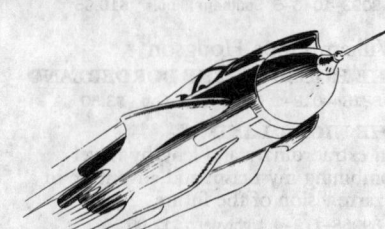

A rocket drawn by Alex Raymond, the creator of Flash Gordon

  IF YOU CAN'T FIND IT, LOOK IN THE INDEX

- **E.E. Smith**
  THE SKYLARK OF SPACE
  First of a tetralogy: the epitome of "space opera"
  0–425–08636–4 Berkley pb $2.95

- **Theodore Sturgeon**
  THE DREAMING JEWELS
  Sturgeon was a preeminent stylist among 1950s science-fiction writers
  0–88184–351–2 Carroll & Graf pb $3.95

  MORE THAN HUMAN
  A mutant humanity—a "gestalt" personality of multiple individuals
  0–345–32721–7 Ballantine pb $3.50

  William Tenn
  OF MEN AND MONSTERS
  On an earth ruled by giant aliens, people learn to function as household pests
  0–345–29523–4 Ballantine pb $2.50

- **A.E. Van Vogt**
  SLAN
  A totalitarian future where telepaths are persecuted
  0–89190–454–9 Amereon $13.95

- **John Wyndham**
  DAY OF THE TRIFFIDS
  Intelligent plants invade Earth, in a novel in the spirit of Wells
  0–345–32817–5 Ballantine pb $2.95

  THE MIDWICH CUCKOOS
  Women of an English village are impregnated by aliens: the basis for the movie *Village of the Damned*
  0–345–28821–1 Ballantine pb $1.95

CONTEMPORARY SCIENCE FICTION

Most of the science fiction being read today was written in the last 20 years. During the 1960s the genre grew phenomenally in quality, quantity, and popularity, and the results have been extraordinarily diverse. The various "streams" of contemporary SF range from the society-building of Ursula K. Le Guin through the hallucinatory dreams of Philip K. Dick to the high-tech extrapolations of Larry Niven—not to mention those who, like the polymath Samuel R. Delany, combine all these tendencies.

Sociological Extrapolations

Some authors use sociology as the basic science for extrapolation, creating future human societies with changed cultures and genetics. Ursula K. Le Guin set the standard with her landmark novel *The Left Hand of Darkness*.

- **Brian Aldiss**
  HELLICONIA SPRING
  The first volume of a trilogy that suggests what sort of culture would evolve on a world whose seasons lasted for millennia
  0–425–08895–2 Berkley pb $3.95

  HELLICONIA SUMMER
  0–425–08650–X Berkley pb $3.95

  HELLICONIA WINTER
  0–425–08994–0 Berkley pb $6.95

- **John Brunner**
  THE CRUCIBLE OF TIME
  0–345–30235–4 Ballantine pb $4.95

  STAND ON ZANZIBAR
  A Hugo winner
  0–345–28845–9 Ballantine pb $2.50

- **Orson Scott Card**
  SONGMASTER
  0–8125–3255–4 Tor pb $3.95

- **C.J. Cherryh**
  CUCKOO'S EGG
  A human raised by aliens
  0–88677–083–1 NAL pb $3.50

  DOWNBELOW STATION
  A complicated spacegoing society with genetically engineered humans
  0–88677–227–3 NAL pb $3.95

- **Ursula K. Le Guin**
  ALWAYS COMING HOME
  An anthropological study of a future culture
  0–553–26280–7 Bantam pb $4.95

  THE DISPOSSESSED
  A complex study of political conflict in the future
  0–06–012563–2 Harper & Row $11.95

  THE LEFT HAND OF DARKNESS
  In this Hugo and Nebula winner, Le Guin hypothesizes a hermaphroditic society and says some pertinent things about sexism along the way
  0–441–47812–3 Berkley pb $3.95

- **Vonda N. McIntyre**
  SUPERLUMINAL
  Romance and adventure among spacefaring pilots
  0–671–60060–5 Pocket pb $3.50

- **Pamela Sargent**
  VENUS OF DREAMS
  A study of those involved in the terraforming of Venus
  0–553–27058–3 Bantam pb $3.95

Hi-Tech

This traditional vein of SF—the story based on hard science, usually revolving around the solution of a scientific puzzle—has become steadily more complex.

- **Poul Anderson**
  ORION SHALL RISE
  0–671–82842–8 Pocket pb $3.95

Illustration of alien creatures of light by Virgil Finlay

- **Gregory Benford**
  Benford devotes much narrative space to the laboratory and those who work in it.
  AGAINST INFINITY
  0–671–45901–5 Pocket pb $3.50

  ARTIFACT
  Two antimatter black holes are loose in the earth's interior
  0–8125–3178–7 Tor pb $4.50

  TIMESCAPE
  A novel built around a complex theory of time travel involving the behavior of tachyons. The theoretical physics presents a considerable challenge to the reader
  0–671–50632–3 Pocket pb $3.95

- **Hal Clement**
  Clement was the main exponent of the high-tech vein back in the 1940s and has successfully extended his work along those lines.
  STILL RIVER
  An expedition charts a strange world with some surprises
  0–345–32916–3 Ballantine $16.95

- **James P. Hogan**
  THE TWO FACES OF TOMORROW
  0–345–32387–4 Ballantine pb $2.95

  VOYAGE FROM YESTERYEAR
  0–345–34246–1 Ballantine pb $3.95

- Donald Moffit

THE GENESIS QUEST
An alien race recreates humanity after its demise
0–345–32474–9 Ballantine pb $3.50

SECOND GENESIS
A sequel to *Genesis Quest*
0–345–33804–9 Ballantine pb $3.50

- Larry Niven

Niven has a flair for outrageous ideas neatly supported by science.

THE INTEGRAL TREES
Posits a colony of gigantic trees that exist in deep space, creating an environment in which other living things can exist: a world without a world, as it were
0–345–32065–4 Ballantine pb $3.95

RINGWORLD
0–345–33392–6 Ballantine pb $4.50

THE SMOKE RING
0–345–30257–5 Ballantine pb $4.50

High Style

Twenty-five years ago the idea of science fiction with literary merit would have met with derision. Writers and readers had traditionally valued concept over style; if the ideas were good, minimal skill in presenting them was acceptable. But since then the level of writing in the genre has risen astonishingly, and many of its practitioners have achieved wide critical recognition.

- J.G. Ballard

Ballard started out as one of the British end-of-civilization novelists and is now recognized as a major writer.

THE BEST SHORT STORIES OF J.G. BALLARD
0–671–61451–7 Pocket pb $4.95

THE CRYSTAL WORLD
Strange jewels threaten to petrify the planet
0–374–52096–8 Farrar, Straus & Giroux pb $7.95

THE DAY OF CREATION
An apparently miraculous river emerges in Africa
0–374–13527–4 Farrar, Straus & Giroux $17.95

THE DROWNED WORLD
The end of civilization, along lines suggested by the title
0–88184–324–5 Carroll & Graf pb $3.95

HIGH RISE
0–88184–400–4 Carroll & Graf pb $3.50

THE TERMINAL BEACH
0–88184–370–9 Carroll & Graf pb $3.50

VERMILION SANDS
0–88184–422–5 Carroll & Graf pb $3.95

- Samuel R. Delany

DHALGREN
A complex novel of a postnuclear world
0–553–25391–3 Bantam pb $4.95

Philip K. Dick
Dick's hip, hallucinogenic novels have achieved cult status since his death in 1982.

BLADE RUNNER
Source of the Ridley Scott film, originally published as *Do Androids Dream of Electric Sheep?*
0–345–30129–3 Ballantine pb $2.95

THE MAN IN THE HIGH CASTLE
A Hugo winner
0–4415–1809–5 Berkley pb $2.95

MARTIAN TIME-SLIP
0–345–34444–8 Ballantine pb $2.95

TIME OUT OF JOINT
0–88184–352–0 Carroll & Graf pb $3.95

THE TRANSMIGRATION OF TIMOTHY ARCHER
0–671–46751–4 Pocket pb $2.95

THE ZAP GUN
0–312–94488–8 St. Martin's pb $7.95

- Thomas M. Disch

CAMP CONCENTRATION
0–88184–386–5 Carroll & Graf pb $3.95

- Stanislaw Lem

THE CYBERIAD: Fables for the Cybernetic Age
Robots roam the cosmos creating beasts and machines
Translated by Michael Kandel
0–15–623550–1 HBJ pb $5.95

SOLARIS
A Polish masterpiece: planet as intelligent organism
0–15–683750–1 HBJ pb $4.95

THE STAR DIARIES
Satirical encounters with civilizations and creatures of deep space
Translated by Michael Kandel
0–15–684905–4 HBJ pb $4.95

- Joanna Russ

THE FEMALE MAN
0–8070–6313–4 Harper & Row pb $7.95

"Look, Flash, our own beloved world!"
Drawing by Alex Raymond

- Gene Wolfe

These four novels constitute the "Book of the New Sun" series, a surrealistic vision of a distant future, described in prose as baroque as the concepts described.

THE SHADOW OF THE TORTURER
0–671–54066–1 Pocket pb $3.50

THE CLAW OF THE CONCILIATOR
0–671–47425–1 Pocket pb $2.95

THE SWORD OF THE LICTOR
0–671–49945–9 Pocket pb $3.50

THE CITADEL OF THE AUTARCH
0–671–49666–2 Pocket pb $3.50

Further Variations

- Brian Aldiss

HOTHOUSE
A surrealist future dominated by the plant world
0–671–55930–3 Pocket pb $2.95

- Piers Anthony

MACROSCOPE
0–380–00209–4 Avon pb $4.50

- Michael Bishop

ANCIENT OF DAYS
0–8125–3197–3 Tor pb $3.95

Algis Budrys
WHO?
Thoughtful cold-war espionage involving a bionic man
0–445–20314–5 Warner pb $3.50

- Orson Scott Card

ENDER'S GAME
0–8125–3355–8 Tor pb $3.95

- Richard Cowper

THE ROAD TO CORLAY
The first of a series
0–671–61213–1 Pocket pb $2.95

- M.J. Engh

ARSLAN
Mideastern military genius conquers the United States
0–87795–884–X Morrow $17.95

- Philip José Farmer

TO YOUR SCATTERED BODIES GO
The first of the "Riverworld" series. A Hugo winner
0–441–82069–7 Berkley pb $3.95

DAYWORLD
A future with room enough only for one day a week per person
0–441–14001–7 Berkley pb $3.95

Jack Finney
TIME AND AGAIN
Wonderfully researched time travel back to New York City in 1880
0–671–24295–4 Simon & Schuster pb $9.95

TO ORDER BOOKS AS GIFTS, SEE PAGE 1

- Leo A. Frankowski
  THE CROSS-TIME ENGINEER
  A modern man in medieval Poland
  0–345–32762–4 Ballantine pb $2.95

- David Gerrold
  THE MAN WHO FOLDED HIMSELF
  A man's relationships with himself at
  different points in time
  0–88411–191–1 Amereon $16.95

  A MATTER FOR MEN
  0–553–27782–0 Bantam pb $4.50

- Ron Goulart
  GALAXY JANE
  A mad romp about the future filming of a
  space opera
  0–425–08684–4 Berkley pb $3.50

- Joe Haldeman
  THE FOREVER WAR
  0–345–32489–7 Ballantine pb $2.95

- Harry Harrison
  THE STAINLESS STEEL RAT
  The first of a satirical series about a future
  anti-hero
  0–441–77924–7 Berkley pb $2.95

  WEST OF EDEN
  An alternate past: mankind against
  intelligent dinosaurs
  0–553–26551–2 Bantam pb $4.50

- Frank Herbert
  DUNE
  The first volume of an enormously
  successful series about an interstellar
  empire
  0–441–17266–0 Berkley pb $4.95

  DUNE MESSIAH
  0–425–07901–5 Berkley pb $7.95

- Sterling E. Lanier
  HIERO'S JOURNEY
  The first part of an unfinished trilogy
  0–345–30841–7 Ballantine pb $3.50

- Keith Laumer
  DINOSAUR BEACH
  0–671–65581–7 Pocket pb $2.95

- Tanith Lee
  DON'T BITE THE SUN
  A fine example of SF humor
  1–55742–044–0 Starmont House $19.95

- Edward Llewellyn
  SALVAGE AND DESTROY
  0–88677–009–2 NAL pb $2.95

- Elizabeth A. Lynn
  THE SARDONYX NET
  A sexually perverse future
  0–425–08635–6 Berkley pb $3.50

- George R. Martin
  TUF VOYAGING
  The varied adventures of an interstellar
  entrepreneur
  0–671–65624–4 Pocket pb $3.50

Julian May
May's four-volume "Saga of Pleistocene
Exile" incorporates time travel, space
travel, alien cultures, telepathy, psi
powers, and the birth of the
Mediterranean in a grand potpourri of
SF themes.
THE MANY-COLORED LAND
0–345–32444–7 Ballantine pb $4.95

THE GOLDEN TORC
0–345–32419–6 Ballantine pb $4.95

THE NONBORN KING
0–345–31421–2 Ballantine pb $3.50

THE ADVERSARY
0–345–31422–0 Ballantine pb $3.50

- Anne McCaffrey
  DRAGONFLIGHT
  The first of a series involving benign aliens
  0–345–33546–5 Ballantine pb $3.95

- Michael Moorcock
  THE CORNELIUS CHRONICLES
  0–380–70255–X Avon pb $3.50

- Larry Niven & Jerry Pournelle
  FOOTFALL
  Invading aliens launch an asteroid at Earth
  0–345–32344–0 Ballantine pb $4.95

  THE MOTE IN GOD'S EYE
  Warfare with an alien race
  0–671–49175–X Pocket pb $3.95

Illustration by Kolliker from a 1942 issue of
"Astounding Science Fiction"

Mercurian salamanders drawn by Virgil
Finlay

- Frederik Pohl
  GATEWAY
  A Nebula winner
  0–345–34690–4 Ballantine pb $3.95

- Jerry Pournelle
  JANISSARIES
  Future mercenaries
  0–441–38291–6 Berkley pb $3.95

- Fred Saberhagen
  BERSERKER
  The first of a series
  0–441–05495–1 Berkley pb $2.95

- Robert Silverberg
  LORD VALENTINE'S CASTLE
  The first volume of the "Majipoor" trilogy,
  a sci-fi saga with fairy-tale trappings
  0–553–27436–8 Bantam pb $4.50

- Norman Spinrad
  BUG JACK BARRON
  0–425–09321–2 Berkley pb $2.95

  THE VOID CAPTAIN'S TALE
  0–671–43483–7 Simon & Schuster $13.95

- James Tiptree, Jr.
  BRIGHTNESS FALLS FROM THE AIR
  A weekend house-party murder mystery on
  another planet
  0–8125–5625–9 Tor pb $3.50

- John Varley
  MILLENNIUM
  0–425–08991–6 Berkley pb $2.95

- James White
  SECTOR GENERAL
  The first of a series based on future
  medical science
  0–345–34627–0 Ballantine pb $2.95

- M.K. Wren
  SHADOW OF THE SWAN
  0–425–09092–2 Berkley pb $3.50

New Writers

If SF's youngest writers have one common
trait, it might be pessimism; the futures they
invent are rarely pleasant ones. A fashionable
label for some recent work—especially that
of William Gibson—is "cyberpunk," a mode

---

characterized by futures featuring direct input into and manipulation of the human mind through electronics and computers.

- **Jim Aikin**
  WALK THE MOONS ROAD
  0–345–32169–3 Ballantine pb $2.95

- **A.A. Attanasio**
  RADIX
  0–553–25406–5 Bantam pb $3.95

- **Greg Bear**
  EON
  Piles outrageous concept on outrageous concept until it reaches epic proportions
  0–812–53159–0 Tor pb $3.95

- **James P. Blaylock**
  HOMONCULUS
  A mad pastiche of 19th-century experimental science
  0–441–34258–2 Berkley pb $2.95

- **David Brin**
  Brin writes novels as speedy and cosmic as the old pulp space operas, but with a modern sensibility and a good deal more content.
  THE POSTMAN
  A sensitive study of the revival of civilization after a nuclear war
  0–553–27874–6 Bantam pb $4.50

  STARTIDE RISING
  0–553–27418–X Bantam pb $4.50

  THE UPLIFT WAR
  Related to *Startide Rising*, although not a sequel
  0–553–27971–8 Bantam pb $4.95

- **Mary Gentle**
  GOLDEN WITCHBREED
  Adventures of a human envoy to a complex alien culture
  0–451–15848–2 NAL pb $4.50

  William Gibson
  COUNT ZERO
  0–441–11773–2 Berkley pb $3.50

  MONA LISA OVERDRIVE
  0–553–05250–0 Bantam $17.95

  NEUROMANCER
  A Hugo and Nebula winner. "State of the art"—*Washington Post*
  0–441–56959–5 Berkley pb $3.95

- **Richard Grant**
  RUMORS OF SPRING
  An ecologically disastrous future related in a giddy style that can be described as neo-Firbank
  0–553–34369–6 Bantam pb $9.95

- **Gwenyth Jones**
  DIVINE ENDURANCE
  Indonesian-flavored postnuclear culture
  0–87795–856–4 Arbor House $15.95

- **Loren MacGregor**
  THE NET
  0–441–56941–2 Berkley pb $2.95

- **Jack McDevitt**
  THE HERCULES TEXT
  0–441–37367–4 Berkley pb $3.50

- **Kim S. Robinson**
  ICEHENGE
  0–441–35854–3 Berkley pb $2.95

  THE PLANET ON THE TABLE
  0–8125–5237–7 Tor pb $3.50

- **Lucius Shepard**
  GREEN EYES
  0–441–30274–2 Berkley pb $2.95

- **Bruce Sterling, editor**
  MIRRORSHADES: The Cyberpunk Anthology
  0–87795–868–8 Arbor House $17.95

- **Michael Swanwick**
  IN THE DRIFT
  Postnuclear-war Philadelphia
  0–441–37072–1 Berkley pb $2.95

- **Howard Waldrop**
  THEM BONES
  0–441–80557–4 Berkley pb $2.95

FANTASY

Fantasy encompasses allegory, surrealism, erotica, fairy tales, science fiction, and almost anything else its creators can dream up. One flourishing subgenre—variously characterized as "pure fantasy," "sword and sorcery," and "high fantasy"—owes much to J.R.R. Tolkien's Middle Earth chronicles, with their elaborately detailed, adult-oriented depiction of a world of working magic and mythical creatures.

- **Poul Anderson**
  THE BROKEN SWORD
  A superb fantasy of an elfin changeling, drawing its inspiration from Norse and Teutonic mythology
  0–671–65382–2 Pocket pb $2.95

  THREE HEARTS AND THREE LIONS
  0–441–80822–0 Berkley pb $2.50

- **Peter S. Beagle**
  THE LAST UNICORN
  Odd, fey odyssey of the last of the species
  0–345–35367–6 Ballantine pb $3.95

- **Marion Zimmer Bradley**
  THE MISTS OF AVALON
  The Arthurian saga from the viewpoint of the women in the legends
  0–345–35049–9 Ballantine pb $10.95

- **C.J. Cherryh**
  THE DREAMSTONE
  An evocation of the fairy folk of Ireland
  0–88677–013–0 DAW pb $2.95

- **L. Sprague De Camp & Fletcher Pratt**
  THE COMPLEAT ENCHANTER
  Adventures in alternate worlds based on *The Faerie Queen,* Norse mythology, and other sources
  0–671–69809–5 Pocket pb $4.50

- **Stephen R. Donaldson**
  THE CHRONICLES OF THOMAS COVENANT
  A fantasy world unusually dark in mood
  0–345–31328–3 Ballantine (boxed set) $23.95

  Volume 1: Lord Foul's Bane
  0–345–34865–6 Ballantine pb $4.95

  Volume 2: The Illearth War
  0–345–31415–8 Ballantine pb $7.95

  Volume 3: The Power That Preserves
  0–345–31416–6 Ballantine pb $7.95

- **David Eddings**
  PAWN OF PROPHECY
  First of "The Belgariad," a series of five novels
  0–345–00684–4 Ballantine pb $3.95

- **Jane Gaskell**
  THE SERPENT
  The first book in the raunchy and sophisticated "Atlan Saga"
  0–87997–990–9 DAW pb $2.95

  H. Rider Haggard
  SHE, KING SOLOMON'S MINES & ALLAN QUARTERMAIN
  She, an 1887 mystical fantasy about an immortal woman in a lost African city, remains fascinating. The other two novels included are more earthbound but are still entertaining
  0–486–20643–2 Dover pb $7.95

  AYESHA: The Return of She
  A Himalayan reincarnation of She-Who-Must-Be-Obeyed
  0–486–23649–8 Dover pb $4.95

- **Barbara Hambly**
  THE TIME OF THE DARK
  0–345–31965–6 Ballantine pb $3.50

- **Robert Holdstock**
  MYTHAGO WOOD
  A World Fantasy Award winner
  0–425–08785–9 Berkley pb $2.95

- **Robert E. Howard**
  CONAN
  The quintessential sword-and-sorcery pulp hero
  0–441–11481–4 Berkley pb $2.95

- **Barry Hughart**
  BRIDGE OF BIRDS
  A World Fantasy Award winner: elegant and amusing chinoiserie
  0–345–32138–3 Ballantine pb $2.95

- **Diana W. Jones**
  ARCHER'S GOON
  0–441–02892–6 Ace pb $2.95

  HOWL'S MOVING CASTLE
  0–688–06233–4 Morrow $10.50

☞ **TO ORDER NEW BOOKS NOT YET LISTED, ASK YOUR BOOKSELLER OR CALL 1-800-882-8770**

SCIENCE FICTION AND FANTASY

"The Ghost Story," a Victorian print from The Delights of Reading *by Otto Bettmann* (Godine)

- Michael Moorcock
ELRIC OF MELNIBONE
The first of a complex series
0–441–20398–1 Berkley pb $2.95

GLORIANA, OR THE UNFULFILLED QUEEN: Being a Romance
Mad and raunchy adventures in an alternate Elizabethan Age
0–445–20862–7 Warner pb $4.95

Mervyn Peake
THE GORMENGHAST TRILOGY
An extraordinary mix of the Gothic and the Dickensian
Introduction by Anthony Burgess
0–87951–144–3 Viking $25.00

- Tim Powers
THE DRAWING OF THE DARK
A fantasy taking place at the Turkish siege of Vienna
0–345–35008–1 Ballantine pb $2.95

- Rosemary Sutcliff
SWORD AT SUNSET
An Arthurian fantasy
0–8125–8852–5 Tor pb $4.50

J.R.R. Tolkien
THE HOBBIT
Prelude to *The Lord of the Rings*
0–345–33968–1 Ballantine pb $4.95

THE FELLOWSHIP OF THE RING
The first of the *Lord of the Rings* trilogy
0–345–33970–3 Ballantine pb $4.95

THE TWO TOWERS
0–345–33971–1 Ballantine pb $4.95

THE RETURN OF THE KING
0–345–33973–8 Ballantine pb $4.95

- Jack Vance
LYONESSE
0–441–50530–9 Berkley pb $3.95

- T.H. White
MISTRESS MASHAM'S REPOSE
Descendants of the Lilliputians on an English estate
0–425–07312–2 Berkley pb $2.95

THE ONCE AND FUTURE KING
The widely popular and influential Arthurian retelling
0–425–09116–3 Berkley pb $4.95

"The Hall at Bag-End, Residence of B. Baggins, Esquire," J.R.R. Tolkien's illustration from The Hobbit (Houghton Mifflin)

- Guy G. Kay
THE SUMMER TREE
The first of a series
0–425–09294–1 Berkley pb $3.50

- Katherine Kurtz
DERYNI RISING
The first of an ongoing series
0–345–34763–3 Ballantine pb $3.95

- Fritz Leiber
SWORDS AND DEVILTRY
The first of a six-volume series
0–441–79191–3 Berkley pb $2.95

- Elizabeth A. Lynn
WATCHTOWER
The first of a trilogy
0–425–08660–7 Berkley pb $2.95

THE DANCERS OF ARUN
0–425–08952–5 Berkley pb $2.95

THE NORTHERN GIRL
0–425–09308–5 Berkley pb $3.50

- Charlotte Macleod
CURSE OF THE GIANT HOGWEED
One of the rare hybrids of fantasy and mystery novel
0–380–70051–4 Avon pb $2.95

- Patricia A. McKillip
McKillip's "Riddle-Master" novels are on a smaller scale than many works in the genre: they might be described as "chamber fantasies."
HARPIST IN THE WIND
0–345–32440–4 Ballantine pb $3.50

HEIR OF SEA AND FIRE
0–345–28882–3 Ballantine pb $2.50

THE RIDDLE-MASTER OF HED
0–345–28881–5 Ballantine pb $2.50

- Robin McKinley
BEAUTY
0–671–60434–1 Pocket pb $2.95

★ FOR COMPLETE ORDERING INFORMATION, SEE PAGE 1

- Tappan Wright
ISLANDIA
A realistic fantasy about an emergent nation and culture in the context of early 20th-century world politics
0–452–25635–6 NAL pb $12.95

- Roger Zelazny
NINE PRINCES IN AMBER
First of the "Amber" series
0–380–01430–0 Avon pb $3.50

SUPERNATURAL FANTASY AND HORROR

- Clive Barker
THE BOOKS OF BLOOD
Stories by a writer praised for the originality of his horrific visions
0–399–13343–7 Putnam $19.95

WEAVEWORLD
Barker's first novel
0–671–64839–X Poseidon $19.95

- Algernon Blackwood
BEST GHOST STORIES OF ALGERNON BLACKWOOD
The best of Blackwood's classic tales, such as *The Willows,* can still frighten
0–486–22977–7 Dover pb $6.95

M.R. James
GHOST STORIES OF AN ANTIQUARY
Contains such classics as *Casting the Runes,* by the master of the traditional English ghost story
0–486–22758–8 Dover pb $3.95

MORE GHOST STORIES OF AN ANTIQUARY
0–486–25700–2 Dover pb $4.95

- Stephen King
CARRIE
0–385–08695–4 Doubleday $16.95
0–451–15071–6 NAL pb $3.95

CHRISTINE
0–670–22026–4 Viking $16.95
0–451–16044–4 NAL pb $4.95

CUJO
0–670–45193–2 Viking $17.95
0–451–16135–1 NAL pb $4.95

THE DEAD ZONE
0–670–26077–0 Viking $17.95
0–451–15575–0 NAL pb $4.95

FIRESTARTER
0–670–31541–9 Viking $17.95
0–451–15031–7 NAL pb $4.50

IT
0–670–81302–8 Viking $22.95
0–451–15927–6 NAL pb $5.95

SALEM'S LOT
0–385–00751–5 Doubleday $19.95
0–451–15065–1 NAL pb $4.50

MISERY
0–670–81364–8 Viking $18.95
0–451–15355–3 NAL pb $4.95

PET SEMATARY
0–451–15775–3 NAL pb $4.95

NIGHT SHIFT
0–385–12991–2 Doubleday $17.95
0–451–16045–2 NAL pb $4.95

THE SHINING
0–451–16091–6 NAL pb $4.95

THE STAND
0–385–12168–7 Doubleday $19.95
0–451–16095–9 NAL pb $5.95

THE TOMMYKNOCKERS
0–399–13314–3 Putnam $19.95

- T.E. Klein
THE CEREMONIES
0–553–27296–9 Bantam pb $4.95

- Dean Koontz
PHANTOMS
0–425–10145–2 Berkley pb $4.95

TWILIGHT EYES
0–425–10065–0 Berkley pb $4.95

WATCHERS
0–425–11203–9 Berkley pb $4.95

- Joseph Sheridan Le Fanu
BEST GHOST STORIES
0–486–20415–4 Dover pb $7.95

GHOST STORIES AND MYSTERIES
0–486–20715–3 Dover pb $6.95

- Fritz Leiber
CONJURE WIFE
This famous novel of witchcraft on campus has been filmed many times
0–441–11749–X Berkley pb $2.95

OUR LADY OF DARKNESS
A World Fantasy Award winner
0–441–64417–1 Berkley pb $2.50

H.P. Lovecraft
Lovecraft's stories are still quite hair-raising, despite, or perhaps because of, their unrestrained purple prose.
THE BEST OF H.P. LOVECRAFT
0–345–35080–4 Ballantine pb $7.95

AT THE MOUNTAINS OF MADNESS & OTHER TALES OF TERROR
0–345–32945–7 Ballantine pb $3.50

THE CASE OF CHARLES DEXTER WARD
Necromancy in New England: one of Lovecraft's most coherent and frightening works
0–345–35490–7 Ballantine pb $2.95

THE DOOM THAT CAME TO SARNATH
0–345–33105–2 Ballantine pb $3.95

THE LURKING FEAR & OTHER STORIES
0–345–32604–0 Ballantine pb $2.95

- Arthur Machen
THE HILL OF DREAMS
0–486–24994–8 Dover pb $5.95

- Richard Matheson
HELL HOUSE
0–446–32624–0 Warner pb $2.95

- Anne Rice
INTERVIEW WITH THE VAMPIRE
A compulsively readable biography of a long-lived drinker of blood
0–345–33766–2 Ballantine pb $4.95

THE VAMPIRE LESTAT
The sequel to *Interview*
0–345–31386–0 Ballantine pb $4.95

THE QUEEN OF THE DAMNED
The third of Rice's best-selling vampire chronicles
0–394–55823–5 Knopf $18.95

- Bram Stoker
DRACULA
0–14–035048–9 Penguin pb $2.50

- Peter Straub
FLOATING DRAGON
0–425–09725–0 Berkley pb $4.50

SHADOWLAND
0–425–09726–9 Berkley pb $4.95

- James Tiptree, Jr.
TALES OF THE QUINTANA ROO
Illustrated by Glennray Tutor
0–87054–152–8 Arkham House $11.95

Bela Lugosi in the 1931 movie of Bram Stoker's Dracula *(photo: Movie Star News)*

➤ **FOR OVERSEAS ORDERING INFORMATION, SEE PAGE 1**

- Jack Williamson
  DARKER THAN YOU THINK
  A vampire novel with a wonderfully
  downbeat ending
  0–312–94079–3 Bluejay pb $8.95

- Chelsea Q. Yarbro
  HOTEL TRANSYLVANIA
  The first of a series
  0–8125–5850–2 Tor pb $3.95

Anthologies

- Everett F. Bleiler, editor
  **A TREASURY OF VICTORIAN GHOST
  STORIES**
  0–684–17823–0 Scribners pb $7.95

  FIVE VICTORIAN GHOST NOVELS
  Includes Riddell's *The Uninhabited House*,
  Meinhold's *The Amber Witch*, Edwards'
  Monsieur Maurice, Lee's *The Phantom
  Lover*, and Beale's *The Ghost of Guir House*
  0–486–22558–5 Dover pb $6.50

- Bennett Cerf, editor
  FAMOUS GHOST STORIES
  0–394–70140–2 Random House pb $4.95

- Richard Dalby, editor
  VICTORIAN GHOST STORIES
  0–88184–473–X Carroll & Graf $18.95

- Alberto Manguel, editor
  **BLACK WATER: The Book of Fantastic
  Literature**
  A magnificent collection of stories to elicit
  both fear and wonder; the authors include
  Max Beerbohm, Jean Cocteau, Ray
  Bradbury, Isak Dinesen, and many others
  0–517–55269–8 Clarkson Potter pb $13.95

HISTORY AND CRITICISM

- Brian Aldiss & David Wingrove
  THE TRILLION YEAR SPREE
  An opinionated but thorough and
  intelligent history by a longtime reader and
  writer of SF
  0–689–11839–2 Atheneum $24.95

- Dougal Dixon
  AFTER MAN: A Zoology of the Future
  This spectacularly illustrated "speculative
  nonfiction" extrapolates on the evolution
  of the earth's animals after the
  disappearance of humanity
  0–312–01162–8 St. Martin's pb $10.95

- Stephen King
  DANSE MACABRE
  A jaunt through horror fiction and films
  0–425–10433–8 Berkley pb $4.95

- Ursula K. Le Guin
  THE LANGUAGE OF THE NIGHT
  0–425–07668–7 Berkley pb $5.95

  Stanislaw Lem
  **MICROWORLDS: Writings on Science
  Fiction and Fantasy**
  0–15–659443–9 HBJ pb $5.95

- H.P. Lovecraft
  **SUPERNATURAL HORROR IN
  LITERATURE**
  An idiosyncratic survey of the supernatural
  up to the 1920s
  0–486–20105–8 Dover pb $3.50

- Michael Moorcock
  FANTASY: The 100 Best Books
  0–88184–335–0 Carroll & Graf $15.95

- Alexei Panshin
  HEINLEIN IN DIMENSION
  Heinlein's writing career through 1969
  Introduction by James Blish
  0–911682–01–5 Advent $10.00
  0–911682–12–0 Advent pb $6.00

- David Pringle
  SCIENCE FICTION: The 100 Best Novels
  An inevitably subjective selection, weighted
  on the side of literary merit
  Foreword by Michael Moorcock
  0–88184–346–6 Carroll & Graf pb $7.95

- Donald H. Tuck
  **ENCYCLOPEDIA OF SCIENCE
  FICTION AND FANTASY**
  A three-volume set
  0–911682–27–9 Advent (set) $85.00

Westerns

CLASSIC WESTERN WRITERS

> It was now the Virginian's turn to bet, or
> leave the game, and he did not speak at
> once.
>   Therefore Trampas spoke. "Your bet,
> you son-of-a–."
>   The Virginian's pistol came out, and
> his hand lay on the table, holding it
> unaimed. And with a voice as gentle as
> ever, the voice that sounded almost like a
> caress, but drawling a very little more
> than usual, so that there was almost a
> space between each word, he issued his
> orders to the man Trampas:—"When you
> call me that, *smile!*"
>
> Owen Wister
> **THE VIRGINIAN**
> 0–14–039065–0 Penguin pb $4.95

- Elliot Arnold
  BLOOD BROTHER
  0–8032–5901–8 Nebraska pb $9.95

- Thomas Berger
  LITTLE BIG MAN
  0–440–34976–1 Dell pb $5.95

- Leigh Brackett
  FOLLOW THE FREE WIND
  0–345–29008–9 Ballantine pb $1.95

- Max Brand
  DESTRY RIDES AGAIN
  0–671–83660–9 Pocket pb $2.50

- W.R. Burnett
  BITTER GROUND
  0–345–34733–1 Ballantine pb $2.50

- Walter Van Tilburg Clark
  THE OX-BOW INCIDENT
  The classic novel of a lynching
  0–451–52239–7 NAL pb $3.50

- Clay Fisher
  THE TALL MEN
  0–553–27644–1 Bantam pb $2.95

- Steve Frazee
  **THE BEST WESTERN STORIES OF
  STEVE FRAZEE**
  Edited by Bill Pronzini & Martin H. Greenberg
  0–8093–1174–7 Southern Illinois $16.95

- Zane Grey
  CODE OF THE WEST
  0–671–50654–4 Pocket pb $2.95

  RIDERS OF THE PURPLE SAGE
  0–671–52766–5 Pocket pb $3.50

  STRANGER FROM THE TONTO
  0–671–45018–2 Pocket pb $2.50

  UNDER THE TONTO RIM
  0–671–60499–6 Pocket pb $2.95

  WESTERN UNION
  0–671–83537–8 Pocket pb $2.50

  WILD HORSE MESA
  0–671–83588–2 Pocket pb $2.95

- Frank Gruber
  THE LONE GUN HAWK
  0–451–15612–9 NAL pb $2.95

- A.B. Guthrie, Jr.
  THE BIG SKY
  Fur traders blaze a trail along the Missouri
  0–395–07762–1 Houghton Mifflin $13.95
  0–553–26683–7 Bantam pb $4.50

- Ernest Haycox
  CANYON PASSAGE
  0–451–11782–4 NAL pb $2.50

- Dorothy M. Johnson
  **THE HANGING TREE & OTHER
  STORIES**
  0–345–32855–8 Ballantine pb $2.50

  A MAN CALLED HORSE
  Eleven stories, including *The Man Who
  Shot Liberty Valance*. "To read her stories is
  to know: this is the way life was lived in
  frontier settlement and in Indian village.
  This is part of the American heritage"—
  Jack Schaefer
  0–345–29069–0 Ballantine pb $1.95

- Elmer Kelton
  THE DAY THE COWBOYS QUIT
  0–87565–053–8 Texas Christian $19.50
  0–87565–054–6 Texas Christian pb $10.95

  THE GOOD OLD BOYS
  0–912646–96–9 Texas Christian $16.95
  0–912646–97–7 Texas Christian pb $9.95

  LLANO RIVER
  0–553–27119–9 Bantam pb $2.95

Alan Ladd in the 1953 movie of Shane *by Jack Schaefer (photo: Movie Star News)*

THE TIME IT NEVER RAINED
0–912646–91–8 Texas Christian $16.95
0–912646–89–6 Texas Christian pb $9.95

THE WOLF AND THE BUFFALO
0–87565–058–9 Texas Christian $17.95
0–87565–059–7 Texas Christian pb $10.95

- **Louis L'Amour**
L'Amour was a legendary figure among western writers, enduringly popular and tremendously prolific. The following are only a few of his many novels.

THE BURNING HILLS
0–553–28210–7 Bantam pb $3.50

DOWN THE LONG HILLS
0–553–24904–5 Bantam pb $2.95

DUTCHMAN'S FLAT
0–553–26188–6 Bantam pb $2.95

THE HAUNTED MESA
Supernatural elements play a part in this story about the Anasazi of the prehistoric Southwest
0–553–05182–2 Bantam $18.95
0–553–27022–2 Bantam pb $4.50

HIGH LONESOME
0–553–25972–5 Bantam pb $2.95

HONDO
0–553–28090–2 Bantam pb $3.50

JUBAL SACKETT
0–553–25673–4 Bantam pb $3.95

LAST STAND AT PAPAGO WELLS
0–553–25807–9 Bantam pb $3.50

LONIGAN
0–553–27536–4 Bantam pb $3.50

RIDE THE DARK TRAIL
0–553–25512–6 Bantam pb $2.95

THE TALL STRANGER
0–553–25876–1 Bantam pb $2.95

- **Tom Lea**
THE WONDERFUL COUNTRY
0–89096–185–9 Texas A&M $15.95

- **Alan LeMay**
THE SEARCHERS
The source for John Ford's classic film
0–515–09229–0 Berkley pb $3.50

- **Frederick Manfred**
CONQUERING HORSE
0–8032–8119–6 Nebraska pb $8.95

KING OF SPADES
0–8032–8121–8 Nebraska pb $7.95

LORD GRIZZLY
"Held me spellbound from beginning to end. I have never in a lifetime of reading about our West met with anything like it"—William Carlos Williams
0–8032–8118–8 Nebraska pb $7.95

RIDERS OF JUDGEMENT
0–8032–8117–X Nebraska pb $6.95

LLANO RIVER
0–553–27119–9 Bantam pb $2.95

- **Nelson Nye**
LONG RUN
0–515–0957–3 Jove pb $2.95

- **Wayne D. Overholser**
THE BEST WESTERN STORIES OF WAYNE D. OVERHOLSER
Edited by Bill Pronzini & Martin H. Greenberg
0–8093–1145–3 Southern Illinois $16.95

RETURN OF THE KID
0–7701–0623–4 Paper Jacks pb $2.95

- **Lewis B. Patten**
THE BEST WESTERN STORIES OF LEWIS B. PATTEN
Edited by Bill Pronzini & Martin H, Greenberg
0–8093–1358–8 Southern Illinois $18.95

- **Charles Portis**
TRUE GRIT
0–451–16002–3 NAL pb $3.95

- **Eugene Manlove Rhodes**
THE BEST NOVELS AND STORIES OF EUGENE MANLOVE RHODES
Edited by Frank V. Dearing
0–8032–3885–1 Nebraska $35.00
0–8032–8928–6 Nebraska pb $12.95

BRANSFORD IN ARCADIA: Or, The Little Eohippus
0–8061–1261–1 Oklahoma $11.95

THE PROUD SHERIFF
0–8061–1426–6 Oklahoma pb $5.95

- **Conrad Richter**
THE SEA OF GRASS
0–394–44397–7 Knopf $13.95
0–345–31778–5 Ballantine pb $3.50

- **Jack Schaefer**
MONTE WALSH
0–8032–4124–0 Nebraska $31.00
0–8032–9121–3 Nebraska pb $7.50

SHANE
0–395–07090–2 Houghton Mifflin $13.95
0–553–27110–5 Bantam pb $2.95

- **Luke Short**
THE MARSHAL OF VENGEANCE
1–55547–254–0 Critics' Choice pb $2.95

- **Owen Wister**
THE VIRGINIAN
0–14–039065–0 Penguin pb $4.95

He was clean-shaven and his face was lean and hard and burned from high forehead to firm, tapering chin. His eyes seemed hooded in the shadow of the hat's brim. He came closer, and I could see that this was because the brows were drawn in a frown of fixed and habitual alertness. Beneath them the eyes were endlessly searching from side to side and forward, checking off every item in view, missing nothing. As I noticed this, a sudden chill, I could not have told why, struck through me there in the warm and open sun.

Jack Schaefer
SHANE
0–553–27110–5 Bantam pb $2.95

CONTEMPORARIES

- Matt Braun
RIO HONDO
0-451-14955-6 NAL pb $3.50

WINDWARD WEST
0-451-14701-4 NAL pb $3.50

- Lou Cameron
THE SPIRIT HORSES
0-441-77809-7 Berkley pb $2.50

- Benjamin Capps
THE TRAIL TO OGALLALA
0-87565-012-0 Texas Christian $16.95
0-87565-013-9 Texas Christian pb $9.95

SAM CHANCE
0-87074-250-7 Southern Methodist $22.50
0-87074-251-5 Southern Methodist pb $10.95

- Dan Cushman
RUSTY IRONS
0-345-32697-0 Ballantine pb $2.50

STAY AWAY, JOE
0-911436-01-4 Stay Away $14.95

- William Decker
THE HOLDOUTS
0-671-42081-X Pocket pb $2.95

- Pete Dexter
DEADWOOD
0-14-009910-7 Penguin pb $4.95

- Loren D. Estleman
BLOODY SEASON
"Estleman's account of events following the O.K. Corral gunfight is the best one I've ever read, by far . . . It's so real you can even smell the horses!"—Elmore Leonard
0-553-05231-4 Bantam $15.95

GUN MAN
0-449-12862-8 Fawcett pb $2.50

MURDOCK'S LAW
0-671-44951-6 Pocket pb $2.95

THE STRANGLERS
0-449-12848-2 Fawcett pb $2.50

Richard Arlen and Gary Cooper in the 1929 screen version of Owen Wister's The Virginian *(photo: Movie Star News)*

"The Earp brothers are businessmen, kid, not penny-dreadful heroes. We've owned saloons in every town from Ellsworth to Tombstone. It may not be heroics but it makes a profit, which is a thing that can be hard to come by in a country that gets dumped on its butt by financial panics every other year and a half, wiped out by blizzards and droughts and a crash in the price of silver. It's all accounting, kid, whether you're a rancher or a hard-rock miner or a saloonkeeper. So you had better get a lot of notions out of your head before you go around begging for somebody to give you a gun you can strap on. A gun's just a tool you use when you haven't got a more profitable way to settle your quarrels."

Brian Garfield
SLIPHAMMER
0-553-26855-4 Bantam pb $2.95

- Brian Garfield
ARIZONA
0-345-33572-4 Ballantine pb $2.50

BUGLE AND SPUR
0-345-33026-9 Ballantine pb $2.50

SLIPHAMMER
Wyatt Earp and his brothers, seen with a disenchanted eye
0-553-26855-4 Bantam pb $2.95

VULTURES IN THE SUN
0-553-26331-5 Bantam pb $2.95

- Elmore Leonard
Before he became one of America's most widely read suspense writers, Leonard was an outstanding western novelist. In either genre his books are unparalleled for their narrative tension and realistic dialogue.
THE BOUNTY HUNTERS
0-553-27099-0 Bantam pb $2.95

ESCAPE FROM FIVE SHADOWS
0-553-27202-0 Bantam pb $2.95

FORTY LASHES LESS ONE
0-553-27625-5 Bantam pb $2.95

GUNSIGHTS
0-553-27337-X Bantam pb $2.95

HOMBRE
0-345-33030-7 Ballantine pb $2.95

LAST STAND AT SABER RIVER
0-553-27097-4 Bantam pb $2.95

THE LAW AT RANDADO
0-553-27201-2 Bantam pb $2.95

VALDEZ IS COMING
0-553-27098-2 Bantam pb $2.95

Three more strides—that was it.

The five came around with weapons in their hands, Sundeen hollering something, and his two men on the ends fell dead in the first sudden explosion from the wall, before they were full around, Bren Early and Moon with revolvers extended, aiming, firing at the scattering, snap-shooting line, Bren holding both the big .44 Russians out in front of him and moving his head right and left to look down the barrels and fire; Moon holding the Greener low against its hard buck and letting go a Double-O charge at a half-kneeling figure and seeing the man's arm fly up with the big-bore report, swinging the Greener on Sundeen and raking his boots with a charge as Sundeen stumbled and Bren Early fired, shooting his hat off, firing again and seeing the man let go of his revolvers and grab his face with both hands as he sank to the ground.

They went over the wall and walked out to where the five lay without moving.

Elmore Leonard
GUNSIGHTS
0-553-27337-X Bantam pb $2.95

- Giles Lutz
THE BLACK DAY
0-441-06682-8 Berkley pb $2.50

- Larry McMurtry
ANYTHING FOR BILLY
McMurtry takes on Billy the Kid
0–671–64268–5 Simon & Schuster $18.95

LONESOME DOVE
A long and constantly absorbing western saga, full of humor and incident
0–671–50420–7 Simon & Schuster $19.95
0–671–62461–X Pocket pb $5.95

- T.V. Olsen
BLOOD RAGE
0–449–13052–5 Fawcett pb $2.50

BRAND OF THE STAR
0–449–13081–9 Fawcett pb $2.50

BREAK THE YOUNG LAND
0–380–75290–5 Avon pb $2.95

THE MAN FROM NOWHERE
0–380–75293–X Avon pb $2.95

SAVAGE SIERRA
0–449–13082–7 Fawcett pb $2.95

- Frank Roderus
LEAVING KANSAS
0–345–32511–7 Ballantine pb $2.50

- Harry Whittington
CHARRO!
0–380–70732–2 Avon pb $2.75

Historical and Romantic Fiction

- Jean M. Auel
The timeless realities of love and war recur in the story of a primitive tribe's struggle for survival in the Ice Age.
THE CLAN OF THE CAVE BEAR
0–517–54202–1 Crown $18.95
0–553–25042–6 Bantam pb $4.95

THE MAMMOTH HUNTERS
0–553–28094–5 Bantam pb $5.50

THE VALLEY OF HORSES
0–517–54489–X Crown $18.95
0–553–25053–1 Bantam pb $4.95

- Maria Bellonci
PRIVATE RENAISSANCE
A fictionalized life of Isabella d'Este who ruled a Renaissance cultural center
Translated by William Weaver
0–688–08188–6 Morrow $24.95

Marion Zimmer Bradley
Adept at every form of light entertainment from science fiction to fantasy romance, Bradley turns to the ancient myths of the fall of Troy and the legends of Arthurian Britain.
THE FIREBRAND
0–671–64177–8 Simon & Schuster $19.95

THE MISTS OF AVALON
0–394–52406–3 Knopf $16.95
0–345–35049–9 Ballantine pb $10.95

- Gillian Bradshaw
THE BEARKEEPER'S DAUGHTER
Byzantine intrigue at the court of Justinian and his powerful and seductive empress, Theodora, who started life as a street performer
0–395–43620–6 Houghton Mifflin $18.95

IMPERIAL PURPLE
A silk weaver is thrust into peril by a request to prepare a purple robe for an imperial usurper
0–395–43635–4 Houghton Mifflin $18.95

- Dee Brown
CONSPIRACY OF KNAVES
The adventures of a traveling theater group during the Civil War
0–14–010602–2 Penguin pb $4.95

SHOWDOWN AT LITTLE BIG HORN
A novel that draws on Brown's expertise in 19th-century Indian lore to retell the story of Custer
0–440–20202–7 Dell pb $2.95

- Bryher
THE COIN OF CARTHAGE
0–15–618407–9 HBJ pb $4.95

- Taylor Caldwell
These love stories do not all have a historical setting, but they explore the larger world of politics and business and are filled with sharp psychological observation.
THE BALANCE WHEEL
0–515–08083–7 Jove pb $4.50

BRIGHT FLOWS THE RIVER
0–449–20655–6 Fawcett pb $5.95

CAPTAINS AND THE KINGS
0–449–20562–2 Fawcett pb $3.95

THE DEVIL'S ADVOCATE
0–515–07864–6 Jove pb $3.50

DIALOGUES WITH THE DEVIL
0–449–21508–3 Fawcett pb $3.50

THE EAGLES GATHER
0–515–07868–9 Jove pb $3.50

THE EARTH IS THE LORD'S
0–515–08111–6 Jove pb $4.50

MELISSA
0–515–07882–4 Jove pb $3.95

TENDER VICTORY
0–446–31404–8 Warner pb $4.95

TESTIMONY OF TWO MEN
0–449–20572–X Fawcett pb $4.95

THIS SIDE OF INNOCENCE
0–446–31248–7 Warner pb $3.95

THE TURNBULLS
0–515–08044–6 Jove pb $4.50

WICKED ANGEL
0–449–23950–0 Fawcett pb $1.95

- Taylor Caldwell & Jess Stearn
I, JUDAS
0–451–13295–5 NAL pb $3.95

THE ROMANCE OF ATLANTIS
0–449–23787–7 Fawcett pb $2.95

- James Clavell
East and West clash in settings ranging from the Tokugawa expulsion of westerners in the 17th century to Japanese expansionism and Iranian revolution in the 20th.
KING RAT
0–440–14546–5 Dell pb $4.95

NOBLE HOUSE
0–385–28737–2 Delacorte $22.95
0–440–16484–2 Dell pb $5.95

SHOGUN
0–385–29224–4 Delacorte $21.95
0–440–17800–2 Dell pb $5.95

TAI-PAN
0–385–29218–X Delacorte $19.95
0–440–18462–2 Dell pb $4.95

WHIRLWIND
0–380–70312–2 Avon pb $5.95

- Eleanor Cooney & David Altieri
THE COURT OF THE LION: A Novel of the Tang Dynasty
0–87795–902–1 Morrow $19.95

- Janet Dailey
CALDER BORN, CALDER BRED
0–671–63786–X Pocket pb $4.50

THE HEIRESS
0–449–13436–9 Fawcett pb $4.95

THE RIVALS
0–316–17140–9 Little, Brown $18.95

- Peter Danielson
His *Children of the Lion* series, about a homeless race at the time of Joseph and the pharaohs that becomes involved in the internal political and religious struggles of Egypt, draws on the colorful evidence of archaeology.
CHILDREN OF THE LION
0–553–26912–7 Bantam pb $4.50

THE GOLDEN PHARAOH
0–553–26885–6 Bantam pb $4.50

LION IN EGYPT
0–553–26594–6 Bantam pb $4.50

LORD OF THE NILE
0–553–27187–3 Bantam pb $4.50

THE PROPHECY
0–553–26325–0 Bantam pb $4.50

THE SHEPHERD KINGS
0–553–26971–2 Bantam pb $4.50

SWORD OF GLORY
0–553–26800–7 Bantam pb $4.50

VENGEANCE OF THE LION
0–553–26769–8 Bantam pb $4.50

- Dorothy Dunnett
Two series—two periods. The Lymond Chronicles follow the adventures of a young Englishman in the 16th-century wars of religion in France. The Niccolò series describes the exploits of a young Florentine merchant of the 15th century.

The Lymond Chronicles

THE GAME OF KINGS
0–446–31459–5 Warner pb $5.95

QUEENS PLAY
0–446–31288–6 Warner pb $3.95

THE DISORDERLY KNIGHTS
0–446–31290–8 Warner pb $3.95

PAWN IN FRANKENCENSE
0–446–31294–0 Warner pb $3.95

THE RINGED CASTLE
0–446–31296–7 Warner pb $4.95

CHECKMATE
0–446–31301–7 Warner pb $4.95

The Niccolò Series

THE SPRING OF THE RAM
0–394–56437–5 Knopf $19.95

NICCOLO RISING
0–440–20072–5 Dell pb $4.95

KING HEREAFTER
0–394–52378–4 Knopf $16.95

• Peter Beresford Ellis
THE RISING OF THE MOON
A strange tale of the invasion of Canada in 1866 by a band of Union officers of Irish-American descent
0–312–00676–4 St. Martin's $19.95

• Thomas Flanagan
Historical expertise went into the creation of these stories of the French invasion of Ireland in the 18th century (*The Year of the French*), and the long and savage political struggles of the 19th century from the Act of Union to Parnell (*The Tenants of Time*).
THE TENANTS OF TIME
0–525–24606–1 Dutton $22.95

THE YEAR OF THE FRENCH
0–03–044591–4 Holt $12.95
0–671–66974–5 Pocket pb $5.95

• C.S. Forester
The Napoleonic Wars were a duel between a tiger and a shark. France dominated the Continent, but Hornblower's exciting shipboard adventures show why Britain ruled the waves.
ADMIRAL HORNBLOWER IN THE WEST INDIES
0–316–28901–9 Little, Brown $17.95

BEAT TO QUARTERS
0–316–28932–9 Little, Brown pb $7.95

COMMODORE HORNBLOWER
0–316–28894–2 Little, Brown $14.95

HORNBLOWER AND THE ATROPOS
0–316–28911–6 Little, Brown $14.95
0–316–28929–9 Little, Brown pb $7.95

HORNBLOWER AND THE HOTSPUR
0–316–28899–3 Little, Brown $14.95
0–316–28928–0 Little, Brown pb $7.95

HORNBLOWER DURING THE CRISIS
0–316–28915–9 Little, Brown $17.95

LIEUTENANT HORNBLOWER
0–316–28907–8 Little, Brown $16.95

LORD HORNBLOWER
0–316–28908–6 Little, Brown $17.95

MR. MIDSHIPMAN HORNBLOWER
0–316–28909–4 Little, Brown $15.95
0–316–28912–4 Little, Brown pb $7.95

SHIP OF THE LINE
0–316–28936–1 Little, Brown pb $7.95

• Robert Graves
Graves combines stunning powers of characterization and storytelling with deep historical knowledge of such diverse areas as mythical Greece, classical Rome, Byzantium, and colonial America.
CLAUDIUS THE GOD
0–394–60812–7 Modern Library $8.95
0–394–72537–9 Random House pb $4.95

COUNT BELISARIUS
0–374–51739–8 Farrar, Straus & Giroux pb $12.95

HERCULES, MY SHIPMATE
0–374–51677–4 Farrar, Straus & Giroux pb $9.95

HOMER'S DAUGHTER
0–89733–059–5 Academy Chicago pb $8.95

I, CLAUDIUS
0–394–60811–9 Modern Library $8.95
0–394–72536–0 Random House pb $5.95

KING JESUS
0–374–18114–4 Farrar, Straus & Giroux $20.00
0–374–51664–2 Farrar, Straus & Giroux pb $6.95

SERGEANT LAMB'S AMERICA
0–89733–213–X Academy Chicago pb $7.95

WIFE TO MR. MILTON
0–14–001024–6 Penguin pb $6.95

• Marek Halter
THE BOOK OF ABRAHAM
Translated by Lowell Bair
0–440–10841–1 Dell pb $4.95

• Georgette Heyer
In these lively and witty romances of the Regency period, feisty country ladies overcome their town rivals and bring to heel the brightest beau.
APRIL LADY
0–425–10529–6 Berkley pb $2.95

ARABELLA
0–425–10523–7 Berkley pb $2.95

BATH TANGLE
0–425–10791–4 Berkley pb $3.50

CHARITY GIRL
0–451–15242–5 NAL pb $2.95

THE GRAND SOPHY
0–425–10528–8 Berkley pb $3.50

THE MASQUERADERS
0–449–23253–0 Fawcett pb $2.50

THE NONESUCH
0–449–23716–8 Fawcett pb $2.50

SPRIG MUSLIN
0–425–10718–3 Berkley pb $2.95

THESE OLD SHADES
0–451–15135–6 NAL pb $2.95
0–449–24000–2 Fawcett pb $1.95

THE TOLL GATE
0–425–10847–3 Berkley pb $3.50

THE UNKNOWN AJAX
0–515–07253–2 Berkley $2.95

VENITA
0–425–10719–1 Berkley pb $3.50

• Ruth B. Hill
HANTA YO: An American Saga
A detailed and deeply moving novel of Indian life before the arrival of the white man
0–446–97857–4 Warner pb $8.95

• Cecilia Holland
THE LORDS OF VAUMARTIN
The adventures of a French nobleman after the disastrous defeat of Crécy
0–395–48828–1 Houghton Mifflin $18.95

• Victoria Holt
The historical settings of Holt's romances range from Elizabethan times to the fall of Marie Antoinette and to the Gothic aspects of Victorian England.
THE CURSE OF THE KINGS
0–449–20951–2 Fawcett pb $3.50

THE DEMON LOVER
0–449–20098–1 Fawcett pb $3.95

THE INDIA FAN
0–385–24600–5 Doubleday $18.95

KING OF THE CASTLE
0–449–20033–7 Fawcett pb $3.95

THE LANDOWER LEGACY
0–449–20727–7 Fawcett pb $4.50

LEGEND OF THE SEVENTH VIRGIN
0–449–21123–1 Fawcett pb $3.95

LORD OF THE FAR ISLAND
0–449–21183–5 Fawcett pb $3.95

THE MASK OF THE ENCHANTRESS
0–449–21084–7 Fawcett pb $3.95

MENFREYA IN THE MORNING
0–449–20107–4 Fawcett pb $2.95

MISTRESS OF MELLYN
0–449–23924–1 Fawcett pb $3.95

MY ENEMY THE QUEEN
0–449–20239–9 Fawcett pb $3.95

THE ROAD TO PARADISE ISLAND
0–449–20888–5 Fawcett pb $4.50

SECRET FOR A NIGHTINGALE
0–449–21296–3 Fawcett pb $4.95

THE SECRET WOMAN
0–449–20878–8 Fawcett pb $3.95

THE SHADOW OF THE LYNX
0–449–20231–3 Fawcett pb $3.95

SILK VENDETTA
0–385–24299–9 Doubleday $17.95

THE SPRING OF THE TIGER
0–385–15261–2 Doubleday $13.95
0–449–20845–1 Fawcett pb $3.95

THE TIME OF THE HUNTER'S MOON
0–449–20511–8 Fawcett pb $3.95

• Susan Howatch
Victorian family sagas unfold in the gloomy, haunted atmosphere of ancient houses in the west of England.
CALL IN THE NIGHT
0–449–21069–3 Fawcett pb $2.95

CASHELMARA
0–449–20623–8 Fawcett pb $4.95

GLITTERING IMAGES
0–394–56206–2 Knopf $18.95

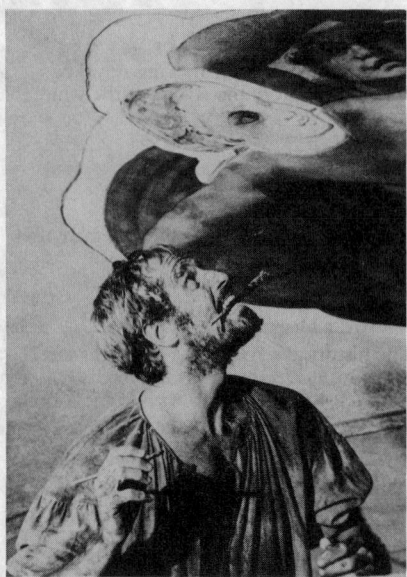

Charlton Heston as Michelangelo in the 1965 movie of Irving Stone's "The Agony and the Ecstasy" (photo: Movie Star News)

PENMARRIC
0–449–20622–X Fawcett pb $3.95

THE SHROUDED WALLS
0–449–21178–9 Fawcett pb $2.95

SINS OF THE FATHERS
0–449–20798–6 Fawcett pb $4.95

THE WAITING SANDS
0–449–20997–0 Fawcett pb $2.95

THE WHEEL OF FORTUNE
0–449–20624–6 Fawcett pb $4.95

• Brenda Jagger
These romance dramas provide a fascinating portrait of the change in 19th-century England from a pastoral to an industrial nation.

DISTANT CHOICES
0–688–07102–3 Morrow $19.95
0–449–21346–3 Fawcett pb $4.50

A SONG TWICE OVER
0–449–21040–5 Fawcett pb $4.50

The Kent Family Chronicles

John Jakes's multivolume family saga ranges from revolutionary and western-expansionist America to the slums of New York during the great immigrations.

• John Jakes
THE BASTARD
0–515–09927–9 Jove pb $4.95

THE REBELS
0–515–09206–1 Jove pb $4.95

THE SEEKERS
0–515–09038–7 Jove pb $4.95

THE FURIES
0–515–09157–X Jove pb $4.95

THE TITANS
0–515–09928–7 Jove pb $5.50

THE WARRIORS
0–515–02323–1 Jove pb $5.50

THE LAWLESS
0–515–09158–8 Jove pb $4.95

THE AMERICANS
0–515–09133–2 Jove pb $4.95

The Civil War Trilogy

John Jakes
NORTH AND SOUTH
0–15–166998–8 HBJ $19.95
0–440–16205–X Dell pb $5.95

LOVE AND WAR
0–15–154496–4 HBJ $19.95
0–440–15016–7 Dell pb $5.95

HEAVEN AND HELL
0–15–131075–0 HBJ $19.95
0–440–20170–5 Dell pb $5.95

• Gary Jennings
Jennings specializes in stunningly detailed first-person accounts of exotic civilizations.

AZTEC
A sweeping chronicle narrated by an ancient Aztec scribe
0–380–55889–0 Avon pb $4.95

THE JOURNEYER
Marco Polo tells of his encounters in his travels across Asia
0–689–11403–6 Atheneum $19.95
0–380–69609–6 Avon pb $4.95

SPANGLE
0–689–11723–X Atheneum $21.95

• M.M. Kaye
These colorful dramas of the Indian Mutiny examine in rich detail the tense relationships between soldiers, wives and children, and the mutinous sepoys.

THE FAR PAVILIONS
0–312–28259–1 St. Martin's $12.95
0–553–22797–1 Bantam pb $4.95

SHADOW OF THE MOON
0–553–27738–3 Bantam pb $5.50

TRADE WIND
0–553–25311–5 Bantam pb $4.95

• Alexander Kent
The Richard Bolitho series celebrates the fighting men of the British navy who swept the seas clear of Napoleon's warships.

COLORS ALOFT
0–399–12988–X Putnam $16.95
0–425–10264–5 Berkley pb $3.50

COMMAND A KING'S SHIP
0–515–07866–2 Jove pb $3.50

ENEMY IN SIGHT!
0–515–08177–9 Jove pb $3.50

HONOR THIS DAY
0–399–13348–8 Putnam $17.95

• Karleen Koen
THROUGH A GLASS DARKLY
A romance tale of early Hanoverian England and the defeated and decadent France of the Regency
0–394–55378–0 Random $19.95
0–380–70416–1 Avon pb $4.95

• Rosalind Laker
TO DANCE WITH KINGS: A Novel of Versailles
A peasant girl and her descendants are linked by destiny with the great Bourbon family, from Louis the Sun King to the tragic Marie Antoinette
0–385–24273–5 Doubleday $18.95

• Morgan Llywelyn
These books are pre-Conquest stories of the Anglo-Saxon and Celtic inhabitants of the British Isles in a magical combination of history and myth.

GRANIA: She-King of the Irish Seas
0–8041–0116–7 Ballantine pb $4.50

THE HORSE GODDESS
0–671–46055–2 Pocket pb $3.95

LION OF IRELAND: The Legend of Brian Boru
0–425–08846–4 Berkley pb $4.95

• Norah Lofts
THE CLAW
0–8125–2116–1 Tor pb $3.95

THE HOUSE AT OLD VINE
0–449–23792–3 Fawcett pb $1.95

JASSY
0–449–24101–7 Fawcett pb $1.95

THE LUTE PLAYER
0–449–22948–3 Fawcett pb $2.95

REQUIEM FOR IDOLS
0–449–24507–1 Fawcett pb $2.50

TO SEE A FINE LADY
0–449–22890–8 Fawcett pb $2.50

A WAYSIDE TAVERN
0–449–20140–6 Fawcett pb $3.50

• Amin Maalouf
LEO AFRICANUS
Exiled with other Jews and Muslims by the Spanish conquest of Granada, Leo's wanderings over North Africa and Asia gain him a position as papal geographer
0–393–02630–2 Norton $17.95

• David Markish
JESTERS
Jewish life in 18th-century Russia through the experiences of three men: a chancellor to Peter the Great, his court jester, and the architect of St. Petersburg
0–8050–0444–0 Henry Holt $19.95

• John Masters
British India is the setting for these tales of adventure and adultery in the closely woven social worlds of native and sahib.

BHOWANI JUNCTION
0–88184–310–5 Carroll & Graf pb $4.50

THE DECEIVERS
0–88184–419–5 Carroll & Graf pb $3.95

NIGHTRUNNERS OF BENGAL
0–88184–355–5 Carroll & Graf pb $4.95

• Colleen McCullough
THE LADIES OF MISSALONGHI
0–06–015739–9 Harper & Row $12.95
0–380–70458–7 Avon pb $3.95

■ TO ORDER BOOKS AS GIFTS, SEE PAGE 1

• Kenneth McKenney
THE CHANGELING
0–380–89686–9 Avon pb $3.50

THESE KINGDOMS
The search for Mayan treasure in the declining days of the Spanish empire when British pirates ruled the Caribbean
0–345–34109–0 Ballantine pb $4.95

• Zena Meyler
SHADOWS ON THE ICE
Ominous signs hover over the gaiety of the Russian aristocracy in the years before the Revolution
1–55785–039–9 Bart pb $4.50

• C.W. Nicol
HARPOON
The struggle of a feudal daimyo to cope with the intrusion of the west in 19th-century Japan
0–399–13177–9 Putnam $22.95
0–451–15307–3 NAL pb $4.95

• Diane Pearson
CSARDAS
0–449–20615–7 Fawcett pb $3.50

SARAH
0–449–20984–9 Fawcett pb $3.50

THE SUMMER OF THE BARSHINSKEYS
0–449–20783–8 Fawcett pb $4.50

• Jean Plaidy
Under her pseudonym, Victoria Holt shows the same command of historical periods, from the great Franco-British House of Plantagenet to the tragic Henrietta Maria, wife of the executed Charles I.
THE BATTLE OF THE QUEENS
0–449–24565–9 Fawcett pb $2.95

BEYOND THE BLUE MOUNTAINS
0–449–24451–2 Fawcett pb $2.95

CAROLINE THE QUEEN
0–399–13123–X Putnam $17.95

THE COURTS OF LOVE: The Story of Eleanor of Aquitaine
0–399–13294–5 Putnam $18.95

THE LADY IN THE TOWER
0–399–13181–7 Putnam $18.95

MYSELF, MY ENEMY
0–449–20648–3 Fawcett pb $3.95

PASSAGE TO PONTEFRACT
0–449–20265–8 Fawcett pb $3.95

PERDITA'S PRINCE
0–399–13307–0 Putnam $17.95

THE PLANTAGENET PRELUDE
0–449–21102–9 Fawcett pb $2.95

THE PRINCE OF DARKNESS
0–425–10853–8 Berkley pb $3.50

THE PRINCESS OF CELLE
0–399–13070–5 Putnam $15.95

QUEEN IN WAITING
0–449–21096–0 Fawcett pb $3.95

QUEEN OF THIS REALM
0–449–20979–2 Fawcett pb $3.95

RED ROSE OF ANJOU
0–449–20630–0 Fawcett pb $3.95

THE SUN IN SPLENDOUR
0–399–12879–4 Putnam $12.95
0–449–20628–9 Fawcett pb $3.95

SWEET LASS OF RICHMOND HILL
0–399–13362–3 Putnam $17.95

THE THIRD GEORGE
0–399–13245–7 Putnam $17.95

UNEASY LIES THE HEAD
0–399–12989–8 Putnam $14.95

VICTORIA VICTORIOUS
0–449–21251–3 Fawcett pb $4.95

THE VOW OF THE HERON
0–449–20264–X Fawcett pb $3.95

• Belva Plain
Family life of 19th- and early 20th-century America in the Caribbean plantations, the Civil War in New Orleans, and the Lower East Side of New York.
CRESCENT CITY
0–440–11549–3 Dell pb $4.95

EDEN BURNING
0–440–12135–3 Dell pb $4.95

EVERGREEN
0–440–13278–9 Dell pb $4.95

THE GOLDEN CUP
0–385–29508–1 Delacorte $17.95
0–440–13091–3 Dell pb $4.95

RANDOM WINDS
0–440–17562–3 Dell pb $4.95

• Mary Renault
Renault uses her wide knowledge of the ancient world to lend historical reality to the great Athenian myths and to depict daily life during the war with Sparta and the conquests of Alexander.
THE BULL FROM THE SEA
0–394–71504–7 Random House pb $4.95

FIRE FROM HEAVEN
0–394–42492–1 Pantheon $15.95
0–394–72291–4 Random House pb $5.95

FUNERAL GAMES
0–394–52068–8 Pantheon $14.50

THE KING MUST DIE
0–394–43195–2 Pantheon $15.95
0–394–75104–3 Random House pb $6.95

THE LAST OF THE WINE
0–394–71653–1 Random House pb $4.95

THE MASK OF APOLLO
0–394–75105–1 Random House pb $6.95

THE PERSIAN BOY
0–394–48191–7 Pantheon $15.95
0–394–75101–9 Random House pb $6.95

THE PRAISE SINGER
0–394–50273–6 Pantheon $12.95
0–394–75102–7 Random House pb $6.95

• Anne Rice
The chronicler of the millenia-old society and the personal lives of vampires can also focus her baroque sensibility on the castrati of the Venetian opera or the mores of decadent New Orleans families.
BELINDA
0–515–09355–6 Jove pb $4.95

CRY TO HEAVEN
0–394–52351–2 Knopf $15.95

THE FEAST OF ALL SAINTS
0–345–33453–1 Ballantine pb $4.95

THE MUMMY: Or Ramses the Damned
0–345–36000–1 Ballantine pb $9.95

INTERVIEW WITH THE VAMPIRE
0–345–33766–2 Ballantine pb $4.95

THE VAMPIRE LESTAT
0–394–53443–3 Knopf $18.95
0–345–31386–0 Ballantine pb $4.95

QUEEN OF THE DAMNED
0–394–55823–5 Knopf $18.95

• Alexandra Ripley
CHARLESTON
0–380–57729–1 Avon pb $4.95

NEW ORLEANS LEGACY
0–446–34211–4 Warner pb $3.95

• Edward Rutherford
SARUM
A brilliant tapestry of English history, tracing the continuity of five Salisbury families from the building of Stonehenge to colonial preeminence in the 19th century
0–8041–0298–8 Ivy pb $5.95

• Michael Shaara
THE BROKEN PLACE
0–07–056377–2 McGraw-Hill $12.95

THE HERALD
0–07–056376–4 McGraw-Hill $11.95

THE KILLER ANGELS: A Novel about the Four Days at Gettysburg
The detailed story of the battle seen through the dispatches of Robert E. Lee and his lieutenant
0–679–50466–4 Random House $19.95
0–345–34810–9 Ballantine pb $4.95

• Robert Skimin
GRAY VICTORY
A fascinating fictional speculation about the possible results of a Confederate victory in the Civil War
0–312–01374–4 St. Martin's $19.95

Jane Smiley
THE GREENLANDERS
Calls up the barren, violent, heroic world of 14th-century Norsemen through the eyes of a Greenland maiden fascinated by a warrior who has learned courtly manners in the south
0–394–55120–6 Knopf $19.95

• Mary Stewart
Stewart specializes in historical legends, among them a retelling of the Arthurian myth from the point of view of Merlin the enchanter.
THE CRYSTAL CAVE
0–449–20644–0 Fawcett pb $4.95

THE GABRIEL HOUNDS
0–449–20729–3 Fawcett pb $2.95

THE HOLLOW HILLS
0–449–20645–9 Fawcett pb $4.95

THE LAST ENCHANTMENT
0–449–20646–7 Fawcett pb $4.95

MARY STEWART'S MERLIN TRILOGY
Includes *The Crystal Cave, The Hollow Hills,* and *The Last Enchantment*
0–688–00347–8 Morrow $17.95

THE MOON-SPINNERS
0–449–20609–2 Fawcett pb $2.95

THUNDER ON THE RIGHT
0–449–20773–0 Fawcett pb $2.95

THE WICKED DAY
A new installment of the Merlin cycle
0–449–36041–2 Fawcett pb $4.95

WILDFIRE AT MIDNIGHT
0–449–20708–0 Fawcett pb $2.50

- Irving Stone

In these fictional biographies of famous men and women of the past, historical events and personalities receive colorful treatment.

THE AGONY AND THE ECSTASY
A life of Michelangelo Buonarroti with a fine portrait of Pope Julius II
0–385–01092–3 Doubleday $19.95
0–451–15947–0 NAL pb $5.95

THE GREEK TREASURE
The lives of Heinrich Schliemann, discoverer of the lost city of Troy, and his wife, Sophia
0–451–13457–5 NAL pb $4.50

IMMORTAL WIFE
0–451–11172–9 NAL pb $3.95

LUST FOR LIFE
A fictionalized biography of Van Gogh
0–385–04270–1 Doubleday $17.95
0–452–25517–1 NAL pb $8.95

THE ORIGIN
A novel based on the life of Charles Darwin
0–385–12064–8 Doubleday $17.95
0–451–13308–0 NAL pb $4.95

THE PRESIDENT'S LADY
A novel about the wife of Andrew Jackson
0–451–15857–1 NAL pb $4.95

- Rosemary Sutcliff

SWORD AT SUNSET
Virtuoso transformation of the legend of Arthur into the historical reality of a Roman-trained Briton trying to save the remnants of Mediterranean civilization from the northern barbarians
0–8125–8852–5 Tor pb $4.50

- Reay Tannahill

THE WORLD, THE FLESH AND THE DEVIL
0–517–56227–8 Crown $17.95
0–8041–0227–9 Ballantine pb $4.95

- Nikolai Tolstoy

THE COMING OF THE KING: A Novel of Merlin
0–553–05269–1 Bantam $18.95

- Sigrid Undset

KRISTIN LAVRANSDATTER
0–394–43262–2 Knopf $34.50

Volume 1: The Bridal Wreath
0–394–75299–6 Random House pb $6.95

Kirk Douglas as Van Gogh in the 1956 movie of Irving Stone's "Lust for Life" (photo: Movie Star News)

Volume 2: The Mistress of Husaby
0–394–75293–7 Random House pb $6.95

Volume 3: The Cross
0–394–75291–0 Random House pb $6.95

- Gore Vidal

Vidal's novels include witty and iconoclastic fictional rewritings of American history, and an imaginary autobiography of the emperor who tried to save Rome from Christianity.

CREATION
A fictional tour of the ancient world
0–394–50015–6 Random House $15.95
0–345–34020–5 Ballantine pb $4.95

JULIAN
0–345–32908–2 Ballantine pb $4.95

BURR
0–394–48024–4 Random House $19.95
0–345–33921–5 Ballantine pb $4.95

1876
0–394–49750–3 Random House $19.95
0–345–34626–2 Ballantine pb $4.95

EMPIRE
0–345–35472–9 Ballantine pb $4.95

LINCOLN
0–345–31221–X Ballantine pb $4.95

WASHINGTON, D.C.
0–345–34236–4 Ballantine pb $4.95

The Great Fiction Bestsellers: 1930–1989

THE '30s

- Hervey Allen

ANTHONY ADVERSE
0–03–028400–7 Henry Holt $12.95

- Sholem Asch

THE NAZARENE
0–88184–072–6 Carroll & Graf $21.95
0–88184–048–3 Carroll & Graf pb $10.95

- Pearl S. Buck

THE GOOD EARTH
0–671–50437–1 Washington Square pb $3.95

- Lloyd C. Douglas

THE MAGNIFICENT OBSESSION
0–395–07634–X Houghton Mifflin $19.95

- Daphne Du Maurier

REBECCA
0–385–04380–5 Doubleday $15.95

- Walter D. Edmonds

DRUMS ALONG THE MOHAWK
0–316–21142–7 Little, Brown $19.95
0–553–27412–0 Bantam pb $3.95

- Hans Fallada

LITTLE MAN, WHAT NOW?
Translated by Eric Sutton
0–89733–086–2 Academy Chicago pb $8.95

● Edna Ferber
CIMARRON
0–449–24114–9 Fawcett pb $1.95

● Ellen Glasgow
THE SHELTERED LIFE
0–15–681690–3 HBJ pb $8.95

VEIN OF IRON
0–15–693476–0 HBJ pb $7.95

● James Hilton
GOODBYE, MR. CHIPS
0–553–25613–0 Bantam pb $2.95

LOST HORIZON
0–688–02007–0 Morrow $13.50
0–671–54148–X Pocket pb $3.95

● Margaret Mitchell
GONE WITH THE WIND
0–380–00109–8 Avon pb $5.95

● J.B. Priestley
ANGEL PAVEMENT
0–226–68210–2 Chicago pb $8.95

● Marjorie Kinnan Rawlings
THE YEARLING
Illustrated by N.C. Wyeth
0–684–18461–3 Macmillan $24.95

● Mary Roberts Rinehart
THE DOOR
0–8217–1895–9 Zebra pb $3.50

● Kenneth Roberts
NORTHWEST PASSAGE
0–449–13838–0 Fawcett pb $3.95

● Mazo De La Roche
THE MASTER OF JALNA
0–449–23932–2 Fawcett pb $1.95

● Franz Werfel
THE FORTY DAYS OF MUSA DAGH
0–88184–015–7 Carroll & Graf pb $9.95

THE '40s

● Taylor Caldwell
THIS SIDE OF INNOCENCE
0–446–31248–7 Warner pb $3.95

● A.J. Cronin
THE GREEN YEARS
0–316–16193–4 Little, Brown pb $6.95

● Lloyd C. Douglas
THE BIG FISHERMAN
0–395–07630–7 Houghton Mifflin $15.95

THE ROBE
Foreword by Andrew Greeley
0–395–07635–8 Houghton Mifflin $19.95
0–317–38798–7 Houghton Mifflin pb $7.95

● John Hersey
A BELL FOR ADANO
0–394–41660–0 Knopf $17.95
0–394–75695–9 Random House pb $6.95

● James Hilton
RANDOM HARVEST
0–88184–125–0 Carroll & Graf pb $4.50

● Laura Z. Hobson
GENTLEMAN'S AGREEMENT
0–89783–010–5 Larlin $16.00

● Richard Llewellyn
HOW GREEN WAS MY VALLEY
0–02–573430–X Macmillan $17.95
0–440–33923–5 Dell pb $4.95

● John P. Marquand
H.M. PULHAM, ESQ.
0–89733–231–8 Academy Chicago pb $9.95

POINT OF NO RETURN
0–89733–174–5 Academy Chicago pb $11.95

● John O'Hara
A RAGE TO LIVE
0–88184–216–8 Carroll & Graf pb $4.95

● Kenneth Roberts
LYDIA BAILEY
0–449–20013–2 Fawcett pb $3.50

OLIVER WISWELL
0–449–24446–6 Fawcett pb $4.95

● Irwin Shaw
THE YOUNG LIONS
0–394–60809–7 Modern Library $7.95

● Betty Smith
A TREE GROWS IN BROOKLYN
0–06–080126–3 Harper & Row pb $5.50

● Lillian E. Smith
STRANGE FRUIT
0–15–185769–5 HBJ $12.95
0–8203–0779–3 Georgia pb $9.95

● Franz Werfel
THE SONG OF BERNADETTE
0–88411–720–0 Amereon $27.95

● Kathleen Winsor
FOREVER AMBER
0–451–14697–2 NAL pb $4.50

● Frank Yerby
THE FOXES OF HARROW
0–385–29512–X Dell pb $6.95

THE '50s

● Eugene Burdick & William J. Lederer
THE UGLY AMERICAN
0–393–00305–1 Norton pb $9.95
0–449–20732–3 Fawcett pb $3.95

● James Gould Cozzens
BY LOVE POSSESSED
0–15–115113–X HBJ $8.50

● Patrick Dennis
AUNTIE MAME
0–8149–0085–2 Vanguard $15.95

● Allen Drury
ADVISE AND CONSENT
0–385–05419–X Doubleday $16.95

● Daphne Du Maurier
THE SCAPEGOAT
0–88184–409–8 Carroll & Graf pb $4.50

● Edna Ferber
GIANT
0–449–24123–8 Fawcett pb $2.95

ICE PALACE
0–449–24124–6 Fawcett pb $1.95

● John Hersey
THE WALL
0–394–45092–2 Knopf $25.00
0–394–75696–7 Random House pb $9.95

● James Jones
FROM HERE TO ETERNITY
0–385–28312–1 Delacorte $19.95
0–440–32770–9 Dell pb $5.95

● MacKinley Kantor
ANDERSONVILLE
0–690–00329–3 Crowell $10.95
0–451–60215–2 NAL pb $4.95

● James A. Michener
HAWAII
0–394–42797–1 Random House $34.50
0–449–13358–0 Fawcett pb $5.95

RETURN TO PARADISE
0–394–44291–1 Random House $24.95
0–449–20650–5 Fawcett pb $4.95

● Nicholas Monsarrat
THE CRUEL SEA
0–394–42090–X Knopf $19.95

● Edwin O'Connor
THE LAST HURRAH
0–316–62659–7 Little, Brown pb $8.95

● John O'Hara
FROM THE TERRACE
0–88184–105–6 Carroll & Graf pb $5.95

TEN NORTH FREDERICK
0–394–44814–6 Random House $14.95
0–88184–173–0 Carroll & Graf pb $4.50

● Boris Pasternak
DOCTOR ZHIVAGO
0–394–42223–6 Pantheon $19.95
0–345–34100–7 Ballantine pb $4.95

James Michener (photo copyright John Kings, courtesy of Random House)

• Ayn Rand
ATLAS SHRUGGED
0–394–41576–0 Random House $29.95
0–451–57486–7 NAL pb $5.95

• Budd Schulberg
THE DISENCHANTED
Introduction by Anthony Burgess
1–55611–027–8 Donald Fine pb $8.95

• Annemarie Selinko
DESIREE
0–688–01448–8 Morrow $17.95

• Nevil Shute
ON THE BEACH
0–434–69919–5 David & Charles $23.95
0–345–31148–5 Ballantine pb $2.95

• Irving Stone
LOVE IS ETERNAL
0–451–14540–2 NAL pb $4.95

• Kay Thompson
ELOISE
Illustrated by Hilary Knight
0–671–22350–X Simon & Schuster $15.95

• Robert Traver
ANATOMY OF A MURDER
0–312–03356–7 St. Martin's pb $8.95

• Leon Uris
BATTLE CRY
0–553–25983–0 Bantam pb $4.50

EXODUS
0–553–25847–8 Bantam pb $4.95

• Herman Wouk
THE CAINE MUTINY
0–671–60425–2 Pocket pb $4.95

MARJORIE MORNINGSTAR
0–671–46016–1 Pocket pb $5.95

THE '60s

• Eugene Burdick & Harvey Wheeler
FAIL-SAFE
0–440–12459–X Dell pb $3.95

• Taylor Caldwell
TESTIMONY OF TWO MEN
0–449–20572–X Fawcett pb $4.95

• James Clavell
TAI-PAN
0–385–29218–X Delacorte $19.95
0–440–18462–2 Dell pb $4.95

• Michael Crichton
THE ANDROMEDA STRAIN
0–394–41525–6 Knopf $18.95
0–440–10199–9 Dell pb $4.50

• Robert Crichton
THE SECRET OF SANTA VITTORIA
0–88184–267–2 Carroll & Graf pb $3.95

• Ian Fleming
THE MAN WITH THE GOLDEN GUN
0–451–58555–1 NAL pb $3.95

YOU ONLY LIVE TWICE
0–451–53480–6 NAL pb $3.50

• Arthur Hailey
AIRPORT
0–440–10066–6 Dell pb $4.50

HOTEL
0–385–03222–6 Doubleday $14.95
0–440–13763–2 Dell pb $4.50

• Fletcher Knebel
VANISHED
0–441–86038–9 Charter pb $3.95

• Giuseppe di Lampedusa
THE LEOPARD
0–394–43291–6 Pantheon $13.50
0–394–74949–9 Pantheon pb $6.95

• Harper Lee
TO KILL A MOCKINGBIRD
0–446–31049–2 Warner pb $3.95

• Ira Levin
ROSEMARY'S BABY
0–394–44308–X Random House $10.95

• Helen MacInnes
THE DOUBLE IMAGE
0–449–20860–5 Fawcett pb $3.95

THE SALZBURG CONNECTION
0–449–20895–8 Fawcett pb $3.95

• Catherine Marshall
CHRISTY
0–380–00141–1 Avon pb $3.95

• Mary McCarthy
THE GROUP
0–15–137280–2 HBJ $8.50
0–380–52134–2 Avon pb $4.95

• Richard McKenna
THE SAND PEBBLES
0–87021–592–2 Naval Institute $21.95

• James A. Michener
CARAVANS
0–394–41849–2 Random House $29.95
0–449–21051–0 Fawcett pb $5.95

THE SOURCE
0–394–41849–2 Random House $34.95
0–449–13803–2 Fawcett pb $5.95

• Robin Moore
THE GREEN BERETS
0–345–33376–4 Ballantine pb $3.95

• John O'Hara
OURSELVES TO KNOW
0–394–43959–7 Random House $14.95

SERMONS AND SODA WATER
0–88184–271–0 Carroll & Graf pb $4.95

• Katherine Anne Porter
SHIP OF FOOLS
0–316–71390–2 Little, Brown pb $7.95

• Chaim Potok
THE CHOSEN
0–449–21344–7 Fawcett pb $4.50

THE PROMISE
0–394–44163–X Knopf $15.50
0–449–20910–5 Fawcett pb $4.50

• Mario Puzo
THE GODFATHER
0–451–14506–2 NAL pb $4.50

• Harold Robbins
THE ADVENTURERS
0–671–53151–4 Pocket pb $4.95

THE CARPETBAGGERS
0–671–52955–X Pocket pb $4.95

THE INHERITORS
0–671–54761–5 Pocket pb $4.95

• Philip Roth
PORTNOY'S COMPLAINT
0–394–44198–2 Random House $15.50
0–449–20291–7 Fawcett pb $4.95

• Terry Southern & Mason Hoffenberg
CANDY
0–14–007027–3 Penguin pb $5.95

• Mary Stewart
THE GABRIEL HOUNDS
0–688–01665–0 Morrow $9.95
0–449–20729–3 Fawcett pb $2.95

THIS ROUGH MAGIC
0–449–20734–X Fawcett pb $3.50

• Irving Stone
THE AGONY AND THE ECSTASY
0–451–59470–1 NAL pb $5.95

• Leon Uris
ARMAGEDDON
0–385–00356–0 Doubleday $17.95
0–440–10290–1 Dell pb $5.95

MILA 18
0–553–24160–5 Bantam pb $4.50

TOPAZ
0–553–73949–2 Bantam pb $4.95

• Gore Vidal
MYRA BRECKINRIDGE & MYRON
0–394–55376–4 Random House $19.95
0–394–75444–1 Random House pb $8.95

• Irving Wallace
THE CHAPMAN REPORT
0–451–13828–7 NAL pb $4.50

THE PLOT
0–671–52523–9 Pocket pb $5.95

THE PRIZE
0–451–13759–0 NAL pb $4.95

• Herman Wouk
DON'T STOP THE CARNIVAL
0–385–02003–1 Doubleday $18.95
0–671–56783–5 Pocket pb $4.95

YOUNGBLOOD HAWKE
0–385–02974–8 Doubleday $21.95
0–671–45472–2 Pocket pb $5.95

➤ **FOR OVERSEAS ORDERING INFORMATION, SEE PAGE 1**

THE '70s

- **Richard Adams**
  WATERSHIP DOWN
  0–02–700030–3 Macmillan $24.95
  0–380–00293–0 Avon pb $4.95

- **Richard Bach**
  ILLUSIONS: The Adventures of a Reluctant Messiah
  0–385–28501–9 Delacorte $14.95
  0–440–34319–4 Dell pb $3.95

  JONATHAN LIVINGSTON SEAGULL
  0–380–01286–3 Avon pb $3.95

  THERE'S NO SUCH PLACE AS FAR AWAY
  Illustrated by Ron Wegen
  0–385–29038–1 Delacorte $14.95

- **Judy Blume**
  WIFEY
  0–671–65245–1 Pocket pb $4.50

- **Taylor Caldwell**
  CAPTAINS AND THE KINGS
  0–449–20562–2 Fawcett pb $3.95

- **James Clavell**
  SHOGUN
  0–385–29224–4 Delacorte $21.95
  0–440–17800–2 Dell pb $5.95

- **Robin Cook**
  COMA
  0–451–15953–5 NAL pb $4.95

- **Margaret Craven**
  I HEARD THE OWL CALL MY NAME
  0–440–34369–0 Dell pb $3.50

- **Michael Crichton**
  THE GREAT TRAIN ROBBERY
  0–440–13099–9 Dell pb $4.50

- **Paul Erdman**
  THE BILLION DOLLAR SURE THING
  0–425–11191–1 Berkley pb $4.50

- **Howard Fast**
  THE ESTABLISHMENT
  0–395–28160–1 Houghton Mifflin $11.95
  0–440–12393–3 Dell pb $4.95

  THE IMMIGRANTS
  0–440–14175–3 Dell pb $4.50

  THE SECOND GENERATION
  0–395–26683–1 Houghton Mifflin $10.95
  0–440–17915–7 Dell pb $4.50

- **Ken Follett**
  EYE OF THE NEEDLE
  0–87795–186–1 Arbor House $17.95
  0–451–15524–6 NAL pb $4.95

  TRIPLE
  0–451–13988–7 NAL pb $4.50

- **John Fowles**
  DANIEL MARTIN
  0–451–12210–0 NAL pb $4.50

- **Sir John Hackett**
  THE THIRD WORLD WAR: August 1985
  0–425–10192–4 Berkley pb $4.95

- **Arthur Hailey**
  THE MONEYCHANGERS
  0–440–15802–8 Dell pb $4.50

  OVERLOAD
  0–440–16754–X Dell pb $4.95

  WHEELS
  0–440–19414–8 Dell pb $4.50

- **Alex Haley**
  ROOTS
  0–385–03787–2 Doubleday $19.95
  0–440–17464–3 Dell pb $5.95

- **Jack Higgins**
  THE EAGLE HAS LANDED
  0–553–27042–7 Bantam pb $4.50

  STORM WARNING
  0–671–66526–X Pocket pb $4.50

- **John Jakes**
  THE BASTARD
  0–515–09927–9 Jove pb $4.95

  THE LAWLESS
  0–515–09189–8 Jove pb $4.95

  THE WARRIORS
  0–515–32323–1 Jove pb $4.95

- **Dan Jenkins**
  SEMI-TOUGH
  0–451–13793–0 NAL pb $3.95

- **Erica Jong**
  FEAR OF FLYING
  0–451–13139–8 NAL pb $3.95

  HOW TO SAVE YOUR OWN LIFE
  0–451–14834–7 NAL pb $4.95

- **M.M. Kaye**
  THE FAR PAVILIONS
  0–312–28259–1 St. Martin's $12.95
  0–553–77359–1 Bantam pb $5.50

- **Avery Korman**
  KRAMER VS. KRAMER
  0–8041–0360–7 Ivy pb $4.95

- **Judith Krantz**
  SCRUPLES
  0–446–34327–7 Warner pb $4.95

- **George Lucas**
  STAR WARS
  0–345–27476–8 Ballantine pb $6.95

- **Robert Ludlum**
  THE HOLCROFT COVENANT
  0–553–26019–7 Bantam pb $4.95

  THE MATARESE CIRCLE
  0–553–25899–0 Bantam pb $4.95

  THE MATLOCK PAPER
  0–440–15538–X Dell pb $4.95

  THE RHINEMANN EXCHANGE
  0–440–15079–5 Dell pb $4.95

- **John D. MacDonald**
  CONDOMINIUM
  0–449–20737–4 Fawcett pb $3.95

- **Helen MacInnes**
  MESSAGE FROM MALAGA
  0–449–20398–0 Fawcett pb $3.50

Robert Ludlum (photo copyright Michelle Ryder, courtesy of Random House)

  PRELUDE TO TERROR
  0–449–13781–X Fawcett pb $3.50

- **Colleen McCullough**
  THE THORN BIRDS
  0–06–012956–5 Harper & Row $19.95
  0–380–01817–9 Avon pb $4.95

- **James A. Michener**
  CENTENNIAL
  0–394–47970–X Random House $34.50
  0–449–14192–X Fawcett pb $5.95

  CHESAPEAKE
  0–394–50079–2 Random House $29.95
  0–449–21158–4 Fawcett pb $5.95

  THE DRIFTERS
  0–394–46200–9 Random House $29.95
  0–449–20522–3 Fawcett pb $5.95

- **Belva Plain**
  EVERGREEN
  0–440–13278–9 Dell pb $4.95

- **Chaim Potok**
  MY NAME IS ASHER LEV
  0–394–46137–1 Knopf $18.95
  0–449–20714–5 Fawcett pb $3.95

- **Mario Puzo**
  FOOLS DIE
  0–451–60193–8 NAL pb $4.95

- **Harold Robbins**
  THE BETSY
  0–671–64414–9 Pocket pb $4.95

  DREAMS DIE FIRST
  0–671–64415–7 Pocket pb $4.95

  THE LONELY LADY
  0–671–66204–X Pocket pb $4.95

  MEMORIES OF ANOTHER DAY
  0–671–55743–2 Pocket pb $4.95

  THE PIRATE
  0–671–64951–5 Pocket pb $4.95

- **Rosemary Rogers**
  THE INSIDERS
  0–380–40576–8 Avon pb $4.50

- Judith Rossner
LOOKING FOR MR. GOODBAR
0–671–66205–8 Pocket pb $4.50

- Erich Segal
OLIVER'S STORY
0–06–013852–1 Harper & Row $13.50

- Irwin Shaw
EVENING IN BYZANTIUM
0–440–13150–2 Dell pb $4.95

- Sidney Sheldon
BLOODLINE
0–688–03196–X Morrow $19.95
0–446–34187–8 Warner pb $4.95

A STRANGER IN THE MIRROR
0–688–03002–5 Morrow $17.95
0–446–34193–2 Warner pb $4.95

- Danielle Steel
THE PROMISE
0–440–17079–6 Dell pb $4.95

- Mary Stewart
THE HOLLOW HILLS
0–449–20645–9 Fawcett pb $4.95

THE LAST ENCHANTMENT
0–449–20646–7 Fawcett pb $4.95

TOUCH NOT THE CAT
0–449–20608–4 Fawcett pb $3.95

- Irving Stone
THE PASSIONS OF THE MIND
0–385–02568–8 Doubleday $19.95
0–451–13456–7 NAL pb $4.95

- J.R.R. Tolkien
THE SILMARILLION
0–395–34646–0 Houghton Mifflin $7.95
0–345–32581–8 Ballantine pb $3.95

- Thomas Tryon
THE OTHER
0–449–01673–6 Dell pb $4.95

- Leon Uris
TRINITY
0–385–03458–X Doubleday $19.95
0–553–25846–X Bantam pb $4.95

- Gore Vidal
BURR
0–345–33921–5 Ballantine pb $4.95

1876
0–394–49750–3 Random House $19.95
0–345–34626–2 Ballantine pb $4.95

- Kurt Vonnegut, Jr.
BREAKFAST OF CHAMPIONS
0–440–13148–0 Dell pb $4.95

JAILBIRD
0–440–15473–1 Dell pb $4.95

SLAPSTICK: Or, Lonesome No More!
0–440–18009–0 Dell pb $4.95

- Joseph Wambaugh
THE BLACK MARBLE
0–440–10644–3 Dell pb $4.95

THE CHOIRBOYS
0–440–11188–9 Dell pb $4.95

- Herman Wouk
WAR AND REMEMBRANCE
0–316–95501–9 Little, Brown $19.95
0–671–67288–6 Pocket pb $5.95

THE WINDS OF WAR
0–316–95500–0 Little, Brown $24.95
0–671–67287–8 Pocket pb $5.95

THE '80s

- V.C. Andrews
FLOWERS IN THE ATTIC
0–671–40453–0 Pocket pb $4.95

GARDEN OF SHADOWS
0–671–64259–6 Pocket $18.95
0–671–64257–X Pocket pb $4.95

HEAVEN
0–671–52658–9 Pocket pb $4.95

IF THERE BE THORNS
0–671–64814–4 Pocket pb $4.95

MY SWEET AUDRINA
0–671–56570–7 Pocket pb $4.95

PETALS ON THE WIND
0–671–64813–6 Pocket pb $4.95

SEEDS OF YESTERDAY
0–671–64815–2 Pocket pb $4.95

- Jeffrey Archer
FIRST AMONG EQUALS
0–671–64314–2 Pocket pb $4.95

KANE AND ABEL
0–449–24376–1 Fawcett pb $4.95

A MATTER OF HONOR
0–671–64159–X Pocket pb $4.95

THE PRODIGAL DAUGHTER
0–671–64276–6 Pocket pb $4.95

- Isaac Asimov
FOUNDATION'S EDGE
0–345–30898–0 Ballantine pb $4.95

THE ROBOTS OF DAWN
0–345–31571–5 Ballantine pb $3.95

- Jean M. Auel
THE CLAN OF THE CAVE BEAR
0–517–54202–1 Crown $18.95
0–553–25042–6 Bantam pb $4.95

THE MAMMOTH HUNTERS
0–553–80945–0 Bantam pb $5.50

THE VALLEY OF HORSES: Earth's Children
0–517–54489–X Crown $18.95
0–553–25053–1 Bantam pb $4.95

- Richard Bach
ONE
0–6880–7802–8 Morrow $16.95

- Arnaud De Borchgrave & Robert Moss
THE SPIKE
0–380–54270–6 Avon pb $3.95

- Barbara Taylor Bradford
ACT OF WILL
0–553–26543–1 Bantam pb $4.95

TO BE THE BEST
0–385–24579–3 Doubleday $19.95

A WOMAN OF SUBSTANCE
0–553–77901–2 Bantam pb $4.95

- Taylor Caldwell
ANSWER AS A MAN
0–449–24467–9 Fawcett pb $3.95

- Tom Clancy
THE CARDINAL OF THE KREMLIN
0–399–13345–3 Putnam $19.95

THE HUNT FOR RED OCTOBER
0–87021–285–0 Naval Institute $14.95
0–425–08383–7 Berkley pb $4.95

PATRIOT GAMES
0–425–10972–0 Berkley pb $4.95

RED STORM RISING
0–425–10107–X Berkley pb $4.95

- Mary Higgins Clark
WEEP NO MORE, MY LADY
0–671–55664–9 Simon & Schuster $17.95
0–440–20098–9 Dell pb $4.95

- Arthur C. Clarke
2010: Odyssey Two
0–345–00661–5 Ballantine pb $3.95

2061: Odyssey Three
0–345–35173–8 Ballantine $17.95

- James Clavell
NOBLE HOUSE
0–385–28737–2 Delacorte $22.95
0–440–16484–2 Dell pb $5.95

WHIRLWIND
0–380–70312–2 Avon pb $5.95

- Jackie Collins
HOLLYWOOD HUSBANDS
0–671–52500–X Simon & Schuster $18.95
0–671–52501–8 Pocket pb $4.95

HOLLYWOOD WIVES
0–671–62425–3 Pocket pb $4.95

LUCKY
0–671–52496–8 Pocket pb $4.95

ROCK STAR
0–671–61881–4 Simon & Schuster $19.95

Jackie Collins (photo by Brian Aris, courtesy of Simon & Schuster)

• Larry Collins & Dominique LaPierre
THE FIFTH HORSEMAN
0–380–54734–1 Avon pb $4.95

• Shirley Conran
LACE
0–671–54755–0 Pocket pb $4.50

• Pat Conroy
THE PRINCE OF TIDES
0–395–35300–9 Houghton Mifflin $19.95
0–553–26888–0 Bantam pb $4.95

• Robin Cook
BRAIN
0–451–11260–1 NAL pb $3.95

SPHINX
0–451–59497–1 NAL pb $4.95

• Stephen Coonts
FINAL FLIGHT
0–385–24555–6 Doubleday $18.95

• Clive Cussler
CYCLOPS
0–671–63184–5 Pocket pb $4.95

TREASURE
0–671–62613–2 Simon & Schuster $18.95

• Stephen R. Donaldson
THE ONE TREE
0–345–34869–9 Ballantine pb $4.95

THE WHITE GOLD WIELDER
0–345–48702–1 Ballantine pb $4.95

• Dominick Dunne
THE TWO MRS. GRENVILLES
0–553–25891–5 Bantam pb $4.50

• Paul Erdman
THE LAST DAYS OF AMERICA
0–671–44717–3 Pocket pb $3.95

• Howard Fast
THE LEGACY
0–440–14720–4 Dell pb $4.50

• Ken Follett
THE KEY TO REBECCA
0–451–55106–1 NAL pb $4.95

LIE DOWN WITH LIONS
0–451–14642–5 NAL pb $4.95

THE MAN FROM ST. PETERSBURG
0–451–54940–2 NAL pb $4.95

• Cynthia Freeman
COME POUR THE WINE
0–553–26090–1 Bantam pb $4.50

NO TIME FOR TEARS
0–553–26092–8 Bantam pb $4.50

• George Gipe
GREMLINS
0–380–89003–8 Avon pb $2.95

• Donald F. Glut
THE EMPIRE STRIKES BACK
0–345–32022–0 Ballantine pb $3.50

• Andrew M. Greeley
THE CARDINAL SINS
0–446–34208–4 Warner pb $4.95

• Arthur Hailey
STRONG MEDICINE
0–440–18366–9 Dell pb $4.50

• Frank Herbert
GOD EMPEROR OF DUNE
0–441–29467–7 Berkley pb $4.95

• Rona Jaffe
CLASS REUNION
0–89621–675–6 Thorndike $18.95
0–440–11288–5 Dell pb $4.50

• John Jakes
THE AMERICANS
0–515–09133–2 Jove pb $4.95

HEAVEN AND HELL
0–15–131075–0 HBJ $19.95

LOVE AND WAR
0–15–154496–4 HBJ $19.95
0–440–15016–7 Dell pb $5.95

NORTH AND SOUTH
0–440–16205–X Dell pb $5.95

• Erica Jong
FANNY
0–451–58903–8 NAL pb $4.95

• Garrison Keillor
LAKE WOBEGON DAYS
0–670–80514–9 Viking $17.95
0–14–009983–2 Penguin pb $4.95

LEAVING HOME: A Collection of Lake Wobegon Stories
0–670–81976–X Viking $18.95

• Stephen King & Peter Straub
THE TALISMAN
0–425–10533–4 Berkley pb $4.95

▶ For the novels of Stephen King, see Science Fiction and Fantasy

• William Kotzwinkle
E.T.: The Extra Terrestrial Storybook
0–399–20936–0 Putnam $6.95

• Judith Krantz
I'LL TAKE MANHATTAN
0–553–26407–9 Bantam pb $4.95

MISTRAL'S DAUGHTER
0–553–25917–2 Bantam pb $4.95

PRINCESS DAISY
0–553–25609–2 Bantam pb $4.95

TILL WE MEET AGAIN
0–517–57026–2 Crown $19.95

• Louis L'Amour
THE HAUNTED MESA
0–553–27022–2 Bantam pb $4.50

JUBAL SACKETT
0–553–77391–4 Bantam pb $4.50

LAST OF THE BREED
0–553–05162–8 Bantam $17.95
0–553–80422–0 Bantam pb $4.50

THE LONESOME GODS
0–553–75186–0 Bantam pb $4.50

THE WALKING DRUM
0–553–70133–1 Bantam pb $4.50

Judith Krantz (photo by Harry Langdon)

• Robert Ludlum
THE AQUITAINE PROGRESSION
0–553–26256–4 Bantam pb $4.95

THE BOURNE IDENTITY
0–553–26011–1 Bantam pb $4.95

THE BOURNE SUPREMACY
0–553–26322–6 Bantam pb $4.95

THE ICARUS AGENDA
0–394–54397–1 Random House $19.95

THE PARSIFAL MOSAIC
0–553–25270–4 Bantam pb $4.95

THE ROAD TO GANDOLFO
0–553–71091–2 Bantam pb $4.95

• John D. MacDonald
FREE FALL IN CRIMSON
0–06–014833–0 Harper & Row $15.00
0–449–32536–6 Fawcett pb $3.95

• Anne McCaffrey
MORETA: Dragonlady of Pern
0–345–29873–X Ballantine pb $3.50

• Colleen McCullough
AN INDECENT OBSESSION
0–06–014920–5 Harper & Row $14.95

• James A. Michener
ALASKA
0–394–55154–0 Random House $22.50

THE COVENANT
0–394–50505–0 Random House $17.95
0–449–14206–1 Fawcett pb $5.95

LEGACY
0–394–56432–4 Random House $16.95

POLAND
0–449–20587–8 Fawcett pb $4.95

SPACE
0–394–50555–7 Random House $17.95
0–449–20379–4 Fawcett pb $5.95

TEXAS
0–394–54154–5 Random House $21.95
0–449–21092–8 Fawcett pb $5.95

- Belva Plain
RANDOM WINDS
0–440–17562–3 Dell pb $4.95

- Mario Puzo
THE SICILIAN
0–553–25282–8 Bantam pb $4.95

- Anne Rice
QUEEN OF THE DAMNED
0–393–55823–5 Knopf $18.95

- Joan Rivers
THE LIFE AND HARD TIMES OF HEIDI ABROMOWITZ
0–440–14721–2 Dell pb $3.50

- Harold Robbins
DESCENT FROM XANADU
0–671–65679–1 Pocket pb $4.95
GOODBYE, JANETTE
0–671–64989–2 Pocket pb $4.95
SPELLBINDER
0–671–65752–6 Pocket pb $4.95

- Rosemary Rogers
LOST LOVE, LAST LOVE
0–380–75515–7 Avon pb $4.50
LOVE PLAY
0–380–81190–1 Avon pb $4.50
SURRENDER TO LOVE
0–380–80630–4 Avon pb $4.50

- Judith Rossner
AUGUST
0–446–32256–3 Warner pb $4.50

- Carl Sagan
CONTACT
0–671–43422–5 Pocket pb $4.95

- Lawrence Sanders
THE EIGHTH COMMANDMENT
0–425–10005–7 Berkley pb $4.95
THE TENTH COMMANDMENT
0–425–10431–1 Berkley pb $4.95
THE THIRD DEADLY SIN
0–425–09961–X Berkley pb $3.50

- Helen H. Santmyer
. . . AND LADIES OF THE CLUB
0–425–10243–2 Berkley pb $5.95

- Dr. Seuss
THE BUTTER BATTLE BOOK
Illustrated by Dr. Seuss
0–394–86580–4 Random House $9.95

- Sidney Sheldon
IF TOMORROW COMES
0–688–04217–1 Morrow $17.95
0–446–32989–4 Warner pb $4.95
MASTER OF THE GAME
0–446–35545–3 Warner pb $5.95
RAGE OF ANGELS
0–688–03687–2 Morrow $12.95
0–446–56611–4 Warner pb $5.95
THE SANDS OF TIME
0–688–06571–6 Morrow $19.95

WINDMILLS OF THE GODS
0–688–06570–8 Morrow $18.95
0–446–35010–9 Warner pb $4.95

- Martin Cruz Smith
GORKY PARK
0–394–51748–2 Random House $13.95
0–345–29834–9 Ballantine pb $3.95

- Danielle Steel
CHANGES
0–440–11181–1 Dell pb $4.95
CROSSINGS
0–440–11585–X Dell pb $4.95
FAMILY ALBUM
0–440–12434–4 Dell pb $4.95
FINE THINGS
0–385–29527–8 Delacorte $18.95
0–440–20056–3 Dell pb $4.95
FULL CIRCLE
0–440–12689–4 Dell pb $4.95
KALEIDOSCOPE
0–385–29594–4 Delacorte $18.95
A PERFECT STRANGER
0–440–16872–4 Dell pb $4.95
REMEMBRANCE
0–385–28872–7 Delacorte $19.95
0–440–17370–1 Dell pb $4.95
THE RING
0–385–28872–7 Delacorte $19.95
0–440–17392–2 Dell pb $4.95
SECRETS
0–440–17648–4 Dell pb $4.95
THURSTON HOUSE
0–440–18532–7 Dell pb $4.95
WANDERLUST
0–385–29463–8 Delacorte $17.95
0–440–19361–3 Dell pb $4.95
ZOYA
0–385–29649–5 Delacorte $19.95

- Trevanian
SHIBUMI
0–345–31180–9 Ballantine pb $4.95

- Scott Turow
PRESUMED INNOCENT
0–374–23713–1 Farrar, Straus & Giroux $18.95
0–446–35098–2 Warner pb $4.95

Danielle Steel (photo copyright Roger Ressmeyer, courtesy of Delacorte)

- Leon Uris
THE HAJ
0–553–24864–2 Bantam pb $4.95
MITLA PASS
0–385–18792–0 Doubleday $19.95

- Helen Van Slyke
A NECESSARY WOMAN
0–446–31312–2 Warner pb $4.50

- Gore Vidal
LINCOLN
0–345–00790–5 Ballantine pb $4.95

- Joan D. Vinge
THE DUNE STORYBOOK
0–399–12949–9 Putnam pb $6.95

- Joseph Wambaugh
THE GLITTER DOME
0–553–27259–4 Bantam pb $4.95

- Tom Wolfe
THE BONFIRE OF THE VANITIES
0–374–11534–6 Farrar, Straus & Giroux $19.95
0–553–27597–6 Bantam pb $5.95

DOMINICK DUNNE:
Ten Novels Which Should Have Been Bestsellers

Timothy Findley
FAMOUS LAST WORDS
Out of print

Molly Keane
GOOD BEHAVIOR
0–394–51818–7 Knopf $10.95
0–525–48224–5 Dutton pb $8.95

Sybil Bedford
A LEGACY
0–912946–26–1 Ecco pb $8.50

Stefan Zweig
BEWARE OF PITY
0–452–25512–0 NAL pb $7.95

John P. Marquand
WICKFORD POINT
0–8446–2666–X Peter Smith $11.95

Rosamond Lehmann
THE BALLAD AND THE SOURCE
0–89984–723–4 Century $32.50

Nancy Mitford
THE PURSUIT OF LOVE
Includes *Love in a Cold Climate*
0–394–60481–4 Modern Library $8.95

James Salter
LIGHT YEARS
0–86547–064–2 North Point pb $12.50

Graham Greene
THE HEART OF THE MATTER
0–14–001789–5 Penguin pb $3.95

Shirley Hazzard
THE TRANSIT OF VENUS
Out of print

 IF YOU CAN'T FIND IT, LOOK IN THE INDEX

- Kathleen E. Woodiwiss
COME LOVE A STRANGER
0–380–89936–1 Avon pb $4.95

  A ROSE IN WINTER
0–380–84400–1 Avon pb $4.95

- Herman Wouk
INSIDE, OUTSIDE
0–316–95504–3 Little, Brown $19.95

Comics

A circulation war between Joseph Pulitzer's *New York World* and William Randolph Hearst's *Journal* led to the birth of the color comic strip. After the *World* added color to *The Yellow Kid,* Hearst countered with his own color comics weekly, billed as "eight pages of polychromatic effulgence that make the rainbow look like a lead pipe." By 1900, cartoonists had established the now-familiar conventions of separate panels, sequential narrative, and dialogue in balloons.

The first successful daily black-and-white strip series began in 1907. Subsequent decades saw the emergence of an incredible variety of strips which have proven to be some of the most enduring and influential creations of American culture: *Little Nemo in Slumberland, Krazy Kat, Little Orphan Annie, Dick Tracy, Popeye, Flash Gordon, Li'l Abner, Prince Valiant, Terry and the Pirates,* among many others.

Comics expanded further in the 1930s with the creation of the comic book, which in short order became the most notorious of American literary forms as the superhero adventures of the 1940s gave way to the crime and horror extravaganzas of the 1950s and, a decade later, to the delirious excesses of *Zap!* and other underground comics. By then comics were an international phenomenon, mutating into dramatically different forms and levels of seriousness in Europe, Asia, and Latin America. Today's "graphic novels" and "graphic albums" explore a constantly expanding range of genres, with a generous dose of the futuristic, the erotic, and the anarchically comic. A work like Art Spiegelman's *Maus,* in which the Holocaust experiences of Spiegelman's father are transmuted into an archetypal drama of stylized cats and mice, testifies to the continuing evolution of the medium.

GENERAL STUDIES AND REFERENCE

- Maurice Horn, editor
THE WORLD ENCYCLOPEDIA OF COMICS
A comprehensive alphabetized survey
0–87754–030–6 Chelsea House $42.50

Frame from the 1905 strip Dreams of the Rarebit Fiend *by Winsor McCay (Dover)*

- Robert M. Overstreet
THE OFFICIAL OVERSTREET COMIC BOOK PRICE GUIDE
Emphasizes the mercenary concerns of comic dealers over historical and aesthetic matters, but still the only book of its kind
0–87637–746–0 Overstreet pb $12.95

- Jeff Rovin
ENCYCLOPEDIA OF SUPERHEROES
Alphabetical entries on more than 1300 crime-fighting characters from comics, literature, TV and films
0–8160–1679–8 Facts On File pb $19.95

  THE ENCYCLOPEDIA OF SUPER VILLAINS
One thousand evildoers from all media, arranged alphabetically
0–8160–1356–X Facts On File $29.95

- Martin Sheridan
CLASSIC COMICS AND THEIR CREATORS
An early account, first published in 1942
0–911160–59–0 Post-Era $14.95

Comics and Society

- Martin Barker
A HAUNT OF FEARS: The Strange History of the British Horror Comics Campaign
The early 1950s crusade which led to Britain's Harmful Publications Act
0–86104–751–6 Longwood pb $7.50

- Ariel Dorfman & Armand Mattelart
HOW TO READ DONALD DUCK: Imperialist Ideology in the Disney Comic
Funny animals as cultural imperialists. First published in Chile in 1971, and banned there since the Pinochet coup
0–88477–023–0 International General pb $9.95

- James B. Gilbert
A CYCLE OF OUTRAGE: America's Reaction to the Juvenile Delinquent in the 1950s
Includes, along with much else related to the rise of American youth culture, a

detailed account of Frederic Wertham's notorious crusade against comic books
0–19–503721–9 Oxford $21.95

Predecessors and Sidelines

- Wilhelm Busch
MAX AND MORITZ
A celebrated German work of illustrated humor
0–486–20181–3 Dover pb $4.95

- Palmer Cox
THE BROWNIES: Their Book
An illustrated children's classic from 1887
0–486–21265–3 Dover pb $4.95

- Robert Jay
THE TRADE CARD IN NINETEENTH-CENTURY AMERICA
A scholarly study of early advertising cards, including 96 color reproductions
0–8262–0619–0 Missouri $30.00

- Harold Schechter
THE BOSOM SERPENT: Folklore and Popular Art
Schechter traces the connection between folklore and such popular forms as comic books and B-movies
0–87745–193–1 Iowa $17.95

COMIC STRIPS

Bill Blackbeard & Martin Williams, editors
THE SMITHSONIAN COLLECTION OF NEWSPAPER COMICS
An outstanding collection of some of the greatest comic strips, beautifully reproduced
Foreword by John Canaday
0–8109–2081–6 Abrams pb $24.95

ART SPIEGELMAN:
Pillars of Comic Book Literacy

Bill Blackbeard & Martin Williams, editors
THE SMITHSONIAN COLLECTION OF NEWSPAPER COMICS
0–8109–2081–6 Abrams pb $24.95

Michael Barrier & Martin Williams, editors
A SMITHSONIAN BOOK OF COMIC BOOK COMICS
0–8109–0696–1 Abrams pb $29.95

Winsor McCay
THE COMPLETE LITTLE NEMO IN SLUMBERLAND
Edited with an introduction by Richard Marshall
0–930193–63–6 Fantagraphics $29.95

DREAMS OF THE RAREBIT FIEND
0–486–21347–1 Dover pb $4.00

Lyonel Feininger
THE KIN-DER-KIDS
0–486–2918–7 Dover pb $6.95

Patrick McDonell & others
KRAZY KAT: The Art of George Herriman
0–8109–1211–2 Abrams $29.95
0–8109–2313–0 Abrams pb $14.95

E.C. Segar
THE COMPLETE E.C. SEGAR POPEYE: Volume 1
0–930193–04–5 Fantagraphics pb $14.95

Chester Gould
DICK TRACY: America's Most Famous Detective
0–8065–1059–5 Citadel pb $12.95

Will Eisner
THE SPIRIT COLOR ALBUMS
0–87816–010–8 Kitchen Sink pb $5.95

Harvey Kurtzman
THE COMPLETE MAD
Four full-color volumes, slipcased, reprinting the first 23 issues of *MAD* comics. For further information apply to Russ Cochran, PO Box 469, West Plains MO, 65775

HARVEY KURTZMAN'S JUNGLE BOOK
0–87816–033–7 Kitchen Sink pb $14.95

Robert Crumb
R. CRUMB'S HEAD COMIX
0–671–66153–1 Simon & Schuster pb $9.95

Art Spiegelman & Françoise Mouly, editors
RAW: Open Wounds from the Cutting Edge of Comics
0–14–012265–6 Penguin pb $14.95

READ YOURSELF RAW
0–394–75551–0 Pantheon pb $14.95

• **Milton Caniff**
THE COMPLETE DICKIE DARE
Caniff's first comic strip, featuring the exploits of Dickie Dare, Dan Flynn, and Kim Sheridan
0–930193–21–0 Fantagraphics pb $12.95

MALE CALL: The Complete War Time Strip, 1942–46
A wartime morale-booster, featuring the adventures of the alluring pin-up girl Miss Lace
Introduction by Bill Mauldin
0–87816–027–2 Kitchen Sink pb $11.95

STEVE CANYON: Fortieth Anniversary Collection
Three complete adventures of the aviator hero
0–87816–032–9 Kitchen Sink pb $7.95

TERRY AND THE PIRATES

Volume 1: Welcome to China
0–918348–20–X NBM pb $6.95

Volume 2: Marooned with Burma
0–918348–23–4 NBM pb $6.95

Volume 3: Dragon Lady's Revenge
0–918348–26–9 NBM pb $5.95

Volume 4: Getting Snared
0–918348–32–3 NBM pb $5.95

Volume 5: Shanghaied
0–918348–35–8 NBM pb $5.95

Volume 6: The Warlord Klans
0–918348–37–4 NBM pb $6.95

Volume 7: The Hunter
0–918348–42–0 NBM pb $6.95

Volume 8: The Baron
0–918348–24–2 NBM pb $6.95

Volume 9: Feminine Venom
0–918348–40–4 NBM pb $6.95

Volume 10: Network of Intrigue
0–918348–60–9 NBM pb $6.95

Volume 11: Gal Got Our Pal
0–918348–63–3 NBM pb $6.95

• **John P. Adams & Richard Marschall**
MILTON CANIFF: Rembrandt of the Comic Strip
Updated edition of a 1946 biography of Caniff, containing many rare illustrations
Introduction by Milton Caniff
0–918348–04–8 NBM pb $6.95

• **Al Capp**
LI'L ABNER
The first in a reprint series devoted to the chronicles of Dogpatch
0–87816–036–1 Kitchen Sink $27.95
0–87816–037–X Kitchen Sink pb $16.95

• **Condo & Raper**
THE OUTBURSTS OF EVERETT TRUE
Everett True, a portly man with a short fuse, has been described as a "living protest against the incarnate irritants that are with us always." This collection first appeared in 1907
0–911572–30–9 Vestal pb $4.95

• **Roy Crane**
WASH TUBBS AND CAPTAIN EASY
Humor and two-fisted adventure, as Wash and his pals Gozzy Gallup and Captain

---

Easy battle Bull Dawson and Shanghai Slug

Volume 1: 1924–1925
0–918348–44–7 NBM pb $16.95

Volume 2: 1925–1926
0–918348–46–3 NBM pb $16.95

Volume 3: 1927–1928
0–918348–51–X NBM pb $16.95

Volume 4: 1928–1930
0–918348–53–6 NBM pb $16.95

• **Will Eisner**
HAWKS OF THE SEAS
This 1930s pirate strip, reproduced here in oversize format, was the first major work of one of the most enduring figures in comics
Introduction by Al Williamson
0–87816–023–X Kitchen Sink pb $12.95

• **Lyonel Feininger**
THE KIN-DER-KIDS: All 31 Strips in Full Color
The Bauhaus painter's contribution to comic strips, which first appeared in the *Chicago Sunday Tribune* in 1906
0–486–23918–7 Dover pb $6.95

• **Hal Foster**
PRINCE VALIANT
Hal Foster's beautifully drawn, long-running medieval epic represents the peak of heroic style in comics. The Fantagraphics editions are full-color reprints in chronological order, of which the volumes listed below are currently available

Volume 28: The Savage Girl
0–930193–12–1 Fantagraphics pb $8.95

Volume 29: Monastery of Demons
0–930193–08–3 Fantagraphics pb $8.95

Volume 30: Arn, Son of Valiant
0–930193–22–9 Fantagraphics pb $9.95

Volume 31: A Joust for Aleta
0–930193–38–5 Fantagraphics pb $9.95

• **Chester Gould**
DICK TRACY: America's Most Famous Detective
Edited by Bill Crouch, Jr.
0–8065–1059–5 Citadel pb $12.95

• **Harold Gray**
THE COMPLETE LITTLE ORPHAN ANNIE: 1931
Harold Gray's original, haunting epic poem of America from the 1920s to the 1950s, delineated in his unmistakable and stunningly effective style

Volume 1
0–930193–39–3 Fantagraphics pb $14.95

Volume 2
0–930193–60–1 Fantagraphics pb $14.95

LITTLE ORPHAN ANNIE
0–486–24420–2 Dover pb $2.75

LITTLE ORPHAN ANNIE IN COSMIC CITY
0–486–24421–0 Dover pb $1.95

LITTLE ORPHAN ANNIE IN THE GREAT DEPRESSION
0–486–23737–0 Dover pb $2.50

• George Herriman
KRAZY AND IGNATZ: The Komplete Kat Komics
0–913035–48–3 Eclipse pb $9.95

• Patrick McDonnell & others
KRAZY KAT: The Art of George Herriman
"From the appearance of *Krazy Kat* before the First World War, it's been widely recognized that Herriman had achieved something not only entrancing on its own terms but also uncannily modern, bearing deep affinities to the spirit and form of crucial styles in vanguard art"—Adam Gopnik, *NY Review of Books*
Introduction by Gilbert Seldes
0–8109–1211–2 Abrams $29.95
0–8109–2313–0 Abrams pb $14.95

Winsor McCay

John Canemaker
WINSOR McCAY: His Life and Art
A lavish survey of a great pioneer of popular art, creator of *Little Nemo in Slumberland, Dreams of the Rarebit Fiend,* and the early animated film *Gertie the Dinosaur*
Foreword by Maurice Sendak
0–89659–687–7 Abbeville $55.00

Winsor McCay
THE COMPLETE LITTLE NEMO IN SLUMBERLAND
Edited with an introduction by Richard Marshall
0–930193–63–6 Fantagraphics $29.95

DREAMS AND NIGHTMARES: Black and White Art of Winsor McCay
0–930193–56–3 Fantagraphics $19.95

DREAMS OF THE RAREBIT FIEND
The surreal effects of eating Welsh rarebit, documented with McCay's usual precision and splendor in a run of strips first collected in 1905
0–486–21347–1 Dover pb $4.00

LITTLE NEMO IN THE PALACE OF ICE
Full-color reproductions of some of the best episodes from *Little Nemo in Slumberland*
0–486–23234–4 Dover pb $5.95

• Richard F. Outcault
BUSTER BROWN
Fifteen episodes from the turn-of-the-century strip, reproduced in the original full colors
0–486–23006–6 Dover pb $3.75

• Alex Raymond, Dashiell Hammett & Leslie Charteris
SECRET AGENT X-9
Not the best of Hammett, and a far cry from his usual hardboiled heroes, but Alex Raymond's artwork is outstanding as always
0–930330–05–6 International Polygonics pb $9.95

• E.C. Segar
THE COMPLETE SEGAR POPEYE
The most popular and enduring comic strip character ever created, presented in oversized format

From Dreams of the Rarebit Fiend *by Winsor McCay (Dover)*

Volume 2
0–930193–04–0 Fantagraphics pb $14.95

Volume 3
0–930193–10–5 Fantagraphics pb $14.95

Volume 4
0–930193–19–9 Fantagraphics pb $14.95

Volume 5
0–930193–29–6 Fantagraphics pb $14.95

Volume 6
0–930193–50–4 Fantagraphics pb $14.95

Volume 7
0–930193–58–X Fantagraphics pb $14.95

Volume 8
0–930193–86–5 Fantagraphics pb $14.95

Brian Walker
THE BEST OF ERNIE BUSHMILLER'S NANCY
A wonderful compilation of one of the most popular and most imaginative comic strips ever
0–8050–0925–6 Henry Holt pb $10.95

COMICS OF THE 1950s AND '60s

• V.T. Hamlin
ALLEY OOP: The Sawalla Chronicles
0–912277–02–5 Ken Pierce pb $5.95

• Johnny Hart & Brant Parker
WIZARD OF ID: Charge!
0–449–12737–0 Fawcett pb $1.95

WIZARD OF ID: Pick a Card, Any Card
0–449–12923–3 Fawcett pb $2.95

• Crockett Johnson
BARNABY: Mr. O'Malley Goes for the Gold
0–345–32880–9 Ballantine pb $2.95

BARNABY: Wanted: A Fairy Godmother
0–345–32673–3 Ballantine pb $2.95

• Walt Kelly
PLUPERFECT POGO
0–671–64220–0 Simon & Schuster pb $10.95

POGO: Even Better
Introduction by Jeff McNelly
0–671–50473–8 Simon & Schuster pb $9.95

POGO: Romances Recaptured
0–671–22184–1 Simon & Schuster pb $9.95

POGO: We Have Met the Enemy and He Is Us
0–671–21260–5 Simon & Schuster pb $7.95

POGO'S DOUBLE SUNDAE
0–671–24139–7 Simon & Schuster pb $9.95

TEN EVER-LOVIN' BLUE-EYED YEARS WITH POGO
0–671–21428–4 Simon & Schuster pb $11.95

• Hank Ketchum
DENNIS THE MENACE: Good Intenshuns
0–449–12730–3 Fawcett pb $1.95

• Charles Saxon, editor
PETER ARNO
0–8253–0401–6 Beaufort pb $14.95

• Charles M. Schulz
HAPPINESS IS A WARM PUPPY
0–886873–11–8 Pharos pb $5.95

YOU'RE ON THE WRONG FOOT AGAIN, CHARLIE BROWN
0–887873–13–4 Pharos pb $5.95

New Yorker Anthologies

THE NEW YORKER ALBUM OF DRAWINGS, 1925–1975
0–14–004968–1 Penguin pb $15.95

THE NEW YORKER CARTOON ALBUM, 1975–1985
0–670–80677–3 Viking $20.00
0–14–008111–9 Penguin pb $14.95

CONTEMPORARY COMIC STRIP ARTISTS AND CARTOONISTS

• Lynda Barry
BIG IDEAS
0–941104–07–9 Real Comet pb $5.95

EVERYTHING IN THE WORLD
0–06–096107–4 Harper & Row pb $7.95

THE FUN HOUSE
0–06–096228–3 Harper & Row pb $8.95

GIRLS AND BOYS
0–941104–00–1 Real Comet pb $5.95

MODERN ROMANCE
0–06–096198–8 Harper & Row pb $8.95

NAKED LADIES, NAKED LADIES, NAKED LADIES
0–941104–13–3 Real Comet pb $9.95

• Berke Breathed
BLOOM COUNTY BABYLON: Five Years of Basic Naughtiness
0–316–10724–7 Little, Brown $24.45
0–316–10309–8 Little, Brown pb $12.45

Roz Chast
THE FOUR ELEMENTS
0–06–096294–1 Harper & Row pb $8.95

MONDO BOXO
0–06–015795–X Harper & Row $15.95

PARALLEL UNIVERSES
0–06–091177–8 Harper & Row pb $8.95

UNSCIENTIFIC AMERICANS
0–385–27622–2 Doubleday pb $9.95

● Howard Cruse
DANCIN' NEKKID WITH THE ANGELS
Funny, moving, superbly drawn vignettes of sex, gay life, drugs, censorship, and other aspects of life in the 1980s
0–87816–028–0 Kitchen Sink pb $25.00

● Jim Davis
THE GARFIELD TREASURY
0–345–32106–5 Ballantine pb $8.95

THE SECOND GARFIELD TREASURY
0–345–33276–8 Ballantine pb $8.95

THE THIRD GARFIELD TREASURY
0–345–32635–0 Ballantine pb $8.95

THE FOURTH GARFIELD TREASURY
0–345–34726–9 Ballantine pb $9.95

● Michael Dougan
EAST TEXAS: Tales from Behind the Pine Curtain
"Michael Dougan's *East Texas* whomps you on the behind and makes your eyeballs bug straight out of your head"—Lynda Barry
0–941104–25–7 Real Comet pb $7.95

● George Gately
HEATHCLIFF
0–515–09242–8 Berkley pb $2.25

HEATHCLIFF RIDES AGAIN
0–515–09383–1 Berkley pb $2.25

● Bill Griffith
ARE WE HAVING FUN YET?: Zippy the Pinhead's 29-Day Guide to Random Activities and Arbitrary Donuts
The syndicated pinhead offers travel tips and helpful hints in 29 "detours." Contains a foldout map of Zip-World
0–525–48184–2 Dutton pb $6.95

KING PIN
0–525–48330–6 Dutton pb $7.95

ZIPPY: Nation of Pinheads
0–915904–71–3 And/Or pb $5.95

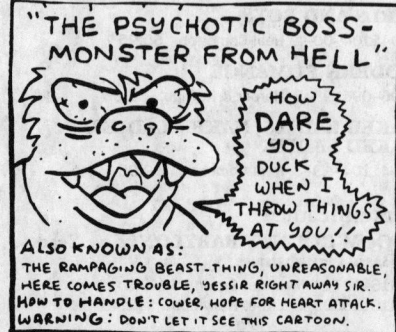

From Matt Groening's Work Is Hell
(*Pantheon*)

Matt Groening
"Matt Groening is the rambunctious, unpredictable, taboo-defying alternative cartoonist who makes Gary Trudeau's *Doonesbury* seem, by comparison, reminiscent of *Mary Worth*."—LA Times

CHILDHOOD IS HELL
0–679–72055–3 Pantheon pb $5.95

LOVE IS HELL
0–394–74454–3 Pantheon pb $5.95

SCHOOL IS HELL
0–394–75091–8 Pantheon pb $5.95

WORK IS HELL
0–394–74864–6 Pantheon pb $5.95

● Cathy Guisewite
A HAND TO HOLD, AN OPINION TO REJECT
0–8362–2092–7 Andrews & McMeel pb $6.95

● William Hamilton
THE MEN WILL FEAR YOU, AND THE WOMEN WILL ADORE YOU
0–312–52965–1 St. Martin's pb $5.95

● Marian Henley
MAXINE
Life and loves of a 1980s "material girl"
0–452–25999–1 NAL pb $6.95

● Nicole Hollander
"Please send me more feminists like the saucy Nicole Hollander, creator of the fiftyish, wisecracking, chain-smoking, beer-swilling Sylvia"—Mordecai Richler, *NY Times*

NEVER TELL YOUR MOTHER THIS DREAM
0–312–56480–5 St. Martin's pb $4.95

NEVER TAKE YOUR CAT TO A SALAD BAR: New Sylvia Cartoons
0–394–75558–8 Random House pb $5.95

THE WHOLE ENCHILADA: A Spicy Collection of Sylvia
0–312–87757–9 St. Martin's pb $11.95

● Edward Koren
ARE YOU HAPPY? & OTHER QUESTIONS LOVERS ASK
0–394–50271–X Pantheon $3.95

● B. Kliban
THE BIGGEST TONGUE IN TUNISIA & OTHER DRAWINGS
0–14–007220–9 Penguin pb $5.95

CAT
0–911104–54–2 Workman pb $3.95

NEVER EAT ANYTHING BIGGER THAN YOUR HEAD & OTHER DRAWINGS
0–911104–67–4 Workman pb $3.95

WHACK YOUR PORCUPINE & OTHER DRAWINGS
0–911104–92–5 Workman pb $3.95

● Mark Kostabi
SADNESS BECAUSE THE VIDEO RENTAL STORE WAS CLOSED & OTHER STORIES
0–89659–800–4 Abbeville $19.95

● Gary Larson
THE FAR SIDE
0–8362–1200–2 Andrews & McMeel pb $5.95

THE FAR SIDE GALLERY
0–8362–2062–5 Andrews & McMeel pb $10.95

THE FAR SIDE GALLERY TWO
0–8362–2085–4 Andrews & McMeel pb $10.95

● Lee Lorenz
THE GOLDEN AGE OF TRASH: Cartoons for the '80s
Pokes at corporate America
0–87701–450–7 Chronicle pb $8.95

● The Mad Peck
MAD PECK STUDIOS: A 20-Year Retrospective
A gathering of work by the underground cartoonist and mad mail-order genius
0–385–23908–4 Doubleday pb $7.95

● Michael Maslin
THE GANG'S ALL HERE
0–671–63536–0 Simon & Schuster pb $5.95

THE MORE THE MERRIER: 110 Cartoons on Life, Love and Further Adventures in Dining
0–671–63535–2 Simon & Schuster pb $5.95

● Russell Myers
BROOM HILDA: The Backward Heimlich
0–449–12992–6 Fawcett pb $2.25

● Jean-Jacques Sempé
THE MUSICIANS
Sixteen color and 49 black-and-white illustrations by the *New Yorker* cover artist
0–89480–099–X Workman pb $14.95

● William Steig
DRAWINGS
Introduction by Lillian Ross
0–374–29031–8 Farrar, Straus and Giroux $19.95

● Gary B. Trudeau
DEATH OF A PARTY ANIMAL
0–8050–0073–9 Henry Holt pb $5.95

DOONESBURY
0–07–065294–5 McGraw-Hill pb $7.95

THE DOONESBURY CHRONICLES
0–03–015256–9 Henry Holt pb $12.95

DOONESBURY DELUXE: Selected Glances Askance
0–8050–0595–1 Henry Holt $22.95
0–8050–0596–X Henry Holt pb $12.95

DOWNTOWN DOONESBURY
0–8050–0354–1 Henry Holt pb $5.95

IN SEARCH OF REAGAN'S BRAIN
0–03–059788–9 Henry Holt pb $5.25

THE PEOPLE'S DOONESBURY: Notes from Underfoot
0–03–049171–1 Henry Holt pb $12.95

READ MY LIPS, MAKE MY DAY, EAT QUICHE AND DIE
0–8362–1845–0 Andrews & McMeel pb $6.95

WE'RE EATING MORE BEETS!
0–8050–0932–9 Henry Holt pb $6.95

● Bill Watterson
CALVIN AND HOBBES
0–8362–2088–9 Andrews & McMeel pb $6.95

☞ **TO ORDER NEW BOOKS NOT YET LISTED, ASK YOUR BOOKSELLER OR CALL 1-800-882-8770**

From Read My Lips, Make My Day, Eat Quiche and Die! *by Gary Trudeau (courtesy of Andrews & McMeel)*

THE ESSENTIAL CALVIN AND HOBBES
0–8362–1805–1 Andrews & McMeel pb $12.95

• Gahan Wilson
GAHAN WILSON'S AMERICA
0–671–62789–9 Simon & Schuster pb $8.95

POLITICAL CARTOONISTS

• Charles Brooks, editor
BEST EDITORIAL CARTOONS OF THE YEAR: 1988 Edition
An annual series compiled with the cooperation of the Association of American Editorial Cartoonists
0–88289–687–3 Pelican pb $9.95

• Jerry Robinson, editor
THE 1970s: Best Editorial Cartoons of the Decade
0–07–053281–8 McGraw-Hill pb $8.95

• Zbynek Zeman
HECKLING HITLER: Caricatures of the Third Reich
A study of anti-Nazi cartoons, with profiles of the artists and numerous illustrations
0–87451–396–0 New England $25.00
0–87451–403–7 New England pb $14.95

• Jules Feiffer
FEIFFER'S CHILDREN
0–8362–2074–9 Andrews & McMeel pb $6.95

JULES FEIFFER'S AMERICA FROM EISENHOWER TO REAGAN
0–394–52846–8 Knopf $25.00
0–394–71279–X Knopf pb $12.95

• Herblock
HERBLOCK AT LARGE: Let's Go Back a Little and Other Cartoons from the Reagan Era
0–394–56569–X Pantheon pb $16.95

• David Low
YEARS OF WRATH: Cartoon History, 1932–1945
A 1949 collection of political cartoons from London's *Evening Standard*, with detailed commentary by Low
0–575–03822–5 David & Charles pb $14.95

• Colin Seymour-Ure & Jom Schoff
DAVID LOW
A full-length appreciation of Britain's preeminent political cartoonist, abundantly illustrated
0–436–44755–X David & Charles pb $20.95

• Bill Mauldin
BILL MAULDIN'S ARMY: Bill Mauldin's Greatest World War II Cartoons
0–89141–180–1 Presidio $25.00
0–89141–159–3 Presidio pb $12.95

LET'S DECLARE OURSELVES WINNERS . . . AND GET THE HELL OUT
0–89141–115–1 Presidio pb $12.95

UP FRONT
The legendary wartime chronicles of Willie and Joe
Introduction by David Halberstam
0–393–08493–0 Norton pb $8.95

• Pat Oliphant
BETWEEN ROCK AND HARD PLACE
0–8362–2084–6 Andrews & McMeel pb $8.95

UP TO THERE IN ALLIGATORS
0–8362–2095–1 Andrews & McMeel pb $8.95

• Dwane Powell
THE REAGAN CHRONICLES: A Cartoon Carnival
A retrospective of the Reagan presidency by a cartoonist who has won the National Headliners Award and the Overseas Press Citation
0–912697–72–5 Algonquin pb $6.95

• Gerald Scarfe
SCARFE BY SCARFE: An Autobiography in Pictures
Drawings, paintings, and sculpture by the caustic British political cartoonist
0–241–11959–6 David and Charles $34.95

• Mark Alan Stamaty
MORE WASHINGTOONS
The further adventures of Senator Bob Forehead, reprinted from *The Village Voice*
0–13–601154–3 Prentice-Hall pb $8.95

AMERICAN COMIC BOOKS

• Michael Barrier & Martin Williams, editors
A SMITHSONIAN BOOK OF COMIC BOOK COMICS
A companion volume to Barrier's earlier comic strip book, magnificently printed
0–8109–0696–1 Abrams $29.95

• Mark J. Estren
THE HISTORY OF UNDERGROUND COMICS
A straightforward, richly illustrated volume with an extraordinary assemblage of hallucinatory raunch from the '60s and '70s
0–914171–11–9 Ronin $17.95

• Ron Goulart
THE GREAT COMIC BOOK ARTISTS
0–312–34557–7 St. Martin's pb $12.95

RON GOULART'S GREAT HISTORY OF COMIC BOOKS
0–8092–5045–4 Contemporary pb $14.95

• Gary Groth & Robert Fiore
THE NEW COMICS
Interviews with Harvey Kurtzman, Art Spiegelman, the Hernandez Brothers, and many more artists
0–425–11366–3 Berkley pb $8.95

• Hal Morgan and Daniel Symmes
AMAZING 3-D
Survey of 3-D comics and movies, with many sample pages and a pair of 3-D glasses with which to view them
0–316–58283–2 Little, Brown pb $14.95

Fritz the Cat, from The Complete Crumb Comics: Volume 3 (*Fantagraphics*)

Superman

John Byrne & Dick Giordano
SUPERMAN: The Man of Steel
New adventures of a Superman revamped for the 1980s
0–345–3509–6 Ballantine pb $12.95

Dennis Dooley & Gary Engle, editors
SUPERMAN AT FIFTY: The Persistence of a Myth
A collection of essays on the definitive superhero
0–940601–00–1 Octavia $16.95

• **Carl Barks**
UNCLE SCROOGE McDUCK: His Life and Times
A sumptuous anthology, beautifully colored, filled with masterpieces by the legendary "good duck artist"
Edited by Edward Summer
Introduction by George Lucas
0–89087–511–1 Celestial Arts $59.95
0–89087–510–3 Celestial Arts pb $34.95

• **Robert Crumb**
THE COMPLETE CRUMB COMICS
Early strips and drawings by the emperor of underground comics. "Makes me proud to be an American"—Kurt Vonnegut Jr.

Volume 1
0–930193–42–3 Fantagraphics pb $12.95

Volume 2
0–930193–62–8 Fantagraphics pb $14.95

Volume 3
0–930193–75–X Fantagraphics pb $14.95

R. CRUMB'S HEAD COMIX
Mr. Natural, Flaky Foont, Fritz the Cat, and the rest of the crew
0–671–66153–1 Simon & Schuster pb $9.95

• **Will Eisner**
THE BUILDING
The interconnections between four individuals involved with a city building under demolition. "A brilliant, graceful graphic novel by the master. It brought tears to my cynical eyes"—Max Allan Collins, *Comic Buyer's Guide*
0–87816–025–6 Kitchen Sink pb $8.95

A CONTRACT WITH GOD
The lives of tenants at 55 Dropsie Avenue in the Bronx during the 1930s
0–87816–018–3 Kitchen Sink pb $7.95

THE DREAMER
This graphic novella is an autobiographical account of Eisner's early publishing experiences
0–87816–015–9 Kitchen Sink $17.50
0–87816–016–7 Kitchen Sink pb $6.95

SIGNAL FROM SPACE
A science-fiction story by the creator of *The Spirit*
0–317–00648–7 Kitchen Sink pb $6.95

THE SPIRIT COLOR ALBUM
Each of these volumes contains 13 Spirit stories in full color

Volume 2
0–87816–010–8 Kitchen Sink pb $5.95

Volume 3
0–87816–011–6 Kitchen Sink pb $5.95

• **Will Eisner, Wallace Wood, & Jules Feiffer**
THE OUTER SPACE SPIRIT
The Spirit's 1952 finale
Introductions by Pete Hamill & Catherine Yronwode
0–87816–007–8 Kitchen Sink $15.95

• **Harvey Pekar**
AMERICAN SPLENDOR
0–385–23195–4 Doubleday pb $7.95

MORE AMERICAN SPLENDOR
The first two volumes of an ongoing autobiographical series, illustrated by Robert Crumb and others. "Pekar has . . . proven that comics can address the ambiguities of daily living, that like the finest fiction they can hold a mirror up to life"—*NY Times*
0–385–24073–2 Doubleday pb $7.95

• **Joe Simon & Jack Kirby**
REAL LOVE: The Best of the Simon & Kirby Love Comics, 1940s–1950s
0–913035–63–7 Eclipse pb $9.95

The "Raw" Artists

Raw magazine has been variously described as "the hippest, artiest, and most intense of the New Comix publications" (*Los Angeles Weekly*), "the best-looking satire magazine in the country today" (*Daily News*), and "a magazine of visual literature, occupying the new terrain outside the comic book world, outside the art world" (*The Village Voice*). Under the editorship of Art Spiegelman and Françoise Mouly, *Raw* has established itself as a prime influence on contemporary graphics and sensibilities.

Art Spiegelman & Françoise Mouly
READ YOURSELF RAW
Reprints from the rare early issues of *Raw,* including work in a variety of surprising formats
0–394–75551–0 Pantheon pb $14.95

Art Spiegelman
MAUS: A Survivor's Tale
In this extraordinary transmutation of his father's memories of the Holocaust, Spiegelman has created a masterpiece of the comics medium. *Maus* was nominated for a National Book Critics Circle Award
0–394–74723–2 Pantheon pb $8.95

Mark Beyer
AGONY
The primitive cartoonist's protagonists experience the "ecstasy of agony" in this beautifully packaged miniature book with one panel per page. "A worldview closer to Kafka's than to Superman's"—C. Carr, *Village Voice*
0–394–75442–5 Pantheon pb $7.95

Charles Burns
HARD-BOILED DEFECTIVE TALES
"The work of Charles Burns is a vision that's both horrifying and hilariously funny"—R. Crumb
0–394–75441–7 Pantheon pb $8.95

Drew & Josh Friedman
ANY SIMILARITY TO PERSONS LIVING OR DEAD IS PURELY COINCIDENTAL
Born-again black humor from the caustic chroniclers of celebrity geeksville
0–930193–15–6 Fantagraphics pb $11.95

Kaz
BUZZBOMB
Frenetic and explosive work by a cartoonist who has appeared in *Weirdo* and *Raw*
0–930193–57–1 Fantagraphics pb $9.95

Gary Panter
JIMBO: Adventures in Paradise
Jimbo confronts the universe, in pages by the *Raw* cartoonist and TV designer (*Pee-Wee's Playhouse*)
0–394–75639–8 Pantheon pb $14.95

AMERICAN GRAPHIC NOVELS

• **Robert Asprin & Lynn Abbey**
THIEVES' WORLD GRAPHICS: Book One
Fantasy humor, adapted from Asprin's novel *Another Fine Myth*
Illustrated by Tim Sale
0–89865–460–2 Starblaze pb $12.95

• **Kyle Baker**
THE COWBOY WALLY SHOW
A show-biz satire tracing the career of "legendary film star" Cowboy Wally
0–385–24122–4 Doubleday pb $8.95

From Maus *by Art Spiegelman (Pantheon)*

"I NEVER THOUGHT I COULD BE SUCH GOOD FRIENDS WITH GIRLS, TO TELL YOU THE TRUTH. I'VE ALWAYS HAD TROUBLE WITH THEM IN ONE WAY OR ANOTHER. MAYBE IT'S THE GIRLS I HUNG OUT WITH, MAYBE IT'S ME, I DON'T KNOW. BUT I REALLY, HONESTLY LIKED HOPEY AND MAGGIE, AND I BELIEVE THEY REALLY, HONESTLY LIKED ME. COOL, HUH?"

From The Lost Women *by Jaime Hernandez (Fantagraphics)*

- **Donald Barthelme & Seymour Chwast**
  SAM'S BAR: An American Landscape
  The regulars at everybody's favorite watering hole, delineated in words and woodcuts by novelist Barthelme and award-winning designer/illustrator Chwast
  0–385–24264–6 Doubleday $15.95

- **Colleen Doran**
  A DISTANT SOIL: The Immigrant Song
  Godlike aliens leave Earth in peace until a 15-year-old girl upsets the balance
  0–89865–514–5 Starblaze pb $6.95

- **John Farris**
  SHATTER
  Collects the first 11 issues of what is said to be the first computer-generated comic book
  0–8125–1780–6 Tor pb $3.95

- **Matt Feazell**
  CYNICALMAN: The Paperback
  Collects Stupid Boy, the Amazing Cynicalman, Cutegirl and other stick-figure characters; a glimpse into the unpredictable world of small-press minicomics
  0–917976–75–4 Thunder Baas pb $7.95

- **John Findley**
  TEX ARCANA
  A black-and-white western fantasy that first appeared in *Heavy Metal*
  0–87416–036–7 Catalan pb $10.95

- **Rick Geary**
  AT HOME WITH RICK GEARY
  Strange humor from *National Lampoon* and elsewhere. "At once an education, a compendium of magic, and a lot of laughs"—Alan Moore
  0–930193–14–8 Fantagraphics pb $9.95

  A TREASURY OF VICTORIAN MURDER
  Graphic novellas of murders researched from 19th-century British newspapers
  0–918348–41–2 NBM pb $6.95

- **Mike Grell**
  JON SABLE, FREELANCE
  A smoothly executed adventure tale, subsequently adapted for television
  0–449–90264–1 Fawcett pb $14.95

Los Brothers Hernandez
LOVE AND ROCKETS
Early issues of *Love and Rockets* collected in book form. "The pure and essential crackle of comic books at their best runs through these pages. Accept no substitute"—Alan Moore

Volume 3
0–930193–31–8 Fantagraphics pb $10.95

Volume 4
0–930193–44–X Fantagraphics pb $10.95

Gilbert Hernandez
THE RETICENT HEART
Eight "Heartbreak Soup" and "Errata Stigmata" stories from *Love and Rockets*. "Mixes Al Capp's blunt carnality with Preston Sturges's compulsive complexities"—*Village Voice*
0–930193–65–2 Fantagraphics pb $10.95

Gilbert Hernandez, Marion Hernandez & Dean Motter
THE RETURN OF MR. X
A science-fiction graphic novel rendered in a style owing much to art deco and German expressionism
0–446–38698–7 Warner pb $8.95

Jaime Hernandez
THE LOST WOMEN & OTHER STORIES
"Mechanics" and "Locas" stories reprinted from the popular comic *Love and Rockets*. "No one has ever caught the punk milieu as well as Jaime Hernandez"—*Louisville Times Scene*
0–930193–66–0 Fantagraphics pb $10.95

- **Rod Kierkegaard, Jr.**
  SHOOTING STARS
  Life on the rock scene
  0–87416–028–6 Catalan pb $12.95

- **Peter Kuper**
  NEW YORK, NEW YORK
  Twelve tales of angst in the Big Apple. "It is Peter Kuper's bent to find the personality lurking within the inanimate and pull it to the surface in all its ironic glory"—*Print Magazine*
  0–930193–54–7 Fantagraphics pb $9.95

- **Harvey Kurtzman & Will Elder**
  GOODMAN BEAVER
  Kurtzman's Candide-like hero encounters Superman, Tarzan, and other media figures in these reprints from the '60s magazine *Help!*
  0–87816–008–6 Kitchen Sink pb $9.95

- **Mark Marek**
  HERCULES AMONGST THE NORTH AMERICANS
  Portrait of the "internationally renowned demi-god and quintessential cosmopolite" as seen on MTV and in *High Times* and *National Lampoon*
  0–14–008215–8 Penguin pb $5.95

- **Frank Miller**
  RONIN
  A dishonored 13th-century samurai resurrected in 21st-century New York: a graphic triumph, with a remarkable contribution by colorist Lynn Varley
  0–446–38674–X Warner pb $12.95

Frank Miller & David Mazzucchelli
BATMAN: Year One
0–446–38923–4 Warner pb $9.95

Frank Miller & others
BATMAN: The Dark Knight Returns
An aged Batman combats '80s-style street crime
0–446–38505–0 Warner pb $12.95

- **Steve Moncuse**
  FISH POLICE
  An underwater fantasy which Harlan Ellison has called "a mystery and a comedy

and a wonky look at a world where what is ain't really what it's supposed to be"
0–446–38739–8 Warner pb $8.95

• Alan Moore & Dave Gibbons
WATCHMEN
A futurist extravaganza, with powerful graphics
0–446–38689–8 Warner pb $14.95

• Alan Moore & others
THE SAGA OF SWAMP THING
0–446–38690–1 Warner pb $10.95

• Pepe Moreno
ZEPPELIN
Fantastic visions of warfare
0–87416–021–9 Catalan pb $10.95

• Wendy & Richard Pini
ELFQUEST
Four volumes of good clean adventurous fun in elfland

Book 1
0–89865–140–9 Starblaze pb $14.95

Book 2
0–89865–245–6 Starblaze pb $14.95

Book 3
0–89865–329–0 Starblaze pb $14.95

Book 4
0–89865–377–0 Starblaze pb $14.95

• Stan Sakai
USAGI YOJIMBO: Book One
The adventures of a samurai rabbit
0–930193–35–0 Fantagraphics pb $9.95

• Dave Stevens
THE ROCKETEER
Action and adventure in 1930s Los Angeles
0–913035–06–8 Eclipse pb $7.95

• Roy Thomas & P. Craig Russell
ELRIC
An adaptation of Michael Moorcock's high-flown fantasy
0–939766–12–4 Marvel pb $5.95

• Doug Wildey
RIO
A western adventure in the classic tradition, with superb artwork by Wildey
0–938965–04–2 Comico pb $8.95

From Usagi Yojimbo *by Stan Sakai* (*Fantagraphics*)

From Lone Wolf and Cub *by Kazuo Koike and Goseki Kojima* (*First*)

• Erick Wujcik, Kevin Eastman & Peter Laird
TEENAGE MUTANT NINJA TURTLES & OTHER STRANGENESS
0–916211–14–2 Palladium pb $9.95

JAPANESE COMICS

"These are the legendary *manga*, the picture books that account for more than a fourth of Japan's publishing and that may yet make literature obsolete. Open one at random and you might find anything—a sleek extraterrestrial landscape, an illustrated treatise on golf or fishing, an episode of torture, an elaborate reconstruction of 16th-century court life or 20th-century gang warfare, a sexy or caricatural romp among high school students—all rendered in a black-and-white so richly varied it makes color beside the point."—*Village Voice*

The world of Japanese comics is only beginning to make its impact felt in America, but the following titles offer some hint of its riches and oddities.

• Shotaro Ishinomori
JAPAN, INC.: Introduction to Japanese Economics (The Comic Book)
A full-scale comic book version of a textbook on the Japanese economy, with a melodramatic plot to speed things along
Introduction by Peter Duus
0–520–06289–2 California pb $10.95

• Kazuo Koike & Goseki Kojima
LONE WOLF AND CUB
The most famous of all Samurai comics: a wandering swordsman's often savage adventures, depicted in brilliantly stylized graphics
0–915419–47–5 First pb $19.95

• Keiji Nakazawa
BAREFOOT GEN: A Cartoon Story of Hiroshima
Nakazawa was a child in Hiroshima when the bomb fell, and in the dense and realistic *Barefoot Gen* he recounts his life up to and including that day
0–86571–095–3 New Society pb $9.95

BAREFOOT GEN: The Day After
A continuation of Nakazawa's autobiographical life-work
Foreword by Barbara Reynolds
0–86571–123–2 New Society pb $8.95

BAREFOOT GEN: Life After the Bomb
The third volume in Nakazawa's continuing series
0–86571–148–8 New Society pb $9.95

• Yoshiro Tatsumi
GOOD-BYE & OTHER STORIES
Life in postwar Japan, rendered with unusual realism
0–87416–056–1 Catalan pb $10.95

• Ian Buruma
BEHIND THE MASK: On Sexual Demons, Sacred Mothers, Transvestites, Gangsters and Other Japanese Cultural Heroes
An analysis of the Japanese psyche as reflected in popular culture: "The violent fantasies of a people forced to be gentle." Much emphasis on comic books
0–452–00738–0 Penguin pb $8.95

Frederik Schodt
MANGA! MANGA!: The World of Japanese Comics
A superbly researched and elegantly written history of Japanese comics, including 96 pages of complete translated stories. "Definitive . . . An unlikely fusion of scholarship, enthusiasm, and wit"—*Village Voice*
0–87011–752–1 Kodansha pb $16.95

EUROPEAN COMICS

• **Donne Avenell & Enrique Romero**
AXA
Erotically-tinged science fiction: the beautiful Axa escapes the safety of the city-domes for a life in the wilds among mutated horrors
0–912277–04–1 Ken Pierce pb $5.95

• **Enki Bilal**
GODS IN CHAOS
Aliens in Paris in the year 2023
0–87416–049–9 Catalan pb $12.95

• **Claire Bretecher**
FRUSTRATION
A satiric portrait of the French middle class
0–8021–3026–7 Grove pb $8.95

Jerome Charyn & François Boucq
THE MAGICIAN'S WIFE
Collaboration between American novelist Charyn and French artist Boucq. "A fascinating work: brilliant, funny, hallucinatory, and, strangest of all, 'realistic' in ways that Charyn's other (prose fiction) work isn't. The drawings are perfectly realized"—Joyce Carol Oates
0–87416–045–6 Catalan pb $14.95

• **Jean-Pierre Dionnet & Enki Bilal**
EXTERMINATOR SEVENTEEN
0–87416–024–3 Catalan pb $11.95

• **Guido Crepax**
THE MAN FROM HARLEM
Crime and jazz in New York during the bebop era
0–87416–040–5 Catalan pb $10.95

• **Jean-Claude Forest & Paul Gillon**
LOST IN TIME: Labyrinths
A 20th-century couple revived in 3000 AD, from the creator of *Barbarella*
0–918348–18–8 NBM pb $8.95

• **Vittorio Giardino**
HUNGARIAN RHAPSODY
A 1938 spy thriller set in Budapest and Paris, drawn with great elegance
0–87416–033–2 Catalan pb $12.95

ORIENT GATEWAY
An Istanbul thriller featuring the hero of *Hungarian Rhapsody*
0–87416–041–3 Catalan pb $12.95

SAM PEZZO, P.I.
A detective adventure in a contemporary setting
0–87416–057–X Catalan pb $8.95

• **Denis Gifford**
THE COMPLETE CATALOGUE OF BRITISH COMICS
An encyclopedic survey with many covers reproduced
0–86350–079–X Viking $24.95

• **Juan Gimenez**
A MATTER OF TIME
Science fiction by an Argentinian artist
Introduction by Carlos Gimenez
0–87416–012–X Catalan pb $8.95

• **Serge Le Tendre & Regis Loisel**
ROXANNA AND THE QUEST FOR THE TIME BIRD: The Temple of Oblivion
0–918348–34–X NBM pb $7.95

• **Loustal & Paringaux**
BARNEY AND THE BLUE NOTE
Downbeat lives and loves in the jazz world, captured in panels of somber beauty
9–072–118–12–X Fantagraphics pb $14.95

• **Milo Manara & Silverio Pisu**
THE APE
An adaptation of the classic Chinese novel *Journey to the West,* concerning the adventures of a magical monkey
0–87416–019–7 Catalan pb $10.95

• **Lorenzo Mattotti**
FIRES
Ecological expressionism as naval officer Lieutenant Absinthe, entranced by a magical island, deserts his ship to save this paradise from destruction
0–87416–048–0 Catalan pb $12.95

• **Nazario**
ANARCOMA
The gay scene in Barcelona, featuring "streetwise transvestite and self-styled detective" Anarcoma
0–87416–000–6 Catalan pb $9.95

• **Hugo Pratt**
CORTO MALTESE IN AFRICA
World War I-era adventures by a popular European comics artist
0–918348–38–2 NBM pb $8.95

• **Hugo Pratt & Milo Manara**
INDIAN SUMMER
An alternately erotic and violent tale of 17th-century New England, focusing on rape, murder, incest, and sadism, with superb color graphics
0–87416–030–8 Catalan pb $17.95

• **Roberto Raviola**
THE SPECIALIST: Full Moon in Dendera
Terrorists and multinationals battle it out in the Middle East
0–87416–044–8 Catalan pb $8.95

• **Marti Riera**
THE CABBIE
Barcelona artist Marti spent three years recapturing the style of Chester Gould's *Dick Tracy* in his own story about a cabdriver, a "prototypical solitary individual, out of touch and helpless in a predatory and hostile world that doesn't have time for people who can't keep up with the Twentieth Century"
Introduction by Art Spiegelman
0–87416–042–1 Catalan pb $10.95

• **Carlos Sampayo & Jose Munoz**
JOE'S BAR
Expressionistic drawings by Munoz illustrate Sampayo's short stories centered on a New York City bar
Introductions by Art Spiegelman & others
0–87416–046–4 Catalan pb $10.95

• **Carlos Sampayo & F. Solano-Lopez**
EVARISTO: Deep City
Violent tales of a Buenos Aires police commissioner in the late 1950s and early 1960s
0–87416–034–0 Catalan pb $10.95

• **Schuiten and Peeters**
THE GREAT WALLS OF SAMARIS
The Belgian artist Schuiten illustrates a haunting tale of the mysterious city Samaris in this large-format graphic novel, first serialized in *Heavy Metal*
0–918348–36–6 NBM pb $9.95

• **Matthias Schultheiss**
BELL'S THEOREM
Eerie science fiction from a West German writer-artist, about a dead scientist's mind resurfacing in an escaped convict
0–87416–037–5 Catalan pb $10.95

• **Stefano Tamburini & Gaetano Liberatore**
RANXEROX IN NEW YORK
Introduction by Richard Corben
0–87416–027–8 Catalan pb $10.95

• **M. Weyland**
ARIA TAKES OFF
A woman warrior in a world dominated by men
0–89865–468–8 Starblaze pb $6.95

Asterix

• **René de Goscinny & Albert Uderzo**
ASTERIX AT THE OLYMPIC GAMES
0–02–497170–7 Macmillan pb $4.95

ASTERIX IN BRITAIN
0–02–506907–1 Macmillan pb $4.95

ASTERIX THE GLADIATOR
0–02–506903–9 Macmillan pb $4.95

ASTERIX THE LEGIONARY
0–02–506909–8 Macmillan pb $4.95

Tintin

The Belgian artist Hergé was one of this century's great storytellers. The Tintin books offer an unending succession of exotic locations, breathless adventures, and brilliant sight gags.

• **Hergé**
THE BLACK ISLAND
0–316–35835–5 Little, Brown pb $6.95

THE BLUE LOTUS
0–316–35856–8 Little, Brown pb $6.95

THE CALCULUS AFFAIR
0–316–35847–9 Little, Brown pb $6.95

THE CASTAFIORE EMERALD
0–316–35842–8 Little, Brown pb $6.95

☛ **FOR ALL OTHER INQUIRIES, PLEASE CALL (212) 333-7900**

From Tintin in America *by Hergé (Little, Brown)*

CIGARS OF THE PHAROAH
0–316–35836–3 Little, Brown pb $6.95

THE CRAB WITH THE GOLDEN CLAWS
0–316–35833–9 Little, Brown pb $6.95

KING OTTOKAR'S SCEPTRE
0–316–35831–2 Little, Brown pb $6.95

PRISONERS OF THE SUN
0–316–35843–6 Little, Brown pb $6.95

RED RACKHAM'S TREASURE
0–316–35834–7 Little, Brown pb $6.95

THE RED SEA SHARKS
0–316–35848–7 Little, Brown pb $6.95

THE SECRET OF THE UNICORN
0–316–35832–0 Little, Brown pb $6.95

THE SEVEN CRYSTAL BALLS
0–316–35840–1 Little, Brown pb $6.95

THE SHOOTING STAR
0–316–35851–7 Little, Brown pb $6.95

TINTIN AND THE PICAROS
0–316–35849–5 Little, Brown pb $6.95

TINTIN IN AMERICA
0–316–35852–5 Little, Brown pb $6.95

TINTIN IN TIBET
0–316–35839–8 Little, Brown pb $6.95

Humor

● Woody Allen
GETTING EVEN
0–394–47348–5 Random House $10.95
0–394–72640–5 Random House pb $2.95

SIDE EFFECTS
0–394–51104–2 Random House $8.95
0–345–34335–2 Ballantine pb $3.50

WITHOUT FEATHERS
0–345–33697–6 Ballantine pb $3.50

● Russell Baker
SO THIS IS DEPRAVITY
0–671–55177–9 Washington Square pb $4.95

● Dave Barry
DAVE BARRY SLEPT HERE
The Pulitzer Prize-winning columnist takes us on a ramble through 200 years of US history—with the dull parts removed
0–394–56541–X Random House $15.95

● Robert Benchley
BENCHLEY LOST AND FOUND
Illustrated by Peter Arno
0–486–22410–4 Dover pb $3.95

THE BENCHLEY ROUNDUP: A Selection by Nathaniel Benchley of His Favorites
Illustrated by Gluyas Williams
0–226–04218–9 Chicago pb $9.95

● Roy Blount, Jr.
ABOUT THREE BRICKS SHY OF A LOAD
0–345–34106–6 Ballantine pb $3.50

CRACKERS
0–345–29805–5 Ballantine pb $3.95

ONE FELL SOUP: Or, I'm Just a Bug on the Windshield of Life
0–14–006892–9 Penguin pb $6.95

WHAT MEN DON'T TELL WOMEN
0–14–007788–X Penguin pb $5.95

● Lenny Bruce
THE UNPUBLISHED LENNY BRUCE
0–89471–260–8 Running Press $19.80
0–89471–259–4 Running Press pb $8.95

● Pedro Carolino
FRACTURED ENGLISH AS SHE IS SPOKE
Introduction by Mark Twain
0–486–22329–9 Dover pb $2.95

● Bill Cosby
FATHERHOOD
0–385–23410–4 Doubleday $14.95
0–425–09772–2 Berkley pb $6.95

● Will Cuppy
THE DECLINE AND FALL OF PRACTICALLY EVERYBODY
Illustrated by William Steig
0–87923–514–4 Godine pb $9.95

● Frank Gannon
YO, POE!
0–670–81481–4 Viking $14.95
0–14–009743–0 Penguin pb $5.95

"I really have no remedy for Sunday afternoon," a drawing by Gluyas Williams, from The Benchley Roundup *(Chicago)*

Veronica Geng
LOVE TROUBLE IS MY BUSINESS
0–06–015969–3 Harper & Row $15.95

PARTNERS
0–06–015295–8 Harper & Row $13.95
0–06–091289–8 Harper & Row pb $6.95

● Cynthia Heimel
BUT ENOUGH ABOUT YOU
0–671–66199–X Simon & Schuster pb $7.95

GRAB HAPPINESS BY THE THROAT: Or, How to Make Friends with Anxiety and Depression
0–671–55264–3 Simon & Schuster $11.95

SEX TIPS FOR GIRLS
0–671–47725–0 Simon & Schuster $7.95

● Garrison Keillor
HAPPY TO BE HERE: Even More Stories and Comic Pieces
0–14–006482–6 Penguin pb $6.95

LAKE WOBEGON DAYS
0–670–80514–9 Viking $17.95
0–14–009983–2 Penguin pb $4.95

LEAVING HOME: A Collection of Lake Wobegon Stories
0–670–81976–X Viking $18.95

● Fran Lebowitz
METROPOLITAN LIFE
0–452–26069–8 NAL pb $7.95

SOCIAL STUDIES
0–671–45047–6 Pocket Books pb $3.50

● Anita Loos
FATE KEEPS ON HAPPENING: Adventures of Lorelei Lee & Other Writings
Edited by Ray P. Corsini
0–396–08398–6 Dodd, Mead pb $3.95

● Jonathan Lynn & Anthony Jay
THE COMPLETE YES MINISTER
0–06–097165–7 Harper & Row pb $9.95

● Don Marquis
ARCHYOLOGY: The Long Lost Tales of Archy and Mehitabel
Illustrated by Edward Gorey
0–02–580410–3 Macmillan $12.95

● Groucho Marx
THE GROUCHO LETTERS: Letters to and from Groucho Marx
0–671–63963–3 Simon & Schuster pb $7.95

● Jackie Mason
THE WORLD ACCORDING TO ME!
0–671–64607–9 Simon & Schuster $16.95

● Monty Python's Flying Circus
THE MEANING OF LIFE
0–394–62474–2 Grove pb $10.95

MONTY PYTHON AND THE HOLY GRAIL
0–458–92970–0 RC&H pb $12.95

● Ogden Nash
I WOULDN'T HAVE MISSED IT: Selected Poems of Ogden Nash
Introduction by Archibald MacLeish
0–316–59830–5 Little, Brown $19.95

 IF YOU CAN'T FIND IT, LOOK IN THE INDEX

OGDEN NASH'S ZOO
0–941434–95–8 Stewart, Tabori & Chang $9.95

YOU CAN'T GET THERE FROM HERE
Illustrated by Maurice Sendak
0–316–59854–2 Little, Brown pb $6.95

Flann O'Brien
THE BEST OF MYLES
Classic humor columns from *The Irish Times,* by the author of *At-Swim-Two-Birds*
0–14–006366–8 Penguin pb $7.95

• Dorothy Parker
THE PORTABLE DOROTHY PARKER
0–14–015074–9 Penguin pb $8.95

• S.J. Perelman
BABY, IT'S COLD INSIDE
0–14–008042–2 Penguin pb $6.95

EASTWARD HA!
0–671–49250–0 Simon & Schuster pb $5.95

THE MOST OF S.J. PERELMAN
0–671–49331–0 Simon & Schuster pb $6.95

THE RISING GORGE
0–14–008041–4 Penguin pb $6.95

THE SWISS FAMILY PERELMAN
0–14–008040–6 Penguin pb $6.95

WESTWARD, HA!: Around the World in 80 Clichés
Illustrated by Al Hirschfeld
0–306–80229–5 Da Capo pb $7.95

Gene Shalit, editor
LAUGHING MATTERS: A Celebration of American Humor
A massive anthology encompassing Will Rogers, Woody Allen, Veronica Geng, Jack Benny, Rube Goldberg, Charles Addams, and many more
0–385–18547–2 Doubleday $24.95

• James Thurber
FABLES FOR OUR TIME & FAMOUS POEMS
0–06–090999–4 Harper & Row pb $6.95

FABLES FOR OUR TIME & FAMOUS POEMS ILLUSTRATED
0–06–014275–8 Harper & Row $11.50

MY LIFE AND HARD TIMES
0–06–080290–1 Harper & Row pb $3.95

A THURBER CARNIVAL
0–394–60474–1 Modern Library $10.95
0–06–090445–3 Harper & Row pb $8.95

• James Thurber & E.B. White
IS SEX NECESSARY?: Or, Why You Feel the Way You Do
0–06–091102–6 Harper & Row pb $6.95

• Calvin Trillin
IF YOU CAN'T SAY SOMETHING NICE
0–89919–531–8 Ticknor & Fields $16.95

• P.G. Wodehouse
CARRY ON, JEEVES
0–14–001174–9 Penguin pb $3.95

THE CODE OF THE WOOSTERS
0–394–72028–8 Random House pb $3.95

THE GOLD BAT & OTHER SCHOOL STORIES
0–14–008080–5 Penguin pb $6.95

HOW RIGHT YOU ARE, JEEVES
0–06–080770–9 Harper & Row pb $3.95

THE INIMITABLE JEEVES
0–14–000933–7 Penguin pb $3.95

JEEVES AND THE FEUDAL SPIRIT
0–06–080666–4 Harper & Row pb $3.95

JEEVES AND THE TIE THAT BINDS
0–06–080667–2 Harper & Row pb $3.50

JEEVES IN THE MORNING
0–06–080658–3 Harper & Row pb $3.95

LIFE AT BLANDINGS, SOMETHING FRESH & SUMMER LIGHTNING
0–14–005903–2 Penguin pb $7.95

LIFE WITH JEEVES, RIGHT HO, JEEVES & THE INIMITABLE JEEVES
0–14–005902–4 Penguin pb $7.95

THE MOST OF P.G. WODEHOUSE
0–671–20349–5 Simon & Schuster pb $12.95

THE RETURN OF JEEVES
0–06–080768–7 Harper & Row pb $3.95

RIGHT HO, JEEVES
0–14–000934–5 Penguin pb $3.95

STIFF UPPER LIP, JEEVES
0–06–080668–0 Harper & Row pb $3.95

SUMMER LIGHTNING
0–14–000995–7 Penguin pb $3.95

THANK YOU, JEEVES
0–06–080657–5 Harper & Row pb $3.95

VERY GOOD, JEEVES
0–14–001173–0 Penguin pb $3.95

VISUAL HUMOR, NOVELTY ITEMS, AND JOKE BOOKS

• Sandra Boynton
A IS FOR ANGRY: An Animal and Adjective Alphabet
0–89480–507–X Workman pb $5.95

• Kevin Cobb
US AND THEM: Or Why America Is Like England, Why England Is Like America and How They Got That Way
Illustrated with photocollages and work by a variety of artists
0–87833–565–X Taylor pb $8.95

• Brian R. Duffy
THE POOR BOY'S GUIDE TO MARRYING A RICH GIRL
0–14–778201–5 Penguin pb $6.95

• Bill Henderson, editor
ROTTEN REVIEWS: A Literary Companion
0–916366–40–5 Pushcart $12.50
0–14–010195–0 Penguin pb $4.95

ROTTEN REVIEWS II: A Literary Companion
0–916366–46–4 Pushcart $12.95

• Tom Hepburn & Selwyn Jacobson
GREAT FISHING LIES OF THE WORLD
"Photo album" of fishing nightmares
0–8431–1988–8 Price Stern Sloan pb $6.95

"In certain moods I love to lapse into song," a drawing by Gluyas Williams, from The Benchley Roundup (*Chicago*)

• Ilene Hochberg
CATMOPOLITAN
0–671–64704–0 Pocket pb $9.95

DOGUE: A Parody of the World's Most Famous Fashion Magazine
1–55562–002–7 Main Street pb $9.95

• Sean Kelly
SPITTING IMAGES
0–15–684819–8 HBJ pb $8.95

• Paul Krassner, editor
BEST OF THE REALIST: The Sixties' Most Outrageously Irreverent Magazine
Cartoons and journalism from the influential and frequently outrageous radical humor periodical
Introduction by Ken Kesey
0–89471–289–6 Running Press $19.80
0–89471–287–X Running Press pb $9.95

• Steven Lukes & Itzhak Galnoor
NO LAUGHING MATTER: A Collection of Political Jokes
0–14–009357–5 Penguin pb $4.95

• Hal Morgan & Kerry Tucker
RUMOR!
0–14–010029–6 Penguin pb $3.50

MORE RUMOR!
0–14–009720–1 Penguin pb $3.50

• Tom Parker
RULES OF THUMB
0–395–34642–8 Houghton Mifflin pb $6.95

RULES OF THUMB II
0–395–42955–2 Houghton Mifflin pb $6.95

• E.O. Parrott, editor
HOW TO BECOME RIDICULOUSLY WELL-READ IN ONE EVENING: A Collection of Literary Encapsulations
0–670–80226–3 Viking $12.95
0–14–007451–1 Penguin pb $5.95

• David Reid & Jonathan Jerald
PURE SILVER: The Second Best of Everything
0–15–679960–X HBJ pb $10.95

• Scott Rice, editor
IT WAS A DARK AND STORMY NIGHT: The Best(?) from the Bulwer-Lytton Contest
0–14–007556–9 Penguin pb $5.95

• Samuel Z. Salant
AN ILLUSTRATED ACCIDENCE AND GALLIMAUFRY OF THE ANGLISH LINGUAGE
Visual puns
1–55562–036–1 Main Street pb $8.95

• Ina Schell
CQ (CANINE QUARTERLY): A Parody of the World's Most Elegant Magazine for Men
1–55562–035–3 Main Street pb $8.95

• Spy Magazine
SEPARATED AT BIRTH?
0–385–24744–3 Doubleday pb $6.95

• Ralph Steadman
SCAR-STRANGLED BANNER
Modern America lampooned in paintings, drawings, and satirical essays
0–88162–314–8 Salem $29.95

• Linda Sunshine
WOMEN WHO DATE TOO MUCH (AND THOSE WHO SHOULD BE SO LUCKY)
0–453–00608–6 NAL $10.95

▣ **TO ORDER BOOKS AS GIFTS, SEE PAGE 1**

PART 5

BOOKS FOR YOUNG READERS

Books for Children Under Five

FIRST BOOKS: Cloth and Board Books for Babies and Toddlers

A book to a baby is a thing to chew on, throw out of the crib, or pull about; and a sturdily made cloth book is an excellent toy. Once children become old enough to make out the pictures, books are satisfying for other reasons. For the toddler, looking at books is a pleasurable activity. "Reading" allows the child to climb into Mommy's or Daddy's lap with the book, cuddle up, and help turn the pages. Small children know that the adult is paying special attention to them; it's a good feeling. With luck the pictures are interesting, too.

The best books are those with uncluttered, self-explanatory pictures and very brief text. Very small children like to hear you "read," but they can't grasp more than one short line at a time. Successful baby books are distinguished by simplicity; bad ones try to do too much or introduce material that young children shouldn't need to understand—and won't anyway.

Glossary for Parents

Several medals and awards are mentioned alongside books in our selection. The awards mean the following:

The American Library Association Awards: Several are awarded each year to worthy children's books in different categories.

The Caldecott Medal: Named after Randolph Caldecott, a 19th-century British illustrator, this is an annual award bestowed by the Children's Services Division of the American Library Association. It is awarded to the best illustrated children's picture book. Several Honor books are chosen as well.

The John Newbery Medal: The companion award to the Caldecott, also given annually by the American Library Association "to the author for the most distinguished contribution to American literature for children."

The Laura Ingalls Wilder Medal: Awarded on occasion by the American Library Association to a living author distinguished by his or her extraordinary lifetime contributions to children's literature.

• Joan Walsh Anglund
BABY'S FIRST BOOK
0–394–87470–6 Random House $2.95

• Sandra Boynton
These quirkily humorous pictures make a pleasant change for adults; the lulling text is just what toddlers want to hear.
BUT NOT THE HIPPOPOTAMUS
0–671–44904–4 Simon & Schuster (boards) $3.95

THE GOING TO BED BOOK
0–671–44902–8 Simon & Schuster (boards) $3.95

MOO BAA LA LA LA
0–671–44901–X Simon & Schuster (boards) $3.95

• Dick Bruna
Dick Bruna's books feature simplified, almost geometric animals and people in bright colors.
ANIMALS
0–8431–1575–0 Price, Stern, Sloan $2.95

FARMER JOHN
0–8431–1526–2 Price, Stern, Sloan $2.95

MIFFY AT THE PLAYGROUND
0–8431–1543–2 Price, Stern, Sloan $2.95

MIFFY AT THE ZOO
0–8431–1532–7 Price, Stern, Sloan $2.95

• Eric Campbell
The Buster books ask the toddler to keep turning the pages so as to build a picture of the hero in his shirt, pants, boots, or whatever. The activity is easy and satisfying.
BUSTER GETS DRESSED
0–8120–5922–0 Barron's $4.95

BUSTER KEEPS WARM
0–8120–5923–9 Barron's $4.95

• Demi
CUDDLY DUCK
0–448–19154–7 Putnam (boards) $6.95

DOWNY DUCKLING
0–448–19153–9 Putnam (boards) $6.95

FLEECY LAMB
0–448–19152–0 Putnam (boards) $6.95

• Rebecca Dickinson
ANIMAL BABIES
Illustrated by Lisa Bonforte
0–307–12116–X Western $3.50

• Christine Dubov
A baby points out the parts of the body in colorful photographs.
ALEKSANDRA, WHERE IS YOUR NOSE?
Photographs by Josef Schneider
0–312–01719–7 St. Martin's $3.95

ALEKSANDRA, WHERE ARE YOUR TOES?
Photographs by Josef Schneider
0–312–01717–0 St. Martin's $3.95

• Kate Duke
BEDTIME
0–525–44207–3 Dutton pb $2.95

CLEAN UP DAY
0–525–44208–1 Dutton pb $2.95

THE PLAYGROUND
0–525–44206–5 Dutton pb $2.95

WHAT BOUNCES?
0–525–44209–X Dutton pb $2.95

• Phoebe Dunn
Very young children may learn to identify these uncluttered images with ease.
BABY'S ANIMAL FRIENDS
0–394–89583–5 Random House (boards) $2.95

BUSY BUSY TODDLERS
0–394–88604–6 Random House $1.95

I'M A BABY
0–394–88605–4 Random House $1.95

• Ed Emberley
The simplest kind of word book introduces toddlers to everyday objects.
FIRST WORDS: Home
0–316–23433–8 Little, Brown (boards) $3.25

FIRST WORDS: Sounds
0–316–23431–1 Little, Brown (boards) $3.25

• Norman Gorbaty
BABY ANIMALS SAY HELLO
0–394–88241–5 Random House $3.95

• Eric Hill
AT HOME
0–394–85638–4 Random House $2.50

BABY BEAR'S BEDTIME
0–394–86572–3 Random House $3.95

GOOD MORNING, BABY BEAR!
0–394–85637–6 Random House $3.95

MY PETS
0–394–85637–6 Random House $2.50

THE PARK
0–394–85636–8 Random House $2.50

UP THERE
0–394–85635–X Random House $2.50

• Tana Hoban
WHAT IS IT?
An ideal first book. A spoon, a bib, a cup—baby's first possessions—are photographed in color and reproduced on sturdy, babyproof pages
0–688–02577–3 Morrow $3.95

• Dorothy Kunhardt
PAT THE BUNNY
First and best of its kind; fashioned after the ever popular toy busy box. The baby-sized activities are easy, varied, and fun
0–307–12000–7 Western $4.95

• Barbro Lindgren
Sam is a funny-looking fellow though you will learn to like him. Unlike some other fictional two-year-olds he possesses annoying qualities as well as charm; there is a wealth of stubborn energy behind his everyday exploits.
SAM'S BALL
Illustrated by Eva Eriksson
0–688–02359–2 Morrow $6.95

SAM'S BATH
Illustrated by Eva Eriksson
0–688–02362–2 Morrow $5.50

SAM'S POTTY
Illustrated by Eva Eriksson
0–688–06603–8 Morrow $6.95

SAM'S TEDDY BEAR
Illustrated by Eva Eriksson
0–688–01270–1 Morrow $5.95

- **Sara Lynn**

  BIG ANIMALS
  0–689–71098–4 Macmillan (boards) $2.95

  CLOTHES
  0–689–71095–X Macmillan (boards) $2.95

  FARM ANIMALS
  0–689–71100–X Macmillan (boards) $2.95

  HOME
  0–689–71097–6 Macmillan (boards) $2.95

  SMALL ANIMALS
  0–689–71099–2 Macmillan (boards) $2.95

  TOYS
  0–689–71096–8 Macmillan (boards) $2.95

- **Jan Ormerod**

  Humor is evident in the situations, which show a realistic baby doing exactly what he likes while a professorial-looking Dad copes good-humoredly.

  DAD'S BACK
  0–688–04126–4 Lee, Lothrop & Shepard $4.95

  MESSY BABY
  0–688–04128–0 Lee, Lothrop & Shepard $4.95

  READING
  0–688–04127–2 Lee, Lothrop & Shepard $4.95

  SLEEPING
  0–688–04129–9 Lee, Lothrop & Shepard $4.95

- **Helen Oxenbury**

  These are commendably uncomplicated board books, dealing with everyday situations the very young will recognize.

  ALL FALL DOWN
  0–02–769040–7 Macmillan $4.95

  CLAP HANDS
  0–02–769030–X Macmillan $4.95

  DRESSING
  0–671–42113–1 Simon & Schuster $3.50

  PLAYING
  0–671–42109–3 Simon & Schuster $3.50

  SAY GOODNIGHT
  0–02–66–769010–5 Macmillan $4.95

  SHOPPING TRIP
  0–8037–7939–9 Dial (boards) $3.50

  TICKLE TICKLE
  0–02–769020–2 Macmillan $4.95

- **Platt & Munk**

  BABY'S THINGS
  Textless photographs show familiar objects in a book that might be one of the first on a child's bookshelf
  0–448–40866–X Putnam $3.95

- **Charlotte Voake**

  FIRST THINGS FIRST: A Baby's Companion
  An illustrated introduction to numbers, colors, ABCs, shapes, and days of the week, with bouncy pictures
  0–316–90510–0 Little, Brown $12.95

- **Shigeo Watanabe**

  Rather purposeful about introducing notions of autonomy and self-reliance—questionable goals for children this young. But the illustrations are nicely done, and the little bear hero is appealing.

  HOW DO I PUT IT ON?
  Illustrated by Yasuo Ohtomo
  0–399–20761–9 Putnam $10.95
  0–399–21040–7 Putnam pb $4.95

  I CAN TAKE A BATH
  Illustrated by Yasuo Ohtomo
  0–399–21362–7 Putnam $10.95

  I CAN TAKE A WALK
  Illustrated by Yasuo Ohtomo
  0–399–21044–X Putnam $8.95
  0–399–21043–1 Putnam pb $3.95

- **Rosemary Wells**

  Max is a sassy baby rabbit whose sister is his bugaboo. The illustrations are amusing, but the relatively advanced vocabulary may put the dialogue beyond the comprehension of many toddlers.

  MAX'S BATH
  0–8037–0162–4 Dial (boards) $3.50

  MAX'S BEDTIME
  0–8037–0160–8 Dial (boards) $3.50

  MAX'S BIRTHDAY
  0–8037–0163–2 Dial (boards) $3.50

  MAX'S BREAKFAST
  0–8037–0161–6 Dial (boards) $3.50

- **Harriet Ziefert**

  ALL CLEAN!
  Illustrated by Henrik Drescher
  0–694–00100–7 Harper & Row $3.95

  ALL GONE!
  Illustrated by Henrik Drescher
  0–694–00098–1 Harper & Row $3.95

  BABY BEN'S BUSY BOOK
  Illustrated by Norman Gorbaty
  0–394–86819–6 Random House (boards) $2.95

  BABY BEN GETS DRESSED
  Illustrated by Norman Gorbaty
  0–394–87025–5 Random House pb $3.95

  BABY BEN'S GO-GO BOOK
  0–394–86820–X Random House $2.95

  BABY BEN'S NOISY BOOK
  Illustrated by Norman Gorbaty
  0–394–86822–6 Random House (boards) $2.95

  SO BUSY!
  Illustrated by Mavis Smith
  0–394–88557–0 Random House $2.95

STORYBOOKS FOR THE TWOS AND THREES

After outgrowing baby books, a child is ready for Margaret Wise Brown's magical bedtime books, written during the 1940s. You can then begin to collect picture books by authors such as Nancy Tafuri and Frank Asch, whose best books have the same effortless and loving quality.

Children just out of the toddling stage like to participate when they are read to by touching the pictures, lifting flaps or finding hidden pictures.

A child of three gets pleasure out of seeing and describing things. The illustrations of trains, buses and cars in Donald Crews's and Byron Barton's books provide a visually stimulating way to keep a child entertained.

- **Janet & Allen Ahlberg**

  EACH PEACH PEAR PLUM
  Set on a summer afternoon in the country, this favorite story reveals a host of nursery rhyme characters
  0–590–33581–2 Scholastic pb $2.95

- **Frank Asch**

  Frank Asch has such an appealingly simple style of illustration that his books will suit the youngest threes, even though his stories have involving plots.

  BEAR'S BARGAIN
  Little Bird will show Bear how to fly, if Bear will show him how to grow bigger
  0–671–66690–8 Prentice-Hall $11.95

  GOODBYE HOUSE
  Aided by a wise daddy, a little bear says goodbye to his first family home
  0–13–360272–9 Prentice-Hall $12.95

  HAPPY BIRTHDAY, MOON
  0–671–66454–9 Prentice-Hall $12.95
  0–13–383696–7 Prentice-Hall pb $4.95

- **Molly G. Bang**

  TEN, NINE, EIGHT
  A counting book, this countdown to bedtime is sufficiently soothing so that the rhymes seem just right for the very young. A Caldecott Honor Book for 1984
  0–688–00906–9 Greenwillow $12.95
  0–14–050543–1 Penguin pb $3.95

- **Byron Barton**

  AIRPLANES
  0–690–04532–8 Harper & Row $9.95
  0–694–00060–4 Harper & Row pb $4.95

  TRAINS
  0–694–00061–2 Harper & Row pb $4.95

- **Margaret Wise Brown**

  A CHILD'S GOOD NIGHT BOOK
  A Caldecott Honor Book for 1944
  Illustrated by Jean Charlot
  0–06–443114–2 Harper & Row pb $3.95

  GOODNIGHT, MOON
  Goodnight socks and goodnight clocks; the sleepy bunny hero of this classic lullaby book has bid goodnight to children since 1947
  Illustrated by Clement Hurd
  0–06–443017–0 Harper & Row pb $3.50

  MARGARET WISE BROWN'S WONDERFUL STORYBOOK
  A Wise Brown collection
  Illustrated by J.P. Miller
  0–307–15777–6 Western $7.95

  THE RUNAWAY BUNNY
  An adventurous little bunny tells his mother he is going to run away; his mother's response makes for an unforgettable fantasy
  Illustrated by Clement Hurd
  0–06–443018–9 Harper & Row pb $3.50

  WAIT TILL THE MOON IS FULL
  A calming little book about how good it is to go to sleep
  Illustrated by Garth Williams
  0–06–020800–7 Harper & Row $11.95

Illustration by Clement Hurd, from Goodnight Moon *by Margaret Wise Brown (Harper & Row)*

● **Eric Carle**

THE VERY BUSY SPIDER
As they listen, children use their fingers to trace the growth of the spider's web until the story reaches its triumphant conclusion
0–399–21166–7 Putnam $14.95

THE VERY HUNGRY CATERPILLAR
Children help the caterpillar turn into a beautiful butterfly by turning half pages or putting small fingers through inviting holes in the stiff pages—a more varied participation than the conventional "lift the flap" books
0–399–20853–4 Putnam $14.95
0–399–21301–5 Putnam (miniature edition) $3.95

● **Nancy White Carlstrom**

BETTER NOT GET WET JESSE BEAR
Illustrated by Bruce Degen
0–02–717280–5 Macmillan $13.95

JESSE BEAR, WHAT WILL YOU WEAR?
"A rose between my toes," suggests Jesse Bear. A rhyming account of Jesse Bear's day, from dawn to dusk—and a very satisfying one
Illustrated by Bruce Degen
0–02–717350–X Macmillan $12.95

● **Tom Cooke**

SESAME STREET HIDE-AND-SEEK SAFARI
Bert and Ernie set off on safari. The children's job is to find the safari animals hidden behind the flaps
0–394–89474–X Random House (boards) $2.95

● **Donald Crews**

Real-looking trains, buses, and trucks, with lots of activity and extremely simple text. Although suitable for older children, Crews's lively illustrations hold the attention of the threes and fours.

FLYING
0–688–04318–6 Greenwillow $11.95

FREIGHT TRAIN
0–688–80165–X Greenwillow $12.95
0–14–050480–X Penguin pb $3.95

SCHOOL BUS
0–688–02807–1 Greenwillow $12.95
0–14–050549–0 Penguin pb $3.95

TRUCK
A Caldecott Honor Book for 1981
0–688–80244–3 Greenwillow $12.95
0–14–050506–7 Penguin $3.95

● **Richard Fowler**

MR. LITTLE'S NOISY BOAT
Mr. Little doesn't know what is wrong with his boat. Children will when they lift the flaps to find out
0–448–18979–8 Putnam pb $9.95

MR. LITTLE'S NOISY CAR
0–448–18977–1 Putnam $10.95

● **Mirra Ginsburg**

GOOD MORNING, CHICK
Illustrated by Byron Barton
0–688–42844–2 Greenwillow $12.95

MUSHROOM IN THE RAIN
A storybook about animals who take refuge under an amazing mushroom, with bold and satisfying illustrations by Jose Aruego and Ariane Dewey
0–02–736241–8 Macmillan $11.95

● **Eric Hill**
Spot is a rotund puppy, and young listeners participate in his adventures by lifting a flap at the appropriate moment.

SPOT GOES TO THE BEACH
0–399–21247–7 Putnam $10.95

SPOT GOES TO THE FARM
0–399–21434–8 Putnam $10.95

SPOT'S BIG BOOK OF WORDS
0–399–21563–8 Putnam $9.95

SPOT'S FIRST CHRISTMAS
0–399–20963–8 Putnam $10.95

SPOT'S FIRST WALK
0–399–20838–0 Putnam $10.95

WHERE'S SPOT?
0–399–21478–X Putnam $11.95
0–399–20758–9 Putnam $10.95

● **Ruth Krauss**

THE CARROT SEED
Illustrated by Crockett Johnson
0–06–023350–8 Harper & Row $10.95
0–06–443210–6 Harper & Row $3.95

● **Helen Oxenbury**
Humorous and sharp-witted as well as kindly, the books in this series are conceived with simple story lines appropriate to three-year-olds. Oxenbury has a good eye for the idiosyncrasies of grown-ups' relations with children so that her stories are consistently interesting.

THE BIRTHDAY PARTY
0–8037–0717–7 Dial $5.95

THE CAR TRIP
0–8037–0009–1 Dial $3.95

THE DANCING CLASS
0–8037–1651–6 Dial $5.95

EATING OUT
0–8037–2203–6 Dial $3.95

FIRST DAY OF SCHOOL
0–8037–0012–1 Dial $5.95

● **Anne & Harlow Rockwell**
Though not as witty as Oxenbury, the prolific Rockwells pay attention to ordinary situations that children are just beginning to master at three and four.

I PLAY IN MY ROOM
0–02–777670–0 Macmillan $8.95

HAPPY BIRTHDAY TO ME
0–02–777680–8 Macmillan $8.95

MY BACK YARD
0–02–777690–5 Macmillan $8.95

Illustration by Crockett Johnson, from The Carrot Seed *by Ruth Krauss (Harper & Row)*

• Nancy Tafuri
EARLY MORNING IN THE BARN
A wordless book, aside from the characteristic sounds of the farm animals, with bold and splendid illustrations. Tafuri's books have just the right balance of clarity and tenderness
0–688–02328–2 Greenwillow $14.95
0–14–050614–4 Penguin pb $3.95

HAVE YOU SEEN MY DUCKLING?
0–688–02797–0 Greenwillow $11.95
0–14–050532–6 Penguin pb $3.95

RABBIT'S MORNING
0–688–04063–2 Greenwillow $11.75

• Charlotte Zolotow
THE SLEEPY BOOK
A bedtime book by an author of consistently excellent work
Illustrated by Ilse Plume
0–06–026967–7 Harper & Row $12.95

NOW WE ARE FOUR: A Picture Book Library

Though parents may be eager to introduce children to the picture book classics of their own childhoods, Madeline and Babar require a bit of sitting still. As they do when crawling, walking or talking, children take their own sweet time before they are ready to listen to the beginning, middle, and end of a story.

• Martha Alexander
AND MY MEAN OLD MOTHER WILL BE SORRY, BLACKBOARD BEAR
0–8037–0126–8 Dial pb $3.50

BLACKBOARD BEAR
Blackboard Bear emerges from a chalk drawing and becomes a little boy's companion. Bear is a wonderful, if silent, friend but he often gets his master into trouble. A nice little fable about the pleasures and dangers of imagination
0–8037–0652–9 Dial $9.95
0–8037–0629–4 Dial pb $3.50

• Judy Barrett
ANIMALS SHOULD DEFINITELY NOT WEAR CLOTHING
A humorous little essay on why camels, hens, lions, and so on look better without it
Illustrated by Ron Barrett
0–689–20592–9 Macmillan $15.95
0–689–70412–7 Macmillan pb $3.95

• Caroline Feller Bauer
MY MOM TRAVELS A LOT
Funny things happen when Mom is away (Dad is in charge)—and nice things, too. The best thing is that Mom always comes back
0–14–050545–8 Viking $3.95

• Ludwig Bemelmans
Bemelmans had a good ear for rhyme and a lovely if wacky illustrative style. Madeline lives in an old house in Paris, and her healthy streak of mischief is a trial to poor Miss Clavell. But she is all indignation

when injustice occurs, especially when animals are the victims.
MADELINE
A Caldecott Honor Book for 1940
0–670–81667–1 Viking (pop-up edition) $13.95
0–670–44580–0 Viking $13.95
0–14–050198–3 Penguin pb $3.95

MADELINE AND THE BAD HAT
0–670–44614–9 Viking $13.95
0–14–050206–8 Penguin pb $3.95

MADELINE IN LONDON
0–670–44648–3 Viking $13.95
0–14–050199–1 Penguin pb $3.95

MADELINE'S RESCUE
Caldecott Medal 1954
0–670–44716–1 Viking $13.95
0–14–050207–6 Penguin pb $3.95

• Norman Bridwell
Clifford behaves as dogs do, but because he is as big and as red as a firehouse, he and his owners are perpetually in trouble. With their few words and simple illustrations Bridwell's picture books are understood even by children under four.
CLIFFORD AT THE CIRCUS
0–590–33588–X Scholastic pb $1.95

CLIFFORD GETS A JOB
0–590–33555–3 Scholastic pb $1.95

CLIFFORD, THE SMALL RED PUPPY
0–590–33583–9 Scholastic pb $1.95

CLIFFORD'S GOOD DEEDS
0–590–33589–8 Scholastic pb $1.95

• Marcia Brown
LET'S GO SWIMMING WITH MR. SILLYPANTS
0–517–56185–9 Crown $9.95

• Margaret Wise Brown
WHEN THE WIND BLEW
An old woman, her toothache, her 17 cats, and her one gray kitten are pleasingly presented
Illustrated by Geoffrey R. Hayes
0–06–020867–8 Harper & Row $11.95

• Ruth Brown
THE BIG SNEEZE
An almost wordless picture book about a sneeze that causes a sequence of unexpected events
0–688–04665–7 Lothrop, Lee & Shepard $13.95

• Eve Bunting
THE MOTHER'S DAY MICE
Mice brothers set off to find the perfect gift in an exceptionally pretty book that also has a nicely consoling point
0–89919–387–0 Clarion $12.95
0–317–69508–8 Clarion pb $4.95

• John Burningham
MR. GUMPY'S MOTOR CAR
0–14–050300–5 Penguin pb $3.50

MR. GUMPY'S OUTING
An eccentric English gentleman is accompanied by the oddest group of people and animals
0–14–050254–8 Penguin pb $3.95

• Rod Campbell
DEAR ZOO
A humorous lift-the-flap book: the author asks the zoo for a pet, and the zoo sends one inappropriate animal after another
0–02–016440–3 Macmillan $8.95
0–317–62180–7 Penguin pb $4.95

• Eric Carle
PAPA, PLEASE GET THE MOON FOR ME
The book unfolds as the story progresses. A younger child will request help with the activity, but the book is fascinating
0–88708–026–X Picture Book Studio $15.95

• Jean de Brunhoff
Babar begins life as an ordinary little elephant. Then, in a series of swiftly drawn events he loses his mother, runs out of the jungle, meets the Old Lady, and learns to dress and think like a human. Thereafter Babar is only short steps away from becoming king and founding Celesteville. Meanwhile, Zephir the monkey and Arthur, Celeste's heedless little brother, are always up to something. A classic for over 50 years.
THE STORY OF BABAR
The first in the series
0–394–86823–4 Random House (oversized) $16.95
0–394–80575–5 Random House $6.95

BABAR AND FATHER CHRISTMAS
0–394–89265–8 Random House $16.95

BABAR AND ZEPHIR
0–394–80579–8 Random House $8.95

BABAR THE KING
0–394–88245–8 Random House $14.95

BABAR AND HIS CHILDREN
0–394–80577–1 Random House $7.95

THE TRAVELS OF BABAR
0–394–87453–6 Random House $15.95

• Laurent de Brunhoff
Laurent de Brunhoff is Jean's son and successor, and his books are pale shadows of the first Babar series. Nevertheless, the characters remain lovable regardless of the plots.
BABAR AND THE GHOST
0–394–94660–X Random House $9.99

BABAR LOSES HIS CROWN
0–394–80045–1 Random House pb $3.95

BABAR VISITS ANOTHER PLANET
0–394–82429–6 Random House pb $4.95

• Jean & Laurent de Brunhoff
BABAR'S ANNIVERSARY ALBUM
Includes six of the Babar Stories
Introduction by Maurice Sendak
0–394–84813–6 Random House $16.95

• Don Freeman
Corduroy is Lisa's toy teddy bear and she takes him everywhere. Of course she loses him too, but he is indestructible.
CORDUROY
0–14–050173–8 Penguin pb $3.95

A POCKET FOR CORDUROY
0–670–56172–X Viking $10.95
0–14–050352–8 Penguin pb $3.95

From The Story of Babar *by Jean de Brun-hoff (Random House)*

● Wanda Gag

MILLIONS OF CATS
Published in 1928, Wanda Gag's classic storybook describes a little old couple who must cope with an explosive feline population when they try to adopt just one cat
0–698–20091–8 Putnam $9.95
0–698–20637–1 Putnam pb $4.95

● Mordicai Gerstein

WILLIAM, WHERE ARE YOU?
A funny hunt for the missing William requires opening turned down pages to see where he has gone
0–517–55644–8 Crown $7.95

● John S. Goodall

Illustrated in a style reminiscent of the Victorian period, Goodall's books are small and densely packed with full and half pages. The trick is to turn the half pages so as to precipitate the action. The books have no text but work beautifully without it. Children four and up will enjoy "reading" these books and will learn to love Paddy Pork, who is a charmer.

PADDY PORK GOES TRAVELING
0–689–50239–7 Macmillan $6.95

PADDY PORK: Odd Jobs
0–689–50293–1 Macmillan $6.95

PADDY TO THE RESCUE
0–689–50330–X Macmillan $8.95

● Anna Grossnickle Hines

IT'S JUST ME, EMILY
Emily pretends she is someone else in a

make believe rhyming game she plays with her mother
0–89919–487–7 Clarion $12.95

● Russell Hoban

Russell Hoban and Lillian Hoban had a long and distinguished collaboration as the author and illustrators of numerous picture books of which the Frances series is the most popular. The Hobans have sensitive ears and eyes for stories that make young children laugh but also provoke questions.

BEST FRIENDS FOR FRANCES
Illustrated by Lillian Hoban
0–06–022327–8 Harper & Row $11.95
0–06–443008–1 Harper & Row pb $2.95

A BIRTHDAY FOR FRANCES
Extraordinary things happen to Frances, a cuddly badger, but Mama and Papa are always there to help
Illustrated by Lillian Hoban
0–06–022338–3 Harper & Row $11.95
0–06–443007–3 Harper & Row pb $2.95

THE LITTLE BRUTE FAMILY
The Brutes are a nasty bunch, until they discover that what they lack is affection. A fable that children will understand
Illustrated by Lillian Hoban
0–02–744110–5 Macmillan $9.95

● Nonny Hogrogian

ONE FINE DAY
A variation on the familiar folk stories in which one action must lead to another so the narrative comes to the proper conclusion. The fun for children is remembering the sequence as the fox loses his tail to an irate old lady and gets it back again. Caldecott Medal 1972
0–02–744000–1 Macmillan $13.95
0–02–043620–3 Macmillan pb $3.95

● Shirley Hughes

ALFIE GIVES A HAND
Alfie doesn't like it when something new happens to him—even when it's a birthday party. But it all turns out to be a lot of fun, and children will enjoy it too
0–688–06521–X Morrow pb $3.95

LUCY AND TOM'S DAY
A very tranquil account of the home life of two young English children
0–14–050068–5 Penguin pb $3.50

SALLY'S SECRET
Another appealingly realistic story, about a little girl playing house in a hidden corner of the garden
0–14–050160–6 Penguin pb $3.50

● Pat Hutchins

ROSIE'S WALK
Rosie the hen is in big trouble from a fox who's trailing right behind her, but she never looks up to notice. Meanwhile the fox meets with a series of comical misadventures every time he tries to close in. An amusing wordless story
0–02–043750–1 Macmillan pb $4.95

Crockett Johnson
HAROLD AND THE PURPLE CRAYON
Harold sets off with his mighty purple

crayon to draw himself an adventure. This masterful little book moves with terrific speed as Harold uses a few brief crayon strokes to put himself in and out of situations
0–06–022935–7 Harper & Row $10.95
0–06–443022–7 Harper & Row pb $2.50

HAROLD'S CIRCUS
0–06–443024–3 Harper & Row pb $2.95

HAROLD'S TRIP TO THE SKY
0–06–443025–1 Harper & Row pb $2.50

● Ezra Jack Keats

GOGGLES!
Caldecott Honor Book 1970
0–02–749590–6 Macmillan $12.95
0–689–71157–3 Macmillan pb $4.50

THE SNOWY DAY
0–14–050182–7 Penguin pb $3.95

WHISTLE FOR WILLIE
Willie wants to whistle so badly but he has to wait to learn. A nice description of the affection between a father and his son
0–14–050202–5 Penguin pb $3.95

● Munro Leaf

THE STORY OF FERDINAND
Ah, Ferdinand the bull, who only wants to sniff the flowers! Children will be happy that Ferdinand sits down during the bullfight and lives out his life in peace
Illustrated by Robert Lawson
0–14–050234–3 Penguin pb $3.95

● Leo Lionni

ALEXANDER AND THE WIND-UP MOUSE
Alexander is a clockwork mouse who wants to be free. His friend is a real mouse who has his own dreams
0–317–53623–0 Knopf pb $2.95

FREDERICK'S FABLES
A collection of six of Lionni's best-loved tales, illustrated with his distinctive collages
0–394–87710–1 Knopf $19.95

SWIMMY
0–317–53621–4 Knopf pb $2.95

● Mercer Mayer

Three small-format, wordless books with precise and humorous observations

From Harold and the Purple Crayon *by Crockett Johnson (Harper & Row)*

✉ TO ORDER BOOKS AS GIFTS, SEE PAGE 1

A BOY, A DOG AND A FROG
0–8037–0763–0 Dial $8.95
0–8037–0769–X Dial pb $2.95

FROG GOES TO DINNER
0–8037–3386–0 Dial $8.95
0–8037–2733–X Dial pb $2.95

FROG, WHERE ARE YOU?
0–8037–2732–2 Dial $8.95
0–8037–2729–1 Dial pb $2.95

THERE'S A NIGHTMARE IN MY CLOSET
And it's not going to stay there, either. Boy and monster make friends, but the ending suggests that other things may be in store
0–8037–8682–4 Dial $11.95
0–8037–8574–7 Dial pb $3.95

THERE'S AN ALLIGATOR UNDER MY BED
Meyer's sequel features a realistic alligator who just happens to live you know where
0–8037–0374–0 Dial $11.95

● Robert McCloskey
BLUEBERRIES FOR SAL
A Caldecott Honor Book for 1949
0–14–050169–X Penguin pb $3.95

MAKE WAY FOR DUCKLINGS
McCloskey comes up with the perfect solution to the problem of bringing up a brood of ducklings in the center of Boston. Caldecott Medal 1942
0–14–050171–1 Penguin pb $3.95

● Emilie McLeod
THE BEAR'S BICYCLE
Illustrated by David McPhail
0–316–56203–3 Little, Brown $12.95
0–316–56206–8 Little, Brown pb $4.95

● A.A. Milne
THE POOH STORY BOOK
Pooh in large format with large print and color illustrations. The book contains one chapter from *Winnie-the-Pooh* and two from *The House at Pooh Corner*, two classics written when young children apparently had a longer attention span and a larger vocabulary
Illustrated by Ernest H. Shepard
0–525–37546–5 Dutton $11.95

● Jill Murphy
FIVE MINUTES' PEACE
Mother Elephant's children won't leave her alone, even when she decides to take a bath. It takes longer than five minutes to get them to understand why Mother needs time off
0–399–21354–6 Putnam $9.95

● Gerald Oakley
HITTY AND HARRIET
Two hens annoyed by their lowly status in the barnyard set off on unforeseen adventures
0–689–30888–4 Macmillan $12.95
0–689–71061–5 Macmillan pb $3.95

● Hiawyn Oram
IN THE ATTIC
A little boy goes up into an attic that isn't there and sees various fantastic sights
Illustrated by Satoshi Kitamura
0–8050–0779–2 Henry Holt $10.95
0–8050–0780–6 Henry Holt pb $3.95

● Doris Orgel
SARAH'S ROOM
An old-fashioned, pleasantly simple rhyming book accompanied by early Sendak illustrations
Illustrations by Maurice Sendak
0–06–024605–7 Harper & Row $8.95

Watty Piper
THE LITTLE ENGINE THAT COULD
I think I can, I think I can. The youngest members of the picture book audience will like the simplified pictures and catchy text
Illustrated by Richard Walz
0–448–18963–1 Putnam $7.95
0–448–40035–9 Putnam (junior edition) $3.95

● Beatrix Potter
Lonely in childhood and youth, Beatrix Potter loved animals. But she was always at great pains to render them accurately and was a fierce critic of her own work. When describing and illustrating her stories she preferred to use places and people (human and animal) she knew. Hence a convincingly rabbitty Peter is chased through an authentic garden by the angry Mr. MacGregor, and we know he is going to put Peter in a pie if he catches him. The authenticity is the reason Beatrix Potter's books fascinate us. She is not the strongest of story tellers, but her fantasies are captivating because she is honest about them.

THE COMPLETE ADVENTURES OF PETER RABBIT
Four of Potter's tales in one volume, with her original illustrations
0–7232–2951–1 Frederick Warne $12.95
0–14–050444–3 Penguin pb $5.95

THE TALE OF PETER RABBIT
0–7232–3460–4 Frederick Warne $4.95
0–7232–3485–X Viking pb $2.25

THE PETER RABBIT POP-UP BOOK
0–7232–2950–3 Viking $11.95

THE TALE OF BENJAMIN BUNNY
0–7232–3463–9 Frederick Warne $4.95
0–7232–3488–4 Frederick Warne pb $2.25

THE TALE OF THE FLOPSY BUNNIES
0–7232–3469–8 Frederick Warne $4.95
0–7232–3494–9 Frederick Warne pb $2.25

THE TALE OF GINGER AND PICKLES
0–7232–3477–9 Frederick Warne $4.95

THE TALE OF JEMIMA PUDDLE-DUCK
0–7232–3468–X Frederick Warne $4.95
0–7232–3493–0 Frederick Warne pb $2.25

THE TALE OF MR. JEREMY FISHER
0–7232–3466–3 Frederick Warne $4.95
0–7232–3491–4 Frederick Warne pb $2.25

THE TALE OF JOHNNY TOWNMOUSE
0–7232–3472–8 Frederick Warne $4.95

THE TALE OF LITTLE PIG ROBINSON
0–7232–3478–7 Frederick Warne $4.95

THE TALE OF PIGLING BLAND
0–7232–3474–4 Frederick Warne $4.95

THE TALE OF SQUIRREL NUTKIN
0–7232–3461–2 Frederick Warne $4.95
0–7232–3486–8 Frederick Warne pb $2.25

THE TALE OF MRS. TIGGY-WINKLE
0–7232–3465–5 Frederick Warne $4.95
0–7232–3490–6 Frederick Warne pb $2.25

THE TALE OF TOM KITTEN
0–7232–3467–1 Frederick Warne $4.95
0–7232–3492–2 Frederick Warne pb $2.25

THE TALE OF TWO BAD MICE
0–7232–3464–7 Frederick Warne $4.95
0–7232–3489–2 Frederick Warne pb $2.25

THE TAILOR OF GLOUCESTER
0–7232–3462–0 Frederick Warne $4.95
0–7232–3487–6 Frederick Warne pb $2.25

● H.A. Rey
These are the five original Curious George books; the others in this lengthy series are by H.A. Rey's daughter, Margaret, and are clearly derivative. The monkey hero is a marvelous invention, a good-humored little guy who gets into real scrapes and bounces back every time.

CURIOUS GEORGE
0–395–15993–8 Houghton Mifflin $10.95
0–395–15023–X Houghton Mifflin pb $3.95

CURIOUS GEORGE GETS A MEDAL
0–395–18559–9 Houghton Mifflin pb $3.95

CURIOUS GEORGE LEARNS THE ALPHABET
0–395–16031–6 Houghton Mifflin $12.95
0–395–13718–7 Houghton Mifflin pb $3.95

CURIOUS GEORGE RIDES A BIKE
0–395–17444–9 Houghton Mifflin pb $3.95

CURIOUS GEORGE TAKES A JOB
0–395–18649–8 Houghton Mifflin pb $3.95

● Anne Rockwell
THE GOLLYWHOPPER EGG
0–689–71072–0 Macmillan pb $3.95

Maurice Sendak
Maurice Sendak won the 1970 Hans Christian Andersen award for his substantial and lasting contributions to children's literature. He has said that he has always had more trouble with the text of his children's books than the pictures, describing how his stories come to him "in bits and pieces of memories that don't seem related for a very long time, but something in me determines they will be closely related: they're going to work together come hell and high water."

IN THE NIGHT KITCHEN
Sendak pushes dream logic to its limit in a hauntingly beautiful book that confronts and transcends some basic anxieties of early childhood
0–06–025489–0 Harper & Row $14.95
0–06–443086–3 Harper & Row pb $4.95

WHERE THE WILD THINGS ARE
Familiarity has tamed the Wild Things somewhat, but young readers are still likely to be startled by the curiously menacing monsters created out of a hodgepodge of mythical and real beasts
0–06–025492–0 Harper & Row $12.95
0–06–443055–3 Harper & Row pb $4.95

Illustration by Maurice Sendak, from Where the Wild Things Are *(Harper & Row)*

• Esphyr Slobodkina
CAPS FOR SALE
A peddler's caps are stolen by a treeful of monkeys in a classic little story book with few words and funny illustrations
0–201–09147–X Harper & Row $8.95
0–06–443143–6 Harper & Row pb $2.95

• Judith Viorst
THE GOOD-BYE BOOK
A little boy tries everything within his power to stop his parents from leaving the house. The author knows what bothers children and what doesn't, and is blessed with an observant sense of humor
Illustrated by Kay Chorao
0–689–31308–X Macmillan $12.95

• Jan Wahl
THE TOY CIRCUS
Illustrated by Tim Bowers
0–15–200609–5 HBJ $13.95

• Rosemary Wells
BENJAMIN AND TULIP
Tulip is the little girl who does whatever she pleases and gets other people into trouble. Benjamin finally realizes what he is up against and acts accordingly. Delightfully observant and humorous
0–8037–2057–2 Dial $8.95

HAZEL'S AMAZING MOTHER
Mother is someone to be relied on, and she arrives on the scene at just the right moment
0–8037–0209–4 Dial $10.95

A LION FOR LEWIS
A serious fantasy in which a little boy becomes unexpectedly powerful
0–8037–4683–0 Dial $9.95
0–8037–0096–2 Dial pb $3.95

TIMOTHY GOES TO SCHOOL
One of the very best books about a child's desire to fit in. Sympathetic and humorous
0–8037–0021–0 Dial pb $3.95

• Brian Wildsmith
GOAT'S TRAIL
Children may peek through pages to discover what will happen next as a rambunctious group of animals run wild through the town
0–394–88276–8 Knopf $10.95

• Barbara Williams
ALBERT'S TOOTHACHE
Illustrated by Kay Chorao
0–525–25368–8 Dutton $11.95
0–525–44363–0 Dutton pb $3.95

• Taro Yashima
UMBRELLA
A little Japanese girl growing up in New York City waits for rain to come so she can try out her new umbrella. An appealingly gentle story
0–14–050240–8 Penguin pb $3.95

• Charlotte Zolotow
MR. RABBIT AND THE LOVELY PRESENT
Illustrated by Maurice Sendak
0–06–026945–6 Harper & Row $12.95
0–06–443020–0 Harper & Row pb $3.50

WHEN I HAVE A LITTLE GIRL
I'm going to let her do all the things you won't let me do, such as …
Illustrated by Hilary Knight
0–06–027045–4 Harper & Row $12.95
0–06–443175–4 Harper & Row pb $2.95

WILLIAM'S DOLL
William wants a doll; when father objects, grandmother comes to the rescue
Illustrated by William Pène du Bois
0–06–027047–0 Harper & Row $11.95
0–06–443067–7 Harper & Row pb $3.95

MAURICE SENDAK: Some Favorite Children's Books

Edward Ardizzone
LITTLE TIM AND THE BRAVE SEA CAPTAIN
0–14–050175–4 Penguin pb $3.95

TIM AND CHARLOTTE
0–19–272118–6 Oxford pb $4.95

William Nicolson
CLEVER BILL
Out of print

THE PIRATE TWINS
Out of print

George MacDonald
THE PRINCESS AND THE CURDIE
0–440–47182–6 Dell pb $4.95

THE PRINCESS AND THE GOBLIN
0–688–06604–6 Morrow $15.00
0–14–035029–2 Penguin pb $2.25

James Marshall
GOLDILOCKS AND THE THREE BEARS
0–8037–0542–5 Dutton $10.95

Lore Segal
TELL ME A MITZI
0–374–37392–2 FS&G $13.95
0–590–41102–0 Scholastic pb $3.95

Tomi Ungerer
THE BEAST OF MONSIEUR RACINE
0–374–30640–0 FS&G $11.95
0–374–40570–0 FS&G pb $4.95

TRADITIONAL STORIES

Little children love the repetition common to the simpler folktales from Europe, Africa, and elsewhere.

• Verna Aardema
BRINGING THE RAIN TO KAPITI PLAIN
An African folktale told in the manner of "The House That Jack Built"
Illustrated by Beatriz Vidal
0–8037–0809–2 Dial $13.95
0–8037–0904–8 Dial pb $3.95

• Jill Bennett
TEENY TINY
This nonsense ghost story invites children to join in the rousing ending
Illustrated by Tomie de Paola
0–399–21293–0 Putnam $8.95

• Jan Brett
GOLDILOCKS AND THE THREE BEARS
The distinctly Russian bears wear their colorful costumes with a half-comic dignity
0–396–08925–9 Dodd, Mead $13.95

• Jane Dyer
GOLDILOCKS AND THE THREE BEARS
0–448–10213–7 Putnam pb $3.95

• Lynn Ferris
GOLDILOCKS AND THE THREE BEARS
0–394–55882–0 Random House $9.95

• Paul Galdone
Galdone's illustrated versions of traditional tales are characteristically jaunty and good-humored.

THE GINGERBREAD BOY
The big animated figures and vivid colors will please the very young
0–395–28799–5 Houghton Mifflin $12.95
0–89919–163–0 Houghton Mifflin pb $4.95

HENNY PENNY
0–395–28800–2 Houghton Mifflin $12.95
0–89919–225–4 Ticknor & Fields pb $4.95

THE MONKEY AND THE CROCODILE: A Jataka Tale from India
Monkey outwits crocodile in this engagingly fast-moving little fable
0–395–28806–1 Houghton Mifflin $13.95
0–89919–524–5 Ticknor & Fields pb $4.95

THE THREE LITTLE PIGS
0–395–28813–4 Houghton Mifflin $12.95
0–89919–275–0 Ticknor & Fields pb $4.95

• Susan Hellard
BILLY GOATS GRUFF: A Lift-the-Flap Book
Children may lift the flaps to see what the troll is doing. A funny version of the Scandinavian folktale
0–399–21291–4 Putnam $10.95

• Gerald McDermott
ANANSI THE SPIDER: A Tale from the Ashanti
A West African folktale retold in simple words and pictured in big geometric illustrations
0–030–88368–1 Henry Holt $11.95

• John Steptoe
MUFARO'S BEAUTIFUL DAUGHTERS
Based on a traditional African tale. Caldecott Honor Book 1988
0–688–04046–2 Lothrop, Lee & Shepard $13.00

• Margot Zemach
THE LITTLE RED HEN
Stars a determined Little Red Hen doing everything for and by herself
0–374–34621–6 Farrar, Straus & Giroux $11.95
0–14–050567–9 Penguin pb $3.50

STORY COLLECTIONS

• Kay Chorao
THE BABY'S STORY BOOK
Since Chorao has a lap book in mind, each story fits into one or two illustrated pages
0–525–44200–6 Dutton $11.95

• Helen Oxenbury, editor
THE HELEN OXENBURY NURSERY STORY BOOK
Rewritten classic tales accompanied by characteristically droll illustrations
0–394–87519–2 Knopf $12.95

• Anne Rockwell
THE THREE BEARS & FIFTEEN OTHER STORIES
The other stories are adaptations of Aesop, Grimm, La Fontaine, and traditional British folktales
0–690–00597–0 Harper & Row $13.95
0–06–440142–1 Harper & Row pb $7.95

• Eric Suben, editor
THE THREE LITTLE PIGS & OTHER NURSERY TALES
Illustrated by Christopher Santoro
0–307–12800–8 Western pb $4.95

TRADITIONAL RHYMES AND POETRY

The poet Jack Prelutsky has said that young children find poetry "as delightful and surprising as being tickled or catching a snowflake on a mitten."

• Lisa Amorso
OLD MOTHER HUBBARD AND HER DOG
0–394–88922–3 Knopf pb $4.95

• Nicola Bayley
AS I WAS GOING UP AND DOWN
Just the sort of comfortable, colorful illustrations that very young children love
0–02–708590–2 Macmillan $8.95

HUSH-A-BYE BABY & OTHER BEDTIME RHYMES
0–02–708610–0 Macmillan $8.95

• Marc Brown, editor
HAND RHYMES
Finger rhymes of several vintages encourage counting, rhyming, and singing
0–525–44201–4 Dutton $11.95

• Kay Chorao
THE BABY'S GOOD MORNING BOOK
Short verse selections appear in the companion volume to *The Baby's Story Book*
0–525–44257–X Dutton $11.95

• Tomie dePaola, editor
TOMIE DEPAOLA'S MOTHER GOOSE
A handsome and comprehensive collection of rhymes
0–399–21258–2 Putnam $17.95

• Cooper Edens, editor
THE GLORIOUS MOTHER GOOSE
The classic rhymes are accompanied by reproductions of illustrations from the 17th century to the present
0–689–31434–5 Atheneum $15.95

• Eugene Field
WYNKEN, BLYNKEN AND NOD
Night sailors Wynken, Blynken, and Nod are pictured as contemporary children in this version of the classic bedtime poem
Illustrated by Susan Jeffers
0–525–44022–4 Dutton $11.95
0–525–44199–9 Dutton pb $3.95

• Paul Galdone
CAT GOES FIDDLE-I-FEE
A retelling of an old English rhyme in which children are introduced to the characteristic sounds of farm animals
0–89919–336–6 Clarion $12.95
0–89919–705–1 Clarion pb $4.95

THREE LITTLE KITTENS
Two rhyming stories accompanied by vigorous illustrations
0–89919–426–5 Clarion $13.95

• Kate Greenaway
A APPLE PIE
A ate it, B bit it, C cut it … Greenaway's pouting little children, charmingly dressed, eat their way through a giant apple pie in a facsimile edition of her 1880s rhyming alphabet book
0–7232–1801–3 Warne $8.95

• Arnold Lobel, editor
THE RANDOM HOUSE BOOK OF MOTHER GOOSE: A Treasury of 306 Timeless Nursery Rhymes
The sometimes bewitching, sometimes bewildering old Mother Goose rhymes come alive for today's children through Lobel's charming illustrations
0–394–86799–8 Random House $14.95

• James Marshall
JAMES MARSHALL'S MOTHER GOOSE
A bright, cartoony collection with plenty of child appeal
0–374–33653–9 Farrar, Straus & Giroux $11.95
0–374–43723–8 Farrar, Straus & Giroux pb $3.95

• A.A. Milne
Pooh was just a teddy bear when he first appeared in print. The hero, Milne's son Christopher Robin, is a small boy doing things small boys did 60 years ago. Contemporary children of the appropriate ages (six and under) won't understand all of it, but the rhymes do keep bouncing along.

THE COLLECTED EDITION: The World of Christopher Robin
The companion volume to *The World of Pooh*; both have new illustrations in color by the artist who created the black-and-white pictures of Pooh, Christopher Robin, and his friends
Illustrated by Ernest H. Shepard
0–525–43348–1 Dutton $26.50

NOW WE ARE SIX
Illustrated by Ernest H. Shepard
0–525–36126–X Dutton $9.95
0–440–46485–4 Dell pb $3.25

WHEN WE WERE VERY YOUNG
Illustrated by Ernest H. Shepard
0–525–42580–2 Dutton $7.95
0–440–49485–0 Dell pb $2.50

• Jennifer Mulherin, editor
POPULAR NURSERY RHYMES
Two hundred illustrations recall past generations of nursery rhyme books
0–448–01346–0 Putnam $8.95

• Iona & Peter Opie
TAIL FEATHERS FROM MOTHER GOOSE
Previously unpublished Mother Goose rhymes, lavishly illustrated by British and American artists
0–316–65081–1 Little, Brown $19.95

• Tracey Campbell Pearson
A APPLE PIE
Illustrated by Tracey Campbell Pearson
0–8037–0252–3 Dial pb $5.95

OLD MACDONALD HAD A FARM
Cheerful illustrations accompany a traditional favorite
Illustrated by Tracey Campbell Pearson
0–8037–0068–7 Dial $9.95
0–8037–0274–4 Dial pb $3.95

• Sarah Pooley
A DAY OF RHYMES
Rhymes for skipping, clapping, and counting out games. Four-, five-, and six-year-olds will enjoy them
0–394–89497–9 Knopf $11.95

• Jack Prelutsky, editor
READ-ALOUD RHYMES FOR THE VERY YOUNG
One of a handful of contemporary poets who write for children, Prelutsky is a distinguished anthologist and the editor of *The Random House Book of Poetry for Children,* the best available collection for elementary school children
Illustrated by Marc Brown
0–394–89833–8 Knopf $19.95

• Alice & Martin Provensen
OLD MOTHER HUBBARD
The Provensens are witty illustrators, and Mother Hubbard's troubles give them plenty of opportunities
0–394–93460–1 Random House $6.00
0–394–83460–7 Random House pb $1.95

• P.K. Roche
JUMP ALL THE MORNING
A collection of rhymes showing daily activities in the life of a small child
0–670–41057–8 Viking $11.95
0–14–050681–0 Penguin pb $3.95

• Caroline Royds
POEMS FOR YOUNG CHILDREN
Illustrated by Inga Moore
0–385–23524–0 Doubleday $9.95

• Robert Louis Stevenson
A CHILD'S GARDEN OF VERSES
0–528–82401–5 Macmillan $12.95
0–528–80073–6 Macmillan pb $8.00

• Olive Wadsworth
OVER IN THE MEADOW
A counting rhyme cheerfully illustrated for the threes and fours
Illustrated by Ezra Jack Keats
0–670–53276–2 Viking $10.95
0–590–40981–6 Scholastic pb $3.95

OVER IN THE MEADOW
With cassette
0–590–63194–2 Scholastic pb $6.95

• Eleanor Wasmuth
Wasmuth's comfortable new editions of traditional rhymes are easily grasped by small fingers
JACK AND JILL
0–671–61729–X Simon & Schuster pb $2.95

HEY DIDDLE DIDDLE
0–671–61726–5 Simon & Schuster pb $2.95

THE OLD WOMAN IN A SHOE
0–671–61728–1 Simon & Schuster pb $2.95

• Brian Wildsmith
BRIAN WILDSMITH'S MOTHER GOOSE
0–19–272180–1 Oxford pb $7.95

ALPHABET AND WORD BOOKS

• Mitsumasa Anno
ANNO'S ALPHABET: An Adventure in Imagination
The alphabet book to buy for a child who is past the letter-learning stage. The pages contain one charming surprise after another—wooden, three-dimensional letters, smoothly rendered illustrations with many fanciful touches
0–690–00540–7 Harper & Row $13.95
0–06–443190–8 Harper & Row pb $5.95

• Kerry Argent & Rod Trinca
ONE WOOLY WOMBAT
An Australian counting and ABC book, full of nice, wacky paintings of koalas, echidnas, and other denizens of the outback
Illustrated by Kerry Argent
0–916291–00–6 Kane/Miller $10.95
0–916291–10–3 Kane/Miller pb $6.95

• Demi
DEMI'S FIND THE ANIMAL ABC
A pretty alphabet book poses puzzles requiring children to find hidden shapes in large, bright pictures
0–448–18970–4 Putnam $9.95

• Kate Duke
THE GUINEA PIG ABC
Rambunctious guinea pigs star in this lively ABC primer
0–525–44058–5 Dutton $10.95
0–525–44274–4 Dutton pb $3.95

• Wanda Gag
THE ABC BUNNY
0–698–20000–4 Putnam $12.95
0–698–20465–4 Putnam pb $4.95

• Arthur Geisert
PIGS FROM A TO Z
A commendably different alphabet book. Pigs build an elaborate tree house, while the reader finds the letters hidden in the curiously drawn black-and-white illustrations
0–395–38509–1 Houghton Mifflin $15.95

• Tana Hoban
26 LETTERS AND 99 CENTS
Bright, colorful photographs provide a simultaneous introduction to the alphabet and to counting money
0–688–06362–4 Greenwillow $13.00

• Arnold Lobel
ON MARKET STREET
This award-winning collaboration introduces the shopkeepers of Market Street, whose elaborate costumes are made up of their wares. Caldecott Honor Book 1982
Illustrated by Anita Lobel
0–688–80309–1 Greenwillow $13.95
0–590–41004–0 Scholastic pb $3.95

• Suse MacDonald
ALPHABATICS
Animated letters invite children to look by moving up, moving down, or even leaving the page. Caldecott Honor Book 1987
0–02–761520–0 Bradbury $15.95

• Annie Owen
ANNIE'S ABC
A cheerful alphabet book filled with objects that children may count as well as name
0–394–89590–8 Knopf $8.95

➤ **FOR OVERSEAS ORDERING INFORMATION, SEE PAGE 1**

Richard Scarry

Crammed with pictures of objects and animals, Scarry's busy world is also a gentle and orderly one. Regardless of any misadventures experienced by his bunny or mouse children, the rows of labelled objects, neat homes, towns, and schools are supremely reassuring.

RICHARD SCARRY'S ABC WORD BOOK
0–394–82339–7 Random House $8.95

RICHARD SCARRY'S BEST WORD BOOK EVER
0–307–15510–2 Western $7.95

RICHARD SCARRY'S BIGGEST WORD BOOK EVER!
0–394–87374–2 Random House $29.95

RICHARD SCARRY'S BUSY BUSY WORLD
0–307–15511–0 Western $8.95

RICHARD SCARRY'S WHAT DO PEOPLE DO ALL DAY?
0–394–81823–7 Random House $9.95

• Sesame Street

THE SESAME STREET ABC BOOK OF WORDS
A straightforward word book based on the activities of the familiar characters. Scenes are designed to reinforce the relationship between letters, the letter sounds, and the words that begin with each letter
Illustrated by Harry McNaught
0–394–88880–4 Random House $8.95

• Dr. Seuss

DR. SEUSS'S ABC
ABC nonsense written and illustrated by the masterful Dr. Seuss
0–394–89784–6 Random House pb $5.95

COUNTING BOOKS

• Mitsumasa Anno

ANNO'S COUNTING BOOK
The landscape fills up as children turn the pages and are asked to count flocks of birds, numbers of houses, and so on
0–690–01287–X Harper & Row $13.95
0–06–443123–1 Harper & Row pb $4.95

• Sandra Boynton

HIPPOS GO BERSERK
Boisterous hippos arrive at a party and must somehow be counted
0–316–10494–9 Little, Brown pb $3.95

• Dick Bruna

I KNOW ABOUT NUMBERS
Characteristic illustrations introduce basic number recognition
0–8431–1547–5 Price Stern Sloan pb $2.95

• David Carter

HOW MANY BUGS IN A BOX?
Odd creatures with witty names pop up and ask to be counted
0–671–64965–5 Simon & Schuster $10.95

• Demi

DEMI'S COUNT THE ANIMALS ONE-TWO-THREE
A companion to Demi's *Find the Animals ABC*
0–448–18980–1 Putnam $9.95

• Lydia Freeman

CORDUROY'S DAY
The toy bear hero of Freeman's story books appears in an affable counting book
Illustrated by Lisa McCue
0–670–80521–1 Viking pb $2.95

• Satoshi Kitamura

WHEN SHEEP CANNOT SLEEP
Woolly the sheep is wide awake, and his night-time adventures give young readers all sorts of things to count
0–374–38311–1 Farrar, Straus & Giroux $9.95
0–374–48359–0 Farrar, Straus & Giroux pb $3.95

• Annie Owen

ANNIE'S ONE TO TEN
This counting primer, liberally sprinkled with hundreds of pictures, doubles as an introduction to arithmetic
0–394–82791–0 Knopf $8.95

• Susan Schade

THE NOISY COUNTING BOOK
Children practice counting grouped objects on the same page. Though slight, the confrontation between the boy and a noisy frog is fun
Illustrated by Jon Buller
0–394–88956–8 Random House pb $3.95

• Maurice Sendak

ONE WAS JOHNNY
Johnny was one, then he became ten, then he became one again. As the house of the once solitary Johnny fills to the ceiling, enjoy Sendak's humorous characterizations
0–06–025540–4 Harper & Row $11.95

• Peter Sis

WAVING
People wave, and others wave back. Children count the participants in these bright illustrations
0–688–07159–7 Greenwillow $11.95

• Nancy Tafuri

ALL YEAR LONG
Children count the days and watch the months and seasons change along with them. This is one counting book children won't tire of easily
0–688–01414–3 Greenwillow $10.25
0–14–050479–6 Penguin pb $3.95

WHO'S COUNTING?
Children count the animals seen by an inquisitive puppy. Another lovely book
0–688–06130–3 Greenwillow $11.75

• Colin West

TEN LITTLE CROCODILES
Crocodiles become larger in numbers, then smaller in numbers in an Australian artist's funny pictures
0–8120–5884–4 Barron's $8.95

SOUNDS, COLORS, AND OTHER CONCEPTS

• Pam Ayres

Rhyming questions provoke guessing games for the threes, fours, and fives.

GUESS WHAT?
Illustrated by Julie Lacome
0–394–99287–3 Knopf $11.00

GUESS WHO?
Illustrated by Julie Lacome
0–394–99288–1 Knopf $11.00

• John Burningham

Sounds made by musical instruments and everyday objects introduce unusual and evocative words to children.

CLUCK BAA
0–670–22580–0 Viking pb $4.95

JANGLE TWANG
0–670–40570–1 Viking pb $4.95

SLAM BANG
0–670–65076–5 Viking pb $4.95

• Tana Hoban

Hoban photographs scenes or objects in close-up, and children find a shape, color or object that fits a prechosen concept. Pre-kindergarten children enter wholeheartedly into the game, and Hoban's sense of the unexpected makes the pictures fun to look at many times over.

I READ SIGNS
0–688–02317–7 Greenwillow $11.75
0–688–07331–X Morrow pb $3.95

IS IT LARGER? IS IT SMALLER?
0–688–04027–6 Greenwillow $11.95

IS IT RED? IS IT YELLOW? IS IT BLUE?
0–688–80171–4 Greenwillow $13.95
0–688–07034–5 Macmillan pb $3.95

IS IT ROUGH? IS IT SMOOTH? IS IT SHINY?
0–688–03823–9 Greenwillow $13.95

• Shirley Hughes

COLORS
Illustrated in a lovely, soft style. Threes to fives will find plenty to look at
0–688–04206–6 Lothrop, Lee & Shepard pb $4.95

• Tony Wells

ALLSORTS
Double pages ask preschool children to sort and group by categories
0–689–71185–9 Macmillan pb $4.95

TRUCKS, CARS, AIRPLANES, AND SO ON

• Joe Mathieu

Two books-with-wheels starring the Sesame Street Muppets

SESAME STREET FIRE TRUCKS
0–394–89952–0 Random House (boards) $2.95

TRUCKS IN YOUR NEIGHBORHOOD
0–394–89951–2 Random House (boards) $2.95

• Anne Rockwell

BIG WHEELS
Bold illustrations feature trucks equipped with clamshells for digging, trucks for farm use, trucks for use in the city
0–525–44226–X Dutton $9.95

PLANES
0–525–44159–X Dutton $9.95

THINGS THAT GO
Pictures grouped to show things that go on water, in the air, on city streets, on farms, and so on
0–525–44266–9 Dutton $10.95

• Richard Scarry

RICHARD SCARRY'S CARS AND TRUCKS AND THINGS THAT GO
0–307–15785–7 Western $7.95

RICHARD SCARRY'S HOP ABOARD, HERE WE GO
0–307–13756–2 Western $6.95

ANIMALS

• Walter Chandoha

PUPPIES AND KITTENS
0–448–40874–0 Putnam pb $3.95

• Judy Dunn

In these charming stories about young animals, the child owners play a prominent role. But because the pigs, lambs, and ducks are pets the books scarcely hint at the real lives of farm animals.

THE LITTLE DUCK
Photographs by Phoebe Dunn
0–394–83247–7 Random House pb $1.95

THE LITTLE KITTEN
Photographs by Phoebe Dunn
0–394–85818–2 Random House pb $1.95

THE LITTLE LAMB
Illustrated by Phoebe Dunn
0–394–83455–0 Random House pb $1.95

THE LITTLE PUPPY
Illustrated by Phoebe Dunn
0–394–86595–2 Random House pb $1.95

THE LITTLE RABBIT
Illustrated by Phoebe Dunn
0–394–84377–0 Random House pb $1.95

• Tana Hoban

A CHILDREN'S ZOO
A petting zoo photographed as though the animals are seen through the eyes of the young visitors
0–688–05202–9 Greenwillow $11.75

• Tish Sommers

A BIRD'S BEST FRIEND
Big Bird gets a puppy and learns what dogs do and don't need
Illustrated by Maggie Swanson
0–307–12018–X Western pb $2.95

• Garth Williams

BABY FARM ANIMALS
0–307–10393–5 Western pb $2.95

EXPLAINING COMMON CHILDHOOD EXPERIENCES

Stan & Janice Berenstain

THE BERENSTAIN BEARS FIRST TIME BOOKS
The Berenstain Bears inhabit a tree house furnished with bunk beds and a piano. Brother and Sister Bear encounter familiar situations and family disputes that Mama and Papa mediate with discipline, understanding, and humor. The series is designed to be read aloud by parents of four- to seven-year olds who are old enough to appreciate cleanliness, neatness, and other virtues.

THE BERENSTAIN BEARS AND THE BAD DREAM
0–394–87341–6 Random House pb $1.95

THE BERENSTAIN BEARS AND THE MESSY ROOM
0–394–88892–8 Random House pb $2.95

THE BERENSTAIN BEARS AND THE SITTER
0–394–88890–1 Random House pb $2.95

THE BERENSTAIN BEARS AND TOO MUCH JUNK FOOD
0–394–87217–7 Random House pb $1.95

THE BERENSTAIN BEARS FORGET THEIR MANNERS
0–394–87333–5 Random House pb $1.95

THE BERENSTAIN BEARS GO TO THE DOCTOR
0–394–848–357 Random House pb $1.95

THE BERENSTAIN BEARS LEARN ABOUT STRANGERS
0–394–87334–3 Random House pb $1.95

• Fred Rogers

FIRST EXPERIENCE BOOKS
Narrated by Mr. Rogers of the PBS television show, the First Experience books are unexpectedly detailed in terms of information and appeal to a wide audience.

GOING TO DAY CARE
0–399–21235–3 Putnam $12.95
0–399–21237–X Putnam pb $5.95

GOING TO THE HOSPITAL
Photographs by Jim Judkis
0–399–21503–4 Putnam $12.95
0–399–21530–1 Putnam pb $5.95

GOING TO THE POTTY
A straight-faced and sensible picture book about toilet training that asks and answers questions from the child's point of view
Illustrated by Jim Judkis
0–399–21296–5 Putnam $12.95
0–399–21297–3 Putnam pb $5.95

THE NEW BABY
Photographs by Jim Judkis
0–399–21236–1 Putnam $12.95
0–399–21238–8 Putnam pb $5.95

Sesame Street

The Sesame Street Growing Up books serve a double function as easy readers.

• Dina Anastasio

BIG BIRD CAN SHARE
Illustrated by Tom Leigh
0–307–12016–3 Western $3.25

• Louisa Campbell

ERNIE GETS LOST
Illustrated by Tom Cooke
0–307–12015–5 Western $3.25

ERNIE GETS LOST
With cassette
0–307–13947–6 Western pb $4.90

• Dan Elliott

GROVER LEARNS TO READ
Grover has to get over the fear that if he learns to read he won't be read to any more
Illustrated by Normand Chartier
0–394–87498–6 Random House $4.95

OSCAR'S ROTTEN BIRTHDAY
Illustrated by Normand Chartier
0–394–84848–9 Random House $4.95

• Sarah Roberts & Joe Mathieu

NOBODY CARES ABOUT ME!
0–394–85177–3 Random House $4.95

• Jocelyn Stevenson

WHEN GROVER MOVED TO SESAME STREET
Illustrated by Tom Cooke
0–307–12017–1 Western $2.95

• Norman Stiles

I'LL MISS YOU, MR. HOOPER
Small children won't remember Mr. Hooper, but they will understand the story as the Sesame Street people help explain that life goes on after grandma, grandpa, or someone close to the child dies
Illustrated by Joe Mathieu
0–394–96600–7 Random House $4.99
0–394–86600–2 Random House pb $3.95

ABOUT CHILDREN'S BOOKS

• Bruno Bettelheim

THE USES OF ENCHANTMENT: The Meaning and Importance of Fairy Tales
A classic study by this distinguished psychologist and interpreter of childhood who links folk tales to children's most pressing emotional needs
0–394–49771–6 Random House $21.95
0–394–72265–5 Random House pb $6.95

Books for Ages Five, Six, and Seven

Though children are still lookers and listeners when they enter kindergarten and first grade, they are advanced verbally and soon become readers. Picture books presenting funny situations are strong favorites, but children of six and seven also enjoy classic fairy tales, folktales, and modern fantasy tales. Many stories that children first meet when they are in preschool or kindergarten remain favorites for two or three years thereafter. The picture books selected are those which children in the early elementary grades can read themselves.

STORY BOOKS

Fantasy

- Bruno Bettelheim & Karen Zelan
ON LEARNING TO READ: The Child's Fascination With Meaning
An evaluation of reading primers and their effects on children
0–394–51592–7 Knopf $13.95
0–394–71194–7 Knopf pb $9.95

- Sheila Egoff, editor
ONLY CONNECT: Readings in Children's Literature
Collection of essays by distinguished authors such as P.L. Travers and C.S. Lewis
0–19–540309–6 Oxford pb $12.95

- Ruth Graves
READING IS FUNDAMENTAL: Guide to Encouraging Young Readers
Over 200 activities collected by the Reading Is Fundamental Organization designed to encourage young children to read. Includes a booklist from baby books up to sixth grade
0–385–23632–8 Doubleday pb $8.95

- Eden Ross Lipson
THE NEW YORK TIMES PARENT'S GUIDE TO THE BEST BOOKS FOR CHILDREN
Cites over 1000 books distinguished by quality rather than popularity. Organized according to reading level
0–8129–1649–2 Random House $22.00
0–8129–1688–3 Random House pb $12.95

- Joanne Oppenheim, editor
CHOOSING BOOKS FOR CHILDREN: How to Choose the Right Book for the Right Child at the Right Time
Over 1500 book reviews collected by lecturers from the Bank Street College of Education for kids from infancy to 12 years old
0–345–32683–0 Ballantine pb $9.95

- Iona & Peter Opie
THE LORE AND LANGUAGE OF SCHOOLCHILDREN
A classic scholarly work
0–19–282059–1 Oxford pb $9.95

- Jim Trelease
THE READ-ALOUD HANDBOOK
A little classic which encourages parents by positive guidance and interesting insights. Booklists included
0–8446–6172–4 Peter Smith $15.75
0–14–046727–0 Penguin pb $8.95

- Judith Barrett
CLOUDY WITH A CHANCE OF MEATBALLS
The little town of Chewandswallow enjoys an edible climate. The weather takes a turn for the worst and the inhabitants of Chewandswallow seek a safe haven
0–689–70749–5 Macmillan pb $3.95

- Quentin Blake
THE STORY OF THE DANCING FROG
A frog befriends a lonely widow and becomes an unexpected celebrity. Blake's long-limbed people are at once graceful and absurd, and the effect is charming
0–394–87033–6 Knopf $10.95

- Anthony Browne
GORILLA
A busy father gives his little girl a toy gorilla as a substitute for a trip to the zoo. The gorilla comes to life and takes her on a nocturnal adventure that may or may not be a dream
0–394–87525–7 Knopf $8.95

- Eve Bunting
SCARY, SCARY HALLOWEEN
Trick-or-treaters are pursued by a mysterious sheeted creature
Illustrated by Jan Brett
0–89919–414–1 Clarion $12.95

- John Burningham
COME AWAY FROM THE WATER, SHIRLEY
Shirley's prosaic parents don't notice that she is having the most extraordinary daydreams. Short on text, but unusually sophisticated for a picture book
0–690–01360–4 Harper & Row $12.95
0–06–443039–1 Harper & Row pb $3.95

- Natalie S. Carlson
SPOOKY AND THE WIZARD'S BATS
Spooky once belonged to a witch, and though he is now just as attached to his family as any other pet cat, he still has magic in him
Illustrated by Andrew Glass
0–688–06280–6 Lee, Lothrop & Shepard $11.75

- Carol Carrick
PATRICK'S DINOSAURS
When Patrick and his older brother visit the zoo, Patrick's brother is too busy showing off to see prehistoric monsters. But Patrick does; giant dinosaurs loom over the elephant house and swim in the zoo's lake until Patrick finally reaches home safely
Illustrated by Donald Carrick
0–89919–402–8 Clarion pb $4.95

WHAT HAPPENED TO PATRICK'S DINOSAURS?
Patrick comes up with an explanation for the dinosaurs' disappearance
Illustrated by Donald Carrick
0–89919–406–0 Clarion $12.95
0–89919–797–3 Clarion pb $4.95

- Roald Dahl
THE ENORMOUS CROCODILE
This bad-tempered crocodile is too greedy for his own good. Children either respond enthusiastically to Dahl's boisterous moralizing, or they just don't find him funny at all
Illustrated by Quentin Blake
0–394–83594–8 Knopf $4.95
0–553–15243–2 Bantam pb $2.95

- Steven Kellogg
THE MYSTERIOUS TADPOLE
A boy's pet tadpole keeps on growing, precipitating a series of ever more outrageous situations
Illustrated by Steven Kellogg
0–8037–6245–3 Dial $12.95
0–8037–6244–5 Dial pb $3.95

- Barbro Lindgren
THE WILD BABY
0–688–00601–9 Greenwillow $12.95

THE WILD BABY GOES TO SEA
The Wild Baby sails off in a wooden boat and turns each danger into an adventure
0–688–01960–9 Greenwillow $11.75

- Arnold Lobel
PRINCE BERTRAM THE BAD
A bad little prince gets his comeuppance from a passing witch but eventually redeems himself
Illustrated by Arnold Lobel
0–590–40265–X Scholastic pb $2.50

- Jan Piénkowski
THE HAUNTED HOUSE
Creepy things spring into action as the reader turns the pages of an inventive mechanical book
0–525–31520–9 Dutton $12.95

- Mary Rayner
GARTH PIG AND THE ICE CREAM LADY
Plump little pig hero Garth Pig doesn't know that the genial ice cream seller is really a hungry wolf
0–689–70495–X Macmillan pb $2.95

● Edith Schreiber-Wicke
CATS' CARNIVAL
Mario, a Venetian boy too young to go to the carnival parties, is invited to one by a mysterious cat in this dreamlike, beautifully illustrated book
Illustrated by Monika Laimgruber
0–87923–627–2 Godine $13.95

● Maurice Sendak
OUTSIDE OVER THERE
Sendak calls this the last book in the trilogy begun by *Where the Wild Things Are* and *In the Night Kitchen*. But this story with its illustrations of fat children and grumpy little girls may puzzle some young readers
0–06–025523–4 Harper & Row $14.95

Dr. Seuss
AND TO THINK THAT I SAW IT ON MULBERRY STREET
Dr. Seuss's first children's book, published in 1937
0–394–84494–7 Random House $9.95

BARTHOLOMEW AND THE OOBLECK
The King arrogantly messes with the weather and causes the precipitation of a horrible substance called oobleck. The pageboy Bartholomew Cubbins can melt the oobleck and bring the King to his senses. Caldecott Medal Honor Book 1950
0–394–90075–8 Random House $8.99
0–394–84539–0 Random House pb $3.95

THE 500 HATS OF BARTHOLOMEW CUBBINS
Bartholomew almost loses his head when the King insists he take off his hat to royalty
0–8149–0388–6 Vanguard $9.95

HORTON HEARS A WHO
When "A person's a person, no matter how small," he or she needs help. Seuss's rhyming story describes a courageous Horton caring for his "person," even though the situation gets him into all kinds of trouble
0–394–80078–8 Random House $8.95

● William Steig
Steig invests his enchanting frogs, mice, and rabbits with a gravity that makes his humor as convincing as his talent for fantasy. One takes great pleasure in the way a Steig picture book looks and sounds.
DOCTOR DE SOTO
A mouse dentist must decide whether his code of ethics requires him to take a fox as a patient. The fox says his tooth hurts terribly but won't our hero end up in those capacious jaws?
0–374–31803–4 Farrar, Straus & Giroux $13.95
0–590–33304–6 Scholastic pb $3.95

GORKY RISES
Gorky the frog experiments with a potion that includes a hefty dash of his father's cologne and all of a sudden he's able to fly. As so often happens in Steig's books, one discovers that magic can have logic of its own
0–374–42784–4 Farrar, Straus & Giroux pb $3.95

From Horton Hears a Who *by Dr. Seuss (Random House)*

SOLOMON THE RUSTY NAIL
Solomon finds he can turn himself into a rusty nail, but the real consequences are unforeseen. This rabbit's adventures make for an inspired nonsense-fantasy
0–374–37131–8 Farrar, Straus & Giroux $13.95
0–374–46903–2 Farrar, Straus & Giroux pb $3.95

SYLVESTER AND THE MAGIC PEBBLE
Sylvester is a young donkey who finds an attractive red pebble and the apparent ability to transform himself at will. Caldecott Medal 1970
0–671–66269–4 Simon & Schuster pb $5.95

● John Steptoe
THE STORY OF THE JUMPING MOUSE
An Indian legend retold to create the character of an unselfish mouse who gives his all and is rewarded by eternal life in a far-off land
0–688–01903–X Lothrop, Lee & Shepard $11.95

● James Thurber
MANY MOONS
A spoiled princess demands the moon and the kingdom is turned upside down as the king's wise men try to get it for her. Then a good-hearted young lad comes along and invents an acceptable solution. Caldecott Medal 1944
0–15–251873–8 HBJ $12.95
0–15–656980–9 HBJ pb $4.95

● Alain Vaes
THE PORCELAIN PEPPER POT
Animated kitchenware enacts a little household drama in this splendidly illustrated book
0–14–050727–2 Penguin pb $4.95

● Chris Van Allsburg
THE GARDEN OF ABDUL GASAZI
A bad-mannered dog breaks into an enchanter's garden and leads a little boy into an adventure. Caldecott Honor Book 1980
0–395–27804–X Houghton Mifflin $15.95

JUMANJI
Two children play a jungle board game that they must finish despite the consequences. There are some scary moments before the children are out of danger. Caldecott Medal 1982
0–395–30448–2 Houghton Mifflin $14.95

● Oscar Wilde
THE SELFISH GIANT
A giant creates a perpetual winter out of his garden because he is too selfish to share it with anyone
Illustrated by Lisbeth Zwerger
0–907–23430–5 Picture Book Studio $14.95

THE SELFISH GIANT
Illustrated by Dom Mansell
0–671–66847–1 Prentice Hall pb $10.95

● Margery Bianco Williams
THE VELVETEEN RABBIT: Or How Toys Become Real
A celebrated fantasy from the 1920s about a toy rabbit who is loved by a boy, cast aside, and changed into a "real" rabbit as a reward for his loyalty and forbearance. Children may cry over it; adults may sense something wrong in the author's failure to castigate the wrongdoers
Illustrated by Michael Hague
0–8050–0209–X Henry Holt $11.95

● Arthur Yorinks
HEY, AL
Al the janitor and his dog are offered a new life in paradise, but the gift is not all that it seems. Caldecott Medal 1987
Illustrated by Richard Egielski
0–374–33060–3 Farrar, Straus & Giroux $13.95

Humor

● Janet & Allan Ahlberg
THE JOLLY POSTMAN
Letters that the reader pulls out of the book are addressed to fairy tale characters. Children familiar with traditional stories will find the idea intriguing
0–316–02036–2 Little, Brown $12.95

● Harry Allard
THE STUPIDS HAVE A BALL
Illustrated by James Marshall
0–395–26497–9 Houghton Mifflin $12.95
0–395–36169–9 Houghton Mifflin pb $3.95

THE STUPIDS STEP OUT
The Stupids put on their sneakers when it's time for bed and vacuum the carpet with a lawn mower. Goofily good-natured, the Stupids will appeal to kids who don't care how silly the jokes are
Illustrated by James Marshall
0–395–25377–2 Houghton Mifflin pb $3.95

● Harry Allard & James Marshall
MISS NELSON HAS A FIELD DAY
The substitute teacher, Coach Swamp, strikes terror in the hearts of the incompetent footballers from homeroom 207
Illustrated by James Marshall
0–395–36690–9 Houghton Mifflin $12.95

MISS NELSON IS MISSING
Miss Nelson's homeroom is inhabited by a bunch of really naughty kids. The situation isn't resolved until nice Miss Nelson

---

becomes horrid Miss Swamp, and some well-behaved children start longing for her return

Illustrated by James Marshall
0–395–40146–1 Houghton Mifflin pb $3.95

MISS NELSON IS MISSING
With cassette
Illustrated by James Marshall
0–395–45737–8 Houghton Mifflin pb $6.95

• Anthony Browne
PIGGYBOOK
Three male slobs turn into pigs in a humorous comment on sex roles in the home
0–394–88416–7 Knopf $9.95

• John Burningham
WOULD YOU RATHER ...
Would you rather be made to eat spider stew or slug dumplings? Would you rather your house were surrounded by snow or by a jungle? A book to provoke laughter and home-grown make-believe
0–690–03917–4 Harper & Row $12.95

• Babette Cole
THE TROUBLE WITH DAD
Cole's book about a loony handyman dad
0–399–21206–X Putnam $12.95
0–399–21467–4 Putnam pb $5.95

THE TROUBLE WITH MOM
Mom has a collection of weird hats. But being a witch as well, can she help doing things to embarrass her children?
0–698–20624–X Putnam pb $5.95

• Jack Gantos
The stories of a well-behaved little girl and her rotten cat Ralph.
ROTTEN RALPH
0–395–29202–6 Houghton Mifflin $4.95

ROTTEN RALPH'S ROTTEN CHRISTMAS
0–395–45346–1 Houghton Mifflin $4.95

ROTTEN RALPH'S TRICK OR TREAT
0–395–48655–6 Houghton Mifflin $4.95

• Steven Kellogg
PINKERTON, BEHAVE!
Pinkerton is an affectionate and awkward Great Dane puppy who will not learn how to behave. The resulting mayhem is the subject of funny illustrations
0–8037–6573–8 Dial $12.95
0–8037–7250–5 Dial pb $3.95

PREHISTORIC PINKERTON
0–8037–0322–8 Dial $12.95

A ROSE FOR PINKERTON
Rose the kitten joins the household and wins the pet show after Pinkerton disrupts one of the show's snootier exhibits
0–8037–7502–4 Dial $12.95
0–8037–0060–1 Dial pb $3.95

• Lee Lorenz
A WEEKEND IN THE COUNTRY
Two friends go off to the country for the weekend but only after telling one another the weird things that they are absolutely positively certain will happen
0–13–947961–9 Prentice Hall $11.95
0–13–948191–5 Simon & Schuster pb $4.95

• Edward Marshall
SPACE CASE
If a scientist granny and a thing from outer space were not enough to cope with, the young hero must also defeat the obnoxious Boober twins
Illustrated by James Marshall
0–8037–8005–2 Dial $12.95
0–8037–8431–7 Dial pb $4.95

MERRY CHRISTMAS, SPACE CASE
The same cast of characters returns for a humorous sequel in which the Boober twins get what they deserve. Both adventures are suitable for young readers
Illustrated by James Marshall
0–8037–0215–9 Dial $10.95

• James Marshall
YUMMERS!
The heroine is Emilie the Pig, whose gustatory adventures are unusual
0–395–39590–9 Houghton Mifflin pb $3.95

YUMMERS TOO: The Second Course
0–395–38990–9 Houghton Mifflin $12.95

• Trinka Hakes Noble
THE DAY JIMMY'S BOA ATE THE WASH
Jimmie's class goes off on a bus trip to a farm, and the boa goes too. The adventures become wilder and funnier as the tall tale progresses
Illustrated by Steven Kellogg
0–8037–1723–7 Dial $12.95
0–8037–0094–6 Dial pb $3.95

• Ellen Raskin
SPECTACLES
Before and after the dreaded visit to the eye doctor. A book characterized by inspired nonsense
0–689–70317–1 Macmillan pb $3.95

• Mary Rayner
MRS. PIG'S BULK BUY
Mrs. Pig is so fed up with the piglets' eating fads that she devises a whole new menu based on their favorite food
0–689–30831–0 Macmillan $10.95
0–689–70771–1 Macmillan pb $3.95

• Amy Schwartz
BEA AND MR. JONES
Bea dislikes school and Mr. Jones is frustrated by his job as an advertising executive. Parent and child swap places—with very surprising results
0–02–781430–0 Bradbury $10.95
0–14–050439–7 Penguin pb $3.95

• Maurice Sendak & Matthew Margolis
SOME SWELL PUP!: Or, Are You Sure You Want A Dog?
A little book that teaches pet care through humor
Illustrated by Maurice Sendak
0–374–37134–2 Farrar, Straus & Giroux $9.95
0–374–46963–6 Farrar, Straus & Giroux pb $3.95

Dr. Seuss
IF I RAN THE CIRCUS
0–394–80080–X Random House $8.95

IF I RAN THE ZOO
Bored with ordinary lions and tigers, the new zoo keeper searches out a

Gusset, a Gherkin, a Gasket, and a Gootch along with some other exotic breeds
0–394–80081–8 Random House $8.95
0–394–84545–5 Random House pb $3.95

SCRAMBLED EGGS SUPER!
Salamagoox eggs mixed with Tittle Topped Goose eggs—not quite fine enough, as we would expect from Seuss's nonsense verse
0–394–84544–7 Random House pb $3.95

YERTLE THE TURTLE & OTHER STORIES
An imperious king insists on climbing on the shoulders of his subjects. The precarious pyramid rests on the back of one small turtle who finally realizes there's no reason to be the fellow at the bottom of the heap
0–394–80087–7 Random House $9.95

• Mitchell Sharmat
GREGORY, THE TERRIBLE EATER
Mom and Dad enjoy the usual goat staples such as tin cans; by their standards Gregory has peculiar eating habits
Illustrated by José Aruego & Ariane Dewey
0–02–782250–8 Macmillan $12.95
0–02–688770–3 Macmillan pb $4.95

• William Steig
SPINKY SULKS
Convinced that his family doesn't love him, Spinky develops a massive case of the sulks
0–374–38321–9 Farrar, Straus & Giroux $13.95

• James Stevenson
COULD BE WORSE
A nice old grandpa is challenged by his grandchildren and comes up with a whopping tale about the things he had to do when he was young
0–688–80075–0 Greenwillow $13.00
0–02–688769–X Macmillan pb $4.95

THERE'S NOTHING TO DO!
Grandpa's description of a wild and wacky visit to his grandparents' farm squelches complaints of boredom
0–688–04698–3 Greenwillow $11.75

WHAT'S UNDER MY BED
Grandpa is awakened and exorcises all the things that are smelly or shaking like jelly
0–688–02325–8 Greenwillow $12.95
0–14–050485–0 Penguin pb $3.95

Kay Thompson
ELOISE
The outrageous six-year-old has delighted several generations of readers since she first took up residence in the Plaza Hotel
Illustrated by Hilary Knight
0–671–22350–X Simon & Schuster $15.95

• Tomi Ungerer
THE BEAST OF MONSIEUR RACINE
Monsieur Racine finds a strange animal digging up his tidy garden and loses his heart to a beast that looks like an old mop with a nose
0–374–30640–0 Farrar, Straus & Giroux $11.95
0–374–40570–0 Farrar, Straus & Giroux pb $4.95

● Bernard Waber

THE HOUSE ON EAST 88TH STREET
A family moves into a New York City brownstone—and finds Lyle the crocodile in the bathtub. The mysterious Lyle is very fond of caviar and was once the star of a sideshow
0–395–19970–0 Houghton Mifflin pb $4.95

LOVABLE LYLE
Lyle has to prove he's lovable when someone in the neighborhood tries to scare him away
0–395–25378–0 Houghton Mifflin pb $4.95

● Audrey Wood

KING BIDGOOD'S IN THE BATHTUB
The court must persuade stubborn King Bidgood to leave his much too comfortable and luxurious bathtub. Caldecott Honor Book 1987
Illustrated by Don Wood
0–15–242730–9 HBJ $13.95

Adventure

● David A. Adler

MY DOG AND THE GREEN SOCK MYSTERY
A friend's dog may or may not be able to solve the mystery of the missing green sock. Beginner readers can tackle Adler's stories on their own
Illustrated by Dick Gackenbach
0–8234–0590–7 Holiday House $12.95

● Edward Ardizzone

LITTLE TIM AND THE BRAVE SEA CAPTAIN
Created in the 50s, Tim is an English boy who lives in a seaside village and has adventures. This one describes Tim's bravery in the face of an unexpectedly frightening sea voyage. Ardizzone's characteristically soft, sketchy style is a pleasure to look at
0–14–050175–4 Penguin pb $3.95

Helen Craig & Katharine Holabird
Angelina is a child mouse and the heroine of a series that begins with her dancing lessons. Despite setbacks along the way, Angelina remains unspoiled when she finally realizes her ambitions.

ANGELINA AND THE PRINCESS
0–517–55273–6 Crown $9.95

ANGELINA AT THE FAIR
0–517–55744–4 Crown $9.95

ANGELINA BALLERINA
0–517–55083–0 Crown $9.95

ANGELINA ON STAGE
0–517–56073–9 Crown $9.95

ANGELINA'S CHRISTMAS
0–517–55823–8 Crown $9.95

● Tomie dePaola

BILL AND PETE
Bill is a Nile crocodile, and Pete the plover is his friend and toothbrush. Threatened with becoming a crocodile suitcase, Bill is rescued by Pete. Bill's adventures are pictured in bold, bright illustrations
0–399–20646–9 Putnam $12.95
0–399–20650–7 Putnam pb $5.95

● Roger Duvoisin

PETUNIA THE SILLY GOOSE STORIES: Five Read-Aloud Classics
Petunia the Goose is a dear friend, but when she helps you out she has the knack of complicating the situation
0–394–88292–X Knopf $15.95

● Roy Gerrard

SIR CEDRIC
Since Sir Cedric the Good is a knight, he defeats sinister opponents and rescues ladies—specifically one Fat Matilda, whom he marries. Gerrard tells his tale in a bouncy rhyming narrative and colorful, eccentric pictures
0–374–36959–3 Farrar, Straus & Giroux $12.95
0–374–46659–9 Farrar, Straus & Giroux pb $3.95

SIR CEDRIC RIDES AGAIN
Sir Cedric and Fat Matilda rescue their daughter from her kidnapper, Black Ned
0–374–36961–5 Farrar, Straus & Giroux $12.95

● Brom Hoban

SKUNK LANE
At the suggestion of his mother and father a young skunk reluctantly sets out on his own and finds that his world is full of unexpectedly interesting people
0–06–022348–0 Harper & Row $9.95

● Steven Kellogg

THE ISLAND OF THE SKOG
On National Rodent Day a tribe of hard-pressed mice decides to set off in search of an uninhabited island. Kellogg's sweet, woolly-headed heroes take possession of their island after a last, scary adventure
0–8037–3842–0 Dial $12.95
0–8037–4122–7 Dial pb $3.95

● Albert Lamorisse

THE RED BALLOON
The adventures of a solitary little boy and his red balloon told in stills made from the sad and charming French film of the same name. In the end the hero escapes a gang of bullies and soars off into the skies of Paris
0–385–00343–9 Doubleday $13.95
0–385–14297–8 Doubleday pb $5.95

● Marjorie W. Sharmat

GILA MONSTERS MEET YOU AT THE AIRPORT
The real and imaginary adventures of a boy who is moving to another part of the country
Illustrated by Byron Barton
0–02–782450–0 Macmillan $13.95
0–14–050430–3 Penguin pb $3.95

● William Steig

BRAVE IRENE
A plucky little girl braves a blizzard to deliver the duchess' ball gown in one of Steig's most successful books for children
0–374–30947–7 Farrar, Straus & Giroux $13.95
0–374–40927–7 Farrar, Straus & Giroux pb $3.95

● Lynd Ward

THE BIGGEST BEAR
Johnny sets out to catch the biggest bear of all. He comes home with a very little bear that grows and grows until it becomes a trial to the entire valley. Caldecott Medal 1953
0–395–15024–8 Houghton Mifflin pb $3.95

Family Stories

● Ina R. Friedman

HOW MY PARENTS LEARNED TO EAT
The young heroine recounts how her mother and father—Japanese and American respectively—met, fell in love, and finally learned to eat with knife and fork as well as chopsticks
Illustrated by Allan Say
0–395–35379–3 Houghton Mifflin $12.95
0–395–44235–4 Houghton Mifflin pb $3.95

● Amy Hest

THE CRACK-OF-DAWN WALKERS
The early risers are a little girl and her grandfather who make the morning's walk into an adventure. There are hints that grandpa won't always be around to enjoy this ordinary ramble through the neighborhood
Illustrated by Amy Schwartz
0–02–743710–8 Macmillan $10.95

THE PURPLE COAT
Grandpa understands a little girl's desire for a different-colored winter coat, in a story set in New York City in the 1940s. The illustrations are fascinating
Illustrated by Amy Schwartz
0–02–743640–3 Macmillan $12.95

● Cynthia Rylant

THE RELATIVES CAME
An ebullient crowd of relatives from West Virginia comes for a visit and reawakens a family's affection. Caldecott Honor Book 1986
Illustrated by Stephen Gammell
0–02–777220–9 Macmillan $12.95

● Eleanor Schick

RAINY SUNDAY
A gray day when nothing happens becomes full of warmth and incident
0–8037–7371–4 Dial pb $2.50

● John Steptoe

DADDY IS A MONSTER … SOMETIMES
Some things make this dad mad and the children know it, though they aren't really afraid of his monster side
0–397–31762–X Harper & Row $12.95
0–06–443042–1 Harper & Row pb $4.95

● Judith Viorst

ALEXANDER AND THE TERRIBLE, HORRIBLE, NO GOOD, VERY BAD DAY
Alexander has one of those days. Viorst makes us laugh but doesn't spoil the story by pasting on a sunny ending
Illustrated by Ray Cruz
0–689–30072–7 Macmillan $11.95
0–689–71173–5 Macmillan pb $2.95

◆ TO ORDER BOOKS AS GIFTS, SEE PAGE 1

ALEXANDER, WHO USED TO BE RICH LAST SUNDAY
Another monologue from Alexander, whose dollar disappears in a series of misadventures
Illustrated by Ray Cruz
0–689–71199–9 Macmillan pb $2.95

• Vera B. Williams
A CHAIR FOR MY MOTHER
After their home is destroyed, a grandmother, mother, and daughter start over with courage and affection. Caldecott Honor Book 1983
0–688–00914–X Greenwillow $13.95
0–688–04074–8 Greenwillow pb $3.95

• Harriet Ziefert
A NEW COAT FOR ANNA
A little girl's mother gets her a new coat. It's an act of courage and determination for a poor family living in Europe after World War II
Illustrated by Anita Lobel
0–394–87426–9 Knopf $11.00
0–394–89861–3 Knopf pb $3.95

Friendships

• Miriam Cohen
Cohen's ongoing saga of Jim and his classmates offers brief, realistic slices of first-grade life, with much humor and surprisingly rounded characterizations
LIAR, LIAR, PANTS ON FIRE!
Illustrated by Lillian Hoban
0–688–04244–9 Greenwillow $11.75
0–440–44755–0 Dell pb $2.95

LOST IN THE MUSEUM
Illustrated by Lillian Hoban
0–688–80187–0 Greenwillow $11.75
0–440–44780–1 Dell pb $2.95

SO WHAT?
Illustrated by Lillian Hoban
0–688–01202–7 Greenwillow $11.75
0–440–40048–1 Dell pb $2.50

STARRING FIRST GRADE
Illustrated by Lillian Hoban
0–688–04029–2 Greenwillow $11.75
0–440–48250–X Dell pb $2.50

WHEN WILL I READ?
Illustrated by Lillian Hoban
0–688–80073–4 Greenwillow $11.75
0–440–49333–1 Dell pb $2.95

• Steven Kellogg
BEST FRIENDS
Louise Jenkins is Katie's best friend—and also a traitor. The theme of best friend turned worst enemy is nicely explored in an amusing book
0–8037–0099–7 Dial $12.95

• James Marshall
George is a bit plodding, Martha is sharp-tongued and decisive. They experience the usual fallings-out and making up common to close friends. They are hippopotami. Marshall's brief and witty text is easy for beginning readers.
GEORGE AND MARTHA
With cassette
0–395–45739–4 Houghton Mifflin pb $6.95

GEORGE AND MARTHA BACK IN TOWN
0–395–35386–6 Houghton Mifflin $10.95

GEORGE AND MARTHA ENCORE
0–395–25379–9 Houghton Mifflin pb $2.95

GEORGE AND MARTHA ONE FINE DAY
0–395–32921–3 Houghton Mifflin pb $3.95

• Lore Segal
MRS. LOVEWRIGHT AND PURRLESS HER CAT
The irritable Mrs. Lovewright becomes a different person once she accepts the friendship of a stubborn cat
0–394–96817–4 Knopf $13.00

• Marjorie Weinman Sharmat
MITCHELL IS MOVING
Mitchell the dinosaur's irresistible desire to move house annoys his resourceful friend Martha, who works out the situation to satisfy them both. First- or second-graders can read this story for themselves
Illustrated by José Aruego & Ariane Dewey
0–02–045260–8 Macmillan pb $3.95

Gabrielle Vincent
Ernest is a fatherly-looking bear, Celestine is a childlike mouse. They inhabit an old-fashioned house in France in amicable fashion and have numerous adventures.
ERNEST AND CELESTINE
0–688–06525–2 Morrow pb $3.95

BRAVO, ERNEST AND CELESTINE!
0–688–00857–7 Greenwillow $10.75

MERRY CHRISTMAS, ERNEST AND CELESTINE
0–688–07330–1 Morrow pb $3.95

SMILE, ERNEST AND CELESTINE
0–688–01247–7 Morrow $10.75

Fairy and Folk Stories

• Verna Aardema
WHY MOSQUITOES BUZZ IN PEOPLE'S EARS: A West African Tale
All the African animals must suffer after a mishap occurs to one of their children. The animal king settles the case, and the scapegoat mosquito is punished. Caldecott Medal 1976
Illustrated by Diane Dillon
0–8037–6089–2 Dial $13.95
0–8037–6088–4 Dial pb $3.95

• Hans Christian Andersen
THE FIR TREE
Sharply defined pictures illustrate the melancholy story of a fir tree who could not wait to grow and leave the forest
Illustrated by Nancy Ekholm Burkert
0–06–443109–6 Harper & Row pb $3.95

THE FIR TREE
Illustrated by Marcel Imsand & Rita Marshall
0–87191–949–4 Creative Education $14.25

THE LITTLE MERMAID
A mermaid falls in love with a prince and makes thankless sacrifices to do so
Adapted by Anthea Bell
0–907234–59–3 Picture Book Studio $14.95

THE NIGHTINGALE
Andersen's story about the selfish emperor and the faithful nightingale set in a landscape populated by villagers and courtiers
Illustrated by Demi
0–15–257428–X HBJ pb $3.95

THE NIGHTINGALE
Zwerger's carefully defined illustrations are usually drawn in soft colors, and her retold fairy stories are very lovely to look at
Illustrated by Lisbeth Zwerger
0–907234–57–7 Picture Book Studio $13.95

THE PRINCESS AND THE PEA
Andersen's little comedy about an ungrateful guest who more than gets away with it
Translated by Anthea Bell
Illustrated by Eve Tharlet
0–88708–052–9 Picture Book Studio $12.95

THUMBELINA
Thumbelina is as small as her name suggests, and her first suitors are equally small and very ugly. But after many tribulations, determined little Thumbelina is rewarded with a husband
Illustrated by Lisbeth Zwerger
0–88708–006–5 Picture Book Studio $13.95

THE UGLY DUCKLING
Edited by Lilian Moore
Illustrated by Daniel San Souci
0–590–40957–3 Scholastic $12.95
0–590–40524–1 Scholastic pb $2.95

THE UGLY DUCKLING
With cassette
Illustrated by Daniel San Souci
0–590–63231–0 Scholastic pb $5.95

THE UGLY DUCKLING
Andersen's masterpiece is the story we like to think is autobiographical
Illustrated by Lorinda Bryan Cavley
0–15–692528–1 HBJ pb $7.95

THE WILD SWANS
An oversized picture book with colored pages. A young woman saves her twelve brothers by putting herself in terrible danger
Retold by Amy Ehrlich
Illustrated by Susan Jeffers
0–8037–9381–2 Dial $12.95
0–8037–0451–8 Dial pb $4.95

Marcia Brown
STONE SOUP
The pleasant old-fashioned story about the miraculous soup pot
0–689–71103–4 Macmillan pb $3.95

STONE SOUP
With cassette
0–87499–053–X Live Oak $19.95

• Tomie dePaola
STREGA NONA
Strega Nona is the local witch. When her foolish assistant Anthony tries to replicate her magic, the results are calamitous—and hilarious. Caldecott Honor Book 1976
0–13–851600–6 Prentice Hall $10.95
0–13–851592–1 Prentice Hall pb $4.95

MERRY CHRISTMAS, STREGA NONA
0–15–253183–1 HBJ $12.95

• Tomie dePaola, editor
TOMIE DEPAOLA'S FAVORITE NURSERY TALES
Children out of the nursery too will enjoy these popular folk stories and fairy tales
0–399–21319–8 Putnam $17.95

• Paul Goble
THE GIFT OF THE SACRED DOG
The horse is the sacred dog, according to Indian lore that dates back to the conquistadors
0–02–736560–3 Bradbury $12.95
0–02–043280–1 Bradbury pb $4.95

• The Brothers Grimm
DEAR MILI: An Old Tale
Illustrated by Maurice Sendak
0–374–31762–3 Farrar, Straus & Giroux $16.95

HANSEL AND GRETEL
The haunting story of the mistreated children is one of those Grimm folktales which both fascinates and frightens. Caldecott Honor Book 1985
Illustrated by Paul O. Zelinsky
0–396–08449–4 Dodd, Mead $12.95

HANSEL AND GRETEL
Illustrated by Susan Jeffers
0–8037–0318–X Dial pb $4.95

LITTLE RED RIDING HOOD
Knopf's Children's Classics series includes favorite stories illustrated rather grandly with full-color pictures
Retold by Arnold Eisen
Illustrated by Lynn B. Ferris
0–394–55883–9 Knopf $9.95

RED RIDING HOOD
A sturdy heroine and a witty ending to the traditional Grimm story. Caldecott Honor Book 1988
Retold and illustrated by James Marshall
0–8037–0344–9 Dial $9.95

RUMPELSTILTSKIN
"The artist envisions the story in a late medieval setting, and he makes the most of it, with a romantic realism that brings each scene to life"—Faith McNulty, *New Yorker*. Caldecott Honor Book 1987
Retold and illustrated by Paul O. Zelinsky
0–525–44265–0 Dutton $12.95

SNOW WHITE AND THE SEVEN DWARFS
Elfish-looking dwarfs appear in line and watercolor illustrations that are lighter in mood than most other artists' renderings of the story
Illustrated by Chihiro Iwasaki
0–88708–012–X Picture Book Studio $13.95

WALT DISNEY'S SNOW WHITE
Disney created Dopey, Sneezy, Doc, and friends out of Grimm's anonymous dwarfs and animated the stepmother queen, whose poisoned apple is one ingredient of a child's imagination
0–307–11055–9 Western pb $1.95

SNOW WHITE AND THE SEVEN DWARFS
A Disney Read-Aloud Film Classic, based on the animated feature
0–517–54325–7 Crown $9.95

• Gail E. Haley
A STORY—A STORY
Spider stories in African folklore describe defenseless men or animals outwitting others or succeeding against great odds. Anansi the spider man is just such a hero as he proves clever enough to purchase a golden box of stories from the sky god. Caldecott Medal Book 1971
0–689–71201–4 Macmillan pb $4.95

Steven Kellogg
CHICKEN LITTLE
The old story given a modern twist
Retold and illustrated by Steven Kellogg
0–688–05690–3 Morrow $13.00

PECOS BILL: A Tall Tale
0–688–05871–X Morrow $13.00

• Gerald McDermott
ARROW TO THE SUN: A Pueblo Indian Tale
0–14–050211–4 Penguin pb $4.95

• Charles Perrault
CINDERELLA
A retelling fashioned from relatively few words. This Cinderella will hold the attention of the fours as well as the fives. Caldecott Medal 1955
Retold and illustrated by Marcia Brown
0–684–12676–1 Macmillan $13.95
0–689–70484–4 Macmillan pb $4.95

CINDERELLA
A subtle retelling in an oversized version
Retold by Amy Ehrlich
Illustrated by Susan Jeffers
0–8037–0205–1 Dial $12.95

THE SLEEPING BEAUTY
Edited and illustrated by Warren Chappell
0–394–48474–6 Random House pb $6.95

• Arthur Ransome, editor
THE FOOL OF THE WORLD AND THE FLYING SHIP: A Russian Tale
The Fool of the World sets off to marry the Czar's daughter and gathers up a crew of foolish people who turn out to possess odd and irreplaceable talents. Caldecott Medal Book 1968
Illustrated by Uri Shulevitz
0–374–32442–5 Farrar, Straus & Giroux $15.95
0–374–42438–1 Farrar, Straus & Giroux pb $4.95

• Pete Seeger
ABIYOYO: South African Lullaby and Folk Story
A little boy and his father make a dreaded giant disappear
Illustrated by Michael Hays
0–02–781490–4 Macmillan $15.95

• Janet Stevens
TORTOISE AND THE HARE
A sassy hare and a lovable tortoise are the heroes of Stevens' funny illustrations
0–823405–10–9 Holiday House $12.95
0–823405–64–8 Holiday House pb $5.95

• Madame de Villeneuve
BEAUTY AND THE BEAST: A Tale of Love's Sacrifice
Illustrated by Etienne Delessert
0–87191–946–X Creative Ed $14.25

BEAUTY AND THE BEAST
Retold and illustrated by Warwick Hutton
0–689–50316–4 Macmillan $11.95

BEAUTY AND THE BEAST
Retold and illustrated by Mercer Mayer
0–689–71151–4 Macmillan pb $5.95

Bible Stories

• Helme Heine
ONE DAY IN PARADISE
A retelling of the Creation by a Caldecott Medal winner
Illustrated by Helme Heine
0–689–50394–6 Macmillan $12.95

• Nonny Hogrogian
NOAH'S ARK
The traditional Biblical text, with the Caldecott Medalist's paintings
0–394–88191–5 Knopf $12.95

• Warwick Hutton
Three retold stories, illustrated with Hutton's luminous watercolor paintings.
ADAM AND EVE
0–689–50433–0 Macmillan $13.95

JONAH AND THE GREAT FISH
0–689–50283–4 Macmillan $13.95

MOSES IN THE BULRUSHES
0–689–50393–8 Macmillan $12.95

• Peter Spier
NOAH'S ARK
A translation of a 17th-century Dutch poem precedes pages of wordless, and glorious, illustrations
0–385–09473–6 Doubleday $12.95
0–385–17302–4 Doubleday pb $4.95

PICTURE BOOKS

Christmas and Hanukkah

• David A. Adler
A PICTURE BOOK OF HANUKKAH
The illustrated story of how the holiday came to be, with suggestions for having a happy Hanukkah
0–8234–0458–7 Holiday House $12.95
0–8234–0574–5 Holiday House pb $5.95

• Raymond Briggs
FATHER CHRISTMAS
Father Christmas grumbles a lot but still gets up and down chimneys. Detailed little pictures are arranged in stories that are really elongated strip cartoons
0–698–20272–4 Putnam $13.95
0–14–050125–8 Penguin pb $3.95

THE SNOWMAN
A wordless book that appeals to older children as well: a boy and a snowman go on a mysterious journey
0–394–88466–3 Random House pb $4.95

• Clement Moore
THE NIGHT BEFORE CHRISTMAS
The beloved story of Old Saint Nick with busy and colorful illustrations
Illustrated by Tomie dePaola
0–8234–0414–5 Holiday House $13.95
0–8234–0417–X Holiday House pb $5.95

THE NIGHT BEFORE CHRISTMAS
A humorous illustrated edition
Illustrated by James Marshall
0–590–33448–4 Scholastic pb $2.95

Dr. Seuss
HOW THE GRINCH STOLE CHRISTMAS
A Christmas classic for over 30 years
0–394–80079–6 Random House $6.95

• Tasha Tudor
A BOOK OF CHRISTMAS
0–399–21475–5 Putnam $12.95

• Chris Van Allsburg
THE POLAR EXPRESS
This picture book about a Christmastime train ride to the North Pole is also a fable about children's belief in inexplicable worlds. Caldecott Medal 1986
0–395–38949–6 Houghton Mifflin $15.95

• Julie Vivas
THE NATIVITY
Vivas gives the Nativity story a contemporary setting and a light-hearted interpretation
0–15–200535–8 HBJ $13.95

• Marcia Williams
THE FIRST CHRISTMAS
A simple retelling, with bright and colorful pictures in a filmstrip format
0–394–80434–1 Random House pb $1.95

• Sophie Windham, illustrator
THE TWELVE DAYS OF CHRISTMAS
Children lift the flaps to find an extraordinary accumulation of Christmas gifts
0–399–21327–9 Putnam pb $13.95

• Jane Breskin Zalben
BENI'S FIRST CHANUKAH
Beni the bear celebrates his first chanukah
0–8050–0479–3 Henry Holt $12.95

Life Then and Now

• Mitsumasa Anno & others
ALL IN A DAY
International illustrators paint a picture of life in eight countries
0–399–21311–2 Putnam $14.95

• Canna Funakoshi
ONE MORNING
A cat enjoys the sights, sounds, and smells of the new morning
Illustrated by Yohi Izawa
0–88708–033–2 Picture Book Studio $10.95

• John S. Goodall
THE STORY OF A CASTLE
The story of an English castle, told in pictures
0–689–50405–5 Macmillan $14.95

THE STORY OF AN ENGLISH VILLAGE
0–689–50125–9 Macmillan $14.95

THE STORY OF A MAIN STREET
0–689–50436–5 Macmillan $14.95

• Donald Hall
OX-CART MAN
A New England farmer gathers the family's produce for the journey to the market town. The story describes a bygone era when families produced food and clothes, and the children helped. Caldecott Medal 1980
Illustrated by Barbara Cooney
0–670–53328–9 Viking $14.95
0–14–050441–9 Penguin pb $4.95

• William Kurelek
A PRAIRIE BOY'S WINTER
A picture book version of the life that Laura Ingalls Wilder, author of *Little House on the Prairie*, might have led had she been a boy and been part of a family that had fewer worries about "getting by." The illustrations are charming
Illustrated by William Kurelek
0–395–17708–1 Houghton Mifflin $13.95
0–395–36609–7 Houghton Mifflin pb $4.95

• Betsy Maestro
THE STORY OF THE STATUE OF LIBERTY
Comic pictures accompany a simple narrative of The Lady's history
Illustrated by Giulio Maestro
0–688–05773–X Lee, Lothrop & Shepard $13.00

• Roxie Munro
Bold and detailed pictures show the exteriors and interiors of celebrated buildings.

THE INSIDE-OUTSIDE BOOK OF NEW YORK CITY
0–396–08513–X Dodd, Mead $13.95

THE INSIDE-OUTSIDE BOOK OF WASHINGTON D.C.
0–525–44298–7 Dutton $12.95

• Cynthia Rylant
NIGHT IN THE COUNTRY
Nighttime sights and sounds by the Caldecott prizewinning author
Illustrated by Mary Szilagyi
0–02–777210–1 Bradbury $13.95

• Uri Shulevitz
RAIN RAIN RIVERS
A deceptively simple picture book depicts rain in town, rain in the country, rain everywhere
0–374–36171–1 Farrar, Straus & Giroux $13.95
0–374–46195–3 Farrar, Straus & Giroux pb $3.95

Peter Spier
PETER SPIER'S RAIN
Another wordless book (with many detailed illustrations) by a distinguished illustrator
0–385–15484–4 Doubleday $12.95
0–385–24105–4 Doubleday pb $6.95

Music and the Arts

• Laurence Krasny Brown & Mark Brown
VISITING THE ART MUSEUM
The whole family goes off to the art museum for the afternoon—and gets a pleasant surprise. Brown draws the art realistically, so kids can find some recognizable masterpieces
0–525–44233–2 Dutton $11.95

Karla Kuskin
THE PHILHARMONIC GETS DRESSED
A charming and ingenious introduction to ordinary people who make music
Illustrated by Marc Simont
0–06–023622–1 Harper & Row $11.95
0–06–443124–X Harper & Row pb $3.95

• Sergei Prokofiev
PETER AND THE WOLF POP-UP-BOOK
Pop-ups create miniature stage sets as Peter saves his animal friends
Illustrated by Barbara Cooney
0–670–80849–0 Viking $13.95

• Jane Yolen, editor
THE LULLABY SONGBOOK
Musical arrangements by Adam Stemple
Illustrated by Charles Mikolaydak
0–15–249903–2 HBJ $13.95

Animals

• Joanna Cole
HUNGRY, HUNGRY SHARKS
Illustrated by Patricia Wynne
0–394–87471–4 Random House pb $2.95

Illustration by Marc Simont, from The Philharmonic Gets Dressed *by Karla Kuskin (Harper & Row)*

● Ruth Heller

CHICKEN'S AREN'T THE ONLY ONES
Bold and attractive illustrations introduce children to the egg-laying creatures, not forgetting such oddities as the duckbilled platypus
0–448–01872–1 Putnam $8.95

HOW TO HIDE A CROCODILE
A picture book that describes the way animals are camouflaged in the wild
0–448–19028–1 Putnam $4.95

● Francine Patterson

KOKO'S KITTEN
Koko the gorilla lives with the animal behaviorist who taught her sign language, and she is able to communicate with humans. A few years ago Koko was given a stray kitten as a pet, and this unusual picture book is a photographed record of her odd but affectionate attachment to it
Photographs by Ronald H. Cohn
0–590–40952–2 Scholastic $10.95
0–590–33812–9 Scholastic pb $3.95

● Norma Simon

CATS DO, DOGS DON'T
Edited by Abby Levine
0–8075–1102–1 Albert Whitman $11.95

● Brian Wildsmith

GIVE A DOG A BONE
0–394–87709–8 Pantheon $10.95

Transportation

● Nina Barbaresi

FAST ROLLING, TOUGH TRUCKS
0–448–09884–9 Putnam pb $5.95

● Mary Blocksman & Dewey Blocksman

EASY TO MAKE SPACESHIPS THAT REALLY FLY
Illustrated by Marisabina Russo
0–671–66301–1 Simon & Schuster $10.95

● Gail Gibbons

FLYING
A straightforward history from ancient times to the present
0–8234–0599–0 Holiday House $12.95

TRUCKS
0–06–443069–3 Harper & Row pb $2.95

● Seymour Reit

THOSE FABULOUS FLYING MACHINES: A History of Flight in Three Dimensions with Punch-Out Plane Model
Illustrated by Randy Weidner
0–02–776020–0 Macmillan $17.95

LEARNING

How Do I Grow?
Where Do Babies Come From?

● Joanna Cole

HOW YOU WERE BORN
0–688–05801–9 Morrow pb $4.95

THE NEW BABY AT YOUR HOUSE
Illustrated by Hella Hammid
0–688–05806–X Morrow $10.25
0–688–07418–9 Morrow pb $4.95

● Sheila Kitzinger

BEING BORN
Stunning micro-photography reveals every step of a baby's development before birth
Illustrated by Lennart Nilsson
0–448–18990–9 Putnam pb $15.95

● Patricia Pearse

SEE HOW YOU GROW
Children open sections of the illustrations to answer questions about where babies come from and how they themselves are developing
Illustrated by Edwina Riddell
0–8120–5936–0 Barron's $10.95

● Clare Smallman & Edwina Riddell

OUTSIDE IN
A companion picture book to *See How You Grow*. This time children lift the flaps to glimpse under the skin and learn the whereabouts of bones, muscles, and organs
0–8120–5760–0 Barron's $10.95

Experiences and
Learning Competence

● Aliki

FEELINGS
Sketches, poems, and anecdotes in a picture book that for a child is second-best to a flesh-and-blood confidant. Funny without making fun of children's fears and attachments
0–688–03831–X Greenwillow $11.25
0–688–06518–X Morrow pb $3.95

● Stan & Janice Berenstain

THE BIKE LESSON
The creators of the Berenstain Bears teach bike skills and safety with their usual good humor
Illustrated by Stan Berenstain
0–394–80036–2 Random House pb $5.95

● Marc Brown & Stephen Krensky

DINOSAURS BEWARE!: A Safety Guide
Pictures of frenetic dinosaurs help kids learn the positives along with the negatives and distinguish rational from irrational fears
0–316–11219–4 Little, Brown pb $5.95

● Marc & Laurene K. Brown

DINOSAURS DIVORCE: A Guide for Changing Families
Dinosaurs act out the roles played by parents and young children in real-life separations
0–316–10996–7 Little, Brown pb $4.95

● Barbara Isenberg & Marjorie Jaffe

ALBERT THE RUNNING BEAR'S EXERCISE BOOK
Albert lives in a zoo, runs marathons, and teaches children good sportsmanship
Illustrated by Diane De Groat
0–89919–294–7 Clarion $13.95
0–89919–318–8 Clarion pb $4.95

● Munro Leaf

SAFETY CAN BE FUN
Amusing artwork doesn't detract from the seriousness of the lessons taught here
0–06–443111–8 Harper & Row pb $3.95

● Jane Resh Thomas

SAYING GOOD-BYE TO GRANDMA
A sensitive portrait of a girl attending her grandmother's funeral
Illustrated by Marcia Sewall
0–89919–645–4 Clarion $13.95

● Judith Viorst

THE TENTH GOOD THING ABOUT BARNEY
Barney is the family cat, and when he dies the children are angry and sad. An unsentimental picture book about necessary losses and grief
Illustrated by Erik Blegvad
0–689–20688–7 Macmillan $12.95
0–689–71203–0 Macmillan pb $3.95

● Ellen Weiss

TELEPHONE TIME: A First Book of Telephone Do's and Don'ts
No-nonsense Ringalinga, the Telephone Fairy, comes up with invaluable advice
Illustrated by Hilary Knight
0–394–88252–0 Random House pb $1.95

Visual Skills

● Mitsumasa Anno

ANNO'S MYSTERIOUS MULTIPLYING JAR
Objects emerge from Anno's handsome jar and start multiplying. Mathematicians call the process factoring. For readers it's a counting game and visual feast combined
0–399–20951–4 Putnam $14.95

● Martin Handford

WHERE'S WALDO?
As wandering Waldo moves from picture to picture, children search the crowded pages to find him. An original idea, and the oversized pictures are great fun
0–316–34293–9 Little, Brown $9.95

FIND WALDO NOW
Waldo wanders through various historical settings, amongst cavemen, Egyptian slaves, and Roman gladiators
0–316–34292–0 Little, Brown $10.95

● David M. Schwartz
HOW MUCH IS A MILLION?
This unconventional counting book takes readers off on adventures asking them to imagine huge numbers rather than enumerate them
Illustrated by Stephen Kellogg
0–688–04049–7 Lothrop, Lee & Shepard $15.00
0–590–33966–4 Scholastic pb $2.95

Activities

● Stan & Janice Berenstain
THE BERENSTAIN BEARS' NATURE GUIDE
A didactic Papa Bear leads Mama and the cubs into the great outdoors. The relevant vocabulary is separately labeled
0–394–86602–9 Random House pb $4.95

THE BERENSTAIN BEARS' SCIENCE FAIR
0–394–86603–7 Random House pb $5.95

● Cynthia H. Neely & Elaine M. Lyerly
MISTER COOKIE BREAKFAST COOKBOOK
Breakfast treats prepared safely by very young cooks
Illustrated by Elaine M. Lyerly
0–88289–493–5 Pelican pb $1.95

● Frederick R. Newman
MOUTHSOUNDS
A favorite pastime featured in an easy-to-read picture book
Illustrated by Marty Norman
0–89480–128–7 Workman pb $6.95

● Aileen Paul
KIDS COOKING WITHOUT A STOVE: A Cookbook for Young Children
Illustrated by Carol Inouye
0–86534–060–9 Sunstone pb $7.95

● Richard Scarry
RICHARD SCARRY'S BEST MAKE-IT BOOK EVER
Projects that children up to first grade can do—for example, a Lowly Worm growth chart and calendar. Includes paper objects to cut out and assemble
0–394–83492–5 Random House pb $8.95

First Reference Books

● Kathleen N. Daly
THE MACMILLAN PICTURE WORDBOOK
Basic vocabulary words with rather conventional illustrations
Illustrated by John Wallner
0–02–725600–6 Macmillan $7.95

From Sammy the Seal *by Syd Hoff (Harper & Row)*

● J. Elliot
THE USBORNE CHILDREN'S ENCYCLOPEDIA
A surprising amount of information is contained in this junior encyclopedia appropriate for first graders and up
Illustrated by Colin King
0–7460–0031–6 EDC $11.95
0–7460–0000–6 EDC pb $9.95

● Robert L. Hillerich, editor
THE AMERICAN HERITAGE PICTURE DICTIONARY
Big pictures introduce 900 words selected from the vocabulary of preschoolers and kindergarten children
Illustrated by Maggie Swanson
0–395–42531–X Houghton Mifflin $7.95

● Stephen Krensky, editor
THE AMERICAN HERITAGE FIRST DICTIONARY
For children learning to read or developing confidence as new readers. Includes the 500 words most frequently used in first reading materials. Also, homographs (spell-alikes) and an illustrated list of homophones (sound-alikes)
Illustrated by George Ulrich
0–395–42530–1 Houghton Mifflin $10.95

● Macmillan
MACMILLAN VERY FIRST DICTIONARY: A Magic World of Words
0–02–761730–0 Macmillan $10.95

● Jacqueline Tivers & Michael Day
THE VIKING CHILDREN'S WORLD ATLAS: An Introductory Atlas for Young People
0–670–21791–3 Viking $8.95
0–14–031874–7 Penguin pb $4.95

Easy Readers

● Sue Alexander
WORLD FAMOUS MURIEL AND THE SCARY DRAGON
Muriel is a tightrope walker who takes on a dragon in this pleasant little fantasy for ambitious beginning readers
Illustrated by Chris L. Demarest
0–316–03134–8 Little, Brown $14.95
0–440–40023–6 Dell pb $2.50

SATURDAY
Grandpa, Grandma and Barney are homey-looking dogs whose Saturday is full of humorous misadventures
Illustrated by Denys Cazet
0–02–717800–5 Bradbury $10.95
0–689–71065–8 Macmillan pb $3.95

SUNDAY
Illustrated by Denys Cazet
0–02–717970–2 Bradbury $11.95

● Philip D. Eastman
ARE YOU MY MOTHER?
A nonsense easy reader from a collaborator of Dr. Seuss. Some odd creatures get asked before the problem is resolved
0–394–80018–4 Random House $5.95

● Linda Haywood
HELLO, HOUSE!
The house talks back in a retelling of an Uncle Remus folktale designed for beginners
Illustrated by Lynn Munsinger
0–394–88864–2 Random House pb $2.95

● Lillian Hoban
ARTHUR'S CHRISTMAS COOKIES
0–06–444055–9 Harper & Row pb $3.50

ARTHUR'S CHRISTMAS COOKIES
With cassette
0–694–00160–0 Harper & Row pb $5.98

ARTHUR'S HONEY BEAR
If growing up means selling a favorite toy, Arthur would rather not do so. An easy reader
0–06–444033–8 Harper & Row pb $3.50

ARTHUR'S HONEY BEAR
With cassette
0–694–00116–3 Harper & Row pb $5.98

● Syd Hoff
Cartoonish early reading books from the 1960s. Both are funny.
DANNY AND THE DINOSAUR
0–06–444002–8 Harper & Row pb $3.50

DANNY AND THE DINOSAUR
With cassette
0–694–00017–5 Harper & Row pb $5.98

SAMMY THE SEAL
0–06–444028–1 Harper & Row pb $3.50

• Pam Zinnemann-Hope
Two illustrated books with simple but pleasant illustrations designed for the very beginner.

FIND YOUR COAT, NED
Illustrated by Kady M. Denton
0–689–50426–8 Macmillan $6.95

LET'S PLAY BALL, NED
Illustrated by Kady M. Denton
0–689–50427–6 Macmillan $6.95

• Theo LeSieg
I WISH THAT I HAD DUCK FEET
A boy's comic fantasies in a 1950s classic. With cassette
Illustrated by Roy McKie
0–394–89777–3 Random House pb $5.95

• Arnold Lobel
FROG AND TOAD ARE FRIENDS
The first book in a tender (and funny) series of stories about an abiding friendship. Short chapters can be read as separate stories to help beginning readers along. Caldecott Honor Book 1971
0–06–444020–6 Harper & Row pb $3.50

FROG AND TOAD ARE FRIENDS
With cassette
0–694–00027–2 Harper & Row pb $5.98

FROG AND TOAD ALL YEAR
0–06–444059–1 Harper & Row pb $3.50

FROG AND TOAD ALL YEAR
With cassette
0–694–00026–4 Harper & Row pb $5.98

DAYS WITH FROG AND TOAD
0–06–444058–3 Harper & Row pb $3.50

DAYS WITH FROG AND TOAD
With cassette
0–694–00025–6 Harper & Row pb $5.98

FROG AND TOAD TOGETHER
0–06–444021–4 Harper & Row pb $3.50

FROG AND TOAD TOGETHER
With cassette
0–694–00028–0 Harper & Row pb $5.98

• Faith McNulty
THE LADY AND THE SPIDER
An unusual early reading book
Illustrated by Bob Marstall
0–06–024191–8 Harper & Row $12.95
0–06–443152–5 Harper & Row pb $3.95

• Edward Marshall
FOX ALL WEEK
Illustrated by James Marshall
0–8037–0062–8 Dial $8.95
0–8037–0008–3 Dial pb $4.95

FOX AND HIS FRIENDS
Illustrated by James Marshall
0–8037–2668–6 Dial pb $3.95

FOX AT SCHOOL
Illustrated by James Marshall
0–8037–2674–0 Dial pb $4.95

• Else Holmelund Minarik
FATHER BEAR COMES HOME
Illustrated by Maurice Sendak
0–06–024230–2 Harper & Row $9.95
0–06–444014–1 Harper & Row pb $3.50

LITTLE BEAR
The consoling illustrations and quiet text make this a classic among easy-to-read books and a splendid read-aloud picture

Illustration by Maurice Sendak, from Little Bear *by Else Holmelund Minarik (Harper & Row)*

book for children up to five. Mother Bear is large, tolerant, and powerful, Baby Bear has big dreams
Illustrated by Maurice Sendak
0–06–444004–4 Harper & Row pb $3.50

LITTLE BEAR
With cassette
Illustrated by Maurice Sendak
0–694–00113–9 Harper & Row pb $5.98

LITTLE BEAR'S VISIT
With cassette
Illustrated by Maurice Sendak
0–694–00032–9 Harper & Row pb $5.98

NO FIGHTING, NO BITING!
Another Minarik title, this time without Little Bear
Illustrated by Maurice Sendak
0–06–444015–X Harper & Row pb $3.50

• Peggy Parish
Amelia Bedelia is the amicable, muddleheaded housekeeper who interprets orders literally by dusting the parlor with talcum, and changing the towels by cutting them up. Of course she is saved by her pie making and general affability. The series will appeal to readers who are past beginner books.

Illustration by Fritz Siebel, from Amelia Bedelia *by Peggy Parish (Harper & Row)*

AMELIA BEDELIA
Illustrated by Fritz Siebel
0–06–024640–5 Harper & Row $9.95

AMELIA BEDELIA AND THE SURPRISE SHOWER
Illustrated by Fritz Siebel
0–06–444019–2 Harper & Row pb $3.50

AMELIA BEDELIA AND THE SURPRISE SHOWER
With cassette
Illustrated by Fritz Siebel
0–694–00161–9 Harper & Row pb $5.98

AMELIA BEDELIA GOES CAMPING
0–688–04057–8 Greenwillow $10.95
0–380–70067–0 Avon pb $2.95

AMELIA BEDELIA HELPS OUT
Illustrated by Lynn Sweat
0–688–80231–1 Greenwillow $11.95
0–380–53405–3 Avon pb $2.95

DINOSAUR TIME
Phonetic pronunciations enable children who are already reading to put the right names to the pictures
Illustrated by Arnold Lobel
0–06–024653–7 Harper & Row $8.95
0–06–444037–0 Harper & Row pb $2.95

• Annabelle Prager
THE SURPRISE PARTY
A surprise birthday party goes awry in a book for first-graders
Illustrated by Tomie dePaola
0–394–89596–7 Random House pb $2.95

• Marjorie Weinman Sharmat
Nate the Great is a popular boy detective whose faithful hound Sludge invariably helps Nate solve his cases.

NATE THE GREAT AND THE FISHY PRIZE
Illustrated by Marc Simont
0–440–40039–2 Dell pb $2.50

NATE THE GREAT AND THE LOST LIST
Illustrated by Marc Simont
0–440–46282–7 Dell pb $2.50

NATE THE GREAT AND THE MISSING KEY
Illustrated by Marc Simont
0–698–20630–4 Putnam $11.95
0–440–46191–X Dell pb $2.50

NATE THE GREAT AND THE SNOWY TRAIL
Illustrated by Marc Simont
0–698–20628–2 Putnam $10.95
0–440–46276–2 Dell pb $2.50

NATE THE GREAT AND THE STICKY CASE
Illustrated by Marc Simont
0–698–20629–0 Putnam $10.95

Dr. Seuss
The master of meaningful nonsense, Dr. Seuss has led millions of American children by the hand and into the world of I Can Read By Myself.

THE CAT IN THE HAT
With cassette
0–394–89218–6 Random House pb $5.95

THE CAT IN THE HAT COMES BACK
With cassette
0–394–88327–6 Random House pb $5.95

FOX IN SOCKS
0–394–80038–9 Beginner $5.95

GREEN EGGS AND HAM
With cassette
0–394–89220–8 Random House pb $5.95

HOP ON POP
With cassette
0–394–89222–4 Random House pb $5.95

OH, THE THINKS YOU CAN THINK
0–394–83129–2 Random House $5.95

OH, SAY CAN YOU SAY?
With cassette
0–394–88769–7 Random House pb $5.95

ONE FISH TWO FISH RED FISH BLUE FISH
With cassette
0–394–89224–0 Random House pb $5.95

• John Stadler
CAT AT BAT
Stadler specializes in short nonsense rhymes matched with his own clever illustrations
0–525–44416–5 Dutton $9.95

HOORAY FOR SNAIL!
0–690–04412–7 Harper & Row $11.95
0–06–443075–8 Harper & Row pb $2.95

• Gene Zion
HARRY AND THE LADY NEXT DOOR
Harry the sometimes grubby dog in an easy-to-read adventure
Illustrated by Margaret B. Graham
0–06–444008–7 Harper & Row pb $3.50

Books for Eights, Nines, and Up

FICTION FOR THE EIGHTS, NINES, AND UP

Children at this age are home-centered, and family fiction is popular. Those who have put picture books behind them still half believe in magic and enjoy fantasy and fairy tales. Children usually become better readers by leaps and bounds and are more than capable of enjoying books by themselves. But they still like to be read to—and why not, when they can listen to *The Little House on the Prairie* or *Abel's Island?*

Family Stories

• Judy Blume
THE ONE IN THE MIDDLE IS THE GREEN KANGAROO
Squeezed in like peanut butter between the oldest and youngest kids of the family, this "middle" child finds ways to make himself visible
0–02–711060–5 Bradbury $10.95

• Ann Cameron
THE STORIES JULIAN TELLS
Julian thinks he knows everything, and his smaller sidekick brother, Huey, believes everything Julian says. And Julian says some very odd things
Illustrated by Ann Strugnell
0–394–89262–3 Knopf pb $2.95

MORE STORIES JULIAN TELLS
Illustrated by Ann Strugnell
0–394–86969–9 Knopf $11.95

JULIAN, SECRET AGENT
Julian in a paperback designed for graduates from easy readers
0–394–81949–7 Random House pb $1.95

• Natalie Savage Carlson
THE HAPPY ORPHELINE
A tribe of French orphans under the supervision of the exceedingly kind Madame Flattot. Little girls will especially enjoy the orphelines' mild adventures
0–440–43455–6 Dell pb $2.75

A BROTHER FOR THE ORPHELINES
0–440–40827–X Dell pb $2.75

Beverly Cleary
Beverly Cleary has been awarded the Laura Ingalls Wilder Medal for 40 years of distinguished writing for children.
RAMONA AND HER FATHER
Energetic eight-year-old Ramona tries to set things right when Dad loses his job, but helping him is much harder than the television says. Written with tenderness as well as humor. Newbery Honor Book 1978
Illustrated by Alan Tiegreen
0–688–22114–9 Morrow $12.95
0–440–47241–5 Dell pb $3.25

RAMONA FOREVER
0–688–03785–2 Morrow $11.75
0–440–47210–5 Dell pb $3.25

RAMONA QUIMBY, AGE EIGHT
Illustrated by Alan Tiegreen
0–688–00477–6 Morrow $12.95
0–440–47350–0 Dell pb $3.25

RAMONA THE BRAVE
Illustrated by Alan Tiegreen
0–688–32015–5 Morrow $12.95
0–440–47351–9 Dell pb $3.25

RAMONA THE PEST
0–440–47209–1 Dell pb $3.25

• Carolyn Haywood
B IS FOR BETSY
Illustrated by Carolyn Haywood & Joe Yakovetic
0–15–204975–4 HBJ $12.95
0–15–611695–2 HBJ pb $4.95

BETSY AND BILLY
Illustrated by Carolyn Haywood & Joe Yakovetic
0–15–206765–5 HBJ $12.95
0–15–611868–8 HBJ pb $4.95

• Johanna Spyri
HEIDI
A freshly illustrated version of the tale of the Swiss orphan, her ornery grandpa, and her beloved mountains
Illustrated by Ruth Sanderson
0–394–53820–X Knopf $18.95

HEIDI
Illustrated by William Sharp
0–448–06012–4 Putnam $12.95
0–448–11012–1 Putnam pb $7.95

• Sydney Taylor
ALL-OF-A-KIND FAMILY
These five little girls are a "stepping stone" family, each one two years apart. Their Lower East Side neighborhood is full of lively people, and the family celebrates the Jewish holidays with much ceremony
Illustrated by Helen John
0–8446–6253–4 Peter Smith $14.00
0–440–40059–7 Dell pb $2.95

ALL-OF-A-KIND FAMILY DOWNTOWN
0–440–42032–6 Dell pb $2.95

• Laura Ingalls Wilder
The Little House series chronicles a childhood in Wisconsin and on the family homestead in De Smet Territory. The family shares the pleasures and dangers of prairie life as well as chores required to make the homestead productive.
LITTLE HOUSE ON THE PRAIRIE
Illustrated by Garth Williams
0–06–026445–4 Harper & Row $13.95
0–317–53651–6 Harper & Row pb $2.95

LITTLE TOWN ON THE PRAIRIE
Illustrated by Garth Williams
0–06–026450–0 Harper & Row $13.95
0–317–53656–7 Harper & Row pb $2.95

LITTLE HOUSE IN THE BIG WOODS
Illustrated by Garth Williams
0–06–026430–6 Harper & Row $13.95
0–317–53650–8 Harper & Row pb $2.95

BY THE SHORES OF SILVER LAKE
Illustrated by Garth Williams
0–06–026416–0 Harper & Row $13.95
0–317–53654–0 Harper & Row pb $2.95

FARMER BOY
Not a Little House book but the story of Wilder's husband's childhood on a farm in New York
Illustrated by Garth Williams
0–06–026425–X Harper & Row $13.95
0–317–53652–4 Harper & Row pb $3.50

THE LONG WINTER
Illustrated by Garth Williams
0–06–026460–8 Harper & Row $13.95
0–317–53655–9 Harper & Row pb $2.95

ON THE BANKS OF PLUM CREEK
Illustrated by Garth Williams
0–06–026470–5 Harper & Row $13.95
0–317–53653–2 Harper & Row pb $2.95

Friendships and Relationships

• Miriam Chaikin
HOW YOSSI BEAT THE EVIL URGE
Illustrated by Petra Mathers
0–06–021185–7 Harper & Row $11.95

YOSSI ASKS THE ANGELS FOR HELP
"Angels, I need two dollars by tomorrow," says Yossi when planning to buy his Hanukkah gifts. A sensible Rebbe helps him in this story about a Yeshiva student and his contemporary Orthodox family
Illustrated by Petra Mathers
0–06–021195–4 Harper & Row $11.95

Illustration by Garth Williams, from Little House on the Prairie *by Laura Ingalls Wilder (Harper & Row)*

• Beverly Cleary

ELLEN TEBBITS
Ellen has to wait until a new little girl moves into town to acquire her very special friend. A quiet, humorous book set in a 50s small town
Illustrated by Louis Darling
0–688–21264–6 Morrow $11.95
0–440–42299–X Dell pb $3.25

HENRY HUGGINS
Henry and his impossibly dirty mutt Ribsy live in Small Town USA, in this old-fashioned and funny book
Illustrated by Louis Darling
0–688–21385–5 Morrow $11.95
0–440–43551–X Dell pb $3.25

RIBSY
In a sequel to *Henry Huggins* the search is on for the beloved, lost Ribsy
0–440–47456–6 Dell pb $3.25

• Judy Delton

PEE WEE SCOUT SERIES
These adventures of a troupe of very young scouts appeal to second- and third-graders and deal humorously with activities they enjoy

CAMP GHOST-AWAY
0–440–40062–7 Dell pb $2.50

COOKIES AND CRUTCHES
0–440–40010–4 Dell pb $2.50

PEANUT-BUTTER PILGRIMS
0–440–40066–X Dell pb $2.50

• Eleanor Estes

THE HUNDRED DRESSES
Every day Wanda comes to school in the same washed-out, blue dress yet she tells the other children she has closets full of clothes. Her Cinderella dreams become real in this story
0–15–642350–2 HBJ pb $4.95

• Paula Fox

MAURICE'S ROOM
Maurice collects things, and not even mean dogs deter him in his own urban treasure hunt
Illustrated by Ingrid Fetz
0–02–735490–3 Macmillan $11.95
0–689–71216–2 Macmillan pb $3.95

• Patricia R. Giff

THE KIDS OF THE POLK STREET SCHOOL
This series introduces second- and third-graders to Ms. Rooney's homeroom at the Polk Street School. Each short, slice-of-life story tells the adventures of one or two members of the class from a child's point of view.

THE BEAST IN MS. ROONEY'S ROOM
Illustrated by Blanche Sims
0–440–40485–1 Dell pb $2.50

DECEMBER SECRETS
Illustrated by Blanche Sims
0–385–29495–6 Delacorte pb $8.95
0–440–41795–3 Dell pb $2.50

FISH FACE
Illustrated by Blanche Sims
0–385–20493–X Delacorte pb $8.95
0–440–42557–3 Dell pb $2.50

PICKLE PUSS
Illustrated by Blanche Sims
0–385–29477–8 Delacorte pb $8.95
0–440–46844–2 Dell pb $2.50

SAY "CHEESE"
Illustrated by Blanche Sims
0–385–29501–4 Delacorte pb $8.95
0–440–47639–9 Dell pb $2.50

SUNNY SIDE UP
Illustrated by Blanche Sims
0–385–29476–X Delacorte pb $8.95
0–440–48406–5 Dell pb $2.50

• Johanna Hurwitz

CLASS CLOWN
Lucas is the smartest kid in Mrs. Hockaday's third grade, but he is always in trouble. Lucas eventually shows just how smart he is in a way that makes everyone happy
Illustrated by Sheila Hamanaka
0–688–06723–9 Morrow $10.95
0–590–41821–1 Scholastic pb $2.50

• Mavis Jukes

BLACKBERRIES IN THE DARK
A boy visits his widowed grandmother soon after the death of a beloved grandpa. A picture book with an ambitious text
Illustrated by Thomas B. Allen
0–394–87599–0 Knopf $10.95
0–440–40647–1 Dell pb $2.50

LIKE JAKE AND ME
Illustrated by Lloyd Bloom
0–394–89263–1 Knopf pb $4.95

• Astrid Lingren

THE CHILDREN OF NOISY VILLAGE
The Swedish farm children in this fictional village are all fast friends. The creator of Pippi Longstocking writes of their goings on
0–14–032609–X Penguin pb $3.95

• Ursula Nordstrom

THE SECRET LANGUAGE
A little girl goes to boarding school, is miserable, makes friends, and learns self-confidence. The calmly written story has a real ring of truth
0–06–440022–0 Harper & Row pb $3.50

• Doris Orgel

MY WAR WITH MRS. GALLOWAY
The humorous account of Rebecca and her baby sitter conceals a surprising ending
Illustrated by Carol Newsom
0–670–50217–0 Viking $9.95
0–14–032171–3 Penguin pb $3.95

• Cynthia Rylant

HENRY AND MUDGE: The First Book of Their Adventures
Illustrated by Sucie Stevenson
0–02–778001–5 Bradbury $10.95

HENRY AND MUDGE UNDER THE YELLOW MOON
Illustrated by Sucie Stevenson
0–02–778004–X Bradbury $10.95

• Jean Van Leeuwen

BENJY THE FOOTBALL HERO
It is anyone's guess as to who will win the fourth grade Superbowl
Illustrated by Gail Owens
0–8037–0189–6 Dial $11.95

• Ilse-Margret Vogel

TIKHON
Inge is a lonely little girl living in Germany just after the First World War. Tikhon is the Russian boy-soldier who takes refuge with her family. They adopt each other, but the situation outside Inge's house is perilous, as the friends discover
0–06–026328–8 Harper & Row $11.95

MY SUMMER BROTHER
0–06–026325–3 Harper & Row $10.95

Fantasy

• James M. Barrie

PETER PAN
Barrie's haunting story remains problematic, and children are either unmoved or are transported by it. The principal characters are troublesome: Peter is boastful, willful, and often cruel; Wendy is bossy and manipulative. Barrie's adult characters are at best foolish, at worse villainous. Nonetheless, it is still capable of magic
Edited and illustrated by Nora Unwin
0–684–13214–1 Macmillan $12.95

PETER PAN
Includes cassette recording by Lynn Redgrave
0–394–89226–7 Random House $13.95

PETER PAN
0–553–21178–1 Bantam pb $2.95

• L. Frank Baum

The first and greatest American fairy story was the *The Wizard of Oz*, and the Oz books make wonderful bedtime story books for children as young as seven or eight and will be read with pleasure by older children as well. *The Land of Oz* and *Ozma of Oz* are in many respects just as inventive as the original title, but a number of the later books pale by comparison.

THE WIZARD OF OZ
The original text whimsically re-illustrated in full color. A lovely gift book for the young Oz reader
Illustrated by Michael Hague
0-03-061661-1 Henry Holt $18.95

THE WIZARD OF OZ
0-345-33590-2 Ballantine pb $2.95
0-14-035001-2 Penguin pb $2.25

THE LAND OF OZ
In a worthy sequel to the Wizard, Baum leaves Dorothy back home in Kansas. New characters include Jack Pumpkinhead, the Saw-Horse, and Mr. H.M. Woggle Bug
Illustrated by John R. Neill
0-528-87188-9 Macmillan pb $3.95

OZMA OF OZ
0-486-24779-1 Dover pb $4.95

DOROTHY AND THE WIZARD IN OZ
Illustrated by John R. Neill
0-486-24714-7 Dover pb $4.95

THE EMERALD CITY OF OZ
0-486-25681-2 Dover pb $6.95

THE PATCHWORK GIRL OF OZ
0-345-33290-3 Ballantine pb $2.95

THE ROAD TO OZ
0-486-25208-6 Dover pb $4.95

• **Joanna Cole**
DOCTOR CHANGE
Doctor Change is a magician whose name is all too appropriate in the eyes of his runaway apprentice
Illustrated by Donald Carrick
0-688-06135-4 Morrow $11.75

• **Roald Dahl**
Dahl's books for children are characterized by a brilliant, loony energy and a violence unusual in contemporary children's fiction. Read-aloud books for the eights and up include three listed below.

CHARLIE AND THE CHOCOLATE FACTORY
A magical tour where the selfish and undeserving are nastily punished and the good are sumptuously rewarded
Illustrated by Joseph Schindelman
0-394-81011-2 Knopf $12.95
0-553-15454-0 Bantam pb $2.75

CHARLIE AND THE GREAT GLASS ELEVATOR
The uncharacteristically tame sequel contains one haunting nightmare image—the elevator that doesn't stop at the top floor
Illustrated by Joseph Schindelman
0-394-82472-5 Knopf $13.95
0-553-15455-9 Bantam pb $2.75

JAMES AND THE GIANT PEACH
Poor James is tormented by two horrible aunts. But with characteristic vigor Dahl devises their horrid fate, while James goes on to extraordinary adventures
Illustrated by Nancy Burkhardt
0-394-81282-4 Knopf $15.95
0-14-032871-8 Penguin pb $3.95

• **Wanda Gag**
THE EARTH GNOME
The king's three daughters must be rescued from underground with the help of the Earth Gnome
Illustrated by Margot Tomes
0-698-20618-5 Putnam $9.95

• **Ruth Stiles Gannett**
MY FATHER'S DRAGON
A little boy tells a story about an island visited by his father, who discovers a dragon endowed with human traits. Newbery Honor Book 1949
0-394-88460-4 Random House $12.95
0-394-89048-5 Knopf pb $3.95

ELMER AND THE DRAGON
Elmer Elevator frees a flying baby dragon from a wild island in a sequel to *My Father's Dragon*
0-394-89049-3 Knopf pb $3.95

THREE TALES OF MY FATHER'S DRAGON
A boxed set of the three stories about Elmer
0-394-89136-8 Knopf pb $11.95

• **Christian Garrison**
THE DREAM EATER
Illustrated by Diane Goode
0-689-71058-5 Macmillan pb $3.95

• **Paul Goble**
THE GIRL WHO LOVED WILD HORSES
Based on Indian legend, the story of a girl who so loves wild horses that she is transformed into a mare. Caldecott Medal 1979
0-02-736570-0 Macmillan $13.95
0-689-71082-8 Macmillan pb $3.95

• **Rudyard Kipling**
The *Just So Stories* are an infectious mix of fable, fantasy, and word play, and beg to be read aloud.

THE BEGINNING OF THE ARMADILLOS
Illustrated by Charles Keeping
0-911745-03-3 Bedrick $9.95

THE CAT THAT WALKED BY HIMSELF
Illustrated by William Stobbs
0-911745-05-X Bedrick $9.95

THE CRAB THAT PLAYED WITH THE SEA
Illustrated by Michael Foreman
0-911745-06-8 Bedrick $9.95

THE ELEPHANT'S CHILD
Illustrated by Louise Brierley
0-87226-030-5 Bedrick $9.95

HOW THE CAMEL GOT HIS HUMP
Illustrated by Quentin Blake
0-87226-029-1 Bedrick $9.95

HOW THE RHINOCEROS GOT HIS SKIN
Illustrated by Jenny Thorne
0-87226-137-9 Bedrick $9.95

JUST SO STORIES
The full text edition illustrated by Kipling himself. Good for older, more ambitious readers, despite some dated racial attitudes
0-14-043302-3 Penguin pb $2.95

• **Irina Korschunow**
ADAM DRAWS HIMSELF A DRAGON
When a miniature dragon appears inside fat, lonely Adam's schoolbag, life changes magically and for the better
Translated by James Skofield
Illustrated by Mary Rahn
0-06-023249-8 Harper & Row $9.95

• **Arnold Lobel**
FABLES
Children will love the bear who dresses up in saucepan headgear and the camel with ballet shoes. Caldecott Medal 1980
0-06-023974-3 Harper & Row $11.95
0-06-443046-4 Harper & Row pb $4.95

• **Hugh Lofting**
Doctor Dolittle understands what animals are saying. He doesn't care about money except for the few pennies needed to feed his many animal house guests. Written in the 1920s, and long out of print, Dolittle has been revised and reissued, so that children can again enjoy these eloquent fantasies about the need to care for others.

THE STORY OF DOCTOR DOLITTLE
0-440-48307-7 Dell pb $2.95

THE VOYAGES OF DOCTOR DOLITTLE
Newbery Medal 1923
0-440-40002-3 Dell pb $3.50

DOCTOR DOLITTLE'S CIRCUS
0-440-40058-9 Dell pb $3.50

DOCTOR DOLITTLE: A Treasury
0-440-41964-6 Dell pb $4.95

• **A.A. Milne**
Milne's quintessentially British fantasy either tends to inspire devotion or leave readers wondering what the fuss is all about. Distinguished by puns and other wordplay, the comedy is invariably deft and amusing. But readers (or listeners) who are not wholehearted members of the Pooh fan club may simply grow tired of all those words.

Children who like Pooh in moderation will enjoy the more straightforward sections, such as the first chapter of *The House at Pooh Corner*, in which Tigger makes his appearance.

Drawing by Ernest H. Shepard, from Winnie the Pooh *by A.A. Milne (Dutton)*

WINNIE-THE-POOH
Illustrated by Ernest H. Shepard
0–525–43035–0 Dutton $9.95

THE HOUSE AT POOH CORNER
Tigger drops in for breakfast, and
Christopher Robin goes away to the place
nobody knows
Illustrated by Ernest H. Shepard
0–525–32302–3 Dutton $9.95
0–440–43795–4 Dell pb $3.25

THE WORLD OF WINNIE-THE-POOH
A collected edition with special color
illustrations
Illustrated by Ernest H. Shepard
0–525–43320–1 Dutton $13.95

• Jill Murphy
THE WORST WITCH
Some pupils are decidedly more promising
than others in this school for witches
0–8052–8019–7 Schocken $7.95
0–380–60665–8 Avon pb $2.50

THE WORST WITCH STRIKES AGAIN
The broomstick-riding heroine is once
again the worst pupil at school. The
illustrations alone are worth the price
0–380–60673–9 Avon pb $2.50

• Graham Oakley
THE CHURCH MOUSE
These church mice have an unusual friend,
a big ginger tomcat. The sevens and up
will enjoy the tongue-in-cheek style
0–689–30058–1 Macmillan $10.95
0–689–70475–5 Macmillan pb $4.95

CHURCH MICE AT CHRISTMAS
0–689–30797–7 Macmillan $10.95
0–689–70767–3 Macmillan pb $4.95

• Pamela K. Service
STINKER FROM SPACE
A short fantasy about a girl, a boy (a
computer whiz, no less), and an alien
forced to take refuge in the body of a
skunk. The alien's return home stretches
the imagination, but younger children
should laugh
0–684–18910–0 Macmillan $11.95

William Steig
ABEL'S ISLAND
Abel is an unlikely Robinson Crusoe.
But there he is, a dandy mouse,
marooned on an uninhabited island.
Steig's text is as elegant as his
illustrations. Newbery Honor Book
1977
0–374–30010–0 FS&G $12.95
0–374–40016–4 FS&G pb $3.50

THE REAL THIEF
0–374–36217–3 FS&G $9.95
0–374–46208–9 FS&G pb $2.95

• George Selden
A CRICKET IN TIMES SQUARE
A lovely little fantasy about a cricket and a
boy whose Italian family runs a Times
Square newsstand. Newbery Honor Book
1961
Illustrated by Garth Williams
0–374–31650–3 Farrar, Straus & Giroux $13.95
0–440–41563–2 Dell pb $2.95

CHESTER CRICKET'S NEW HOME
Illustrated by Garth Williams
0–374–31240–0 Farrar, Straus & Giroux $12.95
0–440–41246–3 Dell pb $2.95

HARRY KITTEN AND TUCKER MOUSE
Animal heroes encounter the perilous New
York City streets as they search for a new
home
Illustrated by Garth Williams
0–374–32860–9 Farrar, Straus & Giroux $11.95

• P.L. Travers
The fearsome British nanny recast as good
fairy: enchantment mixed with never-
speak-with-your-mouth-full.
MARY POPPINS
0–590–08035–0 Scholastic pb $1.95

MARY POPPINS COMES BACK
Illustrated by Mary Shepard
0–15–657683–X HBJ pb $5.95

MARY POPPINS IN THE PARK
Illustrated by Mary Shepard
0–15–657690–2 HBJ pb $4.95

MARY POPPINS OPENS THE DOOR
Illustrated by Mary Shepard & Agnes Sims
0–15–657692–9 HBJ pb $4.95

• Janwillem Van De Wetering
HUGH PINE
A short, charming fable about the
difficulties involved in making decisions for
others; the hero is a porcupine in a red hat
0–395–29459–2 Houghton Mifflin $9.95
0–553–15558–X Bantam pb $2.50

HUGH PINE AND THE GOOD PLACE
0–553–15572–5 Bantam pb $2.50

• Jill Paton Walsh
THE GREEN BOOK
Child refugees travel by spaceship to settle
on an unexplored planet
Illustrated by Lloyd Bloom
0–374–32778–5 Farrar, Straus & Giroux $9.95
0–374–42802–6 Farrar, Straus & Giroux pb $2.95

• E.B. White
E.B. White was awarded the Laura Ingalls
Wilder Medal in 1970 for his lifelong
contributions to children's literature.
CHARLOTTE'S WEB
No pig ever had a truer friend, and no one
was ever as affectionate, loyal and skillful
as Charlotte A. Cavatica, the spider
Illustrated by Garth Williams
0–06–026385–7 Harper & Row $9.95
0–06–440055–7 Harper & Row pb $2.95

STUART LITTLE
Humorous episodes in the life of a mouse
who goes out into the world dressed as a
man
Illustrated by Garth Williams
0–06–026395–4 Harper & Row $9.95
0–06–440056–5 Harper & Row pb $2.95

THE TRUMPET OF THE SWAN
Illustrated by Edward Frascino
0–06–026397–0 Harper & Row $10.95
0–06–440048–4 Harper & Row pb $2.95

Favorite Animal Stories
Fred Gibson
OLD YELLER
0–06–080002–X Harper & Row pb $4.50

Will James
SMOKEY THE COW HORSE
0–689–71171–9 Macmillan pb $3.95

Eric Knight
LASSIE COME-HOME
0–440–40136–4 Dell pb $4.95

Mary O'Hara
MY FRIEND FLICKA
0–06–080902–7 Harper & Row pb $2.95

Majorie Kinnon Rawlings
THE YEARLING
0–684–71878–2 Scribners $9.95
0–020–44931–3 Scribners pb $4.95

Anna Sewell
BLACK BEAUTY
0–448–11007–5 Putnam pb $7.95

Albert Terhune
LAD: A Dog
0–451–14626–3 NAL pb $2.50

Adventure

• David A. Adler
The Cam Jansen mysteries appeal to
second-grade and less confident third-grade
readers but are more ambitious than
conventional easy readers. The stories are
lively and the detective roles evenly divided
between the sexes.
**CAM JANSEN AND THE MYSTERY AT
THE MONKEY HOUSE**
Illustrated by Susanna Natti
0–670–80782–6 Viking $9.95
0–440–40047–3 Dell pb $2.50

**CAM JANSEN AND THE MYSTERY OF
THE BABE RUTH BASEBALL**
Illustrated by Susanna Natti
0–670–20037–9 Viking $9.95
0–440–41020–7 Dell pb $2.50

**CAM JANSEN AND THE MYSTERY OF
THE DINOSAUR BONES**
Illustrated by Susanna Natti
0–670–20040–9 Viking $9.95
0–440–41199–8 Dell pb $2.50

**THE FOURTH FLOOR TWINS AND
THE FORTUNE COOKIE CHASE**
Illustrated by Irene Trivas
0–670–80641–2 Viking $9.95
0–14–032083–0 Penguin pb $3.50

• Nathaniel Benchley
**THE STRANGE DISAPPEARANCE OF
ARTHUR CLUCK**
Illustrated by Arnold Lobel
0–06–020478–8 Harper & Row pb $10.95

• Mary Mapes Dodge
HANS BRINKER: Or, The Silver Skates
0–448–06011–6 Putnam $11.95

• Sid Fleischman
THE WHIPPING BOY
When the bored prince decides to run
away he takes his whipping boy along, but
the adventure soon turns into a
misadventure when the two are kidnapped.
Newbery Medal 1987
Illustrated by Peter Sis
0–688–06216–4 Greenwillow $11.95
0–8167–1038–4 Troll pb $2.95

✉ **TO ORDER BOOKS AS GIFTS, SEE PAGE 1**

• James Herriot
ONLY ONE WOOF
A sweet story about a shy sheepdog and his beloved companion, adapted from Herriot's *All Things Bright and Beautiful*
Illustrated by Peter Barrett
0–312–58583–7 St. Martin's $9.95

• Johanna Hurwitz
THE ADVENTURES OF ALI BABA BERNSTEIN
David changes his name to honor his favorite story book, *The Arabian Nights*. Thereafter his adventures fit his new personality
0–590–42011–9 Scholastic pb $2.50

• Dick King-Smith
BABE THE GALLANT PIG
A clever pig becomes a sheep dog to save himself from becoming a side of bacon
Illustrated by Mary Raynor
0–440–40420–7 Dell pb $2.50

• Joan L. Nixon
BEATS ME, CLAUDE
A tall tale with some unwelcome visitors
Illustrated by Tracey Campbell Pearson
0–670–80781–8 Viking $11.95
0–14–050847–3 Penguin pb $3.95

• Jim & Jane O'Connor
THE GHOST IN TENT 19
The campers in Tent 19 are sent off in search of buried treasure. A short novel for second- or third-graders who aren't ready for chapter books
Illustrated by Richard Williams
0–394–89800–1 Random House pb $1.95

• Anna Sewell
BLACK BEAUTY
Sewell's affecting novel about a horse is adapted by an accomplished children's writer and illustrated by a Caldecott Medal winner. With cassette narrated by Ben Kingsley
Edited by Robin McKinley
Illustrated by Susan Jeffers
0–394–89228–3 Random House $17.95

• Gloria Skurzynski
THE MINSTREL IN THE TOWER
Roger and Alice are captured by highwaymen in this brief novel about a medieval adventure
0–394–99598–8 Random House $6.00
0–394–89598–3 Random House pb $1.95

• David Updike
A WINTER'S JOURNEY
Homer goes to look for his dog in a raging snowstorm and encounters unexpected adventures
Illustrated by Robert A. Parker
0–13–961566–0 Prentice-Hall $12.95

Humor

• Judy Blume
FRECKLE JUICE
When class clown Sharon offers Nicky her secret recipe for freckle juice, Nicky just can't pass up the opportunity
Illustrated by Sonia Lisker
0–440–42813–0 Dell pb $2.50

ALISON LURIE:
Some of the Contemporary Children's Classics That I Most Admire

Alan Arkin
THE LEMMING CONDITION
A brilliant and comic political fable about resistance to mob psychology by the well-known film actor
0–06–020133–9 Harper & Row $11.75

Natalie Babbitt
TUCK EVERLASTING
Suppose you could live forever, would you want to? The legend of the Fountain of Youth updated to 19th-century New England
0–374–37848–7 FS&G $12.95
0–374–48009–5 FS&G pb $3.25

Nina Bawden
CARRIE'S WAR
World War II as seen through the eyes of two children evacuated to the remote countryside; one of many outstanding books by a gifted British author; it has been made into an excellent television film
0–397–31450–7 Harper & Row $12.95
0–14–030689–7 Penguin pb $1.95

Penelope Farmer
A CASTLE OF BONE
A British fantasy which revolves around the discovery of a cupboard that returns whatever is put into it to its original form: a pigskin wallet, for instance, becomes a live pig. A wonderful take with interesting ecological overtones
Out of print

Louise Fitzhugh
HARRIET THE SPY
Though she calls herself a spy, this very independent New York schoolgirl (Brearley) who sometimes takes shocking notes on the behavior of her friends, family, and neighbors could also be a future novelist. When it first appeared, the book was criticised by adults for its frankness, but young readers rapidly made it popular
0–06–021910–6 Harper & Row $12.75
0–440–43447–5 Dell pb $3.50

Russell Hoban
THE MOUSE AND HIS CHILD
The adventures of two linked toys in their long quest to become "self-windin'." The story recalls both *Pinocchio* and the novels of Dickens,

with their large cast of eccentric and sometimes frightening characters
0–06–022378–2 Harper & Row $13.00

Ursula Le Guin
A WIZARD OF EARTHSEA
The first volume of her wonderful and haunting fantasy trilogy for children; as good as anything she has written for adults, or perhaps even better
0–395–27653–5 Houghton Mifflin $12.95
0–553–26250–5 Bantam pb $3.50

Madeleine L'Engle
A WRINKLE IN TIME
Science-fiction, feminism, and faith; a ground-breaking and unbeatable combination; one of the most original children's books of this century
0–374–38613–7 FS&G $13.95
0–440–99805–0 Dell pb $3.25

William Mayne
WINTER QUARTERS
Mayne is one of the most gifted writers for children today; already famous in Britain, he deserves to be better known here. This tale of life among the gypsies, or "travellers," as they prefer to be known, is one of his best and most moving
Out of print

Robert C. O'Brien
MRS. FRISBY AND THE RATS OF NIMH
Animal experimentation and the military-industrial complex as seen through the eyes of a laboratory mouse; an amazing tour de force, much superior to the animated film made from it
0–689–20651–8 Macmillan $14.95
0–689–71068–2 Macmillan pb $3.95

Katherine Paterson
THE GREAT GILLY HOPKINS
A prize-winning and ground-breaking story about foster parents and foster children, both wildly funny and serious in its implications
0–690–03837–2 Harper & Row $12.95
0–06–440201–0 Harper & Row pb $3.50

Cynthia Voigt
HOMECOMING
Five children, abandoned after their mother's death, make their way, mostly on foot, from New England to the Eastern Shore of Maryland in search of a grandmother they have never seen. The author is a keen observer of both landscape and people, and has written several good sequels
0–689–30833–7 Macmillan $13.95

• Michael Bond
A BEAR CALLED PADDINGTON
The first story in a long series about the celebrated bear from Peru dressed in rain hat, duffel coat, and wellies found in London's Paddington Station
Illustrated by Peggy Fortnum
0–395–06636–0 Houghton Mifflin $12.95
0–440–40483–5 Dell pb $2.75

PADDINGTON AT WORK
Illustrated by Peggy Fortnum
0–395–06637–9 Houghton Mifflin $10.95
0–440–40797–4 Dell pb $2.75

PADDINGTON HELPS OUT
Illustrated by Peggy Fortnum
0–395–06639–5 Houghton Mifflin $13.95
0–440–46802–7 Dell pb $2.75

● Shirley Hughes
CHIPS AND JESSIE
Five humorous adventures experienced by best friends
0–688–06402–7 Lothrop, Lee & Shepard $10.25

● Astrid Lindgren
PIPPI LONGSTOCKING
Pippi is the little Swedish girl who lives all by herself with a pet monkey and a big horse. She does exactly as she pleases and has a humorous time doing it
Illustrated by Louis Glanzman
0–670–55745–5 Viking $10.95
0–14–032772–X Penguin pb $3.95

● Betty MacDonald
MRS. PIGGLE WIGGLE
0–06–440148–0 Harper & Row pb $3.50

● Mordecai Richler
JACOB TWO-TWO AND THE DINOSAUR
Jacob Two-Two's exotic pet becomes the subject of a hunt by media-hungry politicians and scientists. A funny and sophisticated story, written with a plainly satirical bite
Illustrated by Norman Eyolfson
0–394–88704–2 Knopf $10.95
0–553–15589–X Bantam pb $2.75

JACOB TWO-TWO MEETS THE HOODED FANG
A short, sharply conceived and verbally adept story about a little boy's bizarrely comic adventure
0–317–64199–9 Bantam pb $2.50

● Glen Rounds
MR. YOWDER, THE PERIPATETIC SIGN PAINTER: Three Tall Tales
Simple but funny illustrated short stories
0–8234–0370–X Holiday House $7.95

FICTION FOR THE TENS AND UP

Families and Relationships

The current crop of fictional children are more adult than adults. They are a resourceful bunch who cope with preadolescence, divorce, family finances, and the inconsistencies of parents and step-parents.

● C.S. Adler
GOOD-BYE, PINK PIG
Lonely Amanda lives with a discontented older brother and a hard-driving mother; her best friend is a pink quartz pig. Amanda inhabits the harsh world of school and home as well as the gentler world of her imagination until changes produce a better life
0–380–70175–8 Avon pb $2.50

● Nina Bawden
THE FINDING
0–688–04979–6 Lothrop, Lee & Shepard $10.25
0–440–40004–X Dell pb $2.95

● Judy Blume
ARE YOU THERE, GOD? IT'S ME, MARGARET
A long monologue about growing and growing up from the viewpoint of an inexperienced half Jewish, half gentile 11-year-old
0–440–40419–3 Dell pb $3.25

STARRING SALLY J. FREEDMAN AS HERSELF
A Jewish girl from New Jersey spends a year growing up in Florida just after the close of World War II. Her daydreams mix with her increasingly shrewd observations about herself, her friends, and family
0–02–711070–2 Bradbury $13.95
0–440–48253–4 Dell pb $3.25

SUPERFUDGE
Voted the most popular children's book of 1983 by the nationwide readers' survey known as Children's Choices
0–525–40522–4 Dutton $10.95
0–440–48433–2 Dell pb $3.25

TALES OF A FOURTH GRADE NOTHING
A nine-year-old is "given" a little sister and soon decides that she is expendable. But some things about little sister are lovable too
Illustrated by Roy Doty
0–525–40720–0 Dutton $10.95
0–440–48474–X Dell pb $2.95

● Betsy Byars
THE BLOSSOMS MEET THE VULTURE LADY
Illustrated by Jacqueline Rogers
0–385–29485–9 Delacorte $13.95
0–440–40677–3 Dell pb $2.75

CRACKER JACKSON
Eleven-year-old Cracker cares very much about his former babysitter, who's in serious trouble. The story deals with problems encountered by responsible children when confronting an unjust adult world
0–670–80546–7 Viking $11.95
0–14–031881–X Penguin pb $3.95

THE NOT-JUST-ANYBODY FAMILY
The maverick Blossom family includes a rodeo rider (Mom) and a boy who flies off the roof when the police come looking for Grandpa—odd heroes dealt with honestly and humorously
0–385–29443–3 Delacorte $13.95
0–440–45951–6 Dell pb $2.95

THE PINBALLS
Called pinballs because they are always being shuffled around, two boys and a girl meet in a group foster home. An odd and healing friendship develops
0–06–441098–7 Harper & Row pb $2.95

● Beverly Cleary
DEAR MR. HENSHAW
A twelve-year-old boy begins a correspondence with his favorite author—not to show off but because he is lonely. Newbery Medal 1983
9–99–753087–X Dell pb $3.25

● Helen Cresswell
ORDINARY JACK: Being the First Part of the Bagthorpe Saga
0–02–725540–9 Macmillan $9.95
0–14–031176–9 Penguin pb $3.95

BAGTHORPES UNLIMITED
Eleven-year-old Jack is the only tolerable member of a family of creative but selfish eccentrics whose erratic behavior makes for numerous satirical situations
0–02–725430–5 Macmillan $9.95
0–14–031178–5 Penguin pb $3.95

● Alice Fleming
WELCOME TO GROSSVILLE
A separated family must move to the other side of the tracks in an unusually honest story about the economic effects of divorce on children
0–684–18289–0 Macmillan $11.95

● Kathryn Forbes
MAMA'S BANK ACCOUNT
0–15–656377–0 HBJ pb $5.95

● Liza Fosburgh
MRS. ABERCORN AND THE BUNCE BOYS
Illustrated by Julie Downing
0–02–735460–1 Macmillan $11.95

● Frank Gilbreth, Jr. & Ernestine Gilbreth Carey
CHEAPER BY THE DOZEN
0–553–25605–X Bantam pb $2.95

● Beverly Keller
DESDEMONA: Twelve Going On Desperate
0–06–440226–6 Harper & Row pb $2.95

NO BEASTS! NO CHILDREN!
Desdemona is one of the resourceful children who cheerfully carry domestic burdens for absent or ineffective parents. Her special burdens are three large dogs, five-year-old twins, and a father looking for a new apartment
0–06–440225–8 Harper & Row pb $2.50

● Norma Klein
MOM, THE WOLFMAN AND ME
Written in the early 70s, Klein's junior novel has a period feel to it, but preteen girls will still enjoy the story of Brett who is afraid her single mom won't be the same if she marries
0–380–00791–6 Avon pb $2.50

● E.L. Konigsburg
JOURNEY TO AN 800 NUMBER
A speedily told story of a miniature preppy and his animal trainer dad
0–689–30901–5 Macmillan $12.95
0–440–44264–8 Dell pb $2.75

● Joseph Krumgold
...AND NOW MIGUEL
A New Mexican 12-year old's rite of passage. Newbery Medal 1954
0–06–440143–X Harper pb $3.50

ONION JOHN
Newbery Medal 1960
0–06–440144–8 Harper pb $2.95

☞ **TO ORDER NEW BOOKS NOT YET LISTED, ASK YOUR BOOKSELLER OR CALL 1-800-882-8770**

• Lois Lenski

STRAWBERRY GIRL

Story of a "strawberry family" in rural 1940s Florida and a way of life that has long disappeared. Newbery Medal 1946

Illustrated by Lois Lenski

0–397–30109–X Harper & Row $13.95

0–440–48347–6 Dell pb $3.25

• Bette Bao Lord

IN THE YEAR OF THE BOAR AND JACKIE ROBINSON

A Chinese immigrant in a working-class Brooklyn neighborhood learns English, the piano, and stickball, in that order

Illustrated by Marc Simont

0–06–024003–2 Harper & Row $11.95

0–06–440175–8 Harper & Row pb $3.50

• Lois Lowry

ANASTASIA KRUPNIK

0–395–28629–8 Houghton Mifflin $12.95

ANASTASIA ON HER OWN

The challenges involved when eleven- or twelve-year-olds take on new responsibilities

0–395–38133–9 Houghton Mifflin $12.95

0–440–40291–3 Dell pb $2.75

SWITCHAROUND

Boy and girl siblings go off on an unexpected visit to their father and are given responsibilities they don't enjoy

0–440–48415–4 Dell pb $2.95

• George Ella Lyon

BORROWED CHILDREN

A twelve-year-old is required to take care of her newborn brother and must leave school. A junior novel set in a black area of Kentucky in the 1930s. "A singular story"—*NY Times*

0–531–05751–8 Orchard Books $12.95

• Patricia MacLachlan

SARAH, PLAIN AND TALL

Sarah answers Papa's advertisement for a mail order bride, but the children are afraid she will not want to stay. Newbery Medal 1986

0–06–024101–2 Harper & Row $9.95

0–06–440205–3 Harper & Row pb $2.50

Illustration by Marc Simont, from In the Year of the Boar and Jackie Robinson *by Bette Bao Lord (Harper & Row)*

• Joan Kane Nichols

ALL BUT THE RIGHT FOLKS

A twelve-year-old black boy spends an unforgettable summer with his white grandmother

0–88045–065–7 Stemmer House $11.95

• Joan Lowery Nixon

MAGGIE, TOO

When Maggie moves in with the grandmother she has hardly ever met, she has many expected and unexpected adjustments to make

0–15–250350–1 HBJ $11.95

AND MAGGIE MAKES THREE

0–15–250355–2 HBJ $12.95

0–440–40127–5 Dell pb $2.50

• Katherine Paterson

BRIDGE TO TERABITHIA

Terabithia is a secret kingdom invented by two unusual children to ease the ordinary hurts of life. The kingdom later becomes a reason for surviving an unexpected tragedy. Newbery Medal 1978

Illustrated by Donna Diamond

0–06–440184–7 Harper & Row pb $2.95

THE GREAT GILLY HOPKINS

A social worker has just about given up on Gilly when she places her with a new and surprising foster family. Gilly's unhappiness is skillfully depicted without condoning her intolerably bad behavior. Newbery Honor Book 1978

0–690–03837–2 Harper & Row $12.95

0–06–440201–0 Harper & Row pb $3.50

• Cynthia Rylant

A BLUE-EYED DAISY

Set in the West Virginia mountains, this imaginative story traces four consecutive seasons in a young girl's life after a mining accident changes her relationship with her father

0–02–777960–2 Bradbury $9.95

0–440–40927–6 Dell pb $2.50

• Virginia Sorensen

MIRACLES ON MAPLE HILL

When a family goes to live on a farm in Pennsylvania they learn to love the land and each other. Newbery Medal 1957

Illustrated by Beth and Joe Krush

0–15–660440–X HBJ pb $5.95

• Noel Stretfield

BALLET SHOES

A British family of orphan girls scrambles to make ends meet by dancing and acting their way to financial independence. A lengthy period-piece but a terrific story

0–440–41508–X Dell pb $3.50

• Laurence Yep

DRAGONWINGS

Moon Shadow comes to San Francisco at the turn of the century to join the father he has never seen. Ordinary Chinese immigrants, they realize an extraordinary dream in a story based on American history. Newbery Honor Book 1975

0–06–440085–9 Harper & Row pb $3.50

Fantasy

• Natalie Babbitt

TUCK EVERLASTING

Tucks are blessed by and doomed to eternal life. A fascinating and engrossing fantasy

0–374–37848–7 Farrar, Straus & Giroux $12.95

0–374–48009–5 Farrar, Straus & Giroux pb $3.50

• Bill Brittain

DEVIL'S DONKEY

Old Magda the witch turns Dan'l Pitt into a donkey and he must struggle to regain human form

Illustrated by Andrew Glass

0–06–020682–9 Harper & Row $12.95

0–06–440129–4 Harper & Row pb $2.95

DR. DREDD'S WAGON OF WONDERS

Alarming things happen in the little New England town of Coven Tree when the straight-talking inhabitants fall victim to Dr. Hugh Dredd's sinister manipulations

Illustrated by Andrew Glass

0–06–020713–2 Harper & Row $11.50

THE WISH GIVER: Three Tales of Coven Tree

Newbery Honor Book 1984

Illustrated by Andrew Glass

0–06–020686–1 Harper & Row $12.95

0–06–440168–5 Harper & Row pb $3.50

• Frances Hodgson Burnett

THE SECRET GARDEN

A turn-of-the-century masterpiece about a little orphan girl who comes to live in a big house in the north of England. An unforgettable evocation of the magic that occurs when people learn to love one another

Illustrated by Tasha Tudor

0–694–00239–9 Harper & Row $8.95

0–06–440188–X Harper & Row pb $2.95

• Oliver Butterworth

THE ENORMOUS EGG

An ordinary hen lays an unusually large egg. The hatchling turns out to be a live dinosaur who grows to full size, causing all kinds of trouble for his young owner

Illustrated by Louis Darling

0–316–11904–0 Little, Brown $14.95

0–440–42337–6 Dell pb $2.95

• Lewis Carroll

The Charles Dodgson who took the pen name Lewis Carroll was a mathematics don at an Oxford college, a composer of amateur nonsense verse, and an excellent but equally unprofessional photographer. However, it was his genius as a fantasist, humorist, and logician that created his legacy to the literature of childhood. Carroll's lunacy lies in the clash of the logical with the illogical. Few other children's books have been read for so long, by so many, and with so much pleasure.

ALICE IN WONDERLAND & ALICE THROUGH THE LOOKING GLASS

The collected edition is a reminder that American children commonly read the first Alice but not the second. Are they put off by the idea of a plot based on a chess game? Or do they find the verbal nonsense

in *Through the Looking Glass* overwhelming?
Illustrated by John Tenniel
0–448–06004–3 Putnam $11.95

ALICE'S ADVENTURES IN WONDERLAND
With muted pictures that hint at Victorian styles
Illustrated by Michael Hague
0–03–002037–9 Henry Holt $14.95

ALICE'S ADVENTURES IN WONDERLAND
Illustrated by Michelle Wiggins
0–394–53227–9 Knopf $16.95

ALICE'S ADVENTURES IN WONDERLAND
With pictures by the author and creator of *Gorilla*
Illustrated by Anthony Browne
0–394–80592–5 Knopf $19.95

• Sylvia Cassedy
BEHIND THE ATTIC WALL
An unrepentant orphan, kicked out of several foster homes, settles with relatives and thereby enters a house of friendly ghosts who become her family
0–690–04336–8 Harper & Row $12.95
0–380–69843–9 Avon pb $2.95

• Grace Chetwin
THE RIDDLE AND THE RUNE
0–02–718312–2 Bradbury $13.95

• Carlo Collodi
THE ADVENTURES OF PINOCCHIO
A recent translation of the black comedy concerning the puppet who wants to become a boy but must first learn hard lessons
Translated & illustrated by Francis Wainwright
0–8050–0027–5 Henry Holt $16.95

PINOCCHIO
0–14–035037–3 Puffin pb $2.25

• Sara & Stephen Corrin, editors
IMAGINE THAT!: Fifteen Fantastic Tales
Illustrated by Jill Bennett
0–571–13843–8 Faber & Faber $12.95

• Julia Cunningham
OAF
A boy sets off with brave animal companions on a treasure hunt armed with the traditional three magical gifts
Illustrated by Peter Sis
0–394–87430–7 Knopf $11.00

• Roald Dahl
THE BFG
A most extraordinary cast of characters including the Queen of England, the Head of the Army, the Head of the Air Force, the orphan Sophie, the Fleshlumper, the Bone Cruncher, the Childchewer, and the BFG (Big Friendly Giant)
Illustrated by Quentin Blake
0–374–30469–6 Farrar, Straus & Giroux $12.95
0–14–034019–X Warne pb $3.95

THE WITCHES
Real witches are very ordinary people, and that is why they are so hard to catch, says the witch-catching, cigar-smoking grandmother heroine of this fantasy about a witches' convention at an otherwise ordinary seaside hotel
Illustrated by Quentin Blake
0–374–38457–6 Farrar, Straus & Giroux pb $13.95
0–14–031730–9 Penguin pb $3.95

• Antoine de Saint-Exupéry
THE LITTLE PRINCE
An excellent translation accompanied by 70 original illustrations by the author
Translated by Katherine Woods
0–15–246503–0 HBJ $9.95
0–15–646511–6 HBJ pb $5.95

• Edward Eager
Eager's fantasy stories appeal because the magic is kindly even when matters are temporarily out of control.
HALF MAGIC
Illustrated by N.M. Bodecker
0–15–233078–X HBJ $10.95
0–15–637990–2 HBJ pb $4.95

MAGIC OR NOT?
0–15–655121–7 HBJ pb $4.95

• Kenneth Grahame
THE RELUCTANT DRAGON
A short and funny fantasy about a reluctant dragon who is engaged to fight by St. George himself
Illustrated by Michael Hague
0–03–064031–8 Henry Holt $11.50
0–8050–0802–0 Henry Holt pb $4.95

THE WIND IN THE WILLOWS
Grahame's lengthy and demanding meditation on freedom is as much about life among river dwellers (animal and human) as it is about the adventures of the incorrigible Mr. Toad. A convincing adventure fantasy
Illustrated by Ernest H. Shepard
Preface by Margaret Hodges
0–684–17957–1 Macmillan $18.95
0–684–18025–1 Macmillan pb $3.95

Drawing by Ernest H. Shepard, from The Wind in the Willows *by Kenneth Grahame (Macmillan)*

• Randall Jarrell
THE ANIMAL FAMILY
The hunter saw it all, but there was no one with him to tell what he had seen. So he found himself a strange and wonderful family. A "timeless and universal story"—*NY Times*. Newbery Honor Book 1965
Illustrated by Maurice Sendak
0–394–81043–0 Pantheon $12.95
0–394–88964–9 Knopf pb $5.95

• Norton Juster
THE PHANTOM TOLLBOOTH
Illustrated by Jules Feiffer
0–394–81500–9 Random House $15.95

• Terry Jones
TERRY JONES' FAIRY TALES
"New" fairy tales by a member of television's "Monty Python's Flying Circus"
Illustrated by Michael Foreman
0–14–031642–6 Penguin pb $7.95

• Richard Kennedy
COLLECTED STORIES
Complicated, sometimes macabre folk tales in which original and traditional elements intertwine. The stories will fascinate older children who enjoy both science fiction and traditional tales
Illustrated by Marcia Sewell
0–317–67705–5 Harper & Row $14.95

• William Kotzwinkle
E.T.: The Storybook of the Green Planet
Illustrated by David Wiesner
0–399–13063–2 Putnam $15.95

• C.S. Lewis
Intended to be read aloud, the *Chronicles of Narnia* will fascinate advanced nine-year-olds with strong narrative and engagingly odd characters. Older children can begin to decipher the mix of Christian theology, Arthurian myth, and classical mythology in these allegorical adventure stories which deal with grander themes than are usual in children's literature.
THE CHRONICLES OF NARNIA
Illustrated by Pauline Baynes
0–02–757740–6 Macmillan (7-book set) $89.95
0–02–044500–8 Macmillan (7-book set) pb $39.95

THE LION, THE WITCH AND THE WARDROBE
Illustrated by Pauline Baynes
0–02–044490–7 Macmillan pb $5.95

PRINCE CASPIAN
Illustrated by Pauline Baynes
0–02–044430–3 Macmillan pb $5.95

THE VOYAGE OF THE DAWN TREADER
0–02–044440–0 Macmillan pb $5.95

THE SILVER CHAIR
Illustrated by Pauline Baynes
0–02–044420–6 Macmillan pb $5.95

THE HORSE AND HIS BOY
Illustrated by Pauline Baynes
0–02–044410–9 Macmillan pb $5.95

THE MAGICIAN'S NEPHEW
Illustrated by Pauline Baynes
0–02–044390–0 Macmillan pb $5.95

THE LAST BATTLE
Illustrated by Pauline Baynes
0–02–044380–3 Macmillan pb $5.95

• Anne Lindbergh Morrow
HUNKY-DORY DAIRY
Illustrated by Julie Brinckloe
0–15–237449–3 HBJ $12.95
9–99–809862–9 Avon pb $2.50

➤ **FOR OVERSEAS ORDERING INFORMATION, SEE PAGE 1**

Illustration by Pauline Baynes, from The Lion, the Witch, and the Wardrobe *by C.S. Lewis (Macmillan)*

- **Robin McKinley**
THE BLUE SWORD
Newbery Honor Book 1983
0–688–00938–7 Greenwillow $13.95

THE OUTLAWS OF SHERWOOD
0–688–07178–3 Greenwillow $11.95

- **Edith Nesbit**
THE FIVE CHILDREN AND IT
Turn-of-the-century stories concerning a tribe of children and the sand-fairy who grants their wishes. The dialogue is dated but the situations are still deliciously funny
0–440–42586–7 Dell pb $4.95

THE FIVE CHILDREN AND IT
Illustrated by H.R. Millar
0–14–035061–6 Penguin pb $2.25

THE STORY OF THE AMULET
0–440–47719–0 Dell pb $4.95

- **Mary Norton**
THE BORROWERS
Pod, Homily, and Arrietty live in a wonderful old house in the country. Rather, they live under the house, in a home of their own furnished with cotton reels, safety pins, and other things filched from the human inhabitants. It's cozy enough but the girl Arrietty is lonely and curious. Where are the other Borrowers or are they the last ones? What does Pa do when Borrowing? A compulsive read, the story of the Borrowers comes close to tragedy when Arrietty befriends a human
Illustrated by Beth & Joe Krush
0–15–209987–5 HBJ $9.95
0–15–613600–7 HBJ pb $4.95

THE BORROWERS AFIELD
Illustrated by Beth & Joe Krush
0–15–210166–7 HBJ $12.95
0–15–613601–5 HBJ pb $4.95

THE BORROWERS AFLOAT
Illustrated by Beth & Joe Krush
0–15–210345–7 HBJ $12.95
0–15–613603–1 HBJ pb $3.95

THE BORROWERS ALOFT
Illustrated by Beth & Joe Krush
0–15–210524–7 HBJ $12.95
0–15–613604–X HBJ pb $3.95

THE BORROWERS AVENGED
Illustrated by Beth & Joe Krush
0–15–210531–X HBJ pb $4.95

- **Robert C. O'Brien**
MRS. FRISBY AND THE RATS OF NIMH
Laboratory rats observe people from their cages, escape, and use their observations to create a society based on human technology. A haunting fantasy about love, loyalty and sacrifice. Newbery Medal 1972
0–689–20651–8 Macmillan $14.95
0–689–71068–2 Macmillan pb $3.95

- **William Pène Du Bois**
THE GIANT
0–440–42994–3 Dell pb $4.95

THE TWENTY-ONE BALLOONS
A balloonist lands abruptly on an uninhabited Pacific island and is welcomed by a colony of formally dressed people living in an advanced civilization. An unlikely, imaginative, and funny parable about what it is like to live on the edge of disaster. Winner of a Newbery Medal in 1947
0–670–73441–1 Viking $12.95
0–14–032097–0 Penguin pb $3.95

- **Phillipa Pearce**
TOM'S MIDNIGHT GARDEN
Provoked by an old lady's memories, a boy travels back into time
0–397–30475–7 Harper & Row $13.95
0–440–48819–2 Dell pb $4.95

- **Mary Rodgers**
FREAKY FRIDAY
Annabel changes into her mother and finds it's tougher being Mom than she'd imagined
0–06–25048–8 Harper & Row $11.95
0–06–440046–8 Harper & Row pb $2.95

A BILLION FOR BORIS
Annabel returns with a new friend in a fantasy sequel to *Freaky Friday*
0–06–025048–8 Harper & Row $11.95
0–06–440075–1 Harper & Row pb $2.95

SUMMER SWITCH
A boy on his way to camp finds himself traveling instead to Hollywood in the body of his scriptwriter father. A captivating fantasy theme explored with characteristic humor
0–06–025058–5 Harper & Row $11.95
0–06–440140–5 Harper & Row pb $2.95

- **Zilpha Keatley Snyder**
BLACK AND BLUE MAGIC
A boy named after Harry Houdini is too clumsy to imitate the stage magic his father once performed but learns about an infinitely more powerful magic from a figure out of the past. A refreshingly unpretentious fantasy
0–440–40053–8 Dell pb $3.25

THE WITCHES OF WORM
Newbery Honor Book 1974
0–440–49727–2 Dell pb $3.25

THE WITCHES OF WORM
Illustrated by Alton Raible
0–689–30066–2 Macmillan $13.95

- **Nancy Willard**
SAILING TO CYTHERA
The first book of the Anatole Series
Illustrated by David McPhail
0–15–269961–9 HBJ pb $5.95

UNCLE TERRIBLE: More Adventures of Anatole
"Her images are invigorating, her fantasy convincing, and she can write on numerous levels simultaneously"—*NY Times*
Illustrated by David McPhail
0–15–292794–8 HBJ pb $5.95

- **Elizabeth Winthrop**
THE CASTLE IN THE ATTIC
A boy learns to deal with a powerful magic associated with the gift of a miniature castle
Illustrated by Trina S. Hyman
0–8234–0579–6 Holiday House $12.95
0–553–15433–8 Bantam pb $2.95

- **Jane Yolen**
THE GIRL WHO CRIED FLOWERS & OTHER TALES
Illustrated by David Palladini
0–690–00216–5 Harper & Row $12.95
0–8052–0666–3 Schocken pb $8.95

- **Jane Yolen & others, editors**
DRAGONS AND DREAMS
0–06–026792–5 Harper & Row $12.50

School

- **Judy Blume**
BLUBBER
Accurately describes the social dynamics of the fifth grade
0–02–711010–9 Bradbury $11.95
0–440–40707–9 Dell pb $2.95

- **Eve Bunting**
SIXTH GRADE SLEEPOVER
0–590–40554–3 Scholastic pb $2.50

- **Barthe DeClements**
NOTHING'S FAIR IN FIFTH GRADE
0–670–51741–0 Viking $11.95
0–590–42316–9 Scholastic pb $2.75

SIXTH GRADE CAN REALLY KILL YOU
Helen spends most of her time bothering her teacher until she realizes that she intends to fail her when the rest of her class graduates
0–670–80656–0 Viking $11.95
0–590–40180–7 Scholastic pb $2.50

- Patricia Reilly Giff
THE ADVENTURES OF CASEY VALENTINE AND HER FRIENDS

THE GIRL WHO KNEW IT ALL
0–440–42855–6 Dell pb $2.75

LEFT-HANDED SHORTSTOP
0–440–44672–4 Dell pb $2.75

RAT TEETH
0–440–47457–4 Dell pb $2.75

THE WINTER WORM BUSINESS
0–440–49259–9 Dell pb $2.75

- Sheila Greenwald
ROSY COLE'S GREAT AMERICAN GUILT CLUB
A funny and pointed story about a club founded by one of the less privileged so that she can understand the lives of a snobbish group of rich girls
Illustrated by Sheila Greenwald
0–316–32709–3 Little, Brown $12.95
0–671–63794–0 Simon & Schuster pb $2.50

- Barbara Park
BUDDIES
Hampered by an unattractive cabin mate, a 13-year-old strives hard for popularity
0–394–86934–6 Knopf $9.95
0–380–69992–3 Avon pb $2.50

Adventure

- Joan Aiken
American by birth and English by adoption, Aiken writes historical adventures that appeal to the child with a sophisticated vocabulary. At her best she recreates the past with an inventive mixture of fact and fantasy.
THE WOLVES OF WILLOUGHBY CHASE
Set squarely within the reign of mythical King James III, this terrific Gothic historical romp is characterized by a runaway plot and inventive wordplay
0–440–49603–9 Dell pb $3.25

BLACK HEARTS IN BATTERSEA
A sequel to *The Wolves of Willoughby Chase*
0–440–40904–7 Dell pb $3.25

NIGHTBIRDS ON NANTUCKET
Aiken's heroine Dido Twite returns in another sequel
0–440–46370–X Dell pb $3.25

- Marion Dane Bauer
ON MY HONOR
Courage and friendship are central to this excellent junior novel about an apparent drowning and a boy's coming to terms with death. Newbery Honor Book 1987
0–440–46633–4 Dell pb $2.50

- John Bellairs
Bellairs writes junior mysteries in the form of Gothic novel thrillers recast for the twelve and under audience.
THE CURSE OF THE BLUE FIGURINE
Johnny Dixon and his friend, professor Childermass, must deal with an Egyptian curse. "A hair-raising, grand-whammy climax ... Susceptible young readers should relish this Gothic spine-tingler"—*NY Times*
0–553–15540–7 Bantam pb $2.95

THE HOUSE WITH A CLOCK IN ITS WALLS
0–8037–3821–8 Dutton $13.95
0–440–43742–3 Dell pb $2.95

THE MUMMY, THE WILL, AND THE CRYPT
The sequel to *The Curse of the Blue Figurine*
0–553–15701–9 Bantam pb $2.95

- James Lincoln Collier & Christopher Collier
WAR COMES TO WILLIE FREEMAN
A tale of the American Revolution. Willie is alone after her father is killed by the British and her brother captured by them. She risks enslavement but shows her bravery amidst fighting between the Patriots and the British
0–440–49504–0 Dell pb $3.25

- Peter Dickinson
THE DANCING BEAR
A long, fascinating novel about a 4th-century runaway slave, a kidnapped heiress, and a dancing bear
0–440–40033–3 Dell pb $4.95

- Elizabeth Enright
GONE-AWAY LAKE
Boy and girl cousins rediscover a lost world when they find two old people left behind by time and circumstance. Newbery Medal 1957
Illustrated by Beth & Joe Krush
0–15–636460–3 HBJ pb $4.95

- Walter Farley
THE BLACK STALLION
The Black Stallion series chronicles the bloodline of a champion. "Everyone loves a winner"—*NY Times*
Illustrated by Keith Ward
0–394–85114–5 Random House $8.95
0–394–83609–X Random House pb $2.95

THE BLACK STALLION AND THE GIRL
0–394–83614–6 Random House pb $2.95

THE BLACK STALLION AND SATAN
0–394–83914–5 Random House pb $2.95

THE BLACK STALLION'S BLOOD BAY COLT
0–394–83915–3 Random House pb $2.95

- John D. Fitzgerald
THE GREAT BRAIN
An eleven-year-old con artist has adventurous schemes
Illustrated by Mercer Mayer
0–440–43071–2 Dell pb $3.25

THE GREAT BRAIN AT THE ACADEMY
0–440–43113–1 Dell $2.95

- Louise Fitzhugh
HARRIET THE SPY
Harriet's hobby is unconventional: she collects material for her novel by spying on her neighbors. She's a heroine with a mind of her own who puzzles and confuses adults yet escapes being bratty
Illustrated by Louise Fitzhugh
0–06–021910–6 Harper & Row $12.95
0–440–43447–5 Dell pb $3.50

From Harriet the Spy *by Louise Fitzhugh (Dell)*

- John R. Gardiner
STONE FOX
A boy takes on responsibility for the family farm when his grandmother falls ill and must help save the farm from foreclosure. Though beautifully written, the ending is hard on a sensitive child. Newbery Medal Winner 1980
Illustrated by Marcia Sewall
0–690–03983–2 Harper & Row $11.95
0–06–440132–4 Harper & Row pb $2.95

- Leon Garfield
Garfield's taut, well-constructed, and inventive historical novels are set in the 18th-century London underworld and aren't for children who are put off by the macabre.
DEVIL-IN-THE-FOG
An eleven-year-old inherits a new world of class and privilege, but his new family is indifferent to him and a stranger's unexpected appearance is clearly menacing
0–440–40095–3 Dell pb $3.25

FOOTSTEPS
0–440–40102–X Dell pb $3.25

SMITH
A twelve-year-old pickpocket steals the motive for a murder and finds himself hunted down for a piece of paper he can't read
0–440–48044–2 Dell pb $4.95

- Rosa Guy
PARIS, PEE WEE, AND BIG DOG
In an adventure story set in New York City things just seem to happen to three boys who set off to enjoy an ordinary Saturday morning
Illustrated by Caroline Binch
0–440–40072–4 Dell pb $2.95

- Marguerite Henry
KING OF THE WIND
Newbery Medal 1949
Illustrated by Wesley Dennis
0–528–82265–9 Macmillan $9.95
0–02–688758–4 Macmillan pb $2.95

MISTY OF CHINCOTEAGUE
Illustrated by Wesley Dennis
0–02–689090–9 Macmillan $12.95
0–02–688759–2 Macmillan pb $2.95

STORMY: Misty's Foal
Illustrated by Wesley Dennis
0–528–82083–4 Macmillan $8.95
0–02–688762–2 Macmillan pb $2.95

• **Hergé**
Tintin is a boy who has sensational adventures in the company of a little white dog and an odd character known as the Captain. Kids still like these unusual cartoon adventure classics.
THE BLACK ISLAND
0–316–35835–5 Little, Brown pb $6.95

EXPLORERS ON THE MOON
0–316–35846–0 Little, Brown pb $6.95

TINTIN IN TIBET
0–316–35839–8 Little, Brown pb $6.95

▶ **For a further listing of the Tintin books, see Comics.**

• **Rudyard Kipling**
THE JUNGLE BOOK
A great adventure story in which animals speak convincingly for themselves. The pictures are edgy and mysterious
Illustrated by Michael Foreman
0–317–62543–8 Viking $13.95

• **Jim Kjelgaard**
BIG RED
A brisk 1945 adventure about a country boy and the training of a champion red setter
Illustrated by Carl Pfeuffer
0–553–15434–6 Bantam pb $2.95

BIG RED
Illustrated by Bob Kuhn
0–8234–0007–7 Holiday House $14.95

OUTLAW RED
Illustrated by Carl Pfeuffer
0–8234–0084–0 Holiday House $14.95
0–553–15686–1 Bantam pb $2.75

• **E.L. Konigsburg**
FROM THE MIXED-UP FILES OF MRS. BASIL E. FRANKWEILER
Two precocious suburban children run away to New York and make their home in the Metropolitan Museum of Art where they become art detectives concerned with the authenticity of a small work by Michelangelo. An original story told with a humorous purposefulness, telling children they are far more resourceful than they usually imagine. Newbery Medal 1968
0–689–20586–4 Macmillan $12.95
0–440–43180–8 Dell pb $2.95

• **Judi Miller**
HOW I KEPT THE U.S. OUT OF WAR
An American ten-year-old is mistaken for a Central European prince and vice versa. Snatches of absurd language and a cast of ineffectual villains make for enjoyable reading
0–553–15522–9 Bantam pb $2.50

• **Beverley Naidoo**
JOURNEY TO JO'BURG: A South African Story
Illustrated by Eric Velasquez
0–397–32168–6 Harper & Row $9.95
0–06–440237–1 Harper & Row pb $2.95

• **Scott O'Dell**
ISLAND OF THE BLUE DOLPHINS
An American Indian girl is left on her tribe's abandoned Pacific island. Her survival and courage are gripping.
Newbery Medal 1961
0–395–06962–9 Houghton Mifflin $12.95
0–440–43988–4 Dell pb $3.25

• **Gary Paulsen**
DOGSONG
An Eskimo boy's life is grim, until he enters a dog-sleigh race. Newbery Honor Book 1986
0–02–770180–8 Bradbury $11.95
0–14–032235–3 Penguin pb $3.95

HATCHET
A small plane goes down in the Canadian wilderness taking with it a 13-year-old boy who must learn how to stay alive. Newbery Honor Book 1987
0–02–770130–1 Bradbury $12.95
0–14–032724–X Penguin pb $3.95

• **Zilpha Keatly Snyder**
THE EGYPT GAME
Newbery Honor Book 1968
0–689–30006–9 Macmillan $13.95
0–440–42225–6 Dell pb $3.25

THE FAMOUS STANLEY KIDNAPPING CASE
A mystery adventure about an unorthodox family
0–440–42485–2 Dell pb $3.50

Illustration by Eric Velasquez, from Beverly Naidoo's Journey to Jo'burg: A South African Story *(Harper & Row)*

• **Donald J. Sobol**
ENCYCLOPEDIA BROWN AND THE CASE OF THE MYSTERIOUS HANDPRINTS
Ten solve-it-yourself mysteries from a long-lived series started in the 1960s
Illustrated by Gail Owen
0–688–04626–6 Morrow $10.95
0–553–15352–8 Bantam pb $2.50

• **Elizabeth George Speare**
THE SIGN OF THE BEAVER
Newbery Honor Book 1984
0–395–33890–5 Houghton Mifflin $12.95
0–440–47900–2 Dell pb $2.95

THE WITCH OF BLACKBIRD POND
Set in 17th-century New England this is a surprisingly unflattering depiction of the unpleasant aspects of the colonists' hard work, thrift and self-sufficiency. Newbery Medal 1959
0–395–07114–3 Houghton Mifflin $13.95
0–440–99577–9 Dell pb $3.25

• **Barbara Brooks Wallace**
PEPPERMINTS IN THE PARLOR
A little girl comes to her wealthy aunt's home to discover terrible and sinister changes. A first-rate novel, peopled by two wicked spinsters, their pathetic elderly guests, and a courageous heroine
0–689–30790–X Macmillan $13.95
0–689–71048–8 Macmillan pb $3.95

• **Johann Wyss**
THE SWISS FAMILY ROBINSON
0–448–06022–1 Putnam $12.95
0–448–11022–9 Putnam pb $7.95

Old Favorites

In recent years many children's classics of earlier generations have been restored to print.

Frances Hodgson Burnett
A LITTLE PRINCESS
0–87923–784–8 Godine $16.95
0–553–21203–6 Bantam pb $2.95

LITTLE LORD FAUNTLEROY
0–553–21202–8 Bantam pb $2.95

Charles Kingsley
THE WATER BABIES
0–14–035035–7 Puffin pb $2.25

George MacDonald
AT THE BACK OF THE NORTH WIND
0–451–52057–2 Signet pb $2.25

THE GOLDEN KEY
Illustrated by Maurice Sendak
Afterword by W.H. Auden
0–374–42590–6 FS&G pb $3.50

Eleanor H. Porter
POLLYANNA
0–14–035023–3 Puffin pb $2.25

Margaret Sidney
FIVE LITTLE PEPPERS AND HOW THEY GREW
0–440–42505–0 Dell pb $4.95

Gene Stratton-Porter
A GIRL OF THE LIMBERLOST
0–451–52181–1 NAL pb $3.95

Jeane Webster
DADDY-LONG-LEGS
0–14–035111–6 Penguin pb $2.95

Kate Douglas Wiggin
REBECCA OF SUNNYBROOK FARM
0–14–035046–2 Puffin pb $2.25

Humor

• Larry Callen
WHO KIDNAPPED THE SHERIFF?
Illustrated by Stephen Gammell
0–87113–008–4 Little, Brown $13.95

• E.A. Hass
INCOGNITO MOSQUITO TAKES TO THE AIR
Adventures based on puns, the story of a private "insecticide" who appears on the David Litterbug show
Illustrated by Don Madden
0–394–87054–9 Random House pb $2.95

• Patricia Hermes
KEVIN CORBETT EATS FLIES
A boy's attempt to set straight a family situation leads to a bizarrely humorous "habit"
Illustrated by Carol Newsom
0–15–242290–0 HBJ $12.95
0–671–66881–1 Simon & Schuster pb $2.95

• Barbara Park
SKINNYBONES
Skinnybones makes up for a diminutive physique with his one-liners. His Little League team hasn't won in years but Skinnybones scores an unexpected success
0–394–84988–4 Knopf $9.95

ALMOST STARRING SKINNYBONES
0–394–89831–1 Knopf $10.95

• Robert Peck
SOUP
The first in a series about the audacious schemes of two boys who live in a small Vermont town in the 1930s. Fun, good-natured, and just a touch nostalgic
Illustrated by Charles Robinson
0–440–48186–4 Dell pb $2.75

SOUP AND ME
Illustrated by Charles Robinson
0–440–48187–2 Dell pb $2.75

SOUP'S DRUM
Illustrated by Charles Robinson
0–440–40003–1 Dell pb $2.95

• D. Marcus Pinkwater
THE HOBOKEN CHICKEN EMERGENCY
A farcical romp initiated by the bringing home of a 266-pound, six-foot-two Thanksgiving chicken
0–13–392499–8 Prentice-Hall $4.95
0–590–11856–0 Scholastic pb $1.50

• Barbara Robinson
THE BEST CHRISTMAS PAGEANT EVER
How the terrible Herdman kids come to be the stars of the Christmas pageant and the consequences. Told for laughs, and lots of them. Children don't seem to mind the sentimental ending
Illustrated by Judith Glynn Brown
0–06–025043–7 Harper & Row $9.95
0–380–48066–2 Avon pb $2.50

• Thomas Rockwell
HOW TO EAT FRIED WORMS
A boy intends to do exactly that in a consistently funny story
9–998–93120–7 Dell pb $2.95

Christmas and Hanukkah

• Charles Dickens
A CHRISTMAS CAROL: Being a Ghost Story of Christmas
An illustrated version that characterizes Scrooge, Tiny Tim, and all the rest as animals
Illustrated by Mercer Mayer
0–02–730310–1 Macmillan $15.95

• O. Henry
THE GIFT OF THE MAGI
An adaptation of the classic Christmas story accompanied by fine illustrations
Illustrated by Lisabeth Zwerger
0–907234–17–8 Picture Book Studio $15.95

• E.T.A. Hoffman
THE NUTCRACKER
The beloved 19th-century Christmas fantasy; Sendak's illustrations suggest the story's more disturbing and fantastic elements
Translated by Ralph Manheim
Illustrated by Maurice Sendak
0–517–55285–X Crown $19.95

• Gian-Carlo Menotti
AMAHL AND THE NIGHT VISITORS
A retelling of the libretto of Menotti's Christmas opera
Illustrated by Michele Lemieux
0–688–05426–9 Morrow $15.00

• Isaac Bashevis Singer
THE POWER OF LIGHT: Eight Stories for Hanukkah
Illustrated by Irene Lieblich
0–374–36099–5 Farrar, Straus & Giroux $13.95

Literary Adaptations

• Barbara Cohen
THE CANTERBURY TALES
Retellings of selections from Chaucer, beautifully illustrated
Illustrated by Trina Hyman
0–688–06201–6 Lothrop, Lee & Shepard $17.95

• Leon Garfield
SHAKESPEARE STORIES
Twelve plays in narrative form, presented without undue simplification and with a strong sense of the dramatic
Illustrated by Michael Foreman
0–8052–3991–X Schocken $18.95

Folktales, Mythology, and Fables

• Aesop
AESOP'S FABLES
Full-color illustrations make this an especially good introduction to Aesop for young children
Illustrated by Michael Hague
0–03–002038–7 Henry Holt $11.95

AESOP'S FABLES
Illustrated by Heidi Holder
0–670–10643–7 Viking $12.95

• Hans Christian Andersen
ANDERSEN'S FAIRY TALES
0–448–11005–9 Putnam pb $10.95

MICHAEL HAGUE'S FAVOURITE HANS CHRISTIAN ANDERSEN FAIRY TALES
The larger print makes the text extremely accessible to young readers. A perfect first Andersen collection for the eights and nines
Illustrated by Michael Hague
0–8050–0659–1 Henry Holt $16.95

• Anonymous
THE ARABIAN NIGHTS
Illustrated by Earle Goodenow
0–448–11006–7 Putnam pb $7.95

• Joanna Cole
BEST LOVED FOLKTALES OF THE WORLD
0–385–18949–4 Doubleday pb $9.95

IF YOU CAN'T FIND IT, LOOK IN THE INDEX

- **Ingri & Edgar P. D'Aulaire**
These classic retellings of Greek and Norse myths are wonderful read-aloud stories for young children and are candidates for an older child's permanent collection.
D'AULAIRE'S BOOK OF GREEK MYTHS
Illustrated by Ingri and Edgar P. D'Aulaire
0–385–01583–6 Doubleday $18.95
0–385–15787–8 Doubleday pb $12.95

D'AULAIRE'S NORSE GODS & GIANTS
0–385–23692–1 Doubleday pb $9.95

- **Amy Ehrlich, editor**
THE RANDOM HOUSE BOOK OF FAIRY TALES
Illustrated by Diane Goode
0–394–85693–7 Random House $14.95

- **Mordicai Gerstein**
TALES OF PAN
Great and ludicrous exploits of the Greek god and his relatives by the author of humorous books for young children
0–06–021996–3 Harper & Row $12.95

- **Jacob & Wilhelm Grimm**
THE JUNIPER TREE: And Other Tales from Grimm
A superior two-volume edition of Grimm's *Household Stories* beautifully translated and matched by evocative line drawings. A marvelous present for an intelligent child
Translated by Lore Segal & Randall Jarrell
Illustrated by Maurice Sendak
0–374–18057–1 Farrar, Straus & Giroux $25.00
0–374–51358–9 Farrar, Straus & Giroux pb $7.95

SNOW-WHITE AND THE SEVEN DWARFS
A fine edition distinguished by an outstanding translation
Translated by Randall Jarrell
Illustrated by Nancy Ekholm Burkert
0–374–37099–0 Farrar, Straus & Giroux $14.95
0–374–46868–0 Farrar, Straus & Giroux pb $5.95

THE TWELVE DANCING PRINCESSES & OTHER TALES FROM GRIMM
Fourteen tales including some of the less familiar ones in a solidly edited, imaginatively illustrated edition
Illustrated by Lidia Postma
0–8037–0237–X Dial $14.95

- **Virginia Hamilton**
THE PEOPLE COULD FLY: American Black Folktales
Twenty-four splendidly illustrated folktales for the more ambitious elevens and twelves. With cassette
Illustrated by Leone & Diane Dillon
Narrated by James Earl Jones
0–394–89183–X Knopf $19.95

- **Joel Chandler Harris**
JUMP: The Adventures of Brer Rabbit
Evocatively illustrated traditional tales retold for contemporary children
Illustrated by Barry Moser
0–15–241350–2 HBJ $15.95

- **Andrew Lang**
THE BLUE FAIRY BOOK
0–14–035090–X Puffin pb $2.95

THE YELLOW FAIRY BOOK
0–14–035089–6 Puffin pb $2.25

- **Alice Low**
THE MACMILLAN BOOK OF GREEK GODS AND HEROES
Illustrated by Arvis Stewart
0–02–761390–9 Macmillan $15.95

- **Scott R. Sanders**
HEAR THE WIND BLOW: American Folksongs Retold
Illustrated by Ponder Goembel
0–02–778140–2 Bradbury $14.95

- **Alvin Schwartz**
SCARY STORIES TO TELL IN THE DARK
Short folk tales that children will enjoy reading at Halloween
Illustrated by Stephen Gammell
0–397–31926–6 Harper & Row $12.95
0–06–440170–7 Harper & Row pb $3.50

MORE SCARY STORIES TO TELL IN THE DARK: Collected and Retold from Folklore
Illustrated by Stephen Gammell
0–397–32081–7 Harper & Row $12.95
0–06–440177–4 Harper & Row pb $3.50

- **Isaac Bashevis Singer**
STORIES FOR CHILDREN
Translated by the author & Elizabeth Shub
0–374–37266–7 Farrar, Straus & Giroux $16.95
0–374–46489–8 Farrar, Straus & Giroux pb $7.95

WHEN SHLEMIEL WENT TO WARSAW AND OTHER STORIES
Eight stories, several based on traditional Jewish tales, written by the master storyteller and Nobel laureate. In the introduction, Singer says, "In my writing there is no basic difference between tales for adults and for young people. The same spirit, the same interest in the supernatural is in all of them"
Illustrated by Margot Zemach
Translated by the author & Elizabeth Shub
0–374–38316–2 Farrar, Straus & Giroux $10.95
0–374–48365–5 Farrar, Straus & Giroux pb $3.95

- **Jane Yolen, editor**
FAVORITE FOLKTALES FROM AROUND THE WORLD
Straightforward translations for children who no longer require a picture on every page
0–394–54382–3 Pantheon $19.95

Devotional Books

- **Miriam Chaikin**
ASK ANOTHER QUESTION: The Story and Meaning of Passover
The history of Passover from the Exodus to today, with explanations of the holiday's songs, rituals, and symbols
Illustrated by Marvin Friedman
0–89919–281–5 Ticknor & Fields $13.95
0–89919–423–0 Ticknor & Fields pb $4.95

LIGHT ANOTHER CANDLE: The Story and Meaning of Hanukkah
Illustrated by Demi
0–395–31026–1 Houghton Mifflin $10.50
0–89919–057–X Ticknor & Fields pb $4.95

- **Michael Hague**
A CHILD'S BOOK OF PRAYERS
Twenty familiar prayers interpreted by Michael Hague's illustrations
0–030–01412–3 Henry Holt $11.95

- **Geoffrey Horn**
BIBLE STORIES FOR CHILDREN
Retellings from the Old and New Testaments with color illustrations
Illustrated by Arvis Stewart
0–02–554060–2 Macmillan $12.95

- **Lore Segal**
THE BOOK OF ADAM TO MOSES
A retelling of Genesis and Exodus. Her narratives will interest children over ten
Illustrated by Leonard Baskin
0–394–86757–2 Knopf $13.95

- **Walter Wangerin, Jr.**
THE BIBLE FOR CHILDREN
0–02–689000–3 Macmillan $9.95

Poetry

- **Arnold Adoff, editor**
MY BLACK ME: A Beginning Book of Black Poetry
0–525–35460–3 Dutton $10.95

- **H.E. Casterline, editor**
JABBERWOCKY & OTHER NONSENSE VERSES
Illustrated by Jean Chandler
0–307–62805–1 Western $13.50

- **Roald Dahl**
ROALD DAHL'S REVOLTING RHYMES
Illustrated by Quentin Blake
0–394–95422–X Knopf $9.95

- **Mark Daniel, editor**
A CHILD'S TREASURY OF POEMS
An anthology of 19th-century and early 20th-century poetry, with 100 full-color and black-and-white reproductions of rarely-seen paintings and engravings. A stunning collection
0–8037–0330–9 Dial $14.95

- **Donald Hall, editor**
THE OXFORD BOOK OF CHILDREN'S VERSE IN AMERICA
For children eleven and up
0–19–503539–9 Oxford $24.95

- **X.J. Kennedy**
THE FORGETFUL WISHING WELL: Poems for Young People
Seventy original poems by an inventive poet who writes wittily about familiar things
Illustrated by Monica Incisa
0–689–50317–2 Macmillan $9.95

- Kenneth Koch & Kate Farrell, editors
TALKING TO THE SUN: An Illustrated Anthology of Poems for Young People
A lavishly illustrated collection with artwork from the collection of the Metropolitan Museum of Art
0–03–005849–X Henry Holt $18.95

- Edward Lear
THE OWL AND THE PUSSY-CAT & OTHER NONSENSE
0–382–09192–2 Silver, Burdett & Ginn $11.95

- Arnold Lobel
THE BOOK OF PIGERICKS
Limericks are easily remembered (and composed) by anyone who is ten or eleven, and Lobel's are amusing
0–06–023982–4 Harper & Row $12.95
0–06–443163–0 Harper & Row pb $4.95

- David McCord
ALL SMALL POEMS
Illustrated by Madelaine Linden
0–316–55519–3 Little, Brown $12.95

- Eve Merriam
HALLOWEEN ABC
Illustrated by Lane Smith
0–02–766870–3 Macmillan $14.95

- Jack Prelutsky
THE RANDOM HOUSE BOOK OF POETRY FOR CHILDREN
Crisp and insightful selections by a prolific writer and poet who understands the television generation
Illustrated by Arnold Lobel
0–394–85010–6 Random House $15.95

THE NEW KID ON THE BLOCK
Illustrated by James Stevenson
0–688–02271–5 Greenwillow $12.95

RIDE A PURPLE PELICAN
Illustrated by Garth Williams
0–688–04031–4 Greenwillow $13.00

TYRANNOSAURUS WAS A BEAST
Illustrated by Arnold Lobel
0–688–06442–6 Greenwillow $11.95

- Beatrice Schenk de Regniers & others, editors
SING A SONG OF POPCORN
An anthology of favorite poems, illustrated by nine Caldecott-winning artists
0–590–40645–0 Scholastic $16.95

- Shel Silverstein
A LIGHT IN THE ATTIC
0–06–025673–7 Harper & Row $14.95

WHERE THE SIDEWALK ENDS: Poems and Drawings
Possibly the most popular book of verse published in the last 20 years; the cautionary verse is exceptionally good
0–06–025667–2 Harper & Row $14.95

- Robert Louis Stevenson
A CHILD'S GARDEN OF VERSES
Written by the author of *Treasure Island* from the memories of a solitary childhood. The centennial edition
Illustrated by Erik Blegvad
0–394–93739–2 Random House pb $1.95

- Wallace Tripp
MARGUERITE, GO WASH YOUR FEET!
A collection of poetic nonsense, illustrated with cartoonish verve. For children eight and up
Illustrated by Wallace Tripp
0–395–35392–0 Houghton Mifflin $15.95

Anthologies

- Joanna Cole & Stephanie Calmenson
THE LAUGH BOOK
Illustrated by Marylin Hafner
0–385–18559–6 Doubleday $14.95

- Clifton Fadiman, editor
THE WORLD TREASURY OF CHILDREN'S LITERATURE
A two-volume set selected and compiled by the well-known anthologist
Illustrated by Leslie Merrill
0–316–27302–3 Little, Brown $40.00

- Judith Hendra, editor
THE ILLUSTRATED TREASURY OF HUMOR FOR CHILDREN
0–448–16429–9 Putnam $12.95

- Margaret Martignoni, editor
ILLUSTRATED TREASURY OF CHILDREN'S LITERATURE
A real bargain—over 40 fairy stories, 70 poems and almost 50 excerpts from stories and junior novels. Plenty for the sevens, eights, nines, and their younger siblings
0–448–04101–4 Putnam $17.95

- Pamela Pollack
THE RANDOM HOUSE BOOK OF HUMOR FOR CHILDREN
Illustrated by Paul O. Zelinsky
0–394–88049–8 Random House $14.95

- Louis & Bryna Untermeyer, editors
THE GOLDEN TREASURY OF CHILDREN'S LITERATURE
9–99–575037–6 Golden $15.95

Jokes, Riddles, and Wordplay

- Alvin Schwartz
THE CAT'S ELBOW & OTHER SECRET LANGUAGES
To speak Cat's Elbow add extra letters to the words. Then look up King Tut and Medieval Greek
Illustrated by Margot Zemach
0–374–41054–2 Farrar, Straus & Giroux pb $3.45

UNRIDDLING: All Sorts of Riddles to Puzzle Your Guessary
A gem among riddle books. To unriddle is the opposite of asking a riddle, by the way
Illustrated by Sue Truesdell
0–06–446057–6 Harper & Row pb $4.95

- Marvin Terban
EIGHT ATE: A Feast of Homonym Riddles
The illustrations are great fun
Illustrated by Giulio Maestro
0–89919–067–7 Clarion $12.95
0–89919–086–3 Clarion pb $4.95

I THINK I THOUGHT & OTHER TRICKY VERBS
Tricky verbs reviewed with the help of amusing illustrations
Illustrated by Giulio Maestro
0–89919–231–9 Clarion $11.95
0–89919–290–4 Clarion pb $4.95

Biography

- David A. Adler
MARTIN LUTHER KING, JR.: Free at Last
Illustrated by Robert Casilla
0–8234–0618–0 Holiday House $12.95
0–8234–0619–9 Holiday House pb $4.95

- Clyde Robert Bulla
POCAHONTAS AND THE STRANGERS
Pocahontas is a little girl, a young woman, and John Smith's bride in this interesting retelling
Illustrated by Peter Burchard
0–590–41711–8 Scholastic pb $2.50

- Ingri & Edgar Parin D'Aulaire
Biographies free of obvious historical clichés (George Washington does not chop down the cherry tree). Children up to nine will appreciate the narratives and brightly crayoned illustrations.
ABRAHAM LINCOLN
Winner of the Caldecott Medal 1940
0–385–24108–9 Doubleday pb $8.95

BENJAMIN FRANKLIN
0–385–24103–8 Doubleday pb $7.95

COLUMBUS
0–385–24106–2 Doubleday pb $8.95

- Margaret Davidson
THE STORY OF JACKIE ROBINSON, THE BRAVEST MAN IN BASEBALL
0–440–40019–8 Dell pb $2.95

- Russell Freedman
LINCOLN: A Photobiography
An ambitious book with far more information than usual in juvenile biographies. The illustrations are from contemporary sources. For attentive readers eleven and up. Newbery Medal 1988
0–89919–380–3 Clarion $15.95

- John Jakes
SUSANNA OF THE ALAMO: A True Story
A 19th-century Texas girl is the heroine of this authentic adventure story
Illustrated by Paul Bacon
0–15–200592–7 HBJ $13.95

- Noemi V. Marri
MARCO POLO
0–382–06983–8 Silver, Burdett & Ginn pb $7.75

- Donald J. Sobol
THE WRIGHT BROTHERS AT KITTY HAWK
Illustrated by Wayne Blickenstaff
0–590–40488–1 Scholastic pb $2.50

- Lina Tridenti
ANNE FRANK
0–382–06987–0 Silver, Burdett & Ginn pb $7.95

"The Women of Our Time" Series

Brief biographies of 20th-century women, allegedly the first such series designed for elementary school children. A commendably eclectic group comprising politicians, sports figures, artists, and others.

David A. Adler
OUR GOLDA: The Story of Golda Meir
Illustrated by Donna Ruff
0–670–53107–3 Viking $10.95
0–14–032104–7 Penguin pb $3.50

Patricia Reilly Giff
MOTHER TERESA: Sister to the Poor
Illustrated by Ted Lewin
0–14–032225–6 Penguin pb $3.50

LAURA INGALLS WILDER: Growing Up in the Little House
Illustrated by Eileen McKeating
0–670–81072–X Viking $10.95

R.R. Knudson
MARTINA NAVRATILOVA: Tennis Power
Illustrated by George Angelini
0–670–80665–X Viking $10.95
0–14–032218–3 Penguin pb $3.50

Milton Meltzer
DOROTHEA LANGE: Life Through the Camera
Photographs by Dorothea Lange
Illustrated by Donna Diamond
0–670–28047–X Viking $10.95

Susan Saunders
MARGARET MEAD: The World Was Her Family
Illustrated by Ted Lewin
0–670–81051–7 Viking $10.95
0–14–032063–6 Penguin pb $3.50

Life Then and Now

• **Aliki**
A MEDIEVAL FEAST
A scrupulously accurate little picture book about a fictional event (a royal visit) and a factual account of what went on in a medieval household
0–690–04245–0 Harper & Row $12.95
0–06–446050–9 Harper & Row pb $4.95

• **Mitsumasa Anno**
ANNO'S U.S.A.
The old, the new, and the fanciful, best enjoyed by children old enough to spot the visual references in exquisitely detailed pictures
0–399–20974–3 Putnam $14.95

• **Melvin Berger**
EARLY HUMANS: A Pop-Up Book
0–399–21476–3 Putnam $13.95

• **Michele Byam**
ARMS AND ARMOR
One of a series of juvenile reference books illustrated throughout by full color photographs. The text is reasonably technical but the pictures will interest children under 14
Photographs by Dave King
0–394–89622–X Knopf $12.95

• **Giovanni Caselli**
AN EGYPTIAN CRAFTSMAN
A royal tomb painter works on a tomb in the Valley of the Kings 3000 years ago
0–87226–100–X Bedrick $9.95

• **Miriam Chaikin**
A NIGHTMARE IN HISTORY: The Holocaust 1933–1945
Chaikin deals with her terrible subject without shrillness. Children ten and up will understand the narrative and contemporary photographs
0–89919–461–3 Clarion $14.95

• **Leonard Everett Fisher**
THE GREAT WALL OF CHINA
The making of an ancient monument described in an illustrated book for children eight and nine
0–02–735220–X Macmillan $12.95

• **Paul Goble**
THE DEATH OF THE IRON HORSE
Trains as they used to be, by a winner of the Caldecott Medal
0–02–737830–6 Bradbury $12.95

• **Quang Nhuong Huynh**
THE LAND I LOST: Adventures of a Boy in Vietnam
Not about the war but about encounters with crocodiles and snakes and other adventures
Illustrated by Mai Vo-Dinh
0–06–024592–1 Harper & Row $12.95
0–06–440183–9 Harper & Row pb $3.50

• **Kinuko Kraft**
JOURNEY TO JAPAN
A nicely illustrated mechanical book with much information
0–670–80119–4 Viking $12.95

• **Joe Lasker**
A TOURNAMENT OF KNIGHTS
A fictional reenactment of a medieval joust in which readers are asked to share the experiences of a young novice matched against a seasoned challenger
0–690–04541–7 Harper & Row $12.95

• **David Macaulay**
Macaulay describes people building great buildings in places as remote as ancient Egypt and as close at hand as today's New York City. The pictures are glorious; detailed pen-and-ink illustrations offer new perspectives each time a page is turned. Macaulay doesn't write (or illustrate) down so younger children may need to ask a fascinated adult to share the books with them.
CASTLE
Caldecott Honor Book 1978
0–395–25784–0 Houghton Mifflin $14.95
0–395–32920–5 Houghton Mifflin pb $6.95
CATHEDRAL: The Story of Its Construction
Caldecott Honor Book 1974
0–395–17513–5 Houghton Mifflin $14.95

CITY: A Story of Roman Planning and Construction
0–395–34922–2 Houghton Mifflin pb $6.95
PYRAMID
0–395–21407–6 Houghton Mifflin $14.95
UNBUILDING
0–395–29457–6 Houghton Mifflin $14.95
0–395–45360–7 Houghton Mifflin pb $6.95
UNDERGROUND
0–395–24739–X Houghton Mifflin $14.95
0–395–34065–9 Houghton Mifflin pb $6.95

• **Betsy Maestro**
THE STORY OF THE STATUE OF LIBERTY
An admirably clear picture-book history
Illustrated by Giulio Maestro
0–688–05773–X Lothrop, Lee & Shepard $13.00

• **Florence Cassen Mayers**
EGYPTIAN ART FROM THE BROOKLYN MUSEUM: An ABC
Photographed treasures briefly described
0–8109–0888–3 Abrams $9.95

• **Kenneth McLeish**
THE SEVEN WONDERS OF THE WORLD
0–521–26538–X Cambridge $11.95

• **Margaret W. Musgrove**
ASHANTI TO ZULU: African Traditions
An alphabet book with a difference. The 26 distinct African tribal customs beautifully pictured in full color span the entire continent. Winner of the Caldecott Medal 1977
Illustrated by Diane & Leo Dillon
0–8037–0357–0 Dial $15.95
0–8037–0308–2 Dial pb $4.95

• **Lila Perl**
BLUE MONDAY AND FRIDAY THE THIRTEENTH: The Stories Behind the Days of the Week
How the days came to be named and what they signify. Library of Congress Children's Book of the Year 1986
Illustrated by Erika Weihs
0–89919–327–7 Clarion $12.95

DON'T SING BEFORE BREAKFAST, DON'T SLEEP IN THE MOONLIGHT: Everyday Superstitions and How They Began
Illustrated by Erika Weihs
0–89919–504–0 Clarion $13.95

• **Alice & Martin Provensen**
THE GLORIOUS FLIGHT ACROSS THE CHANNEL WITH LOUIS BLERIOT
Winner of the Caldecott Medal 1984
0–670–34259–9 Viking $13.95
0–317–63651–0 Penguin pb $4.95

• **Marcia Sewall**
THE PILGRIMS OF PLYMOUTH
A young (fictional) Pilgrim's first-person account of the eventful Mayflower voyage and the settlers' first Thanksgiving
0–689–31250–4 Macmillan $14.95

• Mary J. Shapiro
HOW THEY BUILT THE STATUE OF LIBERTY
Presented as a sketchbook; diagrams and cross-sections show how an engineering miracle came to be
Illustrated by Huck Scarry
0–394–86957–5 Random House $9.95

• Piero Ventura
JOURNEY TO EGYPT
0–670–80099–6 Viking $12.95

Life Sciences

• David Burnie
BIRD
Subjects include the secret of flight and details of birds "at home"
Photographs by Peter Chadwick
0–394–89619–X Knopf $12.95

• Ermanno Cristini & Luigi Puricelli
IN THE POND
0–907234–43–7 Picture Book Studio $11.95

IN THE WOODS
Two wordless picture books introduce younger children to different wild life habitats. An identification key appears at the back of each book
0–907234–31–3 Picture Book Studio $11.95

• Arthur Singer & Alan Singer
STATE BIRDS
Birds and their habitats superbly illustrated with a straightforward text
Commentary by Virginia Buckley
0–525–67177–3 Lodestar $14.95

• Jennifer Owings Dewey
AT THE EDGE OF THE POND
0–316–18208–7 Little, Brown $14.95

• George S. Fitcher
BIRDS OF NORTH AMERICA
Young bird watchers will enjoy this authoritative but simplified field guide produced by the Audubon Society
Illustrated by Arthur Singer
0–394–84771–7 Random House pb $5.95

• Jane Goodall
MY LIFE WITH THE CHIMPANZEES
The English naturalist tells the story of "her" families of wild and endangered chimpanzees
0–671–66095–0 Pocket pb $2.75

• Ada & Frank Graham
BUSY BUGS
A close-up look at 14 "popular" bugs
Illustrated by D.D. Tyler
0–396–08126–6 Dodd, Mead $9.95

• Marguerite Henry
ALL ABOUT HORSES
For children ten and up
0–394–80243–8 Random House $10.95

• Edith Kunhardt
HOW SPEEDY IS A CHEETAH?
Fascinating facts about animals
Illustrated by Richard Roe
0–448–19081–8 Putnam pb $1.95

• Nancy Winslow Parker & Joan Richards Wright
BUGS
In an original approach, this introduction to insects combines facts with humorous rhymes and bright pictures
Illustrated by Nancy Winslow Parker
0–688–06624–0 Greenwillow $11.95
0–688–08296–3 Morrow pb $3.95

• Steve Parker
SKELETON
How animal and human bones and skulls differ. Also, a look at insects and other creatures whose skeletons are outside their bodies
Photographs by Philip Dowell
0–394–89620–3 Knopf $12.95

• David Peters
GIANTS OF LAND, SEA AND AIR: Past and Present
The animals are presented to scale for comparison. To emphasize the point, children must open flaps to measure the bigger creatures
Illustrated by David Peters
0–394–87805–1 Knopf $13.95

• Joyce Pope
DO ANIMALS DREAM?: Children's Questions About Animals Most Often Asked of the Natural History Museum
A fascinating question-and-answer book containing unusual information
0–670–81233–1 Viking $15.95

• Elsa Posell
WHALES AND OTHER SEA MAMMALS
0–516–01663–6 Childrens Press $12.60
0–516–41663–4 Childrens Press pb $3.95

• Helen Rooney Sattler
FISH FACTS AND BIRD BRAINS: Animal Intelligence
Do worms "think?" And what about whales? A proven science writer comes up with just the sort of information that children love to present to adults
Illustrated by Giulio Maestro
0–525–66915–9 Lodestar $12.95

• Peter Seymour
INSECTS: A Close-Up Look
Popular insects presented in a pop-up book about insect anatomy
Illustrated by Jean C. Helmer
0–02–782120–X Macmillan $7.95

Prehistoric Animals

• Aliki
DIGGING UP DINOSAURS
Distinguished by small, delicate illustrations, this is a fascinating account of hunts for extinct monsters and should appeal to a broad age group
0–690–04098–9 Harper & Row $12.95
0–06–445016–3 Harper & Row pb $3.95

DINOSAURS ARE DIFFERENT
Illustrated by Aliki
0–690–04456–9 Harper & Row $12.95
0–06–445056–2 Harper & Row pb $3.95

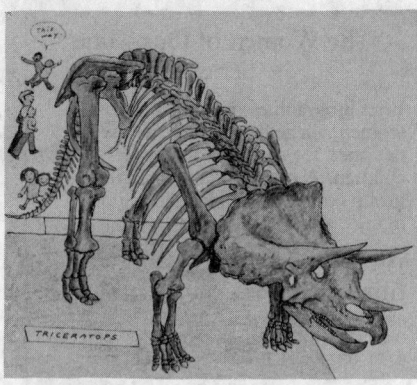
From Dinosaurs Are Different *by Aliki (Harper & Row)*

• Byrd Baylor
IF YOU ARE A HUNTER OF FOSSILS
Illustrated by Peter Parnall
0–684–16419–1 Macmillan $13.95
0–689–70773–8 Macmillan pb $4.95

• Michael J. Benton
THE DINOSAUR ENCYCLOPEDIA
For knowledgeable children older than nine
Illustrated by Jim Channell & others
0–671–51046–0 Simon & Schuster pb $6.95

• Mary Elting
THE MACMILLAN BOOK OF DINOSAURS AND OTHER PREHISTORIC CREATURES
The cleanly written text contains information about the history of discoveries that young enthusiasts might not easily find elsewhere
Illustrated by John Hamberger
0–02–733430–9 Macmillan $14.95
0–02–043000–0 Macmillan pb $8.95

• Patricia Lauber
DINOSAURS WALKED HERE & OTHER STORIES FOSSILS TELL
0–02–754510–5 Bradbury $15.95

• Keith Moseley
DINOSAURS: A Lost World
The pop ups are unusually mobile, and the text is just right for children becoming interested in the subject
Illustrated by Robert Cremins
0–399–21063–6 Putnam $13.95

• Helen Rooney Sattler
DINOSAURS OF NORTH AMERICA
Illustrated by Anthony Rao
0–688–51952–0 Lothrop, Lee & Shepard $14.95
PTEROSAURS: The Flying Reptiles
For children who want more in the way of technical information
Illustrated by Christopher Santoro
0–688–03995–2 Lothrop, Lee & Shepard $13.00

The Universe, Space Flights, and Our Climate

• Franklyn M. Branley
Pleasantly illustrated books for children eight and younger interested in science subjects.
COMETS
Illustrated by Giulio Maestro
0–690–04414–3 Harper & Row $12.95
0–694–00199–6 Harper & Row pb $7.95

HURRICANE WATCH
Illustrated by Giulio Maestro
0–690–04470–4 Harper & Row $11.50
0–06–445062–7 Harper & Row pb $3.95

IS THERE LIFE IN OUTER SPACE?
Illustrated by Don Maddem
0–06–445049–X Harper & Row pb $3.95

JOURNEY INTO A BLACK HOLE
Illustrated by Marc Simont
0–690–04543–3 Harper & Row $12.95
0–06–445075–9 Harper & Row pb $3.95

● Roy A. Gallant
THE MACMILLAN BOOK OF ASTRONOMY
Illustrated by Ron Miller & others
0–02–043230–5 Macmillan pb $8.95

● Clint Hatchett
THE GLOW-IN-THE-DARK NIGHT SKY BOOK
Brief exposure to the light makes the color pictures glow, so that children can take the book outdoors when sky gazing
Illustrated by Stephen Marchesi
0–394–89113–9 Random House $9.95

● Richard Maurer
THE NOVA SPACE EXPLORER'S GUIDE: Where to Go and What to See
Based on photographs from the NASA archives, this guide takes us on a manned moon landing and on the voyages of satellite probes to Mars, Venus, Jupiter, Mercury, and Saturn
0–517–55752–5 Crown $15.95

● Florence Cassen Mayers
THE NATIONAL AIR AND SPACE MUSEUM: An ABC
Photographs of modern and historic aircraft and space vehicles, together with a brief text on air travel and space
0–8109–1859–5 Abrams $9.95

● Sally Ride & Susan Okie
TO SPACE AND BACK
An account of space flight by a crew member of the Space Shuttle who rode, ate, slept, and worked in space
0–688–06159–1 Lothrop, Lee & Shepard $16.95

Illustration by Marc Simont, from Journey into a Black Hole *by Franklyn M. Branley (Harper & Row)*

● Seymour Simon
Big colorful photographs from NASA's archives accompany clear, simple texts. The series will appeal to children up to eleven.
JUPITER
0–688–05796–9 Morrow $13.00
MARS
0–688–06584–8 Morrow $13.00
STARS
0–688–05855–8 Morrow $13.00
THE SUN
0–688–05857–4 Morrow $13.00

● Francis Wilson
THE WEATHER POP-UP BOOK
A seriously written book about climate and its consequences, made more lively by mechanized illustrations. For children over ten
Illustrated by Philip Jacobs
0–671–63699–5 Simon & Schuster $12.95

Earth Science and Chemistry

● Vicki Cobb
SCIENCE EXPERIMENTS YOU CAN EAT
Chemistry demonstrated in kitchen experiments designed for children ten and up
Illustrated by Peter Lippman
0–397–31487–6 Harper & Row $12.95
0–064–46002–9 Harper & Row pb $4.95

● Joanna Cole
Ruled by an eccentric teacher, Cole's imaginary pupils reluctantly accompany Miss Frizzle on trips where fantastical adventures introduce solid scientific information. Second and third graders will enjoy these funny, imaginative, and irreverent science books.
THE MAGIC SCHOOL BUS AT THE WATER WORKS
Illustrated by Bruce Degen
0–590–40361–3 Scholastic $12.95
0–590–40360–5 Scholastic pb $3.95

THE MAGIC SCHOOL BUS INSIDE THE EARTH
Illustrated by Bruce Degen
0–590–40759–7 Scholastic $13.95

● Patricia Lauber
VOLCANO: The Eruption and Healing of Mt. St. Helens
A stunning full-color photo-essay
0–02–75400–8 Bradbury $14.95

● Natural History Museum Staff
ROCKS AND MINERALS
Photographs by Colin Keates & Andreas Einsiedel
0–394–89621–1 Knopf $12.95

● Sara Stein
THE EVOLUTION BOOK: The Story of 4000 Million Years of Life on Earth
An overstuffed paperback encourages children ten and up to observe, experiment, and do projects. Each section introduces a phase in the Earth's evolution and then suggests explanatory observations and experiments
0–89480–927–X Workman pb $11.95

THE SCIENCE BOOK
A companion to *The Evolution Book* that offers many introductory activities in the earth sciences
0–89480–120–1 Workman pb $8.95

Growing Up

● Claire G. Berman
SO WHAT AM I DOING IN A STEP-FAMILY?
The pitfalls and advantages of step-families discussed by a respected authority. For children ten and younger
Illustrated by Dick Wilson
0–8184–0325–X Lyle Stuart $12.00

● Joanna Cole
ASKING ABOUT SEX AND GROWING UP: A Question and Answer Book for Boys and Girls
Includes some harder material, such as AIDS and contraception. Designed for children approaching puberty
Illustrated by Alan Tiegreen
0–688–06927–4 Morrow $11.95
0–688–06928–2 Morrow pb $4.95

● Mary Elting
MACMILLAN BOOK OF THE HUMAN BODY
Illustrated by Kirk Moldoff
0–02–733440–6 Macmillan $15.95
0–02–043080–9 Macmillan pb $8.95

● Jill Krementz
HOW IT FEELS WHEN PARENTS DIVORCE
Illustrated interviews with children presented in their own words; intended for teenagers but helpful for younger children too
0–394–54079–4 Knopf $12.95
0–394–75855–2 Knopf pb $7.95

● Eda LeShan
WHEN GROWNUPS DRIVE YOU CRAZY
Sample topics: When parents forget how old you are; brothers and sisters; favoritism
0–02–756340–5 Macmillan $11.95

● Peter Mayle
WHERE DID I COME FROM
A broadly humorous approach to sex and puberty with comic book illustrations. Includes pages on intercourse
Illustrated by Arthur Robbins & Paul Walter
0–8184–0161–3 Lyle Stuart $12.00
0–8184–0253–9 Lyle Stuart pb $6.95

WHAT'S HAPPENING TO ME: The Answer to the World's Most Embarrassing Questions
Amusing and quite informative
Illustrated by Arthur Robbins & Paul Walter
0–8184–0312–8 Lyle Stuart pb $6.95

● Jonathan Miller
THE HUMAN BODY
Pop-up drawings constructed with "moving" parts allow readers to simulate heart beat and muscle contractions. The sophisticated text is written by Jonathan Miller, M.D., narrator of the TV series *The*

Human Body. Elevens and up tired of junior science texts will enjoy it
Illustrated by Harry Willock
0–670–38605–7 Studio Viking $19.95

Music and Ballet

- **Jill Krementz**
A VERY YOUNG DANCER
A photographic record of a ballet student's first professional appearance in the Christmas production of *The Nutcracker*
0–394–40885–3 Knopf $14.95

- **Donald Mitchell & Roderick Biss, editors**
THE CHILDREN'S SONGBOOK
Illustrated by Errol Le Cain
0–571–10054–6 Faber & Faber pb $7.95

- **Reader's Digest**
THE READER'S DIGEST CHILDREN'S SONGBOOK
Over 130 favorite songs, made easier by numbered notes and chord symbols, suitable for children's voices
0–89577–214–0 Reader's Digest $25.95

- **Jane Rosenberg**
DANCE ME A STORY: Twelve Tales from the Classic Ballets
The plots of great ballets, unfolded with the dancer's point of view in mind
Introduction by Merrill Ashley
0–500–01359–4 Thames & Hudson $19.95

Sports

- **Marty Appel**
THE FIRST BOOK OF BASEBALL
0–517–56726–1 Crown $9.95

- **Michael J. Brown**
SOCCER RULES IN PICTURES
0–399–51267–5 Putnam pb $6.95

- **Red Foley**
RED FOLEY'S BEST BASEBALL BOOK EVER: 1988 Edition
Updated annually, this collection of baseball facts and trivia comes with stickers of many baseball stars
0–671–65725–9 Simon & Schuster pb $7.95

- **G. Jacobs & J.R. McCrory**
BASEBALL RULES IN PICTURES
0–399–51129–6 Putnam pb $6.95

- **Jill Krementz**
Three companion books to *A Very Young Dancer.* Once again, the heroines are serious participants in their chosen sports.
A VERY YOUNG GYMNAST
0–394–50080–6 Knopf $14.95
0–440–49213–0 Dell pb $6.95

A VERY YOUNG RIDER
0–440–49215–7 Dell pb $6.95

A VERY YOUNG SKATER
0–394–50833–5 Knopf $14.95
0–440–49214–9 Dell pb $6.95

- **Gregory Morris**
BASKETBALL BASICS
Illustrated by Tim Engelland
0–13–072223–5 Prentice-Hall pb $4.95

- **Jim Murphy**
BASEBALL'S ALL-TIME ALL-STARS
0–89919–229–7 Houghton Mifflin $10.95

- **Dorothy H. Pinch**
HAPPY HORSEMANSHIP
A guide for riders over ten
0–668–03605–2 Arco pb $5.95

- **J. Allen Queen**
KARATE HANDBOOK
With 200 photographs of students practicing basic karate techniques
0–8069–6286–0 Sterling $12.95
0–8069–6288–7 Sterling pb $6.95

Hobbies

- **Better Homes & Gardens**
BETTER HOMES & GARDENS NEW JUNIOR COOK BOOK
0–696–01145–X Better Homes & Gardens $6.95

- **Christina Björk**
Two unusual, inventive approaches to gardening.
LINNEA IN MONET'S GARDEN
Illustrated by Lena Anderson
91–29–57302–5 R&S $10.95

LINNEA'S WINDOWSILL GARDEN
91–29–59064–7 R&S $11.95

- **Steven Caney**
STEVEN CANEY'S KIDS' AMERICA
Describes Americana from Shaker furniture to tapdancing and suggests projects
0–911104–80–1 Workman pb $11.95

- **Ed Emberley**
ED EMBERLEY'S CRAZY MIXED-UP FACE GAME
0–316–23420–6 Little, Brown pb $13.95

ED EMBERLEY'S BIG GREEN DRAWING BOOK
A step-by-step approach; even children who "can't draw" participate
0–316–23595–4 Little, Brown $9.95
0–316–23596–2 Little, Brown pb $7.95

- **Randy Harelson**
THE KID'S DIARY OF 365 AMAZING DAYS
How-to projects for each day of the year, in an oversized paperback
0–89480–071–X Workman pb $8.95

- **Jill Krementz**
THE FUN OF COOKING
Pumpkin pie, homemade pasta, granola, lemon chicken—and photographed instructions on how to make them
0–394–54808–6 Knopf $18.95

- **Elin McCoy**
SECRET SPACES, IMAGINARY PLACES: Creating Your Own Worlds for Play
The creation of favorite-place spaces (a lemonade stand, a pirate ship) out of household objects
Illustrated by Lynn Sweat
0–02–765460–5 Macmillan $12.95

- **Dokuihtei Nakano**
EASY ORIGAMI
Origami is a good way to learn to follow instructions. The projects include folded paper animals, puppets, and masks
0–670–80382–0 Viking $10.95

- **Helen & Kelly Oechsli**
IN MY GARDEN: A Child's Gardening Book
Illustrated by Kelly Oechsli
0–02–768510–1 Macmillan $12.95

- **Gillian Osband**
THE MESSY BOOK OF THINGS TO MAKE AND DO
Tips on messy fun for messy children who have messy friends and a yard or a play space outdoors
Illustrated by Heather Munro
0–590–40888–7 Scholastic pb $2.50

- **Marjorie Waters**
THE VICTORY GARDEN KIDS BOOK
Illustrated instructions for the gardening season from groundbreaking to the late fall harvest. A special section for adults offers guidelines for working with child gardeners and advice about when not to let children experiment
Photographs by Gary Mottau
Illustrated by George Ulrich
0–395–42730–4 Houghton Mifflin $21.95
0–395–46560–5 Houghton Mifflin pb $12.95

How Things Work

- **Michael & Marcia Folsom**
THE MACMILLAN BOOK OF HOW THINGS WORK
Illustrated by Brad Hammann
0–02–735360–5 Macmillan $15.95
0–689–71139–5 Macmillan pb $8.95

- **David Macaulay**
THE WAY THINGS WORK
An exhaustive, 400-page compendium that explains how all sorts of machines and inventions work
0–395–42857–2 Houghton Mifflin $24.95

- **Jim Murphy**
GUESS AGAIN: More Weird and Wacky Inventions
Guess what they are and then let the author tell you about these 45 odd but exciting inventions
0–02–767720–6 Bradbury $12.95

➤ FOR OVERSEAS ORDERING INFORMATION, SEE PAGE 1

Dictionaries

- **John Grisewood**
  SIMON & SCHUSTER'S ILLUSTRATED YOUNG READERS' DICTIONARY
  0–671–50020–1 Simon & Schuster pb $9.79

- **Houghton Mifflin**
  THE AMERICAN HERITAGE CHILDREN'S DICTIONARY
  Designed for children in grades three to six, with 37,000 entries and many illustrations
  0–395–42529–8 Houghton Mifflin $13.95

- **C.H. Morris**
  MACMILLAN DICTIONARY FOR CHILDREN
  A nicely compact and scrupulously researched illustrated dictionary that is one of the better buys for third- to sixth-graders
  0–02–578790–X Macmillan $13.95

- **Bruce Ogilvie & Douglas Waitley**
  RAND MCNALLY CHILDREN'S ATLAS OF THE WORLD 1989
  0–528–83348–0 Rand McNally $12.95

- **John Paton, editor**
  PICTURE ENCYCLOPEDIA FOR CHILDREN
  One of the few one-volume encyclopedias for children in the middle grades. Straightforward writing and decent illustrations
  0–448–18999–2 Putnam $19.95

- **W.D. Townson**
  PICTURE HISTORY OF THE WORLD
  An introduction to world history and geography with maps and illustrations
  0–448–18988–7 Putnam pb $19.95

- **Merriam Webster**
  THE WEBSTER'S II NEW RIVERSIDE CHILDREN'S DICTIONARY
  Special features include over 250 word histories. For young readers aged eight to twelve
  0–395–37884–2 Houghton Mifflin pb $8.95

- **Angela Wilkes, editor**
  FRENCH PICTURE DICTIONARY
  Designed for children embarking on a second language
  0–8442–1405–1 National Textbook $7.95

- **Jill & David Wright**
  THE SIMON & SCHUSTER YOUNG READERS' ATLAS
  Edited by Wendy Barish
  Illustrated by Mike Saunders & David Wright
  0–671–50657–9 Simon & Schuster pb $6.95

Young Adult Nonfiction

BIOGRAPHY

- **Nathan Aaseng**
  MORE WITH LESS: The Future World of Buckminister Fuller
  Fuller's creations were a mixture of the practical and the prophetic. This brief biography describes his geodesic dome and plans for domed cities of the future
  0–8225–0498–7 Lerner $9.95

- **Maury Allen**
  JACKIE ROBINSON: A Life Remembered
  The story of the first black to break baseball's color barrier, with discussions of Robinson's experiences with bigotry and his impact on civil rights
  0–531–15042–9 Franklin Watts $16.95

- **Maya Angelou**
  ALL GOD'S CHILDREN NEED TRAVELING SHOES
  Black Americans search for an African home in the 1960s
  0–394–75077–2 Random House pb $3.95

- **Joan Benoit & Sally Baker**
  RUNNING TIDE
  Benoit talks about her childhood, college years and Olympic gold medal victory
  0–394–55457–4 Knopf $16.95

- **Josh Clayton-Felt**
  TO BE SEVENTEEN IN ISRAEL: Through the Eyes of an American Teenager
  0–531–10249–1 Franklin Watts $11.95

- **Beverly Cleary**
  A GIRL FROM YAMHILL: A Memoir
  0–688–07800–1 Morrow $14.95

- **Roger Clemens**
  ROCKET MAN: The Roger Clemens Story
  0–8289–0629–7 Viking $15.95

- **Daniel Cohen**
  CARL SAGAN: Superstar Scientist
  Sagan's contributions include his work on the Mars space probes and the "nuclear winter" theory
  0–396–08776–0 Dodd, Mead $12.95

- **Ida Cowen**
  A SPY FOR FREEDOM: The Story of Sarah Aaronsohn
  A brilliant Jewish woman from Britain went to Palestine during World War I to spy and did not return
  0–525–67150–1 Lodestar $14.95

- **Roald Dahl**
  BOY
  The story of Dahl's childhood told with the breakneck humor his fans have learned to expect
  0–14–008917–9 Penguin pb $6.95

- **Jay Daly**
  PRESENTING S.E. HINTON
  A biographical sketch of the author who wrote *The Outsiders* when she was 17
  0–8057–8203–6 Twayne $14.95

- **Jean Fritz**
  THE DOUBLE LIFE OF POCAHONTAS
  "Removes the romantic varnish from legend and turns history into engrossing reality"—Faith McNulty, *New Yorker*
  Illustrated by Ed Young
  0–399–21016–4 Putnam $12.95
  0–14–032257–4 Penguin pb $3.95

  HOMESICK: My Own Story
  A skillfully constructed autobiographical account of Fritz's childhood in pre-Revolutionary China, where the author was both one of the privileged and a foreign devil. A Newberry Honor Book for 1982
  0–440–43683–4 Dell pb $2.95

- **Ron Hansen**
  THE ASSASSINATION OF JESSE JAMES BY THE COWARD ROBERT FORD
  0–345–29626–5 Ballantine pb $3.95

- **Robert T. Hohler**
  "I TOUCH THE FUTURE ...": The Story of Christa McAuliffe
  The astronaut's life from early childhood to the 1986 Challenger disaster
  0–394–55721–2 Random House $16.95
  0–425–11054–0 Berkley pb $4.50

- **Ilse Koehn**
  MISCHLING, SECOND DEGREE: My Childhood in Nazi Germany
  Though one-quarter Jewish, the author posed as an "Aryan" child while her world dissolved into chaos. A first-hand account of World War II
  0–688–84110–4 Greenwillow $12.95

- **Chris May**
  BOB MARLEY
  A biography that describes the musical role of Marley's Rastafarianism and attempts to explain his early death
  0–241–11476–4 David & Charles $9.95

- **Cornelia Meigs**
  INVINCIBLE LOUISA
  A celebrated short biography of Louisa May Alcott, the author of *Little Women*
  0–316–56590–3 Little, Brown $14.95
  0–590–41937–4 Scholastic pb $2.50

- **Laurie Nadel**
  CORAZON AQUINO: Journey to Power
  0–671–63950–1 Messner $9.95

- **Linda Peavy**
  DREAMS INTO DEEDS: Nine Women Who Dared
  Margaret Mead, Babe Didrikson, Jane Addams, and other pioneers
  0–684–18484–2 Macmillan $12.95

- **Blythe Randolph**
  AMELIA EARHART
  0–531–10331–5 Franklin Watts $12.95

- Flip Schulke & Penelope Ortner McPhee
KING REMEMBERED
The story of Martin Luther King's life; with photos
0–393–02256–0 Norton $18.95
0–671–62018–5 Pocket pb $7.95

POETRY AND PLAYS

- Arnold Adoff
SPORTS PAGES
The experiences and dreams of young athletes expressed in verse
0–397–32102–3 Lippincott $11.50

- Maya Angelou
NOW SHEBA SINGS THE SONG
Black women of all ages are evoked in this poem
0–525–24501–4 Dutton $18.95

- Mel Glenn
CLASS DISMISSED: More High School Poems
Original verse describes the things that young adults experience or ponder
0–89919–443–5 Ticknor & Fields $12.95

- Paul B. Janeczko, editor
THIS DELICIOUS DAY
Sixty-five poems by Ogden Nash, John Ciardi, Lilian Moore, and others
0–531–05724–0 Franklin Watts $11.95

- X.J. Kennedy
BRATS
Ingenious and fun
Illustrated by James Watts
0–689–50392–X Macmillan $11.95

- Kenneth Koch, editor
TALKING TO THE SUN: An Illustrated Anthology of Poems for Young People
Illustrated by Kate Farrell
0–03–005849–X Henry Holt $18.95

- Carol Korty
WRITING YOUR OWN PLAYS: Creating, Adapting, Improvising
0–684–18470–2 Scribners $11.95

- Wendy Lamb, editor
MEETING THE WINTER BIKE RIDER & OTHER PRIZE-WINNING PLAYS
Eight plays submitted by young adults to a national contest
0–440955–48–3 Dell pb $3.50

- Myra Cohen Livingston, editor
I LIKE YOU, IF YOU LIKE ME: Poems of Friendship
0–689–50408–X Macmillan $11.95

- Tom McKillip
WHAT'S HAPPENING TO MY LIFE: A Teenage Journey
0–8091–2844–6 Paulist Press pb $6.95

MUSIC AND ART

- Bryan Brewer & Edd Key
THE COMPACT DISK BOOK: A Complete Guide to the Digital Sound of the Future
0–15–620050–3 HBJ $12.95

- Bill Flanagan
WRITTEN IN MY SOUL: Rock's Great Songwriters Talk About Creating Their Music
0–8092–4650–3 Contemporary $11.75

- Pete Fornatale
THE STORY OF ROCK 'N' ROLL
0–688–06277–6 Morrow pb $7.95

- Trudy Hammer
AN ALBUM OF ROCK AND ROLL
0–531–10318–8 Franklin Watts $12.95

- Michael Hurd
THE OXFORD JUNIOR COMPANION TO MUSIC
A reliable junior reference book comprising over 900 photos and 3000 alphabetically arranged definitions
0–1934–302–X Oxford $35.00

- Anthony & H.W. Janson
HISTORY OF ART FOR YOUNG PEOPLE
A concise history from prehistory to the present
0–8109–1098–5 Abrams $29.95

- Larry Kettlekamp
ELECTRONIC MUSICAL INSTRUMENTS: What They Do, How They Work
0–688–02781–4 Morrow $10.50

- Susan Kuklin
REACHING FOR DREAMS: A Ballet from Rehearsal to Opening Night
A backstage look at Alvin Ailey's production of *Speeds*
0–688–06316–0 Lothrop, Lee & Shepard $11.75

- Piero Ventura
GREAT PAINTERS
An oversized, illustrated book translated from Italian
0–399–21115–2 Putnam $19.95

HISTORY AND MYTHOLOGY

- Roger D. Abrahams, editor
AFRO-AMERICAN FOLKTALES: Stories from Black Tradition in the New World
From the African diaspora to the slave holdings of the American South and the Caribbean
0–394–72885–8 Pantheon pb $11.95

- Jules Archer
THE INCREDIBLE SIXTIES: The Stormy Years That Changed America
0–15–238298–4 HBJ $16.95

- John Bierhorst, editor
THE MONKEY'S HAIRCUT & Other Stories Told by the Maya
Twenty-two traditional stories
Illustrated by Robert Andrew Parker
0–688–04269–4 Morrow $13.00

- Rhoda Blumberg
COMMODORE PERRY IN THE LAND OF THE SHOGUN
A much praised recounting of Commodore Perry's forced opening up of 19th-century Japan to the West; a fascinating account of a medieval country and its American "conquerors"
0–688–03723–2 Lothrop, Lee & Shepard $13.00

THE INCREDIBLE JOURNEY OF LEWIS AND CLARK
Tells the story of the explorers who set out to chart the vast wilderness west of the Mississippi
0–688–06512–0 Lothrop, Lee & Shepard $15.00

- Giovanni Castelli
THE FIRST CIVILIZATIONS
A brief social history with descriptions of the ancient world's tools, homes, weapons, and food
0–911745–59–9 Bedrick $14.95

- Kahane Corn & Jacki Moline
MADCAP MEN AND WACKY WOMEN FROM HISTORY
Biographical tidbits about 39 unusual people
0–671–63398–8 Messner $9.95

- Kevin Crossley-Holland
AXE AGE—WOLF AGE: A Selection of Norse Myths
Twenty-one myths explaining creation, the sun, the moon and other events
0–233–97688–4 Dutton $11.95

- Leonard Dinnerstein & David M. Reimers
ETHNIC AMERICANS: A History of Immigration
A brief presentation of an important subject
0–06–041671–8 Harper & Row $15.50

- Carl B. Feldbaum & Ronald J. Bee
LOOKING THE TIGER IN THE EYE: Confronting the Nuclear Threat
A detailed, thoughtful history of modern warfare
0–06–020414–1 Harper & Row $14.95

- William Finnegan
CROSSING THE LINE: A Year in the Land of Apartheid
A white Californian tells of his teaching experiences in South Africa
0–06–091430–0 Harper & Row pb $8.95

- Russell Freedman
INDIAN CHIEFS
Portraits of six chiefs of Western tribes by a renowned authority on American Indian culture
0–8234–0625–3 Holiday House $16.95

- David Goldstein
JEWISH LEGENDS
Its legends reflect the many cultures and places where Judaism flourished
0–87226–045–3 Bedrick $19.95

- W. John Hackwell
SIGNS, LETTERS, WORDS: Archeology Discovers Writing
An archeological study of the steady triumph of the written word, from pictographs to the conquering Latin alphabet
0–684–18807–4 Macmillan $13.95

- Trudy Hammer
THE GROWTH OF CITIES
0–531–10056–1 Franklin Watts $12.95

- Don Lawson
LANDMARK SUPREME COURT CASES
Nine fascinating decisions of historical significance
0–89490–132–X Enslow $13.95

- Edmund Lindop
BIRTH OF THE CONSTITUTION
A concise presentation of its origins and contemporary meanings
0–89490–135–4 Enslow $14.95

- Margot C.J. Mable
THE CONSTITUTION: Reflections of a Changing Nation
0–8050–0335–5 Henry Holt $12.95

VIETNAM THERE AND HERE
Deals not only with the war but also with the emotions and upheavals it caused at home
0–8050–0545–5 Henry Holt $11.95

- Robin McKinley
BEAUTY: The Retelling of the Story of Beauty and the Beast
A 20th-century version of the evocative folk story of a beautiful woman held captive by a beast
0–06–024149–7 Harper & Row $12.95

- Charles Mercer
STATUE OF LIBERTY: Updated Centennial Edition
History of The Lady's creation and construction plus accounts of her refurbishing and the centennial celebration
0–399–20670–1 Putnam $13.95

- Lila Perl
MUMMIES, TOMBS, AND TREASURE
The mysteries of ancient Egypt
0–89919–407–9 Houghton Mifflin $14.95

- Neil Philip, editor
THE SPRING OF BUTTERFLIES & OTHER FOLKTALES
Fourteen folktales representing ten local Chinese populations
Translated by He Liyi
0–688–06192–3 Lothrop $13.00

- Howard Pyle
THE STORY OF THE CHAMPIONS OF THE ROUND TABLE
0–684–18171–1 Macmillan $17.95
0–486–21883–X Dover pb $6.95

THE STORY OF THE GRAIL & THE PASSING OF ARTHUR
American classics; the pictures belong to the golden age of illustrated books
0–684–18483–4 Macmillan $17.95

- Anne Ross
DRUIDS, GODS AND HEROES FROM CELTIC MYTHOLOGY
From ancient Irish folktales to one of the earliest versions of the King Arthur legend
Illustrated by Roger Garland & John Sibbick
0–8052–4014–4 Schocken $16.95

- Cynthia R. Samuels
IT'S A FREE COUNTRY!: A Young Person's Guide to Politics and Elections
0–689–31416–7 Atheneum $12.95

- Ilana Shamir & Shlomo Shavit, editors
THE YOUNG READER'S ENCYCLOPEDIA OF JEWISH HISTORY
0–670–81738–4 Viking $15.95

- Tad Tuleja
CURIOUS CUSTOMS
Amusing stories of our cultural customs
0–517–56654–0 Harmony pb $8.95

- Jane Yolen, editor
FAVORITE FOLKTALES FROM AROUND THE WORLD
For serious readers, a collection of great stories compiled by a noted fantasist
0–394–54382–3 Pantheon $19.95

- Charlotte & David Yue
THE PUEBLO
A well-written book about the ceremonial, spiritual, and cultural life of a pueblo
0–395–38350–1 Houghton Mifflin $12.95

- Melvyn Bernard Zerman
TAKING ON THE PRESS: Constitutional Rights in Conflict
A lively and entertaining discussion of historical legal issues in the context of the Black Panthers, Vietnam, and more
Foreword by Dan Rather
0–690–04301–5 Crowell $11.95

SCIENCE FICTION COLLECTIONS

- Daniel Cohen
THE ENCYCLOPEDIA OF GHOSTS
0–396–08308–0 Dodd, Mead $14.95

- Gardner Dozois, editor
THE YEAR'S BEST SCIENCE FICTION: Fourth Annual Competition
Twenty-seven award-winning short stories
0–312–00710–8 St. Martin's pb $11.95

- Michael Page
ENCYCLOPEDIA OF THINGS THAT NEVER WERE
A comprehensive guide to imaginary peoples, places, and rites of folklore
0–670–81607–8 Viking $25.00

- William E. Warren
THE HEADLESS GHOST: True Tales of the Unexpected
0–13–384280–0 Prentice-Hall $12.95

- Don L. Wulffson
INCREDIBLE TRUE ADVENTURES
One man is caught up by a tornado, another sails around the Arctic in an upside-down ship. . .strange but true
0–396–08799–X Dodd, Mead pb $8.95

COMICS

- Betsy Borns
COMIC LIVES: Inside the World of American Stand-Up Comedy
Jay Leno, Carol Leifer, Richard Lewis, and "Bobcat" Goldthwait, among others
0–671–62620–5 Simon & Schuster pb $8.95

- Ron Goulart
THE GREAT COMIC BOOK ARTISTS
0–312–34557–7 St. Martin's pb $12.95

- Peter Paul Porges
MAD LOBSTERS AND OTHER ABOMINABLE HOUSEBROKEN CREATURES
A *Mad* magazine publication
0–446–32260–1 Warner pb $2.95

- Gary B. Trudeau
CALLING DR. WHOOPEE!
Collection of Doonesbury comics; Trudeau makes nasty fun of Oral Roberts, yuppies, and similar satirical targets
0–8050–0642–7 Henry Holt pb $5.95

NATURE, SCIENCE, AND MATHEMATICS

- Thomas B. Allen, Karen Jensen, & Philip Kopper
EARTH'S AMAZING ANIMALS
Snakes fly, fish walk, and lizards run on water in a colorfully illustrated survey of nature's curiosities
0–912186–48–8 National Wildlife pb $7.50

• Necia H. Apfel
ASTRONOMY PROJECTS FOR YOUNG SCIENTISTS
Build a planetarium, make a telescope, build a theodolite to observe the heavens
0–668–06006–9 Prentice-Hall pb $7.95

• Isaac Asimov
ASIMOV'S GUIDE TO HALLEY'S COMET
Traces the efforts of skywatchers and scientists to understand a great natural phenomenon
0–8027–6204–2 Walker $10.85

• David Attenborough
LIFE ON EARTH
A concise and interesting narrative written for a general audience by the British zoologist and television commentator
0–316–05747–9 Little, Brown $19.95

• N.J. & Jacquelyn Berrill
1001 QUESTIONS ANSWERED ABOUT THE SEASHORE
How crabs breathe, what crabs see, how to find sand eels and grunions, what mollusk shells are made of
0–486–23366–9 Dover pb $5.95

• Maurice Burton
BIRDS
A critical survey of preservation and conservation
0–8160–1063–3 Facts On File $13.95

• Robert & Maurice Burton
BEGINNINGS OF LIFE
Explores the genetics and heredity of plants and animals
0–8160–1070–6 Facts On File $13.95

• Helen C. Challand
SCIENCE PROJECTS AND ACTIVITIES
Includes starting an ant colony and building a camera and telegraph set
0–516–00569–3 Children's Press $14.95

• Diagram Group
FIELD GUIDE TO DINOSAURS: The First Complete Guide to Every Dinosaur Now Known
0–380–83519–3 Avon pb $9.95

• Margery & Howard Facklam
THE BRAIN: Magnificent Mind Machine
Illustrated by Paul Facklam
0–15–211388–6 HBJ $12.95

• Paul Fleisher
SECRETS OF THE UNIVERSE: Discovering the Universal Laws of Science
Laws such as planetary motion and the conservation of matter are explained in relation to everyday objects, telling why and how they work
Illustrated by Patricia A. Keeler
0–689–31266–0 Macmillan $17.95

UNDERSTANDING THE VOCABULARY OF THE NUCLEAR ARMS RACE
0–87518–352–2 Dillon $14.95

• Roy A. Gallant
OUR RESTLESS EARTH
The formation of the Earth, as well as an examination of geologic and climatic changes
0–531–10205–X Franklin Watts $10.95

THE PRIVATE LIVES OF THE STARS
Their birth, life, and death
0–02–737350–9 Macmillan $13.95

• Martin Gardner
AHA! GOTCHA: Paradoxes to Puzzle and Delight
A humorous and engaging collection related to logic, geometry, probability, number, statistics, and time
0–7167–1361–6 Freeman pb $10.95

• Frederick Golden
THE TREMBLING EARTH: Probing and Predicting Quakes
0–684–17884–2 Macmillan $13.95

• Richard Headstrom
SUBURBAN GEOLOGY: An Introduction to the Common Rocks and Minerals of Your Backyard and Local Park
Provides a color key and glossary
0–13–859240–3 Prentice-Hall $16.95

• Judith Herbst
SKY ABOVE AND WORLDS BEYOND
Take a guided trip to the moon, rocket around the solar system, observe comets, meteors, and auroras. Explorations in the future of space travel and the tantalizing search for extraterrestrial life
Illustrated by Richard Rosenblum
0–689–30974–0 Macmillan $14.95

• Jamie Jobb
THE NIGHT SKY BOOK: An Everyday Guide to Every Night
Explore such wonders as constellations, meteors, auroras, and zodiacal light
Illustrated by Linda Bennett
0–316–46551–8 Little, Brown $14.95

• Larry Kettlekamp
THE HUMAN BRAIN
The human brain and nervous system examined with discussions of right brain-left brain concepts and their application to research
0–89490–126–5 Enslow $13.95

• M. Kline, editor
RECENT REVOLUTION IN MATHEMATICS
0–531–10418–4 Franklin Watts $12.95

RECENT REVOLUTION IN PHYSICS
0–531–10066–9 Franklin Watts $12.95

• Pierre Kohler
VOLCANOES AND EARTHQUAKES
A strikingly photographed study
0–8120–3832–0 Barron's pb $4.95

• David Lambert
THE WORLD BEFORE MAN
The decline of the dinosaurs, the evolution of other species, and how we have discovered them
0–8160–1067–6 Facts On File $13.95

• David McKay
SPACE SCIENCE PROJECTS FOR YOUNG SCIENTISTS
0–531–10244–0 Franklin Watts $12.95

• Laurence Pringle
ANIMALS AT PLAY
Two hundred mammals and birds whose play behavior is enchanting and functional
0–15–203554–0 HBJ $12.95

• Chet Raymo
365 STARRY NIGHTS: An Introduction to Astronomy for Every Night of the Year
A full-page map of the stars for each lunar month is followed by helpful hints and explanations of the stars' positions and visibility
0–13–920512–8 Prentice-Hall $12.95

• Reader's Digest
SHARKS, SILENT HUNTERS OF THE DEEP
An illustrated compendium with an index of species and their distinguishing features
0–86438–014–3 Random House $19.95

• Colin A. Ronan
THE SKYWATCHER'S HANDBOOK: Night and Day, What to Look For in the Heavens Above
Colorfully illustrated with material on galaxies, constellations, eclipses, sunspots, mirages, cloud formations, weather maps, equipment, and technology
0–517–55703–7 Crown $13.95

• Eve Stwertka
PSYCHOANALYSIS: From Freud to the Age of Therapy
Freud's revolutionary theories of behavior, emotions and the mind translate directly into today's psychoanalytic practice
0–531–10481–8 Franklin Watts $9.95

• David A. Thomas
MATH PROJECTS FOR YOUNG SCIENTISTS
Suggests research on probability, number theory, and other concepts
0–531–10523–7 Franklin Watts $11.95

• Lyall Watson
THE DREAMS OF DRAGONS & Other Writings on the Edge of Natural History
The real and the mythical: essays on dragons and on extraordinary natural phenomena
0–688–06365–9 Morrow $15.50

• Lawrence White & Ray Brockel
OPTICAL ILLUSIONS
0–531–10220–3 Franklin Watts $10.95

TECHNOLOGY

• Chris Cooper & Jane Insley
HOW DOES IT WORK?
Modern inventions examined
0–8160–1066–8 Facts On File $13.95

• David Feldman
WHY DO CLOCKS RUN CLOCKWISE? AND OTHER IMPONDERABLES: Mysteries of Everyday Life Explained
0–06–015781–X Harper & Row $14.95
0–06–091515–3 Harper & Row pb $7.95

• Kathlyn Gay
ERGONOMICS: Making Products and Places Fit People
0–89490–118–4 Enslow $13.95

• Daniel Isaaman & Jenny Tyler
COMPUTER SPACEGAMES
Fourteen simple microcomputer games and programs
0–86020–683–1 Usborne pb $2.95

• Christopher Lampton
GRAPHICS AND ANIMATION ON THE APPLE II, IIE, IIC
Computer graphics programs explained, with basic information and simple introductions to programs
0–531–10143–6 Franklin Watts $11.95

• Kenneth Lasson
MOUSETRAPS AND MUFFLING CUPS
One hundred brilliant and bizarre US patents are celebrated in a funny book
0–87795–786–X Arbor House pb $9.95

• Dorothy H. Patent
THE QUEST FOR ARTIFICIAL INTELLIGENCE
How computers solve problems and why they sometimes fail, with future applications of artificial intelligence
0–15–264550–0 HBJ $13.95

• Kate Perry
HOW AND WHY WONDER BOOK OF ROBOTS
0–8431–4290–1 Price Stern Sloan pb $1.95

HOBBIES AND ACTIVITIES

• Bina Abling
FASHION SKETCHBOOK
0–87005–562–3 Fairchild $17.50

• Joanne F. Bernstein
TAKING OFF: Travel Tips for a Carefree Trip
What to bring and how to get there, plus a guide to traveling on your own
0–06–446047–9 Lippincott pb $3.95

• Better Homes & Gardens
AFTER SCHOOL COOKING
0–696–01727–X Better Homes pb $5.95

• Percy W. Blandford
24 TABLE SAW PROJECTS
Includes directions for shelves, cabinets, and tables
0–8306–2964–5 TAB pb $6.95

• Jack Botermans
KITE FLIGHT: 40 Models Ready for Takeoff
Complete, easy to follow instructions for making 40 different kites
0–03–008518–7 Henry Holt pb $9.95

• Council on International Education Exchange
THE TEENAGER'S GUIDE TO STUDY, TRAVEL, AND ADVENTURE ABROAD
A comprehensive guide that includes interviews with former student travelers
0–312–02296–4 St. Martin's pb $9.95

• Marianne Ford
COPYCATS AND ARTIFACTS: 42 Creative Artisan Projects to Make
Museum-inspired projects that can be copied by the inexperienced with some adult help
Illustrations by Anna Pugh
0–87923–645–0 Godine pb $14.95

• Elizabeth James & Carol Barkin
THE COMPLETE BABYSITTER'S HANDBOOK
0–671–43800–X Messner $11.50

• Jane Kendon
CROSS-STITCH SAMPLERS
0–312–17681–3 St. Martin's pb $9.95

• Susan E. Meyer
HOW TO DRAW IN PEN AND INK
Figures, landscapes, still lifes, perspective, and composition
0–02–584520–9 Macmillan $24.95
0–02–011920–8 Macmillan pb $12.95

• Dede Napoli
THE STARVING STUDENTS' COOKBOOK
0–446–38145–4 Warner pb $5.95

• Michael Page
ENCYCLOPEDIA OF THINGS THAT NEVER WERE
Describes characters and places in folklore
0–670–81607–8 Viking $25.00

• Dan Ritchard & Kathleen Moloney
VENTRILOQUISM FOR THE TOTAL DUMMY
0–394–75638–X Random House pb $7.95

• Bill Severn
MAGIC FUN FOR EVERYONE
Step-by-step instructions convince beginners to try out simple magic tricks
0–525–24485–9 Dutton $16.95
0–525–48253–9 Dutton pb $8.95

• Peter Smith
THE FIRST PHOTOGRAPHY BOOK
0–85112–846–7 Sterling $14.95

• Ray Smith
THE ARTIST'S HANDBOOK
Techniques include etching, scratchboard, and painting
0–394–55585–6 Knopf $24.95

• Studio D
PICTURE PUZZLES FOR THE SUPER SMART
Logic and spatial skills are put to the test with an intriguing choice of answers
0–8069–7952–6 Sterling pb $4.95

• Stephen Tchudi
SODA POPPERY: The History of Soft Drinks in America with Recipes for Making and Using Soft Drinks Plus Easy Science Experiments
0–684–18488–5 Scribners $13.95

• Phil Wiswell
KID'S GAMES: Traditional Indoor and Outdoor Activities for Children of All Ages
Guessing games, card games, board games, word, number and memory games, games involving running, jumping, and music
0–385–23405–8 Doubleday pb $12.95

GROWTH AND DEVELOPMENT

• Ruth Bell & others
CHANGING BODIES, CHANGING LIVES: A Book for Teens on Sex and Relationships
0–394–50304–X Random House $17.95
0–394–75541–3 Random House pb $12.95

• Judy Blume
LETTERS TO JUDY: What Your Kids Wish They Could Tell You
Confidences on parents, school life, friends, drugs, dating, growth, and development
0–399–13129–9 Putnam $17.95
0–671–62696–5 Putnam pb $4.50

• Susan Cohen
TEENAGE COMPETITION: A Survival Guide
Young adults discuss familiar forms of competition and talk about ways to survive the stresses
0–87131–487–8 Little, Brown $11.95

• Paul Dolmetsch & Gail Mauricette, editors
TEENS TALK ABOUT ALCOHOL AND ALCOHOLISM
0–385–23084–2 Doubleday pb $6.95

• Ellen Erlanger
EATING DISORDERS: A Question and Answer Book About Anorexia Nervosa and Bulimia Nervosa
0–8225–0038–8 Lerner pb $9.95

• Brent Filson
THERE'S A MONSTER IN YOUR CLOSET!
Cartoons and illustrations add to the appeal of this book about phobias
0–671–55496–4 Messner pb $9.50

• Judy Galbraith
THE GIFTED KIDS SURVIVAL GUIDE II
School survival, coping with stress, friendship vs. popularity, and other issues affecting the talented and bright
0–915–793–09–1 Free Spirit pb $9.95

• Margaret Oldroyd Hyde & Elizabeth H. Forsyth
AIDS: What Does It Mean to You?
Includes medical as well as personal information, and a technical glossary
0-8027-6699-4 Walker $12.95

• Chris-Ellyn Johanson
COCAINE: A New Epidemic
A factual presentation on the use, misuse, and abuse of cocaine
0-87754-765-3 Chelsea $17.95

• Eric W. Johnson
PEOPLE, LOVE, SEX, AND FAMILIES: Answers to Questions That Preteens Ask
0-8027-6591-2 Walker $13.95

• Gary F. Kelly
LEARNING ABOUT SEX
0-8120-2432-X Barron's pb $6.95

• Janet Kolehmainen & Sandra Handwerk
TEEN SUICIDE: A Book for Friends, Family, and Classmates
Explores the myths, cites the warning signs, and discusses the availability of help
0-8225-0037-X Lerner $9.95
0-8225-9514-1 Lerner pb $4.95

• Susan Kuklin
FIGHTING BACK
Focusing on volunteers in New York City who offer help and support to people with AIDS, this moving book shows what it is like to be part of the struggle against this disease
0-399-21621-9 Putnam $13.95

• Elaine Landau
DIFFERENT DRUMMER: Homosexuality in America
Teenagers discuss their experiences and feelings about being homosexual
0-671-55497-2 Messner $11.50

• John Langone
BOMBED, BUZZED, SMASHED. . .OR SOBER
0-316-51424-1 Little, Brown $14.95

• Saul Levine & Kathleen Wilcox
DEAR DOCTOR
A question-and-answer introduction to medical topics of interest to young adults
0-688-07094-9 Morrow $12.95
0-688-07095-7 Lothrop pb $6.95

• Jerome Z. Litt
TEEN SKIN: From Head to Toe
A unisex manual of skin care, including inexpensive remedies for common problems
0-345-32462-5 Ballantine pb $3.50

• Bonnie L. Lukes
HOW TO BE A REASONABLY THIN TEENAGE GIRL WITHOUT STARVING, LOSING YOUR FRIENDS, OR RUNNING AWAY FROM HOME
Weight loss and diet control through exercise, nutrition, and psychological means
0-689-31269-5 Atheneum $12.95

• Irma & Arthur Myers
WHY YOU FEEL DOWN AND WHAT YOU CAN DO ABOUT IT
Issues related to depression discussed by a psychotherapist
0-684-17442-1 Macmillan $12.95
0-689-71035-6 Macmillan pb $4.95

• Susan Newman
YOU CAN SAY NO TO A DRINK OR A DRUG: What Every Kid Should Know
0-399-51228-4 Putnam pb $8.95

• Alan E. Nourse
BIRTH CONTROL
Methods and recommendations for birth control for high school students
0-531-10516-4 Franklin Watts $13.95

• Wardell B. Pomeroy
Pomeroy's standard sex education texts dryly present information on dating, petting, intercourse, and physical changes. Each book ends with a question-and-answer section.
BOYS AND SEX
0-440-90753-5 Delacorte pb $3.25
GIRLS AND SEX
0-440-92904-0 Delacorte pb $3.25

• Fred Powledge
YOU'LL SURVIVE!: Late Blooming, Early Blooming, Loneliness, Klutziness, and Other Problems of Adolescence, and How to Live Through Them
0-684-18632-2 Scribners $11.95

• Gail Jones Sanchez & Mary Gerbino
OVEREATING: Let's Talk About It
0-87518-319-0 Dillon pb $9.95

• Dee Snider & Bashe Phillip
DEE SNIDER'S TEENAGE SURVIVAL GUIDE
A member of the rock group Twisted Sister talks about growing up, the search for self-identity, individualism, drugs, and alcohol
0-385-23900-9 Doubleday pb $8.95

• Joyce L. Vedral
MY PARENTS ARE DRIVING ME CRAZY
Typical problems of the under sixteens
0-345-33011-0 Ballantine pb $2.95

• Claudine G. Wirths & Mary Bowman-Kruhm
I HATE SCHOOL: How to Hang in and When to Drop Out
Advice from two psychiatrists on studying, deciding to drop out, and looking for help with personal problems
0-690-04556-5 Harper & Row $11.95

• Peter Ackroyd
MODERN GYMNASTICS
Examines vault, asymmetric bars, balance beam, and floor exercises as well as training and competitions
0-668-06462-5 Prentice-Hall pb $8.95

• Jim Arnosky
FLIES IN THE WATER, FISH IN THE AIR: A Personal Introduction to Fly Fishing
0-688-05834-5 Lothrop $11.95

• Albert Beckles
PEAK PHYSIQUE: Your Lifetime Guide to Muscle and Fitness
Bodybuilding basics, high-intensity training techniques, pro-level training principles, and advanced exercises are included along with a personal record sheet
0-8069-6574-6 Sterling pb $9.95

• Jim Benagh
BASEBALL: The Startling Stories Behind the Records
0-8069-6788-9 Sterling pb $4.95
FOOTBALL: The Startling Stories Behind the Records
0-8069-6858-3 Sterling pb $4.95

• Frank J. Berto
BICYCLING MAGAZINE'S COMPLETE GUIDE TO UPGRADING YOUR BIKE
0-87857-751-3 Rodale pb $14.95
BICYCLING'S COMPLETE GUIDE TO BICYCLE MAINTENANCE AND REPAIR
0-87857-603-7 Bicycle Magazine $19.95
0-87857-604-5 Bicycle Magazine pb $13.95

• Marc Bloom
THE RUNNER'S BIBLE: All You Need to Know to Develop a Running Program
Clothing, equipment, warm-up exercises, getting started, races, marathons, and much more
0-385-18874-9 Doubleday pb $7.95

• David A. Boehm, editor
GUINNESS SPORTS RECORD BOOK 1988–1989
Even scrabble is included in this comprehensive collection
0-8069-6811-7 Sterling $16.95
0-8069-6810-9 Sterling pb $10.95

• Merle O. Butler & Johnny W. Welton
ILLUSTRATED SOFTBALL RULES
0-8092-5521-9 Contemporary pb $5.95

• Tom Cuthbertson
ANYBODY'S BIKE BOOK
0-89815-124-4 Ten Speed pb $7.95
ANYBODY'S SKATEBOARD BOOK
Choosing a board, its assembly, downhill racing, flatland freestyle riding, repairs, and adjustments
0-913668-57-5 Ten Speed pb $3.00

• Ellington Darden
SUPER HIGH-INTENSITY BODYBUILDING
0-399-51220-9 Putnam pb $11.95

• Diagram Group
THE RULE BOOK
An authoritative guide to the history and regulation of most major sports
0–312–00677–2 St. Martin's pb $9.95

• Dan Diamond & Peter McGoey
HOCKEY, THE ILLUSTRATED HISTORY: An Official Publication of the National Hockey League
Heroes, friends, and rivals appear alongside the official summary of the sport's history
0–385–23329–9 Doubleday $19.95

• Charles Einstein
THE FIRESIDE BOOK OF BASEBALL
0–671–63812–2 Simon & Schuster pb $10.95

• Angus G. Garber
END ZONE: A Photographic Celebration of Football
Over 160 photos of equipment, the field, positioning of players, and more
0–8050–0556–0 Henry Holt $15.95

• Robert Gardner
THE YOUNG ATHLETE'S MANUAL
Nutrition, mental attitude, and exercise explored as important aspects of competition
0–671–49369–8 Messner $9.98

• Al Goldis & Rich Wolff
BREAKING INTO THE BIG LEAGUES
For athletes who believe they have major league baseball ability
0–88011–298–0 Leisure pb $10.95

• Susan Kalbfleish
JUMP! THE NEW JUMP ROPE BOOK
An illustrated book on the techniques of jumping rope
0–688–06929–0 Morrow $11.75
0–688–06930–4 Morrow pb $6.95

• Larry Kettelkamp
MODERN SPORTS SCIENCE
How computers can be used in training, and how the body functions in relation to athletic performance
0–688–05494–3 Morrow $11.75

• Jack McDonald
SOMETHING TO CHEER ABOUT: Legends From the Golden Age of Sports
Includes Babe Ruth, Ty Cobb, Joe DiMaggio, Willie Mays, Bob Mathias, and Jack Dempsey
0–15–683804–4 HBJ pb $6.95

• Robert G. Meyer
COMPLETE BOOK OF SOFTBALL: The Loonies' Guide to Playing and Enjoying the Game
0–88011–212–3 Leisure pb $10.95

• Joe Namath
FOOTBALL FOR YOUNG PLAYERS AND PARENTS
0–671–63953–6 Simon & Schuster pb $10.95

• Masatoshi Nakayama
BEST KARATE: Unsu, Sochin, Nijushiho
For advanced karate students
0–87011–734–3 Kodansha pb $11.95

• Robert Pollock
SOCCER FOR JUNIORS: A Guide for Players, Parents, and Coaches
Information on rules, tactics, equipment, injuries, and other topics
0–684–18369–2 Scribners pb $8.95

• J. Allen Queen
KARATE HANDBOOK
An introduction
0–8069–6286–0 Sterling $12.95

• Art Rust, Jr. & Edna Rust
ART RUST'S ILLUSTRATED HISTORY OF THE BLACK ATHLETE
0–385–15140–3 Doubleday pb $10.95

• Robert Schwarz, editor
JUGGLING WITH FINESSE: The Definitive Book of Juggling
Use one to ten balls, learn the proper balance, and start to perform juggling acts
Illustrated by Tuko Fujisaki
0–938981–00–5 Finesse $14.95

• Eugene A. Sloane
THE ALL NEW COMPLETE BOOK OF BICYCLING
0–671–6580–2 Simon & Schuster pb $15.95

COMPLETE BOOK OF ALL-TERRAIN BICYCLES
0–671–53233–2 Simon & Schuster pb $12.95

EUGENE A. SLOANE'S BICYCLE MAINTENANCE MANUAL
0–671–42806–3 Simon & Schuster pb $10.95

CAREERS

• Council on International Educational Exchange
WORK, STUDY, TRAVEL ABROAD 1988–1989
Topics include costs, getting there, and high school student programs
0–312–01539–9 St. Martin's pb $8.95

• Stephen & Howard Figler
ATHLETE'S GAME PLAN FOR COLLEGE AND CAREER
Choosing a college, financing your education, eligibility for college sports, job hunting techniques, dealing with recruiters, and meeting academic requirements
Foreword by Senator Bill Bradley
0–87866–266–9 Peterson's pb $9.95

• Robert W. Macdonald
EXPLORING CAREERS IN THE MILITARY
The advantages and disadvantages of military life described with candor
0–8239–0694–9 Rosen $14.95

• Carolyn Males & Roberta Feigen
LIFE AFTER HIGH SCHOOL: A Career Planning Guide
0–671–54664–3 Messner $10.50

• Rose Neufeld
EXPLORING NON-TRADITIONAL JOBS FOR WOMEN
Photographs by William Neufeld
0–8239–0698–1 Rosen $10.95

• Mary McGowan Slappery
EXPLORING MILITARY SERVICE FOR WOMEN
Information on colleges with ROTC programs, and on the requirements of all the armed services
0–8239–0693–0 Rosen $14.95

• Renee Wittenberg
OPPORTUNITIES IN CHILD CARE CAREERS
The nature of child care today, attributes and skills required, salaries, and working conditions
0–8442–6022–3 VGM Careers $10.95
0–8442–6023–1 VGM Careers pb $7.95

• John H. Woodburn
OPPORTUNITIES IN CHEMISTRY CAREERS
Discussions of genetic engineering and disease control and prevention
0–8442–6137–8 VGM Careers $10.95
0–8442–6138–6 VGM Careers pb $7.95

SCHOOL GUIDES AND GENERAL REFERENCE

• American Heritage
AMERICAN HERITAGE STUDENT'S DICTIONARY
For students aged 12 to 15
0–395–40417–7 Houghton Mifflin $11.95

• John Bartholomew
THE VIKING STUDENT WORLD ATLAS
0–670–81122–X Viking $9.95

• John Baynes
HOW MAPS ARE MADE
0–8160–1691–7 Facts On File $12.95

• Sue R. Brandt
HOW TO WRITE A REPORT
0–531–10216–5 Watts $10.50

• Marilyn Burns
THE I HATE MATHEMATICS! BOOK
0–316–11740–4 Little, Brown $14.95
0–316–11741–2 Little, Brown pb $7.95

MATH FOR SMARTY PANTS: Or Who Says Mathematicians Have Little Pig Eyes
0–316–11738–2 Little, Brown $13.95
0–316–11739–0 Little, Brown pb $7.95

• Bertha Davis
HOW TO WRITE A COMPOSITION
0–531–10042–1 Watts $10.50

• Joan Detz
YOU MEAN I HAVE TO STAND UP AND SAY SOMETHING?
Tips on staying calm, organizing material, and judging an audience
0–689–31221–0 Macmillan $12.95

• Michael W. Ecker
GETTING STARTED IN PROBLEM SOLVING AND MATH CONTESTS
Includes a bibliography and sample exam
0–531–10342–0 Watts $11.95

- Eugene Ehrlich
AMO, AMAS, AMAT AND MORE: How to Use Latin to Your Own Advantage and to the Astonishment of Others
Introduction by William F. Buckley
0–06–181249–8 Harper & Row $17.95

- Nancy Everhart
SO YOU HAVE TO WRITE A TERM PAPER!
Illustrated by Anne Canevari Green
0–531–10427–3 Watts $12.95

- Roy A. Gallant
MEMORY: How It Works and How to Improve It
0–02–736850–5 Macmillan $11.95

- Scott Gelband & others
YOUR COLLEGE APPLICATION
How to assess your strong points and weak ones, with help in gathering and presenting information
0–87447–247–4 College Board pb $9.95

- Sara Gilbert
HOW TO TAKE TESTS
0–688–02469–6 Morrow $10.25
0–688–02470–X Morrow pb $7.50

- Graphic Learning International
THE EARTHBOOK WORLD ATLAS
0–87746–100–7 Graphic Learning $65.00

CONCISE EARTHBOOK WORLD ATLAS
The same information in a smaller, much cheaper format
0–87746–101–5 Graphic Learning $12.95

- Gary R. Gruber
DR. GRUBER'S ESSENTIAL GUIDE TO TEST TAKING FOR KIDS, GRADES 6–7–8–9
0–688–06351–9 Morrow pb $7.95

- William D. Halsey
MACMILLAN DICTIONARY FOR STUDENTS
A concise dictionary; includes maps, glossary of place names, and brief biographies
0–02–761560–X Macmillan $16.95

- Jack McClintock & David Helgren
EVERYTHING IS SOMEWHERE: The Geography Quiz Book
Americans knowledge of geography has been excoriated by the press. Here's a chance to shine at it
0–688–05873–6 Morrow pb $10.95

- Merriam Webster Staff
WEBSTER'S SCHOOL DICTIONARY
0–87779–280–1 Merriam Webster $12.95

- Herbert Meyerand & Jill M. Meyer
HOW TO WRITE
Students organize information, write a first draft, and produce a properly constructed writing project. "The best" for the beginner writer—William Safire, *NY Times*
0–394–75352–6 Random House pb $4.95

- William C. Paxson
THE MENTOR GUIDE TO WRITING TERM PAPERS AND REPORTS
0–451–62612–5 Gallery pb $3.95

- Janet R. Price, Alan H. Levine & Eve Cary
THE RIGHTS OF STUDENTS: The Basic ACLU Guide to a Student's Rights
Issues relating to personal appearance, corporal punishment, sex discrimination, school records, and the right to a public education
0–8093–1423–1 Southern Illinois pb $6.95

- William H. Roberts
THE WRITER'S COMPANION: A Short Handbook
Reviews frequent writing problems, grammar, and research paper composition
0–673–39291–0 Scott-Foresman pb $14.95

- J.I. Rodale
THE SYNONYM FINDER
Updated and revised, containing over 1,000,000 synonyms
Edited by Laurence Urdang
0–446–37029–0 Warner pb $12.95

- Jane Sarnoff
WORDS?: A Book About the Origins of Everyday Words and Phrases
With delightful illustrations
0–684–16958–4 Macmillan $11.95

- Sheila Tobias
SUCCEED WITH MATH
Help for those with math anxiety
0–87447–259–8 Macmillan $12.95

- Vicki Tyler
SCHOLASTIC'S A+ GUIDE TO A BETTER VOCABULARY
Homonyms and synonyms, prefixes and suffixes, completing sentences and the basic rules of spelling
0–590–33962–1 Scholastic pb $2.25

Young Adult Fiction

- C.S. Adler
IN THIS HOUSE, SCOTT IS MY BROTHER
A daughter has a fine relationship with her widower Dad, but his taste in women is lamentable. When he remarries the new stepbrother becomes an unexpected ally
0–02–700140–7 Macmillan $10.95

THE SHELL LADY'S DAUGHTER
Fourteen-year-old Kelly has reached the age when independence must be weighed against her vociferous mother's needs
0–698–20580–4 Putnam $10.95
0–449–70095–X Fawcett pb $1.95

SPLIT SISTERS
Fourteen-year-old Jen and eleven-year-old Case find that they will need to be separated due to their parents' divorce
0–02–700380–9 Macmillan $10.95

- Vivien Alcock
THE CUCKOO SISTER
0–385–29467–0 Delacorte $14.95

TRAVELERS BY NIGHT
0–385–29406–9 Delacorte $14.95

- Louisa May Alcott
LITTLE WOMEN
In 19th-century New England, Jo, Beth, Meg, and Amy March struggle in the face of genteel poverty, keeping their spirits up and their unusually affectionate household going
0–448–11019–9 Putnam pb $9.95
0–553–21275–3 Bantam pb $3.50

- William Armstrong
SOUNDER
A sharecropper steals to feed his family and is forcibly arrested—dividing the family and injuring Sounder, the great coon dog. Set in the 19th-century South, the story shifts to the search by the sharecropper's young son for his missing father and faithful Sounder's role in the boy's odyssey. Newbery Medal 1970
0–06–020143–6 Harper & Row $11.95
0–06–440020–4 Harper & Row pb $2.95

- Christine Arnothy
I AM FIFTEEN—AND I DON'T WANT TO DIE
Christine is caught in the middle of a war-torn city
0–590–40322–2 Scholastic pb $2.50

- Isaac Asimov & others, editors
YOUNG MONSTERS
0–06–020170–3 Harper & Row $12.95
0–06–020169–X Harper & Row pb $7.95

YOUNG WITCHES AND WARLOCKS
0–06–020184–3 Harper & Row $11.95

- Avi
A PLACE CALLED UGLY
Faced with the destruction of his summer home, the hero decides to fight the developers in a story about hard choices and compromises
0–590–41621–9 Scholastic pb $2.50

SOMETIMES I THINK I HEAR MY NAME
0–394–85048–3 Pantheon $9.95

• Edith Bagnold
NATIONAL VELVET
Wishes are granted in this classic story of a skinny girl and a mixed-breed horse who train, fight, and scheme to become winners
0–671–63889–0 Pocket pb $2.75

• Betty Bates
ASK ME TOMORROW
Faced with parental expectations that he will take over the family business, a 16-year-old boy takes refuge in daydreams and escapism
0–8234–0659–8 Holiday $12.95

PICKING UP THE PIECES
0–671–53138–7 Archway pb $2.25

• Clare Bell
RATHA'S CREATURE
A story of discovery, rebellion, and exile set in prehistoric times
0–689–50262–1 Macmillan $12.95

• Judy Blume
FOREVER
0–02–711030–3 Bradbury $12.95
0–671–53225–1 Pocket pb $3.50

JUST AS LONG AS WE'RE TOGETHER
A seventh-grade girl moves to a Connecticut suburb and acquires two unconventional bosom buddies. When her home life alters she needs her new friends more than ever
0–531–05729–1 Orchard $12.95

THEN AGAIN, MAYBE I WON'T
A boy's growing up is interrupted by his parents' new emphasis on social status and his sister's budding sexuality
0–440–48659–9 Dell pb $3.25

TIGER EYES
A father's murder is followed by the bereaved family's visit to unfamiliar relatives. A confessional monologue of sadness mixed with caustic observations and the recounting of a first affair
0–02–711080–X Bradbury $10.95
0–440–98469–6 Dell pb $3.25

• Nancy Bond
A STRING ON THE HARP
When an American boy visiting Wales accidentally discovers the tuning key to the harp of Taliesin, his life is invaded by fragments of the past
0–14–032376–7 Penguin pb $5.95

THE VOYAGE BEGUN
Set on 21st-century Cape Cod riddled by pollution and energy blackouts, where the 16-year-old hero finds himself in a lonely struggle
0–689–50204–4 Macmillan $15.95

• Frank Bonham
DURANGO STREET
Los Angeles gang warfare from the 1960s, as experienced by a boy who must join a gang to survive
0–525–28950–X Dutton $12.95
0–440–92183–X Dell pb $2.75

• Bruce Books
MIDNIGHT HOUR ENCORES
Sib and her father travel around the country so she can meet her hippie mother, who abandoned her when she was born
0–06–020709–4 Harper & Row $13.95

THE MOVES MAKE THE MAN
The one black student to integrate the biggest white school in a North Carolina town meets up with its hero, the school's showcase athlete
0–06–020679–9 Harper & Row $13.95

• Robin F. Brancato
BLINDED BY THE LIGHT
0–394–93721–X Knopf $8.95

FACING UP
A close friendship between teenage boys ends in tragedy after Jep's girlfriend makes reciprocated advances to Dave
0–590–42327–4 Scholastic pb $2.75

SOMETHING LEFT TO LOSE
Three friends are committed to finding out if horoscopes tell the truth
0–394–83183–7 Knopf $6.95

SWEET BELLS JANGLED OUT OF TUNE
0–394–84809–8 Knopf $10.95
0–590–40459–8 Scholastic pb $2.50

UNEASY MONEY
To celebrate his 18th birthday Mike Bronti buys a New Jersey lottery ticket—and wins a fortune
0–394–86954–0 Knopf $11.95

WINNING
A boy wins a different kind of victory after a freak football accident leaves him paralyzed
0–394–80751–0 Knopf pb $2.95

• Robbie Branscum
THE GIRL
An exploited, motherless family in the Arkansas hills grows up battling the odds
0–06–020703–5 Harper & Row $11.50

• Sue Ellen Bridgers
HOME BEFORE DARK
After living in a battered station wagon, Stella has a place she might just call home
0–394–83299–X Bantam $10.95
0–553–27338–8 Bantam pb $2.75

• Eve Bunting
JANET HAMM NEEDS A DATE FOR THE DANCE
Her two best friends have them—and she doesn't
0–89919–408–7 Ticknor & Fields $11.95
0–553–15537–7 Bantam pb $2.75

THE WAITING GAME
Three friends—the trio is the winning force behind their high school's football team—find themselves in competition for scholarship offers
0–397–31941–X Harper & Row $12.95

• Sheila Burnford
THE INCREDIBLE JOURNEY
Separated from their owners, two dogs and a cat trek through 250 miles of dangerous Canadian wilderness to get back home
0–316–11714–5 Little, Brown $14.95
0–553–27442–2 Bantam pb $2.95

• Beverly Butler
LIGHT A SINGLE CANDLE
A girl must learn to live again when she loses her sight at 14
0–396–04709–2 Dodd, Mead $11.95
0–671–61928–4 Archway pb $2.50

• Betsy Byars
THE SUMMER OF THE SWANS
Charlie is an autistic twelve-year-old; Sara his older, protective sister. When Charlie disappears, Sarah's life changes more than she knows
0–670–68190–3 Viking $12.95
0–14–031420–2 Penguin pb $3.95

• Aidan Chambers
BREAKTIME
0–06–021256–X Harper & Row $12.95

DANCE ON MY GRAVE
0–06–091310–X Harper & Row pb $5.95

• Emily Chase
THE GIRLS OF CANBY HALL SERIES
Boarding school friends fight, make up, discuss boys, date boys, read each other's diaries—and so on.

BEST FRIENDS FOREVER
0–590–40083–5 Scholastic pb $2.25

THE BIG CRUSH
0–590–40083–5 Scholastic pb $2.25

MAKE ME A STAR
0–590–40440–7 Scholastic pb $2.25

MAKING FRIENDS
0–590–40327–3 Scholastic pb $2.25

WHO'S THE NEW GIRL?
0–590–40381–8 Scholastic pb $2.25

• Alice Childress
A HERO AIN'T NOTHIN' BUT A SANDWICH
A Harlem adolescent uses heroin regularly. His story is told in a sequence of forceful first-person narratives
0–698–20278–3 Putnam $14.95
0–380–00132–2 Avon pb $2.50

RAINBOW JORDAN
0–698–20531–6 Putnam $13.95
0–380–58974–5 Avon pb $2.95

• John Christopher
THE TRIPODS TRILOGY
A three-volume set including *The White Mountains, The City of Gold and Lead,* and *Pools of Fire*
0–02–042571–6 Macmillan $11.95

THE WHITE MOUNTAINS
In a 21st-century Europe that has regressed to the Middle Ages, villagers live in the shadow of interplanetary Tripods and undergo a surgical puberty rite
0–02–042700–X Macmillan pb $3.95

THE CITY OF GOLD AND LEAD
Further adventures involving the Tripods
0–02–718380–7 Macmillan $12.95
0–02–042701–8 Macmillan pb $3.95

THE POOL OF FIRE
Will and his free compatriots must carry out the destruction of the Master's three great cities before Tripods and Masters utterly destroy the earth
0–02–718350–5 Macmillan $12.95
0–02–042720–4 Macmillan pb $3.95

● Vera Cleaver
SWEETLY SINGS THE DONKEY
Lilly Snowe has had to fight so many battles against poverty that she is already an adult at 14
0–397–32156–2 Harper & Row $12.95
0–06–440233–9 Harper & Row pb $2.95

● Vera & Bill Cleaver
WHERE THE LILIES BLOOM
Eccentric Appalachian children survive the death of their father and subsequent deprivations by bluff and deception
0–397–31111–7 Lippincott $12.95

● Brook Cole
THE GOATS
Two outcasts survive and find inner strength
0–374–32678–9 Farrar, Straus & Giroux $11.95

● James Lincoln Collier & Christopher Collier
MY BROTHER SAM IS DEAD
In a house divided by the Civil War, Tim mediates between his father and his brother, a 17-year-old who loves war and is destroyed by it
0–02–722980–7 Macmillan $13.95
0–590–40737–6 Scholastic pb $2.50

● Susan Cooper
THE DARK IS RISING
An evocative fantasy, set in today's Britain, evokes a pre-Christian world in which humankind's guardians battle a malevolent force seeking its destruction
0–689–30317–3 Macmillan $13.95
0–689–71087–9 Macmillan pb $2.95

SILVER ON THE TREE
The three sequels to *The Dark is Rising* describe further skirmishes in the ongoing conflict between good and evil
0–689–50088–2 Macmillan $13.95
0–689–71152–2 Macmillan pb $2.95

GREENWITCH
0–689–30426–9 Macmillan $13.95
0–689–71088–7 Macmillan pb $2.95

THE GREY KING
0–689–50029–7 Macmillan $13.95
0–689–71089–5 Macmillan pb $2.95

● Robert Cormier
THE BUMBLEBEE FLIES ANYWAY
0–394–86120–5 Knopf $10.95
0–440–90871–X Dell pb $3.25

THE CHOCOLATE WAR
A shy freshman is the pawn of a powerful secret society at a Catholic prep school
0–394–82805–4 Pantheon $13.95
0–440–94459–7 Dell pb $2.95

BEYOND THE CHOCOLATE WAR
0–394–87343–2 Knopf $11.95
0–440–90580–X Dell pb $3.25

I AM THE CHEESE
0–394–83462–3 Pantheon $12.95
0–440–94060–5 Dell pb $2.95

● Gillian Cross
ON THE EDGE
0–8234–0559–1 Holiday $12.95
0–440–96666–3 Dell pb $2.75

● Maureen Daly
SEVENTEENTH SUMMER
A serious love affair, with few cliches and a believable ending
0–671–61931–4 Archway pb $2.95

● Paula Danziger
THE CAT ATE MY GYMSUIT
Overweight, discontented Marcy Lewis finds her orderly world disrupted by an unconventional young English teacher and pursues a new cause zealously
0–385–28183–8 Dell $14.95
0–440–41612–4 Dell pb $2.95

THERE'S A BAT IN BUNK 5
Marcy reappears as a counselor in training under the guidance of her beloved teacher
0–440–98631–1 Dell pb $2.95

● John Donovan
I'LL GET THERE—IT BETTER BE WORTH THE TRIP
Centers on a homosexual encounter
0–06–021718–9 Harper & Row $12.95

● Michael Ende
THE NEVERENDING STORY
A lonely boy of ten ventures into an enchanted world of unicorns, dragons, sprites, and will-o'-the-wisps
0–14–007431–7 Penguin pb $7.95

● Paula Fox
ONE-EYED CAT
Ned's act of careless cruelty alters his perception of his own life and the sacredness of others'. A subtly written book in which one comes to share his burden. A Newbery Honor Book for 1984
0–02–735540–3 Bradbury $11.95
0–440–46641–5 Dell pb $3.50

SLAVE DANCER
Imprisoned aboard a 19th-century slave ship, a young kidnapped deckhand provides the flute music for the obscene slave "dance," performed as exercise by the

shackled captives. A brutal portrait of a small but hellish world
0–02–735560–8 Bradbury $12.95
0–440–96132–7 Dell pb $2.50

● Donald R. Gallo, editor
VISIONS
Nineteen short stories by writers for young adults including Jean Davies Okimoto, Norma Fox Mazer, Ouida Sebestyen, Joan Aiken, and M.E. Kerr
0–385–29588–X Delacorte $16.95

● Nancy Garden
ANNIE ON MY MIND
0–374–30366–5 Farrar, Straus & Giroux $12.95
0–374–40413–5 Farrar, Straus & Giroux pb $3.50

● Joanne Greenberg
I NEVER PROMISED YOU A ROSE GARDEN
0–451–13747–7 NAL pb $2.95

● Bette Greene
SUMMER OF MY GERMAN SOLDIER
A twelve-year-old Jewish girl living in a backwards Arkansas town forms a destructive friendship with a young German prisoner of war. When rebellious Patty hides the enemy-turned-friend, the town's communal wrath is swift and sure
0–8037–8321–3 Dial $14.95
0–553–27247–0 Bantam pb $2.95

● Shep Greene
THE BOY WHO DRANK TOO MUCH
Parental expectations, anxiety, and addiction fill the world of an alcoholic teenager
0–670–18381–4 Viking $11.50

● Eloise Greenfield
SISTER
0–690–00497–4 Harper & Row $13.95

● Rosa Guy
AND I HEARD A BIRD SING
0–385–29563–4 Delacorte $14.95

THE DISAPPEARANCE
Acquitted of murder, a neglected boy is placed with a socially responsible middle-class family, where social tensions are underlined
0–440–92064–7 Dell pb $3.25

THE FRIENDS
0–03–007876–8 Henry Holt $10.95
0–553–27326–4 Bantam pb $2.95

NEW GUYS AROUND THE BLOCK
0–440–95888–1 Dell pb $2.95

● Lynn Hall
THE GIVER
A stifling small town is the setting for an unconsummated love affair between a young girl and a lonely teacher
0–684–18312–9 Macmillan $11.95
0–02–043290–9 Macmillan pb $3.95

● Virginia Hamilton
JUNIUS OVER FAR
Three members of a family travel to the Caribbean to reclaim a lost heritage
0–06–022194–1 Harper & Row $12.95

A LITTLE LOVE
0-399-21046-6 Putnam $12.95
0-425-08424-8 Berkley pb $2.50

M.C. HIGGINS THE GREAT
The unexpected visit of two strangers
threatens a family living in Ohio coal-
mining country
0-02-742480-4 Macmillan $14.95
0-02-043490-1 Macmillan pb $3.95

SWEET WHISPERS, BROTHER RUSH
0-399-20894-1 Putnam $10.95
0-380-64824-5 Avon pb $2.95

A WHITE ROMANCE
A young woman struggles to leave her
girlhood behind and stay free of the
prejudices and fears that surround her
0-399-21213-2 Putnam $14.95

• Ray Harrison
DEATHWATCH
0-684-18425-7 Macmillan $13.95

• Erik Christian Haugaard
THE SAMURAI'S TALE
Of warlords and poets, stable boys and
courtiers, spies and assassins and monks
0-395-34559-6 Houghton Mifflin $12.95

• S.E. Hinton
THE OUTSIDERS
Warfare along class lines begins and ends
bloodily in a memorable book
0-440-96769-4 Dell pb $2.95

RUMBLE FISH
Wildly attached to his older brother Rusty,
James apes a precocity he can't live up to.
The result is a messy round of fights and
escalating troubles
0-440-05919-4 Delacorte pb $6.95

TEX
Tex's carefree Oklahoma days are
numbered as he faces an unexpectedly
violent future
0-385-29020-9 Delacorte $14.95

THAT WAS THEN, THIS IS NOW
Two inseparable 16-year-old boys, and the
experiences and decisions they face
0-440-98652-4 Dell pb $2.95

• Laura Z. Hobson
CONSENTING ADULTS
A fictional homosexual experience told
from the boy's and his parents' viewpoint
0-446-32780-8 Warner pb $3.50

• Felice Holman
SLAKE'S LIMBO
A scrawny, bruised boy takes refuge in the
New York City subway and lives a
hundred days underground
0-684-13926-X Macmillan $12.95
0-689-71066-6 Macmillan pb $3.95

THE WILD CHILDREN
Finding his family gone, the orphaned
Alex starts on a journey that leads him into
the midst of *bezprizorni,* the "wild
children," as the Soviet authorities call
them
0-684-17970-9 Macmillan $12.95

• Irene Hunt
ACROSS FIVE APRILS
Rooted in Kentucky, living in southern
Illinois, Jethro's family doesn't know where
its loyalties lie but is inevitably caught up
in the Civil War. A Newbery Honor Book
0-441-00319-2 Ace pb $2.50

• Stephen Kaufman
**DOES ANYONE HERE KNOW THE WAY
TO THIRTEEN?**
Apprehension turns to self-discovery as a
boy goes through a rite of passage
0-395-35974-0 Houghton Mifflin $11.95

• M.E. Kerr
DINKY HOCKER SHOOTS SMACK!
A witty and touching account of two boys,
two girls, and their relatives living in New
York City in the mercurial early 1970s
0-06-023151-3 Harper & Row $12.95

FELL
John Fell is the new student at elite
Gardner School, but it is not up to him to
keep his name or his hold on a former life
0-06-023267-6 Harper & Row $11.95

HIM SHE LOVES?
0-06-023238-2 Harper & Row $12.95
0-425-09763-3 Berkley pb $2.95

IS THAT YOU, MISS BLUE?
0-553-22767-X Bantam pb $2.25

NIGHT KITES
Two people pay a high price for not fitting
in
0-06-023253-6 Harper & Row $11.50
0-694-05616-2 Harper & Row pb $2.75

• Norma Klein
ANGEL FACE
Family turmoil described by the author of
Mom and The Wolf Man and Me
0-670-12517-2 Viking $13.95
0-449-44504-6 Fawcett pb $2.95

BIZOU
A 13-year-old French girl comes to the
United States to find family and friends
0-449-70252-9 Fawcett pb $2.50

BREAKING UP
Though the family has broken up, the
adults are still icily at war. Meanwhile the
14-year-old heroine is caught up in a first
affair
0-380-55830-0 Avon pb $2.50

• E.L. Konigsburg
THROWING SHADOWS
0-02-044140-1 Macmillan pb $3.95

• Tamela Larimar
BUCK
0-380-75172-0 Avon pb $2.50

• Kathryn Lasky
PAGEANT
A Jewish girl attends an exclusive Christian
girls' school where the Nativity pageant is
acted each year. A shepherd by default for
three years, Sarah Benjamin finally rebels—
with unforeseen consequences
0-02-751720-9 Macmillan $12.95

PRANK
Birdie Flynn, a teenager from East Boston,
struggles against a life of bigotry and
despair
0-02-751690-3 Macmillan $12.95
0-440-97144-6 Dell pb $2.75

• Madeleine L'Engle
A HOUSE LIKE A LOTUS
0-374-33385-8 Farrar, Straus & Giroux $13.95
0-440-93685-3 Dell pb $3.50

A WRINKLE IN TIME
Three children undertake a journey
through time and space in search of their
lost father
0-440-49805-8 Dell pb $3.50

These companion books to *A Wrinkle in
Time* tell of the further journeys of the
Murrys on behalf of universally beneficent
forces.

A SWIFTLY TILTING PLANET
0-440-90158-8 Dell pb $3.25

A WIND IN THE DOOR
0-440-90158-8 Dell pb $2.95

• Ursula K. Le Guin
THE EARTHSEA TRILOGY
A highly praised fantasy creation in which
magic, mythology, and wizardry provoke
adventures reminiscent of Tolkien.

A WIZARD OF EARTHSEA
0-395-27653-5 Houghton Mifflin $12.95
0-553-26250-5 Bantam pb $3.50

THE TOMBS OF ATUAN
0-553-27331-1 Bantam pb $3.50

THE FARTHEST SHORE
0-553-26847-3 Bantam pb $3.50

**VERY FAR AWAY FROM ANYWHERE
ELSE**
A contemporary love story of teenage
exiles who share in a private, believable
universe
0-553-25396-4 Bantam pb $2.50

• Myron Levoy
THREE FRIENDS
An outspoken feminist, a chess prodigy,
and an artist form an unlikely friendship
0-06-023826-7 Harper & Row $12.50

• Robert Lipsyte
THE CONTENDER
Seventeen-year-old dropout Alfred Brook
finds that getting to the top is less
important then how you get there
0-06-023920-4 Harper & Row $12.95
0-694-05602-2 Harper & Row $2.95

ONE FAT SUMMER
A comic "Crisco Kid" finds out how
terrifying and exhilarating a summer can
be
0-06-023896-8 Harper & Row $12.95

• Lois Lowry
FIND A STRANGER, SAY GOOD BYE
An adopted child blessed with intelligence,
good looks, and an affectionate adopted
family sets out to find her natural parents,
aided by only a few scanty clues
0-395-26459-6 Houghton Mifflin $10.95
0-671-64191-3 Pocket pb $2.75

**THE ONE HUNDREDTH THING
ABOUT CAROLINE**
0-440-46625-3 Yearling pb $2.95

RABBLE STARKEY
0-395-43607-9 Houghton Mifflin $12.95
0-440-40056-2 Dell pb $3.25

A SUMMER TO DIE
An account of two girls, one growing up and exploring life, the other dying of leukemia
0–553–27395–7 Bantam pb $2.95

● Margaret Mahy
THE CATALOGUE OF THE UNIVERSE
0–689–50391–1 Macmillan $11.95
0–590–42318–5 Scholastic pb $2.75

THE CHANGEOVER
A New Zealand girl acquires supernatural abilities through her intimacy with a family of witches, but must fight off demonic possession
0–689–50303–2 Macmillan $12.95
0–590–41289–2 Scholastic pb $2.50

THE TRICKSTERS
The story of a warm New Zealand Christmas, a large, intellectual family, and an apparition that can't be explained
0–689–50400–4 Macmillan $13.95
0–590–41513–1 Scholastic pb $2.95

● Sharon Bell Mathis
TEACUP FULL OF ROSES
A black teenager tries to keep his family together
0–14–032328–7 Penguin pb $3.95

● Norma Fox Mazer
A, MY NAME IS AMI
0–590–42433–5 Scholastic pb $2.50

AFTER THE RAIN
Newbery Honor Book 1988
0–688–06867–7 Morrow $11.95

B, MY NAME IS BUNNY
Two 13-year-old girls pledge eternal loyalty in this slice-of-life story about a seesaw friendship
0–590–40930–1 Scholastic $12.95
0–590–40055–X Scholastic pb $2.50

UP IN SETH'S ROOM
0–385–29058–6 Delacorte $13.95
0–440–99190–0 Dell pb $2.95

● Carolyn Meyer
DENNY'S TAPES
The child of interracial parents discovers his past
0–689–50413–6 Macmillan $12.95

● L.M. Montgomery
ANNE OF AVONLEA
0–553–21314–8 Bantam pb $2.95

ANNE OF GREEN GABLES
An orphan is sent to a surly farm family and proves her worth. An American classic
0–448–06030–2 Putnam $12.95
0–451–52113–7 NAL pb $2.50

● Barbara Morgenroth
IN REAL LIFE, I'M JUST KATE
Soap opera actress Kate Rafferty leads the life daydreams are built on—but wants to give it up just the same
0–689–30851–5 Macmillan $9.95

● Walter Dean Myers
FALLEN ANGELS
Seventeen-year-old Richard Perry can't afford college, and street life is harsh. The fictional account of a black conscript's tour of duty in Vietnam
0–590–40942–5 Scholastic $12.95

HOOPS
Seventeen-year-old Lonnie Jackson has the talent to become a great basketball player as he struggles to make his way in a brutal world
0–385–28142–0 Delacorte $13.95

MORTON AND DIDI
0–440–95762–1 Dell pb $2.75

WON'T KNOW TILL I GET THERE
When some good kids stumble into trouble, the judge sentences them to a summer of unpaid service in an old folk's home, in a bouncy story about teenage entrepreneurship
0–670–77862–1 Viking $11.95
0–317–69636–X Penguin pb $3.95

● John Neufeld
LISA, BRIGHT AND DARK
0–87599–153–X S.G. Phillips $14.95
0–451–11983–5 NAL pb $1.95

● Scott O'Dell
ALEXANDRA
0–395–35571–0 Houghton Mifflin $12.95
0–449–70135–2 Fawcett pb $2.25

THE BLACK PEARL
In a pearling seaport off the coast of 19th-century Spanish California, the young Ramón finds that the real and the mythical frequently cross paths
0–395–06961–0 Houghton Mifflin $13.95

CARLOTA
A violent incident throws the heroine's life into confusion and liberates her from her autocratic inheritance
0–395–25487–6 Houghton Mifflin $12.95

THE SERPENT NEVER SLEEPS: A Novel of Jamestown and Pocahontas
Serena Lynn sets sail on the *Sea Ventures*, meets Pocahontas, and plays an important part in the young Jamestown colony
0–395–44242–7 Houghton Mifflin $15.95

SING DOWN THE MOON
0–395–10919–1 Houghton Mifflin $12.95
0–440–97975–7 Dell pb $2.75

● Zibby Oneal
A FORMAL FEELING
An academic family survives a death by making adjustments that the father and brother approve of but that appall the grieving, motherless daughter
0–670–32488–4 Viking $12.95
0–449–70181–6 Fawcett pb $2.25

● Katherine Paterson
JACOB I HAVE LOVED
A beautifully written novel about love and envy between sisters, set in a fascinating and difficult community of crabbers on an island in the Chesapeake Bay
0–690–04078–4 Crowell $12.95
0–380–56499–8 Avon pb $2.95

THE LANGUAGE OF GOLDFISH
People in Northport do not have crazy children, but Carrie is swept up by a force stronger than her mother's social pretensions
0–670–41785–8 Viking $13.95

● Richard Peck
GHOSTS I HAVE BEEN
0–440–42864–5 Dell pb $2.95

PRINCESS ASHLEY
0–385–29561–8 Delacorte $14.95
0–440–20206–X Dell pb $2.95

SECRETS OF THE SHOPPING MALL
0–440–98099–2 Dell pb $2.95

● Stella Pevsner
SMART KID LIKE YOU
Nina lives with her divorced mother while her father remarries. Nina is all set to distance herself from her father—but that's not how it happens
0–590–32735–6 Scholastic pb $1.95

● Marjorie Kinnan Rawlings
THE YEARLING
A classic set in the Florida countryside the author knew and loved
0–684–71878–2 Scribners $9.95
0–020–44931–3 Scribners pb $4.95

● Margaret J. Rostkowski
AFTER THE DANCING DAYS
An inexperienced 13-year-old becomes nurse and confidant at a veterans' hospital for wounded soldiers and discovers how her uncle died in the First World War
0–06–025077–1 Harper & Row $13.95
0–06–440248–7 Harper & Row pb $3.95

● Harriet M. Savitz
RUN DON'T WALK
A marathon for handicapped athletes is the goal of a paralyzed girl
0–451–14627–1 NAL pb $2.25

● Sandra Scoppetone
TRYING HARD TO HEAR YOU
One summer in a girl's life, spent learning about people and herself
0–06–025247–2 Harper & Row $13.95

● Ouida Sebestyen
IOUs
Thirteen-year-old Stowe Garrett confronts some difficult decisions when he finds out his grandfather is dying
0–316–77933–4 Little, Brown $14.95

WORDS BY HEART
At the turn of the century a black girl wins local recognition and a Bible-quoting contest, but her success puts her in risky circumstances
0–316–77931–8 Little, Brown $13.95
0–553–27179–2 Bantam pb $2.95

- Ntozake Shange
BETSEY BROWN
Racial integration as experienced by a middle-class St. Louis family
0–312–07728–9 St. Martin's pb $6.95

- Anne Snyder
GOODBYE, PAPER DOLL
Seventeen-year-old Rosemary Norton struggles with anorexia
0–451–15943–8 NAL pb $2.95

THE BEST THAT MONEY CAN BUY
The cocoon of wealth surrounding a 17-year-old girl rips apart after her father is accused of fraud
0–451–13593–8 NAL pb $2.50

- Carol Snyder
MEMO: To Myself When I Have a Teenage Kid
A 13-year-old girl finds out her mother wasn't so different from her after all
0–399–21087–3 Putnam pb $2.25

- Todd Strasser
FRIENDS TILL THE END
Athletic David befriends a boy dying of leukemia
0–440–92625–4 Dell pb $2.75

- Rosemary Sutcliff
DRAGON SLAYER
A retelling of Beowulf weaves together mythical events in a fine recreation of Anglo-Saxon England
0–14–030254–9 Penguin pb $3.50

- Mildred D. Taylor
ROLL OF THUNDER, HEAR MY CRY
Cassie Logan is raised by a family determined not to surrender their freedom or humanity because they are black
0–8037–7473–7 Dial $14.95
0–553–25450–2 Bantam pb $2.95

- Cynthia Voigt
BUILDING BLOCKS
A fantasy about a boy and his unappreciated father
0–689–31035–8 Macmillan $11.95
0–449–70130–1 Fawcett pb $2.95

COME A STRANGER
0–689–31289–X Macmillan $13.95

HOMECOMING
0–689–30833–7 Macmillan $13.95

DICEY'S SONG
Prematurely responsible for her siblings, Dicey pushes to get herself and the children out of hard times. Newbery Medal 1983
0–689–30944–9 Macmillan $12.95

IZZY, WILLY-NILLY
At 15, Isabel Lingaid is popular, pretty, and a cheerleader. A date's drunk-driving accident changes all of that
0–689–31202–4 Atheneum $14.95
0–449–70214–6 Fawcett pb $2.95

- Maureen C. Wartski
BOAT TO NOWHERE
0–664–32661–7 Westminster $9.95

MY BROTHER IS SPECIAL
0–451–15856–3 NAL pb $2.95

- Nancy Willard
THINGS INVISIBLE TO SEE
An accident brings Clare and Ben closer together
0–394–54058–1 Knopf $16.95
0–553–27652–2 Bantam pb $3.95

- Rita Williams-Garcia
BLUE TIGHTS
An American girl joins an African dance company and discovers her heritage
0–525–67234–6 Lodestar $12.95

- Maia Wojciechowska
TUNED OUT
A boy's first encounter with drugs
0–06–026577–9 Harper & Row $11.95

- Laurence Yep
CHILD OF THE OWL
An assimilated Chinese-American girl joins her thoroughly Chinese grandmother in a tiny San Francisco apartment
0–06–026743–7 Harper & Row $12.95

- Paul Zindel
CONFESSIONS OF A TEENAGE BABOON
Overstuffed with odd characters, this account of a boy's violent coming of age was written by the Pulitzer Prize-winning playwright
0–06–026844–1 Harper & Row $12.95
0–553–27190–3 Bantam pb $2.95

THE GIRL WHO WANTED A BOY: A Story of First Love
0–06–026867–0 Harper & Row $12.95
0–553–26486–9 Bantam pb $2.75

HARRY AND HORTENSE AT HORMONE HIGH
0–06–026864–6 Harper & Row $12.95
0–553–25175–9 Bantam pb $2.95

MY DARLING, MY HAMBURGER
0–06–026824–7 Harper & Row $12.95
0–553–27324–8 Bantam pb $2.95

THE PIGMAN
0–06–026827–1 Harper & Row $13.95
0–553–26321–8 Bantam pb $2.95

THE UNDERTAKER'S GONE BANANAS
0–06–026846–8 Harper & Row $12.95
0–553–27189–X Bantam pb $2.95

PART 6

ART

Art History: General Studies

GENERAL

- Kenneth Clark
CIVILIZATION: A Personal View
0–06–010800–2 Harper & Row $24.95
0–06–090787–8 Harper & Row pb $15.95

- Horst de la Croix & Richard Tansey
GARDNER'S ART THROUGH THE AGES
An excellent two-volume survey, on a par with Janson's *History of Art*; particularly useful for its inclusion of non-Western art. Hardcover edition includes both volumes
0–15–503763–3 HBJ $43.75

Volume 1: Ancient, Medieval and Non-European Art
0–15–503764–1 HBJ pb $29.25

Volume 2: Renaissance and Modern Art
0–15–503765–X HBJ pb $29.25

- E.H. Gombrich
THE STORY OF ART
A concise, readable, and deeply learned narrative account
0–13–850066–5 Prentice-Hall pb $24.95

- Frederick Hartt
ART: A History of Painting, Sculpture and Architecture
A sweeping history, recommended for the quality and scope of its reproductions. This most recent edition includes Far Eastern art
0–8109–1884–6 Abrams $49.50

- H.W. Janson
THE HISTORY OF ART
The standard reference book; a solid, judicious, and complete guide; well illustrated
0–8109–1094–2 Abrams $45.00

REFERENCE

- Ian Chilvers & others, editors
THE OXFORD DICTIONARY OF ART
From Byzantine to Junk Art and beyond, with over 3000 entries on artists, schools, periods, techniques, critical terms, museums, and art historians
0–19–866133–9 Oxford $39.95

- James Hall
DICTIONARY OF SUBJECTS AND SYMBOLS IN ART
Introduction by Kenneth Clark
0–06–430100–1 Harper & Row pb $9.95

- Edward Lucie-Smith
THE THAMES AND HUDSON DICTIONARY OF ART TERMS
A field-guide to the arts, compact and comprehensive
0–500–20222–2 Thames & Hudson pb $9.95

- Peter & Linda Murray
THE PENGUIN DICTIONARY OF ART AND ARTISTS
The last seven centuries, with short biographies and explication of terms. "A vast amount of information, carefully detailed, abreast of current thought and scholarship and easy to read"—*TLS*
0–14–051133–4 Penguin pb $8.95

- Harold Osborne
THE OXFORD COMPANION TO ART
An excellent companion guide and a widely valued handbook
0–19–866107–X Oxford $45.00

THEMES, TECHNIQUES, AND GENRES

- Pascal Bonafoux & others
PORTRAITS OF THE ARTIST: The Self-Portrait in Painting
A thoughtful, superbly illustrated essay on the role and configuration of the self-portrait, from medieval manuscripts to the paintings of Francis Bacon
0–8478–0586–7 Rizzoli $37.50

- Catherine Brisac
A THOUSAND YEARS OF STAINED GLASS
A pictorial survey
0–385–23184–9 Doubleday $40.00

- Ladislas Bugner, general editor
THE IMAGE OF THE BLACK IN WESTERN ART
"Regardless of the complexities and ambiguities of the black image, the artistic heritage from Egyptian and Hellenistic times to the great portraits by Memling, Bosch, and Rembrandt presents an unanswerable challenge to the later racist societies that have relied on dehumanizing caricature as an instrument of social and economic oppression"—*NY Review of Books*. Volume 3 is not yet published

Volume 1: From the Pharaohs to the Fall of the Roman Empire
Text by Amadou-Nahtar M'Bow & others
0–939594–01–3 Harvard $65.00

Volume 2, Part 1: From the Early Christian Era to the Age of Discovery: From the Demonic Threat to the Incarnation of Sainthood
Text by Jean Devisse
0–939594–02–1 Harvard $70.00

Volume 2, Part 2: From the Early Christian Era to the Age of Discovery: Africans in the Christian Ordinance of the World (14th to the 16th Century)
Text by Jean Devisse & Michel Mollat
0–939594–03–X Harvard $80.00

Volume 4, Part 1: From the American Revolution to World War I: Slaves and Liberators
Text by Hugh Honour
0–939594–17–3 Harvard $50.00

Volume 4, Part 2: From the American Revolution to World War I: Black Models and White Myths
Text by Hugh Honour
0–939594–18–X Harvard $50.00

Self-portrait by Samuel F.B. Morse (National Academy of Design)

- Robert Cafritz, Lawrence Gowing & David Rosand
PLACES OF DELIGHT: The Pastoral Landscape
A recent exhibition catalog that traces the pastoral landscape from its Venetian conception through 17th-century Dutch art, Watteau, and Fragonard, and into the modern era
0–517–56979–5 Crown $45.00
0–943044–12–X Crown pb $19.95

- Kenneth Clark
LANDSCAPE INTO ART
A study by the eminent art historian that emphasizes 19th-century developments
0–06–430088–9 Harper & Row pb $12.95

THE NUDE: A Study in Ideal Form
0–691–09792–5 Princeton $73.50
0–691–01788–3 Princeton pb $16.50

- L.M. Delaisse & others
ILLUMINATED MANUSCRIPTS
A lavishly illustrated history
0–7078–0070–6 Sotheby $100.00

- Edward Lucie-Smith
EROTICISM IN WESTERN ART
A compact introduction
0–500–20121–8 Thames & Hudson pb $15.00

- Miriam Milman
TROMPE L'OEIL PAINTING: The Illusion of Reality
A beautifully illustrated, thorough exploration of its history and forms, from the frescoes of antiquity to the photo-realist paintings of the 1970s
0–8478–0817–3 Rizzoli pb $25.00

- Karen Petersen & J.F. Wilson
WOMEN ARTISTS: Recognition and Reappraisal from the Early Middle Ages to the 20th Century
0–06–090387–2 Harper & Row pb $11.50

• John Spike
ITALIAN STILL-LIFE PAINTINGS FROM THREE CENTURIES
Beautiful reproductions of little-known paintings of the 16th to 18th centuries
0–295–96127–9 Washington pb $25.00

• Charles Sterling
STILL-LIFE PAINTING FROM ANTIQUITY TO THE 20TH CENTURY
An important discussion
0–06–438530–2 Harper & Row $27.50

• Clare Sydney
FLOWER PAINTING
Focuses on Chagall, Matisse, and Picasso and their relation to the floral tradition
0–8478–0695–2 Rizzoli pb $19.95

• John Walker
PORTRAITS: 5000 Years
A lavishly illustrated study by the former director of the National Gallery
0–8109–1450–6 Abrams $55.00

Drawings

• Konrad Oberhuber
DRAWINGS DEFINED
Drawings analyzed from every angle by the foremost critic and expert
0–89835–274–6 Abaris $49.50

• Philip Rawson
DRAWING
0–8122–1251–7 Pennsylvania pb $18.95

• Jakob Rosenberg
GREAT DRAUGHTSMEN FROM PISANELLO TO PICASSO
Eight lectures on the master drawings of Leonardo, Raphael, Michelangelo, Dürer, Rembrandt, Watteau, Goya, and Degas
0–674–36200–4 Harvard $20.00

Painting

"Painting is a science, and should be pursued as an inquiry into the laws of nature. Why, then, may not landscape painting be considered a branch of natural philosophy, of which pictures are but the experiments?"— John Constable

• Jean-Luc Duval
OIL PAINTING: From Van Eyck to Rothko
A generously illustrated history
0–8478–0628–6 Rizzoli $37.50

• H.W. & Dora Janson
THE STORY OF PAINTING
0–8105–0491–8 Abrams pb $12.95

• Walter Koschatzky
THE ART OF WATERCOLOR
Analyzes and explains its technique, history, and significance; abundantly illustrated
0–89835–265–7 Abaris $59.50

• Michael Levey
FROM GIOTTO TO CEZANNE: A Concise History of Painting
A compact historical survey focusing on technical developments
0–500–20024–6 Thames & Hudson pb $9.95

• Graham Reynolds
ENGLISH WATERCOLORS
From Turner, Bonnington, and Blake to Edward Lear and Wyndham Lewis
0–941533–43–3 New Amsterdam $35.00

WATERCOLORS: A Concise History
0–500–20109–9 Thames & Hudson pb $9.95

Prints

• Fritz Eichenberg
THE ART OF THE PRINT: Masterpieces, History, Techniques
A lavishly illustrated, up-to-date account
0–8109–0103–X Abrams $55.00

• Arthur M. Hind
AN INTRODUCTION TO A HISTORY OF WOODCUT

Volume 1
0–486–20952–0 Dover pb $7.50

Volume 2
0–486–20953–9 Dover pb $7.50

• Linda Hults
THE PRINT IN THE WESTERN WORLD: An Introductory History
Abundantly illustrated and with a full glossary
0–89835–301–7 Abaris $49.50

• A. Hyatt Mayor
PRINTS AND PEOPLE: A Social History of Printed Pictures
A classic study
0–691–03958–5 Princeton $58.00
0–691–00326–2 Princeton pb $19.95

Sculpture

• Bernard Caysson & others
SCULPTURE: The Great Tradition of Sculpture from the 15th to the 18th Century
A lavishly illustrated and historically sound presentation
0–8478–0882–3 Rizzoli $85.00

• Anne Pingeot & others
SCULPTURE: The Adventure of Modern Sculpture in the 19th and 20th Centuries
Unequaled in scope, with stunning photographs
0–8478–0751–7 Rizzoli $75.00

• Herbert Read
THE ART OF SCULPTURE
0–691–01811–1 Princeton pb $11.50

Walter Neurath Memorial Lecture Series

Kenneth Clark
WHAT IS A MASTERPIECE?
A compelling approach, with reference to works of the 15th to 17th centuries
0–500–27206–9 Thames & Hudson pb $4.95

Lawrence Gowing
THE ORIGINALITY OF THOMAS JONES
0–500–55017–4 Thames & Hudson $12.95

Michael Levey
THE PAINTER DEPICTED: Painters as a Subject in Painting
Engaging thoughts on the historical development of the artist's self-representation
0–500–55013–1 Thames & Hudson $10.95

Stuart Piggott
ANTIQUITY DEPICTED: Aspects of Archaeological Illustration
Records the changing perceptions of antiquity and its artifacts
0–500–55010–7 Thames & Hudson $9.95

Robert Rosenblum
THE ROMANTIC CHILD: From Runge to Sendak
Painting as a mirror of the changing attitudes towards children in the Romantic era
0–500–55020–4 Thames & Hudson $12.95

David Wilson
THE FORGOTTEN COLLECTOR: Augustus Wollaston Franks of the British Museum
The lively and affectionate story of the Keeper of British and Medieval Antiquities and Ethnography who acquired some of the museum's greatest treasures during the 19th century
0–500–55016–6 Thames & Hudson $12.95

MUSEUMS AND COLLECTIONS

• Reinhold Baumstark
LICHTENSTEIN: The Princely Collection
0–8109–1292–9 Abrams $85.00

• Luciano Berti
THE UFFIZI
0–935748–40–7 Scala pb $14.95

• M. Calvesi
TREASURES OF THE VATICAN
0–517–62643–8 Crown $39.95

• Rudolf Distelberger & others
THE KUNSTHISTORICHE MUSEUM, VIENNA
0–935748–50–4 Scala $29.95

• Sir Lawrence Gowing
PAINTINGS IN THE LOUVRE
An extensive, sumptuously illustrated volume. "Gowing is a perfect guide. With a painter's confidence he goes right for the essence of a picture, and he has the language to capture it, strong, fluent and vivid"—John Walsh
0–55670–007–5 Stewart, Tabori & Chang $85.00

• Howard Hibbard
THE METROPOLITAN MUSEUM OF ART
Still the best overall guide to the Met, by the distinguished art historian
0–517–61201–1 Crown $24.95

- Hans Hoetink, editor
THE ROYAL PICTURE GALLERY, THE MAURITSHUIS: Art Treasures of Holland
A sumptuous volume with many cherished examples of Dutch and Flemish art, housed in the The Hague
0–8109–1420–4 Abrams $145.00

- Walter Hopps, editor
THE MENIL COLLECTION: A Selection from the Paleolithic to the Modern Era
0–8109–1440–9 Abrams $49.50

- Paul Magriel & John Spike
A CONNOISSEUR'S GUIDE TO THE MET: The Best of the Metropolitan Museum in Four One-Hour Tours
A practical guide to 100 items in the Metropolitan Museum selected by the eminent art collector
0–394–74857–3 Random House pb $9.95

- John Maxon
THE ART INSTITUTE OF CHICAGO
0–500–20104–8 Thames & Hudson pb $11.95

- Emile Meijer
THE RIJKSMUSEUM
0–935748–63–6 Scala pb $15.95

- David Lawrence Morton
THE TREASURY OF SAN MARCO, VENICE
0–8109–1684–3 Abrams $60.00

- Alfonso Pérez Sánchez & others
THE PRADO
0–935748–75–X Scala $29.95

- Theodore Stebbins & Peter Sutton
MASTERPIECES FROM THE MUSEUM OF FINE ARTS, BOSTON
0–8109–1424–7 Abrams $35.00

- Erich Steingräber
THE ALTE PINAKOTHEK, MUNICH
0–93574--64–6 Scala pb $14.95

- John Walker
THE NATIONAL GALLERY OF ART, WASHINGTON
0–8109–1370–4 Abrams $65.00

- Michael Wilson
THE NATIONAL GALLERY
London's painting treasures
0–935748–57–1 Scala pb $14.95

- James Wood & Katharine Lee
MASTER PAINTINGS FROM THE ART INSTITUTE OF CHICAGO
European and American paintings, from the Renaissance to the 1980s
0–8212–1725–9 NY Graphic Society $34.00

COLLECTORS AND DEALERS

- Joseph Alsop
THE RARE ART TRADITION: A History of Art Collecting and its Linked Phenomena
"What we know about the art market and the history of art dealing is woefully inadequate . . . It has remained for a private scholar who is not an art historian

Honoré Daumier's "L'Amateur" (Metropolitan Museum)

by training to accomplish what we should have done a long time ago"—H.W. Janson
0–06–010091–5 Harper & Row $59.45

- S.N. Behrman
DUVEEN
The life and antics of the controversial dealer responsible for the sale of many great Old Master paintings to American collectors and museums
0–517–54628–0 Crown pb $6.95

- Cara Denison & others
DRAWINGS FROM THE COLLECTION OF MR. AND MRS. EUGENE VICTOR THAW
One of the finest contemporary collections, old masters to moderns
0–87598–082–1 Morgan Library pb $24.95

- René Gimpel
DIARY OF AN ART DEALER
Gimpel was one of the most successful dealers of the early 20th century. His memoirs offer lively portraits of Monet, Braque, and Degas
0–87663–522–2 Universe pb $12.95

- Francis Haskell
REDISCOVERIES IN ART: Some Aspects of Taste, Fashion, and Collecting in England and France
0–8014–9187–8 Cornell pb $16.95

- Christopher Hitchens
IMPERIAL SPOILS: The Curious Case of the Elgin Marbles
The history of the famous ancient Greek sculptures now at the British Museum, and a forceful argument for their return to Greece
0–8090–4189–8 Hill & Wang $19.95

- David Howarth
LORD ARUNDEL AND HIS CIRCLE
0–300–03469–5 Yale $47.50

- Gervase Jackson-Stops, editor
THE TREASURE HOUSES OF BRITAIN: 500 Years of Private Patronage and Art Collecting
The contents of the great English country houses, amassed on grand tours through Europe and selected for the exhibition held at the National Gallery in Washington
0–300–03533–0 Yale pb $29.95

• Raymond Mortimer, editor
BERNARD BERENSON: The Passionate Sightseer
Berenson was renowned as the world's foremost authority on Italian painting. This book gathers selections from his later diaries
0–500–27457–6 Thames & Hudson pb $14.95

• Ernest Samuels
BERNARD BERENSON
A recent biography covering his latter five decades. "Makes for even better reading than one might anticipate, for at the center of it all, beyond our greatest art critic, is art itself"—*NY Times*

Volume 1: The Making of a Connoisseur
0–674–06775–4 Harvard $27.50
0–674–06777–0 Harvard pb $9.95

Volume 2: The Making of a Legend
0–674–06779–7 Harvard $25.00

• Colin Simpson
ARTFUL PARTNERS: Bernard Berenson and Joseph Duveen
0–02–611330–9 Macmillan $22.50

• Charles Smith
AUCTIONS: The Social Construction of Value
A guide to the economic and social dynamics of price, value, and auction prices
0–02–929530–0 Free Press $24.95

• Francis Taylor
PIERPONT MORGAN AS COLLECTOR AND PATRON: 1837-1913
0–87598–033–3 Morgan Library pb $4.00

• John Walker
THE ARMAND HAMMER COLLECTION: Five Centuries of Masterpieces
0–8109–1069–1 Abrams $85.00

EXPERTS' CHOICE: 1000 Years in the Art Trade
A beautifully illustrated account from the former director of the National Gallery in Washington
0–941434–31–1 Stewart, Tabori & Chang $35.00

• Fran Weitzenhoffer
THE HAVEMEYERS: Impressionism Comes to America
A fascinating account of the Havemeyers' superb collection, now at the Metropolitan Museum. Filled with anecdotes about Mary Cassatt and the prominent art dealers of the time, well-illustrated with photographs and works of art
0–8109–1096–9 Abrams $39.95

ARTISTS ON ART

• Robert Goldwater & Marco Treves, editors
ARTISTS ON ART: From the 14th to the 20th Century
0–394–70900–4 Pantheon pb $9.95

• Odilon Redon
TO MYSELF: Notes on Life, Art and Artists
The journals of the French Symbolist painter noted for his delicate, mysterious watercolors
0–8076–1145–X Braziller $16.95

• Sir Joshua Reynolds
DISCOURSES ON ART
The 18th-century artist's view of the relation of genius to the classical rules, presented in its original form to the Royal Academy
0–300–02775–3 Yale pb $15.95

• Auguste Rodin
ART: Conversations with Paul Gsell
"A fascinating document of the Romantic era's way of seeing and thinking about art"—*Print Collector's Newsletter*
0–521–05887–9 California pb $7.95

• Herbert Wellington, editor
THE JOURNALS OF EUGENE DELACROIX
A selection of the artist's subtle and penetrating observations on art, music, literature, and life in mid-19th-century Paris
0–8014–9196–7 Cornell pb $14.95

• James Whistler
THE GENTLE ART OF MAKING ENEMIES
A witty memoir by the expatriate American painter, dandy, and exponent of art for art's sake
0–486–21875–9 Dover pb $6.95

THEORY AND CRITICISM

"I have generally found that persons who had studied painting least were the best judge of it."—William Hogarth

• Rudolf Arnheim
ART AND VISUAL PERCEPTION: A Psychology of the Creative Eye (The New Version)
"A book of first-rate importance . . . Many aspects of the psychology of art are for the first time given scientific basis"—Herbert Read
0–520–02327–7 California $33.00
0–520–02613–6 California pb $12.95

• Moire Barasch
THEORY OF ART FROM PLATO TO WINCKELMANN
A thorough analysis and reassessment of major trends in European art theory
0–8147–1060–3 NYU $50.00
0–8147–1061–1 NYU pb $17.50

• Michael Baxandall
PATTERNS OF INTENTION: On the Historical Explanation of Pictures
Detailed analyses of four works aimed at discovering the artist's original intention; an essential and widely acclaimed work
0–300–03465–2 Yale $25.00
0–300–03763–5 Yale pb $10.95

• John Berger
WAYS OF SEEING
A BBC television series and an engrossing collection of illustrated essays on the perception of artworks
0–14–021631–6 Penguin pb $4.95

• Anita Brookner
THE GENIUS OF THE FUTURE: Essays in French Art Criticism
By the noted British art historian and novelist
0–8014–9540–7 Cornell pb $9.95

• Norman Bryson
VISION AND PAINTING: The Logic of the Gaze
The first comprehensive treatment of art history from a structuralist viewpoint
0–300–02855–5 Yale $25.00
0–300–03583–7 Yale pb $9.95

• Norman Bryson, editor
CALLIGRAM: Essays in New Art History from France
Featuring pieces by Barthes, Baudrillard, Foucault, Kristeva, Marin, and others
0–521–35046–8 Cambridge $39.50
0–521–35927–9 Cambridge pb $12.95

• Jacques Derrida
THE TRUTH IN PAINTING
"Calling into question every certain conclusion, Derrida exposes the impossibility of all final solutions"—*NY Times*
0–226–14323–6 Chicago $49.95
0–226–14324–4 Chicago pb $19.95

• Denis Dutton, editor
THE FORGER'S ART: Forgery and the Philosophy of Art
0–521–04341–3 California $30.00
0–521–05619–1 California pb $12.95

• John Gage
GOETHE ON ART
Goethe founded two art periodicals and ran a series of annual competitions for painting; he drew enthusiastically, and his writings show him to have been a great critic of the arts
0–520–03995–5 California $37.50

• E.H. Gombrich
ART AND ILLUSION: A Study in the Psychology of Pictorial Representation
A milestone in art theory, offering a wide-ranging, highly refined, and lucid view of what Gombrich has called the equation between life and the image; abundantly and shrewdly illustrated
0–691–09785–2 Princeton $63.00
0–691–01750–6 Princeton pb $14.50

MEDITATIONS ON A HOBBY HORSE & OTHER ESSAYS ON THE THEORY OF ART
An important collection of essays and reviews of wide scope and interest
0–226–30215–6 Chicago $14.95

Daniel Halpern, editor
WRITERS ON ARTISTS
Proust on Chardin, Sartre on
Tintoretto, Huxley on El Greco,
Hemingway on Miró, and more
0–86574–339–0 North Point $22.50

• Anne Hollander
MOVING PICTURES
The traditions of Western art in which
paintings, prints, and movies depict
moments of human life. The relation
between originals and prints, between high
art and popular culture
0–394–57400–1 Knopf $29.95

• Erwin Panofsky
MEANING IN THE VISUAL ARTS
The best introduction to the master of
iconological interpretation
0–226–64551–7 Chicago pb $12.50

• Gert Schiff, editor
GERMAN ESSAYS ON ART HISTORY
An introduction to the pioneers, from
Winckelmann to Panofsky
0–8264–0308–5 Continuum $24.50
0–8264–0309–3 Continuum pb $10.95

• Lionello Venturi
HISTORY OF ART CRITICISM
A classic general and critical introduction
to the history of words about images
0–525–47123–5 Dutton pb $4.25

• Rudolf Wittkower
**ALLEGORY AND THE MIGRATION OF
SYMBOLS**
"All students of art history, and
particularly those interested in iconology,
will welcome the present collection"—
Apollo
0–500–27470–3 Thames & Hudson pb $14.95

• Richard Wollheim
ART AND ITS OBJECTS
An acclaimed work examining the
representational properties of art from the
point of view of aesthetics
0–521–22898–0 Cambridge $32.50
0–521–29706–0 Cambridge pb $13.95

PAINTING AS AN ART
An important contribution to our
understanding of how pictures are made;
well illustrated
0–691–09964–2 Princeton $45.00

Prehistoric Art

André Leroi-Gourhan
**THE DAWN OF EUROPEAN ART: An
Introduction to Paleolithic Cave
Painting**
"It is certain that some of our
paleolithic men achieved a mastery of
form in engraving and painting which
implies the existence of a great number
of opportunities to practise it . . . Was
[the artist], at the same time the author
of the decoration and a participant in
the esoteric knowledge, seen as a priest,
a sort of shaman?"
0–521–24459–5 Cambridge $29.95

Mario Ruspoli
**THE CAVE OF LASCAUX: The Final
Photographs**
The famous prehistoric cave paintings
in France photographed before they
were closed to the public
0–8109–1267–8 Abrams $49.50

N.K. Sandars
PREHISTORIC ART IN EUROPE
0–14–056130–7 Penguin pb $18.95

Ann Sieveking
THE CAVE ARTISTS
0–500–02092–2 Thames & Hudson $19.95

Art of Egypt and the Ancient Near East

EGYPT

"Egyptian civilization has long been regarded as the most rigid and conservative ever. Plato said that Egyptian art had
not changed in 10,000 years . . . The basic
pattern of Egyptian institutions, beliefs, and
artistic ideas was formed during the first few
centuries of that vast span of years and kept
reasserting itself until the very end . . . Egyptian art alternates between conservatism and
innovation, but is never static. Some of its
great achievements had a decisive influence
on Greek and Roman art, and thus we can
still feel ourselves linked to the Egypt of
5000 years ago by a continuous, living
tradition."—H.W. Janson, *The History of Art*

• Cyril Aldred
EGYPTIAN ART
Three thousand years of architecture,
painting and sculpture, and their political
and social setting
0–500–18180–2 Thames & Hudson $19.95
0–500–20180–3 Thames & Hudson pb $9.95

• Janine Bourriau
**PHARAOHS AND MORTALS: Egyptian
Art in the Middle Kingdom**
Catalog of an important recent exhibition
held at the Fitzwilliam Museum. The only
introduction to focus on this period
0–521–35319–X Cambridge $49.50

• Jean-Pierre Corteggiani
**THE EGYPT OF THE PHARAOHS: At
the Cairo Museum**
A richly illustrated introduction
0–935748–88–1 Scala $35.00

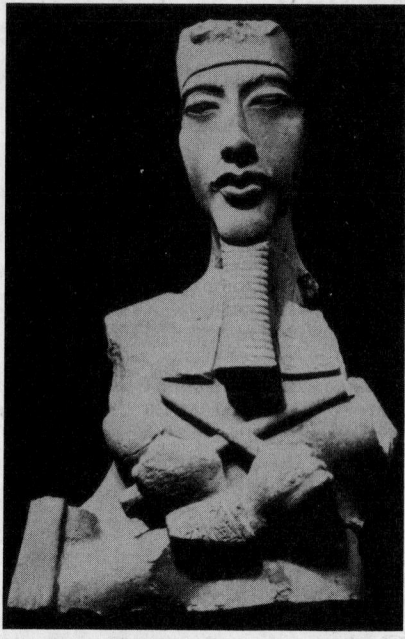
Egyptian bust, c. 15th century BC (Louvre)

• Richard Fazzini
**ANCIENT EGYPTIAN ART: The
Brooklyn Museum**
Sculpture, relief, funerary articles, and
accessories from one of the world's finest
collections. Well illustrated
0–500–23547–3 Thames & Hudson $45.00

• T.G. James & W.V. Davies
EGYPTIAN SCULPTURE
0–674–24161–4 Harvard pb $6.95

• W. Stevenson Smith
**THE ART AND ARCHITECTURE OF
ANCIENT EGYPT**
Art history combined with politics
0–14–056114–5 Penguin pb $18.95

• Donald Spanel
**THROUGH ANCIENT EYES: Egyptian
Portraiture**
An exhibition of Egyptian painting from
the collections of various American
museums
0–295–96692–0 Washington pb $17.50

THE ANCIENT NEAR EAST

• Pierre Amiet
ART OF THE ANCIENT NEAR EAST
Jean Mazenod's photographs of ancient
monuments on site in Lebanon, Syria,
Iraq; and examples of Near Eastern art in
the major museums
0–8109–0638–4 Abrams $125.00

• Henri Frankfort
**ART AND ARCHITECTURE OF THE
ANCIENT ORIENT**
A classic survey of Mesopotamian, Syrian,
Anatolian, and Persian art and architecture,
by a distinguished art historian
0–14–056107–2 Penguin pb $18.95

- Gwendolyn Leick
A DICTIONARY OF ANCIENT NEAR EASTERN ARCHITECTURE
0–415–00240–0 RC&H $49.95

- Seton Lloyd & Hans Muller
ANCIENT ARCHITECTURE: Mesopotamia, Egypt, Crete
0–8478–0692–8 Rizzoli pb $25.00

Mesopotamia

- Leo Bersani & Ulysse Dutoit
THE FORMS OF VIOLENCE: Narrative in Assyrian Art and Modern Culture
0–8052–3973–1 Schocken $19.95

- Malcolm Colledge
PARTHIAN ART
Native and foreign elements examined by the English authority
0–8014–1111–4 Cornell $39.95

- Susan Downey
MESOPOTAMIAN RELIGIOUS ARCHITECTURE: Alexander Through the Parthians
How invading powers modified indigenous art
0–691–03589–X Princeton $55.00

- Julian Reade
ASSYRIAN SCULPTURE
Wall reliefs and three-dimensional sculpture
0–674–05016–9 Harvard pb $6.95

- Harvey Weiss
EBLA TO DAMASCUS: Art and Archaeology of Ancient Syria
One of the few surveys of Syrian archaeology in English
0–86528–029–0 Smithsonian pb $27.50

Ancient Persia

▶ **See also Islamic Art**

- Shinji Fukai
CERAMICS OF ANCIENT PERSIA
0–8348–1523–0 Weatherhill $95.00

- Prudence Harper
THE ROYAL HUNTER: Art of the Sassanian Empire
A well-illustrated exhibition catalog
0–87848–050–1 Asia Society $19.95

- P.R. Mooney
ANCIENT IRAN
A short survey of this refined culture
0–900090–23–5 Longwood pb $6.25

ANCIENT PERSIAN BRONZES IN THE ADAM COLLECTION
0–571–10216–6 Faber & Faber $36.00

Ancient Israel

- Curators of the Israel Museum
TREASURES OF THE HOLY LAND: Ancient Art from the Israel Museum
0–8109–1692–4 Abrams $39.50
0–87099–470–0 Metropolitan Museum pb $19.95

- Stanley Tigerman
THE ARCHITECTURE OF EXILE
An amply illustrated study of Old Testament temple reconstructions, from the paradise garden to Solomon's Temple and the culmination of Ezekiel's vision in the Herodian citadel
0–8478–0902–1 Rizzoli $40.00

Art of the Classical World

GREECE

- John Boardman
GREEK ART
A learned and concise survey; well illustrated
0–500–20194–3 Thames & Hudson pb $11.95

- Reynold Higgins
MINOAN AND MYCENAEAN ART
An illustrated introduction to the statuary, architecture, painting, pottery, and jewelry of the rich Bronze Age culture
0–500–20184–6 Thames & Hudson pb $9.95

- Jerome Pollitt
ART AND EXPERIENCE IN CLASSICAL GREECE
A highly acclaimed study of the visual arts of the classical period (c. 480-323 BC) that draws on philosophy, poetry, and history
0–521–27672–1 Cambridge pb $24.95

ART IN THE HELLENISTIC AGE
An interpretative history of Greek art from the death of Alexander the Great in 323 BC to the end of the 1st century BC
0–521–25712–3 Cambridge $75.00
0–521–27672–1 Cambridge pb $24.95

- Gisela Richter
A HANDBOOK OF GREEK ART
A classic: works in all media, including textiles and furniture, lucidly introduced and thoroughly illustrated
0–306–80298–8 Da Capo pb $17.95

- Martin Robertson
A SHORTER HISTORY OF GREEK ART
A well-illustrated chronological treatment from the Dark Ages through the Hellenistic period
0–521–23629–0 Cambridge $80.00
0–521–28084–2 Cambridge pb $22.95

- Susan Woodford
ART OF GREECE AND ROME
An excellent general introduction with fine illustrations
0–521–29873–3 Cambridge pb $9.95

Greek terracotta vase, 5th century BC (Getty Museum)

Vase Painting

- P.P. Betancourt
THE HISTORY OF MINOAN POTTERY
Considers a wide range of indigenous styles; with fine reproductions
0–691–03579–2 Princeton $60.00
0–691–10168–X Princeton pb $15.95

- John Boardman
ATHENIAN BLACK-FIGURE VASES
"Comprehensive and concise yet never offers less than adequate discussion in crisp, lucid prose"—*TLS*
0–500–20138–2 Thames & Hudson pb $11.95

ATHENIAN RED-FIGURE VASES: The Archaic Period
The painters, styles, and development of the vases decorated using the technique invented in Athens in the 6th century BC
0–500–20143–9 Thames & Hudson pb $11.95

- Sinclair Hood
THE ARTS IN PREHISTORIC GREECE
An amply illustrated introduction to pottery and figurines of the Bronze Age
0–14–056142–0 Penguin pb $18.95

- Joseph Noble
THE TECHNIQUES OF PAINTED ATTIC POTTERY
The definitive work on the methods of the ancient Athenian potters and vase painters, lavishly illustrated
0–500–05047–3 Thames and Hudson $45.00

- Dietrich Von Bothmer
GREEK VASE PAINTING
An excellent introduction, based on the distinguished Metropolitan Museum collection, by its curator
0–87099–488–3 Metropolitan Museum pb $7.95

Sculpture

- John Boardman
GREEK SCULPTURE: The Archaic Period
An informative handbook to works of the 8th-6th centuries BC, reviewing their public function and artistic development
0–500–18166–7 Thames & Hudson pb $19.95

GREEK SCULPTURE: The Classical Period
A comprehensive account, including masterpieces of architectural sculpture
0–500–20198–6 Thames & Hudson pb $11.95

THE PARTHENON AND ITS SCULPTURES
An extraordinary book, with stunning photographs, that includes a history of the planning and construction of the Parthenon
0–292–76498–7 Texas $39.95

• Rhys Carpenter
GREEK SCULPTURE
Focuses on the techniques of the sculptor's craft. Excellent photographs
0–226–09475–8 Chicago pb $12.95

• Pat Getz-Preziosi
EARLY CYCLADIC SCULPTURE: An Introduction
0–89236–101–8 Getty Museum pb $19.95

• Gisela Richter
THE PORTRAITS OF THE GREEKS
The gradual evolution from a generalized to an individual likeness
0–8014–1683–3 Cornell $39.50

Collections

• B.F. Cook
GREEK AND ROMAN ART IN THE BRITISH MUSEUM
All aspects of this superb collection are represented, from Cycladic to Roman antiquities, with copious black-and-white illustrations
0–8120–0903–7 Barron pb $11.95

• Christos Doumas
CYCLADIC ART: Ancient Art of the Aegean from the N.P. Goulandris Collection
0–295–96067–1 Washington pb $15.95

• Pat Getz-Preziosi
EARLY CYCLADIC ART IN NORTH AMERICAN COLLECTIONS
0–295–96552–5 Washington $55.00
0–295–96553–3 Washington pb $29.95

• Cornelius Vermeule
GREEK AND ROMAN SCULPTURE IN AMERICA: Masterpieces in Public Collections in the United States and Canada
From prehistoric Cycladic marble statuettes to late Roman portraits and sarcophagi. Splendid photographs
0–520–04324–3 California $57.50
0–520–04451–7 California pb $25.00

• Dietrich Von Bothmer & Jiri Frel
WEALTH OF THE ANCIENT WORLD: The Nelson Bunker Hunt and William Herbert Hunt Collections
A full catalog of the Hunt Collections, with an essay on collecting ancient art throughout history and special attention to sculpture, vases, and coins
0–912804–14–9 Kimbell Art Museum pb $29.95

The Etruscans

"The Etruscans learned their arts from the Greeks, they admitted Greek artists to work in Etruria and copied their techniques and patterns. It is in the deviations from their models that their character is revealed, such as in painted pottery, where they show a predilection for color, and for the more monstrous elements of the Greek animal frieze style which they sometimes elaborated in an original manner."—John Boardman, *Greek Art*

Otto Brendel
ETRUSCAN ART
A fine introduction
0–14–056143–9 Penguin pb $18.95

Sybille Haynes
ETRUSCAN BRONZES
Solid historical and stylistic background accompanied by fine reproductions
0–85667–195–9 Sotheby $160.00

Maja Sprenger & others
THE ETRUSCANS: Their History, Art and Architecture
A splendid, balanced presentation of major examples, lavishly illustrated
0–8109–0867–0 Abrams $85.00

ROME

• Bernard Andreae
THE ART OF ROME
Roman art in its political, cultural, social, religious, and economic contexts, with superlative illustrations, often reproducing entire monuments
0–8109–0626–0 Abrams $125.00

Etruscan statuette of Zeus, c. 460 BC (Getty Museum)

• George Hanfmann
ROMAN ART: A Modern Survey of the Art of Ancient Rome
A rich introduction by a leading scholar, covering major works of architecture and statuary
0–393–09222–4 Norton pb $13.95

• Martin Henig, editor
A HANDBOOK OF ROMAN ART
0–8014–1539–X Cornell $48.50
0–8014–9242–4 Cornell pb $19.95

• Donald Strong & Roger Ling
ROMAN ART
A broad survey with fine black-and-white illustrations
0–14–056139–0 Penguin pb $18.95

• Mortimer Wheeler
ROMAN ART AND ARCHITECTURE
A survey of architecture, town planning, sculpture and painting, silver, glass, pottery, and other achievements
0–500–20021–1 Thames & Hudson pb $11.95

European Art: Byzantine and Medieval

EARLY CHRISTIAN AND BYZANTINE

• John Beckwith
EARLY CHRISTIAN AND BYZANTINE ART
An accomplished survey of the dissemination of Christian ideals and art throughout the East; with extensive illustrations
0–14–056133–1 Penguin pb $18.95

• David Talbot Rice
ART OF THE BYZANTINE ERA
Emphasizes stylistic developments throughout the Byzantine Empire, including the early Christian centers in Italy and the East; amply illustrated
0–500–20004–1 Thames & Hudson pb $11.95

• Steven Runciman
BYZANTINE STYLE AND CIVILIZATION
An engaging introduction to eleven centuries of artistic production centered in Constantinople
0–14–021827–0 Penguin pb $7.95

• Otto Von Simson
SACRED FORTRESS: Byzantine Art and Statecraft in Ravenna
0–691–04038–9 Princeton $34.50
0–691–00276–2 Princeton pb $12.50

• **Kurt Weitzmann**

THE ICON: Holy Images, 6th to 14th Centuries
The icon was long considered as important as the written word by some—and worthy of destruction by many; includes exquisite color plates of painted and carved works
0–8076–0892–0 Braziller $24.95
0–8076–0893–9 Braziller pb $14.95

LATE ANTIQUE-EARLY CHRISTIAN PAINTING
0–8076–0830–0 Braziller $19.95
0–8076–0831–9 Braziller pb $11.95

MEDIEVAL ART: 600-1400

• **Robert Calkins**

MONUMENTS OF MEDIEVAL ART
A sweeping guide to the major art forms and stylistic developments, emphasizing the significance of works within their historical context
0–8014–9306–4 Cornell pb $14.95

• **Georges Duby**

HISTORY OF MEDIEVAL ART, 980-1440
A thorough survey of the main historical periods by a leading French historian
0–8478–0710–X Rizzoli $45.00

• **Henri Focillon**

THE ART OF THE WEST IN THE MIDDLE AGES
A classic analysis, with an emphasis on the architectural arts

Volume 1: Romanesque
0–8014–9191–6 Cornell pb $14.95

Volume 2: Gothic
0–8014–9192–4 Cornell pb $14.95

• **Whitney Stoddard**

ART AND ARCHITECTURE IN MEDIEVAL FRANCE
Recommended for its historic overviews and attempts to relate artistic production to the political realities of the time. Best on the Gothic period
0–06–430022–6 Harper & Row pb $17.95

• **Marilyn Stokstad**

MEDIEVAL ART
A recent study notable for covering a broad geographical range of artistic production, placing works within their social and aesthetic context. With maps, chronological table, and a glossary
0–06–438555–8 Harper & Row $45.00
0–06–430132–X Harper & Row pb $22.95

• **Paul Williamson, editor**

THE MEDIEVAL TREASURY: The Art of the Middle Ages in the Victoria & Albert Museum
A fully illustrated catalog of one of the world's best collections, with essays sensitive to the original function of the works. Emphasis on liturgical objects and stained glass
0–948107–38–3 Faber & Faber pb $14.95

Late 11th-century Spanish ivory plaque (Metropolitan Museum), from A Connoisseur's Guide to the Met *by Paul Magriel and John Spike (Random House)*

• **George Zarnecki**

ART OF THE MEDIEVAL WORLD: Architecture, Sculpture, Painting, The Sacred Arts
A sweeping survey, from the time of Constantine to the 14th century, with numerous illustrations, a chronological chart, and bibliography
0–13–047514–9 Prentice-Hall $36.95

Contemporary Sources

Cennino Cennini

THE CRAFTSMAN'S HANDBOOK
A valuable source, written by a Florentine painter around 1390; central to understanding the theory and practice of art at that time
Translated by D.V. Thompson
0–486–20054–X Dover pb $3.95

Caecilia Davis-Weyer, editor

EARLY MEDIEVAL ART, 300-1150 AD: Sources and Documents
An informative guide, ranging from theological tracts to painters' instructions
0–8020–6628–3 Toronto pb $9.95

Theresa Frisch, editor

GOTHIC ART, 1140-c.1450: Sources and Documents
The companion volume to Davis-Weyer, recently revised
0–8020–6679–8 Toronto pb $7.95

Theophilus

ON DIVERS ARTS: The Foremost Medieval Treatise on Painting, Glassmaking, and Metalwork
A unique discourse, mostly technical, with a brief commentary on the role of the medieval artist, probably written during the first half of the 12th century by a German author
Translated by John Hawthorne & Cyril Smith
0–486–23784–2 Dover pb $6.50

Early Medieval

• **Janet Backhouse**

THE GOLDEN AGE OF ANGLO-SAXON ART, 966-1066
An excellent exhibition catalog recommended as a general introduction
0–253–13326–2 Indiana $32.50
0–253–21268–5 Indiana pb $20.00

THE LINDISFARNE GOSPELS
A vivid discussion of production, techniques, text, and script, as well as earlier and contemporary works of art, with comprehensive illustrations
0–8014–1354–0 Cornell $29.95

• **John Beckwith**

EARLY MEDIEVAL ART: Carolingian, Ottonian, Romanesque
A concise, authoritative survey of the architecture, painting, sculpture, illuminations, and ivories of the three great periods of early medieval art
0–500–20019–X Thames & Hudson pb $11.95

• **Peter Brown, editor**

THE BOOK OF KELLS
With 48 color and 10 black-and-white illustrations
0–500–27192–5 Thames & Hudson pb $15.95

• **George Henderson**

FROM DURROW TO KELLS: The Insular Gospel Books
New interpretations of the miniatures in the Gospel Books, with black-and-white illustrations
0–500–23474–4 Thames & Hudson $45.00

• **Françoise Henry, editor**

THE BOOK OF KELLS
A lavish book, with 126 color and 70 black-and-white plates
0–394–49475–X Knopf $124.50

• **Ernst Kitzinger**

THE ART OF BYZANTIUM AND THE MEDIEVAL WEST: Selected Studies
A representative work on the reinterpretation of Byzantine motifs in the medieval world
0–253–31055–5 Indiana $27.50

EARLY MEDIEVAL ART
A classic, based on the British Museum collections
0–253–11884–0 Indiana $22.50

• Florentine Mutherich & J.E. Gaehde
CAROLINGIAN PAINTING
A fine introduction to the major
manuscripts of the period, with individual
commentary on the plates
0–8076–0851–3 Braziller $19.95
0–8076–0852–1 Braziller pb $11.95

• Uaininn O'Meadhra
**EARLY CHRISTIAN, VIKING AND
ROMANESQUE ART**
A well-documented survey
91–22–00270–7 Coronet pb $30.00

• Meyer Schapiro
**LATE ANTIQUE, EARLY CHRISTIAN
AND MEDIEVAL ART**
Engaging and lucid scholarly articles on
themes and works from the 8th through
the 15th centuries
0–8076–0927–7 Braziller $25.00

• David Wilson
**ANGLO-SAXON ART: From the 7th
Century to the Norman Conquest**
An important recent survey by a world
expert, with many illustrations
0–87951–976–2 Overlook $75.00

• David Wilson & Ole Klindt-Jensen
VIKING ART
A scholarly study, with black-and-white
illustrations
0–8166–0974–8 Minnesota $29.50
0–8166–0977–0 Minnesota pb $12.95

The Bayeux Tapestry

David Bernstein
**THE MYSTERY OF THE BAYEUX
TAPESTRY**
An investigation of its historical and
iconographic genesis; for all readers
0–226–04400–9 Chicago $29.95

David Wilson, editor
THE BAYEUX TAPESTRY
Scholarly essays accompany a
reproduction of the entire tapestry
0–394–54793–4 Knopf $75.00

Romanesque

• M.F. Hearn
**ROMANESQUE SCULPTURE: The
Revival of Monumental Stone Sculpture in
the 11th and 12th Centuries**
The only existing survey, with a core
bibliography
0–8014–9304–8 Cornell pb $19.50

• Meyer Schapiro
ROMANESQUE ART: Selected Papers
Clearly written, amply illustrated, and of
broad interest
0–8076–0853–X Braziller $30.00

• Hanns Swarzenski
**MONUMENTS OF ROMANESQUE ART:
The Art of Church Treasures**
Excellent illustrations of ivory, gold,
bronze, enamel, and manuscript painting

*Romanesque marble capital from late 11th-
century France depicting Daniel and the lions
(Louvre)*

in northwestern Europe from 800-1200,
with a brief introduction
0–226–78605–6 Chicago $40.00
0–226–78606–4 Chicago pb $8.95

• George Zarnecki
**ENGLISH ROMANESQUE ART, 1066-
1200**
An exhibition catalog and the only book
that covers this period fully. The essays are
organized by media, with extensive
reproductions
0–8390–0338–2 Abner Schram $29.50

Gothic

• Margaret Freeman
THE UNICORN TAPESTRIES
A complete study of the famous late
Gothic tapestries, with many comparative
illustrations
0–87099–147–7 Metropolitan Museum pb $9.95

• Louis Grodecki & Catherine Brisac
GOTHIC STAINED GLASS
A thorough and accessible compendium
with praiseworthy illustrations
0–8014–1809–7 Cornell $75.00

• Adolf Katzenellenbogen
**THE SCULPTURAL PROGRAMS OF
CHARTRES CATHEDRAL: Christ, Mary,
Ecclesia**
An erudite study of the figural sculpture of
the facade
0–393–00233–0 Norton pb $6.95

Emile Mâle
**RELIGIOUS ART IN FRANCE: A
Study of Medieval Iconography and its
Sources**
Mâle's works are central to the study of
Gothic art

Volume 1: The 12th Century
0–691–09912–X Princeton $77.50

Volume 2: The 13th Century
0–691–09913–8 Princeton $79.00

Volume 3: The Late Middle Ages
0–691–09914–6 Princeton $85.00

• Andrew Martindale
GOTHIC ART
A sensible and manageable introduction
0–500–20058–0 Thames & Hudson pb $9.95

• Millard Meiss
**FRENCH PAINTINGS IN THE TIME OF
JEAN DE BERRY: The Limbourgs and
Their Contemporaries**
Manuscript production of 14th- and 15th-
century France studied in its intellectual
context, with stunning reproductions. A
2-volume set
0–8076–0734–7 Braziller (set) $90.00

• Lucy Sandler
GOTHIC MANUSCRIPTS
An introductory essay with copious
reproductions
0–19–921037–3 Oxford $130.00

• Ellen Schultz
**GOTHIC AND RENAISSANCE ART IN
NUREMBERG, 1300-1550**
A profusely illustrated survey, ranging
from early liturgical objects through works
by Dürer
0–87099–466–2 Metropolitan Museum pb $9.95

• Marcel Thomas
**THE GOLDEN AGE: Manuscript Painting
at the Time of Jean, Duke of Berry**
0–8076–0923–4 Braziller $24.95
0–8076–0924–2 Braziller pb $12.95

• Roger Wieck
**TIME SANCTIFIED: The Book of Hours
in Medieval Art and Life**
Lively, well-illustrated discussions suitable
for all readers
0–8076–1189–1 Braziller $45.00

Crafts

• John Beckwith
**IVORY CARVINGS IN EARLY
MEDIEVAL ENGLAND**
A specialized study comprising an
annotated catalog with general essays on
ivories from the 7th through the 12th
centuries; extensive illustrations
0–19–921007–1 Oxford $54.00

• Robert Calkins
**ILLUMINATED BOOKS OF THE
MIDDLE AGES**
Focuses on the nature, use, and structure
of medieval liturgical books, with excellent
color reproductions
0–8014–1506–3 Cornell $52.50
0–8014–9377–3 Cornell pb $24.95

• Marian Campbell
MEDIEVAL ENAMELS
Enamels and goldsmith work from the
Victoria & Albert Museum, from the
Celtic period to the 15th century, with a
concise discussion of history and technique
0–88045–021–5 Stemmer House $9.95

• Christopher De Hamel
**A HISTORY OF ILLUMINATED
MANUSCRIPTS**
Discussed in terms of patronage and
intended readership. Copiously illustrated
0–87923–631–0 Godine $45.00

➤ **FOR OVERSEAS ORDERING INFORMATION, SEE PAGE 1**

- Daniel Thompson
THE MATERIALS AND TECHNIQUES OF MEDIEVAL PAINTING
Manuscripts, laboratory analyses, and information gleaned from medieval sources
Foreword by Bernard Berenson
0–486–20327–1 Dover pb $5.95

- Paul Williamson
INTRODUCTION TO MEDIEVAL IVORY CARVINGS
A solid reference work based primarily on the collection of the Victoria & Albert Museum, with numerous color reproductions
0–88045–006–1 Stemmer House $9.95

Facsimile Editions

Millard Meiss, editor
THE ROHAN MASTER
0–8076–0690–1 Braziller $80.00

THE TRES RICHES HEURES OF JEAN, DUC DE BERRY
0–8076–0512–3 Braziller $80.00
0–8076–1220–0 Braziller pb $24.95

THE VISCONTI HOURS
0–8076–0651–0 Braziller $80.00

John Plummer, editor
THE HOURS OF CATHERINE CLEVE
0–8076–0379–1 Braziller $50.00

The Rise of Italian Painting

- Eve Borsook
THE MURAL PAINTERS OF TUSCANY: From Cimabue to Andrea del Sarto
A substantial study backed by excellent images
0–19–817301–6 Oxford $165.00

- Enzo Carli
SIENESE PAINTINGS
A good introduction to the late medieval School of Siena
0–935748–25–3 Scala pb $13.95

- Bruce Cole
GIOTTO AND FLORENTINE PAINTING, 1280–1375
A basic introduction and a pleasure to read
0–06–430071–4 Harper & Row pb $9.95

- Paul Hills
THE LIGHT OF EARLY RENAISSANCE PAINTING
0–300–03617–5 Yale $32.50

- Millard Meiss
PAINTING IN FLORENCE AND SIENA AFTER THE BLACK DEATH: The Arts, Religion, and Society in the Mid-14th Century
0–691–00312–2 Princeton pb $10.95

- Alastair Smart
THE DAWN OF ITALIAN PAINTING, 1250–1400
0–8014–1124–6 Cornell $47.50

- John White
ART AND ARCHITECTURE IN ITALY, 1250–1400
The fundamental and most reliable survey of the period
0–14–056128–5 Penguin pb $18.95

Italian Artists

"Giotto obscured the fame of Cimabue, as a great light outshines a lesser. Although Cimabue may well be considered the first to have restored the art of painting, Giotto threw open the gates and showed the path to that perfection."—Giorgio Vasari

- James Stubblebine
DUCCIO DI BUONINSEGNA AND HIS SCHOOL
A two-volume portrait of the first great Sienese painter (1278-1319), whose work is influenced by the Byzantine tradition
0–691–03944–5 Princeton (set) $66.00

- John White
DUCCIO: Tuscan Art and the Medieval Workshop
0–500–09135–8 Thames & Hudson $37.50

- Andrew Laddis
TADDEO GADDI: A Critical Reappraisal and Catalogue Raisonné
Mostly black-and-white illustrations of the work of Giotto's pupil
0–8262–0382–5 Missouri $70.00

- Moshe Barasch
GIOTTO AND THE LANGUAGE OF GESTURE
0–521–32454–8 Cambridge $44.50

- Jacqueline & Maurice Guillaud
GIOTTO: The Architecture of Color
An oversize book with beautiful reproductions that imitate the texture of the frescoes
0–517–56702–4 Crown $100.00

Detail of The Crevole Master's "Madonna and Child," from Duccio di Buoninsegna and His School *by James Stubblebine (Princeton)*

European Art: The Renaissance

"The achievements of the Early Renaissance in Italy transformed in a single century not only the visual arts but the nature and purpose of art itself and the social position of the artist more radically than they had been changed in the preceding 1000 years ... The great innovators of central Italy—then, a generation later, those of northern Italy—produced a new art able to represent credibly anything the eye could see, approximating reality in form, space, and color. They infused these optical impressions of the visible world with a sense of inner structure that derived from their own researches in the sphere of proportional, perspective, and anatomical theory, perhaps even more than from their study of antiquity. On this balance between sight and structure depends the beauty of early Renaissance art."—Frederick Hartt, *Art: A History of Painting, Sculpture, Architecture*

- J.J.G. Alexander
ITALIAN RENAISSANCE ILLUMINATIONS
A new style, the predominance of classical texts, and the beginnings of private patronage are discussed and beautifully illustrated
0–8076–0863–7 Braziller $19.95
0–8076–0864–5 Braziller pb $11.95

- Francis Ames-Lewis
DRAWING IN EARLY RENAISSANCE ITALY
0–300–02551–3 Yale $47.00
0–300–02978–0 Yale pb $15.95

- Francis Ames-Lewis & Joanne Wright
DRAWING IN THE ITALIAN RENAISSANCE WORKSHOP
A recent exhibition catalog and good introduction to drawings in relation to contemporary studio practice
0–905209–31–1 Faber & Faber pb $15.95

- James Beck
ITALIAN RENAISSANCE PAINTING
Proposes a new historical framework, grouping painters by generation rather than school, and discussing them in terms of style. An innovative introduction with numerous black-and-white illustrations
0–06–430382–9 Harper & Row $30.00
0–06–430082–X Harper & Row pb $17.95

- Bernard Berenson
ITALIAN PAINTINGS OF THE RENAISSANCE
Essays by the great early critic and connoisseur on the regional schools; abundantly illustrated
0–8014–9195–9 Cornell pb $14.95

Detail of "The Flagellation of Christ" by Piero della Francesca from The Enigma of Piero *by Carlo Ginzburg (Verso)*

● André Chastel
A CHRONICLE OF ITALIAN RENAISSANCE PAINTING
An engaging collection of original documents with striking reproductions, 60 color, 140 black-and-white; perhaps the finest handbook
0–8014–1524–1 Cornell $99.50

● Keith Christiansen & others
PAINTING IN RENAISSANCE SIENA, 1420-1500
The catalog for the recent Metropolitan Museum of Art exhibition
0–8109–1473–5 Abrams $75.00
0–87099–529–4 Metropolitan Museum $45.00
0–87099–530–8 Metropolitan Museum pb $29.50

● Bruce Cole
THE RENAISSANCE ARTIST AT WORK
His methods, materials, studio practice, and social status
0–06–430902–9 Harper & Row $19.50

● Sydney Freedberg
PAINTING IN ITALY, 1500-1600
A solid introduction with numerous illustrations
0–14–056135–8 Penguin pb $18.95

● J.R. Hale, editor
A CONCISE ENCYCLOPEDIA OF THE ITALIAN RENAISSANCE
A sturdy and exhaustive illustrated reference book for the general reader
0–500–23333–0 Thames & Hudson $19.95
0–500–20191–9 Thames & Hudson pb $9.95

● Frederick Hartt
HISTORY OF ITALIAN RENAISSANCE ART: Painting, Sculpture, Architecture
The evolutionary approach; many illustrations, some in color
0–8109–1163–9 Abrams $45.00

● Rosa Letts
THE RENAISSANCE
Accessible, informative, lively, and well-illustrated
0–521–23394–1 Cambridge $24.95
0–521–29957–8 Cambridge pb $9.95

● Michael Levey
EARLY RENAISSANCE
0–14–020914–X Penguin pb $7.95

HIGH RENAISSANCE
A handy survey, with numerous illustrations
0–14–021823–8 Penguin pb $7.95

● Linda Murray
THE HIGH RENAISSANCE AND MANNERISM IN ITALY, THE NORTH, AND SPAIN, 1500-1600
A compact and complete guide; numerous illustrations
0–500–20162–5 Oxford pb $9.95

● Peter & Linda Murray
THE ART OF THE RENAISSANCE
The Renaissance as an international phenomenon; the works of Piero della Francesca, Van Eyck, Mantegna, Bellini, and Dürer figure prominently
0–500–20008–4 Thames & Hudson pb $9.95

● John Pope-Hennessey
THE PORTRAIT IN THE RENAISSANCE
Stimulating and colorful essays by the eminent art historian; with exemplary illustrations
0–691–09795–X Princeton $66.00

● Samuel Sachs, Arthur Rosenauer & others
ITALIAN RENAISSANCE SCULPTURE IN THE TIME OF DONATELLO
An exhibition catalog and the finest recent survey; with many choice illustrations
0–89558–116–7 Detroit Institute pb $22.00

● Richard Turner
THE VISION OF LANDSCAPE IN RENAISSANCE ITALY
Lively and learned essays for specialist and non-specialist alike bring the background matter of Renaissance paintings to the fore
0–691–03849–X Princeton $46.00
0–691–00307–6 Princeton pb $8.50

● Heinrich Wölfflin
CLASSIC ART: An Introduction to the Italian Renaissance
An early study in which the method of appraising individual works by formal analysis is established
0–8014–9193–2 Cornell pb $13.95

RENAISSANCE AND BAROQUE
0–8014–9046–4 Cornell pb $8.95

Theory

● Michael Baxandall
PAINTING AND EXPERIENCE IN 15th CENTURY ITALY: A Primer in the Social History of Style
Pictorial style as an aspect of social history; an excellent introduction to pictorial language, with numerous illustrations
0–19–881329–5 Oxford pb $9.95

● Bruce Cole
ITALIAN ART, 1250-1550: The Relation of Art to Life and Society
Copiously illustrated in black and white
0–06–430162–1 Harper & Row $34.50

● Creighton Gilbert, editor
RENAISSANCE ART
An anthology of classic studies, including essays by Meiss, Panofsky, and Schapiro
0–06–430033–1 Harper & Row pb $7.95

● E.H. Gombrich
STUDIES IN THE ART OF THE RENAISSANCE
Brilliant essays questioning problems of style, patronage, and taste; with fine illustrations

Volume 1: Norm and Form
0–226–30216–4 Chicago pb $14.95

Volume 2: Symbolic Images
0–226–30217–4 Chicago pb $14.95

Volume 3: The Heritage of Apelles
The role of the classical tradition in art, commendably illustrated
0–8014–1012–6 Cornell $34.50

Volume 4: New Light on Old Masters
0–226–30219–9 Chicago $45.00
0–226–30220–2 Chicago pb $17.50

● Millard Meiss
THE PAINTER'S CHOICE: Problems in the Interpretation of Renaissance Art
Illustrated essays on the interrelation of form, subject, meaning, and other aspects, including some Northern examples
0–06–430068–4 Harper & Row pb $9.95

● Erwin Panofsky
RENAISSANCES AND RENASCENCES IN WESTERN ART
Was there a Renaissance and, if so, how did it differ from medieval revivals also called renaissances?
0–06–430026–9 Harper & Row pb $9.95

Contemporary Sources

● Leon Battista Alberti
ON PAINTING
Written in Florence c. 1435, this is the first treatise on the theory of perspective and of history painting
Translated by John Spencer
0–300–00001–4 Yale pb $4.95

● Anthony Blunt, editor
ARTISTIC THEORY IN ITALY, 1450-1600
A collection of original sources showing shifts in the status and aims of artists
0–19–881050–4 Oxford pb $8.95

Engraving by Raphael Morgen after Raphael's "The Madonna of the Grand Duke," from Prints and People *by A. Hyatt Mayor (Princeton)*

• Creighton Gilbert
ITALIAN ART 1400-1500: Sources and Documents
0–13–507947–0 Prentice-Hall pb $25.00

Giorgio Vasari
THE LIVES OF THE ARTISTS
A fine translation of a landmark of art history, important both as a source book and as a work of historiography. Impresario and Michelangelo-idolater, Vasari writes candidly and engagingly
Translated by George Bull

Volume 1
Cimabue watching the young Giotto scratching his first drawings on a stone; Donatello gaping at Brunelleschi's Crucifix; Michelangelo "altering" the nose of the David to fool Soderini
0–14–044500–5 Penguin pb $5.95

Volume 2
Selected lives from the early, high, and late Renaissance
0–14–044460–2 Penguin pb $5.95

T.S.R. Boase
GIORGIO VASARI: The Man and the Book
A comprehensive study of the man himself, his life, career, friendships, influences, ideas, and his contribution to Florentine art under Cosimo I
0–691–10212–0 Princeton pb $22.50

B. Baldwin Brown
VASARI ON TECHNIQUE
Selected passages from *Lives of the Artists*
0–486–20717–X Dover pb $6.50

Perspective

• Samuel Edgerton
THE RENAISSANCE REDISCOVERY OF LINEAR PERSPECTIVE
Excellent essays on Alberti, Brunelleschi, and their antecedents explain and illustrate the keystone of early Renaissance art
0–06–430069–2 Harper & Row pb $7.95

• Michael Kubovy
THE PSYCHOLOGY OF PERSPECTIVE AND RENAISSANCE ART
"A unique study, applying for the first time the special skills of a trained perceptual psychologist to the historical facts of Renaissance art"—Samuel Edgerton
0–521–25376–4 Cambridge $39.50

• John White
THE BIRTH AND REBIRTH OF PICTORIAL SPACE
0–674–07475–0 Harvard pb $14.95

Northern Italy

• Patricia Fortini Brown
VENETIAN NARRATIVE PAINTING IN THE AGE OF CARPACCIO
Paintings for government council chambers and religious fraternities in relation to each other and to social context; beautiful reproductions
0–300–04025–3 Yale $45.00

• David Chambers & Jane Martineau
SPLENDOURS OF THE GONZAGA
Exhibition catalog of the range of art treasures produced for this Mantuan dynasty; generous color plates
0–317–30092–X Faber & Faber pb $25.00

• Michael Dummett
THE VISCONTI-SFORZA TAROT CARDS
A fine example of court art, beautifully reproduced. One of three extant packs of cards devised in 15th-century Italy
0–8076–1140–9 Braziller $30.00
0–8076–1141–7 Braziller pb $15.95

• Rona Goffen
PIETY AND PATRONAGE IN RENAISSANCE VENICE: Bellini, Titian, and Franciscans
"A fine contextual art history, impressive in its research, and highly original"—David Rosand
0–300–03455–5 Yale $45.00

• Jane Martineau & Charles Hope, editors
THE GENIUS OF VENICE, 1500-1600
An exhibition catalog recommended for its lavish coverage of painting, sculpture, drawing, and printmaking
0–8109–0985–5 Abrams $40.00

• Terisio Pignatti
THE GOLDEN CENTURY OF VENETIAN PAINTING
A superb exhibition catalog of works by virtually every great Venetian painter from Bellini to Palma Giovane, with exquisite and often full-page color reproductions
0–8076–0935–8 Braziller $30.00

• David Rosand
PAINTING IN CINQUECENTO VENICE: Titian, Veronese and Tintoretto
A valuable and far-reaching study, masterfully conceived and superbly illustrated
0–300–02626–9 Yale $55.00
0–300–03630–2 Yale pb $24.95

• David Rosand & Michelangelo Muraro
TITIAN AND THE VENETIAN WOODCUT
An exhibition catalog that reproduces and discusses a wide range of printed works
0–88397–067–8 Tuttle pb $14.95

• John Steer
VENETIAN PAINTING: A Concise History
A broad study concentrating on Renaissance works
0–500–20101–3 Thames & Hudson pb $9.95

• Hans Tietze & Erica Tietze-Conrat
THE DRAWINGS OF THE VENETIAN PAINTERS IN THE 15TH AND 16TH CENTURIES
0–87817–254–8 Hacker $90.00

• Harold Wethey
TITIAN AND HIS DRAWINGS: With Reference to Giorgione and Some Close Contemporaries
A comprehensive, finely illustrated account
0–691–04040–0 Princeton $125.00

• Johannes Wilde
VENETIAN ART FROM BELLINI TO TITIAN
"The most intelligent, well-informed, careful, and suggestive introduction to Venetian High Renaissance painting"—*Burlington*
0–19–817331–8 Oxford pb $18.95

Central Italy: Florence and Rome

• Frederick Antal
FLORENTINE PAINTING AND ITS SOCIAL BACKGROUND
Major stylistic developments as related to changing economic and social structures, with numerous black-and-white illustrations
0–674–30668–6 Harvard $19.95

• Sydney Freedberg
PAINTING OF THE HIGH RENAISSANCE IN ROME AND FLORENCE
A comprehensive 2-volume survey recently reissued
0–87817–301–3 Hacker (set) $120.00

• Martin Wackernagel
THE WORLD OF THE FLORENTINE RENAISSANCE ARTISTS: Projects and Patrons, Workshop and Art Market
A classic of art historiography; no illustrations
0–691–03966–6 Princeton $45.00
0–691–10117–5 Princeton pb $18.50

Artists
(alphabetical by subject)

"While he was in Andrea Verrocchio's shop, that master was engaged on a picture of Saint John Baptizing Jesus Christ. Leonardo painted an angel holding some vestments, and, although he was then but a youth, the angel was the best part of the picture. This caused Verrocchio never to touch color again, so much was he chagrined to be outdone by a mere child." —Giorgio Vasari

• Jacqueline & Maurice Guillard
FRA ANGELICO: The Light of the Soul
A vivid presentation of the paintings of the 15th-century Florentine master; artful reproductions
0–517–56340–1 Crown $75.00

• John Pope-Hennessey
FRA ANGELICO
A brief but masterful presentation, essentially a picture book
0–935748–23–7 Scala pb $13.95

• Achille Bonito Oliva
ARCIMBOLDO
A study of the 16th-century Milanese painter, in a deluxe edition with a lively introductory essay by Roland Barthes
0–8478–5309–8 Rizzoli $150.00

• Giles Robertson
GIOVANNI BELLINI
The standard monograph on the first great Venetian painter
0–87817–273–4 Hacker $60.00

• L.D. & Helen Ettlinger
BOTTICELLI
An introductory survey, abundantly illustrated
0–500–18156–X Thames & Hudson $19.95
0–500–20153–6 Thames & Hudson pb $9.95

• Herbert Horne
BOTTICELLI: Painter of Florence
An early classic: the "story" of Botticelli, according to the Pre-Raphaelite imagination
0–691–00323–8 Princeton pb $16.50

• Bruno Santi
BOTTICELLI
A picture book with exquisite reproductions
0–935748–41–5 Scala pb $13.95

• Benvenuto Cellini
AUTOBIOGRAPHY
A vivid picture of the Renaissance sculptor and metalsmith, and an unforgettable evocation of high life and low life in 16th-century Italy
Translated by George Bull
0–14–044049–6 Penguin pb $5.95

• John Pope-Hennessey
CELLINI
A lavish presentation of Cellini's complete works organized according to the phases in his career. Superlative photographs of all major works
0–935748–23–7 Scala pb $13.95

Michelangelo's "Ideal Head of a Woman" (British Museum)

• Diane DeGrazia
CORREGGIO AND HIS LEGACY: 16th-Century Emilian Drawings
The catalog of an important exhibition devoted to the master of sensuous form and color, compiled by an excellent scholar and extensively illustrated
0–89468–072–2 National Gallery of Art $24.95

• Keith Christansen
GENTILE DA FABRIANO
The early 15th-century painter from Venice who also worked in Rome and Florence; fine reproductions
0–8014–1360–5 Cornell $85.00

Kenneth Clark
LEONARDO DA VINCI
A classic, recently reissued with an introduction by Martin Kemp
0–670–80910–1 Viking $24.95

L.D. Ettlinger
THE COMPLETE PAINTINGS OF LEONARDO DA VINCI
A slim and handy picture book with lucid, if brief, introductory text
0–1400–8649–8 Penguin pb $10.95

Charles O'Malley & J.B. Saunders, translators
LEONARDO ON THE HUMAN BODY
Excerpts from Leonardo's writings with fine reproductions of graphic and painted works
0–486–24483–0 Dover pb $11.95

Irma Richter
THE NOTEBOOKS OF LEONARDO DA VINCI
An invaluable source that includes jests, fables, prophecies, as well as reflections on the universe, science, flight, and the arts. Selections from the complete notebooks
0–19–281538–5 Oxford pb $4.95

Jack Wasserman
LEONARDO DA VINCI
Laudable reproductions of all the major works in color, incorporated in a written survey of Leonardo's life and career
0–8109–1285–6 Abrams $19.95

• Marita Horster
ANDREA DEL CASTAGNO: Complete Edition with a Critical Catalogue
A comprehensive study, revealing the artist's brilliance
0–8014–1316–8 Cornell $85.00

• Ana Paolieri
THREE FLORENTINE PAINTERS: Andrea del Castagno, Domenico Veneziano, and Paolo Uccello
0–317–69902–4 Scala pb $13.95

• Michael Hirst
SEBASTIANO DEL PIOMBO
A member of Giorgione's circle in Venice, a close friend of Michelangelo in Rome, and Raphael's chief competition in that city. A thorough consideration of his career, with good black-and-white reproductions
0–19–817308–3 Oxford $84.00

• Carlo Ginzburg
THE ENIGMA OF PIERO
"Includes much valuable research on the involvement of Piero's probable patrons in the great political, religious and cultural events of the time"—*London Review of Books*
0–86091–904–8 Verso pb $12.95

• Jacqueline & Maurice Guillaud
PIERO DELLA FRANCESCA: Poet of Form
Piero's austere, calm lucidity won him belated recognition in the 20th century as one of the greatest Renaissance painters. Beautiful reproductions
0–517–57111–0 Crown $100.00

• Peter Murray
THE COMPLETE PAINTINGS OF PIERO DELLA FRANCESCA
0–14–008647–1 Penguin pb $10.95

• John Pope-Hennessey
LUCA DELLA ROBBIA
The definitive volume on the 15th-century Florentine master, in which all of his sculpture is illustrated and discussed in superb essays
0–8014–1256–0 Cornell $125.00

• H.W. Janson
THE SCULPTURE OF DONATELLO
The standard monograph on the first great Renaissance sculptor
0–691–03528–8 Princeton $61.50

• Ronald Lightbown
DONATELLO AND MICHELOZZO: An Artistic Partnership and its Patrons in the Early Renaissance
A two-volume set
0–19–921024–1 Oxford (set) $74.00

 IF YOU CAN'T FIND IT, LOOK IN THE INDEX

• Richard Krautheimer & Trude Krautheimer-Hess
LORENZO GHIBERTI
The standard monograph on the Florentine master of bronze reliefwork
0–691–03979–8 Princeton $95.00
0–691–00336–X Princeton pb $22.95

• Ettore Camasasca
ANDREA MANTEGNA
Beautiful reproductions set in text, covering the major works and life of the 15th-century Paduan artist
0–935748–11–3 Scala pb $13.95

• Ronald Lightbrown
MANTEGNA
A thorough, thoughtful study with 200 black-and-white photographs and 16 superb full-color plates
0–520–05658–2 California $90.00

• Bruce Cole
MASACCIO AND THE ART OF EARLY RENAISSANCE FLORENCE
0–253–12298–8 Indiana $25.00

John Gere
DRAWINGS BY MICHELANGELO FROM THE BRITISH MUSEUM
0–87598–068–6 Morgan Library pb $12.50

Frederick Hartt
MICHELANGELO
0–8109–1335–6 Abrams $19.95
MICHELANGELO'S SCULPTURE
0–8109–1305–4 Abrams $40.00

Howard Hibbard
MICHELANGELO
An excellent introduction to all areas of Michelangelo's career, with extensive illustrations
0–06–433323–X Harper & Row $20.00

Carlo Pietrangeli & others
THE SISTINE CHAPEL: The Art, the History, and the Restoration
The newly restored frescoes in all their splendor, set against a historical background provided by introductory essays
0–517–56274–X Crown $60.00

David Summers
MICHELANGELO AND THE LANGUAGE OF ART
Analyzes artistic terms and ideas as they were radically reformed by Michelangelo
0–691–03957–7 Princeton $60.00
0–691–10097–7 Princeton pb $24.00

Charles De Tolnay
MICHELANGELO: Sculptor, Painter, Architect
A one-volume condensation of the six-part survey of Michelangelo's artistic output; essential reading, well-illustrated
0–691–03876–7 Princeton $52.50
0–691–00337–8 Princeton pb $21.95

• Innis Shoemaker & Elizabeth Brown
THE ENGRAVINGS OF MARCANTONIO RAIMONDI
A good introduction to Raphael's engraver and the first master of the reproductive print
0–913689–04–1 Spencer Museum pb $18.50

Francis Ames-Lewis
THE DRAFTSMAN RAPHAEL
0–300–03501–2 Yale $35.00

James Beck
RAPHAEL
A beautifully illustrated study
0–8109–0432–2 Abrams $45.00

Richard Cocke
THE COMPLETE PAINTINGS OF RAPHAEL
0–14–009273–0 Penguin pb $10.95

L.D. & Helen Ettlinger
RAPHAEL
0–7148–2303–1 Salem House $75.00

J.A. Gere
DRAWINGS BY RAPHAEL AND HIS CIRCLE
An exhibition catalog of drawings from British and American collections
0–87598–083–X Morgan Library pb $21.95

Paul Joannides
THE DRAWINGS OF RAPHAEL: With a Complete Catalogue
0–520–05087–8 California $125.00

Richard Jones & Nicholas Penny
RAPHAEL
0–300–03061–4 Yale $45.00
0–300–04052–0 Yale pb $19.95

John Pope-Hennessey
RAPHAEL
The Wrightsman lectures given by the eminent art historian, with excellent reproductions
0–8147–0476–X NYU $50.00

• Terisio Pignatti & Francesco Valcanover
TINTORETTO
The life and works of this bold and robust Venetian painter, with 50 color plates and individual commentary
0–8109–1650–9 Abrams $45.00

• Ugo Fasolo
TITIAN
The quintessential Venetian painter, with a brief text and excellent color reproductions
0–935748–09–1 Scala pb $13.95

• David Rosand
TITIAN
A lavishly illustrated examination of the painter's technique, mimetic power, and poetic force, with an essay on his graphic work
0–8109–1654–1 Abrams $45.00

Agnolo Bronzino's "St. John the Baptist," from Circa 1600 *by S.J. Freedberg (Harvard)*

• Richard Cocke
VERONESE'S DRAWINGS: With a Catalogue Raisonné
0–8014–1732–5 Cornell $95.00

Mannerism

• Andre Chastel
THE SACK OF ROME, 1527
Vivid account of the cultural repercussions of a moment, including the spread of the mannerist style; informatively illustrated
0–691–09947–2 Princeton $45.00

• Janet Cox-Rearick
THE DRAWINGS OF PONTORMO: A Catalogue Raisonné with Notes on the Paintings
0–87817–272–6 Hacker $120.00

• Walter Friedlaender
MANNERISM AND ANTI-MANNERISM IN ITALIAN PAINTING
An important essay on the style of Pontormo, Rosso, and Parmigianino and the reaction it generated, with 50 black-and-white illustrations
0–8052–0094–0 Schocken pb $5.95

• Elizabeth Holt
MICHELANGELO AND THE MANNERISTS: The Baroque and 18th Century
A comprehensive documentary history
0–691–03997–6 Princeton $31.50
0–691–00344–0 Princeton pb $9.95

• John Shearman
MANNERISM
Considers a wide variety of works and elucidates the genesis and significance of the term "mannerism"; numerous illustrations
0–14–020808–9 Penguin pb $8.95

NORTHERN EUROPE

• Michael Baxandall
THE LIMEWOOD SCULPTORS OF RENAISSANCE GERMANY, 1475-1525
A critically acclaimed cultural study of three generations of sculptors
0–300–02423–1 Yale $75.00
0–300–02829–6 Yale pb $17.95

• Colin Eisler
EARLY NETHERLANDISH PAINTING
Masterpieces from the Thyssen-Bornemisza Collection, including works by Petrus Christus, Hans Memling, and Rogier van der Weyden, beautifully illustrated
0–85667–353–6 Sothebys $110.00

• Max Friedlaender
FROM VAN EYCK TO BRUEGEL: Early Netherlandish Painting
A standard work by the great connoisseur of Netherlandish pictures, first published in 1916
0–8014–9220–3 Cornell pb $14.95

• John Hand & others
THE AGE OF BRUEGEL: Netherlandish Drawings of the 16th Century
A lavishly illustrated catalog assembled by four renowned scholars
0–521–34196–5 Cambridge $60.00

• Thomas DaCosta Kaufmann
THE SCHOOL OF PRAGUE: Painting at the Court of Rudolph II
Mannerism under Rudolf II, its sources and influence on later Dutch developments; numerous reproductions
0–226–42727–7 Chicago $45.00

• Barbara Lane
THE ALTAR AND THE ALTARPIECE
Discusses the religious paintings of Jan van Eyck, Rogier van der Weyden, Hans Memling, and others, within the context of liturgical ritual, showing how they dramatized the Mass for worshippers
0–06–435000–2 Harper & Row pb $10.95

• Erwin Panofsky
EARLY NETHERLANDISH PAINTING: Its Origins and Character
An important text known for its discussion of perspective and disguised symbolism

Volume 1: Text
0–06–430002–1 Harper & Row pb $19.95

Volume 2: Plates
0–06–430003–X Harper & Row pb $19.95

• Ellen Schultz, editor
GOTHIC AND RENAISSANCE ART IN NUREMBERG, 1300-1500
An exhibition catalog of the varied art of Nuremberg, from liturgical objects to the works of Dürer; copiously illustrated
0–87099–466–2 Metropolitan Museum pb $9.95

• James Snyder
NORTHERN RENAISSANCE ART: Painting, Sculpture, and the Graphic Arts from 1350 to 1575
A strong survey of major, and some minor, developments, with excellent reproductions
0–8109–1081–0 Abrams $45.00

• Walter Strauss, editor
THE BOOK OF HOURS OF THE EMPEROR MAXIMILIAN THE FIRST
Decorated by Albrecht Dürer, Hans Baldung Grien, and Albrecht Altdorfer among others; printed in 1513 at Augsburg. A stunning facsimile reproduction
0–913870–01–3 Abaris $75.00

• Roy Strong
THE CULT OF ELIZABETH: Elizabethan Portraiture and Pagentry
0–520–05840–2 California $45.00
0–520–05841–0 California pb $15.95

• Ellis Waterhouse
PAINTING IN BRITAIN, 1530-1790
A vast survey and an essential reference
0–14–056101–3 Penguin pb $18.95

Artists (alphabetical by subject)

• Jacqueline & Maurice Guillaud
ALTDORFER AND FANTASTIC REALISM IN GERMAN ART
An extraordinary book with superlative reproductions
0–8478–5410–8 Rizzoli $50.00

• Walter Gibson
BOSCH
A compact survey emphasizing the iconography, literary sources, and cultural significance of the visionary Flemish painter. "Probably the best straightforward account of Bosch and his works we shall have for some time"—*TLS*
0–500–20134–X Thames & Hudson pb $11.95

• Jacqueline & Maurice Guillaud
BOSCH: The Garden of Earthly Delights
Another beautiful volume from the Guillauds, printed on onionskin, with hundreds of details of Bosch's great work
0–517–57230–3 Crown $100.00

• Carl Linfert
BOSCH
A beautifully illustrated account of Bosch's work, stressing visual impact rather than iconographic interpretation
0–8109–0043–2 Abrams $45.00

• Walter Gibson
BRUEGEL
A compact and densely illustrated critical introduction and biography of the Flemish master cherished for his charming and enigmatic peasant paintings
0–500–18159–4 Thames & Hudson $19.95
0–500–20156–0 Thames & Hudson pb $11.95

• Arthur Klein, editor
THE GRAPHIC WORLDS OF PIETER BRUEGEL: Reproducing 64 Engravings and a Woodcut after Designs by Pieter Bruegel the Elder
0–486–21132–0 Dover pb $7.95

• Wolfgang Stechow
BRUEGEL
A substantial and finely illustrated volume stressing Bruegel's humanist inclinations;

with individual commentary on over 40 color plates
0–8109–0045–9 Abrams $45.00

• Max Friedlander & Jakob Rosenberg
THE PAINTINGS OF LUCAS CRANACH
A large-format volume with many full-color plates
0–8014–1061–4 Cornell $125.00

• Willi Kurth
THE COMPLETE WOODCUTS OF ALBRECHT DURER
0–486–21097–9 Dover pb $9.95

• Erwin Panofsky
THE LIFE AND ART OF ALBRECHT DURER
"Here is the life, the times, the works of that extraordinary artist whose genius bridged the difficult transition from medieval to Renaissance, effected a union between Mediterranean and northern concepts, and met the challenge of new graphic processes with a magnificence that has never been equaled"—*Kenyon Review*
0–691–00303–3 Princeton pb $20.95

• Alistair Smith
THE COMPLETE PAINTINGS OF DURER
A slim and handy paperback recommended for its reproductions
0–14–009271–4 Penguin pb $10.95

• Walter Strauss, editor
THE COMPLETE ENGRAVINGS, ETCHINGS AND DRYPOINTS OF ALBRECHT DURER
0–486–22851–7 Dover pb $8.95

"Tymotheos" by Jan van Eyck (National Gallery, London)

TO ORDER BOOKS AS GIFTS, SEE PAGE 1

- P. Strieder
ALBRECHT DURER: Drawings, Prints, and Paintings
0–89835–057–3 Abaris $85.00

- Heinrich Wölfflin
DRAWINGS OF DURER
0–486–22352–3 Dover pb $6.95

- Dover Publications
HOLBEIN PORTRAIT DRAWINGS
0–486–24937–9 Dover pb $3.50

- W.L. Gundersheimer, editor
THE DANCE OF DEATH: 41 Woodcuts by Hans Holbein the Younger
A complete facsimile of the 1538 French edition
0–486–22804–5 Dover pb $4.50

- John Rowlands
HOLBEIN: The Paintings of Hans Holbein the Younger
An excellent account of the master of northern Renaissance portraiture
0–87923–578–0 Godine $75.00

- Robert Hughes
THE COMPLETE PAINTINGS OF THE VAN EYCKS
A picture book, with running explanatory text
0–14–009272–2 Penguin pb $10.95

European Art: Baroque and Rococo

- Germain Bazin
BAROQUE AND ROCOCO
The stylistic currents in the arts of Western Europe, from 1600 through 1760. A fast-paced illustrated survey by the Louvre curator
0–500–20018–1 Thames & Hudson pb $11.95

- Julius Held & Donald Posner
17TH AND 18TH CENTURY ART: Baroque Painting, Sculpture and Architecture
A deft, thorough survey with over 1000 illustrations in color and black-and-white, by two major scholars, covering the art of Italy, France, Spain, and the Netherlands
0–13–807339–2 Prentice-Hall $38.95

- Catherine Johnston & others
VATICAN SPLENDOUR: Masterpieces of Baroque Art
Catalog of the 1986 Canadian exhibition stressing the role of the popes and their courts in the formation of 17th-century Italian painting and other arts
0–226–56548–3 Chicago pb $29.95

- Michael Levey
PAINTING AT COURT
0–8147–4950–X NYU $45.00

Caravaggio's "The Lute Player" (Hermitage)

- John Martin
BAROQUE
An engaging search for baroque ideas, attitudes, and assumptions, as opposed to style; numerous black-and-white illustrations
0–06–430077–3 Harper & Row pb $11.95

THE BAROQUE IN ITALY

- Giuliano Briganti & others
THE AGE OF CORREGGIO AND THE CARRACCI: Emilian Painting of the 16th and 17th Centuries
Catalog for the largest and most comprehensive exhibition of Emilian painting, featuring works by Parmigianino, Guercino, Guido Reni, the Carracci, and Correggio
0–521–34019–5 Cambridge $65.00
0–89468–094–3 National Gallery pb $29.95

- Sydney Freedberg
CIRCA 1600: A Revolution of Style in Painting
An accessible account of the shift in style from mannerism to baroque, notable for its sustained attention to individual works and the careers of Annibale Carracci, Caravaggio, and Ludovico Carracci
0–674–13156–8 Harvard $25.00

- Mina Gregori & others
THE AGE OF CARAVAGGIO
The artistic context of the turn of the 17th century, within which Caravaggio worked. Distinguished essays, individual entries and fine reproductions
0–87099–380–1 Metropolitan Museum $40.00
0–87099–382–8 Metropolitan Museum pb $30.00

- Francis Haskell
PATRONS AND PAINTERS: A Study in the Relations Between Italian Art and Society in the Age of the Baroque
A social history of art
0–300–02537–8 Yale $70.00
0–300–02540–8 Yale pb $17.95

- Rudolf Wittkower
ART AND ARCHITECTURE IN ITALY, 1600-1750
A first-rate survey; composed by a master scholar of Italian painting, sculpture, and architecture
0–14–056116–1 Penguin pb $18.95

- Howard Hibbard
BERNINI
A fine brief introduction, which concentrates on Bernini's career as sculptor
0–14–020701–5 Penguin pb $7.95

- Rudolf Wittkower
GIAN LORENZO BERNINI: The Sculptor of the Roman Baroque
A complete catalog introduced by a superlative essay
0–8014–1430–X Cornell $67.50

- Howard Hibbard
CARAVAGGIO
A psychological reading of his life and work; a lucid and well-composed study
0–06–433322–1 Harper & Row $45.00

- Michael Kitson
THE COMPLETE PAINTINGS OF CARAVAGGIO
Useful for reference, with illustrations of all the works, and a survey of the painter's career
0–14–008650–1 Penguin pb $10.95

• Alfred Moir
CARAVAGGIO
Individual entries on 45 exquisite color plates, as well as a biographical essay
0–8109–0757–7 Abrams $45.00

• John Spike & others
GIUSEPPE MARIA CRESPI AND THE EMERGENCE OF GENRE PAINTING IN ITALY
The works by the most innovative Bolognese painter of the first half of the 18th century and his contemporaries, elegantly displayed in this fine exhibition catalog; 50 full page color plates
0–912804–24–6 Kimbell Art Museum $45.00
0–295965–29–0 Kimbell Art Museum pb $24.50

• Richard Spear
DOMENICHINO
A thorough and authoritative two-volume monograph, well documented with mainly black-and-white illustrations
0–300–02359–6 Yale (set) $165.00

• Mary Garrard
ARTEMISIA GENTILESCHI: The Female Hero in Italian Baroque Art
Perhaps the most important woman artist before the modern period, discussed in the first full-length study. Much is made of her unique representations of the female hero—Susanna, Judith, Lucretia, Cleopatra
0–691–04050–8 Princeton $49.50

• John Wilton Ely
THE MIND AND ART OF PIRANESI
Every aspect of Piranesi's life and work, with emphasis on his importance as a pioneer of Roman archaeology
0–500–27477–0 Thames and Hudson pb $24.95

ITALIAN ROCOCO

• Michael Levey
PAINTING IN 18TH-CENTURY VENICE
An enthusiastic account of major developments, arranged by genre; covering painters of Venetian cityscapes such as Canaletto and Guardi, with a culminating chapter on Tiepolo
0–8014–1331–1 Cornell $49.50

GIAMBATTISTA TIEPOLO: His Life and Art
A lavish presentation of the career of the great 18th-century decorative painter and purest exponent of Italian rococo; with color reproductions
0–300–03018–5 Yale $65.00

• J.G. Links
CANALETTO
0–8014–1532–2 Cornell $50.00

• Terisio Piganati
CANALETTO: Selected Drawings
0–271–00105–4 Pennsylvania State $125.00

• Charles J. Bryant
THE ART AND DRAWING OF FRANCESCO GUARDI
0–86650–138–X Gloucester Art $117.85

BAROQUE AND ROCOCO IN FRANCE

• Anthony Blunt
ART AND ARCHITECTURE IN FRANCE, 1500-1700
A good introduction, written by the authority on Poussin; stresses the Italian influence on the development of early French art
0–14–056104–8 Penguin pb $18.95

• Philip Conisbee
PAINTING IN 18TH CENTURY FRANCE
Painting of the last two reigns of the ancien régime, including work of many salon artists; organized by genre and handsomely illustrated
0–8014–1424–5 Cornell $60.00

• Christopher Wright
THE FRENCH PAINTERS OF THE 17TH CENTURY
0–8212–1611–2 NY Graphic Society $29.95

• Georges Brunel
FRANCOIS BOUCHER
The complete works, lavishly illustrated and discussed in the context of the artist's life. Boucher was not only the friend and protégé of Madame de Pompadour and a favored court painter, but also director of the Gobelins tapestry works, and a model-maker for Sèvres porcelain. His mythological scenes were originally censured on moral grounds by the critic Diderot
0–86565–064–0 Vendome $75.00

• Pierre Rosenberg & others
FRANCOIS BOUCHER, 1703-1770
Catalog of the recent retrospective exhibition, with works discussed in general essays by several scholars
0–8109–0743–7 Abrams $60.00

Jean-Baptiste Greuze's "Young Girl Mourning Her Dead Bird" (National Gallery of Scotland), from Painters and Public Life in 18th-Century Paris *by Thomas Crow (Yale)*

• Philip Conisbee
CHARDIN
An agile discussion, taking both contemporary painting and the development of art criticism as a literary genre into account; with excellent reproductions
0–8387–5091–5 Bucknell $55.00

• Pierre Rosenberg
CHARDIN
Exhibition catalog by the Louvre curator; works discussed chronologically and represented by many fine reproductions, including superb details
0–910386–49–8 Indiana pb $32.50

• Gabriel Weisberg & William Talbot
CHARDIN AND THE STILL-LIFE TRADITION IN FRANCE
Championed by Diderot, Chardin revolutionized the ranks of Academic painting. Representative still-life paintings are discussed and beautifully reproduced in this compact exhibition catalog
0–910386–51–X Indiana pb $7.95

• Marcel Roethlisberger
CLAUDE LORRAIN: The Paintings
The catalogue raisonné
0–87817–244–0 Hacker $100.00

• Diane Russell
CLAUDE LORRAIN
A fine introduction; brief discussion with high-quality reproductions
0–8076–1082–8 Braziller pb $19.95

• Hal Opperman
JEAN BAPTISTE OUDRY, 1686-1755
One of the greatest French painters of hunting, animal, and still-life subjects, particularly those with game
0–912804–11–4 Kimbell Art Museum $50.00

• Konrad Oberhuber
POUSSIN: The Early Years in Rome and the Origins of French Classicism
An exhaustive study of influences and developments during the crucial years 1622-1630; with 47 colorplates of the most important early drawings and paintings
0–55595–002–7 Hudson Hills $65.00

• Christopher Wright
POUSSIN PAINTINGS: A Catalogue Raisonné
0–87052–218–3 Hippocrene $60.00

• Donald Posner
WATTEAU
An interpretive study, covering the "Flemish Watteau" of early genre pieces through his theatrical productions and later *fêtes galantes* paintings; beautiful reproductions
0–8014–1571–3 Cornell $75.00

THE BAROQUE IN SPAIN

● Jonathan Brown & John Elliot
A PALACE FOR A KING: The Buen Retiro and the Court of Philip IV
This baroque palace outside Madrid originally housed a collection of over 800 paintings, commissioned from the likes of Velázquez, Zurbarán, Rubens, Poussin, and Claude Lorrain. Art historian and historian collaborate to portray the political and cultural life of the Spanish court
0–300–02507–6 Yale $50.00
0–300–03621–3 Yale pb $16.95

● William Jordan & Sarah Schroth
SPANISH STILL LIFE IN THE GOLDEN AGE, 1600-1650
0–8109–1508–1 Abrams $45.00

● Zahira Veliz, editor
ARTISTS' TECHNIQUES IN GOLDEN AGE SPAIN: Six Treatises in Translation, 1600-1700
An essential source-book, which includes works by Pacheco and Palomino
0–521–32007–0 Cambridge $49.50

● Jonathan Brown
MURILLO AND HIS DRAWINGS
An essay on Murillo as draughtsman followed by a catalogue raisonné; numerous superb illustrations
0–691–03916–X Princeton $47.00

● Craig Felton & William Jordan, editors
JUSEPE DE RIBERA: Lo Spagnoletto
An exhibition catalog with outstanding reproductions
0–295960–22–1 Kimbell Art Museum pb $24.95

Jonathan Brown
DIEGO DE VELAZQUEZ: Painter and Courtier
Velázquez the courtier, official of the royal household of Philip IV, in conflict with Velázquez the artist searching for a new approach to the art of painting. A stunning book by the leading English authority
0–300–03466–0 Yale $55.00

● Enrique Lafuente Ferrai
VELAZQUEZ
0–8478–0948–X Rizzoli pb $25.00

● Enriqueta Harris
VELAZQUEZ
Copious illustrations flesh out the text largely adapted from early biographies of the artist
0–8104–1526–8 Cornell $49.95

● Maurice Serullaz
VELAZQUEZ
A suggestive essay on Velázquez's complex realism, comments on his drawings, and superlative annotated illustrations individually discussed
0–8109–1712–2 Abrams $45.00

● Jonathan Brown & others
ZURBARAN
A recent exhibition catalog, compiled by a team of distinguished scholars, introducing Zurbarán's career with splendid reproductions of his major religious commissions
0–8109–1791–2 Abrams $65.00

THE NETHERLANDS: 1600-1800

● Clifford Ackley
PRINTMAKING IN THE AGE OF REMBRANDT
A thorough look at the types, techniques, and patterns of collection of 17th-century Dutch printmaking; essays followed by entries
0–87846–198–1 NY Graphic Society $70.00

● Svetlana Alpers
THE ART OF DESCRIBING: Dutch Art in the 17th Century
A highly original counterstatement to the view that Dutch imagery is saturated with symbolic meaning; a description of the visual culture within which the art of describing, as opposed to the Italian art of narrative, was produced
0–226–01512–2 Chicago $42.50
0–226–01513–0 Chicago pb $19.95

● Albert Blankert & others
GODS, SAINTS AND HEROES: Dutch Painting in the Age of Rembrandt
An exhibition catalog, presenting the most current analyses of what was the most elevated genre of the period, history painting
0–89468–039–0 National Gallery pb $14.95

● Zirka Filipczak
PICTURING ART IN ANTWERP, 1550-1700
A recent study of art depicting art, with Dutch concepts of self-representation
0–691–04047–8 Princeton $60.00

● Eugene Fromentin
THE MASTERS OF PAST TIME: Dutch and Flemish Painting from Van Eyck to Rembrandt
A classic work, first published in 1876, which contains valuable historiographic background
0–8014–9219–X Cornell pb $14.95

● R.H. Fuchs
DUTCH PAINTING
A fast-paced survey to the 20th century
0–500–18168–3 Thames & Hudson $19.95
0–500–20167–6 Thames & Hudson pb $11.95

● Bob Haak
THE GOLDEN AGE: Dutch Painters of the 17th Century
An excellent survey placing art within its historic and political context; over 1000 illustrations, many unconventional, discussed individually in great detail
0–8109–0956–1 Abrams $75.00

● Madlyn Kahr
DUTCH PAINTING IN THE 17TH CENTURY
A straightforward survey of its most prominent developments
0–06–430087–0 Harper & Row pb $11.95

● Jakob Rosenberg & others
DUTCH ART AND ARCHITECTURE: 1600-1800
Primarily concerned with the 17th century and Rembrandt, Hals, and Vermeer; with numerous black-and-white illustrations
0–14–056127–7 Penguin pb $18.95

● Simon Schama
THE EMBARRASSMENT OF RICHES: An Interpretation of Dutch Culture in the Golden Age
"A model of 'companionate' marriage between art history and social history"— Jonathan Brown
0–394–51075–5 Knopf $39.95
0–520–06147–0 California pb $15.95

● Irina Sokolova, editor
DUTCH AND FLEMISH PAINTINGS FROM THE HERMITAGE
A representative selection recently exhibited in the West, including works by Van Dyck, Jordaens, Rubens, Albert Cuyp, Gerard Dou, and Rembrandt among others. Individual entries accompany the fine reproductions
0–8109–1139–6 Metropolitan Museum $35.00
0–87099–509–X Metropolitan Museum pb $25.00

● Felice Stampfle
RUBENS AND REMBRANDT IN THEIR CENTURY
Superb collection of Flemish and Dutch drawings of the 17th century from the Pierpont Morgan Library
0–87598–069–4 Morgan Library pb $13.50

● Wolfgang Stechow
DUTCH LANDSCAPE PAINTING OF THE 17TH CENTURY
A comprehensive introduction organized by types: Panoramas, Rivers and Canals, The Sea, The Town, and so on. With nearly 400 illustrations
0–87817–268–8 Hacker $60.00
0–8014–9228–9 Cornell pb $14.95

● Peter Sutton & others
MASTERS OF 17TH-CENTURY DUTCH LANDSCAPE PAINTING
A recent exhibition catalog, sumptuously illustrated
0–8122–8105–5 Pennsylvania $49.95
0–87846–282–1 Museum of Fine Arts pb $24.95

● Peter Sutton & Christopher Brown
MASTERS OF 17TH-CENTURY DUTCH GENRE PAINTING
A scholarly exhibition catalog, with numerous illustrations, which includes essays on the limits of realism
0–87633–057–X Philadelphia Museum pb $19.95

● John Walsh & Cynthia Schneider
A MIRROR OF NATURE: Dutch Paintings from the Collection of Mr. and Mrs. Edward William Carter
A superb collection of cabinet-size Dutch landscape, seascape, still-life, and flower

*"Vase of Flowers" by Ambrosius Bosschaert
(Mauritshaus)*

paintings of the highest quality, with many
color plates
0–295–96007–8 Washington pb $32.50

- Christopher Brown
**THE PAINTINGS OF CAREL
FABRITIUS: Complete Edition with a
Catalogue Raisonné**
A complete catalog, with a study of the
short life and experimental work of
perhaps the finest of Rembrandt's pupils
and the supposed master of Vermeer
0–8014–1394–X Cornell $85.00

- Georg Van Der Groot, editor
**FRANS HALS, HIS LIFE, HIS
PAINTINGS: A Critique of His Art**
0–930582–27–6 Gloucester Art $97.75

- Peter Sutton
PIETER DE HOOCH: Complete Edition
An excellent exhaustive account of this
painter of genre scenes, recognizable for
their closeness to Vermeer in the portrayal
of effects of light
0–8014–1339–7 Cornell $99.50

Rembrandt

Svetlana Alpers
**REMBRANDT'S ENTERPRISE: The
Studio and the Market**
A groundbreaking reading of
Rembrandt's relation to his materials,
market, and studio
0–226–01514–9 Chicago $29.95

Pascal Bonafoux
REMBRANDT SELF-PORTRAITS
Fine reproductions of work in a genre
fully exploited by Rembrandt
0–8478–0629–4 Rizzoli $60.00

Kenneth Clark
**AN INTRODUCTION TO
REMBRANDT**
Style, content, and history by the
master of the great *Civilization* series
0–06–430092–7 Harper & Row pb $9.95

Jacqueline & Maurice Guillaud
**REMBRANDT: The Human Form and
Spirit**
A highly innovative production;
meditative texts accompany an
abundance of stunning reproductions
of works in all media; a visual feast
0–517–56341–X Crown $75.00

Bob Haak
REMBRANDT DRAWINGS
A simple, compact, and thoughtful
presentation of selected works
0–87951–051–X Overlook pb $12.95

Ludwig Munz & Bob Haak
REMBRANDT
Recommended for its illustrations,
which are accompanied by an
introductory text
0–8109–1594–4 Abrams $19.95

Jakob Rosenberg
REMBRANDT: Life and Work
A basic study, fluidly written,
organized according to the subject
matter of his work
0–8014–9198–3 Cornell pb $16.95

Gary Schwartz
REMBRANDT: His Life, His Paintings
A controversial attempt to reconstruct
the web of patronage and social
affiliations within which Rembrandt
worked and, according to Schwartz,
failed; close consideration of
Rembrandt's character with
comprehensive illustration of works
0–670–80876–8 Viking $26.00

- Julius Held
**THE OIL SKETCHES OF PETER PAUL
RUBENS: A Critical Catalogue**
A colossal 2-volume work defining one of
the most exciting aspects of Rubens'
artistic production. Exquisite illustrations
of these complete preliminary works
0–691–03929–1 Princeton (set) $160.00

- Lisa Vergara
**RUBENS AND THE POETICS OF
LANDSCAPE**
Invokes the Renaissance notion of the
similarity of painting to poetry to describe
Rubens' use of landscape
0–300–02508–4 Yale $42.50

- Martin Warnke
PETER PAUL RUBENS: Life and Work
A modest and essential introduction to the
master of the baroque
0–8120–2101–0 Barron pb $6.95

- Christopher White
PETER PAUL RUBENS: Man and Artist
Scintillating visual and textual presentation
of Rubens' career within the international
context of the baroque period—a
sumptuous volume
0–300–03778–3 Yale $65.00

- John Rowlands
HERCULES SEGERS
A nicely bound introduction to the work
of the greatest experimental etcher of the

17th century, with numerous color
reproductions of both his prints and
paintings
0–8076–0909–9 Braziller $30.00

- Christopher Brown
VAN DYCK
An impressive art book, filled with
handsome reproductions. Brown maintains
that Van Dyck's precociousness, religiosity,
and love of court life had a significant
influence on the type of pictures he
painted and the way he painted them
0–8014–1537–3 Cornell $50.00

- Alan McNairn
THE YOUNG VAN DYCK
An important contribution, focusing on
Van Dyck's early career in Antwerp and
his relation to Rubens and to Italian art;
illustrated in black and white
0–88884–468–9 Chicago pb $19.95

- Gilles Aillaud & others
VERMEER
Stylistic approaches accompanied by
interesting historical essays on Vermeer's
art, with superlative reproductions
0–8478–0957–9 Rizzoli $85.00

- John Jacob
**THE COMPLETE PAINTINGS OF
VERMEER**
A slim picture book; high-quality
reproductions with an introductory essay
0–14–009274–9 Penguin pb $10.95

- Arthur Wheelock
VERMEER
Beautiful reproductions of all of Vermeer's
art accompanied by an essay on Vermeer's
life and work by the National Gallery
curator
0–8109–1737–8 Abrams $19.95

18TH-CENTURY ENGLAND

- John Hayes
**DRAWINGS OF THOMAS
GAINSBOROUGH**
A two-volume complete catalog, for
general reader and student alike
0–300–01425–2 Yale (set) $125.00
THOMAS GAINSBOROUGH
0–905005–72–4 Salem House pb $20.00

- David Bindman
HOGARTH
A lucid and amply illustrated introduction
0–500–20182–X Thames & Hudson pb $11.95

- Sean Shesgreen, editor
THE ENGRAVINGS OF HOGARTH
The medium through which Hogarth
spread his fame as a social satirist
0–486–22479–1 Dover pb $13.95

- Nicholas Penny, editor
REYNOLDS
Exhibition catalog surveying the artist's
career, milieu, practice, and studio; with
superb reproductions
0–8109–1565–0 Abrams $40.00

European Art: 1750-1900

GENERAL

• Albert Boime
ART IN THE AGE OF REVOLUTION
An important social history of the art of the revolutionary period, 1750-1848, featuring Boucher, Chardin, David, Fragonard, Gainsborough, Reynolds, and many others; amply illustrated in black and white
0-226-06332-1 Chicago $35.00

• Kenneth Clark
THE ROMANTIC REBELLION
An elegant account of classical and romantic art in 18th-century France and England; adapted from the BBC television series
0-06-430167-2 Harper & Row $22.95

• Lorenz Eitner
AN OUTLINE OF 19TH-CENTURY EUROPEAN PAINTING
A series of studies from David through Cézanne, moving deftly from biographical particulars to more general considerations of 19th-century painting; numerous black-and-white illustrations
0-06-432976-3 Harper & Row $30.00
0-06-430126-5 Harper & Row pb $12.95

• Albert Elsen
ORIGINS OF MODERN SCULPTURE: Pioneers and Premises
Essays situating the origins of modern sculpture in the 19th century, and identifying Rodin as the pivotal figure
0-8076-0737-1 Braziller pb $14.95

• H.W. Janson
NINETEENTH-CENTURY SCULPTURE
A comprehensive survey with striking photography
0-8109-1369-0 Abrams $45.00

• Michel Laclotte & others
PAINTINGS AT THE ORSAY MUSEUM
Paris' superb new museum devoted to 19th-century art
0-935748-72-5 Scala $25.00

• Michael Levey
ROCOCO TO REVOLUTION: Major Trends in 18th-Century Painting
Stylistic developments from Watteau's roots in the rococo to the revolutionary ideals of David, Gros, and Goya
0-500-20050-5 Thames & Hudson pb $11.95

• Fritz Novotny
PAINTING AND SCULPTURE IN EUROPE, 1780-1820
An accessible and lively introduction
0-670-53583-4 Viking $50.00
0-14-056120-X Penguin pb $18.95

• Robert Rosenblum
TRANSFORMATIONS IN LATE 18TH-CENTURY ART
Four essays on the background and influence of late 18th-century styles in architecture and painting
0-691-03846-5 Princeton $47.00
0-691-00302-5 Princeton pb $13.95

Robert Rosenblum &
H.W. Janson
NINETEENTH-CENTURY ART
The most up-to-date general survey; a massive volume describing the major movements from 1776 to 1900 and their connection with historical events; considers art outside Paris as well. Plenty of illustrations
0-81090-195-1 Abrams $45.00

• William Vaughan
ROMANTIC ART
A concise and well-illustrated handbook presenting Blake, Friedrich, Goya, and Turner among other artists who, in the late 18th and early 19th centuries, developed an intensely emotional or visionary approach to art
0-500-18160-8 Thames & Hudson $19.95
0-500-20157-9 Thames & Hudson pb $11.95

Specific Movements

• Robert Delevoy
SYMBOLISTS AND SYMBOLISM
The evocative and enigmatic art of the later 19th century; with fine reproductions of works by Klimt, Hodler, Moreau, Beardsley, and others
0-8478-0430-5 Rizzoli pb $25.00

• Michael Gibson
THE SYMBOLISTS
A lavishly presented survey of this major turning point in French painting, seen largely as a reaction against the forces of realism in art and industrialization in society; charts the movement's European scope
0-8109-1516-2 Abrams $85.00

• Robert Goldwater
SYMBOLISM
The earliest scholarly attempt to come to terms with central tendencies in early modern art
0-06-430095-1 Harper & Row pb $10.95

• Hugh Honour
NEO-CLASSICISM
A masterly study of David, Ingres, Canova, and other artists who revived and reformulated the classical tradition
0-14-020978-6 Penguin pb $7.95

• Sven Loevgren
THE GENESIS OF MODERNISM: Seurat, Gauguin, Van Gogh, and French Symbolism in the 1880s
A well-informed account of the early avant-garde movement in its broader artistic context
0-87817-280-7 Hacker $40.00

• Linda Nochlin
REALISM
A pioneering work which defines the mid-century movement throughout Europe
0-14-021305-8 Penguin pb $7.95

• Gabriel Weisberg
THE EUROPEAN REALIST TRADITION: Painting and Drawing, 1830-1900
A revisionist account that reexamines and rehabilitates the radical counterpart to impressionism; many otherwise unstudied works are reproduced
0-910386-60-9 Indiana $50.00
0-253-32084-4 Indiana pb $25.00

Goya

"[Goya's] importance for the Neo-Baroque Romantic painters of France is well attested by the greatest of them all, Eugène Delacroix, who said that the ideal style would be a combination of Michelangelo's art with Goya's."—H.W. Janson, *History of Art*

Pierre Gassier, editor
LIFE AND WORK OF FRANCISCO GOYA
A comprehensive study of Goya's revolutionary ideals and cultural and courtly milieu, embellished with numerous reproductions of works in a variety of media
0-688-61054-4 Morrow $55.00

José Gudiol i Ricart
GOYA
A pictorial introduction to the great Spanish master of intensely realistic and visionary art, with fine color plates, individually discussed, and a basic biographical and critical text
0-8109-0149-8 Abrams $45.00

Fred Licht
GOYA: The Origins of the Modern Temper in Art
A sensitive survey that encompasses political and social influences; important interpretations of several major works
0-06-430123-0 Harper & Row pb $10.95

Perez Sanchez
GOYA AND THE SPIRIT OF THE ENLIGHTENMENT
0-87846-299-6 Little, Brown $55.00
0-87846-300-0 Mus Fine Arts pb $35.00

FRANCE

• Albert Boime
THE ACADEMY AND FRENCH PAINTING IN THE 19TH CENTURY
A behind-the-scenes look at the historical role and influence of the Académie des Beaux-Arts. Generously illustrated in black and white
0-300-03732-5 Yale pb $19.95

Francisco de Goya's "A Young Man with Two Majas," from Drawings from the Collection of Mr. and Mrs. Eugene Victor Thaw *(Morgan Library)*

● Norman Bryson

TRADITION AND DESIRE: From David to Delacroix
A highly original and important study of their complex relations to the past; amply illustrated
0–521–33562–0 Cambridge pb $17.95

WORD AND IMAGE: French Painting of the Ancien Régime
Brilliant and far-ranging interpretation of 18th-century painting in terms of its narrative rather than stylistic aims and developments
0–521–27654–3 Cambridge pb $18.95

● T.J. Clark

THE ABSOLUTE BOURGEOIS: Artists and Politics in France, 1848-1851
"The social history of art as practiced by Mr. Clark is adventurous, unexpected, excitingly conjectural . . . He is startlingly acute about the pictures"—*New Statesman*
0–691–03981–X Princeton $38.00
0–691–00338–6 Princeton pb $12.95

● Thomas Crow

PAINTERS AND PUBLIC LIFE IN 18TH-CENTURY PARIS
A groundbreaking study of the French Academy, state patronage, and the public, focusing on David, Greuze, Watteau, and others
0–300–03354–0 Yale $45.00
0–300–03764–3 Yale pb $16.95

● Michael Fried

ABSORPTION AND THEATRICALITY: Painting and the Beholder in the Age of Diderot
An original interpretation of the evolution of painting in France from the mid-18th century; paintings are viewed in the light of the art criticism of the time
0–520–03758–8 California $42.00

● Walter Friedlaender

DAVID TO DELACROIX
Traces the fundamental tension underlying 19th-century French painting, the opposing currents of classicism and neo-baroque; an elegant and widely acclaimed study
0–674–19401–2 Harvard pb $8.95

● Philippe Grunchec

THE GRAND PRIX DE ROME: Paintings from the Ecole des Beaux-Arts, 1797-1863
The catalog for a fascinating exhibition on the winners of the Prix de Rome and their work
0–88397–075–9 Intl Exhibitions pb $18.50

● Rosalia Shriver

ROSA BONHEUR
A brief and competent introduction to the life and work of an esteemed 19th-century painter; with fine color plates
0–87982–037–3 Art Alliance $24.50

● Anne Wagner

JEAN-BAPTISTE CARPEAUX: Sculptor of the Second Empire
An accomplished study of the principal French sculptor of his day whose work, questioned at the time on moral grounds, was an important precedent for Rodin
0–300–03605–1 Yale $60.00

● Madeleine Hours

COROT
A general essay on the master of classically serene lyricism, with commentary on numerous color plates; many drawings and etchings reproduced
0–8109–0796–8 Abrams $19.95

● Jean Leymarie

COROT
Emphasis on Corot's career as a painter and on his progress toward a "natural way of seeing"; hundreds of handsome and large-format reproductions
0–8478–0815–7 Rizzoli pb $25.00

● Sarah Faunce & Linda Nochlin

COURBET RECONSIDERED
New discoveries and theoretical approaches to his art. Topics discussed include the artist's role in early modernism and his representation of women
0–300–04298–1 Yale $40.00

"Madame de Verninac" by Jacques-Louis David (Louvre)

● Bruno Fourcard

COURBET
A pictorial survey with high-quality reproductions and a brief critical introduction to the greatest 19th-century realist painter
0–517–53285–9 Crown $14.95

● Albert Boime

THOMAS COUTURE AND THE ECLECTIC VISION
The study of a "second-rate figure," elucidating the relation of art to the political and cultural realities of the time
0–300–02158–5 Yale $95.00

● Charles Ramus, editor

DAUMIER: 120 Great Lithographs
A good selection of Daumier's incomparable satire and social observation
0–486–23512–2 Dover pb $6.95

● Robert Rey

DAUMIER
Paintings and graphic works amply reproduced and discussed
0–8109–0834–4 Abrams $19.95

● Anita Brookner

JACQUES-LOUIS DAVID
David in the context of 18th-century ideals, by the eminent British art historian and novelist
0–06–430507–4 Harper & Row $35.00
0–500–27448–7 Thames & Hudson pb $18.95

● Luc de Nanteuil

DAVID
A commendable essay on the career of the versatile neoclassical artist followed by fine, individually discussed, color reproductions
0–8109–0833–6 Abrams $45.00

● Lee Johnson, editor

THE PAINTINGS OF EUGENE DELACROIX: A Critical Catalogue
A complete examination of the early paintings of this important Romantic artist, with a description, history and bibliography of each picture and extensive illustrations. Discusses his training and early influences

Volumes 1 & 2: 1816-1831
Volume 1 is text, and Volume 2 contains 200 plates, mostly black and white
0–19–817314–8 Oxford $235.00

Volumes 3 & 4: 1832-1863
Volume 3 is text, and Volume 4 includes black-and-white plates
0–19–817378–4 Oxford $130.00

Volume 5 & 6: Public Decorations
Volume 5 is text, and Volume 6 is plates, including many previously unpublished sketches
0–19–817380–6 Oxford $195.00

● Pierre Rosenberg

FRAGONARD
A recent and nearly exhaustive exhibition catalog; with innumerable fine repro-ductions and essays on the man, the vicissitudes of his career, his failures and his successes, and the development of his style
0–8109–0921–9 Abrams $85.00

Théodore Gericault's "Head of a Negro," from Drawings from the Collection of Mr. and Mrs. Eugene Victor Thaw (*Morgan Library*)

- **Jacques Thuillier**
  FRAGONARD
  An exciting portrait of the great 18th-century lyric painter, with excellent illustrations, most in color
  0–8478–0885–8 Rizzoli pb $25.00

- **Lorenz Eitner**
  GERICAULT: His Life and Work
  A substantial and comprehensive study of the master of tempestuous romanticism, with excellent illustrations
  0–8014–1468–7 Cornell $85.00

- **Patricia Condon & others**
  IN PURSUIT OF PERFECTION: The Art of Jean-Auguste-Dominique Ingres
  An exemplary exhibition catalog; Ingres' innumerable revisions, copies, versions, and studies of his own works are beautifully illustrated
  0–9612276–0–5 Indiana $45.00

- **Robert Rosenblum**
  INGRES
  Introductory essay on Ingres' career and wide diversity of styles followed by individually discussed full color plates
  0–8109–0195–1 Abrams $45.00

Fred Licht
CANOVA
The Venetian neoclassical sculptor and his work; a sumptuous book. "Antonio Canova was not only the greatest sculptor of his generation; he was the most famous artist of the Western world from the 1790s until long after his death"—H.W. Janson
0–89659–327–4 Abbeville $85.00

Impressionism

"Green, violet, flowing pink. In lively, proliferating brushstrokes, light trembling foliage, zigzag reflections on the water, the wakes of fishing boats and yawls. A heightening of colors, almost of the very odors, in the sap-filled orchards. Couples dancing, the close of a meal, streets decked with flags, boulevards swarming with carriages and pedestrians, ballerinas in the glare of theater spotlights, Sunday promenades on the islands of the Seine—such are the themes of Impressionism."—Pierre Courthion, *Impressionism*

- **Maria & Godfrey Blunden**
  IMPRESSIONISTS AND IMPRESSIONISM
  An elegant blending of critical, historical, and visual aspects of the movement, with an emphasis on the artists, their characters, relations, and lives, as well as their art
  0–8478–0341–4 Rizzoli pb $25.00

- **Pascal Bonafoux**
  THE IMPRESSIONISTS: Portraits and Confidences
  Reconstructs the friendships and the literary and critical correspondences of the period
  0–8478–0732–0 Rizzoli $60.00

- **Richard Bretell & others**
  A DAY IN THE COUNTRY: Impressionism and the French Landscape
  An exhibition catalog focusing on the development of a modernist vision in landscape painting; beautiful illustrations
  0–8109–0827–1 Abrams $40.00

- **T.J. Clark**
  THE PAINTING OF MODERN LIFE: Paris in the Art of Manet and His Followers
  An acclaimed Marxist scholar imaginatively reconstructs the relation of form to content as conveyed in the works and aesthetics of this "bourgeois style"; with numerous illustrations
  0–394–49580–2 Knopf $25.00
  0–691–00275–4 Princeton pb $16.50

- **Pierre Courthion**
  IMPRESSIONISM
  A great compendium of pictures and an introductory critical text; painters from Turner and Corot to the postimpressionist period are represented
  0–8109–2067–0 Abrams pb $14.95

- **Denis Farr & John House**
  IMPRESSIONIST AND POST-IMPRESSIONIST MASTERPIECES FROM THE COURTAULD COLLECTION
  A recent catalog; beautiful reproductions from a spectacular collection. Contains revealing technical analyses
  0–300–03828–3 Yale $35.00
  0–300–03891–7 Yale pb $16.95

- **Robert Herbert**
  IMPRESSIONISM: Art, Leisure and Parisian Society
  By one of the leading scholars of impressionism. The actual context of the movement brilliantly reconstructed, with emphasis on society's relation to artistic practices; handsomely illustrated
  0–300–04262–0 Yale $50.00

- **Charles Moffett**
  IMPRESSIONIST AND POST-IMPRESSIONIST PAINTINGS IN THE METROPOLITAN MUSEUM OF ART
  Perhaps the finest American collection of 19th-century masterworks
  0–8109–1104–3 Abrams $49.50

- **John Rewald**
  THE HISTORY OF IMPRESSIONISM
  Erudite and imaginative; the classic book on the subject, frequently reissued. An account of the developments leading to the first impressionist exhibition of 1874
  0–87070–360–9 NY Graphic Society $50.00

Exhibitions and Critics

"In the course of the 19th century the Salon, which had been a small exhibition of painting and sculpture by the leading artists patronized by the court and nobility, was transformed into a vast public spectacle wherein large numbers of artists sought public as well as private favor, with a few asserting their right to paint as they chose regardless of official or popular approval. Here many of the principles were established and the tactics developed which marked the aggravated relations between the progressive artists and official patronage."—George Heard Hamilton, *Manet and His Critics*

- **Charles Baudelaire**
  ART IN PARIS 1845-1862: Review of Salons and Other Exhibitions
  Criticism by the poet of the major painters of his time—Delacroix, Courbet, Daumier, and his close friend Manet
  0–8014–9227–0 Cornell pb $14.95

"Portrait of Edouard Manet" by Henri Fantin-Latour (Art Institute, Chicago)

THE PAINTER OF MODERN LIFE & OTHER ESSAYS
Brief works championing his illustrious contemporaries, as well as other stimulating essays
0–306–80279–1 Da Capo pb $11.95

• George Heard Hamilton
PAINTING AND SCULPTURE IN EUROPE, 1880-1940
The standard survey of the period, arranged chronologically by artist and covering a broad range of nationalities and styles
0–14–056129–3 Penguin pb $18.95

• John Milner
THE STUDIOS OF PARIS: The Capital of Art in the Late 19th Century
The careers of Parisian artists, their training, and their work—from the most famous painters of the day such as Meissonier to the then largely ignored impressionists
0–300–03990–5 Yale $39.95

• Charles Moffett & others
THE NEW PAINTING: Impressionism, 1874-1900
Impressionism as it was first seen: a recreation of the original Parisian exhibitions in an amply illustrated exhibition catalog
0–8109–1104–3 Abrams $49.50

• Linda Nochlin, editor
IMPRESSIONISM AND POST-IMPRESSIONISM, 1874-1900: Sources and Documents
Illuminating selection assembled by the noted art historian
0–13–452003–3 Prentice-Hall pb $25.00

REALISM AND TRADITION IN ART 1848-1900: Sources and Documents
Important original sources, intelligently compiled and introduced
0–13–766584–9 Prentice-Hall pb $25.00

• Maureen O'Brien
IN SUPPORT OF LIBERTY: European Paintings at the 1883 Pedestal Fund Art Loan Exhibition
Re-creation of an influential exhibition held in New York in 1883 to raise money for the pedestal of the Statue of Liberty; includes works by Corot, Courbet, Tissot, and others
0–943526–14–0 Parrish Art Museum pb $15.00

Jon Whiteley
PUVIS DE CHAVANNES
A discussion of the artist's responses to various contemporary movements: classicism, romanticism, realism, impressionism, symbolism
0–19–921040–3 Oxford $95.00

The Impressionists

• Kirk Varnedoe
GUSTAVE CAILLEBOTTE
The catalog to the exhibition that revived this exciting pivotal figure of the impressionist movement; beautifully illustrated
0–300–03722–8 Yale $39.95

• Gotz Adriani
DEGAS: Pastels, Oil Sketches, Drawings
A superb book on Degas, with 60 color reproductions
0–89659–530–7 Abbeville $75.00

• Jean Sutherland Boggs & others
DEGAS
A lavish catalog for the recent retrospective exhibition, which includes essays by eminent experts, over 280 color and 440 black & white illustrations
0–87099–517–7 Metropolitan Museum $45.00
0–87099–520–0 Metropolitan Museum pb $35.00

• Robert Gordon & Andrew Forge
DEGAS
An impressive volume, organized by subject—theater, horses and riders, portraits, dancers, bathers—and magnificently illustrated
0–8109–1142–6 Abrams $67.50

• Eunice Lipton
LOOKING INTO DEGAS: Uneasy Images of Women and Modern Life
An important and nuanced essay dealing with issues of class, sex, and work which resonate in the paintings of Degas
0–520–05604–3 California $37.50

• Roy McMullen
DEGAS: His Life, Times and Work
A sensitive and scholarly biography of a caustic and difficult genius
0–395–27603–9 Houghton Mifflin $24.95

• Theodore Reff
DEGAS: The Artist's Mind
The foremost Degas scholar explores the psychology of creativity
0–674–19543–4 Harvard pb $16.95

• Denys Sutton
EDGAR DEGAS: Life and Work
Elegant presentation, textual and visual, of the times and career of Degas; by the editor of *Apollo*
0–8478–0733–9 Rizzoli $85.00

• Richard Thomson
DEGAS: The Nudes
The first book to provide a consistent analysis of this aspect of Degas' work
0–500–23509–0 Thames and Hudson $40.00

• Françoise Cachin & others
MANET, 1832-1883
The centennial retrospective exhibition; a massive illustrated volume representing the most up-to-date scholarship on the painter and dandy whom some critics consider the first modern artist
0–8109–1346–1 Abrams $75.00

• Pierre Courthion
MANET
Introductory text accompanying lavish color plates
0–8109–1318–6 Abrams $45.00

• George Heard Hamilton
MANET AND HIS CRITICS
A richly documented study of early impressionism and its reception
0–300–03759–7 Yale pb $11.95

• Anne Coffin Hanson
MANET AND THE MODERN TRADITION
A classic, substantial study of innovative developments in late 19th-century painting
0–300–01954–8 Yale $50.00
0–300–02492–4 Yale pb $17.50

• Phoebe Pool
THE COMPLETE PAINTINGS OF MANET
A handy collection of fine reproductions, with introductory text
0–14–008656–4 Penguin pb $10.95

• Theodore Reff
MANET AND MODERN PARIS: 100 Paintings, Drawings, Prints, and Photographs by Manet and His Contemporaries
Manet in the fascinating context of late 19th-century urbanization; well-illustrated
0–226–70720–2 Chicago $39.95

• Robert Gordon & Andrew Forge
MONET
Thematic organization covering his entire career; with stunning reproductions. "Monet is only an eye—but heavens what an eye!"—Paul Cézanne
0–8109–1312–7 Abrams $75.00

• John House
MONET: Nature into Art
Traces the actual production of Monet's paintings, with fully illustrated discussions of light, color, form, and the limits of naturalism
0–300–03785–6 Yale $45.00

• William Seitz
MONET
Sensitive formal readings of nearly 50 major works, reproduced in color
0–8109–0326–1 Abrams $45.00
0–8109–1341–0 Abrams pb $19.95

• Paul Tucker
MONET AT ARGENTEUIL, 1871-1877
Monet's Parisian leisure subjects considered in relation to the spread of industrialization
0–300–02577–7 Yale $42.50
0–300–03206–4 Yale pb $15.95

• Daniel Wildenstein
MONET'S YEARS AT GIVERNY: Beyond Impressionism
The consummate achievements of Monet's latter period, including the *Water-lilies*
0–8109–1336–4 Abrams $27.50
0–8109–2183–9 Abrams pb $14.95

• Kathleen Adler & Tamar Garb
BERTHE MORISOT
A fundamental biographical and critical study of the impressionist painter and friend of Degas, well illustrated
0–8014–2038–5 Cornell $29.95

• Charles Stuckey & others
BERTHE MORISOT, IMPRESSIONIST
The catalog for the retrospective exhibition, featuring glorious reproductions of paintings, drawings, and

watercolors, assessing Morisot's position within the impressionist movement
0–933920–03–2 Hudson Hills $45.00
0–933920–04–0 Hudson Hills pb $25.00

- Christopher Lloyd
PISSARRO
Exquisite reproductions accompanied by basic introductory text
0–8478–0391–0 Rizzoli $35.00

- John Rewald
PISSARRO
The foremost scholar of impressionism assesses Pissarro's role in the movement; beautiful reproductions
0–8109–0413–6 Abrams $45.00

- John House & others
RENOIR
An exhibition catalog full of fine reproductions; presents important findings of the most current scholarship
0–8109–1575–8 Abrams $40.00

- Walter Pach
RENOIR
A good visual introduction with basic critical text, recommended for its excellent reproductions
0–8109–0446–2 Abrams $45.00
0–8109–1593–6 Abrams pb $19.95

- Barbara White
RENOIR: His Life, Art and Letters
A splendid book, consisting of a monographic study and hundreds of reproductions. "Be a good craftsman; it won't stop you being a genius"—Pierre Auguste Renoir
0–8109–8088–6 Abrams $29.95

Krystyna Matyjaszkiewicz, editor
JAMES TISSOT
An important reintroduction of this long ignored figure; splendidly illustrated
0–89659–516–1 Abbeville $45.00

Michael Wentworth
JAMES TISSOT
A scholarly consideration of his career and influences
0–19–817364–4 Oxford $125.00

Postimpressionism

"Without knowing it, Cézanne, the timid little conventional man sheltering behind his wife and sister and the Jesuit father, was a pure revolutionary. When he said to his models: 'Be an apple! Be an apple!' he was uttering the foreword to the fall not only of Jesuits and the Christian idealists altogether, but to the collapse of our whole way of consciousness, and the substitution of another way."—D.H. Lawrence, *Phoenix I*

- Herschel Chipp, editor
THEORIES OF MODERN ART: A Source Book by Artists and Critics
A rich selection of letters, manifestoes, reviews, interviews, and other writings

Paul Cézanne's "Still Life" (Metropolitan Museum)

related to the study of modern art, from Cézanne to the mid-20th century
0–520–05256–0 California pb $12.95

- Diane Kelder
THE GREAT BOOK OF POST-IMPRESSIONISM
A sumptuous pictorial survey, with complementary introductory text
0–89659–574–9 Abbeville $85.00

- John Rewald
POST-IMPRESSIONISM: From Van Gogh to Gauguin
Companion volume to his renowned *History of Impressionism* and a classic in its own right; covers the period from 1886 to Cézanne's death
0–87070–532–6 NY Graphic Society $60.00

STUDIES IN POST-IMPRESSIONISM
A collection of important and ambitious essays
0–8109–1632–0 Abrams $37.50

- Andre Fermigier
PIERRE BONNARD
Adapted from the recent retrospective exhibition held in Paris; an important contribution with numerous fine reproductions of Bonnard's sensuous, radiant works
0–8109–0041–6 Abrams $45.00
0–8109–0732–1 Abrams pb $19.95

- Michel Terrasse
BONNARD AT LE CANNET
A thrilling account by Bonnard's grandnephew of the artist's production at his favorite working place on the Côte d'Azur; with photographs by Henri Cartier-Bresson
0–394–57166–5 Thames & Hudson $39.95

- Gotz Adriani
CEZANNE WATERCOLORS
0–8109–0784–4 Abrams $65.00

- Richard Kendall, editor
CEZANNE BY HIMSELF
Cézanne as he presented himself, through his own writings, conversations, drawings, watercolors, and paintings
0–8212–1709–7 NY Graphic Society $50.00

- Erle Loran
CEZANNE'S COMPOSITION: Analysis of His Form with Diagrams and Photographs of his Motifs
"An understanding of Cézanne's art more essential than any other I have seen in print"—Clement Greenberg
0–520–05459–8 California pb $15.95

- John Rewald
CEZANNE: A Biography
The newest edition of the classic monograph providing a detailed account of Cézanne's great friendship with the critic and writer Emile Zola; complemented by sumptuous color reproductions
0–8109–0775–5 Abrams $75.00

- William Rubin & others
CEZANNE: The Late Work
Catalog of the blockbuster exhibition, with essays by such art historians as Theodore Reff, John Rewald, and William Rubin
0–87070–278–5 NY Graphic Society $45.00

- Meyer Schapiro
CEZANNE
Penetrating psychologizing interpretation of the modern master of color as form; numerous fine reproductions
0–8109–0052–1 Abrams $45.00

• Robert Goldwater
GAUGUIN
A classic study, with commendable reproductions
0-8109-0137-4 Abrams $45.00

• Christopher Gray
THE SCULPTURE AND CERAMICS OF PAUL GAUGUIN
0-87817-263-7 Hacker $75.00

• Michel Hoog
PAUL GAUGUIN: Life and Work
A magnificently illustrated recent work. "This sumptuous addition to the Gauguin lore may well be the definitive study on the man. Highly recommended for scholar and layman"—*Art Times*
0-8478-0843-2 Rizzoli $85.00

• Marla Prather & Charles Stuckey
GAUGUIN: A Retrospective
The stunning catalog to the recent comprehensive exhibition
0-88363-287-X Levin $60.00

• Belinda Thomson
GAUGUIN
A handy critical introduction, with numerous illustrations
0-500-20220-6 Thames & Hudson pb $11.95

Caroline Boyle-Turner
THE PRINTS OF THE PONT-AVEN SCHOOL: Gauguin and His Circle in Brittany
An exhibition catalog tracing and illustrating the aesthetic and technical experiments among this small circle of artists
0-89659-742-3 Abbeville $35.00

Judy & Charles-Guy Le Paul
GAUGUIN AND THE IMPRESSIONISTS AT PONT-AVEN
The scenic countryside and melancholy peasants of Brittany were important subjects for this small circle of artists in the last quarter of the 19th century; rarely seen paintings, drawings, pastels, and watercolors are augmented with charming fin-de-siècle postcards
0-89659-773-3 Abbeville $95.00

• William Homer
SEURAT AND THE SCIENCE OF PAINTING
A study of Seurat's developments in color and light theory; contemporary scientific advancements as assimilated by the great postimpressionist painter
0-87817-295-5 Hacker $40.00

• John Russell
SEURAT
An engaging critical introduction, with numerous illustrations, by the *New York Times* art critic
0-500-20032-7 Thames & Hudson pb $11.95

• Gotz Adriani
TOULOUSE-LAUTREC
A well-illustrated study of the great painter of bohemian Paris
0-500-09180-3 Thames & Hudson $60.00

• Douglas Cooper
TOULOUSE-LAUTREC
A lucid and well-illustrated introduction, with many individually discussed color plates
0-8109-0512-4 Abrams $45.00
0-8109-1678-9 Abrams pb $19.95

• Denys Sutton
THE COMPLETE PAINTINGS OF TOULOUSE-LAUTREC
A handy, slim volume with good reproductions and basic text
0-14-009275-7 Penguin pb $10.95

• Pierre Cabanne
VAN GOGH
A biographical and critical introduction, with plenty of reproductions
0-500-20092-0 Thames & Hudson pb $9.95

• Ronald Pickvance
VAN GOGH IN ARLES
The latter period from 1888 to 1889 coinciding with Gauguin's visit to Arles and the onset of Van Gogh's mental illness; a comprehensive exhibition catalog of this stirring time
0-8109-1727-0 Abrams $35.00

VAN GOGH IN SAINT-REMY AND AUVERS
The final years of Van Gogh's life, when much of his work was executed in the asylum, beautifully represented in numerous reproductions and discussed in introductory essays
0-8109-1734-3 Abrams $35.00

• Meyer Schapiro
VAN GOGH
A classic and informative study of the man, his work, and troubled life; many fine color reproductions
0-8109-0524-8 Abrams $45.00

• Evert van Uitert
VAN GOGH DRAWINGS
Moving studies of peasants and workers
0-87951-085-4 Overlook $22.50
0-87951-086-2 Overlook pb $12.95

• Belinda Thomson
VUILLARD
A highly accomplished monograph presenting Vuillard as a realist imbued with the aspirations of symbolism; lavishly illustrated
0-89659-883-7 Abbeville $45.00

Rosaline Bacou, editor
ODILON REDON: Pastels
Charts Redon's significant break with his earlier use of charcoal and lithography
0-8076-1180-8 Braziller $65.00

Jean Selz
ODILON REDON
A lucid introduction to the visionary symbolist painter, with numerous color plates of paintings and pastels
0-517-50799-4 Crown $14.95

French Sculptors

• Denys Chevalier
MAILLOL
0-517-02688-0 Crown $14.95

• Aristide Maillol
MAILLOL NUDES: 35 Lithographs
0-486-24000-2 Dover pb $3.50

• John Rewald
ARISTIDE MAILLOL, 1861-1944
A brief study by the foremost scholar of the impressionist movement
0-89207-000-5 Guggenheim pb $9.95

• Bernard Champigneulle
RODIN
A basic critical introduction with numerous illustrations
0-500-20061-0 Thames & Hudson pb $11.95

• Frederic Grunfeld
RODIN: A Biography
Recent acclaimed portrait of the life, loves, and art of the master
0-8050-0279-0 Henry Holt $35.00

• Claude Judrin, editor
RODIN: Watercolors and Drawings
0-500-23368-3 Thames & Hudson $75.00

ENGLAND

• Joseph Burke
ENGLISH ART, 1714-1800
A volume of the excellent Oxford series on the history of English Art, from rococo to romanticism
0-19-817209-5 Oxford $45.00

Henry Fuseli's "Woman Reading" (Kunsthaus, Zurich)

✉ **TO ORDER BOOKS AS GIFTS, SEE PAGE 1**

• Stephen Deuchar
SPORTING ART IN 18TH CENTURY ENGLAND: A Social and Political History
A distinctive genre which became popular in the early 18th century through such artists as George Stubbs
0–300–04116–0 Yale $45.00

• Dennis Farr
ENGLISH ART, 1870-1940
0–19–817208–7 Oxford $59.00
0–19–281855–4 Oxford pb $22.95

• Luke Herrmann
BRITISH LANDSCAPE PAINTING OF THE 18TH CENTURY
Classical, topographical, Italianate, and picturesque traditions are presented in a critical account of a wide range of works; commendable reproductions
0–19–519757–7 Oxford $45.00

• Michael Rosenthal
BRITISH LANDSCAPE PAINTING
0–8014–1489–X Cornell $35.00

• Martin Butlin & Evelyn Joll
THE PAINTINGS OF WILLIAM BLAKE
An extraordinary effort at coordinating the complete works; two volumes, one of text, the second of black-and-white plates
0–300–03276–5 Yale (set) $250.00

• Robert Essick
WILLIAM BLAKE: Printmaker
An account of Blake's entire career as printmaker and publisher, stressing his technical experiments
0–691–03954–2 Princeton $72.00

• Kathleen Raine
WILLIAM BLAKE
A brief but informative introduction; the visionary artist viewed in the context of the Greek revival
0–500–20107–2 Thames & Hudson pb $11.95

• Michael Rosenthal
CONSTABLE
A general survey discussing John Constable's artistic projects in terms of the broader cultural milieu; many paintings, drawings, and watercolors reproduced
0–500–20211–7 Thames & Hudson pb $11.95

CONSTABLE: The Painter and His Landscape
Historical commentary on Constable's East Anglia, where he painted and drew throughout his career; very fine color reproductions
0–300–03014–2 Yale $45.00
0–300–03753–8 Yale pb $25.95

Turner

John Gage
J.M.W. TURNER: A Wonderful Range of Mind
An up-to-date, general study of the great English Romantic landscape painter, with splendid reproductions throughout
0–300–03779–1 Yale $39.95

Luke Herrmann
TURNER: Paintings, Watercolors, Prints and Drawings
A balanced visual survey of Turner's career, complemented by a biographical outline and review of contemporary criticism
0–306–80270–8 Da Capo $22.95

John Walker
TURNER
A discussion of his life and fortunes; nearly 50 fine color plates with individual commentary
0–8109–1679–7 Abrams $19.95

Andrew Wilton
J.M.W. TURNER: France, Italy, Switzerland, Germany
Fine assemblage of the watercolors produced during Turner's frequent European travels
0–8076–1046–1 Braziller $40.00

TURNER AND THE SUBLIME
Exhibition catalog demonstrating Turner's relation to the predominant philosophical concept of the 18th century; excellent reproductions of many major works
0–226–06189–2 Chicago pb $15.95

TURNER IN HIS TIME
Incorporates study of original documents; with hundreds of reproductions
0–8109–1694–0 Abrams $49.50

The Pre-Raphaelites

"It was only one kind of Pre-Raphaelite painting that was so admired in the nineties, whereas ultimately it is the sheer variety of the work produced that impresses. Holman Hunt's symbolic realism, Millais' Tennysonian mood-painting, the colour symbolism and cult of feminine beauty in Rossetti, Burne-Jones' musical and romantic dreams, the modern-life allegories of Madox Brown, indeed the modern moral subjects of them all."—Alan Bowness

• Max Beerbohm
ROSSETTI AND HIS CIRCLE
Beerbohm's famous series of sly and witty caricatures of Rossetti and his contemporaries, including Swinburne, Ruskin, Tennyson, Browning, and the Prince of Wales
0–300–03986–7 Yale $22.50

• Timothy Hilton
THE PRE-RAPHAELITES
A thorough introduction which describes the many aspects of this Romantic, medievalizing movement and its varied responses to Victorian society; Millais, Rossetti, Brown, and Burne-Jones predominate
0–500–20102–1 Thames & Hudson pb $11.95

• Andrew Rose
THE PRE-RAPHAELITES
An important exhibition catalog assembling major monuments of the Victorian movement
0–7148–2166–7 Salem House pb $17.95

• Peter Stansky
REDESIGNING THE WORLD: William Morris, the 1880s, and the Arts and Crafts
0–691–06616–7 Princeton $29.00
0–691–01411–6 Princeton pb $12.95

WILLIAM MORRIS
0–19–287572–8 Oxford $13.95
0–19–287571–X Oxford pb $4.95

• Christopher Wood
OLYMPIAN DREAMERS: Victorian Classical Painters
The resurrection of classical ideals in late 19th-century painting, lucidly discussed and broadly illustrated
0–8390–0354–4 Abner Schram $35.00

NORTHERN EUROPE

• Keith Andrews
THE NAZARENES: A Brotherhood of German Painters in Rome
A study of the early 19th-century movement led by Overbeck and Pforr intended to regenerate German religious art according to late medieval and Renaissance ideals and practice
0–87817–306–4 Hacker $50.00

• Geraldine Norman
BIEDERMEIER PAINTING: Reality Observed in Genre, Portrait and Landscape
Superbly reproduced highlights
0–500–23493–0 Thames & Hudson $45.00

• Robert Rosenblum
MODERN PAINTING AND THE NORTHERN ROMANTIC TRADITION: Friedrich to Rothko
Exploration of a hitherto ignored progression of modern styles, linking German romanticism to expressionism and, in turn, to abstract expressionism; amply illustrated
0–06–430057–9 Harper & Row pb $10.95

• Gert Schiff & Stephen Waetzoldt
GERMAN MASTERS OF THE 19TH CENTURY: Paintings and Drawings from the Federal Republic of Germany
0–517–63013–3 Crown $19.95

• Kirk Varnedoe
NORTHERN LIGHT: Realism and Symbolism in Scandinavian Painting, 1880-1910
A full presentation of the often overlooked early modernist paintings of the North; many beautifully reproduced pictures
0–686–82279–X Brooklyn Museum pb $17.95

VIENNA 1900: Art, Architecture, and Design
0–87070–618–7 NY Graphic Society $50.00

- Jacques Janssens
  ENSOR
  A pictorial and textual introduction to this compelling Belgian expressionist painter
  0–517–53284–0 Crown $14.95

- Diane Lesko
  JAMES ENSOR: The Creative Years
  0–691–04030–3 Princeton $52.50

- Jens Christian Jensen
  CASPAR DAVID FRIEDRICH
  An indispensable introduction to the haunting work of the greatest German Romantic artist; brief and lucid
  0–8120–2102–9 Barron pb $6.95

- Linda Siegel
  CASPAR DAVID FRIEDRICH AND THE AGE OF GERMAN ROMANTICISM
  0–8283–1659–7 Branden $25.00

- Sharon Hirsh
  FERDINAND HODLER
  An engaging and beautifully presented study of the foremost Swiss symbolist landscape painter
  0–8076–1033–X Braziller $50.00

- Angelica Baumer, editor
  GUSTAV KLIMT: Women
  0–8478–0784–3 Rizzoli $50.00

- Alessandra Comini
  GUSTAV KLIMT
  A new treatment of the complex Viennese artist, discussing his sensuous, symbolic work from a "reverse Freudian" angle
  0–8076–0806–8 Braziller pb $14.95

- Johannes Dobai
  GUSTAV KLIMT: Landscapes
  0–8212–1688–0 NY Graphic Society $50.00

- Serge Sabarsky
  GUSTAV KLIMT: Drawings
  0–918825–19–9 Moyer Bell $22.50
  0–918825–20–2 Moyer Bell pb $13.95
  GUSTAV KLIMT: Paintings, Watercolors and Drawings
  0–918825–58–X Moyer Bell $60.00

- Reinhold Heller
  MUNCH: His Life and Work
  0–226–32643–8 Chicago $39.95
  0–226–32644–6 Chicago pb $22.50

- J.P. Hodin
  EDVARD MUNCH
  A widely acclaimed critical study of the great Norwegian artist by a celebrated scholar of expressionism; well illustrated
  0–500–20122–6 Thames & Hudson pb $11.95

- Elizabeth Prelinger
  EDVARD MUNCH: Master Printmaker
  Unravels the technical subtleties of some of Munch's most powerful work: woodcuts, lithographs, and engravings
  0–393–01797–4 Norton $30.00

- Ragna Stang
  EDVARD MUNCH: The Man and His Art
  A comprehensive analysis of Munch's artistic development with substantial new

"Heinrich and Otto Benesch," from Egon Schiele *by Alessandra Comini* (Braziller)

material; profusely illustrated with fine color plates
0–89659–025–9 Abbeville $75.00

- Alessandra Comini
  EGON SCHIELE
  0–8076–0820–3 Braziller pb $14.95

- Erwin Mitsch
  THE ART OF EGON SCHIELE
  An excellent study of the tormented German expressionist with fine reproductions
  1–55595–007–8 Hudson Hills $50.00

Serge Sabarsky, editor
EGON SCHIELE: Paintings, Watercolors, and Drawings
0–918825–02–4 Moyer Bell $49.95
0–918825–47–4 Moyer Bell pb $12.00

- Frank Whitford
  EGON SCHIELE
  0–500–18183–7 Thames & Hudson $19.95
  0–500–20183–8 Thames & Hudson pb $11.95

American Art to 1900

GENERAL STUDIES

"When the United States of America came into being, the leaders and citizens of the young republic faced a formidable identity crisis . . . Creative minds were confronted with the challenge of recording, indeed creating, an accurate 'American' image. This challenge was complicated by the fact that in the young United States, the fine arts of painting and sculpture were regarded with some suspicion and not a little skepticism. To a people engaged daily in the struggle to tame a seemingly endless wilderness, with its attendant physical and psychological hazards, the arts of painting and sculpture were superfluous luxuries."— Elizabeth Milroy, in *A Proud Heritage: Two Centuries of American Art*

- D. Scott Atkinson & others, editors
  A PROUD HERITAGE: Two Centuries of American Art
  Selections from the collections of the Pennsylvania Academy of Fine Arts, Philadelphia; and the Terra Museum of American Art, Chicago
  0–8109–1470–0 Abrams $49.50

• Matthew Baigell
A CONCISE HISTORY OF AMERICAN PAINTINGS AND SCULPTURE
A factual history from colonial times to the present
0–06–430350–0 Harper & Row $39.00

DICTIONARY OF AMERICAN ART
0–06–433254–3 Harper & Row $18.50
0–06–430078–1 Harper & Row pb $10.95

• Milton Brown
AMERICAN ART: Painting, Sculpture, Architecture, Decorative Arts, Photography
0–8109–0658–9 Abrams $49.50

• Wayne Craven
SCULPTURE IN AMERICA
0–87413–225–8 Delaware $60.00

• E. McSherry Fowble
TWO CENTURIES OF PRINTS IN AMERICA, 1680-1880: A Selective Catalogue of the Winterthur Collection
Focuses primarily on prints of historical importance, including views
0–8139–1124–9 Virginia $60.00

• George Groce & David Wallace
NEW YORK HISTORICAL SOCIETY'S DICTIONARY OF ARTISTS IN AMERICA, 1564-1860
A solid and indispensable reference work for students of American art
0–300–00519–9 Yale $62.00

• John McCoubrey, editor
AMERICAN ART, 1700-1960: Sources and Documents
Includes many letters, reviews, and other documentary material
0–13–024521–6 Prentice-Hall pb $26.00

• Daniel Mendelowitz
A HISTORY OF AMERICAN ART
A scholarly narrative history
0–03–089475–1 Holt, Rinehart & Winston pb $39.90

• Vincent Scully
NEW WORLD VISIONS OF HOUSEHOLD GODS AND SACRED PLACES: American Art and the Metropolitan Museum, 1650-1914
0–8212–1647–3 NY Graphic Society $35.00

PAINTING

• Jules David Prown
AMERICAN PAINTING: From the Colonial Period to the Armory Show
An illustrated survey of art created in America before 1913
0–8478–0841–6 Rizzoli $25.00

• Perry Rathbone
AMERICAN PAINTINGS IN THE MUSEUM OF FINE ARTS, BOSTON
Catalog of one of the most important public collections
0–87846–005–5 Tuttle $40.00

Gilbert Stuart's "Francis and Saunders Malbone," from A History of American Painting by James Thomas Flexner (Dover)

• Theodore E. Stebbins, Jr. & Carol Troyen
A NEW WORLD: Masterpieces of American Painting, 1760-1910
Catalog of an important exhibition showing the development of painting in America
0–87846–234–1 Museum of Fine Arts pb $29.95

Watercolors

• Christopher Finch
AMERICAN WATERCOLORS
A survey with emphasis on the late 19th and early 20th centuries
0–89659–654–0 Abbeville $50.00

• Theodore E. Stebbins, Jr.
AMERICAN MASTER DRAWINGS AND WATERCOLORS: A History of Works on Paper from Colonial Times to the Present
0–06–014068–2 Harper & Row $57.50

• Worcester Art Museum
AMERICAN TRADITIONS IN WATERCOLOR
0–89659–674–5 Abbeville $45.00
0–89659–680–X Abbeville pb $24.95

Genre Painting

• Frederick Brandt
AMERICAN MARINE PAINTING
0–917046–01–3 Virginia Museum pb $8.95

• Wayne Craven
DOWN GARDEN PATHS: The Floral Environment in American Art
0–8386–3214–9 Fairleigh Dickinson $30.00

• Lee Edwards
DOMESTIC BLISS: Family Life in American Painting, 1840-1910
0–943651–06–9 Hudson River Museum pb $19.95

• William Gerdts
PAINTERS OF THE HUMBLE TRUTH: Masterpieces of American Still Life, 1801-1939
0–8262–0355–8 Missouri $54.95

• William Gerdts & Mark Thistlewaite
GRAND ILLUSIONS: Historical Painting in America
0–88360–056–0 Amon Carter Museum $21.95

• William Gerdts & Bruce Weber
IN NATURE'S WAYS: American Landscape Painting of the Late 19th Century
0–943411–16–5 Norton Gallery pb $22.95

• David Lubin
ACT OF PORTRAYAL: Eakins, Sargent, James
A study of portraiture, combining art history and cultural history, with many illustrations
0–300–03213–7 Yale $25.00

• Edward Nygren & others
VIEWS AND VISIONS: American Landscape before 1830
0–88675–022–9 Corcoran Gallery $22.95

• John Wilmerding
AMERICAN MARINE PAINTING
The history of American marine painting from the colonial period to the present
0–8109–1861–7 Abrams $40.00

FOLK ART

- **William C. Ketchum, Jr.**
ALL-AMERICAN FOLK ART AND CRAFTS
Generations of American crafts
0–8478–0765–7 Rizzoli $45.00

- **Jean Lipman & Alice Winchester**
THE FLOWERING OF AMERICAN FOLK ART, 1776-1876
The catalog of the Whitney Museum exhibition
0–89471–528–3 Running Press $23.00

- **Jean Lipman & Elizabeth Warren**
YOUNG AMERICA: A Folk-Art History
An excellent survey by the president of the American Museum of Folk Art, essential for collectors, students, and amateurs
0–933920–75–X Hudson Hills $30.00

- **Ian Quimby & Scott Swank, editors**
PERSPECTIVES ON AMERICAN FOLK ART
From a conference held at Winterthur in 1977, which takes a historical look at the collecting of American folk art
0–393–01273–5 Norton $21.95
0–393–95088–3 Norton pb $9.95

- **Roger Ricco & others**
AMERICAN PRIMITIVE: Discoveries in Folk Sculpture
"A veritable museum without walls of outsider art and non-traditional art"—*Maine Antique Digest*
0–394–54467–6 Knopf $75.00

- **Beatrix Rumford, editor**
AMERICAN FOLK PORTRAITS: Paintings and Drawings from the Abby Aldrich Rockefeller Folk Art Center
0–8212–1100–5 NY Graphic Society $39.95

AMERICAN FOLK PAINTINGS: From the Abby Aldrich Rockefeller Folk Art Center
The second volume of the holdings of this noted collection, which includes paintings and drawings other than portraits: landscapes, still lifes, mourning pictures. The work of anonymous painters is included, as well as that of Edward Hicks and Grandma Moses
0–8212–1620–1 NY Graphic Society $70.00

- **Beatrix Rumford & Carolyn Weekley**
TREASURES OF AMERICAN FOLK ART: From the Abby Aldrich Rockefeller Folk Art Center
A study on the development of folk art in America, illustrated with amusing and beautiful objects
0–8212–1726–7 NY Graphic Society $35.00

- **John Michael Vlach**
PLAIN PAINTERS: Making Sense of American Folk Art
Comparative studies of folk knowledge and culture
0–87474–926–3 Smithsonian $45.00

EARLY AMERICAN ART

- **James Thomas Flexner**
AMERICA'S OLD MASTERS
Biographies of Benjamin West, John Singleton Copley, Charles Willson Peale, and Gilbert Stuart
0–07–021285–6 McGraw-Hill pb $9.95

A HISTORY OF AMERICAN PAINTING
A distinguished account from the 17th century to Winslow Homer

Volume 1: First Flowers of Our Wilderness—American Painting, The Colonial Period
The development of painting in colonial America, from the time of the earliest settlements to the American Revolution
0–486–25707–X Dover pb $8.95

Volume 2: The Light of Distant Skies—1760–1835
The search for American identity
0–486–22179–2 Dover pb $8.95

Volume 3: That Wilder Image—The Native School from Thomas Cole to Winslow Homer
The emergence of a distinct national style
0–486–25709–6 Dover pb $8.95

- **William Gerdts & Theodore Stebbins, Jr.**
A MAN OF GENIUS: The Art of Washington Allston, 1779-1834
"The first American painter whose art was an exploration of the visions within his own mind"—Edgar Richardson
0–87846–146–9 Virginia $35.00

- **Lillian Miller & Sidney Hart, editors**
THE SELECTED PAPERS OF CHARLES WILLSON PEALE AND HIS FAMILY: Charles Willson Peale: Artist in Revolutionary America, 1735-1791
Peale was a soldier, inventor, painter of more than 1000 pictures, student of natural history, and founder of one of the first museums in America
0–300–02576–9 Yale $60.00

- **Lillian Miller & others**
REMBRANDT PEALE, 1778-1860: A Life in the Arts
0–910732–19–1 Historical Society pb $10.00

- **Richard McLanathan**
GILBERT STUART: The Father of American Portraiture
0–8109–1501–4 Abrams $35.00

- **Helen Cooper**
JOHN TRUMBULL: The Hand and Spirit of a Painter
Trumbull's work documented the Revolutionary era and its heroes
0–300–02928–4 Yale $50.00
0–300–02932–2 Yale pb $24.95

- **Helmut Von Erffa & Allen Staley**
THE PAINTINGS OF BENJAMIN WEST
Painter of historical subjects and portraits, West moved to England in 1763 and received royal patronage, becoming president of the Royal Academy
0–300–03355–9 Yale $90.00

THE 19TH CENTURY

- **Andres Cosentino & Henry Glassie**
THE CAPITAL IMAGE: Painters in Washington, 1800-1915
0–87474–338–9 Smithsonian $42.00
0–87474–337–0 Smithsonian pb $22.50

- **Lynda R. Hartigan**
SHARING TRADITIONS: Five Black Artists in 19th-Century America
0–87474–513–6 Smithsonian pb $17.50

- **Russell Lynes**
THE ART MAKERS: An Informal History of Painting, Sculpture, and Architecture in 19th Century America
Deals with collecting, art patronage and the relations of the artists with the public
0–486–24239–0 Dover pb $9.95

- **Barbara Novak**
AMERICAN PAINTING OF THE NINETEENTH CENTURY: Realism, Idealism and the American Experience
0–06–430099–4 Harper & Row pb $13.95

NATURE AND CULTURE: American Landscape and Painting, 1825-1875
0–19–502606–3 Oxford $45.00
0–19–502935–6 Oxford pb $25.00

- **Ronald Pisano**
IDLE HOURS: American Leisure Activities, 1865-1914
The work of such artists as Winslow Homer, John Singer Sargent, Thomas Eakins, and Mary Cassatt, describing a time of prosperity and relaxation in America
0–8212–1673–2 NY Graphic Society $65.00

LONG ISLAND LANDSCAPE PAINTING, 1820-1920
0–8212–1597–3 NY Graphic Society $45.00
0–8212–1692–5 NY Graphic Society pb $24.95

- **Richard Wilson & others**
THE AMERICAN RENAISSANCE: 1876-1917
Discusses and illustrates both painting and the decorative arts in the context of social history
0–295–96228–3 Washington pb $14.95

- **John James Audubon**
THE ORIGINAL WATERCOLOR PAINTINGS BY JOHN JAMES AUDUBON FOR THE BIRDS OF AMERICA
Complete reproduction of each of Audubon's 433 original watercolor paintings, from the collection at the New York Historical Society. Large format, beautifully illustrated with a good introduction
0–517–24945–6 Crown $39.95

- **Susanne Low**
AN INDEX AND GUIDE TO AUDUBON'S BIRDS OF AMERICA
A comprehensive cross-indexed concordance to *The Birds of America*, which also deals with variants in plates, and extinct and mystery birds Audubon depicted; with plates for each bird
0–89659–817–9 Abbeville $47.50

 ➤ FOR OVERSEAS ORDERING INFORMATION, SEE PAGE 1

• Lloyd Goodrich
THOMAS EAKINS
A biography of the great realist artist, and
a study of his work in all media
0–674–88490–6 Harvard $90.00

• Elizabeth Johns
**THOMAS EAKINS: The Heroism of
Modern Life**
A detailed account of his work as a
portraitist, centering on five major
paintings
0–691–04022–2 Princeton $50.00

• Alice Ford
EDWARD HICKS: His Life and Art
A large-format picture book
0–89659–570–6 Abbeville $75.00

• Eleanore Mather & Dorothy Miller
**EDWARD HICKS: His Peaceable
Kingdoms and Other Paintings**
The Quaker artist painted more than 50
versions of his *Peaceable Kingdom*, a
biblically inspired work that is regarded as
a masterpiece of American naive painting
0–87413–208–8 Delaware $40.00

• Helen Cooper
WINSLOW HOMER WATERCOLORS
Homer painted over 600 watercolors of
New England, Canada, the Bahamas, Key
West, the Adirondacks and England. His
bold brushwork and colors greatly
influenced later American watercolor artists
0–300–03695–7 Yale $36.00
0–300–03997–2 Yale pb $19.95

• Marc Simpson
**WINSLOW HOMER: Paintings of the
Civil War**
Homer's first paintings, from 1861-71; a
unique view of history through the eyes of
the great American artist
0–938491–15–6 Bedford Arts $39.95

• William Kloss
SAMUEL F.B. MORSE
Emphasizes the artistic side of this painter-
inventor
0–8109–1531–6 Abrams $35.00

• Regina Soria
ELIHU VEDDER
0–8386–6906–9 Fairleigh Dickinson $45.00

• Joshua Taylor & others
**PERCEPTIONS AND EVOCATIONS: The
Art of Elihu Vedder**
0–87474–902–6 Smithsonian $35.00
0–87474–903–4 Smithsonian pb $19.95

The Hudson River School

• Kevin Avery, editor
**AMERICAN PARADISE: The World of the
Hudson River School**
Catalog for the monumental Metropolitan
Museum exhibition: a survey of America's
first indigenous school of painting
0–8109–1165–5 Abrams $49.50

• William Hosley
**THE GREAT RIVER: Art and Society of
the Connecticut River**
0–918333–03–2 Wadsworth Atheneum pb $35.00

• John Howat
**THE HUDSON RIVER AND ITS
PAINTERS**
0–317–54888–3 Apollo $25.00

• Sandra Philips & Linda Weintraub
**CHARMED PLACES: Hudson River
Artists: Their Houses, Studios and Vistas**
0–8109–1041–1 Abrams $29.95

• Gerald Carr
**FREDERIC EDWIN CHURCH: The
Icebergs**
Fascinated by the workings of science and
nature, Church travelled the world to find
the subjects of his dramatic landscapes
0–292–72439–X Texas pb $12.95

• Matthew Baigell
THOMAS COLE
Cole is often considered the ablest of the
early American landscape painters. One of
the founders of the Hudson River School,
he was immensely popular and influential
in his lifetime
0–8230–0648–4 Watson-Guptill pb $16.95

• Howard Merritt
**TO WALK WITH NATURE: The Drawing
of Thomas Cole**
0–943651–11–5 Hudson River Museum pb $10.00

• Ella Foshay & others
JASPER F. CROPSEY: Artist and Architect
Noted for his autumnal landscapes in oil
and watercolor, Cropsey also practiced as
an architect
0–916141–00–4 NY Historical Society pb $19.95

• Kenneth Maddox
**THE UNPREJUDICED EYE: The
Drawings of Jasper Cropsey**
0–943651–07–7 Hudson River Museum pb $10.00

• James Flexner
**ASHER B. DURAND: An Engraver's and a
Farmer's Art**
0–943651–10–7 Hudson River Museum pb $10.00

• Nicolai Cikovsky, Jr. & Michael
Quick
GEORGE INNESS
One of the most prolific landscape painters
of 19th-century America
0–87587–124–0 LA County Museum pb $19.95

• Alfred Werner
INNESS LANDSCAPES
0–8230–2552–7 Watson-Guptill pb $16.95

American Artists Abroad

"I have seen, and heard, much of Cockney
impudence before now; but never expected
to hear a coxcomb ask 200 guineas for
flinging a pot of paint in the public's face."—
John Ruskin, on Whistler

• John Coffey
**TWILIGHT OF ARCADIA: American
Landscape Painters in Rome, 1830-1880**
0–916606–14–7 Bowdoin pb $15.00

"Snowy Owl," from Birds of America *by
John James Audubon (Crown)*

• Margaretta Lovell
VENICE: The American View, 1860-1920
0–88401–044–9 San Francisco Museum pb $19.95

• Adelyn Breeskin
**CASSATT AND HER CIRCLE: Selected
Letters**
Mary Cassatt lived and worked in Paris
from about 1872 and was a friend of many
of the impressionists, especially Edgar
Degas. She is considered the first American
impressionist
0–89659–421–1 Abbeville $19.95

**MARY CASSATT: A Catalogue Raisonné of
the Graphic Work**
0–87474–284–6 Smithsonian $50.00

• Frank Getlein
MARY CASSATT: Paintings and Prints
0–89659–181–6 Abbeville $29.95
0–89659–155–7 Abbeville pb $16.95

• Suzanne Lindsay
MARY CASSATT AND PHILADELPHIA
0–87633–061–8 Philadelphia Museum $14.95

• Nancy Mathews
MARY CASSATT
0–8109–0793–3 Abrams $35.00

• Patricia Hills & others
JOHN SINGER SARGENT
Primarily known for his full-length
portraits of society figures, Sargent was
born in Florence, travelled frequently to
the United States, but settled in London
0–8109–1506–5 Abrams $39.95

• Donelson Hoopes
SARGENT WATERCOLORS
0–8230–4641–9 Watson-Guptill pb $16.95

• Stanley Olson
JOHN SINGER SARGENT: His Portrait
A biographical narrative with discussion of
individual works
0–312–44456–7 St. Martin's $16.95

- Carter Ratcliff
JOHN SINGER SARGENT
Lavishly illustrated account of the career of
the Anglo-American artist
0–89659–673–7 Abbeville pb $39.98

- David Curry
**JAMES McNEILL WHISTLER AT THE
FREER GALLERY OF ART**
Catalog and description of one of the
largest collections of Whistler's work
0–934686–53–X Smithsonian pb $30.00

- Katherine Lochnan
**THE ETCHINGS OF JAMES McNEILL
WHISTLER**
Catalog of the graphic work of the prolific
etcher
0–300–03283–8 Yale pb $17.95

- John Walker
WHISTLER
0–8109–1786–6 Abrams $35.00

- Andrew Young & others
**THE PAINTINGS OF JAMES McNEILL
WHISTLER**
A two-volume catalog of his oil paintings
0–300–02384–7 Yale (set) $250.00

American Impressionism

- Richard Boyle
AMERICAN IMPRESSIONISM
Discussions of Mary Cassatt, Theodore
Robinson, Edmund Tarbell, J. Alden Weir,
and others
0–8212–0597–8 NY Graphic Society $45.00
0–3160–3668–4 NY Graphic Society pb $22.50

- William Gerdts
AMERICAN IMPRESSIONISM
A beautifully illustrated study, by the
eminent art historian
0–89659–451–3 Abbeville $85.00

- Nancy Matthews
**WILLIAM MERRITT CHASE IN THE
COMPANY OF FRIENDS**
The Parrish Art Museum has the most
extensive collection of Chase's work
0–943526–06–X Parrish Art Museum pb $5.00

- Ronald Pisano
WILLIAM MERRITT CHASE
0–8230–5738–0 Watson-Guptill pb $16.95

- Ilene Fort
**THE FLAG PAINTINGS OF CHILDE
HASSAM**
An exhibition catalog of the work of one
of America's foremost impressionists
0–8109–1169–8 Abrams $19.95

- Coe Gallery
**THE REMEMBERED IMAGE:
Prendergast Watercolors, 1896-1906**
0–87663–509–5 Universe pb $12.95

- George Szabo, editor
**MAURICE PRENDERGAST: The Large
Boston Public Garden Sketchbook**
0–8076–1184–0 Braziller $60.00

- Richard Boyle
JOHN TWACHTMAN
One of the most noted American
impressionists, both as a painter and etcher
0–8230–2568–3 Watson-Guptill pb $16.95

- Richard Boyle & others
**TWACHTMAN IN GLOUCESTER: His
Last Years, 1900-1902**
0–87663–526–5 Universe pb $12.95

- Dorothy Young
LIFE & LETTERS OF J. ALDEN WEIR
One of the founders of "The Ten," a
group of American impressionists
organized in 1898
0–306–70097–2 Da Capo $42.50

Sculptors

- Frederick Voss & others
JOHN FRAZEE, 1790-1852: Sculptor
Frazee was one of the earliest American
sculptors. Without formal training, he
became well-known for his marble portrait
busts of prominent Americans of the
period 1825-1835
0–934552–46–0 Boston Athenaeum $15.00

- Michael Richman
**DANIEL CHESTER FRENCH: An
American Sculptor**
The sculptor best known for the Lincoln
Memorial
0–89133–048–8 Preservation Press pb $14.95

- John Dryfhout
**THE WORK OF AUGUSTUS SAINT-
GAUDENS**
Survey of the work of this prolific sculptor
whose career lasted from 1867 to 1907
0–87451–243–3 New England $60.00
0–87451–287–5 New England pb $29.95

*Daniel Chester French's "Gallaudet and His
First Deaf-Mute Pupil," from* 19th-Century
Art *by Robert Rosenblum and H.W. Janson
(Abrams)*

- Burke Wilkinson
**UNCOMMON CLAY: The Life and Works
of Augustus Saint-Gaudens**
The career of the Irish-born, French-
trained American sculptor noted for his
portraiture in marble and bronze and his
civic monuments
0–15–192749–9 HBJ $22.95

REGIONAL ART

- Celeste Adams & others
AMERICA: Art and the West
0–8109–1856–0 Abrams $27.50

- J.L. Aldridge, editor
**THE WESTERN ARTS OF CHARLES M.
RUSSELL**
0–345–34805–2 Ballantine pb $14.95

- Karl Bodmer
KARL BODMER'S AMERICA
Collected works of the artist's visits to the
American frontier in 1832-43. Watercolors
and sketches of such subjects as Prime
Minister Maximillian's expedition up the
Missouri River
0–8032–1185–6 Nebraska $70.00

- Catherine Campbell & Marcia Blaine
**NEW HAMPSHIRE SCENERY: A
Dictionary of 19th-Century Artists of New
Hampshire Mountain Landscapes**
0–914659–12–X Phoenix $25.00

- Paul Fees & Sarah Boehme
**FRONTIER AMERICA: Art and Treasures
of the Old West from the Buffalo Bill
Historical Center**
Paintings, sculptures, and decorative arts
with major holdings of the works of Alfred
Jacob Miller, Remington, Russell, and
other artists of the West
0–8109–0948–0 Abrams $35.00

- William Goetzmann
THE WEST OF THE IMAGINATION
Early 19th-century interpreters of the West
0–393–02370–2 Norton $34.95

- Frederick Renner
**CHARLES M. RUSSELL: Paintings,
Drawings and Sculpture in the Amon G.
Carter Collection**
0–8109–0466–7 Amon Carter Museum $50.00
0–8109–8062–2 Abrams pb $29.95

- Ron Tyler & others
**AMERICAN FRONTIER LIFE: Early
Western Painting and Prints**
0–89659–691–5 Abbeville $45.00

- Robert Workman
**THE EDEN OF AMERICA: Rhode Island
Landscapes, 1820-1920**
0–911517–10–3 RISD pb $18.95

Frederic Remington

Mathew Baigell
**THE WESTERN ART OF FREDERIC
REMINGTON**
0–345–33515–5 Ballantine pb $12.95

Brian Dippie
REMINGTON AND RUSSELL: The Sid Richardson Collection
Catalog of one of the major collections of these two Western artists, now in the Fort Worth Museum
0–292–77-27–8 Texas $29.95

Harold & Peggy Samuels
FREDERIC REMINGTON: A Biography
Remington achieved equal fame as illustrator, painter, and sculptor of the American West
0–292–72451–9 Texas pb $12.95

Michael Shapiro & Peter Hassrick
FREDERIC REMINGTON: The Masterworks
0–8109–1595–2 Abrams $39.95

Allen & Marilyn Splete, editors
FREDERIC REMINGTON: Selected Letters
0–89659–694–X Abbeville $29.95

20th-Century Art

The advent of modern art did not altogether coincide with the advent of the 20th century, but it was in this century that the concept of modern art spread beyond France to become an international phenomenon. As Harold Rosenberg pointed out many years ago, one of the most notable aspects of modern art has been the way it made movements more significant than regional traditions: "Instead of 'the Venetians' or 'the Flemish school,' our era presents practitioners of esthetic isms . . . . In our era it is art movements that make possible continuity of style, that stimulate interchange of ideas and perceptions among artists, that provide new points of departure for individual invention."

GENERAL

• H.H. Arnason
A HISTORY OF MODERN ART: Painting, Sculpture, Architecture, Photography
A thorough, academic survey organized according to the great movements of modern art
0–8109–1097–7 Abrams $49.50

• Dore Ashton, editor
TWENTIETH-CENTURY ARTISTS ON ART
0–394–73489–0 Pantheon pb $14.95

• Riva Castelman
PRINTS OF THE TWENTIETH CENTURY
A survey of this important medium
0–500–20228–1 Thames & Hudson pb $11.95

• Herschel Chipp
THEORIES OF MODERN ART: A Source Book by Artists and Critics
From post-impressionism to the postwar period, Cézanne to Oldenburg
0–520–05256–0 California pb $12.95

• Albert Elsen
ORIGINS OF MODERN SCULPTURE: Pioneers and Premises
An excellent introduction
0–8076–0737–1 Braziller pb $14.95

• Robert Hughes
THE SHOCK OF THE NEW: The Life and Death of Modern Art
A lively and opinionated book by the well-known critic, well-illustrated
0–394–32800–0 Knopf pb $29.95

• Sam Hunter & John Jacobus
AMERICAN ART OF THE TWENTIETH CENTURY: Painting, Sculpture, and Architecture
The standard academic survey
0–8109–0135–8 Abrams $49.50

• Rosalind Krauss
PASSAGES IN MODERN SCULPTURE
A brilliant collection of critical essays
0–262–61033–7 MIT pb $12.50

• Alexander Liberman
THE ARTIST IN HIS STUDIO: The Heroes of Modern Art
A revised edition of this collection of photographs and commentary on the studios of the pioneers of modern art in France. Includes conversations with such artists as Matisse, Braque, Giacometti, and Balthus
0–394–56567–3 Random House $60.00

• Kenneth McLeish
A COMPANION TO THE ARTS IN THE 20TH CENTURY
0–14–051144–X Penguin pb $9.95

• Harold Osborne, editor
THE OXFORD COMPANION TO 20TH-CENTURY ART
0–19–866119–3 Oxford $49.95
0–19–282076–1 Oxford pb $21.50

• Herbert Read
A CONCISE HISTORY OF MODERN PAINTING
0–500–20141–2 Thames & Hudson pb $11.95

• John Russell
THE MEANING OF MODERN ART
An accessible account by the *NY Times* art critic
0–06–430110–9 Harper & Row pb $22.95

• Nikos Stangos, editor
CONCEPTS OF MODERN ART
An invaluable collection of essays
0–06–438535–3 Harper & Row $20.00
0–06–430104–4 Harper & Row pb $10.95

Specific Studies

• Michael Anthonioz
VERVE: The Ultimate Review of Art and Literature
The influential magazine from the 1940s and '50s, whose contributors included Matisse, Picasso, Chagall, Braque, Sartre, Joyce, and Cartier-Bresson
0–8109–1743–2 Abrams $95.00

• William Lieberman
ART OF THE TWENTIES
0–87070–216–5 Museum of Modern Art pb $8.95

• Edward Lucie-Smith
ART OF THE 1930s: The Age of Anxiety
0–317–54948–0 Apollo $35.00

• Jed Perl
PARIS WITHOUT END: On French Art since World War I
0–86547–313–7 North Point $19.95

TWENTIETH-CENTURY BRITISH ART
0–312–00844–9 St. Martin's pb $19.95

• Robert Rosenblum
MODERN PAINTING AND THE NORTHERN ROMANTIC TRADITION: Friedrich to Rothko
0–06–430057–9 Harper & Row pb $10.95

• Maurice Tuchman & Judi Freeman, editors
THE SPIRITUAL IN ART: Abstract Painting, 1890-1985
0–89659–669–9 LA County Museum $55.00
0–87587–130–5 LA County Museum pb $24.95

• Bret Waller & Grace Seiberling
ARTISTS OF LA REVUE BLANCHE: Bonnard, Toulouse-Lautrec, Vallotton, Vuillard
0–295–96211–9 Washington pb $14.95

• Frank Wilford
UNDERSTANDING ABSTRACT ART
0–525–48343–8 Dutton pb $22.50

• Rebecca Zurier
ART FOR THE MASSES, 1911-1917: A Radical Magazine and Its Artists
0–89467–036–0 Yale pb $26.50

American Art

• Milton Brown
AMERICAN PAINTING FROM THE ARMORY SHOW TO THE DEPRESSION
0–691–00301–7 Princeton pb $18.50

THE STORY OF THE ARMORY SHOW
0–89659–795–4 Abbeville $29.95

• Paul Cummings
TWENTIETH-CENTURY AMERICAN DRAWINGS FROM THE WHITNEY MUSEUM OF AMERICAN ART
0–393–02483–0 Norton $29.95

• Gail Levin
TWENTIETH-CENTURY AMERICAN PAINTING: The Thyssen-Bornemisza Collection
The catalog of a fine private collection, beautifully illustrated
0–85667–332–3 Sotheby $95.00

- Barbara Rose
AMERICAN PAINTING: The Twentieth Century
The standard history
0–8478–0716–9 Rizzoli $25.00

CUBISM

Cubism involved two basic tendencies of 20th-century art: the search for an art of pure structure, and (through the use of collage) the direct incorporation of "nonesthetic" elements of the real world. And it arrived at these impulses through the problems of finding two-dimensional equivalents for certain sensations of three-dimensional space.

Pablo Picasso made his first trip from Barcelona to Paris in 1900, which must have been something like mounting a horse in the Middle Ages and getting off in the 20th century. Picasso did a lot of catching up in five years, and in 1906 he painted *Les Demoiselles d'Avignon*, whose sources have been intensely debated ever since. What is certain is that nothing quite like it had been seen before, whatever its debts to Cézanne, primitive Iberian or African carvings, or El Greco. This painting—with its fracturing of pictorial space under a pressure at once intellectual and emotional—seemed to mock Cézanne's commitment to observed nature. Here began the reconstruction of pictorial space out of abstract units which became known as cubism.

- Guillaume Apollinaire
APOLLINAIRE ON ART: Essays and Reviews, 1902-1918
The poet and art critic who introduced Picasso to Braque
0–306–80312–7 Da Capo pb $13.95

- Alfred H. Barr, Jr.
CUBISM AND ABSTRACT ART
The catalog from a historically important exhibition
0–674–17935–8 Harvard pb $17.50

- Douglas Cooper & Gary Tinterow
ESSENTIAL CUBISM
Cooper was both a close friend of many of the cubists and a discerning collector of their work
0–8076–1092–5 Braziller $45.00

- Edward Fry
CUBISM
0–500–20047–5 Thames & Hudson pb $11.95

- John Golding
CUBISM: A History and Analysis, 1907-1914
0–674–17929–3 Harvard $39.95

- Chris Green
CUBISM AND ITS ENEMIES: Modern Movements and Reaction in French Art, 1916-1928
0–300–03468–7 Yale $60.00

Self-portrait by Pablo Picasso (Philadelphia Museum of Art)

Pablo Picasso

- Dore Ashton, editor
PICASSO ON ART: A Selection of Views
0–306–80330–5 Da Capo pb $11.95

- John Berger
THE SUCCESS AND FAILURE OF PICASSO
A bracing antidote to the flattering tone of much writing about Picasso
0–394–73900–0 Pantheon pb $7.95

- Dominique Bozo, editor
THE PICASSO MUSEUM, PARIS: Paintings, Collages, Reliefs, Sculpture, and Ceramics
Excellent plates of the works housed in the newly created museum, the bequest the artist made to the French government in lieu of paying taxes
0–8109–1465–4 Abrams $60.00

- Mary Gedo
PICASSO: Art As Autobiography
0–226–28483–2 Chicago pb $12.50

- Marilyn McCully, editor
A PICASSO ANTHOLOGY: Documents, Criticism, Reminiscences
0–691–04001–X Princeton $31.50
0–691–00348–3 Princeton pb $12.95

- Roland Penrose
PICASSO: His Life and Work
0–520–04182–8 California $37.50
0–520–04207–7 California pb $12.95

- Pablo Picasso
JE SUIS LE CAHIER: The Sketchbooks of Picasso
An intimate view of the artist's work, beautifully reproduced
0–87113–072–6 Atlantic Monthly $65.00

- Edward Quinn & Pierre Daix
THE PRIVATE PICASSO: A Photographic Study
A pictorial and photographic biography
0–8212–1642–2 NY Graphic Society $75.00

- Robert Rosenblum
THE SCULPTURE OF PICASSO
0–938608–08–8 Pace pb $16.00

- William Rubin & Dominique Bozo, editors
PABLO PICASSO: A Retrospective
This exhibition catalog from the Museum of Modern Art includes a fine collection of plates
0–316–70702–3 NY Graphic Society $50.00
0–316–70703–1 NY Graphic Society pb $25.00

- Gertrude Stein
PICASSO: The Complete Writings
A match for Picasso's own idiosyncrasy
0–8070–6657–5 Beacon pb $7.95

The Other Cubists

Picasso was not alone in creating cubism. It resulted from an intense period of collaboration with Georges Braque, during which, as Picasso put it, "it was as if we were husband and wife." The movement soon attracted many adherents, including Juan Gris, in whose hands cubism took a somewhat didactic turn. Strong personalities like Robert and Sonia Delaunay and Fernand Léger were greatly influenced by cubism without ever falling fully under its spell.

- Georges Braque
ILLUSTRATED NOTEBOOKS, 1917-1955
0–486–20232–1 Dover pb $6.00

- Raymond Cogniat
BRAQUE
0–8109–0703–8 Abrams $45.00

- Serge Fauchereau
BRAQUE
0–8478–0794–0 Rizzoli $19.95

- Bernard Zurcher
GEORGES BRAQUE: Life and Work
0–8478–0986–2 Rizzoli $85.00

- Michael Hoog
DELAUNAY
A study of Robert Delaunay's work
0–517–52875–4 Crown $14.95

- Arthur Cohen, editor
SONIA DELAUNAY
0–8109–0292–3 Abrams $65.00

- Mark Rosenthal
JUAN GRIS
0–89659–400–9 Abbeville $45.00

- Gaston Diehl
FERNAND LEGER
0–517–54711–2 Crown $14.95

- Gladys Fabre & others
LEGER AND THE MODERN SPIRIT: An Avant-Garde Alternative to Non-Objective Art
0–295–96072–8 Washington pb $35.00

- Amédée Ozenfant
FOUNDATIONS OF MODERN ART
Theoretical formulations by an artist whose work is sometimes referred to as Purism
0–486–20215–1 Dover pb $8.95

An "accelerated course" in French taste for tourists who are still in need of it ought to begin, in my opinion, with a visit to the *marché aux puces* and end with a visit to the studio of Georges Braque. On the one hand the odds and ends, the secondhand goods produced by several centuries of a unified and centralized culture; on the other, the same objects interpenetrated and flattened out in compositions that have little to do with the well-known genre of the *nature morte* [still life].

Eugenio Montale, 1953

Daniel Halpern, editor
WRITERS ON ARTISTS
0–86547–339–0 North Point $25.00

FAUVISM

One of the fauvists laconically said of the impressionists, "We merely thought their colors were a bit dull." This most ephemeral of major art movements can be isolated to the period 1904-1907, although it reverberated long afterward. Where cubism, at least in its "purer" manifestations, was a structural art of quasi-tactile elements, fauvism was an optical art based on liberating color from any naturalistic function.

- Jean Leymarie
FAUVES AND FAUVISM
0–8478–0815–7 Rizzoli pb $25.00

- Sarah Whitfield
FAUVISM
0–500–20227–3 Thames & Hudson pb $9.95

"Lady in Blue" by Henri Matisse (Philadelphia Museum of Art)

Matisse

"Certainly this one was one who was a great man. Any one could be certain of this thing. Every one would come to be certain of this thing. This one was one certainly clearly expressing something. Any one could come to be certain of this thing. Every one would come to be certain of this thing. This one was one, some were quite certain, one greatly expressing something being struggling. This one was one, some were quite certain, one not greatly expressing something being struggling."—Gertrude Stein on Henri Matisse

- Jack Cowart & Dominique Fourcade
HENRI MATISSE: The Early Years in Nice 1916-1930
The great, often unjustly neglected work of the artist's middle age. Includes 200 colorplates
0–8109–1442–5 Abrams $45.00
0–8109–2366–1 Abrams pb $29.95

- Jack Flam, editor
MATISSE ON ART
The first collection of Matisse's major writings, including transcriptions of interviews and broadcasts
0–525–47490–0 Dutton pb $16.95

MATISSE: The Man and His Art, 1869-1918
0–8014–1840–2 Cornell $75.00

MATISSE: A Retrospective
0–88363–073–7 Levin $75.00

- Jacqueline & Maurice Guillaud
MATISSE: Rhythm and Line
Beautiful quality reproductions
0–517–56339–8 Crown $100.00

- William Lieberman
MATISSE: Fifty Years of His Graphic Art
0–8076–0037–7 Braziller $30.00
0–8076–1022–4 Braziller pb $12.95

- Henri Matisse
JAZZ
One of the century's greatest *livres d'artiste*, reprinted with scrupulous care
Introduction by Riva Castleman
0–8076–1131–X Braziller pb $22.50

- Nicholas Watkins
MATISSE
0–19–520464–6 Oxford $60.00

The Other Fauves

Henri Matisse, André Derain, Raoul Dufy, Georges Rouault, and Maurice Vlaminck were following up, in more extreme ways, on the work of a number of postimpressionist painters, especially Cézanne, Gauguin, and Van Gogh. They aspired to a virtually religious intensity of vision; only in the work of Matisse, however, was this intensity fully attained.

- Gaston Diehl
DERAIN
0–517–03720–3 Crown $14.95

- Alfred Werner
DUFY
0–8109–0083–1 Abrams $45.00
0–8109–0848–4 Abrams pb $19.95

- Pierre Courthion
ROUAULT
0–8109–0459–4 Abrams $45.00

- Jean Selz
VLAMINCK
0–517–03726–2 Crown $14.95

Contemporaries of the Fauves

A number of painters of the same generation as Matisse, such as Bonnard and Vuillard, shared the Fauves' interest in color and pattern, but remained closer to the impressionists' sense of natural light. A more classical turn was taken by the sculptor Aristide Maillol. The slightly younger Amadeo Modigliani as well, in his use of flat planes of color and "primitive" stylization, reflected some of Matisse's impulses.

- André Fermigier
BONNARD
0–8109–0732–1 Abrams $19.95

- Sasha Newman
BONNARD: The Late Paintings
0–500–27400–2 Thames & Hudson $24.95

- William Fifield
MODIGLIANI
A revisionist biography
0–688–08039–1 Morrow pb $3.95

- Alfred Werner
MODIGLIANI
0–8109–1416–6 Abrams $19.95

- Stuart Preston
VUILLARD
0–8109–1706–8 Abrams $19.95

- Belinda Thomson
VUILLARD
0–89659–883–7 Abbeville $45.00

EXPRESSIONISM AND THE BLUE RIDER

Expressionism is less a well-defined approach to picture-making on the order of impressionism or cubism than a recurrent attitude to art, like classicism or romanticism. When we speak more specifically of German expressionist art of the early 20th century, we are speaking primarily of two groups: on the one hand *Die Brücke* (The Bridge), including Ernst Ludwig Kirchner, Emil Nolde, and Max Pechstein, who exhibited together in Dresden between 1905 and 1913; and on the other the group associated with the Munich periodical *Der Blaue Reiter* (The Blue Rider), whose single issue (published in 1912) was edited by Franz Marc and Wassily Kandinsky. Other artists associated with the Blue Rider included Paul Klee and August Macke. In general, the Blue Rider artists were more involved with abstraction than those of *Die Brücke*, and they later provided the core of the painting faculty at the Bauhaus.

After World War I there was a reaction within expressionism against the excessive "inwardness" of older artists in the movement. The narrative, often bitterly satirical works of artists such as Otto Dix and Georg Grosz seemed to herald a "new objectivity" (*Neue Sachlichkeit*)—although the most important of these artists, Max Beckmann, far from embodying objectivity, may be seen as the third great mythographer of modern painting after Picasso and Matisse.

- Wolf-Dieter Dube
THE EXPRESSIONISTS
0-500-20123-4 Thames & Hudson pb $11.95

- Paul Raabe, editor
THE ERA OF GERMAN EXPRESSIONISM
An important documentary sourcebook
0-87951-010-2 Overlook $22.50
0-87951-233-4 Overlook pb $12.95

- Peter Selz
GERMAN EXPRESSIONIST PAINTING
The classic survey of the period
0-520-02515-6 California pb $14.95

- Kirk Varnedoe
VIENNA 1900: Art, Architecture, Design
0-87070-618-7 Museum of Modern Art $50.00

- Peter Vergo
ART IN VIENNA, 1898-1918: Klimt, Kokoschka, Schiele, and Their Contemporaries
0-8014-9226-2 Cornell pb $19.95

- Paul Vogt & others
EXPRESSIONISM: A German Intuition, 1905-1920
0-295-96291-7 Washington pb $19.95

- Frank Whitford
EXPRESSIONIST PORTRAITS
Brings to life a profoundly influential period in modern art, by concentrating on artists, their sitters, and the expression of extreme emotion; sumptuous illustrations
0-89659-780-6 Abbeville $50.00

- John Willett
ART AND POLITICS IN THE WEIMAR PERIOD: The New Sobriety, 1917-1933
0-394-73991-4 Random House pb $14.95

German Expressionists

- Stephen Lackner
MAX BECKMANN: Memories of a Friendship
0-517-55000-8 Crown $14.95

- Carla Schultz-Hoffman & Julia Weiss
MAX BECKMANN: A Retrospective
0-393-01937-3 Norton $100.00

- Fritz Loffler
OTTO DIX: Life and Work
0-8419-0578-9 Holmes & Meier $95.00

- Serge Sabarsky, editor
LYONEL FEININGER: Drawings and Watercolors
0-918825-41-5 Moyer Bell pb $14.00

- Hans Hess
GEORGE GROSZ
0-300-03408-3 Yale $40.00
0-300-03297-8 Yale pb $16.95

- Wassily Kandinsky
CONCERNING THE SPIRITUAL IN ART
Kandinsky's primary statement of his philosophy of art
0-486-23411-8 Dover pb $2.95

- Vivian Barnett & Christian Derouet
KANDINSKY IN PARIS: 1934-1944
0-89207-049-8 Guggenheim pb $19.50

- Clark Poling
KANDINSKY: Russian and Bauhaus Years, 1915-1933
0-89207-044-7 Guggenheim pb $19.50

- Peg Weiss
KANDINSKY IN MUNICH: 1896-1914
0-89207-030-7 Guggenheim pb $19.50

- Paul Klee
THE DIARIES OF PAUL KLEE
Edited by Felix Klee
0-520-00653-4 California pb $12.95

PAUL KLEE ON MODERN ART
A collection of his writing
0-571-06682-8 Faber & Faber pb $5.95

- Will Grohmann
KLEE
0-8109-0228-1 Abrams $45.00
0-8109-1208-2 Abrams pb $19.95

- Carolyn Lancher
PAUL KLEE
Published to accompany the major retrospective held at the Museum of Modern Art
0-870-70403-6 NY Graphic Society $55.00

- Richard Calvocoressi
OSKAR KOKOSCHKA
0-89207-060-9 Guggenheim $38.00
0-89207-059-5 Guggenheim pb $26.00

Expressionism Outside Germany

Expressionism was not limited to German-speaking countries. In Paris some of the fauves came close; Rouault in particular is often referred to as an expressionist. The fantastic paintings of Marc Chagall are closely related, and the impulse reached a particularly intense pitch in the work of Chaim Soutine.

- François Le Targat
CHAGALL
0-8478-0624-3 Rizzoli $19.95

- Raymond Cogniat
SOUTINE
0-517-51136-3 Crown $14.95

- Alfred Werner
SOUTINE
0-8109-1500-6 Abrams $19.95

FUTURISM

Futurism, invented by a well-to-do *littérateur* named F.T. Marinetti, was probably the first important art movement in which publicity came first and art followed. Futurism's romanticizing of speed, dynamism, and the machine could only have arisen in a less developed part of Europe such as Italy, but it did temporarily attract most of the ambitious Italian painters of the pre-war years: Giacomo Balla, Umberto Boccioni, Carlo Carrà, and Gino Severini.

- Pontus Hulten
FUTURISM AND FUTURISMS
The catalog of a mammoth exhibition which attempted to place Italian futurism at the center of the international avant garde. Although it overstated the case, it did point to important connections
0-89659-675-3 Abbeville $85.00

- Giovanni Lista
FUTURISM
0-87663-500-1 Universe pb $9.95

- Caroline Tisdall & Angelo Bozollo
FUTURISM
0-500-18162-4 Thames & Hudson $19.95
0-500-20159-5 Thames & Hudson pb $11.95

Franco Solmi & others
MORANDI
Although Morandi was briefly associated with the Italian metaphysical school of the 1920's, his inscrutable still-lifes put him in a category of his own
0-8478-0930-7 Rizzoli pb $30.00

VORTICISM

Strong affinities with Futurism were shown by the English movement known as vorticism, whose proponents included Wyndham Lewis, Jacob Epstein, Henri Gaudier-Brzeska, and (for a time) David Bomberg. These artists were close to the poet Ezra Pound.

- Richard Cork
VORTICISM AND ABSTRACT ART IN THE FIRST MACHINE AGE
An exhaustive study of the movement

Volume 1: Origins and Development
0-520-03154-7 California $95.00

Volume 2: Synthesis and Decline
0-520-03269-1 California $95.00

 TO ORDER BOOKS AS GIFTS, SEE PAGE 1

DAVID BOMBERG
0–300–03827–5 Yale $100.00
0–300–04194–2 Yale pb $39.95

- Jeremy Lewison, editor
HENRI GAUDIER-BRZESKA, SCULPTOR: 1891-1915
0–87663–992–9 Universe pb $12.50

- Ezra Pound
GAUDIER-BRZESKA: A Memoir
0–8112–0527–4 New Directions pb $7.95

RUSSIAN FUTURISM AND CONSTRUCTIVISM

Russian artists of the early 20th century were attuned to new developments in Paris as well as to Italian futurism, and at the same time were tremendously interested in Russia's icon and folk art traditions, with their innocence of Western naturalism. The result was an artistic ferment from which two primary trends stand out: the purely non-objective tendency which Kasimir Malevich called suprematism, and the utilitarian, antiesthetic direction championed by Vladimir Tatlin and El Lissitsky, which by 1920 was known as constructivism.

- Abrams editors
SOVIET ART, 1920-1930: From the Russian Museum, Leningrad
A recent exhibition of works by Kandinsky, Rodchenko and others not seen by Russians for decades
0–8109–2399–8 Abrams $29.95

- Stephanie Barron & Maurice Tuchman, editors
THE AVANT-GARDE IN RUSSIA, 1910-1930: New Perspectives
An excellent, broad study
0–262–52077–X MIT pb $15.00

- Christina Lodder
RUSSIAN CONSTRUCTIVISM
0–300–03406–7 Yale pb $17.95

- John Milner
VLADIMIR TATLIN AND THE RUSSIAN AVANT-GARDE
0–300–02771–0 Yale $39.95
0–300–03404–0 Yale pb $15.95

MONDRIAN AND DE STIJL

"In the future," wrote the Dutch painter Piet Mondrian, "the tangible embodiment of pictorial values will supplant art. Then we shall no longer need painting, for we shall be in the midst of realized art." Mondrian, along with Theo van Doesburg, edited an influential review called *De Stijl*, whose name became attached to their work, which is also known as neo-plasticism. Their work is notable for its rather Calvinist sobriety and restraint; they restricted their palette to the primary colors red, yellow, and blue, along with black, white, and gray, structured by

Piet Mondrian's "Composition" (Museum of Modern Art), from Modern Art *by Meyer Shapiro (Braziller)*

straight lines and right angles. Their adherence to doctrine was so strict that the two artists fell out in a dispute over the admissibility of diagonals in painting.

- Carel Blotkamp, editor
DE STIJL: The Formative Years
0–262–02247–8 MIT $49.50

- Mildred Friedman, editor
DE STIJL 1917-1931: Visions of Utopia
An important study of the movement
0–89659–257–X Abbeville $39.95
0–89659–255–3 Abbeville pb $29.95

- Harry Holtzman & Martin James, editors
THE NEW ART, THE NEW LIFE: The Collected Writings of Piet Mondrian
0–8057–9957–5 G.K. Hall $60.00

- Hans Jaffe
MONDRIAN
0–8109–1413–1 Abrams $19.95

THE BAUHAUS AND RELATED CONSTRUCTIVISM

Another group, more didactic and experimental, centered around the Bauhaus, the school founded in Weimar by architect Walter Gropius. Among the artists who taught there were Oskar Schlemmer, Lyonel Feininger, and László Moholy-Nagy, as well as some earlier associated with expressionism, like Kandinsky and Klee. A number of the Russian vanguardists arrived after 1922, as the climate for modern art grew chilly at home. Related "constructivist" ideas sprang up elsewhere in Europe as well: in England with the work of Ben Nicholson and the early work of Henry Moore, in Paris with that of Constantin Brancusi.

- Johannes Itten
DESIGN AND FORM
The text of the famous basic course at the Bauhaus
0–442–24039–2 Van Nostrand Reinhold pb $15.95

- Jeremy Lewison
CIRCLE: Constructive Art in Britain, 1934-1940
0–87663–857–4 Universe pb $12.50

- Margit Rowell
THE PLANAR DIMENSION: Europe, 1912-1932
An essential study of international constructivist sculpture
0–295–96290–9 Washington pb $14.95

- Josef Albers
INTERACTION OF COLOR
0–300–01846–0 Yale pb $6.95

- Nicholas Weber
THE DRAWINGS OF JOSEF ALBERS
0–300–03168–8 Yale $37.50
JOSEF ALBERS: A Retrospective
0–8109–1876–5 Abrams $65.00

- Sidney Geist
BRANCUSI: A Study of the Sculpture
An important book
0–87817–290–4 Hacker $40.00

- Radu Varia
BRANCUSI
0–8478–0673–1 Rizzoli $75.00

- David Jenkins
BARBARA HEPWORTH
0–905005–83–X Salem House pb $7.95

"The Kiss," from Brancusi *by Radu Varia (Rizzoli)*

- Clark Poling
KANDINSKY'S TEACHING AT THE BAUHAUS: Color Theory and Analytical Drawing
0–8478–0780–0 Rizzoli $40.00

- Krisztina Passuth
MOHOLY-NAGY
0–500–27449–5 Thames & Hudson pb $24.95

Ann Garrould
HENRY MOORE DRAWINGS
0–8478–0982–X Rizzoli $75.00

William Lieberman
HENRY MOORE: Sixty Years of His Art
0–500–23376–4 Thames & Hudson $24.95

DADA

While fauvism, cubism, and even expressionism can all be seen as modes of pictorial organization, dada (as André Breton said) "is a state of mind." The artists who gathered under the banner of dada came through the years of the Great War with a combination of deadpan nihilism and desperate playfulness that gave their work a new disruptive power—the power of anti-art. The movement was international, with manifestations in Zurich, Berlin, Paris, and even New York.

- Rudolf Kuenzli, editor
NEW YORK DADA
An anthology
0–930279–10–7 Willis, Locker & Owens $22.95
0–930279–09–3 Willis, Locker & Owens pb $12.95

- Robert Motherwell, editor
THE DADA PAINTERS AND POETS
An anthology of original texts
0–674–18500–5 Harvard pb $19.95

- Calvin Tomkins
THE BRIDE AND THE BACHELORS: Five Masters of the Avant-Garde
A study of the aesthetics of Duchamp, Tinguely, John Cage, Robert Rauschenberg, and Merce Cunningham
0–14–004313–6 Penguin pb $7.95

- Serge Fauchereau
HANS ARP
0–8478–0974–9 Rizzoli $19.95

- Jane Hancock & Stefanie Poley, editors
HANS ARP, 1886-1966
0–521–34538–3 Cambridge $65.00

- Ecke Bonk
MARCEL DUCHAMP: Box in a Valise
0–8478–0979–X Rizzoli $65.00

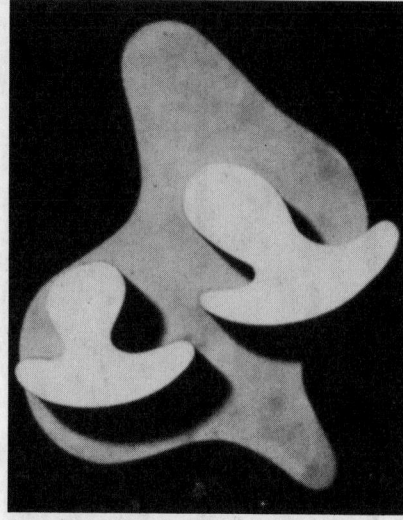

Jean Arp's "Vase-Bust" (Philadelphia Museum of Art)

- Pierre Cabanne
DIALOGUES WITH MARCEL DUCHAMP
"These conversations are more than mere interviews. They are Marcel Duchamp's 'summing up,' and constitute as vivid a self-portrait as we possess of a major twentieth-century artist, thanks to Duchamp's intelligence, scrupulousness, and disdain for the petty"—Robert Motherwell
0–306–80303–8 Da Capo pb $9.95

- Man Ray
SELF PORTRAIT
Afterword by Juliet Man Ray
0–8212–1705–4 NY Graphic Society $35.00

- Neil Baldwin
MAN RAY: American Artist
A new biography
0–517–56001–1 Crown $25.00

- John Elderfield
KURT SCHWITTERS
0–500–27474–6 Thames & Hudson pb $24.95

SURREALISM

Surrealism, which originated among former members of the Paris dada circle, was in a sense an effort to place dada irrationalism on a positive and quasi-scientific footing. More a movement of poets than painters, surrealism produced two distinct pictorial approaches, one based on graphic automatism as an equivalent to automatic writing in poetry (for example, Max Ernst's *frottages* or 'rubbings') while the other sought veristic representations of irrational, dreamlike images, as in the paintings of the Belgian René Magritte.

- Dawn Ades & others
IN THE MIND'S EYE: Dada and Surrealism
0–89659–596–X Abbeville $55.00

- J.H. Matthews
EIGHT PAINTERS: The Surrealist Context
0–8156–2302–X Syracuse pb $12.95

- Gaeton Picon
SURREALISTS AND SURREALISM
0–8478–0486–0 Rizzoli pb $25.00

- André Breton
MANIFESTOES OF SURREALISM
0–472–06182–8 Michigan pb $10.00

- Salvador Dali
DIARY OF A GENIUS
0–13–208521–6 Prentice-Hall pb $10.95

- Robert Descharnes
DALI
0–8109–0222–2 Abrams $49.50

DALI: The Work, the Man
Over 1000 illustrations
0–8109–0825–5 Abrams $145.00

- Max Ernst
MAX ERNST LOPLOP: The Artist in the Third Person
0–8076–1065–8 Braziller $49.00

- Gaston Diehl
MAX ERNST
0–517–50004–3 Crown $14.95

- Robert Rainwater
MAX ERNST: Beyond Surrealism: An Exhibition of the Artist's Books and Prints
0–19–504991–8 Oxford $35.00
0–19–504990–X Oxford pb $19.95

- Michel Foucault
THIS IS NOT A PIPE: Illustrations and Letters by René Magritte
An unusual and distinguished philosophical account of Magritte's work
0–520–04232–8 California $22.00
0–520–04916–0 California pb $7.95

- Pere Gimferrer
MAGRITTE
0–8478–0809–2 Rizzoli $19.95

- Bernard Nöel
MAGRITTE
0–517–53009–0 Crown $14.95

- Joan Miró
JOAN MIRO: A Retrospective
0–300–04073–3 Yale $50.00

- Roland Penrose
MIRO
0–500–20099–8 Thames & Hudson pb $11.95

- Dorothea Tanning
BIRTHDAY
A luminous memoir of the artist's marriage to Max Ernst
0–932499–15–5 Lapis $19.95

Latin American Artists

Luis Cancel, editor
THE LATIN AMERICAN SPIRIT: Art and Artists in the United States, 1920-1970
0–8109–1271–6 Abrams $45.00

Hayden Herrera
FRIDA: A Biography of Frida Kahlo
0–06–091127–1 Harper & Row pb $15.95

Carter Ratcliff
BOTERO
0–89659–146–8 Abbeville $95.00

Edward Sullivan
BOTERO SCULPTURE
0–89659–657–5 Abbeville $125.00

Alma Reed
JOSE CLEMENTE OROZCO
0–87817–204–1 Hacker $50.00

Terri Cohn
DIEGO RIVERA: Selected Works, 1918-1949
0–9605194–4–0 Mexican Museum pb $6.00

Ramon Favela
DIEGO RIVERA: A Retrospective
0–393–02275–7 Detroit Institute $60.00
0–89558–118–3 Detroit Institute pb $30.00

Jose Corredor-Matheos
TAMAYO
0–8478–0855–6 Rizzoli $19.95

Rufino Tamayo
RUFINO TAMAYO: 50 Years of His Painting
0–295–95816–2 Washington $15.00
0–295–95822–7 Washington pb $7.50

"Man on Horseback" by Fernando Botero

AMERICAN ART BEFORE THE 1940s

American art remained relatively provincial up until the 1940s. In the early 20th century two New York-based groups challenged the derivative academic tradition. One centered around Robert Henri, whose socially-oriented naturalism led to the nickname the Ashcan School. More radical and cosmopolitan in outlook were the artists who showed at the 291 Gallery run by photographer Alfred Stieglitz: Arthur Dove, Marsden Hartley, John Marin, and (later) Georgia O'Keefe among them. A group of "synchronists," including Morgan Russell and Stanton McDonald-Wright, practiced an art of color relations comparable to that of the Delaunays in Paris. Among the sculptors active in New York were Gaston Lachaise and Elie Nadelman.

The 1920s

• Gail Levin
SYNCHRONISM AND AMERICAN COLOR ABSTRACTION, 1910-1925
0–8076–0882–3 Braziller $22.50
0–8076–0883–1 Braziller pb $11.95

• Bernard Perlman
PAINTERS OF THE ASHCAN SCHOOL: The Immortal Eight
Interviews of such Ashcan artists as Maurice Prendergast and John Sloan, who worked from the 1870s to the end of World War 1, under the leadership of Robert Henri
0–486–25747–9 Dover pb $9.95

• Jane Myers & Linda Ayres
GEORGE BELLOWS: The Artist and his Lithographs, 1916-1924
0–88360–059–5 Amon Carter Museum $45.00

• Ann Morgan
ARTHUR DOVE: His Life and Work, with a Catalogue Raisonné
0–87413–222–3 Delaware $60.00

• Sasha Newman
ARTHUR DOVE AND DUNCAN PHILLIPS: Artist and Patron
0–686–36420–1 Phillips Collection pb $18.00

• Gail Scott
MARSDEN HARTLEY
0–89659–879–9 Abbeville $55.00

• Robert Henri
THE ART SPIRIT
Henri's writings show why he was such an inspiring teacher, and the center of the Ashcan School
0–06–430138–9 Harper & Row pb $5.95

• William Homer
ROBERT HENRI AND HIS CIRCLE
0–87817–326–9 Hacker $50.00

• Gerald Nordland
GASTON LACHAISE: The Man and His Work
An exhibition catalog devoted to the French sculptor active in New York in the '20s
0–8076–0762–2 Braziller pb $8.95

• MacKinley Helm
JOHN MARIN
0–306–71489–2 Da Capo $39.50

• Klaus Kertess
MARIN IN OIL: 1913-1953
0–943526–15–9 Parrish Art Museum pb $20.00

• Lincoln Kirstein
ELIE NADELMAN
0–87130–034–6 Eakins $85.00

• Lincoln Kirstein, editor
ELIE NADELMAN DRAWINGS
0–87817–045–6 Hacker $25.00

Laurie Lisle
PORTRAIT OF AN ARTIST: A Biography of Georgia O'Keefe
0–8263–0907–0 New Mexico $29.95

National Gallery Curators
GEORGIA O'KEEFE, 1887-1986
0–89468–102–8 National Gallery pb $22.00

Georgia O'Keefe
GEORGIA O'KEEFE
Her paintings with her writings
0–670–33710–2 Viking $75.00

Alfred Stieglitz
GEORGIA O'KEEFE: A Portrait by Alfred Stieglitz
Photographs of the artist taken by her husband Alfred Stieglitz
0–670–51989–8 Viking $45.00

• Elzea Rowland, editor
JOHN SLOAN: Spectator of Life
0–8122–8149–7 Pennsylvania $39.95

The 1930s

By the '30s, a populist school of "American Scene" painters had arisen in opposition to the formal and international aspirations of the avant-garde—among them a former avant-gardist from the Midwest, Thomas Hart Benton. Edward Hopper's idiosyncratically realistic studies of urban solitude and alienation also gained attention. In addition the '30s saw the emergence of a new generation of abstract or quasi-abstract artists, among them Alexander Calder, Stuart Davis, and Isamu Noguchi.

• John Lane & Susan Larsen, editors
ABSTRACT PAINTING AND SCULPTURE IN AMERICA, 1927-1944
An important exhibition catalog devoted to the work and ideas of such American abstract artists as Stuart Davis and George L.K. Morris
0–8109–2278–9 Abrams pb $24.95

- **Thomas Hart Benton**
AN ARTIST IN AMERICA
The artist's own story, with a foreword by Matthew Baigell
0–8262–0394–9 Missouri $25.00
0–8262–0399–X Missouri pb $12.95

- **Henry Adams**
THOMAS HART BENTON: An American Original
An illustrated biography of the artist, written in conjunction with the retrospective exhition of his work
0–394–57153–3 Knopf $60.00

- **John Baur**
THE INLANDER: Life and Work of Charles Burchfield, 1893-1967
0–87413–186–3 Delaware $50.00

- **Michael Gibson**
CALDER
0–87663–541–9 Universe pb $12.95

- **Jean Lipman**
CALDER CREATURES: Great and Small
0–525–48172–9 Dutton pb $10.95
CALDER'S UNIVERSE
0–89471–652–2 Running Press $19.98

- **Jean Lipman & Margaret Aspinwall**
ALEXANDER CALDER AND HIS MAGICAL MOBILES
0–933920–17–2 Hudson Hills $15.00

- **Jane Myers**
STUART DAVIS: Graphic Work and Related Paintings with a Catalogue Raisonné of the Prints
0–88360–054–4 Amon Carter Museum $29.95
0–88360–055–2 Amon Carter Museum pb $14.95

- **Karen Wilkin**
STUART DAVIS
0–89659–755–5 Abbeville $85.00

- **Lloyd Goodrich**
EDWARD HOPPER
0–317–30949–8 Abrams $35.00

Aline Fruhauf's caricature of Stuart Davis, from her book Making Faces (Seven Locks)

- **Gail Levin**
EDWARD HOPPER: The Art and the Artist
0–393–01374–X Norton $50.00
0–393–00082–6 Norton pb $22.50

- **Philip Adams**
WALT KUHN, PAINTER: His Life and Work
0–8142–0258–6 Ohio State $45.00

- **Sam Hunter**
ISAMU NOGUCHI
0–89659–003–8 Abbeville $95.00

- **Isamu Noguchi**
THE ISAMU NOGUCHI GARDEN MUSEUM
0–8109–1374–7 Abrams $35.00

Wanda Corn
GRANT WOOD: The Regionalist Vision
0–300–03103–3 Yale $40.00
0–300–03401–6 Yale pb $16.95

James Dennis
GRANT WOOD: A Study in American Art and Culture
0–8262–0660–3 Missouri pb $29.95

Other Contemporary Artists Active in America

- **Barbara Haskell**
MILTON AVERY
0–06–433320–5 Harper & Row $34.50
0–06–430121–4 Harper & Row pb $18.95

- **Helen Yglesias**
ISABEL BISHOP
0–8478–0976–5 Rizzoli $45.00

- **Lincoln Kirstein**
PAUL CADMUS
0–8478–0767–3 Rizzoli pb $27.50

- **Melvin Lader**
ARSHILE GORKY
0–89659–525–0 Abbeville $29.95
0–89659–528–5 Abbeville pb $19.95

- **Diane Waldman**
ARSHILE GORKY: A Retrospective
0–8109–2309–2 Abrams pb $24.95

- **Ray Kass**
MORRIS GRAVES: Vision of the Inner Eye
0–8076–1068–2 Braziller $35.00

- **Cynthia Goodman**
HANS HOFMANN
0–89659–441–6 Abbeville $29.95
0–89659–442–4 Abbeville pb $19.95

- **Ben Shahn**
THE SHAPE OF CONTENT
0–674–80570–4 Harvard pb $3.95

- **Raphael Soyer**
RAPHAEL SOYER: Life Drawings and Portraits
0–486–25100–4 Dover pb $3.50

Art since 1945

- **R. Alley**
FORTY YEARS OF MODERN ART, 1945-1985
0–295–96759–5 Washington pb $17.95

- **James Casebere**
AMERICAN STILL LIFE, 1945-1982
0–0643–0131–1 Harper & Row pb $19.95

- **Christopher Knight**
ART OF THE SIXTIES AND SEVENTIES
0–317–68251–2 Rizzoli $60.00

- **Edward Lucie-Smith**
AMERICAN ART NOW
0–688–05884–1 Morrow $24.95
MOVEMENTS IN ART SINCE 1945
0–8446–6129–5 Peter Smith $16.75
SCULPTURE SINCE 1945
0–87663–665–2 Universe $39.95

- **Daniel Wheeler**
ART SINCE THE MID-CENTURY
0–86565–083–7 Vendome $45.00
0–13–047598–X Prentice-Hall pb $32.00

ROBERT MOTHERWELL: Some Favorite Books on Modern Art

With two scholarly exceptions, all my recommendations are books either by artists, or filled with quotations from artists, because artists are basically concerned with what their colleagues think and not what the prevailing critical opinion is among literati. My selections are slanted toward the writings of artists themselves, notably:

Margit Rowell, editor
JOAN MIRO: Selected Writings and Interviews
0–8057–0056–7 G.K. Hall $35.00

Jack Flam, editor
MATISSE ON ART
0–525–48227–X Dutton pb $14.95

Robert Motherwell, editor
THE DADA PAINTERS AND POETS
An anthology by the dada painters and poets themselves compiled in the 1940s, which became a classic of counterculture in 20th-century art and was a tremendous influence on the New York school of poets. Allen Ginsberg attributes the existence of "Howl" to reading this book
0–674–18500–5 Harvard pb $19.95

Moreover, the following have extensive quotations from the various artists involved:

Elizabeth Frank
POLLOCK
0–89659–383–5 Abbeville $29.95
0–89659–384–3 Abbeville pb $19.95

➤ **FOR OVERSEAS ORDERING INFORMATION, SEE PAGE 1**

Richard Francis
JASPER JOHNS
0–89659–443–2 Abbeville $29.95
0–89659–444–0 Abbeville pb $19.95

Alexander Liberman
THE ARTIST IN HIS STUDIO
0–394–56567–3 Random House $60.00

Harry Gaugh
WILLEM DE KOONING
0–89659–332–0 Abbeville $29.95
0–89659–333–9 Abbeville pb $19.95

Other selections:

Michael Baxandall
PATTERNS OF INTENTION
A brilliant art history book, concerning such topics as the technique of Chardin, the aesthetics of the Bridge at Firth, and Picasso's artistic and social options as a young man
0–300–03763–5 Yale pb $11.95

Kathleen Howard, editor
THE METROPOLITAN MUSEUM OF ART GUIDE
An inexpensive guide, with 1100 full color illustrations, written by the experts on its staff
Introduction by Philippe de Montebello
0–87099–348–8 MMA $18.50
0–87099–346–1 MMA pb $9.95

Alice Miller
THE DRAMA OF THE GIFTED CHILD
A theoretical book, written by the Swiss psychoanalyst. She is a non-sectarian, whose work strikes every creative person I know to the core, and who, in mid-life, became, through psychoanalytical insight, a very good painter
0–465–09735–9 Basic Books pb $6.95

PICTURES OF A CHILDHOOD
A follow-up book of her own paintings
0–374–23241–5 FS&G $22.50

ABSTRACT EXPRESSIONISM

The origins of the "New York School" of abstract expressionism in the '40s are difficult to disentangle. The most evident influences were surrealist interests in gestural automatism and archetypal subject matter, and a concern for a synthetic treatment of pictorial space derived from cubism and Matisse.

There were two distinct tendencies within the New York School. One reached out to the sublime through large simplified shapes or fields of color, minimal articulations of the unity and flatness of the canvas itself. Clement Greenberg called this approach— exemplified by Barnett Newman, Mark Rothko, Clyfford Still, and Robert Motherwell—"American-type painting." The other broad tendency was what Harold Rosenberg christened "Action Painting": direct paint-

erly gesture channeled fragmentary pictorial impulses into suggestions of sensual volume, activating the canvas as an over-all space ("an arena in which to act," in Rosenberg's words). The painters closer to this second approach included Willem de Kooning, Jackson Pollock, Lee Krasner, and Franz Kline.

Abstract expressionism can best be approached through the writings of its most eloquent champions, Clement Greenberg and Harold Rosenberg.

Clement Greenberg
ART AND CULTURE: Critical Essays
0–8070–6681–8 Beacon pb $10.95

THE COLLECTED ESSAYS AND CRITICISM

Volume 1: Perceptions and Judgments, 1939–1944
0–226–30617–8 Chicago $27.50

Volume 2: Arrogant Purpose, 1945-1949
0–226–30618–6 Chicago $27.50

Harold Rosenberg
THE ANXIOUS OBJECT
0–226–72682–7 Chicago pb $9.95

THE DE-DEFINITION OF ART
0–226–72673–8 Chicago pb $10.95

• Dore Ashton
THE NEW YORK SCHOOL: A Cultural Reckoning
A fine introduction to the cultural milieu of abstract expressionism
0–14–005263–1 Penguin pb $10.95

"New York, N.Y." by Franz Kline (Albright Knox Gallery)

• Michael Auping
ABSTRACT EXPRESSIONISM: The Critical Developments
0–8109–1866–8 Abrams $49.50

• Serge Guilbaut
HOW NEW YORK STOLE THE IDEA OF MODERN ART: Abstract Expressionism, Freedom, and the Cold War
Contests the ideological use to which this art was put
0–226–31038–8 Chicago $22.50
0–226–31039–6 Chicago pb $10.95

• Irving Sandler
THE NEW YORK SCHOOL: The Painters and Sculptors of the Fifties
Including analyses of Gesture Painting, Assemblage, Happenings, Hard-edge, Second Generation/New Academy
0–0643–0094–3 Harper & Row pb $21.95

THE TRIUMPH OF AMERICAN PAINTING: A History of Abstract Expressionism
0–06–430075–7 Harper & Row pb $16.95

• Diane Waldman
ANTHONY CARO
0–89659–230–8 Abbeville $95.00

• Richard Newlin, editor
RICHARD DIEBENKORN: Works on Paper
0–940619–00–8 Houston Fine Art $65.00

• Gerald Nordland
RICHARD DIEBENKORN
0–8478–0870–X Rizzoli $65.00

• Harry Gaugh
WILLEM DE KOONING
0–89659–332–0 Abbeville $29.95
0–89659–333–9 Abbeville pb $19.95

• Harry Gaugh
THE VITAL GESTURE: Franz Kline
0–89659–571–4 Abbeville $55.00

• Barbara Rose
LEE KRASNER: A Retrospective
0–295–96148–1 Washington pb $14.95

• H.H. Arnason & Barbaralee Diamonstein
ROBERT MOTHERWELL
0–8109–1333–X Abrams $75.00

• Dore Ashton & Jack Flam
ROBERT MOTHERWELL
0–89659–387–8 Abbeville $35.00
0–89659–388–6 Abbeville pb $24.95

• Constance & Jack Glenn, editors
ROBERT MOTHERWELL: The Dedalus Sketchbooks
0–8109–2395–5 Abrams pb $24.95

• Barbaralee Diamonstein & David Shirey
LOUISE NEVELSON: Celebration
0–938608–31–2 Pace $75.00

• Brenda Richardson
BARNETT NEWMAN: The Complete Drawings, 1944-1969
0–912298–48–0 Baltimore Museum pb $11.98

• Elizabeth Frank
JACKSON POLLOCK
0–89659–383–5 Abbeville $29.95
0–89659–384–3 Abbeville pb $19.95

• Francis Frascina, editor
POLLOCK AND AFTER: The Critical Debate
This anthology contains material making it possible to begin clarifying Pollock's ambiguous place in modern culture
0–06–433126–1 Harper & Row $20.00

• Jeffrey Potter
TO A VIOLENT GRAVE: An Oral Biography of Jackson Pollock
0–916366–47–2 Pushcart pb $11.95

• Bernice Rose
JACKSON POLLOCK: Drawing into Painting
0–87070–516–4 Museum of Modern Art pb $17.50

• Dore Ashton
ABOUT ROTHKO
0–19–503348–5 Oxford $24.95

• Bonnie Clearwater
MARK ROTHKO: Works on Paper
Introduction by Dore Ashton
0–933920–54–7 Hudson Hills pb $19.95

• Diane Waldman
MARK ROTHKO, 1903-1970: A Retrospective
0–89207–014–5 Guggenheim $38.00
0–686–96878–6 Guggenheim pb $20.00

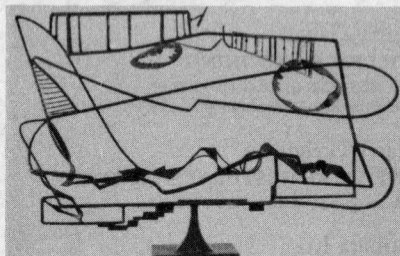

David Smith's "Hudson River Landscape" (Museum of Modern Art)

David Smith

"You know who I am and what I stand for. I have no allegiance, but I stand, and I know what challenge is, and I challenge everything and everybody. And I think that is what every artist has to do. The minute you show a work, you challenge every other artist."—David Smith

Stanley Marcus
DAVID SMITH: The Sculptor and His Work
0–8014–1510–1 Cornell $34.50

Karen Wilkin
DAVID SMITH
0–89659–429–7 Abbeville $29.95
0–89659–430–0 Abbeville pb $19.95

The Second Generation of Abstract Expressionists

De Kooning, Pollock, and Kline inspired a "Second Generation" of abstract expressionists, among them Norman Bluhm and Joan Mitchell, just as the "American-type" painters inspired a school of "color-field" painters such as Helen Frankenthaler and Morris Louis, as well as practitioners of a more geometrically oriented, "hard-edge" or "post-painterly" abstraction, such as Ellsworth Kelly.

• Thomas Krens, editor
HELEN FRANKENTHALER PRINTS: 1961-1979
0–06–434020–1 Harper & Row $25.95
0–06–430103–6 Harper & Row pb $14.95

• John Elderfield
HELEN FRANKENTHALER
0–8109–0916–2 Abrams $125.00

• Richard Axsom & Phylis Floyd
THE PRINTS OF ELLSWORTH KELLY: A Catalogue Raisonné, 1949-1985
0–933920–84–9 Hudson Hills $50.00

• Diane Upright
ELLSWORTH KELLY: Works on Paper
0–8109–1213–9 Abrams $65.00

• John Elderfield
MORRIS LOUIS
0–87070–418–4 NY Graphic Society $40.00

• Diane Upright
MORRIS LOUIS: The Complete Paintings
0–8109–1280–5 Abrams $120.00

• Judith Bernstock
JOAN MITCHELL
0–933920–81–4 Hudson Hills $50.00

• Diane Waldman
KENNETH NOLAND: A Retrospective
0–89207–009–9 Guggenheim pb $18.00

JACK YOUNGERMAN
0–89207–055–2 Guggenheim pb $16.00

AMERICAN ART OF THE 1960s AND '70s

While some artists were refining the breakthroughs of their abstract expressionist predecessors, others, including Jasper Johns, Robert Rauschenberg, and Cy Twombly, were challenging their dominance with a new literalism inspired by dada as well as by the most improvisational and antiformal tendencies within abstract expressionism itself.

• Riva Castleman
PRINTED ART: A View of Two Decades
Surveys the 1960s and '70s
0–87070–541–5 Museum of Modern Art pb $9.95

JASPER JOHNS: A Print Retrospective
0–87070–401–X NY Graphic Society $40.00

• Michael Crichton
JASPER JOHNS
0–8109–1161–2 Abrams $49.50

• David Shapiro
JASPER JOHNS DRAWINGS: 1954-1984
0–8109–1156–6 Abrams $75.00

• Barbara Rose
ROBERT RAUSCHENBERG
An extensive interview with the artist
0–394–75529–4 Random House pb $10.95

• Nan Rosenthal
ROBERT RAUSCHENBERG
0–89659–449–1 Abbeville $29.95
0–89659–450–5 Abbeville pb $16.95

• Calvin Tomkins
OFF THE WALL: Robert Rauschenberg and the Art World of Our Time
An entertaining book by the *New Yorker* critic
0–14–005812–5 Penguin pb $7.95

• Helen Harrison
LARRY RIVERS
0–06–433318–3 Harper & Row pb $23.95

• Harald Szeeman, editor
CY TWOMBLY: Paintings, Works on Paper, Sculpture
0–318–24028–9 TeNeues $55.00

Figurative Painters

Another challenge, although with less immediate impact, came from painters who maintained the European figurative tradition.

• Ann Beattie
ALEX KATZ
Katz can be seen as a forerunner of the Pop Art which emerged in the early '60s
0–8109–1212–0 Abrams $29.95

• Patricia Hills
ALICE NEEL
0–8109–1358–5 Abrams $39.95

• Russell Bowman
PHILIP PEARLSTEIN: The Complete Paintings
0–317–54904–9 Apollo $50.00

• John Perreault
PHILIP PEARLSTEIN: Drawings and Watercolors
0–8109–1496–4 Abrams $45.00

• John Ashbery & others
FAIRFIELD PORTER
0–87846–211–2 Museum of Fine Arts pb $20.00

James Duff & others, editors
AN AMERICAN VISION: Three Generations of Wyeth Art—N.C. Wyeth, Andrew Wyeth, James Wyeth
0–8212–1652–X NY Graphic Society $40.00
0–8212–1656–2 NY Graphic Society pb $22.50

John Wilmerding
ANDREW WYETH: The Helga Pictures
The exhibition catalog for Wyeth's
controversial series of paintings
0–8109–1788–2 Abrams $40.00

Pop Art

The label Pop Art covers an extremely diverse group: Roy Lichtenstein, Claes Oldenburg, James Rosenquist, and Andy Warhol,
and perhaps also Jim Dine and Red Grooms.
Their work was united by its appropriation
of techniques and images from comic strips,
billboards, commercial packaging, and newspaper photography. On the west coast there
were a number of artists (Jess, Wayne Thiebaud, Edward Ruscha), working independently of the New York Pop artists, whose
work paralleled and even anticipated theirs.

- Lucy Lippard
  POP ART
  A classic international survey
  0–500–20052–1 Thames & Hudson pb $11.95

- Brian Wallis & others, editors
  **MODERN DREAMS: The Rise and Fall
  and Rise of Pop**
  0–262–23138–7 MIT $40.00
  0–262–73081–2 MIT pb $25.00

- Simon Watson
  POP
  0–8120–0883–9 Barron's pb $3.50

- Graham Beal & Jim Dine
  JIM DINE: Five Themes
  0–89659–415–7 Abbeville pb $27.50

- Sarah Lafferty & E.A. Cermean
  JIM DINE: Drawings 1973-1987
  0–917562–50–X Contemporary pb $39.95

- David Shapiro
  JIM DINE: Painting What One Is
  0–8109–0367–9 Abrams $65.00

Robert Rauschenberg's "Coca-Cola Plan"
(*Museum of Contemporary Art*), *from* Art of
the Sixties and Seventies *by Christopher
Knight* (*Rizzoli*)

- Carter Ratcliff
  RED GROOMS
  0–89659–403–3 Abbeville $100.00

- Judith Stein, editor
  **RED GROOMS: A Retrospective, 1956-
  1984**
  0–8109–2315–7 Abrams pb $29.95

- Lawrence Alloway
  ROY LICHTENSTEIN
  0–89659–330–4 Abbeville $29.95

- Constance & Jack Glenn, editors
  **ROY LICHTENSTEIN: Landscape
  Sketches, 1984-1985**
  0–8109–1264–3 Abrams $75.00

- Bernice Rose
  **THE DRAWINGS OF ROY
  LICHTENSTEIN**
  0–8109–0849–2 Abrams $39.95

- Calvin Tomkins, editor
  **ROY LICHTENSTEIN: Mural with Blue
  Brushstroke**
  0–8109–2356–4 Abrams pb $19.95

- Claes Oldenburg
  **A BOTTLE OF NOTES AND SOME
  VOYAGES**
  0–8478–0946–3 Rizzoli pb $35.00

- Barbara Rose
  CLAES OLDENBURG
  0–316–14461–4 NY Graphic Society pb $14.50

- Judith Goldman
  JAMES ROSENQUIST
  0–670–80589–0 Viking $20.00

- Dave Hickey & Peter Plagens
  THE WORKS OF EDWARD RUSCHA
  0–933920–21–0 Hudson Hills $35.00
  0–933920–22–9 Hudson Hills pb $20.00

- Sam Hunter & Don Hawthorne
  GEORGE SEGAL
  0–8478–0541–7 Rizzoli $75.00

- Constance Glenn, editor
  **WAYNE THIEBAUD: Private Drawings,
  the Artist's Sketchbook**
  0–8109–1665–7 Abrams $85.00

- Karen Tsujimoto
  WAYNE THIEBAUD
  0–295–96251–8 Washington $40.00
  0–295–96269–0 Washington pb $24.95

"Andy Warhol's influence on the art
world cannot be overstated. He shattered
the whole existing hierarchy of 'artistic'
image, and wiped away the arbitrary
lines that had delineated and confined
'art'. A soup tin, seen with a clear eye, can
be as portentous as a comet."—William
Burroughs

Kynaston McShime, editor
ANDY WARHOL: A Retrospective
The catalog for the recent exhibition
held at the Museum of Modern Art,

Roy Lichtenstein's "Cézanne" (*Museum of
Contemporary Art*), *from* Art of the Sixties
and Seventies *by Christopher Knight*
(*Rizzoli*)

with essays by Robert Rosenblum,
Benjamin H.D. Buchloh and Marco
Livingstone
0–87070–680–2 Little, Brown $50.00

Andy Warhol
THE ANDY WARHOL DIARIES
Edited by Pat Hackett
0–446–51426–8 Warner $29.95

**THE PHILOSOPHY OF ANDY
WARHOL: From A to B and Back
Again**
The muteness of Warhol's art was
surpassed only by the chattiness of his
public persona
0–15–671720–4 HBJ pb $7.95

Andy Warhol & Pat Hackett
POPISM: The Warhol Sixties
0–06–091062–3 Harper & Row pb $12.95

Rainer Crone
**ANDY WARHOL: A Picture Show by
the Artist**
0–8478–0884–X Rizzoli $50.00

Nat Finkelstein
**ANDY WARHOL: The Factory Years,
1964-1967**
0–312–02857–1 St. Martin's pb $19.95

Carter Ratcliff
ANDY WARHOL
0–89659–385–1 Abbeville $29.95
0–89659–386–X Abbeville pb $19.95

Minimalism

Pop Art's studious brother was minimalism.
If the former developed the literalness of the
image, the objects of Donald Judd, Robert
Morris, and, somewhat later, Eva Hesse and
Richard Serra explored the literalness of

forms and materials. The early paintings of Frank Stella were less extreme but perhaps more inventive cousins.

● Kenneth Baker
MINIMALISM
0–89659–887–X Abbeville $39.95

● Lucy Lippard
EVA HESSE
0–8147–4971–2 NYU $50.00
0–8147–4972–0 NYU pb $24.95

● Alicia Legg, editor
SOL LEWITT
0–07070–427–3 Museum of Modern Art $30.00

● Jeremy Lewison
SOL LEWITT: Prints, 1970-1986
0–295–96739–0 Salem House pb $17.50

● Kenworth Moffett
LARRY POONS: Paintings, 1971-1981
0–87846–206–6 Boston Museum pb $5.95

● Ernst-Gerhard Guse & others
RICHARD SERRA
0–317–66842–0 Rizzoli $65.00

● Rosalind Krauss & Douglas Crimp
RICHARD SERRA: Sculpture
0–87070–590–3 Museum of Modern Art pb $27.50

● Frank Stella
WORKING SPACE
The text of Stella's Charles Eliot Norton lectures
0–674–95960–4 Harvard $40.00
0–674–95961–2 Harvard pb $19.95

● Lawrence Rubin, editor
FRANK STELLA: Paintings, 1958-1965
0–941434–92–3 Stewart, Tabori & Chang $75.00

● William Rubin
FRANK STELLA: 1970-1987
0–87070–593–8 NY Graphic Society $45.00

Conceptualism

After minimalism's radical synthesis of the reductive and anti-aesthetic tendencies in modern art, it was only a short step to conceptual art and such related trends as process art and earthworks, which dematerialized the art object or subordinated the work's materiality to the information processed through it, as in the work of Hans Haacke, Bruce Nauman, and Robert Smithson.

● John Beardsley
EARTHWORKS AND BEYOND: Contemporary Art in the Landscape
0–89659–962–0 Abbeville $34.95
0–89659–963–9 Abbeville pb $24.95

● Arakawa & Madeline Gins
ARAKAWA: The Mechanism of Meaning
The writings of an artist, who with great wit presses painting into the service of conceptualism
0–89659–809–8 Abbeville $49.95

● David Bourdon
CHRISTO: Surrounded Islands: 1980-83
0–8109–0790–9 Abrams $85.00
0–8109–2273–8 Abrams pb $14.85

● Dominique Laporte
CHRISTO
0–394–54863–9 Pantheon $19.95

● Jorg Schellmann & Josephine Benecke
CHRISTO: Prints and Objects
0–89659–796–2 Abbeville $35.00

● Brian Wallis, editor
HANS HAACKE: Unfinished Business
0–262–73079–0 MIT pb $15.00

● Coosje Van Bruggen
BRUCE NAUMAN
0–8478–0883–1 Rizzoli $50.00

● Robert Smithson
THE WRITINGS OF ROBERT SMITHSON: Essays with Illustrations
Edited by Nancy Holt
0–8147–3394–8 Columbia $40.00
0–8147–3395–6 Columbia pb $22.50

● Robert Hobbs
ROBERT SMITHSON: Sculpture
0–8014–1324–9 Cornell $38.50

POSTWAR EUROPEAN ART

Major art did not move lock, stock, and barrel from Paris to New York during the Second World War. Many of the artists already listed, including Picasso and Matisse, continued to produce important work in post-war Europe, while a number of somewhat younger artists (including Giacometti and Jean Dubuffet) were only beginning to produce their most characteristic work. In England, Francis Bacon was hitting his stride; in France, Balthus continued to infuse academic technique with his self-consciously perverse sensibility.

● Pierre Alechinsky
PIERRE ALECHINSKY: Les Estampes, 1946-1972
0–915346–17–6 Wofsy $60.00

● Michael Gibson & Pierre Alechinsky
PIERRE ALECHINSKY: Margin and Center
0–89207–061–7 Guggenheim $18.00

● Jean-Clarence Lambert
KAREL APPEL: Works on Paper
Foreword by Marshall McLuhan
0–89659–069–0 Abbeville $95.00

● Pierre Restany & others
KAREL APPEL
0–89659–521–8 Abbeville $95.00

● Jan Van Der Marck
ARMAN
0–89659–423–8 Abbeville $45.00

Dawn Ades & Andrew Forge
FRANCIS BACON
0–8109–0714–3 Abrams $60.00

Michel Leiris
FRANCIS BACON
Bacon's ghostly screaming Pope is as much the embodiment of '50s angst as Warhol's Marilyn is of '60s cool
0–8478–0904–8 Rizzoli $19.95

John Russell
FRANCIS BACON
0–500–18170–5 Thames & Hudson $19.95
0–500–20169–2 Thames & Hudson pb $11.95

David Sylvester
THE BRUTALITY OF FACT: Interviews with Francis Bacon
A rounded view of this complex artist
0–500–27196–8 Thames & Hudson pb $9.95

● Sabine Rewald
BALTHUS
0–8109–0738–0 Abrams $35.00

● Jean-Clarence Lambert
COBRA
The Cobra group (for *Co*penhagen, *Br*ussels, *A*msterdam) followed Dubuffet in accepting the art of children, primitives, and the insane as clues to the direct expression of personal fantasy. The group included Pierre Alechinsky, Karel Appel, and Asger Jorn
0–89659–416–5 Abbeville $95.00

● Jean Dubuffet
ASPHYXIATING CULTURE & OTHER WRITINGS
0–941423–09–3 Four Walls $17.95

Balthus' "André Derain" (Museum of Modern Art), from Writers on Artists *by Daniel Halpern (North Point)*

 IF YOU CAN'T FIND IT, LOOK IN THE INDEX

- Jean Dubuffet & others
JEAN DUBUFFET: 40 Years of His Art
0–935573–02–X Chicago pb $15.00

- Mildred Glimcher & Jean Dubuffet
JEAN DUBUFFET: Towards an Alternative Reality
0–89659–782–2 Abbeville $55.00

- Laurence Gowing
LUCIEN FREUD
0–500–27333–2 Thames & Hudson pb $24.95

- Nicholas Penny & Robert Johnson
LUCIEN FREUD: Works on Paper
0–500–09185–4 Thames & Hudson $40.00

- Robert Hughes
LUCIEN FREUD PAINTINGS
0–500–09179–X Thames & Hudson $40.00

- Valerie Fletcher & others
ALBERTO GIACOMETTI, 1906-1966
0–87474–424–5 Smithsonian $50.00

- James Lord
A GIACOMETTI PORTRAIT
The best introduction to Giacometti: an account of sitting for a portrait by the master
0–374–51573–5 Farrar, Straus & Giroux pb $7.95
GIACOMETTI: A Biography
An ambitious but controversial book; Lord's account has been publicly disavowed by many of the artist's friends and colleagues
0–374–16198–4 Farrar, Straus & Giroux $35.00

- Herbert Matter
ALBERTO GIACOMETTI
0–8109–0999–5 Abrams $60.00

- René Micha
JEAN HELION
0–517–53791–5 Crown $14.95

- Bernard Geysson
SOULAGES
0–517–54105–X Crown $14.95

- Ronald Alley
GRAHAM SUTHERLAND
0–905005–48–1 Salem House pb $14.95

- Roger Berthoud
GRAHAM SUTHERLAND: A Biography
0–571–11882–8 Faber & Faber $26.95

- Anna Agusti
TAPIES: The Complete Works, 1943-1960
0–8478–0980–3 Rizzoli $175.00

- Jose Luis Barrio-Garay
ANTONI TAPIES: 33 Years of His Work
0–914782–11–8 Buffalo Fine Arts pb $15.00

- Steven High
ANTONI TAPIES: Graphic Work, 1947-1987
0–939799–03–0 Portland School of Art pb $7.50

Pop Art and Other Trends

Pop Art was an international phenomenon. The term was actually coined in England, although the most interesting artists associated with the term (such as Kitaj and Hockney) now have little to do with it. In France a group of *Nouveaux Réalistes* (of whom the best known was Yves Klein) took a position similar to Pop. European minimal and conceptual art, too, seem at least as interesting as their American counterparts, although the literature on them is scanty. Especially notable are the Italians, such as Jannis Kounellis, Giulio Paolini, and Michelangelo Pistoletto, whose work was given the tag *arte povera* ("poor art").

- Jorg Schellmann & Bernd Kluser, editors
JOSEPH BEUYS, MULTIPLES: Catalogue Raisonné
0–8147–7813–5 NYU $50.00
0–8147–7814–3 NYU pb $25.00

- Caroline Tisdall
JOSEPH BEUYS
The work of the German artist who continues to have enormous impact
0–500–27454–1 Thames & Hudson pb $24.95

- Benjamin H.D. Buchloh, editor
BROODTHAERS: Writings, Interviews, Photographs
0–262–52135–0 MIT pb $12.50

- Pontus Hulten & others
OYVIND FAHLSTROM
Fahlstrom is one of the most interesting European Pop artists
0–89207–035–8 Guggenheim pb $9.00

- Henry Geldzahler, editor
DAVID HOCKNEY: A Retrospective
0–8109–1167–1 Abrams $49.50

- Nikos Stangos
DAVID HOCKNEY BY DAVID HOCKNEY
0–8109–2409–9 Abrams pb $24.95

- John Ashbery & others
KITAJ: Paintings, Drawings, Pastels
0–500–27303–0 Thames & Hudson pb $19.95

- Institute for the Arts Curators
YVES KLEIN 1928 TO 1962: A Retrospective
0–914412–27–2 Rice pb $25.00

- Pierre Restany
YVES KLEIN, 1928-1962
0–8109–1205–8 Abrams $75.00

- Marcel Joray & Jesus Soto
SOTO
0–8390–0341–2 Abner Schram $145.00

- Pontus Hulten
JEAN TINGUELY: A Magic Stronger Than Death
0–89659–819–5 Abbeville $85.00

- Gaston Diehl
VASARELY
0–517–50800–1 Crown $14.95

THE CONTEMPORARY SCENE

The mid- and late '70s saw a "return to painting" (it had never really gone away) and to the representational image: artists who came to prominence at this time included Jennifer Bartlett, Eric Fischl, Malcolm Morley, Elizabeth Murray, Susan Rothenberg, David Salle, and Julian Schnabel in the U.S.; Georg Baselitz, Anselm Kiefer, and Sigmar Polke in Germany; Francesco Clemente and Enzo Cucchi in Italy. Much of the new work was misnamed neo-expressionism; all of it aroused controversy, both among dogmatic proponents of formalist and reductivist ideas, and among traditionalists who felt these artists were playing fast and loose with traditional values.

- Mark Strand
WILLIAM BAILEY
0–8109–2360–2 Abrams $29.95

- Marge Goldwater & others
JENNIFER BARTLETT
0–89659–519–6 Abbeville $45.00

- John Russell
JENNIFER BARTLETT: In the Garden
0–8109–0709–7 Abrams $39.95

- Roberta Smith
JENNIFER BARTLETT: Rhapsody
0–8109–1577–4 Abrams $39.95

- Mark Rosenthal & Richard Marshall
JONATHAN BOROFSKY
0–8109–0740–2 Abrams $40.00

- Donald Kuspit
LOUISE BOURGEOIS
0–394–74792–5 Random House pb $10.95

- Edward Sullivan
CLAUDIO BRAVO
0–8478–0655–3 Rizzoli $50.00

- Julie Sylvester
JOHN CHAMBERLAIN: A Catalogue Raisonné of the Sculpture, 1954-1985
0–933920–57–1 Rizzoli $50.00

- Judy Chicago
THE DINNER PARTY
0–385–14566–7 Doubleday $24.95
0–385–14567–5 Doubleday pb $12.95

- Michael Auping
FRANCESCO CLEMENTE
0–8109–0772–0 Abrams $39.95

- Rainer Crone & Georgia Marsh
FRANCESCO CLEMENTE
Lengthy interviews with the artist
0–394–74787–9 Random House pb $9.95

Philip Guston with "The Studio," from Musa Mayer's Night Studio (*Knopf*)

• Lisa Lyons & Robert Storr
CHUCK CLOSE
0–8478–0808–4 Rizzoli $45.00
0–8478–0812–2 Rizzoli pb $29.95

• Diane Waldman
ENZO CUCCHI
0–89207–056–0 Guggenheim $20.00

• John Canaday
RICHARD ESTES: The Urban Landscape
0–87846–126–4 NY Graphic Society pb $16.95

• Louis Meisel
RICHARD ESTES: The Complete Paintings, 1966-1985
0–8109–0881–6 Abrams $39.95

• Howard Finster & Tom Patterson
HOWARD FINSTER, STRANGER FROM ANOTHER WORLD: Man of Visions Now on This Earth
Includes 120 color illustrations
0–89659–902–7 Abbeville $35.00

• Donald Kuspit
ERIC FISCHL
Interviews
0–394–74789–5 Random House pb $9.95

• Peter Schjeldahl
ERIC FISCHL
1–55670–052–0 Stewart, Tabori & Chang $75.00

• Robert Doty, editor
JANE FREILICHER: Paintings
0–8008–4301–0 Taplinger $29.95
0–8008–4302–9 Taplinger pb $19.95

• Audrey Flack
AUDREY FLACK ON PAINTING
0–8109–2235–5 Abrams pb $14.95

• Carter Ratcliff
GILBERT AND GEORGE: The Complete Pictures, 1971-1985
0–8478–0779–7 Rizzoli pb $29.95

• Donald Kuspit
LEON GOLUB: Existential-Activist Painter
0–8135–1102–X Rutgers $45.00
0–8135–1124–0 Rutgers pb $12.00

• E.A. Carmean & others
THE SCULPTURE OF NANCY GRAVES
0–933920–77–6 Hudson Hills $50.00

In New York, at least, much new work was inspired by the example of Philip Guston, an abstract expressionist who in 1968 shocked his colleagues by exhibiting canvases employing an ostensibly crude, almost cartoon-like figuration. One hostile critic reviewed these paintings as those of "a mandarin masquerading as a stumblebum," but it now seems clear that Guston's late work represents an extraordinarily rich, deeply moving contribution to American art.

Ross Feld
PHILIP GUSTON
0–8076–0975–7 Braziller $25.00

Musa Mayer
NIGHT STUDIO: A Memoir of Philip Guston by His Daughter
0–394–56377–8 Knopf $30.00

Robert Storr
PHILIP GUSTON
0–89659–665–6 Abbeville $29.95
0–89659–656–7 Abbeville pb $19.95

• Irving Sandler
AL HELD
0–933920–38–5 Hudson Hills $75.00

• Jurgen Harten
A BOOK BY ANSELM KIEFER
Introduction by Theodore E. Stebbins, Jr.
0–8076–1191–3 Braziller $60.00

• Mark Rosenthal
ANSELM KIEFER
3–79130–847–5 Philadelphia Museum pb $40.00

• Carter Ratcliff
ROBERT LONGO
0–8478–0602–2 Rizzoli pb $25.00

• Jed Perl & others
LOUISA MATTHIASDOTTIR: Small Paintings
0–933920–66–0 Hudson Hills $15.00

• Sue Grazel & Kathy Halbreich, editors
ELIZABETH MURRAY: Paintings and Drawings
0–8109–1423–9 Abrams $35.00

• John Handardt
NAM JUNE PAIK
0–393–01609–9 Norton $25.00

• Tom Phillips
A HUMUMENT
0–500–97339–3 Thames & Hudson pb $19.95

• Fiona Irving
DAVID SALLE
0–317–57671–2 Pennsylvania $20.00

• Peter Schjeldahl
DAVID SALLE
Interviews of the artist
0–394–74788–7 Random House pb $9.95

• Julian Schnabel
C.V.J: Nicknames of Maître d's and Other Excerpts from Life
Autobiographical writings
0–394–55313–6 Random House $75.00

• Carter Ratcliff
PAT STEIR: Paintings
0–8109–1503–0 Abrams $29.95
0–8109–2316–5 Abrams pb $14.95

• Barbara Rose
DONALD SULTAN
0–394–74793–3 Random House pb $10.95

Henry Chalfant & James Prigoff
SPRAYCAN ART
0–500–27469–X Thames & Hudson pb $14.95

Martha Cooper & Henry Chalfant
SUBWAY ART
0–03–071963–1 Henry Holt pb $14.95

The Postmodern Condition

A highly ironized approach to geometrical purity and the Duchampian ready-made has generated a good deal of interest in the last few years as symptomatic of the "postmodern" condition.

• Brian Wallis, editor
ART AFTER MODERNISM: Essays on Rethinking Representation
0–87923–563–2 Godine $24.95
0–87923–632–9 Godine pb $15.95

TO ORDER BOOKS AS GIFTS, SEE PAGE 1

BLASTED ALLEGORIES: An Anthology of Artists' Writings
Contributions by Anderson, Nauman, Salle, Smithson, and 40 more
0–262–23128–X MIT $19.95

• Joseph Masheck, editor
POINT ONE: Smart Art
0–930279–01–8 Willis, Locker & Owens pb $7.95

CRITICISM

• Arthur Danto
THE STATE OF THE ART
0–13–770868–8 Prentice-Hall $19.95

• Donald Judd
COMPLETE WRITINGS, 1959-1975
0–8147–4155–X NYU $50.00

• Hilton Kramer
THE REVENGE OF THE PHILISTINES: Art and Culture, 1972-1984
0–02–918470–3 Free Press $25.00

• Rosalind Krauss
THE ORIGINALITY OF THE AVANT-GARDE AND OTHER MODERNIST MYTHS
0–262–61046–9 MIT pb $10.95

• Robert Pincus-Witten
POSTMINIMALISM INTO MAXIMALISM: American Art, 1966-1986
0–8357–1763–1 UMI Research $39.95

• Leo Steinberg
OTHER CRITERIA: Confrontations with 20th-Century Art
0–19–501577–0 Oxford $29.95
0–19–501846–X Oxford pb $25.00

Art and Politics

• John Berger
PERMANENT RED: Essays in Seeing
0–904613–92–5 Writers & Readers pb $6.95

• Peter Fuller
BEYOND THE CRISIS IN ART
0–906495–33–4 Writers & Readers $12.95
0–906495–34–2 Writers & Readers pb $9.95

• Lucy Lippard
FROM THE CENTER: Feminist Essays on Women's Art
0–525–48402–7 Dutton pb $13.95

GET THE MESSAGE?: Activist Essays on Art and Politics
0–525–48037–4 Dutton pb $16.95

THE ART WORLD

Art dealers and collectors have even more impact than critics on the state of art.

• Laura de Coppet & Alan Jones, editors
THE ART DEALERS: Powers Behind the Scene Tell How the Art World Really Works
An informative book of interviews. "A

book for grown-ups about the art world"—Andy Warhol
0–517–55302–3 Crown pb $14.95

• René Gimpel
DIARY OF AN ART DEALER
0–87663–522–2 Universe pb $12.95

• Joan Lukach
HILLA REBAY: In Search of the Spirit in Art
One of the rare books on the career of a museum director
0–8076–1067–4 Braziller $30.00

• Marjorie Phillips
DUNCAN PHILLIPS AND HIS COLLECTION
0–393–01608–0 Norton $35.00
0–393–30041–2 Norton pb $18.95

• Brenda Richardson
DR. CLARIBEL AND MISS ETTA: The Cone Collection of the Baltimore Museum of Art
0–912298–58–8 Baltimore Museum pb $24.95

• Irving Sandler & Amy Newman, editors
DEFINING MODERN ART: Selected Writings of Alfred H. Barr
Essays by the man who played an important role for the Museum of Modern Art
0–8109–0715–1 Abrams $35.00

• Calvin Tomkins
POST- TO NEO-: The Art World of the 1980s
The contemporary scene from the *New Yorker* critic
0–8050–0663–X Henry Holt $19.95

• Tom Wolfe
THE PAINTED WORD
A caustic essay on modern art
0–374–22878–7 Farrar, Straus & Giroux $12.95

PHILOSOPHY AND ART

• Roland Barthes
THE RESPONSIBILITY OF FORMS
Barthes' essays on Cy Twombly are among the best on any contemporary artist
Translated by Richard Howard
0–8090–8075–3 Hill & Wang $22.95
0–8090–1522–6 Hill & Wang pb $9.95

• Gianfranco Baruchello & Henry Martin
HOW TO IMAGINE: A Narrative on Art and Agriculture
0–914232–51–7 McPherson $20.00
0–914232–52–5 McPherson pb $10.00

• David Carrier
ARTWRITING
0–87023–561–3 Massachusetts $20.00
0–87023–562–1 Massachusetts pb $9.95

• Arthur Danto
THE PHILOSOPHICAL DISENFRANCHISEMENT OF ART
0–231–06364–4 Columbia $27.00

THE TRANSFIGURATION OF THE COMMONPLACE: A Philosophy of Art
0–674–90346–3 Harvard pb $8.95

• Hal Foster
RECODINGS: Art, Spectacle, Cultural Politics
0–941920–03–8 Bay $16.95
0–941920–04–6 Bay pb $9.95

• Hal Foster, editor
THE ANTI-AESTHETIC: Essays on Postmodern Culture
0–941920–01–1 Bay pb $8.95

• Nelson Goodman
LANGUAGES OF ART
0–915144–35–2 Hackett $19.50
0–915144–34–4 Hackett pb $9.95

• Karsten Harries
MEANING OF MODERN ART: A Philosophical Interpretation
0–8101–0113–0 Northwestern $19.95
0–8101–0593–4 Northwestern pb $10.95

• Charles Harrison & Fred Orton, editors
MODERNISM, CRITICISM AND REALISM: Alternative Contexts for Art
A good starting point for studying the philosophical background of art
0–06–433319–1 Harper & Row $20.00

• Brian O'Doherty
INSIDE THE WHITE CUBE
0–932499–14–7 Lapis $25.95
0–932499–05–8 Lapis pb $15.95

• Richard Wollheim
ART AND ITS OBJECTS
0–521–29706–0 Cambridge pb $15.95

Primitivism and the Avant-Garde

Two of the most salient aspects of modern art have been its nostalgia for a "primitive" past and its concern with advancing into the future.

Peter Burger
THEORY OF THE AVANT-GARDE
0–8166–1067–3 Minnesota $25.00
0–8166–1068–1 Minnesota pb $12.95

Robert Goldwater
PRIMITIVISM IN MODERN ART
0–674–70490–8 Harvard pb $14.95

Renato Poggioli
THE THEORY OF THE AVANT-GARDE
0–674–88216–4 Harvard pb $8.95

William Rubin, editor
PRIMITIVISM IN TWENTIETH CENTURY ART: Affinity of the Tribal and the Modern
0–87070–518–0 NY Graphic Society $100.00

Arts of Africa

The art of the peoples of sub-Saharan Africa was never a realm apart but an integral aspect of their lives, whether serving religious or secular purposes, tribal or royal institutions. In spite of the interest in "primitive" art that accompanied the modernist movement in the West early in the 20th century, the true scale of achievement of African art has begun to emerge only recently. Archaeologists and art historians have had to overcome the general absence of written records and the tendency of wood objects to decay quickly in the African climate. Today research has revealed much about the significance and history of not only sculpture and masks, the most renowned African arts, but also other forms such as pottery, jewelry, architecture, rock paintings and engravings, costumes, and body art.

- James Baldwin & others
PERSPECTIVES: Angles on African Art
Contributions from a wide selection of American and African curators, historians, and artists
0–8109–1491–3 Abrams $45.00

- William Bascom
AFRICAN ART IN CULTURAL PERSPECTIVE: An Introduction
0–393–09375–1 Norton pb $8.95

- Daniel Biebuyck, editor
TRADITION AND CREATIVITY IN TRIBAL ART
A collection of essays
0–520–01509–6 California $50.00

- Susan Denyer
AFRICAN TRADITIONAL ARCHITECTURE
0–8419–0287–9 Holmes & Meier $44.50
0–8419–0336–0 Holmes & Meier pb $19.50

- Werner Gillon
A SHORT HISTORY OF AFRICAN ART
An excellent introduction to African art, beginning with prehistoric rock paintings and proceeding by region and historical period to take in the major achievements of most African cultures; fully illustrated with black-and-white photographs
0–14–022508–0 Penguin pb $12.95

- Jean Laude
THE ARTS OF BLACK AFRICA
0–520–02358–7 California pb $11.95

- George Preston
SETS, SERIES AND ENSEMBLES IN AFRICAN ART
A study of African art objects which form sets or ensembles by an eminent African art scholar
0–8109–1637–1 Abrams $19.95

- G.W. Sannes
AFRICAN PRIMITIVES: Function and Form in African Masks and Figures
0–8419–0048–5 Holmes & Meier $37.50

- Ladislas Segy
MASKS OF BLACK AFRICA
A popular book, revised since its publication in 1952 under the title *African Sculpture Speaks*
0–486–23181–X Dover pb $10.95

- Roy Sieber & Roslyn Adele Walker
AFRICAN ART IN THE CYCLE OF LIFE
The catalog of the National Museum of African Art
0–87474–822–4 Smithsonian $39.95
0–87474–821–6 Smithsonian pb $24.95

- Robert Farris Thompson
FLASH OF THE SPIRIT: African and Afro-American Art and Philosophy
One of the most provocative scholars writing on the continuity of African art and ritual in the New World
0–394–72369–4 Random House pb $9.95

- Frank Willett
AFRICAN ART: An Introduction
0–500–20103–X Thames & Hudson pb $11.75

"Horn Blower," an African bronze, c. 16th-17th century (Metropolitan Museum), from A Connoisseur's Guide to the Met by Paul Magriel and John Spike (Random House)

- Geoffrey Williams
AFRICAN DESIGNS FROM TRADITIONAL SOURCES
Designs from the Ashanti, Bashongo, Baule, Mangbetu, Mariba, Masai, Ndebele, Toma, and Zulu nations
0–486–22752–9 Dover pb $5.95

Regional Studies

- Emmanuel Asihene
UNDERSTANDING THE TRADITIONAL ART OF GHANA
0–8386–2130–9 Fairleigh Dickinson $18.50

- René Bravmann
ISLAM AND TRIBAL ART IN WEST AFRICA
0–521–29791–5 Cambridge pb $13.95

- Herbert Cole & Chike Amaka
IBO ARTS: Community & Cosmos
Foreword by Chinua Achebe
0–930741–07–2 UCLA Museum $35.00
0–930741–01–3 UCLA Museum pb $19.00

- Margaret Courtney-Clark
NDEBELE: The Art of an African Tribe
0–8478–0685–5 Rizzoli $60.00

- Philip Dark
AN ILLUSTRATED CATALOGUE OF BENIN ART
0–8161–0382–8 G.K. Hall $68.00

- William Fagg
YORUBA BEADWORK: Art of Nigeria
0–85331–443–8 Humanities pb $25.00

- Paul Gebauer
ART OF CAMEROON
A museum catalog of the author's collection; includes notes on each piece and an introduction to Cameroonian culture
0–295–96176–7 Washington pb $14.95

- J. David Lewis-Williams
THE ROCK ART OF SOUTHERN AFRICA
0–521–24460–9 Cambridge $29.95

Collections of African Art

- René Bravmann
THE POETRY OF FORM: Hans and Thelma Lehmann Collection of African Art
0–295–96423–5 Washington pb $14.95

- Theodore Celenko
A TREASURY OF AFRICAN ART FROM THE HARRISON EITELJORG COLLECTION
A richly diverse collection of sculptural figures and masks, presented in beautiful black-and-white and color photographs, with a scholarly text
0–253–11057–2 Indiana $57.50

- Maurice Dedieu & Carl Brasseaux
SENEGAL NARRATIVE PAINTINGS: The Collection of Maurice Dedieu
The rare technique of painting on glass
0–295–96629–7 Washington pb $15.00

- Kate Ezra
ART OF THE DOGON: Selections from the Lester Wunderman Collection
Black-and-white photographs of the elegant wood sculpture, masks, and craftwork of the Dogon region of Mali, with detailed text
0–8109–1874–9 Abrams pb $19.95

- Bryna Freyer
ROYAL BENIN ART: Selections from the National Museum of African Art
Metal sculptural work and other art of the kingdom that flourished in what is now Nigeria from the Middle Ages to the end of the 19th century; with black-and-white illustrations
0–87474–445–8 Smithsonian pb $12.95

- Werner Schmalenbach
AFRICAN ART: The Barbier-Mueller Collection
A large, handsomely and profusely illustrated book that encompasses art from all major black African cultures, with accompanying text by leading scholars
3–7913–0849–1 Prestel $50.00

- Roy Sieber & others
AFRICAN, PACIFIC AND PRE-COLUMBIAN ART IN THE INDIANA UNIVERSITY ART MUSEUM
0–253–30442–3 Indiana $35.00
0–253–20412–7 Indiana pb $20.00

- Robert Farris Thompson
AFRICAN ART IN MOTION: Icon and Act in the Collection of Kathryn Coryton White
0–520–03844–4 California $49.95
0–520–03843–6 California pb $14.95

- Susan Vogel, editor
FOR SPIRITS AND KINGS: African Art from the Paul and Ruth Tishman Collection
0–87099–267–8 Metropolitan Museum $35.00

- Susan Vogel & Francine N'Diaye
AFRICAN MASTERPIECES: From the Musée de l'Homme
0–8109–1825–0 Abrams $40.00

- Allen Wardwell
AFRICAN SCULPTURE: From the University Museum
0–8122–7956–5 Pennsylvania $46.95

Art of Oceania

Terence Barrow
AN ILLUSTRATED GUIDE TO MAORI ART
A survey of the Maori art of New Zealand from the time of Captain Cook's landing in 1769 until 1900; illustrated with old drawings and photographs, and objects in contemporary collections
0–8248–0979–3 Hawaii pb $15.95

Sidney Mead
EXPLORING THE VISUAL ART OF OCEANIA: Australia, Melanesia, Micronesia, and Polynesia
Twenty-six articles by art historians, ethnologists and archaeologists;

illustrated with black-and-white photographs and line drawings
0–8248–0598–4 Hawaii $25.00

Sidney Mead & Bernie Kernot, editors
ART AND ARTISTS OF OCEANIA
A collection of scholarly essays on general themes and specific studies of Melanesian, Micronesian, and Polynesian art and culture
0–9611006–0–5 Ethnographic Arts $39.95

Sidney Mead & others, editors
TE MAORI: Maori Art from New Zealand Collections
0–8109–1344–5 Abrams pb $37.50

Douglas Newton
CROCODILE AND CASSOWARY: Religious Art of the Upper Sepik River, New Guinea
Masks and ornaments from the Museum of Primitive Art in New York, in black-and-white photographs
0–912294–42–6 NY Graphic Society pb $9.95

Peter Sutton
DREAMINGS: The Art of Aboriginal Australia
0–8076–1201–4 Braziller $65.00

Islamic Art and Architecture

"Anyone who visits an ancient Islamic building or a museum exhibition of Islamic art, or who takes a university course in the subject, readily observes the unified decorative schemes, interest in geometry, paucity of figural imagery, and extensive use of color that characterize the family of artistic traditions we call Islamic art. With a little more study one can see that these characteristics develop over the centuries in all the stylistic branches of Islamic art alike, though in disparate ways."—Terry Allen, *Five Essays on Islamic Art*

- Terry Allen
FIVE ESSAYS ON ISLAMIC ART
0–944940–00–5 Solipsist pb $46.00

- Esin Atil
THE AGE OF SULTAN SULEYMAN THE MAGNIFICENT
A large book with color reproductions and photographs of miniature paintings, book illuminations, costumes, painted plates, and other objects from the time of the 16th-century Ottoman emperor
0–8109–1855–2 Abrams $49.50

RENAISSANCE OF ISLAM: Art of the Mamluks
Exhibition catalog devoted to decorative book illuminations and crafts that flourished under the Mamluk sultans of

Egypt from the 13th to the 15th century; color reproductions
0–87474–214–5 Smithsonian $49.95
0–87474–213–7 Smithsonian pb $24.95

- John Brookes
GARDENS OF PARADISE: The History and Design of the Great Islamic Gardens
0–941533–07–7 New Amsterdam $33.00

- Keith Critchlow
ISLAMIC PATTERNS: An Analytical and Cosmological Approach
The cosmological symbolism of typical Islamic art forms
0–500–27071–6 Thames & Hudson pb $12.95

- Toby Falk, editor
TREASURES OF ISLAM
A beautiful book, commendable for its varied selection of paintings, with many color illustrations
0–85667–196–7 Sotheby $49.95

- Oleg Grabar
THE FORMATION OF ISLAMIC ART
Seven related essays on the development of the forms of Islamic art and of Islamic attitudes toward it, illustrated with black-and-white photographs and architectural diagrams
0–300–03969–7 Yale $45.00
0–300–04046–6 Yale pb $16.95

- Marilyn Jenkins
ISLAMIC ART IN THE KUWAIT NATIONAL MUSEUM: The Al-Sabah Collection
Fine color reproductions of manuscripts, bowls, vases, coins, jewelry, and other objects in the Kuwait collection
0–85667–304–8 Sotheby pb $19.95

- Martin Lings
THE QURANIC ART OF CALLIGRAPHY AND ILLUMINATION
A sumptuously illustrated history
0–940793–00–8 Interlink $49.95

- Glenn Lowry & Susan Nemazee
A JEWELER'S EYE: Islamic Arts of the Book from the Vever Collection
Selections from a remarkable collection recently recovered after its disappearance during World War II
0–295–96676–9 Washington $50.00
0–295–96677–7 Washington pb $26.95

- David Talbot Rice
ISLAMIC ART
Well-chosen illustrations and clear, concise prose make this an ideal introductory guide to the whole range of Islamic art: architecture, mosaics, woodwork, carpets and textiles, miniatures, metalwork, and ceramics
0–500–20150–1 Thames & Hudson pb $9.95

ISLAMIC PAINTING
A brief, clear, well-illustrated historical survey of all major areas and schools
0–85224–112–7 Columbia $15.00

- B.W. Robinson & others
ISLAMIC ART IN THE KEIR COLLECTION
Paintings, ceramics, metalwork, and textiles
0–571–13753–9 Faber & Faber $150.00

- Anthony Welch & Stuart Cary Welch
ARTS OF THE ISLAMIC BOOK: The Collection of Prince Sadruddin Aga Khan
Calligraphy, miniatures, and decorative motifs from Islamic books, some of them beautifully reproduced in color, with a shrewd and often witty commentary by one of the most eminent scholars in the field
0–8014–1548–9 Cornell $55.00
0–8014–9882–1 Cornell pb $24.95

ISLAMIC ARCHITECTURE

- Robert Hillenbrand
ISLAMIC ARCHITECTURE: Style, Function and Form
0–85224–391–X Columbia $50.00

- John Hoag
ISLAMIC ARCHITECTURE
A comprehensive, richly illustrated guide to Islamic architecture from Spain to India, emphasizing historical context and showing the unity underlying the diversity
0–8478–0796–7 Rizzoli pb $25.00

- George Michell, editor
ARCHITECTURE OF THE ISLAMIC WORLD: Its History and Social Meaning
A survey with essays by seven leading authorities focusing on form, function, and cultural significance, with over 700 illustrations, including traditional art and diagrams as well as photographs
0–500–34076–5 Thames & Hudson $40.00

ISLAMIC DECORATIVE ARTS

- James Allen
METALWORK OF THE ISLAMIC WORLD: The Aron Collection
0–85667–327–7 Sotheby $95.00

- Esin Atil & others
ISLAMIC METALWORK AT THE FREER GALLERY OF ART
0–934686–54–8 Smithsonian pb $17.50

- Marilyn Jenkins & Manuel Keena
ISLAMIC JEWELRY IN THE METROPOLITAN MUSEUM OF ART
Gold, silver, and gemstone jewelry from the 7th to the 19th centuries, with black-and-white and color illustrations
0–87099–326–7 Metropolitan Museum $28.50
0–87099–327–5 Metropolitan Museum pb $18.50

- Andrew Oliver, Jr.
ANCIENT GLASS: Ancient and Islamic Glass in the Carnegie Museum of Natural History
0–911239–03–0 Carnegie Museum $5.00
0–911239–04–9 Carnegie Museum pb $3.50

- Helen Philon
EARLY ISLAMIC CERAMICS: Catalogue of Islamic Art in the Benaki Museum
A catalog with black-and-white photographs and several color plates of ceramics in the collection of the Benaki Museum in Athens
0–85667–098–7 Sotheby $120.00

PERSIAN ART

- Esin Atil
BRUSH OF THE MASTERS: Drawings from Iran and India
0–934686–29–7 Freer Gallery pb $20.00

- Shinji Fukai
PERSIAN GLASS
A survey by a Japanese scholar, with 89 color plates
0–8348–1515–X Weatherhill $50.00

- Jay & Sumi Gluck
A SURVEY OF PERSIAN HANDICRAFT
0–317–55043–8 Apollo $125.00

- Thomas W. Lentz & Glenn D. Lowry
TIMUR AND THE PRINCELY VISION: Persian Art and Culture in the Fifteenth Century
0–87474–706–6 Smithsonian $75.00

- Arthur Pope
MASTERPIECES OF PERSIAN ART
0–8371–3013–1 Greenwood $38.50

PERSIAN ARCHITECTURE
A survey by one of the leading authorities on Persian art
4–89360–027–3 Tuttle $12.50
4–89360–028–1 Tuttle pb $7.50

- Marianna Simpson
ARAB AND PERSIAN PAINTING IN THE FOGG ART MUSEUM
Black-and-white plates of miniature paintings, book illustrations, and drawings from the 13th to the 19th centuries, with accompanying text
0–916724–10–7 Harvard pb $8.50

Persian Minai bowl, c. 12th-13th century (Metropolitan Museum)

- Mojdeh Stephenson
PERSIAN MINIATURE DESIGNS
0–88045–033–9 Stemmer House pb $5.95

- Olive Watson
PERSIAN LUSTRE WARE
The history of the unique, richly decorated, iridescent pottery of Persia, illustrated with black-and-white and color photographs
0–571–13235–9 Faber & Faber $95.00

East Asian Art

Since the Bronze Age, East Asia has been periodically united and divided by cultural developments. For centuries India and the Himalayas, Southeast and Central Asia, China, Korea, and Japan were bound by the spell of evangelical Buddhism, producing an extraordinary and long-lived international style of figural art. After the 15th century each region found its own identity, yet the various East Asian cultures retained profound and durable affinities.

Western contacts with East Asia go back to the Bronze Age. But the sporadic trade connections, based on such commodities as silk, ivory, precious metals and porcelain, forged only fragile links between the Orient and the West. Although Western curiosity about East Asia was stimulated by the travels of Marco Polo in the 13th century and the Jesuit missionary efforts that began in the 17th century, the modern Western interest in and knowledge of East Asian art and culture dates from the Age of Enlightenment.

By the late 19th century a measured, scientific study of East Asia had developed. The available 20th-century literature on Asian art can be divided into a small body of semi-popular pre-World War II writing based on limited materials, a very small number of postwar popularizations, and a large number of postwar specialized studies.

EAST ASIA: General Works

- Ernest Fenollosa
EPOCHS OF CHINESE AND JAPANESE ART
A classic, dated but still one of the best-written books in the field

Volume 1
0–486–20364–6 Dover pb $6.95

Volume 2
0–486–20365–4 Dover pb $6.95

- Julia Hutt
UNDERSTANDING FAR EASTERN ART
A treatment of the various arts of China, Japan and Korea as products of material culture made by specific techniques for various patrons
Introduction by Margaret Medley
0–525–24521–9 Dutton $29.95
0–525–48295–4 Dutton pb $19.95

- Sherman Lee
A HISTORY OF FAR EASTERN ART
An excellent book for a broad audience, stressing regional Buddhist art and the interplay of Chinese and Japanese art
0–8109–1080–2 Abrams $55.00

- Heinrich Zimmer
THE ART OF INDIAN ASIA: Its Mythology and Transformations
A two-volume work, confined to East Asian art in which Indian influence is

➤ **FOR OVERSEAS ORDERING INFORMATION, SEE PAGE 1**

paramount, focusing on mythology from a Jungian viewpoint
Edited by Joseph Campbell
0–691–09948–0 Princeton (set) $145.00
0–691–01846–4 Princeton pb (set) $39.50

SHERMAN LEE:
A Basic Library of Books on East Asian Art

Pramod Chandra
THE SCULPTURE OF INDIA: 3000 BC-1300 AD

Douglas Barrett & Basil Gray
INDIAN PAINTING

Mary Slusser
NEPAL MANDALA

Laurence Sickman & Alexander Soper
ART AND ARCHITECTURE IN CHINA

James Cahill
CHINESE PAINTING

Robert Van Gulik
CHINESE PICTORIAL ART AS VIEWED BY THE CONNOISSEUR

Margaret Medley
THE CHINESE POTTER

Maggie Keswick
THE CHINESE GARDEN

Langdon Warner
THE ENDURING ART OF JAPAN

J. Matsushita
INK PAINTING
Out of print

Louise Cort
SHIGARAKI, POTTERS' VALLEY

Loraine Kuck
THE WORLD OF THE JAPANESE GARDEN: From Chinese Origins to Modern Landscape Art

---

INDIA

• Ananda Coomaraswamy
HISTORY OF INDIAN AND INDONESIAN ART
An important work, first published in 1928
0–486–25005–9 Dover pb $8.95

• Roy Craven
INDIAN ART: A Concise History
A good introduction to Indian art
0–500–20146–3 Thames & Hudson pb $11.95

• Basil Gray, editor
THE ARTS OF INDIA
0–8014–1425–3 Cornell $56.50

• J.C. Harle
THE ART AND ARCHITECTURE OF THE INDIAN SUBCONTINENT
A very thorough history, fully illustrated
0–14–056049–1 Viking $40.00
0–14–056149–8 Penguin pb $18.95

• Susan & John Huntington
THE ART OF ANCIENT INDIA: Buddhist, Hindu, Jain
A more extensive text than Harle, more copiously but less effectively illustrated
0–8348–0183–3 Weatherhill $80.00

Indian Philosophies of Art

• Ananda Coomaraswamy
THE DANCE OF SIVA: Essays on Indian Art and Culture
A compelling elucidation of the image of Siva, one of the most creative and complex images in the Hindu cosmology
0–486–24817–8 Dover pb $5.95

• B.N. Goswamy
THE ESSENCE OF INDIAN ART
Indian art explained according to the nine *rasas* or sentiments applied to Indian theater
0–295–96641–6 Washington pb $29.95

Tenth-century Indian bronze of Vishnu (Metropolitan Museum)

• Stella Kramrisch
EXPLORING INDIA'S SACRED ART: Selected Writings of Stella Kramrisch
Her greatest achievement in reconciling Eastern and Western attitudes, revealing with passion the magical layers of meaning in the religious art of India
Edited by Barbara Stoler Miller
0–8122–7856–9 Pennsylvania $57.95
0–8122–1134–0 Pennsylvania pb $22.95

• Philip Rawson
THE ART OF TANTRA
A survey of the history and traditions of Tantra
0–500–20166–8 Thames & Hudson pb $11.95

• Heinrich Zimmer
ARTISTIC FORM AND YOGA IN THE SACRED IMAGES OF INDIA
A famous essay written in 1926, with Jungian touches
0–691–07289–2 Princeton $28.00

Sculpture

• Carmel Berkson & others
ELEPHANTA: The Cave of Shiva
A good, brief study of one of the great cave temples in India, presenting the monumental 7th-century images on the island of Elephanta
0–691–00371–8 Princeton pb $19.50

• Pramod Chandra
THE SCULPTURE OF INDIA: 3000 BC-1300 AD
A concise, knowledgeable introduction, backed by a superb selection of sculptures
0–674–79590–3 Harvard $60.00

• Stanislaw Czuma & Rekha Morris
KUSHAN SCULPTURE: Images from Early India
0–910386–82–X Indiana $55.00

• J.C. Harle
GUPTA SCULPTURE: Indian Sculpture of the 4th to the 6th Centuries AD
0–19–817322–9 Oxford $32.50

• R. Nagaswamy
MASTERPIECES OF EARLY SOUTH INDIAN BRONZES
An informative presentation of one of the greatest Indian sculptural achievements
0–940500–90–6 Asia Books $49.95

• Pratapaditya Pal
LIGHT OF ASIA: Buddha Sakyamuni in Asian Art
An exhibition catalog, the most useful introduction to Indian Buddhist art and its expansion to the rest of Asia
0–87587–116–X LA County Museum pb $16.95

Painting

Indian painting can be divided roughly into three major traditions: early wall painting in caves, temples and palaces; medieval manuscript painting and illuminations; and miniature painting of the Mughal and native Rajput courts, characterized by brilliant colors and decorative effects.

"Ten Birds," Indian watercolor, c. 16th-17th century (Musée Guimet)

• **Douglas Barrett & Basil Gray**
INDIAN PAINTING
An excellent survey by two accomplished scholars in the field. Sensitive to the aesthetic qualities of the material, and knowledgeable about its iconography and literary overtones
0–8478–0158–6 Rizzoli pb $25.00

• **Hermann Goetz**
RAJPUT ART AND ARCHITECTURE
3–515–02982–6 Coronet pb $48.50

• **Linda Leach**
INDIAN MINIATURE PAINTINGS AND DRAWINGS: The Cleveland Museum of Art
0–910386–78–1 Indiana $65.00

• **Andrew Topsfield**
AN INTRODUCTION TO INDIAN COURT PAINTING
0–88045–041–X Stemmer House $9.95

• **Stuart Cary Welch**
INDIA: Art and Culture, 1300-1900
Indian painting and decorative arts presented by the great Harvard art historian in a lavish exhibition catalog
0–03–006114–8 Henry Holt $62.95
0–87099–384–4 Metropolitan Museum pb $35.00

SOUTHEAST ASIA AND THE HIMALAYAS

• **Steve van Beek**
AN INTRODUCTION TO THE ARTS OF THAILAND
962–7088–08–0 Tuttle $39.95

• **George Coedes**
ANGKOR
The great and varied art of Cambodia is inadequately served in English, but this book is a helpful introduction to the Khmer civilization and its ancient capital
0–19–638129–0 Oxford pb $9.95

• **Reginald Le May**
A CONCISE HISTORY OF BUDDHIST ART IN SIAM
0–8048–0120–7 Tuttle $30.00

• **Pratapaditya Pal**
ART OF NEPAL: A Catalogue of the Los Angeles County Museum of Art Collection
The most useful single volume on the subject, it includes painting, sculpture, manuscripts, and liturgical objects
0–520–05407–5 California pb $27.50

ART OF TIBET: A Catalogue of the Los Angeles County Museum of Art Collection
A good introduction to a complex subject
0–520–05214–5 California pb $25.00

• **Mary Slusser**
THE NEPAL MANDALA: A Cultural Study of the Kathmandu Valley
A first-hand account in two volumes by a leading scholar of Nepal and the Nepalese, emphasizing the context of the mandala
0–691–03128–2 Princeton (set) $135.00

CHINA

• **Caroline Blunden & Mark Elvin**
A CULTURAL ATLAS OF CHINA
A socio-anthropological compendium useful as background to the study of art
0–87196–132–6 Facts On File $40.00

• **Daisy Lion-Goldschmidt & others**
CHINESE ART: Bronze, Jade, Sculpture, Ceramics
Rich in illustration of all the decorative arts, which do not include painting, calligraphy or architecture
0–87663–014–X Universe $65.00

• **Laurence Sickman & Alexander Soper**
ART AND ARCHITECTURE IN CHINA
A good survey of architecture, sculpture, and painting, leaving out crafts and decorative arts
0–14–056110–2 Penguin pb $18.95

• **Michael Sullivan**
THE ARTS OF CHINA
A balanced and knowledgeable presentation, extending to the early 20th century
0–520–04917–9 California $42.50
0–520–04918–7 California pb $18.95

• **Mary Tregear**
CHINESE ART
An up-to-date survey that is a model of compression
0–19520–189–2 Norton $19.95
0–500–20178–1 Thames & Hudson pb $11.95

• **William Watson**
ART OF DYNASTIC CHINA
A massive compendium, copiously illustrated, with a formidable text
0–8109–0627–9 Abrams $125.00

Neolithic, Bronze and Iron Ages

• **Kwang-Chih Chang**
THE ARCHAEOLOGY OF ANCIENT CHINA
The single most authoritative work on prehistoric, neolithic, and Bronze Age China. Well-illustrated, with a model scholarly text. Written in 1948, before the extraordinary recent archaeological discoveries in China, it serves as a guide to understanding them
0–300–03782–1 Yale $52.00
0–300–03784–8 Yale pb $17.95

SHANG CIVILIZATION
Recommended for understanding the great dynasty in which Chinese writing, bronze technology, and high-fired ceramics were developed
0–300–02428–2 Yale $47.50
0–300–02885–7 Yale pb $13.95

• **Wen Fong, editor**
THE GREAT BRONZE AGE OF CHINA
The catalog for a major exhibition at the Metropolitan Museum, an excellent presentation of both Chinese and Western evaluations of the archaeological discoveries made since the revolution
0–394–51256–1 Knopf $40.00

Late 12th-century Cambodian kneeling female figure (Musée Guimet)

Chinese bronze vessel, c. 13th-11th century BC (Musée Guimet)

• Wang Zhongshu
HAN CIVILIZATION
The best survey of the Han achievements, which established the norms for all future development
0–300–02723–0 Yale $50.00

Painting

• James Cahill
CHINESE PAINTING
A brief work by the pre-eminent scholar and writer in the field. Sensitive to visual problems and attributions, keenly aware of the context of the works
0–8478–0079–2 Rizzoli pb $25.00

• Kodansha Editors
THE ARTS OF CHINA: Paintings in Chinese Museums
0–87011–128–0 Kodansha $89.00

• Sherman Lee, editor
EIGHT DYNASTIES OF CHINESE PAINTING: The Collections of the Nelson Gallery—Atkins Museum, Kansas City, and The Cleveland Museum of Art
A survey of Chinese painting found in the fine collections of the Cleveland Museum and Nelson Gallery with detailed entries on 282 paintings; a useful introduction to the field
0–910386–53–6 Indiana $60.00

• Max Loehr
THE GREAT PAINTERS OF CHINA
A complete and wise overview of the field
0–06–430105–2 Harper & Row pb $18.95

• Torao Miyagawa
CHINESE PAINTING
Extremely well-illustrated, presents a measured Japanese view
0–8348–1527–3 Weatherhill $65.00

• Jerome Silbergeld
CHINESE PAINTING STYLE: Media, Methods, and Principles of Form
A serious, succinct, and clear work
0–295–95921–5 Washington pb $15.00

• Robert Van Gulik
CHINESE PICTORIAL ART AS VIEWED BY THE CONNOISSEUR: Notes of the Means and Methods of Traditional Chinese Connoisseurship of Pictorial Art, Based upon a Study of the Art of Mounting Scrolls in China and Japan
A gold mine of information on mountings, how to paint, collectors' tales, fakes, and more—for the general reader
0–87817–264–5 Hacker $90.00

Chinese Theories of Art

• G. Rowley
PRINCIPLES OF CHINESE PAINTING
A forceful exposition of Chinese principles which are correlated with Western art-historical ideas
0–691–03834–1 Princeton $41.50
0–691–00300–9 Princeton pb $11.50

• Michael Sullivan
THE THREE PERFECTIONS: Chinese Painting, Poetry and Calligraphy
An impeccable distillation of decades of study and viewing with Chinese attitudes always in mind. Well-illustrated in black and white
0–8076–0997–8 Braziller pb $6.95

Translations of ancient Chinese sources are sufficiently available to give an inkling of these indispensable documents.

Susan Bush
CHINESE LITERATI ON PAINTING: Su Shih, 1037-1101 to Tung Ch'i-ch'ang, 1555-1636
Material from the Sung through Ming dynasties
0–674–12425–1 Harvard pb $9.50

Susan Bush & Shih Hsiao-Yen
EARLY CHINESE TEXTS ON PAINTING
Texts from the Han through Yüan dynasties
0–674–22025–0 Harvard pb $20.00

Osvald Siren
THE CHINESE AND THE ART OF PAINTING
From the Han to the Ch'ing dynasty, with a wide selection of texts. The single most useful volume on the subject
0–8052–0057–6 Schocken pb $9.95

Specialized Painting Studies

Buddhist Painting

Buddhist icon paintings, imported from India through Central Asia, were particularly influential in the development of Chinese figure painting.

Kodansha
THE ARTS OF CHINA: Buddhist Cave Temples
0–87011–089–6 Kodansha $89.00

Albert von LeCoq
BUDDHIST TREASURES OF CHINESE TURKESTAN
Introduction by Peter Hopkirk
0–19–583878–5 Oxford pb $13.95

• James Cahill
THE DISTANT MOUNTAINS: Chinese Painting of the Late Ming Dynasty, 1570-1644
Stimulating texts, lavishly illustrated with an excellent selection of classic and innovative works by major and minor masters. The author's knowledge of the subject is unrivaled in the West, and his understanding of Western art adds a dimension to his comments on the development and achievements of the Chinese painters
0–8348–0174–4 Weatherhill $49.95

HILLS BEYOND A RIVER: Chinese Painting of the Yüan Dynasty, 1279-1368
0–8348–0120–5 Weatherhill $37.50

PARTING AT THE SHORE: Chinese Painting of the Early and Middle Ming Dynasty, 1368-1580
0–8348–0128–0 Weatherhill $37.50

• Sherman Lee
CHINESE LANDSCAPE PAINTING
An excellent short introduction to landscape painting, probably China's most significant contribution to the art of painting
0–06–430010–2 Harper & Row pb $7.95

• Chu-tsing Li, editor
THE CHINESE SCHOLAR'S STUDIO: Artistic Life in the Late Ming Period
The social and political context of the later Chinese painters. Illustrations from the Shanghai Museum
0–500–01423–X Thames & Hudson $45.00

• Michael Sullivan
CHINESE LANDSCAPE PAINTING IN THE SUI AND T'ANG DYNASTIES
A detailed and well-illustrated study of the early development of landscape painting
0–520–03558–5 California $49.95

Calligraphy

Some understanding of calligraphy will aid the study of painting, for in Chinese thought and practice the two are inseparable.

• Chiang Yee
CHINESE CALLIGRAPHY: An Introduction to Its Aesthetic and Technique
An easy-to-follow introduction, organized by subject and typology
0–674–12226–7 Harvard pb $10.95

20th-Century Artists

• T.C. Lai
CH'I PAI-SHIH
The work of this artist, known as China's Picasso, is highly prized by collectors and museums
0–295–95315–2 Washington $20.00

A landscape by Wang Hsüeh-hao, 1827

• Jerome Silbergeld
MIND LANDSCAPES: The Paintings of C.C. Wang
A study of the 20th-century landscape painter and collector, whose work is an important bridge between traditional and modern Chinese painting
0–295–96520–7 Washington $40.00

C.C. WANG: Landscape Paintings
Works by the pioneer of modern ink painting
Introduction by James Cahill
0–295–96471–5 Washington $40.00

Ceramics

• Cecile & Michel Beurdeley
A CONNOISSEUR'S GUIDE TO CHINESE CERAMICS
A large handsome book, richly illustrated
0–06–010322–1 Harper & Row $75.00

• Margaret Medley
THE CHINESE POTTER
The best introduction to the subject, a practical history of Chinese ceramics with a delightful text and information on patronage
0–8014–9239–4 Cornell pb $18.95

• Yutaka Mino
ICE AND GREEN CLOUDS: Traditions of Chinese Celadon
An exhibition catalog, which provides a well-documented survey of the celadon tradition of the Sung, Yüan, and early Ming dynasties
0–936260–16–5 Indiana $35.00
0–936260–17–3 Indiana pb $25.00

• Rosemary Scott
IMPERIAL TASTE: Chinese Ceramics from the Percival David Foundation
An important collection of Chinese porcelain which includes masterpieces from the T'ang through Ch'ing dynasties
0–87701–616–X Chronicle $40.00
0–87701–612–7 Chronicle pb $22.95

• Susanne Valenstein
A HANDBOOK OF CHINESE CERAMICS
A thorough compendium, up-to-date and objective; largely limited to the collection of the Metropolitan Museum
0–8109–1170–1 Abrams $50.00

Decorative Arts

Neither Chinese, Korean, nor Japanese makes the unnecessarily sharp distinction made in the West between the "fine" arts and the "decorative" or "minor" arts.

• Harry Garner
CHINESE LACQUER
This succinct book is the best available on the subject of Chinese enamel and lacquer
0–571–11286–2 Faber & Faber $58.00

• Sheila Riddell
DATED CHINESE ANTIQUITIES: 600 to 1650
A useful chronological study of decorative arts from the Sui to the beginning of the Ch'ing dynasty
0–571–09753–7 Faber & Faber $39.95

• William Watson, editor
CHINESE IVORIES: From the Shang to the Ch'ing
0–85667–191–6 Sotheby $50.00

• James Watt
CHINESE JADES FROM HAN TO CH'ING
A splendid, knowledgeable treatment of Chinese jades over the past 2000 years
0–87848–057–9 Asia Society $22.50

Gardens

• Ji Cheng
THE CRAFT OF GARDENS
Published in 1631, this is the earliest manual of Chinese landscape gardening. Includes building design
Introduction by Maggie Keswick
Translated by Alison Hardie
0–300–04182–9 Yale $35.00

• Maggie Keswick
THE CHINESE GARDEN
A persuasive and interesting book, with a section on garden architecture
0–312–13383–9 St. Martin's pb $24.95

• Edwin Morris
THE GARDENS OF CHINA: History, Art, and Meaning
A well-illustrated guide, especially good on botanical matters
0–684–17959–8 Scribners $40.00

KOREA

The understanding of Korean art has been plagued from the beginning of this century: first by Japanese hegemony until World War II, then by the Korean War. There are few available publications on the wonders of Korean art and the importance of its influence as transmitter and catalyst between China and Japan.

• Roger Goepper & Roderick Whitfield
TREASURES FROM KOREA: Art Through Five Thousand Years
A helpful exhibition catalog
0–253–36050–1 Indiana $40.00
0–253–28860–6 Indiana pb $20.00

• Chewon Kim & Kim Lee
ARTS OF KOREA
A very large volume, with almost 300 marvelous illustrations. A commanding work with a knowledgeable text covering all media
0–87011–206–6 Kodansha $89.00

• John Rosenfeld, editor
KOREAN ART TREASURES
Painting, sculpture, metalwork, earthenware, pottery and porcelain,

architecture, and furniture—from the neolithic to the present
0–8109–1214–7 Abrams $80.00

JAPAN

Since 1945, the "Japanese miracle" has been accompanied by an explosion of books on all aspects of Japanese art.

- Vadime & Danielle Elisseeff
  ART OF JAPAN
  An extremely well-illustrated volume
  0–8109–0642–2 Abrams $125.00

- Masao Ishizawa & Ichimatsu Tanaka
  THE HERITAGE OF JAPANESE ART
  A good if brief overview
  0–87011–787–4 Kodansha $35.00

- Sherman Lee
  REFLECTIONS OF REALITY IN JAPANESE ART
  Not primarily historical in approach, this book isolates and interprets opposing tendencies in Japanese art
  0–910386–70–6 Indiana $45.00

- Seiroku Noma
  ARTS OF JAPAN
  A most complete and well-illustrated work. Two volumes in a manageable format
  Volume 1
  0–87011–018–7 Kodansha $95.00
  Volume 2
  0–87011–050–0 Kodansha $95.00

- R. Paine & Alexander Soper
  THE ART AND ARCHITECTURE OF JAPAN
  Good on painting and architecture, but decorative arts are omitted
  0–14–056108–0 Penguin pb $18.95

- Laurence P. Roberts
  A DICTIONARY OF JAPANESE ARTISTS: Painting, Sculpture, Ceramics, Prints, Lacquer
  A reference work for names, alternative names, and brief biographies—indispensable for Westerners
  0–8348–0113–2 Weatherhill $32.50

- Joan Stanley-Baker
  JAPANESE ART
  A survey of painting, calligraphy, decorative arts, and architecture, from the prehistoric period to the present, addressed to novice and connoisseur alike
  0–500–20192–7 Thames & Hudson pb $11.95

- Langdon Warner
  THE ENDURING ART OF JAPAN
  A distillation of Warner's sympathy for Japanese art, particularly fine on sculpture and folk art
  0–8021–3132–8 Grove pb $9.95

"Arashi Ryuzo" by Sharaku, from Japanese Prints *by James Michener (Tuttle)*

Pre-Buddhist Art

The extraordinary sculptural ceramics of Stone Age Japan representing Jomon culture are now known to date to at least 8000-6000 BC. The succeeding Yayoi and Haniwa cultures have commanded the attention of modernists, East and West.

- C. Melvin Aikens & Takayasu Higuchi
  PREHISTORY OF JAPAN
  A useful introduction
  0–12–045280–4 Academic $39.50

- Fujio Miki
  HANIWA
  A good introduction to these surprisingly modern-looking clay sculptures
  0–8348–2714–X Weatherhill $15.00

Painting

- Stephen Addiss
  THE ART OF ZEN: Paintings and Calligraphy by Japanese Monks, 1600-1925
  0–8109–1886–2 Abrams $39.95

- Stephen Addiss & G.C. Hurst
  SAMURAI PAINTERS
  Works by warrior-painters depicting their own particular iconography (eagles, tigers, bamboo) as well as traditional subjects
  0–87011–563–4 Kodansha $24.95

- Akiyama Terukazu
  JAPANESE PAINTING
  A general survey of Japanese painting, the best available introduction to painting as a whole
  0–8478–0132–2 Rizzoli pb $25.00

- James Cahill
  SCHOLAR PAINTERS OF JAPAN: The Nanga School
  A readable and concise introduction to the field. The late Edo literati school *Nanga* has been of particular interest to American museums and collectors, in part because of its derivation from the now fashionable literati painters of China
  0–405–06562–0 Ayer $33.00

- Henri Joly
  LEGENDS IN JAPANESE ART: A Description of Historical Episodes, Legendary Characters, Folklore, Myths, Religious Symbolism
  A general reference work for the complex identification of subjects, motifs and traditions in Japanese art. Its more than 600 pages, with over 700 illustrations, provide the copious information necessary for subject identification
  0–8048–0358–7 Tuttle $60.00

- Miyeko Murase
  TALES OF JAPAN: Scrolls and Prints from the New York Public Library
  A recent exhibition catalog of Japanese illustrated books from the fine collection of the New York Public Library
  0–19–504020–1 Oxford $34.50
  0–19–504021–X Oxford pb $16.95

- Hideo Okudaira
  NARRATIVE PICTURE SCROLLS
  The story-telling handscroll is one of the greatest Japanese artistic achievements. A particularly good survey of many of the best scrolls
  0–8348–2710–7 Weatherhill $15.00

- Leon Zolbrod
  HAIKU PAINTING
  The intimate relationship between *haiku* poems and the abbreviated, often humorous, paintings designed to accompany them
  0–87011–560–X Kodansha $24.95

Yoshiaki Shimizu & John Rosenfield
MASTERS OF JAPANESE CALLIGRAPHY: 8th-19th Century
An exhibition based on American collections, a sound introduction to the subject
0–913720–57–7 Frederic Beil $65.00

Woodblock Prints

The prints of *Ukiyo-e*, pictures of the "floating world", introduced great Japanese art to the West. There is an extensive Western literature available, as *hanga* are the most popular of the art forms outside of Japan.

- James Michener
  JAPANESE PRINTS: From the Early Masters to the Modern
  Michener's love affair with *hanga* is demonstrated by his collection now in the Honolulu Academy of Arts, and by this fluently written book
  0–8048–0314–5 Tuttle $67.50

• Muneshige Narazaki
THE JAPANESE PRINT: Its Evolution and Essence
0–87011–031–4 Kodansha $100.00

Ukiyo-e Artists

Juzo Suzuki & Isaburo Oka
THE DECADENTS
0–87011–098–5 Kodansha pb $13.50

Cynthea Bogel & Israel Goldman
HIROSHIGE: Birds and Flowers
0–8076–1199–9 Braziller $75.00

Sherman Lee
THE SKETCHBOOKS OF HIROSHIGE
Two fan-fold books
Foreword by Daniel Boorstin
0–8076–1105–0 Braziller $45.00

Henry D. Smith, II
HIROSHIGE: 100 Famous Views of Edo
0–8076–1143–3 Braziller $75.00

James Michener, editor
HOKUSAI SKETCHBOOKS: Selections from the Manga
0–8048–0252–1 Tuttle $39.50

Henry D. Smith, II
HOKUSAI: 100 Views of Mount Fuji
0–8076–1195–6 Braziller $35.00

Tuttle Publications
HOKUSAI'S VIEWS OF MOUNT FUJI
Twenty-four prints in miniature, with poems by Easley Stephen Jones
0–8048–0253–X Tuttle $16.95

B.W. Robinson
KUNIYOSHI: The Warrior Prints
0–8104–1488–1 Cornell $55.00

Muneshige Narazaki
SHARAKU
Translated by Bonnie F. Abiko
0–87011–603–7 Kodansha $22.95

Tadashi Kobayashi
UTAMARO
0–87011–503–0 Kodansha $24.95

Ceramics

The Japanese ceramic tradition is divided into two traditions: early earthenware and stoneware, continuing, though transformed, in the tea ceremony wares; and later porcelain beginning in the early 17th century with the direct importation of Chinese porcelains and Korean potters and their wares.

• Louise Cort
SHIGARAKI, POTTERS' VALLEY
A marvelous in-depth study of one of the Six Old Kilns of Japan. Fascinating for history, technology, personalities, and objects
0–87011–382–8 Kodansha $65.00

• Ryoichi Fujioka
SHINO AND ORIBE CERAMICS
Well-illustrated, with a detailed text
0–87011–284–8 Kodansha $27.95

• Soame Jenyns
JAPANESE POTTERY
The most comprehensive survey of the tradition, healthily skeptical of old wives' tales about the origins of kilns and the assumed pedigrees of famous individual tea wares
0–571–08709–4 Faber & Faber $49.95

• Tsugio Mikami
THE ART OF JAPANESE CERAMICS
The best text by a Japanese, an easily handled volume with excellent illustrations
0–8348–1000–X Weatherhill $20.00

• Daniel Rhodes
TAMBA POTTERY: The Timeless Art of a Japanese Village
A fine study by a professional ceramic engineer and potter, with interesting craft insights. Tamba is one of the Six Old Kilns
0–87011–520–0 Kodansha pb $14.95

Kodansha has published a series of slender volumes in large format on the various kilns. Well illustrated, each volume has a brief but informative text.

Motosuke Imaizumi
NABESHIMA
0–87011–415–8 Kodansha $18.95

Gen Kozuro
AGANO AND TAKATORI
0–87011–454–9 Kodansha $18.95

Hiroshi Mizuno
FOLK KILNS I
0–87011–416–6 Kodansha $18.95

Takeshi Murayama
ORIBE
0–87011–530–8 Kodansha $18.95

Takeshi Nagatake
KAKIEMON
0–87011–478–6 Kodansha $19.95

Taroemon Nakazato
KARATSU
0–87011–551–0 Kodansha $19.95

Kichiemon Okamura
FOLK KILNS II
0–87011–477–8 Kodansha $18.95

Yoshiharu Sawade
TOKONAME
0–87011–502–2 Kodansha $18.95

The Tea Ceremony

Alongside Ukiyo-e woodblock prints, the tea ceremony *Cha-no-yu* is Japan's most famous artistic contribution. It is also the most complete and successful means of aesthetic education ever seen, encompassing architec-

ture, ceramics, painting and calligraphy, metalwork, flower arrangement, and garden design.

• Kakuzo Okakura
THE BOOK OF TEA
In this brief but famous work, Okakura claims that Japan cannot be understood without study of the tea ceremony
0–8048–0069–3 Tuttle $10.95

• A.L. Sadler
CHA-NO-YU: The Japanese Tea Ceremony
A reprint of the 1933 classic, this is one of the most helpful publications on the subject—detailed, and by no means too susceptible to the mystique of tea
0–8048–1224–1 Tuttle pb $6.95

Gardens

• David Engel
JAPANESE GARDENS FOR TODAY: A Practical Handbook
This book has a practical emphasis that recommends it to active gardeners
0–8048–0301–3 Tuttle $45.00

• Masao Hayakawa
THE GARDEN ART OF JAPAN
0–8348–1014–X Weatherhill $20.00

• Loraine Kuck
THE WORLD OF THE JAPANESE GARDEN: From Chinese Origins to Modern Landscape Art
0–8348–0029–2 Weatherhill $37.50

Folk Art

The tea ceremony owes part of its greatness to humble folk artists, whether builders, potters, weavers, woodworkers, or painters. A great craft tradition underlies Japanese art.

• Hugo Munsterberg
FOLK ARTS OF JAPAN
0–8048–0190–8 Tuttle $29.50

• Kago Muraoka & Kichiemon Okamura
FOLK ARTS AND CRAFTS OF JAPAN
0–8348–1009–3 Weatherhill $20.00

The Weatherhill and Kodansha Series

Literature about Japanese art has been particularly encouraged by two publishers, Weatherhill/Heibonsha and Kodansha. Both series can be recommended for all readers. The Kodansha series, under the editorship of John Rosenfeld of Harvard, is perhaps more scholarly and detailed.

• Tsugiyoshi Doi
MOMOYAMA DECORATIVE PAINTING
0–8348–1024–7 Weatherhill $20.00

• Toshio Fukuyama
HEIAN TEMPLES: Byodo-In and Chuson-Ji
0–8348–1023–9 Weatherhill $20.00

Kamakura period wooden sculpture of Uyesui Shigefusa, from A History of Far Eastern Art *by Sherman Lee (Abrams)*

- Masao Hayakawa
THE GARDEN ART OF JAPAN
0–8348–1014–X Weatherhill $20.00

- Saburo Ienaga
PAINTING IN THE YAMATO STYLE
0–8348–1016–6 Weatherhill $20.00

- Teiji Itoh
TRADITIONAL DOMESTIC ARCHITECTURE OF JAPAN
0–8348–1004–2 Weatherhill $20.00

- Takeshi Kobayashi
NARA BUDDHIST ART: Todai-Ji
0–8348–1021–2 Weatherhill $20.00

- Tsugio Mikami
THE ART OF JAPANESE CERAMICS
0–8348–1000–X Weatherhill $20.00

- Seiichi Mizuno
ASUKA BUDDHIST ART: Horyu-Ji
0–8348–1020–4 Weatherhill $20.00

- Hiroshi Mizuo
EDO PAINTING: Sotatsu & Korin
0–8348–1011–5 Weatherhill $20.00

- Hisashi Mori
JAPANESE PORTRAIT SCULPTURE
0–87011–286–4 Kodansha $27.95

SCULPTURE OF THE KAMAKURA PERIOD
0–8348–1017–4 Weatherhill $20.00

- Kageo Muraoka & Kichiemon Okamura
FOLK ARTS AND CRAFTS OF JAPAN
0–8348–1009–3 Weatherhill $20.00

- Sensaka Nakagawa
KUTANI WARE
0–87011–322–4 Kodansha $27.95

- Yujiro Nakata
THE ART OF JAPANESE CALLIGRAPHY
0–8348–1013–1 Weatherhill $20.00

- Seiroku Noma
JAPANESE COSTUME AND TEXTILE ARTS
0–8348–1026–3 Weatherhill $20.00

- Yoshitomo Okamoto
THE NAMBAN ART OF JAPAN
0–8348–1008–5 Weatherhill $20.00

- Naomi Okawa
EDO ARCHITECTURE: Katsura and Nikko
0–8348–1027–1 Weatherhill $20.00

- Joji Okazaki
PURE LAND BUDDHIST PAINTINGS
0–87011–287–2 Kodansha $27.95

- Minoru Ooka
TEMPLES OF NARA AND THEIR ART
0–8348–1010–7 Weatherhill $17.50

- Takaaki Sawa
ART IN JAPANESE ESOTERIC BUDDHISM
0–8348–1001–8 Weatherhill $20.00

- Jiro Sugiyama
CLASSIC BUDDHIST SCULPTURE
0–87011–529–4 Kodansha $27.95

- Ichimatsu Tanaka
JAPANESE INK PAINTING: Shubun to Sesshu
0–8348–1005–0 Weatherhill $20.00

- Tsuneo Tanaka
KANO EITOKU
0–87011–295–3 Kodansha $27.95

- Yuzo Yamane
MOMOYAMA GENRE PAINTING
0–8348–1012–3 Weatherhill $20.00

- Yoshiho Yonezawa & Chu Yoshizawa
JAPANESE PAINTING IN THE LITERATI STYLE
0–8348–1019–0 Weatherhill $20.00

EAST AND WEST

The impressionists' use of Japanese prints is well known. The rest of the story of the mutual influence of East and West since the 19th century is still obscure to Westerners. Judgments of modern Chinese or Japanese work in Western styles or in the native manner are still wavering and uncertain.

- Hugh Honour
CHINOISERIE: The Vision of Cathay
0–06–430039–0 Harper & Row pb $6.95

- Michiaki Kawakita
MODERN CURRENTS IN JAPANESE ART
0–8348–1028–X Weatherhill $20.00

- Michael Sullivan
THE MEETING OF EASTERN AND WESTERN ART
Four centuries of interaction between the artists of China and Japan and the artists of Western Europe
0–520–05902–6 California $45.00

- Shuji Takashina & J.T. Rimer
PARIS IN JAPAN: The Japanese Encounter with European Painting
The most recent publication in the field of modern Japanese art
0–295–96700–5 Washington pb $30.00

- Chisaburoh Yamada
DIALOGUE IN ART: Japan and the West
The most complete work on Japan and the West
0–87011–214–7 Kodansha $75.00

Native American Arts

NORTH AMERICA

• David Brose, James Brown & David Penney
ANCIENT ART OF THE AMERICAN WOODLAND INDIANS
0–8109–1827–7 Abrams $35.00
0–8109–2306–8 Abrams pb $29.95

• Ralph Coe
LOST AND FOUND TRADITIONS: Native American Art, 1965-1985
The 400 works discussed include textiles, pottery, baskets, jewelry, and carving; exceptionally good reproductions
0–295–96391–3 Washington $35.00

• Richard Conn
CIRCLES OF THE WORLD: Traditional Art of the Plains Indians
The forms and functions of Plains art, including clothing, jewelry, military and ceremonial regalia, and household objects
0–295–96229–1 Washington pb $14.95

• Christian Feest
NATIVE ARTS OF NORTH AMERICA
A well-ordered overview of the art of 1000 tribes, from Seminole appliqué work of the 1890s to an Arapaho Ghost Dance
0–500–18179–9 Norton $19.95
0–500–20179–X Thames & Hudson pb $11.95

• Jill Furst & Peter Furst
NORTH AMERICAN INDIAN ART
0–8478–0572–7 Rizzoli pb $25.00

• Audrey Hawthorn
KWAKIUTL ART
The definitive catalog, superbly illustrated
0–295–96640–8 Washington pb $29.95

• Jamake Highwater
ARTS OF THE INDIAN AMERICAS, NORTH, CENTRAL AND SOUTH: Leaves from the Sacred Tree
0–06–433330–2 Harper & Row $35.00

SONG FROM THE EARTH: American Indian Painting
0–8212–1091–2 NY Graphic Society pb $16.95

• Robert Inverarity
ART OF THE NORTHWEST COAST INDIANS
0–520–00595–3 California pb $14.95

• Aldona Jonaitis
FROM THE LAND OF THE TOTEM POLES: The Northwest Coast Indian Art Collection at the American Museum of Natural History
The collection housed in the museum's North Pacific Hall, described by Claude Lévi-Strauss as "a magic place where the dreams of childhood hold a rendez-vous, where century-old tree trunks sing and speak"
0–295–96572–X Washington $40.00

• Claude Lévi-Strauss
THE WAY OF THE MASKS
"A fine study of the connections between verbal and plastic objects, it teaches much about Northwest Coast Indian culture, and it applies elegantly structuralist perceptions to carved and painted works of art"—
Journal of American Folklore
Translated by Sylvia Modelski
0–295–96636–X Washington pb $14.95

• Dorothy Ray
ALEUT AND ESKIMO ART: Tradition and Innovation in South Alaska
"A comprehensive survey of Alaskan Eskimo art that is certain to make this book a delight to anyone interested in native American art"—*American Indian Art*
0–295–96410–3 Washington pb $24.95

ESKIMO ART: Tradition and Innovation in North Alaska
An indispensable companion volume to *Aleut and Eskimo Art*
0–295–95518–X Washington pb $35.00

ARTISTS OF THE TUNDRA AND THE SEA
A classic book on the carvers of northwestern Alaska
0–295–95732–8 Washington pb $10.95

• Edwin Wade & Rennard Strickland
MAGIC IMAGES: Contemporary Native American Art
A current survey, featuring the work of 37 contemporary artists including Fritz Scholder and Frank LePena
0–8061–1817–2 Oklahoma pb $16.95

• Andrew Whiteford
NORTH AMERICAN INDIAN ARTS
A handy pocket guide to Indian arts and crafts
0–307–24032–0 Golden Press pb $2.95

MEXICO AND CENTRAL AMERICA

• Ferdinand Anton
ANCIENT PERUVIAN TEXTILES
These textiles, preserved on an unusually large scale, span a period of more than 2500 years. There are 302 illustrations, over 100 of them in color
0–500–01402–7 Norton $40.00

• Michael Coe
LORDS OF THE UNDERWORLD: Masterpieces of Classical Mayan Ceramics
The depicted scenes are linked to a cult of the dead; color fold-out illustrations
0–691–03917–8 Princeton $60.00

• Clemency Chase Coggins & Orrin C. Shane III, editors
CENOTE OF SACRIFICE: Maya Treasures from the Sacred Well at Chichen Itza
More than 300 artifacts; illustrated in black and white, some in color
0–292–71097–6 Texas $40.00
0–292–71098–4 Texas pb $24.50

• Donald Cordry
MEXICAN MASKS
Full treatment of mask-making and mask styles; illustrated in color
0–292–75050–1 Texas $49.95
0–292–75074–9 Texas pb $24.95

• Donald & Dorothy Cordry
MEXICAN INDIAN COSTUMES
Description and analysis; 300 illustrations, some in color
0–292–73426–3 Texas $39.95

• Jorge Enciso
DESIGN MOTIFS OF ANCIENT MEXICO
Silhouette designs from ancient clay stamps
0–486–20084–1 Dover pb $3.95

• Paul Gendrop & Doris Heyden
PRE-COLUMBIAN ARCHITECTURE OF MESOAMERICA
0–8109–1018–7 Abrams $50.00

• Clyde Keeler
CUNA INDIAN ART: The Culture and Craft of Panama's San Blas Islanders
Molas, jewelry, weaving, folk painting, and other arts, mostly illustrated in black and white
0–682–46815–0 Exposition $25.00

• Eduardo Matos Moctezuma
THE GREAT TEMPLE OF THE AZTECS: Treasures of Tenochtitlan
The director of Mexico City's National Museum of Anthropology recounts the 1978 excavation that rediscovered the Aztec capital
0–500–39024–X Norton $29.95

• Arthur Miller
THE MURAL PAINTING OF TEOTIHUACAN
Nearly 400 illustrations; presents virtually all the recorded murals from the classic pre-Aztec site north of Mexico City
0–88402–049–5 Dumbarton Oaks $35.00

• Mary Miller
THE ART OF MESOAMERICA: From Olmec to Aztec
0–500–20203–6 Thames & Hudson pb $11.95

THE MURALS OF BONAMPAK
Maya wall paintings from a site in Chiapas; dances, ceremonies, and scenes of battle; illustrated, with a detailed study
0–691–04033–8 Princeton $67.50

• Zelia Nuttall, editor
THE CODEX NUTTALL: A Picture Manuscript from Ancient Mexico
Color hand-painted facsimile of a Mixtec picture book; the only pre-Columbian codex in an easily affordable edition
0–486–23168–2 Dover pb $10.95

• Zelia Nuttall & Elizabeth Hill Boone, editors
THE BOOK OF THE LIFE OF THE ANCIENT MEXICANS: The Codex Magliabechiano
Another color hand-painted (not photographic) facsimile edition, this time of an Aztec picture book, with interpretive commentary. Two volumes
0–520–04520–3 California (set) $85.00

- **August Panyella**
FOLK ART OF THE AMERICAS
Pictorial encyclopedia; covers Indian and Hispanic crafts of North, South, and Central America
0–8109–0912–X Abrams $50.00

- **Ann Parker & Avon Neal**
MOLAS: Folk Art of the Cuna Indians
The well-known Panamanian stitched-fabric panels; illustrated in color and in black-and-white
0–517–52911–4 Barre $35.00

- **Lee Parsons**
PRE-COLUMBIAN ART
0–06–437000–3 Harper & Row $36.50

- **Tatiana Proskouriakoff**
AN ALBUM OF MAYA ARCHITECTURE
Monochrome paintings by an artist-scholar that show the ancient cities as they might have looked in their prime
0–8061–1351–0 Oklahoma pb $15.95

- **Merle Green Robertson**
THE SCULPTURE OF PALENQUE
The definitive treatment of the classic Maya site; descriptive text by an archaeologist, illustrated with photographs
Volume 1: The Temple of the Inscriptions
0–691–03560–1 Princeton $145.00
Volume 2: The Early Buildings of the Palace and the Wall Paintings
0–691–03568–7 Princeton $145.00

- **Linda Schele & Mary Miller**
THE BLOOD OF KINGS: Dynasty and Ritual in Maya Art
Recent developments in the deciphering of Maya hieroglyphic writing, illustrated with glyph-inscribed art objects
0–8076–1159–X Braziller $50.00

- **Karl Taube**
THE ALBERS COLLECTION OF PRE-COLUMBIAN ART
0–933920–70–9 Hudson Hills $35.00

Pre-Columbian head, c. 600-900, from The Albers Collection of Pre-Columbian Art *by Karl Taube* (Hudson Hills)

Illustration and Popular Graphics

POSTERS

- **Dawn Ades & others**
THE 20TH CENTURY POSTER
0–89659–433–5 Abbeville $55.00
0–89659–434–3 Abbeville pb $24.95

- **John Barnicoat**
POSTERS: A Concise History
The origins of the poster in the murals, folk art, and book illustration of the second half of the 19th century
0–500–20118–8 Thames & Hudson pb $11.95

- **Paul Grushkin**
THE ART OF ROCK: Posters from Presley to Punk
0–89659–584–6 Abbeville $90.00

- **J. Stewart Johnson**
THE MODERN AMERICAN POSTER
20th-century American poster art
0–316–59403–2 Museum of Modern Art pb $16.95

- **Stuart Wrede**
THE MODERN POSTER
0–87070–570–9 NY Graphic Society $50.00

Movie Posters and Lobby Cards

- **Alan Adler, editor**
SCIENCE-FICTION AND HORROR MOVIE POSTERS IN FULL COLOR
0–486–23452–5 Dover pb $8.95

- **Michael Barson, editor**
LOST, LONELY AND VICIOUS: Postcards from the Great Trash Films
0–679–73968–8 Pantheon pb $8.95

- **Mildred Constantine & Alan Fern**
REVOLUTIONARY SOVIET FILM POSTERS
0–8018–1760–9 Johns Hopkins pb $9.95

- **Stephen Rebello & Richard Allen**
REEL ART: Great Posters from the Golden Age of the Silver Screen
0–89659–869–1 Abbeville $75.00

- **Markku Salmi, editor**
NATIONAL FILM ARCHIVE CATALOGUE OF STILLS, POSTERS AND DESIGNS
0–85170–129–9 Illinois pb $29.95

- **Rex Schneider & Christopher Buchman**
MOVIE POSTERS OF THE SILENT FILM ERA
0–916144–61–5 Stemmer House pb $3.95

- **Kathryn Scott**
LOBBY CARDS: The Classic Films
Introduction by Joan Bennett
0–938817–11–6 Pomegranate $29.95

Posters with Specific Themes

- **Nicolas Bailly**
A TOAST TO WINE AND SPIRITS
0–8109–2404–8 Abrams pb $16.95

- **Hayward & Blanche Cirker, editors**
GOLDEN AGE OF THE POSTER
0–486–22753–7 Dover pb $9.95
MASTERPIECES OF THE POSTER FROM THE BELLE EPOQUE: 48 Full-Color Plates from Les Maîtres de L'Affiche
0–486–24549–7 Dover pb $5.95

- **Anthony Crawford, editor**
POSTERS OF WORLD WAR I AND WORLD WAR II
0–8139–0778–0 Virginia $15.00

- **Joseph Czestochowski, editor**
CONTEMPORARY POLISH POSTERS IN FULL COLOR
0–486–23780–X Dover pb $6.95

- **Joseph Darracott, editor**
THE FIRST WORLD WAR IN POSTERS
0–486–22979–3 Dover pb $9.95

- **Jean Delhaye**
ART DECO POSTERS AND GRAPHICS
0–312–05202–2 St. Martin's pb $9.95

- **Chistopher DeNoon**
POSTERS OF THE WPA
0–295–96543–6 Washington $39.95

- **Charles Fox**
AMERICAN CIRCUS POSTERS IN FULL COLOR
0–486–23693–5 Dover pb $8.95

- **Marcel Franciscono & Stephen Prolopoff**
THE MODERN DUTCH POSTER: The First 50 Years
Little-known graphic art, 1890 to 1940
0–262–66061–X MIT $17.50

- **David Kiehl, editor**
AMERICAN ART POSTERS OF THE 1890s
From the collections of the Metropolitan Museum of Art
0–8109–1869–2 Abrams $45.00

- **Sid Latham**
GREAT SPORTING POSTERS OF THE GOLDEN AGE
0–8117–2115–9 Stackpole pb $19.95

- **Walton Rawls**
WAKE UP, AMERICA: World War I and the American Poster
0–89659–888–8 Abbeville $49.95

- **Roger Sainton**
ART NOUVEAU POSTERS AND GRAPHICS
0–312–05274–X St. Martin's pb $9.95

- **Hermann Schardt**
PARIS 1900: The Art of the Poster
0–517–63884–3 Crown $15.95

• Alain Weill
ONE HUNDRED YEARS OF POSTERS OF THE FOLIES BERGERES AND MUSIC HALLS OF PARIS
0–89545–000–3 Images Graphiques $19.95
0–89545–001–1 Images Graphiques pb $8.95

ILLUSTRATION

• Edward Booth-Clibborn
AMERICAN ILLUSTRATION
0–89659–946–9 Abbeville $55.00

• Steven Heller
INNOVATORS OF AMERICAN ILLUSTRATION
0–442–23230–6 Van Nostrand Reinhold $41.95

• Judy Larson
AMERICAN ILLUSTRATION 1890-1925: Romance, Adventure and Suspense
0–919224–47–4 Chicago $24.95

• M. Tamiya
MILITARY ILLUSTRATION
4–7661–0404–8 Books Nippan $24.95

Illustrators

• Irina Pruzhan, editor
LEON BAKST
0–670–81019–3 Viking $35.00

• Erté
ERTE AT NINETY FIVE: The Complete New Graphics
0–525–24560–X Dutton $75.00

NEW ERTE GRAPHICS IN FULL COLOR
0–486–24645–0 Dover pb $6.95

• Marshall Lee
ERTE AT NINETY: The Complete Graphics
0–525–93258–5 Dutton $95.00

• Charles Spencer
ERTE
0–517–54391–5 Crown pb $16.95

• Bruno Ernest
M.C. ESCHER: 29 MASTER PRINTS
0–8109–2268–1 Abrams $16.95

• M.C. Escher
THE GRAPHIC WORKS OF M.C. ESCHER
0–345–32787–X Ballantine pb $12.95

M.C. ESCHER: His Life and Complete Graphic Work
0–8109–0858–1 Abrams $65.00

THE WORLD OF M.C. ESCHER
Time, space and visual reality rearranged according to an ingenious logic
0–8109–8084–3 Abrams $19.95

• Doris Schattschneider & Wallace Walker
M.C. ESCHER KALEIDOCYCLES
Models of Escher's graphics and how they were devised
0–906212–28–6 Tarquin $16.95

• David Larkin, editor
THE FANTASTIC ART OF FRANK FRAZETTA
0–553–34473–0 Bantam pb $14.95

• Charles Gibson
THE GIBSON GIRL AND HER AMERICA
The work of the illustrator who created the turn-of-the-century ideal of feminine beauty
0–486–21986–0 Dover pb $6.95

• Shelley Armitage
JOHN HELD JR., ILLUSTRATOR OF THE JAZZ AGE
A full-length study of the illustrator who immortalized the flapper girls of the 1920s
0–8156–0215–4 Syracuse $37.50

• Fridolf Johnson
ROCKWELL KENT
0–394–41771–2 Knopf $60.00

• Dan Jones
THE PRINTS OF ROCKWELL KENT
0–686–87739–X Wofsy $75.00

• Rockwell Kent
IT'S ME, O LORD: The Autobiography of Rockwell Kent
The story of a major American illustrator of the 1920s and '30s
0–306–77412–7 Da Capo $85.00

• E. Ishioka
TAMARA DE LEMPICKA
4–8–9194049–2 Books Nippan pb $75.00

• Charles Philips
PASSION BY DESIGN: The Art and Times of Tamara de Lempicka
The suavely sophisticated art and eccentric life of a major European illustrator of the 1920s and '30s
0–89659–760–1 Abbeville $29.95

Illustration for "Voyaging," from Rockwell Kent *by Fridolf Johnson (Knopf)*

• Marilyn Cohen
REGINALD MARSH'S NEW YORK: Paintings, Drawings, Prints and Photographs
0–8446–6109–9 Peter Smith $18.25
0–486–24594–2 Dover pb $8.95

• Ann Bridges, editor
ALPHONSE MUCHA: The Complete Graphic Works
0–517–55308–2 Crown pb $10.95

• Coy Ludwig
MAXFIELD PARRISH
One of the most successful and original illustrators of the early 20th century
0–517–15265–7 Crown $14.95

• Maurice Sendak, editor
THE MAXFIELD PARRISH POSTER BOOK
0–517–51402–8 Crown pb $10.95

• Marian Sweeney
MAXFIELD PARRISH PRINTS
0–87233–029–X Bauhan pb $8.95

• Christopher Finch
NORMAN ROCKWELL'S AMERICA
A full display of Rockwell's skill as an illustrator and a commentator on 20th-century life in the United States
0–8109–8071–1 Abrams $19.95

• Norman Rockwell
NORMAN ROCKWELL: Artist and Illustrator
0–8109–8051–7 Abrams $39.95

NORMAN ROCKWELL: My Adventures As an Illustrator
0–8109–1563–4 Abrams $39.95

NORMAN ROCKWELL: A 60-Year Retrospective
0–451–79960–7 NAL pb $8.95

• Norman Rockwell & Fred Bauer
THE FAITH OF AMERICA
0–89659–813–6 Abbeville $19.95

• Boris Vallejo
THE FANTASTIC ART OF BORIS VALLEJO
0–345–35209–2 Ballantine $14.95
0–345–29027–5 Ballantine pb $9.95

BOOK ILLUSTRATION

• Brian Alderson
SING A SONG FOR SIXPENCE: The English Picturebook Tradition and Randolph Caldecott
0–521–33179–X Cambridge $24.95

• Yu-Ying Brown
JAPANESE BOOK ILLUSTRATION
0–7123–0128–3 Longwood pb $8.95

• John Harthan
THE HISTORY OF THE ILLUSTRATED BOOK: The Western Tradition
0–500–23316–0 Thames & Hudson $60.00

- Carol Hogben & Rowan Watson
**FROM MANET TO HOCKNEY: Modern
Artists' Illustrated Books**
0–948107–08–1 Faber & Faber $49.95
0–948107–07–3 Faber & Faber pb $24.95

- Fridolf Johnson, editor
**A TREASURY OF AMERICAN PEN AND
INK ILLUSTRATION: 222 Drawings by
99 Artists, 1890-1930**
0–486–24280–3 Dover pb $6.50

- Susan Meyer
**A TREASURY OF THE GREAT
CHILDREN'S BOOK ILLUSTRATORS**
0–8109–8081–9 Abrams pb $19.95

- Maurice Sendak
**CALDECOTT AND CO.: Notes on Books
and Pictures**
0–374–22598–2 Farrar, Straus & Giroux $18.95

- Gerald Ward
**THE AMERICAN ILLUSTRATED BOOK
IN THE 19TH CENTURY**
0–912724–17–X Winterthur $30.00

Book Illustrators

- Mitsumasa Anno
**THE UNIQUE WORLD OF MITSUMASA
ANNO: Selected Works, 1968-77**
0–399–20743–0 Putnam $19.95

- Edward Hodnett
**FRANCIS BARLOW: First Master of
English Book Illustration**
0–520–03409–0 California $55.00

- Randolph Caldecott, illustrator
**A FIRST CALDECOTT COLLECTION:
The House That Jack Built, A Frog He
Would a Wooing Go**
0–7232–3432–9 Warne $4.95

**A SECOND CALDECOTT
COLLECTION: Sing a Song for Sixpence,
The Three Jovial Hunters**
0–7232–3433–7 Warne $4.95

**A THIRD CALDECOTT COLLECTION:
The Queen of Hearts, The Farmer's Boy**
0–7232–3434–5 Warne $4.95

- Gustave Doré
DORE BIBLE ILLUSTRATIONS
0–486–23004–X Dover pb $8.95

**DORE'S ILLUSTRATIONS FOR
DANTE'S DIVINE COMEDY**
0–486–23231–X Dover pb $5.95

**DORE'S ILLUSTRATIONS FOR DON
QUIXOTE: A Selection of 190 Illustrations
by Gustave Doré**
0–486–24300–1 Dover pb $6.95

- Edward Gorey
AMPHIGOREY
The oblique and macabre black humor of
the contemporary American artist
0–399–50433–8 Putnam pb $12.95

AMPHIGOREY ALSO
0–86553–156–0 Congdon & Weed pb $13.95

AMPHIGOREY TOO
0–399–50420–6 Putnam pb $13.95

*An unused illustration for "The Tale of
Pigling Bland," from* Beatrix Potter *by Judy
Taylor and others* (Warne)

- Jack Hillier
**THE ART OF HOKUSAI IN BOOK-
ILLUSTRATION**
0–520–04137–2 California $125.00

- Audrey Isselbacher
**ILIAZD AND THE ILLUSTRATED
BOOK**
A dynamic figure of the modern movement
who designed and produced innovative
illustrated books
0–87070–396–X Museum of Modern Art pb $10.00

- William Morris
**THE IDEAL BOOK: Essays and Lectures
on the Arts of the Book**
0–520–05625–6 California $15.95

**WILLIAM MORRIS BY HIMSELF:
Designs and Writings**
0–8212–1710–0 Little, Brown $50.00

- Judith Taylor & others
**BEATRIX POTTER, 1866-1943: The
Artist and Her World**
Companion to the Pierpont Morgan
Library exhibition
0–7232–3521–X Warne $35.00
0–7232–3561–9 Warne pb $19.95

- Geoffrey Beare
**THE ILLUSTRATIONS OF W. HEATH
ROBINSON: A Commentary and
Bibliography**
Late-19th-century children's book
illustrator
0–907961–02–9 Spoon River $28.00

- Langston Day
**THE LIFE AND ART OF W. HEATH
ROBINSON**
0–7158–1180–0 Charles River $25.00

- W. Heath Robinson
HEATH ROBINSON AT WAR
0–7156–1318–9 Longwood $13.50

HUMOURS OF GOLF
0–7156–0915–7 Longwood $13.50

INVENTIONS
0–7156–0724–3 Longwood $13.50

RAILWAY RIBALDRY
0–7156–0823–1 Longwood $13.50

- Ronald Searle
**AH YES, I REMEMBER IT WELL . . . :
Paris, 1961-1975**
Drawings by a British illustrator known
for his ornate and whimsical art
0–88162–323–7 Salem $16.95

**ILLUSTRATED WINESPEAK: Ronald
Searle's Wicked World of Winetasting**
0–06–015320–2 Harper & Row $12.95

**RONALD SEARLE'S GOLDEN OLDIES,
1941-1961**
0–318–19320–5 Salem House $16.95

SEARLE'S CATS
0–89815–263–1 Ten Speed pb $9.95

- Selma Lanes
THE ART OF MAURICE SENDAK
The work of a leading contemporary
American children's book illustrator
0–8109–8063–0 Abrams $34.95

- Michael Hancher
**THE TENNIEL ILLUSTRATIONS TO
THE ALICE BOOKS**
0–8142–0408–2 Ohio pb $17.50

CARICATURES

- Jean Cocteau
DRAWINGS
The elegant line drawings of the versatile
French writer
0–486–20781–1 Dover pb $5.95

- Beverly Cox & Denna Anderson
**MIGUEL COVARRUBIAS
CARICATURES**
Jean Harlow, Joe Louis, Haile Selassie,
and many others
0–87474–340–0 Smithsonian $27.50

- David Cuppleditch
**THOMAS NAST: Cartoons and
Illustrations**
The German-born father of American
political cartoons on post-Civil War life
0–486–23067–8 Dover pb $12.50

- David Duncan with Mort Drucker
**FAMILIAR FACES: The Art of Mort
Drucker**
0–94163–02–X Stabur pb $12.95

- Aline Fruhauf
**MAKING FACES: Memoirs of a
Caricaturist**
Drawings of celebrities from the worlds of
theater, music, and fashion; from Maurice
Ravel to Lilian Gish
0–932020–46–1 Seven Locks $19.95

- M. Dorothy George
**HOGARTH TO CRUICKSHANK: Social
Change in Graphic Satire**
A pictorial record of the high, low, and
middle life of 18th- and 19th-century
England
0–670–82116–0 Viking $39.95

- Heinrich Kley
DRAWINGS OF HEINRICH KLEY
The whimsical, surreal comic fantasies of
the 19th-century German artist
Edited by Donald Weeks
0–486–20024–8 Dover pb $4.50

**KLEY-DOSCOPE: The Strange Drawings
of Heinrich Kley**
0–930937–41–4 Winds of the World pb $3.95

MORE DRAWINGS
0–486–20041–8 Dover pb $4.75

"Alfred Knopf," from Miguel Covarrubias Caricatures *by Beverly Cox and Denna Jones Anderson* (Smithsonian)

- David Levine
THE WATERCOLORS OF DAVID LEVINE
Paintings by the preeminent American literary caricaturist
0–295–95817–0 Washington pb $9.00

- Richard Vogler
GRAPHIC WORKS OF GEORGE CRUICKSHANK
Political and social cartoons, 1814-1877
0–486–23438–X Dover pb $8.95

- Judith Wechsler
A HUMAN COMEDY: Physiognomy and Caricature in 19th-Century Paris
0–226–87770–1 Chicago $29.95

ADVERTISING ART

- Mary Black
AMERICAN ADVERTISING POSTERS OF THE 19TH CENTURY
0–486–23356–1 Dover pb $11.95

- William Bockus
ADVERTISING GRAPHICS
0–02–311530–0 Macmillan $32.50

- Clarence Hornung
HANDBOOK OF EARLY ADVERTISING ART
Volume 1: Pictorial
0–486–20122–8 Dover pb $17.95
Volume 2: Typographical and Ornamental
0–486–20123–6 Dover pb $16.95

- Clarence Hornung & Fridolf Johnson
200 YEARS OF AMERICAN GRAPHIC ART
A survey of the printing and advertising arts since the colonial period
0–8076–0791–6 Braziller $25.00

Yasutoshi Ikuta
THE AMERICAN AUTOMOBILE: Advertising from the Antique and Classic Eras
0–87701–522–8 Chronicle $27.50
0–87701–451–5 Chronicle pb $14.95

CRUISE-O-MATIC: Automobile Advertising of the 1950s
0–87701–532–5 Chronicle pb $14.95

- Philip Lemme
AMERICAN STREAMLINE: A Handbook of Neon Advertising Design
0–911380–80–9 Signs of the Times pb $16.95

- Alfredo Marcantonio, editor
IS THE BUG DEAD?
0–941434–24–9 Stewart, Tabori & Chang pb $9.95

- Theodore Menten
ADVERTISING ART IN THE ART DECO STYLE
0–486–23164–X Dover pb $7.95

- Donald Stolz, & others
THE ADVERTISING WORLD OF NORMAN ROCKWELL
Heinz baked beans to Crest toothpaste
0–517–61808–7 Harrison House $19.95

COMMERCIAL DESIGN

- Donald Bush
THE STREAMLINED DECADE: Design in the 1930s
0–8076–0793–2 Braziller pb $14.95

- Ralph Caplan
BY DESIGN: Why There Are No Locks on the Bathroom Doors in the Hotel Louis XIV and Other Object Lessons
0–312–11085–5 St. Martin's $16.95

- Ken Cato
FIRST CHOICE
The world's leading graphic designers select the best of all their work
4–7661–0496–X Books Nippan $75.00

- Adrian Forty
OBJECTS OF DESIRE: Design and Society from Wedgwood to IBM
0–394–75151–5 Pantheon pb $14.95

From Yasutoshi Ikuta's Cruise-O-Matic (Chronicle)

- Thomas Hine
POPULUXE
0–394–54593–1 Knopf $29.95
0–394–74014–9 Knopf pb $16.95

- Leonard Koren
283 USEFUL IDEAS FROM JAPAN: For Entrepreneurs and Everyone Else
0–87701–483–3 Chronicle pb $8.95

- Edward Lucie-Smith
A HISTORY OF INDUSTRIAL DESIGN
0–442–25804–6 Van Nostrand Reinhold $52.95

- Nikolaus Pevsner
PIONEERS OF MODERN DESIGN
0–14–055211–1 Penguin pb $7.95

- Barbara Radice, editor
TERRAZZO
0–8478–5520–1 Rizzoli pb $20.00

- Klaus-Jurgen Sembach
STYLE 1930
0–87663–865–5 Universe pb $14.95

- John Thakara & Peter Dormer, editors
NEW BRITISH DESIGN
0–500–27446–0 Thames & Hudson pb $14.95

- Richard Wilson & others
THE MACHINE AGE IN AMERICA, 1918-1941
0–8109–1421–2 Abrams $39.95

Graphic Design

- Hugh Aldersey-Williams
NEW AMERICAN DESIGN: Products and Graphics for a Post-Industrial Age
0–8478–0992–7 Rizzoli $35.00

- American Artists' Congress Staff
GRAPHIC WORKS OF THE AMERICAN '30s
0–306–80078–0 Da Capo pb $7.95

- Elizabeth Armstrong
TYLER GRAPHICS: The Extended Image
The multifaceted art created at the Tyler workshop
0–89659–750–4 Abbeville $45.00

- Amy E. Arntson
GRAPHIC DESIGN BASICS
0–03–003257–1 Holt, Rinehart & Winston pb $27.95

- Russel Blanchard
GRAPHIC DESIGN
0–13–363226–1 Prentice-Hall pb $34.00

- James Craig & Bruce Barton
THIRTY CENTURIES OF GRAPHIC DESIGN
0–8230–5355–5 Watson-Guptill $24.95

- Ignazia Favata
JOE COLOMBO AND ITALIAN DESIGN OF THE SIXTIES
0–262–06117–1 MIT Press $30.00

- Milton Glaser
GRAPHIC DESIGN
0–87951–188–5 Overlook pb $35.00

Steven Heller & Seymour Chwast
GRAPHIC STYLE: From Victorian to Post-Modern
0–8109–1033–0 Abrams $49.50

SOURCEBOOK OF VISUAL IDEAS
0–442–23271–3 VNR pb $31.95

- Philip Meggs
A HISTORY OF GRAPHIC DESIGN
From cave pictographs to the most modern designs
0–442–26221–3 Van Nostrand Reinhold $41.95

- Gregory Mirow
A TREASURY OF DESIGN FOR ARTISTS AND CRAFTSMEN
0–486–22002–8 Dover pb $4.95

- B. Martin Pedersen
FORTY TWO YEARS OF GRAPHICS COVERS
3–85709–422–2 Watson-Guptill $49.50

- Ettore Sottsass
DESIGN METAPHORS
0–8478–0894–7 Rizzoli pb $12.50

- Bradbury Thompson
THE ART OF GRAPHIC DESIGN
The work of one of the most important 20th-century graphic designers. Designs for magazines, stamps, limited edition books are included in this book elegantly designed by Thompson
0–300–04301–5 Yale $65.00

- Richard Wilde
VISUAL THINKING: Problems and Solutions
0–442–29182–5 Van Nostrand Reinhold $44.95

- Henry Wolf
VISUAL THINKING: Methods for Making Images Memorable
0–931144–47–7 American Showcase $45.00

Graphics: East Asia

- Joseph D'Addetta
TRADITIONAL JAPANESE DESIGN MOTIFS
0–486–24629–9 Dover pb $4.50

A TREASURY OF CHINESE DESIGN MOTIFS
0–486–24167–X Dover pb $5.95

- John Dower
THE ELEMENTS OF JAPANESE DESIGN: A Handbook of Family Crests, Heraldry and Symbolism
0–8348–0143–4 Weatherhill $22.50

- Sandi Fellman, editor
THE JAPANESE TATTOO
0–89659–798–9 Abbeville pb $19.95

- Graphic-Sha Staff, editors
AIRBRUSH ART IN JAPAN
4–7661–0383–1 Books Nippan pb $32.95

- Clarence Hornung, editor
TRADITIONAL JAPANESE STENCIL DESIGNS
0–486–24791–0 Dover pb $5.95

- Owen Jones
CHINESE DESIGN AND PATTERN IN FULL COLOR
0–486–24204–8 Dover pb $6.95

- K. Nagai, editor
GRAPHICS JAPAN
4–7661–0423–4 Books Nippan $79.95

- Ahn Sang-Soo
KOREAN MOTIFS

Volume 1: Geometric Patterns
4–7661–0476–5 Books Nippan $24.95

Volume 2: Floral Patterns
4–7661–0477–3 Books Nippan $24.95

Trademarks and Logos

- Eric Baker & Tyler Blik
TRADEMARKS OF THE '20s AND '30s: A Nostalgic Portfolio of American Trademark Designs
0–87701–360–8 Chronicle pb $12.95

TRADEMARKS OF THE '40s AND '50s
0–87701–485–X Chronicle pb $12.95

- Hayward & Blanche Cirker
MONOGRAMS AND ALPHABETIC DEVICES
0–486–22330–2 Dover pb $7.95

- Hal Morgan
SYMBOLS OF AMERICA
The history, folklore and mystique of the most popular American trademarks and the products they represent
0–670–80667–6 Viking $40.00

> WHAT'S GREAT ABOUT THIS COUNTRY IS THAT AMERICA STARTED THE TRADITION WHERE THE RICHEST CONSUMERS BUY ESSENTIALLY THE SAME THINGS AS THE POOREST. YOU CAN BE WATCHING TV AND SEE COCA-COLA, AND YOU CAN KNOW THAT THE PRESIDENT DRINKS COKE, LIZ TAYLOR DRINKS COKE AND, JUST THINK, YOU CAN DRINK COKE TOO. A COKE IS A COKE, AND NO AMOUNT OF MONEY CAN GET YOU A BETTER COKE THAN THE ONE THE BUM ON THE CORNER IS DRINKING. ALL THE COKES ARE THE SAME AND ALL THE COKES ARE GOOD. LIZ TAYLOR KNOWS IT, THE PRESIDENT KNOWS IT, THE BUM KNOWS IT, AND YOU KNOW IT.
>
> Andy Warhol
> **THE PHILOSOPHY OF ANDY WARHOL: From A to B and Back Again**
> 0–15–671720–4 HBJ pb $7.95

1949 logo for Capitol Records, from Trademarks of the '40s and '50s *by Eric Baker and Tyler Blik* (Chronicle)

Package Design

- David Craig
LUGGAGE LABELS: Mementoes From the Golden Age of Travel
0–87701–531–7 Chronicle pb $14.95

- Graphic-sha Staff, editors
SHOPPING BAGS AND WRAPPING PAPER
4–7661–0482–X Books Nippan $60.00

- Japan Package Design Association
PACKAGE DESIGN IN JAPAN
0–87011–738–6 Kodansha $80.00

- Hideyuki Oka
HOW TO WRAP FIVE MORE EGGS: Traditional Japanese Packaging
0–8348–0108–6 Weatherhill $25.00

- Judi Radice
SHOPPING BAG DESIGN
0–86636–053–0 PBC $55.00

- Philippine de Rothschild
MOUTON ROTHSCHILD: Paintings for the Labels
0–8212–1555–8 NY Graphic Society $39.00
0–8212–1557–4 NY Graphic Society pb $19.95

- Thomas Steele & others
CLOSE COVER BEFORE STRIKING: The Golden Age of Matchbook Art
0–89659–695–8 Abbeville $19.95

- Ellen Stern
THE VERY BEST FROM HALLMARK: Greetings Cards Through the Years
0–8109–1745–9 Abrams $29.95

TYPOGRAPHY

- Kathryn Atkins
MASTERS OF THE ITALIC LETTER: Twenty Exemplars from the 16th Century
0–87923–594–2 Godine $45.00

- Sebastian Carter
TWENTIETH-CENTURY TYPE DESIGNERS
0–8008–7916–3 Taplinger $24.95

- Eric Gill
AN ESSAY ON TYPOGRAPHY
0–87923–762–7 Godine $14.95

- Nicolete Gray
A HISTORY OF LETTERING: Creative Experiment and Letter Identity
0–87923–612–4 Godine $30.00

- Alexander Lawson
ANATOMY OF A TYPEFACE
A study and classification of typefaces, written for the layman. Over 200 illustrations
0–87923–332–X Godine $30.00

- Ruari McLean
THE THAMES AND HUDSON MANUAL OF TYPOGRAPHY
0–500–68022–1 Thames & Hudson pb $11.95

- The Society of Newspaper Design
THE BEST OF NEWSPAPER DESIGN
0–86636–055–7 PBC $55.00

THE BEST OF NEWSPAPER DESIGN 2
0–86636–070–0 PBC $55.00

- Walter Tracy
LETTERS OF CREDIT: A View of Type Design
0–87923–636–1 Godine $27.50

CALLIGRAPHY

- Arthur Baker
ARTHUR BAKER'S FOUNDATIONAL CALLIGRAPHY MANUAL
A basic book by the master calligrapher
0–684–17919–9 Scribners pb $7.95

CALLIGRAPHY
0–486–22895–9 Dover pb $6.95

MASTERING ITALIC CALLIGRAPHY
0–684–18214–9 Scribners pb $7.95

- Emma Butterworth
THE CALLIGRAPHY SOURCEBOOK
0–89471–468–6 Running Press $17.95

- Joan Freeman
LETTERING AND CALLIGRAPHY
0–668–06193–6 Arco $12.95

- Tom Gourdie
BASIC CALLIGRAPHIC HANDS
0–8008–0667–0 Taplinger pb $5.95

MASTERING CALLIGRAPHY
A complete guide for the beginner
0–8230–3021–0 Watson-Guptill pb $12.95

- Peter Jensen
MASTERPIECES OF CALLIGRAPHY: 261 Examples
0–486–24100–9 Dover pb $7.95

- Edward Johnston
LESSONS IN FORMAL WRITING
Out of print or previously unpublished material by Edward Johnston
0–8008–4642–7 Taplinger pb $19.95

- Elizabeth Lucas
CALLIGRAPHY: The Art of Beautiful Writing
0–13–112269–X Prentice-Hall pb $16.95

- Charles Pearce
THE ANATOMY OF LETTERS
Useful manual for beginning and more advanced students
0–8008–0199–7 Taplinger pb $9.95

- Rosemary Sassoon
THE PRACTICAL GUIDE TO CALLIGRAPHY
0–500–27251–4 Thames & Hudson pb $9.25

THE PRACTICAL GUIDE TO LETTERING AND APPLIED CALLIGRAPHY
0–500–27366–9 Thames & Hudson pb $10.95

- Margaret Shepherd
LEARNING CALLIGRAPHY: A Book of Lettering Design and History
0–02–015550–6 Macmillan pb $10.95

- Jacqueline Svaren
WRITTEN LETTERS: 33 Alphabets for Calligraphers
A classic in handy format, 33 alphabets with clear stroke sequence
0–8008–8735–2 Taplinger pb $12.95

- Jan Tschichold
A TREASURY OF CALLIGRAPHY: 219 Great Examples, 1522-1840
0–486–24700–7 Dover pb $9.95

Modern Calligraphy

- Heather Child
THE CALLIGRAPHER'S HANDBOOK
A book of articles, considered one of the outstanding works on contemporary calligraphy
0–8008–1198–4 Taplinger pb $13.95

- Margaret Shepherd
BASICS OF THE NEW CALLIGRAPHY
Instructions on mastering the Basic Block alphabet and variations
0–13–065806–5 Prentice-Hall pb $10.95

MODERN CALLIGRAPHY MADE EASY
Instructions and workbook for the Fundamental Alphabet
0–399–51450–3 Perigree pb $6.95

Photography

In 1839 the painter and inventor L.J.M. Daguerre revealed his discovery of a photographic process (soon to be known as the daguerreotype) to the French Academy. When word reached the public, the academic painter Paul Delaroche memorably proclaimed: "From today, painting is dead!" Meanwhile, across the Channel, the scientist and scholar W.H.F. Talbot was perfecting his own process (the calotype), which was to have a far greater influence on the future of photography: whereas Daguerre's technique made a single shining image on a metal plate, Talbot's process used a paper negative to produce any number of prints. Delaroche was not exactly right about the future of painting, but the new inventions have enormously changed both the history of art and the history of publishing.

HISTORIES AND GENERAL WORKS

- Victor Burgin, editor
THINKING PHOTOGRAPHY
Essays dealing with the theory and practice of photography as a medium of communication, and with the production of meaning in photographs
0–333–27195–5 Humanities pb $17.50

- Centre National de la Photographie (Paris)
EARLY COLOR PHOTOGRAPHY
A volume in the Pantheon Photo Library
0–394–74461–6 Pantheon pb $7.95

- Gisele Freund
PHOTOGRAPHY AND SOCIETY
A reprint of one of the first studies of the relation of this medium to the society which shapes it and is shaped by it, by a sociologist and photographer
0–87923–250–1 Godine $15.00

- Vicki Goldberg
PHOTOGRAPHY IN PRINT
0–8263–1091–5 New Mexico pb $17.95

- Charles Hagen
AMERICAN PHOTOGRAPHERS OF THE DEPRESSION
A volume in the Pantheon Photo Library
0–394–74086–6 Pantheon pb $7.95

- Jean-Claude Lemagny & Andre Rouille, editors
A HISTORY OF PHOTOGRAPHY: Social and Cultural Perspectives
A more theoretical European perspective which results in a challenging but less than comprehensive history
0–521–34407–7 Cambridge $39.50

- Laszlo Moholy-Nagy
PAINTING, PHOTOGRAPHY, FILM
One of the first great theoretical treatises of the 20th century, by the Bauhaus master
0–317–56521–4 MIT pb $10.95

Beaumont Newhall
THE HISTORY OF PHOTOGRAPHY: From 1839 to the Present Day
The revised fifth edition of the first history of photography for the general reader, an authoritative work emphasizing photography as an art
0–87070–380–3 NY Graphic Society $40.00

  IF YOU CAN'T FIND IT, LOOK IN THE INDEX

Beaumont Newhall, editor
PHOTOGRAPHY: Essays and Images— Illustrated Readings in the History of Photography
This anthology of source materials is the companion volume to Newhall's *History*. Classic texts by photographers and critics are illustrated by great images
0–87070–385–4 NY Graphic Society pb $16.95

● Naomi Rosenblum
A WORLD HISTORY OF PHOTOGRAPHY
A massive and richly illustrated volume which includes the work of famous and lesser known photographers, attends to the technical and artistic history of the medium, and emphasizes its tradition of social documentary
Edited by Walton Rawls
0–89659–438–6 Abbeville $49.95

● Aaron Scharf
ART AND PHOTOGRAPHY
A thorough investigation of the relation between photography and its sister arts, examining the influence of painting on photography and vice versa
0–14–006773–6 Penguin pb $13.95

● Robert Sobieszek
MASTERPIECES OF PHOTOGRAPHY FROM GEORGE EASTMAN HOUSE
A lavishly produced treasury from the collection of the International Museum of Photography in Rochester. Rare and magnificent photographs are accompanied by informative texts
0–89659–586–2 Abbeville $125.00

● Edward Steichen
THE FAMILY OF MAN
The photographic bestseller of all time, this book began as an exhibition at the Museum of Modern Art just after World War II
0–671–55412–3 Simon & Schuster $19.95
0–671–55411–5 Simon & Schuster pb $14.95

From Julia Margaret Cameron: Her Life and Work *by Helmut Gernsheim* (*Aperture*)

● John Szarkowski
LOOKING AT PHOTOGRAPHS: 100 Pictures from the Collection of the Museum of Modern Art
Short discussions of these splendid photographs illustrate different aspects of the medium and teach as much about seeing as about photography
0–87070–514–8 NY Graphic Society $40.00
0–87070–515–6 NY Graphic Society pb $27.00

● Alan Trachtenberg
CLASSIC ESSAYS ON PHOTOGRAPHY
0–918172–07–1 Leete's Island $12.95
0–918172–08–X Leete's Island pb $8.95

Movements and Periods

● Van Deren Coke & Diana C. Du Pont
PHOTOGRAPHY—A FACET OF MODERNISM: Photographs from the San Francisco Museum of Modern Art
Great photographs of the 1920s and 1930s with emphasis on German images. The wonderfully graphic design and the intricate use of subconscious imagery of this period are well-represented in this selection of work by many photographers
0–933920–73–3 Hudson Hills $45.00
0–933920–74–1 Hudson Hills pb $25.00

● Agnes St. Cyr De Gouvion & others
TWENTIETH-CENTURY FRENCH PHOTOGRAPHY
0–8478–0943–9 Rizzoli $30.00

● Sally Eauclaire
AMERICAN INDEPENDENTS: 18 Color Photographers
The work of a diverse group of emerging photographers
0–89659–666–4 Abbeville $29.95

THE NEW COLOR PHOTOGRAPHY
A collection of brilliantly colorful work by a variety of photographers
0–89659–190–5 Abbeville $45.00
0–89659–196–4 Abbeville pb $24.95

● Andre Jammes & Eugenia P. Janis
THE ART OF FRENCH CALOTYPE: With a Critical Dictionary of Photographers, 1845-1870
A beautiful book dealing with some of the most exquisite of all early photographs
0–691–04002–8 Princeton $88.00

● Rosalind Krauss & others
L'AMOUR FOU: Photography and Surrealism
An intense and probing study of the photographs of the surrealists. Krauss's formidably theoretical approach comes triumphantly to terms with the difficult and perplexing pictures of these artists
0–89659–576–5 Abbeville $49.95

● Egidio Marzona & Roswitha Fricke, editors
BAUHAUS PHOTOGRAPHY
A charming and light-hearted selection of photographs by famous Bauhaus artists and their students
Foreword by Eugene Prakapas
0–262–13202–8 MIT $37.50
0–262–63109–1 MIT pb $15.00

● Grace Seiberling & Carolyn Bloore
AMATEURS, PHOTOGRAPHY, AND THE MID-VICTORIAN IMAGINATION
An intriguing combination of social history, technical explanation, and pictorial interpretation
0–226–74498–1 Chicago $34.95

● Alfred Stieglitz & others
CAMERA WORK: A Pictorial Guide
Camera Work was Stieglitz's deluxe magazine of photography, promoting an artistic revolution in photography and establishing that medium as a fine art. This volume reprints every photograph published in the magazine, including works by Steichen, Strand, White, Kasebier, Stieglitz himself, and many others
Edited by Marianne F. Margolis
0–486–23591–2 Dover pb $9.95

● W.H. Talbot
PENCIL OF NATURE
0–306–71135–4 Da Capo $95.00

RICHARD AVEDON:
Twelve Recommended Photography Books

Brassai
PARIS BY NIGHT

Hal Hinson
ANDRE KERTESZ: Diary of Light

Henri Cartier-Bresson
HENRI CARTIER-BRESSON: Photographer

Robert Frank
THE AMERICANS

James Agee & Walker Evans
LET US NOW PRAISE FAMOUS MEN

Helmut Gernsheim
JULIA MARGARET CAMERON: Her Life and Photographic Work

Diane Arbus
DIANE ARBUS

Phillip Lopate
LISETTE MODEL

Calvin Tomkins
PAUL STRAND: Sixty Years of Photography

Mark Haworth-Booth & David Mellor
BILL BRANDT: Behind the Camera

Robert Kramer & Beaumont Newhall
AUGUST SANDER: Photographs of an Epoch, 1904-1959

Naomi Rosenblum
A WORLD HISTORY OF PHOTOGRAPHY

From August Sander: Photographs of an Epoch (*Aperture*)

- Emile Zola & François Massin
ZOLA: Photographer
A look at turn-of-the-century Paris, the Universal Exposition of 1900, and Zola's daily life and family through the novelist's own lens
Translated by Lilian Emery Tuck
0–8050–0747–4 Henry Holt $26.95

PHOTOGRAPHERS

- Berenice Abbott
BERENICE ABBOTT
Edited by Julia Van Haften
0–89381–327–3 Aperture $14.95
0–89381–328–1 Aperture pb $9.95

NEW YORK IN THE THIRTIES
A coolly modern appraisal of the city as it was then. Abbott both commemorated old structures and explored the new skyscrapers rising above them in these striking views
0–486–22967–X Dover pb $7.50

- Ansel Adams
ANSEL ADAMS: Classic Images
A selection of great photographs by America's best-loved photographic artist
Introduction by John Szarkowski
0–316–04393–1 NY Graphic Society $29.95

PHOTOGRAPHS OF THE SOUTHWEST
Commentary by Lawrence C. Powell
0–8212–0699–0 NY Graphic Society $45.00
0–316–70261–7 NY Graphic Society pb $25.00

THE PORTFOLIOS OF ANSEL ADAMS
Introduction by John Szarkowski
0–316–71394–5 NY Graphic Society $45.00
0–316–71395–3 NY Graphic Society pb $25.00

SINGULAR IMAGES
A treasury of unusual polaroid work by Adams, including portraits, landscapes and nature studies
Commentary by Edwin Land & others
0–8212–0728–8 NY Graphic Society pb $14.95

YOSEMITE AND THE RANGE OF LIGHT
Adams at his most magnificent. A sustained exploration in masterful photography of the unspoiled landscape of Yosemite
Introduction by Paul Brooks
0–316–96959–1 NY Graphic Society pb $25.00

- Ansel Adams & Mary S. Alinder
ANSEL ADAMS: An Autobiography
Adams tells of his early training as a concert pianist and of his decision to dedicate his life to photography; with plenty of illustrations
0–316–04383–4 NY Graphic Society $60.00

- Andrea Gray
ANSEL ADAMS: An American Place, 1936
0–938262–06–8 Creative Photography pb $19.95

- Robert Adams
ROBERT ADAMS: Los Angeles Spring
Glimpses of spring in seasonless, artificial Los Angeles seen with an eye for the occasional felicitous beauty of urban sprawl
0–89381–220–X Aperture $30.00

SUMMER NIGHTS: Photographs by Robert Adams
The most romantic and emotional of Adams' works, these pictures breathe with the air of summer nights illuminated by street lamps and the stars
0–89381–141–6 Aperture $20.00

Diane Arbus
DIANE ARBUS
This picture book summarizes Arbus' work and contains all her most famous and disturbing images, including her photographs of nudists and freaks
0–912334–40–1 Aperture $40.00
0–912334–41–X Aperture pb $25.00

DIANE ARBUS: Magazine Work
The previously unknown commercial and fashion work by Arbus that launched her career as a photographer
Edited by Thomas W. Southall
Foreword by Doon Arbus & Marvin Israel
0–89381–152–1 Aperture $30.00
0–89381–233–1 Aperture pb $19.95

Patricia Bosworth
DIANE ARBUS: A Biography
Traces in detail the troubled life of an exceptional artist and woman. Bosworth uses Arbus' personal history as a tool for explaining the direction of much of her work
0–394–50404–6 Knopf $17.95
0–380–69927–3 Avon pb $8.95

- Eugene Atget
EUGENE ATGET
0–394–74084–X Pantheon pb $7.95

THE WORK OF ATGET
These four informative volumes are a landmark in photographic history. They represent a dual culmination: the Museum of Modern Art's efforts to preserve their archive of Atget's negatives and prints, and Hambourg's scholarly reconstruction of the meaning and sequence of Atget's prints
Edited by John Szarkowski & Maria M. Hambourg

Volume 1: Old France
0–87070–204–1 NY Graphic Society $40.00

Volume 2: The Art of Old Paris
0–87070–212–2 NY Graphic Society $40.00

Volume 3: The Ancien Régime
0–87070–217–3 NY Graphic Society $40.00

Volume 4: Modern Times
0–316–95418–7 NY Graphic Society $45.00

- James Borcoman
EUGENE ATGET: 1857-1927
0–88884–510–3 Chicago $35.00

- Richard Avedon
IN THE AMERICAN WEST: Photographs, 1979-1984
A chillingly elegant and idiosyncratic documentation of the striking faces of an unlikely cross-section of Americans
0–8109–1105–1 Abrams $49.50

- David Bailey
BLACK AND WHITE MEMORIES: Photographs, 1948-1969
The swinging photographer of '60s London and the model for the protagonist in Antonioni's film *Blow-Up*, Bailey helped revive the glamorous image of the photographic profession
0–460–04539–3 Biblio $35.00

- David Mellor, editor
CECIL BEATON: A Retrospective
Beaton helped to invent glamour as a way of life, and as a photographic style. His pictures and experiences are equally glittering and artificial
0–8212–1632–5 NY Graphic Society $35.00

- Hugo Vickers
CECIL BEATON: A Biography
0–316–90244–6 Little, Brown $25.00
1–55611–021–9 Donald Fine pb $12.95

- Karl Blossfeldt
ART FORMS IN THE PLANT WORLD
Translation and reprint of one of the classic books of the 1920s with close-up botanical studies of common and exotic plants which look like abstract compositions
0–486–24990–5 Dover pb $8.95

- Margaret Bourke-White
THE TASTE OF WAR
Edited by Jonathan Silverman
0–7126–1030–8 David & Charles pb $13.95

- Erskine Caldwell & Margaret Bourke-White
NORTH OF THE DANUBE
0–306–70877–9 Da Capo $35.00

SAY, IS THIS THE U.S.A.?
Reprint of one of the pioneering books of documentary photography of the 1930s
0–306–77434–8 Da Capo $35.00

- Vicki Goldberg
MARGARET BOURKE-WHITE
The biography of one of the first outstanding woman photojournalists. Bourke-White fought her way into a profession previously closed to women, making history first as a *Life* photographer

TO ORDER BOOKS AS GIFTS, SEE PAGE 1

at home, and then on the battlefields of World War II
0–06–015513–2 Harper & Row $25.95

Bill Brandt
BILL BRANDT: Portraits
Brandt's intensity behind the camera resulted in probing portraits that tell as much about what's inside their subjects as outside them
Introduction by Alan Ross
0–292–70740–1 Texas $37.50

SHADOW OF LIGHT
Brandt's greatest images of London, including many from his 1938 book, *A Night in London*
Introduction by Cyril Connolly & Mark Haworth-Booth
0–306–80066–7 Da Capo pb $14.50

Mark Haworth-Booth & David Mellor
BILL BRANDT: Behind the Camera
0–89381–170–X Aperture $25.00

- **Brassaï**
BRASSAI
Introduction by Roger Grenier
0–394–75610–X Pantheon pb $7.95

PARIS BY NIGHT
A reprint of Brassaï's classic 1936 *Paris de Nuit*, one of the most influential photography books of the century
Introduction by Paul Morand
0–394–56327–1 Pantheon $39.95

THE SECRET PARIS OF THE THIRTIES
The illicit night life of the cafés, streets and brothels of Paris captured by an eye at once romantic and cynical
0–394–73384–3 Pantheon pb $17.95

- **Keith F. Davis**
HARRY CALLAHAN: New Color
Rich color views of many places from one of the masters of modern photography whose early work was principally in black and white
0–87529–625–4 Nebraska pb $19.95

From Lisette Model (*Aperture*)

- **Helmut Gernsheim**
JULIA MARGARET CAMERON: Her Life and Photographic Work
The first important study of this remarkable Victorian artist and her poetic work with the camera
0–89381–253–6 Aperture $27.50
0–912334–51–7 Aperture pb $14.50

- **Robert Capa**
ROBERT CAPA: Photographs
"If the pictures aren't good enough, you're not close enough." Capa's famous pronouncement about war photography was also his personal credo. Before he died in action while photographing, he shot a multitude of photographs that forever changed the way photojournalism was practiced under fire
Edited by Cornell Capa & Richard Whelan
0–394–54421–8 Knopf $35.00

- **Richard Whelan**
ROBERT CAPA: A Biography
A better adventure story than many novels, Capa's tumultuous life often seemed to approach fiction
0–345–33449–3 Ballantine pb $5.95

- **Paul Caponigro**
MEGALITHS
Luminous interpretations of the ancient standing stones of the British Isles, photographed over a period of 20 years
0–8212–1616–3 NY Graphic Society $75.00

SEASONS
0–8212–1703–8 NY Graphic Society $35.00

THE WISE SILENCE
Edited by Marianne Fulton
0–8212–1548–5 NY Graphic Society $74.00

- **Helmut Gernsheim**
LEWIS CARROLL: Photographer
0–486–22327–2 Dover pb $6.95

- **Henri Cartier-Bresson**
HENRI CARTIER-BRESSON
A volume in the Pantheon Photo Library
0–394–74083–1 Pantheon pb $7.95

HENRI CARTIER-BRESSON: Photographer
With a commentary by the French poet Yves Bonnefoy
0–8212–0756–3 NY Graphic Society $85.00

HENRI CARTIER-BRESSON IN INDIA
Forward by Mulk Raj Anand
0–500–54124–8 Thames & Hudson $29.95

HENRI CARTIER-BRESSON PHOTOPORTRAITS
Preface by André de Mandiargues
0–500–54109–4 Thames & Hudson $50.00

- **Peter Galassi**
HENRI CARTIER-BRESSON: The Early Work
The first book to place Cartier-Bresson's photographs of fleeting instants in their historical context. Galassi considers his training as a painter as well as the evolution of his photographic style
0–87070–261–0 NY Graphic Society $35.00

- **Alvin Langdon Coburn**
ALVIN LANGDON COBURN, PHOTOGRAPHER: An Autobiography
Coburn was one of the great pictorialist photographers of the Stieglitz circle at the beginning of this century. He left Boston to settle in London where he produced remarkable portraits of famous figures, and—in 1917—some of the first deliberately abstract photographs
Edited by Helmut & Alison Gernsheim
0–486–23685–4 Dover pb $7.95

- **Mike Weaver**
ALVIN LANGDON COBURN: Symbolist Photographer
A probing interpretation of the symbolic meanings deliberately encoded in Coburn's photographs, this study provides a new vision of his work and thought
0–89381–240–4 Aperture $25.00

- **Lynne Cohen**
OCCUPIED TERRITORY
Cohen's deadpan photographs of vernacular interiors are at once disturbing and fascinating. Her lucid views of schools, offices, factories, labs and police training centers are an unparalleled cumulative portrait of North American society
Edited by William A. Ewing
Introduction by David Byrne
0–89381–313–3 Aperture $25.00

- **Bruce Davidson**
SUBWAY
Strikingly vibrant color photographs of the subways of New York by the photographer who first achieved fame through a sensitive documentary portrait of East Harlem in the 1960s
Introduction by Henry Geldzahler
0–89381–231–5 Aperture $29.95

- **Alfred Eisenstaedt**
ABERDEEN: Portrait of a City
Edited by Gregory Vitiello
0–8071–1194–5 Louisiana $19.95

EISENSTAEDT: Martha's Vineyard
Text by Polly Burroughs
0–8487–0739–7 Oxmoor $35.00

EISENSTAEDT ON EISENSTAEDT
0–89659–515–3 Abbeville $25.00

- **Beaumont Newhall**
FREDERICK H. EVANS
Evans' delicate and dusky studies of cathedral interiors are homages to architecture. This study also deals with his non-architectural work
0–912334–49–5 Aperture pb $17.50

Walker Evans
AMERICAN PHOTOGRAPHS
This is a 50th-anniversary recreation of one of the great classics of photographic publishing from the 1930s. Especially notable are Evans' sequencing of images and his insistence that each image be respected on its own terms within the book. The subjects range from Depression-ravaged cities to architectural splendors
0–87070–237–8 MOMA $40.00
0–87070–238–6 MOMA pb $18.95

WALKER EVANS AT WORK
A revealing study of a master photographer's methods and practices, and how they shaped his vision
Introduction by Jerry L. Thompson
0–06–011104–6 Harper & Row $18.95

WALKER EVANS FIRST AND LAST
0–06–011261–1 Harper & Row $34.95

WALKER EVANS: Photographs for the Farm Security Administration, 1935-1938
Many of Evans' most important photographs of the '30s were made in the service of the government's Farm Security Administration, which sought to document the hardships of the Depression and the effects of the aid provided by Roosevelt's New Deal
Introduction by Jerald C. Maddox
0–306–70099–9 Da Capo $39.50
0–306–80008–X Da Capo pb $15.95

James Agee & Walker Evans
LET US NOW PRAISE FAMOUS MEN
0–395–07330–8 Houghton Mifflin $24.95
0–395–29696–X Houghton Mifflin pb $11.95

• Andreas Feininger
ANDREAS FEININGER: Photographer
Introduction by James Enyeart
0–8109–0919–7 Abrams $45.00

THE COMPLETE PHOTOGRAPHER
0–13–162255–2 Prentice-Hall pb $15.95

FEININGER'S CHICAGO: 1941
0–486–23991–8 Dover pb $7.95

IN A GRAIN OF SAND: Exploring Design by Nature
0–87156–763–6 Sierra Club $35.00

INDUSTRIAL AMERICA, 1940-1960: 176 Photographs
0–486–24198–X Dover pb $9.95

NATURE AND ART: A Photographic Exploration
0–486–24539–X Dover pb $9.95

NATURE CLOSE UP: A Fantastic Journey into Reality
0–486–24102–5 Dover pb $9.95

NEW YORK IN THE FORTIES
A close look at the urban texture of New York that finds beauty in the patterns and geometry of modernity
0–486–23585–8 Dover pb $9.95

SHELLS: Forms and Designs of the Sea
0–486–24498–9 Dover pb $8.95

STONE AND MAN: A Photographic Exploration
0–486–23756–7 Dover pb $7.95

• Robert Frank
THE AMERICANS
First published in Paris, then released in this country where it became an underground sensation and finally a classic, this book was the visual bible for the beat generation. The gritty scenes of American cities and roadsides told a story of alienation, segregation, and unexpected beauty, all seen through the eyes of a disaffected European photographer
Introduction by Jack Kerouac
0–394–54977–5 Pantheon $25.00
0–394–74256–7 Pantheon pb $19.95

ROBERT FRANK: Photographs
0–394–55143–5 Pantheon $25.00
0–394–74085–8 Pantheon pb $7.95

• Lee Friedlander
LEE FRIEDLANDER: Portraits
Offbeat but revealing portraits by a photographer best known for his depictions of the "new social landscape" of parking lots, suburbs, and telephone wires
Forward by R.B. Kitaj
0–316–51252–4 NY Graphic Society $60.00

• Alexander Gardner
GARDNER'S PHOTOGRAPHIC SKETCH BOOK OF THE CIVIL WAR
Unlike 20th-century journalists, Gardner and his team of photographers were not able to document actual battles. These pictures show the bodies left on the field after the battle, the buildings destroyed, the fields burned and scarred
0–8446–0104–7 Peter Smith $15.75

• Marni Sandweiss
LAURA GILPIN: An Enduring Grace
0–88360–077–3 Amon Carter $75.00
0–88360–080–3 Amon Carter pb $39.95

• Jim Goldberg
RICH AND POOR
Goldberg photographed people at economic extremes and then invited his subjects to write their thoughts in the margins of the portraits. An often hilarious exposé of raw inequality
0–394–74156–0 Random House pb $18.95

• Nan Goldin
THE BALLAD OF SEXUAL DEPENDENCY
Goldin's pictures of nightclubs and Lower East Side apartments are as saturated with acid color as they are with brittle emotion. Like reports from the front, these pictures chronicle the momentary vicissitudes of a struggle
0–89381–236–6 Aperture $27.95
0–89381–339–7 Aperture pb $19.95

• Jan Groover
JAN GROOVER
Edited by Susan Kismaric
0–87070–309–9 Museum of Modern Art pb $18.50

• Ernst Haas
THE CREATION
0–14–004284–9 Penguin pb $19.95

REALMS OF LIGHT: Selections of Poetry Through the Ages
0–8027–0619–3 Walker $22.50

• Lewis W. Hine
MEN AT WORK
0–486–23475–4 Dover pb $5.00

• Daile Kaplan
LEWIS HINE IN EUROPE, 1918-1919: The Lost Photographs
Best known for his crusading documentary photography in the United States, Hine also worked in Europe. This carefully researched study brings to light a whole new body of work done abroad
0–89659–745–8 Abbeville $50.00

• Geoffrey Holder
ADAM
0–670–81028–2 Viking $29.95

• Yousuf Karsh
KARSH: A 50-Year Retrospective
Portraitist rather than art photographer, Karsh's subjects have included a staggering number of celebrities, heads of state, artists, beauties, and personalities
0–8212–1626–0 Little, Brown pb $25.00

• Andre Kertesz
ANDRE KERTESZ
A volume in the Pantheon Photo Library
0–394–74780–1 Pantheon pb $7.95

KERTESZ ON KERTESZ
0–89659–510–2 Abbeville $25.00

• Hal Hinson
ANDRE KERTESZ: Diary of Light
A large, rich collection of Kertesz's work spanning his entire career
Forward by Cornell Capa
0–89381–256–0 Aperture $125.00

• Weston J. Naef & others
ANDRE KERTESZ OF PARIS AND NEW YORK
The definitive study of this photographer's life and work from the earliest days to the end of his career
0–500–54106–X Thames & Hudson $23.00

• Dorothea Lange
DOROTHEA LANGE: Photographs of a Lifetime
Lange is justly celebrated for achieving the perfect balance between art and documentary in her moving photographs of people living in adversity
Edited by Robert Coles
0–89381–100–9 Aperture $40.00

• Christopher Cox
DOROTHEA LANGE
A volume in the Masters of Photography Series
0–89381–282–X Aperture $14.95
0–89381–283–8 Aperture pb $9.95

• Milton Meltzer
DOROTHEA LANGE: Life Through the Camera
0–670–28047–X Viking $10.95
0–14–032105–5 Penguin pb $3.50

• Eugene P. Janis
THE PHOTOGRAPHY OF GUSTAVE LE GRAY
Technical innovator and magnificent artist, Le Gray was perhaps the greatest of the

French painter-photographers who moved in the Barbizon School circle of the 1850s
0–226–39210–4 Chicago $100.00
0–86559–078–8 Chicago pb $29.95

• **Annie Leibovitz**
PHOTOGRAPHS
Leibovitz made her name working for *Rolling Stone*, where her wild and glitzy portraits of celebrities created images for both the magazine and her subjects
Introduction by Tom Wolfe
0–394–53208–2 Pantheon $35.00
0–394–72597–2 Pantheon pb $15.95

• **Mikael Levin**
SILENT PASSAGE
Tranquil landscape images from Scandinavia, lyrically sequenced and beautifully reproduced. Levin's first book makes an impressive debut
Introduction by Andy Grundberg
Afterword by Mikael Levin
0–55595–008–5 Hudson Hills $20.00

• **Helen Levitt**
IN THE STREET: Chalk Drawings and Messages, New York City, 1938-1948
Levitt's humorous and compassionate photographs of people, particularly children, in urban streets are testaments to the vitality of the human spirit
Introduction by Robert Coles
0–8223–0728–6 Duke $37.50
0–8223–0771–5 Duke pb $20.00

• **George Platt Lynes**
BALLET: 1934-1935
Formal portraits of great dancers costumed for roles in Balanchine's ballets
Introduction by George Balanchine
0–942642–17–1 Twelve Trees $50.00

• **Danny Lyon**
PICTURES FROM THE NEW WORLD
Sociologist, dropout, and gang member, Lyon pioneered the idea and style of photography from within a subculture. His photographs of motorcyclists, prisoners, impoverished Mexicans, and his own family are raw, personal, and not "objective"
0–89381–073–8 Aperture $39.50

• **Sally Mann**
AT TWELVE: Portraits of Young Women
"These photographs offer a subtle and knowing visual statement about that most poignant and vulnerable time, when girls become women . . . Sally Mann is a brilliant observer and artist both"—Robert Coles
0–89381–296–X Aperture $25.00

• **Robert Mapplethorpe**
ROBERT MAPPLETHORPE: Portraits
A luxuriously produced volume of Mapplethorpe's portraits, thought by many to be his finest work. This book emphasizes the elegance of Mapplethorpe's often disturbing vision
Introduction by Susan Sontag
0–942642–14–7 Twelvetrees $50.00

• **Joel Meyerowitz**
CAPE LIGHT: Color Photographs
One of the most enduringly popular of all photography books. Meyerowitz

concentrates on the subtle action of the light of Cape Cod on local architecture and sand
0–87846–132–9 NY Graphic Society $39.00
0–316–12801–5 NY Graphic Society pb $25.00

• **Phillip Lopate**
LISETTE MODEL
Model, a fine photographer in her own right, is best known as the teacher of Diane Arbus. Her very large, aggressive pictures of people in public are by turn glaring, wryly ironic, warm, and vital
Edited by Carol Kismaric & Michael E. Hoffman
0–89381–050–9 Aperture $50.00

• **Laszlo Moholy-Nagy**
MOHOLY-NAGY
Edited by Richard Kostelanetz
0–932360–12–2 R K Editions $75.00
0–932360–11–4 R K Editions pb $50.00

PAINTING, PHOTOGRAPHY, FILM
0–317–56521–4 MIT pb $10.95

• **Andreas Haus**
MOHOLY-NAGY: Photographs and Photograms
Moholy-Nagy's modernist experiments in camera-less "photograms," montage, and abstraction
0–394–50449–6 Pantheon $35.00

• **Krisztina Passuth**
MOHOLY-NAGY
0–500–27449–5 Thames & Hudson pb $24.95

• **Eadward Muybridge**
MUYBRIDGE'S COMPLETE HUMAN AND ANIMAL LOCOMOTION: All 781 Plates from the 1887 Animal Locomotion
Muybridge's use of the camera to analyze the rhythms of motion in man and beast resulted in these photographic sequences. The product of scientific study, they have been widely used by artists
Introduction by Anita V. Mozley

Volume 1
0–486–23792–3 Dover $50.00

Volume 2
0–486–23793–1 Dover $50.00

From Paul Strand: Sixty Years of Photography (*Aperture*)

Volume 3
0–486–23794–X Dover $50.00

ANIMALS IN MOTION
Contains many of the classic sequences, including the celebrated analysis of the horse in motion which conclusively proved that, for a brief moment, no foot touches the ground in a gallop
Edited by Lewis S. Brown
0–486–20203–8 Dover $22.95

• **E. Bradford Burns**
EADWEARD MUYBRIDGE IN GUATEMALA, 1875: The Photographer As Social Recorder
A glimpse of Muybridge's little-known Central American period
0–520–05570–5 California $35.00

• **Arnold Newman**
ARNOLD NEWMAN: Five Decades
Introduction by Arthur Ollman
0–15–107900–5 HBJ $49.95
0–15–607937–2 HBJ pb $24.95

THE GREAT BRITISH
0–297–77611–8 Chicago pb $10.00

ONE MIND'S EYE
0–8212–0732–6 NY Graphic Society pb $29.95

• **Helmut Newton**
HELMUT NEWTON
Introduction by Karl Lagerfeld
0–394–75514–6 Pantheon pb $7.95

PORTRAITS
Introduction by Carol Squiers
0–394–56321–2 Pantheon $39.95

• **Peter Galassi**
NICHOLAS NIXON: Pictures of People
A wide range of quietly compelling, empathetic photographs of strangers and family, the aged and the dying (AIDS patients) as well as the buoyantly healthy
0–87070–437–0 NY Graphic Society $40.00

• **Norman Parkinson**
FIFTY YEARS OF STYLE AND FASHION
0–86565–031–4 Vendome $35.00

WOULD YOU LET YOUR DAUGHTER?
0–394–55086–2 Grove $35.00

• **Irving Penn**
FLOWERS
0–517–54074–6 Crown $50.00

IRVING PENN
Penn's work crosses the border between art and fashion photography again and again, in both directions. His probing of the still life genre is loaded with existential meaning, while his photographs of couturier clothes are pure, brilliant surface
Edited by John Szarkowski
0–316–43451–5 NY Graphic Society $60.00
0–87070–563–6 Museum of Modern Art pb $29.95

• **Eliot Porter**
ELIOT PORTER
One of the first committed color photographers, his splendidly chromatic nature studies and landscapes have pleased a large audience of art and nature lovers
Foreword by Martha A. Sandweiss
0–8212–1675–9 NY Graphic Society $75.00

Man Ray
PHOTOGRAPHS BY MAN RAY:
1920-1934
Man Ray's most striking photographs, including many of his abstract "rayographs" or photograms (camera-less photographs)
0–486–23842–3 Dover pb $8.95

Jean-Hubert Martin
MAN RAY PHOTOGRAPHS
0–500–27473–8 Thames & Hudson pb $24.95

Jed Perl
MAN RAY
A volume in the Masters of Photography Series
0–89381–306–0 Aperture $14.95
0–89381–307–9 Aperture pb $9.95

● Mark Riboud
MARK RIBOUD: Photographs at Home and Abroad
One of the most artistic of the roving photojournalists, his pictures bring a unique vision to exotic locations
0–8109–1566–9 Abrams $40.00

● Jacob Riis
HOW THE OTHER HALF LIVES:
Studies Among the Tenements of New York
A landmark study in investigative photojournalism, Riis's book first appeared nearly 100 years ago. He photographed with the (then new) flash technique inside tenements in the most sordid and dangerous districts of New York
Edited by Sam B. Warner, Jr.
Introduction by C.A. Madison
0–674–41006–8 Harvard $16.50
0–486–22012–5 Dover pb $9.95

● Margaret F. Harker
HENRY PEACH ROBINSON: Master of Photographic Art, 1830-1901
Almost forgotten for many years, Robinson was perhaps the most successful photographer in late 19th-century Britain. His combinations of several negatives into sentimental genre scenes intriguingly prefigure the techniques of many contemporary photographers
0–631–16172–4 Blackwell pb $19.95

● Lucas Samaras
SAMARAS: Photographs, 1969-1986
Altered and manipulated Polaroid and other color photographs that obsessively catalog the motifs of Samaras' elaborate inner life
Edited by Ben Lifson
0–89381–241–2 Aperture $50.00

● Robert Kramer & Beaumont Newhall
AUGUST SANDER: Photographs of an Epoch, 1904-1959
Sander's self-initiated project was to photograph the whole range of society by making portraits of "types" rather than individuals. He systematically recorded the professions of 20th-century Germany: industrialist, artist, secretary, revolutionary, Nazi soldier
0–89381–058–4 Aperture $25.00
0–89381–064–9 Aperture pb $15.00

● Carol Troyen & Erica H. Hirshler
CHARLES SHEELER
Painter as well as photographer, Sheeler stood at the center of the American avant garde during the 1910s and 1920s
Edited by Janet Silver
Introduction by Alan Shestack

Volume 1: Paintings and Drawings
0–87846–284–8 NY Graphic Society $50.00

Volume 2: Photographs
0–87846–285–6 NY Graphic Society $45.00

● W. Eugene Smith
W. EUGENE SMITH
A volume in the Pantheon Photo Library
0–394–74447–0 Pantheon pb $7.95

● Ben Maddow
LET TRUTH BE THE PREJUDICE: The Life and Photographs of W. Eugene Smith
The life and pictures of this maverick of the world of photojournalism. The first master of the photo essay, Smith found that his perfectionism put him at odds with his editors at *Life* and elsewhere
0–89381–179–3 Aperture $50.00

● Edward Steichen
STEICHEN: A Life in Photography
Steichen's long career encompassed the art photography movement of the early years of this century, the photo advertising boom of the '20s and '30s, the war photography of the '40s, and the calmer artistic visions that followed
0–517–55696–0 Crown pb $12.95

● Louis Stettner
EARLY JOYS
Selected street photographs and portraits from Europe and America. Stettner's vision is a grainy and unsentimental one, but these pictures are filled with a quiet affirmation of life
Preface by Brassaï
0–9618482–0–0 Iffland $49.50

● Alfred Stieglitz
ALFRED STIEGLITZ
Edited by Dorothy Norman
0–89381–308–7 Aperture $14.95
0–89381–309–5 Aperture pb $9.95

GEORGIA O'KEEFFE: A Portrait by Alfred Stieglitz
One of the most beautiful series of photographs of all time, these penetrating portraits of one extraordinary artist by another are presented in a very handsome volume
Photographs by Alfred Stieglitz
0–670–51989–8 Viking $45.00

● Aperture Foundation
AMERICA AND ALFRED STIEGLITZ: A Collective Portrait
Essays by Waldo Frank, Lewis Mumford, Dorothy Norman, Paul Rosenfeld, and Harold Rudd
0–89381–040–1 Aperture pb $25.00

From Edward Weston: His Life and Photography (*Aperture*)

● Sue D. Lowe
STIEGLITZ: A Memoir-Biography
Stieglitz's life with his family, his second wife Georgia O'Keefe, and a wide circle of artistic and literary friends make a good story in itself, and an invaluable aid to understanding how modern art arose in America
0–374–26990–4 Farrar, Straus & Giroux $25.50
0–374–51827–0 Farrar, Straus & Giroux pb $14.95

● Dorothy Norman
ALFRED STIEGLITZ: An American Seer
0–89381–035–5 Aperture $35.00

● Paul Strand
PAUL STRAND
Strand's unique position as an apostle of modernism and social change is reflected in his austere studies and portraits of peasants and working class people
0–89381–077–0 Aperture $14.95
0–89381–259–5 Aperture pb $9.95

● Calvin Tomkins
PAUL STRAND: Sixty Years of Photographs
0–912334–81–9 Aperture $35.00
0–912334–82–7 Aperture pb $19.95

● John Thomson
CHINA AND ITS PEOPLE IN EARLY PHOTOGRAPHS
A picturesque excursion in 19th-century photographic sociology in the exotic land of China
Foreword by Janet Lehr
0–486–24393–1 Dover pb $13.95

● George Tice
HOMETOWNS: An American Pilgrimage
Tice started photographing his own territory in New Jersey, making a kind of visual analog of Bruce Springsteen's world. Now, he has branched out to the hometowns of Mark Twain, Jimmy Dean, and Ronald Reagan
0–8212–1713–5 NY Graphic Society $50.00

● Jerry N. Uelsmann
UELSMANN: Process and Perception
Uelsmann's pop surrealism has long been underestimated in terms of both his extraordinary technical virtuosity and his complex dream imagery. This book analyzes his methods and goals
0–8130–0830–1 Florida pb $18.95

➤ **FOR OVERSEAS ORDERING INFORMATION, SEE PAGE 1**

• Peter E. Palmquist
CARLETON E. WATKINS: Photographer of the American West
In the 1860s and 1870s photographer-explorers like Watkins traveled the western wilderness looking for landscape views. Best known for his work in Yosemite, Watkins had an exceptionally diverse career
Forward by Martha Sandweiss
0–8263–0659–4 New Mexico $70.00

Weegee
NAKED CITY
A startlingly rough and intimate portrait of New York and its people, rich and poor, honest and criminal. In the 1940s these pictures fascinated because of their immediacy and then-shocking content
0–306–70724–1 Da Capo $27.50
0–306–80241–4 Da Capo pb $13.50

NAKED HOLLYWOOD
0–306–70728–4 Da Capo $25.00
0–306–80047–0 Da Capo pb $6.95

WEEGEE
0–394–74785–2 Pantheon pb $7.95

WEEGEE'S PEOPLE
0–306–70723–3 Da Capo $27.50
0–306–80242–2 Da Capo pb $13.50

Weegee with Mel Harris
WEEGEE BY WEEGEE: An Autobiography
Only Weegee could do justice to his own life story. A raucous account of a raucous career
0–306–70737–3 Da Capo $22.50

• Edward Weston
EDWARD WESTON
A volume in the Masters of Photography Series
Edited by R.H. Cravens
0–89381–304–4 Aperture $14.95
0–89381–305–2 Aperture pb $9.95

EDWARD WESTON'S CALIFORNIA LANDSCAPES
Weston's beach, desert and farm photographs from the richly productive mature phase of his career
Edited by James L. Enyeart
0–8212–1576–0 NY Graphic Society $100.00

EDWARD WESTON IN MEXICO: 1923-1926
The accomplished early work by one of the masters of modernism in photography
Edited by Amy Conger
0–8263–0666–7 New Mexico pb $15.95

EDWARD WESTON OMNIBUS
Edited by Amy Conger & Beaumont Newhall
0–87905–131–0 Gibbs Smith pb $16.95

• Ben Maddow
EDWARD WESTON: His Life and Photographs
Preface by Cole Weston
0–89381–043–6 Aperture $125.00

• John Szarkowski
WINOGRAND: Figments From the Real World
This book is a full tribute to Gary Winogrand, whose recent death ended a career that began in the 1950s: street photography, series of animals, rodeos, airports, women, and other repeated everyday motifs
0–87070–640–3 NY Graphic Society $45.00

Lewis Carroll's hand-colored photograph of Alice Liddell, 1862 (New York Public Library)

PHOTOJOURNALISM AND HISTORICAL DOCUMENTARY

• Wilbur E. Garrett, editor
ODYSSEY: The Art of Photography at National Geographic
For many decades, *National Geographic* has sponsored the travels of adventurers, usually accompanied by photographers
Introduction by Jane Livingston
0–934738–45–9 Thomasson-Grant $65.00

• Life Magazine
LIFE: The First 50 Years
0–316–52613–4 Little, Brown $50.00
0–316–52614–2 Little, Brown pb $24.95

• John Loengard
LIFE: Classic Photographs
The classic pictures from *Life* magazine that are almost synonymous with visual memory for many Americans, especially from the pre-television era
0–8212–1714–3 NY Graphic Society $24.95

PICTURES UNDER DISCUSSION
0–8174–5539–6 Watson-Guptill $29.95
0–8174–5540–X Watson-Guptill pb $19.95

• Doris C. O'Neil, editor
LIFE: The Second Decade, 1946-1955
0–8212–1581–7 NY Graphic Society $29.95

• Eugene Richards & Christiane Bird
BELOW THE LINE: Living Poor in America
An impassioned look at the reality of life for the poor, homeless and sometimes hopeless people of this wealthy nation. Fine photography movingly deployed to tell a painful story
0–89043–062–4 Consumer Reports $32.00
0–89043–061–6 Consumer Reports pb $20.00

• Paula Richardson Fleming & Judith Luskey
THE NORTH AMERICAN INDIANS
Fascinating historical documents and portraits of Native Americans
0–06–015549–3 Harper & Row $34.50

SPECIAL TOPICS

• Dawn Ades
PHOTOMONTAGE
0–500–20208–7 Thames & Hudson $11.95

• Matthew Brady & Henry W. Elson
THE CIVIL WAR THROUGH THE CAMERA
0–405–12294–2 Ayer $27.50

• Bill Brandt & Mark Haworth-Booth, editors
THE LAND: 20th Century Landscape Photographs
A poetic selection of diverse landscape images selected by a great photographer and a curator
0–306–70753–5 Da Capo $18.50

• William A. Ewing
DANCE AND PHOTOGRAPHY
An energetic survey of the photography of dance. Splashy action photographs predominate
0–8050–0591–9 Henry Holt $50.00

• Anne H. Hoy
FABRICATIONS: Staged, Altered, and Appropriated Photographs
A collection of contemporary photographs using the provocative postmodern methods of artificed subject matter and appropriated imagery
0–89659–751–2 Abbeville $45.00

• Estelle Jussim & Elizabeth Lindquist-Cock
LANDSCAPE AS PHOTOGRAPH
Unusual interpretations of landscape
0–300–03941–7 Yale pb $19.95

• Nissan Perez
FOCUS EAST: Early Photography in the Near East, 1839-1885
This is a comprehensive survey of the practice of photography by many individuals in the Middle East. Scientists, travellers, artists and antiquarians all took up cameras to record the people, objects, and scenery of the Holy Land
0–8109–0924–3 Abrams $49.50

• Cervin Robinson & Joel Herschman
ARCHITECTURE TRANSFORMED: A History of the Photography of Buildings from 1839 to the Present
Essays and reproductions representing the history of architectural photography from the earliest days to the present. A remarkable range of images
0–262–18121–5 MIT $55.00

• Robert A. Sobieszek
THE ART OF PERSUASION: A History of Advertising Photography
A thoughtful study of the evolution of advertising's use of the photographic image. The mutual dependence of advertising and photography are made apparent in the selection of exemplary advertising photographs
0–8109–1469–7 Abrams $40.00

• Constance Sullivan, editor
LEGACY OF LIGHT
Polaroid photographs by an assortment of outstanding contemporary photographers
0–394–56365–4 Knopf $50.00

• Ansel Adams
THE CAMERA
The master photographer explains the camera and its use
0–316–12512–1 NY Graphic Society $25.00

THE NEGATIVE
The negative is the basis of all photographs, and Adams explains what is essential to the making of a good negative
0–316–59931–5 NY Graphic Society $25.00

THE PRINT
Technique is essential to the successful print, and Adams is a great teacher and practitioner of printing
0–316–71930–7 NY Graphic Society $25.00

EXAMPLES: The Making of 40 Photographs
A behind-the-scenes look at what went into the making of 40 of Adams' photographs. His legendary previsualization, zone system and printing technique all combine to produce these celebrated images
0–316–25863–6 NY Graphic Society $45.00

• William Crawford
THE KEEPERS OF LIGHT: A History and Working Guide to Early Photographic Processes
A detailed study of early and unusual photographic processes, including do-it-yourself recipes. Of interest both to practitioners and more casual readers
0–87100–158–6 Morgan & Morgan pb $24.95

ARCHITECTURE
AND
DESIGN

European Architecture to 1900

GENERAL WORKS

- Robert Chitham
CLASSICAL ORDERS OF ARCHITECTURE
A valuable handbook
0–8478–0671–5 Rizzoli pb $19.95

- Banister Fletcher
SIR BANISTER FLETCHER'S HISTORY OF ARCHITECTURE
Revised, expanded edition of the encyclopedic single-volume work. An invaluable reference
0–02–338340–2 Macmillan $90.50

- Spiro Kostof
A HISTORY OF ARCHITECTURE: Settings and Rituals
An eccentric presentation in terms of styles, literature, and social concerns
0–19–503472–4 Oxford $60.00
0–19–503473–2 Oxford pb $29.95

- David Macauley
Large format books with line drawings illustrating the fascinating design of these ancient buildings.
CATHEDRAL: The Story of its Construction
0–395–17513–5 Houghton Mifflin $14.95
0–395–31668–5 Houghton Mifflin pb $6.95
CITY: A Story of Roman Planning and Construction
0–395–34922–2 Houghton Mifflin pb $6.95
PYRAMID
0–395–21407–6 Houghton Mifflin $14.95
0–395–32121–2 Houghton Mifflin pb $6.95

- John Onians
BEARERS OF MEANING: The Classical Orders in Antiquity, the Middle Ages, and the Renaissance
The specific cultural messages borne by the orders, with emphasis on their impact on the urban viewer
0–691–04043–5 Princeton $75.00

Swedish wooden hut, from Architecture: Meaning and Place *by Christian Norberg-Schulz (Rizzoli)*

- Nikolaus Pevsner
DICTIONARY OF ARCHITECTURE
The standard, indispensable reference
0–670–27223–X Viking $27.95

A HISTORY OF BUILDING TYPES
Focuses on the 19th century, from the most ceremonial buildings to the most utilitarian
0–691–09904–9 Princeton $79.00
0–691–01829–4 Princeton pb $24.50

- Helen Powell & David Leatherbarrow
MASTERPIECES OF ARCHITECTURAL DRAWING
The work of some 90 artists and architects over eight centuries
0–89659–326–6 Abbeville $55.00

- Steen Eiler Rasmussen
EXPERIENCING ARCHITECTURE
A classic introduction to the idioms of architecture
0–262–68002–5 MIT pb $6.95

- Witold Rybczynski
THE MOST BEAUTIFUL HOUSE IN THE WORLD
An elegant discussion of what architects do and how we experience space
0–670–81981–6 Viking $18.95

- Mario Salvadori
WHY BUILDINGS STAND UP: The Strength of Architecture
0–07–054482–4 McGraw-Hill pb $9.95

- John Summerson
THE CLASSICAL LANGUAGE OF ARCHITECTURE
Classical idioms from the ancients through the moderns
0–262–69012–8 MIT pb $5.95

- David Watkin
A HISTORY OF WESTERN ARCHITECTURE
An extensively illustrated survey by a distinguished historian
0–500–34100–1 Thames & Hudson $45.00
0–500–27425–8 Thames & Hudson pb $24.95

Theory

- Rudolf Arnheim
DYNAMICS OF ARCHITECTURAL FORM
The principles of Gestalt psychology as they apply to the perception of three-dimensional objects and buildings; by the author of *Art and Visual Perception*
0–520–03305–1 California $29.00
0–520–03551–8 California pb $12.95

- Paul Frankl
PRINCIPLES OF ARCHITECTURAL HISTORY: The Four Phases of Architectural Style, 1420–1900
An historical and critical analysis of the abstract image of the plan and the experience of visual form
0–262–56013–5 MIT pb $9.95

William Chambers' plan for the Pagoda, Kew Gardens (RIBA)

- George Hersey
THE LOST MEANING OF CLASSICAL ARCHITECTURE: Speculations on Ornament from Vitruvius to Venturi
Debates the perennial appeal of classical architecture
0–262–58089–6 MIT pb $9.95

- Christian Norberg-Schulz
ARCHITECTURE: Meaning and Place
A distinguished author of theoretical studies defines architecture in terms of place
0–8478–0847–5 Rizzoli pb $29.95

- Roger Scruton
THE AESTHETICS OF ARCHITECTURE
An inquiry into the concept of beauty by the well-known British philosopher
0–691–00322–X Princeton pb $12.50

• Dora Wiebenson
ARCHITECTURAL THEORY AND PRACTICE FROM ALBERTI TO LEDOUX
A handy anthology, with commentary, of classical theory through the French Enlightenment
0–686–97825–0 Chicago $25.00

GREEK AND ROMAN

"Practically every town of decent size in the Western world has its quota of Doric, Ionic and Corinthian. And some of the great modern buildings, from the Pantheon in Paris, to the Capitol in Washington, to the Imperial Palace in Tokyo, across Southeast Asian countries that have practically nothing to do with classical civilization and back around the world to the government structures of Leningrad, Warsaw, and Brussels, are monumental essays in the use of the orders. Greco-Roman classicism was not only the architecture of the Greeks and the Romans and of their empires, it was also the architecture, mutatis mutandis, of Romanesque Europe and of Byzantium, of the Renaissance and the Baroque, of Neoclassicism, the Baroque Revival, the Beaux Arts, and fascism; and it is even, in a peculiar but strong way, a contributor to postmodernism.—George Hersey, *The Lost Meaning of Classical Architecture*

• John Boardman
THE PARTHENON AND ITS SCULPTURES
A reconstruction of the original position and order of all the Parthenon pieces, with exquisite photographs
0–292–76498–7 Texas $39.95

• Axel Boethius
ETRUSCAN AND EARLY ROMAN ARCHITECTURE
The standard introductory survey
0–14–056144–7 Penguin pb $18.95

• James Walter Graham
THE PALACES OF CRETE
The standard book on Minoan architecture
0–691–00216–9 Princeton pb $14.50

• A.W. Lawrence
GREEK ARCHITECTURE
A classic survey with extensive illustrations
0–14–056111–0 Pelican pb $18.95

• Roland Martin
GREEK ARCHITECTURE
A profusely illustrated study of Minoan Crete and the Mycenaean world, the Greek city-state, and Hellenistic Greece
0–8478–0968–4 Rizzoli pb $25.00

• L. Richardson, Jr.
POMPEII: An Architectural History
Comprehensive, up-to-date, and beautifully illustrated
0–8018–3533–X Johns Hopkins $49.50

• Donald Robertson
GREEK AND ROMAN ARCHITECTURE
A handbook to the progressive achievements of the ancient world
0–521–06104–0 Cambridge $67.50
0–521–09452–6 Cambridge pb $21.95

• J.B. Ward-Perkins
ROMAN ARCHITECTURE
From the Republican period through the early Christian era, surveying all forms of building from marketplaces to aqueducts
0–8478–0972–2 Rizzoli pb $25.00

• Susan Woodford
THE PARTHENON
A lucid and scholarly introduction to the monument and its elaborate sculptural program
0–521–22629–5 Cambridge pb $4.95

Early Christian and Byzantine

William MacDonald
EARLY CHRISTIAN AND BYZANTINE ARCHITECTURE
An introductory work, with fine illustrations
0–8076–0338–4 Braziller pb $7.95

Cyril Mango
BYZANTINE ARCHITECTURE
An informative account, from the early basilicas of the 4th century through the diffusion of the style in 12th-century Europe
0–8478–0615–4 Rizzoli pb $25.00

GOTHIC AND ROMANESQUE

"The spire is the simplest part of the romanesque or gothic architecture, and needs least study in order to be felt. It is a bit of sentiment almost pure of practical purpose. It tells the whole of its story at a glance, and its story is the best that architecture had to tell, for it typified the aspirations of man at the moment when man's aspirations were highest. Yet nine persons out of ten—perhaps 99 in 100—who come within sight of the two spires of Chartres will think it a jest if they are told that the smaller of the two, the simpler, the one that impresses the least, is the one which they are expected to recognize as the most perfect piece of architecture in the world."—Henry Adams, *Mont St. Michel and Chartres*

• Henry Adams
MONT-SAINT MICHEL AND CHARTRES: A Study of 13th-Century Unity
0–691–03971–2 Princeton $40.00
0–691–00335–1 Princeton pb $9.95

• Jean Bony
FRENCH GOTHIC ARCHITECTURE OF THE 12TH AND 13TH CENTURIES
An excellent introduction: effective photography and numerous plans
0–520–02831–7 California $135.00
0–520–05586–1 California pb $39.95

• Robert Branner
GOTHIC ARCHITECTURE
An authoritative account of its genesis and culminating achievements, primarily in France
0–8076–0332–5 Braziller pb $9.95

ST. LOUIS AND THE COURT STYLE IN GOTHIC ARCHITECTURE
The high point of Gothic architecture in mid 13th-century Paris, and its influence throughout Europe
0–302–02753–X Sotheby pb $39.95

• Wolfgang Braunfelds
MONASTERIES OF WESTERN EUROPE: The Architecture of the Orders
A major investigation of the relation of architectural style to liturgy and ritual
0–691–03896–1 Princeton $55.00
0–691–00313–0 Princeton pb $19.95

• Georges Duby
THE AGE OF THE CATHEDRALS: Art and Society, 980–1240
A survey of medieval mentalities as reflected in the architecture of the monastery, the cathedral, and the palace
0–226–16770–4 Chicago pb $11.95

• Louis Grodecki
GOTHIC ARCHITECTURE
A well-illustrated volume tracing its 400-year dominance in Europe; with tables and bibliography
0–8478–0473–9 Rizzoli pb $25.00

• Hans Erich Kubach
ROMANESQUE ARCHITECTURE
A well-illustrated survey
0–8478–0920–X Rizzoli pb $25.00

• Erwin Panofsky
GOTHIC ARCHITECTURE AND SCHOLASTICISM: An Inquiry into the Analogy of the Arts, Philosophy, and Religion in the Middle Ages
How architectural style and structure replicated scholastic definitions of the order and form of thought
0–425–00995–2 NAL pb $10.95

☞ **FOR ALL OTHER INQUIRIES, PLEASE CALL (212) 333-7900**

The Abbey of St. Denis

Caroline Astrid Bruzelius
THE 13TH-CENTURY CHURCH AT ST. DENIS
The structure, chronology, and influence of the 13th-century rebuilding of the great abbey church of St. Denis
0–300–03190–4 Yale $35.00

Sumner McKnight Crosby
THE ROYAL ABBEY OF ST. DENIS: From Its Beginnings to the Death of Suger, 475–1151
0–300–03143–2 Yale $60.00

Erwin Panofsky & Gerda Panofsky-Soergel, editors
SUGER, ABBOT OF SAINT DENIS: Abbot Suger on the Abbey Church of Saint Denis and its Art Treasures
An invaluable anthology of archaeological, historical, and artistic documents
0–691–03936–4 Princeton $41.00
0–691–00314–9 Princeton pb $14.95

The Gothic Cathedral

• Jean Gimpel
THE CATHEDRAL BUILDERS
A vivid, illustrated account of the construction of Gothic cathedrals emphasizing technical, political, and aesthetic considerations
0–06–091158–1 Harper & Row pb $8.95

• Otto von Simson
THE GOTHIC CATHEDRAL
A convincing thesis—that Gothic cathedrals must be understood in terms of the religious experience of the High Middle Ages
0–691–09959–6 Princeton $35.00
0–691–01867–7 Princeton pb $12.95

Chartres

Robert Branner
CHARTRES CATHEDRAL
A thorough introduction to the great cathedral, with critical essays and illustrations
0–393–09851–6 Norton pb $8.95

Emile Mâle
CHARTRES
A basic study of the Gothic period as well as of Chartres itself
0–06–435530–6 Harper & Row $25.95

ITALIAN RENAISSANCE

• Jacob Burckhardt
THE ARCHITECTURE OF THE ITALIAN RENAISSANCE
Impressive for its methodology and cohesive theory of a social and typological history of architecture
0–226–08047–1 Chicago $50.00
0–226–08049–8 Chicago pb $24.95

Andrea Palladio's alternative designs for the Palazzo da Porto Festa, Vicenza (RIBA)

• Peter Murray
THE ARCHITECTURE OF THE ITALIAN RENAISSANCE
A good introduction
0–8052–0807–0 Schocken pb $10.95

RENAISSANCE ARCHITECTURE
From the early experiments of Brunelleschi and Alberti, through the high classicism of Bramante and Raphael and the revolutionary contribution of Michelangelo, this extensively illustrated volume documents the history and influence of Italian architecture
0–8478–0474–7 Rizzoli pb $25.00

• Geoffrey Scott
THE ARCHITECTURE OF HUMANISM: A Study in the History of Taste
An aesthetic theory of the Renaissance style, beautifully written
0–0–393–00734–0 Norton pb $7.95

• Rudolf Wittkower
ARCHITECTURAL PRINCIPLES IN THE AGE OF HUMANISM
Through a study of the theory and practice of Alberti and Palladio, this work proves that the forms of Renaissance architecture were charged with the symbolic values of contemporary humanism
0–312–02082–1 St. Martin's $35.00
0–393–02083–X St. Martin's pb $19.95

• Heinrich Wölfflin
RENAISSANCE AND BAROQUE
A study of independent development in architecture from its maturity during the High Renaissance to its decline in the second half of the 16th century
0–8014–9046–4 Cornell pb $8.95

Contemporary Sources

• Marcus Vitruvius Pollio
THE TEN BOOKS OF ARCHITECTURE
The classic text by the Roman architect and engineer, rediscovered and illustrated during the Renaissance, describes the

classical principles of symmetry, harmony, and proportion
0–486–20645–9 Dover pb $6.95

• Leon Battista Alberti
THE TEN BOOKS OF ARCHITECTURE
Reprint of the 1755 English edition of the original *De Re Aedificatoria.* The first modern work on architecture
0–486–25239–6 Dover pb $14.95

ON THE ART OF BUILDING IN TEN BOOKS
A new English translation, richly annotated and illustrated with prints from the 1550 Italian edition
0–262–01099–2 MIT $45.00

• Andrea Palladio
THE FOUR BOOKS OF ARCHITECTURE
Reprint of the 1738 English edition based on the original 1570 Venetian edition. Discusses the orders, building techniques, public and private buildings, Roman temples, and includes Palladio's own inventions
0–486–21308–0 Dover pb $11.95

• Sebastiano Serlio
THE FIVE BOOKS OF ARCHITECTURE
Incorporating extensive illustrations on geometry and perspective, the orders, building types, and planning, this treatise influenced Europe throughout the Renaissance
0–486–24349–4 Dover pb $14.95

Italian Renaissance Cities

• Giulio Argan
THE RENAISSANCE CITY
0–8076–0521–2 Braziller pb $7.95

• George Holmes
FLORENCE, ROME, AND THE ORIGINS OF THE RENAISSANCE
0–19–822153–3 Oxford pb $19.95

• Paul Letarouilly
EDIFICES DE ROME MODERNE
The result of 35 years of measuring and drawing the domestic, public, and ecclesiastical buildings of the Renaissance, first published in 1848
0–910413–00–2 Princeton Architectural $60.00

• Ralph Lieberman
RENAISSANCE ARCHITECTURE IN VENICE
An illustrated catalog of the most important monuments, with maps
0–89659–310–X Abbeville $45.00

Villas and Gardens

• Harold Acton
VILLAS OF TUSCANY
The English writer and Italian resident describes the life and history of the most typical Tuscan villas
0–500–24121–X Thames & Hudson $45.00

• Marella Agnelli
GARDENS OF THE ITALIAN VILLAS
Private Italian villas today. Beautifully illustrated
0–8478–0825–4 Rizzoli $50.00

• Giorgina Masson
ITALIAN GARDENS
A luxurious new edition of the classic account first published in 1961
1–85149–027–2 Antique Collectors $69.50

• Michelangelo Muraro
VENETIAN VILLAS: The History and Culture
A monumental publication documenting 71 outstanding villas of the Veneto
0–8478–0762–2 Rizzoli $85.00

• J.A. Shepherd & Geoffrey Jellicoe
ITALIAN GARDENS OF THE RENAISSANCE
New edition of the classic 1925 publication comprising a historical survey followed by a descriptive catalog of 26 major gardens, each accompanied by excellent illustrations
0–910413–25–8 Princeton Architectural $45.00

• Edith Wharton
ITALIAN VILLAS AND THEIR GARDENS
A work by the novelist which had a great influence on American landscape architecture of this century
0–306–70817–5 Da Capo $49.50
0–306–80048–9 Da Capo pb $8.95

Architects

• Giovanni Fanelli
BRUNELLESCHI
An illustrated guidebook
0–935748–01–6 Scala pb $13.95

• Paolo Galluzzi, editor
LEONARDO DA VINCI: Engineer and Architect
Includes a large selection of drawings, models, and reconstructions
0–89192–084–8 Northeastern $65.00

• James Ackerman
THE ARCHITECTURE OF MICHELANGELO
A definitive study, with extensive bibliography
0–226–00240–3 Chicago pb $19.95

PALLADIO
A classic introduction to his theory and works
0–14–020845–3 Penguin pb $7.95

• Carolin Constant
THE PALLADIO GUIDE
A succinct guide to all the major edifices
0–910413–10–X Princeton Architectural pb $17.00

• Joseph Farber & Henry Hope Reed
PALLADIO'S ARCHITECTURE AND ITS INFLUENCE: A Photographic Guide
0–486–23922–5 Dover pb $7.95

• Vincent Scully
THE VILLAS OF PALLADIO
A photographic documentation
0–8212–1639–2 NY Graphic Society $45.00

• Deborah Howard
JACOPO SANSOVINO: Architecture and Patronage in Renaissance Venice
Arriving in Venice after the Sack of Rome in 1527, Sansovino introduced the Roman High Renaissance style. His important commissions are perceptively studied and presented
0–300–03890–9 Yale pb $13.95

ENGLISH RENAISSANCE

• James Lees-Milne
THE AGE OF INIGO JONES
0–403–03878–2 Somerset $39.00

• Nikolaus Pevsner & Priscilla Metcalf
THE CATHEDRALS OF ENGLAND

Volume 1: Midland, Eastern and Northern England
0–670–80125–9 Viking $40.00

Volume 2: Southern England
0–670–80124–0 Viking $40.00

• John Summerson
ARCHITECTURE IN BRITAIN, 1530–1830
Introduced into England during the reign of Henry VIII, classical architecture flourished for over 300 years
0–14–0561–03–X Penguin pb $18.95

INIGO JONES
Illuminates the life, culture, and accomplishments of the first English classical architect, who brought the Palladian movement to 17th-century England
0–14–02–0839–9 Penguin pb $7.95

• Rudolf Wittkower
PALLADIO AND ENGLISH PALLADIANISM
A collection of essays on Inigo Jones and the adoption of Renaissance architecture in Britain
0–500–27296–4 Thames & Hudson pb $16.95

Country Houses and Gardens

• Mark Girouard
LIFE IN THE ENGLISH COUNTRY HOUSE
Designed for pleasure as well as status, country houses have created the habits, diversions, and obligations of the English upper classes
0–1400–5406–5 Viking pb $12.95

ROBERT SMYTHSON AND THE ELIZABETHAN COUNTRY HOUSE
The country house is used to discuss the history and ideals of Elizabethan and Jacobean architecture. Richly illustrated
0–300–03134–3 Yale $45.00

• John Harris
THE ARCHITECT AND THE BRITISH COUNTRY HOUSE, 1620–1920
The progress of country house design, including interiors and gardens. Well illustrated with architectural drawings
0–913962–75–9 AIA $19.95

• Roy Strong
THE RENAISSANCE GARDEN IN ENGLAND
The gentlemanly pursuit of gardening in Elizabethan England
0–500–01209–1 Thames & Hudson $24.95

Bay window design by Robert Smythson

BAROQUE AND ROCOCO

Detail of John Vanderlyn's panoramic view of the Gardens of Versailles (Metropolitan Museum)

Italy

- Anthony Blunt

BORROMINI
A comprehensive study of one of the great 17th-century architects
0–674–07925–6 Cambridge pb $17.50

GUIDE TO BAROQUE ROME
An excellent guide to secular and religious buildings and gardens. Illustrated with period prints and plans
0–06–430395–0 Harper & Row $35.00

NEOPOLITAN BAROQUE AND ROCOCO ARCHITECTURE
Illustrated with plans, sections, and original drawings
0–302–02584–7 Harper & Row $125.00

- Franco Borsi

BERNINI
The standard monograph
0–8478–0509–3 Rizzoli $75.00

- Giovanni Battista Cipriani

THE ARCHITECTURE OF ROME: A 19th Century Itinerary
A quality facsimile of over 700 plans and elevations of the major secular and religious buildings, first published in 1835
0–8478–0776–2 Rizzoli $29.95

- Richard Krautheimer

THE ROME OF ALEXANDER VII, 1655–1667
The New Rome as envisioned by Alexander and his architect Bernini
0–691–04032–X Princeton $34.50

- Harold Alan Meek

GUARINO GUARINI AND HIS ARCHITECTURE
Poised between rationalism and mysticism, the principles and buildings of this 17th-century priest, architect, and theologian epitomize a turning point in the history of architecture
0–300–03–989 Yale $55.00

- John Varriano

ITALIAN BAROQUE AND ROCOCO ARCHITECTURE
A general survey incorporating recent research and illustrated with period views, plans, and details
0–19–503547–X Oxford $29.95
0–19–503548–8 Oxford pb $18.95

- Rudolf Wittkower

ART AND ARCHITECTURE IN ITALY, 1600–1750
Largely devoted to the Roman High Baroque, this study also explores Sicily, Turin, Genoa, and Naples
0–14–056116–1 Penguin pb $18.95

France

- William Adams

THE FRENCH GARDEN, 1500–1800
The cultural and aesthetic ideals behind the theory and practice of the geometrical garden
0–8076–0918–8 Braziller $19.95
0–8076–0919–6 Braziller pb $9.95

- Anthony Blunt

ART AND ARCHITECTURE IN FRANCE, 1500–1700
From the earliest influence of the Italian Renaissance and the first original buildings in the Loire valley, French classicism reached its apex with François Mansart
0–14–056104–8 Penguin pb $18.95

FRANCOIS MANSART AND THE ORIGIN OF FRENCH ARCHITECTURE
The architect who perfected the French tradition, and whose work showed little influence from abroad
0–403–07230–1 Somerset $49.00

- Rosalys Coope

SALOMON DE BROSSE & The Development of the Classical Style in French Architecture from 1565 to 1630
A coherent conception of classicism in which the use of the orders produced the first examples of an essentially French character
0–302–02195–7 Harper & Row $65.00

- Michael Dennis

COURT AND GARDEN: From the French Hôtel to the City of Modern Architecture
A detailed, illustrated history of the aristocratic town house developed in Paris between 1500 and 1790
0–262–54051–7 MIT $25.00

Versailles

Robert Berger

IN THE GARDEN OF THE SUN KING: Studies in the Park of Versailles under Louis XIV
0–88402–141–6 Dumbarton Oaks $35.00

VERSAILLES: The Chateau of Louis XIV
It is the garden at Versailles, more than the grandeur of its exteriors or the virtuosity of its interiors, that reveals the complex mythology of the French monarchy
0–271–00412–6 Pennsylvania $30.00

Guy Walton

LOUIS XIV'S VERSAILLES
Gives the nonspecialist an overview of the principal phases of the history of Versailles. Planning, gardens, and art works are studied
0–226–87254–8 Chicago $35.00

Spain

- George Kubler

BUILDING THE ESCORIAL
A chronicle of Philip II's grandiose monastery and palace, built to commemorate victory over the French
0–691–03975–5 Princeton $48.00

- Earl Rosenthal

THE PALACE OF CHARLES V IN GRANADA
A masterful interpretation of imperial iconography
0–691–04034–6 Princeton $83.50

England

- Geoffrey Beard

THE WORK OF JOHN VANBRUGH
His major buildings
0–87663–651–2 St. Martin's $35.00

- Kerry Downes

THE ARCHITECTURE OF WREN
Christopher Wren is considered one of the greatest English architects
0–87663–395–5 St. Martin's $40.00

ENGLISH BAROQUE ARCHITECTURE
A splendidly illustrated historical introduction to the major personalities
0–302–00595–1 Harper & Row $60.00

VANBRUGH
A study of the architect's monumental projects
0–302–02769–6 Harper & Row $95.00

- Marcus Whiffen
THOMAS ARCHER: Architect of the English Baroque
For his free use of curves and his imitation of Bernini and Borromini, Archer has been called the most baroque of English architects
0–912158–23–9 Hennessey $9.95

18TH AND 19TH CENTURIES

General

- James Cracraft
THE PETRINE REVOLUTION IN RUSSIAN ARCHITECTURE
Recounts how modern architectural standards supplanted traditional norms following the massive infusion of foreign expertise initiated by Peter the Great
0–226–11664–6 Chicago $45.00

- James Stevens Curl
THE EGYPTIAN REVIVAL: An Introductory Study of a Recurring Theme in the History of Taste
The first comprehensive account of one of the least familiar stylistic revivals in Western art and architecture
0–04–724001–6 Unwin Hyman $50.00

- Henry-Russell Hitchcock
ARCHITECTURE: The 19th and 20th Centuries
A comprehensive chronology of buildings and standards of taste from 1800 through Le Corbusier's pilgrimage chapel at Ronchamp
0–14–056115–3 Penguin pb $18.95

- Emile Kaufmann
ARCHITECTURE IN THE AGE OF REASON: Baroque and Post-Baroque Architecture in England, Italy and France
A pioneering study of architecture's cultural and philosophical links to the Enlightenment
0–486–21928–3 Dover pb $8.95

- Joseph Rykwert
THE FIRST MODERNS: The Architects of the 18th Century
A personal account, with emphasis on theoretical issues later developed by the modernists
0–262–68039–4 MIT pb $21.95

- John Summerson
THE ARCHITECTURE OF THE EIGHTEENTH CENTURY
An elegant and amply illustrated account of the period of "classic perfection" by England's leading architectural historian
0–500–20202–8 Thames & Hudson pb $11.95

- David Watkin
THE RISE OF ARCHITECTURAL HISTORY
A survey of architectural theory and criticism as it emerged simultaneously in English literature on taste, in French

treatises, and in works by the German founders of the history of art
0–226–87486–9 Chicago pb $8.50

ITALY

- G.B. Piranesi & Herschel Levit
VIEWS OF ROME: Then and Now
0–486–23339–1 Dover pb $8.95

- Andrew Robison
PIRANESI: Early Architectural Fantasies: A Catalogue Raisonné of the Etchings
A thorough account of Piranesi's early prints, with a description of etching techniques, artistic sources, and the nature of his extensive revisions; with many fine reproductions
0–226–72320–8 Chicago $39.95

- John Wilton-Ely
THE MIND AND ART OF GIOVANNI BATTISTA PIRANESI
A comprehensive study of the architecture, architectural fantasies, and vision of antiquity of the great 18th-century artist
0–500–091122–6 Thames & Hudson $50.00

ENGLAND AND SCOTLAND

- Hermann Muthesius
THE ENGLISH HOUSE
A reissue of the classic on 19th-century English architecture originally published in 1904 and still a key work
0–8478–0826–2 Rizzoli $29.95

- Stefan Muthesius
THE ENGLISH TERRACED HOUSE
A survey of townhouse types throughout London and western England
0–300–02871–7 Yale $37.00
0–300–03176–9 Yale pb $15.95

Neoclassicism: Architects

- Joseph & Anne Rykwert
ROBERT AND JAMES ADAM: The Birth of Style
An excellent analysis of the late 18th-century decorative style in England and Scotland
0–8478–0589–1 Rizzoli pb $25.00

- John Harris
SIR WILLIAM CHAMBERS
Chambers differs from other 18th-century architects in the range and depth of his interests and scholarship, epitomized in his treatise on civil architecture of 1759
0–271–00133–X Pennsylvania State $65.00

- Edward McParland
JAMES GANDON: Vitruvius Hibernicus
A disciple of Chambers, Gandon emerged as the leading Dublin architect of the late 18th century, fusing Regency style with Irish neoclassical heritage
0–302–02576–6 Sotheby $125.00

- Terry Friedman
JAMES GIBBS
Gibbs gained recognition as a pioneering neoclassicist for his beautiful London churches and his town and country houses
0–300–03172–6 Yale $65.00

- Michael Wilson
WILLIAM KENT: Architect, Designer, Painter, Gardener, 1685–1748
0–7100–9983–5 RCH $59.00

- Peter Leach
JAMES PAINE
A leading exponent of English Palladianism
0–302–00602–8 Sotheby $95.00

- Pierre de la Ruffinière du Prey
JOHN SOANE: The Making of an Architect
A systematic investigation of Soane's controversial style that combined classical rigor, eccentric hidden spatial devices, and romantic effects of light and shade
0–226–17298–8 Chicago $42.50
0–226–17299–6 Chicago pb $19.95

- John Summerson & others
JOHN SOANE
Essays that identify the principal features of Soane's architecture and set his work in historical context. Richly illustrated with original watercolors and plans
0–312–44462–1 St. Martin's $29.95
0–312–44461–3 St. Martin's pb $19.95

- David Watkin
ATHENIAN STUART: Pioneer of the Greek Revival
The architect who first published full measurements of the buildings of Athens, thus introducing the Greek Revival into England
0–04–720026–X Unwin Hyman $21.95
0–04–720027–8 Unwin Hyman pb $9.95

- Marcus Binney
SIR ROBERT TAYLOR: From Rococo to Neo-Classicism
A key figure in the development of British neoclassicism
0–04–720028–6 Unwin Hyman $19.95
0–04–720031–6 Unwin Hyman pb $9.95

- John Martin Robinson
THE WYATTS: An Architectural Dynasty
The prodigious heterogeneity of the Wyatts' work met the needs of their time and led directly to the eclectic attitudes of the early Victorian period
0–19–817340–7 Oxford $79.00

James Wyatt's Badger Hall (RIBA)

Gothic Revival

• Kenneth Clark
THE GOTHIC REVIVAL: An Essay in the History of Taste
0–06–430048–X Harper & Row pb $7.95

• Charles Eastlake
HISTORY OF THE GOTHIC REVIVAL
Reprint of the first scholarly study of its social, stylistic, and iconographic characteristics
0–89257–035–0 American Life pb $12.00

• John Harris
PUGIN
A look at the way Pugin transformed the Gothic revival
0–912728–72–8 Newbury pb $3.50

• James Lees-Milne
WILLIAM BECKFORD
Beckford's Fonthill Abbey is significant both as architecture and as an expression of its designer's personality
0–8390–0227–0 Abner Schram $18.50

• Michael McCarthy
THE ORIGINS OF THE GOTHIC REVIVAL
Focuses on Horace Walpole, his contemporaries, and two major principles of the Gothic revival: fidelity to historical precedents, and the use of irregularity or lack of symmetry in planning
0–300–03723–6 Yale $45.00

• Alexandra Wedgwood
THE ARCHITECTURAL DRAWING OF A.W.N. PUGIN
0–948107–01–4 Faber & Faber $29.95

Queen Anne and Victorian

• Michael Brooks
JOHN RUSKIN AND VICTORIAN ARCHITECTURE
The influence of early 19th-century architecture on Ruskin, and Ruskin's influence in England and America
0–8135–1205–0 Rutgers $28.00

• Roger Dixon & Stefan Muthesius
VICTORIAN ARCHITECTURE: With a Short Dictionary of Artists
A valuable introduction to the variety of production in Victorian Britain
0–500–20160–9 Thames & Hudson pb $11.95

• Mark Girouard
SWEETNESS AND LIGHT: The Queen Anne Movement, 1860–1900
A lively account of this transitional style and its important contributions to English country house design
0–300–03068–1 Yale pb $17.95

THE VICTORIAN COUNTRY HOUSE
The social and architectural concerns of country life
0–300–02390–1 Yale $50.00
0–300–03472–5 Yale pb $17.95

• Henry-Russell Hitchcock
EARLY VICTORIAN ARCHITECTURE IN GREAT BRITAIN
0–306–80036–5 Da Capo pb $7.95

• Nikolaus Pevsner
STUDIES IN ART, ARCHITECTURE AND DESIGN: Victorian and After
Explores the intricacies of Victorian eclecticism and its vision of the past and the future
0–691–03998–4 Princeton $50.00
0–691–00345–9 Princeton pb $19.50

• John Summerson
THE ARCHITECTURE OF VICTORIAN LONDON
Although lacking a general plan, the rebuilding of London during the 19th century involved almost every section of the city
0–8139–0592–3 Virginia $14.95

Victorian and Edwardian Architects

• Jane Fawcett, editor
SEVEN VICTORIAN ARCHITECTS
William Burn, Philip Charles Hardwick, Sydney Smirke, J.L. Pearson, G.F. Bodley, Alfred Waterhouse, and Edwin Lutyens. An amply illustrated introduction to a generation of historicist styles
0–271–00500–9 Pennsylvania $18.50

• Richard Fellows
SIR REGINALD BLOMFIELD: An Edwardian Architect
Blomfield advocated a tradition of restrained, unselfconscious classicism in his work and writings
0–302–00590–0 Sotheby $29.95

• J. Mordaunt Crook
WILLIAM BURGES AND THE HIGH VICTORIAN DREAM
A study of the English engineer and the tensions created by the Gothic revival in ecclesiastical and private architecture
0–226–12117–8 Chicago $60.00

• J. Mordaunt Crook & C.A. Lennox-Boyd
AXEL HAIG AND THE VICTORIAN VISION OF THE MIDDLE AGES
The Swedish architectural draughtsman, often called the Piranesi of the Gothic revival
0–04–720029–4 Unwin Hyman $19.95

• Christopher Hussey
THE LIFE OF SIR EDWIN LUTYENS
0–907462–59–6 Apollo $49.50

• Jane Brown
GARDENS OF A GOLDEN AFTERNOON: The Story of a Partnership, Edwin Lutyens and Gertrude Jekyll
Surveys 100 gardens designed by the original and eclectic architect and the innovative garden designer Jekyll
0–14–008021–X Penguin pb $12.95

• Robert Irving
INDIAN SUMMER: Lutyens, Baker, and Imperial Delhi
Lutyens relished the imperial grandeur of the Edwardian years, which made him the ideal architect for the monumentality of the Delhi projects
0–300–02422–3 Yale $52.00
0–300–03128–9 Yale pb $17.95

Model of Liverpool Cathedral by Edwin Lutyens

• Andrew Saint
RICHARD NORMAN SHAW
The prolific late Victorian architect surveyed and assessed, with particular attention to his country house designs
0–300–01955–6 Yale $77.00

• Frank Jackson
SIR RAYMOND UNWIN: Architect, Planner and Visionary
Unwin's failure to reconcile medieval nostalgia with bureaucratic control set the stage for later English town planning
0–302–00591–9 Sotheby pb $29.95

• David Gebhard
CHARLES F.A. VOYSEY: Architect
Voysey developed an informal style of country house design
0–912158–54–9 Hennessey $12.95

Arts and Crafts

• William Lethaby
ARCHITECTURE, MYSTICISM, AND MYTH
An evocative account of the importance of mythology for this thinker, teacher, architect, and promoter of the first architectural workshop to gain official recognition in Britain
0–8076–0783–5 Braziller pb $10.00

• Peter Stansky
REDESIGNING THE WORLD: William Morris, the 1880s, and the Arts and Crafts Movement
"Not so much a biography of William Morris as a consideration of him as a political and an esthetic phenomenon"—Quentin Bell
0–691–06616–7 Princeton $29.00
0–691–01411–6 Princeton pb $12.95

The English Landscape Garden

• John Dixon Hunt
WILLIAM KENT: Landscape Garden Designer
The first book devoted to William Kent, precursor of Capability Brown and the most important contributor to the English landscape garden; includes a catalogue raisonné of 115 designs, individually illustrated
0–302–00600–1 Sotheby $60.00

• John Dixon Hunt & Peter Willis, editors

THE GENIUS OF THE PLACE: The English Landscape Garden, 1620–1820
For 200 years, landscape gardens reflected the same changes in attitude about nature, liberty, and order as did literature and painting
0–262–08176–8 MIT $30.00
0–262–58092–6 MIT pb $13.95

• Dorothy Stroud

CAPABILITY BROWN
A monograph on the great 18th-century landscape gardener, with valuable material on his clients
0–571–13405–X Faber & Faber pb $22.95

• Roger Turner

CAPABILITY BROWN AND THE EIGHTEENTH CENTURY ENGLISH LANDSCAPE
A well-illustrated, lively study of Brown and his times
0–8478–0643–X Rizzoli $25.00

FRANCE

• Allan Braham

THE ARCHITECTURE OF THE FRENCH ENLIGHTENMENT
The major developments in architectural thought and practice of the period
0–520–04117–8 California $65.00

• Arthur Drexler, editor

THE ARCHITECTURE OF THE ECOLE DES BEAUX-ARTS
An exhibition catalog featuring some 200 drawings for architectural projects and representing virtually every type of competition and assignment organized by the school
0–262–04053–0 MIT $42.50

• J.C. Lemagny & Dominique De Menil

VISIONARY ARCHITECTS: Boullée, Ledoux, Lequeu
Seminal figures behind the late 18th-century reaction to the excesses of the baroque and rococo
0–914412–21–3 Rice $24.95

• Francois Loyer

PARIS NINETEENTH CENTURY: Architecture and Urbanism
A scholarly and poetic analysis of the relationship between architecture and urbanism
0–89659–885–3 Abbeville $85.00

• Robin Middleton, editor

THE BEAUX-ARTS AND NINETEENTH-CENTURY FRENCH ARCHITECTURE
Offers substantial material for revising the image of 19th-century French architects
0–262–13173–0 MIT $42.50

• David Van Zanten

DESIGNING PARIS: The Architecture of Duban, Labrouste, Duc, and Vaudoyer
Explores the revolution of French architecture that began around 1830 and produced some of the finest examples of French classicism
0–262–22031–8 MIT $35.00

French Architects

• Henri Loyrette

GUSTAVE EIFFEL
"This book is more than just a tale of the great French engineer . . . It is also a history of his most celebrated creation with superb archival photographs of his tower under construction and a thoughtful and well-illustrated essay on the Eiffel Tower as a cultural artifact"—Paul Goldberger
0–8478–0631–6 Rizzoli $40.00

• Christopher Tadgell

ANGE-JACQUES GABRIEL
France's finest 18th-century architect brought the French classical tradition to its ultimate achievement
0–302–02781–5 Sotheby $95.00

• Claude Ledoux

L'ARCHITECTURE
The experimental visionary who struggled to forge an architecture that would at once teach and reform society
0–910413–03–7 Princeton Architectural $60.00

• E.E. Viollet-le-Duc

LECTURES ON ARCHITECTURE
Major documents of 19th-century architectural literature

Volume 1
0–486–25520–4 Dover pb $11.95

Volume 2
0–486–25521–2 Dover pb $11.95

GERMANY

"In general we no longer understand architecture . . . An atmosphere of inexhaustible meaningfulness hung about an ancient building, like a magic veil. Beauty entered the system only secondarily, without impairing the basic feeling of uncanny sublimity, of sanctification by magic or the gods' nearness. At most the beauty tempered the *dread*—but this dread was the prerequisite everywhere."—Friedrich Nietzsche, *Human, All-Too-Human*

• Wolfgang Herrmann

GOTTFRIED SEMPER: In Search of Architecture
First English monograph on one of the leading 19th-century architectural theorists, the most admired architect in Germany of the generation after Schinkel
0–262–08144–X MIT $40.00

• Henry-Russell Hitchcock

GERMAN RENAISSANCE ARCHITECTURE
An authoritative account from the influx of Italian ideas in 1509 to the Thirty Years War of the 17th century
0–691–03959–3 Princeton $83.00

• Christian Otto

SPACE INTO LIGHT: The Churches of Balthasar Neumann
"The master of elegant and ingenious composition. His churches and palaces epitomize the mid 18th-century attitude to life and religion"—Nikolaus Pevsner
0–262–15019–0 MIT $55.00

• David Watkin & Tilman Mellinghoff

GERMAN ARCHITECTURE AND THE CLASSICAL IDEAL
Extensively illustrated account of classicism's impact on palaces, houses, public buildings, and on urban planning throughout the 18th and 19th centuries
0–262–23125–5 MIT $55.00

American Architecture to 1900

This section includes premodern American architecture, with later developments to be found under 20th-Century Architecture. The division is not strict since architects like Frank Lloyd Wright, included here in American Architecture, clearly belong to 20th-Century Architecture as well. Contemporary architectural guides to American cities are also listed here.

GENERAL WORKS

• Wayne Andrews

ARCHITECTURE, AMBITION, AND THE AMERICANS
A social history of American architecture
0–02–900770–4 Free Press $24.95

• Architect's Emergency Committee

GREAT GEORGIAN HOUSES OF AMERICA
A large-format pictorial reference with black-and-white plates

Volume 1
0–486–22491–0 Dover pb $12.95

Volume 2
0–486–22492–9 Dover pb $12.95

• Catherine Beecher & Harriet Beecher Stowe

THE AMERICAN WOMAN'S HOME
A 19th-century work on the relation of women's social status to architectural design
0–917482–04–2 Stowe-Day pb $12.95

• Carl Condit

AMERICAN BUILDING: Materials and Techniques from the Beginning of the Colonial Settlements to the Present
From farm structures to glass-and-steel monuments
0–226–11450–3 Chicago pb $16.95

- Mary Foley
THE AMERICAN HOUSE
A comprehensive guide, with drawings, plans, and photographs
0-06-090831-9 Harper & Row $19.95

- Paul Goldberger
THE SKYSCRAPER
A popular anecdotal account
0-394-71586-1 Knopf pb $16.95

- Alan Gowans
THE COMFORTABLE HOUSE: North American Suburban Architecture, 1890-1930
The post-Victorian vernacular: bungalows, cottages, Mission, Georgian, salt box, Cape Cod, Gothic—many of them ordered from Sears and Montgomery Ward
0-262-07095-2 MIT $35.00

- David Handin
AMERICAN ARCHITECTURE: A Critical History
Covers the main developments from the colonial style through modernism
0-500-20200-1 Thames & Hudson pb $11.95

- Ada Louise Huxtable
ARCHITECTURE ANYONE?: Cautionary Tales of the Building Art
Selections from the work of the Pulitzer Prize-winning *New York Times* architecture critic
0-394-52909-X Random House $27.50

THE TALL BUILDING ARTISTICALLY RECONSIDERED: The Search for a Skyscraper Style
0-394-53773-4 Pantheon $21.95
0-394-74154-4 Pantheon pb $12.95

- Roger Kennedy
ARCHITECTURE, MEN, WOMEN, AND MONEY IN AMERICA, 1600-1860
American domestic architecture in its economic and cultural context
0-394-53579-0 Random House $35.00

- Clay Lancaster
THE AMERICAN BUNGALOW, 1880-1930
A thorough study of the widespread architectural style
0-89659-340-1 Abbeville $39.95

Lewis Mumford

"Mumford is one of the most sensitive critics of the world we see about us; he has been one of the most energetic, sincere and completely devoted apologists of modern architecture in both the US and Great Britain; a 20th-century Ruskin, he has educated a whole generation to the understanding of his enthusiasm and the appreciation of his prejudice."—Colin Rowe

Lewis Mumford
THE BROWN DECADES: A Study of the Arts in America, 1865-1895
Famous appraisal of our "buried Renaissance" in which American art and architecture achieved new power and integrity
0-486-22034-5 MIT $25.00

ROOTS OF CONTEMPORARY AMERICAN ARCHITECTURE
Thirty-seven essays dealing with the mid-19th century onwards and representing the chief critical traditions in today's architecture
0-486-22072-9 Dover pb $8.95

STICKS AND STONES
Investigates the evolution of architectural style in the US and reveals its relationship to broader cultural trends
0-486-20202-X Dover pb $3.95

- Peter Nabokov & Robert Easton
NATIVE AMERICAN ARCHITECTURE
Rich and fully illustrated, with detailed chapters on the wigwam, longhouse, chickee, earthlodge, tipi, pit house, iglu, tent, plank house, hogan, ki, and ramada
0-19-503781-2 Oxford $50.00

- Christian Norberg-Schulz
NEW WORLD ARCHITECTURE
The noted critic's interpretation of American architectural history
0-910413-43-6 Princeton pb $17.50

- William Pierson, Jr. & William Jordy
AMERICAN BUILDINGS AND THEIR ARCHITECTS
The most comprehensive survey available, regularly updated (Volume 3 will be published in the early 1990s)

Volume 1: The Colonial and Neo-Classical Styles
0-19-504216-6 Oxford pb $15.95

Volume 2: Technology and the Picturesque, the Corporate and the Early Gothic Styles
0-19-504217-4 Oxford pb $15.95

Volume 4: Progressive and Academic Ideals at the Turn of the 20th Century
0-19-504218-2 Oxford pb $15.95

Volume 5: The Impact of European Modernism in the Mid-20th Century
0-19-504219-0 Oxford pb $15.95

- Henry Hope Reed
GOLDEN CITY
The controversy between the "modern" and the "classical" tradition with an eloquent denunciation of the former
0-393-00547-X Norton pb $4.95

- William Seale
THE PRESIDENT'S HOUSE: A History
"Before I end my letter, I pray Heaven to bestow the best of Blessings on this House and all that shall hereafter inhabit it. May none but honest and wise Men ever rule under this roof"—John Adams, on his second evening in the damp, unfinished rooms of the White House
0-8109-1490-5 Abrams $39.95

- Robert Stern, editor
AMERICAN ARCHITECTURE: Innovation and Tradition
A well-illustrated sampling of essays
0-8478-0676-6 Rizzoli $25.00

Shaker spiral staircase, Pleasant Hill, Kentucky, from Inner Light: The Shaker Legacy *by June Sprigg (Knopf)*

- Paul Venable Turner
CAMPUS: An American Planning Tradition
From Jefferson's University of Virginia through the modern age, the university campus has witnessed a long tradition of experimentation in design
0-262-70032-8 MIT pb $19.95

- William Ware
THE AMERICAN VIGNOLA: A Guide to the Making of Classical Architecture
Reprint of the highly influential treatise containing measured drawings of the classical orders. First published in 1902
0-393-00839-8 Norton pb $10.95

- Marcus Whiffen
AMERICAN ARCHITECTURE SINCE 1780: A Guide to the Styles
A useful reference work
0-262-23034-8 MIT $30.00
0-262-73057-X MIT pb $9.95

- Marcus Whiffen & Frederick Koeper
AMERICAN ARCHITECTURE
A valuable overview

Volume 1: 1607-1860
0-262-73069-3 MIT pb $12.95

Volume 2: 1860-1976
0-262-73070-7 MIT pb $12.95

- Rebecca Zurier
THE AMERICAN FIREHOUSE
"Fire fighting traditions from the 17th century to the present are enjoyably chronicled and illustrated with numerous photos and prints of firehouses"—*Baltimore Sun*
0-89659-314-2 Abbeville $39.95

➤ FOR OVERSEAS ORDERING INFORMATION, SEE PAGE 1

PREMODERN ARCHITECTURAL STYLES

Colonial

• **Allen Noble**
WOOD, BRICK AND STONE: The North American Landscape
An excellent account of early vernacular architecture

Volume 1: Houses
0–87023–518–4 Massachusetts pb $14.95

Volume 2: Barns and Farm Structures
0–87023–517–6 Massachusetts pb $14.95

Greek Revival

• **Talbot Hamlin**
GREEK REVIVAL ARCHITECTURE IN AMERICA
Argues that the Greek revival was not a revival per se, but a true expression of the national spirit and cultural temperament
0–486–21148–7 Dover pb $9.95

American Renaissance and Victorian

• **Brooklyn Museum Curators**
AMERICAN RENAISSANCE, 1876–1917
Catalog of the important exhibition held at the Brooklyn Museum, with a discussion of architecture, furniture, and design
0–295–96228–3 Washington pb $14.95

• **Edmund Gillon & Clay Lancaster**
VICTORIAN HOUSES: A Treasury of Lesser-Known Examples
Over 100 photographs and individual commentaries
0–486–22966–1 Dover pb $7.95

• **Arnold Lewis & Kate Morgan**
AMERICAN VICTORIAN ARCHITECTURE
Essential documents and monuments reproduced and briefly discussed
0–486–23177–1 Dover pb $10.95

Shingle Style

Vincent Scully
THE ARCHITECTURE OF THE AMERICAN SUMMER: The Flowering of the Shingle Style
An overview of the style from its beginning after the Civil War to its flowering around the turn of the century
0–8478–0769–X Rizzoli $25.00
0–8478–0782–7 Rizzoli pb $14.95

THE SHINGLE STYLE AND THE STICK STYLE: Architectural Theory and Design from Richardson to the Origins of Wright
The definitive study of the complex inspirations and cultural influences fused in the wooden suburban and resort buildings of the 1870s and '80s
0–300–01519–4 Yale pb $17.95

GARDENS AND LANDSCAPE ARCHITECTURE

• **Diana Balmori & others**
BEATRIX FARRAND'S AMERICAN LANDSCAPES: Her Gardens and Campuses
The designer of Dumbarton Oaks and many other important private gardens and public sites
0–89831–003–2 Sagapress $24.95

• **Galen Cranz**
THE POLITICS OF PARK DESIGN: A History of Urban Parks in America
0–262–03086–1 MIT $37.50

• **Frederick Law Olmsted, Jr. & Theodora Kimball**
FORTY YEARS OF LANDSCAPE ARCHITECTURE: Professional Papers of Frederick Law Olmsted
Emphasizes the great Central Park project
0–262–65006–1 MIT pb $9.95

• **Elizabeth Barlow Rogers & others**
REBUILDING CENTRAL PARK: A Management and Restoration Plan
The master design and management plan for America's first large-scale public space, with a history of Olmsted's design
0–262–18127–4 MIT $30.00

REGIONAL ARCHITECTURE

• **Drury Blakeley Alexander**
TEXAS HOMES OF THE NINETEENTH CENTURY
A vivid picture showing Victorian, Spanish, French, and German influences on 200 houses
0–292–73634–7 Texas $39.95

• **Wayne Andrews**
PRIDE OF THE SOUTH: A Social History of Southern Architecture
0–689–70579–4 Atheneum pb $2.95

• **John Drury**
HISTORIC MIDWEST HOUSES
0–226–16551–5 Chicago pb $6.95

• **Hap Hatton**
TROPICAL SPLENDOR: An Architectural History of Florida
0–394–55594–5 Random House $40.00

• **Henry-Russell Hitchcock**
RHODE ISLAND ARCHITECTURE
Rhode Island has some of the finest examples of pre-modern American architecture
0–306–71037–4 Da Capo $37.50

• **Lewis Mumford**
THE SOUTH IN ARCHITECTURE
An eloquent discussion of the South's contribution to the formation of a characteristically American form
0–306–70972–4 Da Capo $25.00

• **Lawrence Speck**
LANDMARKS OF TEXAS ARCHITECTURE
A beautifully illustrated volume that celebrates the variety and vitality of architecture in Texas
0–292–78074–5 Texas $29.95

• **Hermann Valentin von Holst**
COUNTRY AND SUBURBAN HOMES OF THE PRAIRIE SCHOOL PERIOD
A reprint of the 1913 edition of one of American architecture's finest primary sources of residential design. Over 400 photographs and finely rendered plans
0–486–24373–7 Dover pb $5.95

American Cities

"The architects of this land and generation are now brought face to face with something new under the sun—namely that evolution and integration of social conditions, that special grouping of them, that results in a demand for the erection of tall office buildings ... Problem: How shall we impart to this sterile pile, this crude, harsh, brutal agglomeration, this stark, staring exclamation of eternal strife, the graciousness of those higher forms of sensibility and culture that rest on the lower and fiercer passions? How shall we proclaim from the dizzy height of this strange, weird modern housetop the peaceful evangel of sentiment, of beauty, the cult of a higher life?"—Louis Sullivan, 1896

• **Susan & Michael Southworth**
AIA GUIDE TO BOSTON
0–87106–936–9 Globe Pequot pb $14.95

• **Stanley Appelbaum**
THE CHICAGO WORLD'S FAIR OF 1893: A Photographic Record
A brief overview of the fair's plans and concepts, with a discussion of the personalities, rivalries and controversy surrounding its Beaux-Arts architecture
0–486–23990–X Dover pb $6.95

• **Ira Bach**
CHICAGO'S FAMOUS BUILDINGS: A Photographic Guide to the City's Architectural Landmarks and Other Notable Buildings
0–226–03395–3 Chicago $15.00
0–226–03396–1 Chicago pb $7.95

• **Carl Condit**
THE CHICAGO SCHOOL OF ARCHITECTURE: A History of Commercial and Public Building in the Chicago Area, 1875–1925
A thoroughly illustrated work, from William Le Baron's early functional innovations to their imaginative development by Louis Sullivan and Frank Lloyd Wright
0–226–11455–4 Chicago pb $16.95

• **Larry Viskochil**
CHICAGO AT THE TURN OF THE CENTURY IN PHOTOGRAPHS
Historic views from the collections of the Chicago Historical Society
0–486–24656–6 Dover pb $9.95

• John Zukowsky, editor
**CHICAGO ARCHITECTURE,
1872–1922: Birth of a Metropolis**
Catalog of an important recent exhibition
in Paris, highlighting the city's
achievements in both classical revival and
modernist architecture
3–7913–0837–8 Prestel $60.00

• Reyner Banham
LOS ANGELES
In this entertaining book, Banham sets the
works of designers as diverse as Frank
Lloyd Wright, Charles Eames, Richard
Neutra, and Watts Towers constructor
Simon Rodia in their geographical and
man-made contexts
0–14–021178–0 Penguin pb $7.95

• David Gebhard & Robert Winter
**ARCHITECTURE IN LOS ANGELES: A
Complete Guide**
0–87905–087–X Gibbs Smith pb $14.95

• Laura Cerwinske
**TROPICAL DECO: The Architecture and
Design of Old Miami Beach**
Stunning photographs reveal Miami's Art
Deco buildings of the 1920s and '30s
0–8478–0345–7 Rizzoli pb $14.95

• John Andrew Gallery
**PHILADELPHIA ARCHITECTURE: A
Guide to the City**
0–262–56030–5 MIT pb $14.95

• Curt Bruce & Thomas Aidala
GREAT HOUSES OF SAN FRANCISCO
0–394–70773–7 Knopf pb $10.95

• Louis Craig
**THE FEDERAL PRESENCE: Architecture,
Politics, and Symbols in U.S. Government
Building**
A kaleidoscopic survey, tracing the
government's role in shaping America's
built environment, from L'Enfant's plan
for Washington, D.C. to the space-age
technology of Cape Canaveral
0–262–03057–8 MIT $55.00
0–262–53059–7 MIT pb $19.95

• James Goode
**BEST ADDRESSES: A Catalogue of
Washington's Distinguished Apartment
Houses**
A richly illustrated study of the private side
of Washington's architecture, as worthy of
attention as the city's great public
buildings
0–87474–476–8 Smithsonian $45.00

• Bates Lowry
**THE ARCHITECTURE OF
WASHINGTON, D.C.**
Volume 1
0–691–1–002–2 Princeton $160.00
Volume 2
0–691–1–004–9 Princeton $160.00
**BUILDING A NATIONAL IMAGE:
Architectural Drawings for the American
Democracy, 1789–1912**
A beautifully produced volume containing
over 100 color drawings, with lucid

commentary tracing the history of federal
architecture
0–226–49556–6 Chicago $75.00
0–226–49557–4 Chicago pb $45.00

New York City

• Andrew Alpern
**NEW YORK'S FABULOUS LUXURY
APARTMENTS**
Over 100 floor plans and black-and-white
photographs splendidly reveal the
architectural and decorative details of life
at the top
0–486–25318–X Dover pb $7.95

• Stanley Appelbaum
**THE NEW YORK WORLD'S FAIR,
1939–1940**
A history of the people and principles
involved
0–486–23494–0 Dover pb $6.95

• Daniel Badger
**BADGER'S ILLUSTRATED
CATALOGUE OF CAST-IRON
ARCHITECTURE**
A reprint of the 1865 catalog. In many
ways, cast-iron buildings represented the
beginning of mass-production and

*McKim, Mead & White's Columbia Trust
building, New York City*

foreshadowed the modern steel-frame
skyscraper
0–486–24223–4 Dover pb $9.95

• Christine Boyer
**MANHATTAN MANNERS: Architecture
and Style, 1850–1900**
As much social as architectural history, this
handsome volume recreates the era during
which much of Manhattan was built
0–8478–0650–2 Rizzoli $30.00

• Barbaralee Diamonstein
THE LANDMARKS OF NEW YORK
The history and significance of the city's
officially designated landmarks
0–8109–1270–8 Abrams $45.00

• Margot Gayle & Edmund Gillon
**CAST-IRON ARCHITECTURE IN
NEW YORK**
A pictorial anthology of commercial
structures typical of mid-19th-century New
York
0–486–22980–7 Dover pb $8.95

• Edmund Gillon & Henry Hope Reed
**BEAUX-ARTS ARCHITECTURE IN
NEW YORK: A Photographic Guide**
A panoramic view of visual and
documentary importance
0–486–25690–8 Dover pb $8.95

• Paul Goldberger
**THE CITY OBSERVED—NEW YORK: A
Guide to the Architecture of Manhattan**
A well-documented historical tour by the
New York Times architecture critic
0–394–72916–1 Random House pb $12.95

• Carol Herselle Krinsky
ROCKEFELLER CENTER
A historical survey of the great urban
complex
0–19–502404–4 Oxford pb $10.95

• Charles Lockwood
**BRICKS AND BROWNSTONE: The New
York Row House, 1783–1929**
"Informative, genially written history of
the row house. . . . Its floor plans and
other documentation will prove most
useful to hardy souls who would like to
restore an abandoned or crumbling
brownstone"—*NY Times*
0–89659–228–6 Abbeville pb $16.95

• Donald MacKay
**THE BUILDING OF MANHATTAN: How
Manhattan Was Built Overground and
Underground, from the Dutch Settlers to
the Skyscrapers**
A compelling, illustrated account
0–06–015788–7 Harper & Row pb $16.95

• Henry Hope Reed
**THE NEW YORK PUBLIC LIBRARY: Its
Architecture and Decoration**
A lavish and detailed exploration of New
York's great Beaux-Arts landmark
0–393–02317–6 Norton $35.00
0–393–30336–5 Norton pb $16.95

• Donald Martin Reynolds
THE ARCHITECTURE OF NEW YORK CITY: Histories and Views of Important Structures, Sites and Symbols
An art historian's guide to the highlights of New York's history and continued development
0–02–602400–4 Macmillan $29.95

• Robert Stern & others
NEW YORK 1900: Metropolitan Architecture and Urbanism, 1890–1915
A comprehensive guide to the period's architecture with a social and cultural portrait of the city at its most extravagant
0–8478–0511–5 Rizzoli $65.00

NEW YORK 1930: Architecture and Urbanism Between the Two World Wars
The decades when New York was transformed into a city of skyscrapers
0–8478–0618–9 Rizzoli $75.00

• John Tauranac
ELEGANT NEW YORK: The Builders and the Buildings, 1885–1915
A fascinating guide to the grander buildings of Manhattan, superbly photographed
0–89659–458–0 Abbeville $55.00

Elliot Willensky & Norval White
AIA GUIDE TO NEW YORK CITY
Exuberant and opinionated, this recently revised classic is both an encyclopedia of the city's architecture and a high-spirited guide to its multifaceted 350-year history
0–15–104040–0 HBJ $34.95
0–15–603600–2 HBJ pb $21.95

Summer Places and Country Houses

• Donald Curl
MIZNER'S FLORIDA: American Resort Architecture
Picturesque and theatrical buildings from the originator of the Spanish revival in Florida
0–262–03104–3 MIT $37.50
0–262–53068–6 MIT pb $12.95

• Paul Goldberger
THE HOUSES OF THE HAMPTONS
A pictorial examination with commentary; includes many color photographs
0–394–54260–6 Knopf $50.00

• Arnold Lewis
AMERICAN COUNTRY HOUSES OF THE GILDED AGE
A reprint of George Sheldon's 1886 *Artistic Country Seats* describing 93 houses of New England and the middle Atlantic states
0–486–24301–X Dover pb $8.95

• Monica Randall
THE MANSIONS OF LONG ISLAND'S GOLD COAST
Fifty of the most spectacular homes of the North Shore, owned by such families as the Vanderbilts, Whitneys, and Guggenheims; fully illustrated
0–8478–0821–1 Rizzoli pb $19.95

Richard Morris Hunt's Chateau-sur-Mer, Newport, Rhode Island

• John Zukowsky & Robbie Pierce Stimson
HUDSON RIVER VILLAS
An elegant volume illustrating and discussing over 120 villas and estates
0–8478–0613–8 Rizzoli $60.00

INDIVIDUAL ARCHITECTS

• Thomas Hines
BURNHAM OF CHICAGO: Architect and Planner
A skilled administrator who, with his versatile partner Root, had an important share in the evolution of the Chicago school
0–226–34171–2 Chicago pb $14.95

• Hugh Ferriss
THE METROPOLIS OF TOMORROW
Ferriss draws and discusses the skyscraper and presents his romantic vision for a humanistic city
0–910413–11–8 Architectural Press $35.00

• Jean Ferriss Leach
ARCHITECTURAL VISIONS: The Drawings of Hugh Ferriss
Organized in two sections, devoted respectively to visionary designs and actual projects. Includes drawings for the Johnson Wax, Rockefeller Center, and other important buildings
0–8230–7055–7 Watson-Guptill $19.95

• Mardges Bacon
ERNEST FLAGG: Beaux-Arts Architect and Urban Reformer
Architect of the famous Singer building, Flagg's diverse work includes the Corcoran Gallery and much low-cost housing
0–262–02222–2 MIT $42.00

• R. Buckminster Fuller
INVENTIONS: The Patented Works of R. Buckminster Fuller
Fuller's 28 patented inventions are an affirmation of what an innovator can accomplish even in today's mass culture
0–312–43477–4 St. Martin's $40.00

• James O'Gorman & others
THE ARCHITECTURE OF FRANK FURNESS
A catalog of the works of the renowned Philadelphia architect who was Sullivan's first employer
0–8122–7957–3 Pennsylvania $42.50
0–87633–015–4 Philadelphia Museum pb $18.95

• Polly Wynn Allen
BUILDING DOMESTIC LIBERTY: Charlotte Perkin Gilman's Architectural Feminism
A study of the outspoken late 19th-century proponent of the "kitchen-less house," for whom home-sweet-home was a bogus morality for not-so-sweet housekeeping
0–87023–627–X Massachusetts $25.00
0–87023–628–8 Massachusetts pb $11.95

• Richard Oliver
BERTRAM GROSVENOR GOODHUE
Refusing to be influenced by the Beaux-Arts or the new European modernism, Goodhue developed an idiosyncratic and distinctive style
0–262–15024–7 MIT $40.00

• Paul Baker
RICHARD MORRIS HUNT
An analysis of the work of the architect who helped shift American taste in the 1860s and '70s away from English romanticism to French monumentalism
0–262–52109–1 MIT pb $17.50

ARCHITECTURE AND DESIGN

• Suzanne Stein, editor
THE ARCHITECTURE OF RICHARD MORRIS HUNT
A collection of essays with numerous illustrations
0–226–77168–7 Chicago $39.95
0–226–77169–5 Chicago pb $16.95

Jefferson

"But to say that Thomas Jefferson was simply among the first of millions of Americans who designed and built their own homes, or that Monticello is a typical, if somewhat large, example of domestic architecture, is to deny the palpable genius of the man. He was larger than life in most things he did—America's outstanding example of a Renaissance man in an age that produced more than its share."—Jack McLaughlin, *Jefferson and Monticello: The Biography of a Builder*

Fiske Kimball
THOMAS JEFFERSON: Architect
Jefferson's career as a statesman overshadowed his architecture, yet had he done nothing else he would be remembered today for his distinguished buildings
0–306–70965–1 Da Capo $85.00

Jack McLaughlin
JEFFERSON AND MONTICELLO: The Biography of a Builder
National Book Award nominee (1988)
0–8050–0482–3 Holt $29.95

Frederick Nichols, editor
THOMAS JEFFERSON'S ARCHITECTURAL DRAWINGS
A brief catalog with an essay exploring Jefferson's adherence to Palladianism
0–8139–0328–9 Virginia pb $4.95

Frederick Nichols & Ralph Griswold
THOMAS JEFFERSON, LANDSCAPE ARCHITECT
A short catalog, that highlights Jefferson's anti-urban vision
0–8139–0899–X Virginia pb $6.95

• Roth Leland
THE ARCHITECTURE OF McKIM, MEAD & WHITE, 1870–1920
A survey of the New York-based firm that dominated east coast architecture for over 30 years
0–06–438491–8 Harper & Row $40.00

• Sara Holmes Boutelle
JULIA MORGAN, ARCHITECT
Designer and builder of more than 700 structures including Hearst Castle, Morgan was one of America's most accomplished 20th-century architects. This handsome volume documents her life and work with letters, sketches, blueprints, and striking photographs
0–89659–792–X Abbeville $55.00

• Paul Spreiregen
THE ARCHITECTURE OF WILLIAM MORGAN
The innovative architect who used earth as an architectural element to link building and site
0–292–79023–6 Texas $49.50

• Thomas Hines
RICHARD NEUTRA AND THE SEARCH FOR MODERN ARCHITECTURE: A Biography and History
The definitive biography, with critical insights into the genesis of Neutra's practical and aesthetic concepts
0–19–503028–1 Oxford $55.00
0–19–503029–X Oxford pb $29.95

• Esther McCoy
VIENNA TO LOS ANGELES: Two Journeys
Traces the careers of Neutra and Schindler from their early training in Vienna to the erection of their white stucco houses in southern California
0–931228–01–8 Arts & Architecture $17.50
0–931228–02–6 Arts & Architecture pb $10.95

• Richard Neutra
SURVIVAL THROUGH DESIGN
An architectural career develops against the background of the Great Depression in America
0–19–500790–5 Oxford pb $8.95

• Henry-Russell Hitchcock
THE ARCHITECTURE OF H.H. RICHARDSON AND HIS TIMES
Hitchcock was the first to regard Richardson as a pioneer of modern architecture, a man who "created out of a confusion which was actually worse than a mere void the beginnings of a new architecture"—Lewis Mumford
0–262–58005–5 MIT pb $12.95

• Jeffrey Karl Ochsner
H.H. RICHARDSON: Complete Architectural Works
His entire output, represented in plans, drawings, photographs, and descriptions
0–262–65015–0 MIT $29.95

• James O'Gorman
H.H. RICHARDSON: Architectural Forms for an American Society
Based on new biographical material, the author contends that Richardson consciously sought to reflect changing social mores of 19th-century America in his architecture of "big stones"
0–226–62069–7 Chicago $24.95

• Mariana Griswold Van Rensselaer
HENRY HOBSON RICHARDSON AND HIS WORKS
An unabridged republication of the first monograph on Richardson, published in 1888
0–486–22320–5 Dover pb $6.95

• Donald Hofmann
THE ARCHITECTURE OF JOHN WELLBORN ROOT
One of the principal figures of the Chicago school
0–8018–1371–9 Johns Hopkins $28.50

• Steven Ruttenbaum
MANSIONS IN THE CLOUDS: The Skyscraper Palazzi of Emery Roth
The first monograph on the life and work of Roth, architect of many of New York's outstanding skyscrapers of the 1920s and '30s as well as numerous luxury apartment buildings
0–917439–09–0 Balsam $40.00

• Albert Christ-Janer
ELIEL SAARINEN: Finnish-American Architect and Educator
From the multiple legacy of the early modern tradition, Saarinen developed a unique synthesis of romanticism and pragmatism
0–226–10465–6 Chicago pb $17.95

• August Sarnitz
R.M. SCHINDLER, 1887–1953
Born in Vienna, Schindler settled permanently in Los Angeles, where he contributed much to its domestic architecture. This important volume includes original writings and correspondence
0–8478–0921–8 Rizzoli $35.00

Sullivan

Hugh Morrison
LOUIS SULLIVAN: Prophet of Modern Architecture
The first monograph, responsible for the genesis of the Sullivan legend, and still the standard biography
0–393–00116–4 Norton pb $8.95

Paul Sprague
THE DRAWINGS OF LOUIS HENRY SULLIVAN: A Catalogue of the Frank Lloyd Wright Collection at the Avery Architectural Library
Drawings from 1873–1910 that exhibit the full range of Sullivan's exquisite draftsmanship and passion for detail
0–691–03924–0 Princeton $61.00

Louis Sullivan
AUTOBIOGRAPHY OF AN IDEA
Written in Sullivan's later years, these provocative recollections reveal the growth of the organic theory of architecture
0–486–20281–X Dover pb $6.95

KINDERGARTEN CHATS AND OTHER WRITINGS
In which Sullivan's theories about architecture, art, education, and life in general are presented in the classical form of dialogues or "chats" between an architect and a novice
0–486–23812–1 Dover pb $5.00

Robert Twombly
LOUIS SULLIVAN: His Life and Work
A historian's biography that considers the social, economic, and aesthetic background of the father of the American skyscraper
0–226–82006–8 Chicago pb $16.95

IF YOU CAN'T FIND IT, LOOK IN THE INDEX

Rudolph Schindler's 1937 plan for a beach house (RIBA)

• William Morgan
THE ALMIGHTY WALL: The Architecture of Harry Vaughan
A leader of the "Boston Gothicists" in the late 19th century, Vaughan laid the foundations of the last phase of the American Gothic revival
0–262–13187–0 MIT $40.00

• Charles Baldwin
STANFORD WHITE
A pupil of Richardson, and later a partner of McKim Mead & White
0–306–70138–3 Da Capo $45.00
0–306–80031–4 Da Capo pb $6.95

• H. Allen Brooks
THE PRAIRIE SCHOOL: Frank Lloyd Wright and His Midwest Contemporaries
The definitive study of the Prairie School
0–393–00811–8 Norton pb $16.95

• Henry-Russell Hitchcock
IN THE NATURE OF MATERIALS: The Buildings of Frank Lloyd Wright, 1887–1941
The best introduction to the life and work of Wright; reprint of the 1942 edition
0–306–71283–0 Da Capo $39.50
0–306–80019–5 Da Capo pb $14.95

• Grant Manson
FRANK LLOYD WRIGHT TO 1910: The First Golden Age
A companion to Hitchcock's book and a classic in its own right
0–442–26130–6 Van Nostrand Reinhold pb $22.95

• William Storrer
THE ARCHITECTURE OF FRANK LLOYD WRIGHT: A Complete Catalog
The most complete guide available, containing 437 entries with photographs, locations, descriptions, and maps
0–262–69080–2 MIT pb $14.95

• Robert Twombly
FRANK LLOYD WRIGHT: His Life and His Architecture
The definitive biography
0–471–03400–2 John Wiley $41.95

• Frank Lloyd Wright
DRAWINGS, PLANS OF FRANK LLOYD WRIGHT: The Early Period, 1893–1909
A reprint of the famous Wasmuth edition, with numerous photographs and original views
0–486–24457–1 Dover pb $8.95

STUDIES AND EXECUTED BUILDINGS BY FRANK LLOYD WRIGHT
A beautiful volume reproduced from the 1910–1911 Wasmuth portfolios with a selection of drawings of Wright's most remarkable houses of the Oak Park period
0–8478–0687–1 Rizzoli $65.00

> Occasionally a single artist emerges who so profoundly reorganizes the basic assumptions of a period that he deserves to be considered in isolation ... In the formation of modern architecture two figures of this imaginative and intellectual caliber obviously stand out: Le Corbusier and Frank Lloyd Wright.
>
> William Curtis
> **MODERN ARCHITECTURE SINCE 1900**
> 0–13–586694–4 Prentice-Hall pb $42.50

20th-Century Architecture

HISTORY

• Reyner Banham
A CONCRETE ATLANTIS: U.S. Industrial Building and European Modern Architecture
Proposes that the European fascination with technology found its visual sources in the United States, as evidenced by the early writings of Le Corbusier and Gropius
0–262–02244–3 MIT $27.50

THEORY AND DESIGN IN THE FIRST MACHINE AGE
A definitive study of the modern movement that has influenced a generation of students and critics in its treatment of attitudes, themes, and forms
0–262–52058–3 MIT pb $10.95

• Leonardo Benevolo
HISTORY OF MODERN ARCHITECTURE
A chronological account of schools and major figures from the Industrial Revolution to the present day

Volume 1
0–262–52044–3 MIT pb $15.00

Volume 2
0–262–52045–1 MIT pb $17.50

• Peter Blake
THE MASTER BUILDERS: Le Corbusier, Mies van der Rohe, and Frank Lloyd Wright
"If one could have only one book on the general subject, since it illuminates the whole field by attention to the key forces, this would be it"—*Nation*
0–393–00796–0 Norton pb $10.95

• Franco Borsi
THE MONUMENTAL ERA: European Architecture and Design, 1929–1939
"A fascinating and comprehensive study of the stripped classical style as manifested in European buildings from 1929 to 1939"—*Chicago Tribune*
0–8478–0805–X Rizzoli $40.00

- Ulrich Conrads, editor
PROGRAMS AND MANIFESTOES ON 20TH CENTURY ARCHITECTURE
Important for understanding modern architecture in its cultural context
0–262–53030–9 MIT pb $7.95

- William Curtis
MODERN ARCHITECTURE SINCE 1900
A lucid and consistent study of developments in the crucial years of modern architecture
0–13–586694–4 Prentice-Hall pb $42.50

- Dennis & Elizabeth DeWitt
MODERN ARCHITECTURE IN EUROPE: A Guide to Buildings Since the Industrial Revolution
With maps and indexes of building types and architects
0–525–24415–8 Dutton $35.00
0–525–48216–4 Dutton pb $19.95

- Kenneth Frampton
MODERN ARCHITECTURE: A Critical History
An effective combination of key examples with a clear exposition of major issues
0–500–20201–X Thames & Hudson pb $11.95

- Sigfried Giedion
MECHANIZATION TAKES COMMAND
Documents the mechanization of the household from the Middle Ages to the modern period, focusing on the latter
0–393–00489–9 Norton pb $15.95

SPACE, TIME AND ARCHITECTURE: The Growth of a New Tradition
Though its point of view is now challenged, this is still an important interpretation of the history of the modern movement
0–674–83040–7 Harvard $35.00

- Hilde de Haan & Ids Haagsma
ARCHITECTS IN COMPETITION: International Architectural Competitions of the Last 200 Years
An original study presenting the histories of 16 internationally famous buildings commissioned through competitions. Includes rejected entries and many illustrations
0–500–34103–6 Thames & Hudson $65.00

- Vittorio Lampugnani
ENCYCLOPEDIA OF 20TH-CENTURY ARCHITECTURE
A richly illustrated panorama of the major figures and their contributions
0–8109–0860–3 Abrams $24.95
0–8109–2335–1 Abrams pb $16.95

- Nikolaus Pevsner
PIONEERS OF MODERN DESIGN
From William Morris to Walter Gropius, this is the first account of the development of the modern movement in architecture
0–14–055211–1 Penguin pb $7.95

SOURCES OF MODERN ARCHITECTURE AND DESIGN
A brief and well-illustrated survey
0–500–20072–6 Thames & Hudson pb $11.95

- Edward Relph
THE MODERN URBAN LANDSCAPE: 1880 to the Present
0–8018–3559–3 Johns Hopkins $35.00
0–8018–3560–7 Johns Hopkins pb $14.95

- Bernard Rudovsky
ARCHITECTURE WITHOUT ARCHITECTS: A Short Introduction to Non-Pedigreed Architecture
This highly visual presentation of traditional vernacular architectures of the world has had great influence
0–8263–10004–4 New Mexico pb $14.95

- Alberto Sartoris
ELEMENTS OF FUNCTIONALIST ARCHITECTURE
A monumental international compendium of architecture in the 1930s and '40s by a leading proponent of modern architecture
0–8478–1001–1 Rizzoli $85.00

- Vincent Scully
MODERN ARCHITECTURE
A penetrating study by the eminent Yale professor
0–8076–0334–1 Braziller pb $9.95

- Manfredo Tafuri & Francesco Dal Co
MODERN ARCHITECTURE
Emphasizes society's impact on modern architecture and the modern city in the United States and Europe

Volume 1
0–8478–0760–6 Rizzoli pb $25.00

Volume 2
0–8478–0761–4 Rizzoli pb $25.00

CRITICISM

- Alan Colquhoun
ESSAYS IN ARCHITECTURAL CRITICISM: Modern Architecture and Historical Change
Focuses on much-debated buildings and concepts
0–262–03076–4 MIT $37.50
0–262–53063–5 MIT pb $12.50

From Passionate Journey *by Frans Masereel* (*City Lights*)

MODERNITY AND THE CLASSICAL TRADITION: Architectural Essays, 1980–1987
The prominent theoretical concepts—classicism, romanticism, historicism, and rationalism—as they have developed with the changing meaning of history
0–262–03138–8 MIT $25.00

- Kenneth Frampton
LABOR, WORK AND ARCHITECTURE: Critical Essays, 1968–1988
Twenty essays by a highly respected and influential architectural historian and critic
0–8478–0653–7 Rizzoli pb $25.00

MODERN ARCHITECTURE, 1851–1945
Ten incisive essays accompanied by photographs
0–8478–0506–9 Rizzoli $75.00

Volume 1: 1851–1919
0–8478–0507–7 Rizzoli pb $35.00

Volume 2: 1920–1945
0–8478–0508–5 Rizzoli pb $35.00

- Robert Venturi & Denise Scott Brown
THE VIEW FROM THE CAMPIDOGLIO: Selected Essays, 1953–1984
Provides a theoretical base for the shift from modern to postmodern
0–06–438851–4 Harper & Row $25.00

City Planning

- George & Christiane Crasemann Collins, editors
CAMILLO SITTE: The Birth of Modern City Planning
Originally published in 1889, Sitte's work revolutionized urban planning and ushered the discipline into the 20th century; with original drawings and plates
0–8478–0785–1 Rizzoli $40.00

- Le Corbusier
THE CITY OF TOMORROW
A provocative essay, written in 1929, advocating a rationalized environment in which traditional urban features would become obsolete
0–486–25332–5 Dover pb $8.95

FRANCE

"If we eliminate from our hearts and minds all dead concepts in regard to the houses, and look at the question from a critical and objective point of view, we shall arrive at the 'House-Machine,' the mass-production house, healthy (and morally so too) and beautiful in the same way that the working tools and instruments which accompany our existence are beautiful." —Le Corbusier, *Towards a New Architecture*

- Tony Garnier
LA CITE INDUSTRIELLE
An influential book showing Garnier's plans for a utopian community of 35,000, including buildings for industry, housing, and government
0–910413–47–9 Princeton $60.00

- **Dora Wiebenson**
TONY GARNIER: The Cité Industrielle
A brief, illustrated account of Garnier's plans, showing the principles of Beaux Arts town planning influenced by Frank Lloyd Wright
0–8076–0515–8 Braziller pb $7.95

- **Maurice Rheims**
HECTOR GUIMARD
The first complete visual overview of the premier Art Nouveau architect, by the noted art critic
0–8109–0973–1 Abrams $49.50

- **Tim Benton**
THE VILLAS OF LE CORBUSIER, 1920–1930
Includes original drawings and contemporary views
0–300–03780–5 Yale $50.00

- **Maurice Besset**
LE CORBUSIER: To Live with the Light
A fully illustrated monograph containing photographs of the most famous projects as well as drawings and plans, color plates of his paintings, and sketches
0–8478–0816–5 Rizzoli $25.00

- **Le Corbusier**
TOWARDS A NEW ARCHITECTURE
A major work which presents the philosophical, cultural, and visual concerns of the avant-garde and shows how they inform modern design
0–486–25023–7 Dover pb $8.95

VOYAGE TO THE ORIENT
A boxed set of six volumes presenting for the first time a facsimile edition of the early *carnets* recording his travels to the East
0–8478–0910–2 Rizzoli (set) $175.00

- **William Curtis**
LE CORBUSIER: Ideas and Forms
Based on new archival material and focusing on the formative years, architectural ideals, and social realities
0–8478–0726–6 Rizzoli $40.00

- **Deborah Gans**
THE LE CORBUSIER GUIDE
A centennial guide to his buildings with maps, hours, accommodations, and detailed tours
0–910413–23–1 Princeton pb $17.00

- **Jacques Guiton**
THE IDEAS OF LE CORBUSIER: On Architecture and Urban Planning
Le Corbusier promoted his ideas in lectures and speeches, illustrated with his drawings; such material is here reassembled
0–8076–1004–6 Braziller $25.00
0–8076–1005–4 Braziller pb $10.95

- **Charles Jencks**
LE CORBUSIER AND THE TRAGIC VIEW OF ARCHITECTURE
An eccentric study by a theorist of postmodernism who traces the crisis of modern architecture to Le Corbusier's later ideas
0–674–51860–8 Harvard $16.50
0–674–51861–6 Harvard pb $12.50

Walter Gropius' Bauhaus, Dessau

- **Stanislaus Von Moos**
LE CORBUSIER: Elements of a Synthesis
The standard biography
0–262–72008–6 MIT pb $14.95

GERMANY AND AUSTRIA

- **Joan Campbell**
THE GERMAN WERKBUND
The German institution that pursued modern design in all its manifestations, from industrial plant to social housing
0–691–05250–6 Princeton $44.00

- **Franceso Dal Co**
FIGURES OF ARCHITECTURE AND THOUGHT: German Architectural Culture, 1819–1920
Essays focusing on the beginnings of modernism in Germany, its cultural transformations and utopian aspirations
0–8748–0654–5 Rizzoli $25.00

- **Barbara Lane**
ARCHITECTURE AND POLITICS IN GERMANY, 1918–1945
Illuminates the complex interplay of art and culture in the Weimar and Nazi periods
0–674–04350–2 Harvard $18.50

- **William Pehnt**
EXPRESSIONIST ARCHITECTURE IN DRAWINGS
A testimony to the spiritual dimensions of an architecture that aspired to a universality of form
0–442–27384–3 Van Nostrand Reinhold $28.95

The Bauhaus

"Let us create a new guild of craftsmen, without the class distinction which raises an arrogant barrier between craftsmen and artist. Together let us conceive and create the new building of the future, which will embrace architecture and sculpture and painting in one unity and which will rise one day toward heaven from the hands of a million workers like the crystal symbol of a new faith." —Walter Gropius, *Proclamation of the Weimar Bauhaus*

Herbert Bayer & others, editors
BAUHAUS: 1919–1928
Reprint of the catalog for the famous 1938 Museum of Modern Art exhibition, which introduced the central emigrating figures of the Bauhaus—Gropius, Bayer, Albers, Moholy-Nagy, and others—to the American public
0–87070–240–8 MOMA pb $11.50

Howard Dearstyne
INSIDE THE BAUHAUS
A vivid, often anecdotal picture of the influential design school, its curriculum, politics and faculty, by one of the few Americans who studied there
0–8478–0699–5 Rizzoli $40.00
0–8478–0702–9 Rizzoli pb $22.50

Walter Gropius
NEW ARCHITECTURE AND THE BAUHAUS
The international aims of the Bauhaus
0–262–57006–8 MIT pb $5.95

Frank Whitford
BAUHAUS
An introduction tracing the ideas behind the Bauhaus, its teaching methods, and its innovative artists
0–500–20193–5 Thames & Hudson pb $11.95

Hans Wingler
BAUHAUS: Weimar, Dessau, Berlin, Chicago
The standard comprehensive treatment
0–262–23033–X MIT $175.00
0–262–73047–2 MIT pb $30.00

- **Gilbert Herbert**
THE DREAM OF THE FACTORY-MADE HOUSE: Walter Gropius and Konrad Wachsmann
"For anyone seriously interested in the way architecture interacts with the realities of

the marketplace, this impeccably researched case study about the tragic failure of a noble architectural idea should be required reading" —Edward Sekler
0–262–08140–7 MIT $35.00

• Richard Pommer & others
IN THE SHADOW OF MIES: Ludwig Hilberseimer—Architect, Educator, and Urban Planner
The first thorough monograph on this influential urban designer
0–8478–0931–5 Rizzoli pb $19.95

• Giuliano Gresleri
JOSEF HOFFMANN
An analytical survey of the Viennese master's architectural work
0–8478–0554–9 Rizzoli pb $12.50

• Edward Sekler
JOSEF HOFFMANN: The Architectural Work
The large-format catalogue raisonné of a leading member of the Secession movement and the Wiener Werkstätte, with superb color reproductions
0–691–06572–1 Princeton $140.00

• Benedetto Gravagnuolo
ADOLF LOOS: Theory and Works
The first book to present the complete works of this pioneer best known for his attacks on the ornamental style of the Vienna Secession movement
0–8478–0895–5 Rizzoli pb $29.95

• Adolf Loos
SPOKEN INTO THE VOID: Collected Essays, 1897–1900
Loos's polemic writings sought to establish a distinction between architecture and the products of the machine age, between art and everyday culture
0–262–62057–X MIT pb $12.50

• Max Risselada, editor
RAUMPLAN VERSUS PLAN LIBRE: Adolf Loos and Le Corbusier, 1919–1930
Collected essays that analyze their houses for contrasts in the relation of structure to design
0–8478–1000–3 Rizzoli pb $25.00

• Bruno Zevi
ERICH MENDELSOHN
An overview of the celebrated German architect renowned for his manipulation of steel, concrete, and glass; with many drawings, sketches, and fantasy projects
0–8478–0555–7 Rizzoli pb $12.50

• Peter Haiko & Bernd Krimmel, editors
JOSEPH MARIA OLBRICH ARCHITECTURE
The prominent Austrian architect and proponent of the Vienna Secession movement composed these three volumes of designs in Berlin between 1901 and 1908
0–8478–0971–4 Rizzoli $95.00

Mies van der Rohe's ITT building, New York City, from Architecture: Meaning and Place *by Christian Norberg-Schulz (Rizzoli)*

• Iain Boyd Whyte
BRUNO TAUT AND THE ARCHITECTURE OF ACTIVISM
Design in the crisis of modernism that beset German architectural theory in the years after World War I
0–521–23655–X Cambridge $72.50

• Iain Boyd Whyte, editor
THE CRYSTAL CHAIN LETTERS: Architectural Fantasies by Bruno Taut and his Circle
The Crystal Chain was a utopian correspondence, initiated by Taut in 1919, in which a small group of like-minded architects and artists exchanged ideas on the architecture of the future
0–262–23121–2 MIT $32.50

• Franz Schulze
MIES VAN DER ROHE: A Critical Biography
An acclaimed biography with detailed analysis of his relations with Behrens, Johnson, and Wright. Includes many previously unpublished photos
0–226–74059–5 Chicago $39.95

• David Spaeth
MIES VAN DER ROHE
"I believe that true architecture has little or nothing to do with the invention of interesting forms or with personal inclinations. True architecture is always objective and is the expression of the inner structure of our time from which it springs"—Mies van der Rohe. An overview of how Mies's buildings and teachings illustrate the evolution of his thought
Preface by Kenneth Frampton
0–8478–0563–8 Rizzoli pb $25.00

• Wolf Tegethoff
MIES VAN DER ROHE: The Villas and Country Houses
Concrete and brick country houses, built and unbuilt, from 1923 to 1951
0–262–20050–3 MIT $60.00

• John Zukowsky, editor
MIES RECONSIDERED: His Career, Legacy, and Disciples
Essays by contemporary critics, essential for an understanding of his work
0–8478–0771–1 Rizzoli pb $22.50

• Peter Haiko, editor
OTTO WAGNER: Sketches, Projects, and Executed Buildings
Magnificent reproductions of his exquisite sketches and drawings, first published in 1899 and 1922
0–8478–0853–X Rizzoli $85.00

ITALY

• Luciano Caramel & Alberto Longatti
ANTONIO SANT'ELIA: The Complete Works
A leading futurist who proposed a visionary architecture inspired by the images of technology and industrialism. All of his projects were unrealized
0–8478–0964–1 Rizzoli $65.00

• Peter Eisenman
GIUSEPPE TERRAGNI: Transformations, Decompositions, Critiques
In a fascinating series of original diagrams and vintage photographs, Eisenman discloses Terragni's design strategies and compositional methods
0–8478–0772–X Rizzoli $35.00

• Richard Etlin
MODERNISM IN ITALIAN ARCHITECTURE, 1890–1940
A sweeping, generously illustrated study; Etlin explores the changing idea of modernism in Italian architecture over five crucial decades
0–262–05038–2 MIT $39.95

• Thomas Schumacher
THE DANTEUM
Mussolini's unbuilt 1938 commission for a monument to Dante, designed in the Italian rationalist style
0–910413–09–6 Princeton $35.00

• Manfredo Tafuri
HISTORY OF ITALIAN ARCHITECTURE, 1944–1985
Critic/historian Tafuri surveys the rich but fragmented recent history of Italy's architecture
0–262–20067–8 MIT $25.00

THE NETHERLANDS AND BELGIUM

• Sergio Polano
HENDRIK PETRUS BERLAGE: Complete Works
The major Dutch architect and urban planner and his influence
0–8478–0901–3 Rizzoli $65.00

• Klaus-Jurgen Sembach
HENRY VAN DE VELDE
The first full-length study in English of the celebrated Belgian architect known for his

total organic environments and teaching principles
0–8478–0858–0 Rizzoli $50.00

- Nancy Troy
THE DE STIJL ENVIRONMENT
Explores the collaborative effort that produced the group's experiments in color and space
0–262–20046–5 MIT $47.50
0–262–70030–1 MIT pb $19.95

- Wim de Wit, editor
THE AMSTERDAM SCHOOL: Dutch Expressionist Architecture, 1915–1930
Led by the talented de Klerk, the Amsterdam School produced some of the most original and avant-garde designs in the halcyon days of modernism. This book documents all major projects, from renderings of furniture and interiors to completed buildings
0–262–04074–3 MIT $27.50

SCANDINAVIA

- Goran Schildt
ALVAR AALTO: The Early Years
The first of what will be a 3-volume biography of the great Finnish architect, incorporating rare archival material
0–8478–0531–X Rizzoli $40.00

ALVAR AALTO: The Decisive Years
The sequel to *The Early Years* covers the late '20s through 1939
0–8478–0711–8 Rizzoli $40.00

- Goran Schildt, editor
ALVAR AALTO: Sketches
Plans and details tracing the creative origins of architectural projects
0–262–51035–9 MIT pb $12.95

- Claes Caldenby & Olof Hultin, editors
ASPLUND
A fine selection of essays on the admired representative of the '20s classicism known as Swedish Grace
0–8478–0678–2 Rizzoli $45.00

- Stewart Wrede
THE ARCHITECTURE OF ERIK GUNNAR ASPLUND
A discussion of the important but problematic character of Asplund's contributions
0–262–23095–X MIT $42.50
0–262–73068–5 MIT pb $17.95

- Jane Ahlin
SIGURD LEWERENTZ, ARCHITECT
The first Swedish architect to work actively with the Deutscher Werkbund in Germany, where he came into contact with Le Corbusier. Includes fine watercolor reproductions
0–262–01095–X MIT $50.00

THE SOVIET UNION

- Catherine Cooke & Alexander Kudriavtsev
SOVIET ARCHITECTURE
0–312–01281–0 St. Martin's $19.95

- S. O. Khan-Magomedov
PIONEERS OF SOVIET ARCHITECTURE
Written by the leading Soviet architectural historian, this is the most exhaustive presentation of Soviet architecture in any language
0–8478–0744–4 Rizzoli $75.00

Russian Constructivism

- Anatole Kopp
CONSTRUCTIVIST ARCHITECTURE IN THE U.S.S.R.
The constructivists attempted to evolve a training guide for their new concept of the "artist-constructor" following the 1917 revolution
0–312–16599–4 St. Martin's $45.00

- Andrei Gozak & Andrei Leonidov
IVAN LEONIDOV
Documents the hitherto unknown works of Leonidov, unique among Russian avant-garde architects for his bold technological vision and the scale and simplicity of his suprematist-inspired spatial planning
0–8478–0951–X Rizzoli $60.00

- El Lissitsky
RUSSIA: An Architecture for World Revolution
El Lissitsky created a synthesis of functional structures and abstract elements, and often collaborated with western architects and designers
0–262–62047–2 MIT pb $7.95

- Frederick Starr
MELNIKOV: Solo Architect in a Mass Society
In his imaginative use of materials and techniques, Melnikov achieved a formalism in which traditional and vernacular elements are transformed in relation to contemporary social programs
0–691–00331–9 Princeton pb $16.85

- S. O. Khan-Magomedov
RODCHENKO: The Complete Work
The artist's architectural projects plus his photography, graphic, industrial, and stage set designs
0–262–11116–0 MIT $55.00

- John Milner
VLADIMIR TATLIN AND THE RUSSIAN AVANT-GARDE
A good overview with excellent reproductions of paintings, sculpture, and architecture
0–300–02771–0 Yale $39.95
0–300–03404–0 Yale pb $14.95

- Larissa Alekseevna Zhadova
TATLIN
An illustrated study of the influential Soviet artist regarded as the father of Russian constructivism
0–8478–0827–0 Rizzoli $75.00

- S. O. Khan-Magomedov
ALEXANDER VESNIN AND RUSSIAN CONSTRUCTIVISM
The first full-length study of Vesnin in English concentrates on his avant-garde experimentation in various media
0–8478–0773–8 Rizzoli $55.00

SPAIN

- George Collins & Juan Nonell
THE DESIGNS AND DRAWINGS OF ANTONIO GAUDI
Flamboyant and extravagant design is fully reflected in this comprehensively illustrated catalog
0–691–03985–2 Princeton $155.00

- Cesar Martinell
GAUDI, DESIGNER: His Life, His Theories, His Work
84–7031–218–9 International pb $12.95

- Ignasi de Sola-Morales Rubio
GAUDI
The Catalan synthesizer of Gothic, Moorish, and Art Nouveau influences
0–8478–0525–5 Rizzoli $19.95

Contemporary Architecture

- Colin Davies
HIGH TECH ARCHITECTURE
A look at over 40 buildings by architects such as Rogers, Foster, and Piano. Includes the Hong Kong and Shanghai Bank, and the Centre Georges Pompidou
0–8478–0887–4 Rizzoli $45.00
0–8478–0881–5 Rizzoli pb $29.95

- Peter Eisenman & others
FIVE ARCHITECTS: Eisenman, Graves, Gwathmey, Hejduk, Meiser
An exhibition catalog showing the development of American architecture in the 1970s and '80s
Foreword by Philip Johnson
0–19–519795–X Oxford pb $22.50

- Philip Johnson & Mark Wigley
DECONSTRUCTIVIST ARCHITECTURE
An exhibition catalog featuring new works by Libeskind, Koolhaas, Tschumi, Hadid, Eisenman, Gehry, and Himmelbau
0–87070–298–X NY Graphic Society pb $17.95

● Joseph Kleihues & Heinrich Klotz, editors
INTERNATIONAL BUILDING EXHIBITION, BERLIN 1987: Examples of a New Architecture
Discusses and illustrates the designs of the 76 prize-winning architectural firms in the competition for a vast new housing scheme in West Berlin
0–8478–0775–4 Rizzoli pb $40.00

● Ignasi de Sola-Morales Rubio & Anton Gonzalez Capitel
CONTEMPORARY SPANISH ARCHITECTURE: An Eclectic Panorama
The evolution of Spanish architecture over the past three decades
0–8478–0708–8 Rizzoli pb $25.00

● David Stewart
THE MAKING OF A MODERN JAPANESE ARCHITECTURE: 1868 To The Present
0–87011–844–7 Kodansha $60.00

INDIVIDUAL ARCHITECTS

● Tadao Ando
TADAO ANDO: Buildings, Projects, Writings
The internationally acclaimed architect and his unique reinterpretation of the traditional Japanese concepts of nature, light, and form
0–8478–0547–6 Rizzoli pb $19.95

● John Andrews & Jennifer Taylor
JOHN ANDREWS: Architecture, a Performing Art
A proponent of participatory architecture
0–19–550557–3 Oxford $75.00

● Kenneth Frampton, editor
ATELIER 66: The Architecture of Dimitris and Suzana Antonakakis
The firm's projects in Greece since 1966, including apartment buildings, resort hotels, and public projects
0–8478–0623–5 Rizzoli pb $19.95

● Warren James, editor
RICARDO BOFILL: TALLER DE ARQUITECTURA: Buildings and Projects, 1960–1985
A catalogue raisonné and monograph on the work of this important Spanish architect and his multidisciplinary team. Featured are Kafka's Castle, Xanadu, Walden-7, and many other projects
0–8478–0739–8 Rizzoli $45.00
0–8478–0740–1 Rizzoli pb $29.95

● Francesco Dal Co
MARIO BOTTA: Architecture, 1960–1985
Botta's buildings and projects, including his earliest works, with superb illustrations
0–8478–0838–6 Rizzoli $50.00
0–8478–0839–4 Rizzoli pb $35.00

● Carol Herselle Krinsky
GORDON BUNSHAFT OF SKIDMORE, OWINGS AND MERRILL
For many years an executive partner of SOM, Bunshaft is best known for Lever House in Manhattan
0–262–11130–6 MIT $50.00

Richard Meier's Smith House, Darien, Connecticut

● Pierluigi Nicolin
THE DARING FLIGHT: Santiago Calatrava
Structural and formal innovation in the work of the Spanish architect
0–8478–0929–3 Rizzoli pb $35.00

● Werner Seligman & Jorge Silvetti
AMARIO CAMPI AND FRANCO PESSINA
A new monograph of the most talented contemporary architects of the Ticinese school known as "La Tendenza"
0–8478–0799–1 Rizzoli pb $25.00

● Peter Eisenman
HOUSE X
A full documentation of one of Eisenman's experimental houses
0–8478–0355–4 Rizzoli $40.00
0–8478–0346–5 Rizzoli pb $25.00

● Kenneth Frampton & others
THE ARCHITECTURE OF HIROMI FUJI
Twenty-five buildings and projects by a leading Japanese architect
0–8478–0818–1 Rizzoli pb $19.95

● Peter Arnell & Ted Bickford, editors
FRANK GEHRY: Buildings and Projects
The first comprehensive monograph on the renowned California architect
0–8478–0542–5 Rizzoli $45.00
0–8478–0543–3 Rizzoli pb $29.95

● Frank Gehry & others
THE ARCHITECTURE OF FRANK GEHRY
The catalog from the Museum of Modern Art's exhibition
0–8478–0763–0 Rizzoli pb $29.95

● David De Long
BRUCE GOFF: Towards Absolute Architecture
One of the most inventive and eccentric American architects
0–262–04097–2 MIT $50.00

● Werner Blaser, editor
MYRON GOLDSMITH: Concepts and Buildings
The first book to document the 40-year career of the Chicago architect, engineer, and partner with SOM, Mies van der Rohe, and Pierluigi Nervi
0–8478–0790–8 Rizzoli $25.00

● Karen Wheeler & Peter Arnell, editors
MICHAEL GRAVES: Buildings and Projects, 1966–1981
0–8478–0405–4 Rizzoli pb $29.95

● Peter Arnell & Ted Bickford, editors
CHARLES GWATHMEY AND ROBERT SIEGEL, ARCHITECTS
The distinctive designs of the New York-based firm, characterized by a late-Corbusian rationalism and a sensitive use of modern materials
0–06–433285–3 Harper & Row $50.00

● Peter Eisenman
JOHN HEJDUK: Seven Houses
A principal exponent of deconstructivism discusses the experimental works of the Dean of the Cooper Union School of Architecture
0–262–59015–8 MIT pb $15.50

● John Hejduk
MASK OF MEDUSA
A textbook of architectural ideas and a gallery of Hejduk's fantastic designs
0–8478–0567–0 Rizzoli $50.00

● Nory Miller
HELMUT JAHN
The commercial buildings of the Chicago-based architect have made him a celebrity in the world of real estate development
0–8478–0561–1 Rizzoli $45.00
0–8478–0562–X Rizzoli pb $29.95

● Carlton Knight III & Robert A. Stern, editors
PHILIP JOHNSON—JOHN BURGEE: Architecture, 1979–1985
Focuses on 25 major projects, predominantly high-rise buildings and cultural centers
0–8478–0658–8 Rizzoli $45.00

● Louis I. Kahn & Richard Saul Wurman
WHAT WILL BE HAS ALWAYS BEEN: The Words of Louis I. Kahn
Speeches, writings, and conversations
0–8478–0606–5 Rizzoli $45.00
0–8478–0607–3 Rizzoli pb $29.95

● Alex Krieger
THE ARCHITECTURE OF KALLMANN, McKINNELL AND WOOD
A Boston-based firm committed to the ennoblement of the public domain since the early 1960s
0–8478–0339–0 Rizzoli pb $25.00

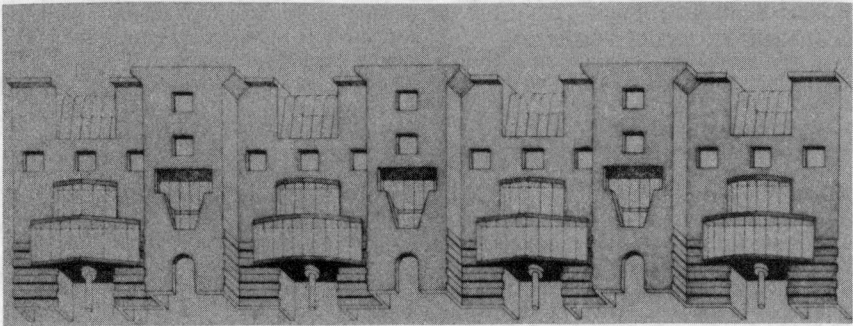

James Stirling's design for New York City townhouses (RIBA)

- Sonia Chao & Trevor Abramson
KOHN PEDERSON FOX: Buildings and Projects, 1976–1986
Talented designers overseeing the widespread commercial application of their generation's design tenets
0–8478–0748–7 Rizzoli $45.00
0–8478–0749–5 Rizzoli pb $29.95

- Rob Krier
ARCHITECTURAL COMPOSITIONS
A theoretical and visual analysis illustrating the creative process that informs Krier's practice and teaching
0–8478–0965–X Rizzoli $60.00

- Wolfgang Pehnt
LUCIEN KROLL: Buildings and Projects
The first monograph in English on the important Belgian architect
0–8478–0866–1 Rizzoli pb $29.95

- Kisho Kurokawa & Francois Chaslin
KISHO KUROKAWA
A leader of the renowned Japanese metabolist movement, Kurokawa first became widely recognized as an outstanding disciple of Kenzo Tange. This first monograph in English offers examples of his works and projects from 1979–1987
0–8478–0909–9 Rizzoli pb $25.00

- Serge Salat & Francoise Labbe
FUMIHIKO MAKI: An Aesthetic of Fragmentation
Works and projects from 1959–1985
0–8478–0905–6 Rizzoli pb $25.00

- Richard Meier
RICHARD MEIER: Architect
Meier's complete architectural works in a single handsome volume
0–8478–0496–8 Rizzoli $60.00
0–8478–0497–6 Rizzoli pb $40.00

- Kenneth Frampton
MITCHELL/GIURGOLA ARCHITECTS
The Philadelphia-New York firm has gained worldwide recognition for its sense of social responsibility
0–8478–0495–X Rizzoli $29.95

- Eugene Johnson
CHARLES MOORE: Buildings and Projects, 1949–1986
A well-illustrated survey of an important American architect and his witty, whimsical buildings
0–8478–0746–0 Rizzoli $45.00
0–8478–0759–2 Rizzoli pb $29.95

- Malcolm Quantrill
REIMA PIETILA: Architecture, Context and Modernism
The Finnish architect's work since the 1950s
0–8478–0635–9 Rizzoli pb $29.95

- José Rafael Moneo, editor
BORIS PODRECCA
The catalog of a recent exhibition documenting over 25 projects by this prominent Viennese architect
0–8478–0836–X Rizzoli pb $15.00

- James Stewart Polshek
JAMES STEWART POLSHEK: Context and Responsibility
A study of the architect's career to date, with photographs, plans, and drawings
0–8478–0876–9 Rizzoli $45.00
0–8478–0877–7 Rizzoli pb $29.95

- Francesco Dal Co, editor
KEVIN ROCHE
Roche's entire career, including a lengthy interview with the architect
0–8478–0677–4 Rizzoli pb $29.95

- Peter Arnell & Ted Bickford, editors
ALDO ROSSI: Buildings and Projects
The first complete monograph
Introduction by Vincent Scully
0–8478–0498–4 Rizzoli $45.00
0–8478–0499–2 Rizzoli pb $29.95

- Aldo Rossi
A SCIENTIFIC AUTOBIOGRAPHY
A charming presentation of the architect's repertoire
0–262–68041–6 MIT pb $10.95

- Francesco Dal Co & Giuseppe Mazzariol, editors
CARLO SCARPA: The Complete Works
Essays on the Venetian craftsman whose work was inspired by Frank Lloyd Wright
0–8478–0591–3 Rizzoli pb $37.50

- Kenneth Frampton, editor
ALVARO SIZA: Poetic Profession
An illuminating introduction to Siza's poetics of space, with Italian/English text
0–8478–0793–2 Rizzoli pb $29.95

- Margaret Reeve & others, editors
ALVARO SIZA: Figures and Configurations, Projects and Buildings, 1986–1988
A catalog of four projects
0–8478–0938–2 Rizzoli pb $20.00

- Robert A. M. Stern
ROBERT A. M. STERN: Buildings and Projects, 1965–1980
The designs and ideas of a leading exponent of postmodernism
0–8478–0400–3 Rizzoli pb $29.95

ROBERT A. M. STERN: Buildings and Projects, 1981–1986
Includes approximately 100 recent works, unrealized designs, and current projects
0–8478–0700–2 Rizzoli $45.00
0–8478–0704–5 Rizzoli pb $29.95

- Peter Arnell & Ted Bickford, editors
JAMES STIRLING: Buildings and Projects
Includes virtually every project by this internationally acclaimed architect, with 1000 illustrations
0–8478–0448–8 Rizzoli $45.00
0–8478–0449–6 Rizzoli pb $29.95

- James Stirling & others
JAMES STIRLING
Stirling's complex work and its concern with a postwar humanism expressed through a technological sensibility
0–312–43987–3 St. Martin's pb $14.95

- Stanislaus Von Moos
VENTURI, RAUCH AND SCOTT BROWN
The Philadelphia firm refined a clear design vocabulary through conventional building technique: function is expressed in terms of ornament and decoration
0–8478–0743–6 Rizzoli $60.00
0–8478–0745–2 Rizzoli pb $37.50

- Antonio Sanmartin, editor
VENTURI, RAUCH AND SCOTT BROWN
A balanced introduction with many reproductions
0–312–00712–4 Saint Martin's pb $29.95

POSTMODERNISM

- Kent Bloomer & Charles Moore
BODY, MEMORY AND ARCHITECTURE
Essays on context and memory in the experience of architecture
0–300–02142–9 Yale pb $12.95

- Paul Goldberger
ON THE RISE: Architecture and Design in a Post-Modern Age
Selections by the *New York Times* critic focusing on the eclecticism of the contemporary scene
0–14–007632–8 Penguin pb $8.95

- Charles Jencks
ARCHITECTURE TODAY
An engaging survey, offering a personal appraisal of late modern and postmodern work, with more than 500 illustrations
0–8109–1883–8 Abrams $75.00

THE LANGUAGE OF POSTMODERN ARCHITECTURE
Described by *Time* as "the main definer of Postmodernism," Jencks attacks the sterility of the modern movement and advocates the more flexible postmodern approach
0–8478–0571–9 Rizzoli $32.50
0–8478–0900–5 Rizzoli pb $29.95

• Heinrich Klotz, editor
POSTMODERN VISIONS: Drawings, Paintings and Models by Contemporary Architects
Winner of the International Architectural Critics' Award, this volume surveys the work of 35 contemporary architects
0–89659–569–2 Abbeville $55.00

• Sir Denys Lasdun
ARCHITECTURE IN AN AGE OF SCEPTICISM: A Practitioner's Anthology
Lasdun questions the basic assumptions of his previous theory and moves toward an idiosyncratic response to current theory
0–19–520445–X Oxford $45.00

• Paolo Portoghesi
POSTMODERN: The Architecture of the Post-Industrial Society
Inspired by the *Strada Novissima* at the 1980 Venice Biennale, an architect/critic explores recent developments
0–8478–0472–0 Rizzoli $29.95

• Aldo Rossi
THE ARCHITECTURE OF THE CITY
Questions the functionalist tenets of the modern movement, thereby setting the stage for the rediscovery of history as an architectural vocabulary and tool
0–262–68043–2 MIT pb $13.50

• Robert A. M. Stern
MODERN CLASSICISM
A personalized analysis of the reversion to a displaced vocabulary of classical forms and a rejection of the austere clarity of modern design
0–8478–0848–3 Rizzoli $45.00

• Robert Venturi
COMPLEXITY AND CONTRADICTION IN ARCHITECTURE
The manifesto that marked the theoretical origin of many postmodernist ideas
Introduction by Vincent Scully
0–87070–282–3 Little, Brown pb $12.95

Detail of Ricardo Bofill's Pyramid, Le Perthus

• Robert Venturi & others
LEARNING FROM LAS VEGAS: The Forgotten Symbolism of Architectural Form
The aesthetic messages conveyed by everyday visual reality
0–262–22020–2 MIT $30.00
0–262–72006–X MIT pb $11.95

• James Wines
DE-ARCHITECTURE
A controversial book of theory, opinion, and critical history on architecture, public art, and community spaces reflecting the philosophy of the architectural group SITE
0–8478–0861–0 Rizzoli $40.00
0–8478–0862–9 Rizzoli pb $25.00

Interior Decoration

"Whenever I pass through a city, I never fail to visit whatever illustrious furnished houses are open to outsiders. Galleries, churches, famous views, landscapes made immortal by the poets, yes, all of these find me far from indifferent; but for houses I have a special weakness. It's not only that I find myself more in touch with the past: the very arrangement of the furnishings acts on me like a spell. The odor of the furniture, of the wax on the floors, of the ancient rooms is as pleasing to me—or even more pleasing—than the scent of meadows in spring."—Mario Praz, *An Illustrated History of Interior Decoration*

GENERAL HISTORIES

• Victoria Ball
ARCHITECTURE AND INTERIOR DESIGN: Europe and America from the Colonial Era to Today
0–471–05161–6 Wiley pb $41.50

• Mark Hampton
ON DECORATING
A collection of *House & Garden* columns by the witty and knowledgeable American decorator, illustrated with his watercolors
0–394–57987–9 Random House $24.95

• John Pile
INTERIOR DESIGN
A wealth of detail and practical information on the basic issues in residential and commercial design. "Its 540 pages and 700 pictures alone make [it] a tome. But, for many amateurs and students of design, the comprehensiveness and insight of the text make it a kind of bible"—*NY Times*
0–8109–1121–3 Abrams $49.50

• Mario Praz
AN ILLUSTRATED HISTORY OF INTERIOR DECORATION: From Pompeii to Art Nouveau
A recent edition of this extraordinary book, first published in 1963, with a charming, scholarly text accompanied by watercolors and paintings. An indispensable reference
0–500–23358–6 Thames & Hudson $75.00

• Peter Thornton
AUTHENTIC DECOR: The Domestic Interior from 1620–1920
A history of decoration in Europe and the United States with period illustrations of furniture placement, porcelain arrangement on sideboards, wall coverings, and more, by the Victoria & Albert Museum curator
0–670–14228–X Viking $60.00

SEVENTEENTH CENTURY INTERIOR DECORATION IN ENGLAND, FRANCE, AND HOLLAND
0–300–02193–3 Yale $97.00
0–300–02776–1 Yale pb $25.00

AMERICAN DECORATION

"Rooms may be decorated in two ways: by a superficial application of ornament totally independent of structure, or by means of architectural features which are part of the organism of every house, inside as well as out."—Edith Wharton, *The Decoration of Houses*

Traditional

• Joseph Bryon
PHOTOGRAPHS OF NEW YORK INTERIORS AT THE TURN OF THE CENTURY
Includes the Astor and other famous residences
0–486–24863–1 Dover pb $9.95

• Helen Griffith
SOUTHERN INTERIORS
Unusual and opulent interiors
0–8487–0740–0 Oxmoor $35.00

• House & Garden
HOUSE & GARDEN'S BEST IN DECORATION
A collection of articles on houses decorated by prominent interior designers, showing the fashionable styles of the 1980s
0–394–56426–X Random House $34.50

• Robert King
THE VANDERBILT HOMES
Houses of the Gilded Age, from Fifth Avenue townhouses inspired by French châteaux to vast cabins in the Adirondacks to 100-room Newport "cottages"
0–8478–1027–5 Rizzoli $45.00

• Philip Langdon
AMERICAN HOUSES
A useful sourcebook, with plans and architectural drawings
0–941434–96–6 Stewart, Tabori & Chang $35.00

• David Larkin & others
COLONIAL: Design and the New World
Interiors and furniture
1–55670–043–1 Stewart, Tabori & Chang $45.00

- **Alison Leopard**
VICTORIAN SPLENDOUR: Recreating America's 19th-Century Interiors
Photographs of recent American houses decorated in the Victorian style. Includes sources for Victoriana and a list of Victorian houses open to the public
0–941434–83–4 Stewart, Tabori & Chang pb $18.95

- **Chris Casson Madden**
INTERIOR VISIONS: Great American Designers and the Showcase House
Where decorators produce rooms viewed by potential clients, and where the latest styles are often created
1–55670–038–5 Stewart, Tabori & Chang $45.00

- **Carleton Varney**
DRAPER TOUCH: The High Life and High Style of Dorothy Draper
Credited with inventing the profession of interior decorating in the United States, Draper's work is still influential today
0–13–219080–X Prentice-Hall $22.50

- **Edith Wharton & Ogden Codman**
THE DECORATION OF HOUSES
In this first American book on interior decoration, Mrs. Wharton explained her preference for French taste over the more prevalent ornate Victorian style
0–393–04468–8 Norton $14.95
0–393–00840–1 Norton pb $10.95

Modern

- **Joan Kron & Suzanne Slesin**
HIGH TECH: The Industrial Style and Sourcebook for the Home
Ideas for a sleek, modern look
0–517–53262 Crown $29.95

- **Tim Street Porter**
FREESTYLE: The New Architecture and Interior Design from Los Angeles
Vibrant colors, clean lines, and often humorous details characterize this style
0–941434–91–5 Stewart, Tabori & Chang $45.00

Rustic

- **Nora Burba**
DESERT SOUTHWEST
0–553–05200–4 Bantam $34.95

- **Mary Ellisor Emmerling**
AMERICAN COUNTRY: A Style and Source Book
A very successful book on country furniture, objects, and decorative touches
0–517–53846–6 Crown $35.00

- **Craig Gilborn**
ADIRONDACK FURNITURE
Imaginative, rustic furniture to inspire the home-carpenter
0–8109–1844–7 Abrams $60.00

- **Chappy Irvine**
FARMHOUSE
0–553–05199–7 Bantam $34.95

- **June Sprigg**
INNER LIGHT: The Shaker Legacy
0–394–53256–2 Knopf $32.00
0–394–73552–8 Knopf pb $22.95

SHAKER: Life, Work, and Art
An informative book on the Shakers and their simple and utilitarian buildings, furniture, and crafts
1–55670–011–3 Stewart, Tabori & Chang $30.00

SHAKER DESIGN
Exhibition catalog from the Whitney Museum
0–393–02338–9 Norton $40.00
0–393–30544–9 Norton pb $25.00

ENGLISH DECORATION

"It is in the country that the Englishman gives scope to his natural feelings . . . He manages to collect around him all the conveniences and elegances of polite life and to banish its restraints. His country seat abounds with every requisite, either for studious retirement, tasteful gratification, or rural exercise. Books, paintings, music, horses, dogs, and sporting implements of all kinds are at hand."—Washington Irving, *Sketch Book*

English mural decoration, 1778 (Victoria and Albert Museum)

Traditional

- **Geoffrey Beard**
CRAFTSMEN AND INTERIOR DECORATION IN ENGLAND, 1660–1820
A dictionary with over 700 names and 6000 entries
0–8419–0703–X Holmes & Meier $125.00

- **Jeremy Cooper**
VICTORIAN AND EDWARDIAN DECOR: From the Gothic Revival to Art Nouveau
0–89659–768–7 Abbeville $60.00

- **Mark Girouard**
LIFE IN THE ENGLISH COUNTRY HOUSE
An architectural history as well as an essential source for understanding the evolution of taste
0–300–02739–7 Yale $45.00
0–14–005406–4 Penguin pb $12.95

- **Thomas Hope**
HOUSEHOLD FURNITURE AND INTERIOR DECORATION: A Classic Style Book of the Regency Period
0–486–21710–8 Dover pb $7.95

- **Gervase Jackson-Stops & James Pipkin**
THE ENGLISH COUNTRY HOUSE: A Grand Tour
Architectural and decorative details in furniture, silver, carpets, clocks, and woodwork
0–8212–1598–1 NY Graphic Society $29.45

- **David Pearce**
THE GREAT HOUSES OF LONDON
A historical survey, beautifully illustrated
0–86565–063–2 Vendome $35.00

- **Doreen Yarwood**
ENGLISH INTERIORS: A Pictorial Guide and Glossary
0–7188–2579–9 Salem House $15.95

Contemporary

- **John Cornforth**
INSPIRATION OF THE PAST: Country House Taste in the 20th Century
How the British country house style has influenced current decorating trends
0–670–80180–1 Viking $30.00

- **Elizabeth Dickson**
THE ENGLISHWOMAN'S BEDROOM
Chintz, ruffles, and dogs
0–88162–087–4 Salem House $27.95

- **David Hicks**
DAVID HICKS STYLE AND DESIGN
The designs of this well-known British decorator incorporate modern elements in traditional settings
0–316–36070–8 Little, Brown $29.95

Min Hogg & Wendy Harrop
INTERIORS
International selections from the British *World of Interiors* magazine. Houses of great style are imaginatively presented
Introduction by Mark Hampton
0–517–57106–4 Crown $40.00

- **Alvilde Lees-Milne & Derry Moore**
THE ENGLISHMAN'S ROOM
The Englishman's often eccentric and highly personal taste
0–88162–214–1 Salem House $27.50

- **Caroline Seebohm**
ENGLISH COUNTRY: Living in England's Private Houses
A guided tour of stately homes as lived-in houses, with separate chapters on the decorative elements
Photographs by Christopher Simon Sykes
0–317–66569–3 Crown $35.00

- **Suzanne Slesin**
ENGLISH STYLE
Everyday living, in everyday houses
0–517–55276–0 Crown $35.00

• John Stefanidis & Mary Henderson
ROOMS: Design and Decoration
The Greek-born decorator's tastes and
style, from an 18th-century country house
to a Greek island villa
0–8478–0962–5 Rizzoli $45.00

Irish

• Sybil Connolly, editor
IN AN IRISH HOUSE
The charm and warmth of Irish houses,
cottages, and castles
Foreword by Molly Keane
0–517–570297 Crown $40.00

• Marianne Heron
IN THE HOUSES OF IRELAND
1–55670–045–8 Stewart, Tabori & Chang $45.00

FRENCH DECORATION

"I have often said to myself that if I were not
a man of letters, if I had not got money,
my chosen profession would have been to
invent interiors for rich people. I should
have loved being allowed to have my own
way by some banker who would have given
me *carte blanche* to work out the decoration
and furniture of a palace with just four bare
walls, using what I could find from dealers,
artists, modern industry, and in my own
head."—Edmond de Goncourt

• Marie-France Boyer & Philippe
Girardeau
**PRIVATE PARIS: The Thirty Most
Beautiful Apartments**
Elegant interiors, from minimal to
cluttered, sophisticated to bohemian
0–89659–922–1 Abbeville $50.00

• Linda Dannenberg & others
**PIERRE DEUX'S NORMANDY: A French
Country Style and Source Book**
"Lush countryside and half-timbered
houses filled with furniture and accessories
indigenous to the area"—*Daily News*
0–517–56079–8 Crown $35.00

• Claude Fregnac & Wayne Andrews
THE GREAT HOUSES OF PARIS
"A superb tour of some of the most
glorious dwellings in the world"—*Chicago
Tribune*
0–670–34972–0 Vendome $50.00

• Pierre Moulin & others
**PIERRE DEUX'S FRENCH COUNTRY: A
Style and Source Book**
The French country look, from the owners
of the successful Provençal store. Includes
photographs of Provence and its gardens
0–517–548787–2 Crown $40.00

• Daphne de Saint-Sauveur
**THE FRENCH TOUCH: Decoration and
Design in the Most Beautiful Homes of
France**
Arranged geographically, from a cottage in
Normandy to a grand apartment in Paris,

*Nineteenth-century French "causeuse," from
Le Moniteur de l'Ameublement*

the houses reflect the styles of decoration
typical of the locale
0–8212–1712–7 NY Graphic Society $35.00

• Suzanne Slesin
FRENCH STYLE
The details of French houses today
0–517–54580–2 Crown $35.00

OTHER DECORATIVE STYLES

• Elizabeth Gaynor
SCANDINAVIAN LIVING DESIGN
Forest manors, cozy cottages, stark modern
houses: important influences on
contemporary European and American
designers
1–55670–009–1 Stewart, Tabori & Chang $40.00

Teiji Itoh
**THE ELEGANT JAPANESE HOUSE:
Traditional Sukiya Architecture**
A beautiful book on what is considered
the culmination of traditional Japanese
domestic architecture
0–8348–1500–1 Tuttle $80.00

Edward Morse
**JAPANESE HOMES AND THEIR
SURROUNDINGS**
The most authoritative description of
Japanese domestic architecture, a classic
first published in 1886
0–8048–0998–4 Tuttle pb $8.50

Suzanne Slesin & others
JAPANESE STYLE
How the Japanese live today: from old
farmhouses to contemporary homes
0–517–56080–1 Crown $35.00

• Catherine Sabino & others
ITALIAN COUNTRY
0–517–56017–8 Crown $35.00

ITALIAN STYLE
From traditional to modern interior design
0–517–54614–0 Crown $35.00

• Suzanne Slesin
CARIBBEAN STYLE
0–517–55611–1 Crown $40.00

GREEK STYLE
From fishermen's houses to holiday villas
0–517–56874–8 Crown $35.00

• William Warren
THAI STYLE
Humble and lavish houses, traditional
Siamese motifs, Chinese- and Indian-
influenced styles, and modern adaptations
0–8478–1043–7 Rizzoli $35.00

20TH-CENTURY DECORATIVE MOVEMENTS

• Stephen Calloway
TWENTIETH CENTURY DECORATION
Arranged chronologically, topics include
the revival of historic styles and the
influence of decorating magazines.
"Authentic contemporary visual data on
how the fashionable, the grand, the artistic
and the self-conscious have set about
decorating their houses"—*TLS*
0–8478–0886–6 Rizzoli $100.00

• Michael Collins
**TOWARDS POST-MODERNISM:
Decorative Arts and Design Since 1851**
The evolution of European and American
decorative arts from the Great Exhibition
of 1851 to contemporary groups like
Memphis. Includes furniture, silver, china,
jewelry, and architectural ornamentation
0–8212–1687–2 NY Graphic Society pb $19.95

• Melanie Fleischmann
**IN THE NEOCLASSICAL STYLE:
Empire, Biedermeier, and the
Contemporary**
0–500–23521–X Thames & Hudson $35.00

• Dan Klein
**DECORATIVE ART, 1880–1980: Arts and
Crafts, Art Nouveau, Art Deco, Postwar
Design**
Glass, furniture, textiles, bronzes, jewelry
0–7148–8025–6 Salem House $50.00

Arts and Crafts

"The teachings of Philip Webb, William
Morris and Charles Eastlake which had in-
spired the Arts and Crafts Movement in
England were heeded in America with en-
thusiasm by Gustav Stickley in the 1890s.
He evolved an extreme variant of the honest
Arts and Crafts manner, the so-called 'Crafts-
man' style."—Peter Thornton, *Authentic
Decor*

• Peter Stansky
**REDESIGNING THE WORLD: William
Morris, the 1880s, and the Arts and Crafts**
Morris' ideas for good design, combined
with social reform, took form in the Arts
and Crafts movement
0–691–06616–7 Princeton $29.00
0–691–01411–6 Princeton pb $12.95

• Tod Volpe & Beth Cathers
**TREASURES OF THE AMERICAN ARTS
AND CRAFTS MOVEMENT, 1890–1920**
A scholarly study, lavishly illustrated with
works by Stickley, Tiffany, Roycroft, and
others
0–8109–1695–9 Abrams $49.50

Art Nouveau

"There has been much laughing at *Art Nouveau,* but no one can deny that, after the last gasp of Neoclassicism in the chaotic eclecticism of the 19th century, this style offered the first kind of decoration with a well-defined personality. . . . The furniture, which in the classic style had been independent cubes and parallelipipeds, was now reabsorbed into the walls, camouflaged, melting into the general decoration of which they became fixed parts."—Mario Praz, *An Illustrated History of Interior Decoration*

- Mario Amaya
  ART NOUVEAU
  0–8052–0784–8 Schocken pb $9.95

- Elena Borisova & Gregory Sternin
  RUSSIAN ART NOUVEAU
  Painting, sculpture, graphic art, and the decorative arts; superb photographs
  0–8478–0994–3 Rizzoli $95.00

- Stephan Madsen
  SOURCES OF ART NOUVEAU
  A complete study of its sources, designers, and continuing influence
  0–306–70733–0 Da Capo $59.50
  0–306–80024–1 Da Capo pb $10.95

- Gabriel Weisberg
  ART NOUVEAU BING: Paris Style, 1900
  Superb reproductions of works designed and made by Siegfried Bing, art dealer and dynamic figure in the decorative arts in Paris
  0–8109–1486–7 Abrams $40.00

- Siegfried Wichmann
  JUGENDSTIL ART NOUVEAU
  Floral and functional forms of the German and Austrian version of art nouveau: a study of its origins, development, and international connections, focusing on the works of Hoffmann, Thonet, and others
  0–8212–1607–4 NY Graphic Society $44.00

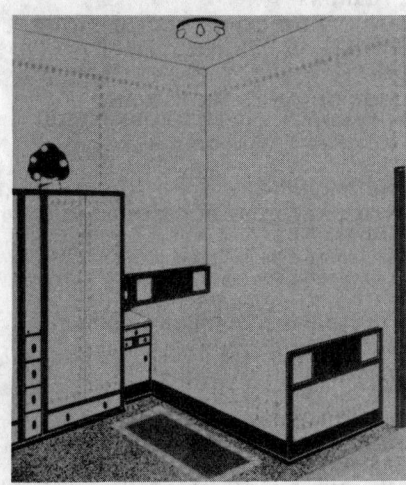

Viennese Secession bedroom, c. 1901, from Authentic Decor *by Peter Thornton* (Viking)

Art Deco

- Peter Adam
  EILEEN GRAY, ARCHITECT/ DESIGNER: A Biography
  0–8109–0996–0 Abrams $39.95

- Victor Arwas
  ART DECO
  0–8109–0691–0 Abrams $49.50

- Jean-Paul Bouillon
  ART DECO, 1900–1940
  Beautiful and extravagant furniture, textiles, interior design, and fine arts
  0–8478–0988–9 Rizzoli $75.00

- Florence Camard
  RUHLMANN: Master of Art Deco
  The great furniture designer
  0–8109–1559–6 Abrams $49.50

- Alastair Duncan
  AMERICAN ART DECO
  0–8109–1850–1 Abrams $49.50

- Alastair Duncan, editor
  THE ENCYCLOPEDIA OF ART DECO
  0–525–24613–4 Dutton $29.95

- Dan Klein & others
  IN THE DECO STYLE
  0–8478–0633–2 Rizzoli $29.95

Modern and Contemporary Design

- Andrea Branzi
  THE HOT HOUSE: Italian New Wave Design
  0–262–02211–7 MIT $30.00
  0–262–52107–5 MIT pb $15.00

- Le Corbusier
  THE DECORATIVE ART OF TODAY
  0–262–62055–3 MIT pb $12.50

- Andrea DiNoto
  ART PLASTIC
  The history of plastic and plastic objects
  0–89659–437–8 Abbeville $45.00
  0–89659–696–6 Abbeville pb $24.95

- Paul Frankl
  NEW DIMENSIONS: The Decorative Arts of Today in Words and Pictures
  Foreword by Frank Lloyd Wright
  0–306–70741–1 Da Capo $42.50

- David Hanks
  THE INTERIORS AND DECORATIVE DESIGNS OF DONALD DESKEY: With Essays by Donald Deskey and Jeffrey Meikle
  0–525–24360–7 Dutton $45.00

- Thomas Hine
  POPULUXE
  0–394–54593–1 Knopf $29.45
  0–394–74014–9 Knopf pb $16.95

- Nikolaus Pevsner
  PIONEERS OF MODERN DESIGN
  0–14–055211–1 Penguin pb $7.95

- Barbara Radice
  MEMPHIS: Research, Experiences, Results, Failures and Successes of New Design
  0–8478–0569–7 Rizzoli $35.00

MARK HAMPTON: Some Favorite Books on Decoration

Peter Inskip & others
EDWIN LUTYENS
0–312–23919–X St. Martin's $35.00
0–312–23918–1 St. Martin's pb $24.95

Michelangelo Muraro
VENETIAN VILLAS
0–8478–0762–2 Rizzoli $85.00

John Cornforth
THE INSPIRATION OF THE PAST: Country House Taste in the 20th Century
0–670–80180–1 Viking $30.00

John Morley
THE MAKING OF THE ROYAL PAVILION
Out of print

Charles McCorquodale
HISTORY OF THE INTERIOR
0–86565–032–2 Vendome $45.00

Mary Gilliatt
DREAM HOUSES
0–316–31364–5 Little, Brown $35.00

Benjamin Blom
McKIM, MEAD & WHITE
Out of print

Gertrude Jekyll
GARDEN ORNAMENT
0–907462–16–2 Antique Collectors $59.50

O. Hill & John Cornforth
ENGLISH COUNTRY HOUSES: Caroline, 1625–1685
0–907462–78–2 Antique Collectors $49.50

James Milne
ENGLISH COUNTRY HOUSES: Baroque, 1685–1715
1–85149–043–4 Antique Collectors $49.50

Christopher Hussey
ENGLISH COUNTRY HOUSES: Early, Middle, and Late Georgian Houses
0–907462–68–5 Apollo $195.00

Mario Praz
AN ILLUSTRATED HISTORY OF INTERIOR DECORATION: From Pompeii to Art Nouveau
0–500–23358–6 Thames & Hudson $75.00

Peter Thornton
AUTHENTIC DECOR: The Domestic Interior from 1620 to 1920
0–670–142228–X Viking $125.00

- Whitney Museum of American Art
HIGH STYLES: 20th-Century American Design
Introduction by Lisa Phillips
0–671–60692–1 Summit $35.00

European Decorative Arts

GENERAL

- Geoffrey De Bellaigue
FURNITURE, CLOCKS AND GILT BRONZES
Fine objects from the Waddesdon Collection, in two volumes
0–7078–0010–2 Sotheby (set) $150.00

- Hugh Honour & John Fleming
DICTIONARY OF THE DECORATIVE ARTS
This excellent book by two art historians includes furniture, jewelry, pottery, and textiles with brief entries on artists, materials, and techniques. An important reference book
0–06–011936–5 Harper & Row $30.00

- Simon Jervis
THE PENGUIN DICTIONARY OF DESIGN AND DESIGNERS
From Renaissance goldsmiths and engravers to Bauhaus designers. The brief biographies include artists and architects from 1450 to the present
0–14–051089–3 Penguin pb $8.95

- Owen Jones
THE GRAMMAR OF ORNAMENT: All 100 Color Plates from the Folio Edition of the Great Victorian Sourcebook of Historic Design
A reference book on style, first published in 1856. Includes Oriental, primitive, classical, medieval, and Renaissance design
0–486–25463–1 Dover pb $10.95

- Philippa Lewis & Gillian Darley
DICTIONARY OF ORNAMENT
0–394–50931–5 Random House $29.95

- Harold Osborne, editor
THE OXFORD COMPANION TO THE DECORATIVE ARTS
An indispensable one-volume reference
0–19–281863–5 Oxford $18.95

Guides for Collectors

- John Marion
SOTHEBY'S INTERNATIONAL PRICE GUIDE: Antiques and Collectibles, 1988–89
Includes 8000 objects from the lower end of the art market, with special features on Americana. A valuable price guide
0–85667–359–5 Sotheby $35.00

- Judith & Martin Miller
MILLER'S INTERNATIONAL ANTIQUE PRICE GUIDE
0–670–82489–5 Viking $24.95

- Rita Reif
RITA REIF'S THE NEW YORK TIMES WORLD GUIDE TO ANTIQUES SHOPPING
International sources for antiques and guides to the antique shops, by the *New York Times* columnist
0–8129–1251–9 Times pb $14.95

- Lucilla Watson
UNDERSTANDING ANTIQUES
0–670–81808–9 Viking $19.95

- Gillian Wilson
SELECTIONS FROM THE DECORATIVE ARTS IN THE J. PAUL GETTY MUSEUM
0–89236–037–2 Getty Museum $39.95
0–89236–050–X Getty Museum pb $29.95

- Mark Wrey, editor
CHRISTIE'S REVIEW OF THE SEASON, 1988
The annual report from the British auction house, with extensive illustrations and record prices
0–7148–8054–X Salem House $50.00

FURNITURE

- Louise Boger
THE COMPLETE GUIDE TO FURNITURE STYLES
From ancient Greece to the present; especially detailed on the great periods of French and English furniture. Over 600 illustrations from important collections
0–684–17641–6 Scribners pb $28.50

- Charles Boyce
DICTIONARY OF FURNITURE
The most comprehensive one-volume dictionary of furniture terminology: styles, manufacture, and makers in all countries
0–8160–1042–0 Facts On File $29.95
0–8050–0752–0 Henry Holt pb $15.95

- Florence De Dampierre
THE BEST OF PAINTED FURNITURE
Furniture from all periods; well-illustrated
0–8478–0804–1 Rizzoli $35.00

Wallace Nutting
FURNITURE TREASURY
The essential reference book on furniture of all types
Volumes 1 & 2
0–02–590980–0 Macmillan $42.50
Volume 3
0–02–591040–X Macmillan $32.50

- Marian Page
FURNITURE DESIGNED BY ARCHITECTS
The work of 26 prominent architects, from Kent and Adams to William Morris and Charles Eames
0–8230–7181–2 Watson-Guptill pb $16.95

Eighteenth-century French chair (Metropolitan Museum)

- Christopher Payne
NINETEENTH CENTURY EUROPEAN FURNITURE
A complete and extensively illustrated guide to the often whimsical 19th-century styles
1–85149–001–9 Antique Collectors $89.50

English Furniture

"Chippendale chairs imparted a lesson of sanity and balance. There was no attempt to conceal the practical purpose of the piece, asserted by its simple solid, straight legs. But on the back of the chair, delicately varied in Rococo or Gothic or exotic motifs and crowned with Cupid's bow, the decorative imagination was expressed."—Mario Praz, *An Illustrated History of Interior Decoration*

- J. Andrews
PRICE GUIDE TO BRITISH ANTIQUE FURNITURE
0–907462–79–0 Antique Collectors $49.50

PRICE GUIDE TO VICTORIAN, EDWARDIAN AND 1920 FURNITURE
0–902028–89–8 Antique Collectors $49.50

- Geoffrey Beard
NATIONAL TRUST BOOK OF ENGLISH FURNITURE
0–670–80141–0 Viking $20.00
0–14–006607–1 Penguin pb $12.95

- Geoffrey Beard & Judith Goodison
ENGLISH FURNITURE, 1500–1840
0–7148–8029–9 Salem House $45.00

- Herbert Cescinsky
ENGLISH FURNITURE FROM GOTHIC TO SHERATON
0–317–54989–8 Apollo $26.00
0–486–21929–1 Dover pb $13.95

- Frances Collard
REGENCY FURNITURE
0–907462–51–0 Antique Collectors $89.50

✉ TO ORDER BOOKS AS GIFTS, SEE PAGE 1

- **Ralph Edwards**
  THE DICTIONARY OF ENGLISH FURNITURE
  Three volumes
  1–85149–037–X Antique Collectors (set) $150.00

- **Ralph Fastnedge**
  SHERATON FURNITURE
  0–907462–47–2 Apollo $49.50

- **George Hepplewhite**
  THE CABINET-MAKER AND UPHOLSTERER'S GUIDE
  A 1794 manual
  0–486–22183–0 Dover pb $6.95

- **F. Lewis Hinckley**
  HEPPLEWHITE, SHERATON AND REGENCY FURNITURE
  0–8147–3446–4 NYU $65.00

  QUEEN ANNE AND GEORGIAN LOOKING GLASSES: Old English and Early American
  0–8147–3447–2 NYU $60.00

- **Thomas Hope**
  HOUSEHOLD FURNITURE AND INTERIOR DECORATION
  Facsimile of the book that announced the Regency style
  0–486–21710–8 Dover pb $7.95

- **Gervase Jackson-Stops, editor**
  THE TREASURE HOUSES OF BRITAIN: 500 Years of Private Patronage and Art Collecting
  Fine and decorative arts from private collections
  0–300–03533–0 Yale pb $35.00

- **Edward Joy**
  ENGLISH FURNITURE, 1800–1851
  A detailed look at the Regency style, and the Classical and Gothic revivals
  0–7063–6676–X David & Charles $65.00

French Furniture

"Under Louis XIV came that sharp distinction between court furniture and bourgeois furniture which lasted up until the Neoclassical period: the bourgeois credenza, used to display handsome pottery, corresponded to the patrician cabinet, used for keeping precious objects."—Mario Praz, *An Illustrated History of Interior Decoration*

- **Yvonne Brunhammer & others**
  L'ART DE VIVRE: Decorative Arts and Design in France, 1789–1989
  The finest in French furniture, tableware, clothes, jewelry, and design
  0–86565–976–1 Vendome $60.00

- **William Rieder**
  FRANCE, 1700–1800
  A small but thorough guide to the decorative arts
  0–87633–052–9 Philadelphia Museum pb $3.50

- **Francis Watson**
  WRIGHTSMAN COLLECTION: Furniture, Snuffboxes, Silver, Porcelain
  Objects from the fine French furniture collection, housed at the Metropolitan Museum
  0–87099–105–1 Metropolitan Museum $65.00

Other European Furniture

- **Antoine Cheneviere**
  THE GOLDEN AGE OF RUSSIAN FURNITURE, 1780–1850
  Extravagant wood furniture, decorated with metals, porcelain, and precious stones. Includes objects from the collections of Catherine the Great
  0–86565–099–3 Rizzoli $60.00

- **Angus Wilkie**
  BIEDERMEIER
  0–89659–749–0 Abbeville $49.95

Modern Furniture

- **Alvar Aalto**
  ALVAR AALTO FURNITURE
  From the first piece (1919) to bentwood creations, with original sketches and designs
  0–262–13206–0 MIT $27.50
  0–262–51040–5 MIT pb $12.50

- **Roger Billcliffe**
  MACKINTOSH FURNITURE
  0–525–24317–8 Dutton $19.95
  0–525–48175–3 Dutton pb $10.95

  CHARLES RENNIE MACKINTOSH: The Complete Furniture, Furniture Drawings and Interior Designs
  0–525–24496–4 Dutton $65.00

- **Arthur Danto**
  397 CHAIRS
  A diverse selection of chairs made in the 1970s and 1980s included in an exhibition at the Architectural League, introduced by "The Seat of the Soul" written by the philosopher and art critic
  0–810901698–3 Abrams $24.95

- **Renato De Fusco**
  LE CORBUSIER, DESIGNER: Furniture, 1929
  An illustrated study
  0–8120–5148–3 Barron's $24.95

- **Denise Domergue**
  ARTISTS DESIGN FURNITURE
  Furniture by contemporary artists
  0–8109–0932–4 Abrams $40.00

- **Peter Dormer**
  THE NEW FURNITURE: Trends and Traditions
  Invaluable on modern furniture, examining its history, with hundreds of international designs
  0–500–23492–2 Thames & Hudson $40.00

- **Marc Emery**
  FURNITURE BY ARCHITECTS: 500 International Masterpieces of 20th-Century Design and Where to Buy Them
  0–8109–0902–2 Abrams $49.50

- **Karl Mang**
  HISTORY OF MODERN FURNITURE
  From the 19th century to the present, including pieces by Thonet and Mies van der Rohe
  0–8109–1066–7 Abrams pb $29.95

- **Christopher Wilk**
  MARCEL BREUER: Furniture and Interior Design
  0–87070–264–5 Museum of Modern Art $22.50
  0–87070–263–7 Museum of Modern Art pb $12.50

PORCELAIN AND POTTERY

"The most beautiful vessels and plates of porcelain that one can describe are made here [in China] . . . And there is plenty there and a great scale, so great that for one Venetian groat you would actually have three bowls so beautiful that none would know how to devise them better."—Marco Polo

▶ **See also East Asian Art**

- **Peter Bradshaw**
  18TH CENTURY ENGLISH PORCELAIN FIGURES
  0–902028–83–9 Antique Collectors $62.50

- **Elisabeth Cameron**
  THE ENCYCLOPEDIA OF POTTERY AND PORCELAIN, 1800–1960
  0–8160–1225–3 Facts On File $40.00

- **A.W. Coysh & R.K. Henrywood**
  THE DICTIONARY OF BLUE AND WHITE POTTERY
  0–907462–06–5 Antique Collectors $69.50

- **Geoffrey de Bellaigue**
  THE LOUIS XVI SERVICE: The Sèvres Porcelain in the Collection of Her Majesty the Queen
  A sumptuous book describing the service made for Marie Antoinette's personal use at Versailles
  0–521–26637–8 Cambridge $195.00

Plate from the "Service Rousseau," decorated by Bracquemond (Musée d'Orsay)

- John Esten
BLUE AND WHITE CHINA
Blue-and-white porcelain from Yüan dynasty China through its European production in the 19th century, describing its influences and changes
0–316–28349–5 Little, Brown $35.00

- Geoffrey Godden
BRITISH PORCELAIN: An Illustrated Guide
0–317–65521–3 David & Charles $75.00

ENGLISH CHINA
0–09–158300–4 David & Charles $65.00

- David Howard
CHINESE ARMORIAL PORCELAIN
By the leading expert in Chinese export porcelain
0–571–09811–8 Faber & Faber $225.00

- Leonard Griffin, Louis & Susan Meisel
CLARICE CLIFF: The Bizarre Affair
The first book on the designs of the Art Deco potter, colorful and informative
0–8109–2323–8 Abrams pb $19.95

- Peter Lane
CERAMIC FORM
Contemporary ceramics and pottery around the world
0–8478–0889–0 Rizzoli $35.00

- Peter Meister & Horst Reber
EUROPEAN PORCELAIN OF THE 18TH CENTURY
0–8014–1443–1 Cornell $95.00

- Herbert, Peter & Nancy Schiffer
CHINESE EXPORT PORCELAIN: Standard Patterns and Forms, 1780–1880
0–916838–01–3 Schiffer $37.50

- Francis & Gillian Watson
MOUNTED ORIENTAL PORCELAIN IN THE J. PAUL GETTY MUSEUM
0–89236–034–8 Getty Museum $49.95

Lamps

- Wolf Uecker
ART NOUVEAU AND ART DECO LAMPS AND CANDLESTICKS
From simple candlesticks to elaborate candelabras and electric lamps
0–89659–668–0 Abbeville $75.00

GLASS

- R.J. Charleston
ENGLISH GLASS AND THE GLASS USED IN ENGLAND, CIRCA 400–1940
0–04–748003–3 Unwin Hyman $40.00

- R.J. Charleston & others
GLASS AND ENAMELS
Illustrated from the superb Waddesdon collection of James de Rothschild, with especially fine examples of French works
0–7078–0066–8 Sotheby $120.00

- Albane Dolez
GLASS ANIMALS: 3500 Years of Artistry and Design
From early Egyptian objects to contemporary designs, including the work of such masters as Gallé and Tiffany
0–8109–1034–9 Abrams $45.00

- Ray & Lee Grover
CARVED AND DECORATED EUROPEAN ART GLASS
0–8048–0707–8 Tuttle $55.00

- James Mackay
GLASS PAPERWEIGHTS
0–7063–6668–9 David & Charles $34.95

- Cyril Manley
DECORATIVE VICTORIAN GLASS
A comprehensive overview with more than 400 illustrated objects, a trademark listing, a chapter on identification, and an index of designs
0–7063–6644–1 David & Charles $34.95

- Harold Newman
AN ILLUSTRATED DICTIONARY OF GLASS
From Roman through modern times
0–500–23262–8 Thames & Hudson $29.95
0–500–27451–7 Thames & Hudson pb $18.95

20th Century Glass

- Victor Arwas
GLASS: Art Nouveau to Art Deco
The work of 120 glassmakers, from 19th-century English cameos to American and European designers of the late 1930s
0–8109–1028–4 Abrams $65.00

- François Charpentier & others
GALLE
The art nouveau glassmaker
0–8109–2390–4 Abrams pb $50.00

- Nicholas Dawes
LALIQUE GLASS
0–517–55835–1 Crown $27.50

SILVER

- Claude Blair
THE HISTORY OF SILVER
0–345–34576–2 Ballantine $40.00

- Vanessa Brett
THE SOTHEBY'S DIRECTORY OF SILVER, 1600–1940
European and American silver, with 2000 illustrations of objects grouped by country and maker
0–85667–193–2 Sotheby $57.50

- Mark Clark & David McFadden
TREASURES FROM THE TABLE: Silver from the Chrysler Museum
Sixteenth- through 20th-century masterpieces from Europe and America, with an essay on table silver
1–55595–011–6 Hudson Hills $35.00

- M. Clayton
THE COLLECTOR'S DICTIONARY OF THE SILVER AND GOLD OF GREAT BRITAIN AND NORTH AMERICA
0–907462–57–X Antique Collectors $89.50

- Philippa Glanville
SILVER IN ENGLAND
0–8419–1139–8 Allen & Unwin $85.00

- Carl Hernmarck
THE ART OF THE EUROPEAN SILVERSMITH, 1430–1830
Two lavishly illustrated volumes
0–85667–034–0 Sotheby $195.00

- John Luddington
STARTING TO COLLECT SILVER
0–907462–48–0 Antique Collectors $49.50

- Harold Newman
AN ILLUSTRATED DICTIONARY OF SILVERWARE
British and American silverware, its decoration, makers, techniques, and styles. From 1500 to the present, with over 2300 entries
0–500–23456–6 Thames & Hudson $39.95

- Ian Pickford
SILVERFLATWARE: English, Irish and Scottish, 1660–1980
0–907462–35–9 Antique Collectors $59.95

- Seymour Wyler
THE BOOK OF OLD SILVER: English, American, Foreign
0–517–00089–X Crown $14.95

OBJETS DE VERTU AND OBJETS D'ART

"It is perhaps not uninstructive to note that we have no English word to describe the class of household ornaments which French speech has provided with at least three designations, each indicating a delicate and almost imperceptible gradation of quality. In place of *bric-à-brac, bibelots, objets d'art,* we have only knickknacks."—Edith Wharton, *The Decoration of Houses*

- Abrams Editors
IVORY: An International History and Illustrated Survey with a Guide for Collectors
0–8109–1118–3 Abrams $67.50

LACQUER: An International History and Illustrated Survey
From the sophisticated wares of 16th-century China and 17th-century Japan to its European and American adaptations
0–8109–1279–1 Abrams $75.00

- Serge Grandjean & others
GOLD BOXES
From the fine Waddesdon Collection of James de Rothschild
0–7078–0023–4 Sotheby $120.00

• Charles Jackson
ENGLISH GOLDSMITHS AND THEIR MARKS: A History of the Goldsmiths and Plate Workers of England, Scotland, and Ireland
0–486–21206–8 Dover $34.95

• Daphne Poskett
MINIATURES: Dictionary and Guide
1–85149–063–9 Antique Collectors $89.50

Christopher Forbes
FABERGE EGGS: Imperial Russian Fantasies
0–8109–2227–4 Abrams pb $12.95

Geza von Habsburg
FABERGE
The extensive catalogue of the 1987 Munich exhibition
0–86565–108–6 Vendome $85.00

Alexander von Solodhoff
THE ART OF CARL FABERGE
The work of the jeweler to the czars, including Easter eggs, bejeweled bell pulls, tiny animals, and boxes
0–517–57124–2 Crown $15.95

RUGS AND CARPETS

• Lee Allane
ORIENTAL RUGS: A Practical Guide
0–500–27517–3 Thames & Hudson pb $14.95

• David Black, editor
THE MACMILLAN ATLAS OF RUGS AND CARPETS: A Comprehensive Guide for the Buyer and Collector
0–02–511120–5 Macmillan $29.95

• M.S. Dimand & Jean Mailey
ORIENTAL RUGS IN THE METROPOLITAN MUSEUM OF ART
0–87099–124–8 Metropolitan Museum $45.00

• Edwin Gans-Ruedin
THE SPLENDOR OF PERSIAN CARPETS
Their manufacture, the meaning of the decorative motifs, and the designs. "An authoritative work made more inviting by the extraordinary beauty of 252 color plates"—*Newsweek*
0–8478–0179–9 Rizzoli $100.00

• Alastair Hull & Nicholas Barnard
LIVING WITH KILIMS
A history of the popular flat-weave rugs from the Middle East, with advice on buying and restoration
0–517–57125–0 Crown $40.00

• Charles Jacobsen
ORIENTAL RUGS: A Complete Guide
0–8048–0451–6 Tuttle $38.95

• Aram K. Jerrehian, Jr.
ORIENTAL RUG PRIMER: Buying and Understanding New Oriental Rugs
Covers each country, with a glossary of terms and color illustrations
0–89471–078–8 Running Press $24.80
0–89471–077–X Running Press pb $12.95

TEXTILES AND WALLPAPER

• Agnes Geijer
A HISTORY OF TEXTILE ART: A Selective Account
0–85667–055–3 Sotheby $29.95

• Monique Lévi-Strauss
THE CASHMERE SHAWL
A history of the exotic shawls from Kashmir, brought to France by officers in Napoleon's Egyptian campaign
0–8109–1045–4 Abrams $65.00

• Charles Oman & Jean Hamilton
WALLPAPERS: An International History and Illustrated Survey from the Victoria & Albert Museum
From the 16th century to the present, divided into three sections: anonymous, pattern books, and designers
0–8109–1778–5 Abrams $85.00

• The Victoria & Albert Museum
ROCOCO SILK, ORNATE WALLPAPERS, INDIAN FLORAL PATTERNS, AND DECORATIVE ENDPAPERS
Three small books with beautiful illustrations of unusual designs from the museum's collections
0–8109–1717–3 Abrams $37.50

• The Victoria & Albert Museum
NOVELTY FABRICS, DESIGNS FOR SHAWLS, JAPANESE STENCILS, THIRTIES FLORAL FABRICS
Fabrics depicting Felix the Cat, cashmere shawls, Japanese patterns, and floral designs are beautifully reproduced in this set of small-sized books
0–8109–1738–6 Abrams $40.00

American Decorative Arts

GENERAL

• G. Bernard & others
THE COUNTRY LIFE ANTIQUES HANDBOOK
Essential information on a vast range of antiques and curios including furniture, china, silver, glass, and other collectibles
0–87226–163–8 Bedrick $39.95

• Doreen Burke, Alice Frelinghuysen & others
IN PURSUIT OF BEAUTY: Americans and the Aesthetic Movement
A Metropolitan Museum exhibition catalog. Includes examples from all the decorative arts of the Aesthetic Movement, 1870–1880
0–8478–0768–1 Rizzoli $65.00
0–87099–468–9 Metropolitan Museum pb $35.00

• Jay Cantor
WINTERTHUR
0–8109–1785–8 Abrams $49.50

• Wendy Cooper
IN PRAISE OF AMERICA: American Decorative Arts, 1650—1830
0–394–50994–3 Knopf $25.00

• Marshall Davidson & Elizabeth Stillinger
THE AMERICAN WING
The Metropolitan Museum's extensive collection of American decorative arts, painting, and sculpture since the 17th century, including period rooms with authentic furnishings
Foreword by Phillipe de Montebello
0–87099–309–7 Metropolitan Museum $24.95
0–87099–238–4 Metropolitan Museum pb $9.95

• Mary Emmerling & Richard Trask
COLLECTING AMERICAN COUNTRY: How to Select, Maintain and Display Country Pieces
0–517–54957–3 Crown $35.00

• Bruce Johnson
ARTS AND CRAFTS: The Early Modernist Movement in American Decorative Arts, 1894–1923
A price guide to the field
0–876–37447–X Ballantine pb $12.95

• Philip Kopper
COLONIAL WILLIAMSBURG
0–8109–0787–9 Abrams $60.00

• Tod Volpe & Beth Cathers
TREASURES OF THE AMERICAN ARTS AND CRAFTS MOVEMENT, 1890–1920
A survey by dealers
0–8109–1695–9 Abrams $49.50

The Knopf Collectors' Guide to American Antiques

"The best, most convenient portable guide I have ever seen—a boon for the general collector"—*Art & Antiques Magazine*

Donald Fennimore
THE KNOPF COLLECTORS' GUIDES TO AMERICAN ANTIQUES: Silver and Pewter
0–394–71527–6 Knopf pb $13.95

William C. Ketchum, Jr.
KNOPF COLLECTORS' GUIDE TO AMERICAN ANTIQUE FURNITURE: Chests, Cupboards, Desks, and Other Pieces
0–394–71270–6 Knopf pb $13.95

Marvin Schwartz
KNOPF COLLECTORS' GUIDE TO AMERICAN ANTIQUE FURNITURE: Chairs, Tables, Sofas, and Beds
0–394–71269–2 Knopf pb $13.95

Shaker Arts

• **Beverley Gordon**
SHAKER TEXTILE ARTS
0–87451–158–5 New England $15.95

• **John Kassay**
THE BOOK OF SHAKER FURNITURE
0–87023–275–4 Massachusetts $60.00

• **Charles Muller & Timothy Rieman**
THE SHAKER CHAIR
A thorough study of its style and production
0–9611116–0–7 Canal $39.95

CRAFTS

• **Charlotte Dinger**
ART OF THE CAROUSEL
Information on painting and restoration as well as a list of the remaining carousels in North America. Over 400 illustrations of the woodcarvings
0–914507–00–1 Carousel Art $40.00

• **Tobin Fraley**
THE CAROUSEL ANIMAL
0–87701–460–4 Chronicle $24.95
0–87701–454–X Chronicle pb $14.95

• **Frederick Fried**
A PICTORIAL HISTORY OF THE CAROUSEL
A large-format book on carousel animals, their history, and the artisans and factories that made them
0–911572–29–5 Vestal $29.95

• **Steve Miller**
THE ART OF THE WEATHERVANE
0–88740–005–1 Schiffer $35.00

Herter Brothers' library table, 1882 (Metropolitan Museum)

• **Katherine Pearson**
AMERICAN CRAFTS: A Source Book for the Home
0–941434–30–3 Stewart, Tabori & Chang $35.00

• **Constance Stapleton**
CRAFTS OF AMERICA: A Guide to the Finest Traditional Crafts Made in the United States
How they are made, who makes them, and where to buy them
0–06–055121–6 Harper & Row $39.95
0–06–096079–5 Harper & Row pb $19.95

• **Frances Thompson**
ANTIQUE BASKETS AND BASKETRY
Who made it, for what purpose, when, and what it is worth
0–087069–427–8 Wallace-Homestead $14.95

Decoys

• **Brad Art & Scott Kimball**
THE FISH DECOY
0–9604906–3–9 Aardvark $50.00

• **Adele Earnest**
THE ART OF THE DECOY: American Bird Carvings
0–916838–62–5 Schiffer $25.00
0–916838–58–7 Schiffer pb $14.95

• **Henry A. Fleckenstein, Jr.**
AMERICAN FACTORY DECOYS
0–916838–53–6 Schiffer $37.50

SHORE BIRD DECOYS
0–916838–32–3 Schiffer $35.00

Quilts

• **Robert Bishop & Carter Houck**
ALL FLAGS FLYING: The Great American Quilt Contest
0–525–24414–X Dutton $24.95
0–525–48214–8 Dutton pb $14.95

• **Dennis Duke & Deborah Harding, editors**
AMERICA'S GLORIOUS QUILTS
A large-format survey, lavishly illustrated
0–68363–487–2 Hugh Levin $75.00

• **Laura Fisher**
QUILTS OF ILLUSION: Tumbling Blocks, Delectable Mountains, Stairway to Heaven, Log Cabin, Windmill Blades, and Other Optical Designs
An illustrated survey of quilts with geometric designs
1–55562–010–8 Main Street $25.00
1–55562–009–4 Main Street pb $15.95

• **Thomas Woodward & Blanche Greenstein**
20TH CENTURY QUILTS, 1900–1950
0–525–48115–X Dutton pb $22.50

FURNITURE

• **Ethel Bjerkoe**
CABINETMAKERS OF AMERICA
0–317–54995–2 Schiffer $22.50

• **Joseph Butler**
FIELD GUIDE TO AMERICAN ANTIQUE FURNITURE: A Unique Visual System for Identifying the Style of Virtually Any Piece of American Antique Furniture
0–8050–0124–7 Henry Holt pb $12.95

• **Sharon Darling**
CHICAGO FURNITURE: Art, Craft and Industry, 1833–1983
Traces the development of design and the economic impact of the industry
0–393–01818–0 Norton $50.00

• **William Elder & Jayne Stokes**
AMERICAN FURNITURE, 1680–1880: From the Collection of the Baltimore Museum
0–912298–62–6 Baltimore Museum $20.00

• **Jonathan Fairbanks & Elizabeth Bates**
AMERICAN FURNITURE: 1620 to the Present
0–399–90096–9 Putnam $12.98

• **Michael Flanigan**
AMERICAN FURNITURE FROM THE KAUFMAN COLLECTION
0–8109–1864–1 Abrams $45.00

➤ FOR OVERSEAS ORDERING INFORMATION, SEE PAGE 1

• P.E. Kane
THREE HUNDRED YEARS OF AMERICAN SEATING FURNITURE: Garvan and Other Collections
0–686–47005–2 Apollo $25.00

• Myrna Kaye
FAKE, FRAUD OR GENUINE: Identifying Authentic American Antique Furniture
0–8212–1666–X NY Graphic Society $29.95

• William C. Ketchum, Jr.
CHESTS, CUPBOARDS, DESKS AND OTHER PIECES
0–394–71270–6 Knopf pb $13.95

• Edgar G. Miller, Jr.
AMERICAN ANTIQUE FURNITURE
Volume 1
0–486–21599–7 Dover pb $14.95
Volume 2
0–486–21600–4 Dover pb $14.95

• Milo Naeve
IDENTIFYING AMERICAN FURNITURE: A Pictorial Guide to Styles and Terms, Colonial to Contemporary
0–393–30580–5 Norton pb $9.95

• Susan Osborn
AMERICAN RUSTIC FURNITURE
0–317–54990–1 Apollo $14.95

• Richard H. Randall, Jr.
AMERICAN FURNITURE IN THE MUSEUM OF FINE ARTS, BOSTON
Introduction by Perry Rathbone
0–87846–003–9 Museum of Fine Arts pb $29.95

• Harold Sack & Max Wilk
AMERICAN TREASURE HUNT: The Legend of Israel Sack
America's first family of antique furniture, who shaped great American museum and private collections
0–316–76593–7 Little, Brown $24.95
0–345–34831–1 Ballantine pb $7.95

• Robert & Harriet Swedberg
AMERICAN OAK FURNITURE STYLES AND PRICES
A brief study
0–87069–492–8 Wallace-Homestead pb $14.95

WICKER FURNITURE STYLES AND PRICES
A brief study
0–87069–409–X Wallace-Homestead pb $12.95

• Gerald W.R. Ward
AMERICAN CASE FURNITURE IN THE MABEL BRADY GARVAN AND OTHER COLLECTIONS AT YALE UNIVERSITY
"Illustrates and documents 233 chests, boxes, desks, sideboards, cupboards, cellarettes, pianos, and even a radio, made between 1650 and 1935"—*Maine Antique Digest*
0–300–03357–5 Yale $60.00

• Gerald W.R. Ward, editor
PERSPECTIVES ON AMERICAN FURNITURE
Essays on regional characteristics of American furniture, its craftsmanship and trade
0–393–02654–X Norton $29.95

Early American Furniture

• Benno Forman
AMERICAN SEATING FURNITURE, 1630–1730: An Interpretive Catalogue
Essential reading from Winterthur. "Chairs as historical documents that tell how the trees were sawed, where the cabinetmakers who made them came from and where they lived, and what kind of customers ordered them"—*Maine Antique Digest*
0–393–02516–0 Norton $75.00

• Brock Jobe & Myrna Kaye
NEW ENGLAND FURNITURE: The Colonial Era
0–395–34406–9 Houghton Mifflin $40.00

• Russell Kettell
PINE FURNITURE OF EARLY NEW ENGLAND
Every aspect and type of Colonial pine furniture. A guide for collectors, with more than 200 examples
0–486–20145–7 Dover $14.95

• John Kirk
EARLY AMERICAN FURNITURE
0–394–70646–3 Knopf pb $11.95

• Albert Sack
FINE POINTS OF FURNITURE: Early America
A classic handbook that compares over 100 types of early American furniture and analyzes their design, craftsmanship, and construction
0–517–00148–9 Crown $12.95

• Charles Santore
THE WINDSOR STYLE IN AMERICA: A Continuing Study of the History and Regional Characteristics of the Most Popular Furniture Form of 18th Century America, 1730–1840
The definitive study, with 275 illustrations and original drawings
0–89471–551–8 Running Press $45.00

• Robert Trent, editor
PILGRIM CENTURY FURNITURE: An Historical Survey
0–87663–239–8 Universe $14.50
0–87663–946–5 Universe pb $7.95

Period Furniture

• David Cathers
FURNITURE OF THE AMERICAN ARTS AND CRAFTS MOVEMENT: Stickley, Roycroft and Mission Oak
0–317–54951–X Apollo $19.95
0–452–25374–8 NAL pb $9.95

• David Cathers, Introduction
STICKLEY CRAFTSMAN FURNITURE CATALOGS
Reprints of two 1910 mission furniture catalogs
0–317–54992–8 Apollo $20.00
0–486–23838–5 Dover pb $7.95

• Michael Donbar
FEDERAL FURNITURE
0–918804–48–5 Taunton $18.95

• Eileen & Richard Dubrow
AMERICAN FURNITURE OF THE 19TH CENTURY, 1840–80
0–686–47035–4 Apollo $30.00

FURNITURE MADE IN AMERICA, 1875–1985
0–916838–66–8 Schiffer $17.95

• Derek Ostergard
BENT WOOD AND METAL FURNITURE, 1850–1940
Ordinary and unusual furniture, including works by Thonet, who revolutionized the workplace and turned traditional shop techniques into mass production
0–295–96409–X Washington $50.00
0–917418–80–8 Federation of Arts pb $35.00

• Robert & Harriet Swedberg
VICTORIAN FURNITURE STYLE AND PRICES
A brief study
0–87069–396–4 Wallace-Homestead pb $14.95

• Christopher Wills
THONET BENTWOOD AND OTHER FURNITURE: The 1904 Illustrated Catalogue and Supplements
One of the firm's rarest catalogs; an invaluable guide for identifying and authenticating vintage Thonet bentwood. Line drawings with descriptions
0–486–24024–X Dover pb $9.95

GLASS

• Bill Edwards
STANDARD ENCYCLOPEDIA OF CARNIVAL GLASS
Over 1000 pieces of glass in full iridescent color. American, English, and Australian examples are all featured in this definitive guide
0–89145–187–0 Collector $24.95

• Robert Koch
LOUIS C. TIFFANY'S GLASS, BRONZES, LAMPS: A Complete Collector's Guide
A source book for identifying and dating thousands of decorative objects
0–517–50568 Crown $19.95

• Ruth Lee
EARLY AMERICAN PRESSED GLASS
0–8048–7004–7 Tuttle $35.00

• Ruth Lee & James Rose
AMERICAN GLASS CUP PLATES
0–8048–7000–4 Tuttle pb $19.75

• Mollie Helen McCain
COLLECTOR'S ENCYCLOPEDIA OF PATTERN GLASS
0–89145–211–7 Collector pb $12.95

• Norman Potter
TIFFANY GLASSWARE
0–517–57123–4 Crown $15.95

- Anne Pullin
GLASS SIGNATURES, TRADEMARKS AND TRADE NAMES
A convenient, comprehensive index to thousands of marks, with benchmark dates given; the entire guide is cross-referenced
0–87069–462–6 Wallace-Homestead pb $12.95

- Albert Revi
AMERICAN CUT AND ENGRAVED GLASS
0–916838–87–9 Schiffer $35.00

NINETEENTH CENTURY GLASS
0–916838–43–9 Schiffer $29.50

- John Shuman
THE COLLECTOR'S ENCYCLOPEDIA OF AMERICAN ART GLASS
0–89145–355–5 Collector $29.95

- Martha Swan
AMERICAN CUT AND ENGRAVED GLASS OF THE BRILLIANT PERIOD
The special vocabulary used to describe motifs and designs, how to judge the age of pieces, and how to assess the value of signatures from the period 1876–1916
0–87069–430–8 Wallace-Homestead $24.95

POTTERY AND PORCELAIN

- E.A. Barber
POTTERY AND PORCELAIN OF THE U.S.
0–87282–010–6 American Life $20.00

- Garth Clark
AMERICAN CERAMICS: 1876 to the Present
How American ceramics evolved from late 19th-century art pottery. With over 200 artists represented, this is the most comprehensive publication on this subject
0–89659–743–1 Abbeville $67.50

- Paul Evans
ART POTTERY OF THE U.S.: An Encyclopedia of Producers and Their Marks
0–9619577–0–0 Feingold & Lewis $45.00

Alice Cooney Frelinghuysen
AMERICAN PORCELAIN, 1770–1920
Published to coincide with an exhibition at the Metropolitan Museum of Art, this book includes outstanding illustrations and a detailed history of stylistic development
0–8109–1887–0 Abrams $60.00

- Lucile Henzke
ART POTTERY OF AMERICA
0–916838–69–2 Schiffer $45.00

- Bob & Sharon Huxford
COLLECTOR'S ENCYCLOPEDIA OF FIESTA
0–89145–354–7 Collector $19.95

- Ellouise Larsen
AMERICAN HISTORICAL VIEWS ON STAFFORDSHIRE CHINA
0–486–23088–0 Dover $17.50
0–486–23055–4 Dover pb $11.95

Cornelius Kierstede's paneled silver bowl, c. 1700-1710 (Metropolitan Museum)

- Elaine Levin
THE HISTORY OF AMERICAN CERAMICS: 1607 to the Present
0–8109–1172–8 Abrams $65.00

- Barbara Perry & others
AMERICAN CERAMICS: The Collection of the Everson Museum of Art
From 9th-century pottery of the Southwest to works by contemporary artists
0–8478–1025–9 Rizzoli $75.00

SILVER

- Kathryn Buhler & Graham Hood
AMERICAN SILVER IN THE YALE UNIVERSITY ART GALLERY
Two volumes
0–317–55087–X Apollo (set) $150.00

- Charles & Mary Carpenter
TIFFANY SILVER
0–396–08338–2 Dodd, Mead pb $13.95

- Stephen Ensko
AMERICAN SILVERSMITHS AND THEIR MARKS
The definitive directory for serious collectors. Over 3000 goldsmiths and silversmiths working from 1650 to 1850 are listed with biographical details, location of shops, and maps of smithing centers
0–486–24428–8 Dover pb $6.00

- Donald Fennimore
THE KNOPF COLLECTORS' GUIDES TO AMERICAN ANTIQUES: Silver and Pewter
The colonial period to the 1950s, a handy guide with color illustrations, descriptions, and prices along with market comments by experts in the field
0–394–71527–6 Knopf pb $13.95

- Graham Hood
AMERICAN SILVER: A History of Style, 1650–1900
0–525–48217–2 Dutton $15.95

- Dorothy Rainwater
ENCYCLOPEDIA OF AMERICAN SILVER MANUFACTURERS
0–88740–046–9 Schiffer pb $19.95

- Barbara & Gerald Ward
SILVER IN AMERICAN LIFE: Selections from the Mabel Brady Garvan and Other Collections at Yale University
0–917418–58–1 Federation of the Arts pb $10.95

- David Warren & others
MARKS OF ACHIEVEMENT: Four Centuries of American Presentation Silver
The events, people, and feats they commemorate, from horse and yacht races to captains of ships, loyal Indian chiefs, and Superbowl trophies
0–8109–1444–1 Abrams $45.00

The Home

Among the practical guides, the Time-Life books are especially recommended for their logical format, excellent illustrations, and well-thought-out instructions. The general books published by the Reader's Digest are invaluable reference guides.

- Tracy Kidder
HOUSE
A popular account of a family building its first home: struggles with builders and contractors, daily frustrations, and ultimate satisfaction
0–380–70176–6 Avon pb $4.50

- Reader's Digest
HOW TO DO JUST ABOUT ANYTHING
A guide to over 1200 small practical problems, arranged alphabetically. Practical advice on such topics as plumbing, gardening, and first aid
0–89577–218–3 Reader's Digest $25.95

- Witold Rybczinski
HOME: A Short History of an Idea
The idea of "the home," the concept of comfort, the effects of invention, and how social and cultural changes influence styles of decoration and furnishing. "Serious, historically minded, and exquisitely readable"—*New Yorker*
0–14–010231–0 Penguin pb $7.95

BUYING A HOUSE

- **Bill Adler**
  THE HOME BUYER'S GUIDE
  0–671–50533–5 Simon & Schuster pb $5.95

- **David Goldstick & Carolyn Janik**
  THE COMPLETE GUIDE TO CO-OPS AND CONDOMINIUMS
  0–452–26092–2 NAL pb $8.95

- **Robert Irwin, editor**
  THE MCGRAW-HILL REAL ESTATE HANDBOOK
  By the author of many successful real estate books
  0–07–032056–X McGraw-Hill $57.95

- **William Klein**
  BEFORE YOU BUY YOUR HOUSE OR APARTMENT
  0–446–38434–8 Warner pb $9.95

Real Estate Financing and Negotiation

- **Sonny Bloch**
  SONNY BLOCH'S INSIDE REAL ESTATE: The Complete Guide to Buying and Selling Your Home, Co-op or Condominium
  Sonny Bloch is the host of successful radio and TV programs on real estate
  1–55584–030–2 Weidenfeld & Nicolson $18.95

- **Suzanne Brangham**
  HOUSEWISE: The Smart Woman's Guide to Buying, Renovating, and Selling Real Estate
  An education in the business and art of home renovation based on personal experience
  0–517–56003–8 Clarkson Potter $18.95

- **George Hoffman**
  HOW TO INSPECT A HOUSE: Exactly What to Look for Before You Buy
  A guide for home buyers on how to save money in professional fees
  0–201–11072–5 Addison-Wesley pb $8.95

- **Robert Irwin**
  MAKING MORTGAGES WORK FOR YOU
  A guide to all types of mortgage financing, with useful payment tables
  0–07–032129–9 McGraw Hill $22.95

- **Robert Minton**
  BANKING ON YOUR HOME: A Consumer's Guide to Home Equity Loans
  How to borrow money against your property
  0–317–54666–X Dow Jones-Irwin $25.00
  0–87094–747–8 Dow Jones-Irwin pb $13.95

BUILDING A HOUSE

As construction becomes increasingly expensive, many people are relying on their own skills to build or enlarge their home. These books, for novice and experienced builder alike, have all been selected for their easy-to-follow, well-diagrammed instructions.

Design and Construction

- **John Cole & Charles Wing**
  FROM THE GROUND UP
  0–316–15112–2 Little, Brown pb $14.95

- **Lupe DiDonno & Phyllis Sperling**
  HOW TO DESIGN AND BUILD YOUR OWN HOUSE
  Illustrated with line drawings, this book concentrates on design, planning, and selection of the best materials and tools
  0–394–75200–7 Knopf pb $16.95

- **Lawrence Grow**
  THE OLD HOUSE BOOK OF CLASSIC COUNTRY HOUSES: Plans for Traditional American Dwellings
  Fifty colonial plans, including such details as doorways, mantels, and cupboards
  1–55562–054–X Main Street pb $8.95

  THE OLD HOUSE BOOK OF COTTAGES AND BUNGALOWS
  Plans for over 100 authentic and charming small country and suburban houses
  1–55562–016–7 Main Street pb $8.95

- **Dennis Holloway & Maureen McIntyre**
  THE OWNER-BUILDER EXPERIENCE: How to Design and Build Your Own Home
  For beginners
  0–87857–643–6 Rodale pb $12.95

- **Frank Jackson**
  PRACTICAL HOUSEBUILDING FOR PRACTICALLY EVERYONE
  0–07–032038–1 McGraw-Hill pb $12.95

- **Morris Krieger**
  HOMEOWNER'S ENCYCLOPEDIA OF HOUSE CONSTRUCTION
  0–07–035497–9 McGraw-Hill $36.50

From Trompe l'Oeil Painting *by Miriam Milman (Rizzoli)*

- **Robert Roskind**
  BUILDING YOUR OWN HOUSE: The First Part from Foundations to Framing
  An award-winning guidebook, well illustrated with diagrams, drawings, and photographs
  0–89815–110–4 Ten Speed pb $17.95

- **Subella**
  HOW TO PLAN, CONTRACT AND BUILD YOUR OWN HOUSE
  0–8306–2806–1 Ten Speed pb $15.95

Additions and Outdoor Buildings

- **Paul Bianchina**
  ADD A ROOM: A Practical Guide to Expanding Your House
  0–8306–1311–0 TAB $27.95
  0–8306–2811–8 TAB pb $17.95

- **D. Dickinson**
  ADDING ON: An Artful Guide to Affordable Residential Additions
  0–07–016814–8 McGraw-Hill $43.50

- **Lawrence Grow**
  COUNTRY ARCHITECTURE
  Old-style designs for carriage houses, garden houses, gazebos, sheds, barns, and other outbuildings
  0–915590–80–8 Main Street pb $9.95

- **Ray Wolf, editor**
  THE BACKYARD BUILDER'S BOOK OF OUTDOOR BUILDING PROJECTS
  Easy-to-build projects such as bird-houses and trellises
  0–87857–696–7 Rodale $24.95

- **May Woods & Arete Warren**
  GLASS HOUSES
  A history of the glass house from the Romans to today, with lavish illustrations of unusual houses, conservatories, and greenhouses
  0–8478–0906–4 Rizzoli $45.00

Renovation

- **Christopher Evers**
  THE OLD-HOUSE DOCTOR
  A guide to treating an old house, with simple, well-illustrated directions for carpentry work; ideas for doors, frames, roofs, rewiring, combating termites, and rehanging wallpaper
  0–87951–239–3 Overlook pb $9.95

- **Lawrence Grow, editor**
  CLASSIC OLD HOUSE PLANS: Three Centuries of American Domestic Architecture
  Floor plans and elevations for a wide variety of houses
  0–915590–41–7 Main Street pb $8.95

  MORE CLASSIC OLD HOUSE PLANS: Authentic Designs for Colonial and Victorian Homes
  "Fun for house plan browsers and practical details for builders and renovators"—
  Washington Post
  0–915590–86–7 Main Street pb $8.95

English floor tile, c. 13th-14th century

- **Shirley Hanson & Nancy Hubby**
  PRESERVING AND MAINTAINING THE OLDER HOME
  0–07–026086–9 McGraw-Hill $27.95

- **Joanna Krotz**
  METROPOLITAN HOME RENOVATION STYLE
  Includes ideas for brownstones, lofts, condominiums, ranches, and Victorian houses
  0–394–54941–4 Random House $40.00
  0–394–75819–6 Random House pb $19.95

- **Martin & Judith Miller**
  PERIOD DETAILS: A Sourcebook for House Restoration
  A useful source; attractively illustrated
  Foreword by Mario Buatta
  0–517–56514–5 Crown $27.50

- **Penny Radford**
  DESIGNER'S GUIDE TO SURFACE FINISHES
  How to renovate walls, floors, ceilings, windows, and trim. A well-organized and attractive book on types of finishes, preparation, and application of new finishes
  0–8230–7144–8 Watson-Guptill $29.95

- **Reader's Digest**
  HOME IMPROVEMENT MANUAL
  A thorough guide to renovating, modernizing, and adding space to a house. Includes American house styles, building codes, estimated costs, and projects for interior and exterior improvements. An essential one-volume reference
  0–89577–132–2 Reader's Digest $25.95

- **Bob Vila & others**
  THIS OLD HOUSE: Restoring, Rehabilitating and Renovating
  0–316–17702–4 Warner pb $19.95

  THIS OLD HOUSE GUIDE TO BUILDING AND REMODELING MATERIALS
  Companion volumes to the Emmy-winning PBS series: practical tips on how to renovate a house on a limited budget
  0–446–38246–9 Warner pb $16.95

Bathrooms

"The idea of locating the water closet and bathtub together in a single room, for the common use of all the family, was an American one ... By the turn of the [19th] century the compact three-fixture bathroom, with the tub placed across the end of the room and the water closet and sink side by side, was commonplace. This was not the case in Europe."—Witold Rybczinski, *Home: A Short History of an Idea*

- **Terence Conran**
  THE BED AND BATH BOOK
  Decorative ideas for the bathroom
  0–517–55940–4 Crown pb $14.95

- **Thomas Cowan**
  BEYOND THE BATH: A Dreamer's Guide
  Fantasy bathrooms
  0–89471–223–3 Running Press pb $8.95

- **Nonie Niesewand**
  CONRAN'S BEDROOMS AND BATHROOMS
  How to improve and redecorate the bedroom, plan efficient closets, and design the bathroom
  0–316–60747–9 Little, Brown pb $7.95

- **Rodale Press**
  BATHS
  Designs for new and remodeled bathrooms of all sizes
  0–87857–640–1 Rodale pb $12.95

Kitchens

- **Terence Conran**
  THE KITCHEN BOOK
  Decorative schemes and workable plans for the kitchen
  0–517–55453–4 Crown pb $14.95

- **Robin Merrill**
  SMALL KITCHENS
  Clever ways to make every corner work, with great ideas for the apartment dweller
  0–671–63354–6 Simon & Schuster $19.95

- **Nonie Niesewand**
  CONRAN'S KITCHENS AND DINING ROOMS
  For small and large kitchens alike, practical and innovative ideas on the latest gadgets and design schemes
  0–316–60746–0 Little, Brown pb $7.95

- **Bo Niles & Juta Ristsoo**
  PLANNING THE PERFECT KITCHEN
  Includes an invaluable planning kit with peel-off appliances and kitchen elements, from the editors of *Country Life* magazine
  0–671–65729–1 Simon & Schuster $19.95

- **Rodale Press**
  KITCHENS
  Many ideas for new and remodeled kitchens, how to choose cabinets, appliances, floors, and lighting
  0–87857–606–1 Rodale pb $12.95

- **Time-Life Books**
  KITCHENS AND BATHROOMS
  0–8094–2386–3 Time-Life $11.95

Floors, Doors, and Windows

- **Amy Zaffarano Rowland**
  HANDCRAFTED DOORS AND WINDOWS
  0–87857–424–7 Rodale pb $12.95

- **Time-Life Books**
  DOORS AND WINDOWS
  0–8094–2406–1 Time-Life $14.95

  FLOORS AND STAIRWAYS
  0–8094–2394–4 Time-Life $14.95

Carpentry

- **Norm Abram**
  THE NEW YANKEE WORKSHOP
  Thirteen handsome and useful projects from the master carpenter, star of the PBS television series
  0–316–00453–7 Little, Brown $29.95
  0–316–00454–5 Little, Brown pb $16.95

- **Hands On Magazine**
  WOODWORKING PROJECTS
  For all skill levels, projects for all parts of the house
  0–87857–615–0 Rodale pb $9.95

  WOODWORKING PROJECTS II
  For beginners and advanced craftsmen, instructions for home decoration and furnishing, and smaller projects
  0–87857–616–9 Rodale pb $9.95

- **Paul Hasluck**
  THE HANDYMAN'S BOOK
  A detailed woodworking manual, published in 1903, with 2500 illustrations, which discusses the tools, workmanship, and all types of furniture of the time
  0–89815–203–8 Ten Speed pb $9.95

- **Bernard Jones**
  THE PRACTICAL WOODWORKER
  0–89815–111–2 Ten Speed $16.95
  0–89815–106–6 Ten Speed pb $9.95

  THE COMPLETE WOODWORKER
  0–89815–034–5 Ten Speed $16.95
  0–89815–022–1 Ten Speed pb $8.95

- **Gaspar Lewis**
  CARPENTRY
  A master carpenter's comprehensive guide to the craft, with over 900 illustrations. Includes sections on tools, materials, rough carpentry, exterior finishing, furniture
  0–8069–6752–8 Sterling $18.95

- **Herbert & Nancy Schiffer**
  WOODS WE LIVE WITH
  A wonderful book identifying and describing the properties of different woods, with actual wood samples. Extremely useful for carpenters and for anyone repairing wood surfaces
  0–916838–10–2 Schiffer $24.95

IF YOU CAN'T FIND IT, LOOK IN THE INDEX

Cabinets and Storage

- Richard Boller
WOODWORKING AND CABINETMAKING
0–02–512800–0 Macmillan $18.95

- James Christ
COMPLETE GUIDE TO MODERN CABINETMAKING
0–13–160177–6 Prentice-Hall $21.00

- Gilly Love
STORAGE SOLUTIONS
A small, well-conceived book in the Conran Home Decoration Series
0–394–74400–4 Random House pb $6.95

- Byron Maguire
CABINETMAKING: From Design to Finish
0–13–109737–7 Prentice-Hall pb $14.95

- Rodale Press
BUILD-IT-BETTER YOURSELF STORAGE AROUND THE HOUSE
Practical and creative ideas for every part of the house, such as TV cabinets, bicycle storage, linen closets, and paper towel holders
0–87857–753–X Rodale $19.95

- Amy Rowland & William Hylton
HANDCRAFTED SHELVES AND CABINETS
Advice from skilled craftsmen on designing and building shelves, dressers, and cabinets
0–87857–482–4 Rodale pb $12.95

Furniture

- Toby Braithwaite
HOW TO RESTORE AND REPAIR FURNITURE
0–8120–5864–X Barron's $24.95

- James Brumbaugh
WOOD FURNITURE: Finishing, Refinishing, Repairing
A good, reliable guide
0–672–23409–2 Macmillan $12.95

- George Buchanan
THE ILLUSTRATED BOOK OF FURNITURE RESTORATION
An English restorer's complete survey covering such subjects as glueing, carving, veneers, frames, faults, joints, upholstery, and setting up a workshop. An easy-to-learn guide for beginners and a useful reference book for professionals
0–06–015558–2 Harper & Row $18.95

- Edith Cramer
EARLY AMERICAN DECORATION MADE EASY: 18 Full-Size Patterns for Furniture and Trays
0–486–24776–7 Dover pb $4.50

- Florence de Dampierre
PAINTED FURNITURE
A picture book, full of ideas, written by a French antique dealer
0–8478–0804–1 Rizzoli $35.00

- Bernard Gladstone
COMPLETE GUIDE TO FURNITURE FINISHING AND REFINISHING
An excellent short guide by a syndicated columnist and *New York Times* editor. Includes stripping, selecting new finishes, preparing furniture, staining techniques
0–671–25603–3 Simon & Schuster pb $8.95

- George Grotz
THE FURNITURE DOCTOR
Best-selling book for amateurs and professionals, covering all manner of repairs and restoration
0–385–17971–5 Doubleday $16.95

- Bruce Johnson
KNOCK ON WOOD: The Insider's Guide to Furniture Repair and Restoration
0–399–12978–2 Putnam $17.95

- Time-Life Books
FURNITURE FINISHES
0–8094–5513–7 Time-Life $19.95

REPAIRING FURNITURE
Mending joints, refinishing, reweaving, upholstering
0–8094–2438–X Time-Life $14.95

Upholstery

"Originally, the upholsterer had been concerned solely with textiles and upholstery coverings, but, being a tradesman and recognizing a business opportunity, he had enlarged his service to include coordination of all interior furnishings and set himself up, according to a 1747 British trade paper, 'as a connoisseur in every article that belongs to a house' . . . By the time that architects realized that they had lost control of the interior arrangement of the house, it was too late. Upholsterers, or interior decorators as they were later called, came increasingly to dominate domestic comfort."—Witold Rybczinski, *Home: A Short History of an Idea*

- James Brumbaugh
UPHOLSTERING
A good, technical guide for laymen and apprentices; each step in the process is clearly explained
0–672–23372–X Macmillan $15.95

- W.L. Gheen
UPHOLSTERY TECHNIQUES ILLUSTRATED
0–8306–0402–2 TAB pb $17.95

- Peter Nesovich
REUPHOLSTERING AT HOME: A Do-It-Yourself Manual for Turning Old Furniture into New Showpieces
0–517–53819–9 Crown pb $9.95

INTERIOR DECORATING

- Kate Corbett-Winder
LAURA ASHLEY LIVING ROOMS
Advice for creating comfortable settings using the Laura Ashley look; floral and striped patterns, copies of period wallpapers, and practical slip-covers
0–517–56857–8 Crown $25.00

- Beth Franks
VERY SMALL LIVING SPACES: Design and Decorating Strategies to Make the Most of What You Have
Imaginative ideas, supplemented with a list of suppliers and sources
0–8050–0520–X Henry Holt $22.95

- Mary Gilliatt
DECORATING BOOK
A complete and useful problem-solving book
0–394–75243–0 Random House pb $19.95

DECORATING ON THE CHEAP
0–89480–354–9 Workman pb $14.95

MARY GILLIATT'S NEW GUIDE TO DECORATING
Each step of the process, from planning to selecting fabrics and furnishings
0–316–31389–8 Little, Brown $40.00

- Linda Gray & Jocasta Innes
THE COMPLETE BOOK OF DECORATING TECHNIQUES
Such decorative techniques as dragging, stencilling, trompe-l'oeil, and marbleizing
0–316–32595–3 Little, Brown $29.95

- Jocasta Innes & Jill Blake
THE CONRAN BASIC BOOK OF INTERIOR DESIGN: A Complete Guide to Decorating and Maintaining Your Home
Good, basic advice from the store chain that has successfully marketed simple, stylish, and durable furnishings
0–670–81772–4 Viking $24.95

- Lorraine & Gabrielle Townsend
OSBORNE & LITTLE: The Decorated Room
A successful London decorating firm offers schemes and details that can add a distinctive look to any room
0–87951–304–7 Overlook $29.95

- Martin & Judith Miller
PERIOD DESIGN AND FURNISHING: A Sourcebook for Home Restoration
How to create period design with furniture, collectibles, wall and floor coverings, paintings, and other objects. Arranged chronologically from Elizabethan to art deco style, the chapters include tips on maintenance and restoration
0–517–57156–0 Crown $30.00

- J. Ronald Reed & Stephanie Culp
THE CRAFTSMAN REVIVAL IN INTERIOR DESIGN: How Today's Artisans Preserve Yesterday's Skills
From decorative moldings and stained-glass windows to hardware and plumbing fixtures—the workmanship of the 19th and early 20th centuries adapted for today
0–8050–0518–8 Henry Holt $29.95

- Julia Hamilton Thomason
CREATIVE IDEAS FOR DECORATING
Decorating for comfort and style; imaginative ideas and simple instructions for projects
0–8487–0689–7 Oxmoor $29.95

MARIO BUATTA: Recommended Books on Interior Decoration

Jocasta Innes
PAINT MAGIC
0–394–75434–4 Random House $19.95

Martin & Judith Miller
PERIOD DETAILS: A Sourcebook for House Restoration
0–517–56514–5 Crown $27.50

Mario Praz
AN ILLUSTRATED HISTORY OF INTERIOR DECORATION: From Pompeii to Art Nouveau
0–500–23358–6 Thames & Hudson $75.00

Edith Wharton & Ogden Codman
THE DECORATION OF HOUSES
0–393–04468–8 Norton $14.95
0–393–00840–1 Norton pb $8.95

House & Garden
HOUSE & GARDEN'S BEST IN DECORATION
0–394–56426–X Random House $34.50

Chris Madden
INTERIOR VISIONS: Great American Designers and the Showcase House
1–55670–038–5 ST&C $45.00

John Fowler & John Cornforth
ENGLISH DECORATION IN THE 18TH CENTURY
Out of print

Herbert Wise
ATTENTION TO DETAIL
0–399–50696–9 Putnam $12.95

John Pile
INTERIOR DESIGN
0–8109–1121–3 Abrams $49.50

Florence de Dampierre
THE BEST OF PAINTED FURNITURE
0–8478–0804–1 Rizzoli $35.00

Wallace Nutting
FURNITURE TREASURY
Volumes 1 & 2
0–02–590980–0 Macmillan $42.50
Volume 3
0–02–591040–X Macmillan $32.50

S.C. Reznikoff
INTERIOR GRAPHIC AND DESIGN STANDARDS
0–8230–7298–3 Watson-Guptill $95.00

English wallpaper pattern

• Derek Walters
FENG SHUI: The Chinese Art of Designing a Harmonious Environment
0–671–65246–X Simon & Schuster $12.95

Fabric

• Caroline Clifton-Mogg
CURTAINS AND BLINDS
From the Conran Home Decorator Series, this useful short book presents a variety of "window treatments"
0–394–74397–0 Random House pb $6.95

• Caroline Clifton-Mogg & Melanie Paine
THE ART AND TECHNIQUE OF DECORATING WITH FABRIC
Five hundred years of curtain and drapery styles. A useful sourcebook, with advice on proportion, awkward window shapes, how to line curtains, make valances, and other projects
0–13–195603–5 Prentice-Hall $27.50

• Donna Lang & Lucretia Robertson
DECORATING WITH FABRIC: A Guide to Sewing for the Home
More than 200 projects; with advice on materials and equipment
0–517–55278–7 Crown $24.95

• Melanie Paine
FABRIC MAGIC
How to use everyday fabrics in imaginative ways. Includes chapters on window treatments, coverings, bedding, what material to buy, and what styles to choose
0–394–55713–1 Random House $29.95

Floors

• Graham Blackburn
FLOORS, WALLS AND CEILINGS
How to repair, refinish, or restore interior surfaces; how to work with professional installers; and a useful buying guide
0–89043–245–7 Consumer Reports pb $12.00

• Akiko Busch
FLOORWORKS
Original designs for floors: inlaid wood, stencil and trompe-l'oeil designs, tiles, and rugs
0–553–05253–5 Bantam $19.95

• Jane Lott
FLOORS AND FLOORING
Another Conran Home Decorator book, describing a wide range of floor materials and designs
0–394–74399–7 Random House pb $6.95

Paint and Wallpaper

• Caroline Cass
MODERN MURALS: Grand Illusions in Interior Decoration
Contemporary mural painting for residential and commercial spaces, now a popular feature in interior decoration
0–8230–3124–1 Watson-Guptill $45.00

• Jocasta Innes
DECORATING WITH PAINT
"Explores overall wall finishes in greater depth and also explains how to marbleize woodwork, apply stencils and mix your own paints" *House Beautiful*
0–517–56280–4 Crown $25.00
0–517–57229–X Crown pb $17.95
PAINT MAGIC
0–394–75434–4 Pantheon $19.95

• Miriam Milman
TROMPE L'OEIL PAINTING: The Illusion of Reality
0–8478–0817–3 Rizzoli pb $25.00

• Isabel O'Neil
THE ART OF THE PAINTED FINISH FOR FURNITURE AND DECORATION
The most complete guide, combining old methods with modern materials and tools. Sections on antiquing, lacquering, and gilding by an expert on decorative paint
0–688–06070–6 Morrow pb $17.95

• Gregg Sandreuter
COMPLETE PAINTERS HANDBOOK: How To Paint Your House—Inside And Out—The Right Way
For the novice painter: advice for the entire process, from selecting tools to cleaning up
0–87857–756–4 Rodale pb $14.95

• Time-Life Books
PAINT AND WALLPAPER
0–8094–2355–3 Time-Life $19.95

Stencilling

• Helen Barnett & Susy Smith
STENCILLING
0–88162–304–0 Salem House $14.95

• Adele Bishop & others
THE ART OF DECORATIVE STENCILING
0–14–046728–9 Penguin pb $17.95

• JoAnne Day
THE COMPLETE BOOK OF STENCILCRAFT
0–486–25372–4 Dover pb $8.95

• Lyn Le Grice
THE ART OF STENCILLING
Offers a large variety of motifs and shows
how stencilling can decorate a room
0–517–56430–0 Crown $22.50

**THE STENCILED HOUSE: An
Inspirational and Practical Guide to
Transforming Your Home**
Instructions for such projects as walls,
floors, chests, and quilts. Lavishly
illustrated
0–671–66670–3 Simon & Schuster $24.95

• Leslie Linsley
FIRST STEPS IN STENCILLING
0–385–23801–0 Doubleday pb $12.95

• Carolyn Warrender & Tessa
Strickland
**CAROLYN WARRENDER'S BOOK OF
STENCILLING: How to Stencil Walls,
Ceiling, Floors, Furniture and Fabrics with
Style and Ease**
Useful advice and inspiration for the
beginner as well as the experienced painter
0–517–57238–9 Crown $25.00

Framing and Hanging Pictures

• Caroline Clifton-Mogg & others
**DISPLAYING PICTURES AND
PHOTOGRAPHS**
0–517–56628–1 Crown $19.95

• Lista Duren
**FRAME IT: A Complete Do-It-Yourself
Guide to Picture Framing**
0–395–24976–7 Houghton Mifflin pb $11.95

• Max Hyder
**MATTING, MOUNTING AND FRAMING
ART**
0–8230–3027–X Watson-Guptill $24.95

• Hal Rogers & Ed Reinhart
**HOW TO MAKE YOUR OWN PICTURE
FRAMES**
0–8230–2451–2 Watson-Guptill $17.50

• Holly Solomon & Alexandra
Anderson
LIVING WITH ART
An attractive book on the pleasures of
collecting and displaying art at home;
practical hints on lighting and framing art,
using examples from houses of collectors—
both modern and antique
0–8478–0960–9 Rizzoli $35.00

Lighting

• Conran Home Decorator
BETTER LIGHTING
A useful short book
0–394–74401–2 Random House pb $6.95

• Edward Effron
**PLANNING AND DESIGNING
LIGHTING**
A clear and comprehensive guide by a
theatrical lighting designer, well illustrated.
0–316–21235–0 Little, Brown $22.95

• Martin Greif
**THE LIGHTING BOOK: A Buyer's Guide
to Locating Almost Every Kind of Lighting
Device**
Over 1000 fixtures of every style and
period
0–915590–81–6 Main Street $22.50
0–915590–82–4 Main Street pb $12.95

HOME REPAIR

• Bernard Gladstone
**SIMON & SCHUSTER COMPLETE
GUIDE TO HOME REPAIR AND
MAINTENANCE**
A comprehensive, recommended book on
such topics as tools, materials, techniques,
energy, security, and saving money
0–671–63940–4 Simon & Schuster pb $12.95

• Gene Logsdon
THE LOW-MAINTENANCE HOUSE
0–87857–718–1 Rodale $19.95

• Reader's Digest
FIX-IT-YOURSELF MANUAL
0–89577–040–7 Random House $21.95

• Time-Life Books
COMPLETE HOME REPAIR MANUAL
0–13–921636–7 Prentice-Hall $24.95

**HOW THINGS WORK IN YOUR HOME:
And What to Do When They Don't**
0–03–003672–0 Henry Holt $24.50
0–8050–0126–3 Henry Holt pb $16.95

Electricity, Plumbing, and Heating

• James Kittle
**HOME ELECTRICAL REPAIR AND
MAINTENANCE**
0–07–034899–5 McGraw-Hill pb $9.95

• Time-Life Books
BASIC WIRING
0–8094–2358–8 Time-Life $14.95

HEATING AND COOLING
0–8094–2378–2 Time-Life $11.95

**KITCHEN AND BATHROOM
PLUMBING**
0–8094–6208–7 Time-Life $17.50

Sydney Cooper & Anne Beller
HOME SECURITY
0–89043–087–X Consumer Reports pb $15.00

Household Appliances and Tools

"The much needed carpet sweeper made its
appearance in the 1860s ... One model
required the user to push the handle up and
down like a pogo stick, another had long
handles which were pumped sideways, like
an enormous pair of shears. The most bizarre
vacuum cleaner consisted of two bellows
which the hapless maid was to wear as shoes,
and which caused the nozzle to suck air as
she walked around the room."—Witold
Rybczinski, *Home: A Short History of an Idea*

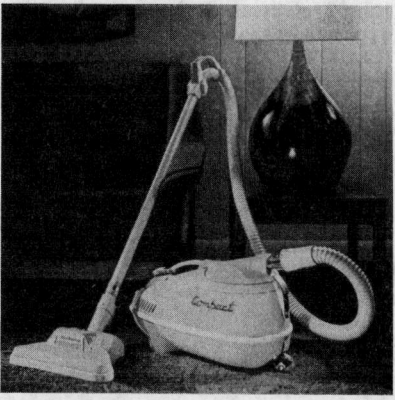

Vacuum cleaner, from Populuxe *by Thomas
Hine (Knopf)*

• Consumer Reports
1989 BUYING GUIDE ISSUE
The ideal reference for household
appliances, tools of any type, electronic
equipment, cars, and a host of other
products
0–89043–270–8 Consumer Reports pb $6.95

• Jackson Day
TOOLS AND HOW TO USE THEM
0–394–73542–0 Knopf $13.95

• Mother Earth News
**THE HOME HARDWARE HANDBOOK:
An Illustrated User's Guide to Common
Tools, Materials, and Supplies**
0–671–65793–3 Simon & Schuster $21.95
0–671–65789–5 Simon & Schuster pb $9.95

• Phyllis Palmore & Nevin Andre
SMALL APPLIANCE REPAIR
0–07–048361–2 McGraw-Hill $25.98

• Evan Powell
**THE COMPLETE GUIDE TO HOME
APPLIANCE REPAIR**
0–06–013384–8 Harper & Row $24.95

• Time-Life Books
MAJOR APPLIANCES
Chapters on tools, refrigerators, electric
ranges, dishwashers, washers, and dryers
0–8094–6204–4 Time-Life $17.50

REPAIRING APPLIANCES
0–8094–3482–2 Time-Life $19.95

HOUSEHOLD HINTS

• Jeff Campbell
THE CLEAN TEAM: Speed Cleaning
A humorous collection of short cuts by the
owner of a cleaning service
0–440–58015–3 Dell pb $5.95

• Monte Florman
**HOW TO CLEAN PRACTICALLY
ANYTHING**
0–89043–058–6 Consumer Reports pb $8.00

• Mablen Jones
TAKING CARE OF CLOTHES
0–312–90355–3 St. Martin's pb $4.95

- John McGowan & Roger Dubern
THE GOOD HOUSEKEEPING ILLUSTRATED BOOK OF HOME MAINTENANCE
0–688–04315–1 Morrow $22.95

- Mary Ellen Pinkham
MARY ELLEN'S BEST OF HELPFUL HINTS
0–446–38121–7 Warner pb $5.95

MARY ELLEN'S BEST OF HELPFUL HINTS: Book Two
0–446–38391–0 Warner pb $5.95

MARY ELLEN'S BEST OF HELPFUL KITCHEN HINTS
Priceless remedies that work
0–446–97212–6 Warner pb $4.50

- Reader's Digest
HOUSEHOLD HINTS AND HANDY TIPS
Comprehensive, well-organized collection of how-to facts and shortcuts
0–89577–276–0 Random House $25.95

- Hermione Sandwith & Sheila Stainton
THE NATIONAL TRUST MANUAL OF HOUSEKEEPING
How to take care of old houses and antique furnishings
0–14–007638–7 Penguin pb $12.95

HOME ENTERTAINING

Etiquette

- Letitia Baldridge
THE AMY VANDERBILT COMPLETE BOOK OF ETIQUETTE
A classic, now updated by a public relations specialist
0–385–14238–2 Doubleday $19.95

- Charlotte Ford
CHARLOTTE FORD'S BOOK OF MODERN MANNERS
Modern manners, which include the protocol of seating divorced and gay friends at the dinner table, and a section for teens
0–671–45769–1 Simon & Schuster pb $11.95

- Elizabeth L. Post
EMILY POST'S ETIQUETTE
The 21st edition brought up to date by a descendant of Emily Post
0–06–181684–1 Harper & Row $25.95

Entertaining

- Lee Bailey
LEE BAILEY'S GOOD PARTIES: Favorite Food, Tableware, Kitchen Equipment, and More to Make Entertaining a Breeze
0–517–55934–X Clarkson Potter $19.95

- Beverly Church & Bethany Bultman
THE JOY OF ENTERTAINING
A well-illustrated reference book with ideas for all kinds of parties and tips on everything from sending invitations to setting the table
0–89659–752–0 Abbeville $39.95

- Ann Tucker Fettner
POTPOURRI, INCENSE AND OTHER FRAGRANT CONCOCTIONS
Recipes for potpourri sachets, scented candles, and more
0–911104–97–6 Workman pb $4.95

- Trish Foley
HAVING TEA: Recipes and Table Settings
Recipes, tips on tea drinking, and presentation
0–517–56007–0 Clarkson Potter $17.95

- James Ginders
NAPKIN FOLDING: 44 Ways to Turn a Square of Linen into a Work of Art
0–517–56632–X Crown pb $6.95

- Susan Kalish
THE ART OF NAPKIN FOLDING
Elegant modern designs for enhancing the table
0–89471–919–X Running Press $24.95

- Barbara Ohrbach
THE SCENTED ROOM: Cherchez's Book of Dried Flowers, Fragrance, and Potpourri
Recipes for a sweet-smelling house, with attractive photographs
0–517–56081–X Crown $17.95

- Martha Stewart
WEDDINGS
Lavish photographs and detailed instructions for more than 40 weddings, including such elements as music, flower arrangement, table decorations, and menus
0–517–55675–8 Crown $50.00

- Martha Stewart & Elizabeth Hawes
ENTERTAINING
This best-selling book provides complete instructions and photographs on how to entertain from four to 400 guests
0–517–54419–9 Clarkson Potter $35.00

- Roger Vergé
ROGER VERGE'S ENTERTAINING IN THE FRENCH STYLE
A beautiful book, with advice for presenting a French meal
0–941434–90–7 Stewart, Tabori & Chang $45.00

Flower Arranging

- Penny Black
THE BOOK OF PRESSED FLOWERS
Pressing, drying, and arranging flowers. This attractive book includes chapters on making pictures and samplers with pressed flowers and leaves
0–671–66071–3 Simon & Schuster $17.95

- Susan Condor
DRIED FLOWERS: Drying and Arranging
Easy-to-follow instructions for making 86 varieties of dried flowers, with new and unusual designs for arranging them
0–87923–719–8 Godine $20.00

- Anne Hamilton & Kathleen White
SILK FLOWERS
A step-by-step guide to making silk roses, chrysanthemums, and other flowers, with

instructions for floral arrangements and bouquets
0–87923–765–1 Godine $22.50

- Malcolm Hillier
DECORATING WITH DRIED FLOWERS
0–517–56923–X Crown $19.95

- Malcolm Hillier & Colin Hilton
THE COMPLETE BOOK OF DRIED FLOWERS
0–671–61939–X Simon & Schuster $19.95

- Madderlake
FLOWERS REDISCOVERED: New Ideas for Using and Enjoying Flowers
A practical book by a well-known florist, beautifully illustrated
0–941434–72–9 Stewart, Tabori & Chang $45.00

- Denise Otis & Ronaldo Maia
DECORATING WITH FLOWERS
Text by a *House & Garden* editor and designs by a prominent New York florist
0–8109–0808–5 Abrams $49.50

- Joanna Sheen
PRESSED FLOWERS
A step-by-step guide, with easy-to-follow instructions and useful information on tools, materials, and techniques
0–87923–766–X Godine $22.50

- Wafu Teshigahara
IKEBANA: A New Illustrated Guide to Mastering the Secrets of Japanese Flower Arranging
0–87011–438–7 Kodansha $16.95

Crafts

- Clois Kicklighter & Ronald Baird
CRAFTS: Illustrated Designs and Techniques
Basic instructions in 39 different crafts from basketry to woodcraft, with 400 projects
0–87006–592–0 Goodheart-Willcox $19.40

- Gene Logsdon
GENE LOGSDON'S PRACTICAL SKILLS: A Revival of Forgotten Crafts, Techniques, and Traditions
Updated traditional projects for the kitchen, workshop, garage, and outdoors
0–87857–577–4 Rodale $24.95

- Katherine Pearson
AMERICAN CRAFTS: A Source Book for the Home
An attractive book of traditional and contemporary designs, including quilts, ceramics, and baskets. The price guide and glossary are useful
0–941434–30–3 Stewart, Tabori & Chang $35.00

- Reader's Digest
CRAFTS AND HOBBIES
An excellent collection of advice for making everything from baskets to mosaics
0–89577–063–6 Reader's Digest $21.95

• Alice Sprintzen
CRAFTS: Contemporary Design and Technique
An introduction to paper, fiber, clay, glass, leather, metal, and scrimshaw. Includes history, techniques, materials, and sources
0–87192–180–4 Davis $22.50

• Carol Sterbenz
AMERICAN COUNTRY FOLK CRAFTS: 50 Country Craft Projects for Decorating Your Home
Includes instructions for quilts, hooked rugs, stuffed animals, and cigar Indians. An attractive gift book
0–8109–1857–9 Abrams $29.95

NEEDLEWORK

• Judy Brittain
THE BANTAM STEP-BY-STEP BOOK OF NEEDLECRAFT
A large book with 6000 monochrome illustrations; chapters on knitting, crochet, embroidery, needlepoint, quilting, and sewing
0–553–34585–0 Bantam pb $24.95

• Jan Eaton
THE COMPLETE STITCH ENCYCLOPEDIA
Four hundred and forty-nine stitches illustrated in color, from Chinese embroidery to American Indian work
0–8120–5731–7 Barron's $19.95

• Linda Parry, editor
A PRACTICAL GUIDE TO CANVAS WORK
A colorful selection of historic embroidery designs from the Victoria & Albert Museum, with instructions on recreating them
1–55562–033–7 Main Street $12.95

• Reader's Digest
COMPLETE GUIDE TO NEEDLEWORK
Well-organized, practical coverage of the subject: embroidery, needlepoint, knitting, macrame, lacework, rug-making, and more
0–89577–059–8 Random House $23.95

• Betty Ring, editor
NEEDLEWORK: An Historical Survey
A pictorial survey of historic samplers, quilts, hooked rugs, and embroidered pictures
0–915590–56–5 Main Street pb $12.95

Crewel Embroidery

• Muriel Baker, editor
HANDBOOK OF AMERICAN CREWEL EMBROIDERY
American crewel pieces, their stitches and techniques
0–8048–0230–0 Tuttle $10.95

• Erica Wilson
CREWEL EMBROIDERY
A best-selling book that presents the fundamentals of crewel work, including instructions for 64 stitches, and examples of fine English and American embroidery
0–684–18383–8 Scribners pb $14.95

Coco Chanel in one of her embroidered designs (photo by Cecil Beaton), from Chanel *by Jean Leymarie (Rizzoli)*

Embroidery

These books include general technique guides and design anthologies. Among the most successful craft writers, both Erica Wilson and Mary Thomas have written on embroidery.

• Y. Chung
THE ART OF ORIENTAL EMBROIDERY: History, Aesthetics, and Techniques
0–684–18040–5 Scribners pb $15.95

• Marion Nichols
ENCYCLOPEDIA OF EMBROIDERY STITCHES INCLUDING CREWEL
One hundred seventy-eight clearly explained stitches
0–486–22929–7 Dover pb $6.95

• Mary Thomas
MARY THOMAS' EMBROIDERY BOOK
0–486–24530–6 Dover pb $4.95

• Erica Wilson
ERICA WILSON'S EMBROIDERY BOOK
0–684–16318–7 Scribners pb $19.95

Lace Making

• Audrey Dean
LEARN LACECRAFT
Lace making and projects for adding lace to linen, clothing, and furnishings
1–55562–030–2 Main Street $11.95

• Birgitta Fuhrmann
BOBBIN LACE: An Illustrated Guide to Traditional and Contemporary Techniques
Clear instructions for making every type of bobbin lace—including history, tools, and patterns
0–486–24902–6 Dover pb $7.95

• Mrs. F. Nevill Jackson
OLD HANDMADE LACE: With a Dictionary of Lace
Well-illustrated study of lace making from ancient Egypt to the late 19th century
0–486–25309–0 Dover pb $9.95

• Elizabeth Minkoff & Margaret Marriage
PILLOW OR BOBBIN LACE: Technique, Patterns, History
This 1907 classic includes a survey of lace in Europe, necessary materials, and basic techniques, along with 50 designs
0–486–25505–0 Dover pb $6.95

Needlepoint

• Muriel Baker, and others
NEEDLEPOINT: Design Your Own
0–684–17733–1 Scribners pb $3.95

• Thérèse de Dillmont
THE COMPLETE ENCYCLOPEDIA OF NEEDLEPOINT
A French classic. "This enormous compendium (nearly 1200 illustrations) dates back to the 19th century and is still a basic reference in its field; the hyperbolic-seeming title is, in reality, a sober, factual description of its scope"—*Washington Post*
0–914294–00–8 Running Press pb $9.95

• Hugh Ehrman, editor
DESIGNER NEEDLEPOINT
Traditional designs from English museums
0–938953–01–X Westminster $22.50

• Kaffe Fassett
GLORIOUS NEEDLEPOINT
Unusual designs for pillows, screens, rugs, and clothes
0–317–61005–8 Crown $24.95

• Hope Hanley
101 NEEDLEPOINT STITCHES AND HOW TO USE THEM
Instructions with black-and-white photographs
0–486–25031–8 Dover pb $4.95

• Maggie Lane
NEEDLEPOINT BY DESIGN: Variations on Chinese Themes
An elegant book
0–684–17315–8 Scribners pb $9.95

- Anna Pearson
NEEDLEPOINT: Stitch by Stitch
A complete course in needlepoint, with projects for all levels
0–345–34055–8 Ballantine $22.50

- Lisbeth Perrone
THE NEW WORLD OF NEEDLEPOINT: 101 Exciting Designs in Bargello, Quickpoint, Grospoint, and other Repeat Patterns
0–394–47265–9 Random House $12.95

- Carol Rome & Georgia Devlin
A NEW LOOK AT NEEDLEPOINT: The Complete Guide to Canvas Embroidery with 80 Different Stitches
0–517–50016–7 Crown pb $8.95

Samplers

- Sarah Don
TRADITIONAL SAMPLERS
0–670–80732–X Viking $16.95

- Dorothea Kay
EMBROIDERED SAMPLERS
0–684–17710–2 Scribners pb $4.95

- Jane Kendon
CROSS-STITCH SAMPLERS
0–312–17681–3 St. Martin's pb $9.95

Sewing

- Jan Eaton
ENCYCLOPEDIA OF SEWING TECHNIQUES
0–8120–5815–1 Barron's $19.95

- Adele Margolis
ENCYCLOPEDIA OF SEWING
A wide range of sewing techniques and problems, listed in alphabetical order
0–440–14989–1 Doubleday $30.00

- Readers Digest
COMPLETE GUIDE TO SEWING
Well-organized and clearly presented
0–89577–026–1 Random House $21.95

The Singer Sewing Series

Singer Sewing
CLOTHING CARE AND REPAIR
0–86573–205–1 De Cosse pb $14.95
MORE SEWING FOR THE HOME
0–86563–236–1 De Cosse pb $11.95
THE PERFECT FIT
0–86573–213–2 De Cosse pb $11.95
SEWING ESSENTIALS
0–86573–202–7 De Cosse pb $11.95
SEWING FOR THE HOME
0–86573–204–3 De Cosse pb $11.95
SEWING FOR STYLE
0–86573–208–6 De Cosse pb $11.95
TIMESAVING SEWING
0–86573–216–7 De Cosse pb $11.95

Smocking

- Dianne Durand
SMOCKING: Techniques, Projects and Designs
Complete instructions from a leading smocking designer
0–486–23788–5 Dover pb $2.50

- Katherine Fisher & Elizabeth Kay
THE CRAFT OF SMOCKING
0–684–16082–X Scribners pb $5.95

Tatting

Tatting is the art of creating delicate hand-made lace by looping and knotting a single thread.

- Elgiva Nicholls
TATTING: Technique and History
A good illustrated guide for beginners and more advanced tatters
0–486–24612–4 Dover pb $3.95

- Anne Orr
ANNE ORR'S CLASSIC TATTING PATTERNS
Ninety patterns for doilies, edgings, and more
0–486–24897–6 Dover pb $2.50

- Rita Weiss
TRADITIONAL TATTING PATTERNS
Doilies, edgings, collars, and other items
0–486–25066–0 Dover pb $2.95

KNITTING AND CROCHETING

General Knitting

- Rhoda Goldberg
THE NEW KNITTING DICTIONARY: 1000 Stitches and Patterns
0–517–55114–4 Crown pb $8.95

- Sally Harding
COTTON KNITTING
How to work with, and care for, cotton knits, with patterns designed for cotton yarns
0–8120–5816–X Barron's $19.95

- Patricia Harste
THE KNIT KIT
An extensive, illustrated sourcebook in notebook form; includes pattern cards
0–394–54789–6 Random House $30.00

- Anne Matthews
THE VOGUE DICTIONARY OF KNITTING STITCHES
Instructions and color illustrations for 450 stitches
0–688–04688–6 Morrow pb $14.95

- Marinella Nava
THE BOOK OF KNITTING
0–312–08942–2 St. Martin's pb $10.95

- Mary Thomas
MARY THOMAS' BOOK OF KNITTING PATTERNS
A classic (1943), with patterns ranging from elementary to complex
0–486–22818–5 Dover pb $5.95
MARY THOMAS' KNITTING BOOK
Everything from winding yarn and the basic stitches to making garments and blocking
0–486–22817–7 Dover pb $4.50

- Barbara Walker
TREASURY OF KNITTING PATTERNS
Includes 500 patterns, modern and traditional
0–684–17314–X Scribners pb $17.95
SECOND TREASURY OF KNITTING PATTERNS
0–684–16938–X Scribners pb $19.95
CHARTED KNITTING DESIGNS: A Third Treasury of Knitting Patterns
These three volumes contain a wealth of patterns with instructions
0–684–17462–6 Scribners pb (set) $19.95

- Erica Wilson
ERICA WILSON'S KNITTING BOOK
Excellent text from the best-known handicraft writer
0–684–18561–X Scribners $24.95

- Elizabeth Zimmerman
KNITTING WITHOUT TEARS
A best-selling guide for beginners
0–684–13505–1 Scribners pb $12.95

Knitting Techniques and Styles

- Melinda Coss & Debby Robinson
THE DISNEY BOOK OF KNITTING
Projects with designs of Disney characters
0–312–01355–8 St. Martin's $19.95

- Kaffe Fassett
GLORIOUS KNITS
Thirty-five original and colorful designs for sweaters, dresses, vests, and shawls from the English designer
0–517–55843–2 Crown $24.95

- Marion Foale
MARION FOALE'S CLASSIC KNITWEAR
For beginners and experienced knitters; patterns for simple, classic sweaters
0–87857–584–7 Rodale pb $12.95

- Bill Gibb
HOLLYWOOD KNITS
Glamorous knitwear designs worn by such stars as Dorothy Lamour and Cary Grant, updated for today
0–345–34661–0 Ballantine pb $11.95

- Ruth Herring & Karen Masters
KNITTING MASTERPIECES
Sweater designs inspired by such works of art as the Mona Lisa, paintings by Monet and Gauguin, and prehistoric cave paintings
0–394–56266–6 Random House $19.95

Celtic interlace pattern, 7th century

- Shelagh Hollingworth
  **THE COMPLETE BOOK OF
  TRADITIONAL ARAN KNITTING**
  0–312–15635–9 St. Martin's $8.95

- Century Hutchinson
  ELLE KNITS
  Stylish knits from the French fashion
  magazine *Elle*
  0–345–33709–3 Ballantine $22.50

- Jill Jago & Jacque Evans
  KNITTING NOSTALGIA
  Still fashionable designs from 1920–1950,
  with patterns
  0–670–80879–2 Viking $17.95

- Linda Ligon
  **HOMESPUN, HANDKNIT: Caps, Socks,
  Mittens and Gloves**
  Handy small projects
  0–934026–26–2 Interweave pb $15.00

- Sheila McGregor
  **THE COMPLETE BOOK OF
  TRADITIONAL FAIRISLE KNITTING**
  0–684–18707–8 Scribners pb $12.95

  **THE COMPLETE BOOK OF
  TRADITIONAL SCANDINAVIAN
  KNITTING**
  0–312–15638–3 St. Martin's pb $10.95

- James Norbury
  **TRADITIONAL KNITTING PATTERNS
  FROM SCANDINAVIA, THE BRITISH
  ISLES, FRANCE, ITALY AND OTHER
  EUROPEAN COUNTRIES**
  Hundreds of patterns, including an
  especially good selection of fisherman's
  sweaters
  0–486–21013–8 Dover pb $5.95

Crochet

- Liz Blackwell
  **A TREASURY OF CROCHET
  PATTERNS**
  0–68416320–9 Scribners $16.95

- Wanda Bonando
  **STITCHES, PATTERNS AND PROJECTS
  FOR CROCHETING**
  A good reference book, in a practical size.
  The stitches are clearly illustrated by color
  photographs
  0–06–091095–X Harper & Row pb $9.95

- Dorling-Kindersley Staff
  PATTERN LIBRARY: Crochet
  A small book, one of a very handy series,
  with patterns presented in color
  photographs
  0–345–32711–X Ballantine pb $6.95

PATTERN LIBRARY: Crochet Medallions
0–345–31875–7 Ballantine pb $5.95

- Rhoda Goldberg
  THE NEW CROCHET DICTIONARY
  Methods, tools, yarns, patterns,
  patchworks, filet, and Afghan crochet
  0–517–55944–7 Crown pb $9.95

- Marinella Nava
  **THE BOOK OF CROCHET: From
  Beginner to Expert**
  From the simplest patterns to complicated
  designs
  0–312–08832–99 St. Martin's pb $12.95

- Anne Orr
  **ANNE ORR'S FILET CROCHET
  DESIGNS**
  By the legendary designer of the 1920s
  0–486–25103–9 Dover pb $2.95

  CROCHET DESIGNS OF ANNE ORR
  0–486–23621–8 Dover pb $2.00

- Maggie Righetti
  CROCHETING IN PLAIN ENGLISH
  Selecting materials, the right tools, how to
  fix mistakes, the basic stitches, assembling,
  and blocking
  0–312–01412–0 St. Martin's pb $12.95

- Rita Weiss, editor
  FAVORITE FILET CROCHET DESIGNS
  Elegant patterns for tablecloths, placemats,
  bedspreads, and the like, described by an
  expert
  0–486–24930–1 Dover pb $2.75

  HEIRLOOM CROCHET DESIGNS
  0–486–25226–4 Dover pb $2.95

- Florence Weinstein
  VICTORIAN CROCHET
  More than 500 patterns for scarves, shawls,
  gloves, and quilts
  0–486–22890–8 Dover pb $8.95

Afghans

- Anne Orr
  **ANNE ORR'S AFGHANS TO CROCHET
  AND KNIT**
  0–486–25440–2 Dover pb $2.50

- Rita Weiss
  CROCHETING AFGHANS
  0–486–23883–0 Dover pb $2.25

  **OLD-FASHIONED AFGHANS TO KNIT
  AND CROCHET**
  Patterns from the 1940s and 1950s, from
  simple to intricate
  0–486–25054–7 Dover pb $2.95

Macramé

Helene Bress
THE CRAFT OF MACRAME
0–684–14723–8 Scribners pb $3.95

Louise Walker
**GRADED LESSONS IN MACRAME,
KNOTTING AND NETTING**
A widely used Victorian manual of
projects such as tassels, bags, belts, and
bead curtains
0–486–22754–5 Dover pb $4.50

QUILTING

- Vicki Brooks & Linda Stokes
  **THE QUILTER'S CATALOG: A Complete
  Guide to Quilting Sources and Supplies**
  An illustrated guide to useful products and
  sources
  1–55562–004–3 Main Street $20.00

- Averil Colby
  QUILTING
  0–684–16058–7 Scribners pb $11.95

- Agnes Frank & Linda Stokes
  **QUILTING FOR BEGINNERS:
  Patchwork and Appliqué Projects for All
  Ages**
  0–915590–73–5 Main Street $22.50
  0–915590–72–7 Main Street pb $14.95

- Dolores Hinson
  QUILTING MANUAL
  Both a how-to manual and a collector's
  guide; with over 400 illustrations
  0–486–23924–1 Dover pb $3.95

- Carter Houck & Myron Miller
  **AMERICAN QUILTS AND HOW TO
  MAKE THEM**
  0–684–16272–5 Scribners pb $18.95

Mrs. Oliver Byrne's quilt, from The Artist
and the Quilt *by Charlotte Robinson
(Knopf)*

- Carol LaBranche
A CONSTELLATION FOR QUILTERS
The star motif, with hundreds of imaginative variations
0–915590–89–1 Main Street pb $14.95

- Leslie Linsley
THE WEEKEND QUILTER
0–312–86016–1 St. Martin's $19.95

- Joan Masters
PICTURE QUILTS
Combining appliqué with quilting to create distinctive pictures
1–55562–012–4 Main Street pb $14.95

- Paula Nadelson & LynNell Hancock
QUILTING TOGETHER: How to Organize, Design, and Make Group Quilts
Quilts designed and executed by several people on one theme; includes antique and contemporary designs and instructions
0–517–568942 Crown $35.00

- Quilt Digest
THE QUILT DIGEST
This up-to-date encyclopedia of quilts and quilting is published annually
0–913327–13–1 Quilt Digest pb $16.95

- Janet Rae
THE QUILTS OF THE BRITISH ISLES
0–525–48341–1 Dutton pb $19.95

- Elsie Svennas
ADVANCED QUILTING
0–684–16612–7 Scribners pb $4.95

- Michele Walker
THE COMPLETE BOOK OF QUILTMAKING
Basic techniques, instructions for over 60 quilts, and advice for designing your own
0–394–55233–4 Knopf $25.00
0–394–74372–5 Knopf pb $15.95

- Rita Weiss & Linda Macho
EASY QUILTING
A two-volume book
0–486–25266–3 Dover pb $8.95

Patchwork

- Nedda Anders
APPLIQUE OLD AND NEW, INCLUDING PATCHWORK AND EMBROIDERY
An excellent book that includes antique and new examples, materials, quilts, and projects for children
0–486–23246–8 Dover pb $3.95

- Beth Gutcheon
THE PERFECT PATCHWORK PRIMER
0–14–046212–0 Penguin pb $10.95

- Dixie Haywood
CRAZY QUILT PATCHWORK: A Modern Approach with 19 Projects
Design-as-you-go method
0–486–25042–3 Dover pb $4.95

- Carol LaBranche
PATCHWORK PICTURES: 1001 Patterns for Piecing
How to piece pictures in cloth
0–915590–70–0 Main Street pb $22.50

- Maggie Lane
MAGGIE LANE'S ORIENTAL PATCHWORK: Elegant Designs for Easy Living
0–684–16907–X Scribners pb $3.95

- Ruby McKim
ONE HUNDRED AND ONE PATCHWORK PATTERNS
Modern and traditional designs; includes quilt folklore
0–486–20773–0 Dover pb $3.95

- Judy Martin
PATCHWORK: Easy Lessons for Quilt Design and Construction
0–684–17945–8 Scribners $15.95

- Linda Parry, editor
A PRACTICAL GUIDE TO PATCHWORK FROM THE VICTORIA & ALBERT MUSEUM
Classic American and British quilts, with instructions for making them
1–55562–032–9 Main Street $12.95

- Lynette Merlin Syme
LEARN PATCHWORK
Basic instruction and tips, with some historical information; well-explained and illustrated
1–55562–015–9 Main Street $11.95

Leslie Linsley
CALICO COUNTRY CRAFT
More than 50 projects
0–312–00867–8 St. Martin's $19.95

WEAVING

- Mary Black
THE KEY TO WEAVING
The classic handbook for beginners, updated
0–02–511170–1 Macmillan $29.95

- Rachel Brown
THE WEAVING, SPINNING AND DYEING BOOK
Complete and specific; highly recommended
0–394–71595–0 Knopf $16.95

- G.H. Oelsner
A HANDBOOK OF WEAVES
A comprehensive guide, with clear text and more than 1800 diagrams
0–486–23169–0 Dover pb $7.95

- Iona Plath
THE HANDWEAVER'S PATTERN BOOK
Over 120 designs for curtains, upholstery, place mats, and other items
0–486–24166–1 Dover pb $4.95

- Else Regensteiner
THE ART OF WEAVING
Covers looms, weaves, patterns, and designs
0–88740–079–5 Schiffer pb $19.95

- John Tovey
THE TECHNIQUE OF WEAVING
0–7134–3851–7 David & Charles pb $13.95

Dyeing

- Elijah Bemiss
THE DYER'S COMPANION
0–486–20601–7 Dover pb $6.50

- Anne Bliss
A HANDBOOK OF DYES FROM NATURAL MATERIALS
0–684–17893–1 Scribners pb $9.95

- Ira Keller
BATIK: The Art and Craft
Covers all aspects for making batik at home, along with a brief history and sample batiks by modern artists
0–8048–0059–6 Tuttle $13.95

- Joyce Storey
THE THAMES & HUDSON MANUAL OF DYES AND FABRICS
Covers the chemical aspects of textile printing for designers and students
0–500–68016–7 Thames & Hudson pb $10.95

BASKET MAKING

- Mara Cary
BASIC BASKETS
0–395–21989–2 Houghton Mifflin pb $10.95

- Frederick Christopher
BASKETRY
0–486–20677–7 Dover pb $2.95

- Carol & Dan Hart
NATURAL BASKETRY
Eight well-diagrammed projects for wicker and twined baskets
0–8230–3155–1 Watson-Guptill pb $12.95

- Virginia Harvey
THE TECHNIQUES OF BASKETRY
0–295–96415–4 Washington pb $12.95

- Pat Laughridge
LET'S WEAVE COLOR INTO BASKETS
A well-presented slim book of attractive designs
0–88740–056–5 Schiffer pb $6.95

BOOKBINDING AND PAPER CRAFTS

- Edith Diehl
BOOKBINDING: Its Background and Technique
A fat volume by the eminent bookbinder; an historical survey and practical guide
0–486–24020–7 Dover pb $12.95

- Arthur Johnson
  THE PRACTICAL GUIDE TO CRAFT BOOKBINDING
  0–500–27360–X Thames & Hudson pb $9.95

  THAMES & HUDSON MANUAL OF BOOKBINDING
  0–500–68021–6 Thames & Hudson pb $10.95

- Francis Kafka
  HOW TO CLOTHBIND A PAPERBACK BOOK: A Step-by-Step Guide for Beginners
  0–486–23837–7 Dover pb $2.25

- Arthur Lewis
  BASIC BOOKBINDING
  0–486–20169–4 Dover pb $3.50

- Aldren Watson
  HAND BOOKBINDING: A Manual of Instruction
  0–02–624430–6 Macmillan $19.95

Marbling

- Anne Chambers
  THE PRACTICAL GUIDE TO MARBLING PAPER
  An attractive book that can be used by beginners
  0–500–27421–5 Thames & Hudson pb $14.95

- Gabriele Grunebaum
  HOW TO MARBLEIZE PAPER
  0–486–24651–5 Dover pb $2.95

- Stuart Spencer
  MARBLING
  0–88162–303–2 Salem House $14.95

Découpage

- Edmund Gillon
  PICTURE SOURCEBOOK FOR COLLAGE AND DECOUPAGE
  0–486–23095–3 Dover pb $7.95

- Hiram Manning
  MANNING ON DECOUPAGE
  Authoritative book by an expert; includes 18th-century techniques. The patterns are lovely
  0–486–24028–2 Dover pb $6.00

- Eleanor Rawlings
  DECOUPAGE: The Big Picture Sourcebook
  0–486–23182–8 Dover pb $7.50

Faith Shannon
PAPER PLEASURE: The Creative Guide to Papercraft
The full range of paper crafts
1–55584–105–8 W&N $16.95

Origami

- Roger Harbin
  NEW ADVENTURES IN ORIGAMI
  0–06–463555–4 Harper & Row pb $5.95

- Isao Honda
  THE WORLD OF ORIGAMI
  0–87040–383–4 Japan Publications pb $14.95

- Kunihiko Kasahara
  ORIGAMI OMNIBUS: Paper-Folding for Everyone
  An encyclopedic work, with large-size print, that includes projects for children as well as experts
  0–87040–696–5 Japan Publications $24.95

- Kunihiko Kasahara & Toshie Takahama
  ORIGAMI FOR THE CONNOISSEUR
  For the more advanced origami maker: 65 ingenious designs including a stegosaurus
  0–87040–670–1 Japan Publications pb $14.95

- Toyoaki Kawai
  COLORFUL ORIGAMI
  0–06–464074–4 Harper & Row pb $7.95

  JAPAN'S CREATIVE ORIGAMI
  0–06–464073–6 Harper & Row pb $7.95

- Eric Kenneway
  COMPLETE ORIGAMI
  One hundred projects for all levels of skill
  0–312–00898–8 St. Martin's pb $9.95

- Florence Sakade
  ORIGAMI: Japanese Paper Folding

  Volume 1
  0–8048–0454–0 Tuttle pb $3.95

  Volume 2
  0–8048–0455–9 Tuttle pb $3.95

  Volume 3
  0–8048–0456–7 Tuttle pb $3.95

GLASS

- Robert Capp & Robert Bush
  GLASS ETCHING: 52 Patterns with Complete Instructions
  0–486–24578–0 Dover pb $2.95

- Anita & Stewart Isenberg
  HOW TO WORK IN STAINED GLASS
  0–8019–7355–4 Chilton pb $19.95

- James McDonell
  STAINED GLASS CRAFT MADE SIMPLE: Step-by-Step Instructions Using the Modern Copper Foil Method
  0–486–24963–8 Dover pb $2.95

- Barbara Norman
  GLASS ENGRAVING
  Methods of engraving, packing, and transportation, along with a short history of glass illustrated by examples of fine glass. For the home engraver
  0–8048–7018–7 Tuttle $16.50

POTTERY

- F. Carlton Ball & Janice Lovoos
  MAKING POTTERY WITHOUT A WHEEL: Texture and Form in Clay
  0–671–60927–0 Prentice-Hall pb $15.95

- Paulus Berensohn
  FINDING ONE'S WAY WITH CLAY: Creating Pinched Pottery and Working with Colored Clays
  0–671–21763–1 Simon & Schuster pb $10.95

- Donald Campbell
  USING THE POTTER'S WHEEL
  0–671–60895–9 Prentice-Hall pb $12.95

- Emanuel Cooper & Derek Royle
  GLAZES FOR THE POTTER
  0–684–17714–5 Scribners pb $3.95

- Robert Fournier
  THE ILLUSTRATED DICTIONARY OF POTTERY DECORATION: Techniques, Materials and History
  0–671–61376–6 Prentice-Hall $29.95

- Frank & Janet Hamer
  THE POTTER'S DICTIONARY OF MATERIALS AND TECHNIQUES
  A comprehensive reference for potters at all levels, well illustrated
  0–8230–4211–1 Watson-Guptill $37.50

- David Hamilton
  THE THAMES & HUDSON MANUAL OF POTTERY AND CERAMICS
  0–500–68007–8 Thames & Hudson pb $10.95

  THE THAMES & HUDSON MANUAL OF STONEWARE AND PORCELAIN
  0–500–68024–8 Thames & Hudson pb $12.95

- Glenn Nelson
  CERAMICS: A Potter's Handbook
  A successful basic manual covering techniques, material, history, and vocabulary
  0–03–064163–2 HR&W $35.00
  0–03–063227–7 HR&W pb $15.75

China Repair

- Echo Evetts
  CHINA MENDING: A Guide to Repairing and Restoration
  0–571–13058–5 Faber & Faber pb $7.95

WOODWORK AND FURNITURE MAKING

- Family Handyman Magazine
  BUILD-IT-BETTER-YOURSELF COUNTRY FURNITURE
  Intermediate skill level, with over 80 projects
  0–87857–629–0 Rodale $21.95

  THE FURNITURE MAKER'S HANDBOOK
  0–684–17313–1 Scribners pb $15.95

  SEVENTY-FIVE FURNITURE PROJECTS YOU CAN BUILD
  0–8306–9921–X TAB $21.95
  0–8306–1122–3 TAB pb $11.95

- John Feirer
  FURNITURE AND CABINET MAKING: A Complete How-to by America's Foremost Expert on Woodworking
  0–684–17965–2 Scribners pb $22.50

Shaker chest and boxes (Metropolitan Museum), from The American Wing *by Marshall Davidson and Elizabeth Stillinger (Knopf)*

- John Feirer & Gilbert Hutchings
ADVANCED WOODWORK AND FURNITURE MAKING
0–684–17475–8 Scribners $35.00

- Alf Martensson
THE BOOK OF FURNITURE MAKING
0–312–08973–2 St. Martin's $25.95

- Thomas Moser
MEASURED SHOP DRAWINGS FOR AMERICAN FURNITURE
Designs and techniques, with illustrations
0–8069–6792–7 Sterling pb $14.95

- Verna Salomonsky
MASTERPIECES OF FURNITURE IN PHOTOGRAPHS AND MEASURED DRAWINGS
0–486–21381–1 Dover pb $7.95

- Harry Smith
THE ART OF MAKING FURNITURE IN MINIATURE
0–525–93249–6 Dutton pb $32.50

Wood-carving

- Fine Woodworking Magazine
CARVING
0–918804–52–3 Taunton pb $7.95

- Paul Hasluck
MANUAL OF TRADITIONAL WOOD CARVING
A thorough and interesting book on traditional woodcarving, with sections on tools, styles, ornamentation; helpful drawings and photographs
0–486–23489–4 Dover pb $8.95

Collectibles

"The collector not only transports himself, as in a dream, to a distant or past world, but also to a better world, in which men are not provided with the things they need any more than in the everyday world, but things themselves are freed from the servitude of having to be useful."—Mario Praz, *An Illustrated History of Interior Decoration*

- Emyl Jenkins
EMYL JENKINS' APPRAISAL BOOK: Identifying, Understanding, and Valuing Your Treasures
Foreword by Samuel Pennington
0–517–57086–6 Crown $24.95

- Ralph & Terry Kovel
KOVEL'S KNOW YOUR COLLECTIBLES
The bestselling guide to evaluating, buying, and caring for collectibles by two of America's foremost experts
0–517–53608–0 Crown $18.95

- John Marion
SOTHEBY'S INTERNATIONAL ANTIQUES PRICE GUIDE: Antiques and Collectibles, 1988–1989
Features over 8000 objects, all illustrated; articles by experts on collecting trends, aimed at the lower end of the market (objects under $1000); and a glossary of terms and financial studies. Biographical details of artists and craftsmen are included
0–85667–359–5 Sotheby $35.00

- Harry Rinker
WARMAN'S ANTIQUES AND THEIR PRICES
With 50,000 listings and more than 1000 photographs
0–911594–15–9 Warman pb $12.95

- Harry Rinker, editor
WARMAN'S AMERICANA AND COLLECTIBLES
0–911594–12–4 Warman pb $13.95

Autographs and Manuscripts

- Mary Benjamin
AUTOGRAPHS: A Key to Collecting
Emphasizes autographs of prominent American presidents and statesmen
0–486–25035–0 Dover pb $9.95

- Edmund Berkley
AUTOGRAPHS AND MANUSCRIPTS: Collector's Manual
A comprehensive manual of the history and fundamentals of autograph collecting
0–684–15622–9 Scribners $24.95

Coins

- Walter Breen
WALTER BREEN'S COMPLETE ENCYCLOPEDIA OF U.S. AND COLONIAL COINS
The definitive reference book, with more than 4000 illustrations
0–385–14207–2 Doubleday $75.00

- Coin World
COIN WORLD ALMANAC
More than 500,000 historical and recent facts and figures for collectors and investors, from the most authoritative American numismatic publication. This 5th edition includes current issues, trends, and record prices
0–88687–324–X Pharos pb $14.95

- Gustave Schon
SIMON & SCHUSTER'S WORLD COIN CATALOGUE
Considered the definitive work: with descriptions and latest prices for more than 11,000 coins minted since 1901
0–671–60416–3 Simon & Schuster pb $14.95

- Scott Travers
COIN COLLECTORS' SURVIVAL MANUAL: An Indispensable Guide for Collectors and Investors
"If followed closely, it should help [readers] do far more than just survive; it should point the way to prosperity"—*NY Times*
0–13–140393–1 Prentice-Hall pb $12.95

- Robert Wolenik
THE COINAGE GUIDE TO COLLECTING AND INVESTING IN COINS
A first-rate introduction, with chapters devoted to scarcity, market trends, and aesthetics. Included is a step-by-step plan for building a collection
0–531–15511–0 Franklin Watts $16.95
0–671–64467–X Simon & Schuster pb $6.95

Dolls and Dollhouses

- Catherine Christopher
COMPLETE BOOK OF DOLL MAKING AND COLLECTING
0–486–22066–4 Dover pb $6.50

- Dorothy Coleman
COLLECTOR'S ENCYCLOPEDIA OF DOLLS
A comprehensive book on dollmakers, clothing, and marks, with over 2000 illustrations

Volume 1: Ancient Times through 1900
0–517–00059–8 Crown $39.95

Volume 2: 1900 through 1930
0–517–55796–7 Crown $55.00

- Barbara Ferguson
THE PAPER DOLL: A Collector's Guide with Prices
0–87069–401–4 Wallace-Homestead pb $14.95

- Flora Jacobs
A HISTORY OF DOLL HOUSES
0–684–14538–3 Scribners pb $14.95

- Wendy Lavitt
THE KNOPF COLLECTORS' GUIDES TO AMERICAN ANTIQUES: Dolls
Includes detailed descriptions and pictures of dolls from the 18th century to the present, as well as advice for the collector
0–394–71542–X Knopf $13.95

- John Schweiter
THE ABC OF DOLL COLLECTING
0–8069–7696–9 Sterling pb $9.95

Maps

- Lloyd Brown
THE STORY OF MAPS
The standard history of cartography, from earliest times to the present
0–486–23873–3 Dover pb $8.95

- Seymour Schwartz & Ralph Ehrenburg
MAPPING OF AMERICA
0–686–62687–7 Abrams $60.00

Movie and TV Memorabilia

- Lee Cotten
ELVIS CATALOG: Memorabilia, Icons and Collectibles Celebrating the King of Rock 'n' Roll
0–385–23705–7 Doubleday $35.00
0–385–23704–9 Doubleday pb $17.95

- Barbara Fenick
COLLECTING THE BEATLES: An Introduction and Price Guide to Fab Four Collectibles, Records, and Memorabilia
0–8092–5393–3 Contemporary pb $14.95

- Chris Gentry & Sally Gibson-Downs
ENCYCLOPEDIA OF TREKKIE MEMORABILIA: Identification and Value Guide
0–89689–066–X Americana pb $16.95

- Bevis Hillier, editor
WALT DISNEY'S MICKEY MOUSE MEMORABILIA: The Vintage Years, 1928–1938
0–8109–1439–5 Abrams $35.00

- Anthony Slide
A COLLECTOR'S GUIDE TO MOVIE MEMORABILIA
0–87069–377–8 Wallace-Homestead $12.95

Music

- Jerry Aycliffe
COLLECTING JUKE BOXES AND SLOT MACHINES
0–89689–055–4 Americana pb $10.95

- David Bowers
ENCYCLOPEDIA OF AUTOMATIC MUSICAL INSTRUMENTS
An extensive book (1000 pages) on music boxes, player pianos, and organs, and all variations of automatic music machines
0–911572–65–1 Vestal pb $45.00

- L.R. Docks
AMERICAN PREMIUM RECORD GUIDE: 78s, 45s, 1915–1965
0–89689–054–6 Americana pb $14.95

- Graham Webb
THE MUSICAL BOX HANDBOOK
A complete listing of makers and agents

Volume 1: Cylinder Boxes
0–911572–36–8 Vestal pb $14.95

Volume 2: Disc Boxes
0–911572–51–1 Vestal pb $15.95

Political Buttons and Memorabilia

- Roger Fischer
TIPPECANOE AND TRINKETS TOO: The Material Culture of American Presidential Campaigns, 1828–1984
0–252–00960–6 Illinois $34.95

- Theodore Hake
POLITICAL BUTTONS

Volume 1: 1789–1916
0–918708–03–6 Hake's Americana pb $20.00

Volume 2: 1920–1976
0–918708–01–X Hake's Americana pb $20.00

Rare Books

- John Carter
ABC FOR BOOK COLLECTORS
An essential reference, with over 450 entries on the vocabulary and conventions of book collecting
0–394–41403–9 Knopf $18.95

- Jack Matthews
COLLECTING RARE BOOKS FOR PLEASURE AND PROFIT
0–8214–0610–8 Ohio $20.95
0–8214–0611–6 Ohio pb $11.95

- G. Uden
UNDERSTANDING BOOK COLLECTING
For the novice and experienced collector: first editions, the condition of books, and other technical aspects, written with great enthusiasm
1–85149–028–0 Antique Collectors pb $19.95

Sports Memorabilia

- Carl Luckey
IDENTIFICATION AND VALUE GUIDE TO OLD FISHING LURES
0–89689–058–9 Americana pb $14.95

- John & Morton Olman
ENCYCLOPEDIA OF GOLF COLLECTIBLES
0–89689–050–3 Americana pb $14.95

- Don Raycraft & Stew Salowitz
COLLECTOR'S GUIDE TO BASEBALL MEMORABILIA
Includes uniforms, bats, gloves, and programs
0–89145–338–5 Collector pb $14.95

- Frank Slocum
CLASSIC BASEBALL CARDS: The Golden Years, 1886–1956
Over 9000 cards reproduced in color, featuring players from the glory days
Foreword by Ted Williams
0–446–51392–X Warner $75.50

Stamps

- Richard Cabeen
STANDARD HANDBOOK OF STAMP COLLECTING
This authoritative guide, often revised, contains everything novice and advanced philatelists need to know, from starting a collection to the fine points of expanding one
0–06–091326–6 Harper & Row pb $9.95

- Herman Herst
FUN AND PROFIT IN STAMP COLLECTING
0–940403–05–6 Linn's Stamp pb $3.95

- James MacKay
THE GUINNESS BOOK OF STAMP FACTS AND FEATS
Facts and trivia by a noted stamp author
0–85112–351–1 Sterling pb $19.95

- Scott Publishing
SCOTT SPECIALIZED CATALOGUE OF UNITED STATES STAMPS
A well-organized reference for collectors and dealers, essential for current market values
0–89487–112–9 Scott pb $23.00

Toys and Games

- Linda Baker
MODERN TOYS, 1930–1980
0–89145–277–X Collector $19.95

- Pierre Carlson
TOY TRAINS: A History From 1840 to 1955
0–06–015614–7 Harper & Row $24.95

- Lee Dennis
WARMAN'S ANTIQUE AMERICAN GAMES, 1840–1940
0–911594–08–6 Warman pb $14.95

- Joseph Doucette & Charles Collins
COLLECTING ANTIQUE TOYS: A Practical Guide
0–02–533010–1 Macmillan $17.95

- Lillian Gottschalk
AMERICAN TOY CARS AND TRUCKS, 1894–1942
0–89659–653–2 Abbeville $85.00

- Everett Grist
ANTIQUE AND COLLECTIBLE MARBLES
0–89145–357–1 Collector pb $9.95

- William Kennedy
TOY SOLDIERS
0–312–01478–3 Saint Martin's $19.95

- Henry Kurtz & Burtt Ehrlich
THE ART OF THE TOY SOLDIER
0–89659–746–6 Abbeville $75.00

- Margaret Mandel
TEDDY BEARS AND STEIFF ANIMALS
0–89145–356–3 Collector $19.95

- Barbro Werkmaster & others
TEDDY BEARS
0–8120–5960–3 Barron's $12.95

- Blair Whitton
THE KNOPF COLLECTORS' GUIDES TO AMERICAN ANTIQUES: Toys
0–394–71526–8 Knopf pb $13.95

- Henry Wiencek
THE WORLD OF LEGO TOYS
0–8109–1790–4 Abrams $29.95
0–8109–2362–9 Abrams pb $17.95

Other

- Jack Martells
BEER CAN COLLECTORS' BIBLE
0–394–28918–8 Ballantine pb $7.95

- Cyril Permutt
COLLECTING OLD CAMERAS
0–306–70855–8 Da Capo Press $29.50

- Robert Overstreet
THE COMIC BOOK PRICE GUIDE
The most comprehensive guide to the market, including a history of comic books
0–517–56103–4 Crown pb $10.95

- Bernard Watney & Homer Babbidge
CORKSCREWS FOR COLLECTORS
0–85667–113–4 Sotheby $29.95

- Scott Bruce
LUNCH BOX: The Fifties and Sixties
0–87701–535–X Chronicle pb $14.95

- Elizabeth Bennion
ANTIQUE MEDICAL INSTRUMENTS
A history of instruments from the Middle Ages through the 19th century
0–520–03832–0 California $67.50

- George LaBarre
COLLECTING STOCKS AND BONDS
A 3-volume work
0–941538–00–1 George LaBarre (set) pb $14.95

- Maurice Rickards
COLLECTING PRINTED EPHEMERA
An introduction to printed ephemera with collecting advice and conservation tips
0–89659–893–4 Abbeville $35.00

- John & Margaret Kaduck
RARE AND EXPENSIVE POSTCARDS
Nearly 1000 rare postcards described and priced
0–87069–407–3 Wallace-Homestead pb $10.95

- Lou McCulloch
CARD PHOTOGRAPHS: A Guide to Their History and Value
0–916838–56–0 Schiffer $30.00

- Gideon Bosker
GREAT SHAKES: Salt and Pepper for All Tastes
Wacky, colorful, collectible shakers, 1920–1950
0–89659–608–7 Abbeville $19.95

- Gillian Walkling
TEA CADDIES
0–317–02535–X Faber & Faber pb $10.95

- Cecil Clutton & George Daniels
WATCHES: A Complete History of the Technical and Decorative Development of the Watch
0–85667–058–8 Sotheby $85.00

- H.G. Harris
COLLECTING AND IDENTIFYING OLD WATCHES
0–87523–190–X Emerson $16.95

- Hugh Tait
CLOCKS AND WATCHES
0–674–13571–7 Harvard pb $6.95

Fashion and Costume

Books on fashion and costume can be divided into histories, picture and photography books, social commentary, biographies, and practical guides. The strength of each area is determined by our current preoccupations. Fashion is perhaps the most capricious business in America, and this trend is reflected in its literature.

The lavish life-style of the 1980s has brought a renewed interest in haute couture, and there are many beautiful books on Coco Chanel, Christian Dior, and Yves Saint-Laurent. There are only occasional works on the imaginative creations of contemporary Japanese and Italian designers, and even fewer books on the street fashion so popular in the 1960s.

The history of fashion and costume is well represented, ranging from studies of court dress to changes in working clothes throughout history. Alison Lurie, Prudence Glynn, and Anne Hollander are among the gifted writers concerned with the meaning of dress.

Articles by today's generation of fashion journalists have yet to be collected, and of the legendary fashion editors only Diana Vreeland's life exists in print.

The current vogue for how-to books is reflected in guides to a more beautiful appearance, a better figure, and a more practical wardrobe—advice often offered by movie stars or models. Men are advised on how to dress for business success or how to appear as gentlemen.

- Charlotte Calasibetta
FAIRCHILD'S DICTIONARY OF FASHION
0–87005–635–2 Fairchild $50.00

ESSENTIAL TERMS OF FASHION: A Collection of Definitions
Both books are useful for those in the fashion profession
0–87005–519–4 Fairchild pb $13.50

- Catherine Houck
THE FASHION ENCYCLOPEDIA: An Essential Guide to Everything You Need to Know about Clothes
0–312–28401–2 St. Martin's pb $13.95

- James Laver
COSTUME AND FASHION
An excellent concise history
0–500–20190–0 Thames & Hudson pb $11.95

- Georgina O'Hara
THE ENCYCLOPEDIA OF FASHION
Introduction by Carrie Donovan
0–8109–0882–4 Abrams $29.95

THE PSYCHOLOGY OF CLOTHES

- Kennedy Fraser
FASHIONABLE MIND: Reflections on Fashion, 1970–1983
Essays describing the sociological reasons for fashion trends and their effects on our culture
0–394–51775–X Knopf $14.50

SCENES FROM THE FASHIONABLE WORLD
Entertaining essays on contemporary fashion from the *New Yorker*
0–394–55483–3 Knopf $17.95

- Prudence Glynn
SKIN TO SKIN: Eroticism in Dress
All ages and cultures, by the former fashion editor of the *Times* (London)
0–19–520391–7 Oxford $39.95

- Ann Hollander
SEEING THROUGH CLOTHES
A classic analysis of the function of clothes
0–14–011084–4 Penguin pb $14.95

- Alison Lurie
THE LANGUAGE OF CLOTHES
Includes chapters on age, status, gender, and pattern. "A delightful book"—Tom Wolfe
0–394–51302–9 Random House $20.00
0–394–71713–9 Random House pb $13.95

TO ORDER BOOKS AS GIFTS, SEE PAGE 1

1950 Dior evening gown (photo by Louise Dahl-Wolfe), from Dior *by Françoise Giroud (Rizzoli)*

- Aileen Ribeiro
DRESS AND MORALITY
A provocative account of the role of dress from ancient Greece to the present
0–8419–1091–X Holmes & Meier $44.50

- Elizabeth Wilson
ADORNED IN DREAMS: Fashion and Modernity
Argues that fashion should not be regarded merely as an illustration of the oppression of women but should be explored for its many cultural and political meanings
0–520–06212–4 California pb $9.95

HISTORY OF FASHION

- François Boucher
TWENTY THOUSAND YEARS OF FASHION: The History of Costume and Personal Adornment
A beautifully illustrated, comprehensive volume
Introduction by Yvonnes Deslandres
0–8109–1693–2 Abrams $45.00

- Diana De Marly
WORKING DRESS: A History of Occupational Clothing
Changes in dress and working conditions, from early agrarian societies through the industrial revolution
0–8419–1111–8 Holmes & Meier $44.50

- Madeleine Ginsburg & others
400 YEARS OF FASHION
Mannequins model fashions from the Victoria & Albert Museum collections
0–00–217189–9 Faber & Faber pb $14.95

- Auguste Racinet
THE HISTORICAL ENCYCLOPEDIA OF FASHION
A recent edition of this classic history, illustrated with 2000 lithographs
0–8160–1976–2 Facts On File $40.00

- Nancy Rexford
WOMEN'S CLOTHING IN AMERICA, 1795–1930
Their design, construction, and evolution
0–8419–0986–5 Holmes & Meier $25.00

- Lynn Schnurnberger
LET THERE BE CLOTHES: 40,000 Years of Fashion From Cro-Magnon to Lacroix
A witty romp through the history of fashion, including fads and trivia
0–89480–833–8 Workman pb $16.95

Specialized Histories

- Martin Battersby
ART DECO FASHION: French Designers, 1908 to 1925
0–312–05181–6 St. Martin's pb $10.95

- Stella Blum, editor
ACKERMANN'S COSTUME PLATES: Women's Fashions in England, 1818–1828
0–486–23690–0 Dover pb $5.95

EIGHTEENTH CENTURY FRENCH FASHION PLATES: 64 Engravings from the Galerie des Modes, 1778–1787
0–486–24331–1 Dover pb $11.95

PARIS FASHIONS OF THE 1890s: A Picture Source Book with 450 Designs Including 24 in Full Color
0–486–24534–9 Dover pb $7.95

VICTORIAN FASHIONS AND COSTUMES FROM HARPER'S BAZAAR, 1898–1967
Fashion plates selected by an eminent authority and former curator of the Metropolitan Museum's Costume Institute
0–486–22990–4 Dover pb $10.95

- Anne Buck
DRESS IN 18TH CENTURY ENGLAND
A vivid picture of those who made, wore, and admired clothes in 18th-century England
0–8419–0517–7 Holmes & Meier $49.50

- Madeleine Ginsburg
VICTORIAN DRESS IN PHOTOGRAPHS
0–8419–0838–9 Holmes & Meier $47.50

- Caroline Goldthorpe
FROM QUEEN TO EMPRESS: Victorian Dress, 1837–1877
The lavishly illustrated catalog for a recent Metropolitan Museum exhibition
0–8109–1178–7 Abrams $19.95

- Jane Mulvagh
THE VOGUE HISTORY OF 20TH-CENTURY FASHION
From the whalebone corset to the freeflowing miniskirt of today
0–670–80172–0 Viking $50.00

- John Peacock
FASHION SKETCHBOOK, 1920–1960
Foreword by Mary Quant
0–500–27090–2 Thames & Hudson pb $9.95

- Aileen Ribeiro
DRESS IN EIGHTEENTH CENTURY EUROPE, 1715–1789
An authoritative study
0–8419–1016–2 Holmes & Meier $49.50

Natalie Rothstein, editor
A LADY OF FASHION: Barbara Johnson's Album of Styles and Fabrics
Barbara Johnson, born in 1783, spent most of her life in fashionable English country houses. In this fascinating album she presents fabric swatches, fashion illustrations, contemporary engravings, flowers, and commentary. Beautifully reproduced facsimile color pages
0–500–01419–1 Thames & Hudson $75.00

HAUTE COUTURE

On Balenciaga:
Its skirt is sculpted in an astounding way into the shape of a spinning top, and formed from row upon row of pinked ruffles, so that the legs would seem to grow out of its heart, like stamens from a black chrysanthemum. To contemplate this dress is to feel an irresistibly mounting gaiety, and finally the viewer is impelled to utter a sort of snort expressing satisfaction in a world that has seen the birth of such a piece of art.

Kennedy Fraser
FASHIONABLE MIND: Reflections on Fashion 1970–1983
0–394–51775–X Knopf $14.50

- Diana De Marly
THE HISTORY OF HAUTE COUTURE, 1850 to 1950
The great houses of Paris and the social climate in which they flourished
0–8419–0586–X Holmes & Meier $49.50

- Caroline Milbank
COUTURE: The Great Designers
Beautifully illustrated essays on the work of 60 couturiers
0–941434–51–6 Stewart, Tabori & Chang $75.00

- Valerie Steele
PARIS FASHION: A Cultural History
Debunks many myths about the fashion industry
0–19–504465–7 Oxford $35.00

- Palmer White
HAUTE COUTURE EMBROIDERY: The Art of Lesage
The family firm that has produced the splendid embroidery for great couturiers from Poiret to Lagerfeld
0–86565–094–2 Rizzoli $50.00

The Couturiers

- Edmonde Charles-Roux
CHANEL AND HER WORLD
Chanel's dashing life and career, elegantly portrayed by the former editor of French *Vogue*
0–86565–024–1 Rizzoli pb $19.95

BILL BLASS:
Some Favorite Books on
Fashion

Diana Vreeland
THE IMPERIAL STYLE: Fashions of
the Hapsburg Era
Out of print

Cecil Beaton
THE BEST OF BEATON
Out of print

Diana De Marly
THE HISTORY OF HAUTE
COUTURE, 1850 to 1950
0-8419-0586-X Holmes & Meier $49.50

Caroline Milbank
COUTURE: The Great Designers
0-941434-51-6 ST&C $75.00

Lois Perschetz
THE DESIGNING LIFE
0-517-55986-2 Clarkson Potter $35.00

Metropolitan Museum Curators
YVES SAINT LAURENT
Out of print

Edmonde Charles-Roux
CHANEL AND HER WORLD
0-86565-024-1 Rizzoli pb $19.95

Michael & Ariane Batterberry
FASHION: The Mirror of History
0-517-38881-2 Outlet $24.95

Barbara Walz & Bernadine Morris
THE FASHION MAKERS
Out of print

Diana Vreeland & Irving Penn
INVENTIVE PARIS CLOTHES,
1909-1939
Out of print

William Packer
THE ART OF VOGUE COVERS,
1909-1940
0-517-55857-2 Outlet $18.95

François Boucher
TWENTY THOUSAND YEARS OF
FASHION: The History of Costume
and Personal Adornment
0-8109-1693-2 Abrams $45.00

Bridget Keenan
DIOR IN VOGUE
Out of print

Christopher Wood
TISSOT
0-212-1635-X NY Graphic Society $60.00

Yvonne Deslandres
POIRET
0-8478-0802-5 Rizzoli $95.00

Nicholas Coleridge
THE FASHION CONSPIRACY: The
Dazzling Inside Story of the Glamorous
World of International High Fashion
0-06-016013-6 Harper & Row $19.95

Max Tilke
COSTUME PATTERNS AND
DESIGNS
0-302-00266-9 Harper & Row $70.00

Milia Davenport
BOOK OF COSTUME
0-517-03716-5 Crown $39.95

Issey Miyake
BODYWORKS
Out of print
EAST MEETS WEST
Out of print

John Fairchild
THE FASHIONABLE SAVAGES
Out of print

Jean Leymarie
CHANEL
0-8478-0874-2 Rizzoli $95.00

Françoise Giroud
DIOR: Christian Dior, 1905 to 1957
0-8478-0860-2 Rizzoli $110.00

- **Yves Saint-Laurent**
YVES SAINT-LAURENT: Images of
Design, 1958-1988
His finest and most influential designs
photographed by Irving Penn, Snowdon,
and Helmut Newton
Introduction by Marguerite Duras
0-394-57326-9 Knopf $100.00

- **Palmer White**
ELSA SCHIAPARELLI
The designer who created "shocking pink"
was every bit as fascinating as her fashions
Introduction by Yves Saint-Laurent
0-8478-0752-5 Rizzoli $45.00

- **Andre Leon Talley**
VALENTINO
The luxurious creations of the Italian
designer who shows in Paris, presented by
an influential *Vogue* editor
0-8478-5417-5 Rizzoli $150.00

BillyBoy
BARBIE: Her Life and Times
Barbie doll dressed by the great
couturiers, as well as the evolution of
Barbie
0-517-56574-9 Crown $25.00

Barbara Guyette
HAUTE COUTURE FOR THE JET
SET TEDDY BEAR
0-87588-265-X Hobby Horse pb $5.95

INTERNATIONAL CONTEMPORARY FASHION

- **Nicholas Coleridge**
THE FASHION CONSPIRACY: The
Dazzling Inside Story of the Glamorous
World of International High Fashion
From Paris salons to Korean sweatshops,
the clothes and those who wear them. An
often scathing attack from a British
journalist
0-06-016013-6 Harper & Row $19.95

- **Richard de Combray & others**
ARMANI
The work of the Italian sportswear king
0-847-5418-3 Rizzoli $150.00

- **Leonard Koren**
NEW FASHION JAPAN
Kimonos, high fashion design, street and
rural dress
0-87011-676-2 Kodansha pb $24.95

- **Thierry Mugler**
THIERRY MUGLER
Innovative photographs taken by the
French designer of his daring creations, in
dramatic poses
Preface by Jack Lang
0-8478-0999-4 Rizzoli $50.00

- **Irving Penn, photographer**
ISSEY MIYAKE
The leader of the Japanese avant-garde.
"Japanese in origin, Western in spirit and,
finally, universal not just in their impact

- **Jean Leymarie**
CHANEL
A handsomely illustrated, behind-
the-scenes view of the early 20th-century
art and fashion worlds in Paris
0-8478-0874-2 Rizzoli $95.00

- **Françoise Giroud**
DIOR: Christian Dior, 1905 to 1957
From his first collection in 1947, which
introduced the New Look, Dior was
recognized as a major figure. This lavish
book, commemorating the 50th
anniversary of the house of Dior, is written
by the former French minister of culture
0-8478-0860-2 Rizzoli $110.00

- **Guillermo de Osma**
MARIANO FORTUNY: His Life and Work
The designer best known for his use of
pleated fabric
0-8478-0641-3 Rizzoli $29.95

- **Meredith Etherington-Smith**
PATOU
0-312-59817-3 St. Martin's $19.95

- **Yvonne Deslandres**
POIRET
A lavishly illustrated book on the turn-
of-the-century designer, known for his use
of strong primary colors and graceful
designs for the corsetless figure
0-8478-0802-5 Rizzoli $95.00

☞ **TO ORDER NEW BOOKS NOT YET LISTED, ASK YOUR BOOKSELLER OR CALL 1-800-882-8770**

but in the ravishing new images of the body they propose"—*Time*
0–8212–1720–8 NY Graphic Society $40.00

- **Jeffrey Trachtenberg**
  RALPH LAUREN: The Man Behind the Mystique
  How the American designer made the Brooks Brothers look into a financial and marketing success
  0–316–85214–7 Little, Brown $19.95

SPECIAL FASHIONS

Fashion by Artists

- **Julie Dale**
  ART TO WEAR
  Original clothes designed and made by artists
  0–89659–664–8 Abbeville $95.00

- **Richard Martin**
  FASHION AND SURREALISM
  Extravagant and ingenious fashion designs; the influence of 1920s and '30s art on designers
  0–8478–0831–9 Rizzoli $45.00

- **Barbara Radice**
  JEWELRY BY ARCHITECTS
  Jewelry by some of the best known post-modern architects, with interviews explaining their designs
  0–8478–0798–3 Rizzoli $35.00

Specific Fashion

- **Gideon Bosker & Jena Lencek**
  MAKING WAVES: Swimsuits and the Undressing of America
  0–87701–398–5 Chronicle pb $19.95

- **Douglas Bullis**
  CALIFORNIA FASHION DESIGNERS: Art and Style
  The lives and work of 35 young contemporary designers
  0–87905–278–3 Gibbs Smith pb $24.95

- **Caroline Hall & Nicholas Drake**
  THE SIXTIES: The Decade in Vogue
  Introduction by David Bailey
  0–13–811647–4 Prentice-Hall $35.00

- **James Mablen**
  GETTIN' IT ON: The Clothing of Rock 'n Roll
  0–89659–686–9 Abbeville $35.00

- **Dyer Spark**
  FIT TO BE TIED
  Vintage neckties
  0–89659–756–3 Abbeville $19.95

- **Thomas Steele**
  THE GREAT AMERICAN T SHIRT
  0–451–79972–0 NAL pb $5.95

  THE HAWAIIAN SHIRT: Its Art and History
  0–89659–419–X Abbeville $19.95

ACCESSORIES

Fashion in Vogue Series

"Each offers a short course not only in its specific design area, but also in fashion history in general. [The author] has filled her books with splashes of art, visual wit and imagination."—*NY Times*

Christina Probert
HATS IN VOGUE SINCE 1910
0–89659–267–7 Abbeville pb $12.95

LINGERIE IN VOGUE SINCE 1910
0–89659–276–6 Abbeville pb $12.95

SHOES IN VOGUE SINCE 1910
0–89659–241–3 Abbeville pb $12.95

SPORTSWEAR IN VOGUE SINCE 1910
0–89659–499–8 Abbeville pb $12.95

SWIMWEAR IN VOGUE SINCE 1910
0–89659–242–1 Abbeville pb $9.95

- **Andrew Baseman**
  THE SCARF
  Couture scarves, gaily printed bandanas, humorous souvenir scarves, extravagant shawls; and ideas for tying and wearing them
  1–55670–061–X Stewart, Tabori & Chang $30.00

- **Fiona Clark**
  HATS
  A history of hat design, including changes in hairdressing and headwear
  0–7134–3774–X Drama Book $15.95

- **Valerie Cumming**
  GLOVES
  A concise history of gloves and their role in social behaviour
  0–7134–1008–6 Drama Book $16.95

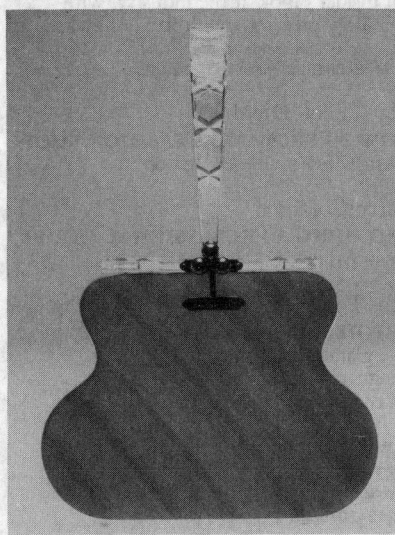

1950s plastic handbag, from A Certain Style *by Robert Gottlieb and Frank Maresca (Knopf)*

- **Vanda Foster**
  BAGS AND PURSES
  The history of pocketbooks carried by men and women
  0–7134–3772–3 Drama Book $15.95

- **Robert Gottlieb & Frank Maresca**
  A CERTAIN STYLE: The Art of the Plastic Handbag, 1949–1959
  0–394–56893–1 Knopf $35.00

- **Alice Mackrell**
  SHAWLS, STOLES, AND SCARVES
  From 1600 to today
  0–7134–4876–8 Drama Book $15.95

- **Cecil Saint-Laurent**
  THE GREAT BOOK OF LINGERIE
  An intriguing history by the witty French author
  0–86565–072–1 Vendome $25.00

- **June Swann**
  SHOES
  A history of footwear
  0–7134–0942–8 Drama Book $15.95

- **Geoffrey Warren**
  FASHION ACCESSORIES, 1500–1960
  An illustrated chronological study of hats, shoes, and gloves
  0–89676–094–4 Drama Book $35.00

Jewelry

- **Vivienne Becker**
  ART NOUVEAU JEWELRY
  0–525–24345–3 Dutton $50.00

- **Barbara Cartlidge**
  TWENTIETH CENTURY JEWELRY
  0–8109–1685–1 Abrams $60.00

- **Corinne Davidov & Ginny Dawes**
  THE BAKELITE JEWELRY BOOK
  0–89659–867–5 Abbeville $35.00

- **Lois Sherr Dubin**
  THE HISTORY OF BEADS: From 30,000 BC to the Present
  An unusual book on the history of beads as a medium of trade, talismans, and adornment. Beautiful color illustrations
  0–8109–0736–4 Abrams $60.00

- **Leslie Field**
  THE QUEEN'S JEWELS: The Personal Collection of Elizabeth II
  The British monarch's unrivaled collection
  0–8109–1525–1 Abrams $29.95

- **John Mack**
  ETHNIC JEWELRY
  Noncommercial jewelry from around the world
  0–8109–0891–3 Abrams $40.00

- **David Marcum**
  THE DOW JONES-IRWIN GUIDE TO FINE GEMS AND JEWELRY
  A price guide
  0–87094–687–0 Dow Jones-Irwin $27.50

- Jane Mulvagh
COSTUME JEWELRY IN VOGUE
0–500–27513–0 Thames & Hudson pb $19.95

- Hans Nadelhoffer
CARTIER: JEWELERS EXTRAORDINARY
The great designers of art deco jewelry
0–8109–0770–4 Abrams $60.00

- Gilles Neret
BOUCHERON: Four Generations of a World Renowned Jeweller
A beautiful book on one of the most daring of the grand French jewelers
0–8478–0987–0 Rizzoli $85.00

- Harold Newman
AN ILLUSTRATED DICTIONARY OF JEWELRY
0–500–27452–5 Thames & Hudson pb $18.95

- Penny Proddow & Debra Healy
AMERICAN JEWELRY
The history of American jewelry, from such early firms as Shreve, Crump & Low to the most modern houses
0–8478–0830–0 Rizzoli $75.00

- Silvie Raulet
ART DECO JEWELRY
"A beautiful and serious tribute to Fouquet, Van Cleef & Arpels, Cartier, and all the others"—*House & Garden*
0–8478–0622–7 Rizzoli $85.00

JEWELRY OF THE 1940s AND 1950s
The heyday of the great houses of Europe, such as Boucheron, Cartier, and Bulgari
0–8478–0935–8 Rizzoli $95.00

VAN CLEEF AND ARPELS
One of the world's great jewelers
0–8478–0754–1 Rizzoli $85.00

- Jody Shields
ALL THAT GLITTERS: The Glory of Costume Jewelry
An amusing look at an art of fantasy
0–8478–0868–8 Rizzoli pb $45.00

MENSWEAR

- Bruce Boyer
ELEGANCE: A Guide to Quality in Menswear
A *Town & Country* writer's advice on stylish dress
0–393–01878–4 Norton $18.95
0–393–30438–8 Norton pb $9.95

- Diana DeMarly
FASHION FOR MEN: An Illustrated History
How men's styles and the masculine ideal have varied through the centuries
0–8419–1013–8 Holmes & Meier $47.50

- Alan Flusser
MAKING THE MAN: The Insider's Guide to Buying and Wearing Men's Clothes
By a prominent menswear designer
0–671–79147–8 Simon & Schuster pb $9.95

- Paul Keers
A GENTLEMAN'S WARDROBE: Classic Clothes and the Modern Man
0–517–56758–X Crown pb $12.95

- Richard Martin
JOCKS AND NERDS: Men's Style in the Twentieth Century
0–8478–1045–3 Rizzoli $45.00

- Ellen Moers
THE DANDY: Brummell to Beerbohm
0–8032–3052–4 Nebraska $23.50
0–8032–8101–3 Nebraska pb $6.50

- John Molloy
DRESS FOR SUCCESS
An enormously successful book. "How to select clothes so they will look efficient, authoritative, and reliable—even when they are incompetent, weak, and shifty"—Alison Lurie
0–446–38552–4 Warner pb $9.95

THE FASHION BUSINESS

"The fashion industry is no more able to preserve a style that men and women have decided to abandon than to introduce one they do not choose to accept. In America, for instance, huge advertising budgets and the wholehearted cooperation of magazines such as *Vogue* and *Esquire* have not been able to save the hat, which for centuries was an essential part of everyone's outdoor (and often of their indoor) costume. It survives now mainly as a utiliatrian protection against weather, as part of ritual dress (at formal weddings, for example) or as a sign of age or individual eccentricity."—Alison Lurie, *The Language of Clothes*

- Barbaralee Diamonstein
FASHION: The Inside Story
An insider's look at the industry, with revealing interviews with top designers
Foreword by Bernardine Morris
0–8478–0610–3 Rizzoli pb $29.95

- Mary Ellen Diehl
HOW TO PRODUCE A FASHION SHOW
0–87005–159–8 Fairchild $15.00

- Larry Goldman
BECOMING A PROFESSIONAL MODEL
0–688–06147–8 Morrow pb $12.95

- Lois Perschetz
THE DESIGNING LIFE
The glamorous home life of fashion designers
0–517–55986–2 Clarkson Potter $35.00

- Melissa Sones
GETTING INTO FASHION: A Career Guide
0–345–30756–9 Ballantine pb $7.95

- Ann Stegemeyer
WHO'S WHO IN FASHION
0–87005–574–7 Fairchild $22.50

People in Fashion

"Once I decided to lay an entire issue of *Vogue* out backward, like a Japanese book, because that's how I thought everyone looked at magazines. You always see people reading that way, flipping a magazine from back to front. We never published it. It would have been a flop. But the basic idea was right."—Diana Vreeland, *D.V.*

- John Fairchild
CHIC SAVAGES: Inside Nouvelle Society—New Money and Haute Couture
An amusing, sometimes scathing, look at the rich fashion followers, from their guru, the publisher of *Women's Wear Daily*
0–671–68334–9 Simon & Schuster $22.95

- Suzy Menkes
THE WINDSOR STYLE
An examination of the fashion and style carefully created by the Duke and Duchess of Windsor
0–88162–321–0 Salem House $34.95

- Anna Piaggi
LAGERFELD'S SKETCHBOOK: Karl Lagerfeld's Illustrated Fashion Journal of Anna Piaggi
The eccentric Italian *Vogue* editor on one of Paris' current favorite designers
1–55584–019–1 Weidenfeld & Nicolson $19.98

- Charles Spencer
ERTE
Biography of the fashion illustrator and costume designer
0–517–54391–5 Clarkson Potter pb $16.95

- Hugo Vickers
CECIL BEATON: A Biography
The entertaining life of the English designer
0–316–90244–6 Little, Brown $25.00
1–55611–021–9 Donald Fine pb $12.95

Barbie in Hermès, from Barbie: Her Life and Times *by BillyBoy (Crown)*

➤ **FOR OVERSEAS ORDERING INFORMATION, SEE PAGE 1**

- Diana Vreeland
D.V.
The eccentric views and sayings of the redoubtable and tremendously influential *Vogue* editor
Edited by George Plimpton & Christopher Hemphill
0–394–73161–1 Random House pb $3.95

- Richard Walker
SAVILE ROW: An Illustrated History
The mecca for fine British tailoring
0–8478–1020–8 Rizzoli $25.00

Fashion Photography

- John Esten & Willis Hartshorn
MAN RAY: Bazaar Years
Fashion and celebrity photographs done by Man Ray for *Harper's Bazaar,* from 1934 to 1942, many previously unpublished
0–8478–1008–9 Rizzoli $35.00
0–8478–1009–7 Rizzoli pb $19.95

David Mellor
CECIL BEATON: A Retrospective
0–8212–1632–5 NY Graphic Society $35.00

Josephine Ross
BEATON IN VOGUE
0–517–56233–2 Crown $45.00

- Valentine Lawford
HORST: His Work and His World
0–394–52171–4 Knopf $55.00

- Kathryn Livingston
FASHION PHOTOGRAPHY: Patrick Demarchelier
One of today's most popular fashion photographers whose work appears regularly in *Vogue*
0–8212–1736–4 Bulfinch $40.00

- John Szarkowski
IRVING PENN
0–316–43451–5 NY Graphic Society $60.00

Fashion Illustration

- Nicholas Drake
FASHION ILLUSTRATION TODAY
More than 20 fashion illustrators from Paris, Milan, New York, and London
0–500–27486–X Thames & Hudson $18.95

- Erté
DESIGNS BY ERTE: Fashion Drawings and Illustrations from Harper's Bazaar
0–486–23397–9 Dover pb $8.95

- Elizabeth Ewing
HISTORY OF TWENTIETH CENTURY FASHION ILLUSTRATION
0–389–20631–8 Barnes & Noble $31.50

- William Packer
FASHION DRAWING IN VOGUE
Includes drawings by Dalí, Botero, and Lepape
Preface by David Hockney
0–500–27528–9 Thames & Hudson pb $24.95

- Sharon Lee Tate
THE COMPLETE BOOK OF FASHION ILLUSTRATION
Well-illustrated and comprehensive
0–06–464085–X Harper & Row pb $15.95

HOW TO DRESS

- Carol Baker
BENETTON COLOR STYLE FILE
A color guide from the successful Italian clothing chain
0–670–81939–5 Viking $19.95

- Emily Cho & Hermine Lueders
IT'S YOU: Looking Terrific Whatever Your Type
A useful what-to-wear guide by a wardrobe consultant
0–345–33164–8 Ballantine pb $7.95

- Patricia Coen & Bryan Milford
CLOSETS: Designing and Organizing the Personalized Closet
How to reorganize your closet and wardrobe
1–55584–096–5 Weidenfeld & Nicolson $22.95
1–55584–097–3 Weidenfeld & Nicolson pb $12.95

- Charlotte Du Cann
VOGUE MODERN STYLE: How To Achieve It
Imaginative ways of dressing with a modern look, illustrated with 200 photographs from British *Vogue*
0–7126–1807–4 David & Charles pb $19.95

- Theodora Faiola & Jo Pullen
MCGRAW-HILL GUIDE TO CLOTHING
0–07–019855–1 McGraw-Hill $26.50

- Mablen Jones
TAKING CARE OF CLOTHES
A most useful guide for taking care of clothes and ensuring that they last
0–312–90355–3 St. Martin's pb $4.95

- John Molloy
THE WOMAN'S DRESS FOR SUCCESS BOOK
Tips on how to get promoted: one way is to wear a gray suit and demure blouse
0–446–38586–7 Warner pb $8.95

- Scott Norman
HOW TO BUY GREAT SHOES THAT FIT
A handy guide written by a Ferragamo salesman
0–688–57048–3 Crown pb $5.95

- Susan Sommers
FRENCH CHIC: How to Dress Like a French Woman
The little secrets of a Frenchwoman's style
0–394–54704–7 Random House $18.95

- Norio Yamanaka
THE BOOK OF KIMONO
A practical guide on how to select, wear, and take care of the kimono
0–87011–785–8 Kodansha pb $11.95

BEAUTY

- Martin Harrison
BEAUTY PHOTOGRAPHY IN VOGUE
Includes work by Helmut Newton, Irving Penn, and Bruce Weber
1–55670–017–2 Stewart, Tabori & Chang $30.00

- Judith Brode Hirsch
THE SPA BOOK: A Guide to the Top 101 Resorts in America
0–399–51491–0 Putnam pb $10.95

- Edwin Morris
FRAGRANCE: The Story of Perfume from Cleopatra to Chanel
An excellent history
0–684–18195–9 Scribners $24.95

- Naomi Sims
ALL ABOUT HEALTH AND BEAUTY FOR THE BLACK WOMAN
Written by a successful black model and cosmetician
0–385–18333–X Doubleday pb $9.95

- Francis Stein & Rochelle Udell
HOT TIPS: 1000 Fashion and Beauty Tricks
Fashion and beauty editors offer their secrets
0–399–50715–9 Putnam pb $9.95

Skin Care

- Joseph Bark
SKIN SECRETS: A Dermatologist's Prescription for Beautiful Skin at Any Age
0–07–003671–3 McGraw-Hill $18.95
0–07–003672–1 McGraw-Hill pb $8.95

- Nelson Lee Novick, M.D.
SUPER SKIN: A Leading Dermatologist's Guide to the Latest Breakthroughs in Skin Care
Includes the effects of sun and aging, rashes, and recent medical breakthroughs
0–517–57035–1 Crown $18.95

Hair and Make-up

- James Stevens Cox
AN ILLUSTRATED DICTIONARY OF HAIRDRESSING AND WIGMAKING
A standard reference
0–7134–4208–5 Drama Book $35.00

- Rex Hilverdink
MAKING UP
A thorough guide to make-up styles and techniques
0–517–55754–1 Crown $19.95

- Louis Licari & Sharon Esche
COLOR YOUR HAIR WITH HAIRCOLOR
The latest in hair coloring by a color specialist, with photos of his celebrity clients
0–399–51498–8 Putnam pb $8.95

- Joey Mills
NEW CLASSIC BEAUTY: A Step-by-Step Guide to Naturally Glamorous Makeup
0–394–56433–2 Random House $19.95

James Tissot's study for "The Last Evening" (Smith College Museum), from Tissot *by Krystyna Matyjaszkiewicz (Abbeville)*

Drama Book Costume Series

Margaret Scott
VISUAL HISTORY OF COSTUME: The 14th and 15th Centuries
0–7134–4857–1 Drama Book $19.95

Jane Ashelford
VISUAL HISTORY OF COSTUME: The 16th Century
0–89676–076–6 Drama Book $19.95

Valerie Cumming
VISUAL HISTORY OF COSTUME: The 17th Century
0–89676–078–2 Drama Book $19.95

Vanda Foster
VISUAL HISTORY OF COSTUME: The 19th Century
0–89676–079–0 Drama Book $19.95

Penelope Byrde
VISUAL HISTORY OF COSTUME: The 20th Century
0–7134–4859–8 Drama Book $19.95

- Lee Pola & Patricia Bozic
CUTTING HAIR AT HOME: Step-by-Step Home Hair-Cutting for the Entire Family
Practical tips for avoiding hairdressers
0–452–60205–8 NAL pb $9.95

Celebrity Secrets

- Christie Brinkley
CHRISTIE BRINKLEY'S OUTDOOR BEAUTY AND FITNESS BOOK
By the star model
0–671–53065–8 Simon & Schuster pb $9.95

- Francesco Scavullo
SCAVULLO WOMEN
The beauty secrets of the photographer's celebrity subjects
0–06–091298–7 Harper & Row pb $14.95

- Raquel Welch
THE RAQUEL WELCH TOTAL BEAUTY AND FITNESS PROGRAM
0–449–90169–6 Fawcett pb $9.95

COSTUME

- Millia Davenport
BOOK OF COSTUME
A recommended book, with excellent illustrations
0–517–03716–5 Crown $39.95

- Carl Kohler
HISTORY OF COSTUME
Detailed illustrated history, up to 1870
0–486–21030–8 Dover pb $7.50

- R. Turner Wilcox
FIVE CENTURIES OF AMERICAN COSTUME
Includes sections on military dress, the costume of the early settlers, and children's clothes
0–684–15161–8 Scribners $27.50

THE MODE IN COSTUME
Illustrated with drawings; includes an amusing section on women's hairdresses
0–684–13913–8 Scribners pb $16.95

Specific Costume

- Chou Hsun & Kao Ch'un-ming
FIVE THOUSAND YEARS OF CHINESE COSTUMES
0–8351–1822–3 China Books $49.95

- Robert La Vine
IN A GLAMOROUS FASHION: The Fabulous Years of Hollywood Costume Design
0–684–16610–0 Scribners $25.00

- Helen Minnich & Shojiro Nomura
JAPANESE COSTUME AND THE MAKERS OF ITS ELEGANT TRADITION
0–8048–0287–4 Tuttle $50.00

P A R T 8

PERFORMING ARTS AND MEDIA

Western Classical Music

REFERENCE

Stanley Sadie, editor
THE NEW GROVE DICTIONARY OF MUSIC AND MUSICIANS
The *Grove Dictionary* began its life in the late 19th century as a personal account of music by Sir George Grove, a confirmed amateur. This sixth edition, published as a 20-volume set, is a new and more factual work with articles ranging from national anthems and Indian ragas to definitive studies of Western musical masters. Some of these have been collected in separate volumes, noted below
0–333–23111–2 Grove $2,100.00

• Christine Ammer
HARPER DICTIONARY OF MUSIC
"Sufficiently comprehensive for amateurs and laymen"—*Saturday Review*
0–06–181020–7 Harper & Row $22.00

• Don M. Randel, editor
THE NEW HARVARD DICTIONARY OF MUSIC
"Drawing on the latest musical research and buttressed by a large group of advisers and readers, Professor Randel has provided concise, accurate, and literate entries pertaining to the entire field of music"—Philip Gossett, University of Chicago
0–674–61525–5 Harvard $35.00

• Michael Kennedy
OXFORD DICTIONARY OF MUSIC
0–19–311333–3 Oxford $39.95

Specialized Works

• Denis Arnold, editor
THE NEW OXFORD COMPANION TO MUSIC
0–19–311316–3 Oxford (2-volume set) $99.00

• Harold Barlow & Sam Morgenstern
A DICTIONARY OF MUSICAL THEMES
An ideal reference guide to 10,000 themes by composers ranging from Adolphe Adam to Efrem Zimbalist
0–517–52446–5 Crown pb $14.95

• Edward Downes
THE GUIDE TO SYMPHONIC MUSIC
0–8027–7177–7 Walker pb $24.95

NEW YORK PHILHARMONIC GUIDE TO THE SYMPHONY
0–8027–0540–5 Walker $50.00

• Edward Greenfield & Robert Layton, editors
THE COMPLETE PENGUIN STEREO RECORD AND CASSETTE GUIDE
0–14–046682–7 Penguin pb $12.95

• Arthur Jacobs
THE NEW PENGUIN DICTIONARY OF MUSIC
0–14–051012–5 Penguin pb $8.95

• Roger Lax & Frederick Smith
THE GREAT SONG THESAURUS
Popular songs from the 16th century to today
0–19–503222–5 Oxford $85.00

• Norman Lebrecht
THE BOOK OF MUSICAL ANECDOTES
Seven hundred eighty-six tales about composers, performers, and their art. For example: "Donizetti, when asked which of his own operas he thought the best, replied, 'How can I say which? A father always has a preference for a crippled child, and I have so many' "
0–02–918710–9 Free Press $24.95

• S.S. Prawer, editor
THE PENGUIN BOOK OF LIEDER
0–14–008123–2 Penguin pb $6.95

• Stanley Sadie, editor
THE NEW GROVE DICTIONARY OF MUSICAL INSTRUMENTS
From "A"—an obsolete Korean barrel drum—to "Zye-zye"—the iron ankle rattle of the Angas people of Nigeria—this three-volume reference work does for instruments what its larger relative did for all of musical life and history
0–943818–05–2 Grove (set) $450.00

• Nicolas Slonimsky, editor
BAKER'S BIOGRAPHICAL DICTIONARY OF MUSICIANS
This is a sparkling, scrupulous account of musicians' lives and works, both familiar and exotic, spiced with Nicolas Slonimsky's personal style
0–317–46604–6 Macmillan $95.00

MUSIC HISTORY

• Gerald Abraham & others, editors
NEW OXFORD HISTORY OF MUSIC
An encyclopedic, integrated survey, detailed and invaluable for both scholars and general readers

Volume 1: Ancient and Oriental Music
0–19–316301–2 Oxford $95.00

Volume 2: Early Medieval Music Up to 1300
0–19–316302–0 Oxford $95.00

Volume 3: Ars Nova and the Renaissance, 1300–1540
0–19–316303–9 Oxford $95.00

Volume 4: The Age of Humanism, 1540–1630
0–19–316304–7 Oxford $95.00

Volume 5: Opera and Church Music, 1630–1750
0–19–316305–5 Oxford $95.00

Volume 6: Concert Music, 1630–1750
0–19–316306–3 Oxford $95.00

Volume 7: The Age of Enlightenment, 1745–1790
0–19–316307–1 Oxford $95.00

Volume 8: The Age of Beethoven, 1790–1830
0–19–316308–X Oxford $95.00

Volume 10: The Modern Age, 1890–1960
0–19–316310–1 Oxford $95.00

• Gerald Abraham
CONCISE OXFORD HISTORY OF MUSIC
The abridged version for readers on all levels
0–19–311319–8 Oxford $60.00
0–19–284010–X Oxford pb $21.95

• Donald Grout & Claude Palisca
A HISTORY OF WESTERN MUSIC
An introductory course in musical history, written with judgment and care
0–393–95627–X Norton $28.95

• Oliver Strunk, editor
SOURCE READINGS IN MUSIC HISTORY
A five-volume series
0–393–09742–0 Norton (set) pb $24.95

Volume 1: Antiquity and the Middle Ages
0–393–09680–7 Norton pb $7.95

Volume 2: The Renaissance Era
0–393–09681–5 Norton pb $5.95

Volume 3: The Baroque Era
0–393–09682–3 Norton pb $9.95

Volume 4: The Classic Era
0–393–09683–1 Norton pb $5.95

Volume 5: The Romantic Era
0–393–09684–X Norton pb $6.95

Middle Ages and Renaissance

• Giulio Cattin
MUSIC OF THE MIDDLE AGES (1)
Devoted to the vast repertory of monophonic music that forms the basis of Europe's musical tradition
0–521–28489–9 Cambridge pb $16.95

• F.A. Gallo
MUSIC OF THE MIDDLE AGES (2)
A study of medieval polyphony examining the links between music and contemporary political, civil, and religious events
0–521–23049–7 Cambridge $39.50
0–521–28483–X Cambridge pb $15.95

• Harry Haskell
THE EARLY MUSIC REVIVAL: A History
"A fine companion to the music and musicians it celebrates"—John Rockwell, *NY Times*
0–500–01449–3 Thames & Hudson $29.95

• Richard Hoppin
MEDIEVAL MUSIC
Ranges from the earliest chants of the Roman church to polyphony in the beginning of the 15th century
0–393–09090–6 Norton $26.95

• Nicholas Kenyon, editor
AUTHENTICITY AND EARLY MUSIC
0–19–816152–2 Oxford $49.95
0–19–816153–0 Oxford pb $14.95

☎ **TO ORDER ANY BOOK IN THIS CATALOG, ASK YOUR BOOKSELLER OR CALL 1-800-882-8770**

• Gustave Reese
MUSIC IN THE MIDDLE AGES
0–393–09750–1 Norton $34.95

• Friedrich Blume
RENAISSANCE AND BAROQUE MUSIC: A Comprehensive Survey
0–393–09710–2 Norton pb $7.95

• Howard Brown
MUSIC IN THE RENAISSANCE
0–13–608497–4 Prentice-Hall pb $26.00

• Gustave Reese & others
THE NEW GROVE HIGH RENAISSANCE MASTERS
0–393–01689–7 Norton $17.95
0–393–30093–5 Norton pb $9.95

• David Fallows
DUFAY
"A lively picture of the world of 15th-century music in which Fallows explains why Dufay goes down with modern audiences, proposes new dates for important works and identifies a lost Mass cycle"—*Times* (London)
0–394–75561–8 Random House pb $10.95

• Denis Arnold
MONTEVERDI
0–8226–0716–6 Littlefield, Adams pb $7.95

THE NEW MONTEVERDI COMPANION
Monteverdi's music was once rarely heard in modern musical life, but he has been rediscovered in recent decades as a profound innovator and creator of operatic masterpieces
0–571–13148–4 Faber & Faber $39.95
0–571–13357–6 Faber & Faber pb $19.95

• Leo Schrade
MONTEVERDI, CREATOR OF MODERN MUSIC
0–306–79565–5 Da Capo $42.50

Baroque

• Denis Arnold & others
THE NEW GROVE ITALIAN BAROQUE MASTERS
Biographical essays and critical assessments of Monteverdi, Frescobaldi, Cavalli, Corelli, A. Scarlatti, Vivaldi, and D. Scarlatti
0–393–01690–0 Norton $17.95
0–393–30094–3 Norton pb $9.95

• Joshua Rifkin & others
THE NEW GROVE NORTH EUROPEAN BAROQUE MASTERS
0–393–01695–1 Norton $17.95
0–393–30099–4 Norton pb $9.95

• Christoph Wolff
THE NEW GROVE BACH FAMILY
If music ever had a dynasty, it was the Bach family. The first important figures were town musicians in the early 17th century; the last, representing the rococo age of the mid-18th century, were the great Johann Sebastian's sons
0–393–01684–6 Norton $16.50
0–393–30088–9 Norton pb $9.95

Johann Sebastian Bach, from The New Grove Bach Family *by Christoph Wolff and others (Norton)*

• Malcolm Boyd
BACH
0–394–75277–5 Random House pb $9.95

• Hans David & Arthur Mendel, editors
THE BACH READER
This classic text reprints documents of the period, accounts by contemporaries, the first published biography by Forkel, and an account of the Bach revival in the mid-19th century
0–393–00259–4 Norton pb $12.95

• Karl & Irene Geiringer
JOHANN SEBASTIAN BACH: The Culmination of an Era
0–19–500554–6 Oxford $24.00

• Philip Spitta
JOHANN SEBASTIAN BACH: His Work and Influence
This survey of Bach's music and life was the first "modern" study of the composer, its two volumes dating from 1873 and 1880. Spitta not only used modern techniques of scholarship, but sensitively attended to the symbolism and spirit of the music, helping to lay the groundwork for the Bach revival

Volume 1
0–486–22278–0 Dover $18.75

Volume 2
0–486–22279–9 Dover $18.75

• Winton Dean & Anthony Hicks
THE NEW GROVE HANDEL
Charts Handel's career before and after he came to England and gives particular attention to the staged works
0–393–01682–X Norton $16.50
0–393–30086–2 Norton pb $9.95

• Ralph Kirkpatrick
DOMENICO SCARLATTI
A biography and musicological study of the baroque composer that reintroduced him to our era, defined a performing style, ordered the works chronologically, and assessed his importance—by one of the premier harpsichordists of the 20th century
0–691–02708–0 Princeton pb $16.50

Classical

The classical composers—Haydn, Mozart, Beethoven, and Schubert—remain at the heart of Western musical culture, while other tastes vary according to fashion. "I do not want to turn Haydn, Mozart, and Beethoven into Hegelians," Charles Rosen writes in his book on the classical style (see below), "but the simplest way to summarize classical form is as the symmetrical resolution of opposing forces. If this seems so broad as to be a definition of artistic form in general, that is because the classical style has largely become the standard by which we judge the rest of music—hence its name."

• Friedrich Blume
CLASSIC AND ROMANTIC MUSIC
The concepts of "classic" and "romantic" in their historical contexts and the range of interpretations they have undergone
0–393–09868–0 Norton pb $8.95

• Hugh Ottaway & Arthur Hutchings
THE PELICAN HISTORY OF MUSIC: Classical and Romantic
0–14–020494–6 Penguin pb $6.95

• Charles Rosen
THE CLASSICAL STYLE: Haydn, Mozart, Beethoven
"The word 'masterpiece' should be used rarely if at all," wrote George Steiner, "but it applies to Charles Rosen's *The Classical Style*." This 1971 book is recognized as the most important and influential work of music criticism in our time. Even the layman will come away ready to hear musical tensions, symmetries, and dramas in new ways
0–393–00653–0 Norton pb $10.95

• Emily Anderson, editor
THE LETTERS OF BEETHOVEN
0–393–02247–1 Norton $75.00

• Martin Cooper
BEETHOVEN: The Last Decade, 1817–1827
0–19–315321–1 Oxford pb $18.95

• Elliot Forbes, editor
THAYER'S LIFE OF BEETHOVEN
A monumental achievement in musical biography. Beethoven was dead just over two decades when Thayer, an American musical amateur and bibliophile, travelled to Europe to extract the truth from the contradictory accounts of the composer's life. Much of the truth he established remains definitive. A two-volume set
0–691–09103–X Princeton (set) $102.00
0–691–02702–1 Princeton (set) pb $19.95

• George Grove
BEETHOVEN AND HIS NINE SYMPHONIES
0–486–20334–4 Dover pb $5.95

• Michael Hamburger, editor and translator
BEETHOVEN: Letters, Journals and Conversations
"A portrait of Beethoven that has the fascination of a documentary film"—*New Yorker*
0–500–27324–3 Thames & Hudson pb $7.95

• Joseph Kerman
THE BEETHOVEN QUARTETS
0–393–00909–2 Norton pb $10.95

• Joseph Kerman & others
THE NEW GROVE BEETHOVEN
0–393–01687–0 Norton $16.50
0–393–30091–9 Norton pb $10.95

• Denis Matthews
BEETHOVEN
"Professor Matthews was an excellent choice to write this much needed, new, concise assessment"—*London Daily Telegraph*
0–394–75562–6 Random House pb $9.95

• Maynard Solomon
BEETHOVEN
This fine example of psychoanalytic biography, by a preeminent—and nonacademic—Beethoven scholar, discerns the psychological themes of the life and connects them with the stylistic transformations of the music
0–02–872240–X Schirmer pb $12.95

• Oscar Sonneck, editor
BEETHOVEN: Impressions by His Contemporaries
0–486–21770–1 Dover pb $4.95

• Hans Keller
THE GREAT HAYDN QUARTETS
0–8076–1167–0 George Braziller $22.50

• H.C. Landon
HAYDN: Chronicle and Works
The definitive modern study of a composer who, as Landon writes, "began in abject poverty, half-trained and largely self-educated . . . rose to be the leading musical figure of Europe in the 1790s and achieved greater popularity in his own lifetime than any composer before him"

Volume 1: The Early Years, 1732–1765
0–253–37001–9 Indiana $85.00

Volume 2: Haydn at Eszterhaza, 1766–1790
0–253–37002–7 Indiana $60.00

Volume 3: Haydn in England, 1791–1795
0–253–37003–5 Indiana $70.00

Volume 4: The Years of "The Creation," 1796–1800
0–253–37004–3 Indiana $75.00

Volume 5: The Late Years, 1801–1809
0–253–37005–1 Indiana $70.00

• Jens Larsen & Georg Feder
THE NEW GROVE HAYDN
Haydn's life and development, and an authoritative listing of his output by two leading scholars
0–393–01681–1 Norton $16.50
0–393–30085–4 Norton pb $9.95

• Emily Anderson
THE LETTERS OF MOZART AND HIS FAMILY
Mozart's letters are among the most extraordinary documents relating to music: whimsical, mordant, graceful, they send us back to the music chastened about our notion of Mozart's divinity, but no less in awe of his achievements
0–393–02248–X Norton $50.00

• Volkmar Braunbehrens
MOZART IN VIENNA, 1781–1791
Translated by Timothy Bell
0–8021–1009–6 Grove $25.00

• Alfred Einstein
MOZART: His Character, His Work
Einstein provides a model for writing about music. He is scholarly, well informed, and precise, but also a critic of grace and worldly insight
0–19–500538–4 Oxford $39.95
0–19–500732–8 Oxford pb $12.95

• Wolfgang Hildesheimer
MOZART
This reflective biography attempts to reveal the man behind the myth without slighting his achievement
0–374–21483–2 Farrar, Straus & Giroux $30.00
0–394–71591–8 Random House pb $6.95

• H. Robbins Landon & Donald Mitchell, editors
A MOZART COMPANION
0–393–00499–6 Norton pb $10.95

• Paul Lang, editor
THE CREATIVE WORLD OF MOZART
0–393–00218–7 Norton pb $5.95

• Stanley Sadie
THE NEW GROVE MOZART
0–393–30084–6 Norton pb $9.95

• Maurice Brown & Eric Sams
THE NEW GROVE SCHUBERT
0–393–01683–8 Norton $16.50
0–393–30087–0 Norton pb $10.95

• Otto Deutsch, editor
FRANZ SCHUBERT'S LETTERS & OTHER WRITINGS
0–8443–0028–4 Vienna House pb $10.00

• George Marek
SCHUBERT: A Biography
A popularly written biography spiced with anecdotes and atmosphere
0–670–62104–8 Viking $19.95

• Charles Osborne
SCHUBERT AND HIS VIENNA
0–394–54111–1 Knopf $18.95

Romantic

The word "romanticism" has become as commonplace in musicological description as the word "classical." The personal, the imagistic, the overtly expressive, the impassioned: these are our associations with romantic music. But the transformation is more central—not just a matter of heart in place of head, but a new function for both. As Claude Lévi-Strauss once suggested, this is the music that has taken over the function of myth in our culture, giving us our gods, detailing our origins, telling tales of our desires and fates.

• Gerald Abraham
ONE HUNDRED YEARS OF MUSIC
0–7156–0703–0 Longwood $40.50
0–7156–0704–9 Longwood pb $13.50

• Jacques Barzun
BERLIOZ AND HIS CENTURY: An Introduction to the Age of Romanticism
"In order to understand the nineteenth century, it is essential to understand Berlioz, and in order to understand Berlioz, it is essential to read Professor Barzun"—W.H. Auden
0–226–03861–0 Chicago pb $9.95

• Martin Cooper
FRENCH MUSIC: From the Death of Berlioz to the Death of Fauré
0–19–316202–4 Oxford pb $10.95

• Alfred Einstein
MUSIC IN THE ROMANTIC ERA
0–393–09733–1 Norton $14.95

• Rey Longyear
NINETEENTH-CENTURY ROMANTICISM IN MUSIC
0–13–622697–3 Prentice-Hall pb $27.00

• Leon Plantinga
ROMANTIC MUSIC: A History of Musical Style
0–393–95196–0 Norton $22.95

• Nicholas Temperley & others
THE NEW GROVE EARLY ROMANTIC MASTERS, I: Chopin, Schumann, and Liszt
"Temperley's . . . discussion treats Chopin's historical position excellently and succinctly"—Charles Rosen, *NY Review of Books*
0–393–01691–9 Norton $17.95
0–393–30095–1 Norton pb $9.95

• John Tyrrell & others
THE NEW GROVE TURN OF THE CENTURY MASTERS: Janácek, Mahler, Strauss, and Sibelius
0–393–01694–3 Norton $17.95
0–393–30098–6 Norton pb $9.95

• John Warrack & others
THE NEW GROVE EARLY ROMANTIC MASTERS, II: Weber, Berlioz, and Mendelssohn
0–393–01692–7 Norton $17.95
0–393–30096–X Norton pb $9.95

Hector Berlioz
MEMOIRS
Berlioz wrote music as if it were programmatic literature; he was also one of music's first men of letters. His description of coming to musical age in France when romanticism was young is an unsurpassed musical autobiography,

---

> a counterpart to the musical
> autobiographies penned in his scores
> 0–486–21563–6 Dover pb $9.95

- Julian Rushton
THE MUSICAL LANGUAGE OF BERLIOZ
This learned treatment of Berlioz's music envisions him outside the mainstream of the musical tradition, owing little to others and leaving few heirs
0–521–24279–7 Cambridge $57.50

- Karl Geiringer
BRAHMS: His Life and Work
"A rare book, equally a product of fine scholarship, a splendid literary gift, and intimate feeling for his subject"—Irving Kolodin
0–306–76093–2 Da Capo $45.00
0–306–80223–6 Da Capo pb $11.95

- Jean-Jacques Eigeldinger
CHOPIN: Pianist and Teacher As Seen by His Pupils
0–521–24159–6 Cambridge $69.50

- James Huneker
CHOPIN: The Man and His Music
This turn-of-the-century American critic wrote about music as if it were a sort of rich confection for the soul
0–486–21687–X Dover pb $4.50

- J.-M. Nectou
GABRIEL FAURE: His Life Through His Letters
0–7145–2768–8 Marion Boyars $40.00

- Sacheverell Sitwell
LISZT
0–486–21702–7 Dover pb $7.50

- Alan Walker
FRANZ LISZT: The Virtuoso Years, 1811–1847
"Splendidly documented, tempered with just the right amount of skepticism about previously accepted work and 'facts' "—Harold C. Schoenberg, *NY Times*
0–394–52540–X Knopf $25.00

- Kurt Blaukopf
GUSTAV MAHLER
0–87910–029–X Limelight pb $12.95

- Norman Lebrecht, editor
MAHLER REMEMBERED
Anecdotes about a composer whose time has, as he himself predicted, finally come
0–393–02572–1 Norton $25.00

- Donald Mitchell
GUSTAV MAHLER: The Early Years
0–520–04141–0 California $42.00
GUSTAV MAHLER: The Wunderhorn Years
0–520–04220–4 California pb $14.95
GUSTAV MAHLER: Songs and Symphonies of Life and Death
0–520–05578–0 California $55.00

- Bruno Walter
GUSTAV MAHLER
0–306–71701–8 Da Capo $32.50

- Nancy Reich
CLARA SCHUMANN: The Artist and the Woman
0–8014–1748–1 Cornell $27.50
0–8014–9388–9 Cornell pb $9.95

- Peter Ostwald
SCHUMANN: The Inner Voices of a Musical Genius
1–55553–014–1 Northeastern pb $12.95

- Leon Plantinga
SCHUMANN AS CRITIC
0–306–70785–3 Da Capo $42.50

- Eric Sams
THE SONGS OF ROBERT SCHUMANN
Introduction by Gerald Moore
0–903873–18–4 Da Capo pb $18.50

- Robert Schumann
ON MUSIC AND MUSICIANS
Virgil Thomson writes, "Robert Schumann is the best music critic who ever lived. He had a composer's understanding of what other composers were up to and of all the differences between originality . . . and mere tastefulness"
0–520–04685–4 California pb $10.95

- Burnett D. James
THE MUSIC OF JEAN SIBELIUS
A musical study of the "voice of the north," who combined the late-romantic appetite for nationalistic music with Nordic detachment and foreboding
0–8386–3070–7 Fairleigh Dickinson $24.50

- Egon Gartenberg
JOHANN STRAUSS: The End of an Era
0–306–80098–5 Da Capo pb $6.95

- Norman Del Mar
RICHARD STRAUSS: A Critical Commentary on His Life and Works
"The three volumes of this magnificent book should be studied by all lovers of late-romantic music, amateurs and professionals alike"—*TLS*
Volume 1
0–8014–9317–X Cornell pb $12.95
Volume 2
0–8014–9318–8 Cornell pb $12.95
Volume 3
0–8014–9319–6 Cornell pb $12.95

- Kurt Wilhelm
RICHARD STRAUSS: An Intimate Portrait
Wilhelm's friendship with Strauss' family and friends has provided much new material for this biography. Many photographs
0–8478–1021–6 Rizzoli $50.00

- John Warrack
CARL MARIA VON WEBER
0–521–29121–6 Cambridge pb $17.95

- John Warrack, editor
CARL MARIA VON WEBER: Writings on Music
0–521–22892–1 Cambridge $77.50

Russian Music

- Gerald Abraham & David Brown
THE NEW GROVE RUSSIAN MASTERS I: Glinka, Borodin, Balakirev, Mussorgsky, Tchaikovsky
0–393–02282–X Norton $17.95
0–393–30102–8 Norton pb $10.95

- Gerald Abraham & Hugh Macdonald
THE NEW GROVE RUSSIAN MASTERS II: Rimsky-Korsakov, Skryabin, Rachmaninov, Prokofiev, Shostakovich
0–393–02283–8 Norton $17.95
0–393–30103–6 Norton pb $10.95

- Rostislav Dubinsky
STORMY APPLAUSE: Making Music in a Worker's State
"Well written and colloquial, it evokes the core of the life of a Soviet musician from the death of Stalin to the time of Mr. Dubinsky's departure from the Soviet Union"—Isaac Stern

- Israel Nestyev
PROKOFIEV
0–8047–0585–2 Stanford $45.00

- Harlow Robinson
SERGEI PROKOFIEV: A Biography
0–670–80419–3 Viking $29.95
1–55778–009–9 Paragon pb $12.95

- Nikolai Rimsky-Korsakov
MY MUSICAL LIFE
0–8443–0024–1 Vienna House $20.00

- Roy Blokker & Robert Dearling
THE MUSIC OF DMITRI SHOSTAKOVICH
0–8386–1948–7 Farleigh Dickinson $22.50

- Christopher Norris
SHOSTAKOVICH: The Man and His Music
0–7145–2778–5 Marion Boyars $25.00

- Dmitri Shostakovich
TESTIMONY: The Memoirs of Dmitri Shostakovich
The composer's bitter, ironic, and scathing memoirs
0–87910–021–4 Limelight pb $11.95

- David Brown
TCHAIKOVSKY: The Early Years, 1840–1874
0–393–07535–4 Norton $24.95
TCHAIKOVSKY: The Crisis Years, 1874–1878
0–393–01707–9 Norton $24.95
TCHAIKOVSKY: The Years of Wandering, 1878–1885
0–393–02311–7 Norton $24.95

Modern French Music

- Elaine Brody
PARIS: The Musical Kaleidoscope, 1875–1925
0–8076–1176–X Braziller $19.95

- Rollo Myers
MODERN FRENCH MUSIC
0–306–76158–0 Da Capo $29.50

- Claude Debussy
LETTERS
"I had dinner with André Gide some time ago," the composer writes in one of his letters. "He's like an old spinster, timid, gracious and polite in the English manner, but he's charming and very swift at coming up with subtle and ingenious ideas. He has a horror of Wagner—a sure sign of a refined intelligence"
0–674–19429–2 Harvard $27.50

- François Lesure & Richard Smith, editors
DEBUSSY ON MUSIC
0–8014–9420–6 Cornell pb $12.95

- Leon Vallas
CLAUDE DEBUSSY: His Life and Works
Traces Debussy's rebellious years at the Conservatoire that culminated in his winning of the Prix de Rome, and his absorption in the bohemian life of Paris
0–486–22916–5 Dover pb $6.50

- Pierre Bernac
FRANCIS POULENC: The Man and His Songs
0–393–02196–3 Norton $25.00

- Roger Nicols
RAVEL REMEMBERED
0–393–02573–X Norton $25.00

- Arbie Orenstein
RAVEL: Man and Musician
0–231–03902–6 Columbia $29.50

- Rollo Myers
ERIK SATIE
0–486–21903–8 Dover pb $4.50

Maurice Ravel by Aline Fruhauf, from her memoir Making Faces *(Seven Locks Press)*

20TH-CENTURY MUSIC

- Theodor Adorno
PHILOSOPHY OF MODERN MUSIC
Adorno, a German Marxist aesthetician associated with the Frankfurt school of philosophers, also studied music composition with Alban Berg. His major contribution has been the idea that the musical score is a social document as well as an aesthetic one
0–8264–0138–4 Continuum pb $10.95

- William Austin
MUSIC IN THE TWENTIETH CENTURY
0–393–09704–8 Norton $33.95

- Richard Burback
TWENTIETH CENTURY MUSIC
0–87196–464–3 Facts On File $40.00

- Aaron Copland
THE NEW MUSIC: 1900–1960
"Like the great composers of the past (Berlioz, Schumann, Debussy), Copland is not concerned with the mechanics of technique but with the ultimate values of meaning and expression"—Alfred Frankenstein
0–393–00239–X Norton pb $7.95

Paul Griffiths
MODERN MUSIC: From Debussy to Boulez
Pierre Boulez is quoted at the beginning of this survey: "In 1945 or 1946, nothing was finished, everything was still to be done." Since then, it seems, everything has been done and little finished. Musical fashion raced through radical serialism and academicism, enlarged playfulness to include chance and randomness, made a fetish of technological innovation and electronic sound. Griffiths gives a nonpartisan account of these developments
0–500–20164–1 Thames & Hudson pb $11.95

- Leonard B. Meyer
MUSIC, THE ARTS, AND IDEAS: Patterns and Predictions in 20th-Century Culture
Meyer, one of the most stimulating thinkers about musical experience, raises as many questions as he answers
0–226–52141–9 Chicago pb $11.00

- Nicholas Slonimsky
MUSIC SINCE 1900
0–684–10550–0 Scribners $75.00

MUSIC SINCE 1900: Supplement
0–684–18438–9 Scribners pb $30.00

20th-Century European Music

- Paul Griffiths & George Perle
THE NEW GROVE SECOND VIENNESE SCHOOL
Traces the development of atonality and the careers of its major practitioners—Schoenberg, Webern, and Berg
0–393–01686–2 Norton $16.50
0–393–30090–0 Norton pb $10.95

- Laszlo Somfai
THE NEW GROVE MODERN MASTERS: Bartók, Stravinsky, Hindemith
0–393–01693–5 Norton $17.95
0–393–30097–8 Norton pb $9.95

- Elliott Antoholetz
THE MUSIC OF BELA BARTOK: A Study of Tonality and Progression in 20th-Century Music
A detailed analysis of Bartók's unorthodox compositional technique, which resulted in an often bizarre mixture of the folkish, the modernist, and the romantic
0–520–04604–8 California $48.50

- Mosco Carner
ALBAN BERG: The Man and the Work
0–8419–0841–9 Holmes & Meier $47.50

- Douglas Jarman
THE MUSIC OF ALBAN BERG
0–520–04954–3 California pb $15.95

- Willi Reich
THE LIFE AND WORK OF ALBAN BERG
0–306–76136–X Da Capo $32.50

- Donald Harris & others, editors
THE BERG-SCHOENBERG CORRESPONDENCE: Selected Letters
Devotion, authority, innovation, reflection—a complex relationship between disciple and master emerges in this unusual collection
0–393–01919–5 Norton $35.00

- David Neumeyer
THE MUSIC OF PAUL HINDEMITH
0–300–03287–0 Yale $35.50

- Carl Dahlhaus
SCHOENBERG AND THE NEW MUSIC
This collection of essays on Schoenberg and related subjects, written as a response to Theodor Adorno's famous book on "new music," rises above arcane musicological issues
0–521–33251–6 Cambridge $44.50

- Charles Rosen
ARNOLD SCHOENBERG
Rosen emphasizes that Schoenberg emerged at a complex moment in music history, at which conservative tonal forms and concepts were combined with avant-garde techniques and revolutionary ambitions
0–691–02706–4 Princeton pb $9.95

- Arnold Schoenberg
STYLE AND IDEA: Selected Writings of Arnold Schoenberg
Among the most important essays about music to be published this century, the

TO ORDER BOOKS AS GIFTS, SEE PAGE 1

sections include Personal Evaluation and Retrospect, Folk Music and Nationalism, Theory and Composition, and Social and Political Matters
0–520–05286–2 California $57.50
0–520–05294–3 California pb $12.95

• Joan Smith
SCHOENBERG AND HIS CIRCLE: A Viennese Portrait
0–02–872620–0 Schirmer $24.95

• Mikhail Druskin
IGOR STRAVINSKY: His Life, Works and Views
0–521–24590–7 Cambridge $29.95

• Paul Horgan
ENCOUNTERS WITH STRAVINSKY: A Personal Record
0–8195–6215–7 Wesleyan pb $14.95

• Igor Stravinsky
AN AUTOBIOGRAPHY
0–393–00161–X Norton pb $7.95

THE POETICS OF MUSIC: In the Form of Six Lessons
0–674–67856–7 Harvard pb $6.95

• Igor Stravinsky & Robert Craft
CONVERSATIONS WITH IGOR STRAVINSKY
0–520–04040–6 California pb $9.95

DIALOGUES
0–520–04650–1 California pb $8.95

EXPOSITIONS AND DEVELOPMENTS
0–520–04403–7 California pb $9.95

MEMORIES AND COMMENTARIES
0–520–04402–9 California pb $8.95

THEMES AND CONCLUSIONS
0–520–04652–8 California pb $9.95

• Pieter Van den Toorn
THE MUSIC OF IGOR STRAVINSKY
The first careful analysis of Stravinsky's oeuvre. Illustrated with nearly 100 musical examples and technical dissections of the major works
0–300–02693–5 Yale $47.50
0–300–03884–4 Yale pb $16.95

• Roman Vlad
STRAVINSKY
0–19–315444–7 Oxford $29.95
0–19–315445–5 Oxford pb $14.95

• Hans & Rosaleen Moldenhauer
ANTON VON WEBERN: A Chronicle of His Life and Work
The definitive biography of Schoenberg's most daring student, who accepted his teacher's method of composing with "twelve tones" but who purged his musical universe of common sensual effects, creating instead an impression of spare, cool space punctuated by bursts of intellect
0–394–47237–3 Knopf $25.00

• David Drew
KURT WEILL: A Handbook
The first detailed guide to the works of Kurt Weill by the British scholar who is now writing the definitive biography
0–520–05839–9 California $45.00

Stravinsky playing "The Rite of Spring," from Jean Cocteau's Drawings *(Dover)*

• Ronald Sanders
THE DAYS GROW SHORT: The Life and Music of Kurt Weill
"Sanders asks readers to join him in taking all of Weill's work seriously—from his 1920s avant-garde orchestral works and *The Threepenny Opera* to the popular but elegant scores for Broadway musicals of the 1940s and 1950s"—*Booklist*
0–87910–043–5 Limelight pb $12.95

20th-Century English Music

• Diana McVeagh & Anthony Payne
THE NEW GROVE TWENTIETH-CENTURY ENGLISH MASTERS: Elgar, Delius, Vaughan-Williams, Tippett, Holst, Walton, and Britten
0–393–02285–4 Norton $22.95
0–393–30351–9 Norton pb $11.95

• Peter Evans
THE MUSIC OF BENJAMIN BRITTEN
0–8166–0836–9 Minnesota $29.50

• Christopher Palmer, editor
THE BRITTEN COMPANION
0–521–27844–9 Cambridge pb $12.95

• Eric White
BENJAMIN BRITTEN: His Life and Operas
0–520–04894–6 California pb $14.95

• Arnold Whittall
THE MUSIC OF BRITTEN AND TIPPETT: Studies in Themes and Techniques
0–521–23523–5 Cambridge $52.50

• Lionel Carley
DELIUS: A Life in Letters, 1862–1908
The British-born composer with German parentage received his musical education in Florida
0–674–19570–1 Harvard $37.00

• Christopher Palmer
DELIUS: Portrait of a Cosmopolitan
0–8419–0274–7 Holmes & Meier $34.50

• Michael Kennedy
PORTRAIT OF ELGAR
"The comments on the music are informed, perceptive and fired by great enthusiasm"—*Classical Music Weekly*
0–19–284017–7 Oxford pb $14.95

• Jerrold Moore
EDWARD ELGAR: A Creative Life
"Shows us Elgar through a large, clear pane, offering a view that is fully and scrupulously lit"—*The Times* (London)
0–19–315447–1 Oxford $85.00

• Imogen Holst
GUSTAV HOLST: A Biography
The daughter of the composer, herself a musician, composer, and critic, relates her father's life
0–19–315458–7 Oxford $35.00

• Ian Kemp
TIPPETT: The Composer and His Music
0–9–2873–23–0 Da Capo $39.50

• Susanna Walton
WILLIAM WALTON: Behind the Facade
0–19–315156–1 Oxford $22.95

Music Since 1945

• Carlos Chavez
TOWARD A NEW MUSIC: Music and Electricity
0–306–70719–5 Da Capo $29.50

• Paul Griffiths
MODERN MUSIC: The Avant-Garde since 1945
0–8076–1018–6 Braziller pb $10.95

A GUIDE TO ELECTRONIC MUSIC
0–500–27203–4 Thames & Hudson pb $7.95

• Michael Nyman
EXPERIMENTAL MUSIC: Cage and Beyond
Experimental music of the last four decades has discarded the major axioms of Western musical performance and composition. Nyman sympathetically surveys the various experiments and experimentalists
0–02–871660–4 Schirmer pb $10.95

• Tom Schnabel
STOLEN MOMENTS: Conversations with Contemporary Musicians
Interviews ranging across all styles of music to illustrate the diversity of contemporary practice; the subjects include John Adams, Kiri Te Kanawa, Sunny Ade, Philip Glass, Michael Feinstein, Wayne Shorter, Richard Stoltzman, Nina Simone, and many others. "This is a book of conversations with people I have most admired and wanted to meet"—David Byrne
0–918226–22–8 Acrobat pb $13.95

• Ellen Schwartz
ELECTRONIC MUSIC: A Listener's Guide
0–306–76260–9 Da Capo $29.50

• Elliott Schwartz & Barney Childs, editors
CONTEMPORARY COMPOSERS ON CONTEMPORARY MUSIC
Published in 1967
0–306–77587–5 Da Capo $45.00

• Pierre Boulez
ORIENTATIONS
The avant-garde composer and one-time conductor of the New York Philharmonic takes on his own and others' music. "Our musical life, in so far as it is an affair of famous performers and works that belong in museums, is a rapidly dying culture and one which will die ever more rapidly if it receives a blow or two. And we must hasten its death because culture has nothing to do with these sham phenomena of knowledge"
0–674–64375–5 Harvard $32.50

• Joan Peyser
BOULEZ
A psychological portrait that connects Boulez's cool, aloof intellect with the fashions of postwar musical life
0–02–871810–0 Schirmer pb $6.95

• Paul Griffiths
BOULEZ
A short and scholarly survey of Boulez's music
0–19–315442–0 Oxford pb $14.95

OLIVIER MESSIAEN AND THE MUSIC OF TIME
0–8014–1813–5 Cornell $26.95

• Robin Maconie
THE WORKS OF KARLHEINZ STOCKHAUSEN
0–7145–2706–8 Marion Boyars pb $20.00

• Karl H. Worner
STOCKHAUSEN: His Life and Work
0–520–03272–1 California pb $6.95

20th-Century American Music

• H. Wiley Hitchcock & Stanley Sadie, editors
THE NEW GROVE DICTIONARY OF AMERICAN MUSIC
A four-volume set
0–943818–36–2 Grove $595.00

• H. Wiley Hitchcock
MUSIC IN THE UNITED STATES: A Historical Introduction
0–13–608407–9 Prentice-Hall pb $25.00

• William Austin
THE TWENTIETH-CENTURY AMERICAN MASTERS
Studies of Barber, Bernstein, Cage, Carter, Copland, Cowell, Gershwin, Ives, Sessions, and Thomson
0–393–01698–6 Norton $19.95
0–393–30353–5 Norton pb $12.95

• John Rockwell
ALL-AMERICAN MUSIC: Composition in the Late 20th Century
The critic for the *New York Times* weaves a skein giving equal place to Milton Babbitt and Keith Jarrett, Ernst Krenek and Talking Heads, Elliott Carter and Stephen Sondheim
0–394–51163–8 Knopf $19.95

• Leonard Bernstein
THE JOY OF MUSIC
Probably the most popular, clear, and entertaining explanation of music ever published, with essays on such subjects as why Beethoven's music is like the mountains, what makes a hit tune, and how American musical comedies work
0–671–39721–4 Simon & Schuster pb $9.95

THE UNANSWERED QUESTION: Six Talks at Harvard
Bernstein takes on linguistics, theory, and 20th-century music. Amid fireworks and fancy footwork, he discusses the primacy of tonal music and the failure of many of the works of our century
0–674–92001–5 Harvard pb $14.95

• Peter Gradenwitz
LEONARD BERNSTEIN
0–85496–510–6 St. Martin's $21.95

• John Cage
Cage's playful, maddening musical escapades have their textual counterpart in these books, containing his poems, koans, diaries, and meditations on his favorite subject (mushrooms). Many selections were composed using "chance" operations; all were composed to shock, unsettle, or inspire.
EMPTY WORDS
"John Cage is one of those few contemporaries who do important work in more than one art"—*NY Times Book Review*
0–8195–6067–7 Wesleyan pb $12.95

M: Writings '67–'72
0–8195–6035–9 Wesleyan pb $10.95

SILENCE: Lectures and Writings
0–8195–6028–6 Wesleyan pb $12.95

A YEAR FROM MONDAY: New Lectures and Writings
0–8195–6002–2 Wesleyan pb $12.95

X: Writings '79–'82
0–8195–6098–7 Wesleyan pb $17.95

• Richard Kostelanetz
CONVERSING WITH CAGE
Witticisms and twists of logic from the avant-garde master of the random and iconoclastic. "I was with de Kooning once in a restaurant," John Cage tells his valiant interviewer, "and he said, 'If I put a frame around these bread crumbs, that isn't art.' And what I'm saying is that it is"
0–87910–104–0 Limelight $22.95
0–87910–100–8 Limelight pb $13.95

• Allen Edwards
FLAWED WORDS AND STUBBORN SOUNDS: A Conversation with Elliott Carter
The important contemporary American composer discusses his style, his career, and the state of American musical life, and offers hints for understanding his difficult music
0–393–02159–9 Norton pb $7.95

• David Schiff
THE MUSIC OF ELLIOTT CARTER
An indispensable source
0–903873–07–9 Da Capo pb $22.50

• Else & Kurt Stone, editors
THE WRITINGS OF ELLIOTT CARTER: An American Composer Looks at Modern Music
0–253–36720–4 Indiana $20.00

• Arthur Berger
AARON COPLAND
0–306–76266–8 Da Capo $22.50

• Neil Butterworth
THE MUSIC OF AARON COPLAND
Preface by André Previn
0–87663–495–1 Universe $20.00

• Aaron Copland
MUSIC AND IMAGINATION
"Aaron Copland is a notable contemporary example of the 'initial composer,' the man who can write about music with the same

☞ TO ORDER NEW BOOKS NOT YET LISTED, ASK YOUR BOOKSELLER OR CALL 1-800-882-8770

persuasiveness that he writes music itself"—*Saturday Review*
0-674-58915-7 Harvard pb $4.95

WHAT TO LISTEN FOR IN MUSIC
Introduction by William Schuman
0-07-013091-4 McGraw-Hill $17.95
0-451-62687-7 NAL pb $4.95

• Aaron Copland & Vivian Perlis
COPLAND: 1900 Through 1942
"A valuable, readable, endearing record of his achievement"—*NY Times*
0-312-01149-0 St. Martin's pb $12.95

• Philip Glass
MUSIC BY PHILIP GLASS
Autobiographical sketches with photos and score segments
0-06-091536-6 Harper & Row pb $12.95

• Edward Jablonski
GERSHWIN: A Biography
The best biography available on the Jewish immigrants' son who transformed American concert and show music
0-385-19431-5 Doubleday $21.95

• Charles Schwartz
GERSHWIN: His Life and Music
0-306-80096-9 Da Capo pb $11.95

• Peter Burkholder
CHARLES IVES: The Ideas Behind the Music
"Peter Burkholder digs beneath the surface to unearth the philosophies behind Ives' works, and he does so with originality and vitality"—Vivian Perlis
0-300-03885-2 Yale pb $8.95

• Henry & Sidney Cowell
CHARLES IVES AND HIS MUSIC
0-306-76125-4 Da Capo $35.00

• Charles Ives
ESSAYS BEFORE A SONATA, THE MAJORITY & OTHER WRITINGS
Ives wrote these idiosyncratic and cantankerous essays as preface for his Second Piano Sonata. Each essay—*Emerson, Hawthorne, The Alcotts,* and *Thoreau*—corresponds to a movement of the sonata. The other writings further demonstrate Ives' singular vision
0-393-00528-3 Norton pb $7.95

• Vivian Perlis
CHARLES IVES REMEMBERED
One of the dozens of raconteurs recalls: "The *Universe Symphony,* the unfinished one, he didn't intend to finish. He told me that anybody else could add to it if they felt like it . . . Maybe someday they'll do it [as he envisioned], with orchestras here and there on the hills, and different choruses all around the countryside." This is an extraordinary book of recollections about one of the most storied of all composers
0-393-00825-8 Norton pb $3.95

Ned Rorem
THE PARIS AND NEW YORK DIARIES
One of America's finest composers for the voice displays his literary skill in diaries as worldly, and occasionally racy, as his music
0-86547-109-6 North Point pb $15.00

THE LATER DIARIES: 1961–1972
0-86547-117-7 North Point pb $16.00

THE NANTUCKET DIARY: 1973–1985
0-86547-259-9 North Point $30.00

SETTLING THE SCORE: Essays on Music
0-15-180895-3 HBJ $29.95

• A. Oldsstead
CONVERSATIONS WITH ROGER SESSIONS
1-55553-010-9 Northeastern $21.95

• Roger Sessions
MUSICAL EXPERIENCE OF COMPOSER, PERFORMER, LISTENER
0-691-09116-1 Princeton $21.00
0-691-02703-X Princeton pb $9.95

QUESTIONS ABOUT MUSIC
0-393-00571-2 Norton pb $6.95

ROGER SESSIONS ON MUSIC: Collected Essays
0-691-09126-9 Princeton $42.00
0-691-10074-8 Princeton pb $14.50

• Virgil Thomson
SELECTED LETTERS OF VIRGIL THOMSON
These letters reconfirm his reputation for common-sense, wit, innocence, and mordant irony
Edited by Tim & Vanessa Page
0-671-62117-3 Simon & Schuster $24.95

Musical Personalities

Leonie Rosenstiel
NADIA BOULANGER: A Life in Music
Boulanger was one of the most influential teachers of this century; her students included Virgil Thomson, Aaron Copland, and Elliot Carter
0-393-01495-9 Norton $24.95

Arthur Gold & Robert Fizdale
MISIA
Biography of Misia Sert, a vibrant figure in the worlds of music and dance in the early 20th century
0-394-48710-9 Knopf $16.95

Nicholas Slonimsky
PERFECT PITCH
"Now I have reached the Age of Absurdity," writes this mischievous musical chronicler, "I refuse to believe I am 93. Have I really outlived Tolstoy and Goethe? I don't even have a white beard or bushy eyebrows to attest my age." An entertaining romp, not without its sadness over grand ambitions and abilities expended on trivia
0-19-315155-3 Oxford $21.95

• Jacques Barzun, editor
THE PLEASURES OF MUSIC
An anthology of writing about music and musicians that includes fiction by E.T.A. Hoffman, Bernard Shaw, and Charles Dickens, criticism by Thomas DeQuincey and Martin Luther, and scores of other essays and musical proclamations
0-226-03854-8 Chicago pb $10.95

• Carl Dahlhaus
This important historian and philosopher asks how music history is interpreted, why music was considered romantic when fine arts were considered realist, and how music changed with the coming of modernity.
AESTHETICS OF MUSIC
0-521-28007-9 Cambridge pb $11.95

FOUNDATIONS OF MUSIC HISTORY
0-521-29890-3 Cambridge pb $12.95

REALISM IN NINETEENTH-CENTURY MUSIC
0-521-27841-4 Cambridge pb $10.95

• Evan Eisenberg
THE RECORDING ANGEL
Philosophical riffs and eccentric profiles defining the experience of music on record
0-14-011338-X Penguin pb $7.95

• H.L. Mencken
H.L. MENCKEN ON MUSIC
Edited by Louis Cheslock
0-02-871550-0 Schirmer pb $3.95

• Leonard B. Meyer
EMOTION AND MEANING IN MUSIC
"Clears the air of many confused notions . . . and lays the groundwork for exhaustive study of the basic problem of music theory and aesthetics, the relationship between pattern and meaning"—*Journal of Music Theory*
0-226-52139-7 Chicago pb $9.00

• Sam Morgenstern
COMPOSERS ON MUSIC
0-394-73040-2 Pantheon pb $14.95

• Ernest Newman
ESSAYS FROM THE WORLD OF MUSIC
0-7145-3548-6 Riverrun pb $14.95

• Andrew Porter
MUSIC OF THREE SEASONS
"If the experience of a concert or an opera is evanescent, the values involved in that experience can be of permanent interest, and Porter [music critic for *The New Yorker*] demonstrates an uncanny ability to present those permanent values in readable prose"—*Washington Post*
0-374-51551-4 Farrar, Straus & Giroux pb $14.95

• George Bernard Shaw
COLLECTED MUSIC CRITICISM
A four-volume set with everything from disposable juvenilia to expert soap-box proclamations on the music of his time
0-8443-0063-2 Vienna House $75.00

THE GREAT COMPOSERS: Reviews and Bombardments
A selection of Shaw's music criticism, which in its color, conflict, and posturing complements his plays
0–520–03266–7 California pb $10.95

THE PERFECT WAGNERITE
A semi-socialist, semi-messianic reading of the Ring
0–486–21707–8 Dover pb $3.95

• Victor Zuckerkandl
In elegant prose, Zuckerkandl speculates on how music works, and what happens between the written notes that makes them so compelling.
THE SENSE OF MUSIC
0–691–02700–5 Princeton pb $12.95

SOUND AND SYMBOL

Volume 1: Music and the External World
0–691–01759–X Princeton pb $13.95

Volume 2: Man and Music
0–691–01812–X Princeton pb $13.95

MUSICAL FORMS

• Alfred Einstein
THE ITALIAN MADRIGAL
A three-volume set
0–691–09112–9 Princeton $135.00

• William Newman
Newman's works are an encyclopedic survey of the central musical form of our tradition—its revolution and importance.
THE SONATA IN THE CLASSIC ERA
0–393–95286–X Norton $22.50

THE SONATA IN THE BAROQUE ERA
0–393–95275–4 Norton $18.95

THE SONATA SINCE BEETHOVEN
0–8078–1121–1 North Carolina $35.00

• Charles Rosen
SONATA FORMS
"To familiar and unfamiliar music alike Rosen brings not only an uncommonly refined ear and sensibility, but also, again and again, unerring insight into just the features that make the music special and fine"—Joseph Kerman, NY Review of Books
0–393–30219–9 Norton pb $10.95

• Denis Stevens, editor
A HISTORY OF SONG
Scholars on song ranging from the Middle Ages to modern Czechoslovakia. "The best yet in English on the subject of the secular art song"—Library Journal
0–393–00536–4 Norton pb $11.95

• Donald Tovey
ESSAYS IN MUSICAL ANALYSIS: Concertos and Choral Works
Tovey's essays on more than 250 compositions remain models of criticism and analysis that work for both lay reader and scholar
0–19–315149–9 Oxford pb $14.95

ESSAYS IN MUSICAL ANALYSIS: Symphonies and Other Orchestral Works
0–19–315147–2 Oxford pb $12.50

MUSIC THEORY

• Walter Piston
HARMONY
0–393–95480–3 Norton $28.95

ORCHESTRATION
Analysis of orchestration, covering instrumentation of primary and secondary melodies, part writing, chords, and contrapuntal techniques
0–393–09740–4 Norton $21.95

• Heinrich Schenker
This most influential Viennese scholar (1868–1935) was remarkable for his insights into how we hear music, his discernment of a universal structural line in all tonal music, and his reform of musical analysis.
HARMONY
0–226–73734–9 Chicago pb $8.95

COUNTERPOINT
0–393–09728–5 Norton $15.95

FREE COMPOSITION
0–02873–180–8 Macmillan $45.00

Joseph Kerman
LISTEN
0–87901–127–0 Worth $33.95

Maurice Lieberman
EAR TRAINING AND SIGHT SEEING
0–393–09519–3 Norton pb $14.95

Joseph Machlis
THE ENJOYMENT OF MUSIC
A widely used text introducing students and new listeners to musical history and ideas
0–393–95300–9 Norton $29.95

INTRODUCTION TO CONTEMPORARY MUSIC
0–393–09026–4 Norton $28.95

Howard Shanet
LEARN TO READ MUSIC
0–671–21027–0 S&S pb $7.95

INSTRUMENTAL HISTORY AND PERFORMERS

• David Munrow
INSTRUMENTS OF THE MIDDLE AGES AND RENAISSANCE
0–19–321321–4 Oxford pb $16.95

• Harold Schoenberg
THE VIRTUOSI: Great Performers from Paganini to Pavarotti
"A fine, fascinating account of world-famous executants from the eighteenth century to the present"—New Yorker
0–394–75532–4 Vintage pb $12.95

Keyboard Music

• Willi Apel
THE HISTORY OF KEYBOARD MUSIC TO 1700
0–253–32795–4 Indiana $39.50

• C.P.E. Bach
ESSAY ON THE TRUE ART OF PLAYING KEYBOARD INSTRUMENTS
This classic 18th-century manual by J.S. Bach's son influenced generations of pianists and remains a guide to the playing of the music of the period
0–393–09716–1 Norton $23.95

• Alfred Cortot
FRENCH PIANO MUSIC
0–306–70896–5 Da Capo $27.50

• Dieter Hildebrandt
PIANOFORTE: A Romance of the Piano
A history of the single most important instrument in the musical life of the 19th century
Introduction by Anthony Burgess
0–8076–1182–4 Braziller $19.95

• F.E. Kirby
SHORT HISTORY OF KEYBOARD MUSIC
0–02–917330–2 Free Press $24.95

• William Newman
THE PIANIST'S PROBLEMS
0–306–80269–4 Da Capo pb $10.95

• Bernard Sonnaillion
KING OF INSTRUMENTS: A History of the Organ
0–8478–0582–4 Rizzoli $65.00

• David Sudnow
WAYS OF THE HAND
An ethnographer and sociologist gives a "phenomenological account" of his learning to improvise in a jazz style at the keyboard. His epigram is from Heidegger; his accounts are riffs on the miracle of playing
0–674–94833–5 Harvard $15.00

• Peter Williams & Barbara Owen
THE ORGAN
0–393–30516–3 Norton pb $14.95

• Konrad Wolff
MASTERS OF THE KEYBOARD: Individual Style Elements in the Piano Music of Bach, Haydn, Mozart, Beethoven, and Schubert
0–253–33690–2 Indiana $22.50

Pianists

• David Dubal
REFLECTIONS FROM THE KEYBOARD: The World of the Concert Pianist
Conversations with pianists about technique, music, and life onstage
0–671–49240–3 Summit $19.95

• Wilson Lyle
A DICTIONARY OF PIANISTS
Biographical notes on 4000 pianists
0–02–919250–1 Schirmer $35.00

➤ FOR OVERSEAS ORDERING INFORMATION, SEE PAGE 1

- Elyse Mach
GREAT PIANISTS SPEAK FOR THEMSELVES
A 2-volume set with an introduction by Georg Solti
0–396–08850–3 Dodd, Mead pb $18.95

- Linda Noyle
PIANISTS ON PLAYING: Interviews with Twelve Concert Pianists
0–8108–1953–8 Scarecrow $20.00

- Harold Schoenberg
THE GREAT PIANISTS
Schoenberg's learning and scholarship are worn lightly but carefully in this exuberant book about the great virtuosos. Behind the irresistible anecdotes and lore is the *New York Times* critic's impassioned advocacy for the powers of performance and personality
0–671–63837–8 Simon & Schuster pb $13.95

THE GREAT PIANISTS FROM MOZART TO THE PRESENT
0–671–28999–3 Simon & Schuster pb $12.95

- Joseph Horowitz
CONVERSATIONS WITH ARRAU
A detailed and probing series of interviews with a performing artist. The Chilean pianist Claudio Arrau talks about psychoanalysis, musical training, pianistic technique, and the prerogatives of interpretation. Other musicians talk about him
0–394–51390–8 Knopf $19.95

- Jonathan Cott
CONVERSATIONS WITH GLENN GOULD
Listening to the late great pianist talk is like listening to him play. Gould combines whimsy, eccentricity, glittering brilliance, profound insight, and immense silliness
0–316–15776–7 Little, Brown pb $7.95

- Otto Friedrich
GLENN GOULD: A Life and Variations
"One of the great biographies of an artist's mind and personality of this or any other period. A passionate, spellbinding story"— Robert Craft
0–394–57771–X Random House $22.50

- Tim Page, editor
THE GLENN GOULD READER
"I'm a Streisand freak and make no bones about it. With the possible exception of Elisabeth Schwarzkopf, no vocalist has brought me greater pleasure or more insight into the interpreter's art." Gould on art: "I feel that art should be given the chance to phase itself out. I think that we must accept the fact that art is not inevitably benign, that it is potentially destructive." Gould on any subject is worth reading
0–394–54067–0 Knopf $25.00

- Artur Schnabel
MY LIFE AND MUSIC
A memoir by the pianist who set new standards for the performance of Beethoven, Mozart and Schubert
0–486–25571–9 Dover pb $6.95

Glenn Gould (photo by Don Hunstein), from The Glenn Gould Reader, *edited by Tim Page (Knopf)*

String Instruments

- Alberto Bachmann
AN ENCYCLOPEDIA OF THE VIOLIN
Introduction by Eugene Ysaye
0–306–80004–7 Da Capo pb $11.95

- David Boyden
HISTORY OF VIOLIN PLAYING: From its Origins to 1761 and Its Relationship to the Violin and Violin Music
0–19–316315–2 Oxford $99.00

- Elizabeth Cowling
THE CELLO
0–684–14784–X Scribners pb $4.95

- Paul Griffiths
THE STRING QUARTET
0–500–27183–9 Thames & Hudson pb $10.95

- Yehudi Menuhin
THE VIOLIN AND VIOLA
0–02–871410–5 Macmillan $19.95
0–02–871350–8 Macmillan pb $9.95

String Players

- Margaret Campbell
THE GREAT CELLISTS
From the 17th century to the present, this comprehensive study traces the individual lives of cellists as well as the influence of national schools and musical traditions on the modern players such as Yo Yo Ma and Jaqueline du Pré
0–943955–09–2 David & Charles $24.95

- Boris Schwartz
THE GREAT MASTERS OF THE VIOLIN
Paganini was thought to have a pact with the devil; Vivaldi was an ordained priest— and both were masters of this instrument so often linked to images demonic and divine. Schwartz, a scholar, teacher, and great lover of the violin, presents the history of the instrument from its

invention to the latest generation of fiddlers
Foreword by Yehudi Menuhin
0–671–22598–7 Simon & Schuster $25.00
0–671–60461–9 Simon & Schuster pb $13.95

- David Blum
THE ART OF QUARTET PLAYING: The Guarneri Quartet in Conversation with David Blum
0–8014–9456–7 Cornell pb $9.95

CASALS AND THE ART OF INTERPRETATION
Introduction by Paul Tortelier
0–520–04032–5 California pb $11.95

- Artur Weschler-Vered
JASCHA HEIFETZ
0–02–934480–8 Schirmer $16.95

- Yehudi Menuhin
THE COMPLEAT VIOLINIST
0–671–61294–8 Summit $15.95

- Graham Wade
SEGOVIA: A Celebration of the Man and His Music
0–8052–8147–9 Schocken pb $6.95

- Joseph Szigeti
SZIGETI ON THE VIOLIN
0–486–23763–X Dover pb $5.00

Woodwind, Brass, and Percussion Instruments

- Anthony Baines
BRASS INSTRUMENTS: Their History and Development
0–684–16668–2 Scribners pb $14.95

- James Blades
PERCUSSION INSTRUMENTS AND THEIR HISTORY
0–571–18081–7 Faber & Faber pb $35.00

- Adam Carse
  MUSICAL WIND INSTRUMENTS: A History of the Wind Instruments Used in European Orchestras, from the Later Middle Ages to the Present
  0–306–80005–5 Da Capo pb $9.95

- James Galway
  FLUTE
  0–02–871380–X Macmillan $19.95
  0–02–871400–8 Macmillan pb $9.95

- Barry Tuckwell
  HORN
  0–02–871530–6 Macmillan $19.95
  0–02–871560–8 Macmillan pb $9.95

Conductors

- James Camner
  GREAT CONDUCTORS IN HISTORIC PHOTOGRAPHS: 193 Portraits
  0–486–24397–4 Dover pb $6.95

- Bernard Jacobson
  CONDUCTORS ON CONDUCTING
  0–914366–09–2 Vanguard $17.95

- Thomas Beecham
  A MINGLED CHIME: An Autobiography
  0–306–70791–8 Da Capo $39.50

- Paul Robinson
  THE ART OF THE CONDUCTOR: Bernstein
  0–8149–0865–9 Vanguard pb $10.95

- Peter Heyworth
  OTTO KLEMPERER: His Life and Times, 1885–1933
  0–521–24293–2 Cambridge $39.50

- Paul Robinson
  SOLTI
  0–8149–0802–0 Vanguard pb $10.95

- Abram Chasins
  LEOPOLD STOKOWSKI: A Profile
  0–306–80146–9 Da Capo pb $8.95

- Joseph Horowitz
  UNDERSTANDING TOSCANINI: How He Became an American Culture-God and Helped Create a New Audience for Old Music
  A controversial account that holds Toscanini and the marketing geniuses who promoted him largely responsible for the decline of musical life
  0–394–52918–9 Knopf $30.00
  0–8166–1678–7 Minnesota pb $12.95

- Harvey Sachs
  TOSCANINI
  A sober and careful biography by an admiring writer
  0–397–01320–5 Harper & Row $17.95
  0–06–091473–4 Harper & Row pb $10.95

OPERA

- Harold Barlow & Sam Morgenstern
  A DICTIONARY OF OPERA AND SONG THEMES
  Eight thousand themes from the most important operas and songs
  0–517–52503–8 Crown $15.95

- Catherine Clément
  OPERA, OR THE UNDOING OF WOMEN
  A feminist approach to opera's tragic heroines
  0–8166–1655–8 Minnesota pb $13.95

- Peter Conrad
  ROMANTIC OPERA AND LITERARY FORM
  0–520–04508–4 California pb $9.95

  A SONG OF LOVE AND DEATH: The Meaning of Opera
  0–671–67263–0 Poseidon pb $9.95

- Milton Cross
  THE NEW MILTON CROSS' COMPLETE STORIES OF THE GREAT OPERAS
  0–385–04324–4 Doubleday $19.95

- Milton Cross & Karl Kohrs
  THE NEW MILTON CROSS' MORE STORIES OF THE GREAT OPERAS
  0–385–14776–7 Doubleday $21.95

- David Hamilton, editor
  THE METROPOLITAN OPERA ENCYCLOPEDIA: A Comprehensive Guide to the World of Opera
  0–671–61732–X Simon & Schuster $35.00

- Earl of Harewood, editor
  THE DEFINITIVE KOBBE'S OPERA BOOK
  An essential companion for the opera lover, giving basic information about composers and performance history, with crystalline summaries of even the most impossibly operatic plots
  0–399–13180–9 Putnam $35.00

- Arthur Jacobs & Stanley Sadie
  THE LIMELIGHT BOOK OF OPERA
  0–87910–044–3 Limelight pb $12.95

Joseph Kerman
OPERA AS DRAMA
Kerman is literate and controversial in a field long dominated by writers who are neither. This is still the most important book of opera criticism written by an American; its most famous line: calling *Tosca* a "shabby little shocker"
0–520–06273–6 California $25.00

- Paul Lang
  THE EXPERIENCE OF OPERA
  0–393–00706–5 Norton pb $8.95

- Charles Osborne
  THE DICTIONARY OF THE OPERA
  0–671–49218–7 Simon & Schuster $22.95
  0–671–62801–1 Simon & Schuster pb $10.95

- Paul Robinson
  OPERA AND IDEAS: From Mozart to Strauss
  Robinson brings opera into the history of ideas while displaying subtle insight into musical details
  0–06–015450–0 Harper & Row $22.95

- Harold Rosenthal & John Warrack, editors
  THE CONCISE OXFORD DICTIONARY OF OPERA
  0–19–311321–X Oxford pb $13.95

- Stanley Sadie
  OPERA
  0–393–02506–3 Norton $39.95

- Gary Schmidgall
  LITERATURE AS OPERA
  Places major operatic works in a literary context, (discussing, for example, Beaumarchais, Dryden, Milton, and Pope) and applies literary analysis to *Le Nozze di Figaro*
  0–19–502706–X Oxford pb $11.95

- Henry W. Simon
  100 GREAT OPERAS AND THEIR STORIES
  0–385–05448–3 Doubleday pb $9.95

Opera Histories

- Edward Dent
  FOUNDATIONS OF ENGLISH OPERA
  0–306–70905–8 Da Capo $32.50

  THE RISE OF ROMANTIC OPERA
  0–521–29659–5 Cambridge pb $12.95

- Robert Donington
  THE RISE OF OPERA
  0–684–17165–1 Scribners $45.00

- Donald Grout & Hermine Williams
  A SHORT HISTORY OF OPERA
  0–231–06192–7 Columbia $39.00

- Ethan Mordden
  OPERA ANECDOTES
  Mordden recounts a famous miscue: "Backstage at *Lohengrin* before his first entrance, Leo Slezak was bemused to see the swan-boat take off just before he got into it; a stagehand had jumped the cue. As the boat glided into the opera without its silver knight, Slezak turned to someone and asked, 'What time's the next swan?' "
  0–19–503600–X Oxford $21.95

- Ira Nowinski
  A SEASON AT GLYNDEBOURNE
  Photographer Nowinski pays a pictorial tribute to England's most famous opera festival
  0–7470–2407–3 David & Charles $55.00

- Leslie Orrey
  OPERA: A Concise History
  0–500–20217–6 Thames & Hudson pb $11.95

- Richard Traubner
  OPERETTA: A Theatrical History
  0–19–520778–5 Oxford pb $16.95

Martin Mayer
THE MET: One Hundred Years of Grand Opera
0–671–47087–6 Simon & Schuster $35.00

Martin Sokol
THE NEW YORK CITY OPERA: An American Adventure
Introduction by Beverly Sills
0–02–612280–4 Macmillan $24.95

Opera Composers and Their Operas

- Andrew Porter
  THE NEW GROVE MASTERS OF ITALIAN OPERA
  0–393–01685–4 Norton $16.50
  0–393–30089–7 Norton pb $7.95

- Herbert Weinstock
  VINCENZO BELLINI: His Life and His Operas
  0–394–41656–2 Knopf $20.00

- William Ashbrook
  DONIZETTI AND HIS OPERAS
  0–521–27663–2 Cambridge pb $21.95

- William Mann
  THE OPERAS OF MOZART
  0–19–520397–6 Oxford $17.95

- William Ashbrook
  THE OPERAS OF PUCCINI
  0–8014–1820–8 Cornell $34.50
  0–8014–9309–9 Cornell pb $9.95

- Mosco Carner
  PUCCINI: A Critical Biography
  0–8419–0302–6 Holmes & Meier $55.00

- Stendhal
  LIFE OF ROSSINI
  Translated by Richard Coe
  0–7145–0632–X Riverrun pb $11.95

- Herbert Weinstock
  ROSSINI: A Biography
  0–87910–071–0 Limelight $32.50
  0–87910–102–4 Limelight pb $19.95

- Julian Budden
  THE OPERAS OF VERDI
  Volume 1: From Oberto to Rigoletto
  0–19–520449–2 Oxford pb $16.95
  Volume 2: From Il Trovatore to La Forza del Destino
  0–19–520450–6 Oxford pb $16.95
  Volume 3: From Don Carlo to Falstaff
  0–19–520451–4 Oxford pb $16.95

- Charles Osborne
  THE COMPLETE OPERAS OF VERDI
  0–306–80072–1 Da Capo pb $12.95
  VERDI: A Life in the Theatre
  0–88064–106–1 Fromm pb $11.95

- Frank Walker
  THE MAN VERDI
  Introduction by Philip Gossett
  0–226–87132–0 Chicago pb $9.95

Photograph from Verdi: A Life in the Theatre *by Charles Osborne (Knopf)*

- William Weaver, translator
  SEVEN VERDI LIBRETTOS
  Includes *Rigoletto, Il Trovatore, La Traviata, Un Ballo in Maschera, Aida, Otello,* and *Falstaff*
  0–393–00852–5 Norton pb $12.95

- William Weaver & Martin Chusid, editors
  THE VERDI COMPANION
  0–393–01215–8 Norton $22.95
  0–393–30443–4 Norton pb $10.95

- Barry Billington
  WAGNER
  0–394–75279–1 Random House pb $9.95

- John & Carl Dahlhaus
  THE NEW GROVE WAGNER
  0–393–01688–9 Norton $17.95
  0–393–30092–7 Norton pb $7.95

- Thomas Mann
  THOMAS MANN PRO AND CONTRA WAGNER
  0–226–50335–6 Chicago pb $10.95

- Ernest Newman
  THE LIFE OF RICHARD WAGNER
  A classic biography by any standard, this detailed study by a music critic and historian stands out in the literature on Wagner for its range and subtlety
  Volume 1
  0–521–29094–5 Cambridge pb $18.95
  Volume 2
  0–521–29095–3 Cambridge pb $18.95
  Volume 3
  0–521–29096–1 Cambridge pb $18.95
  Volume 4
  0–521–29097–X Cambridge pb $18.95

- Friedrich Nietzsche & Richard Wagner
  THE NIETZSCHE-WAGNER CORRESPONDENCE
  Translated by Caroline Kerr
  Edited by Elizabeth Foerster-Nietzsche
  0–87140–230–0 Norton pb $10.95

- Curt Von Westernhagen
  THE FORGING OF THE RING
  0–521–21293–6 Cambridge $44.50

- Richard Wagner
  THE DIARY OF RICHARD WAGNER
  Edited by J. Bergfeld
  0–521–23311–9 Cambridge pb $21.95
  MY LIFE
  Translated by Andrew Gray
  Edited by Mary Whittall
  0–521–35900–7 Cambridge pb $24.95
  SELECTED LETTERS OF RICHARD WAGNER
  0–393–02500–4 Norton $35.00

Cambridge Opera Handbooks

Although librettos are not included, the handbooks listed below treat each opera from a historical and musicological viewpoint, including discussions of the opera's performances and evaluations of the text and score. Each title includes a full discography.

- Douglas Jarman
  ALBAN BERG: WOZZECK
  0–521–28481–3 Cambridge pb $14.95

- Ian Kemp
  HECTOR BERLIOZ: LES TROYENS
  0–521–34813–7 Cambridge pb $14.95

- Donald Mitchell
  BENJAMIN BRITTEN: DEATH IN VENICE
  0–521–31943–9 Cambridge pb $13.95
  BENJAMIN BRITTEN: THE TURN OF THE SCREW
  0–521–28356–6 Cambridge pb $9.95

- Roger Nichols & Richard Langham Smith
  CLAUDE DEBUSSY: PELLEAS ET MELISANDE
  0–521–31446–1 Cambridge pb $14.95

- John Whenham, editor
  CLAUDIO MONTEVERDI: ORFEO
  0–521–28477–5 Cambridge pb $12.95

- Thomas Bauman
  W.A. MOZART: THE ABDUCTION FROM THE SERAGLIO
  0–521–31060–1 Cambridge pb $12.95

- Julian Rushton
  W.A. MOZART: DON GIOVANNI
  0–521–29663–3 Cambridge pb $9.95

- Tim Carter
  W.A. MOZART: THE MARRIAGE OF FIGARO
  0–521–31606–5 Cambridge pb $12.95

☞ **FOR ALL OTHER INQUIRIES, PLEASE CALL (212) 333-7900**

- Mosco Carner
  GIACOMO PUCCINI: TOSCA
  0–521–29661–7 Cambridge pb $11.95

- Paul Griffiths
  IGOR STRAVINSKY: THE RAKE'S PROGRESS
  0–521–28199–7 Cambridge pb $8.95

- James Hepokoski
  GIUSEPPE VERDI: FALSTAFF
  0–521–28016–8 Cambridge pb $11.95
  GIUSEPPE VERDI: OTELLO
  0–521–27749–3 Cambridge pb $12.95

- Patricia Howard
  C.W. VON GLUCK: ORPHEUS AND EURYDICE
  0–521–29664–1 Cambridge pb $8.95

- Lucy Beckett
  RICHARD WAGNER: PARSIFAL
  0–521–29662–5 Cambridge pb $11.95

Riverrun Press Opera Guides

This series, published in association with the English National Opera and The Royal Opera, is intended to prepare the audience prior to performance. In addition to a complete libretto, each book contains numerous photographs, essays, and musical analyses.

- Nicholas John, series editor
  GEORGES BIZET: CARMEN
  0–7145–3937–6 Riverrun pb $4.95
  MODESTE MUSSORGSKY: BORIS GODUNOV
  0–7145–3922–8 Riverrun pb $4.95
  GIACOMO PUCCINI: LA BOHEME
  0–7145–3938–4 Riverrun pb $4.95
  GIACHOMO ROSSINI: THE BARBER OF SEVILLE & MOSES
  0–7145–4080–3 Riverrun pb $8.95
  RICHARD STRAUSS: SALOME & ELEKTRA
  0–7145–4131–1 Riverrun pb $6.95
  GIUSEPPE VERDI: RIGOLETTO
  0–7145–3939–2 Riverrun pb $7.95
  GIUSEPPE VERDI: SIMON BOCCANEGRA
  0–7145–4064–1 Riverrun pb $5.95
  RICHARD WAGNER: THE FLYING DUTCHMAN
  0–7145–3920–1 Riverrun pb $4.95
  RICHARD WAGNER: THE MASTERSINGERS OF NUREMBERG
  0–7145–3961–9 Riverrun pb $4.95
  RICHARD WAGNER: THE RHINEGOLD
  0–7145–4078–1 Riverrun pb $5.95
  RICHARD WAGNER: THE TWILIGHT OF THE GODS (GOTTERDAMMERUNG)
  0–7145–4063–3 Riverrun pb $5.95

Gilbert & Sullivan

Ian Bradley, editor
THE ANNOTATED GILBERT AND SULLIVAN
0–14–070848–0 Penguin pb $10.95

George Dunn, editor
GILBERT AND SULLIVAN DICTIONARY
0–306–70007–7 Da Capo $25.00

Charles Hayter
GILBERT AND SULLIVAN
0–312–00446–X St. Martin's $19.95

Alan Jefferson
THE COMPLETE GILBERT AND SULLIVAN OPERA GUIDE
0–87196–857–6 Facts On File $24.95

Audrey Williamson
GILBERT AND SULLIVAN OPERA
0–7145–2766–1 Marion Boyars $19.95
0–7145–2767–X Marion Boyars pb $9.95

Opera Stars

- James Camner, editor
  THE GREAT OPERA STARS IN HISTORIC PHOTOGRAPHS: 343 Portraits from the 1850s to the 1940s
  0–486–23575–0 Dover pb $9.95
  STARS OF THE OPERA, 1950–1985, IN PHOTOGRAPHS
  0–486–25240–X Dover pb $9.95

- Rubert Christansen
  PRIMA DONNA: A History
  0–670–80482–7 Viking $19.95
  0–14–008378–2 Penguin pb $6.95

- Angus Heriot
  CASTRATI IN OPERA
  0–306–80003–9 Da Capo pb $5.95

- John Ardoin
  CALLAS AT JUILLIARD: The Master Classes
  0–394–56367–0 Knopf $22.50
  THE CALLAS LEGACY: A Biography of a Career
  0–684–16343–8 Scribners pb $3.95

- George Jellinek
  CALLAS: Portrait of a Prima Donna
  0–486–25047–4 Dover pb $7.95

- Arianna Stassinopoulos
  MARIA CALLAS: The Woman Behind the Legend
  0–345–30179–X Ballantine pb $3.95

- Howard Greenfeld
  CARUSO
  0–306–80215–5 Da Capo pb $9.95

- Placido Domingo
  MY FIRST FORTY YEARS
  0–394–52329–6 Knopf $15.95

Maria Callas in the title role of "Anna Bolena" (courtesy of La Scala, Milan)

- Dietrich Fischer-Dieskau
  REVERBERATIONS: The Memoirs
  Translated by Ruth Hein
  0–88064–137–1 Fromm $24.95

- Howard Vogt
  FLAGSTAD: Singer of the Century
  0–436–55800–9 David & Charles $39.95

- Marilyn Horne & Jane Scovell
  MARILYN HORNE: My Life
  0–689–11401–X Atheneum $16.95

- Mayer Martin
  GRANDISSIMO PAVAROTTI
  0–385–23138–5 Doubleday $40.00

- Luciano Pavarotti with William Wright
  PAVAROTTI: My Own Story
  0–446–30179–5 Warner pb $3.95

- Beverly Sills with Lawrence Linderman
  BEVERLY: An Autobiography
  0–553–26647–0 Bantam pb $4.95

- Quaintance Eaton
  SUTHERLAND AND BOYNTON: An Intimate Biography
  0–396–08945–3 Dodd, Mead $21.95

LEONARD BERNSTEIN:
Books I Can't Live Without

CORINTHIANS I & II

Vladimir Nabokov
LOLITA

William Shakespeare
THE COMPLETE WORKS

Lewis Carroll
COMPLETE WORKS

Helen Gardner, editor
THE NEW OXFORD BOOK OF ENGLISH VERSE, 1250–1950

Richard Ellmann, editor
THE NEW OXFORD BOOK OF AMERICAN VERSE

T.S. Eliot
FOUR QUARTETS

John Keats
THE COMPLETE POEMS

E.M. Kirkpatrick, editor
CHAMBERS TWENTIETH-CENTURY DICTIONARY

James Merrill
THE CHANGING LIGHT AT SANDOVER

American Popular Music

SONGWRITERS

• Alec Wilder
AMERICAN POPULAR SONG: The Great Innovators, 1900–1950
Wilder, himself a fine composer and songwriter, has a sharp mind and a cultivated writing style
0–19–501445–6 Oxford $39.95
0–19–501925–3 Oxford pb $12.95

• Edward Jablonski
HAROLD ARLEN: Happy with the Blues
A life of the songwriter from his early days in midwestern vaudeville to the Broadway stage. Known primarily as the musical force behind *The Wizard of Oz*, Arlen maintained a lifelong passion for the blues
0–306–80274–0 Da Capo pb $10.95

• Deena Rosenberg
THE BROTHERS GERSHWIN
A lively study of the creative styles of the Gershwins, who reshaped American popular music with an admixture of classical and black influences
0–689–11493–1 Atheneum $25.00

• Robert Kimball & Dorothy Hart, editors
THE COMPLETE LYRICS OF LORENZ HART
An invaluable encyclopedic document, covering the 30-year output of a great American songwriter/ lyricist
0–394–54680–6 Knopf $39.50

• Michael Freedland
JEROME KERN: A Biography
Along with Berlin and the Gershwins, Kern defined the American musical theater in its formative years. A celebratory and informative overview of his career
0–88186–700–4 Parkwest pb $6.95

• Charles Schwartz
COLE PORTER: A Biography
Comprehensive biography of perhaps the wittiest stylist of the golden age of popular song. Illustrated, with a listing of recordings and stage-production history
0–306–80097–7 Da Capo pb $8.95

• Robert Kimball, editor
THE COMPLETE LYRICS OF COLE PORTER
0–394–53214–7 Knopf $29.50
0–394–72764–9 Knopf pb $14.95

• Bryan Appleyard
RICHARD RODGERS: A Biography
0–571–13976–0 Faber & Faber pb $22.95

• Tony Thomas
HARRY WARREN AND THE HOLLYWOOD MUSICAL
How vaudeville and the Broadway stage came to Hollywood in the 1930s, seen through the career of a little-known but influential early practitioner
0–8065–0468–4 Lyle Stuart $14.95

SINGERS

• Whitney Balliett
AMERICAN SINGERS
Profiles of popular singers, by the *New Yorker*'s jazz writer
0–19–504610–2 Oxford $19.95

• Gene Lees
THE SINGERS AND THE SONG
Lees is a longtime jazz writer and also a lyricist with several songs to his credit. These are his meditations on the performers and the milieu of American non-rock popular singers
0–19–504293–X Oxford $18.95

• Henry Pleasants
THE GREAT AMERICAN POPULAR SINGERS
Musings by a veteran critic
0–671–54098–X Simon & Schuster $19.95

• Laurence J. Zwisohn
BING CROSBY: A Lifetime of Music
Song-by-song and first-source index to all Crosby's recordings. Valuable for this discography
Introduction by James Van Heusen
0–686–15969–1 Palm Tree pb $8.95

• Gail Lumet Buckley
THE HORNES: An American Family
This fascinating six-generation chronicle by Lena Horne's daughter provides unique documentation of an upper-middle-class black family in America
0–452–25959–2 NAL pb $8.95

• Lena Horne & Richard Schickel
LENA
An entertaining autobiography of one of the first successful black singer-actresses
0–87910–066–4 Limelight pb $8.95

• Peggy Lee
MISS PEGGY LEE: An Autobiography
1–556–11112–6 Donald I. Fine $18.95

• James Haskins
MABEL MERCER: A Biography
0–689–11595–4 Atheneum $19.95

• Kitty Kelley
HIS WAY: The Unauthorized Biography of Frank Sinatra
The controversial and best-selling portrait of a true American icon is full of juicy details, though at times almost too well researched. Glitz aside, it is an important document about a giant of contemporary popular culture
0–553–05137–7 Bantam $21.95
0–553–26515–6 Bantam pb $6.95

Lena Horne, from The Hornes: An American Family *by Gail Lumet Buckley (Knopf)*

• Mel Tormé
IT WASN'T ALL VELVET: An Autobiography
0–670–82289–2 Viking $18.95

Donald Spoto
LENYA: A Life
0–316–80725–7 Little, Brown $19.95

Margaret Crosland
PIAF
This first rather sensational English biography still captures something of the passion, irony, and despair of the French torch-singer's life
0–88064–069–3 Fromm pb $8.95

Country and Folk Music

GENERAL SURVEYS

• Charles T. Brown
MUSIC USA: America's Country and Western Tradition
A useful introduction to musical styles from honky-tonk to country-pop and to leading artists in the postwar country-and-western music scene
0–13–608167–3 Prentice-Hall pb $14.95

• Judie Eremo, editor
COUNTRY MUSICIANS: Their Music and How They Made It
Portraits of the Carter Family, Charlie Daniels, Waylon Jennings, Merle Travis, Willie Nelson, and many others, culled from interviews and articles
0–8021–0008–2 Grove $22.95
0–8021–3003–8 Grove pb $12.95

• Chet Hagan
GRAND OLE OPRY: The Official History
0–8021–0543–9 Henry Holt pb $19.95

• Bill C. Malone
COUNTRY MUSIC, U.S.A.
A well-documented, scholarly history by the foremost authority on country music, covering the entire lifespan of the genre, with bibliography and discography
0–292–71095–X Texas $24.95
0–292–71096–8 Texas pb $14.95

• Bill C. Malone & Judith McCullough, editors
STARS OF COUNTRY MUSIC: Uncle Dave Macon to Johnny Rodriguez
Full-length studies of the 23 most important figures from the last 50 years of country music
0–252–00527–9 Illinois $22.50

• Alanna Nash
BEHIND CLOSED DOORS: Talking with the Legends of Country Music
Interviews with Roy Acuff, Merle Haggard, Loretta Lynn, Tammy Wynette, and many others
0–679–72102–9 Knopf pb $14.95

• William W. Savage
SINGING COWBOYS AND ALL THAT JAZZ: A Short History of Popular Music in Oklahoma
0–8061–1648–X Oklahoma $16.95

• Myron Tassin & Jerry Henderson
FIFTY YEARS AT THE GRAND OLE OPRY
A tribute to one of the longest-running and most influential musical radio programs in America, with celebrity and fan photos
Foreword by Minnie Pearl
0–88289–089–1 Pelican pb $6.00

FOLK TRADITIONS

The work of John Lomax and, later, his son Alan set a precedent for musicologists and folklorists that continues today. For almost a century they have located, transcribed and researched thousands of cowboy ballads, Negro hymns and blues songs, and regional vocal traditionals from every corner of the United States.

John Lomax & Alan Lomax
COWBOY SONGS AND OTHER FRONTIER BALLADS
0–02–061260–5 Macmillan pb $16.95

THE FOLK SONGS OF NORTH AMERICA
0–385–03772–4 Doubleday pb $15.95

• Vance Randolph
OZARK FOLKSONGS
An abridgment of Randolph's immense collection of music and lyrics from the South and Midwest, not just from the Ozark region
Edited by Norm Cohen
0–252–00815–4 Illinois $42.50
0–252–00952–5 Illinois pb $14.95

• Art & Margo Rosenbaum
FOLK VISIONS AND VOICES: Traditional Music and Song in North Georgia
A thorough collection of African-American music and lyrics from the Deep South
Foreword by Pete Seeger
0–8203–0682–7 Georgia $27.50

• Anne Warner
TRADITIONAL AMERICAN FOLK SONGS FROM THE ANNE AND FRANK WARNER COLLECTION
An authoritative anthology of songs primarily from areas of North and South Carolina
Foreword by Alan Lomax
0–8156–2313–5 Syracuse $48.00
0–8156–0185–9 Syracuse pb $25.95

Bluegrass

Robert Cantwell
BLUEGRASS BREAKDOWN: The Making of the Old Southern Sound
A useful introduction to the sources of bluegrass music, its instruments, performers, and subgenres
0–252–01054–X Illinois $19.95

Marilyn Kochman, editor
THE BIG BOOK OF BLUEGRASS
Interviews with leading contemporary bluegrass artists taken from *Frets* magazine with essays on instruments and the development of bluegrass styles
Foreword by Earl Scruggs
0–688–02940–X Morrow $25.00
0–688–02942–6 Morrow pb $14.95

Neil V. Rosenberg
BLUEGRASS: A History
Charts the growth of bluegrass from its minstrel roots in the early 1900s to the present, with a focus on Bill Malone, the "Father of Bluegrass"
0–252–00265–2 Illinois $24.95

INDIVIDUAL ARTISTS

• Elizabeth Schlappi
ROY ACUFF: The Smoky Mountain Boy
Biography of a quintessential country-and-western singer-songwriter
Edited by James Calhoun
0–88289–144–8 Pelican pb $13.95

• Woody Guthrie
BOUND FOR GLORY
Guthrie's colorful autobiography paints a saga of America from the 1920s to the 1950s
Introduction by Pete Seeger
0–452–25483–3 NAL pb $6.95

Photograph from Woody Guthrie: A Life *by Joe Klein (Knopf)*

TO ORDER BOOKS AS GIFTS, SEE PAGE 1

- **Joe Klein**
  WOODY GUTHRIE: A Life
  First-rate, well-illustrated biography of the man and his times
  0–394–50152–7 Knopf $15.95
  0–345–29628–1 Ballantine pb $8.95

- **Roger M. Williams**
  SING A SAD SONG: The Life of Hank Williams
  A dispassionate, sometimes overly grim but powerful look at a short and tragic life
  0–252–00861–8 Illinois pb $9.95

- **Al Stricklin with Jon McConal**
  MY YEARS WITH BOB WILLS
  Pianist and close friend Stricklin tells candidly of his years with Wills's Texas Playboys
  0–89015–240–3 Eakin $14.95

- **Charles Townsend**
  SAN ANTONIO ROSE: The Life and Music of Bob Wills
  The definitive chronicle of Bob Wills, the creator and most talented exponent of country jazz
  0–252–01362–X Illinois pb $14.95

REFERENCE

- **Fred Dellar, Alan Cackett & Roy Thompson**
  THE HARMONY ILLUSTRATED ENCYCLOPEDIA OF COUNTRY MUSIC
  The most thorough and useful overview of the country-and-western music scene
  0–517–56503–X Crown pb $13.95

- **Melvin Shestack**
  COUNTRY MUSIC ENCYCLOPEDIA
  This slightly outdated reference work contains useful biographies and information on more than 200 artists
  0–690–01220–9 Crowell pb $7.95

Lester Young and bassist Nick Fenton (photo courtesy of the Frank Driggs Collection), from Jazz Giants: A Visual Retrospective edited by K. Abé (Billboard)

Jazz

"What is jazz? If you have to ask, you'll never know."

This famous rejoinder, attributed to both Louis Armstrong and Fats Waller, hasn't stopped legions of writers from trying to define, analyze, criticize and codify this most democratic and American of musical forms. Jazz resists definition because it is more an attitude toward playing music than a canon of specific techniques or repertoire. The music called jazz has its roots in the cross-pollination that occurred when the musical forms that African slaves brought to America began modifying, and being modified by, the forms they encountered in the New World. Thus, it is primarily a music of encounter and contrast, music of the action of one rhythm on another, one musician's style on another's. It is truly a New World, American, and profoundly democratic music, in that its finest moments occur when a balance is achieved between the individual musician's stylistic demands and the direction of the group.

SURVEYS OF JAZZ HISTORY

- **Joachim Berendt**
  THE JAZZ BOOK: From Ragtime to Fusion and Beyond with a New American Discography
  An excellent survey, updated and translated by Dan Morgenstern, head of the Institute of Jazz Studies at Rutgers University
  0–88208–141–1 Lawrence Hill pb $9.95

- **Linda Dahl**
  STORMY WEATHER: The Music and Lives of a Century of Jazzwomen
  A groundbreaking study of women musicians in a male-dominated musical world. Many interviews and photos
  0–394–72271–X Pantheon pb $12.95

  > **Leonard Feather**
  > **FROM SATCHMO TO MILES**
  > Feather has been an active chronicler of jazz since the late '30s
  > 0–306–80302–X Da Capo pb $9.95
  >
  > **THE JAZZ YEARS: Ear Witness to an Era**
  > 0–306–80296–1 Da Capo pb $10.95

- **André Francis**
  JAZZ
  A serious study of the major players by an important European critic
  0–306–70812–4 Da Capo $22.50

- **Nat Hentoff, editor**
  JAZZ: New Perspectives on the History of Jazz by Twelve of the World's Foremost Jazz Critics and Scholars
  A useful collection of essays edited by a sensitive and knowledgeable writer
  0–306–80002–0 Da Capo pb $10.95

Charlie Parker (photo courtesy of the Arthur Zimmerman Collection), from Jazz Giants: A Visual Retrospective edited by K. Abé (Billboard)

- **Francis Newton**
  THE JAZZ SCENE
  An English critic's social history of jazz
  0–306–70685–7 Da Capo $29.50

- **Nat Shapiro & Nat Hentoff, editors**
  HEAR ME TALKIN' TO YA: The Story of Jazz by the Men Who Made It
  This invaluable anecdotal history, told in interview snippets by many of the heroes of early jazz, is the source of many oft-repeated quotes
  0–486–21726–4 Dover pb $7.95

- **Marshall W. Stearns**
  THE STORY OF JAZZ
  This standard one-volume history provides a reliable chronology of the music's history and major figures
  0–19–500115–X Oxford $24.95
  0–19–501269–0 Oxford pb $11.95

- **Barry Ulanov**
  A HISTORY OF JAZZ IN AMERICA
  An ambitious study by a fine critic, covering the period through the early '50s
  0–306–70427–7 Da Capo $39.50

- **Martin Williams**
  The dean of American jazz writers, Williams combines a lucid style with a sensitive and serious attitude.
  JAZZ HERITAGE
  0–19–505071–1 Oxford pb $8.95

  THE JAZZ TRADITION
  An influential critical examination of the major streams in the music
  0–19–503291–8 Oxford pb $8.95

  THE SMITHSONIAN HISTORY OF JAZZ
  0–394–33545–7 Knopf pb $16.00

Blues and Gospel

Blues and gospel music represent the profane and the sacred sides of the same coin: both are folk forms. The blues are usually a rhythmic statement of romantic complaint, gospel a rhythmic statement of religious hope or faith. Both idioms had a large influence on the feeling of jazz.

● Samuel B. Charters
THE COUNTRY BLUES
A groundbreaking although sometimes inaccurate study of the major figures of rural blues by a dedicated early student
0–306–80014–4 Da Capo pb $9.95

THE LEGACY OF THE BLUES: Art and Lives of Twelve Great Bluesmen
0–306–80054–3 Da Capo pb $8.95

● Helen Oakley Dance
STORMY MONDAY: The T-Bone Walker Story
A jazz-influenced blues guitarist and singer whose career began in the '40s, Walker influenced many others, notably B.B. King and Chuck Berry
Foreword by B.B. King
0–8071–1355–7 LSU $24.95

● David Evans
BIG ROAD BLUES: Tradition and Creativity in the Folk Blues
0–306–80300–3 Da Capo $14.95

● William Ferris
BLUES FROM THE DELTA
Introduction by Billy Taylor
0–306–80327–X Da Capo pb $10.95

● Laurraine Goreau
JUST MAHALIA, BABY: The Mahalia Jackson Story
0–88289–441–2 Penguin pb $13.95

● W.C. Handy
FATHER OF THE BLUES
The autobiography of a dominant figure in black music shows how black folklore became assimilated into the mainstream of American popular culture
0–306–76241–2 Da Capo $37.50

● W.C. Handy, editor
BLUES: An Anthology
An update of the 1926 collection of early blues tunes, with notes and an introduction by the man referred to as the "father of the blues"
0–306–76244–7 Da Capo $37.50

● Sheldon Harris
BLUES WHO'S WHO
A valuable encyclopedic reference book by an expert
0–306–80155–8 Da Capo pb $29.50

● Daphne Duval Harrison
BLACK PEARLS: Blues Queens of the 1920s
0–8135–1279–4 Rutgers $19.95

Anthony Heilbut
THE GOSPEL SOUND: Good News and Bad Times
The definitive study of the world of gospel music
0–87910–034–6 Limelight pb $12.95

● James Weldon Johnson & J. Rosamond Johnson
THE BOOKS OF AMERICAN NEGRO SPIRITUALS
Early anthology of spirituals, arranged for voice and piano, with commentary by one of the most important black poets of the early 20th century
0–306–80074–8 Da Capo pb $11.95

● Charles Keil
URBAN BLUES
An important survey of electric blues traditions
0–226–42960–1 Chicago pb $2.95

● Kip Lornell
HAPPY IN THE SERVICE OF THE LORD: Afro-American Gospel Quartets in Memphis
0–252–01523–1 Illinois $19.95

VIRGINIA'S BLUES, GOSPEL, AND COUNTRY RECORDS, 1902–1943
0–8131–1658–9 Kentucky $27.00

● John Lovell, Jr.
BLACK SONG: The Forge and the Flame
A sweeping study of the Afro-American spiritual
0–913729–53–1 Paragon pb $12.95

● George Mitchell
BLOW MY BLUES AWAY
A study of contemporary Mississippi delta bluesmen, illustrated with the author's own photos
0–306–76173–4 Da Capo $29.50

● Robert Palmer
DEEP BLUES
A first-rate study of the blues styles and major performers of the Mississippi delta. Meticulously researched by a leading writer in the field
0–14–006223–8 Penguin pb $7.95

● Mike Rowe
CHICAGO BLUES: The City and the Music
Detailed study of the electric blues tradition of the most important urban blues center
0–306–80145–0 Da Capo pb $8.95

● Charles Sawyer
THE ARRIVAL OF B.B. KING: The Authorized Biography
The life and work of one of the major figures in postwar blues
0–306–80169–8 Da Capo pb $9.95

Ragtime

In vogue around the turn of the century, ragtime was a syncopated music played by solo pianists, brass bands, and other instrumental combinations. It formed the rhythmic basis of the early New Orleans band music that constituted jazz's first flowering.

● Edward A. Berlin
RAGTIME: A Musical and Cultural History
0–520–05219–6 California pb $9.95

● Rudi Blesh & Harriet Janis
THEY ALL PLAYED RAGTIME
A classic, if somewhat outdated, study of the form, its composers and performers
0–8256–0091–X Oak pb $9.95

● John E. Hasse
RAGTIME: Its History, Composers, Music
0–02–872650–2 Macmillan pb $17.95

● William Schafer & Johannes Riedel
THE ART OF RAGTIME: Form and Meaning of an Original Black American Art
0–306–80057–8 Da Capo pb $8.95

● Terry Waldo
THIS IS RAGTIME
0–306–76229–3 Da Capo $29.50

Early Jazz: New Orleans and Beyond

Jazz's early years were a process of sorting out many questions: how ensembles would play together, what a solo instrumentalist's role was, what was appropriate repertoire. Much of the most important experimentation went on in New Orleans, home of jazz's first great soloist, Louis Armstrong, and its first great composer, Jelly Roll Morton. But the sound was heard all over the country and, eventually, the world. Before the 1920s were out, many regions and sensibilities had put their distinctive stamps on the music.

● Rudi Blesh
SHINING TRUMPETS
An early history of jazz and its major and minor figures
0–306–80029–2 Da Capo pb $9.95

● H.O. Brunn
THE STORY OF THE ORIGINAL DIXIELAND JAZZ BAND
Close-up on the white New Orleans band that made first jazz recordings
0–306–70892–2 Da Capo $32.50

● Jack V. Buerkle & Danny Barker
BOURBON STREET BLACK: The New Orleans Black Jazzman
A flavorful memoir by a New Orleans guitarist who has played in many different settings in a 60-year career
0–19–501832–X Oxford pb $6.95

• Samuel B. Charters
JAZZ: New Orleans 1885–1963
Unique and fascinating biographical
reference to the musicians of New Orleans
0–306–76189–0 Da Capo $22.50

• Richard Hadlock
JAZZ MASTERS OF THE TWENTIES
Informative portraits of major figures of
the period
0–306–80328–3 Da Capo pb $10.95

• Donald M. Marquis
**IN SEARCH OF BUDDY BOLDEN: First
Man of Jazz**
Investigative reportage on a legendary,
little-documented New Orleans progenitor
of jazz
0–8071–0356–X LSU $16.95

• Nathan W. Pearson, Jr.
GOIN' TO KANSAS CITY
0–252–01336–0 Illinois $24.95

• Frederick Ramsey & Charles Edward
Smith
JAZZMEN
Reprint of a 1939 collection of lyrical
essays about the people and places of early
jazz, especially New Orleans and Chicago.
An enjoyable period piece
0–87190–039–7 Limelight pb $9.95

• Al Rose & Edmond Souchon
NEW ORLEANS JAZZ: A Family Album
A beautifully illustrated guided tour to
great and obscure alike, from earliest times
to the present
0–8071–1173–2 LSU pb $19.95

• William J. Schafer & Richard B. Allen
**BRASS BANDS AND NEW ORLEANS
JAZZ**
0–8071–0282–2 LSU pb $8.95

> Gunther Schuller
> **EARLY JAZZ: Its Roots and Musical
> Development**
> A classic study by a musician and
> composer trained in European music as
> well as jazz. Sensitive and scholarly
> analysis of the music's first flowering
> 0–19–504043–0 Oxford pb $9.95

• Martin Williams
JAZZ MASTERS OF NEW ORLEANS
Portraits of jazz pioneers by a
knowledgeable writer
0–306–80093–4 Da Capo pb $9.95

Swing and Big Band

Through the 1920s, arrangers and band-
leaders such as Fletcher Henderson, Don
Redman, and Duke Ellington transferred
the formulas worked out in New Orleans
ensembles to the standard dance band ensembles. They produced and refined a big-
band jazz style that ripened, in the 1930s,
into the swing era, a period of unprecedented appreciation of jazz-based music.

• Stanley Dance
THE WORLD OF SWING
Knowledgeable and enthusiastic, Dance
presents witty portraits of musicians he
knows and understands well
0–306–80103–5 Da Capo pb $10.95

• Drew Page
**DREW'S BLUES: A Sideman's Life with
the Big Bands**
0–8071–0686–0 LSU $19.95

> Gunter Schuller
> **THE SWING ERA: The Development
> of Jazz, 1933–1945**
> The long-awaited second volume in
> Schuller's monumental history of jazz
> 0–19–504312–X Oxford $32.50

• George T. Simon
THE BIG BANDS
A study by a former editor of the jazz
journal *Metronome*
0–02–872430–5 Schirmer pb $12.95

• Rex Stewart
JAZZ MASTERS OF THE THIRTIES
A great trumpet player from the Ellington
and Fletcher Henderson bands paints
unusual portraits of his contemporaries and
peers, in a penetrating, anecdotal style
Introduction by Martin Williams
0–306–80159–0 Da Capo pb $9.95

Bebop and Post-Bop

Sometime around 1940, a number of musicians began experimenting with the musical
assumptions under which jazz had been
operating for over a decade. In informal
sessions, they began working out a new
approach, which became known as bebop,
stressing fluency of execution, harmonic sophistication, quick reflexes, and mordant
wit. Through the 1950s, musicians, many of
them half a generation younger than bop's
founders, continued to refine and expand the
new possibilities introduced by the boppers.

• Leonard Feather
INSIDE JAZZ
Originally published during bebop's
heyday, this remains an entertaining
introduction to the jazz revolution of the
late '40s, by a champion of what was then
the "new" jazz
0–306–80076–4 Da Capo pb $7.95

• Ira Gitler
JAZZ MASTERS OF THE FORTIES
A flavorful survey of the main figures, by a
longtime writer and enthusiast
0–306–80224–4 Da Capo pb $9.95

**SWING TO BOP: An Oral History of the
Transition in Jazz in the 1940s**
An oral-history approach to the
transitional period between the big-band
era and the bop era
0–19–505070–3 Oxford pb $9.95

• Joe Goldberg
JAZZ MASTERS OF THE FIFTIES
This worthy sequel to the Gitler volume
includes portraits of Thelonious Monk,
Miles Davis, and others
0–306–80197–3 Da Capo pb $9.95

• A.B. Spellman
**FOUR LIVES IN THE BEBOP
BUSINESS**
Four realistic portraits of musicians of the
1950s (some becoming major figures in
the 1960s) and their tribulations: Ornette
Coleman, Cecil Taylor, Jackie McLean,
and Herbie Nichols. Outstanding
0–87910–042–7 Limelight pb $11.95

The '60s and Since

As happened when the swing era ripened,
musicians in the late 1950s and early '60s
began to feel restive with the vocabulary that
had been standard since 1945. Some experimented with totally free-form playing (with
no preestablished harmonic or rhythmic basis), some became traditionalists, and some
tried to incorporate so-called rock elements
into jazz.

• Ekkehard Jost
FREE JAZZ
Analysis of the musical approaches of the
'60s, including thoughts on John Coltrane,
Ornette Coleman, Cecil Taylor, and other
avant-garde figures
0–306–76140–8 Da Capo $27.50

• John Litweiler
**THE FREEDOM PRINCIPLE: Jazz After
1958**
Thoughts on the changes in the '60s, by
one of the most informed critics of the
period
0–87975–157–6 Prometheus $17.95

• Barry McRae
THE JAZZ CATACLYSM
Study of the transitional period that
resulted in the free jazz revolution of the
1960s
0–306–76240–4 Da Capo $25.00

• Ben Sidran
BLACK TALK
Introduction by Archie Shepp
0–306–80184–1 Da Capo pb $8.95

• Martin Williams
**JAZZ MASTERS IN TRANSITION,
1957–1969**
Probing portraits of important musicians
of the turbulent avant-garde years
0–306–80175–2 Da Capo pb $9.95

ESSAYS AND REVIEWS

• Amiri Baraka
Baraka (aka LeRoi Jones) is a prominent
black poet and playwright who has written
consistently about jazz, championing
particularly the "new thing," or avant-

garde, players of the '60s. His essays are opinionated and thought-provoking.

BLUES PEOPLE: Negro Music in White America
0–688–18474–X Morrow pb $9.95

THE MUSIC: Reflections on Jazz and Blues
0–688–04388–7 Morrow $22.95

- Whitney Balliett
Balliett, for over 30 years a knowledgeable and eloquent contributor to *The New Yorker,* at his best brings a fine fiction writer's eye to portraits of musicians, singers, and songwriters.

AMERICAN MUSICIANS: 56 Portraits in Jazz
0–19–503758–8 Oxford $27.95

IMPROVISING: 16 Jazz Musicians and Their Art
0–19–502149–5 Oxford $21.95

JELLY ROLL, JABBO AND FATS: 19 Portraits in Jazz
0–19–503425–2 Oxford pb $8.95

NEW YORK NOTES: A Journal of Jazz in the '70s
0–306–80037–3 Da Capo pb $8.95

NIGHT CREATURE: A Journal of Jazz, 1975–1980
0–19–502908–9 Oxford $21.95

THE SOUND OF SURPRISE
0–306–77543–3 Da Capo $29.50

- Rudi Blesh
COMBO USA
Entertaining portraits of swing-era musicians
0–306–79568–X Da Capo $29.50

- Hayden Carruth
SITTING IN: Selected Writings on Jazz, Blues, and Related Topics
A distinguished poet's thoughts on the music
0–87745–153–2 Iowa $22.50

- Stanley Dance
JAZZ ERA: The Forties
Biographies of major figures of this era
0–306–76191–2 Da Capo $27.50

- Francis Davis
IN THE MOMENT: Jazz in the 1980's
Interesting, somewhat overblown pieces, mostly reviews, by a younger critic for *The Atlantic*
0–19–504090–2 Oxford $24.95

- Leonard Feather
FROM SATCHMO TO MILES
Anecdotal collection of essays on major figures
0–306–80302–X Da Capo pb $9.95

Gary Giddins
Portraits, critical essays, and occasional pieces by the most knowledgeable young jazz critic
RHYTHM-A-NING: Jazz Tradition and Innovation in the '80s
0–19–504214–X Oxford pb $8.95

RIDING ON A BLUE NOTE: Jazz and American Pop
0–19–503213–6 Oxford pb $9.95

- Ted Gioia
THE IMPERFECT ART: Reflections on Jazz and Modern Culture
0–19505343–5 Oxford $16.95

- Nat Hentoff
THE JAZZ LIFE
Combines social criticisms with Hentoff's knowledge of musicians' lives
0–306–80088–8 Da Capo pb $8.95

- André Hodéir
JAZZ: Its Evolution and Essence
The groundbreaking French critic and musician applies academic structural criteria; an influential book when first published in the 1950s
0–394–17525–5 Grove pb $7.95

TOWARD JAZZ
0–306–80264–3 Da Capo pb $9.95

- Max Jones
TALKING JAZZ
Short sketches and interviews with many of the heroes of early jazz, by a British critic
0–393–024994–6 Norton $19.95

- Orrin Keepnews
THE VIEW FROM WITHIN: Jazz Writings, 1948–1987
The articulate and knowledgeable Keepnews, who founded the Riverside and Milestone labels, has been one of the most significant record producers in jazz
0–19–505284–6 Oxford $19.95

- Philip Larkin
ALL WHAT JAZZ: A Record Diary
Distinguished British poet's collection of highly opinionated reviews from the 1960s
0–374–10340–2 Farrar, Straus & Giroux $19.95
0–374–51908–0 Farrar, Straus & Giroux pb $9.95

- Neil Leonard
JAZZ: Myth and Religion
0–19–504249–2 Oxford $19.95

- Marian McPartland
ALL IN GOOD TIME
Essays by the jazz pianist and radio interview host
0–19–504871–7 Oxford $14.95

- Paul Oliver
BLUES OFF THE RECORD: Thirty Years of Blues
0–306–80321–6 Da Capo pb $13.95

SCREENING THE BLUES
0–306–80344–5 Da Capo pb $11.95

- Robert Reisner
THE JAZZ TITANS
Sketches of major jazz musicians
0–306–70866–3 Da Capo $25.00

- Martin Williams, editor
THE ART OF JAZZ: Ragtime to Bebop
Afterword by Gunther Schuller
0–306–80134–5 Da Capo pb $8.95

Benny Goodman by Ronald Searle, from The Image of America in Caricature and Cartoon *by Ron Tyler (Amon Carter Museum/cartoon courtesy University of Texas)*

JAZZ PANORAMA
A mixed bag of essays and interviews from the short-lived but excellent magazine *The Jazz Review,* ranging from the earliest jazz to the "new thing" of the '60s
0–306–79574–4 Da Capo $32.50

- Valerie Wilmer
JAZZ PEOPLE
Verbal and photographic portraits whose subjects include Billy Higgins, Jimmy Heath, Randy Weston, Archie Shepp, and others
0–306–76269–2 Da Capo $21.50

- Al Young
BODIES AND SOUL: Musical Memoirs
Memories of Duke Ellington, Hank Williams, Nat Cole, and Ray Charles
0–916870–39–1 Creative Arts pb $6.95

KINDS OF BLUE: Musical Memoirs
A companion volume to *Bodies and Soul*
0–916870–82–0 Creative Arts pb $7.95

THINGS AIN'T WHAT THEY USED TO BE
From the tango to the bossa nova, Young pinpoints the past through the power of music
0–88739–024–2 Creative Arts pb $8.95

JAZZ APPRECIATION AND THEORY

- **John Chilton**
  TEACH YOURSELF JAZZ
  0–679–12225–7 David McKay pb $6.95

- **Jerry Coker**
  IMPROVISING JAZZ
  Standard, useful guide to the theory behind jazz improvisation
  0–671–62829–1 Simon & Schuster pb $8.95

- **Martin Williams**
  WHERE'S THE MELODY?: A Listener's Introduction to Jazz
  The best book on jazz appreciation for the layman
  0–306–80183–3 Da Capo pb $8.95

THE JAZZ SCENE

- **Roy Carr, Brian Case & Fred Dellar**
  THE HIP: Hipsters, Jazz and the Beat Generation
  An interesting, multiformat nostalgia book—but only peripherally useful as a look at the '50s jazz scene
  0–571–13809–8 Faber & Faber pb $14.95

- **Samuel B. Charters & Leonard Kunstadt**
  JAZZ: A History of the New York Scene
  A colorful survey of the New York scene of the 1920s, '30s, and '40s, from contemporary sources
  0–306–80225–2 Da Capo pb $9.95

- **Ted Fox**
  SHOWTIME AT THE APOLLO
  Fascinating history of the major Harlem venue for black performing artists in New York City
  0–03–060534–2 Holt pb $9.95

- **Max Gordon**
  LIVE AT THE VILLAGE VANGUARD
  An anecdotal memoir by the owner of New York City's longest-lived jazz club
  Introduction by Nat Hentoff
  0–306–80160–4 Da Capo pb $8.95

- **Arnold Shaw**
  FIFTY SECOND STREET: The Street of Jazz
  Entertaining, episodic history of the heyday of New York's block-long entertainment center during the 1930s and '40s, where every musician of interest played at one time or another
  0–306–80068–3 Da Capo pb $8.95

- **Frederick S. Starr**
  RED AND HOT: The Fate of Jazz in the Soviet Union, 1917–1980
  0–19–503163–6 Oxford $21.95
  0–87910–026–5 Limelight pb $9.95

VISUAL BOOKS

- **K. Abé, editor**
  JAZZ GIANTS: A Visual Retrospective
  0–8230–7536–2 Billboard $60.00

- **William Claxton**
  JAZZ
  A beautifully produced large-format book of photos by a preeminent photographer
  0–942642–28–7 Twelvetrees $40.00

- **Frank Driggs & Harris Lewine**
  BLACK BEAUTY, WHITE HEAT: A Pictorial History of Classic Jazz, 1920–1950
  A lavish, large-format pictorial book; rare photos, record labels, handbills, and more from jazz's "golden age," 1920–1950
  0–688–03771–2 Morrow $50.50

- **Carol Friedman & Gary Giddins**
  A MOMENT'S NOTICE: Photographs of American Jazz Musicians
  First-rate portraits of musicians in the 1970s and '80s, with text by Giddins
  0–02–872040–7 Schirmer $21.95

- **Milt Hinton & David Berger**
  BASS LINE: The Stories and Photographs of Milt Hinton
  0–87722–518–4 Temple $35.95

- **Carol Reiff**
  NIGHTS IN BIRDLAND: Jazz Photographs 1954–60
  Moody portraits, mostly shot during the mid- and late '50s, at various jazz clubs
  Introduction by Jack Kerouac
  0–671–63281–7 Simon & Schuster pb $10.95

- **Valerie Wilmer**
  THE FACE OF BLACK MUSIC
  Work by one of the most prominent jazz photographers of the 1960s
  0–306–80039–X Da Capo pb $9.95

STUDIES OF INDIVIDUAL ARTISTS
(alphabetical by subject)

Louis Armstrong

The first great jazz soloist, and the man who set the rules, as trumpeter and singer, for everyone who came after, regardless of instrument, Armstrong was also one of America's most beloved entertainers.

Louis Armstrong
SATCHMO: My Life in New Orleans
Full of the sound of Armstrong's voice, characteristic humor, and vitality; covers the period up until he left New Orleans for Chicago
0–306–80276–7 Da Capo pb $9.95

James Lincoln Collier
LOUIS ARMSTRONG: An American Genius
Collier's characteristic armchair psychoanalytic approach is misleading and unbalanced
0–19–503727–8 Oxford pb $9.95

Gary Giddins
SATCHMO
An astute and lavishly illustrated portrait
0–385–24428–2 Doubleday pb $24.95

Robert Goffin
HORN OF PLENTY: The Story of Louis Armstrong
A portrait covering Satchmo's career through the mid-1940s
0–306–77430–5 Da Capo $32.50

Max Jones & John Chilton
LOUIS: The Louis Armstrong Story, 1900–1971
The best single volume available about Armstrong
0–306–80324–0 Da Capo pb $10.95

Hugues Panassié
LOUIS ARMSTRONG
Thin but affectionate biography by a Frenchman who was one of the first jazz critics
0–306–79611–2 Da Capo $25.00
0–306–80116–7 Da Capo pb $7.95

- **Danny Barker**
  A LIFE IN JAZZ
  Edited by Alyn Shipton
  0–19–505479–2 Oxford pb $9.95

- **Charlie Barnet & Stanley Dance**
  THOSE SWINGING YEARS: The Autobiography of Charlie Barnet
  Autobiography of a well-known bandleader and saxophonist of the swing era
  Foreword by Billy May
  0–8071–1128–7 LSU $19.95

- **Count Basie with Albert Murray**
  GOOD MORNING BLUES: The Autobiography of Count Basie
  Portrait of jazz giant, pianist, bandleader, covering his more than 50-year career in great detail
  0–917657–89–6 Donald Fine pb $10.95

- **Stanley Dance**
  THE WORLD OF COUNT BASIE
  An overview of Basie and his band members, by a first-rate historian of the era
  0–306–80245–7 Da Capo pb $10.95

- **Sidney Bechet**
  TREAT IT GENTLE: An Autobiography
  One of the best jazz autobiographies, lyrical and even poetic in spots, covering the career of the great clarinetist and soprano saxophonist from the beginnings through the early 1950s
  Foreword by Desmond Flower
  0–306–80086–1 Da Capo pb $8.95

• John Chilton
SIDNEY BECHET: The Wizard of Jazz
Biography by a well-known English critic
0–19–520623–1 Oxford pb $24.95

• Barney Bigard
WITH LOUIS AND THE DUKE
Memoir by the great New Orleans clarinetist who played with Armstrong and Ellington
0–19–520637–1 Oxford pb $8.95

• Buck Clayton with Nancy M. Elliott
BUCK CLAYTON'S JAZZ WORLD
The career of the great trumpeter and arranger, famous primarily for his star role with Count Basie's band
Introduction by Humphrey Littleton
0–19–520535–9 Oxford $24.95

• C.O. Simpkins
COLTRANE
0–933121–20–2 Black Classic pb $11.95

• J.C. Thomas
CHASIN' THE TRANE
0–306–80043–8 Da Capo pb $9.95

• Eddie Condon with Thomas Sugrue
WE CALLED IT MUSIC
Entertaining reminiscence by guitarist, bandleader, and raconteur focuses on the 1920s and '30s, with anecdotes and opinions on all the major figures of the time, as well as rare photos
0–306–76276–6 Da Capo $35.00

• Jack Chambers
MILESTONES: The Music and Times of Miles Davis
The preeminent trumpet stylist who came up in the 1940s under the tutelage of Charlie Parker, Davis pointed the way toward a more moody, "cool" approach to playing. One of the most influential musicians of the postwar era
Volume 1: To 1960
0–688–02635–4 Morrow $17.95
Volume 2: Since 1960
0–688–04646–0 Morrow $17.95

• Vladimir Simosko & Barry Tepperman
ERIC DOLPHY: A Musical Biography and Discography
Biography of the important saxophonist who helped shape the new styles of the 1960s
0–306–80107–8 Da Capo pb $7.95

Duke Ellington

Ellington's career spanned over 50 years, during which he became jazz's most important composer and bandleader. He was a magnetic personality, a unique pianist, and a cultural figure of the highest significance in America.

James Lincoln Collier
DUKE ELLINGTON
A controversial recent biography
0–19–503770–7 Oxford $19.95

Stanley Dance
THE WORLD OF DUKE ELLINGTON
Portraits of Ellington, his sidemen, and aides-de-camp, illustrated with fine pictures, by a writer who traveled with the band and knew them for decades
Foreword by Duke Ellington
0–306–80136–1 Da Capo pb $9.95

Duke Ellington
MUSIC IS MY MISTRESS
A uniquely flavored book of reminiscences and anecdotes by the man himself. Loosely structured, but entertaining and liberally illustrated
0–306–80033–0 Da Capo pb $12.95

Mercer Ellington & Stanley Dance
DUKE ELLINGTON IN PERSON
A revealing, candid memoir by Ellington's son, himself a talented composer, arranger, and trumpeter
0–306–80104–3 Da Capo pb $9.95

Peter Gammond, editor
DUKE ELLINGTON: His Life and Music
Essays on various Ellingtonian topics by 14 critics and musicians
0–306–70874–4 Da Capo $29.50

Derek Jewell
DUKE: A Portrait of Duke Ellington
0–393–00973–4 Norton pb $4.95

Barry Ulanov
DUKE ELLINGTON
The first full-length biography of Ellington, by one of the best and brightest critics of the 1940s and '50s, covers the maestro's career to the late '40s
0–306–70727–6 Da Capo $35.00

• Dizzy Gillespie with Al Fraser
TO BE OR NOT TO BOP: Memoirs of Dizzy Gillespie
Cofounder of bebop, trumpeter, entertainer, and musical thinker of the highest caliber, DG is still active after 50 years. In this memoir he pulls few punches
0–306–80236–8 Da Capo pb $13.95

• Stanley Baron, editor
BENNY: King of Swing
The clarinetist and bandleader Benny Goodman, called the King of Swing during the 1930s, played a major role as a popularizer of the big-band jazz sound
0–306–80289–0 Da Capo pb $14.95

• Raymond Horricks
STEPHANE GRAPPELLI
A slim but readable portrait of the great French violinist
0–306–802570–0 Da Capo pb $8.95

• Hampton Hawes with Don Asher
RAISE UP OFF ME: A Portrait of Hampton Hawes
The candid and sometimes harrowing autobiography of the excellent West Coast pianist Hampton Hawes, detailing his struggles with heroin addiction
Introduction by Gary Giddins
0–306–80101–9 Da Capo pb $7.95

• Stanley Dance
THE WORLD OF EARL HINES
Pianist and bandleader, Hines advanced the piano's continued role as a solo instrument during the late 1920s and '30s, and continued to perform through the 1970s. His big band of the early '40s was an incubator for the bebop sound, featuring such innovators as Charlie Parker and Dizzy Gillespie. Dance has compiled lively portraits of Hines and his musical associates
0–306–80182–5 Da Capo pb $10.95

• Raymond Horricks
QUINCY JONES
0–87052–215–9 Hippocrene $12.95

• Carol Easton
STRAIGHT AHEAD: The Story of Stan Kenton
An important bandleader and figurehead of the "Progressive Jazz" movement of the 1940s, Kenton inspired and showcased important musicians such as Lee Konitz and Zoot Sims
0–306–80152–0 Da Capo pb $7.95

• George T. Simon
GLENN MILLER AND HIS ORCHESTRA
The celebrated bandleader of the late 1930s was never a significant force in jazz, but rather an important popularizer
Introduction by Bing Crosby
0–306–80129–9 Da Capo pb $10.95

• Janet Coleman & Al Young
MINGUS/MINGUS
Bassist and composer Charles Mingus was very influential in the 1950s and '60s as a bandleader as well. His volatile personality and opinions made him a visible figure to the public at large
0–88739–067–6 Creative Arts $14.95

Charles Mingus (photo by Tadayuki Naito), from his autobiography Beneath the Underdog *(Penguin)*

- Charles Mingus
BENEATH THE UNDERDOG
Compelling, turbulent autobiography
0–14–003880–9 Penguin pb $5.95

- Brian Priestley
MINGUS: A Critical Biography
0–306–80217–0 Da Capo pb $9.95

Charlie Parker

One of the inventors of modern jazz, Parker redefined the soloist's language and, by extension, the notion of how groups played together.

Gary Giddins
CELEBRATING BIRD: The Triumph of Charlie Parker
A large-format book, lavishly illustrated and with a perceptive text
0–688–05951–1 Morrow pb $12.95

Robert G. Reisner, editor
BIRD: The Legend of Charlie Parker
Illustrated series of interviews with Parker's associates, friends and fans: a multi-faceted picture of a protean genius
0–306–80069–1 Da Capo pb $9.95

- Art Pepper & Laurie Pepper
STRAIGHT LIFE
The autobiography of the troubled West Coast saxophonist Art Pepper, detailing his sexual and pharmaceutical preoccupations. A fascinating, if sometimes depressing, look into the jazz scene of a certain time and place
0–02–872010–5 Schirmer pb $9.95

- Alan Groves
BUD POWELL: His Life and Times
Powell, a contemporary of Parker and Gillespie, plagued with personal problems through his life, was a virtuoso pianist who defined modern jazz playing during the 1940s and '50s
0–87663–530–3 Universe pb $10.95

- Charles Delaunay
DJANGO REINHARDT
A biography by an important early French critic of the European Gypsy guitarist who brought a unique, lyrical sensibility to the jazz of the 1930s, and who often recorded with American musicians such as Coleman Hawkins and Rex Stewart
0–306–80171–X Da Capo pb $9.95

- Artie Shaw
THE TROUBLE WITH CINDERELLA
The entertaining, colorful autobiography of a much-married, highly individualistic clarinetist and bandleader
0–306–80091–8 Da Capo pb $9.95

Ella Fitzgerald and Dizzy Gillespie in 1948 (photo by William Gottlieb), from Jazz Giants: A Visual Retrospective *edited by K. Abé (Billboard)*

- Willie "The Lion" Smith with George Hoefer
MUSIC ON MY MIND: The Memoirs of an American Pianist
Autobiography of the legendary pianist and raconteur, a giant of the stride piano school of the 1920s
Foreword by Duke Ellington
0–306–70684–9 Da Capo $32.50
0–306–80087–X Da Capo pb $9.95

- Jay D. Smith & Len Guttridge
JACK TEAGARDEN: The Story of a Jazz Maverick
Teagarden was one of the most important trombonists in early jazz, and a fine singer with extremely natural blues phrasing
0–306–80322–4 Da Capo pb $9.95

Fats Waller

The master of stride piano, and a popular entertainer in the 1930s, Waller composed such perennially popular songs as "Honeysuckle Rose," "Squeeze Me," and "Ain't Misbehavin'."

Ed Kirkeby
AIN'T MISBEHAVIN': The Story of Fats Waller
A workmanlike biography by Fats's manager
0–306–80015–2 Da Capo pb $8.95

Maurice Waller & Anthony Calabrese
FATS WALLER
A biographical memoir by Waller's son
0–02–872710–X Schirmer pb $6.95

SINGERS

- Sid Colin
ELLA: The Life and Times of Ella Fitzgerald
One of the best-loved jazz singers, Ella Fitzgerald began her career in the 1930s with the Chick Webb band. Her melodically inventive, hornlike phrasing is universally admired by musicians
0–241–11754–2 David & Charles $19.95

- John Chilton
BILLIE'S BLUES
Holiday's phrasing and sensibility made her one of the most influential of all jazz singers
0–306–80363–1 Da Capo pb $12.95

- Billie Holiday with William Dufty
LADY SINGS THE BLUES
A raw, powerful autobiography
0–14–006762–0 Penguin pb $6.95

- John White
BILLIE HOLIDAY: Her Life and Times
0–87663–528–1 Universe pb $10.95

- Frank C. Taylor
ALBERTA HUNTER: A Celebration in Blues
An early blues and popular singer of the 1920s, Hunter traveled the world, eventually retiring to become a nurse. Her reemergence and resumption of active performance was one of the most appreciated popular music events of the 1970s
0–07–063172–7 McGraw-Hill pb $8.95

- Albert Murray
STOPPING THE BLUES
0–306–80362–3 Da Capo pb $11.95

- Anita O'Day with George Eells
HIGH TIMES, HARD TIMES
0–87910–118–0 Limelight pb $12.95

Bessie Smith

Bessie Smith was the greatest female blues singer of the 1920s. Her powerful voice and deep emotion are evident on her many recorded performances, with accompaniments by jazz musicians such as Louis Armstrong and James P. Johnson.

Edward Brooks
THE BESSIE SMITH COMPANION
A study of all of the great blues singer's recordings, with biographical material as well
0–306–76202–1 Da Capo $27.50

Elaine Feinstein
BESSIE SMITH
0–670–80642–0 Viking pb $13.95

• Jim Haskins
QUEEN OF THE BLUES: A Biography of Dinah Washington
The great blues, ballad, and jazz singer was beloved of musicians and fans for her powerful emotional delivery and distinctive style
0–688–04846–3 Morrow $16.95

• Leslie Gourse
EVERY DAY: The Story of Joe Williams
Williams gained fame as a blues and ballad singer with Count Basie's orchestra
0–306–80275–9 Da Capo pb $9.95

REFERENCE

• Brian Case, Stan Britt & Chrissi Murray
THE HARMONY ILLUSTRATED ENCYCLOPEDIA OF JAZZ
0–517–56442–4 Crown $22.95
0–517–56443–2 Crown pb $13.95

• John Chilton
WHO'S WHO OF JAZZ
Biographical entries; very useful and authoritative
0–306–76271–4 Da Capo $29.50
0–306–80243–0 Da Capo pb $11.95

• Leonard Feather
THE ENCYCLOPEDIA OF JAZZ
Important book of biographies, musical examples, and fascinating peripheral material; covers period through 1960
0–306–80214–7 Da Capo pb $18.95

• Leonard Feather & Ira Gitler
THE ENCYCLOPEDIA OF JAZZ IN THE '70s
A further update
Introduction by Quincy Jones
0–306–80290–2 Da Capo pb $16.95

• Steve Harris
JAZZ ON COMPACT DISC
Useful alphabetical guide
0–517–56688–5 Crown pb $13.95

• Max Harrison, Charles Ford & Eric Thacker
THE ESSENTIAL JAZZ RECORDS, VOLUME ONE: Ragtime to Swing
Idiosyncratic, exhaustively annotated, opinionated guide by three British critics
0–306–80236–7 Da Capo pb $14.95

• Len Lyons
THE 101 BEST JAZZ ALBUMS: A History of Jazz on Records
0–688–08720–5 Morrow pb $12.95

• David Meeker
JAZZ IN THE MOVIES
0–306–76147–5 Da Capo $35.00

• Paul Oliver, Max Harrison & William Bolcom
THE NEW GROVE GOSPEL, BLUES AND JAZZ
0–393–01696–X Norton $22.95
0–393–30100–1 Norton pb $11.95

• Frederick Ramsey, Jr.
A GUIDE TO LONG-PLAY JAZZ RECORDS
Interesting mainly to hard-core collectors and researchers, this surveys records from 1948–1953
0–306–70891–4 Da Capo $27.50

Rock

GENERAL CRITICISM AND CONSUMER GUIDES

• Lester Bangs
PSYCHOTIC REACTIONS AND CARBURETOR DUNG: An Anthology of Writings by Lester Bangs
The critics' critic, who died in 1982 at age 33, was funny and illuminating
Edited by Greil Marcus
0–394–53896–X Knopf $19.95
0–679–72045–6 Random House pb $9.95

• Julie Burchill & Tony Parsons
"THE BOY LOOKED AT JOHNNY": The Obituary of Rock and Roll
"It's either the best exposé of rock I've ever read—a cult book?—or it's the biggest con that's ever been published"—*Tribune* (UK). It's all three
Introduction by Lenny Kaye
0–571–12992–7 Faber & Faber pb $8.95

• Simon Frith
SOUND EFFECTS: Youth, Leisure and the Politics of Rock 'n' Roll
Acclaimed, influential study of rock and roll's cultural and economic impact
0–394–74811–5 Pantheon pb $11.95

• Simon Frith & Howard Horne
ART INTO POP
Of interest to fans of the British Invasion and just about everything else worthwhile since
0–416–41540–7 RC&H pb $9.95

• Paul Gambaccini
THE TOP 100 ROCK 'N' ROLL ALBUMS OF ALL TIME
A large international panel's 100 best LPs selected for this large-format, full-color mainstream roundup. Few surprises: Huey Lewis but no Led Zep
0–517–56561–7 Crown pb $12.95

• Greil Marcus
MYSTERY TRAIN: Images of America in Rock 'n' Roll Music
A revised edition of what is probably the single most influential work of rock criticism
0–525–47708–X Dutton pb $11.95

• Dave Marsh & John Swenson, editors
THE NEW ROLLING STONE RECORD GUIDE
A 1983 update of the first and best-selling consumer guide to LPs
0–394–72107–1 Random House pb $13.95

• Robert Pattison
THE TRIUMPH OF VULGARITY: Rock Music in the Mirror of Romanticism
0–19–503876–2 Oxford $19.95

• David Prakel
ROCK 'N' ROLL ON COMPACT DISC
Technically oriented guide
0–517–56687–7 Crown pb $13.95

• Dave Rimmer
LIKE PUNK NEVER HAPPENED: Culture Club and the New Pop
Nominally the story of Boy George and Culture Club's meteoric rise, this is an incisive examination of the machinations behind pop success in the '80s
0–571–13739–3 Faber & Faber pb $9.95

• Ira Robbins, editor
THE NEW TROUSER PRESS RECORD GUIDE
Indispensable guide to a wide range of newer genres (hardcore, rap, punk, electronic), edited by the founder of the sadly missed *Trouser Press* magazine
0–02–036370–2 Macmillan pb $16.95

• Linda Sandahl
ROCK FILMS: A Viewer's Guide to Three Decades of Musicals, Concerts, Documentaries, and Soundtracks
0–8160–1576–7 Facts On File pb $14.95

• John Schaefer
NEW SOUNDS: A Listener's Guide to New Music
Sophisticated, entertaining guide: everything from Pink Floyd, Philip Glass, and Windham Hill, to ethnic music from around the globe
0–06–055054–6 Harper & Row $24.95
0–06–097081–2 Harper & Row pb $10.95

• Bill Shapiro
THE CD ROCK 'N' ROLL LIBRARY: 30 Years of Rock 'n' Roll on Compact Disc
0–8362–7947–6 Andrews & McMeel pb $8.95

- Michael Shore, editor
MUSIC VIDEO: A Consumer's Guide
Informative reviews of more than 900 commercially available long-format music-video programs. The only work of its type
0–345–33346–2 Ballantine pb $9.95

- John Street
REBEL ROCK: The Politics of Popular Music
An English writer's informed and persuasive argument for why rock really matters
0–631–14345–9 Blackwell pb $14.95

- John A. Walker
CROSS-OVERS: Art into Pop/Pop into Art
Extensively illustrated study of the connections between pop music and the visual arts
1–85178–016–5 Routledge pb $16.95

HISTORY AND PROFILES

- Carl Belz
THE STORY OF ROCK
An early history
0–19–501554–1 Oxford $29.95

- Pamela Des Barres
I'M WITH THE BAND: Confessions of a Groupie
Charming, funny, and surprisingly likable memoirs of an ex-groupie
0–688–06602–X Morrow $17.95
0–515–09712–8 Berkley pb $3.95

- Bill Flanagan
WRITTEN IN MY SOUL: Conversations with Rock's Great Songwriters
An exemplary collection of interviews with Springsteen, Bono of U2, Dylan, Van Morrison, Keith Richards, Joni Mitchell, and others
0–8092–4650–3 Contemporary pb $11.95

- Pete Fornatale
THE STORY OF ROCK 'N' ROLL
Informative, illustrated historical overview for younger readers
Foreword by Graham Nash
0–688–06276–8 Morrow $11.95
0–688–06277–6 Morrow pb $7.95

- Ted Fox
IN THE GROOVE: The People Behind the Music
These twelve in-depth interviews with leading record producers provide an insider's history of pop music
Foreword by Doc Pomus
0–312–41166–9 St. Martin's $18.95

- Charlie Gillett
THE SOUND OF THE CITY: The Rise of Rock and Roll
An expanded 1984 revision of a landmark survey of rock and roll history—the music, the performers, and the business
0–394–72638–3 Pantheon pb $7.95

- John Javan & Bob Shannon
BEHIND THE HITS: Inside Stories of Classic Pop and Rock & Roll
0–446–38171–3 Warner pb $10.95

- Roman Kozak
THIS AIN'T NO DISCO: The Story of CBGB
An illustrated anecdotal history of the New York City club that was the cradle of punk and new wave
Photos by Ebet Roberts
0–571–12956–0 Faber & Faber pb $9.95

- Jack McDonough
SAN FRANCISCO ROCK: The Illustrated History of San Francisco Rock Music
Beautifully produced, generously illustrated history of Bay Area rock, from the '60s to the present
0–877–01–286–5 Chronicle pb $16.95

- Jim Miller, editor
THE ROLLING STONE ILLUSTRATED HISTORY OF ROCK & ROLL
Heavy on facts, strong on analysis, and amply illustrated, the best historical overview to date charts rock's history in over 80 critical essays
0–394–73938–8 Random House pb $19.95

- Arnold Shaw
THE ROCKIN' FIFTIES
0–306–80301–1 Da Capo pb $10.95

- Joe Smith
OFF THE RECORD: An Oral History of Popular Music
Record company executive and longtime insider Smith presents the history of popular music in a series of anecdotes from Paul McCartney, Bob Dylan, Tony Bennett, Woody Herman, Jerry Lee Lewis, Mick Jagger, Ray Charles, and others
0–446–51232–X Warner $22.95

- Nick Tosches
UNSUNG HEROES OF ROCK 'N' ROLL
Twenty-six portraits of rock's lesser-known but important pioneers. Aptly subtitled "The birth of rock 'n' roll in the dark and wild years before Elvis"
0–684–18149–5 Scribners pb $8.95

- Artemy Troitsky
BACK IN THE U.S.S.R.
Fascinating history of rock behind the Iron Curtain, by a Soviet journalist banned from the official press for suggesting a liberal attitude toward the music
0–571–12997–8 Faber & Faber pb $9.95

- Ed Ward, Geoffrey Stokes & Ken Tucker
ROCK OF AGES: The Rolling Stone History of Rock & Roll
In this ambitious and informative decade-by-decade history the results are uneven, though Ward's account of rock's early years is recommended
0–671–54438–1 Simon & Schuster $24.95
0–671–63068–7 Simon & Schuster pb $14.95

- Ian Whitcomb
AFTER THE BALL: Pop Music from Rag to Rock
A '60s rock star's enjoyable examination of pop music in the pre-rock years
0–87910–063–X Limelight pb $9.95

BLACK MUSIC

- David Bianco
HEAT WAVE: The Motown Fact Book
Every Motown lover's dream: complete discographies, illustrated artist and label principal profiles
0–87650–204–4 Pierian $35.00

- Ted Fox
SHOWTIME AT THE APOLLO
Extensively illustrated history of the legendary Harlem theater and the artists who performed there
0–03–060534–2 Henry Holt pb $9.95

- Nelson George
THE DEATH OF RHYTHM AND BLUES
Leading black music critic's controversial argument for the revival and preservation of black popular music outside the white-dominated music industry
0–394–55238–5 Pantheon $18.95

WHERE DID OUR LOVE GO?: The Rise and Fall of the Motown Sound
An informative history of the label, which clearly empathizes with those out of the spotlight
0–312–01109–1 St. Martin's pb $9.95

Peter Guralnick
SWEET SOUL MUSIC: Rhythm and Blues and the Southern Dream of Freedom
Must reading for every serious rock fan, Guralnick's account of soul music's rise and fall—artistic and economic—is revealing
0–06–096049–3 Harper & Row pb $14.95

Aretha Franklin (photo courtesy of the Frank Driggs Collection), from The Death of Rhythm and Blues *by Nelson George (Pantheon)*

• Steven Hager
HIP HOP: The Illustrated History of Break Dancing, Rap Music and Graffiti
The first published study of the hip-hop movement. Authoritative and well written
0–312–37317–1 St. Martin's pb $8.95

• Michael Haralambos
SOUL MUSIC: The Birth of a Sound in Black America
Important study of the decline of the blues and the rise of soul as the dominant black music form in the '60s
0–306–80246–5 Da Capo pb $7.95

• Gerri Hirshey
NOWHERE TO RUN: The Story of Soul Music
Hirshey's powerful account of soul music is dominated by the voices of her subjects (including Aretha Franklin, James Brown, Wilson Pickett)
0–8129–1111–3 Times Books $17.95

Otis Redding (courtesy of Stax Records), from Nelson George's The Death of Rhythm and Blues *(Pantheon)*

• Arnold Shaw
BLACK POPULAR MUSIC IN AMERICA: From the Spirituals, Minstrels, and Ragtime to Soul, Disco, and Hip-Hop
To date, the most comprehensive history of black popular music
0–02–872310–4 Schirmer $19.95

HONKERS AND SHOUTERS
Lively, revealing history of rhythm and blues, covering not only the artists and their music but the industry that so shamelessly exploited them
0–002–061740–2 Collier pb $10.95

GROUPS AND INDIVIDUAL ARTISTS
(alphabetical by subject)

• Joan Baez
AND A VOICE TO SING WITH
Acclaimed autobiography of the singer/activist
0–671–40062–2 Summit $19.95
0–452–26094–9 NAL pb $8.95

• Brad Elliott
SURF'S UP: The Beach Boys on Record, 1961–1981
Extensive discography
0–87650–118–8 Pierian $29.50

• Steven Gaines
HEROES AND VILLAINS: The True Story of the Beach Boys
The group's music plays dimly in the background of this page-turning pathography
0–451–15033–3 NAL pb $4.50

• David Leaf
THE BEACH BOYS: The Spirit of America
0–88715–013–6 Putnam pb $9.95

• Peter Brown & Steven Gaines
THE LOVE YOU MAKE: An Insider's Story of the Beatles
Sensationalistic, best-selling account by longtime Beatles associate Brown. Filled with hot gossip
0–451–12797–8 Penguin pb $4.50

• Harry Castleman & Walter Podrazik
ALL TOGETHER NOW: The First Complete Beatles Discography, 1961–1975
Exactly what it says, with information on chart positions, musicians, and the four Beatles' involvement in musical projects outside the group
0–87650–075–0 Pierian $29.50

THE BEATLES AGAIN
Supplements and updates *All Together Now*
0–87650–089–0 Pierian $16.50

• Richard Di Lello
THE LONGEST COCKTAIL PARTY
The author was part of the Apple press office between 1968 and 1970
0–87650–155–2 Pierian $19.50

• Brian Epstein
A CELLARFUL OF NOISE
By the man who discovered, managed, and guided the Beatles until his death from a drug overdose in August 1967
0–87650–169–2 Pierian $16.50

• Barbara Fenick
COLLECTING THE BEATLES: An Introduction and Price Guide to the Fab Four Collectibles, Records, and Memorabilia
0–8092–5393–3 Contemporary pb $14.95

• Chet Flippo
YESTERDAY: The Unauthorized Biography of Paul McCartney
The only serious work on McCartney in print. Less than a fifth is devoted to Paul's career post-Beatles, but that includes new information
0–385–23482–1 Doubleday $18.95

• Albert Goldman
THE LIVES OF JOHN LENNON
This controversial best-seller delivers less than it promises (few facts here haven't been published before), and Goldman is sloppy with even the most basic information
0–688–04721–1 Morrow $22.95

• Dezo Hoffmann
THE FACES OF JOHN LENNON
Nicely produced black-and-white photos of Lennon, 1962 to 1970
0–07–029306–6 McGraw-Hill pb $9.98

• John Lennon
IN HIS OWN WRITE
Lennon's first volume of drawings, poetry, and prose was a best-seller when published in 1964
0–06–097123–1 Harper & Row pb $4.95

SKYWRITING BY WORD OF MOUTH
Posthumous collection of Lennon's writings. Playful, witty, irreverent. Includes "The Ballad of John and Yoko" and other short works
Afterword by Yoko Ono
0–06–015656–2 Harper & Row $12.95
0–06–091444–0 Harper & Row pb $6.95

A SPANIARD IN THE WORKS
Lennon's second zany collection. Also a joy
0–06–097122–3 Harper & Row pb $4.95

Mark Lewisohn
THE BEATLES' RECORDING SESSIONS: The Official Abbey Road Studio Session Notes, 1962–1970
Offers new information on the group's creative processes, countless great photos, and an enlightening interview with Paul
Introduction by Paul McCartney
0–517–570661 Crown $24.95

• Wilfrid Mellers
TWILIGHT OF THE GODS: The Music of the Beatles
The classical and academic take on the Beatles' music
0–02–871390–7 Schirmer pb $9.95

• Philip Norman
SHOUT! The Beatles in Their Generation
Generally considered the best group biography. An international best-seller
0–446–32255–5 Warner pb $4.95

• May Pang with Henry Edwards
LOVING JOHN: The Untold Story
Pang, the Lennons' assistant and John's lover, accompanied him on his 18-month "lost weekend" during which he separated from Yoko. Not altogether trashy
0–446–37916–6 Warner pb $8.95

✉ TO ORDER BOOKS AS GIFTS, SEE PAGE 1

- Tim Riley
TELL ME WHY: A Beatles Commentary
Invaluable track-by-track analysis of the recordings
0–394–55061–7 Knopf $19.95

- Andrew Solt & Sam Egan
IMAGINE: John Lennon
This lavishly produced tribute to Lennon features rare photographs with statements by John and by those who knew him. Tie-in to 1988 movie of the same name
Foreword by Yoko Ono
Preface by David L. Wolper
0–02–630910–6 Macmillan $39.95

- Carol D. Terry
HERE, THERE AND EVERYWHERE: The First International Beatles Bibliography, 1962–1982
0–87650–163–3 Pierian $39.50

- Elizabeth Thomson & David Gutman, editors
THE LENNON COMPANION: 25 Years of Comment
A collection of 60 essays and articles from a wide range of sources (a few written especially for this collection)
0–02–872591–3 Schirmer $19.95

Chuck Berry
CHUCK BERRY: The Autobiography
Rock's first poet wrote this book without a ghostwriter. He is characteristically engaging, witty, and cool, though not totally revealing
0–517–56666–4 Crown $17.95
0–671–67159–6 Simon & Schuster pb $8.95

- Howard A. Dewitt
CHUCK BERRY: Rock 'n' Roll Music
A critical biography, with international discography
0–87650–171–4 Pierian $16.50

- James Brown with Bruce Tucker
JAMES BROWN: The Godfather of Soul
This oral-history-style book raises as many questions as it answers. Brown's tough guardedness is natural, but leaves you hoping for a glimpse into his heart
0–02–517430–4 Macmillan $18.95

- Eric Burdon
I USED TO BE AN ANIMAL, BUT I'M ALL RIGHT NOW
Ex-Animals' lead singer's life up to his friend Jimi Hendrix's death in 1970. Many books are better written, but few as painfully frank
0–571–12952–8 Faber & Faber $19.95
0–571–13492–0 Faber & Faber pb $9.95

- Judy Collins
TRUST YOUR HEART: An Autobiography
0–395–41285–4 Houghton Mifflin $17.95

David Crosby with Carl Gottlieb
LONG TIME GONE: The Autobiography of David Crosby
This graphic autobiography combines Gottlieb's history of the '60s scene, accounts of the events from Joni Mitchell, Graham Nash, Crosby's doctors, and others, and Crosby's own story of his 25-year career and concurrent descent into drug addiction
0–385–24530–0 Doubleday $18.95

- Dave Zimmer
CROSBY, STILLS AND NASH: The Authorized Biography
The rare rock biography that benefits from all of authorization's advantages (access) and none of the drawbacks (it's honest)
Photography by Henry Diltz
0–312–17660–0 St. Martin's pb $13.95

- Dion DiMucci with Davin Seay
THE WANDERER: Dion's Story
The singer's life from the Bronx circa 1958 and the Belmonts to heroin addiction and alcoholism, on to recovery and God. Honest, and one of the few accounts of the white doo-wop/teen-idol genre
0–688–07841–9 Morrow $16.95

- Jerry Hopkins & Daniel Sugerman
NO ONE HERE GETS OUT ALIVE
This top-selling, sensational biography of the Doors and the group's late charismatic leader, Jim Morrison, helped fuel their revival and crystallize the myth
0–446–34268–8 Simon & Schuster pb $4.95

- Jim Morrison
THE LORDS AND THE NEW CREATURES
Posthumous collection of poetry. Morrison considered himself a serious writer first, then a rock star
0–671–21044–0 Simon & Schuster pb $4.95
WILDERNESS: The Lost Writings of Jim Morrison
0–394–56434–0 Random House $12.95

Bob Dylan
LYRICS: 1962–1985
Well-produced collection of Dylan's lyrics
0394–54278–9 Knopf pb $21.95

- Wilfrid Mellers
A DARKER SHADE OF PALE: A Backdrop to Bob Dylan
The renowned musicologist's study
0–19–503622–0 Oxford pb $8.95

- Robert Shelton
NO DIRECTION HOME: The Life and Music of Bob Dylan
Comprehensive and definitive, this is the best Dylan biography to date, despite the author's respectful reluctance to turn some interesting stones
0–345–34721–8 Ballantine pb $5.95

- Bob Spitz
DYLAN: A Biography
0–07–060330–8 McGraw-Hill $19.95

- Eric Tamm
BRIAN ENO: His Music and the Vertical Color of Sound
0–571–12958–7 Faber & Faber pb $9.95

- Bob Geldof with Paul Vallely
IS THAT IT?: The Autobiography
A minor rock star with the Boomtown Rats, Geldof earned international prominence (and a Nobel Peace Prize nomination) for his work with the historic Band Aid project and Live Aid concert on behalf of world hunger
0–345–35197–5 Ballantine pb $5.95

- David Henderson
'SCUSE ME WHILE I KISS THE SKY: The Life of Jimi Hendrix
The definitive biography of a true rock genius
0–553–25985–7 Bantam pb $4.50

- John Goldrosen & John Beecher
REMEMBERING BUDDY: The Definitive Biography of Buddy Holly
Thoroughly researched tribute to Holly's brief but influential career, with a wealth of rare photos
0–14–010363–5 Penguin pb $21.95

- Nelson George
MICHAEL JACKSON
This best-selling pop biography contains lots of facts, little analysis, no sex or drugs. One of the few rock biographies that's safe for kids
0–440–15593–2 Dell pb $3.50

- Michael Jackson
MOONWALK
The Gloved One's celebrated auto-biography neither explains nor dilutes his mystique. Jackson typically drops his guard (accuses his father of physical abuse) but keeps us reading between the lines for the real story. Lots of photos, many in color
0–385–24712–5 Doubleday $15.95

- Carol Terry
SEQUINS AND SHADES: The Michael Jackson Reference Guide
With six indexes, complete US and UK discographies, and bibliographies, the ultimate reference work
0–87650–205–2 Pierian $39.50

- Stephen Davis
HAMMER OF THE GODS: The Led Zeppelin Saga
This 1985 best-seller on the much-maligned but incredibly popular heavy-metal band offered little new information. Lots of sex and drugs
0–688–04507–3 Morrow $15.95
0–345–33516–3 Ballantine pb $4.95

- Paul Taylor, editor
IMPRESARIO: Malcolm McLaren and the British New Wave
0–262–70035–2 MIT pb $14.95

- Martin Torgoff
AMERICAN FOOL: The Roots and Improbable Rise of John Cougar Mellencamp
Low on objectivity, high on detail, but redeemed by the star's candid observations

on the journey from smalltown ne'er-do-well to respected artist
0–312–02319–7 St. Martin's pb $10.95

• Edward Reilly & others
THE MONKEES: A Manufactured Image
They all laughed at this made-for-TV band during its mid-'60s heyday; in 1986, MTV reruns and a new hit record made them hip
0–87650–236–2 Pierian $39.50

• Jerry Hopkins
YOKO ONO
The first biography of the avant-garde musician/artist
0–02–553950–7 Macmillan $17.95

• Howard Banney
RETURN TO SENDER: The First Complete Discography of Elvis Tribute and Novelty Records, 1956–1986
This says more about us than about the King
0–87650–238–9 Pierian $39.50

• Stanley Booth
ELVIS PRESLEY'S GRACELAND
0–317–42627–3 Aperture $20.00

• Lee Cotten
THE ELVIS CATALOG: Memorabilia, Icons, and Collectibles Celebrating the King of Rock 'n' Roll
Reliable Elvis biography illustrated with a wealth of collectibles and information on approximate values
0–385–23705–7 Doubleday $35.00
0–385–23704–9 Doubleday pb $17.95

• Elaine Dundy
ELVIS AND GLADYS
The best-written, most reliable account of Elvis and his family up to his beloved mother's death in 1958
0–440–11132–3 Dell pb $4.50

• Larry Geller & Joel Spector with Patricia Romanowski
"IF I CAN DREAM": Elvis's Own Story
Geller began as Presley's hairdresser but quickly became his friend and spiritual guide. Partly based on Geller's secret diary of Presley's last months and notes for Presley's planned autobiography
0–671–65922–7 Simon & Schuster $19.95

• Jerry Hopkins
ELVIS: The Final Years
One of the first accounts of the King's last years. Still a good read, despite subsequent new info
0–425–09880–X Berkley pb $4.50

• Ernst Jorgensen & others
RECONSIDER BABY: The Definitive Elvis Sessionography, 1954–1977
0–87650–220–6 Pierian $29.50

• J.B. Leviton & Ger J. Rijff
ELVIS CLOSE-UP: Rare Intimate Photographs of Elvis Presley in 1956
0–671–66955–9 Simon & Schuster pb $12.95

An Elvis doll from Jane and Michael Stern's Elvis World *(Knopf)*

• Jill Pearlman & Wayne White
ELVIS FOR BEGINNERS
This "documentary comic book" is a concise and witty account of the social, economic, and cultural forces that led to the Presley phenomenon
0–86316–110–3 Writers & Readers pb $6.95

• Jane & Michael Stern
ELVIS WORLD
Those who take offense at the Sterns' poking fun at Elvis imitators should remember that he'd probably be laughing at them too. Between these faux gold lamé covers lies the map to all that is Elvis
0–394–55619–4 Knopf $34.50

• Roger G. Taylor, editor
ELVIS IN ART
0–312–01381–7 St. Martin's $19.95

• Dirk Vellenga with Mick Farren
ELVIS AND THE COLONEL
Detailed, unsympathetic account of the life and deals of Andres van Kuijk, or, as Elvis knew him, Colonel Tom Parker
0–385–29521–9 Delacorte $17.95

• Red West & others
ELVIS: What Happened?
Published just weeks before Presley's death in 1977, three ex-employees expose Elvis's drug abuse in this so-called "bodyguard" book
0–345–30635–X Ballantine pb $3.95

• Fred L. Worth & Steve D. Tamerius
ELVIS: His Life From A to Z
A compendium of Elvis trivia, full of facts for fans
0–8092–4528–0 Contemporary $35.00

• Smokey Robinson with David Ritz
SMOKEY: Inside My Life
Robinson was Motown's all-purpose player: brilliant producer, songwriter, singer, and corporate vice-president. Smokey discusses his career, extramarital affairs, and cocaine addiction
0–07–053209–5 McGraw-Hill $18.95

• Felix Aepelli
HEART OF STONE: The Definitive Rolling Stones Discography
0–87650–192–7 Pierian $29.50

• Stanley Booth
THE TRUE ADVENTURES OF THE ROLLING STONES
Booth began this in 1969 as an authorized group biography. A personal firsthand account of the Stones during the American tour that culminated in Altamont
0–394–74110–2 Vintage pb $6.95

• Dezo Hoffman
THE ROLLING STONES: The Early Years
Photographs of the band in the early days
Introduction by Mick Jagger
0–07–029305–8 McGraw-Hill pb $9.95

• Jessica MacPhail
YESTERDAY'S PAPERS: The Rolling Stones in Print, 1964–1984
0–87650–209–5 Pierian $39.50

• Philip Norman
THE LIFE AND GOOD TIMES OF THE ROLLING STONES
0–517–57464–0 Crown $24.95

• Ron Wood with Bill German
RON WOOD: The Works
This charming collection of the Stones's guitarist's art and reminiscences offers as many juicy anecdotes about his band as we're likely to get for a while
0–06–096098–1 Harper & Row pb $15.95

• Patrick Humphries
PAUL SIMON: Still Crazy After All These Years
Tells all about the music but little about the man
0–385–24908–X Doubleday $17.95

• Mark Ribowsky
HE'S A REBEL: The Truth about Phil Spector—Rock and Roll's Legendary Madman
0–525–24727–0 Dutton $18.95

• Robert Hilburn
SPRINGSTEEN
A safe, somewhat bland account of the Boss's career. Recommended for those new to Bruce
0–684–18703–5 Scribners pb $17.95

• Dave Marsh
BORN TO RUN: The Bruce Springsteen Story
An informative best-seller, this 1981 revision covers Springsteen's career up to *The River* LP
0–440–10694–X Dell pb $4.95

• Mary Wilson with Patricia
Romanowski & Arghus Juilliard
DREAMGIRL: My Life as a Supreme
Best-selling autobiography of an original
Supreme. "Never has a Motown veteran
spoken out as a first-person witness from
inside Hitsville"—*NY Times*
0–312–90759–1 St. Martin's pb $4.95

• Jerome Davis
TALKING HEADS
This group history ends with the 1984
concert film *Stop Making Sense* and
concentrates on leader David Byrne's art
influences and early years
0–394–74131–5 Random House pb $6.95

• David Gans
TALKING HEADS
0–380–89954–X Avon pb $9.95

• Talking Heads with Fred Olinsky
WHAT THE SONGS LOOK LIKE
Over 50 works of art inspired by Talking
Heads' music, by such artists as Basquiat,
Haring, Rauschenberg, and Wegman
0–06–055117–8 Harper & Row $35.00
0–06–096205–4 Harper & Row pb $14.95

• Otis Williams with Patricia
Romanowski
TEMPTATIONS
The Temptations' founder combines
autobiography with a warm history of the
legendary group
0–399–13313–5 Putnam $24.95

• Tina Turner with Kurt Loder
I, TINA
A frank autobiography of the '60s soul star
whose dazzling 1983 comeback was a
personal and professional triumph
0–380–70097–2 Avon pb $4.50

• Edmond Dunphy
**UNFORGETTABLE FIRE: The Story
of U2**
Though acclaimed by the press, rock
cognoscenti had a field day pointing out
errors in this biography of the important
Irish band
0–446–51469–4 Warner $16.50
0–446–38974–9 Warner pb $9.95

• Beverly Mendheim
**RITCHIE VALENS: The First Latino
Rocker**
This intelligent and definitive biography
also discusses the Latino influence on rock
0–916950–79–4 Bilingual Press pb $10.00

• Dave Marsh
**BEFORE I GET OLD: The Story of
The Who**
Marsh combines a fan's passion, a critic's
insight, and a historian's quest for the facts
in this important account of the English
group
0–312–07155–8 St. Martin's pb $10.95

• John Swenson
STEVIE WONDER
A thoroughly researched, thoughtful, and
well-written profile of the real genius of
Motown
0–06–097067–7 Harper & Row pb $12.95

REFERENCE

• David Bianco, editor
**WHO'S NEW WAVE IN MUSIC: An
Illustrated Encyclopedia, 1976–1982**
0–87650–173–0 Pierian $29.50

• John Blair
**THE ILLUSTRATED DISCOGRAPHY
OF SURF MUSIC, 1961–1965**
Second edition, revised
0–87650–174–9 Pierian $29.50

• Fred Bronson
**THE BILLBOARD BOOK OF NUMBER
ONE HITS: 2nd Edition**
The stories behind every single to hit the
top of the chart from 1955 to 1987
0–8230–7545–1 Watson-Guptill pb $16.95

• Mike Clifford
**THE HARMONY ILLUSTRATED
ENCYCLOPEDIA OF ROCK: 6th Edition**
Lavishly illustrated, featuring Pete Frame's
wonderful genealogy charts. Reliable, but
with an English slant
0–517–57164–1 Harmony pb $14.95

• Bob George & Martha De Foe
**VOLUME: International Discography of
the New Wave**
A 1982 guide to everything new wave
from AA to Zytacoreantirtum, plus
fanzines, sources, clubs, record companies
0–7119–0050–7 Omnibus pb $10.95

• Brock Helander
**THE ROCK WHO'S WHO: A Complete
Guide to the Great Artists and Albums of
30 Years, from Rockabilly to New Wave**
Though Helander devotes inordinate space
to the marginally important, this is reliable,
with full discographies
0–02–871250–1 Schirmer $25.00
0–02–871920–4 Schirmer pb $16.95

Terry Hounsome
ROCK RECORD: 3rd Edition
The most extensive general rock album
discography. Extensively cross-indexed
with information on over 45,000 LPs
and 78,000 musicians (sidemen
included)
0–8160–1754–9 Facts On File pb $14.95

• Barry Lazell, editor
**MOVERS AND SHAKERS: An A–Z of the
People Who Made Rock Happen**
0–8230–7608–3 Watson-Guptill pb $16.95

• Jerry Osborne
**THE OFFICIAL PRICE GUIDE TO
RECORDS: 8th Edition**
Rock, pop, soul, country records, all listed
and valued by release year and label. A
must for collectors and those who insure
their collections
876–370810–4 Ballantine pb $16.95

• Jerry Osborne, Perry Cox &
Joe Lindsay
**THE OFFICIAL PRICE GUIDE TO
MEMORABILIA OF ELVIS PRESLEY
AND THE BEATLES**
876–37080–6 Ballantine pb $10.95

Jon Pareles & Patricia
Romanowski, editors
**THE ROLLING STONE
ENCYCLOPEDIA OF ROCK & ROLL**
With over 1300 entries, discographies,
personnel chronologies, and chart
positions, this 1983 encyclopedia is still
the most comprehensive around
0–671–43457–8 Summit $24.95
0–671–44071–3 Summit pb $12.95

• Joel Whitburn
**THE BILLBOARD BOOK OF TOP 40
ALBUMS**
0–8230–7513–3 Watson-Guptill pb $16.95

**THE BILLBOARD BOOK OF TOP 40
HITS: 3rd Edition**
0–8230–7546–X Watson-Guptill pb $16.95

• Fred L. Worth
**ROCKFACTS: The Ultimate Book of Rock
& Roll Trivia**
Lots of trivia—and a few errors—in this
oddly organized first volume of a proposed
two-volume set
0–8160–1099–4 Facts On File $22.95
0–8160–1145–1 Facts On File pb $14.95

VISUAL BOOKS

• Roger Dean & David Howells
**THE ULTIMATE ALBUM COVER
ALBUM**
A dazzling survey of album cover art
0–13–935750–5 Prentice-Hall pb $19.95

• Paul Grushkin
**THE ART OF ROCK: Posters from Presley
to Punk**
Lavish presentation of over 1500 color
reproductions from the archivist's
collection
0–89659–584–6 Abbeville $90.00

Michael Ochs
**ROCK ARCHIVES: A Photographic
Journey Through the First Two Decades
of Rock and Roll**
A 1988 revised edition of the best
photo history of popular music from
the '40s to the late '60s with over 1000
rare and wonderful black-and-white
photos
Introduction by Peter Guralnick
0–385–19434–X Doubleday pb $17.95

• Guy Peelaert & Nik Cohn
ROCK DREAMS
A classic visual commentary on the legends
of rock and roll: the Stones in Nazi regalia
fondling young girls; Jim Morrison taking
his last bath; the Beatles having tea with
the queen
0–394–52870–0 Knopf $19.95
0–394–71000–2 Knopf pb $10.95

THE MUSIC INDUSTRY

• Simon Garfield
MONEY FOR NOTHING: Greed and Exploitation in the Music Industry
Scathing exposé of how the music business really works
0–571–12972–2 Faber & Faber $18.95
0–571–12980–3 Faber & Faber pb $9.95

• Dave Marsh
THE FIRST ROCK & ROLL CONFIDENTIAL REPORT: Inside the Real World of Rock and Roll
Marsh's newsletter, *Rock & Roll Confidential,* is more controversial, political, and investigative than any rock magazine
0–394–74070–X Pantheon pb $12.95

• Peter McIan & Larry Wichman
THE MUSICIAN'S GUIDE TO HOME RECORDING
A technical yet accessible guide
0–671–65754–2 Linden $24.95
0–671–60189–X Simon & Schuster pb $14.95

• Bob Monaco & James Riordan
THE PLATINUM RAINBOW: How to Succeed in the Music Business Without Selling Your Soul
Straightforward, basic primer though lacking in hard legal advice
0–8092–4813–1 Contemporary pb $9.95

• Cousin Brucie (Morrow) with Laura Baudo
COUSIN BRUCIE!: My Life in Rock 'n' Roll Radio
Memoirs of the ever-popular radio personality
0–688–06615–1 Morrow $16.95

• Diane Sward Rapaport
HOW TO MAKE AND SELL YOUR OWN RECORD: 3rd Edition
The best guide of its type available
0–399–51430–9 Perigee pb $14.95

• Rick Sklar
ROCKING AMERICA: How the All-Hit Radio Stations Took Over
An insider's story behind the rise and fall of the WABC-AM Musicradio format that changed rock radio forever
0–312–68798–2 St. Martin's pb $7.95

Janis Joplin, from The Rolling Stone Illustrated History of Rock and Roll *(Random House/photo by Herb Greene)*

Other Musical Traditions

• Jeremy Marre & Hannah Charlton
BEATS OF THE HEART: Popular Music of the World
A pictorial and socio-political guide to the changing face of native music from Africa, India, South America, Japan, North America and the Caribbean
0–394–74258–3 Pantheon pb $13.95

• John Storm Roberts
BLACK MUSIC OF TWO WORLDS
0–688–05278–9 Riverrun pb $5.95
0–9614458–0–7 Original Music pb $5.95

AFRICAN MUSIC

• Muff Anderson
MUSIC IN THE MIX: The Story of South African Popular Music
An adventurous look at the interrelation of cultural politics and indigenous black music traditions from the 1930s to the present
0–86975–218–9 Ohio pb $11.95

• Francis Bebey
AFRICAN MUSIC: A People's Art
An authoritative and informative overview of native African musical styles, instruments, and traditions, with an essential pre-Afro-pop discography
Translated by Josephine Bennett
0–88208–050–4 Chicago Review pb $9.95

• Rose Brandel
THE MUSIC OF CENTRAL AFRICA
Ethnological study of music as a vital social factor
0–306–76222–6 Da Capo $39.50

• John M. Chernoff
AFRICAN RHYTHM AND AFRICAN SENSIBILITY: Aesthetics and Social Action in African Musical Idioms
Travelogue and sociological investigation, based on travels in Ghana in the early 1970s
0–226–10345–5 Chicago pb $12.00

• John Collins
MUSIC MAKERS OF WEST AFRICA
The explosive development of contemporary African pop styles such as juju, highlife, and Afro-beat over the past two decades
0–89410–076–9 Three Continents pb $10.00

• Ronnie Graham
THE DA CAPO GUIDE TO CONTEMPORARY AFRICAN MUSIC
For both layman and expert, this is the only available reliable reference on modern African music, arranged by country, region, and artist, with a good index
0–306–80325–9 Da Capo pb $13.95

• Miriam Makeba with James Hall
MAKEBA: My Story
0–452–26234–8 NAL pb $8.95

• Joseph H. Nketia
THE MUSIC OF AFRICA
0–393–09249–6 Norton pb $9.95

MUSIC OF THE AMERICAS

• David P. Appleby
THE MUSIC OF BRAZIL
Discusses—from a decidedly Western perspective—traditional musical forms as they relate to more conventional composers such as Villa-Lobos
0–292–75068–4 Texas $25.00
0–292–75111–7 Texas pb $10.95

• Billy Bergman & others
HOT SAUCES: Latin and Caribbean Pop
A well-informed introduction to representative artists in soca, reggae, salsa, tropicalista, merengue, and many other styles
0–688–02193–X Morrow pb $7.95

• John Broven
SOUTH TO LOUISIANA: The Music of the Cajun Bayous
A history of Louisiana's Cajun, zydeco, and swamp-pop traditions, enlivened with a true fan's passion
0–88289–300–9 Pelican $19.95

• Dick Hebdige
CUT 'N' MIX: Culture, Identity and Caribbean Music
A well-researched study focusing on the evolution of contemporary Jamaican music
0–906890–99–3 RC&H pb $10.95

• Jacqueline H. McMahan
THE SALSA BOOK
0–9612150–2–X Olive $12.95
0–9612150–3–8 Olive pb $9.95

• John Storm Roberts
THE LATIN TINGE: The Impact of Latin American Music on the United States
Documents 100 years of Caribbean musical traditions and their influence on current Western pop music
0–19–502564–4 Oxford $18.95
0–9614458–1–5 Riverrun pb $9.95

• Keith Q. Warner
KAISO: The Trinidad Calypso
Analysis of the calypso as a prevalent and integral form of unwritten literature
0–89410–025–4 Three Continents $24.00
0–89410–026–2 Three Continents pb $12.00

Reggae

Stephen Davis & Peter Simon
REGGAE BLOODLINES
Precursor to *Reggae International* and first American attempt to grasp Jamaican music, covering artists from Toots and The Maytals to Bob Marley
0–385–12330–2 Doubleday pb $10.95

➤ **FOR OVERSEAS ORDERING INFORMATION, SEE PAGE 1**

Bob Marley (photo courtesy of Peter Simon), from Reggae International *edited by Stephen Davis and Peter Simon*

REGGAE INTERNATIONAL
Illustrated essays and interviews by various writers on reggae, its subgenres, ska, rock-steady, dub, and their effect on world music and culture
0–394–71313–3 Knopf pb $14.95

Jonathan Runge
RUM AND REGGAE: What's Hot and What's Not in the Caribbean
0–312–01509–7 St. Martin's pb $9.95

Timothy White
CATCH A FIRE: The Life of Bob Marley
A straightforward landmark portrait that clearly defines Marley's tremendous influence on US and British music of the 1970s and later
0–03–063531–4 Henry Holt $16.95
0–03–062109–7 Henry Holt pb $9.95

Malika L. Whitney & Dermott Hussey
BOB MARLEY: Reggae King of the World
Though this biography is biased and often inaccurate, it is still a compelling firsthand document
Foreword by Rita Marley
0–525–48088–9 Dutton $14.95

ASIAN MUSIC

These titles have been recommended by The Asia Society.

• Rewi Alley
PEKING OPERA
This slim volume contains synopses of 15 classic Chinese operas and a brief history of the Opera's long-standing reputation
0–8351–1617–4 China Books pb $19.95

• James Araki
THE BALLAD DRAMA OF MEDIEVAL JAPAN
0–8048–1279–9 Tuttle pb $4.50

• Leela Floyd
INDIAN MUSIC
Introduction to the instruments, history, and tonal scales of classical Indian music, tailored for a Western audience
0–19–321330–3 Oxford pb $7.95

• Eta Harich-Schneider
A HISTORY OF JAPANESE MUSIC
0–19–316203–2 Oxford $89.00

• Jennifer Lindsay
JAVANESE GAMELAN
A basic guide to the instruments, unique musical scale and history of *gamelan*, a form that relies primarily on percussion
0–19–580413–9 Oxford pb $9.95

• William Malm
SIX HIDDEN VIEWS OF JAPANESE MUSIC
Informative studies on the subtle role of music in Japanese society, culture, and mores
0–520–05727–9 California $37.50

JAPANESE MUSIC AND MUSICAL INSTRUMENTS
0–8048–0308–0 Tuttle $37.50

• Huang Shang
TALES FROM PEKING OPERA
An anthology of the traditional tales and myths on which the standard Chinese operas were based
0–8351–1399–X China Books pb $6.95

• Robert van Gulik
THE LORE OF THE CHINESE LUTE
A short, exquisite study of the most sophisticated element in medieval Chinese music by one of few Westerners held in high esteem by Chinese experts
0–8048–0869–4 Tuttle $21.00

Dance

HISTORIES

• Jack Anderson
BALLET AND MODERN DANCE: A Concise History
0–916622–43–6 Princeton Book pb $14.95

• Susan Au
BALLET AND MODERN DANCE
0–500–20219–2 Thames & Hudson pb $11.95

• Mary Clarke
BALLERINA: The Art of Women in Classical Ballet
0–916622–71–1 Princeton Book $30.00

• Selma Cohen, editor
DANCE AS A THEATRE ART: Source Readings in Dance History from 1581 to the Present
0–06–041315–8 Harper & Row pb $17.95

• Lynne Emery
BLACK DANCE: From 1619 to Today
The standard history
0–916622–63–0 Princeton Book pb $19.95

• Lincoln Kirstein
DANCE: A Short History of Classic Theatrical Dancing
A brilliant and unsettling history, from primitive times to America's golden age
0–87127–019–6 Princeton Book pb $15.95

• Paul Magriel, editor
CHRONICLES OF THE AMERICAN DANCE: From the Shakers to Martha Graham
Fascinating documents from colonial to modern times
0–306–77566–2 Da Capo $35.00
0–306–80082–9 Da Capo pb $7.95

Queen Elizabeth dancing la volta with the Earl of Leicester, from Pre-Classic Dance Forms *by Louis Horst (Princeton Book)*

• Parmenia Migel
THE BALLERINAS: From the Court of Louis XIV to Pavlova
An unusual history, focusing on the female dancer
0–306–80115–9 Da Capo pb $9.95

• Natalia Roslavleva
THE ERA OF RUSSIAN BALLET
A standard book, spanning the era of Didelot to the 1960s
0–306–79536–1 Da Capo $37.50

• Walter Terry
THE DANCE IN AMERICA
0–306–76059–2 Da Capo $32.50

PRE-19TH CENTURY

The Ancient World Through the Middle Ages

• Lillian Lawler
THE DANCE IN ANCIENT GREECE
0–8195–6057–X Wesleyan pb $10.95

• John Stevens
WORDS AND MUSIC IN THE MIDDLE AGES: Song, Narrative, Dance and Drama, 1050–1350
0–521–33904–9 Cambridge pb $24.95

• Maria-Gabriele Wosien
SACRED DANCE
0–500–81006–0 Thames & Hudson pb $11.95

The Renaissance Through the 17th Century

• Antonio Cornazano
THE BOOK ON THE ART OF DANCING
A 15th-century treatise
0–903102–56–0 Princeton Book $14.95

• Mabel Dolmetsch
DANCES OF ENGLAND AND FRANCE FROM 1450–1600: With Their Music and Authentic Manner of Performance
A classic
0–306–80025–X Da Capo pb $6.95

• John Playford
ENGLISH DANCING MASTER: Or, Plaine and Easie Rules for the Dancing of Country Dances, with the Tune to Each Dance
A guide to music and dances of 17th-century England
0–903102–80–3 Princeton Book pb $9.95

The 18th Century

• John Guthrie
HISTORICAL DANCES FOR THE THEATRE: The Pavan and the Minuet
A guide for dancers, with notation and musical scores
0–903102–68–4 Princeton Book pb $14.95

• Wendy Hilton
DANCE OF COURT AND THEATER: The French Noble Style 1690–1725
A classic
0–916622–09–6 Princeton Book $39.95

• Soame Jenyns
THE ART OF DANCING: A Poem in Three Cantos
A period guide in verse to 18th-century dance
0–903102–36–6 Princeton Book pb $7.95

• Jean Noverre
LETTERS ON DANCING AND BALLET
A major document by a great choreographer
0–87127–006–4 Princeton Book pb $14.95

• Richard Ralph
THE LIFE AND WORKS OF JOHN WEAVER
The first English dance historian
0–87127–139–7 Princeton Book $125.00

THE 19TH CENTURY

This was the moment when the ballerina rose onto pointe and the ballet as we know it rose into being. Romantic ballet—ethereal in atmosphere, tragic in theme—dominated the century, as both a positive influence and a springboard for rebellion.

• Edwin Binney
GLORIES OF THE ROMANTIC BALLET
Features 130 prints
0–903102–83–8 Princeton Book pb $17.95

• Carlo Blasis
THE CODE OF TERPSICHORE
The 1831 masterwork of an Italian dancer, famous for codifying the *danse d'école*
0–87127–055–2 Princeton Book pb $20.95

• Théophile Gautier
GAUTIER ON DANCE
The 19th-century poet and novelist Gautier was also a major dance critic
0–903102–94–3 Princeton Book $85.00

• Ivor Guest
FANNY CERRITO: The Life of a Romantic Ballerina
0–903102–09–0 Princeton Book pb $9.95

JULES PERROT
Portrait of the French virtuoso dancer and choreographer
0–87127–140–0 Princeton Book $39.95

THE ROMANTIC BALLET IN PARIS
0–903102–45–5 Princeton Book $39.95

VICTORIAN BALLET GIRL: The Tragic Story of Clara Webster
A 19th-century dancer who died in a theater fire
0–306–76043–6 Da Capo $25.00

• Charles Heath
BEAUTIES OF THE OPERA AND BALLET
Facsimile of a charming period album telling the plot of the major romantic works. Illustrated with intricate line drawings
0–306–70844–2 Da Capo $25.00

Ballets

• Cyril Beaumont
THE BALLET CALLED GISELLE
An indispensable handbook with an account of the changes to the choreography of *Giselle* over the century
0–87127–022–6 Princeton Book pb $14.95

THE BALLET CALLED SWAN LAKE
An essential companion volume
0–87127–128–1 Princeton Book pb $14.95

• Roland Wiley
TCHAIKOVSKY'S BALLETS: Swan Lake, Sleeping Beauty, Nutcracker
Includes extensive and provocative discussions of the music and the Maryinsky Theater productions
0–19–315314–9 Oxford $59.00

THE 20TH CENTURY

Ballet in our time has been dominated by Diaghilev's universally influential Ballets Russes and by George Balanchine. The rise of modern dance in America and Germany was a dramatic reaction by individual rebels to a classical tradition perceived as monolithic.

Diaghilev and the Ballets Russes

• Alexandre Benois
REMINISCENCES OF THE RUSSIAN BALLET
An informative and perceptive memoir by a founder and leading designer of the Ballets Russes, whose connection with the company ended in 1914
0–306–77426–7 Da Capo $45.00

• Richard Buckle
DIAGHILEV
The standard biography
0–689–70664–2 Atheneum pb $14.95

• Arnold Haskell & Walter Nouvel
DIAGHILEFF: His Artistic and Private Life
A good biography by a childhood friend of the maestro
0–306–80085–3 Da Capo pb $6.95

• Peter Lieven
THE BIRTH OF BALLETS-RUSSES
A useful account
0–486–22962–9 Dover pb $6.95

• Nesta MacDonald
DIAGHILEV OBSERVED
The only Diaghilev history currently in print with the company's repertoire as its focus
0–903102–14–5 Princeton Book $69.95

George Balanchine and the New York City Ballet

• Merrill Ashley & Larry Kaplan
DANCING FOR BALANCHINE
0–525–24280–5 Dutton $29.95

• Richard Buckle & John Taras
GEORGE BALANCHINE: Ballet Master
One of the best available studies: Buckle had unique access to company material and to the Kirstein diaries and also conducted interviews in the United States and the Soviet Union
0–394–53906–0 Random House $29.95

• Lincoln Kirstein
PORTRAIT OF MR. B: Photographs of George Balanchine with an Essay
A photographic portfolio of the choreographer from childhood to old age, onstage and off
Foreword by Peter Martins
0–670–56633–0 Viking pb $12.95

THIRTY YEARS: The New York City Ballet
0–394–73615–X Knopf pb $6.95

UNION JACK: The New York City Ballet
A lively souvenir volume, commemorating this 1977 Balanchine ballet
Photographs by Martha Swope
0–87130–047–8 Eakins pb $6.95

• Joseph Mazo
DANCE IS A CONTACT SPORT
A portrait of the New York City Ballet during the early 1970s by a young dancer who observed Balanchine's way of thinking, teaching, and relating to his dancers
0–306–80044–6 Da Capo pb $9.95

• Moira Shearer
BALLETMASTER: A Dancer's View of George Balanchine
0–399–13184–1 Putnam $18.95

• Bernard Taper
BALANCHINE: A Biography
0–8129–1136–9 Times Books $19.95
0–520–06059–8 California pb $12.95

Ballet Companies and Schools

• Jack Anderson
THE ONE AND ONLY: The Ballet Russe de Monte Carlo
An account of the company that Leonide Massine co-founded with Sergei Denham
0–87127–127–3 Princeton Book $29.95

• Clive Barnes
INSIDE AMERICAN BALLET THEATRE
0–306–80192–2 Da Capo pb $11.95

• Anthony Crickmay
A PORTRAIT OF THE ROYAL BALLET
Photographic portraits of each member of the Royal Ballet, along with a brief history of the company by its director
Introduction by Anthony Dowell
0–948397–04–7 David & Charles $29.95

• Jennifer Dunning
BUT FIRST A SCHOOL: The First 50 Years of the School of American Ballet
The official history
0–670–80407–X Viking $20.00

• Sophia Golovkina
THE BOLSHOI BALLET SCHOOL
An introduction to the famous school by its current director, with many color photographs
0–86622–497–1 TFH $19.95

• Charles Payne
THE AMERICAN BALLET THEATRE
A definitive and fascinating historical portrait of the company and its management under Lucia Chase
0–394–49835–6 Knopf $39.95

• Kirsten Ralov, editor
THE BOURNONVILLE SCHOOL
A study of this technique, described by one of the Royal Danish Ballet's leading Bournonville experts
0–903102–44–7 Princeton Book $19.95

• Juri Slonimsky
SOVIET BALLET
0–306–71897–9 Da Capo $39.50

Cynthia Gregory in "Swan Lake" (photo by B. Leidersdorf), from American Ballet Theatre *by Charles Payne (Knopf)*

• Agrippina Vaganova
BASIC PRINCIPLES OF CLASSICAL BALLET
A lively discussion of the classic technique that distinguishes Soviet ballet and the Kirov school
0–486–22036–2 Dover pb $3.50

• Katherine Walker & Sarah Woodcock
THE ROYAL BALLET
0–306–80176–0 Da Capo pb $10.95

• Joan White, editor
TWENTIETH-CENTURY DANCE IN BRITAIN: A History of Five Dance Companies
0–903102–85–4 Princeton Book pb $14.95

Ballet Dancers and Choreographers

• Mikhail Baryshnikov & Martha Swope
BARYSHNIKOV AT WORK
With photographs by Martha Swope
0–394–73587–0 Knopf pb $17.95

• A.H. Franks
SVETLANA BERIOSOVA: A Biography
0–306–79537–X Da Capo $25.00

• Alexandra Danilova
CHOURA: The Memoirs of Alexandra Danilova
Lively memoirs, written with Holly Brubach
0–394–50539–5 Knopf $20.00

• Agnes De Mille
DANCE TO THE PIPER & PROMENADE HOME
A two-part autobiography by the influential theatrical choreographer
Introduction by Cynthia Gregory
0–306–80161–2 Da Capo pb $10.95

• Ninette De Valois
COME DANCE WITH ME: A Memoir, 1898–1956
0–306–79616–3 Da Capo $29.50

• Cyril Beaumont
MICHEL FOKINE AND HIS BALLETS
0–87127–120–6 Princeton Book pb $14.95

• Dawn Horwitz
MICHEL FOKINE
0–8057–9603–7 G.K. Hall $20.95

• Margot Fonteyn
MARGOT FONTEYN: Autobiography
0–394–48570–X Knopf $16.95

• Tamara Geva
SPLIT SECONDS: A Remembrance
Best on Balanchine
0–87910–006–0 Limelight pb $8.95

• Tamara Karsavina
THEATRE STREET: The Reminiscences of Tamara Karsavina
0–903102–47–1 Princeton Book $29.95

• Gelsey Kirkland & Greg Lawrence
DANCING ON MY GRAVE
A sobering look at the difficult life of a
ballerina, with some startling revelations
0–385–19964–3 Doubleday $17.95
0–515–09465–X Berkley pb $4.50

• Mathilde Kschessinska
**DANCING IN PETERSBURG: The
Memoirs of Kschessinska**
0–306–77433–X Da Capo $37.50

• Lydia Kyasht
ROMANTIC RECOLLECTIONS
0–306–77572–7 Da Capo $25.00

• Edward Thorpe
**KENNETH MACMILLAN: The Man and
the Ballets**
Foreword by Ninette De Valois
0–241–11694–5 David & Charles $35.95

• Richard Austin
NATALIA MAKAROVA
0–903102–34–X Princeton Book $24.95

• Alicia Markova
MARKOVA REMEMBERS
Largely pictorial
0–316–54625–9 Little, Brown $24.95

• Steven Caras
PETER MARTINS: Prince of the Dance
A photographic portfolio of the dancer's
New York City Ballet career
Introduction by Francis Mason
0–8109–2324–6 Abrams pb $14.95

• Peter Martins with Robert Cornfield
FAR FROM DENMARK
As dancers' memoirs go, this one is
unusually strong: hardheaded, direct, and
dryly amusing
0–316–54855–3 Little, Brown $24.95

• Nancy Van Norman Baer
**BRONISLAVA NIJINSKA: A Dancer's
Legacy**
An excellent catalog
0–87663–895–7 San Francisco Museum pb $14.95

Paul Magriel, editor
**NIJINSKY, PAVLOVA, DUNCAN:
Three Lives in Dance**
If you were to buy only one work
about 20th-century dancers, you might
consider this one. It depicts the three
legendary muses of the century of
whom there is little or (in Nijinsky's
case) no film footage
0–306–80035–7 Da Capo pb $12.95

• Romola Nijinsky, editor
THE DIARY OF VASLAV NIJINSKY
0–520–00945–2 California pb $8.95

• Clive Barnes
NUREYEV
0–9609736–2–1 Helene Obolensky $35.00

• Keith Money
ANNA PAVLOVA: Her Life and Art
0–394–42786–6 Knopf $55.00

• V. Svetloff
ANNA PAVLOVA
0–486–23047–3 Dover pb $8.95

• Mary Clarke
ANTOINETTE SIBLEY
Introduction by Frederick Ashton
0–903102–64–1 Princeton Book $29.95

• Barbara Newman
**ANTOINETTE SIBLEY: Reflections of a
Ballerina**
0–09–164000–8 David & Charles $24.95

• Wayne Sleep
VARIATIONS ON WAYNE SLEEP
0–434–70756–2 David & Charles pb $12.95

Modern Dance

• Jack Anderson
THE AMERICAN DANCE FESTIVAL
0–8223–0683–2 Duke $27.95

• Sally Banes
**TERPSICHORE IN SNEAKERS: Post-
Modern Dance**
The definition of "postmodern dance"
0–8195–6160–6 Wesleyan pb $15.95

• Jean Brown, editor
THE VISION OF MODERN DANCE
Interviews with choreographers
0–916622–12–6 Princeton Book pb $12.95

• Gay Cheney
**BASIC CONCEPTS IN MODERN
DANCE: A Creative Approach**
0–916622–76–2 Princeton Book pb $10.95

• Selma Cohen, editor
**THE MODERN DANCE: Seven Statements
of Belief**
Seven choreographers plan imaginary
versions of a dance about the prodigal son
0–8195–6003–0 Wesleyan pb $12.95

• Elizabeth Kendall
**WHERE SHE DANCED . . . : American
Dancing, 1880–1930**
Essays on the creators of modern dance
0–394–40029–1 Knopf $14.95

• Don McDonagh
**THE RISE AND FALL AND RISE OF
MODERN DANCE**
0–87690–013–9 Dutton pb $7.95

• Louise Steinman
**THE KNOWING BODY: Elements of
Contemporary Performance and Dance**
Includes evaluations of performance artists
Meredith Monk and Spalding Gray,
among others
0–87773–322–8 Shambhala pb $14.95

Modern Dancers, Choreographers,
and Schools

"I am a thief—and I glory in it—I steal from
the present and from the glorious past—and
I stand in the dark of the future as a glorying
and joyous thief—There are so many wonderful things of the imagination to pilfer—
so I stand accused—I am a thief—but with
this reservation—I think I know the value of
what I steal and I treasure it for all time—not
as a possession but as a heritage and as
legacy."—*The Notebooks of Martha Graham*

• Oscar Schlemmer & others
THE THEATER OF THE BAUHAUS
Authoritative overview by participants
Introduction by Walter Gropius
0–8195–6020–0 Wesleyan pb $12.95

• Merce Cunningham & Jacqueline
Lesschaeve
**THE DANCER AND THE DANCE: Merce
Cunningham in Interviews**
A probing statement about dance-making
0–7145–2809–9 Marion Boyars $27.50

• James Klosty, editor
MERCE CUNNINGHAM
Superb photographs by Klosty and pieces
by Cunningham's colleagues (among them:
Carolyn Brown, Robert Rauschenberg,
and Lincoln Kirstein)
0–8791–0055–9 Limelight pb $19.95

• Isadora Duncan
ART OF THE DANCE
0–87830–005–8 Theatre Arts $19.95

• Ilya Schneider
ISADORA DUNCAN: The Russian Years
Foreword by Frederick Ashton
0–306–80142–6 Da Capo pb $6.95

• Margaret Harris
LOIE FULLER: Magician of Light
Introduction by Martin Battersby
0–917046–06–4 Virginia Museum of Arts pb $6.95

• Merle Armitage, editor
MARTHA GRAHAM: The Early Years
0–306–80084–5 Da Capo pb $7.95

• Barbara Morgan
**MARTHA GRAHAM: 16 Dances in
Photographs**
A powerful and sympathetic book of dance
photographs
0–87100–176–4 Morgan & Morgan $40.00

• Ernestine Stodelle
**DEEP SONG: The Dance Story of Martha
Graham**
This biography by a former modern dancer
focuses on Graham's art, glossing over the
more tempestuous moments of her life
0–02–872520–4 Macmillan $27.00

• Doris Humphrey
THE ART OF MAKING DANCES
0–8021–3078–9 Grove pb $9.95

• Marcia Siegel
**DAYS ON EARTH: The Dance of Doris
Humphrey**
A provocative and illuminating biography
0–300–03856–9 Yale $30.00

• Helen Caldwell
MICHIO ITO: The Dancer and His Dances
0–520–03219–5 California $30.00

- Murray Louis
INSIDE DANCE
Introduction by Alwin Nikolais
Foreword by Marcel Marceau
0–312–41872–8 St. Martin's pb $7.95

Ted Shawn and Ruth St. Denis

Ted Shawn
ONE THOUSAND AND ONE ONE NIGHT STANDS
0–306–80095–0 Da Capo pb $6.95

Jane Sherman
SOARING: The Diary and Letters of a Denishawn Dancer in the Far East, 1925–1926
Very revealing
0–8195–4093–5 Wesleyan $19.00

Jane Sherman & Barton Mumaw
BARTON MUMAW, DANCER: From Denishawn to Jacob's Pillow and Beyond
0–87127–138–9 Princeton Book $29.95

- Paul Taylor
PRIVATE DOMAIN: An Autobiography
0–394–51683–4 Knopf $22.95
0–86547–322–6 North Point pb $12.95

- Mary Wigman
THE LANGUAGE OF DANCE
Essays by the German dancer/choreographer, considered by many to be the founder of modern dance in Europe
0–8195–6037–5 Wesleyan pb $12.95

Ruth St. Denis in "Radha" (New York Public Library: Tilden Foundation), from Elizabeth Kendall's Where She Danced: American Dancing, 1880-1930 *(Knopf)*

- Kay Ambrose
CLASSICAL DANCES AND COSTUMES OF INDIA
0–312–14263–3 St. Martin's $22.50

- Brendan Breathnach
FOLK MUSIC AND DANCES OF IRELAND
0–85342–509–4 Irish Book pb $5.95

- Katherine Dunham
DANCES OF HAITI
Foreword by Claude Lévi-Strauss
0–934934–17–7 UCLA $22.50
0–934934–11–8 UCLA pb $14.50

- Angna Enters
ON MIME
A summary of wisdom accumulated by one of the celebrated mimes of the 20th century
0–8195–6056–1 Wesleyan pb $9.95

- K. Bharatha Iyer
DANCE DRAMAS OF INDIA AND THE EAST
0–86590–029–9 Apt Books $40.00

- Andrei Lopvkohv
CHARACTER DANCE
A collection of essays by Soviet specialists
0–903102–90–0 Princeton Book pb $15.95

- Han Man-yong
KOREAN DANCE-THEATER AND CINEMA
0–89209–017–0 Pace International $20.00

- Mary Swift
ART OF THE DANCE IN THE U.S.S.R.
0–268–00305–X Notre Dame $24.95

Dance and Anthropology

- Judith Hanna
DANCE, SEX, AND GENDER: Signs of Identity, Dominance, Defiance, and Desire
0–226–31551–7 Chicago pb $15.95

THE PERFORMER-AUDIENCE CONNECTION: Emotion to Metaphor in Dance and Society
0–292–76480–4 Texas pb $11.95

TO DANCE IS HUMAN: A Theory of Nonverbal Communication
0–226–31549–5 Chicago pb $14.95

- Anya Royce
MOVEMENT AND MEANING: Creativity and Interpretation in Ballet and Mime
0–253–33888–3 Indiana $27.50

Dance and Music

- Louis Horst
PRE-CLASSIC DANCE FORMS
A famous statement of principles by an influential teacher of music to dancers and a key composer and musical adviser for Martha Graham
0–916622–51–7 Princeton Book pb $10.95

- Minna Lederman, editor
STRAVINSKY IN THE THEATRE
A revealing collection of essays emphasizing Stravinsky and the ballet, from Nijinsky to Balanchine
0–306–80022–5 Da Capo pb $9.95

- Elizabeth Sawyer
DANCE WITH THE MUSIC: The World of the Ballet Musician
A discussion of musicality in dancing by a longtime dance accompanist. Enthusiastic about the musical instincts of Antony Tudor, cool on Balanchine
0–521–31925–0 Cambridge pb $19.95

- Humphrey Searle
BALLET MUSIC: An Introduction
A rapid history, best on pre-World War I periods
0–486–22917–3 Dover pb $5.95

Social and Folk Dancing

- Irene Castle
CASTLES IN THE AIR
Memoirs of the ballroom dancer who, with her husband Vernon, popularized the Castle Walk, the Foxtrot, and other social dances
Introduction by Ginger Rogers
0–306–80122–1 Da Capo pb $6.95

- Hank Greene
SQUARE AND FOLK DANCING: A Complete Guide
0–06–015325–3 Harper & Row $18.50

- Carol Wallace & others
DANCE: A Very Social History
Essays by several authors, with lovely color illustrations
0–8478–0819–X Rizzoli $25.00

Scenic and Costume Design

- Irina Pruzhan
LEON BAKST: Set and Costume Designs
Includes Bakst's celebrated creations for the Ballets Russes
0–670–81019–3 Viking $35.00

- Jean Rosenthal & Lael Wertenbaker
THE MAGIC OF LIGHT: The Craft and Career of Jean Rosenthal, Pioneer in Lighting for the Modern Stage
0–316–93120–9 Little, Brown $24.50

- Roy Strong, Ivor Guest & Richard Buckle
DESIGNING FOR THE DANCER
From costume in the Ballet de Cour to Barry Kay and Liz Da Costa
0–87663–570–2 Universe pb $10.00

Tap, Jazz, Broadway, and Hollywood

Arlene Croce
THE FRED ASTAIRE AND GINGER
ROGERS BOOK
Indispensable: enlightening, passionate,
fun, and well illustrated
0–525–48371–3 Dutton pb $12.95

Sarah Giles
FRED ASTAIRE: His Friends Talk
0–385–24741–9 Doubleday $30.00

John Mueller
ASTAIRE DANCING: The Musical
Films
A film-by-film guide to Astaire's dance
career in the movies, with instructive
analyses of the dances
0–394–51654–0 Knopf $45.00

● **Richard Kislan**
HOOFING ON BROADWAY: A History of
Show Dancing
Well-organized and informative
0–13–809484–5 Prentice-Hall $19.95

● **Serge Leslie**
A DANCER'S SCRAPBOOK
A memory book about Doris Niles,
Broadway dancer of the 1920s and '30s
1–85273–001–3 Princeton Book $34.95

● **Marshall Stearns & Jean Stearns**
JAZZ DANCE: The Story of American
Vernacular Dance
The basic history, full of facts
0–02–872510–7 Schirmer pb $12.95

● **Robert Toll**
ON WITH THE SHOW!: The First
Century of American Show Business
0–19–502057–X Oxford $27.50

● **Diana Washbourne**
BASIC TAP DANCING
An illustrated guide to tap fundamentals
0–14–046503–0 Penguin pb $3.95

DANCE CRITICISM

● **Jack Anderson**
CHOREOGRAPHY OBSERVED
Anderson is a poet and dance critic for the
New York Times
0–87745–172–9 Iowa $27.50

● **Alexander Bland**
OBSERVER OF THE DANCE: 1958–1982
Alexander Bland is the pen name for
English critics Mary Clarke and Clement
Crisp
Introductions by Margot Fonteyn & others
0–903102–91–9 Princeton Book $39.95

● **Selma Cohen**
NEXT WEEK, SWAN LAKE: Reflections
on Dance and Dances
A book-length essay on dance aesthetics
0–8195–6110–X Wesleyan pb $12.95

● **Roger Copeland & Marshall Cohen**
WHAT IS DANCE?: Readings in Theory
and Criticism
A comprehensive anthology, which
addresses the major intellectual and
aesthetic issues of dance
0–19–503197–0 Oxford pb $13.95

● **A.V. Coton**
WRITINGS ON DANCE 1938–1968
An important British dance critic during
the birth of the Sadler's Wells (now the
Royal) Ballet
0–903102–20–X Princeton Book pb $19.95

● **Arlene Croce**
GOING TO THE DANCE
Reviews from the mid-1970s by one of the
very best dance critics in America, with
special attention to Balanchine
0–394–70826–1 Knopf pb $8.95

SIGHT LINES
New pieces from the '80s
0–394–56164–3 Knopf $19.95

● **Edwin Denby**
DANCE WRITINGS
One of the finest volumes of dance
criticism from the 1930s through the
1960s
0–394–54416–1 Knopf $40.00
0–394–74984–7 Knopf pb $18.95

● **Gordon Fancher & Gerald Myers,**
editors
PHILOSOPHICAL ESSAYS ON DANCE:
With Responses from Choreographers,
Critics and Dancers
Dance critics and philosophers square off
0–87127–126–5 Princeton Book pb $14.95

● **Susan Leigh Foster**
READING DANCING: Bodies and
Subjects in Contemporary Dance
A controversial study of dance texts,
influenced by semiotics
0–520–05549–7 California $37.50

● **James Friedman**
THE DANCER AND OTHER
AESTHETIC OBJECTS
0–9604232–0–6 Balletmonographs pb $8.50

● **Margaret H'Doubler**
DANCE: A Creative Art Experience
A classic for teachers
0–299–01520–3 Wisconsin $20.00
0–299–01524–6 Wisconsin pb $8.95

● **Louis Horst & Carroll Russell**
MODERN DANCE FORMS IN
RELATION TO THE OTHER MODERN
ARTS
A classic by an early Martha Graham
adviser
0–916622–52–5 Princeton Book $10.95

● **Deborah Jowitt**
TIME AND THE DANCING IMAGE
Historical essays on the image and role of
the dancer in 19th- and 20th-century
Western choreography
0–688–04910–9 Morrow $22.95

● **Lincoln Kirstein**
BALLET: Bias and Belief
0–87127–133–8 Princeton Book $39.95

● **André Levinson**
BALLET OLD AND NEW
Levinson was a brilliant, deeply
conservative critic, born in Russia, where
he witnessed the end of Imperial Ballet.
He emigrated to Europe following the
Revolution. He is especially interesting for
his dislikes, which include the modernist
phase of Diaghilev's Ballets Russes, and
the style of Isadora Duncan
0–87127–130–3 Princeton Book pb $15.95

● **Myron Nadel & Constance Miller,**
editors
THE DANCE EXPERIENCE: Readings in
Dance Appreciation
0–87663–972–4 Universe pb $8.95

● **Betty Redfern**
DANCE, ART AND AESTHETICS
0–903102–73–0 Princeton Book pb $19.95

● **Maxine Sheets-Johnstone, editor**
ILLUMINATING DANCE: Philosophical
Explorations
A collection of essays
0–8387–5063–X Bucknell $26.50

● **Marcia Siegel**
THE SHAPES OF CHANGE: Images of
American Dance
Analyses of 20th-century choreography for
American themes and techniques
0–520–04212–3 California pb $10.95

● **Walter Sorell**
DANCE IN ITS TIME
0–231–06391–1 Columbia pb $16.50

● **Cobbett Steinberg, editor**
DANCE ANTHOLOGY
Elegant selections ranging from D.H.
Lawrence on the dance of the Hopi to
Arlene Croce on Baryshnikov
0–452–260280 NAL pb $12.95

DANCE PRINTS, PHOTOGRAPHS, AND FILMS

● **Robert Coe**
DANCE IN AMERICA
A companion volume to the PBS show
0–525–24325–9 Dutton $29.95

● **Dance Films**
MODERN DANCE AND BALLET ON
FILM AND VIDEO: A Catalog
0–317–41588–3 Dance Films $19.95

● **Marian Eames**
DANCING IN PRINTS: A Portfolio
Assembled from the Archives of the Dance
Collection, 1634–1870
Large, individual prints make this a fine
gift
0–87104–060–3 NY Public Library $25.00

✕ **TO ORDER BOOKS AS GIFTS, SEE PAGE 1**

- **William Ewing**
DANCE AND PHOTOGRAPHY
Striking dance images from the past 150 years, assembled by the curator of the influential "Fleeting Image" exhibition of the 1970s
0–8050–0591–9 Henry Holt $50.00

- **Fred Fehl, photographer**
STARS OF THE BALLET AND DANCE IN PERFORMANCE PHOTOGRAPHS
For nearly half a century, Fehl has been photographing professional dancers in performance, showing a keen eye for the dance content of his images
0–486–24492–X Dover pb $9.95

- **John Fraser**
PRIVATE VIEW: Inside Baryshnikov's American Ballet Theater
Photographs by Eve Arnold
0–5553–05321–3 Bantam $30.00

- **Ethan Hoffman, photographer**
BUTOH: Dance of the Dark Soul
Vivid color pictures of the avant-garde Japanese dance form that originated during the 1960s, with contributions from Mark Holburn, Tatsumi Hijikata, and Yukio Mishima
0–89381–216–1 Aperture $40.00

- **Lotte Jacobi**
THEATER AND DANCE PHOTOGRAPHS
Haunting German expressionist-style pictures of German and American modern dancers
Introduction by Cornell Capa
0–914378–93–7 Countryman pb $10.95

- **George Platt Lynes, photographer**
BALLET 1934–1955
Splendid images from the 1930s and 1940s, including many of Balanchine ballets, by one of the greatest theatrical photographers of the century
Introduction by George Balanchine
0–942642–17–1 Twelvetrees $50.00

- **Jack Woody, editor**
GEORGE PLATT LYNES: Photographs 1931–1955
Includes the notorious and beautiful nude versions of the "Orpheus and Dark Angel" sequence from Balanchine's *Orpheus*. Contributions by George Balanchine, Lincoln Kirstein, and Glenway Wescott
0–942642–00–7 Twelvetrees $45.00

- **Parmenia Migel**
GREAT BALLET STARS IN HISTORIC PHOTOGRAPHS: 249 Portraits from 1855–1955
0–486–24865–8 Dover pb $9.95
GREAT BALLET PRINTS OF THE ROMANTIC ERA
0–486–24050–9 Dover pb $9.95

- **Paul Padgette, photographer**
THE DANCE PHOTOGRAPHY OF CARL VAN VECHTEN
0–02–872680–4 Macmillan $35.00

- **Jack Rennert & Walter Terry**
100 YEARS OF DANCE POSTERS
0–380–00485–2 Avon pb $8.50

BODY SCIENCE, KINESICS, AND TECHNIQUE

- **Ray Birdwhistell**
KINESICS AND CONTEXT: Essays on Body Motion Communication
0–8122–1012–3 Pennsylvania pb $17.95

- **Kenneth Laws**
THE PHYSICS OF DANCE
A physicist anatomizes the engineering of classic ballet
Photographs by Martha Swope
0–02–873360–6 Schirmer pb $14.95

- **Thalia Mara**
FIRST STEPS IN BALLET: Basic Exercises at the Barre
An old and reliable book
0–916622–53–3 Princeton Book pb $6.95
SECOND STEPS IN BALLET: Basic Center Exercises
0–916622–54–1 Princeton Book pb $6.95
THIRD STEPS IN BALLET: Basic Allegro Steps
0–916622–55–X Princeton Book pb $6.95
FOURTH STEPS IN BALLET: On Your Toes! Basic Pointe Work
0–916622–56–8 Princeton Book pb $6.95

- **Anna Paskevska**
BOTH SIDES OF THE MIRROR: The Science and Art of Ballet
0–87127–135–4 Princeton Book pb $14.95

- **Muriel Stuart**
THE CLASSIC BALLET: Basic Technique and Terminology
The diagrams highlighting proper body placement are extremely helpful
Introduction by Lincoln Kirstein
0–394–40820–9 Random House $24.50

- **Mabel Todd**
THINKING BODY: A Study of Balancing Forces of Dynamic Man
0–87127–014–5 Princeton Book pb $15.95

- **Stuart Wright**
THE DANCER'S GUIDE TO INJURIES OF THE LOWER EXTREMITY: Diagnosis, Treatment, and Care
0–8453–4782–9 Associated University $18.95

BEING A DANCER

- **Toni Bentley**
WINTER SEASON: A Dancer's Journal
The day-to-day life of a member of New York City Ballet's corps
0–394–72398–8 Random House pb $4.95

- **Dance Theater Workshop**
POOR DANCER'S ALMANAC: A Survival Manual for Choreographers, Managers and Dancers
Dance Theater Workshop is a leading center for experimental dance
0–9611382–0–3 DTW pb $15.00

- **Suzanne Gordon**
OFF BALANCE: The Real World of Ballet
Interesting glimpses of the kind of competition the aspiring dancer faces, and some of the pitfalls of the profession
0–394–51985–X Pantheon $15.95
0–07–023770–0 McGraw-Hill pb $7.95

- **Marian Horosko & Judith Kupersmith**
THE DANCER'S SURVIVAL MANUAL: Everything You Need to Know About Being a Dancer . . . Except How to Dance
Horosko writes a popular monthly column in *Dance* magazine; Kupersmith is a psychologist known for her work with performing artists
Foreword by Robert Joffrey
0–06–055084–8 Harper & Row $21.95
0–06–096199–6 Harper & Row pb $10.95

- **Ellen Jacob**
DANCING: A Guide for the Dancer You Can Be
0–937180–00–9 Danceways pb $11.95

- **Allegra Kent**
THE DANCER'S BODY BOOK
Advice from the former New York City Ballet star
0–688–01539–5 Morrow pb $9.50

REFERENCE

- **George Balanchine & Francis Mason**
101 STORIES OF THE GREAT BALLETS
Contains entries on more than 400 works, with extensive discussion of differences between major productions. Also offers an excellent chronology of ballet, and several essays by and interviews with Balanchine
0–385–03398–2 Doubleday pb $9.95

- **Mary Clark & Clement Crisp**
BALLET GOER'S GUIDE
0–394–51307–X Knopf $22.50

- **Barbara Cohen-Stratyner**
BIOGRAPHICAL DICTIONARY OF DANCE
The only one-volume US encyclopedia on the subject in print. Especially recommended for entries on popular dancing
0–02–870260–3 Schirmer $75.00

- **Gail Grant**
TECHNICAL MANUAL AND DICTIONARY OF CLASSICAL BALLET
0–486–21843–0 Dover pb $2.95

- **Horst Koegler**
THE CONCISE OXFORD DICTIONARY OF BALLET
0–19–311330–9 Oxford pb $17.95

- **Walter Terry**
THE BALLET GUIDE
Thumbnail sketches and stories of the ballets
0–396–08098–7 Dodd, Mead pb $13.95

Theater

Although performance is the most evanescent of arts, the institution of theater and some of its literature have endured remarkably. The Rodgers and Hart musical of *The Boys from Syracuse,* for instance, was a culmination of more than 2300 years of stealing and borrowing: it was inspired by *The Comedy of Errors,* which Shakespeare took from Plautus, who in turn adapted it from a Greek model. And the text of Euripides' tragedy *The Bacchae,* that most joyful of pagan plays, has been partially preserved in a medieval version in which the god Dionysus is transformed into the suffering Christ.

HISTORY

• Oscar G. Brockett
THE THEATRE: An Introduction
For the serious student, by the most comprehensive and academically sound of contemporary American historians
0–03–021676–1 Henry Holt $35.50

• Oscar G. Brockett & Mark Pape
WORLD DRAMA
0–03–057668–7 Holt, Rinehart & Winston pb $24.95

• Robert W. Corrigan
THE WORLD OF THE THEATRE
0–673–15107–7 Scott, Foresman $22.95

• Phyllis Hartnoll
THE THEATRE: A Concise History
Provides a good overview with pictures
0–500–20073–4 Thames & Hudson pb $11.95

• A.M. Nagler
SOURCE BOOK IN THEATRICAL HISTORY
A classic anthology of writing about the theater by its practitioners
0–486–20515–0 Dover pb $9.95

• Richard Southern
THE SEVEN AGES OF THE THEATRE
Still one of the more readable and thought-provoking books about the great periods of Western theater, from the Greeks to the 20th century
0–8090–0534–4 Hill & Wang pb $9.95

• Glynne Wickham
A HISTORY OF THE THEATRE
A sound history by an outstanding British theater scholar
0–521–30651–5 Cambridge pb $29.95

Ancient

• John Jones
ON ARISTOTLE AND GREEK TRAGEDY
A difficult but important book about the (mis)interpretation of Aristotle as it affects our understanding of Greek drama
0–8047–1092–9 Stanford $27.50
0–8047–1093–7 Stanford pb $7.95

H.D. F. Kitto
GREEK TRAGEDY: A Literary Study
Cogent and passionately argued essays about the meaning of drama in the mid-20th century
0–416–68900–0 RC&H $15.95

• Bernard Knox
WORD AND ACTION: Essays on the Ancient Theater
0–8018–3409–0 Johns Hopkins pb $12.95

• Ericka Simon
THE ANCIENT THEATRE
Short and sweet
0–416–32530–0 RC&H pb $7.95

Medieval and Elizabethan

Among the hundreds of books written about Shakespeare and his contemporaries, this brief selection concentrates on practical aspects of understanding and staging plays of this period.

• Gerald E. Bentley
THE PROFESSIONS OF DRAMATIST AND PLAYER IN SHAKESPEARE'S TIME, 1590–1642
0–691–01426–4 Princeton pb $14.50

• Grigori Kozintzev
KING LEAR: The Space of Tragedy
A diary by the Soviet film director who filmed *Lear*
Translated by Mary Mackintosh
0–520–03392–2 California $32.50

• A.M. Nagler
SHAKESPEARE'S STAGE
A succinct introduction to a hotly debated and ever-evolving subject
0–300–02689–7 Yale pb $9.95

• Simon Shepherd
MARLOWE AND THE POLITICS OF ELIZABETHAN THEATRE
0–312–51546–4 St. Martin's $29.95

• Richard Southern
MEDIEVAL THEATRE IN THE ROUND
Combining scholarship with theatrical horse sense, this book has influenced the revival of interest in producing medieval drama
0–87830–085–6 Theatre Arts $19.95

• Peter Thomson
SHAKESPEARE'S THEATRE
0–7102–0382–9 RC&H pb $12.95

Britain and Ireland

• Sally Beauman
THE ROYAL SHAKESPEARE COMPANY: A History of Ten Decades
An account of one of the world's most important companies for Shakespearean and modern productions
0–19–212209–6 Oxford $29.95

• Terry Browne
PLAYWRIGHTS' THEATRE: The English Stage Company at the Royal Court
Founded by George Devine in 1956, the English Stage Company became the chief producer of the most important British and European playwrights for the next two decades
0–273–00758–0 Wesleyan pb $8.50

• Christopher Fitz-Simon
THE IRISH THEATRE
0–500–01300–4 Thames & Hudson $24.95

• Ronald Hayman
BRITISH THEATRE SINCE 1955: A Reassessment
0–19–219127–6 Oxford $19.95

• Peter Kavanagh
THE STORY OF THE ABBEY THEATRE
0–915032–29–5 National Poetry $25.00
0–915032–30–9 National Poetry pb $12.95

• Charles Marowitz & others, editors
NEW THEATRE VOICES OF THE FIFTIES AND SIXTIES: Selections from "Encore" Magazine 1956–1963
With its global perspective, *Encore* was the most important English theater magazine of the day
0–413–48900–0 RC&H $22.00
0–413–48910–8 RC&H pb $10.95

• George Rowell & Anthony Jackson
THE REPERTORY MOVEMENT: A History of Regional Theatre in Britain
0–521–31919–6 Cambridge pb $14.95

Europe

• Alba Amoia
THE ITALIAN THEATRE TODAY: Twelve Interviews
0–87875–107–6 Whitston $12.50

• André Antoine
MEMORIES OF THE THEATRE-LIBRE
Antoine (1858–1943) founded the art-theater movement which spread from Paris to other European cities. One of the fathers of modern theater, he helped establish Ibsen's realistic social dramas
Edited by H.D. Albright
0–87024–034–X Miami $12.95

• Marvin Carlson
THE ITALIAN STAGE: From Goldoni to D'Annunzio
Goldoni reformed the moribund *commedia dell'arte,* which has had a lasting influence on many forms of comedy, such as improvisation, slapstick, and children's theater; D'Annunzio was a forerunner of Italian fascism
0–89950–000–5 McFarland $25.95

• Ruby Cohn
FROM DESIRE TO GODOT: Pocket Theater of Postwar Paris
0–520–05825–9 California $25.00

• Bohdan Drozdowsky, editor
TWENTIETH-CENTURY POLISH THEATRE
More experimental and less realistic than other Eastern European countries, the

☞ **TO ORDER NEW BOOKS NOT YET LISTED, ASK YOUR BOOKSELLER OR CALL 1-800-882-8770**

Polish theater has had a major impact on Western drama
0–7145–3738–1 Riverrun $16.95

● Pierre L. Ducharte
ITALIAN COMEDY: The Improvisation, Scenarios, Lives, Attributes, Portraits and Masks of the Illustrious Characters of the Commedia Dell'arte
A reprint of this 1929 account of the *commedia dell'arte*
0–486–21679–9 Dover pb $9.95

● Wallace Fowlie
DIONYSUS IN PARIS: A Guide to Contemporary French Theater
0–8446–0096–2 Peter Smith $11.50

● Mel Gordon
THE GRAND GUIGNOL: Theatre of Fear and Terror
A graphically illustrated account of the notorious theater of shock and cruelty that flourished in Paris from 1897 to 1962
0–941693–08–2 Amok pb $12.95

● Vladimir Nemirovitch-Dantchenko
MY LIFE IN THE RUSSIAN THEATRE
Unlike Stanislavski, with whom he co-founded the Moscow Art Theatre, Nemirovich-Dantchenko actually understood Chekhov's plays. This is an important book about the Russian theater
0–87830–520–3 Theatre Arts pb $3.50

● Konstantin Rudnitsky
RUSSIAN AND SOVIET THEATER: 1905–1932
A full graphic presentation of decades of experiment
0–8109–1596–0 Abrams $75.00

From The Grand Guignol *by Mel Gordon (Amok Press)*

● Nahma Sandrow
VAGABOND STARS: A World History of Yiddish Theater
So, enjoy!
0–87910–060–5 Limelight pb $13.95

● Leroy R. Shaw, editor
THE GERMAN THEATER TODAY: A Symposium
0–292–73250–3 Texas $11.95

● August Strindberg
OPEN LETTERS TO THE INTIMATE THEATER
Between 1907 and 1913, Stockholm's Intima Teatern staged some two dozen of Strindberg's chamber plays and changed the course of modern drama
Translated by Walter Johnson
0–295–74055–8 Washington $15.00

● John Willett
THE THEATRE OF THE WEIMAR REPUBLIC
An account by an English critic of the Weimar period (1920–33), from Reinhardt to the expressionists, from the Bauhaus to Piscator, Brecht, and Kurt Weill
0–8419–0759–5 Holmes & Meier $45.00

Africa

● David B. Coplan
IN TOWNSHIP TONIGHT!
A marvelous book about the urban performing arts in South Africa
0–582–64401–1 Longman $32.95
0–582–64400–3 Longman pb $13.95

● Mineke Schipper
THEATER AND SOCIETY IN AFRICA
Provides the social context for the development of African theater
Translated by Ampie Coetzee
0–86975–135–2 Ohio pb $8.95

● Russell Vandenbroucke
TRUTHS THE HAND CAN TOUCH: The Theater of Athol Fugard
0–930452–45–3 Theatre Comm pb $12.50

Asia

● James R. Brandon
THEATER IN SOUTHEAST ASIA
0–674–87587–7 Harvard pb $9.95

● J.I. Crump
CHINESE THEATER IN THE DAYS OF KUBLAI KHAN
The book on classical Chinese theater
0–8165–0656–6 Arizona pb $14.95

● Kunio Komparu
THE NOH THEATER: Principles and Perspectives
A detailed account of Noh's techniques and fundamental structures
0–8348–1529–X Weatherhill $32.50

● Colin Mackerras, editor
CHINESE THEATER: From Its Origins to the Present Day
0–8248–0813–4 Hawaii $19.95

● Arthur Miller
SALESMAN IN BEIJING
An account of a Chinese production of *Death of a Salesman*
0–670–61601–X Viking $17.95

● Leonard C. Pronko
THEATER EAST AND WEST: Perspectives Toward a Total Theater
The classic introductory book by Professor Pronko, who both teaches and produces Eastern theater
0–520–02622–5 California pb $7.95

● Constantine Tung & Colin MacKerras
DRAMA IN THE PEOPLE'S REPUBLIC OF CHINA
0–88706–389–6 SUNY $54.50
0–88706–390–X SUNY pb $16.95

North America

● Brooks Atkinson
BROADWAY
A consequential history (published in 1970) by the dean of New York critics
0–87910–047–8 Limelight pb $14.95

● Brooks Atkinson & Al Hirschfeld
THE LIVELY YEARS: 1920–1973
Each of Hirschfeld's caricatures is worth more than a thousand words
0–306–80234–1 Da Capo pb $9.95

● Gerald M. Berkowitz
NEW BROADWAYS: Theater Across America, 1950–1980
The phenomenal rise of residential companies in every region of America
0–8476–7031–7 Rowman & Littlefield $29.95

Harold Clurman
THE FERVENT YEARS: The Group Theater and the Thirties
A firsthand history and passionate manifesto by a founder of one of the most important theater groups in America between the wars
Introduction by Stella Adler
0–306–80186–8 Da Capo pb $10.95

● David Garfield
THE ACTORS STUDIO: A Player's Place
A controversial history of the studio that has trained some of the best-known figures in American theater and film, especially in the 1940s and '50s
0–02–012310–8 Macmillan pb $9.95

● Stanley Green
THE GREAT CLOWNS OF BROADWAY
0–19–503471–6 Oxford $21.95

● Otis Guernsey
CURTAIN TIMES: The New York Theater, 1965–1987
A detailed survey of all the productions during this period
Illustrated by Al Hirschfeld
0–936839–23–6 Applause pb $16.95

- Errol Hill
THE THEATRE OF BLACK AMERICANS
A standard work by the leading authority in the field
0–936839–27–9 Applause pb $12.95

- Foster Hirsch
A METHOD TO THEIR MADNESS: The History of the Actors Studio
0–306–80268–6 Da Capo pb $11.95

- Jorge A. Huerta
CHICANO THEATER: Themes and Forms
A critical survey of this nascent and lively ethnic theater by a leading scholar and activist
0–916950–25–5 Bilingual Review pb $10.95

- Judith Malina, editor
THE DIARIES OF JUDITH MALINA, 1947–1957
The first ten years of the Living Theater, by its co-founder
0–394–53132–9 Grove $27.50
0–394–62450–5 Grove pb $11.95

- Carlton W. & Barbara J. Molette
BLACK THEATER: Premise and Presentation
0–932269–94–X Wyndham Hall pb $17.95

- Ethan Mordden
THE AMERICAN THEATER
"Mordden is an extraordinarily gifted and delightful critic with a sure eye and ear for the essence and significance of a play and the skill to render its meaning in a few smart, but never smart alecky, sentences"—*American Literature*
0–19–502959–3 Oxford $32.95

William Redfield
LETTERS FROM AN ACTOR
A gossipy and useful account of the famous 1964 Gielgud production of *Hamlet* with Richard Burton on Broadway
0–87910–007–9 Limelight pb $7.95

- Charles W. Stein, editor
AMERICAN VAUDEVILLE AS SEEN BY ITS CONTEMPORARIES
Good source material about the outstanding personalities in vaudeville
0–306–80256–2 Da Capo pb $11.95

- Robert C. Toll
Toll's books present entertaining accounts of popular entertainment in America.
BLACKING UP: The Minstrel Show in 19th-Century America
0–19–502172–X Oxford pb $8.95

THE ENTERTAINMENT MACHINE: American Show Business in the 20th-Century
0–19–503081–8 Oxford $35.00
0–19–503232–2 Oxford pb $12.95

- Joseph W. Zeigler
REGIONAL THEATER: The Revolutionary Stage
0–306–80056–X Da Capo pb $6.95

Contemporary and Avant-Garde

- Eileen Blumenthal
JOSEPH CHAIKIN
0–521–28589–5 Cambridge pb $13.95

Stefan Brecht
THE THEATRE OF VISIONS: Robert Wilson
Wilson, primarily a visual artist, has changed the way we perceive space and time in the theater
3–518–02488–4 RC&H pb $13.00

Contemporary Arts Center, Cincinnati Staff
ROBERT WILSON: The Theater of Images
A volume prepared in collaboration with the Byrd Hoffman Foundation of New York
Introduction by John Rockwell
0–06–091138–7 Harper & Row pb $14.95

- Rose Lee Goldberg
PERFORMANCE ART: From Futurism to the Present
Traces the roots of this marriage of art and theater from early in the century to the present
0–8109–2371–8 Abrams pb $12.95

- Ronald Hayman
THEATER AND ANTI-THEATER: New Movements Since Beckett
0–19–520089–6 Oxford $29.95

Bonnie Marranca & Gautam Dasgupta, editors
THEATRE OF THE RIDICULOUS
0–933826–00–1 PAJ pb $5.95

- James Roose-Evans
EXPERIMENTAL THEATRE: From Stanislavsky to Peter Brook
0–87663–564–8 Universe pb $8.95

- Richard Schechner
THE END OF HUMANISM: Writings on Performance
Schechner, one of the most honest and readable of contemporary critics, has practiced what he theorizes and vice versa
0–933826–18–4 PAJ $18.95
0–933826–19–2 PAJ pb $6.95

- Rodney Simard
POSTMODERN DRAMA: Contemporary Playwrights in America and Britain
0–8191–4195–X American Theatre pb $12.00

Theater and Politics

- Stephan Brecht
QUEER THEATRE
3–518–02489–2 RC&H pb $9.00

- Robert Brustein
REVOLUTION AS THEATRE: Essays on Radical Style
0–87140–238–6 Liveright pb $1.95

- Hallie Flanagan
ARENA
An important account of the Federal Theatre Project of the 1930s by the woman who ran it
Foreword by John Houseman
0–87910–033–8 Limelight pb $12.95

- Malcolm Goldstein
THE POLITICAL STAGE: American Drama and Theater of the Great Depression
0–19–501745–5 Oxford $29.95

- Catherine Itzin
STAGES IN THE REVOLUTION: Political Theatre in Britain Since 1968
This book by a leading feminist in England chronicles the second wave of Britain's Angry Generation
0–413–39180–9 RC&H $24.00

- Helene Keyssar
FEMINIST THEATRE
0–394–54631–8 Grove $22.50
0–394–62059–3 Grove pb $7.95

- John O'Connor & Lorraine Brown, editors
THE FEDERAL THEATRE PROJECT
Foreword by John Houseman
0–413–46770–8 RC&H $19.95

- Maria L. Piscator
THE PISCATOR EXPERIMENT: The Political Theatre
0–8093–0458–9 Southern Illinois pb $3.50

The Musical Theater

- Gerald Bordman
AMERICAN MUSICAL COMEDY: From Adonis to Dreamgirls
Adonis was the first musical comedy (1884) to rack up more than 500 performances on Broadway; Bordman charts almost 100 years in the evolution of this genre
0–19–503104–0 Oxford $24.95

AMERICAN MUSICAL REVUE: From The Passing Show to Sugar Babies
A complete account and annotated list of all Broadway revues, from 1894 on
0–19–503630–1 Oxford $24.95

AMERICAN MUSICAL THEATRE: A Chronicle
"Much more than a source book. It is fun to read"—John S. Wilson, *NY Times*
0–19–502356–0 Oxford $49.95
0–19–504045–7 Oxford pb $19.95

AMERICAN OPERETTA: From H.M.S. Pinafore to Sweeney Todd
Links the American musical to its European roots and predecessors
0–19–502869–4 Oxford $24.95

- Martin Gottfried
BROADWAY MUSICALS
0–8109–8060–6 Abrams $24.95

- Stanley Green
BROADWAY MUSICALS OF THE '30s
A complete list, including discography and film versions; many illustrations
Introduction by Brooks Atkinson
0–306–80165–5 Da Capo pb $14.95

➤ FOR OVERSEAS ORDERING INFORMATION, SEE PAGE 1

BROADWAY MUSICALS—SHOW BY SHOW
More facts than one is ever likely to need about musicals from *The Black Crook* (1866) to *Les Miz*
0–88188–761–7 Hal Leonard pb $19.95

THE WORLD OF MUSICAL COMEDY
A history mainly of Broadway in its golden age
0–306–80207–4 Da Capo pb $19.95

• Otis L. Guernsey, editor
BROADWAY SONG AND STORY: Playwrights, Lyricists, Composers Discuss Their Hits
Conversations about the creation of musicals
Introduction by Terrence McNally
0–396–08753–1 Dodd, Mead $22.95

• Foster Hirsch
HAROLD PRINCE AND THE AMERICAN MUSICAL THEATER
Forewords by Harold Prince & Stephen Sondheim
0–521–33314–8 Cambridge $29.95

• Al Kasha & Joel Hirschhorn
NOTES ON BROADWAY: Conversations with the Great Songwriters
0–8092–5162–0 Contemporary $22.95

Ethan Mordden
BROADWAY BABIES: The People Who Made the American Musical
Brings to life the great personalities who created the Broadway musical, from Florenz Ziegfeld to Harold Prince and Stephen Sondheim; with an extensive discography
0–19–503345–0 Oxford $24.95
0–19–505425–3 Oxford pb $7.95

• Sheridan Morley
SPREAD A LITTLE HAPPINESS: The First Hundred Years of the British Musical
A heavily illustrated history of the past 100 years
0–500–01398–5 Thames & Hudson $29.95

• P.G. Wodehouse & Guy Bolton
BRING ON THE GIRLS!: The Impossible Story of Our Life in Musical Comedy and the Pictures to Prove It
First published in 1953, this is a tongue-in-cheek account of this duo's flops and hits in the 1920s and '30s
0–87910–011–7 Limelight pb $7.95

SELECTED MEMOIRS AND BIOGRAPHIES

• Eve Arden
THREE PHASES OF EVE: An Autobiography
0–312–80267–6 St. Martin's $17.95
0–312–01521–6 St. Martin's pb $9.95

• Gene Fowler
GOOD NIGHT, SWEET PRINCE: The Life and Times of John Barrymore
0–916515–56–7 Mercury pb $12.95

Two of Craig's "Black Figures" from Gordon Craig *by Edward Craig (Limelight)*

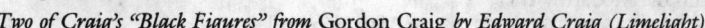

• Anne Baxter
INTERMISSION
0–345–34016–7 Ballantine pb $3.50

• Cornelia Otis Skinner
MADAME SARAH
1–557–78107–9 Paragon House pb $9.95

• Melvyn Bragg
RICHARD BURTON: A Life
0–316–10595–3 Little, Brown $22.95

• Noel Coward
AN AUTOBIOGRAPHY

Volume 1: Present Indicative
0–306–80112–4 Da Capo pb $9.95

Volume 2: Future Indefinite
0–306–80126–4 Da Capo pb $9.95

• Edward Gordon Craig
INDEX TO THE STORY OF MY DAYS
The son of Ellen Terry Craig (1872–1966) was one of the great visionary designers of the modern theater
0–521–28070–2 Cambridge pb $15.95

• Edward Craig
GORDON CRAIG: The Story of His Life
"A remarkable record of this extraordinary man"—John Gielgud
0–87910–030–3 Limelight pb $12.95

• Eva Le Gallienne
THE MYSTIC IN THE THEATRE: Eleonora Duse
One great actress pays tribute to another
0–8093–0631–X Southern Illinois pb $24.95

• John Gielgud
AN ACTOR IN HIS TIME
0–14–005636–X Penguin pb $4.95

EARLY STAGES
0–916515–57–5 Mercury pb $11.95

• Ruth Gordon
SHADY LADY
0–8217–1187–3 Zebra pb $3.50

Alec Guinness
BLESSINGS IN DISGUISE
A delightfully modest memoir by an actor equally versatile on stage and screen
0–446–38426–7 Warner pb $9.95

• Tyrone Guthrie
A LIFE IN THE THEATRE
The memoirs of the great director who founded both Canada's Shakespeare Festival and the Guthrie Theatre in Minneapolis
0–87910–048–6 Limelight pb $10.95

• Alfred Rossi
ASTONISH US IN THE MORNING: Tyrone Guthrie Remembered
Some of the great actors and designers who worked with Guthrie recall and evaluate his achievement
0–8143–1669–7 Wayne State $29.95
0–8143–1670–0 Wayne State pb $9.95

• Uta Hagen
SOURCES: A Memoir
0–933826–54–0 Performing Arts $19.95
0–933826–55–9 Performing Arts pb $7.95

• Peter Hall
PETER HALL'S DIARIES
These not-always-discreet journals reveal Hall's highs and lows at the helm of Britain's National Theatre
Edited by John Goodwin
0–87910–045–1 Limelight pb $12.95

• Hugh Fordin
GETTING TO KNOW HIM: A Biography of Oscar Hammerstein II
This 1977 biography, based on archives and interviews, is introduced by Stephen Sondheim
0–8044–6200–3 Ungar pb $13.95

• John Houseman
FRONT AND CENTER
Houseman founded the Mercury Theatre in the 1930s with Orson Welles, and the Acting Company when he was seventy, before starting a whole new acting career

---

as the curmudgeonly law professor in the TV series *Paper Chase*
0–671–41391–0 Simon & Schuster pb $9.95

• Joseph Jefferson
THE AUTOBIOGRAPHY OF JOSEPH JEFFERSON
This beguiling book (1890) by one of the greatest and best-loved actors of the 19th century is still a landmark in American theatrical writing
Edited by Alan S. Downer
0–674–05350–8 Harvard $24.50

Elia Kazan
A LIFE
A revealing and human self-portrait of the director, novelist, and womanizer, from the early days of the Group Theatre, through the McCarthy era (when he named names), to his mature reflections
0–394–55953–3 Knopf $24.95

• Simon Callow
CHARLES LAUGHTON: A Difficult Actor
0–8021–3169–7 Grove pb $8.95

• Anne Edwards
VIVIEN LEIGH
0–671–55220–1 Pocket pb $4.95

• Hugo Vickers
VIVIEN LEIGH: A Biography
0–316–90245–4 Little, Brown $22.95

• Donald Spoto
LENYA: A Life
0–316–80725–7 Little, Brown $19.95

• Jerome Lawrence
ACTOR: The Life and Times of Paul Muni
A detailed biography of the Yiddish character actor who conquered Broadway and Hollywood
0–573–69034–0 Samuel French pb $9.50

• Arthur Miller
TIMEBENDS: A Life
0–8021–0015–5 Grove $25.00
0–06–097178–9 Harper & Row pb $10.95

• Sheridan Morley
THE GREAT STAGE STARS: Distinguished Theatrical Careers of the Past and Present
A survey of great actors of past and present
0–8160–1401–9 Facts On File $24.95

• Anthony Holden
LAURENCE OLIVIER
0–689–11536–9 Macmillan $22.50

• Laurence Olivier
CONFESSIONS OF AN ACTOR: An Autobiography
0–14–006888–0 Penguin pb $5.95

• John Lahr
PRICK UP YOUR EARS: The Biography of Joe Orton
A graphic portrait of the gay British playwright, tragically murdered at 34 by his lover
0–394–75305–4 Random House pb $4.95

• José Quintero
IF YOU DON'T DANCE THEY BEAT YOU
This 1974 autobiography by the director of the major O'Neill revivals deals with an important period of American theater in the 1950s and '60s
0–312–02222–0 St. Martin's pb $10.95

• Martin Duberman
PAUL ROBESON
0–394–52780–1 Random House $24.95

• Alan Schneider
ENTRANCES: An American Director's Journey
The reminiscences of the great American director of Albee, Beckett, and others, who met his untimely death in a London accident
Preface by Edward Albee
0–670–80608–0 Viking $25.00
0–87910–067–2 Limelight pb $17.95

• Don Shewey & Susan Shacter
CAUGHT IN THE ACT: New York Actors Face to Face
0–453–00523–3 NAL $24.50
0–452–25991–6 NAL pb $12.95

• Constantin Stanislavski
MY LIFE IN ART
0–87830–550–5 Theatre Arts pb $12.95

• Nina Auerbach
ELLEN TERRY: Player in Her Time
0–393–30582–1 Norton pb $10.95

• Kathleen Tynan
THE LIFE OF KENNETH TYNAN
0–688–08906–2 Morrow $15.50

DRAMATIC THEORY AND CRITICISM

• Adolpho Appia
THE WORK OF LIVING ART & MAN IS THE MEASURE OF ALL THINGS
Two seminal works by the French-Swiss artist who revolutionized lighting design at the turn of the century
0–87024–305–5 Miami $15.00

• Antonin Artaud
THE THEATER AND ITS DOUBLE
A work that deeply influenced the absurdists, and inspired the Theater of Cruelty in the 1960s
Translated by Mary C. Richards
0–8021–5030–6 Grove pb $8.95

• Bertold Brecht
BRECHT ON THEATRE
Theoretical writings by Brecht that have vastly influenced modern drama and theatrical practice
Translated by John Willett
0–8090–0542–5 Hill & Wang pb $8.95

Peter Brook
THE EMPTY SPACE
"What I treasure most in the book is that it always harks back to the artistic, social, psychological, practical basis of the theater as a concern of cultural significance"—Harold Clurman
0–689–70558–1 Atheneum pb $6.95

• Marvin Carlson
THEORIES OF THE THEATRE: A Historical and Critical Survey from the Greeks to the Present
An overview of the aesthetic and philosophical movements that have shaped (mainly) Western theater
0–8014–9337–4 Cornell pb $14.95

• Barrett H. Clark
EUROPEAN THEORIES OF THE DRAMA
Contains important and little-known texts for the critic and scholar
0–517–50539–8 Crown $19.95

• Gordon Craig
ON THE ART OF THE THEATRE
A classic manifesto (1911) by one of the visionaries of the modern theater
0–87830–570–X Theatre Arts pb $8.95

• Martin Esslin
AN ANATOMY OF DRAMA
A straightforward introduction to dramatic analysis and the whole theatrical experience
0–8090–0550–6 Hill & Wang pb $7.95

THE FIELD OF DRAMA: How the Signs of Drama Create Meaning on Stage and Screen
Relates the theory of semiotics to a practical understanding of the dramatic media
0–413–53530–4 RC&H $16.95

• Richard Kostelanetz
THE THEATRE OF MIXED MEANS
The impact of audiovisual technology on the theater
0–932360–289 RK Editions pb $15.00

• Michel Saint-Denis
THEATRE: The Rediscovery of Style
Lectures by the great French-English director and teacher ranging from the French classical tradition to acting, directing, and designing in the modern realistic theater
Introduction by Laurence Olivier
0–87830–523–8 Theatre Arts pb $7.95

• Richard Schechner
BETWEEN THEATER AND ANTHROPOLOGY
Foreword by Victor Turner
0–8122–1225–8 Pennsylvania pb $16.95

• James Schevill
BREAKOUT: In Search of New Theatrical Environments
0–8040–0574–5 Ohio $18.00
0–8040–0640–7 Ohio pb $4.95

• J.L. Styan
ELEMENTS OF DRAMA
A clear introduction, illustrated with examples from the works of the great modern dramatists
0–521–09201–9 Cambridge pb $15.95

MODERN DRAMA IN THEORY AND PRACTICE
The most complete work on the subject

Volume 1
0–521–29628–5 Cambridge pb $9.95

Volume 2
0–521–29629–3 Cambridge pb $9.95

Volume 3
0–521–29630–7 Cambridge pb $10.95

• Peter Szondi
THEORY OF THE MODERN DRAMA
Writing in 1963, this German critic ties together the many strands of 20th-century European theater from Ibsen to existentialism
Edited by Michael Hays
Foreword by Jochen Schulte-Sasse
0–8166–1285–4 Minnesota pb $10.95

• Victor Turner
FROM RITUAL TO THEATRE: The Human Seriousness of Play
Essays on comparative symbology, social dramas, dramatic ritual/ritual drama, and more
0–933826–16–8 Performing Arts $17.95
0–933826–17–6 Performing Arts pb $8.95

• J. Michael Walton, editor
CRAIG ON THEATRE
0–413–49540–X RC&H $21.00
0–413–47220–5 RC&H pb $10.95

Essays and Criticism

• Eric Bentley
THE LIFE OF THE DRAMA
0–689–70011–3 Atheneum pb $7.95

WHAT IS THEATRE?
Reviews and critical comments from Bentley's best period as a critic
0–87910–012–5 Limelight pb $10.95

• C.W.E. Bigsby
A CRITICAL INTRODUCTION TO 20TH-CENTURY AMERICAN DRAMA

Volume 1: 1900–1940
0–521–27116–9 Cambridge pb $16.95

Volume 2: Tennessee Williams, Arthur Miller, Edward Albee
0–521–25811–1 Cambridge $44.50
0–521–27717–5 Cambridge pb $16.95

Volume 3: Beyond Broadway
0–521–26256–9 Cambridge $42.50
0–521–27896–1 Cambridge pb $15.95

• Herbert Blau
TAKE UP THE BODIES: Theater at the Vanishing Point
Blau is perhaps the most complex thinker writing about the American theater
0–252–01245–3 Illinois pb $10.95

BLOODED THOUGHT: Occasions of Theatre
0–933826–39–7 Performing Arts pb $6.95

• Peter Brook
THE SHIFTING POINT: Theatre, Film, Opera, 1946–1987
The great director's reflections and reminiscences about his diverse projects over the past 40 years
0–06–039073–5 Harper & Row $22.00

• John R. Brown
MODERN BRITISH DRAMATISTS: New Perspectives
0–13–588021–1 Prentice-Hall $19.95

Robert Brustein
THE THEATRE OF REVOLT: An Approach to the Modern Drama
Early studies in the modern movement: Ibsen, Strindberg, Chekhov, Shaw, Brecht, Pirandello, O'Neill, and Genet
0–316–11287–9 Little, Brown pb $12.45

WHO NEEDS THEATRE?
His latest collection of essays and reviews
0–87113–206–0 Atlantic Monthly pb $18.95

• Joseph Chaikin
THE PRESENCE OF THE ACTOR
0–689–70338–4 Atheneum pb $8.95

• Robert W. Corrigan
THE MAKING OF THEATRE: From Drama to Performance
0–673–15403–3 Scott, Foresman pb $13.50

• Martin Esslin
THE THEATRE OF THE ABSURD
The most influential book about the revolution in modern drama wrought by Beckett, Ionesco, Genet, Adamov, and other writers in the 1950s
0–14–055228–6 Penguin pb $7.95

• Francis Fergusson
THE IDEA OF A THEATER: The Art of Drama in Changing Perspective
This influential study, first published in 1949, started a reevaluation of the purpose of theater and the revival of noncommercial theater in America. The ten plays analyzed range from *Oedipus Rex* to *Murder in the Cathedral*
0–691–01288–1 Princeton pb $9.50

• Richard Gilman
THE MAKING OF MODERN DRAMA
Gilman's study focuses on Büchner, Ibsen, Strindberg, Chekhov, Pirandello, Brecht, Beckett, and Handke. "It moves toward the deepest sources of some great plays, so it deepens their effect on us"—Stanley Kauffman
0–306–80293–7 Da Capo pb $10.95

• Eugène Ionesco
NOTES AND COUNTERNOTES
Translated by Donald Watson
0–7145–0044–5 Riverrun pb $9.95

• Walter Kerr
TRAGEDY AND COMEDY
This 1967 book by the eminent newspaper critic is more readable and insightful than most academic books
Introduction by William Alfred
0–306–80249–X Da Capo pb $9.95

• Jan Kott
SHAKESPEARE OUR CONTEMPORARY
This important political interpretation of Shakespeare's plays has influenced Peter Brook and a host of Eastern European directors active in America today
Introduction by Martin Esslin
0–393–00736–7 Norton pb $9.95

THE THEATER OF ESSENCE
A stimulating collection of essays ranging from Shakespeare and Ibsen to Japanese theater, Grotowski, and Peter Brook
Introduction by Martin Esslin
0–8101–0665–5 Northwestern pb $10.95

• Bonnie Marranca
THEATREWRITINGS
Includes essays on the avant-garde theater and performance art, and surprisingly fresh insights into Lillian Hellman, Pirandello, and Chekhov
0–933826–67–2 Performing Arts $19.95
0–933826–68–0 Performing Arts pb $8.95

• Arthur Miller
THE THEATER ESSAYS OF ARTHUR MILLER
Edited by Robert A. Martin
0–14–004903–7 Penguin pb $9.95

• John Peter
VLADIMIR'S CARROT: Modern Drama and the Modern Imagination
The most recent studies of postwar avant-garde drama by the critic of the *Times* (London)
0–226–66265–9 Chicago $24.95

• George Bernard Shaw
DRAMATIC CRITICISM: 1895–98
Shaw's famous reviews set a still unmatched standard for verbal pyrotechnics, subjectivity, and sheer entertainment
Introduction by J.F. Matthews
0–8371–5234–8 Greenwood $29.95

THE ART AND PRACTICE OF THEATER

Playwriting

• George P. Baker
DRAMATIC TECHNIQUE
The classic book by the father of American playwriting
0–306–80030–6 Da Capo pb $8.95

• Eric Bentley
THINKING ABOUT THE PLAYWRIGHT
Essays and reviews by the distinguished
critic
0-8101-0733-3 Northwestern pb $14.95

• Toby Cole, editor
**PLAYWRIGHTS ON PLAYWRITING:
The Meaning and Making of Modern
Drama**
A broad and useful selection
Introduction by John Gassner
0-8090-0529-8 Hill & Wang pb $7.95

• Lajos Egri
THE ART OF DRAMATIC WRITING
This compelling book from the 1940s is
still a staple of many university courses;
some writers have claimed that reading
Egri changed their lives
0-671-21332-6 Simon & Schuster pb $10.95

• Lee A. Morrow & Frank Pike
**CREATING THEATRE: The Professionals'
Approach to New Plays**
Interviews dealing with aspects of play
development once the playwright has
mailed out the script
0-394-74279-6 Random House pb $9.95

Directing

• Edward Braun
**THE THEATRE OF MEYERHOLD:
Revolution on the Modern Stage**
0-413-41120-6 RC&H pb $22.00

• Michael Chekhov
**TO THE DIRECTOR AND
PLAYWRIGHT**
The playwright's nephew synthesizes some
of the most important ideas in the modern
theater
Edited by Charles Leonard
0-87910-018-4 Limelight pb $9.95

• Harold Clurman
ON DIRECTING
This historically interesting and amusing
book tells how Clurman got the young
Marlon Brando to stop mumbling, and
more
0-02-526410-9 Macmillan $13.95
0-02-013350-2 Macmillan pb $10.95

• Nikolai M. Gorchakov
STANISLAVSKY DIRECTS
This pupil kept notes and diaries between
1924 and 1936, while Stanislavsky lectured
and worked on five productions
Translated by Miriam Goldina
0-87910-051-6 Limelight pb $10.95

• Charles Marowitz
**PROSPERO'S STAFF: Acting and
Directing in the Contemporary Theatre**
0-253-34622-3 Indiana $22.50

• David Selbourne, editor
**THE MAKING OF A MIDSUMMER
NIGHT'S DREAM**
An eyewitness backstage account of Peter
Brook's famous production
0-413-53230-5 RC&H pb $12.95

• Konstantin Stanislavsky
**STANISLAVSKY ON THE ART OF THE
STAGE**
Translated with an introduction by David Magarshack
0-571-08172-X Faber & Faber pb $11.95

• Alexander Tairov
NOTES OF A DIRECTOR
Tairov (1885–1950), one of the great anti-
naturalistic directors of the Russian
theater, did much of his work in
opposition to the party line
0-87024-309-8 Miami pb $9.95

Professional Training and Advice

• Simon Callow
BEING AN ACTOR
An introspective and helpful book by an
English actor about his trade
0-312-07276-7 St. Martin's $13.95

• Ronald Hayman
HOW TO READ A PLAY
A straightforward introduction to dramatic
analysis
0-8021-3042-9 Grove pb $7.95

• Gordon Hunt
HOW TO AUDITION
0-06-463490-6 Harper & Row pb $6.95

• Katinka Matson
**THE WORKING ACTOR: A Guide to the
Profession**
0-14-046343-7 Penguin pb $4.95

• Michael Shurtleff
**AUDITION: Everything an Actor Needs to
Know**
Introduction by Bob Fosse
0-553-27295-0 Bantam pb $4.95

Acting

• Brian Bates
**THE WAY OF THE ACTOR: A Path to
Knowledge and Power**
A psychologist who worked at the Royal
Academy of Dramatic Arts compares actors
to shamans and seers who possess special
powers
0-87773-384-8 Shambhala $15.95
0-87773-441-0 Shambhala pb $9.95

• Robert L. Benedetti
THE ACTOR AT WORK
0-13-003732-X Prentice-Hall $34.00

• Richard Boleslavsky
ACTING: The First Six Lessons
A classic that bridges the Russian tradition
and the American "Method"
0-87830-000-7 Theatre Arts $16.95

• Michael Chekhov
**LESSONS FOR THE PROFESSIONAL
ACTOR**
Another classic work
Edited by Deirdre Hurst du Prey
Introduction by Mel Gordon
0-933826-79-6 Performing Arts $19.95
0-933826-80-X Performing Arts pb $8.95

• Toby Cole & Helen K. Chinoy,
editors
ACTORS ON ACTING
A store of historical information and
experiences
0-517-50299-2 Crown $12.95
0-517-54048-7 Crown pb $9.95

• Uta Hagen & Haskel Frankel
RESPECT FOR ACTING
An acclaimed book by the distinguished
actress
0-02-547390-5 Macmillan $16.95

• Bertram Joseph
ACTING SHAKESPEARE
One of the best practical books on
Shakespeare
0-87830-522-X Theatre Arts pb $7.95

• Joshua Karton, editor
FILM SCENES FOR ACTORS
These useful paperbacks are based on the
premise that film acting is best practiced
with scenes from great scenarios
Volume 1
0-553-25434-0 Bantam pb $4.95
Volume 2
0-553-26804-X Bantam pb $4.95

• Robert Lewis
ADVICE TO THE PLAYERS
One of the major exponents of "Method"
acting reveals a lifetime of experience
Introduction by Harold Clurman
0-06-012615-9 Harper & Row $14.95

• Sanford Meisner & Dennis Longwell
SANFORD MEISNER ON ACTING
A detailed transcription of a great acting
teacher's classes and methods
0-394-75059-4 Random House pb $8.95

• Sonia Moore
**THE STANISLAVSKI SYSTEM: The
Professional Training of an Actor**
Introduction by Joshua Logan
Preface by John Gielgud
0-14-046660-6 Penguin pb $4.95

From Passionate Journey *by Franz Masereel
(City Lights)*

🐛 **IF YOU CAN'T FIND IT, LOOK IN THE INDEX**

- Laurence Olivier
  ON ACTING
  0–671–64562–5 Simon & Schuster pb $8.95

- Frank Pike & Thomas G. Dunn
  SCENES AND MONOLOGUES FROM THE NEW AMERICAN THEATER
  0–451–62547–1 NAL pb $4.95

Constantin Stanislavksi
CREATING A ROLE
Translated by Elizabeth R. Hapgood
Edited by Hermine I. Popper
0–87830–024–4 Theatre Arts $16.95
0–87830–981–0 RC&H pb $14.95

AN ACTOR PREPARES
0–87830–001–5 Theatre Arts $18.95
0–87830–983–7 RC&H pb $14.95

BUILDING A CHARACTER
0–87830–012–0 Theatre Arts $16.95
0–87830–982–9 RC&H pb $14.95

- Lee Strasberg
  A DREAM OF PASSION: The Development of the Method
  The "Method" from the horse's mouth
  0–316–81870–4 Little, Brown $16.50

Design

- Arnold Aronson
  AMERICAN SET DESIGN
  0–930452–39–9 Theatre Comm pb $16.95

- Jarka Burian
  THE SCENOGRAPHY OF JOSEF SVOBODA
  The Czech designer has exercised great international influence in theater and opera
  0–8195–6032–4 Wesleyan pb $12.95

- Robert Edmond Jones
  THE DRAMATIC IMAGINATION
  One of the few classics about design by the man who dominated American stage design between the wars
  0–87830–035–X Theatre Arts pb $8.95

- Oren W. Parker & Harvey K. Smith
  SCENE DESIGN AND STAGE LIGHTING
  0–03–064248–5 Holt, Rinehart & Winston $29.95

- Frank Rich & Lisa Aronson
  THE THEATRE ART OF BORIS ARONSON
  A richly illustrated tribute to one of the great stage designers
  0–394–52913–8 Knopf $75.00

- Terry Thomas
  CREATE YOUR OWN STAGE SETS
  0–13–189077–8 Prentice-Hall pb $9.95

Stagecraft and Administration

- Lehman Engel
  GETTING THE SHOW ON: The Complete Guidebook
  0–02–87080–3 Macmillan $14.95

- Joann Green
  THE SMALL THEATRE HANDBOOK: A Guide to Management and Production
  0–916782–19–0 Harvard Common $11.95
  0–916782–20–4 Harvard Common pb $8.95

- Francis Reid
  THE STAGING HANDBOOK
  0–87830–160–7 Theatre Arts $14.95

GIFT AND PICTURE BOOKS

- Stanley Appelbaum, editor
  THE NEW YORK STAGE: Famous Productions in Photographs
  A fascinating collection of stills
  0–486–23241–7 Dover pb $8.95

- Daniel Blum
  A PICTORIAL HISTORY OF THE AMERICAN THEATRE, 1860–1985
  Edited by John Willis
  0–517–56258–8 Crown $29.95

- Fred Fehl & others
  ON BROADWAY
  Fehl's performance photographs from the 1940s and '50s are enhanced by quotes, reminiscences, and anecdotes
  0–292–76010–8 Texas $29.95
  0–306–80125–6 Da Capo pb $13.50

Peter Hay
THEATRICAL ANECDOTES
"Not only a source of amusement and wit, this book also encapsulates most of the social history of the theatre in England and America"—Martin Esslin
0–19–503818–5 Oxford $19.95

- George Perry
  THE COMPLETE PHANTOM OF THE OPERA
  Contains Andrew Lloyd Weber's libretto, much peripheral information, and photos
  0–8050–0657–5 Henry Holt $24.95

SELECTED DRAMA ANTHOLOGIES

- Sylvan Barnet, editor
  EIGHT GREAT COMEDIES
  Includes *The Clouds, Mandragola, Twelfth Night, The Miser, The Beggar's Opera, The Importance of Being Earnest, Uncle Vanya,* and *Arms and the Man*
  0–451–62364–9 NAL pb $4.95

- Harold Clurman, editor
  NINE PLAYS OF THE MODERN THEATER
  Includes *Waiting for Godot, The Visit, Tango, The Caucasian Chalk Circle, The Balcony, Rhinoceros, American Buffalo, The Birthday Party,* and *Rosencrantz and Guildenstern Are Dead*
  0–8021–5032–2 Grove pb $16.95

- Ramon L. Delgado, editor
  THE BEST SHORT PLAYS OF 1988
  1–55783–026–6 Applause pb $10.95

- Julia Miles, editor
  THE WOMEN'S PROJECT: Seven New Plays by Women
  0–933826–07–9 Performing Arts pb $9.95

  WOMEN'S PROJECT 2: Five New Plays by Women
  0–933826–74–5 Performing Arts pb $8.95

- Eileen J. Ostrow, editor
  CENTER STAGE: An Anthology of 21 Contemporary Black American Plays
  Introduction by Sandra L. Richards
  0–9605208–0–5 Sea Urchin pb $19.95

- Michelene Wandor & Mary Remnant, editors
  PLAYS BY WOMEN

  Volume 1
  0–413–50020–9 RC&H pb $10.95

  Volume 2
  0–413–51030–1 RC&H pb $10.95

  Volume 3
  0–413–54300–5 RC&H pb $10.95

  Volume 4
  0–413–56740–0 RC&H pb $10.95

  Volume 5
  0–413–41570–8 RC&H pb $10.95

  Volume 6
  0–413–14080–6 RC&H pb $13.95

REFERENCE

- Martin Banham, editor
  THE CAMBRIDGE GUIDE TO WORLD THEATRE
  0–521–26595–9 Cambridge $49.50

- Gerald Bordman
  THE OXFORD COMPANION TO AMERICAN THEATRE
  An encyclopedia of the major figures, plays, historical trends from colonial times to the present
  0–19–503443–0 Oxford $49.95

- Walter P. Bowman & Robert H. Ball
  THEATRE LANGUAGE: A Dictionary
  0–87830–551–3 Theatre Arts pb $8.95

- Steve Fletcher & Norman Jopling, editors
  THE BOOK OF A THOUSAND PLAYS
  Essential information about *Hamlet, Death of a Salesman, Damn Yankees,* and hundreds of other frequently performed plays
  0–8160–2121–X Facts On File $24.95

- Stanley Green
  ENCYCLOPEDIA OF THE MUSICAL THEATRE
  Contains complete listings of productions and personalities of the British and American musical to the 1970s
  0–306–80113–2 Da Capo pb $14.95

- Phyllis Hartnoll, editor
THE OXFORD COMPANION TO THE THEATRE
Despite some shortcomings, this encyclopedia is the most up-to-date reference book about world theater
0-19-211546-4 Oxford $49.95

- Lee A. Morrow
THE TONY AWARD BOOK: Four Decades of Great American Theater
0-89659-771-7 Abbeville $55.00

- Isabelle Stevenson
THE TONY AWARD: A Complete Listing of Winners and Nominees with a History of the American Theater Wing
0-517-56664-8 Crown $14.95

ROBERT BRUSTEIN: Favorite Books on the Theater

Aristotle
ARISTOTLE'S POETICS
0-393-95216-9 Norton pb $5.95

Eric Bentley
THE PLAYWRIGHT AS THINKER: A Study of Drama in Modern Times
0-15-672041-8 HBJ pb $9.95

Anton Chekhov
THE OXFORD CHEKHOV

Volume 1: Short Plays
0-19-211349-6 Oxford $44.00

Volume 2: Platonov, Ivanov, The Seagull
0-19-211347-X Oxford $44.00

Volume 3: Uncle Vanya, The Three Sisters, The Cherry Orchard, The Wood Demon
0-19021339-9 Oxford $44.00

Francis Fergusson
THE IDEA OF A THEATER
0-691-06143-2 Princeton $33.50
0-691-01288-1 Princeton pb $10.95

Henrik Ibsen
CORRESPONDENCE
0-8383-1098-2 Haskell $49.95

Jan Kott
SHAKESPEARE OUR CONTEMPORARY
0-393-00736-7 Norton pb $9.95

Friedrich Nietzsche
THE BIRTH OF TRAGEDY
0-394-70369-3 Random House pb $5.95

George Bernard Shaw
DRAMATIC CRITICISM: 1895-98
0-8371-5234-8 Greenwood $29.95

Stark Young
THE FLOWER IN DRAMA AND GLAMOUR: Theater Essays and Criticisms
0-374-98840-4 Hippocrene $19.00

Film

When the pioneering filmmaker Louis Lumière abandoned movie production at the turn of the century, he dismissed the medium as being without commercial potential. By the 1920s, movies were established as both the primary form of mass entertainment and, for many visionaries, as "the art of the 20th century."

Three decades ago, film history consisted largely of Griffith, Chaplin, and the Odessa Steps; a close-up was a close-up, montage was montage, and that was about all the theory you needed to get by. Around 1960, new elements emerged in rapid succession: the New Wave, the auteur theory, the pop obsession with Hollywood imagery, the breaching of censorship barriers, the surfacing of the underground. With the elevation of film studies to full academic stature came an industry devoted to churning out monographs, filmographies, and theoretical treatises: a flood that shows no signs of abating. The trick is to uncover, amid heaps of glorified fan mail, cut-and-paste nostalgia, and dutifully dull scholarship, the smaller pile of books that really prompt a refreshment of vision.

INTRODUCTIONS AND GENERAL HISTORIES

The movies do not lend themselves to broad overview. Large-scale histories suffer from the fact that there are simply too many movies. Even the best of such surveys tend to rely on convenient generalizations and relentless pigeonholing to tie together their disparate subject matter. The following reasonably up-to-date books do their best with a thankless task.

- Erik Barnouw
DOCUMENTARY: A History of the Non-Fiction Film
A useful supplement, since most histories focus on fiction films
0-19-503301-9 Oxford pb $9.95

- David Bordwell & Kristin Thompson
FILM ART: An Introduction
A serviceable tour of the film-studies syllabus, incorporating recent critical trends
0-394-35237-8 Knopf pb $22.95

- Ivan Butler
SILENT IMAGE: Rediscovering the Silent Cinema
0-8044-2078-5 Ungar $24.95

- Gerald Mast
A SHORT HISTORY OF THE MOVIES
0-672-61521-5 Pegasus pb $20.00

- James Monaco
HOW TO READ A FILM
A useful introductory study of the art and technology of film, with an extensive bibliography
0-19-502806-6 Oxford pb $15.95

- Eric Rhode
A HISTORY OF THE CINEMA: From Its Origins to 1970
Rhode was a long-term contributor to the English magazine *Sight and Sound*
0-306-80233-3 Da Capo pb $13.95

- David Shipman
THE STORY OF CINEMA: A Complete Narrative History from the Beginnings to the Present
Preface by Ingmar Bergman
0-312-76280-1 St. Martin's pb $19.95

NATIONAL CINEMAS

France

- Richard Abel
FRENCH CINEMA: The First Wave, 1915-1929
A densely researched, groundbreaking study
0-691-00813-2 Princeton pb $27.50

- Roy Armes
FRENCH CINEMA
0-19-520471-9 Oxford $32.00
0-19-520472-7 Oxford pb $12.95

Mary Lea Bandy, editor
REDISCOVERING FRENCH FILM
A series of interesting and unusual essays, published in conjunction with the Museum of Modern Art's memorable French film series
Introduction by Richard Roud
0-316-72935-3 NY Graphic Society pb $15.50

- James Monaco
THE NEW WAVE: Truffaut, Godard, Chabrol, Rohmer, Rivette
0-19-502246-7 Oxford pb $10.95

- Anthony Slide
FIFTY CLASSIC FRENCH FILMS, 1912-1982: A Pictorial Record
0-486-25256-6 Dover pb $11.95

Germany

- Timothy Corrigan
NEW GERMAN FILM: The Displaced Image
Critical studies of films by Wenders, Herzog, Syberberg, Schlöndorff, Fassbinder, and Kluge
0-292-71087-9 Texas pb $10.95

   IF YOU CAN'T FIND IT, LOOK IN THE INDEX

Lotte Eisner
THE HAUNTED SCREEN
Eisner was the great chronicler of
German expressionism, its roots and its
impact
Translated by Roger Greaves
0–520–02479–6 California pb $11.95

- Thomas Elsaesser
NEW GERMAN CINEMA: A History
0–8135–1392–8 Rutgers pb $14.95

- John Kobal
**GREAT FILM STILLS OF THE
GERMAN SILENT ERA**
0–486–24195–5 Dover pb $8.95

- Siegfreid Kracauer
**FROM CALIGARI TO HITLER: A
Psychological History of the German Film**
Kracauer uncovers proto-Nazi elements in
the classics of German expressionism
0–691–02505–3 Princeton pb $9.95

- John Sandford
THE NEW GERMAN CINEMA
0–389–20015–8 Barnes & Noble $27.50
0–306–80177–9 Da Capo pb $13.95

Great Britain

- Roy Armes
**A CRITICAL HISTORY OF BRITISH
CINEMA**
0–19–520043–8 Oxford $45.00

- Charles Barr
EALING STUDIOS
The story of the studio that produced such
successful comedies as *Passport to Pimlico*
and *Kind Hearts and Coronets*
0–87951–101–X Overlook $19.95
0–87951–147–8 Overlook pb $13.95

- Charles Barr, editor
**ALL OUR YESTERDAYS: 90 Years of
British Cinema**
An entertaining collection of essays, with
many illustrations
0–85170–179–5 Illinois pb $19.95

- Michael Korda
CHARMED LIVES
A memoir of Alexander, Zoltan, and
Vincent Korda, by the latter's son
0–394–41954–5 Random House $15.00
0–380–53017–1 Avon pb $3.95

- Anthony Slide
**FIFTY CLASSIC BRITISH FILMS,
1932–1982**
0–486–24860–7 Dover pb $11.95

Italy

- Peter Bondanella
**ITALIAN CINEMA: From Neorealism to
the Present**
0–8044–6061–2 Harper & Row pb $14.95

- Mira Liehm
**PASSION AND DEFIANCE: Italian Film
from 1942 to the Present**
0–520–05744–9 California pb $12.95

Akira Kurosawa, from his book Something Like an Autobiography *(photo by Akihide Tamura,
courtesy of Knopf)*

- Millicent Marcus
**ITALIAN FILM IN THE LIGHT OF
NEOREALISM**
0–691–10208–2 Princeton pb $17.50

- Roger Witcombe
THE NEW ITALIAN CINEMA
0–19–520381–X Oxford $24.95

Japan

- Joseph L. Anderson & Donald Richie
THE JAPANESE FILM: Art and Industry
This recently revised study remains the best
survey
Foreword by Akira Kurosawa
0–691–00792–6 Princeton pb $14.50

- Audie Bock
JAPANESE FILM DIRECTORS
Includes studies of Ozu, Mizoguchi,
Kurosawa, and Oshima
0–87011–714–9 Kodansha pb $14.95

- Noel Burch
**TO THE DISTANT OBSERVER: Form
and Meaning in Japanese Cinema**
An intellectually dense, graphically
beautiful book; Burch gives preference to
pre-war films, which he considers more
original in style
0–520–03877–0 California pb $12.95

- David Desser
**EROS PLUS MASSACRE: An
Introduction to the Japanese New Wave
Cinema**
A thematic survey of Japan's New Wave,
focusing on the work of such directors as
Oshima, Shinoda, Imamura, and Yoshida
0–253–20469–0 Indiana pb $12.95

- Joan Mellen
**THE WAVES AT GENJI'S DOOR: Japan
Through Its Cinema**
A predominantly social analysis
0–394–73278–2 Pantheon pb $8.95

- Donald Richie
THE JAPANESE MOVIE
0–87011–489–1 Kodansha $22.95

- Tadao Sato
CURRENTS IN JAPANESE CINEMA
Essays on a variety of topics by one of
Japan's leading film critics
Translated by Gregory Barrett
0–87011–815–3 Kodansha pb $13.95

- Alain Silver
THE SAMURAI FILM
0–87951–246–6 Overlook pb $12.95

Other Countries

When one talks of cinema, one talks of
American cinema. The influence of cinema is the influence of American cinema,
which is the most aggressive and widespread aspect of American culture
throughout the world. For this reason,
every discussion of cinema made outside
Hollywood must begin with Hollywood.

Roy Armes
**THIRD WORLD FILM MAKING AND
THE WEST**
0–520–05690–6 California $17.95

- Brian McFarlane
AUSTRALIAN CINEMA
0–231–06728–3 Columbia $27.50

- Eric Reade
**HISTORY AND HEARTBURN: The Saga
of Australian Film, 1896–1978**
0–8386–3082–0 Fairleigh Dickinson $60.00

- Graham Shirley & Brian Adams
**AUSTRALIAN CINEMA: The First 80
Years**
0–312–06126–9 St. Martin's $27.50

- Randal Johnson
**CINEMA NOVO X 5: Masters of
Contemporary Brazilian Film**
0–292–71090–9 Texas pb $22.50

- Randal Johnson & Robert Stam,
editors
BRAZILIAN CINEMA
0–292–70767–3 Texas pb $12.95

• Jay Leyda
DIANYING—ELECTRIC SHADOWS: An Account of Films and the Film Audience in China
0–262–62030–8 MIT pb $7.95

• Michael Chanan
THE CUBAN IMAGE: Cinema and Cultural Politics in Cuba
0–253–21261–8 Indiana pb $12.95

• Istvan Nemeskurty
A SHORT HISTORY OF THE HUNGARIAN CINEMA
963–13–1101–5 Zoetrope pb $4.95

• Julianne Burton, editor
CINEMA AND SOCIAL CHANGE IN LATIN AMERICA
0–292–72454–3 Texas pb $10.95

• Carl J. Mora
MEXICAN CINEMA: Reflections of a Society
0–520–04287–5 California $37.50

• Mira Liehm & Antonin Liehm
THE MOST IMPORTANT ART: Soviet and East European Film After 1945
0–520–04128–3 California pb $10.95

• Neya Zorkaya
THE ILLUSTRATED HISTORY OF SOVIET CINEMA
0–87052–560–3 Hippocrene $25.00

• Virginia Higginbotham
SPANISH FILM UNDER FRANCO
0–292–77603–9 Texas pb $9.95

• Roy Armes
THIRD WORLD FILM MAKING AND THE WEST
The first fully comprehensive account of film production in Third World countries which, though usually ignored and marginalized in histories of "world cinema," now produce well over half of the world's films
0–520–05690–6 California pb $17.95

FILM IN AMERICA

• Kenneth Anger
HOLLYWOOD BABYLON
The famously scurrilous account of filmland scandals by the director of *Scorpio Rising*

Volume 1
0–440–15325–5 Doubleday pb $6.95

Volume 2
0–452–25721–2 NAL pb $12.95

• Steven Bach
FINAL CUT: Dreams and Disaster in the Making of Heaven's Gate
0–451–40036–4 NAL pb $4.95

• Tino Balio
UNITED ARTISTS: The Company Built by the Stars
0–299–06944–3 Wisconsin pb $14.95

UNITED ARTISTS: The Company That Changed the Film Industry
Carries on Balio's account of the studio from 1951 onward
0–299–11440–6 Wisconsin $32.50

• Tino Balio, editor
THE AMERICAN FILM INDUSTRY
A large compendium of academic essays on industry structure and filmmaking practices
0–299–09874–5 Wisconsin pb $14.95

• Rudy Behlmer, editor
INSIDE WARNER BROTHERS: 1935–1951
Film history recreated most entertainingly through a selection of in-house memos
0–670–80478–9 Viking $19.95
0–671–63135–7 Simon & Schuster pb $8.95

• Andrew Bergman
WE'RE IN THE MONEY
The novelist and director writes sympathetically of Depression-era movies
0–06–131948–1 Harper & Row pb $5.95

• Paul F. Boller, Jr. & Ronald L. Davis
HOLLYWOOD ANECDOTES
0–345–35654–3 Ballantine pb $10.95

• David Bordwell & others
THE CLASSICAL HOLLYWOOD CINEMA: Film Style and Mode of Production to 1960
The technical norms that conditioned American movies between 1917 and 1960. By far the most comprehensive book of its kind, it typifies current concern for ordinary rather than extraordinary films
0–231–06055–6 Columbia pb $25.00

• Kevin Brownlow
THE PARADE'S GONE BY . . .
A beautifully designed book about the glories of silent filmmaking
0–520–03068–0 California pb $17.95

• Larry Ceplair & Steven Englund
THE INQUISITION IN HOLLYWOOD: Politics in the Film Community, 1930–1960
An exceptionally detailed account of the background of Hollywood's political wars
0–520–04886–5 California pb $12.95

Greta Garbo, from The Parade's Gone By . . . *by Kevin Brownlow (Knopf)*

• Tom Dardis
SOME TIME IN THE SUN: The Hollywood Years of F. Scott Fitzgerald, William Faulkner, Nathaniel West, Aldous Huxley, and James Agee
0–87910–116–4 Limelight pb $12.95

• John Gregory Dunne
THE STUDIO
A study of 20th Century-Fox
0–87910–031–1 Limelight pb $7.95

• William Everson
THE AMERICAN SILENT FILM
0–19–503208–X Oxford pb $9.95

• Stephen Farber & Marc Green
OUTRAGEOUS CONDUCT: Art, Ego, and the Twilight Zone Case
An account of the investigation into the death of Vic Morrow and two child actors on the set of *The Twilight Zone: The Movie*, which led to the indictment of director John Landis and others
0–87795–948–X Arbor House $18.95

• Joel W. Finler
THE HOLLYWOOD STORY
0–517–56576–5 Crown $35.00

Otto Friedrich
CITY OF NETS
A collage-portrait of Hollywood in the 1940s, constructed from a wide range of anecdotes that Friedrich weaves together ingeniously
0–06–091439–4 Harper & Row pb $10.95

• Neal Gabler
AN EMPIRE OF THEIR OWN: How the Jews Invented Hollywood
An examination of the careers of Samuel Goldwyn, Louis B. Mayer, and other movie producers, showing how they successfully imposed their fantasies of American life
0–517–56808–X Crown $24.95

• David McClintick
INDECENT EXPOSURE: A True Story of Hollywood and Wall Street
The lowdown on the David Begelman scandal
0–440–14007–2 Dell pb $5.95

• Barry Norman
THE STORY OF HOLLYWOOD
"Brings a fresh outlook to an always fascinating saga with firsthand observations that make it come to life"—Leonard Maltin
0–453–00589–6 NAL $19.95

• Andrew Sarris
THE AMERICAN CINEMA: Directors and Directions, 1929–1968
Sarris' influential rating of American directors, from the "pantheon" on down, with filmographies up to 1968; a classic statement of the auteurist position
0–226–73500–1 Chicago pb $11.95

✉ TO ORDER BOOKS AS GIFTS, SEE PAGE 1

• Thomas Schatz
THE GENIUS OF THE SYSTEM:
Hollywood Filmmaking in the Studio Era
A study of how the Hollywood system really worked, with emphasis on Warner Brothers, MGM, Universal, and Selznick International
0–394–53979–6 Pantheon $24.95

• P. Adams Sitney
VISIONARY FILM: The American Avant-Garde, 1943–1978
0–19–502486–9 Oxford pb $14.95

• Raymond W. Stedman
THE SERIALS: Suspense and Drama by Installment
0–8061–1695–1 Oklahoma pb $14.95

• John Taylor
STORMING THE MAGIC KINGDOM:
Wall Street, the Raiders, and the Battle for Disney
0–345–35407–9 Ballantine pb $9.95

• Tony Thomas & Aubrey Solomon
THE FILMS OF 20TH CENTURY-FOX
Year-by-year synopses and stills
0–8065–0958–9 Citadel $34.95

• Mason Wiley & Damien Bona
INSIDE OSCAR: The Unofficial History of the Academy Awards
0–345–34777–3 Ballantine pb $15.95

• Robin Wood
HOLLYWOOD FROM VIETNAM TO REAGAN
Wood combines formal analysis with an intensely political reading of recent American film
0–231–05777–6 Columbia pb $12.50

GENRES AND THEMES

• Jeanine Basinger
THE WORLD WAR II COMBAT FILM:
Anatomy of a Genre
An analytical study of *The Dirty Dozen, Tora Tora Tora!*, and many others
0–231–05953–1 Columbia pb $14.95

• Donald Bogle
TOMS, COONS, MULATTOES, MAMMIES AND BUCKS
A historical overview of how Hollywood has portrayed blacks
0–8264–0416–2 Harper & Row pb $14.95

• Stanley Cavell
PURSUITS OF HAPPINESS: The Hollywood Comedy of Remarriages
0–674–73906–X Harvard pb $8.95

• Mary Anne Doane
THE DESIRE TO DESIRE: The Woman's Film of the 1940s
"Insightful elaboration of the mechanics of the assertion and denial of desire in the four subgenres of the woman's film"—*Film Quarterly*
0–253–20433–X Indiana pb $12.50

• Derek Elley
THE EPIC FILM: Myth and History
Elley takes on all the costume spectacles, from *Samson and Delilah* to *Hercules and the Captive Women*, and produces an amusing yet remarkably serious book
0–7100–9993–2 RC&H pb $13.95

• George MacDonald Fraser
THE HOLLYWOOD HISTORY OF THE WORLD
0–688–07520–7 Morrow $24.95

• Barry Gifford
THE DEVIL THUMBS A RIDE & Other Unforgettable Films
Quick recaps of dozens of *film noir* classics and near-classics, along with some unclassifiably bizarre items, narrated with much verve and humor
0–8021–3078–X Grove pb $7.95

• Stanley Green
ENCYCLOPEDIA OF THE MUSICAL FILM
0–19–505421–0 Oxford pb $13.95

• Phil Hardy
THE ENCYCLOPEDIA OF HORROR MOVIES
0–06–055050–3 Harper & Row $34.50

• James Harvey
ROMANTIC COMEDY: In Hollywood from Lubitsch to Sturges
An enthusiastic and knowledgeable survey of screwball and other trends of the 1930s and 1940s, with beautifully reproduced stills
0–394–50339–2 Knopf $35.00

• Molly Haskell
FROM REVERENCE TO RAPE: The Treatment of Women in the Movies
0–226–31885–0 Chicago pb $14.95

• Foster Hirsch
THE DARK SIDE OF THE SCREEN:
Film Noir
0–306–80203–1 Da Capo pb $14.95

• Robert P. Kolker
A CINEMA OF LONELINESS: Penn, Kubrick, Scorsese, Spielberg, Altman
0–19–503390–7 Oxford pb $16.95

• Jeffrey Richards
SWORDSMEN OF THE SCREEN: From Douglas Fairbanks to Michael York
0–7100–0681–0 RC&H pb $10.95

• Alan Rosenthal
THE DOCUMENTARY CONSCIENCE: A Casebook in Filmmaking
0–520–04022–8 California pb $11.95

• Alan Rosenthal, editor
NEW CHALLENGES FOR DOCUMENTARY
0–520–05724–4 California pb $18.95

• Vito Russo
THE CELLULOID CLOSET:
Homosexuality in the Movies
A groundbreaking study of overt and covert homosexual themes in Hollywood films
0–06–090871–8 Harper & Row pb $10.95

• Linda J. Sandahl
ROCK FILMS: A Viewer's Guide to Three Decades of Musicals, Concerts, Documentaries and Soundtracks
0–8160–1576–7 Facts On File pb $14.95

• Paul Schrader
TRANSCENDENTAL STYLE IN FILM:
Ozu, Bresson, Dreyer
0–306–80335–6 Da Capo pb $11.95

• Ted Sennett
LUNATICS AND LOVERS: The Golden Age of Hollywood Comedy
0–87910–041–9 Limelight pb $10.95

• Alain Silver & Elizabeth Ward, editors
FILM NOIR: An Encyclopedic Reference to the American Style
"Some 300 American movies distinguished by a somber and cynical mood, morose anti-heroes, and low-key photography are surveyed in a well-researched and deftly analytical work"—*American Cinematographer*
0–87951–326–8 Overlook pb $17.95

• Vivian Sobchack
SCREENING SPACE: The American Science Fiction Film
A detailed and subtle survey, with many illustrations. "Her writing style is clear, witty and concise as she shapes new definitions of the SF film"—*Film Bulletin*
0–8044–6886–9 Ungar pb $14.95

DIRECTORS

Making a film means, first of all, to tell a story. That story can be an improbable one, but it should never be banal. It must be dramatic and human. What is drama, after all, but life with the dull bits cut out.—Alfred Hitchcock

François Truffaut
HITCHCOCK
0–671–52601–4 Simon & Schuster $19.95

• Ellen Cumano
FILM FORUM: 35 Top Filmmakers Discuss Their Craft
Cumano intercuts separate interviews in order to create a compendium on film technique
0–312–28933–2 St. Martin's pb $9.95

• Eric Sherman
DIRECTING THE FILM: Film Directors on Their Art
The filmmaking process from start to finish, in the words of 75 directors
0–918226–15–5 Acrobat pb $14.95

- Edwin T. Arnold & Eugene L. Miller
THE FILMS AND CAREER OF ROBERT ALDRICH
A biographical and critical study of the director of *Kiss Me Deadly* and *Vera Cruz*, written in close collaboration with Aldrich
0–87049–504–6 Tennessee $24.95

- Robert Benayoun
THE FILMS OF WOODY ALLEN
A nice compendium of Allen stills illustrate a rather humorless text by the editor of the French film magazine *Positif*
Translated by Alexander Walker
0–517–56928–0 Crown pb $16.95

- Thierry de Navacelle
WOODY ALLEN ON LOCATION
0–688–06643–7 Morrow $18.95

- Michelangelo Antonioni
THAT BOWLING ALLEY ON THE TIBER: Tales of a Director
Stories, sketches, and ideas for films
Translated by William Arrowsmith
0–19–504224–7 Oxford pb $8.95

- Ingmar Bergman
THE MAGIC LANTERN: An Autobiography
0–670–81911–5 Viking $19.95

- Stig Bjorkman & others
BERGMAN ON BERGMAN: Interviews with Ingmar Bergman
0–671–22157–4 Simon & Schuster pb $9.95

- Robert P. Kolker
BERNARDO BERTOLUCCI
0–19–520492–1 Oxford $21.95

- Michel Ciment
JOHN BOORMAN
Superbly designed graphic analysis of recurring patterns in such films as *Point Blank, Zardoz*, and *Excalibur*
0–571–13831–4 Faber & Faber $49.95

- J. Francisco Aranda
LUIS BUNUEL: A Critical Biography
0–306–80028–4 Da Capo pb $9.95

- Luis Buñuel
MY LAST SIGH
0–394–72501–8 Random House pb $6.95

- Raymond Durgnat
LUIS BUNUEL
0–520–03424–4 California pb $8.95

- Frank Capra
THE NAME ABOVE THE TITLE: An Autobiography
0–394–71205–6 Random House pb $9.95

- Susan Dworkin
DOUBLE DE PALMA: A Film Study with Brian De Palma
0–937858–43–9 Newmarket pb $8.95

David Bordwell
THE FILMS OF CARL-THEODOR DREYER
An exceptionally rigorous and intelligent formal analysis, elegantly illustrated
0–520–04450–9 California pb $14.95

- Sergei Eisenstein
IMMORAL MEMORIES: An Autobiography
0–395–36569–4 Houghton Mifflin pb $13.95
NOTES OF A FILM DIRECTOR
0–486–22392–2 Dover pb $7.95

- Robert Katz
LOVE IS COLDER THAN DEATH: The Life and Times of Rainer Werner Fassbinder
A gossipy, *Hollywood Babylon*-style account of the German director's tumultuous life
0–394–53456–5 Random House $19.95

- Hollis Alpert
FELLINI: A Life
1–55778–000–5 Paragon pb $9.95

- Paul Rotha
ROBERT J. FLAHERTY: A Biography
0–8122–7887–9 Pennsylvania $28.95

- Tag Gallagher
JOHN FORD: The Man and His Films
Thoroughgoing review of Ford's films, elaborately researched
0–317–67094–8 California pb $14.95

- Joseph McBride & Michael Wilmington
JOHN FORD
0–306–80016–0 Da Capo pb $9.95

- Raymond Durgnat
FRANJU
A study of the director of *Le Sang des Bêtes* and *Eyes Without a Face*
0–520–00367–5 California pb $5.95

- Kevin Brownlow
NAPOLEON: Abel Gance's Silent Classic
Detailed presentation of the silent masterpiece that Brownlow helped reconstruct
0–394–72116–0 Knopf pb $14.95

- Jean Narboni & Tom Milne, editors
GODARD ON GODARD
A compendium of Godard's inimitably paradoxical pronouncements
0–306–80259–7 Da Capo pb $10.95

- Joseph McBride
HAWKS ON HAWKS
The director looks back at his career in this series of late interviews
0–520–04552–1 California pb $9.95

- Gerald Mast
HOWARD HAWKS, STORYTELLER
0–19–503233–0 Oxford pb $10.95

- Timothy Corrigan
THE FILMS OF WERNER HERZOG
0–416–41070–7 RC&H pb $14.95

- Marshall Deutelbaum & Leland Poague, editors
A HITCHCOCK READER
A collection of essays illustrating the range of intellectual response that Hitchcock's work is currently eliciting
0–8138–0892–8 Iowa State pb $19.95

- Leonard J. Luff
HITCHCOCK AND SELZNICK
An absorbing account of the often troubled collaboration that produced *Rebecca, Notorious,* and other films
1–55584–272–0 Weidenfeld & Nicholson pb $11.95

- Tania Modleski
THE WOMEN WHO KNEW TOO MUCH: Hitchcock and Feminist Theory
0–416–01711–8 RC&H pb $10.95

- Eric Rohmer & Claude Chabrol
HITCHCOCK: The First 44 Films
Dated, but extremely influential; an often outrageous instance of the *Cahiers du Cinéma* style at its most unrestrained
Translated by Stanley Hochman
0–8044–6749–8 Ungar pb $8.95

- William Rothman
HITCHCOCK: The Murderous Gaze
Sharply focused readings of selected films in terms of recurrent obsessive images
0–674–40411–4 Harvard pb $14.00

- Donald Spoto
THE ART OF ALFRED HITCHCOCK
The best general study of Hitchcock's work
0–385–15569–7 Doubleday pb $15.95
THE DARK SIDE OF GENIUS: The Life of Alfred Hitchcock
In case anyone wonders, Hitchcock was not the happiest of men. Spoto spells out the grimmer side of his career and in the process casts new light on many details of his films
0–316–80723–0 Little, Brown $24.50
0–345–31462–X Ballantine pb $4.95

- François Truffaut
HITCHCOCK
A pioneering book of interviews that can also serve as an introduction to film technique
Translated by Helen G. Scott
0–671–52601–4 Simon & Schuster $19.95
0–671–20346–0 Simon & Schuster pb $11.50

- John Huston
AN OPEN BOOK
0–345–25444–9 Ballantine pb $3.95

- Michel Ciment
KAZAN ON KAZAN
0–670–41187–6 Viking $10.00

- Tom Dardis
KEATON: The Man Who Wouldn't Lie Down
0–87910–117–2 Limelight pb $14.95

- Buster Keaton & Charles Samuels
  BUSTER KEATON: My Wonderful World of Slapstick
  Introduction by Dwight Macdonald
  0–306–80178–7 Da Capo pb $9.95

- Akira Kurosawa
  SOMETHING LIKE AN AUTOBIOGRAPHY
  Reminiscences by the director of *Seven Samurai* and *Ran*
  Translated by Audie E. Bock
  0–394–50938–2 Knopf $15.00
  0–394–71439–3 Random House pb $8.95

- Donald Richie
  THE FILMS OF AKIRA KUROSAWA
  0–520–05191–2 California pb $15.95

- Lotte H. Eisner
  FRITZ LANG
  Eisner, a friend of Lang, covers all his films, with much attention to technical aspects
  0–306–80271–6 Da Capo pb $13.95

- Stephen Jenkins, editor
  FRITZ LANG: The Image and the Look
  New theoretical takes on what the semiotically-minded contributors prefer to call "the Lang text"
  0–85170–108–6 Illinois pb $14.95

- Spike Lee
  SPIKE LEE'S GOTTA HAVE IT: Inside Guerrilla Filmmaking
  The making of *She's Gotta Have It*, with the complete screenplay
  0–671–64417–3 Simon & Schuster pb $9.95

- Spike Lee & Lisa Jones
  UPLIFT THE RACE: The Construction of School Daze
  How *School Daze* was made, with the complete screenplay
  0–671–64418–1 Simon & Schuster pb $9.95

- Michel Ciment
  CONVERSATIONS WITH LOSEY
  0–416–40120–1 RC&H pb $16.95

- William Paul
  ERNST LUBITSCH'S AMERICAN COMEDY
  0–231–05681–8 Columbia pb $14.50

- Lotte Eisner
  MURNAU
  A definitive study of the great German director
  0–520–02285–8 California $35.00

- David Bordwell
  OZU AND THE POETICS OF CINEMA
  0–691–00822–1 Princeton pb $25.00

- Donald Richie
  OZU: His Life and Films
  0–520–03277–2 California pb $8.95

Michael Powell
A LIFE IN MOVIES: An Autobiography
A long, anecdotal, immensely diverting autobiography by the director of *The Red Shoes* and *Black Narcissus*, touching on many aspects of early film history and the rise of the British film industry
0–394–55935–5 Knopf $24.95

- Raymond Durgnat
  JEAN RENOIR
  0–520–02743–4 California pb $9.95

- Christopher Faulkner
  THE SOCIAL CINEMA OF JEAN RENOIR
  0–691–06673–6 Princeton $28.00

- Alexander Sesonske
  JEAN RENOIR: The French Years, 1924–1939
  A painstaking account of what many would consider the major phase of Renoir's career. The director wrote of this book: "With Sesonske's book I have my arch of triumph"
  0–674–47355–8 Harvard $29.50
  0–674–47360–4 Harvard pb $10.95

- James Monaco
  ALAIN RESNAIS
  0–19–520038–1 Oxford pb $8.95

- Peter Brunette
  ROBERTO ROSSELLINI
  A detailed study that does justice to the full variety of Rossellini's career, from the early Neorealist classics to the late history films
  0–19–504989–6 Oxford pb $14.95

- James Curtis
  BETWEEN FLOPS: A Biography of Preston Sturges
  The alternately troubled and hilarious life of one of the great American originals, director of *The Lady Eve* and *The Miracle of Morgan's Creek*
  0–87910–027–3 Limelight pb $9.95

- Andrei Tarkovsky
  SCULPTING IN TIME: Reflections on the Cinema
  Translated by Kitty Hunter-Blair
  0–292–77624–1 Texas pb $17.95

- Don Allen
  FINALLY TRUFFAUT
  A film-by-film guide to the late director's career
  0–8253–0336–2 Beaufort pb $12.95

- François Truffaut
  THE FILMS IN MY LIFE
  Reviews and essays reprinted from *Cahiers du Cinéma* and other publications
  0–671–24663–1 Simon & Schuster pb $9.95

  TRUFFAUT BY TRUFFAUT
  A lavishly illustrated assemblage of Truffaut's writings, arranged to form a sort of autobiography
  0–8109–1689–4 Abrams $50.00

- Andrzej Wajda
  DOUBLE VISION: My Life in Film
  0–8050–0451–3 Henry Holt $17.95

- Stephen Koch
  STARGAZER: Andy Warhol's World and His Films
  0–7145–1037–8 Marion Boyars pb $11.95

- Barbara Leaming
  ORSON WELLES: A Biography
  A long and absorbing account of Welles' very eventful life
  0–670–52895–1 Viking $19.95
  0–14–009620–5 Penguin pb $4.95

- Pauline Kael
  THE CITIZEN KANE BOOK: Raising Kane
  Kael's acerbic essay introduces the complete screenplay of *Citizen Kane*
  0–87910–016–8 Limelight pb $16.95

- Maurice Zolotow
  BILLY WILDER IN HOLLYWOOD
  0–87910–070–2 Limelight pb $12.95

MOVIE STARS

Arlene Croce
THE FRED ASTAIRE AND GINGER ROGERS BOOK
The definitive account of the Astaire-Rogers cycles, and one of the most stylish and intelligent of film books
0–525–48371–3 Dutton pb $12.95

Sarah Giles
FRED ASTAIRE: His Friends Talk
Photographs interspersed with interviews with family, friends, and colleagues
0–385–24741–9 Doubleday $30.00

John Mueller
ASTAIRE DANCING: The Musical Films
A serious, copiously illustrated analysis of the Astaire style
0–394–51654–0 Knopf $45.00

- Lauren Bacall
  LAUREN BACALL BY MYSELF
  0–394–41308–3 Knopf $12.95
  0–345–33321–7 Ballantine pb $3.95

- Wolfgang Fuchs
  HUMPHREY BOGART
  A detailed filmography with many pictures
  3–8228–0032–5 Taco pb $13.95

- David Stenn
  CLARA BOW: Runnin' Wild
  0–385–24125–9 Doubleday $18.95

- Charles Higham
  BRANDO: The Unauthorized Biography
  0–453–00543–8 NAL $18.95
  0–451–15394–4 NAL pb $4.50

Fred Astaire in "Blue Skies," from Astaire Dancing: The Musical Films *by John Mueller (Knopf)*

- Melvyn Bragg
  RICHARD BURTON: A Life
  0–316–10595–3 Little, Brown $22.95

- Robert LaGuardia
  MONTY: A Biography
  The troubled life of Montgomery Clift
  1–55611–110–X Donald Fine pb $8.95

- Bette Davis with Michael Herskowitz
  THIS 'N' THAT
  0–425–10624–1 Berkley pb $3.95

- David Dalton & Ron Cayen
  JAMES DEAN: American Icon
  Introduction by Martin Sheen
  0–312–43958–X St. Martin's $29.95
  0–312–43962–8 St. Martin's pb $18.95

- Dennis Stock
  JAMES DEAN REVISITED
  0–87701–471–X Chronicle pb $14.95

- Yvonne De Carlo with Doug Warren
  YVONNE: An Autobiography
  0–312–00217–3 St. Martin's $17.95

- Kirk Douglas
  THE RAGMAN'S SON: An Autobiography
  0–671–63717–7 Simon & Schuster $21.95

- Ronald Fields
  W.C. FIELDS: A Life in Film
  0–312–85312–2 St. Martin's pb $14.95

- Rizzoli
  GRETA GARBO: Portraits, 1920–1951
  A monumental display of glamour
  photography at its finest
  0–8478–0688–X Rizzoli pb $29.95

- Lillian Gish
  THE MOVIES, MR. GRIFFITH, AND ME
  0–916515–40–0 Mercury House pb $9.95

- Charles Higham & Roy Moseley
  CARY GRANT: The Lonely Heart
  0–15–115787–1 HBJ $18.95

- Allan Hunter
  GENE HACKMAN
  0–312–02579–3 St. Martin's $17.95

- Rock Hudson & Sara Davidson
  ROCK HUDSON: His Own Story
  0–688–06472–8 Morrow $16.95
  0–380–70292–4 Avon pb $4.50

- Simon Callow
  CHARLES LAUGHTON: A Difficult Actor
  0–8021–1047–9 Grove $18.95

- Myrna Loy & James Kotsilabas-Davis
  MYRNA LOY: Being and Becoming
  1–55611–101–0 Donald Fine pb $9.95

- Maxine Marx
  GROWING UP WITH CHICO
  0–87910–059–1 Limelight pb $8.95

- Groucho Marx
  GROUCHO AND ME: The Autobiography of Groucho Marx
  0–671–67881–0 Simon & Schuster pb $8.95

  THE GROUCHO LETTERS: Letters to and from Groucho Marx
  0–671–63963–3 Simon & Schuster pb $7.95

  MEMOIRS OF A MANGY LOVER
  0–671–67941–4 Simon & Schuster pb $8.95

- Harpo Marx with Rowland Barber
  HARPO SPEAKS!
  0–87910–036–2 Limelight pb $13.95

Randall Riese & Neal Hitchens, editors
THE UNABRIDGED MARILYN: Her Life from A to Z
0–86553–167–6 Congdon & Weed pb $14.95

James Spada
MONROE: Her Life in Pictures
0–385–17940–5 Doubleday pb $17.95

Gloria Steinem
MARILYN
Photographs by George Barris
0–452–25982–7 NAL pb $20.95

Anthony Summers
GODDESS: The Secret Lives of Marilyn Monroe
0–451–40014–3 NAL pb $4.95

- John Griggs
  THE FILMS OF GREGORY PECK
  0–8065–1025–0 Lyle Stuart pb $12.95

- Debbie Reynolds & David Patrick Columbia
  DEBBIE: My Life
  0–688–06633–X Morrow $18.95

- Martin Bauml Duberman
  PAUL ROBESON
  0–394–52780–1 Random House $24.95

- Al Diorio
  BARBARA STANWYCK: A Biography
  0–425–09455–3 Berkley pb $3.95

- Mamie Van Doren with Art Aveillie
  PLAYING THE FIELD
  0–425–11251–9 Berkley pb $3.95

- Marianne Robin-Tani
  ROBIN WILLIAMS
  0–312–91023–1 St. Martin's pb $3.50

- Fay Wray
  ON THE OTHER HAND: A Life Story
  0–312–02265–4 St. Martin's $16.95

- Doug McClelland
  STARSPEAK: Hollywood on Everything
  0–571–12981–1 Faber & Faber pb $14.95

John Wayne in a 1931 photo by William A. Fraker

- Danny Peary, editor
CLOSE-UPS: Intimate Profiles of Movie Stars
An overflowing assortment of articles, photos, and trivia tidbits
0–671–65758–5 Simon & Schuster pb $13.95

OTHER CREATIVE CONTRIBUTORS

- Nestor Almendros
A MAN WITH A CAMERA
Almendros talks about his collaboration with Eric Rohmer, Terrence Malick, and other directors
Translated by Rachel P. Belash
Preface by François Truffaut
0–374–51966–8 Farrar, Straus & Giroux pb $8.95

- A. Scott Berg
GOLDWYN: A Biography
0–394–51059–3 Knopf $24.95

- Robert L. Carringer
THE MAKING OF CITIZEN KANE
Carringer focuses less on the singular genius of Orson Welles and more on the interplay between the director and his creative partners. Full of fascinating technical details
0–520–05876–3 California pb $11.95

- Richard Corliss
TALKING PICTURES: Screenwriters in the American Cinema
Introduction by Andrew Sarris
0–87951–159–1 Overlook pb $10.95

- Mark Evans
SOUNDTRACK: The Music of the Movies
0–306–80099–3 Da Capo pb $9.95

- Aljean Harmetz
THE MAKING OF THE WIZARD OF OZ
A study of all aspects of the film's production, from technical trickery to studio politics
0–87910–000–1 Limelight pb $12.95

- Patrick McGilligan
BACKSTORY: Interviews with Screenwriters of Hollywood's Golden Age
The screenwriters interviewed provide a frequently acerbic account of what went on behind the camera
0–520–05689–2 California pb $12.95

- Kris Malkiewicz
FILM LIGHTING
Interviews with leading cinematographers and gaffers
Illustrated by Leonard Konopelski
0–671–62271–4 Prentice-Hall pb $19.95

- Leonard Maltin
THE ART OF THE CINEMATOGRAPHER: A Survey and Interviews with Five Masters
0–486–23686–2 Dover pb $7.95

- Ralph Rosenblum & Robert Karen
WHEN THE SHOOTING STOPS . . . THE CUTTING BEGINS: A Film Editor's Story
0–306–80272–4 Da Capo pb $9.95

- Dennis Schaefer & Larry Salvato
MASTERS OF LIGHT: Conversations with Contemporary Cinematographers
0–520–05336–2 California pb $12.95

- Thomas G. Smith
INDUSTRIAL LIGHT AND MAGIC: The Art of Special Effects
0–345–32263–0 Ballantine $60.00

- Tom Stempel
FRAMEWORK: A History of Screenwriting in the American Film
Foreword by Philip Dunne
0–8264–0411–1 Ungar $22.95

Animation

Jerry Beck & Will Friedwald
LOONEY TUNES AND MERRIE MELODIES: A Complete Illustrated Guide to the Warner Bros. Cartoons
0–8050–0894–2 Henry Holt pb $14.95

Leslie Cabarga
THE FLEISCHER STORY
0–306–80313–5 Da Capo pb $16.95

Shamus Culhane
ANIMATION FROM SCRIPT TO SCREEN
0–312–02162–3 St. Martin's $17.95

Christopher Finch
THE ART OF WALT DISNEY: From Mickey Mouse to the Magic Kingdoms
0–8109–8052–5 Abrams $39.95

Jeff Lenburg
THE ENCYCLOPEDIA OF ANIMATED CARTOON SERIES
0–306–80191–4 Da Capo pb $14.95

Leonard Maltin
OF MICE AND MAGIC: A History of American Animated Cartoons
0–452–25993–2 NAL pb $14.95

Richard Schickel
THE DISNEY VERSION
"The story of how Disney built an empire on corrupt popular culture . . . becomes a revealing part of American cultural history. Schickel makes it an important story"—Pauline Kael
0–671–54714–3 Simon & Schuster pb $10.95

Stephen Schneider
THAT'S ALL FOLKS: The Art of the Warner Brothers Animation
Introduction by Ray Bradbury
0–8050–0889–6 Henry Holt $39.95

DESIGN AND GLAMOUR

- Margaret J. Bailey
THOSE GLORIOUS GLAMOROUS YEARS: Classic Hollywood Costume Design of the 1930s
0–8065–1065–X Citadel pb $15.95

- David Fahey & Linda Rich
MASTERS OF STARLIGHT: Photographers in Hollywood
Decades of the best portraits and candid shots
0–345–35509–1 Ballantine $50.00

- Howard Mandelbaum & Eric Myers
SCREEN DECO: A Celebration of High Style in Hollywood
A beautifully illustrated survey of art deco design in '30s Hollywood
0–312–01087–7 St. Martin's pb $15.95

- Richard Schickel
STRIKING POSES
A rich gathering of Hollywood glamour photography at its most sublimely unreal. "How wonderfully produced the book is"—Olivia De Havilland
1–55670–024–5 Stewart, Tabori & Chang pb $16.95

- Michael Webb, editor
HOLLYWOOD: Legend and Reality
Hollywood wasn't just movies; it was a mode of perceiving the universe. Webb's book offers up some of the artifacts that sprang from that inimitably gaudy mode of perception
0–8212–1589–2 NY Graphic Society pb $19.95

SCREENPLAYS

Collections

- Woody Allen
FOUR FILMS OF WOODY ALLEN
Includes *Annie Hall, Interiors, Manhattan,* and *Stardust Memories*
0–394–52443–8 Random House $20.00
0–394–71229–3 Random House pb $10.95

THREE FILMS OF WOODY ALLEN
Includes *Zelig, Broadway Danny Rose,* and *The Purple Rose of Cairo*
0–394–75304–6 Random House pb $12.95

Busby Berkeley and the Gold Diggers of 1933 (photo courtesy of the Kobal Collection), from The Genius of the System *by Thomas Schatz (Pantheon)*

• Ingmar Bergman
FOUR SCREENPLAYS
Includes *Smiles of a Summer Night, The Seventh Seal, Wild Strawberries,* and *The Magician*
0–671–67833–7 Simon & Schuster pb $12.95

THE MARRIAGE SCENARIOS
Includes *Scenes from a Marriage, Face to Face,* and *Autumn Sonata*
0–679–72032–4 Pantheon pb $9.95

PERSONA & SHAME
Translated by Alan Blair
0–7145–0757–1 Marion Boyars pb $6.95

• Luis Buñuel
L'AGE D'OR & AN ANDALUSIAN DOG
0–8044–6068–X Ungar pb $7.95

THE EXTERMINATING ANGEL, NAZARIN & LOS OLVIDADOS
0–8044–6072–8 Ungar pb $12.95

• Jean Cocteau
BLOOD OF A POET & THE TESTAMENT OF ORPHEUS
0–7145–0580–3 Marion Boyars pb $7.95

• Horton Foote
THE TRIP TO BOUNTIFUL, TENDER MERCIES & TO KILL A MOCKINGBIRD
0–8021–1124–6 Grove $19.95
0–8021–3125–5 Grove pb $9.95

• Harold Pinter
FIVE SCREENPLAYS
Includes *The Servant, The Pumpkin Eater, Accident, The Go-Between,* and *The Quiller Memorandum*
0–394–17802–5 Grove pb $17.50

THE FRENCH LIEUTENANT'S WOMAN & OTHER SCREENPLAYS
0–413–48680–X RC&H pb $13.95

• Eric Rohmer
SIX MORAL TALES
Treatments in novelized form for *My Night at Maud's, Claire's Knee,* and the rest of the cycle
0–8044–6748–X Ungar pb $10.95

• Preston Sturges
FIVE SCREENPLAYS BY PRESTON STURGES
Includes *The Great McGinty, Christmas in July, The Lady Eve, Sullivan's Travels,* and *Hail the Conquering Hero*
Edited by Brian Henderson
0–520–05442–3 California $40.00
0–520–05564–0 California pb $19.95

• Sam Thomas, editor
BEST AMERICAN SCREENPLAYS
Includes *All Quiet on the Western Front, Meet John Doe, Casablanca, Miracle on 34th Street, Rebel Without a Cause, Bonnie and Clyde, The Graduate, Butch Cassidy and the Sundance Kid, Sounder, On Golden Pond, Arthur,* and *The Candidate*
0–517–55542–5 Crown $24.95

• John Waters
TRASH TRIO
Includes *Pink Flamingoes, Desperate Living,* and *Flamingoes Forever*
0–394–75986–9 Random House pb $10.95

Individual Films
(alphabetical by title)

• Louis Malle
AU REVOIR LES ENFANTS
Translated by Anselm Hollo
0–8021–3114–X Grove pb $6.95

• Sergei Eisenstein
THE BATTLESHIP POTEMKIN
Translated by Gillon R. Aitken
0–571–12559–X Faber & Faber pb $9.95

• Luis Buñuel & Jean-Claude Carrière
BELLE DE JOUR
0–8044–6071–X Ungar pb $9.95

• Orson Welles & Oja Kodar
THE BIG BRASS RING: An Original Screenplay
An unfilmed screenplay about political corruption and betrayal
0–944166–01–6 Santa Teresa $45.00

• Lawrence Kasdan & Barbara Benedek
THE BIG CHILL
0–312–00009–X St. Martin's pb $8.95

• Jean-Luc Godard
BREATHLESS
Edited by Dudley Andrew
0–8135–1253–0 Rutgers pb $12.00

• Howard Hawks
BRINGING UP BABY
Edited by Gerald Mast
0–8135–1341–3 Rutgers pb $14.00

• Les Blank
BURDEN OF DREAMS
Edited by James Bogan
0–938190–17–2 North Atlantic pb $12.95

• Derek Jarman
CARAVAGGIO
0–500–27419–3 Thames & Hudson pb $8.98

• Orson Welles
CHIMES AT MIDNIGHT
Edited by Bridget Gellert Lyons
0–8135–1339–1 Rutgers pb $14.00

• Casey Robinson
DARK VICTORY
Edited by Bernard F. Dick
0–299–08764–6 Wisconsin pb $8.95

• François Truffaut
DAY FOR NIGHT
Translated by Sam Flores
0–936839–56–2 Applause Theatre pb $7.95

• James Seymour & Rian James
42ND STREET
Edited by Rocco Fumento
0–299–08104–4 Wisconsin pb $8.95

• François Truffaut
THE 400 BLOWS
0–936839–55–4 Applause Theatre pb $7.95

• Stanley Kubrick, Michael Herr & Gustav Hasford
FULL METAL JACKET
0–394–75823–4 Knopf pb $16.95

• Erwin Gelsey & others
GOLD DIGGERS OF 1933
Edited by Arthur Hove
0–299–08084–6 Wisconsin pb $6.95

• Woody Allen
HANNAH AND HER SISTERS
0–394–74749–6 Random House pb $5.95

• Marguerite Duras
HIROSHIMA, MON AMOUR
Translated by Richard Seaver
0–8021–3104–2 Grove pb $7.95

• Hans-Jürgen Syberberg
HITLER: A Film from Germany
Translated by Joachim Neugroschel
Preface by Susan Sontag
0–374–51565–4 Farrar, Straus & Giroux pb $10.95

• Sheridan Gibney & others
I AM A FUGITIVE FROM A CHAIN GANG
Edited by John O'Connor
0–299–08754–9 Wisconsin pb $8.95

• John Berger & Alain Tanner
JONAH WHO WILL BE TWENTY-FIVE IN THE YEAR 2000
Translated by Michael Palmer
0–913028–3 North Atlantic pb $9.95

• John Huston & others
JUAREZ
Edited by Paul Vanderwood
0–299–08744–1 Wisconsin pb $8.95

• François Truffaut & Suzanne Schiffman
THE LAST METRO
Edited by Mirella Affron & E. Rubinstein
0–8135–1066–X Rutgers pb $11.00

- Howard Koch
LETTER FROM AN UNKNOWN WOMAN
Edited by Virginia Wexman
0–8135–1160–7 Rutgers pb $12.00

- Francis Faragoh & Robert E. Lee
LITTLE CAESAR
Edited by Gerald Peary
0–299–08454–X Wisconsin pb $8.95

- Rainer Werner Fassbinder
THE MARRIAGE OF MARIA BRAUN
Edited by Joyce Rheuban
0–8135–1130–5 Rutgers pb $11.00

- Ranald MacDougall & Catherine Turney
MILDRED PIERCE
Edited by Albert LaValley
0–299–08374–8 Wisconsin pb $6.95

- Howard Koch
MISSION TO MOSCOW
Edited by David Culbert
0–299–08384–5 Wisconsin pb $8.95

- Hanif Kureishi
MY BEAUTIFUL LAUNDRETTE
0–571–13981–7 Faber & Faber pb $8.95

- Samuel G. Engel & Winston Miller
MY DARLING CLEMENTINE
Edited by Robert Lyons
0–8135–1051–1 Rutgers pb $11.00

- Casey Robinson
NOW, VOYAGER
Edited by Jeanne Allen
0–299–09794–3 Wisconsin pb $8.95

- Harvey Thew & others
THE PUBLIC ENEMY
Edited by Henry Cohen
0–299–08464–7 Wisconsin pb $8.95

- Akira Kurosawa & others
RAN
0–87773–387–2 Shambhala pb $19.95

- Hanif Kureishi
SAMMY AND ROSIE GET LAID
0–14–011262–6 Penguin pb $6.95

- Seton I. Miller & Howard Koch
THE SEA HAWK
Edited by Rudy Behlmer
0–299–09014–0 Wisconsin pb $6.95

- Claude Lanzmann
SHOAH: An Oral History of the Holocaust
Preface by Simone De Beauvoir
Introduction by Elie Wiesel
0–394–74329–6 Pantheon pb $6.95

- François Truffaut
SMALL CHANGE
Translated by Anselm Hollo
0–936839–51–1 Applause Theatre pb $6.95

THE STORY OF ADELE H.
0–394–17908–0 Grove pb $2.50

- Graham Greene
THE THIRD MAN
0–571–12634–0 Faber & Faber pb $9.95

- Orson Welles
TOUCH OF EVIL
Edited by Terry Comito
0–8135–1097–X Rutgers pb $11.00

- Ivan Goff & Ben Roberts
WHITE HEAT
Edited by Patrick McGilligan
0–299–09674–2 Wisconsin pb $8.95

- Noel Langley & others
THE WIZARD OF OZ: The Screenplay
Edited with an introduction by Michael Patrick Hearn
0–385–29760–2 Delacorte pb $9.95

- Robert Buckner & Edmund Joseph
YANKEE DOODLE DANDY
Edited by Patrick McGilligan
0–299–08474–4 Wisconsin pb $8.95

FILM THEORY

Film theory once centered on the silent era. The writings of Eisenstein, Pudovkin, Arnheim, and Balazs retained their dominance for decades, and new technical developments like color and wide screen were viewed mostly as commercial aberrations rather than new formal opportunities. Then came André Bazin and the young Turks of *Cahiers du Cinéma* to stir things up, and in their wake a host of structuralists, semioticians, and (especially influential in recent years) feminists. As a result, every analytical truism has been called into question. Nearly everything written about film in recent years bears the imprint of French post-structuralist thought, if only at second or third hand. This is not always a blessing, since it requires continual immersion in terms like "syntagmatic parallelism" and "maximization of the diegetic effect," but there is no question that the semiotic approach has illuminated film in unexpected ways through its reading of narrative codes and generic structures. In the process, attention has shifted from high-minded prescriptions of what cinema ought to do, to focus instead on precise notation of what it actually does.

Early Classics

- Rudolf Arnheim
FILM AS ART
0–520–00035–8 California pb $7.95

André Bazin
WHAT IS CINEMA?
A classic collection of essays: brilliant, deeply influential, and often beautifully written
Translated by Hugh Gray

Volume 1
0–520–00092–7 California pb $8.95

Volume 2
0–520–02255–6 California pb $8.95

- Sergei Eisenstein
FILM FORM
0–15–630920–3 HBJ pb $8.95

THE FILM SENSE
0–15–630935–1 HBJ pb $8.95

- Dziga Vertov
KINO-EYE: The Writings of Dziga Vertov
Edited by Annette Michelson
0–520–05630–2 California pb $11.95

Contemporary Theory

- David Bordwell
NARRATION IN THE FICTION FILM
0–299–10174–6 Wisconsin pb $14.95

- Leo Braudy
THE WORLD IN A FRAME: What We See in Films
0–226–07155–3 Chicago pb $9.95

- Noel Burch
THEORY OF FILM PRACTICE
0–691–00329–7 Princeton pb $8.95

- Stanley Cavell
THE WORLD VIEWED: Reflections on the Ontology of Film
0–674–96196–X Harvard pb $6.95

- Teresa De Lauretis
ALICE DOESN'T: Feminism, Semiotics, Cinema
0–253–20316–3 Indiana pb $10.95

- Gilles Deleuze
CINEMA ONE: Movement-Image
Translated by Hugh Tomlinson & Barbara Habberjam
0–8166–1400–8 Minnesota pb $13.95

- Gerald Mast & Marshall Cohen, editors
FILM THEORY AND CRITICISM: Introductory Readings
0–19–503573–9 Oxford $18.95

- Christian Metz
FILM LANGUAGE: A Semiotics of the Cinema
Translated by Michael Taylor
0–19–501762–5 Oxford $35.00

THE IMAGINARY SIGNIFIER: Psychoanalysis and the Cinema
Translated by Celia Britton & others
0–253–20380–5 Indiana pb $10.95

- Philip Rosen
NARRATIVE, APPARATUS, IDEOLOGY: A Film Theory Reader
0–231–05881–0 Columbia pb $14.50

FILM REVIEWERS

Before there were film critics, there were movie reviewers. They had the advantage of working not from a theoretical matrix but out of the daily experience of seeing. If that experience induced little beyond sleepy cynicism in most, a handful turned a journalistic necessity into a minor art form.

Jim Hillier, editor
CAHIERS DU CINEMA: The 1950s—Neo-Realism, Hollywood, New Wave
The prime years of the most influential of all film magazines; staff writers included Godard, Truffaut, Rohmer, Rivette, and Chabrol
0–674–09060–8 Harvard $22.50
0–674–09061–6 Harvard pb $7.95

CAHIERS DU CINEMA: The 1960s—New Wave, New Cinema, Reevaluating Hollywood
In the 1960s *Cahiers* grew steadily more politicized, and in the process many of its original positions were modified or abandoned altogether
0–674–09062–4 Harvard $25.00

• Pauline Kael
HOOKED
0–525–24705–X Dutton $24.95
0–525–48429–9 Dutton pb $14.95

TAKING IT ALL IN
0–03–069362–4 Henry Holt $25.00
0–03–069361–6 Henry Holt pb $14.95

WHEN THE LIGHTS GO DOWN
0–03–056842–0 Henry Holt pb $9.95

• Stanley Kauffmann
BEFORE MY EYES: Film Criticism and Comment
Essays by the longtime reviewer for *The New Republic*
0–306–80179–5 Da Capo pb $9.95

Poster for "Metropolis," from Fritz Lang *by Lotte Eisner (Da Capo)*

• Dwight MacDonald
ON MOVIES
Introduction by John Simon
0–306–80150–7 Da Capo pb $11.95

• Andrew Sarris
POLITICS AND CINEMA
0–231–04034–2 Columbia $27.00

DO IT YOURSELF

Here are some useful titles for the novice filmmaker.

• Daniel Arijon
GRAMMAR OF THE FILM LANGUAGE
0–240–50779–7 Focal Press $65.00

• Roger Crittenden
THE THAMES AND HUDSON MANUAL OF FILM EDITING
0–500–67023–4 Thames & Hudson $18.95
0–500–68023–X Thames & Hudson pb $10.95

Edward Dmytryk
ON FILM EDITING
0–240–51738–5 Focal Press pb $11.95

ON SCREEN DIRECTING
0–240–51716–4 Focal Press pb $11.95

ON SCREEN WRITING
0–240–51753–9 Focal Press pb $11.95

• Syd Field
SCREENPLAY: The Foundations of Screenwriting
0–440–57647–4 Doubleday pb $8.95

• Paul N. Lazarus
THE MOVIE PRODUCER: A Handbook for Producing and Picture-Making
0–06–463724–7 Harper & Row pb $7.95

• Alec Nisbett
THE TECHNIQUE OF THE SOUND STUDIO
0–240–51100–X Focal Press pb $29.95

• Karel Reisz & Gavin Millar
TECHNIQUE OF FILM EDITING
0–240–50846–7 Focal Press pb $21.95

• Eric Sherman
FRAME BY FRAME: A Handbook for Creative Filmmaking
0–918226–12–0 Acrobat pb $19.95

• Raymond Spottiswoode, editor
THE FOCAL ENCYCLOPEDIA OF FILM AND TELEVISION TECHNIQUES
0–240–50654–5 Focal Press $85.00

REFERENCE

Finally there are the lists. Movies and list-making naturally go together, from the ritual of ten-best choices to the current spate of encyclopedic reference works geared to the VCR owner. The following are some of the standouts in a crowded field.

• Leslie L. Halliwell
Halliwell's thick and well-researched volumes are extremely useful for their data, although the author's opinions are, to say the least, questionable.
HALLIWELL'S FILMGOER'S COMPANION
0–684–19063–X Scribners $42.50
0–684–18410–9 Scribners pb $16.95

HALLIWELL'S FILM AND VIDEO GUIDE: Sixth Edition
Alphabetical film-by-film entries notable for their detailed credits listings
0–684–19051–6 Scribners pb $19.95

• Pauline Kael
FIVE THOUSAND ONE NIGHTS AT THE MOVIES: A Guide from A to Z
Makes no attempt to be comprehensive, but Kael's thumbnail critiques are irresistibly readable even when they annoy
0–03–000442–X Henry Holt pb $12.95

• Ephraim Katz
THE FILM ENCYCLOPEDIA
Remarkably comprehensive: now somewhat dated, but still the best one-volume data source
0–399–50601–2 Putnam pb $16.95

Leonard Maltin
LEONARD MALTIN'S TV MOVIES AND VIDEO GUIDE, 1989
Maltin's annual publication is far and away the best film-by-film reference guide, with an amazing quantity of information in its tightly-packed descriptions. Its only shortcoming is its relative neglect of foreign films
0–452–26147–3 NAL pb $12.95

• Danny Peary
GUIDE FOR THE FILM FANATIC
A breezy ramble through the repertoire of "cult" films
0–671–61081–3 Simon & Schuster pb $13.95

• Michael Weldon
THE PSYCHOTRONIC ENCYCLOPEDIA OF FILM
A guided tour of sleaze, splatter, and exploitation that is both a paradigm of post-punk sensibility and an extraordinary job of research in the lower reaches of filmmaking
0–345–34345–X Ballantine pb $17.95

• Ronald Bergan & Robyn Karney
THE HOLT FOREIGN FILM GUIDE
Credits, synopses, and critical assessments of more than 2000 foreign-language films
0–8050–0991–4 Henry Holt $39.95

Journalism

The first newspaper in America, *Publick Occurrences,* was founded in 1690: it lasted one issue before Massachusetts authorities shut it down for impertinence. Two thirds of the history of American journalism had been recorded before the storied William Randolph Hearst commandeered his first daily a century ago.

Still, it is this recent century that engages most of our attention, for in its new prominence, what was once referred to only as "the newspaper business" has become a giant industry, a profession, and a social-political institution.

▶ See also 20th-Century American Essays and Journalism

HISTORY

• Michael & Edwin Emery
THE PRESS AND AMERICA: An Interpretive History of the Mass Media
A standard textbook, thick and informative
0–13–699059–2 Prentice-Hall $41.00

• Thomas G. Leonard
THE POWER OF THE PRESS: The Birth of American Political Reporting
Eclectic essays on political journalism from colonial days to the early 1900s
0–19–505184–X Oxford pb $7.95

• Michael Schudson
DISCOVERING THE NEWS: A Social History of American Newspapers
Stimulating essays focusing on the concept of objectivity
0–465–01666–9 Basic Books pb $9.95

• Anthony Smith
GOODBYE, GUTENBERG: The Newspaper Revolution of the 1980s
The new history: how computers are radically changing the way the news is made and purveyed
0–19–503006–0 Oxford pb $9.95

• Mitchell Stephens
A HISTORY OF THE NEWS: From the Drum to the Satellite
0–670–81378–8 Viking $24.95

The Age of the Printer: 1690–1800

The first century of American journalism was an era of tiny, perishable newspapers trying to make their way in a culture that was not sure it needed the press.

• Leonard W. Levy
THE EMERGENCE OF A FREE PRESS
The major study on the origins of the major force in American journalism: freedom of the press
0–19–504240–9 Oxford pb $9.95

• Arthur M. Schlesinger, Jr.
PRELUDE TO INDEPENDENCE: The Newspaper War on Britain 1764–1776
The pivotal role of the press in the American Revolution
Foreword by Charles Akers
0–930350–13–8 Northeastern pb $9.95

• Jeffrey Smith
PRINTERS AND PRESS FREEDOM: The Ideology of Early American Journalism
0–19–505144–0 Oxford $28.00

The Age of the Editor: 1800–1880

The 19th century brought a transition from newspapers for the few—the political and commercial elite—to newspapers for the many. The vehicle for expansion was news: it was either entertaining or useful, or, occasionally, both.

News for amusement came on the scene with the penny press of the 1830s. The multifeatured newspaper that we know today arrived with Horace Greeley's *New York Tribune* in the 1840s. And the Civil War, a major turning point in the history of the American press, created a monstrous appetite that newspapers and other news media are still trying to sate.

• Douglas Fermer
JAMES GORDON BENNETT AND THE NEW YORK HERALD
Biography of the man who invented—and corrupted—news as we know it
0–312–43955–5 St. Martin's $29.95

• Morton Keller
THE ART AND POLITICS OF THOMAS NAST
The illustrator is better remembered than any editor of the post-Civil War era
0–19–501929–6 Oxford pb $12.95

• Louis M. Starr
BOHEMIAN BRIGADE
How the Civil War, and the reporters who covered it, created a 19th-century news revolution
Foreword by James Boylan
0–299–11344–2 Wisconsin pb $13.50

The Age of the Reporter: Since 1880

Although such innovators as Joseph Pulitzer, William Randolph Hearst, and E.W. Scripps were more famous names, reporters became the key figures in the new urban journalism of the 1880s. They remained the workhorses of the press for the next century. As police reporters, war correspondents, and tenacious investigators, they created the legends of American journalism.

• Whitman Bassow
THE MOSCOW CORRESPONDENTS: Reporting on Russia from the Revolution to Glasnost
How an elite group of 300 Western reporters has operated in Moscow and

Drawing by Gustave Doré

almost single-handedly shaped our perceptions of the Soviet Union, from a former Moscow bureau chief of *Newsweek*
0–688–04392–5 Morrow $18.95

• Barbara Belford
BRILLIANT BYLINES: A Biographical Anthology of Notable Newspaperwomen in America
Outstanding survey of women in American journalism based on two dozen profiles of reporters from the 19th century to the present
0–231–05496–3 Columbia $35.00

• Timothy Crouse
THE BOYS ON THE BUS: Riding with the Campaign Press Corps
A biting, irreverent behind-the-scenes look at coverage of the 1972 presidential campaign. "Crouse takes a big bite out of the hand that feeds news to America"—Hunter Thompson
0–345–34015–9 Ballantine pb $3.95

• Sally Foreman Griffith
HOMETOWN NEWS: William Allen White and the Emporia Gazette
A biography of the famous small-town journalist and a social history of small-town life
0–19–505589–6 Oxford $24.95

• David Halberstam
THE POWERS THAT BE
The definitive work on the emergence of the mass media in postwar America, from CBS to the *Washington Post*
0–440–36997–5 Doubleday pb $6.95

• Phillip Knightley
THE FIRST CASUALTY: From the Crimea to Vietnam—The War Correspondent as Hero, Propagandist, and Myth Maker
On war correspondents of all nationalities, told with more gusto than accuracy
0–15–631130–5 HBJ pb $5.95

- Stephen R. MacKinnon & Oris Friesen
CHINA REPORTING: An Oral History of American Journalism in the 1930s and 1940s
A fascinating glimpse into one of the American press's first experiences with world revolution
0–520–05843–7 California $20.00

BIOGRAPHIES AND MEMOIRS

- William Macadams
BEN HECHT: The Man Behind the Legend
0–684–18980–1 Scribners $22.50

- Antoinette May
WITNESS TO WAR: A Biography of Marguerite Higgins
The life of the flamboyant Pulitzer Prize-winning overseas correspondent
0–8253–0161–0 Beaufort $17.95
0–14–007597–6 Penguin pb $6.95

- Ira Berkow
RED: A Biography of Red Smith
Affectionate portrait of the late admired sports writer, by a colleague
0–8129–1203–9 Random House $17.95
0–07–004852–5 McGraw-Hill pb $4.95

- Andrew Patner
I.F. STONE: A Portrait
"What a lovely portrait of our epoch's greatest journalist"—Studs Terkel
0–394–55808–1 Pantheon $15.95

- Raymond Sokolov
WAYWARD REPORTER: The Life of A.J. Liebling
0–916870–63–4 Creative Arts pb $10.95

First-Person Accounts

- Russell Baker
THE GOOD TIMES
0–688–06170–2 Morrow $19.95

- Carl Bernstein & Bob Woodward
ALL THE PRESIDENT'S MEN
The journalistic bible of the 1970s and '80s, the story about the Watergate investigation that changed history and made investigative reporting the new standard for the American press
0–446–32264–4 Warner pb $4.50

- Henry Brandon
SPECIAL RELATIONSHIPS: A Foreign Correspondent's Memoirs from Roosevelt to Reagan
0–689–11588–1 Atheneum $19.95

- Edna Buchanan
THE CORPSE HAD A FAMILIAR FACE: Covering Miami, America's Hottest Beat
Tales of the front lines, both amusing and horrifying, from the nation's top crime reporter and 1986 Pulitzer Prize winner
0–394–55794–8 Random House $17.95

- Nicholas Daniloff
TWO LIVES, ONE RUSSIA
Daniloff is the *US News & World Report* journalist whose arrest by the KGB became an international incident
0–395–44601–5 Houghton Mifflin $19.95

- Hedley Donovan
ROOSEVELT TO REAGAN: A Reporter's Encounters with Nine Presidents
0–06–039067–0 Harper & Row pb $8.95

- Ben Hecht
A CHILD OF THE CENTURY
The tumultuous life of the journalist, playwright, and screenwriter
Introduction by Sidney Zion
0–917657–41–1 Donald Fine pb $11.95

- H.L. Mencken
A CHOICE OF DAYS
Selections from the Sage of Baltimore's autobiographical volumes, including *Newspaper Days*
Edited by Edward L. Galligan
0–394–50795–9 Knopf $12.95
0–394–74760–7 Random House pb $7.95

- Harrison E. Salisbury
A TIME OF CHANGE: A Reporter's Tale of Our Time
0–06–039083–2 Harper & Row $19.95

JOURNEY FOR OUR TIMES: A Memoir
0–06–039006–9 Harper & Row $22.50

- George Seldes
WITNESS TO A CENTURY: Encounters with the Noted, the Notorious, and the Three SOB's
0–345–35329–3 Ballantine pb $12.95

- Vincent Sheean
PERSONAL HISTORY
A durable classic on a journalist's prewar days in Europe
Introduction by Norman Corwin
0–8065–1004–8 Lyle Stuart pb $9.95

- William L. Shirer
TWENTIETH-CENTURY JOURNEY: A Memoir, a Life and the Times
The chronicler of the Nazi era gives a personal account of the century's toughest reporting challenge

Volume 1: The Start, 1904–1930
0–553–34204–5 Bantam pb $12.95

Volume 2: The Nightmare Years, 1930–1940
0–316–78703–5 Little, Brown $24.95

- Red Smith
TO ABSENT FRIENDS
0–451–14387–6 NAL pb $4.95

- Theodore H. White
IN SEARCH OF HISTORY: A Personal Adventure
0–446–34657–8 Warner pb $6.95

- Donald Woods
ASKING FOR TROUBLE
First-person account from the South African reporter who exposed the death of Stephen Biko
0–689–70718–5 Atheneum pb $9.95

- Sidney Zion
READ ALL ABOUT IT
0–425–07209–6 Berkley pb $9.95

KEN AULETTA: Some Useful Books for a Journalist

Herbert Gans
DECIDING WHAT'S NEWS: A Study of CBS Evening News, NBC Nightly News, Newsweek and Time
Serves as a reminder that journalists should try to talk to not just "the knowns" in our phone books, but "the unknowns" as well
0–394–74354–7 Random House pb $9.95

Timothy Crouse
THE BOYS ON THE BUS: Riding with the Campaign Press Corps
A wry account of the dangers, and joys, of pack journalism
0–345–34015–9 Ballantine pb $3.95

Ronald Steel
WALTER LIPPMAN AND THE AMERICAN CENTURY
A wonderful portrait of one of journalism's giants, a man who strove to put things in a larger context. But, also, a man who sometimes grew too close to the powerful
0–316–81190–4 Little, Brown $24.50

Robert Caro
THE POWER BROKER: Robert Moses and the Fall of New York
Combines good reporting and good writing, and reminds that no interesting public figure is a stick figure
0–394–48076–7 Knopf $34.50
0–394–72024–5 Random House pb $18.95

Michael Barone & Grant Ujifusa
THE ALMANAC OF AMERICAN POLITICS
If writing about national politics, this is a treasure chest of useful facts and information
0–89234–038–X National Journal pb $39.95

Bureau of the Census
STATISTICAL ABSTRACT OF THE UNITED STATES
If writing about America (about families, jobs, drop-outs, suburban growth, nearly anything) this is where you find the facts
0–318–22591–3 USGPO $29.00

Any Government Budget: Politicians make speeches about their priorities; their budget defines their true priorities

Any Trollope novel: A pleasurable reminder that people (their personality, their vanity, their insecurities, their panic, their greed) often shape events far more than facts or historical forces

TO ORDER BOOKS AS GIFTS, SEE PAGE 1

THE NEWSPAPER BARONS

- **Ellis Cose**
  THE PRESS: Inside America's Most Powerful Newspaper Empires—From the Newsrooms to the Boardrooms
  0–688–07403–0 Morrow $19.95

- **Deborah Davis**
  KATHARINE THE GREAT: Katharine Graham and the Washington Post
  0–915765–43–8 National Press $17.95

- **Richard Kluger**
  THE PAPER: The Life and Death of the New York Herald Tribune
  A richly detailed account of the great New York daily from its 19th-century birth to its death in 1967
  0–394–50877–7 Knopf $24.95
  0–394–75565–0 Random House pb $16.95

- **Michael Leapman**
  ARROGANT AUSSIE: The Rupert Murdoch Story
  A look at the man behind the British tabloids and the incessant controversy surrounding him
  0–8184–0370–5 Lyle Stuart $14.95

- **Peter Prichard**
  THE MAKING OF McPAPER: The Inside Story of USA Today
  Allen Neuharth's obsession to create a national newspaper. "A biography as colorful as the weather map in *USA Today*"—James J. Kilpatrick
  Foreword by Charles Kuralt
  0–8362–7939–5 Andrews & McMeel $19.95

- **W.A. Swanberg**
  CITIZEN HEARST
  "Best biography yet on a strange, complicated man who was an important part of American life for so long"—*Saturday Review*
  0–684–17147–3 Scribners pb $7.95

- **Charles Whited**
  KNIGHT: A Publisher in the Tumultuous Century
  The life and times of the founder of the

Félix Vallotton's "The Era of the Press" in The Dreyfus Affair: Art, Truth and Justice *(The Jewish Museum)*

Knight-Ridder media chain, by a longtime *Miami Herald* columnist
0–525–24723–8 Dutton $21.95

The New York Times

- **Susan W. Dryfoos**
  IPHIGENE: My Life and The New York Times—The Memoirs of Iphigene Ochs Sulzberger
  0–8129–1700–6 Times Books $22.50

- **Joseph C. Goulden**
  FIT TO PRINT: A.M. Rosenthal and His Times
  0–8184–0474–4 Lyle Stuart $21.95

- **Gay Talese**
  THE KINGDOM AND THE POWER
  A somewhat dated but revealing behind-the-scenes portrait of the *Times*
  0–440–34525–1 Dell pb $6.95

The Wall Street Journal

- **Jerry M. Rosenberg**
  INSIDE THE WALL STREET JOURNAL: The History and the Power of Dow Jones and Company and America's Most Influential Newspaper
  0–02–604860–4 Macmillan $16.95

- **Edward E. Scharff**
  WORLDLY POWER: The Making of The Wall Street Journal
  From a single-page trade sheet to one of the most important American dailies. "A rich mine of insider's lore"—*Business Week*
  0–8253–0359–1 Beaufort $18.95
  0–452–25917–7 NAL pb $9.95

The Binghams of Louisville

- **Sallie Bingham**
  PASSION AND PREJUDICE: A Family Memoir
  The heiress who set in motion the events that led to the dissolution of the Bingham communications empire tells her version of the family's saga
  0–394–55851–0 Knopf $22.95

- **Marie Brenner**
  HOUSE OF DREAMS: The Bingham Family of Louisville
  "Brenner's narrative weaves exceptionally intimate portraits. . .with riveting historical accounts of the Binghams' active and influential role in 20th century America"—David McClintick
  0–394–55831–6 Random House $19.95

- **David L. Chandler & Mary V. Chandler**
  THE BINGHAMS OF LOUISVILLE: The Dark History Behind One of America's Great Fortunes
  0–517–56895–0 Crown $17.95

THE TELEVISION AGE

- **Gwenda Blair**
  ALMOST GOLDEN: Jessica Savitch and the Selling of Television News
  The rise, compromises, and untimely death

of one of the most successful women in TV news
0–671–63285–X Simon & Schuster $18.95

- **Peter J. Boyer**
  WHO KILLED CBS?: How America's Number-One News Network Went Down the Tubes
  Recent troubles at the once-mighty network of Murrow, Rather, and Cronkite under Van Gordon Sauter and Laurence Tisch. "The definitive story of how cynicism and pettiness nearly destroyed a great news organization"—Jonathan Alter, *Newsweek*
  0–394–56034–5 Random House $18.95

- **Christine Craft**
  TOO OLD, TOO UGLY AND NOT DEFERENTIAL TO MEN: An Anchorwoman's Courageous Battle Against Sex Discrimination
  Notes on women in TV news, from the anchorwoman who won a landmark sex-discrimination case
  Foreword by Larry King
  0–914629–65–4 St. Martin's $17.95

- **Linda Ellerbee**
  AND SO IT GOES: Adventures in Television
  One of TV newsdom's most irreverent fixtures lets loose on the TV news industry
  0–425–10237–8 Berkley pb $4.50

- **Edward J. Epstein**
  NEWS FROM NOWHERE: Television and the News
  A devastating 1973 critique of network news. "The best book ever written about any aspect of television"—Richard Schickel, *Harper's*
  0–394–71998–0 Random House pb $5.50

- **Ed Joyce**
  PRIME TIMES, BAD TIMES
  An account of infighting and chaos behind the scenes at CBS by the former president of CBS News
  0–385–23923–8 Doubleday $19.95

- **Barbara Matusow**
  THE EVENING STARS: The Making of the Network News Anchor
  0–345–31714–9 Ballantine pb $3.95

- **Peter McCabe**
  BAD NEWS AT BLACK ROCK: The Sell-Out of CBS News
  One of a spate of recent works on behind-the-scenes troubles at CBS News
  0–87795–907–2 Arbor House $17.95

- **Alanna Nash**
  GOLDEN GIRL: The Story of Jessica Savitch
  One of two recent biographies on the ill-fated anchorwoman
  0–525–24667–3 Dutton $18.95

- **Gil Noble**
  BLACK IS THE COLOR OF MY TV TUBE
  The autobiographical odyssey of a star black reporter, one of the first in the industry, during the 1960s
  0–8184–0297–0 Lyle Stuart $12.00

• Daniel Paisner
THE IMPERFECT MIRROR: Inside Stories of Television Newswomen
A profile of the status of the profession, based on interviews with 50 newswomen
0–688–074999–5 Morrow $18.95

• Lewis J. Paper
EMPIRE: William S. Paley and the Making of CBS
The story of CBS and its founder and longtime head
0–312–02572–6 St. Martin's pb $12.95

• Joseph Persico
EDWARD R. MURROW: An American Original
1–07–049480–0 McGraw-Hill $24.95

• Eric Sevareid
NOT SO WILD A DREAM
0–689–70578–6 Atheneum pb $8.95

• Robert Slater
THIS. . .IS CBS: A Chronicle of 60 Years
More on the fascination with CBS, from its birth in 1928 to the takeover pressure of the 1980s
0–13–919234–4 Prentice-Hall $19.95

• Ann M. Sperber
MURROW: His Life and Times
Biography of the century's leading pioneer in broadcast journalism
0–553–34384–X Bantam pb $12.95

• Mike Wallace with Gary P. Gates
CLOSE ENCOUNTERS: Mike Wallace's Own Story
0–425–08269–5 Berkley pb $4.50

MAGAZINE JOURNALISM

For nearly a century, magazines have been a major force in American journalism, expanding its role far beyond the expectations of the earliest newspaper editors. After the rise of the popular ten-cent magazine in the 1890s, magazine journalism soon struck a rich vein in what was first called the "literature of exposure," and then dubbed "muckraking" by Theodore Roosevelt.

In due course, the news magazine became the dominant form. *Time* was created by Henry Luce—who placed himself in the public eye as the proponent of "the American Century"—and his forgotten partner, Briton Hadden.

The Muckrakers

• Justin Kaplan
LINCOLN STEFFENS: A Biography
0–671–22035–7 Simon & Schuster pb $12.95

• Jessica Mitford
POISON PENMANSHIP: The Gentle Art of Muckraking
Afterword by Carl Bernstein
0–394–50260–4 Random House pb $13.95

Ida Tarbell
THE HISTORY OF THE STANDARD OIL COMPANY
An abridged edition of a famous exposé
0–393–00496–1 Norton pb $7.95

Kathleen Brady
IDA TARBELL: Portrait of a Muckraker
0–399–31023–1 Putnam $17.95

Life

• Loudon Wainwright
THE GREAT AMERICAN MAGAZINE: An Inside History of Life
"As definitive as a book will ever need to be about the magazine's impact on the society, its achievement and swift decline"—*LA Times*
0–394–45987–3 Knopf $19.95
0–345–34776–5 Ballantine pb $5.95

The New Yorker and Literary Journalists

• Scott Elledge
E.B. WHITE: A Biography
0–393–01771–0 Norton $22.50
0–393–30305–5 Norton pb $9.95

• Brendan Gill
HERE AT THE NEW YORKER
0–88184–350–4 Carroll & Graf pb $12.95

• E.J. Kahn
ABOUT THE NEW YORKER AND ME: A Sentimental Journey
0–14–011428–9 Penguin pb $9.95

YEAR OF CHANGE: More About The New Yorker and Me
Kahn's yearlong daily journal includes many personal and literary reminiscences, with an inside view of the crisis following the departure of longtime editor William Shawn
0–670–82411–9 Viking $19.95

• Gigi Mahon
THE LAST DAYS OF THE NEW YORKER
The story of the sale of the magazine to S.I. Newhouse in 1985
0–07–039635–3 McGraw-Hill $18.95

• David Seideman
THE NEW REPUBLIC: A Voice of Modern Liberalism
Covers the first 25 years of the magazine and its responses to major historical events from labor strikes to Stalinism
Foreword by Martin Peretz
0–275–92016–X Praeger pb $9.95

• Norman Sims, editor
THE LITERARY JOURNALISTS: The New Art of Personal Reportage
Interviews and excerpts from literary journalism's leading stylists, including Joan Didion, John McPhee, Sara Davidson, and Tracy Kidder
0–345–31081–0 Ballantine pb $8.95

ALTERNATIVE JOURNALISM

In recent years, the term "alternative journalism" has become synonymous with the underground press and its variants, which emerged in the 1960s and have played a major role in providing an outlet for the American left and progressive causes, as well as non-traditional writing styles.

Led by such stylists as Tom Wolfe in the 1960s and '70s, the "new journalism" emerged as a rule-breaking means of conveying fact with the artistry of fiction. Less a political trend than an artistic one, the new journalism found a way to present factual information that was as ground-breaking as the work of the dissident press before it.

• Charles Flippen
LIBERATING THE MEDIA: The New Journalism
0–87491–361–6 Acropolis pb $9.95

• Michael L. Johnson
NEW JOURNALISM: The Underground Press, the Artists of Nonfiction, and Changes in the Established Media
0–7006–0085–X Kansas pb $9.95

• Diane Kruchkow & Curt Johnson, editors
GREEN ISLE IN THE SEA: An Informal History of the Alternative Press, 1960–85
0–913204–15–3 December pb $12.50

• Abe Peck
UNCOVERING THE SIXTIES: The Life and Times of the Underground Press
0–394–52793–3 Pantheon $22.95
0–394–71217–X Pantheon pb $12.95

• Tom Wolfe & E.W. Johnson
THE NEW JOURNALISM
0–06–047183–2 Harper & Row pb $19.95

JOURNALISM TODAY

• The Associated Press
THE ASSOCIATED PRESS STYLEBOOK AND LIBEL MANUAL: The Journalist's Bible
0–201–10433–4 Addison-Wesley pb $10.95

• David Broder
BEHIND THE FRONT PAGE: A Candid Look at How the News Is Made
"More wisdom and insight in each brilliant chapter than is available in six semesters at the finest journalism school"—Martin F. Nolan, *Boston Globe*
0–671–44943–5 Simon & Schuster $18.95
0–671–65721–6 Simon & Schuster pb $8.95

• Lou Cannon
REPORTING: An Inside View
Notes from the seasoned *Washington Post* political reporter
0–930302–13–3 California Journal pb $9.95

- John Chancellor & Walter R. Mears
THE NEWS BUSINESS: Getting and Writing the News as Two Top Journalists Do It
0–06–015104–8 Harper & Row $12.95
0–451–62309–6 NAL pb $3.95

- Martin Mayer
MAKING NEWS
Behind-the-scenes look at how and why news is made in America today
0–385–18983–4 Doubleday $18.95

- Melvin Mencher
NEWS REPORTING AND WRITING
The fourth edition of a largely anecdotal, first-rate textbook
0–697–04369–X William Brown $32.50

- Kay Mills
A PLACE IN THE NEWS: From the Women's Pages to the Front Pages
The recent rise of women in newspapers
0–396–08932–1 Dodd, Mead $19.95

- Clint C. Wilson & Felix Gutierrez
MINORITIES AND MEDIA: Diversity and the End of Mass Communication
Charts the slow progress in the hiring and promotion of minorities in the newsroom
0–8039–2454–2 Sage $28.00
0–8039–2455–0 Sage pb $14.00

The National Press Corps

Although most national news organizations retain a New York base, the heaviest permanent mass of journalists is the national press corps in Washington. The press has assumed increasing importance with the centralization of American politics in the White House.

- Sam Donaldson
HOLD ON, MR. PRESIDENT
Chatty autobiography of the contentious ABC newsman
0–394–55393–4 Random House $17.95
0–449–21520–2 Fawcett pb $4.95

- Stephen Hess
THE WASHINGTON REPORTERS
0–8157–3593–6 Brookings Institute pb $9.95

- Larry Speakes with Robert Pack
SPEAKING OUT: The Reagan Presidency from Inside the White House
Kiss-and-tell from Reagan's former press secretary
0–684–18929–1 Scribners $19.95

Critical Studies

- Ben H. Bagdikian
THE MEDIA MONOPOLY
0–8070–6171–9 Beacon pb $10.95

- Daniel J. Boorstin
IMAGE: A Guide to Pseudo-Events in America
0–689–70280–9 Atheneum pb $7.95

- Herbert J. Gans
DECIDING WHAT'S NEWS: A Study of CBS Evening News, NBC Nightly News, Newsweek and Time
"Gans does a hell of a job in demolishing the myths of an anti-establishment press"— *Washington Monthly*
0–394–74354–7 Random House pb $9.95

- Todd Gitlin
THE WHOLE WORLD IS WATCHING: Mass Media in the Making and Unmaking of the New Left
Inside look at the new shape of the opposition in a media-saturated society
0–520–03889–4 California $27.50
0–520–04024–4 California pb $10.95

- Tom Goldstein
THE NEWS AT ANY COST: How Journalists Compromise Their Ethics to Shape the News
0–671–62251–X Simon & Schuster pb $8.95

- Edward S. Herman & Noam Chomsky
MANUFACTURING CONSENT: The Political Economy of the Mass Media
The authors argue that an underlying elite consensus largely structures all facets of the news
0–394–54926–0 Pantheon $24.95
0–679–72034–0 Random House pb $14.95

- S. Robert Lichter, Stanley Rothman & Linda S. Lichter
THE MEDIA ELITE: America's New Powerbrokers
Study of personality and bias among America's broadcast and print journalists
0–917561–11–2 Adler & Adler $19.95

- A.J. Liebling
THE PRESS
Introduction by Alexander Cockburn
0–394–74849–2 Pantheon pb $6.95

- Robert K. Manoff & Michael Schudson, editors
READING THE NEWS
0–394–74649–X Pantheon pb $9.95

From Passionate Journey *by Franz Masereel (City Lights)*

- Michael Parenti
INVENTING REALITY: Politics and the Mass Media
The press meets the Reagan era
0–312–43474–X St. Martin's pb $14.00

- William A. Rusher
THE COMING BATTLE FOR THE MEDIA: Curbing the Power of the Media Elite
The publisher of the *National Review* argues that the press has retained a decidedly liberal slant
0–688–06433–7 Morrow $18.95

- David Shaw
PRESS WATCH: A Provocative Look at How Newspapers Report the News
Disquisitions by the media monitor of the *LA Times*
0–02–610030–4 Macmillan $15.95

- Gaye Tuchman
MAKING NEWS: A Study in the Construction of Reality
Sociological study of mass media and American culture
0–02–932960–4 Free Press pb $11.95

The Press and the Government

- Peter Braestrup
BIG STORY: How the American Press and Television Reported and Interpreted the Crisis of Tet 1968 in Vietnam and Washington
0–300–02807–5 Yale pb $11.95

- Daniel Hallin
THE UNCENSORED WAR: The Media and Vietnam
Detailed account of what Americans read and watched during the Vietnam War
0–19–503814–2 Oxford $24.95

- Mark Hertsgaard
ON BENDED KNEE: The Press and the Reagan Presidency
How the press failed to report what was really going on in the Reagan administration, as a result of government manipulation and voluntary self-censorship
0–374–25197–5 Farrar, Straus & Giroux $22.50

- Deborah Lipstadt
BEYOND BELIEF: The American Press and the Coming of the Holocaust
How the press failed to overcome official indifference to the Holocaust
0–02–919160–2 Free Press $24.95

- William E. Porter
ASSAULT ON THE MEDIA: The Nixon Years
0–472–06301–4 Michigan pb $6.95

- Peter Stoler
THE WAR AGAINST THE PRESS: Politics, Pressure and Intimidation in the '80s
0–396–08757–4 Dodd, Mead $17.95

- John Tebbel & Sarah M. Watts
THE PRESS AND THE PRESIDENCY: From George Washington to Ronald Reagan
0–19–503628–X Oxford $29.95

• Kathleen J. Turner
LYNDON JOHNSON'S DUAL WAR:
Vietnam and the Press
Johnson's ultimately unsuccessful struggle
to gain the support of the press for the
war in Vietnam
0–226–81732–6 Chicago pb $9.95

Censorship and Freedom of the Press

▶ **See also Law**

• Renata Adler
RECKLESS DISREGARD: Westmoreland
v. CBS et. al.; Sharon v. Time
0–394–52751–8 Knopf $16.95
0–394–75525–1 Random House pb $6.95

• Burton Benjamin
FAIR PLAY: CBS, General Westmoreland,
and How a Television Documentary Went
Wrong
A new study of *The Uncounted Enemy: A*
Vietnam Deception and the press freedom
issues it raised; by the man who led CBS's
own investigation into the documentary's
production
Introduction by Walter Cronkite
0–06–015928–6 Harper & Row $17.95

• Kevin Boyle, editor
ARTICLE 19 WORLD REPORT 1988:
Information, Freedom, and Censorship
A compendium of censorship laws and
practices in 50 countries, compiled by the
human-rights organization Article 19
Preface by William Shawcross
0–8129–1801–0 Times Books $22.50

• Fred Friendly
MINNESOTA RAG
Near v. *Minnesota*, an epoch-making case
about a scandal sheet
0–394–71241–2 Random House pb $6.50

• Rodney Smolla
SUING THE PRESS: Libel, the Media,
and Power
From *Carol Burnett* v. *The National*
Enquirer to *Westmoreland* v. *CBS*, a study
of trends in recent libel cases
0–19–505192–0 Oxford pb $8.95

THE PRACTITIONERS: A Sampler

The list below includes collections of various types of journalism—news articles, columns, magazine pieces—from a wide range of American and foreign journalists.

• Jimmy Breslin
THE WORLD ACCORDING TO
BRESLIN
Columns from the *Herald Tribune*
0–89919–310–2 Ticknor & Fields $15.95
0–07–007649–9 McGraw-Hill pb $4.95

• Alexander Cockburn
CORRUPTIONS OF EMPIRE
A collection of columns and articles on the
Reagan era, from a master of alternative
journalism
0–86091–940–4 Verso pb $13.95

• Alistair Cooke
AMERICA OBSERVED: The Newspaper
Years of Alistair Cooke
A collection of articles written when
Cooke served as chief American
correspondent for the *Manchester*
Guardian, 1946–1972
0–394–57432–0 Knopf $19.95

• Oriana Fallaci
INTERVIEW WITH HISTORY
A collection of fascinating interviews with
world leaders by a top journalist
0–395–25223–7 Houghon Mifflin pb $9.95

• William E. Geist
CITY SLICKERS
A collection of the author's "About New
York" columns from the *New York Times*
0–14–011580–3 Penguin pb $7.95

• Martha Gellhorn
THE FACE OF WAR
0–87113–211–7 Atlantic Monthly pb $9.95
THE VIEW FROM THE GROUND
0–87113–212–5 Atlantic Monthly pb $9.95

• Bob Greene
AMERICAN BEAT
0–14–007320–5 Penguin pb $7.95
JOHNNY DEADLINE, REPORTER: The
Best of Bob Greene
0–88229–361–3 Nelson-Hall $21.95

• Christopher Hitchens
PREPARED FOR THE WORST
A collection of critical essays from such
publications as *The Nation, TLS,* and
Harper's
0–8090–7857–0 Farrar, Straus & Giroux $19.95

• Edward Klein & Don Erickson,
editors
ABOUT MEN
Selections from the *New York Times*
column on male experience
Foreword by Russell Baker
0–671–61116–X Simon & Schuster $17.95

• Nancy R. Newhouse, editor
HERS—THROUGH WOMEN'S EYES:
Essays from the "Hers" Column of The
New York Times
0–06–097028–6 Harper & Row pb $7.95

• Anna Quindlen
LIVING OUT LOUD
A collection from the popular syndicated
New York Times "Life in the '30s" column
0–394–56964–4 Random House $17.95

• Dora Russell
THE DORA RUSSELL READER: 57 Years
of Writing and Journalism
0–86358–020–3 RC&H pb $8.95

• Robert Scheer
THINKING TUNA FISH, TALKING
DEATH: Essays on the Pornography of
Power
0–8090–9316–2 Hill & Wang $19.95

THE FOREIGN PRESS

• Madeleine K. Albright
POLAND: The Role of the Press in
Political Change
0–275–91559–X Praeger pb $9.95

• William Finnegan
DATELINE SOWETO
The story of the courageous reporters for
the Johannesburg *Star* and the risks they
take to tell the full story of life in the black
townships and bantustans of South Africa
0–06–015932–4 Harper & Row $18.95

• Ellen Mickiewicz
MEDIA AND THE RUSSIAN PUBLIC
0–275–90682–5 Praeger $33.95
0–275–91515–8 Praeger pb $16.95
SPLIT SIGNALS: Television and Politics
in the Soviet Union
The first in-depth look at Soviet television
and its place in Gorbachev's glasnost
campaign focuses on the popularity of
news reports. The main Soviet news
broadcast *Vremya* (Time) is seen by 150
million viewers nightly
0–19–505463–6 Oxford $22.95

• Richard Pollak
UP AGAINST APARTHEID: The Role and
the Plight of the Press in South Africa
0–8093–1013–9 Southern Illinois $16.95

• Angus Roxburgh
PRAVDA: Inside the Soviet News Machine
The history and operations of the official
Soviet newspaper whose title means
"truth"
0–8076–1186–7 Braziller $19.95

VISUAL IMAGES: Big Books for the Coffee Table

• Marianne Fulton
EYES OF TIME: Photojournalism in
America
A beautiful book featuring some of the
extraordinary photographs that have
shaped America's vision of the news
0–8212–1657–0 NY Graphic Society $40.00

• Life Magazine
LIFE: The First Fifty Years
A mostly pictorial retrospective
0–316–52613–4 Little, Brown $50.00
0–316–52614–2 Little, Brown pb $24.95

• Phelps Dewey
HEADLINES: Front-Page News from the
San Francisco Chronicle, 1865–1988
Reproductions of front pages from the San
Francisco daily record momentous events
of local and national history
0–87701–542–2 Chronicle $24.00

➤ **FOR OVERSEAS ORDERING INFORMATION, SEE PAGE 1**

• Frederick S. Voss
MAN OF THE YEAR: A Time Honored Tradition
A beautifully reproduced volume featuring highlights of the *Time* magazine covers honoring the "Man of the Year," a tradition begun in 1927
Foreword by Alan Fern
0–87474–949–2 Smithsonian pb $12.95

LEWIS LAPHAM:
Grub Street—New and Old

Honoré de Balzac
LOST ILLUSIONS
0–14–044251–0 Penguin pb $7.95

Guy de Maupassant
BEL AMI
0–14–044315–0 Penguin pb $5.95

George Gissing
NEW GRUB STREET
0–14–043032–6 Penguin pb $6.95

William Dean Howells
A HAZARD OF NEW FORTUNES
0–452–00768–2 NAL pb $5.95

Upton Sinclair
BRASS CHECK
0–405–01696–4 Ayer $25.50

H.L. Mencken
NEWSPAPER DAYS, 1899 to 1906
0–404–20176–8 AMS $37.50

A.J. Liebling
THE PRESS
0–394–74849–2 Pantheon pb $6.95

Anthony Trollope
PHINEAS FINN
0–19–281587–3 Oxford pb $6.96

Evelyn Waugh
SCOOP
0–316–92610–8 Little, Brown pb $7.95

Edward R. Murrow (copyright Karsh, Ottawa)

Radio

HISTORIES AND REFERENCE WORKS

Erik Barnouw
A HISTORY OF BROADCASTING IN THE UNITED STATES

Volume 1: A Tower in Babel: To 1933
0–19–500474–4 Oxford $45.00

Volume 2: The Golden Web: 1933 to 1953
0–19–500475–2 Oxford $45.00

Volume 3: The Image Empire: From 1950
0–19–501259–3 Oxford $45.00

• Michael Barson, editor
FLYWHEEL, SHYSTER AND FLYWHEEL: The Marx Brothers' Lost Radio Show
Scripts from the early 1930s
0–679–72036–7 Pantheon pb $9.95

• Susan J. Douglas
INVENTING AMERICAN BROADCASTING, 1899–1922
0–8018–3832–0 Johns Hopkins pb $14.95

• Peter Fornatale & Joshua E. Mills
RADIO IN THE TELEVISION AGE
Begins where the golden age of radio left off. "An adventure story with heroes of its own"—*Newsday*
0–87951–172–9 Viking pb $9.95

• Gene Fowler & Bill Crawford
BORDER RADIO
The colorful story of Mexican border radio stations that commanded a national audience from the 1930s to the 1960s
Foreword by Wolfman Jack
0–87719–066–6 Texas Monthly $18.95

• Dennis Gifford
THE GOLDEN AGE OF RADIO: British Radio, An Illustrated Companion
0–7134–4234–4 David & Charles $35.95

• J. Fred MacDonald
DON'T TOUCH THAT DIAL
0–88229–528–4 Nelson-Hall $24.95
0–88229–673–6 Nelson-Hall pb $13.95

Lorenzo Wilson Milam
SEX AND BROADCASTING: A Handbook on Building a Radio Station for the Community
The fourth edition of a popular book on independent broadcasting. "[Milam] wrote his book . . . to give practical advice to anyone who shares his passion for broadcasting, anyone mad enough to build a radio station for love, not money. The book is firmly grounded in practicalities . . . but it is also wiser and funnier than almost any other book in the field"—*TLS*
0–917320–01–8 Mho & Mho Works pb $12.95

• David Rothel
WHO WAS THAT MASKED MAN?: The Story of the Lone Ranger
0–498–02538–1 Oak Trees $19.50

• Rick Sklar
ROCKING AMERICA: How the All-Hit Radio Stations Took Over, An Insider's Story
0–312–68798–2 St. Martin's pb $7.95

BIOGRAPHIES AND MEMOIRS

• Robert Taylor
FRED ALLEN: His Life and Wit
0–316–83388–6 Little, Brown $19.95

• LeRoy R. Bannerman
NORMAN CORWIN AND RADIO: The Golden Years
0–8173–0274–3 Alabama $28.50

• Larry King & Emily Yoffe
LARRY KING
0–671–41138–1 Simon & Schuster $14.95

• Cyra McFadden
RAIN OR SHINE: A Family Memoir
Memoir about McFadden's father, a country-and-western radio personality
0–394–51937–X Knopf $16.95

• Bruce Morrow with Laura Baudo
COUSIN BRUCIE: My Life in Rock 'n' Roll Radio
0–688–06615–1 Morrow $16.95

• Anthony Slide
GREAT RADIO PERSONALITIES IN HISTORIC PHOTOGRAPHS
0–911572–72–4 Vestal pb $11.95

Television

• Kevin Allman
TV TURKEYS: An Outrageous Look at the Most Preposterous Shows Ever on Television
From *My Mother the Car* (about a woman's reincarnation in the form of her son's Model T) to *Skippy, The Bush Kangaroo,* Australia's answer to Lassie
0–399–51404–X Perigree pb $9.95

• Erik Barnouw
TUBE OF PLENTY: The Evolution of American Television
0–19–501949–0 Oxford $22.50
0–19–503092–3 Oxford pb $11.95

• George Brandt, editor
BRITISH TELEVISION DRAMA
0–521–29384–7 Cambridge pb $15.95

• Tim Brooks
THE COMPLETE DIRECTORY TO PRIME-TIME TV STARS
0–345–31866–8 Ballantine pb $14.95

⇨ **TO ORDER ANY BOOK IN THIS CATALOG, ASK YOUR BOOKSELLER OR CALL 1-800-882-8770**   **647**

• Tim Brooks & Earle Marsh
THE COMPLETE DIRECTORY TO PRIME-TIME NETWORK TELEVISION SHOWS 1946 TO THE PRESENT
A well-researched reference book, packed with information on the casts and broadcasting history of each program listed. "The Guinness Book of World Records, The Encyclopedia Britannica of Television"—*TV Guide*
0–345–00552–X Ballantine pb $14.95

TV IN THE SIXTIES
Nostalgia, with many pictures
0–345–31866–8 Ballantine pb $3.50

TV'S GREATEST HITS
0–345–31865–X Ballantine pb $3.50

• Max Allan Collins & John Javna
THE BEST OF CRIME AND DETECTIVE TV: The Critics' Choice
0–517–57055–6 Crown pb $9.95

• Jane Feuer & Paul Kerr
MTM: Quality Television
A detailed appraisal of the rise and subsequent decline of the Mary Tyler Moore Studios, which, under the leadership of Grant Tinker created such programs as *The Mary Tyler Moore Show, Lou Grant, The White Shadow, Hill Street Blues,* and *St. Elsewhere*
0–85170–162–0 Illinois $30.50
0–85170–163–9 Illinois pb $19.95

• Todd Gitlin
INSIDE PRIME-TIME
Critical essays on such shows as *Lou Grant* and *Hill Street Blues* by one of the country's finest writers about television
0–394–73787–3 Pantheon pb $9.95

• William Hawes
AMERICAN TELEVISION DRAMA: The Experimental Years
0–8173–0276–X Alabama $29.95

• John Javna
THE BEST OF SCIENCE FICTION TV: The Critics' Choice
0–517–56650–8 Crown pb $8.95

CULT TV: A Viewer's Guide to the Shows America Can't Live Without
0–312–17848–4 St. Martin's pb $12.95

THE TV THEME SONG SINGALONG SONGBOOK

Volume 1
0–312–78215–2 St. Martin's pb $6.95

Volume 2
0–312–78218–7 St. Martin's pb $5.95

• Marvin Kitman
I AM A VCR: A Book About Sex, Violence, Dynasty and Dallas, Roone Arledge and Larry Hagman, Rock and Roll and Jiggling, Hero Cars, and the Rest of TV
0–394–56001–9 Random House $17.95

• J. Fred MacDonald
WHO SHOT THE SHERIFF? The Rise and Fall of the Television Western
0–275–92326–6 Praeger $35.00

• Alex McNeil
TOTAL TELEVISION: A Comprehensive Guide to Programming from 1948 through 1979
0–14–007377–9 Penguin pb $14.95

• Leonard Maltin
TV MOVIES AND VIDEO GUIDE 1988 EDITION
An alphabetized listing of over 17,500 films and videos
0–451–15619–6 Signet pb $5.95

• Alvin H. Marill
MOVIES MADE FOR TELEVISION: The Telefeature and the Mini-Series, 1964–1986
0–918432–85–5 NY Zoetrope pb $19.95

• Richard Meyers
THE TV DETECTIVES
0–498–02576–4 Barnes $25.00
0–498–02236–6 Barnes pb $14.95

• Jeff Rovin
TV BABYLON
Titillating and scandalous stories about real-life TV stars
0–451–14782–0 Signet pb $3.95

• Steve Ryan & David Schwartz
THE ENCYCLOPEDIA OF TELEVISION GAME SHOWS
0–918432–87–1 NY Zoetrope $39.95

• Christopher Schemering
THE SOAP OPERA ENCYCLOPEDIA
Both daytime and nighttime soaps, illustrated with photographs
0–345–32459–5 Ballantine pb $8.95

• Cobbett Steinberg
TV FACTS
0–87196–733–2 Facts On File $40.00

• Joseph H. Udelson
THE GREAT TELEVISION RACE: A History of the American Television Industry
0–8173–0082–1 Alabama $18.95

• Vince Waldron
CLASSIC SITCOMS: An Illustrated Celebration of the Best of Prime-Time Comedy in the Past Four Decades
0–02–622770–3 Macmillan $27.50

THE SHOWS

• John Cleese & Connie Booth
THE COMPLETE FAWLTY TOWERS
0–394–57301–3 Pantheon pb $11.95

• Peter Crescenti & Bob Columbe
THE OFFICIAL HONEYMOONERS' TREASURY
Introduction by Audrey Meadows
0–399–51201–2 Putnam pb $3.95

• Gerry Davis
THE TODAY SHOW BOOK
The first 35 years
0–688–06766–2 Morrow $17.95
0–688–06545–7 Morrow pb $7.95

• Stephen Davis
SAY KIDS, WHAT TIME IS IT?: Notes From the Peanut Gallery
The *Howdy Doody Show* story, from the son of the show's head writer and director
0–316–17662–1 Little, Brown $16.95

• Mark Dawidziak
THE COLUMBO PHILE: A Casebook
0–89296–376–X Mysterious $24.95

• Dave Gerrold
THE WORLD OF STAR TREK
A hard-to-find compendium of the cult series
0–312–94463–2 Blue Jay pb $9.95

• Joey Green
THE UNOFFICIAL GILLIGAN'S ISLAND HANDBOOK
Big print, plot synopses, lots of photographs about one of the dopiest shows ever on TV
0–446–38668–5 Warner pb $8.95

• Jon Hestland
THE MAN FROM U.N.C.L.E. BOOK
TV's answer to James Bond
Introduction by Robert Vaughn
0–312–00052–9 St. Martin's pb $12.95

• Suzy Kalter
THE COMPLETE BOOK OF DALLAS: Behind the Scenes at the World's Favorite Television Show
0–8109–0836–0 Abrams pb $14.95

THE COMPLETE BOOK OF M*A*S*H
0–8109–8083–5 Abrams pb $19.95

• Brian Kelleher & Diana Merrill
THE PERRY MASON TV SHOW BOOK
0–312–00669–1 St. Martin's pb $12.95

• Jeff Lenburg & others
THE THREE STOOGES SCRAPBOOK
0–8065–0946–5 Citadel pb $12.95

• Frank Lovece & Jules Franco
HAILING TAXI
A tribute to the long-running series
0–13–372103–5 Prentice-Hall pb $12.95

• Donna McCrohan & Peter Crescenti
THE HONEYMOONERS' LOST EPISODES
0–89480–157–0 Workman pb $8.95

• Donna McCrohan
THE HONEYMOONERS' COMPANION
0–89480–022–1 Workman pb $7.95

ARCHIE AND EDITH, MIKE AND GLORIA: The Tumultuous History of All in the Family
0–317–66192–2 Workman pb $7.95

• Ric Meyers
MURDER ON THE AIR: Television's Great Mystery Series
0–89296–977–6 Mysterious pb $12.95

• Ted Sennett
YOUR SHOW OF SHOWS
The golden age of TV comedy, with Sid Caesar, Imogene Coca, and others
0–306–80235–0 Da Capo pb $10.95

- Jeff Sorenson
  THE TAXI BOOK: The Complete Guide to TV's Most Lovable Hacks
  0–312–00691–8 St. Martin's pb $10.95

- Jeff Weingrad & Doug Hill
  SATURDAY NIGHT: A Backstage History of Saturday Night Live
  Jealousies and politicking behind the scenes
  0–688–05099–9 Morrow $17.95
  0–394–75053–5 Random House pb $8.95

- Matthew White & Jaffer Ali
  THE OFFICIAL PRISONER COMPANION
  0–446–38744–4 Warner pb $9.95

- Stephen Whitfield & Gene Roddenberry
  THE MAKING OF STAR TREK
  0–345–34019–1 Ballantine pb $4.95

- Mark Scott Zicree
  THE TWILIGHT ZONE COMPANION
  0–553–34362–9 Bantam pb $11.95

CELEBRITY BIOGRAPHIES AND AUTOBIOGRAPHIES

- Charles Higham
  LUCY: The Real Life of Lucille Ball
  0–312–50004–1 St. Martin's pb $3.95

- Bob Woodward
  WIRED: The Short Life and Fast Times of John Belushi
  The excesses of the *Saturday Night Live* star, the struggle for control over his career by agents, managers, and family, and his sudden death from an overdose of cocaine and heroin, by the *Washington Post* editor and coauthor of *All The President's Men*
  0–317–54722–4 Pocket Books pb $4.95

- Milton Berle
  B.S. I LOVE YOU: 60 Funny Years with the Famous and the Infamous
  Reminiscences—mostly involving the fabled Friars Club—by one of television's first and biggest stars
  0–07–004913–0 McGraw-Hill $17.95

  Carol Burnett
  ONE MORE TIME
  The comedienne's chaotic upbringing and her early career
  0–394–55254–7 Random House $18.95
  0–380–70449–8 Avon pb $4.50

- Paul Corkery
  CARSON: The Unauthorized Biography
  0–942101–02–2 Randt pb $3.95

- Laurence Leamer
  KING OF THE NIGHT: The Life of Johnny Carson
  0–688–07404–9 Morrow $19.95

Carol Burnett with Gary Moore in Neil Simon's "Princess of Monrovia" sketch (photo courtesy of CBS, Irv Haberman), from her autobiography One More Time *(Random House)*

- Joan Collins
  PAST IMPERFECT
  The life and romances of the *Dynasty* villainess
  0–425–07786–7 Berkley pb $3.95

- Fred Cordova
  JOHNNY CAME LATELY
  The autobiography of the *Tonight Show* executive producer and onetime director of such films as *Bedtime for Bonzo*
  0–671–55849–8 Simon & Schuster $17.95

- Patty Duke with Kenneth Turan
  CALL ME ANNA: The Autobiography of Patty Duke
  The child star's lonely childhood
  0–553–05209–8 Bantam $17.95

- James Bacon
  HOW SWEET IT IS: The Jackie Gleason Story
  0–312–90229–8 St. Martin's pb $4.50

- Caroline Latham
  THE DAVID LETTERMAN STORY
  531–15032–1 Franklin Watts pb $3.95

TELEVISION AND SOCIETY

- Michael J. Arlen
  LIVING-ROOM WAR
  0–14–006081–2 Penguin pb $6.95

  THE CAMERA AGE: Essays on Television
  0–374–11822–1 Farrar, Straus & Giroux $13.95

- Geoffrey Barlow & Alison Hill, editors
  VIDEO VIOLENCE AND CHILDREN
  The effects of televised mayhem on children
  0–312–84571–5 St. Martin's $19.95

- Razelle Frankl
  TELEVANGELISM: The Marketing of Popular Religion
  The rise of TV ministries and an explanation of their methods, power, and popularity
  0–8093–1299–9 Southern Illinois $22.50

- Todd Gitlin
  THE WHOLE WORLD IS WATCHING: Mass Media in the Making and Unmaking of the New Left
  An extended essay on television and politics by the Berkeley professor and one of the finest critics and writers about television
  0–520–03889–4 California $27.50

- Todd Gitlin, editor
  WATCHING TELEVISION
  A wide-ranging, hit-or-miss collection of essays about TV by a mix of academics, journalists, and critics
  0–394–54496–X Pantheon $19.95
  0–394–74651–1 Pantheon pb $9.95

- Patricia Greenfield
  MIND AND MEDIA: The Effects of Television Video Games and Computers
  Illustrated
  0–674–57620–9 Harvard $13.50
  0–674–57621–7 Harvard pb $4.95

- Hal Himmelstein
  TELEVISION, MYTH AND THE AMERICAN MIND
  0–275–91190–X Praeger $40.95
  0–275–91788–6 Praeger pb $17.95

- Bob Hodge & David Tripp
  CHILDREN AND TELEVISION: A Semiotic Approach
  0–8047–1352–9 Stanford $32.50

- Jerry Mander
  FOUR ARGUMENTS FOR THE ELIMINATION OF TELEVISION
  0–688–08274–2 Morrow pb $7.95

- Kate Moody
  GROWING UP ON TELEVISION: A Report to Parents
  With an introduction by Norman Cousins
  0–07–042871–9 McGraw-Hill pb $6.95

- Horace Newcomb, editor
  TELEVISION: The Critical View
  "Essays on music television, sitcoms, and the ideological structures of television from a variety of approaches including semiotics, communication theory, and institutional analysis"—*Film Quarterly*
  0–19–504175–5 Oxford pb $16.95

- Robert Sklar
  PRIME-TIME AMERICA: Life On and Behind the Television Screen
  0–19–503046–X Oxford pb $6.95

- Jim Spence with Dave Diles
  UP CLOSE AND PERSONAL
  An insider's vengeful account of Roone
  Arledge, Howard Cosell, and the rise of
  ABC sports
  0–689–11943–7 Atheneum $19.95

- Martin Williams
  TV: The Casual Art
  Essays by a well-known jazz critic
  0–19–502992–5 Oxford $19.95

- Raymond Williams
  **RAYMOND WILLIAMS ON
  TELEVISION: The Culture of Television**
  A collection of Williams' essays for *The
  Listener*
  Edited by Alan O'Connor
  0–415–02627–X RC&H pb $14.95

- Marie Winn
  **THE PLUG-IN DRUG: Television,
  Children and the Family**
  0–14–007698–0 Penguin pb $6.95

  **UNPLUGGING THE PLUG-IN DRUG:
  Help Your Children Kick the TV Habit**
  0–670–81887–9 Viking $18.95

THE BUSINESS OF TELEVISION

- Christopher Byron
  **THE FANCIEST DIVE: What Happened
  When the Giant Media Empire of Time-Life
  Leapt Without Looking into the Age of
  High-Tech**
  The corporate misadventures that led to
  HBO
  0–393–02261–7 Norton $16.95

- Richard Levinson & William Link
  **OFF-CAMERA: Conversations with the
  Makers of Prime-Time Television**
  Interviews with Norman Lear (*All in the
  Family, The Jeffersons, Maude*), Larry
  Gelbart, (*M*A*S*H*) and others,
  conducted by the creators of *Columbo* and
  Murder, She Wrote
  0–452–25873–1 NAL pb $8.95

- George Mair
  **INSIDE HBO: The Billion Dollar War
  Between HBO and the Home Video
  Revolution**
  0–396–08420–6 Dodd, Mead $17.95

- Horace Newcomb & Robert S. Alley
  **THE PRODUCER'S MEDIUM:
  Conversations with Creators of American
  TV**
  0–19–503583–6 Oxford pb $8.95

- Huntington Williams III
  **BEYOND CONTROL: The Rise and Fall of
  ABC**
  How ABC rose to number one in the
  1970s with *Roots, Happy Days,* and
  Charlie's Angels, and subsequently fell into
  an abyss that resulted in a historic
  takeover; by an ABC insider
  0–689–11818–X Atheneum $19.95

TECHNICAL AND HOW-TO

- Howard Blumenthal
  **TELEVISION PRODUCING AND
  DIRECTING**
  0–06–463700–X Harper & Row pb $12.95

- Martin S. Dick
  **THE OUT-OF-CONTROL ROOM: A
  Hilarious Look at TV Production**
  A firsthand account
  0–9618502–0–5 Sugma pb $9.25

- Syd Field
  **SCREENPLAY: The Foundations of
  Screenwriting**
  One of the most popular books on
  screenwriting, particularly helpful for
  understanding script structure
  0–440–57647–4 Doubleday pb $8.95

  THE SCREENWRITER'S WORKBOOK
  A practical, step-by-step guide
  0–440–58225–3 Doubleday pb $8.95

  **STAY TUNED: An Inside Look at the
  Making of Prime-Time Television**
  0–312–76136–8 St. Martin's pb $11.95

- Peter E. Mayeux
  **WRITING FOR THE BROADCAST
  MEDIA**
  0–205–08343–9 Allyn & Bacon $26.95

- Linda Seger
  **MAKING A GOOD SCRIPT GREAT: A
  Guide to Writing and Re-Writing**
  The most useful and instructive book on
  screenwriting
  0–396–08935–6 Dodd, Mead $15.95
  0–396–08953–4 Dodd, Mead pb $10.95

- Bob Shanks
  **THE PRIMAL SCREEN: How to Write,
  Sell and Produce Movies For Television**
  General information about optioning
  properties, wooing studio execs, pitch
  meetings, etc.
  0–393–01993–4 Norton $16.95
  0–449–90229–3 Fawcett pb $9.95

ADVERTISING

- Michael J. Arlen
  THIRTY SECONDS
  Probably the best-written account of how
  a commercial is made, by the novelist and
  New Yorker essayist
  0–374–27576–9 Farrar, Straus & Giroux $9.95
  0–14–005810–9 Penguin pb $6.95

- Erik Barnouw
  **THE SPONSOR: Notes on a Modern
  Potentate**
  Advertising and sponsorship and their
  influence
  0–19–502614–4 Oxford pb $8.95

- Edwin Diamond & Stephen Bates
  **THE SPOT: The Rise of Political
  Advertising on Television**
  Illustrated
  0–262–04095–6 MIT $25.00
  0–262–54049–5 MIT pb $10.95

IF YOU CAN'T FIND IT, LOOK IN THE INDEX

PART 9

WORLD HISTORY
AND
CURRENT AFFAIRS

The Varieties of Civilization

"History is a discipline widely cultivated among nations and races. It is eagerly sought after. The men in the street, the ordinary people, aspire to know it. Kings and leaders vie for it.

Both the learned and the ignorant are able to understand it. For on the surface history is no more than information about political events, dynasties, and occurrences of the remote past, elegantly presented and spiced with proverbs. It serves to entertain large, crowded gatherings and brings to us an understanding of human affairs. It shows how changing conditions affect [human affairs], how certain dynasties came to occupy an ever wider space in the world, and how they settled the earth until they heard the call and their time was up.

The inner meaning of history, on the other hand, involves speculation and an attempt to get at the truth, and deep knowledge of the how and why of events. History, therefore, is firmly rooted in philosophy. It deserves to be accounted a branch of it."— Ibn Khaldûn, *The Muqaddimah: An Introduction to History* (late 14th century)

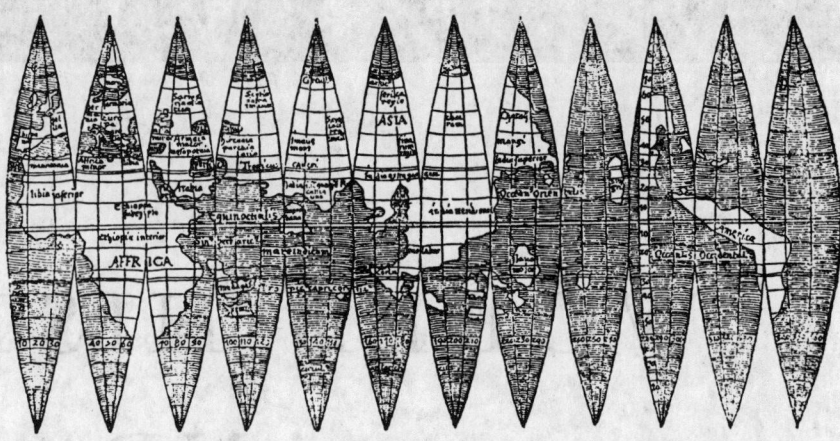

Woodcut gores for a 1507 globe, from The Mapmakers *by John Noble Wilford* (*Knopf*)

WORLD HISTORIES

• **John A. Garraty & Peter Gay, editors**
THE COLUMBIA HISTORY OF THE WORLD
A magnificent synthesis; published in 1972
0–06–011432–0 Harper & Row $9.95

• **Bernard Grun**
THE TIMETABLES OF HISTORY: A Horizontal Linkage of People and Events
Based on Werner Stein's *Kulturfahrplan*
0–671–24988–6 Simon & Schuster pb $19.95

• **William H. McNeill**
THE RISE OF THE WEST: A History of the Human Community
Traces the fundamental interrelations among different cultures throughout history, challenging the idea that separate civilizations evolved on largely independent paths
0–226–56144–5 Chicago pb $15.00

• **R.R. Palmer & Joel Colton**
A HISTORY OF THE MODERN WORLD
Now in its sixth printing, this is a terrific textbook; the focus is on Europe since the Renaissance
0–394–53396–8 Knopf $45.00

• **J.M. Roberts**
THE PELICAN HISTORY OF THE WORLD
The whole story, in one compact paperback volume. "Unbelievably accurate in its facts and almost incontestable in its judgments"—A.J.P. Taylor
0–14–022785–7 Penguin pb $11.95

The Mapmakers

Daniel J. Boorstin
THE DISCOVERERS: A History of Man's Search to Know His World and Himself
The bestselling story of the "men of discovery" and the illusions of knowledge which lay as barriers in their paths
0–394–72625–1 Random House pb $9.95

John Noble Wilford
THE MAPMAKERS: The Story of the Great Pioneers in Cartography from Antiquity to the Space Age
0–394–75303–8 Random House pb $13.95

Readings in Western Civilization

• **John W. Boyer & Julius Kirshner, editors**
UNIVERSITY OF CHICAGO READINGS IN WESTERN CIVILIZATION
A widely-used, authoritative collection of source materials

Volume 1: The Greek Polis
Edited by Arthur W.H. Adkins & Peter White
0–226–06935–4 Chicago pb $8.95

Volume 2: Late Republic and Principate
Edited by Walter Emil Kaegi, Jr. & Peter White
0–226–06937–0 Chicago pb $8.95

Volume 3: The Church in the Roman Empire
Edited by Karl F. Morrison
0–226–06939–7 Chicago pb $7.95

Volume 4: Medieval Europe
Edited by Julius Kirshner & Karl F. Morrison
0–226–06943–5 Chicago pb $11.95

Volume 5: The Renaissance
Edited by Eric Cochrane & Julius Kirshner
0–226–06945–1 Chicago pb $11.95

Volume 6: Early Modern Europe: Crisis of Authority
Edited by Eric Cochrane, Charles M. Gray & Mark A. Kishlansky
0–226–06948–6 Chicago pb $14.95

Volume 7: The Ancien Régime and the French Revolution
Edited by Keith Michael Baker
0–226–06950–8 Chicago pb $11.95

Volume 8: Nineteenth-Century Europe: Liberalism in an Age of Industrialization
Edited by Jan Goldstein & John W. Boyer
0–226–06952–4 Chicago pb $13.95

Volume 9: Twentieth-Century Europe
Edited by John W. Boyer & Jan Goldstein
0–226–06954–0 Chicago pb $14.95

• **William H. McNeill**
HISTORY OF WESTERN CIVILIZATION: A Handbook
0–226–56160–7 Chicago pb $17.95

John Carey, editor
EYEWITNESS TO HISTORY
An engaging collection of snapshots great and small: Rome burns, AD 64; dinner with Attila the Hun, c. AD 450; the murder of Thomas à Becket, December 29, 1170; Marie Antoinette at the opera, July 1792; the conquest of Everest, May 29, 1953; and more
0–674–28750–9 Harvard $24.95

The 20th Century

• **Raymond Aron**
THE CENTURY OF TOTAL WAR
0–8191–4563–7 University Press pb $15.50

• **Karl-Dietrich Bracher**
THE AGE OF IDEOLOGIES: A History of Political Thought in the Twentieth Century
By the author of the highly praised *German Dictatorship*
Translated by Ewald Osers
0–312–01230–6 St. Martin's pb $11.95

• **Clifton Daniels & others, editors**
CHRONICLE OF THE 20TH CENTURY
A detailed and beautifully-illustrated guide to the major events and players in recent world history
0–13–133703–3 Prentice-Hall $49.95

• **Paul Johnson**
MODERN TIMES: The World from the Twenties to the Eighties
A tour de force from a British neo-conservative, stressing the dangers of the consolidation of state power
0–06–091210–3 Harper & Row pb $11.95

- William R. Keylor
**THE TWENTIETH-CENTURY WORLD:
An International History**
Properly sets Europe in a global context
0–19–503370–1 Oxford pb $13.95

- Greil Marcus
**LIPSTICK TRACES: A Secret History of
the Twentieth Century**
The "counterhistory" of hidden cultural
movements
0–674–53580–4 Harvard $29.95

- W.W. Rostow
**RICH COUNTRIES AND POOR
COUNTRIES: Reflections from the Past,
Lessons for the Future**
0–8133–0497–0 Westview $34.50

CULTURAL POLITICS

- Benedict Anderson
**IMAGINED COMMUNITIES: Reflections
on the Origin and Spread of Nationalism**
The sense of *nationality*, the personal and
cultural feeling of belonging to a nation.
Anderson probes the impact of print
during the Reformation, the independence
movements of 18th-century America, the
Meiji Restoration, and more
0–86091–759–2 Verso pb $11.95

- Alfred W. Crosby
**ECOLOGICAL IMPERIALISM: The
Biological Expansion of Europe, 900-1900**
0–521–32009–7 Cambridge $29.95

- Franklin L. Ford
**POLITICAL MURDER: From Tyrannicide
to Terrorism**
0–674–68636–5 Harvard pb $9.95

- E.J. Hobsbawm
BANDITS
0–394–74850–6 Pantheon pb $4.95

PRIMITIVE REBELS
0–393–00328–0 Norton pb $7.95

- Barrington Moore, Jr.
**PRIVACY: Studies in Social and Cultural
History**
0–87332–269–X Sharpe pb $12.95

**REFLECTIONS ON THE CAUSES OF
HUMAN MISERY**
0–8070–1531–8 Beacon pb $7.95

**THE SOCIAL ORIGINS OF
DICTATORSHIP AND DEMOCRACY**
0–8070–5075–X Beacon pb $12.95

- Conor Cruise O'Brien
**GOD'S LAND: Reflections on Religion and
Nationalism**
Old Testament Canaan, Joan of Arc,
Puritan Massachusetts, and National Prayer
Breakfasts all come under the author's
sardonic gaze
0–674–35510–5 Harvard $15.95

ECONOMIC HISTORY

- William Ashworth
**A SHORT HISTORY OF THE
INTERNATIONAL ECONOMY SINCE
1850**
0–582–49383–8 Longman pb $15.95

- Carlo M. Cipolla
**BEFORE THE INDUSTRIAL
REVOLUTION: European Economy and
Society, 1000-1700**
0–393–01343–X Norton $16.95
0–393–95115–4 Norton pb $9.95

- Carlo M. Cipolla, editor
**THE ECONOMIC HISTORY OF WORLD
POPULATION**
0–06–491138–1 Barnes & Noble $26.50

- Philip D. Curtin
**CROSS-CULTURAL TRADE IN WORLD
HISTORY**
Silk from China to Rome, African ivory,
the Indian Ocean spice trade: the colorful
world of exchange over two millennia
0–521–26931–8 Cambridge pb $10.95

- Paul M. Hoenberg & Lynn Hollen
Lees
**THE MAKING OF URBAN EUROPE,
1000-1950**
A landmark in historiography, tracing the
social, economic and political changes
within Europe's cities, as well as the
evolving relationships between town and
country and among the different urban
centers
0–674–54361–0 Harvard pb $10.95

- Karl Polanyi
**THE GREAT TRANSFORMATION: The
Political and Economic Origins of Our
Time**
0–8070–5679–0 Beacon pb $10.95

- W.W. Rostow
**THE STAGES OF ECONOMIC
GROWTH**
0–521–09650–2 Cambridge pb $15.95

- Pierre Vilar
**A HISTORY OF GOLD AND MONEY,
1450-1920**
By the historian whose *La Catalogne dans
l'Espagne Moderne* has been hailed as a
major work. "This book has deservedly
become a classic"—*New Society*
Translated by Judith White
0–86091–798–3 Verso pb $15.95

- Carolyn Webber & Aaron Wildavsky
**A HISTORY OF TAXATION AND
EXPENDITURE IN THE WESTERN
WORLD**
Five thousand years of taxing and
spending, from Mesopotamia to Reagan's
America. "A model of analytic history"—
James W. Felser, Yale University
0–671–63321–X Simon & Schuster pb $14.95

- William Woodruff
**THE IMPACT OF WESTERN MAN: A
Study of Europe's Role in the World
Economy, 1750-1960**
0–8191–2486–9 University Press pb $17.95

INTELLECTUAL HISTORY

- Franklin L. Baumer
**MAIN CURRENTS OF WESTERN
THOUGHT: Readings in Western
European Intellectual History from the
Middle Ages to the Present**
0–300–02233–6 Yale pb $17.95

**MODERN EUROPEAN THOUGHT:
Continuity and Change in Ideas, 1600-1950**
0–02–306450–1 Macmillan $26.95

- Jacob Bronowski & Bruce Mazlish
**THE WESTERN INTELLECTUAL
TRADITION: From Leonardo to Hegel**
0–06–133001–9 Harper & Row pb $10.95

Alan Bullock
THE HUMANIST TRADITION
The Renaissance, the Enlightenment,
the 19th-century definitions of
humanism, and the elements of a new
humanism in the 20th century. Highly
recommended reading by a gifted
political historian; illustrated
0–393–30421–3 Norton pb $10.95

- Klaus K. Klostermaier
A SURVEY OF HINDUISM
Accessible and comprehensive coverage of
what is sometimes regarded as the seed of
world religion
0–88706–809–X SUNY pb $18.95

- Dominick LaCapra & Steven L.
Kaplan, editors
**MODERN EUROPEAN INTELLECTUAL
HISTORY: Reappraisals and New
Perspectives**
0–8014–9881–3 Cornell pb $16.95

- Hugh McLeod
**RELIGION AND THE PEOPLE OF
WESTERN EUROPE, 1789-1970**
0–19–215832–5 Oxford $17.95
0–19–289101–4 Oxford pb $9.95

- Frank E. & Fritzie P. Manuel
**UTOPIAN THOUGHT IN THE
WESTERN WORLD**
0–674–93186–6 Harvard pb $12.95

- Robert Nisbet
HISTORY OF THE IDEA OF PROGRESS
0–465–03028–9 Basic Books pb $12.95

- Benjamin Schwartz
**THE WORLD OF THOUGHT IN
ANCIENT CHINA**
The golden age of Chinese thought
between the 6th and 3rd centuries BC
0–674–96190–0 Harvard $29.50

- Roland N. Stromberg
**AFTER EVERYTHING: Western
Intellectual History Since 1945**
0–312–01120–2 St. Martin's pb $14.95

**EUROPEAN INTELLECTUAL HISTORY
SINCE 1789**
0–13–292046–8 Prentice-Hall $26.95

PERSPECTIVES IN HISTORY

• **William J. Baker**
SPORTS IN THE WESTERN WORLD
"Every . . . sporting event, from amateur Olympics to professional media hype [is] presented in this thorough, well-composed chronicle"—*Best Sellers*
0–252–06042–3 Illinois pb $14.95

• **Paul F. Boller, Jr. & John George**
THEY NEVER SAID IT: A Book of Fake Quotes, Misquotes, and Misleading Attributions
0–19–505541–1 Oxford $15.95

• **François Boucher**
TWENTY THOUSAND YEARS OF FASHION: The History of Costume and Personal Adornment
A profusely illustrated survey
0–8109–1693–2 Abrams $45.00

• **Leo Braudy**
THE FRENZY OF RENOWN: Fame and Its History
By the author of *The World in a Frame: What We See in Films*
0–19–505178–5 Oxford pb $13.95

• **Alain Corbin**
THE FOUL AND THE FRAGRANT: Odor and the French Social Imagination
An offbeat look at the 18th and 19th centuries. "Reminds us that social history, too long sanitized and too often abstract, must make room for the senses"—Michael Burns, *LA Times Book Review*
0–674–31176–0 Harvard pb $10.95

• **John R. Gillis**
YOUTH AND HISTORY: Tradition and Change in European Age Relations, 1770 to the Present
0–12–785264–6 Academic $19.95

• **Mark Girouard**
CITIES AND PEOPLE
An ideal survey; beautifully illustrated
0–300–03968–9 Yale pb $19.95

• **Emmanuel Le Roy Ladurie**
TIMES OF FEAST, TIMES OF FAMINE: A History of Climate Since the Year 1000
Translated by Barbara Bray
0–374–52122–0 Noonday pb $14.95

• **Colleen McDannell & Bernhard Lang**
HEAVEN: A History
"A whistle-stop tour . . . of the extraordinary things Christians and others have believed about life and death"—John Barton, *London Review of Books*
0–300–04346–5 Yale $29.95

• **Lewis Mumford**
THE CITY IN HISTORY: Its Origins, Its Transformations and Its Prospects
A classic study of the development and degeneration of cities by the eminent cultural philosopher
0–15–618035–9 HBJ pb $12.95

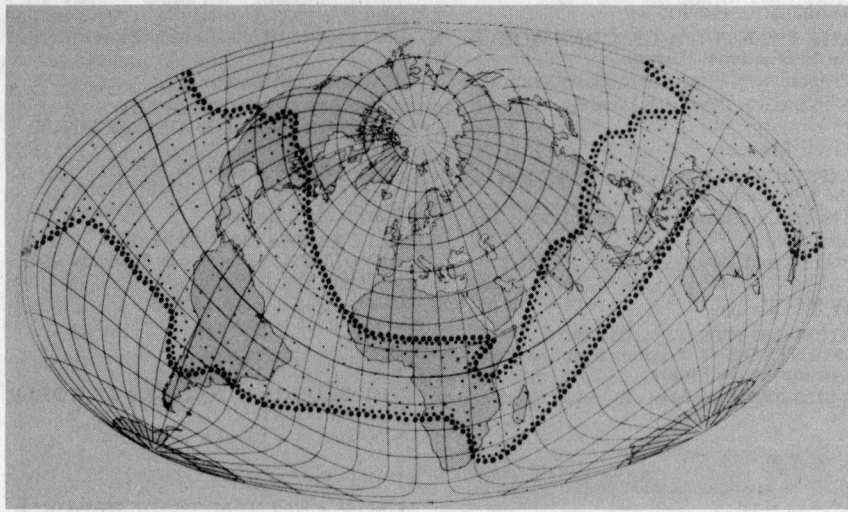

The hoe-cultivation belt, from The Structures of Everyday Life *by Fernand Braudel* (*Harper & Row*)

• **John T. Noonan Jr.**
BRIBES: The Intellectual History of a Moral Idea
A 4000-year history of an idea central to democratic government
0–520–06154–3 California pb $14.95

• **Roderick Phillips**
PUTTING ASUNDER: A History of Divorce in Western Society
0–521–32434–3 Cambridge $39.50

• **Roy Porter**
A SOCIAL HISTORY OF MADNESS: The World Through the Eyes of the Insane
An illuminating and provocative discussion of the experiences of both the famous and the obscure with psychiatric treatment and confinement, including George III, Schumann, Nietzsche, Nijinsky, Artaud, Plath
Edited by Mark Polizzotti
1–55584–185–6 Weidenfeld & Nicolson $18.95

• **William H. White**
CITY: Rediscovering Its Center
0–385–05458–0 Doubleday $24.95

• **Hans Zinsser**
RATS, LICE AND HISTORY
0–316–98890–1 Atlantic Monthly $12.95
0–316–98896–0 Little, Brown pb $7.95

Sexuality and Private Life

• **Philippe Ariès**
CENTURIES OF CHILDHOOD: A Social History of Family Life
Translated by Robert Baldick
0–394–70286–7 Random House pb $8.95

• **Philippe Ariès & André Bejin, editors**
WESTERN SEXUALITY: Practice and Precept in Past and Present Times
Essays from French, Italian, and English scholars on the western models of marriage, love within and outside marriage, and changing sexual practices
Translated by Anthony Forster
0–631–14989–9 Blackwell pb $12.95

• **Philippe Ariès & Georges Duby, editors**
A HISTORY OF PRIVATE LIFE
Stimulating essays by historians and literary critics. "One of the most arresting, original and rewarding historical surveys to be published in many years"—Bernard Knox, *Atlantic*
Translated by Arthur Goldhammer

Volume 1: From Pagan Rome to Byzantium
Edited by Paul Veyne
0–674–39975–7 Harvard $35.00

Volume 2: Revelations of the Medieval World
Edited by Georges Duby
0–674–39976–5 Harvard $39.50

Volume 3: Passions of the Renaissance
Edited by Roger Chartier
0–674–39977–3 Harvard $39.50

• **John D'Emilio & Estelle B. Freedman**
INTIMATE MATTERS: A History of Sexuality in America
0–06–015855–7 Harper & Row $24.95
0–06–091550–1 Harper & Row pb $9.95

• **Michel Feher & others, editors**
FRAGMENTS FOR A HISTORY OF THE HUMAN BODY
Essays by leading social historians; published by Zone books and distributed by MIT Press. "Michel Feher has assembled an all-star Euro-crit team, with MVPs like Julia Kristeva, Jean Starobinski, and Jean-Pierre Vernant, to perform an exhaustive physical exam: no body part is left unpoked"—Albert Mobilio, *VLS*

Volume 1: Zone 3
0–942299–23–X Zone pb $19.95

Volume 2: Zone 4
0–942299–24–8 Zone pb $19.95

Volume 3: Zone 5
0–942299–28–0 Zone pb $19.95

• **Gerard Kent & Gert Helema, editors**
THE PURSUIT OF SODOMY: Male Homosexuality in Renaissance and Enlightenment Europe
0–918393–49–3 Harrington Park pb $22.95

IF YOU CAN'T FIND IT, LOOK IN THE INDEX

- Paul Robinson
THE MODERNIZATION OF SEX:
Havelock Ellis, Alfred Kinsey, William
Masters and Virginia Johnson
0–8104–9539–3 Cornell pb $9.95

Food and Pharmaceuticals

- K.C. Chang, editor
FOOD IN CHINESE CULTURE
"Solid facts and insights into the meaning
and historical background of Chinese
dishes, food customs and symbolism,
utensils, culinary aesthetics"—*NY Times
Book Review*
0–300–02759–1 Yale pb $13.95

- Henry Hobhouse
**SEEDS OF CHANGE: Five Plants That
Transformed Mankind**
How quinine, sugar cane, tea, cotton and
the potato changed the course of human
history. "Infused with witty speculation
and the courage to suggest new ways at
looking at the cause and effect of world
events"—*Smithsonian*
0–06–091440–8 Harper & Row pb $8.95

- Lydia Mez-Mangold
A HISTORY OF DRUGS
An illustrated history of drugs and the
science of pharmacy, from Mesopotamia to
the present
0–389–20638–5 Barnes & Noble $25.00

- Sidney W. Mintz
**SWEETNESS AND POWER: The Place of
Sugar in Modern History**
How Europe and America transformed
sugar from a rare foreign luxury to a staple
of modern life
0–14–009233–1 Penguin pb $7.95

- Redcliffe Salaman
**THE HISTORY AND SOCIAL
INFLUENCE OF THE POTATO**
0–521–31623–5 Cambridge pb $17.95

- Reay Tannahill
FOOD IN HISTORY
A fascinating social history dealing with
nutrition, staples, luxuries like sugar,
coffee, tea, and liquors, banquets,
restaurants, trade, and regional peculiarities
0–517–57186–2 Crown $19.95

- Margaret Visser
**MUCH DEPENDS ON DINNER: The
Extraordinary History and Mythology,
Allure and Obsessions, Perils and Taboos,
of an Ordinary Meal**
0–8021–0023–6 Grove $19.95

Women

- Bonnie S. Anderson & Judith Zinsser
**A HISTORY OF THEIR OWN: Women in
Europe From Prehistory to the Present**
Volume 1:
0–06–015850–6 Harper & Row $27.50
0–06–091452–1 Harper & Row pb $12.95
Volume 2:
0–06–015899–9 Harper & Row $27.50

- Renate Bridenthal, Claudia Koonz &
Susan M. Stuard
**BECOMING VISIBLE: Women in
European History**
0–395–41950–6 Houghton Mifflin pb $23.50

- Vern & Bonnie Bullough
**WOMEN AND PROSTITUTION: A Social
History**
0–87975–372–2 Prometheus pb $16.95

- Janice Delaney & others
**THE CURSE: A Cultural History of
Menstruation**
"By providing a broad cultural reading . . .
the authors make an important feminist
and scholarly statement about women and
the continuing impact of 'menstrual
politics' "—Paula A. Treichler
0–252–01240–2 Illinois $29.95
0–252–01452–9 Illinois pb $10.95

- Antonia Fraser
THE WARRIOR QUEENS
0–394–54939–2 Knopf $22.95

Men at Arms

- Frances Gies
THE KNIGHT IN HISTORY
Demythologizes the knight throughout
European history
0–06–091413–0 Harper & Row pb $8.95

- Michael Howard
WAR IN EUROPEAN HISTORY
0–19–289095–6 Oxford pb $9.95

- Paul Kennedy
**THE RISE AND FALL OF THE GREAT
POWERS: Economic Change and Military
Conflict, 1500-2000**
0–394–54674–1 Random House $24.95
0–679–72019–7 Random House pb $12.95

- V.G. Kiernan
THE DUEL IN EUROPEAN HISTORY
The evolution of the duel from medieval
times
0–19–822566–0 Oxford $49.95

- William H. McNeill
**THE PURSUIT OF POWER: Technology,
Armed Force, and Society Since A.D. 1000**
0–226–56158–5 Chicago pb $11.95

- Geoffrey Parker
**THE MILITARY REVOLUTION: Military
Innovation and the Rise of the West, 1500-
1800**
"Illuminates virtually every aspect of
warfare in this watershed period"—Gordon
A. Craig, *NY Review of Books*
0–521–32607–9 Cambridge $29.95

- Richard A. Preston & Sydney F. Wise
**MEN IN ARMS: A History of Warfare and
Its Interrelationships with Western Society**
0–03–045681–9 HR&W pb $25.95

▶ See also Historical and Political Atlases in the
Reference section of Practical Advice

- Geoffrey Barraclough, editor
**THE TIMES ATLAS OF WORLD
HISTORY**
0–8437–1129–9 Hammond $85.00
**THE TIMES CONCISE ATLAS OF
WORLD HISTORY**
Illustrated by John Bartholomew & Son
0–8437–1133–7 Hammond pb $24.95

- Hermann Kinder & Werner
Hilgemann
**THE ANCHOR ATLAS OF WORLD
HISTORY**
Volume 1: From the Stone Age to the Eve
of the French Revolution
0–385–06178–1 Doubleday pb $9.95
Volume 2: From the French Revolution to
the American Bicentennial
0–385–13355–3 Doubleday pb $9.95

- Colin McEvedy
**THE PENGUIN ATLAS OF AFRICAN
HISTORY**
0–14–051083–4 Penguin pb $8.95
**THE PENGUIN ATLAS OF MEDIEVAL
HISTORY**
0–14–051152–0 Penguin pb $7.95
**THE PENGUIN ATLAS OF MODERN
HISTORY: To 1815**
0–14–051153–9 Penguin pb $6.95
**THE PENGUIN ATLAS OF NORTH
AMERICAN HISTORY: To 1870**
0–14–051128–8 Penguin pb $6.95
**THE PENGUIN ATLAS OF RECENT
HISTORY**
0–14–051154–7 Penguin pb $6.95

- Colin McEvedy & Richard Jones
**THE ATLAS OF WORLD POPULATION
HISTORY**
0–14–051076–1 Penguin pb $7.95

Archaeology

Archaeology is the systematic study of the material remains of human behavior in the past. Stuart Piggot called it "the science of rubbish," and it is by carefully examining bits of pottery, sword handles, and scraps of papyrus that an archaeologist is able to piece together the habits of a society that may have disappeared millenia before.

To make full use of their finds, archaeologists have developed a battery of techniques. Some, like thermoluminescence and cobalt dating, are extremely sophisticated; others are merely a matter of common sense. One useful technique resulted from the identification of certain types of pottery with certain eras. Now, any dig is carefully conducted so that the pottery at the various strata can date other objects on the same level.

Assyrian palace relief, from The Forms of Violence *by Leo Bersani and Ulysse Dutoit (Schocken)*

Books on context and dating techniques have much of the same fascination as Sherlock Holmes's explanation of his "methods." Whether ancient societies were nomadic cattle-herders or were ruled in the name of god-kings by priestly bureaucracies, we have few written records. All we know must be deduced from their bronze implements and broken chariot wheels, their circles of monumental stone. Although this does not yield history, it allows us to paint a haunting picture of the way of life of many strange, distant peoples now gone forever.

GENERAL ARCHAEOLOGY

• Lewis R. Binford
IN PURSUIT OF THE PAST: Decoding the Archaeological Record
The introduction of computer techniques and the search for new explanations of cultural evolution
0–500–27494–0 Thames & Hudson pb $14.95

• Warwick Bray & David Trump
THE PENGUIN DICTIONARY OF ARCHAEOLOGY
References to all areas of archaeological interest—Baal, the Yang Shao culture of neolithic China, the nutcracker men of prehistoric Africa—as well as explanations of the specialized vocabulary
0–14–051116–4 Penguin pb $8.95

• C.W. Ceram
GODS, GRAVES, AND SCHOLARS: The Story of Archaeology
Communicates the excitement of a science that requires the nerves of an adventurer and the mind of a first-rate detective
0–394–42661–4 Knopf $24.95

• Brian M. Fagan
ARCHAEOLOGY: A Brief Introduction
The goals of archaeology, problems of finding and excavating sites, of dating artifacts and reconstructing cultures from them
0–673–39719–X Scott, Foresman pb $10.95

• Robert J. Wenke
PATTERNS IN PRE-HISTORY: Humankind's First Three Million Years
0–19–503442–2 Oxford $18.95

• H.V. Winstone
UNCOVERING THE ANCIENT WORLD
The great discoveries and the eccentrics who made them
0–8160–1578–3 Facts On File $29.95

The Sea Remembers

George Bass, editor
SHIPS AND SHIPWRECKS OF THE AMERICAS: A History Based on Underwater Archaeology
A richly illustrated picture book
0–500–05049–X Thames & Hudson $40.00

Peter Throckmorton, editor
THE SEA REMEMBERS: Shipwrecks and Archaeology
Stories of the salvage of shipwrecks from the 14th century BC to the Titanic illustrate methods of marine archaeology
1–55584–093–0 W&N $29.95

ARCHAEOLOGICAL TECHNIQUES AND PHILOSOPHY

• Jacob Bronowski
THE ASCENT OF MAN
The charm and eloquence of Bronowski's writing are complemented by plentiful illustrations from the popular television series
0–316–10933–9 Little, Brown $24.95

• John A.J. Cowlett
ASCENT TO CIVILIZATION: The Archaeology of Early Man
Our primitive beginnings at the remote and dimmest edge of human existence in Africa. Elaborately mapped and illustrated
0–394–72266–3 Knopf pb $19.95

• Riane Eisler
THE CHALICE AND THE BLADE
Posits the golden age as a lost "Goddess culture," and how its end, amid chaotic conditions, bifurcated human cultural evolution
0–06–250287–5 Harper & Row pb $16.95

• Ian Hodder
READING THE PAST: Current Approaches to Interpretation in Archaeology
A controversial adaptation of new semiotic approaches to the archaeological recreation of cultures
0–521–33960–X Cambridge pb $9.95

• Jane McIntosh
THE PRACTICAL ARCHAEOLOGIST
Explains in clear and practical detail how we know about the past and how our knowledge is increasing
0–8160–1814–6 Facts On File pb $12.95

• Ralph Merrifield
THE ARCHAEOLOGY OF RITUAL AND MAGIC
Examines the *longue durée* of ritual below cultural and ideological change, from pristine animism to rationalistic thought
0–941533–26–3 New Amsterdam pb $15.95

• Bruce Norman
FOOTSTEPS: Nine Archaeological Journeys of Romance and Discovery
Illustrated stories of nine archaeological adventurers who uncovered some of the most famous cities of antiquity in India, America, and Mesopotamia; illustrated
0–88162–324–5 Salem House $29.95

• Philip Rahtz
INVITATION TO ARCHAEOLOGY
"Today's garbage is tomorrow's archaeology." An introduction to the methods enlivened with the quirks of some of the methodologists
0–631–14106–5 Blackwell $24.95
0–631–14107–3 Blackwell pb $8.95

• Bruce G. Trigger
GORDON CHILDE: Revolutions in Archaeology
0–231–05038–0 Columbia $31.00

TIME AND TRADITIONS
0–231–04548–4 Columbia $28.00

• Ruth Whitehouse & John Wilkins
THE MAKING OF CIVILIZATION: History Discovered Through Archaeology
A brilliant picture of the emerging patterns of authority. Focuses on the study of urban centers from Mohenjo-Daro in the Indus Valley to the ancient Middle Eastern cultures to Tenochtitlán in Mexico; illustrated
0–394–72685–5 Knopf pb $18.95

TO ORDER BOOKS AS GIFTS, SEE PAGE 1

LANGUAGE AND WRITING

Archaeology also builds up its pictures of lost peoples from fragments of writing, whether ritual inscriptions or palace inventories, on stone or papyrus, and from whatever traces it can find of the once vast oral tradition.

• David Diringer
THE BOOK BEFORE PRINTING:
Ancient, Medieval and Oriental
0–486–24243–9 Dover pb $10.95

• I.J. Gelb
THE STUDY OF WRITING
This history of the evolution of writing and its relationship to speech, art, and religion includes discussions of primitive petroglyphs, and various systems from the Sumerian to the Japanese syllabary
0–226–28606–1 Chicago pb $12.00

• Jack Goody
THE INTERFACE BETWEEN THE WRITTEN AND THE ORAL
Considers this complex interplay in three ways: as internal to certain societies; in relationship between oral and written societies; and in the linguistic life of the individual
0–521–33794–1 Cambridge pb $14.95

• W. John Hackwell
SIGNS, LETTERS, WORDS: Archaeology Discovers Writing
The evolution of writing and its impact on civilization
Illustrated by W. John Hackwell
0–684–18807–4 Scribners pb $13.95

• Colin Renfrew
ARCHAEOLOGY AND LANGUAGE: The Puzzle of Indo-European Origins
A remarkable synthesis of archaeology and linguistics. Renfrew pushes the earliest date of the Indo-European occupation of Europe back to 6000 BC and demonstrates its agricultural character. Highly recommended
0–521–35432–3 Cambridge $29.95

Reading the Past

The series Reading the Past is published jointly by University of California Press and the British Museum. Amply illustrated, these books serve as excellent introductions to the writing systems of the ancient world.

John Chadwick
LINEAR B AND RELATED SCRIPTS
The script of the Minoan bureaucracy: its discovery and interpretation
0–520–06019–9 California pb $7.95

B.F. Cook
GREEK INSCRIPTIONS
0–520–06113–6 California pb $7.95

W.D. Davies
EGYPTIAN HIEROGLYPHS
Explanation of their principles, origins, development, and use, as well as the history of their decipherment
0–520–06287–6 California pb $7.95

O.A. Dilke
MATHEMATICS AND MEASUREMENT
Classical and preclassical techniques of mapping, surveying, measurement, and mathematics in trade and astrology
0–520–06072–5 California pb $7.95

R.I. Page
RUNES
0–520–06114–4 California pb $7.95

C.B. Walker
CUNEIFORM
The writing system of Mesopotamia, its origins and development, the scribes who used it and their libraries, and its modern decipherment
0–520–06115–2 California pb $7.95

THE ARCHAEOLOGY OF CIVILIZATIONS

Asia

• Edmund Capon
ART AND ARCHAEOLOGY IN CHINA
Splendid catalog to an Australian exhibition, beautifully illustrated and printed
0–262–03064–0 MIT pb $11.95

• Chang Kwang-chih
THE ARCHAEOLOGY OF ANCIENT CHINA
From paleolithic times to the regional cultures that emerged around 1000 BC whose interaction laid the foundations for the dynastic civilizations
0–300–03784–8 Yale pb $17.95

SHANG CIVILIZATION
This study illuminates the independent origins of Chinese civilization
0–300–02885–7 Yale pb $13.95

• Roger Hicks
HIDDEN TIBET: The Land and Its People
A photographic record of life in Tibet as it has been lived for thousands of years
1–85230–030–2 Element Books pb $16.95

• Peter Hopkirk
FOREIGN DEVILS ON THE SILK ROAD: The Search for the Lost Cities and Treasures of Chinese Central Asia
0–87023–435–8 Massachusetts pb $13.95

• David N. Keightly
SOURCES OF SHANG HISTORY: The Oracle-Bone Inscriptions of Bronze Age China
Inscriptions carved on cattle scapulas and turtle shells dating from the second

millenium BC are used to delineate the ethos of the first dynasty
0–520–05455–5 California pb $22.50

• M. Aurel Stein
RUINS OF DESERT CATHAY
An archaeologist and explorer traces the ancient silk routes to the West and the path of Marco Polo

Volume 1
0–486–25351–1 Dover pb $14.95

Volume 2
0–486–25404–6 Dover pb $14.95

• Foster Stockwell & Tang Bowen, editors
RECENT DISCOVERIES IN CHINESE ARCHAEOLOGY
0–8351–1377–9 China Books pb $9.95

Mesopotamia

• Seton Lloyd
THE ARCHAEOLOGY OF MESOPOTAMIA: From the Old Stone Age to the Persian Conquest
A succinct introduction to the most impressive finds of the pioneering excavations
0–500–79009–4 Thames & Hudson pb $11.95

FOUNDATIONS IN THE DUST: The Story of Mesopotamian Exploration
Knits the lives and work of the great Assyriologists from Layard to Woolley into an exciting narrative
0–500–05038–4 Thames & Hudson $19.95

• Leonard Woolley
UR OF THE CHALDEES: A Revised and Updated Edition of Sir Leonard Woolley's Excavations at Ur by P.R.S. Moorey
The brilliant archaeologist and raconteur tells in his own inimitable fashion the story of the discovery and re-creation of the birthplace of Abraham's father
0–8014–1518–7 Cornell $29.95

Egypt

• Howard Carter & A.C. Mace
THE DISCOVERY OF THE TOMB OF TUTANKHAMEN
The original story by the discoverer and excavator
0–486–23500–9 Dover pb $6.50

Animal form of Seth, Slayer of Osiris, from The Mythic Image *by Joseph Campbell* (*Princeton*)

- **Thomas Hoving**
  TUTANKHAMEN: The Untold Story
  No honor among scientists is the moral of this tale of passion and pettiness surrounding the discovery of the only treasure tomb to have survived the depredations of 33 centuries
  0–671–24370–5 Simon & Schuster pb $12.95

- **T.G. James**
  EXCAVATING IN EGYPT
  Egyptian civilization and the explorations that uncovered it
  0–226–39192–2 Chicago pb $14.95

Northern Europe

- **Charles Blinderman**
  THE PILTDOWN INQUEST
  0–87975–359–5 Prometheus $22.95

- **Aubrey Burl**
  MEGALITHIC BRITTANY
  0–500–01364–0 Thames & Hudson pb $18.95

- **Rodney Castleden**
  THE STONEHENGE PEOPLE: An Exploration of Life in Neolithic Britain, 4100-2000 BC
  Investigates the purpose of the building, how the huge bluestones were hauled from the sacred mountains of the west to Salisbury Plain, and the customs of the builders
  0–7102–0968–1 RC&H $27.50

- **Christopher Chippindale**
  STONEHENGE COMPLETE
  Everything important, interesting, or odd that has been written, painted, imagined, or discovered about the most extraordinary ancient building
  0–8014–9451–6 Cornell pb $24.95

- **Barry Cunliffe**
  DANEBURY: Anatomy of an Iron Age Hillfort
  Illustrated
  0–7134–0998–3 RC&H $29.95

- **P.V. Glob**
  THE BOG PEOPLE: Iron-Age Man Preserved
  0–8014–9527–X Cornell pb $12.95

- **Roger Joussaume**
  DOLMENS FOR THE DEAD: Megalith-Building Throughout the World
  The ancient chamber-tombs constructed with huge untrimmed rocks provide information about burial rites, social organization, and religious customs of prehistoric Europe. Illustrated
  Translated by Anne & Christopher Chippindale
  0–8014–2156–X Cornell $29.95

- **Mario Ruspoli**
  THE CAVES OF LASCAUX: The Final Photographs
  The "Sistine Chapel" of the cavemen, discovered by two boys in France in 1940, was closed in 1980 to protect the paintings from corrosion and decay. For three years before the cave was sealed, the great Italian photographer recorded these breathtaking works 17,000 years old
  0–8109–1267–8 Abrams $49.50

Britain from Celt to Angle

▶ See also Great Britain and Ireland

- **C.J. Arnold**
  AN ARCHAEOLOGY OF THE EARLY ANGLO-SAXON KINGDOMS
  0–415–03248–2 RC&H pb $17.95

- **T.B. Barry**
  THE ARCHAEOLOGY OF MEDIEVAL IRELAND
  0–415–01104–3 RC&H pb $14.95

- **Frank Delany**
  THE CELTS
  The pre-history of an ancient race scattered from the plains of Hungary to the coasts of Brittany and Ireland; a photographic essay
  0–316–17993–0 Little, Brown $24.95

- **Peter Harbison**
  PRE-CHRISTIAN IRELAND: From the First Settlers to the Early Celts
  The latest thinking on the astronomical significance of the megalithic tombs and the social implications of the great Bronze Age hoards; interwoven with up-to-date accounts of recent excavations at Rathgall and Navan Fort. Illustrated
  0–500–02110–4 Thames & Hudson $24.95

- **George Henderson**
  FROM DURROW TO KELLS
  0–500–23474–4 Thames & Hudson $45.00

- **Robert O'Driscoll, editor**
  THE CELTIC CONSCIOUSNESS
  A collection of the judicial and poetic texts that remain from early times
  0–8076–1136–0 Braziller $22.50

- **Stuart Piggott**
  THE DRUIDS
  0–500–27363–4 Thames & Hudson pb $11.95

- **Ward Rutherford**
  CELTIC MYTHOLOGY: The Nature and Influence of Celtic Mythology from Druidism to Arthurian Legend
  0–85030–551–9 Aquarian Press pb $9.95

- **John Sharkey**
  CELTIC MYSTERIES
  0–500–81009–5 Thames & Hudson pb $11.95

- **Charles Thomas**
  CELTIC BRITAIN
  0–500–02107–4 Thames & Hudson $22.50

American Southwest

▶ See also Native American Cultures: North America

- **George J. Gumerman**
  A VIEW FROM BLACK MESA: The Changing Face of Archaeology
  0–8165–0848–8 Arizona $18.95

- **Alfred Vincent Kidder**
  AN INTRODUCTION TO THE STUDY OF SOUTHWESTERN ARCHAEOLOGY
  Combines an overall summary of Pueblo archaeology with an excellent account of the work at Kidder's Pecos site
  Introduction by Irving Rouse
  0–300–00140–1 Yale pb $15.95

- **Robert H. & Florence C. Lister**
  THOSE WHO CAME BEFORE: Southwestern Archeology in the National Park System
  Photographs by David Muench
  0–911408–62–2 SW Parks & Monuments pb $12.95

- **John C. McGregor**
  SOUTHWESTERN ARCHAEOLOGY
  0–252–00989–4 Illinois pb $16.95

Central and South America

▶ See also Native American Cultures: Central and South America

- **Ignacio Bernal**
  A HISTORY OF MEXICAN ARCHAEOLOGY: The Vanished Civilizations of Middle America
  0–500–79008–6 Thames & Hudson pb $9.95

- **Michael D. Coe**
  THE MAYA
  Revised edition
  0–500–27455–X Thames & Hudson pb $11.95

- **Nigel Davies**
  THE AZTECS: A History
  From their rude beginnings to their rise to domination over a large part of Mesoamerica and their defeat at the hands of the conquistadores
  0–8061–1691–9 Oklahoma pb $13.95

  THE TOLTECS: Until the Fall of Tula
  This personal hypothesis unifies the fragmentary archaeological remains of the predecessors of the Aztecs in Central America
  0–8061–2071–1 Oklahoma pb $16.95

  VOYAGERS TO THE NEW WORLD
  Asks whether pre-Columbian cultures provide evidence for the independent origins of symbols or for cultural diffusionism through ancient contacts with Europe
  0–8263–0880–5 New Mexico pb $10.95

- **Brian M. Fagan**
  THE GREAT JOURNEY: The Peopling of Ancient America
  The veteran archaeologist provides a plausible explanation and an exciting account of how America was first peopled
  0–500–05045–7 Thames & Hudson $19.95

- **Charles Gallenkamp**
  MAYA: The Riddle and Rediscovery of a Lost Civilization
  The wonders of a people who built cities, temples, and palaces, possessed sophisticated mathematical and scientific knowledge, and mysteriously disappeared at the height of their power
  0–14–008831–8 Penguin pb $7.95

- Evan Hadingham
  LINES TO THE MOUNTAIN GODS:
  Nazca and the Mysteries of Peru
  0–394–54235–5 Random House $22.00

- Norman Hammond
  ANCIENT MAYA CIVILIZATION
  From the discovery of the ancient Maya
  centers deep in the forests of central
  America to the rise and fall of classic
  Mayan civilization
  0–8135–0906–8 Rutgers pb $15.00

- L. Bruce Hunter
  A GUIDE TO ANCIENT MEXICAN
  RUINS
  Part fun guide, part cultural history of the
  ruins of the Toltec, Zapotec, Mixtec, and
  Aztec peoples
  0–8061–1407–X Oklahoma pb $9.95

- J.L. King
  ANCIENT MEXICO: An Overview
  An engaging introduction to Mexico
  before the Spanish conquest by a leading
  Mexican archaeologist
  0–8263–0817–1 New Mexico pb $7.95

- Eduardo Matos Moctezuma
  THE GREAT TEMPLE OF THE
  AZTECS: Treasures of Tenochtitlán
  The site of present-day Mexico City
  0–500–39024–X Thames & Hudson $29.95

- Tony Morrison
  PATHWAYS TO THE GODS: The Mystery
  of the Andes Lines
  Who built the Nasca lines that extend for
  up to 20 miles on a desolate Peruvian
  plain, and why? This popular book by a
  BBC producer incorporates work by
  Gerald Hawkins of the Smithsonian and
  Maria Reiche, who has worked in Peru
  since the 1940s
  0–89733–282–2 Academy Chicago pb $9.95

- Dennis Tedlock, translator
  POPOL VUH: The Definitive Edition of
  the Mayan Book of the Dawn of Life and
  the Glories of Gods and Kings
  With a commentary based on the ancient
  knowledge of the modern Quiche Maya
  0–671–61771–0 Simon & Schuster pb $9.95

- Peter Tompkins
  MYSTERIES OF THE MEXICAN
  PYRAMIDS
  Their history since their first sighting by
  Cortés, the attempts to solve the mystery
  of their construction, and the variety of
  theories about their purpose from
  mathematical instruments to foci for
  cosmic and telluric forces
  0–06–091366–5 Harper & Row pb $15.95

Island Peoples

Peter Bellwood
THE POLYNESIANS: Prehistory of an
Island People
Fully informative about the culture that
colonized the Pacific islands, with a
discussion of the stone monuments of
Easter Island and the art of wood
carving
0–500–27450–9 Thames & Hudson pb $10.95

Early Sumerian Eye Goddess figurines, c. 3500-3000 BC, from The Mythic Image *by Joseph Campbell* (Princeton)

Thor Heyerdahl
THE MALDIVE MYSTERY: The
Search for Ancient Civilizations in the
Remote Islands of the Indian Ocean
Explores the islands whose wealth of
remains is due to their immersion in
three great cultures—the Hindu, the
Buddhist, and the Islamic
0–345–34727–7 Ballantine pb $4.95

The Ancient Near East

Some of the most spectacular achievements
of archaeology have been among the
ruins of the great civilizations that flourished
between the valley of the Tigris and the
Euphrates and the Mediterranean coast.
From this arid land sprang Sumer, Assyria,
and Babylon, the first known civilizations,
whose achievements in writing, technical
invention, and religion gave an impetus to
subsequent, more familiar cultures.

- Henri Frankfort
  KINGSHIP AND THE GODS: A Study of
  Ancient Near Eastern Religion As the
  Integration of Society and Nature
  The differences between the social and
  religious forms developed in the natural
  fertility of the Nile valley and the more
  arid Mesopotamian plains
  Preface by Samuel N. Kramer
  0–226–26011–9 Chicago pb $16.95

- Henri Frankfort & others, editors
  THE INTELLECTUAL ADVENTURE OF
  ANCIENT MAN: An Essay on Speculative
  Thought in the Ancient Near East
  How abstract reasoning evolved from the
  primitive poetic mind that divined invisible
  agencies behind each natural phenomenon
  0–226–26008–9 Chicago pb $12.95

- Cyrus H. Gordon
  THE ANCIENT NEAR EAST
  Focuses on ancient Canaan as the
  geographical crossroads of eastern
  Mediterranean life
  0–393–00275–6 Norton pb $8.95

- William W. Hallo & William K.
  Simpson
  THE ANCIENT NEAR EAST: A History
  A parallel history of ancient Egypt and the
  ancient Near East for general readers
  0–15–502755–7 HBJ pb $18.95

- S.H. Hooke
  MIDDLE EASTERN MYTHOLOGY:
  From the Assyrians to the Hebrews
  The variety and similarity of ancient myths
  and their influence on the Bible
  0–14–020546–2 Penguin pb $5.95

- Amelie Kuhrt & Susan Sherwin-
  White, editors
  HELLENISM IN THE EAST: Greek and
  Non-Greek Civilizations from Syria to
  Central Asia After Alexander
  The continuity of Mesopotamian
  civilizations under the Seleucid successors
  of Alexander
  0–520–06054–7 California $35.00

- Georges Roux
  ANCIENT IRAQ
  Covers with a light but exact touch the
  political, cultural, and economic history
  from the prehistoric to the Christian
  period
  0–14–020828–3 Penguin pb $6.95

● Carol G. Thomas
**THE EARLIEST CIVILIZATIONS:
Ancient Greece and the Near East, 3000-200
B.C.**
Alexander's conquest of the East is only
one incident in the seesaw history of the
relationship between the two cultures
0–8191–2598–9 University Press $30.50
0–8191–2599–7 University Press pb $13.50

MESOPOTAMIA

The Mesopotamian city-state of Sumer
disappeared from the annals of history
until quite recently. It is not even mentioned
in the Bible. But since its discovery in the
course of digs by Assyriologists, it has become one of the marvels of archaeology: a
complete civilization based on a complex
irrigation system, it also invented the potter's
wheel, the wagon wheel, the sailboat,
bronze-casting, and a system of writing on
clay used all over the Near East for 2000
years.

● Thorkild Jacobsen
**THE TREASURES OF DARKNESS: A
History of Mesopotamian Religion**
A study based on Sumerian mythological
literature
0–300–02291–3 Yale pb $10.95

● Samuel N. Kramer
**THE SUMERIANS: Their History, Culture
and Character**
The doyen of Sumerologists uses the
ancient texts to demonstrate the common
humanity of the forgotten civilization
0–226–45238–7 Chicago pb $12.95

● Sabatino Moscati, editor
THE PHOENICIANS
Illustrated. "Includes a rich series of texts
by archeologists, linguists and ancient
historians discussing the latest
discoveries"—Kenan T. Erim, *NY Times
Book Review*
0–89659–892–6 Abbeville $125.00

● Joan Oates
BABYLON
From Sargon to Hammurabi, and the
Babylonian view of the Greek occupation
of Mesopotamia
0–500–27384–7 Thames & Hudson pb $11.95

● A. Leo Oppenheim
**ANCIENT MESOPOTAMIA: Portrait of a
Dead Civilization**
City life, the scribes, kings, and "scientists"
of ancient Mesopotamia
0–226–63187–7 Chicago pb $15.00

● H.W. Saggs
**EVERYDAY LIFE IN BABYLONIA AND
ASSYRIA**
Cultural history from 2000 to 500 BC
0–88029–127–3 Hippocrene $17.95

● Leonard Woolley
THE SUMERIANS
The great British archaeologist describes
the people whose achievements influenced
the course of Western civilization for 2000

years before their very name faded from
historical records
0–393–00292–6 Norton pb $7.95

EGYPT

Ancient Egypt's history has a longer span
than western Europe from the time of
Julius Caesar to our own day. Yet the power
of the priestly bureaucracy that upheld the
god-king was such that in all that time very
little change can be discerned. By its very
strangeness, this religion fascinates us; and
the excavators of the great tombs built to
preserve the body for its other-worldly journey have revealed many of its mysteries. The
excellent studies of Egyptian religion are
matched by many works giving detailed
accounts of the daily life of the people.

History

● Cyril Aldred
**EGYPT TO THE END OF THE OLD
KINGDOM**
Using a wealth of art objects, Aldred
recreates Egypt under Pharaonic rule, a
refinement of the African worship of an
omnipotent, rain-making god-king
0–500–29001–6 Thames & Hudson pb $10.95

● Alan K. Bowman
**EGYPT AFTER THE PHARAOHS: 332
B.C.-642 A.D.**
A history of Egypt in decline under the
Macedonian and Roman empires, until the
Muslim invasion
0–520–05930–1 California $29.95

● W.B. Emery
ARCHAIC EGYPT
Archaeology and history of the unification
period during the First and Second
dynasties
0–14–020462–8 Penguin pb $6.95

● George Steindorff & Keith C. Seele
**WHEN EGYPT RULED THE EAST: From
the Eighteenth to the Twentieth Dynasty**
The period of Egypt's greatest imperial
expansion after the overthrow of the
Hyksos, the invading Asiatic shepherd
kings
0–226–77199–7 Chicago pb $10.50

● L.A. Waddell
**EGYPTIAN CIVILIZATION: Its
Sumerian Origin and Real Chronology**
0–317–53201–4 Noontide pb $10.00

Culture and Society

● Cyril Aldred
THE EGYPTIANS
A popular and instructive introduction to
their history and culture by the British art
historian
0–500–27345–6 Thames & Hudson pb $11.95

● T.G. James
**PHARAOH'S PEOPLE: Scenes from Life
in Imperial Egypt**
Social history of the scribes and farmers
0–226–39193–0 Chicago $20.00
0–226–39194–9 Chicago pb $10.95

● Jill Kamil
**THE ANCIENT EGYPTIANS: A Popular
Introduction to Life in the Pyramid Age**
977–424–051–0 Columbia pb $18.50

COPTIC EGYPT: A History and Guide
977–424–104–5 Columbia pb $15.00

● Pierre Montet
**EVERYDAY LIFE IN EGYPT IN THE
DAYS OF RAMESES THE GREAT**
Life in Egypt during the reign of the
pharaoh most likely to have tangled with
Moses
0–8122–1113–8 Pennsylvania pb $17.95

● John Romer
**ANCIENT LIVES: The Story of the
Pharaoh's Tombmakers**
The tombmakers lived outside Thebes in a
tight-packed village filled with experts of
special life-style and values, craftsmen who
made the figures of the gods
0–03–000733–X Henry Holt $18.95

● Mirian Stead
EGYPTIAN LIFE
0–674–24151–7 British Museum pb $8.95

● John A. Wilson
THE CULTURE OF ANCIENT EGYPT
0–226–90152–1 Chicago pb $7.95

Akhenaten

Cyril Aldred
AKHENATEN: King of Egypt
The king who tried to replace the
entrenched religious bureaucracy with
his own worship of the sun disk
0–500–05048–1 Thames & Hudson $29.95

Donald B. Redford
AKHENATEN: The Heretic King
Eunuch king, disguised woman,
mentor of Moses? These are only some
of the speculations surrounding this
potent but obscure monarch. Scholar
and general reader alike will benefit
from this fresh portrait
0–691–03567–9 Princeton $42.50
0–691–00217–7 Princeton pb $14.50

Pyramids, Mummies, and Obelisks

● Carol Andrews
EGYPTIAN MUMMIES
0–674–24152–5 Harvard pb $8.95

● I.E.S. Edwards
THE PYRAMIDS OF EGYPT
The rise and decline of the massive
funerary monuments, from the step-
pyramids and mastabas of the early
dynasties to the attempt to foil grave
robbers with the cliff-tombs of the Valley
of the Kings
0–670–80153–4 Viking $25.00
0–14–022549–8 Penguin pb $6.95

- Labib Habachi

THE OBELISKS OF EGYPT: Skyscrapers of the Past
977–424–022–7 Columbia pb $15.00

- Kurt Mendelssohn

THE RIDDLE OF THE PYRAMIDS
A new society was created by the massive organization required to build pyramids
0–500–05015–5 Thames & Hudson $24.95
0–500–27388–X Thames & Hudson pb $12.95

- Peter Tompkins

SECRETS OF THE GREAT PYRAMID
Adventures and discoveries of the explorers and scientists who, for 200 years, have been probing the mysteries of the Great Pyramid of Cheops
0–06–014327–4 Harper & Row pb $26.00

Beliefs and Knowledge

- Robert Armour

GOD AND MYTHS OF ANCIENT EGYPT
977–424–113–4 Columbia pb $15.00

- Bob Brier

ANCIENT EGYPTIAN MAGIC
An up-to-date account of the role of the magician in every aspect of Egyptian life—from mummification to love potions
0–688–00796–1 Morrow pb $10.95

- Rosalie David

THE ANCIENT EGYPTIANS: Religious Beliefs and Practices
The influence of religion on medicine and education as well as on temple rituals and funerary customs
0–7100–0878–3 RC&H pb $19.95

- Derek D. Price

SCIENCE SINCE BABYLON
0–300–01798–7 Yale pb $9.95

- A.J. Spencer

DEATH IN ANCIENT EGYPT
The origin and development of burial practices
0–14–022294–4 Penguin pb $7.95

- Barbara Watterson

THE GODS OF ANCIENT EGYPT
Myths surrounding 30 major Egyptian deities
0–8160–1111–7 Facts On File $21.95

LANGUAGE, CIPHERS, AND HIEROGLYPHICS

- Carol Andrews

THE BRITISH MUSEUM BOOK OF THE ROSETTA STONE
The decipherment of this text from the time of Ptolemy Epiphanes (196 BC) by Champollion was the key to understanding hieroglyphics
0–87226–033–X Bedrick $12.95
0–87226–034–8 Bedrick pb $5.95

- E.A. Wallis Budge

EGYPTIAN LANGUAGE: Easy Lessons in Egyptian Hieroglyphics with Sign List
0–486–21394–3 Dover pb $5.00

From Egyptian Wall Paintings *by Charles K. Wilkinson* (*Metropolitan Museum*)

EGYPTIAN HIEROGLYPHIC DICTIONARY

Volume 1
0–486–23615–3 Dover pb $13.95

Volume 2
0–486–23616–1 Dover pb $13.95

- Edward Chiera

THEY WROTE ON CLAY: The Babylonian Tablets Speak Today
A friendly view of the Mesopotamian cultures through the written word and the professional scribes
Edited by G.G. Cameron
0–226–10425–7 Chicago pb $9.95

- Cyrus H. Gordon

FORGOTTEN SCRIPTS: Their Ongoing Discovery and Decipherment
The cryptologist's story of ancient languages now includes the recently discovered Eblaite
0–465–02484–X Basic Books pb $16.95

REFERENCE

- John Baines & Jaromir Malek

ATLAS OF ANCIENT EGYPT
0–87196–334–5 Facts On File $40.00

- Michael Grant

ANCIENT HISTORY ATLAS
Europe and the Mediterranean world, including Egypt and the Near East
0–915262–73–8 Dust pb $10.00

- George Hart

A DICTIONARY OF EGYPTIAN GODS AND GODDESSES
Gives full information in an attractive format with line drawings of the Egyptian symbols and images of their deities
0–7102–0167–2 RC&H pb $12.95

- Christine Hobson

THE WORLD OF THE PHARAOHS: A Complete Guide to Ancient Egypt
Foreword by Thomas Logan
0–500–05046–5 Thames & Hudson $19.95

- Manfred Lurker

GODS AND SYMBOLS OF ANCIENT EGYPT: An Illustrated Dictionary
Edited by Peter A. Clayton
0–500–11018–2 Thames & Hudson $19.95
0–500–27253–0 Thames & Hudson pb $11.95

- William J. Murnane

THE PENGUIN GUIDE TO ANCIENT EGYPT
More than a practical guide for the tourist of antiquities, it is full of fascinating historical and archaeological information
0–14–046326–7 Penguin pb $12.95

PALESTINE AND THE BIBLE

The archaeology of the Bible has a special interest, since for many people it is not merely a question of recreating a dead past but also of assisting in the exposition of living faiths. A number of works in this field employ the archaeological discoveries to interpret the biblical text. This combination of text and artifact can yield rich results both in corroborating biblical accounts and adding to our understanding of the ancient societies. The evidence provided by the remains of devastated cities can bring to light information on both Solomon's monopoly of the Palestinian metal industry and the invasion of Canaan in Exodus.

• Yohanan Aharoni
THE ARCHAEOLOGY OF THE LAND OF ISRAEL
An Israeli archaeologist's view, with detailed reference to his own excavations
Translated by Anson F. Rainey
0–664–24430–0 Westminster pb $18.95

• Tim Dowley, editor
DISCOVERING THE BIBLE
What archaeology can and cannot tell us about the Bible
0–8028–3624–0 Eerdmans $14.95

• John Finegan
LIGHT FROM THE ANCIENT EAST
The material world inhabited by the prophets and the apostles
Volume 1
0–691–00208–8 Princeton pb $19.95
Volume 2
0–691–00207–X Princeton pb $19.95

• Werner Keller
THE BIBLE AS HISTORY
Classic textbook in this genre
0–553–27943–2 Bantam pb $5.95

• Kathleen M. Kenyon
ARCHAEOLOGY IN THE HOLY LAND
An excavator's creative suggestions about the culture of the societies of Palestine from pre-historic times until the end of the Hebrew kingdoms
0–393–01285–9 Norton pb $10.95

• John Van Seters
IN SEARCH OF HISTORY: Historiography in the Ancient World and the Origins of Biblical History
A comparison of Hebraic historiographical traditions with Greek and Near Eastern historians
0–300–03633–7 Yale pb $13.95

Reference

• Yohanon Aharoni & Michael Avi-Yonah
THE MACMILLAN BIBLE ATLAS
Illustrates both Old and New Testaments
0–02–500590–1 Macmillan $29.95

• Gonzalo Baez-Camargo
ARCHAEOLOGICAL COMMENTARY ON THE BIBLE
Interesting attempt to correlate archaeological findings with biblical exegesis
0–385–17969–3 Doubleday pb $9.95

• Gaalyah Cornfeld & David N. Freedman, editors
ARCHAEOLOGY OF THE BIBLE, BOOK BY BOOK: An Up-to-Date Archaeological Commentary on the Bible
Maps, drawings, and photographs on almost every page of the book illustrate the physical and cultural setting of the Old and New Testaments
0–06–061587–7 Harper & Row pb $19.95

• Luc Grollenberg
THE PENGUIN SHORTER ATLAS OF THE BIBLE
Translated by M.F. Hedlund
0–14–051056–7 Penguin pb $8.95

• Samuel Heilman
A WALKER IN JERUSALEM
Award-winning guide with detailed itinerary for various tours in Jerusalem area
0–671–54433–0 Summit $18.95

• Hilla & Max Jacoby, photographers
THE LAND OF ISRAEL
A topographical and geographical emphasis
Introduction by Heinrich Böll
0–500–24101–5 Thames & Hudson $25.00

• Jerome Murphy-O'Connor
THE HOLY LAND: An Archaeological Guide from Earliest Times to 1700
A popular, accurate introductory guide, easily used
0–19–285158–6 Oxford pb $10.95

• James B. Pritchard, editor
THE HARPER ATLAS OF THE BIBLE
Includes maps of Near East areas relevant to biblical text
0–06–181883–6 Harper & Row $49.95

CITIES AND SITES

• Graham Davies, editor
MEGIDDO
The spectacular fortifications of Solomon's "chariot city" have been a rich source of information on the period of the kings
0–8028–0247–8 Eerdmans pb $8.95

• Christos G. Doumas
THERA, POMPEII OF THE ANCIENT AEGEAN: Excavations at Akrotiri, 1967-1979
0–500–39016–9 Thames & Hudson $29.95

• Kenan Grim
APHRODISIAS: City of Venus Aphrodite
Fine illustrations bring this ancient center of marble sculpture to life
0–8160–1541–4 Facts On File $50.00

• Kenneth G. Holum & others
KING HEROD'S DREAM: Caesarea on the Sea
Exquisite photographic reconstruction of one of the great cities of Roman Palestine—planned and built by Herod
0–393–02493–8 Norton $35.00

• Aicha Ben Abed Ben Khader & David Soren
CARTHAGE: A Mosaic of Ancient Tunisia
Stunning photographs of a site that dates back to the Phoenicians and holds memories of Dido, Hannibal, and Saint Augustine
0–393–02549–7 Norton $35.00

• F.E. Peters
JERUSALEM: The Holy City in the Eyes of Chroniclers, Visitors, Pilgrims, and Prophets from the Days of Abraham to the Beginnings of Modern Times
Reactions of visitors through the ages in their own words
0–691–07300–7 Princeton $37.00

• James B. Pritchard
GIBEON, WHERE THE SUN STOOD STILL: The Discovery of a Biblical City
The author's discoveries on the ancient site. "Pritchard writes lucidly . . . and with just the right leaven of the dry digger's wit"—*Washington Post*
0–691–03517–2 Princeton $31.00
0–691–00210–X Princeton pb $9.50

• David Soren & Jamie James
KOURION: The Search for a Lost Roman City
The Roman port on Cyprus, buried by an earthquake in AD 365, yields its secrets in this pictorially beautiful work of exploration
0–385–24141–0 Doubleday pb $21.95

• Veronica Tatton-Brown
ANCIENT CYPRUS
The unique and distinctive culture of Cyprus developed from its position at the crossroads of Mediterranean cultures. With color and black-and-white illustrations
0–674–03307–8 British Museum pb $8.95

• Yigael Yadin
MASADA: Herod's Fortress and the Zealots' Last Stand
"I can only assure the reader that if he is at all interested in the subject, he will find this book enthralling"—Edmund Wilson
0–394–43542–7 Random House $25.00

The Dead Sea Scrolls

The most epochal find of recent times: the texts of the Jewish monastic community that flourished in the age of Augustus and whose tenets have been suggested as the source of Christian thought. But the scrolls are also valuable in their own right. The story of their discovery is no less fabulous than the texts themselves with their protagonists, the Righteous Teacher and the Wicked Priest, and the millennial "War of the Children of Darkness against the Children of Light."

Theodor H. Gaster
THE DEAD SEA SCRIPTURES
Annotated translations of the major documents
0–385–08859–0 Doubleday pb $8.95

Geza Vermes
THE DEAD SEA SCROLLS: Qumran in Perspective
Their discovery, authentication, and dating, and the evidence they provide of the beliefs and practices of the Essene community
0–8006–1435–6 Fortress pb $9.95

THE DEAD SEA SCROLLS IN ENGLISH
The intention and meaning of the genres with translations of the basic texts
0–14–022779–2 Penguin pb $6.95

Edmund Wilson
ISRAEL AND THE DEAD SEA SCROLLS
Superbly written discussion of the special meaning the scrolls have for the Israeli state whose birth was almost contemporaneous with the first discoveries
0–19–500665–8 Oxford $22.50
0–374–51341–4 FS&G pb $9.50

Yigael Yadin
THE TEMPLE SCROLL: The Hidden Law of the Dead Sea Sect
The Israeli general and scholar describes the difficulties of acquiring the famous scroll that consists partly of practical plans for building a temple and partly of communications from God
0–394–54498–6 Random House $24.50

Ancient Greece

The study of ancient Greek history has, for centuries, provided the West with political models. In addition to describing diplomacy and war, Greek historians speculated on the effect of the political structure on behavior, and their speculations gave subsequent generations a language with which to debate their own policies.

This tradition is still alive. Gore Vidal recently suggested that rulers on both sides of the iron curtain might benefit from study of Thucydides on the Peloponnesian War in which a dashing, expansionist Athens broke itself against the stolid rock of militarist Sparta. The debate engendered by these opposed systems swayed to and fro for 2400 years and continues to thread its way through modern history.

Although support is almost unanimous today for democratic Athens, questions persist about the nature of a democracy based on slavery. The following books are thus part of an ongoing argument about our own place in the larger world of political participation.

General Political History

• Andrew R. Burn
PELICAN HISTORY OF GREECE
An elegantly written introduction that does not neglect the telling detail. Includes excellent maps and chronological tables
0–14–020792–9 Penguin pb $6.95

• J.K. Davies
DEMOCRACY AND CLASSICAL GREECE
The problem of sources for ancient history complements the investigation of what made Greece a cultural continuum but a political patchwork
0–8047–1226–3 Stanford pb $8.95

• I.E. Edwards, C.J. Gadd & N.G. Hammond, editors
CAMBRIDGE ANCIENT HISTORY
Volume 1, Part 1: Prolegomena and Prehistory
0–521–29821–0 Cambridge pb $39.50

Volume 1, Parts 2A & 2B: Early History of the Middle East
0–521–29822–9 Cambridge pb $44.50

Volume 2, Part 1: The Middle East and the Aegean Region, c. 1800-1380 BC
0–521–29823–7 Cambridge pb $44.50

Volume 2, Parts 2A & 2B: The Middle East and the Aegean Region, c. 1380-1000 BC
0–521–29824–5 Cambridge pb $44.50

• John Fine
THE ANCIENT GREEKS: A Critical History
The most current one-volume overview of history and culture based on up-to-date findings and interpretations
0–674–03311–6 Harvard $39.50
0–674–03314–0 Harvard pb $15.95

• Michael Grant
THE RISE OF THE GREEKS
0–684–18536–9 Scribners $27.50
0–02–032781–1 Macmillan pb $14.95

• Peter Green
ANCIENT GREECE: An Illustrated History
Arid landscape contrasted with the sensuousness of art and philosophy
0–500–27161–5 Thames & Hudson pb $11.95

• Aubrey de Selincourt
THE WORLD OF HERODOTUS
"Lovingly written and beautifully achieved"—*Christian Science Monitor*
0–86547–070–7 Northpoint pb $12.00

General Cultural History

• Antony Andrewes
THE GREEKS
Greek society in archaic and classical times
0–393–00877–0 Norton pb $8.95

• John Boardman, Jasper Griffin & Oswyn Murray, editors
THE OXFORD HISTORY OF THE CLASSICAL WORLD: Greece and the Hellenistic World
Thirty contributors whose essays range from the Homeric hero to the twilight of the classical pantheon
0–19–872112–9 Oxford $49.95
0–19–282165–2 Oxford pb $18.95

• Kenneth Dover
THE GREEKS
"A resilient, satirical, cheeky people who wanted clear and sane answers to the questions Why? and Why not?"—from the Introduction
0–292–72723–2 Texas $17.95
0–292–72724–0 Texas $8.95

• M.I. Finley
ANCIENT GREEKS
The Dark Ages following the destruction of Mycenae, the tyrants and lawgivers of Archaic Greece, and the achievements and final decline of the city-state
0–14–020812–7 Penguin pb $6.95

ASPECTS OF ANTIQUITY
A vivid historical imagination illuminates these essays on everything from the authenticity of the Trojan War to an apology for Diocletian's persecutions
0–14–021509–3 Penguin pb $6.95

THE WORLD OF ODYSSEUS
"Finley's magnificent work has long been one of the treasures of my library"—Mary Renault
0–14–020570–5 Penguin pb $6.95

• Michael Grant
THE ANCIENT MEDITERRANEAN
0–452–00949–9 NAL pb $9.95

• Simon Hornblower
THE GREEK WORLD, 479-323 BC
The great age of Greece begins with the defeat of Xerxes at Salamis and culminates with Alexander's incursion into Nepal
0–416–74990–9 Methuen $29.95
0–416–75000–1 Methuen pb $11.95

• J.W. Roberts
CITY OF SOKRATES: A Social History of Classical Athens
The paradoxes of Athens at its zenith, with particular attention to the part played by the drama and public ceremonies
0–7100–9805–7 Methuen $29.95
0–7102–1102–3 Methuen pb $13.95

Early Greece and Minoan Periods

Arthur Evans' discovery of the palace of Minos at Knossos on Crete revealed that a great maritime civilization had flourished in the Mediterranean from 2000 to 1400 BC.

• W.R. Biers
ARCHAEOLOGY OF GREECE
The physical remains interpreted against the political and social background of the period between the age of the Homeric heroes and the era of the first colonies
0–8014–4406–0 Cornell $17.95

• John Boardman
THE GREEKS OVERSEAS: Their Early Colonies and Trade
0–500–27233–6 Thames & Hudson pb $12.95

Painting on a Greek jar, 5th century BC, from The Image of the Black in Western Art, Volume 1: From the Pharoahs to the Fall of the Roman Empire *by Amadou-Mahtar M'Bow (Harvard)*

● Gerald Cadogan
PALACES OF MINOAN CRETE
The great Minoan buildings, site by site, from the palace at Knossos to the country manors, with an account of archaeology's imaginative recreations of the society
0–416–73160–0 Methuen pb $11.95

● Y. John Chadwick
LINEAR B AND RELATED SCRIPTS
How the script of the Minoan bureaucracy was discovered, deciphered, and interpreted. The diagrams of hieroglyphics and their meanings are especially helpful
0–520–06019–9 California pb $7.95

THE MYCENEAN WORLD
0–521–29037–6 Cambridge pb $14.95

● M.I. Finley
EARLY GREECE: The Bronze and Archaic Ages
Reconstructs the lost cultures of Crete and Troy from archaeological and mythical evidence
0–393–01569–6 Norton $14.95
0–393–30051–X Norton pb $5.95

● Reynold Higgins
MINOAN AND MYCENEAN ART
0–500–20184–6 Thames & Hudson pb $11.95

● R.F. Hoddinott
THE THRACIANS
0–500–02099–X Thames & Hudson pb $19.95

● Paul MacKendrick
THE GREEK STONES SPEAK: The Story of Archaeology in Greek Lands
0–393–30111–7 Norton pb $12.95

● N.K. Sandars
THE SEA PEOPLES: Warriors of the Ancient Mediterranean, 1250 to 1150
The collapse of the ancient Mediterranean civilizations centered around Crete and Egypt is still unexplained. Here, the evidence for northern invaders who adapted to marine warfare is given full exposition
0–500–27387–1 Thames & Hudson pb $11.95

● Aubrey Snodgrass
ARCHAIC GREECE
The baronial conflicts of the Homeric ages left less written history than our own Middle Ages. This portrait of a violent yet creative culture is composed of archaeological and artistic findings
0–520–04373–1 California pb $10.95

● William Taylor
THE MYCENEANS
0–500–02103–1 Thames & Hudson $19.95

● Emily T. Vermeule
GREECE IN THE BRONZE AGE
From the first inhabitants to the fall of the Mycenean palace-towns in the 13th century BC, with special attention to the tragic encounter between the Minoan and Mycenean empires
0–226–85354–3 Chicago pb $16.95

● Michael Wood
IN SEARCH OF THE TROJAN WAR
Archaeological detective work at Hissarlik, the site of ancient Troy, comes up with some unexpected discoveries
0–8160–1355–1 Facts On File $14.95
0–452–25960–6 NAL pb $12.95

The Greek Wars

● John M. Cook
THE PERSIAN EMPIRE
Greece's greatest antagonist from its founding by Cyrus to Alexander's defeat of Darius and the burning of Persepolis
0–8052–3846–8 Schocken $30.00

● L.F. Fitzhardinge
THE SPARTANS
Numerous illustrations support the argument that under all that warrior-code bluster the Spartans were really creative art lovers
0–500–27364–2 Thames & Hudson pb $10.95

● Donald Kagan
THE OUTBREAK OF THE PELOPONNESIAN WAR
These four volumes, by a distinguished historian at Yale, re-examine Thucydides' *History of the Peloponnesian War*
0–8014–0501–7 Cornell $42.50

THE ARCHIDAMIAN WAR
0–8014–0889–X Cornell $39.50

THE PEACE OF NICIAS AND THE SICILIAN EXPEDITION
0–8014–1367–2 Cornell $39.50

THE FALL OF THE ATHENIAN EMPIRE
0–8014–1935–2 Cornell $39.50

Macedon and Alexander

● J.R. Ellis
PHILIP II AND MACEDONIAN IMPERIALISM
Treads cautiously through the controversies surrounding Alexander's father—great man or brute?—and the process by which he brought Macedon from the periphery to the center of the ancient world
0–500–40028–8 Thames & Hudson $19.95

● J.R. Hamilton
ALEXANDER THE GREAT
Emphasis on the Macedonian Alexander—his hard drinking and political cunning—and his limited influence on the spread of Hellenism
0–8229–6084–2 Pittsburgh pb $9.95

● Mary Renault
THE NATURE OF ALEXANDER
A biography by the famous novelist. "The perfect companion to her Alexander novels"—*Wall Street Journal*
0–394–73825–X Pantheon pb $5.95

● W.W. Tarn
ALEXANDER THE GREAT
A reprint of the 1948 classic
0–89005–388–X Ares $30.00

● Ulrich Wilcken
ALEXANDER THE GREAT
Alexander as the military missionary for the spread of Hellenism through the Persian and Egyptian monarchies
0–393–00381–7 Norton pb $10.95

The Hellenistic World

An overlooked but important aspect of the ancient Greeks is their 200-year domination of Asia Minor, the Middle East, Egypt, and Persia. Though politically disunited, they achieved hegemony for the cultural products of Athenian democracy, which spread out from the great centers of Antioch and Alexandria.

● Michael Grant
FROM ALEXANDER TO CLEOPATRA: The Hellenistic World
An easily digestible history of the ancient past
0–684–17780–3 Scribners $19.95
0–684–17819–2 Scribners pb $14.95

● Peter Green
ALEXANDER TO ACTIUM: An Essay on the Historical Evolution of the Hellenistic Age
Spans an entire age—past the fall of the Roman republic and the emergence of Augustus as sole ruler of the Mediterranean
0–520–05611–6 California $40.00

● Moses Hadas
HELLENISTIC CULTURE
This highly original history traces Greek influence on the Middle Eastern cultures, with special attention to Judaism and striking insights into similarities between the classical tragedians and the Bible
0–393–00593–3 Norton pb $5.95

● Arnaldo Momigliano
ALIEN WISDOM: The Limits of Hellenization
The dean of ancient historiographers considers the conflict between Greek culture and its Middle Eastern opponents
0–521–20876–9 Cambridge $29.95

ANCIENT GREECE

- F.W. Walbank
THE HELLENISTIC WORLD
This excellent introduction to the post-conquest period includes the individual kingdoms of the Attalids, Ptolemies, and Seleucids, and the remarkable achievements of Alexandrian astronomy and literary scholarship
0–674–38725–2 Harvard pb $8.95

ANCIENT GREEK SOURCES

M.I. Finley, editor
PORTABLE GREEK HISTORIANS
Selections from Herodotus, Thucydides, Xenophon, and Polybius provide an introduction to the first historians
0–14–015065–X Penguin pb $7.95

A.N.W. Saunders, translator
GREEK POLITICAL ORATORY
A record of Athenian politics through the speeches of its greatest orators from Pericles to Demosthenes
0–14–144223–5 Penguin pb $6.95

- Arrian
THE CAMPAIGNS OF ALEXANDER
Alexander as heroic leader, magnanimous and brilliant, by a Greek historian of the Age of the Antonines
Translated by Aubrey De Selincourt
0–14–044253–7 Penguin pb $5.95

- Herodotus
THE HISTORY
Father of history; father of lies—Herodotus has both reputations. The new translation upholds the reputation of this bestiary of ancient customs, which becomes a history of Greek resistance to the invasion of the Persian king Xerxes in 480 BC
Translated by David Grene
0–226–32772–8 Chicago pb $7.95

THE PERSIAN WARS
Translated by George Rawlinson
Introduction by R.B. Godolphin
0–394–30954–5 Random House pb $6.95

- Pausanias
GUIDE TO GREECE
Translated by Peter Levi

Volume 1: Central Greece
0–14–044225–1 Penguin pb $7.95

Volume 2: Southern Greece
0–14–044226–X Penguin pb $7.95

- Plutarch
THE AGE OF ALEXANDER
The will to power of Alexander's generals and the courage of those who opposed them
Translated by Ian Scott-Kilvert
0–14–044286–3 Penguin pb $5.95

PLUTARCH'S LIVES
Translated by John Dryden
Revised by Arthur H. Clough
0–394–60407–5 Modern Library $10.95

PLUTARCH ON SPARTA
0–14–044463–7 Penguin pb $3.95

THE RISE AND FALL OF ATHENS: Nine Greek Lives
The gritty personalities of the men who made Athens great and led her to defeat
Translated by Ian Scott-Kilvert
0–14–044102–6 Penguin pb $5.95

- Quintus Curtius Rufus
THE HISTORY OF ALEXANDER
Alexander as the favorite of fortune corrupted by his heady successes, portrayed by a Roman aristocrat of the early empire
Translated by John Yardley
Introduction by Heckel Waldemar
0–14–044412–2 Penguin pb $6.95

- Thucydides
HISTORY OF THE PELOPONNESIAN WAR
Seapower was the key to Greek victory in the Persian War, and the Athenians used the navy to dominate other Greek states until the tragic conflict with Sparta destroyed her empire. This unflinching record by an exiled Athenian general established a standard for accurate history writing
Translated by Rex Warner
0–14–044039–9 Penguin pb $5.95

- Xenophon
A HISTORY OF MY TIMES
Life in the defeated Athenian Empire, with personal reminiscences of Plato and Socrates
Translated by Rex Warner
0–14–044175–1 Penguin pb $6.95

THE MARCH UP COUNTRY: A Modern Translation of the Anabasis
Stranded in the heart of the Persian Empire, a Greek contingent fights its way north from Babylon to the Black Sea
Translated by W.H. Rouse
0–472–06095–3 Michigan pb $9.95

THE PERSIAN EXPEDITION
An excellent translation of the *Anabasis*
Translated by Rex Warner
0–14–044007–0 Penguin pb $6.95

ROBERT FAGLES: A Short Course in Greek Literature

Homer
THE ILIAD OF HOMER
Translated by Richmond Lattimore
0–226–46940–9 Chicago pb $8.95

THE ODYSSEY
Translated by Richmond Lattimore
0–06–090479–8 Harper & Row pb $5.95

Hesiod
THEOGONY & WORKS AND DAYS
Translated by Apostolos N. Athanassakis
0–8018–2998–4 Johns Hopkins $20.00
0–8018–2999–2 Johns Hopkins pb $8.95

Guy Davenport, translator
ARCHILOCHOS, SAPPHO, ALKMAN: Three Lyric Poets of the Seventh Century B.C.
0–520–03823–1 California $30.00
0–520–05223–4 California pb $10.95

Peter Jay, editor
THE GREEK ANTHOLOGY
0–14–044285–5 Penguin pb $6.95

Pindar
PINDAR'S VICTORY SONGS
Translated by Frank Nisetich
0–8018–2350–1 Johns Hopkins $42.50
0–8018–2356–0 Johns Hopkins $14.95

Aeschylus
THE ORESTEIA
Translated by Robert Fagles
Introduction & notes by W.B. Stanford
0–670–52832–3 Viking $20.00
0–14–044333–9 Penguin pb $3.95

Sophocles
THE THREE THEBAN PLAYS
Translated by Robert Fagles
Introductions & notes by Bernard Knox
0–670–69805–9 Viking $25.00
0–14–044425–4 Penguin pb $2.95

Euripides
THREE TRAGEDIES
Includes *Electra*, *The Phoenician Women*, and *The Bacchae*
Translated by Emily Vermeule, Elizabeth Wyckoff & William Arrowsmith
Edited by David Grene & Richmond Lattimore
0–226–30784–0 Chicago pb $6.50

Aristophanes
THREE COMEDIES
Includes *The Birds*, *The Clouds*, and *The Wasps*
Edited by William Arrowsmith
0–472–06153–4 Michigan pb $9.95

Herodotus
THE HISTORIES
Translated by David Grene
0–226–32772–8 Chicago pb $7.95

Thucydides
THE PELOPONNESIAN WAR
Translated by Rex Warner
0–14–044039–9 Penguin pb $5.95

Plato
FIVE DIALOGUES
Translated by G.M. Grube
0–915145–23–5 Hackett $22.50
0–915145–22–7 Hackett pb $4.75

THE REPUBLIC
Translated by Francis Cornford
0–19–500364–0 Oxford pb $4.95

Aristotle
THE POETICS
Translated by Gerald Else
0–472–06166–6 Michigan pb $8.95

TOPICS IN ANCIENT GREEK HISTORY

Arts

- Charles Rowan Beye
ANCIENT GREEK LITERATURE AND SOCIETY
Greek literature from the epic as source of the mytho-poetic tradition to the

Minoan amphora, from The Oxford Companion to Art *edited by Harold Osborne*

Hellenistic institutions of education and the library
0–8014–9444–3 Cornell pb $9.95

• John Boardman
GREEK SCULPTURE
Excellent introduction to the art form whose influence reaches from Japanese Buddhism to European neoclassicism
0–500–20198–6 Thames & Hudson pb $11.95

• Emile Brehier
HISTORY OF PHILOSOPHY: The Hellenistic and Roman Age
The post-Aristotelian systems of thought are disentangled in this account of Stoicism, Epicureanism, skepticism, Neoplatonism, Hellenism, and Christianity
Translated by Wade Baskin
0–226–07221–5 Chicago pb $7.00

• Jeffrey M. Hurwit
ART AND CULTURE OF EARLY GREECE, 1100–480 BC
Illustrated introduction to the cultural context of art from the Archaic period to the eve of the Persian War in its political and philosophical background
0–8014–9401–X Cornell $16.95

• Jacqueline de Romilly
A SHORT HISTORY OF GREEK LITERATURE
0–226–14311–2 Chicago pb $9.95

• Susan Woodford
AN INTRODUCTION TO GREEK ART
"Imparts a radiant lustre to the Greeks and their artistic creations, drawn from her special sensitivity to their inner spirit"—D.G. Mitter, Harvard University Art Museums
0–8014–9480–X Cornell pb $17.95

THE PARTHENON
0–521–22629–5 Cambridge pb $4.95

Religion

• Walter Burkert
GREEK RELIGION
Without priestly organizations, revelatory Ur-texts, or monastic orders, the Greeks used ritual and myth as a force for continuity
0–674–36281–0 Harvard pb $10.95

HOMO NECANS: The Anthropology of Ancient Greek Ritual and Myth
How the ritual sacrifice of animals achieved sacred status
Translated by Peter Bing
0–520–05875–5 Campus pb $10.95

STRUCTURE AND HISTORY IN GREEK MYTHOLOGY
A rare combination of fine scholarship with imagination and humor
0–520–04770–2 California pb $11.95

• Marcel Detienne & Jean-Pierre Vernant
THE CUISINE OF SACRIFICE AMONG THE GREEKS
0–226–14353–8 Chicago pb $14.95

• E.R. Dodds
THE GREEKS AND THE IRRATIONAL
The sources of Greek rationalism are to be found in primitive modes of thought
0–520–00327–6 California pb $10.95

• Joseph Fontenrose
THE DELPHIC ORACLES: Its Responses and Operations with a Catalogue of Responses
A collection of all the known responses of this famous oracle, and an analysis of their aims and accuracy that refutes their transcendental claims
0–520–04359–6 Berkley pb $12.95

PYTHON: A Study of Delphic Myth
0–520–04091–0 California pb $10.95

• L. Kerenyi
THE GODS OF THE GREEKS
From the castration of Uranus to affairs between nymphs and satyrs—stories of all the most important Greek myths
0–500–27048–1 Thames & Hudson pb $9.95

• Jon D. Mikalson
ATHENIAN POPULAR RELIGION
Religious beliefs of Athens in the fifth and fourth centuries BC drawn from contemporary sources—state decrees, sacred laws, religious dedications, and epitaphs
0–8078–4194–3 North Carolina pb $8.95

• Paul Veyne
DID THE GREEKS BELIEVE IN THEIR MYTHS?: An Essay on the Constitutive Imagination
"Brilliant and exhilarating"—*TLS*
0–226–85434–5 Chicago pb $10.95

Women in Antiquity

• Paul Friedrich
THE MEANING OF APHRODITE
The goddess of love as a complex figure at the border of sexuality and abstinence
0–226–26483–1 Phoenix Women's Studies pb $8.95

• G.E.R. Lloyd
SCIENCE, FOLKLORE AND IDEOLOGY
Scientific views and ideals of the ruling elite as they supported their opinions of female social and biological inferiority
0–521–27307–2 Cambridge $18.95

• Sarah B. Pomeroy
GODDESSES, WHORES, WIVES, AND SLAVES: Women in Classical Antiquity
0–8052–0530–6 Schocken pb $8.95

• Philip E. Slater
THE GLORY OF HERA: Greek Mythology and the Greek Family
Matriarchal dominance in Greek society both encouraged and stymied the male child's urge to heroic behavior
0–8070–5795–9 Beacon $14.95

Politics and Ideas

The Greek rationalist methodology that intuited the atom and measured the circumference of the earth remains an outstanding contribution to civilization. Though progress has overtaken most of their discoveries, the extent of the knowledge the Greeks acquired before the fall of the classical world can still amaze us.

• Marshall Clagett
GREEK SCIENCE IN ANTIQUITY
How human reason and ingenuity first ordered and mastered the experience of natural phenomena
0–02–091880–1 Macmillan pb $4.95

• A.H. Jones
ATHENIAN DEMOCRACY
The merits and demerits of ancient Athens: cradle of democracy or slave society ruled by effete intellectuals?
0–8018–3380–9 Johns Hopkins pb $8.95

• G.E.R. Lloyd
EARLY GREEK SCIENCE: Thales to Aristotle
0–393–00583–6 Norton pb $5.95

GREEK SCIENCE AFTER ARISTOTLE
The Greeks were the first to explain natural phenomena in naturalistic terms. Lloyd places their scientific achievement in its social setting and discusses the motives of individual thinkers
0–393–00780–4 Norton pb $5.95

• D.R. Ricks
EARLY GREEK ASTRONOMY TO ARISTOTLE
The astronomy of Homer and Hesiod, of the pre-Socratics, of Plato, Eudoxus, and Aristotle
0–8014–9310–2 Cornell pb $10.95

• S. Sambursky
THE PHYSICAL WORLD OF THE GREEKS
How much the Greeks knew, how they thought, and the limitations of their knowledge
0–691–02411–1 Princeton pb $8.95

PHYSICS OF THE STOICS
The Stoic continuum theory is described

TO ORDER BOOKS AS GIFTS, SEE PAGE 1

and traced to earlier sources, and the more rigorous elaborations are discussed
0–691–02412–X Princeton pb $8.95

I.F. Stone
THE TRIAL OF SOCRATES
The most emphatic treatment of the trial of Socrates as a political event, with the twist that the philosopher had it coming
0–316–81758–9 Little, Brown $18.95

Private Life and Recreation

• **K.J. Dover**
GREEK HOMOSEXUALITY
"A landmark study . . . With philological brilliance and scholarly objectivity, he presents facts that can no longer be ignored"—Erich Segal
0–674–36270–5 Harvard pb $12.95

• **Michel Foucault**
THE USE OF PLEASURE: History of Sexuality, Volume 2
A brilliant amateur's foray into the precincts of the classical world revises our conception of both ancient and modern sexuality
Translated by Robert Hurley
0–394–54349–1 Pantheon $17.45
0–394–72952–8 Random House pb $5.95

• **J.C. Gosling & C.C. Taylor**
THE GREEKS ON PLEASURE
A collection that spans responses from the stern Stoic to the epicene Epicurean
0–19–824775–3 Oxford pb $17.95

• **Ian Jenkins**
GREEK AND ROMAN LIFE
0–674–36307–8 Harvard pb $8.95

• **Eva C. Keals**
THE REIGN OF THE PHALLUS: Sexual Politics in Ancient Athens
A profusely illustrated history of the war of the sexes, showing the forms taken by the male claim to gender dominance and the intense countermovement on the stage, in public debate, and on the streets
0–06–091129–8 Harper & Row pb $14.95

• **H.I. Marrou**
HISTORY OF EDUCATION IN ANTIQUITY
0–299–08814–6 Wisconsin pb $12.95

• **Bernard Sergent**
HOMOSEXUALITY IN GREEK MYTH
The practice of homosexuality in ancient Greece was different from its modern manifestations
Translated by Arthur Goldhammer
Preface by Georges Dumézil
0–8070–5700–2 Beacon $24.95

• **Bennett Simon**
MIND AND MADNESS IN ANCIENT GREECE: The Classical Roots of Modern Psychiatry
Seeks the origins of contemporary psychiatric theory in Homer, Plato, the tragedians, and the Hippocratic writings
0–8014–9202–5 Cornell pb $12.95

• **Waldo E. Sweet**
SPORT AND RECREATION IN ANCIENT GREECE
Foreword by Erich Segal
0–19–504126–7 Oxford $29.95
0–19–504127–5 Oxford pb $8.95

Society and Economy

• **Lionel Casson**
SHIPS AND SEAMANSHIP IN THE ANCIENT WORLD
Traces the art and technology of Mediterranean vessels and navigation from 3000 BC to the heyday of the Byzantine fleets
0–691–00215–0 Princeton pb $19.50

• **M.I. Finley**
THE ANCIENT ECONOMY
Modern terms cannot be automatically used to describe the Greek economy. Finley finds a middle path to illuminate it without distortion
0–520–05452–0 California pb $11.95

ANCIENT SLAVERY AND MODERN IDEOLOGY
This comparison of ancient slave societies with their modern counterparts opens a perspective on the history of slavery that transcends particular historical eras
0–14–022500–5 Penguin pb $7.95

• **Yvon Garlan**
SLAVERY IN ANCIENT GREECE
The best recent book on the complex interweaving of slave and freeborn members of ancient society, where both often worked side by side and joined the same craft clubs
0–8014–9504–0 Cornell pb $12.95

• **John Morrison & John Coates**
THE ATHENIAN TRIREME: The History and Reconstruction of an Ancient Greek Warship
0–521–32202–2 Cambridge $42.95
0–521–31100–4 Cambridge pb $12.95

• **Brent D. Shaw & Richard P. Saller, editors**
ECONOMY AND SOCIETY IN ANCIENT GREECE
0–14–022520–X Penguin pb $7.95

The Greek City

• **John M. Camp**
THE ATHENIAN AGORA: Excavations in the Heart of Classical Athens
0–500–39021–5 Thames & Hudson $29.95

• **Numa de Coulanges**
THE ANCIENT CITY: A Classic Study of the Religious and Civil Institutions of Ancient Greece and Rome
Foreword by Arnaldo Momigliano & S.C. Humphreys
0–8018–2304–8 Johns Hopkins pb $7.95

• **A.H. Jones**
THE GREEK CITY FROM ALEXANDER TO JUSTINIAN
Cities in the Old World seem either timeless or to have swollen up from small settlements. But two of the greatest were founded by powerful commanders—Alexandria and Constantinople. These

quintessentially Greek cities are among the many discussed in this fascinating work
0–19–814842–9 Oxford pb $29.95

• **Robin Osborne**
CLASSICAL LANDSCAPE WITH FIGURES: The Ancient Greek City and Its Countryside
0–911378–73–1 Sheridan House $34.95

• **R.E. Wycherly**
HOW THE GREEKS BUILT CITIES
Urban architectural forms reflect the inner nature growing out of the needs, ways of life, traditions, and ideas of the citizens
0–393–00814–2 Norton pb $7.95

THE STONES OF ATHENS
Studies the architectural and monumental remains in the light of the literature
0–691–03553–9 Princeton $47.50
0–691–10059–4 Princeton pb $16.50

Greek Influence

• **Martin Bernal**
BLACK ATHENA, THE AFRO-ASIATIC ROOTS OF CLASSICAL CIVILIZATION, Volume 1: The Fabrication of Ancient Greece, 1785-1985
Argues that the Egyptian and Middle Eastern sources of Greek civilization were downplayed in the interests of the northern peoples who proclaimed themselves heirs to Greek scientific thought
0–8135–1276–X Rutgers $45.00
0–8135–1277–8 Rutgers pb $15.00

• **Richard Jenkyns**
THE VICTORIANS AND ANCIENT GREECE
0–674–93686–8 Harvard $32.00
0–674–93687–6 Harvard pb $10.95

• **Hugh Lloyd-Jones**
BLOOD FOR THE GHOSTS: Classical Influences in the Nineteenth and Twentieth Centuries
0–8018–3017–6 Johns Hopkins $32.50

REFERENCE

• **Robert Graves**
THE GREEK MYTHS
Volume 1
0–14–020508–X Penguin pb $4.95

Greek workers quarrying for clay in the 6th century BC, from The Oxford History of the Classical World *edited by John Boardman and others*

Volume 2
0–14–020509–8 Penguin pb $4.95

● Peter Levi
ATLAS OF THE GREEK WORLD
0–87196–448–1 Facts On File $40.00

● Betty Radice
WHO'S WHO IN THE ANCIENT WORLD
"One person's pointers to some of the classical names that have kept their vitality—as poetic symbols, themes in music, painting, or drama, or forces in the western unconscious"—from the author's introduction
0–14–051055–9 Penguin pb $7.95

● Richard J.A. Talbert
ATLAS OF CLASSICAL HISTORY
Maps, diagrams, and commentary: from the Bronze Age to Constantine
0–415–03463–9 RC&H pb $17.95

Mary Renault

Mary Renault's novels of ancient Greece, mostly narrated in the first person, are notable for their richly-detailed evocations of history and mythology and their 20th-century knowledge of anthropology and psychology.

Mary Renault
THE KING MUST DIE
Fascinating story set in the Minoan period as Theseus, mythical king of Athens, saves the city from its annual tribute of young men and maidens for sacrifice to the Minotaur
0–394–43195–2 Pantheon $15.50
0–394–75104–3 Random House pb $6.95

THE BULL FROM THE SEA
More adventures of Theseus—his life-and-death struggle with and eventual unquenchable passion for Hippolyta, queen of the Amazons
0–394–71504–7 Random House pb $4.95

FUNERAL GAMES
0–394–52068–8 Pantheon $14.50

THE LAST OF THE WINE
A young Athenian actor tells of his troupe's exciting travels through Greece during the Peloponnesian War
0–394–71653–1 Random House pb $6.95

THE MASK OF APOLLO
0–394–75105–1 Random House pb $5.95

THE PERSIAN BOY
A first-person account by a beautiful young captive of the Macedonian Army who becomes the catamite of the conqueror Alexander
0–394–48191–7 Pantheon $15.95
0–394–75101–9 Random House pb $6.95

THE PRAISE SINGER
0–394–50273–6 Pantheon $12.95

Ancient Rome

Imperial Rome's achievement was enormous. No empire has ever conquered so many peoples by force and established stable rule over them for so long. Modern nations that would have fallen under Rome's mandate run from Great Britain to Turkey and from Syria to Morocco. The edifice as a whole lasted for more than 400 years, and the Byzantine eastern portion survived the barbarian invasions and the power of Islam until 1453. Even in its death, Rome left as a legacy to Europe an ideal of unity that has influenced politicians and political theorists to the present.

But it had a dreadful cost. First, the republican government that presided over most of the conquests was insufficient to govern the immense territorial acquisitions and gave way after civil war to the despotic rule of a single man—the emperor. And second, the stable administration was imposed and maintained by military brutalities, the uprooting of whole populations, and genocide.

Its costs show up in a continuous dark commentary from the Roman historians themselves to current writers. Beginning with Tacitus and Suetonius, the value of the imperial settlement has been brought into doubt. Historians of this school look back to the republic, the period of Rome's greatest expansion, to study the source of its power and the reasons for its fall. And in our own age of destructive demagoguery, they find the character of Julius Caesar, the first to establish single rule on a populist base, particularly controversial.

● Perry Anderson
PASSAGES FROM ANTIQUITY TO FEUDALISM
A British Marxist history of the empire and the barbarian invaders by the author of *Lineages of the Absolutist State*
0–86091–709–6 Verso pb $15.95

● R.H. Barrow
THE ROMANS
A brief but excellent introduction which proposes that the Roman genius is of vital importance for understanding ourselves
0–14–020196–3 Penguin pb $5.95

● John Boardman, Jasper Griffin & Oswyn Murray
THE ROMAN WORLD
This collection of essays forms an agreeable and informative introduction to all aspects of life in ancient Rome
0–19–282166–0 Oxford pb $18.95

● Michael Grant
HISTORY OF ROME
The rise and fall. Illustrated with useful maps, family trees, and lists of emperors
0–02–345610–8 Macmillan pb $26.00

The Etruscans and Early Rome

● Axel Boethius
ETRUSCAN AND EARLY ROMAN ARCHITECTURE
From 1400 BC to the Hellenized buildings of Pompeii and Herculaneum
0–14–056144–7 Penguin pb $18.95

● Otto J. Brendel
ETRUSCAN ART
Aristocratic family life; elegant bronzes and personal portraits
0–14–056143–9 Penguin pb $18.95

● Michael Grant
THE ETRUSCANS
0–684–16724–7 Scribners $17.50

● Emmeline Richardson
THE ETRUSCANS: Their Art and Civilization
The genius of a mysterious people who borrowed from Greece and influenced Rome
0–226–71235–4 Chicago pb $9.50

● H.H. Scullard
THE ETRUSCAN CITIES AND ROME
0–8014–0373–1 Cornell $36.50

The Emperor Vespasian (69-79 AD), from The Oxford History of the Classical World *edited by John Boardman and others*

Republic to Empire

● Michael Crawford
THE ROMAN REPUBLIC
Its history and constitution from its establishment after the fall of the kings in

---

the 6th century BC to the triumph of Augustus
0–674–77931–2 Harvard pb $7.95

- Henry T. Rowell
ROME IN THE AUGUSTAN AGE
0–8061–0956–4 Oklahoma pb $8.95

- H.H. Scullard
FROM THE GRACCHI TO NERO: A History of Rome from 133 B.C. to A.D. 68
Populist resistance to patrician power leads to the first imperial dynasty
0–416–32890–3 Methuen $33.00
0–416–32900–4 Methuen pb $18.95

- Ronald Syme
THE ROMAN REVOLUTION
A classic from the 1930s, still essential on the revolution that overturned the republic and established the empire after Antony and Cleopatra's defeat at Actium in 31 BC
0–19–881001–6 Oxford pb $10.95

- Colin Wells
THE ROMAN EMPIRE
Balances a description of central government against life in the provinces
0–8047–1238–7 Stanford pb $10.95

Late Empire

"But the empire of the Romans filled the world, and, when that empire fell into the hands of a single person, the world became a safe and dreary prison for his enemies. The slave of imperial despotism, whether he was condemned to drag his gilded chain in Rome and the senate, or to wear out a life of exile on the barren rock of Seriphus or the frozen banks of the Danube, expected his fate in silent despair. To resist was fatal, and it was impossible to fly. On every side he was encompassed with a vast extent of sea and land, which he could never hope to traverse without being discovered, seized and restored to his irritated master. Beyond the frontiers, his anxious view could discover nothing, except the ocean, inhospitable deserts, hostile tribes of barbarians, of fierce manners and unknown language, or dependent kings, who would gladly purchase the emperor's protection by the sacrifice of an obnoxious fugitive. 'Wherever you are,' said Cicero to the exiled Marcellus, 'remember that you are equally within the power of the conqueror.' "—Edward Gibbon, *The Decline and Fall of the Roman Empire*

- Diana Bowder
THE AGE OF CONSTANTINE AND JULIAN
Diocletian's successors adopt his system of government but struggle over the official status of Christianity
0–06–490601–9 Barnes & Noble $32.50

- Peter Brown
THE MAKING OF LATE ANTIQUITY
In an epoch-making shift, the civic culture of the Antonines gives way to the religious cultism of the late empire
0–674–54320–3 Harvard $16.00

- Jacob Burckhardt
THE AGE OF CONSTANTINE THE GREAT
Translated by Moses Hadas
0–520–04680–3 California pb $11.95

- J.B. Bury
HISTORY OF THE LATER ROMAN EMPIRE: From the Death of Theodosius I to the Death of Justinian
The tragic history from the struggle between the two barbarians, Alaric and Stilicho, for the fate of Rome, to its recovery by Belisarius under the Byzantine emperor Justinian

Volume 1
0–486–20398–0 Dover pb $7.95

Volume 2
0–486–20399–9 Dover pb $7.95

- A.H. Jones
THE LATER ROMAN EMPIRE, 284–602: A Social, Economic, and Administrative Survey
The classic study, available for the first time in paperback. One of the most eminent ancient historians surveys social, economic, and administrative developments from the restructuring of the empire by Diocletian to its collapse in the West in 476

Volume 1
0–8018–3348–5 Johns Hopkins $39.50
0–8018–3353–1 Johns Hopkins pb $24.50

Volume 2
0–8018–3349–3 Johns Hopkins $49.50
0–8018–3354–X Johns Hopkins pb $19.50

- Ramsey MacMullen
CORRUPTION AND DECLINE OF ROME
Deep familiarity with the history and customs of the Roman Empire gives weight and color to the latest theory of its fall
0–300–04313–9 Yale $27.50

- Stephen Williams
DIOCLETIAN AND THE ROMAN RECOVERY
After the disastrous invasions and civil wars of the third century, Diocletian restores stability through a drastic change in the system of government
0–416–01151–9 Methuen $19.95

ANCIENT ROMAN SOURCES

"All over the field Roman soldiers lay dead in their thousands, horse and foot mingled, as the shifting phases of the battle, or the attempt to escape had brought them together. Here and there wounded men smeared with blood, recovering consciousness in the morning cold, were dispatched by a quick blow as they struggled to rise from amongst the corpses; others with the sinews in their thighs and behind the knees sliced through, bared their throats and necks and begged anyone to spill what little blood they had left. Some had their heads buried in the ground, having choked themselves to death by digging holes and smothering their

faces in the earth. Strangest of all was a Numidian, with nose and ears horribly lacerated, still breathing, pinned beneath the body of a Roman who, when his sword-arm failed, had died tearing his foe in bestial fury with his teeth."—Livy, *Hannibal in Italy*

- Julius Caesar
THE BATTLE FOR GAUL
Translated by Anne & Peter Wiseman
Illustrated by Barry Cunliffe
0–87923–306–0 Godine $24.95
0–87923–561–6 Godine pb $12.95

THE CIVIL WAR
After conquering Gaul, Caesar turns his armies against the Senate
Translated by Jane F. Mitchell
0–14–044187–5 Penguin pb $5.95

- Cassius Dio
THE ROMAN HISTORY: The Reign of Augustus
Augustan politics by a professional politican in 2nd-century Rome
Translated by Ian Scott-Kilvert
Introduction by John Carter
0–14–044448–3 Penguin pb $6.95

- Flavius Josephus
THE JEWISH WAR
The rebellion against Roman power whose failure initiated the Diaspora—by a leader of the Jews
Translated by G.A. Williamson
Edited by E. Mary Smallwood
0–14–044420–3 Penguin pb $7.95

THE WORKS OF JOSEPHUS
The tenacious struggle against total domination by one of the empire's victims
0–913573–86–8 Hendrickson $19.95

- Titus Livy
THE EARLY HISTORY OF ROME
From the mythic times of Romulus to the hardships of recovery after the sack of Rome by the Gauls
Translated by Aubrey De Selincourt
0–14–044104–2 Penguin pb $5.95

ROME AND ITALY
Early Roman expansion into surrounding territory
0–14–044388–6 Penguin pb $5.95

THE WAR WITH HANNIBAL
Rome's most dangerous hour. How the early republic survived invasion by Carthage, her greatest rival for control of the Mediterranean
Translated by Aubrey De Selincourt
0–14–044145–X Penguin pb $6.95

ROME AND THE MEDITERRANEAN
Roman armies move east to confront the rulers of the remnants of Alexander's empire in Macedonia, Syria, and Egypt
Translated by Henry Bettenson
0–14–044318–5 Penguin pb $6.95

- Ammianus Marcellinus
THE LATER ROMAN EMPIRE (A.D. 353–378)
The end of the western empire in the words of the last pagan historian
Edited by Walter Hamilton
Introduction by Andrew Wallace-Hadrill
0–14–044406–8 Penguin pb $7.95

- Plutarch

THE FALL OF THE ROMAN REPUBLIC: Six Roman Lives
Dramatic portraits of the men who struggled for power and possession in the power vacuum of the crumbling Roman republic
Translated by Rex Warner
0–14–044084–4 Penguin pb $6.95

MAKERS OF ROME
Contains the lives of Coriolanus, Fabius Maximus, Marcellus, Cato the Elder, Tiberius Gracchus, Gaius Gracchus, Sertorius, Brutus, and Mark Antony
Translated by Ian Scott-Kilvert
0–14–044158–1 Penguin pb $5.95

- Polybius

POLYBIUS ON ROMAN IMPERIALISM
The noble Greek hostage whose history combines the excitement of the war against Hannibal with still-valid insights into the reasons for Roman dominance
Translated by Evelyn S. Shuckburgh
Edited by Alvin H. Bernstein
0–89526–902–3 Regnery pb $10.95

THE RISE OF THE ROMAN EMPIRE
More engrossing reading about the growth of Roman power; an expert translation
Translated by Ian Scott-Kilvert
0–14–044362–2 Penguin pb $8.95

- Procopius

THE SECRET HISTORY
The seamy underside of the Byzantine court—fascinating reading
Translated by G.A. Williamson
0–14–044182–4 Penguin pb $6.95

THE SECRET HISTORY
Translated by Richard Atwater
Foreword by A.E. Boak
0–472–08728–2 Michigan pb $4.95

- Sallust

THE JUGURTHINE WAR & THE CONSPIRACY OF CATILINE
Perils at home and abroad. Marius becomes the first Roman to turn his armies against the Senate: Cicero defends the republic against the designs of yet another disgruntled young aristocrat
Translated by S.A. Handford
0–14–044132–8 Penguin pb $4.95

- Suetonius

THE TWELVE CAESARS
Madness and perversity among the supremely powerful
Translated by Robert Graves
0–14–044072–0 Penguin pb $4.95

THE TWELVE CAESARS: An Illustrated Edition
Translated by Robert Graves
0–14–005416–2 Penguin pb $18.95

- Tacitus

COMPLETE WORKS
Edited by Moses Hadas
0–394–30953–7 Random House pb $7.50

AGRICOLA & GERMANIA
A patrician soldier's exemplary career and wistful regret for Rome's lost primitivism in a study of the ancient Germans
Translated by Hugh Mattingly
0–14–044241–3 Penguin pb $4.95

ANNALS OF IMPERIAL ROME
This ironic depiction of the gradual loss of freedom among Romans under the first emperors includes memorable vignettes of Messalina's career and the failed plot against Nero
Translated by Michael Grant
0–14–044060–7 Penguin pb $7.95

THE HISTORIES
AD 69: the year of the four emperors. Chaos following Nero's suicide allows Tacitus to deploy his narrative verve on the events of the civil war
Translated by Kenneth Wellesley
0–14–044150–6 Penguin pb $5.95

- Anthony R. Birley, translator & editor

LIVES OF THE LATER CAESARS
The unsolved mystery of their authorship does not detract from the fascination of these brief biographies of some of the greatest emperors—Trajan, Hadrian, and Marcus Aurelius
0–14–044308–8 Penguin pb $5.95

ROMAN PORTRAITS
(alphabetical by subject)

"Whenever Britannicus was seated at his meal, it was a settled rule that an attendant should taste his food and liquor. To preserve this custom, and prevent detection by the attendant's death, an innocent beverage, without any infusion that could hurt, was tried by the proper officer, and presented to the prince. He found it too hot, and returned it. Cold water, in which the poison had been mixed, was immediately poured into the cup. Britannicus drank freely; the effect was violent, and, in an instant, it seized the powers of life: his limbs were palsied, his breath was suppressed, and his utterance failed. The company were thrown into consternation. Some rushed out of the room, but others, who had more discernment, stayed, though in astonishment, with their eyes fixed on Nero, who lay stretched at ease on his couch, with an air of innocence, and without emotion."—Tacitus, *Annals of Imperial Rome*

Michael Grant
THE ROMAN EMPERORS
The whole gamut—from Augustus to Romulus Augustulus, the last barbarian puppet ruler deposed in 476. A magnificent collection of biographical cameos, illustrated with ancient contemporary portraits
0–684–18388–9 Scribners $25.00

- Ramsey MacMullen

CONSTANTINE
Did he adopt Christianity out of sincere conviction or political expediency?
0–7099–4685–6 Methuen pb $14.95

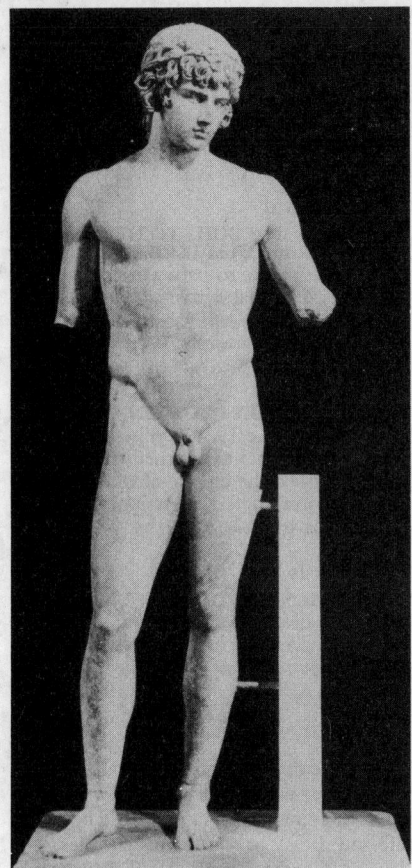

Statue of Antinous, the Emperor Hadrian's lover, who drowned in mysterious circumstances in the River Nile in AD 130

- Royston Lambert

BELOVED AND GOD
An investigation of the mysterious death of Hadrian's lover Antinous, in the Nile; the cult of his memory recreates the *fin de siècle* mood of Rome's Silver Age
0–8216–2003–7 Meadowland pb $9.95

- Stuart Perowne

HADRIAN
Most cultured of the emperors, Hadrian wrote verse and built cities to his lost love, Antinous, but arbitrarily executed Roman senators
0–7099–4048–3 Methuen pb $12.95

- Ernle Bradford

HANNIBAL: The General from Carthage
The great leader who almost changed the course of history by attacking the Roman republic in its infancy
0–07–007064–4 McGraw-Hill $14.95

- Robert Browning

THE EMPEROR JULIAN
Constantine's lonely nephew, survivor of a political bloodbath, turns against his uncle's religion and becomes the last pagan ruler in AD 360
0–520–03731–6 California pb $7.95

➤ **FOR OVERSEAS ORDERING INFORMATION, SEE PAGE 1**

• Arthur D. Kahn
THE EDUCATION OF JULIUS CAESAR: A Biography, a Reconstruction
The conqueror as hero. Followers of Caesar felt "fulfilled as human beings"
0-8052-4009-8 Schocken $28.00

• Zvi Yavetz
JULIUS CAESAR AND HIS PUBLIC IMAGE
Exposes the myth of Caesar as enlightened despot
0-8014-1440-7 Cornell $29.95

• Miriam T. Griffin
NERO: The End of a Dynasty
Nero was only the stepson of the emperor Claudius. Through the machinations of his mother, Agrippina, he was declared successor to the throne over the claim of Britannicus, the real heir. Matricide and this playboy's tragic flaws led to his own early suicide and the fall of the Julio-Claudian dynasty
0-300-04034-2 Yale pb $13.95

• John Leach
POMPEY THE GREAT
The tragic career of Caesar's son-in-law and greatest rival. His defeat by Caesar at Pharsalus in 48 BC while leading the senatorial forces meant the end of the republic
0-7099-4127-7 Methuen pb $12.95

• Anthony R. Birley
SEPTIMIUS SEVERUS: The African Emperor
0-300-04467-4 Yale $29.95

• Arthur Keaveney
SULLA: The Last Republican
Bloodthirsty oligarch or dedicated patriot? The dictator who tried to restore the republic in the face of attempts by military leaders to seize power
0-7099-3104-2 Methuen pb $14.95

• Barbara Levick
TIBERIUS THE POLITICIAN
The vexing question of the second emperor: a morose and self-indulgent sadist governing through corrupt favorites? Or a maligned and lonely man looking for ways to rule the largest empire in history?
0-7099-4132-3 Methuen pb $16.95

TOPICS IN ROMAN HISTORY

"Constantine promoted the spread of Christianity beyond the frontiers, still more within them. He tried to reclaim heretics and schismatics. His motive, however, was not to save souls but, one almost might say, bodies. He aimed at the prosperity of his reign and realm through ensuring to God acceptable worship, and by prosperity he evidently had in mind quite material well-being: an end to civil war, security along the borders, plentiful crops for a plentiful population—in short, peace, and its products. Few of the essential elements of Christian belief interested Constantine very much—neither God's mercy nor man's sinfulness, neither damnation nor salvation, neither brotherly love, nor, needless to say, humility. Ardent in his convictions he remained nevertheless oblivious to their moral implications."—Ramsey MacMullen, *Christianizing the Roman Empire*

Religion

• Peter Brown
AUGUSTINE OF HIPPO: A Biography
A comprehensive biography of this late-ancient Christian founding father
0-520-01411-1 California pb $11.95

THE BODY AND SOCIETY: Men, Women and Sexual Renunciation in Early Christianity
0-231-06100-5 Columbia $45.00

THE CULT OF THE SAINTS: Its Rise and Function in Latin Christianity
The saints succeed the ancient heroes
0-226-07622-9 Chicago pb $7.95

SOCIETY AND THE HOLY IN LATE ANTIQUITY
0-520-04305-7 California $32.50

• Franz Cumont
ASTROLOGY AND RELIGION AMONG THE GREEKS AND ROMANS
Star worship, mystery religions, and Near Eastern cults and their impact
0-486-20581-9 Dover pb $4.50

THE MYSTERIES OF MITHRA
A 1911 study about the Persian religion that gave us Sunday and Christmas and almost beat out Christianity for dominance in the Roman Empire
Translated by Thomas J. McCormack
0-486-20323-9 Dover pb $5.95

• Jean Danielou & H.I. Marrou
THE FIRST SIX HUNDRED YEARS
A European view of the ancient roots of Christianity
0-8091-0275-7 Paulist Press $22.95

• E.R. Dodds
PAGAN AND CHRISTIAN IN AN AGE OF ANXIETY: Some Aspects of Religious Experience from Marcus Aurelius to Constantine
0-393-00545-3 Norton pb $6.95

• John Ferguson
THE RELIGIONS OF THE ROMAN EMPIRE
A variegated picture of religious life as its importance increased during the 2nd and 3rd centuries
0-8014-9311-0 Cornell pb $8.95

• Robin Lane Fox
PAGANS AND CHRISTIANS
0-394-55495-7 Knopf $35.00
0-06-062852-9 Harper & Row pb $16.95

• Georg Luck, editor
ARCANA MUNDI: Magic and the Occult in the Greek and Roman Worlds
A collection of ancient texts translated, annotated, and introduced by Luck. A first-rate comprehensive sourcebook and introduction to magic as practiced by witches and sorcerers, magi and astrologers
0-8018-2523-7 Johns Hopkins $32.50
0-8018-2548-2 Johns Hopkins pb $12.95

• Ramsey MacMullen
CHRISTIANIZING THE ROMAN EMPIRE
The social forces involved in the spread of Christianity, from supernatural contests between rival wonder-workers to imperial coercion under Constantine
0-300-03216-1 Yale $22.50
0-300-03642-6 Yale pb $9.95

PAGANISM IN THE ROMAN EMPIRE
The movement from rationalism to eastern occultism prepares the way for Christianity
0-300-02984-5 Yale pb $9.95

• R.M. Ogilvie
ROMANS AND THEIR GODS IN THE AGE OF AUGUSTUS
Religion in the early empire was tolerant but failed because the world changed from rationalist to mystic
0-393-00543-7 Norton pb $5.95

• Jaroslav Pelikan
THE EXCELLENT EMPIRE
The award-winning historian finds common ground between the believer Augustine and the sceptic Gibbon. Full-color illustrations from antiquity and the Renaissance
0-06-254636-8 Harper & Row $18.95

• Robert L. Wilken
THE CHRISTIANS AS THE ROMANS SAW THEM
The views of the most cogent pagan opponents of Christianity, from the philosopher Celsus to Julian the Apostate, in a mix of social and intellectual history
0-300-03066-5 Yale $25.00

Women

• J.P. Balsdon
ROMAN WOMEN: Their History and Habits
From first ladies of the empire to the Roman housewife, with portraits of the powerful wives and mothers who made imperial policy
0-06-464062-0 Harper & Row pb $7.95

• Marjorie W. Bingham & Susan H. Gross
WOMEN IN ANCIENT GREECE AND ROME
0-914227-00-9 Glenhurst pb $8.95

• Eva Cantarella
PANDORA'S DAUGHTERS: The Role and Status of Women in Greek and Roman Antiquity
Draws upon the evidence of myth, ritual, and literature to question whether women were actually subjugated to the extent that the laws imply
Translated by Maureen B. Fant
Foreword by Mary R. Lefkowitz
0-8018-3385-X Johns Hopkins pb $9.95

• Mary R. Lefkowitz & Maureen B. Fant
WOMEN'S LIFE IN GREECE AND ROME: A Source Book in Translation
"The texts are well and widely chosen, and newly translated . . . The modern reader can enter the ancient world through this text"—Peter Parsons, *London Review of Books*
0–8018–2866–X Johns Hopkins pb $12.00

• Merlin Stone
ANCIENT MIRRORS OF WOMANHOOD: A Treasury of Goddess and Heroine Lore from Around the World
Illustrated by Cynthia Stone
0–8070–6719–9 Beacon pb $11.95

Arts

• Richard Brilliant
VISUAL NARRATIVES: Story-Telling in Etruscan and Roman Art
0–8014–9387–0 Cornell pb $12.95

• C. Wade Meade
RUINS OF ROME: A Guide to the Classical Antiquities
0–936638–00–1 Palatine $18.95
0–936638–01–X Palatine pb $10.95

• Jocelyn Toynbee
ROMAN MEDALLIONS
A reprint of the 1944 edition
0–89722–212–1 American Numismatic $40.00

• J.B. Ward-Perkins
ROMAN IMPERIAL ARCHITECTURE
The Hellenistic tradition revolutionized by the Roman invention of concrete. Fully illustrated
0–14–056145–5 Penguin pb $18.95

• Mortimer Wheeler
ROMAN ART AND ARCHITECTURE
A wide range of Roman artistic achievement through plentiful and apt illustrations
0–500–20021–1 Thames & Hudson pb $11.95

Social Life

• Philippe Ariès, Georges Duby & Paul Veyne, editors
A HISTORY OF PRIVATE LIFE, Volume 1: From Pagan Rome to Byzantium
The first of three volumes. "A generous sampler of the delectable fruits of Annales historiography"—*New Republic*
0–674–39975–7 Harvard $35.00

• Keith R. Bradley
SLAVES AND MASTERS IN THE ROMAN EMPIRE: A Study in Social Control
0–19–520607–X Oxford pb $8.95

• Jerome Carcopino
DAILY LIFE IN ANCIENT ROME: The People and the City at the Height of the Empire
Splendor and squalor, spectacle and daily routine, recreated from archaeological findings and ancient literature
Translated by E.O. Lorimer
0–300–00031–6 Yale pb $9.95

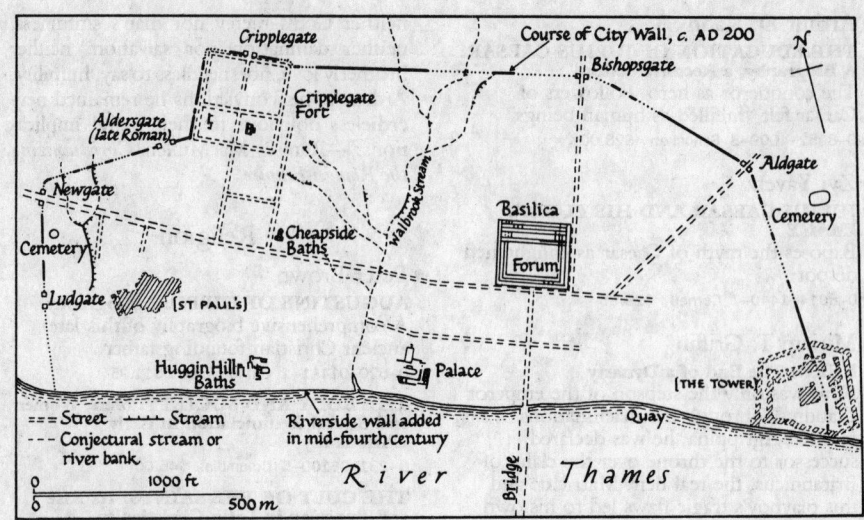

Map of Roman London, early 2nd century, *from* The Oxford Illustrated History of Britain *edited by Kenneth O. Morgan*

• M.I. Finley
ANCIENT SLAVERY AND MODERN IDEOLOGY
Moral, social, and economic underpinning of ancient slave societies compared with modern counterparts
0–14–022500–5 Penguin pb $7.95

• Thomas Hope
COSTUMES OF THE GREEKS AND ROMANS
Early 19th-century classic line renderings of authentic costumes of many classes and occupations, including armor and household objects
0–486–20021–3 Dover pb $6.95

• William C. McDermott & Anne E. Orentzel
ROMAN PORTRAITS: The Flavian-Trajanic Period
Biographical sketches of aristocrats of early imperial Rome give a unique view of daily social and intellectual life
0–8262–0275–6 Missouri $17.50

• K.D. White
GREEK AND ROMAN TECHNOLOGY
From farm implements to hydraulic engineering. Includes illustrations and helpful diagrams
0–8014–1439–3 Cornell $44.50

• Thomas Wiedemann
GREEK AND ROMAN SLAVERY
New translations of 243 texts and inscriptions on slavery from 5th- and 4th-century Greece and Rome
0–415–02972–4 RC&H pb $17.95

Cities

• Christopher Hibbert
ROME: The Biography of a City
This combination of portrait, history, and guidebook captures the seductive beauty of the Eternal City. Lavishly illustrated
0–14–007078–8 Penguin pb $14.95

• Richard Krautheimer
THREE CHRISTIAN CAPITALS: Topography and Politics
Rome, Milan, and Constantinople. Architectural masterpieces illuminate the shaping of life by power politics and religious beliefs
0–520–04541–6 California $38.00
0–520–06034–2 California pb $10.95

• Peter Marsden
ROMAN LONDON
Roman layout of the city, Boadicea's attack, and the repeated destruction and rebuilding during Saxon times
0–500–27293–X Thames & Hudson pb $10.95

• John E. Stambaugh
THE ANCIENT ROMAN CITY
The details and texture of daily existence—apartment houses and street vendors, taverns and graffiti, water deliverymen and dry cleaners
0–8018–3574–7 Johns Hopkins $30.00
0–8018–3692–1 Johns Hopkins pb $12.95

The Melting-Pot Empire

• Anthony R. Birley
LIFE IN ROMAN BRITAIN
0–7134–3643–3 Batsford pb $18.95

• Peter Blair
ROMAN BRITAIN AND EARLY ENGLAND, 55 B.C. TO A.D. 871
The transition from Roman rule to Saxon England, using archaeological and written sources
0–393–00361–2 Norton pb $8.95

• David Braund
ROME AND THE FRIENDLY KING: The Character of Client Kingship
0–312–69210–2 St. Martin's $22.95

• Walter Goffart
BARBARIANS AND ROMANS, A.D. 418-584: The Techniques of Accommodation
How the Germans settled within the frontiers of the western empire
0–691–10231–7 Princeton pb $14.50

- Martin Goodman
THE RULING CLASS OF JUDAEA: The Origins of the Jewish Revolt Against Rome, A.D. 66-70
0–521–33401–2 Cambridge $39.50

- Justine Randers-Pherson
BARBARIANS AND ROMANS: The Birth Struggle of Europe, A.D. 400-700
Province-by-province account of the transformation of late antiquity into the Middle Ages under the impact of the northern invaders
0–8061–1818–0 Oklahoma $32.50

- H.H. Scullard
ROMAN BRITAIN: Outpost of the Empire
0–500–27405–3 Thames & Hudson pb $10.95

Military

- Arthur Ferrill
THE FALL OF THE ROMAN EMPIRE: The Military Explanation
0–500–27495–9 Thames & Hudson pb $12.95

- Edward Luttwak
THE GRAND STRATEGY OF THE ROMAN EMPIRE
"Detailed insights into the working of Roman military organization, in strategy and tactics"—E. Badian
0–8018–2158–4 Johns Hopkins pb $8.95

Reference

- Diana Bowder, editor
WHO WAS WHO IN THE ROMAN WORLD
Thorough name reference, with supplementary lists of Homeric heroes, historical outlines, royal family trees, and plentiful maps
0–8014–1358–3 Cornell $35.00
0–671–50160–7 Washington Square pb $8.95

- Tim Cornell & John Matthews
ATLAS OF THE ROMAN WORLD
Detailed maps, colorful illustrations, informative text: more than an atlas, a glimpse of a world
0–87196–652–2 Facts On File $40.00

- Michael Grant
ANCIENT HISTORY ATLAS
0–915262–73–8 Durst pb $10.00

- Colin McEvedy
THE PENGUIN ATLAS OF ANCIENT HISTORY
0–14–051151–2 Penguin pb $6.95

- Betty Radice
WHO'S WHO IN THE ANCIENT WORLD
"One person's pointers to some of the classical names that have kept their vitality—as poetic symbols, themes in music, painting, or drama, or forces in the western unconscious"—from the introduction
0–14–051055–9 Penguin pb $7.95

- Richard J.A. Talbert
ATLAS OF CLASSICAL HISTORY
Maps, diagrams, and commentary: from the Bronze Age to Constantine
0–415–03463–9 RC&H pb $17.95

Gibbon

Edward Gibbon (1737-1794) devoted his life to what is still the only work on Rome that starts with Marcus Aurelius in AD 161 and continues to the fall of Constantinople in 1453, from the height of empire to the eve of Columbus' voyage, taking in the history of peoples from the Orkneys to Turkestan.

Edward Gibbon
THE HISTORY OF THE DECLINE AND FALL OF THE ROMAN EMPIRE
Bury's scholarly edition is still unsurpassed; his footnotes and appendixes are a compendium of classical knowledge in themselves. A seven-volume reprint
Edited by John B. Bury
0–404–02820–9 AMS (set) $300.00

THE HISTORY OF THE DECLINE AND FALL OF THE ROMAN EMPIRE
This convenient edition contains the complete original work

Volume 1
0–394–60401–6 Modern Library $12.95

Volume 2
0–394–60402–4 Modern Library $12.95

Volume 3
0–394–60403–2 Modern Library $12.95

THE HISTORY OF THE DECLINE AND FALL OF THE ROMAN EMPIRE
Whet your appetite with this one-volume abridgment, but don't miss the main course
Edited by Dero A. Saunders & Charles A. Robinson, Jr.
0–14–043189–6 Penguin pb $6.95

MEMOIRS OF MY LIFE
"Decency and ignorance cast a veil over the mystery of generation, but I may relate that after floating nine months in a liquid element I was painfully transported into the vital air." Gibbon's autobiography offers a glimpse into the cool, poised mind of the 18th century
Edited by Betty Radice
0–14–043217–5 Penguin pb $4.95

Patricia B. Craddock
EDWARD GIBBON: Luminous Historian, 1772-1794
The long-awaited second volume of this masterly biography relates the 20 years of work on the Decline and Fall to the incidents of Gibbon's own life
0–8018–3720–0 Johns Hopkins $29.95

Historiography

- M.I. Finley
ANCIENT HISTORY: Evidence and Models
0–670–80970–5 Viking $17.95

- Simon Hornblower
THUCYDIDES
0–8018–3529–1 Johns Hopkins $25.00

- Arnaldo Momigliano
ESSAYS IN ANCIENT AND MODERN HISTORIOGRAPHY
"The most important edition of 'shorter writings'. . . in the fields of historiography and classical civilization"—Karl Christ, History and Theory
0–8195–5010–8 Wesleyan pb $25.00

Historical Fiction

- Lion Feuchtwanger
JOSEPHUS: A Historical Romance
The Jewish general who became a Roman historian
0–689–70345–7 Atheneum pb $12.95

- Robert Graves
COUNT BELISARIUS
Labyrinthine politics surround the Byzantine general's recovery of Rome from the Goths
0–374–51739–8 Farrar, Straus & Giroux pb $12.50
I, CLAUDIUS
The early life of the clownish uncle of Caligula who became emperor
0–394–72536–0 Random House pb $5.95
CLAUDIUS THE GOD
The husband of Messalina and Agrippina attains divinity
0–394–72537–9 Random House pb $4.95

- Allan Massie
LET THE EMPEROR SPEAK: A Novel of Caesar Augustus
0–385–24156–9 Doubleday $18.95

- Gore Vidal
JULIAN
The Apostate portrayed with sympathetic irony by the author of Hollywood
0–345–32908–2 Ballantine pb $4.95

- Thornton Wilder
THE IDES OF MARCH
Intimate portrait of Caesar in the months before his assassination
0–06–091403–3 Harper & Row pb $7.95

- Marguerite Yourcenar
MEMOIRS OF HADRIAN
Sophisticated world-weariness of the most cultured emperor
0–374–20728–3 Farrar, Straus & Giroux $17.95
0–374–50348–6 Farrar, Straus & Giroux pb $10.95

Medieval and Renaissance Europe

The term "Middle Ages," possibly first used as early as 1469, originally described that period of history between the decline of learning in late antiquity and the "Renaissance" of classical studies in 15th-century Italy. Since then, the period has acquired various reputations, good and bad: "medieval" may suggest "superstitious," "unenlightened," "backward," and "feudal," but equally "pious," "faithful," "chivalrous," "noble," and "romantic."

Few would now attempt to color these thousand years of history with a single brush. Instead, recent scholarship has stressed the changes within the medieval epoch. The most popular current chronology recognizes three major divisions of medieval history, each with its own principal themes. The early Middle Ages, extending roughly from the fall of the Roman Empire in the West to c. 1000, witnessed the formation of a new cultural community in the European West, comprised of Latins, Germans, Celts, Slavs, and others; each of these peoples retained its own cultural character but all of them came to share common values and attitudes. This was "the making of Europe."

In the central period of medieval history, from about 1000 to 1350, the European community was profoundly reorganized and took on many of the social and cultural traits it would retain through the Renaissance and Reformation, up until the economic and political revolutions of the 18th and 19th centuries. The central Middle Ages, in other words, created "traditional" Europe.

Finally, the late period, from c. 1350 to 1500, was a time of many spectacular disasters, brought on by plagues, famines, and incessant wars. Out of this age of crisis and readjustment, Europe declined in population but gained a more powerful technology (through printing, guns, sails, and other inventions), a richer culture (with a revival of things classical), and more effective political institutions (best embodied by the "new" national monarchies). By the late 15th century, Europe was equipped for its great worldwide expansion in the early modern period. The discovery of America in 1492 is only one of several dates used to mark the end of the Middle Ages, but it may be the best. The discovery opened Europe to a wider world and thereby changed it, and the world, forever.

GENERAL HISTORIES

• Richard Barber
THE PENGUIN GUIDE TO MEDIEVAL EUROPE
Europe's great medieval monuments in their political, religious, and social contexts
0–14–046633–9 Penguin pb $11.95

Thirteenth-century knight, from The Oxford Illustrated History of Britain *edited by Kenneth O. Morgan*

• Philippe Contamine
WAR IN THE MIDDLE AGES
War in all its aspects—technological, economic, political, and cultural
0–631–14469–2 Blackwell pb $14.95

• Robert Fossier, editor
THE CAMBRIDGE ILLUSTRATED HISTORY OF THE MIDDLE AGES, 350-950
Translated by Janet Sondheimer
0–521–26644–0 Cambridge $49.50

• W.H. Frend
THE RISE OF CHRISTIANITY
0–8006–1931–5 Fortress $24.95

• C. Warren Hollister
MEDIEVAL EUROPE: A Short History
A well-written introduction
0–394–34186–4 Random House $16.95

• Bryan Holme
MEDIEVAL PAGEANT
A beautifully illustrated panorama
Introduction by Timothy Husband
0–500–01421–3 Thames & Hudson $24.95

• George Holmes
THE OXFORD ILLUSTRATED HISTORY OF MEDIEVAL EUROPE
Balanced treatment of Europe, north and south, with admirable use of visual monuments
0–19–820073–0 Oxford $35.00

• Maurice Keen
THE PELICAN HISTORY OF MEDIEVAL EUROPE
Assumes no previous knowledge of the subject and yet engages the reader in a stimulating discussion of the period's most important issues
0–14–021085–7 Penguin pb $6.95

• Archibald R. Lewis & Timothy J. Runyan
EUROPEAN NAVAL AND MARITIME HISTORY, 300-1500
The seas, northern and southern, in times of peace and war
0–253–32082–8 Indiana $22.50

• Henri Pirenne
ECONOMIC AND SOCIAL HISTORY OF MEDIEVAL EUROPE
A much-criticized classic by one of this century's major historians; still worth exploring
Translated by I.E. Clegg
0–15–627533–3 HBJ pb $5.95

• C.W. Previte-Orton, editor
THE SHORTER CAMBRIDGE MEDIEVAL HISTORY
A useful tool for checking dates, facts, and figures

Volume 1: The Later Roman Empire to the 12th Century
0–521–20962–5 Cambridge $74.50

Volume 2: The 12th Century to the Renaissance
0–521–20963–3 Cambridge $74.50

Sources and Documents

• Ernest F. Henderson, editor
SELECT HISTORICAL DOCUMENTS OF THE MIDDLE AGES
0–8196–0149–7 Biblio pb $15.00

• David Herlihy, editor
MEDIEVAL CULTURE AND SOCIETY
An overture to peasants and poets in the Documentary History of Western Civilization series
0–06–131340–8 Harper & Row pb $10.95

• James B. Ross and Mary M. McLaughlin, editors
THE PORTABLE MEDIEVAL READER
0–14–015046–3 Penguin pb $9.95

CULTURAL AND INTELLECTUAL HISTORY

• J.H. Burns, editor
THE CAMBRIDGE HISTORY OF MEDIEVAL POLITICAL THOUGHT, c. 350—c. 1450
An invaluable work of reference, less successful as a synthesis
0–521–24324–6 Cambridge $89.50

• Peter Dronke
A HISTORY OF 12TH-CENTURY WESTERN PHILOSOPHY
0–521–25896–0 Cambridge $69.95

• Richard Erdoes
AD 1000: Living on the Brink of Apocalypse
0–06–250295–6 Harper & Row $19.95

 IF YOU CAN'T FIND IT, LOOK IN THE INDEX

• Charles H. Haskins
**THE RENAISSANCE OF THE
TWELFTH CENTURY**
Argues that the Middle Ages had a
"Renaissance," too
0–674–76075–1 Harvard pb $8.95

• Ernest H. Kantorowicz
**THE KING'S TWO BODIES: A Study of
Medieval Political Theology**
A classic analysis of the overlap between
medieval religious and political ideas
0–691–02018–3 Princeton pb $16.50

Jacques Le Goff

"One economic system replaces another
only after it has passed through a long
and varied obstacle course. History is
people and the instigators of capitalism
were usurers: merchants of the future,
sellers of time . . . These men were Christians but it was not the *earthly* consequences of the Church's condemnation
of usury that restrained them; it was the
agonizing fear of Hell. In a society where
all conscience was a religious conscience,
obstacles were first of all—or finally—
religious. The hope of escaping Hell,
thanks to purgatory, permitted the usurer to propel the economy and society of
the thirteenth century ahead toward
capitalism."—*Your Money or Your Life:
Economy and Religion in the Middle Ages*

Jacques Le Goff
THE BIRTH OF PURGATORY
Suggests that purgatory was
transformed from a state to a place in
the 12th century, even as a new
"spiritual accounting" entered the
practice of penitence
Translated by Arthur Goldhammer
0–226–47083–0 Chicago pb $13.95

**TIME, WORK, AND CULTURE IN
THE MIDDLE AGES**
Collected essays, illustrating the use of
anthropological concepts and methods
Translated by Arthur Goldhammer
0–226–47081–4 Chicago pb $13.95

**YOUR MONEY OR YOUR LIFE:
Economy and Religion in the Middle
Ages**
A brief monograph by the co-director
of the journal *Annales-sociétés-civilisations*
Translated by Patricia Ranum
0–942299–14–0 Zone $18.95

• Robert S. Lopez
THE BIRTH OF EUROPE
Lively portrayal of human progress in the
Middle Ages
0–87131–132–1 M. Evans pb $7.95

• Alexander Murray
**REASON AND SOCIETY IN THE
MIDDLE AGES**
How a new rationalism and precision
informed intellectual life in the central
medieval period
0–19–821985–7 Oxford pb $19.95

• George J. Ovitt
**THE RESTORATION OF PERFECTION:
Labor and Technology in Medieval Culture**
An original exploration of the relationship
between speculations on the nature of the
universe and technological innovation
0–8135–1235–2 Rutgers $32.00

• Donald Weinstein & Rudolph M. Bell
**SAINTS AND SOCIETY: The Two Worlds
of Western Christendom, 1000 to 1700**
An innovative effort to recapture styles of
medieval piety through the computer-
assisted analysis of saints' lives. "Highly
recommended reading for all students of
medieval and early modern religion"—
American Historical Review
0–226–89056–2 Chicago pb $13.95

Heloise and Abelard

• Etienne Gilson
HELOISE AND ABELARD
0–472–06038–4 Michigan pb $8.95

• Betty Radice, translator
**THE LETTERS OF ABELARD AND
HELOISE**
Includes Abelard's *History of My
Misfortunes*, four personal letters, two
hymns, and other correspondences
0–14–044297–9 Penguin pb $4.95

SOCIAL AND ECONOMIC HISTORY

• Philippe Ariès & Georges Duby,
editors
A HISTORY OF PRIVATE LIFE
Stimulating essays by historians and
literary critics. "One of the most arresting,
original and rewarding historical surveys to
be published in many years"—Bernard
Knox, *Atlantic*
Translated by Arthur Goldhammer

Volume 1: From Pagan Rome to Byzantium
Edited by Paul Veyne
0–674–39975–7 Harvard $35.00

**Volume 2: Revelations of the Medieval
World**
Edited by Georges Duby
0–674–39976–5 Harvard $39.50

Volume 3: Passions of the Renaissance
Edited by Roger Chartier
0–674–39977–3 Harvard $39.50

• Marc Bloch
**FRENCH RURAL HISTORY: An Essay on
Its Basic Characteristics**
A master historian makes the seemingly
dull countryside come alive
Translated by Janet Sondheimer
0–520–01660–2 California pb $12.95

• John Boswell
**CHRISTIANITY, SOCIAL TOLERANCE,
AND HOMOSEXUALITY: Gay People in
Western Europe from the Beginning of the
Christian Era to the 14th Century**
An erudite examination of Christian
attitudes toward homosexuality, arguing
that tolerance changed into intolerance as
the Middle Ages progressed
0–226–06711–4 Chicago pb $12.95

**THE KINDNESS OF STRANGERS: The
Abandonment of Children in Western
Europe from Late Antiquity to the
Renaissance**
0–394–57240–8 Pantheon $24.95

• Jean Chapelot & Robert Fossier
**VILLAGE AND HOUSE IN THE
MIDDLE AGES**
A collaborative effort by an archaeologist
and a historian, covering all of Europe and
many types of buildings, with additional
discussion of landscapes
Translated by Henry Cleere
0–520–04669–2 California $45.00

• John Cummins
**THE HOUND AND THE HAWK: The
Practice and Meaning of Medieval Hunting**
The cosmos of medieval hunting and
falconry, from the practical concern for
technique to the belief that the hunt would
save the huntsman from damnation
0–312–02716–8 St. Martin's $29.95

• Georges Duby
**THE KNIGHT, THE LADY AND THE
PRIEST: The Making of Modern Marriage
in Medieval France**
The dispute between the aristocracy of
northern France and the Church in the
12th century over the rules of marriage.
"An important book for anyone interested
in the origins of contemporary sexual roles
and mores"—*LA Times Book Review*
Translated by Barbara Bray
0–394–71331–1 Pantheon pb $9.95

**RURAL ECONOMY AND COUNTRY
LIFE IN THE MEDIEVAL WEST**
A survey of European farming from c. 800
to 1400, with special attention to France
Translated by Cynthia Postan
0–87249–347–4 South Carolina pb $12.95

• Frances & Joseph Gies
LIFE IN A MEDIEVAL CITY
A well-written social history
0–06–090880–7 Harper & Row pb $6.95

**MARRIAGE AND THE FAMILY IN THE
MIDDLE AGES**
A readable summary of recent work
0–06–015791–7 Harper & Row $22.50

Christine de Pisan building the City, from
The Book of the City of Ladies *by
Christine de Pisan (Persea/Braziller)*

📖 **TO ORDER BY FAX, SEE PAGE 1**

• Jean Gimpel
THE MEDIEVAL MACHINE: The Industrial Revolution of the Middle Ages
An enthusiastic account of medieval technological innovations
0–14–004514–7 Penguin pb $7.95

• Jack Goody
THE DEVELOPMENT OF THE FAMILY AND MARRIAGE IN EUROPE
An anthropologist looks at medieval marriages, with strange, wonderful, and debatable conclusions
0–521–24739–X Cambridge $47.50
0–521–28925–4 Cambridge pb $16.95

• Robert S. Gottfried
DOCTORS AND MEDICINE IN MEDIEVAL ENGLAND, 1340-1530
0–691–05481–9 Princeton $45.00

• David Herlihy
MEDIEVAL HOUSEHOLDS
The making of modern households in medieval Europe
0–674–56376–X Harvard pb $12.95

• Peter Levi
THE FRONTIERS OF PARADISE: A Study of Monks and Monasteries
A professor of poetry's respectful homage to the life of the spirit
1–55584–197–X Weidenfeld & Nicolson $16.95

• Alan Macfarlane
MARRIAGE AND LOVE IN ENGLAND: Modes of Reproduction, 1300-1800
Extravagant claims for the social modernity of early medieval England
0–631–15438–8 Blackwell $15.95

• Michel Mollat
THE POOR IN THE MIDDLE AGES: An Essay in Social History
The ever-present poor, viewed under multiple aspects
Translated by Arthur Goldhammer
0–300–02789–3 Yale $32.50

• David Nicholas
THE DOMESTIC LIFE OF A MEDIEVAL CITY: Women, Children, and the Family in Fourteenth-Century Ghent
"A book to be reckoned with in any global interpretation of medieval social or family history"—David Herlihy
0–8032–3310–8 Nebraska $28.95

THE METAMORPHOSIS OF A MEDIEVAL CITY: Ghent in the Age of the Arteveldes, 1302-1390
Ghent was the largest city in the Low Countries, the wealthiest and most industrialized region in northern Europe. Nicholas's is the fullest description ever compiled on the economic life of the city
0–8032–3314–0 Nebraska $35.00

• Henri Pirenne
MEDIEVAL CITIES: Their Origins and the Revival of Trade
By an old master of economic history, to be admired more than believed
Translated by F.D. Halsey
0–691–00760–8 Princeton pb $9.95

• M.M. Postan
MEDIEVAL TRADE AND FINANCE
Reprinted studies by the most prominent English economic historian of the past generation
0–521–08745–7 Cambridge $52.50

• Eileen Power
MEDIEVAL PEOPLE
A classic reconstruction of individual lives—nobles, merchants, monks, and others
0–06–463253–9 Harper & Row pb $6.95

• Jacques Rossiaud
MEDIEVAL PROSTITUTION
Prostitutes and pimps in southeast France, used to launch sweeping comments on medieval sexual culture
Translated by Lydia G. Cochrane
0–631–15141–9 Blackwell $24.95

• Richard Ungar
THE SHIP IN THE MEDIEVAL ECONOMY, 600-1600
A study of ship construction, with differences noted between Mediterranean and northern regions and changes in design as the Middle Ages progressed
0–7735–0526–1 Toronto $25.00

• Lynn White, Jr.
MEDIEVAL RELIGION AND TECHNOLOGY: Collected Essays
Archaeology, iconography, etymology, travel literature, and practical experience relate technology to the values of Western medieval culture
0–520–05896–8 California pb $11.95

MEDIEVAL TECHNOLOGY AND SOCIAL CHANGE
Beautiful essays on warfare, stirrups, plows, and cranks
0–19–500266–0 Oxford pb $7.95

Women

• Rudolph M. Bell
HOLY ANOREXIA
Psychological portraits of more than 250 Italian women from the 13th century to the present. "According to Bell, the demon that spurs self-starvation in women is an ever-elusive ideal: in modern America, 'bodily health, thinness, and self-control'; in medieval Christendom, 'spiritual health, fasting, and self-denial.' In both cases, anorexia represents a woman's 'war against bodily urges' in a search for autonomy from a suffocating, male-dominated society"—*Kirkus Reviews*
Epilogue by William N. Davis
0–226–04205–7 Chicago pb $11.95

• Judith M. Bennett
WOMEN IN THE MEDIEVAL ENGLISH COUNTRYSIDE: Gender and Household in Brigstock before the Plague
There was no "golden age" for women in the early medieval society
0–19–504094–5 Oxford $36.00

• Judith C. Brown
IMMODEST ACTS: The Life of a Lesbian Nun in Renaissance Italy
The story of an abbess who had an affair with a nun, reconstructed from the archives of a church investigation
0–19–504225–5 Oxford pb $7.95

• Caroline W. Bynum
HOLY FEAST AND HOLY FAST: The Religious Significance of Food to Medieval Women
The subjects of this book were "extravagant in their bodily self-denial and self-immolation, and their craving for the Eucharist of the Holy Feast was the complement to their extreme fasting practice, their Holy Fast"—*NY Review of Books*
0–520–05722–8 California $32.50
0–520–06329–5 California pb $12.95

• Penny Schine Gold
THE LADY AND THE VIRGIN: Image, Attitude, and Experience in 12th Century France
Images of women that have endured into the modern era: the secular image of the dame of romance and the religious image of Notre Dame, the Virgin Mary
Foreword by Catharine R. Stimpson
0–226–30088–9 Chicago pb $9.95

• Martha C. Howell
WOMEN, PRODUCTION AND PATRIARCHY IN LATE MEDIEVAL CITIES
Working women at Leiden and Cologne, viewed in Marxist perspective
0–226–35503–9 Chicago $25.00

• Julius Kirshner & Suzanne F. Wemple
WOMEN OF THE MEDIEVAL WORLD: Essays in Honor of John H. Mundy
Collected essays on aspects of women's lives, with an early medieval focus
0–631–15492–2 Blackwell pb $15.95

The bath and steam room were places of relaxation, where people went not only to cleanse their bodies but also to talk, rest, and amuse themselves. What better place for amorous encounters of every kind? Some baths had such bad reputations that it was generally considered disreputable to work in a bathhouse or as a masseuse. The erotic connotations of water color the descriptions of furtive encounters at the baths of Bourbon-l'Archambault in *Flamenca*, an Occitanian poem of guilty love. The immodest and the innocent met in the baths; bathers were scrutinized, judged, desired, seduced. The exchanges of glances that must have taken place are not hard to imagine.

Georges Duby, editor
A HISTORY OF PRIVATE LIFE: Volume 2, Revelations of the Medieval World
Translated by Arthur Goldhammer
0–674–39976–5 Harvard $39.50

✉ **TO ORDER BOOKS AS GIFTS, SEE PAGE 1**

- Ian Maclean
THE RENAISSANCE NOTION OF WOMAN: A Study in the Fortunes of Scholasticism and Medical Science in European Intellectual Life
0–521–27436–2 Cambridge pb $12.95

- Eileen Power & M.M. Poston
MEDIEVAL WOMEN
Nuns, burgesses, and women workers in England
0–521–09946–3 Cambridge pb $9.95

RELIGIOUS HISTORY

- Rosalind & Christopher Brooke
POPULAR RELIGION IN THE MIDDLE AGES
An effort to recover the religion of common folk in the central Middle Ages
0–500–27381–2 Thames & Hudson pb $10.95

- Norman Cohn
THE PURSUIT OF THE MILLENNIUM: Revolutionary Millenarians and the Mystical Anarchists of the Middle Ages
Popular religious and social movements from the 11th to the 16th century. "A work of the first water . . . of great originality and power"—Isaiah Berlin
0–19–500456–6 Oxford pb $11.95

- Meister Eckhart
MEISTER ECKHART: A Modern Translation
The great German mystic, urging us to kindle the "divine spark" within us
Translated by R.P. Blakeny
0–06–130008–X Harper & Row pb $9.95

- Amos Funkenstein
THEOLOGY AND THE SCIENTIFIC IMAGINATION FROM THE MIDDLE AGES TO THE 17TH CENTURY
Late medieval theology as a pathway to the scientific revolution
0–691–08408–4 Princeton $47.50

- Thomas à Kempis
ON THE IMITATION OF CHRIST
The programmatic statement as to what constitutes the *devotio moderna*
Translated by Leo Shirley-Price
0–14–044027–5 Penguin pb $3.95

- Emmanuel Le Roy Ladurie
MONTAILLOU: The Promised Land of Error
A sometimes shocking and always moving picture of a community in the Pyrenees, and of the lives, beliefs, and behavior of its people
Translated by Barbara Bray
0–394–72964–1 Random House pb $7.95

- Steven Ozment
THE AGE OF REFORM (1250-1550): An Intellectual and Religious History of Late Medieval and Reformation Europe
0–300–02760–5 Yale pb $15.95

- Steven Runciman
THE MEDIEVAL MANICHEE: A Study of the Christian Dualist Heresy
0–521–06166–0 Cambridge $39.50
0–521–28926–2 Cambridge pb $15.95

"The Visitation," late 12th-century French or Flemish (British Museum)

Jewry

- Riccardo Calimani
THE GHETTO OF VENICE
The history of one of Western Europe's most important Jewish communities
Translated by Katherine Wolfthal
0–87131–484–3 M. Evans $19.95

- Jeremy Cohen
THE FRIARS AND THE JEWS: The Evolution of Medieval Anti-Judaism
Reasons for and results of the mendicant antagonism against the Jews
0–8014–9266–1 Cornell pb $10.95

THE MEDIEVAL AESTHETIC

- Henry Adams
MONT-SAINT-MICHEL AND CHARTRES
Introduction by Raymond Carney
0–14–039054–5 Penguin pb $6.95

- Robert Branner
THE CATHEDRAL OF BOURGES: And Its Place in Gothic Architecture
A monographic approach to one of the mightiest of the Gothic structures
0–262–52130–X MIT pb $15.00

- Wolfgang Braunfelds
MONASTERIES OF WESTERN EUROPE: The Architecture of the Orders
The relation of style to liturgy and ritual
0–691–00313–0 Princeton pb $19.95

- Andreas Capellanus
THE ART OF COURTLY LOVE
The theory of love, famed for its statement that true love is incompatible with marriage
Translated by John J. Parry
0–393–09848–6 Norton pb $7.95

- Georges Duby
THE AGE OF THE CATHEDRALS: Art and Society, 980-1420
Translated by Eleanor Levieux & Barbara Thompson
0–226–16770–4 Chicago pb $11.95

HISTORY OF MEDIEVAL ART
0–8478–0710–X Rizzoli $45.00

Johan Huizinga
THE WANING OF THE MIDDLE AGES: A Study of the Forms of Life, Thought and Art in France and the Netherlands in the 14th and 15th Centuries
Impressions by a master of the history of style. "Not a systematic study of [the bourgeoisie's] way of life, but tells one more about them, perhaps, than any other single work"—Maurice Keen
0–312–85540–0 St. Martin's $25.00
0–385–09288–1 Doubleday pb $6.95

- C.S. Lewis
ALLEGORY OF LOVE: A Study of Medieval Tradition
0–19–281220–3 Oxford pb $9.95

- Erwin Panofsky
GOTHIC ARCHITECTURE AND SCHOLASTICISM: An Inquiry into the Analogy of the Arts, Philosophy and Religion in the Middle Ages
How architectural style provided tangible equivalents to scholastic definitions of the order and form of thought
0–452–00933–2 NAL pb $9.95

- Marilyn Stokstad
MEDIEVAL ART
Surveys over a thousand years of western art and architecture, from ancient Rome to the age of exploration; hundreds of illustrations
0–06–430132–X Harper & Row pb $22.95

- David L. Warner, editor
THE SEVEN LIBERAL ARTS IN THE MIDDLE AGES
0–253–20397–X Indiana pb $8.95

THE EARLY MIDDLE AGES

▶ See also Ancient Rome

The Barbarians and the Barbarian Kingdoms

Simon Keynes & Michael Lapidge, translators
ALFRED THE GREAT
Includes Asser's contemporaneous *Life of King Alfred* and other writings of the period
0–14–044409–2 Penguin pb $6.95

Gregory of Tours
THE HISTORY OF THE FRANKS
The dominating source of early Frankish history
Translated by Lewis Thorpe
0–14–044295–2 Penguin pb $7.95

• Geoffrey Barraclough
THE CRUCIBLE OF EUROPE: The Ninth and Tenth Centuries in European History
0–520–03118–0 California pb $8.95

• Thomas S. Burns
A HISTORY OF THE OSTROGOTHS
A reconstruction of the culture and a tracking of the movements of a principal Germanic people
0–253–32831–4 Indiana $29.95

• Frank Delaney
THE CELTS
The basis of a BBC television program exploring the extraordinarily extensive sites of prehistoric Celtic culture, from Austria to Ireland
0–316–17993–0 Little, Brown $24.95

• Patrick J. Geary
BEFORE FRANCE AND GERMANY: The Creation and Transformation of the Merovingian World
An illuminated look at a dark epoch
0–19–504457–6 Oxford $29.95

• Otto Maenchen-Heifer
THE WORLD OF THE HUNS: Studies in Their History and Culture
The dark world of nomads who, through their migrations, churned up a world
0–520–01596–7 California $50.00

• Lucien Musset
THE GERMANIC INVASIONS: The Making of Europe, A.D. 400-600
Effective synthesis of what is now believed about the early Germans and their wanderings
0–271–01198–X Pennsylvania State $28.95

• Edward K. Rand
FOUNDERS OF THE MIDDLE AGES
Polished essays on late-ancient teachers
0–486–20369–7 Dover pb $7.95

• Katherine Scherman
THE BIRTH OF FRANCE: Warriors, Bishops and Long-Haired Kings
How Celts, Romans, and Franks created medieval France
1–55778–174–5 Paragon pb $14.95

• E.A. Thompson
WHO WAS ST. PATRICK?
The life of the apostle of Ireland written with engaging skepticism
0–312–87084–1 St. Martin's $21.95

• J.M. Wallace-Hadrill
THE LONG-HAIRED KINGS AND OTHER STORIES IN FRANKISH HISTORY
The roots of royal authority in Frankland, now reprinted in a scholarly series from Toronto
0–8020–6500–7 Toronto pb $8.50

• Michael Wood
IN SEARCH OF THE DARK AGES
Early English history through biographies of principal figures, from Boadicea to William the Conqueror
0–8160–1686–0 Facts On File $22.95

Charlemagne and the Making of Europe

Einhard & Notker the Stammerer
TWO LIVES OF CHARLEMAGNE
Translated by Lewis Thorpe
0–14–044213–8 Penguin pb $4.95

• Heinrich Fichtenau
THE CAROLINGIAN EMPIRE
A survey of Carolingian Europe, stressing oppression and depression; available in a reprint edition
Translated by Peter Munz
0–8020–6367–5 Toronto pb $9.95

• Judith Herrin
THE FORMATION OF CHRISTENDOM
The emergence of early medieval culture, with many bows to the East
0–691–05482–7 Princeton $34.95

• Richard Hodges & David Whitehouse
MOHAMMED, CHARLEMAGNE AND THE ORIGINS OF EUROPE: The Pirenne Thesis in the Light of Archaeology
A pioneering effort to apply archeological evidence to historical problems. "Succeeds ... not only in integrating archaeology with traditionally researched history but also interweaving European and Islamic history in the early medieval period"— *American Historical Review*
0–8014–9262–9 Cornell pb $9.95

• Pierre Riché
DAILY LIFE IN THE WORLD OF CHARLEMAGNE
The few sources of the Carolingian world expertly gathered, sifted, and interpreted
Translated by Jo Ann McNamara
0–8122–1096–4 Pennsylvania $17.95

• Suzanne F. Wemple
WOMEN IN FRANKISH SOCIETY: Marriage and the Cloister, 500-900
Finds a deterioration of women's status as the early Middle Ages progressed
0–8122–1209–6 Pennsylvania $21.95

The battle rages, spreads throughout the hosts:
Count Roland pays no heed to his own safety,
but plies his lance as long as its shaft holds—
with fifteen blows it's splintered and is useless—
and then unsheathes his good sword Durendal.
He spurs his horse and goes against Chernuble:
he breaks the helmet on which rubies gleam;
he slices downward through the coif and hair
and cuts between the eyes, down through his face
the shiny hauberk made of fine-linked mail,
entirely through the torso to the groin,
and through the saddle trimmed with beaten gold.
The body of the horse slows down the sword,
which, seeking out no joint, divides the spine:
both fall down dead upon the field's thick grass.
He says then: "Coward, you have come in vain!
Mohammed will not give you any help;
no glutton such as you will win this fight."
THE SONG OF ROLAND
Translated by Robert Harrison
0–451–62623–0 NAL pb $3.95

Byzantium

Anna Comnena
THE ALEXIAD OF ANNA COMNENA
A biography of Alexius I (1081-1118) by his daughter, who demonstrates a gift for fast-moving narrative and shrewd character sketches
Translated by E.R.A. Sewter
0–14–044215–4 Penguin pb $7.95

• Deno J. Geanakoplos, editor
BYZANTIUM: Church, Society, and Civilization Seen through Contemporary Eyes
A gold mine of sources on the Byzantine church, society, and civilization, knit together with an analytical commentary
0–226–28461–1 Chicago pb $18.95

• Cyril Mango
BYZANTINE ARCHITECTURE
A lavishly illustrated architectural study
0–8109–1004–7 Abrams $50.00
0–8478–0615–4 Rizzoli pb $25.00

• D.M. Nicol
THE END OF THE BYZANTINE EMPIRE
0–8419–0644–0 Holmes & Meier $22.50
0–8419–5826–2 Holmes & Meier pb $14.95

• John Julius Norwich
BYZANTIUM: The Early Centuries
The Byzantine Empire during the five centuries before the emergence of

Charlemagne's Holy Roman Empire; with
32 pages of illustrations
0–394–53778–5 Knopf $29.95

• Michael Psellus
FOURTEEN BYZANTINE RULERS
A translation of the *Chronographia*, tracing
the decline of Byzantium, by an adviser,
friend, and tutor to successive emperors
Translated by E.R.A. Sewter
0–14–044169–7 Penguin pb $7.95

• Steven Runciman
**BYZANTINE STYLE AND
CIVILIZATION**
0–14–021827–0 Penguin pb $7.95

Vikings and Normans

• Johannes Brondsted
**THE VIKINGS: The Background to a
Fierce and Fascinating Civilization**
Origins of the Vikings, their industries and
equipment, ships and armies, daily life, and
religious beliefs
0–14–020459–8 Penguin pb $6.95

• R. Allen Brown
**NORMANS AND THE NORMAN
CONQUEST**
0–317–43358–X Longwood $36.00

• Gwyn Jones
A HISTORY OF THE VIKINGS
The best recent survey
0–19–285139–X Oxford pb $12.95

**THE NORSE ATLANTIC SAGA: Being
the Norse Voyages of Discovery and
Settlement of Iceland, Greenland, America**
0–19–285160–8 Oxford pb $9.95

• Peter H. Sawyer
**FROM ROMAN BRITAIN TO NORMAN
ENGLAND**
A spirited survey by an advocate of the
Anglo-Saxons and Vikings
0–312–30783–7 St. Martin's $27.50

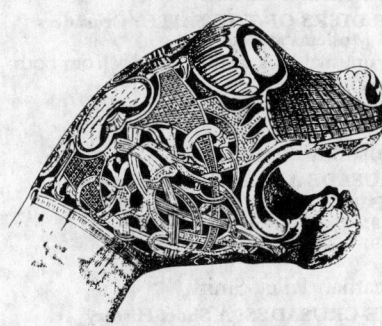

*Ninth-century post from a Viking ship burial,
from* The Oxford Companion to Art, *edited
by Harold Osborne*

KINGS AND VIKINGS
A critical appraisal of the difficult sources
that illuminate the Vikings
0–416–74190–8 Methuen pb $13.95

Culture

"The 'Carolingian Renaissance' was only a
beginning. As such it deserves a good deal of
criticism. It has been called a movement
lacking in breadth, almost entirely clerical
and extending to no more than a few hundred clerks in the whole of Europe. An
eminent historian like Henri Pirenne has
actually described it as a decline, on the
grounds that earlier centuries had possessed
a greater number of educated laymen, although this was merely the tail-end of Roman society, and without issue. Western
society was to be rebuilt on different foundations and the extraordinarily primitive
conditions of its physical survival sufficiently
explain that only a very few men should have
had the leisure and inclination to devote
themselves to intellectual pursuits.

It has also been called a movement lacking
in originality, without any real philosophical
and scientific thought, cut off by its ignorance of languages from all access to the
superior cultural world of the Greeks, and,
furthermore, incapable even if it had possessed such access, of benefiting from it for
lack of intellectual ambitions and techniques
of thought.

This is true. These are the inherent weaknesses of a new beginning. But the great
merit of the Carolingian Renaissance was
that it was a beginning at all." —Philippe
Wolff, *The Awakening of Europe*

• G.R. Evans
**THE THOUGHT OF GREGORY THE
GREAT**
The thought of Gregory the Great was
normative for medieval society
0–521–30904–2 Cambridge $42.50
0–521–36826–X Cambridge pb $10.95

• Walter Goffart
**THE NARRATORS OF BARBARIAN
HISTORY (A.D. 550–800): Jordanes,
Gregory of Tours, Bede, and Paul the
Deacon**
Critical appraisals of the four historians to
whom we owe nearly all our knowledge of
early medieval political history
0–691–05514–9 Princeton $39.50

• Jean Leclercq
**LOVE OF LEARNING AND DESIRE
FOR GOD: A Study of Monastic Culture**
A modern monk admires early monastic
culture
0–8232–0407–3 Fordham pb $10.00

• Jean LeClercq & others
**THE SPIRITUALITY OF THE MIDDLE
AGES**
Medieval mysticism, by one familiar with
the art
0–8164–2373–3 Harper & Row $19.95

• Pierre Riché
**EDUCATION AND CULTURE IN THE
BARBARIAN WEST: Sixth Through
Eighth Centuries**
Comprehensive survey of formal education
under chiefly monastic auspices
Translated by J.J. Contreni
0–87249–376–8 South Carolina pb $14.95

• Philippe Wolff
**THE AWAKENING OF EUROPE: The
Growth of European Culture from the 9th
Century to the 12th**
A fine introduction
0–14–021001–6 Penguin pb $6.95

THE HIGH MIDDLE AGES: Empire and Papacy

• Geoffrey Barraclough
THE MEDIEVAL PAPACY
0–393–95100–6 Norton pb $9.95

THE ORIGINS OF MODERN GERMANY
In fact a history of medieval Germany,
stressing real rather than ideological factors
in its development
0–393–30153–2 Norton pb $12.95

• Horst Fuhrmann
**GERMANY IN THE HIGH MIDDLE
AGES**
Translated by Timothy Reuter
0–521–26638–6 Cambridge $32.50
0–521–31980–3 Cambridge pb $9.95

• Francis Oakley
**THE WESTERN CHURCH IN THE
LATER MIDDLE AGES**
0–8014–1208–0 Cornell $32.50
0–8014–9347–1 Cornell pb $9.95

• Paolo Prodi
**THE PAPAL PRINCE: One Body and Two
Souls—The Papal Monarchy in Early
Modern Europe**
0–521–32259–6 Cambridge $49.50

Feudal Institutions

• Marc Bloch
FEUDAL SOCIETY
Without question, one of the most
influential works of history written in the
20th century
Translated by L.A. Manyon

Volume 1
0–226–05978–2 Chicago pb $8.95

Volume 2
0–226–05979–0 Chicago pb $7.95

• Georges Duby
THE CHIVALROUS SOCIETY
Essays on feudal organization and culture
in the central Middle Ages
Translated by Cynthia Postan
0–520–04271–9 California pb $11.95

**THE THREE ORDERS: Feudal Society
Imagined**
A lengthy examination of feudal ideas on
social order, extending into the 17th
century
Translated by Arthur Goldhammer
0–226–16772–0 Chicago pb $12.95

• François L. Ganshof
FEUDALISM
The best short introduction available
Translated by Philip Grierson
0–06–131058–1 Harper & Row pb $6.95

- Carl Stephenson
MEDIEVAL FEUDALISM
An easy introduction
Translated by Julia E. Edmondson
0–8014–9013–8 Cornell pb $6.95

Chivalry

- Georges Duby
WILLIAM MARSHAL: The Flower of Chivalry
In large part a paraphrase of and comment on a contemporary *chanson de geste*
Translated by Richard Howard
0–394–75154–X Pantheon pb $6.95

- Frances Gies
THE KNIGHT IN HISTORY
A short, graceful introduction to medieval knighthood
0–06–015339–3 Harper & Row $16.95
0–06–091413–0 Harper & Row pb $8.95

- Maurice Keen
CHIVALRY
An admiring account that finds in medieval chivalry the model for modern views of officers and gentlemen. "A rich book, making effective use of all sorts of documents. Mr. Keen moves easily across Europe in search of the international spirit of chivalry"—David Herlihy, *NY Times Book Review*
0–300–03360–5 Yale pb $13.95

The Feudal Principalities of England and France

▶ See also Great Britain and Ireland

Bede
THE HISTORY OF THE ENGLISH CHURCH AND PEOPLE
The one indisputable masterpiece of early medieval Latin letters
Translated by Leo Shirley-Price
0–14–044042–9 Penguin pb $4.95

- David J. Bernstein
THE MYSTERY OF THE BAYEUX TAPESTRY
A study (with illustrations) of the only monumental pictorial record of political events to survive from the early Middle Ages
0–226–04400–9 Chicago $29.95

- Robert Fawtier
THE CAPETIAN KINGS OF FRANCE: Monarchy and Nation, 987-1328
Capetian kings and their government to the accession of Philip VI
0–312–11900–3 St. Martin's pb $16.00

- Elizabeth Hallam, editor
THE PLANTAGENET CHRONICLES
Brilliant combination of translated chronicles, informative essays and beautiful illustrations
Introduction by H.R. Trevor-Roper
1–55584–018–3 Weidenfeld & Nicolson $35.00

From The Bayeux Tapestry *edited by David M. Wilson* (*Knopf*)

THE FOUR GOTHIC KINGS: The Turbulent History of Medieval England and the Plantagenet Kings (1216-1377)
A continuation of *The Plantagenet Chronicles* covering the reigns of Henry III, Edward I, Edward II, and Edward III
Introduction by H.R. Trevor-Roper
1–55584–171–6 Weidenfeld & Nicolson $35.00

- Joseph R. Strayer
THE REIGN OF PHILIP THE FAIR
The study by a master American medievalist of the great French king
0–691–10089–6 Princeton pb $16.50

- Geoffrey of Monmouth
THE HISTORY OF THE KINGS OF BRITAIN
Translated by Lewis Thorpe
0–14–044170–0 Penguin pb $5.95

Spain

- Roger Collins
THE BASQUES
Summarizes modern historical discoveries concerning the oldest surviving people of Europe
0–631–13478–6 Blackwell $29.95

EARLY MEDIEVAL SPAIN: Unity in Diversity, 400-1000
A look at one of Europe's most important countries, too often neglected in English publications
0–312–01354–X St. Martin's pb $12.95

- David Wasserstein
THE RISE AND FALL OF THE PARTY-KINGS: Politics and Society in Islamic Spain, 1002-1086
0–691–05436–3 Princeton $37.00

The Crusades

"If an outsider were to strike any of your kin down, would you not avenge your blood-relative? How much more ought you to avenge your God . . . whom you see re-proached, banished from his estates, cruci-fied?" —Baldric of Bourgueil, late 11th century, cited in Jonathan Riley-Smith, *The Crusades: A Short History*

▶ See also The Islamic World to World War I

Geoffrey de Villehardouin & Jean de Joinville
CHRONICLES OF THE CRUSADES
Firsthand accounts by two noblemen who took part in the French Crusades
Translated by Margaret R.B. Shaw
0–14–044124–7 Penguin pb $6.95

- Edward Burman
THE TEMPLARS: Knights of God
The dramatic history of one of three great military religious orders founded during the crusades, to its violent suppression by Philip IV of France in 1307
0–85030–396–6 Thorsons pb $9.95

- Ronald C. Finucane
SOLDIERS OF THE FAITH: Crusaders and Moslems at War
An unusual look at the crusades from both warring camps
0–312–74256–8 St. Martin's $19.95

- Benjamin Z. Kedar
CRUSADE AND MISSION: European Approaches Toward the Muslims
0–691–05424–X Princeton $28.00
0–691–10246–5 Princeton pb $14.95

- Jonathan Riley-Smith
THE CRUSADES: A Short History
An excellent and brief one-volume account
0–300–03905–0 Yale $25.00

- Steven Runciman
THE FALL OF CONSTANTINOPLE, 1453
The exciting story of the siege that destroyed Byzantium and put the capstone on the Ottoman empire
0–521–09573–5 Cambridge pb $16.95

HISTORY OF THE CRUSADES
The standard work. "The best scholarly survey of the subject by a single author"—*English Historical Review*

Volume 1: The First Crusade and the Foundation of the Kingdom of Jerusalem
0–521–34770–X Cambridge pb $14.95

Volume 2: The Kingdom of Jerusalem and the Frankish East, 1100-1187
0–521–34771–8 Cambridge pb $14.95

Volume 3: The Kingdom of Acre and the Later Crusades
0–521–34772–6 Cambridge pb $14.95

THE SICILIAN VESPERS: A History of the Mediterranean World in the Later Thirteenth Century
The career and vast oriental ambitions of Charles of Anjou
0–521–28652–2 Cambridge pb $18.95

Medieval Portraits

• Amy Kelley
ELEANOR OF AQUITAINE AND THE FOUR KINGS
0–674–24254–8 Harvard pb $9.95

• Paul M. Kendall
LOUIS XI: The Universal Spider
Best-seller in France. "A thoroughly satisfactory biography"—*New Yorker*
0–393–30260–1 Norton pb $9.95

• W.L. Warren
HENRY II
"A fine work by a professional historian who can write"—A.L. Rowse
0–520–03494–5 California pb $14.95

THE 14TH CENTURY: Black Death and Economic Depression

• T.H. Aston and C.H. Philpin, editors
THE BRENNER DEBATE: Agrarian Class Structure and Economic Development in Pre-Industrial Europe
Spirited disputes over whether excess population or class oppression led to the great population collapse of the late Middle Ages
0–521–34933–8 Cambridge pb $14.95

• Ann G. Carmichael
PLAGUE AND THE POOR IN RENAISSANCE FLORENCE
A study not only of plague but of the common causes of death; part of the Cambridge History of Medicine Series
0–521–26833–8 Cambridge $32.50

• Robert S. Gottfried
THE BLACK DEATH: Natural and Human Disaster in Medieval Europe
"Marks a distinct intellectual advance . . . a powerful reminder of how drastically ecological balances can be upset"—William H. McNeill
0–02–912630–4 Macmillan $24.95
0–02–912370–4 Free Press pb $9.95

• William H. McNeill
PLAGUES AND PEOPLES
An important essay whose focus is larger than the 14th century
0–385–12122–9 Doubleday pb $6.95

A widowed tenant pictured in a 14th-century tax document, from A History of Private Life, Volume 2 *edited by Georges Duby* (Harvard)

• Barbara Tuchman
A DISTANT MIRROR: The Calamitous 14th Century
"What Mrs. Tuchman does superbly is to tell *how* it was"—Lawrence Stone
0–394–40026–7 Knopf $25.00
0–345–34957–1 Ballantine pb $12.95

Wars and Revolts

Jean Froissart
CHRONICLES
Sometimes described as the historian of the Hundred Years War, Froissart (1337-1410) was one of the first great journalists
Translated by Geoffrey Brereton
0–14–044200–6 Penguin pb $6.95

• Christopher Allmand
THE HUNDRED YEARS WAR: England and France at War, 1300-1450
0–521–26499–5 Cambridge $34.50
0–521–31923–4 Cambridge pb $9.95

• Charles Ross
THE WARS OF THE ROSES: A Concise History
The gloom of 15th-century England has been too often exaggerated
0–500–27407–X Thames & Hudson pb $11.95

• Desmond Seward
THE HUNDRED YEARS WAR: The English in France, 1337-1453
A short account, with much attention given to the war's effects on England
0–689–70628–6 Atheneum pb $10.95

RENAISSANCE ITALY AND THE COMING OF HUMANISM

Lucrezia Borgia
THE PRETTIEST LOVE LETTERS IN THE WORLD: Letters Between Lucrezia Borgia and Pietro Bembo, 1503-1519
Good examples of the refined, learned, and supposedly Platonic relationship across sexual lines in a Renaissance court
0–87923–716–3 Godine $25.00

Francesco Guicciardini
THE HISTORY OF ITALY
A well-translated abridgment of Guicciardini's four-volume masterpiece
Translated by Sidney Alexander
0–691–00800–0 Princeton pb $13.50

MAXIMS AND REFLECTIONS
0–8122–1037–9 Pennsylvania pb $11.95

Niccolò Machiavelli
THE PRINCE
Translated by George Bull
0–14–044107–7 Penguin pb $2.25

• Hans Baron
CRISIS OF THE EARLY ITALIAN RENAISSANCE: Civic Humanism and Republican Liberty in an Age of Classicism and Tyranny
0–691–00752–7 Princeton pb $19.95

• Michael Baxandall
PAINTING AND EXPERIENCE IN FIFTEENTH-CENTURY ITALY
Early Renaissance painting as a reflection of the society from which it evolved
0–19–282144–X Oxford pb $9.95

• Thomas G. Bergin & Jennifer Speake, editors
ENCYCLOPEDIA OF THE RENAISSANCE
Brief entries on persons, places, events, and literary works, covering all of Europe from about 1300 to 1650
0–8160–1315–2 Facts On File $45.00

• William J. Bouwsma
VENICE AND THE DEFENSE OF REPUBLICAN LIBERTY: Renaissance Values in the Age of the Counter Reformation
A new look at the Renaissance, focusing on the Venetian republic. "One of the most important contributions to Renaissance historiography in recent memory"—*Journal of Modern History*
0–520–05221–8 California pb $12.95

• Gene Brucker
GIOVANNI AND LUSANNA
In 1455, Lusanna, a beautiful Florentine woman of the artisan class, brought suit against her wealthy, high-born lover Giovanni, who had contracted to marry a young aristocrat. "At its core, this splendid study is about stubborn love and the forms of law, and the impossiblity of each to accommodate the ultimate claims of the other"—A. Bartlett Giamatti
0–520–06328–7 California pb $7.95

RENAISSANCE FLORENCE
"There is no other book about Florence in this period which combines such a broad range of archival sources—family records, records of church and state—with standard literary sources in such an original and effective way"—*American Historical Review*
0–520–04695–1 California pb $10.95

THE SOCIETY OF RENAISSANCE FLORENCE: A Documentary Study
Excerpts from original documents that reveal something about the emotions, passions, and temperaments of Renaissance

Florentines, from family squabbles to prostitution to business fortunes
0–06–131607–5 Harper & Row pb $7.95

● Jacob Burckhardt
THE CIVILIZATION OF THE RENAISSANCE IN ITALY
The programmatic argument that Renaissance Italy was the birthplace of the modern world. "In analyzing the mind, the trend of thought of the Renaissance, and its movements as a whole, nobody has surpassed him"—*New Statesman*
Translated by S.G.C. Middlemore

Volume 1: The State as a Work of Art; The Development of the Individual; The Revival of Antiquity
0–06–090459–3 Harper & Row pb $5.95

Volume 2: The Discovery of the World of Man; Society and Festivals; Morality and Religion
0–06–090460–7 Harper & Row pb $6.95

● Peter Burke
THE ITALIAN RENAISSANCE: Culture and Society in Italy
Unusual approaches to usual subjects
0–691–09431–4 Princeton $38.50
0–691–02838–9 Princeton pb $12.50

● Ernst Cassirer & others, editors
THE RENAISSANCE PHILOSOPHY OF MAN
Excerpts on classical humanism, Platonism, and Aristotelianism from Petrarch, Valla, Ficino, Pico, Pomponazzi, and Vives
0–226–09604–1 Chicago pb $10.95

● Ivan Cloulas
THE BORGIAS
A popular biography of the celebrated family and a runaway best-seller in Europe
0–531–15101–8 Watts $24.95

A Florentine reader from the late 15th century, in A History of Private Life, *Volume 2 edited by Georges Duby (Harvard)*

● David Coffin
THE VILLA IN THE LIFE OF RENAISSANCE ROME
The change in function of the country residence from a productive farm to a center of pleasurable relaxation
0–691–00279–7 Princeton pb $19.95

● Rachel Erlanger
THE UNARMED PROPHET: Savonarola in Florence
A fresh interpretation of Savonarola as a 15th-century ayatollah
0–07–019602–8 McGraw-Hill $19.95

● A. Bartlett Giamatti
THE EARTHLY PARADISE AND THE RENAISSANCE EPIC
"An original approach to Spenser and Milton . . . This is comparative literature as it ought to be done"—*NY Review of Books*
0–393–30573–2 Norton pb $8.95

● Felix Gilbert
MACHIAVELLI AND GUICCIARDINI: Politics and History in Sixteenth-Century Florence
0–393–30123–0 Norton pb $9.95

● Richard A. Goldthwaite
THE BUILDING OF RENAISSANCE FLORENCE: An Economic and Social History
A splendid view of the city's 16th-century architectural transformation
0–8018–2977–1 Johns Hopkins pb $11.95

● J.R. Hale
RENAISSANCE EUROPE: The Individual and Society, 1480-1520
0–520–03471–6 California pb $10.95

WAR AND SOCIETY IN RENAISSANCE EUROPE, 1450-1620
0–8018–3196–2 Johns Hopkins pb $10.95

● J.R. Hale, editor
CONCISE ENCYCLOPAEDIA OF THE ITALIAN RENAISSANCE
0–500–20191–9 Thames & Hudson pb $11.95

● Denys Hay
EUROPE IN THE FOURTEENTH AND FIFTEENTH CENTURIES
0–582–48343–3 Longman pb $16.95

THE ITALIAN RENAISSANCE IN ITS HISTORICAL BACKGROUND
0–521–21321–5 Cambridge $47.50
0–521–29104–6 Cambridge pb $12.95

● George Holmes
FLORENCE, ROME, AND THE ORIGINS OF THE RENAISSANCE
0–19–822153–3 Oxford pb $19.95

● Christiane Klapisch-Zuber
WOMEN, FAMILY, AND RITUAL IN RENAISSANCE ITALY
A living picture of the Tuscan household—its size and composition, its values and priorities—drawn from the detailed records of tax collectors, as well as business and household accounts
Translated by Lydia G. Cochrane
Foreword by David Herlihy
0–226–43926–7 Chicago pb $13.95

● Frederic C. Lane
VENICE: A Maritime Republic
0–8018–1445–6 Johns Hopkins $32.50
0–8018–1460–X Johns Hopkins pb $14.95

● John Larner
ITALY IN THE AGE OF DANTE AND PETRARCH: 1216-1380
0–582–49149–5 Longman pb $18.95

● Mary McCarthy
THE STONES OF FLORENCE
There is no better guide to the monuments of the city and their cultural history
0–15–685081–8 HBJ pb $19.95

● Charles R. Mack
PIENZA: The Creation of a Renaissance City
Rebuilt by Pius II as a Renaissance model, the small hill town embodied the theoretical propositions of Brunelleschi and Alberti
0–8014–1699–X Cornell $39.95

● Lauro Martines
POWER AND IMAGINATION: City-States in Renaissance Italy
0–394–50112–8 Random House pb $15.95

● Iris Origo
THE MERCHANT OF PRATO
Documents and letters recreating the life of Datini, a Florentine merchant-banker. Includes 20 pages of illustrations
0–87923–596–9 Godine pb $14.95

● Peter Partner
RENAISSANCE ROME: A Portrait of a Society, 1500-1559
0–520–03945–9 California pb $11.95

● Mark Phillips
THE MEMOIR OF MARCO PARENTI: A Life in Medici Florence
The public and private life of a 15th-century silk merchant. "Combines very careful and sound scholarship with intellectual originality and a remarkable sense for literary presentation"—Felix Gilbert
0–691–00833–7 Princeton pb $9.95

● J.H. Plumb
THE ITALIAN RENAISSANCE
0–8281–0485–9 Houghton Mifflin pb $9.95

● John Ruskin
THE STONES OF VENICE
An original and illuminating commentary on the city's monuments
0–306–80244–9 Da Capo pb $9.95

● Kate Simon
A RENAISSANCE TAPESTRY: The Gonzaga of Mantua
Colorful if impressionistic history of the dukes of Mantua, from the 15th century to the Napoleonic epoch
0–06–015847–6 Harper & Row $22.50
0–06–091558–7 Harper & Row pb $8.95

● Roberto Weiss
THE RENAISSANCE DISCOVERY OF CLASSICAL ANTIQUITY
0–631–16077–9 Blackwell $15.95

Zocoli, Venetian women's footwear of the 16th century, from The Structures of Everyday Life *by Fernand Braudel (Harper & Row)*

The Medicis

J.R. Hale
FLORENCE AND THE MEDICI: The Pattern of Control
The rebuilding of the city seen through the policies and patronage of the powerful family
0–500–27301–4 Thames & Hudson pb $11.95

Christopher Hibbert
THE HOUSE OF MEDICI: Its Rise and Fall
0–688–05339–4 Morrow pb $12.95

Erasmus and the Northern Renaissance

"Here a new watchword comes to the fore: back to the sources! It is not merely an intellectual, philological requirement; it is equally an ethical and aesthetic necessity of life. The original and pure, all that is not yet overgrown or has not passed through many hands, has such a potent charm. Erasmus compared it to an apple which we ourselves pick off the tree. To recall the world to the ancient simplicity of science, to lead it back from the now turbid pools to those living and most pure fountain-heads, those most limpid sources of gospel doctrine—thus he saw the task of divinity."—Johan Huizinga, *Erasmus and the Age of Reformation*

- **Desiderius Erasmus**
ERASMUS ON HIS TIMES: A Shortened Version of the Adages of Erasmus
Edited by Margaret Mann Phillips
0–521–09413–5 Cambridge pb $11.95

THE ESSENTIAL ERASMUS
Includes *The Praise of Folly, The Complaint of Peace, An Inquiry Concerning Faith*, and other writings
Edited by John P. Dolan
0–452–00673–2 NAL pb $3.95

THE PRAISE OF FOLLY
The great satirical work by the renowned northern humanist
Translated by Betty Radice
0–14–044240–5 Penguin pb $5.95

- **Roland H. Bainton**
ERASMUS OF CHRISTENDOM
0–684–15380–7 Scribners $20.00

- **M.A. Screech**
ERASMUS: Ecstasy and The Praise of Folly
"To the familiar portrait of Erasmus as critic and mischievous observer of his time, as humourist, as philological custodian of the Ancients and as international pacificist, Screech has added the dimension of Erasmus as a guide to the human soul"—Margaret Mann Phillips, *Colloque Erasmien de Liège*
0–14–055235–9 Peregrine pb $7.95

Introductions to Modern European History

- **J.H. Hexter, Richard Pipes & others**
PERSPECTIVES IN WESTERN CIVILIZATION: The Struggle for Empire to Europe in the Modern World
An excellent textbook on European history, designed for college freshmen and written for the common reader
0–06–043835–5 Harper & Row pb $14.95

- **R.R. Palmer & Joel Colton**
A HISTORY OF THE MODERN WORLD
The sixth edition of a classic textbook whose focus is on Europe since the Renaissance
0–394–53396–8 Knopf $45.00

The Norton History of Modern Europe

This series, edited by Felix Gilbert, offers a uniformly well-written set of introductions to the major periods of European history.

Eugene F. Rice, Jr.
THE FOUNDATIONS OF EARLY MODERN EUROPE, 1460-1559
From the development of movable metal type, perfected in Mainz about 1450, through the English Reformation
0–393–09898–2 Norton pb $7.95

Richard S. Dunn
THE AGE OF RELIGIOUS WARS, 1559-1689
Chapters include "Calvinism Versus Catholicism in Western Europe" and "The Century of Genius," with discussions of Newton, Montaigne, Pascal, Hobbes, Rubens, Velázquez, Bernini, and Rembrandt
0–393–09021–3 Norton pb $9.95

Leonard Krieger
KINGS AND PHILOSOPHERS, 1689-1789
0–393–09905–9 Norton pb $10.95

Isser Woloch
EIGHTEENTH CENTURY EUROPE: Tradition and Progress, 1715-1789
0–393–95214–2 Norton pb $9.95

Charles Breunig
THE AGE OF REVOLUTION, 1789-1850
0–393–09143–0 Norton pb $9.95

Norman Rich
THE AGE OF NATIONALISM AND REFORM, 1850-1890
Chapters include "The Intellectual and Cultural Climate" and "The Course of Reform: Great Britain and Russia"
0–393–09183–X Norton pb $8.95

Felix Gilbert
THE END OF THE EUROPEAN ERA: 1890 to the Present
The "present" is 1983
0–393–95440–4 Norton pb $12.95

The People of Europe

- **Luigi Barzini**
THE EUROPEANS
The eminent journalist on the imperturbable British, the mutable Germans, the quarrelsome French, the flexible Italians, the careful Dutch, and the baffling Americans
0–14–007150–4 Penguin pb $7.95

THE ITALIANS
Their manners and morals. "Searching into every corner of Italian life and scrutinizing every cliché concerning it, from the charm of the people (an illusion, he maintains), to the consolations of *La Dolce Vita* (another one), Mr. Barzini has written an invaluable and astringent guidebook to his country"—*New Yorker*
0–689–70540–9 Atheneum pb $9.95

- **Gordon A. Craig**
THE GERMANS
The paradoxes that have produced great music, art, literature—and Hitler
0–399–12436–5 Putnam $15.95
0–452–00622–8 NAL pb $8.95

- **Moses Khorenats'i**
HISTORY OF THE ARMENIANS
Translated by R.W. Thomson
0–674–39571–9 Harvard $30.00

- **Flora Lewis**
EUROPE: A Tapestry of Nations
0–671–66829–3 Simon & Schuster pb $10.95

- **Hedrick Smith**
THE RUSSIANS
0–8129–1086–9 Times Books $24.95
0–345–31746–7 Ballantine pb $4.95

• Theodore Zeldin
THE FRENCH
Penetrating observations by Britain's
master of modern French social history
0–394–72421–6 Random House pb $9.95

REGIONAL AND NATIONAL HISTORIES

▶ **See also Great Britain and Ireland & Russian and Soviet Studies**

Eastern Europe and Poland

• Neal Ascherson
THE STRUGGLES FOR POLAND
An illustrated companion to the PBS
documentary covering the broad sweep of
Poland's tragic past
0–394–55997–5 Random House $19.95

• Norman Davies
**GOD'S PLAYGROUND: A History of
Poland**
"The best introduction available to the
incredible imbroglio of Polish history"—
Stanislaw Baranczak, *New Republic*

Volume 1: The Origins to 1795
0–231–05351–7 Columbia pb $21.00

Volume 2: 1795 to the Present
0–231–05353–3 Columbia pb $21.00

**HEART OF EUROPE: A Short History of
Poland**
Starting with the Solidarity movement and
working back to the 18th-century
partitions, a view of Poland as the
geographical and symbolic heart of Europe
0–19–285152–7 Oxford pb $10.95

Polish soldier, early 17th century

• Francis Dvornik
**THE SLAVS IN EUROPEAN HISTORY
AND CIVILIZATION**
0–8135–0403–1 Rutgers pb $15.00

• R.F. Leslie
**THE HISTORY OF POLAND SINCE
1863**
0–521–27501–6 Cambridge pb $21.95

• Robin Okey
**EASTERN EUROPE: Feudalism to
Communism, 1740-1985**
An excellent synthesis
0–8166–1561–6 Minnesota pb $13.95

• E. Garrison Walters
**THE OTHER EUROPE: Eastern Europe to
1945**
0–8156–2440–9 Syracuse pb $16.95

France

• Fernand Braudel
**THE IDENTITY OF FRANCE, Volume 1:
History and Environment**
Unique insights into the making of
modern France by a student of the
Mediterranean and its history. Two further
volumes, already published in France, will
appear next year. "Positively glows with
love, even personal touches of nostalgia"—
NY Times
0–06–016021–7 Harper & Row $25.00

• G. de Bertier de Sauvigny &
David H. Pinkney
HISTORY OF FRANCE
Translated by James Friguglietti
0–88273–425–3 Forum pb $19.95

Alfred Cobban
A HISTORY OF MODERN FRANCE
An excellent survey by the late British
historian

Volume 1: 1715-1799
0–14–020403–2 Penguin pb $6.95

Volume 2: 1799-1870
0–14–020525–X Penguin pb $5.95

Volume 3: 1871-1962
0–14–020711–2 Penguin pb $6.95

• Pierre Goubert
THE COURSE OF FRENCH HISTORY
A useful synthesis by the author of *Louis
XIV and Twenty Million Frenchmen*
Translated by Maarten Ultee
0–531–15054–2 Watts $26.95

• Roger Price
**AN ECONOMIC HISTORY OF MODERN
FRANCE: 1730-1914**
0–312–23322–1 St. Martin's $27.50

• Charles Tilly
THE CONTENTIOUS FRENCH
A social historian on urban and provincial
uprisings throughout the modern period
0–674–16695–7 Harvard $25.00

• Gordon Wright
FRANCE IN MODERN TIMES
0–393–95582–6 Norton pb $17.95

The Cambridge History of
Modern France

Each volume in the Cambridge History
is a translation from the series *Nouvelle
histoire de la France contemporaine*, which
has been published by Editions du Seuil,
Paris, since 1972. The series forms an
up-to-date history of France since the
Bourbon Restoration.

André Jardin & André-Jean
Tudesq
**RESTORATION AND REACTION,
1815-1848**
Translated by Elborg Forster
0–521–35855–8 Cambridge pb $16.95

Maurice Agulhon
**THE REPUBLICAN EXPERIMENT,
1848-1852**
Translated by Janet Lloyd
0–521–28988–2 Cambridge pb $12.95

Alain Plessis
**THE RISE AND FALL OF THE
SECOND EMPIRE, 1852-1871**
Translated by Jonathan Mandelbaum
0–521–35856–6 Cambridge pb $10.95

Jean-Marie Mayeur & Madeleine
Rebérioux
**THE THIRD REPUBLIC FROM ITS
ORIGINS TO THE GREAT WAR,
1871-1914**
Translated by J.R. Foster
0–521–35857–4 Cambridge pb $14.95

Philippe Bernard & Henri Dubief
**THE DECLINE OF THE THIRD
REPUBLIC, 1914-1938**
Translated by Anthony Forster
0–521–25240–7 Cambridge $54.50
0–317–69895–8 Cambridge $14.95

Jean-Pierre Azema
**FROM MUNICH TO THE
LIBERATION, 1938-1944**
Translated by Janet Lloyd
0–521–27238–6 Cambridge pb $15.95

Jean-Pierre Rioux
THE FOURTH REPUBLIC, 1944-1958
Translated by Godfrey Rogers
0–521–25238–5 Cambridge $59.50

Germany

• V.R. Berghahn
**MODERN GERMANY: Society, Economy
and Politics in the Twentieth Century**
A crisp account beginning with the rapid
industrialization of the pre-World War I
era and focusing on social and economic
developments
0–521–34748–3 Cambridge pb $10.95

• David Childs
GERMANY SINCE 1918
0–312–32628–9 St. Martin's $25.00

• Hajo Holborn

A HISTORY OF MODERN GERMANY
The standard survey of German history. A "massive and unmatched reconstruction of the German Past"—Fritz Stern

Volume 1: The Reformation
0–691–00795–0 Princeton pb $14.50

Volume 2: 1648-1840
"The first major work in English on the subject in which adequate attention is given to various facets of German historical development and particularly to economic factors"—L.L. Snyder, *Annals of the American Academy*
0–691–00796–9 Princeton pb $11.50

Volume 3: 1840-1945
"In this third volume, Holborn has demonstrated once more his comprehensive knowledge of political, cultural and social history of his native country and his well-balanced, fair, and keen judgments on conditions and leading figures"—*Library Journal*
0–691–00797–7 Princeton pb $14.50

• Fritz Stern

DREAMS AND DELUSIONS: The Drama of German History
"Stern writes with all the poignancy of one who loves German civilization deeply and is determined to fathom how it could have done such terrible violence to others, and to itself"—David P. Calleo, *Foreign Affairs*
0–394–55995–9 Knopf $19.95
0–394–75772–6 Random House pb $10.95

Greece and the Balkans

• Richard Clogg

A SHORT HISTORY OF MODERN GREECE
Greece's turbulent history, from the decline of the Byzantine Empire through the 1980s
0–521–32837–3 Cambridge $44.50
0–521–33804–2 Cambridge pb $12.95

• R.J. Crampton

A SHORT HISTORY OF MODERN BULGARIA
From Bulgaria's liberation from the Ottoman Empire in 1878 to the present; a good introduction
0–521–27323–4 Cambridge pb $12.95

• Barbara Jelavich

HISTORY OF THE BALKANS

Volume 1: Eighteenth and Nineteenth Centuries
0–521–25249–0 Cambridge $57.50
0–521–27458–3 Cambridge pb $19.95

Volume 2: Twentieth Century
0–521–27459–1 Cambridge pb $19.95

• Fred Singleton

A SHORT HISTORY OF THE YUGOSLAV PEOPLES
0–521–27485–0 Cambridge pb $13.95

The Habsburg Empire, Modern Austria, and Hungary

• Jorg K. Hoensch

A HISTORY OF MODERN HUNGARY, 1867-1986
From the Compromise of 1867 to the upheavals of 1956, and into the 1980s
Translated by Kim Traynor
0–582–01484–0 Longman $37.95

• Barbara Jelavich

MODERN AUSTRIA: Empire and Republic, 1800-1986
Political history and foreign policy, from the Congress of Vienna to the 1986 elections
0–521–31625–1 Cambridge pb $12.95

• Robert A. Kann

A HISTORY OF THE HABSBURG EMPIRE, 1526-1918
An essential one-volume survey
0–520–04206–9 California pb $15.95

• William O. McCagg, Jr.

A HISTORY OF HABSBURG JEWS, 1670-1918
Draws on a wide range of European sources to offer the first history of this community to be written since the 19th century
0–253–33189–7 Indiana $27.50

• A.J.P. Taylor

THE HABSBURG MONARCHY, 1809-1918: A History of the Austrian Empire and Austria Hungary
First published in 1941 and still essential reading for all students of the period. "A very good book indeed, brilliant, acid and penetrating"—Alan Bullock
0–226–79145–9 Chicago pb $10.00

Italy

• M.I. Finley, Denis Mack Smith & Christopher Duggan

A HISTORY OF SICILY
0–670–81725–2 Viking $24.95

• H. Hearder & D.P. Waley

A SHORT HISTORY OF ITALY
0–521–09394–5 Cambridge pb $15.95

• William H. McNeill

VENICE: The Hinge of Europe, 1081-1797
0–226–56149–6 Chicago pb $18.95

• Denis Mack Smith

ITALY: A Modern History
Authoritative study by the leading English-speaking historian of modern Italy
0–472–07051–7 Michigan $29.50

Spain

Unfortunately, Stanley G. Paine's two-volume of *History of Spain and Portugal* (University of Wisconsin Press) is out of print.

• Raymond Carr

SPAIN: 1808-1975
Economic, political, and social history to the death of Franco; with an extensive bibliographical essay
0–19–822128–2 Oxford pb $26.00

• John Crow

SPAIN—THE ROOT AND THE FLOWER: An Interpretation of Spain and the Spanish People
An older, idiosyncratic study
0–520–05123–8 California $37.50
0–520–05133–5 California pb $12.95

Other Countries

• T.K. Derry

A HISTORY OF MODERN NORWAY, 1814-1972
The most comprehensive survey of modern Norway available in English
0–19–822503–2 Oxford $47.00

• Adam Hopkins

HOLLAND: Its History, Paintings and People
Holland's extraordinary social and artistic achievements
Photographs by Tim Stephens
0–571–14681–3 Faber & Faber $30.00
0–571–14682–1 Faber & Faber pb $12.95

• E.H. Kossman

THE LOW COUNTRIES, 1750-1940
A comparative approach to why Belgium and the Netherlands, despite many similarities, embarked on different courses of development
0–19–822108–8 Oxford $59.00

• S.J. Shaw

HISTORY OF THE OTTOMAN EMPIRE AND MODERN TURKEY

Volume 1: Empire of the Gazis
0–521–29163–1 Cambridge pb $24.95

Volume 2: Reform, Revolution, and Republic
0–521–29166–6 Cambridge pb $24.95

Early Modern Europe

• H.G. Koenigsberger & George L. Mosse

EUROPE IN THE SIXTEENTH CENTURY
0–582–48345–X Longman pb $16.95

• David Maland

EUROPE IN THE SEVENTEENTH CENTURY
0–312–26775–4 St. Martin's pb $15.95

• John F. New

THE RENAISSANCE AND REFORMATION: A Short History
0–394–34199–6 Random House pb $15.95

• Theodore K. Rabb

THE STRUGGLE FOR STABILITY IN EARLY MODERN EUROPE
0–19–501956–3 Oxford pb $10.95

• Geoffrey Treasure

THE MAKING OF MODERN EUROPE, 1648-1780
0–416–72370–5 Methuen pb $16.95

• H.R. Trevor-Roper

THE GOLDEN AGE OF EUROPE: From Elizabeth I to the Sun King
The consolidation of nation states and the wars of religion. Contributions include H.G. Koenigsberger on the Thirty Years War and Henry Willetts on Poland and the evolution of Russia. Over 270 full-color and black-and-white illustrations, photos, and maps
0–517–64836–9 Outlet $15.95

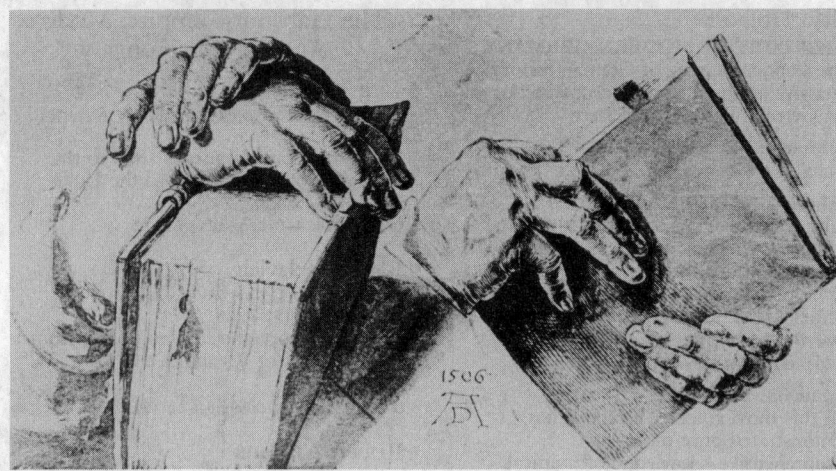

Woodcut by Albrecht Dürer, from Delights of Reading *by Otto L. Bettmann* (*Godine*)

REFORMATION AND COUNTER-REFORMATION

▶ See also Great Britain and Ireland; for theology and doctrine, see Christianity

• John Bossy

CHRISTIANITY IN THE WEST, 1400-1700
A systematic exposition of pre-Reformation Christianity and the forces that undermined it
0–19–289162–6 Oxford pb $9.95

• Owen Chadwick

THE REFORMATION
Part of the Pelican History of the Church series
0–14–020504–7 Penguin pb $5.95

• Eric Cochrane

FLORENCE IN THE FORGOTTEN CENTURIES, 1527-1800: A History of Florence and the Florentines in the Age of the Grand Dukes
0–226–11151–2 Chicago pb $7.95

• A.G. Dickens

THE COUNTER-REFORMATION
How the Catholic Church sought to regain its spiritual dominion after the abuses of the Renaissance papacy
0–393–95086–7 Norton pb $9.95

A late 15th-century woodcut foretelling the wreck of the Church

THE ENGLISH REFORMATION
0–8052–0177–7 Schocken pb $9.95

REFORMATION AND SOCIETY IN SIXTEENTH-CENTURY EUROPE
A first-rate introductory study
0–15–576455–1 HBJ pb $14.50

• Hans Hillerbrand, editor

THE PROTESTANT REFORMATION
Excerpts from Luther, Calvin, and Zwingli, plus additional documents tracing the Reformation through the Anabaptists and developments in England
0–06–131342–4 Harper & Row pb $9.95

• R. Po-chia Hsia

THE GERMAN PEOPLE AND THE REFORMATION
Essays on how the religious schisms of 16th-century Europe affected the lives of ordinary Germans
0–8014–2064–4 Cornell $39.95
0–8014–9485–0 Cornell pb $12.95

• Steven Ozment, translator & editor

MAGDALENA AND BALTHASAR: An Intimate Portrait of Life in Sixteenth-Century Europe Revealed in the Letters of a Nuremberg Husband and Wife
0–300–04378–3 Yale pb $9.95

WHEN FATHERS RULED: Family Life in Reformation Europe
0–674–95120–4 Harvard $18.50
0–674–95121–2 Harvard pb $8.95

• Lewis W. Spitz

THE PROTESTANT REFORMATION, 1517-1559: The Rise of Modern Europe
The Reformation's expansion in the four decades following Luther's 95 theses, a period, the author argues, of more radical change than the Renaissance
0–06–013958–7 Harper & Row $22.95

• Donald J. Wilcox

IN SEARCH OF GOD AND SELF: Renaissance and Reformation Thought
0–88133–276–3 Waveland pb $12.95

Religion and Capitalism

• Max Weber

THE PROTESTANT ETHIC AND THE SPIRIT OF CAPITALISM
Weber's classic argument, first published in 1904, that the spread of Protestantism directly affected the rise of the capitalist ethic. "What really emerges from a reading of Weber's essay is the feeling that economic facts and institutions are cultural phenomena, more or less responsive to the ethical aspirations of men"—*New Republic*
0–02–424860–6 Scribners pb $15.50

• Gordon Marshall

IN SEARCH OF THE SPIRIT OF CAPITALISM: An Essay on Max Weber's Protestant Ethic Thesis
0–231–05498–X Columbia $31.00
0–231–05499–8 Columbia pb $14.00

• R.H. Tawney

RELIGION AND THE RISE OF CAPITALISM
Tawney evaluates Weber's theory of the Protestant ethic and suggests a revision, providing an account of conscious and unconscious attitudes about business in the early modern period
0–8446–1446–7 Peter Smith $12.95

The Printing Revolution

Peter Burke
POPULAR CULTURE IN EARLY MODERN EUROPE
0–06–131928–7 Harper & Row pb $8.95

Elizabeth L. Eisenstein
THE PRINTING REVOLUTION IN EARLY MODERN EUROPE
Eisenstein sees print *qua* print as the genius of modern history
0–521–25858–8 Cambridge $42.50
0–521–27735–3 Cambridge pb $10.95

THE PRINTING PRESS AS AN AGENT OF CHANGE
A shorter statement of the same thesis, with pictures
0–521–29955–1 Cambridge $24.95

Lucien Febvre & Henri-Jean Martin
THE COMING OF THE BOOK: The Impact of Printing, 1450-1800
In the 40 years between the Gutenberg Bible and the close of the 15th century, more than 20 million printed volumes were manufactured in Europe; between 1500 and 1600, between 150 and 200 million. Febvre and Martin's classic study conveys the revolutionary impact of printing on early modern Europe. "One of the most exciting scholarly books ever written on printing"—H.R. Trevor-Roper
Translated by David Gerard
Edited by Goeffrey Nowell-Smith & David Wootton
0-86091-797-5 Verso pb $15.95

Janet Ing
JOHANN GUTENBERG AND HIS BIBLE
Illustrated
0-945074-00-X Typophiles $27.50

Reformers and Revolutionaries

• William J. Bouwsma
JOHN CALVIN: A Sixteenth Century Portrait
"By intense reading in Calvin's work [Bouwsma] has come up with a 20th-century psychological scheme, giving a genuinely new insight into the man and into the 16th century as a whole"—*NY Times*
0-19-504394-4 Oxford $24.95
0-19-505951-4 Oxford pb $8.95

• Martin Luther
MARTIN LUTHER: Selections from His Writings
Edited by John Dillenberger
0-385-09876-6 Doubleday pb $8.95

• Roland H. Bainton
HERE I STAND: A Life of Martin Luther
0-451-62404-1 NAL pb $4.95

• Erik Erikson
YOUNG MAN LUTHER
The origins of Luther's rebelliousness and later authoritarianism; one of the most successful forays into psychobiography, by the author of *Childhood, Youth and Crisis*
0-393-00170-9 Norton pb $5.95

• Ernest G. Schwiebert
LUTHER AND HIS TIMES: The Reformation from a New Perspective
0-570-03246-6 Concordia $26.95

• G.R. Potter
ZWINGLI
0-521-27888-0 Cambridge pb $18.95

John Calvin as a young man

DEMONS, WITCHCRAFT, AND MAGIC

• Norman Cohn
EUROPE'S INNER DEMONS: An Enquiry Inspired by the Great Witch-Hunt
The waves of mass fear, hate, and persecution that have periodically swept over Europe
0-452-00900-6 NAL pb $9.95

• Carlo Ginzburg
THE CHEESE AND THE WORMS: The Cosmos of a Sixteenth-Century Miller
A miller in Italy burned as a heretic under the Inquisition. "By the end of the book, the reader who has followed Dr. Ginzburg in his wanderings through the labyrinthine mind of the miller of Friuli will take leave of this strange and quirky old man with genuine regret"—*NY Review of Books*
Translated by John & Anne Tedeschi
0-14-006046-4 Penguin pb $7.95

THE NIGHT BATTLES: Witchcraft and Agrarian Cults in the Sixteenth and Seventeenth Centuries
The Inquisition's persecution of a simple peasant society deeply rooted in fertility cults
Translated by John & Anne Tedeschi
0-14-007688-3 Penguin pb $8.95

• R. Po-chia Hsia
THE MYTH OF RITUAL MURDER: Jews and Magic in Reformation Germany
Throughout the 16th century, German Jews were persecuted for the alleged ritual murders of Christian children, whose blood was erroneously believed to have played a role in Jewish magical rites
0-300-04120-9 Yale $27.50

• Michael Kunze
HIGHROAD TO THE STAKE: A Tale of Witchcraft
"A vivid story of a witch trial ... Deeply moving, fascinating"—Wendy Doniger O'Flaherty, *NY Times*
0-226-46212-9 Chicago pb $12.95

• Jeffrey B. Russell
A HISTORY OF WITCHCRAFT: Sorcerers, Heretics and Pagans
0-500-27242-5 Thames & Hudson pb $11.95

• Geoffrey Scarre
WITCHCRAFT AND MAGIC IN SIXTEENTH AND SEVENTEENTH CENTURY EUROPE
As many as 100,000 people, most of them women, were condemned to death for witchcraft in early modern Europe. This 80-page essay, aimed at students of European history, investigates patterns of deviance and social control
0-391-03505-3 Humanities pb $8.50

• Keith Thomas
RELIGION AND THE DECLINE OF MAGIC
A highly acclaimed study of English attitudes in the 16th and 17th centuries. "If magic is to be defined as the employment of ineffective techniques to allay anxiety when effective ones are not available, then we must recognise that no society will ever be free from it"—Keith Thomas
0-684-14542-1 Scribners pb $19.95

• H.R. Trevor-Roper
THE EUROPEAN WITCH CRAZE IN THE SIXTEENTH AND SEVENTEENTH CENTURIES & OTHER ESSAYS
Includes three additional essays on the Reformation and social change; the general crisis of the 17th century; and the religious origins of the Enlightenment
0-06-131416-1 Harper & Row pb $7.95

THE EXPANSION OF EUROPE: Empire and Commerce

▶ For the European exploration of the Americas, see US History to the Civil War

Exploration

• Helen Delpar
THE DISCOVERERS: An Encyclopedia of Explorers and Exploration
0-07-016264-6 McGraw-Hill $63.50

• J.H. Elliott
THE OLD WORLD AND THE NEW: 1492-1650
0-521-09621-9 Cambridge pb $8.95

• Samuel Eliot Morison
ADMIRAL OF THE OCEAN SEA: A Life of Christopher Columbus
The achievements and tribulations of the explorer
Illustrated by Erwin Raisz & Bertram Greene
0-930350-37-5 Northeastern pb $14.95

• J.H. Parry
THE AGE OF RECONNAISSANCE: Discovery, Exploration, and Settlement, 1450-1650
0-520-04234-4 California $37.50
0-520-04235-2 California pb $11.95

*Indians carrying burdens for the Spanish,
from* Lines to the Mountain Gods: Nazca
and the Mysteries of Peru *by Evan
Haddingham (Oklahoma)*

● G.V. Scammell
**THE WORLD ENCOMPASSED: The First
European Maritime Empires, c. 800-1650**
0–520–04422–3 California $45.00

● Norman J. Thrower, editor
**SIR FRANCIS DRAKE AND THE
FAMOUS VOYAGE, 1577-1580: Essays
Commemorating the Quadricentennial of
Drake's Circumnavigation of the Earth**
Preface by Prince Philip
0–520–04876–8 California $40.00

The Colonial Empires

▶ See also Latin America and the Caribbean

● C.R. Boxer
THE DUTCH SEABORNE EMPIRE
In the 17th century the Dutch dominated
trade. Ships traveled as far as modern day
New York and Nagasaki, and settlements
were founded in Indonesia and South
Africa
0–14–021600–6 Penguin pb $8.95

● William B. Cohen
**THE FRENCH ENCOUNTER WITH
AFRICANS: White Response to Blacks,
1530-1880**
0–253–34922–2 Indiana $25.00

● Bailey W. Diffie & George D. Winius
**FOUNDATIONS OF THE PORTUGUESE
EMPIRE, 1415-1850**
Edited by Boyd C. Shafer
0–8166–0850–4 Minnesota pb $10.95

● Lyle N. McAlister
**SPAIN AND PORTUGAL IN THE NEW
WORLD, 1492-1700**
0–8166–1218–8 Minnesota pb $15.95

● J.H. Parry
THE SPANISH SEABORNE EMPIRE
0–394–44650–X Knopf $15.95

The Triumph of Capitalism

Fernand Braudel
**CIVILIZATION AND CAPITALISM:
Fifteenth to Eighteenth Centuries**
An ambitious 3-volume effort to
explore the roots of capitalist culture by
one of the great French historians of
the postwar era. "A masterpiece of
modern scholarship, *Civilization and
Capitalism* belongs beside the great
histories of Thucydides and Jacob
Burckhardt—and beside the great
treatises of social theory by Karl Marx
and Max Weber"—*Newsweek*
Translated by Siân Reynolds

**THE STRUCTURES OF EVERYDAY
LIFE**
0–06–014845–4 Harper & Row $35.00
0–06–091294–4 Harper & Row pb $19.95

THE WHEELS OF COMMERCE
0–06–015091–2 Harper & Row $35.00
0–06–015091–2 Harper & Row pb $16.95

**THE PERSPECTIVE OF THE
WORLD**
0–06–091296–0 Harper & Row pb $16.95

● J. De Vries
**THE ECONOMY OF EUROPE IN AN
AGE OF CRISIS: 1600-1750**
0–521–21123–9 Cambridge $37.50
0–521–29050–3 Cambridge pb $10.95

● Rodney Hilton, Maurice Dobb &
others
**THE TRANSITION FROM FEUDALISM
TO CAPITALISM**
Participants in the "transition debate" of
the early 1950s include Maurice Dobb,
Paul Sweezy, and Christopher Hill. Their
contributions are reprinted here, along
with essays by Pierre Vilar and Eric
Hobsbawm
0–86091–701–0 Verso pb $10.95

● Albert O. Hirschman
**THE PASSIONS AND THE INTERESTS:
Political Arguments for Capitalism Before
Its Triumph**
The debate over the justification of
economic gain (and hence capitalism) in
this era
0–691–00357–2 Princeton pb $8.95

● E.L. Jones
**THE EUROPEAN MIRACLE:
Environments, Economies and Geopolitics
in the History of Europe and Asia**
0–521–33449–7 Cambridge $39.50
0–521–28055–9 Cambridge pb $12.95

● Peter Kriedte
**PEASANTS, LANDLORDS AND
MERCHANT CAPITALISTS: Europe and
the World Economy, 1500-1800**
0–521–25755–7 Cambridge $34.50

● Harry A. Miskimin
**THE ECONOMY OF EARLY
RENAISSANCE EUROPE**
0–521–29021–X Cambridge pb $10.95

● Immanuel Wallerstein
HISTORICAL CAPITALISM
A condensation of Wallerstein's
monumental study of capitalism as an
integrated, historical entity, "the modern
world system"
0–86091–761–4 Verso pb $9.95

THE THIRTY YEARS WAR, 1618-1648

A series of protracted wars, the Thirty
Years War was something of a European
civil war between the Habsburg Empire and
other powers. It consisted of four phases:
the Bohemian (1618-1625), the Danish
(1625-1629), the Swedish (1630-1635),
and the Swedish-French (1635-1648). Is it
an accident that it peaked—as did the English Civil War—at the same time as the fall
of the Ming dynasty in China (1644)? From
Bourbon France to Tokugawa Japan, Europe and Asia experienced a midcentury
upheaval that some historians call "the crisis
of the 17th century."

● Pam Gems
QUEEN CHRISTINA
The conversion to Catholicism of Gustavus
Adolphus' daughter and her abdication of
the Swedish throne in 1654 after a reign
of over two decades
0–9508443–0–6 Methuen pb $4.95

● Geoffrey Parker
EUROPE IN CRISIS, 1598-1648
A general history of a period of constant
conflict beginning with the death of Felipe
II and culminating in the Thirty Years War
0–8014–9209–2 Cornell pb $7.95

● Geoffrey Parker, editor
THE THIRTY YEARS' WAR
A valuable collection of essays
0–415–02534–6 RC&H pb $15.95

● Geoffrey Parker & Lesley M. Smith,
editors
**THE GENERAL CRISIS OF THE
SEVENTEENTH CENTURY**
Essays in the heated debate over the
existence and nature of a political and
economic "general crisis" in Europe in the
17th century
0–7102–0545–7 Methuen pb $9.95

● J.V. Polisensky
**WAR AND SOCIETY IN EUROPE,
1618-1648**
0–521–21659–1 Cambridge $39.50

● Michael Roberts
**THE SWEDISH IMPERIAL
EXPERIENCE, 1560-1718**
Sweden's important role in European
affairs in the 17th century
0–521–27889–9 Cambridge pb $13.95

● Henrik Tikkanen
THE THIRTY YEARS' WAR
Translated by George & L.T. Blecher
0–8032–9407–7 Nebraska pb $8.95

• C.V. Wedgwood
THE THIRTY YEARS WAR
The wars that virtually decimated
Germany. An excellent guide to the
military and diplomatic complexities of a
struggle that saw Catholic France side with
Lutheran Sweden against Catholic Austria
0–416–32020–1 Methuen pb $15.95

SPAIN: Golden Age and Decline

• Fernand Braudel
**THE MEDITERRANEAN AND THE
MEDITERRANEAN WORLD IN THE
AGE OF PHILIP II**
A magisterial example of *Annales* history,
stressing the importance of geography,
climate, and population as influences on
political and military events and
culminating in the struggle for mastery in
the Mediterranean between Turks and
Spaniards
Translated by Siân Reynolds

Volume 1
0–06–090566–2 Harper & Row pb $12.95

Volume 2
0–06–090567–0 Harper & Row pb $13.95

• Marcelin Defourneaux
**DAILY LIFE IN SPAIN IN THE
GOLDEN AGE**
Translated by Newton Branch
0–8047–1029–5 Stanford pb $9.95

• J.H. Elliott
**THE COUNT-DUKE OF OLIVARES: The
Statesman in an Age of Decline**
Don Gaspar de Gusmán, count-duke of
Olivares, right-hand adviser to Philip IV
and archrival of Richelieu. "The finest
biography ever written on a Spanish
statesman"—Raymond Carr, *NY Review of
Books*
0–300–03390–7 Yale $37.50
0–300–04499–2 Yale pb $19.95

Philip II by Sánchez Coello, from The
Spanish Armada *by Colin Martin and
Geoffrey Parker (Norton)*

A gunner discharging his cannon, from The
Spanish Armada *by Colin Martin &
Geoffrey Parker (Norton)*

IMPERIAL SPAIN: 1469-1716
The essential work in English on this
period by the leading authority
0–452–00782–8 NAL pb $10.95

**THE REVOLT OF THE CATALANS: A
Study in the Decline of Spain, 1598-1640**
0–521–27890–2 Cambridge pb $24.95

SPAIN AND ITS WORLD, 1500-1700
0–300–04217–5 Yale $27.50

• Henry Kamen
**INQUISITION AND SOCIETY IN SPAIN
IN THE SIXTEENTH AND
SEVENTEENTH CENTURIES**
0–253–33015–7 Indiana $27.50

SPAIN, 1469-1714: A Society of Conflict
0–582–49226–2 Longman pb $18.50

• John Lynch
SPAIN UNDER THE HABSBURGS

**Volume 1: Empire and Absolutism, 1516-
1598**
0–8147–5009–5 NYU pb $15.00

Volume 2: Spain and America, 1598-1700
0–8147–5010–9 NYU pb $15.00

• Peter Pierson
PHILIP II OF SPAIN
0–500–87003–9 Thames & Hudson pb $16.95

The Spanish Armada

The armada that Philip II launched
against England in 1588 consisted of
130 ships, weighing nearly 60,000 tons
and carrying 2400 pieces of artillery and
30,000 men.

David Howarth
**THE VOYAGE OF THE ARMADA:
The Spanish Story**
The voyage of the *armada católica*,
from the Spanish—as opposed to
English—point of view
0–14–006315–3 Penguin pb $8.95

Colin Martin & Geoffrey Parker
THE SPANISH ARMADA
0–393–02607–8 Norton $27.50

Garrett Mattingly
THE ARMADA
0–395–48682–3 Houghton Mifflin $29.95
0–395–08366–4 Houghton Mifflin pb $9.95

Peter Padfield
**ARMADA: A Celebration of the Four
Hundredth Anniversary of the Defeat of
the Spanish Armada, 1588-1988**
0–87021–006–8 Naval Institute $24.95

No region of the Mediterranean was free
from the scourge. Catalonia, Calabria
and Albania, all notorious regions in this
respect, by no means had a monopoly of
brigandage. It cropped up everywhere in
various guises, political, social, economic,
terrorist; at the gates of Alexandria in
Egypt or of Damascus and Aleppo; in the
countryside round Naples, where watch
towers were built to warn of brigands
and in the Roman Campagna, where
brush fires were sometimes ordered to
smoke out bands of robbers who found
abundant cover there; even in a state so
apparently well-policed as Venice. When
the sultan's army marched along the
Stambul road to Adrianople, Nis, Belgrade and on into Hungary, it left behind
along the roadside scores of hanged brigands whom it had disturbed in their lairs.

Fernand Braudel
**THE MEDITERRANEAN AND THE
MEDITERRANEAN WORLD IN THE
AGE OF PHILIP II: Volume 2**
0–06–090567–0 Harper & Row pb $13.95

EARLY MODERN FRANCE

• Theodore-Agrippa d'Aubigné
HIS LIFE, TO HIS CHILDREN
A Huguenot partisan, the poet Theodore-
Agrippa d'Aubigné (1552-1630) fought in
the wars of religion until the pacification
imposed by Henry IV, whom he had
served as a squire. *His Life, To His Children*
is filled with battles, rescues, duels, escapes
from prison, betrayals, and love intrigues.
Intimate views of Catherine de Medicis,
Marguérite de Valois, and Henry III
recommend this "first modern
autobiography"
Translated by John Nothnagle
0–8032–1682–3 Nebraska $20.00

• David Buisseret
HENRY IV
Flippantly remarking that "Paris is worth a
mass," Henry converted to Catholicism,
bringing the Bourbons to the throne in
1589 and establishing a dynasty that
would rule, not without interruption, until
1830
0–04–944012–8 Unwin Hyman $37.95

• Natalie Zemon Davis
**FICTION IN THE ARCHIVES: Pardon
Tales and Their Tellers in Sixteenth-
Century France**
"Her original and detailed exploration of
the stories French men and women told to
save their lives challenges the conventional
boundaries between fiction and truth"—
Stephen Greenblatt
0–8047–1412–6 Stanford $22.50

THE RETURN OF MARTIN GUERRE
"One can only admire Natalie Davis for the major work of historical reconstruction she has performed without any kind of ideological bias . . . The movie was great but Natalie Davis' book is even better"—Emmanuel Le Roy Ladurie, *NY Review of Books*
0–674–76690–3 Harvard $17.50
0–674–76691–1 Harvard pb $7.95

SOCIETY AND CULTURE IN EARLY MODERN FRANCE
Eight essays from the social historian at Princeton
0–8047–0972–6 Stanford pb $11.95

● Barbara B. Diefendorf
PARIS CITY COUNCILLORS IN THE SIXTEENTH CENTURY: The Politics of Patrimony
The social and economic process that made houses and miniature castles fashionable
0–691–05362–6 Princeton $35.00

Lucien Febvre
LIFE IN RENAISSANCE FRANCE
A splendid account of life at the court of Francis I (1515-1547), and of the new aristocracy of parvenus by the great 20th-century French historian
Translated by Marian Rothstein
0–674–53180–9 Harvard pb $6.95

THE PROBLEM OF UNBELIEF IN THE SIXTEENTH CENTURY: The Religion of Rabelais
Translated by Beatrice Gottlieb
0–674–70826–1 Harvard pb $11.95

● Robert M. Kingdon
MYTHS ABOUT THE ST. BARTHOLOMEW'S DAY MASSACRES, 1572-1576
How the new medium of print was used by Protestants to perpetuate the myths and propaganda that helped shape reaction to the catastrophe
0–674–59831–8 Harvard $30.00

● R.J. Knecht
FRANCIS I
Contemporary of Henry VIII, Charles V, and Suleiman the Magnificent, François I presided over Renaissance France. "A model of what a dense historical biography should be"—*Times* (London)
0–521–27887–2 Cambridge pb $15.95

● Emmanuel Le Roy Ladurie
CARNIVAL IN ROMANS
0–8076–0928–5 Braziller $20.00
0–8076–0991–9 Braziller pb $8.95

● Robert Mandrou
INTRODUCTION TO MODERN FRANCE, 1500-1640: An Essay in Historical Psychology
More from the *Annales* school and its interpretation of the *mentalité*, or collective outlook, of different classes
Translated by R.E. Hallmark
0–8419–0245–3 Holmes & Meier $35.00

● Robert Muchembled
POPULAR CULTURE AND ELITE CULTURE IN FRANCE: 1400-1750
How the popular mind-set blended Christian and pagan elements; its chief preoccupations being the practice of sorcery, the encouragement of fertility, the unleashing of pent-up sexuality, and the assurance of a bountiful harvest
Translated by Lydia Cochrane
0–8071–1218–6 LSU $32.50

● Nancy L. Roelker
QUEEN OF NAVARRE, JEANNE D'ALBRET, 1528-1572
0–674–74150–1 Harvard $34.50

● J.H. Salmon
RENAISSANCE AND REVOLT: Essays in the Intellectual and Social History of Early France
0–521–32769–5 Cambridge $49.50

● David Thomson
RENAISSANCE PARIS
An architectural history
0–520–05359–1 California pb $15.95

Louis XIII and Richelieu

● Ruth Kleinman
ANNE OF AUSTRIA: Queen of France
Louis XIII's wife, Louis XIV's mother, Cardinal Mazarin's secret lover. "Traditionally scholars have dismissed Anne as almost a nonentity—lazy, fat, stupid, and of little influence in the government. Kleinman offers convincing revisions of each of these assumptions"—*Choice*
0–8142–0429–5 Ohio State pb $12.95

● A. Lloyd Moote
LOUIS XIII, THE JUST
The hapless monarch of Dumas' *The Three Musketeers* in a new biography. "A powerfully convincing portrait of one of the most inarticulate kings in European history"—Orest Ranum
0–520–06485–2 California $29.95

● Victor L. Tapié
FRANCE IN THE AGE OF LOUIS XIII AND RICHELIEU
Translated by D.M. Lockie
0–521–26924–5 Cambridge pb $15.95

● C.V. Wedgwood
RICHELIEU AND THE FRENCH MONARCHY
More on Louis XIII's Machiavellian minister, whose spies and agents covered Europe no less than his police network covered France; a good introduction for the nonspecialist
0–02–038240–5 Macmillan pb $5.95

Louis XIV and the Ancien Régime

Lenin wrote that the old regime has no beginning, only an end. And for Tocqueville, two generations before him, the roots of the great French Revolution were to be located in the centralizing power of Louis XIV's efficiently run state.

Louis XIV by Charles Le Brun

● Maurice Ashley
LOUIS XIV AND THE GREATNESS OF FRANCE
0–02–901080–2 Free Press pb $12.95

● Nancy Nichols Barker
BROTHER TO THE SUN KING: Philippe, Duke of Orléans
0–8018–3791–X Johns Hopkins $24.95

● Olivier Bernier
LOUIS XIV: A Royal Life
0–385–19785–3 Doubleday $19.95

● Paul Fréart de Chantelou
DIARY OF THE CAVALIERE BERNINI'S VISIT TO FRANCE
In 1665, the 66-year-old Bernini arrived in Paris commissioned to redesign the Louvre. Chantelou, assigned by the king to attend him, kept a diary of the visit
0–691–04028–1 Princeton $49.95

● Pierre Goubert
THE FRENCH PEASANTRY IN THE SEVENTEENTH CENTURY
Translated by Ian Patterson
0–521–26007–8 Cambridge $42.50
0–521–31269–8 Cambridge pb $13.95

LOUIS XIV AND TWENTY MILLION FRENCHMEN
Rather than focusing on the glitter of Versailles, an *Annales* historian portrays the ordinary men and women of the age
0–394–71751–1 Random House pb $4.95

● Cecil Gould
BERNINI IN FRANCE: An Episode in Seventeenth-Century History
0–691–03994–1 Princeton $30.50

● W.H. Lewis
THE SPLENDID CENTURY
First published in 1953, this book offers the lighter side of history: courtly life in the age of Louis XIV
0–688–06009–9 Morrow pb $12.95

➤ FOR OVERSEAS ORDERING INFORMATION, SEE PAGE 1

• Louis Marin
PORTRAIT OF THE KING
The image and symbols of royalty in Louis' France, from an historian and semiotician
Translated by Martha M. Houle
0–8166–1604–3 Minnesota pb $14.95

• Roland Mousnier
THE INSTITUTIONS OF FRANCE UNDER THE ABSOLUTE MONARCHY, 1598-1789
Challenges both Marxist and *Annales* writers by arguing that the need for greater revenues, due to constant warfare, forced the monarchy to move from a system of administration in which offices were owned privately to one in which administrators were employed by the king. For Mousnier, the powers of government were left in the hands of clerks and functionaries, and it was these minor bureaucrats who were the chief beneficiaries of the French Revolution

Volume 1: Society and the State
Translated by Brian Pearce
0–226–54327–7 Chicago $55.00

Volume 2: The Organs of State and Society
Translated by Arthur Goldhammer
0–226–54328–5 Chicago $55.00

• John Noone
THE MAN BEHIND THE MASK
An inquiry into the legend of the Man in the Iron Mask. "As a result of Mr. Noone's expert guidance, we come to realize that what began in the late 17th century as a standard rumor, as various attempts at understanding a report supported by a few more or less dubious shreds of evidence, became . . . rumor historicized, a belief so often repeated that, in one version or another, it was part of the general conception of Louis XIV's reign"—Joan DeJean, *NY Times Book Review*
0–312–02400–2 St. Martin's $35.00

• Orest Ranum
PARIS IN THE AGE OF ABSOLUTISM
Originally published in 1969 and still a good introduction
0–253–19677–9 Indiana $20.00
0–253–20238–8 Indiana pb $6.95

• Jonathan D. Spence
THE QUESTION OF HU
The story of one man who came from China to France in the 1720s
0–394–57190–8 Knopf $18.95

Marie Antoinette

Olivier Bernier
SECRETS OF MARIE ANTOINETTE: A Collection of Letters
Ten years (1770-1780) of revealing correspondences between Marie Antoinette and her mother, Empress Maria Theresa of Austria
0–88064–064–2 Fromm pb $10.95

Joan Haslip
MARIE ANTOINETTE
The "Austrian woman" of Revolutionary fame was less than 15 when she married the future Louis XVI, only 38 when she died
1–555–84183–X W&N $19.95

Who for instance could guess that at Versailles it was the height of bad manners to knock at a door? You must scratch it with the little finger of the left hand, growing the finger nail long for that purpose. Or who could know that you must not *tutoyer* an intimate friend in any place where the King was present? That if the lackey of a social superior brought you a message, you had to receive him standing, and bare-headed? You have mastered the fact that you must not knock on a door, so when you go to make your first round of calls in the great houses in the town, you scratch: wrong again, you should have knocked.

W.H. Lewis
THE SPLENDID CENTURY
0–688–06009–9 Morrow pb $12.95

THE NETHERLANDS

• Pieter Geyl
THE REVOLT OF THE NETHERLANDS, 1555-1609
Holland created itself as a nation in a prolonged resistance to the ambitions of Catholic Spain. This is a masterful account by a great Dutch historian, originally written in 1932
0–06–492382–7 Barnes & Noble $26.50
0–06–492383–5 Barnes & Noble pb $9.95

• Jonathan Israel
THE DUTCH REPUBLIC AND THE HISPANIC WORLD, 1606-1661
Illustrated
0–19–821998–9 Oxford pb $19.95

"Woman Reading," from Rembrandt Etchings *(Dover)*

• Geoffrey Parker
THE DUTCH REVOLT
An admirable, compact study first published in 1977
0–8014–1136–X Cornell $35.00

• Herbert H. Rowen
JOHN DE WITT: Statesman of the True Freedom
0–521–30391–5 Cambridge $37.50

THE PRINCES OF ORANGE: The Stadholders in the Dutch Republic
First published in 1988
0–521–34525–1 Cambridge $39.50

• Simon Schama
THE EMBARRASSMENT OF RICHES: An Interpretation of Dutch Culture in the Golden Age
A generously illustrated analysis, of interest to students both of art history and social history. "With wit and intense curiosity [Schama] teases out the meaning of every aspect of Dutch 17th-century life, from its ideas about sea monsters to its obsessions with hygiene"—Robert Hughes
0–394–51075–5 Knopf $39.95
0–520–06147–0 California pb $15.95

AUSTRIA AND THE GERMAN-SPEAKING STATES

Austria

• Derek Beales
JOSEPH II: In the Shadow of Maria Theresa, 1741-1780
The apprenticeship of "the most radical of the Enlightened despots" traces the development of Joseph's strange personality; the first of two planned volumes
0–521–24240–1 Cambridge $49.50

• Edward Crankshaw
MARIA THERESA
The mother of Joseph II and Marie-Antoinette ruled Austria from 1740 to 1780
0–689–70708–8 Atheneum pb $10.95

• R.J. Evans
THE MAKING OF THE HAPSBURG MONARCHY: 1550-1700
The role of the Counter-Reformation and regional diversity in the emergence of the Habsburg state
0–19–873085–3 Oxford pb $24.95

Prussia

• Robert B. Asprey
FREDERICK THE GREAT: The Magnificent Enigma
Flutist, poet, military tactician, and one of the most enigmatic rulers of the modern period. "A solid, glamorous biography"— *Kirkus Reviews*
0–89919–840–6 Ticknor & Fields pb $12.95

• Gordon A. Craig
THE POLITICS OF THE PRUSSIAN ARMY, 1640-1945
A pioneer study of 1955 arguing against the popular belief that "the Germans are by nature subservient to authority, militaristic, and aggressive." For Craig these qualities "are not inherent in the German character but are rather—as Franz Neumann has written—'products of a structure which vitiated the attempts to create a viable democracy'"
0-19-500257-1 Oxford pb $12.95

• Christopher Duffy
FREDERICK THE GREAT: A Military Life
Solid military history with superb battle maps and tactical analysis
0-415-00276-1 RC&H pb $16.95

• Sidney B. Fay & Klaus Epstein
THE RISE OF BRANDENBURG-PRUSSIA TO 1786
How the energetic efforts of its Hohenzollern rulers made possible the rise of Brandenburg-Prussia from a small frontier state with scant resources to a powerful kingdom with a strong army
0-89874-377-X Krieger pb $6.50

• Gerhard Ritter
FREDERICK THE GREAT: A Historical Profile
Not a biography but a series of essays; this translation is based on the third edition of 1954
Translated with an introduction by Peter Paret
0-520-01074-4 California $29.50
0-520-02775-2 California pb $9.95

THE OTTOMAN EMPIRE

▶ **See also The Islamic World to World War I**

• Norman Itzkowitz
OTTOMAN EMPIRE AND ISLAMIC TRADITION
0-226-38806-9 Chicago pb $6.00

• Lord Kinross
THE OTTOMAN CENTURIES: The Rise and Fall of the Turkish Empire
0-688-08093-6 Morrow pb $14.95

• Bernard Lewis
THE MUSLIM DISCOVERY OF EUROPE
A great historian uses journals, letters, diaries, dispatches, and books to reveal a 700-year-old relationship
0-393-30233-4 Norton pb $9.95

• Peter F. Sugar
SOUTHEASTERN EUROPE UNDER OTTOMAN RULE, 1354-1804
0-295-96033-7 Washington pb $12.95

THE SCIENTIFIC REVOLUTION

The scientific revolution did more than dislodge the earth from the astronomic centrality it had held since antiquity. By Newton's death in 1725, the scientific method had become firmly established as a means of seeking truth. It was widely believed that the universe was governed by uniform laws that the human mind could ascertain. From there it was a short step to the Enlightenment and the discovery of similar laws for human society as well.

▶ **See also Science and Technology**

• Marie Boas
SCIENTIFIC RENAISSANCE, 1450-1630
Excellent on the relation of magic to science and in its treatment of Galileo's trial
0-06-130583-9 Harper & Row pb $9.95

• I. Bernard Cohen
THE BIRTH OF A NEW PHYSICS
A terse survey of astronomy from Copernicus to Newton. Students with some math will profit from the extensive formulas and diagrams
0-393-01994-2 Norton $17.95
0-393-30045-5 Norton pb $7.95

• Thomas Goldstein
THE DAWN OF MODERN SCIENCE: From the Arabs to Leonardo da Vinci
0-395-48924-5 Houghton Mifflin pb $9.95

• G. Holton
THE SCIENTIFIC IMAGINATION
0-521-21700-8 Cambridge pb $15.95

• Margaret C. Jacob
THE CULTURAL MEANING OF THE SCIENTIFIC REVOLUTION
The road from the scientific revolution to the industrial revolution
0-87722-536-2 Temple $34.95
0-394-32799-3 Knopf pb $10.50

• Alexandre Koyre
FROM THE CLOSED WORLD TO THE INFINITE UNIVERSE
0-8018-0347-0 Johns Hopkins pb $10.95

• Thomas S. Kuhn
THE COPERNICAN REVOLUTION: Planetary Astronomy in the Development of Western Thought
The best account of the thought, background, and impact of Copernicus
0-674-17103-9 Harvard pb $9.95

• Robert Mandrou
FROM HUMANISM TO SCIENCE: 1480-1700
Intellectual developments and their social context, from Erasmus to Newton. "Skillfully told and many themes—literary, theological, philosophical, social and economic—are woven together into a convincing narrative"—*Classical Review*
Translated by Brian Pearce
0-14-022079-8 Penguin pb $6.95

Galileo and Newton

• Galileo Galilei
DIALOGUE CONCERNING THE TWO CHIEF WORLD SYSTEMS, PTOLEMAIC AND COPERNICAN
0-520-00450-7 California pb $12.95

• Maurice A. Finocchiaro, translator & editor
THE GALILEO AFFAIR: A Documentary History
Galileo was tried and condemned as a heretic by the Inquisition in 1633, an episode in the history of science that remains a subject of controversy
0-520-06662-6 California pb $12.95

• Pietro Redondi
GALILEO: Heretic
Translated by Raymond Rosenthal
0-691-08451-3 Princeton $29.95

• Gale E. Christianson
IN THE PRESENCE OF THE CREATOR: Isaac Newton and His Times
0-02-905190-8 Free Press $19.95

• Richard S. Westfall
NEVER AT REST: A Biography of Isaac Newton
0-521-27435-4 Cambridge pb $24.95

THE AGE OF ENLIGHTENMENT

Though France was certainly its epicenter, the Enlightenment was a cosmopolitan movement, disrespectful of national boundaries. By the 1770s, to be "enlightened" meant to be in the forefront of intellectual thought throughout the Western world.

▶ **See also Western Philosophy & Modern Political Thought**

• M.S. Anderson
EUROPE IN THE EIGHTEENTH CENTURY, 1713-1783
An excellent short introduction
0-582-49389-7 Longman pb $23.95

• Harvey Chisick
THE LIMITS OF REFORM IN THE ENLIGHTENMENT
0-691-05305-7 Princeton $30.00

• Gerald Cragg
THE CHURCH AND THE AGE OF REASON
0-14-020505-5 Penguin pb $4.95

• Robert Darnton
THE BUSINESS OF ENLIGHTENMENT: A Publishing History of the Encyclopédie, 1775-1800
One of several important books from a historian whose intriguing approach has shed new light on 18th-century France
0-674-08785-2 Harvard $32.00

THE GREAT CAT MASSACRE
A venture into popular culture in the Enlightenment age, which tells a good deal about the collective mentality of the working and other classes
0-394-72927-7 Random House pb $7.95

An elephant visits a library for a truncated reading lesson: an 18th-century engraving from The Delights of Reading *by Otto L. Bettmann (Godine)*

THE LITERARY UNDERGROUND OF THE OLD REGIME
The underbelly of the Enlightenment: how Grub Street served as the ideological precursor of the radicalism of the Great Revolution
0–674–53656–8 Harvard $20.00
0–674–53657–6 Harvard pb $7.95

MESMERISM AND THE END OF THE ENLIGHTENMENT IN FRANCE
0–674–56950–4 Harvard $16.50
0–674–56951–2 Harvard pb $8.95

• Robert Darnton & Daniel Roche, editors
REVOLUTION IN PRINT: The Press in France, 1775-1800
Journals, almanacs, pamphlets, posters, song sheets, board games, ration cards, money—anything that made an impression on a population largely incapable of reading the declarations of their rights
0–520–06431–3 California pb $24.95

• Peter Gay
THE ENLIGHTENMENT: An Interpretation
A massive compendium of the ideas of major and minor figures revolving around the theme of their reevaluation of the culture of classical antiquity

Volume 1: The Rise of Modern Paganism
0–393–00870–3 Norton pb $12.95

Volume 2: The Science of Freedom
0–393–00875–4 Norton pb $14.95

• Norman Hampson
THE ENLIGHTENMENT: An Evaluation of its Assumptions, Attitudes and Values
Argues that the Enlightenment set out to free mankind from superstition and pessimism and establish a reasonable world of experiment and progress. Yet by 1760,

in the works of Rousseau, Kant, and Goethe, there was a new awareness of self that had eluded their predecessors
0–14–021004–0 Penguin pb $6.95

• George Rudé
EUROPE IN THE EIGHTEENTH CENTURY: Aristocracy and the Bourgeois Challenge
A succinct account of institutions, economies, war, and the circulation of ideas in terms of social pressures and needs. Rudé pays particular attention to the role of popular protest as a factor of change
0–674–26921–7 Harvard pb $10.95

• Samia I. Spencer, editor
FRENCH WOMEN AND THE AGE OF ENLIGHTENMENT
Introduction by Elizabeth Fox-Genovese
0–253–32481–5 Indiana $35.00

• Franco Venturi
THE END OF THE OLD REGIME IN EUROPE, 1768-1776
From the Greek uprising of 1770 and the Pugachev revolt in Russia to the crisis of reform in France and the outbreak of the American Revolution. "Venturi presents a panorama of Europe during the critical years when the Old Regime in many countries drifted toward its end. The skillful and fluent translation by Burr Litchfield makes the book a pleasure to read"—R.R. Palmer
Translated by R. Burr Litchfield
0–691–05564–5 Princeton $34.95

The Thought of the Philosophes

• A. Owen Aldridge
VOLTAIRE AND THE CENTURY OF LIGHT
0–691–06287–0 Princeton $53.50

• A.J. Ayer
VOLTAIRE
Voltaire's acerbic wit and iconoclasm have merited a highly sympathetic biography by the leading philosopher-logician of our era
0–394–54798–5 Random House $19.95

• Keith M. Baker
CONDORCET: From Natural Philosophy to Social Mathematics
0–226–03533–6 Chicago $17.00

• Carl Becker
THE HEAVENLY CITY OF THE EIGHTEENTH-CENTURY PHILOSOPHERS
A provocative essay from the 1920s that portrays the 18th-century writers as utopians substituting their own cosmogony and dogma for the older Christian ones; faulted by many commentators for giving inadequate credit to the philosophes for their pragmatism, but still a pleasure to read
0–300–00017–0 Yale pb $7.95

• Ernst Cassirer
THE PHILOSOPHY OF THE ENLIGHTENMENT
Powerful insights derived from considerations of specific figures from Bayle to Kant
Translated by F. Koelin & J. Pettegrove
0–691–01963–0 Princeton pb $10.50

THE QUESTION OF JEAN-JACQUES ROUSSEAU
A succinct Kantian interpretation aimed at scholars and students alike
Translated & edited by Peter Gay
0–300–04329–5 Yale pb $7.95

• Maurice Cranston
JOHN LOCKE: A Biography
The definitive biography of Locke's multifaceted personality
0–19–283044–9 Oxford pb $12.95

• Peter Gay
VOLTAIRE'S POLITICS
0–300–04096–2 Yale $40.00
0–300–04095–4 Yale pb $15.95

• Paul Hazard
EUROPEAN THOUGHT IN THE EIGHTEENTH CENTURY: From Montesquieu to Lessing
0–8446–2226–5 Peter Smith $16.50

• Margaret C. Jacob
THE RADICAL ENLIGHTENMENT: Pantheists, Freemasons and Republicans
0–04–901029–8 Unwin Hyman pb $14.95

• Haydn Mason
VOLTAIRE: A Biography
0–8018–2611–X Johns Hopkins $22.50

• Harry Payne
THE PHILOSOPHES AND THE PEOPLE
0–300–01907–6 Yale $26.00

- Leon Pompa
VICO: A Study of the New Science
0–521–20584–0 Cambridge $34.50

- Jean Starobinski
JEAN-JACQUES ROUSSEAU:
Transparency and Obstruction
"The greatness of *Transparency and Obstruction* consists in its ability to draw the disconnected threads of Rousseau's life and works into one supremely coherent interpretation and to show how his personal drama opened a route into the major concerns of the 19th and 20th centuries"—Robert Darnton, *NY Review of Books*
Translated by Arthur Goldhammer
0–226–77128–8 Chicago pb $19.95

- Ira Wade
THE STRUCTURE AND FORM OF THE FRENCH ENLIGHTENMENT

Volume 1: Esprit Philosophique
0–691–05256–5 Princeton $71.00

Volume 2: Esprit Révolutionnaire
0–691–05257–3 Princeton $45.00

- Arthur M. Wilson
DIDEROT
Definitive biography of the celebrated literary figure of the Enlightenment
0–19–501506–1 Oxford $45.00

- D. Winch
ADAM SMITH'S POLITICS
How the philosophes tried to curtail economic restrictions
0–521–29288–3 Cambridge pb $13.95

A Sampler of Enlightenment Works

Condorcet
SKETCH FOR A HISTORICAL PICTURE OF THE PROGRESS OF THE HUMAN MIND
0–88355–838–6 Hyperion $22.00

Denis Diderot
RAMEAU'S NEPHEW & D'ALEMBERT'S DREAM
0–14–044173–5 Penguin pb $6.95

Thomas Jefferson
WRITINGS
Includes Jefferson's *Autobiography, A Summary View of the Rights of British America, Notes on the State of Virginia, Public Papers, Addresses, Messages and Replies, Miscellany* and *Letters*
0–940450–16–X Library of America $30.00

Jean-Jacques Rousseau
THE ESSENTIAL ROUSSEAU
Translated by Lowell Bair
Introduction by Matthew Josephson
0–452–00674–0 NAL pb $4.95

Voltaire
THE PORTABLE VOLTAIRE
Edited by B.R. Redman
0–14–015041–2 Penguin pb $8.95

Perhaps the most outspoken *libelle*—a pamphlet so sensational and so widely read that it became virtually a prototype of the genre—was the work that especially horrified Voltaire: *Le Gazetier cuirassé* by Charles Theveneau de Morande. Morande mixed specific calumny and general declamation in brief, punchy paragraphs, which anticipated the style of gossip columnists in the modern yellow press. He promised to reveal "behind-the-scenes secrets" (*secrets des coulisses*) in the tradition of the *chronique scandaleuse*. But he provided more than scandal . . .

This sexual sensationalism conveyed a social message: the aristocracy had degenerated to the point of being unable to reproduce itself; the great nobles were either impotent or deviant; their wives were forced to seek satisfaction from their servants, representatives of the more virile lower classes; and everywhere among *les grands* incest and venereal disease had extinguished the last sparks of humanity.

Robert Darnton
THE LITERARY UNDERGROUND OF THE OLD REGIME
0–674–53656–8 Harvard $20.00
0–674–53657–6 Harvard pb $7.95

The French Revolution and Napoleon

"In 1789 France fell into revolution, and the world has never since been the same. The French Revolution was by far the most momentous upheaval of the whole revolutionary age. It replaced the 'old regime' with 'modern society,' and at its extreme phase it became very radical, so much so that all later revolutionary movements have looked back to it as a predecessor to themselves. At the time, in the age of the Democratic or Atlantic Revolution from the 1760s to 1848, the role of France was decisive . . .

The French Revolution, unlike the Russian or Chinese revolutions of the twentieth century, occurred in what was in many ways the most advanced country of the day. France was the center of the intellectual movement of the Enlightenment. French science then led the world. French books were read everywhere, and the newspapers and political journals which became very numerous after 1789 carried a message which hardly needed translation. French was a kind of international spoken language in the educated and aristocratic circles of many countries. France was also, potentially before 1789 and actually after 1793, the most powerful country in Europe."—R.R. Palmer & Joel Colton, *A History of the Modern World*

- Geoffrey Best
WAR AND SOCIETY IN REVOLUTIONARY EUROPE, 1770-1870
A good attempt at international history, first published in 1982
0–19–520501–4 Oxford pb $11.95

- Geoffrey Best, editor
THE PERMANENT REVOLUTION: The French Revolution and Its Legacy, 1789-1989
Essays on the Revolution's legacy, from the practice of nationalism to the pursuit of human rights, to the ways people make revolutions. Contributors include Conor Cruise O'Brien, George Steiner, Norman Hampson, and Eugen Weber
0–226–04428–9 Chicago pb $10.95

- Norman Hampson
THE FIRST EUROPEAN REVOLUTION, 1776-1815
0–393–95096–4 Norton pb $9.95

- E.J. Hobsbawm
THE AGE OF REVOLUTION: 1789-1848
Surveys the two great revolutions of this era: the political revolution of France and the economic revolution of Britain. Highly recommended is the brilliant chapter on the French Revolution
0–451–62362–2 NAL pb $4.95

- R.R. Palmer
THE AGE OF THE DEMOCRATIC REVOLUTION: A Political History of Europe and America, 1760-1800
A pioneer study offering rich comparative insights between the French Revolution and developments in America and elsewhere in Europe; a "bourgeois" response to Hobsbawm's "Marxist" interpretation. An excellent introduction to the Revolution is also provided in Palmer and Colton's *History of the Modern World*

Volume 1: The Challenge
0–691–00569–9 Princeton pb $16.50

Volume 2: The Struggle
0–691–00570–2 Princeton pb $16.50

THE WORLD OF THE FRENCH REVOLUTION
0–06–131620–2 Harper & Row pb $7.95

- John Roberts
REVOLUTION AND IMPROVEMENT: The Western World, 1775-1847
0–520–03076–1 California $42.50

- D.M.G. Sutherland
FRANCE 1789-1815: Revolution and Counter-Revolution
How counterrevolutionary movements affected the course of the Revolution and led to the failure of constitutional government; a good overview
0–19–520513–8 Oxford pb $13.95

THE REVOLUTION: 1789-1799

- Jean-Paul Bertaud
THE ARMY OF THE FRENCH REVOLUTION
The foremost expert on the army of the Revolution, the first to be composed primarily of draftees in a war of national

---

survival. Integrates military and social history to show how the army, as a "school for the republic," paved the way for Napoleon
Translated by R.R. Palmer
0–691–05537–8 Princeton $45.00

● Olivier Blanc

LAST LETTERS: Prisons and Prisoners of the French Revolution
Correspondence by those about to face the guillotine
0–374–18386–4 Farrar, Straus & Giroux $22.50
0–374–52188–3 Farrar, Straus & Giroux pb $9.95

WORDS OF FIRE, DEEDS OF BLOOD: The Mob, the Monarchy, and the French Revolution
0–316–09206–1 Little, Brown $21.95

● J.F. Bosher

THE FRENCH REVOLUTION
An excellent new narrative account by a professor at York University, Ontario, and a student of the late Alfred Cobban. Includes a valuable chronology of events and a who's who in the French Revolution
0–393–02588–8 Norton $24.95

● Chronicle Books

CHRONICLE OF THE FRENCH REVOLUTION
More than 700 pages long, this lavishly illustrated volume follows the progress of the Revolution through pictures and day-by-day accounts for general readers
0–13–133729–7 Chronicle $55.00

● Richard Cobb

THE PEOPLE'S ARMIES
"A kind of documentary film of what revolutionary France looked like, how different citizens behaved, what the attack on Catholicism meant in obscure villages, how food supplies were organized, and what revolutionary orthodoxy implied in the remoter provinces"—Norman Hampson, *NY Review of Books*
Translated by Marianne Elliott
0–300–02728–1 Yale $55.00
0–300–04042–3 Yale pb $17.95

● Richard Cobb & Colin Jones

VOICES OF THE FRENCH REVOLUTION
Produced in the style of the popular *Plantagenet Chronicles*, this volume includes original documents (diaries, newspaper articles, private letters) to convey the events that made up the Revolution
0–88162–338–5 Salem House $29.95

● William Doyle

THE OXFORD HISTORY OF THE FRENCH REVOLUTION
Covers the period 1789-1799
0–19–822781–7 Oxford $29.95

● Christopher Hibbert

THE DAYS OF THE FRENCH REVOLUTION: The Day-to-Day Story of the Revolution
Exciting reading with genuine cinematic appeal
0–688–00746–5 Morrow pb $10.95

The return of the royal family to Paris under armed escort after their attempt to flee the country, June 22, 1791

● Lynn Hunt

POLITICS, CULTURE AND CLASS IN THE FRENCH REVOLUTION
An intriguing new approach emphasizing the importance of rhetoric, ritual, and ceremony in the Revolution
0–520–05740–6 California pb $10.95

● P.M. Jones

THE PEASANTRY IN THE FRENCH REVOLUTION
This book fills a gap in the literature of the Revolution. Jones agrees with Georges Lefebvre's view that the peasantry held center stage during the early years of the Revolution; but he departs from Lefebvre's thesis that the peasantry's participation ran counter to the Revolution's capitalist thrust
0–521–33716–X Cambridge pb $14.95

● Georges Lefebvre

THE COMING OF THE FRENCH REVOLUTION
A brief classic from the 1930s by the greatest authority on 18th-century French rural history. Lefebvre carries the events from the Aristocratic Reaction of 1787 to October 1789
Translated by R.R. Palmer
0–691–00751–9 Princeton pb $8.95

THE FRENCH REVOLUTION
A solid account that remains unmatched

Volume 1: From Its Origins to 1793
Translated by Elizabeth M. Evans
0–231–08598–2 Columbia pb $16.00

Volume 2: From 1793 to 1799
Translated by John H. Stewart & James Friguglietti
0–231–08599–0 Columbia pb $16.00

● Darline G. Levy & others, editors

WOMEN IN REVOLUTIONARY PARIS, 1789-1795
0–252–00855–3 Illinois pb $15.95

● Mona Ozouf

FESTIVALS AND THE FRENCH REVOLUTION
"With enormously rich original materials, she has fashioned a means of understanding revolutionary culture through its symbolic forms"—Lynn Hunt
Translated by Alan Sheridan
0–674–29883–7 Harvard $37.50

● R.R. Palmer

TWELVE WHO RULED
The executive committee of the National Convention—The Committee of Public Safety—and the Reign of Terror, 1793-94
0–691–00761–6 Princeton pb $8.95

● John Paxton

COMPANION TO THE FRENCH REVOLUTION
A-to-Z coverage of names, dates, places, and definitions from the storming of the Bastille to the Napoleonic era
0–8160–1116–8 Facts On File $24.95

● Jean Starobinski

1789: The Emblems of Reason
Exciting analysis of the painting and sculpture the revolutionaries used to purvey their new ideas
Translated by Barbara Bray
0–262–69122–1 MIT pb $14.95

● J.M. Thompson

THE FRENCH REVOLUTION
A clear and factual account, over 40 years old. "The most precise and satisfying history of the French Revolution for many years to come"—A.J.P. Taylor
0–631–11921–3 Blackwell pb $14.95

19th-Century Classics

"His hands are tied, his head bare; the fatal moment is come. He advances to the edge of the Scaffold, his face very red, and says: 'Frenchmen, I die innocent: it is from the Scaffold and near appearing before God that I tell you so. I pardon my enemies; I desire that France—' A General on horseback, Santerre or another, prances out, with uplifted hand: 'Tambours!' The drums drown the voice. 'Executioners, do your duty!' The Executioners, desperate lest themselves be murdered (for Santerre and his Armed Ranks will strike, if they do not), seize the hapless Louis: six of them desperate, him singly desperate, struggling there; and bind him to their plank. Abbé Edgeworth, stopping, bespeaks him: 'Son of Saint Louis, ascend to Heaven.' The Axe clanks down; a King's Life is shorn away. It is Monday, the 21st of January 1793. He was aged Thirty-eight years four months and twenty-eight days."—Thomas Carlyle, *The French Revolution*

Thomas Carlyle
THE FRENCH REVOLUTION
Originally published in 1837; this is a reprint of the 1900 edition
0–8495–0880–0 Arden (2-volume set) $115.00

THE FRENCH REVOLUTION
Edited by K.J. Fielding & David Sorensen
0–19–281843–0 Oxford pb $13.95

Jules Michelet
HISTORY OF THE FRENCH REVOLUTION
Translated by Charles Cocks
Introduction by Gordon Wright
0–226–52333–0 Chicago pb $14.95

Specialized Series from Cambridge University Press

• Michel Vovelle
THE FALL OF THE FRENCH MONARCHY, 1787-1792
A sophisticated chronology from the ancien régime to the fall of the monarchy on August 10, 1792; by a leading undoctrinaire Marxist
Translated by Susan Burke
0–521–28916–5 Cambridge pb $16.95

• Marc Bouloiseau
THE JACOBIN REPUBLIC, 1792-1794
Despite the excesses of the Reign of Terror, the Jacobins initiated the modernization of French civil society
Translated by Jonathan Mandelbaum
0–521–28918–1 Cambridge pb $14.95

• Denis Woronoff
THE THERMIDOREAN REGIME AND THE DIRECTORY, 1794-1799
Translated by Julian Jackson
0–521–28917–3 Cambridge pb $14.95

INTERPRETING THE REVOLUTION

• William Doyle
ORIGINS OF THE FRENCH REVOLUTION
The second edition of this clear and thoughtful book originally released in 1981. "A synthesis worthwhile for any historian or educated reader"—*Journal of Modern History*
0–19–822284–X Oxford pb $14.95

• Emmet Kennedy
A CULTURAL HISTORY OF THE FRENCH REVOLUTION
A comprehensive cultural history of painting, music, fiction, theater, science, education, philosophy, and religion. Includes 95 illustrations
0–300–04426–7 Yale $35.00

Alexis de Tocqueville

Best known in the United States as the author of *Democracy in America*, Tocqueville was also a lifelong student of the French Revolution. Recently a large body of scholarship has affirmed his place in the English-speaking world, and he now stands in the company of great political thinkers, with Aristotle, Hobbes, Locke, Rousseau, and Marx.

Alexis de Tocqueville
THE OLD REGIME AND THE FRENCH REVOLUTION
Still the greatest interpretive work on the subject and a masterpiece of historical thinking. "One of the very few 19th-century studies of the French Revolution that have not been rendered obsolete by the work of later historians"—John Gross, *NY Times*
Translated by Stuart Gilbert
Edited by J.P. Mayer & A.P. Kerr
0–385–09260–1 Doubleday pb $5.95

Robert Boesche
THE STRANGE LIBERALISM OF ALEXIS DE TOCQUEVILLE
"Uncommonly provocative and culturally annotated"—George Armstrong Kelly, *New Republic*
0–8014–1964–6 Cornell $29.95

André Jardin
TOCQUEVILLE: A Biography
A concise and balanced treatment of Tocqueville's public views, this is the first full-scale modern biography. Originally published in France in 1984
Translated by Lydia Davis
0–374–27836–9 FS&G $35.00

R.R. Palmer
THE TWO TOCQUEVILLES, FATHER AND SON: Hervé and Alexis de Tocqueville on the Coming of the French Revolution
0–691–05495–9 Princeton $28.50

L'école de Marx

For Marxists, the French Revolution was the great bourgeois revolution in which a "feudal" aristocracy was deposed by a revolutionary bourgeois capitalist class. The shortcomings of this thesis are articulated in works by Alfred Cobban and François Furet, listed below.

• Richard Cobb
PARIS AND ITS PROVINCES, 1792-1802
The people of Paris and the surrounding countryside in the revolutionary era
0–19–212195–2 Oxford pb $25.00

• George C. Comninel
RETHINKING THE FRENCH REVOLUTION: Marxism and the Revisionist Challenge
A sociologist suggests that Marxists have lapsed into abstractions on the question of the transition from feudalism to capitalism. He argues instead for a return to the principles of historical materialism that found their mature expression in *Capital*
Foreword by George Rudé
0–86091–179–9 Verso $34.95

• Georges Lefebvre
THE GREAT FEAR OF 1789: Rural Panic in Revolutionary France
The frenzy that swept the countryside in the summer of '89 and brought down the old regime by force
0–691–00793–4 Princeton pb $8.50

• Albert Soboul
THE SANS-CULOTTES: The Popular Movement and Revolutionary Government, 1793-1794
The *sans-culottes* were primarily artisans, master craftsmen, shopkeepers, small merchants, and domestic servants, those who for the most part wore long trousers, not the breeches of the aristocracy
0–691–00782–9 Princeton pb $11.50

• George Rudé
THE CROWD IN THE FRENCH REVOLUTION
Riots and riot makers as a key component in the Revolution
0–19–500370–5 Oxford pb $9.95

Anti-Marxist Views

"Though the Jacobins, as every history relentlessly points out, were great respecters of property, their war was a war against commercial capitalism. They may not have intended it that way at the beginning, but their incessant rhetoric against 'rich egoists' and the incrimination of the commercial and financial elites in federalism meant that, in practice, mercantile and industrial enterprise—unless it had been pulled into the service of the military—was itself attacked. Not surprisingly, then, it was the great growth areas of eighteenth-century France—the Atlantic and Mediterranean ports, the textile towns of the north and the east, the great metropolis of Lyon—which were the major casualties of the Revolution. The 'bourgeoisie' which Marxist history long be-

TO ORDER BOOKS AS GIFTS, SEE PAGE 1

lieved to be the essential beneficiaries of the Revolution was, in fact, its principal victim."—Simon Schama, *Citizens: A Chronicle of the French Revolution*

• Alfred Cobban
THE SOCIAL INTERPRETATION OF THE FRENCH REVOLUTION
A provocative, iconoclastic lecture of the early 1960s by the distinguished English historian. "Stimulating and challenging to all those who have so far accepted the orthodox 'bourgeois versus aristocrat' theory"—*Times Educational Supplement*
0–521–09548–4 Cambridge pb $12.95

• François Furet
INTERPRETING THE FRENCH REVOLUTION
The Revolution in light of contemporary experience and the writings of Tocqueville and Cochin; a brilliant and challenging response to the grip of academic Marxism
Translated by Elborg Forster
0–521–28049–4 Cambridge pb $13.95

MARX AND THE FRENCH REVOLUTION
Translated by Deborah Kan Furet
0–226–27338–5 Chicago $34.95

• Simon Schama
CITIZENS: A Chronicle of the French Revolution
How "subjects" became "citizens" and how the France of the old regime, far from dying of infirmity, was a dynamic society obsessed with novelty and technology
0–394–55948–7 Knopf $29.95

While in Europe, I often amused myself with contemplating the characters of the then reigning sovereigns of Europe. Louis XVI. was a fool, of my own knowledge, and in despite of the answers made at his trial. The King of Spain was a fool, and of Naples the same. They passed their lives in hunting, and despatched two couriers a week, one thousand miles, to let each other know what game they had killed the preceding days. The King of Sardinia was a fool. All these were Bourbons. The Queen of Portugal, a Braganza, was an idiot by nature. And so was the King of Denmark. Their sons, as regents, exercised the powers of government. The King of Prussia, successor to the great Frederick, was a mere hog in body as well as in mind. Gustavus of Sweden, and Joseph of Austria, were really crazy, and George of England you know was in a straight waistcoat. There remained, then, none but old Catherine, who had been too lately picked up to have lost her common sense. In this state Buonaparte found Europe; and it was this state of its rulers which lost it with scarce a struggle.

from a letter to Governor John Langdon, dated March 5, 1810 in

Thomas Jefferson
WRITINGS
0–940450–16–X Library of America $30.00

THE REVOLUTION AND THE WORLD

• T.C. Blanning
THE FRENCH REVOLUTION IN GERMANY: Occupation and Resistance in the Rhineland, 1792-1802
Nationalism, as it later came to be known, developed as a resistance movement to the internationalism of the Revolution
0–19–822564–4 Oxford $59.00

• Crane Brinton
THE ANATOMY OF REVOLUTION
A provocative effort to compare the English, American, French, and Russian revolutions
0–394–70044–9 Random House pb $5.95

• Ian R. Christie
WARS AND REVOLUTIONS: Britain, 1760-1815
0–674–94761–4 Harvard pb $9.95

• Friedrich Meinecke
THE AGE OF GERMAN LIBERATION, 1795-1815
The perspective of a great German historian
Translated by Peter Paret & Helmut Fischer
0–520–03454–6 California pb $8.95

• Simon Schama
PATRIOTS AND LIBERATORS: Revolution in the Netherlands, 1780-1813
The definitive study of the Batavian republic and the kingdom of Holland, by the author of *Citizens: A Chronicle of the French Revolution*
0–394–48516–5 Knopf $20.00

THE AGE OF NAPOLEON

▶ See also Military Affairs

• Louis Bergeron
FRANCE UNDER NAPOLEON
The most important contribution of recent scholarship, this is a strong analysis of French society and the nature of the Napoleonic system; originally published in France as *L'Épisode napoléonien: Aspects intérieurs, 1799-1815*
Translated by R.R. Palmer
0–691–00789–6 Princeton pb $10.95

• David Chandler
THE MILITARY MAXIMS OF NAPOLEON
Napoleon's thoughts on the art of war, tactics, strategies, command, and other military giants
0–02–897171–X Macmillan $19.95

• John R. Elting
SWORDS AROUND A THRONE: Napoleon's Grande Armée
An American military historian's view of Napoleonic warfare
0–02–909501–8 Free Press $35.00

• J. Christopher Herold
THE AGE OF NAPOLEON
A colorful popular account
0–317–40584–5 Houghton Mifflin pb $9.95

• George F. Nafziger
NAPOLEON'S INVASION OF RUSSIA
Assembling an army of nearly 600,000, the largest force under a single command seen in Europe until that time, Napoleon crossed the Russian frontier on June 23, 1812. Nafziger's study includes 16 maps and appendices with invaluable and hard-to-find documents
Foreword by David Chandler
0–89141–322–7 Presidio $45.00

• G.E. Rothenberg
THE ART OF WARFARE IN THE AGE OF NAPOLEON
Insights into the character of warfare of the age and Napoleon's military style
0–253–31076–8 Indiana $22.50
0–253–20260–4 Indiana pb $9.95

The Congress of Vienna

Henry A. Kissinger
A WORLD RESTORED: Metternich, Castlereagh and the Problems of Peace, 1812-1822
Shrewd insights into the reconstruction of Europe following the collapse of Napoleonic France
0–395–17229–2 Houghton Mifflin pb $11.95

Harold Nicolson
THE CONGRESS OF VIENNA: A Study of Allied Unity, 1812-1822
Fascinating study of the 19th-century peace settlement by an author who was present at Versailles after World War I
0–15–622061–X HBJ pb $7.95

BIOGRAPHY

• Henri Troyat
ALEXANDER OF RUSSIA: Napoleon's Conqueror
Popular history
0–88064–059–6 Fromm pb $11.95

• R.B. Rose
GRACCHUS BABEUF: The First Revolutionary Communist
Babeuf's "Conspiracy of Equals" was put down and Babeuf was tried and executed in 1797
0–8047–0949–1 Stanford $39.00

• J. Christopher Herold, editor
THE MIND OF NAPOLEON: A Selection of His Written and Spoken Words
0–231–08523–0 Columbia pb $17.50

• R. Ben Jones
NAPOLEON: Man and Myth
0–8419–0441–3 Holmes & Meier pb $12.50

• Georges Lefebvre
NAPOLEON: From Eighteen Brumaire to Tilsit, 1799-1807
Translated by Henry F. Stockhold
0–231–02558–0 Columbia $39.00

NAPOLEON: From Tilsit to Waterloo, 1807-1815
Translated by J.E. Anderson
0–231–03313–3 Columbia $41.00

Napoleon by Délaroche

Prince Blücher von Wahlstadt by George Dawe

The Duke of Wellington by Sir Thomas Lawrence

• Norman Mackenzie
THE ESCAPE FROM ELBA: The Fall and Flight of Napoleon, 1814-1815
The emperor's exile and triumphant return to the Tuileries—and his final defeat
0–19–215863–5 Oxford $24.95

Felix Markham
NAPOLEON
An excellent short biography
0–451–62273–1 NAL pb $4.50

• J.M. Thompson
NAPOLEON BONAPARTE
Was Napoleon the last warrior king, the first modern dictator, or a Byronic hero pursuing an essentially personal ambition?
0–631–16414–6 Blackwell $29.95

• Ernest J. Knapton
EMPRESS JOSEPHINE
0–674–25201–2 Harvard pb $7.95

• Norman Hampson
DANTON
The charismatic revolutionary's tale of espionage, corruption, high politics, and low intrigue rivals the best historical novels
0–8419–0408–1 Holmes & Meier $32.50
0–631–16116–3 Blackwell pb $12.95
THE LIFE AND OPINIONS OF MAXIMILIEN ROBESPIERRE
A narrator and three people of sharply contrasting views—a civil servant, a member of the Communist party, and a clergyman—explore the mind of the notorious revolutionary leader
0–631–16226–7 Blackwell pb $14.95

• J.M. Thompson
ROBESPIERRE
Modern students cannot isolate Robespierre from his impact on Lenin's revolution and the revolutions of the 20th century. This classic, unrivaled biography was first published in 1935
0–631–15504–X Blackwell $34.95

• Duff Cooper
TALLEYRAND
An old regime bishop whose political agility kept him on top—through the Revolution, the Empire, and the Restoration. First published in 1932
0–88064–065–0 Fromm pb $9.95

19th-Century Europe

Revolution and Napoleonic rule raised the political consciousness of much of Europe's lower middle class, which found itself actively seeking self-government, freedom, and an end to foreign domination. At the same time, another revolution as cataclysmic as the French Revolution began to take form. As the Industrial Revolution spread, so too did socialism and other movements for social reform.

• Theodore S. Hamerow
THE BIRTH OF A NEW EUROPE: State and Society in the Nineteenth Century
The rise of the working and middle classes, the growth of literacy and the extension of the ballot, and the profound transformation brought about by the Industrial Revolution
0–8078–4239–7 North Carolina pb $14.95

• David Thomson
EUROPE SINCE NAPOLEON
0–394–30529–9 Knopf $26.00

REVOLUTION AND REACTION: 1815-1848

• Maurice Agulhon
THE REPUBLICAN EXPERIMENT, 1848-1852
0–521–28988–2 Cambridge pb $12.95

• Louis Chevalier
LABORING CLASSES AND DANGEROUS CLASSES IN PARIS DURING THE FIRST HALF OF THE NINETEENTH CENTURY
The most important social history of Paris during the age of Balzac
Translated by F. Jellinek
0–691–00783–7 Princeton pb $14.95

• Clive Church
EUROPE IN 1830
A good bird's-eye view
0–04–940067–3 Unwin Hyman $29.95

- Lewis Namier
1848: THE REVOLUTION OF THE INTELLECTUALS
The great Polish-born historian of the politics of 18th-century England on the Revolution in Central Europe. First published in 1946
0–85672–358–4 Longwood pb $8.00

- Priscilla Robertson
THE REVOLUTIONS OF 1848: A Social History
0–691–00756–X Princeton pb $11.50

- Peter N. Stearns
1848: The Revolutionary Tide in Europe
The 1815 settlement imposed on France lasted until revolutions broke out all over Europe. First published in 1974, this remains the best introduction
0–393–09311–5 Norton pb $9.95

- J.R. Talmon
ROMANTICISM AND REVOLT
The idealism of the reformers and revolutionaries set in the context of Romanticism
0–393–95081–6 Norton pb $9.95

- Alice Hanson
MUSICAL LIFE IN BIEDERMEIER VIENNA
With the fall of the old regime, the culture of the bourgeoisie begins to dominate in Europe
0–521–25799–9 Cambridge $44.50

- William Weber
MUSIC AND THE MIDDLE CLASS: The Social Structure of Concert Life in London, Paris, and Vienna Between 1830 and 1848
0–8419–0218–6 Holmes & Meier $24.50

Romanticism: A Sample

Hector Berlioz
MEMOIRS OF HECTOR BERLIOZ
Translated by David Cairns
0–393–00698–0 Norton pb $8.95

Marilyn Butler
ROMANTICS, REBELS, AND REACTIONARIES: English Literature and Its Background, 1760 to 1830
0–19–289132–4 Oxford pb $8.95

Rupert Christiansen
ROMANTIC AFFINITIES: Portraits from an Age, 1780-1830
0–399–13310–0 Putnam $18.95

Eugène Delacroix
THE JOURNAL OF EUGENE DELACROIX
Translated by Lucy Norton
Edited by Herbert Wellington
0–8014–9196–7 Cornell pb $14.95

Hugh Honour
ROMANTICISM
Lavishly illustrated and a good introduction
0–06–430089–7 Harper & Row pb $12.95

Philip W. Martin
BYRON: A Poet Before His Public
0–521–24186–3 Cambridge $42.50
0–521–28766–9 Cambridge pb $13.95

The Industrial Revolution

▶ **See also Great Britain and Ireland**

- Asa Briggs
THE POWER OF STEAM: An Illustrated History of the World's Steam Age
By the author of *Victorian People* and *Victorian Things*. Includes 200 illustrations
0–226–07497–8 Chicago pb $10.00

- David S. Landes
THE UNBOUND PROMETHEUS: Technological Change and Industrial Development in Western Europe from 1750 to the Present
Landes's study is widely regarded as a classic
0–521–09418–6 Cambridge pb $14.95

- Sidney Pollard
PEACEFUL CONQUEST: The Industrialization of Europe, 1760-1970
The three stages of industrial development on the Continent
0–19–877095–2 Oxford pb $14.95

19TH-CENTURY FRANCE

"I have taken as models the political institutions that once before, at the turn of the century, in similar circumstances, gave new strength to a shaken society and raised France to the height of prosperity and grandeur. I have taken as models the institutions that, instead of vanishing at the first outbreak of popular disturbances, were toppled only by the coalition of all of Europe against us. In short, I asked myself: since France has been functioning for the past fifty years only thanks to the administrative, military, judiciary, religious and financial organizations of the Consulate and the Empire, why should we not also adopt the political institutions of that period? As the creation of the same mind, they must surely embody the same national character and the same practical usefulness."—Louis Bonaparte (later Napoleon III), 14 January 1852, quoted in Alain Plessis, *The Rise and Fall of the Second Empire, 1852-1871*

- John Bierman
NAPOLEON III AND HIS CARNIVAL EMPIRE
The public and private life of the adventurer who presided over France in the age of Offenbach and impressionism
0–312–01827–4 St. Martin's $24.95

- Jean-Denis Bredin
THE AFFAIR: The Case of Alfred Dreyfus
Translated by Jeffrey Mehlman
0–8076–1109–3 Braziller $24.95

- J.P. Bury
FRANCE, 1814-1940
0–416–37930–3 Methuen pb $15.95

- Judith Devlin
THE SUPERSTITIOUS MIND: French Peasants and the Supernatural in the Nineteenth Century
0–300–03710–4 Yale $32.50

- François Furet & Jacques Ozouf
READING AND WRITING: Literacy in France from Calvin to Jules Ferry
From the Protestant Reformation to the New Imperialism
0–521–27402–8 Cambridge pb $21.95

- Joan Ungersma Halperin
FELIX FENEON: Aesthete and Anarchist in Fin-de-Siècle Paris
An influential art critic and publisher of Mallarmé and Rimbaud, Fénéon was an anarchist propagandist for workers' rights. This first major biography in any language includes 140 black-and-white illustrations and 20 colorplates
Foreword by Germaine Brée
0–300–04300–7 Yale $35.00

- Alistair Horne
THE FALL OF PARIS: The Siege and the Commune, 1870-71
After the Franco-Prussian War, the defeated French government used the guns of their conquerors to subdue a revolt of the people of Paris
0–14–005210–0 Penguin pb $7.95

- André Jardin & André-Jean Tudesq
RESTORATION AND REACTION, 1815-1848
Translated by Elborg Forster
0–521–35855–8 Cambridge pb $16.95

- J.R. Jennings
GEORGES SOREL: The Character and Development of His Thought
Foreword by Theodore Zeldin
0–312–32458–8 St. Martin's $25.00

- Norman L. Kleeblatt, editor
THE DREYFUS AFFAIR: Art, Truth and Justice
A catalog and commentary of the Jewish Museum exhibition
0–520–05939–5 California $29.95

Louis Philippe caricatured as a pear by Charles Philipon

★ **FOR COMPLETE ORDERING INFORMATION, SEE PAGE 1**

● Roger Magraw
FRANCE 1815-1914: The Bourgeois Century
The consolidation of bourgeois strength after 1789
0–19–520510–3 Oxford $32.50
0–19–520503–0 Oxford pb $11.95

● Michael Marrinan
PAINTING POLITICS FOR LOUIS-PHILIPPE: Art and Ideology in Orléanist France, 1830-1848
The depiction of revolutionary themes in the world of the *Comédie Humaine*, with special attention paid to Guizot's role in choosing revolutionary subjects for public buildings
0–300–03853–4 Yale $45.00

● Charles Marville
PHOTOGRAPHS OF PARIS AT THE TIME OF THE SECOND EMPIRE
0–933444–39–7 French Institute pb $10.00

● Jean-Marie Mayeur & Madeleine Rebérioux
THE THIRD REPUBLIC FROM ITS ORIGINS TO THE GREAT WAR, 1871-1914
Part of the Cambridge History of Modern France
Translated by J.R. Foster
0–521–35857–4 Cambridge pb $14.95

● John M. Merriman
THE RED CITY: Limoges and the French Nineteenth Century
One hundred years in the life of Limoges, France's first socialist city: the story of urban transformation, political radicalism, and the making of a powerful working class. "A city could not hope to have a better biographer"—*Contemporary French Civilization*
0–19–505682–5 Oxford pb $14.95

● David H. Pinkney
DECISIVE YEARS IN FRANCE, 1840-1847
"Pinkney's book is, without question, a major contribution to the field"—W.W. Rostow
0–691–05467–3 Princeton $33.50

NAPOLEON III AND THE REBUILDING OF PARIS
The Paris of the boulevards was the creation of the Second Empire
0–691–05136–4 Princeton $29.00
0–691–00768–3 Princeton pb $10.50

● Alain Plessis
THE RISE AND FALL OF THE SECOND EMPIRE, 1852-1871
A period of plentiful but dear money. An age that saw the creation of *Les Misérables*, *Olympia*, and the French protectorate over Cambodia. Plessis's recent study is a good attempt to reveal the period's rich complexity
Translated by Jonathan Mandelbaum
0–521–25242–3 Cambridge $37.50
0–521–35856–6 Cambridge pb $10.95

● Charles Rearick
PLEASURES OF THE BELLE EPOQUE: Entertainment and Festivity in Turn-of-the-Century France
0–300–04381–3 Yale pb $17.95

Claude Monet's "Le Banc" (1873), from The Painting of Modern Life: Paris in the Art of Manet and His Followers *by T.J. Clark (Knopf)*

● Jerrold Seigel
BOHEMIAN PARIS: Culture, Politics, and the Boundaries of Bourgeois Life, 1830-1930
An excellent cultural history of the classic era of bohemian life, from Baudelaire to the surrealists
0–14–009440–7 Penguin pb $9.95

● Debora Silverman
ART NOUVEAU IN FIN-DE-SIECLE FRANCE
Republican politicians, museum curators, wealthy collectors, and luxury artisans in an allied quest for stylistic innovation based on the rediscovery of the 18th-century rococo arts
0–520–06322–8 California $35.00

● Richard D. Sonn
ANARCHISM AND CULTURAL POLITICS IN FIN DE SIECLE FRANCE
Argues that beneath the apparent disorder of the period lay a real solidarity, supported by the institutions maintained by the anarchists themselves. Moral, intellectual, and aesthetic bonds formed a subculture, making French anarchism in the 1890s more than the expression of utopian ideals or terrorist violence; with 14 illustrations
0–8032–4175–5 Nebraska $29.95

● Eugen Weber
FRANCE, FIN DE SIECLE
"The epoch immortalized by Marcel Proust in *Remembrance of Things Past* has now found a historian equal to the task of capturing its tones and textures"—Lynn Hunt, *LA Times Book Review*
0–674–31812–9 Harvard $22.50

● Roger L. Williams
MORTAL NAPOLEON III
0–691–05192–5 Princeton $25.00

What the people of this period liked in their furniture was … first of all a symbol of status. The poor had virtually no furniture; even the middle classes took a long time to collect more than bare essentials—a bed, a table and cheap chairs. It was natural that the taste of an age of increasing prosperity, obsessed by social climbing, should have expressed itself in the collection of objects and bric-a-brac, simply to indulge its pleasure in the ownership of property, and that it should have favoured in particular furniture that was solid, impressive and that gave evidence of the hard work and money that had gone into it. Since furniture was above all property, people wanted theirs to look as much like the furniture of the rich as possible. There were alternative ways of gaining status, but when it came to exhibiting one's wealth, it was hard to fool one's neighbours. The people of this period tried hard, nevertheless, to do so; they tried to make their homes—or at least their sitting-rooms—into miniature versions of châteaux. But they favoured the old and the fake-old also because it had the essential quality of property, permanence and investment value.

Theodore Zeldin
FRANCE, 1848-1945: Taste and Corruption
0–19–285100–4 Oxford pb $10.95

● Theodore Zeldin
A master of the new social history, Theodore Zeldin offers understanding of everyday life by studying such topics as family life, education, psychology, crime, newspapers, sport, clothing, and food. His talent for the telling detail is remarkable.

➤ **FOR OVERSEAS ORDERING INFORMATION, SEE PAGE 1**

FRANCE, 1848-1945

Volume 1: Anxiety and Hypocrisy
0–19–285106–3 Oxford pb $10.95

Volume 2: Intellect and Pride
0–19–285096–2 Oxford pb $10.95

Volume 3: Taste and Corruption
0–19–285100–4 Oxford pb $10.95

Volume 4: Politics and Anger
0–19–285082–2 Oxford pb $10.95

Volume 5: Ambition and Love
0–19–285090–3 Oxford pb $10.95

19TH-CENTURY GERMANY

• Theodore S. Hamerow
RESTORATION, REVOLUTION, REACTION: Economics and Politics in Germany, 1815-1871
The German states during the years in which Austria and Prussia competed for leadership, and in which economic ties prepared the way for political unification
0–691–00755–1 Princeton pb $10.95

• Michael Howard
THE FRANCO-PRUSSIAN WAR: The German Invasion of France, 1870-71
0–416–30750–7 Methuen pb $16.95

• James J. Sheehan
GERMAN LIBERALISM IN THE NINETEENTH CENTURY
0–226–75208–9 Chicago pb $12.50

Bismarck

Otto von Bismarck (1815-1898) was the chief architect of the German Empire created in 1871. Skillfully marshalling popular support, he conducted victorious wars against Austria (in 1866) and France (in 1870) and made Prussia the cornerstone of a Germany that would dominate Europe until World War I.

Otto von Bismarck

• Edward Crankshaw
BISMARCK
"A psychologically convincing and wonderfully readable account of a great and evil man"—Isaiah Berlin
0–14–006344–7 Penguin pb $8.95

• Erich Eyck
BISMARCK AND THE GERMAN EMPIRE
0–393–00235–7 Norton pb $8.95

• Theodore S. Hamerow
OTTO VON BISMARCK: A Historical Assessment
0–669–82008–3 Heath pb $10.95

• George O. Kent
BISMARCK AND HIS TIMES
A solid, up-to-date approach
0–8093–0859–2 Southern Illinois pb $8.95

• Fritz Stern
GOLD AND IRON: Bismarck, Bleichroder and the Building of the German Empire
Bismarck's modus operandi after unification; the story of a Jewish banker and the creator of the Second Reich. "A major contribution to our understanding of some of the great themes of modern European history—the relations between Jews and Germans, between economics and politics, between banking and diplomacy"—James Joll, *NY Times Book Review*
0–394–49545–4 Knopf $25.00
0–394–74034–3 Random House pb $14.95

• A.J.P. Taylor
BISMARCK: The Man and the Statesman
First published in 1955. Performs "the difficult task of compressing the most earth-shattering career between Napoleon and Hitler into fewer than 300 pages with conspicuous success"—*TLS*
0–394–70387–1 Random House pb $4.95

Friedrich Nietzsche

"Nietzsche was seventeen when Bismarck came to power and went insane a year before the Iron Chancellor was dismissed from office. Nietzsche's time is the Bismarckian era. It was during Bismarck's rise to power and through the climactic events of the 1860s that Nietzsche and his generation came of age politically."—Peter Bergmann, *Nietzsche: The Last Antipolitical German*

Friedrich Nietzsche
THE PORTABLE NIETZSCHE
Includes selections from *Twilight of the Idols*, *The Anti-Christ*, and *Nietzsche Contra Wagner*
Edited by Walter Kaufman
0–14–015062–5 Penguin pb $7.95

Peter Bergmann
NIETZSCHE: The Last Antipolitical German
0–253–34061–6 Indiana $29.50

Alexander Nehamas
NIETZSCHE: Life as Literature
0–674–62426–2 Harvard pb $9.95

Peter Sloterdijk
THINKER ON STAGE: Nietzsche's Materialism
For Sloterdijk Nietzsche is not "an exacting philologist behind a lectern but rather a thinker on stage, acting out a defiant psychodrama on universal suffering"
Translated by Jamie Owen Daniel
0–8166–1764–3 Minnesota $29.50
0–8166–1765–1 Minnesota pb $12.95

J.P. Stern
A STUDY OF NIETZSCHE
0–521–28380–9 Cambridge pb $16.95

The Second Reich

• Michael Balfour
THE KAISER AND HIS TIMES
0–393–00661–1 Norton pb $10.95

• David Blackbourn & Geoffrey Eley
THE PECULIARITIES OF GERMAN HISTORY: Bourgeois Society and Politics in Nineteenth-Century Germany
Reevaluation of the assumptions thought to distinguish modern German history from that of other nations
0–19–873057–8 Oxford pb $14.95

• Geoffrey Eley
FROM UNIFICATION TO NAZISM: Reinterpreting the German Past
0–04–943038–6 Unwin Hyman $44.95
0–04–943039–4 Unwin Hyman pb $14.95

• Fritz Fischer
FROM KAISERREICH TO THIRD REICH: Elements of Continuity in German History, 1871-1945
Essays include "Steel and Rye," " 'War Socialism' Without Reform," and "The Army and the Power-State Tradition"
Translated by Roger Fletcher
0–04–943044–0 Unwin Hyman pb $9.95

• Hans-Ulrich Wehler
THE GERMAN EMPIRE, 1871-1918
Translated by Kim Traynor
0–907582–32–X St. Martin's pb $14.95

19TH-CENTURY AUSTRIA AND THE HABSBURGS

• Edward Crankshaw
THE FALL OF THE HOUSE OF HABSBURG
Emperor Franz Josef and the last decades of the Austro-Hungarian Empire
0–14–006459–1 Penguin pb $8.95

• Istvan Deak
THE LAWFUL REVOLUTION: Louis Kossuth and the Hungarians, 1848-1849
0–231–04602–2 Columbia $37.00

- Alexander Gerschenkron & others, editors
AN ECONOMIC SPURT THAT FAILED: Four Lectures on Austrian Economic History
0–691–04216–0 Princeton $26.50

- A.J.P. Taylor
THE HABSBURG MONARCHY, 1809-1918: A History of the Austrian Empire and Austria-Hungary
0–226–79145–9 Chicago pb $10.00

> 1900 was both a milestone and a turning point in the history of Budapest. It has a meaning that is more than chronological. It provides a contrast with Vienna 1900 and Paris 1900—two capital cities of capital importance for the culture of the Western world—about which so many books have been written. The *belle époque* is a pleasant nostalgic phrase, but the crisis of an older France and the breaking away from the ideas, ideals and standards of the nineteenth century had begun in Paris fifteen or even twenty-five years before 1900. In Vienna, too, 1900 was the end of the Austrian *fin-de-siècle*, with many of its interesting artistic and intellectual symptoms and alarming manifestations. In Budapest, *le mal* (if it was a *mal-de-siècle*) was only about to begin.
>
> John Lukacs
> **BUDAPEST 1900: A Historical Portrait of a City and Its Culture**
> 1–55584–060–4 W&N $20.95

19TH-CENTURY ITALY

- Christopher Duggan
FASCISM AND THE MAFIA
Examines private papers, police files, and trial proceedings in the period from 1860 through the 1920s and concludes that the idea of the Mafia is a fiction, the result of political calculation and real misunderstanding of the behavior of Sicilians
0–300–04372–4 Yale $27.50

- Salvatore Saladino
ITALY FROM UNIFICATION TO 1919: Growth and Decay of a Liberal Regime
0–88295–762–7 Harlan Davidson pb $9.95

- Gaetano Salvemini
MAZZINI
A classic biography of Giuseppe Mazzini (1805-1872), republican and democrat, Romantic intellectual and publicist, and founder of the "Young Italy" society
0–8047–0496–1 Stanford $17.50

- Denis Mack Smith
CAVOUR AND GARIBALDI 1860: A Study in Political Conflict
The astute prime minister of Piedmont and the swashbuckling Sicilian soldier-hero. First published in 1954 and now reissued with a new preface, this remains the single most important contribution by an English-speaking historian to the study of the Risorgimento. Devoted to seven essential months in 1860, the work examines the events between the Sicilian

rebellion in April and the absorption of all the south into the Italian kingdom of Victor Emmanuel in November
0–521–30356–7 Cambridge $49.50
0–521–31637–5 Cambridge pb $19.95

- Stuart Woolf
A HISTORY OF ITALY, 1700-1860: The Social Constraints of Political Change
0–416–80890–5 Methuen pb $23.00

OTHER COUNTRIES

- Richard Clogg, editor
THE STRUGGLE FOR GREEK INDEPENDENCE: Essays to Mark the 150th Anniversary of the Greek War of Independence
0–208–01303–2 Shoe String $27.50

- Charles & Barbara Jelavich
THE ESTABLISHMENT OF THE BALKAN NATIONAL STATES, 1804-1920
0–295–96413–8 Washington pb $15.00

- John Lynch
THE SPANISH-AMERICAN REVOLUTIONS, 1808-1826
0–393–02349–4 Norton $24.95
0–393–95537–0 Norton pb $9.95

- Juhani Paasivirta
FINLAND AND EUROPE: The Period of Autonomy and International Crises in 1808-1914
Translated by Anthony F. & Sirka B. Upton
Edited by D.G. Kirby
0–8166–1046–0 Minnesota $29.50

THE RISE OF MARXISM

▶ See also Modern Political Thought

- W. Kamenka, editor
THE PORTABLE KARL MARX
Includes *The Communist Manifesto*, *The German Ideology*, selections from *Capital*, letters, and other documents
0–14–015096–X Penguin pb $9.95

- Robert C. Tucker, editor
THE MARX-ENGELS READER
A comprehensive anthology including *The Communist Manifesto*, selections from *Capital*, *The Grundrisse*, and other writings
0–393–09040–X Norton pb $11.95

- George Lichtheim
MARXISM: An Historical and Critical Study
Balanced study by a humanist Marxist reveals strengths and weaknesses of a major 19th-century mode of thought
0–231–05425–4 Columbia pb $16.00

- David McLellan
MARXISM AFTER MARX
An essential text by a leading figure in the field of Marxist studies
0–395–31541–7 Houghton Mifflin pb $9.95

- David McLellan, editor
MARX: The First Hundred Years
0–312–50126–9 St. Martin's $22.50

Biography

- David McLellan
FRIEDRICH ENGELS
Edited by Frank Kermode
0–14–004935–5 Penguin pb $5.95

- Gary P. Steenson
KARL KAUTSKY, 1854-1938: Marxism in the Classical Years
0–8229–3377–2 Pittsburgh $29.95

- Isaiah Berlin
KARL MARX: His Life and Environment
The classic study, newly revised
0–19–520052–7 Oxford pb $8.95

- Jerrold Seigel
MARX'S FATE: The Shape of a Life
0–691–05259–X Princeton $44.50

- H.F. Peters
RED JENNY: A Life with Karl Marx
0–312–00005–7 St. Martin's $14.95

Socialist and Labor Movements

- Tony Judt
MARXISM AND THE FRENCH LEFT: Studies on Labour and Politics in France, 1830-1981
Essays on labor, socialism, and communism in France
0–19–821929–6 Oxford $29.95

- Annie Kriegel
THE FRENCH COMMUNISTS: Profile of a People
Translated by Elaine Halperin
0–226–45290–5 Chicago $27.00

- V.R. Lorwin
THE FRENCH LABOR MOVEMENT
0–674–32200–2 Harvard $22.50

May Day cartoon of a German worker shaking hands with a Russian worker after the 1905 revolution, from The Age of Empire, 1875-1914 *by Eric Hobsbawm (Pantheon)*

• Bernard H. Moss
THE ORIGINS OF THE FRENCH LABOR MOVEMENT: Socialism of Skilled Workers, 1830-1940
0–520–04101–1 California $30.00

• Carl E. Schorske
GERMAN SOCIAL DEMOCRACY, 1905-1918: The Development of the Great Schism
0–674–35125–8 Harvard pb $8.95

• Edmund Wilson
TO THE FINLAND STATION
The roots of modern radicalism, from Fourier and Saint-Simon to Lenin
0–374–51045–8 Farrar, Straus & Giroux pb $12.95

IDEAS, CULTURE, AND SOCIETY

• Theodor Adorno
IN SEARCH OF WAGNER
Reflections on the scores and staging methods of Wagner's operas, the composer's social character, and the ideological impulses of his creativity
Translated by Rodney Livingstone
0–86091–796–7 Verso pb $11.95

• Jacques Barzun
CLASSIC, ROMANTIC AND MODERN
0–226–03852–1 Chicago pb $9.95

DARWIN, MARX, WAGNER: Critique of a Heritage
Focuses on 1859: the year of *The Origin of Species*, *Critique of Political Economy*, and *Tristan and Isolde*
0–226–03859–9 Chicago pb $12.95

• Owen Chadwick
THE SECULARIZATION OF THE EUROPEAN MIND IN THE NINETEENTH CENTURY
0–521–29317–0 Cambridge pb $14.95

• Gordon A. Craig
THE TRIUMPH OF LIBERALISM: Zurich in the Golden Age, 1830-1869
How Switzerland, especially Zurich, became a model in the struggle for political freedom
0–684–19062–1 Scribners $24.95

• Bram Dijkstra
IDOLS OF PERVERSITY: Fantasies of Feminine Evil in Fin-de-Siècle Culture
An exploration of pervasive turn-of-the-century misogyny in the work of hundreds of artists and writers, from Zola to Renoir to Darwin
0–19–505652–3 Oxford pb $14.95

• Peter Gay
THE BOURGEOIS EXPERIENCE: Victoria to Freud

Volume 1: Education of the Senses
Sexuality in the bourgeois age
0–19–503352–3 Oxford $27.00
0–19–503728–6 Oxford pb $10.95

Volume 2: The Tender Passion
Bourgeois theories of love, homosexuality, and sublimation
0–19–503741–3 Oxford $27.95

• H. Stuart Hughes
CONSCIOUSNESS AND SOCIETY: The Reorientation of European Social Thought, 1890-1930
For all its limitations, this remains the best introduction to the intellectual revolution of the period
0–394–70201–8 Random House pb $7.95

• William M. Johnston
THE AUSTRIAN MIND: An Intellectual and Social History, 1848-1938
0–520–04955–1 California pb $12.95

• John Lukacs
BUDAPEST 1900: A Historical Portrait of a City and Its Culture
1–55584–060–4 W&N $20.95

• Franco Moretti
THE WAY OF THE WORLD: The Bildungsroman in European Culture
"Youth" as the new hero of 19th-century society and the symbol of modernity in works of Goethe, Austen, Balzac, Stendhal, Dickens, Flaubert, and George Eliot
Translated by Albert Sbragia
0–86091–891–2 Verso pb $16.95

Fin-de-Siècle Vienna

George E. Berkley
VIENNA AND ITS JEWS: The Tragedy of Success, 1880-1980s
Foreword by Harry Zohn
0–8191–6816–5 ABT $24.95

Peter Gay
FREUD, JEWS AND OTHER GERMANS: Masters and Victims in Modernist Culture
Especially strong on the virulence of anti-Semitism; by the author of *Voltaire's Politics*
0–19–502258–0 Oxford $24.95
0–19–502493–1 Oxford pb $9.95

Paul Hofmann
THE VIENNESE: Splendor, Twilight, and Exile
Hitler, Herzl, Freud, Mahler, Klimt, and Kokoschka all called Vienna home. This lively study by a veteran *New York Times* correspondent covers Vienna from the waltz and psychoanalysis to Nazism and Zionism
0–385–23974–2 Doubleday $22.50

Frederic Morton
A NERVOUS SPLENDOR: Vienna, 1888-1889
0–14–005667–X Penguin pb $7.95

Carl E. Schorske
FIN-DE-SIECLE VIENNA: Politics and Culture
0–394–74478–0 Random House pb $12.95

Hilde Spiel
VIENNA'S GOLDEN AUTUMN: From the Watershed Year 1866 to Hitler's Anschluss, 1938
1–555–84136–8 W&N $22.50

Larry Wolff
POSTCARDS FROM THE END OF THE WORLD: Child Abuse in Freud's Vienna
0–689–11883–X Atheneum $18.95

Freud

▶ See also Psychology for a full list of works by and about Freud

• Peter Gay
FREUD: A Life for Our Time
A National Book Award nominee (1988)
0–393–02517–9 Norton $25.00

• Octave Mannoni
FREUD: The Theory of the Unconscious
This intellectual biography traces in order of appearance Freud's central concepts and provides a summary of each of his major works
Translated by Renaud Bruce
0–86091–834–3 Verso pb $13.95

• Philip Rieff
FREUD: The Mind of a Moralist
Offers an excellent entry into Freud's thinking
0–226–71639–2 Chicago pb $13.95

THE NEW IMPERIALISM

"If France took the whole of Africa," an English colonial critic suggested in 1857, "I do not see what harm she would do us or anybody else save herself." Yet within 15 years, Benjamin Disraeli challenged Britain to "be a great country, an Imperial country, a country where your sons, when they rise, rise to paramount positions and obtain not merely the esteem of their countrymen, but command the respect of the world." By World War I about one-quarter of the world's land surface was carved up as colonies among a half-dozen states. This was the era of the "new imperialism."

The books that follow cover not only Europe's colonial expansion in the late 19th century, but newer forms of political and economic imperialism as they developed in the 20th century.

▶ See also Economics & Great Britain and Ireland

• Winfried Baumgart
IMPERIALISM: The Idea and Reality of British and French Colonial Expansion, 1880-1914
Survey of the various theories of imperialism
Translated by B.V. Mast
0–19–873040–3 Oxford $38.00
0–19–873041–1 Oxford pb $12.95

White tea party in India with native retinue, from The Age of Empire, 1875-1914 *by Eric Hobsbawm (Pantheon)*

J.A. Hobson
IMPERIALISM
The term "imperialism" exploded into general use in the 1890s. When the British Liberal J.A. Hobson wrote his study in 1902 it was "on everybody's lips . . . and used to denote the most powerful movement in the current politics of the western world." Hobson stressed economic motivations and the need for outlets for "surplus capital" as the cause of expansion
Introduction by P. Siegelman
0–472–06103–8 Michigan pb $11.95

V.I. Lenin
IMPERIALISM: The Highest Stage of Capitalism
A radical "student" of Hobson, Lenin argued a decade later that the new imperialism had economic roots in a new *phase* of capitalism, which resulted in "the territorial division of the world among the great capitalist powers"
0–7178–0098–9 International pb $2.75

• **Raymond Betts**
UNCERTAIN DIMENSIONS: Western Overseas Empires in the Twentieth Century
0–8166–1308–7 Minnesota $22.50
0–8166–1309–5 Minnesota pb $11.95

• **Ronald Robinson & John Gallagher**
AFRICA AND THE VICTORIANS: The Official Mind of Imperialism
0–333–05552–7 Humanities pb $19.95

• **Tony Smith**
THE PATTERN OF IMPERIALISM: The United States, Great Britain and the Late-Industrializing World Since 1815
0–521–28076–1 Cambridge pb $13.95

• **A.P. Thornton**
IMPERIALISM IN THE TWENTIETH CENTURY
0–8166–0993–4 Minnesota pb $13.95

The Colonial Empires

▶ **See also Africa**

• **Paul H. Clyde & Burton F. Beers**
THE FAR EAST: A History of Western Impacts and Eastern Responses, 1830-1975
0–13–302968–9 Prentice-Hall $48.00

• **Ernest S. Dodge**
ISLANDS AND EMPIRES: Western Impact on the Pacific and East Asia
0–8166–0788–5 Minnesota $17.50

• **E.J. Hobsbawm**
THE AGE OF EMPIRE, 1875-1914
"Few, if any, present practitioners of the historian's craft can equal the astonishing range and dazzling craft of Mr. Hobsbawm's scholarship"—*NY Times Book Review*
0–394–56319–0 Pantheon $22.95
0–679–72175–4 Random House pb $12.95

• **David Levering Lewis**
THE RACE TO FASHODA
Fast-paced story of the European scramble for Africa
1–55584–058–2 Weidenfeld & Nicolson $24.95

• **Roger Owen**
THE MIDDLE EAST IN THE WORLD ECONOMY, 1800-1914
0–416–14270–2 Methuen $45.00

• **Woodruff D. Smith**
THE GERMAN COLONIAL EMPIRE
0–8078–1322–2 North Carolina $27.50

• **Henry S. Wilson**
THE IMPERIAL EXPERIENCE IN SUB-SAHARAN AFRICA
0–8166–0797–4 Minnesota $20.00

• **Eric R. Wolf**
EUROPE AND THE PEOPLE WITHOUT HISTORY
A cross-disciplinary study of European colonialism looking outward from "native" societies
Illustrated by Noel L. Diaz
0–520–04459–2 California $35.95
0–520–04898–9 California pb $12.95

20th-Century Europe to the Second World War

• **H. Stuart Hughes & James Wilkinson**
CONTEMPORARY EUROPE: A History
An intelligent textbook to Europe since 1914; now in its sixth edition
0–13–169947–4 Prentice-Hall $42.00

• **James Joll**
EUROPE SINCE 1870: An International History
0–06–043415–5 Harper & Row pb $26.95

• **Robert O. Paxton**
EUROPE IN THE TWENTIETH CENTURY
0–15–524719–0 HBJ $35.95

WORLD WAR I

"No power had any over-all, conscious designs for war in 1914. Nowhere, even in the summer of 1914, was a calculated, advance decision made for global war. Rather, the powers, as a result of Sarajevo, became involved in a series of moves and countermoves . . . that stage by stage, step by step, imperceptibly at times, and hardly ever with any true vision of the consequences, placed them in a position from which there was no way back to the negotiating table."—Joachim Remak, *The Origins of World War I*

Diplomatic Background

A.J.P. Taylor
THE STRUGGLE FOR MASTERY IN EUROPE: 1848-1918
In the period between the fall of Metternich and the advent of Wilson and Lenin, nationalism, tempered by the balance of power, dominated European relations. "One of the glories of 20th-century writing"—*Observer*
0–19–822101–0 Oxford $52.00
0–19–881270–1 Oxford pb $14.95

- Oron J. Hale
THE GREAT ILLUSION, 1900-1914
Excellent on diplomacy but also a general history of the Edwardian Age in Europe and England
0–06–131578–8 Harper & Row pb $9.95

- Georges Haupt
SOCIALISM AND THE GREAT WAR:
The Collapse of the Second International
The politics of the International Socialist Bureau Against the Dangers of War, 1900-1914
0–19–827184–0 Oxford $29.95

- James Joll
THE ORIGINS OF THE FIRST WORLD WAR
The most informative current assessment, taking newer interpretations into consideration
0–582–49016–2 Longman pb $17.50

- George F. Kennan
THE DECLINE OF BISMARCK'S EUROPEAN ORDER: Franco-Russian Relations, 1875-1890
A search for the origins of Europe's "delicious euphoria" over the outbreak of war. Kennan is "at his best when revealing how human frailties played havoc with national interests"—Theodore Zeldin
0–691–00784–5 Princeton pb $14.50

- Paul Kennedy
THE RISE OF THE ANGLO-GERMAN ANTAGONISM: 1860-1914
Reaches beyond diplomatic history to compare the two societies and the changes that led to unbearable friction between them. "An imaginatively researched, innovative study of one of the most important historical questions of the pre-1914 period"—Fritz Stern
0–948660–06–6 Ashfield pb $22.95

- Arno J. Mayer
THE PERSISTENCE OF THE OLD REGIME: Europe to the Great War
A challenge to conventional wisdom, arguing that Europe remained in the grasp of a fundamentally feudal and nobilitarian system on the eve of the war
0–394–71117–3 Pantheon pb $7.95

- Joachim Remak
THE ORIGINS OF WORLD WAR I
0–03–082839–2 Henry Holt pb $13.95

- Barbara Tuchman
THE PROUD TOWER
Patricians and anarchists: Europe and America in the years before the Great War
0–02–620300–6 Macmillan $22.95
0–553–25602–5 Bantam pb $5.95

The Great War

▶ **See also Great Britain and Ireland**

- Byron Farwell
THE GREAT WAR IN AFRICA, 1914-1918
0–393–02369–9 Norton $18.95

The grim result of the Somme offensive of 1916, from The Oxford Illustrated History of Britain *edited by Kenneth O. Morgan*

- B.H. Liddell Hart
THE REAL WAR, 1914-1918
A largely military history, written in 1930 by the famous wartime strategist
0–316–52505–7 Little, Brown pb $11.95

- Keith Robbins
THE FIRST WORLD WAR
The major battles against the backdrop of cultural, literary, and diplomatic developments
0–19–289149–9 Oxford pb $10.95

- Harold Elk Straubing, editor
THE LAST MAGNIFICENT WAR: Rare Journalistic and Eyewitness Accounts of World War I
1–55778–030–7 Paragon House $24.95

- Tim Travers
THE KILLING GROUND: The British Army, the Western Front and the Emergence of Modern Warfare, 1900-1918
0–04–942205–7 Unwin Hyman $34.95

- Barbara W. Tuchman
THE GUNS OF AUGUST
"Let the man on the right brush the channel with his sleeve": with the breakdown of negotiations, the Germans sweep through Belgium and threaten Paris. The first months of World War I on both fronts
0–02–620310–3 Macmillan $19.95
0–553–25401–4 Bantam pb $5.95

- Denis Winter
DEATH'S MEN: Soldiers of the Great War
The individual British soldier, in the trenches with five million of his countrymen
0–14–005215–1 Penguin pb $6.95

The Cost of War

- Gerd Hardach
THE FIRST WORLD WAR, 1914-1918
The war economies of the belligerents
0–520–04397–9 California pb $9.95

- Jurgen Kocka
FACING TOTAL WAR: German Society, 1914-1918
Translated by Barbara Weinberger
0–674–29031–3 Harvard $22.50

- John A. Thayer
ITALY AND THE GREAT WAR: Politics and Culture, 1870-1914
0–299–03280–9 Wisconsin $37.50

- Robert Wohl
THE GENERATION OF 1914
An attempt to regain the true story of a generation "lost" to myth
0–674–34466–9 Harvard pb $9.95

The Armenian Massacre

The chaos of World War I allowed the Ottoman Empire to suppress the nationalist aspirations of one of its constituent peoples through mass deportations into the desert, causing the deaths of hundreds of thousands. The surviving Armenians became one of the world's scattered peoples.

Michael Arlen
PASSAGE TO ARARAT
0–374–22989–9 FS&G pb $8.95

Gerard Chalian & Yves Ternon
THE ARMENIANS: From Genocide to Resistance
0–86232–160–3 Humanities pb $9.95

Richard G. Hovannisian, editor
THE ARMENIAN GENOCIDE IN PERSPECTIVE
0–88738–096–4 Transaction $29.95
0–88738–636–9 Transaction pb $14.95

Christopher J. Walker
ARMENIA: The Survival of a Nation
0–312–04944–7 St. Martin's $31.95

The Peace of Paris

● Michael Dockrill & J. Douglas Goold
PEACE WITHOUT PROMISE: Britain and the Peace Conferences, 1919-1923
0–208–01909–X Shoe String $27.50

● John Meynard Keynes
THE ECONOMIC CONSEQUENCES OF THE PEACE
Introduction by Robert Lekachman
0–14–011380–0 Penguin pb $7.95

● Walter A. McDougall
FRANCE'S RHINELAND POLICY, 1914-1924: The Last Bid for a Balance of Power in Europe
0–691–05268–9 Princeton $45.50

● Stanley Weintraub
A STILLNESS HEARD ROUND THE WORLD: The End of the Great War, Armistice 1918
The "sausage machine" grinds to an exhausted halt
0–19–505208–0 Oxford pb $9.95

A BROKEN WORLD: The Interwar Years

Despite the ravages of war, the Europe of 1919 seemed more "a broken world," in Raymond Sontag's phrase, than a Europe destroyed. Yet the hope that the Europeans could pick up where they had left off in 1914 and once again find prosperity was shattered by the Great Depression and the ascension of Hitler in 1933. The Depression cast its political shadow over the entire decade, passing the threat—and often the triumph—of dictatorship over much of the Continent.

● Perry Anderson
CONSIDERATIONS ON WESTERN MARXISM
The nature and evolution of Marxist theory that developed after the Russian Revolution. "By far the best available intellectual history of European Marxism"—*New Society*
0–86091–720–7 Verso pb $9.95

● Modris Eksteins
RITES OF SPRING: The Great War and the Birth of the Modern Age
A cultural history of the influence of World War I on western society, opening with the premiere performance of Stravinsky's *Le Sacre du Printemps* in Paris and ending with Hitler committing suicide in his Berlin bunker while his officers danced in the cafeteria
0–395–49856–2 Houghton Mifflin $21.95

● John A. Garraty
THE GREAT DEPRESSION
Compares the responses of the major nations, noting some paradoxical similarities between the democratic New Deal and the Nazi experience
0–15–136903–8 HBJ $17.95
0–385–24085–6 Doubleday pb $9.95

"Ventriloquist (Caller in the Moor)" (1923), from Paul Klee *by Sabine Rewald (Metropolitan Museum/Abrams)*

● Felix Gilbert
A EUROPEAN PAST: Memoirs, 1905-1945
A historian's early years. By the editor of *The Norton History of Modern Europe*
0–393–02552–7 Norton $19.95

● Charles S. Maier
RECASTING BOURGEOIS EUROPE: Stabilization in France, Germany and Italy in the Decade After World War I
How the elites held on to power in the turmoil of the postwar period
0–691–10025–X Princeton pb $16.95

● Sally Marks
THE ILLUSION OF PEACE: International Relations, 1918-1933
0–312–40635–5 St. Martin's pb $14.95

● Raymond Sontag
A BROKEN WORLD, 1919-1939
The interwar years in the Harper Torch Series
0–06–131651–2 Harper & Row pb $9.95

● Marc Trachtenberg
REPARATION IN WORLD POLITICS: France and European Economic Diplomacy, 1916-1923
A lucid examination of the complicated war debts-reparations question
0–231–04786–X Columbia $38.00

Paris Was Yesterday

● Joel Colton
LEON BLUM: Humanist in Politics
France's first socialist prime minister; by the co-author, with R.R. Palmer, of *A History of the Modern World*
0–8223–0762–6 Duke pb $16.95

● Janet Flanner
PARIS WAS YESTERDAY: 1925-1939
Notes from *The New Yorker*'s "Genêt"
Edited by Irving Drutman
0–15–670990–2 Penguin pb $8.95

● Herbert Tint
FRANCE SINCE 1918
0–312–30315–7 St. Martin's $25.00

The Rise of Italian Fascism

● Victoria De Grazia
THE CULTURE OF CONSENT: Mass Organization of Leisure in Fascist Italy
What the regime meant in practice to the average Italian
0–521–23705–X Cambridge $39.50

● Denis Mack Smith
MUSSOLINI: A Biography
Authoritative and accessible, and rapidly becoming the standard English biography. "While his book may not be psychohistory in the strict sense of the term, there hovers in the background of his account the sort of informed professional understanding that has inspired the best work in that genre"—H. Stuart Hughes
0–394–50694–4 Knopf $20.00
0–394–71658–2 Random House pb $12.95

● John F. Pollard
THE VATICAN AND ITALIAN FASCISM, 1929-1932: A Study in Conflict
0–521–26870–2 Cambridge $37.50

Antonio Gramsci
AN ANTONIO GRAMSCI READER
Edited with an introduction by David Forgacs
0–8052–0924–7 Schocken pb $12.95

LETTERS FROM PRISON
A founder of the Italian Communist party and one of this century's major Marxist theorists, Gramsci composed these moving and brilliant letters between 1926 and 1937
Translated & with an introduction by Lynne Lawner
0–374–52182–4 FS&G pb $8.95

Central and Eastern Europe Between the Wars

● Ivo Banac
THE NATIONAL QUESTION IN YUGOSLAVIA: Origins, History, Politics
"Succeeds in disentangling the astonishing complexities of the Yugoslav situation between 1918 and 1921, and points convincingly to the likely causes of the dramatic developments that followed the creation of Europe's last great multinational state"—Istvan Deak, *NY Review of Books*
0–8014–9493–1 Cornell pb $14.95

● Joseph Rothschild
EAST CENTRAL EUROPE BETWEEN THE TWO WORLD WARS
0–295–95357–8 Washington pb $14.95

● Hugh Seton-Watson
EASTERN EUROPE BETWEEN THE WARS: 1918-1941
0–8133–7092–2 Westview pb $53.50

"Forward, Red Soldiers!" A 1919 Hungarian revolutionary poster, from Art and Politics in the Weimar Period *by John Willet (Pantheon)*

• Rebecca West

BLACK LAMB AND GREY FALCON
West's exhaustive and fascinating travel diary of a 1937 voyage through Yugoslavia
0–14–006355–2 Penguin pb $14.95

Rosa Luxemburg

Elzbieta Ettinger
ROSA LUXEMBURG: A Life
Biography of the Polish-born communist leader who was murdered in 1919
0–8070–7006–8 Beacon $24.95

Norman Geras
THE LEGACY OF ROSA LUXEMBURG
Confronts and refutes Luxemburg's views on the Russian Revolution and socialist democracy
0–86091–780–0 Verso pb $13.95

J.P. Nettl
ROSA LUXEMBURG
Introduction by Hannah Arendt
0–8052–0890–9 Schocken pb $14.95

1919 woodcut commemorating Rosa Luxemburg, from Art and Politics in the Weimar Period *by John Willet (Pantheon)*

THE THIRD REICH

• Karl-Dietrich Bracher

THE GERMAN DICTATORSHIP: The Origins, Structure, and Effects of National Socialism
According to Fritz Stern, probably the most authoritative account
Translated by Jean Steinberg
Introduction by Peter Gay
0–275–83780–7 Henry Holt pb $24.00

• Gordon A. Craig

GERMANY, 1866-1945
A superb synthesis by a leading historian of politics and diplomacy
0–19–822113–4 Oxford $39.95
0–19–502724–8 Oxford pb $16.95

Portraits of Weimar

• Otto Friedrich

BEFORE THE DELUGE: A Portrait of Berlin in the 1920s
"Where art and riot flourished side by side and incredibility was the normal state of things"—*Atlantic*
0–88064–054–5 Fromm pb $12.95

• Peter Gay

WEIMAR CULTURE: The Outsider as Insider
0–06–131482–X Harper & Row pb $7.95

• Walter Laqueur

WEIMAR: A Cultural History
An age of experimentation, from Brecht to Klee to Einstein
0–399–50346–3 Putnam pb $8.95

• John Willett

ART AND POLITICS IN THE WEIMAR PERIOD: The New Sobriety, 1917-1933
From the German typographic revolution to the Brecht-Weill partnership. "An original and challenging book, thoroughly researched and aptly illustrated"—*Times* (London)
0–394–73991–4 Pantheon pb $14.95

Why Hitler Came to Power

• Theodore Abel

WHY HITLER CAME INTO POWER
Foreword by Thomas Childers
0–674–95200–6 Harvard pb $10.95

• David Abraham

THE COLLAPSE OF THE WEIMAR REPUBLIC: Political Economy and Crisis
Reissued version of the controversial analysis of the fall of Weimar and rise of Hitler
0–8419–1083–9 Holmes & Meier $45.00
0–8419–1084–7 Holmes & Meier pb $17.50

• Thomas Childers

THE NAZI VOTER: The Social Foundations of Fascism in Germany, 1919-1933
Statistical analysis that illuminates upper- and lower-middle-class electoral support for the Nazis
0–674–95200–6 Harvard pb $10.95

• Theodor Eschenburg

THE ROAD TO DICTATORSHIP: Germany 1918-1933
The "hundred days" of political and military manipulations that went on around Hindenburg culminating in Hitler's accession to the chancellorship
Translated by Lawrence Wilson
0–85496–117–8 St. Martin's pb $7.00

• Charles Bracelen Flood

HITLER: The Path to Power
Offers new information about the young Hitler and the country he transformed
0–395–35312–2 Houghton Mifflin $29.95

• Sebastian Haffner

THE AILING EMPIRE: Germany from Bismarck to Hitler
By the author of *The Meaning of Hitler*
0–88064–136–3 Fromm $18.95

• Michael H. Kater

THE NAZI PARTY: A Social Profile of Members and Leaders, 1919-1945
0–674–60655–8 Harvard $27.00
0–674–60656–6 Harvard pb $12.50

• Peter H. Merkl

THE MAKING OF A STORMTROOPER
0–691–07620–0 Princeton $25.00

• A.J. Nicholls

WEIMAR AND THE RISE OF HITLER
A good introduction
0–312–86067–6 St. Martin's pb $14.00

• Fritz Stern

DREAMS AND DELUSIONS: National Socialism in the Drama of the German Past
0–394–75772–6 Random House pb $10.95

• Henry A. Turner, Jr.

GERMAN BIG BUSINESS AND THE RISE OF HITLER
The other side of the great debate: Argues that while big business supported many conservative movements, it did not directly support the Nazi accession to power
0–19–503492–9 Oxford $35.00
0–19–504235–2 Oxford pb $10.95

Life, Death, and Politics in the Third Reich

• Bernt Engelmann

IN HITLER'S GERMANY: Everyday Life in the Third Reich
Interviews with the "silent" generation
Translated by Krishna Winston
Foreword by Studs Terkel
0–8052–0864–X Schocken pb $8.95

• Henry Grosshans

HITLER AND THE ARTISTS
How Hitler's perverse notions of cultural advancement led to clashes with many of Germany's major artists; illustrated
0–8419–0746–3 Holmes & Meier $34.50

• Klaus Hildebrand
THE THIRD REICH
A German scholar tackles the "repellent subject" and analyzes the politics of the era
Translated by P.S. Falla
0–04–943033–5 Unwin Hyman $34.95
0–04–943032–7 Unwin Hyman pb $12.95

• David Irving
GORING: A Biography
Reichsmarschal, drug addict, and onetime mental patient, Hermann Göring was Hitler's alter ego and chosen successor. This is the first full-length biography of him and the only one in print
0–688–06606–2 Morrow $22.95

• Claudia Koonz
MOTHERS IN THE FATHERLAND: Women, Family Life and Nazi Ideology, 1919-1945
How the Nazis mobilized women in their support
0–312–54933–4 St. Martin's $25.00
0–312–02256–5 St. Martin's pb $14.95

• Richard Mandell
THE NAZI OLYMPICS
A look at the 1936 Munich Olympics, one of the most bizarre episodes in modern sports
0–252–01325–5 Illinois pb $9.95

• George L. Mosse
NAZI CULTURE
Choice selections from the newspapers, the literature, and the public pronouncements of the age
0–8052–0668–X Schocken pb $9.95

• Robert N. Proctor
RACIAL HYGIENE: Medicine Under the Nazis
The links between science and politics in the rise of the Third Reich; highly recommended
0–674–74580–9 Harvard $34.95

• Joachim Remak, editor
THE NAZI YEARS: A Documentary History
0–671–62830–5 Simon & Schuster pb $8.95

• David Schoenbaum
HITLER'S SOCIAL REVOLUTION: Class and Status in Nazi Germany, 1933-1939
Argues that Hitler, by leveling classes, accomplished a social revolution
0–393–00993–9 Norton pb $9.95

• William L. Shirer
THE RISE AND FALL OF THE THIRD REICH
A popular and widely read journalistic account
0–671–42813–6 Simon & Schuster pb $17.95

• Ronald Smelser
ROBERT LEY: Hitler's Labour Front Leader
The architect of the German Labor Front. Corrupt and alcoholic, Ley typified the criminal mentality of the Nazi elite
0–85496–161–5 St. Martin's $35.00

• Albert Speer
INSIDE THE THIRD REICH
An insider's account of Hitler's machine, to be read with caution
0–02–037500–X Macmillan pb $10.95

HITLER: Studies in Tyranny

• Alan Bullock
HITLER: A Study in Tyranny
A solid biography; tells as much about the times as the man. "Remains the best biography of Adolf Hitler in English"— Gordon A. Craig, *NY Review of Books*
0–06–131123–5 Harper & Row pb $13.95

• William Carr
HITLER: A Study in Personality and Politics
0–7131–6462–X Edward Arnold pb $16.95

Joachim C. Fest
THE FACE OF THE THIRD REICH: Portraits of the Nazi Leadership
Translated by Michael Bullock
0–394–73407–6 Pantheon pb $9.50
HITLER
"An enormous mural of sorcery, conquest, war and destruction"— *Nation*
Translated by Richard & Clara Winston
0–394–72023–7 Random House pb $14.95

• Sebastian Haffner
THE MEANING OF HITLER
The psychological and historical forces that shaped the mind of Hitler and made his rise possible
Translated by Ewald Osers
0–674–55775–1 Harvard pb $7.95

• Adolf Hitler
MEIN KAMPF
Hitler's blueprint for National Socialism, composed while he was in prison in the 1920s
0–395–07801–6 Houghton Mifflin $17.95
0–395–08362–1 Houghton Mifflin pb $9.95

• J.P. Stern
HITLER: The Führer and the People
0–520–02952–6 California pb $9.95

• John Toland
ADOLF HITLER
0–345–33848–0 Ballantine pb $12.95

• H.R. Trevor-Roper
THE LAST DAYS OF HITLER
0–02–038010–0 Macmillan pb $7.95

• Zbynek Zeman
HECKLING HITLER: Caricatures of the Third Reich
A leading authority of the art of propaganda assembles the best political caricatures of Hitler and his henchmen; 178 illustrations in all
0–87451–403–7 New England pb $14.95

FASCISM AND TOTALITARIANISM

"Totalitarianism is the antithesis of liberalism and its most implacable enemy. It rejects the philosophical principles on which the liberal order rests. It denies the ultimate worth of the individual, valuing him only insofar as he is useful to the state or national community . . . It also denies the fundamental harmony of human interests, stressing instead the universality of conflict, whether social, national, or racial. From the point of view of these assumptions, totalitarianism is a conservative creed. It is a mass-oriented movement, harnessing the emotions and aspirations of the multitude not to satisfy them but, with their help, to destroy resistance to total power whether at home or abroad. It is conservative in its aims and radical in its means."—Richard Pipes, *Western Civilization: The Struggle for Empire to Europe in the Modern World*

• Hannah Arendt
THE ORIGINS OF TOTALITARIANISM
0–15–670153–7 HBJ pb $10.95

• F.L. Carsten
THE RISE OF FASCISM
0–520–04307–3 California $28.00
0–520–04643–9 California pb $11.95

• H.R. Kedward
FASCISM IN WESTERN EUROPE, 1900-1945
0–8147–4551–2 NYU $25.00

• Walter Laqueur, editor
FASCISM—A READER'S GUIDE: Analysis, Interpretations and Bibliography
An academic guide to the accumulated wisdom on fascism
0–520–03033–8 California $45.50
0–520–03642–5 California pb $11.95

From Mussolini *by Denis Mack Smith* (*Knopf*)

- George L. Mosse
THE CRISIS OF GERMAN IDEOLOGY:
Intellectual Origins of the Third Reich
The development and institutionalization
of the ideas behind National Socialism
0–8052–0669–8 Schocken pb $7.95

- Stanley G. Payne
FASCISM: A Comparative Approach
Toward a Definition
0–299–08060–9 Wisconsin $25.00
0–299–08064–1 Wisconsin pb $8.95

- Fritz Stern
THE POLITICS OF CULTURAL
DESPAIR: A Study in the Rise of the
Germanic Ideology
The development of Nazi ideology, as
evidenced by the writings of three German
cultural critics, Paul de Lagarde, Julius
Langbehn, and Moeller van den Bruck
0–520–02626–8 California pb $10.95

THE SPANISH CIVIL WAR

Gerald Brenan
THE SPANISH LABYRINTH
0–521–09107–1 Cambridge pb $14.95

- Valentine Cunningham, editor
SPANISH FRONT: Writers on the Civil
War
Excerpts from Trotsky, Woolf, Auden,
Eliot, Orwell, Mann, Hemingway, and
others
0–19–282006–0 Oxford pb $8.95

- Ronald Fraser
BLOOD OF SPAIN: An Oral History of
the Spanish Civil War
0–394–73854–3 Pantheon pb $12.95

- J. Fusi
FRANCO: A Biography
Introduction by Raymond Carr
0–06–433127–X Harper & Row $25.00

- Gabriel Jackson
THE SPANISH REPUBLIC AND THE
CIVIL WAR, 1931-1939
Polished, detailed account, sympathetic to
the liberal Republican cause
0–691–00757–8 Princeton pb $14.95

- Nancy MacDonald
HOMAGE TO THE SPANISH EXILES:
Voices from the Spanish Civil War
Introduction by Mary McCarthy
0–898–85325–7 Insight $24.95

- George Orwell
HOMAGE TO CATALONIA
Memoirs of fighting for the Republicans
Introduction by Lionel Trilling
0–15–642117–8 HBJ pb $4.95

- Stanley G. Payne
FALANGE: A History of Spanish Fascism
0–8047–0059–1 Stanford pb $10.95

THE FRANCO REGIME, 1936-1975
0–299–11070–2 Wisconsin $30.00

- Paul Preston
THE COMING OF THE SPANISH CIVIL
WAR: Reform, Reaction and Revolution in
the Second Republic
0–416–35720–2 Methuen pb $13.95

- R. Dan Richardson
THE COMINTERN ARMY: The
International Brigades and the Spanish
Civil War
0–8131–1439–X Kentucky $20.00

- Peter Stansky & William Abrahams
JOURNEY TO THE FRONTIER: Two
Roads to the Spanish Civil War
0–226–77111–3 Chicago pb $12.50

- Hugh Thomas
THE SPANISH CIVIL WAR
0–06–014278–2 Harper & Row $40.50

- Ann Wilson, editor
THE SPANISH CIVIL WAR: A History in
Pictures
Introduction by Raymond Carr
0–393–30499–X Norton pb $12.95

The Second World War

GENERAL HISTORIES

- Peter Calvocoressi & others
TOTAL WAR: Causes and Courses of the
Second World War
A superb account covering all the theaters
of the war. Hardcover version is a newly
revised edition that incorporates
information from official documents
released in the past 15 years
0–394–57811–2 Pantheon $39.95
0–14–021422–4 Penguin pb $10.95

Winston S. Churchill
THE SECOND WORLD WAR
The complete set
Introduction by John Keegan
0–395–07541–6 Houghton Mifflin (set) $177.95

Volume 1: The Gathering Storm
The origins of, and entry into, the war
and Churchill's appointment as prime
minister at age 65
0–395–07537–8 Houghton Mifflin $29.95
0–395–41055–X Houghton Mifflin pb $9.95

Volume 2: Their Finest Hour
The months from May to December
1940
0–395–07536–X Houghton Mifflin $29.95
0–395–41056–8 Houghton Mifflin pb $9.95

Volume 3: The Grand Alliance
1941: the year of the sinking of the
Bismarck, Hitler's invasion of Russia,
Pearl Harbor, and the formation of the
"Grand Alliance"
0–395–07538–6 Houghton Mifflin $29.95
0–395–41057–6 Houghton Mifflin pb $9.95

Volume 4: The Hinge of Fate
The turning of the tide in the Pacific
and North Africa
0–395–07539–4 Houghton Mifflin $29.95
0–395–41058–4 Houghton Mifflin pb $9.95

Volume 5: Closing the Ring
Allied efforts up to the Normandy
invasion
0–395–07535–1 Houghton Mifflin $29.95
0–395–41059–2 Houghton Mifflin pb $9.95

Volume 6: Triumph and Tragedy
From the D-Day landings to the
Japanese surrender
0–395–07540–8 Houghton Mifflin $29.95
0–395–41060–6 Houghton Mifflin pb $9.95

- D. Fodor
THE NEUTRALS
Those who stayed at peace in a world at
war
0–8094–3432–6 Silver, Burdett & Ginn $23.95

- Edwin P. Hoyt
THE GI'S WAR: The Story of American
Soldiers in Europe in World War II
0–07–030627–3 McGraw-Hill $24.95

- Robert Leckie
DELIVERED FROM EVIL: The Saga of
World War II
A one-volume history that makes excellent
use of first-person testimonies
0–06–015812–3 Harper & Row $29.95
0–06–091535–8 Harper & Row pb $12.95

- B.H. Liddell Hart
HISTORY OF THE SECOND WORLD
WAR
A survey by the late British military
historian
0–399–50445–1 Putnam pb $16.95

- Graham Lyons, editor
THE RUSSIAN VERSION OF THE
SECOND WORLD WAR
A challenge to the West's conventional
wisdom about the course of the war,
constructed from Soviet texts and historical
writing
0–87196–136–9 Facts On File $19.95

- John MacDonald
GREAT BATTLES OF WORLD WAR II
A beautifully illustrated book, filled with
maps, photographs, and computer graphics
that recreate the most vital combats of the
war, including Dunkirk, Midway,
Guadalcanal, El Alamein, Stalingrad,
Normandy, Okinawa, and others
0–02–577350–X Macmillan $35.00
0–02–044463–X Macmillan pb $19.95

- Bill Mauldin
BILL MAULDIN'S GREATEST WORLD
WAR II CARTOONS
These cartoons follow "Willie" and "Joe"
from training camp to the war and back
home
0–89141–159–3 Presidio pb $12.95

• Alan S. Milward
WAR, ECONOMY AND SOCIETY: 1939-1945
The war years with a focus on economic issues
0–520–03942–4 California pb $12.95

• The New Yorker
THE NEW YORKER BOOK OF WAR PIECES: London, 1939-Hiroshima, 1945
A re-release of the classic collection of war reportage, first published in 1947. Includes A.J. Liebling on the civic pride of Hull, the most-bombed city in England; Janet Flanner on "Paris, Germany—The Capital of Limbo"; and John Hersey on Lt. John F. Kennedy, survivor of PT-109
0–8052–4049–7 Schocken $24.95
0–8052–0901–8 Schocken pb $12.95

• Ernie Pyle
ERNIE'S WAR: The Best of Ernie Pyle's World War II Dispatches
Bulletins from the front by the noted war correspondent
0–671–64452–1 Simon & Schuster pb $9.95

• David Scherman, editor
LIFE GOES TO WAR: A Pictorial History of World War II
Brilliant work by the world's great photojournalists
0–671–79077–3 Simon & Schuster pb $14.95

• I.F. Stone
THE WAR YEARS, 1939-1945
Part of the *Nonconformist History of Our Times* series
0–316–81771–6 Little, Brown $18.95

• C.J. Sulzberger
WORLD WAR II
"An objective and engrossing commentary"—*San Francisco Chronicle*
0–8281–0331–3 Houghton Mifflin pb $9.95

• Studs Terkel
THE GOOD WAR: An Oral History of World War II
Interviews with men and women, whites, blacks, and Asians, combat soldiers, officers, and those who stayed at home
0–394–53103–5 Pantheon $19.95

• Gerhard L. Weinberg
WORLD IN THE BALANCE: Behind the Scenes of World War II
"The dean of American historians specializing in the history of Nazi Germany has written a book that will benefit anyone interested in modern history"—*History Teacher*
0–87451–217–4 New England pb $7.00

• Gordon Wright
THE ORDEAL OF TOTAL WAR, 1939-1945
Originally published in the late 1960s, this remains an excellent survey of the war's military, diplomatic, social, technological, and psychological ramifications; highly recommended
0–06–131408–0 Harper & Row pb $8.95

Hitler and Stalin in David Low's 1939 cartoon, from The Deadly Embrace *by Anthony Read and David Fisher* (Norton)

The War on Radio

Edward R. Murrow
THIS IS LONDON
Transcripts of Murrow's radio broadcasts from England recall the early days of the war—the invasion of Poland, the war in Norway, the London blitz
0–8052–0882–8 Schocken pb $7.95

George Orwell
ORWELL: The War Commentaries
The lost texts of Orwell's weekly radio commentaries, transmitted from December 1941 to February 1943. "Provides a fresh perspective on how a major literary talent and significant socialist thinker perceived one of the climactic events of our time"—*Booklist*
Edited by W.J. West
0–8052–0889–5 Schocken pb $8.95

THE ROAD TO WAR

• Anthony Adamthwaite
THE MAKING OF THE SECOND WORLD WAR
0–04–940057–6 Unwin Hyman pb $11.95

• Robert Dallek
FRANKLIN D. ROOSEVELT AND AMERICAN FOREIGN POLICY, 1932-1945
A full-scale history of American diplomacy during FDR's presidency
0–19–502894–5 Oxford pb $12.95

• Robert Divine
THE RELUCTANT BELLIGERENT: American Entry into World War II
0–394–34171–6 Random House pb $10.00

• Waldo Heinrichs
THRESHOLD OF WAR: Franklin D. Roosevelt and American Entry into World War II
Roosevelt emerges as a cautious and deliberate leader in this narrative of the climactic months leading up to Pearl Harbor
0–19–504424–X Oxford $21.95

• Eberhard Jackel
HITLER'S WORLD VIEW: A Blueprint for Power
Foreword by Franklin L. Ford
0–674–40425–4 Harvard pb $6.95

• Gordon Martel, editor
THE ORIGINS OF THE SECOND WORLD WAR RECONSIDERED: The A.J.P. Taylor Debate after Twenty-Five Years
0–04–940085–1 Unwin Hyman pb $14.95

• Anthony Read & David Fisher
THE DEADLY EMBRACE: Hitler, Stalin, and the Nazi-Soviet Pact, 1939-1941
0–393–02528–4 Norton $25.00

• Norman Rich
HITLER'S WAR AIMS: Ideology, the Nazi State, and the Course of Expansion
A good overview by a shrewd historian of diplomacy
0–393–00802–9 Norton pb $10.95

• E.M. Robertson, editor
THE ORIGINS OF THE SECOND WORLD WAR
0–312–58870–4 St. Martin's pb $13.00

• A.J.P. Taylor
THE ORIGINS OF THE SECOND WORLD WAR
Taylor's influential work remains a controversial one, arguing that responsibility for the war and its devastation is too complex an issue to be blamed entirely on Hitler
0–689–70658–8 Atheneum pb $9.95

➤ **FOR OVERSEAS ORDERING INFORMATION, SEE PAGE 1**

• Christopher Thorne
THE APPROACH OF WAR, 1938-1939
0–312–04655–3 St. Martin's $14.95

• Gerhard L. Weinberg
THE FOREIGN POLICY OF HITLER'S GERMANY: Starting World War II, 1937-1939
0–226–88513–5 Chicago pb $10.95

THE WAR AT HOME: The United States

• John Morton Blum
V WAS FOR VICTORY: Politics and American Culture During World War II
0–15–693628–3 HBJ pb $7.95

• David Brinkley
WASHINGTON GOES TO WAR
0–394–51025–9 Knopf $18.95

• Sherna Berger Gluck
ROSIE THE RIVETER REVISITED: Women, the War and Social Change
An oral history of the women who went to work to help with the war effort and the lives they led after the war ended
0–452–00911–1 Meridian pb $8.95

• William A. Klingaman
1941: Our Lives in a World on the Edge
0–06–015948–0 Harper & Row $24.50

• Allen W. Koop
STARK DECENCY: German Prisoners of War in a New England Village
0–87451–458–4 New England $18.00
0–87451–468–1 New England pb $8.95

• Geoffrey Perret
DAYS OF SADNESS, YEARS OF TRIUMPH: The American People, 1939-1945
0–299–10394–3 Wisconsin pb $13.95

• Leila J. Rupp
MOBILIZING WOMEN FOR WAR: German and American Propaganda, 1939-1945
0–691–04649–2 Princeton $31.50

• K.R.M. Short, editor
FILM AND RADIO PROPAGANDA IN WORLD WAR II
0–87049–386–8 Tennessee $27.95

• Elfrieda Shukert & Barbara Scibetta
WAR BRIDES OF WORLD WAR II
Based on interviews with 2000 of the estimated one million foreign women who married Americans during and after the war
0–89141–309–X Presidio $18.95

The American Concentration Camps

In one of the ugliest episodes in wartime America, some 120,000 Japanese-Americans were evacuated from their homes and relocated to internment camps in the months following the attack on Pearl Harbor. Renewed attention to the subject—culminating in reparations payments offered to the remaining victims by the US government—has produced books that focus both on the politics and human consequences of the internment.

• John Armor & Peter Wright
MANZANAR
A largely photographic account of life in the camps
Commentary by John Hersey
Photographs by Ansel Adams
0–8129–1727–8 Times Books $27.00

• Deborah Gesensway
BEYOND WORDS: Images from America's Concentration Camps
The authors "have collected from attics, basements, and college libraries prison paintings by internees, ranging from comic caricatures to desolate landscapes . . . The result is not only beyond words, it is even beyond newsreels, since the moving hand of art is always present"—*NY Times Book Review*
0–8014–1919–0 Cornell $29.95
0–8014–9522–9 Cornell pb $18.95

• Peter Irons
JUSTICE AT WAR: The Inside Story of the Japanese American Internment
The role of the Justice Department and interviews with participants, including the three defendants in the cases that reached the Supreme Court
0–19–503273–X Oxford $24.95
0–19–503497–X Oxford pb $11.95

• Michi Weglyn
YEARS OF INFAMY: The Untold Story of America's Concentration Camps
0–688–07996–2 Morrow $19.95

THE WAR IN EUROPE

General Military Accounts

• F.W. Von Mellenthin
PANZER BATTLES
0–345–32158–8 Ballantine pb $4.95

• Shelby L. Stanton
ORDER OF BATTLE: U.S. Army, World War II
Covers all the theaters of the war
0–89141–195–X Presidio $60.00

• Charles Whiting
POOR BLOODY INFANTRY: 1939-1945
0–09–172380–9 David & Charles $34.95

Germany

▶ See also 20th-Century Europe to the Second World War for a complete list on Nazi Germany

• Robert Goldston
THE LIFE AND DEATH OF NAZI GERMANY
Short, popular account of the Nazi era
0–449–30030–7 Fawcett pb $3.95

• Claudia Koonz
MOTHERS IN THE FATHERLAND: Women, Family Life and Nazi Ideology, 1919-1945
Traces the role of women in the massive German war effort
0–312–54933–4 St. Martin's $25.00
0–312–02256–5 St. Martin's pb $14.95

• James Lucas
WORLD WAR II THROUGH GERMAN EYES
0–85368–863–X Sterling $24.95

• Albert Seaton
THE GERMAN ARMY, 1933-1945
0–452–00739–9 NAL pb $8.95

• William L. Shirer
THE RISE AND FALL OF THE THIRD REICH
The popular journalistic account; readers should also consult Joachim Fest's *Hitler*
0–671–42813–6 Simon & Schuster pb $17.95

• Marie Vassiltchikov
BERLIN DIARIES, 1940-1945
Edited by Anne Freedgood
0–394–75777–7 Random House pb $8.95

Britain

▶ See also Great Britain and Ireland

• David Fraser
AND WE SHALL SHOCK THEM: The British Army in the Second World War
0–340–27085–3 David & Charles $30.95

• Paul Fussell
WARTIME: Understanding and Behavior in the Second World War
0–19–503797–9 Oxford $20.00

• Tom Harrison
LIVING THROUGH THE BLITZ
A record of life in wartime London. "Provides for the first time an accurate analysis of morale in the blitzed cities, freed at last from the accretions of patriotic legend"—*New Society*
0–8052–0892–5 Schocken pb $11.95

• Warren F. Kimball, editor
CHURCHILL AND ROOSEVELT: The Complete Correspondence
An encyclopedic collection covering every aspect of the war years. Together with Kimball's commentary, the three volumes of letters provide a major interpretive account of Anglo-American diplomacy
0–691–05649–8 Princeton (set) $160.00
0–691–00817–5 Princeton (set) pb $65.00

• A.J.P. Taylor
ENGLISH HISTORY, 1914-1945
0–19–500304–7 Oxford pb $16.95

Italy

• Henry Adams
ITALY AT WAR
An extensively illustrated history of Mussolini's attempt to recreate the Roman Empire
0–8094–3424–5 Silver, Burdett & Ginn $23.95

London's Tower Bridge silhouetted in a 1940 bombing, from Life: The First Fifty Years *edited by Phillip B. Kunhardt, Jr. (Little, Brown)*

• Maria de Blasio
THE OTHER ITALY: Italian Resistance in World War II
A focus on Jews, women, and the Catholic clergy who rose up against the Church's official indifference
0–393–02568–3 Norton $18.95

• MacGregor Knox
MUSSOLINI UNLEASHED, 1939-1941: Politics and Strategy in Fascist Italy's Last War
0–521–23917–6 Cambridge $42.50

• Iris Origo
WAR IN VAL D'ORCIA: An Italian War Diary, 1943-1944
Foreword by Denis Mack Smith
0–87923–500–4 Godine $14.95
0–87923–476–8 Godine pb $8.95

France

• Jean-Pierre Azema
FROM MUNICH TO THE LIBERATION, 1938-1944
Part of the first-rate Cambridge History of Modern France series
Translated by Janet Lloyd
0–521–25237–7 Cambridge $44.50
0–521–27238–6 Cambridge pb $15.95

• Marguerite Duras
THE WAR: A Memoir
0–394–75039–X Pantheon pb $6.95

• A.J. Liebling
THE ROAD BACK TO PARIS
The New Yorker goes to war
1–55778–106–0 Paragon pb $8.95

• Robin Mackness
MASSACRE AT ORADOUR
More than 1000 men, women, and children were killed in the 1944 massacre at the French village of Oradour-sur-Glâne
Introduction by John Fowles
0–394–57002–2 Random House $17.95

• Robert O. Paxton
VICHY FRANCE: Old Guard and New Order, 1940-1944
"With the publication of *Vichy France,* [the] conventional apologia for Vichy is revealed for what it has always been: an alibi that made it easier for a generation of Frenchmen to live with themselves. Paxton's study tells us as much of the truth about Vichy as we are likely to have for a long time"—Nicholas Wahl, Princeton University
0–231–05427–0 Columbia pb $15.00

• John F. Sweets
CHOICES IN VICHY FRANCE: The French under Nazi Occupation
Popular responses to, and rejections of, Nazism in Clermont-Ferrand, near the Occupation capital
0–19–503751–0 Oxford $24.95

THE POLITICS OF RESISTANCE IN FRANCE, 1940-1944: A History of the Mouvements Unis de la Résistance
0–87580–061–0 Northern Illinois $15.00

Poland

• Josef Garlinski
POLAND IN THE SECOND WORLD WAR
A comprehensive account from September 1, 1939 to the war's end
0–87052–372–4 Hippocrene pb $14.95

• Richard C. Lukas
THE FORGOTTEN HOLOCAUST: The Poles Under German Occupation, 1939-1944
0–8131–1566–3 Kentucky $24.00

• Steven Zaloga & Victor Madej
THE POLISH CAMPAIGN OF 1939
An account of the Polish invasion from the perspective of the Polish Army; challenges the idea that the German victory was an easy one
0–88254–994–4 Hippocrene $19.95

• J.K. Zawodny
DEATH IN THE FOREST: The Story of the Katyn Forest Massacre
First written in 1962, this is the story of the murder of more than 10,000 Polish officers who were captured when the Soviets invaded Poland in 1939
0–87052–563–8 Hippocrene pb $8.95

Russia

• Vladimir Karpov
RUSSIA AT WAR, 1941-45
Highlights every major campaign with stunning photographs from the military archives of the Soviet Union; includes 320 illustrations
Edited by Caroline Schofield
Introduction by Harrison E. Salisbury
0–86565–077–2 Vendome $30.00

• Alexander Werth
RUSSIA AT WAR, 1941-1945
The classic history of the Soviet Union at war; precise, literate, thought-provoking, and a must for the student of World War II
0–88184–084–X Carroll & Graf pb $15.95

The Resistance

• Basil Davidson
SCENES FROM THE ANTI-NAZI WAR: Fighting Back, 1940-45
A British officer recalls his experiences with the partisans in Yugoslavia and northern Italy
0–853–45588–0 Monthly Review pb $6.50

• Jorgen Haestrup
EUROPEAN RESISTANCE MOVEMENTS, 1939-1945: A Complete History
0–930466–36–5 Meckler $45.00

• Peter Hoffmann
GERMAN RESISTANCE TO HITLER
0–674–35085–5 Harvard $25.00
0–674–35086–3 Harvard pb $9.95

A HISTORY OF GERMAN RESISTANCE, 1933-1945
The elements within Germany, mostly conservative and cut off from any popular base, whose activities culminated in the unsuccessful attempt to assassinate Hitler on July 20, 1944
Translated by Richard Barry
0–262–58038–1 MIT pb $15.00

• Margaret L. Rossiter
WOMEN IN THE RESISTANCE
0–275–91812–2 Praeger pb $13.95

- Inge Scholl
WHITE ROSE: Munich, 1942-1943
The story of courageous Catholic teenagers who opposed Hitler, by the sister of Sophie Scholl, one of the executed leaders of the group
Translated by Arthur R. Schultz
0–8195–6086–3 Wesleyan pb $9.95

- Yuri Suhl
THEY FOUGHT BACK: The Story of the Jewish Resistance in Nazi Europe
Confronts the myth of Jewish passivity in the Holocaust
0–8052–0479–2 Schocken pb $11.95

THE WAR IN EUROPE: The Western Front

The Opening Campaigns

- Marc Bloch
STRANGE DEFEAT: A Statement of Evidence Written in 1940
A moving testimonial by a distinguished medievalist, shot for his Resistance activities
Translated by Gerard M. Hopkins
0–393–00371–X Norton pb $6.95

- Len Deighton
BLITZKRIEG: From the Rise of Hitler to the Fall of Dunkirk
0–345–29426–2 Ballantine pb $9.95

- John R. Elting
BATTLES FOR SCANDINAVIA
Lavishly illustrated story of the war in the north: Finland, Norway, the Russian convoys, and the *Tirpitz*
0–8094–3395–8 Time-Life $19.95

- Alistair Horne
TO LOSE A BATTLE: France 1940
Essentially a chronicle of the vital period from May 9 to 22. Horne places the Battle of France in historical context, tracing the events of the 1920s and 1930s that led to disaster
0–14–005042–6 Penguin pb $7.95

- James Leasor
GREEN BEACH
The controversial story of the 1942 raid on Dieppe, where thousands of Allied forces, mostly Canadian, were killed in a devastating amphibious assault that served as a rehearsal for D-Day
0–931933–21–8 Richardson & Steirman pb $8.95

- Walter Lord
THE MIRACLE OF DUNKIRK
Was Dunkirk a defeat, a moral victory, or a lost opportunity? Lord explores the series of crises that led to encirclement and escape at a small town on the Belgian seacoast
0–14–005085–X Penguin pb $7.95

- Patrick Turnbull
DUNKIRK: Anatomy of Disaster
0–8419–0396–4 Holmes & Meier $35.00

The Battle of Britain

- Len Deighton
FIGHTER: The True Story of the Battle of Britain
Introduction by A.J.P. Taylor
0–394–42757–2 Knopf $16.95

- Alfred Price
THE HARDEST DAY: Battle of Britain, August 18, 1940
A blow-by-blow account, accompanied by photographs, of a turning point in the lengthy air battle
0–85368–831–1 Sterling $24.95

- Peter Townsend
THE ODDS AGAINST US: Memoirs of Aerial Combat at Night During the Battle of Britain
0–688–04290–2 Morrow $16.95

The Sinking of the Bismarck

- Russell Grenfell
THE BISMARCK EPISODE
The sinking of the 42,000-ton Bismarck in May 1941 was both a military and psychological victory
0–8446–4024–7 Peter Smith $11.50

- Burkhard Von Mullenheim-Rechberg
BATTLESHIP BISMARCK: A Survivor's Story
0–87021–096–3 Naval Institute $19.95

D-Day and the Normandy Campaign

- Stephen E. Ambrose
PEGASUS BRIDGE: June 6, 1944
0–671–67156–1 Simon & Schuster pb $7.95

- Gordon Harrison
UNITED STATES ARMY IN WORLD WAR II: European Theater of Operations, Cross-Channel Attack
The army's official history of D-Day
0–318–22740–1 USGPO $29.00

- Max Hastings
OVERLORD: D-Day, June 6, 1944
Describes the magnificence of the German defense and explodes postwar myths about the ease of Allied victory. Without neglecting the generalship involved, Hastings evokes the experience of the campaign by studying the weapons, training, and ability of the ordinary soldier
0–671–46029–3 Simon & Schuster $17.95

- John Keegan
SIX ARMIES IN NORMANDY: From D-Day to the Liberation of Paris
Highly recommended account
0–14–005293–3 Penguin pb $7.95

- Henry Maule
CAEN: The Brutal Battle and Breakout from Normandy
A look at a key operation of the campaign; part of the Battle Standards Series
0–7153–9200–X David & Charles pb $10.95

- Cornelius Ryan
THE LONGEST DAY
The oral history of June 6, 1944
0–671–62228–5 Pocket pb $4.50

From D-Day to V-E Day

- William B. Breuer
OPERATION DRAGOON: The Allied Invasion of the South of France
Operation Dragoon involved 1000 ships, 3000 aircraft, and one million troops
0–89141–307–3 Presidio $17.95

- John S.D. Eisenhower
THE BITTER WOODS
A gripping account of the Battle of the Bulge
0–89839–106–7 Battery $29.95

- Ken Hechler
THE BRIDGE AT REMAGEN
The story of the first Allied bridgehead over the Rhine
0–345–27891–7 Ballantine pb $1.95

- Charles B. MacDonald
A TIME FOR TRUMPETS: The Untold Story of the Battle of the Bulge
"Moving beyond one's expectations"—*NY Times Book Review*
0–553–34226–6 Bantam pb $11.95

- Robert A. Miller
AUGUST 1944
A day-by-day account of a crucial turning point
0–89141–316–2 Presidio $17.95

- Cornelius Ryan
A BRIDGE TOO FAR
Operation Market Garden called for the taking of five bridges. Four were taken and held; the last, over the Rhine at Arnhem, was a scene of tragedy for the Allies and an important holding action for the Germans
0–671–54117–X Simon & Schuster pb $4.95

THE LAST BATTLE
0–671–54116–1 Simon & Schuster pb $5.95

- Russell F. Weigley
EISENHOWER'S LIEUTENANTS: The Campaign of France and Germany, 1944-1945
Inspired by Freeman's Civil War classic, *Lee's Lieutenants*, this is a magnificent, scholarly approach, from the daily activity on the front to the problems of setting and achieving objectives in an incompletely unified Allied camp
0–253–13333–5 Indiana $25.00

- Charles Whiting
THE BATTLE OF HURTGEN FOREST: The Untold Story of a Disastrous Campaign
The battle for the forest near Aachen in late 1944 and early 1945 was a costly one for the GIs, who amassed 33,000 casualties
0–517–56675–3 Crown $18.95

48 HOURS TO HAMMELBURG
The German POW camp was the site of a
rescue mission by Patton's troops in the
spring of 1945
0–515–07737–2 Berkley pb $2.95

HITLER'S WEREWOLVES
0–515–07297–4 Berkley pb $2.95

THE WAR IN EUROPE:
The Eastern Front

- Alan Clark
**BARBAROSSA: The Russian-German
Conflict, 1941-1945**
0–688–04268–6 Morrow pb $12.95

- Bryan I. Fugate
**OPERATION BARBAROSSA: Strategy
and Tactics on the Eastern Front, 1941**
The opening of the war in Russia to the
Battle of Moscow, including analyses of
pre-invasion planning by both sides
0–89141–197–6 Presidio $22.50

- Leon Goure
THE SIEGE OF LENINGRAD
Leningrad had lost half of its three million
residents to more than two years of
constant shelling, bombing, famine, and
disease by the time the Germans retreated
in January 1944
0–8047–0115–6 Stanford $39.50

- Janusz Piekalkiewicz
MOSCOW, 1941: The Frozen Offensive
Reconstructs and analyzes Hitler's eastern
campaign, using news reports, military
dispatches, and media accounts
0–89141–204–2 Presidio $20.00

**OPERATION CITADEL: Kursk and Orel,
the Greatest Tank Battle of the Second
World War**
At Kursk, the Russians met and won a
milestone victory from the Germans on an
open plain in good weather, conditions
that, until then, had meant certain triumph
for the panzers
Translated by Michaela Nierhaus
0–89141–254–9 Presidio $25.00

- Theodore Plievier
STALINGRAD
At Stalingrad, the most bitterly contested
conflict of the war, the tide turned in
Russia's favor. Trapped as much by their
own mistakes as by Zhukov's superb
counteroffensive, the Germans lost an army
and their hope of final victory. Plievier's is
a German perspective on the great battle
Translated by Richard & Clara Winston
0–88184–108–0 Carroll & Graf pb $8.95

- Harrison E. Salisbury
**THE NINE HUNDRED DAYS: The Siege
of Leningrad**
0–306–80253–8 Da Capo pb $14.95

- Earl F. Ziemke
**STALINGRAD TO BERLIN: The German
Defeat in the East**
A major study of the Soviet-German
conflict, first published by the US Army
Center of Military History; with numerous
maps and illustrations
0–88029–059–5 Hippocrene $24.95

The Battle of Stalingrad, 1942 (Photo by Georgi Zelma)

This scene of filth and suffering in that
yard of the Red Army House was my last
glimpse of Stalingrad. I remembered the
long anxious days of the summer of
1942, and the nights of the London blitz,
and the photographs of Hitler, smirking
as he stood on the steps of the Madeleine
in Paris, and the weary days of '38 and
'39 when a jittery Europe would tune in
to Berlin and hear Hitler's yells accompanied by the cannibal roar of the German mob. And there seemed a rough but
divine justice in those frozen cesspools
with their diarrhoea, and those horses'
bones, and those starved yellow corpses
in the yard of the Red Army House at
Stalingrad.

Alexander Werth
RUSSIA AT WAR, 1941-1945
0–88184–084–X Carroll & Graf pb $15.95

THE MEDITERRANEAN WAR

North Africa

- Correlli Barnett
THE DESERT GENERALS
0–253–20379–1 Indiana pb $11.50

- Ernle Bradford
SIEGE: Malta, 1940-1943
A tiny island only 60 miles from Italy,
Malta endured attack and siege for three
years, refusing to surrender to the
combined efforts of Italy and Germany
0–688–04781–5 Morrow $19.95

- Richard Collier
WAR IN THE DESERT
0–8094–2474–6 Time-Life $14.95

- Michael Glover
**AN IMPROVISED WAR: The Abyssinian
Campaign of 1940-1941**
A reappraisal of the campaign in Ethiopia,
the first Allied victory of the war
0–87052–456–9 Hippocrene $29.50

- S.W. Pack
INVASION NORTH AFRICA, 1942
Brief illustrated account of America's first
amphibious attack in the European theater
0–684–15921–X Scribners $12.95
0–684–17243–7 Scribners pb $4.95

Italy

- William B. Breuer
**DROP ZONE SICILY: Allied Airborne
Strike, July 1943**
A well-written account, based on
interviews with officers and enlisted men
Introduction by James Gavin
0–89141–196–8 Presidio $15.95

- William O. Darby & William H.
Baumer
WE LED THE WAY: Darby's Rangers
An American Ranger company at war in
the Mediterranean; a firsthand account
0–515–09511–7 Berkley pb $3.50

- John Ellis
**CASSINO: The Hollow Victory—The
Battle for Rome, January-June 1944**
The emphasis here is on the ordinary
combat soldier. Ellis also describes the
ineptitude and bickering in the Allied
camp that brought the Cassino campaign
to the edge of failure
0–07–019427–0 McGraw-Hill $19.95

- Carlo D'Este
**BITTER VICTORY: The Battle for Sicily,
1943**
A new account of the huge amphibious
assault known as "Operation Husky"
0–525–24471–9 Dutton $27.50

British infantry capture an enemy tank, North Africa, 1941 (Photo by Lenart Chetwyn)

- Norman Lewis
NAPLES '44
"A British officer's . . . eloquent journal of a year in Allied-occupied Naples"—*NY Times*
0–394–72300–7 Pantheon pb $7.95

- Janusz Piekalkiewicz
CASSINO: Anatomy of the Battle
0–918678–32–3 Historical Times $19.95

- Gen. Johannes Steinhoff
MESSERSCHMITTS OVER SICILY
A personal account of the Luftwaffe's two-month campaign in Sicily, by the former chairman of NATO's military committee, who was a major in the Luftwaffe in 1944
0–933852–57–6 Nautical & Aviation $19.95

- Raleigh Trevelyan
THE FORTRESS: A Diary of Anzio and After
0–907675–52–2 Seven Hills pb $10.95

- Charles Whiting
THE LONG MARCH ON ROME: The Forgotten War
0–7126–1439–7 David & Charles pb $22.95

THE PACIFIC WAR

Overviews

- John Costello
THE PACIFIC WAR, 1941-1945: The First Comprehensive One-Volume Account of the Causes and Conduct of World War II in the Pacific
0–688–01620–0 Morrow pb $14.95

- David Day
THE GREAT BETRAYAL: Britain, Australia, and the Onset of the Pacific War, 1939-1942
Though Australian troops fought in Europe, Britain failed to protect Australia's vulnerable western coast as the Pacific war escalated
0–393–02685–X Norton $19.95

- John Dower
WAR WITHOUT MERCY: Race and Power in the Pacific War
Racial hatred in the Pacific on both sides of the fighting
0–394–50030–X Pantheon $22.50
0–394–75172–8 Pantheon pb $9.95

- Thomas R. Havens
VALLEY OF DARKNESS: The Japanese People and World War II
0–8191–5495–4 University Press pb $12.50

- Saburo Ienaga
THE PACIFIC WAR, 1931-1945
A harsh critique of Japanese aggression by a leading Japanese scholar
Translated by Frank Baldwin
0–394–73496–3 Pantheon pb $7.95

- Akira Iriye
POWER AND CULTURE: The Japanese-American War, 1941-1945
0–674–69580–1 Harvard $25.00
0–674–69582–8 Harvard pb $9.95

- James W. Morley, editor
JAPAN'S ROAD TO THE PACIFIC WAR: The China Quagmire
Translated by James B. Crowley
0–231–05522–6 Columbia $42.00

- Hiroo Onoda
NO SURRENDER: My Thirty-Year War
Onoda, a lieutenant in the Philippines, spent 29 years in the jungle before learning that the war was over
Translated by Charles S. Terry
0–87011–240–6 Kodansha pb $8.50

- Ronald H. Spector
EAGLE AGAINST THE SUN: The American War with Japan
0–394–74101–3 Random House pb $9.95

- Christopher Thorne
ALLIES OF A KIND: The United States, Britain, and the War Against Japan, 1941-1945
A massive study of the Pacific war, in its foreign policy, strategic, racial, and commercial aspects
0–19–520173–6 Oxford pb $13.95

- John Toland
THE RISING SUN: The Decline and Fall of the Japanese Empire: 1936-1945
A Pulitzer Prize-winning study that pays equal attention to the Japanese and American sides
0–553–26435–4 Bantam pb $6.95

- Peter Williams & David Wallace
UNIT 731: Japan's Secret Biological Warfare in World War II
0–02–935301–7 Free Press $22.95

Pearl Harbor

- Harry Albright
JAPAN'S FATAL BLUNDER: The True Story Behind Japan's Attack on December 7, 1941
A new account by an American officer involved in the Hawaiian defense
0–87052–507–7 Hippocrene $17.95

- Lee Kennett
FOR THE DURATION: The United States Goes to War
0–684–18239–4 Scribners $15.95

- Walter Lord
DAY OF INFAMY
0–553–26777–9 Bantam pb $4.50

> Gordon W. Prange
> **AT DAWN WE SLEPT: The Untold Story of Pearl Harbor**
> Perhaps the best book on the subject
> 0–14–006455–9 Penguin pb $14.95

- John J. Stephan
HAWAII UNDER THE RISING SUN: Japan's Plans for Conquest after Pearl Harbor
"Will give a fresh perspective on the place of the Hawaiian islands in Japanese strategy and war aims"—*History*
0–8248–0872–X Hawaii $16.95

- John Toland
INFAMY: Pearl Harbor and Its Aftermath
Argues that FDR and others had prior knowledge of the Japanese attack
0–425–09040–X Berkley pb $5.50

The Philippines

- James & William Belote
CORREGIDOR: The Saga of a Fortress
0–515–07738–0 Berkley pb $2.95

- E.M. Flanagan
CORREGIDOR: The Rock Force Assault
The airborne operation that defeated the Japanese on this heavily fortified island in early 1945
0–89141–319–7 Presidio $18.95

Manila, after Warsaw the most devastated Allied city of World War II, from In Our Image: America's Empire in the Philippines *by Stanley Karnow (Random House)*

- Donald Knox
DEATH MARCH: The Survivors of Bataan
Preface by Stanley L. Falk
0–15–625224–4 HBJ pb $11.95

- Manny Lawton
SOME SURVIVED
A true account of a survivor of the Bataan death march
Introduction by John Toland
0–912697–13–X Algonquin $16.95
0–446–34934–8 Warner pb $3.95

Midway

- Mitsuo Fuchida & Masatke Okumiya
MIDWAY: The Battle that Doomed Japan
At Midway, Japan lost air superiority over the Pacific, and effective naval superiority as well
0–345–34691–2 Ballantine pb $3.50

- Gordon W. Prange & others
MIRACLE AT MIDWAY
0–07–050672–8 McGraw-Hill $19.95
0–14–006814–7 Penguin pb $10.95

The Island War

- Harry Gailey
"HOWLIN' MAD" VS. THE ARMY: Conflict in Command, Saipan 1944
The controversy that began when USMC Lt. Gen. Holland McTyeire "Howlin' Mad" Smith relieved Army Maj. Gen. Ralph Smith of his command during the July 1944 battle for Saipan
0–89141–242–5 Presidio $17.95

THE LIBERATION OF GUAM: 21 July-10 August, 1944
0–89141–324–3 Presidio $16.95

PELELIU: 1944
0–933852–41–X Nautical & Aviation $21.95

- Brig. Gen. Samuel B. Griffith II
THE BATTLE FOR GUADALCANAL
The capture of the island by American marine and naval forces
0–933852–04–5 Nautical & Aviation $19.95

Edwin P. Hoyt
Hoyt, a popular American military historian, chronicles the battles of the Pacific war in a series of books, arranged here in chronological order.
BLUE SKIES AND BLOOD: The Battle of the Coral Sea
0–515–08896–X Berkley pb $3.50

TO THE MARIANAS: War in the Central Pacific, 1944
0–380–65839–9 Avon pb $3.95

THE BATTLE OF LEYTE GULF
Over the course of three days in October 1944, the Japanese Fleet was essentially destroyed
0–515–09230–4 Berkley pb $3.95

THE KAMIKAZES
The full story of the suicide pilots
0–515–08066–7 Berkley pb $3.50

- Don Jones
OBA, THE LAST SAMURAI: Saipan, 1944-1945
0–89141–245–X Presidio $16.95

- Richard F. Newcomb
IWO JIMA
0–553–27547–X Bantam pb $3.95

- Bill D. Ross
IWO JIMA: Legacy of Valor
0–8149–0895–0 Vanguard $25.00
0–394–74288–5 Random House pb $9.95

- Eugene Sledge
WITH THE OLD BREED AT PELELIU AND OKINAWA
A memoir
0–89141–119–4 Presidio $15.95

The Mainland War

- Won-loy Chan
BURMA: The Untold Story
A memoir from "Charlie" Chan, a combat intelligence officer and Japanese language specialist
0–89141–266–2 Presidio $14.95

- Charlton Ogburn
THE MARAUDERS
0–688–01625–1 Morrow pb $6.50

- Barbara Tuchman
STILWELL AND THE AMERICAN EXPERIENCE IN CHINA
A veteran China hand after two tours of duty between the wars, "Vinegar Joe" Stilwell was appointed Chief-of-Staff to Chiang Kai-Shek and commander of the US forces on the Asian mainland in 1942; his refusal to defer to Chiang, or to condone the corruption of the Kuo Min Tang, led to his recall in 1944
0–02–620290–5 Macmillan $21.95
0–553–25798–6 Bantam pb $6.95

THE WAR IN THE AIR

- Clay Blair
RIDGWAY'S PARATROOPERS: The American Airborne in World War II
0–688–06754–9 Morrow pb $15.95

- Eric Brown, Capt., RN (Ret.)
DUELS IN THE SKY: World War II Naval Aircraft in Combat
0–87021–063–7 Naval Institute $19.95

- Gerard M. Devlin
PARATROOPER: The Saga of the U.S. Army and Marine Parachute and Glider Combat Troops During World War II
Foreword by William P. Yarborough
0–312–59652–9 St. Martin's pb $14.95

- Max Hastings
VICTORY OVER EUROPE: D-Day to VE Day
Photographs by George Stevens
0–316–81334–6 Little, Brown $25.00

- Capt. Richard C. Knott, USN (Ret.)
BLACK CAT RAIDERS OF WORLD WAR II
The black-painted planes that attacked Japanese ships as night raiders
0–933852–18–5 Nautical & Aviation $20.95

- Samuel W. Mitcham, Jr.
MEN OF THE LUFTWAFFE
The men of the German Air Force, including Göring, Richtofen, Kesselring, and Udet
0–89141–308–1 Presidio $18.95

TO ORDER BOOKS AS GIFTS, SEE PAGE 1

● Wilbur H. Morrison
FORTRESS WITHOUT A ROOF: The Allied Bombing of the Third Reich
0–312–90179–8 St. Martin's pb $4.95

● Williamson Murray
LUFTWAFFE
An account of its downfall
0–933852–45–2 Nautical & Aviation $24.95

● Hatsuho Naito
THUNDER GODS: The Kamikaze Pilots Tell Their Stories
Translated by Mayumi Ichikawa
Foreword by James Michener
0–87011–909–5 Kodansha $18.95

● Michael O'Leary
USAAF FIGHTERS OF WORLD WAR II IN ACTION
0–7137–1839–0 Sterling $39.95

● Janusz Piekalkiewicz
THE AIR WAR, 1939-1945
Translated by Jan Van Heurck
0–7137–1132–9 Sterling $29.95

● P.R. Reid
COLDITZ: The Full Story
The German fortress where hundreds of Allied flyers were imprisoned
0–312–00578–4 St. Martin's $18.95
0–312–91019–3 St. Martin's pb $4.50

● Ronard Schaffer
WINGS OF JUDGMENT: American Bombing in World War II
War's terrible choices ensured that Dresden, Berlin, and dozens of other cities would not survive, but that Rome and Florence would be preserved
0–19–505640–X Oxford pb $9.95

● Michael Sherry
THE RISE OF AMERICAN AIR POWER: The Creation of Armageddon
0–300–03600–0 Yale $29.95

THE WAR AT SEA

● William Breuer
DEVIL BOATS: The PT War Against Japan
The US Navy's PT boats and their successes in the southwest Pacific
Foreword by Rear Admiral John D. Bulkeley
0–89141–269–7 Presidio $16.95

● Paul S. Dull
A BATTLE HISTORY OF THE IMPERIAL JAPANESE NAVY: 1941-1945
A well-researched general history
0–87021–097–1 Naval Institute $24.95

● Wolfgang Frank
THE SEA WOLVES
0–345–29504–8 Ballantine pb $2.50

● Richard Hough
THE LONGEST BATTLE: The War at Sea, 1939-1945
0–688–07953–9 Morrow pb $9.95

● Edwin P. Hoyt
THE CARRIER WAR
0–380–75360–X Avon pb $3.50

● Jeter A. Isely & Philip Crowl
U.S. MARINES AND AMPHIBIOUS WAR
A first-rate account of all the marine actions in the Pacific
0–686–31000–4 Marine Corps Association $15.95

● Geoffrey Jones
DEFEAT OF THE WOLF PACKS
How American forces ultimately triumphed over the German U-boats
0–89141–314–6 Presidio $16.95

● Samuel Eliot Morison
THE TWO-OCEAN WAR: A Short History of the United States Navy in the Second World War
0–316–58366–9 Little, Brown $35.00

HISTORY OF THE UNITED STATES NAVAL OPERATIONS IN WORLD WAR TWO
0–316–58300–6 Little, Brown (set) $367.50

Volume 1: The Battle of the Atlantic, 1939-1943
0–316–58301–4 Little, Brown $27.50

Volume 2: Operations in North African Waters, October 1942-June 1943
0–316–58302–2 Little, Brown $25.00

Volume 3: The Rising Sun in the Pacific, 1931-April 1942
0–316–58303–0 Little, Brown $27.50

Volume 4: Coral Sea, Midway and Submarine Actions, May 1942-August 1942
0–316–58304–9 Little, Brown $27.50

Volume 5: The Struggle for Guadalcanal, August 1942-February 1943
0–316–58305–7 Little, Brown $25.00

Volume 6: Breaking the Bismarck's Barrier, 22 July 1942-May 1944
0–316–58306–5 Little, Brown $25.00

Volume 7: Aleutians, Gilberts and Marshalls, June 1942-April 1944
0–316–58307–3 Little, Brown $25.00

Volume 8: New Guinea and the Marianas, March 1944-August 1944
0–316–58308–1 Little, Brown $25.00

Volume 9: Sicily-Salerno-Anzio, January 1943-June 1944
0–316–58316–2 Little, Brown $25.00

Volume 10: The Atlantic Battle Won, May 1943-May 1945
0–316–58310–3 Little, Brown $25.00

Volume 11: The Invasion of France and Germany, 1944-1945
0–316–58311–1 Little, Brown $25.00

Kamikaze pilot, from The Rising Sun: The Decline and Fall of the Japanese Empire, 1936-1945 *by John Toland (*Bantam*)*

Volume 12: Leyte, June 1944-January 1945
0–316–58317–0 Little, Brown $25.00

Volume 13: The Liberation of the Philippines—Luzon, Mindanao, the Visayas, 1944-1945
0–316–58313–8 Little, Brown $25.00

Volume 14: Victory in the Pacific, 1945
0–316–58314–6 Little, Brown $25.00

Volume 15: Supplement and General Index
0–316–58315–4 Little, Brown $25.00

● R. Adm. Richard H. O'Kane, USN (Ret.)
WAHOO: The Patrols of America's Most Famous World War II Submarine
The successes of the USS *Wahoo* recreated by the man who was the sub's exec for many of its war patrols
0–89141–301–4 Presidio $18.95

● Janusz Piekalkiewicz
SEA WAR, 1939-1945
0–7137–1665–7 Sterling $29.95

● Barrie Pitt
BATTLE OF THE ATLANTIC
0–316–84737–2 Little, Brown pb $14.95

● Robert Sherrod
HISTORY OF MARINE CORPS AVIATION IN WORLD WAR II
By a former correspondent for *Time* and *Life*
0–933852–58–4 Nautical & Aviation $24.95

● Edward Stafford
THE BIG E
0–87021–036–X Naval Institute $23.95
0–345–31504–9 Ballantine pb $4.95

● John Terraine
THE U-BOAT WARS, 1916-1945
With a strong analysis of the Battle of the Atlantic
0–399–13291–0 Putnam $22.95

● Dan van der Valt
THE ATLANTIC CAMPAIGN: An Epic History of World War II's Struggle at Sea
0–06–015967–7 Harper & Row $25.00

SPIES AND CODE-BREAKERS

● Aline, Countess of Romanones
THE SPY WORE RED: My Adventures as an Undercover Agent in World War II
A first-person account of the Brooklyn-born model sent to wartime Madrid to uncover high-society intelligence links to Hitler
0–394–55665–8 Random House $18.95

● Ralph Bennett
ULTRA IN THE WEST
0–684–17750–1 Scribners pb $6.95

● Anthony C. Brown
BODYGUARD OF LIES
0–553–34016–6 Bantam pb $12.95

• William Brueur

HITLER'S UNDERCOVER WAR: The Nazi Espionage Invasion of the U.S.A
When Hitler began rearming Germany he concluded that "the USA is the decisive factor." This is a fast-paced narrative of how the FBI worked with US Navy and Army intelligence to dismantle the Nazi spy machine
0–312–02620–X St. Martin's $19.95

THE SECRET WAR WITH GERMANY: Deception, Espionage, and Dirty Tricks, 1939-1945
A chronological history of wartime espionage, including the German spies who were caught because they didn't know British pub hours; the theft of the Warzburg radar; how ULTRA broke the highest German code; and many other events
0–89141–298–0 Presidio $17.95

• W.J. Holmes

DOUBLE-EDGED SECRETS
How the Japanese codes were broken
0–87021–162–5 Naval Institute $13.95

• David Kahn

HITLER'S SPIES: German Military Intelligence in World War II
0–02–052440–4 Macmillan pb $14.95

• Edwin T. Layton, Roger Pineau & John Costello

AND I WAS THERE: Pearl Harbor and Midway—Breaking the Secrets
0–688–04883–8 Morrow $19.95
0–688–06968–1 Morrow pb $10.95

• Ronald Lewin

THE AMERICAN MAGIC: Codes, Ciphers and the Defeat of Japan
0–14–006471–0 Penguin pb $7.95

• J.C. Masterman

THE DOUBLE-CROSS SYSTEM
The astonishing story of how British intelligence used German spies to feed false information to their masters
0–345–29743–1 Ballantine pb $2.50

• G.W. Prange, D.M. Goldstein & K.V. Dillon

TARGET TOKYO: The Story of the Sorge Spy Ring
0–07–050678–7 McGraw-Hill pb $4.95

• William Stephenson

A MAN CALLED INTREPID
The Canadian-born millionaire's adventures as Britain's chief of intelligence in the Western hemisphere; a best-seller (1979)
0–345–31023–3 Ballantine pb $4.95

• F.W. Winterbotham

THE ULTRA SECRET
0–06–014678–8 Harper & Row pb $10.00

• John Winton

ULTRA AT SEA: How Breaking the Nazi Code Affected Allied Naval Strategy During World War II
Especially good on how the Allies acquired Nazi special intelligence and used it to find and destroy battleships like the *Tirpitz* and *Bismarck*
0–688–08546–6 Morrow $18.95

Code Names

TORCH: used in Allied North African campaign for landings on Mediterranean and Atlantic coasts in 1942
ULTRA: for information gleaned from decrypting German enciphered wireless traffic
UNDERTONE: for Seventh US Army drive to break through the West Wall and establish a bridgehead over the Rhine in the vicinity of Worms-Mainz, March-April 1945
UTAH: for Normandy beach assaulted by troops of US VII Corps on D-Day
V-1: Vergeltungswaffe, vengeance weapon. The first-generation pilotless bomb or German rocket
VERITABLE: for the 21st Army Group plan for attack by Canadian forces between the Maas and the Rhine, February 1945
WADHAM: for the Allied invasion threat against the Cotentin Peninsula in 1943
WIDEWING: for SHAEF headquarters, located at Bushy Park outside London
ZEPPELIN: for Allied deception plan that threatened an invasion of the Balkans to divert German divisions from Normandy before the D-Day invasion

Adapted from the Glossary of Terms and Acronyms in

David Eisenhower
EISENHOWER: At War, 1943-1945
0–394–75533–2 Random House pb $12.95

THE END OF THE WAR

Europe

• Keith Sainsbury

THE TURNING POINT: Roosevelt, Stalin, Churchill, and Chiang Kai-shek, 1943—The Moscow, Cairo, and Teheran Conferences
An important study of the first meeting of the wartime leaders and the early decisions that would affect the postwar map
0–19–285172–1 Oxford pb $13.95

• John Toland

THE LAST ONE HUNDRED DAYS
The events on both fronts from January 27 to May 8, 1945 in the German homeland and in the Allied Councils, and the final collapse of the Third Reich
0–553–34518–4 Bantam pb $12.95

• H.R. Trevor-Roper

THE LAST DAYS OF HITLER
By a leading British historian
0–02–038010–0 Macmillan pb $7.95

• John W. Wheeler-Bennett & Anthony Nicholls

THE SEMBLANCE OF PEACE: The Political Settlement After the Second World War
0–393–00709–X Norton pb $4.95

The Pacific: Hiroshima and Nagasaki

▶ See also Japan

• Gar Alperovitz

ATOMIC DIPLOMACY: Hiroshima and Potsdam
0–14–008337–5 Penguin pb $8.95

• Arnold C. Brackman

THE OTHER NUREMBERG: The Untold Story of the Tokyo War Crimes Trials
0–688–07957–1 Morrow pb $9.95

• Damage of the Atomic Bombs in Hiroshima and Nagasaki Committee

HIROSHIMA AND NAGASAKI: The Physical, Medical, and Social Effects of the Atomic Bombings
The most current scientific data compiled in Japan
0–465–02987–6 Basic Books pb $15.95

• Herbert Feis

ATOMIC BOMB AND THE END OF WORLD WAR II
0–691–01057–9 Princeton pb $8.95

• John Hersey

HIROSHIMA
Hersey's masterpiece tells what happened on August 6, 1945, through the memories of survivors
0–679–72103–7 Random House pb $3.95

• William Lawren

THE GENERAL AND THE BOMB: A Biography of General Leslie R. Groves, Director of the Manhattan Project
0–396–08761–2 Dodd, Mead $21.95

Richard Rhodes
THE MAKING OF THE ATOMIC BOMB
"The comprehensive history of the bomb and also a work of literature"—Tracy Kidder
0–671–44133–7 Simon & Schuster $22.95
0–671–65719–4 Simon & Schuster pb $12.95

• Martin J. Sherwin

A WORLD DESTROYED: Hiroshima and the Origins of the Arms Race
0–394–75204–X Random House pb $9.95

• Peter Wyden

DAY ONE: Before Hiroshima and After
0–446–34006–5 Warner pb $3.95

MEMOIRS AND BIOGRAPHIES

• A.J.P. Taylor

THE WAR LORDS
The five great leaders of the war: Churchill, Hitler, Mussolini, Roosevelt, and Stalin
0–14–004638–0 Penguin pb $6.95

The High Command

- **Omar N. Bradley & Clay Blair**
  A GENERAL'S LIFE: An Autobiography
  Bradley, whose concern for his men won him the title "the GI's general," commanded forces in North Africa, Sicily, Normandy, and the European campaign, and was one of Eisenhower's most trusted subordinates
  0–671–41024–5 Simon & Schuster pb $15.95

- **Charles de Gaulle**
  THE COMPLETE WAR MEMOIRS OF CHARLES DE GAULLE, 1940-1946
  De Gaulle's strategic theories were ignored by his superiors even after his briefly successful counterattack during the Battle of France in 1940. Unable to convince his compatriots to continue the fight, he fled to England and retained his position as French leader in the Allied ranks. This edition is superbly rendered by a translator of Baudelaire
  Translated by Richard Howard
  0–306–80227–9 Da Capo pb $14.95

- **C.R. Messenger, editor**
  HITLER'S GLADIATOR: The Life of SS-Obergruppenführer and General der Waffen-SS Sepp Dietrich
  "Sepp" Dietrich managed to combine a career as a fanatic Nazi with that of a successful panzer commander. He was executed in 1945 for atrocities carried out during the Battle of the Bulge
  0–08–031207–1 Pergamon $26.95

- **David Eisenhower**
  EISENHOWER: At War, 1943-1945
  As Allied Commander in North Africa and Europe, Eisenhower was renowned both for his strategic judgment and his ability to keep diverse and aggressive subordinates working in harness. This is a great study, revealing afresh the major issues of the war; by the general's grandson
  0–394–41237–0 Random House $29.95
  0–394–75533–2 Random House pb $12.95

- **Dwight D. Eisenhower**
  CRUSADE IN EUROPE
  A massive, detailed account
  0–306–70768–3 Da Capo $45.00
  0–306–80109–4 Da Capo pb $10.95

- **Merle Miller**
  IKE THE SOLDIER: As They Knew Him
  An intimate portrait based on hundreds of interviews
  0–399–13201–5 Putnam $24.95
  0–399–51483–X Putnam pb $13.95

- **Heinz Guderian**
  PANZER LEADER
  Memoirs of this century's leading tank strategist and a fascinating, sometimes horrifying portrait of military life in Hitler's Germany
  0–89201–076–2 Zenger $25.00

- **Charles Burdick & Hans-Adolf Jacobsen, editors**
  THE HALDER WAR DIARY, 1939-1942
  The German Army's chief of staff follows the war effort through his dismissal in 1942 and offers an intimate view of Hitler as commander
  0–89141–302–2 Presidio $35.00

- **E.B. Potter**
  BULL HALSEY: A Biography
  0–87021–146–3 Naval Institute $21.95

- **Correlli Barnett, editor**
  HITLER'S GENERALS
  Includes Rommel, Model, Student, and Beck
  1–55584–161–9 Weidenfeld & Nicolson $24.95

- **Alan Bullock**
  HITLER: A Study in Tyranny
  A solid biography; tells as much about the times as the man
  0–06–131123–5 Harper & Row pb $13.95

- **Edwin P. Hoyt**
  HITLER'S WAR
  The progress of the war from Hitler's point of view
  0–07–030622–2 McGraw-Hill $22.95

- **Ronald Lewin**
  HITLER'S MISTAKES
  A biting analysis
  Introduction by Stephen Ambrose
  0–688–07289–5 Morrow pb $6.95

- **Kenneth Macksey**
  HITLER AS A COMMANDER
  A chronicle of Hitler as strategist, analyzing his downfall from the rapid conquest of Western Europe to the collapse of the Reich
  0–8050–0860–8 Henry Holt $24.95

- **John Toland**
  ADOLF HITLER
  "The first book that anyone who wants to learn about Hitler or the war in Europe must read!"—*Newsweek*
  0–345–33848–0 Ballantine pb $12.95

General MacArthur, with Philippine Commonwealth President Sergio Osmeña, comes ashore at Leyte, from In Our Image: America's Empire in the Philippines *by Stanley Karnow (Random House)*

- **William Manchester**
  AMERICAN CAESAR: Douglas MacArthur, 1880-1964
  The US commander-in-chief in the Pacific: enigmatic, charismatic, revered and despised, but never ignored
  0–440–30424–5 Doubleday pb $6.95

- **Forrest C. Pogue**
  GEORGE C. MARSHALL
  Recognized early in his career as a military genius, Marshall was appointed US Army Chief of Staff on the eve of the war. After Pearl Harbor, he played a vital part in keeping the war effort centered on a European victory by means of a second front
  Edited by Gordon Harrison
  Foreword by Omar Bradley

  Volume 1: Education of a General, 1889-1939
  0–670–33685–8 Viking $24.95

  Volume 2: Ordeal and Hope, 1939-1943
  0–670–33686–6 Viking $24.95

  Volume 3: Organizer of Victory, 1943-1945
  0–670–33694–7 Viking $29.95

- **Nigel Hamilton**
  MONTY
  Montgomery of Alamein, the most controversial of British generals, is best remembered for his first great victory at El Alamein and for Operation Market Garden, an operation that attained many of its objectives but ended in catastrophe at Arnhem. The first volume of *Monty* is out of print

  Volume 2: Master of the Battlefield—Monty's War Years, 1942-1944
  0–07–025806–6 McGraw-Hill $25.95

  Volume 3: Field Marshal—The Final Years, 1944-1976
  0–07–025807–4 McGraw-Hill $29.95

- **E.B. Potter**
  NIMITZ
  Biography of the commander of the US Pacific Fleet
  0–87021–492–6 Naval Institute $21.95

- **Martin Blumenson**
  PATTON: The Man Behind the Legend, 1885-1945
  Individual to the point of eccentricity, this cavalry officer-turned-commander's outbursts and mannerisms won him fame, but almost destroyed his career. Though he showed an awesome ability to advance rapidly against the enemy, he has been accused of sacrificing his men for eye-catching victories
  0–688–06082–X Morrow $17.95

  THE PATTON PAPERS 1: 1885-1940
  0–395–12706–8 Houghton Mifflin $39.50

  THE PATTON PAPERS 2: 1940-1945
  0–395–18498–3 Houghton Mifflin $40.00

- **George S. Patton**
  WAR AS I KNEW IT
  The principles forged from the general's fighting experience in three wars
  0–395–08074–6 Houghton Mifflin $17.95
  0–553–25991–1 Bantam pb $4.95

- Ronald Lewin
ROMMEL: As Military Commander
Most famous for his brilliant campaigns in the desert, Rommel fought an excellent holding battle in France until wounded by Allied aircraft. He committed suicide at the Führer's orders after being implicated in the anti-Nazi plot of the summer of 1944
0–345–28797–5 Ballantine pb $2.50

- Desmond Young
ROMMEL: The Desert Fox
0–688–06771–9 Morrow pb $9.95

- Robert A. Divine
ROOSEVELT AND WORLD WAR II
0–14–021191–8 Penguin pb $5.95

- Eric Larrabee
COMMANDER IN CHIEF: Franklin Delano Roosevelt, His Lieutenants and Their War
0–671–66382–8 Simon & Schuster pb $12.95

- Hiroyuki Agawa
THE RELUCTANT ADMIRAL: Yamamoto and the Imperial Navy
Convinced by several visits to the US that America's industrial strength was bound to prevail in a prolonged war, Yamamoto's strategy—typified by the attack on Pearl Harbor—emphasized knock-out blows against the US Navy, designed to force America to early negotiations
Translated by John Bester
0–87011–355–0 Kodansha $16.95
0–87011–512–X Kodansha pb $7.95

- Georgi K. Zhukov
MARSHAL ZHUKOV'S GREATEST BATTLES
One of the best tacticians of the war, perhaps of the century, describes his war against the Germans
Translated by Theodore Shabad
Edited by Harrison E. Salisbury
0–06–014786–5 Harper & Row pb $7.95

The Men in the Field

- Henry Berry
SEMPER FI, MAC
0–425–09724–2 Berkley pb $4.50

- Tom Blackburn & Eric Hamel
THE JOLLY ROGERS: The Story of Tom Blackburn and Navy Fighting Squadron VF-17
0–517–57075–0 Crown $18.95

- Gregory Boyington
BAA BAA BLACK SHEEP
0–553–26350–1 Bantam pb $3.95

- John Comer
COMBAT CREW: A True Story of Flying and Fighting in World War II
The air war over Germany, as seen from a B-17
0–688–07614–9 Morrow $16.95

- Keith Douglas
ALAMEIN TO ZEM ZEM
A memoir of the North Africa Campaign
Edited by Desmond Graham
0–19–281267–X Oxford pb $9.95

- Allan Mayer
GASTON'S WAR: The True Story of a Hero of the Resistance in World War II
The life of Gaston Vandermeerssche, a would-be soldier who led a Dutch underground network and ultimately survived his capture and torture by the Nazis
0–89141–291–3 Presidio $17.95

- John Muirhead
THOSE WHO FALL
A B-17 pilot's memoir of the air war over Italy
0–394–54983–X Random House $18.95
0–671–64944–2 Simon & Schuster pb $4.50

- Audie Murphy
TO HELL AND BACK
The classic combat journal of the most famous American GI
0–553–24297–0 Bantam pb $3.95

- Colonel R. Bruce Porter with Eric Hammel
ACE!: A Marine Night Fighter Pilot in World War II
0–935553–01–0 Pacifica Press $22.95

- C.F. Rawnsley & Robert Wright
NIGHT FIGHTER
Rawnsley flew combat sorties almost continuously from 1939 to 1945 as the radar operator in a two-man night fighter
0–345–31025–X Ballantine pb $2.95

- Mark Scott & Semoyn Krasilshchik
YANKS MEET REDS: Recollections of US and Soviet Vets from the Linkup in World War II
American and Soviet veterans offer eyewitness accounts from the Elbe River in 1945
0–88496–276–8 Capra pb $9.95

- John Verney
GOING TO THE WARS
Witty, literate memoirs of Verney's service in the Near East as a member of a yeomanry regiment and his secret mission behind the lines in Sardinia
0–907746–30–6 Longwood pb $7.50

- Bob Whinney
THE U-BOAT PERIL: An Anti-Submarine Commander's Story
0–7137–1821–8 Sterling $24.95

The Holocaust

The growing field of "Holocaust Studies" not only includes several first-rate general histories, but a wide range of memoirs, works of fiction, criticisms of Allied inaction, and philosophical ruminations, as well. Among the best surveys are two relatively recent works: Lucy Dawidowicz's *The War Against the Jews, 1933-1945* (1975), and Martin Gilbert's *The Holocaust* (1985).

Much of the work listed below transcends the strict boundaries of historical research.

An increasing flow of survivors' memoirs translates cold numbers into deeply personal tales. Several volumes have collected the artwork of the victims themselves. Novelists (as well as filmmakers) have also taken on the difficult task of exploring the psychic and physical brutality of the Nazi era.

▶ See also Judaism, The Second World War, Modern Hebrew Literature & Yiddish Literature

- Lucy S. Dawidowicz
THE HOLOCAUST AND THE HISTORIANS
Why many of the world's historians have paid little attention to Hitler's mass murder of the Jews
0–674–40566–8 Harvard $17.95
0–674–40567–6 Harvard pb $7.95

A HOLOCAUST READER
0–87441–236–6 Behrman House pb $10.95

THE WAR AGAINST THE JEWS, 1933-1945
A narrative account of the attempted extermination of the Jews, from the death squads to the ghettoes and death camps
0–02–908030–4 Free Press $23.95
0–553–34532–X Bantam pb $11.95

- Gerald Fleming
HITLER AND THE FINAL SOLUTION
An exhaustive examination that documents Hitler's direct responsibility for the "Final Solution"
0–520–06022–9 California pb $9.95

- François Furet, editor
UNANSWERED QUESTIONS: Nazi Germany and the Genocide of the Jews
Historians include Raul Hilberg, Yehuda Bauer, Pierre Vidal-Naquet; topics include the origins of the genocide, its relation to the principles of fascism, the gas chambers, and the question of Jewish "passivity" in the face of annihilation
0–8052–4051–9 Schocken $24.95
0–8052–0908–5 Schocken pb $15.95

- Martin Gilbert
THE HOLOCAUST: The History of the Jews of Europe During the Second World War
A definitive narrative weaving historical research and survivors' testimony into one of the most gripping accounts of the Nazi genocide
0–03–062416–9 Henry Holt $24.95

THE MACMILLAN ATLAS OF THE HOLOCAUST
Detailed maps show week-by-week progress of the Nazi attempt to exterminate the Jews
0–306–80218–X Da Capo pb $13.95

- Ian Hancock
THE PARIAH SYNDROME: An Account of Gypsy Slavery and Persecution
An illuminating account by a Gypsy of his people's oppression, including the murder of at least half a million Gypsies at the hands of the Nazis
0–89720–079–9 Karoma pb $17.95

- Raul Hilberg

THE DESTRUCTION OF THE EUROPEAN JEWS
This massive account, first published in 1961, is filled with facts, figures, and a thorough dissection of how the genocide was carried out. In Hilberg's words, it is "not a book about the Jews. It is a book about people who destroyed the Jews." Harcover version is a 3-volume set
0–8419–0832–X Holmes & Meier (set) $159.50
0–8419–0910–5 Holmes & Meier pb $14.95

- Michael R. Marrus

THE HOLOCAUST IN HISTORY
0–87451–425–8 New England $16.50

- Arno J. Mayer

WHY DID THE HEAVENS NOT DARKEN?: The "Final Solution" in History
Controversial account suggests that Nazi anti-Semitism did not become genocidal until well into World War II, when the foundering of the all-out campaign against Russia triggered the "Final Solution"
0–394–57154–1 Pantheon $29.95

- Richard Plant

THE PINK TRIANGLE: The Nazi War Against Homosexuals
The origins, growth, and terrible consequences—homosexuals were the lowest rung in the concentration-camp hierarchy—of homophobia in Hitler's Germany
0–8050–0600–1 Henry Holt pb $9.95

- Leon Poliakov

HARVEST OF HATE: The Nazi Program for the Destruction of the Jews of Europe
A good introduction to the origins and mechanics of the Holocaust by a leading expert on anti-Semitism
0–8052–5006–9 Schocken pb $12.95

As well as the six million Jews who were murdered, more than ten million other non-combatants were killed by the Nazis. Under the Nazi scheme, Poles, Czechs, Serbs and Russians were to become subject peoples; slaves, the workers of the New Order. The Jews were to disappear altogether. It was the Jews alone who were marked out to be destroyed in their entirety: every Jewish man, woman and child, so that there would be no future Jewish life in Europe. Against the eight million Jews who lived in Europe in 1939, the Nazi bureaucracy assembled all the concerted skills and mechanics of a modern state: the police, the railways, the civil service, the industrial power of the Reich; poison gas, soldiers, mercenaries, criminals, machine guns, artillery; and over all, a massive apparatus of deception.

Martin Gilbert

THE HOLOCAUST: The History of the Jews of Europe During the Second World War
0–03–062416–9 Henry Holt $24.95

The main deportation railroads to Auschwitz, from The Macmillan Atlas of the Holocaust *by Martin Gilbert (Da Capo)*

- Simon Wiesenthal

EVERY DAY REMEMBRANCE DAY: A Chronicle of Jewish Martyrdom
The noted Nazi-hunter's documentation, in the form of a 365-day calendar, of Jewish suffering and persecution throughout history; many of the events occurred between 1939 and 1945
0–8050–0098–4 Henry Holt $25.00

HOLOCAUST EXPERIENCES: From Paris to Warsaw

The Nazi domination of Europe meant a Holocaust not only of death factories but also of ghettoes, murderous roving bands, mass shootings, deportations, starvation, and hiding.

- Jacques Adler

THE JEWS OF PARIS AND THE FINAL SOLUTION: Communal Response and Internal Conflict, 1940-1944
"As objective as it is horrifying, a work which historians of the occupation were lacking"—*Vingtième Siecle*
0–19–504305–7 Oxford $32.50

- Haim Avni

SPAIN, THE JEWS, AND FRANCO
Based on new materials detailing the Franco regime's aid of refugees from Nazism
Translated by Emanuel Shimoni
0–8276–0188–3 JPS $19.95

- Leonard Baker

DAYS OF SORROW AND PAIN: Leo Baeck and the Berlin Jews
The wartime biography of the great Berlin rabbi who ultimately survived the concentration camps
0–19–502800–7 Oxford pb $9.95

- Randolph L. Braham

THE POLITICS OF GENOCIDE: The Holocaust in Hungary
A definitive study, in two volumes
0–231–04496–8 Columbia (set) $112.00

- Terrence Des Pres

THE SURVIVOR: An Anatomy of Life in the Death Camps
0–19–502703–5 Oxford pb $8.95

Lucjan Dobroszycki, editor
THE CHRONICLE OF THE LODZ GHETTO, 1941-1944
The painstakingly detailed diary of life and administration in Europe's second largest ghetto, reduced from 163,177 people in 1941 to 877 in 1944. A chilling document
0-300-03924-7 Yale pb $19.95

• Ilya Ehrenburg & Vasily Grossman, editors
THE BLACK BOOK
A documentary of the Holocaust in the Soviet Union told through letters, diaries, articles, and eyewitness accounts
Translated by John Glad & James S. Levine
0-89604-031-3 Holocaust $24.95
0-89604-032-1 Holocaust pb $14.95

• Konnilyn Feig
HITLER'S DEATH CAMPS: The Sanity of Madness
An "unsparing compilation of the collective camp experience . . . written with sensitivity, power, and emotion"—*American Historical Review*
0-8419-0676-9 Holmes & Meier $44.50
0-8419-0675-0 Holmes & Meier pb $34.50

• Leonard Gross
THE LAST JEWS IN BERLIN
The Jews who called themselves "U-boats" and their capture and survival underground
0-671-65724-0 Simon & Schuster pb $8.95

• Yisrael Gutman
THE JEWS OF WARSAW, 1939-1943: Ghetto, Underground, Revolt
The outstanding example of Jewish resistance dramatically reconstructed
Translated by Ina Friedman
0-253-33174-9 Indiana $40.00
0-253-20511-5 Indiana pb $17.50

• Shimon Huberband
KIDDUSH HASHEM: Jewish Religious and Cultural Life in Poland During the Holocaust
Told by a Warsaw rabbi
Translated by David E. Fishman
Edited by Jeffrey S. Gurock & Robert S. Hirt
0-88125-118-6 Ktav $35.00
0-88125-121-6 Ktav pb $19.95

• Michael R. Marrus & Robert O. Paxton
VICHY FRANCE AND THE JEWS
A landmark study, focusing on the long denial of French collaboration in Hitler's "Final Solution"
0-8052-0741-4 Schocken pb $12.95

• Susan Zuccotti
THE ITALIANS AND THE HOLOCAUST: Persecution, Rescue and Survival
How and why 85 percent of Italy's Jews survived World War II
0-465-03621-X Basic Books pb $9.95

Murderous Science

Robert Jay Lifton
THE NAZI DOCTORS: Medical Killing and the Psychology of Genocide
"Breaks through the frontiers of historiography to provide a convincing psychological interpretation of the Third Reich and the crimes of National Socialism"—Neal Ascherson, *NY Review of Books*
0-465-04904-4 Basic Books $22.95
0-465-04905-2 Basic Books pb $12.95

Benno Muller-Hill
MURDEROUS SCIENCE: Elimination by Scientific Selection of Jews, Gypsies and Others, Germany 1933-1945
The macabre connection between science and genocide in Nazi Germany
0-19-261555-6 Oxford $24.95

FIRST PERSON ACCOUNTS

First-person accounts—Anne Frank's diary of a hidden life in occupied Holland, Primo Levi's chronicle of humanity gone haywire at Auschwitz—do what most histories cannot: they distill the horror of mass murder into the story of a single tortured life.

• Wladyslaw Bartoszewski
THE WARSAW GHETTO: A Christian's Testimony
Memoir of a Polish Catholic who served as liaison between Jewish leaders in the ghetto and the Polish underground
Foreword by Stanislaw Lem
0-8070-5602-2 Beacon $14.95

• Bruno Bettelheim
THE INFORMED HEART: Autonomy in a Mass Age
The noted psychologist and educator, a prisoner at Dachau and Buchenwald in 1938-39, offers psychological parallels between life in the camps and the loss of self in today's "mass society"
0-02-903200-8 Free Press $20.75

• Lucy S. Dawidowicz
FROM THAT TIME AND PLACE: A Memoir, 1938-1947
By the author of *The War Against the Jews, 1933-1945*
0-393-02674-4 Norton $21.95

• Alexander Donat
THE HOLOCAUST KINGDOM: A Memoir
"Never—and I include such books as *The Wall*—has the story of the Warsaw Ghetto been told as understandably, as vividly"—Meyer Levin
0-8052-5001-8 Schocken pb $12.95

Anne Frank
ANNE FRANK: The Diary of a Young Girl
0-385-04019-9 Doubleday $18.95
0-671-61760-5 Washington Square pb $4.50

THE DIARY OF ANNE FRANK: The Critical Edition
An exhaustively detailed version of the acclaimed diary, including material not found in the standard edition
Translated by Arnold J. Pomerans
Edited by Netherlands State Institute for War Documentation
0-385-24023-6 Doubleday $30.00

Miep Gies with Alison L. Gold
ANNE FRANK REMEMBERED: The Story of the Woman Who Helped to Hide the Frank Family
0-671-54771-2 Simon & Schuster $17.95
0-671-66234-1 Simon & Schuster pb $6.95

• Anton Gill
THE JOURNEY BACK FROM HELL: Conversations with Concentration Camp Survivors
0-688-08847-3 Morrow $22.95

• Abraham I. Katsh, editor & translator
SCROLL OF AGONY: The Warsaw Diary of Chaim A. Kaplan
The first-person account of a Hebrew school principal, discovered hidden in a kerosene can 20 years after the Warsaw ghetto uprising
0-02-034000-1 Macmillan pb $6.95

• Eugen Kogon
THE THEORY AND PRACTICE OF HELL
Classic and occasionally gruesome anatomy of life and political resistance at Buchenwald
0-425-07761-6 Berkley pb $4.50

• Primo Levi
SURVIVAL IN AUSCHWITZ: The Nazi Assault on Humanity
"Documentary evidence of the first order of the inhumanity of man to man in our time"—*American Journal of Sociology*
0-02-034310-8 Macmillan pb $4.95

• Louis J. Micheels
DOCTOR 117641: A Holocaust Memoir
A memoir of Auschwitz and the Dachau death march
0-300-04398-8 Yale $19.95

• Henry Orenstein
I SHALL LIVE: Surviving Against All Odds, 1939-1945
A survivor of five concentration camps tells how he saved himself by posing as a mathematician and becoming a member of a group of Jewish "superbrains" organized with the Gestapo's blessing to help Hitler win the war
0-671-66782-3 Simon & Schuster pb $8.95

• Samuel Pisar
OF BLOOD AND HOPE
0-02-006310-5 Macmillan pb $9.95

• Emmanuel Ringelblum
NOTES FROM THE WARSAW GHETTO: The Journal of Emmanuel Ringelblum
Day-to-day eyewitness account of the destruction of Europe's largest ghetto, by its archivist, who was executed with his wife and son in 1944
0-8052-0460-1 Schocken pb $9.95

- Sylvia Rothchild, editor
VOICES FROM THE HOLOCAUST
Interviews with survivors
Foreword by Elie Wiesel
0–452–00860–3 Meridian pb $10.95

- Samuel Willenberg
SURVIVING TREBLINKA
0–631–16261–5 Blackwell $19.95

> Now everyone is busy scraping the bottom of his bowl with his spoon so as not to waste the last drops of the soup; a confused, metallic clatter, signifying the end of the day. Silence slowly prevails and then, from my bunk on the top row, I see and hear old Kuhn praying aloud, with his beret on his head, swaying backwards and forwards violently. Kuhn is thanking God because he has not been chosen.
>
> Kuhn is out of his senses. Does he not see Beppo the Greek in the bunk next to him, Beppo who is twenty years old and is going to the gas chamber the day after tomorrow and knows it and lies there looking fixedly at the light without saying anything and without even thinking any more? Can Kuhn fail to realize that next time it will be his turn? Does Kuhn not understand that what has happened today is an abomination, which no propitiatory prayer, no pardon, no expiation by the guilty, which nothing at all in the power of man can ever clean again.
>
> If I was God, I would spit at Kuhn's prayer.
>
> Primo Levi
> **SURVIVAL IN AUSCHWITZ: The Nazi Assault on Humanity**
> 0–02–034310–8 Macmillan pb $4.95

RESCUE AND RESISTANCE

Uplifting tales of those who risked their lives to resist persecution and murder range from the efforts of individuals, like Sweden's Raoul Wallenberg, who used his position to save thousands of Hungarian Jews, to Denmark's collective action to resist Hitler. They also tell of the Jewish partisans whose underground activities challenge the notion that the Jews marched to their graves like "sheep to the slaughter."

- Robert Abzug
INSIDE THE VICIOUS HEART: Americans and the Liberation of Nazi Concentration Camps
0–19–503597–6 Oxford $24.95
0–19–504236–0 Oxford pb $8.95

- Ruth Andreas-Friedrich
BERLIN UNDERGROUND, 1938-1945
1–55778–159–1 Paragon pb $12.95

- Len Crome
UNBROKEN: Resistance and Survival in the Concentration Camps
The efforts of communist and socialist prisoners, told through the experiences of a theater group member
0–8052–4064–0 Schocken $18.95
0–8052–0881–X Schocken pb $7.95

- Philip Hallie
LEST INNOCENT BLOOD BE SHED
How a French village under the Occupation organized to save Jews
0–06–132051–X Harper & Row pb $8.95

- Kati Marton
WALLENBERG
The Swedish aristocrat who rescued thousands of Hungarian Jews later disappeared mysteriously
0–345–30364–4 Ballantine pb $3.95

- Samuel P. & Pearl M. Oliner
THE ALTRUISTIC PERSONALITY: Rescuers of Jews in Nazi Europe
Interviews with 700 people who did—and did not—save European Jews, aimed at discovering what led people to risk their lives to save others
0–02–923830–7 Free Press $24.95

- Hannah Senesh
HANNAH SENESH: Her Life and Diary
The Zionist pioneer who was executed by the Nazis for resistance activities in Europe
0–8052–0410–5 Schocken pb $9.95

- Yuri Suhl
THEY FOUGHT BACK: The Story of the Jewish Resistance in Nazi Europe
Confronts the myth of Jewish passivity
0–8052–0479–2 Schocken pb $11.95

- Nechama Tec
WHEN LIGHT PIERCED THE DARKNESS: Christian Rescue of Jews in Nazi-Occupied Poland
Based on 500 case histories of people who risked death to open their doors to Jews; by a Polish Jew aided by Christians
0–19–505194–7 Oxford pb $8.95

- Leni Yahil
THE RESCUE OF DANISH JEWRY: Test of a Democracy
How conquered Denmark and neutral Sweden saved Jews from the "Final Solution" in a dramatic episode in October 1943
Translated by Morris Gradel
0–8276–0232–4 JPS pb $9.95

WHILE SIX MILLION DIED: The World and the Holocaust

The response of the world—particularly the United States and its allies—to the plight of Europe's Jews has become a major source of research and controversy. In 1966 Arthur Morse's *While Six Million Died* demonstrated that more than simple disbelief led to Allied inaction. Since then, led by the pioneering work of historian David Wyman, many factors have been blamed for the apa-

How Danish refugees from the Nazis were ferried to safety in Sweden, September 1943, from The Macmillan Atlas of the Holocaust *by Martin Gilbert (Da Capo)*

thetic response to Hitler's ongoing murder of Jews: anti-Semitism, opposition to immigration, the silence of the Catholic church, insecurity and ineffective leadership among American Jews, Britain's troubles in Palestine, and even Franklin Roosevelt's own indifference.

- Leonard Dinnerstein
AMERICA AND THE SURVIVORS OF THE HOLOCAUST
Chronicles the postwar mistreatment of refugees and their arrival in the United States. "The shocking story of antisemitism, neglect, and heroic effort is laid bare here"—*Publishers Weekly*
0–231–04177–2 Columbia pb $16.00

- Henry L. Feingold
THE POLITICS OF RESCUE: The Roosevelt Administration and the Holocaust, 1938-1945
"Neither an apologia for nor an indictment of the Roosevelt Administration, but rather a balanced and persuasive account of what it did and might have done about rescuing Europe's Jews"—*American Historical Review*
0–8052–5019–0 Schocken pb $12.95

- Seymour Maxwell Finger, editor
AMERICAN JEWRY DURING THE HOLOCAUST
A report sponsored by the American Jewish Commission on the Holocaust
0–8419–7506–X Holmes & Meier pb $35.00

- Martin Gilbert
AUSCHWITZ AND THE ALLIES
A disturbing chronicle of Allied inaction
0–03–057058–1 Henry Holt pb $9.95

- Walter Laqueur
**THE TERRIBLE SECRET: Suppression of
the Truth about Hitler's "Final Solution"**
"After reading this book, with its proof of
how much was known, I am astonished at
our state of ignorance then"—*NY Times
Book Review*
0–14–006136–3 Penguin pb $7.95

- Walter Laqueur & Richard Breitman
BREAKING THE SILENCE
The story of Edward Schulte, the German
industrialist who in 1942 broke the silence
to the Allies on the extermination of the
Jews
0–671–63315–5 Simon & Schuster pb $8.95

- Deborah Lipstadt
**BEYOND BELIEF: The American Press
and the Coming of the Holocaust**
How the press failed to overcome official
indifference to the Holocaust
0–02–919160–2 Free Press $24.95

- Haskel Lookstein
**WERE WE OUR BROTHERS'
KEEPERS?: The Public Response of
American Jews to the Nazis, 1938-1944**
Could America's Jews have done more to
save their brethren in Europe? By a noted
rabbi
0–394–75598–7 Random House pb $8.95

- John F. Morley
**VATICAN DIPLOMACY AND THE JEWS
DURING THE HOLOCAUST, 1939-1943**
What the Catholic Church did—and did
not—do; by a Catholic priest
0–87068–701–8 Ktav $35.00

- Arthur D. Morse
**WHILE SIX MILLION DIED: A Chronicle
of American Apathy**
An early (1966) account of America's
failure to rescue Europe's Jews
0–87951–973–8 Overlook pb $9.95

- Bernard Wasserstein
**BRITAIN AND THE JEWS OF EUROPE,
1939-1945**
Focuses on Britain's near-total wartime ban
on Jewish refugee immigration and its
restrictive immigration policy in Palestine;
by a first-rate historian
0–19–282185–7 Oxford pb $12.95

David S. Wyman
**THE ABANDONMENT OF THE
JEWS**
The definitive account of American
apathy to the Jewish plight in the
Holocaust. "We will not see a better
book on this subject in our lifetime"—
Leonard Dinnerstein, *Journal of
American History*
Introduction by Elie Wiesel
0–394–74077–7 Pantheon pb $8.95

**PAPER WALLS: America and the
Refugee Crisis, 1938-1941**
How unemployment, nationalism, anti-
Semitism, and fear of members of the
fifth column posing as refugees allowed
only a small number of Jews to find
refuge in the United States; first
published in 1968
0–394–73659–1 Pantheon pb $8.95

ART AND LITERATURE

- Joseph P. Czarnecki
LAST TRACES: The Lost Art of Auschwitz
Paintings, drawings, poems, and other art
works from victims of the death camp
Introduction by Chaim Potok
0–689–12022–2 Atheneum $35.00

- Judith E. Doneson
**THE HOLOCAUST IN AMERICAN
FILM**
Argues that the presentation of the
Holocaust has been influenced by such
American social issues as McCarthyism,
civil rights, Vietnam, and black-Jewish
tensions
0–8276–0284–7 JPS $22.95

- Yaffa Eliach
HASIDIC TALES OF THE HOLOCAUST
Over 85 stories of Hasidim, their
destruction and survival, in the form of
classic Hasidic tales
0–19–503199–7 Oxford $24.95
0–679–72043–X Random House pb $7.95

- Albert H. Friedlander, editor
**OUT OF THE WHIRLWIND: A Reader of
Holocaust Literature**
Selections from Anne Frank, Abraham
Joshua Heschel, Leo Baeck, Elie Wiesel,
Rolf Hochhuth, and others
0–8052–0517–9 Schocken pb $11.95

- Annette Insdorf
**INDELIBLE SHADOWS: Film and the
Holocaust**
Foreword by Elie Wiesel
0–521–37810–9 Cambridge pb $12.95

- Alfred Kantor
**THE BOOK OF ALFRED KANTOR: An
Artist's Journal of the Holocaust**
Over 150 watercolors and drawings create
an illustrated diary of a 22-year-old Czech
artist's years at three concentration camps
0–8052–0825–9 Schocken pb $16.95

- Claude Lanzmann
SHOAH: An Oral History of the Holocaust
Complete text of the landmark film
Foreword by Simone de Beauvoir
0–394–74329–6 Pantheon pb $6.95

- Eleanor Mlotek & Malke Gottlieb,
editors
WE ARE HERE: Songs of the Holocaust
Forty songs, most of them written in
ghettoes and concentration camps,
reflecting both the despair and hope of
Holocaust victims
Translated by Roslyn Bresnick-Perry
Illustrated by Tsirl Waletzky
Foreword by Elie Wiesel
0–88254–857–3 Hippocrene $10.00

- Anne Roiphe
**A SEASON FOR HEALING: Reflections
on the Holocaust**
0–671–66753–X Summit $17.95

- Hana Volavkova, editor
**I NEVER SAW ANOTHER BUTTERFLY:
Children's Drawings and Poems from
Terezin Concentration Camp, 1942-1944**
Translated by Jeanne Nemcova
0–8052–0598–5 Schocken pb $6.95

Holocaust Fiction: A Sampler

- Saul Bellow
MR. SAMMLER'S PLANET
0–670–49322–8 Viking $12.95
0–14–007317–5 Penguin pb $6.95

- Leslie Epstein
KING OF THE JEWS
0–452–25823–5 NAL pb $7.95

- John Hersey
THE WALL
Hersey's diary of life and death in the
Warsaw Ghetto
0–394–45092–2 Knopf $25.00

- Rolf Hochhuth
THE DEPUTY
A play depicting the Catholic Church's
failures to intercede on behalf of the Jews
Translated by Richard & Clara Winston
0–394–17125–X Grove pb $7.95

- Thomas Keneally
SCHINDLER'S LIST
A German's efforts to save Jews
0–14–006784–1 Penguin pb $6.95

- André Schwarz-Bart
THE LAST OF THE JUST
Translated by Stephen Becker
0–689–70365–1 Atheneum pb $12.95

- Art Spiegelman
MAUS: A Survivor's Tale
A cartoonist tries to come to terms with
his father's life in Hitler's Europe through
a cat-and-mouse fable of Nazis and Jews
0–394–74723–2 Pantheon pb $8.95

- William Styron
SOPHIE'S CHOICE
A young American southerner comes of
age through his relationship with a non-
Jewish Polish survivor whose experience at
Auschwitz has doomed her
0–394–46109–6 Random House $29.95
0–553–27749–9 Bantam pb $5.50

- Leon Uris
MILA 18
More on the Warsaw Ghetto, from the
author of *QBVII* and *Exodus*
0–553–24160–5 Bantam pb $4.50

Elie Wiesel

Beginning with the publication of his first
novel *Night*, a loosely fictionalized account
of his haunted memories of Auschwitz, Wiesel has recorded the tragedy both of death
and of survival. His recent books have
branched into the realms of Soviet Jews,
Hasidism, and Biblical studies; several of his

IF YOU CAN'T FIND IT, LOOK IN THE INDEX

nonfiction works can be found in the Judaism chapter. Wiesel won the 1986 Nobel Peace Prize.

- Elie Wiesel
THE ACCIDENT
0–8090–1525–0 Hill & Wang pb $5.95

A BEGGAR IN JERUSALEM
0–8052–0778–3 Schocken pb $8.95

DAWN
An Auschwitz survivor faces his own life-and-death dilemma as a member of the Zionist underground
0–553–22536–7 Bantam pb $2.95

THE GATES OF THE FOREST
A young survivor of the Nazis travels a strange, folkloric path through the underground forests of Europe
0–8052–0698–1 Schocken pb $7.95

LEGENDS OF OUR TIME
Wiesel recounts the deeds and visions of extraordinary people
0–8052–0714–7 Schocken pb $7.95

NIGHT
Perhaps the best single volume in print on the Holocaust
0–553–27253–5 Bantam pb $3.50

THE NIGHT TRILOGY: Night, Dawn, The Accident
0–8090–1537–4 Hill & Wang pb $9.95

THE OATH
The sole survivor of a pogrom takes an oath of silence but roams the earth years later in search of someone to release him from the burden of silence
0–8052–0808–9 Schocken pb $8.95

ONE GENERATION AFTER
Stories and writings reflecting on the legacy of the Holocaust, as Wiesel returns to the village of his youth
0–8052–0713–9 Schocken pb $6.95

THE TRIAL OF GOD: A Play in Three Acts
In 1649 in Shamgorod, three actors and the three survivors of a pogrom attempt to stage a trial of God for what He allowed to happen to His people in this "tragic farce"
0–8052–0809–7 Schocken pb $7.95

TWILIGHT
0–671–64407–6 Summit $17.95

ZALMEN, OR THE MADNESS OF GOD
Dealing with the courage to cry out against oppression and isolation, this play is a metaphor for Soviet Jewry
0–8052–0777–5 Schocken pb $7.95

THE POSTWAR TRIALS AND THE NAZI HUNTERS

- Hannah Arendt
EICHMANN IN JERUSALEM: A Report of the Banality of Evil
Haunting reflections on Eichmann's role in the "Final Solution," written during his war-crimes trial in Jerusalem
0–14–004450–7 Penguin pb $6.95

West Berlin in 1965, from Europe in the Twentieth Century *by Robert O. Paxton (HBJ)*

- Chuck Ashman & Robert Wagman
THE NAZI HUNTERS
Focuses on Simon Wiesenthal and the Klarsfelds, in addition to identifying war criminals now in hiding
0–88687–357–6 Pharos $18.95

- Robert E. Conot
JUSTICE AT NUREMBERG
A dramatic account of the trial
0–88184–032–7 Carroll & Graf pb $11.95

- Bradley Smith
THE ROAD TO NUREMBERG
0–465–07056–6 Basic Books $14.95

- Ann Tusa & John Tusa
THE NUREMBERG TRIAL
A detailed narrative history, focusing on the mechanics of international law
0–07–065511–1 McGraw-Hill pb $9.95

Epilogue: Children of the Holocaust

- Helen Epstein
CHILDREN OF THE HOLOCAUST: Conversations with Sons and Daughters of Survivors
How the Holocaust has affected the children of survivors
0–14–011284–7 Penguin pb $7.95

- Peter Sichrovsky
BORN GUILTY: Children of Nazi Families
Oral histories probe the legacy of Nazism in 14 families. "In some ways cuts closer to the core of the Nazi system than anything else on the subject"—Howard Fast
0–465–00742–2 Basic Books $17.95

STRANGERS IN THEIR OWN LAND: Young Jews in Germany and Austria Today
0–14–009965–4 Penguin pb $5.95

Postwar Europe and Current Affairs

▶ See also International Relations and Strategic Studies

- Hans Magnus Enzensberger
EUROPE, EUROPE: Forays into a Continent
A leading West German writer's portraits of contemporary Spain, Portugal, Sweden, Italy, Poland, and Hungary
Translated by Marin Chalmers
0–394–55819–7 Pantheon $18.95

- Michael J. Hogan
THE MARSHALL PLAN: America, Britain, and the Reconstruction of Western Europe, 1947-1952
0–521–25140–0 Cambridge $34.50

- H. Stuart Hughes
SOPHISTICATED REBELS: The Political Culture of European Dissent, 1968-1987
What happened to the revolutionary spirit after 1968? Hughes suggests that dissenters learned their lesson and began to pursue their goals in patient, realistic, limited fashion
0–674–82130–0 Harvard $20.00

- Jane Kramer
EUROPEANS
An elegant and witty series of essays by a *New Yorker* contributor. Chapters include "Being German," "Danton and Robespierre," and "Mitterand's Monarchy"
0–374–14939–9 Farrar, Straus & Giroux $22.95

UNSETTLING EUROPE
The "new" Europe of migrants, refugees, and political exiles, including rural Italians, Ugandan Asians driven to England, and French Algerians in France
0–374–52183–2 Farrar, Straus & Giroux pb $7.95

• **Michael R. Marrus**
THE UNWANTED: European Refugees in the Twentieth Century
Those displaced by the Nazis, the Spanish Civil War, the Cold War, and other 20th-century crises
0–19–503615–8 Oxford $27.95

• **Alan S. Milward**
THE RECONSTRUCTION OF WESTERN EUROPE, 1945-51
An economic history of the reconstruction and a search for the origins of the Great Boom of the 1950s and 1960s
0–520–06035–0 California pb $15.95

• **Robert O. Paxton**
EUROPE IN THE TWENTIETH CENTURY
0–15–524719–0 HBJ $35.95

• **Roland N. Stromberg**
AFTER EVERYTHING: Western Intellectual History Since 1945
0–312–01120–2 St. Martin's pb $14.95

European Communism

Fernando Claudin
THE COMMUNIST MOVEMENT: From Comintern to Cominform
A Marxist looks at international communism under Lenin and Stalin; a 2 volume set
Translated by Brian Pearce
0–85345–366–7 Monthly Review $27.00

Carl Marzani
THE PROMISE OF EUROCOMMUNISM
Introduction by John Cammett
0–88208–110–1 Lawrence Hill $16.95
0–88208–111–X Lawrence Hill pb $8.95

THE SOVIET BLOC

▶ **See also Russian and Soviet Studies**

• **Timothy Garton Ash**
THE POLISH REVOLUTION: Solidarity
0–684–18114–2 Scribners $17.95
0–394–72907–2 Random House pb $10.95

• **Rudolf Bahro**
THE ALTERNATIVE IN EASTERN EUROPE
In contrast to much dissident writing in Russia and Eastern Europe, this work constitutes a major theoretical synthesis in the great tradition of German Marxism. "The most important book on socialist theory to have appeared since the Second World War"—*Tribune* (London)
Translated by David Fernbach
0–86091–734–7 Verso pb $17.95

• **J.F. Brown**
EASTERN EUROPE AND COMMUNIST RULE
The former director of Radio Free Europe considers domestic and foreign policy issues in the Warsaw Pact nations as well as Yugoslavia and Albania
0–8223–0841–X Duke pb $17.95

Prague, August 1968. The sign says: "Dubček Hurray! USSR go home," from Europe in the Twentieth Century *by Robert O. Paxton (HBJ)*

• **Helene Carrer d'Encausse**
BIG BROTHER: The Soviet Union and Soviet Europe
From the postwar "Stalinization" of Eastern Europe to the continuing eruptions of nationalism to the age of Gorbachev; from a noted French political scientist
Translated by George Holoch
0–8419–1043–X Holmes & Meier pb $24.50

• **Karen Dawisha**
EASTERN EUROPE, GORBACHEV AND REFORM: The Great Challenge
Soviet policy in a region with political ties to Moscow and cultural ties with the West
0–521–35560–5 Cambridge $29.95
0–521–35663–6 Cambridge pb $12.95

• **Charles Gati**
HUNGARY AND THE SOVIET BLOC
0–8223–0747–2 Duke pb $14.95

• **Sandor Kopacsi**
IN THE NAME OF THE WORKING CLASS
The Budapest police chief's account of the 1956 Hungarian uprising
0–802–10010–4 Grove $17.95

• **Joseph Rothschild**
RETURN TO DIVERSITY: A Political History of East Central Europe Since World War II
The challenges to a monolithic Eastern Europe—from the Yugoslavia of the 1940s to the Poland of the 1980s
0–19–504574–2 Oxford $24.95

• **Dennison Rusinow**
THE YUGOSLAV EXPERIMENT, 1948-1974
0–520–03304–3 California $46.50
0–520–03730–8 California pb $10.50

• **Jurgen Tampke**
THE PEOPLE'S REPUBLICS OF EASTERN EUROPE
0–312–60035–6 St. Martin's $22.50

• **Lech Walesa**
A WAY OF HOPE: An Autobiography
0–8050–0668–0 Henry Holt $19.95

• **Duncan Wilson**
TITO'S YUGOSLAVIA
0–521–22655–4 Cambridge $37.50

THE NEW GERMANYS

• **Douglas Botting**
FROM THE RUINS OF THE REICH: Germany, 1945-1949
"A portrait of hell, complete with all the details"—*NY Times*
0–452–00816–6 Meridian pb $9.95

• **Norman Gelb**
THE BERLIN WALL: Kennedy, Khrushchev, and a Showdown in the Heart of Europe
The politics of the wall and the people whose lives it transformed
0–8129–1218–7 Times Books $19.95
0–671–65787–9 Simon & Schuster pb $8.95

• **Sabine Reichel**
WHAT DID YOU DO IN THE WAR, DADDY?: Growing Up German
"Outspoken, pugnacious, penned in prose that cuts like a knife, this autobiographical sketch records how one German woman came to grips with her country's Nazi past and her parents' deafening silence"—*Publishers Weekly*
0–8090–9685–4 Hill & Wang $19.95

• Henry A. Turner, Jr.
THE TWO GERMANIES SINCE 1945: East and West
From the Nazi surrender to the Bundestag elections of 1987
0–300–04415–1 Yale pb $9.95

> We assumed that the West Germans were "ours," even as the Sovietized East Germans were "theirs." We knew that the Germans needed our protection for their security. And in the process we forgot that Bonn was intended as a *provisorium*, that the federal constitution anticipated the time when the two Germanys would be reunited "in peace and freedom." We also forgot that NATO was originally intended to contain the Soviets openly—and the Germans, discreetly . . .
>
> For several decades we forgot "the German question," as did so many Germans. We assumed that Adenauer's original option for Western integration and indefinite postponement of reunification would last forever. We did not anticipate that once the FRG had become the most powerful country in Europe west of the USSR, that once it had become somewhat disenchanted with the dream of Europe or the model of America, it would recall Germany's historic unity, it would remember that it uniquely is a powerful state with the deepest national grievance.
>
> Fritz Stern
> **DREAMS AND DELUSIONS: National Socialism in the Drama of the German Past**
> 0–394–75772–6 Random House pb $10.95

The German Democratic Republic

• David Childs
THE GDR: Moscow's German Ally
0–04–445095–8 Unwin Hyman pb $17.95

• Gregory W. Sandford
FROM HITLER TO ULBRICHT: The Communist Reconstruction of East Germany, 1945-46
0–691–05367–7 Princeton $30.00

The Federal Republic of Germany

• John Ardagh
GERMANY AND THE GERMANS: An Anatomy of Society Today
The engaging British journalist asks, Are the Germans still plagued by their famous love of order and obeying rules, and is this a strength or weakness? Chapters include "The Economic Miracle," "Turks and 'Other Guests,'" and "How Stable a Democracy?"
0–06–015839–5 Harper & Row $24.95
0–06–091532–3 Harper & Row pb $10.95

• Ralf Dahrendorf
SOCIETY AND DEMOCRACY IN GERMANY
A German sociologist attempts to describe the "whole" of his own society
0–393–00953–X Norton pb $10.95

• Ian Derbyshire
POLITICS IN WEST GERMANY: From Schmidt to Kohl
An up-to-date political history covering the most recent events, policies, and political personalities. Includes a valuable glossary and appendices
0–550–20740–6 Chambers pb $8.95

• Marion Donhoff
FOE INTO FRIEND: The Makers of the New Germany from Konrad Adenauer to Helmut Schmidt
0–312–29692–4 St. Martin's $20.00

• Lewis J. Edinger
WEST GERMAN POLITICS
Politics and policy in the West Germany of the 1980s, in light of history and the democracies of the West
0–231–06090–4 Columbia $32.50
0–231–06091–2 Columbia pb $11.00

• Richard J. Evans
IN HITLER'S SHADOW: West German Historians and the Attempt to Escape from the Nazi Past
Analyzes the new revisionism that soft-peddles German responsibility for Nazi war atrocities
0–394–57686–1 Pantheon $16.95
0–679–72348–X Pantheon pb $6.95

• Werner Hulsberg
THE GERMAN GREENS: A Social and Political Profile
0–86091–897–1 Verso pb $15.95

• Walter Laqueur
GERMANY TODAY: A Personal Report
0–316–51453–5 Little, Brown $16.95

• Helmut Schmidt
MEN AND POWER: A Political Memoir
Reflections from the former West German chancellor (1974-1982) on such leaders as Deng, Brezhnev, Gorbachev, Thatcher, Kissinger, Carter, and Reagan
Introduction by Henry Kissinger
0–394–56994–6 Random House $24.95

• Gordon Smith
DEMOCRACY IN WESTERN GERMANY: Parties and Politics in the Federal Republic
The third edition of Smith's study has been expanded to include developments since 1983
0–8419–1103–7 Holmes & Meier $29.50
0–8419–1096–0 Holmes & Meier pb $16.95

Kurt Waldheim

Richard Bassett
AUSTRIA AND WALDHEIM
The Waldheim controversy, by a London *Times* correspondent
0–670–82173–X Viking $19.95

Robert Edwin Herzstein
WALDHEIM: The Missing Years
0–877–95959–5 Morrow $18.95

• Louis P. De Menil
WHO SPEAKS FOR EUROPE: The Case of De Gaulle
0–312–87025–6 St. Martin's $19.95

• Richard F. Kuisel
CAPITALISM AND THE STATE IN MODERN FRANCE: Renovation and Economic Management in the Twentieth Century
0–521–23474–3 Cambridge $49.50
0–521–27378–1 Cambridge pb $15.95

• Jean LaCouture
CHARLES DE GAULLE: The Rebel
Translated by Patrick O'Brien
0–8419–0927–X Holmes & Meier pb $19.50

• Maurice Larkin
FRANCE SINCE THE POPULAR FRONT: Government and Politics, 1936-1986
The evolution of French political life from the short-lived ministries of the Third and Fourth Republics to the greater stability of the Fifth Republic. Close attention is given to key figures and the crises of 1940, 1958, and 1968
0–19–873035–7 Oxford pb $19.95

• Bernard Ledwidge
DE GAULLE
0–312–19127–8 St. Martin's $17.95

• Jean-Pierre Rioux
THE FOURTH REPUBLIC, 1944-1958
Translated by Godfrey Rogers
0–521–25238–5 Cambridge $59.50

• Charles Tilly
THE CONTENTIOUS FRENCH
A social historian on urban and provincial uprisings throughout the modern period
0–674–16695–7 Harvard $25.00

Recent History and Current Affairs

• John Ardagh
FRANCE TODAY
Among the many topics Ardagh treats are the position of women, the role of education, Club Mediterranée, *nouvelle cuisine*, and the cinema. This revised edition of *France in the 1980s* is by the author of *Germany and the Germans*
0–14–010098–9 Penguin pb $7.95

• Ian Derbyshire
POLITICS IN FRANCE: From Giscard to Mitterand
A compact volume designed for students of politics, journalists, and political commentators
0–550–20744–9 Cambridge pb $8.95

• Daniel Singer
IS SOCIALISM DOOMED?: The Meaning of Mitterrand
The collapse of the Socialist party during Mitterrand's first term
0–19–504925–X Oxford $27.95

France-Amérique

Raymonde Carroll
CULTURAL MISUNDERSTANDINGS: The French-American Experience
A native of Tunisia, educated in France and the US, probes the clash of cultures in such topics as party manners, child-rearing, privacy, and using the telephone
Translated by Carol Volk
0–226–09497–9 Chicago $19.95

J.B. Duroselle
FRANCE AND THE UNITED STATES: From the Beginnings to the Present Day
This edition originally published in 1978
Translated by Derek Coltman
0–226–17408–5 Chicago $18.00

POSTWAR ITALY

• Donald Blackmer
UNITY IN DIVERSITY: Italian Communism and the Communist World
0–262–02030–0 MIT $37.50

• John Haycroft
ITALIAN LABYRINTH: An Authentic and Revealing Portrait of Italy in the 1980s
With a population of 57 million, Italy has few natural resources, except its people; yet in the period 1957-1967, Italy became the seventh leading industrial country in the world
0–14–006918–6 Penguin pb $6.95

• H. Stuart Hughes
PRISONERS OF HOPE: The Silver Age of the Italian Jews, 1924-1974
0–674–70727–3 Harvard $17.95

• Joseph La Palombara
DEMOCRACY, ITALIAN STYLE
The foremost authority on the subject looks at the apparent chaos and stability of Italian democracy. "Journalists and diplomats should read this book. So should the tourists who flock to Italy each summer"—*London Review of Books*
0–300–04411–9 Yale pb $11.95

• Frederic Spotts & Theodor Wieser
ITALY: A Difficult Democracy
An explanation of democracy in the least-understood major European state
0–521–30451–2 Cambridge $39.50
0–521–31511–5 Cambridge pb $10.95

POSTWAR SPAIN AND PORTUGAL

• Raymond Carr & Juan P. Fusi
SPAIN: Dictatorship to Democracy
The end of Francoism and Spain's abrupt jump into modernity
0–04–946014–5 Unwin Hyman pb $14.95

• Hugo G. Ferreira & Michael W. Marshall
PORTUGAL'S REVOLUTION: Ten Years On
0–521–32204–9 Cambridge $37.50

• John Hooper
THE SPANIARDS: A Portrait of the New Spain
Life in post-Franco Spain
0–14–009808–9 Penguin pb $6.95

• Paul Preston
THE TRIUMPH OF DEMOCRACY IN SPAIN
0–416–36350–4 Methuen $32.00

POSTWAR GREECE AND TURKEY

• Richard Clogg
PARTIES AND ELECTIONS IN GREECE: The Search for Legitimacy
The antecedents of the present party system and the structure of the parties currently in power
0–8223–0823–1 Duke pb $16.95

A SHORT HISTORY OF MODERN GREECE
From the Greeks under Ottoman rule to democracy in the 1980s. Second edition
0–521–33804–2 Cambridge pb $12.95

• Richard Clogg, editor
GREECE IN THE 1980s
In 1981 Greece became the Common Market's tenth member, perhaps the most momentous step in her history since independence 150 years ago
0–312–34714–6 St. Martin's $27.50

• Nicholas Gage
ELENI
0–394–52093–9 Random House $19.50
0–345–32494–3 Ballantine pb $4.95

HELLAS: A Portrait of Greece
0–394–55694–1 Random House $17.95

• Dankwart A. Rustow
TURKEY: America's Forgotten Ally
Turkey's crucial role in American global strategy and the dynamic changes taking place within Turkish society
0–87609–023–4 Foreign Relations $14.95

Great Britain and Ireland

INTRODUCTORY WORKS

England

• Asa Briggs
A SOCIAL HISTORY OF ENGLAND: From the Romans to Mrs. Thatcher
0–14–007492–9 Penguin pb $9.95

An English town, c. 1505, from An Introduction to a History of Woodcut *by Arthur Hind (Dover)*

• Christopher Hibbert
THE ENGLISH: A Social History, 1066-1945
By the popular historian of the French Revolution and the Indian Mutiny
0–393–02371–0 Norton $39.95

• Paul Johnson
A HISTORY OF THE ENGLISH PEOPLE
Two thousand years of English history told by the conservative author of *Modern Times*. "This is a John Bull of a book, the sort of book that Cobbett might have written"—A.J.P. Taylor
0–06–132075–7 Harper & Row pb $10.95

• Trevor O. Lloyd
THE BRITISH EMPIRE, 1558-1983
0–19–873024–1 Oxford $34.50
0–19–873025–X Oxford pb $16.95

• Kenneth O. Morgan, editor
THE OXFORD ILLUSTRATED HISTORY OF BRITAIN
This beautifully produced volume traces the British Isles and people from earliest times to the present and includes contributions by ten British historians
0–19–822684–5 Oxford $35.00
0–19–285174–8 Oxford pb $16.95

• G.M. Trevelyan
A SHORTENED HISTORY OF ENGLAND
A somewhat dated but good old-fashioned Whig historical survey
0–14–010241–8 Penguin pb $7.95

• R.K. Webb
MODERN ENGLAND: From the Eighteenth Century to the Present
A comprehensive text designed for the American reader and probably the best introduction for this period
0–06–046974–9 Harper & Row pb $21.95

Kenneth Baker, editor
THE FABER BOOK OF ENGLISH HISTORY IN VERSE
Works of Shakespeare, Milton, Swift, Blake, Eliot, Larkin, and others
0–571–14882–4 Faber & Faber $25.00

Scotland and Wales

• Paul Coones & John Patten
THE PENGUIN GUIDE TO THE LANDSCAPE OF ENGLAND AND WALES
From the Mesolithic period and Bronze Age to the 20th century
0–14–008626–9 Penguin pb $9.95

• J.D. Mackie
A HISTORY OF SCOTLAND
A fine, brief synthesis
0–14–020671–X Penguin pb $5.95

• Fitzroy Maclean
A CONCISE HISTORY OF SCOTLAND
Illustrated
0–500–27224–7 Thames & Hudson pb $11.95

• Kenneth O. Morgan
REBIRTH OF A NATION: Wales, 1880-1980
0–19–821736–6 Oxford $35.00
0–19–821760–9 Oxford pb $12.95

• Jan Morris
THE MATTER OF WALES: Epic Views of a Small Country
Seen through the eyes of Owen Glendower, a 15th-century Welsh patriot who briefly united Wales in a war of independence
0–19–504221–2 Oxford pb $8.95

IRELAND

• Thomas Bartlett & others
IRISH STUDIES: A General Introduction
0–389–20806–X Barnes & Noble pb $11.50

• J.C. Beckett
THE MAKING OF MODERN IRELAND, 1603-1923
0–394–43473–0 Knopf $17.95

A SHORT HISTORY OF IRELAND
Beginning in the 5th century, when St. Patrick converted the island to Christianity, and moving into the world of modern politics and society
0–09–168741–1 David & Charles pb $13.95

• Karl Bottingheimer
IRELAND AND THE IRISH: A Short History
From the Celtic and Viking inheritance to the "Irish abroad," with a concluding chapter on Irish literature
0–231–04611–1 Columbia pb $14.50

• Denis Donoghue
WE IRISH: Essays on Irish Literature and Society
Essays include "The European Joyce," "De Valera's Day," and "O'Casey in His Letters"
0–394–55451–5 Knopf $18.95
0–520–06425–0 California pb $10.95

R.F. Foster
MODERN IRELAND, 1600-1972
"Sure to become the standard against which similar books are judged for a long time to come"—Andrew M. Greeley, *NY Times Book Review*
0–7139–9010–4 Viking $34.50

R.F. Foster, editor
THE OXFORD ILLUSTRATED HISTORY OF IRELAND
The latest in the acclaimed *Oxford Illustrated History* series
0–19–822970–4 Oxford $35.00

• Peter & Fiona Somerset Fry
A HISTORY OF IRELAND
Useful and balanced outline to the present day; illustrated
0–415–00878–6 RC&H $29.95

• Henry Glassie
PASSING THE TIME IN BALLYMENONE: Culture and History of an Ulster Community
A remarkable study revealing the complexity of traditional culture in a small agricultural community. Glassie provides everything: political ballads, potato farming, parlor decorations, jokes, and much more
0–8122–7823–2 Pennsylvania $18.95

• Paul Johnson
IRELAND, LAND OF TROUBLES: A History from the Twelfth Century to the Present Day
0–8419–0758–7 Holmes & Meier $24.50

• Oliver MacDonagh
STATES OF MIND: A Study of Anglo-Irish Conflict, 1780-1980
0–04–941015–6 Unwin Hyman pb $11.95

• Oliver MacDonagh & others, editors
IRISH CULTURE AND NATIONALISM, 1750-1950
0–312–43595–9 St. Martin's pb $27.50

• T.W. Moody & F.X. Martin, editors
THE COURSE OF IRISH HISTORY
0–85342–710–0 Alpha pb $24.95

• Frank Murphy, editor
THE BOG IRISH: Who They Were and How They Lived
0–14–008439–8 Penguin pb $6.95

• John O'Beirne Ranelagh
A SHORT HISTORY OF IRELAND
0–521–28889–4 Cambridge pb $10.95

• Kathleen J. Ryan & Bernard Share, editors
IRISH TRADITIONS
Introduction by James Plunkett
0–8109–1109–4 Abrams $39.95

• Roger Stalley
THE CISTERCIAN MONASTARIES OF IRELAND
0–300–04546–8 Yale pb $29.95

• Niall Toibin, editor
THE IRISH RECITER: Ballads, Poems and Recitations for Every Occasion
0–85640–369–5 Longwood pb $6.50

• Niall Williams & Christine Breen
O COME YE BACK TO IRELAND: Our First Year in County Clare
0–939149–07–9 Soho Press $16.95
0–939149–22–2 Soho Press pb $8.95

TOPICS IN BRITISH HISTORY

Social Life

• Margaret Baker
FOLKLORE AND CUSTOMS OF RURAL ENGLAND
How ancient beliefs, superstitions, and rituals live on
0–7153–9249–2 David & Charles pb $11.95

• Ronald Blythe
AKENFIELD: Portrait of an English Village
A classic focusing on one village on the Suffolk coast
0–394–73847–0 Pantheon pb $7.95

• Antonia Fraser
THE WEAKER VESSEL: Woman's Lot in Seventeenth-Century England
By the author of *The Warrior Queens*
0–394–73251–0 Random House pb $9.95

• John R. Gillis
FOR BETTER, FOR WORSE: British Marriages, 1600 to the Present
"Aspires to be the most comprehensive treatment to date of the history of marriage in a major Western society, and may well have succeeded"—*Kirkus Reviews*
0–19–504556–4 Oxford pb $12.95

• Geoffrey Hughes
WORDS IN TIME: A Social History of the English Vocabulary
The fascinating origin of words: "blurb" comes from "Miss Linda Blurb" who appeared on an American book cover around 1900; and more
0–631–15832–4 Blackwell $24.95

• Peter Laslett
THE WORLD WE HAVE LOST: England Before the Industrial Age
0–02–367860–7 Macmillan pb $24.00

• Alan Macfarlane
MARRIAGE AND LOVE IN ENGLAND: 1300-1840
0–631–15438–8 Blackwell pb $15.95

• Richard Muir
THE ENGLISH VILLAGE
A 1980 best-seller with 174 illustrations, 22 in color
0–500–27213–1 Thames & Hudson pb $9.95

• Lawrence Stone
FAMILY, SEX AND MARRIAGE IN ENGLAND, 1500-1800
0–06–131979–1 Harper & Row pb $10.95

A 17th-century maypole, from The Oxford Illustrated History of Britain *edited by Kenneth O. Morgan*

● Lawrence & Jeanne C. Stone
AN OPEN ELITE?: England, 1540-1880
A test of the long-held notion that landed society was opened to infiltration by families newly made rich through trade, office, or the professions
0–19–285149–7 Oxford pb $12.95

● John K. Walton & James Walvin, editors
LEISURE IN BRITAIN, 1780-1939
0–7190–1946–X St. Martin's pb $12.50

Town and Country

● Christopher Brooke & Roger Highfield
OXFORD AND CAMBRIDGE
A cultural and architectural history
0–521–30139–4 Cambridge $49.50

● Gordon E. Cherry
CITIES AND PLANS: The Shaping of Urban Britain in the Nineteenth and Twentieth Centuries
0–7131–6562–6 Edward Arnold $26.95

● Mark Girouard
ROBERT SMYTHSON AND THE ELIZABETHAN COUNTRY HOUSE
England eagerly receives the architecture of Italy and makes it its own
0–300–02389–8 Yale pb $15.95

VICTORIAN PUBS
A photographic essay: interiors and exteriors of gin palaces, many still in existence today
0–300–03199–8 Yale $37.50
0–300–03201–3 Yale pb $17.95

Sea Power

● Paul M. Kennedy
THE RISE AND FALL OF BRITISH NAVAL MASTERY
The author of *The Rise and Fall of the Great Powers* surveys his subject from the Tudors to the present day. "A work of the first importance"—*International Historical Review*
0–948660–01–5 Ashfield pb $17.50

● G.E. Manwaring & Bonamy Dobrée
MUTINY: The Floating Republic
While England was at war with France, the Navy mutinied in 1797. The uprising was remarkable for its Jacobin-like

organization and rigid discipline, and it led to long overdue reforms
0–09–173154–2 David & Charles pb $15.95

REFERENCE

● James S. Curl
ENGLISH ARCHITECTURE: An Illustrated Glossary
Over 2000 entries
0–7153–8887–8 David & Charles $24.95

● Christopher Haigh
THE CAMBRIDGE HISTORICAL ENCYCLOPEDIA OF GREAT BRITAIN AND IRELAND
0–521–25559–7 Cambridge $37.50

● Elizabeth Longford, editor
THE OXFORD BOOK OF ROYAL ANECDOTES
"Absolutely jam-packed with tempting tidbits"—*Library Journal*
0–19–214153–8 Oxford $19.95

● Alan & Victoria Palmer
WHO'S WHO IN BLOOMSBURY
0–312–01630–1 St. Martin's $29.95

WHO'S WHO IN SHAKESPEARE'S ENGLAND
Over 700 biographies of leading figures in the arts, politics, the church, the court, the secret service, as well as the theater and literary world
0–312–87096–5 St. Martin's $32.50

● Nigel Saul
THE BATSFORD COMPANION TO MEDIEVAL ENGLAND
0–389–20359–9 Barnes & Noble $28.50

The Pelican History of England

This first-rate, popularly priced series spans the entire course of English history and is useful for students and general readers alike.

Ian Richmond
ROMAN BRITAIN
0–14–020315–X Penguin pb $5.95

Dorothy Whitelock
THE BEGINNINGS OF ENGLISH SOCIETY
0–14–020245–5 Penguin pb $5.95

Doris Mary Stenton
ENGLISH SOCIETY IN THE EARLY MIDDLE AGES
0–14–020252–8 Penguin pb $5.95

A.R. Myers
ENGLAND IN THE LATE MIDDLE AGES
0–14–020234–X Penguin pb $5.95

S.T. Bindoff
TUDOR ENGLAND
0–14–020212–9 Penguin pb $5.95

J.P. Kenyon
STUART ENGLAND
0–14–022552–8 Penguin pb $5.95

J.H. Plumb
ENGLAND IN THE EIGHTEENTH CENTURY
0–14–020231–5 Penguin pb $5.95

David Thomson
ENGLAND IN THE NINETEENTH CENTURY
0–14–020197–1 Penguin pb $5.95

ENGLAND IN THE TWENTIETH CENTURY
0–14–020691–4 Penguin pb $5.95

HIGHLIGHTS OF MEDIEVAL ENGLAND AND IRELAND

At the height of the Plantagenet (Norman) dynasty, the kings of England considered their holdings in France as valuable as anything they ruled in Britain. For the medieval period, therefore, the history of England cannot be separated from that of France.
▶ **See also Archaeology & Medieval and Renaissance Europe**

Arthur's Britain

Leslie Alcock
ARTHUR'S BRITAIN: History and Archaeology
0–14–021396–1 Penguin pb $7.95

Geoffrey Ashe
THE LANDSCAPE OF KING ARTHUR
Lovely photographs of landscapes Arthur would have known, with comments by a leading Arthurian scholar
0–8050–0711–3 Henry Holt $24.95

Norma Lorre Goodrich
KING ARTHUR
A medieval scholar searches archaeology, history, and romance for the truth of the Arthurian legend
0–06–097182–7 Harper & Row pb $10.95

MERLIN
Passages from ancient sources brought together in a fascinating narrative recreate the magical thinking of the early Middle Ages
0–06–097183–5 Harper & Row pb $10.95

● David J. Bernstein
THE MYSTERY OF THE BAYEUX TAPESTRY
Illustration of the Conquest woven by the wives and daughters of the Norman barons
0–226–04400–9 Chicago $29.95

● R. Allen Brown
NORMANS AND THE NORMAN CONQUEST
0–317–43358–X Longwood $36.00

• M.T. Clanchy
ENGLAND AND ITS RULERS, 1066-1547: Foreign Lordship and National Identity
0–389–20423–4 Barnes & Noble $27.50

• Helen Clarke
THE ARCHAEOLOGY OF MEDIEVAL ENGLAND
0–631–15293–8 Blackwell pb $16.95

• Kevin Crossley-Holland, editor
THE ANGLO-SAXON WORLD: An Anthology
0–19–281632–2 Oxford pb $6.95

• John Harvey
CATHEDRALS OF ENGLAND AND WALES
The most up-to-date source on the architecture of the 13th, 14th, and 15th centuries
0–7134–5871–2 David & Charles pb $29.95

• Peter Harbison
PRE-CHRISTIAN IRELAND: From the First Settlers to the Early Celts
0–500–02110–4 Thames & Hudson $24.95

• R.H. Hilton & T.H. Aston
THE ENGLISH RISING OF 1381
Essays presenting the most recent interpretation of the Peasants' War
0–521–35930–9 Cambridge pb $10.95

• Michael Richter
MEDIEVAL IRELAND: The Enduring Tradition
Translated by Brian Store
0–312–02338–3 St. Martin's $35.00

• Michael Wood
IN SEARCH OF THE DARK AGES
Biographies of principal figures, from Boadicea to William the Conqueror
0–8160–1686–0 Facts On File $22.95

The Making of the English Constitution

• Stanley B. Chrimes
AN INTRODUCTION TO THE ADMINISTRATIVE HISTORY OF MEDIEVAL ENGLAND
A clear exposition of the medieval bureaucracy: the use of the royal seals, the growth of the Exchequer and the financial systems, of the Chancery, the Chamber, and the Wardrobe
0–631–12141–2 Blackwell pb $9.95

• Elizabeth Hallam
DOMESDAY BOOK THROUGH NINE CENTURIES
The making of the great survey and why it was preserved
0–500–25097–9 Thames & Hudson $24.95

• Bryce Lyon
A CONSTITUTIONAL AND LEGAL HISTORY OF MEDIEVAL ENGLAND
0–393–95132–4 Norton $16.95

Prince Harold with members of his court, from The Bayeux Tapestry *edited by David M. Wilson (Knopf)*

• Austin Lane Poole
FROM DOMESDAY BOOK TO MAGNA CARTA, 1087-1216
Part of the Oxford History of England Series
0–19–821707–2 Oxford $52.00

Medieval Portraits
(alphabetical by author)

• Frank Barlow
EDWARD THE CONFESSOR
0–520–05319–2 California pb $11.95

THOMAS BECKET
0–520–05920–4 California $30.00

• J.G. Bellamy
ROBIN HOOD: An Historical Enquiry
0–253–35015–8 Indiana $19.50

• David C. Douglas
WILLIAM THE CONQUEROR: The Norman Impact Upon England
0–520–00350–0 California pb $11.95

• Chris Given-Wilson & Alice Curteis
THE ROYAL BASTARDS OF MEDIEVAL ENGLAND
Despite ecclesiastical disapproval, noble bastardy was not a major barrier to success. Chapters include "Sex, Love and Illegitimacy" and "The Bastards of Richard I and King John"
0–7102–0939–8 RC&H pb $13.95

• Donald R. Howard
CHAUCER: His Life, His Works, His World
Soldier, diplomat, courtier, but above all poet. "Lavish and detailed"—*NY Review of Books*
0–525–24400–X Dutton $29.95
0–449–90341–9 Fawcett pb $12.95

• Amy Kelly
ELEANOR OF AQUITAINE AND THE FOUR KINGS
The strong-willed woman who married two kings and gave birth to two others
0–674–24254–8 Harvard pb $8.95

• Paul Murray Kendall
WARWICK THE KINGMAKER
During the War of the Roses, Richard Neville, Earl of Warwick, lived in more than regal splendor and exercised more than regal power. "The definitive biography"—Garrett Mattingly
0–393–30380–2 Norton pb $9.95

• Michael Prestwich
EDWARD I
The first comprehensive account
0–520–06266–3 California $29.95

• Charles Ross
RICHARD III
Richard ruled for only 26 months, but remains one of the most controversial English monarchs. Ross argues that his resort to violent means and illegal actions to attain his ends was, in his day, by no means unique
0–520–05075–4 California pb $9.95

• Desmond Seward
HENRY V: The Scourge of God
A new interpretation of the victor of Agincourt and a striking departure from the Shakespearean myth
0–670–81174–2 Viking $19.95

• W.L. Warren
HENRY II
The king best remembered for his struggles with Thomas Becket and Eleanor of Aquitaine. "A fine work by a professional historian who can write"—A.L. Rowse
0–520–03494–5 California pb $14.95

KING JOHN
0–520–03643–3 California pb $10.95

THE TUDORS: 1485-1603

The years 1485 and 1603 are strictly political anchors, demarcating control of the crown by a Welsh family over three generations. The underlying social and economic developments that carried England into the modern world are not easily confined to specific years.

- Richard Barber
  THE PASTONS: The Letters of a Family in the Wars of the Roses
  Pre-Tudor England, through the letters of its gentry
  0–14–057002–0 Penguin pb $6.95

- John Guy
  TUDOR ENGLAND
  A recent study
  0–19–873088–8 Oxford $35.00

- Charles Ross
  THE WARS OF THE ROSES: A Concise History
  Suggests that the gloom of 15th-century England has been too often exaggerated
  0–500–27407–X Thames & Hudson pb $11.95

- Conrad Russell
  THE CRISIS OF PARLIAMENTS: English History, 1509-1660
  An excellent synthesis that departs from the traditional dynastic periodization
  0–19–501442–1 Oxford pb $11.95

- Alan G. Smith
  THE EMERGENCE OF A NATION STATE: The Commonwealth of England, 1529-1660
  0–582–48974–1 Longman pb $18.95

- Penry Williams
  THE TUDOR REGIME
  0–19–822678–0 Oxford pb $16.95

Muriel St. Clare Byrne, editor
THE LISLE LETTERS: An Abridgement
A collection of letters written to and from Viscount Lisle; a revealing mirror of life at the beginning of the Tudor period
0–226–08810–3 Chicago pb $12.95

From the Reformation Through the Reign of Elizabeth I

Though the major effect of the English Reformation was largely political, it could not have happened had England not felt the spiritual crisis of the century. The rise of Calvinism in the form of Puritanism was as much a part of the process as Henry VIII's theatrics.

▶ **For books on the Spanish Armada, see Early Modern Europe**

- A.G. Dickens
  THE ENGLISH REFORMATION
  The best single-volume treatment
  0–8052–0177–7 Schocken pb $9.95

- G.R. Elton
  ENGLAND UNDER THE TUDORS
  0–416–70690–8 Methuen pb $19.95

REFORM AND REFORMATION: England, 1509-1558
Politics and administration, by the period's leading authority
0–674–75248–1 Harvard pb $9.95

- Wallace T. MacCaffrey
  QUEEN ELIZABETH AND THE MAKING OF POLICY, 1572-1588
  Includes the religious issues that continued to divide the country
  0–691–10112–4 Princeton pb $22.50

- A.L. Rowse
  THE ENGLAND OF ELIZABETH
  0–299–07724–1 Wisconsin pb $14.50

- Roy Strong
  THE CULT OF ELIZABETH: Elizabethan Portraiture and Pageantry
  With 94 black-and-white photos and four color plates
  0–520–05841–0 California pb $15.95

- R.B. Wernham
  THE MAKING OF ELIZABETHAN FOREIGN POLICY, 1558-1603
  0–520–03974–2 California pb $9.95

Biography

- Eric Ives
  ANNE BOLEYN
  "A lush look at Tudor court life, with its elegant official celebrations, its moves from castle to castle, its cut-throat games of one-upsmanship and faction"—*Washington Book Review*
  0–631–16065–5 Blackwell pb $12.95

- Carolly Erickson
  THE FIRST ELIZABETH
  0–671–41746–0 Summit $19.95
  0–671–50393–6 Summit pb $10.95

- Alison Plowden
  ELIZABETH TUDOR AND MARY STUART: Two Queens in One Island
  0–389–20518–4 Barnes & Noble $28.50

Anne Boleyn, from Thomas More *by Richard Marius (Knopf)*

Henry VIII, from Thomas More *by Richard Marius (Knopf)*

- Jasper Ridley
  ELIZABETH I: The Shrewdness of Virtue
  Hesitant, indecisive, and contradictory, the Virgin Queen as a consummate politician
  0–670–81526–8 Viking $24.95
  0–88064–110–X Fromm pb $11.95

- Lacey Baldwin Smith
  ELIZABETH TUDOR: Portrait of a Queen
  0–316–80153–4 Little, Brown pb $7.95

- Carolly Erickson
  GREAT HARRY: The Extravagant Life of Henry VIII
  "Carefully researched, skillfully constructed and full of those telling details that are an essential ingredient of the narrator's art"—Christopher Hibbert
  0–671–50392–8 Summit pb $12.95

- Jasper Ridley
  HENRY VIII: The Politics of Tyranny
  "Demolishes the characterizations of . . . [Henry VIII] as a promising young humanist gradually corrupted by such powerful and evil bureaucrats as Cardinal Wolsey and Thomas Cromwell"—*NY Times*
  0–670–80699–4 Viking $24.95

- J.J. Scarisbrick
  HENRY VIII
  The standard, solid biography
  0–520–01130–9 California pb $9.95

- Carolly Erickson
  BLOODY MARY
  Henry VIII's daughter by Catherine of Aragon married Philip II of Spain and attempted to reestablish a Catholic monarchy. Persecuted Protestants gave her the infamous nickname
  0–312–08508–7 St. Martin's pb $10.95

- Antonia Fraser
  MARY QUEEN OF SCOTS
  The tragic life of Elizabeth's Catholic rival, whom Elizabeth put to death in 1587
  0–440–35476–5 Dell pb $6.95

• Richard Marius
THOMAS MORE: A Biography
Henry VIII's martyred chancellor and
"man for all seasons." Scholarly but
accessible
0–394–45982–2 Knopf $22.95

THE CENTURY OF REVOLUTION

"In order to close this part of British history,
it is also necessary to relate the dissolution
of the monarchy in England: That event
soon followed upon the execution of the
monarch. When the peers met, on the day
appointed in their adjournment, they entered upon business, and sent down some
votes to the commons, of which the latter
deigned not to take the least notice. In a few
days, the lower house passed a vote, that
they would make no more addresses to the
house of peers, nor receive any from them;
and that that house was useless and dangerous, and was therefore to be abolished. A
like vote passed with regard to the monarchy
. . . The commons ordered a new great seal
to be engraved, on which that assembly was
represented, with this legend, ON THE
FIRST YEAR OF FREEDOM, BY GOD'S
BLESSING, RESTORED, 1648. The
forms of all public business were changed,
from the king's name, to that of the keepers
of the liberties of England. And it was
declared high treason to proclaim, or any
otherwise acknowledge Charles Stuart, commonly called prince of Wales."—David
Hume, *A History of England*, Volume 5

• G.E. Aylmer
**REBELLION OR REVOLUTION?:
England, 1640-1660**
Argues that the revolution came from the
middle class and the Puritans; rebellion
from both aristocratic and popular
elements
0–19–289212–6 Oxford pb $10.95

• Peter Beresford Ellis
**HELL OR CONNAUGHT: The
Cromwellian Colonisation of Ireland**
Following the execution of Charles I in
1649 Cromwell reduced the last bastions
of royal support at Drogheda and
Wexford, and redistributed confiscated
estates among parliamentary supporters
0–312–36715–5 St. Martin's $25.00

Christopher Hill
**THE CENTURY OF REVOLUTION,
1603-1714**
England on the path to Parliamentary
rule, literary achievement, religious
toleration, and scientific
accomplishment. An ideal introduction
0–393–01573–4 Norton $19.95
0–393–30016–1 Norton pb $7.95

A study for a portrait of Charles I, by Van Dyck

**THE EXPERIENCE OF DEFEAT:
Milton and Some Contemporaries**
The response among intellectuals and
religious leaders to the failure of the
English Revolution
0–670–30208–2 Viking $16.95
0–14–55203–0 Penguin pb $7.95

**THE INTELLECTUAL ORIGINS OF
THE ENGLISH REVOLUTION**
The forces that prepared men's minds
for revolutionary change
0–19–822635–7 Oxford pb $18.95

**REFORMATION TO INDUSTRIAL
REVOLUTION**
Part of the Pelican Economic History
of Britain series
0–14–020897–6 Penguin pb $6.95

**SOME INTELLECTUAL
CONSEQUENCES OF THE ENGLISH
REVOLUTION**
0–299–08144–3 Wisconsin pb $8.95

**A TINKER AND A POOR MAN: John
Bunyan and his Church, 1628-1688**
The first biography in many decades of
the controversial literary genius of the
English Revolution
0–394–57242–4 Knopf $22.95

**THE WORLD TURNED UPSIDE
DOWN: Radical Ideas During the
English Revolution**
Diggers, Ranters, Quakers, Levellers—
and the social and theological impulses
that gave rise to them. The "worm's
eye view" of the Civil War
0–14–055147–6 Penguin pb $6.95

• Ronald Hutton
**THE RESTORATION: A Political and
Religious History of England and Wales,
1658-1667**
The transformation of Cromwell's
commonwealth into the restoration
monarchy
0–19–285183–7 Oxford pb $12.95

• J.P. Kenyon
THE CIVIL WARS OF ENGLAND
"The key question is this: how did a small,
poor, underpopulated nation, which had
no regular army and no evident military
tradition later than the fifteenth century,
whose manufacturing industry was
minuscule, whose parliaments prior to
1640 had insisted time and again on the
poverty of the taxpaying classes—how did
this nation raise, equip, pay and sustain
very substantial armies, reaching by 1644 a
level of well over 30,000 men on each
side, fight two civil wars with considerable
skill and sophistication, and emerge in the
1650s as a formidable military power, to
be reckoned with in the councils of
Europe?"—from the Introduction
0–394–55259–8 Knopf $22.95

• R.C. Richardson
**THE DEBATE ON THE ENGLISH
REVOLUTION**
This second edition includes a valuable
bibliographic guide
0–415–01167–1 RC&H pb $22.95

• Lawrence Stone
**THE CAUSES OF THE ENGLISH
REVOLUTION, 1529-1642**
A good introduction to the great debate
on the English Civil War
0–06–131678–4 Harper & Row pb $5.95

**THE CRISIS OF THE ARISTOCRACY,
1558-1641**
Argues that the relative decline of the
aristocracy—not the rise or fall of the
gentry—was the fundamental social change
in pre-Civil War England
0–19–500274–1 Oxford pb $11.95

• H.R. Trevor-Roper
**CATHOLICS, ANGLICANS AND
PURITANS: Seventeenth Century Essays**
New essays on Nicholas Hill, the Atomist;
Laudianism and political power; James

Ussher, Archbishop of Armagh; the Great Tew circle; Milton in politics
0–226–81228–6 Chicago $27.50

• David Underdown
REVEL, RIOT AND REBELLION: Popular Politics and Culture in England, 1603-1660
A pioneering synthesis linking festive culture with political allegiance
0–19–285193–4 Oxford pb $10.95

• Michael Walzer
THE REVOLUTION OF THE SAINTS: A Study in the Origins of Radical Politics
0–674–76786–1 Harvard pb $7.95

• C.V. Wedgwood
HISTORY AND HOPE: Essays on History and the English Civil War
0–525–24740–8 Dutton $25.00

Sources

• John Aubrey
AUBREY'S BRIEF LIVES
Miniportraits of figures great and small: Descartes, William Penn, Shakespeare, and Thomas Wolsey. Disjointed, inaccurate, ribald, and invariably entertaining
Edited by Oliver Lawson Dick
0–14–043079–2 Penguin pb $7.95

• Richard Gough
THE HISTORY OF MYDDLE
The life of a small community in Stuart England
Edited with an introduction by David Hey
0–14–043314–7 Penguin pb $6.95

• Samuel Pepys
THE SHORTER PEPYS
"Pepys's diary is the cheerful self-report, not of the man eminent in naval history, nor of the historical witness, but of the unobjectionable hedonist"—Geoffrey Grigson
Edited by Robert Latham
0–520–03426–0 California $37.50

THE LATER STUARTS AND THE GLORIOUS REVOLUTION

• G.N. Clark
THE LATER STUARTS, 1660-1714
A classic particularly good on old-fashioned politics
0–19–821702–1 Oxford $52.00

• Tim Harris
LONDON CROWDS IN THE REIGN OF CHARLES II: Propaganda and Politics from the Restoration until the Exclusion Crisis
0–521–32623–0 Cambridge $42.50

• J.R. Jones
COURT AND COUNTRY: England, 1658-1714
A valuable study of a crucial component in English politics
0–674–17535–2 Harvard pb $9.95

THE REVOLUTION OF 1688 IN ENGLAND
Analyzes James II's schemes to pack his ministry and even the universities with men drawn from his inner circle. The birth of an heir apparent and the fears that a Catholic dynasty would rule England far into the future triggered the revolt. Originally published in 1972
0–393–09998–9 Norton pb $9.95

• Thomas Babington Macaulay
THE HISTORY OF ENGLAND
The classic Whig history of the 1850s celebrates the constitutional legacy of the Glorious Revolution and spans the period 1685-1702
Edited, abridged & with an introduction by H.R. Trevor-Roper
0–14–043133–0 Penguin pb $6.95

• Sir Patrick MacRory
THE SIEGE OF DERRY
The failure of King James II to capture Londonderry prepared the way for the final defeat of Stuart hopes at the Boyne in 1690
0–19–285182–9 Oxford pb $12.95

• David Ogg
ENGLAND IN THE REIGN OF CHARLES II
Published in 1955 and still the best introduction to the Restoration
0–19–285142–X Oxford pb $14.95
ENGLAND IN THE REIGNS OF JAMES II AND WILLIAM III
0–19–881154–3 Oxford pb $13.95

• W.A. Speck
THE RELUCTANT REVOLUTIONARIES: Englishmen and the Revolution of 1688
The year that marked a decisive, though not inevitable, movement toward a mixed, constitutional monarchy
0–19–822768–X Oxford $39.95
STABILITY AND STRIFE: England 1714-1760
The best synthesis for the period, incorporating political, economic and social developments
0–674–83350–3 Harvard pb $9.95

• G.M. Trevelyan
THE ENGLISH REVOLUTION, 1688-1689
Suggests that the Revolution strengthened conservatism but that its results made it a turning point in history. "The traditional Whig view at its best—the view of Locke, Burke, and Macaulay"—*Guardian*
0–19–500263–6 Oxford pb $6.95

• Henri & Barbara van der Zee
1688: Revolution in the Family
How the Glorious Revolution was an intimate family affair
0–670–80820–2 Viking $19.95

THE 18TH CENTURY

• John Cannon
THE ARISTOCRATIC CENTURY: The Peerage of Eighteenth Century England
0–521–33566–3 Cambridge pb $13.95

• J.C.D. Clark
ENGLISH SOCIETY 1688-1832: Ideology, Social Structure and Political Practice During the Ancien Regime
Revises the Marxist claim that the Civil War and 1688 saw the triumph of the bourgeoisie; a shrewd analysis for advanced students
0–521–31383–X Cambridge pb $16.95
REVOLUTION AND REBELLION: State and Society in England in the Seventeenth and Eighteenth Centuries
Reviews the polemics around the rise of capitalism and democracy in England
0–521–33710–0 Cambridge pb $9.95

• Daniel Defoe
A TOUR THROUGH THE WHOLE ISLAND OF GREAT BRITAIN
Businessman, journalist, soldier, and spy, Defoe toured Britain from 1724 to 1726. "Far the best authority for early 18th-century England"—Dorothy George
0–14–043066–0 Penguin pb $7.95

• Dorothy George
HOGARTH TO CRUIKSHANK: Social Change in Graphic Satire
Big, illustrated, and lots of fun
0–670–82116–0 Viking $39.95

David Hume
THE HISTORY OF ENGLAND
From the Invasion of Julius Caesar to the Revolution in 1688

Volume 1
From Early Britain to King John
0–86597–021–1 Liberty Classics $15.00
0–86597–022–X Liberty Classics pb $7.50

Volume 2
From Henry III to Richard III
0–86597–026–2 Liberty Classics $15.00
0–86597–027–0 Liberty Classics pb $7.50

Volume 3
From Henry VII to Mary
0–86597–028–9 Liberty Classics $15.00

Volume 4
Elizabeth I
0–86597–030–0 Liberty Classics $15.00

Volume 5
James I to Charles I
0–86597–032–7 Liberty Classics $15.00

Volume 6
From the Commonwealth to the Glorious Revolution
0–86597–034–3 Liberty Classics $15.00

• Derek Jarrett
ENGLAND IN THE AGE OF HOGARTH
0–300–03609–4 Yale pb $11.95

• Bruce Lenman
THE JACOBITE RISING IN BRITAIN, 1689-1746
0–8419–7004–1 Holmes & Meier $34.50

• Richard Pares
KING GEORGE III AND THE POLITICIANS
"Full of wit and gaiety, enlivened with anecdote and a delight to read"—A.J.P. Taylor
0–19–881130–6 Oxford pb $17.95

- J.H. Plumb
THE GROWTH OF POLITICAL STABILITY IN ENGLAND, 1675-1725
"By providing this illuminating introduction to the political scene when Walpole first entered the Commons, he has done much to clear up the complexities of a very confusing period and lay the basis for a new interpretation"—Dorothy Marshall
0–391–01908–2 Humanities pb $15.00

- Roy Porter
MIND-FORG'D MANACLES: A History of Madness in England from the Restoration to the Regency
Argues that before the advent of the public asylum all was not apathy, cruelty, and corruption. "A brilliant British answer to Foucault"—Elaine Showalter
0–674–57617–9 Harvard $38.50

- E.P. Thompson
WHIGS AND HUNTERS: The Origin of the Black Act
Insights into justice in early 18th-century England
0–394–73086–0 Pantheon pb $9.50

- E.P. Thompson & others
ALBION'S FATAL TREE: Crime and Society in Eighteenth-Century England
0–394–73085–2 Pantheon pb $9.50

- T.H. White
THE AGE OF SCANDAL: An Excursion Through a Minor Period
0–19–281948–8 Oxford pb $8.95

Biography

- Edward Gregg
QUEEN ANNE
The last of the Stuarts, who had over a dozen children and survived them all
0–7448–0018–8 Methuen pb $9.95

- Stanley Ayling
EDMUND BURKE: His Life and Opinions
The first full-scale biography in 50 years, published in 1989
0–312–02686–2 St. Martin's $19.95

- Charles Carlton
CHARLES I: The Personal Monarch
0–7448–0016–1 Methuen pb $8.95

- Maurice Ashley
CHARLES I AND OLIVER CROMWELL: A Study in Contrasts and Comparisons
0–413–16270–2 Methuen $22.50

- J.R. Jones
CHARLES II: Royal Politician
0–04–942196–4 Unwin Hyman $34.95

- Carolly Erickson
BONNIE PRINCE CHARLIE
With his band of Highland rebels the Young Pretender threatened the English heartland in 1745
0–688–06087–0 Morrow $19.95

- Fitzroy Maclean
BONNIE PRINCE CHARLIE
Authoritative biography by a British wartime hero with Highland roots
0–689–12047–8 Atheneum $24.95

- Antonia Fraser
CROMWELL: The Lord Protector
0–917657–90–X Donald Fine pb $11.95

- Christopher Hill
GOD'S ENGLISHMAN: Oliver Cromwell and the English Revolution
"For good or for evil," writes Hill, "Oliver Cromwell presided over the great decisions which determined the future course of English and world history. Marston Moor, Naseby, Preston, Worcester—and regicide—ensured that England was to be ruled by Parliaments and not by absolute kings"
0–06–131666–0 Harper & Row pb $7.95

- S.J. Houston
JAMES I
0–582–35208–8 Longman pb $7.95

- Flora Fraser
EMMA: Lady Hamilton
Lord Nelson's mistress, set against the glamor and scandal of 18th-century European society
1–557–78008–0 Paragon pb $10.95

- Brian W. Hill
ROBERT HARLEY: Speaker, Secretary of State, and Prime Minister
A pioneer of parliamentary government, Harley turned the "country" Tories into an effective opposition in the reigns of William III and Anne
0–300–04284–1 Yale $35.00

- Maurice Cranston
JOHN LOCKE: A Biography
Pioneer of clinical medicine, diplomat, scientist, theologian—and England's foremost philosopher of liberalism and toleration
0–19–283044–9 Oxford pb $12.95

- Winston S. Churchill
MARLBOROUGH AND HIS TIMES
The colorful biography of Sir Winston's military ancestor, John Churchill, Duke of Marlborough, who built Blenheim Palace out of profits from the War of the Spanish Succession
0–684–17674–2 Scribners $40.00

- Tom Pocock
HORATIO NELSON
A recent popular biography, especially of interest to those intrigued by that Hamilton woman
0–394–57056–1 Knopf $22.95

- Oliver Warner
A PORTRAIT OF LORD NELSON
The contrast between the naval hero's public and private life
0–14–008068–6 Penguin pb $6.95

- Peter Quennell
FOUR PORTRAITS: Boswell, Gibbon, Sterne, and Wilkes
An age revealed through four linked biographies
0–09–173149–6 David & Charles pb $13.95

The Lure of London

Dorothy George
LONDON LIFE IN THE EIGHTEENTH CENTURY
This classic of social history written in 1925 describes life among the capital's poor
0–89733–147–8 Academy Chicago pb $8.95

Christopher Hibbert
LONDON: The Biography of a City
A profusely illustrated history, with a guide to historic London
0–14–005247–X Penguin pb $14.95

Peter Jackson
GEORGE SCHARF'S LONDON: Sketches and Watercolours of a Changing City, 1820-50
Working in pencil sketches, lithographs, and watercolors, Scharf captured the vitality of everyday life, from hawkers and musicians to the new London Zoo. With 187 black-and-white plates
0–7195–4379–7 David & Charles $34.95

Henry Mayhew
LONDON LABOUR AND THE LONDON POOR
Portraits of Dickens' London, first published in 1861
0–14–043241–8 Penguin pb $7.95

George Rudé
HANOVERIAN LONDON, 1714-1808
0–520–01778–1 California $40.00

John Summerson
GEORGIAN LONDON
The Russells, the Grosvenors, and the Harleys, among other landlords, shaped the contours of some of London's loveliest spots. This revised edition of a 1945 classic reveals the taste and industry of a great age; 23 color and 140 black-and-white plates
0–7126–2095–8 David & Charles $45.00

THE 19TH CENTURY AND THE INDUSTRIAL REVOLUTION

"Were we to characterize this age of ours by any single epithet we should be tempted to call it, above all others, the Mechanical Age . . . The same habit regulates not our modes of action alone but our modes of thought and feeling. Men are grown mechanical in head and in heart as well as in hand."—Thomas Carlyle, *Signs of the Times* (1829)

Horatio Nelson by John Francis Rigaud (Granger Collection), from Horatio Nelson *by Tom Pocock (Knopf)*

● Carolly Erickson
OUR TEMPESTUOUS DAY: A History of Regency England
"[Makes] the peculiar mix of gaiety, turbulence and sheer British doughtiness that was the Regency era read like a whopping good novel"—*NY Times*
0–688–07292–5 Morrow pb $8.95

● C.P. Hill
BRITISH ECONOMIC AND SOCIAL HISTORY: 1700-1982
0–7131–7382–3 Edward Arnold pb $19.95

● E.J. Hobsbawm
INDUSTRY AND EMPIRE: The Making of Modern English Society
Britain's heady ride as the world's first industrial power, and the years that followed
0–14–020898–4 Penguin pb $6.95

● Harold Perkin
THE ORIGINS OF MODERN ENGLISH SOCIETY, 1780-1880
Bold and provocative; the birth of the new class society and its mid-Victorian maturity
0–7448–0026–9 Methuen pb $12.50

● E.P. Thompson
THE MAKING OF THE ENGLISH WORKING CLASS
A pioneer study of working class culture in the Romantic Age
0–394–70322–7 Random House pb $13.95

● Raymond Williams
CULTURE AND SOCIETY: 1780-1950
From Edmund Burke and William Cobbett to F.R. Leavis and George Orwell. "Digs into the ideological layers that envelop modern politics. Written from an independent Left standpoint, this critical history . . . is exactly to the point of contemporary discussions of value"—Harold Rosenberg
0–231–05701–6 Columbia pb $12.50

The Industrial Revolution

"The Industrial Revolution marks the most fundamental transformation of human life in the history of the world recorded in written documents. For a brief period it coincided with the history of a single country, Great Britain. An entire world economy was thus built on, or rather around, Britain, and this country therefore temporarily rose to a position of global influence and power unparalleled by any state of its relative size before or since, and unlikely to be paralleled by any state in the foreseeable future. There was a moment in the world's history when Britain can be described, if we are not too pedantic, as its only workshop, its only massive importer and exporter, its only carrier, its only imperialist . . . "—E.J. Hobsbawm, *Industry and Empire*

● Maxine Berg
THE AGE OF MANUFACTURES, 1700-1820: Industry, Innovation, and Work in Britain
0–19–520500–6 Oxford pb $12.95

● Phyllis Deane
THE FIRST INDUSTRIAL REVOLUTION
0–521–29609–9 Cambridge pb $14.95

● Gertrude Himmelfarb
THE IDEA OF POVERTY: England in the Early Industrial Age
0–394–72607–3 Random House pb $12.95

● E.J. Hobsbawm
THE AGE OF REVOLUTION: 1789-1848
Surveys the two great revolutions of this era: the political revolution of France and the economic revolution of Britain
0–451–62362–2 NAL pb $4.95

● Peter Mathias
THE FIRST INDUSTRIAL NATION: An Economic History of Britain, 1700-1914
0–416–33300–1 Methuen pb $14.95

"London Scavenger," an engraving from an 1848 newspaper, reproduced in The Oxford Illustrated History of Britain *edited by Kenneth O. Morgan*

Protest, Reform and The New Economic Thought

● John Bowditch & Clement Ramsland, editors
VOICES OF THE INDUSTRIAL REVOLUTION: Selected Readings from the Liberal Economists and Their Critics
0–472–06053–8 Michigan pb $8.95

● Thomas Carlyle
PAST AND PRESENT
"It is a moral, political, historical, and a most questionable red-hot indignant thing," Carlyle wrote of this volume, "for my heart is sick to look at the things now going on in England." Carlyle's principal contemporary social criticism, first published in 1843
Edited by Richard D. Altick
0–8147–0562–6 NYU pb $15.00

● William Cobbett
RURAL RIDES
A series of fact-finding tours made on horseback bears witness to the death struggle of old rural England. "Reads as if a character from Fielding had adventured his way through the world created by Dickens"—George Woodcock in his introduction
0–14–043023–7 Penguin pb $5.95

● Seamus Deane
THE FRENCH REVOLUTION AND ENLIGHTENMENT IN ENGLAND, 1789-1832
The revolution's impact on English thought
0–674–32240–1 Harvard $25.00

● Friedrich Engels
THE CONDITION OF THE WORKING CLASS IN ENGLAND
Engels' finest hour: a masterpiece of committed reporting on the appalling living and working conditions in industrialized Manchester
Edited with an introduction by Victor Kiernan
0–14–044486–6 Penguin pb $6.95

● Robert Heilbroner
THE WORLDLY PHILOSOPHERS: The Lives, Times, and Ideas of the Great Economic Thinkers
A sampling of the debate at the time, including the dim view of labor's prospects offered by the economic liberals of the Manchester school
0–671–63318–X Simon & Schuster pb $9.95

● E.J. Hobsbawm & George Rudé
CAPTAIN SWING: A Social History of the Great English Agricultural Uprising of 1830
0–393–00793–6 Norton pb $8.95

● David Jones
CHARTISM AND THE CHARTISTS
0–312–13090–2 St. Martin's $25.00

● Steven Marcus
ENGELS, MANCHESTER, AND THE WORKING CLASS
Applies critical literary techniques to Victorian responses to the Industrial Revolution
0–393–30237–7 Norton pb $6.95

TO ORDER BOOKS AS GIFTS, SEE PAGE 1

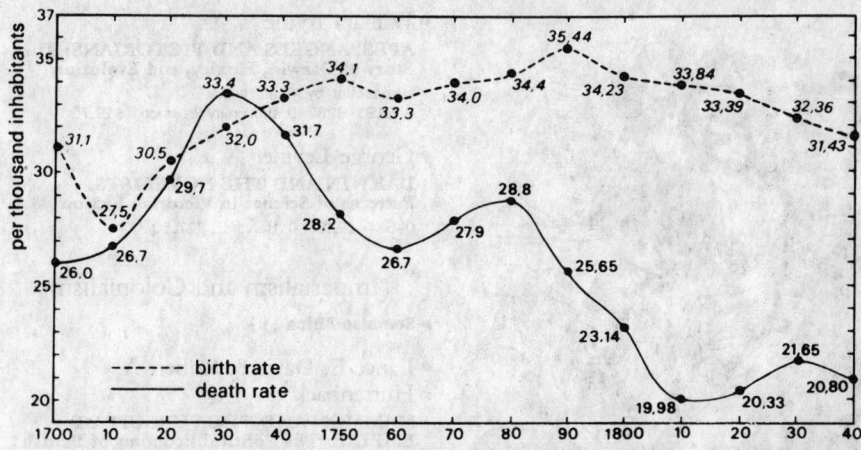

Birth and death rates in England (1700-1840): the "demographic revolution" was largely created by the increase in industry after the 1730s, from The Perspective of the World *by Fernand Braudel (Harper & Row)*

• Dorothy Thompson
THE CHARTISTS: Popular Politics in the Industrial Revolution
Mass pressures for widening suffrage and for other reforms brought England close to revolution
0–394–72474–7 Pantheon pb $13.95

• D.G. Wright
POPULAR RADICALISM: The Working-Class Experience, 1780-1880
Argues that most radical workingmen aimed at manhood suffrage rather than insurrection; a major proletarian revolution was never a real possibility
0–582–49440–0 Longman pb $13.95

THE VICTORIAN ERA

• Peter Bailey
LEISURE AND CLASS IN VICTORIAN ENGLAND: Rational Recreation and the Contest for Control, 1830-1885
An illustrated social history
0–416–02142–5 RC&H pb $15.95

MUSIC HALL: The Business of Pleasure
0–335–15129–9 Taylor & Francis pb $19.00

• Virginia Berridge & Griffith Edwards
OPIUM AND THE PEOPLE: Opiate Use in Nineteenth-Century England
0–300–03804–6 Yale pb $13.95

• Asa Briggs
THE AGE OF IMPROVEMENT, 1783 TO 1867
0–582–49100–2 Longman $17.95

THE COLLECTED ESSAYS OF ASA BRIGGS
"An unrivaled panorama of the range and riches of Victorian life"—David Cannadine

Volume 1: Words, Numbers, Places, People
Insights into local politics, class, media, and language in early Victorian England
0–252–06004–0 Illinois pb $14.95

Volume 2: Images, Problems, Standpoints, Forecasts
Spans such diverse subjects as public health, George Eliot, cholera, and the popularity of William Morris
0–252–06005–9 Illinois pb $14.95

VICTORIAN PEOPLE: A Reassessment of Persons and Themes, 1851-1867
This revised and illustrated edition includes Briggs's famous essays on the Crystal Palace Exposition and Disraeli's "Leap in the Dark"
0–226–07488–9 Chicago pb $11.95

VICTORIAN THINGS
The meaning of objects in the Victorian Age: cameras and spectacles, matches, hats, postage stamps, telephones, and typewriters
0–226–07483–8 Chicago $29.95

• G. Kitson Clark
THE MAKING OF VICTORIAN ENGLAND
Insight into the mid-Victorian religious scene and its concern for the outward maintenance of piety
0–689–70049–0 Atheneum pb $6.95

• Peter Clarke
LIBERALS AND SOCIAL DEMOCRATS
0–521–28651–4 Cambridge pb $15.95

• Wolf von Eckardt & others
OSCAR WILDE'S LONDON: A Scrapbook of Vices and Virtues, 1880-1900
0–385–09703–4 Doubleday pb $24.95

• Robert Ensor
ENGLAND, 1870-1914
First published in 1936 and still remarkable for its appeal to students and general readers alike
0–19–821721–8 Oxford pb $16.95

• Gertrude Himmelfarb
MARRIAGE AND MORALS AMONG THE VICTORIANS
Essays include "Godwin's Utopia," "Who Now Reads Macaulay?" and "Disraeli: The Tory Imagination"
0–394–75290–2 Random House pb $9.95

• Derek Jarrett
THE SLEEP OF REASON: Fantasy and Reality from the Victorian Age to the First World War
The momentous change of attitude and ideas about man, God, and the universe in the English-speaking world
0–06–016049–7 Harper & Row $22.50

• Steven Marcus
THE OTHER VICTORIANS: A Study of Sexuality and Pornography in Mid-Nineteenth Century England
0–393–30236–9 Norton pb $7.95

• Roderick Marshall
WILLIAM MORRIS AND HIS EARTHLY PARADISES
0–8076–1012–7 Braziller $22.50

• James Morris
THE PAX BRITTANICA TRILOGY

HEAVEN'S COMMAND: An Imperial Progress
0–15–640006–5 HBJ pb $9.95

PAX BRITTANICA: The Climax of an Empire
0–15–671466–3 HBJ pb $9.95

FAREWELL THE TRUMPETS: An Imperial Retreat
0–15–630286–1 HBJ pb $9.95

• Henry Pelling
POPULAR POLITICS AND SOCIETY IN LATE VICTORIAN BRITAIN
0–391–01205–3 Macmillan $26.00

• F.M.L. Thompson
THE RISE OF RESPECTABLE SOCIETY: A Social History of Victorian Britain, 1830-1900
0–674–77285–7 Harvard $30.00

• Gaye Tuchman with Nina E. Fortin
EDGING WOMEN OUT: Victorian Novelists, Publishers, and Social Change
"How male writers invaded and took over this white-collar occupation is the phenomenon investigated in this bombshell of a book"—*Publishers Weekly*
0–300–04316–3 Yale $29.95

• G.M. Young
VICTORIAN ENGLAND: Portrait of an Age
0–19–500259–8 Oxford pb $9.95

Ireland under the Union

• Thomas Gallagher
PADDY'S LAMENT—IRELAND, 1846-1847: Prelude to Hatred
The potato famine and its place in Irish resentment of England
0–15–670700–4 HBJ pb $7.95

• Tom Garvin
NATIONALIST REVOLUTIONARIES IN IRELAND, 1858-1928
Suggests that the elite who came to power after 1921 were heavily influenced not only by old agrarian grievances but also by contemporary Catholic abhorrence of the Protestant and secular world
0–19–820134–6 Oxford $48.00

• Gifford Lewis
SOMERVILLE AND ROSS: The World of the Irish R.M.
The relationship between the two cousins responsible for *The Real Charlotte* and *The Irish R.M.*; beautifully illustrated
0–14–008262–X Penguin pb $10.95

A riot in a potato store in Ireland during the great famine of the 1840s

● **F.S.L. Lyons**
**CULTURE AND ANARCHY IN
IRELAND 1819-1939: The Ford Lectures**
Cultural diversity as an agent of anarchy
0–19–822493–1 Oxford $29.95

● **Kerby A. Miller**
**EMIGRANTS AND EXILES: Ireland and
the Irish Exodus to North America**
0–19–505187–4 Oxford pb $13.95

● **Joel Mokyr**
**WHY IRELAND STARVED: A
Quantitative and Analytical History of the
Irish Economy, 1800-1850**
Illustrated
0–04–941014–8 Unwin Hyman pb $18.95

● **T.W. Moody**
**DAVITT AND IRISH REVOLUTION:
1846-1882**
0–19–820069–2 Oxford pb $18.95

● **Austen Morgan**
**JAMES CONNOLLY: A Political
Biography**
0–7190–2519–2 St. Martin's $49.95

● **Robert Nicholson**
**THE ULYSSES GUIDE: Tours Through
Joyce's Dublin**
A guide for Joyceans, with maps, detailed
directions, and information on the
"unnoticed" activities of the original
Bloomsday
0–413–60900–6 RC&H pb $9.95

● **Eunan O'Halpin**
**THE DECLINE OF THE UNION:
British Government in Ireland, 1892-1920**
0–8156–2425–5 Syracuse $33.00

Women in Love

Gay Daly
PRE-RAPHAELITES IN LOVE
Diaries and letters reveal the stormy
relations between the artists and the
women they loved
0–89919–450–8 Ticknor & Fields $24.95

Flora Fraser, editor
**MAUD: The Illustrated Diary of a
Victorian Woman**
0–87701–429–9 Chronicle $19.95

Janet H. Murray
**STRONG-MINDED WOMEN & Other
Lost Voices of Nineteenth-Century
England**
An anthology of letters, journals, and
articles on everything from education
to sex to fashion
0–394–71044–4 Pantheon pb $11.95

Phyllis Rose
**PARALLEL LIVES: Five Victorian
Marriages**
Five couples, each with a famous
writer: Thomas Carlyle, John Stuart
Mill, Charles Dickens, John Ruskin,
and George Eliot
0–394–52432–2 Knopf $11.95
0–394–72580–8 Random House pb $6.95

Martha Vicinus, editor
**SUFFER AND BE STILL: Women in
the Victorian Age**
0–253–20168–3 Indiana pb $9.95

The Darwinian Revolution

● **Gertrude Himmelfarb**
**DARWIN AND THE DARWINIAN
REVOLUTION**
0–393–00455–4 Norton pb $11.95

● **William Irvine**
**APES, ANGELS AND VICTORIANS: The
Story of Darwin, Huxley, and Evolution**
Introduction by Julian Huxley
0–8191–3282–9 University Press pb $19.75

● **George Levine**
**DARWIN AND THE NOVELISTS:
Patterns of Science in Victorian Fiction**
0–674–19285–0 Harvard $27.50

Imperialism and Colonialism

▶ **See also Africa**

● **Lance E. Davis & Robert A.
Huttenback**
**MAMMON AND THE PURSUIT OF
EMPIRE: The Political Economy of British
Imperialism, 1860-1912**
Abridged
0–521–35723–3 Cambridge pb $12.95

● **Colin Eldridge, editor**
**BRITISH IMPERIALISM IN THE
NINETEENTH CENTURY**
0–312–10299–2 St. Martin's $29.95

● **Byron Farwell**
**MR. KIPLING'S ARMY: All the Queen's
Men**
Victoria's upstairs-downstairs army—the
smallest ever to hold an empire
0–393–30444–2 Norton pb $8.95

QUEEN VICTORIA'S LITTLE WARS
Worldwide military expeditions protected
Britons and British interests. In the
process, the British Empire quadrupled
0–393–30235–0 Norton pb $9.95

● **E.J. Hobsbawm**
THE AGE OF EMPIRE, 1875-1914
The third part of Eric Hobsbawm's trilogy
(following *The Age of Revolution* and *The
Age of Capital*) spans the entire world in
this period and is aimed at "the educated
non-expert"
0–394–56319–0 Pantheon $22.95
0–679–72175–4 Random House pb $12.95

● **Alan Moorehead**
THE WHITE NILE
First published in 1960 and now reissued
with beautiful color plates
0–394–71445–8 Random House pb $13.95

● **Thomas Pakenham**
THE BOER WAR
The costliest, bloodiest, and most
humiliating war that Britain fought
between 1815 and 1914; Pakenham's
study is as fast-moving as a novel
0–394–42742–4 Random House $29.95

● **Bernard Porter**
**THE LION'S SHARE: A Short History of
British Imperialism, 1850-1983**
The tail wagging the dog—Britain
controlled by her need to hold on to her
empire
0–582–49387–0 Longman pb $15.95

- Norman Rich
WHY THE CRIMEAN WAR?: A Cautionary Tale
A recent study by a perceptive diplomatic historian
0–87451–328–6 New England $25.00

- Ronald Robinson & John Gallagher
AFRICA AND THE VICTORIANS: The Official Mind of Imperialism
0–333–05552–7 Humanities pb $19.95

- Tony Smith
THE PATTERN OF IMPERIALISM: The United States, Great Britain and the Late-Industrializing World Since 1815
0–521–28076–1 Cambridge pb $13.95

- Cecil Woodham-Smith
THE REASON WHY
Trained against Napoleon, the British general staff had little understanding of mid-century warfare—a deficiency made amply clear in the famous Charge of the Light Brigade
0–525–48269–5 Dutton pb $7.95

EMINENT VICTORIANS

- Lytton Strachey
EMINENT VICTORIANS
A classic from 1918—four biographical essays that pierced the bubble of high Victorianism by revealing the private lives behind the public personalities
Introduction by Michael Holroyd
0–14–000649–4 Penguin pb $6.95

Walter Bagehot

Editor of *The Economist* from 1861 until his death in 1877, Walter Bagehot brought fresh insights into the psychological underpinnings of political action. Many regard *The English Constitution* (1867) as still the best introduction to English political culture.

Walter Bagehot
THE ENGLISH CONSTITUTION
0–8014–9023–5 Cornell pb $8.95

H.J. Hanham, editor
THE NINETEENTH CENTURY CONSTITUTION, 1815-1914
Includes original documents and criticism
0–521–07351–0 Cambridge $49.50
0–521–09560–3 Cambridge pb $19.95

- Ruddock Mackay
BALFOUR: Intellectual Statesman
Focuses on the prime minister's work in education and defense and offers new insights into British foreign policy
0–19–212245–2 Oxford $34.50

Then there is my lord Boodle, of considerable reputation with his party, who has known what office is and who tells Sir Leicester Dedlock with much gravity, after dinner, that he really does not see to what the present age is tending. A debate is not what a debate used to be; the House is not what the House used to be; even a Cabinet is not what it formerly was. He perceives with astonishment that supposing the present government to be overthrown, the limited choice of the Crown, in the formation of a new ministry, would lie between Lord Coodle and Sir Thomas Doodle—supposing it to be impossible for the Duke of Foodle to act with Goodle, which may be assumed to be the case in consequence of the breach arising out of that affair with Hoodle. Then, giving the Home Department and the leadership of the House of Commons to Joodle, the Exchequer to Koodle, the Colonies to Loodle, and the Foreign Office to Moodle, what are you to do with Noodle? You can't offer him the presidency of the Council; that is reserved for Poodle. You can't put him in the Woods and Forests; that is hardly good enough for Quoodle. What follows? That the country is shipwrecked, lost, and gone to pieces (as is made manifest to the patriotism of Sir Leicester Dedlock) because you can't provide for Noodle!

Charles Dickens
BLEAK HOUSE
0–19–254503–5 Oxford $9.95

- John D. Rosenberg
CARLYLE AND THE BURDEN OF HISTORY
Illustrates how the author of *The French Revolution* was a great epic poet whose natural medium was prose and for whom history was prophecy, biography, and social criticism
0–674–09754–8 Harvard $22.50

- Robert Blake
DISRAELI
Dizzy entered Parliament in 1837 and, in the 1840s, published two novels which created a sensation. He later headed the government from 1874 to 1880 in a ministry marked by imperialism and social reform; the solid, standard biography
0–88184–296–6 Carroll & Graf pb $14.50

- Philip Magnus
KING EDWARD VII
The Francophile who spent 60 years as Prince of Wales and only nine as king
0–14–002658–4 Penguin pb $5.95

- P.J. Jagger, editor
GLADSTONE, POLITICS AND RELIGION
Essays with contributions by Michael Foot and Robert Blake
0–312–32763–3 St. Martin's $22.50

William Gladstone reading in his study (National Portrait Gallery, London)

- Peter Stansky
GLADSTONE: A Progress in Politics
Head of the Liberal Party and Prime Minister four times—viewed largely through his Parliamentary speeches
0–393–00037–0 Norton pb $5.95

- John H. Waller
GORDON OF KHARTOUM: The Saga of a Victorian Hero
A modern biography relying on recently available letters and diaries
0–689–11812–0 Atheneum $29.95

- Bentley B. Gilbert
DAVID LLOYD GEORGE: A Political Life
Prime Minister of a coalition government during World War I, Lloyd George later presided over the decline of the Liberal party
0–8142–0432–5 Ohio State $40.00

- John Clive
MACAULAY: The Shaping of the Historian
A National Book Award winner
0–674–54005–0 Harvard pb $13.95

- Philip Henderson
WILLIAM MORRIS: His Life, Work and Friends
Craftsman and poet, businessman and socialist
0–233–97855–0 Andre Deutsch $17.95

- E.P. Thompson
WILLIAM MORRIS: Romantic to Revolutionary
0–8047–1509–2 Stanford pb $19.95

- Julia Briggs
A WOMAN OF PASSION: The Life of E. Nesbit, 1858-1924
Biography of a founding member of the Fabian Society
0–941533–03–4 New Amsterdam $27.95

● E.V. Quinn & J.M. Prest, editors
DEAR MISS NIGHTINGALE: A Selection of Benjamin Jowett's Letters to Florence Nightingale, 1860-1893
0–19–822953–4 Oxford $69.00

● Mrs. Oliphant
THE AUTOBIOGRAPHY OF MRS. OLIPHANT
Author of nearly 100 books, Mrs. Oliphant brought up a large family and cultivated friendships with Tennyson, Carlyle, and Leslie Stephen
0–226–62651–2 Chicago pb $9.95

● Muriel Chamberlain
LORD PALMERSTON
Foreign minister in several Whig cabinets throughout the 1830s and '40s, Palmerston became prime minister of a Whig-Peelite administration during the Crimean War and remained in office until his death in 1865
0–8132–0663–4 Catholic University $22.95
0–8132–0664–2 Catholic University pb $8.95

● Barbara Castle
SYLVIA AND CHRISTABEL PANKHURST
The story of two leaders of the suffragist movement
0–14–008761–3 Penguin pb $4.95

● Brian Roberts
CECIL RHODES: Flawed Colossus
A new biography of the imperialist's imperialist
0–393–02576–6 Norton $22.50

Michael Holroyd
BERNARD SHAW: 1856-1898—The Search for Love
The young Shaw fashions the persona by which the world would know him, achieving fame as music and theater critic, political activist, orator, and dramatist
0–394–52577–9 Random House $24.95

● Noel Annan
LESLIE STEPHEN: The Godless Victorian
0–226–02106–8 Chicago pb $14.95

● Kitty Muggeridge & Ruth Adam
BEATRICE WEBB: A Life, 1858-1943
0–89733–088–9 Academy Chicago pb $7.95

Victoria

● Christopher Hibbert
QUEEN VICTORIA IN HER LETTERS
0–14–057027–6 Penguin pb $7.95

● Elizabeth Longford
VICTORIA R.I., ILLUSTRATED EDITION: A Picture Book
0–06–012672–8 Harper & Row $15.00

● Lytton Strachey
QUEEN VICTORIA
First published in 1921. "A masterpiece"— *New Statesman*
0–15–675696–X HBJ pb $10.95

● Stanley Weintraub
VICTORIA: An Intimate Biography
The new, highly acclaimed account
0–525–24469–7 Dutton $26.95
0–525–48420–5 Dutton pb $13.95

THE 20TH CENTURY

● Robert Blake
THE DECLINE OF POWER, 1915-1964
From the disintegration of the Liberal Party to the election of Harold Wilson's Labour government
0–19–520480–8 Oxford $24.95

● David Dimbleby & David Reynolds
AN OCEAN APART: The Relationship Between Britain and America in the Twentieth Century
"An excellent account"—Paul M. Kennedy
0–394–56968–7 Random House $24.95
0–679–72190–8 Random House pb $12.95

● Alfred F. Havighurst
BRITAIN IN TRANSITION: The Twentieth Century
0–226–31970–9 Chicago pb $16.95

● Trevor O. Lloyd
EMPIRE TO WELFARE STATE: English History, 1906-1985
0–19–822134–7 Oxford pb $19.95

● Keith Robbins
THE ECLIPSE OF A GREAT POWER: Modern Britain, 1870-1975
A first-rate survey
0–582–48972–5 Longman pb $16.95

The Edwardian Era

● George Dangerfield
THE STRANGE DEATH OF LIBERAL ENGLAND
A brilliant narrative of the troubled years 1909-1914; first published in 1935
0–89733–332–2 Academy Chicago pb $8.95

● Aaron L. Friedberg
THE WEARY TITAN: Britain and the Experience of Relative Decline, 1895-1905
Highly praised scholarship in theory and history
0–691–05532–7 Princeton $29.95

● Gregory D. Phillips
THE DIEHARDS: Aristocratic Society and Politics in Edwardian England
0–674–20555–3 Harvard $18.50

● Robert Roberts
THE CLASSIC SLUM: Salford Life in the First Quarter of the Century
Manchester two generations after Engels
0–14–021692–8 Penguin pb $6.95

The Titanic

Michael Davie
TITANIC: The Death and Life of a Legend
0–394–55816–2 Knopf $19.95

John P. Eaton & Charles A. Maas
TITANIC: Destination Disaster: The Legends and the Reality
An illustrated account including recent photographs of the wreck
0–393–30492–2 Norton pb $10.95

Charles Pellegrino
HER NAME, "TITANIC": The Real Story of the Sinking and Finding of the Unsinkable Ship
The disaster re-examined through the recently discovered findings
0–07–049280–8 McGraw-Hill $18.95

Wyn Craig Wade
THE TITANIC
Called by some critics the definitive story
0–14–009635–3 Penguin pb $4.95

Armaggedon, 1914-1918

" 'You say the news from home must seem trivial compared with my experience out here,' wrote Noakes. 'Please don't get that impression. Out here news of home is like food and drink to us, however trivial. Indeed, this life is like a dream and the old life is the only reality. We live on memories. Our constant thought is—what are they doing home.' The parcels would give more tangible backing. Contents might range from the over-ripe partridge and a bunch of violets, which Ellis once got, through to the home-made cakes, Oxo cubes, chocolate bars and cigarettes which were the more common staple. The contents of all parcels naturally were shared out equally among mates. The thought was the private and valuable part."—Denis Winter, *Death's Men: Soldiers of the Great War*

● Hilary Bailey
VERA BRITTAIN
Biography of the author of *Testament of Youth*, a classic account of life in wartorn England
0–14–008003–1 Penguin pb $4.95

● John Bourne
BRITAIN AND THE GREAT WAR, 1914-1918
0–7131–6592–8 Edward Arnold pb $14.95

● Vera Brittain
TESTAMENT OF YOUTH
A classic memoir of Britain's war years
0–14–012251–6 Penguin pb $10.95

● Paul Fussell
THE GREAT WAR AND MODERN MEMORY
The British literary response to the upheaval of war
0–19–502171–1 Oxford pb $9.95

● Robert Graves
GOODBYE TO ALL THAT
Grave's "bitter leave-taking of England" at 33, in an autobiography about coming of age in the trenches of World War I
0–385–09330–6 Doubleday pb $6.95

David Lloyd George visiting Indian soldiers on the French front in 1916, from The Oxford Illustrated History of Britain *edited by Kenneth O. Morgan*

- Lyn MacDonald

THE ROSES OF NO MAN'S LAND
Nurses and doctors in the great war
0–689–70810–6 Atheneum pb $12.95

SOMME
0–689–70812–2 Atheneum pb $14.95

THEY CALLED IT PASSCHENDAELE
Five summer and autumn months in 1917
0–689–70811–4 Atheneum pb $12.95

- Arthur Marwick

THE DELUGE: British Society and the First World War
The home front: how the Great War forever changed British life
0–393–00523–2 Norton pb $8.95

- Alan Moorehead

GALLIPOLI
The disastrous Allied campaign in Turkey
0–06–013025–3 Harper & Row $15.95
0–345–33088–9 Random House pb $3.95

- Zara Steiner

BRITISH ORIGINS OF WORLD WAR I
0–312–09818–9 St. Martin's $22.50
0–312–09819–7 St. Martin's pb $14.00

- Edwin Campion Vaughan

SOME DESPERATE GLORY: The World War I Diary of a British Officer
0–671–67904–X Simon & Schuster pb $8.95

- Robert Wohl

THE GENERATION OF 1914
The haunted memories of survivors
0–674–34466–9 Harvard pb $9.95

- Stanley Weintraub

A STILLNESS HEARD ROUND THE WORLD: The End of the Great War, Armistice 1918
0–19–505208–0 Oxford pb $9.95

- Denis Winter

DEATH'S MEN: Soldiers of the Great War
0–14–005215–1 Penguin pb $6.95

Britain Between the Wars

- Paul Fussell

ABROAD: British Literary Traveling Between the Wars
0–19–502767–1 Oxford $22.95
0–19–503068–0 Oxford pb $8.95

In Wigan I stayed for a while with a miner who was suffering from nystagmus. He could see across the room but not much further. He had been drawing compensation of twenty-nine shillings a week for the past nine months, but the colliery company were now talking of putting him on "partial compensation" of fourteen shillings a week . . . Watching this man go to the colliery to draw his compensation, I was struck by the profound differences that are still made by *status*. Here was a man who had been half blinded in one of the most useful of all jobs and was drawing a pension to which he had a perfect right, if anybody has a right to anything. Yet he could not, so to speak, *demand* this pension—he could not, for instance, draw it when and how he wanted it. He had to go to the colliery once a week at a time named by the company, and when he got there he was kept waiting about for hours in the cold wind. For all I know he was also expected to touch his cap and show gratitude to whomever paid him; at any rate he had to waste an afternoon and spend sixpence in bus fares. It is very different for a member of the bourgeoisie, even such a down-at-heel member as I am. Even when I am on the verge of starvation I have certain rights attaching to my bourgeois status. I do not earn much more than a miner earns, but I do at least get it paid into my bank in a gentlemanly manner and can draw it out when I choose. And even when my account is exhausted the bank people are still passably polite.

George Orwell
THE ROAD TO WIGAN PIER
0–15–676750–3 HBJ pb $4.95

- Robert Graves & Alan Hodge

THE LONG WEEKEND: A Social History of Great Britain, 1918 to 1939
0–393–00217–9 Norton pb $10.95

- Samuel Hynes

THE AUDEN GENERATION: Literature and Politics in England in the 1930s
0–691–01395–0 Princeton pb $11.50

- George Orwell

THE ROAD TO WIGAN PIER
The human suffering of the Depression and a great work of documentary reporting
Foreword by Victor Gollancz
0–15–676750–3 HBJ pb $4.95

- Tom Ryall

ALFRED HITCHCOCK AND THE BRITISH CINEMA
During the ten years that the Cinematograph Films Act of 1927 was in force, British directors, actors, and technicians enjoyed continuous employment, and Hitchcock created some of his early masterpieces, among them *The 39 Steps*, *Sabotage*, and *Young and Innocent*
0–252–01374–3 Illinois $24.95

- John Stevenson

BRITISH SOCIETY, 1914-1945
0–14–022084–4 Penguin pb $5.95

- A.J.P. Taylor

ENGLISH HISTORY, 1914-1945
0–19–500304–7 Oxford pb $16.95

- Wesley K. Wark

THE ULTIMATE ENEMY: British Intelligence and Nazi Germany, 1933-1939
0–8014–1821–6 Cornell $32.50

- Christopher Warwick

ABDICATION
The abdication of Edward VIII in 1936 to marry the woman he loved
0–283–99351–0 Sidgwick & Jackson $24.95

Winston Churchill

There is, unfortunately, no convenient single biography. Churchill's life must be pieced together, perhaps in too much detail, by several volumes. His *The Second World War*, for which he won the Nobel Prize in 1953, remains a perennial favorite.

- Winston S. Churchill

THE SECOND WORLD WAR
A series without peer, written in the grand style by a statesman-historian from a unique perspective
0–395–07541–6 Houghton Mifflin (set) $177.95

Volume 1: The Gathering Storm
0–395–07537–8 Houghton Mifflin $29.95
0–395–41055–X Houghton Mifflin pb $9.95

Volume 2: Their Finest Hour
0–395–07536–X Houghton Mifflin $29.95
0–395–41056–8 Houghton Mifflin pb $9.95

Volume 3: The Grand Alliance
0–395–07538–6 Houghton Mifflin $29.95
0–395–41057–6 Houghton Mifflin pb $9.95

Volume 4: The Hinge of Fate
0–395–07539–4 Houghton Mifflin $29.95
0–395–41058–4 Houghton Mifflin pb $9.95

Volume 5: Closing the Ring
0–395–07535–1 Houghton Mifflin $29.95
0–395–41059–2 Houghton Mifflin pb $9.95

Volume 6: Triumph and Tragedy
0–395–07540–8 Houghton Mifflin $29.95
0–395–41060–6 Houghton Mifflin pb $9.95

- John Colville

THE FRINGES OF POWER: 10 Downing Street Diaries, 1939-1955
The diaries of Churchill's wartime private secretary
0–393–30411–6 Norton pb $12.95

- Martin Gilbert

CHURCHILL: The Wilderness Years
The basis of an engaging PBS series
0–395–31869–6 Houghton Mifflin $16.95

WINSTON S. CHURCHILL
Half of Martin Gilbert's massive and authoritative study is out of print

Volume 3: Challenge of War, 1914-1916
0–395–13153–7 Houghton Mifflin $40.00

Volume 5: The Prophet of Truth, 1922-1939
0–395–25104–4 Houghton Mifflin $40.00

Volume 7: Road to Victory, 1941-1945
0–395–37859–1 Houghton Mifflin $40.00

Volume 8: Never Despair, 1945-1965
0–395–41918–2 Houghton Mifflin $40.00

- William Manchester
THE LAST LION: Winston Spencer Churchill

Volume 1: Visions of Glory, 1874-1932
0–316–54503–1 Little, Brown $24.50

Volume 2: Alone, 1932-1940
An acclaimed addition to Manchester's ongoing work
0–316–54512–0 Little, Brown $24.95

- Ted Morgan
CHURCHILL: Young Man in a Hurry, 1874-1915
A popular account by the biographer of FDR and Somerset Maugham
0–671–25304–2 Simon & Schuster pb $10.95

▶ For the British experience during World War II see The Second World War

POSTWAR BRITAIN

- Correlli Barnett
THE PRIDE AND THE FALL
Argues that the upper classes' anti-entrepreneurial attitudes led to the country's decline, and that a moral failure after 1945 led to "a dark reality of a segregated, subliterate, unskilled, unhealthy and institutionalized proletariat hanging on the nipple of state materialism"
0–02–901851–X Free Press $24.95

- Robert Chesshyre
THE RETURN OF A NATIVE REPORTER
A journalist's late 1980s observations, written after a four year absence
0–670–81734–1 Viking $18.95

- Dennis Kavanagh
THATCHERISM AND BRITISH POLITICS: The End of Consensus
The dissolution of the Labour/Conservative postwar consensus
0–19–827521–8 Oxford pb $12.95

- Brian Lapping
END OF EMPIRE
Britain emerged from World War II so impoverished that it could no longer defend its colonies. Lapping's is the best survey of Britain's withdrawal from imperial status
0–312–25071–1 St. Martin's $24.95
0–312–25072–X St. Martin's pb $14.95

- Arthur Marwick
BRITISH SOCIETY SINCE 1945
"What went wrong" in postwar Britain
0–14–021906–4 Penguin pb $6.95

- Kenneth O. Morgan
LABOUR IN POWER: 1945-1951
The government that shaped the welfare state
0–19–285150–0 Oxford pb $13.95

LABOUR PEOPLE: Leaders and Lieutenants, Hardie to Kinnock
Illustrated
0–19–822929–1 Oxford $28.00

"Mr. and Mrs. Clark Percy" by David Hockney (Tate Gallery)

- Anthony Sampson
THE CHANGING ANATOMY OF BRITAIN
"An invaluable reference for anyone who wants to understand Britain today"—*Washington Post Book World*
0–394–72425–9 Random House pb $8.95

- Alan Sked & Chris Cook
POST-WAR BRITAIN: A Political History
0–14–022594–3 Penguin pb $7.95

Working Class Accounts

- Beverly Bryan, Stella Dadzie & Suzanne Scafe
THE HEART OF THE RACE: Black Women's Lives in Britain
What life has been like for African-Caribbean women in Britain over the past 40 years
0–86068–361–3 Virago pb $7.95

- Jocelyn Cornwell
HARD-EARNED LIVES: Accounts of Health and Illness from East London
A case-study examination of families and households
0–422–78580–6 Tavistock pb $12.95

20TH-CENTURY BIOGRAPHY

- Harold Oxbury, editor
GREAT BRITONS: Twentieth Century Lives
More than 600 figures of particular significance
0–19–211599–5 Oxford $29.95

- Philip Norman
SHOUT!: The Beatles in Their Generation
An international best-seller
0–446–32255–5 Warner pb $4.95

- John Campbell
ANEURIN BEVAN AND THE MIRAGE OF BRITISH SOCIALISM
A new biography of the postwar leader of British Labour's left wing
0–393–02452–0 Norton $25.95

- Alan Bullock
ERNEST BEVIN: Foreign Secretary, 1945-1951
By the author of *Hitler, A Study in Tyranny*
0–393–01825–3 Norton $37.50

- Quentin Crisp
THE NAKED CIVIL SERVANT
Autobiography of the flamboyant civil servant who chose to flaunt his homosexuality in the conventional world of 1930s London
0–452–25413–2 NAL pb $6.95

- Robert Rhodes James
ANTHONY EDEN: A Biography
An authorized biography of the prime minister and three-time foreign minister who opposed appeasement, helped establish the United Nations, and led Britain through the Suez crisis of 1956
0–07–032285–6 McGraw-Hill $22.95

- Roy Harrod
THE LIFE OF JOHN MAYNARD KEYNES
0–393–30024–2 Norton pb $10.95

- Robert Skidelsky
JOHN MAYNARD KEYNES: Hopes Betrayed, 1883-1920
A well-received biography
0–670–40810–7 Viking $24.95

- Malcom Brown & Julia Cave
A TOUCH OF GENIUS: The Life of T.E. Lawrence
1–55778–203–2 Paragon $22.95

- J.M. Wilson
LAWRENCE OF ARABIA
The British secret agent who played a legendary part in the Arab Awakening. This new biography contains previously unpublished photographs, letters, and other documents
0–689–11934–8 Macmillan $21.95

- Alistaire Horne
HAROLD MACMILLAN, POLITICIAN, 1894-1956
0–670–80502–5 Viking $24.95

- Philip Ziegler
MOUNTBATTEN
Engaging portrait of Britain's last viceroy to India. "Just the right balance between the life and the times"—*NY Review of Books*
0–06–097022–7 Harper & Row pb $10.95

- Anthony Holden
LAURENCE OLIVIER: A Biography
Published in 1988; includes a chronological list of all Olivier's performances
0–689–11536–9 Macmillan $19.95

- Caroline Moorehead
FREYA STARK
Biography of one of the great 20th-century travelers
0–14–008108–9 Penguin pb $4.95

- Michael Holroyd
LYTTON STRACHEY: A Biography
Highly recommended
0–14–058031–X Penguin pb $10.95

• Kenneth Harris
THATCHER
A journalist's enthusiastic portrait of the first prime minister in 160 years to win three consecutive general elections
0–316–34837–6 Little, Brown $19.95

• Martin Stannard
EVELYN WAUGH: The Early Years, 1903-1939
A life of wit, bravado, and colorful escapades; but in Waugh's own phrase, a "sad story" of one who was melancholy at heart
0–393–02450–4 Norton $24.95

• Fay Weldon
REBECCA WEST
0–14–008002–3 Penguin pb $4.95

• Phyllis Rose
WOMAN OF LETTERS: A Life of Virginia Woolf
0–15–698190–4 HBJ pb $8.95

The Royal Family
"The populace cannot understand the bureaucracy; it can only worship the national idols."—Bernard Shaw, "Maxims for Revolutionists" in *Man and Superman*

Michael Bloch
THE SECRET FILE OF THE DUKE OF WINDSOR: The Private Papers, 1937-1972
0–06–016090–X Harper & Row $19.95

John Cannon & Ralph Griffiths
THE OXFORD ILLUSTRATED HISTORY OF THE BRITISH MONARCHY
The crown's full history since Anglo-Saxon times. Includes 130 color illustrations, 270 black-and-white pictures, six color maps, and ten genealogies
0–19–822786–8 Oxford $39.95

Charles Higham
THE DUCHESS OF WINDSOR: The Secret Life
More details for those with insatiable appetites for royal goings-on
0–07–028801–1 McGraw-Hill $17.95

Brian Hoey
MONARCHY: Behind the Scenes with the Royal Family
0–312–01475–9 St. Martin's $15.95

Anthony Holden
KING CHARLES III: A Biography
1–55584–309–3 W&N $19.95

Paul James & Peter Russell
AT HOME WITH THE ROYAL FAMILY
0–06–015697–X Harper & Row $17.95

Robert Lacey
MAJESTY
Elizabeth II, by the master of postwar biography of British royalty
0–380–01842–X Avon pb $4.95

PRINCESS
The Lady Di story
0–8129–6329–6 Times pb $9.95

QUEEN MOTHER
The ever-popular Elizabeth, mother of the current queen and queen consort to George VI
0–316–51167–6 Little, Brown $17.95

John Pearson
THE SELLING OF THE ROYAL FAMILY
How the Windsors and the gossip they spawn have become big business
0–515–09276–2 Jove pb $4.50

Roy Strong
CECIL BEATON: The Royal Portraits
Revealing portraits of the Windsors from 1930 to 1979
0–671–67033–6 Simon & Schuster $35.00

IRELAND DIVIDED

Backed by German aid during the First World War, Sinn Fein, the military arm of the Irish independence movement, rebelled against British rule in 1916. In 1922 a settlement was reached, and Ireland was divided. Within a few years southern Ireland broke political relations with Britain and became an independent republic.

• Sally Belfrage
LIVING WITH WAR: A Belfast Year
0–670–81811–9 Viking $19.95

• J. Bowyer Bell
THE SECRET ARMY: The IRA from 1916-1979
By an expert on terrorism
0–262–52090–7 MIT pb $15.00

• David Beresford
TEN MEN DEAD: The Story of the 1981 Irish Hunger Strike
Ten who chose to perish "for a cause more ancient than the gray walls of Long Kesh prison"; by a reporter for *The Guardian*
Introduction by Peter Maas
0–871–13269–9 Atlantic Monthly $18.95

• Paul Bew & Henry Patterson
THE BRITISH STATE AND THE ULSTER CRISIS
Challenges the belief that Britain has maintained a coherent imperialist stretegy in Northern Ireland
0–86091–815–7 Verso pb $9.95

• Kevin Boyle & Tom Hadden
IRELAND: A Positive Proposal
A bold challenge to current despair over Northern Ireland, offering a practical solution
0–14–052362–6 Penguin pb $5.95

• Terence Brown
IRELAND: A Social and Cultural History, 1922 to the Present
"Gaelic, peasant Ireland may still inspire idealists and delight tourists. Terence Brown shows how its influence . . . no longer dominates the essential Ireland of the later 20th century"—*Times Educational Supplement*
0–8014–9349–8 Cornell $12.95

• John Darby, editor
NORTHERN IRELAND: The Background to the Conflict
A dispassionate collection of essays pointing to accommodation in the subtle relations between Catholics and Protestants
0–8156–2417–4 Syracuse pb $12.95

• Jack Holland
THE AMERICAN CONNECTION: U.S. Guns, Money, and Influence in Northern Ireland
"Compulsory reading for those who wish to understand the place and influence of Irish-American nationalism on Anglo-Irish affairs"—*Boston Globe*
0–14–008495–9 Penguin pb $7.95

• Dermot Keogh
IRELAND AND EUROPE, 1919-1948
0–389–20803–5 Barnes & Noble $28.50

• John Stalker
THE STALKER AFFAIR
0–670–82262–0 Viking $19.95
0–14–011051–8 Penguin pb $7.95

Russian and Soviet Studies

OVERVIEWS OF RUSSIAN AND SOVIET HISTORY

• Stephen F. Cohen
RETHINKING THE SOVIET EXPERIENCE: Politics and History since 1917
A survey that challenges the West's conventional wisdom on Soviet affairs
0–19–503468–6 Oxford $21.95
0–19–504016–3 Oxford pb $6.95

• Robert V. Daniels
RUSSIA: The Roots of Confrontation
Examines the traditional love/hate relationship between the Russian national character and the influence of the West
0–674–77966–5 Harvard pb $8.95

• Mikhail Heller & Aleksandr M. Nekrich
UTOPIA IN POWER: The History of the Soviet Union from 1917 to the Present
Survey by two Soviet-educated scholars who emigrated to the West. "Portrays a moral struggle that we would be wrong to ignore, and bears testimony to courage and

commitment to truth that we would do well to emulate"—*NY Times*
0–671–64535–8 Summit pb $12.95

• Lionel Kochan & Richard Abraham
THE MAKING OF MODERN RUSSIA
A colorful and lively introduction to Russian history from the 10th-century principality of Kiev to Secretary Brezhnev
0–14–022488–2 Penguin pb $7.95

• Fitzroy Maclean
PORTRAIT OF THE SOVIET UNION
Illustrated companion volume to the television series
0–8050–0891–8 Henry Holt $23.95

• Olga Narkiewicz
SOVIET LEADERS: From the Cult of Personality to Collective Rule
0–312–74857–4 St. Martin's $32.50

• Alec Nove
AN ECONOMIC HISTORY OF THE USSR
The growing pains of a giant—the dramatic economic expansion of the Soviet Union in the 20th century
0–14–021403–8 Penguin pb $7.95

• Nicholas V. Riasanovsky
A HISTORY OF RUSSIA
Abundantly detailed history with the imprimatur of a leading academic press
0–19–503361–2 Oxford $29.50

• Leonard Schapiro
THE COMMUNIST PARTY OF THE SOVIET UNION
From Lenin to Brezhnev, the first comprehensive study of the Party by an outsider
0–394–70745–1 Random House pb $11.95

RUSSIAN STUDIES
Essays on topics from law to literature from one of the West's leading Soviet authorities
Edited by Ellen Dahrendorf
0–14–009376–1 Penguin pb $9.95

Early 16th-century sledges in Russia

• Albert & Joan Seaton
THE SOVIET ARMY: 1917 to the Present
0–452–00906–5 Meridian pb $9.95

• J.N. Westwood
ENDURANCE AND ENDEAVOUR: Russian History, 1812-1986
The defeat of Napoleon paradoxically created the forces of nationalism and radicalism that overthrew the Romanov dynasty and led to the Soviet state
0–19–822146–0 Oxford $54.00
0–19–822145–2 Oxford pb $19.95

Cultural and Intellectual History

• James H. Billington
THE ICON AND THE AXE: An Interpretive History of Russian Culture
"Will do more to make Russia understandable to the west than 50 cultural exchange sorties"—Elizabeth Janeway, *Books Today*
0–394–70846–6 Random House pb $13.95

• W.J. Leatherbarrow & D.C. Offord, translators & editors
A DOCUMENTARY HISTORY OF RUSSIAN THOUGHT: From the Enlightenment to Marxism
The gentry revolutionaries, the liberal westernizers, and the revolutionary populists; over 20 writers, social and political critics included, among them Belinsky, Herzen, Chernyshevsky, Dostoevsky, Bakunin, and Plekhanov
0–87501–018–0 Ardis $35.00
0–87501–019–9 Ardis pb $15.95

• Suzanne Massie
LAND OF THE FIREBIRD: The Beauty of Old Russia
A cultural history of pre-revolutionary Russia, with color pictures
0–671–46059–5 Simon & Schuster pb $17.95

• Nikolai Tolstoy
THE TOLSTOYS: Twenty-Four Generations of Russian History
A heavily illustrated view of Russian history through the eyes of its most creative family
0–688–06674–7 Morrow pb $10.95

• Adam B. Ulam
IDEOLOGIES AND ILLUSIONS: Revolutionary Thought from Herzen to Solzhenitsyn
Russia's vibrant intellectual tradition: from the aristocratic friend of the people of the 19th century to the dissident arch-foe of communism today
0–674–44310–1 Harvard $19.50

• Andrzej Walicki
A HISTORY OF RUSSIAN THOUGHT: From the Enlightenment to Marxism
"The value of Walicki's book resides . . . in his ability to see the development of individual thinkers against a complex background and to relate them to earlier and later aspects of the movement"—Philip Pomper, *Russian History*
0–8047–1026–0 Stanford $45.50
0–8047–1132–1 Stanford pb $11.95

After the destruction of the Byzantine-inspired culture of Kiev by the Mongols in the 13th century, the Russian national identity reasserted itself through the gradual expansion of Moscow, a small fort-settlement town in the central plain.

• Basil Dmytryshyn, editor
MEDIEVAL RUSSIA: A Source Book, 900-1700
Illuminating documents reveal the laws and manners of primitive Russia until the time of Peter the Great
0–03–086441–0 Henry Holt $25.95

• John Fennell
THE CRISIS OF MEDIEVAL RUSSIA, 1200-1304
Mongol rule, though not oppressive, threatened the development of native self-government for over 100 years, until the first Muscovite victory at Kulikovo in 1380. Part of the Longman History of Russia Series
0–582–48150–3 Longman pb $16.95

• Charles J. Halperin
RUSSIA AND THE GOLDEN HORDE: The Mongol Impact on Medieval Russian History
Argues that the Russian-Tatar relationship was complex, multifaceted, and by no means always hostile
0–253–20445–3 Indiana pb $7.95

• Richard Hellie
SLAVERY IN RUSSIA, 1450-1725
Makes us aware of the importance of slavery in early modern Russia by presenting comparisons with other slave-owning societies
0–226–32648–9 Chicago pb $20.00

• Vladimir Nabokov, translator
THE SONG OF IGOR'S CAMPAIGN
0–87501–061–X Ardis pb $4.50

• Vladimir Volkoff
VLADIMIR: The Russian Viking
The powerful prince of Kiev, descendant of northern warrior-traders, who adopted the religion and culture of Byzantium in the 10th century
0–87951–234–2 Overlook pb $10.95

An alliance with the powerful monasteries enabled Ivan III, the Grand Duke of Moscow, to free himself from Tatar overlordship in the 15th century and, by adopting the imperial rank of Czar, establish an extreme version of autocratic divine right.

Peter the Great by Sir Godfrey Kneller, from Peter the Great *by Robert Massie* (Ballantine)

● **W. Bruce Lincoln**
THE ROMANOVS: Autocrats of All the Russias
Dynastic struggles following the death of Ivan the Terrible ended in 1613 with the accession of the Romanov family, which held supreme power until 1917
0–385–27908–6 Doubleday pb $16.95

● **Benson Bobrick**
FEARFUL MAJESTY: The Life and Reign of Ivan the Terrible
0–399–13256–2 Putnam $22.95

● **Francis Carr**
IVAN THE TERRIBLE
The heir of the first Czar brought Muscovite expansion into new conflicts with the Tatars in the south and the Poles and Lithuanians in the west; but his psychopathic personality inaugurated a reign of terror that culminated in the murder of his only son
0–389–20150–2 Barnes & Noble $27.50

● **Henri Troyat**
IVAN THE TERRIBLE
A popular and reliable biography of one of the greatest expansionist czars, much admired by Stalin
Translated by Joan Pickham
0–425–08481–7 Berkley pb $3.95

Peter the Great

The reign of Peter the Great (1682-1725) ushered in one of the most productive and influential transformations in modern European history. It was Peter who broke the independent armed bands of the Streltsy, defeated the Swedes at Poltava, expanded Russia to the Baltic, and moved the capital from Moscow to the new city of St. Petersburg.

Vasili Klyuchevsky
PETER THE GREAT
An influential view by a 19th-century liberal Russian historian
Translated by Liliana Archibald
0–8070–5647–2 Beacon pb $11.95

Robert Massie
PETER THE GREAT
A vivid, popular account used as the basis of the NBC mini-series
0–345–29806–3 Ballantine pb $9.95

B. H. Sumner
PETER THE GREAT AND THE EMERGENCE OF RUSSIA
0–02–037760–6 Macmillan pb $4.95

● **Isabel de Madariaga**
RUSSIA IN THE AGE OF CATHERINE THE GREAT
The enlightenment continued under the reign of the German-born empress whose plans for social and intellectual progress won the praise of Voltaire and Jeremy Bentham
0–300–02843–1 Yale pb $17.95

● **John T. Alexander**
CATHERINE THE GREAT: Life and Legend
A well-researched biography that judiciously examines the myths, Catherine's sexual voracity among others, that sprang up around this great ruler
0–19–505236–6 Oxford $24.95

● **Henri Troyat**
CATHERINE THE GREAT
Mother, lover, victorious expansionist, empress of all the Russias, presented in an entertaining narrative
Translated by Joan Pinkham
0–425–07981–3 Berkley pb $4.50

ALEXANDER OF RUSSIA: Napoleon's Conqueror
The leader of the religious reaction against the French revolutionary doctrines of liberty and reason
0–88064–059–6 Fromm pb $11.95

Czar Nicholas I afraid he has overextended himself in the Crimean War, from Daumier: 120 Great Lithographs *edited by Charles F. Ramus* (Dover)

● **Robert Massie**
NICHOLAS AND ALEXANDRA
A popular biography of the last Romanovs, an inward-looking family unable to cope with the forces that brought the Bolsheviks to power
0–689–10177–5 Atheneum $29.95
0–440–36358–6 Dell pb $6.95

● **Peter Kurth**
ANASTASIA: The Riddle of Anna Anderson
How genuine were her claims to be a daughter of the czar who survived the massacre at Ekaterinaburg?
0–316–50717–2 Little, Brown pb $10.95

It was a dream-like ride in the unreal glow of the northern night. The men marched without knowing exactly where they were going, nor what they were going to do, but their enthusiasm was totally engaged in this mad adventure, mingling as it did light and shade, duty and revolution, truth and illusion. At the head of the slow procession, a woman, perhaps the goddess of war. Behind her, the Orlov brothers and many officers, all of whom seemed to be in love with her. The military band played stirring tunes. And when it stopped, the soldiers struck up old marching songs, broken by happy shouts and whistles. Always the same cry: "Long live our little mother Catherine!" Each time she heard her name yelled by these rough throats, she quivered with almost sexual joy. That was what she needed: a people which would be for her like a many-shaped lover, always ardent and always submissive.

Henri Troyat
CATHERINE THE GREAT
Translated by Joan Pinkham
0–425–07981–3 Berkley pb $4.50

THE OLD REGIME

● **Paul Avrich**
RUSSIAN REBELS, 1600-1800
Bolotnikov, Stenka Razin, Bulavin, and Pugachev—the four great Cossack-led peasant rebellions that shook the throne of the Romanovs
0–393–00836–3 Norton pb $7.95

● **Victoria E. Bonnell, editor**
THE RUSSIAN WORKER: Life and Labor under the Tsarist Regime
Personal accounts by sales clerks and textile mill and factory workers
0–520–04837–7 California $35.95
0–520–05059–2 California pb $10.95

● **Jeffrey Brooks**
WHEN RUSSIA LEARNED TO READ: Literacy and Popular Literature, 1861-1917
"The popular books that entertained and instructed, reflected, and helped shape the values of millions of newly literate Russians, particularly during the last three decades of the Romanov empire"—Maurice Friedberg, *Political Science Quarterly*
0–691–00821–3 Princeton pb $12.95

• Kyril FitzLyon & Tatiana Browning
BEFORE THE REVOLUTION: Russia and Its People Under the Czars
A photographic journey
0–87951–167–2 Overlook pb $12.95

• Richard Pipes
RUSSIA UNDER THE OLD REGIME
The rise of the Russian state from its medieval origins to the 1880s, when the assassination of Alexander II led, according to Pipes, to the formation of a police state that survived the Leninist revolution. Controversial and highly recommended
0–02–395700–X Macmillan $24.50

• Marc Raeff
UNDERSTANDING IMPERIAL RUSSIA: State and Society in the Old Regime
The Russia of the czars, both in its own right and as a basis for the emergence of the Soviet Union
Translated by Arthur Goldhammer
0–231–05842–X Columbia $27.00
0–231–05843–8 Columbia pb $14.00

• G.T. Robinson
RURAL RUSSIA UNDER THE OLD REGIME: A History of the Landlord-Peasant World and a Prologue to the Peasant Revolution of 1917
0–520–01075–2 California pb $11.95

• Hugh Seton-Watson
THE RUSSIAN EMPIRE, 1801-1917
From Alexander I to the Abdication of Nicholas II. As the Russian Empire expanded into Western Europe, India, and the dominions of Turkey, internal dissension reached critical proportions
0–19–822152–5 Oxford pb $29.95

Roots of Revolution

"You are not alone, workers and peasants of Russia! If you succeed in overthrowing, crushing and destroying the tyrants of feudal, police-ridden landlord and tsarist Russia your victory will serve as a signal for a world struggle against the tyranny of capital."—V.I. Lenin, 1905, quoted in Eric Hobsbawm, *The Age of Empire*

• Abraham Ascher
THE REVOLUTION OF 1905: Russia in Disarray
The army stayed loyal during the massive popular revolution following Russia's defeat by Japan, but the constitutional reforms only staved off 1917
0–8047–1436–3 Stanford $39.50

• Isaiah Berlin
RUSSIAN THINKERS
This collection of essays includes the famous "The Hedgehog and the Fox," as well as comparisons of Herzen and Bakunin
0–14–022260–X Penguin pb $7.95

• Victoria E. Bonnell
ROOTS OF REBELLION: Workers' Politics and Organizations in St. Petersburg and Moscow, 1900-1914
0–520–04740–0 California $42.00
0–520–05114–9 California pb $11.95

Mikhail Bakunin, photographed by Nadar

• Nikolai Chernyshevsky
WHAT IS TO BE DONE?
This novel of love and sacrifice by one of the Old Regime's most famous critics is a primary text of Russian feminism and socialism
Translated & edited by K. Feuer
0–87501–017–2 Ardis pb $6.95

• Edward Crankshaw
THE SHADOW OF THE WINTER PALACE: The Drift to Revolution, 1825-1917
Smooth narrative account of the febrile fumblings of the Old Regime in the face of growing discontent
0–14–004622–4 Penguin pb $7.95

• Robert Edelman
PROLETARIAN PEASANTS: The Revolution of 1905 in Russia's Southwest
A case study of a peasant revolt in the Ukraine
0–8014–9473–7 Cornell pb $9.95

• Abbott Gleason
YOUNG RUSSIA: The Genesis of Russian Radicalism in the 1860s
"Certainly the best and most readable account of the early stages of Russian radicalism"—Walter M. Pintner, Cornell University
0–226–29961–9 Chicago pb $12.00

• Aileen Kelly
MIKHAIL BAKUNIN: A Study in the Psychology and Politics of Utopianism
Argues that Bakunin's self-deception allowed him to utilize mass movements as an outlet for his own personal goals and frustrations
0–300–03874–7 Yale pb $14.95

• Anatole G. Mazour
THE FIRST RUSSIAN REVOLUTION, 1825: The Decembrist Movement
The failed attempt at aristocratic reforms by officers returning from France is seen as the beginning of the movement that toppled czarism
0–8047–0081–8 Stanford $32.50
0–8047–0082–6 Stanford pb $10.95

• Hans Rogger
RUSSIA IN THE AGE OF MODERNISATION AND REVOLUTION: 1881-1917
0–582–48912–1 Longman pb $19.50

• Franco Venturi
ROOTS OF REVOLUTION: A History of the Populist and Socialist Movements in Nineteenth-Century Russia
The classic history of the ideas and ideologists of czarist Russia includes considerations of Herzen, Bakunin, and Chernyshevsky. Widely considered a classic in its field
Translated by Francis Haskell
Introduction by Isaiah Berlin
0–226–85270–9 Chicago pb $20.00

World War I

• D.C. Lieven
RUSSIA AND THE ORIGINS OF THE FIRST WORLD WAR
0–312–69608–6 St. Martin's $27.50
0–312–69611–6 St. Martin's pb $14.00

• W. Bruce Lincoln
IN WAR'S DARK SHADOW: The Russians Before the Great War
The age of the Triple Entente with a militarily unprepared Russia backing France against Germany despite the pressure of internal disorder
0–671–62821–6 Simon & Schuster pb $10.95

PASSAGE THROUGH ARMAGEDDON: The Russians in War and Revolution, 1914-1918
"Events canter across the pages of *Passage Through Armageddon* faster than Cossack cavalrymen chasing a Bolshevik"—*NY Times Book Review*
0–671–64560–9 Simon & Schuster pb $14.95

George F. Kennan
RUSSIA AND THE WEST UNDER LENIN AND STALIN
A classic by the former Ambassador of the United States to the Soviet Union. "Surely one of the most important books since the end of the last war"—Edmund Wilson
0–451–62460–2 NAL pb $4.95

RUSSIA LEAVES THE WAR: Soviet-American Relations, 1917-1920
From the Bolshevik revolution to Russia's exit from World War I, by one of America's leading diplomats and historians. Winner of the Pulitzer Prize and the National Book Award
0–393–30214–8 Norton pb $12.95

THE REVOLUTION

An army demoralized by its failure against Germany and a czar absent from the capital paved the way for the first revolution in February, 1917. The subsequent leadership vacuum allowed the highly-motivated Bolsheviks under Lenin's direction to take control of the government in October.

▶ **TO ORDER BOOKS AS GIFTS, SEE PAGE 1**

E.H. Carr
THE BOLSHEVIK REVOLUTION
An unrivaled account from a
sympathetic and leftwing perspective

Volume 1
Analyzes the events from 1898 to
1917, the provisional constitution, and
the Bolshevik takeover
0–393–30195–8 Norton pb $11.95

Volume 2
The civil war, the revolt of the
peasantry, and the decline of industrial
output leads to greater repression and
the New Economic Policy
0–393–30197–4 Norton pb $11.95

Volume 3
The foreign policy of the new
communist state as it faces the stress of
international confrontation
0–393–30199–0 Norton pb $12.95

THE RUSSIAN REVOLUTION
A condensation of Carr's massive study
of the revolution from Lenin to Stalin
0–02–905140–1 Free Press $18.95

• **William H. Chamberlin**
**THE RUSSIAN REVOLUTION, 1917-
1921**
An old, but still impressive narrative by the
former Christian Science Monitor
correspondent in Moscow
Edited by Diane Koenker

**Volume 1: 1917-1919, From the Overthrow
of the Tsar to the Assumption of Power by
the Bolsheviks**
0–691–00814–0 Princeton pb $12.50

**Volume 2: 1919-1921, From the Civil War
to the Consolidation of Power**
0–691–00815–9 Princeton pb $14.50

• **Sheila Fitzpatrick**
THE RUSSIAN REVOLUTION
The entire revolutionary period, from
1905 to Stalin
0–19–219162–4 Oxford $21.95
0–19–289148–0 Oxford pb $7.95

• **Abbott Gleason & others, editors**
**BOLSHEVIK CULTURE: Experiment and
Order in the Russian Revolution**
0–253–20513–1 Indiana pb $14.95

• **Robert Goldston**
THE RUSSIAN REVOLUTION
Short, popularized account of the
Bolshevik revolution
0–449–30025–0 Fawcett pb $2.95

• **Tim McDaniel**
**AUTOCRACY, CAPITALISM, AND
REVOLUTION IN RUSSIA**
New synthesis of "class" and "mass"
explanations for the revolution shows how
the cross-purposes of capitalism and
autocracy hindered reform
0–520–06071–7 California pb $14.95

• **Leonard Schapiro**
**THE RUSSIAN REVOLUTIONS OF
1917: The Origins of Modern Communism**
"If the reader wants to know how the
Russian Revolution took place and what
happened in its early aftermath, there is no

better place to begin than this little
book"—Robert C. Tucker
0–465–07155–4 Basic Books pb $10.95

• **Daniel H. Kaiser**
**THE WORKERS' REVOLUTION IN
RUSSIA, 1917: The View from Below**
0–521–34166–3 Cambridge $32.50
0–521–34971–0 Cambridge pb $8.95

• **Harrison E. Salisbury**
**BLACK NIGHT, WHITE SNOW: Russia's
Revolutions, 1905-1917**
A journalist's account of Russian politics
and society as the reign of the Romanovs
crumbled
0–306–80154–X Da Capo pb $14.95

• **Harold Shukman, editor**
**THE BLACKWELL ENCYCLOPEDIA OF
THE RUSSIAN REVOLUTION**
An illustrated volume offering a
comprehensive chronology and biographies
of key figures
0–631–15238–5 Blackwell $65.00

• **Richard Stites, editor**
**REVOLUTIONARY DREAMS: Utopian
and Experimental Life in the Russian
Revolution**
The emotional and expressive realm of the
revolution in artistic artifacts, science
fiction, fantasy cities, invented rituals, and
literary utopias
0–19–505536–5 Oxford $35.00

Red October: 1917

• **Robert V. Daniels**
**RED OCTOBER: The Bolshevik
Revolution of 1917**
Views the Bolshevik success as the product
of fortunate accident rather than historical
necessity
0–8070–5644–8 Beacon $25.00
0–8070–5645–6 Beacon pb $11.95

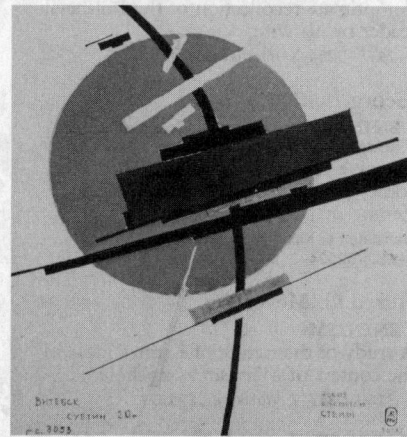

Nikolai Suetin's "Design for a Mural," from
Soviet Art of the 1920s-1930s: From the
Russian Museum, Leningrad (*Abrams*)

• **Paul Dukes**
**OCTOBER AND THE WORLD:
Perspectives on the Russian Revolution**
0–312–58096–7 St. Martin's $20.00

• **Marc Ferro**
**OCTOBER 1917: A Social History of the
Russian Revolution**
A noteworthy contribution to the newer
social history of the revolution
0–7100–0534–2 Methuen $35.00

• **John Reed**
TEN DAYS THAT SHOOK THE WORLD
The American radical journalist's
eyewitness account of the Bolshevik seizure
of power records the excitement of the
October days and the beginnings of his
own disillusionment
Edited by Bertram D. Wolfe
0–394–70719–2 Random House pb $4.95

The Fate of the Revolution

• **Paul Avrich**
KRONSTADT 1921
The brutal suppression of the sailors' revolt
against the Bolshevik regime they had
helped bring to power
0–393–00724–3 Norton pb $6.95

• **Walter Laqueur**
THE FATE OF THE REVOLUTION
The mutations of Russian historiography
on the Revolution
0–02–034080–X Collier pb $10.95

• **Rosa Luxemburg**
**THE RUSSIAN REVOLUTION: Leninism
or Marxism?**
Shortly before her murder by the German
right in 1919, the Polish Marxist wrote
this sympathetic but skeptical investigation
into the genuineness of Bolshevik Marxism
Introduction by Bertram D. Wolfe
0–472–06057–0 Michigan pb $6.95

• **Alfred G. Meyer**
COMMUNISM
The changes and distortions of Marxism in
its Soviet application
0–394–33163–X Random House pb $10.50

• **Richard Pipes**
**THE FORMATION OF THE SOVIET
UNION: Communism and Nationalism,
1917-1923**
0–674–30950–2 Harvard $27.00

• **Leonard Schapiro**
**THE ORIGIN OF THE COMMUNIST
AUTOCRACY: Political Opposition in the
Soviet State—First Phase, 1917-1922**
How Lenin and the Bolsheviks held on to
power without large popular support
0–674–64452–2 Harvard pb $12.50

• **Theodore H. Von Laue**
**WHY LENIN? WHY STALIN? A
Reappraisal of the Russian Revolution,
1900-1930**
0–397–47200–5 Harper & Row pb $12.50

Women and Revolution

Barbara A. Engel
MOTHERS AND DAUGHTERS: Women of the Intelligentsia in Nineteenth Century Russia
In contrast to Turgenev's *Fathers and Sons*, this book provides a corrective to the underrated contribution of Russian women to radical thought
0–521–25125–7 Cambridge $39.50
0–521–31301–5 Cambridge pb $12.95

Gail W. Lapidus
WOMEN IN SOVIET SOCIETY: Equality, Development, and Social Change
0–520–03938–6 California pb $9.95

Richard Stites
THE WOMEN'S LIBERATION MOVEMENT IN RUSSIA: Feminism, Nihilism, and Bolshevism, 1860-1930
An engrossing account that crosses over traditional chronological boundaries
0–691–10058–6 Princeton pb $19.95

Christine Sutherland
THE PRINCESS OF SIBERIA: The Story of Maria Volkonsky
Biography of the wife of an exiled Decembrist who accompanied her husband to the Siberian wilderness
0–374–51961–7 FS&G pb $8.95

BIOGRAPHY: The Revolutionary Era

• **Adam B. Ulam**
THE BOLSHEVIKS
Engaging biographical account focusing on the school teacher's son, Vladimir Ilyich Ulyanov (1870-1924), better known as Lenin; an ideal introduction to the period
0–02–038100–X Macmillan pb $11.95

• **Stephen F. Cohen**
BUKHARIN AND THE BOLSHEVIK REVOLUTION: A Political Biography, 1888-1938
Bukharin's rise and fall, focusing on the period from Lenin's death in 1924 to Stalin's rise in 1929
0–19–502697–7 Oxford pb $14.95

• **Roy A. Medvedev**
NIKOLAI BUKHARIN: The Last Years
Poignant and dramatic account by a disaffected Soviet historian of the man Lenin called "deservedly the favorite of the Party." Bukharin's reputation was rehabilitated in 1988 after his humiliation and execution by Stalin in 1938
0–393–30110–9 Norton pb $6.50

• **Richard Abraham**
ALEXANDER KERENSKY: The First Love of the Revolution
A biography of the leading politician during the chaos between the czar's abdication in March, and the Bolshevik takeover in October, 1917
0–231–06108–0 Columbia $30.00

Lenin in 1887, the year he graduated from gymnasium, from Lenin: A Biography *by Ronald W. Clark (Harper & Row)*

• **Ronald W. Clark**
LENIN: A Biography
The most recent biography shows the man beneath the revolutionary
0–060–15802–6 Harper & Row $27.95

• **Christopher Hill**
LENIN AND THE RUSSIAN REVOLUTION
A postwar, leftwing work of the biographer of Oliver Cromwell. "Brings out Lenin's purposefulness, realism, commonsense, will-power, and pugnacity"—*Daily Telegraph* (London)
0–14–021297–3 Penguin pb $5.95

• **N.K. Krupskaya**
REMINISCENCES OF LENIN
An intimate recollection of the Bolshevik leader by his wife
0–7178–0254–X International pb $4.95

• **Georg Lukács**
LENIN: A Study on the Unity of his Thought
To stave off criticism, Lukács attributes some of his own transcendentalism to Lenin
Translated by Nicholas Jacobs
0–262–62024–3 MIT pb $4.95

• **Alfred G. Meyer**
LENINISM
A study of the nature of Lenin's ideas in the context of Marxism as a whole
0–8133–0387–7 Westview $21.00

• **Robert Tucker, editor**
THE LENIN ANTHOLOGY
A comprehensive and authoritative anthology of the most influential communist writings after Marx's own
0–393–09236–4 Norton pb $14.95

• **Warren Lerner**
KARL RADEK: The Last Internationalist
Communism's brilliant publicist who fell victim to Stalin's purge of the Old Bolsheviks
0–8047–0722–7 Stanford $20.00

Trotsky

Despite his success as minister of war and creator of the Red Army, Trotsky was outmaneuvered by Stalin, exiled to the West, and eventually assassinated in Mexico.

• **Isaac Deutscher**
Three volumes worth reading both for their literary style and insights into the revolutionary mentality.
THE PROPHET ARMED: Trotsky, 1879-1921
0–19–281064–2 Oxford pb $10.95
THE PROPHET UNARMED: Trotsky, 1921-1929
0–19–281065–0 Oxford pb $10.95
THE PROPHET OUTCAST: Trotsky, 1929-1940
0–19–281066–9 Oxford pb $10.95

• **Irving Howe**
LEON TROTSKY
A useful, brief guide by an intellectual of the American left
0–14–005067–1 Penguin pb $4.95

• **Leon Trotsky**
HISTORY OF THE RUSSIAN REVOLUTION
0–913460–83–4 Pathfinder $22.95
MY LIFE
Considerable literary merit enhances the interest of this autobiography of a revolutionary written in 1930, the year after Trotsky's expulsion from the Soviet Union
0–87348–144–5 Pathfinder pb $12.95
THE REVOLUTION BETRAYED
Despite the bitterness of recent exile an objective view prevails in this critique of Stalin's revival of Russian absolutism
Translated by Max Eastman
0–87348–226–3 Pathfinder pb $7.95

THE STALIN ERA

• **Robert Conquest**
HARVEST OF SORROW: Soviet Collectivization and the Terror-Famine
A graphic portrayal of the political ruthlessness with which Stalin stifled opposition and imposed his collectivization and industrialization programs
0–19–504054–6 Oxford $22.95
STALIN AND THE KIROV MURDER
Stalin's Reichstag fire: a political murder on his own orders gave Stalin the opportunity to inaugurate the treason trials that liquidated his old comrades-in-arms; by the author of *The Great Terror*, now out of print
0–19–505579–9 Oxford $16.95

• Eugenia Semyonovna Ginzburg
JOURNEY INTO THE WHIRLWIND
Memoir of years in prison and labor camps under Stalin
0–15–646509–4 Harvest pb $9.95

• Alex De Jonge
STALIN AND THE SHAPING OF THE SOVIET UNION
"This eloquent, engrossing chronicle surpasses its genre"—*NY Times*
0–688–07291–7 Morrow pb $12.95

• Moshe Lewin
THE MAKING OF THE SOVIET SYSTEM: Essays in the Social History of Interwar Russia
0–394–72900–5 Pantheon pb $14.95

RUSSIAN PEASANTS AND SOVIET POWER: A Study of Collectivization
0–393–00752–9 Norton pb $11.95

• Roy Medvedev
LET HISTORY JUDGE: The Origins and Consequences of Stalinism
A revised and enlarged edition
Translated & edited by George Shriver
0–231–06350–4 Columbia $57.50

LET HISTORY JUDGE: The Origins and Consequences of Stalinism
A ringing indictment by a leading dissident
Edited by Georges Haupt & David Joravsky
0–394–71928–X Random House pb $9.95

• Suzanne Rosenberg
A SOVIET ODYSSEY
A young Communist woman's tortuous encounter with Stalinist Siberia offers a rare glimpse of both Soviet life and the Stalinist era
0–19–540654–0 Oxford $19.95

• Karlo Stajner
SEVEN THOUSAND DAYS IN SIBERIA
New autobiographical account of 20 years of imprisonment during Stalin's purges
Translated by Joel Agee
0–374–26126–1 Farrar, Straus & Giroux $30.00

• Robert C. Tucker, editor
STALINISM: Essays in Historical Interpretation
0–393–05608–2 Norton $19.95
0–393–00892–4 Norton pb $10.95

Portraits of Stalin

"Stalin's head had 'a solid peasant look about it,' but his face was pock-marked and his teeth uneven. His eyes were dark brown with a tinge of hazel. He had a stiff left arm and shoulder, the result of an accident when he was about ten. His torso was short and narrow and his arms were too long. Like many ambition-driven men he was very short, only about five feet two inches. He raised himself an inch or so by specially built shoes, and at the May Day and 7 November parades stood on a wooden slab which gave him another inch or two."—Robert Conquest, *The Great Terror*

• Isaac Deutscher
STALIN: A Political Biography
Deutscher's scholarship is colored by his sympathies for some of Stalin's accomplishments
0–19–500273–3 Oxford pb $16.95

• Milovan Djilas
CONVERSATIONS WITH STALIN
Memoir by one of Tito's top aides, ousted from the Communist Party in 1954
Translated by Michael B. Petrovich
0–15–622591–3 Harvest pb $5.95

• Daniel Rancour-Leferrière
THE MIND OF STALIN: A Psychoanalytic Study
Psychoanalysis used to answer a host of questions: What did Stalin's paranoia and narcissism mean in the Soviet context? What were his attitudes toward women and homosexuals? Why did he trust Hitler? What were the psychological consequences of his bodily defects? This is a complex and original study
0–87501–053–9 Ardis $17.95

• Robert C. Tucker
STALIN AS REVOLUTIONARY, 1879-1929: A Study in History and Personality
Focuses on the formative years and the maneuverings which led Stalin to become Lenin's successor
0–393–05487–X Norton $12.95
0–393–00738–3 Norton pb $11.95

• Adam B. Ulam
STALIN: The Man and His Era
A mammoth portrait of Stalin and the development of the Soviet state
0–8070–7001–7 Beacon pb $15.95

World War II

▶ **For a complete list see The Second World War**

Vladimir Karpov
RUSSIA AT WAR, 1941-45
While the Nazis incurred 80 percent of their losses on the eastern front, the Russians paid a staggering price for their victory: 20 million killed, 30 million wounded, 25 million left homeless. This volume highlights every major campaign with magnificent photographs from the military archives of the Soviet Union. Includes 320 illustrations
Edited by Caroline Schofield
Introduction by Harrison K. Salisbury
0–86565–077–2 Vendome $30.00

• Graham Lyons, editor
THE RUSSIAN VERSION OF THE SECOND WORLD WAR
A challenge to the West's conventional wisdom about the course of the war, constructed from Soviet texts and historical writing
0–87196–136–9 Facts On File $19.95

• Anthony Read & David Fisher
THE DEADLY EMBRACE: Hitler, Stalin, and the Nazi-Soviet Pact, 1939-1941
"The story of the 'monstrous chess game' the two dictators . . . proceeded to play, using whole countries as pieces while preparing for a battlefield confrontation that would exceed anything before or since in bloodshed"—*Publishers Weekly*
0–393–02528–4 Norton $25.00

• Alexander Werth
RUSSIA AT WAR, 1941-1945
A military history of the initial collapse of the Russian armies before the German invaders, and the stubborn resistance and brilliant tactics that led them to the doors of the shattered Reichstag
0–88184–084–X Carroll & Graf pb $15.95

Origins of the Cold War

"With Communists we cannot say it with flowers . . . The cold war must be fought with as much energy and singlemindedness as the shooting war . . ."—Harold Macmillan, House of Commons, 23 March 1949

• John Lewis Gaddis
THE LONG PEACE: Inquiries into the History of the Cold War
Argues for the stability of the system of confrontation prevailing since Yalta
0–19–504336–7 Oxford $24.95

THE UNITED STATES AND THE ORIGINS OF THE COLD WAR, 1941-1947
A post-revisionist analysis of American policy
0–231–08302–5 Columbia pb $15.00

• Charles R. Morris
IRON DESTINIES, LOST OPPORTUNITIES: The Arms Race Between the USA and the USSR, 1947-1987
The story in clear nontechnical language, free of acronyms and military jargon
0–06–039082–4 Harper & Row $22.95

• Michael Parenti
THE SWORD AND THE DOLLAR: Imperialism, Revolution and the Arms Race
Emphasizes the role of American-based corporations in determining US foreign policy
0–312–02295–6 St. Martin's $16.95

• Adam B. Ulam
THE RIVALS: America and Russia Since World War II
0–14–004309–8 Penguin pb $8.95

SOVIET SOCIETY TODAY

• James H. Bater
THE SOVIET SCENE: A Geographical Pespective
A survey of the Soviet Union's economy, resources, population, and politics aimed at the non-specialist
0–7131–6420–4 Edward Arnold pb $16.95

- Stephen F. Cohen
SOVIETICUS: American Perceptions and Soviet Realities
Collected columns from *The Nation*
0–393–30338–1 Norton pb $7.95

- James Cracraft, editor
THE SOVIET UNION TODAY: An Interpretive Guide
Thirty experts address history, politics, armed forces, economy, science and technology, culture and society
0–226–11663–8 Chicago pb $12.50

- Mikhail Heller
COGS IN THE WHEEL: The Formation of Soviet Man
"Conveys more of the essence and life of Soviet history than a dozen products of academic political science"—Robert Conquest
0–394–56926–1 Knopf $22.95

- Geoffrey Hoskins
THE FIRST SOCIALIST SOCIETY: A History of the Soviet Union from Within
"For the general reader a very good introduction to the phantasmagoric history of the Communist state and for the specialist, a valuable aid"—*TLS*
0–674–30441–1 Harvard pb $10.95

- Basile Kerblay
MODERN SOVIET SOCIETY
A comprehensive study moving through the physical environment and population trends in the USSR, social and family structures, politics, and cultural values; with international comparisons to France, the United States and Japan
Foreword by Moshe Lewin
0–394–71111–4 Pantheon pb $9.95

- Inger Thorup Lauridsen & Per Dalgaard, editors
THE BEAT GENERATION AND THE RUSSIAN NEW WAVE
Like the Beat Generation, the Russian New Wave came to maturity during the Cold War. Their confessional literature is reflected here in interviews with writers Allen Ginsberg, Andrei Voznesensky, Vassily Aksyonov, Gary Snyder, Lawrence Ferlinghetti, and Bella Akhmadulina
0–87501–034–2 Ardis $19.95

- Ellen Mickiewicz
SPLIT SIGNALS: Television and Politics in the Soviet Union
An in-depth look at Soviet television tells how Gorbachev has used the medium as part of his glasnost campaign
0–19–505463–6 Oxford $24.95

- Michael Paul Sacks & Jerry Pankhurst, editors
UNDERSTANDING SOVIET SOCIETY
0–04–445036–2 Unwin Hyman $39.95
0–04–445048–6 Unwin Hyman pb $15.95

- Richard Sakwa
SOVIET POLITICS: An Introduction
Sakwa's twin themes: continuity and change, and the tension between ideology and practice
0–415–00506–X RC&H pb $14.95

Lenin and Stalin in 1922, from Lenin: A Biography *by Ronald W. Clark (Harper & Row)*

The Forces of Control

- John Barron
KGB TODAY: The Hidden Hand
A former naval intelligence officer's chronicle of the inner circles of the KGB
0–425–10408–7 Berkley pb $6.95

- Andrew Cockburn
THE THREAT: Inside the Soviet Military Machine
"A huge contribution to our understanding of our potential adversary, and of our own security needs"—James Fallows
0–394–72379–1 Random House pb $4.95

- William R. Corson & Robert T. Crowley
THE NEW KGB: Engine of Soviet Power
Two former senior intelligence officers share the insights gained from 68 years of combined experience
0–688–06669–0 Morrow pb $10.95

- Tom Gervasi
THE MYTH OF SOVIET MILITARY SUPREMACY
Attempts to provide an antidote to the scare tactics of supporters of a strong US defense budget
0–06–091378–9 Harper & Row pb $10.95

- Amy W. Knight
THE KGB: Police and Politics in the Soviet Union
How the secret police holds the key to glasnost and other changes in Soviet politics. "A well-informed and sober history of the security police as a political institution from 1917 through 1987"—*NY Times Book Review*
0–04–445035–4 Unwin Hyman $34.95

Problems of Development

- Joseph S. Berliner
SOVIET INDUSTRY FROM STALIN TO GORBACHEV: Studies in Management and Innovation
Essays written over 35 years analyzing the structural problems that have hampered Soviet economic performance since the Stalin Revolution
0–8014–2170–5 Cornell $34.50

- Viktor Haynes & Marko Bojcun
THE CHERNOBYL DISASTER
First-hand accounts from survivors and rescue-workers evoke the terror of living through the disaster
0–7012–0816–3 Random House pb $11.95

- Alec Nove
THE SOVIET ECONOMIC SYSTEM
An introduction to the Soviet economy, updated to include an analysis of Gorbachev's proposed reforms
0–04–497025–0 Unwin Hyman pb $17.95

- James E. Oberg
UNCOVERING SOVIET DISASTERS: Exploring the Limits of Glasnost
A sober look at the Soviet's supposed technological superiority. A free-world authority on Soviet technological secrets uncovers a host of accidents, including a 1979 anthrax outbreak and the 1960 explosion of a Mars probe, among others
0–394–56095–7 Random House $19.95

- Judy Shelton
THE COMING SOVIET CRASH: Gorbachev's Desperate Pursuit of Credit in Western Financial Markets
The extent of the Soviet Union's current financial problems and how the US and the West should resist the temptation to offer it subsidized credit
0–02–928581–X Free Press $22.50

From Khrushchev to Gorbachev

- Seweryn Bialer
THE SOVIET PARADOX: External Expansion, Internal Decline
Brezhnev's legacy, Gorbachev's ascent to power, and the centrifugal inner forces threatening glasnost
0–394–54095–6 Knopf $22.95
0–394–75288–0 Random House pb $9.95

STALIN'S SUCCESSORS: Leadership, Stability and Change in the Soviet Union
The maintainance of stability through a combination of harsh authoritarian rule and political flexibility
0–521–28906–8 Cambridge pb $13.95

- Christopher Creighton & Noel Hynd
THE KHRUSHCHEV OBJECTIVE
0–385–18013–6 Doubleday $17.95

- Dusko Doder
SHADOWS AND WHISPERS: Power Politics Inside the Kremlin from Brezhnev to Gorbachev
0–14–010526–3 Penguin pb $7.95

- Mark Frankland
THE SIXTH CONTINENT: Mikhail Gorbachev and the Soviet Union
A British journalist elucidates the responses of Soviet pressure groups to glasnost, from old line party members to the myriad ethnic interests
0–06–091534–X Harper & Row pb $8.95

- Mikhail Gorbachev
PERESTROIKA: New Thinking for Our Country and the World
The glasnost czar's own blueprint for domestic and world reform
0–060–39085–9 Harper & Row $19.95

➤ **FOR OVERSEAS ORDERING INFORMATION, SEE PAGE 1**

• Alan B. Sherr
THE OTHER SIDE OF ARMS CONTROL: Soviet Objectives in the Gorbachev Era
0–04–445063–X Unwin Hyman pb $17.95

• Martin Walker
THE WAKING GIANT: Gorbachev's Russia
"The most original and thought-provoking book on contemporary Soviet society and politics to have appeared for a decade"— *London Review of Books*
0–679–73954–8 Pantheon pb $8.95

• Alexander Yanov
THE RUSSIAN CHALLENGE AND THE YEAR 2000
A harsh warning about the dangers to both Russia and the west if Gorbachev's reforms fail, from an exile of Brezhnev's Russia
0–631–15334–9 Blackwell $24.95

Today's Soviet Union: Popular Reading

Nicholas Daniloff
TWO LIVES, ONE RUSSIA
The journalist whose arrest by the KGB became an international incident
0–395–44601–5 Houghton Mifflin $19.95

Robert G. Kaiser
RUSSIA: The People and the Power
Sympathetic attempt to convey the common humanity beneath our political differences
0–671–50324–3 Washington Square pb $5.95

Andrea Lee
RUSSIAN JOURNAL
Penetrating observations by a young American in pre-Gorbachev Russia
0–394–51891–8 Random House $13.00
0–394–71127–0 Random House pb $4.95

David K. Shipler
RUSSIA: Broken Idols, Solemn Dreams
The impact of Gorbachev on the lives of ordinary Russians; revised and expanded
0–8129–1788–X Times Books $22.50

Hedrick Smith
THE RUSSIANS
0–8129–1086–9 Times $24.95
0–345–31746–7 Ballantine pb $4.95

Vladimir Solovyov & Elena Klepikova
BEHIND THE HIGH KREMLIN WALLS
Two former Russian journalists' behind-the-scenes account of high stakes politics in today's USSR, including Gorbachev's political and personal life, the rise of Kremlin "mafias," and KGB plots
0–425–09716–1 Berkley pb $3.95

David K. Willis
KLASS: How Russians Really Live
The everyday world of perks and privileges of the Soviet elite, by a former Moscow correspondent for the *Christian Science Monitor*
0–380–70263–0 Avon pb $4.50

Dissidents

▶ See also Jewish History

• Elena Bonner
ALONE TOGETHER
Memoir of persecution by the wife of physicist Andrei Sakharov
0–394–75538–3 Random House pb $8.95

• Stephen F. Cohen, editor
AN END TO SILENCE: Uncensored Opinion in the Soviet Union
Excerpts from Roy Medvedev's underground magazine, *Political Diary*, circulated between 1964 and 1971
0–393–30127–3 Norton pb $9.95

• Martin Gilbert
THE JEWS OF HOPE: The Plight of Soviet Jewry Today
0–1400–8510–6 Penguin pb $7.95

• Lionel Kochan, editor
THE JEWS IN SOVIET RUSSIA SINCE 1917
Various aspects of Jewish life under communism, from reactions to Bolshevism to today's refuseniks
0–19–281199–1 Oxford pb $9.95

• Edward D. Lozansky, editor
ANDREI SAKHAROV AND PEACE
An anthology of writings by the dissident physicist and his supporters
0–380–89819–5 Avon pb $8.95

• Joshua Rubenstein
SOVIET DISSIDENTS: Their Struggle for Human Rights
Revised edition of a slightly dated but comprehensive overview, covering such topics as Sakharov, Jewish emigration, and the independent Soviet peace movement that emerged in 1982; by a member of Amnesty International
0–8070–3215–8 Beacon pb $10.95

• Michael Scammell
SOLZHENITSYN: A Biography
The biography of the exiled author
0–393–30378–0 Norton pb $14.95

• Natan Sharansky
FEAR NO EVIL
Autobiographical account by the most famous Jewish refusenik of his voyage through Soviet prisons and ultimately to Israel
Translated by Stefani Hoffman
0–394–55878–2 Random House $19.95

• Aleksandr Solzhenitsyn
THE GULAG ARCHIPELAGO
Through a mixture of individual stories and clear overviews, the novelist recreates

---

life in the thousands of prisons of the world within a world
0–06–080332–0 Harper & Row pb $5.95

THE GULAG ARCHIPELAGO 2
0–06–080345–2 Harper & Row pb $4.95

THE GULAG ARCHIPELAGO 3
0–06–080396–7 Harper & Row pb $3.95

• Romnald Spasowski
THE LIBERATION OF ONE
Autobiography of the highest-ranking Soviet official to defect to the West
0–15–651280–7 Harvest pb $14.95

THE SOVIET UNION ABROAD

• Seweryn Bialer, editor
DANGEROUS RELATIONS: The Soviet Union in World Politics, 1970-1982
0–19–503237–3 Oxford $29.95
0–19–503424–4 Oxford pb $8.95

THE DOMESTIC CONTEXT OF SOVIET FOREIGN POLICY
0–8133–0504–7 Westview $40.00
0–8133–0505–5 Westview pb $17.95

• Herbert J. Ellison, editor
SOVIET POLICY TOWARD WESTERN EUROPE: Implications for the Atlantic Alliance
0–295–96035–3 Washington $30.00
0–295–96036–1 Washington pb $14.95

• Jerry Hough
RUSSIA AND THE WEST: Gorbachev and the Politics of Reform
0–671–61839–3 Simon & Schuster $19.95

• Efraim Karsh
THE SOVIET UNION AND SYRIA
Explores the keen sense of national interest on both sides of the relationship; published in 1988
0–415–03030–7 RC&H pb $14.95

• Jeri Laber & Barnett Rubin
A NATION IS DYING: Afghanistan Under the Soviets, 1979-1987
The human rights side of eight years of Soviet intervention
0–8101–0771–6 Northwestern $26.95
0–8101–0772–4 Northwestern pb $10.95

• Wolfgang Leonhard
THE KREMLIN AND THE WEST: A Realistic Approach
Advocates more attention to the internal affairs and domestic strategies of the USSR's political elite than to strictly military affairs
Translated by Houchang Chehabi
0–393–30527–9 Norton pb $8.95

• Richard Pipes
SURVIVAL IS NOT ENOUGH: Soviet Realities and America's Future
"A trenchant analysis of the connection between Soviet domestic and foreign policy"—Robert C. McFarlane
0–671–60614–X Simon & Schuster pb $9.95

WORLD HISTORY AND CURRENT AFFAIRS

• Donald Zagoria, editor
SOVIET POLICY IN EAST ASIA
An analysis of Soviet policies in economic, political and military sectors by a selection of well-known specialists
0–300–02738–9 Yale $32.00
0–300–03239–0 Yale pb $13.95

The Soviet Bloc

▶ **See also Postwar Europe and Current Affairs**

• Zbigniew K. Brzezinski
SOVIET BLOC: Unity and Conflict
A 1967 analysis of the factions of world communism from the man who would become Jimmy Carter's National Security Adviser
0–674–82545–4 Harvard $35.00
0–674–82548–9 Harvard pb $13.50

• Karen Dawisha
EASTERN EUROPE, GORBACHEV AND REFORM: The Great Challenge
Soviet policy in a region with political ties to Moscow and cultural ties with the West
0–521–35560–5 Cambridge $29.95
0–521–35663–6 Cambridge pb $12.95

Gypsies

The word *Gypsy* derives from *Egypt*, where many people mistakenly thought Gypsies originated. In fact, the Gypsies (or *Rom* in their own language, *Romanés*) started out in northern India. Beginning around the 10th century, many of them left in several waves, moving westward into Europe. No one knows exactly why they left India (though there are countless theories), but the routes as well as the times of their various migrations can be traced through linguistic evidence.

Being outsiders, Gypsies were persecuted everywhere they went, by enslavement, systematic deportation, and massacre. Officially freed in the mid-19th century, the Gypsies have endured programs of forced assimilation in many countries, as well as unofficial pressures to abandon their culture. As Jean-Pierre Liégeois has remarked, "the Gypsies, moving about in their nomadic groups, were seen as physically threatening and ideologically disruptive. Their very existence constituted dissidence." Violence against Gypsies reached a peak during the Second World War when the Nazis attempted to wipe out the entire Gypsy race in Europe. At least half a million Gypsies perished in the Holocaust.

The following list of books deal with both historical and contemporary issues.

• Thomas Acton
GYPSIES
A politically aware overview of the culture, history, and struggles of the many different groups of Gypsies. Written for young people
0–382–06645–6 Silver Burdett $16.00

• Marilyn Brown
GYPSIES AND OTHER BOHEMIANS: The Myth of the Artist in Nineteenth-Century France
Examines the bourgeois myth of bohemianism by studying the portrayal of "real bohemians." The author discusses the ways artists used Gypsies as a complex metaphor for their own lives and aims
0–83571704–6 UMI Research $44.95

• Rena Gropper
GYPSIES IN THE CITY: Culture Patterns and Survival
Written by an anthropologist who has done fieldwork with the Gypsies since 1947, this account of Gypsies in New York City is full of intimate information not available elsewhere
0–87850–008–1 Darwin $19.95

• Ian Hancock
THE PARIAH SYNDROME: An Account of Gypsy Slavery and Persecution
An illuminating account by a Gypsy of his people's oppression, concentrating primarily on slavery in Eastern Europe and on the Holocaust
0–89720–079–9 Karoma pb $17.95

• Josef Koudelka & Willy Guy
GYPSIES
Sixty of Koudelka's intense black-and-white photographs, most of them taken among isolated Gypsy settlements in East Slovakia. Willy Guy's succinct essay provides historical and political background
0–89381–215–3 Aperture pb $19.95

Jean-Pierre Liégeois
GYPSIES: An Illustrated History
An excellent and insightful history illustrated with black-and-white photographs
0–86356–025–3 Interlink pb $15.00

• Merrill F. McLane
PROUD OUTCASTS: The Gypsies of Spain
An uncomplicated, anecdotal glimpse of the author's experiences with the Gypsies of Spain, especially those of Guadix
0–938813–03–X Carderock pb $10.95

• David Mayall
GYPSIE-TRAVELLERS IN NINETEENTH CENTURY SOCIETY
Reconstructs the Gypsy lifestyles of the period and examines the negative stereotypes that arose as a result of conflict
0–521–32297–5 Cambridge $49.50

• George Nickels
THE GYPSY SEASON
A biography of the author's father, Angelo Nickels, a professional Russian Gypsy dancer, and his fight against the injustice of an extortion racket in the 1920s and 1930s. Includes information on Romani values and customs
0–87949–187–6 Ashley $16.95

• Judith Okely
THE TRAVELLER-GYPSIES
English Gypsy culture as seen by a social anthropologist who spent years in the field
0–521–28870–3 Cambridge pb $14.95

• Bertha B. Quintana & Lois G. Floyd
QUE GITANO!: Gypsies of Southern Spain
Through observation and interviews, an anthropologist and a psychologist examine the culture of the Sacro Monte Gypsies and their critical views of American culture
0–88133–217–8 Waveland pb $7.50

• David Sibley
OUTSIDERS IN URBAN SOCIETY
Social geographer's account of the Gypsy/non-Gypsy struggle in northern England
0–312–59192–6 St. Martin's $26.00

• Anne Sutherland
GYPSIES: The Hidden Americans
Describes a predominantly Kalderash community in California (here called Barvale). The book is brought to life by the major contribution of social worker Jan Tompkins
0–88133–235–6 Waveland pb $9.95

• Marlene Sway
FAMILIAR STRANGERS: Gypsy Life in America
0–252–01512–6 Illinois $19.95

• Nebojsa-Bato Tomasevic & Rajko Djuric
GYPSIES OF THE WORLD
Text and photographs (300 in color) illustrate the authors' journey through India, Turkey, and other countries with large Gypsy populations
Photographs by Dragoljub Zamurovic
0–8050–0924–8 Henry Holt $50.00

• Diane Tong
GYPSY FOLKTALES
An international collection of 80 stories, many never before published; with an insert of 16 black-and-white photographs of Greek Gypsies
0–15–138310–3 HBJ $19.95
0–15–637989–9 HBJ pb $12.95

• Jan Yoors
CROSSING: A Journal of Survival and Resistance in World War II
An impassioned account of the author's recruitment by the British into World War II Resistance work and his subsequent enlisting of Lowara and Churara Gypsies in anti-Nazi activities
0–88133–364–6 Waveland pb $8.95

THE GYPSIES
A lyrical celebration of life on the road with a group of Lowara horse traders
0–88133–305–0 Waveland pb $8.95

752 📷 **TO ORDER ANY BOOK IN THIS CATALOG, ASK YOUR BOOKSELLER OR CALL 1-800-882-8770**

Jewish History

"Jewish history can be presented as a succession of climaxes and catastrophes. It can also be seen as an endless continuum of patient study, fruitful industry and communal routine, much of it unrecorded . . . Over 4,000 years the Jews proved themselves not only great survivors but extraordinarily skillful in adapting to the societies among which fate thrust them, and in gathering whatever human comforts they had to offer. No people has been more fertile in enriching poverty or humanizing wealth, or in turning misfortune to creative account. This capacity springs from a moral philosophy both solid and subtle, which has changed remarkably little over the millennia precisely because it has been seen to serve the purposes of those who share it. Countless Jews, in all ages, have groaned under the burden of Judaism. But they have continued to carry it because they have known, in their hearts, that it carried them. The Jews were survivors because they possessed the law of survival."—Paul Johnson, *A History of the Jews*

"Jews in a synagogue" (1648), *from* Rembrandt Etchings (*Dover*)

GENERAL HISTORIES

• H.H. Ben-Sasson, editor
A HISTORY OF THE JEWISH PEOPLE
Six Hebrew University scholars trace the history of the Jews. "Breaks new ground for a one-volume history, both in its range and in its authority"—*Commentary*
0–674–39730–4 Harvard $60.00
0–674–39731–2 Harvard pb $18.95

• David Biale
POWER AND POWERLESSNESS IN JEWISH HISTORY
"A brave work attacking a metahistory of the Jewish people and unmasking propagandists and those who would mystify rather than write the truth"—*Jewish Exponent*
0–8052–4015–2 Schocken $18.95
0–8052–0841–0 Schocken pb $8.95

• Max I. Dimont
JEWS, GOD AND HISTORY
"By far the liveliest popular history of the Jewish people that I have ever read"—Richard B. Morris
0–451–14694–8 NAL pb $4.95

• Abba Eban
HERITAGE: Civilization and the Jews
Handsomely illustrated companion volume to the television documentary
0–671–44103–5 Summit $35.00
0–671–62881–X Summit pb $16.95

MY PEOPLE: The Story of the Jews
"Israel's Foreign Minister, who has been called a blend of Shakespeare and Churchill, gives his personal evaluation of the forces, events and personalities that shaped Jewish destiny"—Walter Berkov, *Cleveland Plain Dealer*
0–394–72759–2 Random House pb $14.95

• Paul Johnson
A HISTORY OF THE JEWS
This survey of 4000 years emphasizes the impact of Jewish genius and imagination on the world. Beautifully written
0–06–015698–8 Harper & Row $24.95

• Franz Kobler, editor
LETTERS OF JEWS THROUGH THE AGES
The history of Jews, through their correspondence

Volume 1
0–85222–212–2 Hebrew Publishing pb $7.95

Volume 2
0–85222–213–0 Hebrew Publishing pb $7.95

• Paul Mendes-Flohr & Jehuda Reinharz
THE JEW IN THE MODERN WORLD: A Documentary History
A collection of original source materials
0–19–502631–4 Oxford $35.00
0–19–502632–2 Oxford pb $18.95

• Chaim Potok
WANDERINGS: Chaim Potok's History of the Jews
0–394–50110–1 Knopf $40.00

• Cecil Roth
A HISTORY OF THE JEWS: From the Earliest Times Through the Six Day War
Focuses on social, religious and cultural development; from the noted British scholar
0–8052–0009–6 Schocken pb $10.95

• Leo W. Schwarz, editor
GREAT AGES AND IDEAS OF THE JEWISH PEOPLE
A collection of essays
0–394–60413–X Modern Library $10.95

• Yosef Hayim Yerushalmi
ZAKHOR: Jewish History and Jewish Memory
Essays on Jewish collective memory; winner of the National Jewish Book Award for history (1982)
0–8052–0878–X Schocken pb $8.95

Reference

• Joseph Alpher, editor
ENCYCLOPEDIA OF JEWISH HISTORY
Detailed and illustrated entries on the major figures, places, and events of Jewish history
0–8160–1220–2 Facts On File $35.00

• Martin Gilbert
ATLAS OF JEWISH HISTORY
Jewish history, migration and life through the ages, told through 121 maps
Cartography by Arthur Banks
0–88029–018–8 Hippocrene $17.95

• David C. Gross
THE JEWISH PEOPLE'S ALMANAC
An unconventional compendium of facts about Jewish history, culture, and religion
Illustrated by Robert Leydenfrost
0–87052–583–2 Hippocrene pb $14.95

BIBLICAL AND ANCIENT HISTORY

• Yohanan Aharoni
THE LAND OF THE BIBLE: A Historical Geography
Translated by Anson F. Rainey
0–664–24266–9 Westminster pb $19.95

• Michael Avi-Yonah
THE JEWS UNDER ROMAN AND BYZANTINE RULE: A Political History of Palestine from the Bar Kokhba War to the Arab Conquest
0–8052–3580–9 Schocken $23.00

• Elias Bickerman
FROM EZRA TO THE LAST OF THE MACCABEES: Foundations of Post-Biblical Judaism
Examines the elements that shaped the Jewish people after their return from the Babylonian exile
0–8052–0036–3 Schocken pb $7.95

THE JEWS IN THE GREEK AGE
0–674–47490–2 Harvard $30.00

• John Bright
A HISTORY OF ISRAEL
A sophisticated history of the ancient period
0–664–21381–2 Westminster $18.95

• Louis Finkelstein
AKIBA: Scholar, Saint and Martyr
The definitive story of perhaps the most famous Jewish martyr of all time, Rabbi Akiba ben Joseph
0–689–70230–2 Atheneum pb $9.95

• Michael Grant
THE HISTORY OF ANCIENT ISRAEL
0–02345620–5 Macmillan pb $25.00

Flavius Josephus
THE JEWISH WAR
Translated by G.A. Williamson
Edited by E. Mary Smallwood
0–14–044420–3 Penguin pb $7.95

• Jacob Neusner
A HISTORY OF THE JEWS IN BABYLONIA: The Parthian Period
0–89130–738–9 Scholars pb $21.00

THE PHARISEES: Rabbinic Perspectives
0–88125–067–8 Ktav pb $19.95

• James Parkes
CONFLICT OF THE CHURCH AND THE SYNAGOGUE: A Study in the Origins of Antisemitism
0–689–70151–9 Atheneum pb $9.95

• Emil Schurer
A HISTORY OF THE JEWISH PEOPLE IN THE TIME OF JESUS
An abridgment of Schurer's monumental history detailing the political history of Palestine from the Maccabean revolt to the fall of Jerusalem
Edited by Nahum Glatzer
0–8052–0008–8 Schocken pb $11.95

• Victor Tcherikover
HELLENISTIC CIVILIZATION AND THE JEWS
Translated by S. Applebaum
0–689–70248–5 Atheneum pb $12.95

• Max Weber
ANCIENT JUDAISM
"No one who has occupied himself with the study of Israelite culture can fail to admire the great sweep, the prevailing accuracy, and the true sensitivity of Weber's sociological analysis"—
Commentary
Translated & edited by Don Martindale & Hans Gerth
0–02–934130–2 Free Press pb $14.95

• Edmund Wilson
ISRAEL AND THE DEAD SEA SCROLLS
Reconstructs the discovery of the Dead Sea Scrolls in the late 1940s
0–374–51341–4 Farrar, Straus & Giroux pb $9.25

THE MIDDLE AGES

• Israel Abrahams
JEWISH LIFE IN THE MIDDLE AGES
0–689–70001–6 Atheneum pb $9.95

• Eliyahu Ashtor
THE JEWS OF MOSLEM SPAIN
A definitive study of Jewish life under Moslem rule
Translated by Aaron Klein and Jenny Machlowitz Klein

Volume 1
0–8276–0017–8 JPS $19.95

Volume 2
Focuses on Granada, Cordova, Seville and Saragossa in the 11th century
0–8276–0100–X JPS $19.95

Volume 3
Focuses on the waning years of Moslem rule
0–8276–0237–5 JPS $19.95

• Yitzhak F. Baer
GALUT
Introduction by Jacob Neusner
0–8191–5783–X University Press $9.75

HISTORY OF THE JEWS IN CHRISTIAN SPAIN
0–8276–0115–8 JPS pb (2-volume set) $20.00

• Riccardo Calimani
THE GHETTO OF VENICE
The history of one of west Europe's most important Jewish communities
Translated by Katherine Wolfthal
0–87131–484–3 Evans $19.95

• Jeremy Cohen
THE FRIARS AND THE JEWS: The Evolution of Medieval Anti-Judaism
Reasons for and results of the mendicant antagonism against the Jews
0–8014–9266–1 Cornell pb $10.95

• Mark R. Cohen, editor and translator
THE AUTOBIOGRAPHY OF A 17TH-CENTURY VENETIAN RABBI: Leon Modena's Life of Judah
A fascinating account of an intellectual figure in the early modern Italian Jewish community
0–691–05529–7 Princeton $39.95
0–691–00824–8 Princeton pb $14.95

• Gluckel of Hameln
THE MEMOIRS OF GLUCKEL OF HAMELN
This fascinating diary of a 17th-century German-Jewish mother and businesswoman is the only document of its kind. Though this edition omits some important material, overall it offers an unparalleled literary and historical view of the author's times
0–8052–0464–4 Schocken pb $6.95

• Nathan Hanover
THE ABYSS OF DESPAIR
Recounts the brutal 17th-century Chmielnicki massacres
Translated by Abraham J. Mesch
Introduction by William B. Helmreich
0–87855–927–2 Transaction pb $19.95

• Abraham Joshua Heschel
MAIMONIDES
Translated by Joachim Neugroschel
0–374–19874–8 Farrar, Straus & Giroux $15.00

• Bernard W. Lewis
THE JEWS OF ISLAM
"Lewis refuses . . . simplistic approaches and tries to explain the complex and often contradictory history of Jewish-Muslim relations over fourteen hundred years"—
Norman A. Stillman, *NY Review of Books*
0–691–00807–8 Princeton pb $8.95

• Jacob R. Marcus
THE JEW IN THE MEDIEVAL WORLD: A Source Book, 315-1791
An anthology of original source materials
0–689–70133–0 Atheneum pb $14.95

• Therese & Mendel Metzger
JEWISH LIFE IN THE MIDDLE AGES: Illuminated Hebrew Manuscripts of the 13th to the 16th Century
A reconstruction of Jewish life in Europe as seen by Jews and Christians; copiously illustrated
0–89009–839–5 Chartwell $29.98

• Leon Nemoy, translator
KARAITE ANTHOLOGY: Excerpts from the Early Literature
A collection of writings covering the thought and beliefs of the influential sect, to about 1500
0–300–00792–2 Yale $45.00

• Benzion Netanyahu
DON ISAAC ABRAVANEL: Statesman and Philosopher
Biography of a leading figure of the Jewish community in Spain (1437-1508)
0–8276–0213–8 JPS pb $6.95

• Abraham A. Neuman
THE JEWS IN SPAIN: Their Social, Political and Cultural Life During the Middle Ages
Originally written in 1942, this work highlights the parallels between the fate of the Jews of medieval Spain and those of 20th-century Europe; a 2-volume set
0–374–96061–5 Hippocrene (set) $54.50

• Cecil Roth
A HISTORY OF THE MARRANOS
The Jews of Inquisition Spain were forced to convert to Christianity but many maintained a secret Jewish life
0–8052–0463–6 Schocken pb $10.95

THE JEWS IN THE RENAISSANCE
0–8276–0103–4 JPS pb $8.95

• Gershom Scholem
SABBATAI SEVI: The Mystical Messiah
A detailed and authoritative account of the messianic 17th-century Sabbatian

Illustration from Yiddish Folktales *edited by Beatrice Silverman Weinreich (Pantheon)*

movement from its inception to its founder's death
Translated by R. Zwi Werblowski
0–691–01809–X Princeton pb $22.50

- Norman A. Stillman
THE JEWS OF ARAB LANDS: A History and Source Book
"Clarifies two seemingly opposite interpretations of Muslim-Jewish relations—that Jewish life under Islam was the antithesis of medieval European persecution, and that the Jews were a persecuted minority in the Mideast"—
Kirkus Reviews
0–8276–0198–0 JPS $11.95

MODERN EUROPE

Enlightenment, Reform, Assimilation

- Jean-Denis Bredin
THE AFFAIR: The Case of Alfred Dreyfus
Translated by Jeffrey Mehlman
0–8076–1109–3 Braziller $24.95
0–8076–1175–1 Braziller pb $12.95

- Isaac Deutscher
THE NON-JEWISH JEW
0–932870–18–X Alyson pb $5.95

- Todd Endelman
THE JEWS OF GEORGIAN ENGLAND, 1714-1830: Tradition and Change in a Liberal Society
The road of Jewish immigrants into society and activities long closed to them; winner of the National Jewish Book Award
0–8276–0119–0 JPS $14.50

- Moses Hadas, editor
SOLOMON MAIMON: An Autobiography
Fascinating account of a key iconoclastic figure in the Jewish Enlightenment who traded the life of a tiny Polish village for intellectual encounters with with the great thinkers of his day
0–8052–0150–5 Schocken pb $4.95

- Jacob Katz
OUT OF THE GHETTO: The Social Background of Jewish Emancipation, 1770-1870
The effect of the transition into society-at-large on both Jews and Gentiles
0–8052–0601–9 Schocken pb $8.95

- William O. McCagg, Jr.
A HISTORY OF HABSBURG JEWS, 1670-1918
0–253–33189–7 Indiana $27.50

- Raphael Mahler
HASIDISM AND THE JEWISH ENLIGHTENMENT: Their Confrontation in Galicia and Poland in the First Half of the Nineteenth Century
A major study of the bitter struggle between the Hasidim and the adherents of the *Haskalah*, or Jewish Enlightenment, during a watershed period
Translated by Eugene Orenstein & Aaron & Jenny Machlowitz Klein
0–8276–0233–2 JPS $29.95

- Michael R. Marrus
THE POLITICS OF ASSIMILATION: The French Jewish Community at the Time of the Dreyfus Affair
0–19–822591–1 Oxford pb $19.95

- Michael A. Meyer
RESPONSE TO MODERNITY: A History of the Reform Movement in Judaism
0–19–505167–X Oxford $39.95

- Max Wiener
ABRAHAM GEIGER AND LIBERAL JUDAISM: The Challenge of the Nineteenth Century
0–87820–800–3 Ktav pb $9.95

Eastern Europe

- Chimen Abramsky & others
THE JEWS IN POLAND
Essays by important historians covering centuries of Jewish life in Poland
0–631–16582–7 Blackwell pb $16.95

- David Altschuler, editor
THE PRECIOUS LEGACY: Judaic Treasures from the Czechoslovak State Collection
Beautifully-illustrated companion volume to an exhibit of the art and artifacts of the Czechoslovakian Jewish community
0–671–49448–1 Summit $40.00
0–671–49498–8 Summit pb $17.95

- Lucy S. Dawidowicz
THE GOLDEN TRADITION: Jewish Life and Thought in Eastern Europe
An anthology tracing the daily and inner worlds of Eastern European Jewry from its origins to its destruction in World War II
0–8052—768–6 Schocken pb $11.95

- Lucjan Dobroszycki & Barbara Kirshenblatt-Gimblett
IMAGE BEFORE MY EYES: A Photographic History of Jewish Life in Poland, 1864-1939
Reconstructs Jewish life in Poland through a fascinating collection of photographs
0–8052–3607–4 Schocken $29.95
0–805–0634–5 Schocken pb $19.95

- Celia Heller
ON THE EDGE OF DESTRUCTION: Jews of Poland Between the Two World Wars
An excellent account of the social trends in Europe's largest Jewish community before the Holocaust
0–8052–0651–5 Schocken pb $8.95

- Abraham Joshua Heschel
THE EARTH IS THE LORD'S: The Inner World of the Jew in Eastern Europe
0–374–51469–0 Farrar, Straus & Giroux pb $6.95

- Jack Kugelmass & Jonathan Boyarin, translators & editors
FROM A RUINED GARDEN: The Memorial Books of Polish Jewry
Excerpts from the many "memorial books" of Jewish towns in Eastern Europe written by survivors after World War II.
"Kugelmass and Boyarin have done a splendid job of combing the vast memorial book literature to select the most revealing accounts of life in interbellum Poland"—
Barbara Kirshenblatt-Gimblett
0–8052–0789–9 Schocken pb $8.95

- Ezra Mendelsohn
THE JEWS OF EAST-CENTRAL EUROPE BETWEEN THE WORLD WARS
A much-needed, first-rate study of interwar Jewish life and community
0–253–33160–9 Indiana $27.50
0–253–20418–6 Indiana pb $12.95

Isaac Bashevis Singer
IN MY FATHER'S COURT
A memoir of Singer's boyhood in Eastern Europe
0–374–17560–8 FS&G pb $10.95

I.J. Singer
OF A WORLD THAT IS NO MORE
Reminiscences of Polish-Jewish life, from the well-known Yiddish writer and older brother of Isaac Bashevis Singer
0–571–14685–6 Faber & Faber pb $7.95

- Henry J. Tobias
THE JEWISH BUND IN RUSSIA FROM ITS ORIGINS TO 1905
0–8047–0764–2 Stanford $39.50

- Roman Vishniac
POLISH JEWS: A Pictorial Record
Portraits taken by a master photographer on the eve of the Holocaust
Introduction by Abraham Joshua Heschel
0–8052–0910–7 Schocken pb $11.95

A VANISHED WORLD
Extraordinary collection of photographs, many of them taken secretly, of Eastern European Jews in the shtetl and the ghetto on the eve of the Holocaust
0–374–28247–1 Farrar, Straus & Giroux $65.00
0–374–52023–2 Farrar, Straus & Giroux pb $19.95

• Mark Zborowski & Elizabeth Herzog
LIFE IS WITH PEOPLE: The Culture of the Shtetl
A somewhat sentimentalized but detailed account of daily life in small Jewish towns
Introduction by Margaret Mead
0–8052–0020–7 Schocken pb $11.95

ANTI-SEMITISM

• David Berger, editor
HISTORY AND HATE: The Dimensions of Anti-Semitism
Essays by experts on different eras of Jewish history
0–8276–0267–7 JPS $14.95

• Jacob Katz
EXCLUSIVENESS AND TOLERANCE: Studies in Jewish-Gentile Relations in Medieval and Modern Times
0–87441–365–6 Behrman House pb $8.95

FROM PREJUDICE TO DESTRUCTION: Anti-Semitism, 1700-1933
Blends the history of ideas with social analysis, viewing modern anti-Semitism as a direct outgrowth of traditional, Christian anti-Semitism
0–674–32507–9 Harvard pb $8.95

• Bernard W. Lewis
SEMITES AND ANTI-SEMITES
"A brilliant, dispassionate investigation of the historical roots of contemporary anti-Semitic passions"—Samuel Lewis, former US ambassador to Israel
0–393–30420–5 Norton pb $7.95

• Barnet Litvinoff
THE BURNING BUSH: Anti-Semitism and World History
0–525–24602–9 Dutton $22.50

• Leon Poliakov
HARVEST OF HATE: The Nazi Program for the Destruction of the Jews of Europe
0–8052–5006–9 Schocken pb $12.95

HISTORY OF ANTI-SEMITISM
A definitive survey of anti-Semitism, from its earliest times to its eruption in Nazi Europe

Volume 1: From the Time of Christ to the Court Jews
0–8149–0186–7 Vanguard $22.50

Volume 2: From Mohammed to the Marranos
Translated by Natalie Gerardi
0–8149–0701–6 Vanguard $22.50

Volume 3: From Voltaire to Wagner
0–8149–0762–8 Vanguard $22.50

Volume 4: Suicidal Europe, 1870-1933
0–8149–0872–1 Vanguard $22.50

• Jean-Paul Sartre
ANTI-SEMITE AND JEW
A challenge to anti-Semitism from a non-Jewish point of view. "One of the most brilliant psychological analyses of the marginal Jew and the fanatical anti-Semite that has ever been published"—Sidney Hook
0–8052–3004–1 Schocken pb $6.95

Jews being burned alive in Cologne during massacres prompted by the approach of the Black Death (14th century)

• Joshua Trachtenberg
THE DEVIL AND THE JEWS: The Medieval Conception of the Jew and Its Relation to Modern Anti-Semitism
Traces anti-Semitism to the medieval view of the Jew as a devil; first published in 1943
Foreword by Marc Saperstein
0–8276–0227–8 JPS pb $9.95

THE ORIGINS OF ZIONISM

▶ See also The Contemporary Middle East

• Shlomo Avineri
THE MAKING OF MODERN ZIONISM: The Intellectual Origins of the Jewish State
Profiles of the early leaders of Zionism, from Herzl to Jabotinsky to Ben-Gurion
0–465–04331–3 Basic Books pb $7.95

• Bernard Avishai
THE TRAGEDY OF ZIONISM: Revolution and Democracy in the Land of Israel
0–374–52044–5 Farrar, Straus & Giroux pb $8.95

• Martin Buber
ISRAEL AND THE WORLD: Essays in a Time of Crisis
0–8052–0066–5 Schocken pb $6.50

ON ZION: The History of an Idea
Essays focusing on Buber's vision of an egalitarian, binational state that was not simply political, but "must be born in the soul"
0–8052–0812–7 Schocken pb $5.95

• Benjamin Halpern
A CLASH OF HEROES: Brandeis, Weizmann and American Zionism
0–19–504062–7 Oxford 32.50

• Arthur Hertzberg, editor
THE ZIONIST IDEA: A Historical Analysis and Reader
A strong introductory essay leads off this authoritative anthology of Zionist thought
0–689–70093–8 Atheneum pb $7.95

• Walter Laqueur
A HISTORY OF ZIONISM
The classic historical analysis of Zionism
0–8052–0523–3 Schocken pb $12.95

• Amnon Rubenstein
THE ZIONIST DREAM REVISITED: From Herzl to Gush Emunim and Back
The shifts in Israel's political ideology
0–8052–0835–6 Schocken pb $8.95

• Leon Simon, editor
SELECTED ESSAYS OF AHAD HA-AM
"Ahad Ha-am," meaning "one of the nation," was the pseudonym of Asher Ginzberg, who saw a homeland in Palestine as a spiritual center of the Jewish people
0–318–14661–4 JPS pb $8.95

• David Vital
THE ORIGINS OF ZIONISM
A two-part history of Zionist thought and politics; this volume ends with the First Zionist Congress (1897)
0–19–827439–4 Oxford pb $18.95

ZIONISM: The Formative Years
0–19–827443–2 Oxford $49.95

RUSSIA AND THE SOVIET UNION

▶ See also Russian and Soviet Studies

• Salo Baron
THE RUSSIAN JEW UNDER TSARS AND SOVIETS
0–8052–0838–0 Schocken pb $14.95

• Bella & Marc Chagall
BURNING LIGHTS: A Unique Double Portrait of the Warm World of Russian Jewry
A memoir with text by Bella Chagall and 36 drawings by Marc Chagall recalls their young lives in the Russian-Jewish market town of Vitebsk
0–8052–0863–1 Schocken pb $6.95

• Martin Gilbert
THE JEWS OF HOPE: The Plight of Soviet Jewry Today
A top historian's personal report of Soviet Jewry in the early 1980s
0–1400–8510–6 Penguin pb $7.95

Cover of a 1926 collection of poetry and prose by Hebrew writers in the Soviet Union, from A Sign and a Witness *by Leonard Singer Gold (Oxford)*

✉ **TO ORDER BOOKS AS GIFTS, SEE PAGE 1**

SHCHARANSKY: Hero of Our Time
Biography of the Refusenik whose sufferings in the Soviet Union became an international cause
0–670–81418–0 Viking $24.95

● Zvi Gitelman
A CENTURY OF AMBIVALENCE: The Jews of Russia and the Soviet Union, 1881 to the Present
A photographic panorama
0–8052–4034–9 Schocken $39.95

● Louis Greenberg
THE JEWS IN RUSSIA: The Struggle for Emancipation
Two volumes of Greenberg's magisterial work have been combined into this one edition, covering the years from 1772 to 1817
Edited by Mark Wischnitzer
0–8052–0525–X Schocken pb $11.95

● Lionel Kochan
JEWS IN SOVIET RUSSIA SINCE 1917
Various aspects of Jewish life under communism, from reactions to Bolshevism to today's Refuseniks
0–19–281199–1 Oxford pb $9.95

● Benjamin Pinkus
THE JEWS OF THE SOVIET UNION: A History of a National Minority
0–521–34078–0 Cambridge $34.50

● Natan Sharansky
FEAR NO EVIL
Autobiographical account by the most famous Jewish Refusenik of his voyage through Soviet prisons and ultimately to Israel
Translated by Stefani Hoffman
0–394–55878–2 Random House $19.95

● Elie Wiesel
THE JEWS OF SILENCE: A Personal Report on Soviet Jewry
Wiesel's 1966 report on Soviet Jewry first focused the West's attention on the plight of the Refuseniks
Afterword by Martin Gilbert
0–8052–0826–7 Schocken pb $8.95

THE JEWS IN AMERICA

General Histories

● Stephen Birmingham
THE REST OF US
The story of the Eastern European Jews in America
0–316–09647–4 Little, Brown $19.95
0–425–08074–9 Berkley pb $4.50

● Ze'ev Chafets
MEMBERS OF THE TRIBE: On the Road in Jewish America
Chafets returns to the US after 20 years to meet with everyone from the last Cajun Jews on the Bayou, to a congregation of orthodox Black Jews, to a San Francisco gay synagogue, to a woman who wears a Jewish star around her neck to ward off anti-Semites
0–553–05308–6 Bantam $18.95

● Steven M. Cohen
AMERICAN MODERNITY AND JEWISH IDENTITY
0–422–77750–1 RC&H pb $12.95

● Neil M. & Ruth Schwartz Cowan
OUR PARENTS' LIVES: The Americanization of Eastern European Jews
An oral history of the immigrant experience in the early 20th century
0–465–05425–0 Basic Books $19.95

● Max I. Dimont
THE JEWS IN AMERICA
0–671–25412–X Simon & Schuster pb $8.95

● Leonard Fein
WHERE ARE WE: The Inner Life of America's Jews
"Trenchant, iconoclastic, at times scathing, at times rich with praise, this book is must reading for anyone concerned with the current condition of American Jewry"—Chaim Potok
0–06–015872–7 Harper & Row $19.95

● Henry L. Feingold
ZION IN AMERICA: The Jewish Experience from Colonial Times to the Present
A good introductory survey
0–88254–592–2 Hippocrene pb $10.95

● Nathan Glazer
AMERICAN JUDAISM
Edited by Daniel J. Boorstin
0–226–29843–4 Chicago pb $9.95

● Calvin Goldscheider & Alan S. Zuckerman
THE TRANSFORMATION OF THE JEWS
0–226–30147–8 Chicago $24.95
0–226–30148–6 Chicago pb $10.95

● Peter Grose
ISRAEL IN THE MIND OF AMERICA
America's complex relationship with Zionism
0–8052–0767–8 Schocken pb $9.95

● Ben Halpern
THE AMERICAN JEW: A Zionistic Analysis
Includes a new postscript in which Halpern reviews his conclusions in light of the events of the last quarter century
0–8052–0742–2 Schocken pb $6.95

● Arthur Hertzberg
BEING JEWISH IN AMERICA: The Modern Experience
A collection of essays
0–8052–0654–X Schocken pb $7.95

Illustration from Yiddish Folktales *edited by Beatrice Silverman Weinreich (Pantheon)*

● Abraham J. Karp
HAVEN AND HOME: A History of the Jews in America
"Karp uses a rich store of documents to their fullest . . . There are also engaging stories about Jewish labor leaders, gangsters, politicians and figures in the arts"—Ari L. Goldman, *NY Times Book Review*
0–8052–3920–0 Schocken $24.95
0–8052–0817–8 Schocken pb $9.95

● Jonathan Kaufman
BROKEN ALLIANCE: The Turbulent Times Between Blacks and Jews in America
A tapestry of the difficulties of the post-Civil Rights era, told by a *Boston Globe* reporter through a series of biographical portraits
0–684–18699–3 Scribners $19.95

● Kenneth Libo & Irving Howe
WE LIVED THERE TOO: In Their Own Words, Pioneer Jews and the Westward Movement of America, 1630-1930
A large coffee-table picture book with text, documenting the westward journeys of American Jews
0–312–85867–1 St. Martin's pb $13.95

● Jacob Neusner
ISRAEL IN AMERICA: A Too-Comfortable Exile?
"Approaches the complex question of whether Jewishness is religious or ethnic with relentless honesty"—*NY Times Book Review*
0–8070–3602–1 Beacon $14.95
0–8070–3603–X Beacon pb $8.95

● Dan A. Oren
JOINING THE CLUB: A History of Jews at Yale
0–300–03330–3 Yale $32.00

● Marc Lee Raphael
PROFILES IN AMERICAN JUDAISM: The Reform, Conservative, Orthodox, and Reconstructionist Traditions in Historical Perspective
The differing paths of American Judaism
0–06–066802–4 Harper & Row pb $12.95

● Harriet & Fred Rochlin
PIONEER JEWS: A New Life in the Far West
A picture book with text. "The stereotype of the urban Jew is vigorously, and even exuberantly, rejected in this colorful history"—*Chicago Sun Times*
0–395–42639–1 Houghton Mifflin pb $12.95

● Stuart E. Rosenberg
THE NEW JEWISH IDENTITY IN AMERICA
"A serious and informed book, for thinking readers"—Franklin H. Littell, Temple University
0–88254–997–9 Hippocrene $19.95

● Allon Schoener
THE AMERICAN JEWISH ALBUM: 1654 to the Present
A large picture book tracing 300 years of history
0–8478–0592–1 Rizzoli $25.00

• Charles E. Silberman
A CERTAIN PEOPLE: American Jews and Their Lives Today
0–671–62877–1 Summit pb $9.95

• Howard Simons
JEWISH TIMES: Voices of the American Jewish Experience
An oral history based on more than 200 interviews
0–395–44680–5 Houghton Mifflin $22.95

• Chaim I. Waxman
AMERICA'S JEWS IN TRANSITION
0–87722–321–1 Temple $29.95
0–87722–329–7 Temple pb $14.95

Orthodoxy

• Lis Harris
HOLY DAYS: The World of a Hasidic Family
"What is special about Lis Harris is her combination of openness and skepticism toward her subject. *Holy Days* is a deeply felt and informative introduction to an appealing sect of fundamentalist faith"— *NY Times*
0–671–46296–2 Summit $18.95
0–02–020970–3 Macmillan pb $8.95

• William N. Helmreich
THE WORLD OF THE YESHIVA: An Intimate Portrait of Orthodox Jewry
Penetrating study of life in Orthodox Jewish education
0–02–914640–2 Free Press $22.95
0–300–03715–5 Yale pb $15.95

Assimilation and Intermarriage

• Steven M. Cohen
AMERICAN ASSIMILATION OR JEWISH REVIVAL?
As American Jews grow further from their European pasts are they becoming more American or are they undergoing a great revival?
0–253–30608–6 Indiana $27.50

• Paul Cowan
AN ORPHAN IN HISTORY
The now-classic odyssey of an assimilated Jew toward the embrace of his roots. "At a time when many are seeking answers in all sorts of paths—religious, mystical, and political—Paul Cowan managed to find them, and himself, in his own history"— Richard F. Shepard, *NY Times*
0–553–26030–8 Bantam pb $3.95

• Paul & Rachel Cowan
MIXED BLESSINGS: Marriages Between Jews and Christians
0–385–19502–8 Doubleday $18.95

• Egon Mayer
LOVE AND TRADITION: Marriage Between Jews and Christians
Sociologist Mayer interviewed hundreds of intermarried couples and their children and assesses their motivations and religious identities
0–306–42043–0 Plenum $17.95
0–8052–0828–3 Schocken pb $8.95

Illustration from Yiddish Folktales *edited by Beatrice Silverman Weinreich (Pantheon)*

Anti-Semitism in America

• Leonard Dinnerstein
THE LEO FRANK CASE
The infamous case of the southern Jewish man blamed and lynched for the murder of a factory girl
0–8203–0965–6 Georgia pb $12.95

UNEASY AT HOME: Antisemitism and the American Jewish Experience
0–231–06252–4 Columbia $25.00

• David A. Gerber, editor
ANTI-SEMITISM IN AMERICAN HISTORY
0–252–01214–3 Illinois $29.95

• Harold E. Quinley & Charles Y. Glock
ANTI-SEMITISM IN AMERICA
0–02–925640–2 Free Press $14.95

The Lower East Side and the Jews of New York

The production of Yiddish periodicals in New York City, the hub of the Yiddish-American universe, was accelerated by the rising immigration. Between 1885 and 1914 over 150 daily, weekly, monthly, quarterly, and festive journals and yearbooks appeared. The yearnings for free expression, suppressed in the Old World, erupted in the New. Self-discovered authors, journalists, and humbler enthusiasts bewitched by the printed page, turned groggy with printer's ink and the perturbations in their own brains. The passion to educate and uplift, political and literary zeal, appetites for literary immortality and momentary fame, ideological divergencies, and the commercial instinct drove the presses at a furious pace.

Moses Rischin
THE PROMISED CITY: New York's Jews, 1870-1914
0–674–71502–0 Harvard $24.50
0–674–71501–2 Harvard pb $9.95

• Abraham Cahan
THE RISE OF DAVID LEVINSKY
The classic novel, by the editor of the *Jewish Daily Forward*, of material success and the elusive quest for happiness in the New World
0–06–131912–0 Harper & Row pb $8.50

• Arthur A. Goren
NEW YORK JEWS AND THE QUEST FOR COMMUNITY
Covers the attempts of early 20th-century New York Jews to form a central communal structure
0–231–03422–9 Columbia $34.00
0–231–08368–8 Columbia pb $17.00

• Irving Howe
WORLD OF OUR FATHERS
The classic, beautifully-written account of the Jewish migration from Europe to the United States, with detailed looks at everything from Yiddish theater to the Jewish labor movement
0–15–146353–0 HBJ $29.95
0–671–49252–7 Simon & Schuster pb $12.95

• Jenna Weissman Joselit
OUR GANG: Jewish Crime and the New York Jewish Community, 1900-1940
0–253–15845–1 Indiana $19.95
0–253–20314–7 Indiana pb $9.95

• Isaac Metzker, editor
A BINTEL BRIEF
Letters from the *Jewish Daily Forward* bring the Lower East Side to life
0–87441–345–1 Behrman House pb $6.95

• Moses Rischin
THE PROMISED CITY: New York's Jews, 1870-1914
Authoritative account of the Lower East Side experience, covering secularization, economic success, the labor movement, and Yiddish theater
0–674–71502–0 Harvard $24.50
0–674–71501–2 Harvard pb $9.95

• Ronald Sanders
THE DOWNTOWN JEWS: Portraits of an Immigrant Generation
0–486–25510–7 Dover pb $9.95

SHORES OF REFUGE: One Hundred Years of Jewish Emigration
Covers Jewish migrations since 1881 from Russia and Eastern Europe to both the US and Palestine. "Ronald Sanders proves more than ever before that he is the most sensitive, best informed, and most graphic American historian of the 20th-century Jewish experience"—Alfred Kazin
0–8050–0563–3 Henry Holt $27.95
0–8052–0916–6 Schocken pb $14.95

• Sydney Stahl Weinberg
THE WORLD OF OUR MOTHERS: The Lives of Jewish Immigrant Women
Oral histories of more than 40 women. Though some became professionals while others never learned to read, they all shared a cultural heritage
0–8078–1762–7 Chapel Hill $22.95

OTHER JEWISH EXPERIENCES

• Phyllis Cohen Albert
CONTEMPORARY FRENCH JEWRY
0–8419–0933–4 Holmes & Meier pb $14.50

Illustration from Yiddish Folktales *edited by Beatrice Silverman Weinreich (Pantheon)*

● Avigdor Dagan & others, editors
THE JEWS OF CZECHOSLOVAKIA
A trilogy, from the founding of the first republic in 1918 to the advent of communism in 1948

Volume 1
0-8276-0146-8 JPS $29.95

Volume 2
0-8276-0146-8 JPS $29.95

Volume 3
Covers the Holocaust and the rebuilding of the Jewish community after the war
0-8276-0230-8 JPS $29.95

● Daniel J. Elazar
THE OTHER JEWS: The Sephardim Today
Covers the Sephardic communities in Europe, Africa, Asia, the Pacific, the Caribbean, Latin America and North America, as well as the sometimes troubled relationship between Sephardim and Ashkenazim
0-465-05365-3 Basic Books $21.95

● Harriet Pass Freidenreich
THE JEWS OF YUGOSLAVIA: A Quest for Community
A study of a Jewish community born after World War I
0-8276-0122-0 JPS $14.95

● Shlomo Hillel
OPERATION BABYLON: The Story of the Rescue of the Jews of Iraq
Traces the rescue of 125,000 Iraqi Jews between 1947 and 1952
0-385-23597-6 Doubleday $19.95

● Zion Mansour Ozeri
YEMENITE JEWS: A Photographic Essay
Scenes of Yemenite jewelers, blacksmiths, farmers, weddings, funerals and holidays
0-8052-3980-4 Schocken $19.95

● Michael Pollak
MANDARINS, JEWS, AND MISSIONARIES: The Jewish Experience in the Chinese Empire
The Jews of Kaifeng China
0-8276-0229-4 JPS pb $12.95

● Dan Ross
ACTS OF FAITH: A Journey to the Fringes of Jewish Identity
Portraits of communities whose Jewishness is often disputed, including the Portuguese Marranos, the Mashadi Jews of Iran, Israel's Samaritans, the Chinese Jews of Kaifeng, and the Bene Israel of India
Foreword by Raphael Patai
0-8052-0759-7 Schocken pb $8.95

● Howard Morley Sachar
DIASPORA: An Inquiry into the Contemporary Jewish World
A survey of recent Jewish history outside the US and Israel
0-06-015403-9 Harper & Row $27.50

● Claire Safran
SECRET EXODUS: The Untold Story of How Operation Moses Saved the Lost Tribe of Ethiopian Jews
0-13-798182-1 Prentice-Hall $17.95

● Sidney Shapiro, editor
JEWS IN OLD CHINA
Fascinating essays by Chinese scholars about the Jewish presence in China as early as the 8th century BC; translated and compiled by Shapiro
0-87052-553-0 Hippocrene pb $8.95

● Robert Weisbrot
THE JEWS OF ARGENTINA: From the Inquisition to Peron
An important Jewish community from early to latter-day persecutions
0-8276-0114-X JPS $12.50

BIOGRAPHY

● Eli N. Evans
JUDAH P. BENJAMIN: The Jewish Confederate
Born in St. Croix, raised in South Carolina, and educated at Yale, Benjamin was Attorney General, Secretary of War, and Secretary of State for the Confederacy in the American Civil War
0-02-908880-1 Free Press $24.95

● Gershom Scholem
WALTER BENJAMIN: The Story of a Friendship
A memoir of the friendship between two noted scholars
Translated by Harry Zohn
0-8276-0197-2 JPS $13.95
0-8052-0870-4 Schocken pb $9.95

● Amos Elon
HERZL
The authoritative biography of the founder of modern Zionism, by a leading Israeli intellectual. "A convincing, highly readable account"—*Choice*
0-8052-0790-2 Schocken pb $12.95

● Shlomo Avineri
MOSES HESS: Prophet of Communism and Zionism
"A compact, lucid study of a notable thinker of the 19th century whose insight reached into the 20th"—*Journal of Jewish Studies*
0-8147-0587-1 NYU $15.00

● Anita Shapira
BERL: The Biography of a Socialist Zionist, Berl Katznelson, 1887-1944
The story of a founder of the Israeli labor movement, from the Pale to the kibbutz
0-521-25618-6 Cambridge $29.95

● Julius Lester
LOVESONG: Becoming a Jew
A personal account of a black intellectual's conversion to Judaism
0-8050-0588-9 Henry Holt $17.95

● Ralph G. Martin
GOLDA: Golda Meir, The Romantic Years
A new biography of Meir's early years, including her American childhood and growth as a Zionist
0-684-19017-6 Scribners $19.95

● Arthur Hertzberg
MENDELSSOHN
Biography of the leading figure of the Jewish Enlightenment
0-8021-1131-9 Grove $15.95

● Jonathan D. Sarna
JACKSONIAN JEW: The Two Worlds of Mordecai Noah
0-8419-0567-3 Holmes & Meier $35.00

● Nahum N. Glatzer
FRANZ ROSENZWEIG: His Life and Thought
An intellectual biography of a key Jewish theologian of progressive Judaism
0-8052-0021-5 Schocken pb $8.95

● Derek Wilson
ROTHSCHILD: A Story of Wealth and Power
A new account of the leading French family
0-684-19018-4 Scribners $27.50

From Hannah Senesh: Her Life and Diary *(Schocken)*

- Gershom Scholem
FROM BERLIN TO JERUSALEM:
Memories of My Youth
The early life of a foremost scholar of
Jewish mysticism
0–8052–0871–2 Schocken pb $9.95

- Dan V. Segre
MEMOIRS OF A FORTUNATE JEW: An
Italian Story
An odyssey through fascist Italy and the
founding of Israel
0–917561–32–5 Farrar, Straus & Giroux $16.95
0–440–20188–8 Dell pb $4.95

- Hannah Senesh
HANNAH SENESH: Her Life and Diary
A major hero in Israel, Senesh was a
pioneer Zionist, killed by the Nazis at the
age of 23 after a failed attempt to rescue
Hungarian Jews
Translated by Marta Cohn
Introduction by Abba Eban
0–8052–0410–5 Schocken pb $9.95

JEWISH CULTURE

▶ **See also Yiddish Language and Literature,**
Modern Hebrew Literature, & Judaism

- Nathan Ausubel, editor
A TREASURY OF JEWISH FOLKLORE
0–517–50293–3 Crown $18.95

A TREASURY OF JEWISH HUMOR
A wonderful collection of stories, poems,
jokes and words of wisdom by leading
Jewish writers
0–87131–546–7 Evans pb $14.95

- Joseph L. Baron, editor
A TREASURY OF JEWISH
QUOTATIONS
0–87668–894–6 Jason Aronson $25.00

- Neal Gabler
AN EMPIRE OF THEIR OWN: How the
Jews Invented Hollywood
0–517–56808–X Crown $24.95

- Leonard Singer Gold, editor
A SIGN AND A WITNESS: 2,000 Years of
Hebrew Books and Illuminated Manuscripts
0–19–505619–1 Oxford $24.95

- Jay Greenspan
HEBREW CALLIGRAPHY: A Step-by-
Step Guide
Easy-to-follow instructions and detailed
drawings help beginners learn one of the
oldest of Jewish arts
0–8052–0664–7 Schocken pb $8.95

- Joseph Gutmann
HEBREW MANUSCRIPT PAINTING
A vast range of illustrations of Jewish
customs and holiday observances in
manuscripts from Germany, Spain, Italy,
and Islamic countries
0–8076–0891–2 Braziller pb $12.95

- Louis Harap
THE IMAGE OF THE JEW IN
AMERICAN LITERATURE: From Early
Republic to Mass Immigration
Analyzes stereotypes and portrayals of Jews
through the 19th century
0–8276–0054–2 JPS $10.00

- A.Z. Idelsohn
JEWISH MUSIC
0–8052–0165–3 Schocken pb $12.50

- Benzion Kaganoff
A DICTIONARY OF JEWISH NAMES
0–8052–0643–4 Schocken pb $8.95

- Norman L. Kleeblatt & Vivian B.
Mann
TREASURES OF THE JEWISH
MUSEUM
The art and artifacts in the Jewish Museum
collection in New York; beautifully
illustrated
0–87663–890–6 Universe pb $19.95

- Raphael Patai
THE JEWISH MIND
0–684–16321–7 Scribners pb $15.95

- David G. Roskies
AGAINST THE APOCALYPSE: Responses
to Catastrophe in Modern Jewish Culture
The Holocaust in the context of
generations of Jewish response to
persecutions. "Densely argued, richly
allusive, exemplary in its far-ranging
scholarship"—*TLS*
0–674–00916–9 Harvard pb $9.95

THE LITERATURE OF DESTRUCTION:
Jewish Responses to Catastrophe
0–8276–0314–2 JPS $34.95

- Ruth Rubin, editor
A TREASURY OF JEWISH FOLKSONG
Lullabies, love songs, Sabbath and holiday
tunes, Israeli songs and other traditional
songs in English, Hebrew, and Yiddish
Piano settings by Ruth Post
Illustrated by T. Herzl Rome
0–8052–0528–4 Schocken pb $12.50

- Howard Schwartz, editor
MIRIAM'S TAMBOURINE: Jewish
Folktales from Around the World
Fifty folktales, from the Jewish version of
Snow White to the tales of the Ba'al Shem
Tov
0–19–282136–9 Oxford pb $10.95

- Geoffrey Wigoder
SYNAGOGUES THROUGH THE AGES
0–06–069401–7 Harper & Row $35.00

- Leon I. Yudkin
JEWISH WRITING AND IDENTITY IN
THE TWENTIETH CENTURY
0–312–44234–3 St. Martin's $22.50

The Islamic World to World War I

Islamic civilization began with Muhammad in the 7th century: new forms of polity, religion, and culture were established—first in the Middle East between 600 and 1200; then, in much of the rest of Central and Southern Asia, North Africa, Sub-Saharan Africa, and Eastern Europe. Today, Islam is the religion of 900 million people and it is expanding rapidly in Asia, Africa, and the Americas.

Islam's success has inspired pride and faith among its numerous adherents, but it has also provoked suspicion, fear, and contempt from outsiders. Ever since the Middle Ages, Europeans have been trying to comprehend, and to contend with, this intimate, ambivalent adversary. As soldiers confronted Muslim warriors on the battlefields of Spain and Palestine, medieval scholars translated the Qur'an and Islamic philosophy into Latin. From the 15th to the 18th centuries, Europeans anguished over the threat of the Ottoman Empire, but delighted in Oriental fashion and taste.

In the 18th century, the tide was reversed: Europeans began to push back the Ottoman Empire and to conquer formerly Muslim lands. Even today, the legacy of colonialism, the struggle between Israel and the Arabs, and the Islamic revival make the confrontation between Islam and the West a passionate issue.

- C. Brockelmann
HISTORY OF THE ISLAMIC PEOPLES
This reliable short history provides the
standard version in convenient form
0–7100–0521–0 Methuen pb $16.95

- Frederick M. Denny
ISLAM AND THE MUSLIM
COMMUNITY
An interpretation of the doctrines,
devotional practices, and institutions which
provides a ready understanding of current
world events involving Muslims
0–06–061875–2 Harper & Row pb $7.95

- Gerhard Endress
AN INTRODUCTION TO ISLAM
0–231–06580–9 Columbia pb $16.00

- Alfred Guillaume
ISLAM
0–14–020311–7 Penguin pb $6.95

- Philip K. Hitti
A HISTORY OF THE ARABS
The best one-volume political and cultural
history of Islam, from its origins in the 7th
century until the end of Ottoman rule
0–312–37520–4 St. Martin's pb $26.00

➤ **FOR OVERSEAS ORDERING INFORMATION, SEE PAGE 1**

• Marshall G. Hodgson

THE VENTURE OF ISLAM: Conscience and History in World Civilization
Hodgson is particularly sensitive to cultural and literary issues and to the meaning of Islamic religious discourse. This work resounds with his idiosyncratic and brilliant voice; winner of the Ralph Waldo Emerson Award

Volume 1: The Classical Age of Islam
0–226–34683–8 Chicago pb $15.95

Volume 2: The Expansion of Islam in the Middle Period
0–226–34684–6 Chicago pb $18.00

Volume 3: The Gunpowder Empire and Modern Times
0–226–34685–4 Chicago pb $15.95

• P.M. Holt & others, editors

CAMBRIDGE HISTORY OF ISLAM
This sturdy and reliable reference work by western scholars is an excellent source; a 4-volume set
0–521–08755–4 Cambridge pb (set) $90.00

Volume 1A: Central Islamic Lands From Pre-Islamic Times to the First World War
0–521–29135–6 Cambridge pb $29.95

Volume 1B: Central Islamic Lands Since 1918
0–521–29136–4 Cambridge pb $24.95

Volume 2A: The Indian Subcontinent, Africa and the Muslim West
0–521–29137–2 Cambridge pb $24.95

Volume 2B: Islamic Society and Civilization
0–521–29138–0 Cambridge pb $32.95

• Ira M. Lapidus

A HISTORY OF ISLAMIC SOCIETIES
0–521–22552–3 Cambridge $42.50

• Maxime Rodinson

THE ARABS
A great scholar's study of the Arabs from their first eruption into history to their complex presence in the contemporary world
Translated by Arthur Goldhammer
0–226–72356–9 Chicago pb $6.95

EUROPE AND THE MYSTIQUE OF ISLAM
Translated by Roger Veinus
0–295–96485–5 Washington pb $9.95

ISLAM AND CAPITALISM
An orientalist's fundamental challenge to Max Weber's thesis that capitalism is grounded in western Protestantism
Translated by Brian Pearce
0–292–73816–1 Texas pb $9.95

• Edward W. Said

ORIENTALISM
A ground-breaking work on how modes of discourse affect the object of study, with particular reference to the western "scientific" approach to Islam
0–394–74067–X Random House pb $8.95

SOURCES

Al-Tabari

This 10th-century compilation remains the indispensable source for Islam's early history, as well as for the declining years of the Persian Empire. Working in the traditional form of the "universal history," Al-Tabari recounts human history from an Islamic view, from Creation, Adam and Eve, the Flood, and the Prophets to the birth of Islam and the growth of the Islamic empire. The SUNY series is the first attempt to translate this enormous work—perhaps the greatest work of classical Arab historiography—into English. It is still incomplete; this list provides a sampling of the volumes now available.

• Al-Tabari

THE HISTORY OF AL-TABARI

Volume 1: From Creation to the Flood
Translated by Franz Rosenthal
0–88706–562–7 SUNY $49.95

Volume 4: The Ancient Kingdoms
Translated by Moshe Perlmann
0–88706–181–8 SUNY $39.50
0–88706–182–6 SUNY pb $16.95

Volume 6: Muhammad at Mecca
Translated by W. Montgomery Watt & M.V. McDonald
0–88706–706–9 SUNY $44.50
0–88706–707–7 SUNY pb $14.95

Volume 7: The Foundation of the Community: Muhammad at Al-Madinah, AD 622-626
Translated by W. Montgomery Watt & M.V. McDonald
0–88706–344–6 SUNY $44.50
0–88706–345–4 SUNY pb $16.95

Volume 9: The Last Years of the Prophet, AD 630-632
Translated by Ismail K. Poonawalla
0–88706–691–7 SUNY $44.50
0–88706–692–5 SUNY pb $19.95

Volume 25: The Later Marwanids
0–88706–569–4 SUNY $49.50
0–88706–570–8 SUNY pb $19.95

Volume 27: The Abbasid Revolution, AD 743-750
Translated & edited John A. Williams
0–87395–884–5 SUNY $44.50

Volume 30: The Abbasid Caliphate in Equilibrium: The Caliphates of Musa Al-Hadi and Harun Al-Rashid, AD 785-809
Translated by C.E. Bosworth
0–88706–564–3 SUNY $49.50
0–88706–566–X SUNY pb $24.50

Volume 35: The Crisis of the Abbasid Caliphate, AD 862-869
0–87395–883–7 SUNY $44.50

Volume 38: The Return of the Caliphate to Baghdad, AD 892-915
Translated by Franz Rosenthal
0–87395–876–4 SUNY $44.50

Other Sources

• Ibn Khaldûn

THE MUQADDIMAH: An Introduction to History
The 14th-century philosophy of history by the Tunisian statesman and scholar who has been called the first social scientist; a 3-volume set
Translated by Franz Rosenthal
0–691–09797–6 Princeton (set) $170.00

THE MUQADDIMAH: Abridged Edition
A single volume abridgement of the masterpiece. "Should make the essential ideas of Ibn Khaldûn accessible to a wide circle of readers"—*Times Literary Supplement*
Translated by Franz Rosenthal
Edited by N.J. Dawood
0–691–09946–4 Princeton $28.00
0–691–01754–9 Princeton pb $13.95

• Usamah Ibn Minqidh

AN ARAB-SYRIAN GENTLEMAN AND WARRIOR IN THE PERIOD OF THE CRUSADES: Memoirs of Usamah Ibn Munqidh
Translated by Philip K. Hitti
0–691–07746–0 Princeton $32.50
0–691–02269–0 Princeton pb $9.95

• Hilal Al-Sabi

RUSUM DAR AL-KHILA FAH (RULES AND REGULATIONS OF THE ABBASID COURT)
Edited by Elie A. Salem
0–8156–6046–4 Syracuse $19.95

MUHAMMAD AND THE QUR'AN

• Michael Cook

MUHAMMAD
A concise summary, from the Past Masters series
0–19–287605–8 Oxford pb $4.95

• Emile Dermenghem

MUHAMMAD AND THE ISLAMIC TRADITION
0–87951–130–3 Overlook $18.95

• Muhammad Marmaduke Pickthall, translator

THE MEANING OF THE GLORIOUS KORAN
A literal translation in which each verse is followed by a brief explanation of its historical and religious meaning
0–451–62641–9 NAL pb $4.95

• Maxime Rodinson

MUHAMMAD
An outstanding biography by the French orientalist which avoids slighting either the spiritual or the material aspects of the prophet's greatness
Translated by Anne Carter
0–394–73822–5 Pantheon pb $10.50

• W. Montgomery Watt

MUHAMMAD: Prophet and Statesman
0–19–881078–4 Oxford pb $7.95

بسم الله الرحمن الرحيم

"In the name of God, the Compassionate, the Merciful," calligraphy by Ibn al-Buwwāb from his Qur'ān of 1000 AD

EARLY ISLAMIC HISTORY

These books are good general surveys from the beginning of the Muslim era (AD 622) to 1258.

• Bernard Lewis
THE ARABS IN HISTORY
An inquiry into the definition and characteristics of many civilizations and races
0–06–131029–8 Harper & Row pb $6.95

THE ASSASSINS: A Radical Sect in Islam
A basic introduction to one of history's most intriguing sects, which threatened the Abbasid Empire with syllogism and dagger
0–19–520550–2 Oxford pb $8.95

• Bernard Lewis, translator & editor
ISLAM: From the Prophet Muhammad to the Capture of Constantinople
A collection of documents from the great ages of Islamic history

Volume 1: Politics and War
0–19–505087–8 Oxford pb $9.95

Volume 2: Religion and Society
0–19–505088–6 Oxford pb $10.95

• J.J. Saunders
A HISTORY OF MEDIEVAL ISLAM
The rise and fall of the caliphate and its relationship with the Christian world. The mission of Muhammad, the Arab conquests, the rise and decline of the empire of the caliphs, the coming of the Seljuk Turks, the Crusades, the Mongol invasions, and the character of the great Arabic civilization, which contributed directly to the European Renaissance
0–7100–0050–2 RC&H pb $13.95

Arab Conquests and the Caliphate

• C.E. Bosworth
THE ISLAMIC DYNASTIES
0–85224–402–9 Edinburgh pb $10.00

Iranian steel war mask, from Timur and the Princely Vision: Persian Art and Culture in the Fifteenth Century *by Thomas W. Lentz and Glenn D. Lowry (Smithsonian)*

• Fred M. Donner
THE EARLY ISLAMIC CONQUESTS
Donner holds that the success of the invasion of Syria and Iran was due to the internal dynamics of Islam rather than to accidental or deterministic historical forces
0–691–10182–5 Princeton pb $19.95

• M.A. Shaban
ISLAMIC HISTORY
Stresses economic and political matters with fresh, but sometimes controversial, interpretations

Volume 1: AD 600 to 750: A New Interpretation
0–521–29131–3 Cambridge pb $16.95

Volume 2: The Abbasid Revolution
0–521–29534–3 Cambridge pb $14.95

After the Dynasties

• Clifford E. Bosworth
THE LATER GHAZNAVIDS: Splendor and Decay, the Dynasty in Afghanistan and Northern India
0–231–04428–3 Columbia $29.00

THE CAMBRIDGE HISTORY OF IRAN
An excellent history, the third and fifth volumes of which are unfortunately out of print.

Volume 1: The Land of Iran
Edited by W.B. Fisher
0–521–06935–1 Cambridge $97.50

Volume 2: The Median and Archaemenian Periods
Edited by Ilya Gershevitch
0–521–20091–1 Cambridge $110.00

Volume 4: From the Arab Invasion to the Saljuqs
Edited by R.N. Frye
0–521–20093–8 Cambridge $95.00

Volume 6: The Timurid and Sefavid Periods
Edited by Peter Jackson & Laurence Lockhart
0–521–20094–6 Cambridge $105.00

• Robert Irwin
THE MIDDLE EAST IN THE MIDDLE AGES: The Early Mamluk Sultanate, 1250-1382
0–8093–1286–7 Southern Illinois $26.95

THE CRUSADES

• Francesco Gabrieli, editor & translator
ARAB HISTORIANS OF THE CRUSADES
The "other side" of the Holy War
Translated from the Italian by E.J. Costello
0–520–05224–2 California pb $12.95

• Malcolm Cameron Lyons & D.E.P. Jackson
SALADIN: The Politics of the Holy War
"The best book yet written about him in English"—*TLS*
0–521–31739–8 Cambridge pb $16.95

• Amin Maalouf
THE CRUSADES THROUGH ARAB EYES
0–8952–0833–X Schocken pb $8.95

• Steven Runciman
HISTORY OF THE CRUSADES
The standard work. "The best scholarly survey of the subject by a single author"—*English Historical Review*

Volume 1: The First Crusade and the Foundation of the Kingdom of Jerusalem
0–521–34770–X Cambridge pb $14.95

Volume 2: The Kingdom of Jerusalem and the Frankish East, 1100-1187
0–521–34771–8 Cambridge pb $14.95

Volume 3: The Kingdom of Acre and the Later Crusades
0–521–34772–6 Cambridge pb $14.95

Wearing no turban, his head shaved as a sign of mourning, the venerable qadi Abu Sa'ad al-Harawi burst with a loud cry into the spacious diwan of the caliph al-Mustanzir Billah, a throng of companions, young and old, trailing in his wake. Noisily assenting to his every word, they, like him, offered the chilling spectacle of long beards and shaven skulls. A few of the court dignitaries tried to calm him, but al-Harawi swept them aside with brusque disdain, strode resolutely to the center of the hall, and then, with the searing eloquence of the seasoned preacher declaiming from his pulpit, proceeded to lecture all those present, without regard to rank.

"How dare you slumber in the shade of complacent safety," he began, "leading lives as frivolous as garden flowers, while your brothers in Syria have no dwelling place save the saddles of camels and the bellies of vultures? Blood has been spilled! Beautiful young girls have been shamed, and must now hide their sweet faces in their hands! Shall the valorous Arabs resign themselves to insult, and the valiant Persians accept dishonor?"

Amin Maalouf
THE CRUSADES THROUGH ARAB EYES
0–8052–0833–X Schocken pb $8.95

THE RISE AND FALL OF THE OTTOMANS

▶ **See also Medieval and Renaissance Europe & Early Modern Europe**

The Ottoman Empire emerged in the early 14th century under the legendary Osman I, reached its apogee in the 16th century under Suleiman the Magnificent, whose forces threatened the gates of Vienna, and gradually diminished thereafter until Mehmed VI, who was sent into exile by Mustafa Kemal (Atatürk) in the 20th century.

• **Franz Babinger**
MEHMED THE CONQUEROR AND HIS TIME
Translated by Ralph Manheim
Edited by William Hickman
0–691–09900–6 Princeton $57.00

• **M.A. Cook, editor**
THE HISTORY OF THE OTTOMAN EMPIRE TO 1730
As late as the 1680s the Ottomans threatened Vienna; only in the 18th century was a marked decline evident
0–521–20891–2 Cambridge $47.50

• **Godfrey Goodwin**
A HISTORY OF OTTOMAN ARCHITECTURE
0–500–27429–0 Thames & Hudson pb $24.95

• **Norman Itzkowitz**
THE OTTOMAN EMPIRE AND ISLAMIC TRADITION
A brief history that emphasizes the Ottomans' own conception of their historical experience
0–226–38806–9 Chicago pb $6.00

• **Lord Kinross**
THE OTTOMAN CENTURIES: The Rise and Fall of the Turkish Empire
The best one-volume history by the man Arnold Toynbee calls "a master of character-drawing and a master of narrative"
0–688–08093–6 Morrow pb $14.95

• **Steven Runciman**
THE FALL OF CONSTANTINOPLE, 1453
The exciting story of the siege that destroyed Byzantium and put the capstone on the Ottoman Empire
0–521–09573–5 Cambridge pb $16.95

Islamic Dominions

• **Jamil M. Abun Nasr**
A HISTORY OF THE MAGHRIB IN THE ISLAMIC PERIOD
0–521–33184–6 Cambridge $59.50
0–521–33767–4 Cambridge pb $24.95

• **W. Montgomery Watt & Pierre Cachia**
A SHORT HISTORY OF ISLAMIC SPAIN
Recalls some of the most glorious political and cultural achievements in the history of the peninsula, which have been almost forgotten since the Christian recovery
0–85224–332–4 Columbia pb $10.00

THE MEDIEVAL MIDDLE EASTERN WORLD

Economy

• **E. Ashtor**
A SOCIAL AND ECONOMIC HISTORY OF THE NEAR EAST IN THE MIDDLE AGES
Part of the Near East Center Series
0–520–02962–3 California $45.00

• **Henri Pirenne**
MOHAMMED AND CHARLEMAGNE
The Belgian historian's famous and unusual recreation of the period; a bold thesis on the Islamic contribution to the decline of the western economy after Rome fell
0–389–20134–0 Barnes & Noble pb $17.95

Community and Society

• **Ross E. Dunn**
THE ADVENTURES OF IBN BATTUTA: A Muslim Traveler of the Fourteenth Century
This entertaining account of the remarkable traveler provides a detailed picture of the 14th-century Islamic world
0–520–06743–6 California pb $12.95

• **S.D. Goitein**
JEWS AND ARABS: Their Contacts Through the Ages
0–8052–0464–4 Schocken pb $8.95

• **Ralph S. Hattox**
COFFEE AND COFFEEHOUSES: The Origins of a Social Beverage in the Medieval Near East
The early history of coffee from its use in Sufi rituals to its widespread consumption in medieval Muslim coffeehouses
0–295–96231–3 Washington pb $12.50

• **Ira M. Lapidus**
MUSLIM CITIES IN THE LATER MIDDLE AGES
0–521–27762–0 Cambridge pb $16.95

• **Bernard Lewis**
THE JEWS OF ISLAM
"Lewis refuses . . . simplistic approaches and tries to explain the complex and often contradictory history of Jewish-Muslim relations over 1400 years"—Norman A. Stillman, *NY Review of Books*
0–691–00807–8 Princeton pb $8.95

• **Roy P. Mottahedeh**
LOYALTY AND LEADERSHIP IN AN EARLY ISLAMIC SOCIETY
0–691–05296–4 Princeton $27.00
0–691–10191–4 Princeton pb $12.50

Reference

• **Michael Dempsey & Norman Barrett**
ATLAS OF THE ARAB WORLD
0–87196–779–0 Facts On File $16.95

• **H.A. Gibb & J.H. Kramers**
SHORTER ENCYCLOPEDIA OF ISLAM
Focuses on religious issues
0–8014–0150–X Cornell $88.50

• **Francis Robinson**
ATLAS OF THE ISLAMIC WORLD SINCE 1500
0–87196–629–8 Facts On File $40.00

The Contemporary Middle East

• **Ghazi A. Algosaibi**
ARABIAN ESSAYS
Meditations on literature and politics by a Saudi patrician
0–7103–0126–X KPI pb $10.95

• **Jere L. Bacharach**
A MIDDLE EAST STUDIES HANDBOOK
The indispensable reference containing a historical atlas, Islamic calendar, conversion tables, list of dynasties, time charts, identification of acronyms, and sociolinguistic spread-sheets
0–295–96144–9 Washington pb $12.50

• **M.A. Bakalla**
ARABIC CULTURE: Through Its Language and Literature
A non-specialized introduction to all aspects of the subject from the Arabian Nights to modern Arab poetesses, from proverbs to literary criticism
0–7103–0027–1 KPI pb $11.95

• **Jimmy Carter**
THE BLOOD OF ABRAHAM: Insights into the Middle East
The former president's analysis of the area of his greatest success and greatest failure
0–395–41498–9 Houghton Mifflin pb $7.95

• **Elizabeth & Robert A. Fernea**
THE ARAB WORLD: Personal Encounters
Anecdotes of the anthropologists' experiences counteract the stereotypes
0–385–23973–4 Doubleday pb $9.95

• **Thomas L. Friedman**
FROM BEIRUT TO JERUSALEM
A personal account of the conflicts between Arab and Israeli by the Pulitzer Prize-winning correspondent
0–374–15894–0 Farrar, Straus & Giroux $19.95

• **Clifford Geertz**
ISLAM OBSERVED: Religious Development in Morocco and Indonesia
The anthropologist draws conclusions about the nature of religious belief from the development of a single creed, Islam, in two quite different civilizations
0–226–28511–1 Chicago pb $6.95

• **Hamilton A.R. Gibb**
STUDIES IN THE CIVILIZATION OF ISLAM
"Combines the grace of Burckhardt with a hard-headed understanding of the material realities"—Roy P. Mottadeh
0–691–00786–1 Princeton pb $13.95

• **Charles Glass**
TRIBES WITH FLAGS: A Dangerous Passage Through the Chaos of the Middle East
The American television correspondent who escaped from his pro-Iranian captors in 1987 writes of the diversity and vitality of life in the Middle East, based on his

travels from the Turkish coast through Syria, Israel, Jordan, and Lebanon
0–87113–267–2 Atlantic Monthly $19.95

• Arthur Goldschmidt, Jr.
A CONCISE HISTORY OF THE MIDDLE EAST
Conversational, direct, and trenchant history with incisive but sympathetic critiques of all the parties involved; revised edition
0–8133–0472–5 Westview $23.95

• David Lamb
THE ARABS: Journey beyond the Mirage
Inside the Arab world, in the journalistic tradition of John Gunther
0–394–54433–1 Random House $19.95

• Walter Laqueur & Barry Rubin, editors
THE ISRAEL-ARAB READER: A Documentary History of the Middle East Conflict
An illuminating collection of statements representing a wide range of views
0–87196–873–8 Facts On File $29.95
0–14–022588–9 Penguin pb $9.95

• V.S. Naipaul
AMONG THE BELIEVERS: An Islamic Journey
This record of the novelist's travels through Iran, Pakistan, Malaysia and Indonesia is a profound inquiry into life, culture and ferment in Islam
0–394–71195–5 Random House pb $8.95

• David Pryce-Jones
THE CLOSED CIRCLE: An Interpretation of the Arabs
Argues that the disorder of the postwar Arab world is not the legacy of colonialism, but of a tribal culture with complex blends of shame, honor, and power-challenging difficult for Westerners to understand
0–06–016047–0 Harper & Row $25.00

• Barbara Tuchman
BIBLE AND SWORD: England and Palestine from the Bronze Age to Balfour
Traces a crucial relationship through the Crusades, the need to secure passage to India, and the impassioned tourism of the 19th century
0–345–31427–1 Ballantine pb $10.95

CONTEMPORARY POLITICS AND SOCIETY

• Fouad Ajami
THE ARAB PREDICAMENT: Arab Political Thought and Practice since 1967
"Ajami understands Arab politics; though angry and impatient with its short-comings, he empathizes with it; though passionate, he writes with insight and clarity"—*Middle East Journal*
0–521–23914–1 Cambridge $32.50
0–521–27063–4 Cambridge pb $11.95

• John L. Esposito
VOICES OF RESURGENT ISLAM
Muslim and non-Muslim scholars of history, religion and political science offer direct access to the nature and agenda of contemporary Islam
0–19–503340–X Oxford pb $13.95

• Albert Hourani
ARABIC THOUGHT IN THE LIBERAL AGE, 1798-1939
Demonstrates how two streams of thought, one aiming to restore the social principles of Islam, the other justifying the separation of religion and politics, merge to create contemporary nationalisms
0–521–25837–5 Cambridge $54.50
0–521–27423–0 Cambridge pb $17.95

• Edward Mortimer
FAITH AND POWER: The Politics of Islam
0–394–71173–4 Random House pb $8.50

Daniel Pipes
IN THE PATH OF GOD: Islam and Political Power
Well-informed, non-academic, and over-all an excellent introduction to contemporary Islam
0–465–03452–7 Basic Books pb $12.95

• Edward W. Said
COVERING ISLAM: How the Media and the Experts Determine How We See the Rest of the World
0–394–74808–5 Pantheon pb $8.95

• Wilfred C. Smith
ISLAM IN MODERN HISTORY
0–691–03030–8 Princeton $39.00
0–691–01991–6 Princeton pb $10.95

• Robin Wright
SACRED RAGE: The Wrath of Militant Islam
A Middle East correspondent approaches Islamic fundamentalism through first-hand knowledge of Beirut, Damascus, and Teheran, combined with interviews of guerrillas and religious leaders
0–671–62811–9 Simon & Schuster pb $8.95

Women

• Soraya Altorki
WOMEN IN SAUDI ARABIA: Ideology and Behavior Among the Elite
0–231–06183–8 Columbia pb $13.00

• Lois Beck & Nibbi Keddie, editors
WOMEN IN THE MUSLIM WORLD
Explores women's lives in countries ranging from Morocco to Iran, Indonesia, and China
0–674–95481–5 Harvard $16.50

• Elizabeth Warnock Fernea
WOMEN AND THE FAMILY IN THE MIDDLE EAST: New Voices of Change
A progress report: essays, stories, life histories, poems, and documents
0–292–75529–5 Texas pb $11.95

• Sarah Graham-Brown
IMAGES OF WOMEN: The Portrayal of Women in Photography of the Middle East, 1860-1950
0–231–06826–3 Columbia $40.00

• Nadia Hijab
WOMANPOWER: The Arab Debate on Women at Work
0–521–26443–X Cambridge $42.50
0–521–26992–X Cambridge pb $11.95

• Fatima Mernissi
BEYOND THE VEIL: Male-Female Dynamics in Modern Muslim Society
An exploration of the suppression of female sexuality in the Muslim tradition, and the disorienting effect of modern life; revised edition
0–253–20423–2 Midland pb $7.95

• Minou Reeves
FEMALE WARRIORS OF ALLAH: Women and the Islamic Revolution
0–525–24712–2 Dutton $18.95

Society

• Akbar S. Ahmad
TOWARDS AN ISLAMIC ANTHROPOLOGY
0–317–52455–0 New Era pb $7.50

• Dale F. Eickelman
THE MIDDLE EAST: An Anthropological Approach
0–13–582289–0 Prentice-Hall pb $27.95
MOROCCAN ISLAM: Tradition and Society in a Pilgrimage Center
0–292–75062–5 Texas pb $12.95

• Ira M. Lapidus
A HISTORY OF ISLAMIC SOCIETIES
0–521–22552–3 Cambridge $42.50

EGYPT

• Sana Hasan
ENEMY IN THE PROMISED LAND: An Egyptian's Journey into Israel
The bold and moving account of a young Harvard graduate's experiences among her people's enemies in the early 1970s
0–8052–0853–4 Schocken pb $8.95

• Mohamed H. Heikal
CUTTING THE LION'S TAIL: Suez Through Egyptian Eyes
0–87795–919–6 Arbor House $18.95

IF YOU CAN'T FIND IT, LOOK IN THE INDEX

- Peter M. Holt
EGYPT AND THE FERTILE CRESCENT, 1516-1922: A Political History
The internal politics of the Ottoman Empire in Egypt, and the fate of its subsequent subsidiaries
0–8014–9079–0 Cornell pb $11.95

- Derek Hopwood
EGYPT: Politics and Society, 1945-1984
0–04–956014–X Unwin Hyman pb $13.95

- Thomas W. Lippman
EGYPT AFTER NASSER: Sadat, Peace, and the Mirage of Prosperity
1–55778–041–2 Paragon $22.95

- Anwar al-Sadat
IN SEARCH OF IDENTITY: An Autobiography
0–06–132071–4 Harper & Row pb $9.95

- Jehan Sadat
A WOMAN OF EGYPT
0–671–54071–8 Simon & Schuster $19.50
0–671–67305–X Simon & Schuster pb $8.95

- Afaf L. Sayyid-Marsot
A SHORT HISTORY OF MODERN EGYPT
Discusses the central paradox of Egyptian identity—the continuity of the people and the land, and alienation from a succession of foreign rulers
0–521–27234–3 Cambridge pb $10.95

- Huda Shaarawi
HAREM YEARS: The Memoirs of an Egyptian Feminist, 1879-1924
A first-hand account of the private world of a Cairo harem by the founder of the Egyptian Feminist Union, who publicly removed her veil in a Cairo railroad station in 1923
Translated & edited by Margot Badran
0–935312–71–4 Feminist Press $33.00
0–935312–70–6 Feminist Press pb $9.95

- Ghali Shoukri
EGYPT, PORTRAIT OF A PRESIDENT: Sadat's Road to Jerusalem
0–86232–062–3 Humanities $38.75
0–86232–072–0 Humanities pb $12.50

- P.J. Vatikiotis
THE HISTORY OF EGYPT
From the founder of modern Egypt to the political and religious dissent that caused Sadat's violent end
0–8018–3325–6 Johns Hopkins $45.00
0–8018–3326–4 Johns Hopkins pb $16.95

NASSER AND HIS GENERATION
0–312–55938–0 St. Martin's $29.95

- John Waterbury
THE EGYPT OF NASSER AND SADAT: The Political Economy of Two Regimes
Probes the failure of the socialist transformation of Egypt under two presidents
0–691–10147–7 Princeton pb $16.95

IRAN

- Said Amir Arjomand
THE SHADOW OF GOD AND THE HIDDEN IMAM: Religion, Political Order, and Societal Change in Shi'ite Iran from the Beginning to 1890
Influenced by Max Weber, this is both a history and sociology of the long relationship between Shi'ism and political organization
0–226–02782–1 Chicago $28.00
0–317–57640–2 Chicago pb $14.95

- Sayyed Mohammed Ali Jamalzadeh
ISFAHAN IS HALF THE WORLD: Memories of a Persian Boyhood
Life in Iran at the turn of the century in the family of an enlightened Muslim clergyman
0–691–10186–8 Princeton pb $17.50

- Donald Wilber
IRAN PAST AND PRESENT: From Monarchy to Islamic Republic
Encyclopedic coverage through two millennia, from earliest times to Iran's present day combination of industrial state and theocracy
0–691–00025–5 Princeton pb $12.50

The Iranian Revolution

- Ervand Abrahamian
THE IRANIAN MOJAHEDIN
Probes the social background of their leadership, the Marxist influence of their interpretation of Islam, and why they failed to gain political power in the early stages of the Revolution
0–300–04423–2 Yale $27.50

- Said Amir Arjomand
THE TURBAN FOR THE CROWN: The Islamic Revolution in Iran
0–19–504257–3 Oxford $21.95

- Ryszard Kapuscinski
SHAH OF SHAHS
Verbal snapshots capture the theater of the popular Islamic revolution that toppled the Shah
Translated by W.R. Brand & K. Mroczkowska-Brand
0–15–181483–X HBJ pb $12.95

- Nikki R. Keddie & Yann Richard
ROOTS OF REVOLUTION: An Interpretive History of Modern Iran
"If one has a limited time to gain an appreciation of the revolutionary force of Islam in Iran, it should be spent here"—Scott Armstrong, *Washington Post Book World*
0–300–02606–4 Yale $37.50
0–300–02611–0 Yale pb $10.95

- Barry Rubin
PAVED WITH GOOD INTENTIONS: The American Experience in Iran
How the USA was transformed from Iranian savior to world-devouring Satan
0–19–502805–8 Oxford $25.00
0–14–005964–4 Penguin pb $7.95

- William Shawcross
THE SHAH'S LAST RIDE: The Fate of an Ally
Dying of cancer and abandoned by the US, the exiled Shah flees from doctor to doctor, from country to country. A brilliant account
0–671–55231–7 Simon & Schuster $19.95

- Amir Taheri
NEST OF SPIES: America's Journey to Disaster in Iran
An Iranian journalist traces the roots of America's experience to mistakes of the Roosevelt and Truman administrations and, based on new information, to US covert operations in Iran from 1979 to 1987
0–394–57566–0 Pantheon $18.95

The Islamic Republic

- Shaul Bakhash
THE REIGN OF THE AYATOLLAHS: Iran and the Islamic Revolution
"The most authoritative and comprehensive account of the Iranian revolution yet to appear"—Gary Sick
0–465–06887–1 Basic Books $18.95
0–465–06888–X Basic Books pb $11.95

- Cheryl Benard & Zalmay Khalilzad
THE GOVERNMENT OF GOD: Iran's Islamic Republic
0–231–05376–2 Columbia $30.00
0–231–05377–0 Columbia pb $14.50

- Richard Cottam
IRAN AND THE UNITED STATES: A Cold War Case Study
A State Department veteran traces the flaws in the US relationship with Iran, culminating in the arms-for-hostages scandal
0–8229–5407–9 Pittsburgh pb $12.95

- Dilip Hiro
IRAN UNDER THE AYATOLLAHS
"A competent sensible narrative of the eventful last half dozen years . . . written with colour and excitement"—*Observer*
0–7100–9924–X RC&H $39.95
0–7102–1123–6 RC&H pb $16.95

- Roy Mottahedeh
THE MANTLE OF THE PROPHET: Religion and Politics in Contemporary Iran
0–394–74865–4 Pantheon pb $9.95

The Hostage Crisis: 1979-1981

Moorhead Kennedy
THE AYATOLLAH IN THE CATHEDRAL: Reflections of a Hostage
A blow-by-blow account of the embassy takeover and a scathing indictment of American foreign policy by a former hostage
Afterword by Louisa Kennedy
0–8090–2765–8 Hill & Wang $17.95
0–8090–1533–1 Hill & Wang pb $8.95

Gary Sick
ALL FALL DOWN
The principal White House aide for Iran during the crisis exposes the rivalry that kept the Carter administration from forging a coherent policy
0–14–008837–7 Penguin pb $8.95

Tim Wells
444 DAYS: The Hostages Remember
0–15–132803–X HBJ $19.95

IRAQ

• Frederick Axelgard
IRAQ IN TRANSITION: A Political, Economic, and Strategic Perspective
0–8133–0352–4 Westview pb $26.00

• Samir al-Khalil
REPUBLIC OF FEAR: The Politics of Modern Iraq
0–520–06442–9 California $25.00

• Christine Moss-Helms
IRAQ: Eastern Flank of the Arab World
Analyzes the power of tradition, the rise of the Ba'ath Socialist party, and the war with Iran
0–8157–3556–1 Brookings $28.95

• Tim Niblock
IRAQ: The Contemporary State
0–312–43585–1 St. Martin's $27.50

• Reeva S. Simon
IRAQ BETWEEN THE TWO WORLD WARS: The Creation and Implementation of a Nationalist Ideology
0–231–06074–2 Columbia $31.00

The Gulf War

• M.S. El Azhary, editor
THE IRAN-IRAQ WAR: An Historical, Economic and Political Analysis
0–312–43583–5 St. Martin's $25.00

• Majid Khadduri
THE GULF WAR: The Origins and Implications of the Iraq-Iran Conflict
Hostilities over boundaries, religion, and ethnic groups, particularly since World War II, get close attention from a military expert and Arab scholar at Johns Hopkins
0–19–504529–7 Oxford $24.95

The minaret of the "Malwiyyah" at Samarra, Iraq, the largest ancient mosque still extant, from The Concise Encyclopedia of Islam *by Cyril Glasse (Harper & Row)*

• Edgar O'Ballance
THE GULF WAR: 1980-1987
0–08–034747–9 Pergamon $32.00

ISRAEL

▶ **For books about the origins of Zionism, see also Jewish History**

• Ben Halpern
THE IDEA OF A JEWISH STATE
0–674–44201–6 Harvard $34.50

• Howard M. Sachar
A HISTORY OF ISRAEL

Volume 1: From the Rise of Zionism to Our Time
0–394–73679–6 Knopf $16.95

Volume 2: From the Aftermath of the Yom Kippur War
0–19–504386–3 Oxford $19.95

• Nadav Safran
ISRAEL: The Embattled Ally
This in-depth story of Israel since its founding focuses on its relationship with the US and includes a brilliant analysis of Kissinger's Israel policy
0–674–46881–3 Harvard $32.00
0–674–46882–1 Harvard pb $12.50

• A.B. Yehoshua & Frederic Brenner
ISRAEL
A beautiful coffee-table book commemorating Israel's history and 40th anniversary
0–06–015959–6 Harper & Row $39.50

Independence, 1948

• Larry Collins & Domonique Lapierre
O JERUSALEM!
Best-selling account of the day-to-day story of the founding of the state of Israel in 1948
0–671–66241–4 Simon & Schuster pb $10.95

• Uri Dan
TO THE PROMISED LAND: The Birth of Israel, 40th Anniversary
A photographic journey through the formative events
0–385–24597–1 Doubleday $24.95

• Simha Flapan
THE BIRTH OF ISRAEL: Myths and Realities
A critic of Zionism argues that many so-called historical facts of the early history of modern Israel are really propaganda myths
0–394–55888–X Pantheon $18.95

• Jon Kimche & David Kimche
THE SECRET ROADS: The Illegal Migration of a People
0–88355–329–5 Hyperion $23.00

• Jehuda Reinharz
CHAIM WEIZMANN: The Making of a Zionist Leader
0–19–503446–5 Oxford $35.00
0–19–505069–X Oxford pb $12.95

• Shabtai Teveth
BEN-GURION: The Burning Ground, 1886-1948
0–395–35409–9 Houghton Mifflin $29.95

Israel Since 1948

• Bernard Avishai
THE TRAGEDY OF ZIONISM: Revolution and Democracy in the Land of Israel
0–374–52044–5 Farrar, Straus & Giroux pb $8.95

• Benjamin Beit-Hallahmi
THE ISRAELI CONNECTION: Who Israel Arms and Why
Analysis of today's Israel as arms dealer, including its secret alliance with South Africa
0–394–55922–3 Pantheon $18.95

• Saul Bellow
TO JERUSALEM AND BACK
The novelist's personal account of a 1975 journey
0–14–007273–X Penguin pb $6.95

• Amos Elon
ISRAELIS: Founders and Sons
0–14–022476–9 Penguin pb $7.95

• Peter Grose
ISRAEL IN THE MIND OF AMERICA
0–394–51658–3 Knopf $17.95
0–8052–0767–8 Schocken pb $9.95

■ TO ORDER BOOKS AS GIFTS, SEE PAGE 1

- Leslie Hazleton
JERUSALEM, JERUSALEM: A Memoir of War and Peace, Passion and Politics
"Lays open the heart of Israel with the skill and healing power of a surgeon"—T.D. Allman
0–14–010244–2 Penguin pb $7.95

- Conor Cruise O'Brien
THE SIEGE: The Saga of Israel and Zionism
Sweeping, in-depth account of the exodus to Palestine after the Holocaust and the subsequent struggle for the preservation of Israel
0–671–60044–3 Simon & Schuster $24.95

- Abraham Rabinovich
THE BATTLE FOR JERUSALEM: 20th Anniversary Edition
A *Jerusalem Post* reporter reconstructs the events of June 5-7, 1967
Foreword by Teddy Kollek
0–8276–0287–1 JPS $29.95
0–8276–0285–5 JPS pb $14.95

THE BOATS OF CHERBOURG: The Secret Israeli Operation That Revolutionized Naval Warfare
0–8050–0680–X Seaver $19.95

JERUSALEM ON EARTH: People, Passions, and Politics in the Holy City
0–02–925740–9 Free Press $19.95

- Amnon Rubinstein
THE ZIONIST DREAM REVISITED
0–8052–3886–7 Schocken $14.95
0–8052–0835–6 Schocken pb $8.95

- Naomi Shepherd
TEDDY KOLLEK: Mayor of Jerusalem
0–06–039084–0 Harper & Row $16.95

- Avraham Tamir
A SOLDIER IN SEARCH OF PEACE: An Inside Look at Israel's Strategy
0–06–039088–3 Harper & Row $22.50

- Edward Tivnan
THE LOBBY: Jewish Political Power and American Foreign Policy
Analysis of the touchy question of whether lobbying by the American Israeli Public Affairs Committee (AIPAC) serves the nation's best interests or has led to a dangerous, blind-faith support of Israel
0–671–50153–4 Simon & Schuster $19.95

- Milton Viorst
SANDS OF SORROW: Israel's Journey From Independence
"A thoroughly challenging analysis by a sensitive observer, of an Israel torn by its dreams, its ideals, its ambitions, and the politics of its American protector"— Ronald Steel
0–06–015707–0 Harper & Row $19.95

- Robert Wistrich, editor
THE LEFT AGAINST ZION: Communism, Israel and the Middle East
0–85303–193–2 Biblio $25.00
0–85303–199–1 Biblio pb $9.95

ARABS, ISRAELIS, AND THE PALESTINIAN QUESTION

- American Friends Service Committee
A COMPASSIONATE PEACE: A Future for Israel and the Palestinians
An updated version of the 1981 work by a Harvard educator, based on recent travels
Edited by Everett Mendelsohn
0–8090–3576–6 Hill & Wang $18.95
0–8090–1536–6 Hill & Wang pb $8.95

- Arieh L. Avneri
THE CLAIM OF DISPOSSESSION: Jewish Land Settlement and the Arabs, 1878-1948
0–87855–964–7 Transaction pb $12.95

- Noam Chomsky
THE FATEFUL TRIANGLE: The United States, Israel and the Palestinians
A critical look at the situation in Israel that blames the US for what some perceive as the intransigence of Israeli government policies towards the Palestinians
0–89608–188–5 South End $30.00
0–89608–187–7 South End pb $13.00

- Pauline Cutting
CHILDREN OF THE SIEGE
A western doctor's 18 months in a Palestinian refugee camp in Beirut
0–312–02557–2 St. Martin's $15.95

- Uri Davis
ISRAEL: An Apartheid State
A prominent Israeli academic illustrates the legal provisions that institutionalize racial discrimination and considers the positions of various Israeli opposition movements
0–86232–317–7 Humanities $39.95
0–86232–318–5 Humanities pb $10.50

- David Grossman
THE YELLOW WIND
An Israeli writer's account of relations between Arab and Jew in Israel's occupied territories. "A tormented account that describes the ways in which the Occupation humiliates and contorts both its Arab victims and the Israeli rulers"— *Newsweek*
Translated by Haim Watzman
0–374–29345–7 Farrar, Straus & Giroux $17.95
0–385–29736–X Delta pb $8.95

- Yehoshafat Harkabi
ISRAEL'S FATEFUL HOUR
A former chief of Israeli military intelligence argues that his country's only alternative is to begin unconditional negotiations with the PLO
0–06–016039–X Harper & Row $22.50

- Mark Heller
A PALESTINIAN STATE: The Implications for Israel
A researcher at the Institute for Strategic Studies, Tel Aviv, argues that Israel's security may depend on the creation of a Palestinian state
0–674–65222–3 Harvard pb $7.95

- Chaim Herzog
THE ARAB-ISRAEL WARS: War and Peace in the Middle East
A largely military overview of more than three decades of Arab-Israeli warfare
0–394–71746–5 Random House pb $8.95

- J.C. Hurewitz
THE STRUGGLE FOR PALESTINE
0–8052–0524–1 Schocken pb $10.95

- Ann Mosely Lesch & Mark Tessler
ISRAEL, EGYPT, AND THE PALESTINIANS: From Camp David to Intifada
0–253–33320–2 Indiana $45.00
0–253–20512–3 Indiana pb $17.50

- Ian Lustick
ARABS IN THE JEWISH STATE: Israel's Control of a National Minority
0–292–70347–3 Texas $22.50

- Paul R. Mendes-Flohr, editor
A LAND OF TWO PEOPLES: Martin Buber on Jews and Arabs
0–19–503165–2 Oxford $39.95
0–19–503426–0 Oxford pb $8.95

- Benny Morris
THE BIRTH OF THE PALESTINIAN REFUGEE PROBLEM, 1947-1949
This 1988 book by an Israeli historian draws on previously unavailable sources to argue that neither the official Arab version—that Arabs were driven wholesale from their homes by Israeli terror—nor the official Israeli version—that Arab leaders broadcast orders for all Arabs to leave Palestine—is without serious omissions and historical distortions
0–521–33028–9 Cambridge $39.50
0–521–33889–1 Cambridge pb $14.95

- Raphael Patai
THE SEED OF ABRAHAM: Arabs and Jews in Conflict
0–684–18752–3 Scribners pb $11.95

- Rosemary Radford Ruether & Herman J. Ruether
THE WRATH OF JONAH: The Crisis of Religious Nationalism in the Israeli-Palestinian Conflict
0–06–066873–7 Harper & Row $19.95

- Maxime Rodinson
ISRAEL: A Colonial-Settler State?
The French scholar of the left argues that Palestinian opposition to Israel is that of colonized to colonizer
0–913460–23–0 Pathfinder pb $5.95

- Edward W. Said
AFTER THE LAST SKY: Palestinian Lives
Photographs by Jean Mohr
0–394–74469–1 Pantheon pb $17.95

THE QUESTION OF PALESTINE
An illumination of the tragic conflict from a Palestinian point of view
0–394–74527–2 Random House pb $6.95

• Edward W. Said & Christopher Hitchens, editors
BLAMING THE VICTIMS: Spurious Scholarship and the Palestinian Question
Argues that academics have tended to dismiss the claims and even the existence of Palestinians
0–86091–175–6 RC&H $39.95
0–86091–887–4 RC&H $13.95

• David Shipler
ARAB AND JEW: Wounded Spirits in a Promised Land
The origins of the prejudices currently intensified by war, terrorism, and religious fervor
0–8129–1273–X Times Books $22.50
0–14–010376–7 Penguin pb $8.95

• Avi Shlaim
COLLUSION ACROSS THE JORDAN: King Abdullah, the Zionist Movement, and the Partition of Palestine
Working from recently declassified documents, Shlaim tells of the clandestine diplomacy and collusion that left Palestinian Arabs without a homeland
0–231–06838–7 Columbia $40.00

The PLO

• Helena Cobban
THE PALESTINIAN LIBERATION ORGANISATION: People, Power, and Politics
A Beirut correspondent shows the importance of Al-Fatah in the development of the PLO
0–521–27216–5 Cambridge pb $9.95

• Alan Hart
ARAFAT: A Political Biography
The first American edition
0–253–32711–3 Indiana $39.95
0–253–20516–6 Indiana pb $18.95

• Shireen Hunter, editor
THE PLO AFTER TRIPOLI
0–8191–5929–8 University Press pb $6.95

• Rashid Khalidi
UNDER SIEGE: P.L.O. Decisionmaking During the 1982 War
Inside view of the complex internal negotiations and military maneuvers behind the PLO evacuation of Beirut
0–231–06186–2 Columbia $30.00
0–231–06187–0 Columbia pb $12.50

• Shaul Mishal
THE PLO UNDER ARAFAT: Between Gun and Olive Branch
0–300–03709–0 Yale $25.00

Gaza and the West Bank

• Meron Benvenisti
CONFLICTS AND CONTRADICTIONS
0–394–53647–9 Random House $15.50

• Paul Cossali & Clive Robson
STATELESS IN GAZA
0–86232–508–0 Humanities $29.95
0–86232–509–9 Humanities pb $9.95

• Rafik Halabi
THE WEST BANK STORY
A Druse veteran of the Israeli Defense Forces balances a condemnation of Israeli policy with an attack on PLO "murder and sabotage"
Translated by Ina Friedman
0–15–695724–8 HBJ pb $7.95

• David Newman, editor
THE IMPACT OF GUSH EMUNIM: Politics and Settlement in the West Bank
0–312–40972–9 St. Martin's $35.00

• Don Peretz
THE WEST BANK: An Historical, Political, Social and Economic Survey
0–8133–0297–8 Westview pb $26.50

• Hillel Schenker, "New Outlook" & "Al Fajr," editors
LAND ON FIRE: A West Bank/Gaza Reader
1–55774–030–5 Adama $19.95
1–55774–042–9 Adama pb $12.95

JORDAN

• Uriel Dann
KING HUSSEIN AND THE CHALLENGE OF ARAB RADICALISM: Jordan, 1955-1967
The unlikely story of the durability of Jordan and its Hashemite king in the growing years of Arab radicalism
0–19–505498–9 Oxford $29.95

• James Lunt
HUSSEIN OF JORDAN: Searching for a Just and Lasting Peace—A Political Biography
By a confidant of the king
0–688–06498–1 Morrow $19.95

• Shaul Mishal
WEST BANK-EAST BANK: The Palestinians in Jordan, 1949-1967
0–300–02191–7 Yale $20.00

LEBANON

• Fouad Ajami
THE VANISHED IMAM: Musa al Sadr and the Shia of Lebanon
The myth created by the disappearance of a modern-day Imam leads to the revival of militant Shi'ism in Lebanon
0–8014–9416–8 Cornell pb $8.95

BEIRUT: The Fragmented City
A 50-page essay on the tragic price of war in one of the most favored cities in Arab culture, with photographs of hidden death and life in the ruins
Photographs by Eli Reed
0–393–30507–4 Norton $19.95

• Robert Brenton Betts
THE DRUZE
This thousand-year-old religious sect concentrated in the mountains of Lebanon, Syria, and Israel has been a key player in the Middle East power struggle—despite the fact that its adherents are non-Muslim Arabs
0–300–04100–4 Yale $22.50

• Richard A. Gabriel
OPERATION PEACE FOR GALILEE: The Israeli-P.L.O. War in Lebanon
This accurate and impartial account by an American intelligence officer provides excellent military history complete with detailed maps
0–8090–1504–8 Hill & Wang pb $7.95

• Walid Khalidi
CONFLICT AND VIOLENCE IN LEBANON: Confrontation in the Middle East
Offers a clear picture of the politics and events leading up to and including the Israeli invasion
0–87674–038–7 Harvard pb $9.95

• Jonathan C. Randal
GOING ALL THE WAY: Christian Warlords, Israeli Adventurers and the War in Lebanon
0–670–42259–2 Viking $16.95

• Kamal Salibi
A HOUSE OF MANY MANSIONS: The History of Lebanon Reconsidered
0–520–06517–4 California $22.50

• Jacobo Timerman
THE LONGEST WAR: Israel in Lebanon
The Argentine editor's critical account passionately conveys the heart-rending that the war caused in Israel itself
Translated by Miguel Acoca
0–394–71471–7 Random House pb $4.95

NORTH AFRICA AND THE MEDITERANNEAN

Algeria

• Jamil M. Abun-Nasr
A HISTORY OF THE MAGHRIB IN THE ISLAMIC PERIOD
0–521–33184–6 Cambridge $59.50
0–521–33767–4 Cambridge pb $24.95

• Alistair Horne
A SAVAGE WAR OF PEACE: Algeria, 1954-1962
French and Algerians both receive full measure in this harrowing narration of one of the most tragic of the post-colonial wars
0–14–010191–8 Penguin pb $8.95

• William Spencer
ALGIERS IN THE AGE OF THE CORSAIRS
0–8061–1334–0 Oklahoma $14.95
0–8061–1705–2 Oklahoma pb $7.95

Frantz Fanon
A DYING COLONIALISM
How the native Algerians modified their colonized characteristics during the struggle to eject the French colonials
0–8021–5027–6 Grove pb $12.50

THE WRETCHED OF THE EARTH
A brilliant, harrowing examination of the role of violence in effecting social change
0–8021–5083–7 Grove pb $6.95

Cyprus

- Christopher Hitchens
  HOSTAGE TO HISTORY: Cyprus from the Ottomans to Kissinger
  0–374–52184–0 Noonday pb $7.95

Libya

- Jonathan Bearman
  QADDHAFI'S LIBYA
  The tumultuous clash between a tribal culture and the social forces that are changing a backward society into a modern militant Arabic state
  0–86232–433–5 Humanities $42.95
  0–86232–434–3 Humanities pb $12.50

- René Lemarchand, editor
  THE GREEN AND THE BLACK: Qadhafi's Policies in Africa
  An effort to move beyond the "mad-dog" syndrome as an explanation of Qadhafi's foreign policy
  0–253–32678–8 Indiana $29.95

Morocco and Tunisia

- Tony Hodges
  WESTERN SAHARA: The Roots of a Desert War
  The journalist's study of the war between the Polisario guerrillas and the western-backed Moroccan regime
  0–88208–152–7 Lawrence Hill pb $14.95

- Dwight L. Ling
  MOROCCO AND TUNISIA: A Comparative History
  0–8191–0873–1 University Press pb $13.25

- Douglas Porch
  THE CONQUEST OF THE SAHARA
  The dark side of France's "civilizing mission" and a rich tale of extravagant hopes, genius and foolhardiness
  0–88064–061–8 Fromm pb $11.95

- Norma Salem
  HABIB BOURGUIBA, ISLAM AND THE CREATION OF TUNISIA
  0–7099–3319–3 RC&H $28.00

- Michel Vieuchange
  SMARA: The Forbidden City
  The diary of a young French adventurer who gave his life in the exploration of the ruins of this ancient Moroccan city
  0–88001–146–7 Ecco pb $9.50

SAUDI ARABIA

- Michael Field
  THE MERCHANTS: The Big Business Families of Saudi Arabia and the Gulf States
  Investigates the inner workings of the powerful and secretive international trade empires of Arabia
  0–87951–226–1 Overlook pb $10.95

- Robert Lacey
  THE KINGDOM
  The inside story of the family at the top of a feudal economy based on oil-production, where computer printouts begin by praising the lord, and princesses are beheaded for adultery
  0–380–61762–5 Avon pb $5.95

- Sandra Mackey
  THE SAUDIS: Inside the Desert Kingdom
  0–395–41165–3 Houghton Mifflin $19.95

- Jeffrey Robinson
  YAMANI: The Inside Story of the Man Who Ran OPEC
  The rise and fall of the world famous oil minister
  0–87113–323–7 Atlantic Monthly $18.95

- Nadav Safran
  SAUDI ARABIA: The Ceaseless Quest for Security
  This demystification of Saudi policy is based upon the rulers' sense of domestic precariousness
  0–674–78985–7 Harvard $25.00
  0–8014–9484–2 Cornell pb $15.95

SYRIA

- John F. Devlin
  SYRIA: A Modern State in an Ancient Land
  Takes us into the Syrian theater of the Arab confrontation with modernity, and shows how Syria has regained its political equilibrium under Asad
  0–8133–0021–5 Croom-Helm pb $17.95

- Derek Hopwood
  SYRIA 1945-1986: Politics and Society
  "Relates the important features of the country's history, supplemented by brief discussions of significant institutions . . . Probably the best available book of its type"—*Library Journal*
  0–04–445046–X Unwin Hyman pb $14.95

- Patrick Seale
  ASAD: The Struggle for the Middle East
  A pro-Syrian account of how Asad developed from a simple country boy into a politician of great subtlety. "A thriller, a textbook and an invaluable contemporary history"—John le Carré
  0–520–06667–7 California $25.00

  THE STRUGGLE FOR SYRIA: A Study in Post-War Arab Politics
  How the great powers' attempts to control the newly-independent Arab states and the recent defeat in Palestine contributed to Syria as it is today
  0–300–03944–1 Yale $45.00
  0–300–03970–0 Yale pb $15.95

TURKEY

- Marjorie Housepian Dobkin
  SMYRNA 1922: The Destruction of a City
  The tragedy of the final expulsion of Greeks from Asia Minor
  0–87338–359–1 Kent State pb $14.00

An Istanbul market, from The Wheels of Commerce *by Fernand Braudel (Harper & Row)*

Bernard Lewis
THE EMERGENCE OF MODERN TURKEY
A brief and lucid interpretation by the well-known orientalist
0–19–500344–6 Oxford pb $12.95

- Peter Mansfield
  THE OTTOMAN EMPIRE AND ITS SUCCESSORS
  0–312–59010–5 St. Martin's $18.95
  0–312–58975–1 St. Martin's pb $11.95

- S.J. Shaw
  HISTORY OF THE OTTOMAN EMPIRE AND MODERN TURKEY
  Volume 1
  0–521–29163–1 Cambridge pb $24.95
  Volume 2
  0–521–29166–6 Cambridge pb $24.95

- Vamik D. Volkan & Norman Itzkowitz
  THE IMMORTAL ATATURK: A Psychobiography
  The young Kemal's search for a father-figure, his agonizing transition from soldier to politician, and his emergence as Atatürk, the father-in-chief of modern Turkey
  0–226–86389–1 Chicago pb $14.95

Africa

GENERAL HISTORIES

● **A. Adu Boahen**
AFRICAN PERSPECTIVES ON COLONIALISM
How Africans saw the colonial enterprise
0–8018–3456–2 Johns Hopkins $22.00

● **Denis Boyles**
AFRICAN LIVES: White Lies, Tropical Truth, Darkest Gossip, and Rumblings of Rumor—from Chinese Gordon to Beryl Markham, and Beyond
Provocative, informed, humorous, journalistic—and invariably entertaining
1–55584–034–5 Weidenfeld & Nicolson $18.95

● **Donald Crummey, editor**
BANDITRY, REBELLION AND SOCIAL PROTEST IN AFRICA
A trendsetting look at decades of African protest in cultural phenomena such as work songs, stealing, and feigning illnesses
0–435–08011–3 Heinemann $27.50

● **Philip D. Curtin**
THE ATLANTIC SLAVE TRADE: A Census
This definitive summary vastly revised previous estimates of the traffic in people
0–299–05404–7 Wisconsin pb $12.95

CROSS-CULTURAL TRADE IN WORLD HISTORY
A broad synthesis with a partial focus on Africa; an excellent example of the new global history
0–521–26931–8 Cambridge pb $10.95

Basil Davidson

Basil Davidson's expertise ranges from long-lost African civilizations to post-colonial liberation movements. *The New York Review of Books* calls him "the most effective popularizer of African history and archeology outside Africa, and certainly the one best trusted in Black Africa itself."

Basil Davidson
THE AFRICAN GENIUS: An Introduction to African Social and Cultural History
0–316–17432–7 Little, Brown pb $10.95

THE AFRICAN SLAVE TRADE
Between the 15th and 19th centuries, perhaps 50 million men, women, and children were captured, brought, or kidnapped from Africa by European slave traders. This is an expanded edition of Davidson's classic account
0–316–17438–6 Little, Brown pb $10.95

LET FREEDOM COME: Africa in Modern History
The culmination of decades of study of Africa's hard fight for independence
0–316–17437–8 Little, Brown pb $10.95

THE LOST CITIES OF AFRICA
Revised and reissued. "A book which must inspire all Africans to a pride in our past"—Kwame Nkrumah
0–316–17431–9 Little, Brown pb $10.95

● **Cheikh Anta Diop**
THE AFRICAN ORIGIN OF CIVILIZATION
African nationalist broadside against historians who sought to sever Egypt from Black Africa; bursting with energy and hyperbole
Translated & edited by Mercer Cook
0–88208–022–9 Lawrence Hill pb $9.95

● **W.E.B. DuBois**
THE WORLD AND AFRICA
The activist's personal and learned "Inquiry into the Part Which Africa has Played in Western History," which had a major impact on Afro-American thought
0–527–25340–5 UNIPUB-Kraus $21.00

● **Bill Freund**
THE MAKING OF CONTEMPORARY AFRICA: The Development of African Society Since 1800
A materialist's sweeping view; focuses on the means of production and the relationship between capital and labor in development
0–253–33660–0 Indiana $25.00
0–253–28600–X Indiana pb $9.95

● **Nicholas Harman**
BWANA STOKESI AND HIS AFRICAN CONQUEST
An Irish missionary's true adventures in love and politics in East and Central Africa. The Belgians eventually hanged him
0–224–01998–8 Salem House $18.95

● **Joseph E. Harris**
AFRICANS AND THEIR HISTORY
A black American professor summarizes the literature
0–451–62556–0 NAL pb $4.95

● **John Iliffe**
THE AFRICAN POOR: A History
That rare commodity in African history, an excellent synthesis. Includes sections on the urban poor, South African townships, and leprosy
0–521–34415–8 Cambridge $49.50
0–521–34877–3 Cambridge pb $14.95

● **Bogumil Jewsiewicki & David Newbury**
AFRICAN HISTORIOGRAPHY
An overview of history and future directions
0–8039–2498–4 Sage $29.95

● **Robert July**
AN AFRICAN VOICE: The Role of the Humanities in Africa
Intellectual life, theater and learning, all emphasizing Africans as thinkers
0–8223–0717–0 Duke $22.50
0–8223–0769–3 Duke pb $10.95

● **David Lamb**
THE AFRICANS
A *Los Angeles Times* correspondent's impressions of 46 countries
0–394–51887–X Random House $17.95
0–394–75308–9 Random House pb $8.95

● **Mark R. Lipschutz & R. Kent Rasmussen**
DICTIONARY OF AFRICAN HISTORICAL BIOGRAPHY
An acclaimed reference work expanded and updated to include entries on over 800 people important in sub-Saharan history up to 1980
0–520–06611–1 California pb $12.95

● **Paul E. Lovejoy**
TRANSFORMATIONS IN SLAVERY: A History of Slavery in Africa
Africans enslaving Africans: for prestige, reproduction, or labor? A significant addition to the debate
0–521–28646–8 Cambridge pb $15.95

● **Phyllis M. Martin & Patrick O'Meara, editors**
AFRICA
A compendium of essays on politics, culture, history
0–253–30211–0 Indiana $40.00
0–253–20392–9 Indiana pb $14.95

● **Ali A. Mazrui**
THE AFRICANS: A Triple Heritage
Companion to the controversial PBS series; an eclectic illustrated journey
0–316–55200–3 Little, Brown $29.95
0–316–55201–1 Little, Brown pb $17.95

● **Roland Oliver & Anthony Atmore**
AFRICA SINCE 1800
The third edition of a standard text, focusing on the great civilizations and states of the 19th century
0–521–29975–6 Cambridge pb $13.95

Roland Oliver & J.D. Fage
A SHORT HISTORY OF AFRICA
This excellent introduction has now reached its sixth edition
0–14–022759–8 Penguin pb $6.95

● **Ronald Robinson & John Gallagher**
AFRICA AND THE VICTORIANS: The Official Mind of Imperialism
The imperialist scramble as a series of paranoid reactions to political developments in Africa. Its themes set off an explosive debate
0–333–05552–7 Humanities pb $19.95

● **Walter Rodney**
HOW EUROPE UNDERDEVELOPED AFRICA
Sweeping Marxist history and indictment
0–88258–096–5 Howard pb $6.95

● **Patricia W. Romero, editor**
LIFE HISTORIES OF AFRICAN WOMEN
Stories from seven regions, collected by noted specialists
0–948660–04–X Humanities $29.95
0–948660–05–8 Humanities pb $12.50

➤ **FOR OVERSEAS ORDERING INFORMATION, SEE PAGE 1**

• Alex Shoumatoff
AFRICAN MADNESS
A staff writer at *The New Yorker* chronicles contemporary Africa. Chapters include "The Woman Who Loved Gorillas," "The Last of the Dog-headed Men," "The Emperor Who Ate His People," and "In Search of the Source of AIDS"
0–394–56914–8 Knopf $18.95

• Sanford J. Ungar
AFRICA: The People and Politics of an Emerging Continent
Readable and well-presented
0–671–42010–0 Simon & Schuster $21.95
0–671–62809–7 Simon & Schuster pb $12.95

• Jan Vansina
KINGDOMS OF THE SAVANNAH
A 1966 survey that broke ground for a generation of historians
0–299–03664–2 Wisconsin pb $14.95

ORAL TRADITION AS HISTORY
The pioneer of oral historiography speaks, drawing heavily from his knowledge of Africa
0–299–10214–9 Wisconsin pb $9.95
0–8014–9583–0 Cornell pb $9.95

Philip Snow
THE STAR RAFT: China's Encounter with Africa
A relationship that began with Chinese merchants in search of markets on the east coast of Africa in the 17th century and continued through the era of Mao, when Africans looked to China as a model for their own independence struggles
1–55584–184–8 W&N $18.95
0–8014–9583–0 Cornell pb $9.95

UNESCO General History of Africa

Many scholars consider the UNESCO volumes the most important development in African historiography. Under the aegis of the United Nations, an editorial reading committee of 36 prominent specialists supervises an international project of which half the total staff is African. Each volume includes roughly 30 chapters. In addition to Western historians, Eastern Europeans, Africans, and Middle Easterners—many of them rarely seen in the English-language press—have contributed heavily.

Volume 1: Methodology and African Prehistory
Edited by J. Ki-Zerbo
0–520–03912–2 California $35.00

Volume 2: Ancient Civilizations of Africa
Edited by G. Mokhtar
0–520–03913–0 California $35.00

Volume 3: Africa from the Seventh to the Eleventh Century
Edited by M. El-Fasi
0–520–03914–9 California $35.00

Volume 4: Africa from the Twelfth to the Sixteenth Century
Edited by D.T. Niane
0–520–03915–7 California $35.00

Volume 5: Africa from the Sixteenth to the Eighteenth Century
Edited by B.A. Ogot
0–520–03916–5 California $35.00

Volume 6: The Nineteenth Century Until 1880
Edited by J.F. Ade Ajayi
0–520–03917–3 California $35.00

Volume 7: Africa Under Colonial Rule, 1880-1935
Edited by A. Adu Boahen
0–520–03918–1 California $35.00

Volume 8: Africa Since the Ethiopian War, 1935-1975
Edited by A.A. Mazrui
0–520–03920–3 California $35.00

RELIGION AND CULTURE

The extraordinary diversity of African civilization makes generalization difficult. The following books represent only a small sampling of the riches of African thought and culture.

• William Bascom
AFRICAN ART IN CULTURAL PERSPECTIVE: An Introduction
0–393–09375–1 Norton pb $8.95

• Francis Bebey
AFRICAN MUSIC: A People's Art
0–88208–050–4 Chicago Review pb $9.95

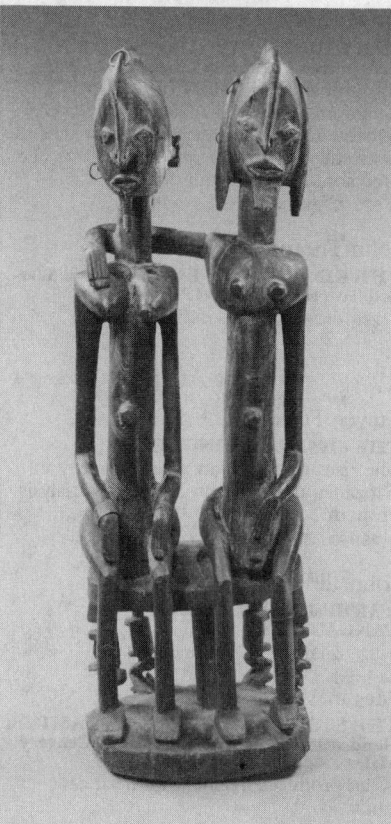

From The Art of the Dogon *by Kate Ezra (Metropolitan Museum/Abrams)*

• John M. Chernoff
AFRICAN RHYTHM AND AFRICAN SENSIBILITY: Aesthetics and Social Action in African Musical Idioms
An acclaimed study of the contexts of African music
0–226–10345–5 Chicago pb $12.00

• Werner Gillon
A SHORT HISTORY OF AFRICAN ART
An excellent introduction, covering the major achievements of most African cultures
0–14–022508–0 Penguin pb $12.95

• Judith Gleason
OYA: In Praise of the Goddess
A study of a major Yoruba deity whose devotees are also found in Brazil, the Caribbean, and the US
0–877–73430–5 Shambhala pb $12.95

• Ronnie Graham
THE DA CAPO GUIDE TO CONTEMPORARY AFRICAN MUSIC
An indispensable reference book covering the spectrum of contemporary popular music
0–306–80325–9 Da Capo pb $13.95

• Marcel Griaule
CONVERSATIONS WITH OGOTEMMELI: An Introduction to Dogon Religious Ideas
A classic exposition of Dogon cosmology as expressed in every aspect of daily life
0–19–519821–2 Oxford pb $9.95

• Paul Irwin
LIPTAKO SPEAKS: History from Oral Tradition in Africa
0–691–05309–X Princeton $28.00

• John Middleton
LUGBARA RELIGION: Ritual and Authority among East African People
0–87474–667–1 Smithsonian pb $14.95

• Oyekan Owomoyela
AFRICAN LITERATURES: An Introduction
0–918456–18–5 African Studies $12.00

• Mineke Schipper
THEATER AND SOCIETY IN AFRICA
0–86975–135–2 Ohio pb $8.95

• Robert Farris Thompson
FLASH OF THE SPIRIT: African and Afro-American Art and Philosophy
Traces the ramifications of African aesthetic concepts in New World traditions
0–394–72369–4 Random House pb $9.95

• Victor Turner
THE FOREST OF SYMBOLS: Aspects of Ndembu Ritual
The work of a great anthropologist
0–8014–9101–0 Cornell pb $12.95

REVELATION AND DIVINATION IN NDEMBU RITUAL
0–8014–9158–4 Cornell pb $10.95

European Explorers in Africa

Mary Kingsley
TRAVELS IN WEST AFRICA
One of the best late-19th-century explorers' accounts
0-8070-7105-6 Beacon pb $12.95

Alan Moorehead
THE WHITE NILE
A narrative treatment of Sudan's history. "Once more Alan Moorehead has shown his mastery of panorama, his power of bringing clear detail and physical life to a large and confusing subject . . . He appears to have visited every inch of the scene himself and puts it before us with simplicity and power"—V.S. Pritchett
0-394-71445-8 Random House pb $13.95

Henry M. Stanley
THROUGH THE DARK CONTINENT: Or the Sources of the Nile Around the Great Lakes of Equatorial Africa and Down the Livingstone River to the Atlantic Ocean

Volume 1
0-486-25667-7 Dover pb $9.95

Volume 2
0-486-25668-5 Dover pb $9.95

REGIONAL HISTORIES

West Africa

• Michael Crowder
WEST AFRICA: An Introduction to its History
0-582-60003-0 Addison-Wesley pb $8.95

• Finn Fuglestad
A HISTORY OF NIGER, 1850-1960
One of the few histories in English of a former French colony
0-521-25268-7 Cambridge $44.50

• Mary Smith
BABA OF KARO
Classic biography of the very full life of a Nigerian woman
0-300-02734-6 Yale $32.00
0-300-02741-9 Yale pb $9.95

• Robert Smith
KINGDOMS OF THE YORUBA
Now in its third edition, this is an outstanding synthesis for anthropolgists and historians, and for students at all college levels
0-299-11600-X Wisconsin $39.75
0-299-11604-2 Wisconsin pb $14.95

Central Africa

• David Birmingham & Phyllis Martin, editors
HISTORY OF CENTRAL AFRICA

Volume 1
Precolonial history, the Kongo Kingdom, Great Zimbabwe and more
0-582-64674-X Longman pb $18.95

Thirteenth-century king waited upon by Muslim ambassadors and slaves, from a late 18th-century Ethiopian manuscript

Volume 2
The best of its sort for the colonial period. Draws on new work concerning the role of ecology in history
0-582-64676-6 Longman pb $17.95

• Karen Fields
REVIVAL AND REBELLION IN COLONIAL CENTRAL AFRICA
Provocative account of religious violence. Was the colonial regime a theocracy?
0-691-09409-8 Princeton $43.00

• Gwyn Prins
THE HIDDEN HIPPOPOTAMUS: A Reappraisal in African History
A highly praised history of the Lozi Kingdom of Central Africa. Using every possible source, the author reconstructs the domestic and foreign policy decisions of a precolonial African kingdom
0-521-22915-4 Cambridge $57.50

• John Thornton
THE KINGDOM OF KONGO: Civil War and Transition, 1641-1718
0-299-09290-9 Wisconsin $25.00

East Africa

• Steven Feierman
THE SHAMBAA KINGDOM
The rise and fall of an inland dynasty in Tanzania, using a Lévi-Straussian analysis of myth
0-299-06360-7 Wisconsin $30.00

• John Iliffe
A MODERN HISTORY OF TANGANYIKA
0-521-29611-0 Cambridge pb $24.95

• Megan Vaughan
THE STORY OF AN AFRICAN FAMINE: Gender and Famine in Twentieth-Century Malawi
What produces famine? A crucial case study
0-521-32917-5 Cambridge $37.50

Northern Africa

▶ For other countries of North Africa, see also The Contemporary Middle East

• David Levering Lewis
THE RACE TO FASHODA
Fast-paced story of the European scramble for Africa at the end of the 19th century and the African reaction
1-55584-058-2 Weidenfeld & Nicolson $24.95

• Douglas Porch
THE CONQUEST OF THE SAHARA
Beau Geste as it really was: heat, dust, the Tuareg, and politics
0-394-53086-1 Knopf $18.95
0-88064-061-8 Fromm pb $11.95

• David Robinson
THE HOLY WAR OF UMAR TAL: The Western Sudan in the Mid-Nineteenth Century
Scholarly use of sources in tandem with an enthralling narrative of Islamic holy war in West Africa
0-198-22720-5 Oxford $55.00

Southern Africa

• Peter Becker
THE PATHFINDERS: The Saga of Exploration in Southern Africa
This unusual work unselfconsciously adopts the viewpoint of Dutch and English colonizers
0-670-80126-7 Viking $17.95
0-14-007478-3 Penguin pb $7.95

• Michael Crowder
THE FLOGGING OF PHINEHAS McINTOSH: A Tale of Colonial Folly and Injustice, Bechuanaland, 1933
An untoward incident illuminates the nature of the imperial enterprise in southern Africa
0-300-04098-9 Yale $27.50

• Terence O. Ranger
REVOLT IN SOUTHERN RHODESIA, 1896-97
Insurrection in colonial Africa from the African side. Factually flawed yet

Chief Regolo Moquepera with his two sons and some of his wives, c. 1900

tremendously influential, especially in Zimbabwe
0–435–94800–8 Heinemann pb $15.00

● Laurens Van der Post
THE LOST WORLD OF THE KALAHARI
Photographs by David Coulson
0–688–08608–X Morrow $39.95
0–15–653706–0 HBJ pb $8.95

TESTAMENT TO THE BUSHMEN
0–670–80065–1 Viking $20.00
0–14–007579–8 Penguin pb $10.95

A WALK WITH A WHITE BUSHMAN
0–688–07264–X Morrow $18.95

CURRENT AFFAIRS IN AFRICA

Political scientists have traditionally structured their writing on Africa around a series of politico-economic theories. Today, more weight is given to the actions of Africans as participants in their own political and social fortunes—or misfortunes, as the case may be.

● Molefi Kete Asante
AFROCENTRICITY
0–8654–3067–5 Africa World Press pb $9.95

● Gwendolyn Carter
CONTINUITY AND CHANGE IN SOUTHERN AFRICA
An important political scientist's analysis of contemporary affairs
0–918456–57–6 African Studies pb $9.95

INTERNATIONAL POLITICS IN SOUTHERN AFRICA
0–253–34285–6 Indiana $32.50
0–253–20281–7 Indiana pb $9.95

● Patrick Chabal
AMILCAR CABRAL
The best biography of the West African revolutionary
0–521–24944–9 Cambridge $49.50
0–521–27113–4 Cambridge pb $18.95

● Basil Davidson
NO FIST IS BIG ENOUGH TO HIDE THE SKY: The Liberation of Guinea-Bissau and Cape Verde
The fight against the Portuguese, updated and revised since Cabral's assasination in 1973
Foreword by Amilcar Cabral
0–905762–93–2 Humanities $27.50
0–905762–89–4 Humanities pb $9.95

● Lucy Ecreevey, editor
WOMEN FARMERS IN AFRICA: Rural Development in Mali and the Sahel
Critical essays approach development in the driest of agricultural landscapes
0–8156–2358–5 Syracuse $29.95
0–8156–2359–3 Syracuse pb $14.95

● Frantz Fanon
THE WRETCHED OF THE EARTH
The classic and shattering anticolonial handbook from Algeria
0–8021–5083–7 Grove pb $7.95

● William J. Foltz & Henry S. Bienan, editors
ARMS AND THE AFRICAN
A Council on Foreign Relations study on the Soviet, American, and South African militarization of Africa
0–300–03925–5 Yale pb $9.95

● Prosser Gifford & William Roger Louis, editors
DECOLONIZATION AND AFRICAN INDEPENDENCE: The Transfers of Power, 1960-1980
0–300–04070–9 Yale $50.00

● Nancy Hafkin & Edna G. Bay, editors
WOMEN IN AFRICA: Studies in Social and Economic Change
0–8047–0906–8 Stanford $30.00
0–8047–1011–2 Stanford pb $9.95

● Tony Hodges
WESTERN SAHARA: The Roots of a Desert War
The first full story of the politics, mineral riches, and foreign powers on the scene, and other stakes in Western Sahara's fight to reverse Morocco's annexation of 1975
0–88208–152–7 Lawrence Hill pb $14.95

● Madeline Kalb
THE CONGO CABLES: The Cold War in Africa from Eisenhower to Kennedy
US doings in the Katanga secession and Lumumba affair
0–02–560620–4 Macmillan $19.95

● Gaim Kibreab
REFLECTIONS ON THE AFRICAN REFUGEE PROBLEM
0–86543–006–3 Africa World Press $25.00
0–86543–007–1 Africa World Press pb $7.95

● E. Wayne Nafziger
INEQUALITY IN AFRICA: Political Elites, Proletariat, Peasants and the Poor
0–521–31703–7 Cambridge pb $12.95

● Kwame Nkrumah
NEO-COLONIALISM: The Last Stage of Imperialism
Ghana's angry prophet in a Leninist mode
0–7178–0140–3 International pb $4.95

● Julius K. Nyerere
UJAMAA: Essays on Socialism
Ujamaa and African socialism by the leader of Tanzania
0–19–501474–X Oxford pb $6.95

● Peter Anyang' Nyongo
POPULAR STRUGGLES FOR DEMOCRACY IN AFRICA
0–86232–737–7 Humanities pb $15.95

● Nzongola-Ntalaja
REVOLUTION AND COUNTER REVOLUTION IN AFRICA: Essays in Contemporary Politics
Excellent survey of a thorny issue
0–86232–750–4 Humanities $42.95
0–86232–751–2 Humanities pb $12.95

● Mort Rosenblum & Doug Williamson
SQUANDERING EDEN: Africa at the Edge
Environmental politics
0–15–184860–2 HBJ $19.95

● Richard Sandbrook & Judith Barker
THE POLITICS OF AFRICA'S ECONOMIC STAGNATION
Who profits and who loses
0–521–31961–7 Cambridge pb $11.95

● Carol Spindel
IN THE SHADOW OF THE SACRED GROVE
An account of a yearlong stay in a remote Ivory Coast village
0–679–72214–9 Random House pb $8.95

● Immanuel Wallerstein
AFRICA AND THE MODERN WORLD
A collection of articles from the past two decades. Wallerstein evolved his "world system" theory out of his Africanist

background, later supplemented by his reading of Fernand Braudel

0–86543–021–7 Africa World Press $32.00
0–86543–022–5 Africa World Press pb $10.95

- Crawford Young
IDEOLOGY AND DEVELOPMENT IN AFRICA
Masterful synthesis by the premier political scientist working in Central Africa

0–300–02744–3 Yale $40.00
0–300–03096–7 Yale pb $13.95

A NATIONAL FOCUS

Angola

- Ryszard Kapuscinski
ANOTHER DAY OF LIFE
A journey to the besieged center of Angola's civil war

Translated by W.R. Brand & K. Mroczkowsa-Brand
0–15–107563–8 HBJ $14.95

- John Stockwell
IN SEARCH OF ENEMIES: A CIA Story
0–393–00926–2 Norton pb $8.95

A wrecked billboard on the way into town offers a chance to rest your eyes: "In Pereira d'Eça," it says, "Stop at the Black Swan Inn. Air-Conditioning—Home Cooking—Garden—Bar—Attractive Prices." The traveller along the sterile and monotonous road from Luanda to Windhoek—2230 kilometers—can find a comfortable stopping place here. May I impart a word of advice to the weary wayfarer? Don't stop in this town tonight. Not these days. Times have changed and the promised comfort is lacking. There may be water, indeed, but there are no lights. It's dark. The moon doesn't rise. There are only stars, but somehow distant ones, faint and not very helpful. It's not a good place to sleep, because the houses have been smashed and looted. Nor is the cuisine to be recommended. On the concrete floor of the inn, in a puddle of dried blood, lies a butchered goat that has already begun to reek. Anyone who's hungry carves out a hunk of meat with a bayonet and roasts it over the bonfire.

Ryszard Kapuscinski
ANOTHER DAY OF LIFE
0–15–107563–8 HBJ $14.95

Côte d'Ivoire

- Barbara Lewis
THE IVORY COAST
0–86531–023–8 Westview $26.50

Eritrea

- James Firebrace & Stuart Holland
NEVER KNEEL DOWN: Drought, Development and Liberation in Eritrea
Results of a British fact-finding mission to Eritrea, land of brutal war, drought, and famine

Preface by Neil Kinnock
0–932415–00–8 Red Sea Press $29.95
0–932415–01–6 Red Sea Press pb $9.95

- Robert Machida
ERITREA: The Struggle for Independence
The roots of the costly 25-year civil war in the African Horn by an American who lived in Ethiopia in the 1970s

0–932415–24–5 Red Sea Press pb $5.95

Ethiopia

- Ruth Gruber
RESCUE: The Exodus of the Ethiopian Jews
The saga of the Israeli airlift during the worst of the famine

0–689–11771–X Atheneum $19.95

- John W. Harbeson
THE ETHIOPIAN TRANSFORMATION: The Quest for the Post-Imperial State
"A very full historical account of the coup which overthrew Haile Selassie, the stages of the revolution which followed, and an assessment of the policies—particularly land reform—of the successor regime"—*Foreign Affairs*

0–8133–7418–9 Westview $32.50

- Kurt Jansson, Michael Harris, & Angela Pemrose
THE ETHIOPIAN FAMINE
The directors of the UN and Oxfam relief efforts offer their views on the natural and political causes of the famine

0–86232–745–8 Humanities pb $12.50

- Ryszard Kapuscinski
THE EMPEROR: Downfall of an Autocrat
The Polish journalist's depiction of the outrageous pomp and decadence at the Ethiopian court, through interviews with Haile Selassie's servants

Translated by W.R. Brand & K. Mroczkowsa-Brand
0–394–72376–7 Random House pb $5.95

- Edmond J. Keller
REVOLUTIONARY ETHIOPIA: From Empire to People's Republic
The historical roots, development, and results of the Ethiopian revolution of 1974. Essential for understanding the politics of Ethiopia's famine

0–253–35014–X Indiana $35.00

Ghana

- David Rooney
KWAME NKRUMAH: A Political Kingdom in the Third World
Africa's first post-colonial black ruler who led Ghana to independence in 1957 and whose career ended ignominiously in a military coup

0–312–02479–7 St. Martin's $29.95

Jomo Kenyatta

Kenya

- Jomo Kenyatta
FACING MOUNT KENYA
0–394–70210–7 Random House pb $5.50

- Thomas T. Spear
KENYA'S PAST: An Introduction to Historical Methods in Africa
History where there are no documents

0–582–64695–2 Longman pb $13.95

- David Throup
THE ECONOMIC AND SOCIAL ORIGINS OF MAU MAU
The great explosion of African violence in Kenya, 1954

0–8214–0883–6 Ohio $29.95
0–8214–0884–4 Ohio pb $15.95

Kwame Nkrumah

IF YOU CAN'T FIND IT, LOOK IN THE INDEX

Mozambique

• Joseph Hanlon
MOZAMBIQUE: The Revolution Under Fire
Vignettes of daily life along with numerous photos and maps make sense of the complex story of droughts, policy blunders, and civil war with South Africa-backed troops; by a veteran BBC correspondent
0–86232–244–8 Humanities $29.95
0–86232–245–6 Humanities pb $12.50

Nigeria

• Thomas J. Biersteker
MULTINATIONALS, THE STATE, AND CONTROL OF THE NIGERIAN ECONOMY
Who wields corporate power in Africa's most populous and influential nation?
0–691–07728–2 Princeton $45.00
0–691–02261–5 Princeton pb $12.50

• Michael Crowder
THE STORY OF NIGERIA
0–571–04946–X Faber & Faber $17.95

• Richard A. Joseph
DEMOCRACY AND PREBENDAL POLITICS IN NIGERIA: The Rise and Fall of the Second Republic
0–521–34136–1 Cambridge pb $42.50

Sudan

• P.M. Holt & M.W. Daly
A HISTORY OF THE SUDAN: From the Coming of Islam to the Present Day
0–582–00406–3 Longman pb $17.50

Uganda

• Holger Bernt Hansen & Michael Twaddle, editors
UGANDA NOW
A recent (1988) collection of essays. Christine Obbo's contribution traces the roots of Uganda's social and political violence to the colonial period
0–8214–0896–8 Ohio $29.95
0–8214–0897–6 Ohio pb $15.95

• Jan Jorgensen
UGANDA: A Modern History
Published in 1981
0–312–82786–5 St. Martin's $29.95

• Amii Omara-Otunnu
POLITICS AND THE MILITARY IN UGANDA, 1890-1985
0–312–00046–4 St. Martin's $35.00

Zaire

• Paul Hyland
THE BLACK HEART: A Voyage Into Central Africa
A voyage up the Congo through the heart of Zaire
0–8050–0433–5 Henry Holt $22.95

• Nzongola-Ntalaja, editor
THE CRISIS IN ZAIRE: Myths and Realities
0–86543–024–1 Africa World Press pb $11.95

• Michael G. Schatzberg
THE DIALECTICS OF OPPRESSION IN ZAIRE
Argues that scarcity and insecurity have become twin motors of a dialectic of oppression, resulting in coercion, corruption, exploitation, and fear
0–253–31703–7 Indiana $25.00

• Helen Winternitz
EAST ALONG THE EQUATOR: A Journey Up the Congo
Rendezvous with Zaire's secret police in a modern-day Conradian "journey upriver"
0–87113–162–5 Atlantic Monthly pb $7.95

Zimbabwe

• Andre Astrow
ZIMBABWE: A Revolution That Lost Its Way?
Yes, indeed, writes this socialist and critic
0–86232–140–9 Humanities $35.00
0–86232–141–7 Humanities pb $9.95

• Ian Hancock
WHITE LIBERALS, MODERATES AND RADICALS IN RHODESIA, 1953-1980
0–312–86778–6 St. Martin's $25.00

• David Martin & Phyllis Johnson
THE STRUGGLE FOR ZIMBABWE
Introduction by Robert Mugabe
0–85345–599–6 Monthly Review pb $8.95

• Terence O. Ranger
PEASANT CONSCIOUSNESS AND GUERRILLA WAR IN ZIMBABWE
Why do African peasants rise up to fight and die? Ranger's most recent and sophisticated conclusions
0–520–05588–8 California pb $12.95

• Colin Stoneman, editor
ZIMBABWE'S INHERITANCE
0–312–89883–5 St. Martin's $27.50

SOUTH AFRICA: History

World interest, together with the long tradition of scholarship from within South Africa itself, has resulted in abundant material. At its best, South African history absorbs the reader in its tragedy and yet is uplifting in its depiction of black struggles to persevere.

• William Beinart & Colin Bundy, editors
HIDDEN STRUGGLES IN RURAL SOUTH AFRICA
An anthology of the newest work on millenarianism and revolt
0–520–05779–1 California $40.00
0–520–05780–5 California pb $11.95

• Belinda Bozzoli
CLASS, COMMUNITY AND CONFLICT: South African Perspectives
From a 1984 history symposium in South Africa
0–86975–281–2 Ohio pb $22.95

• Colin Bundy
THE RISE AND FALL OF THE SOUTH AFRICAN PEASANTRY
What happened to Africans—farmers all—as the Boers commanded the building of modern South Africa
0–520–03754–5 California $42.50

• John W. Cell
THE HIGHEST STAGE OF WHITE SUPREMACY
The development of segregation in the US South compared with apartheid in South Africa
0–521–24096–4 Cambridge $44.50
0–521–27061–8 Cambridge pb $11.95

• T.R.H. Davenport
SOUTH AFRICA: A Modern History
An excellent survey, now in its third edition
0–8020–6312–8 Toronto pb $19.95

• Richard Elphick
KHOIKHOI AND THE FOUNDING OF SOUTH AFRICA
The vanished people who inhabited the Cape of Africa in 1652, when the Dutch first settled there
0–86975–230–8 Ohio pb $14.95

• Emanoel Lee
TO THE BITTER END: A Photographic Account of the Boer War, 1899-1902
Stark black-and-white photos and a sophisticated text
0–670–80143–7 Viking $20.00
0–14–007237–3 Penguin pb $10.95

• J.D. Omer-Cooper
A HISTORY OF SOUTHERN AFRICA
A solid history in an attractive format
0–435–08010–5 Heinemann $20.00

• Charles van Onselen
STUDIES IN THE SOCIAL AND ECONOMIC HISTORY OF THE WITWATERSRAND, Volume 1: New Babylon
A lavish portrayal of vice, control, and interracial contact in a turn-of-the-century gold town
0–582–64383–X Longman pb $9.95

• Thomas Pakenham
THE BOER WAR
An excellent narrative account. With 9 maps and 32 pages of black-and-white illustrations
0–394–42742–4 Random House $29.95

• Brian Roberts
CECIL RHODES: Flawed Colossus
0–393–02576–6 Norton $22.50

❏ **TO ORDER BY FAX, SEE PAGE 1**

• Robert I. Rotberg with Miles F. Shore
THE FOUNDER: Cecil Rhodes and the Pursuit of Power
The clergyman's son from Hertfordshire, who went to South Africa at the age of 20 because of poor health, and became one of the great diamond magnates of his day. "Without Rhodes's historical invervention, neither colonial Rhodesia nor modern South Africa would have been possible, but neither would Zimbabwe—or whatever emerges in South Africa when the present system goes"—Geoffrey Wheatcroft, *NY Times Book Review*
0–19–504968–3 Oxford $35.00

• Anthony Sampson
BLACK AND GOLD
0–394–55581–3 Pantheon $19.95

• Leonard M. Thompson
THE POLITICAL MYTHOLOGY OF APARTHEID
How the Afrikaner people have interpreted history to sustain their notion of destiny
0–300–03368–0 Yale $30.00
0–300–03512–8 Yale pb $10.95

• Marq de Villiers
WHITE TRIBE DREAMING: Apartheid's Bitter Roots as Witnessed by Eight Generations of an Afrikaner Family
A liberal Afrikaner on the story of his own family and such leaders as Paul Kruger, Louis Botha, Jan Smuts, and James Hertzog
0–670–81794–5 Viking $21.95
0–14–010270–1 Penguin pb $8.95

• Geoffrey Wheatcroft
THE RANDLORDS: South Africa's Robber Barons and the Mines that Forged a Nation
Corporate raiding, South Africa style. Rhodes, Oppenheim, and the founders of today's world gold-producing and diamond-marketing network
0–689–11795–7 Atheneum $17.95
0–671–63993–5 Simon & Schuster pb $9.95

• Francis Wilson
LABOUR IN THE SOUTH AFRICAN GOLD MINES: 1911-1969
0–521–08303–6 Cambridge $44.50

• Monica Wilson & Leonard M. Thompson, editors
A HISTORY OF SOUTH AFRICA TO 1870
Originally published as volume 1 of the Oxford History of South Africa, this groundbreaking work has been supplied with new illustrations. Highly recommended
0–86531–581–7 Westview $49.00
0–86531–582–5 Westview pb $21.00

• Nigel Worden
SLAVERY IN DUTCH SOUTH AFRICA
0–521–25875–8 Cambridge $44.50

Zulu

In the 1820s, a small polity controlled first by Dingiswayo and then by his protégé, Shaka, swept up southeastern Africa in a brilliant conquest. Modifying hunting techniques into a modern form of warfare completely unlike "ritualized" battle, Shaka forged a large military state. Known and feared throughout southern Africa, the Zulu kingdom persisted until 1879, when the English defeated a large contingent of troops and divided the domain.

Robert B. Edgerton
LIKE LIONS THEY FOUGHT
The most memorable contact between whites and Zulus: wars of rampant destruction
0–02–908910–7 Free Press $22.95

Thomas Mofolo
CHAKA: An Historical Romance
A novel written in Sotho in the 1920s using the techniques of the oral tradition
Translated by F.H. Dutton
0–19–724172–7 Oxford $26.00

Donald R. Morris
THE WASHING OF THE SPEARS: The Rise and Fall of the Zulu Nation
Popular and gripping story of African empire
0–671–63108–X Simon & Schuster $21.95
0–671–62822–4 Simon & Schuster pb $13.95

E.A. Ritter
SHAKA ZULU
A rendition based on the royal Zulu account
0–14–004826–X Penguin pb $6.95

Marks's Marxist History

Even detractors admit that Shula Marks's anthologies are major contributions to mainstream South African historiography. The works listed below contain well-researched stories of conquest, power, ideology, and struggle, collected and critiqued by the editors. Many of the contributors have published longer academic works on their particular topics.

• Shula Marks & Anthony Atmore, editors
ECONOMY AND SOCIETY IN PRE-INDUSTRIAL SOUTH AFRICA
0–582–64656–1 Longman pb $12.95

• Shula Marks & Stanley Trapido, editors
THE POLITICS OF RACE, CLASS AND NATIONALISM IN TWENTIETH CENTURY SOUTH AFRICA
0–582–64490–9 Longman pb $24.95

• Heribert Adam & Kogila Moody
SOUTH AFRICA WITHOUT APARTHEID
Controversial liberal argument for a democratic "corporate federalism" compromise with Afrikaners
0–520–05769–4 California $25.00
0–06–250052–X California pb $9.95

• Cedric de Beer
THE SOUTH AFRICAN DISEASE: Apartheid Health and Health Services
South Africa stopped keeping track of black mortality when the statistics became embarrassing
0–86543–038–1 Africa World Press $19.95
0–86543–039–X Africa World Press $7.95

• Jeffrey Butler, Richard Elphick & David Welsh, editors
DEMOCRATIC LIBERALISM IN SOUTH AFRICA: Its History and Prospects
The roots of, and potential for, the nonviolent opposition
0–8195–5165–1 Wesleyan $35.00
0–8195–6197–5 Wesleyan pb $12.95

• Kevin Danaher
IN WHOSE INTEREST? A Guide to U.S.-South Africa Relations
"Succinct and crystal-clear analysis of the misadventures of US policy"—Immanuel Wallerstein
0–89758–038–9 Policy Studies pb $11.95

• Stephen Davis
APARTHEID'S REBELS: Inside South Africa's Hidden War
The military side of the fight by the African National Congress (ANC), told in even prose by a former State Department officer
0–300–03992–1 Yale pb $8.95

• William Finnegan
DATELINE SOWETO
An account of the reporters for the Johannesburg *Star* and the risks they take to report on black life in the townships
0–06–015932–4 Harper & Row $18.95

• Don Foster & Dennis Davis
DETENTION AND TORTURE IN SOUTH AFRICA: Psychological, Legal and Historical Studies
Interviews with nearly 200 survivors form the basis of this meticulous and credible report
0–312–00785–X St. Martin's $29.95

• Stanley Greenberg
LEGITIMATING THE ILLEGITIMATE: State, Markets and Resistance in South Africa
A rather academic but unmatched account of government policy, ideology, and struggles among the rulers of South Africa
0–520–06010–5 California $37.50
0–520–06011–3 California pb $12.95

• Joseph Hanlon
APARTHEID'S SECOND FRONT: South Africa's War Against Its Neighbors
A look at the rarely seen military and economic attacks since the early 1980s in Lesotho, Zimbabwe, Mozambique, Malawi, and Angola
0–14–052370–7 Penguin pb $4.95

BEGGAR YOUR NEIGHBORS
South Africa's extrusion of its conflict onto foreign soil, including first-hand reports on terrorism in Mozambique
0–253–33131–5 Indiana $35.00
0–253–20452–6 Indiana pb $12.95

• Joseph Lelyveld
MOVE YOUR SHADOW
Lelyveld served two tours of duty in South Africa for the *New York Times* and wrote this insightful and erudite work
0–8129–1237–3 Times Books $18.95

• William Minter
KING SOLOMON'S MINES REVISITED
How Western interests lock into apartheid
0–465–03723–2 Basic Books $21.95

• Roger Omond & Joseph Hanlon
THE SANCTIONS HANDBOOK: For or Against?
A fair and complete presentation of arguments
0–14–052388–X Penguin pb $6.95

• Elizabeth Schmidt
DECODING CORPORATE CAMOUFLAGE
Argues that moral business investment in South Africa is impossible
Foreword by Congressman Ronald Dellums
0–89758–022–2 Policy Studies pb $5.95

• Lyle Tatum, editor
SOUTH AFRICA: Challenge and Hope
Topical introduction to apartheid and resistance
0–8090–8750–2 Hill & Wang $15.95
0–8090–1530–7 Hill & Wang pb $7.95

• Mark A. Uhlig, editor
APARTHEID IN CRISIS: Perspectives on the Coming Battle for South Africa
A chorus of voices includes Andries Treurnicht, the Rightist "Dr. No," and Nelson Mandela, speaking from Pollsmoor prison
0–394–74455–1 Random House pb $5.95

• Donald Woods
BIKO
The book that inspired the film *Cry Freedom*
0–8050–0385–1 Henry Holt pb $4.95

SOUTH AFRICAN DISPATCHES: Letters to My Countrymen
The famed journalist's columns in prose as clear as spring water
Introduction by Alan Paton
0–8050–0783–0 Henry Holt pb $9.95

Nelson Mandela

Mary Benson
NELSON MANDELA: The Man and the Movement
Fine biography of the man whose picture cannot be printed in South Africa
Foreword by Desmond Tutu
0–393–30322–5 Norton pb $7.95

Jacques Derrida & Mustapha Tilli, editors
FOR NELSON MANDELA
Essays, poems, and tributes by Derrida, Sontag, Beckett, and others
0–8050–0581–1 Henry Holt $17.95

Nelson Mandela
THE STRUGGLE IS MY LIFE
Speeches and writings from before his imprisonment and an account of his life afterwards
0–87348–663–3 Pathfinder pb $8.95

Winnie Mandela
PART OF MY SOUL WENT WITH HIM
Her life, her cause, and moving reflections on her husband
0–393–02215–3 Norton $14.95
0–393–30290–3 Norton pb $5.95

Steve Biko

Personal Accounts

• Steve Biko
I WRITE WHAT I LIKE
The essays and letters of the black student leader. "You are either alive and proud or you are dead," wrote Biko, shortly before his death
0–06–250055–4 Harper & Row pb $8.95

• William Finnegan
CROSSING THE LINE: A Year in the Land of Apartheid
Sensitive portrayal of the African and Indian victims of apartheid
0–06–015570–1 Harper & Row $22.95
0–06–091430–0 Harper & Row pb $8.95

• Graham Leach
SOUTH AFRICA: No Easy Path to Peace
The former BBC correspondent for South Africa tracks some of the significant political events he witnessed
0–413–15330–4 Methuen pb $7.95

• Mark Mathabane
KAFFIR BOY: The True Story of a Black Youth's Coming of Age in Apartheid South Africa
0–451–15799–0 NAL pb $4.95

• James North
FREEDOM RISING: War and Peace in Southern Africa
A book about people, from one man's five-year journey through South Africa
0–02–589940–6 Macmillan $19.95
0–452–25805–7 NAL pb $8.95

• Molapatene Collins Ramusi
SOWETO, MY LOVE: A Testimony to Black Life in South Africa
A political memoir of the struggle for a free black South Africa
0–8050–0263–4 Henry Holt $22.95

Pictorials

• Omar Badsha, editor
SOUTH AFRICA: The Cordoned Heart
Photo essays by 20 prominent photographers working in South Africa
Text by Francis Wilson
Foreword by Desmond Tutu
0–393–02341–9 Norton $25.00
0–393–30335–7 Norton pb $14.95

• Peter Kallaway & Patrick Pearson
JOHANNESBURG: Images and Continuities—A History of Working-Class Life Through Pictures, 1885-1935
Fascinating archival photos with explanations
0–86975–303–7 Ohio pb $19.95

• Peter Magubane
SOWETO: The Fruit of Fear
Haunting, stark photographs of the Soweto uprising
0–8028–3631–3 Eerdmans $29.95
0–8028–0248–6 Eerdmans pb $14.95

• Gavin Younge
ART OF THE SOUTH AFRICAN TOWNSHIPS
The political struggles of South Africa told through its extraordinary black art
Foreword by Desmond Tutu
0–8478–0973–0 Rizzoli pb $17.95

The Indian Subcontinent

Following the standard practice of its time with respect to European history, the first edition of the *Oxford History of India* divided its subject into three categories: ancient (prehistoric, Vedic, Classical), medieval (Islamic), and modern (British). Although these categories are even more inappropriate for India than they are for Europe, they have been employed here to some extent because they reflect very well the relative availability of books on successive periods of Indian history. General interest surveys of ancient and classical Indian cultures are extremely hard to come by; the situation is better for the Islamic period, and there is a relative abundance of material on the British and post-Independence era.

Given such uneven distribution, the reader interested in either the full sweep of Indian history or in a detailed understanding of particular events is forced to rely on texts that are not properly considered historical. The following list, therefore, contains books on Indian religions, essays in sociology, surveys of art history, a standard work of literary criticism, and a novel—all of which provide valuable historical information.

- **A.L. Basham, editor**
  A CULTURAL HISTORY OF INDIA
  Essays on the whole range of Indian cultural history, from noted contributors
  0–19–561520–4 Oxford $29.95

- **Louis Dumont**
  HOMO HIERARCHIUS: The Caste System and Its Implications
  The most thorough and sophisticated analysis of the caste system ever written. A landmark in Indian studies and also an example of French rationalism
  Translated by Basia Gulati
  0–226–16963–4 Chicago pb $17.00

Ainslee Embree, editor
SOURCES OF INDIAN TRADITION: Volume 1
The first of two volumes of the standard, widely used compilation of primary Indian sources, newly revised and reissued. This volume covers the premodern period
0–231–06651–1 Columbia pb $17.00

Stephen Hay, editor
SOURCES OF INDIAN TRADITION: Volume 2
The second volume of the newly revised *Sources*, with much new material and short but illuminating introductions on each phase of the modern era
0–231–06415–2 Columbia pb $16.00

- **Wilhelm Halbfass**
  INDIA AND EUROPE: An Essay in Understanding
  The intellectual encounter of India and the West from pre-Alexandrian antiquity to the present. Examines India's role in European philosophical thought and the impact of the West on India
  0–88706–795–6 SUNY pb $19.95

- **J.C. Harle**
  ART AND ARCHITECTURE OF THE INDIAN SUBCONTINENT
  A thoroughgoing and enormously erudite survey of Indian art, replete with information on intellectual, cultural, and social life
  0–14–056149–8 Penguin pb $18.95

- **Vincent Smith**
  THE OXFORD HISTORY OF INDIA
  The original text of the standard history, revised and edited in places, but left largely intact. An excellent survey now in its fourth edition
  Edited by Percival Spear
  0–19–561297–3 Oxford pb $12.95

- **Romila Thapar**
  A HISTORY OF INDIA: Volume 1
  The first of a two-volume overview of Indian history, written by the foremost historian of ancient India
  0–14–020769–4 Penguin pb $6.95

- **Percival Spear**
  A HISTORY OF INDIA: Volume 2
  The second volume covers the Islamic and modern periods and is a good place for the novice to begin exploring
  0–14–020770–8 Penguin pb $6.95

- **Stanley Wolpert**
  A NEW HISTORY OF INDIA
  A highly readable account that places modern Indian developments in their historical context. An excellent starting point for readers unfamiliar with India
  0–19–505636–1 Oxford pb $29.95
  0–19–505637–X Oxford pb $14.95

Tapan Raychaudhuri & Irfan Habib
THE CAMBRIDGE ECONOMIC HISTORY OF INDIA, Volume 1: c. 1200–c. 1750
Both volumes in this survey are first-rate and highly recommended. This volume has 9 maps
0–521–22692–9 Cambridge $100.00

Dharma Kumar & Meghnad Desai
THE CAMBRIDGE ECONOMIC HISTORY OF INDIA, Volume 2: c. 1751–c. 1970
With 12 maps and 20 diagrams
0–521–22802–6 Cambridge $112.50

FROM PREHISTORIC INDIA TO THE CLASSICAL PERIODS

- **Bridget & Raymond Allchin**
  THE RISE OF CIVILIZATION IN INDIA AND PAKISTAN
  The standard historical text on pre-Aryan India, incorporating all of the current archaeological evidence
  0–521–28550–X Cambridge $21.95

- **A.K. & Nivedita Coomaraswamy**
  MYTHS OF THE HINDUS AND BUDDHISTS
  A very engaging retelling of Indian myths; co-authored by the renowned art historian, A.K. Coomaraswamy
  0–486–21759–0 Hawaii pb $6.95

- **Stephen Darian**
  THE GANGES IN MYTH AND HISTORY
  The sacred river of Indian religion and its interaction with man
  0–824–80509–7 Hawaii $12.00

- **Diana Eck**
  BANARAS: City of Light
  A beautiful book about Hinduism's holiest city
  0–691–02023–X Princeton pb $10.95

- **J.L. Jaini**
  OUTLINES OF JAINISM
  A well-written, straightforward account of one of the major offshoots of the Vedantic tradition
  0–88355–801–7 Hyperion $21.00

- **G.L. Posselh, editor**
  THE HARAPAN CIVILIZATION
  A beautifully produced book examining the first of India's urban cultures
  0–85668–211–X Humanities $45.00

- **Jean W. Sedlar**
  INDIA AND THE GREEK WORLD: A Study in the Transmission of Culture
  An enormously erudite and suggestive study of an elusive subject
  0–8476–6173–3 Rowman & Littlefield $35.00

- **Romila Thapar**
  FROM LINEAGE TO STATE: Social Formations of the Mid-First Millennium B.C. in the Ganges Valley
  An ingenious discussion of the formation of classical Indian society, using a wide variety of sources
  0–19–561394–5 Oxford $24.95

- **Robert C. Zaehner**
  HINDUISM
  The best available single-volume treatment of the subject
  0–19–888012–X Oxford pb $8.95

☞ **TO ORDER NEW BOOKS NOT YET LISTED, ASK YOUR BOOKSELLER OR CALL 1-800-882-8770**

Harvest in 16th-century India, from The Structures of Everyday Life *by Fernand Braudel (Harper & Row)*

THE ISLAMIC PERIOD

- **Aziz Ahmad**
  AN INTELLECTUAL HISTORY OF ISLAMIC INDIA
  A survey of the subject designed to buttress the separatist argument that led to the formation of Pakistan
  0–85224–274–3 Columbia pb $10.00

- **Richard Eaton**
  THE SUFIS OF BIJAPUR, 1300-1700: The Social Roles of Sufis in Medieval India
  A highly praised account of religious and political life in the pre-Mughal kingdoms of the Deccan
  0–691–03110–X Princeton $44.50

- **Ainslee Embree, editor**
  ALBERUNI'S INDIA
  The first and still the best traveller's account of India, written in the 11th century by Alberuni, the great Persian astronomer and mathematician attached as a chronicler to the Indian campaigns of Mahmud of Ghazni
  0–393–00568–2 Norton pb $2.95

- **H.A.R. Gibb**
  MOHAMMEDANISM: A Historical Survey
  A short, very useful introduction to Islamic history
  0–19–500245–8 Oxford pb $6.95

- **Rumer Godden**
  GULBADAN: Portrait of a Rose Princess at the Mughal Court
  A biography of a Mughal princess by the distinguished novelist. Includes beautiful reproductions of Mughal miniatures
  0–670–35756–1 Viking $14.95

- **Ifran Habib**
  AN ATLAS OF THE MUGHAL EMPIRE
  A prime source of statistics and geographical information about one of the most powerful empires the world has ever known
  0–19–560379–6 Oxford $75.00

- **S.M. Ikram**
  A HISTORY OF MUSLIM CIVILIZATION IN INDIA AND PAKISTAN
  An admirably balanced narrative survey of Islam in India, written by one of the foremost intellectuals of Pakistan
  0–317–46089–7 Kazi $25.00

- **Stephen Charles Neill**
  A HISTORY OF CHRISTIANITY IN INDIA
  Although peripheral to the major developments of Indian history, the arrival of Christianity in India is contemporaneous with the writing of the first Gospels. These two volumes explore this fascinating subject in great depth

  Volume 1: The Beginnings to 1707
  0–521–24351–3 Cambridge $90.00

  Volume 2: 1707-1858
  0–521–30376–1 Cambridge $90.00

Raghu & Usha Rai
TAJ MAHAL
Perhaps the most opulent and splendid of the Mughal Empire's legacies, the Taj Mahal in Agra is a center of Muslim worship and India's most famous site. This handsome picture book features a text by Usha Rai, a feature writer for *The Times of India*, and photographs by Raghu Rai, a regular contributor to *National Geographic*
0–86565–078–0 Vendome $65.00

- **Khushwant Singh**
  A HISTORY OF THE SIKHS
  An excellent, nonacademic work by the greatest Sikh writer of this century
  0–691–00805–1 Princeton (set) pb $27.00

  Volume 1
  0–691–00803–5 Princeton pb $14.50

  Volume 2
  0–691–00804–3 Princeton pb $14.50

THE BRITISH PERIOD

The British period has an enormous literature associated with it. The following list provides representative samples of this writing; it is not meant to be exhaustive. Readers interested in exploring further should consult the excellent bibliographies in the surveys listed above.

- **C.A. Bayly**
  INDIAN SOCIETY AND THE MAKING OF THE BRITISH EMPIRE
  One of the best contemporary historians of India examines the internal forces that made British rule possible
  0–521–25092–7 Cambridge $29.95

- **Philip Davies**
  SPLENDOR OF THE RAJ: British Architecture in India, 1660-1947
  0–14–009247–1 Penguin pb $10.95

- **Henry Dodwell**
  DUPLEIX AND CLIVE: Beginning of Empire
  The genesis of the divide-and-rule policy of British expansion placed in the context of both Indian political environments and the worldwide rivalry between England and France
  0–7146–1125–5 Biblio $29.50

- **Ranajit Guha**
  ELEMENTARY ASPECTS OF PEASANT INSURGENCY IN COLONIAL INDIA
  The work of a major historian on the subject
  0–19–561517–4 Oxford $24.95

- **Christopher Hibbert**
  THE GREAT MUTINY: India 1857
  Popular reading by the author of *The Days of the French Revolution*
  0–14–004752–2 Penguin pb $7.95

- **Francis Ingall**
  THE LAST OF THE BENGAL LANCERS
  The last days of the Raj—the 1930s and '40s—through the memoirs of a brigadier in the sixth Duke of Connaught's Own Bengal Lancers
  0–89141–203–4 Presidio $17.95

- **Philip Mason**
  THE MEN WHO RULE INDIA
  A widely read and widely praised book about the powers and personalities behind British expansion and administration
  0–393–01946–2 Norton pb $27.50

- **James Mill**
  THE HISTORY OF BRITISH INDIA
  The great English utilitarian's account of the history of the East India company, written while he was employed as that organization's secretary—a post later held by his son, John Stuart Mill
  Edited by William Thomas
  0–226–52555–4 Chicago $35.00

★ **FOR COMPLETE ORDERING INFORMATION, SEE PAGE 1**

From Banaras: City of Light *by Diana L. Eck* (*Princeton*)

• Geoffrey Moorhouse

INDIA BRITANNICA
A celebration of the British Empire in
India. Good light reading
0–06–015115–3 Harper & Row $22.95

• James Morris

**HEAVEN'S COMMAND: An Imperial
Progress**
The story of various military campaigns by
a well-known journalist. The chapters on
the Indian Rebellion of 1857 are quite
enjoyable
0–15–640006–5 HBJ pb $10.95

• Percival Spear

**THE OXFORD HISTORY OF MODERN
INDIA: 1749-1975**
An elegantly written but conventional
account that tends to avoid the knottier
problems of British rule
0–472–07141–6 Michigan $24.95

• Eric Stokes & C.A. Bayly

**THE PEASANT ARMED: The Indian
Revolt of 1857**
A fresh and convincing account of the
causes and consequences of the most
violent event of the British period
0–19–821570–3 Oxford $55.00

• Raleigh Trevelyan

**THE GOLDEN ORIOLE: A 200-Year
History of an English Family in India**
0–670–81184–X Viking $24.95

• Pratapaditya Pal & Vidya Dehejia

**FROM MERCHANTS TO EMPERORS:
British Artists and India, 1757-1930**
0–8014–9386–2 Cornell pb $29.95

• Stanley Wolpert

**TILAK AND GOKHALE: Revolution and
Reform in the Making of Modern India**
A study of the forefathers of the Indian
Independence movement, written in
Wolpert's customarily lucid prose
0–520–03339–6 California $38.50

Women of the Raj

Marian Fowler

**BELOW THE PEACOCK FAN: First
Ladies of the Raj**
Four women removed from the ease of
Victorian England to the turbulence of
India in the 19th century: Emily Eden,
Charlotte Canning, Edith Lytton, and
Mary Curzon. "Witty, pungent, boldly
irreverent and totally absorbing"—
London Free Press
0–670–80748–6 Viking $19.95
0–14–008233–6 Penguin pb $7.95

Margaret MacMillan

WOMEN OF THE RAJ
0–500–01420–5 Thames & Hudson $17.95

NATIONALISM AND INDEPENDENCE

General Histories

• Chester Bowles

**THE VIEW FROM NEW DELHI: Selected
Speeches and Writings**
Materials drawn from the American
diplomat's tenures as Ambassador to India
in the Truman, Kennedy, and Johnson
administrations
0–300–01233–0 Yale $25.00

• Judith M. Brown

**MODERN INDIA: The Origins of a South
Asian Democracy**
A highly intelligent and valuable survey of
the modern era
0–19–913124–4 Oxford $49.95
0–19–822859–7 Oxford pb $14.95

• Larry Collins & Dominique LaPierre

FREEDOM AT MIDNIGHT
A journalistic account of Partition by the
authors of *Is Paris Burning?*, based on
extensive interviews with the last viceroy,
Lord Louis Mountbatten
0–380–00693–6 Avon pb $5.95

• Sarvepalli Gopal

JAWAHARLAL NEHRU: A Biography
The authorized biography of the
nationalist leader and first prime minister
of India

Volume 1
0–674–47310–8 Harvard $29.50

Volume 2
0–674–47311–6 Harvard $27.00

Volume 3
0–674–47312–4 Harvard $24.50

• Henry D. Hodson

**THE GREAT DIVIDE: Britain—India—
Pakistan**
The story of the Partition of British India
told from the point of view of a British
liberal who was given extensive access to
many of the major participants
0–19–577340–3 Oxford $32.00

• Stanley Kochanek

**THE CONGRESS PARTY OF INDIA: The
Dynamics of a One-Party Democracy**
The political structure of independent
India
0–691–03013–8 Princeton $47.50

• Ved Mehta

**A FAMILY AFFAIR: India under Three
Prime Ministers**
Mehta brings his characteristic insight to
this examination of India's ruling dynasty
0–19–503118–0 Oxford $22.95

• Anil Seal

**THE EMERGENCE OF INDIAN
NATIONALISM**
A revisionist account, influenced largely by
the Namierite school of British history
0–521–09652–9 Cambridge $15.95

• Milton Singer

**WHEN A GREAT TRADITION
MODERNIZES**
An examination of the continuities and
changes within Indian society
0–226–76102–9 Chicago $21.00

• Khushwant Singh

TRAIN TO PAKISTAN
A novel that examines the effects of
Partition on a small Punjabi village. A
classic in the literature
0–8021–5023–3 Grove pb $5.95

Gandhi

Mohandas K. Gandhi

**AUTOBIOGRAPHY: The Story of My
Experiments With Truth**
A 20th-century classic by any standard
0–486–24593–4 Dover pb $7.95

THE ESSENTIAL GANDHI
A well-chosen selection of Gandhi's
writings
Edited by Louis Fischer
0–394–71466–0 Random House pb $5.95

➤ **FOR OVERSEAS ORDERING INFORMATION, SEE PAGE 1**

Erik Erikson

GANDHI'S TRUTH: On the Origins of a Militant Nonviolence
The famous psychoanalytic approach to Gandhi's career
0–393–00741–3 Norton pb $5.95

Louis Fischer

THE LIFE OF MAHATMA GANDHI
A biography that concerns itself more with Gandhi's spiritual achievements than with his political achievements
0–06–091038–0 Harper & Row pb $11.95

Ved Mehta

MAHATMA GANDHI AND HIS DISCIPLES
A neutral, somewhat skeptical account of Gandhi and the civil disobedience movement
0–14–004571–6 Penguin pb $6.95

Current Affairs

• Paul Brass & Marcus Franda, editors
RADICAL POLITICS IN SOUTH ASIA
An examination of left-wing politics in India, Pakistan, Bangladesh, and Sri Lanka
0–262–02099–8 MIT $32.50

• Rolf Caseen
INDIA: Population, Economy, Society
The country's population problem and its impact on the society
0–8419–0648–3 Holmes & Meier pb $19.50

• Pranay Gupte
VENGEANCE: India After the Assassination of Indira Gandhi
Indira Ghandi was murdered in 1984 by two of her security guards who acted in revenge for her part in the storming of the Golden Temple in Amritsar, a Sikh shrine. Part political travelogue and part autobiography, Gupte's book is a detailed portrait of Indians and India
0–393–02230–7 Norton pb $3.95

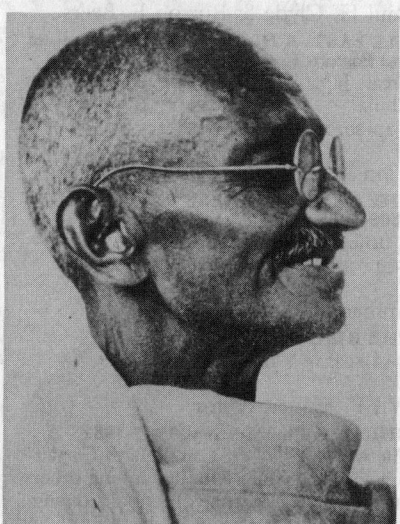

Mahatma Gandhi

• V.S. Naipaul
INDIA: A Wounded Civilization
0–394–72463–1 Random House pb $4.95

• Baldey Nayar
MINORITY POLITICS IN THE PUNJAB
Background to the current violence in the Punjab
0–691–03036–7 Princeton $40.00

PAKISTAN

Carved out of the northwestern provinces of the Indian subcontinent, the predominantly Muslim state of Pakistan came into existence in 1947. Since independence, political parties have functioned only intermittently and martial law has been periodically imposed, keeping Pakistan always one step away from an established democracy.

Closely tied with the United States, Pakistan is often perceived as a buffer against communism, and was effectively used to channel arms to the Afghan rebels against the Soviet-backed Kabul regime.

• Benazir Bhutto
DAUGHTER OF DESTINY: An Autobiography
Autobiography of the first woman elected prime minister of a Muslim nation
0–671–66983–4 Simon & Schuster $19.95

• S.M. Ikram
A HISTORY OF MUSLIM CIVILIZATION IN INDIA AND PAKISTAN
By one of the leading intellectuals of modern Pakistan
0–317–46089–7 Kazi $25.00

• S.F. Mahmud
A CONCISE HISTORY OF INDO-PAKISTAN
0–19–577385–3 Oxford pb $10.95

• David G. Mandelbaum
WOMEN'S SECLUSION AND MEN'S HONOR: Sex Roles in North India, Bangladesh, and Pakistan
0–8165–1043–1 Arizona $21.95

• Sara Suleri
MEATLESS DAYS
0–226–77980–7 Chicago $17.95

• Stanley Wolpert
JINNAH OF PAKISTAN: A Life
A succinct, detailed, and highly readable account of Jinnah the politician, and of the creation of Pakistan
0–19–503412–0 Oxford $27.95

BANGLADESH

The history of Bangladesh is linked to its larger neighbor, India. In the partition of the subcontinent in 1947, the 90 percent Muslim province of East Bengal became East Pakistan. It was not until 1971 that Bangladesh, with the help of India, emerged as an independent nation.

Modern Bangladesh has been plagued by a series of coups and countercoups, with parliamentary democracy being periodically suspended and martial law imposed.

• Craig Baxter
BANGLADESH: A New Nation in an Old Setting
Part of the Profiles on Nations of Contemporary Asia series
0–86531–630–9 Westview $30.50

• Marcus Franda
BANGLADESH: The First Decade
0–8364–0891–8 South Asia $24.00

AFGHANISTAN

The mountainous terrain of the Himalayan foothills has helped to preserve the independence of the Islamic population (15,000,000 at last count) for hundreds of years. For the British Empire it was the turbulent North-West frontier. The Soviet Union is the most recent expansionist power to retreat before the hardiness and pugnacity of the inhabitants.

• Raja Anwar
THE TRAGEDY OF AFGHANISTAN: A First-Hand Account
Conversations in an Afghan prison with leaders of both factions of Afghan communism provide the basis of this readable analysis
Translated by Khalid Hasan
0–86091–208–6 Verso $29.95

• Henry S. Bradsher
AFGHANISTAN AND THE SOVIET UNION
0–8223–0556–9 Duke $37.50
0–8223–0690–5 Duke pb $12.95

• Sandy Gall
BEHIND RUSSIAN LINES: An Afghan Journal
0–312–07260–0 St. Martin's $22.50

• Edward Girardet
AFGHANISTAN: The Soviet War
0–312–00923–2 St. Martin's $25.00

• Jan Goodwin
CAUGHT IN THE CROSSFIRE
Disguised as a man, this *Ladies Home Journal* editor traveled in secret behind enemy lines to observe Afghan rebels in their fight against Soviet troops
0–525–24493–X Dutton $18.95

• Anthony Hyman
AFGHANISTAN UNDER SOVIET DOMINATION, 1964-1981
0–312–00927–5 St. Martin's $29.95

• Jeri Laber & Barnett Rubin
A NATION IS DYING: Afghanistan Under the Soviets
0–8101–0772–4 Northwestern pb $10.95

Head of a barbarian, Afghanistan, c. 3rd-4th century (Musée Guimet)

- Doris Lessing
THE WIND BLOWS AWAY OUR WORDS
The novelist's first-hand account of the Afghan resistance
0–394–75504–9 Random House pb $5.95

- Nancy & Richard Newell
THE STRUGGLE FOR AFGHANISTAN
0–8014–9236–X Cornell pb $10.95

- Olivier Roy
ISLAM AND RESISTANCE IN AFGHANISTAN
0–521–32833–0 Cambridge $24.95

Sri Lanka

After nearly four and a half decades of foreign domination, beginning with the Portuguese and followed by the Dutch and the British, Sri Lanka (formerly Ceylon) became an independent state in 1948.

Located off the southern tip of India, the island enjoyed uninterrupted progress until recently. The minority (Hindu) Tamil population (20 percent) claims that its demands for equal opportunies in the (Buddhist) Sinhalese-dominated state have not been dealt with fairly. Since 1983, the country has been torn by civil war, and an actual partition of the island looms as a far from distant possiblity.

- Pranay Gupte
SRI LANKA: Unrest in Paradise
0–87131–529–7 Evans $17.95

- Nigel Palmer
SRI LANKA
0–500–24120–1 Thames & Hudson $29.95

- K.M. De Silva
A HISTORY OF SRI LANKA
0–520–04320–0 California $48.00

China

GENERAL HISTORIES

- Arthur Cotterell
CHINA: A Concise Cultural History
0–452–00950–2 NAL pb $10.95

- Molly Coye & Jon Livingston, editors
CHINA: Yesterday, and Today
0–553–23876–0 Bantam pb $5.95

- John K. Fairbank & Edwin O. Reischauer
EAST ASIA: Tradition and Transformation
This book remains the most widely used introduction to the history and culture of East Asia
0–395–25812–X Houghton Mifflin $45.50

- Jacques Gernet
A HISTORY OF CHINESE CIVILIZATION
An elegantly written one-volume history, which defines the political, social, and intellectual trends from China's past and present
0–521–24130–8 Cambridge $54.50
0–521–31647–2 Cambridge pb $19.95

- Madge Huntington
A TRAVELLER'S GUIDE TO CHINESE HISTORY
A popular account aimed at the general reader
0–8050–0097–6 Henry Holt pb $11.95

- Conrad Schirokauer
A BRIEF HISTORY OF CHINESE AND JAPANESE CIVILIZATIONS
A sweeping bird's-eye view of the cultural and political history of the two great Asian powers
0–15–505569–0 HBJ pb $31.50

- Robert Temple
THE GENIUS OF CHINA: 3000 Years of Science, Discovery, and Invention
A captivating tour through China's long history of scientific achievement; beautifully illustrated with paintings, photos, and diagrams
0–671–67407–2 Simon & Schuster pb $14.95

- Lyman P. Van Slyke
YANGTZE: Nature, History, and the River
The great river that flows through Chinese history yields up its natural and cultural secrets in this multi-strand narrative
0–201–08894–0 Addison-Wesley $14.95

Imperial China

- Rene Grousset
THE RISE AND SPLENDOUR OF THE CHINESE EMPIRE
The cultural peaks and dominant personalities of the great dynasties
0–520–00525–2 California pb $12.95

A charioteer of the Qin dynasty (221-206 BC), from The Great Bronze Age of China edited by Wen Fong (Knopf/Metropolitan Museum)

- Charles Hucker
CHINA TO 1850: A Short History
Brisk and reliable introduction to the pre-modern era
0–8047–0957–2 Stanford $15.00
0–8047–0958–0 Stanford pb $6.95

Modern China

- Marc Blecher
CHINA: Politics, Economics and Society
0–931477–81–6 Lynne Rienner pb $12.95

- Jean Chesneaux
CHINA: The People's Republic, 1949-1976
Concentrates on the main problems of the People's Republic—Soviet influence, technological inferiority, the new bureaucracy, and conservative resistance
0–394–73623–0 Pantheon pb $5.95

- Paul H. Clyde & Burton F. Beers
FAR EAST: A History of Western Impacts and Eastern Responses (1830-1975)
Treats Japan and Southeast Asia as well as China
0–13–302968–9 Prentice-Hall $48.00

- John K. Fairbank
THE GREAT CHINESE REVOLUTION: 1800-1985
A brilliant recent summary
0–317–53310–X Harper & Row $20.95

- Immanuel Hsu
THE RISE OF MODERN CHINA
0–19–503218–7 Oxford $32.00

- W.J.F. Jenner, editor
CHINA: A Photohistory, 1937-1987
The work of Robert Capa, Henri Cartier-Bresson, and Marc Riboud, among others, makes up an exquisite collection showing the idiosyncratic face of China at work and play
Introduction by Jonathan D. Spence
0–394–57281–5 Pantheon $34.95

• Maurice Meisner
MAO'S CHINA AND AFTER
The most comprehensive of the new texts, and the strongest and most provocative in its treatment of politics and ideology
0–02–920870–X Free Press $24.95
0–02–920880–7 Free Press pb $12.95

• Mark Selden, editor
THE PEOPLE'S REPUBLIC OF CHINA: A Documentary History of Revolutionary Change
Traces the shifting contours of China's political economy
0–85345–532–5 Monthly Review pb $15.00

• Jonathan D. Spence
THE GATE OF HEAVENLY PEACE: The Chinese and Their Revolution, 1895-1980
A century of change, through portraits of revolutionary leaders. "A magical symphony that tells us as no conventional history could of the agony of a nation in awesome labor"—Harrison E. Salisbury
0–14–006279–3 Penguin pb $8.95

Reference

• Caroline Blunden & Mark Elvin
CULTURAL ATLAS OF CHINA
The major changes over time with a combination of maps and compact discussion
0–87196–132–6 Facts On File $40.00

• Brian Hook, editor
THE CAMBRIDGE ENCYCLOPEDIA OF CHINA
Exhaustive reference work brings a sense of fun to its subject
0–521–23099–3 Cambridge $42.50

• Hugh B. O'Neill
COMPANION TO CHINESE HISTORY
Handy reference combining a who's who, a gazetteer, a chronology, and a mini-atlas
0–8160–1825–1 Facts On File pb $14.95

Han dynasty funerary sculpture

• The Times (London)
THE TIMES ATLAS OF CHINA
This up-to-date set of maps is thorough, reliable and informative
0–7230–0118–9 Van Nostrand $20.95

The Cambridge History of China

The Cambridge History of China spans the course of Chinese history and provides a scholarly treatment with exhaustive references. New volumes will appear annually.
THE CAMBRIDGE HISTORY OF CHINA

Volume 1: The Ch'in and Han Empires, 221 BC-220 AD
Edited by Denis Twitchett & Michael Loewe
0–521–24327–0 Cambridge $120.00

Volume 3: Sui and T'ang China, 589-906, Part 1
Edited by Denis Twitchett
0–521–21446–7 Cambridge $130.00

Volume 7: Ming China, 1368-1644, Part 2
Edited by Denis Twitchett & Frederick W. Mote
0–521–24332–7 Cambridge $110.00

Volume 10: Late Ch'ing 1800-1911, Part 1
Edited by John K. Fairbank
0–521–21447–5 Cambridge $120.00

Volume 11: Late Ch'ing 1800-1911, Part 2
Edited by John K. Fairbank
0–521–22029–7 Cambridge $120.00

Volume 12: Republican China 1912-1949, Part 1
Edited by John K. Fairbank
0–521–23541–3 Cambridge $137.50

Volume 13: Republican China 1912-1949, Part 2
Edited by John K. Fairbank & Albert Feurwerker
0–521–24338–6 Cambridge $115.00

Volume 14: The People's Republic of China, 1949-1976
Edited by Roderick MacFarquhar & John K. Fairbank
0–521–24336–X Cambridge $100.00

ARCHAEOLOGY AND EARLY CHINESE CIVILIZATION

• Chang Kwang-chih
THE ARCHAEOLOGY OF ANCIENT CHINA
The 3000-year-old Shang dynasty is accessible through the remains of its strangely-wrought bronzes and its talismanic bones. A masterful study
0–300–03782–1 Yale $52.00
0–300–03784–8 Yale pb $17.95

• Arthur Cotterell
THE FIRST EMPEROR OF CHINA: The Story Behind the Terracotta Army of Mount Li
The discovery of thousands of life-size terracotta soldiers guarding the grave of Ch'in-shih Huang-ti, first uncovered in 1974, revealed rows of infantry, chariots, and cavalry. This volume explores the

historical impact of the emperor and examines the excavated figures in detail
0–14–011567–6 Penguin pb $12.95

• David Keightley, editor
THE ORIGINS OF CHINESE CIVILIZATION
Wide-ranging essays by leading archaeologists and historians reflecting the current state of archaeology
0–520–04230–1 California pb $18.95

• Michael Loewe
EVERYDAY LIFE IN EARLY IMPERIAL CHINA
Engaging portrait of manners in the Han dynasty (206 BC-AD 221) when the patterns were being set for the political, literary, and artistic character of China
0–88029–177–X Dorset $16.95

• Zewen Luo & others
THE GREAT WALL OF CHINA: In History and Legend
A pioneering joint study by Chinese and Western scholars of the only man-made monument visible from the moon
0–8351–1454–6 China Books pb $12.95

• Zhongshu Wang
HAN CIVILIZATION
An archaeological survey
0–300–02723–0 Yale $50.00

• Burton Watson, translator
COURTIER AND COMMONER IN ANCIENT CHINA: Selections from the History of Former Han by Pan Ku
An early Chinese history, demonstrating the richness of the written historical tradition
0–231–08354–8 Columbia pb $15.00

RECORDS OF THE HISTORIAN
Selections from Ssu-ma Ch'ien's *Shih Chi*, one of the great early Chinese histories on the founding of the Han dynasty
0–231–03321–4 Columbia pb $17.50

SELECTIONS FROM THE TSO CHUAN: China's Oldest Narrative History
A literary and historical masterpiece of the 3rd century BC
0–231–06714–3 Columbia $32.50

TOPICS IN IMPERIAL CIVILIZATION

Dynastic Politics

• John Chaffee
THE THORNY GATES OF LEARNING IN SUNG CHINA
The stability and conservatism of Chinese government was achieved by the Confucian ideal of a highly-developed bureaucracy. Chaffee focuses on its effectiveness in the Sung dynasty
0–521–30207–2 Cambridge $44.50

• Patricia Ebrey, editor
CHINESE CIVILIZATION AND SOCIETY: A Sourcebook
The power of the oligarchic families suppressed under the Han empire revived during the Period of Division
0–02–908760–0 Free Press $19.95

• Ho Ping-ti
THE LADDER OF SUCCESS IN IMPERIAL CHINA: Aspects of Social Mobility, 1368-1911
More than 35,000 case histories from the Imperial archives went into this picture of the struggle for personal improvement during the Ming and Ch'ing dynasties
0–231–05161–1 Columbia pb $16.00

• Charles Hucker
THE CHINESE STATE IN MING TIMES
0–8165–0033–2 Stanford pb $3.50

• Franz Michael
THE ORIGIN OF MANCHU RULE IN CHINA
The last imperial dynasty (the Ch'ing, 1644-1911), resulted from the seizure of the throne by an ethnic minority from the northern Chinese border
0–374–95605–7 Hippocrene $16.00

• Ichisadu Miyazaki
CHINA'S EXAMINATION HELL: The Civil Service Examination of Imperial China
For two millennia, the bureaucracy was the only outlet for rising talent. This book details types of questions from the ferocious exams, the psychological and financial burdens on the students, and such problems as nepotism and cheating
0–300–02639–0 Yale pb $8.95

• Frederic Wakeman
THE GREAT ENTERPRISE: The Manchu Reconstruction of Imperial Order in 17th Century China
Winner of the Bancroft Prize; a 2-volume work
0–520–04804–0 California (set) $75.00

• Karl Wittfogel
ORIENTAL DESPOTISM: A Comparative Study of Total Power
A controversial argument that the bureaucratic apparatus and centralized state arose from the need to control water resources
0–394–74701–1 Random House pb $8.95

• Arthur Wright & Denis Twitchett, editors
PERSPECTIVES ON THE T'ANG
Informed entrée to the world of T'ang institutional and economic history
0–300–02674–9 Yale pb $14.95

Biographies and Memoirs

• Marco Polo
THE TRAVELS OF MARCO POLO
The Italian trader who followed the Silk Road opened by the Mongol invasion and became the adviser of Khubilai Khan

dictated his adventures in a Venetian prison
Translated by Ronald Latham
0–14–044057–7 Penguin pb $4.95

• Morris Rossabi
KHUBILAI KHAN: His Life and Time
The first and greatest of the Mongol rulers of China. He sent letters to the pope through Marco Polo, but burned the Taoist sacred books, and installed ignorant Mongol soldiers over mandarin administrators
0–520–05913–1 California $29.95

• Jonathan D. Spence
EMPEROR OF CHINA: Self-Portrait of K'ang-hsi
Selections from the writings of one of the great emperors, a contemporary of Louis XIV and Peter the Great. His border treaty with Russia was the first ever between China and a western power
0–679–72074–X Random House pb $18.95

• Richard Strassberg
THE WORLD OF K'UNG SHANG-JEN: A Man of Letters in Early Ch'ing China
The world of a Confucian scholar/official
Introduction by Cyril Birch
0–231–05530–7 Columbia $39.00

Chinese Thought

▶ **See also Asian Religion and Philosophy**

• Joseph Levenson
CONFUCIAN CHINA AND ITS MODERN FATE: A Trilogy
Studies the continuity of the classical dilemmas of Chinese history—the intellectual and ethical tradition, and the tensions between the monarchy and the bureaucracy
0–520–00736–0 California $40.00
0–520–00737–9 California pb $16.95

• Daniel C. Overmyer
RELIGIONS OF CHINA
A concise and agreeable sketch of the interaction of the three vibrant ways of thought—Confucian, Taoist and Buddhist—of one of the oldest traditions
0–06–066401–0 Harper & Row pb $47.95

• Benjamin Schwartz
THE WORLD OF THOUGHT IN ANCIENT CHINA
The most important recent study investigates the thinkers—including Confucius—of the golden age of Chinese thought between the 6th and 3rd centuries BC
0–674–96190–0 Harvard $29.50

• Max Weber
THE RELIGION OF CHINA: Confucianism and Taoism
How institutions founded on ethical systems affect the organization of people within the society
0–02–934440–9 Free Press $19.95

• Arthur Wright
BUDDHISM IN CHINESE HISTORY
Traces the rise of an imported religion that attained strength enough to challenge the Confucian orthodoxy for two millennia
0–8047–0548–8 Stanford pb $6.95
CONFUCIANISM AND CHINESE CIVILIZATION
The system of moral order that restored Chinese society again and again to long periods of stability and creative achievement
0–8047–0891–6 Stanford pb $10.95

Culture, Society, and Economy

• Chao Kang
MAN AND LAND IN CHINESE HISTORY: An Economic Analysis
Agriculture from ancient to modern times
0–8047–1271–9 Stanford $35.00

• Mark Elvin
PATTERN OF THE CHINESE PAST: A Social and Economic Interpretation
A controversial interpretation of China's longterm development trajectory
0–8047–0826–6 Stanford $35.00
0–8047–0876–2 Stanford pb $10.95

Jacques Gernet
DAILY LIFE IN CHINA ON THE EVE OF THE MONGOL INVASION, 1250-1276
A fascinating account of Chinese customs, beliefs, institutions, and the splendid lifestyle of Hangchow, the capital of the doomed Sung dynasty
0–8047–0720–0 Stanford pb $7.95

• Ray Huang
1587, A YEAR OF NO SIGNIFICANCE: The Ming Dynasty in Decline
"Cleverly constructed and deliberately paradoxical. If 1587 is of no significance in the larger view, it is nevertheless full of incident, and each incident carries promise of future drama"—Jonathan D. Spence
0–300–02884–9 Yale pb $11.95

• Li Chu-tsing, editor
THE CHINESE SCHOLAR'S STUDIO: Artistic Life in the Late Ming Period
The social and political context in which the Ming painters worked
0–500–01423–X Thames & Hudson $45.00

• Susan Naquin & Evelyn S. Rawski
CHINESE SOCIETY IN THE EIGHTEENTH CENTURY
"[An] interesting and well-informed survey of China between about 1680 and 1820"—W.J.F. Jenner, *Asian Affairs*
0–300–03848–8 Yale $30.00
0–300–04602–X Yale pb $12.95

• Evelyn S. Rawski
EDUCATION AND POPULAR LITERACY IN CH'ING CHINA
0–472–08753–3 Michigan $16.50

A Chinese mandarin, 18th century, from The Structures of Everyday Life *by Fernand Braudel (Harper & Row)*

- Madeleine Zelin

THE MAGISTRATE'S TALE: Rationalizing Fiscal Reform in Eighteenth Century Ch'ing China
A lucid explanation of Ch'ing economy and finance
0–520–04930–6 California $42.00

China and the West

Michel Beurdley
GIUSEPPE CASTIGLIONE: A Jesuit Painter at the Court of the Chinese Emperors
Father Castiglione painted landscapes, portraits, and interiors to embellish the Italianate palaces of the Ch'ing emperor, Ch'ien-lung
0–8048–0987–9 Tuttle $25.00

George Dunne
GENERATION OF GIANTS: The Story of the Jesuits in China in the Last Days of the Ming Dynasty
French Jesuit missionaries in the 17th and 18th centuries introduced the latest European developments in astronomy, mathematics and cartography to the Chinese court
0–268–00109–X Notre Dame $24.95

Jacques Gernet
CHINA AND THE CHRISTIAN IMPACT: A Conflict of Cultures
The theological concepts with which the Jesuits attempted to supplant traditional Chinese beliefs
0–521–31319–8 Cambridge pb $19.95

Jonathan D. Spence
THE MEMORY PALACE OF MATTEO RICCI
"Bodhisattva" Ricci was the first Jesuit to realize that the Chinese literati could be reached by introducing the arts and sciences of Europe
0–670–46830–4 Viking $19.95
0–14–008098–8 Penguin pb $7.95

THE QUESTION OF HU
The experiences of a Chinese exile in early 18th-century France
0–394–57190–8 Knopf $18.95

TO CHANGE CHINA: Western Advisors in China, 1620-1960
0–14–005528–2 Penguin pb $7.95

THE END OF IMPERIAL POWER

So remote were Chinese perceptions of the West that in less than 50 years, between the embassy of Lord MacCartney in 1793 and the outbreak of the Opium War in 1839, Britain went from being "a small barbarian island where the women wear their hair loose" to being a dominant power in China. The Chinese were never to catch up. The consequences were futile popular rebellions against the encroachments of 19th-century imperialism and the eventual collapse of the Ch'ing dynasty in 1911. After the failure of the Republic to control the feuding warlords, whatever stability Chiang Kai-shek might have imposed was destroyed by the Japanese invasion of 1932.

- Guy Alitto

THE LAST CONFUCIAN: Liang Shu-ming and the Chinese Dilemma of Modernity
Presents the conservative thinker as an opponent of the alienation of technological society
0–520–05318–4 California pb $12.95

- Jerome Ch'en

CHINA AND THE WEST: Society and Culture, 1815-1937
The story of China's desperate attempts to assimilate and resist western influences backed by irresistible firepower
0–253–12032–2 Indiana $25.00

- Jean Chesneaux, editor

POPULAR MOVEMENTS AND SECRET SOCIETIES IN CHINA, 1840-1950
Runaway inflation, government corruption, and foreign invasion created huge popular uprisings with messianic overtones throughout the 19th century
0–8047–0790–1 Stanford $35.00

- Joseph W. Esherik

THE ORIGINS OF THE BOXER UPRISING
The revolt against European imperialism was not inspired by antagonism to the dynasty but by resentment of alien

influence. Winner of the John K. Fairbank Prize in East Asian History
0–520–06459–3 California pb $14.95

- Peter Fay

THE OPIUM WAR: 1840-1842
"Gunboat diplomacy" solved the problem of Britain's trade deficit with China by compelling the Peking government to accept Indian opium in exchange for Chinese products
0–393–00823–1 Norton pb $9.95

- Peter Fleming

THE SIEGE AT PEKING
A sympathetic but basically western account of the Boxer uprising that pinned Europeans in their embassies for almost two months in 1900
0–19–583735–5 Oxford pb $9.95

- Christopher Hibbert

THE DRAGON WAKES: China and the West, 1793-1911
The clash of two proud and alien civilizations; by the popular author of *The English: A Social History, 1066-1945*
0–14–006646–2 Penguin pb $8.95

- David Johnson & others

POPULAR CULTURE IN LATE IMPERIAL CHINA
0–520–06172–1 California pb $12.95

- Philip Kuhn

REBELLION AND ITS ENEMIES IN LATE IMPERIAL CHINA: Militarization and Social Structure, 1796-1864
The gradual erosion of central power led to the temporary success of the T'ai P'ing rebellion whose motives ranged from mystical to social reformist. It prohibited drugs and alcohol, and asserted equality of the sexes
0–674–74954–5 Harvard pb $9.95

- Elizabeth Perry

REBELS AND REVOLUTIONARIES IN NORTH CHINA, 1845-1945
A study of three rebellions, in the area from which Mao marched on Peking, shows the importance of topography and peasant support for guerrilla movements
0–8047–1175–5 Stanford pb $10.95

- Eva Jane Price

CHINA JOURNAL, 1889-1900: An American Missionary Family During the Boxer Rebellion
Exhumed after 100 years from an attic in Iowa, these letters and journals by the wife of an American missionary show the arduous but joyful process of bridging two different cultures
Notes & annotations by Robert H. Felsing
Foreword by Harrison E. Salisbury
0–684–18951–8 Scribners $22.50

- Frederic Wakeman

THE FALL OF IMPERIAL CHINA
Combines a description of the cycle of the dynasties with a history of the decline and fall of the Ch'ing under European pressure
0–02–933690–2 Free Press $19.95

• Arthur Waley
THE OPIUM WAR THROUGH CHINESE EYES
These superbly translated diaries, autobiographies, and confessions of the Chinese participants are animated by brief connecting narratives
0–8047–0611–5 Stanford pb $8.95

• Mary Wright
THE LAST STAND OF CHINESE CONSERVATISM: The T'ung-Chih Restoration, 1862-1874
A useful starting point for exploring the tensions in Chinese politics and statecraft as the Ch'ing dynasty confronted the unfamiliar challenge of imperialism
0–8047–0475–9 Stanford $40.00
0–8047–0476–7 Stanford pb $12.95

Biography

• Edward Behr
THE LAST EMPEROR
The poignant tale of the child emperor whose fate it was to live through the turbulent times after his dynasty had succumbed to the modernizing forces of the 20th century
0–553–34474–9 Bantam pb $9.95

• Jung Chang with Jon Holliday
MADAME SUN YAT-SEN
Daughter of the mighty Soong family, sister of Mme Chiang Kai-shek, and Honorary President of the People's Republic, Ching-ling was a major influence in altering the traditional roles of Chinese women
0–14–008455–X Penguin pb $4.95

• John Maxwell Hamilton
EDGAR SNOW: A Biography
The life of the American midwesterner whose love for China and the oppressed gained him access to the inner circle around Mao both before and after his rise to power
0–253–31909–9 Indiana $25.00

• Jonathan D. Spence
THE DEATH OF WOMAN WANG
The plight of a Chinese peasant woman
0–14–005121–X Penguin pb $5.95

• Aisin Gioro (Henry) Pu Yi
FROM EMPEROR TO CITIZEN
The autobiography of the last emperor, dethroned in 1912 when he was only six, a Japanese puppet during the Second World War, and eventually "reeducated" by the Communist government
Translated by W.J.F. Jenner
0–19–282099–0 Oxford pb $10.95

• H.R. Trevor-Roper
THE HERMIT OF PEKING
A forger and confidence-man who sold bridges and battleships, the mysterious Edmund Backhouse died in Peking in 1944; an impoverished Chinese scholar, leaving his papers to form the basis of Hugh Trevor-Roper's true but improbable tale
0–88064–063–4 Fromm pb $10.95

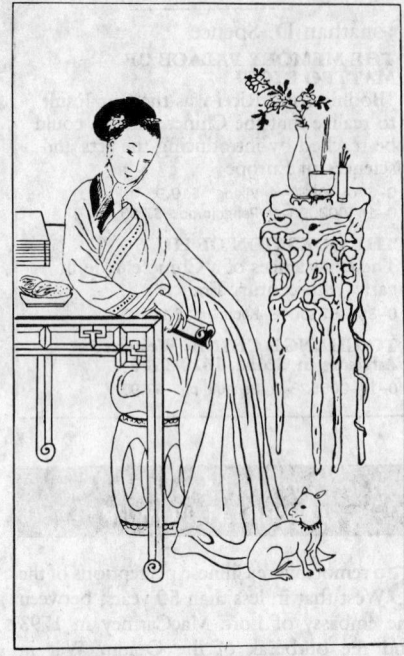

Tz'u-hsi, Empress Dowager

• Marina Warner
THE DRAGON EMPRESS: Life and Times of Tz'u-hsi, 1835-1908, Empress Dowager of China
A popular biography of the powerful matriarch who rose from the family of a minor mandarin to preside over the fall of the Manchu dynasty
0–689–70714–2 Atheneum pb $9.95

REPUBLICAN AND NATIONALIST CHINA

• Sherman Cochran & others, editors
ONE DAY IN CHINA: May 21, 1936
0–300–02834–2 Yale $35.00
0–300–03400–8 Yale pb $11.95

• Lloyd E. Eastman
FAMILY, FIELD, AND ANCESTORS: Constancy and Change in China's Social and Economic History, 1550-1949
Rejects the suddenness of revolutionary change for the belief that the forces that moulded modern China began in the 16th century
0–19–505270–6 Oxford pb $12.95

• Shinkichi Eto & Harold Schiffrin
1911 REVOLUTION IN CHINA
The events leading up to the revolution that overthrew the Ch'ing dynasty and established the Republic under the leadership of Sun Yat Sen
0–86008–349–7 Columbia $27.50

• Edward Friedman
BACKWARD TOWARD REVOLUTION: The Chinese Revolutionary Party
0–520–03279–9 California pb $10.95

• Harold Schiffrin
SUN YAT SEN AND THE ORIGINS OF THE CHINESE REVOLUTION
A Chinese Lenin without a Bolshevik party. During a long exile in Honolulu and London he planned the revolution, but lost control in 1911 to the military
0–520–01142–2 California $35.50

• Stirling Seagrave
THE SOONG DYNASTY
The popular account of the influential merchant clan that set policy for nationalist China by marrying its daughters to Sun Yat Sen, Chiang Kai-shek, and the finance czar, H.H. Kung
0–06–091318–5 Harper & Row pb $9.95

• James Sheridan
CHINA IN DISINTEGRATION: The Republican Era in Chinese History, 1912-1949
Stimulating narrative of the chaotic years of the warlords, the Japanese invasion, and the rise of Mao
0–02–928650–6 Free Press $15.95

CHINESE WARLORD: The Career of Feng Yu-hsiang
"Tracing the career of the colorful 'Christian general,' it also analyzes the essence of warlordism"—John K. Fairbank
0–8047–0146–6 Stanford pb $10.95

• Tien Hung-mao
GOVERNMENT AND POLITICS IN KUOMINTANG CHINA: 1927-1937
0–8047–0812–6 Stanford $22.50

• C. Martin Wilbur
SUN YAT-SEN: Frustrated Patriot
After losing control of the revolution to the forces of reaction, Sun founded the Kuomintang and formed an alliance with the communists in an attempt to provide stability for China
0–231–04036–9 Columbia $34.00

• Ernest Young
THE PRESIDENCY OF YUAN SHIH-K'AI: Liberalism and Dictatorship in Early Republican China
An analysis of the changing contours of state power and policy from the late Ch'ing through the Republic
0–472–08995–1 Michigan $17.50

THE COMMUNIST REVOLUTION

The corruption of the Kuomintang under Chiang Kai-shek and its failure to withstand the Japanese effectively undermined its support before and during the Second World War. Mao and the communists, however, had survived annihilation at the hands of the KMT by the Long March from Kiangsi province to Yenan, a distance of 6000 miles. They flourished at their new base, where they initiated popular land reforms, and soon became strong enough to cause serious losses to the Japanese. After the war their disciplined and confident troops expelled Chiang and his followers to the island of

■ **TO ORDER BOOKS AS GIFTS, SEE PAGE 1**

Formosa (Taiwan) and began the reconstruction of mainland China along the lines of the Russian example.

▶ **See also The Second World War**

• Lucien Bianco
ORIGINS OF THE CHINESE REVOLUTION: 1915-1949
Sets China in the context of revolutions since 1789 while finally relating it to roots in the peasantry
0–8047–0827–4 Stanford pb $8.95

• John Boyle
CHINA AND JAPAN AT WAR: 1937-1945
The politics of collaboration
0–8047–0800–2 Stanford $35.00

• Jean Chesneaux
THE CHINESE LABOR MOVEMENT
The leading study of labor and the communist movement
0–8047–0644–1 Stanford $45.00

• Edwin Hoyt
THE RISE OF THE CHINESE REPUBLIC: From the Last Emperor to Deng Xiaoping
Fast-paced narrative covers all the bases from the 1911 revolution to the tentative capitalist ventures of the 1980s
0–07–030619–2 McGraw-Hill $19.95

• Harold Isaacs
TRAGEDY OF THE CHINESE REVOLUTION
Valuable work by an excellent scholar
0–8047–0416–3 Stanford pb $12.95

• Chalmers Johnson
PEASANT NATIONALISM AND COMMUNIST POWER: The Emergence of Revolutionary China, 1937-1945
0–8047–0073–7 Stanford $28.50
0–8047–0074–5 Stanford pb $9.95

• Suzanne Pepper
CIVIL WAR IN CHINA: The Political Struggle, 1945-1949
"A dramatic account of how Chiang, who seemed in 1945 to have the Mandate of Heaven, could in less than four years lose every shred of it to the communists"—*American Political Science Review*
0–520–04085–6 California pb $10.95

• Harrison E. Salisbury
THE LONG MARCH
The Long March permitted the retreating communist forces to survive the nationalist onslaught and position themselves for the anti-Japanese resistance. This is a well-written account, based on interviews conducted by the *NY Times* correspondent 50 years after the march
0–317–56827–2 McGraw-Hill pb $7.95

• Benjamin Schwartz
CHINESE COMMUNISM AND THE RISE OF MAO
Argues that the success of the Chinese revolution depended less on Moscow or orthodox communist principles than on flexible responses to changing situations
0–674–12251–8 Harvard $17.50
0–674–12260–7 Harvard pb $7.95

Mao

Mao Zedong
THE WRITINGS OF MAO: September 1949-December 1955
The first of a projected five volumes in an authoritative collection
Edited by Michael Y.M. Kau & John Leung
0–87332–391–2 Sharpe $90.00

Roderick MacFarquhar & others, editors
THE SECRET SPEECHES OF CHAIRMAN MAO: From the Hundred Flowers to the Great Leap Forward
0–674–79673–X Harvard pb $15.00

Stuart R. Schram
THE THOUGHT OF MAO TSE-TUNG
A pioneering collection, presenting both the original texts and their official, revised versions
0–521–32549–8 Cambridge $44.50
0–521–31062–8 Cambridge pb $14.95

Stuart R. Schram, editor
CHAIRMAN MAO TALKS TO THE PEOPLE: Talks and Letters, 1956-1971
0–394–70641–2 Pantheon pb $5.75

Edgar Snow
RED STAR OVER CHINA
A journalistic classic on the early Communist movement, including the autobiography of Mao as told to Snow in 1936
Introduction by John K. Fairbank
0–394–47524–0 Grove pb $11.95

The People's Republic

• B. Michael Frolic
MAO'S PEOPLE: Sixteen Portraits of Life in Revolutionary China
0–674–54846–9 Harvard $18.50
0–674–54845–0 Harvard pb $6.95

• John Gittings
THE ROLE OF THE CHINESE ARMY
0–19–500160–5 Oxford $19.95

• Harry Harding
ORGANIZING CHINA: The Problem of Bureaucracy, 1949-1976
0–8047–1080–5 Stanford $42.50

• William A. Joseph
THE CRITIQUE OF ULTRA-LEFTISM IN CHINA, 1958-1981
0–8047–1208–5 Stanford $35.00

• Witold Rodzinski
THE PEOPLE'S REPUBLIC OF CHINA: A Concise Political History
Poland's ambassador to China sorts out the facts from the myths and the propaganda
0–02–926872–9 Free Press pb $9.95

• Franz Schurmann
IDEOLOGY AND ORGANIZATION IN COMMUNIST CHINA
How the Chinese communists substituted their own ideas and methods for the traditional social system
0–520–01153–8 California pb $10.95

The Cultural Revolution

In 1966 Mao instigated a new phase of the revolution with the intention of rooting out all vestiges of traditional culture. The Red Guard, an organization of fanatical teenagers who had grown up since 1949, were permitted to attack foreigners, including the Russians, as well as any member of the older generation whose education marked him as elitist. The result was disastrous. Many of the government's most effective administrators were deprived of their posts, and ignorant youths put in their place. Much of China's cultural heritage was obliterated, and a generation of scholars cut off at the root. The mindless destruction only came to an end with Mao's death in 1976.

• Anita Chan, Richard Madsen & Jonathan Unger
CHEN VILLAGE: The Recent History of a Peasant Community in Mao's China
Based on refugee interviews, the political history of a south China rural community from the Socialist Education Movement through the Cultural Revolution
0–520–05618–3 California pb $10.95

• Lowell Dittmer
LIU SHAO-CH'I AND THE CHINESE CULTURAL REVOLUTION: The Politics of Mass Criticism
The most prominent of the old guard who suffered humiliation and disgrace during the Cultural Revolution
0–520–02957–7 California pb $12.95

• Roderick MacFarquhar
THE ORIGINS OF THE CULTURAL REVOLUTION
Personality conflicts, the Sino-Soviet break, and the horrendous failure of the Great Leap Forward all contributed to the human tragedy

Volume 1: Contradictions Among the People, 1956-1957
0–231–03841–0 Columbia $37.00
0–231–08385–8 Columbia pb $17.50

Volume 2: The Great Leap Forward, 1958-1960
0–231–05716–4 Columbia $40.00
0–231–05717–2 Columbia pb $17.50

• Anne F. Thurston
ENEMIES OF THE PEOPLE: The Ordeals of the Intellectuals in China's Great Cultural Revolution
The harrowing stories of 49 victims of the Red Guard adds a human dimension to this lucid introduction to the origin and course of Mao's greatest folly
0–674–25375–2 Harvard pb $10.95

• Tsou Tang
THE CULTURAL REVOLUTION AND POST-MAO REFORMS: A Historical Perspective
An informed overview locating China's tumultuous political transformations against the background both of the imperial state and contemporary Leninist states
0–226–81513–7 Chicago $32.50

CHINA AFTER MAO

Following Mao's death and the arrest of the "Gang of Four," China embarked on the most profound socio-economic transformation since the collectivization, nationalization and commune formation of 1955-58. The emergence of a broadly based, student-led democracy movement in May, 1989, and the brutal suppression of it left the ultimate fate of the economic reform program and of the Communist regime itself in doubt. The books listed below precede this latest turning-point in Chinese history.

• A. Doak Barnett & Ralph N. Clough
MODERNIZING CHINA: Post-Mao Reform and Development
0–8133–0332–X Westview $34.00
0–8133–0333–8 Westview pb $14.95

• Michel Chossudovsky
TOWARDS CAPITALIST RESTORATION?: Chinese Socialism after Mao
0–312–81134–9 St. Martin's $29.95
0–312–81135–7 St. Martin's pb $12.95

• Uli Franz
DENG XIAOPING
A biography that probes early party infighting and reviews the mix of economic pragmatism and communist orthodoxy of the most powerful of Mao's successors. Franz's study predates the events of 1989
Translated by Tom Artin
0–15–125177–0 HBJ $21.95

• John Gardner
CHINESE POLITICS AND THE SUCCESSION TO MAO
Inner sanctum power-plays for the party succession, from the ill-fated Lin Biao, shot down while fleeing to Russia, to the eventual emergence of Deng Xiaoping
0–8419–0809–5 Holmes & Meier pb $15.50

• Immanuel C.Y. Hsu
CHINA WITHOUT MAO: The Search for a New Order
Focuses on the defeat of the Gang of Four that ushered in the pragmatic combination of market forces with the socialist economy
0–19–503134–2 Galaxy pb $7.95

• Elisabeth J. Perry & Christine Wong, editors
THE POLITICAL ECONOMY OF REFORM IN POST-MAO CHINA
0–674–68590–3 Harvard pb $14.00

Orville Schell
DISCOS AND DEMOCRACY: China in the Throes of Reform
0–385–26187–X Doubleday pb $9.95

TO GET RICH IS GLORIOUS: China in the '80s
Presents China as a land of cultural schizophrenia where Holiday Inns coexist with ancient temples, and successful capitalists are the new heroes
0–451–62437–8 NAL pb $3.95

• Mark Selden & Victor Lippit, editors
THE TRANSITION TO SOCIALISM IN CHINA
Reform in the 1980s against the background of the revolutionary transformation of the 1950s and 1960s
0–87332–212–6 Sharpe $30.00
0–87332–216–9 Sharpe pb $14.95

Democracy and Dissent

• Randle Edwards & Andrew Nathan
HUMAN RIGHTS IN CONTEMPORARY CHINA
0–231–06180–3 Columbia $29.00

• Merle Goldman
CHINA'S INTELLECTUALS: Advice and Dissent
A good introduction to the role of the intellectuals in the People's Republic
0–674–11970–3 Harvard $21.00

LITERARY DISSENT IN COMMUNIST CHINA
Covers the attempt of the party to control literary output before the Cultural Revolution
0–674–53625–8 Harvard $24.50

• Merle Goldman, Timothy Cheek & Carol Hamrin, editors
CHINA'S INTELLECTUALS AND THE STATE: In Search of a New Relationship
0–674–11972–X Harvard pb $14.00

• Liang Heng & Judith Shapiro
WARM WINDS, COLD WINDS: Intellectual Life in China Today
The struggle in the arts, religion, and the press to renew China's literary heritage after decades of repression
0–8195–5162–7 Wesleyan $17.95
0–8195–6168–1 Wesleyan pb $12.95

• Liu Pin-an
PEOPLE OR MONSTERS? & OTHER STORIES AND REPORTAGE FROM CHINA AFTER MAO
Introduction by Leo Ou-fan Lee
0–253–34329–1 Indiana $20.00
0–253–20313–9 Indiana pb $7.95

• Andrew Nathan
CHINESE DEMOCRACY
The work of a top scholar
0–394–51386–X Knopf $22.50
0–520–05933–6 California pb $10.95

Americans in China

Fox Butterfield
CHINA: Alive in the Bitter Sea
Insights into the lives of lovers, farmers, workers, and intellectuals by the first journalist permitted to live in Beijing since the revolution
0–553–34502–8 Bantam pb $12.95

Mark Salzman
IRON AND SILK
The Chinese adventures of a young martial arts master "produce the gulp of feeling you might get from an unusually fine short story" (NY Times)
0–394–75511–1 Random House pb $5.95

CONTEMPORARY CHINESE SOCIETY

• Godwin C. Chu & Frances L.K. Hsu
CHINA'S NEW SOCIAL FABRIC
Argues that the enormous conservatism of local communities in Chinese culture is still the glue that holds the new state together
0–7103–0050–6 KPI pb $16.95

• Elisabeth Croll
THE FAMILY RICE BOWL: Food and Domestic Economy in China
A comprehensive and thoughtful critical introduction to the country's economic development since 1949
0–86232–124–7 Humanities $29.95
0–86232–125–5 Humanities pb $12.50

• William Hinton
FANSHEN: A Documentary of Revolution in a Chinese Village
Arresting narrative of history's impact on the patterns of life in a typical village, from adulterous liaisons to the backbreaking task of tilling the soil
0–394–70465–7 Random House pb $14.95

SHENFAN: The Continuing Revolution in a Chinese Village
0–394–72378–3 Random House pb $10.95

Boys in Beijing, 1988 (Photo by Freya Read)

☞ **TO ORDER NEW BOOKS NOT YET LISTED, ASK YOUR BOOKSELLER OR CALL 1-800-882-8770**

"Ten huge buildings designed in an undistinguished Western-influenced style were erected in Peking in 1958-59, and Tiananmen Square was vastly enlarged to be a setting for mass rallies. Beside the square was one of the biggest of the ten monsters, the Great Hall of the People, seen above through the massive portico of another, the joint Museums of Chinese History and of the Chinese Revolution." Photo and caption from China: A Photohistory, 1937-1987 *edited by W.J.F. Jenner (Pantheon/photo copyright Marc Riboud 1965)*

• Christopher Howe

CHINA'S ECONOMY: A Basic Guide
"For the non-specialist reader, this is the best up-to-date survey of the Chinese economy available"—Nicholas Lardy, Yale University
0–465–01100–4 Basic Books pb $8.95

• Nicholas Lardy

ECONOMIC GROWTH AND DISTRIBUTION IN CHINA
0–521–21904–3 Cambridge $39.50

• Victor Lippit

THE ECONOMIC DEVELOPMENT OF CHINA
Early 20th-century economics and the attempt at socialist development since 1949
0–87332–403–X Sharpe $39.95
0–87332–404–8 Sharpe pb $16.95

• Steven Mosher

BROKEN EARTH: The Rural Chinese
"For readers wishing to go beyond the tales of happy workers and barefoot doctors, this book is highly recommended"—Boston Herald
0–02–921720–2 Free Press pb $9.95

• Rhoads Murphey

THE FADING OF THE MAOIST VISION: City and Country in China's Development
0–416–60201–0 RC&H pb $14.95

• Leo Orleans

EVERY FIFTH CHILD: The Population of China
0–8047–0819–3 Stanford pb $15.00

• Lynn Pan

THE NEW CHINESE REVOLUTION
A western-educated Shanghai woman observes at first hand China's capitulation to the consumer culture of brand names and fast food
0–8092–4610–4 Contemporary $19.95

• William L. Parish & Martin K. Whyte

VILLAGE AND FAMILY IN CONTEMPORARY CHINA
A good introduction to both city and countryside
0–226–64590–8 Chicago $30.00
0–226–64591–6 Chicago pb $15.00

• Dwight H. Perkins & Shahid Yusuf

RURAL DEVELOPMENT IN CHINA
0–8018–3261–6 Johns Hopkins $25.00
0–8018–3066–4 Johns Hopkins pb $14.50

• Thomas G. Rawski

ECONOMIC GROWTH AND EMPLOYMENT IN CHINA
0–19–520151–5 Oxford $22.00
0–19–520152–3 Oxford pb $8.95

• Ruth & Victor W. Sidel

THE HEALTH OF CHINA
0–8070–2161–X Beacon pb $11.95

• Vaclav Smil

THE BAD EARTH: Enviromental Degradation in China
A devastating critique of China's environmental policies
0–87332–230–4 Sharpe $35.00

• Andrew G. Walder

COMMUNIST NEO-TRADITIONALISM: Work and Authority in Chinese Industry
An exploration of the changing economic, social, and political position of the working class
0–520–05439–3 California $40.00

• Zhang Xinxin & Sang Ye

CHINESE LIVES: An Oral History of Contemporary China
Sixty ordinary Chinese people, ranging from prison guard to hairdresser, talk about their own lives and hard times
Preface by Studs Terkel
0–679–72056–1 Pantheon pb $9.95

Women and the Family

Several recent books provide overviews of the changing position of Chinese women in the 20th century, who are engaged in the often conflicting issues of feminism and socialist revolution.

• Phyllis Andors

THE UNFINISHED LIBERATION OF CHINESE WOMEN, 1949-1980
0–253–36022–6 Indiana $22.50

• Elisabeth Croll

CHINESE WOMEN SINCE MAO
0–87332–267–3 Sharpe pb $13.95

• Kay A. Johnson

WOMEN, THE FAMILY AND PEASANT REVOLUTION IN CHINA
What happens when the Party's commitment to leading a peasant revolution clashes with the liberation of women
0–226–40187–1 Chicago $25.00
0–226–40189–8 Chicago pb $11.95

• Ono Kazuko

CHINESE WOMEN IN A CENTURY OF REVOLUTION, 1850-1950
The only comprehensive history of women in China, from the Taiping rebellion to the People's Republic
0–8047–1497–5 Stanford pb $10.95

• William Kessen, editor

CHILDHOOD IN CHINA
Detailed observations of children's behavior successfully convey the feeling of childhood in the People's Republic
0–300–01917–3 Yale pb $10.95

• Alice P. Lin

GRANDMOTHER HAD NO NAME
A Chinese-born New York professional's confrontation with the inequities of gender and culture in her own heritage
0–8351–2034–1 China Books pb $9.95

• Mary Sheridan & Janet W. Salaff

LIVES: Chinese Working Women
Among other moving portraits from China, Hong Kong and Taiwan, the life of a woman who went from nun to peasant to Hakka stevedore symbolizes the flux of modern history
0–253–20319–8 Indiana pb $8.95

• Judith Stacey
PATRIARCHY AND SOCIALIST REVOLUTION IN CHINA
The limits of women's liberation
0–520–04825–3 California $37.50
0–520–04826–1 California pb $9.95

• Margery Wolf & Roxane Witke, editors
WOMEN IN CHINESE SOCIETY
0–8047–0874–6 Stanford $25.00

FOREIGN RELATIONS

• Graeme Browning
IF EVERYONE BOUGHT ONE SHOE: American Capitalism in Communist China
An examination of the inhospitability of the People's Republic to foreign business
0–8090–3735–1 Hill & Wang $18.95

• Harry Harding
CHINA'S FOREIGN RELATIONS IN THE 1980s
0–300–03207–2 Yale $27.50
0–300–03628–0 Yale pb $9.95

• Orville Schell
WATCH OUT FOR THE FOREIGN GUESTS!: China Encounters the West
0–394–74899–9 Pantheon pb $3.95

• George Segal
CHINA DEFENDING
0–19–827470–X Oxford $44.00

• Philip Snow
THE STAR RAFT: China's Encounter with Africa
From the first contact in the 15th century to the recent riots against African students, the relationship has been a volatile mix of friendly altruism and political opportunism; illustrated
1–555–84184–8 Weidenfeld & Nicolson $19.95
0–8014–9583–0 Cornell pb $9.95

• Jay Taylor
CHINA AND SOUTHEAST ASIA: Peking's Relations with Revolutionary Movements
0–275–91468–2 Praeger pb $18.95

• Allen S. Whiting
CHINA CROSSES THE YALU: The Decision to Enter the Korean War
0–8047–0627–1 Stanford $30.00
0–8047–0629–8 Stanford pb $8.95

• Michael Yahuda
TOWARDS THE END OF ISOLATIONISM: China's Foreign Policy after Mao
0–312–81141–1 St. Martin's $25.00
0–312–81142–X St. Martin's pb $11.95

Dragon and Eagle

• John K. Fairbank
CHINABOUND: A Fifty Year Memoir
China memories from the Harvard scholar
0–06–039028–X Harper & Row pb $10.00

Children on a bus in Inner Mongolia, 1988 (Photo by Freya Read)

CHINA WATCH
A collection of Fairbank's expert musings on the peculiar relationship between the US and China
0–674–11765–4 Harvard $26.00

THE UNITED STATES AND CHINA
A popular work which offers both an overview of Chinese society and a history of Sino-American relations
0–674–92438–X Harvard pb $9.95

• John K. Fairbank, editor
THE MISSIONARY ENTERPRISE IN CHINA AND AMERICA
19th-century Americans in China
0–674–57655–1 Harvard $27.00

• Michael Hunt
THE MAKING OF A SPECIAL RELATIONSHIP: The United States and China to 1914
0–231–05516–1 Columbia $40.00

• Ernest May & John K. Fairbank
AMERICA'S CHINA TRADE IN HISTORICAL PERSPECTIVE
A reassessment of the Sino-American relationship from the perspective of investment and trade
0–674–03075–3 Harvard $21.00

• Michael Schaller
THE UNITED STATES AND CHINA IN THE TWENTIETH CENTURY
A brief and incisive overview
0–19–502598–9 Oxford $16.95
0–19–502599–7 Oxford pb $8.95

THE U.S. CRUSADE IN CHINA, 1938-1945
"A sordid tale of America's disastrous military, economic, diplomatic and political ambiguity towards China, of cynical maneuverings of Nationalist and Communist, and of missed opportunities"—*LA Times*
0–231–04455–0 Columbia pb $15.00

• Barbara Tuchman
STILWELL AND THE AMERICAN EXPERIENCE IN CHINA
"The most informative book the American public has ever had on the difficulties and failures of the American relationship with China"—Edwin O. Reischauer
0–02–620290–5 Macmillan $21.95
0–553–25798–6 Bantam pb $6.95

MEMOIRS

• Nien Cheng
LIFE AND DEATH IN SHANGHAI
"The most powerful account yet of the Cultural Revolution . . . [it] echoes Kafka and Solzhenitsyn"—*Washington Post*
0–394–55548–1 Grove $19.95
0–14–010870–X Penguin pb $8.95

• Frank Ching
ANCESTORS: 900 Years in the Life of a Chinese Family
A correspondent for the *New York Times* traces his family blood line
0–449–90353–2 Fawcett pb $12.95

• Gao Yuan
BORN RED: A Chronicle of the Cultural Revolution
The view from an elite school
0–8047–1368–5 Stanford $39.50
0–8047–1369–3 Stanford pb $7.95

• Liang Heng & Judith Shapiro
SON OF THE REVOLUTION
Liang Heng recounts his participation in the Cultural Revolution as a youth from an intellectual family set adrift by the political upheavals since 1957
0–394–52568–X Knopf $15.00
0–394–72274–4 Random House pb $7.95

• David & Nancy D. Milton
THE WIND WILL NOT SUBSIDE: Years in Revolutionary China, 1964-1969
Story from the perspective of Americans in China struggling with the Cultural Revolution
0–394–70936–5 Pantheon pb $7.95

• Helen Foster Snow
MY CHINA YEARS
First-hand account of the prewar years and the revolution by the woman whose successful industrial cooperatives—the gung-hos—enlarged American English vocabulary
0–688–07525–8 Morrow pb $9.95

• Daiyun Yue & Carolyn Wakeman
TO THE STORM: The Odyssey of a Revolutionary Chinese Woman
A painstaking account of the torture and turmoil inflicted on intellectuals during the Cultural Revolution. The author has since been restored to the Party and continues to teach at Beijing University
0–520–05580–2 California $25.00
0–520–06029–6 California pb $10.95

➤ **FOR OVERSEAS ORDERING INFORMATION, SEE PAGE 1**

TIBET

- **A.T. Grunfeld**
THE MAKING OF MODERN TIBET
An introduction to China's stormy
relations with Tibet
0–87332–415–3 Sharpe $35.00

- **André Guibaut**
TIBETAN VENTURE
The story of the disastrous French
anthropological expedition during the
Second World War
0–19–584214–6 Oxford pb $7.95

Tibetan musicians

- **Hugh E. Richardson**
TIBET AND ITS HISTORY
The only complete history in English
0–87773–376–7 Random House pb $10.95

- **David Snellgrove & Hugh
Richardson**
A CULTURAL HISTORY OF TIBET
0–394–74380–6 Shambhala pb $15.95

- **Chogyam Trungpa**
BORN IN TIBET
This autobiography of a Tibetan lama
includes the gripping tale of his escape
from invading Chinese troops in 1959
0–394–74219–2 Shambhala pb $9.95

The Steppes of Central Asia

C.R. Bawden
**THE MODERN HISTORY OF
MONGOLIA**
The first English chronicle from the
colonial age to modern times; links the
saga of Genghis Khan with the present-
day Mongolian People's Republic
0–7103–0326–2 KPI pb $19.95

René Grousset
**THE EMPIRE OF THE STEPPES: A
History of Central Asia**
0–8135–1304–9 Rutgers pb $20.00

Japan

- **Ruth Benedict**
**THE CHRYSANTHEMUM AND THE
SWORD: Patterns of Japanese Culture**
A study dating from the 1940s, by a
leading anthropologist
0–452–00916–2 NAL pb $8.95

- **Robert C. Christopher**
THE JAPANESE MIND
0–449–90120–3 Fawcett pb $7.95

- **John Whitney Hall**
JAPAN: From Prehistory to Modern Times
An excellent synthesis with a useful
glossary and chronology. This 1971
edition carries the story up until the 1960s
0–385–28478–0 Dell pb $12.95

- **Ivan Morris**
**THE NOBILITY OF FAILURE: Tragic
Heroes in the History of Japan**
A witty and penetrating study of how
defenders of lost causes have been the most
enduring Japanese heroes
0–374–52120–4 Farrar, Straus & Giroux pb $14.95

- **Edwin O. Reischauer**
JAPAN: The Story of a Nation
A sympathetic survey by the best-known
American Japan specialist
0–394–51362–2 Knopf $15.95

**THE JAPANESE TODAY: Change and
Continuity**
An updated and greatly expanded edition
of *The Japanese*; one of the most popular
overviews
0–674–47181–4 Harvard $25.00

- **George Sansom**
JAPAN: A Short Cultural History
0–8047–0954–8 Stanford pb $14.95

- **Edward G. Seidensticker**
THIS COUNTRY, JAPAN
A translator of Japanese literature offers
rich insights on themes ranging from
classical fiction to taxi drivers
0–87011–229–5 Kodansha $16.95
0–87011–641–X Kodansha pb $5.95

- **Kurt Singer**
**MIRROR, SWORD AND JEWEL: The
Geometry of Japanese Life**
Singer taught at Tokyo Imperial University
in the 1930s; his book remains a classic
analysis of Japanese society
0–87011–460–3 Kodansha pb $5.25

- **Robert J. Smith**
**JAPANESE SOCIETY: Tradition, Self and
the Social Order**
0–521–31552–2 Cambridge pb $10.95

*A caricature of a scribe in the Sutra Copying
Bureau, dated 745, from* Japan: A Short
Cultural History *by G.B. Sansom (Stanford)*

- **Richard Storry**
A HISTORY OF MODERN JAPAN
0–14–020475–X Penguin pb $6.95

- **Conrad Totman**
JAPAN BEFORE PERRY: A Short History
0–520–04134–8 California pb $10.95

- **H. Paul Varley**
JAPANESE CULTURE: A Short History
A summary of artistic, social, and political
forces
Illustrated by Joe Shulman
0–8048–1493–7 Tuttle pb $7.95

Okinawa

- **Mitsugu Sakihara**
**A BRIEF HISTORY OF OKINAWA:
Based on the Omoro Soshi**
A social history of the kingdom of
Ryukyu, relying heavily on ancient poems
recorded between the 12th and 17th
centuries
0–8248–1130–5 Hawaii pb $25.00

TRADITIONAL CULTURE

- **Martin Collcutt, Marius Jansen, &
Isao Kumakura**
THE CULTURAL ATLAS OF JAPAN
0–8160–1927–4 Facts On File $40.00

Religion

▶ **See also Asian Religion and Philosophy**

- **Joseph M Kitagawa**
**ON UNDERSTANDING JAPANESE
RELIGION**
0–691–07313–9 Princeton $47.00
0–691–10229–5 Princeton pb $14.95

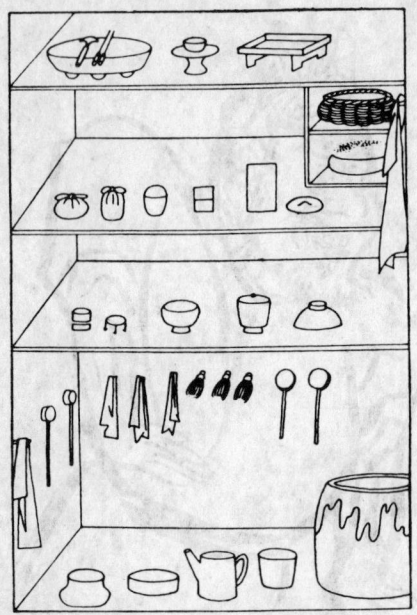

The arrangement of utensils, from Cha-no-yu: The Japanese Tea Ceremony *by A.L. Sadler (Tuttle)*

- Oliver Statler
JAPANESE PILGRIMAGE
The story of a traditional Buddhist pilgrimage, incorporating the author's own experiences
0–688–04834–X Hawaii pb $6.95

- D.T. Suzuki
ZEN AND JAPANESE CULTURE
An elegant book by Zen's best-known interpreter
0–691–01770–0 Princeton pb $10.95

Martial Arts

- Yagyu Munenori
THE SWORD AND THE MIND
Traditional treatises on swordsmanship
Translated by Hiroaki Sato
0–87951–209–1 Overlook $16.95
0–87951–256–3 Overlook pb $8.95

- Oscar Ratti & Adele Westbrook
SECRETS OF THE SAMURAI: A Survey of the Martial Arts of Feudal Japan
A long and comprehensive guide
0–8048–0917–8 Tuttle $39.95

- Yamamoto Tsunetomo
HAGAKURE: The Book of the Samurai
"The most influential of all samurai treatises"—Ivan Morris
Translated by William S. Wilson
0–87011–378–X Kodansha $18.95

The Japanese Way

Peter Grilli
FURO: The Japanese Bath
The history and traditions of a fundamental aspect of Japanese tradition, accompanied by superb photography
Photographs by Dana Levy
Foreword by Isamu Noguchi
0–87011–601–0 Kodansha $45.00

Ishimura Hayao & Maruyama Nobuhiko
ROBES OF ELEGANCE: Japanese Kimonos of the Sixteenth through Twentieth Centuries
Introduction by Richard S. Schneiderman
0–88259–955–0 North Carolina $29.95

Donald Richie
A TASTE OF JAPAN, FOOD FACT AND FABLE: What the People Eat, Customs and Etiquette
"In his very entertaining way, Mr. Richie makes you feel familiar with the basic vocabulary you need to really experience and enjoy Japanese food the way the Japanese do"—Alice Waters
0–87011–675–4 Kodansha $18.95

A.L. Sadler
CHA-NO-YU: The Japanese Tea Ceremony
An old but detailed account
0–8048–1224–1 Tuttle pb $7.95

Oliver Statler
JAPANESE INN: A Reconstruction of the Past
The succeeding generations of a family of innkeepers, recounted in novelistic style; one of the best introductory books on Japanese tradition
0–8248–0818–5 Hawaii pb $8.95

Junichiro Tanizaki
IN PRAISE OF SHADOWS
A brief and indispensable essay on traditional aesthetics by one of Japan's greatest modern writers
0–918172–02–0 Leete's Island pb $3.95

JAPAN TO 1600

After achieving a high state of civilization by the middle of the first millennium, Japanese society remained at the mercy of warring feudal overlords until final unification under the Tokugawa shogunate in 1603.

- George Sansom
Sansom's monumental work is still the most complete general history of Japan to the Meiji Restoration.
A HISTORY OF JAPAN TO 1334
0–8047–0523–2 Stanford pb $12.95

A HISTORY OF JAPAN, 1334-1615
0–8047–0525–9 Stanford pb $12.95

A HISTORY OF JAPAN, 1615-1867
0–8047–0527–5 Stanford pb $8.95

Heian Period: 794-1185

- Ivan Morris
THE WORLD OF THE SHINING PRINCE
A splendid recreation of the court society that created *The Tale of Genji* and other literary masterpieces
0–14–055083–6 Penguin pb $7.95

Kamakura, Muromachi, and Shokuhō Periods: 1185-1600

- Kenneth A. Grossberg
JAPAN'S RENAISSANCE: The Politics of the Muromachi Bakufu
The Muromachi, or Ashikaga, period spans the era from 1338 to 1573. The term *bakufu* refers both to the headquarters of the shogun and to the shogunate as a system of government
0–674–47251–9 Harvard $20.00

- John Whitney Hall, Nagaharo Keiji & Kozo Yamamura, editors
JAPAN BEFORE TOKUGAWA: Political Consolidation in Economic Growth, 1500 to 1650
0–691–10216–3 Princeton pb $16.50

- John Whitney Hall & Takeshi Toyoda, editors
JAPAN IN THE MUROMACHI AGE
0–520–02888–0 California $38.50

- Jeffrey P. Mass
THE DEVELOPMENT OF KAMAKURA RULE, 1180-1250: A History with Documents
0–8047–1003–1 Stanford $32.50

Glossary

shogun: from the 12th through the 19th century, the chief military figure of Japan.
shōyū: soy sauce.
tennō: emperor.
tenryō: the territory held directly by the Tokugawa shogun.
tozama: "allied daimyo" of the Tokugawa shogun; i.e., those who pledged allegiance as peers of the Tokugawa shogun.
uji: aristocratic lineage consisting of a main family and an extended group of branches.
uji-gami: deity worshipped as the guardian or founding spirit by the members of an aristocratic lineage.
ukiyo: "fleeting world," the stylish world of the urban entertainment quarters. Also "floating world."
za: trade or commercial guild in medieval Japan.
zaibatsu: the "business clique," the great commercial-industrial cartels which emerged during the 1920s.

Adapted from the Glossary in

John Whitney Hall
JAPAN: From Prehistory to Modern Times
0–385–28478–0 Dell pb $12.95

The Mongol Invasions, 1274-1281, after a contemporary scroll, from Japan: A Short Cultural History *by G.B. Sansom (Stanford)*

• Jeffrey P. Mass & William B. Hauser, editors

THE BAKUFU IN JAPANESE HISTORY
The techniques through which military overlords from the Heian period to the Meiji Restoration turned the emperor into a puppet
0–8047–1278–6 Stanford $34.00

THE TOKUGAWA PERIOD: 1600-1868

Political and Economic History

• Peter Arnesen

THE MEDIEVAL JAPANESE DAIMYO
The term *daimyo* refers to those local magnates (after the 15th century) with territory producing 50,000 bushels or more of rice
0–300–02341–3 Yale $32.50

• Mary E. Berry

HIDEYOSHI
Toyotomi Hideyoshi, who built Osaka Castle and invaded Korea, ruled supreme in Japan from 1590 until his death in 1598
0–674–39025–3 Harvard $32.00

• Herbert P. Bix

PEASANT PROTEST IN JAPAN: 1590-1884
A superb reconstruction of rural class conflict
0–300–03485–7 Yale $32.50

• C.R. Boxer

THE CHRISTIAN CENTURY IN JAPAN: 1549-1650
The failure of Christianity after its initial successes to resist Japanese isolationist tendencies
0–520–02702–7 California $49.50

• Nakae Chomin

A DISCOURSE BY THREE DRUNKARDS ON GOVERNMENT
An early Japanese view of the West
Translated by Nobuko Tsukui
0–8348–0192–2 Weatherhill pb $12.50

• James L. McClain

KANAZAWA: A Seventeenth-Century Japanese Castle Town
0–300–02736–2 Yale $27.50

• Tetsuo Najita

VISIONS OF VIRTUE IN TOKUGAWA JAPAN: The Kaitokudō Merchant Academy of Osaka
A study of the development of the merchant discourse on political economy during the 18th century
0–226–56804–0 Chicago $37.50
0–226–56805–9 Chicago pb $16.95

• Thomas C. Smith

THE AGRARIAN ORIGINS OF MODERN JAPAN
0–8047–0530–5 Stanford $25.00
0–8047–0531–3 Stanford pb $8.95

NAKAHARA: Family Farming and Population in a Japanese Village, 1717-1830
With Smith's *Agrarian Origins*, this is a classic study of the early modern period
0–8047–0928–9 Stanford $22.50

TOKUGAWA IEYASU: Shogun
In 1603, the year James VI of Scotland became James I of England, Ieyasu took the title of Shogun and established the Tokugawa line
0–89346–210–1 Heian pb $9.95

• Stephan Vlastos

PEASANT PROTESTS AND UPRISINGS IN TOKUGAWA JAPAN
0–520–04614–5 California $27.50

• Anne Walthall

SOCIAL PROTEST AND POPULAR CULTURE IN 18TH-CENTURY JAPAN
0–8165–0961–1 Arizona $19.95

The Collapse of the Tokugawa Shogunate

"Three years before the East India Company lost its Indian hunting-ground, Commodore Perry with his black ships peremptorily battered down the walls that for so long had kept Japan in self-imposed isolation. After 1854, the self-confidence and inner legitimacy of the Bakufu (Tokugawa Shogunate regime) were rapidly undermined by a conspicuous impotence in the face of the penetrating West. Under the banner of Sonnō Jōi (Revere the Sovereign, Expel the Barbarians), a small band of middle-ranking samurai . . . finally overthrew it in 1868. Among the reasons for their success was an exceptionally creative absorption, especially after 1860, of the new Western military science systematized since 1815 by Prussian and French staff professionals. They were thus able

to make effective use of 7300 ultra-modern rifles (most of them American Civil War scrap), purchased from an English arms-merchant."—Benedict Anderson, *Imagined Communities: Reflections on the Origin and Spread of Nationalism*

W.G. Beasley

THE MEIJI RESTORTATION
The classic study
0–8047–0815–0 Stanford $55.00

Albert M. Craig

CHOSHU IN THE MEIJI RESTORATION
The small bands of middle level samurai instrumental in the fall of the Tokugawa shogunate were drawn from the Satsuma and Chōshū *han*. This is the second edition of a valuable study
0–674–12850–8 Harvard $25.00

Marius B. Jansen

SAKAMOTO RYOMA AND THE MEIJI RESTORATION
Highly educated, like many of his peers, Sakamoto Ryōmo was a key player in ending Tokugawa rule
0–8047–0784–7 Stanford pb $20.00

Conrad Totman

THE COLLAPSE OF THE TOKUGAWA BAKUFU: 1862-1868
0–8248–0614–X Hawaii $25.00

Society, Culture, and Ideas

• Robert N. Bellah

TOKUGAWA RELIGION
An influential attempt to apply the sociological theories of Talcott Parsons to Japanese thought
0–02–902460–9 Free Press pb $10.95

"The Kitchen Scene" by Utamaro (1753-1806), from Tales of Japan: Scrolls and Prints from the New York Public Library *by Miyako Murase (New York Public Library)*

- Donald Keene
  THE JAPANESE DISCOVERY OF EUROPE, 1720-1830
  A well-told history of Japan's sometimes contradictory approaches to the West
  0–8047–0669–7 Stanford pb $9.95

- Tetsuo Najita
  JAPAN: The Intellectual Foundations of Modern Japanese Politics
  Incisive and original
  0–226–56803–2 Chicago pb $8.00

- Peter Nosco, editor
  CONFUCIANISM AND TOKUGAWA CULTURE
  0–691–07286–8 Princeton $34.50

- Noel Perrin
  GIVING UP THE GUN: Japan's Reversion to the Sword, 1543-1879
  A rare instance of the rejection of superior military technology for cultural reasons
  0–897–23773–2 Godine pb $12.95

FROM THE MEIJI RESTORATION TO THE END OF EMPIRE: 1868-1945

What the Japanese wanted from the West was primarily science, technology, and organization. They were content enough with the innermost substance of their culture, their moral ideas, their family life, their arts and amusements, their religious conceptions, though even in these they showed an uncommon adaptability. Essentially it was to protect their internal substance, their Japanese culture, that they took over the external apparatus of Western civilization.

R.R. Palmer & Joel Colton
A HISTORY OF THE MODERN WORLD
0–394–53396–8 Random House $40.00

- Peter Duus
  THE RISE OF MODERN JAPAN
  0–395–20665–0 Houghton Mifflin $33.50

John K. Fairbank, Edwin O. Reischauer & Albert M. Craig
EAST ASIA: Tradition and Transformation
This remains the most influential text by the foremost American experts on China and Japan
0–395–25812–X Houghton Mifflin $45.95

- Mikiso Hane
  MODERN JAPAN: A Historical Survey
  "Hane has a keen eye for vivid small events as well as for the great triumphs and tragedies in Japan's emergence as a great power"—John W. Dower
  0–8133–0315–X Westview $49.00

  PEASANTS, REBELS AND OUTCASTS: The Underside of Modern Japan
  A spirited guide to the dark side of Japan's drive to empire and to the life of the lower

An umbrella maker in the 1880s photographed by Kusakabe Kimbei, from Japan: Photographs 1854-1905 *by Clark Worswick (Knopf)*

classes, themes once largely ignored by Western historians
0–394–71040–1 Pantheon pb $11.50

- Janet E. Hunter
  A CONCISE DICTIONARY OF MODERN JAPANESE HISTORY
  0–520–04557–2 California pb $14.95

- Marius B. Jansen
  JAPAN AND ITS WORLD: Two Centuries of Change
  0–691–05310–3 Princeton $16.50

- Jon Livingston & others, editors
  THE JAPAN READER
  A collection of documents tracing Japan's history since the late 19th century

  Volume 1
  0–394–70668–4 Pantheon pb $11.95

  Volume 2
  0–394–70669–2 Pantheon pb $11.95

- Barrington Moore, Jr.
  SOCIAL ORIGINS OF DICTATORSHIP AND DEMOCRACY
  See chapter five
  0–8070–5075–X Harper & Row pb $12.95

- E.H. Norman
  ORIGINS OF THE MODERN JAPANESE STATE: Selected Writings of E.H. Norman
  Norman, the pioneer Western scholar of modern Japan, wrote these influential studies in the 1940s
  Edited by John W. Dower
  0–394–70927–6 Pantheon pb $8.95

Politics and Political Movements

- John Crump
  THE ORIGINS OF SOCIALIST THOUGHT IN JAPAN
  0–312–58872–0 St. Martin's $35.00

- Richard Deacon
  KEMPEI TAI: A History of the Japanese Secret Service
  0–8253–0131–9 Beaufort $14.95

- Thomas M. Huber
  THE REVOLUTIONARY ORIGINS OF MODERN JAPAN
  0–8047–1048–1 Stanford $28.50

- Sharon Minichiello
  RETREAT FROM REFORM: Patterns of Political Behavior in Interwar Japan
  0–8248–0778–2 Hawaii $18.00

- Tetsuo Najita, editor
  CONFLICT IN MODERN JAPANESE HISTORY: The Neglected Tradition
  Pathbreaking essays on an underestimated theme
  0–691–05364–2 Princeton pb $17.00

Society and Culture

- Irokawa Daikichi
  THE CULTURE OF THE MEIJI PERIOD
  Probes the *mentalité* of peasants and rustic intellectuals
  Translation edited by Marius B. Jansen
  0–691–06634–5 Princeton $35.50

- Yukichi Fukuzawa
  AUTOBIOGRAPHY
  The story of the founder of Keiō University and one of Meiji Japan's great Westernizers
  Translated by Eiichi Kiyooka
  0–231–08373–4 Columbia $16.50

- Carol Gluck
  JAPAN'S MODERN MYTHS: Ideology in the Late Meiji Period
  A study of the invention of Japanese "national" traits when the country decided to modernize in the last quarter of the 19th century
  0–691–00812–4 Princeton pb $12.50

- Mikiso Hane, translator & editor
  REFLECTIONS ON THE WAY TO THE GALLOWS: Rebel Women in Pre-War Japan
  Translations of memoirs, diaries, and essays by women in protest movements
  0–520–06259–0 California $22.50

- Johannes Hirschmeier
  THE ORIGINS OF ENTREPRENEURSHIP IN MEIJI JAPAN
  0–674–64475–1 Harvard $24.50

- Germaine Hoston
  MARXISM AND THE CRISIS OF DEVELOPMENT IN PRE-WAR JAPAN
  Penetrating analysis of Marxist controversy in political thought and historiography during the 1920s and '30s
  0–691–07722–3 Princeton $40.00
  0–691–10206–6 Princeton pb $15.95

- Earl H. Kinmonth
  THE SELF-MADE MAN IN MEIJI JAPANESE THOUGHT: From Samurai to Salary Man
  0–520–04159–3 California $40.00

- Donald T. Roden
  SCHOOLDAYS IN IMPERIAL JAPAN: A Study in the Culture of a Student Elite
  Lively and well-documented
  0–520–03910–6 California $40.00

- Jay Rubin
  INJURIOUS TO PUBLIC MORALS: Writers and the Meiji State
  0–295–96043–4 Washington $35.00

- Edward G. Seidensticker
  LOW CITY, HIGH CITY: Tokyo from Edo to the Earthquake, 1867-1923
  A history of Tokyo's refined and low-life quarters in the era before the Great Earthquake of 1923
  0–394–50730–4 Knopf $20.00

- Sharon L. Sievers
  FLOWERS IN SALT: The Beginnings of Feminist Consciousness in Modern Japan
  0–8047–1382–0 Stanford pb $8.95

- Robert J. Smith & Ella L. Wiswell
  THE WOMEN OF SUYE MURA
  Presents first-hand observations of the condition of rural women in the 1930s
  0–226–76345–5 Chicago pb $11.00

- Eleanor Westney
  IMITATION AND INNOVATION: The Transfer of Western Organizational Patterns to Meiji Japan
  Historical study by a sociologist of adaptation of western models of police, military, and the press
  0–674–44437–X Harvard $25.00

Imperial Japan and the Pacific War

▶ **See also The Second World War**

- Hiroyuki Agawa
  THE RELUCTANT ADMIRAL: Yamamoto and the Imperial Navy
  A biography of Japan's best military mind who agreed to the attack on Pearl Harbor although he foresaw the disastrous consequences
  Translated by John Bester
  0–87011–355–0 Kodansha pb $16.95

- Michael A. Barnhart
  JAPAN PREPARES FOR TOTAL WAR: The Search for Economic Security, 1919-1941
  Illuminates Japan's drive for a world empire in the first half of the 20th century
  0–8014–1915–8 Cornell $29.95

- John Costello
  THE PACIFIC WAR, 1941-1945
  0–688–01620–0 Morrow pb $14.95

- John W. Dower
  WAR WITHOUT MERCY: Race and Power in the Pacific War
  A history of anti-Japanese attitudes in America and anti-Western attitudes in Japan. "A cautionary tale for all peoples, now and in the future"—*Foreign Affairs*
  0–394–50030–X Pantheon $22.50
  0–394–75172–8 Pantheon pb $9.95

- Masayo Duus
  TOKYO ROSE: Orphan of the Pacific
  A fact-based account of the seductive radio star
  Translated by Peter Duus
  Introduction by Edwin O. Reischauer
  0–87011–607–X Kodansha pb $4.95

- Thomas R. Havens
  VALLEY OF DARKNESS: The Japanese People and World War II
  0–8191–5495–4 University Press pb $13.50

- Saburo Ienaga
  THE PACIFIC WAR, 1931-1945
  A harsh critique of Japanese aggression by a leading Japanese scholar
  Translated by Frank Baldwin
  0–394–73496–3 Pantheon pb $7.95

- Akira Iriye
  POWER AND CULTURE: The Japanese-American War, 1941-1945
  0–674–69580–1 Harvard $25.00
  0–674–69582–8 Harvard pb $9.95

- Ramon Myers & Mark Peattie, editors
  THE JAPANESE COLONIAL EMPIRE: 1895-1945
  0–691–10222–8 Princeton pb $19.95

- Hiroo Onoda
  NO SURRENDER: My Thirty-Year War
  Onoda, a lieutenant in the Philippines, spent 29 years in the jungle before learning that the war was over
  Translated by Charles Terry
  0–87011–240–6 Kodansha pb $8.25

- Ronald H. Spector
  EAGLE AGAINST THE SUN: The American War with Japan
  0–394–74101–3 Random House pb $9.95

- John J. Stephan
  HAWAII UNDER THE RISING SUN: Japan's Plans for Conquest after Pearl Harbor
  "Will give a fresh perspective on the place of the Hawaiian islands in Japanese strategy and war aims"—*History*
  0–8248–0872–X Hawaii $16.95

- Richard Storry
  JAPAN AND THE DECLINE OF THE WEST IN ASIA, 1894-1942
  0–312–44050–2 St. Martin's $25.00

- Christopher Thorne
  ALLIES OF A KIND: The United States, Britain, and the War Against Japan, 1941-1945
  A massive study of the Pacific war, in its foreign policy, strategic, racial, and commercial aspects
  0–19–520173–6 Oxford pb $13.95

- John Toland
  THE RISING SUN: The Decline and Fall of the Japanese Empire, 1936-1945
  A Pulitzer Prize-winning study that pays equal attention to the Japanese and American sides
  0–553–26435–4 Bantam pb $6.95

The Ginza in Tokyo, from a 1930s postcard

☐ **TO ORDER BY FAX, SEE PAGE 1**

The Atomic Bomb

• Gar Alperovitz
ATOMIC DIPLOMACY: Hiroshima and Potsdam
0–14–008337–5 Penguin pb $8.95

• Damage of the Atomic Bombs in Hiroshima and Nagasaki Committee
HIROSHIMA AND NAGASAKI: The Physical, Medical, and Social Effects of the Atomic Bombings
The most current scientific data compiled in Japan
0–465–02987–6 Basic Books pb $15.95

• John W. Dower & John Junkerman, editors
THE HIROSHIMA MURALS: The Art of Iri Maruki and Toshi Maruki
Iri and Toshi Maruki devoted their lives to depicting the horrors of war, as in the 15 enormous murals reproduced here
0–87011–735–1 Kodansha $29.95

• Japan Broadcasting Corporation
UNFORGETTABLE FIRE: Pictures Drawn by Atomic Bomb Survivors
0–394–74823–9 Pantheon pb $11.95

• Robert Jay Lifton
DEATH IN LIFE: Survivors of Hiroshima
A classic psychological study of the emotional scars left by the bomb
0–465–01582–4 Basic Books pb $12.95

A soldier in Hiroshima, from Looking the Tiger in the Eye: Confronting the Nuclear Threat *by Ronald J. Bee and Carl B. Feldbaum (Harper & Row/photo: National Archives)*

• Keiji Nakazawa
BAREFOOT GEN: A Cartoon Story of Hiroshima
Nakazawa survived the Hiroshima bombing and grew up to become one of Japan's leading comic book creators
0–86571–094–5 New Society $29.95
0–86571–095–3 New Society pb $9.95

• Arata Osada, editor
CHILDREN OF HIROSHIMA
0–85066–228–1 Taylor & Francis $30.00
0–85066–216–8 Taylor & Francis pb $16.00

• Martin J. Sherwin
A WORLD DESTROYED: Hiroshima and the Origins of the Arms Race
The best analysis of the decision to drop the bomb
0–394–75204–X Random House pb $9.95

• Peter Wyden
DAY ONE: Before Hiroshima and After
0–446–34006–5 Warner pb $3.95

The American Occupation

• Arnold C. Brackman
THE OTHER NUREMBERG: The Untold Story of the Tokyo War Crimes Trials
0–688–04783–1 Morrow $19.95
0–688–07957–1 Morrow pb $9.95

• John W. Dower
EMPIRE AND AFTERMATH: Yoshida Shigeru and the Japanese Experience, 1878-1954
Illuminates the period by focusing on Yoshida Shigeru, who played a major role in shaping Japan's response to the postwar years
0–674–25126–1 Harvard pb $14.00

• Kazuo Kawai
JAPAN'S AMERICAN INTERLUDE
0–226–42775–7 Chicago pb $14.00

• Michael Schaller
THE AMERICAN OCCUPATION OF JAPAN: The Origins of the Cold War in Asia
"Recounts in fine detail the five years during which the autocratic MacArthur vied with Washington for dominance in Japan and a role in world affairs"—
Philadelphia Inquirer
0–19–505190–4 Oxford pb $9.95

• Saburo Shiroyama
WAR CRIMINAL: The Life and Death of Hirota Koki
Hirota was the only civilian among the convicted war criminals executed in 1948; Shiroyama suggests that he was denied full justice
Translated by John Bester
0–87011–368–2 Kodansha pb $6.50

• Robert E. Ward & Sakamoto Yoshizaku
DEMOCRATIZING JAPAN: The Allied Occupation
Differing Japanese and American perceptions regarding the nature of the occupation
0–8248–0883–5 Hawaii $31.00

OVERVIEWS OF CONTEMPORARY JAPAN

• Roger Buckley
JAPAN TODAY
0–521–27832–5 Cambridge pb $8.95

• Rokuro Hidaka
THE PRICE OF AFFLUENCE: The Dilemma of Contemporary Japan
A sociological analysis critical of the effects of the "economic miracle"
Translated by Gavan McCormack
0–87011–655–X Kodansha $14.95

• Peter Tasher
THE JAPANESE
Japan in the 1980s
0–525–24675–4 Dutton $19.95

Karel van Wolferen
THE ENIGMA OF JAPANESE POWER: People and Politics in a Stateless Nation
A Dutch journalist who lives in Tokyo probes the "elusive state," "Japanese culture as ideology," and "the system as religion" in an intriguing new look at one of the world's economic superpowers. "Forceful and important"—James Fallows, *Atlantic*
0–394–57796–5 Knopf $24.95

International Relations

• Herbert J. Ellison, editor
JAPAN AND THE PACIFIC QUADRILLE: The Major Powers in East Asia
Essays exploring the relationships among Japan, China, the United States, and the Soviet Union
0–8133–7314–X Westview pb $33.50

• Jon Halliday & Gavan McCormack
JAPANESE IMPERIALISM TODAY
A left-wing perspective; published in 1973
0–85345–311–X Monthly Review pb $7.95

• Thomas R. Havens
FIRE ACROSS THE SEA: The Vietnam War and Japan, 1965-1975
A chronicle of Japan's important anti-Vietnam War movement
0–691–05491–6 Princeton $37.50
0–691–00811–6 Princeton pb $17.50

Domestic Politics

• David E. Apter & Nagayo Sawa
AGAINST THE STATE: Politics and Social Protest in Japan
0–674–00920–7 Harvard $24.50
0–674–00921–5 Harvard pb $9.95

• Gerald L. Curtis
THE JAPANESE WAY OF POLITICS
A comprehensive study of party politics in today's Japan
0–231–06680–5 Columbia $35.00

• Margaret A. McKean
ENVIRONMENTAL PROTEST AND CITIZEN POLITICS IN JAPAN
Clarifies an important area of conflict in contemporary Japan
0–520–04115–1 California $32.50

• Joe Moore
JAPANESE WORKERS AND THE STRUGGLE FOR POWER, 1945-1947
Moore effectively demolishes the myth of the docile Japanese worker
0–299–09320–4 Wisconsin $23.95

• T.J. Pempel
POLICY AND POLITICS IN JAPAN: Creative Conservatism
Presents a useful selection of Japanese documents
0–87722–250–9 Temple pb $16.95

TO ORDER BOOKS AS GIFTS, SEE PAGE 1

ECONOMICS AND BUSINESS

• James C. Abegglen & George
Stalk, Jr.
**KAISHA, THE JAPANESE
CORPORATION: The New Competitors in
World Business**
Abegglen, a long-time resident of Tokyo,
is a leading authority on Japanese business
0–465–03711–9 Basic Books $23.95
0–465–03712–7 Basic Books pb $12.95

• Rodney Clark
THE JAPANESE COMPANY
0–300–02646–3 Yale pb $12.95

• Michael A. Cusumano
**THE JAPANESE AUTOMOBILE
INDUSTRY: Technology and Management
at Nissan and Toyota**
0–674–47255–1 Harvard $25.00

• William H. Davidson
**THE AMAZING RACE: Winning the
Technorivalry with Japan**
0–471–88711–0 John Wiley $22.95

• Ronald Dore
**FLEXIBLE RIGIDITIES: Industrial Policy
and Structural Adjustment in the Japanese
Economy, 1970-1980**
0–8047–1328–6 Stanford $32.50
0–8047–1465–7 Stanford pb $10.95

• Mark W. Fruin
**KIKKOMAN: Company, Clan, and
Community**
0–674–50340–6 Harvard $35.00

• David Halberstam
THE RECKONING
Detroit versus Japan's automakers
0–688–04838–2 Morrow $19.95
0–380–70447–1 Avon pb $5.95

• Shotaro Ishinomori
**JAPAN, INC.: Introduction to Japanese
Economics (The Comic Book)**
Contemporary economics in comic book
form, complete with heroes, villains, and
even a bit of sex and violence
Introduction by Peter Duus
0–520–06288–4 California $25.00
0–520–06289–2 California pb $10.95

• Chalmers Johnson
**MITI AND THE JAPANESE MIRACLE:
The Growth of Industrial Policy, 1925-
1975**
The classic study of Japanese economic
planning; dense but worth the effort
0–8047–1128–3 Stanford $32.50
0–8047–1206–9 Stanford pb $11.95

• Kodansha
**THE BEST OF JAPAN: Innovations,
Present and Future**
Presents 260 award-winning products and
services, chosen by the Japan Economic
Journal; an impressive glimpse of future
technology
0–87011–801–3 Kodansha pb $24.95

• Yutaka Kosai & Yoshitaro Ogino
**THE CONTEMPORARY JAPANESE
ECONOMY**
Translated by Ralph Thompson
0–87332–273–8 Sharpe $37.50
0–87332–274–6 Sharpe pb $16.95

• Thomas K. McCraw, editor
**AMERICA VS. JAPAN: A Comparative
Study**
A useful collection of essays on the
differences between Japanese and American
economic strategy
0–87584–139–2 Harvard Business School $29.95

• Michio Morishima
**WHY HAS JAPAN SUCCEEDED?:
Western Technology and the Japanese Ethos**
0–521–26903–2 Cambridge pb $12.95

• Akio Morita & Edwin M. Reingold
**MADE IN JAPAN: Akio Morita and the
Sony Corporation**
The autobiography of Sony's founder, one
of the rare flashy personalities in Japanese
business
0–452–25987–8 NAL pb $9.95

• Kenichi Ohmae
**BEYOND NATIONAL BORDERS:
Reflections on Japan and the World**
Ohmae, a McKinsey and Co. consultant, is
probably Japan's best-selling non-fiction
writer; here he argues that the Japanese
must "internationalize" and stop thinking
they are unique
1–55623–017–6 Dow Jones-Irwin $20.95

**TRIAD POWER: The Coming Shape of
Global Competition**
Ohmae contends that companies,
consumers, and cultures are becoming the
same around the world, and that Japan,
the US, and Europe must become more
tightly integrated
0–02–923470–0 Free Press $21.95

• Terutomo Ozawa
**MULTINATIONALISM, JAPANESE
STYLE: The Political Economy of Outward
Dependency**
An introduction to the conglomerates now
making their challenge on a global scale
0–691–04221–7 Princeton $31.50
0–691–00367–X Princeton pb $12.95

• Clyde V. Prestowitz, Jr.
**TRADING PLACES: How We Allowed
Japan to Take the Lead**
A former US trade negotiator argues that
the Japanese still view trade as "strategic
competition" (more plainly, as war) and
that the US must respond in kind
0–465–08680–2 Basic Books $19.95

• Tatsuro Uchino
**JAPAN'S POSTWAR ECONOMY: An
Insider's View of Its History and Its Future**
Japanese perspectives on the Japanese
economy, written by a former government
planner. Highly accessible
Translated by Mark Harbison
0–87011–595–2 Kodansha $17.95

• Raymond Vernon
**TWO HUNGRY GIANTS: The United
States and Japan in the Quest for Oil and
Ores**
0–674–91470–8 Harvard $19.50

Management and Labor

• Ronald Dore
**BRITISH FACTORY-JAPANESE
FACTORY: The Origins of National
Diversity in Employment Relations**
0–520–02495–8 California pb $12.95

• Kunio Odaka
**TOWARD INDUSTRIAL DEMOCRACY:
Management and the Workers in Modern
Japan**
0–674–89816–8 Harvard $18.50

• Kenichi Ohmae
**THE MIND OF THE STRATEGIST: The
Art of Japanese Business**
0–07–047595–4 McGraw-Hill $24.95

• Jared Taylor
**SHADOWS OF THE RISING SUN: A
Critical View of the Japanese Miracle**
0–688–04827–7 Morrow pb $9.95

• Lester C. Thurow, editor
**THE MANAGEMENT CHALLENGE:
Japanese Views**
Of the many recent studies of Japanese
management, this is one of the most
insightful
0–262–20053–8 MIT $20.00

CONTEMPORARY SOCIETY
AND CULTURE

• Theodore C. Bestor
NEIGHBORHOOD TOKYO
An anthropologist considers the uses of
tradition in contemporary urban Japan
0–8047–1439–8 Stanford $35.00

• Ian Buruma
**BEHIND THE MASK: On Sexual Demons,
Sacred Mothers, Transvestites, Gangsters
and Other Japanese Cultural Heroes**
A journalist's witty and vivid examination
of Japanese popular culture, including its
more outrageous movies and comic books
0–452–00738–0 NAL pb $8.95

• Winston Davis
**DOJO: Magic and Exorcism in Modern
Japan**
A lively study of one of Japan's new
religions, Sukyo Mahikari
0–8047–1053–8 Stanford $27.50
0–8047–1131–3 Stanford pb $10.95

• David Desser
**EROS PLUS MASSACRE: An
Introduction to the Japanese New Wave
Cinema**
0–253–20469–0 Indiana pb $12.95

• Takeo Doi
THE ANATOMY OF DEPENDENCE
A book the Japanese themselves take very
seriously as a key to their character, written
by a leading psychologist
Translated by John Bester
0–87011–494–8 Kodansha pb $4.95

THE ANATOMY OF SELF
Doi's most recent work deals with the role
of the individual in Japan
0–87011–761–0 Kodansha $16.95

● Ronald Dore

TAKING JAPAN SERIOUSLY: A Confucian Perspective on Leading Economic Issues
Emphasizes the Confucian roots of many of Japan's accomplishments
0–8047–1350–2 Stanford $35.00
0–8047–1401–0 Stanford pb $11.95

● Norie Huddle, Michael Reich & Nahum Stiskin

ISLAND OF DREAMS: Environmental Crisis in Japan
Afterword by Ralph Nader
0–87047–027–2 Schenkman $22.95
0–87047–028–0 Schenkman pb $15.95

● David Kaplan & Alec Dubro

YAKUZA: The Explosive Account of Japan's Criminal Underworld
A study of the gangsters whom foreigners often overlook when perceiving an all-harmonious Japan
0–02–033990–9 Macmillan pb $8.95

● Robert Jay Lifton

SIX LIVES, SIX DEATHS
0–300–02600–5 Yale pb $12.95

● Chie Nakane

JAPANESE SOCIETY
"Miss Nakane has distilled into 150 pages a gin-crisp, clear, and fresh primer on what is Japanese about modes of human relating in Japan . . . . If you have time for just one book on Japan, try this one"—*Asian Student*
0–520–02154–1 California pb $9.95

Haru M. Reischauer

SAMURAI AND SILK: A Japanese and American Heritage
Several generations of a Japanese aristocratic family, by the wife of Edwin O. Reischauer. "Beautifully written, with a sense of intimacy that only first-hand experience and family traditions could confer"—John Gross, *NY Times*
0–674–78800–1 Harvard $20.00
0–674–78801–X Harvard pb $10.95

● Frederik L. Schodt

MANGA! MANGA!: The World of Japanese Comics
Superbly detailed not only on comics but on their social context and significance
Introduction by Osamu Tezuka
0–87011–752–1 Kodansha pb $16.95

● Shunsuke Tsurumi

A CULTURAL HISTORY OF POSTWAR JAPAN, 1945-1980
Touches on everything from comic books to the war crimes trial
0–7103–0259–2 RC&H $45.00

AN INTELLECTUAL HISTORY OF WARTIME JAPAN, 1931-1945
A wide-ranging and provocative survey
0–7103–0072–7 RC&H $39.95

A frame of Shinji Mizushima's "Dokaben," from Manga! Manga!: The World of Japanese Comics *by Frederik L. Schodt (Kodansha)*

● Merry White

THE JAPANESE OVERSEAS: Can They Go Home Again?
Examines the cultural isolation faced by overseas Japanese workers when they return home
0–02–935091–3 Free Press $19.95

Education

● Joy Hendry

BECOMING JAPANESE: The World of the Pre-School Child
0–8248–1092–9 Hawaii $18.00

● Thomas P. Rohlen

JAPAN'S HIGH SCHOOLS
A remarkably full and comprehensive account
0–520–04863–6 California pb $11.95

● Merry White

THE JAPANESE EDUCATIONAL CHALLENGE: A Commitment to Children
A vivid study of what makes Japanese schools work as well as they do
0–02–933800–X Free Press $18.95
0–02–933801–8 Free Press pb $9.95

Rural Society

● Ronald Dore

SHINOHATA: Portrait of a Japanese Village
An acclaimed portrait of rural life
0–394–73843–8 Pantheon pb $6.50

● Tadashi Fukutake

JAPANESE RURAL SOCIETY
Fukutake is the most prominent writer on Japanese society
Translated by Ronald Dore
0–8014–9127–4 Cornell pb $9.95

Women and the Family

● Gail L. Bernstein

HARUKO'S WORLD: A Japanese Farm Woman and Her Community
0–8047–1174–7 Stanford $25.00
0–8047–1287–5 Stanford pb $7.95

● Kittredge Cherry

WOMANSWORD: What Japanese Words Say about Women
The role of women in Japanese culture, as exemplified in the meaning and usage of 80 words
0–87011–794–7 Kodansha pb $13.95

● Liza Crichfield Dalby

GEISHA
Tales from an American woman who worked as a geisha; both scholarly and enthralling
0–394–72893–9 Random House pb $9.95

● Shidzue Ishimoto

FACING TWO WAYS: The Story of My Life
Edited by Barbara Molony
0–8047–1239–5 Stanford $42.50

● Joyce Lebra & others, editors

WOMEN IN CHANGING JAPAN
0–8047–0971–8 Stanford pb $10.95

● Takie S. Lebra

JAPANESE WOMEN: Constraint and Fulfillment
0–8248–0868–1 Hawaii $18.95
0–8248–1025–2 Hawaii pb $9.50

● Tomoko Yamazaki

THE STORY OF YAMADA WAKA: From Prostitute to Feminist Pioneer
The remarkable story of a feminist activist of interwar years
Translated by Ann Kostant & Wakako Hironaka
0–87011–733–5 Kodansha $16.95

Foreigners in Japan

Pat Barr

THE COMING OF THE BARBARIANS: A Story of Western Settlement in Japan, 1853-1870
An anecdotal account of the first decades of contact with the West after the 17th-century isolation
0–14–009577–2 Penguin pb $7.95

Isabella L. Bird

UNBEATEN TRACKS IN JAPAN
An indomitable Victorian traveler explores remote corners of Japan, much to the surprise of the inhabitants
0–8070–7015–7 Beacon pb $9.95

Michael Cooper, editor

THEY CAME TO JAPAN: An Anthology of European Reports on Japan, 1543-1640
0–520–04509–2 California pb $12.95

John D. Morley

PICTURES FROM THE WATER TRADE: Adventures of a Westerner in Japan
An unusual exploration of the night life of contemporary Tokyo
0–06–097041–3 Harper & Row pb $7.95

Robert A. Rosenstone
MIRROR IN THE SHRINE: American Encounters with Meiji Japan
Three very different Westerners: the missionary William Elliot Griffis, the scientist Edward S. Morse, and the writer Lafcadio Hearn
0–674–57641–1 Harvard $25.00

Philipp Von Siebold
MANNERS AND CUSTOMS OF THE JAPANESE IN THE NINETEENTH CENTURY
Based on first-hand observations in the 1820s
0–8048–1081–8 Tuttle pb $6.75

Clara A. Whitney
CLARA'S DIARY: An American Girl in Meiji Japan
Whitney, a missionary's daughter, began this highly detailed diary at age 15
Introduction by William Steele
0–87011–470–0 Kodansha pb $8.95

Korea

"**K**oreans call their country Choson . . . 'The Land of the Morning Calm'. Despite the country's indigenous name, the history of Korea has been anything but calm with successive invasions by the Chinese, the Mongols and the Japanese. Today's division of Korea has added a new dimension to this turbulent past . . . Following the destruction of the Korean War, the economy remained very weak for a decade . . . Following a military coup in 1961, South Korea enjoyed both political stability and economic growth which, within 20 years, turned the Republic of Korea into an advanced industrial country . . . From less than $40 million in 1961, exports rose to about $455 million in 1968 . . . to over $15 billion in 1979; per capita national income during the same period increased from $82 per annum to about $1500. The GNP jumped from $2 billion to $60 billion . . . The ROK had become in effect an advanced industrial country, second only to Japan in the Far East."—David Rees, *A Short History of Modern Korea*

ONE NATION: To 1945

• Isabella L. Bird
KOREA AND HER NEIGHBOURS
Nineteenth-century Korea observed by an intrepid traveler
0–8048–1489–9 Tuttle pb $11.50

• Bong-Youn Choy
KOREA: A History
0–8048–0249–1 Tuttle $21.50

• Martin Duchler
CONFUCIAN GENTLEMEN AND BARBARIAN ENVOYS: The Opening of Korea, 1875-1885
A well-written account of a crucial decade in modern Korean history
0–295–95552–X Washington $27.50

• Woo-Keun Han
THE HISTORY OF KOREA
"A survey of Korean history which is clearly in a class by itself"—*Library Journal*
Translated by Kyung-Shik Lee
Edited by Grafton K. Mintz
0–8248–0334–5 Hawaii pb $11.95

• Jattyun Kim Haboush
A HERITAGE OF KINGS: One Man's Monarchy in the Confucian World
"Elegant biographical study of Yongjo, one of Korean's most illustrious and yet tragic kings"—Laura Kendall
0–231–06656–2 Columbia $35.00

• William E. Henthorn
HISTORY OF KOREA
0–02–914460–4 Free Press $19.95
0–02–914610–0 Free Press pb $12.95

• Jeong-Hak Kim
THE PREHISTORY OF KOREA
Translated by Richard J. & Kazue Pearson
0–8248–0552–6 Hawaii $20.00

• Key-Hiuk Kim
THE LAST PHASE OF THE CONFUCIAN WORLD ORDER: Korea, Japan, and the Chinese Empire, 1860-1882
An important, original study of international politics and diplomacy
0–520–03556–9 California $40.00

"Korean Man" by Rubens, c. 1616 (Getty Museum)

• Ki-Baik Lee
A NEW HISTORY OF KOREA
A meticulously indexed book, strong on the development of Korean culture. "The best and most comprehensive general history of Korea published to date"— *History*
Translated by Edward Wagner & Edward Schultz
0–674–61575–1 Harvard $25.00
0–674–61576–X Harvard pb $12.95

• David Rees
A SHORT HISTORY OF MODERN KOREA
A leading authority traces the progress of the country from its origins to present times
0–87052–575–1 Hippocrene $16.95

• Simon Winchester
KOREA
0–13–516626–8 Prentice-Hall $17.95

THE KOREAN WAR

• Bevin Alexander
KOREA: The First War We Lost
0–87052–135–7 Hippocrene $24.95

• Clay Blair
THE FORGOTTEN WAR: America in Korea, 1950-1953
0–8129–1670–0 Times Books $29.95
0–385–26033–4 Doubleday pb $16.95

• James Cotton & Ian Neary, editors
THE KOREAN WAR IN HISTORY
0–391–03497–9 Humanities Press $39.95

• Bruce Cumings
THE ORIGINS OF THE KOREAN WAR: Liberation and the Emergence of Separate Regimes
An in-depth examination of the road into and out of war
0–691–10113–2 Princeton pb $24.50

• J.C. Goulden
KOREA: The Untold Story of the War
A popular history
0–07–023580–5 McGraw-Hill pb $14.95

• Jon Halliday
KOREA: The Unknown War
A generously illustrated, thorough and authoritative book. Uses extensive interviews as the main source
0–394–55366–7 Pantheon $19.95

• Max Hastings
THE KOREAN WAR
A preeminent military historian draws from the accounts of more than 200 veterans to chart the first war the US could not win. "Must reading for any American who wants to understand some of the watershed events of the post World War II period"—Richard M. Nixon
0–671–52823–8 Simon & Schuster $22.95

• Burton Kaufman
THE KOREAN WAR: The Challenges in Crisis, Credibility and Command
0–394–34154–6 Knopf pb $10.50

• Donald Knox
THE KOREAN WAR: Pusan to Chosin—An Oral History
"A fast-paced, in-the-trenches look at the war"—*Baltimore Sun*
0–15–147288–2 HBJ $24.95
0–317–56663–6 HBJ pb $10.95

THE KOREAN WAR: Uncertain Victory
Edited by Alfred Coppel
0–15–147289–0 HBJ $29.95
0–15–647200–7 HBJ pb $10.95

• Peter Lowe
THE ORIGINS OF THE KOREAN WAR
0–582–49278–5 Longman pb $17.50

• Callum A. MacDonald
KOREA: The War Before Vietnam
0–02–919621–3 Free Press $24.95

• Matthew B. Ridgway
THE KOREAN WAR: How We Met the Challenge
The general who took over from MacArthur in 1951 "deals harshly with those who shout 'There is no substitute for victory' without really knowing what victory means" (J.M. Allison, *Saturday Review*)
0–306–80267–8 Da Capo pb $12.95

• I.F. Stone
THE HIDDEN HISTORY OF THE KOREAN WAR, 1950-1951
"It took guts to publish this book in the McCarthy era"—*Baltimore Sun*
0–316–81773–2 Little, Brown $17.95
0–316–81770–8 Little, Brown pb $8.95

KOREA DIVIDED

Politics and Society

• William J. Barnds, editor
THE TWO KOREAS IN EAST ASIAN AFFAIRS
0–8147–0988–5 NYU $30.00

• Patricia M. Bartz
SOUTH KOREA
0–19–874008–5 Oxford $49.95

• Brian Bridges
KOREA AND THE WEST
Examines the political culture and economic development of the two Koreas, as well as the state of the military balance in the peninsula
0–7102–1110–4 RC&H $12.95

• Ralph N. Clough
EMBATTLED KOREA: The Rivalry for International Support
The history of Korea's division and the competition between Seoul and Pyongyang
0–8133–7324–7 Westview $32.50

• Harold C. Hinton
KOREA UNDER NEW LEADERSHIP: The Fifth Republic
An appreciative work detailing the accomplishments of the current regime
0–275–91006–7 Praeger $35.95

• James Hoare & Susan Pares
KOREA: An Introduction
An introductory book presenting a full picture of the country and its 40 million inhabitants
0–7103–0299–1 RC&H pb $12.95

• Russell Warren Howe
THE KOREANS: Passion and Grace
A detailed primer on modern-day Korea by an aficionado of two decades
0–15–647185–X HBJ pb $12.95

• Laurel Kendall & Mark Peterson, editors
KOREAN WOMEN: View from the Inner Room
0–910825–02–5 East Rock $20.00

• Kim Dae Jung
PRISON WRITINGS
A trenchant view of the dictatorship and the tumultuous politics of South Korea by the long incarcerated opposition leader
0–520–05482–2 California $25.00

• Byung C. Koh
THE FOREIGN POLICY SYSTEMS OF NORTH AND SOUTH KOREA
0–520–04805–9 California $37.50

• Chong-Sik Lee
KOREAN WORKERS' PARTY: A Short History
Edited by R.F. Staar
0–8179–6852–0 Hoover Institute pb $7.95

• Donald MacDonald
THE KOREANS: Contemporary Politics and Society
0–8133–0515–2 Westview $34.95

• John Merrill
D.P.R. KOREA: Politics, Economics and Society
A brief but up-to-date introduction to the country's various sectors, plus an analysis of its international relations
0–86187–424–2 Columbia $35.00
0–86187–425–0 Columbia pb $12.50

• Joo-Hong Nam
AMERICA'S COMMITMENT TO SOUTH KOREA: The First Decade of the Nixon Doctrine
0–87296–020–X Si-sa-yong-o-sa $20.00

• Edward Olsen
U.S. POLICY AND THE TWO KOREAS
The military, commercial, and political interests of the United States in North and South Korea
0–8133–0593–4 Westview pb $11.95

• J.K. Park & B.C. Koh, editors
THE FOREIGN RELATIONS OF NORTH KOREA: A New Perspective
0–8133–0569–1 Westview $43.00

• David I. Steinberg
THE REPUBLIC OF KOREA: Economic Transformation and Social Change
0–86531–720–8 Westview $34.50

• Dae-Sook Suh
KOREAN COMMUNISM, 1945-1980: A Reference Guide to the Political System
A heavily documented sourcebook which maps out the history and evolution of the movement
0–8248–0740–5 Hawaii $35.00

KIM IL SUNG: The North Korean Leader
0–231–06572–8 Columbia $45.00

• John Sullivan & Roberta Foss, editors
TWO KOREAS, ONE FUTURE: A Report Prepared for the American Friends Service Committee
Among the best recent evaluations of the dilemmas facing a divided and volatile nation
0–8191–6049–0 University Press $25.00
0–8191–6050–4 University Press pb $11.50

• Nym Wales & Kim San
SONG OF ARIRAN: A Korean Communist in the Chinese Revolution
This portrait of a Korean revolutionary in China between 1920 and 1940 highlights the interconnection of Asian revolutionary movements
0–87867–022–X Ramparts pb $6.95

• Jon Woronoff
KOREA'S ECONOMY: Man-Made Miracle
The role of central government planning in the "miraculous" process
0–89209–214–9 Si-sa-yong-o-sa $12.00

Culture

• Stanley H. Barkan, editor
SOUTH KOREAN POETS OF RESISTANCE
Translated by Ko Won
0–89304–607–8 Cross-Cultural pb $5.00

• Chongwha Chung, editor
KOREAN CLASSICAL LITERATURE: An Anthology
0–7103–0279–7 RC&H $22.50

Musicians and dancer, an 18th-century Korean genre scene

➤ **FOR OVERSEAS ORDERING INFORMATION, SEE PAGE 1**

- Laurel Kendall
THE LIFE AND HARD TIMES OF A KOREAN SHAMAN: Of Tales and the Telling of Tales
An innovative re-creation of the dramatic life story of a woman many times wronged by men, finally claimed by the spirits, and now a practicing yarn-spinning shaman and ritual specialist
0–8248–1136–4 Hawaii $23.00
0–8248–1145–3 Hawaii pb $9.95

SHAMANS, HOUSEWIVES AND OTHER RESTLESS SPIRITS: Women in Korean Ritual Life
A reconsideration of Korean notions of family and kin through an analysis of women's beliefs and practices
0–8248–1142–9 Hawaii pb $9.95

- Richard E. Kim
LOST NAMES: Scenes from a Boyhood in Japanese-Occupied Korea
0–87663–678–4 Universe $14.95

- Han Man-yong & others
KOREAN DANCE, THEATER, AND CINEMA
0–89209–017–0 Pace International $20.00

- John Rosenfield, editor
KOREAN ART TREASURES
0–8109–1214–7 Abrams $80.00

- Yushin Yoo
KOREA THE BEAUTIFUL: Treasures of the Hermit Kingdom
0–942091–01–9 Golden Pond $24.95

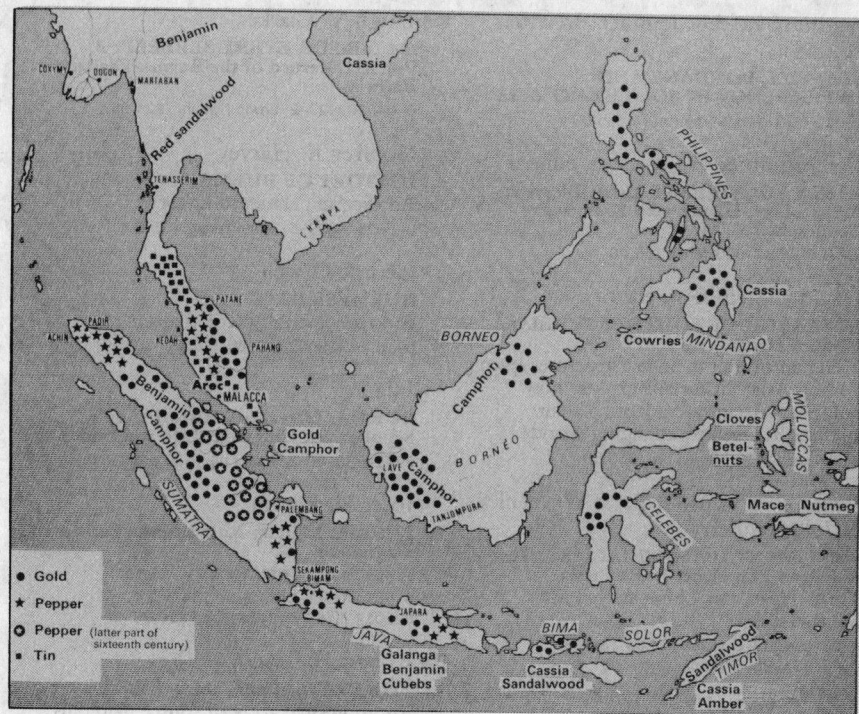

The wealth of the East Indies, from Perspectives of the World *by Fernand Braudel (Harper & Row)*

Southeast Asia and the Philippines

"What does the future hold for Indochina? Judging by recent history the years ahead can bring more suffering and perhaps more bloodshed. China is determined to tame Vietnam and establish its own supremacy in Southeast Asia—a goal for which it has only partial support from ASEAN and the West. Vietnam is determined to maintain the dominance it has achieved by military might and deprivation of its own people. Unless there is willingness in both Peking and Hanoi to lower their sights, Indochina will not know peace . . . A heavy responsibility—and opportunity—however lies with the United States. An ironic turn of the wheel has again placed Washington in the position of arbiter in Asia. It is best placed to guarantee a new balance of power in Southeast Asia."—Nayan Chanda, *Brother Enemy: A History of Indochina Since the Fall of Saigon*

- Ian Buruma
GOD'S DUST: A Modern Asian Journey
Deep familiarity with customs of both east and west makes Buruma one of the most qualified observers of the thriving Pacific Rim. *God's Dust* is a tour of Burma, Thailand, the Philippines, Malaysia, Singapore, Taiwan, South Korea, and Japan
0–374–16458–4 Farrar, Straus & Giroux $17.95

- John Cady
THE HISTORY OF POSTWAR SOUTHEAST ASIA: Independence Problems
0–8214–0160–2 Ohio $30.00
0–8214–0175–0 Ohio pb $15.00

THE SOUTHEAST ASIAN WORLD
0–88273–502–0 Forum pb $6.95

- Nayan Chanda
BROTHER ENEMY: A History of Indochina Since the Fall of Saigon
A close examination of both the truth and the significance of the Third Indochina War authoritatively written in the form of a highly readable narrative
0–02–049361–4 Macmillan pb $12.95

- Ernest S. Dodge
ISLANDS AND EMPIRES: Western Impact on the Pacific and East Asia
0–8166–0788–5 Minnesota $17.50

- Daniel G. Hall
A HISTORY OF SOUTH EAST ASIA
0–312–38642–7 St. Martin's pb $15.95

- Peter Hayes & others
AMERICAN LAKE: Nuclear Peril in the Pacific
Why World War III is more likely to begin in the Pacific than in the Middle East or Europe
0–14–009396–6 Penguin pb $6.95

- Akira Iriye
THE WORLD OF ASIA
0–88273–500–4 Forum pb $17.95

- Staffan B. Linder
THE PACIFIC CENTURY: Economic and Political Consequences of Asian-Pacific Dynamism
0–8047–1294–8 Stanford $22.50
0–8047–1305–7 Stanford pb $7.95

- Donald G. McCloud
SYSTEM AND PROCESS IN SOUTHEAST ASIA: The Evolution of a Region
0–86531–588–4 Westview pb $16.95

- Clark Neher
POLITICS IN SOUTHEAST ASIA
0–87047–011–6 Schenkman pb $15.95

- Milton Osborne
SOUTHEAST ASIA: An Illustrated Introduction
0–86861–668–0 Unwin Hyman pb $11.95

- Lucian W. & Mary W. Pye
ASIAN POWER AND POLITICS: The Cultural Dimensions of Authority
"Will be the subject of much scholarly debate"—*Foreign Affairs*
0–674–04979–9 Harvard pb $12.95

- Anthony Reid
SOUTHEAST ASIA IN THE AGE OF COMMERCE 1450-1680: The Lands Below the Winds, Volume 1
A total history encompassing a fascinating gamut of social and cultural structures from diet to law to sex to war; volume 2 forthcoming
0–300–03921–2 Yale $25.00

• Anthony Reid & Jennifer Brewster, editors
SLAVERY, BONDAGE AND DEPENDENCY IN SOUTHEAST ASIA
0–312–72812–3 St. Martin's $35.00

• R.B. Smith & W. Watson, editors
EARLY SOUTH EAST ASIA: Essays in Archaeology, History and Historical Geography
0–19–713587–0 Oxford $55.00

• David J. Steinberg, editor
IN SEARCH OF SOUTHEAST ASIA: A Modern History
Using an overall thematic structure, seven leading Asian historians explore how Southeast Asians are adapting their cultures to a swiftly changing world
0–8248–1110–0 Hawaii pb $18.50

• James C. Thomson, Peter W. Stanley & John C. Perry
SENTIMENTAL IMPERIALISTS: The American Experience in East Asia
Treats Japan and China as well as Southeast Asia
0–06–014282–0 Harper & Row $18.50
0–06–131998–8 Harper & Row pb $8.95

• Paul T. Welty
THE ASIANS: Their Heritage and Their Destiny
0–06–047001–1 Harper & Row pb $17.95

• Lea E. Williams
SOUTHEAST ASIA: A History
Considers men and movements of influence in Southeast Asia: Sukarno, Ho Chi Minh, Ferdinand Marcos, and the Viet Minh
0–19–502000–6 Oxford pb $12.95

BURMA

Independent in 1948 after more than a century of British rule, and with a more remote history of Chinese domination, this large Buddhist state has been a "nominally civilian" one-party Socialist Democratic Republic since 1974. Its secretive stance—visitors may sojourn no longer than one closely watched week—means that little is known of this land with a rice-and-teak economy, apart from its regime's brutal repression of all dissent.

• Michael Aung-Thwin
PAGAN: The Origins of Modern Burma
0–8248–0960–2 Hawaii $25.00

• John Cady
THE UNITED STATES AND BURMA
0–674–92320–0 Harvard $21.00

• Won-loy Chan
BURMA: The Untold Story
0–89141–266–2 Presidio $14.95

• Hugh V. Clarke
A LIFE FOR EVERY SLEEPER: A Pictorial Record of the Burma-Thailand Railway
0–04–909023–2 Unwin Hyman $24.95

• Godfrey E. Harvey
HISTORY OF BURMA
An excellent standard history
0–88254–839–5 Hippocrene $35.00

• George Orwell
BURMESE DAYS
A novel of English colonialism
0–15–614850–1 HBJ pb $5.95

• Hla Pe
BURMA: Literature, Historiography, Scholarship, Language, Life and Buddhism
9971–988–00–3 Gower pb $29.95

• Josef Silverstein
BURMA: Military Rule and the Politics of Stagnation
A study of contemporary Burma
0–8014–0911–X Cornell $34.95
0–8014–9863–5 Cornell pb $10.95

• Robert H. Taylor
THE STATE IN BURMA
An impressive array of source materials helps to unravel the history of Burma's political development since the early 1960s when the military took power
0–8248–1141–0 Hawaii $32.00

CAMBODIA

Between the splendors of the Khmer Angkor empire (800-1220) and the infamies of the Pol Pot/Khmer Rouge regime (1975-1979) Cambodia also knew a century of French rule, until independence under King Sihanouk in 1953. Efforts to steer clear of the Vietnam War were thwarted by United States interventions in the early 1970s. War with one foe or another has remained a fact of life ever since, although the bloodshed appeared to peak under Pol Pot, who annihilated as much as one third of the entire population of six million.

• David A. Ablin & Marlowe Hood, editors
THE CAMBODIAN AGONY
Specialists in Indochinese politics address the major issues confronting the country in the aftermath of the Pol Pot regime, which provoked the most radical social upheaval in any country in recorded history
0–87332–421–8 Sharpe $35.00

• Elizabeth Becker
WHEN THE WAR WAS OVER: Cambodia's Revolution and the Voices of Its People
The definitive book on the Cambodian revolution. "An extraordinary synthesis of journalism and scholarship"—Strobe Talbott
0–671–64559–5 Simon & Schuster pb $9.95

Fragment of a demonic head, Khmer, c. 1200 (Musée Guimet)

• David P. Chandler & Ben Kiernan, editors
REVOLUTION AND ITS AFTERMATH IN KAMPUCHEA: Eight Essays
0–938692–05–4 Yale pb $14.00

• George Coedes
ANGKOR: An Introduction
The work of a great scholar
0–19–638129–0 Oxford pb $9.95

• Richard Dudman
FORTY DAYS WITH THE ENEMY
The story of a journalist held captive by guerrillas in Cambodia
0–87140–259–9 Liveright pb $2.50

• Craig Etcheson
THE RISE AND DEMISE OF DEMOCRATIC KAMPUCHEA
0–86531–650–3 Westview $41.50

• Someth May
CAMBODIAN WITNESS: The Autobiography of Someth May
Introduction by James Fenton
0–394–54804–3 Random House $17.95

• Haing Ngor & Roger Warner
HAING NGOR: A Cambodian Odyssey
0–02–589330–0 Macmillan $19.95

• Sydney H. Schanberg
THE DEATH AND LIFE OF DITH PRAN
Source of the Oscar-winning *The Killing Fields*
0–14–008457–6 Penguin pb $5.95

• William Shawcross
SIDESHOW: Kissinger, Nixon and the Destruction of Cambodia
The Nixon administration's furtive tactics in Cambodia. "Portrays the surreal world of power severed from morality"—*NY Times*
0–671–64103–4 Simon & Schuster pb $12.95

- Molyda Szymusiak
THE STONES CRY OUT: A Cambodian Childhood, 1975-1980
A young girl's arrival at puberty in a time of madness. "Evokes as no other account before the chaos and cruelty of one nation's season in hell"—*Newsweek*
Translated by Linda Coverdale
0–8090–1534–X Hill & Wang pb $8.95

- Michael Vickery
CAMBODIA: 1975-1982
Fluent in all Khmer patois, Vickery based his study on discussions with hundreds of refugees
0–89608–190–7 South End $25.00
0–89608–189–3 South End pb $10.00

HONG KONG

"Hong Kong seldom was a very characteristic British possession. In its affairs we see reflected not only the decline of a historical genre—it is the last great *European* colony, too—but the shifting aspirations of communism and capitalism, the resurgence of the new Asia, the rising power of technology. As it prepares to withdraw at last from the British imperium, it is like a mirror to the world, or perhaps a geomancer's compass."—Jan Morris, *Hong Kong*

- Joseph Y.S. Cheng
HONG KONG: In Search of a Future
0–19–583747–9 Oxford pb $17.95

- Bruce Bueno de Mesquita & others
FORECASTING POLITICAL EVENTS: The Future of Hong Kong
0–300–03519–5 Yale $30.00

- Lau Siu-Kai
SOCIETY AND POLITICS IN HONG KONG
0–312–73892–7 St. Martin's $25.00

- Norman J. Miners
THE GOVERNMENT AND POLITICS OF HONG KONG
An authoritative reference on the administration of the Crown Colony; includes an up-to-date discussion of the changes following the 1984 Sino-British agreement on Hong Kong's restoration to the mainland
0–19–584171–9 Oxford $29.95
0–19–584062–3 Oxford pb $13.95
HONG KONG UNDER IMPERIAL RULE, 1912-1941
0–19–584171–9 Oxford $35.00

- Jan Morris
HONG KONG
A great travel writer's montage of imperial history and modern capitalism shows the precipitous contrasts between primitive poverty and outrageous wealth
0–394–55097–8 Random House $19.95

INDONESIA

Currently fifth in world population, with more than 170 million people scattered across some 13,000 islands, Indonesia is potentially the richest state in Southeast Asia. Moslem by the 15th century, it is now the world's largest Islamic republic. Dutch occupation culminated in membership in the Netherlands kingdom after World War I, until Sukarno proclaimed independence in 1945. His Sino-Soviet-oriented "guided (i.e., non-parliamentary) democracy" was ousted by General Suharto in 1967 after a series of virulent anti-communist purges claiming, it is said, over a quarter of a million victims. The Suharto regime boasts political—and economic—stability, with more open policies toward both China and the West.

- Susan Abeyasekere
JAKARTA: A History
0–19–582688–4 Oxford $36.00

- Karl D. Jackson & Lucian W. Pye, editors
POLITICAL POWER AND COMMUNICATIONS IN INDONESIA
0–520–04205–0 California pb $11.95

- Hamish McDonald
SUHARTO'S INDONESIA
An up-to-date and timely book on the republic and its restructuring
0–8248–0781–2 Hawaii pb $5.95

- Robin Osborne
INDONESIA'S SECRET WAR: The Guerilla Struggle in Irian Jaya
0–86861–519–6 Unwin Hyman pb $12.95

- Anthony Reid
THE BLOOD OF THE PEOPLE: Revolution and the End of Traditional Rule in Northern Sumatra
0–19–580399–X Oxford $39.95

- M.C. Ricklefs
A HISTORY OF MODERN INDONESIA
0–253–19593–4 Indiana $25.00

LAOS

After enjoying a heyday in the late 17th century, the Lao kingdom declined, eventually suffering the ignominy of incorporation into French Indochina until 1953. A monarchic regime was finally overthrown in 1975 by Pathet-Lao communists. The educated elite fled while others ended up in "re-education centers," from which many never re-emerged.

- Arthur Dommen
LAOS: Keystone of Indochina
0–86531–771–2 Westview $38.00

- Martin Goldstein
AMERICAN POLICY TOWARD LAOS
0–8386–1131–1 Fairleigh Dickinson $30.00

- Paul Langer & Joseph Zasloff
NORTH VIETNAM AND THE PATHET LAO: Partners in the Struggle for Laos
0–674–62675–3 Harvard $20.00

- Martin Stuart-Fox, editor
CONTEMPORARY LAOS: Studies in the Politics and Society of the Lao People's Republic
0–312–16676–1 St. Martin's $29.95

- Joseph Westermeyer
POPPIES, PIPES, AND PEOPLE: Opium and Its Use in Laos
0–520–04622–6 California $37.50

MALAYSIA, SINGAPORE, AND BRUNEI

The original Federation of Malaysia, created in 1963 after nearly 100 years of British rule, included Singapore as well as Sabah and Sarawak. Singapore withdrew in 1965.

- S. Husin Ali
THE MALAYS: Their Problems and Future
0–686–79033–2 Heinemann pb $8.50

- Barbara & Leonard Andaya
A HISTORY OF MALAYSIA
0–312–38121–2 St. Martin's pb $14.95

- R.S. Milne & Diane Mauzy
MALAYSIA: Tradition, Modernity, and Islam
0–8133–0011–8 Westview $33.50

- James Minchin
NO MAN IS AN ISLAND: A Study of Singapore's Lee Kuan Yew
A critical biography
0–86861–906–X Unwin Hyman $34.95

- Janet Salaff
STATE AND FAMILY IN SINGAPORE: Structuring an Industrial Society
A detailed analysis of the dramatic shift in emphasis from labor-intensive to capital-intensive society, based on a methodology of interview and follow-up
0–8014–2140–3 Cornell $37.50

- C.M. Turnbull
A HISTORY OF SINGAPORE, 1819-1975
A re-issued edition (1989)
0–19–588911–8 Oxford $29.95

A SHORT HISTORY OF MALAYSIA, SINGAPORE, AND BRUNEI
Retraces the human evolution of the area from the present day back to the first occupation 50,000 years ago, with glossary, good bibliography, maps and tables
9971–947–06–4 Three Continents pb $15.00

- Richard Winstedt
THE MALAYS: A Cultural History
9–97199–015–6 Three Continents $25.00

THE PHILIPPINES

The sprawling archipelago was propelled into the limelight in early 1986 with the ouster of the Marcos regime by the popular rebellion led by Corazon Aquino, widow of the opposition leader Benigno Aquino assassinated in 1983. Following over three centuries of Spanish rule, the islands were ceded to the United States in 1898 and did not gain independence until after World War II. Sporadic leftist activism plagued each corrupt presidency since, and communist insurgency continues to be a threat to the present government.

- Sandra Burton
  IMPOSSIBLE DREAM: The Marcoses, the Aquinos, and the Unfinished Revolution
  0–446–51398–9 Random House $24.95

- Claude Buss
  CORY AQUINO AND THE PEOPLE OF THE PHILIPPINES
  "From his presence behind the scenes and his access to the movers and shakers of the period, he weaves a political tale with skill and understanding"—Philip Habib
  0–916318–25–7 Stanford Alumni $16.95
  0–916318–24–9 Stanford Alumni pb $9.95

- William Chapman
  INSIDE THE PHILIPPINE REVOLUTION: The New People's Army and Its Struggle for Power
  0–393–02461–X Norton $18.95

- Richard Z. Chesnoff
  THE PHILIPPINES
  A beautiful picture book
  Photographs by Larry Secrist
  0–8109–1475–1 Abrams $29.95

- Leonard Davis
  THE PHILIPPINES: People, Poverty and Politics
  0–312–00412–5 St. Martin's $35.00

- Gerald N. Hill
  THE AQUINO ASSASSINATION: The True Story and Analysis
  0–912133–04–X Hilltop pb $8.95

- Stanley Karnow
  IN OUR IMAGE: America's Empire in the Philippines
  An excellent history of US involvement in the Philippines by the author of *Vietnam: A History*
  0–394–54975–9 Random House $21.50

- Benedict J. Kerkvliet
  THE HUK REBELLION: A Study of Peasant Revolt in the Philippines
  0–520–04635–8 California pb $14.95

- Monina A. Mercado, editor
  PEOPLE POWER: An Eyewitness History of the Philippines Revolution of 1986
  0–86316–131–6 Writers & Readers pb $19.95

Corazon Aquino campaigns for the presidency in 1986, from In Our Image: America's Empire in the Philippines *by Stanley Karnow (Random House/photo:UPI-Bettmann Newsphotos)*

- R.J. May & Francisco Nomenzo, editors
  THE PHILIPPINES AFTER MARCOS
  0–312–60419–X St. Martin's $29.95

- E. San Juan
  CRISIS IN THE PHILIPPINES: The Making of a Revolution
  An insider's scrutiny of the relentless avalanche of political events which culminated in the slaying of the opposition leader Aquino
  Foreword by George Wald
  0–89789–085–X Bergin & Garvey $34.95
  0–89789–093–0 Bergin & Garvey pb $16.95

- Daniel B. Schirmer & Stephen R. Shalom, editors
  THE PHILIPPINES READER: A History of Colonialism, Neocolonialism, Dictatorship, and Resistance
  The grassroots quest and struggle for true social justice
  0–89608–276–8 South End $30.00
  0–89608–275–X South End pb $16.00

- James C. Scott
  WEAPONS OF THE WEAK: Everyday Forms of Peasant Resistance
  0–300–03641–8 Yale pb $14.95

- David J. Steinberg
  THE PHILIPPINES: A Singular and a Plural Place
  0–86531–751–8 Westview pb $15.95

The Marcoses

Sagas of footwear and excessive spending sprees have tended to obscure darker aspects of the dictatorship, such as its national web of repression and torture, and the real extent of the Marcoses' systematic looting.

- Raymond Bonner
  WALTZING WITH A DICTATOR: The Marcoses and the Making of American Policy
  Extraordinary detective work, interviews with scores of officials and the sifting of more than 12,000 pages of previously classified US documents have produced a vivid account of 25 years of Philippine-American relations
  0–394–75835–8 Random House pb $11.95

- John Bresnan, editor
  CRISIS IN THE PHILIPPINES: The Marcos Era and Beyond
  "The background behind the newspaper headlines and television segments"— Stanley Karnow
  0–691–05490–8 Princeton $35.00
  0–691–00810–8 Princeton pb $10.95

In Tacloban [Imelda] built a monument to herself, christening it the Santo Niño Shrine. Everyone in Tacloban called it "the Imelda Shrine". Set in a formal garden shaded by royal palms, the $30 million pink concrete palace looked like the box her shoes came in, furnished by someone who thought the Romanovs ordered Fabergé eggs by the dozen. The guest suites contained elaborate dioramas, crèche scenes depicting immortal moments in the First Lady's life: Imelda bestowing the wonders of modern technology on her "little brown people"; Imelda with Mao Tse-tung; Imelda with Muammar Khadafy. These miniatures were how she wanted to be remembered, not for three thousand pairs of size eight and a half shoes, five hundred size 38 brassieres, and two hundred size 42 girdles.

Sterling Seagrave
THE MARCOS DYNASTY: The Incredible Inside Story
0–06–015815–8 Harper & Row $22.50

 IF YOU CAN'T FIND IT, LOOK IN THE INDEX

• Carmen Navarro Pedrosa
IMELDA MARCOS: The Rise and Fall of One of the World's Most Powerful Women
0–312–00058–8 St. Martin's $15.95

• Beth D. Romulo
INSIDE THE PALACE: The Rise and Fall of Ferdinand and Imelda Marcos
0–399–13253–8 Putnam $18.95

TAIWAN

"Taiwan ... is a modern nation, albeit without official independence. This has created a problem of identity which is quite different in kind from the divisions of many centuries ago: How can a modern Chinese state identify itself with Chinese civilization if it is not 'China'? The temporary answer is to hold up the illusion that it is."—Ian Buruma, *God's Dust: A Modern Asian Journey*

• Ralph Crozier
KOXINGA AND AND CHINESE NATIONALISM: History, Myth and the Hero
The legendary 17th-century naval hero who fled China during the Manchu invasion for Taiwan, where he fought the Dutch and set up a Chinese bureaucracy
0–67405–566–2 Harvard pb $11.00

• John Fei
GROWTH WITH EQUITY: The Taiwan Case
An economic study
0–19–520115–9 Oxford $27.50

• Thomas Gold
STATE AND SOCIETY IN THE TAIWAN MIRACLE
0–87332–349–1 Sharpe $37.50

• Samuel Ho
ECONOMIC DEVELOPMENT OF TAIWAN: 1860-1970
0–300–02087–2 Yale $52.50

• George Kerr
FORMOSA BETRAYED
The Japanese occupation of Taiwan
0–8248–0323–X Da Capo $55.00

• Victor Li
THE FUTURE OF TAIWAN: A Difference of Opinion
0–87332–173–1 Sharpe $45.00

• Burton Pasternak
KINSHIP AND COMMUNITY IN TWO CHINESE VILLAGES
0–8047–0823–1 Stanford $17.50

THAILAND

The populous Buddhist kingdom is the only Southeast Asian country never to have been occupied by a European colonial power. (In the later 19th century it served as a buffer between French Indochina and British Burma.) Representative government was introduced in the 1930s, diminishing the absolute nature of the monarchy. The last decade has been punctuated by coups large and small. The country's already serious domestic problems—inflation, crime and widespread social unrest—have been compounded by an influx of refugees from neighboring Cambodia.

• Carl Bock
TEMPLES AND ELEPHANTS: Travels in Siam in 1881-1882
0–19–582623–X Oxford pb $9.95

• David Elliott
THAILAND: Origins of Military Rule
Foreword by Malcolm Caldwell
0–905762–11–8 Humanities pb $8.95

• Charles Keyes
THAILAND: Buddhist Kingdom As Modern Nation State
"An excellent introduction to the politics and society of Thailand"—*Choice*
0–86531–138–2 Westview $35.00

• Paul & Elaine Lewis
PEOPLES OF THE GOLDEN TRIANGLE: Six Tribes in Thailand
0–500–97314–8 Thames & Hudson $35.00

Head of Buddha, Thai, 14th-century (Musée Guimet)

• Clark Neher, editor
MODERN THAI POLITICS: From Village to Nation
0–87073–916–6 Schenkman $22.50
0–87073–917–4 Schenkman pb $12.50

• Jack Potter
THAI PEASANT SOCIAL STRUCTURE
0–226–67635–8 Chicago $22.00

• Ross Prizzia
THAILAND IN TRANSITION: The Role of Oppositional Forces
0–8248–0977–7 Hawaii pb $9.00

• B.J. Terwiel
A HISTORY OF MODERN THAILAND
0–7022–1902–9 Queensland pb $17.95

David K. Wyatt
THAILAND: A Short History
The history of the Thai people from the early centuries AD to 1982. The standard account
0–300–03054–1 Yale $35.00
0–300–03582–9 Yale pb $13.95

VIETNAM

Under Chinese suzerainty until the 15th century, Vietnam was unified by France in 1887. Divided after Ho Chi Minh's triumph at Dien Bien Phu in 1954, and finally reunified in 1975 after two further decades of war, populous and impoverished Vietnam is again embroiled in conflict. It is on the offensive in Cambodia against remnants of Pol Pot's forces, and on the defensive in the north against the threat of Chinese invasion. The West perceives Vietnam as a land of unflinching zealotry, a view enhanced by Boat People and reports of religious pogroms.

▶ **See also The Vietnam War**

• David Dellinger
VIETNAM REVISITED: From Covert Action to Invasion to Reconstruction
"An account both historical and personal of Vietnam's recent history [which] makes necessary reading for a society that seems bent on repeating its most tragic crimes"—Rev. William Sloane Coffin
0–89608–320–9 South End $25.00
0–89608–319–5 South End pb $9.00

• William Duiker
VIETNAM SINCE THE FALL OF SAIGON
0–89680–133–0 Ohio pb $12.00

• James P. Harrison
THE ENDLESS WAR: 50 Years of Struggle in Vietnam
0–02–914040–4 Free Press $21.95

• Hue-Tam Ho Tai
MILLENARIANISM AND PEASANT POLITICS IN VIETNAM
0–674–57555–5 Harvard $32.00

Stanley Karnow
VIETNAM: A History
A first-rate survey of the American era in Vietnam
0–14–007324–8 Penguin pb $12.95

• **Tim Page**
TEN YEARS AFTER: Vietnam Today
In 1985 the author set out to exorcise the ghosts of the war—in photos
Introduction by William Shawcross
0–394–56464–2 Knopf $30.00
0–394–75654–1 Knopf pb $18.95

• **Douglas Pike**
VIETNAM AND THE SOVIET UNION: Anatomy of an Alliance
Analysis of a liaison currently tainted by mistrust, uncertainty, and a lack of shared perceptions, save a mutual attitude toward a common neighbor, China
0–8133–0470–9 Westview $32.50

• **Keith W. Taylor**
THE BIRTH OF VIETNAM
0–520–04428–2 California $47.50

Australia, New Zealand, and Polynesia

AUSTRALIA

"I grew up with a skimpy sense of colonial Australia. Convict history was ignored in schools and little taught in universities—indeed, the idea that the convicts might *have* a history worth telling was foreign to Australians in the 1950s and 1960s. Even in the mid-1970s only one general history of the System (as transportation, assignment and secondary punishment in colonial Australia were loosely called) was in print: A.G.L. Shaw's pioneering study *Convicts and the Colonies*. An unstated bias rooted deep in Australian life seemed to wish that 'real' Australian history had begun with Australian respectability—with the flood of money from gold and wool, the opening of the continent, the creation of an Australian middle class. Behind the bright diorama of Australia Felix lurked the convicts, some 160,000 of them, clanking their fetters in the penumbral darkness. But on the feelings and experiences of these men and women, little was written. They were statistics, absences, and finally embarrassments."—Robert Hughes, *The Fatal Shore*

• **Jan Bassett, editor**
THE OXFORD DICTIONARY OF AUSTRALIAN HISTORY
0–19–554422–6 Oxford $14.95

• **Manning Clark**
A SHORT HISTORY OF AUSTRALIA
A soundly researched account ranging from the first scattered aboriginal settlements to Australia's latterday emergence as a prosperous and dynamic power
0–451–62561–7 NAL pb $4.95

• **D. Pike**
AUSTRALIA: The Quiet Continent
A succinct, brightly written history spanning the entire period from 1788 to the 1960s, with two introductory chapters setting the stage
0–521–07745–1 Cambridge $37.50

• **Lloyd Robson**
A SHORT HISTORY OF TASMANIA
An informative study of the beautiful island state, from its discovery by the Dutch mariner Tasman in 1642 to its troubled road to modernity in the 1980s
0–19–554651–2 Oxford pb $14.95

• **Ross Terrill**
THE AUSTRALIANS
A contemporary 22,000-mile journey of rediscovery. "Sweeps along on its author's playful and insatiable curiosity to convey a brief, intense intimacy with something large and strange and changeable"—*LA Times Book Review*
0–671–54441–1 Simon & Schuster $19.95
0–671–66239–2 Simon & Schuster pb $8.95

Aboriginal History

"There have been two versions of Australian history since 1788. Most Australians and their governments have based their understanding on the school history books, in which Australia was 'founded' (not taken or conquered) in 1788; and Australian law assumes that there was no law before that date. But new techniques of research, and new ways of using old ones, are literally 'uncovering' what happened over an enormous range of time, probably at least 400 centuries of 'prehistory' before the 1.91 centuries of recorded history based on documents written by the whites."—*Handbook for Aboriginal and Islander History*

• **Geoffrey Blainey**
TRIUMPH OF THE NOMADS: A History of Aboriginal Australia
A recent and necessary examination of the complex society of the continent's earliest indigenous inhabitants, honored more by time than by their European co-habitants
0–87951–043–9 Overlook $22.95
0–87951–084–6 Overlook pb $11.95

• **Michael C. Howard, editor**
WHITEFELLA BUSINESS: Aborigines in Australian Politics
A timely look at a recent phenomenon
0–915980–48–7 Study of Human Issues $17.50

Aborigines of Botany Bay react to Cook's expedition in 1773, from The Fatal Shore *by Robert Hughes (Random House)*

• **M.J. Meggitt**
DESERT PEOPLE: A Study of the Walbiri Aborigines of Central Australia
Looks at local organization, family and kinship, descent lines, initiations and death
0–226–51822–1 Chicago $22.50

• **Sally Morgan**
MY PLACE
An exploration of the author's aboriginal roots. "Sally Morgan's extraordinary work is about a quest for the past of one person and one family, an individual past which turns out to be a communal past, which is, in turn, the history of a people"—*NY Times*
0–8050–0911–6 Seaver $19.95

• **W. Lloyd Warner**
BLACK CIVILIZATION: A Social Study of an Australian Tribe
Fieldwork carried out in the 1920s by a cultural anthropologist among the Murngin in the farthest Australian north. "The first to deal with amplitude of the structure and supernaturalism of a tropical Australian people"—from the foreword
0–8446–0954–4 Peter Smith $13.50

• **J.P. White & J.F. O'Connell, editors**
A PREHISTORY OF AUSTRALIA, NEW GUINEA AND SAHUL: International Edition
0–12–746750–5 Academic $24.95

19th-Century Australia

• **Paul Carter**
THE ROAD TO BOTANY BAY: An Exploration of Landscape and History
"An impressive exploration on the nature of emptiness, place-names, convict behaviour and history itself—a remapping of the European settlement of Australia"—Murray Bail
0–394–57035–9 Knopf $22.95

TO ORDER BOOKS AS GIFTS, SEE PAGE 1

Marcus Clarke
HIS NATURAL LIFE
A celebrated 19th-century Australian
novel about a wronged convict, with
vivid descriptions of the then untamed
and boundless hinterland
0–14–043051–2 Penguin pb $7.95

• **Alexander Harris**
SETTLERS AND CONVICTS
A 19th-century account by an "emigrant
mechanic" of somewhat mysterious
identity and one of the liveliest extant
records of early colonial life as seen by an
ordinary man
Foreword by C.M. Clark
0–522–83944–4 International pb $10.50

• **Margaret Hazzard**
**PUNISHMENT SHORT OF DEATH: A
History of the Penal Settlement at Norfolk
Island**
0–908090–64–1 International $25.00

• **Robert Hughes**
THE FATAL SHORE
"Hughes has a story to tell as vivid, large-
scale and appalling as anything by Dickens
or Solzhenitsyn, but one that's virtually
unknown—until the writing of this
splendid book"—Susan Sontag
0–394–50668–5 Knopf $24.95
0–394–75366–6 Random House pb $10.95

• **Geoffrey C. Ingleton**
**TRUE PATRIOTS ALL: Or News from
Early Australia As Told in a Collection of
Broadsides**
An exuberant journalistic litany of
murders, executions, piracies, mutinies,
villainies, and more
0–8048–1545–3 Tuttle $34.95

The Oxford History of Australia

Beverley Kingston, editor
**THE OXFORD HISTORY OF
AUSTRALIA, Volume 3: 1860-1900**
0–19–554611–3 Oxford $39.95

Stuart F. MacIntyre, editor
**THE OXFORD HISTORY OF
AUSTRALIA, Volume 4: 1901-1942**
0–19–554612–1 Oxford $36.00

Geoffrey Bolton, editor
**THE OXFORD HISTORY OF
AUSTRALIA, Volume 5: 1942-1986**
0–19–554613–X Oxford $39.95

• **Alan Moorehead**
COOPER'S CREEK
The tragic story of the disastrous Burke-
Wills 1860 expedition in quest of a
legendary "inland sea" in the heart of the
desert outback
0–87113–168–4 Atlantic Monthly pb $7.95

Flogging a convict at Moreton Bay in 1836, from The Fatal Shore *by Robert Hughes*
(Random House)

• **L.L. Robson**
CONVICT SETTLERS OF AUSTRALIA
A period inquiry into the "Origin and
Character of the Convicts Transported to
New South Wales and Van Diemen's Land
1787-1852"
0–522–83994–0 International pb $10.00

20th-Century Australia

Akin to Canada in its continental vastness,
modern Australia, with just 16 million inhabitants, boasts a population slightly
smaller than the greater New York area.

• **Joseph Camilleri**
**THE AUSTRALIA-NEW ZEALAND-U.S.
ALLIANCE: Regional Security in the
Nuclear Age**
A thorough examination of the widening
gap between US interests and those of the
two Pacific partners. "Provides the reader
with a balanced and nuanced discussion of
the issues that underlie the ANZUS
controversy"—Richard Falk
0–8133–0615–9 Westview $29.95

• **John Carroll**
**INTRUDERS IN THE BUSH: The
Australian Quest for Identity**
A collection of essays focusing on a search
for the roots of Australian myth in art,
literature, and popular culture
0–19–554308–4 Oxford pb $16.95

• **Ann Curthoys & John Merritt, editors**
**BETTER DEAD THAN RED: Australia's
First Cold War**
The many ways in which the conflict
between communism and anti-communism
permeated Australian society between 1945
and 1960, with special emphasis on trade
unionism and the peace and other social
movements
0–04–909022–4 Unwin Hyman $34.95

• **David Day**
**THE GREAT BETRAYAL: Britain,
Australia, and the Onset of the Pacific War,
1939-1942**
Although Australian troops fought in
Europe in World War II, Britain failed to

protect Australia's vulnerable western coast
as the Pacific war escalated
0–393–02685–X Norton $19.95

• **Ross Fitzgerald**
**FROM 1915 TO THE EARLY 1980s: A
History of Queensland**
Sequel to an earlier history offering an
uncompromising look at the state's history
set against the labor dominance up to
1957 and the subsequent conservative
monopoly
0–7022–1957–6 Queensland pb $18.95

• **Shirley Graham & Brian Adams**
**AUSTRALIAN CINEMA: The First 80
Years**
0–312–06126–9 St. Martin's $27.50

• **Herman Kahn & Thomas Pepper**
**WILL SHE BE ALRIGHT?: The Future of
Australia**
Can Australia's prospects be taken as a
model for the rest of the world? This and
other questions are discussed by two
directors of the Hudson Institute think
tank
0–7022–1568–6 Queensland $25.00
0–7022–1569–4 Queensland pb $9.95

• **William S. Livingston & W. Roger
Louis, editors**
**AUSTRALIA, NEW ZEALAND, AND
THE PACIFIC ISLANDS SINCE THE
FIRST WORLD WAR**
A sharp analysis of transformations
wrought by three principal factors:
dwindling British power, rising United
States influence, and various forms of
nationalism
0–292–70344–9 Texas $20.00

• **Lenore Manderson, editor**
AUSTRALIAN WAYS
0–86861–703–2 Unwin Hyman $24.95
0–86861–671–0 Unwin Hyman pb $12.95

• **Dennis Phillips**
**AMBIVALENT ALLIES: Myth and Reality
in the Australian-American Relationship**
0–14–009220–X Penguin pb $7.95

• B.A. Santamaria
AUSTRALIA AT THE CROSSROADS: Reflections of an Outsider
A blunt critique of the machinations of financial speculators by a conservative-*cum*-radical
0–522–84345–X International pb $17.95

NEW ZEALAND

Discovered by the Dutch in 1642 and formally annexed by Britain two centuries later, New Zealand has been a self-governing sliver of Britishness since 1852. It bears a similarity to the Scandinavian democracies in its pioneering championship of social welfare programs, some of which date back to the turn of the century. As an outspoken exponent of anti-nuclear environmentalism, it shamed the French government over the Greenpeace/Rainbow Warrior incident, and is currently in collision with the United States over nuclear-armed naval ships.

• Dora Alves
ANTI-NUCLEAR ATTITUDES IN NEW ZEALAND AND AUSTRALIA
0–318–19999–8 USGPO pb $2.95

• Angela Ballara
PROUD TO BE WHITE: A Survey of Pakaha Prejudice in New Zealand
0–86863–292–9 International pb $14.95

• Mary A. Barker
STATION LIFE IN NEW ZEALAND
Introduction by Fiona Kidman
0–8070–7029–7 Beacon pb $9.95

• Terence Barrow
AN ILLUSTRATED GUIDE TO MAORI ART
An anthropologist explains Maori art symbols, the everyday function of art objects and the place of art in Maori society, with good illustrations
0–8248–0979–3 Hawaii pb $15.95

• Jonathan Boston & Martin Holland, editors
THE FOURTH LABOUR GOVERNMENT
0–19–558161–X Oxford pb $22.50

• Gary Hawke
THE MAKING OF NEW ZEALAND: An Economic History
0–521–26226–7 Cambridge $52.50

• Charles Higham
THE MAORIS
0–521–21931–0 Cambridge pb $4.95

• Brian Mackrell
HARIRU WIKITORIA!: An Illustrated History of the Maori Tour of England, 1863
0–19–558072–9 Oxford pb $27.00

• Richard Mulgan
DEMOCRACY AND POWER IN NEW ZEALAND: A Study in New Zealand Politics
0–19–558106–7 Oxford pb $18.95

• W.H. Oliver, editor
THE OXFORD HISTORY OF NEW ZEALAND
0–19–558063–X Oxford pb $34.95

• Margaret Orbell
THE NATURAL WORLD OF THE MAORI
0–911378–52–9 Sheridan House $45.00

• Geoffrey Palmer
UNBRIDLED POWER: A Study of New Zealand's Constitution and Government
0–19–558170–9 Oxford pb $27.50

• K. Sinclair
HISTORY OF NEW ZEALAND
0–14–020344–3 Penguin pb $7.95

POLYNESIA

The umbrella term describes the area of Oceania which contains the principal island nations of Samoa, Tonga, Fiji, and the Solomons, as well as the Hawaiian islands and French Polynesia, where Kanak autonomy claims have exposed the persistence of colonialism. The South Seas are studded with some 25,000 islands in all—and a total population of 1.5 million.

• Antony Alpers
THE WORLD OF THE POLYNESIANS SEEN THROUGH THEIR MYTHS AND LEGENDS, POETRY, AND ART
0–19–558142–3 Oxford pb $10.95

• John C. Beaglehole
THE EXPLORATION OF THE PACIFIC
Delves into the driving ideas behind the exploration of the Pacific, and describes the epic voyages of Magellan, Drake, Mendaña, Quiros, Tasman and others
0–8047–0310–8 Stanford $35.00
0–8047–0311–6 Stanford pb $9.95

• Peter Bellwood
THE POLYNESIANS: Prehistory of an Island People
0–500–27450–9 Thames & Hudson pb $10.95

• William Bligh
MUTINY ON BOARD H.M.S. BOUNTY
0–451–52293–1 NAL pb $3.50

• Ian Cameron
LOST PARADISE: The Exploration of the Pacific
0–88162–275–3 Salem House $24.95

Captain Cook

John C. Beaglehole
THE LIFE OF CAPTAIN JAMES COOK
A classic study and the first full-scale biography to do justice to the exploits and achievements of the intrepid navigator and explorer
0–8047–0848–7 Stanford $39.50

James Cook
EXPLORATIONS OF CAPTAIN JAMES COOK IN THE PACIFIC, AS TOLD BY SELECTIONS OF HIS OWN JOURNALS, 1768-1779
Detailed excerpts from the logs of one of the 18th century's most important and colorful circumnavigators
Edited by A. Grenfell Price
0–486–22766–9 Dover pb $6.50

Sydney Parkinson
JOURNAL OF A VOYAGE TO THE SOUTH SEAS IN H.M.S. ENDEAVOUR
Parkinson was a Quaker, youthful, eager and virtuous, who was engaged as a botanical draftsman in Cook's 1768-1771 voyage. He died in passage but bequeathed a primary authority on the circumnavigation
Edited by Christine Holmes
0–904573–51–6 Longwood $20.00

Lynne Withey
VOYAGES OF DISCOVERY: Captain Cook and the Exploration of the Pacific
0–688–05115–4 Morrow $19.95
0–520–06564–6 California pb $12.95

• Thomas Harding & Ben Wallace
CULTURES OF THE PACIFIC
0–02–913800–0 Free Press pb $14.95

• David Howarth
TAHITI: A Paradise Lost
0–14–008095–3 Penguin pb $7.95

• K.R. Howe
WHERE THE WAVES FALL: A New South Sea Islands History from First Settlement to Colonial Rule
0–8248–1186–0 Hawaii $29.95

• Edward Joesting
HAWAII: An Uncommon History
0–393–00907–6 Norton pb $10.95

• Patrick V. Kirch
THE EVOLUTION OF THE POLYNESIAN CHIEFDOMS
0–521–25332–2 Cambridge $49.50

• David Lewis
WE, THE NAVIGATORS: The Ancient Art of Landfinding in the Pacific
0–8248–0394–9 Hawaii pb $9.95

• Alan Moorehead
THE FATAL IMPACT: The Invasion of the South Pacific, 1767-1840
Focus on three distinct sites—lush Tahiti, the temperate east coast of Australia, and the bleak south polar regions
Foreword by Manning Clark
0–06–015800–X Harper & Row $25.00

• Marshall Sahlins
ISLANDS OF HISTORY
"Deeply grounded in his mastery of Polynesian ethnography, but also wide-ranging in its comparative references, in

Pacific history and in broad statements of historical/anthropological method"—*TLS*
0–226–73358–0 Chicago pb $8.95

- Bernard Smith
EUROPEAN VISION AND THE SOUTH PACIFIC
An illustrated book surveying the work of artists attached to voyages of exploration
0–300–04479–8 Yale pb $24.95

- Robert Louis Stevenson
IN THE SOUTH SEAS: The Marquesas, Paumotus and Gilbert Islands
0–7103–0140–5 RC&H pb $12.95

- Peter Worsley
THE TRUMPET SHALL SOUND: A Study of Cargo Cults in Melanesia
0–8052–0156–4 Schocken pb $8.95

- Ronald Wright
ON FIJI ISLANDS
A travel writer's keen observations on the "Cannibal Isles"
0–14–009551–9 Penguin pb $7.95

Military Affairs

▶ **See also International Relations and Strategic Studies**

MILITARY HISTORY

Histories of specific wars can be found throughout the various history chapters, including The Second World War, The Civil War and Reconstruction, and The Vietnam War. The books below provide overviews of military history in the world and in the United States.

General Histories

- Raymond Aron
THE CENTURY OF TOTAL WAR
0–8191–4563–7 University Press pb $15.50

- Ian R. Becket, editor
ROOTS OF COUNTERINSURGENCY: Armies and Guerrilla Warfare, 1900-1945
The rise of guerrilla warfare in the first half of the century, and the conventional military's responses to it
0–7137–1922–2 Blandford $29.95

- R. Ernest & Trevor N. Dupuy
THE ENCYCLOPEDIA OF MILITARY HISTORY: From 3500 B.C. to the Present
0–06–181235–8 Harper & Row $39.95

- Victor Davis Hanson
THE WESTERN WAY OF WAR: Infantry Battle in Classical Greece
What happened on the battlefields of ancient Greece, and how those battles have affected war to the present day
Introduction by John Keegan
0–394–57188–6 Knopf $19.95

English archers training with the longbow, late 13th century, from A Distant Mirror *by Barbara Tuchman (Knopf)*

- Michael Howard
WAR IN EUROPEAN HISTORY
Short and authoritative study of warfare as it has developed from the Middle Ages to the present
0–19–289095–6 Oxford pb $9.95

- Paul Kennedy
THE RISE AND FALL OF THE GREAT POWERS: Economic Change and Military Conflict, 1500-2000
0–394–54674–1 Random House $24.95
0–679–72019–7 Random House pb $12.95

- Michael T. Klare & Peter Kornbluh, editors
LOW INTENSITY WARFARE: Counterinsurgency, Proinsurgency, and Antiterrorism in the '80s
The American answer to revolution and unrest in the Third World, as seen by nine experts who trace the evolution, costs, and future of this new military strategy; with sections on Vietnam, El Salvador, the Philippines, and Afghanistan
0–394–74653–8 Random House pb $8.95

- John Laffin
BATTLEFIELD ARCHAEOLOGY
Using examples in France, Belgium, Turkey, and Israel, the author explains battlefield archaeology as the art of knowing where to dig and what to look for
0–87052–449–6 Hippocrene $22.50

- Lloyd Lindo
FORCES '89
A guide to military affairs around the globe, covering the workings of the USS Nimitz, developments in military medicine, spy equipment, armored vehicles, and other subjects
0–933852–85–1 Nautical & Aviation $17.95

- William H. McNeill
THE PURSUIT OF POWER: Technology, Armed Force, and Society Since A.D. 1000
Society's conflicts and dilemmas from the cross-bow to the nuclear missile; the arms race as the motor of progress. "A grand synthesis . . . that tells us almost as much

about the history of butter as the history of guns"—*Washington Post Book World*
0–226–56158–5 Chicago pb $11.95

- Alfred Thayer Mahan
THE INFLUENCE OF SEA POWER UPON HISTORY, 1660-1805
The book that inspired America's entry into the battleship era
0–89141–312–X Presidio $40.00
0–486–25509–3 Dover pb $11.95

- Robert L. O'Connell
OF ARMS AND MEN: A History of War, Weapons and Aggression
From prehistoric times to the nuclear age, focusing on how social and economic conditions interact with weapons and the tactics employed in warfare
0–19–505359–1 Oxford $24.95

- Shelley Saywell
WOMEN IN WAR
Their stories as guerrillas, spies, soldiers, saboteurs, nurses, and other roles, from World War II to the Falkland Islands War
0–670–80348–0 Viking $17.95

Today's Wars

Jon Lee Anderson & Scott Anderson
WAR ZONES: Voices from the World's Killing Grounds
Civilians tell how war affects daily life in Uganda, Sri Lanka, Israel, El Salvador, and Northern Ireland
0–396–08915–1 Dodd, Mead $21.95

James Nachtwey
A WORLD AT WAR: Photographs, 1981-88
Pictures of war in Northern Ireland, Nicaragua, El Salvador, Guatemala, Lebanon, the West Bank and Sinai, Sub-Saharan Africa, the Philippines, Korea, Sri Lanka, and Afghanistan
Introduction by Robert Stone
0–500–54152–3 Thames & Hudson $35.00

American Military History

● James L. Abrahamson
AMERICA ARMS FOR A NEW CENTURY: The Making of a Great Military Power
0–02–900190–0 Free Press $21.95

● Daniel P. Bolger
AMERICANS AT WAR: 1975-1986, An Era of Violent Peace
0–89141–303–0 Presidio $24.95

● Lawrence D. Cress
CITIZENS IN ARMS: The Army and Militia in American Society to the War of 1812
0–8078–1508–X North Carolina $27.50

● R. Ernest Dupuy & Trevor N. Dupuy
THE MILITARY HERITAGE OF AMERICA
Foreword by Douglas MacArthur
0–915979–00–4 Hero $29.95

● Irwin Hass
AMERICA'S HISTORIC BATTLEFIELDS
A guide for both history students and travelers, organized by geographic region
0–87052–239–6 Hippocrene $14.95

● Charles E. Heller & William A. Stofft, editors
AMERICA'S FIRST BATTLES, 1776-1950
0–7006–0276–3 Kansas $29.95
0–7006–0277–1 Kansas pb $14.95

● Maj. Gen. Jeanne Holm, USAF (Ret.)
WOMEN IN THE MILITARY: An Unfinished Revolution
A historical account of women in the American military
0–89141–262–X Presidio pb $12.95

● Edwin P. Hoyt
AMERICA'S WARS
By a leading American military historian
0–07–030618–4 McGraw-Hill $24.95

● Robert Leckie
THE WARS OF AMERICA
Foreword by Richard B. Morris
0–06–012571–3 Harper & Row $35.95

● Allan R. Millett & Peter Maslowski
FOR THE COMMON DEFENSE: A Military History of the United States, 1607-1983
A good survey
0–02–921580–3 Free Press $24.95

● Susan D. Moeller
SHOOTING WAR: Photography and the American Experience of Combat
A visual and historical account
0–465–07777–3 Basic Books $25.95

● Geoffrey Perret
A COUNTRY MADE BY WAR: A Story of America's Rise to Power
Traces not only the history of America at war, but how the American style of combat has affected the nation's political and cultural life
0–394–55398–5 Random House $22.50

● Russell F. Weigley
THE AMERICAN WAY OF WAR: A History of U.S. Military Strategy and Policy
0–253–28029–X Indiana pb $12.95

● T. Harry Williams
A HISTORY OF AMERICAN WARS: From Colonial Times to World War I
Americans at war, by the biographer of Huey Long
0–394–51167–0 Knopf $25.00

Atlases

● Arthur Banks
ATLAS OF ANCIENT AND MEDIEVAL WARFARE
Includes 154 new maps
Introduction by Lord Chalfont
0–88254–698–8 Hippocrene $25.00

● David G. Chandler
ATLAS OF MILITARY STRATEGY
0–02–905750–7 Free Press $29.95

● Martin Gilbert
ATLAS OF THE FIRST WORLD WAR
Covers all aspects of the war in 159 maps
Cartography by Arthur Banks
Introduction by Viscount Montgomery of Alamein
0–88029–020–X Hippocrene $17.95

● Simon Goodenough
WAR MAPS
0–517–66470–4 St. Martin's $18.95

● John Keegan & Andrew Wheatcroft
ZONES OF CONFLICT: An Atlas of Future Wars
A tour of 40 potentially volatile spots on every continent and in outer space, by a respected British military analyst and an award-winning illustrator. The text and maps highlight the terrain and strategic importance of each area, and likely offensive and defensive battle tactics
0–671–60115–6 Simon & Schuster $18.95
0–671–62411–3 Simon & Schuster pb $10.95

Arthur Banks
A WORLD ATLAS OF MILITARY HISTORY, 1860-1945
An emphasis on the American Civil War, World War I and World War II
0–88254–454–3 Hippocrene $22.50

Tom Hartman with John Mitchell
A WORLD ATLAS OF MILITARY HISTORY, 1945-1984
A map and text history of conflicts in the Middle East, Africa, India, China, Korea, Southeast Asia, Central and South America, and Europe
0–87052–000–8 Hippocrene $24.95
0–306–80316–X Da Capo pb $14.95

Theory and Strategy

● Carl Von Clausewitz
ON WAR
0–14–044427–0 Penguin pb $5.95

● James F. Dunnigan
HOW TO MAKE WAR: A Comprehensive Guide to Modern Warfare
0–688–07979–2 Morrow pb $14.95

● Trevor N. Dupuy
UNDERSTANDING WAR: History and Theory of Combat
By the co-author of *The Encyclopedia of Military History*
0–913729–57–4 Paragon $24.95

● Archer Jones
THE ART OF WAR IN THE WESTERN WORLD
0–252–01380–8 Illinois $34.95

● John Keegan
THE FACE OF BATTLE
0–14–004897–9 Penguin pb $6.95

THE MASK OF COMMAND
0–670–45988–7 Viking $18.95

● Sun Tzu
THE ART OF WAR
Written in China more than 2000 years ago, this series of aphoristic essays is the first known study of the planning and conduct of military operations
Translated with an introduction by Samuel B. Griffith
0–19–501540–1 Oxford $15.95

Soldiers

● Richard Garrett
P.O.W.: The Uncivil Face of War
A history of prisoners of war through first-hand accounts, from the Hundred Years War to the present
0–7153–9201–8 David & Charles pb $7.95

● J. Glenn Gray
THE WARRIORS: Reflections on Men in Battle
0–06–090580–8 Harper & Row pb $7.95

● John Keegan & Richard Holmes
SOLDIERS: A History of Men in Battle
0–670–80969–1 Viking $22.95

A feudal warrior, from Japan: A Short Cultural History *by G.B. Sansom (Stanford)*

➤ **FOR OVERSEAS ORDERING INFORMATION, SEE PAGE 1**

• Anthony Mockler
THE NEW MERCENARIES: The History of the Hired Soldier from the Congo to the Seychelles
0–913729–72–8 Paragon House $24.95

• Richard Severo & Lewis Milford
THE WAGES OF WAR: When America's Soldiers Came Home—From Valley Forge to Vietnam
A comprehensive history of how our fighting men have been treated after war
0–671–54325–3 Simon & Schuster $19.95

WARS THROUGH THE AGES

▶ See also The Second World War, The Civil War and Reconstruction & The Vietnam War

Ancient Warfare

• Donald W. Engels
ALEXANDER THE GREAT AND THE LOGISTICS OF THE MACEDONIAN ARMY
"Careful analyses of terrain, climate and supply . . . are combined in a masterly fashion to help account for Alexander's strategic decisions"—*NY Review of Books*
0–520–04272–7 California pb $10.95

• Arthur Ferrill
THE FALL OF THE ROMAN EMPIRE: The Military Explanation
0–500–27495–9 Thames & Hudson pb $12.95

• Edward N. Luttwak
THE GRAND STRATEGY OF THE ROMAN EMPIRE
"Brings detailed insights into the working of Roman military organization, in strategy and tactics"—E. Badian
0–8018–2158–4 Johns Hopkins pb $8.95

• N.K. Sandars
THE SEA PEOPLES: Warriors of the Ancient Mediterranean, 1250-1150
The collapse of the ancient Mediterranean civilizations centered in Crete and Egypt is still unexplained. Here, the evidence for northern invaders who adapted to marine warfare is given full exposition
0–500–27387–1 Thames & Hudson pb $11.95

• Chester G. Starr
THE INFLUENCE OF SEA POWER IN ANCIENT HISTORY
0–19–505667–1 Oxford pb $8.95

• Arthur Terrill
THE ORIGINS OF WAR: From the Stone Age to Alexander the Great
0–500–27427–4 Thames & Hudson pb $10.95

• Michael Wood
IN SEARCH OF THE TROJAN WAR
Archaeological detective work at the site of ancient Troy comes up with some unexpected discoveries
0–8160–1355–1 Facts On File $14.95
0–452–25960–6 NAL pb $12.95

The Middle Ages

• Michael Bennett
THE BATTLE OF BOSWORTH
The battle of 1485 that ended Richard III's short reign and established the Tudor dynasty
0–312–06972–3 St. Martin's $29.95

• Malcolm Billings
THE CROSS AND THE CRESCENT: A History of the Crusades
The pageantry and clash of battle, the toll of disease; from the first crusade to Napoleon's taking of Malta. Over 200 illustrations
0–8069–6904–0 Sterling $19.95

• Philippe Contamine
WAR IN THE MIDDLE AGES
A sophisticated study of war in all its aspects—technological, economic, political and cultural. Highly recommended
0–631–14469–2 Blackwell pb $14.95

• Ronald C. Finucane
SOLDIERS OF THE FAITH: Crusaders and Moslems at War
0–312–74256–8 St. Martin's $19.95

• Tim Newark
CELTIC WARRIORS
Two thousand years of Celtic warfare. Famous warlords include Arthur, Macbeth, Hugh O'Neill, and the leaders of the clans of Scotland and Ireland
Illustrated by Angus McBride
0–7137–1690–8 Sterling $24.95
0–7137–2043–3 Blandford pb $12.95

MEDIEVAL WARLORDS
Illustrated by Angus McBride
0–7137–1816–1 Sterling $24.95

• Stephen Turnbull
SAMURAI WARRIORS
0–7137–1767–X Sterling $24.95

The 18th Century and The Napoleonic Era

• Rodney Atwood
THE HESSIANS: Mercenaries from Hessen-Kassel in the American Revolution
0–521–22884–0 Cambridge $39.50

• Scott Bowden
ARMIES AT WATERLOO
Introduction by Gunther E. Rothenberg
0–913037–02–8 Empire Games $34.95

• Christopher Duffy
THE FORTRESS IN THE AGE OF VAUBAN AND FREDERICK THE GREAT, 1660-1789
0–7100–9648–8 RC&H $50.00

THE MILITARY EXPERIENCE IN THE AGE OF REASON
From the Great Northern War and the War of the Austrian Succession to the contest between Britain and France in North Africa; a new study by a leading British historian
0–689–11993–3 Atheneum $24.95

> All the tall men with moustaches are placed in the first rank, with due attention being paid in the dressing to a uniformity of appearance—thus we do not like to place an old soldier next to a much younger one, or someone with a thin, half-starved face next to an individual with a strong countenance. The flanks are most in evidence when the soldiers march past, and so they must be covered by our most handsome men with good faces. Men who have moustaches, but are less good looking, are placed in the second rank, but if there are not enough moustaches to fill the whole rank, they must be positioned on one of the flanks. The shortest men go to the third rank, and the tallest men without moustaches to the fourth.
>
> from a Brunswick drill book of 1751 quoted in
>
> Christopher Duffy
> **THE MILITARY EXPERIENCE IN THE AGE OF REASON**
> 0–689–11993–3 Atheneum $24.95

• David Chandler
THE CAMPAIGNS OF NAPOLEON: The Mind and Method of History's Greatest Soldier
0–02–523660–1 Free Press $60.00

THE MILITARY MAXIMS OF NAPOLEON
Napoleon's thoughts on the art of war, tactics, strategies, and command
0–02–897171–X Macmillan $19.95

• John R. Elting
SWORDS AROUND A THRONE: Napoleon's Grande Armée
An American historian's view of Napoleonic warfare
0–02–909501–8 Free Press $35.00

• Paddy Griffith & others
WELLINGTON COMMANDER: The Iron Duke's Generalship
0–907319–08–4 Faber & Faber $45.00

• Philip J. Haythornthwaite
NAPOLEON'S MILITARY MACHINE
How the ragged armies of the French Revolution were transformed into the era's best fighting force. This is a big, lavishly illustrated book
0–87052–549–2 Hippocrene $35.00

• John Lynn
BAYONETS OF THE REPUBLIC: Motivation and Tactics in the Army of Revolutionary France
0–252–01091–4 Illinois $24.95

• George F. Nafziger
NAPOLEON'S INVASION OF RUSSIA
Assembling an army of nearly 600,000, the largest force under a single command seen in Europe until that time, Napoleon crossed the Russian frontier on June 23, 1812 in a campaign that culminated in the Battle of Borodino on September 7. Includes 16 maps and appendices with valuable documents
Foreword by David Chandler
0–89141–322–7 Presidio $45.00

• Dudley Pope
LIFE IN NELSON'S NAVY
0–87021–346–6 Naval Institute $15.95

• G.E. Rothenberg
THE ART OF WARFARE IN THE AGE OF NAPOLEON
0–253–31076–8 Indiana $22.50
0–253–20260–4 Indiana pb $9.95

• Oliver Warner
A PORTRAIT OF LORD NELSON
0–14–008068–6 Penguin pb $6.95

• Richard Woodman
DECISION AT TRAFALGAR
0–8027–0993–1 Walker $16.95

Wars of Imperialism

• Michael Barthorp
WAR ON THE NILE: Britain, Egypt and the Sudan, 1882-1898
0–7137–1858–7 Sterling pb $12.95

THE ZULU WAR: A Pictorial History
0–7137–1469–7 Sterling pb $12.95

• David L. Bullock
ALLENBY'S WAR: The Palestine-Arabian Campaigns, 1916-1918
Far from the Western front a campaign of mobility brought Edmund Allenby a crushing victory over the Turks. Bullock assesses Lawrence of Arabia and the unleashing of Arab nationalism
0–7137–1869–2 Blandford $24.95

• David Clammer
THE ZULU WAR
The massacre of the British at Isandhlwana and the defense at Rorke's Drift; includes maps, photographs, and illustrations
0–7153–9246–8 David & Charles pb $7.95

• R.M. Connaughton
THE WAR OF THE RISING SUN AND TUMBLING BEAR: A Military History of the Russo-Japanese War, 1904-1905
Bloody battles in the rugged Korean and Manchurian landscape offered a glimpse of what would come in 1914
0–415–00906–5 RC&H $49.95

• John H. Waller
GORDON OF KHARTOUM: The Saga of a Victorian Hero
0–689–11812–0 Atheneum $29.95

• Philip Warner
KITCHENER: The Man Behind the Legend
0–689–11805–8 Atheneum $15.95

• John R. Young
THE FRENCH FOREIGN LEGION: The Inside Story of the World Famous Fighting Force
0–500–27382–0 Thames & Hudson pb $14.95

World War I

▶ See also 20th-Century Europe to the Second World War, Great Britain and Ireland, US History since 1877, & Russian and Soviet Studies

• Richard P. Hallion
RISE OF THE FIGHTER AIRCRAFT: 1914-1918
"Destroys the standard belief that the war in the skies above Belgium and France was an impotent sideshow"—*LA Times*
0–933852–42–8 Nautical & Aviation $22.95

• B.H. Liddell Hart
THE REAL WAR, 1914-1918
A largely military history, written in 1930 by the famous wartime strategist
0–316–52505–7 Little, Brown pb $11.95

• Dwight R. Messimer
MERCHANT U-BOAT: Adventures of the Deutschland, 1916-1918
The secret wartime activities of the cargo U-boat
0–87021–771–2 Naval Institute $24.95

• Alan Moorehead
GALLIPOLI
The disastrous Allied campaign in Turkey
0–345–33088–9 Ballantine pb $3.95

• John H. Morrow, Jr.
GERMAN AIRPOWER IN WORLD WAR I
0–8032–3076–1 Nebraska $24.50

• Richard Muller
WORLD WAR I FLYING ACE
Illustrated by George Pratt
0–553–27231–4 Bantam pb $2.50

• Douglas Porch
THE MARCH TO THE MARNE: The French Army, 1871-1914
0–521–23883–8 Cambridge $57.50

• Myron J. Smith, Jr.
WORLD WAR I IN THE AIR: A Bibliography and Chronology
0–8108–0990–7 Scarecrow $22.50

• Tim Travers
THE KILLING GROUND: The British Army, The Western Front and The Emergence of Modern Warfare, 1900-1918
0–04–942205–7 Unwin Hyman $34.95

• Edwin Campion Vaughan
SOME DESPERATE GLORY: The World War I Diary of a British Officer
Hidden for more than 40 years, Vaughan's trench journal reads like a novel
0–671–67904–X Simon & Schuster pb $8.95

Denis Winter
DEATH'S MEN: Soldiers of the Great War
Highly recommended
0–14–005215–1 Penguin pb $6.95

ARMIES OF THE WORLD

The US Army

• Edward M. Coffman
THE OLD ARMY: A Portrait of the American Army in Peacetime, 1784-1898
The only comprehensive study of the people who made up the "garrison world" in the peacetime intervals between the War for Independence and the Spanish-American War, particularly the lonely men of Northern cities for whom enlistment was "a choice of evils"
0–19–503750–2 Oxford $35.00

• Richard H. Kohn
EAGLE AND SWORD: The Beginnings of the Military Establishment in America
0–02–918350–2 Free Press pb $12.95

• Ivan Prashker
DUTY, HONOR, VIETNAM: Twelve Men of West Point
"A unique, penetrating study of one of America's most important institutions. Ivan Prashker interviews deftly and writes with . . . genuine warmth"—Mario Puzo
1–55710–015–2 Morrow $19.95

• Col. Charles M. Simpson III, USA (Ret.)
INSIDE THE GREEN BERETS: The First Thirty Years—A History of the U.S. Army Special Forces
0–89141–163–1 Presidio $16.95

• Shelby L. Stanton
GREEN BERETS AT WAR: U.S. Army Special Forces in Asia, 1956-1975
A complete combat history, including many obscure and remote battlefields
0–89141–238–7 Presidio $18.95

• Russell F. Weigley
HISTORY OF THE UNITED STATES ARMY
0–253–20323–6 Indiana pb $10.95

The US Navy

• Robert G. Albion
THE MAKERS OF NAVAL POLICY, 1798-1947
Edited by Rowena Reed
0–87021–360–1 Naval Institute $22.95

• Edward L. Beach, USN (Ret.)
THE UNITED STATES NAVY: A Two-Hundred Year History
An affectionate history by the author of *Run Silent, Run Deep*. Winner of the Theodore and Franklin D. Roosevelt Naval History Prize
0–395–43289–8 Houghton Mifflin pb $12.95

• Paolo E. Coletta
THE AMERICAN NAVAL HERITAGE IN BRIEF
0–8191–5596–9 University Press $34.50
0–8191–5597–7 University Press pb $24.95

- R. Adm. R.W. King, editor
  NAVAL ENGINEERING AND AMERICAN SEA POWER
  A history of American maritime technology
  0–933852–73–8 Nautical & Aviation $29.95

- Jack Sweetman, editor
  AMERICAN NAVAL HISTORY: An Illustrated Chronology of the U.S. Navy and Marine Corps, 1775 to the Present
  0–87021–290–7 Naval Institute $29.95

The US Marines

- Agostino von Hassell
  WARRIORS: The United States Marines
  A photographic journal of the Marines, based on 60,000 miles of travel over eight years
  0–943231–08–6 Howell $38.00

- Peter B. Mersky
  U.S. MARINE CORPS AVIATION: 1912 to the Present
  0–933852–39–8 Nautical & Aviation $22.95

- Allan R. Millett
  SEMPER FIDELIS: The History of the U.S. Marine Corps
  0–02–921590–0 Free Press $35.00
  0–02–921570–6 Free Press pb $18.95

- Robert J. Moskin
  THE U.S. MARINE CORPS STORY
  The second edition of a popular text book
  0–07–043457–3 McGraw-Hill pb $14.95

- John de St. Jorre
  THE MARINES
  "The beating heart of the U.S. Marine Corps"—Stephen Coonts. Beautifully illustrated
  Photographs by Anthony Edgeworth
  0–385–23683–2 Doubleday $40.00

Other US Forces

- Ernest K. Gann
  THE BLACK WATCH: The True Inside Story of America's Most Elite and Secret Air Corps
  The story of the U.S. Air Force's intelligence pilots and planes of the 99th Squadron
  0–394–57507–5 Random House $18.95

- Robert E. Johnson
  GUARDIANS OF THE SEA: A History of the U.S. Coast Guard, 1915 to the Present
  0–87021–720–8 Naval Institute $23.95

- John K. Mahon
  HISTORY OF THE MILITIA AND THE NATIONAL GUARD OF THE UNITED STATES
  0–02–919750–3 Free Press $24.95

- Gregory J.W. Urwin
  THE UNITED STATES CAVALRY: An Illustrated History
  Illustrations by Ernest L. Reedstrom
  0–7137–1219–8 Sterling $24.95
  0–7137–1817–X Sterling pb $12.95

One of the 196,000 flights of the Berlin Airlift (June 1948-May 1949)

THE UNITED STATES INFANTRY: An Illustrated History, 1775-1918
A clear explanation of infantry tactics, a showcase of the leaders, and a detailed account of the regiments—regulars, green militiamen, and volunteers
Illustrated by Darby Erd
0–7137–1757–2 Blandford $24.95

US Military Leadership

- Edgar F. Puryear, Jr.
  NINETEEN STARS: A Study in Military Character and Leadership
  MacArthur, Marshall, Eisenhower, and Patton
  Foreword by Forrest C. Pogue
  0–89141–148–8 Presidio pb $12.95

  STARS IN FLIGHT: A Study in Air Force Character and Leadership
  The careers of the first five chiefs of staff of the Air Force: Arnold, Spaatz, Twining, Vandenberg, and White
  0–89141–127–5 Presidio $14.95
  0–89141–128–3 Presidio pb $8.95

- William J. Wood
  LEADERS AND BATTLES: The Art of Military Leadership
  Military lessons based on the experiences of such men as Dan Morgan at Cowpens, Anthony Wayne at Stony Point, Bouquet at Bushy Run, and others
  0–89141–185–2 Presidio $16.95

Great Britain

- Frank Hilton
  THE PARAS
  An overview of the elite British unit
  0–563–20099–5 Presidio $18.95

- Charles Messenger
  THE HISTORY OF THE BRITISH ARMY
  Battles, regimental organization, the social origins of officers and rank and file, and technological changes
  0–89141–267–0 Presidio $25.00

- Anthony Preston
  HISTORY OF THE ROYAL NAVY IN THE TWENTIETH CENTURY
  An illustrated history of the third most powerful navy in the world, from the launching of HMS Dreadnaught in 1906 through the Falklands War
  0–89141–283–2 Presidio $25.00

Soviet Union

- David C. Isby
  TEN MILLION BAYONETS: Inside the Armies of the Soviet Union
  The flaws and strengths of the Red Army with insights into military life in the Soviet Union, including recruitment, daily routine, training, the role of women, and combat capability
  0–85368–774–9 Arms & Armour $19.95

• Brian Moynahan
CLAWS OF THE BEAR: The History of the Red Army from the Revolution to the Present
A general history, from the army's desertion of the czar in 1917, through the Civil War, victory in World War II, and its role in the postwar world
0–395–51076–7 Houghton-Mifflin $24.95

• Albert Seaton
THE HORSEMEN OF THE STEPPES: The Story of the Cossacks
A history of the unique fighting force, from its origins as the mounted Tatar hordes of Ghengis Khan to its fall in the Russian Revolution
0–87052–141–1 Hippocrene $22.50

• Albert & Joan Seaton
THE SOVIET ARMY: 1917 to the Present
0–452–00906–5 Meridian pb $9.95

AIR POWER

▶ **See also Boats, Cars, Planes, and Trains**

• Michael S. Sherry
THE RISE OF AMERICAN AIR POWER: The Creation of Armageddon
An in-depth history of American strategic bombing
0–300–03600–0 Yale $29.95

Aircraft

• Enzo Angelucci
THE AMERICAN FIGHTER: A Definitive Illustrated Guide to All American Aircraft from 1917 to the Present
0–317–60354–X Crown $40.00

• J.M. Bruce
BRITAIN'S FIRST WARPLANES
0–85368–852–4 Sterling $24.95

• Chris Chant, editor
ENCYCLOPEDIA OF MODERN AIRCRAFT ARMAMENT
Includes numerous photos and illustrations
0–85059–862–1 Sterling $29.95

• Robert F. Dorr
U.S. JET FIGHTERS SINCE 1945
From the first battle use of the F-80C encountering MiG-14s over Korea to the F-4D Phantoms battling MiG-19s over Vietnam, to the recent F-14 Tomcats over the Gulf of Sidra; 198 photographs
0–7137–1948–6 Blandford $14.95

AN ILLUSTRATED GUIDE TO THE MODERN U.S. AIR FORCE
0–668–05497–2 Arco pb $10.95

• Hans Halberstadt
AIRBORNE: Assault from the Sky
0–89141–279–4 Presidio pb $12.95

• George Hall
TOP GUN: The Navy's Fighter Weapons School
0–89141–261–1 Presidio pb $12.95

• George Hall, editor
TOTAL FORCE: Flying with America's Reserve and Guard
Beautifully illustrated by color photos
Introduction by Barry Goldwater
0–934738–33–5 Thomasson-Grant $39.95

• C.J. Heatley III
FORGED IN STEEL: U.S. Marine Corps Aviation
Color photographs of the A-4 Skyhawk, "Whiskey" Cobra helicopter, F-18 fighter and many others
Introduction by John Glenn
0–943231–00–0 Howell $37.00

• Robert Jackson
NATO AIR POWER
A heavily illustrated guide
0–89141–294–8 Presidio $25.00

• Nick Kotz
WILD BLUE YONDER: Money, Politics, and the B-1 Bomber
0–394–55700–X Pantheon $19.95

• Piet Hein Meijering
SIGNED WITH THEIR HONOR: Air Chivalry During the Two World Wars
1–55778–116–8 Paragon $24.95

• Peter B. Mersky
U.S. MARINE CORPS AVIATION: 1912 to the Present
From the Western Front through Vietnam and beyond
0–933852–39–8 Nautical & Aviation $22.95

• Russell Miller
THE SOVIET AIR FORCE AT WAR
Part of the Epic of Flight series
0–8094–3372–9 Silver, Burdett & Ginn $21.95

• Michael O'Leary
U.S. SKY SPIES SINCE WORLD WAR I
0–7137–1555–3 Sterling $24.95
0–7137–1692–4 Sterling pb $12.95

• John W. Taylor, editor
JANE'S ALL THE WORLD'S AIRCRAFT '88-'89
0–7106–0867–5 Jane's $165.00

• Michael Taylor & David Mondey
THE GUINNESS BOOK OF AIRCRAFT
A compendium of flying facts
0–85112–355–4 Guinness $19.95

• Anthony Thornborough
USAF PHANTOMS
Over 125 photographs and charts illustrate the majestic Phantom's weapons systems and power plants
0–85368–887–7 Arms & Armour $19.95

• Bryce Walker
FIGHTING JETS
Part of the Epic of Flight Series
0–8094–3363–X Silver, Burdett & Ginn $21.50

• Andrew W. Waters
ALL THE U.S. AIR FORCE PLANES, 1907-1983
A reference guide that covers such topics as designers, attack planes, bombers, cargo transports, electronics aircraft, jet fighters, helicopters, amphibians, pursuit planes,

reconnaissance planes, experimental aircraft, and many others
0–87052–031–8 Hippocrene pb $14.95

• David Wragg
AIRLIFT: A History of Military Air Transport
A heavily illustrated history that includes the C-130 Hercules and helicopters in Vietnam and the British "air bridge" in the Falklands
0–89141–282–4 Presidio $25.00

Helicopters

• Paul Beaver
MODERN MILITARY HELICOPTERS
0–85059–893–1 Sterling pb $7.95

• Kenneth Munson & Alex Lumsden
COMBAT HELICOPTERS SINCE 1942
0–7137–1755–6 Sterling pb $12.95

• Cdr. Howard Wheeler, USN
ATTACK HELICOPTERS
The use of helicopters in Vietnam and Afghanistan, technology in NATO countries, and other subjects
0–933852–52–5 Nautical & Aviation $22.95

Space

• Curtis Peebles
GUARDIANS: Strategic Reconnaissance Satellites
A guide to military satellites and space systems, including history, development, technology, and data
0–89141–284–0 Presidio $28.95

World War II Aircraft

• Enzo Angelucci & Paolo Matricardi
COMBAT AIRCRAFT OF WORLD WAR II
0–517–56786–5 Crown $17.95

• John M. Emory
THE SOURCE BOOK OF WORLD WAR II AIRCRAFT
0–7137–1722–X Sterling $39.95

• Philip Kaplan & Rex Smith
ONE LAST LOOK: A Sentimental Journey to the Eighth Air Force Heavy Bomber Bases of World War II in England
0–89659–404–1 Abbeville $30.00

• Mark Meyer
CLASSICS: U.S. Aircraft of World War II
Color photographs of the classic planes, by a *Time* magazine photographer
Text by Walter J. Boyne
0–9616878–6–X Howell $45.00

• David Mondey
THE CONCISE GUIDE TO AXIS AIRCRAFT OF WORLD WAR II
0–600–35027–4 Presidio pb $12.95

• Thomasson-Grant
GHOSTS: Vintage Aircraft of World War II
0–934738–29–7 Thomasson-Grant $36.00

Spitfire

Jeffrey Quill
SPITFIRE: A Test Pilot's Story
0–295–96152–X Washington $19.95

Jerry Scutts
SPITFIRE IN ACTION
0–89747–092–3 Squadron Signal pb $5.95

TANKS AND ARMORED VEHICLES

• **Noel Ayliffe-Jones**
WORLD TANKS AND RECONNAISSANCE VEHICLES SINCE 1945
Covers developments in different countries, as well as firepower, anti-tank guided weapons, and projections of future developments
0–88254–978–2 Hippocrene $19.95

• **Christopher F. Foss, editor**
JANE'S MAIN BATTLE TANKS
Guide to one of the pre-eminent weapons of modern war
0–7106–0372–X Jane's $22.00

• **R.P. Hunnicutt**
FIREPOWER: A History of the American Heavy Tank
A heavily illustrated volume tracing the development of the heavy tank from the Mark VIII through the M103-A2
0–89141–304–9 Presidio $40.00

PATTON: A History of the American Main Battle Tank
Foreword by Donn A. Starry
0–89141–230–1 Presidio $60.00

SHERMAN: A History of the American Medium Tank
The Allies' most important tank during World War II is still in service; heavily illustrated
0–89141–080–5 Presidio $60.00

• **Samuel M. Katz**
ISRAELI TANK BATTLES: Yom Kippur to Lebanon
Many photos, maps and an explanatory text trace the armored combat of the Israeli force for nine years
0–85368–868–0 Sterling $24.95

• **Charles Messenger**
ANTI-ARMOUR WARFARE
An experienced tank commander shows how today's anti-armor battle might be fought
0–87052–152–7 Hippocrene $19.95

• **A.J. Smithers**
A NEW EXCALIBUR: The Development of the Tank, 1909-1939
The inventors, engineers, soldiers and politicians who developed the tank as a new instrument of warfare following the stalemates of World War I
0–436–47520–0 Hippocrene $29.95

RUDE MECHANICALS: An Account of Tank Maturity During the Second World War
The sequel to *A New Excalibur* covers Britain's decline in tank capability between the wars
0–87052–499–2 Hippocrene $39.95

Tanks of World War II

• **Ray Bonds, editor**
AN ILLUSTRATED GUIDE TO WORLD WAR II TANKS AND FIGHTING VEHICLES
The armored vehicles that won and lost the war, their history and technology, lavishly illustrated
0–668–05232–5 Arco pb $9.95

• **George Forty**
GERMAN TANKS OF WORLD WAR II
0–7137–1634–7 Sterling $24.95

M4 SHERMAN
An illustrated history of the mainstay of the US armored divisions in World War II
0–7137–1678–9 Sterling $24.95

U.S. TANKS OF WORLD WAR II IN ACTION
0–7137–1818–8 Sterling pb $14.95

SHIPS AND SEA WARFARE

• **G. Albrecht, editor**
WEYER'S WARSHIPS OF THE WORLD, 1988-89
More than 600 drawings and 900 photos of ships in all the world's navies; in English and German
Foreword by Norman Polmar
0–933852–75–4 Nautical & Aviation $78.95

• **James J. Colledge**
SHIPS OF THE ROYAL NAVY: An Historical Index
0–678–05514–9 Augustus Kelley (set) $75.00

Volume 1: Major Ships
0–678–05300–6 Augustus Kelley $50.00

Volume 2: Navy-Built Trawlers, Drifters, Tugs and Requisitioned Ships
0–678–05301–4 Augustus Kelley $37.50

• **Peter Garrison**
CV: Carrier Aviation
The story of the aircraft carrier that changed the face of war at sea; third edition
Photographs by George Hall
0–89141–299–9 Presidio pb $12.95

• **Edwyn Gray**
SUBMARINE WARRIORS
0–89141–325–1 Presidio $18.95

• **Harold Hahn**
SHIPS OF THE AMERICAN REVOLUTION AND THEIR MODELS
0–87021–653–8 Naval Institute $29.95

• **Hans Hansen**
SHIPS OF THE GERMAN FLEET, 1848-1945
0–87021–654–6 Naval Institute $24.95

• **John Jordan**
AN ILLUSTRATED GUIDE TO THE MODERN U.S. NAVY
Today's navy, from submarine to aircraft carrier
0–668–05505–7 Arco pb $10.95

• **John E. Moore, editor**
JANE'S FIGHTING SHIPS, 1988-89
0–7106–0858–6 Jane's $150.00

JANE'S NATO WARSHIPS HANDBOOK
0–7106–0377–0 Jane's pb $13.95

JANE'S WARSAW PACT WARSHIPS HANDBOOK
0–7106–0400–9 Jane's pb $11.95

• **Brian Lavery**
THE ARMING AND FITTING OF ENGLISH SHIPS OF WAR, 1600-1815
0–87021–009–2 Naval Institute $37.95

• **Emanuel Raymond Lewis**
SEACOAST FORTIFICATIONS OF THE UNITED STATES
A history of the Army's coast artillery from colonial times to the end of World War II
0–89141–257–3 Presidio pb $9.95

• **John E. Moore & Richard Compton-Hall**
SUBMARINE WARFARE: Today and Tomorrow
0–917561–21–X Adler & Adler $22.95

• **Malcolm Muir**
THE IOWA CLASS BATTLESHIPS
US battleships in war and peace
0–7137–1732–7 Sterling $19.95

World War II Ships

• **Erminio Bagnasco**
SUBMARINES OF WORLD WAR II
0–87021–962–6 Naval Institute $32.95

• **Jonathan Crane**
SUBMARINE: Life in the British Submarine Service
0–87021–687–2 Naval Institute $14.95

• **Richard Humble**
U.S. FLEET CARRIERS OF WORLD WAR II
0–7137–1819–6 Sterling pb $14.95

• **Norman Polmar & Dorr B. Carpenter**
SUBMARINES OF THE IMPERIAL JAPANESE NAVY
0–87021–682–1 Naval Institute $34.95

ARMS AND ARMAMENT

The technology of weapons and armor is a fascinating byway of military studies. The development of arms, their strategic and tactical employment, construction and identification are the subject of hundreds of books and monographs. This selection is a representative collection of arms and armor through the ages.

- Bernard Blake, editor
JANE'S WEAPON SYSTEMS, 1988-89
0-7106-0855-1 Jane's $187.50

- Christopher F. Foss, editor
JANE'S ARMOUR AND ARTILLERY, 1988-89
0-7106-0863-2 Jane's $127.50

- Ian V. Hogg, editor
JANE'S INFANTRY WEAPONS, 1988-89
0-7106-0857-8 Jane's $165.00

MILITARY PISTOLS AND REVOLVERS
0-85368-807-9 Sterling $24.95

- Ian V. Hogg & John Weeks
MILITARY SMALL ARMS OF THE 20TH CENTURY
0-910676-87-9 DBI pb $16.95

- James Ladd & Keith Molton
CLANDESTINE WARFARE: Weapons and Equipment of the SOE and OSS
A largely photographic history of the devices used by the British Special Operations Executive and the American Office of Strategic Services during World War II
0-7137-1822-6 Blandford $24.95

- George Markham
GUNS OF THE ELITE: Special Forces Firearms, 1940 to the Present
0-85368-866-4 Sterling $24.95

- Peter Newark
SABRE AND LANCE: An Illustrated History of Cavalry
0-7137-1813-7 Sterling $29.95

- A.V.B. Norman & Don Pottinger
ENGLISH WEAPONS AND WARFARE, 449-1660
A heavily illustrated history, featuring numerous drawings of such weapons as the sword, crossbow, longbow, halberd, pike, and pistol
0-88029-044-7 Hippocrene $14.95

- Carl P. Russell
GUNS ON THE EARLY FRONTIERS: A History of Firearms from Colonial Times Through the Years of the Western Fur Trade
0-8032-8903-0 Nebraska pb $10.95

- J.W. Ryan
GUNS, MORTARS AND ROCKETS
0-08-028325-X Pergamon pb $13.50

- Leroy Thompson & Rene Smeets
GREAT COMBAT HANDGUNS
0-7137-1444-1 Sterling $29.95

High Technology and Chemical Weapons

- Ronald W. Clark
WAR WINNERS
The impact of science and technology on war, from the Civil War to Vietnam; heavily illustrated
0-283-98503-8 Presidio $14.95

- Richard S. Friedman & others
ADVANCED TECHNOLOGY WARFARE
0-517-55851-3 Crown pb $12.95

- T.J. Gander
NUCLEAR, BIOLOGICAL AND CHEMICAL WAR
Traces the historical background, operation and effects of the various kinds of nuclear devices, war chemicals, and biological agents
0-87052-451-8 Hippocrene $22.50

- Chuck Hansen
U.S. NUCLEAR WEAPONS: The Secret History
A large picture book
0-517-56740-7 Orion $29.95

- William Moore
GAS ATTACK!: Chemical Warfare 1915-1918 and Afterwards
A history of gas warfare from its first use by the Germans in 1915 in Flanders to the Gulf War
0-87052-455-0 Hippocrene $22.50

UNIFORMS AND INSIGNIA

- J.R. Bender & Richard D. Law
UNIFORMS, ORGANIZATION AND HISTORY OF THE AFRIKAKORPS
Foreword by Walter Nehring
0-912138-09-2 James R. Bender $24.95

- J.R. Bender & Warren W. Odegard
UNIFORMS, ORGANIZATION AND HISTORY OF THE PANZERTRUPPE
0-912138-18-1 James R. Bender $24.95

- Peter Cochrane
SCOTTISH MILITARY DRESS
0-7137-1738-6 Sterling $24.95

- John R. Elting, editor
MILITARY UNIFORMS IN AMERICA
Includes more than 60 color plates in each volume. Volume 2 is unavailable

Volume 1: The Era of the American Revolution, 1755-1795
0-89141-025-2 Presidio $40.00

Volume 3: Long Endure—The Civil War Period, 1852-1867
0-89141-143-7 Presidio $40.00

Volume 4: The Modern Era, from 1868
0-89141-292-1 Presidio $40.00

- Liliane & Fred Funcken
ARMS AND UNIFORMS: The Napoleonic Wars

Volume 1
0-13-046228-4 Prentice-Hall pb $9.95

Volume 2
0-13-046244-6 Prentice-Hall pb $9.95

- Boris Mollo
UNIFORMS OF THE IMPERIAL RUSSIAN ARMY
Illustrated by John Mollo
0-7137-1939-7 Sterling pb $12.95

- Leroy Thompson
UNIFORMS OF THE INDO-CHINA AND VIETNAM WARS
0-7137-1264-3 Sterling $29.95

UNIFORMS OF THE SOLDIERS OF FORTUNE
Illustrated by Ken J. McSwan
0-7137-1328-3 Sterling pb $14.95

- Gordon Williamson
THE IRON CROSS: A History, 1813-1957
0-7137-1460-3 Sterling $19.95

War Games

Bruce Quarrie
ARMORED WARGAMING
Covers the history and development of tank warfare, plus playing rules and tactics for the war games enthusiast
0-85059-936-9 Sterling pb $9.99

BEGINNER'S GUIDE TO WARGAMING
0-85059-852-4 Sterling pb $9.00

REFERENCE

- David Chandler, editor
THE DICTIONARY OF BATTLES
0-8050-0441-6 Henry Holt pb $24.95

- Dan Cragg
THE NCO GUIDE
0-8117-2168-X Stackpole pb $14.95

- Lawrence P. Crocker
THE ARMY OFFICER'S GUIDE
0-8117-2188-4 Stackpole pb $17.95

- Trevor N. Dupuy & others
DICTIONARY OF MILITARY TERMS
0-8242-0717-3 H.W. Wilson $35.00

- Max Hastings, editor
THE OXFORD BOOK OF MILITARY ANECDOTES
0-19-214107-4 Oxford $19.95
0-19-520528-6 Oxford pb $8.95

- John MacDonald
GREAT BATTLEFIELDS OF THE WORLD
Introduction by Len Deighton
Foreword by John Hackett
0-02-583110-0 Macmillan $35.00

- John Sweetman
A DICTIONARY OF EUROPEAN LAND BATTLES: From the Earliest Times to 1945
0-02-931700-2 Macmillan $24.95

Historiography

THE CLASSICS

- **Lord Bolingbroke**
  HISTORICAL WRITINGS
  With aristocratic panache, the 18th-century statesman parlays history into a weapon against his political enemy, Robert Walpole
  Edited by Isaac Kramnick & John Clive
  0–226–06346–1 Chicago pb $3.50

- **Jacob Burckhardt**
  REFLECTIONS ON HISTORY
  A cultural historian for whom art and literature are as important as political institutions
  Introduction by Gottfried Dietze
  0–913966–37–1 Liberty Fund pb $9.00

- **Thomas Carlyle**
  PAST AND PRESENT
  Carlyle's prophetic tone castigates the materialistic Victorians by contrasting their worldview with the organic quality of medieval life
  Edited by Richard D. Altick
  0–8147–0562–6 NYU pb $15.00

  SELECTED WRITINGS
  Edited by Alan Shelston
  0–14–043065–2 Penguin pb $7.95

- **Wilhelm Dilthey**
  INTRODUCTION TO THE HUMAN SCIENCES: An Attempt to Lay a Foundation for the Study of Society and History
  The great 19th-century German theorist attempted to attain objectively valid interpretations of the inner life of past cultures
  Translated & edited by Ramon J. Betanzos
  0–8143–1897–5 Wayne State $49.95
  0–8143–1898–3 Wayne State pb $19.95

- **Francesco Guicciardini**
  MAXIMS AND REFLECTIONS
  The Florentine historian was one of the first to make the distinction between history and romance
  0–8122–1037–9 Pennsylvania pb $19.95

- **G.W.F. Hegel**
  LECTURES ON THE PHILOSOPHY OF HISTORY
  History as the rational process of the spirit of world freedom from the ancient Orient through classical Greece to 19th-century Europe
  Translated by J. Sibree
  Introduction by C.J. Friedrich
  0–486–20112–0 Dover pb $6.95

  LECTURES ON THE PHILOSOPHY OF WORLD HISTORY: Reason in History
  Edited by D. Forbes & H.B. Nisbet
  0–521–20566–2 Cambridge $37.50
  0–521–28145–8 Cambridge pb $16.95

- **Ibn Khaldûn**
  THE MUQADDIMAH: Abridged Edition
  A single volume abridgement of the 14th-century masterpiece of Islamic historiography. "Should make the essential

Jules Michelet, photographed by Nadar

ideas of Ibn Khaldûn accessible to a wide circle of readers"—*TLS*
Translated by Franz Rosenthal
Edited by N.J. Dawood
0–691–09946–4 Princeton $28.00
0–691–01754–9 Princeton pb $13.95

- **Niccolò Machiavelli**
  THE PORTABLE MACHIAVELLI
  Contains *The Prince*, excerpts from *The Discourses* (Machiavelli's commentary on Roman history), and other writings
  Translated by Mark Musa & Peter Bondanella
  0–14–015092–7 Penguin pb $8.95

- **Charles de Montesquieu**
  THE SPIRIT OF THE LAWS
  The first structuralist shows the variety of political constitutions by collecting and categorizing historical evidence from all times and places
  0–02–849270–6 Hafner pb $13.95

- **Friedrich Nietzsche**
  THE USE AND ABUSE OF HISTORY
  Deeply influenced by Emerson, the philosopher criticizes the 19th-century dependence on history at the expense of living in the present
  Translated by Adrian Collins
  Introduction by J. Kraft
  0–02–323730–9 Macmillan pb $5.50

  UNTIMELY MEDITATIONS
  Translated by R.J. Hollingdale
  0–521–24740–3 Cambridge $32.50
  0–521–28927–0 Cambridge pb $10.95

- **Oswald Spengler**
  THE DECLINE OF THE WEST
  This World War I-inspired meditation on the doom of Western civilization is still interesting for its depiction of the centralization of control over the culture industry; available as a complete set or in an abridged edition
  Edited by Helmut Werner
  0–394–60488–1 Modern Library $7.95

  THE DECLINE OF THE WEST
  0–394–42178–7 Knopf (set) $74.50

  Volume 1
  0–394–42179–5 Knopf $39.50

Volume 2
0–394–42176–0 Knopf $35.00

- **Alexis de Tocqueville**
  JOURNEYS TO ENGLAND AND IRELAND
  Introduction by J.P. Mayer
  0–88738–716–0 Transaction pb $19.95

  RECOLLECTIONS OF THE FRENCH REVOLUTION OF 1848
  Edited with an introduction by J.P. Mayer
  Preface by Fernand Braudel
  0–88738–658–X Transaction pb $24.95

  TOCQUEVILLE'S AMERICA: The Great Quotations
  Edited by Frederick Kershner, Jr.
  0–8214–0753–8 Ohio pb $5.95

▶ **For more on Tocqueville see also The French Revolution and Napoleon & Modern Political Thought**

- **Arnold Toynbee**
  A STUDY OF HISTORY: Abridgement of Volumes 1-6
  An enormous sweep over nations and epochs firmly situates Western civilization in the last five minutes of the clock of history
  Abridged by D.C. Somervell

  Volume 1
  0–19–505080–0 Oxford pb $12.95

  Volume 2
  0–19–505081–9 Oxford pb $12.95

- **Giambattista Vico**
  THE NEW SCIENCE OF GIAMBATTISTA VICO
  This groundbreaking 18th-century work was the first to break with the theory of progress and treat the internal dynamics of primitive cultures
  Translated by Thomas G. Bergin & Max Fisch
  0–8014–9265–3 Cornell pb $12.95

- **Voltaire**
  PHILOSOPHY OF HISTORY
  A vivacious attempt to span early world history in terms of cultural rather than political developments
  0–8065–0078–6 Lyle Stuart pb $3.50

THE GREAT TRADITION

- **Harry E. Barnes**
  HISTORY OF HISTORICAL WRITING
  A still useful but somewhat dated guide to historians from classical times to the 1930s
  0–486–20104–X Dover pb $7.50

- **Geoffrey Barraclough**
  AN INTRODUCTION TO CONTEMPORARY HISTORY
  0–14–020827–5 Penguin pb $5.95

  MAIN TRENDS IN HISTORY
  Part of a UNESCO project on the human sciences, it is optimistic about eventually discovering a scientific basis for historical studies
  0–8419–0505–3 Holmes & Meier pb $14.95

• Isaiah Berlin
AGAINST THE CURRENT: Essays in the History of Ideas
Essays on iconoclastic thinkers including Machiavelli, Vico, Herder, Herzen, and Sorel
0–670–10944–4 Viking $16.95

CONCEPTS AND CATEGORIES: Philosophical Essays
0–14–005805–2 Penguin pb $6.95

• Herbert Butterfield
THE WHIG INTERPRETATION OF HISTORY
One of the earliest books to question the 19th-century interpretation of Britain's constitutional development
0–393–00318–3 Norton pb $6.95

• John Cannon, editor
THE BLACKWELL DICTIONARY OF HISTORIANS
More than 200 contributors have created an authoritative work, including extensive entries on more than 500 historians from Herodotus to the present and numerous historiographical essays on a wide range of topics
0–631–14708–X Blackwell $75.00

• Norman F. Cantor & Richard I. Schneider
HOW TO STUDY HISTORY
Excellent practical guide for the beginner
0–88295–709–0 Harlan Davidson pb $9.95

• E.H. Carr
WHAT IS HISTORY?
Classic by a great British historian of the Russian Revolution
0–394–70391–X Random House pb $5.50

• John Clive
NOT BY FACT ALONE: Essays on the Writing and Reading of History
Reveals the "tricks of the trade," especially as used by such masters as Tocqueville, Carlyle, Macaulay, Michelet, and Burckhardt
0–394–48953–5 Knopf $27.50

• R.G. Collingwood
THE IDEA OF HISTORY
Collingwood is the best English exponent of historical idealism: that the meaning of history is created by human imagination
Edited by T.M. Knox
0–19–500205–9 Oxford pb $9.95

• Will & Ariel Durant
LESSONS OF HISTORY
0–671–41333–3 Simon & Schuster $16.95

• Robert W. Fogel & G.R. Elton
WHICH ROAD TO THE PAST?: Two Views of History
Illuminating discussion between a leading practitioner of the new quantitative methods and a defender of traditional history
0–300–03278–1 Yale pb $8.95

• Pieter Geyl
THE USE AND ABUSE OF HISTORY
0–208–00827–6 Shoe String $16.50

• Gertrude Himmelfarb
THE NEW HISTORY AND THE OLD
A highly critical look at the trends of recent decades
0–674–61580–8 Harvard $20.00

• Richard Hofstadter
THE PROGRESSIVE HISTORIANS: Turner, Beard, Parrington
"The greatest [historian] of his generation"—Fritz Stern
0–226–34818–0 Chicago pb $7.95

• Johan Huizinga
MEN AND IDEAS: History, the Middle Ages, the Renaissance
Historiography from the author of *The Waning of the Middle Ages*
Introduction by Bert F. Hoselitz
0–691–05422–3 Princeton $37.00
0–691–00802–7 Princeton pb $10.95

• John Kenyon
THE HISTORY MEN: The Historical Profession in England since the Renaissance
Entertaining biographies are supplemented by a clear grasp of abiding controversial issues
0–8229–5900–3 Pittsburgh pb $14.95

• Leonard Krieger
RANKE: The Meaning of History
0–226–45349–9 Chicago $31.00

• William H. McNeill
MYTHISTORY AND OTHER ESSAYS
By an American exponent of global history
0–226–56135–6 Chicago $19.95

• Maurice Mandelbaum
PHILOSOPHY, HISTORY, AND THE SCIENCES: Selected Critical Essays
A variety of views by the great opponent of relativism
0–8018–3112–1 Johns Hopkins $37.50

• Frank E. Manuel
SHAPES OF PHILOSOPHICAL HISTORY
Cultivated lectures on the patterns that man has tried to find in history from Daniel to Immanuel Kant
0–8047–0248–9 Stanford $13.50

• Friedrich Meinecke
MEN AND EVENTS: Historical Essays
0–374–97997–9 Hippocrene $20.00

• Arnaldo Momigliano
ESSAYS IN ANCIENT AND MODERN HISTORIOGRAPHY
Urbane and erudite studies of the great classical historians
0–8195–5010–8 Wesleyan pb $25.00

• Fritz Stern, editor
THE VARIETIES OF HISTORY: From Voltaire to the Present
A canny selection of seminal texts in the history of historiography
0–394–71962–X Random House pb $9.95

• Barbara Tuchman
PRACTICING HISTORY: Selected Essays
The popular historian discourses on working methods and on current events from Japan to Israel
0–394–52086–6 Knopf $16.50
0–345–30363–6 Ballantine pb $8.95

• C.V. Wedgwood
HISTORY AND HOPE: Essays on History and the English Civil War
Articles and lectures dating from 1942 to 1978 and published in 1989. "Rewarding reading for historians and history buffs alike"—*Publishers Weekly*
0–525–24740–8 Dutton $25.00

• Robin W. Winks, editor
THE HISTORIAN AS DETECTIVE: Essays on Evidence
A variety of historians apply their deductive talents to the elucidation of mysteries from medieval murders to Edgar Allan Poe thrillers
0–06–131933–3 Harper & Row pb $10.95

• C. Vann Woodward
THE BURDEN OF SOUTHERN HISTORY
0–8071–0837–5 LSU $25.00
0–8071–0133–8 LSU pb $8.95

THINKING BACK: The Perils of Writing History
0–8071–1304–2 LSU $12.95
0–8071–1377–8 LSU pb $6.95

NEW DIRECTIONS

• Perry Anderson
IN THE TRACKS OF HISTORICAL MATERIALISM
A Marxist questions the direction of his own methodology
0–226–01788–5 Chicago $15.00

• Stephen Bann
THE CLOTHING OF CLIO: A Study of the Representation of History in Nineteenth Century Britain and France
0–521–25616–X Cambridge $44.50

• Robert H. Canary & Henry Kozicki, editors
THE WRITING OF HISTORY: Literary Form and Historical Understanding
Language is the new subjectivity: these essays show how rhetorical tropes distort the historian's desire to reproduce reality
0–299–07570–2 Wisconsin $32.50

• Peter Gay
FREUD FOR HISTORIANS
0–19–503586–0 Oxford $19.95
0–19–504228–X Oxford pb $8.95

• Lionel Gossman
THE EMPIRE UNPOSSESS'D: An Essay on Gibbon's "Decline and Fall"
0–521–23453–0 Cambridge $24.95

• J.H. Hexter
ON HISTORIANS: Reappraisals of Some of the Masters of Modern History
0–674–63427–6 Harvard pb $9.95

REAPPRAISALS IN HISTORY: New Views on History and Society in Early Modern Europe
Traditional techniques wielded with particular dexterity cast new light on social and cultural problems in the 16th and 17th centuries
0–226–33233–0 Chicago pb $13.00

- **E.J. Hobsbawm & Terence Ranger, editors**
THE INVENTION OF TRADITION
Just how old are traditions? These essays will tell you precisely when the tartan was invented and describe the mixture of Ali Baba and Lohengrin that was hoked up for the great 1870 durbar at Delhi
0–521–24645–8 Cambridge $39.50
0–521–26985–7 Cambridge pb $10.95

- **Lynn Hunt, editor**
THE NEW CULTURAL HISTORY
0–520–06429–1 California pb $9.95

- **Georg Iggers**
NEW DIRECTIONS IN EUROPEAN HISTORIOGRAPHY
Excellent coverage of the current trends—*Annales*, Modern German, Marxist—with some historical background
0–8195–6071–5 Wesleyan pb $12.95

- **Georg Iggers, editor**
THE GERMAN CONCEPTION OF HISTORY
0–8195–6080–4 Wesleyan pb $14.95

- **Dominick LaCapra**
HISTORY AND CRITICISM
Attempts to locate ways of doing history that will incorporate new rhetorical criticism while retaining a sense of the difference of the past
0–8014–1788–0 Cornell $21.95
0–8014–9324–2 Cornell pb $6.95

HISTORY, POLITICS, AND THE NOVEL
0–8014–2033–4 Cornell $22.50

- **David Lowenthal**
THE PAST IS A FOREIGN COUNTRY
An illustrated personal investigation into the persistence of the past in our daily lives through architecture, sculpture, and the sites of great events
0–521–22415–2 Cambridge $29.95
0–521–29480–0 Cambridge pb $13.95

- **Georg Lukács**
THE HISTORICAL NOVEL
Translated by Hannah & Stanley Mitchell
0–8032–7910–8 Nebraska pb $8.95

- **R.S. Neale**
WRITING MARXIST HISTORY: British Society, Economy and Culture Since 1700
0–631–14051–4 Blackwell $55.00

- **Karl R. Popper**
THE POVERTY OF HISTORICISM
The most famous attack on history-writing in which theories overwhelm facts
0–744–80052–8 RC&H pb $8.95

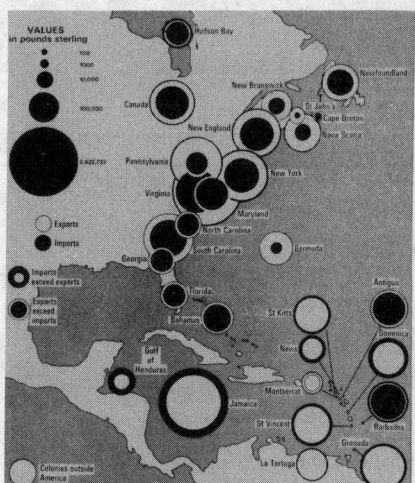
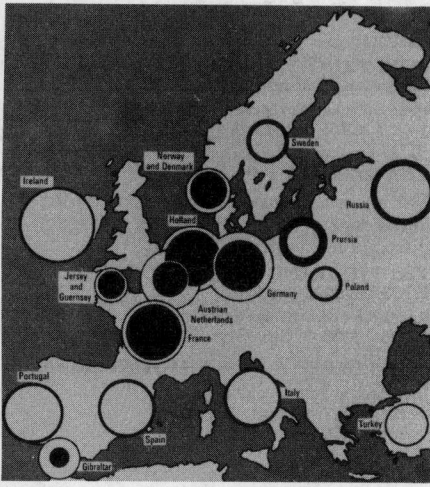

Great Britain's trade with the world in 1792, from The Perspective of the World *by Fernand Braudel (Harper & Row)*

- **Paul Ricoeur**
TIME AND NARRATIVE
Translated by Kathleen McLaughlin & David Pellauer

Volume 1
0–226–71331–8 Chicago $25.00

Volume 2
0–226–71333–4 Chicago $25.00

Volume 3
0–226–71335–0 Chicago $29.95

- **Lawrence Stone**
THE PAST AND PRESENT
0–7102–1253–4 RC&H $49.95
0–7102–1193–7 RC&H pb $16.95

- **Paul Thompson**
THE VOICE OF THE PAST: Oral History
Oral history records the lives of ordinary people through their own voices
0–19–219230–2 Oxford $39.95
0–19–289216–9 Oxford pb $12.95

- **Jan Vansina**
ORAL TRADITION AS HISTORY
Traditional African narratives are used to map a non-European past
0–299–10214–9 Wisconsin pb $9.75

- **Hayden White**
The foremost proponent of history as a rhetorical form, rather than a representation of reality, makes a series of powerful arguments in the following books:

THE CONTENT OF THE FORM: Narrative Discourse and Historical Representation
0–8018–2937–2 Johns Hopkins $26.50

METAHISTORY: The Historical Imagination in Nineteenth-Century Europe
Hegel, Michelet, Ranke, Tocqueville, Burckhardt, Marx, Nietzsche, and Croce
0–8018–1761–7 Johns Hopkins pb $11.95

TROPICS OF DISCOURSE: Essays in Cultural Criticism
0–8018–2741–8 Johns Hopkins pb $10.95

Annales

The highly influential French school, named for its own periodical, *Annales—sociétés—civilisations* has a methodological rather than a political orientation. Its early focus was on the *mentalité*, the cultural and religious particularity of past periods, derived from little-used documents such as heresy trial records and private letter caches. Later writers developed the idea of the *longue durée* as a supplement to the interpretation of political, military, and constitutional events. They analyzed the effect of geological, social, and technological changes spanning hundreds and even thousands of years.

- **Marc Bloch**
THE HISTORIAN'S CRAFT
These essays by one of the group's earliest members have an unpretentious touch
0–394–70512–2 Random House pb $4.50

- **Fernand Braudel**
ON HISTORY
The most famous member of the school discusses the method used in such works as *The Structures of Everyday Life*
Translated by Sarah Matthews
0–226–07151–0 Chicago pb $8.95

- **Michel de Certeau**
THE WRITING OF HISTORY
0–231–05574–9 Columbia $40.00

- **Roger Chartier**
CULTURAL HISTORY: Between Practices and Representations
Translated by Lydia Cochrane
0–8014–2223–X Cornell $29.95

- **François Furet**
IN THE WORKSHOP OF HISTORY
Essays on the Enlightenment, the French Revolution, and anti-Semitism in France
Translated by Jonathan Mandelbaum
0–226–27336–9 Chicago $27.50

• Jacques Le Goff & Pierre Nora, editors
CONSTRUCTING THE PAST: Essays in Historical Methodology
Introduction by Colin Lucas
0–521–25976–2 Cambridge $42.50

• Emmanuel Le Roy Ladurie
The historian who used Inquisition records in his depiction of a 13th-century village discusses his working methods.
THE MIND AND METHOD OF THE HISTORIAN
Translated by Siân & Ben Reynolds
0–226–47325–2 Chicago pb $12.95

THE TERRITORY OF THE HISTORIAN
Translated by Siân & Ben Reynolds
0–226–47327–9 Chicago $26.00
0–226–47328–7 Chicago pb $11.95

• Paul Veyne
WRITING HISTORY
An empiricist formulation of the aims and intentions of the *Annales* school
Translated by Mina Moore-Rinvolucri
0–8195–5067–1 Wesleyan $30.00
0–8195–6076–6 Wesleyan pb $14.95

BIOGRAPHIES AND CRITICAL STUDIES

• Hugh Tulloch
ACTON
0–312–02726–5 St. Martin's $24.95

• Elisabeth Labrousse
BAYLE
0–19–287541–8 Oxford $12.95

• A.L. Le Quesne
CARLYLE
0–19–287563–9 Oxford $16.95

• John D. Rosenberg
CARLYLE AND THE BURDEN OF HISTORY
An eloquent and suggestive study
0–674–09754–8 Harvard $22.50

• Richard Ollard
CLARENDON: A Biography
0–689–11731–0 Atheneum $22.50

• J.W. Burrow
GIBBON
0–19–287553–1 Oxford $13.95
0–19–287552–3 Oxford pb $4.95

• John Clive
MACAULAY: The Shaping of the Historian
0–674–54005–0 Harvard pb $13.95

• Felix Gilbert
MACHIAVELLI AND GUICCIARDINI: Politics and History in Sixteenth-Century Florence
0–393–30123–0 Norton pb $9.95

• Quentin Skinner
MACHIAVELLI
0–19–287516–7 Oxford pb $4.95

• G.R. Elton
F.W. MAITLAND
0–300–03528–4 Yale $18.00

• Peter Singer
MARX
0–19–287510–8 Oxford pb $4.95

• Judith Shklar
MONTESQUIEU
0–19–287649–X Oxford $18.95
0–19–287648–1 Oxford pb $4.95

• André Jardin
TOCQUEVILLE: A Biography
A concise and balanced treatment of Tocqueville's public views, and a useful source for all students
0–374–27836–9 Farrar, Straus & Giroux $35.00

• William H. McNeill
ARNOLD J. TOYNBEE: A Life
"A rare treat . . . Poignant and perceptive"—*Library Journal*
0–19–505863–1 Oxford $24.95

• Peter Burke
VICO
0–19–287619–8 Oxford $14.95
0–19–287618–X Oxford pb $4.95

➤ **FOR OVERSEAS ORDERING INFORMATION, SEE PAGE 1**

HISTORY OF THE AMERICAS

Native American Cultures: North America

"Despite vast study by scientists and a voluminous literature of modern knowledge about Indians, still common are ignorance and misconceptions, many of them resulting from the white man's continuing inability to regard Indians save from his own European-based point of view. Today most Indians on both continents have been conquered and enfolded within the conquerors' own cultures; but the span of time since the various phases of the conquest ended has been short, and numerous Indians still cling to traits that are centuries, if not millennia, old and cannot be quickly shed."—Alvin M. Josephy, Jr., *The Indian Heritage of America*

GENERAL WORKS

▶ **See also Native American Literature**

- William Brandon
INDIANS
A strong, compact narrative
0–8281–0301–1 Houghton Mifflin pb $9.95

- Angie Debo
A HISTORY OF THE INDIANS OF THE UNITED STATES
0–8061–1888–1 Oklahoma pb $13.95

- Harold E. Driver
INDIANS OF NORTH AMERICA
One of the most useful overviews; this revised edition incorporates recent archaeological findings and devotes much space to the 20th century
0–226–16467–5 Chicago pb $16.95

- Alvin M. Josephy, Jr.
THE INDIAN HERITAGE OF AMERICA
An encyclopedic work by one of the best historians of Indian America, surveying tribal cultures region by region
0–394–30315–6 Knopf pb $5.95

- Philip Kopper
THE SMITHSONIAN BOOK OF NORTH AMERICAN INDIANS: Before the Coming of the Europeans
Features 293 full-color illustrations
0–8109–1510–3 Abrams $39.95

- Ruth M. Underhill
RED MAN'S AMERICA: A History of Indians in the United States
Illustrated by Marianne Stoller
0–226–84165–0 Chicago pb $13.95

- Carl Waldman
ATLAS OF THE NORTH AMERICAN INDIAN
Contains over 100 maps, with an extensive text treating prehistory, culture, wars, land cessions, and contemporary issues
Illustrated by Molly Braun
0–87196–850–9 Facts On File $29.95

Bear mask, c. 1920 (courtesy Philbrook Art Center), from The Arts of the North American Indian: Native Traditions in Evolution *edited by Edwin L. Wade (Hudson Hills)*

ENCYCLOPEDIA OF NATIVE AMERICAN TRIBES
Appropriate for both adult and young readers
Illustrated by Molly Braun
0–8160–1421–3 Facts On File $35.00

- Jack Weatherford
INDIAN GIVERS: How the Indians of the Americas Transformed the World
Contributions in business, government, medicine, architecture, agriculture, and many other social and cultural affairs
0–517–56969–8 Crown $17.95

- Clark Wissler
INDIANS OF THE UNITED STATES: Four Centuries of Their History and Culture
Unusual in that it traces the tribes by language family rather than by culture area
0–385–02019–8 Doubleday pb $6.50

Prehistory

Michael Coe, Dean Snow & Elizabeth Benson
ATLAS OF ANCIENT AMERICA
A guide to the Americas before Columbus
0–8160–1199–0 Facts On File $40.00

Brian M. Fagan
THE GREAT JOURNEY: The Peopling of Ancient America
A piece of archaeological detective work uncovering the evidence of ancient migrations; many illustrations
0–500–05045–7 Thames & Hudson $19.95

Jesse D. Jennings, editor
ANCIENT NORTH AMERICANS
A reliable basic source
0–7167–1428–0 W.H. Freeman $29.95

Paul S. Martin, George I. Quimby & Donald Collier
INDIANS BEFORE COLUMBUS: 20,000 Years of North American History Revealed by Archaeology
0–226–50782–3 Chicago pb $6.95

EARLY PAINTINGS AND PHOTOGRAPHS

- George Catlin
LETTERS AND NOTES ON THE MANNERS, CUSTOMS AND CONDITIONS OF THE NORTH AMERICAN INDIANS
The classic early account of life among the Plains Indians

Volume 1
0–486–22118–0 Dover pb $7.95

Volume 2
0–486–22119–9 Dover pb $7.95

- Edward S. Curtis
THE NORTH AMERICAN INDIANS: Photographs by Edward S. Curtis
0–912–334–34–7 Aperture pb $25.00

- David Hunt & others
KARL BODMER'S AMERICA
Indian life in the 1830s, recorded by a great painter. Contains 257 color plates with commentary by David Hunt, Marsha Gallagher, and William Orr
Introduction by William H. Goetzmann
0–8032–1185–6 Nebraska $70.00

- Christopher M. Lyman
THE VANISHING RACE AND OTHER ILLUSIONS: Photographs of Indians by Edward S. Curtis
Introduction by Vine Deloria, Jr.
0–394–71029–0 Pantheon pb $14.95

- William Webb & Robert Weinstein
DWELLERS AT THE SOURCE: Southwestern Indian Photographs of A.C. Vroman, 1895–1904
0–8263–1009–5 New Mexico pb $24.95

REGIONAL AND TRIBAL STUDIES

Northeast and Great Lakes

- Cadwallader Colden
THE HISTORY OF THE FIVE INDIAN NATIONS
An 18th-century account of the Iroquois League
0–8014–9086–3 Cornell pb $6.95

- Edmund J. Danziger, Jr.
THE CHIPPEWAS OF LAKE SUPERIOR
0–8061–1487–8 Oklahoma $21.95

- George T. Hunt
WARS OF THE IROQUOIS: A Study in Intertribal Trade Relations
0–299–00164–4 Wisconsin pb $14.50

- Isabel T. Kelsay
JOSEPH BRANT, 1743–1807: Man of Two Worlds
The Mohawk chief who sided with the British during the American Revolution
0–8156–0182–4 Syracuse $40.00
0–8156–0208–1 Syracuse pb $17.50

• Helen H. Tanner, editor
ATLAS OF GREAT LAKES INDIAN HISTORY
Contains 33 newly researched maps. "Far and away one of this century's landmark works on American Indian history—absolutely indispensible . . . A quantum leap forward in the study and understanding of the Indian past"—Alvin M. Josephy, Jr.
Cartography by Miklos Pinther
0–8061–1515–7 Oklahoma $75.00
0–8061–2056–8 Oklahoma pb $29.95

• Bruce G. Trigger
THE CHILDREN OF AATAENTSIC: A History of the Huron People to 1660
A remarkably detailed work that attempts to avoid the Eurocentric bias of earlier writers
0–7735–0626–8 Toronto $70.00
0–7735–0627–6 Toronto pb $24.95

Southeastern

• Angie Debo
THE RISE AND FALL OF THE CHOCTAW REPUBLIC
0–8061–1247–6 Oklahoma pb $11.95

• John Ehle
TRAIL OF TEARS: The Rise and Fall of the Cherokee Nation
0–385–23953–X Doubleday $19.95

• Grant Foreman
INDIAN REMOVAL: The Emigration of the Five Civilized Tribes of Indians
The forced removals to Indian Territory in the 1830s
0–8061–0019–2 Oklahoma $21.95
0–8061–1172–0 Oklahoma pb $12.95

• Charles Hudson
THE SOUTHEASTERN INDIANS
0–87049–187–3 Tennessee $29.95
0–87049–248–9 Tennessee pb $12.95

• Duane H. King, editor
THE CHEROKEE INDIAN NATION: A Troubled History
0–87049–227–6 Tennessee $14.95

• Edwin C. McReynolds
THE SEMINOLES
Including an account of the removal from Florida to Indian Territory
0–8061–1255–7 Oklahoma pb $11.95

• Theda Perdue
SLAVERY AND THE EVOLUTION OF CHEROKEE SOCIETY, 1540–1866
0–87049–259–4 Tennessee $19.95
0–87049–530–5 Tennessee pb $9.95

Plains, Plateau, and Great Basin

• Norman Bancroft-Hunt & Forman Werner
THE INDIANS OF THE GREAT PLAINS
0–688–01215–9 Morrow $25.00

• Donald J. Berthrong
THE SOUTHERN CHEYENNES
Takes their history up to the present
0–8061–1199–2 Oklahoma pb $14.95

• Edwin T. Denig
FIVE INDIAN TRIBES OF THE UPPER MISSOURI: Sioux, Arickaras, Assiniboines, Crees and Crows
A firsthand account by a fur trader who married an Assiniboine woman and lived among various tribes from 1833 to 1858
Edited by John Ewers
0–8061–1308–1 Oklahoma pb $8.95

• John Ewers
THE BLACKFEET: Raiders on the Northwestern Plains
An ethnic history to 1930, including all three divisions of the Blackfeet: Piegan, Blood, and Siksika
0–8061–1836–9 Oklahoma pb $12.95

• George B. Grinnell
THE FIGHTING CHEYENNES
Nineteenth-century wars with other tribes and subsequently with whites
Introduction by Stanley Vestal
0–8061–0347–7 Oklahoma $29.95
0–8061–1839–3 Oklahoma pb $14.95

• George E. Hyde
SPOTTED TAIL'S FOLK: A History of the Brule Sioux
0–8061–1380–4 Oklahoma pb $12.95

RED CLOUD'S FOLK: A History of the Oglala Sioux Indians
The migration of the Oglala Sioux from the upper Mississippi to the Powder River in Montana
Foreword by Royal B. Hassrick
0–8061–1520–3 Oklahoma pb $9.95

• Alvin M. Josephy, Jr.
THE NEZ PERCE INDIANS AND THE OPENING OF THE NORTHWEST
0–8032–2555–5 Nebraska $31.50
0–8032–7551–X Nebraska pb $14.95

• Robert H. Lowie
INDIANS OF THE PLAINS
A concise survey, first published in 1954
Foreword by Harry L. Shapiro
0–8032–2858–9 Nebraska $21.00
0–8032–7907–8 Nebraska pb $7.95

• Mildred P. Mayhall
THE KIOWAS
0–8061–0987–4 Oklahoma pb $12.95

• William E. Unrau
THE KANSA INDIANS: A History of the Wind People, 1673–1873
From first contact with whites to migration and settlement in eastern Kansas
Foreword by R. David Edmunds
0–8061–1965–9 Oklahoma pb $10.95

Southwestern

• Frank Hamilton Cushing
ZUNI: Selected Writings of Frank Hamilton Cushing
Cushing stayed at Zuni pueblo from 1879 to 1884, the first professional anthropologist to live among his subjects. His writings are of far more than historical interest
Edited by Jesse Green
0–8032–2100–2 Nebraska $28.50
0–8032–7007–0 Nebraska pb $9.95

• Bertha P. Dutton
AMERICAN INDIANS OF THE SOUTHWEST
A history of the Apache, Navajo, and Pueblo peoples, updated with information on current issues
0–8263–0704–3 New Mexico pb $15.95

• Frank C. Lockwood
THE APACHE INDIANS
"Undoubtedly the best account for the general reader"—*Christian Science Monitor*
0–8032–2878–3 Nebraska $26.50
0–8032–7925–6 Nebraska pb $9.95

• Dan L. Thrapp
VICTORIO AND THE MIMBRES APACHES
The Mimbres from their first American contacts in 1849 to the massacre of 1880, with a biography of their war leader Victorio
0–8061–1645–5 Oklahoma pb $13.95

• Ruth M. Underhill
THE NAVAJOS
0–8061–1816–4 Oklahoma pb $9.95

• Frank Waters
THE BOOK OF THE HOPI
0–14–004527–9 Penguin pb $8.95

California

• John Fahey
THE KALISPEL INDIANS
The history of a hunting people
0–8061–2000–2 Oklahoma $18.95

Baking bread in Narrow Creek Canyon, New Mexico, from In America *by Eve Arnold* (Knopf)

• Robert F. Heizer & Albert B. Elsasser
THE NATURAL WORLD OF THE CALIFORNIA INDIANS
This highly detailed guide situates the Indians within the interlocked, self-sustaining ecosystem they inhabited and summarizes the destruction of their ways
0–520–03896–7 California pb $10.95

• Robert F. Heizer & Theodora Kroeber, editors
ISHI THE LAST YAHI: A Documentary History
0–520–04366–9 California pb $9.95

• Robert F. Heizer & M. A. Whipple, editors
THE CALIFORNIA INDIANS: A Source Book
0–520–01770–6 California $38.00
0–520–02031–6 California pb $15.95

• Theodora Kroeber
ISHI IN TWO WORLDS: A Biography of the Last Wild Indian in North America
0–520–03152–0 California $25.00
0–520–03153–9 California pb $10.95

• Joaquin Miller
LIFE AMONGST THE MODOCS:
Unwritten History
An account by the 19th-century San Francisco poet
Edited by Alan Rosenus
Afterword by William Everson
0–913522–13–9 Urion $19.95
0–913522–12–0 Urion pb $8.95

• Keith A. Murray
THE MODOCS AND THEIR WAR
Describes the beliefs that led the Modocs of northern California to war in 1872
0–8061–1331–6 Oklahoma pb $8.95

• Stephen Powers
TRIBES OF CALIFORNIA
Introduction by Robert F. Heizer
0–520–03023–0 California $40.00
0–520–03172–5 California pb $11.95

Northwest Coast

• Franz Boas
KWAKIUTL ETHNOGRAPHY
An anthropological classic
Edited with an introduction by Helen Codere
0–226–06237–6 Chicago pb $11.00

• Stanley Walens
FEASTING WITH CANNIBALS: An Essay on Kwakiutl Cosmology
0–691–09392–X Princeton $19.00

Northern Canadian and Arctic Peoples

• Don E. Dumond
THE ESKIMOS AND ALEUTS: Their Archaeology and Early History
"One of the most provocative holistic statements of Arctic prehistory"—*Alaska Journal*
0–500–27479–7 Thames & Hudson pb $11.95

• William W. Fitzhugh & Susan Kaplan
INUA: Spirit World of the Bering Sea Eskimo
0–87474–430–X Smithsonian $39.95
0–87474–429–6 Smithsonian pb $19.95

• Diamond Jenness
THE INDIANS OF CANADA
0–8020–6326–8 Toronto pb $15.95

PEOPLE OF THE TWILIGHT
0–226–39653–3 Chicago pb $9.95

• Richard K. Nelson
HUNTERS OF THE NORTHERN ICE
Introduction by William S. Laughlin
0–226–57176–9 Chicago pb $12.95

• Ulli Steltzer
INUIT: The North in Transition
0–226–77247–0 Chicago pb $22.50

INDIAN-WHITE RELATIONS

"In ordinary conversation, Apaches address each other in low, softly modulated tones and at a pace they consider measured and deliberate. By comparison, they say, they are forcefully struck by the speech of Anglo-Americans, which is regularly described as being too fast, too loud, and too 'tense.' . . . Among themselves, Apaches associate these . . . phenomena with the expression of criticism and indignant self-assertion—with the voice of a woman scolding a child, for example, or with that of a man responding to an insult. As a result, Anglo-Americans, even when speaking in a manner that they consider genial and relaxed, may easily give the impression of being vexed and irate. Most Apaches recognize this disjunction and on occasions find it amusing, as when they observe, 'Whitemen are angry even when they're friendly.'"—Keith H. Basso, *Portraits of "The Whiteman"*

• Keith H. Basso
PORTRAITS OF "THE WHITEMAN": Linguistic Play and Cultural Symbols Among the Western Apache
Investigates a complex form of joking in which Apaches stage carefully crafted imitations of Anglo-Americans
0–521–22640–6 Cambridge $24.95
0–521–29593–9 Cambridge pb $10.95

• Robert F. Berkhofer, Jr.
THE WHITE MAN'S INDIAN: Images of the American Indian from Columbus to the Present
0–394–72794–0 Random House pb $8.50

• Peter Nabokov, editor
NATIVE AMERICAN TESTIMONY: An Anthology of Indian and White Relations
Preface by Vine Deloria, Jr.
0–06–131993–7 Harper & Row pb $7.95

• Francis P. Prucha
THE GREAT FATHER: The United States Government and the American Indians
An abridgment of Prucha's massive study. "The most important history ever published about the formulation of federal Indian policies in the United States"—*Minnesota History*
0–8032–3675–1 Nebraska $27.50
0–8032–8712–7 Nebraska pb $9.95

THE INDIANS IN AMERICAN SOCIETY: From the Revolutionary War to the Present
The transformation from self-sufficiency into dependency
0–520–05503–9 California $20.00

• Edward H. Spicer
CYCLES OF CONQUEST: The Impact of Spain, Mexico and the United States on Indians of the Southwest, 1533–1960
0–8165–0021–5 Arizona pb $14.95

• Raymond W. Stedman
SHADOWS OF THE INDIAN: Stereotypes in American Culture
Examples drawn from literature, art, and popular culture
Foreword by Rennard Strickland
0–8061–1963–2 Oklahoma pb $14.95

The Early Period

"Every European 'discoverer' had Indian guides. Every European colonizer had Indian instruction and assistance. Ethnocentric semantics have hidden the chief role of Indians in the creation of American society by reserving exclusively for Europeans the honorable title of 'pioneer' and contrasting it to the lowly status of 'native,' but the European vanguard were pupils in the Indian school. Indians brought to their symbiotic partnership with Europeans the experience and knowledge of millennia of genuine pioneering. What American society owes to Indian society, as much as to any other source, is the mere fact of its existence."—Francis Jennings, *The Invasion of America*

• James Axtell
THE EUROPEAN AND THE INDIAN: Essays in the Ethnohistory of Colonial North America
A blend of history and anthropology, drawing on archaeology, linguistics, literature, and art
0–19–502903–8 Oxford $27.50
0–19–502904–6 Oxford pb $9.95

THE INVASION WITHIN: The Contest of Cultures in Colonial North America
"The best introduction now available to the problem of cultural conversion in the New World"—William Cronon
0–19–503596–8 Oxford $38.00

• Alvar Nuñez Cabeza de Vaca
ADVENTURES IN THE UNKNOWN INTERIOR OF AMERICA
The ill-fated Nervaez expedition to Florida; an astonishing narrative of early American exploration
Translated with notes by Cyclone Covey
0–8263–0656–X New Mexico pb $8.95

• Frederick Drimmer, editor
CAPTURED BY THE INDIANS: Fifteen Firsthand Accounts, 1750–1870
Excerpted (and in some cases modernized) narratives, presenting a remarkable diversity of experiences
0–486–24901–8 Dover pb $6.95

 IF YOU CAN'T FIND IT, LOOK IN THE INDEX

- Richard Drinnon
FACING WEST: The Metaphysics of Indian-Hating and Empire-Building
0–452–00632–5 NAL pb $10.95

- Francis Jennings
THE AMBIGUOUS IROQUOIS EMPIRE: The Covenant Chain Confederation of Indian Tribes with English Colonies
0–393–30302–0 Norton pb $12.95

EMPIRE OF FORTUNE: Crowns, Colonies, and Tribes in the Seven Years War in America
0–393–02537–3 Norton $27.50

THE INVASION OF AMERICA: Indians, Colonialism, and the Cant of Conquest
A startlingly revised picture of Puritans and Indians
0–393–00830–4 Norton pb $9.95

- Bruce E. Johansen
FORGOTTEN FOUNDERS: How the American Indians Helped Shape Democracy
"Rarely has a book given me more information and a worse conscience. It tells what one should know of how the first Americans governed themselves and in many ways set an example for the Europeans"—John Kenneth Galbraith
0–916782–90–5 Harvard Common pb $8.95

- Bernard W. Sheehan
SAVAGISM AND CIVILITY
0–521–22927–8 Cambridge $44.50
0–521–29723–0 Cambridge pb $10.95

SEEDS OF EXTINCTION: Jeffersonian Philanthropy and the American Indian
0–393–00716–2 Norton pb $8.95

- Wiley Sword
PRESIDENT WASHINGTON'S INDIAN WAR: The Struggle for the Old Northwest, 1790–1795
The little-known story of how the United States gained control in modern-day Ohio, Illinois, Indiana, Wisconsin, and Michigan
0–8061–1864–4 Oklahoma $24.95

INDIAN WARS

- Stephen E. Ambrose
CRAZY HORSE AND CUSTER
Parallel lives converging at the Little Bighorn
0–452–00869–7 NAL pb $9.95

- Merrill D. Beal
I WILL FIGHT NO MORE FOREVER: Chief Joseph and the Nez Perce War
0–295–74009–4 Washington pb $10.95

- Jason Betzinez & Wilbur S. Nye
I FOUGHT WITH GERONIMO
The memoirs of Betzinez, Geronimo's cousin, who survived until 1959. "The Apache wars from the inside looking out"—Angie Debo, *NY Times*
Illustrated by J. Franklin Whitman, Jr.
0–8032–1204–6 Nebraska $19.95
0–8032–6086–5 Nebraska pb $7.95

- John G. Bourke
AN APACHE CAMPAIGN IN SIERRA MADRE: An Account of the Expedition in Pursuit of the Hostile Chiricahua Apaches in the Spring 1883
Crook's pursuit of Geronimo from Arizona to Mexico in 1883
Foreword by Joseph C. Porter
0–8032–6085–7 Nebraska pb $4.95

ON THE BORDER WITH CROOK
"Capt. John G. Bourke understood the Apache people and the Apache country . . . as a soldier, as a scholar, and as a man with eager sympathies for nearly all things human"—J. Frank Dobie
0–8032–5741–4 Nebraska pb $11.95

- Dee Brown
BURY MY HEART AT WOUNDED KNEE: An Indian History of the American West
0–03–085322–2 Henry Holt $18.95

- Evan S. Connell
SON OF THE MORNING STAR: Custer and the Little Bighorn
A complex and beautifully written exploration that arrives not at one truth but a multitude of sometimes contradictory realities
0–06–097161–4 Harper & Row pb $9.95

- George A. Custer
MY LIFE ON THE PLAINS: Or, Personal Experiences with Indians
Covers 1867–69, including the battle of the Washita
0–8061–1357–X Oklahoma pb $7.95

- R. David Edmunds
THE SHAWNEE PROPHET
"Previous historians have stressed the role of Tecumseh in the creation of an anti-American confederacy in the years before 1912. Edmunds demonstrates that Tecumseh's brother Tenskwatawa, the Prophet, launched the movement and dominated it for several years"—*Montana*
0–8032–6711–8 Nebraska pb $7.95

TECUMSEH AND THE QUEST FOR INDIAN LEADERSHIP
0–316–21151–6 Little, Brown $14.95

- Stan Hoig
THE SAND CREEK MASSACRE
0–8061–1147–X Oklahoma pb $7.95

- Alvin M. Josephy, Jr.
THE PATRIOT CHIEFS: A Chronicle of American Indian Resistance
0–14–004219–9 Penguin pb $6.95

- David Humphreys Miller
CUSTER'S FALL: The Indian Side of the Story
Starting in the 1930s, Miller collected firsthand accounts from 71 Indian survivors of the Battle of the Little Bighorn
0–8032–3098–2 Nebraska $23.95
0–8032–8129–3 Nebraska pb $7.95

Sitting Bull's war shield, an illustration by the author, from Custer's Fall *by David Humphreys Miller (University of Nebraska/Bison)*

- John Sugden
TECUMSEH'S LAST STAND
How tribes of the Old Northwest joined with the British to resist American expansion during the War of 1812
0–8061–1944–6 Oklahoma $19.95

Sitting Bull. Sitting Bull.
In English this name sounds a little absurd, and to whites of the nineteenth century it was still more so; they alluded to him as Slightly Recumbent Gentleman Cow.

Exact translation from the Sioux is impossible, but his name may be better understood if one realizes how Plains Indians respected and honored the bull buffalo. Whites considered this animal to be exceptionally stupid. Col. Dodge states without equivocation that the buffalo is the dullest creature of which he has any knowledge. A herd of buffalo would graze complacently while every member was shot down. He himself shot two cows and thirteen calves while the survivors grazed and watched. He and others in his party had to shout and wave their hats to drive the herd away so the dead animals could be butchered.

Indians, however, regarded buffalo as the wisest and most powerful of creatures, nearest to the omnipresent Spirit. Furthermore, if one says in English that somebody is sitting it means he is seated, balanced on the haunches; but the Sioux expression has an additional sense, not equivalent to but approximating the English words *situate* and *locate* and *reside*.

Thus, from an Indian point of view, the name Sitting Bull signified a wise and powerful being who had taken up residence among them.

Evan S. Connell
SON OF THE MORNING STAR
0–06–097161–4 Harper & Row pb $9.95

- Robert M. Utley
THE INDIAN FRONTIER OF THE AMERICAN WEST, 1846–1890
0–8263–0716–7 New Mexico pb $13.95

☐ **TO ORDER BY FAX, SEE PAGE 1**

FRONTIERSMEN IN BLUE: The United States Army and the Indian, 1848–1865
0–8032–9550–2 Nebraska pb $10.95

FRONTIER REGULARS: The United States Army and the Indian, 1866–1891
The final drive of the Regular Army to open the West
0–8032–9551–0 Nebraska pb $12.95

● Robert M. Utley & Wilcomb E. Washburn
INDIAN WARS
0–8281–0202–3 Houghton Mifflin pb $9.95

● Paula Gunn Allen
THE SACRED HOOP: Recovering the Feminine in American Indian Traditions
0–8070–4601–9 Beacon pb $10.95

● Russel L. Barsh & James Y. Henderson
THE ROAD: Indian Tribes and Political Liberty
0–520–04636–6 California pb $9.95

● Gretchen M. Bataille & Kathleen Mullen Sands
AMERICAN INDIAN WOMEN: Telling Their Lives
"A unique and intimate record. All [21 autobiographies] signal Native American women's diversity and unity"—*Library Journal*
0–8032–1159–7 Nebraska $19.95
0–8032–6082–2 Nebraska pb $7.95

● Menno Boldt
THE QUEST FOR JUSTICE: Aboriginal Peoples and Aboriginal Rights
0–8020–2572–2 Toronto $45.00
0–8020–6589–9 Toronto pb $18.95

● Vine Deloria, Jr.
BEHIND THE TRAIL OF BROKEN TREATIES: An Indian Declaration of Independence
The events and issues surrounding the 1973 occupation of Wounded Knee
0–292–70754–1 Texas pb $10.95

CUSTER DIED FOR YOUR SINS
0–380–00250–7 Avon pb $3.50

● Vine Deloria, Jr., editor
AMERICAN INDIAN POLICY IN THE TWENTIETH CENTURY
The present realities and future possibilities of American Indian policy, from a historical and legal point of view
0–8061–1897–0 Oklahoma $17.95

● Vine Deloria, Jr. & Clifford M. Lytle
AMERICAN INDIANS, AMERICAN JUSTICE
0–292–73833–1 Texas $19.95
0–292–73834–X Texas pb $9.95

THE NATIONS WITHIN: The Past and Future of American Indian Sovereignty
0–394–72566–2 Pantheon pb $12.95

● Peter Iverson, editor
THE PLAINS INDIANS OF THE TWENTIETH CENTURY
A pioneering anthology that emphasizes the maintenance of tribal identity despite many changes and adaptations
0–8061–1866–0 Oklahoma $21.95
0–8061–1959–4 Oklahoma pb $9.95

● Alvin M. Josephy, Jr.
NOW THAT THE BUFFALO'S GONE: A Study of Today's American Indian
The histories of seven Indian tribes serve to illustrate Indian-white relations, including racial stereotyping, self-determination, and control of tribal affairs and resources
0–394–46672–1 Knopf $17.95
0–8061–1915–2 Oklahoma pb $11.95

RED POWER: The American Indians' Fight for Freedom
A documentary history of the American Indian movement of the 1960s, exploring such areas as employment, education, health, and land rights
0–8032–7563–3 Nebraska pb $7.50

● Kenneth Lincoln & Al L. Slagle
THE GOOD RED ROAD: Passages into Native America
Travels through contemporary Indian lands lead into a consideration of history
Foreword by Alfonso Ortiz
0–06–250516–5 Harper & Row $17.95

● Peter Matthiessen
INDIAN COUNTRY
0–670–39787–3 Viking $17.95

● L.G. Moses & Raymond Wilson, editors
INDIAN LIVES: Essays on Nineteenth and Twentieth Century Native American Leaders
0–8263–0814–7 New Mexico $19.95
0–8263–0815–5 New Mexico pb $9.95

Maggie Six-Shooter and her granddaughter, Sioux living on the Pine Ridge Reservation in South Dakota, from Now That the Buffalo's Gone *by Alvin M. Josephy, Jr. (Knopf/photo copyright Richard Erdoes)*

Ecology and Economy

● William Cronon
CHANGES IN THE LAND: Indians, Colonists, and the Ecology of New England
"Demonstrates beyond dispute how lands and peoples changed each other when Europeans arrived in 'New England.' This is analytical history of a very high order"—Francis Jennings
0–8090–0158–6 Hill & Wang pb $7.95

● Wayne Gard
THE GREAT BUFFALO HUNT
"Gard tells the story of that unparalleled slaughter with authority, illuminating anecdotes, and the disgust it so fully merits"—*New Yorker*
0–8032–5067–3 Nebraska pb $11.95

● J. Donald Hughes
AMERICAN INDIAN ECOLOGY
0–87404–070–1 Texas Western $20.00

● Calvin Martin
KEEPERS OF THE GAME: Indian-Animal Relationship and the Fur Trade
A controversial study suggesting that Indian attitudes toward animals were disrupted by trade with the whites
Introduction by Nancy Lurie
0–520–03519–4 California $27.50
0–520–04637–4 California pb $11.95

● Virgil J. Vogel
AMERICAN INDIAN MEDICINE
Medicinal practices and theories of disease, with a listing of Indian contributions to pharmacology
0–8061–0863–0 Oklahoma $34.50

Religion and Mythology

● Hartley Burr Alexander
THE WORLD'S RIM: Great Mysteries of the North American Indians
Foreword by Clyde Kluckhohn
0–8032–5003–7 Nebraska pb $7.95

● John Bierhorst
THE MYTHOLOGY OF NORTH AMERICA
"Even in synopsis, many of the stories are moving and fascinating; and Bierhorst's descriptions of the background and history, the connections and crossovers of the myths and mythologies, and his glimpses of the world views of the various peoples and regions, are lucid and thoughtful"—Ursula K. Le Guin
0–688–06666–6 Morrow pb $6.95

● Henry W. Bowden
AMERICAN INDIANS AND CHRISTIAN MISSIONS: Studies in Cultural Conflict
0–226–06812–9 Chicago pb $7.95

● Joseph E. Brown, editor
THE SACRED PIPE: Black Elk's Account of the Seven Rites of Oglala Sioux
0–8061–0272–1 Oklahoma $18.95
0–14–003346–7 Penguin pb $4.95

• Vine Deloria, Jr.
GOD IS RED
0–440–33044–0 Doubleday pb $4.50

• Jamake Highwater, editor
THE PRIMAL MIND: Vision and Reality in Indian America
American Indian traditions contrasted with Western culture. "An intellectual passion and eloquence approaching poetry"—Weston LaBarre
0–452–00966–9 NAL pb $8.95

• Joseph G. Jorgensen
THE SUN DANCE RELIGION: Power for the Powerless
0–226–41086–2 Chicago pb $14.95

• David Humphreys Miller
GHOST DANCE
The Lakota spiritual awakening of the 1890s, seen largely from the Indian point of view
0–8032–8130–7 Nebraska pb $8.95

• James Mooney
THE GHOST-DANCE RELIGION AND THE SIOUX OUTBREAK OF 1890
A contemporary investigation of the roots of the last great Indian uprising; dated but ethnographically fascinating
Edited by Anthony F. Wallace
0–226–53517–7 Chicago pb $14.00

• John G. Neihardt
BLACK ELK SPEAKS: Being the Life Story of a Holy Man of the Oglala Sioux
Introduction by Vine Deloria, Jr.
0–8032–3301–9 Nebraska $16.50

• William K. Powers
OGLALA RELIGION
The durability of Oglala beliefs in the face of overwhelming obstacles
0–8032–8706–2 Nebraska pb $6.95

• Dennis & Barbara Tedlock, editors
TEACHINGS FROM THE AMERICAN EARTH: Indian Religion and Philosophy
0–87140–0979–9 Liveright pb $8.95

• Ray A. Williamson
LIVING THE SKY: The Cosmos of the American Indian
Astronomy and Native American beliefs
0–8061–2034–7 Oklahoma pb $14.95

Music and Dance

• Reginald Laubin & Gladys Laubin
INDIAN DANCES OF NORTH AMERICA: Their Importance to Indian Life
Includes descriptions, costumes, and musical accompaniment; illustrated with paintings, drawings, and photographs
Foreword by Louis R. Bruce
0–8061–1319–7 Oklahoma $34.50

Language

"It has not been possible so far to determine how many different languages and dialects have been spoken in the Americas. Many tongues have become extinct. But linguistic scholar Morris Swadesh believes that when the whites arrived in the New World, Indians were speaking some 2200 different languages, many of them possessing regional variations. Other students have estimated that there were at least 200 mutually unintelligible languages among the native peoples north of Mexico, at least another 350 in Mexico and Central America, and considerably more than 1000 in the Caribbean and South America."—Alvin M. Josephy, Jr., *The Indian Heritage of America*

John Rydjord
INDIAN PLACE NAMES: Their Origin, Evolution, and Meanings, Collected in Kansas from the Siouan, Algonquian, Shoshonean, Caddoan, Iroquoian, and Other Tongues
0–8061–0801–0 Oklahoma $27.95
0–8061–1763–X Oklahoma pb $10.95

Travel

• Arnold Marquis
A GUIDE TO AMERICA'S INDIANS: Ceremonials, Reservations, and Museums
Basic information for the traveler
0–8061–1148–8 Oklahoma pb $14.95

• Ralph Shanks & Lisa W. Shanks
NORTH AMERICAN INDIAN TRAVEL GUIDE
0–930268–07–5 Costano pb $14.95

Native American Cultures: Central and South America

MEXICO AND CENTRAL AMERICA: General Works

▶ **See also Latin America and the Caribbean**

• Anthony F. Aveni
SKYWATCHERS OF ANCIENT MEXICO
Archaeoastronomy of Mesoamerica; illustrated
0–292–77557–1 Texas $35.00
0–292–77578–4 Texas pb $17.50

• Michael D. Coe
MEXICO
A brief introduction to the archaic cultures, the Olmecs, the classic civilizations of Teotihuacán and Monte Alban, and the postclassic Toltecs and Aztecs
0–500–27328–6 Thames & Hudson pb $10.95

• Nigel Davies
THE ANCIENT KINGDOMS OF MEXICO
0–14–022232–4 Penguin pb $6.95

Red clay figure with canine headdress, c. AD 1-150, from the Acatlán region, Mexico (Metropolitan Museum)

• Munro S. Edmonson
THE BOOK OF THE YEAR: Middle American Calendrical Systems
Source book on the ancient calendars of Mexico and Guatemala
0–87480–288–1 Utah $40.00

• Carl Lumholtz
UNKNOWN MEXICO: Explorations in the Sierra Madre and Other Regions, 1890–1898
Pioneering ethnography by the Norwegian explorer and naturalist; a primary source for Tarahumara and Huichol studies

Volume 1
0–486–25364–3 Dover pb $14.95
Volume 2
0–486–25413–5 Dover pb $14.95

• William & Claudia Madsen
A GUIDE TO MEXICAN WITCHCRAFT
Compact description for the general reader, with emphasis on modern Aztecs, or Nahuas, of central Mexico
0–912434–10–4 Ocelot pb $4.50

THE OLMEC, TOLTEC, AND MIXTEC

• Michael D. Coe & Richard A. Diehl
IN THE LAND OF THE OLMEC
Results of a large-scale expedition to explore the age and nature of the Olmec, in volumes respectively titled *The Archaeology of San Lorenzo Tenochtitlán* and *The People of the River*; illustrated
0–292–77549–0 Texas (2-volume set) $100.00

• Nigel Davies
THE TOLTECS: Until the Fall of Tula
An accurate history of a pre-Aztec people about whom there is a great deal of controversy
0–8061–2071–1 Oklahoma pb $16.95

• Jacques Soustelle
THE OLMECS: The Oldest Civilization in Mexico
0–8061–1962–4 Oklahoma pb $10.95

• Ronald Spores
THE MIXTECS IN ANCIENT AND COLONIAL TIMES
0–8061–1884–9 Oklahoma $29.98

THE AZTEC

• Hernando Ruiz de Alarcón
AZTEC SORCERERS IN SEVENTEENTH-CENTURY MEXICO: The Treatise on Superstitions
The principal source of Aztec incantations and medical lore, in an edition designed for the general reader
Translated by Michael Coe & Gordon Whittaker
0–942041–06–2 Texas pb $21.00

TREATISE ON THE HEATHEN SUPERSTITIONS THAT TODAY LIVE AMONG THE INDIANS NATIVE TO THIS NEW SPAIN, 1629
A more scholarly edition of Alarcón's treatise on Aztec sorcery
Translated by J. Richard Andrews & Ross Hassig
0–8061–2031–2 Oklahoma pb $16.95

• Johanna Broda & others
THE GREAT TEMPLE OF TENOCHTITLAN: Center and Periphery in the Aztec World
The nature and significance of the Templo Mayor, the great double pyramid excavated in Mexico City from 1978 to 1982. Includes black-and-white photographs
0–520–05602–7 California $38.00

• Burr Cartwright Brundage
THE FIFTH SUN: Aztec Gods, Aztec World
Examines the cults of the major gods and goddesses in search of unifying themes
0–292–72438–1 Texas pb $9.95

THE JADE STEPS: A Ritual Life of the Aztecs
Interpretive description of calendrical festivals, cult images, ritual warfare, and human sacrifice
0–87480–247–4 Utah $22.50

• Alfonso Caso
THE AZTECS: People of the Sun
A popular introduction to Aztec religion, illustrated with full-color paintings by Miguel Covarrubias
0–8061–0414–7 Oklahoma $24.95

• Diego Durán
BOOK OF THE GODS AND RITES AND THE ANCIENT CALENDAR
A 16th-century missionary's account of Aztec ceremonies and calendrical lore
0–8061–1201–8 Oklahoma pb $12.95

• Charles Gibson
THE AZTECS UNDER SPANISH RULE: A History of the Indians of the Valley of Mexico, 1519–1810
Strong on economic issues and political life
0–8047–0912–2 Stanford pb $17.95

• Fernando Horcasitas
THE AZTECS THEN AND NOW
Concise introduction to the Aztecs of ancient and modern times; illustrated
0–912434–22–8 Ocelot pb $7.50

• Benjamin Keen
THE AZTEC IMAGE IN WESTERN THOUGHT
Detailed study of Aztec influences in Western art, literature, and philosophy from the Renaissance to the present; illustrated
0–8135–0698–0 Rutgers $50.00

• Miguel León-Portilla
THE BROKEN SPEARS: The Aztec Account of the Conquest of Mexico
Compiled from Sahagún's Florentine Codex and other 16th-century sources
0–8070–5499–2 Beacon pb $9.95

• Jacques Soustelle
DAILY LIFE OF THE AZTECS ON THE EVE OF THE SPANISH CONQUEST
Customs, manners, life cycle, and daily round
0–8047–0721–9 Stanford pb $8.95

The Florentine Codex

The Florentine Codex is a primary source for Aztec studies. This complete English-Nahuatl edition is available in 12 books plus an introductory volume. The illustrations by native artists are reproduced in black and white. Of particular interest are volumes 3 and 12.

Bernardino de Sahagún
THE FLORENTINE CODEX: General History of the Things of New Spain
The complete set
0–87480–082–X Utah $350.00

Volume 3: Origins of the Gods
0–87480–002–1 Utah $17.50

Volume 12: Conquest of Mexico
0–87480–096–X Utah $27.50

THE MAYA

• Michael D. Coe
THE MAYA
A general introduction, with emphasis on the ancient Maya
0–500–57745–5 Thames & Hudson pb $11.95

• Sylvanus G. Morley & George W. Brainerd
THE ANCIENT MAYA
A comprehensive introduction, now in its fourth revision; illustrated
0–8047–1137–2 Stanford $38.50
0–8047–1288–3 Stanford pb $14.95

• Linda Scheke & Mary E. Miller
BLOOD OF KINGS: Dynasty and Ritual in Maya Art
0–8076–1159–X Braziller $50.00

• John L. Stephens
INCIDENTS OF TRAVEL IN YUCATAN
The classic 19th-century account of visits to the jungle-covered Maya ruins; illustrated with engravings by Frederick Catherwood

Volume 1
0–486–20926–1 Dover pb $4.95

Volume 2
0–486–20927–X Dover pb $4.95

• Dennis Tedlock, translator
POPOL VUH
The newest translation of the Quiche Maya classic combines anthropological and literary values
0–671–45241–X Simon & Schuster $19.95
0–671–61771–0 Simon & Schuster pb $9.95

• J. Eric Thompson
MAYA HIEROGLYPHIC WRITING: An Introduction
Specialists find chapter twelve out of date, but Thompson's massive, well-illustrated treatment remains the best introduction to the subject
0–8061–0958–0 Oklahoma $32.50

MAYA HISTORY AND RELIGION
Collected scholarly articles on demography, cultural boundaries, tobacco use, trade relations, rituals, and creation myths
0–8061–0884–3 Oklahoma $26.95

THE RISE AND FALL OF MAYA CIVILIZATION
General description of the ancient Maya
0–8061–0301–9 Oklahoma $24.95

Mayan Culture in the Modern Period

• Victoria Reifler Bricker
RITUAL HUMOR IN HIGHLAND CHIAPAS
Fiesta lore of the modern Tzotzil-speaking Indians of southern Mexico
0–292–77029–4 Texas pb $8.95

• Robert M. Carmack, editor
HARVEST OF VIOLENCE: The Maya Indians and the Guatemalan Crisis
Articles by a dozen specialists documenting the effects of civil war on the Guatemalan Maya of the 1980s
0–8061–2132–7 Oklahoma $21.95

Mayan female whistle figurine from Jaina, Coastal Campeche (AD 600-900), from The Albers Collection of Pre-Columbian Art *by Karl A. Taube (Hudson Hills)*

• Gary Gossen
CHAMULAS IN THE WORLD OF THE SUN: Time and Space in a Maya Oral Tradition
Native classification of oral genres in the Tzotzil Maya community of Chamula, Chiapas; includes samples of myths, folktales, gossip, and word games
0–88133–091–4 Waveland pb $11.95

• Victor Perera & Robert D. Bruce
THE LAST LORDS OF PALENQUE: The Lacandon Mayas of the Mexican Rain Forest
0–520–05309–5 California pb $10.95

• Ricardo Pozas
JUAN THE CHAMULA: An Ethnological Recreation of the Life of a Mexican Indian
Composite life story of a typical Tzotzil Maya
0–520–01027–2 California pb $6.95

• Nelson Reed
THE CASTE WAR OF YUCATAN
Revitalization and rebellion among the 19th-century Maya
0–8047–0165–2 Stanford pb $10.95

• Evan Z. Vogt
THE ZINACANTECOS OF MEXICO: A Modern Maya Way of Life
Concise ethnography of the Tzotzil Maya of Zinacantan, Chiapas, by the director of the Harvard Chiapas Project
0–03–084016–3 HR&W pb $13.00

OTHER SPECIFIC STUDIES

• David Burckhalter
THE SERIS
Photographic essay on a small Sonoran tribe
0–8165–0517–9 Arizona pb $7.50

• Carlos Castaneda
THE TEACHINGS OF DON JUAN: A Yaqui Way of Knowledge
Personal (not tribal) lore of a Yaqui mystic as perceived by a young writer-anthropologist; first in a series of best-selling books
0–520–02258–0 California pb $9.95

• N. Ross Crumrine
THE MAYO INDIANS OF SONORA: A People Who Refuse to Die
General history and ethnography, highlighting recent revitalization movements
0–8165–0605–1 Arizona $12.50
0–8165–0473–3 Arizona pb $5.95

• James Dow
THE SHAMAN'S TOUCH: Otomi Indian Symbolic Healing
0–87480–257–1 Utah pb $13.95

• Bernard L. Fontana
TARAHUMARA: Where the Night Is the Day of the Moon
Description for the lay reader of an important Indian culture of northwest Mexico; illustrated with photographs
0–87358–443–0 Northland pb $21.95

• Mary W. Helms
ASANG: Adaptations to Culture Contact in a Miskito Community
Ethnography of an important Indian culture of eastern Nicaragua
0–8130–0298–2 Florida pb $12.00

• Barbara G. Myerhoff
PEYOTE HUNT: The Sacred Journey of the Huichol Indians
Description of the pilgrimage to collect peyote, with an overview of Huichol religion
0–8014–9137–1 Cornell pb $9.95

• Joseph W. Whitecotton
THE ZAPOTECS: Princes, Priests, and Peasants
History of the pre-Columbian, early colonial, and 20th-century Zapotec Indians of Oaxaca
0–8061–1914–4 Oklahoma pb $9.95

Guidebooks

• C. Bruce Hunter
A GUIDE TO ANCIENT MAYA RUINS
0–8061–1992–3 Oklahoma pb $12.95

A GUIDE TO ANCIENT MEXICAN RUINS
0–8061–1407–X Oklahoma pb $9.95

• Joyce Kelly
THE COMPLETE VISITOR'S GUIDE TO MESOAMERICAN RUINS
Illustrated with photographs, drawings, and maps
0–8061–1566–1 Oklahoma $39.95

SOUTH AMERICA: General Works

Threatened more than ever by technological change and rampant land development, the native cultures of South America remain little known. The wide-ranging titles below (history, anthropology, travel literature, ecology, and even fiction) present many aspects of a complex situation.

• José M. Arguedas
DEEP RIVERS
Translated by Frances H. Barraclough
0–292–71533–1 Texas pb $9.95

YAWAR FIESTA
Based on his own experiences growing up in the Andes, *Yawar Fiesta* and *Deep Rivers* are two of this leading Peruvian anthropologist's major fictional works
Translated by Frances H. Barraclough
0–292–79601–3 Texas $19.95
0–292–79602–1 Texas pb $8.95

• Ellen B. Basso
IN FAVOR OF DECEIT: A Study of Tricksters in an Amazonian Society
Based on years of research with the Kalapalo Indians of Brazil, this work is the first study of a trickster tradition in a native South American culture
0–8165–1022–9 Arizona $40.00

A MUSICAL VIEW OF THE UNIVERSE: Kalapalo Myth and Ritual Performances
Filled with brilliant texts and original analyses
0–8122–7931–X Pennsylvania $39.95

• Catherine Caufield
IN THE RAINFOREST: Report from a Strange, Beautiful, Imperiled World
One of the best discussions of the destruction of rainforests
0–394–52701–1 Knopf $16.95
0–226–09786–2 Chicago pb $11.95

• Napolean A. Chagnon
YANOMAMO: The Fierce People
The controversial study of South America's largest remaining group of hunters and gatherers
0–03–062328–6 HR&W pb $10.95

• Pierre Clastres
SOCIETY AGAINST THE STATE: Essays in Political Anthropology
A classic work now back in print
0–942299–00–0 MIT $18.95

• Jon Christopher Crocker
VITAL SOULS: Bororo Cosmology, Natural Symbolism and Shamanism
One of several ethnographies emerging from Harvard's Central Brazil Project of the 1960s
0–8165–0877–1 Arizona $29.95

• Marlene Dobkin de Rios
VISIONARY VINE: Hallucinogenic Healing in the Peruvian Amazon
0-88133-093-0 Waveland pb $8.95

• Thomas Gregor
MEHINAKU: The Drama of Daily Life in a Brazilian Indian Village
0-226-30744-1 Chicago $24.00
0-226-30746-8 Chicago pb $13.00

• David M. Guss
TO WEAVE AND SING: Art, Symbol, and Narrative in the South American Rainforest
0-520-06427-5 California $37.50

• Michael Harner
THE JIVARO: People of the Sacred Waterfalls
The standard ethnography of Ecuador's Shuar people, famous for their custom of shrinking heads
0-520-05065-7 California pb $10.95

• John Hemming
AMAZON FRONTIER: The Defeat of the Brazilian Indians
0-674-01725-0 Harvard $29.95

RED GOLD: The Conquest of the Brazilian Indians, 1500–1760
0-674-75107-8 Harvard $37.00

• Claude Lévi-Strauss
TRISTES TROPIQUES
The now-classic account of Lévi-Strauss's sole field expedition to northern Brazil in the late 1930s. "One of the great books of our century . . . rigorous, subtle, bold in thought [and] beautifully written"—Susan Sontag
0-671-45850-7 Washington Square pb $4.95

• Jacques Lizot
TALES OF THE YANOMAMI: Daily Life in the Venezuela Forest
Written as a rebuttal of Chagnon's *Yanomamo*: a compelling story
0-521-31451-8 Cambridge pb $10.95

• Peter Matthiessen
AT PLAY IN THE FIELDS OF THE LORD
A brilliant fictional account of life in the western Amazon and the emerging conflict of the forces gathered there
0-394-75083-7 Random House pb $6.95

• Betty J. Meggers
AMAZONIA: Man and Culture in a Counterfeit Paradise
In one of the most enduring studies of the Amazonian basin, Meggers applies a cultural ecological approach to an analysis of seven diverse groups
0-88295-609-4 Harlan Davidson pb $10.95

• Yolanda & Robert F. Murphy
WOMEN OF THE FOREST
An analysis of the Mundurucu of Brazil with particular attention to the role of women
0-231-06089-0 Columbia pb $12.00

• June Nash
WE EAT THE MINES AND THE MINES EAT US: Dependency and Exploitation in Bolivian Tin Mines
0-231-04711-8 Columbia pb $17.50

• Michel Perrin
THE WAY OF THE DEAD INDIANS: Guajiro Myths and Symbols
A passionate interpretation of Guajiro life as seen through its myths
Translated by Michael Fineberg
0-292-79039-2 Texas pb $12.95

• Gerardo Reichel-Dolmatoff
AMAZONIAN COSMOS: The Sexual and Religious Symbolism of the Tukano Indians
A rare blend of psychoanalysis, structuralism, semiotics, and ecology that makes Reichel-Dolmatoff unique in South American anthropology
0-226-70732-6 Chicago pb $7.95

• Michael Sallnow
PILGRIMS OF THE ANDES: Regional Cults in Cusco
An extremely readable history of several of Peru's most popular religious cults
0-87474-826-7 Smithsonian $29.95

• Tobias Schneebaum
KEEP THE RIVER ON YOUR RIGHT
Fascinating account of an artist's exploration in the Peruvian Amazon
0-8021-3133-6 Grove pb $7.95

• Michael Taussig
SHAMANISM, COLONIALISM, AND THE WILD MAN: A Study in Terror and Healing
A rare and stimulating combination of in-depth fieldwork experience with current ideas in literary criticism, performance theory, and self-reflexive anthropology
0-226-79012-6 Chicago $29.95

• Gary Urton, editor
ANIMAL MYTHS AND METAPHORS IN SOUTH AMERICA
A good introduction to eight of South America's most interesting anthropologists
0-87480-205-9 Utah pb $17.50

• Norman E. Whitten, Jr.
SICUANGA RUNA: The Other Side of Development in Amazonian Ecuador
A sophisticated account of cultural resilience and adaptation
0-252-01117-1 Illinois $24.95

• Ronald Wright
CUT STONES AND CROSSROADS: A Journey in the Two Worlds of Peru
An intelligent and informative travelogue through the Andes
0-14-009565-9 Penguin pb $7.95

Inca wall at Ollantaytambo

THE INCAS

• Hiram Bingham
LOST CITY OF THE INCAS
The classic account of Bingham's discovery of Machu Picchu in 1911
0-689-70014-8 Atheneum pb $6.95

• Bernabé Cobo
HISTORY OF THE INCA EMPIRE
Based on Father Bernabé Cobo's early 17th-century text, *Historia del Nuevo Mundo*
Translated by Roland Hamilton
Foreword by John H. Rowe
0-292-73008-X Texas $20.00
0-292-73025-X Texas pb $10.95

• John Hemming
THE CONQUEST OF THE INCAS
The first of Hemming's impressive volumes of the European occupation of South America
Illustrated by K.C. Jordan
0-15-622300-7 HBJ pb $12.95

• Alfred Metraux
THE HISTORY OF THE INCAS
Translated by George Ordish
0-8052-0248-X Schocken pb $9.95

• Frank Salomon
NATIVE LORDS OF QUITO IN THE AGE OF THE INCAS: The Political Economy of North-Andean Chiefdoms
How Ecuador was affected by Inca expansion in pre-conquest times
0-521-30299-4 Cambridge $47.50

• Irene Silverblatt
MOON, SUN, AND WITCHES: Gender Ideologies and Class in Inca and Colonial Peru
The women's world in the Peruvian Andes before and after the Spanish Conquest and Inquisition
0-691-02258-5 Princeton pb $14.50

• Victor W. Von Hagen, editor
THE INCAS OF PEDRO DE CIEZA DE LEON
A chronicle of 17 years of travel in Peru during the 16th century; originally published in 1553
Translated by Harriet de Onís
0-8061-0433-3 Oklahoma $32.50

➤ **FOR OVERSEAS ORDERING INFORMATION, SEE PAGE 1**

US History to the Civil War

This chapter and the two that follow are devoted to a basic outline of social and political history, from America's exploration and settlement to the present. Subsequent chapters deal with aspects of the national experience and current scene whose inclusion here might hamper the general flow of events.

GENERAL HISTORIES

• Daniel J. Boorstin
THE AMERICANS
A highly original work, less a textbook history than a fascinating, somewhat conservative interpretation. A 3-volume set
0–394–49588–8 Random House (set) $77.95

Volume 1: The Colonial Experience
0–394–41506–X Random House $24.95
0–394–70513–0 Random House pb $8.95

Volume 2: The Democratic Experience
0–394–48724–9 Random House $24.95
0–394–70358–8 Random House pb $8.95

Volume 3: The National Experience
0–394–41453–5 Random House $24.95
0–394–71011–8 Random House pb $10.95

• Hugh Brogan
THE LONGMAN/PELICAN HISTORY OF THE UNITED STATES OF AMERICA
One of the best recent surveys happens to be by a British historian
0–688–06467–1 Morrow $25.00
0–14–022527–7 Penguin pb $7.95

• James MacGregor Burns
THE AMERICAN EXPERIMENT

Volume 1: The Vineyard of Liberty
0–394–50546–8 Knopf $22.95

Volume 2: The Workshop of Democracy
0–394–51275–8 Knopf $24.95
0–394–74320–2 Random House pb $12.95

Volume 3: The Crosswinds of Freedom
From Roosevelt to Reagan
0–394–51276–6 Knopf $29.95

• Peter N. Carroll & David W. Noble
THE FREE AND THE UNFREE: A New History of the United States
The story of Native Americans, blacks, immigrants, religious minorities, and women
0–14–022827–6 Pelican pb $7.95

• Alistair Cooke
ALISTAIR COOKE'S AMERICA
A text-and-pictures overview of the American past and present, from the nation's favorite Briton-turned-American
0–394–73449–1 Knopf pb $24.95

• Marshall B. Davidson
500 YEARS OF LIFE IN AMERICA: An Illustrated History
0–8109–8077–0 Abradale $19.95

• Carl N. Degler
OUT OF OUR PAST: The Forces That Shaped Modern America
A good introduction
0–06–131985–6 Harper & Row pb $11.95

• Richard D. Heffner, editor
A DOCUMENTARY HISTORY OF THE UNITED STATES
A selection and interpretation of more than 50 documents, from the Declaration of Independence to Ronald Reagan's 1985 inaugural address
0–451–62413–0 NAL pb $4.95

• Maldwyn A. Jones
THE LIMITS OF LIBERTY: American History, 1607–1980
0–19–913130–9 Oxford pb $18.95

• Samuel Eliot Morison
THE OXFORD HISTORY OF THE AMERICAN PEOPLE
A graceful narrative by a first-rate historian, first published in 1965 and written for the general public; recreates American ways of life through social and economic developments rather than political events

Volume 1
0–451–62600–1 NAL pb $4.95

Volume 2
0–451–62408–4 NAL pb $4.95

Volume 3
0–451–62446–7 NAL pb $4.95

• Page Smith
A PEOPLE'S HISTORY OF THE UNITED STATES
Nearly 10,000 pages of popular narrative history, focusing on politics and economics. An 8-volume set
0–07–909019–2 McGraw-Hill (set) $195.00

A PEOPLE'S HISTORY OF THE UNITED STATES
Includes Volumes 1 and 2; other volumes forthcoming
0–14–095354–X Penguin pb $29.95

• Howard Zinn
A PEOPLE'S HISTORY OF THE UNITED STATES
"A brilliant and moving history . . . from the point of view of those who have been exploited politically and economically"—*Library Journal*
0–06–090792–4 Harper & Row pb $9.95

Larry Gonick
THE CARTOON GUIDE TO U.S. HISTORY

Volume 1: 1585–1865
0–06–460420–9 Barnes & Noble pb $5.95

Volume 2: 1865–Now
0–06–460421–7 Barnes & Noble pb $6.95

Richard Shenkman
LEGENDS, LIES, AND CHERISHED MYTHS OF AMERICAN HISTORY
A heretical look at the truth behind historical myths, including the Liberty Bell, Betsy Ross, Eli Whitney, Johnny Appleseed, and George Washington
0–688–06580–5 Morrow $15.95

Richard Shenkman & Kurt Reiger
ONE-NIGHT STANDS WITH AMERICAN HISTORY: Odd, Amusing, and Little-Known Incidents
J. Edgar Hoover refused to allow people to walk on his shadow; in 1721, women were in such short supply that the government of France shipped 25 prostitutes to the colonies
0–688–01399–6 Morrow pb $7.95

Carl Sifakis
AMERICAN ECCENTRICS: 140 of the Greatest Human Interest Stories Ever Told
0–87196–788–X Facts On File $19.95

John & Claire Whitcomb
O SAY CAN YOU SEE: Unexpected Anecdotes About American History
More amusing anecdotes, arranged in list format
0–688–08664–0 Morrow pb $8.95

Present History

• Joel Garreau
THE NINE NATIONS OF NORTH AMERICA
Rewrites the map of modern-day America by dividing it into nine nations, including MexAmerica, Dixie, and the Breadbasket, and analyzes each region's prospects for the future
0–380–57885–9 Avon pb $8.95

• Neal R. Peirce & Jerry Hagstrom
THE BOOK OF AMERICA: Inside 50 States Today
A thick state-by-state guide
0–446–38036–9 Warner pb $14.95

TEXTBOOKS

Practicing a kind of "affirmative action" historiography, the better college textbooks make room for labor, families, and neglected minorities, often in special sections. Furthermore, college publishers are free of much of the self-censorship that plagues the high school market, subject as it is to the demands of powerhouse state textbook adoption committees.

• John Morton Blum, William S. McFeely, Edmund S. Morgan & others
THE NATIONAL EXPERIENCE
A political emphasis

Volume 1: A History of the United States to 1877
0–15–565665–1 HBJ pb $24.00

Volume 2: A History of the United States since 1865
0–15–565666–X HBJ pb $25.50

• Frances FitzGerald
AMERICA REVISED
A biting critique of how textbooks portray the American past
0–394–74439–X Random House pb $3.95

• John A. Garraty
A SHORT HISTORY OF THE AMERICAN NATION
A well-written text by a noted Columbia historian
0–06–042415–X Harper & Row pb $20.00

Volume 1: To 1877
0–06–042294–7 Harper & Row pb $12.95

Volume 2: Since 1865
0–06–042295–5 Harper & Row pb $12.95

• Samuel Eliot Morison, Henry Steele Commager & William E. Leuchtenburg
THE GROWTH OF THE AMERICAN REPUBLIC

Volume 1
0–19–502593–8 Oxford $26.00

Volume 2
0–19–502594–6 Oxford $26.00

A CONCISE HISTORY OF THE AMERICAN REPUBLIC
An abbreviated version of *The Growth of the American Republic,* revised to include the Carter and Reagan administrations; available in a 1 or 2-volume edition
0–19–503179–2 Oxford $49.95
0–19–503180–6 Oxford pb $23.00

Volume 1: To 1877
0–19–503181–4 Oxford pb $18.95

Volume 2: Since 1865
0–19–503182–2 Oxford pb $18.95

• Mary B. Norton, William M. Tuttle, Jr., Howard Chudacoff & others
A PEOPLE AND A NATION: A History of the United States
A social emphasis
0–395–35953–8 Houghton Mifflin $38.00

• George B. Tindall
AMERICA: A Narrative History

Volume 1
0–393–95356–4 Norton pb $11.95

Volume 2
0–393–95358–0 Norton pb $11.95

Reference

• Robert H. Ferrell & Richard Natkiel
ATLAS OF AMERICAN HISTORY
Informed text, historical paintings, and color photos. The maps range from the Atlantic trade in 1770 to presidential elections from 1800 to 1980
0–8160–1028–5 Facts On File $24.95

• Frank Freidel & others
THE HARVARD GUIDE TO AMERICAN HISTORY
Provides a sense of the full sweep of American history books, in and out of print
0–674–37555–6 Harvard $20.00

• John A. Garraty
1,001 THINGS EVERYONE SHOULD KNOW ABOUT AMERICAN HISTORY
History made fun for the layman, presented in the form of a numerical listing of major names, dates, places and events
0–385–24432–0 Doubleday $19.95

• Richard B. Morris & others, editors
ENCYCLOPEDIA OF AMERICAN HISTORY
0–06–181605–1 Harper & Row $29.95

• Arthur M. Schlesinger, Jr., editor
THE ALMANAC OF AMERICAN HISTORY
Illustrated with more than 200 line drawings and maps; describes major events in an easy-to-locate format with contributions from five leading historians
0–399–51082–6 Putnam pb $13.95

• Laurence Urdang, editor
THE TIMETABLES OF AMERICAN HISTORY
0–671–25246–1 Simon & Schuster pb $18.95

ESSAYS AND REFLECTIONS

• Daniel J. Boorstin
HIDDEN HISTORY: Exploring Our Secret Past
Essays from the Pulitzer Prize-winning historian
0–679–72223–8 Random House pb $9.95

• Henry Steele Commager
THE EMPIRE OF REASON: How Europe Imagined and America Realized the Enlightenment
A classic, wide-ranging guide to the roots of the American Revolution, including political, artistic, scientific, and other developments
0–19–503062–1 Oxford pb $9.95

• Richard Hofstadter
THE AMERICAN POLITICAL TRADITION AND THE MEN WHO MADE IT
Essays on some of the outstanding political leaders in American history
Foreword by Christopher Lasch
0–394–48880–6 Knopf $21.95
0–679–72315–3 Random House pb $7.95

• Michael Kammen
PEOPLE OF PARADOX: An Inquiry Concerning the Origins of American Civilization
How the 17th- and 18th-century colonies helped form a style and temper that foreshadows our own
0–19–502803–1 Oxford pb $9.95

• Max Lerner
AMERICA AS A CIVILIZATION: Life and Thought in the United States Today
The 30th-anniversary edition with a postscript chapter, "The New America 1957–1987." "Lerner has depicted with great wisdom and imagination the various facets of American Civilization"—Reinhold Niebuhr
0–8050–0355–X Henry Holt pb $19.95

• Seymour Martin Lipset
THE FIRST NEW NATION: The United States in Historical and Comparative Perspective
0–393–00911–4 Norton pb $8.95

Philippe Galle's "America," (1581) from Make Way! Two Hundred Years of American Women in Cartoons *by Monika Franzen and Nancy Ethiel (Chicago Review Press)*

• David M. Potter
PEOPLE OF PLENTY: Economic Abundance and the American Character
0–226–67633–1 Chicago pb $8.00

• Arthur M. Schlesinger, Jr.
THE CYCLES OF AMERICAN HISTORY
0–395–37887–7 Houghton Mifflin $22.95
0–395–45400–X Houghton Mifflin pb $11.95

Caricature and Cartoon

Monika Franzen & Nancy Ethiel
MAKE WAY! 200 YEARS OF AMERICAN WOMEN IN CARTOONS
1–556–52023–9 Chicago Review pb $9.95

Ron Tyler
THE IMAGE OF AMERICA IN CARICATURE AND CARTOON
0–88360–052–8 Amon Carter pb $14.95

THE EUROPEAN DISCOVERY OF AMERICA

• John Bakeless
AMERICA AS SEEN BY ITS FIRST EXPLORERS: The Eyes of Discovery
0–486–26031–3 Dover pb $8.95

• Gordon Brotherston
IMAGE OF THE NEW WORLD: The American Continent Portrayed in Native Texts
0–500–01206–7 Thames & Hudson $19.95

• Christopher Columbus
THE DIARIO OF CHRISTOPHER COLUMBUS'S FIRST VOYAGE TO AMERICA, 1492–1493
"The single most important piece of Columbus scholarship to appear in a long, long time"—Robert Fuson, University of South Florida
Translated & edited by Oliver Dunn & James E. Kelley, Jr.
0–8061–2101–7 Oklahoma $57.50

• Helen Delpar
THE DISCOVERERS: An Encyclopedia of Explorers and Exploration
0–07–016264–6 McGraw-Hill $59.95

• Barry Fell
SAGA AMERICA: A Startling New Theory on the Old World Settlement of America Before Columbus
Argues that pre-Columbian America was continuously settled by Europeans and North Africans from the 4th century BC to about AD 1000
0–8129–6324–5 Times Books pb $8.95

• Gianni Granzotto
CHRISTOPHER COLUMBUS
A tale of royal intrigue and great sea adventure
Translated by Stephen Sartarelli
0–8061–2100–9 Oklahoma pb $9.95

• C.H. Haring
THE SPANISH EMPIRE IN AMERICA
0–15–684701–9 HBJ pb $7.95

• Gwyn Jones
THE NORSE ATLANTIC SAGA: Being the Norse Voyages of Discovery and Settlement to Iceland, Greenland, America
0–19–285160–8 Oxford pb $9.95

• Magnus Magnusson & Hermann Palsson, translators
THE VINLAND SAGAS: The Norse Discovery of America
Includes the *Graenlendinga Saga* and *Eirik's Saga*
0–14–044154–9 Penguin pb $5.95

• D.W. Meinig
THE SHAPING OF AMERICA: A Geographical Perspective on 500 Years of History
A historical geographer charts how the colonial era saw diverse ethnic and religious groups create a set of distinct regional societies
0–300–03882–8 Yale pb $19.95

• Samuel Eliot Morison
ADMIRAL OF THE OCEAN SEA: A Life of Christopher Columbus
0–316–58354–5 Atlantic Monthly $29.95
0–930350–37–5 New England pb $14.95

THE EUROPEAN DISCOVERY OF AMERICA: The Northern Voyages
A gripping account of every voyage to the New World before 1600, by the historian who dominates the field
0–19–501377–8 Oxford $35.00

THE EUROPEAN DISCOVERY OF AMERICA: The Southern Voyages
The second part of this monumental study focuses on Latin America, the Caribbean, Bermuda, Florida, and California
0–19–501823–0 Oxford $35.00

THE GREAT EXPLORERS: The European Discovery of America
A popular condensation of Morison's two longer volumes
0–19–504222–0 Oxford pb $14.95

SAILOR HISTORIAN: The Best of Samuel Eliot Morison
An anthology of 34 selections
0–395–50074–5 Houghton Mifflin pb $9.95

• Ivan Van Sertima
THEY CAME BEFORE COLUMBUS: The African Presence in Ancient America
0–394–40245–6 Random House $19.95

• S. Lyman Tyler
TWO WORLDS: The Indian Encounter with the European, 1492–1509
0–87480–297–0 Utah $25.00

• Alvar Nuñez Cabeza de Vaca
ADVENTURES IN THE UNKNOWN INTERIOR OF AMERICA
The story of the ill-fated Nervaez expedition to Florida; one of the most astonishing narratives of early American exploration
Translated with notes by Cyclone Covey
0–8263–0656–X New Mexico pb $8.95

• Erik Wahlgren
THE VIKINGS AND AMERICA
0–500–02109–0 Thames & Hudson $22.50

• Gwyn A. Williams
MADOC: The Making of a Myth
An overview and analysis of the long-standing Welsh myth, now largely discredited, that Madoc, son of Prince Owain Gwynedd, settled in North America in the 12th century
0–19–285178–0 Oxford pb $8.95

THE NEW COLONIES

Early American settlements are a natural subject for historians interested in social, particularly family, life. Increased sensitivity about race has not only led to outstanding studies of the first confrontation of Native Americans, whites, and blacks, but has also increased our perception of the social and ideological origins of the Revolutionary War.

• James Axtell
THE EUROPEAN AND THE INDIAN: Essays in the Ethnohistory of Colonial North America
0–19–502904–6 Oxford pb $9.95

THE INVASION WITHIN: The Contest of Cultures in Colonial North America
0–19–504154–2 Oxford pb $11.95

• Bernard Bailyn
THE PEOPLING OF BRITISH NORTH AMERICA: An Introduction
Three fine essays exploring the migration of Europeans to North America
0–394–55392–6 Knopf $16.95
0–394–75779–3 Random House pb $5.95

VOYAGERS TO THE WEST: A Passage in the Peopling of America on the Eve of the Revolution
Using such research techniques as computerized demographic analysis, Bailyn explores the lives and attitudes of colonial Americans in this Pulitzer Prize-winning book
0–394–51569–2 Knopf $30.00
0–394–75778–5 Random House pb $14.95

• T.H. Breen
PURITANS AND ADVENTURERS: Change and Persistence in Early America
Essays on how the local origins of English colonists influenced their attitudes, and on contrasts between the settlements in Massachusetts and Virginia
0–19–502728–0 Oxford $22.50
0–19–503207–1 Oxford pb $11.95

• Bruce & William Catton
THE BOLD AND MAGNIFICENT DREAM: America's Founding Years, 1492–1815
A sweeping narrative history
0–385–00341–2 Doubleday pb $6.50

• William Cronon
CHANGES IN THE LAND: Indians, Colonists, and the Ecology of New England
"Combines ecological and cultural analysis into a cogent, sophisticated, and balanced study of Indian-white contact"—Richard White, Michigan State University
0–8090–0158–6 Hill & Wang pb $7.95

• Philip Greven
THE PROTESTANT TEMPERAMENT: Patterns of Child-rearing, Religious Experience, and the Self in Early America
"Interdisciplinary historical effort, in which children and women are deemed significant, in which the rituals of the home are understood to be intimately connected with the tactics of church and state"—Ann Douglas, *NY Times Book Review*
0–226–30830–8 Chicago pb $14.95

• Oscar & Lillian Handlin
LIBERTY AND POWER: 1600–1760
0–06–039059–X Harper & Row $16.95

• David Freeman Hawke
EVERYDAY LIFE IN EARLY AMERICA
People seen in the vividness and hardship of their daily lives: living in cramped houses, drinking too much, governed by superstition, subject to epidemics, and coping with the guerrilla tactics of the Indians
0–06–015856–5 Harper & Row $16.95
0–06–091251–0 Harper & Row pb $7.95

• Francis Jennings
THE AMBIGUOUS IROQUOIS EMPIRE: The Covenant Chain Confederation of Indian Tribes with English Colonies
0–393–30302–0 Norton pb $12.95

EMPIRE OF FORTUNE: Crowns, Colonies, and Tribes in the Seven Years War in America
0–393–02537–3 Norton $27.50

THE INVASION OF AMERICA: Indians, Colonialism, and the Cant of Conquest
A startlingly revised and richly documented picture of Puritans and Indians in the 17th century. "Will surprise many readers with its revelations"—Dee Brown
0–393–00830–4 Norton pb $9.95

● Benjamin Woods Labaree
AMERICA'S NATION-TIME: 1607–1789
0–393–00821–5 Norton pb $8.95

● Gary B. Nash
RACE, CLASS AND POLITICS: Essays on American Colonial and Revolutionary Society
0–252–01313–1 Illinois pb $15.95

RED, WHITE, AND BLACK: The Peoples of Early America
0–13–769786–4 Prentice-Hall pb $23.50

● Howard Peckham
COLONIAL WARS, 1689–1762
0–226–65314–5 Chicago pb $9.00

● Richard C. Simmons
THE AMERICAN COLONIES FROM SETTLEMENT TO INDEPENDENCE
0–393–00999–8 Norton pb $10.95

● John Smith
CAPTAIN JOHN SMITH: A Select Edition of His Writings
A handsome edition of the writings of the redoubtable chronicler of the Jamestown settlement. Includes Smith's observations on relations with the Indians and the future of colonization
Edited by Karen Ordahl Kupperman
0–8078–4208–7 North Carolina pb $10.95

● Clarence L. Ver Steeg
THE FORMATIVE YEARS: 1607–1763
"Ver Steeg's central concern is with the forces that converted 'transplanted Englishmen' into 'provincial Americans' . . . [He] shows how cultural conditioning, not mere geography, caused the pattern of New England settlement to differ from that in Virginia. At the same time, in analyzing how abundant land, expanding trade, and immigration modified the European heritage, he persuasively argues that Frederick Jackson Turner's frontier hypothesis . . . is valid when applied to the settlement of the Old West"—from the Foreword by David Herbert Donald
0–8090–0137–3 Hill & Wang pb $8.50

● Stephen S. Webb
1676: The End of American Independence
Argues that the colonists had lost their freedom to the British Empire a century before the Revolutionary War
0–674–25220–9 Harvard pb $10.95

● Louis B. Wright, editor
THE ATLANTIC FRONTIER: Colonial American Civilization, 1607–1763
0–8014–9043–X Cornell pb $10.95

Puritan Lives

Though Puritanism was fundamentally a religious movement, books about the Puritan experience are listed here because of its adherents' extraordinary influence on all of American society.

● Charles Cohen
GOD'S CARESS: The Psychology of Puritan Religious Experience
0–19–503973–4 Oxford $34.50

● George Francis Dow
EVERYDAY LIFE IN THE MASSACHUSETTS BAY COLONY
Furniture, clothing, sports, trade, medicine, crime and punishment, and manners, with detailed lists of such things as inventories of shops and homes
0–486–25565–4 Dover pb $9.95

● Philip F. Gura
A GLIMPSE OF SION'S GLORY: Puritan Radicalism in New England, 1620–1660
Challenges Perry Miller's view of 17th-century Puritan ideology as a monolithic "New England mind," documenting a rich heterogeneity of radical dissent and its influence on subsequent American political, religious, and social thought and practice
0–8195–5095–7 Wesleyan $30.00
0–8195–6154–1 Wesleyan pb $14.95

● Michael G. Hall
THE LAST AMERICAN PURITAN: The Life of Increase Mather
0–8195–5128–7 Wesleyan $35.00

● Alan Heimert & Andrew Delbanco, editors
THE PURITANS IN AMERICA: A Narrative Anthology
A collection of documents and narrative, some of which are reprinted here for the first time in 300 years
0–674–74066–1 Harvard pb $9.95

Perry Miller
THE NEW ENGLAND MIND: The Seventeenth Century
"An authoritative description of Puritanism, the most subtle and most fully coherent intellectual system which has ever functioned as the official code of an American regional society"—Henry Nash Smith
0–674–61306–6 Harvard pb $10.95

THE NEW ENGLAND MIND: From Colony to Province
"The historical process whereby Puritan became Yankee—as part of that larger process whereby the Reformation became the Enlightenment"—*Christian Science Monitor*
0–674–61301–5 Harvard pb $10.95

● Edmund S. Morgan
THE GENTLE PURITAN: A Life of Ezra Stiles, 1727–1795
0–393–30126–5 Norton pb $9.95

Cotton Mather

THE PURITAN FAMILY: Religion and Domestic Relations in Seventeenth Century New England
0–06–131227–4 Harper & Row pb $7.95

ROGER WILLIAMS: The Church and the State
0–393–30403–5 Norton pb $5.95

VISIBLE SAINTS: The History of a Puritan Idea
0–8014–9041–3 Cornell pb $6.95

● Darrett B. Rutman
WINTHROP'S BOSTON: A Portrait of a Puritan Town, 1630–1649
The difference between the ideal that guided the Winthrop migration of 1630 and the reality of the settled community and its institutional development
0–393–00627–1 Norton pb $7.95

● Kenneth Silverman
THE LIFE AND TIMES OF COTTON MATHER
"This elusive, often maligned, but key figure of early America is presented as the complex and extremely interesting person that he was"—Emory Elliott, Princeton University
0–231–06125–0 Columbia pb $18.00

● David E. Stannard
THE PURITAN WAY OF DEATH: A Study in Religion, Culture, and Social Change
Probes the idea of death and the problem of mortality in Puritan and modern America
0–19–502521–0 Oxford pb $8.95

● Harry S. Stout
THE NEW ENGLAND SOUL: Preaching and Religious Culture in Colonial New England
The first comprehensive analysis of preaching in colonial New England examines more than 2000 sermons spanning five generations of ministers
0–19–503958–0 Oxford $32.50

The Witches of New England

John Putnam Demos
ENTERTAINING SATAN: Witchcraft and the Culture of Early New England
An outstanding work on the social and psychological roots of witchcraft, including case histories of various episodes
0–19–503378–7 Oxford pb $12.95

Chadwick Hansen
WITCHCRAFT AT SALEM
Argues that witchcraft actually was practiced in 17th-century New England. "A story that departs significantly from the traditional version . . . undermines the work of generations of American historians who could make sense of the witchcraft trials only by seeing evidence of fraud, malice, and the harsh moral politics that marked Puritanism"—*NY Times Book Review*
0–8076–1137–9 Braziller pb $8.95

Carol F. Karlsen
THE DEVIL IN THE SHAPE OF A WOMAN: Witchcraft in Colonial New England
"The assumptions, explicit and implicit, that governed the everyday relationships of men and women in early New England"—Edmund S. Morgan
0–393–02478–4 Norton pb $22.95
0–679–72184–3 Random House pb $10.95

Marion L. Starkey
THE DEVIL IN MASSACHUSETTS: A Modern Enquiry into the Salem Witch Trials
Modern psychiatry takes on the notorious trials of 1692; first published in 1949
0–385–03509–8 Doubleday pb $6.95

New York

Although the following titles may appear specialized, they help place the colonial experience within the framework of early modern social history.

• Sung Bok Kim
LANDLORD AND TENANT IN COLONIAL NEW YORK: Manorial Society, 1664–1775
A scholarly appraisal of the relationship between tenants and the great manorial landlords; concludes that tenants were well off and that little class conflict existed
0–8078–4168–4 North Carolina pb $14.95

• Robert C. Ritchie
THE DUKE'S PROVINCE: A Study of New York Politics and Society, 1664–1691
Explores the pluralism—and sometimes conflict—of early New York society as the basis of struggles for power
0–8078–1292–7 North Carolina $27.50

The Southern Colonies

• T.H. Breen
TOBACCO CULTURE: The Mentality of the Great Tidewater Planters on the Eve of Revolution
"Breen's major contribution is to delineate the 'mentality' of the great planters of the period when private and public distress converged"—Peter S. Onuf, *William & Mary Quarterly*
0–691–00596–6 Harvard pb $9.95

• T.H. Breen & Stephen Innes
MYNE OWNE GROUND: Race and Freedom on Virginia's Eastern Shore, 1640–1676
The story of several blacks who amassed property, established plantations, and lived for several generations as free members of Virginia society
0–19–502727–2 Oxford $19.95
0–19–503206–3 Oxford pb $9.95

• Rhys Isaac
THE TRANSFORMATION OF VIRGINIA, 1740–1790
Pulitzer Prize-winning social history on the effect of religious revival and political revolution
0–8078–1489–X North Carolina $29.50
0–8078–4116–1 North Carolina pb $9.95

• Thomas Jefferson
NOTES ON THE STATE OF VIRGINIA
Edited by William Peden
0–393–00647–6 Norton pb $9.95

• Allan Kulikoff
TOBACCO AND SLAVES: The Development of Southern Cultures in the Chesapeake, 1680–1800
The changing social relations, among both blacks and whites, explored in a "true synthesis dealing with the entire Chesapeake region"—*Register of the Kentucky Historical Society*
0–8078–1671–X North Carolina $30.00

• Kenneth A. Lockridge
THE DIARY AND LIFE OF WILLIAM BYRD II OF VIRGINIA, 1674–1744
0–8078–1736–8 North Carolina $19.95

• Edmund S. Morgan
AMERICAN SLAVERY, AMERICAN FREEDOM: The Ordeal of Colonial Virginia
0–393–09156–2 Norton pb $8.95

• Gerald W. Mullin
FLIGHT AND REBELLION: Slave Resistance in Eighteenth Century Virginia
0–19–501788–9 Oxford pb $8.95

• Darrett B. Rutman & Anita H. Rutman
A PLACE IN TIME: Middlesex County, Virginia, 1650–1750
0–393–01801–6 Norton $19.95
0–393–30318–7 Norton pb $8.95

• Peter H. Wood
BLACK MAJORITY: Negroes in Colonial South Carolina from 1670 Through the Stono Rebellion
0–393–00777–4 Norton pb $9.95

The Great Awakening

• Jonathan Edwards
SELECTED WRITINGS OF JONATHAN EDWARDS
Edited by Harold P. Simonson
0–8044–6132–5 Ungar pb $7.95

• Edwin S. Gaustad
THE GREAT AWAKENING IN NEW ENGLAND
0–8446–1491–2 Peter Smith $13.75

• Perry Miller
JONATHAN EDWARDS
0–87023–328–9 Massachusetts pb $11.95

THE ORIGINS OF THE AMERICAN REVOLUTION

"But what do we mean by the American Revolution? Do we mean the American war? The Revolution was effected before the war commenced. The Revolution was in the minds and hearts of the people; a change in their religious sentiments, of their duties and obligations . . . This radical change in the principles, opinions, sentiments, and affections of the people was the real American Revolution."—John Adams to Hezekiah Niles, 1818, quoted in Bernard Bailyn, *The Ideological Origins of the American Revolution*

• Fred Anderson
A PEOPLE'S ARMY: Massachusetts Soldiers and Society in the Seven Years War
This fine example of the "new military history" gauges the impact of the French and Indian War on a generation of colonists
0–393–95520–6 Norton pb $6.95

Bernard Bailyn
THE IDEOLOGICAL ORIGINS OF THE AMERICAN REVOLUTION
A landmark study that examines pamphlet literature and stresses the role of Whig thought in the emergence of revolutionary consciousness. "One cannot claim to understand the Revolution without having read this book"—*NY Times Book Review*
0–674–44301–2 Harvard pb $8.95
THE ORDEAL OF THOMAS HUTCHINSON
A fine biography of the unpopular governor of Massachusetts, 1771–1774
0–674–64161–2 Harvard pb $9.95

• Richard Hofstadter
AMERICA AT 1750: A Social History
0–394–46589–X Knopf $14.95
0–394–71795–3 Random House pb $4.95

• Linda K. Kerber
WOMEN OF THE REPUBLIC: Intellect and Ideology in Revolutionary America
0–393–30345–4 Norton pb $8.95

• Benjamin Woods Labaree
THE BOSTON TEA PARTY
The dumping of tea into Boston Harbor on the night of December 16, 1773, as a protest against the trade monopoly of the British East India Company was a major turning point in the road to revolution. "A brilliant and scholarly demonstration of the way a single act of violence can affect the course of history"—Julian P. Boyd, editor, *The Papers of Thomas Jefferson*
0–930350–05–7 Northeastern pb $10.95

• Pauline Maier
FROM RESISTANCE TO REVOLUTION: Colonial Radicals and the Development of American Opposition to Britain, 1765–1776
0–394–71937–9 Random House pb $5.95

• John C. Miller
THE ORIGINS OF THE AMERICAN REVOLUTION
"The full story of the decade before the Revolution is here recounted with uniformly crisp phrasing, incisive comment, and apt quotation"—*Yale Review*
0–8047–0594–1 Stanford pb $16.95

Edmund S. Morgan
THE BIRTH OF THE REPUBLIC, 1763–89
A brief account
0–226–53759–5 Chicago pb $6.95

THE CHALLENGE OF THE AMERICAN REVOLUTION
Essays on events and ideas that formed the background to revolution, with a controversial interpretation of slavery and class conflict
0–393–00876–2 Norton pb $5.95

THE GENIUS OF GEORGE WASHINGTON
The Third George Rogers Clark Lecture
0–393–00060–5 Norton pb $5.95

INVENTING THE PEOPLE: The Rise of Popular Sovereignty in England and America
0–393–02505–5 Norton $18.95

Edmund S. & Helen M. Morgan
THE STAMP ACT CRISIS: Prologue to Revolution
0–02–035280–8 Macmillan pb $8.95

• Gary B. Nash
THE URBAN CRUCIBLE: Social Change, Political Consciousness and the Origins of the American Revolution
An attempt to tie the Revolution in part to social conflict among the colonists themselves
0–674–93059–2 Harvard pb $10.95

• Alan Rogers
EMPIRE AND LIBERTY: American Resistance to British Authority, 1755–1763
0–520–02275–0 California $36.50

• Clinton Rossiter
THE FIRST AMERICAN REVOLUTION: The American Colonies on the Eve of Independence
0–15–631121–6 HBJ pb $6.95

Toppling a statue of King George III in Boston

• Arthur M. Schlesinger, Jr.
PRELUDE TO INDEPENDENCE: The Newspaper War on Britain, 1764–1776
The pivotal role of the press in the American Revolution
Foreword by Charles Akers
0–930350–13–8 Northeastern pb $9.95

• Robert W. Tucker & David C. Hendrickson
THE FALL OF THE FIRST BRITISH EMPIRE: Origins of the War of American Independence
0–8018–2780–9 Johns Hopkins $39.50

• Garry Wills
INVENTING AMERICA: Jefferson's Declaration of Independence
An adept and controversial analysis compares Jefferson's original draft with the final accepted version—thereby challenging many long-cherished assumptions about both the man and the document
0–394–72735–5 Random House pb $9.50

THE REVOLUTIONARY WAR

• John R. Alden
THE AMERICAN REVOLUTION, 1775–1783
0–06–133011–6 Harper & Row pb $9.95

THE SOUTH IN THE REVOLUTION, 1763–1789
0–8071–0003–X LSU $30.00
0–8071–0013–7 LSU pb $9.95

• Edward Countryman
THE AMERICAN REVOLUTION
"A balanced view of how the Revolution was made by a variety of social groups . . . and how, in turn, these groups were transformed by the Revolutionary experience"—Gary B. Nash, UCLA
Edited by Eric Foner
0–8090–0162–4 Hill & Wang pb $7.95

• Jonathan R. Dull
A DIPLOMATIC HISTORY OF THE AMERICAN REVOLUTION
A good introduction. Interested readers should also look at R.R. Palmer's *The Age of the Democractic Revolution* for the European context of the war
0–300–03419–9 Yale $25.00

• Jack P. Greene, editor
COLONIES TO NATION, 1763–1789: A Documentary History of the American Revolution
0–393–09229–1 Norton pb $14.95

• Henry Lumpkin
FROM SAVANNAH TO YORKTOWN: The American Revolution in the South
A history of British military attempts to suppress rebellion in the South
0–913729–48–5 Paragon pb $9.95

• D.J. MacLeod
SLAVERY, RACE AND THE AMERICAN REVOLUTION
0–521–09877–7 Cambridge pb $13.95

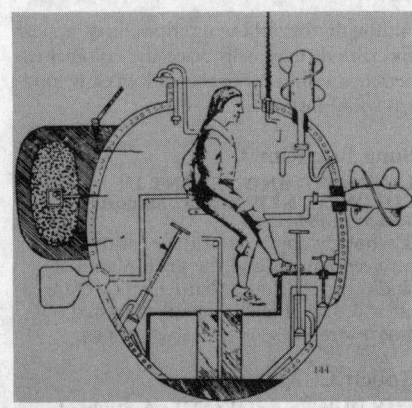

Diagram showing the operator's position inside the world's first combat submarine, "The Turtle," which saw action in 1776

TO ORDER BOOKS AS GIFTS, SEE PAGE 1

- Robert Middlekauff
THE GLORIOUS CAUSE: The American Revolution, 1763–1789
Proves that traditional narrative on a grand scale is still one of the most rewarding offerings of history
0–19–503575–5 Oxford pb $14.95

- Richard B. Morris
THE PEACEMAKERS: The Great Powers and American Independence
How Franklin, Jay, and Adams confronted Europe's diplomats and negotiated the Peace of Paris and the end of the Revolutionary War
0–930350–36–7 New England pb $10.95

- Jack N. Rakove
THE BEGINNINGS OF NATIONAL POLITICS: An Interpretive History of the Continental Congress
0–8018–2864–3 Johns Hopkins pb $11.95

- Kenneth Silverman
A CULTURAL HISTORY OF THE AMERICAN REVOLUTION: Painting, Music, Literature and the Theatre in the Colonies and the United States from the Treaty of Paris to the Inauguration of George Washington, 1763–1789
"Makes a good case for his major thesis, that this period saw the first burst of creative energy directed toward high culture in America"—Edmund S. Morgan, *NY Review of Books*
0–231–06295–8 Columbia pb $19.50

- Page Smith
Smith's sweeping histories are massive (*A New Age Now Begins* runs more than 1800 pages; his eight-volume *People's History of the United States* runs nearly 10,000) but energetic, aimed at a general audience concerned more with detail and the flow of events than with more sophisticated interpretation.
A NEW AGE NOW BEGINS: A People's History of the American Revolution
"He has, so far as I can judge, left no source, printed or manuscript, unread, he has really absorbed them, eschewing footnotes, at which the public will rejoice"—Samuel Eliot Morison. A 2-volume set
0–07–059097–4 McGraw-Hill (set) $24.95

THE CONSTITUTION: A Documentary and Narrative History
0–688–08349–8 Morrow pb $15.95

THE NATION COMES OF AGE: A People's History of the Ante-Bellum Years
0–07–059018–4 McGraw-Hill $24.95

- Barbara W. Tuchman
THE FIRST SALUTE
The author of *The Guns of August* and *A Distant Mirror* brings her talents to an episode of the Revolutionary War, showing how not only England and America were affected by the Revolution, but the rest of Europe as well
0–394–55333–0 Knopf $22.95

- Gordon S. Wood
THE CREATION OF THE AMERICAN REPUBLIC, 1776–1787
An important study emphasizing the role of ideas and their influence on founding the new nation
0–393–00644–1 Norton pb $10.95

Humor

- George Washington & Marvin Kitman
GEORGE WASHINGTON'S EXPENSE ACCOUNT
The Father of Our Nation meets an acerbic TV critic, via the strange doings of Washington's Revolutionary expense accounts
0–06–097185–1 Harper & Row pb $8.95

Revolutionary Lives

John D. Dann, editor
THE REVOLUTION REMEMBERED: Eyewitness Accounts of the War for Independence
0–226–13624–8 Chicago pb $12.95

A.J. Langguth
PATRIOTS: The Men Who Started the American Revolution
0–671–52375–9 Simon & Schuster $22.95
0–671–67562–1 Simon & Schuster pb $9.95

Benjamin Quarles
THE NEGRO IN THE AMERICAN REVOLUTION
0–8078–0833–4 North Carolina $24.00

George F. Scheer & Hugh F. Rankin
REBELS AND REDCOATS: The American Revolution Through the Eyes of Those Who Fought and Lived It
"I know of no book where either the professional student or the general reader can attain, in one vivid apprehension, a more stimulating sense of what it truly was to have been there, of what it meant for humanity, patriot or redcoat, to have fought there"—Perry Miller
0–306–80307–0 Da Capo pb $14.95

I must soon quit the Scene, but you may live to see our Country flourish, as it will amazingly and rapidly after the War is over. Like a Field of young Indian Corn, which long Fair weather and Sunshine had enfeebled and discolored, and which in that weak State, by a Thunder Gust, of violent Wind, Hail, and Rain, seem'd to be threaten'd with absolute Destruction; yet the Storm being past, it recovers fresh Verdure, shoots up with double Vigour, and delights the Eye, not of its Owner only, but of every observing Traveller.

Letter to George Washington, dated Passy, March 5, 1780, in

Benjamin Franklin
WRITINGS
0–940450–29–1 Library of America $35.00

THE MAKING OF THE CONSTITUTION

Long preoccupied by the motives of the members of the Philadelphia Convention, historians now seem uncertain about the precise mix of economic interests, democratic values, and conservative intentions that spurred the framers.

▶ See also Law

- Charles A. Beard
AN ECONOMIC INTERPRETATION OF THE CONSTITUTION OF THE UNITED STATES
With a new introduction by Forrest McDonald. The famous thesis, first published in 1913, that the document was shaped by men whose commercial interests were served by its provisions
0–02–902480–3 Free Press pb $10.95

- Richard Beeman & others, editors
BEYOND CONFEDERATION: Origins of the Constitution and American National Identity
Essays that probe the ideological background of the Constitution, the rigors of its writing and ratification, and the problems it provoked and faced immediately afterward
0–8078–1719–8 North Carolina $25.00
0–8078–4172–2 North Carolina pb $8.95

- Catherine Drinker Bowen
MIRACLE AT PHILADELPHIA: The Story of the Constitutional Convention, May to September 1787
Foreword by Warren E. Burger
0–316–10378–0 Little, Brown $18.95
0–316–10398–5 Little, Brown pb $8.95

- Christopher & James Lincoln Collier
DECISION IN PHILADELPHIA: The Constitutional Convention of 1787
A popular retelling
0–345–34652–1 Ballantine pb $4.95

James Madison (portrait by Asher B. Durand, courtesy of The New-York Historical Society)

• **Merrill Jensen**
THE NEW NATION: A History of the United States During the Confederation, 1781–1789
Although somewhat dated, this interpretive account gives an excellent background of the period by a recognized scholar
Foreword by Richard B. Morris
0–930350–15–4 Northeastern $26.95
0–930350–14–6 Northeastern pb $12.95

• **Michael Kammen**
A MACHINE THAT WOULD GO OF ITSELF: The Constitution in American Culture
"Identifies the place of the Constitution 'in the public consciousness and symbolic life of the American people' "—Stanley N. Katz, *Washington Post Book World*
0–394–75600–2 Random House pb $9.95

• **Michael Kammen, editor**
THE ORIGINS OF THE AMERICAN CONSTITUTION: A Documentary History
Key Federalist papers and anti-Federalist writings
0–14–008744–3 Penguin pb $6.95

• **James Madison, Alexander Hamilton & John Jay**
THE FEDERALIST PAPERS
The brilliant essays in defense of the Constitution, considered by later generations as sacred as the Constitution itself
Edited by Isaac Kramnick
0–14–044495–5 Penguin pb $7.95

• **Jackson Turner Main**
THE ANTI-FEDERALISTS: Critics of the Constitution, 1781–1788
0–393–00760–X Norton pb $9.95

• **Forrest McDonald**
NOVUS ORDO SECLORUM: The Intellectual Origins of the Constitution
"A realistic, tough-minded book about the role of ideas among practical men of affairs at a pivotal and difficult moment in human history"—Michael Kammen
0–7006–0311–5 Kansas pb $9.95

Alexander Hamilton (portrait by John Trumbull, courtesy of The New-York Historical Society)

John Jay (portrait by Joseph Wright, courtesy of The New-York Historical Society)

• **Charles L. Mee, Jr.**
THE GENIUS OF THE PEOPLE
A popular account of the Constitutional Convention
0–06–015702–X Harper & Row $19.95
0–06–091478–5 Harper & Row pb $8.95

• **Richard B. Morris**
THE FORGING OF THE UNION, 1781–1789
Treats the Confederation as an extraordinary, if brief, interlude of trial and experimentation
0–06–015733–X Harper & Row $22.95
0–06–091424–6 Harper & Row pb $8.95

• **Clinton Rossiter**
1787: The Grand Convention
"No one has so successfully captured the human elements of the gathering at Philadelphia"—from the Foreword by Richard B. Morris
0–393–30404–3 Norton pb $8.95

• **David B. Szatmary**
SHAYS' REBELLION: The Making of an Agrarian Insurrection
A brief account of the 1786 rebellion that played a key role in strengthening the public desire for a strong, constitutional federal government
0–87023–419–6 Massachusetts pb $9.95

• **Carl Van Doren**
THE GREAT REHEARSAL: The Story of the Making and Ratifying of the Constitution of the United States
A very readable day-to-day account
0–14–008965–9 Penguin pb $6.95

THE NEW NATION

• **Henry Adams**
HISTORY OF THE UNITED STATES DURING THE ADMINISTRATIONS OF JEFFERSON AND MADISON
A masterpiece of American historical writing
Edited by Earl Harbert

Volume 1: The Administrations of Thomas Jefferson
0–940450–34–8 Library of America $27.50

Volume 2: The Administrations of James Madison
0–940450–35–6 Library of America $27.50

• **Daniel J. Boorstin**
THE LOST WORLD OF THOMAS JEFFERSON
The ideas of "the Jeffersonian Circle"—the concepts of God, nature, toleration, education—and their underlying world view
0–226–06496–4 Johns Hopkins pb $12.95

• **Roger H. Brown**
THE REPUBLIC IN PERIL, 1812
0–393–00578–X Norton pb $7.95

• **Harry L. Coles**
THE WAR OF 1812
A compact history
0–226–11350–7 Chicago pb $10.00

• **Marcus Cunliffe**
THE NATION TAKES SHAPE, 1789–1837
Provides excellent background and analysis of the period
0–226–12667–6 Chicago pb $9.00

• **Noble E. Cunningham, Jr.**
THE JEFFERSONIAN REPUBLICANS: The Formation of Party Organization, 1789–1801
0–8078–0730–3 North Carolina $30.00

• **George Dangerfield**
THE AWAKENING OF AMERICAN NATIONALISM, 1815–1828
By the author of *The Strange Death of Liberal England*. "It is the special virtue of Mr. Dangerfield's brilliant synthesis of the period that he manages to keep the focus on this central theme—the contest between the economic nationalism expounded by Henry Clay and John Quincy Adams and the democratic nationalism exemplified by the partisans of Andrew Jackson"—from the Introduction by Henry Steele Commager & Richard B. Morris
0–06–133061–2 Harper & Row pb $12.95

• **Ralph Ketcham**
PRESIDENTS ABOVE PARTY: The First American Presidency, 1789–1829
0–8078–4179–X North Carolina pb $9.95

• **Ernest R. May**
THE MAKING OF THE MONROE DOCTRINE
The doctrine was as much the work of England's Canning as America's John Quincy Adams
0–674–54340–8 Harvard $21.00

• **Thomas P. Slaughter**
THE WHISKEY REBELLION: Frontier Epilogue to the American Revolution
It took 13,000 soldiers in 1794 to crush the first large-scale resistance to federal law under the Constitution
0–19–505191–2 Oxford pb $9.95

• Marshall Smelser
THE DEMOCRATIC REPUBLIC, 1801–1815
An introduction to the era of Jefferson, Madison, Randolph, Burr, and Pickering; part of the New American Nation Series
Introduction by Henry Steele Commager & Richard B. Morris
0–06–131406–4 Harper & Row pb $10.95

• Barbara Clark Smith
AFTER THE REVOLUTION: The Smithsonian History of Everyday Life in the Eighteenth Century
An illustrated guidebook to the real lives of America's new citizens, based on a Smithsonian exhibit
0–394–54381–5 Pantheon pb $13.95

• Robert H. Wiebe
THE OPENING OF AMERICAN SOCIETY: From the Adoption of the Constitution to the Eve of Disunion
By the author of *The Search for Order*
0–394–72965–X Random House pb $12.95

• James S. Young
THE WASHINGTON COMMUNITY: 1800–1828
Fascinating study of the difficulties of establishing a truly representative national government
0–231–08381–5 Columbia pb $12.50

The United States were supposed to have stabbed England in the back at the moment when her hands were tied, when her existence was in the most deadly peril and her anxieties were most heavy. England never could forgive treason so base and cowardice so vile. That Madison had been from the first a tool and accomplice of Bonaparte was thenceforward so fixed an idea in British history that time could not shake it. Indeed, so complicated and so historical had the causes of war become that no one even in America could explain or understand them, while Englishmen could see only that America required England as the price of peace to destroy herself by abandoning her naval power, and that England preferred to die fighting rather than to die by her own hand. The American party in England was extinguished; no further protest was heard against the war; and the British people thought moodily of revenge.

"England Angry 1812–1813" in

Henry Adams
HISTORY OF THE UNITED STATES OF AMERICA DURING THE ADMINISTRATIONS OF JAMES MADISON
0–940450–35–6 Library of America $27.50

ANTEBELLUM AMERICA AND THE AGE OF JACKSON

Historians have had a special affinity for the Jacksonian era because it seemed to parallel the politics of the mid-20th century: Andrew Jackson and Franklin Roosevelt both represented the forces of democracy in the battle against special privilege. Histori-

ans now see that a more complex pattern of social conflict spurred the vigorous public life of the 1830s. They've begun to wonder, too, just how democratic the vaunted "Jacksonian democracy" really was.

• David Brion Davis, editor
ANTEBELLUM AMERICAN CULTURE: An Interpretive Anthology
Traces such social changes as reform movements, abolitionism, utopianism, and revivals
0–669–01476–1 Heath $19.95

• Richard E. Ellis
THE UNION AT RISK: Jacksonian Democracy, States' Rights and the Nullification Crisis
"Shows how the states-rights bulwark of Jefferson's yeoman republic became the bulwark of slavery"—Charles Sellers
0–19–503785–5 Oxford $34.00

• Grant Foreman
INDIAN REMOVAL: The Emigration of the Five Civilized Tribes of Indians
The 1830s forced removals to Indian territory
0–8061–0019–2 Oklahoma $21.95
0–8061–1172–0 Oklahoma pb $12.95

• Marvin Meyers
JACKSONIAN PERSUASION: Politics and Belief
0–8047–0506–2 Stanford pb $9.95

• Edward Pessen
JACKSONIAN AMERICA: Society, Personality, and Politics
In Pessen's own words, "The time has come for a comprehensive reexamination of the Jacksonian era." A strong statement of newer research on "the inegalitarian society"
0–252–01237–2 Illinois pb $13.50

• Robert V. Remini
ANDREW JACKSON AND THE BANK WAR
Remini is the leading authority of the Jacksonian era. His prize-winning biography of Jackson is listed below
0–393–09757–9 Norton pb $6.95

ANDREW JACKSON AND THE COURSE OF AMERICAN DEMOCRACY
0–06–015279–6 Harper & Row $27.50

• Charles E. Rosenberg
THE CHOLERA YEARS: The United States in 1832, 1849, and 1866
"A masterful analysis of the moral and social interest attached to epidemic disease"—Steven Shapin, *TLS*
0–226–72677–0 Chicago pb $9.95

• Arthur M. Schlesinger, Jr.
THE AGE OF JACKSON
The classic analogy between the New Deal and the Jacksonian era
0–316–77344–1 Little, Brown $22.50
0–316–77343–3 Little, Brown pb $10.95

• Daniel E. Sutherland
THE EXPANSION OF EVERYDAY LIFE: 1840–1870
0–06–016023–3 Harper & Row $18.95

• Alexis de Tocqueville
DEMOCRACY IN AMERICA
"America," Tocqueville wrote to John Stuart Mill, "was only my framework; democracy was my subject." A 1960s translation of Tocqueville's masterpiece
Translated by George Lawrence
0–394–42186–8 Knopf $35.00
0–06–091522–6 Harper & Row pb $14.95

DEMOCRACY IN AMERICA
Francis Bowen's revised translation of the 19th-century version by Henry Reeve

Volume 1
0–394–70110–0 Random House pb $6.95

Volume 2
0–394–70111–9 Random House pb $4.95

• Paul A. Varg
U.S. FOREIGN RELATIONS, 1820–1860
0–87013–212–1 Michigan State $15.00

The Mexican War

• John S.D. Eisenhower
SO FAR FROM GOD: The U.S. War with Mexico, 1846–48
"A brilliant match of painstaking scholarship and engrossing interpretation"—James A. Michener
0–394–56051–5 Random House $24.95

• Robert W. Johannsen
TO THE HALLS OF THE MONTEZUMAS: The Mexican War in the American Imagination
0–19–503518–6 Oxford $29.95
0–19–504981–0 Oxford pb $11.95

• Otis A. Singletary
THE MEXICAN WAR
0–226–76061–8 Chicago pb $9.95

Gore Vidal's Historic America

Gore Vidal
BURR
0–345–33921–5 Ballantine pb $4.95

LINCOLN
"He is in Vidal's version at once more complex, mysterious and enigmatic, more implacably courageous and, finally, more tragic than the conventional public images, the marble man of the memorial"—George Garrett, *Chicago Tribune*
0–345–00790–5 Ballantine pb $4.95

1876
0–345–34626–2 Ballantine pb $4.95

EMPIRE
0–345–35472–9 Ballantine pb $4.95

WASHINGTON, D.C.
0–345–34236–4 Ballantine pb $4.95

SLAVERY AND BLACK LIVES

• Terry Alford
PRINCE AMONG SLAVES
0–19–504223–9 Oxford pb $8.95

The Battle of Resaca de la Palma, from So Far from God: The U.S. War with Mexico, 1846-48 *by John S.D. Eisenhower (Random House)*

• **Ira Berlin**
SLAVES WITHOUT MASTERS: The Free Negro in the Antebellum South
How the thousands of Southern blacks who enjoyed freedom before the Civil War tried to maintain their liberty within the grip of the slave system
0–19–502905–4 Oxford pb $10.95

• **John W. Blassingame**
THE SLAVE COMMUNITY: Plantation Life in the Ante-Bellum South
0–19–502563–6 Oxford pb $10.95

• **Leonard P. Curry**
THE FREE BLACK IN URBAN AMERICA, 1800–1850: The Shadow of the Dream
0–226–13125–4 Chicago pb $12.50

• **David Brion Davis**
THE PROBLEM OF SLAVERY IN THE AGE OF REVOLUTION
0–8014–9156–8 Cornell pb $12.95

THE PROBLEM OF SLAVERY IN WESTERN CULTURE
0–19–505639–6 Oxford pb $13.95

SLAVERY AND HUMAN PROGRESS
A complete survey covering slavery from the early expansion of Europe to the present
0–19–503439–2 Oxford $29.95
0–19–503733–2 Oxford pb $9.95

• **Stanley M. Elkins**
SLAVERY: A Problem in American Institutional and Intellectual Life
0–226–20477–4 Chicago pb $12.95

• **Robert W. Fogel**
WITHOUT CONSENT OR CONTRACT: The Rise and Fall of American Slavery
0–393–01887–3 Norton $22.50

• **Elizabeth Fox-Genovese**
WITHIN THE PLANTATION HOUSEHOLD: Black and White Women in the Old South
Argues that class and race did affect women's experiences and that slaves and slaveholders were never linked in sisterhood
0–8078–4232–X North Carolina pb $12.95

Eugene D. Genovese
ROLL, JORDAN, ROLL: The World the Slaves Made
An enduring classic. "Genovese's great gift is his ability to penetrate the minds of both slaves and masters, revealing not only how they viewed themselves and each other, but also how their contradictory perceptions interacted"— David Brion Davis, *NY Times Book Review*
0–394–71652–3 Random House pb $14.95

THE WORLD THE SLAVEHOLDERS MADE: Two Essays in Interpretation
0–8195–6204–1 Wesleyan pb $12.95

• **Michael P. Johnson & James L. Roark**
BLACK MASTERS: A Free Family of Color in the Old South
0–393–01906–3 Norton $22.50
0–393–30314–4 Norton pb $9.95

• **Leslie H. Owens**
THIS SPECIES OF PROPERTY: Slave Life and Culture in the Old South
0–19–502245–9 Oxford pb $9.95

• **Albert J. Raboteau**
SLAVE RELIGION: The Invisible Institution in the Antebellum South
Slave religion from its African roots through its reinterpretation under Christianity
0–19–502705–1 Oxford pb $11.95

• **C. Duncan Rice**
THE RISE AND FALL OF BLACK SLAVERY
0–8071–0257–1 LSU pb $10.95

• **Mechal Sobel**
TRABELIN' ON: The Slave Journey to an Afro-Baptist Faith
A religious history of the slaves and free blacks of antebellum America. "Takes seriously the religion of black people and shows its creative power to construct a sacred cosmos"—Andrew E. Murray, *Journal of American History*
0–691–00603–2 Princeton pb $12.95

• **Kenneth M. Stampp**
THE PECULIAR INSTITUTION
0–394–44015–3 Knopf $17.95
0–394–70253–0 Random House pb $7.95

• **Thomas L. Webber**
DEEP LIKE THE RIVERS: Education in the Slave Quarter Community, 1831–1865
0–393–00998–X Norton pb $10.95

If, therefore, it be an infidel Society, it is so only in the sense in which Jesus was a blasphemer, and the Apostles were "pestilent and seditious fellows, seeking to turn the world upside down." It is infidel to Satan, the enslaver; it is loyal to Christ, the redeemer. It is infidel to a Gospel which makes man the property of man; it is bound up with the Gospel which requires us to love our neighbors as ourselves, and to call no man master. It is infidel to a Church which receives to its communion the "traffickers in slaves and the souls of men"; it is loyal to the Church which is not stained with blood, nor polluted by oppression . . . It is infidel to all blood-stained compromises, sinful concessions, unholy compacts, respecting the system of slavery; it is devotedly attached to whatever is honest, straightforward, invincible for the right.

From William Lloyd Garrison, "The 'Infidelity' of Abolition" (1860), quoted in

David Brion Davis, editor
ANTEBELLUM AMERICAN CULTURE: An Interpretive Anthology
0–669–01476–1 Heath $19.95

➤ **FOR OVERSEAS ORDERING INFORMATION, SEE PAGE 1**

REFORMERS AND ABOLITIONISTS

- Robert H. Abzug
  PASSIONATE LIBERATOR: Theodore Dwight Weld and the Dilemma of Reform
  A study of the most effective abolition leader, co-founder of the American Anti-Slavery Society, husband of Angelina Grimké, and teacher at Oberlin College. Abzug probes Weld's stormy religious conversion, his entry into the world of reform, and his rejection of public life
  0–19–502771–X Oxford $27.50

- Kathleen L. Barry
  SUSAN B. ANTHONY: A Biography of a Singular Feminist
  0–8147–1105–7 NYU $27.95

- Arthur Bestor
  BACKWOODS UTOPIAS: The Sectarian Origins and the Owenite Phase of Communitarian Socialism in America, 1663–1829
  0–8122–1004–2 Pennsylvania pb $13.95

- Merton L. Dillon
  THE ABOLITIONISTS: The Growth of a Dissenting Minority
  0–393–00957–2 Norton pb $8.95

- Ann Douglas
  THE FEMINIZATION OF AMERICAN CULTURE
  Traces today's culture back to its Victorian roots
  0–385–24241–7 Doubleday pb $10.95

- Barbara L. Epstein
  THE POLITICS OF DOMESTICITY: Women, Evangelism, and Temperance in Nineteenth-Century America
  0–8195–6184–3 Wesleyan pb $12.95

Frederick Douglass (portrait courtesy of The National Portrait Gallery), from Fifty American Faces by Margaret C.S. Christman (Smithsonian)

John Brown (portrait by Ole Peter Hansen Balling, courtesy of The National Portrait Gallery), from Fifty American Faces by Margaret C.S. Christman (Smithsonian)

- Nathan I. Huggins
  SLAVE AND CITIZEN: The Life of Frederick Douglass
  0–316–38001–6 Little, Brown pb $14.95

- Paul E. Johnson
  A SHOPKEEPER'S MILLENNIUM: Society and Revivals in Rochester, New York, 1815–1837
  0–8090–0136–5 Hill & Wang pb $7.95

- Stephen B. Oates
  TO PURGE THIS LAND WITH BLOOD: A Biography of John Brown
  Hanged for leading an armed insurrection in 1859, Brown had planned to found an abolitionist republic and wage guerrilla war on slavery
  0–87023–458–7 Massachusetts pb $14.95

- James B. Stewart
  HOLY WARRIORS: The Abolitionists and American Slavery
  0–8090–0123–3 Hill & Wang pb $6.95

- Alice Felt Tyler
  FREEDOM'S FERMENT: Phases of American Social History from the Revolution to the Outbreak of the Civil War
  Particularly good in tracing the reform movements of the pre-Civil War years
  0–06–131074–3 Harper & Row pb $8.95

- Ronald G. Walters
  AMERICAN REFORMERS, 1815–1860
  0–8090–0130–6 Hill & Wang pb $6.95

  THE ANTISLAVERY APPEAL: American Abolitionism after 1830
  0–393–95444–7 Norton pb $5.95

The Romantic Age

Van Wyck Brooks
THE FLOWERING OF NEW ENGLAND, 1815–1865
0–395–30522–5 Houghton Mifflin pb $7.95

Lawrence Buell
NEW ENGLAND LITERARY CULTURE: From Revolution Through Renaissance
0–521–37801–X Cambridge pb $17.95

F.O. Matthiessen
AMERICAN RENAISSANCE: Art and Expression in the Age of Emerson and Whitman
A famous account, first published in 1941, with chapters on Emerson, Thoreau, Hawthorne, Melville, and Whitman
0–19–500759–X Oxford pb $18.95

David S. Reynolds
BENEATH THE AMERICAN RENAISSANCE: The Subversive Imagination in the Age of Emerson and Melville
0–394–54448–X Knopf $35.00

Louise Hall Tharp
THE PEABODY SISTERS OF SALEM
A biography both of three influential women and of the New England golden era of Emerson, Channing, and Thoreau
0–316–83919–1 Little, Brown pb $8.95

BIOGRAPHY

- Lester J. Cappon
  THE ADAMS-JEFFERSON LETTERS: The Complete Correspondence Between Thomas Jefferson and Abigail and John Adams
  Begins in 1777, ceases in 1801 after Jefferson's defeat of Adams for the presidency, resumes in 1812, and continues until the death of both on July 4, 1826
  0–8078–4230–3 North Carolina pb $17.95

- Phyllis Lee Levin
  ABIGAIL ADAMS: A Biography
  The life of the famous First Lady who married one president and mothered another, told with the help of her own writings
  0–345–35473–7 Ballantine pb $10.95

- Paul C. Nagel
  THE ADAMS WOMEN: Abigail and Louisa Adams, Their Sisters and Daughters
  0–19–503874–6 Oxford $24.95

  DESCENT FROM GLORY: Four Generations of the John Adams Family
  0–19–503172–5 Oxford $29.95
  0–19–503445–7 Oxford pb $12.95

- Leonard L. Richards
  THE LIFE AND TIMES OF CONGRESSMAN JOHN QUINCY ADAMS
  Story of "Old Man Eloquent," "the conscience of New England," and the "archest enemy of slavery that ever existed"—the only ex-president to serve in Congress
  0–19–504026–0 Oxford $19.95
  0–19–505427–X Oxford pb $8.95

John Adams (portrait by Asher B. Durand, courtesy of The New-York Historical Society)

• Peter Shaw
THE CHARACTER OF JOHN ADAMS
0–393–00856–8 Norton pb $7.95

• Stephen Burroughs
MEMOIRS OF STEPHEN BURROUGHS
The shady colonial character whose alleged indiscretions included impersonating a minister on the eve of Shays' Rebellion, counterfeiting, and committing robbery and rape
1–55553–035–4 Northeastern pb $14.95

• John Niven
JOHN C. CALHOUN AND THE PRICE OF THE UNION
0–8071–1451–0 LSU $24.95

• Clement Eaton
HENRY CLAY AND THE ART OF AMERICAN POLITICS
0–673–39335–6 Scott, Foresman pb $7.95

• Benjamin Franklin
WRITINGS
Includes *Boston and London, 1722–1726; Philadelphia, 1726–1757; London, 1757–1775; Paris, 1776–1785; Philadelphia, 1785–1790; Poor Richard's Almanack, 1733–1758; The Autobiography*
0–940450–29–1 Library of America $35.00

• Catherine Drinker Bowen
THE MOST DANGEROUS MAN IN AMERICA: Scenes from the Life of Benjamin Franklin
"The book, like the man, is astute and delightful"—*New Yorker*
0–316–10379–9 Little, Brown pb $8.95

• Claude-Anne Lopez & Eugenia W. Herbert
THE PRIVATE FRANKLIN: The Man and His Family
"Seen not as a scientist, philosopher, and a statesman, but as a son, brother, husband, uncle, father, and grandfather"—*Library Journal*
0–393–30227–X Norton pb $7.95

• Esmond Wright
FRANKLIN OF PHILADELPHIA
0–674–31809–9 Harvard $25.00

• Forrest McDonald
ALEXANDER HAMILTON
A serious biography focusing on Hamilton's abilities and accomplishments as the first Secretary of the Treasury
0–393–30048–X Norton pb $10.95

• David S. Lifton
THE RAVEN: A Biography of Sam Houston
A Pulitzer Prize-winning biography of the rebel elected president of the Republic of Texas in 1836
Introduction by Henry Steele Commager
0–292–77040–5 Texas pb $10.95

• Robert V. Remini
THE LIFE OF ANDREW JACKSON
A new one-volume version of Remini's prizewinning 3-volume biography of Jackson, portrayed here as heroic and larger-than-life
0–06–015904–9 Harper & Row $27.95

• John William Ward
ANDREW JACKSON: Symbol for an Age
How Jackson's image as a victorious general, rough-hewn frontiersman and man of iron will made him the legendary figure of his age
0–19–500699–2 Oxford pb $8.95

• Thomas Jefferson
WRITINGS
Includes the *Autobiography; A Summary of the Rights of British America; Notes on the State of Virginia; Public Papers; Addresses, Messages, and Replies; Miscellany;* and *Letters*
0–940450–16–X Library of America $30.00

• Fawn M. Brodie
THOMAS JEFFERSON: An Intimate History
Highly controversial biography that makes much of Jefferson's relationship with his slave mistress, Sally Hemmings
0–553–27335–3 Bantam pb $6.95

• Noble E. Cunningham, Jr.
IN PURSUIT OF REASON: The Life of Thomas Jefferson
0–8071–1375–1 LSU $24.95

• Dumas Malone
JEFFERSON THE VIRGINIAN
0–316–54474–4 Little, Brown $25.00
0–316–54472–8 Little, Brown pb $12.95

JEFFERSON AND THE RIGHTS OF MAN
0–316–54473–6 Little, Brown $25.00
0–316–54470–1 Little, Brown pb $12.95

JEFFERSON AND THE ORDEAL OF LIBERTY
0–316–54475–2 Little, Brown $25.00
0–316–54469–8 Little, Brown pb $12.95

JEFFERSON THE PRESIDENT: First Term, 1801–1805
0–316–54467–1 Little, Brown $25.00
0–316–54466–3 Little, Brown pb $12.95

JEFFERSON THE PRESIDENT: Second Term, 1805–1809
0–316–54465–5 Little, Brown $25.00
0–316–54464–7 Little, Brown pb $12.95

JEFFERSON AND HIS TIME: The Sage of Monticello
0–316–54463–9 Little, Brown $25.00
0–316–54478–7 Little, Brown pb $12.95

• Jack McLaughlin
JEFFERSON AND MONTICELLO: The Biography of a Builder
0–8050–00482–3 Henry Holt $29.95

• Merrill D. Peterson
THOMAS JEFFERSON AND THE NEW NATION
0–19–501909–1 Oxford pb $18.95

• Stephen B. Oates
WITH MALICE TOWARD NONE: The Life of Abraham Lincoln
"An admirable job in portraying Lincoln's life and character, the conquest of his deficiencies and the out-maneuvering of political jackals"—*Publishers Weekly*
0–451–62314–2 NAL pb $4.95

▶ For other books about Lincoln, see The Civil War and Reconstruction

• Esther Forbes
PAUL REVERE AND THE WORLD HE LIVED IN
A Pulitzer Prize-winning biography (1943); part of the American Heritage Library
0–395–08370–2 Houghton Mifflin pb $9.95

• Donald B. Cole
MARTIN VAN BUREN AND THE AMERICAN POLITICAL SYSTEM
The first New Yorker to be president, and the archetype of the American party politician
0–691–04715–4 Princeton $50.00

• John D. Alden
GEORGE WASHINGTON: A Biography
0–440–32836–5 Doubleday pb $5.95

• Marcus Cunliffe
GEORGE WASHINGTON: Man and Monument
A compact study
0–451–62461–0 NAL pb $3.95

• James T. Flexner
GEORGE WASHINGTON

Volume 1: The Force of Experience, 1732–1775
0–316–28597–8 Little, Brown $25.00

Volume 2: In the American Revolution, 1775–1783
0–316–28595–1 Little, Brown $25.00

Volume 3: And the New Nation, 1783–1793
0–316–28600–1 Little, Brown $25.00

Volume 4: Anguish and Farewell, 1793–1799
0–316–28602–8 Little, Brown $25.00

• Barry Schwartz
GEORGE WASHINGTON: The Making of an American Symbol
0-02-928141-5 Free Press $22.50

• Irving H. Bartlett
DANIEL WEBSTER
In the grand style of the elder Pitt, Webster was one of America's greatest orators, a commanding figure of the US Senate
0-393-00996-3 Norton pb $8.95

• Robert F. Dalzell, Jr.
DANIEL WEBSTER AND THE TRIAL OF AMERICAN NATIONALISM, 1843-1852
0-393-00782-0 Norton pb $4.95

Merrill D. Peterson
THE GREAT TRIUMVIRATE: Webster, Clay, and Calhoun
A sweeping biography of the foremost statesmen who personified their respective regions in antebellum America. "[Peterson's] details enable us to recognize how little the practices of parliamentary democracy have changed"—*New Yorker*
0-19-503877-0 Oxford $27.95

The Civil War and Reconstruction

The literature of the Civil War—the "American Iliad," as Gore Vidal calls it—is enormous. Much of it is popular military history for the enthusiast. The titles here are only a sample of a much larger field, which is best surveyed in a good library. Many of these books, while exploring the larger context of the war, focus on specific events and highlight their cataclysmic effects on the young nation. *Battle Cry of Freedom* relates how George Ticknor, a retired Harvard professor, wrote in 1869 that the Civil War created a "great gulf between what happened before in our century and what has happened since, or what is likely to happen hereafter. It does not seem to me as if I were living in the country in which I was born."

SURVEYS OF THE CIVIL WAR ERA: 1845-1877

• James M. McPherson
BATTLE CRY OF FREEDOM: The Era of the Civil War
Starting with the war with Mexico, McPherson traces the contradictions and confusions that separated North and South to the point of war—and carries the story to Appomattox. A national best-seller and winner of the Pulitzer Prize
0-19-503863-0 Oxford $30.00
0-345-35942-9 Ballantine pb $14.95

THE NEGRO'S CIVIL WAR: How American Negroes Felt and Acted During the War for the Union
0-252-00949-5 Illinois pb $9.95

STRUGGLE FOR EQUALITY: Abolitionists and the Negro in the Civil War and Reconstruction
0-691-04566-6 Princeton pb $44.50
0-691-00555-9 Princeton pb $14.95

• Roy Nichols & Eugene Berwanger
THE STAKES OF POWER: 1845-1877
0-8090-0151-9 Hill & Wang pb $7.95

• Richard H. Sewell
A HOUSE DIVIDED: Sectionalism and Civil War, 1848-1865
"The North and South may not have been distinct cultures, but by mid-century each section *thought* of itself as possessing a distinct and superior way of life, one shaped most profoundly by the absence or presence of human bondage"—Richard H. Sewell
0-8018-3531-3 Johns Hopkins $29.50
0-8018-3532-1 Johns Hopkins pb $9.95

• Page Smith
TRIAL BY FIRE: A People's History of the Civil War and Reconstruction
0-07-058571-7 McGraw-Hill $29.95

• Edmund Wilson
PATRIOTIC GORE: Studies in the Literature of the American Civil War
Essays whose subjects include Ulysses S. Grant, William T. Sherman, Mary Chesnut, and many others
Foreword by C. Vann Woodward
0-930350-61-8 Northeastern pb $14.95

GENERAL HISTORIES OF THE WAR: 1861-1865

• Bruce Catton
THE CENTENNIAL HISTORY OF THE CIVIL WAR IN THREE VOLUMES
A solid military history, especially in its evaluation of civil and military leaders, written from a somewhat Northern view

Volume 1: Coming Fury
How and why the war began
0-385-09813-8 Doubleday $17.95
0-671-54308-3 Washington Square pb $5.95

Volume 2: Terrible Swift Sword
From the aftermath of First Bull Run to Antietam—the second phase, when men still tried to fight a war of moderation
0-385-02614-5 Doubleday $17.95
0-671-61933-0 Washington Square pb $5.95

Volume 3: Never Call Retreat
From Fredericksburg in the East, Stones River in the West, through Vicksburg, Gettysburg, and Georgia to Appomattox and Lincoln's assassination
0-671-63883-1 Washington Square pb $5.95

William C. Davis, editor
TOUCHED BY FIRE: A Photographic Portrait of the Civil War
0-316-17664-8 Little, Brown $50.00

• Shelby Foote
THE CIVIL WAR: A Narrative
A panoramic military study, slightly biased toward the Confederate viewpoint

Volume 1: Fort Sumter to Perryville
0-394-74623-6 Random House pb $15.95

Volume 2: Fredericksburg to Meridian
0-394-74621-X Random House pb $15.95

Volume 3: Red River to Appomattox
0-394-74622-8 Random House pb $15.95

• Margaret Leech
REVEILLE IN WASHINGTON, 1860-1865
A Pulitzer Prize-winning (1942) history of Washington, DC, during the war
0-88184-254-0 Carroll & Graf pb $11.95

• John MacDonald
GREAT BATTLES OF THE CIVIL WAR
A glorious picture book that uses computer graphics to recreate the great battles
0-02-577300-3 Macmillan $39.95

• Phillip Shaw Paludan
A PEOPLE'S CONTEST: The Union and the Civil War, 1861-1865
Chapters include "Congress and the Capitalists" and "Frankenstein and Everyman: Sherman, Grant, and Modern War"
0-06-015903-0 Harper & Row $27.95

• Walton Rawls, editor
GREAT CIVIL WAR HEROES AND THEIR BATTLES
With over 200 illustrations, 150 in color
0-89659-522-6 Abbeville $45.00

Reference

• Mark M. Boatner III
THE CIVIL WAR DICTIONARY
Over 4000 entries including 2000 biographical sketches, major battles, lesser engagements and skirmishes, weapons, military terms and definitions; 86 specially prepared maps and diagrams; all carefully cross-referenced
0-8129-1689-1 David McKay $29.95

• John S. Bowman, editor
THE CIVIL WAR ALMANAC
0-886-87401-7 St. Martin's pb $14.95

• Patricia L. Faust, editor
HISTORICAL TIMES ILLUSTRATED ENCYCLOPEDIA OF THE CIVIL WAR
0-06-181261-7 Harper & Row $39.95

• E.B. Long with Barbara Long
THE CIVIL WAR DAY BY DAY: An Almanac, 1861-1865
0-306-80255-4 Da Capo pb $19.95

THE GATHERING STORM

"As to the policy I 'seem to be pursuing,' as you say, I have not meant to leave any one in doubt. I would save the Union. I would save it the shortest way under the Constitution. The sooner the national authority can be restored, the nearer the Union will be 'the Union as it was.' If there be those who would not save the Union unless they could at the same time save slavery, I do not agree with them. If there be those who would not save the Union unless they could at the same time destroy slavery, I do not agree with them. My paramount objective in this struggle is to save the Union, and is not either to save or to destroy slavery. If I could save the Union without freeing any slave, I would do it; and if I could save it by freeing some and leaving others alone, I would also do that. What I do about slavery, and the colored race, I do because I believe it helps to save the Union; and what I forbear, I forbear because I do not believe it would help to save the Union."—Abraham Lincoln in a letter to Horace Greeley, editor of the New York *Tribune,* published August 22, 1862

Paul M. Angle, editor
CREATED EQUAL?: The Complete Lincoln-Douglas Debates of 1858
0–226–02085–1 Chicago pb $20.00

Robert W. Johannsen, editor
THE LINCOLN-DOUGLAS DEBATES OF 1858
0–19–500921–5 Oxford pb $11.95

• **David Herbert Donald**
CHARLES SUMNER AND THE COMING OF THE CIVIL WAR
One of the more radical and important early Republican leaders
0–226–15633–8 Chicago pb $12.50

LINCOLN RECONSIDERED: Essays on the Civil War Era
0–394–70190–9 Random House pb $5.95

• **Eric Foner**
FREE SOIL, FREE LABOR, FREE MEN: The Ideology of the Republican Party Before the Civil War
A significant reevaluation of the causes of the war
0–19–501352–2 Oxford pb $8.95

• **George B. Forgie**
PATRICIDE IN THE HOUSE DIVIDED: A Psychological Interpretation of Lincoln and His Age
0–393–00035–4 Norton pb $5.95

• **Oscar & Lillian Handlin**
ABRAHAM LINCOLN AND THE UNION
0–673–39340–2 Scott, Foresman pb $7.95

• **Michael F. Holt**
THE POLITICAL CRISIS OF THE 1850s
0–393–95370–X Norton pb $7.95

The eagle before and after President Buchanan, from an 1861 cartoon in The Image of America in Caricature and Cartoon *by Ron Tyler (Amon Carter Museum)*

• **David M. Potter with Don Fehrenbacher**
THE IMPENDING CRISIS, 1848–1861
An often brilliant political history of the collision of North and South over slavery
0–06–131929–5 Harper & Row pb $12.95

• **Kenneth M. Stampp**
THE CAUSES OF THE CIVIL WAR
Blends the conclusions of historians with the writings of contemporaries. Excerpts from the Lincoln-Douglas debates and vivid commentaries by Horace Greeley, John C. Calhoun, and Jefferson Davis are included in this revised edition
0–671–62237–4 Simon & Schuster pb $6.95

THE IMPERILED UNION: Essays on the Background of the Civil War
The long-standing controversy about the cause and inevitability of the sectional crisis as well as other key questions
0–19–502991–7 Oxford pb $9.95

• **Charles B. Strozier**
LINCOLN'S QUEST FOR UNION: Public and Private Meanings
"It will become *all* one thing," Lincoln wrote in June 1858, "or *all* the other." Strozier balances psychoanalytic insight with rigorous scholarship to trace Lincoln's maturity and to show how "a house divided" referred both to himself and the nation
0–252–01377–8 Illinois pb $9.95

THE CONFEDERACY

• **Clement Eaton**
HISTORY OF THE SOUTHERN CONFEDERACY
0–02–908710–4 Free Press pb $14.95

• **Lacy K. Ford, Jr.**
ORIGINS OF SOUTHERN RADICALISM: The South Carolina Upcountry, 1800–1860
This new study analyzes the circumstances and values of white society in a hotbed of proslavery Southern radicalism
0–19–504422–3 Oxford $39.95

• **Rod Gragg, editor**
THE ILLUSTRATED CONFEDERATE READER
A collection of personal experiences and eyewitness accounts by Southern soldiers and civilians
0–06–015798–4 Harper & Row $27.50

• **Mark E. Neely, Jr. & others**
THE CONFEDERATE IMAGE: Prints of the Lost Cause
The popular lithographs and engravings cherished by Southerners after the Civil War
0–8078–1742–2 North Carolina $32.50
0–8078–4197–8 North Carolina pb $14.95

• **William Robert Taylor**
CAVALIER AND YANKEE: The Old South and American National Character
A highly recommended study
0–674–10440–4 Harvard pb $10.95

• **Emory Thomas**
THE CONFEDERATE NATION, 1861 TO 1865
"A serious, scholarly, readable work . . . that rounds up modern scholarship and offers a fresh and detached view of the whole subject"—C. Vann Woodward, *New Republic*
0–06–131965–1 Harper & Row pb $9.95

• **Frank E. Vandiver**
THEIR TATTERED FLAGS: The Epic of the Confederacy
0–89096–355–X Texas A&M pb $12.95

THE LEADERS

Lincoln

• **Gabor Boritt & Norman O. Forness, editors**
THE HISTORIAN'S LINCOLN: Pseudohistory, Psychohistory and History
Different views of Lincoln and his place in American history
0–252–01527–4 Illinois $24.95

• **LaWanda Cox**
LINCOLN AND BLACK FREEDOM: A Study in Presidential Leadership
An award-winning analysis of Lincoln's objectives and priorities for Reconstruction with special focus on Louisiana, which became a showcase of wartime reconstruction efforts
0–252–01173–2 Illinois pb $8.95

• **Don Fehrenbacher**
PRELUDE TO GREATNESS: Lincoln in the 1850s
0–8047–0119–9 Stanford $20.00
0–8047–0120–2 Stanford pb $7.95

• **William Henry Herndon**
LIFE OF LINCOLN
First published in 1889. "William H. Herndon had a closer acquaintance with his law partner, Abraham Lincoln, and a better understanding of his complex pesonality than any other student ever had. For this reason, for all its limitations, Herndon's *Lincoln* remains a classic—the essential book that any serious student of Abraham Lincoln must read"—David Herbert Donald, Harvard University
0–306–80195–7 Da Capo pb $13.95

 IF YOU CAN'T FIND IT, LOOK IN THE INDEX

Abraham Lincoln

- **Stephen B. Oates**
ABRAHAM LINCOLN: The Man Behind the Myths
0–06–015304–0 Harper & Row $19.95

WITH MALICE TOWARD NONE: The Life of Abraham Lincoln
"An admirable job in portraying Lincoln's life and character, the conquest of his deficiencies and the out-maneuvering of political jackals"—*Publishers Weekly*
0–06–013283–3 Harper & Row $16.95
0–451–62314–2 NAL pb $4.95

- **Benjamin P. Thomas**
ABRAHAM LINCOLN: A Biography
Well-balanced, critical, scholarly
0–394–60468–7 Modern Library $10.95

Earlier in the summer I occasionally saw the President and his wife, toward the latter part of the afternoon, out in a barouche, on a pleasure ride through the city . . . They pass'd me once very close, and I saw the President in the face fully, as they were moving slowly, and his look, though abstracted happen'd to be directed steadily in my eye. He bow'd and smiled, but far beneath his smile I noticed well the expression I have alluded to. None of the artists or pictures has caught the deep, though subtle and indirect expression of this man's face. There is something else there. One of the great painters of two or three centuries ago is needed.

from "Specimen Days" in

Walt Whitman
COMPLETE POETRY AND COLLECTED PROSE
0–940450–02–X Library of America $27.50

Confederates and Yankees

- **T. Harry Williams**
P.G.T. BEAUREGARD: Napoleon in Gray
Though given important commands throughout the war, from Charleston to the Carolinas, the status of a Lee or Jackson somehow eluded "the Hero of Sumter"
0–8071–0831–6 LSU $24.95

- **Michael Ballard**
A LONG SHADOW: Jefferson Davis and the Final Days of the Confederacy
0–87805–295–X Mississippi $22.50

- **Clement Eaton**
JEFFERSON DAVIS: The Sphinx of the Confederacy
A graduate of West Point, Davis was respected for his humane treatment of his slaves. Unfortunately for the South, he neither excelled as a military thinker, nor delegated authority effectively
0–02–908700–7 Free Press $25.95

Ulysses S. Grant
PERSONAL MEMOIRS OF U.S. GRANT
Written as he was dying, Grant's autobiography is a powerful account of his failings and triumphs. Mark Twain called Grant's memoirs "the best of any general's since Caesar"
Introduction by William S. McFeely
0–306–80172–8 Da Capo pb $13.95

- **William S. McFeely**
GRANT: A Biography
Winner of the Pulitzer Prize for biography (1982)
0–393–30046–3 Norton pb $14.95

- **Nancy Scott & Dwight Anderson**
THE GENERALS: Ulysses S. Grant and Robert E. Lee
An engrossing full-scale biography, tracing their lives from childhood to their fateful meeting at Appomattox
0–394–52106–4 Knopf $24.95
0–394–75985–0 Random House pb $12.95

- **James I. Robertson, Jr.**
GENERAL A.P. HILL: The Story of a Confederate Warrior
One of "Lee's Lieutenants," Hill was an excellent subordinate who saw action in every major conflict in the eastern theater
0–394–55257–1 Random House $24.95

- **Frank E. Vandiver**
MIGHTY STONEWALL
A recent biography of General "Stonewall" Jackson
0–89096–384–3 Texas A&M $27.50
0–89096–391–6 Texas A&M pb $13.95

- **Thomas Lee Connelly**
THE MARBLE MAN: Robert E. Lee and His Image in American Society
0–8071–0474–4 LSU pb $9.95

- **Charles Bracelen Flood**
LEE: The Last Years
The story of Lee's efforts to heal the wounds of war
0–395–34637–1 Houghton Mifflin pb $9.95

- **Douglas S. Freeman**
LEE
0–684–17427–8 Scribners pb $18.95

LEE'S LIEUTENANTS: A Study in Command
A history of the war in the East and the Army of North Virginia, including biographies of dozens of high-ranking officers. Its complex appreciation of tactics and strategies makes it a classic study of battle and the issues of command. A 3-volume set
0–684–17926–1 Scribners (set) $90.00

Volume 1: Manassas to Malvern Hill
0–684–18748–5 Scribners pb $16.95

Volume 2: Cedar Mountain to Chancellorsville
0–684–18749–3 Scribners pb $16.95

Volume 3: Gettysburg to Appomattox
0–684–18750–7 Scribners pb $16.95

- **William Piston**
LEE'S TARNISHED LIEUTENANT: James Longstreet and His Place in Southern History
Despite errors at Seven Pines and Second Manassas, Longstreet justified Lee's confidence in him at Antietam and Fredericksburg, but showed little aptitude for independent command
0–8203–0907–9 Georgia $24.95

Robert E. Lee in his house in Richmond eleven days after he surrendered to Grant, from Alistair Cooke's America *(Knopf)*

• Stephen W. Sears

GEORGE B. McCLELLAN: The Young Napoleon

At 35, he commanded all the Northern armies; at 37, he was nominated for the presidency by the Democratic party. McClellan's importance in shaping the cause of the Union during the Civil War was—Sears argues—matched only by Lincoln, Grant, and Sherman

0–89919–264–5 Ticknor & Fields $24.95

• Stephen W. Sears, editor

THE CIVIL WAR PAPERS OF GEORGE B. McCLELLAN: Selected Correspondence, 1860–1865

An as-it-happened narrative, with an appeal extending beyond specialists' interests

0–89919–337–4 Ticknor & Fields $29.95

• Gary W. Gallagher

STEPHEN DODSON RAMSEUR: Lee's Gallant General

Based largely on the letters of a young Confederate officer at war, this is a study of one of the South's most talented commanders

0–8078–1627–2 North Carolina $19.95

• George Green Shackelford

GEORGE WYTHE RANDOLPH AND THE CONFEDERATE ELITE

A grandson of Thomas Jefferson, Randolph became secretary of war in 1862. This study reveals his role in recruiting a technocracy to run the war economy

0–8203–0998–2 Georgia $25.00

• Paul A. Hutton

PHIL SHERIDAN AND HIS ARMY

Though his career got off to a slow start, "Little Phil" proved an audacious and effective commander, breaking the Confederate line at Chattanooga and conducting a devastating campaign along the Shenandoah in '64–'65

0–8032–2329–3 Nebraska $35.50
0–8032–7227–8 Nebraska pb $14.95

• William Tecumseh Sherman

MEMOIRS OF WILLIAM TECUMSEH SHERMAN

"Sherman's story of his march on the South must be one of the most articulate and engrossing ever written by an important general. It creates the appalled suspense of a kind of Grand Guignol horror, as we follow this intrepid and disciplined man, in many ways so sympathetic, going further and further in destructiveness, and recounting the process with the utmost exactitude and without the slightest compunction"—Edmund Wilson

0–306–80213–9 Da Capo pb $13.95

• Emory M. Thomas

BOLD DRAGOON: The Life of J.E.B. Stuart

Combining bravery, panache, and good humor with a thorough professionalism, Stuart dazzled friend and foe with his striking raids and "rides around McClellan"

0–06–015566–3 Harper & Row $22.95
0–394–75775–0 Random House pb $8.95

THE SOLDIERS

• Nat Brandt

THE MAN WHO TRIED TO BURN NEW YORK

Focuses on the trial of Robert Cobb Kennedy, the last Confederate hanged for spying

0–8156–0227–8 Syracuse pb $9.95

• Dudley Taylor Cornish

THE SABLE ARM: Black Troops in the Union Army, 1861–1865

Black soldiers fought in every theater of the war, and by its end they made up one-tenth of the Union army

Foreword by Herman Hattaway

0–7006–0345–X Kansas $25.00
0–7006–0328–X Kansas pb $9.95

• Henry Kyd Douglas

I RODE WITH STONEWALL

Evokes the day-by-day sense of Confederate army life

0–8078–0337–5 North Carolina $19.95

• B.P. Gallaway

THE RAGGED REBEL: A Common Soldier in W.H. Parsons' Texas Cavalry, 1861–1865

A young Texas farmer in the Confederate cavalry

0–292–77024–3 Texas $19.95

• Thomas Wentworth Higginson

ARMY LIFE IN A BLACK REGIMENT

A classic by the preacher-soldier who commanded the First South Carolina, composed of runaway slaves

0–87928–022–0 Corner House $20.00
0–393–30157–5 Norton pb $7.95

• Gerald F. Linderman

EMBATTLED COURAGE: The Experience of Battle in the American Civil War

0–02–919760–0 Free Press $22.50
0–02–919761–9 Free Press pb $11.95

• Reid Mitchell

CIVIL WAR SOLDIERS: Their Expectations and Their Experiences

A fresh use of unpublished sources to recreate the war's immediacy. "I come to the letters and diaries left by Civil War soldiers with the questions I would have asked the writers if they had been alive . . . What was it like to be in battle? Were you frightened; how did you overcome your fear? How did you face death—how did you give meaning to violence and destruction?"

0–670–81742–2 Viking $19.95

• Thomas W. Osborn

THE FIERY TRAIL: A Union Officer's Account of Sherman's Last Campaigns

Foreword by William S. McFeely

0–87049–500–3 Tennessee $22.50

• John Ransom

JOHN RANSOM'S ANDERSONVILLE DIARY

Introduction by Bruce Catton

0–8397–4300–9 Eriksson $16.95
0–425–10554–7 Berkley pb $3.95

"Union Cavalryman" by Winslow Homer (courtesy of The Cooper-Hewitt Museum), from 500 Years of Life in America *by Marshall B. Davidson (Abradale/Abrams)*

• James Robertson, Jr.

SOLDIERS BLUE AND GRAY

An in-depth treatment of Civil War soldier life

0–87249–572–8 South Carolina $24.95

• Kevin H. Siepel

REBEL: The Life and Times of John Singleton Mosby

A guerrilla fighter of the Confederacy. "Decent, solid, popular biography"— *Village Voice*

0–312–01507–0 St. Martin's pb $8.95

• Stephen Z. Starr

THE UNION CAVALRY IN THE CIVIL WAR

The cavalry's transformation from a misused, incompetent branch of the service into the cutting edge of the Union forces

Volume 1: From Fort Sumter to Gettysburg
0–8071–0484–1 LSU $35.00

Volume 2: The War in the East, from Gettysburg to Appomattox, 1863–1865
0–8071–0859–6 LSU $35.00

Volume 3: The War in the West, 1861–1865
0–8071–1209–7 LSU $35.00

• Bell Irvin Wiley

These two classic studies are valuable for their discussion of volunteerism.

THE LIFE OF BILLY YANK: The Common Soldier of the Union
0–8071–0476–0 LSU pb $9.95

THE LIFE OF JOHNNY REB: The Common Soldier of the Confederacy
0–8071–0475–2 LSU pb $9.95

TO ORDER BOOKS AS GIFTS, SEE PAGE 1

E.H. Hampton of the 58th North Carolina wrote the widow of a comrade that her husband had only been wounded in the hand, and that the real cause of his death was the doctor's neglect; "the doctor was very mean to him and did not treat him right." A federal cavalryman told his wife, "When a person is sick in camp they might as well dig a hole and put him in as to take him to one of thee (sic) infernal hells called hospitals." One man in his regiment had died neglected, while nearby hospital attendants played euchre. After the war another soldier vividly remembered a one-eyed man in the ambulance corps who neglected the wounded to rob the dead.

Reid Mitchell
CIVIL WAR SOLDIERS: Their Expectations and Their Experiences
0–670–81742–2 Viking $19.95

THE CIVILIANS

• John R. Brumgardt, editor
CIVIL WAR NURSE: The Diary and Letters of Hannah Ropes
The chief nurse of the Union Hospital in Washington, DC, describes her experiences and comments on notable political personalities
0–87049–280–2 Tennessee $14.50

Mary Chesnut
MARY CHESNUT'S CIVIL WAR
A spirited diary by the wife of a leading South Carolina Confederate
Edited by C. Vann Woodward
0–300–02979–9 Yale pb $16.95

Elisabeth Muhlenfeld
MARY BOYKIN CHESNUT: A Biography
Foreword by C. Vann Woodward
0–8071–0852–9 LSU $27.50

Mary Chesnut

• Gerry van der Heuvel
CROWNS OF THORNS AND GLORY: Mary Todd Lincoln and Varina Howell Davis, The Two First Ladies of the Civil War
Utterly different in many respects and on opposite sides of a war-torn border, they shared private and public pressures that few could comprehend
0–525–24599–5 Dutton $19.95

• Robert Manson Myers
THE CHILDREN OF PRIDE: A True Story of Georgia and the Civil War
Abridged edition of the award-winning collection of letters of a Georgia plantation family; tells of the Old South and its destruction
0–300–04053–9 Yale pb $14.95

• Elizabeth Brown Pryor
CLARA BARTON: Professional Angel
Barton organized an agency for getting medical supplies and care to the soldiers. In 1869 she went to Switzerland as a member of the Red Cross and succeeded in 1882 in having the US sign the Geneva agreement
0–8122–1273–8 Pennsylvania pb $18.95

Theodore Rosengarten
TOMBEE: Portrait of a Cotton Planter with the Journal of Thomas Chaplin
The biography of one of the wealthiest men of antebellum America, interwoven with the complexities of Southern slavery, the Civil War, and emancipation
0–688–05412–9 Morrow $22.95
0–07–053821–2 McGraw-Hill pb $12.95

• John Rozier, editor
THE GRANITE FARM LETTERS: The Civil War Correspondence of Edgeworth and Sallie Bird
The letters of a Georgia plantation family span the entire Civil War era. From Sallie Bird in Gordonsville, Virginia, to her daughter Saida: "I believe if I were a man I would never lay down my arms in this glorious struggle, till the fiendish invader was driven back step-by-step from our soil"
Foreword by Theodore Rosengarten
0–8203–1042–5 Georgia $24.95

• Louis M. Starr
BOHEMIAN BRIGADE
How the Civil War, and the reporters who covered it, created a 19th-century news revolution
0–299–11340–X Wisconsin $35.00
0–299–11344–2 Wisconsin pb $13.50

• Justin G. & Linda Levitt Turner
MARY TODD LINCOLN: Her Life and Letters
A balanced view of an often misunderstood character, presented largely through her own letters. "Most convincing portrait of Mary Todd Lincoln yet written"—*LA Times*
Introduction by Fawn M. Brodie
0–88064–073–1 Fromm pb $12.95

BATTLES AND CAMPAIGNS: The War in the East

Bull Run and the Peninsular Campaign

• Joseph P. Cullen
THE PENINSULAR CAMPAIGN 1862: McClellan and Lee Struggle for Richmond
"In ten days I shall be in Richmond," McClellan boasted in 1862. But Lee emerged as the South's military genius while McClellan, "the Little Napoleon," earned his reputation for procrastination and politicking
0–8117–1220–6 Stackpole pb $3.50

• William C. Davis
BATTLE AT BULL RUN: A History of the First Major Campaign of the Civil War
The first—and what many thought would be the last—conflict of the war shattered the innocence of both victor and vanquished
0–8071–0867–7 LSU pb $9.95

Antietam

• Jay Luvaas & Harold W. Nelson
THE U.S. ARMY WAR COLLEGE GUIDE TO THE BATTLE OF ANTIETAM: The Maryland Campaign of 1862
0–06–097160–6 Harper & Row pb $8.95

• James V. Murfin
THE GLEAM OF BAYONETS: The Battle of Antietam and Robert E. Lee's Maryland Campaign, September 1862
0–8071–0990–8 LSU pb $9.95

• Stephen W. Sears
LANDSCAPE TURNED RED: The Battle of Antietam
McClellan's victory cost him his command, Lee's defeat added to his already shining reputation, and Lincoln had the military success he needed for emancipation
0–89919–172–X Ticknor & Fields $17.95

Gettysburg

• Edwin B. Coddington
THE GETTYSBURG CAMPAIGN: A Study in Command
0–684–18152–5 Scribners $22.95

• Jay Luvaas & Harold W. Nelson
THE U.S. ARMY WAR COLLEGE GUIDE TO THE BATTLE OF GETTYSBURG
0–06–097096–0 Harper & Row pb $8.95

• Harry W. Pfanz
GETTYSBURG: The Second Day
An exhaustive—almost 600 pages—inquiry into the critical engagement of the brutal, decisive battle of the war, by a former military historian at Gettysburg National Park. With 60 illustrations and 13 maps
0–8078–1749–X North Carolina $34.95

William T. Sherman (photo c. 1890 by George Cox, courtesy of The National Portrait Gallery)

The Shenandoah Valley

• Jeffry D. Wert
FROM WINCHESTER TO CEDAR CREEK: The Shenandoah Campaign of 1864
Using regimental histories, diaries, letters, and soldiers' memoirs, Wert traces one of the lesser-known campaigns of the war
0–937339–11–3 South Mountain $22.50
0–671–67806–X Simon & Schuster pb $10.95

Sherman's March

John G. Barrett
SHERMAN'S MARCH THROUGH THE CAROLINAS
"A scholarly and temperate account of a part of the Civil War which even yet can hardly be viewed without emotion"—*NY Times Book Review*
0–8078–0701–X North Carolina pb $19.95

Burke Davis
SHERMAN'S MARCH: The First Full-Length Narration of General William T. Sherman's Devastating March Through Georgia and the Carolinas
Taking off from their victories in Tennessee, the Union forces moved southeast to Atlanta, then north through the Carolinas, to menace Richmond from the south
0–394–75763–7 Random House pb $7.95

Joseph T. Glatthaar
THE MARCH TO THE SEA AND BEYOND: Sherman's Troops in the Savannah and Carolina Campaigns
0–8147–3008–6 NYU pb $10.00

James Lee McDonough & James Pickett Jones
WAR SO TERRIBLE: Sherman and Atlanta
Sherman's troops, 62,000 strong, cut a 60-mile swath of destruction through Georgia, destroying crops, tearing up rails, heating them, and twisting them into "Sherman's hairpins"
0–393–02497–0 Norton $19.95

James Reston, Jr.
SHERMAN'S MARCH AND VIETNAM
A fascinating analysis of Sherman's philosophy and practice of total war
0–02–036360–5 Macmillan pb $10.95

The Road to Appomattox

• Bruce Catton
GRANT TAKES COMMAND
Along with *Grant Moves South* (see below), the best military biography of the war
0–316–13210–1 Little, Brown $25.00

A STILLNESS AT APPOMATTOX
0–671–53143–3 Washington Square pb $5.95

• William A. Frassanito
GRANT AND LEE: The Virginia Campaigns, 1864–1865
Includes contemporary photographs
0–684–18704–3 Scribners pb $13.95

• William G. Robertson
BACK DOOR TO RICHMOND: The Bermuda Hundred Campaign, April–June 1864
0–87413–303–3 Delaware $38.50

• Richard Wheeler
WITNESS TO APPOMATTOX
Eyewitness accounts of the final days of the war
0–06–016078–0 Harper & Row $19.95

BATTLES AND CAMPAIGNS: The War in the West

• Bruce Catton
GRANT MOVES SOUTH
Particularly good on Grant at Vicksburg
0–316–13207–1 Little, Brown $25.00

• Ray C. Colton
THE CIVIL WAR IN THE WESTERN TERRITORIES: Arizona, Colorado, New Mexico, and Utah
The story of a little-known arena
0–8061–1902–0 Oklahoma pb $8.95

• William C. Davis
THE ORPHAN BRIGADE: The Kentucky Confederates Who Couldn't Go Home
0–8071–1077–9 LSU pb $9.95

• Jay Monaghan
CIVIL WAR ON THE WESTERN BORDER, 1854–1865
The bloody first phase of the war began at least six years before the First Bull Run with the conflict between the proslavery elements from Missouri and the New England abolitionists who migrated to Kansas
0–8032–3091–5 Nebraska $35.00
0–8032–8126–9 Nebraska pb $9.95

Shiloh

More Americans fell at Shiloh in two days than in all the battles of the Revolution, the War of 1812, and the Mexican War combined.

• James L. McDonough
SHILOH: In Hell Before Night
"The best book devoted entirely to Shiloh yet to be published"—Thomas Connelly, *Journal of American History*
0–87049–199–7 Tennessee $18.95
0–87049–232–2 Tennessee pb $9.95

• David Miller
THE ROAD TO SHILOH
0–8094–4712–6 Time-Life $19.95

The Battle for Tennessee

Next to Virginia, Tennessee saw more military action than any state during the Civil War.

• Thomas Lee Connelly
ARMY OF THE HEARTLAND: The Army of Tennessee, 1861–1862
0–8071–0404–3 LSU $25.00

AUTUMN OF GLORY: The Army of Tennessee, 1862–1865
0–8071–0445–0 LSU $30.00

CIVIL WAR TENNESSEE
Short, historically accurate, and easy to read
0–87049–261–6 Tennessee pb $3.50

• Larry J. Daniels
CANNONEERS IN GRAY: The Field Artillery of the Army of Tennessee, 1861–1865
The difficulties of artillery warfare in the western theater
0–8173–0203–4 Alabama $21.50

• Stanley F. Horn
THE DECISIVE BATTLE OF NASHVILLE
The battle that ended the Confederacy's last offensive action and removed the Confederate Army of Tennessee from the field as an effective fighting force
0–87049–087–7 Tennessee $14.50

• James Lee McDonough
CHATTANOOGA: A Death Grip on the Confederacy
"More vivid, more human, than can be gathered from a history book chapter or a historical marker"—*Southern Living*
0–87049–425–2 Tennessee $19.95

STONES RIVER: Bloody Winter in Tennessee
"Attractive to any Civil War buff"—Timothy D. Johnson, *Alabama Historian*
0–87049–301–9 Tennessee $18.95
0–87049–373–6 Tennessee pb $9.95

- James Lee McDonough & Thomas Lee Connelly
FIVE TRAGIC HOURS: The Battle of Franklin
In a single day in November 1864, nearly 2000 Confederates lost their lives in a senseless attack against a well-fortified Union position
0–87049–396–5 Tennessee $19.95

Vicksburg

With the garrison reduced to eating rats, Vicksburg fell on July 4, 1863, a day after the end of Gettysburg. Its loss gave Union gunboats control of the Mississippi, and isolated Texas and Arkansas from the Confederacy.

- Earl S. Miers
THE WEB OF VICTORY: Grant at Vicksburg
0–8071–1199–6 LSU pb $9.95

THE WAR AT SEA

- William C. Davis
DUEL BETWEEN THE FIRST IRONCLADS
0–8071–0868–5 LSU pb $9.95

Against the warnings of Seward and the misgivings of Admiral Porter, who accompanied him, Abraham Lincoln arrived by ship in Richmond. When he stepped on the wharf, a dozen joyous Negroes flung themselves at his feet, one white-haired old man exclaiming, "Bless the Lord, the great Messiah!" Lincoln, embarrassed but controlled, replied, "Don't kneel to me. That is not right. You must kneel to God only . . ."

"About four in the afternoon," a Southern woman wrote to her daughter, "a salute of thirty-four guns was fired. A company of mounted dragoons advanced up the street, escorting an open carriage drawn by four horses in which Mr. Lincoln sat and a naval officer, followed by an escort of cavalry. They drove straight to Mr. Davis's house, cheered all the way by Negroes, and returned the way they came. I had a good look at Mr. Lincoln. He seemed tired and old—and I must say, with due respect to the President of the United States, I thought him to be the ugliest man I had ever seen."

Eli N. Evans
JUDAH P. BENJAMIN: The Jewish Confederate
0–02–908880–1 Free Press $24.95

- Charles G. Summersell
CSS ALABAMA: Builder, Captain, and Plans
Built at Liverpool despite Britain's official neutrality, this Confederate raider took 69 Union ships in two years, traveling from Indochina to Cherbourg, before she was sunk by the USS *Kearsarge*
0–8173–0209–3 Alabama $39.50

- Maxine Turner
NAVY GRAY: A Story of the Confederacy Navy on the Chatahoochee and Apalachicola Rivers
In developing ironclad ships and torpedo boats, Confederate planners possessed vision but lacked the means to make their plans succeed on a daily operational level
0–8173–0316–2 Alabama $24.95

THE OUTCOME

- Richard E. Beringer, Herman Hattaway & others
WHY THE SOUTH LOST THE CIVIL WAR
Argues that the erosion of nationalism and morale, more than defeat in battle, led to the South's collapse. "The wholesale desertion that took away 40 percent of the Confederate armies east of the Mississippi in the fall and early winter of 1864–65 showed that, before a full-scale resort to guerrilla warfare loomed as the alternative, a critical number of Confederates had given to the cause all that their commitment warranted"—from the Epilogue
0–8203–0815–3 Georgia $29.95

- David Herbert Donald, editor
WHY THE NORTH WON THE CIVIL WAR
Foreword by U.S. Grant III
0–02–031660–7 Macmillan pb $4.95

- Edward Hagerman
THE AMERICAN CIVIL WAR AND THE ORIGINS OF MODERN WARFARE
The Civil War's commanders had to abandon the Napoleonic tradition and create new forms of tactical organization. Hagerman argues that their armies were the first to confront the full impact of mid-19th-century industrial technology on weapons, trench warfare, and logistics
0–253–30546–2 Indiana $37.50

- William Hanchett
THE LINCOLN MURDER CONSPIRACIES
Debunks the many conspiracy theories that have flourished since Lincoln's assassination
0–252–01361–1 Illinois pb $9.95

- Herman Hattaway & Archer Jones
HOW THE NORTH WON: A Military History of the Civil War
The importance of organization, management, and execution in the winning

Ulysses S. Grant (1864 photo by Matthew Brady, courtesy of The National Portrait Gallery)

of battles, with insights for both the novice and the experienced reader
Illustrated by Jerry Vanderlinde
0–252–00918–5 Illinois $27.50

• William A. Tidwell & others
COME RETRIBUTION: The Confederate Secret Service and the Assassination of Lincoln
New evidence that Lincoln's death emerged from a Confederate plot
0–87805–348–4 Mississippi $17.95

RECONSTRUCTION

• Michael L. Benedict
THE IMPEACHMENT AND TRIAL OF ANDREW JOHNSON
The Republicans failed by a single vote to impeach Lincoln's successor
0–393–09418–9 Norton pb $5.95

• Fawn Brodie
THADDEUS STEVENS, SCOURGE OF THE SOUTH
0–393–00331–0 Norton pb $7.95

• Dan T. Carter
WHEN THE WAR WAS OVER: The Failure of Self-Reconstruction in the South, 1865–1867
0–8071–1204–6 LSU pb $9.95

• Richard Nelson Current
THOSE TERRIBLE CARPETBAGGERS: A Reinterpretation
A revision of the traditional image of the carpetbaggers as evil moneygrubbers, demonstrating that many were highly educated, had served well in the Union army, and, in some cases, brought their own money to help refurbish the war-torn South
0–19–504872–5 Oxford $24.95

• David Herbert Donald
THE POLITICS OF RECONSTRUCTION, 1863–1867
"Calling for a 'fresh general approach to the entire Reconstruction era,' he

undertakes to employ 'techniques more frequently used in behavioral sciences' in an analysis of Republican factionalism in the House of Representatives"—C. Vann Woodward
0–674–68953–4 Harvard pb $5.95

• W.E.B. DuBois
THE SOULS OF BLACK FOLK
The second chapter of DuBois' famous work focuses on a history of the Reconstruction era "so far as it relates to the American Negro"
0–396–07757–9 Dodd, Mead $10.95
0–451–51953–1 NAL pb $3.95

Eric Foner
RECONSTRUCTION: America's Unfinished Revolution, 1863–1877
"With this book, Mr. Foner becomes the pre-eminent historian of Reconstruction"—William S. McFeely. Winner of the Los Angeles Times Book Award
0–06–015851–4 Harper & Row $29.95
0–06–091453–X Harper & Row pb $14.95

• Gaines M. Foster
GHOSTS OF THE CONFEDERACY: Defeat, the Lost Cause, and the Emergence of the New South
Argues that, contrary to folklore, Southerners accepted their loss, embraced reunification, and helped to foster sectional reconciliation
0–19–505420–2 Oxford pb $10.95

• Eric L. McKitrick
ANDREW JOHNSON AND RECONSTRUCTION
Challenges the long-standing idea of Johnson as a misunderstood statesman, arguing that he was a small-minded, vindictive, stubborn man whose rigid determination to defy Northern majority opinion thwarted the postwar reunion of North and South
0–19–505707–4 Oxford pb $13.95

• Michael Perman
EMANCIPATION AND RECONSTRUCTION, 1862–1879
The attempt to establish a two-party political system in the South. Suggests that the key to Reconstruction politics can be found in the factions that developed within the two parties
0–88295–836–4 Harlan Davidson pb $9.50

THE ROAD TO REDEMPTION: Southern Politics, 1869–1879
0–8078–1526–8 North Carolina $29.50
0–8078–4141–2 North Carolina pb $7.95

• Kenneth M. Stampp
THE ERA OF RECONSTRUCTION: 1865–1877
Discards many popular notions, arguing that the radical governments—despite their shortcomings—were more democratic than any the South had known; that their record included a substantial list of achievements, and that "scalawag" and "carpetbagger" are not altogether justified terms
0–394–70388–X Random House pb $5.50

• Daniel E. Sutherland
THE CONFEDERATE CARPETBAGGERS
The story of the Confederate expatriates who settled in Northern and Midwestern cities to recoup their shattered fortunes
0–8071–1470–7 LSU pb $16.95

• C. Vann Woodward
ORIGINS OF THE NEW SOUTH, 1877–1913
A Brancroft Prize winner
0–8071–0019–6 LSU pb $9.95

US History since 1877

• Gabriel Kolko
MAIN CURRENTS IN MODERN AMERICAN HISTORY
A New Left viewpoint on the years since the Civil War
0–394–72512–3 Pantheon pb $11.50

• Walter LaFeber & others
THE AMERICAN CENTURY: A History of the United States since the 1890s
0–394–35116–9 Knopf pb $22.95

• Arthur S. Link
AMERICAN EPOCH: A History of the United States since 1900
A solid textbook introduction to the period, updated since it first appeared in 1955

Volume 1
0–394–36204–7 Knopf $18.50

Volume 2
0–394–36205–5 Knopf $18.50

Remains of a plantation house near Fredericksburg (*photo courtesy of The Library of Congress*), *from* Battle Cry of Freedom *by James M. McPherson* (*Oxford*)

➤ **FOR OVERSEAS ORDERING INFORMATION, SEE PAGE 1**

• Tom Tiede
AMERICAN TAPESTRY: Eyewitness Accounts of the Twentieth Century
An oral history that includes a witness at the Scopes trial, the first man to detonate an atomic bomb, and the first woman to vote
0–88687–359–2 Pharos $19.95

THE GILDED AGE AND THE PROGRESSIVE ERA

Once, historians neatly divided the period from the end of Reconstruction to World War I: a corrupt "Gilded Age" in the late 19th century, replete with greedy robber-baron industrialists and corrupt politicians, was followed around 1900 by a generation-long "Progressive Era," marked by crusading reformism and good government. In recent years, the dividing line has been blurred. The Gilded Age no longer seems so simplistic; reform clearly began before the turn of the century. And something called "Progressivism" may never have existed at all.

▶ **For books about immigration in this period, see American People and Places**

• Kenneth D. Ackerman
THE GOLD RING: Jim Fisk, Jay Gould, and Black Friday 1869
0–396–09065–6 Dodd, Mead $21.95

• Jane Addams
TWENTY YEARS AT HULL HOUSE
The most famous settlement house, founded in Chicago in 1889
0–451–51955–8 Signet pb $3.95

• Louis Auchincloss
THE VANDERBILT ERA: Profiles of a Gilded Age
0–684–19112–1 Scribners $19.95

• William Bronson
THE EARTH SHOOK, THE SKY BURNED: A Moving Record of America's Great Earthquake and Fire, San Francisco, April 18, 1906
0–87701–389–6 Chronicle pb $12.95

• Sean Dennis Cashman
AMERICA IN THE GILDED AGE: From the Death of Lincoln to the Rise of Theodore Roosevelt
Personalities and events in the age of industry, immigration, urbanization, and the politics of Reconstruction and Populism
0–8147–1418–8 NYU pb $17.50

AMERICA IN THE AGE OF THE TITANS
An interdisciplinary journey through the Progressive Era
0–8147–1411–0 NYU pb $17.50

Andrew Carnegie on the cover of "Life" in 1905 (courtesy of The National Portrait Gallery)

• Lawrence Goodwyn
THE POPULIST MOMENT: A Short History of the Agrarian Revolt in America
An abridged version of Goodwyn's massive *Democratic Promise*; a major reinterpretation of the most important reform movement of the late 19th century
0–19–502417–6 Oxford pb $9.95

• John Steele Gordon
THE SCARLET WOMAN OF WALL STREET: Jay Gould, Jim Fisk, Cornelius Vanderbilt, and the Erie Railway Wars
1–55584–212–7 Weidenfeld & Nicolson $22.95

• Lewis L. Gould
REFORM AND REGULATION: American Politics from Roosevelt to Wilson
0–394–35413–3 Knopf pb $12.00

• Richard Hofstadter
THE AGE OF REFORM: From Bryan to F.D.R.
A classic, Pulitzer Prize-winning (1956) work
0–394–41442–X Knopf $16.95
0–394–70095–3 Random House pb $5.95

SOCIAL DARWINISM IN AMERICAN THOUGHT
A major analysis of the social philosophies of the intellectual movements of the Gilded Age and Progressive Era
0–8070–5461–5 Beacon pb $10.95

• Gabriel Kolko
THE TRIUMPH OF CONSERVATISM: A Reinterpretation of American History, 1900–1916
Argues that Progressivism was a profoundly conservative effort to maintain existing political and social relations in a new economic context
0–02–916650–0 Free Press pb $11.95

• David Lowe, editor
THE GREAT CHICAGO FIRE IN EYEWITNESS ACCOUNTS AND SIXTY-THREE CONTEMPORARY PHOTOGRAPHS AND ILLUSTRATIONS
0–486–23771–0 Dover pb $5.95

David McCullough
McCullough's epic style brings to life the dramatic stories often shunned by academic historians. The following volumes cover the tremendous engineering feats of the Panama Canal and Brooklyn Bridge, a disastrous flood, and the boyhood of one of the century's most colorful presidents.
THE GREAT BRIDGE: The Epic Story of the Building of the Brooklyn Bridge
A classic account of one of the greatest engineering feats of all time
0–671–45711–X Simon & Schuster pb $14.95

THE JOHNSTOWN FLOOD
More than 2000 people were killed on May 31, 1889, when a dam built to create a lake for an exclusive summer resort collapsed
0–671–20714–8 Simon & Schuster pb $8.95

MORNINGS ON HORSEBACK
A biography of the young Teddy Roosevelt
0–671–44754–8 Simon & Schuster pb $12.95

THE PATH BETWEEN THE SEAS: The Creation of the Panama Canal, 1870–1914
The best-selling account of the elaborate construction effort and political history of the canal
0–671–24409–4 Simon & Schuster pb $13.95

• Michael E. McGerr
THE DECLINE OF POPULAR POLITICS, 1865–1928
"The transformation from popular to elitist politics . . . [An] essential [book] about changes in American political behavior during the late 19th and early 20th centuries"—*Pennsylvania Magazine of History and Biography*
0–19–503682–4 Oxford $24.95

• George E. Mowry
THE ERA OF THEODORE ROOSEVELT AND THE BIRTH OF MODERN AMERICA: 1900–1912
0–06–133022–1 Harper & Row pb $10.95

• Nell Irvin Painter
STANDING AT ARMAGEDDON: The United States, 1877–1919
A history of politics and labor that pays due attention to the dispossessed, including the working class, women, and blacks
0–393–02405–9 Norton $25.00
0–393–30588–0 Norton pb $9.95

• Jacob Riis
HOW THE OTHER HALF LIVES
The tenements of turn-of-the-century New York
0–674–41006–8 Harvard $16.50
0–486–22012–5 Dover pb $9.95

• Milton Rugoff
AMERICA'S GILDED AGE: Intimate Portraits from an Era of Extravagance and Change, 1850–1890
0–8050–0852–7 Henry Holt $24.95

• **Carroll Smith-Rosenberg**
DISORDERLY CONDUCT: Visions of Gender in Victorian America
How and why male-female relations, families, sex, and social custom changed as the US embarked on industrialization
0–394–53545–6 Knopf $19.95
0–19–504039–2 Oxford pb $9.95

• **John G. Sproat**
THE BEST MEN: Liberal Reformers in the Gilded Age
0–226–76990–9 Chicago pb $9.95

• **Lincoln Steffens**
THE AUTOBIOGRAPHY OF LINCOLN STEFFENS, Volume 2
Steffens' famous articles on corruption in America's big cities first appeared in *McClure's* in 1902. Volume 1 is out of print
0–15–609396–0 HBJ pb $9.95

• **Alan Trachtenberg**
THE INCORPORATION OF AMERICA: Culture and Society in the Gilded Age
0–8090–014504 Hill & Wang pb $6.95

• **Harvey Wasserman**
HARVEY WASSERMAN'S HISTORY OF THE UNITED STATES
0–941423–10–7 4 Walls 8 Windows pb $6.95

• **Richard Samuel West**
SATIRE ON STONE: The Political Cartoons of Joseph Keppler
America's leading political cartoonist of the 1880s; includes reproductions of 170 cartoons, many republished for the first time
Foreword by Jim Borgman
0–252–01497–9 Illinois $39.95

• **Robert H. Wiebe**
THE SEARCH FOR ORDER: 1877–1920
A provocative argument about the transformation of America from a collection of isolated "island communities" at the end of Reconstruction into a centralized, bureaucratized organizational society by the First World War
0–8090–0104–7 Hill & Wang pb $7.95

THE SEGMENTED SOCIETY: An Introduction to the Meaning of America
0–19–502006–5 Oxford pb $5.95

The Sporting Society

"Every other form of entertainment revealed the same quality of commercialization. Sport, even 'amateur' competition, became big business. Professional baseball teams played to capacity crowds, and so too did boxers and wrestlers. Intercollegiate football attracted millions of spectators, and high-school basketball tournaments became events of statewide importance. Few Americans saw any connection between the exaltation of competitive sports and the low standards of public education."—Samuel Eliot Morison, Henry Steele Commager & William E. Leuchtenburg in *The Growth of the American Republic* (Volume 2)

Eliot Asinof
EIGHT MEN OUT: The Black Sox and the 1919 World Series
The Black Sox scandal of 1919 tarnished one of America's most cherished institutions
0–8050–0346–0 Henry Holt pb $9.95

Michael T. Isenberg
JOHN L. SULLIVAN AND HIS AMERICA
How an outlaw in an outlawed sport became one of America's first national celebrities; as much a history of national culture in the Gilded Age as a story of a boxing hero
0–252–01381–6 Illinois $24.95

THE ROAD TO WORLD POWER

• **Robert L. Beisner**
TWELVE AGAINST EMPIRE: The Anti-Imperialists, 1898–1900
The leaders of the protest against the Spanish-American War, including William James, Charles Eliot Norton, Andrew Carnegie, and Benjamin Harrison
0–226–04171–9 Chicago pb $9.95

• **Walter LaFeber**
THE NEW EMPIRE: An Interpretation of American Expansion, 1860–1898
0–8014–9048–0 Cornell pb $10.95

THE PANAMA CANAL: The Crisis in Historical Perspective
0–19–502360–9 Oxford $24.95
0–19–502511–3 Oxford pb $8.95

• **Gerald F. Linderman**
THE MIRROR OF WAR: American Society and the Spanish-American War
0–472–57500–7 Michigan pb $12.95

• **H. Wayne Morgan**
AMERICA'S ROAD TO EMPIRE: The War with Spain and Overseas Expansion
0–394–34198–8 Random House pb $8.95

• **G.J.A. O'Toole**
THE SPANISH WAR: An American Epic, 1898
Narrative history of the turning point that ended an era of isolation and inaugurated a

William Howard Taft, the first US civilian governor of the Philippines, from In Our Image: America's Empire in the Philippines *by Stanley Karnow (Random House)*

---

system of alliances and spheres of influence whose legacy is still felt
0–393–30304–7 Norton pb $7.95

• **Richard E. Welch, Jr.**
RESPONSE TO IMPERIALISM: The United States and the Philippine-American War, 1899–1902
0–8078–4177–3 North Carolina pb $9.95

World War I

America's brief involvement in World War I resulted in considerably fewer casualties than those suffered by Europe, but the war had a powerful impact. The books below describe both the horrors of combat and the social changes that swept the nation.

• **Edward M. Coffman**
THE WAR TO END ALL WARS: The American Military Experience in World War I
Vividly recounts the short but often horrifying experience of US soldiers
0–299–10964–X Wisconsin pb $12.50

• **Robert H. Ferrell**
WOODROW WILSON AND WORLD WAR I: 1917–1921
A good general history, particularly strong on the logistics of the war effort
0–06–091216–2 Harper & Row pb $8.95

• **Ross Gregory**
THE ORIGINS OF AMERICAN INTERVENTION IN THE FIRST WORLD WAR
0–393–09980–6 Norton pb $6.95

David M. Kennedy
OVER HERE: The First World War and American Society
A wide-ranging social history covering such topics as the repression of dissent; the special implications of the war for intellectuals, blacks, and workers; and the quality of Wilson's presidential leadership
0–19–502729–9 Oxford $27.50
0–19–503209–8 Oxford pb $9.95

• **N. Gordon Levin**
WOODROW WILSON AND WORLD POLITICS: America's Response to War and Revolution
0–19–500803–0 Oxford pb $10.95

• **Paul L. Murphy**
WORLD WAR I AND THE ORIGIN OF CIVIL LIBERTIES IN THE UNITED STATES
How the prosecution of more than 2000 cases under the Espionage and Sedition Acts led to a new and widespread movement to protect civil liberties
0–393–95012–3 Norton pb $7.95

• **Walton Rawls**
WAKE UP, AMERICA!: World War I and the American Poster
A glorious coffee-table book filled with reproductions of the posters that captured the American imagination
Foreword by Maurice Richards
0–89659–888–8 Abbeville $49.95

- Barbara W. Tuchman
THE ZIMMERMANN TELEGRAM
How and why the US entered the war
0–345–32425–0 Ballantine pb $7.95

- Neil A. Wynn
FROM PROGRESSIVISM TO PROSPERITY: World War I And American Society
A British historian's analysis of how World War I pushed America into the 20th century
0–8419–1107–X Holmes & Meier pb $19.95

THE ROARING TWENTIES

Although the decade still appears flashy and excessive, it is now more commonly seen as a bridge between the Progressive Era and the New Deal—perhaps because of the ongoing rehabilitation of Herbert Hoover, a more compelling figure than he appeared in traditional views.

- Frederick Lewis Allen
ONLY YESTERDAY: An Informal History of the 1920s
A classic, first published in 1931
0–06–080004–6 Harper & Row pb $5.95

- John Brooks
ONCE IN GOLCONDA: A True Drama of Wall Street, 1920–38
0–525–48166–4 Dutton pb $11.95

- Paul A. Carter
THE TWENTIES IN AMERICA
0–88295–717–1 Harlan Davidson pb $8.50

- Norman Clark
DELIVER US FROM EVIL: An Interpretation of American Prohibition
0–393–09170–8 Norton pb $6.95

THE DRY YEARS
0–295–96466–9 Washington pb $12.95

- Paula S. Fass
THE DAMNED AND THE BEAUTIFUL: American Youth in the 1920s
The explosive changes that took place as the Roaring Twenties broke with Victorian traditions
0–19–502492–3 Oxford pb $11.95

- Ray Ginger
SIX DAYS OR FOREVER?: Tennessee vs. John Thomas Scopes
The full story of the "Monkey Trial" of 1925
0–19–519784–4 Oxford pb $8.95

- Isabel Leighton
THE ASPIRIN AGE, 1919–1941
0–671–20062–3 Simon & Schuster pb $12.95

- Geoffrey Perret
AMERICA IN THE TWENTIES: A History
Emphasizes the '20s not as roaring but as the decade of the Klan, the Wobblies, Sacco and Vanzetti, the Scopes trial, and Teapot Dome
0–671–25108–2 Simon & Schuster pb $9.95

Marathon dancing in Venice, California, early 1920s, from Los Angeles: An Illustrated History *by Bruce Henstell (Knopf)*

- Robert Sobel
THE GREAT BULL MARKET: Wall Street in the 1920s
0–393–09817–6 Norton pb $6.95

Marion Frankfurter & others, editors
LETTERS OF SACCO AND VANZETTI
0–8065–0894–9 Lyle Stuart pb $8.95

William Young & David E. Kaiser
POSTMORTEM: New Evidence in the Case of Sacco and Vanzetti
0–87023–479–X Massachusetts pb $10.95

THE GREAT DEPRESSION AND THE NEW DEAL

- James Agee & Walker Evans
LET US NOW PRAISE FAMOUS MEN
The classic portrait of America's southern tenant farmers at the nadir of the Great Depression, with text by Agee and photographs by Evans
0–395–48901–6 Houghton Mifflin $24.95
0–395–48897–4 Houghton Mifflin pb $12.95

- Dale Maharidge & Michael Williamson
AND THEIR CHILDREN AFTER THEM
Author Maharidge and photographer Williamson spent three years tracking down the original subjects (and their descendants) of *Let Us Now Praise Famous Men*. Includes 95 black-and-white photos
0–394–57766–3 Pantheon $22.95

- Frederick Lewis Allen
SINCE YESTERDAY—THE 1930s IN AMERICA: September 3, 1929 to September 3, 1939
Another classic, from 1939. "Conveys the impression of the American people telling their own story in autobiographical form"—*NY Times*
0–06–091322–3 Harper & Row pb $8.95

The Federal Writers' Project

Ann Banks, editor
FIRST PERSON AMERICA
Many of the nation's finest young writers interviewed ordinary Americans for the Federal Writers' Project; this sampling offers a rewarding glimpse of America during the Depression and the era of World War II
0–394–74796–8 Random House pb $6.50

Archie Hobson, editor
REMEMBERING AMERICA: A Sampler of the WPA Guide Series
The Federal Writers' Project put thousands of people to work to create a portrait of everyday life. Here are over 500 passages of folklore, local history, social commentary, and humor, taken from the original American Guide series of travel books
0–02–033280–7 Macmillan pb $11.95

Geoffrey O'Gara
A LONG ROAD HOME: A Journey Through Today's America with the 1930s American Guides
Retraces the steps of the writers who contributed to the American Guide series in the '30s to see what has become of their America
0–393–0264–3 Norton $18.95

• Anthony Badger
THE NEW DEAL: The Depression Years, 1933–1940
0–8090–7260–2 Farrar, Straus & Giroux $19.95
0–374–52174–3 Farrar, Straus & Giroux pb $9.95

• Robert Bendiner
JUST AROUND THE CORNER: A Highly Selective History of the Thirties
Fred Allen, John L. Lewis, Huey Long, Father Coughlin, Fiorello La Guardia, Mae West, and others
0–525–48273–3 Dutton pb $10.95

• Irving Bernstein
A CARING SOCIETY: The New Deal, the Worker and the Great Depression
0–395–33116–1 Houghton Mifflin $22.95

• Alan Brinkley
VOICES OF PROTEST: Huey Long, Father Coughlin and the Great Depression
Two major demagogues and their genius for voicing—and manipulating—the needs and hopes of ordinary people ruined by the Depression
0–394–71628–0 Random House pb $8.95

• Robert Dallek
FRANKLIN D. ROOSEVELT AND AMERICAN FOREIGN POLICY, 1932–1945
The first full-scale history of American diplomacy during the Roosevelt presidency
0–19–502457–5 Oxford $39.95
0–19–502894–5 Oxford pb $12.95

• Kenneth S. Davis
FDR: The New Deal Years, 1933–1937
An excellent synthesis
0–394–52753–4 Random House $29.50

• John A. Garraty
THE GREAT DEPRESSION
The author, an historian at Columbia University, puts the Depression in its worldwide context
0–15–136903–8 HBJ $17.95

• Steve Fraser & Gary Gerstle, editors
THE RISE AND FALL OF THE NEW DEAL ORDER, 1930–1980
Essays that "demonstrate afresh how the New Deal continues to influence twentieth-century American politics and political economy"—Jordan A. Schwarz
0–691–04761–8 Princeton $25.00

• Ludovic Kennedy
THE AIRMAN AND THE CARPENTER: The Lindbergh Kidnapping and the Framing of Richard Hauptmann
The Lindbergh kidnapping and murder was one of the biggest news stories of the decade
0–670–80606–4 Viking $18.95
0–14–008994–2 Penguin pb $7.95

• Joseph P. Lash
DEALERS AND DREAMERS: A New Look at the New Deal
By the author of *Eleanor and Franklin*
0–385–18716–5 Doubleday $24.95

North Dakota, 1937, by Russell Lee, from First Person America: Eighty Life History Narratives Collected by the Federal Writer's Project *edited by Ann Banks*

• William E. Leuchtenburg
FRANKLIN D. ROOSEVELT AND THE NEW DEAL, 1932–1940
After 25 years still the best one-volume account of the period
0–06–133025–6 Harper & Row pb $7.95

IN THE SHADOW OF FDR: From Harry Truman to Ronald Reagan
"Shrewdly sets forth the special cruelty of the dilemma Roosevelt's successors have all faced: 'If he did not walk in FDR's footsteps, he ran the risk of having it said that he was not a Roosevelt but a Hoover. Yet to the extent that he did copy FDR, he lost any chance of marking out his own claim to recognition' "—*NY Times Book Review*
0–8014–9303–X Cornell pb $8.95

THE PERILS OF PROSPERITY
Entertaining and highly recommended account of the transformation of America from a decentralized, agrarian nation into the urban, industrialized capital of the world
0–226–47369–4 Chicago pb $8.50

• Robert S. McElvaine
THE GREAT DEPRESSION: America, 1929–1941
A comprehensive narrative account of all aspects of the Depression
0–8129–6343–1 Times Books pb $9.95

• Robert S. McElvaine, editor
DOWN AND OUT IN THE GREAT DEPRESSION: Letters from the Forgotten Man
0–8078–4099–8 North Carolina pb $9.95

• Dr. Ben L. Reitman, editor
BOXCAR BERTHA: An Autobiography
The lowlife misadventures of the famed vagabond of the 1930s
0–941693–06–6 Amok Press pb $7.95

• Albert U. Romasco
THE POLITICS OF RECOVERY: Roosevelt's New Deal
Explores conflict within the administration, changing attitudes of business towards the New Deal, the NRA, relief policy, and FDR's changing political goals
0–19–503248–9 Oxford $24.95

THE POVERTY OF ABUNDANCE: Hoover, the Nation, the Depression
How American leaders, following Hoover's suggestions, tried to master the economic collapse
0–19–500760–3 Oxford pb $7.95

• Arthur M. Schlesinger, Jr.
THE AGE OF ROOSEVELT
Schlesinger halted this admiring work after three volumes

THE CRISIS OF THE OLD ORDER
0–395–48903–2 Houghton Mifflin pb $11.95

THE COMING OF THE NEW DEAL
0–395–48905–9 Houghton Mifflin pb $11.95

THE POLITICS OF UPHEAVAL
0–395–48904–0 Houghton Mifflin pb $11.95

• Harvard Sitkoff, editor
FIFTY YEARS LATER: The New Deal Evaluated
0–394–33548–1 Knopf pb $11.95

• Joseph E. Stevens
HOOVER DAM: An American Adventure
Nearly 5000 workers toiled around the clock through the worst years of the Depression to build the dam that would harness the Colorado River and transform the West
0–8061–2115–7 Oklahoma $24.95

• Studs Terkel
HARD TIMES: An Oral History of the Great Depression
0–394–74691–0 Pantheon pb $8.95

► For books on the American experience in World War II, see The Second World War

---

 IF YOU CAN'T FIND IT, LOOK IN THE INDEX

1945 TO THE PRESENT: The "American Century"

In 1941 Henry Luce, the founder of *Time*, called on a powerful United States to become "the Good Samaritan of the entire world," and proclaimed this the "American Century."

- **Stephen Ambrose**
  RISE TO GLOBALISM: American Foreign Policy since 1938
  The fifth edition includes analyses of SDI, the Iran-Contra affair, the Nicaraguan revolution, international terrorism, superpower summits, and other recent developments
  0–14–022826–8 Penguin pb $8.95

- **William Henry Chafe**
  THE UNFINISHED JOURNEY: America since World War II
  Highlights the paradoxes of postwar reform and reaction, and shows how things might have been different
  0–19–503639–5 Oxford $35.00
  0–19–503640–9 Oxford pb $16.95

- **John Patrick Diggins**
  THE PROUD DECADES: America in War and Peace, 1941–1960
  This portrait of a triumphant America gives "the overview we have needed of that mid-century shift that changed the course of American life—even before we entered the Sixties"—Walter LaFeber
  0–393–02548–9 Norton $19.95

- **James Gilbert**
  ANOTHER CHANCE: Postwar America, 1945–1968
  Edited by R. Jackson Wilson
  0–87722–224–X Temple $29.95

- **Otis L. Graham, Jr.**
  TOWARD A PLANNED SOCIETY: From Roosevelt to Nixon
  The beginnings and development of national growth policies and machinery
  0–19–502181–9 Oxford pb $8.95

Patton, Eisenhower, and US servicemen in Germany, 1945, from The American Century *by Walter LaFeber and others (Knopf)*

- **Godfrey Hodgson**
  AMERICA IN OUR TIME: From World War II to Nixon—What Happened and Why
  0–394–72517–4 Random House pb $14.50

- **Jonathan Kwitny**
  ENDLESS ENEMIES: The Making of an Unfriendly World
  0–14–008093–7 Penguin pb $8.95

- **William Manchester**
  THE GLORY AND THE DREAM: A Narrative History of America, 1932–1972
  "This fluent, likable, can't-put-it-down narrative history of America from the Bonus Army to Watergate is popular history in our special tradition"—Alfred Kazin, *NY Times Book Review*
  0–553–34589–3 Bantam pb $17.95

- **Frederick F. Siegel**
  TROUBLED JOURNEY: From Pearl Harbor to Ronald Reagan
  A survey of American political life, focusing on the still-unresolved legacy of the New Deal
  0–8090–0155–1 Hill & Wang pb $9.95

I.F. Stone
A NONCONFORMIST HISTORY OF OUR TIMES
The late editor of *I.F. Stone's Weekly*—founded as a dissenting voice at the height of the McCarthy era—was one of the most enduring fixtures of American radical journalism. The books below comprise the best of Stone's essays, articles, and columns from a variety of publications.

THE WAR YEARS, 1939–1945
0–316–81771–6 Little, Brown $18.95

THE HIDDEN HISTORY OF THE KOREAN WAR, 1950–1951
0–316–81773–2 Little, Brown $17.95
0–316–81770–8 Little, Brown pb $8.95

THE TRUMAN ERA, 1945–1952
0–316–81761–9 Little, Brown $17.95
0–316–81772–4 Little, Brown pb $8.95

THE HAUNTED FIFTIES, 1953–1963
0–316–81764–3 Little, Brown $19.95

IN A TIME OF TORMENT, 1961–1967
0–316–81762–7 Little, Brown $19.95
0–316–81750–3 Little, Brown pb $9.95

- **Theodore H. White**
  AMERICA IN SEARCH OF ITSELF: The Making of the President, 1956–1980
  A summation of White's presidential series, tracing the evolution of postwar society
  0–446–37098–3 Warner pb $9.95

THE TRUMAN AND EISENHOWER YEARS

- **Stephen E. Ambrose**
  EISENHOWER

  Volume 1: Soldier, General of the Army, President-Elect, 1890–1952
  0–671–44069–1 Simon & Schuster $24.95

  Volume 2: The President
  0–671–49901–7 Simon & Schuster $24.95

- **Robert Donovan**
  CONFLICT AND CRISIS: The Presidency of Harry S. Truman, 1945–1948
  A veteran Washington correspondent on Truman's first administration
  0–393–00924–6 Norton pb $11.95

  TUMULTUOUS YEARS: The Presidency of Harry S. Truman, 1949–1953
  0–393–30164–8 Norton pb $9.95

- **Eric F. Goldman**
  THE CRUCIAL DECADE AND AFTER: America, 1945–1960
  0–394–70183–6 Random House pb $4.95

- **Fred I. Greenstein**
  THE HIDDEN-HAND PRESIDENCY: Eisenhower as Leader
  0–465–02951–5 Basic Books pb $10.95

- **William L. O'Neill**
  AMERICAN HIGH: The Years of Confidence, 1945–1960
  0–02–923679–7 Free Press pb $9.95

The Cold War

▶ See also International Relations, American Politics and Foreign Policy & Russian and Soviet Studies

- **Gar Alperovitz**
  ATOMIC DIPLOMACY: Hiroshima to Potsdam
  A revisionist history that argues that the reason for bombing Hiroshima and Nagasaki was less to defeat the Japanese than to "make the Russians more manageable"
  0–14–00–8337–5 Penguin pb $8.95

- **Michael R. Beschloss**
  MAYDAY: Eisenhower, Khrushchev and the U-2 Affair
  "Enough new material and insight to command the attention of serious scholars"—*Foreign Affairs*
  0–006–091407–6 Harper & Row pb $8.95

- **McGeorge Bundy**
  DANGER AND SURVIVAL: Choices About the Bomb in the First Fifty Years
  A highly praised history, from the discovery of fission in 1938 to the summits of 1988
  0–394–52278–8 Random House $24.95

- **Robert A. Divine**
  EISENHOWER AND THE COLD WAR
  How Ike shaped the nation's foreign policy during eight critical years
  0–19–502824–4 Oxford pb $7.95

- **Herbert Feis**
  THE ATOMIC BOMB AND THE END OF WORLD WAR II
  0–691–01057–9 Princeton pb $8.95

- **Fraser J. Harbutt**
  THE IRON CURTAIN: Churchill, America and the Origins of the Cold War
  0–19–503817–7 Oxford $24.95

● Walter LaFeber
AMERICA, RUSSIA, AND THE COLD WAR: 1945–1984
0–394–34391–3 Knopf pb $13.50

● Thomas G. Paterson
ON EVERY FRONT: The Making of the Cold War
0–393–95014–X Norton pb $6.95

● Michael Schaller
THE AMERICAN OCCUPATION OF JAPAN: The Origins of the Cold War in Asia
Argues that the reconstruction of postwar Japan shaped not only that country's future but also US policy throughout postwar Asia, leading up to the interventions in China, Korea, and Vietnam
0–19–503626–3 Oxford $24.95

The Korean War

Historians have recently shown a revival of interest in the Korean War. Several detailed accounts chronicle the first major conflict of the Cold War, which took more than three million Korean and 30,000 American lives.

● Clay Blair
THE FORGOTTEN WAR: America in Korea, 1950–1953
A voluminous, detailed military history
0–8129–1670–0 Times Books $29.95

● Jon Halliday
KOREA: The Unknown War
An illustrated companion to the television series
0–394–55366–7 Pantheon $19.95

● Max Hastings
THE KOREAN WAR
0–671–66834–X Simon & Schuster pb $10.95

● Burton Kaufman
THE KOREAN WAR
0–394–34154–6 Knopf pb $10.50

● Donald Knox
THE KOREAN WAR: Pusan to Chosin, An Oral History
The first six months, told almost entirely in the words of American participants
0–15–147288–2 HBJ $24.95

THE KOREAN WAR: Uncertain Victory
The second volume of Knox's oral history
Additional text by Alfred Coppel
0–15–1147289–0 HBJ $29.95

● John W. Spanier
THE TRUMAN-MACARTHUR CONTROVERSY AND THE KOREAN WAR
0–393–00279–9 Norton pb $7.95

● James L. Stokesbury
A SHORT HISTORY OF THE KOREAN WAR
A brief introduction for the layman. "Enough battle detail to produce a flesh-and-blood book, not just a diplomatic and strategic overview"—Harry Levins, *St. Louis Post-Dispatch*
0–688–06377–2 Morrow $18.95

The McCarthy Era

More than 30 years after his death, McCarthy has few admirers, but the abiding questions of his era—the morality of informing, the threat of native radicalism, the persecution of Communist sympathizers, the question of ultimate guilt—remain at the heart of political debate.

● Carl Bernstein
LOYALTIES: A Son's Memoir
The coauthor of *All the President's Men* tells his own story of life in a family all but destroyed by McCarthyism
0–671–64942–6 Simon & Schuster $18.95

● Robert Griffith
THE POLITICS OF FEAR: Joseph R. McCarthy and the Senate
0–87023–555–9 Massachusetts pb $10.95

● Lillian Hellman
SCOUNDREL TIME
Introduction by Garry Wills
0–316–35515–1 Little, Brown $15.95

● Albert E. Kahn
THE MATUSOW AFFAIR: Memoir of a National Scandal
Harvey Matusow was a star witness for McCarthy and HUAC but later recanted his testimony
Introduction by Angus Cameron
0–918825–38–5 Moyer Bell $18.95
0–918825–85–7 Moyer Bell pb $9.95

● Stanley I. Kutler
THE AMERICAN INQUISITION: Justice and Injustice in the Cold War
0–8090–0157–8 Hill & Wang pb $7.95

● Victor Navasky
NAMING NAMES
The definitive liberal account of the HUAC hearings, focusing on the morality of informing
0–14–005942–3 Penguin pb $8.95

1954 *"Punch" cartoon of Joseph McCarthy, from* The Image of America in Caricature and Cartoon *by Ron Tyler (Amon Carter Museum)*

● David M. Oshinsky
A CONSPIRACY SO IMMENSE: The World of Joe McCarthy
A detailed account recreating (often with actual dialogue) many of the Wisconsin senator's probes into government agencies
0–02–923490–5 Free Press $24.95
0–02–923760–2 Free Press pb $10.95

● Richard Rovere
SENATOR JOE MCCARTHY
A brief, analytic account, first published in 1959. "This portrait is . . . a more subtle one, perhaps, than anyone else has given us"—Donald Malcolm, *New Yorker*
0–06–131970–8 Harper & Row pb $5.95

● Joseph Sharlitt
FATAL ERROR: The Miscarriage of Justice that Sealed the Rosenbergs' Fate
0–684–19059–1 Scribners $24.95

● Christopher Simpson
BLOWBACK: America's Recruitment of Nazis and Its Effect on the Cold War
The hushed-up story of postwar recruitment of Nazis (particularly scientists), and the government-approved immigration of ex-Nazis
1–55584–106–6 Weidenfeld & Nicolson $19.95

● James Wechsler
THE AGE OF SUSPICION
0–917657–38–1 Donald Fine pb $10.95

The Hiss Case

Whittaker Chambers
WITNESS
The autobiographical account of one of the most controversial episodes of the McCarthy era
Preface by Robert Novak
0–89526–789–6 Regnery pb $11.95

Alger Hiss
RECOLLECTIONS OF A LIFE
Hiss's apprenticeship with Justice Oliver Wendell Holmes, his early days in the New Deal, his trip to the Yalta Conference with FDR, and his trial and life in prison
0–8050–0612–5 Henry Holt $19.95

Allen Weinstein
PERJURY: The Hiss-Chambers Case
The definitive account
0–394–49546–2 Knopf $20.00

CAMELOT: The Kennedy Years

● James G. Blight & David A. Welch
ON THE BRINK: Americans and Soviets Reexamine the Cuban Missile Crisis
0–374–22634–2 Farrar, Straus & Giroux $24.95

● Abram Chayes
THE CUBAN MISSILE CRISIS
0–19–519758–5 Oxford pb $5.95

TO ORDER BOOKS AS GIFTS, SEE PAGE 1

• Peter Collier & David Horowitz
THE KENNEDYS: An American Drama
0–446–32702–6 Warner pb $4.95

• Leo Damore
SENATORIAL PRIVILEGE: The Chappaquiddick Coverup
0–89526–564–8 Regnery $21.95

• Doris Kearns Goodwin
THE FITZGERALDS AND THE KENNEDYS: An American Saga
Best-selling account of the famous immigrant families and the political power they wielded
0–312–90933–0 St. Martin's pb $5.95

• Jim F. Heath
DECADE OF DISILLUSIONMENT: The Kennedy-Johnson Years
0–253–31670–7 Indiana $25.00
0–253–20201–9 Indiana pb $7.95

• Trumbull Higgins
THE PERFECT FAILURE: Kennedy, Eisenhower, and the CIA at the Bay of Pigs
0–393–30563–5 Norton pb $7.95

• Robert Kennedy
ROBERT KENNEDY IN HIS OWN WORDS: The Unpublished Recollections of the Kennedy Years
Foreword by Arthur Schlesinger, Jr.
0–553–05316–7 Bantam $22.50
0–553–34661–X Bantam pb $13.95

THIRTEEN DAYS: A Memoir of the Cuban Missile Crisis
0–451–62514–5 NAL pb $3.95

• Philip B. Kunhardt
LIFE IN CAMELOT: The Kennedy Years
Life magazine meets JFK
0–316–21089–7 Little, Brown $40.00

• Robert MacNeil
THE WAY WE WERE: 1963, The Year Kennedy Was Shot
A coffee-table book filled with crisp pictures
0–88184–433–0 Carroll & Graf $39.95

• William Manchester
ONE BRIEF, SHINING MOMENT: Remembering Kennedy
A retrospective and tribute to JFK, by a writer who knew him well
0–316–54491–4 Little, Brown $25.00
0–316–54511–2 Little, Brown pb $16.95

• Jack Newfield
ROBERT KENNEDY: A Memoir
A moving portrait by a veteran reporter; recently reissued
0–452–26064–7 NAL pb $7.95

• Lewis J. Paper
JOHN F. KENNEDY: The Promise and the Performance
Introduction by Senator Bill Bradley
0–306–80114–0 Da Capo pb $9.95

• Herbert S. Parmet
JFK: The Presidency of John F. Kennedy
A reevaluation of the public and private man. "Highly recommended for those who ask what book(s) on the subject they

should read first"—Gaddis Smith, *Foreign Affairs*
0–14–007054–0 Penguin pb $7.95

• Arthur M. Schlesinger, Jr.
One of America's best-known historians, Schlesinger embodies the liberal tradition of historical writing. Known for his interpretations of the Jacksonian and New Deal eras—and for linking their democratic traditions—Schlesinger is also a chief defender of the Kennedy legacy.

A THOUSAND DAYS: John F. Kennedy in the White House
An admiring look
0–449–30021–8 Fawcett pb $4.95

ROBERT KENNEDY AND HIS TIMES
0–345–32547–8 Ballantine pb $4.95

• Garry Wills
THE KENNEDY IMPRISONMENT: A Meditation on Power
0–671–45854–X Simon & Schuster pb $3.95

• Jules Witcover
EIGHTY-FIVE DAYS: The Last Campaign of Robert Kennedy
Introduction by Senator Edward M. Kennedy
0–688–07859–1 Morrow pb $10.95

The Kennedy Assassination

• David W. Belin
FINAL DISCLOSURE: The Full Truth About the Assassination of President Kennedy
The Warren Commission's chief investigator takes apart the many conspiracy theories and attempts to prove that Oswald was the sole killer
0–684–18976–3 Scribners $19.95

• John H. Davis
MAFIA KINGFISH: Carlos Marcello and the Assassination of John F. Kennedy
0–07–015779–0 McGraw-Hill $19.95

• Henry Hurt
REASONABLE DOUBT: An Investigation into the Assassination of John F. Kennedy
"A powerful case for conspiracy with . . . methodical, meticulous re-examination of the evidence"—*San Francisco Chronicle*
0–8050–0360–6 Henry Holt pb $9.95

• Michael L. Kurtz
CRIME OF THE CENTURY: The Kennedy Assassination from a Historian's Perspective
Analyzes investigations into the assassination, outlines major areas of controversy, argues that the most popular conspiracy theories fail to fit the facts, and offers a new theory of the assassination
0–87049–332–9 Tennessee $29.95
0–87049–479–1 Tennessee pb $14.95

• David S. Lifton
BEST EVIDENCE: Disguise and Deception in the Assassination of John F. Kennedy
A meticulously detailed, best-selling argument for a conspiracy to murder JFK
0–88184–438–1 Carroll & Graf pb $11.95

• David Scheim
CONTRACT ON AMERICA: The Mafia Murder of President John F. Kennedy
0–933503–30–X Shapolsky $19.95

CIVIL RIGHTS

▶ **See also African-American Studies**

Martin Luther King, Jr. in Jackson, Mississippi, 1966

• Taylor Branch
PARTING THE WATERS: America in the King Years, 1954–1963
A powerful, scrupulously detailed account of the early civil rights years
0–671–46097–8 Simon & Schuster $24.95

• Seth Cagin & Philip Dray
WE ARE NOT AFRAID: The Murder of Goodman, Schwerner, and Chaney and the Civil Rights Campaign for Mississippi
The lynching of three civil rights workers; the real-life version of the events fictionalized in the film *Mississippi Burning*
0–02–520260–X Macmillan $24.95

• Doug McAdam
FREEDOM SUMMER
In 1964, over 1000 mostly white college students arrived in Mississippi as part of a campaign to register black voters. By summer's end, four had died and hundreds had endured bombings, beatings, and arrests
0–19–504367–7 Oxford $24.95

• Stephen B. Oates
LET THE TRUMPET SOUND: The Life of Martin Luther King, Jr.
0–06–014993–0 Harper & Row $24.95
0–451–62350–9 NAL pb $4.95

• Juan Williams
EYES ON THE PRIZE: America's Civil Rights Years, 1954–1965
Illustrated accompaniment to the PBS television series
Introduction by Julian Bond
0–670–81412–1 Viking $24.95
0–14–009653–1 Penguin pb $10.95

LBJ

Robert A. Caro
THE PATH TO POWER: The Years of Lyndon Johnson
A highly praised, exhaustive account by a Pulitzer prize-winning author
0–394–49973–5 Knopf $29.95
0–394–71654–X Random House pb $9.95

Merle Miller
LYNDON: An Oral Biography
0–345–34529–0 Ballantine pb $5.95

THE SIXTIES

"By the time the decade reached its end with episodes like the Weatherman rampage in Chicago, 'the Sixties' represented not just a span of time but an impetuous, extreme spirit—youthful and reckless, searching and headstrong, foolhardy, romantic, willing to try almost anything ... The spirit of ecstatic freedom proved impossible to sustain. The Movement collapsed, leaving behind a congeries of smaller single-issue movements, demanding peace in Vietnam, dignity for blacks, liberation for women, respect for homosexuality, reverence for the balance of nature. Frustrated revolutionists built bombs, turning reveries of freedom into cruel, ineffectual outbursts of terrorism. And one by one, the political pilgrims who had created 'the Sixties' fell back to earth."—James Miller, *"Democracy Is in the Streets": From Port Huron to the Siege of Chicago*

▶ See also The Vietnam War

● **Scott L. Bills**
KENT STATE/MAY 4: Echoes Through a Decade
The killing of four students—three of them bystanders—at a college protest was the climactic event of a tumultuous decade; this anthology offers essays and interviews with those touched by the violence
0–87338–360–5 Kent State pb $12.00

● **John H. Bunzel, editor**
POLITICAL PASSAGES: Journeys of Change Through Two Decades
Essays reflecting on the legacy of the '60s, by such writers as Carol Iannone, Michael Novak, Ronald Radosh, and Richard Rodriguez
0–02–904921–0 Free Press $21.95

● **Peter Clecak**
AMERICA'S QUEST FOR THE IDEAL SELF: Dissent and Fulfillment in the '60s and '70s
Argues for one extended period, marked by a quest for individual self-fulfillment
0–19–503226–8 Oxford $29.95
0–19–503544–5 Oxford pb $12.95

● **Peter Collier & David Horowitz**
DESTRUCTIVE GENERATION: Second Thoughts About the '60s
The authors of *The Kennedys* argue that the leftist ideology of the 1960s damaged the nation
0–671–66752–1 Simon & Schuster $18.95

● **Jack Curry**
WOODSTOCK: The Summer of Our Lives
1–55584–040–X Weidenfeld & Nicolson $19.95

● **Morris Dickstein**
GATES OF EDEN: American Culture in the Sixties
A new edition of the work originally published in 1977, tracing '60s culture from the beat poets of the '50s through the work of people like Bob Dylan, Norman Mailer, Ralph Ellison, and the Rolling Stones
0–14–011617–6 Penguin pb $8.95

● **Todd Gitlin**
THE SIXTIES: Years of Hope, Days of Rage
"Brilliant in its understanding of the New Left as a genuinely American insurgency, rooted in the mass culture of the '50s; and brave for its revealingly self-critical analysis of why that movement faded all too soon"—Barbara Ehrenreich
0–553–05233–0 Bantam $19.95
0–553–34601–6 Bantam pb $12.95

● **Richard N. Goodwin**
REMEMBERING AMERICA: A Voice from the Sixties
A look back at the political leaders, from one who knew them well
0–316–32024–2 Little, Brown $19.95

● **Tom Hayden**
REUNION: A Memoir
A memoir from a leader of the student movement and a founder of SDS
0–394–56533–9 Random House $22.50

● **Joel Makower**
WOODSTOCK: The Oral History
0–385–24716–8 Doubleday $24.95
0–385–24717–6 Doubleday pb $14.95

Robert Kennedy on the campaign trail, from The Year of the Barricades *by David Caute (Harper and Row)*

● **Allen J. Matusow**
THE UNRAVELING OF AMERICA: A History of Liberalism in the 1960s
"May well be *the* definitive analysis"—Bill Youngblood, *Fort Worth Star Telegram*
0–06–015224–9 Harper & Row $22.95

● **Kim McQuaid**
THE ANXIOUS YEARS: America in the Vietnam-Watergate Era
0–465–00389–3 Basic Books $19.95

● **James Miller**
"DEMOCRACY IS IN THE STREETS": From Port Huron to the Siege of Chicago
A wonderful account of the student movement and the rise and fall of the SDS
0–671–53056–6 Simon & Schuster $19.95
0–671–66235–X Simon & Schuster pb $9.95

● **Charles R. Morris**
A TIME OF PASSION: America 1960–1980
What went wrong in the transition of the solutions of the '60s—The Great Society and containment—into the failures of the New Economics and Vietnam
0–14–008643–9 Penguin pb $7.95

● **Joan & Robert K. Morrison**
FROM CAMELOT TO KENT STATE: The Sixties Experience in the Words of Those Who Lived It
0–8129–1715–4 Times Books pb $12.95

● **Geoffrey O'Brien**
DREAM TIME: Chapters from the Sixties
"Recovers lost sensibilities—splendors and miseries both—and makes them sing"—Todd Gitlin
0–670–81844–5 Viking $15.95
0–14–010362–7 Penguin pb $7.95

● **William L. O'Neill**
COMING APART: An Informal History of America in the 1960s
0–8129–6223–0 Times Books pb $9.95

● **Charles Perry**
HAIGHT-ASHBURY: A History
0–394–74144–7 Random House pb $5.95

● **Jay Stevens**
STORMING HEAVEN: LSD and the American Dream
Charts LSD's brief but convulsive reign in America, from CIA projects of chemical warfare to Timothy Leary's turning on
0–06–097172–X Harper & Row pb $9.95

● **Milton Viorst**
FIRE IN THE STREETS: America in the 1960s
The era of sit-ins, riots, the Chicago convention, and freedom rides
0–671–42814–4 Simon & Schuster pb $14.95

● **Peter O. Whitmer with Bruce van Wyngarden**
AQUARIUS REVISITED: Seven Who Created the Sixties Counterculture that Changed America
The decade dissected through the lives and ideas of William Burroughs, Allen Ginsberg, Ken Kesey, Timothy Leary, Norman Mailer, Tom Robbins, and Hunter S. Thompson
0–02–627670–4 Macmillan $19.95

1968

David Caute
THE YEAR OF THE BARRICADES: 1968
0–06–015870–0 Harper & Row $24.95

David Farber
CHICAGO '68
The full story of the epochal event told from three perspectives: Yippies, antiwar protesters, and Mayor Daley and his police
0–226–23800–8 Chicago $19.95

Ronald Fraser, editor
1968: A Student Generation in Revolt
An oral history of the student rebellions that gripped the world, linking the sit-ins of Berkeley to protests in Prague, Paris, and Beijing
0–394–54599–0 Pantheon $24.95
0–679–73953–X Pantheon pb $14.95

Charles Kaiser
1968 IN AMERICA: Music, Politics, Chaos, Counterculture, and the Shaping of a Generation
1–55584–242–9 W&N $19.95

Irwin Unger & Debi Unger
TURNING POINT: 1968
A view of the year that changed America
0–684–18696–9 Scribners $24.95

NIXON, FORD, AND CARTER

• **Stephen E. Ambrose**
NIXON, Volume 1: The Education of a Politician, 1913–1962
0–671–65722–4 Simon & Schuster pb $10.95

• **Fawn M. Brodie**
RICHARD NIXON: The Shaping of His Character
0–674–76880–9 Harvard pb $10.95

• **John Dean**
BLIND AMBITION
Watergate from the perspective of the presidential counsel who spilled many of the beans
0–671–82343–4 Simon & Schuster pb $2.95

Seymour Hersh
THE PRICE OF POWER: Kissinger in the Nixon White House
0–671–50688–9 Summit pb $9.95

Henry A. Kissinger
THE WHITE HOUSE YEARS
0–316–49661–8 Little, Brown $29.95

• **J. Anthony Lukas**
COMMON GROUND: A Turbulent Decade in the Lives of Three American Families
0–394–41150–1 Knopf $19.95
0–394–74616–3 Random House pb $9.95

Raymond Depardon's *"Sioux City (U.S.A.), September 1968," from* Eyes of Time: Photojournalism in America *by Marianne Fulton and others (New York Graphic Society/Little, Brown)*

NIGHTMARE: The Underside of the Nixon Years
The whole Watergate story, from Nixon's first wiretaps of his associates to his resignation
0–14–011229–4 Penguin pb $10.95

• **Joe McGinniss**
THE SELLING OF THE PRESIDENT, 1968
How Nixon was successfully repackaged by advertising advisers during the 1968 presidential campaign
0–14–011240–5 Penguin pb $7.95

• **Walter Russell Mead**
MORTAL SPLENDOR: The American Empire in Transition
America's decline since the mid-1960s traced by "a post-Toynbee historian with a view as tough-minded and Olympian"—*Boston Globe*
0–395–46809–4 Houghton Mifflin pb $9.95

• **Bruce Oudes, editor**
FROM: THE PRESIDENT: Richard Nixon's Secret Files
0–06–015953–7 Harper & Row $17.95

• **William Safire**
BEFORE THE FALL: An Inside View of the Pre-Watergate White House
Anecdotes and observations of the siege mentality of the Nixon administration by the speechwriter-turned-*New York Times* columnist
0–306–80334–8 Da Capo pb $15.95

• **Jonathan Schell**
OBSERVING THE NIXON YEARS
Pieces that appeared in *The New Yorker* in the late 1960s, plus an analysis of the effect of Vietnam and the Watergate break-in on American politics
0–394–57495–8 Pantheon $19.95

THE TIME OF ILLUSION
Beautifully analyzes Nixon's administration
0–394–72217–5 Random House pb $6.50

• **Garry Wills**
LEAD TIME: A Journalist's Education
Essays from 1968 to 1982, covering such topics as Nixon, Vietnam, Pope John Paul II, and Muhammad Ali
0–14–006968–2 Penguin pb $8.95

NIXON AGONISTES
A first-rate analysis of a troubled presidency, perhaps the finest of Wills's commentaries on recent commanders-in-chief
0–451–62399–1 NAL pb $5.95

• **Bob Woodward & Carl Bernstein**
ALL THE PRESIDENT'S MEN
How two green *Washington Post* reporters toppled a presidency
0–671–64644–3 Simon & Schuster pb $6.95

THE FINAL DAYS
Nixon's last days in the White House and his struggle against resignation
0–671–64645–1 Simon & Schuster pb $7.95

The Carter Presidency

▶ See also The Contemporary Middle East

Jimmy Carter
KEEPING FAITH: Memoirs of a President
0–553–34571–0 Bantam pb $13.95

Clark R. Mollenhoff
THE PRESIDENT WHO FAILED: Carter Out of Control
Analyzes the weaknesses in Carter's presidential style which led to his unpopularity and electoral defeat
0–02–921750–4 Macmillan $19.95

Gaddis Smith
MORALITY, REASON AND POWER: American Diplomacy in the Carter Years
A Yale historian's analysis of Carter's foreign policy
0–8090–0168–3 Hill & Wang pb $8.95

THE REAGAN YEARS

• Annelise Anderson & Dennis L. Bark, editors
THINKING ABOUT AMERICA: The United States in the 1990s
Essays in foreign and domestic policy, including the Middle East, debt, and taxes, from a wide range of experts
0–8179–8752–5 Hoover pb $14.95

• Martin Anderson
REVOLUTION
A White House insider chronicles the Reagan revolution in government
0–15–177087–5 HBJ $19.95

• Laurence I. Barrett
GAMBLING WITH HISTORY: Ronald Reagan in the White House
"A meaty account of the infighting and strategies at the top of the Administration"—*NY Times*
0–14–007275–6 Penguin pb $8.95

• Sidney Blumenthal & Thomas Byrne Edsall, editors
THE REAGAN LEGACY: An Unfinished Revolution
Seven writers analyze the Reagan years, including the politicizing of the justice system, foreign policy, and the uncertain prospects for liberalism
0–394–56555–X Pantheon $22.95
0–394–75970–2 Pantheon pb $11.95

• Hodding Carter
THE REAGAN YEARS
Notes on the Reagan presidency from a noted journalist and former Carter administration spokesman
0–8076–1209–X Braziller $17.50

• Mark Green & Gail MacColl
RONALD REAGAN'S REIGN OF ERROR
An amusing anthology of flubs and misstatements
0–394–75644–4 Pantheon pb $6.95

• William Greider
THE EDUCATION OF DAVID STOCKMAN AND OTHER AMERICANS
0–525–48276–8 Dutton pb $6.95

• Jeanne K. Kirkpatrick
DICTATORSHIPS AND DOUBLE STANDARDS
0–671–49266–7 Simon & Schuster pb $8.95

• Jane Mayer & Doyle McManus
LANDSLIDE: The Unmaking of the President, 1984–1988
0–395–45185–X Houghton Mifflin $21.95

• Kevin B. Phillips
POST-CONSERVATIVE AMERICA: People, Politics and Ideology in a Time of Crisis
0–394–71438–5 Random House pb $7.95

• Richard Reeves
AMERICAN JOURNEY: Traveling with Tocqueville in Search of Democracy in America
A journalist retraces Tocqueville's famous 1831 journey to analyze the state of American culture in the 1980s
0–671–47067–1 Simon & Schuster pb $9.95

• Donald T. Regan
FOR THE RECORD: From Wall Street to Washington
0–15–163966–3 HBJ $21.95

• Bob Schieffer & Gary Paul Gates
THE ACTING PRESIDENT: Ronald Reagan and the Men Who Helped Him Create the Illusion that Held America Spellbound
0–525–24572–1 Dutton $18.95

• David Stockman
THE TRIUMPH OF POLITICS: Why the Reagan Revolution Failed
0–06–015560–4 Harper & Row $21.95

• Studs Terkel
One of our century's most adept chroniclers, Terkel practically invented oral history, using the words of ordinary men and women to illustrate the tenor of the times.
AMERICAN DREAMS: Lost and Found
0–394–50793–2 Pantheon $14.95
0–345–32993–7 Ballantine pb $4.95

DIVISION STREET: America
Terkel's first oral history presents the voices of a highly diverse cross-section of Americans
0–394–71009–6 Pantheon pb $5.95

THE GREAT DIVIDE: Second Thoughts on the American Dream
Yuppies, Wall Street greed, right-wing fundamentalism, and other puzzling facets of today's America
0–394–57053–7 Pantheon $18.95

• George F. Will
One of the best-known political commentators of the Reagan era, Will's reputation is based both on his eloquence and his conservative outlook.
THE MORNING AFTER: American Successes and Excesses, 1981–1986
0–02–934430–1 Free Press $19.95
0–02–055450–8 Macmillan pb $9.95

THE NEW SEASON: A Spectator's Guide to the 1988 Election
0–671–64837–3 Simon & Schuster $17.95
0–671–66275–9 Simon & Schuster pb $7.95

• Garry Wills
REAGAN'S AMERICA
With a new chapter on the legacy of the Reagan Era
0–14–010557–3 Penguin pb $8.95

BIOGRAPHY

• Hedley Donovan
ROOSEVELT TO REAGAN: A Reporter's Encounters with Nine Presidents
0–06–039067–0 Harper & Row pb $8.95

• Philippa Strum
LOUIS D. BRANDEIS: Justice for the People
0–8052–0884–4 Schocken pb $14.95

• Kendrick A. Clements
WILLIAM JENNINGS BRYAN: Missionary Isolationist
0–87049–364–7 Tennessee $23.95

• Lawrence Levine
DEFENDER OF THE FAITH: William Jennings Bryan—The Last Decade, 1915–1925
0–674–19542–6 Harvard pb $11.95

• Donald R. McCoy
CALVIN COOLIDGE: The Quiet President
"McCoy [shows] that Coolidge was a fair-minded, sincere, assiduous, and idealistic president"—*American Historical Review*
0–7006–0351–4 Kansas pb $14.95

• Mike Royko
BOSS: Richard J. Daley of Chicago
A sardonic portrait by the Chicago columnist which presents Chicago's mayor from 1955 to 1976 as the quintessential big-city boss
0–452–26167–8 NAL pb $7.95

• Virginia Foster Durr
OUTSIDE THE MAGIC CIRCLE: The Autobiography of Virginia Foster Durr
The metamorphosis of a Southern belle into a New Deal liberal and champion of civil rights
Foreword by Studs Terkel
0–671–63855–6 Simon & Schuster pb $9.95

• Stephen E. Ambrose
EISENHOWER

Volume 1: Soldier, General of the Army, President-Elect, 1890–1952
0–671–44069–1 Simon & Schuster $24.95

Volume 2: The President
0–671–49901–7 Simon & Schuster $24.95

▶ For Eisenhower the general, see The Second World War

• Piers Brendon
IKE: His Life and Times
"The most provocative and readable one-volume life of Eisenhower in print"—Michael Beschloss
0–06–015508–6 Harper & Row $21.95

➤ **FOR OVERSEAS ORDERING INFORMATION, SEE PAGE 1**

• Dwight D. Eisenhower
THE EISENHOWER DIARIES
Edited by Robert H. Ferrell
0–393–01432–0 Norton $19.95

• Barry M. Goldwater with Jack Casserly
GOLDWATER
Autobiography of the man who lost to LBJ in a landslide but inaugurated the "new conservatism" that led to the electoral triumph of Ronald Reagan
0–385–23947–5 Doubleday $21.95

• Woody Guthrie
BOUND FOR GLORY
0–452–25483–3 NAL pb $6.95

• Joe Klein
WOODY GUTHRIE: A Life
0–394–50152–7 Knopf $15.95

• W. A. Swanberg
CITIZEN HEARST: A Biography of William Randolph Hearst
"Best biography yet on a strange, complicated man"—*Saturday Review*
0–684–17147–3 Scribners pb $7.95

• David Burner
HERBERT HOOVER: The Public Life
0–394–46134–7 Knopf $17.95

• George H. Nash
THE LIFE OF HERBERT HOOVER: The Humanitarian, 1914–1917
0–393–02550–0 Norton $25.00

• Richard G. Powers
SECRECY AND POWER: The Life of J. Edgar Hoover
0–02–925060–9 Free Press $27.95
0–02–925061–7 Free Press pb $12.95

• Carl Solberg
HUBERT HUMPHREY: A Biography
0–393–01806–7 Norton $19.95

• Michael R. Beschloss
KENNEDY AND ROOSEVELT: The Uneasy Alliance
The stormy friendship between FDR and Joseph P. Kennedy
0–06–097095–2 Harper & Row pb $8.95

• Ronald Steel
WALTER LIPPMANN AND THE AMERICAN CENTURY
0–316–81190–4 Little, Brown $25.00

• T. Harry Williams
HUEY LONG
Full-scale biography of Louisiana's "Kingfish"; the nonfiction version of *All the King's Men*
0–394–74790–9 Random House pb $14.95

• Wilfrid Sheed
CLARE BOOTH LUCE
0–425–05978–2 Berkley pb $7.95

• William Manchester
AMERICAN CAESAR: Douglas MacArthur, 1880–1964
0–316–54498–1 Little, Brown $25.00

Herbert Hoover in a 1940 caricature by Emidio Angelo, from The Image of America in Caricature and Cartoon *by Ron Tyler (Amon Carter Museum)*

• Michael Schaller
DOUGLAS MACARTHUR: The Far Eastern General
0–19–503886–X Oxford $19.95

• William Manchester
DISTURBER OF THE PEACE: The Life of H.L. Mencken
The best biography of the exuberant iconoclast who did much to establish the cultural tone of the 1920s
0–87023–543–5 Massachusetts $25.00
0–87023–544–3 Massachusetts pb $9.95

• Robert A. Caro
THE POWER BROKER: Robert Moses and the Fall of New York
A first-rate biography of the controversial builder who left a permanent imprint on the New York City area
0–394–48076–7 Knopf $34.50
0–394–72024–5 Random House pb $18.95

• Ann M. Sperber
MURROW: His Life and Times
Biography of the century's leading pioneer in broadcast journalism
0–553–34384–X Bantam pb $12.95

• Joann Robinson
ABRAHAM WENT OUT: A Biography of A.J. Muste
Biography of the noted peace, labor, and civil rights activist
0–87722–560–5 Temple pb $14.95

• Donald Smythe
PERSHING: General of the Armies
0–253–34381–X Indiana $27.50

• Frank E. Vandiver
BLACK JACK: The Life and Times of John J. Pershing
A 2-volume set
0–89096–024–0 Texas A&M (set) $47.50

• Roger A. Bruns
THE DAMNDEST RADICAL: The Life and World of Ben Reitman, Chicago's Celebrated Social Reformer, Hobo King, and Whorehouse Physician
0–252–00984–3 Illinois $24.95

• Martin Bauml Duberman
PAUL ROBESON
A full-scale biography
0–394–52780–1 Knopf $24.95

• Joseph Alsop
FDR: A Centenary Remembrance, 1882–1945
0–671–45891–4 Washington Square pb $3.50

• Frank Freidel
FRANKLIN D. ROOSEVELT

Volume 1: The Apprenticeship
0–316–29304–0 Little, Brown $15.00

Volume 2: The Ordeal
0–316–29305–9 Little, Brown $15.00

Volume 3: The Triumph
0–316–29306–7 Little, Brown $15.00

Volume 4: Launching the New Deal
0–316–29303–2 Little, Brown $15.00
0–316–29302–4 Little, Brown pb $8.95

• Ted Morgan
FDR: A Biography
Strong on FDR's private life and on newer issues of his administration, including refugee policy toward European Jews and the internment of Japanese Americans during World War II. "FDR appears in grand form, much as he was in life: a magnificent leader but flawed man"—*Wall Street Journal*
0–671–45495–1 Simon & Schuster $22.95
0–671–62812–7 Simon & Schuster pb $12.95

Eleanor and Franklin

Joseph P. Lash
ELEANOR AND FRANKLIN
0–451–14076–1 NAL pb $5.95

ELEANOR: The Years Alone
0–393–07361–0 Norton $14.95
0–452–00771–2 NAL pb $10.95

LOVE, ELEANOR: Eleanor Roosevelt and Her Friends, The Early Years
0–07–036486–9 McGraw-Hill pb $9.95

A WORLD OF LOVE: Eleanor Roosevelt and Her Friends, 1943–1962
0–07–036487–7 McGraw-Hill pb $9.95

• William H. Harbaugh
THE LIFE AND TIMES OF THEODORE ROOSEVELT
A reappraisal of the first of the modern presidents
0–19–519822–0 Oxford pb $12.95

• Edmund Morris
THE RISE OF THEODORE ROOSEVELT
The popular biography by Reagan's official biographer; excellent on Roosevelt's personality, but weaker on his politics
0–345–33902–9 Ballantine pb $10.95

• Robert & Michael Meeropol
WE ARE YOUR SONS: The Legacy of Ethel and Julius Rosenberg
The updated version includes the recollections of the Rosenbergs' sons, arguments for their parents' innocence, and a fascinating collection of letters written by the couple from prison
0–252–01263–1 Illinois $27.50

Eleanor Roosevelt in 1958, from World Celebrities in Ninety Photographic Portraits *by Fred Stein (Dover)*

- **Ilene Philipson**
  ETHEL ROSENBERG: Beyond the Myths
  0–531–15057–7 Franklin Watts $18.95

- **Oscar Handlin**
  AL SMITH AND HIS AMERICA
  A sympathetic portrait of the four-term New York governor, the first Roman Catholic to run for president
  1–55553–021–4 Northeastern pb $10.95

- **Porter McKeever**
  ADLAI STEVENSON: His Life and Legacy
  0–688–06661–5 Morrow $24.50

- **Roy Jenkins**
  TRUMAN
  A British statesman outlines Truman's achievements as a Free World leader in the perilous years of the Cold War. "Combines graceful portraiture with astute and dispassionate judgment"—Arthur Schlesinger, Jr.
  0–06–091422–X Harper & Row pb $7.95

- **Margaret Truman**
  HARRY S. TRUMAN
  Best-selling biography by the late president's daughter
  0–688–03924–3 Morrow pb $10.95

  BESS W. TRUMAN
  0–515–08973–7 Berkley pb $4.50

- **John M. Cooper, Jr.**
  THE WARRIOR AND THE PRIEST: Woodrow Wilson and Theodore Roosevelt
  A comparative biography of the two dominant figures whose sophistication and character—and struggles with each other—set the tone for political debate for much of the century
  0–674–94751–7 Harvard pb $9.95

- **Alexander L. & Juliette L. George**
  WOODROW WILSON AND COLONEL HOUSE: A Personality Study
  The complex interrelationship of Wilson and his closest adviser, blending historical research and psychoanalytic theory
  0–486–21144–4 Dover pb $6.95

- **Arthur S. Link**
  WOODROW WILSON AND THE PROGRESSIVE ERA: 1910–1917
  "In it Wilson is much less the demigod and more the rational, eloquent, stubborn, and human party leader who was forced into the role of war leader despite himself"—Robert S. Maxwell, *Journal of Southern History*
  0–06–133023–X Harper & Row pb $9.95

American Regional History: The West and the South

▶ **See also Natural History**

THE WESTERN FRONTIER: Overviews

"Americans had a safety valve for social danger, a bank account on which they might continually draw to meet losses. This was the vast unoccupied domain that stretched from the borders of the settled area to the Pacific Ocean ... No grave social problem could exist while the wilderness at the edge of civilizations opened wide its portals to all who were oppressed, to all who with strong arms and stout heart desired to hew out a home and a career for themselves. Here was an opportunity for social development continually to begin over again, wherever society gave signs of breaking into classes. Here was a magic fountain of youth in which America continually bathed and was rejuvenated."—Frederick Jackson Turner, quoted in Henry Nash Smith, *Virgin Land: The American West as Symbol and Myth*

▶ **See also Native American Cultures: North America**

- **Richard A. Bartlett**
  THE NEW COUNTRY: A Social History of the American Frontier, 1776–1890
  A spirited account focusing on settlement of the country, the settlers' racial and ethnic composition, agriculture, transportation, and the nature of frontier society
  0–19–502021–9 Oxford pb $12.95

- **Ray A. Billington**
  THE FAR WESTERN FRONTIER, 1830–1860
  Its impact on those who opened it; for general readers as well as scholars
  0–06–133012–4 Harper & Row pb $8.95

- **Bernard DeVoto**
  DeVoto's trilogy tells the story of the emigrants, soldiers, refugees, heroes, villains, and bystanders of the antebellum West.
  THE COURSE OF EMPIRE
  0–395–51014–7 Houghton Mifflin pb $9.95

  THE YEAR OF DECISION, 1846
  0–395–50079–6 Houghton Mifflin pb $9.95

  ACROSS THE WIDE MISSOURI
  A Bancroft Prize-winning chronicle of the Rocky Mountain fur trade during its climax and decline; part of the American Heritage Library
  0–395–08374–5 Houghton Mifflin pb $9.95

- **Allan W. Eckert**
  Eckert's six-part series traces the full story of the westward expansion.
  THE CONQUERORS
  0–316–20865–5 Little, Brown $24.50

  THE FRONTIERSMEN
  0–316–20856–6 Little, Brown $24.50

  GATEWAY TO EMPIRE
  0–316–20861–2 Little, Brown $24.50

  TWILIGHT OF EMPIRE
  0–316–20886–8 Little, Brown $24.95

  WILDERNESS EMPIRE
  0–316–20864–7 Little, Brown $24.50

  WILDERNESS WAR
  0–316–20875–2 Little, Brown $24.50

- **Howard R. Lamar**
  THE READER'S ENCYCLOPEDIA OF THE AMERICAN WEST
  Over 2400 entries on its people, places, institutions, and ideas; a magnificent, endlessly entertaining reference work
  0–06–015726–7 Harper & Row $30.00

- **Richard Slotkin**
  THE FATAL ENVIRONMENT: The Myth of the Frontier in the Age of Industrialization
  How the frontier myth was used by proponents of industrial capitalism
  0–8195–6183–5 Wesleyan pb $14.95

  REGENERATION THROUGH VIOLENCE: The Mythology of the American Frontier, 1600–1860
  Frontier mythology as it shaped the nation's literature
  0–8195–6034–0 Wesleyan pb $14.95

- **Henry Nash Smith**
  VIRGIN LAND: The American West As Symbol and Myth
  "The rise and decline of the conception of the West as an agrarian utopia—the myth of the 'garden of the world' "—*Nation*
  0–674–93955–7 Harvard pb $7.95

- **Frederick Jackson Turner**
  THE FRONTIER IN AMERICAN HISTORY
  In 1893, Turner was the first to theorize that the frontier, with its endless possibilities for social regeneration, gave America its uniquely individualistic and democratic society
  0–8165–0946–8 Arizona pb $10.95

- **Dale Van Every**
  THE AMERICAN FRONTIER
  A comprehensive and dramatic four-volume record
  1754–1774: Forth to the Wilderness
  0–688–07522–3 Morrow pb $9.95
  1775–1783: A Company of Heroes
  0–688–07523–1 Morrow pb $9.95

1784–1803: Ark of Empire
0–688–07949–0 Morrow pb $9.95

1804–1845: The Final Challenge
0–688–08256–4 Morrow pb $9.95

● Walter P. Webb
THE GREAT FRONTIER
The frontier of America as only part of a vast movement to colonize all of the world's unexploited, habitable regions
Introduction by Arnold J. Toynbee
0–8032–9711–4 Nebraska pb $9.95

ART OF THE WEST

● Elizabeth Cunningham & others
MASTERPIECES OF THE AMERICAN WEST
Selections from the Anschutz Collection include works of George Catlin, Alfred Jacob Miller, Georgia O'Keeffe, Albert Bierstadt, and George Bellows
0–8032–6329–5 Nebraska pb $25.00

● William H. & William N. Goetzmann
THE WEST OF THE IMAGINATION
0–393–02370–2 Norton $34.95

● David C. Hunt
THE LEGACY OF THE WEST
Profiles 247 artworks, including those of George Catlin, Seth Eastman, Alfred Jacob Miller, Frederic Remington, Gutzon Borglum, and William R. Leigh
0–936364–08–4 Nebraska pb $18.95

● Eliot Porter
THE WEST
A wonderful collection of photographs of the entire region, from Big Sur to Olympic National Park
0–8212–1711–9 Little, Brown $60.00

● Ron Tyler & others
AMERICAN FRONTIER LIFE: Early Western Painting and Prints
Intelligent essays, with 78 full-color illustrations
0–89659–691–5 Abbeville $45.00

WESTERN EXPLORATIONS

● William H. Goetzmann
EXPLORATION AND EMPIRE: The Explorer and the Scientist in the Winning of the American West
0–393–00881–9 Norton pb $14.95

● David Freeman Hawke
THOSE TREMENDOUS MOUNTAINS: The Story of the Lewis and Clark Expeditions
"Makes clear the scientific value of the expedition without in any way dulling its impact as high and heroic adventure"—
New Yorker
0–393–30289–X Norton pb $7.95

Meriwether Lewis & William Clark
THE JOURNALS OF LEWIS AND CLARK
A one-volume abridgment of the account by the explorers who saw the American West before white settlement
Edited by Bernard DeVoto
0–395–08380–X Houghton Mifflin pb $9.95
THE JOURNALS OF LEWIS AND CLARK
Edited & with an introduction by Frank Bergon
0–14–017006–5 Penguin pb $8.95

● Francis Parkman, Jr.
THE OREGON TRAIL
The classic account of Parkman's 1846 expedition
Edited by David Levin
0–14–039042–1 Penguin pb $4.95

● Zebulon M. Pike
THE EXPEDITIONS OF ZEBULON MONTGOMERY PIKE

Volume 1
0–486–25254–X Dover pb $11.95

Volume 2
0–486–25255–8 Dover pb $11.95

● John Wesley Powell
THE EXPLORATION OF THE COLORADO RIVER AND ITS CANYONS
The classic first-hand account
0–14–017000–6 Penguin pb $6.95

● Wallace Stegner
BEYOND THE HUNDREDTH MERIDIAN: John Wesley Powell and the Second Opening of the West
"The one-armed Civil War hero who explored the great canyons of the Colorado River and then launched a political struggle for a sensible water policy for the West was certainly larger than life"—*Accent*
Introduction by Bernard DeVoto
0–8032–9128–0 Nebraska pb $12.50

AMERICA MOVES WEST

● Leonard J. Arrington
GREAT BASIN KINGDOM: An Economic History of the Latter-Day Saints, 1830–1900
0–8032–5006–1 Nebraska pb $13.95

● Robert G. Athearn
HIGH COUNTRY EMPIRE: The High Plains and Rockies
0–8032–5008–8 Nebraska pb $6.50

● Will Baker
MOUNTAIN BLOOD
Tales from the West include *The Beautician and the One-Legged Man* and *The Legend of Great Uncle Jim and the Woman Behind It All.* "Unlike anything you've ever read . . . unless you still have warm memories of early Bret Harte and Mark Twain"—*Arts Journal, North Carolina*
0–8203–0819–6 Georgia $14.95
0–671–66096–9 Simon & Schuster pb $7.95

● Thomas James
THREE YEARS AMONG THE INDIANS AND MEXICANS
A first-hand account of exploration and trade
Introduction by A.P. Nasatir
0–8032–7556–0 Nebraska pb $5.95

● Julie Roy Jeffrey
FRONTIER WOMEN: The Trans-Mississippi West, 1840–1880
How women took on roles normally reserved for men, yet clung to the Victorian values that defined their era
0–8090–0141–1 Hill & Wang pb $7.95

● David Lavender
THE GREAT WEST
0–8281–0303–8 Houghton Mifflin pb $9.95

LAND OF GIANTS: The Drive to the Pacific Northwest, 1750–1950
0–8032–2854–6 Nebraska $32.50
0–8032–7905–1 Nebraska pb $11.95

WESTWARD VISION: The Story of the Oregon Trail
The efforts of emigration societies, missionaries, and early pioneers and the routes they took to the "Promised Land"
Illustrated by Marian Ebert
0–8032–2866–X Nebraska $27.95
0–8032–7915–9 Nebraska pb $9.95

● Kenneth Libo & Irving Howe
WE LIVED THERE TOO: In Their Own Words, Pioneer Jews and the Westward Movement of America, 1630–1930
A large picture book with text
0–312–85867–1 St. Martin's pb $13.95

☞ **FOR ALL OTHER INQUIRIES, PLEASE CALL (212) 333-7900**

"The Tetons and the Snake River" (*copyright The Ansel Adams Publishing Rights Trust*), *from* Ansel Adams: Letters and Images, 1916-1984 (*New York Graphic Society/Little, Brown*)

Entrepreneurs

- Hiram Martin Chittenden
  THE AMERICAN FUR TRADE OF THE FAR WEST
  A classic history, nearly a century old
  Introduction and notes by Stallo Vinton
  Volume 1
  0–8032–6320–1 Nebraska pb $10.95
  Volume 2
  0–8032–6321–X Nebraska pb $9.95

- David Dary
  ENTREPRENEURS OF THE OLD WEST
  The "silent army" of merchants, outfitters, land speculators, railroad builders, and other entrepreneurs who linked America's East and West
  0–8032–6572–7 Nebraska pb $11.95

- J. Valerie Fifer
  AMERICAN PROGRESS: The Growth of the Transport, Tourist, and Information Industries in the Nineteenth-Century West
  How the West was sold and transformed into a center of tourism and settlement
  0–87106–732–3 Globe Pequot $29.95

- Maury Klein
  UNION PACIFIC: The Birth of a Railroad, 1862–1893
  The personalities and events behind the construction of the first transcontinental railway and the birth of one of the nation's biggest corporations
  0–385–17728–3 Doubleday $27.50

- Peter C. Newman
  COMPANY OF ADVENTURERS: The Story of the Hudson's Bay Company
  0–14–010139–X Penguin pb $7.95
  CAESARS OF THE WILDERNESS: The Story of the Hudson's Bay Company
  0–14–011456–4 Penguin pb $8.95

- Gerald McFarland
  A SCATTERED PEOPLE: An American Family Moves West
  A vivid personal history of one family's migration over almost two centuries
  0–14–009366–4 Penguin pb $8.95

- Sandra L. Myres
  WESTERING WOMEN AND THE FRONTIER EXPERIENCE, 1800–1915
  0–8263–0626–8 New Mexico pb $13.95

- Rodman Paul
  THE FAR WEST AND THE GREAT PLAINS IN TRANSITION, 1859–1900
  How a multi-ethnic group of settlers forged into the Rockies, the plains, and the desert mountains of Nevada and Utah in the era following the California gold rush
  0–06–015836–0 Harper & Row $24.95

- Harriet Rochlin
  PIONEER JEWS: A New Life in the Far West
  A colorful account filled with rare period photographs
  0–395–31832–7 Houghton Mifflin $17.95
  0–395–42639–1 Houghton Mifflin pb $12.95

- Lillian Schlissel
  WOMEN'S DIARIES OF THE WESTWARD JOURNEY
  Introduction by Carl Degler
  0–8052–0747–3 Schocken pb $10.95

- Lillian Schlissel & others
  FAR FROM HOME: Families of the Westward Journey
  Letters and diaries tell the stories of three families who ventured west
  Preface by Robert Coles
  0–8052–4052–7 Schocken $19.95

- George R. Stewart
  ORDEAL BY HUNGER: The Story of the Donner Party
  The true story of the group that set out for California in 1846, and, trapped by winter in the High Sierras, turned cannibal
  0–8032–9171–X Nebraska pb $7.95

- Irving Stone
  MEN TO MATCH MY MOUNTAINS
  The great popularizer's saga of the winning of the West
  0–425–10544–X Berkley pb $9.95

- R.B. Stratton
  THE CAPTIVITY OF THE OATMAN GIRLS
  A best-seller when it first appeared in 1857, this recounts the massacre of the Oatman family on the Santa Fe Trail and the captivity of two of their daughters
  0–8032–9139–6 Nebraska pb $7.95

- John D. Unruh, Jr.
  THE PLAINS ACROSS: The Overland Emigrants and the Trans-Mississippi West, 1840–60
  Foreword by Doyce Nunis
  0–252–00968–1 Illinois pb $8.95

- Walter P. Webb
  THE GREAT PLAINS
  0–8032–9702–5 Nebraska pb $9.95

Fred Reinfeld
PONY EXPRESS
0–8032–5786–4 Nebraska pb $4.95

Raymond W. Settle & Mary L. Settle
SADDLES AND SPURS: The Pony Express Saga
0–8032–5765–1 Nebraska pb $8.95

LEGENDARY FIGURES AND PLACES

- Duncan Aikman
  CALAMITY JANE AND THE LADY WILDCATS
  First published in 1927, this account also tells of Belle Starr, Madame Moustache, Poker Alice Tubbs, and Carrie Nation
  Introduction by Watson Parker
  0–8032–5911–5 Nebraska pb $8.95

- M. Morgan Estergreen
  KIT CARSON: A Portrait in Courage
  0–8061–1601–3 Oklahoma pb $9.95

- Thelma S. Guild & Harvey L. Carter
  KIT CARSON: A Pattern for Heroes
  "The authors show how Carson gradually evolved from antagonist to friend of the Indian"—*American West*
  0–8032–2118–5 Nebraska $23.95

- John Wesley Hardin
  THE LIFE OF JOHN WESLEY HARDIN AS WRITTEN BY HIMSELF
  Introduction by Robert G. McCubbin
  0–8061–1051–1 Oklahoma pb $6.95

    IF YOU CAN'T FIND IT, LOOK IN THE INDEX

• Tom Horn
LIFE OF TOM HORN, GOVERNMENT SCOUT AND INTERPRETER, WRITTEN BY HIMSELF, TOGETHER WITH HIS LETTERS AND STATEMENTS BY HIS FRIENDS: A Vindication
Introduction by Dean Krakel
0–8061–1044–9 Oklahoma pb $7.95

• Joseph C. Rosa & Robin May
BUFFALO BILL AND HIS WILD WEST: A Pictorial Biography
0–7006–0398–0 Kansas $27.50
0–7006–0399–9 Kansas pb $14.95

• Don Russell
THE LIVES AND LEGENDS OF BUFFALO BILL
0–8061–1537–8 Oklahoma pb $14.95

• Glenn Shirley
BELLE STARR AND HER TIMES: The Literature, the Facts and the Legends
0–8061–1713–3 Oklahoma $19.95

Davy Crockett

David Crockett
A NARRATIVE OF THE LIFE OF DAVID CROCKETT OF THE STATE OF TENNESSEE
Readers "should find this carefully researched and authoritative edition, which extricates the man from the myth, a valuable addition to the frontier history, biography, and literature of Tennessee and America"— Robert E. Dalton, *Tennessee Historical Quarterly*
0–87049–119–9 Tennessee $16.95
0–87049–533–X Tennessee pb $7.95

Richard Boyd Hauck
DAVY CROCKETT: A Handbook
Includes an introductory biography and a look at how plays, movies, TV, biographies, historical novels, and his own autobiography have perpetuated Crockett's image
0–8032–7230–8 Nebraska pb $6.95

Michael A. Lofaro, editor
DAVY CROCKETT: The Man, the Legend, the Legacy
0–87049–459–7 Tennessee $24.95
0–87049–507–0 Tennessee pb $12.95

James A. Shackford
DAVID CROCKETT: The Man and the Legend
Introduction by Michael Lofaro
0–8078–4163–3 North Carolina pb $10.95

Outlaws and Vigilantes

• Pearl Baker
THE WILD BUNCH AT ROBBERS ROOST
A history of the famous hideout in the Utah desert that often sheltered the notorious Wild Bunch in the 1890s
0–8032–1210–0 Nebraska $19.95
0–8032–6089–X Nebraska pb $7.95

• John Boessenecker
BADGE AND BUCKSHOT: Lawlessness in Old California
The true stories of the once-famous peace officers and outlaws of old California, including Ben Thorn, the iron-willed but scandal-plagued sheriff of Calaveras County; the Coates-Frost feud, which left 14 men dead; and Captain Ingram's Rangers, who raided stagecoaches during the Civil War
0–8061–2097–5 Oklahoma $22.95

• Larry C. Bradley
JESSE JAMES: The Making of a Legend
An account of the much-mythicized Missouri bandit
0–9604370–0–2 Larren pb $8.95

• Thomas J. Dimsdale
THE VIGILANTES OF MONTANA
A 19th-century account of the coming of law and order
0–8061–1379–0 Oklahoma pb $6.95

• Pat Garrett
THE AUTHENTIC LIFE OF BILLY THE KID
The original biography of one of the Old West's most famous outlaws, by the man who shot him
0–8061–1195–X Oklahoma pb $6.95

• W. Hattich
TOMBSTONE, IN HISTORY, ROMANCE AND WEALTH
Foreword by John D. Gilchriese
0–8061–1753–2 Oklahoma $14.95

• Paula Mitchell Marks
AND DIE IN THE WEST: The Story of the O.K. Corral Gunfight
A detailed narrative account of the celebrated gunfight of 1881
0–688–07288–7 Morrow $20.95

• Roger D. McGrath
GUNFIGHTERS, HIGHWAYMEN AND VIGILANTES: Violence on the Frontier
McGrath's "comparisons between crime rates in the East and on the frontier, in the present and the past, are both unique and convincing, and . . . [his] criticisms of other writers on frontier violence are telling"—Ralph Mann, *New Mexico Historical Review*
0–520–06026–1 California pb $11.95

• A.S. Mercer
THE BANDITTI OF THE PLAINS
Foreword by William H. Kittrell
0–8061–1315–4 Oklahoma pb $7.95

• Bill O'Neal
ENCYCLOPEDIA OF WESTERN GUNFIGHTERS
0–8061–1508–4 Oklahoma $27.95

• John Rollin Ridge (Yellow Bird)
THE LIFE AND ADVENTURES OF JOAQUIN MURIETA, THE CELEBRATED CALIFORNIA BANDIT
Introduction by Henry Jackson
0–8061–0312–4 Oklahoma $14.95
0–8061–1429–0 Oklahoma pb $6.95

• Phillip W. Steele
JESSE AND FRANK JAMES: The Family History
0–88289–653–9 Pelican pb $6.95

• Stephen Tatum
INVENTING BILLY THE KID: Visions of the Outlaw in America, 1881–1981
How the myth of Billy the Kid affected American culture
0–8263–0823–6 New Mexico pb $10.95

• Jon Tuska
BILLY THE KID: A Handbook
"This is an excellent book—the best to date on the Kid and the making of the legend"—*Western Historical Quarterly*
0–8032–9406–9 Nebraska pb $7.95

• Robert M. Utley
HIGH NOON IN LINCOLN: Violence on the Western Frontier
The story of the 1878 Lincoln County War of New Mexico
0–8263–0981–X New Mexico $22.50

Cattlemen and Miners

• Andy Adams
THE LOG OF A COWBOY: A Narrative of the Old Trail Days
0–8032–1000–0 Nebraska $29.50
0–8032–5000–2 Nebraska pb $5.95

• Nannie T. Alderson & Helena H. Smith
A BRIDE GOES WEST
Memoir of ranching life in Montana
Illustrated by J. Cosgrove, Jr.
0–8032–5001–0 Nebraska pb $5.95

• Lewis Atherton
THE CATTLE KINGS
0–8032–5759–7 Nebraska pb $8.95

• Robert R. Dykstra
THE CATTLE TOWNS
Social and political diversions in the early days of Dodge City and Abilene
0–8032–6561–1 Nebraska pb $10.95

• Anne Ellis
THE LIFE OF AN ORDINARY WOMAN
Tales from Colorado mining camps
0–8032–6704–5 Nebraska pb $7.95

• Teresa Jordan
COWGIRLS: Women of the American West
An oral history of 28 contemporary women
0–385–14511–X Doubleday pb $10.95

• Thomas J. Noel
THE CITY AND THE SALOON: Denver, 1858–1916
0–8032–3306–X Nebraska $17.50
0–8032–3354–7 Nebraska pb $6.95

• Malcolm J. Rohrbough
ASPEN: The History of a Silver-Mining Town, 1879–1893
"How the mining frontier of the Colorado Rockies 'worked,' from its shaky first days,

A Texas cowboy breaking in a new mount, 1909 (courtesy of the Erwin E. Smith Collection, Library of Congress)

to its boom years, to ghost town"—Walter Nugent, University of Notre Dame
0–19–504064–3 Oxford $19.95

• Charles A. Siringo
A TEXAS COWBOY: Or, Fifteen Years on the Hurricane Deck of a Spanish Pony
0–8032–9111–6 Nebraska pb $8.95

• Duane A. Smith
ROCKY MOUNTAIN MINING CAMPS: The Urban Frontier
The overnight change from mining camps to towns and the urban problems that came with it
0–8032–5792–9 Nebraska pb $7.95

• Fay E. Ward
THE COWBOY AT WORK: All About His Job and How He Does It
A detailed account by an experienced practitioner
Foreword by John R. Erickson
0–8061–2051–7 Oklahoma pb $14.95

WARS AND CONFLICTS

• Harry Sinclair Drago
THE GREAT RANGE WARS: Violence on the Grasslands
The bloodiest range conflicts in Texas, Arizona, New Mexico, Wyoming, and Montana in the late 19th century
0–8032–6563–8 Nebraska pb $9.95

• Elizabeth A. Johns
STORMS BREWED IN OTHER MEN'S WORLDS: The Confrontation of Indians, Spanish, and French in the Southwest, 1540–1795
0–8032–7554–4 Nebraska pb $13.50

• Robert M. Utley
FRONTIERSMEN IN BLUE: The United States Army and the Indian, 1848–1865
0–8032–4550–5 Nebraska $31.00
0–8032–9550–2 Nebraska pb $10.95

FRONTIER REGULARS: The United States Army and the Indian, 1866–1891
The final, massive drive by the Regular Army to subdue and control the Indians
0–8032–9551–0 Nebraska pb $12.95

• Robert M. Utley & Wilcomb E. Washburn
INDIAN WARS
A well-told one-volume history
0–8281–0202–3 Houghton Mifflin pb $9.95

• Robert Wooster
THE MILITARY AND UNITED STATES INDIAN POLICY, 1865–1903
0–300–03972–7 Yale $22.50

The Custer Legend

• Stephen E. Ambrose
CRAZY HORSE AND CUSTER
Parallel lives converging at the Little Bighorn
0–452–00934–0 NAL pb $10.95

• Evan S. Connell
SON OF THE MORNING STAR: Custer and the Little Bighorn
A complex and beautifully written exploration, arriving not at one truth but at a multitude of sometimes contradictory realities
0–06–097161–4 Harper & Row pb $9.95

• George A. Custer
MY LIFE ON THE PLAINS: Or Personal Experiences with Indians
Covers the years 1867–69, including the Battle of the Washita
0–8061–1357–X Oklahoma pb $7.95

• W.A. Graham
THE CUSTER MYTH: A Source Book of Custeriana
Accounts from military journals, pamphlets, frontier newspapers, Arikawa and Crow scouts and the Sioux, all

offering their version of what really happened to Custer and his troops
0–8032–7016–X Nebraska pb $14.95

• Jay Monaghan
CUSTER: The Life of General George Armstrong Custer
0–8032–3056–7 Nebraska $31.95
0–8032–5732–5 Nebraska pb $10.95

• Robert M. Utley
CAVALIER IN BUCKSKIN: George Armstrong Custer and the Western Military Frontier
0–8061–2150–5 Oklahoma $19.95

• Frederic F. Van de Water
GLORY-HUNTER: A Life of General Custer
"A complex and unsparing analysis"— William Rose Benet, *Saturday Review of Literature*
0–8032–9607–X Nebraska pb $10.95

THE MAKING OF WESTERN STATES

Texas

• José Enrique De La Peña
WITH SANTA ANNA IN TEXAS: A Personal Narrative of the Revolution
Based on the diary of a captain in the Mexican Army, perhaps the best eyewitness account of the fall of the Alamo
Translated by Carmen Perry
Introduction by Llerena Friend
0–89096–001–1 Texas A&M $16.95

• T.R. Fehrenbach
LONE STAR: A History of Texas and the Texans
Particularly good on the early days
0–02–032170–8 Macmillan pb $12.95

• David Montejano
ANGLOS AND MEXICANS IN THE MAKING OF TEXAS, 1836–1986
0–292–77566–0 Texas $29.95
0–292–77596–2 Texas pb $12.95

• John M. Myers
THE ALAMO
0–8032–5779–1 Nebraska pb $5.95

California

• Richard E. Lingenfelter
DEATH VALLEY AND THE AMARGOSA: A Land of Illusion
"Death Valley is a wilderness of extremes—the lowest, the driest, the hottest—and not surprisingly, its human history represents one more extreme, a bumptious, sleazy, hilarious Wild West Show"—Mark Munro, *Boston Globe*
0–520–06356–2 California pb $15.95

TO ORDER BOOKS AS GIFTS, SEE PAGE 1

● Kevin Starr
AMERICANS AND THE CALIFORNIA DREAM, 1850–1915
"Demonstrates how idea, myth, misconception and hope shaped and often distorted a developing society"—*LA Times*
0–19–501644–0 Oxford $25.00
0–19–504233–6 Oxford pb $12.95

INVENTING THE DREAM: California Through the Progressive Era
Part two of Starr's cultural history focuses on the emergence of southern California as a regional culture in its own right
0–19–503489–9 Oxford $24.95
0–19–504234–4 Oxford pb $10.95

Other States

● Robert G. Athearn
THE COLORADANS
0–8263–0623–3 New Mexico pb $12.95

● Warren A. Beck
NEW MEXICO: A History of Four Centuries
0–8061–0533–X Oklahoma $24.95

● Odie Falk
ARIZONA: A Short History
0–8061–1222–0 Oklahoma pb $9.95

● Edwin C. McReynolds & others
OKLAHOMA: The Story of Its Past and Present
0–8061–0509–7 Oklahoma $16.95

● Paul C. Nagel
MISSOURI: A Bicentennial History
0–393–05633–3 Norton $14.95

● K. Ross Toole
MONTANA: An Uncommon Land
0–8061–1890–3 Oklahoma pb $8.95

THE 20TH-CENTURY WEST

● Robert G. Athearn
THE MYTHIC WEST IN TWENTIETH-CENTURY AMERICA
0–7006–0304–2 Kansas $25.00
0–7006–0377–8 Kansas pb $9.95

● Philip L. Fradkin
SAGEBRUSH COUNTRY: Land and the American West
A history of the Uinta National Forest that stretches through Utah, Wyoming, and Colorado, linking the past with such current issues as water rights, tensions between government and developers, and between conservationists and local residents
0–394–52935–9 Knopf $22.95

● Patricia Nelson Limerick
THE LEGACY OF CONQUEST: The Unbroken Past of the American West
A new interpretation, demonstrating strong continuities between the trappers, traders, Indians, farmers, oilmen, cowboys, and sheriffs of the old West and the economic realities of today's West
0–393–30497–3 Norton pb $9.95

● Ann M. Low
DUST BOWL DIARY
An autobiography of a girl growing up on a stock farm in North Dakota during the late 1920s and 1930s. "A lovingly detailed, sometimes humorous and often painful account"—*LA Times Book Review*
0–8032–2864–3 Nebraska $20.00
0–8032–7913–2 Nebraska pb $7.95

● Richard Lowitt
THE NEW DEAL AND THE WEST
How the New Deal combatted droughts, dust storms, locusts, and the Depression
Foreword by Martin Ridge
0–253–34005–5 Indiana $25.00

● John McPhee & Christopher Merrill, editors
OUTCROPPINGS
Anthology of McPhee's writings about the West
Photographs by Tom Till
0–87905–262–7 Peregrine Smith $29.95

● Gerald D. Nash
THE AMERICAN WEST IN THE TWENTIETH CENTURY: A Short History of an Urban Oasis
0–8263–0464–8 New Mexico pb $11.95

● Marc Reisner
CADILLAC DESERT: The American West and Its Disappearing Water
"A savagely witty history of America's reckless depletion of its water resources"—*Newsday*
0–14–010432–1 Penguin pb $9.95

● Peter Wiley & Robert Gottlieb
EMPIRES IN THE SUN: The Rise of the New American West
"A good old-fashioned muckraking journey through the slimy greed-and-growth politics of the American Southwest"—Edward Abbey
0–8165–0911–5 Arizona pb $10.95

● Donald Worster
RIVERS OF EMPIRE: Water, Aridity, and the Growth of the American West
0–394–75161–2 Pantheon pb $12.95

New Lands, New Men

John Burroughs & others
ALASKA: The Harriman Expedition, 1899
The original tales of the explorers who sailed from Seattle to the Bering Strait in the famed expedition financed by railroad magnate Edward Henry Harriman; copiously illustrated
0–486–25109–8 Dover pb $11.95

William H. Goetzmann
NEW LANDS, NEW MEN: America and the Second Great Age of Discovery
Explorations from the 17th to the 19th centuries of the Pacific Northwest, as well as the oceans, Japan, and the polar regions. "Ultimately a tale of high adventure—both in the physical and intellectual sense"—*Texas Monthly*
0–14–009733–3 Penguin pb $7.95

Claus M. Naske & Herman E. Slotnick
ALASKA: A History of the 49th State
0–8061–2099–1 Oklahoma $27.95

Robert E. Peary
THE NORTH POLE: Its Discovery in 1909 Under the Auspices of the Peary Arctic Club
0–486–25129–2 Dover pb $9.95

John Edward Weems
PEARY: The Explorer and the Man
Introduction by Sir Edmund Hillary
0–87477–469–1 Tarcher pb $11.95

THE SOUTH: Overviews

The South remains the strongest regional specialty in American historiography. The literature of Southern history is not only vast but also includes some of the most important historical writing we have.

► Books about the Confederacy can be found in The Civil War and Reconstruction; for slavery and the southern colonies see US History to the Civil War & African-American Studies

● Edward D.C. Campbell, Jr.
THE CELLULOID SOUTH: Hollywood and the Southern Myth
0–87049–327–2 Tennessee $24.95

● Wilbur Joseph Cash
THE MIND OF THE SOUTH
0–394–43623–7 Knopf $17.95
0–394–70098–8 Random House pb $3.95

● Carl N. Degler
PLACE OVER TIME: The Continuity of Southern Distinctiveness
0–8071–0299–7 LSU $12.95
0–8071–1031–1 LSU pb $5.95

● David C. Roller & Robert W. Twyman, editors
THE ENCYCLOPEDIA OF SOUTHERN HISTORY
0–8071–0575–9 LSU $90.00

● Charles Reagan Wilson & William Ferris, editors
ENCYCLOPEDIA OF SOUTHERN CULTURE
A monumental effort compiling the work of more than 800 scholars and writers. "Mirrors the very best of what has lately come to be called 'the new South' "—Alex Haley
0–8078–1823–2 North Carolina $59.95

● C. Vann Woodward
THE BURDEN OF SOUTHERN HISTORY
Outstanding essays by the South's most famous historian
0–8071–0837–5 LSU $25.00
0–8071–0133–8 LSU pb $7.95

THE ANTEBELLUM SOUTH

• **Edward L. Ayers**
**VENGEANCE AND JUSTICE: Crime and
Punishment in the 19th-Century American
South**
0–19–503383–3 Oxford $38.00
0–19–503988–2 Oxford pb $11.95

• **Carol Bleser**
THE HAMMONDS OF REDCLIFFE
0–19–502920–8 Oxford $25.00
0–19–504984–5 Oxford pb $8.95

• **Carol Bleser, editor**
**SECRET AND SACRED: The Diaries of
James Henry Hammond, a Southern
Slaveholder**
0–19–505308–7 Oxford pb $22.95

• **Steven A. Channing**
**CRISIS OF FEAR: Secession in South
Carolina**
0–393–00730–8 Norton pb $7.95

• **Avery O. Craven**
**EDMUND RUFFIN, SOUTHERNER: A
Study in Secession**
The ardent Southern nationalist who fired
the first shot at Fort Sumter and killed
himself after Appomattox
0–8071–0104–4 LSU pb $9.95

• **Drew G. Faust**
**JAMES HENRY HAMMOND AND THE
OLD SOUTH: A Design for Mastery**
0–8071–1048–5 LSU $32.50
0–8071–1248–8 LSU pb $8.95

• **Martha McCulloch-Williams**
**DISHES AND BEVERAGES OF THE
OLD SOUTH**
A facsimile of the original (1913). " 'Must'
reading for anyone who wants to
understand the history and culture of the
real South"—Stephen A. Smith
Introduction by John Egerton
0–87049–580–1 Tennessee $14.95

• **Frank L. Owsley**
PLAIN FOLK OF THE OLD SOUTH
Foreword by Grady McWhiney
0–8071–1062–0 LSU $22.50
0–8071–1063–9 LSU pb $6.95

• **Steven M. Stowe**
**INTIMACY AND POWER IN THE OLD
SOUTH: Ritual in the Lives of the Planters**
0–8018–3388–4 Johns Hopkins $29.50

• **Bertram Wyatt-Brown**
**HONOR AND VIOLENCE IN THE OLD
SOUTH**
0–19–504241–7 Oxford $24.95
0–19–504242–5 Oxford pb $7.95

The Slave South

• **William J. Cooper, Jr.**
**THE SOUTH AND THE POLITICS OF
SLAVERY, 1828–1856**
0–8071–0385–3 LSU $37.50
0–8071–0775–1 LSU pb $8.95

*Ralph E.W. Earl's 1824 "The Ephraim Hubbard Foster Family" (courtesy of the Cheekwood Fine
Arts Center), from* The Art of the Old South: Painting, Sculpture, Architecture, and the
Products of Craftsmen *by Jessie Poesch (Knopf)*

• **Alison G. Freehling**
**DRIFT TOWARD DISSOLUTION: The
Virginia Slavery Debate of 1831–1832**
0–8071–1035–3 LSU $32.50

• **Eugene D. Genovese**
**THE WORLD THE SLAVEHOLDERS
MADE: Two Essays in Interpretation**
A comparative history of slavery and the
Virginia pro-slavery ideologue George
Fitzhugh
0–819–56204–1 Wesleyan pb $12.95

• **Kenneth S. Greenberg**
**MASTERS AND STATESMEN: The
Political Culture of American Slavery**
0–8018–2762–0 Johns Hopkins $22.50

• **J. Mills Thornton**
**POLITICS AND POWER IN A SLAVE
SOCIETY: Alabama, 1800–1860**
0–8071–0259–8 LSU $40.00
0–8071–0891–X LSU pb $12.95

AFTER SLAVERY: Origins of The New South

• **David Carlton**
**MILL AND TOWN IN SOUTH
CAROLINA, 1880–1920**
0–8071–1042–6 LSU $32.50
0–8071–1059–0 LSU pb $14.95

• **Charles L. Flynn, Jr.**
**WHITE LAND, BLACK LABOR: Caste
and Class in Late 19th-Century Georgia**
0–8071–1097–3 LSU $27.50

• **Gaines M. Foster**
**GHOSTS OF THE CONFEDERACY:
Defeat, the Lost Cause and the Emergence
of the New South, 1865–1913**
0–19–504213–1 Oxford $34.00

• **Steven Hahn**
**THE ROOTS OF SOUTHERN
POPULISM: Yeoman Farmers and the
Transformation of the Georgia Upcountry,
1850–1890**
0–19–503249–7 Oxford $34.50
0–19–503508–9 Oxford pb $12.95

• **Louis D. Rubin, Jr., editor**
**I'LL TAKE MY STAND: The South and
the Agrarian Tradition**
0–8071–0357–8 LSU pb $9.95

• **Barton C. Shaw**
**THE WOOL-HAT BOYS: Georgia's
Populist Party**
0–8071–1148–1 LSU $25.00

• **Altina L. Waller**
**FEUD: Hatfields, McCoys, and Social
Change in Appalachia, 1860–1900**
The legendary struggle as a symbol of
economic and social struggle between local
interests and outside industrialists
0–8078–4216–8 Chapel Hill pb $12.50

C. Vann Woodward
**ORIGINS OF THE NEW SOUTH,
1877–1913**
Still overshadows its entire field more
than 30 years after publication. A
landmark of American historical writing
0–8071–0009–9 LSU $30.00
0–8071–0019–6 LSU pb $9.95

• **Gavin Wright**
**OLD SOUTH, NEW SOUTH: Revolutions
in the Southern Economy since the Civil
War**
Why the New South took so long to rise
again and how it has become the nation's
fastest-growing region since World War II
0–465–05193–6 Basic Books $19.95
0–465–05194–4 Basic Books pb $9.95

- Gavin Wright, editor
THE POLITICAL ECONOMY OF THE COTTON SOUTH
0–393–09038–8 Norton pb $7.95

THE NEW SOUTH

- Pete Daniel
STANDING AT THE CROSSROADS: Southern Life in the 20th Century
0–8090–8821–5 Hill & Wang $19.95
0–8090–0167–5 Hill & Wang pb $7.95

- Richard H. King
A SOUTHERN RENAISSANCE: The Cultural Awakening of the American South, 1930–1955
0–19–502664–0 Oxford $22.50
0–19–503043–5 Oxford pb $8.95

- Jack T. Kirby
RURAL WORLDS LOST: The American South, 1920–1960
0–8071–1360–3 LSU pb $16.95

- Alexander P. Lamis
THE TWO-PARTY SOUTH
0–19–505680–9 Oxford $34.00

- A.J. Liebling
EARL OF LOUISIANA
Foreword by T. Harry Williams
0–8071–0203–2 LSU pb $8.95

- Anne C. Loveland
LILLIAN SMITH: A Southerner Confronting the South
0–8071–1343–3 LSU $24.95

- William A. Percy
LANTERNS ON THE LEVEE: Recollections of a Planter's Son
Introduction by Walker Percy
0–8071–1184–8 LSU $19.95
0–8071–0072–2 LSU pb $9.95

- John S. Reed
THE ENDURING SOUTH: Subcultural Persistence in Mass Society
Foreword by Edwin M. Yoder, Jr.
0–8078–4162–5 North Carolina pb $7.95

North Carolina textile worker in the 1970s

- Daniel J. Singal
THE WAR WITHIN: From Victorian to Modernist Thought in the South, 1919–1945
0–8078–1505–5 North Carolina $30.00
0–8078–4087–4 North Carolina pb $15.95

- George B. Tindall
THE EMERGENCE OF THE NEW SOUTH, 1913–1945
0–8071–0010–2 LSU $30.00
0–8071–0020–X LSU pb $12.95

Southern Places

- Harry M. Caudill
NIGHT COMES TO THE CUMBERLANDS: A Biography of a Depressed Area
The impoverished people and land in a region of Appalachia where coal mining is king. "The story of how this rich and beautiful land was changed into an ugly, poverty-ridden place of desolation"—*NY Times*
0–316–13212–8 Little, Brown pb $9.95

- Robert E. Corlew
TENNESSEE: A Short History
The second edition of this work traces the state from its beginnings to 1978, offering a searching appraisal of its development and future
0–87049–302–7 Tennessee pb $14.50

- Harley E. Jolley
THE BLUE RIDGE PARKWAY
An illustrated history and guide
0–87049–100–8 Kentucky pb $7.95

- Lawrence H. Larsen
THE URBAN SOUTH: A History
0–8131–0309–6 Kentucky $23.00

- Oxmoor House
GREAT AMERICAN HOMES
A 4-volume set of text and photographs focusing on the great mansions of the Old South; volumes are Historic Charleston, Mansions of the Virginia Gentry, Plantations of the Old South, and Old New Orleans
0–8487–0754–0 Little, Brown (set) $60.00

- William S. Powell
NORTH CAROLINA THROUGH FOUR CENTURIES
A single volume on the events and people that have shaped the history of the Tarheel state
0–8078–1846–1 North Carolina $24.95

- Robert Tallant
MARDI GRAS . . . AS IT WAS
A tour of Mardi Gras traditions, first published in 1947
0–88289–722–5 Penguin pb $7.95

- William S. Ward
A LITERARY HISTORY OF KENTUCKY
0–87049–577–1 Tennessee $34.95
0–87049–578–X Tennessee pb $17.50

American People and Places

IMMIGRATION

"So we come finally to a paradox in assessing the impact of immigration. Clearly, it has enhanced the variety of American culture. Its diversifying influence is imprinted in the American ideal of nationality, in the American religious pattern, and in the sheer presence of so many different human types. On the other hand, the diversities have given way time and again to pressures for uniformity, which have come not just from older Americans but which immigrants and their children have also shaped and inspired. Through the systems of mass production and mass communications, America and its immigrants assimilated one another within an urban, technological culture that overrode distinctions of place, class, and ethnic type.

Yet the distinctions were never obliterated, the assimilation never wholly satisfying or complete. Today many Americans are rebuilding ethnic identities, and are discovering that America no longer looks as monolithic as it did a few years ago. Other societies have had a simpler experience with immigrant groups, either absorbing them or acquiescing in their separateness. In American life these contrary impulses mingle, their tensions unresolved, their implications still unfolding."—John Higham, *Send These to Me: Immigrants in Urban America*

- John Bodnar
THE TRANSPLANTED: A History of Immigrants in Urban America
Summarizes the newer view that immigrants maintained a separate identity rooted in their national traditions
0–253–20416–X Indiana pb $8.95

- David M. Brownstone & others
ISLAND OF HOPE, ISLAND OF TEARS
An oral history of some of the nearly 15 million people who passed through Ellis Island
0–14–008820–2 Penguin pb $7.95

- Lewis A. Coser
REFUGEE SCHOLARS IN AMERICA: Their Impact and Their Experiences
0–300–03193–9 Yale $29.50

- Leonard Dinnerstein & others
NATIVES AND STRANGERS: Ethnic Groups and the Building of America
The role of blacks, Indians, and immigrant minorities in transforming colonial society into the nation of the 1970s
0–19–502426–5 Oxford $24.95
0–19–502427–3 Oxford pb $10.95

• Nathan Glazer & Daniel P. Moynihan
BEYOND THE MELTING POT: The Negroes, Puerto Ricans, Jews, Italians, and Irish of New York City
0–262–57022–X MIT pb $10.95

Oscar Handlin
BOSTON'S IMMIGRANTS: A Study in Acculturation
An early landmark study (1941) of ethnic acculturation. "The first historical case study of the impact of immigrants upon a particular society and of the adjustment of the immigrants to that society"—*American Journal of Sociology*
0–674–07980–9 Harvard $27.00
0–674–07985–X Harvard pb $9.95

THE UPROOTED: The Story of the Great Migrations that Made the American People
The Pulitzer Prize-winning story (1952) of immigrant lives, cut off from their heritage by distance and American culture
0–316–34313–7 Little, Brown pb $9.95

Jakob Mithelstadt and family, Russian Germans en route to North Dakota, in a 1905 photograph by Augustus Sherman (courtesy of The American Museum of Immigration at the Statue of Liberty)

• John Higham
SEND THESE TO ME: Immigrants in Urban America
Essays on Jewish immigration, anti-Semitism, and other topics
0–8018–2438–9 Johns Hopkins pb $10.95

• Dirk Hoerder, editor
STRUGGLE A HARD BATTLE: Essays on Working-Class Immigrants
0–87580–112–9 Northern Illinois $25.00
0–87580–533–7 Northern Illinois pb $9.50

• Maldwyn Allen Jones
AMERICAN IMMIGRATION
A survey from 1607 to 1959, analyzing the forces that uprooted Europeans and their roles in America's sectional conflicts, labor movements, westward expansion, and foreign policy
0–226–40632–6 Chicago pb $10.00

• Thomas Kessner
THE GOLDEN DOOR: Italian and Jewish Immigrant Mobility in New York City, 1880–1915
How two immigrant groups, with differing results, used New York not only as an entry port but also as a stepping-stone to Americanization
0–19–502116–9 Oxford $22.50
0–19–502161–4 Oxford pb $10.95

• Thomas Kessner & Betty Boyd Caroli
TODAY'S IMMIGRANTS, THEIR STORIES: A New Look at the Newest Americans
0–19–503000–1 Oxford $19.95
0–19–503270–5 Oxford pb $8.95

• Stanley Lieberson
A PIECE OF THE PIE: Black and White Immigrants Since 1880
0–520–04362–6 California pb $14.95

• David M. Reimers
STILL THE GOLDEN DOOR: The Third World Comes to America
Charts the shift in immigration that has brought an influx of newcomers from the Third World
0–231–05771–7 Columbia pb $14.50

• Al Santolini
NEW AMERICANS, AN ORAL HISTORY: Immigrants and Refugees in the U.S. Today
By the author of *Everything We Had*
0–670–81583–7 Viking $19.95

• Ronald Takaki, editor
FROM DIFFERENT SHORES: Perspectives on Race and Ethnicity in America
0–19–504187–9 Oxford pb $14.95

• Stephan Thernstrom, Ann Orlov & Oscar Handlin, editors
HARVARD ENCYCLOPEDIA OF AMERICAN ETHNIC GROUPS
A splendid resource on American immigration and ethnicity
0–674–37512–2 Harvard $90.00

• Marvin Trachtenberg
THE STATUE OF LIBERTY: The Centenary Edition of a Classic History and Guide
Beautifully illustrated
0–14–008493–2 Penguin pb $12.95

• Doris Weatherford
FOREIGN AND FEMALE: Immigrant Women in America, 1840–1930
"If their superstitions ring strange in our ears, if their vulnerability seems pathetic, Weatherford's work shows us their enormous resiliency, their dogged determination to find a better life"—from the Foreword by Lillian Schlissel
0–8052–4017–9 Schocken $18.95

• Thomas Wheeler, editor
IMMIGRANT EXPERIENCE: The Anguish of Becoming American
Personal narratives on the immigrant experience
0–14–021575–1 Penguin pb $5.95

ETHNIC AND RACE RELATIONS

• Derrick Bell
AND WE ARE NOT SAVED: The Elusive Quest for Racial Reform
0–465–00328–1 Basic Books $19.95

• Leslie W. Dunbar, editor
MINORITY REPORT: What Has Happened to Blacks, Hispanics, American Indians, and Other Minorities in the Eighties
Seven civil rights veterans chronicle the status of political power, economic clout, and social mobility for America's minorities
0–394–72513–1 Pantheon pb $9.95

• Nathan Glazer
AFFIRMATIVE DISCRIMINATION: Ethnic Inequality and Public Policy
0–674–00730–1 Harvard pb $8.95

• Fred R. Harris & Roger W. Wilkins
QUIET RIOTS: Race and Poverty in the United States
An update on the Kerner Report finds segregation more pronounced, poverty deeper, and unemployment doubled in America's inner cities
0–394–57473–7 Pantheon $19.95
0–679–72100–2 Random House pb $8.95

➤ **FOR OVERSEAS ORDERING INFORMATION, SEE PAGE 1**

- Ivan H. Light
  ETHNIC ENTERPRISE IN AMERICA:
  Business and Welfare among Chinese,
  Japanese, and Blacks
  0–520–01738–2 California $33.00
  0–520–02485–0 California pb $9.95

- Gunnar Myrdal
  AN AMERICAN DILEMMA
  A classic dissertation on race relations
  considered in moral terms, viewing racism
  as a kind of caste system
  Volume 1
  0–394–73042–9 Pantheon pb $5.95
  Volume 2
  0–394–73043–7 Pantheon pb $5.95

- National Advisory Commission on
  Civil Disorders
  THE KERNER REPORT
  The findings that shocked the nation in
  1968 are still valid today
  Introductions by Fred R. Harris & Tom Wicker
  0–679–72078–2 Pantheon pb $8.95

- Thomas F. Pettigrew
  THE SOCIOLOGY OF RACE
  RELATIONS: Reflection and Reform
  0–02–925110–9 Free Press pb $17.95

- Richard Polenberg
  ONE NATION DIVISIBLE: Class, Race
  and Ethnicity in the United States Since
  1938
  "Deftly manipulates a wide variety of
  materials, from the perplexing statistical
  profiles provided by government surveys to
  the work of social scientists Gunnar
  Myrdal, Ashley Montagu, and David
  Riesman, to the poetry of Nikki Giovanni
  and the fiction of Joseph Heller"—Alan M.
  Kraut, *Washington Star*
  0–14–021246–9 Penguin pb $7.95

- Thomas Sowell
  ETHNIC AMERICA: A History
  0–465–02075–5 Basic Books pb $9.95

- Robin M. Williams, Jr.
  MUTUAL ACCOMMODATION: Ethnic
  Conflict and Cooperation
  A realistic, though somewhat upbeat,
  appraisal of the prospects for an integrated
  but pluralistic America, by a Cornell social
  scientist
  0–8166–0845–8 Minnesota pb $10.95

Nativism, Bigotry, and the Extreme Right

- David M. Chalmers
  HOODED AMERICANISM: The History
  of the Ku Klux Klan
  "Chalmers has steeped himself in the
  details of the KKK organization,
  personalities, and intrigue, and particularly
  their relation to the entire nation"—
  American Historical Review
  0–8223–0772–3 Duke pb $12.95

- James Coates
  ARMED AND DANGEROUS: The Rise of
  the Survivalist Right
  "Introduces us to the world of those who
  live by the gun, and who plan to succeed
  the rest of us by surviving the coming

Apocalypse and rebuilding a pure Aryan
race"—Christopher Hitchens, *Newsday*
0–374–52125–5 Farrar, Straus & Giroux pb $8.95

- Kevin Flynn & Gary Gerhardt
  THE SILENT BROTHERHOOD: Inside
  America's Racist Underground
  0–02–910312–6 Free Press $22.95

- John Higham
  STRANGERS IN THE LAND: Patterns of
  American Nativism, 1860–1920s
  A scholarly study of restrictive immigration
  0–8135–1308–1 Rutgers pb $12.00

- William L. Katz
  THE INVISIBLE EMPIRE: Ku Klux Klan
  Impact on History
  The KKK from its birth in 1866 to the
  present, and its relation to government
  institutions
  0–940880–15–6 Open Hand $17.95
  0–940880–14–8 Open Hand pb $9.95

- Dennis King
  LYNDON LAROUCHE AND THE NEW
  AMERICAN FASCISM
  A brilliant piece of investigative reporting
  0–385–23880–0 Doubleday $19.95

- Thomas Martinez with John Guinther
  BROTHERHOOD OF MURDER
  An inside account of going undercover to
  expose a racist hate movement
  0–07–040699–5 McGraw-Hill $17.95

- Harold E. Quinley & Charles Y.
  Cook
  ANTI-SEMITISM IN AMERICA
  0–02–925640–2 Free Press $14.95

- Paul Roberts
  AN AMERICAN FUHRER: Lyndon
  LaRouche and the Politics of Paranoia
  Traces LaRouche's beginnings as a
  Trotskyite labor leader to his current
  position of great influence, his neo-Nazi
  affiliations, and his presidential ambitions
  0–312–02161–5 St. Martin's $16.95

- Stephen Singular
  TALKED TO DEATH: The Life and
  Murder of Alan Berg
  0–688–06154–0 Morrow $17.95

- Wyn Craig Wade
  THE FIERY CROSS: The Ku Klux Klan in
  America
  History and photos with emphasis on the
  Klan's changing methods, actions, targets,
  and survival
  0–671–41476–3 Simon & Schuster $19.95
  0–671–65723–2 Simon & Schuster pb $10.95

THE MELTING POT

African-Americans

▶ **See also African-American Studies**

- Lerone Bennett, Jr.
  BEFORE THE MAYFLOWER: A History
  of Black America
  0–87485–029–0 Johnson $25.00
  0–14–007214–4 Penguin pb $9.95

- August Meier & Elliott Rudwick
  FROM PLANTATION TO GHETTO
  Black history from the slave trade through
  the civil rights era
  0–8090–0122–5 Hill & Wang pb $8.95

- Benjamin Quarles
  THE NEGRO IN THE MAKING OF
  AMERICA
  0–02–036140–8 Macmillan pb $5.95

Asian-Americans

- Yuji Ichioka
  THE ISSEI: The World of the First
  Generation Japanese Immigrants,
  1885–1924
  0–02–915370–0 Free Press $22.95

- Peter Irons
  JUSTICE AT WAR: The Inside Story of
  the Japanese-American Internment
  The imprisonment of thousands of
  Japanese-Americans whose loyalty was
  questioned during World War II
  0–19–503273–X Oxford $24.95
  0–19–503497–X Oxford pb $11.95

- Maxine Hong Kingston
  CHINA MEN
  "Captures the emotional truth of the
  Chinese-American experience far better
  than any conventional history"—*Newsday*
  0–679–72328–5 Random House pb $7.95

  THE WOMAN WARRIOR: Memoirs of a
  Girlhood Among Ghosts
  National Book Critics' Circle Award
  winner (1976). "Dizzying, elemental, a
  poem turned into a sword"—*NY Times*
  0–679–72188–6 Random House pb $6.95

- Peter Kwong
  THE NEW CHINATOWN
  0–374–52121–2 Farrar, Straus & Giroux pb $7.95

From Chinese-American Portraits: Personal
Histories, 1828-1988 *by Ruthanne Lum
McCunn (Chronicle)*

• Ruthanne Lum McCunn
CHINESE-AMERICAN PORTRAITS:
Personal Histories, 1828–1988
Illustrated
0–87701–580–5 Chronicle $29.95
0–87701–491–4 Chronicle pb $16.95

• H. Brett Melendy
ASIANS IN AMERICA
Focuses on Filipinos, Koreans, and East
Indians
0–88254–513–2 Hippocrene pb $9.95

CHINESE AND JAPANESE AMERICANS
0–88254–901–4 Hippocrene pb $7.95

• Victor & Brett De Bary Nee
LONGTIME CALIFORN': A Documentary
Study of an American Chinatown
A fascinating portrait of San Francisco's
Chinatown
0–8047–1336–7 Stanford pb $10.95

• Ronald Takaki
STRANGERS FROM A DIFFERENT
SHORE: A History of Asian-Americans
A popular, comprehensive history
0–316–83109–3 Little, Brown $22.95

• Shih-shan Henry Tsai
THE CHINESE EXPERIENCE IN
AMERICA
0–253–31359–7 Indiana $29.95
0–253–20387–2 Indiana pb $9.95

German-Americans

• Jay P. Dolan
THE IMMIGRANT CHURCH: New
York's Irish and German-Catholics,
1815–1865
Foreword by Martin E. Marty
0–268–01151–6 Notre Dame pb $7.95

• Frederick C. Luebke
BONDS OF LOYALTY: German-Americans
and World War I
German immigrants found that latent
tensions erupted into manifest hostilities at
the outbreak of war, though most
German-Americans remained loyal to their
adopted country
0–87580–514–0 Northern Illinois pb $6.00

Hispanic-Americans

• Rodolfo Acuna
OCCUPIED AMERICA: A History of
Chicanos
0–06–040163–X Harper & Row pb $17.95

• Ted Conover
COYOTES
Disguised as a Mexican alien, the author
followed the harrowing path through
today's underground railroad, over the
American border, and into the world of
illegal aliens
0–394–75518–9 Random House pb $6.95

• Nan Elsasser, Kyle MacKenzie &
others
LAS MUJERES: Conversations from a
Hispanic Community
An oral history of four generations of New
Mexico Hispanic women
0–912670–70–3 Feminist Press pb $9.95

• Rodolfo O. de la Garza & others
THE MEXICAN AMERICAN
EXPERIENCE: An Interdisciplinary
Anthology
0–292–75088–9 Texas $25.00
0–292–75083–8 Texas pb $14.95

• Douglas Kent Hall
THE BORDER: Life on the Line
A beautifully illustrated panorama of life
and its struggles on the Mexican border
0–89659–685–0 Abbeville $35.00

• Lester D. Langley
MEXAMERICA: Two Countries, One
Future
0–517–56732–6 Crown $19.95

• Matt S. Meier & Feliciano Rivera
THE CHICANOS: A History of Mexican
Americans
0–8090–1365–7 Hill & Wang pb $9.95

• Ricardo Romo
EAST LOS ANGELES: History of a Barrio
0–292–72041–6 Texas pb $8.95

• Thomas Weyr
HISPANIC USA: Breaking the Melting Pot
A portrait of the minority that, by 1995,
will be the nation's largest
0–06–039066–2 Harper & Row $19.95

The Sanctuary Movement

Ann Crittenden
SANCTUARY: A Story of American
Conscience and Law in Collision
The movement that, in defiance of law,
has provided a haven for Central
American refugees
1–55584–039–6 W&N $21.95

Miriam Davidson
CONVICTIONS OF THE HEART: Jim
Corbett and the Sanctuary Movement
0–8165–1034–2 Arizona $19.95

Irish-Americans

• Stephen Birmingham
REAL LACE: America's Irish Rich
0–425–08789–1 Berkley pb $3.95

• Bob Callahan, editor
THE BIG BOOK OF AMERICAN IRISH
CULTURE
A glorious coffee-table book filled with
pictures and commentary
0–670–81825–9 Viking $29.95
0–14–010326–0 Penguin pb $12.95

• Dennis Clark
THE IRISH IN PHILADELPHIA: Ten
Generations of Urban Experience
0–87722–227–4 Temple pb $12.95

• Andrew M. Greeley
THE IRISH-AMERICANS: The Rise to
Money and Power
Argues that "Irish-Catholic Americans have
become the most successful educational,
occupational, and economic gentile ethnic
group in America"—*NY Times Book Review*
0–446–38558–1 Warner pb $8.95

• Jack Holland
THE AMERICAN CONNECTION: U.S.
Guns, Money, and Influence in Northern
Ireland
0–14–008495–9 Penguin pb $7.95

• Lawrence J. McCaffrey
THE IRISH DIASPORA IN AMERICA
0–8132–0593–X Catholic University pb $8.95

• Kerby A. Miller
EMIGRANTS AND EXILES: Ireland and
the Irish Exodus to North America
An outstanding recent work that
emphasizes the pain of migration
0–19–505187–4 Oxford pb $13.95

Italian-Americans

• John W. Briggs
AN ITALIAN PASSAGE: Immigrants to
Three American Cities, 1890–1930
0–300–02095–3 Yale $37.50

• Linda Brandi Cateura
GROWING UP ITALIAN: How Being
Brought Up as an Italian-American Helped
Shape the Characters, Lives, and Fortunes
of Twenty-Four Celebrated Americans
Profiles include Yogi Berra, Tony Bennett,
Gay Talese, Ellie Smeal, Mario Cuomo,
and others
0–688–07952–0 Morrow pb $7.95

• Donna R. Gabaccia
FROM SICILY TO ELIZABETH
STREET: Housing and Social Change
among Italian Immigrants, 1880–1930
0–87395–768–7 SUNY $44.50
0–87395–769–5 SUNY pb $18.95

• Humbert S. Nelli
FROM IMMIGRANTS TO ETHNICS:
The Italian Americans
0–19–503200–4 Oxford $29.95

• Virginia Yans-McLaughlin
FAMILY AND COMMUNITY: Italian
Immigrants in Buffalo, 1880–1930
0–8014–1036–3 Cornell $27.50
0–252–00916–9 Illinois pb $8.95

Jewish-Americans

▶ **See also Jewish History**

• Irving Howe
WORLD OF OUR FATHERS
0–15–146353–0 HBJ $29.95
0–671–49252–7 Simon & Schuster pb $12.95

• Ronald Sanders
THE DOWNTOWN JEWS: Portraits of an
Immigrant Generation
0–486–25510–7 Dover pb $9.95

• Sydney Stahl Weinberg
THE WORLD OF OUR MOTHERS: The
Lives of Jewish Immigrant Women
0–8078–1762–7 North Carolina $22.95

Other Groups

• John J. Bukowczyk
AND MY CHILDREN DID NOT KNOW
ME: A History of the Polish-American
0–253–30701–5 Indiana $27.50
0–253–20391–0 Indiana pb $8.95

◉ **TO ORDER ANY BOOK IN THIS CATALOG, ASK YOUR BOOKSELLER OR CALL 1-800-882-8770**

New York City's Hester Street, c. 1900, from The American Century *by Walter LaFeber and others (Knopf)*

• Odd Lovell
THE PROMISE OF AMERICA: A History of the Norwegian-American People
0–8166–1334–6 Minnesota pb $16.95

• Robert Mirak
TORN BETWEEN TWO LANDS: Armenians in America, 1890-World War I
0–674–89541–X Harvard pb $12.95

• Gregory Orfalea
BEFORE THE FLAMES: A Quest for the History of Arab-Americans
Orfalea's search for identity took him on a ten-year odyssey from Los Angeles to his family's ancestral village in Syria
0–292–70748–7 Texas $22.50

• Ted Pejovich
THE STATE OF CALIFORNIA: Growing Up Foreign in the Backyards of Eden
Memoir of a bilingual boyhood among immigrant migrant farmers in California's Santa Clara Valley
0–394–56863–X Knopf $16.95

• Marlene Sway
FAMILIAR STRANGERS: Gypsy Life in America
How their family structure, religion, system of justice, economic practices, and culture have prevented their assimilation
0–252–01512–6 Illinois $19.95

CLASS IN AMERICA

"Class distinctions in America are so complicated and subtle that foreign visitors often miss the nuances and sometimes even the existence of a class structure. So powerful is 'the fable of equality,' as Frances Trollope called it when she toured America in 1832, so embarrassed is the government to confront the subject—in the thousands of measurements pouring from its bureaus, social class is not officially recognized—that it's easy for visitors not to notice the way the class system works. A case in point is the experience of Walter Allen, the British novelist and literary critic. Before he came over here to teach at a college in the 1950s, he imagined that 'class scarcely existed in America, except, perhaps, as divisions between ethnic groups or successive waves of immigrants.' But living a while in Grand Rapids opened his eyes: there he learned of the snob power of New England and the pliability of the locals to the long-wielded moral and cultural authority of old families."—Paul Fussell, *Class*

• Paul Fussell
CLASS: A Guide Through the American Status System
A witty guide to its signs, symbols, and customs
0–345–31816–1 Ballantine pb $3.95

• Lewis H. Lapham
MONEY AND CLASS IN AMERICA: Notes and Observations on our Civil Religion
The editor of *Harper's* dissects Americans' endless quest for self-gratification through wealth
1–55584–109–0 Weidenfeld & Nicolson $18.95

• Michael J. Weiss
THE CLUSTERING OF AMERICA
The class-dominated landscape of America's neighborhoods, from "Blue Blood Estates" to ghettos
0–06–015790–9 Harper & Row $22.50

Social Mobility

• Matthew Edel, Eliott Sclar & Daniel Luria
SHAKY PALACES: Home Ownership and Social Mobility in Boston, 1870–1970
0–231–05627–3 Columbia pb $19.00

• Frank Levy
DOLLARS AND DREAMS: The Changing American Income Distribution
Argues that a family's chances of attaining the middle-class dream have declined significantly since 1973
0–393–30557–0 Norton pb $7.95

• Stephan Thernstrom
THE OTHER BOSTONIANS: Poverty and Progress in the American Metropolis, 1880–1970
A classic study of social mobility
0–674–64495–6 Harvard $24.50
0–674–64496–4 Harvard pb $10.95

POVERTY AND PROGRESS: Social Mobility in a Nineteenth-Century City
An exciting social history that uses census records and other previously neglected sources to recover the lives of ordinary people
0–674–69500–3 Harvard $22.50
0–674–69501–1 Harvard pb $8.95

THE UPPER CLASS

• Nelson W. Aldrich, Jr.
OLD MONEY: The Mythology of America's Upper Class
"A revealing document not just about one social class in America but about class itself"—Richard Sennett
0–394–57036–7 Knopf $19.95
0–679–72224–6 Random House pb $8.95

• Michael Patrick Allen
THE FOUNDING FORTUNES
0–525–24569–3 Dutton $22.50
0–525–48484–1 Dutton pb $12.95

• E. Digby Baltzell
PHILADELPHIA GENTLEMEN: The Making of a National Upper Class
A first-rate study of the rise of the Eastern urban aristocracy
0–8122–7765–1 Pennsylvania $16.95

THE PROTESTANT ESTABLISHMENT
An interesting study of the role of upper-class anti-Semitism
0–300–03917–4 Yale $35.00
0–300–03818–6 Yale pb $13.95

PURITAN BOSTON AND QUAKER PHILADELPHIA
The leading families of two leading cities—and how they have differed throughout their history
0–02–901320–8 Free Press $24.95

• Stephen Birmingham
AMERICA'S SECRET ARISTOCRACY
An inside view of America's oldest and foremost families and their clubs, estates, schools, sports, marriages, and financial empires
0–316–09650–4 Little, Brown $18.95

"One of the Codfish Aristocracy": an 1849 caricature of a New York Opera subscriber (courtesy The New-York Historical Society)

- Frederic C. Jaher
THE URBAN ESTABLISHMENT: Upper Strata in Boston, New York, Charleston, Chicago and Los Angeles
An encyclopedic study full of fascinating data
0–252–00827–8 Illinois $42.50
0–252–00932–0 Illinois pb $14.95

- Ferdinand Lundberg
THE RICH AND THE SUPER RICH: A Study in the Power of Money Today
A reissue of the classic first published in 1968
0–8184–0486–8 Lyle Stuart $14.95

- Vance Packard
THE ULTRA RICH: How Much is Too Much?
What it means to be "ultra rich" and some prescriptions for change in the American system of rewards; based on interviews with 30 extraordinarily wealthy men and women
0–316–68752–9 Little, Brown $22.95

- Ronald Story
HARVARD AND THE BOSTON UPPER CLASS
0–8195–6135–5 Wesleyan pb $12.95

THE MIDDLE CLASS

- Loren Baritz
THE GOOD LIFE: The Meaning of Success for the American Middle Class
The middle class throughout American history, from immigrant settlements to the consumer-driven 1980s
0–394–54947–3 Knopf $19.95

- Burton J. Bledstein
THE CULTURE OF PROFESSIONALISM: The Middle Class and the Development of Higher Education in America
0–393–05574–4 Norton $12.95
0–393–00891–6 Norton pb $9.95

- Barbara Ehrenreich
FEAR OF FALLING: The Inner Life of the Middle Class
0–394–56692–5 Pantheon $18.95

From Populuxe *by Thomas Hines (Knopf)*

- John S. Gilkeson, Jr.
MIDDLE-CLASS PROVIDENCE, 1820–1940
Focuses on middle-class voluntary associations of the period
0–691–04734–0 Princeton $29.95

- Karen Halttunen
CONFIDENCE MEN AND PAINTED WOMEN: A Study of Middle-Class Culture in America, 1830–1870
0–300–02835–0 Yale $30.00
0–300–03788–0 Yale pb $10.95

- Colleen McDannell
THE CHRISTIAN HOME IN VICTORIAN AMERICA, 1840–1900
0–253–31376–7 Indiana $25.00

- Katherine S. Newman
FALLING FROM GRACE: The Experience of Downward Mobility in the American Middle Class
Until recently America's middle class believed it could only move up the social ladder
0–02–923121–3 Free Press $22.95

THE POOR

"If we strip away the rhetoric of the right and the left, a surprising consensus emerges. There is broad agreement that America has developed an underclass, although some would prefer another term. There is sharp disagreement about the causes of this underclass, but rarely about its effects. Those on the right tend to use words like 'pathology,' 'passivity,' and 'hostility'; those on the left tend to speak of 'despair,' 'hopelessness,' and 'alienation'—different words that often mean the same thing. As Jacob Riis warned more than a century ago, a 'few generations' of slum life might produce monsters. For the first time in America's relatively young history, the ghetto has become a permanent home for too many broken families. For some, upward mobility is a lie, and organized society is the enemy; for others, the temporary crutch of welfare has turned into a straitjacket of permanent dependency. Whether you are compassionate or scared, the underclass should command your attention."—Ken Auletta, *The Underclass*

- Ken Auletta
THE UNDERCLASS
0–394–52343–1 Random House $17.50
0–394–71388–5 Random House pb $7.95

- R.H. Bremner
FROM THE DEPTHS: The Discovery of Poverty in the United States
0–8147–0055–1 NYU $15.00

Robert Coles
CHILDREN OF CRISIS
Volume 1: A Study of Courage and Fear
0–316–15154–8 Little, Brown pb $19.95

Volume 2: Migrants, Sharecroppers, Mountaineers
The difficult lives of the eastern coastal migrant farmers, the tenant farmers of southern plantations, and the coalminers of Appalachia
0–316–15176–9 Little, Brown pb $19.95

Volume 3: The South Goes North
0–316–15177–7 Little, Brown pb $19.95

Volume 4: Eskimos, Chicanos, Indians
0–316–15162–9 Little, Brown pb $19.95

Volume 5: Privileged Ones: The Well-Off and Rich in America
0–316–15150–5 Little, Brown pb $19.95

- Michael Harrington
THE OTHER AMERICA: Poverty in the United States
This classic portrait caused a sensation when it first appeared in 1962, and deeply influenced New Left politics; revised edition
0–14–021308–2 Pelican pb $6.95

THE NEW AMERICAN POVERTY
Harrington's 1980s reassessment of poverty in America
0–03–062157–7 Henry Holt $17.95
0–14–008112–7 Penguin pb $7.95

- Eugene Richards
BELOW THE LINE: Living Poor in America
A haunting collection of portraits by a master photographer
0–89043–062–4 Consumer Reports pb $20.00

- Ruth Sidel
WOMEN AND CHILDREN LAST: The Plight of Poor Women in Affluent America
A fine study of the "feminization of poverty"
0–14–010013–X Penguin pb $6.95

The Homeless

- Jonathan Kozol
RACHEL AND HER CHILDREN: Homeless Families in America
A harrowing portrait by the author of *Death at an Early Age*
0–517–56730–X Crown $16.95
0–449–90339–7 Fawcett pb $8.95

- National Mental Health Association, editors
HOMELESS IN AMERICA
A book of stark, beautifully reproduced black-and-white photographs
0–87491–888–X Acropolis $29.95

- Richard H. Ropers
THE INVISIBLE HOMELESS: A New Urban Ecology
This new study shows that at least 250,000 people nationwide are homeless on any given night
0–89885–406–7 Human Sciences $24.95

IF YOU CAN'T FIND IT, LOOK IN THE INDEX

Homeless woman, New York City, 1979, from The American Century *by Walter LaFeber and others (Knopf)*

• **E. Fuller Torrey, M.D.**
NOWHERE TO GO: The Tragic Odyssey of the Homeless Mentally Ill
"You'll see how ignorance, myth, cruelty and greed affected state hospitals, prisons and agencies, how the broken promises of community health centers and a diminished low-income housing supply dumped hundreds of thousands of these Americans into the streets, makeshift shelters and untold misery"—Ralph Nader
0–06–015993–6 Harper & Row $18.95

WELFARE AND SOCIAL POLICY

• **Fred Block & others**
THE MEAN SEASON: The Attack on the Welfare State
"A compelling revelation of America's dirty little secret: that our welfare state is the cheapest in the western world and under outrageous attack for excessive generosity at a time when it is needed more than ever"—Michael Harrington
0–394–74450–0 Pantheon pb $8.95

• **Stuart Butler & Anna Kondratas**
OUT OF THE POVERTY TRAP: A Conservative Strategy for Welfare Reform
Proposals from two experts in domestic policy for the Heritage Foundation
0–02–905061–8 Free Press $17.95

• **Forrest Chisman & Alan Pifer**
GOVERNMENT FOR THE PEOPLE: The Federal Social Role—What It Is, What It Should Be
Challenges widely held assumptions about social security, social spending, welfare, and other aspects of social policy
0–393–30526–0 Norton pb $9.95

• **Sheldon H. Danziger & Daniel H. Weinberg, editors**
FIGHTING POVERTY: What Works and What Doesn't
Economists, sociologists and political scientists assess the antipoverty policies of the last 20 years
0–674–30085–8 Harvard $29.50
0–674–30086–6 Harvard pb $10.95

• **Leslie W. Dunbar**
THE COMMON INTEREST: How Our Social Welfare Policies Don't Work and What We Can Do About Them
0–394–56558–4 Pantheon $22.95
0–679–73965–3 Pantheon pb $9.95

• **David T. Ellwood**
POOR SUPPORT: Poverty in the American Family
0–465–05996–1 Basic Books $19.95

• **Nathan Glazer**
THE LIMITS OF SOCIAL POLICY
0–674–53443–3 Harvard $22.50

• **Michael B. Katz**
IN THE SHADOW OF THE POOR-HOUSE: A Social History of Welfare in America
Suggests that America has the resources and competence to eliminate poverty, hunger, and bad housing through creative public policy
0–465–03225–7 Basic Books $22.95
0–465–03226–5 Basic Books pb $11.95

• **Charles Murray**
LOSING GROUND: American Social Policy, 1950–1980
Argues that the ambitious programs of the Great Society not only didn't work but actually made things worse
0–465–04232–5 Basic Books pb $12.95

Frances Fox Piven & Richard A. Cloward
THE NEW CLASS WAR: Reagan's Attack on the Welfare State and Its Consequences
0–394–70647–1 Pantheon pb $6.95

REGULATING THE POOR: The Functions of Public Welfare
"The central thesis is crucial for understanding the dramatic rise in welfare rolls that has been taking place in recent years"—Herbert Gans
0–394–71743–0 Pantheon pb $6.95

Walter I. Trattner, editor
SOCIAL WELFARE OR SOCIAL CONTROL?: Some Historical Reflections on "Regulating the Poor"
A historical critique that takes issue with the social control thesis offered by Piven and Cloward, who offer a spirited rebuttal
0–87049–374–4 Tennessee $18.95
0–87049–375–2 Tennessee pb $9.95

• **Lisbeth B. Schorr with Daniel Schorr**
WITHIN OUR REACH: Breaking the Cycle of Disadvantage
Foreword by Judith Viorst
0–385–24243–3 Doubleday $19.95
0–385–24244–1 Doubleday pb $9.95

• **Susan Sheehan**
A WELFARE MOTHER
A New York City welfare mother and her nine children, based on a *New Yorker* article. "The best, most honest and most informative examination of the welfare industry I've seen anywhere"—David Brinkley
0–451–62682–6 NAL pb $3.95

• **William Julius Wilson**
THE TRULY DISADVANTAGED: The Inner City, the Underclass and Public Policy
0–226–90130–0 Chicago $19.95

URBAN AMERICA

• **Alexander B. Callow, Jr., editor**
AMERICAN URBAN HISTORY: An Interpretive Reader with Commentaries
Thirty-two essays examine the development of cities from colonial times to the present, addressing the question of whether American urban history reflects our national history or whether it developed on a divergent path
0–19–502981–X Oxford pb $14.95

• **Charles N. Glaab & A. Theodore Brown**
A HISTORY OF URBAN AMERICA
Interpretive essays on the processes of urbanization, organized around social, political, and economic themes
0–02–344120–8 Macmillan pb $27.00

• **David R. Goldfield & Blaine A. Brownell**
URBAN AMERICA: From Downtown to No Town
0–395–27397–8 Houghton Mifflin pb $28.95

• **Jane Jacobs**
THE DEATH AND LIFE OF GREAT AMERICAN CITIES
0–394–70241–7 Random House pb $6.95

• **Zane L. Miller**
THE URBANIZATION OF MODERN AMERICA: A Brief History
0–15–593657–3 HBJ pb $14.95

• **Leo Schnore, editor**
THE NEW URBAN HISTORY: Quantitative Explorations by American Historians
0–691–04624–7 Princeton $28.00

• **Jon C. Teaford**
THE TWENTIETH-CENTURY AMERICAN CITY
A slim, scholarly volume contrasting the promise and reality of urban life
0–8018–3096–6 Johns Hopkins pb $8.95

• **William N. Whyte**
CITY: Rediscovering the Center
0–385–05458–0 Doubleday $24.95

Special Studies

• Gunther Barth
CITY PEOPLE: The Rise of Modern City Culture in 19th-Century America
0–19–503194–6 Oxford pb $9.95

• Thomas Bender
TOWARD AN URBAN VISION: Ideas and Institutions in Nineteenth-Century America
Explores the distinctive "urban vision" that sought to reconcile America's rural heritage with its new industrial life
0–8018–2925–9 Johns Hopkins pb $9.95

• Richard M. Bernard & Bradley R. Rice, editors
SUNBELT CITIES: Politics and Growth since World War II
0–292–77580–6 Texas pb $12.95

• Kenneth Fox
METROPOLITAN AMERICA: Urban Life and Urban Policy in the United States, 1940–1980
This comprehensive history emphasizes the interaction between government policy and metropolitan development
0–87805–283–6 Mississippi $27.50

• Roberta Brandes Gratz
THE LIVING CITY
The rejuvenation of urban areas demonstrates the successes that come from "thinking small in a big way"
0–671–63337–6 Simon & Schuster $19.95

• Ira Katznelson
CITY TRENCHES: Urban Politics and the Patterning of Class in the United States
0–226–42673–4 Chicago pb $12.00

• William H. & Jane H. Pease
THE WEB OF PROGRESS: Private Values and Public Styles in Boston and Charleston, 1828–1843
"Enriches our understanding of both cities and highlights the distinctive influences that shaped each of them"—Richard P. McCormick, Rutgers University
0–19–503467–8 Oxford $36.00

From Here Is New York *by E.B. White, illustrated by Alison Seiffer (Warner)*

• David Schuyler
THE NEW URBAN LANDSCAPE: The Redefinition of City Form in 19th-Century America
The failed effort to use public space and recreation to reform cramped urban life
0–8018–3231–4 Johns Hopkins $29.50

• Richard C. Wade
URBAN FRONTIER: The Rise of Western Cities, 1790–1830
0–674–93075–4 Harvard $25.00

• Sam Bass Warner, Jr.
THE PRIVATE CITY: Philadelphia in Three Periods of Its Growth
0–8122–1243–6 Pennsylvania pb $12.95

• Olivier Zunz
THE CHANGING FACE OF INEQUALITY: Urbanization, Industrial Development, and Immigrants in Detroit, 1880–1920
0–226–99458–9 Chicago pb $16.95

Suburbia

• Henry C. Binford
THE FIRST SUBURBS: Residential Communities on the Boston Periphery, 1815–1860
Argues that peripheral communities began to modernize before mass transportation linked the city to the outskirts
0–226–05158–7 Chicago $25.00

• Robert A. Fishman
BOURGEOIS UTOPIAS: The Rise and Fall of Suburbia
From its origins in 18th-century London to its fall in the sprawl of Los Ángeles
0–465–00748–1 Basic Books $19.95
0–465–00747–3 Basic Books pb $9.95

Kenneth T. Jackson
CRABGRASS FRONTIER: The Suburbanization of America
A Bancroft Prize-winning study. "Among the many interpretations, attacks, sociological reviews and other accounts of suburbia's spread since 1945, Mr. Jackson's stands out as the most comprehensive"—Grady Clay, *NY Times Book Review*
0–19–503610–7 Oxford $24.95
0–19–504983–7 Oxford pb $9.95

• Zane L. Miller
SUBURB: Neighborhood and Community in Forest Park, Ohio, 1935–1976
0–87049–289–6 Tennessee $24.95

• John R. Stilgoe
BORDERLAND: Origins of the American Suburb, 1820–1939
A highly praised new study
0–300–04257–4 Yale $35.00

• Sam Bass Warner, Jr.
STREETCAR SUBURBS: The Process of Growth in Boston, 1870–1900
0–674–84210–3 Harvard $15.00
0–674–84211–1 Harvard pb $8.95

Housing

The following books on domestic architecture imaginatively use houses to explore family life and broader social conflicts, particularly in the late 19th and early 20th centuries.

• Clifford E. Clark, Jr.
THE AMERICAN FAMILY HOME, 1800–1960
0–8078–1675–2 North Carolina $29.95
0–8078–4151–X North Carolina pb $14.95

• David Handlin
AMERICAN ARCHITECTURE: A Critical History
0–500–20200–1 Thames & Hudson pb $11.95

• Dolores Hayden
THE GRAND DOMESTIC REVOLUTION: A History of Feminist Designs for American Homes, Neighborhoods, and Cities
0–262–58055–1 MIT pb $11.95

• Ronald Lawson & Mark Naison, editors
THE TENANT MOVEMENT IN NEW YORK CITY, 1904–1984
0–8135–1158–5 Rutgers $35.00
0–8135–1203–4 Rutgers pb $15.00

• Irving Welfeld
WHERE WE LIVE: The American Home and the Social, Political and Economic Landscape, from Slums to Suburbs
0–671–63869–6 Simon & Schuster $18.95

• Gwendolyn Wright
BUILDING THE DREAM: A Social History of Housing in America
An original, lucid exploration of the relationship between the way we build our homes and our images of ourselves
0–262–73064–2 MIT pb $12.50

AMERICAN CITIES
(alphabetical by subject)

▶ **See also Travel Photography**

• Webb Garrison
THE LEGACY OF ATLANTA: A Short History
0–934601–14–3 Peachtree pb $7.95

• Joseph E. Garland
BOSTON'S NORTH SHORE: Being an Account of Life Among the Noteworthy, Fashionable, Wealthy, Eccentric and Ordinary, 1823–1890
0–316–30425–5 Little, Brown $27.50

BOSTON'S GOLD COAST: The North Shore, 1890–1929
The sequel
0–316–30430–1 Little, Brown $27.50

• Sam Bass Warner, Jr.
TO DWELL IS TO GARDEN: A History of Boston's Community Gardens
1–55553–007–9 New England $18.95

• Robert Cromie
A SHORT HISTORY OF CHICAGO
0–938530–28–3 Lexikos pb $9.95

TO ORDER BOOKS AS GIFTS, SEE PAGE 1

North Michigan Avenue (photo by Stephen Deutch, 1960), from Chicago *by Studs Terkel (Pantheon)*

● Michael H. Ebner
CREATING CHICAGO'S NORTH SHORE: A Suburban History
0–226–18205–3 Chicago $29.95

● Harold M. Mayer & Richard C. Wade
CHICAGO: Growth of a Metropolis
0–226–51274–6 Chicago pb $19.95

● Studs Terkel
CHICAGO
0–394–55337–3 Pantheon pb $11.95

● Sam Acheson
DALLAS YESTERDAY
0–87074–160–8 SMU $16.95

● Frank B. & Arthur M. Woodford
ALL OUR YESTERDAYS: A Brief History of Detroit
0–8143–1381–7 Wayne State pb $6.50

● David G. McComb
HOUSTON: A History
0–292–73020–9 Texas pb $10.95

● Michael J. McDonald & William Bruce Wheeler
KNOXVILLE, TENNESSEE: Continuity and Change in an Appalachian City
0–87049–393–0 Tennessee $16.95

● Scott L. Bottles
LOS ANGELES AND THE AUTOMOBILE: The Making of the Modern City
0–520–05795–3 California $27.50

● Bruce Henstell
LOS ANGELES: An Illustrated History
0–394–50941–2 Knopf $25.00

SUNSHINE AND WEALTH: Los Angeles in the '20s and '30s
0–87701–275–X Chronicle pb $12.95

● John Walton Caughey & LaRee Caughey
LOS ANGELES: Biography of a City
Collection of historical and literary essays
0–520–03410–4 California pb $6.95

● T.D. Allman
MIAMI: City of the Future
0–87113–102–1 Atlantic Monthly $22.50
0–87113–227–3 Atlantic Monthly pb $5.95

● Joan Didion
MIAMI
0–671–64664–8 Simon & Schuster $17.95
0–671–66820–X Simon & Schuster pb $7.95

● David Rieff
GOING TO MIAMI: Exiles, Tourists, Refugees in the New America
0–14–011091–7 Penguin pb $7.95

● John Lukacs
PHILADELPHIA: Patricians and Philistines
0–374–23161–3 Farrar, Straus & Giroux $17.50

● Russell F. Weigley & others, editors
PHILADELPHIA: A Three Hundred Year History
0–393–01610–2 Norton $17.95

● Tom Cole
A SHORT HISTORY OF SAN FRANCISCO
0–938530–00–3 Lexikos pb $9.95

● Mel Scott
THE SAN FRANCISCO BAY AREA: A Metropolis in Perspective
The area's growth and development along with planning ideas for the future; illustrated
0–520–05512–8 California pb $18.95

● Ruth Silverman
SAN FRANCISCO OBSERVED: A Photographic Portfolio from 1850 to the Present
0–87701–388–8 Chronicle pb $14.95

● Ashbel Green, editor
THE CITY OF WASHINGTON: An Illustrated History
0–394–73550–1 Knopf pb $15.95

● Constance M. Green
WASHINGTON: A History of the Capital
0–691–00585–0 Princeton pb $15.95

● David L. Lewis
DISTRICT OF COLUMBIA: A Bicentennial History
0–393–05601–5 Norton $14.95

● Robert Reed
OLD WASHINGTON, D.C., IN EARLY PHOTOGRAPHS
0–486–23869–5 Dover pb $9.95

New York City

● Brian J. Cudahy
UNDER THE SIDEWALKS OF NEW YORK: The Story of the World's Greatest Subway System
An illustrated history
0–8289–0685–8 Stephen Greene $19.95

● Paul A. Gilje
THE ROAD TO MOBOCRACY: Popular Disorder in New York City, 1763–1834
0–8078–1743–0 Chapel Hill $32.00

● Jeff Kisseloff
YOU MUST REMEMBER THIS: An Oral History of Manhattan from the 1890s to World War II
0–15–187988–5 HBJ $29.95

● Edward I. Koch
MAYOR!
Discourses on politics, from New York's outspoken mayor
0–446–34305–6 Warner pb $4.95

POLITICS
0–446–32300–4 Warner pb $4.95

The Chrysler building, from New York, 1930 *by Robert Stern (Rizzoli)*

• Geoffrey Moorhouse
IMPERIAL CITY: New York
0–8050–0915–9 Henry Holt $21.95

• Jack Newfield & Wayne Barrett
CITY FOR SALE: Ed Koch and the Betrayal of New York
Traces the web of scandals that has gripped the city's government
0–06–016060–8 Harper & Row $22.50

• Rebecca Shanor
THE CITY THAT NEVER WAS
Photographs, drawings, and histories of 30 urban improvement plans that would have changed the look of New York City
0–670–80558–0 Viking $35.00

• Martin Shefter
POLITICAL CRISIS—FISCAL CRISIS: The Collapse and Revival of New York City
The definitive study of the 1975 fiscal crisis that drove New York City to the brink of bankruptcy, by a Cornell political scientist
0–465–05875–2 Basic Books $21.95
0–465–05876–0 Basic Books pb $9.95

• Leonard Wallock, editor
NEW YORK: Culture Capital, 1940–1965
Beautifully illustrated essays
0–8478–0990–0 Rizzoli $65.00

• Elliot Willensky
WHEN BROOKLYN WAS THE WORLD: 1920–1957
A well-illustrated backward glance
0–517–55858–0 Crown $19.95

African-American Studies

• Lerone Bennett, Jr.
BEFORE THE MAYFLOWER: A History of Black America
Traces black American history from the West African empires through the 1970s; includes useful chronological tables and biographies
0–87485–029–0 Johnson $25.00
0–14–007214–4 Penguin pb $9.95

• Mary Frances Berry & John W. Blassingame
LONG MEMORY: The Black Experience in America
0–19–502909–7 Oxford $35.00
0–19–502910–0 Oxford pb $14.95

• Allison Blakely
RUSSIA AND THE NEGRO: Blacks in Russian History and Thought
"Opens the field of Soviet scholarship to further investigations, fresh insights, and interpretations by those scholars who see the Negro's role in world affairs as a theme of unheralded significance"—Albert Parry
0–88258–146–5 Howard $17.95

• Oliver C. Cox
CASTE, CLASS, AND RACE
A cross-cultural view that tackles such times and places as India, the Middle Ages, and contemporary America
0–85345–116–8 Monthly Review pb $10.00

• W.E.B. DuBois
WRITINGS
This volume contains DuBois' most important historical and autobiographical writings, including *The Suppression of the African Slave-Trade*, *The Souls of Black Folk*, and *Dusk of Dawn*
Edited by Nathan Huggins
0–940450–33–X Library of America $27.50

• John Hope Franklin & Alfred Moss, Jr.
FROM SLAVERY TO FREEDOM: A History of Negro Americans
0–394–32256–8 Knopf pb $19.95

• Vincent Harding
THERE IS A RIVER: The Black Struggle for Freedom in America
0–15–189342–X HBJ $19.95

• William Loren Katz
BLACK INDIANS: A Hidden Heritage
Crispus Attucks, Cherokee Bill, and the "Dusky Demon" are among the figures in this chronicle of the little-known history of the black-Native American alliance
0–689–31196–6 Atheneum $15.95

• Gerda Lerner, editor
BLACK WOMEN IN WHITE AMERICA: A Documentary History
0–394–71880–1 Random House pb $9.95

• August Meier & Elliott Rudwick
FROM PLANTATION TO GHETTO
A survey of black history with particular emphasis on how ideas and protests were shaped by two forces: the rural plantation and the city ghetto
0–8090–0122–5 Hill & Wang pb $8.95

• Benjamin Quarles
THE NEGRO IN THE MAKING OF AMERICA
A best-selling history beginning with the arrival of slave ships in the early 17th century
0–02–036140–8 Macmillan pb $5.95

THE NEGRO IN THE AMERICAN REVOLUTION
0–393–00674–3 Norton pb $7.95

• Ivan van Sertima
THEY CAME BEFORE COLUMBUS: The African Presence in Ancient America
A provocative and detailed account of African explorers
0–394–40245–6 Random House $19.95

Encyclopedias and Picture Books

• Nancy Cunard, editor
NEGRO: An Anthology
A broad examination of black life in the Americas, Europe and Africa; first published in 1934
Abridged with an introduction by Hugh Ford
0–8044–6095–7 Ungar pb $24.95

Phillis Wheatley, from Before the Mayflower: A History of Black America *by Lerone Bennett, Jr. (Penguin)*

• Denise Dennis & Susan Willmarth
BLACK HISTORY FOR BEGINNERS
History in comic book form covering many aspects of black life in America often omitted from textbooks
0–86316–069–7 Writers & Readers $14.95
0–86316–068–9 Writers & Readers pb $7.95

• W. Augustus Low & Virgil A. Clift
ENCYCLOPEDIA OF BLACK AMERICA
Offers a variety of special sections, including slavery, folklore, religion, education, the NAACP, and the Black Panther party
0–07–038834–2 McGraw-Hill $99.00
0–306–80221–X Da Capo pb $32.50

• J.A. Rogers
WORLD'S GREAT MEN OF COLOR
An encyclopedia of notable figures since the 18th century. Entries include Pushkin, Alexandre Dumas, and Marcus Garvey

Volume 1
0–02–081300–7 Macmillan pb $11.95

Volume 2
0–02–081310–4 Macmillan pb $11.95

• Richard Wright, editor
TWELVE MILLION BLACK VOICES: A Folk History of the Negro in the U.S.
A Wright essay accompanies stunning photographs of blacks in the 1930s, depicting sharecroppers and city-dwellers alike
Photographs by Edwin Rosskam
0–938410–44–X Thunder's Mouth pb $15.95

Slavery

▶ **A full selection of books on slavery is listed in US History to the Civil War**

• Ira Berlin
SLAVES WITHOUT MASTERS: The Free Negro in the Antebellum South
How southern blacks tried to maintain and expand their liberty within the grip of the slave system
0–19–502905–4 Oxford pb $10.95

☞ **TO ORDER NEW BOOKS NOT YET LISTED, ASK YOUR BOOKSELLER OR CALL 1-800-882-8770**

- Ira Berlin & others, editors
THE BLACK MILITARY EXPERIENCE
Part of the *Freedom, A Documentary History of Emancipation, 1861–1867* series
0–521–22984–7 Cambridge $47.50

THE DESTRUCTION OF SLAVERY
Part of the same series as above
0–521–22979–0 Cambridge $42.50

- John W. Blassingame
THE SLAVE COMMUNITY: Plantation Life in the Antebellum South
0–19–502562–8 Oxford $27.95
0–19–502563–6 Oxford pb $10.95

- Elizabeth Fox-Genovese
WITHIN THE PLANTATION HOUSEHOLD: Black and White Women of the South
0–8078–1808–9 North Carolina $34.95
0–8078–4232–X North Carolina pb $12.95

- Eugene D. Genovese
ROLL, JORDAN, ROLL: The World the Slaves Made
"Genovese's great gift is his ability to penetrate the minds of both slaves and masters, revealing not only how they viewed themselves and each other, but also how their contradictory perceptions interacted"—David Brion Davis, *NY Times Book Review*
0–394–71652–3 Random House pb $14.95

- James M. McPherson
THE NEGRO'S CIVIL WAR: How American Negroes Felt and Acted During the War for the Union
0–252–00949–5 Illinois pb $9.95

- Sterling Stuckey
SLAVE CULTURE: Nationalist Theory and the Foundations of Black America
0–19–505664–7 Oxford pb $10.95

- Deborah Gray White
AR'N'T I A WOMAN?: Female Slaves in the Plantation South
An important study of the women who faced the double burdens of sexism and racism
0–393–30406–X Norton pb $6.95

The history of the American Negro is the history of this strife,—this longing to attain self-conscious manhood, to merge his double self into a better and truer self. In this merging he wishes neither of the older selves to be lost. He would not Africanize America, for America has too much to teach the world and Africa. He would not bleach his Negro soul in a flood of white Americanism, for he knows that Negro blood has a message for the world. He simply wishes to make it possible for a man to be both a Negro and an American, without being cursed and spit upon by his fellows, without having the doors of Opportunity closed roughly in his face.

The Souls of Black Folk in

W.E.B. DuBois
WRITINGS
0–940450–33–X Library of America $27.50

The South since Emancipation

- Gerald D. Jaynes
BRANCHES WITHOUT ROOTS: The Genesis of the Black Working Class, 1862–1882
0–19–503619–0 Oxford $36.00

Leon F. Litwack
BEEN IN THE STORM SO LONG: The Aftermath of Slavery
Explores the lives of ex-slaves and their masters to uncover the mutual dependency of blacks and whites during and after the Civil War
0–394–50099–7 Knopf $20.00

- Nell Irvin Painter
EXODUSTERS: Black Migration to Kansas After Reconstruction
By the author of *Standing at Armageddon*
0–7006–0288–7 Kansas pb $7.95

- Howard N. Rabinowitz
RACE RELATIONS IN THE URBAN SOUTH, 1865–1890
Introduction by C. Vann Woodward
0–252–00811–1 Illinois pb $10.95

- Roger Ransom & Richard Sutch
ONE KIND OF FREEDOM
Includes 432 tables
0–521–21450–5 Cambridge $49.50
0–521–29203–4 Cambridge pb $14.95

- Booker T. Washington & W.E.B. DuBois
THE NEGRO IN THE SOUTH
0–8216–0183–0 Birch Lane pb $7.95

The North

America's northern industrial cities have long seemed to glisten with opportunity for southern blacks and West Indians; their northward migration and the subsequent rise of the urban ghetto marked a turning point in the nation's political and social history. From the cultural mecca of 1920s Harlem to the controversial gentrification of 1980s slums, black neighborhoods have played a leading role in the shape and economy of American cities.

- Dennis C. Dickerson
OUT OF THE CRUCIBLE: Black Steelworkers in Western Pennsylvania, 1875–1980
0–88706–306–3 SUNY pb $16.95

- Arnold R. Hirsch
MAKING THE SECOND GHETTO: Race and Housing in Chicago, 1940–1960
0–521–31506–9 Cambridge pb $11.95

- David M. Katzman
BEFORE THE GHETTO: Black Detroit in the Nineteenth Century
0–252–00562–7 Illinois pb $8.95

- Elliot Liebow
TALLY'S CORNER
The classic sociological study of black street life
0–316–52514–6 Little, Brown pb $7.95

- August Meier & Elliott Rudwick
BLACK DETROIT AND THE RISE OF THE UAW
Blacks battle to become a part of unionized labor
0–19–502561–X Oxford $22.50

- Sylvester Monroe & Peter Goldman
BROTHERS: A Story of Courage and Survival Against the Odds of Today's Society
Mid-1980s profiles of half a dozen men from Chicago's South Side ghetto
0–688–07622–X Morrow $18.95

- James M. McPherson
THE ABOLITIONIST LEGACY: From Reconstruction to the NAACP
0–691–10039–X Princeton pb $18.50

- Allan H. Spear
BLACK CHICAGO: The Making of a Negro Ghetto, 1890–1920
0–226–76857–0 Chicago pb $10.95

- Joe W. Trotter, Jr.
BLACK MILWAUKEE: The Making of an Industrial Proletariat, 1915–45
How factory jobs were a step up from sharecropping and house service
0–252–01124–4 Illinois $24.95

The Making of Harlem

Jervis Anderson
THIS WAS HARLEM: A Cultural Portrait, 1900–1950
The bright side of Harlem as it became a black enclave, including jazz and avant-garde music, experimental writing, liberal politics, interracial social life, and a reputation as a black American Paris
0–374–51757–6 FS&G pb $13.95

Houston A. Baker, Jr.
MODERNISM AND THE HARLEM RENAISSANCE
0–226–03525–5 Chicago pb $9.95

Kenneth B. Clark
DARK GHETTO: Dilemmas of Social Power
A sweeping overview of housing, schools, psychology, and the politics of the Harlem ghetto, by a leading sociologist of race
Foreword by Gunnar Myrdal
0–06–131317–3 Harper & Row pb $7.95

Nathan I. Huggins
HARLEM RENAISSANCE
The first full-scale story of 1920s Harlem in the context of American history, including artistic, cultural, political, and social developments
0–19–501665–3 Oxford pb $12.95

Gilbert Osofsky
HARLEM: The Making of a Ghetto, 1890–1930
How an upper-middle-class white neighborhood was turned into a ghetto by discriminatory realtors
0–06–131572–9 Harper & Row pb $8.95

THE CIVIL RIGHTS MOVEMENT AND BEYOND

Often regarded as a time of unprecedented alliance between blacks and whites, the civil rights decade marked a full-scale war on racial inequality that had been long in preparation. The Rev. Martin Luther King, Jr.'s 1963 March on Washington, with 200,000 in attendance, was among the highlights of an inspirational movement that placed intense pressure on the federal government, whose most significant response to the growing unrest of those years was the Civil Rights Act of 1964.

- Harry S. Ashmore
HEARTS AND MINDS: A Personal Chronicle of Race in America
The civil rights movement as seen by the former editor of the *Arkansas Gazette,* whose editorials advocating integration won him a Pulitzer Prize
Introduction by Harold Fleming
0–932020–58–5 Seven Locks pb $14.95

- William R. Beardslee
THE WAY OUT MUST LEAD IN: Life Histories in the Civil Rights Movement
The author, active in the 1960s civil rights struggle, follows up on the movement a decade later, portraying such people as John Lewis, chairman of the Student Nonviolent Coordinating Committee (SNCC) and Mrs. Washington, a plantation worker
0–88208–153–5 Lawrence Hill $14.95
0–88208–120–9 Lawrence Hill pb $7.95

- Taylor Branch
PARTING THE WATERS: America in the King Years, 1954–1963
A powerful account of the early civil rights years
0–671–46097–8 Simon & Schuster $24.95

- Seth Cagin & Philip Dray
WE ARE NOT AFRAID: The Murder of Goodman, Schwerner, and Chaney and the Civil Rights Campaign for Mississippi
The lynching of three civil rights workers
0–02–520260–X Macmillan $24.95

- Stokely Carmichael & Charles V. Hamilton
BLACK POWER: The Politics of Liberation in America
0–394–70033–3 Random House pb $5.95

- Clayborne Carson
IN STRUGGLE: SNCC and the Black Awakening of the 1960s
0–674–44725–5 Harvard $27.00
0–674–44726–3 Harvard pb $9.95

- William Henry Chafe
CIVILITIES AND CIVIL RIGHTS: Greensboro, North Carolina, and the Black Struggle for Freedom
0–19–502625–X Oxford $24.95
0–19–502919–4 Oxford pb $9.95

Martin Luther King, Jr., addressing a mass meeting of bus boycotters, from Eyes on the Prize: America's Civil Rights Years *by Juan Williams (Penguin/photo by Dan Weiner)*

Ward Churchill & Jim Vander Wall
AGENTS OF REPRESSION: The FBI's Secret Wars Against the Black Panther Party and the American Indian Movement
0–89608–293–8 South End $15.00

Kenneth O'Reilly
"RACIAL MATTERS": The FBI's Secret File on Black America, 1960–1972
0–02–923681–9 Free Press $24.95

- James Farmer
LAY BARE THE HEART: The Autobiography of the Civil Rights Movement
The founder of the Congress of Racial Equality portrays himself, Martin Luther King, Jr., Malcolm X, John F. Kennedy, and others amid the hopes and frustrations of the 1950s and '60s
0–452–25803–0 NAL pb $8.95

- James Forman
SAMMY YOUNGE, JR: The First Black College Student to Die in the Black Liberation Movement
Argues that nonviolence ended as a tactic in the quest for civil rights after Younge was murdered in an Alabama gas station
0–940880–12–1 Open Hand $16.95
0–940880–13–X Open Hand pb $9.95

- Jonathan Kaufman
BROKEN ALLIANCE: The Turbulent Times Between Blacks and Jews in America
0–684–18699–3 Scribners $19.95

- Aldon D. Morris
THE ORIGINS OF THE CIVIL RIGHTS MOVEMENT: Black Communities Organizing for Change
0–02–922120–X Free Press $24.95
0–02–922130–7 Free Press pb $9.95

- Howell Raines
MY SOUL IS RESTED: Movement Days in the Deep South Remembered
Resisters and civil rights leaders tell of their lives; with testimonies from Bull Connor, Martin Luther King, Jr., George Wallace, and Rosa Parks
0–14–006753–1 Penguin pb $7.95

- Jo Ann Gibson Robinson
THE MONTGOMERY BUS BOYCOTT AND THE WOMEN WHO STARTED IT: The Memoir of Jo Ann Gibson Robinson
An autobiographical account of one of the most successful tactics of the civil rights era
Edited by David J. Garrow
0–87049–527–5 Tennessee pb $12.95

- Pete Seeger & Robert S. Reiser
EVERYBODY SAYS FREEDOM: The Civil Rights Movement in Words, Pictures, and Song
0–393–02646–9 Norton $29.95
0–393–30604–6 Norton pb $18.95

- Thomas Sowell
CIVIL RIGHTS: Rhetoric or Reality?
A critical look at the movement by the author of *The Economics and Politics of Race*
0–688–06269–5 Morrow pb $5.95

Juan Williams
EYES ON THE PRIZE: America's Civil Rights Years, 1954–1965
Excellent, illustrated accompaniment to the PBS series
Introduction by Julian Bond
0–670–81412–1 Viking $24.95
0–14–009653–1 Penguin pb $10.95

➤ **FOR OVERSEAS ORDERING INFORMATION, SEE PAGE 1**

RACE RELATIONS

• James Baldwin
THE PRICE OF THE TICKET: Collected Nonfiction, 1948–1985
Black-white relations, as seen by the master essayist
0–312–64306–3 St. Martin's $29.95

• Derrick Bell
AND WE ARE NOT SAVED: The Elusive Quest for Racial Justice
Freedom and full rights are still not realities for African-Americans, according to a Harvard law professor
0–465–00328–1 Basic Books $19.95
0–456–00329–X Basic Books pb $9.95

• Joseph Boskin
SAMBO: The Rise and Demise of an American Jester
"A major contribution to the study of stereotypes, the history of theatrical and other entertainments in America, and the analysis of material culture in the United States"—*Philadelphia Inquirer*
0–19–504074–0 Oxford $22.95

• Harold Cruse
PLURAL BUT EQUAL: Blacks and Minorities in America's Plural Society
0–688–04486–7 Morrow $22.95

• George Davis & G. Watson
BLACK LIFE IN CORPORATE AMERICA: Swimming in the Mainstream
Life in the executive suite as seen by a corporate manager with Xerox and a former *Washington Post* reporter
0–385–14702–3 Doubleday pb $7.95

• Kevin Flynn & Gary Gerhardt
THE SILENT BROTHERHOOD: Inside an American Racist Conspiracy
0–02–910312–6 Free Press $22.95

• George M. Frederickson
THE BLACK IMAGE IN THE WHITE MIND: The Debate on Afro-American Character and Destiny, 1817–1914
0–8195–6188–6 Wesleyan pb $14.95

WHITE SUPREMACY: A Comparative Study in American and South African History
0–19–502759–0 Oxford $39.95
0–19–503042–7 Oxford pb $10.95

• A. Leon Higginbotham
IN THE MATTER OF COLOR: Race and the American Legal Process, The Colonial Period
0–19–502387–0 Oxford $35.00
0–19–502745–0 Oxford pb $14.95

• Winthrop D. Jordan
WHITE OVER BLACK: American Attitudes Toward the Negro, 1550–1812
0–393–00841–X Norton pb $12.95

• Bart Landry
THE NEW BLACK MIDDLE CLASS
0–520–06465–8 California pb $9.95

Mississippi, 1939, from Bearing Witness: A Photographic Chronicle of American Life *by Michael Lesy (Pantheon/photo courtesy of Marion Post Wolcott)*

• Stanley Lieberson
A PIECE OF THE PIE: Black and White Immigrants Since 1880
0–520–04362–6 California pb $14.95

• Bernard Magubane
THE TIES THAT BIND: African-American Consciousness of Africa
A startling analysis of black self-prejudice
0–86543–036–5 Africa World $32.00
0–86543–037–3 Africa World pb $9.95

Gunnar Myrdal
AN AMERICAN DILEMMA
A classic dissertation on race relations in America by a noted Swedish scholar

Volume 1
0–394–73042–9 Pantheon pb $5.95

Volume 2
0–394–73043–7 Pantheon pb $5.95

• Thomas F. Pettigrew
THE SOCIOLOGY OF RACE RELATIONS: Reflection and Reform
0–02–925110–9 Free Press pb $17.95

• Alphonso Pinkney
THE MYTH OF BLACK PROGRESS
A statistically rich refutation of the argument that African-Americans have progressed greatly since the 1964 Civil Rights Act in income, employment, educational access, and growth of a middle class
0–521–25983–5 Cambridge $19.95
0–521–31047–4 Cambridge pb $9.95

• Howard Schuman, Charlotte Steeh & Lawrence Bobo
RACIAL ATTITUDES IN AMERICA: Trends and Interpretations
0–674–74574–4 Harvard $25.00

• Thomas Sowell
THE ECONOMICS AND POLITICS OF RACE
Provocative analysis of the relative significance of race in society, both in the US and elsewhere
0–688–04832–3 Morrow pb $6.95

• Joel Williamson
A RAGE FOR ORDER: Black-White Relations in the American South Since Emancipation
0–19–504025–2 Oxford pb $9.95

• William Julius Wilson
THE DECLINING SIGNIFICANCE OF RACE: Blacks and Changing American Institutions
0–226–90129–7 Chicago pb $9.95

THE TRULY DISADVANTAGED: The Inner City, the Underclass and Public Policy
0–226–90130–0 Chicago $19.95

• C. Vann Woodward
AMERICAN COUNTERPOINT: Slavery and Racism in the North-South Dialogue
0–19–503269–1 Oxford pb $7.95

THE STRANGE CAREER OF JIM CROW
A brief but outstanding account of segregation
0–19–501805–2 Oxford pb $7.95

• Bruce M. Wright
BLACK ROBES, WHITE JUSTICE
A black New York City judge and poet investigates racism in the American legal system
0–8184–0422–1 Lyle Stuart $15.95

The Kerner Report

National Advisory Commission on Civil Disorders
THE KERNER REPORT
The conclusions of the famous report that shocked the nation in 1968 are still valid today
Introductions by Fred R. Harris & Tom Wicker
0–679–72078–2 Pantheon pb $8.95

Fred R. Harris & Roger W. Wilkins
QUIET RIOTS: Race and Poverty in the United States
An update of the Kerner Report finds segregation more pronounced, poverty deeper, and unemployment doubled in America's inner cities
0–394–57473–7 Pantheon $19.95
0–679–72100–2 Pantheon pb $8.95

Facing Violence

• Robert Sam Anson
BEST INTENTIONS: The Education and Killing of Edmund Perry
The story of an Exeter student from Harlem killed by a white policeman in an alleged holdup attempt
0–394–55274–1 Random House $17.95
0–394–75707–6 Random House pb $6.95

• James Baldwin
THE EVIDENCE OF THINGS NOT SEEN
The Atlanta serial murders of the 1980s moved Baldwin to write about collective responsibility in the trial of the black man accused
Introduction by William Styron
0–8050–0138–7 Henry Holt pb $4.95

• Dan T. Carter
SCOTTSBORO: A Tragedy of the American South
0–8071–0498–1 LSU pb $9.95

• William I. Hair
CARNIVAL OF FURY: Robert Charles and the New Orleans Race Riot of 1900
0–8071–1348–4 LSU pb $8.95

• Elliott M. Rudwick
RACE RIOT AT EAST ST. LOUIS, JULY 2, 1917
0–252–00951–7 Illinois pb $9.95

• Howard Smead
BLOOD JUSTICE: The Lynching of Mack Charles Parker
A chilling reconstruction of a Mississippi lynching and the subsequent FBI investigation
0–19–504121–6 Oxford $22.95
0–19–505429–6 Oxford pb $7.95

• Stephen J. Whitfield
A DEATH IN THE DELTA: The Story of Emmett Till
In August 1955, 14-year-old Emmett Till was lynched for allegedly making a pass at a white woman, but an all-white jury acquitted the white defendants
0–02–935121–9 Free Press $19.95

Now, if what I have tried to sketch has any validity, it becomes thoroughly clear, at least to me, that any Negro who is born in this country and undergoes the American educational system runs the risk of becoming schizophrenic. On the one hand he is born in the shadow of the stars and stripes and he is assured it represents a nation which has never lost a war. He pledges allegiance to that flag which guarantees "liberty and justice for all." He is part of a country in which anyone can become president, and so forth. But on the other hand he is also assured by his country and his countrymen that he has never contributed anything to civilization—that his past is nothing more than a record of humiliations gladly endured. He is assured by the republic that he, his father, his mother, and his ancestors were happy, shiftless, watermelon-eating darkies who loved Mr. Charlie and Miss Ann, that the value he has as a black man is proven by one thing only—his devotion to white people. If you think I am exaggerating, examine the myths which proliferate in this country about Negroes.

James Baldwin, "A Talk to Teachers" in

Rick Simonson & Scott Walker, editors
THE GRAYWOLF ANNUAL FIVE: Multi-Cultural Literacy
1–55597–114–8 Graywolf pb $8.50

POLITICAL THEORY AND MOVEMENTS

• Molefi K. Asante
THE AFROCENTRIC IDEA
0–87722–483–8 Temple $24.95

• Sheila Collins
THE RAINBOW CHALLENGE: The Jackson Campaign and the Future of U.S. Politics
A former officer and organizer examines the inner politics of the Rainbow Coalition
0–85345–690–9 Monthly Review $27.00
0–85345–691–7 Monthly Review pb $11.00

• Harold Cruse
CRISIS OF THE NEGRO INTELLECTUAL: A Historical Analysis of the Failure of Black Leadership
A forceful and disturbing book that has sacrificed none of its relevance since its first printing in 1967
0–688–03886–7 Morrow pb $10.95

• Frantz Fanon
THE WRETCHED OF THE EARTH
This "bible" of American black activists since the 1960s focuses on the rage and subsequent violent history of the Algerian revolution
Translated by Constance Farrington
Preface by Jean-Paul Sartre
0–802–15083–7 Grove pb $7.95

• James Forman
SELF-DETERMINATION: An Examination of the Question and Its Application to African-American People
An argument for black empowerment by a former civil rights leader; also surveys the role of political parties in the quest for self-determination
0–940880–09–1 Open Hand $15.95
0–940880–08–3 Open Hand pb $7.95

• C. Eric Lincoln
RACE, RELIGION AND THE CONTINUING AMERICAN DILEMMA
The wins and losses of blacks in politics, by the author of the 1960s classic *The Black Muslims*
0–8090–8016–8 Hill & Wang $17.95
0–8090–0163–2 Hill & Wang pb $8.95

• Wilson J. Moses
THE GOLDEN AGE OF BLACK NATIONALISM, 1850–1925
0–19–520639–8 Oxford pb $8.95

• Mark Naison
COMMUNISTS IN HARLEM DURING THE DEPRESSION
Blunders and heady adventures; winner of the American Political Science Association Ralph Bunche Award (1984)
0–252–00644–5 Illinois $27.95
0–394–62301–0 Grove pb $9.95

• Caryl Phillips
THE EUROPEAN TRIBE
An Oxford-educated black West Indian describes Europeans as the primitives in today's cultural and economic conflicts
0–374–14935–6 Farrar, Straus & Giroux $15.95

• William K. Tabb
THE POLITICAL ECONOMY OF THE BLACK GHETTO
Argues that a colonial relationship exists between ghettoes and the larger society
0–393–09930–X Norton pb $5.95

CULTURE

Family

• Andrew Billingsley
BLACK FAMILIES IN WHITE AMERICA
A classic, now more than 20 years old. "The first book to debunk the myths and mythologies surrounding the black family"—Joyce A. Ladner, Howard University
0–671–67162–6 Simon & Schuster pb $8.95

• E. Franklin Frazier
BLACK BOURGEOISIE: The Rise of a New Middle Class in the United States
This 1957 analysis of America's black middle class made "black bourgeoisie" as loaded a term as "yuppie" is today
0–02–910580–3 Free Press pb $12.95
0–02–095600–2 Macmillan pb $5.95

THE NEGRO FAMILY IN THE UNITED STATES
From slavery through 1939, by a leading scholar
0–226–26141–7 Chicago pb $9.00

• Herbert G. Gutman
THE BLACK FAMILY IN SLAVERY AND FREEDOM, 1750–1925
"Gutman has successfully challenged the traditional view that slavery virtually destroyed the Afro-American family"—John Hope Franklin
0–394–72451–8 Random House pb $14.95

Women

▶ **See also Women's Studies**

• Angela Davis
WOMEN, RACE AND CLASS
0–394–71351–6 Random House pb $5.95

• Paula Giddings
IN SEARCH OF SISTERHOOD: Delta Sigma Theta and the Challenge of the Black Sorority Movement
A history of black women in American political, social, and economic affairs
0–688–05775–6 Morrow $16.95

WHEN AND WHERE I ENTER: The Impact of Black Women on Race and Sex in America
Portraits of such figures as Mary McLeod Bethune and Fannie Lou Hamer and their struggles
0–553–34561–3 Bantam pb $9.95

• Gloria T. Hull & others, editors
ALL THE WOMEN ARE WHITE, ALL THE BLACKS ARE MEN, BUT SOME OF US ARE BRAVE: Black Women's Studies
A collection for the general reader covering such topics as political theory, essays on major writers, and racism in higher education
0–912670–95–9 Feminist Press pb $12.95

• Jacqueline Jones
LABOR OF LOVE, LABOR OF SORROW: Black Women, Work and the Family from Slavery to the Present
Bancroft Prize winner
0–394–74536–1 Random House pb $10.95

Marian Anderson in 1959, from World Celebrities in Ninety Photographic Portraits *by Fred Stein (Dover)*

Religion

• Albert B. Cleage, Jr.
BLACK CHRISTIAN NATIONALISM: New Directions for the Black Church
By the famous Detroit minister who shared platforms with Malcolm X
0–941205–01–0 Luxor pb $10.00

• E. Franklin Frazier & C. Eric Lincoln
THE NEGRO CHURCH IN AMERICA & THE BLACK CHURCH SINCE FRAZIER
Two important works
0–8052–0387–7 Schocken pb $7.95

• Albert J. Raboteau
SLAVE RELIGION: The Invisible Institution in the Antebellum South
Slave religion from its African roots through its reinterpretation under Christianity
0–19502705–1 Oxford pb $11.95

• Mechal Sobel
TRABELIN' ON: The Slave Journey to an Afro-Baptist Faith
"Sobel takes seriously the religion of black people and shows its creative power to construct a sacred cosmos"—Andrew E. Murray, *Journal of American History*
0–691–00603–2 Princeton pb $12.95

• Robert Weisbrot
FATHER DIVINE AND THE STRUGGLE FOR RACIAL EQUALITY
Edited by August Meier
0–252–00973–8 Illinois $22.95

• Gayraud S. Wilmore
BLACK RELIGION AND BLACK RADICALISM: An Interpretation of the Religious History of Afro-American People
0–88344–032–6 Orbis pb $13.95

The Black Aesthetic

• Houston A. Baker, Jr.
AFRO-AMERICAN POETICS: Revisions of Harlem and the Black Aesthetic
0–299–11500–3 Wisconsin $19.95

BLUES, IDEOLOGY, AND AFRO-AMERICAN LITERATURE: A Vernacular Theory
0–226–03538–7 Chicago pb $8.95

• Donald Bogle
TOMS, COONS, MULATTOES, MAMMIES AND BUCKS: An Interpretive History of Blacks in American Film
0–8264–0146–2 Crossroad pb $14.95

• J.L. Dillard
BLACK ENGLISH: Its History and Usage in the United States
0–394–71872–0 Random House pb $7.95

• Ted Fox
SHOWTIME AT THE APOLLO
A history of America's foremost launchpad for black talent, from Lena Horne to Richard Pryor
0–03–060534–2 Henry Holt pb $9.95

• Henry Louis Gates, Jr.
THE SIGNIFYING MONKEY: A Theory of Afro-American Literary Criticism
0–19–503463–5 Oxford $29.95

• Nelson George
WHERE DID OUR LOVE GO?: The Rise and Fall of the Motown Sound
A fascinating look at black capitalism and the Detroit sound that changed American popular music
0–312–01109–1 St. Martin's pb $9.95

• Ira Gitler
SWING TO BOP: An Oral History of the Transition in Jazz in the 1940s
"An era when black musicians tried innovatively to wrest control of their music from white big-band leaders"—Mel Watkins, *American Visions*
0–19–505070–3 Oxford pb $9.95

• Jim Haskins
COTTON CLUB
A history of Harlem's famous nightclub showcase and its gangster-owners, white-only patrons, and black entertainers
0–452–25598–8 NAL pb $9.95

• Charles Johnson
BEING AND RACE: Black Writing Since 1970
0–253–31165–9 Indiana $15.95

• Spike Lee
THE CONSTRUCTION OF SCHOOL DAZE
A hilarious journal of the behind-the-scenes politics of filming a satire of fraternity life at an eminent black college; includes screenplay and photos
0–671–64418–1 Simon & Schuster pb $9.95

SPIKE LEE'S SHE'S GOTTA HAVE IT: Inside Guerrilla Filmmaking
The making of Lee's first feature, filmed in Brooklyn
Foreword by Nelson George
0–671–64417–3 Simon & Schuster pb $9.95

• Lawrence W. Levine
BLACK CULTURE AND BLACK CONSCIOUSNESS: Afro-American Folk Thought from Slavery to Freedom
0–19–502374–9 Oxford pb $9.95

• Alan Pomerance
REPEAL OF THE BLUES: How the Black Entertainers Influenced Civil Rights
0–8065–1105–2 Citadel $17.95

• Gunther Schuller
EARLY JAZZ: Its Roots and Musical Development
A classic study by a musician trained in European music as well as jazz
0–19–504043–0 Oxford pb $9.95

THE SWING ERA: The Development of Jazz, 1933–1945
The long-awaited second volume in Schuller's history
0–19–504312–X Oxford $32.50

• Marshall & Jean Stearns
JAZZ DANCE: The Story of Vernacular Dance
0–02–872510–7 Schirmer pb $14.95

• Robert Farris Thompson
FLASH OF THE SPIRIT: African and Afro-American Art and Philosophy
0–394–72369–4 Random House pb $9.95

Folklore

Nearly every American black writer has touched on some aspect of folk culture. Zora Neale Hurston, a pioneering feminist and cultural anthropologist, incorporated a great deal of folk material into her writing, as did Langston Hughes. Its impression can be seen in the work of such early writers as Paul Laurence Dunbar and Jean Toomer, as well as in the contemporary contributions of Ishmael Reed, Alice Walker, and Toni Morrison.

- Roger D. Abrahams, editor
AFRO-AMERICAN FOLKTALES: Stories from Black Traditions in the New World
"This fine collection will contribute significantly toward making the traditional stories of the African subcontinent more accessible"—*LA Times*
0–394–72885–8 Pantheon pb $11.95

- Harold Courlander
A TREASURY OF AFRO-AMERICAN FOLKLORE
0–517–52348–5 Crown $14.95

- Daryl C. Dance
LONG GONE: The Mecklenberg Six and the Theme of Escape in Black Folklore
0–87049–512–7 Tennessee $18.95

SHUCKIN' AND JIVIN': Folklore from Contemporary Black Americans
0–253–35220–7 Indiana $27.50
0–253–20265–5 Indiana pb $12.50

- J. Frank Dobie, editor
COFFEE IN THE GOURD
0–87074–039–3 Southern Methodist $11.95

- Joel Chandler Harris
UNCLE REMUS: His Songs and His Sayings
Edited by Robert Hemenway
0–14–039014–6 Penguin pb $5.95

- Langston Hughes & Arna Bontemps, editors
THE BOOK OF NEGRO FOLKLORE
0–396–08197–5 Dodd, Mead pb $12.95

- Zora Neale Hurston
MULES AND MEN
This classic was the first substantial collection of folktales by a black writer
Illustrated by Miguel Covarrubias
0–253–33932–4 Indiana $25.00
0–253–20208–6 Indiana pb $8.95

- Bruce Jackson
WAKE UP DEAD MAN: Afro-American Worksongs from Texas Prisons
0–674–94546–8 Harvard $24.50
0–674–94547–6 Harvard pb $9.95

- Bessie Jones & Bess L. Hawes
STEP IT DOWN: Games, Plays, Songs, and Stories from the Afro-American Heritage
0–8203–0960–5 Georgia pb $10.95

W.E.B. DuBois

- Jane Livingston & John Beardsley
BLACK FOLK ART IN AMERICA, 1930–1980
Foreword by Peter C. Marzio
0–87805–398–0 Mississippi $35.00
0–87805–158–9 Mississippi pb $24.95

- Jakie L. Pruett & Everett B. Cole
AS WE LIVED: Stories Told by Black Story Tellers
0–89015–309–4 Eakins $9.95

- Michael P. Smith
SPIRIT WORLD: Pattern in the Expressive Folk Culture of Afro-American New Orleans
Introduction by Nicholas R. Spitzer
0–9613133–0–7 Urban Folklife pb $14.00

- Geneval Smitherman
TALKIN' AND TESTIFYING: The Language of Black America
0–8143–1805–3 Wayne State pb $12.95

BLACK VOICES, BLACK LIVES

Classic Autobiographies

- William L. Andrews, editor
SISTERS OF THE SPIRIT: Three Black Women's Autobiographies of the 19th Century
Three preachers of Christian Gospel who helped to launch a feminist revolution in American religious life
0–253–28704–9 Indiana pb $8.95

TO TELL A FREE STORY: The First Century of Afro-American Autobiography, 1760–1864
"Imaginatively combines literary criticism, anthropological theory and history to provide a detailed, nuanced, and persuasive reading of Afro-American autobiography from its origins in the 18th century through emancipation"—Julius S. Scott, *Journal of Southern History*
0–252–06033–4 Indiana pb $10.95

- John Hope Franklin, editor
THREE NEGRO CLASSICS
Includes Booker T. Washington's *Up From Slavery*, W.E.B. DuBois's *The Souls of Black Folk*, and James Weldon Johnson's *The Autobiography of an Ex-Coloured Man*
0–380–01581–1 Avon pb $4.95

- Maya Angelou
GATHER TOGETHER IN MY NAME
0–394–48692–7 Random House $15.95
0–553–26066–9 Bantam pb $3.95

HEART OF A WOMAN
0–553–24689–5 Bantam pb $3.95

I KNOW WHY THE CAGED BIRD SINGS
0–394–42986–9 Random House $18.95
0–553–27937–8 Bantam pb $4.50

- Sara Brooks
YOU MAY PLOW HERE: The Narrative of Sara Brooks
Edited by Thordis Simonsen
Introduction by Robert Coles
0–393–02257–9 Norton $12.95
0–671–63848–3 Simon & Schuster pb $6.95

IF YOU CAN'T FIND IT, LOOK IN THE INDEX

• Claude Brown
MANCHILD IN THE PROMISED LAND
Painfully honest autobiography of growing up in Harlem in the 1940s and 1950s
0–02–517320–0 Macmillan $20.95
0–451–15741–9 NAL pb $4.95

Frederick Douglass
NARRATIVE OF THE LIFE OF FREDERICK DOUGLASS, AN AMERICAN SLAVE
0–14–039012–X Penguin pb $3.95

• W.E.B. DuBois
AUTOBIOGRAPHY OF W.E.B. DUBOIS: A Soliloquy of Viewing My Life from the Last Decade of Its First Century
0–7178–0234–5 International pb $8.95

• Nikki Giovanni
GEMINI: An Extended Autobiographical Statement on My First Twenty-Five Years of Being a Black Poet
0–14–004264–4 Penguin pb $4.95

• Marita Golden
MIGRATIONS OF THE HEART
0–345–34669–6 Ballantine pb $3.50

• Dick Gregory with Robert Lipsyte
NIGGER
From poverty to celebrity status as a comedian and civil rights activist
0–671–62611–6 Washington Square pb $3.95

• John Howard Griffin
BLACK LIKE ME
A white writer chemically darkened his skin and traveled through the mid-1950s South; his journal, a longtime bestseller, offers chilling revelations
0–395–25102–8 Houghton Mifflin $16.95
0–451–15530–0 NAL pb $3.95

• John L. Gwaltney
DRYLONGSO: A Self-Portrait of Black America
These eloquent and, at times, disturbing testimonies, conducted in the early 1970s with "drylongso" or ordinary people, are among the most illuminating of core black culture
0–394–74713–5 Random House pb $7.95

• Lorraine Hansberry
TO BE YOUNG, GIFTED AND BLACK
Autobiography of the youngest winner of the New York Drama Critics Award (at age 29) for *A Raisin In the Sun;* adapted by her husband, Robert Nemiroff
Introduction by James Baldwin
0–451–15952–7 NAL pb $4.95

• Langston Hughes
THE BIG SEA
Part One of the autobiography of the man Richard Wright called "*the* jazz poet" covers Hughes' life after graduation from Columbia University, waiting tables in Paris, and in the Harlem Renaissance
Introduction by Amiri Baraka
0–938410–33–4 Thunder's Mouth pb $10.95

I WONDER AS I WANDER
The second part of Hughes' autobiography covers his 1930s travels to Cuba, Haiti, Russia, Japan, and civil-war Spain
0–938410–36–9 Thunder's Mouth pb $10.95

• Zora Neale Hurston
DUST TRACKS ON A ROAD
Introduction by Larry Neal
Foreword by Robert E. Hemenway
0–252–01047–7 Illinois pb $8.95

• Martin Luther King, Jr.
STRIDE TOWARD FREEDOM: The Montgomery Story
0–06–250490–8 Harper & Row $8.95

• Mary King
FREEDOM SONG: A Personal Story of the 1960s Civil Rights Movement
0–688–08251–3 Morrow pb $12.95

• Malcolm X with Alex Haley
THE AUTOBIOGRAPHY OF MALCOLM X
A personal account of internal politics in the Nation of Islam, by its most famous minister
0–345–35068–5 Ballantine pb $4.95

BY ANY MEANS NECESSARY
Edited by George Breitman
0–87348–150–X Path Press pb $7.95

SELECTED SPEECHES AND STATEMENTS
Edited by George Breitman
0–8021–3051–8 Grove pb $8.95

• Paul Robeson
HERE I STAND
Robeson's major autobiographical and political statement, from 1958
Introduction by Sterling Stuckey
0–8070–6445–9 Beacon pb $8.95

• Philip S. Foner, editor
PAUL ROBESON SPEAKS
A collection of Robeson's writings, from his graduation oration at Rutgers in 1919 to pieces on the color bar, South Africa, and black history
0–8065–0815–9 Lyle Stuart pb $9.95

• Theodore Rosengarten
ALL GOD'S DANGERS: The Life of Nate Shaw
An award-winning oral history of a sharecropper in the post-Civil War South
0–394–72245–0 Random House pb $12.95

• Booker T. Washington
UP FROM SLAVERY
0–14–039051–0 Penguin pb $3.95

• Richard Wright
AMERICAN HUNGER
A passionate tale of coming-of-age in the Communist party
0–06–014768–7 Harper & Row $13.95
0–06–090991–9 Harper & Row pb $7.95

Voices from Slavery

"To the slave mother, New Year's day comes laden with peculiar sorrows. She sits on her cold cabin floor, watching the children who may all be torn from her the next morning; and often does she wish that she and they might die before the day dawns. She may be an ignorant creature, degraded by the system that has brutalized her from childhood; but she has a mother's instincts, and is capable of feeling a mother's agonies."—from *Linda: Incidents in the Life of a Slave Girl*, cited in Marion Wilson Starling, *The Slave Narrative: Its Place in American History*

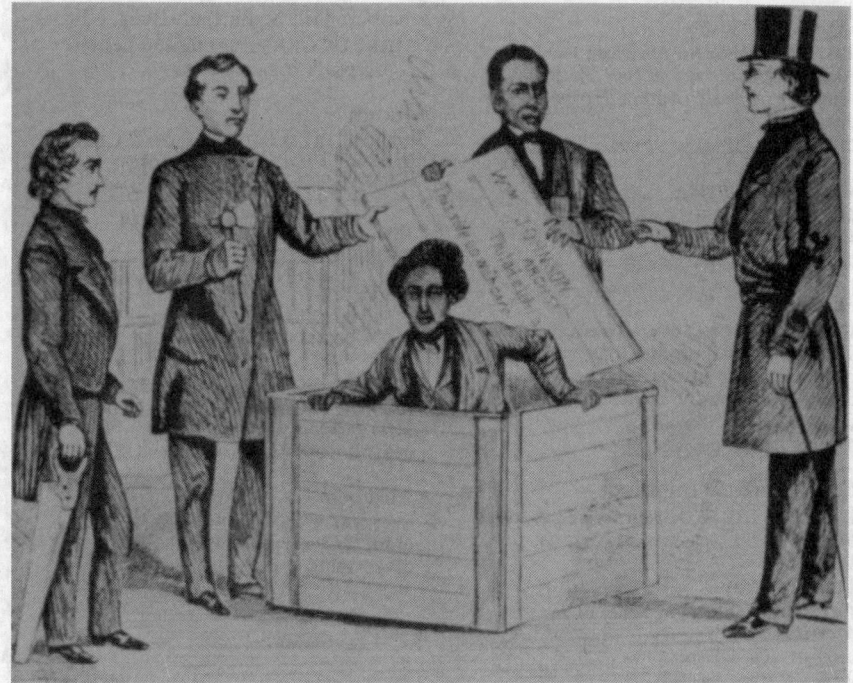

Henry "Box" Brown's escape from slavery, from Before the Mayflower: A History of Black America *by Lerone Bennett, Jr.* (Penguin)

• John W. Blassingame, editor
SLAVE TESTIMONY: Two Centuries of Letters, Speeches, Interviews, and Autobiographies
The largest annotated and authenticated account of slaves ever published in one volume
0–8071–0273–3 LSU pb $14.95

• Linda Brent
INCIDENTS IN THE LIFE OF A SLAVE GIRL
Edited by L. Maria Child
Preface by Walter Teller
0–15–644350–3 HBJ pb $6.95

• Charlotte L. Forten
THE JOURNAL OF CHARLOTTE L. FORTEN: A Free Negro in a Slave Era
Edited by Ray A. Billington
0–393–00046–X Norton pb $8.95

• Henry Louis Gates, Jr., editor
CLASSIC SLAVE NARRATIVES
0–451–62726–1 NAL pb $4.95

• James Mellon, editor
BULLWHIP DAYS: The Slaves Remember
The Federal Writers' Project of the mid-1930s dispatched interviewers to collect the memories of the dwindling number of former slaves; 29 of these narrative oral histories plus other writings make up this new collection
1–55584–210–0 Weidenfeld & Nicolson $25.00

• Marion Wilson Starling
THE SLAVE NARRATIVE: Its Place in American History
The testimonies of 6000 blacks, before, during, and after slavery
0–88258–165–1 Howard pb $12.95

Family Chronicles

• Gail L. Buckley
THE HORNES: An American Family
An affectionate saga of the "black bourgeois" family of Lena Horne, by her daughter
0–452–25959–2 NAL pb $8.95

• James P. Comer
MAGGIE'S AMERICAN DREAM: The Life and Times of a Black Family
0–453–00588–8 NAL $18.95

• Alex Haley
ROOTS: The Saga of an American Family
The book that spurred a major television production and inspired interest among blacks in tracing the roots of their African heritage
0–440–17464–3 Doubleday pb $5.95

• Sara Lawrence Lightfoot
BALM IN GILEAD: Journey of a Healer
0–201–09312–X Addison-Wesley $18.95

• Pauli Murray
PROUD SHOES: The Story of an American Family
0–06–013109–8 Harper & Row $13.95
0–06–091398–3 Harper & Row pb $7.95

• Dorothy Spruill Redford with Michael D'Orso
SOMERSET HOMECOMING: Recovering a Lost Heritage
Redford's research ultimately led to two homecomings, in 1986 and 1988
0–385–24245–X Doubleday $18.95
0–385–24246–8 Doubleday pb $9.95

• John Edgar Wideman
BROTHERS AND KEEPERS
Beginning with their childhood in a Pittsburgh ghetto, the author charts his own life as a Rhodes scholar and college professor, and that of his brother Robby, given a life sentence for murder
0–14–008267–0 Penguin pb $6.95

Leaders and Activists

• Barbara Reynolds
AND STILL WE RISE
Interviews with a cross-section of 50 black role models, including Angela Davis, the late Harold Washington, and Ray Charles
0–944347–02–9 USA Today Books $14.95

• J. Gregory Payne & Scott C. Ratzan
TOM BRADLEY: The Impossible Dream
How a black athlete and cop became mayor of America's second-largest city
Introduction by Alex Haley
0–915677–29–6 Roundtable $18.95
0–7701–0653–6 Paper Jacks pb $4.95

• Waldo E. Martin
THE MIND OF FREDERICK DOUGLASS
0–8078–4148–X North Carolina pb $9.95

• Manning Marable
W.E.B. DUBOIS: Black Radical Democrat
0–8057–7750–4 G.K. Hall $24.95

• Robert Hill & Barbara Blair, editors
MARCUS GARVEY: Life and Lessons
0–520–06214–0 California $25.00

• Judith Stein
THE WORLD OF MARCUS GARVEY: Race and Class in Modern Society
0–8071–1236–4 LSU $25.00

• Nell Irvin Painter
THE NARRATIVE OF HOSEA HUDSON: His Life As a Negro Communist in the South
0–674–60110–6 Harvard $29.50
0–674–60111–4 Harvard pb $10.95

• Jesse Jackson
A TIME TO SPEAK: The Autobiography of Jesse Jackson
0–317–64227–8 Simon & Schuster $17.95

• Elizabeth O. Colton
THE JACKSON PHENOMENON: The Man, the Power, the Myth
0–385–26070–9 Doubleday $19.95

• Ernest R. House
JESSE JACKSON AND THE POLITICS OF CHARISMA: The Rise and Fall of the PUSH/Excel Program
A look beyond charismatic myth into Jackson's leadership, focusing on his crusade to save America's black youth
0–8133–0767–8 Westview $23.95

• Adolph L. Reed
THE JESSE JACKSON PHENOMENON: The Crisis of Purpose in Afro-American Politics
0–300–03543–8 Yale $22.50
0–300–03552–7 Yale pb $8.95

David J. Garrow
BEARING THE CROSS: Martin Luther King, Jr., and the Southern Christian Leadership Conference, 1955–1968
0–688–04794–7 Morrow $22.95
0–394–75623–1 Random House pb $10.95

THE FBI AND MARTIN LUTHER KING, JR.
0–393–01509–2 Norton $15.95
0–14–006486–9 Penguin pb $7.95

Stephen B. Oates
LET THE TRUMPET SOUND: The Life of Martin Luther King, Jr.
0–451–62350–9 NAL pb $4.95

• Anne Moody
COMING OF AGE IN MISSISSIPPI
A memoir of lynchings, economic hardship, and other abuses of plantation life, and the civil rights movement of the 1960s
0–440–31488–7 Dell pb $4.50

• Jervis A. Anderson
A. PHILIP RANDOLPH: A Biographical Portrait
The rise of a young radical street orator in Harlem to national labor leader of sleeping-car porters
0–520–05505–5 California pb $11.95

• Assata Shakur
ASSATA: An Autobiography
As a leader of the Black Panther party in 1973, Assata Shakur was charged with murder in a shootout with state troopers; she later escaped from prison, went underground and, based in Cuba, wrote this memoir about prison and the life that led her to join the Panthers
0–88208–221–3 Lawrence Hill $18.95
0–88208–222–1 Lawrence Hill pb $9.95

• Roger Wilkins
A MAN'S LIFE: An Autobiography
The life of the former US Assistant Attorney General and Pulitzer Prize-winning journalist
0–671–22673–8 Simon & Schuster $17.95
0–671–49268–3 Simon & Schuster pb $7.95

• Roy Wilkins with Tom Mathews
STANDING FAST: The Autobiography of Roy Wilkins
The civil rights leader and a major force in the NAACP
0–14–007373–6 Penguin pb $7.95

- John Hope Franklin
GEORGE WASHINGTON WILLIAMS: A Biography
The self-made intellectual, long over-looked, who wrote the first history of blacks in America
0–226–26083–6 Chicago $24.95
0–226–26084–4 Chicago pb $12.95

Scientists and Educators

- Daisy Bates
THE LONG SHADOW OF LITTLE ROCK
Memoir of a key figure in the fight to integrate Central High in Little Rock
0–938626–74–4 Arkansas $18.95

- Linda O. McMurry
GEORGE WASHINGTON CARVER: Scientist and Symbol
0–19–503205–5 Oxford pb $9.95

- Septima Clark
READY FROM WITHIN: Septima Clark and the Civil Rights Movements
A South Carolina teacher fired for joining the NAACP in 1965 went on to organize "freedom" schools and register voters
Edited by Cynthia S. Brown
0–931125–04–9 Wild Trees pb $8.95

- Kenneth R. Manning
BLACK APOLLO OF SCIENCE: The Life of Ernest Everett Just
The zoologist at Woods Hole, Massachusetts
0–19–503498–8 Oxford pb $10.95

- Benjamin E. Mays
BORN TO REBEL: An Autobiography by Benjamin E. Mays
Born the son of a sharecropper in 1894, Mays rose to become president of Morehouse College in Atlanta
Introduction by Orville V. Burton
0–8203–0880–3 Georgia $30.00
0–8203–0881–1 Georgia pb $14.95

- Louis R. Harlan
BOOKER T. WASHINGTON: The Making of a Black Leader, 1856–1901
The man, his era, and the problem of living in the face of racial injustice; Pulitzer Prize winner (1984)
0–19–501915–6 Oxford pb $11.95

BOOKER T. WASHINGTON: The Wizard of Tuskegee, 1901–1915
The second half of Harlan's masterful biography
0–19–504229–8 Oxford pb $11.95

Artists and Literary Figures

- Henry Crowder & Hugo Speck
AS WONDERFUL AS ALL THAT?: Henry Crowder's Memoir of His Affair with Nancy Cunard, 1928–1935
A black musician's memoir of globe-trotting with Nancy Cunard, and how it changed their lives
Introduction & epilogue by Robert L. Allen
0–931125–05–7 Wild Trees pb $9.95

Richard Wright, from World Celebrities in Ninety Photographic Portraits *by Fred Stein (Dover)*

- Arnold Rampersad
THE LIFE OF LANGSTON HUGHES

Volume 1: I, Too, Sing America, 1902–1941
0–19–505426–1 Oxford pb $9.95

Volume 2: I Dream a World, 1941–1967
0–19–504519–X Oxford $24.95

- Wayne F. Cooper
CLAUDE McKAY, REBEL SOJOURNER IN THE HARLEM RENAISSANCE: A Biography
0–8071–1310–7 LSU $29.95

- Cynthia E. Kerman & Richard Eldridge
THE LIVES OF JEAN TOOMER: A Hunger for Wholeness
Includes a literary analysis of the poet's work as well as a dramatic account of his life, including his move to enroll in the University of Wisconsin as a white, and his subsequent quest for a raceless identity
0–8071–1354–9 LSU $29.95

- Margaret Walker
RICHARD WRIGHT: A Portrait of the Man, a Critical Look at His Work
The life of the literary giant, by a contemporary
0–446–71001–6 Warner $22.00

Athletes and Entertainers

- Arthur R. Ashe, Jr.
A HARD ROAD TO GLORY: A History of the African-American Athlete
A sport-by-sport narrative account, including an extensive reference section on the successes of black athletes

Volume 1: 1619–1918
0–446–71006–7 Warner $29.95

Volume 2: 1919–1945
0–446–71007–5 Warner $39.95

Volume 3: Since 1946
0–446–71008–3 Warner $39.95

- Josephine Baker & Jo Bouillon
JOSEPHINE
The dramatic story of the American dancer who became the toast of Paris in the

1920s, and a spy for the Allies in World War II
Translated by Mariana Fitzpatrick
1–55778–108–7 Paragon pb $9.95

- William J. Baker
JESSE OWENS: An American Life
"The story of the ultimate black American sports hero and how he was used and abused"—Marty Glickman
0–02–901760–2 Free Press pb $9.95

- Joe Louis Barrow, Jr. & Barbara Munder
JOE LOUIS: 50 Years of an American Hero
"Perhaps Louis's primary contribution was in positively representing what could be done if blacks were allowed to compete fairly with whites under the same set of rules"—from the Foreword by Arthur R. Ashe, Jr.
0–07–003955–0 McGraw-Hill $18.95

- Chris Mead
CHAMPION: Joe Louis, Black Hero in White America
0–14–009285–4 Penguin pb $6.95

- Gil Noble
BLACK IS THE COLOR OF MY TV TUBE
The autobiographical odyssey of a star black reporter, one of first in the industry during the 1960s
0–8184–0297–0 Lyle Stuart $12.00

Martin Bauml Duberman
PAUL ROBESON
A major biography
0–394–52790–1 Knopf $24.95

- Susan Robeson
THE WHOLE WORLD IN HIS HANDS: A Pictorial Biography of Paul Robeson
A beautifully illustrated book by his grandchild
0–8065–0977–5 Lyle Stuart pb $12.95

- Jim Haskins & N.R. Mitgang
MR. BOJANGLES: The Biography of Bill Robinson
The famous tap dancer, who starred with Shirley Temple in *The Little Colonel*
0–688–07203–8 Morrow $17.95

- Robert Waldron
OPRAH!
National bestseller on the TV star, Oprah Winfrey
0–517–67712–1 St. Martin's pb $3.98

Soldiers

▶ See also The Civil War and Reconstruction & The Vietnam War

- Stanley Goff, Robert Sanders & Clark Smith
BROTHERS: Black Soldiers in Nam
0–425–10648–9 Berkley pb $3.50

• Thomas Wentworth Higginson
ARMY LIFE IN A BLACK REGIMENT
A classic of Civil War literature by the
preacher-soldier who led the First South
Carolina
0–87928–022–0 Corner House $20.00
0–393–30157–5 Norton pb $6.95

• Wallace Terry
**BLOODS: An Oral History of the Vietnam
War by Black Veterans**
0–345–31197–3 Ballantine pb $4.50

• James Yates
**MISSISSIPPI TO MADRID: Memoir of a
Black American in the Abraham Lincoln
Brigade**
0–940880–20–2 Open Hand pb $9.95

American Politics and Foreign Policy

▶ **See also International Relations and Strategic
Studies & Modern Political Thought**

POLITICAL HISTORY

• Richard F. Bensel
**SECTIONALISM AND AMERICAN
POLITICAL DEVELOPMENT, 1880–1980**
0–299–09834–6 Wisconsin pb $14.95

• Daniel J. Boorstin
**THE GENIUS OF AMERICAN
POLITICS**
0–226–06491–3 Chicago pb $7.00

• James W. Clarke
**AMERICAN ASSASSINS: The Darker Side
of Politics**
0–691–07637–5 Princeton $28.00
0–691–02221–6 Princeton pb $10.50

• Alonzo L. Hamby
**LIBERALISM AND ITS
CHALLENGERS: F.D.R. to Reagan**
0–19–503418–X Oxford $32.00
0–19–503419–8 Oxford pb $13.95

• Louis Hartz
**THE LIBERAL TRADITION IN
AMERICA: An Interpretation of American
Political Thought since the Revolution**
0–15–651269–6 HBJ pb $10.95

• Samuel P. Hays
**AMERICAN POLITICAL HISTORY AS
SOCIAL ANALYSIS**
Pathbreaking essays on the social base of
political behavior and the structure of
modern society
0–87049–276–4 Tennessee $36.95

• Richard Hofstadter
**THE AMERICAN POLITICAL
TRADITION**
Insightful essays on outstanding political
leaders by one of the great postwar
historians
0–394–48880–6 Knopf $21.95
0–679–72315–3 Random House pb $7.95

• Morris Janowitz
**THE LAST HALF-CENTURY: Societal
Change and Politics in America**
0–226–39306–2 Chicago $35.00
0–226–39307–0 Chicago pb $16.00

• Robert Kelley
**THE CULTURAL PATTERN IN
AMERICAN POLITICS: The First
Century**
The ethnic and religious roots of political
behavior
0–8191–1825–7 University Press pb $13.25

V.O. Key, Jr.
**SOUTHERN POLITICS IN STATE
AND NATION**
A new edition of a massive work
originally published in 1949
0–87049–435–X Tennessee pb $14.95

• Alpheus Thomas Mason & Gordon E.
Baker, editors
**FREE GOVERNMENT IN THE
MAKING: Readings in American Political
Thought**
A comprehensive collection of documents;
updated to include the role of women and
minorities
0–19–503524–0 Oxford $29.95

• Richard L. McCormick
**THE PARTY PERIOD AND PUBLIC
POLICY: American Politics from the Age
of Jackson to the Progressive Era**
An important recent work
0–19–503860–6 Oxford $32.50

• Thomas K. McCraw
**PROPHETS OF REGULATION: Charles
Francis Adams, Louis D. Brandeis, James
M. Landis, Alfred E. Kahn**
A Pulitzer Prize-winning study (1984)
using biography to probe the development
of government economic regulation
0–674–71607–8 Harvard $22.95
0–674–71608–6 Harvard pb $9.95

• Wilson E. Nelson
**THE ROOTS OF AMERICAN
BUREAUCRACY, 1830–1900**
A short, thoughtful meditation
0–674–77945–2 Harvard $27.00

• Shelley Ross
**FALL FROM GRACE: Sex, Scandal and
Corruption in American Politics from 1702
to the Present**
Strange but true tales: New York's
governor Lord Cornbury, who wore
hooped skirts and women's accessories as a
tribute to Queen Anne; Grover Cleveland's
illegitimate child; and many others
0–345–35381–1 Ballantine pb $9.95

DEMOCRATS AND REPUBLICANS

• Jerome Clubb, William H. Flanigan
& Nancy Zingale
**PARTISAN REALIGNMENT: Voters,
Parties, and Government in American
History**
0–8039–1445–8 Sage $29.95

*Thomas Hart Benton's "Political Conven-
tion," from 500 Years of Life in America by
Marshall B. Davidson (Abradale/Abrams)*

• Thomas Ferguson & Joel Rogers
**RIGHT TURN: The Decline of the
Democrats and the Future of American
Politics**
"Ferguson and Rogers' study of the
relationship between key business leaders
and officials of the Democratic Party, and
of policy decisions tied to these
relationships, sheds new light on the dark
side of democracy, where money
determines public policy"—Thomas Byrne
Edsall
0–8090–0170–5 Hill & Wang pb $8.95

• Ralph M. Goldman
**DILEMMA AND DESTINY: The
Democratic Party in America**
The party's history and prospects,
including a portrait of what it and America
may look like in 2032
Foreword by Arthur Hoppe
0–8191–4384–7 University Press pb $8.95

**SEARCH FOR CONSENSUS: The Story
of the Democratic Party**
0–87722–152–9 Temple $34.95

• Xandra Kayden & Eddie Mahe, Jr.
**THE PARTY GOES ON: The Persistence
of the Two-Party System in the United
States**
0–465–05451–X Basic Books pb $8.95

• Robert Kuttner
**THE LIFE OF THE PARTY: Democratic
Prospects in 1988 and Beyond**
Charts the party's recent decline in
presidential politics and offers an agenda
for its resurgence
0–14–009877–1 Penguin pb $7.95

• Alexander P. Lamis
THE TWO-PARTY SOUTH
The transformation of the Old South
dominated by a conservative Democratic
party into today's two-party New South;
includes analyses of the 1984 and 1986
elections
0–19–505680–9 Oxford $34.00

• David R. Mayhew
**PLACING PARTIES IN AMERICAN
POLITICS: Organization, Electoral
Settings, and Government Activity in the
Twentieth Century**
A serious academic study, by a Yale scholar
0–691–02249–6 Princeton pb $11.50

☞ **TO ORDER NEW BOOKS NOT YET LISTED, ASK YOUR BOOKSELLER OR CALL 1-800-882-8770**

- Robert A. Rutland
  THE DEMOCRATS: From Jefferson to Carter
  0–8071–0574–0 LSU $22.50

- Fred Schwengel
  THE REPUBLICAN PARTY: Its Heritage and History
  An illustrated commemorative volume
  0–87491–883–9 Acropolis pb $12.95

- James L. Sundquist
  DYNAMICS OF THE PARTY SYSTEM: Alignment and Realignment of Political Parties in the United States
  0–8157–8225–X Brookings pb $12.95

Voting

- Paul Kleppner
  WHO VOTED?: The Dynamics of Electoral Turnout, 1870–1980
  0–275–90661–2 Praeger $35.95

- Frances Fox Piven & Richard A. Cloward
  WHY AMERICANS DON'T VOTE
  The authors argue that our electoral system works to keep it that way
  0–394–55396–9 Pantheon $19.95
  0–679–72318–8 Pantheon pb $9.95

THE CONGRESS

"The principle of the independence of the states triumphed in the formation of the Senate, and that of the sovereignty of the nation in the composition of the House of Representatives. Each state was to send two senators to Congress, and a number of representatives proportional to its population. It results from this arrangement that the state of New York has at the present day thirty-three representatives, and only two senators; the state of Delaware has two senators, and only one representative; the state of Delaware is therefore equal to the state of New York in the Senate, while the latter has thirty-three times the influence of the former in the House of Representatives. Thus the minority of the nation in the Senate may paralyze the decisions of the majority represented in the other house, which is contrary to the spirit of constitutional government."—Alexis de Tocqueville, *Democracy in America,* volume 1

- Congressional Quarterly
  THE POWERS OF CONGRESS
  A useful guidebook to congressional powers and limits
  0–87187–242–0 Congressional Quarterly pb $9.95

- Robert Goehlert & John Sayre
  THE UNITED STATES CONGRESS
  0–02–911900–6 Free Press $50.00

- Gary C. Jacobson & Samuel Kernell
  STRATEGY AND CHOICE IN CONGRESSIONAL ELECTIONS
  Assesses various factors that influence the outcome of congressional races
  0–300–03077–0 Yale pb $5.95

- Loch K. Johnson
  A SEASON OF INQUIRY: Congress and Intelligence
  "Especially useful in underlining the complexities in major oversight efforts"—Morris Ogul, University of Pittsburgh
  0–534–10597–1 Wadsworth pb $14.50

- David R. Mayhew
  CONGRESS: The Electoral Connection
  0–300–01777–4 Yale $25.00
  0–300–01809–6 Yale pb $7.95

- Walter Oleszek
  CONGRESSIONAL PROCEDURES AND THE POLICY PROCESS
  0–87187–477–6 CQ pb $15.95

- George E. Reedy
  THE U.S. SENATE: Paralysis or Search for Consensus?
  0–451–62608–7 NAL pb $4.95

- Philip M. Stern
  THE BEST CONGRESS MONEY CAN BUY
  How members of Congress are becoming more dependent on PACs and special interests for campaign funds. "A cogent and coherent account of the corrupting influence of political money on Congress"—Daniel Schorr
  0–394–56628–9 Pantheon $18.95

- James L. Sundquist
  THE DECLINE AND RESURGENCE OF CONGRESS
  0–8157–8224–1 Brookings $34.95
  0–8157–8223–3 Brookings pb $15.95

THE PRESIDENCY

- James David Barber
  THE PULSE OF POLITICS: The Rhythm of Presidential Elections in the Twentieth Century
  A 1974 study by a leading student of the presidency
  0–393–01341–3 Norton $14.95

- Paul F. Boller, Jr.
  PRESIDENTIAL ANECDOTES
  Revealing stories from Washington to Reagan
  0–14–006349–8 Penguin pb $8.95

  PRESIDENTIAL CAMPAIGNS
  Entertaining history of the showdowns for the nation's highest office
  0–19–503722–7 Oxford pb $7.95

- Carl M. Brauer
  PRESIDENTIAL TRANSITIONS: Eisenhower Through Reagan
  How five newly elected presidents created their administrations
  0–19–505655–8 Oxford pb $9.95

- Marcus Cunliffe
  THE PRESIDENCY
  0–8281–1217–7 Houghton Mifflin $19.95
  0–8281–1202–9 Houghton Mifflin pb $9.95

- Roger A. Fischer
  TIPPECANOE AND TRINKETS TOO: The Material Culture of American Presidential Campaigns
  A richly illustrated collection of campaign memorabilia
  0–252–00960–6 Illinois $34.95

- Kathleen Hall Jamieson
  ELOQUENCE IN AN ELECTRONIC AGE: The Transformation of Political Speechmaking
  The impact of TV and radio on political oratory
  0–19–503826–6 Oxford $24.95

  PACKAGING THE PRESIDENCY
  Chronicles the strategies for winning voters' hearts and ballots, focusing on the elections from Eisenhower to Reagan
  0–19–505656–6 Oxford $12.95

- Kathleen Hall Jamieson & David S. Birdsell
  PRESIDENTIAL DEBATES: Their Power, Problems and Promise
  Includes numerous suggestions for improving debates
  0–19–505539–X Oxford $19.95

- Barbara Kellerman
  THE POLITICAL PRESIDENCY: The Practice of Leadership from Kennedy Through Reagan
  How six presidents handled the most important domestic policy issues
  0–19–503457–0 Oxford $22.50
  0–19–504037–6 Oxford pb $12.95

- Harold J. Laski
  THE AMERICAN PRESIDENCY: An Interpretation
  First published in 1940 and still essential. "One of the best books ever written about the institutions of another country by a foreign observer"—Kingsley Martin, *New Statesman and Nation*
  0–87855–821–7 Transaction pb $12.95

1940 campaign poster (courtesy of The New-York Historical Society)

- Richard P. McCormick
THE PRESIDENTIAL GAME: The Origins of American Presidential Politics
The origins of presidential politics and why the selection process has become something quite different from that intended by the framers of the Constitution
0–19–503455–4 Oxford pb $10.95

Richard E. Neustadt
PRESIDENTIAL POWER: The Politics of Leadership from FDR to Carter
0–02–386670–5 Macmillan $20.50

- LuAnn Paletta & Fred L. Worth
THE WORLD ALMANAC OF PRESIDENTIAL FACTS
A chatty catalog of presidential lore, noting astrological signs, college affiliations, home addresses, namesakes, favorite meals, club memberships, pets, nicknames, and favorite books
0–88687–326–6 World Almanac pb $9.95

- Edward Pessen
THE LOG CABIN MYTH: The Social Backgrounds of the Presidents
0–300–03754–6 Yale pb $10.95

- Richard M. Pious
THE AMERICAN PRESIDENCY
0–465–00184–X Basic Books pb $15.95

- George E. Reedy
THE TWILIGHT OF THE PRESIDENCY: From Johnson to Reagan
How the president's isolation from all below him affects politics and the nation
0–451–62510–2 NAL pb $4.50

- Clinton Rossiter
THE AMERICAN PRESIDENCY
A widely consulted introduction to its history and political culture, by the late Cornell professor
Introduction by Michael Nelson
0–8018–3545–3 Johns Hopkins pb $9.95

- William Seale
THE PRESIDENT'S HOUSE: A History
0–8109–1490–5 Abrams $39.95

- John Tebbel & Sarah M. Watts
THE PRESS AND THE PRESIDENCY: From George Washington to Ronald Reagan
0–19–503628–X Oxford $29.95

First Families

- Paul F. Boller, Jr.
PRESIDENTIAL WIVES
Includes a biographical essay on each First Lady, followed by a selection of revealing anecdotes. "Just before Inauguration Day, Mrs. Eisenhower received a beautiful embossed invitation to the inaugural ball. 'What should we do about this,' she asked Ike. 'Turn it down,' he said with a straight face. 'Tell them we've got another engagement.'"
0–19–503763–4 Oxford $19.95

- Betty Boyd Caroli
FIRST LADIES
Wives from Martha to Nancy come alive through their backgrounds, successes, and failures; including Jane Pierce, who prayed her husband would lose the election, Edith Wilson, who virtually became president herself after her husband's stroke, and Pat Nixon, who perfected what some have called "the robot image"
0–19–505654–X Oxford pb $8.95

- Peter Hay
ALL THE PRESIDENTS' LADIES: Anecdotes of the Women Behind the Man in the White House
Organized by topic, this book looks at First Ladydom from policy-making to love lives to household maintenance
0–670–81395–8 Viking $19.95

- Diana Dixon Healy
AMERICA'S FIRST LADIES: Private Lives of the Presidential Wives
Concise portraits of each First Lady
0–689–11873–2 Atheneum $18.95

- E.H. Gwynne Thomas
THE PRESIDENTIAL FAMILIES: From George Washington to Ronald Reagan
0–87052–590–5 Hippocrene $22.50

Recent Presidential Elections

- Elizabeth Drew
ELECTION JOURNAL: Political Events of 1987–88
A brilliant account of the 1988 presidential election by *The New Yorker*'s Washington correspondent
0–688–08332–3 Morrow $19.95

- Thomas Ferguson
HIDDEN ELECTION: Politics and Economics in the 1980 Presidential Campaign
0–394–74958–8 Pantheon pb $6.95

- Robert Scheer
WHAT HAPPENED?: The Story of Election 1980
0–394–41482–9 Random House $14.95

- Paul Simon
WINNERS AND LOSERS: The Race for the Presidency 1988
An account of the election, by one of its failed candidates
0–8264–0428–6 Crossroad $17.95

CURRENT POLITICAL THOUGHT AND ISSUES

- James David Barber & Barbara Kellerman
WOMEN IN AMERICAN POLITICS
0–13–962267–5 Prentice-Hall pb $28.00

- David Broder
CHANGING OF THE GUARD: Power and Leadership in America
0–14–005940–7 Penguin pb $7.95

- William F. Buckley, Jr.
ON THE FIRING LINE: The Public Life of Our Public Figures
Dialogues with Galbraith, Mailer, Wolfe, Dukakis, Reagan, Capote, Hoffa and others, based on Buckley's long-running television show
Introduction by Alistair Cooke
0–394–57568–7 Random House $22.50

- Walter Dean Burnham
THE CURRENT CRISIS IN AMERICAN POLITICS
0–19–503219–5 Oxford $29.95
0–19–503220–9 Oxford pb $10.95

- Joshua Cohen & Joel Rogers
ON DEMOCRACY: Toward a Transformation of American Society
"The best extant statement of what's wrong with America—progressive diagnosis and progressive prescription—in the tradition of Debs and FDR, through the lens of the leading political philosophers of our time"—Duncan Kennedy, Harvard Law School
0–14–006781–7 Penguin pb $7.95

- Sheila D. Collins
THE RAINBOW CHALLENGE: The Jackson Campaign and the Future of U.S. Politics
"A thorough, incisive critique of the complex role of race and class in American politics"—Manning Marable
0–85345–691–7 Monthly Review pb $11.00

- Robert A. Dahl
WHO GOVERNS?: Democracy and Power in an American City
A classic study of how local American government really works, first published in 1961 and based on a study of New Haven politics
0–300–00051–0 Yale pb $10.95

- G. William Domhoff
WHO RULES AMERICA NOW?: A View for the Eighties
The sequel to *Who Rules America?* argues that our political and economic scene is run by a privileged elite
0–671–62235–8 Simon & Schuster pb $9.95

- Thomas Byrne Edsall
THE NEW POLITICS OF INEQUALITY
A *Washington Post* reporter examines how control of the nation's tax and spending policies is increasingly falling into the hands of the affluent
0–393–30250–4 Norton pb $5.95

- Myron Peretz Glazer & Penina Migdal Glazer
THE WHISTLE-BLOWERS: Exposing Corruption in Government and Industry
A full-scale study of the people who have put their careers and lives on the line to expose dangerous or illegal situations
0–465–09173–3 Basic Books $19.95

- Mark Green
THE OTHER GOVERNMENT: The Unseen Power of Washington Lawyers
0–393–00865–7 Norton pb $3.95

- Allen D. Hertzke
REPRESENTING GOD IN WASHINGTON: The Role of Religious Lobbies in the American Polity
0–87049–553–4 Tennessee $29.50
0–87049–570–4 Tennessee pb $14.95

- Irving Louis Horowitz
IDEOLOGY AND UTOPIA IN THE UNITED STATES, 1956–1976
Topics include political assassination, government-sponsored research, and covert operations
0–19–502107–X Oxford pb $10.95

- Samuel P. Huntington
AMERICAN POLITICS: The Promise of Disharmony
Examines the gap between American political ideals and actual performance
0–674–03021–4 Harvard pb $8.95

- Brooks Jackson
HONEST GRAFT: Big Money and the American Political Process
How Political Action Committees are altering the shape of American politics, by a *Wall Street Journal* investigative reporter
0–394–56452–9 Knopf $18.95

- Walter Karp
LIBERTY UNDER SIEGE: American Politics, 1976–1988
An outspoken political history arguing that there has been a major assault on American liberties, including a systematic intimidation of the press, the return of big money to politics, lifetime censorship of political officials, invasion of privacy, and the expansion of secret government
0–8050–0859–4 Henry Holt $19.95

- Steven Kelman
MAKING PUBLIC POLICY: A Hopeful View of American Government
Why the system works better than most Americans believe; by a professor at the John F. Kennedy School of Government
0–465–04335–6 Basic Books pb $9.95

- Charles Krauthammer
CUTTING EDGES: Making Sense of the '80s
Pieces from *The New Republic, The Washington Post,* and *Time,* on such subjects as nuclear deterrence, Jane Fonda, abortion, and pornography
1–55778–125–7 Paragon pb $9.95

- Burdett Loomis
THE NEW AMERICAN POLITICIAN: Ambition, Entrepreneurship, and the Changing Face of Political Life
0–465–04997–4 Basic Books $19.95

Theodore J. Lowi
THE END OF LIBERALISM: The Second Republic of the United States
0–393–09000–0 Norton pb $11.95

- Richard P. Nathan
SOCIAL SCIENCE IN GOVERNMENT: Uses and Misuses
0–465–07911–3 Basic Books $18.95

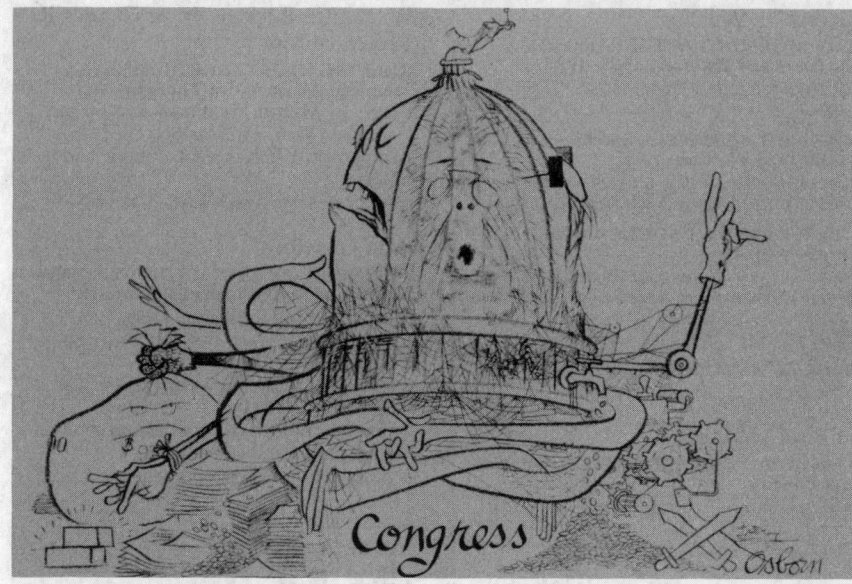

"Congress" by Robert Osborne from The Image of America in Caricature and Cartoon *by Ron Tyler (Amon Carter Museum/cartoon courtesy The Swann Collection)*

- H.G. Nicholas
THE NATURE OF AMERICAN POLITICS
Traces the evolution of the American political process, including an assessment of its current participation and manipulation
0–19–827482–3 Oxford pb $11.95

- Richard M. Nixon
LEADERS
0–446–90488–0 Warner pb $3.95

1999: Victory Without War
0–671–65992–8 Simon & Schuster $19.95
0–671–67834–5 Pocket pb $8.95

NO MORE VIETNAMS
0–380–70119–7 Avon pb $4.50

REAL PEACE
0–316–61149–2 Little, Brown $16.95

THE REAL WAR
0–446–51201–X Warner $12.50
0–446–32280–6 Warner pb $4.95

- Bradley H. Patterson, Jr.
THE RING OF POWER: The White House Staff and Its Expanding Role in Government
0–465–07025–6 Basic Books $19.95

- Eric Redman
THE DANCE OF LEGISLATION
A case study of the complexity of American legislative politics, tracing the drafting and passing of a single piece of legislation, the National Health Service Bill; by a former Senate aide
0–671–21746–1 Simon & Schuster pb $9.95

- Michael Rogin
RONALD REAGAN, THE MOVIE: & Other Episodes in Political Demonology
"A dazzling, heady . . . exploration of 'the countersubversive tradition and political demonology' in America since colonial times"—Phillip French, *Observer*
0–520–06469–0 California pb $10.95

- Larry J. Sabato
THE RISE OF POLITICAL CONSULTANTS
How consultants have come to play a major role in electoral politics
0–465–07039–6 Basic Books pb $11.95

- Arthur M. Schlesinger, Jr.
THE VITAL CENTER: The Politics of Freedom
Schlesinger's treatise on maintaining the balance between extremes in American politics, first published in 1949
0–306–80323–2 Da Capo pb $10.95

- Jonathan E. Schwarz
AMERICA'S HIDDEN SUCCESS: A Reassessment of Public Policy from Kennedy to Reagan
"Shows that America's political and economic institutions have performed much better than commonly thought"—Aaron Wildavsky, UC/Berkeley
0–393–30447–7 Norton pb $6.95

- Harold Seidman & Robert S. Gilmour
POLITICS, POSITION AND POWER: From the Positive to the Regulatory State
An inside view of the federal administration as it affects and is affected by competing forces for power, position, and political advantage; revised edition
0–19–503991–2 Oxford pb $13.95

- Gail Sheehy
CHARACTER: America's Search for Leadership
0–688–08072–3 Morrow $17.95

- Hedrick Smith
THE POWER GAME: How Washington Works
0–394–55447–7 Random House $24.95

- Susan J. Tolchin & Martin Tolchin
DISMANTLING AMERICA: The Rush to Deregulate
0–19–503577–1 Oxford pb $8.95

• George F. Will
**THE MORNING AFTER: American
Successes and Excesses, 1981–1986**
0–02–934430–1 Free Press $19.95
0–02–055450–8 Macmillan pb $9.95

**THE NEW SEASON: A Spectator's Guide
to the 1988 Election**
0–671–64837–3 Simon & Schuster $17.95
0–671–66275–9 Simon & Schuster pb $7.95

**STATECRAFT AS SOULCRAFT: What
Government Does**
0–671–42733–4 Simon & Schuster $13.95
0–671–42734–2 Simon & Schuster pb $7.95

• Garry Wills
REAGAN'S AMERICA
0–14–010557–3 Penguin pb $8.95

• James Q. Wilson
**AMERICAN GOVERNMENT: Institutions
and Policies**
A best-selling textbook now in its fourth
edition
0–669–15430–X Heath $27.00

Jargon is a vital element of the Washington game. Washington jargon is impenetrable and often deliberately so, to exclude all but the initiated.

For starters: unless you're President Reagan, you can't be a major player in budget politics unless you know the difference between constant dollars and current dollars, between outlays and obligations, between the baseline and the out-years; you can't enter the arena of arms control without some grasp of launchers, throwweight, and RVs ... You will also know that bogeys are the spending targets the secretary of Defense gives the armed services and that beamsplitters are the nearly invisible TelePromTers that flash the text of a speech to the president as he turns his head from side to side.

Hedrick Smith
**THE POWER GAME: How
Washington Works**
0–394–55447–7 Random House $24.95

Conservatism and the New Right

Ronald Reagan's stunning victory in 1980 and his enduring popularity have made this field a bustling one: the books below range from celebratory to highly critical.

• Martin Anderson
REVOLUTION
Notes on the Reagan revolution by an administration insider who traces the movement back to Goldwater
0–15–177087–5 HBJ $19.95

• Sidney Blumenthal
**OUR LONG NATIONAL DAYDREAM: A
Political Pageant of the Reagan Era**
0–06–015973–1 Harper & Row $18.95

**THE RISE OF THE COUNTER-
ESTABLISHMENT: From Conservative
Ideology to Political Power**
0–8129–1205–5 Times Books $19.95
0–06–097140–1 Harper & Row pb $9.95

• William F. Buckley, Jr. & Charles R.
Kesler, editors
**KEEPING THE TABLETS: Modern
American Conservative Thought**
Essays by Milton Friedman, Leo Strauss, George F. Will, Thomas Sowell, Jeane Kirkpatrick, Whittaker Chambers, and others
0–06–096285–2 Harper & Row pb $15.95

• Alan Crawford
**THUNDER ON THE RIGHT: The "New
Right" and the Politics of Resentment**
0–394–74862–X Pantheon pb $3.95

• Louis Filler, editor
**A DICTIONARY OF AMERICAN
CONSERVATISM**
Entries on politicians, parties, programs, and triumphs and setbacks
0–8065–1087–0 Citadel pb $12.95

• Irving Kristol
**REFLECTIONS OF A
NEOCONSERVATIVE: Looking Back,
Looking Ahead**
A political autobiography, including an analysis of the development of neoconservative politics
0–465–06873–1 Basic Books pb $9.95

• Michael W. Miles
**THE ODYSSEY OF THE AMERICAN
RIGHT**
0–19–502774–4 Oxford $27.50

• Gillian Peele
**REVIVAL AND REACTION: The Right in
Contemporary America**
0–19–821132–5 Oxford pb $14.95

• Kevin B. Phillips
**POST-CONSERVATIVE AMERICA:
People, Politics and Ideology in a Time of
Crisis**
0–394–71438–5 Random House pb $7.95

Liberals and the Left

• Mike Davis & Michael Sprinker
**RESHAPING THE U.S. LEFT: Popular
Struggles in the 1980s**
Essays on the successes and current activities of leftist groups, including the Central America solidarity campaigns, the sanctuary movement, the women's peace movement, and labor struggles
0–86091–909–9 Verso pb $17.95

• Michael Harrington
**THE NEXT LEFT: The History of the
Future**
What the American Left can do in the aftermath of the Reagan era, by a leading American socialist
0–8050–0792–X Henry Holt pb $8.95

• Robert Lekachman
**VISIONS AND NIGHTMARES: America
After Reagan**
A liberal analysis of both Democratic and

Republican policies and an agenda for an anticonservative coalition
0–02–073710–6 Macmillan pb $9.95

• Robert B. Reich
**TALES OF A NEW AMERICA: The
Anxious Liberal's Guide to the Future**
"The reigning myths of the Reagan era lie in shambles after his searching probe"—
Commonweal
0–394–75706–8 Random House pb $8.95

FOREIGN POLICY AND DIPLOMATIC HISTORY

Overviews

• Thomas A. Bailey
**A DIPLOMATIC HISTORY OF THE
AMERICAN PEOPLE**
Surveys social, political, economic, and diplomatic developments from colonial times to post-World War II, in a lively prose style
0–13–214726–2 Prentice-Hall $47.00

• William H. Becker & Samuel F. Wells
**ECONOMICS AND WORLD POWER: An
Assessment of American Diplomacy Since
1789**
0–231–04370–8 Columbia $45.00
0–231–04371–6 Columbia pb $14.00

• Jerald A. Combs
**AMERICAN DIPLOMATIC HISTORY:
Two Centuries of Changing Interpretations**
0–520–04590–4 California $47.50
0–520–05893–3 California pb $11.95

• Alexander De Conde
**A HISTORY OF AMERICAN FOREIGN
POLICY**

**Volume 1: Growth to World Power,
1700–1914**
0–02–327970–2 Macmillan pb $23.00

Woodrow Wilson and Raymond Poincaré before the opening of the 1919 Paris Peace Conference

---

☎ **TO ORDER ANY BOOK IN THIS CATALOG, ASK YOUR BOOKSELLER OR CALL 1-800-882-8770**

Volume 2: Global Power, 1900 to the Present
0–02–327980–X Macmillan pb $23.00

• **Robert H. Ferrell**
AMERICAN DIPLOMACY
0–393–09309–3 Norton $24.95

• Howard Jones
THE COURSE OF AMERICAN DIPLOMACY: From the Revolution to the Present
0–534–10600–5 Dorset $38.00

• George F. Kennan
AMERICAN DIPLOMACY
Expanded edition of the master diplomat's lectures on topics from "The War With Spain" to "Diplomacy in the Modern World"
0–226–43147–9 Chicago pb $6.95

• Henry A. Kissinger
AMERICAN FOREIGN POLICY
0–393–05641–4 Norton pb $9.95

Walter LaFeber
THE AMERICAN AGE: United States Foreign Policy at Home and Abroad Since 1750
0–393–95611–3 Norton $25.00

• Thomas G. Paterson & others
AMERICAN FOREIGN POLICY: A History
Volume 1
0–669–12664–0 Heath pb $14.50
Volume 2
0–669–12665–9 Heath pb $20.95

20th-Century Diplomacy

• Stephen Ambrose
RISE TO GLOBALISM: American Foreign Policy Since 1938
The fifth edition includes analyses of the Iran-Contra affair, the Nicaraguan revolution, international terrorism, superpower summits, and other recent developments
0–14–022826–8 Penguin pb $8.95

• C.J. Bartlett
THE RISE AND FALL OF THE PAX AMERICANA: U.S. Foreign Policy in the Twentieth Century
0–312–68355–3 St. Martin's $23.00

• Cecil V. Crabb & Kevin W. Mulcahy
PRESIDENTS AND FOREIGN POLICY MAKING: From FDR to Reagan
Six case studies trace changes in the structure of America's foreign policy apparatus
0–8071–1362–X LSU pb $15.95

• Robert H. Ferrell
AMERICAN DIPLOMACY: The 20th Century
0–393–95609–1 Norton pb $10.95

• Lloyd C. Gardner
A COVENANT WITH POWER: America and World Order from Wilson to Reagan
0–19–503357–4 Oxford $22.95

• Robert D. Schulzinger
AMERICAN DIPLOMACY IN THE 20TH CENTURY
A comprehensive survey blending historical narrative with analysis of how and why policy is made
0–19–503373–6 Oxford pb $13.95

Interpretations

• Gregory A. Fossedal
THE DEMOCRATIC IMPERATIVE: Exporting the American Revolution
A conservative approach arguing that democracy can serve as both a goal and instrument of foreign policy
0–465–09801–0 Basic Books $19.95

• Michael H. Hunt
IDEOLOGY AND U.S. FOREIGN POLICY
A reinterpretation of American diplomatic history, arguing that foreign policy has been based on an ideology that has a basic hostility toward social revolutions
0–300–03717–1 Yale $25.00
0–300–04369–4 Yale pb $8.95

• Jonathan Kwitny
ENDLESS ENEMIES: The Making of an Unfriendly World
Suggests that interventionist activities have consistently undermined America's foreign policy goals
0–14–008093–7 Penguin pb $8.95

• Frances Moore Lappé & others
BETRAYING THE NATIONAL INTEREST
Argues that foreign aid undermines the political and economic stability of the Third World and therefore poses a threat to global security
0–802–13027–5 Grove pb $8.95

• Harry Magdoff
THE AGE OF IMPERIALISM: The Economics of U.S. Foreign Policy
How the American "empire" influences a complex system of military spending and foreign aid, and an international monetary and banking system that keeps other nations bound to the United States
0–85345–101–X Monthly Review pb $7.50

• Ernest R. May
THE LESSONS OF THE PAST: The Use and Misuse of History in American Foreign Policy
The misapplication of historical precedent in four policy decisions since World War II and how presidents and their advisers justified their actions
0–19–501698–X Oxford $18.95
0–19–501890–7 Oxford pb $8.95

• David D. Newsom
DIPLOMACY AND THE AMERICAN DEMOCRACY
0–253–31816–5 Indiana $25.00
0–253–20470–4 Indiana pb $9.95

• William Pfaff
BARBARIAN SENTIMENTS: How the American Century Ends
Assesses nationalism and ideology in the modern age and how both the Soviet Union and the United States have

misinterpreted national movements in Asia, the Middle East, and Central America
0–8090–6665–3 Hill & Wang $19.95

• Emily Rosenberg
SPREADING THE AMERICAN DREAM: American Economic and Cultural Expansion, 1890–1945
"An essential book for anyone attempting to understand . . . why at times the spreading American dream has plunged other countries into nightmare"—Marilyn B. Young, New York University
0–8090–0146–2 Hill & Wang pb $7.95

• Barry Rubin
SECRETS OF STATE: The State Department and the Struggle over U.S. Foreign Policy
The current policy-making apparatus and the influence of individual decision makers from Roosevelt to Kissinger
0–19–505010–X Oxford pb $8.95

• Sanford J. Ungar, editor
ESTRANGEMENT: America and the World
A dozen experts shed light on America's increasingly uneasy relations with its allies, adversaries, and nations of the Third World
0–19–503707–3 Oxford $22.95

• William Appleman Williams
EMPIRE AS A WAY OF LIFE: An Essay on the Causes and Character of America's Present Predicament, Along with a Few Thoughts About an Alternative
Argues that American history has been based for centuries on continual and unlimited expansion and on seeking dominion over internal and external foes
0–19–502766–3 Oxford $22.95
0–19–503045–1 Oxford pb $8.95

THE TRAGEDY OF AMERICAN DIPLOMACY
A classic examination of the profound contradictions between America's ideals and its actual uses of power, from the Open Door Notes of 1898 to the Bay of Pigs of 1961
0–393–30493–0 Norton pb $9.95

Viewed from one perspective, it can hardly be said that the dilemmas facing the United States are unique. Which country in the world, one is tempted to ask, is *not* encountering problems in evolving a viable military policy, or in choosing between guns and butter investment? From one perspective, however, the American position is a very special one. For all its economic and perhaps military decline, it remains, in Pierre Hassner's words "the decisive actor in every type of balance and issue."

Paul Kennedy
THE RISE AND FALL OF THE GREAT POWERS: Economic Change and Military Conflict, 1500–2000
0–394–54674–1 Random House $24.95
0–679–72019–7 Random House pb $12.95

☞ **FOR ALL OTHER INQUIRIES, PLEASE CALL (212) 333-7900**

SPECIAL TOPICS IN AMERICAN FOREIGN POLICY

• George Black
THE GOOD NEIGHBOR: How the U.S. Wrote the History of Central America and the Caribbean
0–394–75965–6 Pantheon pb $9.95

• Raymond Bonner
WALTZING WITH A DICTATOR: The Marcoses and the Making of American Policy
0–8129–1326–4 Times Books $19.95
0–394–75835–8 Random House pb $11.95

• Richard E. Feinberg
THE INTEMPERATE ZONE: The Third World Challenge to U.S. Foreign Policy
0–393–30143–5 Norton pb $7.95

• Fitzhugh Green
AMERICAN PROPAGANDA ABROAD: From Benjamin Franklin to Ronald Reagan
A historical survey of propaganda, focusing on the United States Information Agency
0–87052–579–4 Hippocrene $16.95

• Roy Gutman
BANANA DIPLOMACY: The Making of American Policy in Nicaragua, 1981–1987
0–671–60626–3 Simon & Schuster $19.95
0–671–68294–6 Simon & Schuster pb $9.95

• Michael J. Hogan
THE MARSHALL PLAN: America, Britain and the Reconstruction of Western Europe, 1947–1952
0–521–37840–0 Cambridge pb $15.95

• William G. Hyland, editor
THE REAGAN FOREIGN POLICY: A Foreign Affairs Reader
Includes articles by Shultz, Nixon, Schlesinger, Kennan, McNamara, Bundy, Tower, and others
0–452–00889–1 NAL pb $9.95

• Stanley Karnow
IN OUR IMAGE: America's Empire in the Philippines
The author of *Vietnam: A History* portrays America's 19th- and 20th-century empire builders, the role of the Philippines in establishing the US as a great Pacific power, and the continuing legacy of American involvement in the nation of Marcos and Aquino
0–394–54975–9 Random House $24.95

• Gabriel Kolko
CONFRONTING THE THIRD WORLD: United States Foreign Policy, 1945–1980
Argues that the pattern of US action, or inaction, was fashioned by the ideological framework within which successive administrations operated
0–394–57138–X Pantheon $24.95
0–394–75933–8 Pantheon pb $15.95

• Walter LaFeber
INEVITABLE REVOLUTIONS: The United States in Central America
0–393–30212–1 Norton pb $7.95

Marshall and Molotov, 1947

THE PANAMA CANAL: The Crisis in Historical Perspective
0–19–502360–9 Oxford $24.95
0–19–502511–3 Oxford pb $8.95

• Anthony Lake
SOMOZA FALLING: A Case Study in the Making of U.S. Foreign Policy
Based on the 1978 Nicaraguan crisis
0–395–41983–2 Houghton Mifflin $18.95

• William J. Lederer & Eugene Burdick
THE UGLY AMERICAN
0–393–00305–1 Norton pb $9.95

• Thomas L. McNaugher
ARMS AND OIL: U.S. Military Strategy and the Persian Gulf
An assessment of US prospects for securing its interests in the Gulf in the aftermath of the Soviet invasion of Afghanistan and the Iranian revolution; offers a military strategy
0–8157–5623–2 Brookings pb $10.95

• Constantine C. Menges
INSIDE THE NATIONAL SECURITY COUNCIL: The True Story of the Making and Unmaking of Reagan's Foreign Policy
A behind-the-scenes account of events and issues
0–671–64996–5 Simon & Schuster $19.95

• Bernard S. Morris
COMMUNISM, REVOLUTION, AND AMERICAN POLICY
A revised edition of the author's influential 1966 study *International Communism and American Policy*
0–8223–0760–X Duke pb $12.95

• Robert A. Pastor
CONDEMNED TO REPETITION: The United States and Nicaragua
"The first extensive insider's account of U.S. policy-making toward Nicaragua during the crucial four-year period that began in 1977"—*Washington Post Book World*
0–691–02291–7 Princeton pb $12.95

• Thomas G. Paterson
MEETING THE COMMUNIST THREAT: Truman to Reagan
A distinguished diplomatic historian traces why and how Americans have perceived and exaggerated the Communist threat, with devastating critiques of Kennedy's foreign policy, Reagan's rewriting of the Vietnam War, and Congress' inability to oversee the CIA's covert activities
0–19–504533–5 Oxford $24.95

• Dennis Phillips
AMBIVALENT ALLIES: Myth and Reality in the Australian-American Relationship
0–14–009220–X Penguin pb $7.95

• John Prados
PRESIDENTS' SECRET WARS: CIA and Pentagon Covert Operations from World War II Through Iranscam
0–688–07759–5 Morrow pb $9.95

• Holly Sklar
WASHINGTON'S WAR ON NICARAGUA
0–89608–296–2 South End $30.00
0–89608–295–4 South End pb $15.00

The Iran-Contra Scandal

• Ben Bradlee, Jr.
GUTS AND GLORY: The Rise and Fall of Oliver North
1–556–11053–7 Donald Fine $21.95

• Joel Brinkley & Stephen Engelberg, editors
IRAN-CONTRA AFFAIR
The abridged version of the congressional report investigating the Iran-Contra Affair, including the minority view
0–8129–1695–6 Times Books pb $9.95

• Leslie Cockburn
SECRET WAR: The White House, the Contras and Nicaragua
An in-depth study, the result of a two-year investigation by a CBS News producer
0–87113–169–2 Atlantic Monthly $18.95

• Senators William S. Cohen & George J. Mitchell
MEN OF ZEAL
0–670–82252–3 Viking $19.95

• Michael A. Ledeen
PERILOUS STATECRAFT
0–684–18994–1 Macmillan $19.95

• Neil C. Livingstone & Terrell E. Arnold
BEYOND THE IRAN-CONTRA CRISIS: The Shape of U.S. Anti-Terrorism Policy in the Post-Reagan Era
0–669–16467–4 Lexington pb $16.95

• Jonathan Marshall & others
THE IRAN-CONTRA CONNECTION: Secret Teams and Covert Operations in the Reagan Era
Views the Iran-Contra affair as a function of ongoing CIA and extra-CIA operations including drug-trafficking, gun-running, government-toppling, and assassination
0–89608–291–1 South End pb $11.00

• Jane Mayer & Doyle McManus
LANDSLIDE: The Unmaking of the President, 1984–1988
0–395–45185–X Houghton Mifflin $21.95

 IF YOU CAN'T FIND IT, LOOK IN THE INDEX

• Bill Moyers
THE SECRET GOVERNMENT: The Constitution in Crisis
Both a history of events culminating in the Iran-Contra affair and an analysis of the threat posed by the growth of the secret government; based on the PBS documentary
Introduction by Henry Steele Commager
0–932020–61–5 Seven Locks $16.95
0–932020–60–7 Seven Locks pb $9.95

• The New York Times, editors
THE TOWER COMMISSION REPORT
Full text of the report on the Iran-Contra scandal
0–553–26968–2 Times Books pb $5.50

• Samuel Segev
THE IRANIAN TRIANGLE: The Untold Story of Israel's Role in the Iran-Contra Affair
0–02–928341–8 Free Press $22.50

THE CIA, FBI, AND ESPIONAGE

► See also Espionage

• Philip Agee
INSIDE THE COMPANY: CIA Diary
An uncensored account, written by a former "deep cover" agent
0–553–26012–X Bantam pb $5.95

• Ward Churchill & Jim Vander Wall
AGENTS OF REPRESSION: The FBI's Secret Wars Against the Black Panther party and the American Indian Movement
0–89608–293–8 South End $15.00

• Cecil B. Currey
EDWARD LANSDALE: The Unquiet American
0–395–38510–5 Houghton Mifflin $24.95

• Edward J. Epstein
DECEPTION: The Invisible War Between the KGB and the CIA
An investigative reporter's chronicle of intelligence and counterintelligence officers caught in the "war of the moles" that nearly ruined the CIA in the 1970s
0–671–41543–3 Simon & Schuster $19.95

• Howard Frazier, editor
UNCLOAKING THE CIA
An unsanitized and uncensored look at CIA activities
0–02–910590–0 Free Press $14.95

• Darrell Garwood
UNDER COVER: 35 Years of CIA Deception
An exposé of how the CIA subverted the law and deceived the public in postwar America
0–394–62073–9 Grove pb $3.95

• Rhodri Jeffreys-Jones
AMERICAN ESPIONAGE: From Secret Service to CIA
0–02–916360–9 Free Press $17.00

THE CIA AND AMERICAN DEMOCRACY
0–300–04149–7 Yale $25.00

• Jonathan Kwitny
THE CRIMES OF PATRIOTS: A True Tale of Dope, Dirty Money, and the CIA
0–393–02387–7 Norton $19.95
0–671–66637–1 Simon & Schuster pb $7.95

• Peter Maas
MANHUNT
The search for the renegade CIA agent Edwin P. Wilson, who supplied arms to Libya
0–515–09014–X Berkley pb $3.95

• Victor Marchetti & John D. Marks
THE CIA AND THE CULT OF INTELLIGENCE
An exposé, using previously classified and suppressed information, written by a former CIA senior official and an ex-State Department intelligence expert
0–394–48239–5 Knopf $16.95

• Nathan Miller
SPYING FOR AMERICA: The Hidden History of U.S. Intelligence
1–55778–186–9 Paragon $24.95

Herbert Mitgang
DANGEROUS DOSSIERS: Exposing the Secret War Against America's Greatest Authors
Documents FBI and CIA surveillance of writers from William Faulkner to Carl Sandburg. "Enthralling study of the FBI's campaign against artistic and intellectual liberty"—*NY Newsday*
0–317–65633–3 Donald Fine $18.95
0–345–35801–5 Ballantine pb $4.95

• Richard G. Powers
SECRECY AND POWER: The Life of J. Edgar Hoover
0–02–925060–9 Free Press $27.95

• Thomas Powers
THE MAN WHO KEPT THE SECRETS: Richard Helms and the CIA
One of the best books ever written on the inner circles of American intelligence
0–394–50678–2 Knopf $22.00

• John Ranelagh
THE AGENCY: The Rise and Decline of the CIA
A comprehensive history of the CIA, from its early years to its scandal-ridden present
0–671–63994–3 Simon & Schuster pb $12.95

• Jeffrey Richelson
AMERICAN ESPIONAGE AND THE SOVIET TARGET
Detailed account of how the US spies on the USSR
0–688–06753–0 Morrow $18.95

• Bradley F. Smith
THE SHADOW WARRIORS: OSS and the Origins of the CIA
How the CIA emerged from the Office of Strategic Services of World War II
0–465–07756–0 Basic Books $20.95

• Stansfield Turner
SECRECY AND DEMOCRACY: The CIA in Transition
Turner's too-hot-to-publish story of his four years as head of the CIA; over 100 passages from the book were shredded by CIA censors
0–06–097025–1 Harper & Row pb $7.95

• Ernest Volkman & Bonnie Baggett
SECRET INTELLIGENCE: The Inside Story of America's Espionage Empire
A history and status report on the CIA and other intelligence operations; companion volume to the PBS series
0–385–24590–4 Doubleday $19.95

• Robin W. Winks
CLOAK AND GOWN: Scholars in the Secret War, 1939–1961
0–688–08665–9 Morrow pb $14.95

• Bob Woodward
VEIL: The Secret Wars of the CIA, 1981–1987
The best-selling account of William Casey's CIA
0–671–60117–2 Simon & Schuster $21.95
0–671–66159–0 Simon & Schuster pb $4.95

MEMOIRS AND BIOGRAPHIES

► For biographies of recent presidents and numerous other political figures see also US History since 1877

• Zbigniew Brzezinski
POWER AND PRINCIPLE: Memoirs of the National Security Adviser, 1977–1981
"Fascinating as an insight into how a crucial part of government works, intimidating as a reflection of what it takes to go forth in bureaucratic wars, and appealing in its candor"—Flora Lewis, *NY Times*
0–374–51877–7 Farrar, Straus & Giroux pb $11.95

• J. William Fulbright
THE PRICE OF EMPIRE
The former chairman of the Senate Foreign Relations Committee writes on his career and the history of foreign relations, and offers advice for the future
0–394–57224–6 Pantheon $17.95

• Waldo H. Heinrichs, Jr.
AMERICAN AMBASSADOR: Joseph C. Grew and the Development of United States Diplomatic Tradition
0–19–504159–3 Oxford pb $12.95

• Walter Isaacson & Evan Thomas
THE WISE MEN: Six Friends and the World They Made
How Robert Lowell, John McCloy, Averell Harriman, Charles Bohlen, George Kennan, and Dean Acheson shaped American policy in the postwar world
0–671–65712–7 Simon & Schuster pb $12.95

• George F. Kennan
SKETCHES FROM A LIFE
The esteemed diplomat on the cities and countries in which he has served, based on his private diaries
0–394–57504–0 Pantheon $22.95

MEMOIRS

Volume 1: 1925–1950
0–394–71624–8 Pantheon pb $8.95

Volume 2: 1950–1963
0–394–71626–4 Pantheon pb $7.95

• Tip O'Neill with William Novak
MAN OF THE HOUSE: The Life and Political Memoirs of Speaker Tip O'Neill
0–394–55201–6 Random House $19.95

• Thomas E. Schoenbaum
WAGING PEACE AND WAR: Dean Rusk in the Truman, Kennedy and Johnson Years
0–671–60351–5 Simon & Schuster $22.95

• Morris Udall
TOO FUNNY TO BE PRESIDENT
0–8050–0593–5 Henry Holt $17.95

Texts and Reference

• Michael Barone & Grant Ujifusa
THE ALMANAC OF AMERICAN POLITICS: 1990
0–89234–043–6 National Journal $56.95
0–89234–044–4 National Journal pb $44.95

• Richard M. Pious
AMERICAN POLITICS AND GOVERNMENT
0–07–050121–1 McGraw-Hill $33.95

• Edward C. Smith & Arnold J. Zurcher
DICTIONARY OF AMERICAN POLITICS
0–06–480803–3 Barnes & Noble $19.95
0–06–463261–X Harper & Row pb $7.95

American Labor and Radical Movements

Heavily influenced by European scholarship, a "new labor history" emerged in the 1960s, shifting attention from unions and organized labor to working-class life and culture itself.

▶ See also Women's Studies

GENERAL HISTORIES

• Paul Buhle & Alan Dawley, editors
WORKING FOR DEMOCRACY: American Workers from the Revolution to the Present
Essays by Eric Foner, Nell Irvin Painter, David Montgomery, Barbara Meyer Wertheimer, Manning Marable, and others
0–252–01220–8 Illinois $19.95
0–252–01221–6 Illinois pb $6.95

• Philip S. Foner
ORGANIZED LABOR AND THE BLACK WORKER, 1619–1981
"The best one-volume study"—*Black Scholar*
0–7178–0601–4 International $17.00
0–7178–0594–8 International pb $6.50

• Philip S. Foner, editor
HISTORY OF THE LABOR MOVEMENT IN THE UNITED STATES
A Marxist-oriented narrative

Volume 1: From Colonial Times to the Foundation of the American Federation of Labor
0–7178–0376–7 International pb $6.95

Volume 2: From the Foundation of the American Federation of Labor to the Emergence of American Imperialism
0–7178–0388–0 International pb $4.95

Volume 3: The Policies and Practices of the American Federation of Labor, 1900–1909
0–7178–0389–9 International pb $4.95

Volume 4: The Industrial Workers of the World, 1905–1917
0–7178–0396–1 International pb $4.95

Volume 5: The AFL in the Progressive Era, 1910–1915
0–7178–0562–X International pb $4.95

Volume 6: On the Eve of America's Entrance into World War I, 1915–1916
0–7178–0595–6 International pb $5.95

Volume 7: Labor and World War I, 1914–1918
0–7178–0627–8 International pb $9.95

Volume 8: Postwar Struggles, 1918–1920
0–7178–0652–9 International pb $8.95

• Richard B. Morris, editor
A HISTORY OF THE AMERICAN WORKER
From colonial settlement to the modern labor movement, told in six essays
0–691–04697–2 Princeton pb $30.50
0–691–00593–1 Princeton pb $8.50

• Henry Pelling
AMERICAN LABOR
Still a valuable brief survey; by a British historian of the Labour party
0–226–65393–5 Chicago pb $9.00

• Joseph G. Rayback
A HISTORY OF AMERICAN LABOR
First published in 1959
0–02–925850–2 Free Press pb $17.95

• Samuel Yellen
AMERICAN LABOR STRUGGLES, 1877–1934
Ten decisive confrontations between owners and workers; first published in 1936
0–913460–33–8 Pathfinder pb $9.95

• Robert Zieger
AMERICAN WORKERS, AMERICAN UNIONS, 1920–1985
0–8018–3126–1 Johns Hopkins $25.00
0–8018–3128–8 Johns Hopkins pb $9.95

Essays

• David Brody
WORKERS IN INDUSTRIAL AMERICA: Essays on the 20th Century Struggle
0–19–502491–5 Oxford pb $10.95

• Michael H. Frisch & Daniel J. Walkowitz
WORKING CLASS AMERICA: Essays on Labor, Community and American Society
Ten original essays in the "new" labor history
0–252–00954–1 Illinois $10.95

• James R. Green, editor
WORKERS' STRUGGLES, PAST AND PRESENT: A "Radical America" Reader
Essays first published in the journal *Radical America* between 1967 and 1982
0–87722–293–2 Temple $34.95
0–87722–315–7 Temple pb $16.95

Herbert G. Gutman
POWER AND CULTURE: Essays in the American Working Class
A final collection from the late historian
Edited by Ira Berlin
0–394–56026–4 Pantheon $29.95
WORK, CULTURE, AND SOCIETY IN INDUSTRIALIZING AMERICA
0–394–72251–5 Random House pb $8.95

• Herbert G. Gutman & Donald H. Bell, editors
THE NEW ENGLAND WORKING CLASS AND THE NEW LABOR HISTORY
0–252–01301–8 Illinois pb $12.95

• Daniel J. Leab, editor
THE LABOR HISTORY READER
An anthology from the journal *Labor History*
Introduction by David Brody & Herbert G. Gutman
0–252–01198–8 Illinois pb $12.50

• David Montgomery
WORKERS' CONTROL IN AMERICA: Studies in the History of Work, Technology, and Labor Struggles
0–521–22580–9 Cambridge $32.50
0–521–28006–0 Cambridge pb $9.95

• Charles Stephenson & Robert Asher, editors
LIFE AND LABOR: Dimensions of Working-Class History
0–88706–173–7 SUNY $44.50
0–88706–172–9 SUNY pb $14.95

THE EARLY YEARS: From Crafts to Industry

• Stephen Innes
WORK AND LABOR IN EARLY AMERICA
"Especially strong in detailing the process of work and the consciousness of workers in rural America"—Allan Kulikoff, University of Northern Illinois
0–8078–4236–2 Chapel Hill pb $9.95

✉ TO ORDER BOOKS AS GIFTS, SEE PAGE 1

Laundry workers on strike in Brooklyn, New York (photo courtesy of The Library of Congress), from First Person America *edited by Ann Banks (Knopf)*

● Bruce Laurie
ARTISANS INTO WORKERS: Labor in Nineteenth-Century America
A new study blending the institutional focus of the "old" labor history with the broader concerns of the "new" labor history
0–8090–2752–6 Hill & Wang $18.95
0–374–52153–0 Hill & Wang pb $8.95

WORKING PEOPLE OF PHILADELPHIA, 1800–1850
The patterns of belief, culture, and political identification
0–87722–168–5 Temple $29.95
0–87722–292–4 Temple pb $14.95

● W.J. Rorabaugh
THE CRAFT APPRENTICE: From Franklin to the Machine Age in America
0–19–503647–6 Oxford $34.00
0–19–505189–0 Oxford pb $9.95

● Steven J. Ross
WORKERS ON THE EDGE: Work, Leisure and Politics in Industrializing Cincinnati, 1788–1890
0–231–05521–8 Columbia pb $16.50

● Charles G. Steffen
THE MECHANICS OF BALTIMORE: Workers and Politics in the Age of Revolution, 1763–1812
Urban craftsmen in early American political life
0–252–01088–4 Illinois $24.95

● Sean Wilentz
CHANTS DEMOCRATIC: New York City and the Rise of the American Working Class, 1788–1850
An important and beautifully written work by a Princeton historian
0–19–504012–0 Oxford pb $10.95

In a little room in this big, black shed—a little room not twenty feet square—forty boys are picking their lives away. The floor of the room is an inclined plane, and a stream of coal pours constantly in. They work here, in this little black hole, all day and every day, trying to keep cool in summer, trying to keep warm in winter, picking away among the black coals, bending over till their little spines are curved, never saying a word all the live-long day. These little fellows go to work in this cold dreary room at seven o'clock in the morning and work till it is too dark to see any longer. For this they get $1 to $3 a week. Not three boys in this roomful could read or write. Shut in from everything that is pleasant, with no chance to learn, with nothing to do but work, grinding their little lives away in this dusty room, they are no more than the wire screens that separate the great lumps of coal from the small. They had no games; when their day's work is done they are too tired for that. They know nothing but the difference between slate and coal.

The breaker room in the Hickory Colliery near St. Clair, Pennsylvania, described by a contemporary (1877) in

Milton Meltzer
BREAD AND ROSES: The Struggle of American Labor, 1865–1915
0–451–62396–7 NAL pb $3.95

INDUSTRIAL AMERICA: To 1920

● Paul Avrich
THE HAYMARKET TRAGEDY
On May 4, 1886, in Chicago, center for the campaign for the eight-hour work day, seven policemen were killed when a bomb was hurled into the ranks of an anarchist protest meeting
0–691–04711–1 Princeton $36.50
0–691–00600–8 Princeton pb $9.95

● Jeremy Brecher
STRIKE!
A sympathetic history
0–8467–0364–5 South End pb $9.00

● David Brody
LABOR IN CRISIS: The Steel Strike of 1919
0–252–01373–5 Illinois pb $8.95

STEELWORKERS IN AMERICA: The Non-Union Era
From the decline of the Amalgamated Association in the late 1880s to the prosperity of the pre-Depression years
0–06–131485–4 Harper & Row pb $7.95

● Stanley Buder
PULLMAN: An Experiment in Industrial Order and Community Planning, 1880–1930
The fate of the company town rocked by the great strike of 1894
0–19–500838–3 Oxford pb $10.95

● Dan Clawson
BUREAUCRACY AND THE LABOR PROCESS: The Transformation of U.S. Industry, 1860–1920
0–85345–543–0 Monthly Review pb $10.00

● Alan Dawley
CLASS AND COMMUNITY: The Industrial Revolution in Lynn
"The author brilliantly examines the structure and culture of Lynn shoemakers, their relations with the owners, changes in their work situation due to the displacement of craft skills by factory machines, local and vocational distribution of property and income, social and geographical mobility"—*Historian*
0–674–13395–1 Harvard pb $8.95

● Thomas Dublin
WOMEN AT WORK: The Transformation of Work and Community in Lowell, Massachusetts, 1826–1860
Winner of the Bancroft prize; deals with the first generation of American women to face the demands of industrial capitalism
0–231–04166–7 Columbia $29.50
0–231–04167–5 Columbia pb $14.00

● Melvyn Dubofsky
INDUSTRIALISM AND THE AMERICAN WORKER, 1865–1920
Edited by John Hope Franklin & Abraham Eisenstadt
0–88295–831–3 Harlan Davidson pb $8.95

● Leon Fink
WORKINGMEN'S DEMOCRACY: The Knights of Labor and American Politics
Uses community studies to raise broader critical issues about the Knights
0–252–01256–9 Illinois pb $10.95

● Philip S. Foner, editor
AMERICAN LABOR SONGS OF THE NINETEENTH CENTURY
0–252–00187–7 Illinois $29.95

THE GREAT LABOR UPRISING OF 1877
Argues that what began as a railroad workers' strike became the first "general strike" in American history
0–913460–57–5 Pathfinder pb $6.95

• Jacquelyn Dowd Hall, James Leloudis & others
LIKE A FAMILY: The Making of a Southern Cotton Mill World
Life in the early mills and the technological changes that transformed them
0–8078–4196–X North Carolina pb $12.95

• Dirk Hoerder, editor
AMERICAN LABOR AND IMMIGRANT HISTORY 1877–1920s: Recent European Research
0–252–00963–0 Illinois $28.95

• Ira Katznelson & Aristide R. Zolberg, editors
WORKING-CLASS FORMATION: 19th-Century Patterns in Western Europe and the United States
How and when the idea of class became central to the ideologies and actions of working people, and the political consequences of that consciousness
0–691–10207–4 Princeton pb $15.50

• Milton Meltzer
BREAD AND ROSES: The Struggle of American Labor, 1865–1915
An illustrated history that draws heavily on contemporary and eyewitness accounts
0–451–62396–7 NAL pb $3.95

• Gwendolyn Mink
OLD LABOR AND NEW IMMIGRANTS IN AMERICAN POLITICAL DEVELOPMENT: Union, Party and State, 1875–1920
Traces the political implications of union leaders' attitudes toward immigrants
0–8014–1863–1 Cornell $29.95

• David Montgomery
BEYOND EQUALITY: Labor and the Radical Republicans, 1862–1872
A landmark study
0–252–00915–0 Illinois pb $9.95

THE FALL OF THE HOUSE OF LABOR: The Workplace, the State, and American Labor Activism, 1865–1925
0–521–22579–5 Cambridge $27.95

• Jonathan Prude
THE COMING OF INDUSTRIAL ORDER: Town and Factory Life in Rural Massachusetts, 1810–1860
0–521–31396–1 Cambridge pb $13.95

• Leon Stein
THE TRIANGLE FIRE
An account of the infamous New York City sweatshop fire that killed 146 people, most of them young women, in 1911
0–88184–126–9 Carroll & Graf pb $7.95

• Daniel J. Walkowitz
WORKER CITY, COMPANY TOWN: Iron and Cotton-Worker Protest in Troy and Cohoes, New York, 1855–1884
Why labor was assertive in one place and quiescent in another
0–252–00667–4 Illinois $24.95
0–252–00915–0 Illinois pb $9.95

• Anthony F.C. Wallace
ROCKDALE: The Growth of an American Village in the Early Industrial Revolution
0–393–00991–2 Norton pb $12.95

ST. CLAIR: A Nineteenth-Century Coal Town's Experience with a Disaster Prone Industry
The anthracite colliery and the workingman's town that was totally dependent on it
0–394–52867–0 Knopf $30.00
0–8014–9900–3 Cornell pb $12.95

The Wobblies

The Industrial Workers of the World—or Wobblies, as they came to be known—was the first labor organization committed to the idea that a giant union of all workers could crush the capitalist system. Though it lasted less than two decades, the IWW has long since remained a preeminent symbol of radical American unionism.

Philip S. Foner
THE CASE OF JOE HILL
Joe Hill, a Wobbly poet and organizer accused of murder and executed in Salt Lake City on November 19, 1915, became a martyr
0–7178–0022–9 International pb $2.75

Joyce Kornbluh, editor
REBEL VOICES: An IWW Anthology
0–88286–118–2 Charles Kerr pb $18.95

Anne Huber Tripp
THE IWW AND THE PATERSON SILK STRIKE OF 1913
0–252–01382–4 Illinois $29.95

20TH-CENTURY HISTORIES AND STUDIES

• Stanley Aronowitz
FALSE PROMISES: The Shaping of American Working-Class Consciousness
First published in 1973
0–07–002316–6 McGraw-Hill pb $5.95

WORKING CLASS HERO: A New Strategy for Labor
"Aronowitz thinks that old-fashioned union doctrine is killing the labor movement. Unions should turn to the left for their own good. They should form a new progressive bloc and in general become a real social movement"—Paul Berman, *Mother Jones*
0–915361–13–2 Adama pb $12.95

• David Bensman & Roberta Lynch
RUSTED DREAMS: Hard Times in a Steel Community
"Traces the history of Chicago's Southeast Side, the growth and demise of its neighborhoods, and the steel industry in relation to global competition"—Phyllis Janik, *Chicago Tribune*
0–520–06302–3 California pb $8.95

• Irving Bernstein
THE LEAN YEARS: A History of the American Worker, 1920–1933
0–306–80202–3 Da Capo pb $11.95

A CARING SOCIETY: The New Deal, the Worker and the Great Depression
0–395–33116–1 Houghton Mifflin $22.95

• Cletus E. Daniel
BITTER HARVEST: A History of California Farmworkers, 1870–1941
0–520–04722–2 California pb $10.95

• Ronald W. Edsforth
CLASS CONFLICT AND CULTURAL CONSENSUS: The Making of a Mass Consumer Society in Flint, Michigan
0–8135–1184–4 Rutgers $40.00
0–8135–1105–4 Rutgers pb $12.00

A 1913 suffrage cartoon: "The Minimum Wage: Has She Earned It?" from Make Way! 200 Years of American Women in Cartoons *by Monika Franzen and Nancy Ethiel (Chicago Review Press)*

- Richard Feldman & Michael Betzold, editors
END OF THE LINE: Autoworkers and the American Dream
An illustrated oral history
1–55584–170–8 Weidenfeld & Nicolson $19.95

- David Gartman
AUTO SLAVERY: The Labor Process in the American Automobile Industry, 1897–1950
0–8135–1181–X Rutgers $42.00
0–8135–1104–6 Rutgers pb $20.00

- Michael Goldfield
THE DECLINE OF ORGANIZED LABOR IN THE UNITED STATES
0–226–30103–6 Chicago pb $12.95

- William B. Gould IV
A PRIMER ON AMERICAN LABOR LAW
An overview of its background, historical development, basic principles, and current status
0–262–57063–7 MIT pb $10.95

- James R. Green
THE WORLD OF THE WORKER: Labor in Twentieth-Century America
"The first truly integrated synthesis of the working-class experience which incorporates the work place, the union and political activism . . . but which goes beyond this to include the role of immigrants, blacks . . . women, the neighborhood, and the family"—John H.M. Laslett
Edited by Eric Foner
0–8090–0132–2 Hill & Wang pb $7.95

- Tamara K. Hareven & Randolph Langenbach
AMOSKEAG: Life and Work in an American Factory-City
An illustrated history of the full cycle of life in the New Hampshire town that housed what was once the world's largest textile factory
0–394–73855–1 Pantheon pb $10.95

- Charles C. Heckscher
THE NEW UNIONISM: Employee Involvement in the Changing Corporation
A call for a new system of "associational" unionism
0–465–05098–0 Basic Books $22.95

- Ira Katznelson
CITY TRENCHES: Urban Politics and the Patterning of Class in the United States
"The most persuasive analysis I have ever encountered of . . . the sources and nature of political turmoil in American cities during the 1960s, and how political order was restored at the end of that turbulent decade"—Martin Shefter, Cornell University
0–226–42673–4 Chicago pb $12.00

- Nelson Lichtenstein
LABOR'S WAR AT HOME: The CIO in World War II
"A brilliant peek into the origins of the postwar welfare-warfare state"—Melvyn Dubofsky
0–521–23472–7 Cambridge $34.50

- Alice Lynd & Staughton Lynd, editors
RANK AND FILE: Personal Histories of Working Class Organizers
Organizers from World War I to the present
0–85345–752–2 Monthly Review pb $10.00

- Mark H. Maier
CITY UNIONS: Managing Discontent in New York City
A history of New York's municipal unions and the rise of collective bargaining from 1896 to the present
0–8135–1229–8 Rutgers pb $12.00

- August Meier & Elliott Rudwick
BLACK DETROIT AND THE RISE OF THE UAW
"By ignoring the conventional lines between labor and black history, Meier and Rudwick have found an unexplored middle ground—the net of relations between the black community and the white economic institutions"—David Brody, University of California at Davis
0–19–502561–X Oxford $22.50
0–19–502895–3 Oxford pb $9.95

- Ronald W. Schatz
THE ELECTRICAL WORKERS: A History of Labor at General Electric and Westinghouse, 1923–60
The rise and decline of unionism at two technologically advanced corporations
0–252–01031–0 Illinois $24.95

- Nancy Lynn Schwartz
THE HOLLYWOOD WRITERS' WARS
0–07–055791–8 McGraw-Hill pb $8.95

- Studs Terkel
WORKING
Oral histories of blue- and white-collar workers
0–345–32569–9 Ballantine pb $5.95

- Christopher L. Tomlins
THE STATE AND THE UNIONS: Labor Relations, Law, and the Organized Labor Movement in America, 1880–1960
"Combines a sure knowledge of the labor movement with a profound understanding of the origins of modern labor law"—Stanley N. Katz, Princeton University
0–521–31452–6 Cambridge pb $13.95

Sociological Studies

- Robert Blauner
ALIENATION AND FREEDOM: The Factory Worker and His Industry
0–226–05811–5 Chicago pb $8.00

- Michael Burawoy
MANUFACTURING CONSENT: Changes in the Labor Process under Monopoly Capitalism
An unorthodox Marxist theory of the capitalist labor process, based in part on the author's experiences as a machine operator in a Chicago factory
0–226–08038–2 Chicago pb $11.00

- William Form
DIVIDED WE STAND: Working-Class Stratification in America
0–252–01168–6 Illinois $29.95

- David M. Gordon, Richard Edwards & Michael Reich
SEGMENTED WORK, DIVIDED WORKERS: The Historical Transformation of Labor in the United States
0–521–23721–1 Cambridge $42.50
0–521–28921–1 Cambridge pb $13.95

- David Halle
AMERICA'S WORKING MAN: Work, Home and Politics among Blue-Collar Property Owners
Based on interviews at an automated chemical plant in New Jersey
0–226–31365–4 Chicago $24.95
0–226–31366–2 Chicago pb $14.95

- Robert Howard
BRAVE NEW WORKPLACE
Suggests that computerization has not eliminated social conflict and inequality in the workplace
0–14–009434–2 Penguin pb $6.95

- Rosabeth M. Kanter
THE CHANGE MASTERS: Innovation for Productivity in the American Corporation
0–671–52800–9 Simon & Schuster pb $10.95

- William Kornblum
BLUE COLLAR COMMUNITY
The complex social organization of the South Chicago steel-mill community
Foreword by Morris Janowitz
0–226–45038–4 Chicago pb $6.50

- Seymour Martin Lipset, editor
UNIONS IN TRANSITION: Entering the Second Century
0–917616–74–X ICS $29.95
0–917616–73–1 ICS pb $12.95

- Lillian Rubin
WORLDS OF PAIN: Life in the Working Class Family
0–465–09724–3 Basic Books pb $10.95

- Richard Sennett & Jonathan Cobb
THE HIDDEN INJURIES OF CLASS
A classic work on the conflicts of blue-collar America
0–394–71940–9 Random House pb $5.95

SOCIALISTS, COMMUNISTS, AND RADICALS

- Paul Avrich
ANARCHIST PORTRAITS
A collection of portraits of anarchists in America, Russia and Europe; American topics include "Proudhon and America," "Sacco and Vanzetti: The Italian Anarchist Background," and "Mollie Steimer: An Anarchist Life"
0–691–04753–7 Princeton $27.50

- Daniel Bell
MARXIAN SOCIALISM IN THE UNITED STATES
0–691–02155–4 Princeton pb $11.50

- Mari Jo Buhle
WOMEN AND AMERICAN SOCIALISM, 1870–1920
"Throws new light not only on the history of socialism in this period but on temperance, populism, labor, social purity, and even on progressivism"—Eli Zaretsky, *Reviews in American History*
0–252–00873–1 Illinois $24.95
0–252–01045–0 Illinois pb $10.95

- Paul Buhle
MARXISM IN THE USA, 1870 TO THE PRESENT DAY
0–86091–141–1 Verso pb $29.95

- David Caute
THE FELLOW-TRAVELERS: Intellectual Friends of Communism
The revised edition of Caute's highly praised work
0–300–04195–0 Yale $45.00
0–317–67274–6 Yale pb $17.95

- Richard H. Crossman, editor
THE GOD THAT FAILED
The classic statement of disillusionment with communism
Foreword by Norman Podhoretz
0–89526–867–1 Gateway pb $8.95

- Theodore Draper
AMERICAN COMMUNISM AND SOVIET RUSSIA
A classic history of the American Communist party to 1930. "A definitive source volume and analysis of the Stalinization of American communism"— Michael Harrington, *Commonweal*
0–394–74308–3 Random House pb $3.95

THE ROOTS OF AMERICAN COMMUNISM
0–374–92342–6 Hippocrene $37.50

- Richard Flacks
MAKING HISTORY: The Radical Tradition in American Life
0–231–04832–7 Columbia $35.00

- Philip S. Foner, editor
MOTHER JONES SPEAKS: Collected Writings and Speeches
0–913460–89–3 Anchor pb $16.95

- James R. Green
GRASS-ROOTS SOCIALISM: Radical Movements in The Southwest, 1895–1943
0–8071–0367–5 LSU $32.50
0–8071–0773–5 LSU pb $9.95

Irving Howe
SOCIALISM AND AMERICA
Six essays from a leading American intellectual
0–15–683520–7 HBJ pb $5.95

Irving Howe & Lewis Coser
THE AMERICAN COMMUNIST PARTY: A Critical History
0–306–70636–9 Da Capo $59.50

- Maurice Isserman
IF I HAD A HAMMER . . . : The Death of the Old Left and the Birth of the New Left
0–456–03195–1 Basic Books pb $8.95

- Mark E. Kann
MIDDLE-CLASS RADICALISM IN SANTA MONICA
"Though superficially a narrow study of 'radicalism in one city,' it actually says more about the nature of, and prospects for, the American Left today than any book I can remember"—Philip Green, Smith College
0–87722–526–5 Temple pb $12.95

- Roger Keeran
THE COMMUNIST PARTY AND THE AUTO WORKERS' UNIONS
"The first . . . to separate the genuine achievement of the communists in the labor movement during the New Deal both from the hagiography of . . . admirers . . . and from the knee-jerk anticommunism of the right"—John H.M. Laslett
0–7178–0639–1 International pb $8.95

- Harvey Klehr
THE HEYDAY OF AMERICAN COMMUNISM: The Depression Decade
"The definitive treatment"—Seymour Martin Lipset
0–465–02945–0 Basic Books $27.00

FAR LEFT OF CENTER: The American Radical Left Today
0–88738–217–7 Transaction $29.95

- John H.M. Laslett & Seymour Martin Lipset, editors
FAILURE OF A DREAM?: Essays in the History of American Socialism
Revised edition
0–520–04452–5 California pb $12.95

- Bruce C. Nelson
BEYOND THE MARTYRS: A Social History of Chicago's Anarchists
Focuses on the rank-and-file workers whose lives exploded in the Haymarket tragedy
0–8135–1345–6 Rutgers pb $15.00

- Bertell Ollman & Edward Vernoff, editors
THE LEFT ACADEMY: Marxist Scholarship on American Campuses
0–07–047552–0 McGraw-Hill pb $8.95

THE LEFT ACADEMY: Marxist Scholarship on American Campuses, Volume 3
0–275–92117–4 Praeger pb $14.95

- James Weinstein
THE DECLINE OF SOCIALISM IN AMERICA: 1912–1925
A recently reissued history
0–8135–1069–4 Rutgers pb $12.00

- Rebecca Zurier
ART FOR THE MASSES: A Radical Magazine and Its Graphics, 1911–1917
A large coffee-table book with handsome reproductions analyzes how *The Masses*

used pictures to convey its political message
Introduction by Leslie Fishbein
0–87722–513–3 Temple $29.95

- Melvyn Dubofsky & Warren Van Tine, editors
LABOR LEADERS IN AMERICA
Profiles include Samuel Gompers, Eugene V. Debs, Sidney Hillman, A. Philip Randolph, Jimmy Hoffa, and Cesar Chavez
0–252–01343–3 Illinois $14.95

- Paul Avrich
AN AMERICAN ANARCHIST: The Life of Voltairine de Cleyre
"Avrich has greatly enriched our knowledge and understanding of life as it was for hundreds of ordinary men and women who dared to stand for a new order"—*Choice*
0–691–04657–3 Princeton $36.00

- Nick Salvatore
EUGENE V. DEBS: Citizen and Socialist
Winner of the Dunning and Bancroft prizes. "This book's distinction is its exploration of Debs's social milieu, its analysis of his tortured passage from right-wing craft unionism to left-wing socialism, and its penetrating insights into the failure of socialism in America"—William N. Harbaugh, *New Republic*
0–252–00967–3 Illinois $24.95
0–252–01148–1 Illinois pb $9.95

- Elizabeth Gurley Flynn
MY FIRST LIFE, 1906–1926: An Autobiography
0–7178–0368–6 International pb $5.95

- Rosalyn Baxandall
WORDS ON FIRE: The Life and Writing of Elizabeth Gurley Flynn
The heroine of left-wing causes (1890–1964)
0–8135–1240–9 Rutgers $35.00
0–8135–1241–7 Rutgers pb $15.00

- Emma Goldman
LIVING MY LIFE

Volume 1
0–486–22543–7 Dover pb $8.95

Volume 2
0–486–22544–5 Dover pb $8.95

- Alice Wexler
EMMA GOLDMAN IN AMERICA
"A magnificent job in integrating the public myth with the intimate life"— *Chicago Tribune*
0–8070–7003–3 Beacon pb $10.95

- Harold Livesay
SAMUEL GOMPERS AND ORGANIZED LABOR IN AMERICA
0–673–39345–3 Scott, Foresman pb $7.95

➤ **FOR OVERSEAS ORDERING INFORMATION, SEE PAGE 1**

Emma Goldman upon her deportation in 1919 (photo by Augustus Sherman, courtesy of The American Museum of Immigration at the Statue of Liberty)

- Melvyn Dubofsky & Warren Van Tine
  JOHN L. LEWIS: A Biography
  0–252–01349–2 Illinois $29.95
  0–252–01287–9 Illinois pb $11.95

- Steve Nelson
  STEVE NELSON, AMERICAN RADICAL
  0–8229–3441–8 Pittsburgh $29.95

- John Barnard
  WALTER REUTHER AND THE RISE OF THE AUTOWORKERS
  0–673–39320–8 Scott, Foresman pb $7.95

- Dorothy Gallagher
  ALL THE RIGHT ENEMIES: The Life and Murder of Carlo Tresca
  The 1943 murder of the noted socialist-turned-anarchist has never been solved
  0–8135–1310–3 Rutgers $24.95

Topics in American Studies

ECONOMIC HISTORY

▶ See also Economics & Business, Industry, and Finance

- Michael A. Bernstein
  THE GREAT DEPRESSION: Delayed Recovery and Economic Change in America, 1929–1939
  A serious economic analysis of the Depression years
  0–521–34048–9 Cambridge $29.95
  0–521–37985–7 Cambridge pb $10.95

- Thomas C. Cochran
  FRONTIERS OF CHANGE: Early Industrialism in America
  0–19–502875–9 Oxford $21.95
  0–19–503284–5 Oxford pb $9.95

- Milton Friedman & Anna Jacobson Schwartz
  A MONETARY HISTORY OF THE UNITED STATES, 1867–1960
  "The numerical account is dexterously and gracefully interwoven with a history of monetary institutions, legislation, policies, personalities, and politics"—James Tobin, *American Economic Review*
  0–691–00354–8 Princeton pb $25.00

- Edward C. Kirkland
  HISTORY OF AMERICAN ECONOMIC LIFE
  0–89197–215–3 Irvington pb $18.95

- John J. McCusker & Russell R. Menard
  THE ECONOMY OF BRITISH AMERICA, 1607–1789
  0–8078–4165–X North Carolina pb $14.95

- Douglass C. North
  ECONOMIC GROWTH OF THE UNITED STATES, 1790–1860
  0–393–00346–9 Norton pb $7.95

- Edwin J. Perkins
  THE ECONOMY OF COLONIAL AMERICA
  0–231–06338–5 Columbia $30.00
  0–231–06339–3 Columbia pb $13.00

- Barry W. Poulson
  ECONOMIC HISTORY OF THE UNITED STATES
  0–02–396220–8 Macmillan $39.00

- Martin J. Sklar
  THE CORPORATE RECONSTRUCTION OF AMERICAN CAPITALISM, 1890–1916: The Market, the Law and Politics
  0–521–31382–1 Cambridge pb $15.95

- Herbert Stein
  PRESIDENTIAL ECONOMICS: The Making of Economic Policy from Roosevelt to Reagan and Beyond
  0–8447–3656–2 American Enterprise pb $12.95

Farming in America

- Wendell Berry
  THE UNSETTLING OF AMERICA: Culture and Agriculture
  0–87156–772–5 Sierra pb $7.95

- Cletus E. Daniel
  BITTER HARVEST: A History of California Farmworkers, 1870–1941
  0–520–04722–2 California pb $10.95

- Pete Daniel
  BREAKING THE LAND: The Transformation of Cotton, Tobacco, and Rice Cultures since 1880
  0–252–01391–3 Illinois pb $12.95

- Gilbert C. Fite
  THE FARMERS' FRONTIER, 1865–1900
  Foreword by Ray A. Billington
  0–8061–2063–0 Oklahoma pb $12.95

- Steven Hahn & Jonathan Prude, editors
  THE COUNTRYSIDE IN THE AGE OF CAPITALIST TRANSFORMATION
  0–8078–4139–0 North Carolina pb $9.95

- Gene Logsdon
  THE LAST DAYS OF A FARMER: A Personal Account
  A first-person account tracing the decline of traditional rural life in America
  0–86547–377–3 North Point $18.95

- Howard S. Russell
  A LONG, DEEP FURROW: Three Centuries of Farming in New England
  Edited and abridged by Mark Lapping
  0–87451–214–X New England pb $15.95

- Theodore Saloutos
  THE AMERICAN FAMRER AND THE NEW DEAL
  0–8138–1076–0 Iowa State $27.95

- John L. Shover
  FIRST MAJORITY, LAST MINORITY: The Transforming of Rural Life in America
  0–87580–056–4 Northern Illinois $15.00
  0–87580–522–1 Northern Illinois pb $7.00

Business History

Alfred D. Chandler, Jr.
THE VISIBLE HAND: The Managerial Revolution in American Business
A Pulitzer Prize winning study of the emergence of large-scale organizations
0–674–94051–2 Harvard $32.00
0–674–94052–0 Harvard pb $12.95

STRATEGY AND STRUCTURE: Chapters in the History of the American Industrial Enterprise
An influential study of corporate reorganization
0–262–53009–0 MIT pb $9.95

- Alfred D. Chandler, Jr. & Herman Daems, editors
  MANAGERIAL HIERARCHIES: Comparative Perspectives on the Rise of the Modern Industrial Enterprise
  The beginnings of a more comparative economic history
  0–674–54741–1 Harvard pb $8.95

- Thomas V. DiBacco
  MADE IN THE U.S.A.: The History of American Business
  0–06–091466–1 Harper & Row pb $8.95

- Gerald Gunderson
  THE WEALTH CREATORS: An Entrepreneurial History of the United States
  0–525–24729–7 Dutton $18.95

- Jonathan Hughes
  THE VITAL FEW: The Entrepreneur and American Economic Progress
  0–19–504038–4 Oxford pb $11.95

- Glenn Porter
  THE RISE OF BIG BUSINESS
  0–88295–750–3 Harlan Davidson pb $7.95

The Business Barons

● Peter Collier & David Horowitz
THE FORDS: An American Epic
The dramatic conflict among three generations of Fords as seen against the backdrop of an industrial empire
0–671–66951–6 Simon & Schuster pb $9.95

THE ROCKEFELLERS: An American Dynasty
0–671–67788–8 Simon & Schuster $22.95
0–671–67445–5 Simon & Schuster pb $9.95

● John Ensor Harr & Peter J. Johnson
THE ROCKEFELLER CENTURY: Three Generations of America's Greatest Family
"Each one emerges as a man of significant stature and compelling interest"—Robert L. Payton, University of Virginia
0–684–18936–4 Scribners $29.95

● Matthew Josephson
THE ROBBER BARONS: The Great American Capitalists, 1861–1901
0–15–676790–2 HBJ pb $7.95

● Maury Klein
THE LIFE AND LEGEND OF JAY GOULD
Gould portrayed as far more complex and sympathetic than the amoral, daring investor and railroad czar of popular image
0–8018–2880–5 Johns Hopkins $34.50

● Robert Lacey
FORD: The Men and the Machine
A lively history of the Ford family and auto dynasty, from the author of numerous books on modern British royalty; illustrated
0–345–34312–3 Ballantine pb $5.95

● Caroline Latham & David Agresta
DODGE DYNASTY: The Car and the Family that Rocked Detroit
A sweeping history, from John and Horace Dodge's boyhood in southwestern Michigan to their business triumphs and personal scandals
0–15–125320–X HBJ $18.95

● Robert Lenzner
THE GREAT GETTY
Popular biography of the man long known as the world's richest magnate
0–451–14699–9 Signet pb $4.95

● Harold C. Livesay
AMERICAN MADE: Men Who Shaped the American Economy
An interesting set of biographical vignettes
0–673–39346–1 Scott, Foresman pb $14.00

ANDREW CARNEGIE AND THE RISE OF BIG BUSINESS
The short version of Carnegie's life
0–673–39344–5 Scott, Foresman pb $7.95

● Russell Miller
THE HOUSE OF GETTY
0–8050–0323–1 Henry Holt pb $4.95

● Joseph F. Wall
ANDREW CARNEGIE
The long version of Carnegie's life
0–19–501282–8 Oxford $39.95

R.H. Macy's first store, at 6th Avenue and 14th Street, New York, c. 1869 (courtesy of The Smithsonian Institution)

History of Consumerism

Though it is difficult to avoid clichés about the spread of conformity and the stimulation of unnecessary demands, several historians have written works that provide fresh insights into American culture.

● Susan P. Benson
COUNTER CULTURES: Saleswomen, Managers and Customers in American Department Stores, 1890–1940
0–252–01252–6 Illinois $27.50

● Richard W. Fox & T. Jackson Lears, editors
THE CULTURE OF CONSUMPTION: Critical Essays in American History, 1860–1960
0–394–71611–6 Pantheon pb $10.50

● Daniel Horowitz
THE MORALITY OF SPENDING: Attitudes Toward the Consumer Society in America, 1875–1940
0–8018–2530–X Johns Hopkins $32.50

● David E. Shi
THE SIMPLE LIFE: Plain Living and High Thinking in American Culture
0–19–504013–9 Oxford pb $8.95

History of Advertising

● Stuart Ewen
CAPTAINS OF CONSCIOUSNESS
0–07–019846–2 McGraw-Hill pb $6.95

● Stephen Fox
THE MIRROR MAKERS: A History of Twentieth-Century American Advertising
0–394–73246–4 Random House pb $4.95

● Roland Marchand
ADVERTISING THE AMERICAN DREAM: Making Way for Modernity, 1920–1940
How advertising manipulated modern art and photography to promote an enduring consumption ethic
0–520–05253–6 California $42.50
0–520–05885–2 California pb $15.95

● Daniel Pope
THE MAKING OF MODERN ADVERTISING
0–465–04325–9 Basic Books $18.95

HISTORY OF SCIENCE AND TECHNOLOGY

▶ **See also Science and Technology & Medicine**

Industrial Revolutions

● Brooke Hindle
EMULATION AND INVENTION
The invention of the steamboat and the telegraph, in their social and psychological contexts; with illustrations. "What is surprising is that both Robert Fulton and Samuel Finley Breese Morse began their careers as artists . . . Mr. Hindle sees invention and art as being related . . . He makes a good case"—*New Yorker*
0–8147–3409–X NYU $27.50
0–393–30113–3 Norton pb $5.95

● Brooke Hindle & Steven Lubar
ENGINES OF CHANGE: The American Industrial Revolution, 1790–1860
0–87474–540–3 Smithsonian $29.95
0–87474–539–X Smithsonian pb $14.95

● David A. Hounshell
FROM THE AMERICAN SYSTEM TO MASS PRODUCTION, 1800–1932: The Development of Manufacturing Technology in the United States
0–8018–3158–X Johns Hopkins pb $14.95

● David A. Hounshell & John Kenly Smith, Jr.
SCIENCE AND CORPORATE STRATEGY: DuPont R&D, 1902–1980
A corporate history of the role of research in the development of DuPont products
0–521–32767–9 Cambridge $39.50

- Thomas P. Hughes
  AMERICAN GENESIS: A Century of Technological Enthusiasm, 1870–1970
  0–670–81478–4 Viking $24.95

- Otto Mayr & Robert C. Post, editor
  YANKEE ENTERPRISE: The Rise of the American System of Manufactures
  0–87474–634–5 Smithsonian $22.50
  0–87474–631–0 Smithsonian pb $12.50

- David F. Noble
  AMERICA BY DESIGN: Science, Technology, and the Rise of Corporate Capitalism
  0–19–502618–7 Oxford pb $10.95

  FORCES OF PRODUCTION: A Social History of Industrial Automation
  "Approaches technology from a leftist perspective, a viewpoint that is largely lacking in the existing historical literature"—Philip M. Boffey, *NY Times Book Review*
  0–394–51262–6 Knopf $22.95
  0–19–504046–5 Oxford pb $12.95

- Richard G. Wilson & others
  THE MACHINE AGE IN AMERICA, 1918–1941
  A beautifully illustrated history
  0–8109–1421–2 Abrams $39.95

Inventions

- Hugh G. Aitken
  THE CONTINUOUS WAVE: Technology and American Radio, 1900–1932
  0–691–02390–5 Princeton pb $19.95

  SYNTONY AND SPARK: The Origins of Radio
  0–691–02392–1 Princeton pb $13.95

- Grace R. Cooper
  THE SEWING MACHINE: Its Invention and Development
  0–87474–330–3 Smithsonian $29.95

- John Ellis
  THE SOCIAL HISTORY OF THE MACHINE GUN
  "It's hard to imagine a more stimulating way to study human destructiveness"—Christopher Lehmann-Haupt, *NY Times*
  Foreword by Edward C. Ezell
  0–8018–3358–2 Johns Hopkins pb $9.95

- Siegfried Giedion
  MECHANIZATION TAKES COMMAND
  0–393–00489–9 Norton pb $15.95

- Reese V. Jenkins
  IMAGES AND ENTERPRISE: Technology and the American Photographic Industry, 1839–1925
  Technological changes that culminated in George Eastman's creation of the Kodak system of amateur photography in the 1880s
  0–8018–1588–6 Johns Hopkins $35.00
  0–8018–3549–6 Johns Hopkins pb $16.95

A 19th-century wooden mouse trap (courtesy of The New-York Historical Society)

Planes, Trains, and Automobiles

- Roger Bilstein
  FLIGHT IN AMERICA: From the Wrights to the Astronauts
  "From technological trends and research and development to the effect of air travel on the expansion of major league baseball in the 1950s and 1960s . . . A superior work"—William F. Trimble, *Journal of American History*
  0–8018–2973–9 Johns Hopkins $39.50
  0–8018–3561–5 Johns Hopkins pb $12.95

- Edward W. Constant, II
  THE ORIGINS OF THE TURBOJET REVOLUTION
  0–8018–2222–X Johns Hopkins $35.00

- Tom Crouch
  A DREAM OF WINGS: Americans and the Airplane, 1875–1905
  0–393–01385–5 Norton $15.95

  THE BISHOP'S BOYS: A Life of Wilbur and Orville Wright
  Focuses on the brothers' early family life and their technological innovation in the context of its time
  0–393–02660–4 Norton $22.50

- James J. Flink
  THE AUTOMOBILE AGE
  A sweeping social history of the car and its impact on American society
  0–262–06111–2 MIT $25.00

- Fred Howard
  ORVILLE AND WILBUR: A Biography of the Wright Brothers
  0–345–35393–5 Ballantine pb $12.95

- John Hoyt Williams
  A GREAT AND SHINING ROAD: The Epic Story of the Transcontinental Railroad
  0–8129–1668–9 Times Books $22.50

- Jeana Yeager & Dick Rutan, with Phil Patton
  VOYAGER
  First-person account by the pilots who designed and flew the pioneering plane
  0–06–097197–5 Harper & Row pb $8.95

The Space Age

▶ **See also Astronomy**

- Michael Collins
  LIFTOFF: The Story of America's Adventure in Space
  The American space program, by an astronaut
  0–8021–1011–8 Grove $25.00

- Walter A. McDougall
  THE HEAVENS AND THE EARTH: A Political History of the Space Age
  From the utopian fantasies of 19th-century rocketry pioneers to the debate over Star Wars. "It clears up the story of the space race and connects it to the central public issues of our time—i.e., the political organization of technological and social change"—William H. McNeill
  0–465–02887–X Basic Books $25.95
  0–465–02888–8 Basic Books pb $11.95

- Paul B. Stares
  THE MILITARIZATION OF SPACE: U.S. Policy, 1945–1984
  The change from relatively peaceful exploration of space to the beginnings of a new militarization in the late 1970s
  0–8014–1810–0 Cornell $29.95
  0–8014–9471–0 Cornell pb $10.95

- Tom Wolfe
  THE RIGHT STUFF
  0–374–25033–2 Farrar, Straus & Giroux $15.95
  0–553–27556–9 Bantam pb $4.95

Technology and Culture

- John F. Kasson
  CIVILIZING THE MACHINE: Technology and Republican Values in America, 1776–1900
  The collision of culture and machine—of the utopian world of Emerson with the factories of Lowell, Massachusetts—in industrializing America
  0–14–004415–9 Penguin pb $7.95

- Leo Marx
  THE MACHINE IN THE GARDEN: Technology and the Pastoral Ideal in America
  0–19–500738–7 Oxford pb $9.95

- Cecelia Tichi
  SHIFTING GEARS: Technology, Literature, Culture in Modernist America
  0–8078–1715–5 North Carolina $35.00
  0–8078–4167–6 North Carolina pb $14.95

- James A. Ward
  RAILROADS AND THE CHARACTER OF AMERICA, 1820–1887
  "A solid contribution"—William S. Greever, *Lexington Quarterly*
  0–87049–498–8 Tennessee pb $14.95

A 1957 Cadillac Park Avenue sedan

Science and Medicine

• Robert V. Bruce
THE LAUNCHING OF MODERN AMERICAN SCIENCE
"Admirably details how American science was transformed in the mid-nineteenth century from an enterprise of disparate local amateurs to an organized cadre of nationally—and nationalistically—ambitious professionals"—Daniel J. Kevles, California Institute of Technology
0–394–55394–2 Knopf $30.00

• John Duffy
THE HEALERS: A History of American Medicine
0–252–00743–3 Illinois pb $9.95

• Robert Fuller
AMERICANS AND THE UNCONSCIOUS
0–19–504027–9 Oxford $24.95

• John S. Haller, Jr.
AMERICAN MEDICINE IN TRANSITION, 1840–1910
0–252–00806–5 Illinois $34.95

• Daniel J. Kevles
IN THE NAME OF EUGENICS: Genetics and the Uses of Human Heredity
0–394–50702–9 Knopf $22.95
0–520–05763–5 California pb $10.95

THE PHYSICISTS: The History of a Scientific Community in Modern America
0–674–66655–0 Harvard pb $12.95

• Sally G. Kohlstedt
THE FORMATION OF THE AMERICAN SCIENTIFIC COMMUNITY: The American Association for the Advancement of Science, 1848–1860
0–252–00419–1 Illinois $24.95

• Regina M. Morantz-Sanchez
SYMPATHY AND SCIENCE: Women Physicians in American Medicine
0–19–503627–1 Oxford $24.95
0–19–504985–3 Oxford pb $10.95

• Nathan Reingold, editor
SCIENCE IN NINETEENTH-CENTURY AMERICA: A Documentary History
0–226–70947–7 Chicago pb $12.50

• Nathan Reingold & Ida H. Reingold, editors
SCIENCE IN AMERICA: A Documentary History, 1900–1939
0–226–70946–9 Chicago $37.50

• Paul Starr
THE SOCIAL TRANSFORMATION OF AMERICAN MEDICINE
0–465–07934–2 Basic Books $24.95
0–465–07935–0 Basic Books pb $13.95

• Morris J. Vogel & Charles E. Rosenberg, editors
THE THERAPEUTIC REVOLUTION: Essays on the Social History of American Medicine
0–8122–7773–2 Pennsylvania $14.95

Plagues and Epidemics

Mark Caldwell
THE LAST CRUSADE: The War on Consumption, 1872–1954
0–689–11810–4 Atheneum $22.50

James Patterson
THE DREAD DISEASE: Cancer and Modern American Culture
0–674–21625–3 Harvard $25.95

Charles E. Rosenberg
THE CHOLERA YEARS: The United States in 1832, 1849, and 1866
"A masterful analysis of the moral and social interest attached to epidemic disease, providing generally applicable insights into how the connections between social change, changes in knowledge, and changes in technical practice may be conceived"—Steven Shapin, *TLS*
0–226–72677–0 Chicago pb $9.95

Randy Shilts
AND THE BAND PLAYED ON: Politics, People, and the AIDS Epidemic
0–312–00994–1 St. Martin's $24.95
0–14–011369–X Penguin pb $12.95

INTELLECTUAL HISTORY

Guided by Christopher Lasch's extraordinary set of essays *The New Radicalism in America, 1889–1963,* now more than 20 years old, many of the newer works focus more on a history of intellectuals than on particular ideas. Some of the studies of slavery and racism (particularly the works of David Brion Davis) suggest the rich possibilities for intellectual history. The list below represents a mix of both newer works and some employing an older approach that should not be ignored.

▶ **See also Education**

• Sacvan Bercovitch
THE AMERICAN JEREMIAD
0–299–07350–5 Wisconsin $32.50
0–299–07354–8 Wisconsin pb $11.95

• Leslie Cohen Berlowitz & others, editors
AMERICA IN THEORY
Sixteen prominent thinkers examine the myths and theories that make up the idea of modern America
0–19–505396–6 Oxford $24.95

• Norman Birnbaum
THE RADICAL RENEWAL: The Politics of Ideas in Modern America
0–394–52315–6 Pantheon $17.95
0–394–70659–5 Random House pb $8.95

• Daniel J. Boorstin
THE LOST WORLD OF THOMAS JEFFERSON
The concepts of the Jeffersonian Circle: God, nature, equality, toleration, education, and government, and the worldview that underlies them
0–226–06496–4 Chicago pb $12.95

Benjamin Franklin (painting by John Trumbull, courtesy Yale University Art Gallery)

IF YOU CAN'T FIND IT, LOOK IN THE INDEX

• Paul Boyer
BY THE BOMB'S EARLY LIGHT:
American Thought and Culture at the Dawn
of the Atomic Age
Documents "how the bomb figured in the
nation's public discourse and popular
mythology between 1945 and 1950 . . . an
era brought vividly back to life in this rich
and disturbing chronicle"—*Newsweek*
0–394–74767–4 Pantheon pb $11.95

• Charles Capper & David A.
Hollinger, editors
THE AMERICAN INTELLECTUAL
TRADITION
An anthology of substantial selections from
prominent American thinkers since the
17th century
0–19–505774–0 Oxford (2-volume set) $45.00

Volume 1
Covers the period up to 1865
0–19–504461–4 Oxford pb $14.95

Volume 2
From 1865 to the present
0–19–504462–2 Oxford pb $12.95

• Patricia Kline Cohen
A CALCULATING PEOPLE: The Spread
of Numeracy in Early America
How numeracy shaped the character of
society, through episodes including the
controversial inauguration of the census in
Jamestown and the West Indies colonies
and the furor over errors in the 1840
census
0–226–11283–7 Chicago $22.50
0–226–11284–5 Chicago pb $9.95

• Henry Steele Commager
THE AMERICAN MIND: An
Interpretation of American Thought and
Character since the 1880s
0–300–00046–4 Yale pb $12.95

• David Brion Davis
FROM HOMICIDE TO SLAVERY:
Studies in American Culture
A leading historian on slavery probes such
subjects as capital punishment, the cowboy
as American hero, violence in American
literature, and the rise of antislavery
movements
0–19–505418–0 Oxford pb $10.95

• John Patrick Diggins
THE LOST SOUL OF AMERICAN
POLITICS: Virtue, Self-Interest, and the
Foundations of Liberalism
0–226–14877–7 Chicago pb $15.95

• Howard M. Feinstein
BECOMING WILLIAM JAMES
"William, while perhaps raising an
eyebrow here and there, would have
welcomed it and praised it lavishly"—
R.W.B. Lewis, *TLS*
0–8014–1617–5 Cornell $24.95
0–8014–9373–0 Cornell pb $10.95

• Frances FitzGerald
CITIES ON A HILL
Four communities—San Francisco's gay
community, Jerry Falwell's Lynchburg, a
Florida retirement community, and the
guru-inspired Rajneeshpuram—and their
common manifestation of the American

visionary drive to shake the past and build
anew
0–671–55209–0 Simon & Schuster $19.95
0–671–64561–7 Simon & Schuster pb $9.95

• James B. Gilbert
WORK WITHOUT SALVATION:
America's Intellectual and Industrial
Alienation, 1880–1910
0–8018–1954–7 Johns Hopkins $20.00

Richard Hofstadter
ANTI-INTELLECTUALISM IN
AMERICAN LIFE
1964 Pulitzer Prize winner. "A rich,
complex, shifting picture of the life of
the mind in a society dominated by the
ideal of practical success"—Robert Peel,
Christian Science Monitor
0–394–41535–3 Knopf $13.95
0–394–70317–0 Random House pb $8.95

• David A. Hollinger
IN THE AMERICAN PROVINCE: Studies
in the History and Historiography of Ideas
0–253–32933–7 Indiana $22.50

• Russell Jacoby
THE LAST INTELLECTUALS: American
Culture in the Age of Academe
Analyzes the disappearance of the
nonacademic intellectual—people like
Dwight MacDonald, Lewis Mumford, and
Edmund Wilson—in an age dominated by
suburbanization and gentrification
0–465–03812–3 Basic Books $18.95
0–374–52175–1 Farrar, Straus & Giroux pb $8.95

• Paul Johnson
INTELLECTUALS
0–06–016050–0 Harper & Row $22.50

• Harry Kalven, Jr.
A WORTHY TRADITION: Freedom of
Speech in America
0–06–015810–7 Harper & Row $35.00

• James T. Kloppenberg
UNCERTAIN VICTORY: Social
Democracy and Progressivism in European
and American Thought, 1870–1920
Pivotal intellectual figures—William James,
John Dewey, Dilthey, Green, Sidgwick,
Fouillée—and their influence on the next
generation—Lippmann, Bernstein, Weber,
and others
0–19–503749–9 Oxford $42.00

Christopher Lasch
THE CULTURE OF NARCISSISM
Trenchant critique of "the dotage of
bourgeois society"
0–446–32104–4 Warner pb $4.95

THE NEW RADICALISM IN
AMERICA, 1889–1963: The Intellectual
As a Social Type
0–393–30319–5 Norton pb $7.95

• Henry F. May
THE END OF AMERICAN INNOCENCE:
A Study of the First Years of Our Own
Time, 1912–1917
Traces the intellectual and cultural
transformations associated with the 1920s
to their origins
0–19–502528–8 Oxford pb $12.95

THE ENLIGHTENMENT IN AMERICA
0–19–502367–6 Oxford pb $11.95

• Perry Miller
LIFE OF THE MIND IN AMERICA:
From the Revolution to the Civil War
0–15–651990–9 HBJ pb $7.95

• Roderick Nash
WILDERNESS AND THE AMERICAN
MIND
0–300–02905–5 Yale $40.00
0–300–02910–1 Yale pb $12.95

• Vernon Louis Parrington
MAIN CURRENTS IN AMERICAN
THOUGHT

Volume 1: The Colonial Mind, 1620–1800
0–8061–2080–0 Oklahoma pb $14.95

Volume 2: The Romantic Revolution in
America, 1800–1860
0–8061–2081–9 Oklahoma pb $14.95

Volume 3: The Beginnings of Critical
Realism in America, 1860–1920
0–8061–2082–7 Oklahoma pb $14.95

• Lewis Perry
INTELLECTUAL LIFE IN AMERICA: A
History
The background and roles of intellectuals
in different eras of American history
0–226–66101–6 Chicago pb $14.95

• Merrill D. Peterson
THE JEFFERSON IMAGE IN THE
AMERICAN MIND
0–19–501539–8 Oxford $27.50
0–19–500698–4 Oxford pb $12.95

Henry Adams

☐ **TO ORDER BY FAX, SEE PAGE 1**

• R. Jackson Wilson
FIGURES OF SPEECH: American Writers and the Literary Marketplace, from Benjamin Franklin to Emily Dickinson
Was publication, as Emily Dickinson wrote, "the auction of the mind"? Wilson suggests that the writers he studies were never free from the tensions that the new capitalism evoked
0–394–49696–5 Knopf $24.95

New York Intellectuals

• Thomas Bender
NEW YORK INTELLECT: A History of Intellectual Life in New York City, From 1750 to the Beginnings of Our Time
From Walt Whitman to Edmund Wilson, and 18th-century coffeehouses to modern universities
0–8018–3639–5 Johns Hopkins pb $10.95

• Alexander Bloom
PRODIGAL SONS: The New York Intellectuals and Their World
The Jewish intellectuals who were raised in New York, educated at Columbia and City College, and turned to radical politics in the 1930s, became established writers and scholars in postwar America, and by the 1950s were the nation's dominant intellectuals
0–19–505177–7 Oxford pb $11.95

• Alan M. Wald
THE NEW YORK INTELLECTUALS: The Rise and Decline of the Anti-Stalinist Left from the 1930s to the 1980s
0–8078–1716–3 North Carolina $32.50
0–8078–4169–2 North Carolina pb $12.95

CULTURAL AND SOCIAL HISTORY

▶ **For American folklore see Mythology and Folklore**

• Erik Barnouw
TUBE OF PLENTY: The Evolution of American Television
0–19–503092–3 Oxford pb $11.95

• Raymonde Carroll
CULTURAL MISUNDERSTANDINGS: The French-American Experience
Translated by Carol Volk
0–22609497–9 Chicago $19.95

• Gilbert Chase
AMERICA'S MUSIC: From the Pilgrims to the Present
The third edition of a classic, first published in 1955
Foreword by Richard Crawford
Essay by William Brooks
0–252–00454–X Illinois $29.95

• Duncan Emrich
FOLKLORE ON THE AMERICAN LAND
A handsome reissue of a noted anthology, covering language, legends, tales, beliefs and superstitions
0–316–23721–3 Little, Brown pb $12.95

Bob Hope, Mrs. Khrushchev, and Frank Sinatra in Hollywood, 1959 (photo by Burt Glinn), from The Fifties: Photographs of America *edited by Magnum Photos Staff (Pantheon)*

• Martin Green
NEW YORK 1913: The Armory Show and the Paterson Silk Pageant
The 1913 Armory Show revolutionized America's artistic and cultural worlds by importing the European modernism that displaced traditional and academic art, and became an emblem of the new radicalism of the pre-World War I years
0–684–18993–3 Scribners $24.95

• Neil Harris
THE ARTIST IN AMERICAN SOCIETY: The Formative Years, 1790–1860
0–226–31754–4 Chicago pb $12.95

• Jackson Lears
NO PLACE OF GRACE: Antimodernism and the Transformation of American Culture, 1880–1920
0–394–50816–5 Pantheon pb $10.95

• Harvey A. Levenstein
REVOLUTION AT THE TABLE: The Transformation of the American Diet
How social, economic, and political forces have changed America's eating habits
0–19–504365–0 Oxford $21.95

• Russell Lynes
THE TASTEMAKERS: The Development of American Popular Taste
0–486–23993–4 Dover pb $6.95

• Anne L. Macdonald
NO IDLE HANDS: The Social History of American Knitting
With illustrations
0–345–33906–1 Ballantine $19.95

• Karal Ann Marling
GEORGE WASHINGTON SLEPT HERE: Colonial Revivals and American Culture
0–674–34951–2 Harvard $39.95

• Lary May
SCREENING OUT THE PAST: The Birth of Mass Culture and the Motion Picture Industry
0–226–51173–1 Chicago pb $11.95

• Lary May, editor
RECASTING AMERICA: Culture and Politics in the Age of Cold War
Essays by leading scholars on the convergence of politics and cultural change in postwar America
0–226–51175–8 Chicago $49.95
0–226–51176–6 Chicago pb $15.95

• Ted Morgan
ON BECOMING AMERICAN
Reflections on American identity by the French aristocrat who converted to Americanism and became a Pulitzer Prize-winning author
1–55778–070–6 Paragon pb $8.95

• Debora Silverman
SELLING CULTURE: Bloomingdale's, Diana Vreeland and the Aristocracy of Taste in Reagan's America
"Illuminates the mixture of fantasy and corruption that is the distinctive mark of both the aristocratic revival in fashion and the Reagan presidency"—Michael Rogin
0–394–55109–5 Pantheon $17.95
0–394–74303–2 Pantheon pb $8.95

• Robert Sklar
MOVIE-MADE AMERICA: A Cultural History of American Movies
0–394–72120–9 Random House pb $11.95

• Robert Blair St. George, editor
MATERIAL LIFE IN AMERICA, 1600–1860
Essays by leading scholars on folklore, anthropology, decorative arts, and related subjects provide a multifaceted portrait of early American life
1–55553–020–6 Northeastern pb $25.00

• Ronald Sukenick
DOWN AND IN: Life in the Underground
The world of American underground culture
0–688–06589–9 Morrow $17.95
0–02–008731–4 Macmillan pb $10.95

• John Tebbel
BETWEEN COVERS: The Rise and Transformation of Book Publishing in America
0–19–504189–5 Oxford $29.95

✉ **TO ORDER BOOKS AS GIFTS, SEE PAGE 1**

- Alan Trachtenberg
READING AMERICAN PHOTOGRAPHS: Images as History from Mathew Brady to Walker Evans
The role of photographers in shaping the American perception of the past
0–8090–8037–0 Hill & Wang $25.00

- Richard Weiss
THE AMERICAN MYTH OF SUCCESS: From Horatio Alger to Norman Vincent Peale
0–252–06043–1 Illinois pb $9.95

LEISURE

- Donna Braden
LEISURE AND ENTERTAINMENT IN AMERICA
Includes hundreds of black-and-white and color illustrations
0–8143–2153–4 Wayne State $39.95
0–8143–2154–2 Wayne State pb $19.95

- Lewis A. Erenberg
STEPPIN' OUT: New York Nightlife and the Transformation of American Culture, 1890–1930
From the Gay '90s through the Jazz Age, New York nightlife was both a symbol and catalyst of America's liberation from the Victorian period
0–226–21515–6 Chicago pb $11.95

- John M. Findlay
PEOPLE OF CHANCE: Gambling in American Society from Jamestown to Las Vegas
0–19–503740–5 Oxford $22.95

- John F. Kasson
AMUSING THE MILLIONS: Coney Island at the Turn of the Century
An excellent short illustrated history of the meaning of the amusement park
0–8090–0133–0 Hill & Wang pb $7.95

- Kathy Peiss
CHEAP AMUSEMENTS: Working Women and Leisure in Turn-of-the-Century New York
With colorful details about dance styles, silent-movie plots, and amusement parks, this book shows how working women spent their free time and money
0–87722–389–0 Temple $29.95

- W.J. Rorabaugh
THE ALCOHOLIC REPUBLIC: An American Tradition
The changes in drinking patterns between 1790 and 1840 and the psychological factors that helped produce the temperance movement
0–19–502584–9 Oxford $29.95
0–19–502990–9 Oxford pb $9.95

- Roy Rosenzweig
EIGHT HOURS FOR WHAT WE WILL: Workers and Leisure in an Industrial City, 1870–1920
A superb study with implications far beyond its subject of Worcester, Massachusetts
0–521–31397–X Cambridge pb $10.95

Ask the *bartender* (1855) *to set 'em up* (1851)! Do you want only *a snifter* (1848), or do you prefer a drink precisely measured by a *jigger* (1836) . . . ? Ask for a *long drink* (1828), unless you prefer your whiskey *straight* (1862; the English word was *neat*). Would you like an *eggnog* (1775), a *mint-julep* (1809), or some kind of *cobbler* (1840), for example, a *sherry cobbler* (1841)? . . . The world-famous *cocktail*—destined to become one of the most prolific American inventions, linguistic or otherwise—came not from a later effete era, but from that same Gothic Age. Its first recorded use, in the Hudson, New York, *Balance (and Columbian Repository)* on May 13, 1806, explained: "*Cock tail,* then, is a stimulating liquor, composed of spirits of any kind, *sugar, water,* and *bitters*—it is vulgarly called *bittered sling* . . . It is said, also, to be of great use to a democratic candidate: because, a person having swallowed a glass of it, is ready to swallow any thing else."

Daniel J. Boorstin
THE AMERICANS: The Democratic Experience
0–394–48724–9 Random House $24.95

Sports in American Society

- Edwin H. Cady
THE BIG GAME: College Sports and American Life
"Scrutinizes the values of a strong athletic program to the academic community, the proper methods of recruitment . . . and offers some solutions to the countless problems that big time athletics generate"—*Choice*
0–87049–254–3 Tennessee $24.95

- Elliott J. Gorn
THE MANLY ART: Bare-Knuckle Prize Fighting in America
"First-rate social history rendered in felicitious prose . . . Gorn masterfully blends boxing and social history"—*Chicago Sun-Times*
0–8014–9582–2 Cornell pb $9.95

- Harvey Green
FIT FOR AMERICA: Health, Fitness, Sport and American Society
0–8018–3642–5 Johns Hopkins pb $10.95

- Allen Guttmann
FROM RITUAL TO RECORD: The Nature of Modern Sports
0–231–08369–6 Columbia pb $14.00

- Richard D. Mandell
SPORT: A Cultural History
0–231–05470–X Columbia $35.00
0–231–05471–8 Columbia pb $15.00

- Donald J. Mrozek
SPORT AND AMERICAN MENTALITY, 1880–1910
"A fine example of the social history of sport"—Allen Guttmann, *American Historical Review*
0–87049–394–9 Tennessee $29.95
0–87049–395–7 Tennessee pb $12.95

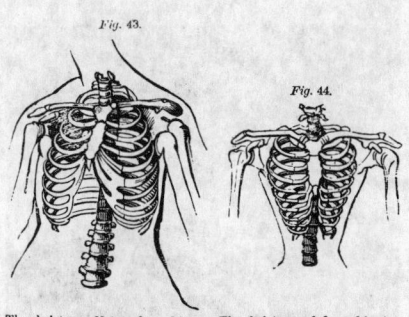

Fig. 43.

Fig. 44.

The skeleton as Nature formed it.   The skeleton as deformed by Art.

From Catherine Beecher's 1856 "Physiology and Calisthenics," reproduced in Fit for America *by Harvey Green*

- Steven A. Riess, editor
THE AMERICAN SPORTING EXPERIENCE: A Historical Anthology of Sport in America
0–88011–210–7 Leisure $20.00

- Jeffrey T. Sammons
BEYOND THE RING: The Role of Boxing in American Society
An ambitious work tracing the history of heavyweight boxing from an illegal activity to a vaunted big business, and how it reflects social change
0–252–01473–1 Illinois $24.95

RELIGION IN AMERICA

- S.E. Ahlstrom
A RELIGIOUS HISTORY OF THE AMERICAN PEOPLE
0–300–01762–6 Yale pb $22.95

- William A. Clebsch
FROM SACRED TO PROFANE AMERICA: The Role of Religion in American History
0–89130–517–3 Scholars pb $9.95

- Winthrop Hudson
RELIGION IN AMERICA: An Historical Account of the Development of American Religious Life
0–02–357820–3 Macmillan $24.00

- Martin E. Marty
MODERN AMERICAN RELIGION, Volume 1: The Irony of It All, 1893–1919
0–226–50893–5 Chicago $24.95

PILGRIMS IN THEIR OWN LAND
0–316–54867–7 Little, Brown $25.00
0–14–008268–9 Penguin pb $8.95

- Henry F. May
IDEAS, FAITHS, AND FEELINGS: Essays on American Intellectual and Religious History, 1952–1982
0–19–503235–7 Oxford $25.00
0–19–503236–5 Oxford pb $9.95

- William G. McLoughlin
REVIVALS, AWAKENING, AND REFORM: An Essay on Religion and Social Change in America, 1607–1977
0–226–56092–9 Chicago pb $9.00

"Methodist Church, Provincetown" by Edward Hopper, 1930, from American Drawings and Watercolors from the Wadsworth Atheneum *by Judith A. Barter (Hudson Hills)*

• R. Laurence Moore
RELIGIOUS OUTSIDERS AND THE MAKING OF AMERICANS
0–19–503663–8 Oxford $32.50
0–19–505188–2 Oxford pb $8.95

• Rosemary R. Ruether & Rosemary S. Keller, editors
WOMEN AND RELIGION IN AMERICA: 1900–1968
0–06–066833–4 Harper & Row $26.95

• Mark Silk
SPIRITUAL POLITICS: Religion and America since World War II
"Demonstrates at once the pervasiveness of evangelical religion and politics in American life and the paradoxes that have resulted since 1945 from the nation's alleged commitment to the 'Judeo-Christian' tradition"—Daniel Aaron
0–671–43910–3 Simon & Schuster $19.95
0–671–67563–X Simon & Schuster pb $8.95

Early America

▶ For the Great Awakening, see US History to the Civil War

• Thomas J. Curry
THE FIRST FREEDOMS: Church and State in America to the Passage of the First Amendment
0–19–503661–1 Oxford $32.00
0–19–505181–5 Oxford pb 10.95

• Edwin S. Gaustad
FAITH OF OUR FATHERS: Religion and the New Nation
The history of the origins of separation of church and state, and the ambivalence between a "nation under God" and the need for religious liberty
0–06–250347–2 Harper & Row $15.95

• Leonard W. Levy
THE ESTABLISHMENT CLAUSE: Religion and the First Amendment
0–02–918750–8 Macmillan $16.95

• David S. Lovejoy
RELIGIOUS ENTHUSIASM IN THE NEW WORLD: Heresy to Revolution
0–674–75864–1 Harvard $27.00

• Ronald L. Numbers & Jonathan M. Butler, editors
THE DISAPPOINTED: Millerism and Millenarianism in the 19th Century
0–253–34299–6 Indiana $29.95

• James Turner
WITHOUT GOD, WITHOUT CREED: The Origins of Unbelief in America
0–8018–3407–4 Johns Hopkins pb $12.95

Special Studies

• Priscilla J. Brewer
SHAKER COMMUNITIES, SHAKER LIVES
"Draws from sociology, statistics, social history, and cultural history to provide a well-reasoned, thoroughly researched analysis of the dynamics of Shaker development and decline"—*Choice*
0–87451–400–2 New England pb $12.95

• John Heineman & Anson Shupe
THE MORMON CORPORATE EMPIRE: The Eye-Opening Report on the Church and Its Political and Financial Agenda
0–8070–0407–3 Beacon pb $11.95

• James J. Hennesey
AMERICAN CATHOLICS: A History of the Roman Catholic Community in the United States
0–19–502946–1 Oxford $29.95
0–19–503268–3 Oxford pb $11.95

John A. Hostetler
AMISH SOCIETY
The third edition of a noted work on Amish culture, religious beliefs, community and family life, and interactions with outsiders
0–8018–2334–X Johns Hopkins pb $9.95

Donald R. Kraybill
THE RIDDLE OF AMISH CULTURE
0–8018–3681–6 Johns Hopkins $35.00
0–8018–3682–4 Johns Hopkins pb $8.95

• Winthrop S. Hudson
AMERICAN PROTESTANTISM
0–226–35803–8 Chicago pb $4.95

• William R. Hutchinson
THE MODERNIST IMPULSE IN AMERICAN PROTESTANTISM
One of the most authoritative writers on American religion traces liberal thought in American Protestantism from the 1870s to the 1930s
0–674–58058–3 Harvard $22.50
0–19–503084–2 Oxford pb $9.95

• Anne Devereaux Jordan
THE SEVENTH-DAY ADVENTISTS: A History
A history of the movement that began with the Millerites, who awaited Christ's

Second Coming, and of the prophetess Ellen Gould Harmon White
0–87052–562–X Hippocrene $14.95

• Joseph M. Murphy
SANTERIA: An African Religion in America
"His engaging picture of Santeria, the Yoruba religion now practiced in the United States by way of Cuba, is fresh, startling, then strangely attractive and even inspiring"—Harvey Cox, Harvard Divinity School
0–8070–1014–6 Beacon $19.95

• Marc Lee Raphael
PROFILES IN AMERICAN JUDAISM: The Reform, Conservative, Orthodox and Reconstructionist Traditions in Historical Perspective
0–06–066802–4 Harper & Row $12.95

• Bruce A. Rosenberg
CAN THESE BONES LIVE?: The Art of the American Folk Preacher
"One can see the folk artist in action, feel his imagery, his language unfold in a dynamic process of interaction between his audience and himself, one aiding and stimulating the other in a mutual ritual"—David C. Fowler
0–252–01415–4 Illinois $39.95
0–252–01416–2 Illinois pb $14.95

• Jan Shipps
MORMONISM: The Story of a New Religious Tradition
0–252–01417–0 Illinois pb $9.95

Revivals and Evangelicalism

• Michael D'Antonio
FALL FROM GRACE: The Failed Crusade of the Christian Right
An analysis of Christian fundamentalism, from *Newsday*'s religious affairs correspondent
0–374–11551–6 Farrar, Straus & Giroux $18.95

• Carol Flake
REDEMPTORAMA: Culture, Politics and the New Evangelicalism
0–14–008265–4 Penguin pb $7.95

• Gregor T. Goethals
THE TV RITUAL: Worship at the Video Altar
0–8070–3223–9 Beacon pb $12.95

• Eric W. Gritsch
BORN AGAINISM: Perspectives on a Movement
0–8006–1625–1 Fortress pb $3.95

• Jeffrey Hadden & Anson Shupe
TELEVANGELISM: Power and Politics on God's Frontier
0–8050–0778–4 Henry Holt $19.95

• David E. Harrell, Jr.
ALL THINGS ARE POSSIBLE: The Healing and Charismatic Revivals in Modern America
0–253–10090–9 Indiana $20.00
0–253–20221–3 Indiana pb $9.95

- Samuel S. Hill & Dennis E. Owen
  **THE NEW RELIGIOUS-POLITICAL
  RIGHT IN AMERICA**
  0-687-27867-8 Abingdon pb $10.95

- James D. Hunter
  **AMERICAN EVANGELICALISM:
  Conservative Religion and the Quandary of
  Modernity**
  0-8135-0985-8 Rutgers pb $9.95

  **EVANGELICALISM: The Coming
  Generation**
  0-226-36082-2 Chicago $19.95
  0-226-36083-0 Chicago pb $11.95

- George M. Marsden
  **FUNDAMENTALISM AND AMERICAN
  CULTURE: The Shaping of Twentieth-
  Century Evangelicalism, 1870–1925**
  0-19-503083-4 Oxford pb $9.95

- Larry Martz with Ginny Carroll
  **MINISTRY OF GREED: The Inside Story
  of the Televangelists and their Holy Wars**
  The story of Jim and Tammy Faye Bakker
  and the PTL wars
  1-55584-216-X Weidenfeld & Nicolson $18.95

- Patsy Sims
  **CAN SOMEBODY SHOUT AMEN!: Inside
  the Tents and Tabernacles of American
  Revivalists**
  0-312-01397-3 St. Martin's $15.95

Biography

- Robert Coles
  DOROTHY DAY: A Radical Devotion
  The author writes as a close friend of Day,
  the radical Catholic woman who fed,
  clothed, and befriended the destitute for
  over 50 years
  0-201-02829-8 Addison-Wesley $17.95

*Dorothy Day (photo by Bob Fitch), from By
Little and by Little: The Selected Writings
of Dorothy Day edited by Robert Ellsberg
(Knopf)*

- Robert M. Miller
  **HARRY EMERSON FOSDICK: Preacher,
  Pastor, Prophet**
  0-19-503512-7 Oxford $36.00

- Michael Mott
  **THE SEVEN MOUNTAINS OF THOMAS
  MERTON**
  Biography of the scholar and Trappist
  monk
  0-395-40451-7 Houghton Mifflin pb $12.95

- David E. Harrell, Jr.
  ORAL ROBERTS: An American Life
  Scrupulously objective, this biography also
  vividly conveys the changes in American
  Pentecostal culture over the past 50 years
  0-253-15844-3 Indiana $29.95

- Leonard J. Arrington
  BRIGHAM YOUNG: American Moses
  0-252-01296-8 Illinois pb $14.95

HISTORY OF FAMILY LIFE

Moving beyond demographic issues such
as family size and structure, recent
writings on the family explore its complex
relationships with the economy and the
state.

- Carl N. Degler
  **AT ODDS: Women and the Family in
  America from the Revolution to the Present**
  A major work on the closely intertwined
  history of women and the family and the
  tensions between them
  0-19-502657-8 Oxford $29.95
  0-19-502934-8 Oxford pb $12.95

- John Putnam Demos
  **PAST, PRESENT, AND PERSONAL: The
  Family and the Life Course in American
  History**
  The changing nature of fatherhood, the
  experience of middle age in colonial times
  and the present, and the historian's role in
  discussions of present-day policy-making
  0-19-504766-4 Oxford pb $8.95

- Michael Gordon, editor
  **THE AMERICAN FAMILY IN SOCIAL-
  HISTORICAL PERSPECTIVE**
  A fine collection of essays illustrating the
  variety of recent historiography
  0-312-02313-8 St. Martin's pb $19.95

- Tamara K. Hareven, editor
  **TRANSITIONS: The Family and the Life
  Course in Historical Perspectives**
  0-12-325150-8 Academic $27.50

- Christopher Lasch
  **HAVEN IN A HEARTLESS WORLD: The
  Family Besieged**
  The more the family is needed as a refuge,
  the less it serves as one
  0-465-02884-5 Basic Books pb $9.95

- Steven Mintz & Susan Kellogg
  **DOMESTIC REVOLUTIONS: A Social
  History of Domestic Family Life**
  An overview of changes in the family in
  the last 300 years, including a look at
  today's family
  0-02-921290-1 Free Press $22.50
  0-02-921291-X Free Press pb $11.95

- Daniel Patrick Moynihan
  FAMILY AND NATION
  0-15-130143-3 HBJ $12.95
  0-15-630140-7 HBJ pb $5.95

- Donald M. Scott & Bernard Wishy,
  editors
  **AMERICA'S FAMILIES: A Documentary
  History**
  As told through letters, diaries, popular
  songs, and marriage contracts
  0-06-090903-X Harper & Row pb $3.98

Special Studies

- John Putnam Demos
  **LITTLE COMMONWEALTH: Family Life
  in Plymouth Colony**
  Roles and relationships within the family
  in the early Pilgrim communities
  0-19-501355-7 Oxford pb $6.95

- Marian Wright Edelman
  **FAMILIES IN PERIL: An Agenda for
  Social Change**
  The president of the Children's Defense
  Fund charts such growing problems for
  both whites and blacks as teen pregnancy,
  joblessness, and single-parent households,
  and offers suggestions for widespread
  change
  0-674-29228-6 Harvard $15.00

- Linda Gordon
  **HEROES OF THEIR OWN LIVES: The
  Politics and History of Family Violence,
  Boston, 1880–1960**
  0-670-81909-3 Viking $24.95

- Robert L. Griswold
  **FAMILY AND DIVORCE IN
  CALIFORNIA, 1850–1890: Victorian
  Illusions and Everyday Realities**
  A study of 400 divorce cases with insights
  into family values, sexuality, parenthood,
  and domestic violence
  0-87395-633-8 SUNY $44.50

- Michael Grossberg
  **GOVERNING THE HEARTH: Law and
  the Family in Nineteenth-Century America**
  0-8078-1646-9 North Carolina $32.00

- Tamara K. Hareven
  **FAMILY TIME AND INDUSTRIAL
  TIME: The Relationship Between the
  Family and Work in a New England
  Industrial Community**
  0-521-23094-2 Cambridge $57.50
  0-521-28914-9 Cambridge pb $19.95

- Barry Levy
  **QUAKERS AND THE AMERICAN
  FAMILY: British Settlement in the
  Delaware Valley**
  Argues that the Quakers played a pivotal
  role in the development of American
  family ideology and the belief that morally
  self-sufficient nuclear households must

serve as the foundation of a republican society
0–19–504975–6 Oxford $24.95

• Elaine Tyler May
GREAT EXPECTATIONS: Marriage and Divorce in Post-Victorian America
Why did the divorce rate rise by 2000 percent between 1867 and 1929? May analyzed over 1000 divorce cases across the country to provide quantitative and personal accounts
0–226–51170–7 Chicago pb $8.00

HOMEWARD BOUND: American Families in the Cold War Era
0–405–03054–8 Basic Books $20.95

• Mary P. Ryan
CRADLE OF THE MIDDLE CLASS: The Family in Oneida County, New York, 1790–1865
0–521–23200–7 Cambridge $32.50
0–521–27403–6 Cambridge pb $11.95

• Richard Sennett
FAMILIES AGAINST THE CITY: Middle-Class Homes of Industrial Chicago, 1872–1890
0–674–29226–X Harvard pb $8.95

• Daniel Blake Smith
INSIDE THE GREAT HOUSE: Planter Family Life in 18th-Century Chesapeake Society
A key period that saw a change from a patriarchal, authoritarian, and emotionally restrained family into a more intimate, child-centered family life marked by close emotional bonds and growing autonomy
0–8014–1313–3 Cornell $32.50
0–8014–9380–3 Cornell pb $10.95

• Winifred D. Wandersee
WOMEN'S WORK AND FAMILY VALUES, 1920–1940
0–674–95535–8 Harvard $21.00

RITES OF PASSAGE

Courtship

• Beth L. Bailey
FROM FRONT PORCH TO BACK SEAT: Courtship in 20th-Century America
0–8018–3609–3 Johns Hopkins $18.95

• Ellen K. Rothman
HANDS AND HEARTS: A History of Courtship in America
Focusing on the years from 1770 to 1920, Rothman traces such practices as engagements, wedding gifts, honeymoons, free choice in marriage, and the value given to romantic love in marriage
0–674–37160–7 Harvard pb $8.95

Youth

• James B. Gilbert
A CYCLE OF OUTRAGE: America's Reaction to the Juvenile Delinquent in the 1950s
0–19–503721–9 Oxford $21.95

• Paul Goodman
GROWING UP ABSURD
0–394–70032–5 Random House pb $4.95

• N. Ray Hiner & Joseph M. Hawes
GROWING UP IN AMERICA: Children in Historical Perspective
0–252–01218–6 Illinois pb $9.95

• Joseph F. Kett
RITES OF PASSAGE: Adolescence in America, 1790 to the Present
0–465–07044–2 Basic Books pb $10.95

• David Nasaw
CHILDREN OF THE CITY: At Work and at Play
0–19–504015–5 Oxford pb $8.95

• Ray Raphael
THE MEN FROM THE BOYS: Rites of Passage in Male America
0–8032–3888–6 Nebraska $19.95

• Marie Winn
CHILDREN WITHOUT CHILDHOOD
0–394–51136–0 Pantheon $13.50
0–14–007105–9 Penguin pb $6.95

Aging

• Daniel Callahan
SETTING LIMITS: Medical Goals in an Aging Society
Argues that society must limit the money spent on care that is merely life-extending and concentrate on relief for the suffering
0–671–22477–8 Simon & Schuster $18.95

• Ken Dychtwald & Joe Flower
AGE WAVE: The Challenges and Opportunities of an Aging America
0–87477–441–1 Tarcher $17.95

• Beth H. Hess & Elizabeth W. Marbum, editors
GROWING OLD IN AMERICA: New Perspectives on Old Age
Essays on public policy, history, and the sociology of aging
0–87855–998–1 Transaction pb $14.95

• Philip Longman
BORN TO PAY: The New Politics of Aging in America
"Adds a fresh perspective on America's failure to invest in the economic well-being of our future generations"—Peter G. Peterson
0–395–38369–2 Houghton Mifflin $17.95

• Alan Pifer & Lydia Bronte, editors
OUR AGING SOCIETY: Paradox and Promise
How the aging population can be turned into a public asset instead of a problem
0–393–30334–9 Norton pb $12.95

HISTORY OF SEXUALITY

➤ **See also Women's Studies & Gay Studies**

Florenz Ziegfeld's soubrette, Anna Held, c. 1897 (photo by W.M. Morrison)

• Allan M. Brandt
NO MAGIC BULLET: A Social History of Venereal Disease in the United States Since 1880
Includes a section on AIDS
0–19–503469–4 Oxford $27.95
0–19–504237–9 Oxford pb $9.95

• John Costello
VIRTUE UNDER FIRE: How World War II Changed Our Social and Sexual Attitudes
How the brutality of war and women's economic emancipation in wartime America set the stage for postwar social change
0–316–73968–5 Little, Brown $17.95
0–88064–070–7 Fromm pb $9.95

John D'Emilio & Estelle B. Freedman
INTIMATE MATTERS: A History of Sexuality in America
0–06–015855–7 Harper & Row $24.95
0–06–091550–1 Harper & Row pb $9.95

• John S. & Robin M. Haller
THE PHYSICIAN AND SEXUALITY IN VICTORIAN AMERICA
0–252–00207–5 Norton pb $29.95

Birth Control and Abortion

• David M. Kennedy
BIRTH CONTROL IN AMERICA: The Career of Margaret Sanger
0–300–01495–3 Yale pb $11.95

• Judith W. Leavitt
BROUGHT TO BED: Childbearing in America, 1750–1950
Birthing, obstetrics, and medicine, and the influence of women on the history of childbearing
0–19–505690–6 Oxford pb $9.95

➤ **FOR OVERSEAS ORDERING INFORMATION, SEE PAGE 1**

- **Ellen Messer & Kathryn E. May**
  BACK ROOMS: Voices from the Illegal Abortion Era
  Frontline tales from women who had backroom abortions before *Roe v. Wade*
  Foreword by Marge Piercy
  0–312–01732–4 St. Martin's $16.95
  0–671–68202–4 Simon & Schuster pb $8.95

- **James C. Mohr**
  ABORTION IN AMERICA: The Origins and Evolution of National Policy, 1800–1900
  0–19–502616–0 Oxford pb $9.95

- **James Reed**
  THE BIRTH CONTROL MOVEMENT AND AMERICAN SOCIETY: From Private Vice to Public Virtue
  0–691–09404–7 Princeton $38.50
  0–691–02830–3 Princeton pb $12.50

Prostitution

- **Jacqueline Barnhart**
  THE FAIR BUT FRAIL: Prostitution in San Francisco, 1849–1900
  0–87417–102–4 Nevada $15.95

- **Anne M. Butler**
  DAUGHTERS OF JOY, SISTERS OF MISERY: Prostitutes in the American West, 1865–90
  "Butler has portrayed the stark realities of prostitution in the American West with sensitivity and insight"—*Southwest Review*
  0–252–01466–9 Illinois pb $9.95

- **Marion S. Goldman**
  GOLD DIGGERS AND SILVER MINERS: Prostitution and Social Life on the Comstock Lode
  0–472–09332–0 Michigan pb $12.95

- **Barbara Meil Hobson**
  UNEASY VIRTUE: The Politics of Prostitution and the American Reform Tradition
  "How and why we regulate prostitution, who America's prostitutes were, and how our practice and attitudes contrast with those of Europe"—Caroll Smith-Rosenberg, University of Pennsylvania
  0–465–08868–6 Basic Books $20.95

- **Ruth Rosen**
  THE LOST SISTERHOOD: Prostitution in America, 1900–1918
  A vivid study of an era in which prostitution became a widespread concern of the American public
  0–8018–2664–0 Johns Hopkins $28.50
  0–8018–2665–9 Johns Hopkins pb $9.95

- **Gitta Sereny**
  THE INVISIBLE CHILDREN: Child Prostitution in America, West Germany and Great Britain
  Twelve runaways and their lives on the streets as the newest breed of prostitute
  0–394–53389–5 Knopf $17.95

CURRENT AFFAIRS: Drug Abuse

- **Shana Alexander**
  THE PIZZA CONNECTION: Lawyers, Money, Drugs, Mafia
  0–55584–027–2 Weidenfeld & Nicolson $19.95

- **David T. Courtwright & others**
  ADDICTS WHO SURVIVED: An Oral History of Narcotic Use in America, 1923–1965
  Life in the drug subculture during the era of strict narcotic control
  Foreword by Claude Brown
  0–87049–587–9 Tennessee $24.95

- **Paul Eddy with Hugo Sabogul & Sara Walden**
  THE COCAINE WARS
  Three investigative reporters follow the story from the jungles of South America where the coca is grown to the streets of Miami where drug money has corrupted at least one in every ten policemen
  0–393–02579–9 Norton $18.95

- **Guy Gugliotta & Jeff Leen**
  KINGS OF COCAINE
  Based on an award-winning series in the *Miami Herald*, the story of the Medellín cartel, the powerful Colombian narcotics ring that controls as much as 80 percent of the world cocaine market
  0–671–64957–4 Simon & Schuster $18.95

- **Abbie Hoffman with Jonathan Silvers**
  STEAL THIS URINE TEST: Fighting Drug Hysteria in America
  The late author of *Steal This Book* argues that the current wave of drug testing is an unconstitutional and dangerous assault, comparable to the loyalty oaths of the 1950s
  0–14–010400–3 Penguin pb $5.95

- **David F. Musto, M.D.**
  THE AMERICAN DISEASE: Origins of Narcotic Control
  A history of the relationship between public outcry against drugs and prohibitive drug laws, including today's anti-drug campaigns
  0–19–505211–0 Oxford pb $11.95

- **Elaine Shannon**
  DESPERADOS: Latin Drug Lords, U.S. Lawmen, and the War America Can't Win
  0–670–81026–6 Viking $19.95

The Vietnam War

"In human terms at least, the war in Vietnam was a war that nobody won—a struggle between victims. Its origins were complex, its lessons disputed, its legacy still to be assessed by future generations. But whether a valid venture or a misguided endeavor, it was a tragedy of epic dimensions."—Stanley Karnow, *Vietnam: A History*

GENERAL HISTORIES

- **Thomas D. Boettcher**
  VIETNAM: The Valor and the Sorrow
  0–316–10083–8 Little, Brown $29.95
  0–316–10081–1 Little, Brown pb $16.95

- **Michael Charlton & Anthony Montcrieff**
  MANY REASONS WHY: The American Involvement in Vietnam
  Includes firsthand accounts by George Ball, William Colby, Daniel Ellsberg, Nguyen Cao Ky, Dean Rusk, and others
  Foreword by George Herring
  0–8090–0172–1 Farrar, Straus & Giroux pb $9.95

- **Dick Durrance**
  WHERE WAR LIVES: A Photographic Journal of Vietnam
  Introduction by Ron Kovic
  0–8090–9692–7 Hill & Wang $35.00
  0–374–52129–8 Farrar, Straus & Giroux pb $14.95

- **Marvin E. Gettleman & others, editors**
  VIETNAM AND AMERICA: A Documentary History
  Documents from World War II to America's defeat in 1975
  0–394–62277–4 Grove pb $14.95

- **Stanley Karnow**
  VIETNAM: A History
  A best-selling 800-page panorama
  0–01400–7324–8 Penguin pb $12.95

- **James P. Harrison**
  THE ENDLESS WAR: Vietnam's Struggle for Independence
  A leading Sinologist covers all sides, including some of the fullest characterizations of the Vietnamese; with a new preface
  0–231–06909–X Columbia pb $14.50

- **George C. Herring**
  AMERICA'S LONGEST WAR: The United States and Vietnam, 1950–1975
  Focuses on the geopolitical and cultural effects; a favorite on university campuses
  0–394–34185–6 Random House pb $11.95

- **Gabriel Kolko**
  ANATOMY OF A WAR: Vietnam, the United States and the Modern Historical Experience
  0–394–74761–5 Pantheon pb $12.95

- **Guenter Lewy**
  AMERICA IN VIETNAM
  0–19–502732–9 Oxford pb $10.95

• Michael MacLear

THE TEN-THOUSAND DAY WAR
The basis for a TV documentary shown in 90 countries, by the first American to report from Hanoi and to interview American POWs
0-312-79094-5 St. Martin's $16.95

• Harry Maurer

STRANGE GROUND: Americans in Vietnam, 1945-1975, An Oral History
0-8050-0919-1 Henry Holt $29.95

• Gareth Porter, editor

VIETNAM: A History in Documents
Introduction by Gloria Emerson
0-452-00637-6 NAL pb $9.95

• Grace Sevy

THE AMERICAN EXPERIENCE IN VIETNAM: A Reader
0-8061-2211-0 Oklahoma $24.95

• William S. Turley

THE SECOND INDOCHINA WAR: A Short Political and Military History, 1954-1975
0-8133-0308-7 Westview $32.50
0-451-62546-3 NAL pb $4.95

• William Appleman Williams & others, editors

AMERICA IN VIETNAM
Public attitudes, government deceptions, and the media's impact on public support for the war; based on documents from the CIA, the media, Congress, and the government
0-393-30555-4 Norton pb $9.95

THE POLITICS

• Larry Berman

LYNDON JOHNSON'S WAR
0-393-02636-1 Norton $18.95

PLANNING A TRAGEDY: The Americanization of the War in Vietnam
0-393-95326-2 Norton $7.95

• Gloria Emerson

WINNERS AND LOSERS: Battles, Retreats, Gains, Losses, and Ruins from a Long War
A *New York Times* correspondent interviews soldiers and draft dodgers, veterans, and their parents, at home and in Nam
0-14-008216-6 Penguin pb $7.95

• Bernard B. Fall

STREET WITHOUT JOY
A military and political history of the pre-American conflict; first published in 1961
0-8052-0330-3 Schocken pb $9.95

• Frances FitzGerald

FIRE IN THE LAKE: The Vietnamese and the Americans in Vietnam
A prizewinning 1973 classic (Pulitzer, National Book Award, and Bancroft) looks at US intervention from the vantage point of Vietnamese culture and society
0-679-72394-3 Random House pb $8.95

• Lloyd C. Gardner

APPROACHING VIETNAM: From World War II Through Dienbienphu
Analyzes events from 1941 to 1954. "Illuminates not only the origins of the Vietnam War, but the creation of the postwar world"—Ronald Steel
0-393-30578-3 Norton pb $9.95

• Leslie Gelb & Richard K. Betts

THE IRONY OF VIETNAM: The System Worked
One of the best scholarly reviews of American political decision making on the war through 1968
0-8157-3072-1 Brookings $28.95
0-8157-3071-3 Brookings pb $10.95

• David Halberstam

THE BEST AND THE BRIGHTEST
The founding of Kennedy's "Camelot" and how America's "best and brightest" designed a disastrous war
0-14-006983-6 Penguin pb $9.95

THE MAKING OF A QUAGMIRE
A personal account of Vietnam in 1961-62 with an inside look at the press in conflict with officialdom
0-394-36860-6 Knopf pb $9.95

• Ellen J. Hammer

A DEATH IN NOVEMBER: America in Vietnam, 1963
Three weeks before the assassination of President Kennedy, South Vietnamese president Ngo Dinh Diem and his brother were assassinated in a military coup that transformed the Vietnam conflict into an American war
0-19-520640-1 Oxford pb $9.95

• Townsend Hoopes

THE LIMITS OF INTERVENTION
0-393-30427-2 Norton pb $7.95

• Nguyen Tien Hung & Jerrold L. Schecter

THE PALACE FILE: The Remarkable Story of the Secret Letters from Nixon and Ford to the President of South Vietnam and the American Promises that Were Never Kept
0-06-091572-2 Harper & Row pb $10.95

• George Kahin

INTERVENTION: How America Became Involved in Vietnam
Edited by Ashbel Green
0-394-54367-X Knopf $24.95

• Myra McPherson

LONG TIME PASSING: Vietnam and the Haunted Generation
0-451-13607-1 NAL pb $4.95

• Herbert Y. Schandler

LYNDON JOHNSON AND VIETNAM: The Unmaking of a President
An authoritative reconstruction of the events leading to LBJ's decision to stop escalating the war and not seek reelection
0-691-02222-4 Princeton pb $11.50

From The Year of the Barricades: 1968 *by David Caute (Harper & Row)*

• Neil Sheehan

A BRIGHT SHINING LIE: John Paul Vann and America in Vietnam
A magisterial view of the war, told through the life of John Paul Vann, the colonel who was "the closest thing the US had to Lawrence of Arabia"
0-394-48447-9 Random House $24.95

• Kathleen J. Turner

LYNDON JOHNSON'S DUAL WAR: Vietnam and the Press
0-226-81732-6 Chicago pb $9.95

The Antiwar Movement

Many general histories include accounts of the antiwar movement and the drift of public opinion against escalating the conflict. Readers should also consult the many recent books on the 1960s, listed in US History since 1877, for broader views of the protests and politics.

• Norman Mailer

THE ARMIES OF THE NIGHT
A first-person account of the momentous 1967 march on the Pentagon
0-451-14070-2 NAL pb $4.95

• Melvin Small

JOHNSON, NIXON, AND THE DOVES
A history of the antiwar movement
0-8135-1288-3 Rutgers pb $12.00

• Nancy Zaroulis & Gerald Sullivan

WHO SPOKE UP?: American Protest Against the War in Vietnam, 1963-1975
0-03-005603-9 Henry Holt pb $10.95

THE BATTLEFIELD

• John S. Bowman

WORLD ALMANAC OF THE VIETNAM WAR
A road map of events and a survey of military action, with biographies of leading officers and government officials and 250 photos
0-88687-272-3 St. Martin's pb $14.95

- Phillip B. Davidson
VIETNAM AT WAR: The History, 1946–1975
A new overview of the fighting, from planning and management to the battlefield, with special attention to the strategies of senior North Vietnamese general Vo Nguyen Giap
0–891–41–306–5 Presidio $27.50

- Van Tien Dung
OUR GREAT SPRING VICTORY: An Account of the Liberation of the South
The war from the side of the senior North Vietnamese general
0–85345–409–4 Monthly Review $15.00

- Ellen Frey-Wouters & Robert S. Laufer
LEGACY OF A WAR: The American Soldier in Vietnam
0–87332–562–1 Sharpe pb $19.95

- Michael Herr
DISPATCHES
The ground war through the eyes of a first-time war correspondent; highly recommended
0–380–01976–0 Avon pb $3.95

- Andrew F. Krepinevich, Jr.
THE ARMY AND VIETNAM
A US Army major analyzes the American military's flawed reliance on the conventional warfare tactics of World War II
0–8018–2863–5 Johns Hopkins $32.50

- Jonathan Schell
THE REAL WAR: The Classic Reporting on the Vietnam War
Reports from attack helicopters, bombing runs, and refugee camps, originally published in *The New Yorker*
0–394–75550–2 Pantheon pb $7.95

- Harry G. Summers, Jr.
VIETNAM WAR ALMANAC
Over 440 articles on battles, weapons, military units and key concepts, with maps and photos
0–8160–1017–X Facts On File $24.95

Strategy

- James W. Gibson
THE PERFECT WAR: The War We Couldn't Lose and How We Did
How American planners slipped into the never-never land of technology and lost touch with reality on the battlefield
0–87113–063–7 Atlantic Monthly $24.95
0–394–75704–1 Random House pb $12.95

- Bruce Palmer, Jr.
THE 25-YEAR WAR: America's Military Role in Vietnam
A four-star general and deputy to Westmoreland reviews key wins and losses
0–671–61178–X Simon & Schuster pb $8.95

- Harry G. Summers, Jr.
ON STRATEGY: A Critical Analysis of the Vietnam War
A leading American colonel explains his ideas on strategy and tells how the US could have won the war
0–89141–156–9 Presidio $14.95

Campaigns and Controversies

- Mark Clodfelter
THE LIMITS OF AIR POWER: The American Bombing of Vietnam
0–02–905990–9 Free Press $22.95

- Eric Hammel
KHE SANH: Siege in the Clouds
An oral history
0–517–57268–0 Crown $25.95

- Keith William Nolan
INTO LAOS
The last major US offensive in Vietnam—invading Laos to crush enemy supply routes
0–89141–247–6 Presidio $18.95
0–440–20044–X Doubleday pb $4.95

- Don Oberdorfer
TET: Turning point in the Vietnam War
Retraces the surprise attacks that ripped across South Vietnam during the Vietnamese New Year in 1968
0–306–80210–4 Da Capo pb $9.95

- Robert Pisor
THE END OF THE LINE: The Siege of Khe Sanh
Uses the experience of American GIs trapped for 70 days on the plains of Khe Sanh to focus on key questions of US overall military theory and practice, especially General Westmoreland's
0–345–33112–5 Ballantine pb $3.95

"We took the gooks' weapons off them and stacked the bodies next to each other. You ever see them safari pictures, when they go to Africa and they kill an elephant? The hunter steps on the elephant and he puts his rifle on it, like a picture of Teddy Roosevelt with a water buffalo. This is what it was like in Nam. They shot up the bodies, then they would pile the bodies up. Then they would call over the news people, like NBC news or CBS. They wasn't out there when we was shooting, but they was out there when it was over for the body count. They took pictures of the bodies strewed out there and the Americans standing around. It was like a trophy. Hey, this is trophy day. What is the hunter's kill?"

Quoted in

Mark Baker
NAM: The Vietnam War in the Words of the Men and Women Who Fought There
0–688–01224–8 Morrow pb $7.95

- James Reston, Jr.
SHERMAN'S MARCH AND VIETNAM
Retraces Sherman's "scorched earth" retreat through Georgia and compares it to the US carpet-bombing of Vietnam in order to explore the moral question of terror against civilians
0–02–602300–8 MacMillan pb $14.95

- Admiral Elmo Zumwalt, Jr., Lt. Elmo Zumwalt III & John Pehkanan
MY FATHER, MY SON
Zumwalt ordered the use of Agent Orange; his son, who was among the soldiers in the sprayed jungles, developed cancer, and his grandchild was born with brain dysfunction.
0–440–15973–3 Doubleday pb $4.50

Personal Battle Accounts

- Mark Baker
NAM: The Vietnam War in the Words of the Men and Women Who Fought There
0–688–01224–8 Morrow pb $7.95

- Matthew Brennan
BRENNAN'S WAR
A member of Blue Platoon of first squadron, 9th Calvary—nicknamed the "headhunters" because of their high kill rate—relives the action of 1965–69
0–89141–236–0 Presidio $17.95

- Philip D. Chinnery
LIFE ON THE LINE: Stories of Vietnam Air Combat
Includes many photos
0–312–02599–8 St. Martin's $17.95

- Lynda Van Devanter & Christopher Morgan
HOME BEFORE MORNING: The Story of an Army Nurse in Vietnam
The traumatic awakening and homecoming of a high school cheerleader who joined the army to nurse the "boys dying for democracy"
0–446–35147–4 Warner pb $4.95

- Frederick Downs
THE KILLING ZONE: My Life in the Vietnam War
Detailed characterizations of men under combat
0–425–10436–2 Berkley pb $3.95

- Bernard Edelman, editor
DEAR AMERICA: Letters Home From Vietnam
Companion to the HBO TV special
0–671–65684–8 Simon & Schuster pb $4.50

- W.D. Ehrhart
VIETNAM PERKASIE
Autobiography by a marine sergeant who became a poet of the war
0–89950–076–5 McFarland pb $13.95

- Ron Kovic
BORN ON THE FOURTH OF JULY
Paralyzed from the waist down in combat, Kovic relates his conversion from warrior and victim to antiwar activist
0–671–52792–4 Simon & Schuster pb $3.95

Troops move up to Chu Phong Mountain, 1965 (photo by Tim Page)

- Robert Mason
CHICKENHAWK: A Shattering Personal Account of the Helicopter War in Vietnam
By a veteran of a thousand combat flights
0–670–21582–1 Viking $17.95
0–14–007218–7 Penguin pb $4.95

- Edward F. Murphy
VIETNAM MEDAL OF HONOR HEROES
The actions that earned medals for 100 soldiers, plus a list of all Vietnam Medal of Honor recipients
0–345–33890–1 Ballantine pb $8.95

- Tim O'Brien
IF I DIE IN A COMBAT ZONE
Combat in the sniper-filled tunnels and the minefields of My Lai
0–440–34311–9 Dell pb $4.50

- Al Santoli
EVERYTHING WE HAD: An Oral History of the Vietnam War By 33 American Soldiers Who Fought It
0–345–32279–7 Ballantine pb $3.95

- Wallace Terry
BLOODS: An Oral History of the Vietnam War by Black Veterans
Blacks left the civil rights movement at home to meet racism, drugs, and special Communist propaganda in Vietnam
0–345–31197–3 Ballantine pb $4.50

- John Trotti
PHANTOM OVER VIETNAM
A fighter pilot tells how it felt
0–891–41188–7 Presidio $17.95

- Keith Walker
A PIECE OF MY HEART: The Stories of Twenty-Six American Women Who Served in Vietnam
0–891–41–241–7 Ballantine pb $18.95

- Kim Willenson, with correspondents of Newsweek
THE BAD WAR: An Oral History of the Vietnam Conflict
From the "grunt" to White House aide Alexander Haig and antiwar activist Joan Baez
0–452–26063–9 NAL pb $8.95

Bantam Illustrated History

These 18 books make up the new Illustrated History of the Vietnam War series:

- James R. Arnold
ARMOR
The M-113 personnel carrier and the M-48 tank proving themselves
0–553–34347–5 Bantam pb $6.95

ARTILLERY
The unique development of a system linking hilltop fire support bases
0–553–34319–X Bantam pb $6.95

RANGERS
The life of the jungle fighter
0–553–34509–5 Bantam pb $6.95

- F. Clifton Berry, Jr.
AIR CAV
The story of the 1st Air Cavalry, pioneers in air mobility
0–553–34569–9 Bantam pb $6.95

CHARGERS
The 196th Infantry Brigade, lightly equipped and highly mobile for hand-to-hand combat
0–553–34347–5 Bantam pb $6.95

GADGET WARFARE
Some of the often bizarre tools created for the war
0–553–34547–8 Bantam pb $6.95

SKY SOLDIERS
Life with the 173rd Airborne, the first major US ground combat unit to launch offensive operations with parachute attacks in Vietnam
0–553–34507–9 Bantam pb $6.95

STRIKE AIRCRAFT
The men and machines behind aerial combat
0–553–34508–7 Bantam pb $6.95

- John L. Cook
DUST OFF
0–553–34550–8 Bantam pb $6.95

- Robert F. Dorr
SKYRAIDER
How a World War II piston-engine plane fought in the jet-age war
0–553–43548–6 Bantam pb $6.95

- Mike Ewing
KHE SANH
Americans under siege
0–553–34458–7 Bantam pb $6.95

- Edward C. Ezell
PERSONAL FIREPOWER
The behind-the-scenes arms race changed the way the war was fought
0–553–34549–4 Bantam pb $6.95

- John Forbes & Robert Williams
RIVERINE FORCE
The story of the brown water navy's attempt to secure South Vietnam's 3500 miles of waterways
0–553–34317–3 Bantam pb $6.95

- Tom Mangold & John Penycate
TUNNEL WARFARE
A harrowing account of the "tunnel rats" who entered 200 miles of secret tunnel networks around Saigon for hand-to-hand combat
0–553–343–18–1 Bantam pb $6.95

- Edward Marolda
CARRIER OPERATIONS
A look at the Seventh Fleet, the landing and takeoff strips for the heaviest bombing of the war
0553–34348–3 Bantam pb $6.95

- Michael O'Leary & John Guilmartin
HELICOPTERS
For the first time helicopters were an essential part of war
0–553–34506–0 Bantam pb $6.95

- Edwin H. Simmons
MARINES
The first troops to land and last to leave
0–553–34448–X Bantam pb $6.95

- Jack Shulimson
TET-1968
0–553–34582–6 Bantam pb $6.95

THE CAMBODIAN CONFLICT

- Elizabeth Becker
WHEN THE WAR WAS OVER: Cambodia's Revolution and the Voices of Its People
A *Washington Post* reporter covers the revolution and destruction that followed the Khmer Rouge
0–671–64559–5 Simon & Schuster pb $9.95

- William Shawcross
SIDESHOW: Kissinger, Nixon and the Destruction of Cambodia
Politics and intrigue in the last stages of the war; secret bombing raids and the role of Kissinger, Nixon, and other high officials
0–671–64103–4 Simon & Schuster pb $12.95

THE QUALITY OF MERCY: Cambodia, Holocaust and Modern Conscience
The sequel to *Sideshow* focuses on the 1979 Cambodian famine and the world's response to it
0–671–44022–5 Simon & Schuster pb $4.98

- Molyda Szymusiak
THE STONES CRY OUT: A Cambodian Childhood, 1975–1980
War from the rarely heard voice of a child. "A story of terror, struggle and death, sprinkled with moments of tenderness"— *NY Times*
0–8090–1534–X Hill & Wang pb $8.95

The Killing Fields

Haing Ngor & Roger Warner
HAING NGOR: A Cambodian Odyssey
The real-life story of the Cambodian doctor who starred in *The Killing Fields*
0–02–589330–0 Macmillan $19.95

Sydney H. Schanberg
THE DEATH AND LIFE OF DITH PRAN
The relationship between Schanberg, the *New York Times* correspondent in Cambodia, and his assistant, who fell into the hands of the Khmer Rouge; the basis for the film *The Killing Fields*
0–14–008457–6 Penguin pb $5.95

THE AFTERMATH

• **Loren Baritz**
BACKFIRE: A History of How American Culture Led Us into Vietnam and Made Us Fight the Way We Did
Suggests that Americans let go of old myths and expanded their self-knowledge as a result of Vietnam—an experience as important as the military losses and lessons of the war
0–345–33121–4 Ballantine pb $3.95

• **William Broyles, Jr.**
BROTHERS IN ARMS: A Journey from War to Peace
One of the first vets to return to Nam in 1984, Broyles confronted old enemy soldiers, families, and battle sites to find peace of mind
0–394–54911–2 Knopf $17.95

• **Geoffrey Clifford**
VIETNAM: The Land We Never Knew
A former army helicopter pilot shot this beautiful collection of color photos of contemporary Vietnam
0–87701–597–X Chronicle $29.95
0–87701–597–X Chronicle pb $18.95

• **David Dellinger**
VIETNAM REVISITED: From Covert Action to Invasion to Reconstruction
A sympathetic eye on Vietnam, based on a 1985 visit by a leading activist of the 1960s
0–89608–320–9 South End $25.00

• **Peter Goldman & Tony Fuller**
CHARLIE COMPANY: What Vietnam Did to Us
A *Newsweek* team meets 65 soldiers who recall their life in Nam and at home in 1981–82
0–345–31496–4 Ballantine pb $3.95

• **Bob Greene**
HOMECOMING: When the Soldiers Returned from Vietnam
The best-selling columnist asked readers who were Vietnam vets if they had ever been spat upon. The fascinating letters he received are collected here
0–399–13386–0 Putnam $17.95

• **Laura Palmer**
SHRAPNEL IN THE HEART: Letters and Remembrances from the Vietnam Veterans Memorial
"Helps restore humanity to a generation of young Americans who were depersonalized and dehumanized by the political passions of an unpopular war"—Ted Koppel
0–394–56027–2 Random House $17.95
0–394–75988–5 Random House pb $7.95

• **Al Santoli**
TO BEAR ANY BURDEN
An oral history by Americans and Southeast Asians
0–345–33188–5 Ballantine pb $3.95

• **Jan Scruggs & Joel Swerdlow**
TO HEAL A NATION: The Vietnam Veterans Memorial
The inside story of building the memorial in Washington, by a leading participant. An oversized book with many photos and a list of the Americans killed in Vietnam
0–06–015404–7 Harper & Row pb $6.00

• **John Wheeler**
TOUCHED WITH FIRE: The Future of the Vietnam Generation
The vet who helped create Washington's Vietnam Veterans Memorial examines the cultural issues provoked by the war
0–380–69886–2 Avon pb $3.98

LITERATURE: Fiction and Poetry

• **James Amos**
THE MEMORIAL: A Novel of the Vietnam War
0–517–56971–X Crown $19.95

• **Jimmy Breslin**
TABLE MONEY
Vietnam memories haunt troubled, hard-drinking Congressional Medal of Honor winner
0–14–010046–6 Penguin pb $4.95

• **Philip Caputo**
INDIAN COUNTRY
0–553–05187–3 Bantam $18.95
0–553–27029–X Bantam pb $4.95

• **Charles Darden**
NO BUGLES, NO DRUMS
A favorite of vets for pinning down the way it felt
0–380–69260–0 Avon pb $3.50

• **John M. Del Vecchio**
THE THIRTEENTH VALLEY
The day-by-day progress of a platoon over two weeks on an operation
0–553–26020–0 Bantam pb $4.95

• **Graham Greene**
THE QUIET AMERICAN
Suspense, romance and international intrigue during the French occupation of Vietnam
0–14–001792–5 Penguin pb $4.95

• **Jon Hasford**
THE SHORT TIMERS
The inspiration for Stanley Kubrick's *Full Metal Jacket*
0–553–27945–9 Bantam pb $3.95

• **Larry Heinemann**
PACO'S STORY
The lone survivor of an attack that killed his 90-man company returns to civilian life as a Valium-popping dishwasher in a small-town cafe. Winner of the National Book Award (1987)
0–374–22847–7 Farrar, Straus & Giroux $15.95
0–14–010085–7 Penguin pb $4.50

• **Franklin Allen Leib**
THE FIRE DREAM
"The battle scenes are hair-raising, and honor—a concept that has been sadly unfashionable for a long time—returns sounding wonderful"—*Kirkus Reviews*
0–89141–334–0 Presidio $19.95

• **Steve Mason**
JOHNNY'S SONG: Poetry of a Vietnam Veteran
0–671–66381–X Simon & Schuster pb $6.95

• **Tim O'Brien**
GOING AFTER CACCIATO
A soldier dreams he and his platoon pursue a deserter on a fantastic voyage to Paris
0–440–32965–5 Doubleday pb $4.95

• **Nicholas Proffitt**
GARDENS OF STONE
Surreal images of Vietnam blur past and present, dreams and reality
0–88184–312–1 Carroll & Graf pb $4.50

• **Elizabeth Ann Scarborough**
THE HEALER'S WAR
A novel about the life of a military nurse in Vietnam
0–385–24828–8 Doubleday $17.95

• **James Webb, Jr.**
FIELDS OF FIRE
0–553–25679–3 Bantam pb $4.50

• **Stephen Wright**
MEDITATIONS IN GREEN: A Novel of Vietnam
The corruption and decay of Spec. 4 Griffin, who had planned to glide through the war untouched
0–684–18010–3 Scribners $14.95
0–684–18973–9 Scribners pb $8.95

Canada

The world's second-largest nation (in area) has a population smaller than California's; 90 percent of the 25 million Canadians occupy just 10 percent of the land. The theory "fewer people, less bother," may help explain Canada's relatively smooth political ride over the past two centuries. A slight tremor was registered in 1967 when De Gaulle uttered his *"Vive le Québec libre!"* exhortation, after which separatist sentiment occasionally developed into urban terrorist episodes. Fifteen years later, the Constitution Act formalized the already existing state of independence from Britain.

In more recent times, there have been problems related to a significant influx of immigrants, more than five million in all since World War II. A certain amount of regional push-and-pull has brought an acceleration of domestic redistribution policies. Internationally, Canada has matured from a somewhat subservient posture into a role of more self-assertive nationhood—particularly in relation to the United States.

GENERAL HISTORIES

● P.W. Fox, editor
POLITICS: Canada
0–07–549211–3 McGraw-Hill pb $19.95

● R. Cole Harris, editor
HISTORICAL ATLAS OF CANADA 1: From the Beginning to 1800
Seventy full-color double-page plates illuminate the impact of the Europeans on Canada, paying close attention to individual frontier settlements. Volumes on the 19th and 20th centuries are forthcoming
0–8020–2495–5 Toronto $100.00

Jacques Cartier

● Kenneth MacNaught
THE PENGUIN HISTORY OF CANADA
The British dominion from Champlain, the first French explorer, to Trudeau, the last French prime minister
0–14–011033–X Penguin pb $7.95

● William L. Morton
THE CANADIAN IDENTITY
An interpretation of the history and distinctive national character of Canadians and their attitudes towards Britain and America
0–8020–6139–7 Toronto pb $9.95

● R.T. Naylor
CANADA IN THE EUROPEAN AGE, 1453–1919
0–919573–70–3 New Star $39.95
0–919573–69–X New Star pb $19.95

● Doug Owram
PROMISE OF EDEN: The Canadian Expansionist Movement and the Idea of the West
How 19th-century opinions about the Northwest changed from despising it as an inhospitable region to seeing it as a land of opportunity
0–8020–6385–3 Toronto $13.95

● John Porter
VERTICAL MOSAIC: An Analysis of Social Class and Power in Canada
0–8020–6055–2 Toronto pb $16.95

● Ogden Tanner
THE CANADIANS
The romance of the Canadian Northwest; part of the Time-Life Old West Series
0–8094–1543–7 Silver, Burdett & Ginn $19.95

● George Woodcock
THE CANADIANS
An illustrated story of the weaving of different races into a people; by a leading Canadian student of European history
0–674–09335–6 Harvard $22.50

Colonial Times

● James Axtell
THE INVASION WITHIN: The Contest of Cultures in Colonial North America
Relations between root cultures in Canada—Indian, French, and English
0–19–504154–2 Oxford pb $11.95

● Pierre Berton
THE INVASION OF CANADA: 1812–1813
A popular history of the War of 1812 and what led up to it
0–14–010855–6 Penguin pb $4.95

FLAMES ACROSS THE BORDER: 1813–1814
A continuation of *The Invasion of Canada*
0–14–010888–2 Penguin pb $4.95

● Peter C. Newman
COMPANY OF ADVENTURERS: The Story of the Hudson's Bay Company
The expansion into the North American wilderness of the world's largest trading company
0–14–010139–X Penguin pb $7.95

CAESARS OF THE WILDERNESS: The Story of the Hudson's Bay Company
The eventful tale of the trading post that systematically conquered the vast territory that is modern Canada
0–14–011456–4 Penguin pb $8.95

● Francis Parkman
FRANCE AND ENGLAND IN NORTH AMERICA
Two great empires maneuver for dominance on hostile and unfamiliar terrain; a classic of 19th-century historical writing, despite its obvious biases
Edited by David Levin

Volume 1
0–940450–10–0 Library of America $30.00
Volume 2
0–940450–11–9 Library of America $30.00

● Bruce Trigger
NATIVES AND NEWCOMERS: Canada's Heroic Age Reconsidered
A major Canadian anthropologist reinterprets the history of New France. "A landmark, a milestone, epochal in its field"—*Toronto Star*
0–7735–0594–6 Toronto $35.00
0–7735–0595–4 Toronto pb $18.95

● Robert Wheeler
A TOAST TO THE FUR TRADE: A Picture Essay on Its Material Culture
Edited by Ardis Wheeler
Illustrated by David Christofferson
0–9614362–0–4 Wheeler $24.95
0–9614362–1–2 Wheeler pb $15.95

Immigrants and the West

"In 1869 the Northwest Territories reverted to the Crown . . . In the whole of this western empire there was a settled population of about 7000. Fort Garry, on the present site of Winnipeg, was the hub of settlement. Its population of slightly more than 5000 was composed of Métis (mixed Indian and white), scattered English-speaking farmers, a handful of Americans . . . and a small group of very active Canadians."—Kenneth McNaught, *The Penguin History of Canada*

● Patrick Dunae
GENTLEMEN EMIGRANTS: From the British Public Schools to the Canadian Frontier
0–295–95862–6 Washington $16.95

● Bruce S. Elliott
IRISH MIGRANTS IN THE CANADAS: A New Approach
A focus on a single social group illuminates the migration process from the Atlantic Coast to the Ottawa Valley and the Huron Tract
0–7735–0607–1 Toronto $35.00

● Gerald Friesen
THE CANADIAN PRAIRIES: A History
Immigrant farm families, native leaders, Alberta oil barons, and political reformers in a lively, judicious history of the prairie West; illustrated
0–8020–2513–7 Toronto $24.95

✉ TO ORDER BOOKS AS GIFTS, SEE PAGE 1

Canada at War

World War II claimed 42,000 Canadian lives, a figure slightly smaller than in World War I. Canada's thriving war economy enabled her to offer valuable aid to Britain.

- **Ken Bell**
THE WAY WE WERE
The combat photographer presents side-by-side photographs of Canadian battle sites from Normandy to the Rhine as they were then and as they are now
0–8020–3990–1 Toronto $39.95

- **A.M.J. Hyatt**
GENERAL SIR ARTHUR CURRIE: A Military Biography
Currie, the "amateur" soldier of the First World War, had all the instincts of a professional, and he used them to minimize the destruction of the young troops under his command
0–8020–2603–6 Toronto $24.95

- **Desmond Morton & Glenn Wright**
WINNING THE SECOND BATTLE: Canadian Veterans and the Return to Civilian Life, 1915–1930
"Readers may be astonished," the authors argue, "to find veterans as the focus and the origin of many of the institutions of our modern industrial society. The re-establishment of veterans became a justification for a National Employment Service. If veterans were entitled to income maintenance and medical care, how could legitimate boundaries be set without, at some point, including the entire citizenry?"
0–8020–5705–5 Toronto $40.00
0–8020–6634–8 Toronto pb $17.95

- **Thomas P. Socknat**
WITNESS AGAINST WAR: Pacifism in Canada, 1900–1945
Study of a small but forceful minority in Canadian society, radicalized by the First World War and the peace movement of the interwar years
0–8020–5704–7 Toronto $35.00
0–8020–6632–1 Toronto pb $16.95

- **C.P. Stacey & Barbara M. Wilson**
THE HALF-MILLION: The Canadians in Britain, 1939–1946
Photographs and cartoons supplement this story of the admirable relationship that grew out of the wartime encounter between two quite different peoples
0–8020–5757–8 Toronto $24.95

FRENCH CANADA AND QUEBEC

- **William D. Coleman**
THE INDEPENDENCE MOVEMENT IN QUEBEC: 1945–1980
The coalition that united the francophone business class, middle class, and organized labor in the aftermath of the "Quiet Revolution"
0–8020–6542–2 Toronto pb $13.95

- **John Fitzmaurice**
QUEBEC AND CANADA: Past, Present and Future
0–312–65921–0 St. Martin's $37.50

Samuel de Champlain

- **Richard Handler**
NATIONALISM AND THE POLITICS OF CULTURE IN QUEBEC
Experimental ethnography through rhetorical analysis brings history, sociology, and philosophy to bear on this vexing problem
0–299–11510–0 Wisconsin $39.50
0–299–11514–3 Wisconsin pb $15.95

- **Jane Jacobs**
THE QUESTION OF SEPARATISM: Quebec and the Struggle over Sovereignty
A general view that includes a comparison with the separation between Norway and Sweden
0–394–50981–1 Random House pb $8.95

CANADA TODAY

- **David Bercuson**
SACRED TRUST?: Brian Mulroney and the Conservative Party in Power
0–385–25060–6 Doubleday $19.95

- **Robert Bothwell, Ian Drummond & John English**
CANADA, 1900–45
How the everyday lives of Canadians were shaped by the state and by concrete developments in the economy. The authors examine the political currents running through Canada during two wars and assess their impact on social and cultural institutions
0–8020–5690–3 Toronto $27.50

CANADA SINCE 1945: Politics, Power and Provincialism
A general history of the postwar years
0–8020–6672–0 Toronto $18.95

- **Dawn Fuller**
THE HEART OF JOSHUA
A personal account of a mother's struggle against her infant's heart problems that

also looks into the relative merits of Canadian and US health systems
0–8020–5764–0 Toronto $30.00
0–8020–6675–5 Toronto pb $12.95

- **Hugh Johnston**
THE VOYAGE OF THE KOMAGATA MARU: The Sikh Challenge to Canada's Colour Bar
0–19–561164–0 Oxford $22.00

- **Angela Miles & Geraldine Finn, editors**
FEMINISM IN CANADA: From Pressure to Politics
0–919619–02–9 Black Rose $22.95

- **Thomas Pawlick**
A KILLING RAIN: The Global Threat of Acid Precipitation
0–87156–823–3 Random House pb $15.95

- **Arthur Siegel**
POLITICS AND THE MEDIA IN CANADA
0–07–077866–3 McGraw-Hill pb $11.95

- **Suzanne Zeller**
INVENTING CANADA: Early Victorian Science and the Idea of a Transcontinental Nation
The role of science in the expansion of a local into a transcontinental state
0–8020–2644–3 Toronto $35.00
0–8020–6606–2 Toronto pb $15.95

Canada and the United States

William R. Duggan
OUR NEIGHBOURS UPSTAIRS: The Canadians
A personal view by an old "Canadian hand" in the foreign office
0–88229–667–1 Nelson-Hall pb $13.95

Denis Smith
DIPLOMACY OF FEAR: Canada and the Cold War, 1941–1948
Canada carves its own pathway through the shifting alliances of Allied and postwar politics
0–8020–5770–5 Toronto $35.00
0–8020–6684–4 Toronto pb $15.95

Charles Taylor
SNOW JOB: Canada, the United States and Vietnam, 1954–1973
0–88784–619–X Toronto pb $7.95

Memoirs and Personal Reminiscences

- **Mordecai Richler**
HOME SWEET HOME: My Canadian Album
A collection of lighthearted views of the novelist's native land
0–394–53756–4 Knopf $16.95

- **Laura Goodman Salverson**
CONFESSIONS OF AN IMMIGRANT'S DAUGHTER
0–8020–6434–5 Toronto $15.00

The Constitution

The last legislative link with Britain was severed in 1982 when Queen Elizabeth signed the Constitution Act. Until then (since the British North America Act of 1867), approval from Parliament in London had been required for any constitutional amendment.

● C.E.S. Franks
THE PARLIAMENT OF CANADA
A recent Gallup poll found that a majority of Canadians had little or no interest in Parliament, considering it neither important nor effective. Franks examines the theories of parliamentary government and the proposed reforms to the Senate and the electoral system
0–8020–6651–8 Toronto pb $15.00

CULTURE AND SOCIETY

● Alan Filewood
COLLECTIVE ENCOUNTERS: Documentary Theatre in English Canada
0–8020–6669–0 Toronto $14.95

● Northrop Frye
DIVISIONS ON THE GROUND: Essays on Canadian Culture
The old maestro draws universal applications from Canadian topics
0–88784–093–0 University Press $19.95

● A.B. McKillop
CONTOURS OF CANADIAN THOUGHT
Explores the thought of a number of English-Canadian thinkers from the 1860s to the 1920s. Chapters include "Evolution, Ethnology, and the Poetic Fancy" and "Science, Authority, and the American Empire"
0–8020–6652–6 Toronto pb $12.95

● Edmund Wilson
O CANADA: An American's Notes on Canadian Culture
0–374–98650–9 Octagon $18.00

Latin America and the Caribbean

GENERAL WORKS

● Leslie Bethel, editor
THE CAMBRIDGE HISTORY OF LATIN AMERICA
"A superb work of reference"—Raymond Carr, *NY Review of Books*

Volume 1: Colonial Latin America
0–521–23223–6 Cambridge $82.50

Volume 2: Colonial Latin America
0–521–24516–8 Cambridge $87.50

Volume 3: From Independence to c. 1870
0–521–23224–4 Cambridge $95.00

Inca quipu-keeper from Lines to the Mountain Gods *by Evan Hadingham (Oklahoma)*

Volume 4: c. 1870 to 1930
0–521–23225–2 Cambridge $77.50

Volume 5: c. 1870 to 1930
0–521–24517–6 Cambridge $87.50

● E. Bradford Burns
LATIN AMERICA: A Concise Interpretive History
A lively examination that focuses on the post-independence era
0–13–524356–4 Prentice-Hall pb $26.00

● John Crow
THE EPIC OF LATIN AMERICA
Dated but offers solid information and is still fun to read
0–520–03776–6 California pb $15.95

● Benjamin Keen & Mark Wasserman
A HISTORY OF LATIN AMERICA
A comprehensive overview
0–395–35942–2 Houghton Mifflin pb $25.50

● George Pendle
THE PENGUIN HISTORY OF LATIN AMERICA
"A beginner's guide to the continent . . . lively and full of anecdote"—*Financial Times*
0–14–020620–5 Penguin pb $6.95

● Eric Williams
FROM COLUMBUS TO CASTRO: The History of the Caribbean
0–394–71502–0 Random House pb $11.95

THE PRE-COLUMBIAN ERA

▶ **See also Native American Cultures: Central and South America**

● Nigel Davies
THE ANCIENT KINGDOMS OF MEXICO
0–14–022232–4 Penguin pb $6.95

● Norman Hammond
ANCIENT MAYA CIVILIZATION
An up-to-date survey of recent research
0–8135–0906–8 Rutgers pb $15.00

● Alfred Metraux
THE HISTORY OF THE INCAS
Translated by George Ordish
0–8052–0248–X Schocken pb $9.95

● R.C. Padden
THE HUMMINGBIRD AND THE HAWK: Conquest and Sovereignty in the Valley of Mexico, 1503–1541
A graphic, controversial interpretation of Aztec history and society. "A book in the tradition of the great 19th-century histories: impressive in its form and style, it moves inexorably to its tragic conclusion"—*New Yorker*
0–06–131898–1 Harper & Row pb $8.95

● Jacques Soustelle
DAILY LIFE OF THE AZTECS ON THE EVE OF THE SPANISH CONQUEST
0–8047–0721–9 Stanford pb $8.95

Well before daybreak of the opening day, legionnaires prepared the victims, who were put in close single file down the steps of the great pyramid, through the city, out over the causeways, and as far as the eye could see. For the average person viewing the spectacle from his roof top, it would appear that the victims stretched in lines to the ends of the earth. The bulk of the unfortunates were from hostile provinces and the swollen ranks of slavery. On the pyramid's summit four slabs had been set up, one at the head of each staircase, for Tlacaellel and the three kings of the Triple Alliance, all of whom were to begin the affair as sacrificial priests. All was in readiness; the lines of victims were strung out for miles, with great reservoirs at their ends, thousands of trapped humans milling about like cattle, awaiting their turn in the line that was about to move. Suddenly, the brilliantly arrayed kings appeared on the platform and silence fell over the city . . . great snakeskin drums began to throb, announcing that the lines could now begin to move. The lambs were slaughtered with machine-like precision; as the knife wielders fell exhausted, they were replaced by fresh priests who lifted the heavy blade and let it fall in precise and measured strokes until their arms grew weary; others stepped in without losing a beat. A refinement of mass sacrificial technique was apparent; it took but seconds to dispatch each victim.

R.C. Padden
THE HUMMINGBIRD AND THE HAWK: Conquest and Sovereignty in the Valley of Mexico, 1503–1541
0–06–131898–1 Harper & Row pb $8.95

● Garcilaso de la Vega, the Inca
ROYAL COMMENTARIES OF THE INCAS AND GENERAL HISTORY OF PERU
Born in 1539, Garcilaso de la Vega was the illegitimate son of a Spanish cavalier and an Inca princess. His work is an

account of the origin, growth, and destruction of the Inca Empire, from its legendary birth until the death in 1572 of its last independent ruler
Translated by Harold V. Livermore
Foreword by Arnold J. Toynbee
0–292–77038–3 Texas pb $14.95

• Eric Wolf
SONS OF THE SHAKING EARTH
A brilliant account of the history and society of Mesoamerica
0–226–90500–4 Chicago pb $8.00

THE CONQUEST

• David Carrasco
QUETZALCOATL AND THE IRONY OF EMPIRE: Myths and Prophecies in the Aztec Tradition
0–226–09489–8 Chicago pb $10.00

• Hernando Cortés
LETTERS FROM MEXICO
Written to Charles V between 1519 and 1526, *Cartas de Relación* is a unique rendition of the conquest of Mexico by the conqueror himself
Translated by Anthony R. Pagden
Introduction by J.H. Elliott
0–300–03799–6 Yale pb $14.95

• Bernal Diaz Del Castillo
THE CONQUEST OF NEW SPAIN
Magnificent narrative of the march from the coast, Montezuma's death, and the eventual capture of the capital of Mexico by one who served under Cortés
Translated by J.M. Cohen
0–14–044123–9 Penguin pb $5.95

• Miguel Léon-Portilla
THE BROKEN SPEARS: The Aztec Account of the Conquest of Mexico
0–8070–5499–2 Beacon pb $9.95

• John Lynch
SPAIN UNDER THE HABSBURGS
Volume 1: Empire and Absolutism, 1516–1598
0–8147–5009–5 Columbia pb $15.00
Volume 2: Spain and America, 1598–1700
0–8147–5010–9 Columbia pb $15.00

• William H. Prescott
HISTORY OF THE CONQUEST OF MEXICO & THE CONQUEST OF PERU
Two classics in one volume, dating from the 1840s
0–394–60471–7 Modern Library $15.95

• Garcilaso de la Vega, the Inca
THE FLORIDA OF THE INCA
Garcilaso de la Vega recounts de Soto's march through the jungles, swampland, and forests between Florida and the Mississippi Valley; the first complete English translation since its publication in Spanish nearly four centuries ago
Translated by John & Jeannette Varner
0–292–72434–9 Texas pb $14.95

• Jon Manchip White
CORTES AND THE DOWNFALL OF THE AZTEC EMPIRE
0–88184–461–6 Carroll & Graf pb $10.95

1521: Florida
PONCE DE LEON

He was old, or felt he was. There wouldn't be enough time, nor would the weary heart hold out. Juan Ponce de León wanted to discover and win the unconquered world that the Florida islands had announced. He wanted to dwarf the memory of Christopher Columbus by the grandeur of his feats.

Here he landed, following the magic river that crosses the garden of delights. Instead of the fountain of youth, he has met this arrow that penetrates his breast. He will never bathe in the waters that restore energy to the muscles and shine to the eyes without erasing the experience of the mature spirit.

The soldiers carry him in their arms toward the ship. The conquered captain murmurs complaints like a newborn baby, but his years remain many and he is still aging. The men carrying him confirm without astonishment that here a new defeat has occurred in the continuous struggle between the alwayses and the nevers.

Eduardo Galeano
MEMORY OF FIRE
Volume 1: Genesis
Translated by Cedric Belfrage
0–394–74730–5 Pantheon pb $9.95

THE COLONIAL PERIOD

• Charles Gibson
SPAIN IN AMERICA
A survey tailored to the particular interests of American readers
0–06–133077–9 Harper & Row pb $7.95

• C.H. Haring
THE SPANISH EMPIRE IN AMERICA
The transfer of Spanish modes of government and society to the New World and their evolution in a remote and different environment
0–15–684701–9 HBJ pb $7.95

• James Lockhart & Stuart Schwartz
EARLY LATIN AMERICA: A History of Colonial Spanish America and Brazil
0–521–29929–2 Cambridge pb $14.95

• Lyle N. McAlister
SPAIN AND PORTUGAL IN THE NEW WORLD, 1492–1700
0–8166–1216–1 Minnesota $35.00
0–8166–1218–8 Minnesota pb $14.95

The Age of Piracy

B.R. Burg
SODOMY AND THE PIRATE TRADITION: English Sea Rovers in the Seventeenth-Century Caribbean
The sexual mores and practices of English buccaneers in the 17th century
0–8147–1073–5 NYU pb $12.50

Robert C. Ritchie
CAPTAIN KIDD AND THE WAR AGAINST THE PIRATES
0–674–09501–4 Harvard $20.00

Frank Sherry
RAIDERS AND REBELS: The Golden Age of Piracy
0–688–04684–3 Morrow $19.95
0–688–07515–0 Morrow pb $9.95

Specialized Studies

• C.R. Boxer
THE GOLDEN AGE OF BRAZIL, 1659–1750: Growing Pains of a Colonial Society
0–520–01550–9 California pb $12.95

• Nancy M. Farriss
MAYA SOCIETY UNDER COLONIAL RULE: The Collective Enterprise of Survival
0–691–10158–2 Princeton pb $19.50

• Charles Gibson
THE AZTECS UNDER SPANISH RULE: A History of the Indians of the Valley of Mexico, 1519–1810
Detailed and scholarly, one of the great works of Latin American history
0–8047–0912–2 Stanford pb $17.95

• Colin M. MacLachlan & Jaime E. Rodriguez
THE FORGING OF THE COSMIC RACE: A Reinterpretation of Colonial Mexico
0–520–04280–8 California pb $7.95

• Stanley J. & Barbara H. Stein
COLONIAL HERITAGE OF LATIN AMERICA: Essays on Economic Dependence in Perspective
Six essays on colonial institutions and social attitudes. "The value of this book lies in the demonstration that the peculiar form of direct colonial dependence of Latin America . . . was almost inevitably succeeded by the neocolonialism of the nineteenth and twentieth centuries"—E.J. Hobsbawm, *NY Review of Books*
0–19–501292–5 Oxford pb $9.95

• William B. Taylor
DRINKING, HOMICIDE, AND REBELLION IN COLONIAL MEXICAN VILLAGES
How Indians adjusted to Spanish rule
0–8047–1112–7 Stanford pb $5.95

SLAVERY

▶ **See also US History to the Civil War & African-American Studies**

• Richard S. Dunn
SUGAR AND SLAVES: The Rise of the Planter Class in the English West Indies, 1624–1713
The settlers of St. Christopher, Barbados, Nevis, Montserrat, Antigua, and Jamaica in the early colonial era
0–393–00692–1 Norton pb $9.95

• David Eltis
ECONOMIC GROWTH AND THE ENDING OF THE TRANSATLANTIC SLAVE TRADE
"No other scholar . . . rivals Eltis in tracing the connections between industrialization in Europe and coerced labor in the Americas; . . . in deciphering the covert activities of large multinational slaving firms; in mastering the details of slave ship tonnage, mortality, and voyage time; or in moving on a global scale from the plantations of Cuba and Brazil back to the sophisticated African slave-trading networks extending from Upper Guinea to Mozambique"—David Brion Davis, *NY Review of Books*
0–19–504135–6 Oxford $39.95

• Herbert S. Klein
AFRICAN SLAVERY IN LATIN AMERICA AND THE CARIBBEAN
The evolution of slavery in Europe, Africa, and America, and the life and culture of some twelve million African slaves over five centuries
0–19–503837–1 Oxford $22.95

• Katia M. de Queiros Mattoso
TO BE A SLAVE IN BRAZIL, 1500–1888
"A stunning tale of social and economic relations, of extraordinary cruelty occasionally mitigated by human circumstances"—Shepard Foreman, *NY Times*
Translated by Arthur Goldhammer
0–8135–1154–2 Rutgers $35.00

• Richard Price
MAROON SOCIETIES: Rebel Slave Communities in the Americas
0–8018–2247–5 Johns Hopkins pb $12.95

• Rebecca J. Scott
SLAVE EMANCIPATION IN CUBA: The Transition to Free Labor, 1860–1899
The underlying social process that led to the end of a very profitable institution
0–691–10157–4 Princeton pb $14.95

INDEPENDENCE

"Whereas out of the North American struggle against the English, thirteen colonies became one United States, the Spanish American insurrections and wars prepared the way not for unity but for the emergence of seventeen separate republics. It has been argued that if Spanish American emancipation had been delayed for just fifty years, until railways could be built, such national fragmentation might have been avoided."—George Pendle, *The Penguin History of Latin America*

• David Bushnell & Neill Macaulay
THE EMERGENCE OF LATIN AMERICA IN THE NINETEENTH CENTURY
A clear summary of, and guide to, the politics of the continent
0–19–504464–9 Oxford pb $11.95

• Raymond Carr
SPAIN, 1808–1939
Good background reading for all students of Latin America
0–19–822128–2 Oxford pb $26.00

• C.L.R. James
THE BLACK JACOBINS: Toussaint L'Ouverture and the San Domingo Revolution
The role of the famous revolutionary in the first area in Latin America to cut its ties with the Old World. James's classic first appeared in 1938
0–394–70242–5 Random House pb $6.95

• Peggy Liss
ATLANTIC EMPIRES: The Network of Trade and Revolution, 1713–1826
The network of commerce, revolution, and ideology that bound Britain and Iberia to their colonies in the Americas
0–8018–2742–6 Johns Hopkins $37.50

• John Lynch
THE SPANISH-AMERICAN REVOLUTIONS, 1808–1826
0–393–02349–4 Norton $24.95
0–393–95537–0 Norton pb $9.95

• J.L. Salcedo-Bastardo
BOLIVAR: A Continent and a Destiny
A concise account of the Liberator's career and its relevance to contemporary Latin America
Translated & edited by Annella McDermott
0–391–03399–9 Humanities pb $12.50

Simón Bolívar

Toussaint L'Ouverture, from Before the Mayflower: A History of Black America *by Lerone Bennett, Jr. (Penguin)*

1794: Mountains of Haiti
TOUSSAINT

He came on the scene two years ago. In Paris they call him the *Black Spartacus*.

Toussaint L'Ouverture has the body of a tadpole and lips that occupy almost all of his face. He was a coachman on a plantation. An old black man taught him to read and write, to cure sick horses, and to talk to men; but he learned on his own how to look not only with his eyes, and he knows how to see flight in every bird that sleeps.

Eduardo Galeano
MEMORY OF FIRE

Volume 2: Faces and Masks
Translated by Cedric Belfrage
0–394–75167–1 Pantheon pb $9.95

ARGENTINA

Four times the size of Texas, Argentina is Latin America's second-largest nation, and one of the most prosperous. In the 20th century, however, Argentina has been beset by serious problems. Conservative administrations alternating with military rule produced a sequence of fierce dictatorships spanning much of the century. This pattern was only recently broken by the victory of the moderate, civilian left in 1983. The national economy has suffered from high inflation and a massive foreign debt, casting the political stability of the country in doubt.

• David Bushnell
REFORM AND REACTION IN THE PLATINE PROVINCES, 1810–1852
Post-independence era Argentina
0–8130–0757–7 Florida pb $14.00

• D.C. Platt & Guido Di Tella, editors
ARGENTINA, AUSTRALIA AND CANADA: Studies in Comparative Development, 1870–1965
0–312–04868–8 St. Martin's $29.95

➤ **FOR OVERSEAS ORDERING INFORMATION, SEE PAGE 1**

- Robert A. Potash
THE ARMY AND POLITICS IN ARGENTINA, 1928–1945: Yrigoyen to Perón
With its companion volume below, a study of one of the most important institutions in modern Argentina—the military
0–8047–0683–2 Stanford $32.50

THE ARMY AND POLITICS IN ARGENTINA, 1945–1962: Perón to Frondizi
0–8047–1056–2 Stanford $39.50

David Rock
ARGENTINA, 1560–1987: From Spanish Colonization to Alfonsín
Supplemented by a glossary of Spanish terms and a comprehensive bibliography. "Without question this is the best general history of Argentina in the English language"—Thomas L. Whigham, *Latin America in Books*
0–520–06178–0 California pb $12.95

- Kristin Hoffman Ruggiero
AND HERE THE WORLD ENDS: The Life of an Argentine Village
A vivid narrative of contemporary rural life, revealing on a small scale the larger values of people living on the periphery of the modern world
0–8047–1379–0 Stanford $32.50

- Domingo F. Sarmiento
LIFE IN THE ARGENTINE REPUBLIC IN THE DAYS OF THE TYRANTS: Or Civilization and Barbarism
A classic polemic against gaucho rule in the 19th century
Translated by Mary T. Mann
0–02–851650–8 Macmillan pb $10.95

Juan and Eva Perón

- Donald C. Hodges
ARGENTINA, 1943–1987: The National Revolution and Resistance
The tactics, strategy, and ideology of the Peronist movement. This revised edition includes chapters on the impact of the Nicaraguan revolution and the return of democracy
0–8263–1056–7 New Mexico pb $13.95

- Joseph Page
PERON: A Biography
Juan Perón ruled Argentina from 1946 to 1955. After an 18-year exile in Spain, he returned for a third term as president in 1973. He died a year later
0–394–52297–4 Random House $24.50

- Nicholas Fraser & Marysa Navarro
EVA PERON
"A fascinating, frightening, straightforward look at the ways a private mythology integrated a public personality"—*Cleveland Plain Dealer*
0–393–01457–6 Norton $17.95
0–393–30238–5 Norton pb $7.95

Demonstration in 1983 on behalf of the "disappeared" in Argentina, from The Humanist Tradition in the West *by Alan Bullock (Norton)*

- V.S. Naipaul
THE RETURN OF EVA PERON
Naipaul's meditation on the Evita phenomenon is co-featured in this volume along with *The Killings in Trinidad*
0–394–74675–9 Random House pb $5.95

- Julie M. Taylor
EVA PERON: The Myths of a Woman
Saint, revolutionary, or whore? "An anthropologist's concise and brilliant examination of . . . a woman who broke with Argentine tradition and became a political figure in her own right"—*New Yorker*
0–226–79144–0 Chicago pb $6.95

Los Desaparecidos

In 1976 the military deposed Juan Perón's widow, Isabel, from power and proceeded to wage war against so-called subversives. Over 30,000 people "disappeared." Another 10,000 were executed. After enduring a seven-year reign of terror and a brief, disastrous war with Britain over the Falkland Islands, the Argentine people established a democratic government under Raúl Alfonsín.

- Argentine National Commission on the Disappeared
NUNCA MAS: The Report of the Argentine National Commission on the Disappeared
Introduction by Ronald Dworkin
0–374–22350–5 Farrar, Straus & Giroux $22.50

- Andrew Graham-Yooll
A MATTER OF FEAR: Portrait of an Argentinian Exile
0–88208–145–4 Lawrence pb $7.95

- John Simpson & Jana Bennett
THE DISAPPEARED AND THE MOTHERS OF THE PLAZA
The mothers of the Plaza de Mayo defied government threats by holding weekly silent protests in one of Buenos Aires' great squares
0–312–21229–1 St. Martin's $17.95

- Jacobo Timerman
PRISONER WITHOUT A NAME, CELL WITHOUT A NUMBER
"Ranks with Hannah Arendt's *Eichmann in Jerusalem* in its examination of the totalitarian mind, the role of anti-Semitism, and the silence"—Eliot Fremont-Smith, *Village Voice*
Translated by Toby Talbot
0–394–51448–3 Knopf $12.00
0–394–75131–0 Random House pb $3.95

Las Malvinas: The Falklands

- Max Hastings & Simon Jenkins
THE BATTLE FOR THE FALKLANDS
Military and naval history reminiscent of Barbara Tuchman's *The Guns of August*
0–393–30198–2 Norton pb $10.95

BRAZIL

Occupying almost half the South American continent, Brazil, with its population of over 150 million, is custodian of the mighty Amazon, whose continued maintenance is a matter of worldwide concern. For these and other reasons, Brazil is rightly perceived as a world power to be reckoned with in the 21st century. However, it has not only vast, untapped resources but also one of the world's highest external debts and a similarly alarming rate of inflation. Vibrant and youthful, the nation is seen as a symbol of the future, yet half the population lives in poverty, a condition associated with decades of military and dictatorial rule. The current civilian government was voted in by a democratic election in 1985.

- Roderick V. Barman
  BRAZIL: The Forging of a Nation, 1798–1852
  A new study, published in 1988, that challenges prevailing interpretations by suggesting a more traumatic birth for the Brazilian state
  0–8047–1437–1 Stanford $42.50

- José Maria Bello
  A HISTORY OF MODERN BRAZIL, 1889–1964
  Based on the 1959 fourth edition, the last to appear in the author's lifetime
  Translated by James L. Taylor
  Concluding chapter by Rollie E. Poppino
  0–8047–0240–3 Stanford pb $10.95

- E. Bradford Burns
  A HISTORY OF BRAZIL
  Lively and authoritative; the best single-volume history
  0–231–04749–5 Columbia pb $19.00

- Charles Wagley
  INTRODUCTION TO BRAZIL
  Dated but still an excellent entry into the continent's largest country
  0–231–03543–8 Columbia pb $17.50

Brazilian Society

Euclides da Cunha
REBELLION IN THE BACKLANDS
The brutal campaigns against religious mystic Antonio Conselheiro
Translated by Samuel Putnam
0–226–12444–4 Chicago pb $12.95

Gilberto Freyre
THE MANSIONS AND THE SHANTIES: The Making of Modern Brazil
Translated by Harriet de Onís
0–520–05681–7 California pb $14.95

THE MASTERS AND THE SLAVES: A Study in the Development of Brazilian Civilization
Translated by Samuel Putnam
0–520–05665–5 California pb $14.95

ORDER AND PROGRESS: Brazil from Monarchy to Republic
The rise and fall of patriarchal society by an acclaimed anthropologist of Brazil
Translated by Rod W. Horton
0–520–05682–5 California pb $14.95

Specialized Studies

- Michael L. Conniff & Frank D. McCann, editors
  MODERN BRAZIL: Elites and Masses in Historical Perspective
  Essays on the rural folk, urban workers, immigrants, and the mass media. "The clearest impression I have found in a single work of the origins, evolution, and present

status of class and cultural distinctions within Brazilian society"—Rollie E. Poppino, University of California, Davis
0–8032–3131–8 Nebraska $33.95

- Peter Evans
  DEPENDENT DEVELOPMENT: The Alliance of Multinational, State, and Local Capital in Brazil
  The most important examination of economic development in the past two decades
  0–691–02185–6 Princeton pb $9.95

- Alex Shoumatoff
  THE CAPITAL OF HOPE: Brasilia and Its People
  0–8263–0959–3 New Mexico pb $10.95

- Alfred Stepan
  RETHINKING MILITARY POLITICS: Brazil and the Southern Cone
  0–691–07750–9 Princeton $25.00
  0–691–02274–7 Princeton pb $9.95

- Alfred Stepan, editor
  DEMOCRATIZING BRAZIL: Problems of Transition and Consolidation
  0–19–505151–0 Oxford $35.00
  0–19–505152–1 Oxford pb $14.95

- Steven Topik
  THE POLITICAL ECONOMY OF THE BRAZILIAN STATE, 1889–1930
  Demonstrates that well before the disruption of the export economy of 1929, the Brazilian state was one of the most interventionist in Latin America
  0–292–76500–2 Texas $25.00

The Amazon

Henry Walter Bates
THE NATURALIST ON THE RIVER AMAZONS
First published in 1863. "It remains the basic text, one of the monuments of scientific travel writing"—Alex Shoumatoff
0–14–017011–1 Penguin pb $8.95

John Hemming
AMAZON FRONTIER: The Defeat of the Brazilian Indians
A survey from the mid-18th century to the present
0–674–01725–0 Harvard $29.95

José Toribio Medina, editor
THE DISCOVERY OF THE AMAZON
Classic account of Orellana's 16th-century expedition
0–486–25589–1 Dover pb $9.95

Alex Shoumatoff
THE RIVERS AMAZON
0–87156–771–7 Sierra Club pb $8.95

Roger D. Stone
DREAMS OF AMAZONIA
The destruction of the jungles through unplanned exploitation
0–14–009573–X Penguin pb $6.95

Military Rule in Brazil

- Joan Dassin, editor
  TORTURE IN BRAZIL: A Report by the Archdiocese of São Paulo
  A report on the use of torture by Brazilian military governments from 1964 to 1979, secretly prepared by the Archdiocese of São Paulo
  Translated by Jaime Wright
  0–394–74456 Random House pb $10.95

- Phyllis R. Parker
  BRAZIL AND THE QUIET INTERVENTION, 1964
  "A convincing criticism of US Latin American policy"—Latin America in Books
  0–292–78507–0 Texas $14.50

- Thomas L. Skidmore
  THE POLITICS OF MILITARY RULE IN BRAZIL, 1964–85
  A best-seller in Brazil
  0–19–503898–3 Oxford $29.95

CHILE

Under the thumb of General Pinochet since the 1973 overthrow of the Marxist Allende government, dissenting Chileans finally merged in 1988 to form a coalition concerted enough to reject Pinochet's quest for an extended mandate. It remains to be seen whether the junta's brand of messianic right-wing ideology will prevail.

- Genara Arriagada
  PINOCHET: The Politics of Power
  An in-depth account of Pinochet's manipulation of Chile's political machinery, press and military
  0–04–497061–7 Unwin Hyman $34.95
  0–04–497062–5 Unwin Hyman pb $12.95

- Nathaniel Davis
  THE LAST TWO YEARS OF SALVADOR ALLENDE
  0–8014–1791–0 Cornell $26.50

- Thomas Hauser
  MISSING: The Execution of Charles Horman
  The death of an American in the aftermath of the Chilean coup; the basis for the Costa-Gavras film
  0–671–66432–8 Simon & Schuster pb $6.95

- Brian Loveman
  CHILE: The Legacy of Hispanic Capitalism
  Tension between the Hispanic tradition in Chile and later outside factors—European capitalism, liberalism, Marxism, and the influence of the United States. "The best single volume on Chilean history"—Charles Bergquist
  0–19–505219–6 Oxford pb $14.95

• Paul E. Sigmund
THE OVERTHROW OF ALLENDE AND THE POLITICS OF CHILE, 1964–1976
A detailed account of Allende's government, the Frei government that preceded it, the 1973 coup that ended it, and the Pinochet government that succeeded it
0–8229–5287–4 Pittsburgh pb $14.95

• Jacobo Timerman
CHILE: Death in the South
Translated by Robert Cox
0–394–53838–2 Knopf $15.95

• Peter Winn
WEAVERS OF REVOLUTION: The Yarur Workers and Chile's Road to Socialism
A reinterpretation of the Allende era through analysis of the dramatic seizure of the Yarur cotton mill in Santiago and its widely felt repercussions for Allende's revolution
0–19–503960–2 Oxford $22.95

MEXICO

• J. Bazant
A CONCISE HISTORY OF MEXICO FROM HIDALGO TO CARDENAS, 1805–1940
From the era of independence through the administration of Lázaro Cárdenas, the president who affirmed Mexico's control of its own natural resources, nationalized its oil industry, and distributed millions of acres to the peasants
0–521–29173–9 Cambridge pb $14.95

• Michael C. Meyer & William L. Sherman
THE COURSE OF MEXICAN HISTORY
Revised 1986 edition; a lavishly illustrated textbook distinguished by coverage of the pre-Columbian period and emphasis on social and cultural development
0–19–504201–8 Oxford pb $19.95

• Henry Bamford Parkes
HISTORY OF MEXICO
Originally published in 1938 and most recently revised in 1969. "A remarkably well-balanced and sound interpretation"— *New Republic*
0–395–08410–5 Houghton Mifflin pb $9.70

From the Conquest to the 20th Century

• Jonathan Kandell
LA CAPITAL: The Biography of Mexico City
An anecdotal rather than analytical narrative, focusing on personalities— Cortés, Archduke Maximilian, Porfirio Díaz, Diego Rivera—rather than on economic or political issues
0–394–54069–7 Random House $24.95

• Jacques Lafaye
QUETZALCOATL AND GUADALUPE: The Formation of the Mexican National Consciousness, 1531–1813
"Published in France in 1974, and now excellently translated by Benjamin Keen,

Death of the Niños, from So Far From God: The U.S. War with Mexico *by John S.D. Eisenhower (Random House)*

[this book] is likely to establish itself immediately as a classic of Mexican history, but it is also of exceptional interest for all those concerned with the now fashionable *histoire des mentalités*, and with understanding how a 'national consciousness' develops"—J.H. Elliott, *NY Review of Books*
Foreword by Octavio Paz
0–226–46788–0 Chicago pb $14.95

• Laurens B. Perry
JUAREZ AND DIAZ: Machine Politics in Mexico
Two of Mexico's greatest 19th-century leaders placed against a political backdrop
0–87580–058–0 Northern Illinois $25.00

• Nelson Reed
THE CASTE WAR OF YUCATAN
The great Maya revolt against Mexican authority in the middle of the 19th century
0–8047–0165–2 Stanford pb $7.95

• Patricia Seed
TO LOVE, HONOR, AND OBEY IN COLONIAL MEXICO: Conflicts over Marriage Choice, 1574–1821
Focuses on nearly the entire colonial period in Mexico City
0–8047–1457–6 Stanford $39.50

The Revolutionary Period

• John Mason Hart
REVOLUTIONARY MEXICO: The Coming and Process of the Mexican Revolution
For Hart the revolution broke out during a global crisis and a wave of nationalistic revolution: in Iran (1905), Russia (1905), and China (1911)
0–520–05995–6 California $35.00

• Friedrich Katz
THE SECRET WAR IN MEXICO: Europe, the United States, and the Mexican Revolution
A tour de force exposition of diplomacy and domestic events. "The interplay among

the revolutionary factions, the powers, and foreign investors in Mexico is analyzed in all its complexity"—Helen Delpar, *The Americas*
0–226–42589–4 Chicago $20.00

• Alan Knight
THE MEXICAN REVOLUTION
A prize-winning study

Volume 1: Porfirians, Liberals and Peasants
0–521–24475–7 Cambridge $54.50

Volume 2: Counter-Revolution and Reconstruction
0–521–24475–7 Cambridge $54.50

• John Reed
INSURGENT MEXICO
By the author of *Ten Days That Shook the World*
0–14–006881–3 Penguin pb $4.95

• Ramon E. Ruiz
THE GREAT REBELLION: Mexico 1905–1924
Entertaining mini-biographies
0–393–95129–4 Norton pb $13.95

• John Womack, Jr.
ZAPATA AND THE MEXICAN REVOLUTION
Displays great sympathy for the peasants who made the revolution and their hero who embodied it
0–394–70853–9 Random House pb $10.95

1918: The Mountain of Morelos
RAVAGED LAND, LIVING LAND

The hogs, the cows, the chickens, are they Zapatistas? And the jugs, the pans, the stewpots, what of them? Government troops have exterminated half the population of Morelos in these years of stubborn peasant war, and taken away everything. Only stones and charred stalks remain in the fields; the wreckage of a house, a woman heaving a plow. Of the men, any not dead or exiled have become outlaws.

But the war continues. The war will continue as long as corn sprouts in secret mountain crannies, as long as Zapata's eyes flash.

Eduardo Galeano
MEMORY OF FIRE

Volume 3: Century of the Wind
Translated by Credric Belfrage
0–394–75726–2 Pantheon pb $10.95

Regional Elites

• Alex M. Saragoza
THE MONTERREY ELITE AND THE MEXICAN STATE, 1880–1940
The "Grupo Monterrey," the business elite that transformed the city into the "Pittsburgh" of Mexico
0–292–71113–1 Texas $30.00

• Mark Wasserman
CAPITALISTS, CACIQUES, AND REVOLUTION: The Native Elite and Foreign Enterprise in Chihuahua, Mexico, 1854–1911
Revolution in the northern state south of the Río Bravo and home of Mexico's most powerful regional family during the 19th and early 20th centuries
0–8078–1580–2 North Carolina $27.00

Contemporary Mexico

• Casanova P. Gonzalez
DEMOCRACY IN MEXICO
A devastating critique of the Mexican system
0–19–501533–9 Oxford pb $7.95

• Nora Hamilton
THE LIMITS OF STATE AUTONOMY: Post-Revolutionary Mexico
0–691–02211–9 Princeton pb $9.95

• Lester D. Langley
MEXAMERICA: Two Countries, One Future
0–517–56732–6 Crown $19.95

• Patrick Oster
THE MEXICANS: A Personal Portrait of a People
A journey into the United States' number-three trading partner and number-one source of illegal drugs; published in 1989
0–688–08193–2 Morrow $19.95

• Robert A. Pastor & Jorge G. Castañeda
LIMITS TO FRIENDSHIP: The United States and Mexico
Explores the mutual mistrust and misconceptions that have characterized international relations. "Valuable, timely and fascinating"—*NY Times*
0–394–55840–5 Knopf $24.95

• Alan Riding
DISTANT NEIGHBORS: Portrait of the Mexicans
An excellent study by a former *New York Times* resident correspondent
0–394–50005–9 Knopf $18.95
0–394–74015–7 Random House pb $4.95

Aspects of Mexican Culture

Octavio Paz
ALTERNATING CURRENT
0–8050–0188–3 Henry Holt $14.95
0–8050–0187–5 Henry Holt pb $7.95

• Oscar Lewis
THE CHILDREN OF SANCHEZ
"The stories were taken down by tape-recorder, over a period of years, and under various circumstances. The result is a moving, strange tragedy, not an interview, a questionnaire, or a sociological study"—Elizabeth Hardwick
0–394–70280–8 Random House pb $10.95

FIVE FAMILIES: Mexican Case Studies in the Culture of Poverty
"He was the first anthropologist to insist that there was a culture of poverty which deserved careful ethnographic study, and he invented the method of seeing individuals as they presented themselves within families"—from the Introduction by Margaret Mead
0–465–09705–7 Basic Books pb $10.95

• Carl J. Mora
MEXICAN CINEMA: Reflections of a Society, 1896–1988
Updated with a new concluding chapter
0–520–04304–9 California pb $10.95

• Patrick Romanell
THE MAKING OF THE MEXICAN MIND: A Study in Recent Mexican Thought
Dated but still the only work of its kind
0–268–00165–0 Notre Dame pb $7.95

NATIONS OF SOUTH AMERICA

Bolivia

• Robert Devlin & Michael Mortimore
EXTERNAL DEBT IN BOLIVIA
0–8133–7366–2 Westview $29.50

• Herbert S. Klein
BOLIVIA: The Evolution of a Multi-Ethnic Society
The preeminent American historian of Bolivia discusses one of the most colorful and dramatic nations in South America
0–19–503011–7 Oxford $24.95
0–19–503012–5 Oxford pb $10.95

• Eric Lawlor
IN BOLIVIA
In the tradition of Paul Theroux, a dark and funny journey. Lawlor views Bolivia as a grand opera—with a tragic plot
0–394–75836–6 Random House pb $7.95

Colombia

Colombia is now dominated by the nation-wide violence caused by the thriving drug industry—the homicide rate is more than five times that of the United States. So it is all the more noteworthy that the country is one of the few in Latin America to function as a democracy.

• Bruce Bagley
STATE AND SOCIETY IN CONTEMPORARY COLOMBIA: Beyond the National Front
Published in 1988
0–8133–7207–0 Westview $26.00

• Robert Davis, editor
A HISTORICAL DICTIONARY OF COLOMBIA
0–8108–0999–0 Scarecrow $13.50

Ecuador

• David W. Schodt
ECUADOR: An Andean Enigma
A good survey of a country often neglected in discussions of Latin America
0–8133–0230–7 Westview $26.50

• Mark J. Van Aken
KING OF THE NIGHT: Juan José Flores and Ecuador, 1824–1864
General Juan José Flores rose from humble origins in Venezuela to attain eminence in the wars of independence and the first presidency of Ecuador
0–520–06277–9 California $40.00

Paraguay

• Augusto Roa Gastos
SON OF MAN
An illuminating novel of early 20th-century Paraguay
Foreword by Ariel Dorfman
0–85345–733–6 Monthly Review pb $7.50

• R.B. Cunninghame Graham
A VANISHED ARCADIA: Being Some Account of the Jesuits in Paraguay in 1607–1767
From their arrival in South America in 1550 until their expulsion in 1767, the Jesuits sought to defend the Guaraní Indian against enslavement by European settlers. Threats of relocation led to an uprising, and the Indian army was destroyed in 1756. This tragic story provides the background to Roland Joffe's film *The Mission*
0–7126–1887–2 David & Charles pb $13.95

• Paul H. Lewis
PARAGUAY UNDER STROESSNER
Stroessner, who engineered a successful coup in 1954, enjoyed eight consecutive terms of "unrelenting dictatorship" until his ouster in February 1989
0–8078–1437–7 North Carolina $25.00

• Harris G. Warren
PARAGUAY AND THE TRIPLE ALLIANCE: The Postwar Decade, 1869–1878
0–292–76445–6 Texas $23.50
0–292–76444–8 Texas pb $11.50

Peru

• Henry F. Dobyns & Paul L. Doughty
PERU: A Cultural History
0–19–502089–8 Oxford $22.50

• Abraham F. Lowenthal
THE PERUVIAN EXPERIMENT: Continuity and Change under Military Rule
Evaluates the Peruvian military coup of 1968
0–691–00214–3 Princeton pb $11.50

• Cynthia McClintock & Abraham F. Lowenthal, editors
THE PERUVIAN EXPERIMENT RECONSIDERED
Essays on Peru, 1968–1980
0–691–02214–3 Princeton pb $10.50

  IF YOU CAN'T FIND IT, LOOK IN THE INDEX

The processing of coca leaves in a coca-paste pit, from Cocaine: White Gold Rush in Peru *by Edmundo Morales (Arizona)*

- **Edmundo Morales**
  COCAINE: White Gold Rush in Peru
  A look inside the underground industry
  0–8165–1066–0 Arizona $24.95

- **Ronald Wright**
  CUT STONES AND CROSSROADS: A Journey in the Two Worlds of Peru
  A traveler's account
  0–14–009565–9 Penguin pb $7.95

Uruguay

- **Martin Weinstein**
  URUGUAY: Democracy at the Crossroads
  How the "Switzerland of Latin America" fell into stagnation and dictatorship and then regained its constitutional democracy
  0–86531–290–7 Westview $29.95

Venezuela

- **John V. Lombardi**
  VENEZUELA: The Search for Order, the Dream of Progress
  From the 16th century to the present, with special attention to the creative period 1750–1850. Presents a positive case for the political stability that has evolved out of Venezuela's increased recent prosperity
  0–19–503013–3 Oxford pb $12.95

THE CARIBBEAN

- **Franklin W. Knight**
  THE CARIBBEAN: The Genesis of a Fragmented Nationalism
  Five centuries of economic and social development, emphasizing such areas as the slave-run plantation economy, US influence, and the effect of Castro's revolution
  0–19–502243–2 Oxford pb $11.95

- **Franklin W. Knight & Colin A. Palmer, editors**
  THE MODERN CARIBBEAN
  Thirteen original essays by experts
  0–8078–4240–0 North Carolina pb $12.95

- **Gordon K. Lewis**
  THE GROWTH OF THE MODERN WEST INDIES
  The British and former British West Indian territories from the First World War through the 1960s
  0–85345–130–3 Monthly Review pb $10.00

  MAIN CURRENTS IN CARIBBEAN THOUGHT: The Historical Evolution of Caribbean Society in Its Ideological Aspects, 1492–1900
  How European, African, and Asian ideas became Creolized and Americanized, creating an entirely new ideology. "Written with verve, imagination and passion"— *TLS*
  0–8018–3492–9 Johns Hopkins pb $12.95

- **V.S. Naipaul**
  THE LOSS OF ELDORADO: A History
  The early history of Trinidad
  0–394–72124–1 Random House pb $5.95

- **Catherine A. Sunshine**
  THE CARIBBEAN: Survival, Struggle and Sovereignty
  A comprehensive introduction to the region, organized thematically
  0–89608–304–7 South End pb $11.00

- **Clive Y. Thomas**
  THE POOR AND THE POWERLESS: Economic Policy and Change in the Caribbean
  A historical overview and contemporary analysis of development strategies in five English-speaking Caribbean countries
  0–85345–744–1 Monthly Review pb $12.00

CUBA

- **Hugh Thomas**
  CUBA: The Pursuit of Freedom, 1762–1969
  A monumental work and perhaps the best general view of Cuban history
  0–06–014259–6 Harper & Row pb $35.00

José Martí

The writings of the late-19th century political journalist and activist José Martí had a profound influence on 20th-century Cuban politics. From 1881 to 1895 Martí lived most of the time in New York, where his initial sympathy for American democracy was transformed into an ardent hostility toward capitalism and most of its cultural implications.

José Martí

INSIDE THE MONSTER: Writings on the United States and American Imperialism
0–85345–359–4 Monthly Review $16.50
0–85345–403–5 Monthly Review pb $5.95

ON ART AND LITERATURE: Critical Writings
Includes essays on Goya, Emerson, Whitman, Pushkin, and Wilde
Edited with an introduction by Philip S. Foner
0–85345–590–2 Monthly Review pb $10.00

OUR AMERICA: Writings on Latin America and the Struggle for Cuban Independence
0–85345–414–0 Monthly Review $16.50
0–85345–495–7 Monthly Review pb $7.50

Cuba Under Communism

- **Nestor T. Carbonell**
  AND THE RUSSIANS STAYED: A Personal Portrait of the Sovietization of Cuba
  Assesses the current situation among the emigrés as it traces and indicts Soviet involvement inside Cuba
  0–688–07213–5 Morrow $19.95

- **Edward Gonzalez**
  CUBA UNDER CASTRO: The Limits of Charisma
  0–395–14067–6 Houghton Mifflin $19.95

- **Che Guevara**
  GUERRILLA WARFARE
  Guevara's works and the application of his theories to guerrilla campaigns in Central and South America; with useful maps and chronologies
  Introduction & Case Studies by Brian Loveman & Thomas M. Davies, Jr.
  0–8032–7010–0 Nebraska pb $10.95

- **Oscar & Ruth M. Lewis & Susan M. Rigdon**
  FOUR MEN LIVING THE REVOLUTION: An Oral History of Contemporary Cuba
  0–252–00628–3 Illinois $32.50

  FOUR WOMEN LIVING THE REVOLUTION: An Oral History of Contemporary Cuba
  With its companion volume, examines everyday life in Cuba
  0–252–00805–7 Illinois pb $12.95

- **Carmelo Mesa-Lago**
  THE ECONOMY OF SOCIALIST CUBA: A Two-Decade Appraisal
  A Cuban exile's evenhanded examination of the Revolution's economic performance
  0–8263–0585–7 New Mexico pb $10.95

- Ramon E. Ruiz
CUBA: The Making of a Revolution
Argues that the revolution did not represent a sharp break with the past but grew out of events that had been developing for well over half a century
0–393–00513–5 Norton pb $6.95

- Tad Szulc
FIDEL: A Critical Portrait
The most thorough biography of the dictator to date; a critical assessment filled with good gossip and insights
0–688–04645–2 Morrow $19.95
0–380–69956–7 Avon pb $5.95

- Armando Valladares
AGAINST ALL HOPE: The Prison Memoirs of Armando Valladares
A harrowing personal account of political imprisonment by a Cuban poet who spent 22 years in Castro's prisons
0–394–53425–5 Knopf $18.95
0–345–34403–0 Ballantine pb $4.95

HAITI

- Elizabeth Abbott
HAITI: The Duvaliers and Their Legacy
"This is the best in-depth book on the Haitian situation that I have ever read"—Graham Greene
0–07–046029–9 McGraw-Hill $19.95

- James Ferguson
PAPA DOC, BABY DOC: Haiti and the Duvaliers
0–631–16579–7 Blackwell pb $9.95

- David Nicholls
FROM DESSALINES TO DUVALIER: Race, Colour and National Independence in Haiti
0–521–22177–3 Cambridge $59.50

HAITI IN CARIBBEAN CONTEXT: Ethnicity, Economy and Revolt
0–312–35659–5 St. Martin's $27.50

- Amy Wilentz
THE RAINY SEASON: Haiti Since Duvalier
0–671–64186–7 Simon & Schuster $18.95

> People repeated an old Haitian joke. Jean-Claude has just married the detested Michèle, the story goes, and in honeymooning with her has ended his nine-year honeymoon with the Haitian people. He is in a helicopter, while below him thousands of peasants wave their arms at him and shout. "I can't hear what they're saying," Jean-Claude complains to his pilot. "Go lower, I want to hear what my people are calling out to me." Reluctantly the pilot loses altitude until finally Jean-Claude can hear the collective voice of his people. "Jump!" they are shouting in unison. "Jump, Jean-Claude, jump!"
>
> Elizabeth Abbott
> **HAITI: The Duvaliers and their Legacy**
> 0–07–046029–9 McGraw-Hill $19.95

JAMAICA

- Leonard E. Barrett, Sr.
THE RASTAFARIANS: Sounds of Cultural Dissonance
The best study of this controversial social and religious force. This updated edition includes new information on the impact of the deaths of Haile Selassie and Bob Marley
0–8070–1027–8 Beacon pb $11.95

- Daryl C. Dance
FOLKLORE FROM CONTEMPORARY JAMAICA
With brief critical introductions to each chapter, photographs, and original drawings
0–87049–436–8 Tennessee $24.95
0–87049–566–6 Tennessee pb $12.95

- Melanie Creag Dreher
WORKING MEN AND GANJA: Marijuana Use in Rural Jamaica
0–89727–025–8 ISHI $21.00

- Barry Floyd
JAMAICA: An Island Microcosm
Illustrated
0–312–43953–9 St. Martin's $19.95

- Michael Kaufman
JAMAICA UNDER MANLEY: Dilemmas of Socialism and Democracy
0–88208–204–3 Lawrence Hill pb $9.95

- Michael Manley
THE POLITICS OF CHANGE: A Jamaican Testament
0–88258–049–3 Howard pb $11.95

UP THE DOWN ESCALATOR: Development and the International Economy—A Jamaican Case Study
0–88258–112–0 Howard $19.95

PUERTO RICO

- Raymond Carr
PUERTO RICO: A Colonial Experiment
A dispassionate and disturbing analysis of Puerto Rico's relations with its imperial rulers from the time it was a Spanish colony to the present
0–394–72431–3 Random House pb $12.95

- Arturo Morales Carrión & others
PUERTO RICO: A Political and Cultural History
The Puerto Rican search for identity
0–393–30193–1 Norton pb $10.95

- César Andreu Iglesias, editor
MEMOIRS OF BERNARDO VEGA: A Contribution to the History of the Puerto Rican Community in New York
Oral history of a Puerto Rican laborer in the early 1900s
Translated by Juan Flores
0–85345–656–9 Monthly Review pb $10.00

- Sidney Mintz
WORKER IN THE CANE: A Puerto Rican Life History
0–393–00731–6 Norton pb $9.95

- Edward Rivera
FAMILY INSTALLMENTS: Memories of Growing Up Hispanic
A family's journey from a small Puerto Rican village to New York City. "An intense, living drama of the Puerto Rican diaspora"—Geraldo Rivera
0–14–006726–4 Penguin pb $6.95

- Pedro Juan Soto
SPIKS
Six short stories. "A work of protest as well as compassion, the kind of writing that has almost ceased to exist in the U.S., and whose role is partially filled here now by nonfiction"—William Kennedy, *New Republic*
Translated by Victoria Ortiz
0–85345–331–4 Monthly Review pb $6.00

- Iris M. Zavala & Rafael Rodriguez, editors
THE INTELLECTUAL ROOTS OF INDEPENDENCE: An Anthology of Puerto Rican Political Essays
Thirty-five essays on 19th- and 20th-century colonialism
0–85345–521–X Monthly Review pb $8.50

CENTRAL AMERICA

- Victor Bulmer-Thomas
THE POLITICAL ECONOMY OF CENTRAL AMERICA SINCE 1920
A scholarly study of the five Central American republics by the coeditor of the *Journal of Latin American Studies*
0–521–34839–0 Cambridge pb $16.95

- Thomas M. Leonard
THE UNITED STATES AND CENTRAL AMERICA, 1944–1949: Perceptions of Political Dynamics
0–8173–0190–9 Alabama $21.95

- Stephen G. Rabe
EISENHOWER AND LATIN AMERICA: The Foreign Policy of Anticommunism
In portraying Eisenhower as a virulent cold warrior, the author challenges the revisionists who consider him a model of diplomatic restraint. "Should become the standard account"—Walter LaFeber
0–8078–4204–4 North Carolina pb $9.95

- Ralph L. Woodward, Jr.
CENTRAL AMERICA: A Nation Divided
This revised edition covers events since 1976, including US withdrawal of control from the Panama Canal, the Nicaraguan revolution, and civil war in El Salvador
0–19–503593–3 Oxford pb $11.95

Recent Developments

- Phillip Berryman
INSIDE CENTRAL AMERICA: The Essential Facts Past and Present on El Salvador, Nicaragua, Honduras, Guatemala, and Costa Rica
0–394–72943–9 Pantheon pb $5.95

TO ORDER BOOKS AS GIFTS, SEE PAGE 1

● Morris Blachman, William LeoGrande
& William Sharpe, editors
**CONFRONTING REVOLUTION:
Security Through Diplomacy in Central
America**
The impact of outside intervention in
Central America
0–394–74453–5 Pantheon pb $12.95

● James Chace
**ENDLESS WAR: How We Got Involved in
Central America and What Can Be Done**
0–394–72779–7 Random House pb $3.95

● Martin Diskin, editor
**TROUBLE IN OUR BACKYARD: Central
America and the United States in the
Eighties**
0–394–52295–8 Pantheon $19.50
0–394–71589–6 Pantheon pb $9.95

● Marcelo M. Suarez-Orozco
**CENTRAL AMERICAN REFUGEES AND
U.S. HIGH SCHOOLS: A Psychosocial
Study of Motivation and Achievement**
Looks at students from El Salvador,
Guatemala, and Nicaragua in major
American cities to explain why so many
Central American immigrant youths stay in
school and succeed, and why their success
rate is greater than other ethnic groups
0–8047–1498–3 Stanford $37.50

EL SALVADOR

● Robert Armstrong & Janet Shenk
EL SALVADOR: The Face of Revolution
0–89608–137–0 South End pb $9.00

● Roque Dalton
MIGUEL MARMOL
Testimony of a revolutionary,
documenting historical and political events
of El Salvador during the first decades of
the 20th century
0–915306–68–9 Curbstone $19.95
0–915306–67–0 Curbstone pb $12.95

● Joan Didion
SALVADOR
"Didion has that rare gift, the ability to
take in the essence of a country through
her pores"—Robert E. White, former
ambassador to El Salvador
0–671–50174–7 Washington Square pb $5.95

● Marvin E. Gettleman, David
Mermelstein & others, editors
**EL SALVADOR: Central America in the
New Cold War**
0–394–62345–2 Grove pb $12.95

GUATEMALA

● George Black, Milton Jamail &
Norma Stoltz Chinchilla
GARRISON GUATEMALA
From the democratic revolution of 1944 to
the present
0–85345–665–8 Monthly Review $25.00
0–85345–666–6 Monthly Review pb $9.00

● Elizabeth Burgos-Debray, editor
**I . . . RIGOBERTA MENCHU: An Indian
Woman in Guatemala**
The stuff of everyday life in a Guatemalan
Indian community. "A fascinating and
moving description of the culture of an
entire people"—*Times* (London)
0–86091–788–6 Verso pb $11.95

● Jonathan L. Fried & others, editors
**GUATEMALA IN REBELLION:
Unfinished History**
0–85345–665–8 Monthly Review $25.00
0–85345–666–6 Monthly Review pb $9.00

● Richard H. Immerman
**THE CIA IN GUATEMALA: The Foreign
Policy of Intervention**
The US role in the overthrow of the
democratic government of Guatemala in
1954; a tension-packed account
0–292–71083–6 Texas pb $9.95

● Stephen Schlesinger & Stephen
Kinzer
**BITTER FRUIT: The Untold Story of the
American Coup in Guatemala**
"Tells, for the first time, the whole squalid
story"—Jim Miller, *Newsweek*
0–385–18354–2 Doubleday pb $8.95

NICARAGUA

▶ See also American Politics and Foreign Policy

● Donald C. Hodges
**INTELLECTUAL FOUNDATIONS OF
THE NICARAGUAN REVOLUTION**
Argues that Nicaragua's leaders today are
neither doctrinaire Marxist-Leninists nor
reform-minded social democrats but,
rather, representatives of a Latin American
New Left that incorporates features of
both; by the author of *Argentina,
1943–1987: The National Revolution and
Resistance*
0–292–73838–2 Texas $27.50
0–292–73843–9 Texas pb $11.50

● Anthony Lake
**SOMOZA FALLING: A Case Study in the
Making of U.S. Foreign Policy**
The 1978 Nicaraguan crisis
0–395–41983–2 Houghton Mifflin $18.95

● Neill Macaulay
THE SANDINO AFFAIR
Augusto Sandino, the rebel leader,
anarcho-syndicalist, and opponent of US
intervention, was murdered in 1934 by the
National Guard, on the order of its leader,
Anastasio Somoza García
0–8223–0696–4 Duke pb $12.50

William Walker
Robert Houston
THE NATION THIEF
Fact-based novel about William Walker
0–345–31897–8 Ballantine pb $3.50

William Walker
THE WAR IN NICARAGUA
Reprint of the 1860 edition. The
journalist, surgeon, and soldier of
fortune who became commander-in-
chief of the Nicaraguan army
0–8165–0882–8 Arizona pb $11.95

The Current Scene

● E. Bradford Burns
**AT WAR IN NICARAGUA: The Reagan
Doctrine and the Politics of Nostalgia**
A polemic against Reagan administration
policy and a concise history of US-
Nicaraguan relations from the beginning of
this century
0–06–055074–0 Harper & Row pb $14.95

● Omar Cabezas
**FIRE FROM THE MOUNTAIN: The
Making of a Sandinista**
Translated by Kathleen Weaver
Foreword by Carlos Fuentes
0–452–25844–8 NAL pb $7.95

● Shirley Christian
NICARAGUA: Revolution in the Family
"If you decided to read just one blow-by-
blow account of recent Nicaraguan events,
this should be it"—*Philadelphia Inquirer*
0–394–74457–8 Random House pb $8.95

● Forrest D. Colburn
**POST-REVOLUTIONARY NICARAGUA:
State, Class, and the Dilemmas of Agrarian
Policy**
0–520–05524–1 California $25.00
0–520–06166–7 California pb $8.95

*Augusto Sandino, leader of the Nicaraguan
revolution, 1928, from* The American
Century *by Walter LaFeber and others
(Knopf)*

- Joseph Collins & others
NICARAGUA: What Difference Could a Revolution Make?
Challenges Washington's perception of food and farming in the new Nicaragua
0–8021–3067–4 Grove pb $11.95

- Peter Davis
WHERE IS NICARAGUA?
By the winner of the Academy Award for *Hearts and Minds*. The form of the chronicle, Davis suggests, is one suggested by Richard Hofstadter: "part narrative, part personal essay, part systematic empirical inquiry, part speculative philosophy"
0–671–54618–X Simon & Schuster $19.95
0–671–65720–8 Simon & Schuster pb $8.95

- Christopher Dickey
WITH THE CONTRAS: A Reporter in the Wilds of Nicaragua
0–671–53298–7 Simon & Schuster $18.95
0–671–63313–9 Simon & Schuster pb $6.95

- Richard L. Harris & Carlos M. Vilas, editors
NICARAGUA: A Revolution under Siege
0–86232–484–X Humanities pb $9.95

- Robert A. Pastor
CONDEMNED TO REPETITION: The United States and Nicaragua
"[Pastor] combines a scholar's expertise at research with the firsthand knowledge of a participant"—William M. LeoGrande
0–691–07752–5 Princeton $24.95
0–691–02286–0 Princeton pb $12.50

- Peter Rosset & John Vandermeer, editors
NICARAGUA: Unfinished Revolution
Critics and defenders of the Sandinistas; well-argued on both sides
0–394–62143–3 Grove pb $12.95

PANAMA

- Graham Greene
GETTING TO KNOW THE GENERAL
0–671–55679–7 Washington Square pb $3.95

- Basil & Anne Hedrick
A HISTORICAL DICTIONARY OF PANAMA
0–8108–0347–X Scarecrow pb $10.00

- Ulrich Keller, editor
THE BUILDING OF THE PANAMA CANAL IN HISTORIC PHOTOGRAPHS
0–486–24408–3 Dover pb $8.95

- David McCullough
THE PATH BETWEEN THE SEAS: The Creation of the Panama Canal, 1870–1914
0–671–24409–4 Simon & Schuster pb $13.95

ASPECTS OF LATIN AMERICA

Economic Development

There is an enormous controversy over the origins of Latin American underdevelopment. The three essential books are:

- Fernando H. Cardoso & Enzo Faletto
DEPENDENCY AND DEVELOPMENT IN LATIN AMERICA
The most persuasive elucidation of the "dependency" approach. Suggests that the dependency of Latin America stems not merely from the domination of the world market over national and "enclave" economies, but also from the more complex interaction of economic drives, political structures, social movements, and historically conditioned alliances
Translated by Marjory Mattingly Urquidi
0–520–03527–5 California pb $10.95

- André Gunder Frank
CAPITALISM AND UNDERDEVELOPMENT IN LATIN AMERICA
The most radical exposition of the theory that the North Atlantic countries exploited Latin America
0–85345–093–5 Monthly Review pb $10.00

- Celso Furtado
ECONOMIC DEVELOPMENT OF LATIN AMERICA
0–521–29070–8 Cambridge pb $16.95

Religion

- Phillip Berryman
LIBERATION THEOLOGY
A sympathetic exposition by an American Catholic antiwar activist and former priest
0–394–74652–X Pantheon pb $6.95

- Penny Lernoux
CRY OF THE PEOPLE: The Struggle for Human Rights in Latin America—The Catholic Church in Conflict with U.S. Policy
Argues that the metamorphosis of the Catholic Church is the most significant development in Latin America since the Cuban revolution. "Powerful and important . . . Lernoux writes with intelligence and passion"—*Nation*
0–14–006047–2 Penguin pb $7.95

- Daniel H. Levine
RELIGION AND POLITICS IN LATIN AMERICA: The Catholic Church in Venezuela and Colombia
0–691–02200–3 Princeton pb $13.95

Politics

- Charles Bergquist
LABOR IN LATIN AMERICA: Comparative Essays on Chile, Argentina, Venezuela, and Colombia
0–8047–1311–1 Stanford pb $14.95

- John A. Booth & Mitchell A. Seligson, editors
POLITICAL PARTICIPATION IN LATIN AMERICA
"Must reading for those interested in Latin American politics"—*Journal of Developing Areas*
Volume 1: Citizen and State
0–8419–0376–X Holmes & Meier pb $14.00
Volume 2: Politics and the Poor
0–8419–0406–7 Holmes & Meier pb $14.00

- John J. Johnson
POLITICAL CHANGE IN LATIN AMERICA: The Emergence of the Middle Sectors
A classic that looked to the middle class as the key to Latin American democracy. Discredited in the 1960s and 1970s, it is now making a comeback
0–8047–0528–3 Stanford $15.00

- Brian Loveman & Thomas M. Davies, Jr., editors
THE POLITICS OF ANTIPOLITICS: The Military in Latin America
The first edition of this work brought into vogue the idea of "antipolitics"—the rejection of "politics" in favor of military rule and "personalist" factions. Two countries, El Salvador and Guatemala, have been added to the five—Argentina, Bolivia, Brazil, Chile, and Peru—in this expanded edition
0–8032–2884–8 Nebraska $37.95
0–8032–7928–0 Nebraska pb $15.95

- C.O. Maolian, editor
LATIN AMERICAN POLITICAL MOVEMENTS
Seven hundred legal and illegal political parties, guerrilla movements, and other organizations active in continental and insular Latin America
0–8160–1410–8 Facts On File $24.95

- Bruce Marcus & Michael Taber, editors
MAURICE BISHOP SPEAKS: The Grenada Revolution, 1979–83
A collection of speeches from the late prime minister
0–87348–612–9 Pathfinder pb $9.95

- Guillermo O'Donnell & Philippe C. Schmitter, editors
TRANSITIONS FROM AUTHORITARIAN RULE: Comparative Perspectives
Up-to-date essays on political developments
0–8018–3192–X Johns Hopkins pb $10.95
TRANSITIONS FROM AUTHORITARIAN RULE: Tentative Conclusions about Uncertain Democracies
0–8018–2682–9 Johns Hopkins pb $6.95

- John A. Peeler
LATIN AMERICAN DEMOCRACIES
0–8078–4153–6 North Carolina pb $8.95

- Alfred Stepan
RETHINKING MILITARY POLITICS: Brazil and the Southern Cone
0–691–07750–9 Princeton $25.00
0–691–02274–7 Princeton pb $9.95

- Gary W. Wynia
THE POLITICS OF LATIN AMERICAN DEVELOPMENT
One of the best overviews
0–521–27842–2 Cambridge pb $12.95

International Relations and Finance

- Timothy Ashby
THE BEAR IN THE BACKYARD: Moscow's Caribbean Strategy
0–669–14768–0 Lexington $22.95

- Cole Blasier
THE GIANT'S RIVAL: The USSR and Latin America
Focuses on the post-1970 period. "This is a book that Americans interested in Latin America and puzzled by the Reagan Administration's events there definitely should read"—Wayne S. Smith, *NY Times*
0–8229–3576–7 Pittsburgh $24.95
0–8229–5400–1 Pittsburgh pb $9.95

- Pedro-Pablo Kuczynski
LATIN AMERICAN DEBT
The debt crisis from the high inflation and cheap credit of the 1970s through 1987, when the total amount owed by all Latin American countries was five times their combined earnings from exports. By a former Peruvian cabinet member and investment banker
0–8018–3660–3 Johns Hopkins pb $12.95

- Penny Lernoux
IN BANKS WE TRUST
Exposes the dirty dealing of banking institutions in Latin America
0–14–008794–X Penguin pb $7.95

- John D. Martz
UNITED STATES POLICY IN LATIN AMERICA: A Quarter Century of Crisis and Challenge, 1961–1986
Topics include Johnson's invasion of the Dominican Republic, Nixon's actions against the Marxist regime in Chile, and Carter's negotiation of the Panama Canal treaties
0–8032–3097–4 Nebraska $28.95

- Lars Schoultz
HUMAN RIGHTS AND UNITED STATES POLICY TOWARD LATIN AMERICA
From the early 1960s through 1980
0–691–02204–6 Princeton pb $11.50

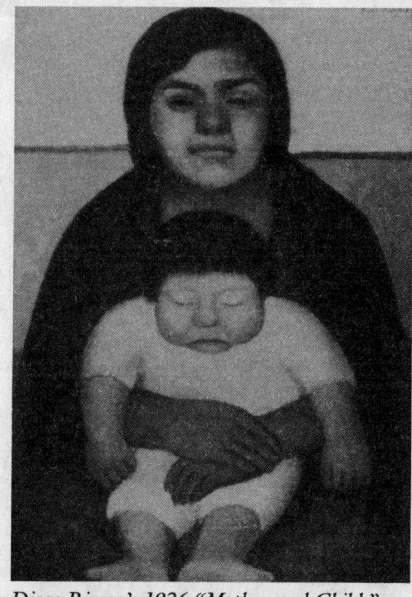

Diego Rivera's 1926 "Mother and Child," from The Latin American Spirit: Art and Artists in the United States (*Abrams*)

- Barbara Stallings
BANKER TO THE THIRD WORLD: U.S. Portfolio Investment in Latin America, 1900–1986
"Stands out for its historical perspective, useful collection of data, sound economic analysis, and cool understanding. It is at the same time scholarly and accessible"— Charles P. Kindleberger
0–520–06164–0 California pb $12.95

- Augusto Varas, editor
SOVIET-LATIN AMERICAN RELATIONS IN THE 1980s
Authoritative, moderate, and richly researched essays by ten Latin Americans
0–8133–7401–4 Westview $29.95

Social Thought, Culture, and Aesthetics

- Julianne Burton, editor
CINEMA AND SOCIAL CHANGE IN LATIN AMERICA
Twenty interviews with key figures of Latin American cinema, covering three decades and ranging from Argentina to Mexico
0–292–72453–5 Texas $22.50
0–292–72454–3 Texas pb $10.95

- Jan Carew
FULCRUMS OF CHANGE: Origins of Racism in the Americas and Other Essays
The Guyanese poet and novelist on racism, exile, and imperialism
0–86543–033–0 Africa World pb $9.95

- Aimé Césaire
DISCOURSE ON COLONIALISM
Political essays by the Martiniquais poet and revolutionary
Translated by Joan Pinklam
0–85345–226–6 Monthly Review pb $6.00

- Ariel Dorfman
THE EMPIRE'S OLD CLOTHES: What the Lone Ranger, Babar, and Other Innocent Heroes Do to Our Minds
Translated by Clark Hansen
0–394–71486–5 Pantheon pb $8.95

- Marie-Lise Garzarian Gautier
INTERVIEWS WITH LATIN AMERICAN WRITERS
Conversations with Mario Vargas Llosa, Isabel Allende, Manuel Puig, and others
0–916583–32–5 Dalkey Archive $19.95

- John Krich
EL BEISBOL: Travels Through the Pan-American Pastime
"The notion of baseball as an international sport is a comforting one; it is our most benevolent, least expensive and most accessible export. It is neutral but not neutered, peaceful but not passive. John Krich has taken this idea and headed south with it"—Tom Miller, *NY Times Book Review*
0–87113–303–2 Atlantic Monthly $18.95

- Jacinto Quirarte, Marimar Benitez & others
THE LATIN AMERICAN SPIRIT: Art and Artists in the United States, 1920–1970
What the Latin American presence has meant to the art of the United States. Works of the Uruguayan Torres-García, the Colombian Fernando Botero, and the Chilean Matta among many others included; 230 illustrations with 100 plates in full color
Introduction by Luis R. Cancel
0–8109–1271–6 Abrams $45.00

- José Enrique Rodó
ARIEL
First published in 1900 in Uruguay, *Ariel* is Latin America's most famous essay on esthetic and philosophical sensibility, as well as its most discussed treatise on hemispheric relations
Translated by Margaret Sayers Peden
Prologue by Carlos Fuentes
0–292–70395–3 Texas $16.95
0–292–70396–1 Texas pb $7.95

RELIGION
AND
PHILOSOPHY

World Religion

"Let us consider the deepest and most fundamental element in all strong and sincerely felt religious emotion . . . Let us follow it up with every effort of sympathy and imaginative intuition wherever it is to be found, in the lives of those around us, in sudden, strong ebullitions of personal piety . . . in the fixed and ordered solemnities of rites and liturgies, and again in the atmosphere that clings to old religious monuments and buildings, to temples and to churches. If we do so we shall find we are dealing with something for which there is only one appropriate expression, 'mysterium tremendum.' The feeling of it may at times come sweeping like a gentle tide, pervading the mind with a tranquil mood of deepest worship . . . It may burst in sudden eruption up from the depths of the soul with spasms and convulsions, and lead to the strangest excitements, to intoxicated frenzy, to transport, and to ecstasy . . . It may become the hushed, trembling, and speechless humility of the creature in the presence of—whom or what? In the presence of that which is a *mystery* inexpressible and above all creatures."—Rudolf Otto in *The Idea of the Holy*

Under this heading we have grouped general and comparative studies of religion, and books that focus on such special topics as mysticism, religious skepticism, and the occult. Books dealing specifically with the major world faiths will be found under a series of separate headings immediately following this introductory section.

CLASSICS OF WESTERN RELIGIOUS THOUGHT

- **Martin Buber**
I AND THOU
A classic of religious existentialism
Translated by Walter Kauffman & S.G. Smith
0–684–15575–3 Scribners $25.00
0–684–71725–5 Scribners pb $8.95
0–684–18254–8 Macmillan pb $4.95

- **William James**
THE VARIETIES OF RELIGIOUS EXPERIENCE
A wide-ranging masterpiece that highlights the personal, subjective, and mystical aspects of religion—an approach that coincides with contemporary tastes
0–14–039034–0 Penguin pb $4.95

- **Moses Maimonides**
THE GUIDE OF THE PERPLEXED
A reconciliation of the Old Testament and Aristotle by the great 12th-century Jewish philosopher
Translated by Shlomo Pines
Introduction by Leo Strauss
Volume 1
0–226–50230–9 Chicago pb $15.95
Volume 2
0–226–50231–7 Chicago pb $15.95

- **Rudolf Otto**
THE IDEA OF THE HOLY
First published in Germany in 1917, this influential work set the agenda for much of 20th-century theology by attempting to isolate an irreducible, nonrational sense of mystery in religious experience
Translated by John W. Harvey
0–19–500210–5 Oxford pb $8.95

- **Blaise Pascal**
PENSEES
The 17th-century mathematician's great work consists of aphoristic notes toward a defense of Christian faith. Pascal is most eloquent in confronting the fragility of human reason
Translated by A.J. Krailsheimer
0–14–044171–9 Penguin pb $4.95

- **Evelyn Underhill**
MYSTICISM
This 1911 book is still the best introduction to the subject, offering copious quotations from mystical texts in all the major traditions, placing mysticism in relation to psychology, theology, and symbolism, and tracing the characteristic stages of spiritual illumination
0–452–00840–9 NAL pb $12.95

- **Simone Weil**
WAITING FOR GOD
Reflections on the spiritual life by the brilliant and ill-fated French Catholic convert
0–06–090295–7 Harper & Row pb $6.95

Our normal waking consciousness, rational consciousness as we call it, is but one special type of consciousness, whilst all about it, parted from it by the filmiest of screens, there lie potential forms of consciousness entirely different. We may go through life without suspecting their existence; but apply the requisite stimulus, and at a touch they are there in all their completeness, definite types of mentality which probably somewhere have their field of application and adaptation. No account of the universe in its totality can be final which leaves these other forms of consciousness quite disregarded. How to regard them is the question—for they are so discontinuous with ordinary consciousness. Yet they may determine attitudes though they cannot furnish formulas, and open a region though they fail to give a map. At any rate they forbid a premature closing of our accounts with reality.

William James
THE VARIETIES OF RELIGIOUS EXPERIENCE
0–14–039034–0 Penguin pb $4.95

GENERAL SURVEYS AND STUDIES

- **Robert O. Ballou, editor**
THE PORTABLE WORLD BIBLE
Selections from the scriptures of major world religions
0–14–015005–6 Penguin pb $8.95

- **Jan De Vries**
PERSPECTIVES IN THE HISTORY OF RELIGIONS
An excellent survey of literary, philosophical, anthropological, and psychological views of religion since ancient times
Translated with an introduction by Kees W. Bolle
0–520–03300–0 California pb $7.95

- **Mircea Eliade**
A HISTORY OF RELIGIOUS IDEAS
A monumental work, one of the crowning achievements of the great Romanian scholar who died in 1986. In these three volumes Eliade traces religious development from prehistory to the Reformation

Volume 1: From the Stone Age to the Eleusinian Mysteries
Translated by Willard R. Trask
0–226–20400–6 Chicago $27.50
0–226–20401–4 Chicago pb $16.95

Volume 2: From Gautama Buddha to the Triumph of Christianity
Translated by Willard R. Trask
0–226–20402–2 Chicago $27.50
0–226–20403–0 Chicago pb $16.95

Volume 3: From Muhammad to the Age of Reforms
Translated by Alf Hiltebeitel & Diane Apostolos-Cappadona
0–226–20404–9 Chicago $27.50
0–226–20405–7 Chicago pb $16.95

- **Michael Novak**
ASCENT OF THE MOUNTAIN, FLIGHT OF THE DOVE: An Invitation to Religious Studies
One of the best brief introductions, by a Catholic scholar
0–06–066322–7 Harper & Row pb $7.95

- **Geoffrey Parrinder, editor**
WORLD RELIGIONS: From Ancient History to the Present
Clear, historically comprehensive accounts by leading scholars, profusely illustrated
0–87196–129–6 Facts on File $29.95
0–8160–1289–X Facts on File pb $15.95

- **Ninian Smart**
THE RELIGIOUS EXPERIENCE OF MANKIND
This illustrated historical survey by an eminent comparative religion scholar is widely used as a college text
0–684–18077–4 Scribners $30.00
0–02–412130–4 Macmillan pb $24.50

- **Huston Smith**
THE RELIGIONS OF MAN
A good introductory account of the beliefs of the major world religions
0–06–090043–1 Harper & Row pb $7.95

Religious Poetry

Karen Armstrong, editor
TONGUES OF FIRE: An Anthology of Religious and Poetic Experience
A collection that ranges widely over world poetry, from ancient to contemporary, in order to illustrate different modes of spiritual experience
0–14–058566–4 Penguin pb $7.95

TO ORDER ANY BOOK IN THIS CATALOG, ASK YOUR BOOKSELLER OR CALL 1-800-882-8770

F. Forrester Church &
Terrence J. Mulry, editors
**THE MACMILLAN BOOK OF
EARLIEST CHRISTIAN HYMNS**
Hymns, songs, and liturgy from various
strands of early Christian tradition
0–02–525581–9 Macmillan $19.95

Peter Levi, editor
**THE PENGUIN BOOK OF ENGLISH
CHRISTIAN VERSE**
A large and well-chosen anthology
0–14–058602–4 Penguin pb $7.95

Peter Levi, translator
THE PSALMS
0–14–044319–3 Penguin pb $6.95

Lucien Stryk & Takashi Ikemoto,
editors
**THE PENGUIN BOOK OF ZEN
POETRY**
Poems from the Chinese and Japanese
0–14–058599–0 Penguin pb $6.95

COMPARATIVE RELIGION

• Arthur J. Arberry
RELIGION IN THE MIDDLE EAST
A great Middle Eastern scholar provides
detailed historical accounts of major and
minor religious developments. A two-
volume set
0–521–07400–2 Cambridge $110.00
Volume 1
0–521–20543–3 Cambridge $62.50
Volume 2
0–521–20544–1 Cambridge $59.50

• Julia Ching
CONFUCIANISM AND CHRISTIANITY
Ching discusses where the two religions
agree or fundamentally differ on matters of
God, meditation, ethics, and conscience,
and sketches the historical encounters
between the faiths
0–87011–303–8 Kodansha $16.95

• Mary Douglas
**PURITY AND DANGER: An Analysis of
the Concepts of Pollution and Taboo**
0–7448–0011–0 RC&H pb $6.95

**NATURAL SYMBOLS: Explorations in
Cosmology**
A British anthropologist's incisive
comments on religion and social order
0–394–71105–X Random House pb $7.95

ELAINE PAGELS:
Early Western Religion

Herbert Musurillo
**THE ACTS OF THE CHRISTIAN
MARTYRS**
Original sources in Greek and Latin
together with excellent translations. I
find these accounts powerful and
moving; they also describe the social,
political, and religious pressure on
Christians during the early centuries
0–19–826806–8 Oxford $52.00

Hans Jonas
GNOSTIC RELIGION
The classic early study of the Gnostic
religion written from an Existentialist
viewpoint before the discovery of a
major library of gnostic sources at Nag
Hammadi in Upper Egypt in 1945
0–8070–5799–1 Beacon pb $10.95

James Robinson, editor
THE NAG HAMMADI LIBRARY
The complete collection of early
Christian sources discovered at Nag
Hammadi, including *The Gospel of
Thomas* and *The Gospel of Mary
Magdalene*
0–06–066934–9 Harper & Row $24.95
0–06–066933–0 Harper & Row pb $11.50

Bentley Layton
THE GNOSTIC SCRIPTURES
A recent translation of many major
gnostic sources, well-annotated with
good historical commentary
0–385–17447–0 Doubleday pb $35.00

Howard Clark Kee
**JESUS IN HISTORY: An Approach to
the Study of the Gospels**
A lucid presentation of sources for
study of the gospels, and of ways that
scholarly view of the New Testament
have changed in the past hundred years
0–15–547382–4 HBJ pb $13.00

Victor Tcherikover
**HELLENISTIC CIVILIZATION AND
THE JEWS**
An illuminating, detailed study of
pressures for assimilation—and
resistance to it—among Jews of the
Hellenistic era
Translated by S. Applebaum
0–689–70248–5 Atheneum pb $12.95

E.R. Dodds
**PAGAN AND CHRISTIAN IN AN
AGE OF ANXIETY: Some Aspects of
Religious Experience from Marcus
Aurelius to Constantine**
0–393–00545–3 Norton pb $5.95

Rosemary Ruether
**FAITH AND FRATRICIDE: The
Theological Roots of Anti-Semitism**
A ground-breaking book by a Roman
Catholic scholar who charges—quite
convincingly—that anti-Jewish attitudes
are built into the history of the New
Testament itself
0–8164–2263–X Harper & Row pb $8.95

Elisabeth Fiorenza, editor
**IN MEMORY OF HER: A Feminist
Theological Reconstruction of Christian
Origins**
A highly provocative and influential
work that is transforming feminist
thinking about the Bible
0–8245–0493–3 Crossroad $22.50
0–8245–0667–7 Crossroad pb $13.95

Helen Waddell
THE DESERT FATHERS
Translation of an ancient collection of
anecdotes about the radical desert
hermits of Egypt
0–472–06008–2 Michigan pb $7.95

Thomas Merton
WISDOM OF THE DESERT
Sayings of the 4th-century desert
priests, well translated by a 20th-
century Cistercian monk and poet
0–8112–0102–3 New Directions pb $4.95

Marcus Aurelius
MEDITATIONS
Marcus Aurelius, philosopher-emperor
of Rome (c. 160), wrote these
reflections on human character, power,
and mortality at night, mostly while
camped with his soldiers on campaign
Translated by Maxwell Staniforth
0–14–044140–9 Penguin pb $4.95

Lucius Apuleius
THE GOLDEN ASS
A humorous, first person account of
one man's "conversion" to the worship
of the goddess Isis and his initiation
into her mysteries in the second-
century Roman empire
Translated by Robert Graves
0–374–50532–2 FS&G pb $7.95

Augustine
**THE CONFESSIONS OF ST.
AUGUSTINE**
The aging bishop of Hippo reflects on
his past life in the light of his Christian
conversion
0–8010–0118–8 Baker pb $4.95

Peter Brown
AUGUSTINE OF HIPPO
The definitive biography of the teacher
who became, for better and worse, the
most influential teacher in the history
of Christianity
0–88029–098–6 Hippocrene $22.50

And, two books that I've written
myself:

Elaine Pagels
THE GNOSTIC GOSPELS
The meaning of an ancient library
found near Nag Hammadi in upper
Egypt, including many early Christian
sources attributed to Jesus and his
disciples
0–394–50278–7 Random House $14.45
0–394–74043–2 Random House pb $3.95

ADAM, EVE AND THE SERPENT
Which is about the ideological
transformation within the first few
Christian centuries from an emphasis
on human freedom and dignity to an
assertion of universal human sinfulness
0–394–52140–4 Random House $17.95

• Mircea Eliade
THE SACRED AND THE PROFANE: The Nature of Religion
Eliade's incomparably fluent exploration of recurrent themes in world religions—an excellent introduction
Translated by Willard R. Trask
0–15–679201–X HBJ pb $4.95

• Peter Levi
THE FRONTIERS OF PARADISE: A Study of Monks and Monasteries
Levi, a poet and classical scholar, focuses chiefly on European traditions, offering many anecdotes and exploring unusual aspects of monastic culture
1–55584–197–X Weidenfeld & Nicolson $16.95

• Geoffrey Parrinder
SEX IN THE WORLD'S RELIGIONS
A concise survey of sexual attitudes, taboos, and practices
0–19–520202–3 Oxford pb $9.95

• F.E. Peters
THE CHILDREN OF ABRAHAM: Judaism, Christianity, Islam
A study of the development of three intertwined and often mutually suspicious faiths, with discussions of scripture, mysticism, asceticism, and theology
0–691–07267–1 Princeton $25.00
0–691–02030–2 Princeton pb $10.95

• Ninian Smart
WORLDVIEWS: Crosscultural Explorations in Human Beliefs
Smart is one of the most eminent 20th-century scholars in the field of comparative religion
0–02–412010–3 Macmillan pb $13.50

RELIGIONS OF TRADITIONAL CULTURES

▶ **See also Anthropology**

• Walter Burkert
GREEK RELIGION
"A masterpiece, packed with learning but also rich in ideas and connections of every sort. . . . Nobody else could have produced an account of the subject of comparable range and power"—*NY Review of Books*
0–674–36281–0 Harvard pb $10.95

HOMO NECANS: The Anthropology of Ancient Greek Sacrificial Ritual and Myth
Translated by Peter Bing
0–520–05875–5 California pb $10.95

• Holger Kalweit
DREAMTIME AND INNER SPACE: The World of the Shaman
A survey of shamanism in Africa, Australia, Asia, Siberia, and the Americas, and a comparison with modern scientific studies of altered consciousness
Foreword by Elisabeth Kübler-Ross
0–87773–406–2 Shambhala pb $14.95

• Arnold Van Gennep
RITES OF PASSAGE
A classic French study of the ceremonies marking life crises
Translated by Monika Vizedon & Gabrielle Caffee
0–226–84849–3 Chicago pb $6.95

MYSTICISM

• Arthur C. Danto
MYSTICISM AND MORALITY: Oriental Thought and Moral Philosophy
A closely argued account of Buddhism, Taoism, and Hinduism and their divergence from Western moral teachings
0–231–06639–2 Columbia pb $12.50

• Mircea Eliade
THE TWO AND THE ONE
Eliade explores the paradoxical relationship between "oneness" and dualism
Translated by J.M. Cohen
0–226–20389–1 Chicago pb $10.00

• John Ferguson
ENCYCLOPEDIA OF MYSTICISM AND MYSTERY RELIGIONS
A well-illustrated reference with concise entries on major mystics, concepts of mysticism, and mystical religions
0–8245–0429–1 Crossroad pb $9.95

• Frank C. Happold
MYSTICISM
A good entry to the subject combining general remarks with an anthology of crucial texts
0–14–020568–3 Penguin pb $6.95

• William Johnston
THE INNER EYE OF LOVE: Mysticism and Religion
0–06–064201–7 Harper & Row pb $8.95

• Geoffrey Parrinder
MYSTICISM IN THE WORLD'S RELIGIONS
A survey of the varieties of mystical experience and interpretation
0–19–502185–1 Oxford pb $6.95

• Walter T. Stace
MYSTICISM AND PHILOSOPHY
Philosophical problems raised by mystical experience
Foreword by Jacob Needleman
0–87477–416–0 Tarcher pb $11.95

• R.C. Zaehner
MYSTICISM: Sacred and Profane
A cross-cultural study comparing mystical experiences with experiences induced by drugs
0–19–500229–6 Oxford pb $7.95

Mystery Religions

Samuel Angus
THE MYSTERY RELIGIONS
A classic in the history of religion
0–486–23124–0 Dover pb $6.95

Walter Burkert
ANCIENT MYSTERY CULTS
The most eminent contemporary historian of ancient Greek religion discusses the cults of Demeter, Dionysus, the Great Mother, Isis, and Mithras, and describes initiation rituals, priestly organization, and secret rites
0–674–03386–8 Harvard $20.00

Marvin W. Meyer, editor
THE ANCIENT MYSTERIES: A Sourcebook
Sacred texts of the ancient mystery religions, including the cults of the Great Mother, Isis and Osiris, Dionysus, Mithras, and Jewish and Christian mysteries. "This will be for many students the lifting of the veil for which they were looking"—James Robinson
0–06–065576–3 Harper & Row pb $14.95

Isis is, in fact, the female principle of Nature, and is receptive of every form of generation, in accord with which she is called by Plato the gentle nurse and the all-receptive, and by most people has been called by countless names, since, because of the force of Reason, she turns herself to this thing or that and is receptive to all manner of shapes and forms. She has an innate love for the first and most dominant of all things, which is identical with the good, and this she yearns for and pursues; but the portion which comes from evil she tries to avoid and to reject, for she serves them both as place and means of growth, but inclines always towards the better and offers to it opportunity to create from her and to impregnate her with effluxes and likenesses in which she rejoices and is glad that she is made pregnant and teeming with these creations. For creation is the image of being in matter, and the thing created is a picture of reality.

Plutarch, *On Isis and Osiris* in

Marvin W. Meyer, editor
THE ANCIENT MYSTERIES: A Sourcebook
0–06–065576–3 Harper & Row pb $14.95

PHILOSOPHY AND RELIGION

• Charles Hartshorne
OMNIPOTENCE AND OTHER THEOLOGICAL MISTAKES
A critique of mainstream theology by a leading exponent of "process philosophy"
0–87395–771–7 SUNY pb $10.95

• Leszek Kolakowski
RELIGION: If There Is No God . . . On God, the Devil, Sin and Other Worries of the So-Called Philosophy of Religion
Kolakowski wrestles with the contradictions between reason and eros, skepticism and mysticism, and exhaustion and eternity
Edited by Frank Kermode
0–19–520429–8 Oxford pb $8.95

• John Macquarrie
EXISTENTIALISM
An introduction to the most important tendency in 20th-century religious thought
0–14–021569–7 Penguin pb $6.95

TWENTIETH CENTURY RELIGIOUS THOUGHT
A lucid overview of modern religious philosophy and theology
0-684-17334-4 Scribners pb $18.95

• Wayne Proudfoot
RELIGIOUS EXPERIENCE
An argument against the theological tendency to detach religion from its contexts in history, society, and individual psychology
0-520-05143-2 California $35.00

SKEPTICISM AND ATHEISM

• Paul Blanshard, editor
CLASSICS OF FREE THOUGHT
An introduction to the tradition of skeptical humanism
0-87975-421-4 Prometheus pb $12.95

• Roger E. Greeley, editor
THE BEST OF ROBERT INGERSOLL
Selections from the work of the eloquent 19th-century American agnostic
0-87975-209-2 Prometheus pb $13.95

• Paul Kurtz
IN DEFENSE OF SECULAR HUMANISM
Kurtz is a leading philosophical champion of scientific skepticism
0-87975-228-9 Prometheus pb $12.95

• H.L. Mencken
PREJUDICES: A Selection
These essays by the great American journalist include some of his sardonic writings on religion
Edited by James T. Farrell
0-394-70058-9 Random House pb $4.95

• Friedrich Nietzsche
TWILIGHT OF THE IDOLS & THE ANTICHRIST
Despite its polemical title and tone, *The Antichrist* is a serious effort to identify the cultural and psychological conditions for Christianity, Buddhism, and priestly religion
0-14-044207-3 Penguin pb $3.95

• Bertrand Russell
WHY I AM NOT A CHRISTIAN & Other Essays on Religion and Related Subjects
Engaging essays by the great English philosopher on religion and the varieties of skepticism
0-671-20323-1 Simon & Schuster pb $8.95

• Morton Smith
JESUS THE MAGICIAN
Makes an always interesting if not entirely compelling case for the theory that Jesus was primarily a magician and faith healer
0-06-067413-X Harper & Row pb $10.95

PSYCHOLOGY AND RELIGION

• Joseph F. Byrnes
THE PSYCHOLOGY OF RELIGION
The best overview of 20th-century theories of religion and of psychological research on religious experience
0-02-903580-5 Free Press $27.95

• Sigmund Freud
THE FUTURE OF AN ILLUSION
Psychoanalysis as the most powerful argument against the consolations of religion
Edited by James Strachey
0-393-01120-8 Norton $10.95
0-393-00831-2 Norton pb $3.95

MOSES AND MONOTHEISM
Freud speculates that modern science developed out of the asceticism fostered by monotheism
0-394-70014-7 Random House pb $4.95

• Erich Fromm
PSYCHOANALYSIS AND RELIGION
0-300-00089-8 Yale pb $5.95

• Carl G. Jung
MODERN MAN IN SEARCH OF A SOUL
On the need for a spiritual revival in the modern world
0-15-661206-2 HBJ pb $4.95

• Abraham H. Maslow
RELIGIONS, VALUES, AND PEAK-EXPERIENCES
Religion and self-actualization
0-14-004262-8 Penguin pb $4.95

• Donald Meyer
THE POSITIVE THINKERS: Religion As Pop Psychology from Mary Baker Eddy to Oral Roberts
0-394-73899-3 Pantheon pb $5.95

• Ann & Barry Ulanov
RELIGION AND THE UNCONSCIOUS
A scholarly exposition of religious psychology, from a Jungian perspective
0-664-24657-5 Westminster pb $14.95

RELIGION AND SOCIETY

• Peter L. Berger
THE SACRED CANOPY: Elements of a Sociological Theory of Religion
An influential contemporary attempt at a theory of religion in its social context
0-385-07305-4 Doubleday pb $5.95

• Emile Durkheim
THE ELEMENTARY FORMS OF THE RELIGIOUS LIFE
A classic study that explains the function of the totem and introduces a distinction between sacred and profane religion
Translated by Joseph W. Swain
0-02-908010-X Free Press pb $16.95

• Max Weber
THE SOCIOLOGY OF RELIGION
A theory of religion in society by the master in the field
Translated by Ephraim Fischoff
0-8070-4193-1 Beacon pb $10.95

WOMEN AND RELIGION

• Carol P. Christ & Judith Plaskow
WOMANSPIRIT RISING: A Feminist Reader in Religion
An anthology of feminist scholarship
0-06-061385-8 Harper & Row pb $9.95

• Christine Downing
THE GODDESS: Mythological Images of the Feminine
Female figures in Greek myth
0-8245-0624-3 Crossroad pb $11.95

• Elisabeth S. Fiorenza, editor
IN MEMORY OF HER: A Feminist Theological Reconstruction of Christian Origins
0-8245-0667-7 Crossroad pb $13.95

• Gerda Lerner
THE CREATION OF PATRIARCHY
Patriarchal religion in ancient Europe
0-19-505185-8 Oxford pb $8.95

• Barbara H. Rigney
LILITH'S DAUGHTERS: Women and Religion in Contemporary Fiction
0-299-08960-6 Wisconsin $17.50

• Rosemary Ruether & Eleanor McLaughlin
WOMEN OF SPIRIT
Women in the history of religion
0-671-24805-7 Simon & Schuster pb $11.95

• Marina Warner
ALONE OF ALL HER SEX: The Myth and the Cult of the Virgin Mary
The relationship between images of Mary in church iconography and doctrine and the subordinate role of women endorsed by the church. "Explores the cult in all its ramifications, peeling aside each successive accretion of doctrine and devotion in order to examine its moral, social, and emotional implications"—Keith Thomas, *NY Review of Books*
0-394-71155-6 Random House pb $12.95

In medieval miracle stories, statues and paintings, in accordance with iconodule belief, are constantly coming to life. In many the Virgin weeps, as she did in 1953 in Syracuse and elsewhere more recently; in one, a Saracen is converted when her breasts become flesh and flow with oil; in a very popular tale, a woman begs the Virgin to spare her dying child, and to make sure seizes the Christ child from her arms as a hostage and only returns him to his mother on the recovery of her own child. In yet another miracle, the Virgin breaks out in a sweat as she tries to restrain her son's almighty and vengeful arm from striking a sinner down.

Marina Warner
ALONE OF ALL HER SEX: The Myth and the Cult of the Virgin Mary
0-394-71155-6 Random House pb $12.95

RELIGION IN THE MODERN WORLD

- **Robert N. Bellah**
BEYOND BELIEF: Essays on Religion in a Post-Traditional World
By a leading American sociologist of religion
0–06–060775–0 Harper & Row pb $8.95

- **Harvey Cox**
RELIGION IN THE SECULAR CITY: Toward a Post-Modern Theology
The significance of developments in American religious life since the 1960s
0–671–52805–X Simon & Schuster pb $8.95

- **Victor Frankel**
MAN'S SEARCH FOR MEANING
"A moving, compressed account of a psychiatrist's reflections on his experiences in Auschwitz and their implications"— Elaine Pagels
0–671–24422–1 Simon & Schuster pb $5.95

- **Andrew M. Greeley**
UNSECULAR MAN: The Persistence of Religion
The endurance of religious questioning from prehistoric times to the technological age
0–8052–0794–5 Schocken pb $8.95

- **Michael Harrington**
THE POLITICS AT GOD'S FUNERAL: The Spiritual Crisis of Western Civilization
The breakdown of values resulting from the erosion of religious certainties
0–14–007689–1 Penguin pb $7.95

Cults

- **Willa Appel**
CULTS IN AMERICA: Programmed for Paradise
An even-handed approach with a psychological emphasis, focusing on conversion techniques
0–80–500524–2 Henry Holt pb $7.95

- **David Bromley & Anson Shupe**
STRANGE GODS: The Great American Cult Scare
Challenges the alarmist view
0–8070–1109–6 Beacon pb $9.95

- **Robert S. Ellwood**
ALTERNATIVE ALTARS: Unconventional and Eastern Spirituality in America
Psychological and historical accounts of visionary religions in America
0–226–20620–3 Chicago pb $5.50

- **Robert S. Ellwood & Harry Partin**
RELIGIOUS AND SPIRITUAL GROUPS IN MODERN AMERICA
An excellent survey of recent eccentric groups, including spiritualists, theosophists, Gurdjieff, Zen, neopagans, Scientology, and others
0–13–773309–7 Prentice Hall pb $24.00

- **Irving Hexham & Karla Poewe**
UNDERSTANDING CULTS AND NEW RELIGIONS
A psychological explanation of cults as more magical and therapeutic than religious
0–8028–0170–6 Eerdmans pb $8.95

J. Gordon Melton
Melton's works provide the best guide to individual groups and their beliefs.
A BIOGRAPHICAL DICTIONARY OF AMERICAN CULT AND SECT LEADERS
0–8240–9037–3 Garland $41.95
THE ENCYCLOPEDIC HANDBOOK OF CULTS IN AMERICA
0–8240–9036–5 Garland $26.95

- **Hugh Milne**
BHAGWAN: The God That Failed
The full story of Bhagwan Shree Rajneesh
0–312–00106–1 St. Martin's pb $15.95

- **Shiva Naipaul**
JOURNEY TO NOWHERE: A New World Tragedy
An excellent journalistic account of Jim Jones and the Jonestown tragedy
0–14–006189–4 Penguin pb $6.95

THE OCCULT, WITCHCRAFT, AND THE DEVIL

- **Margot Adler**
DRAWING DOWN THE MOON: Witches, Druids, Goddess-Worshippers, and Other Pagans in America Today
A thorough and sympathetic account of contemporary neopagan groups
0–8070–3253–0 Beacon pb $14.95

- **Ioan P. Couliano**
EROS AND MAGIC IN THE RENAISSANCE
Magic as a manipulative psychology of motives, especially erotic ones
Translated by Margaret Cook
Foreword by Mircea Eliade
0–226–12315–4 Chicago $34.95
0–226–12316–2 Chicago pb $13.95

- **Nevill Drury**
ENCYCLOPEDIA OF MYSTICISM AND THE OCCULT
A sympathetic guide to occult and mystical concepts, rites, and practitioners
0–06–062093–5 Harper & Row $24.95
0–06–062094–3 Harper & Row pb $14.95

- **Mircea Eliade**
OCCULTISM, WITCHCRAFT, AND CULTURAL FASHION: Essays in Comparative Religions
Fascinating discourses on the occult, Gnosticism, Tantric Buddhism, and contemporary culture
0–226–20392–1 Chicago pb $9.00

- **Jeffrey Burton Russell**
A HISTORY OF WITCHCRAFT: Sorcerers, Heretics and Pagans
0–500–27242–5 Thames & Hudson pb $11.95

THE PRINCE OF DARKNESS: Radical Evil and the Power of Good in History
A one-volume study of a topic Russell has covered in extraordinary depth in his magisterial four-volume treatment, listed below
0–8014–2014–8 Cornell $21.95

THE DEVIL: Perceptions of Evil from Antiquity to Primitive Christianity
This and its successors constitute a definitive history of the idea and image of the Devil
0–8014–0938–1 Cornell $32.50
0–8014–9409–5 Cornell pb $10.95
SATAN: The Early Christian Tradition
0–8014–1267–6 Cornell $32.50
0–8014–9413–3 Cornell pb $10.95
LUCIFER: The Devil in the Middle Ages
0–8014–1503–9 Cornell $29.95
0–8014–9429–X Cornell pb $12.95
MEPHISTOPHELES: The Devil in the Modern World
0–8014–1808–9 Cornell $24.95

- **Kurt Seligmann**
THE HISTORY OF MAGIC AND THE OCCULT
Magic, astrology, and alchemy in Western culture
0–517–55129–2 Crown pb $9.95

Curious connections exist between Satan and Santa Claus (Saint Nicholas). The Devil lives in the far north and drives reindeer; he wears a suit of red fur; he goes down chimneys in the guise of Black Jack or the Black Man covered in soot; as Black Peter he carries a large sack into which he pops sins or sinners (including naughty children); he carries a stick or cane to thrash the guilty (now he merely brings candy canes); he flies through the air with the help of strange animals; food and wine are left out for him as a bribe to secure his favors. The Devil's nickname (!) "Old Nick" derives directly from Saint Nicholas. Nicholas was often associated with fertility cults, hence with fruit, nuts, and fruitcake, his characteristic gifts.

Jeffrey Burton Russell
THE PRINCE OF DARKNESS: Radical Evil and the Power of Good in History
0–8014–2014–8 Cornell $21.95

REFERENCE WORKS

- **Mircea Eliade, editor**
THE ENCYCLOPEDIA OF RELIGION
The most comprehensive and culturally sympathetic reference work on religion in English; a 16-volume set
0–02–909480–1 Macmillan (set) $1,100.00

- **John R. Hinnells, editor**
A HANDBOOK OF LIVING RELIGIONS
0–14–022342–8 Penguin pb $8.95

THE PENGUIN DICTIONARY OF RELIGIONS
A compact and extremely useful reference source on religious history, doctrines, terminology
0–14–051106–7 Penguin pb $7.95

• J. Gordon Melton, editor
ENCYCLOPEDIA OF AMERICAN RELIGIONS
The most thorough guide, taking in everything from mainstream denominations to obscure flying saucer cults, and often as entertaining as it is authoritative
0–8103–2841–0 Gale $175.00

• Geoffrey Parrinder
DICTIONARY OF NON-CHRISTIAN RELIGIONS
A comprehensive illustrated guide to Hinduism, Buddhism, and Islam, as well as to classical paganism, Judaism, African, Australian, and Native American religions
0–7175–0972–9 Dufour $22.50

MIRCEA ELIADE

Mircea Eliade (1907–1986) has been one of the most influential writers on comparative religion and mythology in this century. For the convenience of readers who wish to explore his entire work, as an author and as an editor, we present a fuller listing of those titles currently available, including memoirs and works of fiction.

• Mircea Eliade
THE FORGE AND THE CRUCIBLE: The Origins and Structures of Alchemy
Translated by Stephen Corrin
0–226–20390–5 Chicago pb $9.00

FROM PRIMITIVES TO ZEN: A Thematic Sourcebook in the History of Religions
An anthology of written and oral texts
0–06–062134–6 Harper & Row $13.95

A HISTORY OF RELIGIOUS IDEAS

Volume 1: From the Stone Age to the Eleusinian Mysteries
Translated by Willard R. Trask
0–226–20400–6 Chicago $27.50
0–226–20401–4 Chicago pb $16.95

Volume 2: From Guatama Buddha to the Triumph of Christianity
Translated by Willard R. Trask
0–226–20402–2 Chicago $27.50
0–226–20403–0 Chicago pb $16.95

Volume 3: From Muhammad to the Age of Reforms
Translated by Alf Hiltebeitel & Diane Apostolos-Cappadona
0–226–20404–9 Chicago $27.50
0–226–20405–7 Chicago pb $16.95

MYTH AND REALITY
0–06–131369–6 Harper & Row pb $6.95

MYTHS, DREAMS, AND MYSTERIES: The Encounter Between Contemporary Faiths and Archaic Realities
0–06–131943–0 Harper & Row pb $6.95

THE MYTH OF THE ETERNAL RETURN
Translated by Willard R. Trask
0–691–01777–8 Princeton pb $8.95

MYTHS, RITES, SYMBOLS: A Mircea Eliade Reader
Edited by Wendell C. Beane & William G. Doty

Volume 1
0–06–131955–4 Harper & Row pb $5.95

Volume 2
0–06–090511–5 Harper & Row pb $5.95

OCCULTISM, WITCHCRAFT, AND CULTURAL FASHION: Essays in Comparative Religions
0–226–20392–1 Chicago pb $9.00

ORDEAL BY LABYRINTH: Conversations with Claude-Henri Rocquet
0–226–20388–3 Chicago pb $8.95

PATANJALI AND YOGA
0–8052–0491–1 Schocken pb $7.95

PATTERNS IN COMPARATIVE RELIGION
0–452–00728–3 NAL pb $10.95

THE QUEST: History and Meaning in Religion
0–226–20386–7 Chicago pb $10.00

RITES AND SYMBOLS OF INITIATION: The Mysteries of Birth and Rebirth
0–06–131236–3 Harper & Row pb $6.95

THE SACRED AND THE PROFANE: The Nature of Religion
Translated by Willard R. Trask
0–15–679201–X HBJ pb $5.95

SHAMANISM: Archaic Techniques of Ecstasy
Translated by Willard R. Trask
0–691–01779–4 Princeton pb $14.50

SYMBOLISM, THE SACRED AND THE ARTS
Edited by Diane Apostolos-Cappadona
0–8245–0865–3 Crossroad pb $10.95

THE TWO AND THE ONE
Translated by J.M. Cohen
0–226–20389–1 Chicago pb $10.00

YOGA: Immortality and Freedom
Translated by Willard R. Trask
0–691–01764–6 Princeton pb $12.50

ZALMOXIS: The Vanishing God
0–226–20385–9 Chicago pb $16.00

Memoirs and Fiction

AUTOBIOGRAPHY
Translated by Mac L. Ricketts

Volume 1: Journey East, Journey West 1907–1937
0–06–062142–7 Harper & Row $17.50
0–06–062144–3 Harper & Row pb $9.95

Volume 2: 1937–1960, Exile's Odyssey
0–226–20411–1 Chicago $19.95

THE FORBIDDEN FOREST
Translated by Mac L. Ricketts & Mary P. Stevenson
0–268–00943–0 Notre Dame $25.00

NO SOUVENIRS: Journals, 1957–1969
0–06–062141–9 Harper & Row $15.00
0–06–062143–5 Harper & Row pb $7.95

THE OLD MAN AND THE BUREAUCRATS
Translated by Mary P. Stevenson
0–226–20410–3 Chicago pb $7.95

TALES OF THE SACRED AND THE SUPERNATURAL
0–664–24391–6 Westminster pb $7.95

TWO STRANGE TALES
Translated by William A. Coates
0–87773–386–4 Shambhala pb $6.95

YOUTH WITHOUT YOUTH: Three Fantastic Novellas
Translated by Mac L. Ricketts
0–8142–0457–0 Ohio State $18.95

In the beginning there was nothing but mere appearance, nothing really existed. It was a phantasm, an illusion that our father touched; something mysterious it was that he grasped. Nothing existed. Through the agency of a dream our father, He-who-is-appearance-only, Nainema, pressed the phantasm to his breast and then was sunk in thought.

Not even a tree existed that might have supported this phantasm and only through his breath did Nainema hold this illusion attached to the thread of a dream. He tried to discover what was at the bottom of it, but he found nothing . . .

He tied the emptiness to the dream-thread and pressed the magical glue-substance upon it. Thus by means of his dream did he hold it like the fluff of raw cotton.

He seized the bottom of the phantasm and stamped upon it repeatedly, allowing himself finally to rest upon the earth of which he had dreamt.

The earth-phantasm was now his. Then he spat out saliva repeatedly so that the forest might arise. He lay upon the earth and set the covering of heaven above it. He drew from the earth the blue and white heavens and placed them above.

A belief of the Uitoto of Colombia, South America

Mircea Eliade, editor
FROM PRIMITIVES TO ZEN: A Thematic Sourcebook in the History of Religions
0–06–062134–6 Harper & Row $13.95

Mythology and Folklore

GENERAL INTRODUCTIONS

• Thomas Bulfinch
BULFINCH'S MYTHOLOGY
The enduringly popular 19th-century retelling of Greek, Roman, and medieval myths and legends
0–394–60437–7 Modern Library $11.95

THE AGE OF FABLE
The first and best-known volume of Bulfinch's famous work, focusing on Greek and Roman mythology; illustrated
Introduction by Joseph Campbell
0–14–005643–2 Penguin pb $18.95

• Joseph Campbell
Campbell's work combines scholarship, Jungian depth psychology, and inspirational writing, and remains an immensely popular introduction. His approach reflects the continuing relevance of mythological symbols even—or especially—in our secular, mythless age.

THE FLIGHT OF THE WILD GANDER
Fairy tales and myths interpreted in relation to science, psychology, religion, and modern life
0–89526–914–7 Regnery pb $8.95

THE HERO WITH A THOUSAND FACES
This best-seller attempts to discover an archetypal "monomyth" within the myths of various cultures
0–691–09743–7 Princeton $41.50
0–691–01784–0 Princeton pb $9.95

HISTORICAL ATLAS OF WORLD MYTHOLOGY
A multivolume survey, abundantly illustrated

**Volume 1: The Way of the Animal Powers
Part 1: Mythologies of the Primitive Hunters and Gatherers**
0–06–096348–4 Harper & Row pb $24.95

Part 2: Mythologies of the Great Hunt
0–06–096349–2 Harper & Row pb $24.95

**Volume 2: The Way of the Seeded Earth
Part 1: The Sacrifice**
0–06–096350–6 Harper & Row pb $24.95

Part 2: Mythologies of the Primitive Planters: The North Americans
0–06–096351–4 Harper & Row pb $24.95

Part 3: Mythologies of the Primitive Planters: The Middle and Southern Americas
0–06–096352–2 Harper & Row pb $24.95

THE INNER REACHES OF OUTER SPACE: Metaphor As Myth and As Religion
A distillation of the author's lifework
0–06–055152–6 Harper & Row $18.95
0–06–096353–0 Harper & Row pb $8.95

THE MASKS OF GOD
Campbell's major work of comparative mythology

Volume 1: Primitive Mythology
0–14–004304–7 Penguin pb $8.95

Volume 2: Oriental Mythology
0–14–004305–5 Penguin pb $8.95

Volume 3: Occidental Mythology
0–14–004306–3 Penguin pb $8.95

Volume 4: Creative Mythology
0–14–004307–1 Penguin pb $8.95

• Joseph Campbell & M.J. Abadie
THE MYTHIC IMAGE
Mythological art from all cultures and periods, with commentary
0–691–01839–1 Princeton pb $19.95

• Joseph Campbell with Bill Moyers
THE POWER OF MYTH
A transcript of the popular television series
0–385–24773–7 Doubleday $27.50
0–385–24774–5 Doubleday pb $19.95

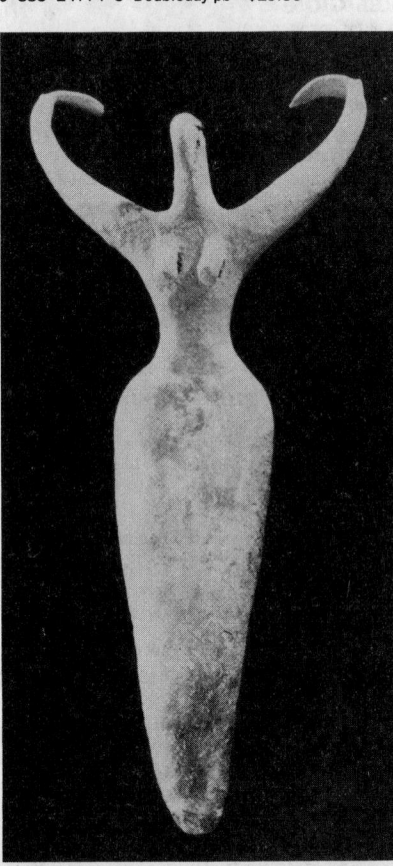

Ancient bird deity (The Brooklyn Museum), from The Power of Myth *by Joseph Campbell with Bill Moyers (Doubleday)*

• Ernst Cassirer
LANGUAGE AND MYTH
An important study of the relation of myth, language, and thought, by a German neo-Kantian philosopher
Translated by Susanne K. Langer
0–486–20051–5 Dover pb $2.95

• Giorgio de Santillana & Hertha von Dechend
HAMLET'S MILL: An Essay on Myth and the Frame of Time
A highly original examination of the origins of human knowledge and the relation of myth to science
0–87645–008–7 Harvard Common pb $15.00

• Alan Dundes, editor
SACRED NARRATIVE: Reading in the Theory of Myth
A valuable collection edited by a leading contemporary folklorist
0–520–05192–0 California pb $12.95

• Mircea Eliade
Although resolutely empirical in his approach to history and anthropology, Eliade suggests that particular historical patterns all point to a universal and ahistorical experience of the sacred.
MYTH AND REALITY
Creation, renewal, and end-of-the-world myths and their related significance; a good summation of Eliade's principal ideas
0–06–131369–6 Harper & Row pb $6.95

THE MYTH OF THE ETERNAL RETURN
An influential study of history and mythical time; using Eastern European folk materials, Eliade traces the transmutation of historical events into myths
Translated by Willard R. Trask
0–691–01777–8 Princeton pb $8.95

MYTHS, DREAMS AND MYSTERIES: The Encounter Between Contemporary Faiths and Archaic Realities
Myth, psychoanalysis, and the relations between myth and modern society
0–06–131943–0 Harper & Row pb $6.95

• James G. Frazer
THE GOLDEN BOUGH
Frazer's bold and pioneering study of ancient European myths, published in 1890 and subsequently revised and expanded, may have lost its revolutionary effect on contemporary readers—precisely because its ideas have been thoroughly absorbed into our culture, most visibly in the work of Sigmund Freud and the poetry of T.S. Eliot
Edited and abridged by Theodore Gaster
0–451–62052–1 NAL pb $6.95

THE GOLDEN BOUGH
Frazer's complete classic in a 13-volume set. Includes *The Magic Art and the Evolution of Kings; Taboo and the Perils of the Soul; The Dying God; Adonis, Attis, Osiris; Spirits of the Corn and of the Wild; The Scapegoat; Balder the Beautiful; The Fire Festivals of Europe and the Doctrines of the Eternal Soul; Bibliography and General Index;* and *Aftermath: A Supplement*
0–312–33215–7 St. Martin's $375.00

• Robert Graves
THE WHITE GODDESS: A Historical Grammar of Poetic Myth
An eccentric and engaging study of poetry and its relation to muses and myths, mainly Celtic and Greek; in the author's words, "a very difficult book, as well as a very queer one"
0–374–50493–8 Farrar, Straus & Giroux pb $9.95

• Carl G. Jung & Carl Kerenyi
ESSAYS ON A SCIENCE OF MYTHOLOGY: The Myths of the Divine Child and the Mysteries of Eleusis
Two central mythological themes and their relation to the unconscious
0–691–01756–5 Princeton pb $7.50

☞ **TO ORDER NEW BOOKS NOT YET LISTED, ASK YOUR BOOKSELLER OR CALL 1-800-882-8770**

- **G.S. Kirk**
  MYTH: Its Meaning and Functions in Ancient and Other Cultures
  The relation of myth to the unconscious and to folklore and ritual, the theory of structuralism, and the influence of Near Eastern mythology on Greek thought
  0–520–02389–7 California pb $11.95

- **Samuel Noah Kramer, editor**
  MYTHOLOGIES OF THE ANCIENT WORLD
  Essays by ten leading scholars, including Cyrus Gordon on Canaan, Derk Bodde on China, and Miguel Leon-Portilla on Mexico
  0–385–09567–8 Doubleday pb $6.95

> When the sun god Re, the king of mankind and the gods, had grown very old, he learned that upstream and in the desert man was plotting against him. Therefore, he summoned his council of gods which included the males, Shu, Geb, and Nunu, and the females, Tefnut, Nut, and the Eye of Re. This was done secretly, lest man should know about it. On the advice of the gods, Re sent his Eye, in the form of the goddess Hathor, to kill mankind. When she came back rejoicing, after having accomplished part of her task, Re repented and decided to spare the rest of mankind. He ordered red beer to be poured out onto the fields during the night, and then when the bloodthirsty Eye came back in the morning, she found the red beer pleasant for her heart. She became intoxicated and failed to recognize men. Thus, adds the narrator, originated the custom of preparing intoxicating drinks on the Feast of Hathor.
>
> Rudolf Anthes in
>
> Samuel Noah Kramer, editor
> **MYTHOLOGIES OF THE ANCIENT WORLD**
> 0–385–09567–8 Doubleday pb $6.95

- **Claude Lévi-Strauss**
  MYTH AND MEANING
  A structuralist interpretation
  0–8052–0622–1 Schocken pb $5.95

- **Jacques Merleau-Ponty, Bruno Morando, & Helen Weaver**
  THE REBIRTH OF COSMOLOGY
  0–8214–0606–X Ohio pb $9.95

- **Carl Olson, editor**
  THE BOOK OF THE GODDESS
  A source book of essays on the female deities of Eastern and Western cultures, including the Sophia of the Gnostics, the Virgin Mary, and the Hindu goddesses
  0–8245–0689–8 Crossroad pb $12.95

Barbara C. Sproul
PRIMAL MYTHS: Creating the World
"A representative, well-chosen collection, from good sources, well presented for use either as an introduction to the study of mythology or as a convenient reference work and

refresher of memory"—Joseph Campbell
0–06–067501–2 Harper & Row pb $12.95

- **Giambattista Vico**
  THE NEW SCIENCE
  Vico's 1725 treatise was the first modern study of myth, foreshadowing later anthropological views: "The fables of the gods are true histories of customs"
  0–8014–9265–3 Cornell pb $12.95

- **Heinrich Zimmer**
  THE KING AND THE CORPSE
  Tales of the soul's conquest of evil, culled from Eastern and Western folk literature and retold by the renowned Indologist and Jungian
  Edited by Joseph Campbell
  0–691–01778–6 Princeton pb $7.95

THE ANCIENT WORLD: Egypt and Mesopotamia

Egypt

- **E.A. Wallis Budge**
  THE GODS OF THE EGYPTIANS: Studies in Egyptian Mythology
  A major study, covering the myths of Thoth and Isis, the Book of the Dead, the cult of Osiris, and the mythological associations of animals and birds. Many illustrations

  Volume 1
  0–486–22055–9 Dover pb $10.95

  Volume 2
  0–486–22056–7 Dover pb $10.95

  OSIRIS
  A comprehensive study of the Egyptian deity and the associated iconography and religious practices

  Volume 1
  0–486–22780–4 Dover pb $7.95

  Volume 2
  0–486–22781–2 Dover pb $7.95

- **Hasan M. El-Shamy, editor**
  FOLKTALES OF EGYPT
  Foreword by Richard M. Dorson
  0–226–20625–4 Chicago pb $10.95

- **Veronica Ions**
  EGYPTIAN MYTHOLOGY
  0–911745–07–6 Peter Bedrick $18.95

- **Manfred Lurker**
  THE GODS AND SYMBOLS OF ANCIENT EGYPT: An Illustrated Dictionary
  Edited by Peter A. Clayton
  0–500–11018–2 Thames & Hudson $19.95
  0–500–27253–0 Thames & Hudson pb $11.95

Mesopotamia

- **John Gray**
  NEAR EASTERN MYTHOLOGY
  An illustrated survey
  0–87226–004–6 Peter Bedrick $18.95

- **S.H. Hooke**
  MIDDLE EASTERN MYTHOLOGY
  A compact summary of the mythology of the Egyptians, Babylonians, Assyrians, Hittites, Canaanites, and Hebrews, in the light of 20th-century archaeological discoveries. Hooke also discusses influences on early Christianity
  0–14–020546–2 Penguin pb $5.95

CLASSICAL MYTHOLOGY: Ancient Greece and Rome

- **Walter Burkert**
  STRUCTURE AND HISTORY IN GREEK MYTHOLOGY AND RITUAL
  Prehistoric patterns of meaning in Greek rites and myths, by an eminent historian
  0–520–03771–5 California $35.00
  0–520–04770–2 California pb $10.95

- **Michael Grant**
  MYTHS OF THE GREEKS AND ROMANS
  An admirable retelling of the classical myths, with illustrations ranging from Greek art to Picasso
  0–451–62693–1 NAL pb $5.95

- **Robert Graves**
  THE GREEK MYTHS
  The scattered elements of these classical myths are organized into fluent narratives, with copious indexes, cross-references, and discussions of problems of historical and anthropological interpretation

  Volume 1
  0–14–020508–X Penguin pb $4.95

  Volume 2
  0–14–020509–8 Penguin pb $4.95

Pierre Grimal
THE DICTIONARY OF CLASSICAL MYTHOLOGY
The complete story of every mythic figure and type—gods and mortals, centaurs, satyrs, nymphs, and dryads—with illustrations from classical art, maps, and genealogical charts. "It will indeed be a learned reader who does not find something he did not previously know on almost every page"—TLS
0–631–13209–0 Blackwell $50.00

- **Rhoda A. Hendricks, translator**
  CLASSICAL GODS AND HEROES: Myths as Retold by the Ancient Authors
  Selections from Hesiod, Ovid, Sophocles, Catullus, and others, with glossary and maps
  0–688–05279–7 Morrow pb $7.95

- **C. Kerenyi**
  THE GODS OF THE GREEKS
  The Greek myths, humanistically reinterpreted in terms of their continued relevance to contemporary life
  0–500–27048–1 Thames & Hudson pb $9.95

Odysseus threatening Circe on a fourth-century cup from Thebes, in The Oxford History of the Classical World *edited by John Boardman and others*

• G.S. Kirk
THE NATURE OF GREEK MYTHS
A systematic examination, including an overview of the leading theories and speculation on the transition from mythology to philosophy
0–14–021783–5 Penguin pb $5.95

• H.J. Rose
A HANDBOOK OF GREEK MYTHOLOGY
A complete, clear, and scholarly guide, now in its sixth edition
0–525–48414–0 Dutton pb $8.95

• Gustav Schwab
GODS AND HEROES
A 19th-century German compendium of myths and legends drawn from Greek and Roman literature
0–394–73402–5 Pantheon pb $9.95

• Michael Stapleton
THE ILLUSTRATED DICTIONARY OF GREEK AND ROMAN MYTHOLOGY
Classical gods and heroes, with summaries of the literary works in which they appear
Introduction by Stewart Perowne
0–87226–063–1 Peter Bedrick $17.95

EUROPEAN MYTHOLOGY

• Hans P. Duerr
DREAMTIME: Concerning the Boundary Between Wilderness and Civilization
An eccentric, original, and learned meditation on myth, witchcraft, folk custom, philosophy, and anthropology
0–631–15548–1 Blackwell pb $14.95

• Georges Dumézil
THE STAKES OF THE WARRIOR
The tragic warrior-hero as a crucial figure in Indo-European mythology
Translated by David Weeks
0–520–04834–2 California $29.50

• Marija Gimbutas
GODDESSES AND GODS OF OLD EUROPE, 7000 TO 3500 BC: Myths, Legends, and Cult Images
0–520–04655–2 California pb $15.95

British

• Katherine M. Briggs
BRITISH FOLKTALES
A wide-ranging collection of stories and legends organized by type
0–394–73993–0 Pantheon pb $7.95

Tom Thumb, from Folk Tales of the British Isles *edited by Kevin Crossley-Holland, illustrated by Hannah Firman (Pantheon)*

Kevin Crossley-Holland, editor
FOLKTALES OF THE BRITISH ISLES
Sixty-seven stories from Celtic, English, and Norse traditions, including fairy tales, heroic tales, nursery stories, and legends of giants
0–394–56328–X Pantheon $22.95
0–394–75553–7 Pantheon pb $11.95

• Charles Kightly
THE FOLK HEROES OF BRITAIN
The Arthurian knights, Robin Hood, and others
0–500–25082–0 Thames & Hudson $19.95
0–500–27325–1 Thames & Hudson pb $10.95

Celtic

• Richard Cavendish
KING ARTHUR AND THE GRAIL
The history of legends of the Round Table and the Holy Grail from their origins in Celtic mythology to their Norman transformations
0–8008–4466–1 Taplinger pb $6.95

• Patrick K. Ford, editor & translator
THE MABINOGI & OTHER MEDIEVAL WELSH TALES
Celtic literature unadulterated by the French Arthurian romances, constituting the core of the ancient Welsh mythological cycle
0–520–03414–7 California pb $10.95

• Jeffrey Gantz, translator
EARLY IRISH MYTHS AND SAGAS
The oral traditions of the Iron Age Celts
0–14–044397–5 Penguin pb $4.95

THE MABINOGION
Eleven medieval Welsh stories first recorded in the early 14th century, in an excellent modern translation
0–14–044322–3 Penguin pb $3.95

After some time had passed, however, there fell upon the island of Britain three plagues the like of which no one had ever seen. The first of these was the arrival of a people called the Corannyeid, the extent of whose knowledge was such that there was no conversation anywhere in the island, however hushed, that they did not hear, provided the wind caught it; consequently no harm could be done to them. The second plague was a scream that was heard every May Eve over every hearth in the island; it pierced the hearts of the people and terrified them so that men lost their colour and strength, women suffered miscarriages, children lost their senses, and animals and trees and soil and water all became barren. The third plague was this: however much provision had been prepared in the king's courts, though it might be a year's supply of food and drink, none of it ever remained after the first night. The first plague was evident to all, but no one knew the meaning of the other two, and therefore they had more hope of being delivered from the first than from the second or third.

Jeffrey Gantz, translator
THE MABINOGION
0–14–044322–3 Penguin pb $3.95

• Henry Glassie, editor
IRISH FOLKTALES
0–394–74637–6 Pantheon pb $11.95

• Kenneth Hartstone Jackson, editor
A CELTIC MISCELLANY
Prose and verse from six Celtic languages, including bardic elegies, heroic tales, and the literature of love
0–14–044247–2 Penguin pb $5.95

• Proinsias MacCana
CELTIC MYTHOLOGY
0–87226–002–X Peter Bedrick $18.95

• W.B. Yeats, editor
FAIRY AND FOLK TALES OF IRELAND
Fairies, leprechauns, ghosts, witches, princesses, devils, and others, compiled by Yeats in the 1880s
Foreword by Benedict Kiely
0–02–055640–3 Macmillan pb $9.95

➤ **FOR OVERSEAS ORDERING INFORMATION, SEE PAGE 1**

Italian

Italo Calvino
ITALIAN FOLKTALES
Lovers, saints, rogues, kings, peasants, and animals, in tales from every region of Italy, retold by the distinguished novelist
Translated by George Martin
0–15–145770–0 HBJ $27.50
0–394–74909–X Pantheon pb $11.95

Jewish

• Nathan Ausubel, editor
A TREASURY OF JEWISH FOLKLORE
0–517–50293–3 Crown $14.95

• Raphael Patai
ON JEWISH FOLKLORE
0–8143–1707–3 Wayne State $29.95

• Howard Schwartz
ELIJAH'S VIOLIN & OTHER JEWISH FAIRY TALES
Illustrated by Linda Heller
0–06–015108–0 Harper & Row pb $14.95

MIRIAM'S TAMBOURINE: Jewish Folktales from Around the World
Foreword by Dov Noy
Illustrated by Lloyd Bloom
0–02–929260–3 Free Press $24.95

• Beatrice Weinreich & Leonard Wolf, editors
YIDDISH FOLKTALES
0–394–54618–0 Pantheon $21.95

Norse and Germanic

• Peter C. Asbjornsen & Jorgen Moe
NORWEGIAN FOLK TALES
0–394–71054–1 Pantheon pb $7.95

• Kevin Crossley-Holland, editor
THE NORSE MYTHS
A vivid new rendering
0–394–50048–2 Pantheon $16.45
0–394–74846–8 Pantheon pb $8.95

• H.R. Ellis Davidson
GODS AND MYTHS OF NORTHERN EUROPE
A renowned scholar explores Viking mythology, relating cultic practices to daily life and speculating on the eclipse of pagan beliefs by Christianity
0–14–020670–1 Penguin pb $5.95

SCANDINAVIAN MYTHOLOGY
A survey of Norse myths, with photographs of Viking art, artifacts, ships
0–87226–041–0 Peter Bedrick $18.95

Georges Dumézil
GODS OF THE ANCIENT NORTHMEN
A pioneering study of Indo-European civilization, tracing its central principles of order, prowess, and well-being as revealed in Norse myths
Translated by Einar Haugen
0–520–02044–8 California $34.00
0–520–03507–0 California pb $11.95

• Jacob & Wilhelm K. Grimm
GRIMM'S TALES FOR YOUNG AND OLD: The Complete Stories
A fine new translation
Translated by Ralph Manheim
0–385–18950–8 Doubleday pb $11.95

• Lee M. Hollander, translator
THE POETIC EDDA
An early collection of Norse myths, composed between 800 and 1100, recounting the creation and twilight of the gods, tales of Sigurd and Odin, and much more; Hollander's translation attempts to capture the texture and rhythm of the original
0–292–76499–5 Texas pb $12.95

• Elias Lönnrot, editor
THE KALEVALA
The Finnish national epic, compiled in the 19th century from cycles of traditional stories
Translated by Francis Magoun
0–674–50010–5 Harvard pb $10.95

• Snorri Sturluson
THE PROSE EDDA OF SNORRI STURLUSON: Tales from Norse Mythology
The Norse gods, as told by the 13th-century Icelandic poet
Translated by Jean I. Young
0–520–01232–1 California pb $7.95

Russian and Slavic

• Alexander Afanasyev, editor
RUSSIAN FOLK TALES
A classic collection
Translated by Robert Chandler
Illustrated by Ivan Bilibin
0–87773–090–9 Shambhala pb $9.95

Siberian shaman (The Smithsonian Institution), from The Power of Myth *by Joseph Campbell with Bill Moyers (Doubleday)*

• Elizabeth Warner
HEROES, MONSTERS AND OTHER WORLDS FROM RUSSIAN MYTHOLOGY
0–8052–4007–1 Schocken $15.95

THE NON-WESTERN WORLD

African

• Harold Courlander
A TREASURY OF AFRICAN FOLKLORE
Tales, legends, sayings, and humor from a wide range of African cultures
0–517–51670–5 Crown $14.95

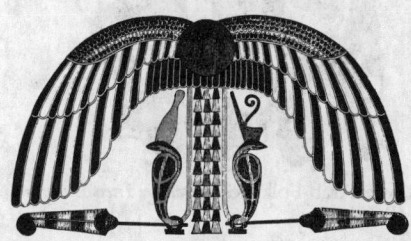

• Bernard B. Dadié
THE BLACK CLOTH: A Collection of African Folk Tales
Stories rich in humor and inventiveness, retold by the distinguished Ivory Coast poet, novelist, and statesman
Translated by Karen C. Hatch
Foreword by E'-Kia Mphahlele
0–87023–556–7 Massachusetts $20.00
0–87023–557–5 Massachusetts pb $9.95

• Leo Frobenius & Douglas C. Fox
AFRICAN GENESIS
An important introduction to African culture, including the famous "Gassire's Lute"
0–913666–77–7 Turtle Island pb $8.95

• Judith Gleason
OYA: In Praise of the Goddess
A study of a major Yoruba deity whose devotees are also found in Brazil, the Caribbean, and the United States
0–877–73430–5 Shambhala pb $12.95

• Geoffrey Parrinder
AFRICAN MYTHOLOGY
Illustrated with photographs of African artwork
0–87226–042–9 Peter Bedrick $18.95

• Paul Radin, editor
AFRICAN FOLKTALES
Stories from sub-Saharan Africa including those of the Hausa, the Bantu, the Bushmen, and the Zulu, compiled by a distinguished American anthropologist
0–8052–0732–5 Schocken pb $11.95

Arab

• Iner Bushnaq, editor
ARAB FOLKTALES
"Beautifully edited, translated, and annotated"—Edward W. Said
0–39475–179–5 Pantheon pb $11.95

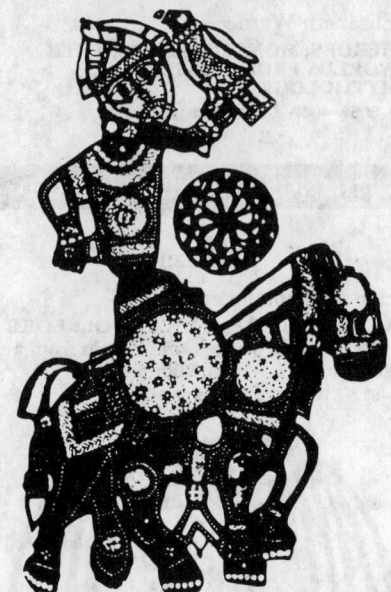

From Arab Folktales *edited by Inea Bushnaq (Pantheon)*

There is in the Koran a whole *sura,* or chapter, named for the Djinn. Indeed, just as God created man from potter's clay, so he formed the Djinn from a smokeless fire. He sent the prophet to enlighten both worlds of sentient beings, that of the Ins, or humans, and that of the Djinn, or spirits. Much of the excitement in the tales of magic lies in the removal of the boundary between the two worlds. Whether they are potential helpers to be wooed or dangerous enemies to be overcome, the spirits are as much a part of the landscape as the heroes. When a merchant watering his camels pulls a handsome youth up from the bottom of the well with his rope, or when a prince hunting in the wilderness comes upon a girl whose hair shines like threads of gold, the question "Are you Ins or are you Djinn?" is asked as a matter of course.

Iner Bushnaq, editor
ARAB FOLKTALES
0–39475–179–5 Pantheon pb $11.95

Chinese

• Yin-Lien Chin & others
TRADITIONAL CHINESE FOLKTALES
0–87332–507–9 M.E. Sharpe $17.95

• Anthony Christie
CHINESE MYTHOLOGY
0–87226–015–1 Peter Bedrick $18.95

• Wolfram Eberhard, editor
FOLKTALES OF CHINA
Seventy-nine traditional stories from Eberhard's classic 1937 collection, along with six from modern China, with historical notes and bibliography
0–226–18193–6 Chicago pb $9.95

• Moss Roberts, editor
CHINESE FAIRY TALES AND FANTASIES
0–394–73994–9 Pantheon pb $9.95

Indian

• Brenda E.F. Beck & others, editors
FOLKTALES OF INDIA
Nearly 100 tales from 14 languages, arranged by theme
Foreword by A.K. Ramanujan
0–226–04080–1 Chicago $29.95

• David Kinsley
HINDU GODDESSES: Visions of the Divine Feminine in the Hindu Religious Tradition
0–520–06339–2 California pb $10.95

Wendy D. O'Flaherty
DREAMS, ILLUSION AND OTHER REALITIES
The role of dreams and dreaming in Indian religion, philosophy, literature, and art
0–226–61855–2 Chicago pb $15.95

WOMEN, ANDROGYNES, AND OTHER MYTHICAL BEASTS
Sexual symbolism and themes in Indian myth and ritual. "An important, provocative and original work . . . splendid translations, and exegesis of so many, and so different, Sanskrit texts"—Mircea Eliade
0–226–61849–8 Chicago $27.50
0–226–61850–1 Chicago pb $10.95

Wendy D. O'Flaherty, translator
HINDU MYTHS
A kaleidoscopic survey with selections from the Vedas, the medieval pantheon, and the mythology of Krishna and the minor gods
0–14–044306–1 Penguin pb $5.95

• Heinrich Zimmer
MYTHS AND SYMBOLS IN INDIAN ART AND CIVILIZATION
0–691–01778–6 Princeton pb $7.95

Japanese

• Lafcadio Hearn
A JAPANESE MISCELLANY
Folktales, ghost stories, and sketches and impressions of Japan as Hearn knew it in the 1890s
0–8048–0307–2 Tuttle pb $5.75

• Fanny H. Mayer, translator & editor
ANCIENT TALES IN MODERN JAPAN: An Anthology of Japanese Folk Tales
0–253–30710–4 Indiana $27.50

• Juliet Piggott
JAPANESE MYTHOLOGY
Mythological art with historical background and a selection of myths, legends, and tales
0–911745–09–2 Peter Bedrick $18.95

• Royall Tyler
JAPANESE TALES
0–394–52190–0 Pantheon $19.95

• Post Wheeler
TALES FROM THE JAPANESE STORYTELLERS AS COLLECTED IN THE HO-DAN ZO
Edited by Harold G. Henderson
0–8048–1132–6 Tuttle pb $3.95

Oceanian

• Padraic Colum
LEGENDS OF HAWAII
Nineteen native tales skillfully retold by an Irish poet and fiction writer
0–300–03923–9 Yale pb $9.95

• Antony Alpers
THE WORLD OF THE POLYNESIANS SEEN THROUGH THEIR MYTHS AND LEGENDS, POETRY, AND ART
0–19–558142–3 Oxford pb $10.95

• Leinani Melville
CHILDREN OF THE RAINBOW: The Religions, Legends and Gods of Pre-Christian Hawaii
An attempt to reconstruct the religious beliefs and oral poetry of the early Hawaiians
0–8356–0002–5 Theosophical pb $5.95

Tibetan

• Fredrick & Audrey Hyde-Chambers
TIBETAN FOLK TALES
Over 30 legends and tales, including creation myths, parables, and the epic of the warrior king Gesar of Ling
Illustrated by Kusho Ralla
0–394–74886–7 Shambhala pb $8.95

• Alexandra David-Neel & Lama Yongden, translators
THE SUPERHUMAN LIFE OF GESAR OF LING
The Tibetan folk epic of supernatural adventure
0–87773–412–7 Shambhala pb $14.95

THE WESTERN HEMISPHERE

African-American

• Roger D. Abrahams, editor
AFRO-AMERICAN FOLKTALES
0–394–72885–8 Pantheon pb $11.95
▶ **See also African-American Studies**

American

• Kemp Battle
GREAT AMERICAN FOLKLORE: Legends, Tales, Ballads, and Superstitions from All Across America
Nearly 700 pages of diverse material
0–671–68281–4 Simon & Schuster pb $12.95

• Walter Blair
TALL TALE AMERICA: A Legendary History of Our Humorous Heroes
0–226–05596–5 Chicago pb $9.95

Jan H. Brunvand

Brunvand's journeys into the byways of urban folklore to explore apocryphal—and often horrific—things usually described as having happened to "a friend of a friend."

THE CHOKING DOBERMAN & Other "New" Urban Legends
0–393–30321–7 Norton pb $6.95

THE MEXICAN PET: More "New" Urban Legends and Some Old Favorites
0–393–30542–2 Norton pb $6.95

THE VANISHING HITCHHIKER: American Urban Legends and Their Meanings
0–393–95169–3 Norton pb $7.95

- ## Richard M. Dorson
  AMERICA IN LEGEND: Folklore from the Colonial Period to the Present
  0–394–70926–8 Pantheon pb $14.95

- ## Alan Dundes & Carl R. Pagter
  WORK HARD AND YOU SHALL BE REWARDED: Urban Folklore from the Paperwork Empire
  A serious but entertaining survey of contemporary materials that proliferate through photocopying rather than oral tradition
  0–253–20207–8 Indiana pb $6.95

  WHEN YOU'RE UP TO YOUR ASS IN ALLIGATORS: More Urban Folklore from the Paperwork Empire
  A follow-up to *Work Hard and You Shall Be Rewarded*
  0–8143–1867–3 Wayne State pb $9.95

- ## Mary & Herbert Knapp
  ONE POTATO, TWO POTATO: The Folklore of American Children
  0–393–09039–6 Norton pb $7.95

- ## Vance Randolph
  OZARK MAGIC AND FOLKLORE
  A noted study first published in 1947
  0–486–21181–9 Dover pb $6.50

Caribbean

- ## Paule Barton
  THE WOE SHIRT
  A collection of Caribbean folktales
  Translated by Howard Norman
  0–915308–36–3 Graywolf pb $5.00

- ## Daryl C. Dance
  FOLKLORE FROM CONTEMPORARY JAMAICANS
  The first comprehensive anthology, with critical annotation, glossary, photos, and maps
  0–87049–436–8 Tennessee $24.95

Wade Davis

PASSAGE OF DARKNESS: The Ethnobiology of the Haitian Zombie
A controversial account of Davis' attempt to explain the zombie phenomenon. "Davis broke into that amazing world for the first time and what he found has, I think, possible transoceanic resonance . . . He has

written of one of the most fascinating and most misunderstood phenomena of all the Black Americas"—Robert Farris Thompson
0–8078–4210–9 North Carolina pb $9.95

Maya Deren

DIVINE HORSEMEN: The Living Gods of Haiti
A study of voodoo owing much to the experiences of the author, a leading experimental filmmaker of the 1940s
Foreword by Joseph Campbell
0–914232–63–0 McPherson pb $10.00

Alfred Metraux

VOODOO IN HAITI
All in all, the best study
0–8052–0341–9 Schocken pb $11.95

Native American

- ## John Bierhorst
  THE MYTHOLOGY OF NORTH AMERICA
  A systematic survey of heroes, goddesses, and spirits, from the Arctic regions to the Southwest. Illustrated
  0–688–06666–6 Morrow pb $6.95

- ## Frank H. Cushing
  ZUNI FOLK TALES
  0–8165–0986–7 Arizona pb $12.95

- ## Emilio Abreu Gomez
  CANEK: History and Legend of a Maya Hero
  Translated by Mario L. Davila & Carter Wilson
  0–520–03148–2 California $27.50
  0–520–03982–3 California pb $5.95

- ## Edwin S. Hall, Jr.
  THE ESKIMO STORYTELLER: Folktales from Noatak, Alaska
  0–87049–160–1 Tennessee $34.95

- ## Barry Lopez
  GIVING BIRTH TO THUNDER, SLEEPING WITH HIS DAUGHTER: Coyote Builds North America
  A retelling of some of the many myths and tales about Coyote
  0–8362–0726–2 Andrews & McMeel $8.95

- ## Lawrence Millman
  A KAYAK FULL OF GHOSTS: Eskimo Tales
  0–88496–267–9 Capra pb $9.95

- ## Irene Nicholson
  MEXICAN AND CENTRAL AMERICAN MYTHOLOGY
  0–87226–003–8 Peter Bedrick $18.95

- ## Harold Osborne
  SOUTH AMERICAN MYTHOLOGY
  0–87226–043–7 Peter Bedrick $18.95

- ## Marion Wood
  SPIRITS, HEROES AND HUNTERS FROM NORTH AMERICAN INDIAN MYTHOLOGY
  Illustrated by John Sibbick
  0–8052–3792–5 Schocken $16.95

FOLKLORE

- ## Bruno Bettelheim
  THE USES OF ENCHANTMENT: The Meaning and Importance of Fairy Tales
  0–394–49771–6 Knopf $21.95
  0–394–72265–5 Random House pb $6.95

- ## Joanna Cole
  BEST LOVED FOLKTALES OF THE WORLD
  Over 200 stories, arranged geographically, including *Snow White, The Indian Cinderella,* and *The Magic Orange Tree*
  0–385–18949–4 Doubleday pb $12.95

Richard M. Dorson, editor

FOLKLORE AND FOLKLIFE: An Introduction
An excellent work by an eminent American scholar
0–226–15871–3 Chicago pb $15.95

FOLKTALES TOLD AROUND THE WORLD
Brings together the work of field workers, folklorists, and storytellers, with an emphasis on contemporary folk narrative
0–226–15874–8 Chicago pb $15.00

- ## Duncan Emrich
  FOLKLORE ON THE AMERICAN LAND
  An absorbing collection of legends, songs, proverbs, street cries, and other lore
  0–316–23721–3 Little, Brown pb $12.45

- ## Max Luthi
  THE EUROPEAN FOLKTALE: Form and Nature
  A classic attempt to define the essential laws of the genre
  0–253–20393–7 Indiana pb $7.95

  THE FAIRY TALE AS ART FORM AND PORTRAIT OF MAN
  The traditional fairy tale examined aesthetically and anthropologically; Luthi considers whether such tales project a particular image of the human world
  Translated by Jon Erickson
  0–253–20420–8 Indiana pb $7.95

  ONCE UPON A TIME: On the Nature of Fairy Tales
  Essays on such celebrated stories as *Hansel and Gretel, Sleeping Beauty,* and *Rapunzel*
  0–253–20203–5 Indiana pb $5.95

- ## Odell Shepard
  THE LORE OF THE UNICORN
  Hunts the mythical creature through world literature; anecdotal and scholarly
  0–06–090721–5 Colophon pb $5.95

- ## Stith Thompson
  THE FOLKTALE
  An important study of European, Middle Eastern, Indian, and North American stories, classified by theme
  0–520–03537–2 California pb $10.95

- ## Jack Zipes
  BREAKING THE MAGIC SPELL: Radical Theories of Folk and Fairy Tales
  0–292–70725–8 Texas $15.00
  0–416–01001–6 RC&H pb $10.95

Asian Religion and Philosophy

Western interest in the religions of Asia has a long history; Greek ambassadors reported on Indian religious observances in the 3rd century BC, and references to Buddhism can be found in early Christian writings. European colonial and missionary efforts after the 16th century led to increased contact, and the intellectual sympathy for Chinese culture and the climate of tolerance that came out of the Enlightenment fostered a desire to understand Eastern traditions on their own terms. In the 19th century, the study of Asian languages and the progress of historical and philological disciplines prepared the way for the immense increase in the knowledge of Asian religions in our own time.

INTRODUCTIONS AND SURVEYS

- **Yong C. Kim**
  ORIENTAL THOUGHT: An Introduction to the Philosophical and Religious Thought of Asia
  0–8226–0365–9 Littlefield, Adams pb $6.95

- **Joseph M. Kitagawa**
  RELIGIONS OF THE EAST
  An excellent comparative study
  0–664–24837–3 Westminster pb $7.95

- **Hajime Nakamura**
  WAYS OF THINKING OF EASTERN PEOPLES: India, China, Tibet, Japan
  An introduction by an eminent Japanese scholar
  Edited by Philip P. Wiener
  0–8248–0078–8 Hawaii pb $12.95

- **Geoffrey Parrinder**
  AN INTRODUCTION TO ASIAN RELIGIONS
  A concise guide to doctrines and practices across the continent
  0–19–519858–1 Oxford pb $7.95

THE INDIAN TRADITIONS

- **Ainslie T. Embree & Stephen Hay, editors**
  SOURCES OF INDIAN TRADITION
  A new edition of an anthology that has become a classic. "A serious, careful, dependable book, broader and more varied even than the old *Sources* . . . This is *the* primary study of Indian civilization"—Wendy D. O'Flaherty
  Volume 1
  0–231–06651–1 Columbia pb $17.00
  Volume 2
  0–231–06415–2 Columbia pb $16.00

- **M. Hiriyana**
  THE ESSENTIALS OF INDIAN PHILOSOPHY
  A straightforward exposition of the philosophies advanced in the Vedas and Upanishads and the six systems (*darsanas*) of classical Indian philosophy; also includes introductions to Buddhist and Jain thought
  0–04–181023–6 Unwin Hyman pb $11.95

- **Robert Lingat**
  THE CLASSICAL LAW OF INDIA
  Translated by J. Duncan Derrett
  0–520–01898–2 California $40.00

- **Sarvepalli Radhakrishnan & Charles A. Moore, editors**
  A SOURCE BOOK IN INDIAN PHILOSOPHY
  "This long-awaited book gives a splendid coverage of indispensable source material in Indian philosophy"—Dale Riepe
  0–691–01958–4 Princeton pb $13.95

- **Heinrich Zimmer**
  PHILOSOPHIES OF INDIA
  Wide-ranging and profound, Zimmer's famous study remains a modern classic in Asian studies
  Edited by Joseph Campbell
  0–691–01758–1 Princeton pb $12.50

HINDUISM

Classic Texts

- **Cornelia Dimmitt, editor**
  CLASSICAL HINDU MYTHOLOGY: A Reader in the Sanskrit Puranas
  Extracts from the Puranas—encyclopedic repositories of Hindu myths, legends, and customs—with excellent introductory material
  Translated by J.A. Van Buitenen
  0–87722–122–7 Temple pb $19.95

- **Juan Mascaro, translator**
  THE UPANISHADS
  A fine translation of the most important and original text of Indian religious thought
  0–14–044163–8 Penguin pb $3.50

- **Wendy D. O'Flaherty, translator**
  THE RIG VEDA
  A new, authoritative translation of selected hymns from the earliest of the Vedas
  0–14–044402–5 Penguin pb $6.95

- **J.A. Van Buitenen, translator & editor**
  THE BHAGAVADGITA IN THE MAHABHARATA: A Bilingual Edition
  This sacred poem, part of the epic *Mahabharata*, is a dialogue between Krishna and the warrior Arjuna on the conflict between action and contemplation. Van Buitenen's superb translation is presented with facing Sanskrit text
  0–226–84662–8 Chicago pb $9.95

Krishna as the Butter Thief (Nelson Gallery-Atkins Museum), from History of Far Eastern Art *by Sherman E. Lee (Abrams)*

OM. In the centre of the castle of Brahman, our own body, there is a small shrine in the form of a lotus-flower, and within can be found a small space. We should find who dwells there, and we should want to know him.

And if anyone asks, "Who is he who dwells in a small shrine in the form of a lotus-flower in the centre of the castle of Brahman? Whom should we want to find and to know?" we can answer:

"The little space within the heart is as great as this vast universe. The heavens and the earth are there, and the sun, and the moon, and the stars; fire and lightning and winds are there; and all that now is and all that is not: for the whole universe is in Him and He dwells within our heart."

Juan Mascaro, translator
THE UPANISHADS
0–14–044163–8 Penguin pb $3.50

- **R.C. Zaehner, translator**
  THE BHAGAVAD-GITA
  Another highly recommended translation of the great sacred poem
  0–19–501666–1 Oxford pb $12.95

General Studies

- **Paul Deussen**
  THE PHILOSOPHY OF THE UPANISHADS
  The classic introduction to the subject
  0–486–21616–0 Dover pb $8.50

- **Eliot Deutsch**
  ADVAITA VEDANTA: A Philosophical Reconstruction
  An interpretation of the religious and philosophical system of Sankara, perhaps India's greatest religious figure
  0–8248–0271–3 Hawaii pb $5.95

🐸 IF YOU CAN'T FIND IT, LOOK IN THE INDEX

- Mircea Eliade
YOGA: Immortality and Freedom
Eliade's encyclopedic work examines the
yogic tradition in all its ramifications
Translated by Willard R. Trask
0–691–01764–6 Princeton pb $12.50

> From the time of the Upaniṣads India
> rejects the world as it is and devaluates
> life as it reveals itself to the eyes of the
> sage—ephemeral, painful, illusory. Such
> a conception leads neither to nihilism nor
> pessimism. *This* world is rejected, *this* life
> depreciated, because it is known that
> *something else* exists, beyond becoming,
> beyond temporality, beyond suffering. In
> religious terms, it could almost be said
> that India rejects the *profane* cosmos and
> *profane* life, because it thirsts for a *sacred*
> world and a *sacred* mode of being.
>
> Mircea Eliade
> **YOGA: Immortality and Freedom**
> Translated by Willard R. Trask
> 0–691–01764–6 Princeton pb $12.50

- Ainslie T. Embree, editor
THE HINDU TRADITION
Selected readings from the tradition,
modestly annotated
0–394–71702–3 Random House pb $5.95

- John S. Hawley & Donna M. Wulff,
editors
**THE DIVINE CONSORT: Radha and the
Goddesses of India**
An anthology examining feminine aspects
of divinity in the Indian tradition. "A
shower of insights on the male/female
polarity itself, in all its subtlety, tensions,
and potential glory"—Huston Smith
0–8070–1303–X Beacon pb $12.95

- Wendy D. O'Flaherty
**THE ORIGINS OF EVIL IN HINDU
MYTHOLOGY**
Enriched, like all this author's works, by
remarkable insight and erudition. "The
range and number of myths handled is
dazzling . . . A major contribution to the
study of religion in general and Hinduism
in particular"—*TLS*
0–520–04098–8 California pb $10.95

SIVA: The Erotic Ascetic
A detailed survey of the major mythic
themes, centered on the paradox of the
god's dual role as ascetic and heroic lover
0–19–520250–3 Oxford pb $9.95

- Milton Singer, editor
KRISHNA: Myths, Rites, and Attitudes
0–226–76101–0 Chicago pb $12.00

- Margaret & James Stutley
**HARPER'S DICTIONARY OF
HINDUISM: Its Mythology, Folklore,
Philosophy, Literature and History**
0–06–067767–8 Harper & Row pb $16.95

- R.C. Zaehner
HINDUISM
A lucid, topical presentation of major
themes in the tradition
0–19–888012–X Oxford pb $8.95

Modern Trends

- Philip H. Ashby
MODERN TRENDS IN HINDUISM
An overview of the principal strands of
Hinduism in contemporary Indian society
0–231–03768–6 Columbia $25.00

- Margaret Chatterjee
GANDHI'S RELIGIOUS THOUGHT
0–268–01011–0 Notre Dame pb $9.95

- Mohandas K. Gandhi
**AUTOBIOGRAPHY: The Story of My
Experiments with Truth**
"An absorbing book that stands alone in
frankness and plain honesty . . . Its place
among the classics of autobiography
cannot be in doubt"—*New Statesman*
0–486–24593–4 Dover pb $6.95

- Christopher Isherwood
RAMAKRISHNA AND HIS DISCIPLES
A good book for the beginner
0–87481–037–X Vedanta pb $9.95

- Robert A. McDermott, editor
**SIX PILLARS: Introduction to the Major
Works of Sri Auribindo**
0–89012–001–3 Anima pb $5.95

BUDDHISM AS A PAN-ASIAN RELIGION

- W. Theodore De Bary, editor
**THE BUDDHIST TRADITION: In India,
China and Japan**
Readings from the various literatures of
Buddhism with brief introductions and
annotations
0–394–71696–5 Random House pb $7.50

- Hans W. Schumann
BUDDHISM
An outstanding primer of Buddhist
thought that includes a sympathetic
treatment of the main schools of Mahayana
Buddhism
0–8356–0457–8 Theosophical pb $7.95

- Lucien Stryk, editor
**THE WORLD OF THE BUDDHA: An
Introduction to Buddhist Literature**
Ecumenical and well-selected. "A fine
reference book for both the beginning and
advanced student"—*Choice*
0–8021–3095 Grove pb $12.95

BUDDHISM IN INDIA

Classic Texts

- Edward Conze, translator
BUDDHIST SCRIPTURES
The selections are arranged by topic and
are taken almost entirely from Sanskrit
Buddhist texts
0–14–044088–7 Penguin pb $5.95

- E.B. Cowell, editor
BUDDHIST MAHAYANA TEXTS
Recommended for its translation of the
three chief scriptures of Pure Land
Buddhism
0–486–25552–2 Dover pb $8.95

- Juan Mascaro, translator
THE DHAMMAPADA
One of the loveliest texts of Buddhist
literature, treasured for its aphoristic moral
instructions, in a translation sensitive to its
literary quality
0–14–044284–7 Penguin pb $3.50

- D.T. Suzuki, translator
**THE LANKAVATARA SUTRA: A
Mahayana Text**
Contains material central to the Yogacara
wing of Buddhist thought
0–7100–2165–8 RC&H $27.00

- Henry C. Warren
BUDDHISM IN TRANSLATIONS
A classic anthology of Pali texts
0–689–70200–0 Atheneum pb $7.95

- Alex & Hideko Wayman, translators
**THE LION'S ROAR OF QUEEN
SRIMALA: A Buddhist Scripture on the
Tathagatagarbha Theory**
0–231–03726–0 Columbia $23.00

General Studies

- Edward Conze
BUDDHISM: Its Essence and Development
An overview of the main themes of the
tradition and its historical development
0–06–130058–6 Harper & Row pb $6.95

- Herbert V. Guenther, translator
**THE LIFE AND TEACHING OF
NAROPA**
A good discussion of the Tantric practices
of the 11th-century mystic Naropa and his
followers
0–87773–356–2 Shambhala pb $9.95

- Winston L. King
**IN THE HOPE OF NIBBANA: The Ethics
of Theravada Buddhism**
An examination of Buddhist ethics
founded on Theravada sources
0–87548–230–9 Open Court $22.95

- Walpola Rahula
WHAT THE BUDDHA TAUGHT
An excellent overview of basic Buddhist
thought from the perspective of the
Theravada school
Foreword by Paul Demieville
0–802–13031–3 Grove pb $8.95

- Richard H. Robinson & Willard L.
Johnson
**THE BUDDHIST RELIGION: A
Historical Introduction**
An excellent survey, with an extensive
bibliography
0–534–01027–X Wadsworth pb $15.75

- David Snellgrove
INDO-TIBETAN BUDDHISM: Indian Buddhists and Their Tibetan Successors
Focuses on late Indian Buddhism and its transmission to Central Asia and Tibet

Volume 1
0–87773–311–2 Shambhala pb $18.95

Volume 2
0–87773–379–1 Shambhala pb $18.95

- Nyanaponika Thera
THE HEART OF BUDDHIST MEDITATION
Outlines the Theravada program of meditation and the practice of "mindfulness" (*satipatthana*)
0–87728–073–8 Samuel Weiser pb $9.95

OTHER RELIGIONS OF INDIA

Sikhism

- Owen W. Cole & Piara S. Sambhi
THE SIKHS: Their Religious Beliefs and Practices
0–7100–8843–4 RC&H pb $13.95

- W.H. McLeod
THE EVOLUTION OF THE SIKH COMMUNITY: Five Basic Essays
0–19–826529–8 Oxford $36.00

THE SIKHS: History, Religion and Society
0–231–06814–X Columbia $25.00

Jainism

- Colette Caillat
THE JAIN COSMOLOGY
0–517–54662–0 Crown $55.00

- Padmanabh S. Jaini
THE JAINA PATH OF PURIFICATION
Written chiefly from the perspective of the Digambara school; a fine introduction to the tradition
0–520–03459–7 California $35.95

Zoroastrianism

The Persian Zoroastrians who settled in India in the latter half of the first millennium became known as Parsis. The following are a few general works on the Zoroastrian tradition and its Indian vicissitudes.

- Mary Boyce
THE ZOROASTRIANS: Their Religious Beliefs and Practices
A general study, incorporating contemporary scholarship, on the Indian Zoroastrian tradition
0–7102–0156–7 RC&H pb $17.95

- Mary Boyce, editor
ZOROASTRIANISM
A highly recommended history aimed at the more advanced student
0–389–20478–1 Barnes & Noble pb $23.50

- R.C. Zaehner
THE TEACHINGS OF THE MAGI
A long-valued introduction to Zoroastrian doctrine
0–19–519857–3 Oxford pb $7.95

THE CHINESE TRADITIONS

William T. De Bary, editor
SOURCES OF CHINESE TRADITION
Selections from major Chinese religious, philosophical, and literary texts with commentary. An invaluable reference

Volume 1
0–231–08602–4 Columbia pb $17.00

Volume 2
0–231–08603–2 Columbia pb $14.50

- Wing-tsit Chan, editor
A SOURCE BOOK IN CHINESE PHILOSOPHY
"Heroically [the editor] translates his philosophers himself, with the result that for the first time the entire map is seen through a consistent eye"—Robert Payne
0–691–01964–9 Princeton pb $13.50

- Herrlee G. Creel
CHINESE THOUGHT FROM CONFUCIUS TO MAO TSE-TUNG
0–226–12030–9 Chicago pb $10.95

- Fung Yu-Lan
A HISTORY OF CHINESE PHILOSOPHY
The classic history
Translated by Derk Bodde

Volume 1
0–691–02021–3 Princeton pb $16.95

Volume 2
0–691–02022–1 Princeton pb $22.00

- Henri Maspero
CHINA IN ANTIQUITY
A chronicle of early social and religious life by one of the foremost 20th-century sinologists
0–87023–296–7 Massachusetts pb $15.00

- Frederick W. Mote
THE INTELLECTUAL FOUNDATIONS OF CHINA
A concise introduction to early philosophical thought
0–394–31042–X Knopf pb $7.00

- Arthur Waley
THREE WAYS OF THOUGHT IN ANCIENT CHINA
For generations this has been the classic introduction to Confucianism, Taoism, and "Realism" (Legalism). "The book is full of memorable phrases and amusing aphorisms. It reveals a world at once close to us and very far away"—Peter Quennell, *New Statesman*
0–8047–1169–0 Stanford pb $7.95

- Max Weber
THE RELIGION OF CHINA
Weber, the master sociologist of religion, argues in this famous work that China's religious ethic impeded the development of a rational capitalist economy
0–02–934440–9 Free Press $19.95

CONFUCIANISM

"The Master said, Be of unwavering good faith, love learning, if attacked be ready to die for the good Way. Do not enter a State that pursues dangerous courses, nor stay in one where the people have rebelled. When the Way prevails under Heaven, then show yourself; when it does not prevail, then hide. When the Way prevails in your own land, count it a disgrace to be needy and obscure; when the Way does not prevail in your land, then count it a disgrace to be rich and honoured."—Confucius, *The Analects*, translated by Arthur Waley

Classic Texts

- Confucius
THE ANALECTS
The best of the modern translations of the aphorisms of Confucius, superbly illustrated
Translated by D.C. Lau
0–14–044348–7 Penguin pb $4.95

THE ANALECTS OF CONFUCIUS
An excellent translation published in 1939, with a good introduction and biography of Confucius
Translated by Arthur Waley
0–679–72296–3 Random House pb $6.95

THE CONFUCIAN ANALECTS, THE GREAT LEARNING & THE DOCTRINE OF THE MEAN
Three of the so-called Four Books (the fourth being the *Mencius*) that formed the core of the official Confucian curriculum
Edited by James Legge
0–486–22746–4 Dover pb $8.95

- C.F. Baynes & Richard Wilhelm, translators
I CHING, OR THE BOOK OF CHANGES
Confucius' attention to this divination text (he allegedly wrote its most important commentary) ensured its central role in Chinese thought
0–691–09750–X Princeton $17.50

- Mencius
MENCIUS
The best modern translation of the second most influential thinker in the Confucian tradition
Translated by D.C. Lau
0–14–044228–6 Penguin pb $6.95

- Burton Watson, translator & editor
BASIC WRITINGS OF MO TZU, HSUN TZU & HAN FEI TZU
A fine translation of the classical neo-Confucian thinker Mo Tzu, the Confucian reformist Hsun Tzu, and the legalist Han Fei Tzu
0–231–02515–7 Columbia $21.00

■ **TO ORDER BOOKS AS GIFTS, SEE PAGE 1**

- Chu Hsi & Lu Tsu-Ch'ien
**REFLECTIONS ON THINGS AT HAND:
The Neo-Confucian Anthology**
A collection assembled in the 12th century
by Chu Hsi, the Neo-Confucian
movement's foremost figure. His thought
defined the official state orthodoxy until
the creation of the Republic of China in
1912
Translated by Wing-tsit Chan
0–231–06037–8 Columbia pb $17.00

General Studies

- Wing-tsit Chan, editor
CHU HSI AND NEO-CONFUCIANISM
0–8248–0961–0 Hawaii $30.00

- Julia Ching
**TO ACQUIRE WISDOM: The Way of
Wang Yang-Ming**
A detailed account of the intellectual
development of an important Neo-
Confucian thinker
0–231–03938–7 Columbia $31.50

- William T. De Bary
**NEO-CONFUCIAN ORTHODOXY AND
THE LEARNING OF THE HEART-MIND**
0–231–05229–4 Columbia pb $15.00

- Herbert Fingarette
CONFUCIUS: The Secular As Sacred
A penetrating and highly original
interpretation of Confucian thought,
particularly concerned with the centrality
of ritual in everyday life
0–06–131682–2 Harper & Row pb $6.95

TAOISM

"**B**ut to wear out your brain trying to make
things into one without realizing that
they are all the same—this is called 'three in
the morning.' What do I mean by 'three in
the morning'? When the monkey trainer was
handing out acorns, he said, 'You get three
in the morning and four at night.' This made
all the monkeys furious. 'Well, then,' he said,
'you get four in the morning and three at
night.' The monkeys were all delighted.
There was no change in the reality behind
the words, and yet the monkeys responded
with joy and anger. Let them, if they want
to. So the sage harmonizes with both right
and wrong and rests in Heaven the Equal-
izer. This is called walking two roads."—
Chuang Tzu, *The Complete Works*, translated
by Burton Watson

Classic Texts

- Lao Tzu
**THE TAO TE CHING: The Book of
Meaning and Life**
The Taoist classic, probably the work of a
number of writers over a long period, but
attributed to a contemporary of Confucius
called Lao Tzu ("the Old Man")
Translated by Richard Wilhelm
1–85063–011–9 RC&H pb $5.95

TAO TE CHING: A New English Version
A recent rendering by Stephen Mitchell,
known for his translations of Rilke and the
Book of Job
0–06–016001–2 Harper & Row $15.95

- Arthur Waley
**THE WAY AND ITS POWER: A Study of
the Tao Te Ching and Its Place in Chinese
Thought**
A highly recommended translation of the
Tao Te Ching with an excellent
introduction
0–802–15085–3 Grove pb $10.95

- Chuang Tzu
**THE COMPLETE WORKS OF
CHUANG TZU**
A delightful translation of this classic
Taoist text, preserving all the humor,
paradox, and deliberate ambiguity of the
original
Translated by Burton Watson
Foreword by William T. De Bary
0–231–03147–5 Columbia $37.50

CHUANG TZU: Basic Writings
Extracts from the complete works, listed
above
Translated by Burton Watson
0–231–08606–7 Columbia pb $10.00

CHUANG TZU: The Inner Chapters
Translated by A.C. Graham
0–04–99013–0 Unwin Hyman pb $12.95

- Thomas Cleary, translator
**THE BOOK OF BALANCE AND
HARMONY**
A hitherto untranslated collection of
essays, poems, and songs about the secrets
of Taoism
0–86547–363–3 North Point pb $10.95

General Studies

- Herrlee G. Creel
**WHAT IS TAOISM?: & Other Studies in
Chinese Cultural History**
0–226–12047–3 Chicago pb $12.95

- Max Kaltenmark
LAO-TZU AND TAOISM
A brief survey by an eminent French
scholar
0–8047–0689–1 Stanford pb $6.95

- Thomas Merton
THE WAY OF CHUANG TZU
A sympathetic account by the Catholic
scholar and poet
0–8112–0103–1 New Directions pb $5.95

- Holmes Welch
TAOISM: The Parting of the Way
A wonderful brief introduction, containing
much material on religious Taoism not
easily found elsewhere and emphasizing
the gulf between the Taoist mysticism and
Taoist practice
0–8070–5973–0 Beacon pb $7.95

CHINESE BUDDHISM

Classic Texts

- Thomas Cleary, translator
**THE FLOWER ORNAMENT
SCRIPTURE: A Translation of the
Avatamsaka Sutra**
A massive composite work whose vision of
the interrelatedness of all phenomena was
central to the emerging worldview of
Chinese Buddhism. "The consummation of
Buddhist thought, Buddhist sentiment,
and Buddhist experience"—D.T. Suzuki

Volume 1
0–87773–304–X Shambhala $59.95

Volume 2
0–87773–299–X Shambhala $59.95

Volume 3
0–87773–300–7 Shambhala $59.95

- Leon Hurvitz, translator
**SCRIPTURE OF THE LOTUS BLOSSOM
OF THE FINE DHARMA: The Lotus
Sutra**
A faithful and elegant translation of one of
the most popular scriptures in East Asian
Buddhism
0–231–03920–4 Columbia pb $16.00

- A.F. Price & Wong Mou-Lam,
translators
**THE DIAMOND SUTRA & THE SUTRA
OF HUI NENG**
Two texts of crucial importance to
Mahayana and Zen Buddhism
Forewords by W.Y. Evans-Wentz & Christmas
Humphreys
0–394–73019–4 Shambhala pb $9.95

General Studies

- Kenneth Ch'en
**BUDDHISM IN CHINA: A Historical
Survey**
The standard account, unsurpassed for its
panaromic scope
0–691–00015–8 Princeton pb $14.50

*Chinese Buddha from the T'ang Dynasty
(The Metropolitan Museum), in*
A Connoisseur's Guide to the Met *by
Paul Magriel and John T. Spike (Vintage)*

• Kogen Mizuno
THE BUDDHIST SUTRAS: Origin, Development, Transmission
Development of the codified and edited discourses of the Buddha with particular attention to the Chinese Buddhist canon
4–333–01028–4 Tuttle pb $8.95

• Arthur F. Wright
BUDDHISM IN CHINESE HISTORY
A short, clearly written work for the general reader. "Throws light on the renewed process of borrowing and adaptation taking place in China today"—Derk Bodde
0–8047–0546–1 Stanford $15.00
0–8047–0548–8 Stanford pb $6.95

THE JAPANESE TRADITIONS

Robert N. Bellah
TOKUGAWA RELIGION
A classic study by the leading American sociologist of religion. In the manner of Max Weber, Bellah traces the origins of Japanese modernization to the religious ethos of the Tokugawa period (1600–1868). "Remains a landmark reference in Japanese studies . . . [by a] sensitive and critical interpreter of modernization"—Tetsuo Najita, University of Chicago
0–02–902460–9 Free Press pb $9.95

• Carmen Blacker
THE CATALPA BOW: A Study of Shamanistic Practices in Japan
A comprehensive account based on both literary evidence and observation of contemporary activity
0–04–398008–2 Unwin Hyman pb $15.95

• William T. De Bary
SOURCES OF JAPANESE TRADITION
An essential collection of annotated religious and philosophical writings
Volume 1
0–231–08604–0 Columbia pb $17.00
Volume 2
0–231–08605–9 Columbia pb $16.00

• Byron H. Earhart
THE RELIGIONS OF JAPAN: Many Traditions Within One Sacred Day
A brief analysis taking both historical and thematic approaches
0–06–062112–5 Harper & Row pb $7.95

• Joseph M. Kitagawa
RELIGION IN JAPANESE HISTORY
The standard account by one of the most perceptive modern interpreters
0–231–02834–2 Columbia $40.00

• Sokyo Ono
SHINTO: The Kami Way
A brief exposition of Japan's earliest religious traditions
0–8048–0525–3 Tuttle $8.95

Portrait of Daruma by Sesshu, from History of Far Eastern Art *by Sherman E. Lee (Abrams)*

JAPANESE BUDDHISM

• Yoshita S. Hakeda, translator
KUKAI: Major Works, Translated with an Account of His Life and a Study of His Thought
An introduction to the 8th-century scholar and saint, one of the most influential figures in Japanese Buddhism. "Hakeda's achievement in arriving at these lively and intelligible translations is of the highest order"—Choice
0–231–05933–7 Columbia pb $14.00

• Taiko Yamasaki
SHINGON: Japanese Esoteric Buddhism
A comprehensive history of Japanese Tantrism
Foreword by Carmen Blacker
0–877–73443–7 Shambhala pb $19.95

ZEN AND CH'AN

Western interest in Zen Buddhism (and its Chinese precursor Ch'an) is reflected in the immense English-language literature on the subject. Listed below are some reliable introductory works.

• Robert Aitken
THE MIND OF CLOVER: Essays in Zen Buddhist Ethics
Applications of Zen to the modern world. "Clear, down to earth, and excellently crafted while full of depth, Zen spirit, and humanity"—Religious Studies Review
0–86547–158–4 North Point pb $11.50

• Thomas Cleary, translator
THE ORIGINAL FACE: An Anthology of Rinzai Zen
A collection of sayings, poems, sermons, and other writings of the best-known Japanese Rinzai masters
0–8021–1703–8 Grove pb $4.95

• Dōgen
MOON IN A DEWDROP: Writings of Zen Master Dōgen
Twenty-four texts by the founder of the Soto sect
0–86547–185–1 North Point $35.00
0–86547–186–X North Point pb $15.95
ZEN MASTER DOGEN: An Introduction with Selected Writings
"Incisive translations of twelve heuristic selections from Dōgen's major work, *The Eye Storehouse of the True Law* (*Shobogenzo*), and three independent writings explaining his basic religious viewpoint. The background chapters, excellent footnotes, and glossary entice the reader"—*Choice*
0–8348–0116–7 Weatherhill pb $9.95

• Heinrich Dumoulin
ZEN BUDDHISM: A History
A rich and detailed account of the roots of the Zen tradition and its ramifications throughout Asia. Only the first volume, covering India and China, is so far available in English
Volume 1: India and China
0–02–908260–9 Macmillan pb $14.95

• A.V. Grimstone, editor
TWO ZEN CLASSICS: Mumonkan & Hekiganroku
A translation of two of the most influential and popular *koan* collections
Translated by Katsuki Sekida
0–8348–0131–0 Weatherhill $13.50
0–8348–0130–2 Weatherhill pb $8.95

• Eugen Herrigel
ZEN IN THE ART OF ARCHERY
A perennially popular title
0–679–72297–1 Random House pb $5.95

• Huang Po
THE ZEN TEACHING OF HUANG PO ON THE TRANSMISSION OF THE MIND
A classic of Ch'an Buddhism, dating from the T'ang dynasty
Translated by John Blofeld
0–394–17217–5 Grove pb $9.95

• Kenneth Kraft, editor
ZEN: Tradition and Transition
An anthology dealing with the whole range of modern developments in Zen. The contributors include Burton Watson, Philip Yampolsky, Chang Shen-yen, and Albert Low
0–8021–1022–3 Grove $16.95

• Isshu Miura & Ruth F. Sasaki
THE ZEN KOAN
A well-documented study of the form's history
0–15–699981–1 HBJ pb $7.95

- Paul Reps, editor
ZEN FLESH, ZEN BONES: A Collection of Zen and Pre-Zen Writings
A lively anthology of *koans* that has entertained and stimulated generations of students
0–385–08130–8 Doubleday pb $4.95

- Sōiku Shigematsu
A ZEN FOREST: Sayings of the Masters
Over 1200 Chinese and Japanese aphorisms from the *Zenrin Kushu* (Zen Forest Saying Anthology)
Foreword by Gary Snyder
0–8348–0159–0 Weatherhill $19.95

A ZEN HARVEST: Japanese Folk Zen Sayings
Short poems related to the Zen tradition of *jakugo* (capping-phrase exercises): "Ears/ Hear and eyes/ See,/ Then what does/ Mind do?"
0–86547–328–5 North Point pb $12.95

Ummon said, "The world is vast and wide. Why do you put on your seven-piece robe at the sound of the bell?"
Mumon's Comment: In studying Zen, you should not be swayed by sounds and forms. Even though you attain insight when hearing a voice or seeing a form, this is simply the ordinary way of things. Don't you know that the real Zen student commands sounds, controls forms, is clear-sighted at every event and free on every occasion?
Granted you are free, just tell me: Does the sound come to the ear or does the ear go to the sound? If both sound and silence die away, at such a juncture how could you talk of Zen? While listening with your ear, you cannot tell. When hearing with your eye, you are truly intimate.

from *Mumonkan* in

A.V. Grimstone, editor
TWO ZEN CLASSICS: Mumonkan & Hekiganroku
Translated by Katsuki Sekida
0–8348–0131–0 Weatherhill $13.50

- Lucien Stryk & Takashi Ikemoto, translators & editors
ZEN POEMS OF CHINA AND JAPAN: The Crane's Bill
One hundred fifty poems ranging from the 9th to the 19th century. "A fine chronological anthology of Buddhist writings"—*Choice*
0–8021–3019–4 Grove pb $7.95

- D.T. Suzuki
ESSAYS IN ZEN BUDDHISM
First published in the 1920s, these essays helped introduce Zen to the West
0–394–17230–2 Grove pb $11.95

AN INTRODUCTION TO ZEN BUDDHISM
A widely consulted guide by the leading expositor of Zen to the West
Foreword by C.G. Jung
0–802–13055–0 Grove pb $4.95

MANUAL OF ZEN BUDDHISM
Prayers, sutras, and sayings that have long been part of the Zen tradition
0–8021–3065–8 Grove pb $10.95

ZEN AND JAPANESE CULTURE
One of the most influential of Suzuki's books
0–691–01770–0 Princeton pb $10.95

- Shunryu Suzuki
ZEN MIND
"A primer on what Zen is and how a person can begin to practice it"—*Publishers Weekly*
0–8348–0079–9 Weatherhill pb $5.95

- Philip B. Yampolsky, translator
THE PLATFORM SUTRA OF THE SIXTH PATRIARCH
"Without sacrificing scholarly accuracy, Yampolsky has produced a lucid and idiomatic translation which even the layman can enjoy"—*Literature East and West*
0–231–08361–0 Columbia pb $16.00

SOUTHEAST ASIAN RELIGION

- Robert C. Lester
THERAVADA BUDDHISM IN SOUTHEAST ASIA
A good, clearly written survey of Theravada Buddhist doctrine and the function of religion in the societies of mainland Southeast Asia
0–472–06184–4 Michigan pb $9.95

- Clifford Geertz
THE RELIGION OF JAVA
An authoritative work on modern Javanese religion by a powerful and original thinker
0–226–28510–3 Chicago pb $14.00

- Raphael Israeli, editor
THE CRESCENT IN THE EAST
Essays on Islam in Malaysia, Indonesia, and the Philippines
0–391–02099–4 Humanities $14.50

TIBETAN RELIGION

- Stephan Beyer
THE CULT OF TARA: Magic and Ritual in Tibet
A lucid and sophisticated analysis of the cult of the great savioress, demonstrating the way in which religious and magical elements complement each other in religious ritual
Introduction by Kees Bolle
0–520–03635–2 California pb $14.95

- W.Y. Evans-Wentz, translator & editor
TIBETAN YOGA AND SECRET DOCTRINES
The best work by a popular but not always reliable interpreter of Tibetan religion
0–19–500278–4 Oxford pb $12.95

- Francesca Fremantle & Chögyam Trungpa, translators
THE TIBETAN BOOK OF THE DEAD: The Great Liberation Through Hearing in the Bardo
Although it is by no means the central work of the Tibetan Buddhist tradition (whatever its estimation in the West), this work remains a fascinating account of Tibetan beliefs about the state immediately following death and preceding the next rebirth
0–87773–074–1 Shambhala pb $9.95

- Herbert V. Guenther, translator
THE JEWEL ORNAMENT OF LIBERATION
An exposition of the principles and practice of Tibetan Buddhism. "The book remains the classic text of all Buddhists"—Chögyam Trungpa
0–87773–78–3 Shambhala pb $14.95

- Geshe K. Gyatso
THE CLEAR LIGHT OF BLISS
An exposition of one of the central meditative practices of the advanced Anuttarayoga Tantras
Translated by Tenzin Norbu
Edited by Chris Colb & Jonathan Landow
0–86171–005–3 Wisdom Publications pb $10.95

- Frederick & Audrey Hyde-Chambers
TIBETAN FOLK TALES
A wonderful collection of edifying tales and stories filled with the imagery and symbolism of Tibetan Buddhism
Illustrated by Kusho Ralla
0–394–74886–7 Shambhala pb $8.95

- Lobsang P. Lhalunga, translator
THE LIFE OF MILAREPA
A rendering of a popular Tibetan biography of perhaps the best-known and most venerated of all Buddhists in Tibet
0–394–72696–0 Shambhala pb $13.95

- David Snellgrove & Hugh Richardson
THE CULTURAL HISTORY OF TIBET
A superb survey by two accomplished scholars of Tibetan history and religion
0–394–74380–6 Shambhala pb $12.95

- R.A. Stein
TIBETAN CIVILIZATION
An authoritative study with a useful table of key terms
Translated by J.E. Driver
0–8047–0806–1 Stanford $32.50

- Chögyam Trungpa & others, translators
THE LIFE OF MARPA THE TRANSLATOR
A biography of the 11th-century founder of the Practice Lineage of the Kagyu order
0–877–73377–5 Shambhala pb $12.95

INNER ASIAN TRADITIONS

- **Mircea Eliade**
SHAMANISM: Archaic Techniques of Ecstasy
Eliade's study of shamanism is one of his greatest and most influential works. He takes a global approach to the subject but focuses particularly on the traditions of North and Central Asia
Translated by Willard R. Trask
0–691–01779–4 Princeton pb $14.50

- **Walther Heissig**
THE RELIGIONS OF MONGOLIA
An authoritative study that focuses on the non-Buddhist component of Mongol religion
0–520–03857–6 California $31.00

> Healer and psychopomp, the shaman is these because he commands the techniques of ecstasy—that is, because his soul can safely abandon his body and roam at vast distances, can penetrate the underworld and rise to the sky. Through his own ecstatic experience he knows the roads of the extraterrestrial regions. He can go below and above because he has already been there. The danger of losing his way in these forbidden regions is still great; but sanctified by his initiation and furnished with his guardian spirits, the shaman is the only human being able to challenge the danger and venture into a mystical geography.
>
> Mircea Eliade
> SHAMANISM: Archaic Techniques of Ecstasy
> Translated by Willard R. Trask
> 0–691–01779–4 Princeton pb $14.50

Judaism

The following books focus primarily on Judaism as both a religion and a way of life. Books that explore the various other aspects of Jewish existence can be found in the chapters on Jewish History, Hebrew Literature, Yiddish Literature, the Holocaust, and the Contemporary Middle East.

THE BIBLE

The volumes of biblical translation and commentary listed below reflect a continuing discussion over biblical interpretation. The Five Scrolls were edited by scholars who are identified with Reform Judaism; the commentaries contained in the Soncino Books of the Bible are an anthology of Orthodox interpretation. The authors in the section of commentaries represent their own individual views; none of them speaks for a party.

- **Jewish Publication Society, editors**
TANAKH: A New Translation of the Holy Scriptures According to the Traditional Hebrew Text
All three volumes collected in a new English translation prepared by scholars from the three main branches of American Judaism; also available as individual volumes
0–8276–0252–9 JPS $21.95

  THE TORAH: The Five Books of Moses
  0–8276–0015–1 JPS $10.95

  THE PROPHETS: Nevi'im
  0–8276–0096–8 JPS $10.95

  THE WRITINGS: Ketubim
  0–8276–0202–2 JPS $10.95

- **Herbert N. Bronstein & Albert H. Friedlander, editors**
THE FIVE SCROLLS
The Reform movement's Hebrew and English version of the five biblical books that form the basis for major festivals: Ecclesiastes, Esther, Song of Songs, Ruth, and Lamentations
0–916694–80–1 CCAR $19.95

- **A. Cohen, editor**
THE SONCINO BOOKS OF THE BIBLE
An excellent Hebrew-English Bible in 14 volumes with extensive commentary, from Soncino, the noted press
0–900689–11–1 Soncino (set) $165.00

- **Everett Fox, translator**
IN THE BEGINNING: A New English Rendition of the Book of Genesis
A translation that brings the reader closer to the literary style and Hebrew voice of the Bible than do traditional versions
0–8052–3870–0 Schocken $14.95

  NOW THESE ARE THE NAMES: A New English Rendition of the Book of Exodus
  "Fox has succeeded in capturing the poetic beauty and power of the original Bible version"—*Library Journal*
  0–8052–4020–9 Schocken $16.95

- **J.H. Hertz**
THE PENTATEUCH & HAFTORAHS
Torah readings grouped with their Haftorah readings, in Hebrew and English
0–900689–21–8 Soncino $27.50

> **Stephen Mitchell, translator**
> **THE BOOK OF JOB**
> An acclaimed new translation that highlights *Job*'s literary qualities. "Stephen Mitchell's version of *Job* succeeds in conveying a rush, a momentum, that are insistent, at times awesome, and often the bearers of a new insight into the meaning and power of the unique original"—W.S. Merwin
> 0–86547–270–X North Point pb $12.50

- **W. Gunther Plaut & Bernard J. Bamberger**
THE TORAH: A Modern Commentary
A Reform-movement edition of the Five Books of Moses
0–8074–0055–6 UAHC $30.00

Biblical Commentary

- **Robert Alter**
THE ART OF BIBLICAL NARRATIVE
A commentary on the Bible as a literary work. "Alter's book may open up the Bible to those who usually avoid it, and offer new insights to those who know it well"— Elaine Pagels, *New Republic*
0–465–00424–5 Basic Books $14.95
0–465–00427–X Basic Books pb $9.95

- **Martin Buber**
ON THE BIBLE: Eighteen Studies
A collection summarizing the central themes of the great 20th-century humanist's encounters with biblical writings
Edited by Nahum N. Glatzer
Introduction by Harold Bloom
0–8052–3796–8 Schocken $17.95
0–8052–0691–4 Schocken pb $8.95

- **Louis Ginzberg**
LEGENDS OF THE JEWS
A classic collection of biblical stories and legends
0–8276–0148–4 JPS (7-volume set) $95.00

- **Nahum N. Glatzer, editor**
THE DIMENSIONS OF JOB: A Study and Selected Readings
An anthology of essays from Jewish, Christian, and humanist points of view
0–8052–0378–8 Schocken $7.95

- **Robert Gordis**
KOHELETH: The Man and His World—A Study of Ecclesiastes
A thorough analysis of the book of Ecclesiastes in the context of both the literature of its time and its relevance to modern thought
0–8052–0166–1 Schocken pb $10.95

- **Abraham Joshua Heschel**
THE PROPHETS
"Heschel seeks not so much to expound the message of the prophets against the background of their times and to fix their place in the history of Israel's religion, as to explore the phenomenon of prophecy as such, to analyze its fundamental presuppositions and the nature of prophetic inspiration"—John Bright, *Westminster Bookman*

  Volume 1: An Introduction
  0–06–131421–8 Harper & Row pb $7.95

  Volume 2
  0–06–131557–5 Harper & Row pb $7.95

- **Yehezkel Kaufmann**
THE RELIGION OF ISRAEL: From Its Beginnings to the Babylonian Exile
Analyzes major concepts, the work of the classical prophets, and the origins of the Torah
Translated and abridged by Moshe Greenberg
0–8052–0364–8 Schocken pb $13.95

➤ FOR OVERSEAS ORDERING INFORMATION, SEE PAGE 1

ARTHUR HERTZBERG: Essential Books in Judaica

Jewish Publication Society, editors
TANAKH: A New Translation of the Holy Scriptures According to the Traditional Hebrew Text
0–8276–0252–9 JPS $21.95

Leo Baeck
THE ESSENCE OF JUDAISM
0–8052–0006–1 Schocken pb $8.50

Yitzhak Baer
GALUT
0–8191–5783–X University Press pb $10.95

H.H. Ben-Sasson, editor
A HISTORY OF THE JEWISH PEOPLE
0–674–39730–4 Harvard $60.00
0–674–39731–2 Harvard pb $18.95

Martin Buber
ON JUDAISM
0–8052–0343–5 Schocken pb $7.95

Herbert Danby, translator & editor
THE MISHNAH
0–19–815402–X Oxford $55.00

Moses Hadas, editor
SOLOMON MAIMON: An Autobiography
0–8052–0150–5 Schocken pb $4.95

Arthur Hertzberg, editor
THE ZIONIST IDEA: A Historical Analysis and Reader
0–689–70093–8 Atheneum pb $7.95

Abraham Joshua Heschel
THE EARTH IS THE LORD'S: The Inner World of the Jew in Eastern Europe
0–374–51469–0 FS&G pb $6.95

C.G. Montefiore & H. Loewe, editors
A RABBINIC ANTHOLOGY
0–8052–0442–3 Schocken pb $16.95

Louis I. Newman
THE HASIDIC ANTHOLOGY: Tales and Teachings of the Hasidim
0–8052–0836–4 Schocken pb $12.95

Gershom Scholem
KABBALAH
0–452–00887–5 NAL pb $11.95

Joseph B. Soloveitchik
HALAKHIC MAN
Translated by Lawrence Kaplan
0–8276–0222–7 JPS $12.95

Elie Wiesel
NIGHT
0–553–27253–5 Bantam pb $3.50

● **Chaim Pearl**
RASHI
Rabbi Solomon Ben Isaac (1040–1105) is the foremost Jewish Bible commentator of all time; this intellectual biography is part of the new Jewish Thinkers series
0–8021–1063–0 Grove $15.95

David Rosenberg, editor
CONGREGATION: Writers Read the Jewish Bible
Reflections on each book of the Bible from Mordecai Richler, Isaac Bashevis Singer, Cynthia Ozick, Anne Roiphe, James Atlas, and others
0–15–146350–6 HBJ $29.95

● **Samuel Sandmel**
THE HEBREW SCRIPTURES: An Introduction to Their Literature and Religious Ideas
0–19–502369–2 Oxford pb $16.95

● **Nahum M. Sarna**
UNDERSTANDING GENESIS: The Heritage of Biblical Israel
"The most comprehensive and careful interpretation of the Bible's initial book in light of the extrabiblical sources bearing upon it"—*Journal of Biblical Literature*
0–8052–0253–6 Schocken pb $8.95

EXPLORING EXODUS: The Heritage of Biblical Israel
Sarna demonstrates the significance of Israel's revolutionary monotheism by analyzing how and why the biblical text represents an original departure in religious imagination
0–8052–3982–0 Schocken $18.95
0–8052–0830–5 Schocken pb $8.95

● **Shalom Spiegel**
THE LAST TRIAL: On the Legend and Lore of the Command to Abraham to Offer Isaac As a Sacrifice—The Akedah
A learned book on a key episode in the demonstration of Jewish faith that figured strongly in the Hebrew liturgy of the 12th and 13th centuries
0–87441–290–0 Behrman House pb $7.95

The sacrifice of Isaac, from Yiddish Folktales *edited by Beatrice Silverman Weinreich (Pantheon)*

● **Elie Wiesel**
MESSENGERS OF GOD: Biblical Portraits and Legends
Original thoughts on the stories of Adam, Cain and Abel, the sacrifice of Isaac, Jacob and the angel, Joseph, Moses, Job, and others
0–671–52333–3 Summit $16.95
0–671–54134–X Summit pb $8.95

FIVE BIBLICAL PORTRAITS
Portraits of Saul, Jonah, Jeremiah, Elijah, and Joshua
0–268–00962–7 Notre Dame pb $6.95

LATER ANTIQUITY

● **Edgar Goodspeed**
THE APOCRYPHA: An American Translation
Includes such key works as Maccabees I and II, The Wisdom of Solomon, and the Book of Judith
Introduction by Moses Hadas
0–394–70163–1 Random House pb $5.95

● **G. Vermes**
THE DEAD SEA SCROLLS IN ENGLISH
A translation of the Hebrew and Aramaic documents discovered in the 1940s and dating from 200 BCE to the 1st century CE, offering unparalleled insights into post-biblical Jewish life; a revised and updated edition
0–14–022779–2 Penguin pb $6.95

THE TALMUD

"Historically speaking, the Talmud is the central pillar of Jewish culture. This culture is many faceted, but each of its numerous aspects is connected in some way with the Talmud. This is true not only of the literature that deals directly with the interpretation or continuation of the Talmud, but also of all other types of Jewish creativity. Halakhic literature is, of course, based entirely on the Talmud, but most original Jewish philosophy has also drawn inspiration from it in one way or another. It is impossible to approach biblical exegesis or Jewish or esoteric philosophy without knowledge of the Talmud. Even works that have no ostensible connection with talmudic literature—like poetry or prayers—are inspired by it in various ways. The student who claims to understand the significance and intention of material will realize, after close perusal of this literature, how barren are the attempts to absorb Jewish knowledge while ignoring its basic sources."—Adin Steinsaltz, *The Essential Talmud*

● **Philip Blackman, translator**
THE MISHNAH
The entire, fully indexed work, in Hebrew and English; a 7-volume set
0–910818–00–2 Judaica Press (set) $85.00

● **Abraham Cohen**
EVERYMAN'S TALMUD
A classic, straightforward introduction to the fundamental concepts of the Talmud
0–8052–0497–0 Schocken pb $12.95

● Herbert Danby, translator & editor
THE MISHNAH
The standard reference work, a one-volume translation of the entire Mishnah by a noted Christian scholar
0–19–815402–X Oxford $55.00

● Isadore Epstein, editor
THE SONCINO TALMUD
The full Talmud—Mishnah and commentary—in English. An 18-volume set
0–900689–22–6 Soncino (set) $375.00

● R. Travers Herford, editor
THE ETHICS OF THE TALMUD: Sayings of the Fathers
Aphorisms of the great rabbis on Jewish law and the human condition
0–8052–0023–1 Schocken pb $7.95

● Jacob Neusner
THE MISHNAH: A New Translation
A formal-analytical rendering of the entire Mishnah, keeping as close to a literal translation as possible, by a leading scholar
0–300–03065–7 Yale $55.00

● Solomon Schechter
ASPECTS OF RABBINIC THEOLOGY: Major Concepts of the Talmud
An introduction to rabbinic views
Introduction by Louis Finkelstein
0–8052–0015–0 Schocken pb $8.95

● Adin Steinsaltz
THE ESSENTIAL TALMUD
A clear and intelligent guide to the history, structure and content, and method of the Talmud
0–465–02063–1 Basic Books pb $9.95

● Ephraim E. Urbach
THE SAGES: The World and Wisdom of the Rabbis of the Talmud
A landmark examination of the ancient texts that form the basis for the rabbinic code of ethics and the conduct of daily life
Translated by Israel Abrahams
0–674–78523–1 Harvard pb $18.95

The Shulhan Arukh

Solomon Ganzfried
CODE OF JEWISH LAW
A one-volume English edition of the 16th-century guide to orthodox Jewish law (the Kitzur Shulhan Arukh)
Translated by Hyman E. Goldin
0–88482–423–3 Hebrew Publishing $19.50

EARLY PHILOSOPHICAL TEXTS

● Israel Abrahams, editor
HEBREW ETHICAL WILLS
A collection of the traditional "ethical wills" in which parents instruct their children in the morality and wisdom of life
Translated by Israel Abrahams
Foreword by Judah Goldin
0–8276–0082–8 JPS pb $12.95

● J. David Bleich
WITH PERFECT FAITH: The Foundations of Jewish Belief
A collection of medieval philosophical writings
0–87068–452–3 Ktav pb $20.00

● Erwin R. Goodenough
AN INTRODUCTION TO PHILO JUDAEUS
The life and writings of the ancient philosopher Philo of Alexandria (20 BCE–50 CE)
0–8191–5335–4 University Press pb $12.75

● Judah Halevi
THE KUZARI: An Argument for the Faith of Israel
The Jewish religion presented in the form of an argument before a medieval king; a classic work from the foremost Jewish poet and thinker of the Middle Ages
0–8052–0075–4 Schocken pb $6.95

● Moses Maimonides
THE GUIDE OF THE PERPLEXED
A reconciliation of the Old Testament and Aristotle by the great 12th-century Jewish philosopher
Translated by Shlomo Pines
Introduction by Leo Strauss

Volume 1
0–226–50230–9 Chicago pb $15.95
Volume 2
0–226–50231–7 Chicago pb $15.95

● Isadore Twersky, editor
A MAIMONIDES READER
Excerpts from the great medieval philosopher, including pieces from his two greatest works: *Guide of the Perplexed* and *Mishneh Torah*
0–87441–206–4 Behrman House pb $10.95

MYSTICISM AND HASIDISM

Mysticism and Kabbalah

● Adolphe Franck
THE KABBALAH
A readily comprehensible overview of the mystical texts
0–8065–0708–X Citadel pb $6.95

Gershom Scholem
KABBALAH
The history and basic ideas of the Kabbalah, plus detailed entries on a wide range of concepts and personalities in the mystical literature; by the leading authority on Jewish mysticism
0–452–00887–5 NAL pb $11.95

MAJOR TRENDS IN JEWISH MYSTICISM
A collection of lectures on the features of the movement that began in antiquity and continues in Hasidism today
0–8052–0005–3 Schocken pb $10.95

THE MESSIANIC IDEA IN JUDAISM & Other Essays on Jewish Spirituality
Scholem explores the complex relationship between mysticism and Messianism in Jewish thought
0–8052–0362–1 Schocken pb $8.95

● Ben Shahn
THE ALPHABET OF CREATION: An Ancient Legend from the Zohar
A great artist retells this passage from the mystical work of the 14th-century scholar Moses de Leon
0–8052–0359–1 Schocken pb $5.95

● Isaiah Tishby, editor
THE WISDOM OF THE ZOHAR
Translated by David Goldstein
0–19–710043–0 Oxford (3-volume set) $198.00

● Joshua Trachtenberg
JEWISH MAGIC AND SUPERSTITION: A Study in Folk Religion
0–689–70234–5 Atheneum pb $10.95

● Herbert Weiner
NINE AND ONE HALF MYSTICS: The Kabbalah Today
"Rabbi Weiner ranks with Martin Buber and Gershom Scholem as a most profound (and also delightful) exponent of his spiritual tradition"—Alan Watts
0–02–068160–7 Macmillan pb $8.95

Hasidism

● Arnold Band, translator & editor
NAHMAN OF BRATSLAV: The Tales
Thirteen tales from a Hasidic master
0–8091–2103–4 Paulist Press pb $9.95

● Dan Ben-Amos & Jerome R. Mintz, editors
IN PRAISE OF THE BAAL SHEM TOV
A collection of legends about the 18th-century founder of Hasidism, the "Master of the Good Name," originally published in Hebrew in 1814
0–8052–0758–9 Schocken pb $9.95

● Martin Buber
THE LEGEND OF THE BAAL-SHEM
0–8052–0233–1 Schocken pb $8.95

TALES OF THE HASIDIM

Volume 1: The Early Masters
0–8052–0001–0 Schocken pb $9.95

Volume 2: The Later Masters
0–8052–0002–9 Schocken pb $9.95

THE ORIGIN AND MEANING OF HASIDISM
Compares Hasidism with Biblical prophecy, Spinoza, Freud, Christianity, Zen Buddhism, and more
0–391–03549–5 Humanities pb $15.00

● Samuel H. Dresner
ZADDIK: The Doctrine of the Zaddik According to the Writings of Rabbi Yaakov Yosef of Polnoy
Preface by Abraham Joshua Heschel
0–8052–0437–7 Schocken pb $4.95

• Arthur Green & Barry W. Holtz,
editors and translators
**YOUR WORD IS FIRE: The Hasidic
Masters on Contemplative Prayer**
"Hints as to the various rungs of inner
prayer and how they are attained," based
on the teachings of such Hasidic masters as
the Baal Shem Tov and the Maggid Dov
Baer of Meidzyrzec
0–8052–0842–9 Schocken pb $7.95

• Louis I. Newman, editor
**THE HASIDIC ANTHOLOGY: Tales and
Teachings of the Hasidim**
Translations of writings and documents
covering the history and practice of
Hasidic life
0–8052–0836–4 Schocken pb $12.95

• Elie Wiesel
**SOULS ON FIRE: Portraits and Legends
of Hasidic Masters**
Writings about the Hasidic sects. "These
tales, although they are the kernel of a
highly developed form of Jewish
mysticism, have a basic human interest that
transcends the dividing lines of religion"—
Alan Pryce-Jones, *Washington Post*
0–671–45210–X Summit $17.50
0–671–44171–X Summit pb $8.95

ANTHOLOGIES OF BASIC TEXTS

• Samuel Caplan & Harold Ribalow,
editors
THE GREAT JEWISH BOOKS
An introduction to the major works, with
brief excerpts from the Bible, the Talmud,
Maimonides, the Zohar, the Shulhan
Arukh, Herzl, and many others
0–8180–1135–1 Western pb $10.95

• Nahum Glatzer, editor
**THE JUDAIC TRADITION: Jewish
Writing From Antiquity to the Modern Age**
A comprehensive collection including
selections from ancient, medieval, and
modern Judaism on topics ranging from
the nature of God to the politics of
modern Zionism. "An outstanding
anthology of Jewish thought, full of
substance and yet highly readable and well
organized"—Emil L. Fackenheim
0–87668–984–5 Jason Aronson $35.00
0–87441–344–3 Behrman House pb $12.50

• Barry Holtz, editor
**BACK TO THE SOURCES: Reading the
Classic Jewish Texts**
"The best and most comprehensive
introduction available"—Harold Bloom
0–671–45467–6 Summit $24.95
0–671–60596–8 Summit pb $12.95

• C.G. Montefiore & H. Loewe, editors
A RABBINIC ANTHOLOGY
0–8052–0442–3 Schocken pb $16.95

*Moses' stone tablets pictured by Leonard
Baskin, from* The Book of Adam to Moses
by Lore Segal (Knopf)

MODERN THEOLOGY AND PHILOSOPHY

Overviews

Arthur A. Cohen & Paul Mendes-
Flohr, editors
**CONTEMPORARY JEWISH
RELIGIOUS THOUGHT**
An ample collection: 140 essays from
such major figures as Emil Fackenheim,
Jacob Neusner, Gerson Cohen, and
others
0–02–906040–0 Free Press pb $24.95

Nahum Glatzer, editor
**MODERN JEWISH THOUGHT: A
Source Reader**
Excerpts from the major figures,
including Mendelssohn, Geiger, Baeck,
Buber, Rosenzweig, Kaplan,
Fackenheim, Heschel, and others
0–8052–0542–X Schocken pb $7.50

Julius Guttmann
**PHILOSOPHIES OF JUDAISM: A
History of Jewish Philosophy from
Biblical Times to Franz Rosenzweig**
A complete, thick, and authoritative
survey. "At once a history of Jewish
philosophy and a profound
philosophical treatment of Judaism"—
John E. Smith, Yale University
0–8052–0402–4 Schocken pb $13.50

• Leo Baeck
THE ESSENCE OF JUDAISM
The foremost theological work of Baeck
(1873–1956), the German Reform Rabbi
and leader of Progressive Judaism who
survived Theresienstadt
0–8052–0006–1 Schocken pb $8.50

• Eugene B. Borowitz
LIBERAL JUDAISM
0–8074–0264–8 UAHC pb $8.95

• Martin Buber
I AND THOU
A classic of religious existentialism
Translated by Walter Kauffman & S.G. Smith
0–684–15575–3 Scribners $25.00
0–684–71725–5 Scribners pb $8.95
0–684–18254–8 Macmillan pb $4.95

ON JUDAISM
Twelve essays, dating from 1909 to 1951,
including "Judaism and Mankind," "Myth
in Judaism," and "The Dialogue Between
Heaven and Earth"
0–8052–0343–5 Schocken pb $7.95

TWO TYPES OF FAITH
Buber's major work on the interplay of
Judaism and Christianity, viewing the
former as a faith based on trust,
represented by the tradition of the Torah,
and the latter based on belief in truth,
represented by Christ as revealed in the
New Testament
0–02–084180–9 Macmillan pb $7.95

• Emil L. Fackenheim
TO MEND THE WORLD
A major work on post-Holocaust spiritual
survival by a German-born rabbi and
Jewish philosopher
0–8052–0699–X Schocken pb $12.95

**WHAT IS JUDAISM?: An Interpretation
for the Present Age**
An introduction to what Judaism can mean
in the aftermath of the Holocaust and the
rise of the Israeli state
0–671–46243–1 Summit $18.95
0–02–032191–0 Macmillan pb $9.95

• Hafetz Hayyim
**AHAVATH CHESED: The Love of
Kindness As Required by God**
A very important work on the fundamental
Jewish concept of kindness by one of the
greatest religious leaders of Eastern
Europe's Jews, Rabbi Israel Meir ha-
Kohen, better known as the Hafetz
Hayyim
Translated by Leonard Oschry
0–87306–110–1 Philipp Feldheim $11.95

• Samuel Heilmann
**THE GATE BEHIND THE WALL: A
Pilgrimage to Jerusalem**
A scholar's reacquaintance with original
Jewish texts and thought on his voyage
through the Holy City
0–671–52489–5 Summit $15.95

• Abraham Joshua Heschel
**BETWEEN GOD AND MAN: An
Interpretation of Judaism**
An anthology of key writings by a leading
modern Jewish philosopher
Edited by Fritz A. Rothschild
0–02–914510–4 Free Press pb $10.95

**GOD IN SEARCH OF MAN: A Philosophy
of Judaism**
0–374–51331–7 Farrar, Straus & Giroux pb $12.95

**MAN IS NOT ALONE: A Philosophy of
Religion**
0–374–51328–7 Farrar, Straus & Giroux pb $9.95

• Louis Jacobs
THE BOOK OF JEWISH BELIEF
0–87441–379–6 Behrman House pb $7.95

• Mordecai M. Kaplan

DYNAMIC JUDAISM: The Essential Writings of Mordecai M. Kaplan
An anthology of works by the founder of the Reconstructionist movement that offers clear insight into Kaplan's thought and the philosophy of the fourth major branch of American Judaism
Edited by Emanuel S. Goldsmith & Mel Scult
0–8052–0786–4 Schocken pb $12.95

JUDAISM AS A CIVILIZATION
Kaplan's major work on the principles of Reconstructionist Judaism
0–8276–0194–8 JPS pb $14.95

• Moses Luzzatto

THE PATH OF THE JUST
Moral guidelines from a major Hebrew poet, kabbalist, and ethical thinker of the 18th century
0–87306–114–4 Philipp Feldheim $12.95
0–87306–115–2 Philipp Feldheim pb $9.95

• Franz Rosenzweig

ON JEWISH LEARNING
Essays on Jewish education by a leading 20th-century German-Jewish theologian who flirted with conversion but ultimately was reconciled to Judaism
Edited & with an introduction by Nahum N. Glatzer
0–8052–0843–7 Schocken pb $5.95

THE STAR OF REDEMPTION
Translated by William W. Hallo
Foreword by Nahum N. Glatzer
0–268–01718–2 Notre Dame pb $12.95

• Abba Hillel Silver

WHERE JUDAISM DIFFERS: An Inquiry into the Distinctiveness of Judaism
A key work by a noted American rabbi and Zionist leader (1893–1963)
0–02–037221–3 Macmillan pb $9.95

The core of Judaism is right conduct to other people. The Talmud . . . tells that a Gentile came to the Rabbi Hillel and asked to be taught all Judaism while standing on one foot. Hillel's colleague, Shammai, had driven the man from his door, taking the question for a baiting impertinence. Hillel amiably replied, "What is offensive to you do not do to others. The rest is commentary. Now carry on your studies." The man became a convert.

The core of a nuclear reactor, or of an apple, or of a religion, is not all of it. We make few core decisions day by day. Life is too packed with running trivialities, with mechanical repetition. Judaism does not let that part of life go. It weaves commitment, and therefore at least formal significance, all through one's day.

Herman Wouk

THIS IS MY GOD: The Jewish Way of Life
0–316–95507–8 Little, Brown $17.95

• Joseph B. Soloveitchik

HALAKHIC MAN
A basic theological statement on the importance of halakhah, or law, in Jewish life
Translated by Lawrence Kaplan
0–8276–0222–7 JPS $12.95

• Herman Wouk

THIS IS MY GOD: The Jewish Way of Life
A new edition, updated and including "Israel at Forty: The Land and the Faith"
0–316–95507–8 Little, Brown $17.95

HOW-TO:
Ritual and Practice

The Basics of Judaism

• Marc D. Angel

THE RHYTHMS OF JEWISH LIVING: The Sephardic Approach
0–87203–126–8 Hermon $14.95

• Michael Asheri

LIVING JEWISH: The Lore and Law of the Practicing Jew
A guidebook to Jewish life and ritual noting differences in beliefs and customs among the Orthodox and Reform, Sephardim and Ashkenazim
0–396–08263–7 Dodd, Mead pb $9.95

Hayim Halevy Donin

TO BE A JEW
A comprehensive guide to Jewish law and life from a modern Orthodox perspective, covering everything from prayer to birth control
0–465–08624–1 Basic Books $17.95

TO PRAY AS A JEW: A Guide to the Prayer Book and the Synagogue Service
Includes texts of prayers and songs
0–465–08628–4 Basic Books $17.95

• David C. Gross

1,001 QUESTIONS AND ANSWERS ABOUT JUDAISM
"Ideal for busy people seeking ready answers on the basic questions of Judaism and the Jewish people"—Rabbi Alexander Schindler, President, Union of American Hebrew Congregations
0–87052–446–1 Hippocrene pb $8.95

• Aryeh Kaplan

JEWISH MEDITATION: A Practical Guide
"A guide to Jewish prayer and meditation that is both grounded in the tradition and genuinely mind-expanding"—William Novak
0–8052–0781–3 Schocken pb $9.95

• Morris N. Kertzer

WHAT IS A JEW?
Questions and answers on Jewish life, religion, and culture ranging from birth control to Jewish attitudes toward the New Testament
0–02–086350–0 Macmillan pb $5.95

• Alfred J. Kolatch

THE JEWISH BOOK OF WHY
A question-and-answer approach to the fundamental tenets and practices of Judaism
0–8246–0256–0 Jonathan David $13.95

THE SECOND JEWISH BOOK OF WHY
A sequel, addressing more complex and controversial issues of modern Jewish life
0–8246–0305–2 Jonathan David $13.95

• Arthur Kurzweil

FROM GENERATION TO GENERATION: How to Trace Your Jewish Genealogy and Personal History
Foreword by Elie Wiesel
0–8052–0706–6 Schocken pb $9.95

• Helen Latner

THE BOOK OF MODERN JEWISH ETIQUETTE
The practical aspects of Jewish life, including behavior, home ceremonies, and coping with Christmas
0–06–097054–5 Harper & Row pb $9.95

• Simeon J. Maslin, editor

GATES OF MITZVAH: A Guide to the Jewish Life Cycle
A Reform handbook on birth, childhood, education, marriage, death, mourning, and other aspects of life
0–916694–53–4 CCAR pb $7.95

• Dennis Prager & Joseph Telushkin

THE NINE QUESTIONS PEOPLE ASK ABOUT JUDAISM
"The intelligent skeptic's guide to Judaism"—Herman Wouk
0–671–62261–7 Simon & Schuster pb $7.95

• Milton Steinberg

BASIC JUDAISM
A succinct and clearly-written exposition of Judaism's fundamental concepts and practices. "A book for Jew and Gentile alike: indeed for all men who continue to wrestle with the ultimate questions of man's destiny"—Lewis Mumford
0–87668–975–6 Jason Aronson $20.00
0–15–610698–1 HBJ pb $4.95

Sabbath and Holidays

• S.Y. Agnon

DAYS OF AWE: A Treasury of Tradition, Legends and Learned Commentaries Concerning Rosh Ha-Shanah, Yom Kippur and the Days Between
A hymn to the High Holy Days, by a major novelist
Introduction by Judah Goldin
0–8052–0100–9 Schocken pb $9.95

• Theodor H. Gaster

FESTIVALS OF THE JEWISH YEAR: A Modern Interpretation and Guide
0–688–06008–0 Morrow pb $7.95

• Abraham Joshua Heschel

THE SABBATH: Its Meaning for Modern Man
A brief discourse on the Sabbath as a symbol of Judaism's sanctification of time
0–374–51267–1 Farrar, Straus & Giroux pb $5.95

IF YOU CAN'T FIND IT, LOOK IN THE INDEX

- Peter S. Knobel, editor
  THE GATES OF THE SEASONS: A Guide to the Jewish Year
  Holidays, festivals, the Sabbath, and other special days, from the perspective of the Reform movement
  0–916694–92–5 CCAR pb $9.95

- Hayyim Schauss
  THE JEWISH FESTIVALS: History and Observance
  The background and meaning of the major Jewish holidays, including a calendar of dates for the next two decades
  0–8052–0413–X Schocken pb $9.95

- Michael Strassfeld
  JEWISH HOLIDAYS
  An informative guide from the coauthor of the popular Jewish Catalog series
  Illustrated by Betsy P. Teutsch
  Commentaries by Arnold Eisen
  0–06–015406–3 Harper & Row $24.95

- Arthur Waskow
  SEASONS OF OUR JOY: A Celebration of Modern Jewish Renewal
  A "New Age" guide to Jewish holidays
  0–553–01369–6 Bantam pb $8.95

Passover

- Herbert Bronstein, editor
  A PASSOVER HAGGADAH: The New Union Haggadah
  Prepared by the Central Conference of American Rabbis
  0–14–004871–5 Penguin pb $14.95

- Nahum Glatzer, editor
  THE PASSOVER HAGGADAH
  Illustrated with woodcuts from the first illuminated Haggadah, Prague, 1526
  0–8052–0624–8 Schocken pb $3.95

- David Goldstein, editor
  THE ASHKENAZI HAGGADAH
  The Passover Haggadah has been, for centuries, the inspiration for some of the most beautiful Hebrew illuminated manuscripts, including this splendid one
  0–8109–1819–6 Abrams $75.00

- Raphael Loewe, editor
  THE RYLANDS HAGGADAH: A Medieval Sephardi Masterpiece in Facsimile
  A replication of a 14th-century edition of an original Sephardic Haggadah housed in Manchester, England
  0–8109–1568–5 Abrams $95.00

Family and Household

- David M. Feldman
  MARITAL RELATIONS, BIRTH CONTROL, AND ABORTION IN JEWISH LAW
  A systematic ethical study tracing its subjects through sources in religious law and rabbinic interpretation, and comparing the Jewish tenets with Christian views. "A landmark in comparative ethics"—James Gustafson, *Christian Century*
  0–8052–0438–5 Schocken pb $8.95

- Blu Greenberg
  HOW TO RUN A TRADITIONAL JEWISH HOUSEHOLD
  0–671–41700–2 Simon & Schuster $19.95

- S.B. Levi & Sylvia R. Kaplan
  GUIDE FOR THE JEWISH HOMEMAKER
  A practical handbook for maintaining a Jewish home and family, including preparations for the Sabbath, holidays, and other special occasions, blending traditional and contemporary views
  0–8052–0087–8 Schocken pb $7.95

Women

- Rachel Biale
  WOMEN AND JEWISH LAW: An Exploration of Women's Issues in Halakhic Sources
  "A rare book in Jewish women's studies, combining a scholarly review of halakhah [law] with the presentation of a thoughtful feminist opinion"—*Washington Jewish Week*
  0–8052–3887–5 Schocken $18.95
  0–8052–0810–0 Schocken pb $8.95

- Susannah Heschel, editor
  ON BEING A JEWISH FEMINIST: A Reader
  "Superb collection . . . on the feminist side of Judaism and the woman as 'outsider' "—Jack Nusan Porter
  0–8052–0745–7 Schocken pb $10.95

- Elizabeth Koltun, editor
  THE JEWISH WOMAN: New Perspectives
  An anthology organized from the viewpoint of the new women's consciousness
  0–8052–0532–2 Schocken pb $8.95

- Susan W. Schneider
  JEWISH AND FEMALE: Choices and Changes in Our Lives Today
  0–671–42103–4 Simon & Schuster $19.95

Children

- Anita Diamant
  THE JEWISH BABY BOOK
  Includes a section on names for Jewish children
  0–671–63935–8 Summit $16.95

- Hayim Halevy Donin
  TO RAISE A JEWISH CHILD: A Guide for Parents
  "The 'Jewish Dr. Spock' offers parents warm, contemporary but traditional advice"—*Baltimore Jewish Times*
  0–465–08626–8 Basic Books $15.95

- Harold S. Kushner
  WHEN CHILDREN ASK ABOUT GOD
  By the best-selling author of *When Bad Things Happen to Good People*
  0–8052–0879–8 Schocken pb $6.95

Marriage and Weddings

- Anita Diamant
  THE NEW JEWISH WEDDING
  An overview of traditional practice and its

variations for those who want to fashion their own ceremony
0–671–49527–5 Summit $16.95
0–671–62882–8 Summit pb $7.95

- Lilly S. Routtenberg & Ruth R. Seldin
  THE JEWISH WEDDING BOOK
  A straightforward guide
  0–8052–0186–6 Schocken pb $6.95

Self-Help

- Harold S. Kushner
  WHEN BAD THINGS HAPPEN TO GOOD PEOPLE
  A best-selling guide to crisis management, from a noted rabbi
  0–8052–3773–9 Schocken $13.95
  0–380–60392–6 Avon pb $3.95

- Maurice Lamm
  THE JEWISH WAY IN DEATH AND MOURNING
  Practical and spiritual guidelines
  0–8246–0126–2 Jonathan David pb $8.95

- Jack Riemer, editor
  JEWISH REFLECTIONS ON DEATH
  Essays by Elie Wiesel, Abraham Joshua Heschel, Joseph B. Soloveitchik, Milton Steinberg, Max Lerner, Jacob Neusner, and others
  Foreword by Elisabeth Kübler-Ross
  0–8052–0516–0 Schocken pb $5.95

Travel

- Alan M. Tigay, editor
  THE JEWISH TRAVELER: Hadassah Magazine's Guide to the World's Jewish Communities and Sights
  A wealth of information on kosher restaurants, places of worship, Jewish community centers, historical sights, and Jewish life
  0–385–23451–1 Doubleday pb $10.95

Resources

- Ruth S. Frank & William Wollheim
  THE BOOK OF JEWISH BOOKS: A Reader's Guide to Judaism
  A wonderful bibliography of Jewish books, arranged by subject, with detailed and authoritative descriptions; also includes useful chapters on how to build a Jewish library and a list of Jewish book stores
  0–06–063009–4 Harper & Row pb $10.95

- Michael Strassfeld, Sharon Strassfeld, & Richard Siegel
  THE FIRST JEWISH CATALOG: A Do-It Yourself Kit
  A best-selling volume offering practical guidelines on everything from keeping kosher to crocheting *kippot*
  0–8276–0042–9 JPS pb $12.95

  THE SECOND JEWISH CATALOG: Sources and Resources
  0–8276–0084–4 JPS pb $12.95

  THE THIRD JEWISH CATALOG: Creating Community
  0–8276–0183–2 JPS pb $12.95

Christianity

BIBLES AND APOCRYPHA

• Cambridge University Press
THE HOLY BIBLE: King James Version
With presentation page, concordance, eight maps in color, and gazetteer; bound in black imitation leather
0-521-16110-X Cambridge $29.95

• Alexander Jones, editor
THE JERUSALEM BIBLE: Reader's Edition
A monument of modern Catholic scholarship, published in 1966; one of the most readable translations
0-385-01189-X Doubleday pb $16.95

• George M. Lamsa, translator
THE HOLY BIBLE: From the Ancient Eastern Text
A translation from the ancient Aramaic text
0-06-064922-4 Harper & Row $49.95
0-06-064923-2 Harper & Row pb $20.95

• Richmond Lattimore, translator
THE FOUR GOSPELS & THE REVELATION
A beautiful rendition by the distinguished translator of Greek classics
0-671-50441-X Washington Square pb $3.95

THE ACTS & LETTERS OF THE APOSTLES
Another Lattimore rendering of high literary quality
0-374-10082-9 Farrar, Straus & Giroux $16.00

• Bruce M. Metzger & others, editors
THE NEW OXFORD ANNOTATED BIBLE
The Revised Standard Version, with footnoted commentary
0-19-528-3244 Oxford $29.95

THE NEW OXFORD BIBLE WITH THE APOCRYPHA
0-19-528-3481 Oxford $32.95

> Again Jesus said: Truly truly I tell you, I am the gate for the sheep. All those who came before me are thieves and robbers; but the sheep did not listen to them. I am the gate. Whoever enters through me shall be saved and go in and out and find pasturage. The thief does not come except to steal and slaughter and destroy; I came so that they may have life, and have abundance. I am the good shepherd. The good shepherd lays down his life for the sheep.
>
> Richmond Lattimore, translator
> **THE FOUR GOSPELS & THE REVELATION**
> 0-671-50441-X Washington Square pb $3.95

• J.B. Phillips, translator
THE NEW TESTAMENT IN MODERN ENGLISH
Effective precisely because of its almost matter-of-fact tone
0-02-596970-6 Macmillan $12.95
0-02-088490-7 Macmillan pb $8.95

• Henry Wansbrough, editor
THE NEW TESTAMENT OF THE NEW JERUSALEM BIBLE
A contemporary Catholic translation
0-385-23706-5 Doubleday pb $6.95

Apocrypha and Other Texts

• Willis Barnstone, editor
THE OTHER BIBLE
Jewish Pseudepigrapha, Christian Apocrypha, Gnostic scriptures, the Kabbalah, and the Dead Sea Scrolls
0-06-250031-7 Harper & Row $27.95
0-06-250030-9 Harper & Row pb $15.95

• James H. Charlesworth, editor
OLD TESTAMENT PSEUDEPIGRAPHA
Jewish and Hellenistic texts that served as sources or are otherwise related to the canonical Old Testament scriptures
0-385-19491-9 Doubleday (2-volume set) $80.00

Volume 1: Apocalyptic Literature and Testaments
0-385-09630-5 Doubleday $40.00

Volume 2: Expansions of the Old Testament and Legends, Wisdom and Philosophical Literature, Prayers, Psalms and Odes, Fragments of Lost Judeo-Hellenistic Worlds
0-385-18813-7 Doubleday $40.00

• Theodor H. Gaster, translator
THE DEAD SEA SCRIPTURES
A selection of the Essene texts and other scriptures that were found in caves near the Dead Sea in 1947 and subsequent years, and that reveal much about sectarian religious life in ancient Judaea
0-385-08859-0 Doubleday pb $8.50

CLASSICS

• George Appleton, editor
THE OXFORD BOOK OF PRAYER
0-19-282108-3 Oxford pb $8.95

• St. Augustine
THE CITY OF GOD
The first Christian philosophy of history, a monumental response to pagan interpretations of the decline of Rome. Augustine's exposition of predestination and the two symbolic cities, heavenly and earthly, profoundly influenced subsequent Christian thought
Edited by David Knowles
0-14-044426-2 Penguin pb $12.95

THE CONFESSIONS
Augustine's spiritual autobiography, tracing his passage from boyhood sin through Manichaeanism to Christian conversion
Translated by R.S. Pine-Coffin
0-14-044114-X Penguin pb $4.95

• Oxford University Press
THE BOOK OF COMMON PRAYER & ADMINISTRATION OF THE SACRAMENTS: According to the Use of the Church of England
The liturgy of the Anglican communion, originally adopted in 1549
0-19-130601-0 Oxford $11.95

• John Bunyan
THE PILGRIM'S PROGRESS
The classic allegory of Christian's journey through danger and temptation to the Celestial City, in plain and powerful prose
Edited by Roger Sharrock
Foreword by F.R. Leavis
0-14-043004-0 Penguin pb $2.95

• St. Francis of Assisi
THE LITTLE FLOWERS OF ST. FRANCIS
A compilation of anecdotes (some apocryphal) that convey the joyful faith of the medieval saint
Translated by Raphael Brown
0-385-07544-8 Doubleday pb $5.95

• Thomas à Kempis
THE IMITATION OF CHRIST
After the Bible, this 15th-century devotional work, distinguished by its simplicity and spiritual purity, is probably the most influential Christian book ever written
Translated by Leo Sherley-Price
0-14-044027-5 Penguin pb $3.95

• Søren Kierkegaard
These writings by the founder of existentialist religious thought emphasize the risk and irrationality of faith.
A KIERKEGAARD ANTHOLOGY
The 19th-century philosopher's austere vision of religion
Edited by Robert Bretall
0-691-01978-9 Princeton pb $9.95

ATTACK UPON "CHRISTENDOM"
Translated by Walter Lowrie
Introduction by H.A. Johnson
0-691-01950-9 Princeton pb $8.95

FEAR AND TREMBLING
Translated by Alastair Hannay
0-14-044449-1 Penguin pb $4.95

• Peter Levi, editor
THE PENGUIN BOOK OF ENGLISH CHRISTIAN VERSE
0-14-058602-4 Penguin pb $7.95

• C.S. Lewis
THE ESSENTIAL C.S. LEWIS
0-02-019550-8 Macmillan pb $12.95

THE SCREWTAPE LETTERS
Letters from a senior devil to a junior one on the ways good Christians may be tempted into sin
0-553-26369-2 Bantam pb $3.50

SURPRISED BY JOY: The Shape of My Early Life
An engagingly candid autobiographical account of the author's early life and conversion to Christianity
0-15-187011-X HBJ $12.95
0-15-687011-8 HBJ pb $5.95

- Thomas Merton
THE SEVEN STOREY MOUNTAIN
The autobiography of the influential
American Catholic poet, scholar, and monk
0–15–680679–7 HBJ pb $7.95

  A VOW OF CONVERSION
0–374–28535–7 Farrar, Straus & Giroux $17.95

- John Henry Newman
APOLOGIA PRO VITA SUA
Newman's eloquent account of his search
for an authentic tradition of Christian
faith, which took him from the Oxford
Movement within the Church of England
to the Roman Catholic Church
Edited by David DeLaura
0–393–09766–8 Norton pb $12.95

  **AN ESSAY IN AID OF A GRAMMAR OF
ASSENT**
A theological classic on the nature of faith
and knowledge
Introduction by Nicholas Lash
0–268–01000–5 Notre Dame pb $10.95

- Blaise Pascal
PENSEES
A masterpiece of skepticism and faith
0–14–044171–9 Penguin pb $3.95

- Friedrich Schleiermacher
**ON RELIGION: Speeches to Its Cultured
Despisers**
One of the most important works of
Protestant theology; an attempt to
reconcile Christianity and Romanticism by
finding the essence of religion in the
suggestions of infinity that permeate
everyday existence
Introduction by Rudolph Otto
0–06–130036–5 Harper & Row pb $8.95

- Leo Tolstoy
**THE KINGDOM OF GOD IS WITHIN
YOU**
Tolstoy's plea for Christian anarchism, and
a scathing attack on the state and
militarism
Translated by Constance Garnett
Foreword by Martin Green
0–8032–4411–8 Nebraska $27.95
0–8032–9404–2 Nebraska pb $8.50

- Simone Weil
WAITING FOR GOD
Searching spiritual autobiography by a
brilliant and austere Catholic convert
Translated by Emma Craufurd
0–06–090295–7 Harper & Row pb $6.95

Early Christian Writings

- Henry Bettenson, translator
**THE EARLY CHRISTIAN FATHERS:
A Selection from the Writings of the
Fathers from St. Clement of Rome to
St. Athanasius**
0–19–283009–0 Oxford pb $9.95

- F. Forrester Church & Terrence J.
Mulry, editors
**THE MACMILLAN BOOK OF EARLIEST
CHRISTIAN HYMNS**
0–02–525581–9 Macmillan $19.95

  **THE MACMILLAN BOOK OF EARLIEST
CHRISTIAN PRAYERS**
0–02–525570–3 Macmillan $17.95

- Thomas Merton
THE WISDOM OF THE DESERT
0–8112–0102–3 New Directions pb $4.95

- Maxwell Staniforth, translator
**EARLY CHRISTIAN WRITINGS: The
Apostolic Fathers**
A selection of doctrinal and controversial
works by the earliest Christian theologians
0–14–044475–0 Penguin pb $5.95

CHRISTIAN MYSTICISM

There is the soul's day and God's day. A
day, whether six or seven ago, or more
than six thousand years ago, is just as
near to the present as yesterday. Why?
Because all time is contained in the
present Now-moment. Time comes of
the revolution of the heavens and day
began with the first revolution. The
soul's day falls within this time and consists of the natural light in which things
are seen. God's day, however, is the complete day, comprising both day and night.
It is the real Now-moment, which for the
soul is eternity's day, on which the Father
begets his only begotten Son and the soul
is reborn in God. Whenever this birth
occurs, it is the soul giving birth to the
only begotten Son.

Meister Eckhart
**MEISTER ECKHART: A Modern
Translation**
Translated by R.F. Blakeney
0–06–130008–X Harper & Row pb $8.95

- Patrick Grant, editor
**A DAZZLING DARKNESS: An Anthology
of Western Mysticism**
0–8028–0088–2 Eerdmans pb $9.95

- St. John of the Cross
THE DARK NIGHT OF THE SOUL
One of the greatest works of mystical
literature, by the 16th-century Spanish
monk and poet
0–385–02930–6 Doubleday pb $5.95

- Julian of Norwich
REVELATIONS OF DIVINE LOVE
This mystical text by Julian (or Juliana) of
Norwich, a 14th-century Englishwoman,
combines profound theology and
superlative literary art
Translated by Clifton Wolters
0–14–044177–8 Penguin pb $4.95

- Jean LeClercq & others
**THE SPIRITUALITY OF THE MIDDLE
AGES**
A study of medieval mysticism by a French
Catholic monk and scholar
0–8164–2373–3 Harper & Row $19.95

- Clifton Wolters, translator
**THE CLOUD OF UNKNOWING &
OTHER WORKS**
A classic mystical work, written
anonymously in England in the 14th
century
0–14–044385–1 Penguin pb $3.95

HISTORY

Surveys

- Paul Johnson
A HISTORY OF CHRISTIANITY
A clear, vigorous survey by an English
Catholic journalist and scholar. "The best
one-volume history of Christianity ever
done"—*Christian Century*
0–689–70591–3 Atheneum pb $13.95

- Kenneth S. Latourette
A HISTORY OF CHRISTIANITY
A superb scholarly work that pays ample
attention to the Eastern church

  Volume 1: Beginnings to 1500
0–06–064952–6 Harper & Row pb $14.95

  Volume 2: Reformation to the Present
0–06–064953–4 Harper & Row pb $14.95

- Williston Walker & others
**A HISTORY OF THE CHRISTIAN
CHURCH**
A classic textbook, recently revised, with a
clear, concise presentation of historical and
theological developments
0–0242–3870–8 Scribners $35.00

Orthodox

- John Meyendorff
**THE ORTHODOX CHURCH: Its Past
and Its Role in the World Today**
A good survey of the history of Eastern
Orthodoxy with a straightforward
presentation of basic doctrine and its
contemporary implications
0–913836–81–8 St. Vladimir's pb $8.95

- Timothy Ware
THE ORTHODOX CHURCH
A history covering the last 2000 years, and
a survey of the doctrines and rituals of
contemporary Orthodoxy
0–14–020592–6 Penguin pb $5.95

Roman Catholic

- William V. Bangert
**A HISTORY OF THE SOCIETY OF
JESUS**
Edited by George E. Ganss
0–912422–73–4 Norton $21.00
0–912422–74–2 Norton pb $17.50

- Thomas Bokenkotter
**A CONCISE HISTORY OF THE
CATHOLIC CHURCH**
By a Catholic scholar
0–385–13015–5 Doubleday pb $7.50

  **ESSENTIAL CATHOLICISM: Dynamics
of Faith and Belief**
0–385–23243–8 Doubleday pb $10.95

- Jay P. Dolan
**THE AMERICAN CATHOLIC
EXPERIENCE: A History from Colonial
Times to the Present**
0–385–15207–8 Doubleday pb $12.95

Protestant

- **John Dillenberger & Claude Welch**
  PROTESTANT CHRISTIANITY:
  Interpreted Through Its Development
  A history with an emphasis on doctrine
  0–02–329601–1 Macmillan pb $20.00

- **Martin E. Marty**
  PROTESTANTISM IN THE UNITED
  STATES: Righteous Empire
  History and interpretation by a prolific
  authority on contemporary American
  religion
  0–02–376500–3 Macmillan $17.50

- **Stephen Neill**
  ANGLICANISM
  0–19–520033–0 Oxford pb $11.95

Histories of the Bible

- **Cambridge University Press**
  THE CAMBRIDGE HISTORY OF THE
  BIBLE
  A three-volume set
  0–521–29018–X Cambridge pb (set) $47.50

  Volume 1: From the Beginnings to Jerome
  Edited by P.R. Ackroyd & C.F. Evans
  0–521–09973–0 Cambridge pb $23.95

  Volume 2: The West from the Fathers to
  the Reformation
  Edited by G.W. Lampe
  0–521–29017–1 Cambridge pb $24.95

  Volume 3: The West from the Reformation
  to the Present Day
  Edited by S.L. Greenslade
  0–521–29016–3 Cambridge pb $21.95

- **F.F. Bruce**
  THE HISTORY OF THE BIBLE IN
  ENGLISH
  0–19–520088–8 Oxford pb $8.95

Beginnings and Early History

- **Peter Brown**
  THE CULT OF THE SAINTS: Its Rise
  and Function in Latin Christianity
  0–226–07622–9 Chicago pb $7.95

- **E.R. Dodds**
  PAGAN AND CHRISTIAN IN AN AGE
  OF ANXIETY: Some Aspects of Religious
  Experience from Marcus Aurelius to
  Constantine
  0–393–00545–3 Norton pb $6.95

- **Eusebius**
  THE HISTORY OF THE CHURCH
  FROM CHRIST TO CONSTANTINE
  The first chronicle of the Christian church,
  written in the early 4th century by the
  bishop of Palestine, and concentrating on
  the Eastern church and the defeat of heresy
  Translated by G.A. Williamson
  0–14–044138–7 Penguin pb $5.95

- **W.H. Frend**
  THE RISE OF CHRISTIANITY
  A monumental, richly detailed history of
  the first 600 years of Christianity, from its
  Jewish origins to the formation of the
  medieval church, with special attention to

heresy, schism, theology, and social and
political background. Illustrated
0–8006–1931–5 Fortress pb $24.95

- **Hyam Maccoby**
  THE MYTHMAKER: Paul and the
  Invention of Christianity
  A provocative work arguing that Jesus
  remained a faithful Jew and that
  Christianity was created by Paul, who
  synthesized it out of Gnosticism and other
  Hellenistic cults
  0–06–015582–5 Harper & Row $17.95

- **Wayne A. Meeks**
  THE FIRST URBAN CHRISTIANS: The
  Social World of the Apostle Paul
  Who were the Christians to whom Paul
  preached? What were their class, ethnic,
  and family backgrounds, their
  neighborhoods, daily life, and view of the
  world? Meeks offers answers to these
  questions
  0–300–02876–8 Yale $32.00
  0–300–03244–7 Yale pb $10.95

- **Elaine Pagels**
  ADAM, EVE, AND THE SERPENT
  The evolution of Christian thought—from
  an early emphasis on freedom to the
  asceticism and determinism that prevailed
  through the writings of Augustine—as
  reflected in orthodox and Gnostic
  interpretations of the story of Adam and
  Eve
  0–394–52140–4 Random House $17.95

- **E.P. Sanders**
  PAUL AND PALESTINIAN JUDAISM: A
  Comparison of Patterns of Religion
  Paul's ideas in the context of the
  contemporary Judaism he renounced
  0–8006–1899–8 Fortress pb $24.95

Gnosticism

Gnosticism has aroused a great deal of interest since the discovery of the Nag Hammadi
documents in Egypt in 1945. It has been
compared to existentialism, certain contemporary cults, and almost anything else that
has seemed particularly pessimistic or extreme.

- **John Dart**
  THE JESUS OF HERESY AND
  HISTORY: The Discovery and Meaning of
  the Nag Hammadi Gnostic Library
  "A highly readable, non-technical
  introduction to one of the truly great
  manuscript discoveries of the 20th
  century"—*Christianity Today*
  0–06–061694–6 Harper & Row pb $10.95

- **Charles W. Hedrick, Sr., & Robert**
  Hodgson, Jr.
  NAG HAMMADI, GNOSTICISM, AND
  EARLY CHRISTIANITY
  Emphasizes the significance of these texts
  0–913573–16–7 Hendrickson pb $14.95

In a world in which Christians not only
were free to follow their faith but were
officially encouraged to do so, Augustine
came to read the story of Adam and Eve
very differently than had the majority of
his Jewish and Christian predecessors.
What they had read for centuries as a
story of human freedom became, in his
hands, a story of human bondage. Most
Jews and Christians had agreed that God
gave humankind in creation the gift of
moral freedom, and that Adam's misuse
of it brought death upon his progeny.
But Augustine went further: Adam's sin
not only caused our mortality but cost us
our moral freedom, irreversibly corrupted our experience of sexuality (which
Augustine tended to identify with original sin), and made us incapable of genuine political freedom.

Elaine Pagels
ADAM, EVE, AND THE SERPENT
0–394–52140–4 Random House $17.95

- **Hans Jonas**
  THE GNOSTIC RELIGION
  A comprehensive study of the tenets of
  Gnosticism, with copious excerpts from
  original texts and a chapter comparing
  Gnosticism with existentialism
  0–8070–5799–1 Beacon pb $10.95

- **Marvin W. Meyer, translator**
  THE SECRET TEACHINGS OF JESUS:
  Four Gnostic Gospels
  *The Secret Book of James, The Gospel of
  Thomas, The Book of Thomas,* and *The Secret
  Book of John* from the Nag Hammadi
  discoveries
  0–394–52959–6 Random House $15.45

- **Elaine Pagels**
  THE GNOSTIC GOSPELS
  A superb study of Gnostic texts and ideas
  in the context of early Christianity
  0–394–74433–0 Random House $16.45
  0–394–74043–2 Random House pb $3.95

James M. Robinson, editor
THE NAG HAMMADI LIBRARY
The complete Gnostic texts found at
Nag Hammadi. "We have to do here
with an understanding of existence, an
answer to the human dilemma, an
attitude toward society, that is worthy
of being taken quite seriously by
anyone able and willing to grapple with
such ultimate issues. This basic stance
has until now been known almost
exclusively through the myopic view of
heresy-hunters, who often quote only
to refute or ridicule. Thus the coming
to light of the Nag Hammadi library
gives unexpected access to the Gnostic
stance as Gnostics themselves presented
it. It provides new roots for the
uprooted"—from the introduction
0–06–066934–9 Harper & Row pb $24.95

• Kurt Rudolph
GNOSIS: The Nature and History of Gnosticism
An authoritative study of the doctrines and rites of Gnostic sects and their enduring influence on Christianity
0–06–067017–7 Harper & Row $28.95
0–06–067018–5 Harper & Row pb $14.95

Middle Ages and Renaissance

• The Venerable Bede
THE HISTORY OF THE ENGLISH CHURCH AND PEOPLE
The story of the Anglo-Saxons and their conversion to Christianity, written in the 8th century by the first great English historian
Translated by Leo Sherley-Price
0–14–044042–9 Penguin pb $4.95

• Rosalind & Christopher Brooke
POPULAR RELIGION IN THE MIDDLE AGES
0–500–27381–2 Thames & Hudson pb $10.95

• Judith Herrin
THE FORMATION OF CHRISTENDOM
An ambitious study of Christianity in the Dark Ages. "An extraordinarily significant contribution to the study of the late antique and early mediaeval Mediterranean world"—G.W. Bowersock
0–691–05482–7 Princeton $34.95

• Malcolm Lambert
MEDIEVAL HERESY: Popular Movements from Bogomil to Hus
0–8419–0298–4 Holmes & Meier $54.50

• Steven Runciman
THE MEDIEVAL MANICHEE: A Study of the Christian Dualist Heresy
0–521–28926–2 Cambridge pb $13.95

English 12th-century ivory cross (The Cloisters, Metropolitan Museum of Art)

Reformation

• Roland H. Bainton
THE REFORMATION OF THE SIXTEENTH CENTURY
A lucid account of the various Protestant Reformers and their churches with an emphasis on doctrine and ideas
Introduction by Jaroslav Pelikan
0–8070–1301–3 Beacon pb $9.95

• Hans Hillerbrand
THE REFORMATION: A Narrative History Related by Contemporary Observers and Participants
0–8010–4185–6 Baker pb $13.95

• George H. Williams
THE RADICAL REFORMATION
A detailed history of the Anabaptists and other radical sects that emerged from the Reformation
0–664–20372–8 Westminster $24.95

Modern

• Ronald A. Knox
ENTHUSIASM
The classic account of visionary and evangelical sects and movements, mainly English, during the 17th and 18th centuries
0–87061–080–5 Christian Classics pb $22.95

• Claude Welch
PROTESTANT THOUGHT IN THE NINETEENTH CENTURY
An intellectual history covering Protestantism's response to romanticism, Darwinism, biblical criticism, and socialism, and discussing such thinkers as Schleiermacher, Emerson, Kierkegaard, William James, and Weber
Volume 1:
0–300–04200–0 Yale pb $12.95
Volume 2:
0–300–04201–9 Yale pb $12.95

• Wilton Wynn
OUR NAME IS PETER: John, Paul and John Paul II—Three Who Changed the Church
0–394–55762–X Random House $18.95

Third World

• Enrique Dussel
THE HISTORY OF THE CHURCH IN LATIN AMERICA: Colonialism to Liberation
A complete account with an emphasis on theology and the emergence of liberation theology
0–8028–3548–1 Eerdmans $21.95

• Penny Lernoux
THE CRY OF THE PEOPLE: The Struggle for Human Rights in Latin America—The Catholic Church in Conflict with US Policy
Consequences of the Church's shift from supporting to opposing conservative Latin American regimes
0–14–006047–2 Penguin pb $7.95

• Stephen Neill
A HISTORY OF CHRISTIAN MISSIONS
The best general account of such Christian efforts
0–14–022736–9 Penguin pb $5.95

North America

• S.E. Ahlstrom
RELIGIOUS HISTORY OF THE AMERICAN PEOPLE
0–300–01762–6 Yale pb $22.95

• Robert T. Handy
A HISTORY OF THE CHURCHES IN THE UNITED STATES AND CANADA
0–19–502531–8 Oxford pb $8.95

• Martin Luther King, Jr.
STRIDE TOWARD FREEDOM: The Montgomery Story
King's account of the bus boycott demonstrates that the political movement for civil rights was impelled by religious convictions
0–06–250490–8 Harper & Row pb $8.95

• Albert J. Raboteau
SLAVE RELIGION: The Invisible Institution in the Antebellum South
0–19–502705–1 Oxford pb $11.95

• George M. Marsden
FUNDAMENTALISM AND AMERICAN CULTURE: The Shaping of Twentieth-Century Evangelicalism
The rise of fundamentalism as a separate force in American Christianity between 1870 and 1925
0–19–503083–4 Oxford pb $9.95

• Jan Shipps
MORMONISM: The Story of a New Religious Tradition
0–252–01417–0 Illinois pb $9.95

BIOGRAPHY

The Life of Jesus

• Gaalyah Cornfeld
THE HISTORICAL JESUS: A Scholarly View of the Man and His World
Jesus in the context of contemporaneous Palestinian Judaism
0–02–528200–X Macmillan $16.95

• John Drane
JESUS AND THE GOSPELS
0–06–062066–8 Harper & Row pb $9.95

• Ian Wilson
JESUS: The Evidence
Argues that historical documentation tends to support the Gospel narratives
0–06–069433–5 Harper & Row $17.95
0–06–250973–X Harper & Row pb $9.95

Saints

- Donald Attwater, editor
THE PENGUIN DICTIONARY OF
SAINTS
This concise and reliable guide to 750
saints includes biographies, feast days,
dates of canonization, symbols in art, and a
glossary of hagiographic terms
0–14–051123–7 Penguin pb $7.95

- Peter Brown
AUGUSTINE OF HIPPO: A Biography
0–520–01411–1 California pb $11.95

- Alban Butler
BUTLER'S LIVES OF THE SAINTS
A revised and abridged version of the
18th-century classic
Edited by Michael Walsh
0–06–069251–0 Harper & Row $20.95

- G.K. Chesterton
SAINT THOMAS AQUINAS
A short, vigorous informal biography
0–385–09002–1 Doubleday pb $3.95

- Monica Furlong
THERESE OF LISIEUX
The life of the Carmelite nun who was
canonized in 1925. "Piercingly perceptive,
alive, witty"—Nina Auerbach
0–394–75360–7 Pantheon pb $7.95

- Michael Grant
SAINT PAUL
A provocative study by a leading scholar of
the period that attempts to put Paul's life
and conversion into historical perspective
0–684–14682–7 Scribners pb $5.95

- Julien Green
GOD'S FOOL: The Life and Times of
Francis of Assisi
A biography by an outstanding French
novelist
0–06–063464–2 Harper & Row pb $7.95

- Anthony Kenny
THOMAS MORE
0–19–287573–6 Oxford pb $4.95

- St. Ignatius Loyola
THE AUTOBIOGRAPHY OF ST.
IGNATIUS LOYOLA
Edited by John C. Olin
0–06–131783–7 Harper & Row pb $6.95

Protestants

- Roland H. Bainton
HERE I STAND: A Life of Martin Luther
A well-known book by the dean of
Protestant historians
0–451–62443–5 NAL pb $4.95

- Fawn M. Brodie
NO MAN KNOWS MY HISTORY: The
Life of Joseph Smith
The best biography of Mormonism's
founder
0–394–46967–4 Knopf $21.95

- V.H. Green
JOHN WESLEY
An excellent account of the founder of
Methodism
0–8191–6461–5 University Press pb $9.75

- François Wendel
CALVIN: Origins and Development of His
Religious Thought
Translated by Philip Mairet
0–939464–44–6 Labyrinth pb $14.95

20th Century

- Ederhard Bethge
DIETRICH BONHOEFFER
A study of the life and thought of the
German Lutheran theologian martyred by
the Nazis
0–06–060771–8 Harper & Row pb $19.95

- Richard Fox
REINHOLD NIEBUHR
A biography of the most important
modern American Protestant thinker
0–06–250343–X Harper & Row pb $10.95

- Richard Gilman
FAITH, SEX, MYSTERY: A Memoir
A self-revealing account of the author's
conversion to Catholicism and his
subsequent loss of faith. "A haunting and
courageous work"—Robert Stone
0–14–010587–5 Penguin pb $7.95

- David E. Harrell, Jr.
ORAL ROBERTS: An American Life
This scrupulously objective biography
vividly conveys the changes in American
Pentecostal culture over the past 50 years
0–253–15844–3 Indiana $29.95
0–06–250381–2 Harper & Row pb $12.95

- Peter Hebblethwaite
POPE JOHN XXIII: Shepherd of the
Modern World
0–385–23537–2 Doubleday pb $10.95

- Michael Mott
THE SEVEN MOUNTAINS OF THOMAS
MERTON
"A stunning portrait of a complex and holy
man"—Boston Globe
0–395–40451–7 Houghton-Mifflin pb $12.95

- Stephen B. Oates
LET THE TRUMPET SOUND: The Life
of Martin Luther King, Jr.
0–06–014993–0 Harper & Row $24.95
0–451–62350–9 NAL pb $4.95

- Dan Wakefield
RETURNING: A Spiritual Journey
An autobiographical account of how a
middle-aged novelist and screenwriter
recovered his faith after years of drift,
drinking, and personal crisis
0–385–23722–7 Doubleday $17.95
0–14–011727–X Penguin pb $7.95

THEOLOGY AND DOCTRINE

The following titles will provide the reader
with introductions to and summaries of
the major Christian thinkers, although
clearly no attempt can be made to represent
all views.

▶ See also Western Philosophy

History of Doctrine

- Rudolf Bultmann
JESUS AND THE WORD
A 1926 work by one of the most
influential of modern Protestant
theologians
0–684–17596–7 Scribners $20.00

- J.N. Kelly
EARLY CHRISTIAN DOCTRINES
The development of Christian belief and
dogma from the early Fathers to the 5th
century
0–06–064334–X Harper & Row $10.95

- Colleen McDannell & Bernhard Lang
HEAVEN: A History
The evolution of the doctrines and
concepts of Heaven in Christian thought
0–300–04346–5 Yale $29.95

- John Macquarrie
PRINCIPLES OF CHRISTIAN
THEOLOGY
A clear, incisive discussion of the major
themes of Christian thought as applied to
problems of contemporary life
0–02–374510–X Scribners pb $26.00

- John Meyendorff
BYZANTINE THEOLOGY: Historical
Trends and Doctrinal Themes
The best guide to the development of
orthodoxy
0–8232–0967–9 Fordham pb $10.00

- Jaroslav Pelikan
THE CHRISTIAN TRADITION: A
History of the Development of Doctrine
A comprehensive treatment, written by a
master

Volume 1: Emergence of the Catholic
Tradition, 100–600
0–226–65370–6 Chicago $25.00
0–226–65371–4 Chicago pb $12.95

Volume 2: The Spirit of Eastern
Christendom, 600–1700
0–226–65372–2 Chicago $25.00
0–226–65373–0 Chicago pb $10.95

Volume 3: The Growth of Medieval
Theology, 600–1300
0–226–65374–9 Chicago $27.50
0–226–65375–7 Chicago pb $12.95

Volume 4: Reformation of Church and
Dogma, 1300–1700
0–226–65376–5 Chicago $27.50
0–226–65377–3 Chicago pb $14.95

JESUS THROUGH THE CENTURIES:
His Place in the History of Culture
A brilliant work that traces the image of
Jesus in art, literature, church doctrine,
philosophy, and secular affairs. "Unique
among current publications in bridging
scholarly and popular discourse on the

From Jaroslav Pelikan's Jesus Through the Centuries: His Place in the History of Culture *(Yale)*

prophet from Nazareth over the past 2000 years . . . A sweeping visual and conceptual panorama"—*NY Times*
0–300–03496–2 Yale $25.00
0–06–097080–4 Harper & Row pb $9.95

● Ernst Troeltsch
THE SOCIAL TEACHING OF THE CHRISTIAN CHURCHES
A highly influential history of Christian ethical ideals, by a contemporary of Max Weber
Translated by Olive Wyon
Volume 1
0–226–81298–7 Chicago pb $17.00
Volume 2
0–226–81299–5 Chicago pb $17.00

Theology

● St. Thomas Aquinas
SELECTED WRITINGS OF ST. THOMAS AQUINAS
An introduction to the most important scholastic philosopher, whose theological works defined traditional Roman Catholic doctrine. Includes *The Principles of Nature, On Being and Essence, On the Virtues in General,* and *On Free Choice*
Translated by Robert P. Goodwin
0–0234–5050–9 Macmillan pb $5.50

● Karl Barth
DOGMATICS IN OUTLINE
A summary of *Church Dogmatics,* Barth's systematic, multivolume exposition of neo-orthodoxy, one of the great theological works of the 20th century
0–06–130056–X Harper & Row pb $5.95

One of the many Renaissance portraits of Jesus as Universal Man to combine magnificently several of the motifs and "images" that we have been discussing throughout this book is *The Savior* by Kyriakos Theotokopoulos, whom posterity calls El Greco. The model for the portrait was a Jewish young man in Toledo, for El Greco wanted to take seriously the Jewishness of Jesus . . . This Jesus is indeed a historical figure, and he is indeed Jewish; but he has been pictured in a way that also stands in the tradition of the Byzantine icon, as the Jesus of the Transfiguration. And all of this has been suffused with the spirit of the Spanish Christ-mysticism of the sixteenth century, in whose atmosphere El Greco worked. The result is a remarkable synthesis of several artistic, mystical, and theological traditions—a synthesis that makes its presence felt throughout the Renaissance perspective on Jesus as the Universal Man.

Jaroslav Pelikan
JESUS THROUGH THE CENTURIES: His Place in the History of Culture
0–300–03496–2 Yale $25.00

EVANGELICAL THEOLOGY: An Introduction
A good introduction to Barth's thought, containing lectures he delivered before his retirement from the chair of theology at Basel and giving a succinct account of his views on the nature and method of this form of theology
Introduction by Grover Foley
0–8028–1819–6 Eerdmans pb $14.95

● Dietrich Bonhoeffer
THE COST OF DISCIPLESHIP
Based on the Sermon on the Mount, this work by the German Lutheran theologian martyred by the Nazis challenges the tendencies toward "cheap grace"
0–02–083850–6 Macmillan pb $5.95

● John Calvin
THE INSTITUTES OF CHRISTIAN RELIGION
Calvin's central presentation of his Reformation theory
Edited by Tony Lane & Hilary Osborne
0–8010–2524–9 Baker Book House pb $7.95

● Hans Kung
ON BEING A CHRISTIAN
What it means to be a Christian today in a world of science, technology, political and personal crisis; a challenging statement of faith by a controversial German Catholic theologian
0–385–19286–X Doubleday pb $10.95

● Martin Luther
MARTIN LUTHER: Selections from His Writings
A sampling of Luther's theological, exegetical, and polemical works
Edited by John Dillenberger
0–385–09876–6 Doubleday pb $8.95

● Reinhold Niebuhr
THE ESSENTIAL REINHOLD NIEBUHR: Selected Essays and Addresses
Taken from the writings of the most influential 20th-century American Protestant thinker. Niebuhr was particularly concerned with the relation between religion and the political and social order
Edited by Robert M. Brown
0–300–03464–4 Yale $25.00

● Friedrich Schleiermacher
THE CHRISTIAN FAITH
The book that initiated modern Protestant theology, by the great 19th-century German theologian
0–567–02239–0 Fortress $24.95

● Pierre Teilhard de Chardin
THE PHENOMENON OF MAN
The principal exposition of Teilhard's evolutionary theology
0–06–090495–X Harper & Row pb $8.95

● Paul Tillich
THE DYNAMICS OF FAITH
The best introduction to Tillich's existentialist theology
0–06–130042–X Harper & Row pb $7.95

Contemporary Issues

● Leonardo Boff
LIBERATING GRACE
An exposition of liberation theology by a Brazilian theologian who has been embroiled in controversy with the Vatican
Translated by John Drury
0–88344–282–5 Orbis pb $11.95

● Dietrich Bonhoeffer
LETTERS AND PAPERS FROM PRISON
Writings from a Nazi prison by the martyred German theologian
0–02–083920–0 Macmillan pb $7.95

● William Sloane Coffin
LIVING THE TRUTH IN A WORLD OF ILLUSIONS
0–06–061512–5 Harper & Row $12.95

● Deane W. Ferm, editor
CONTEMPORARY AMERICAN THEOLOGIES: A Critical Survey
0–8164–2341–5 Harper & Row pb $8.95

THIRD WORLD LIBERATION THEOLOGIES: A Reader
Essays and documents by Christian political militants from Latin America, Africa, and Asia
0–88344–516–6 Orbis pb $16.95

● Langdon Gilkey
SOCIETY AND THE SACRED: Toward a Theology of Culture in Decline
0–8245–0089–X Crossroad $18.95

● Andrew Greeley
HOW TO SAVE THE CATHOLIC CHURCH
0–670–38475–5 Viking $16.95

ANDREW GREELEY'S WORLD: An Anthology of Critical Essays, 1986–88
0–446–38989–7 Warner pb $12.95

• Penny Lernoux
PEOPLE OF GOD: The Struggle for World Catholicism
0–670–81529–2 Viking $19.95

• Malachi Martin
THE JESUITS: The Society of Jesus and the Betrayal of the Roman Catholic Church
The author, a conservative American Catholic, argues that the Jesuits, after a long history of serving the papacy, have been transformed in the last 20 years into a radical conspiracy against the traditional church and the West
0–671–65716–X Simon & Schuster pb $8.95

• Mary & Sidney Nolan
CHRISTIAN PILGRIMAGE IN MODERN WESTERN EUROPE
A commanding exploration of religious shrines in modern Roman Catholicism, ranging from a discussion of obscure chapels to the world-famous shrines at Rome, Lourdes, and Fátima
0–8078–1814–3 North Carolina $34.95

• Mary J. Weaver
THE NEW CATHOLIC WOMEN: A Contemporary Challenge to Traditional Religious Authority
A good synthesis of feminist historical and theological themes
0–06–069287–1 Harper & Row $18.95

• Gayraud S. Wilmore
BLACK RELIGION AND BLACK RADICALISM: An Interpretation of the Religious History of Afro-American People
0–88344–032–6 Orbis pb $13.95

REFERENCE

• David Barrett, editor
WORLD CHRISTIAN ENCYCLOPEDIA: A Comparative Survey of Churches and Religions in the Modern World, A.D. 1900 to 2000
A monumental guide to contemporary Christianity, with information and statistics on all churches and sects for every country
0–19–572435–6 Oxford $185.00

• F.L. Cross & Elizabeth A. Livingstone
THE OXFORD DICTIONARY OF THE CHRISTIAN CHURCH
A standard work, concise, scholarly, and thorough, with more than 6000 árticles on important figures, events, movements, and ideas in Eastern and Western Christianity
0–19–211545–6 Oxford $65.00

• J.N. Kelly
THE OXFORD DICTIONARY OF POPES
The lives of all the popes about whom information is available
0–19–213964–9 Oxford $29.95

• Franklin H. Littell
THE MACMILLAN ATLAS HISTORY OF CHRISTIANITY
Maps illustrating the development of the Christian churches from their beginnings to the 20th century
0–02–573140–8 Macmillan $24.95

Theology

• Van A. Harvey
A HANDBOOK OF THEOLOGICAL TERMS
Three hundred short essays, mainly Protestant in approach, that help penetrate the language of contemporary theology
0–02–085430–7 Macmillan pb $5.95

• Karl Rahner
A DICTIONARY OF THEOLOGY
A guide to modern Catholic theology, with short articles on major concepts and dogmas as well as summaries of biblical and theological texts; includes policies and biblical interpretations sanctioned by Vatican II
0–8245–0691–X Crossroad pb $17.95

The Bible

• Mathew Black & H.H. Rowley
PEAKE'S COMMENTARY ON THE BIBLE
0–8407–5019–6 Thomas Nelson $39.95

• Raymond E. Brown, editor
THE JEROME BIBLICAL COMMENTARY
A useful guide by 50 Roman Catholic scholars that covers the entire Bible and the Apocrypha and utilizes the principles of modern biblical criticism
0–13–509612–X Prentice-Hall $59.95

• George A. Buttrick & Keith R. Crim, editors
THE INTERPRETER'S DICTIONARY OF THE BIBLE
The standard dictionary: defines every proper name, place, and episode in the Bible; explains concepts, doctrines, and rituals; includes maps, pronunciation guides, and bibliographies. Contributions, generally Protestant in approach, from 253 scholars
0–687–19268–4 Abingdon (5-volume set) $119.95

• Peter Calvocoressi, editor
WHO'S WHO IN THE BIBLE
0–14–051212–8 Penguin pb $7.95

• Keith R. Crim & others, editors
THE INTERPRETER'S DICTIONARY OF THE BIBLE: Supplementary Volume
An updated, cross-referenced supplement to the above
0–687–19269–2 Abingdon $24.95

• Charles M. Laymon, editor
THE INTERPRETER'S ONE-VOLUME COMMENTARY ON THE BIBLE
A succinct exposition with clearly written contributions from 70 Protestant scholars on geography, historical background and chronology, biblical languages, units of measurement and money, and many maps and charts
0–687–19299–4 Abingdon $26.95

• Mark Levine & Eugene Rachlis, editors
THE COMPLETE BOOK OF BIBLE QUOTATIONS
0–671–49864–9 Simon & Schuster pb $12.95

• William Smith
SMITH'S BIBLE DICTIONARY
0–8407–5542–2 Thomas Nelson $9.95
0–8407–3085–3 Thomas Nelson pb $6.95

• Robert Young
YOUNG'S ANALYTICAL CONCORDANCE TO THE BIBLE
The classic concordance, originally published in 1879, with 311,000 references, and with the original Hebrew and Greek words listed under each English entry; includes a guide to the pronunciation of proper names
0–8028–8084–3 Eerdmans $19.95

Islam

In this section will be found titles relating directly to the history, doctrines, and practice of Islam as a religion. In view of the difficulty of making such a separation of the religious from the social and cultural, the following headings should also be consulted for a fuller picture: The Islamic World, The Contemporary Middle East, Arabic Literature, Persian Literature, and Islamic Art and Architecture.

Islamic belief has a reputation for being easily understood and while under careful study it turns out to have its due share of complexity, in fact its most essential elements can be set forth rather simply. It is the very point of islâm to own the supremacy of one single God, Who is identified as the God of Abraham and of Moses and of Jesus, and Whose name in Arabic is Allâh. To make this supremacy meaningful, faith must specify. God is the Creator of the world and of mankind in it; and He will finally bring the world to an end and, reviving at the Last Judgment all men and women that have ever lived, will punish them in Hell or reward them in Paradise according to whether they have obeyed His will in their lifetimes. To give God's supremacy concrete content, faith must specify further. God has sent prophets, such as Moses and Jesus, to summon various peoples to obedience, which consists in worshipping Him alone and in dealing justly with one's fellow men. The last and greatest of these prophets, whose message is to all the world and supersedes that of any previous prophet, was Muhammad of Arabia (d. 632 CE), whose precepts and example all men and women are henceforth bound to follow, individually and collectively.

Marshall Hodgson
THE VENTURE OF ISLAM: Conscience and History in a World Civilization, Volume 1
0–226–34683–8 Chicago pb $15.95

GENERAL STUDIES

- **Arthur J. Arberry**
  ASPECTS OF ISLAMIC CIVILIZATION AS DEPICTED IN THE ORIGINAL TEXTS
  A very useful anthology by a great translator
  0–472–06130–5 Michigan pb $9.95

- **Kenneth Cragg**
  THE CALL OF THE MINARET
  0–88344–207–8 Orbis pb $14.95

- **Victor Danner**
  THE ISLAMIC TRADITION
  An insightful presentation by an academic Orientalist and religious thinker
  0–916349–16–0 Amity House pb $13.95

- **Charles Le Gai Eaton**
  ISLAM AND THE DESTINY OF MAN
  0–88706–163–X SUNY $16.95

- **John L. Esposito**
  ISLAM: The Straight Path
  0–19–504399–5 Oxford pb $9.95

- **Hamilton A. Gibb**
  MOHAMMEDANISM: An Historical Survey
  An authority noted for his powers of synthesis and lucid, succinct exposition masterfully presents the subject
  0–19–500245–8 Oxford pb $5.95

Cyril Glassé
THE CONCISE ENCYCLOPEDIA OF ISLAM
Easy to understand and the most complete one-volume reference on the ideas, history, theology, beliefs, practices, and customs of the Islamic world. Almost 1200 entries, fully cross-referenced, illustrated, containing maps, diagrams, and educational aids. Hundreds of quotations, poems, and prayers illuminate the text
Introduction by Huston Smith
0–06–063123–6 Harper & Row $59.45

- **Alfred Guillaume**
  ISLAM
  A reliable and scholarly introduction
  0–14–020311–7 Penguin pb $6.95

- **Philip K. Hitti**
  ISLAM: A Way of Life
  A useful and lively introduction, part history, part cultural study
  0–8092–6155–3 Regnery pb $7.95

- **Fazlur Rahman**
  ISLAM
  A highly respected Muslim scholar explains his religion
  0–226–70281–2 Chicago pb $10.95

THE QUR'AN

Muslims believe the Qur'an (or Koran) to be God's very words revealed to Muhammad. It is the basis and immutable reference point of Islamic civilization. Many Muslims turn to it daily to guide their actions.

- **Ahmad Ali, translator**
  AL-QUR'AN: A Contemporary Translation
  A new scholarly version
  0–691–02046–9 Princeton pb $9.95

- **Arthur J. Arberry**
  THE KORAN INTERPRETED
  A brilliant, not always literal rendition of the original
  0–02–083260–5 Princeton pb $9.95

- **N.R. Dawood, translator**
  THE KORAN
  An accessible prose version, with the traditional order of chapters changed
  0–14–044052–6 Penguin pb $4.95

- **Muhammad Marmaduke Pickthall, translator**
  THE MEANING OF THE GLORIOUS KORAN
  A literal rendering in which many chapters are preceded by a brief explanation of their historical and religious meaning. Pickthall follows the most widely accepted traditional commentaries. The most reliable translation from a religious point of view
  0–451–62641–9 NAL pb $4.95

- **Fazlur Rahman**
  MAJOR THEMES IN THE QUR'AN
  A clear explanation of the Qur'an's view of man and the world, by a respected Muslim scholar who taught in the West
  0–88297–027–5 Bibliotheca pb $16.00

THE LIFE AND CAREER OF MUHAMMAD

- **Michael Cook**
  MUHAMMAD
  An entry in the publisher's Past Masters series
  0–19–287605–8 Oxford pb $4.95

- **Emile Dermenghem**
  MUHAMMAD AND THE ISLAMIC TRADITION
  0–87951–130–3 Overlook $16.95

- **Martin Lings**
  MUHAMMAD
  A fresh and direct life of the Prophet based upon the most authoritative early biography and traditions. The story comes to life for the modern reader
  0–89281–170–6 Inner Traditions pb $12.95

- **Maxime Rodinson**
  MUHAMMAD
  A perceptive skeptical biography
  Translated by Anne Carter
  0–394–73822–5 Pantheon pb $10.95

- **Annemarie Schimmel**
  AND MUHAMMAD IS HIS MESSENGER: The Veneration of the Prophet in Islamic Piety
  0–8078–4128–5 North Carolina pb $9.95

19th-century Turkish calligraphy, "Muhammad is the Messenger of God," from And Muhammad Is His Messenger *by Annemarie Schimmel (North Carolina)*

- **W. Montgomery Watt**
  MUHAMMAD: Prophet and Statesman
  A concise biography by a leading scholar of Muhammad's career
  0–19–881078–4 Oxford pb $7.95

ISLAMIC THEOLOGY AND LAW

- **Avicenna**
  AVICENNA ON THEOLOGY
  Translated by Arthur J. Arberry
  0–88355–676–6 Hyperion $15.00

- **Noel Coulson**
  A HISTORY OF ISLAMIC LAW
  An engrossing study that reveals the background and brings Islamic law to life
  0–85224–354–5 Columbia pb $10.00

- **Ignaz Goldziher**
  INTRODUCTION TO ISLAMIC THEOLOGY AND LAW
  Scholarly, important essays by a distinguished Islamicist
  0–691–10099–3 Princeton pb $15.95

- **Al-Ghazali**
  THE FAITH AND PRACTICE OF AL-GHAZALI
  Translations from the writings of one of the greatest figures in Islamic history, including his semi-autobiographical "Deliverance from Error"
  Translated by W. Montgomery Watt
  0–686–18610–9 Kazi pb $5.95

  ON THE DUTIES OF BROTHERHOOD
  0–686–83895–5 Kazi pb $8.95

  THE JUST BALANCE
  0–317–01603–2 Kazi pb $5.50

  INNER DIMENSIONS OF ISLAMIC WORSHIP
  Translated by Mukhtar Holland
  0–86037–125–5 New Era pb $6.95

ISLAMIC PHILOSOPHY

• Henry Corbin
AVICENNA AND THE VISIONARY RECITAL
Translated by Willard Trask
0–88214–213–5 Spring pb $16.50

CYCLICAL TIME AND ISMAILI GNOSIS
Studies in a form of Gnosticism that developed within the medieval Islamic world
0–7103–0048–4 Methuen pb $13.95

• Majid Fakhry
A HISTORY OF ISLAMIC PHILOSOPHY
A widely used study of the subject
0–231–05533–1 Columbia pb $16.00

• Oliver Leaman
AN INTRODUCTION TO MEDIEVAL ISLAMIC PHILOSOPHY
0–521–28911–4 Cambridge pb $14.95

Tughrā calligraphy, "May God Bless the Unlettered Prophet," by Annemarie Schimmel from her book And Muhammad Is His Messenger *(North Carolina)*

THE SHI'A

The Shi'a, a sect constituting roughly ten percent of the Islamic world, is itself divided into several groups. Recent events have brought the Shi'a, or Shi'ites, to prominence on the world scene.

• Henry Corbin
SPIRITUAL BODY AND CELESTIAL EARTH: From Mazdean Iran to Shi'ite Iran
Translated by Nancy Pearson
0–691–09937–5 Princeton $44.50

• Reinhold Loeffler
ISLAM IN PRACTICE: Religious Beliefs in a Persian Village
0–88706–679–8 SUNY pb $16.95

• Wilfred Madelung
RELIGIOUS TRENDS IN EARLY ISLAMIC IRAN
An expert leads the reader into the little-known world where ancient Iranian ideas influenced nascent Shi'ism
0–88706–701–8 SUNY pb $9.95

• Moojan Momen
AN INTRODUCTION TO SHI'I ISLAM: The History and Doctrines of Twelver Shi'ism
A very informative, factual, up-to-date study with valuable insights into the underlying dynamics of Iranian current events
0–300–03531–4 Yale pb $15.95

• Matti Moosa
EXTREMIST SHIITES: The Ghulat Sects
Extremely informative on the beliefs and practices of the Ahl'i Haqq and the Nusayris. The latter, although a small minority, are the dominant group in the Syrian government today
0–8156–2411–5 Syracuse $37.50

• Abdulaziz A. Sachedina
ISLAMIC MESSIANISM: The Ideal of the Mahdi in Twelver Shi'ism
0–87395–458–0 SUNY pb $19.95

SUFISM

Sufism is the mysticism of Islam. Rich in poetry, music, and intellectual ideas, the Sufis have walked (as al-Ghazali wrote) "in the light of prophecy" and have continuously inspired Islamic civilization. They are much studied today in the West.

• Arthur J. Arberry
THE DOCTRINE OF THE SUFIS
A translation of the writings of a medieval Sufi, al-Kalabadhi
0–521–29218–2 Cambridge pb $13.95

• R.W. Austin, editor
IBN-AL-ARABI: The Bezels of Wisdom
An authentic look into the thoughts of a 13th-century Arab mystic from Spain
Preface by Titus Burckhardt
0–8091–0313–3 Paulist Press pb $12.95

• Henry Corbin
CREATIVE IMAGINATION IN THE SUFISM OF IBN ARABI
Translated by Ralph Manheim
0–691–01828–6 Princeton pb $13.95

• Victor Danner & Wheeler Thackston
IBN 'ATA ILLAH & KWAJA ABDULLAH ANSARI: The Book of Wisdom & Intimate Conversations
Two classics of Sufism. The aphorisms in particular may be called the greatest of Sufi writing, renowned from Morocco to Indonesia
0–8091–0279–X Paulist Press $12.95
0–8091–2182–4 Paulist Press pb $8.95

• Ibn Abbad of Ronda
LETTERS ON THE SUFI PATH
A Muslim mystic's advice and instruction to disciples on the spiritual path. Ranks

with the Philokalia in its depth and inspiration
Translated by John Renard, S.J.
Preface by Annemarie Schimmel
0–8091–2730–X Paulist Press pb $9.95

• Ahmad Ghazzali
SAWANIH: Inspiration from the World of Pure Spirits—The Oldest Persian Sufi Treatise on Love
0–7103–0091–3 KPI $29.95

• Martin Lings
A SUFI SAINT OF THE TWENTIETH CENTURY: Shaikh Ahmad al-'Alawi, His Spiritual Heritage and Legacy
An unusual, compelling, and intimate introduction to the life of the greatest Sufi of modern times, who had more than 200,000 disciples from North Africa to Malaysia. A rare insight into the activity of an authentic and impeccably orthodox Sufi order that today lives not only in the East but also in Europe and America
0–520–02486–9 California pb $8.95

• Louis Massignon
THE PASSION OF AL-HALLAJ: Mystic and Martyr of Islam
This fascinating study of a mysterious figure opens the door onto the astonishingly brilliant intellectual richness of 10th-century Baghdad. Scholarly, demanding, and immensely instructive
0–691–09910–3 Princeton (4-volume set) $135.00
0–691–10203–1 Princeton pb $24.50

• Sayyed H. Nasr
SUFI ESSAYS
0–87395–389–4 SUNY pb $10.95

• Reynold A. Nicholson
THE MYSTICS OF ISLAM: An Introduction to Sufism
0–8052–0492–X Schocken pb $5.95

• Jalal ad-Din Rumi
OPEN SECRET: Versions of Rumi
New translations of a Sufi poet, by a poet and Persian scholar in collaboration
Translated by John Moyne & Coleman Barks
0–939660–06–7 Threshold pb $7.00

THE SUFI PATH OF LOVE
Translated by William C. Chittick
0–87395–724–5 SUNY pb $12.95

UNSEEN RAIN: Quatrains of Rumi
About 200 quatrains, in fresh versions by the translators of *Open Secret*
Translated by John Moyne & Coleman Barks
0–939660–16–4 Threshold pb $8.00

• Annemarie Schimmel
MYSTICAL DIMENSIONS OF ISLAM
A sensitive and scholarly account of the history, doctrines, and practices of Sufism. "Beautifully written. The best and most comprehensive study on Islamic mysticism in the English language"—*Religious Studies Review*
0–8078–1271–4 North Carolina pb $9.95

• Margaret Smith
RABI'A THE MYSTIC AND HER FELLOW SAINTS IN ISLAM
0–521–31863–7 Cambridge pb $14.95

THE WAY OF THE MYSTICS: The Early Christian Mystics and the Rise of the Sufis
0-19-519967-7 Oxford pb $6.95

Behind all created beauty the mystic sees a witness to the source of eternal beauty—the ruby is the heart of the stone, which has been transformed into a priceless jewel through patience and shedding its blood; the emerald is powerful like the mystical leader, blinding the eyes of the serpents or the enemies of faith. The millstone turns in its restless journey like the Sufi, and the waterwheel sighs like the lover who is separated from his home and his friend. Rain is God's mercy, which revives the heart that has become lowly as dust; sun is His glory, to be contemplated through the multicolored prisms of created things. The breeze of His loving-kindness makes the growing boughs and buds dance, and the storm of His wrath uproots the dried-up bushes and trees that lack the sap of love.

Annemarie Schimmel
MYSTICAL DIMENSIONS OF ISLAM
0-8078-1271-4 North Carolina pb $9.95

Western Philosophy

Philosophy begins, according to Aristotle, in wonder. From this auspicious beginning, it has arrived at some odd places—at the position, for instance, that the book you are holding in your hand has no physical existence (and neither does your hand). Even odder is that the history of philosophy consists of a long series of unsuccessful efforts to put an end to philosophy. Most philosophers have begun by trying to solve all major philosophical problems, and many of them have ended by announcing that they have done so. But few people—and no other philosophers—have agreed with them.

When we get beyond everyday routines, we are all likely to run up against mysteries that evoke perplexity and wonder. We are all capable of pondering the nature of knowledge, choice, mind, language; what it means to call an act good or evil or a painting beautiful; whether the soul is immortal or God exists. What philosophers have always attempted to do is to think clearly, precisely, and thoroughly about questions that most of us think about sporadically and vaguely.

Thus philosophy can be read as a way of thinking that offers a sense of clarification and cautious consolidation, a means of examining, testing, and ordering our values and beliefs. Conceived in this way, philosophy may live up to its original meaning: love of wisdom.

INTRODUCTIONS TO PHILOSOPHY

- Morris R. Cohen & Ernest Nagel
AN INTRODUCTION TO LOGIC
0-15-645125-5 HBJ pb $6.95

- John Hospers
AN INTRODUCTION TO PHILOSOPHICAL ANALYSIS
0-13-491697-2 Prentice Hall $35.00

- Thomas Nagel
WHAT DOES IT ALL MEAN?: A Very Short Introduction to Philosophy
0-19-505216-1 Oxford pb $5.95

- Richard H. Popkin & Avrum Stroll
PHILOSOPHY AND CONTEMPORARY PROBLEMS: A Reader
0-03-061701-4 Holt, Rinehart & Winston pb $29.50

- John H. Randall, Jr. & Justus Buchler
PHILOSOPHY: An Introduction
0-06-460041-6 Harper & Row pb $7.95

- Jack B. Rogers & Forrest Baird
INTRODUCTION TO PHILOSOPHY: A Case Study Approach
0-06-066997-7 Harper & Row pb $12.95

- Robert C. Solomon
ETHICS: A Brief Introduction
0-07-059658-1 McGraw-Hill pb $16.95

INTRODUCING PHILOSOPHY: A Text with Readings
0-15-541560-3 HBJ pb $22.95

- Karsten J. & Paula R. Struhl, editors
PHILOSOPHY NOW: An Introductory Reader
0-394-31852-8 Random House pb $12.95

ENCYCLOPEDIAS AND HISTORIES OF PHILOSOPHY

- A.J. Ayer
PHILOSOPHY IN THE TWENTIETH CENTURY
A history by a leading analytical philosopher
0-394-50454-2 Random House $22.00
0-394-71655-8 Random House pb $8.95

- Frederick J. Copleston
A HISTORY OF PHILOSOPHY
A superb, scrupulously objective account of the major figures and movements of Western philosophy by an English Jesuit scholar

Book 1: Volumes 1-3
0-385-23031-1 Doubleday pb $17.95

Book 2: Volumes 4-6
0-385-23032-X Doubleday pb $17.95

Book 3: Volumes 7-9
0-385-23033-8 Doubleday pb $17.95

- Paul Edwards, editor
THE ENCYCLOPEDIA OF PHILOSOPHY
An incomparable four-volume reference work, containing excellent entries on major thinkers and issues
0-02-894950-1 Free Press (set) $350.00

- David Furley
THE GREEK COSMOLOGISTS, Volume 1: The Formation of the Atomic Theory and Its Earliest Critics
The first installment of a scholarly study of the philosophical materialism that began with Democritus
0-521-33328-8 Cambridge $34.50

- W.K. Guthrie
A HISTORY OF GREEK PHILOSOPHY

Volume 1: The Earlier Presocratics and the Pythagoreans
0-521-29420-7 Cambridge pb $27.95

Volume 2: The Presocratic Tradition from Parmenides to Democritus
0-521-29421-5 Cambridge pb $24.95

Volume 3: The Fifth-Century Enlightenment

Part 1: The Sophists
0-521-09666-9 Cambridge pb $19.95

Part 2: Socrates
0-521-09667-7 Cambridge pb $15.95

Volume 4: Plato, The Man and His Dialogues: Earlier Period
0-521-31101-2 Cambridge pb $19.95

Volume 5: The Later Plato and the Academy
0-521-31102-0 Cambridge pb $20.95

Volume 6: Aristotle, An Encounter
0-521-23573-1 Cambridge $85.00

- D.W. Hamlyn
HISTORY OF WESTERN PHILOSOPHY
"Well crafted and readable . . . neither laden with footnotes nor weighed down with technical language . . . a general guide to three millennia of philosophizing in the West"—TLS
0-670-80243-3 Viking $19.95
0-14-022540-4 Penguin pb $6.95

- Karl Jaspers
PHILOSOPHY
Translated by E.B. Ashton

Volume 1:
0-226-39489-1 Chicago $19.00

Volume 2:
0-226-39491-3 Chicago $21.00

Volume 3:
0-226-39494-8 Chicago $14.00

- Bruce Kuklick
THE RISE OF AMERICAN PHILOSOPHY: Cambridge, Massachusetts, 1860-1930
The Harvard philosophy department and its hegemony
0-300-02413-4 Yale pb $15.95

- Bertrand Russell
A HISTORY OF WESTERN PHILOSOPHY
A characteristically lucid, incisive, and often droll account, stressing the historical

context and the social and political implications of philosophical ideas
0–671–20158–1 Simon & Schuster pb $15.95

Anne Fremantle, editor
THE AGE OF BELIEF: The Medieval Philosophers
0–452–00720–8 NAL pb $3.95

Giorgio di Santillana, editor
THE AGE OF ADVENTURE: The Renaissance Philosophers
0–452–00851–4 NAL pb $8.25

Stuart Hampshire, editor
THE AGE OF REASON: The Seventeenth Century Philosophers
0–452–00698–8 NAL pb $3.50

Isaiah Berlin, editor
THE AGE OF ENLIGHTENMENT: The Eighteenth Century Philosophers
0–452–00904–9 NAL pb $5.95

Henry D. Aiken, editor
THE AGE OF IDEOLOGY: The Nineteenth Century Philosophers
0–452–00792–5 NAL pb $3.50

Morton White, editor
THE AGE OF ANALYSIS: The Twentieth Century Philosophers
0–452–00830–1 NAL pb $6.95

THE PRESOCRATICS

The chief Presocratic philosophers, whose work survives only in fragments, were concerned with the basic stuff, the underlying unity, of the universe. Thales thought it was water, Anaximander "the boundless." This culminated in the drastic monism of the Eleatic school, notably in the contention of Parmenides that only unchanging being exists and that all motion and plurality are illusory; his follower Zeno tried to prove the point with his famous paradoxes. The mysterious aphorisms of Heraclitus, on the other hand, suggest that all is ceaseless change and that everything contains and becomes its opposite.

• Jonathan Barnes, translator & editor
EARLY GREEK PHILOSOPHY
0–14–044461–0 Penguin pb $6.95

• Charles H. Kahn, editor
THE ART AND THOUGHT OF HERACLITUS: An Edition of the Fragments with Translation and Commentary
0–521–28645–X Cambridge pb $19.95

• G.S. Kirk, John E. Raven & Malcolm Schofield
THE PRESOCRATIC PHILOSOPHERS
A new edition of the standard critical history, including a comprehensive selection of texts; several chapters have been rewritten to reflect recent research
0–521–27455–9 Cambridge pb $19.95

Commentaries

• Jonathan Barnes
THE PRESOCRATIC PHILOSOPHERS
A rigorous and precise study of pre-Socratic ideas. "Lovers of the Presocratics will welcome this highly personal, vigorous and stimulating survey of the field"—Charles H. Kahn, *Journal of Philosophy*
0–7100–9200–8 RC&H pb $19.95

• Martin Heidegger
EARLY GREEK THINKING
According to Heidegger, Western philosophy not only begins with the Presocratics but culminates in ideas that are close to theirs
Translated by David Krell & Frank Capuzzi
0–06–063842–7 Harper & Row pb $8.95

One cannot step twice into the same river, nor can one grasp any mortal substance in a stable condition, but it scatters and again gathers; it forms and dissolves, and approaches and departs.

Heraclitus in

G.S. Kirk, John E. Raven & Malcolm Schofield
THE PRESOCRATIC PHILOSOPHERS
0–521–27455–9 Cambridge pb $19.95

SOCRATES

Socrates apparently wrote nothing. He described himself as a gadfly, and since he was executed on a charge of corrupting the young, it is safe to assume that his sly and relentless questioning, as depicted in Plato's early dialogues, really was the "Socratic method." The ethical intensity of Plato's Socrates—the injunction "know thyself" and the conviction that virtue is a form of knowledge—also rings true. Whatever his precise teachings, Socrates has been most influential as a supreme example of the committed philosophical spirit.

Commentaries

• Gerasimos X. Santas
SOCRATES
A systematic study of Socrates' methods of constructing philosophical questions and definitions
0–7100–9327–6 RC&H pb $10.95

• I.F. Stone
THE TRIAL OF SOCRATES
An attempt to understand the execution of Socrates from a point of view sympathetic to the democratic Athenian state
0–316–81758–9 Little, Brown $18.95

• Gregory Vlastos, editor
THE PHILOSOPHY OF SOCRATES: A Collection of Critical Essays
0–268–01537–6 Notre Dame pb $10.95

PLATO

Plato was a rationalist among poets and a poet among rationalists, who presented his most rigorous thought in beautifully written dialogues. This severe moralist who would have banned most forms of poetry, art, and music from his ideal city has always appealed to poets, aesthetes, and visionaries, for he was akin to them all.

• Plato
THE COLLECTED DIALOGUES OF PLATO
Edited by Edith Hamilton & Huntington Cairns
0–691–09718–6 Princeton $27.50

EARLY SOCRATIC DIALOGUES
The moral teachings of Socrates
Edited and with an introduction by Trevor J. Saunders
0–14–044447–5 Penguin pb $5.95

GORGIAS
On the moral shortcomings of rhetoric, and a defense of justice against the idea that might makes right
Translated by W. Hamilton
0–14–044094–1 Penguin pb $4.95

THE LAST DAYS OF SOCRATES
Includes *Euthyphro, Apology, Crito, Phaedo*. The speeches and teachings of Socrates at the time of his trial, and the doctrine of the immortality of the soul
Translated by Hugh Tredennick
0–14–044037–2 Penguin pb $3.95

THE LAWS
A late work offering detailed practical legislation for a real, not ideal, state, ranging from education and elections to games and diet
Translated by T.J. Saunders
0–14–044222–7 Penguin pb $5.95

PHAEDRUS & LETTERS VII & VIII
The psychology of love
Translated by Walter Hamilton
0–14–044275–8 Penguin pb $4.95

PHILEBUS
The good in relation to pleasure and intelligence
Translated by Robin A. Waterfield
0–14–044395–9 Penguin pb $4.95

THE PORTABLE PLATO
Edited by Scott Buchanan
0–14–015040–4 Penguin pb $8.95

PROTAGORAS & MENO
In the *Protagoras* Socrates argues about goodness and pleasure with a celebrated Sophist, and in the *Meno* he offers a conception of what we knew before birth
Translated by W.K. Guthrie
0–14–044068–2 Penguin pb $3.95

THE REPUBLIC
Plato's most famous work, presenting the Allegory of the Cave, the Theory of Forms, and the blueprint for an ideal state ruled by philosophers
Translated by H.D. Lee
0–14–044048–8 Penguin pb $3.95

THE REPUBLIC
The great 19th-century translation, the most distinguished for its literary style
Translated by Benjamin Jowett
0–394–70128–3 Random House pb $3.95

TO ORDER BOOKS AS GIFTS, SEE PAGE 1

THE REPUBLIC
Translated by Allan Bloom
0–465–06936–3 Basic Books pb $10.95

THE SYMPOSIUM
A classic discussion of love as the desire for eternal beauty
Translated by Walter Hamilton
0–14–044024–0 Penguin pb $2.95

THEAETETUS
A brilliant and rigorous inquiry into the nature of thought and knowledge, notably rejecting the view that sense perception is knowledge
Edited with an introduction by Robin A. Waterfield
0–14–044450–5 Penguin pb $5.95

TIMAEUS & CRITIAS
Plato's cosmology and natural science; the *Timaeus* contains the earliest known form of the Atlantis legend
Translated by H.D. Lee
0–14–044261–8 Penguin pb $4.95

THE WORKS OF PLATO
Edited with an introduction by Irwin Edman
0–394–30971–5 Modern Library pb $6.95

> But I suggest, gentlemen, that the difficulty is not so much to escape death; the real difficulty is to escape from doing wrong, which is much fleeter of foot. In this present instance I, the slow old man, have been overtaken by the slower of the two, but my accusers, who are clever and quick, have been overtaken by the faster: by iniquity. When I leave this court I shall go away condemned by you to death, but they will go away convicted by Truth herself of depravity and wickedness . . . No doubt it was bound to be so, and I think the result is fair enough.
>
> Socrates, in *The Apology*, in
> Plato
> **THE LAST DAYS OF SOCRATES**
> Translated by Hugh Tredennick
> 0–14–044037–2 Penguin pb $3.95

● Julia Annas
AN INTRODUCTION TO PLATO'S REPUBLIC
Plato as philosophical educator rather than dogmatist
0–19–827429–7 Oxford pb $9.95

● R.M. Hare
PLATO
A brief, elegant summary of the major arguments, from the Past Masters series
0–19–287586–8 Oxford $14.95
0–19–287585–X Oxford pb $4.95

● Martha C. Nussbaum
THE FRAGILITY OF GOODNESS: Luck and Ethics in Greek Tragedy and Philosophy
An important study of Greek culture encompassing literature as well as philosophical ethics
0–521–27702–7 Cambridge pb $19.95

● Leo Strauss
STUDIES IN PLATONIC POLITICAL PHILOSOPHY
Edited by Thomas L. Pangle
Foreword by Joseph Cropsey
0–226–77700–6 Chicago pb $8.95

ARISTOTLE

Aristotle has been such a monumental presence in Western philosophy that he is almost as difficult to approach as he is to get around. He was the chief influence not only on medieval scholastic philosophy but also on all philosophy of a realist or empiricist tendency right up through 20th-century "ordinary language" philosophy. The great systematizer and classifier, he was called "the master of those who know" by Dante. Yet his surviving works consist solely of lecture notes, arranged in arbitrary order by editors. His dialogues, Platonic in tone, are lost. Aristotle's philosophy should be approached in the inquisitive, investigative spirit in which it was written.

● Aristotle
THE COMPLETE WORKS OF ARISTOTLE: The Revised Oxford Translation
Edited by Jonathan Barnes
0–691–09950–2 Princeton (2-volume set) $79.00

A NEW ARISTOTLE READER
Edited by J.L. Ackrill
0–691–02043–4 Princeton pb $13.95

THE POCKET ARISTOTLE
Edited by Justin Kaplan
0–671–46377–2 Washington Square pb $5.95

ARISTOTLE'S POETICS
Aristotle's theory of tragedy as catharsis has been of crucial importance to subsequent literary theory
Translated by S.H. Butcher
Introduction by Frances Fergusson
0–8090–0527–1 Hill & Wang pb $4.95

THE ATHENIAN CONSTITUTION
Translated by P.J. Rhodes & Martin Hurlimann
0–14–044431–9 Penguin pb $4.95

DE ANIMA: On the Soul
The relation of the soul to God and to intellectual and imaginative capacity
Translated by Hugh Lawson-Tancred
0–14–044471–8 Penguin pb $5.95

THE NICOMACHEAN ETHICS
Ethics as an imprecise practical science; virtue as the mean between extremes
Translated by Sir David Ross
Revised translation by J.L. Ackrill & J.O. Urmson
0–19–281518–0 Oxford pb $4.95

POLITICS
Treats man the political animal, and surveys the various kinds of states and their advantages and disadvantages
0–14–044421–1 Penguin pb $4.95

● J.L. Ackrill, editor
ARISTOTLE THE PHILOSOPHER
Shows why contemporary philosophers still draw from and return to Aristotle
0–19–289118–9 Oxford pb $9.95

● Jonathan Barnes
ARISTOTLE
Barnes places Aristotle in historical context, as a controversial political figure and a member of Plato's philosophical school
0–19–287581–7 Oxford pb $4.95

● Jonathan Lear
ARISTOTLE: The Desire to Understand
A lucid introduction and guide to Aristotle's central doctrines
0–521–34762–9 Cambridge pb $12.95

STOICS AND EPICUREANS

● Epicurus
EPICURUS: The Extant Remains, with a Short Critical Apparatus
Far from epicurean in the modern sense, Epicurus lived on bread and cheese and taught moderation and tranquility as the path to happiness
Translated by Cyril Bailey
0–88355–789–4 Hyperion $35.00

● Lucretius
THE NATURE OF THINGS
An eloquent poetic exposition of materialism and atheism
Translated by F.O. Copley
0–393–09094–9 Norton pb $6.95

THE WAY THINGS ARE: The "De Rerum Natura" of Titus Lucretius Carus
Translated by Rolfe Humphries
0–253–20125–X Indiana pb $6.95

● Seneca
LETTERS FROM A STOIC
The austere ideal of passionless virtue developed by the Stoics was never more eloquently urged than by the Roman essayist and dramatist Seneca
Edited by Robin Campbell
0–14–044210–3 Penguin pb $6.95

THE STOIC PHILOSOPHY OF SENECA: Essays and Letters
Edited by Moses Hadas
0–393–00459–7 Norton pb $6.95

● Marcus Aurelius
THE MEDITATIONS
These meditations by the ruler of antiquity's proudest empire are humble reflections on the limits of human attainment and the importance of self-mastery
Translated by Maxwell Staniforth
0–14–044140–9 Penguin pb $4.95

Commentaries
● John M. Rist
STOIC PHILOSOPHY
Stoic thought from Aristotle to Marcus Aurelius
0–521–29201–8 Cambridge pb $15.95

PLOTINUS

Some 600 years after Plato's death, Plotinus turned Platonic philosophy into something more mystical, rarefied, and elaborate. His hierarchical chain of being still continues to influence Christian thought and literature.

● Plotinus
THE ENNEADS
The complete works, in three bilingual volumes from the Loeb Classics

Volume 1
0–674–99484–1 Harvard $13.95

Volume 2
0–674–99486–8 Harvard $13.95

Volume 3
0–674–99487–6 Harvard $13.95

THE ESSENTIAL PLOTINUS:
Representative Treatises from the Enneads
Translated by Elmer O'Brien
0–914144–09–3 Hackett pb $4.95

AUGUSTINE

The last great philosopher of classical antiquity and the first great philosopher of the Middle Ages, Augustine assimilated Neoplatonism and retained a tincture of his youthful Manichaeanism while formulating a Christian philosophy based on original sin and predestination.

● Augustine
THE CITY OF GOD
The first Christian philosophy of politics and history, divorcing the community of the faithful from identification with any particular political order
Translated by Henry Bettenson
0–14–044426–2 Penguin pb $12.95

THE CONFESSIONS
The classic spiritual autobiography
Translated by R.S. Pine-Coffin
0–14–044114–X Penguin pb $4.95

● Peter Brown
AUGUSTINE OF HIPPO: A Biography
An acclaimed study
0–520–01411–1 California pb $11.95

● Henry Chadwick
AUGUSTINE
"Deep learning and lucidity make this a finely balanced and authoritative introduction to Augustine's thought"—
TLS
0–19–287534–5 Oxford pb $4.95

● Karl Jaspers
PLATO AND AUGUSTINE
From Jaspers' monumental *The Great Philosophers*
Translated by Karl Manheim
0–15–672035–3 HBJ pb $4.95

● Elaine Pagels
ADAM, EVE AND THE SERPENT
A brilliant reinterpretation of the ascendancy of Augustine, considered as having discarded the early Christian ideal of freedom
0–394–52140–4 Random House $17.95

ST. THOMAS AQUINAS

By fully assimilating Aristotle into Scholastic philosophy, Thomas Aquinas achieved the great synthesis in medieval thought; and throughout his comprehensive, systematic philosophy he sought to reconcile opposing arguments. In the 19th century his philosophy was accepted by the church as the main philosophical basis of Catholic doctrine.

● Thomas Aquinas
THE POCKET AQUINAS
Edited by V. Bourke
0–671–60171–7 Washington Square pb $4.95

SELECTED WRITINGS OF ST. THOMAS AQUINAS
Includes *The Principles of Nature, On Being and Essence, On the Virtues in General*, and *On Free Choice*
Translated by Robert P. Goodwin
0–02–345050–9 Macmillan pb $5.50

● Frederick C. Copleston
AQUINAS
A sympathetic account, stressing modern implications
0–14–020349–4 Penguin pb $5.95

● Anthony Kenny
AQUINAS
A short study comprising an account of Aquinas' life and works and his significance for philosophy; a summary of major metaphysical concepts; and an account of his philosophy of mind
0–19–287500–0 Oxford pb $4.95

● Paul E. Sigmund, editor
ST. THOMAS AQUINAS ON POLITICS AND ETHICS
Contains new translations of central selections from *The Summa Against the Gentiles, On Kingship or The Governance of Rulers*, and *The Summa of Theology*. Selected critical interpretations trace Aquinas' influence on Roman Catholicism during the Renaissance, on 19th- and 20th-century papal social thought, and on contemporary Christian Democratic political parties in Europe and Latin America
0–393–95243–6 Norton pb $7.95

OTHER MEDIEVAL PHILOSOPHERS

Boethius

Boethius, a Christian Platonist who also drew on Aristotle, was the archetypal philosopher for the Middle Ages. Accused of treason, he wrote his *Consolation of Philosophy* while in prison awaiting execution.

● Boethius
THE CONSOLATION OF PHILOSOPHY
Translated by V.E. Watts
0–14–044208–1 Penguin pb $4.95

St. Anselm

An originator of Scholastic philosophy, the 11th-century philosopher Anselm is best known as the inventor of the ontological proof for the existence of God, which holds that it is an essential part of God's perfection that he exist.

● St. Anselm
BASIC WRITINGS
Edited by Sidney N. Deane
Introduction by Charles Hartshorne
0–87548–109–4 Open Court pb $8.95

Duns Scotus

The American philosopher C.S. Pierce, influenced by his theory of universals, called the 13th-century Franciscan Scholastic one of the most profound metaphysicians who ever lived.

● Duns Scotus
PHILOSOPHICAL WRITINGS: A Selection
Translated by Allan Wolter & Marilyn M. Adams
0–87220–019–1 Hackett $28.50
0–87220–018–3 Hackett pb $7.95

● Martha & William Kneale
THE DEVELOPMENT OF LOGIC
A history of logic particularly useful for its treatment of Duns Scotus
0–19–824773–7 Oxford pb $16.95

William of Ockham

The greatest Scholastic logician, William of Ockham is best known for Ockham's razor, the widely neglected principle that philosophers, while explaining things, should not multiply logical entities: "What can be done with fewer assumptions is done in vain with more."

● William of Ockham
OCKHAM'S THEORY OF PROPOSITIONS: Part II of the Summa Logicae
Translated by Alfred J. Freddoso & Henry Schurman
0–268–01496–5 Notre Dame pb $9.95

OCKHAM'S THEORY OF TERMS
Translated by Michael J. Loux
0–268–00551–6 Notre Dame pb $9.95

RENAISSANCE PHILOSOPHERS

Marsilio Ficino

The radiant and serene Platonism that pervades much of European Renaissance literature is largely due to Ficino, founder of the Platonic Academy in Florence. By making the first complete translation of Plato's dialogues and assimilating ancient Neoplatonism into his own thought, Ficino conveyed Platonic philosophy to modern Europe, especially the idea of love as presented in the *Symposium*.

● Marsilio Ficino
THE BOOK OF LIFE
Translated by Charles Boer
0–88214–212–7 Spring pb $14.50

Giovanni Pico della Mirandola

Believing that a measure of truth could be found in all philosophies, Pico drew on not only Aristotle, the Scholastics, and Plato, but also on Jewish Kabbalists and Renaissance Hermetic philosophers. His most famous and influential work, *The Oration on the Dignity of Man,* strikes a modern note through its uncompromising insistence on human freedom, by which man can sink to the lowest levels of existence or rise to the divine.

- Giovanni Pico della Mirandola
ORATION ON THE DIGNITY OF MAN
Translated by A. Robert Caponigri
0–89526–925–2 Regnery pb $4.95

Giordano Bruno

The most famous and iconoclastic figure in Renaissance philosophy, Giordano Bruno was its only martyr. Arrested by the Inquisition, he languished in prison for eight years until 1600, when he was burned alive for heresy. A caustic critic of the static cosmos presented in Scholastic philosophy, Bruno evoked a universe containing an infinite number of worlds, a divine unity in which all opposites are reconciled. This pantheism edged into the occult: Bruno was an ardent champion of magic, hermetic philosophy, and astrology.

- Giordano Bruno
THE ASH WEDNESDAY SUPPER
90–2797–581–7 Mouton de Gruyter $30.95

- Frances Yates
GIORDANO BRUNO AND THE HERMETIC TRADITION
0–226–95003–4 Chicago pb $17.00

BACON

The first great English essayist, Francis Bacon was also the first philosophical advocate of the scientific experimental method, which he said could give mankind mastery over nature.

- Francis Bacon
THE ESSAYS
A few years after Montaigne invented the essay in French, Bacon composed his terse, epigrammatic, and shrewdly perceptive meditations, introducing the form into English literature
Edited by John Pitcher
0–14–043216–7 Penguin pb $5.95

THE ADVANCEMENT OF LEARNING: Book One
0–485–12605–2 Humanities pb $14.95

THE NEW ORGANON & RELATED WRITINGS
Bacon's revolutionary philosophy of science
Edited by Fulton H. Anderson
0–02–303380–0 Bobbs-Merrill pb $9.00

- Anthony Quinton
FRANCIS BACON
A short study that focuses on Bacon as a strict philosopher, not the universal dabbler
0–19–287524–8 Oxford pb $4.95

HOBBES

Thomas Hobbes considered human life in its natural state to be "solitary, poor, nasty, brutish, and short." His moral psychology is materialistic and egotistic, and his political theory is based on a social contract by which individuals establish an absolute authority that can provide them with security.

- Thomas Hobbes
LEVIATHAN
Edited by C.B. Macpherson
0–14–043195–0 Penguin pb $5.95

I became aware that, while I decided thus to think that everything was false, it followed necessarily that I who thought thus must be something; and observing that this truth: *I think, therefore I am,* was so certain and so evident that all the most extravagant suppositions of the sceptics were not capable of shaking it, I judged that I could accept it without scruple as the first principle of the philosophy I was seeking.

from *Discourse on Method* in

René Descartes
DISCOURSE ON METHOD & THE MEDITATIONS
0–14–044206–5 Penguin pb $3.95

DESCARTES

René Descartes broke radically with the Scholastic tradition by means of introspective analysis and systematic doubt. The prototype of the modern philosopher, he was the first to acknowledge that philosophy had lost ground to science as a description of the world.

- René Descartes
DISCOURSE ON METHOD & THE MEDITATIONS
Translated by F.E. Sutcliffe
0–14–044206–5 Penguin pb $3.95

PHILOSOPHICAL WORKS
Edited by S. Haldane & G.R. Ross

Volume 1
0–521–09416–X Cambridge pb $16.95

Volume 2
0–521–09417–8 Cambridge pb $14.95

THE PHILOSOPHICAL WRITINGS
Translated by John Cottingham & Dugald Murdoch

Volume 1
0–521–28807–X Cambridge pb $12.95

Volume 2
0–521–28808–8 Cambridge pb $12.95

- Bernard Williams
DESCARTES: The Project of Pure Enquiry
0–14–022006–2 Penguin pb $7.95

SPINOZA

The Dutch thinker Baruch Spinoza is a gigantic figure, but few readers know his work at first hand. It repays study: his beautifully designed systems of ethics and metaphysics are built on profound insights.

- Baruch Spinoza
THE COLLECTED WORKS OF SPINOZA, Volume 1
Edited by Edwin Curley
0–691–07222–1 Princeton $52.50

ETHICS
Translated by George Eliot
Edited by James Hogg
3–7052–0574–9 Longwood pb $15.00

ON THE IMPROVEMENT OF THE UNDERSTANDING
0–486–20250–X Dover pb $6.95

THEOLOGICO-POLITICAL TREATISE: Political Treatise
Translated by R.H. Elwes
0–486–20249–6 Dover pb $6.95

- Stuart Hampshire
SPINOZA
0–14–020253–6 Penguin pb $6.95

- Richard H. Popkin
THE HISTORY OF SCEPTICISM FROM ERASMUS TO SPINOZA
"Demonstrates conclusively and in fascinating detail how the transmission of ancient scepticism was a vital factor in the formation of modern thought"—M.F. Burnyeat
0–520–03876–2 California pb $11.95

- Leo Strauss
SPINOZA'S CRITIQUE OF RELIGION
Translated by E.M. Sinclair
0–8052–0704–X Schocken pb $8.50

- Harry A. Wolfson
THE PHILOSOPHY OF SPINOZA: Unfolding the Latent Processes of His Reasoning
"Wolfson has tracked Spinoza to his lair in a work of scholarship and erudition hard to duplicate . . . He argues his thesis with persuasion and wit . . . and writes in a style that is a model of clarity"—*New Republic*
0–674–66595–3 Harvard pb $17.50

LOCKE

John Locke is equally important as the founder of British empiricism and the champion of political liberalism. The philosopher who best embodies the clarity and rationality of the Enlightenment, he is very much present in contemporary philosophical and political debates.

• **John Locke**
AN ESSAY CONCERNING HUMAN UNDERSTANDING
Locke's major work in philosophy
0–452–00941–3 NAL pb $9.95

TWO TREATISES OF GOVERNMENT
The theory of government based on mutual consent and natural rights
0–451–62586–2 NAL pb $4.95

John Locke by David Levine

• **John Dunn**
LOCKE
0–19–287560–4 Oxford pb $4.95

• **J.L. Mackie**
PROBLEMS FROM LOCKE
Locke posed questions about knowledge and perception that philosophers are still trying to resolve
0–19–875036–6 Oxford pb $14.95

LEIBNIZ

Gottfried Wilhelm Leibniz is an intimidating intellectual figure. Metaphysicians are humbled by his work in formal logic, logicians by his contributions to geology (he is the first to hypothesize that the earth was molten in its early state), geologists by his innovations in mathematics (he invented the calculus).

• **Gottfried Wilhelm Leibniz**
LOGICAL PAPERS: A Selection
Translated by G.H. Parkinson
0–19–824306–5 Oxford $34.95

MONADOLOGY & OTHER PHILOSOPHICAL ESSAYS
0–02–406970–1 Macmillan pb $8.95

NEW ESSAYS ON HUMAN UNDERSTANDING
Edited by Peter Remnant & Jonathan Bennett
0–521–28539–9 Cambridge pb $14.95

THE POLITICAL WRITINGS OF LEIBNIZ
Edited by Patrick Riley
0–521–35380–7 Cambridge $39.50

• **Nicholas Rescher, editor**
LEIBNIZ: An Introduction to His Philosophy
0–8191–5217–X University Press pb $11.50

VICO

Rejecting the mathematical ideal of knowledge advanced by Descartes, Giambattista Vico replaced it with history: we can understand history better than nature, he contended, because we have made it. Ignored in his own time, he became a strong influence on such diverse writers as Michelet, Marx, and James Joyce.

• **Giambattista Vico**
THE AUTOBIOGRAPHY OF GIAMBATTISTA VICO
Translated by Max H. Fisch & Thomas G. Bergin
0–8014–9088–X Cornell pb $8.95

THE NEW SCIENCE OF GIAMBATTISTA VICO
Vico's chief work, in which he expounds his new historical science and a cyclical theory of history
Translated by Max H. Fisch & Thomas G. Bergin
0–8014–9265–3 Cornell pb $12.95

VICO: Selected Writings
Edited and translated by Leon Pompa
0–521–28014–1 Cambridge pb $14.95

• **Peter Burke**
VICO
Puts Vico in a historical context—as Vico would have done in discussing another thinker
0–19–287618–X Oxford pb $4.95

BERKELEY

To be is to be perceived, George Berkeley taught; inanimate things exist only as they are perceived by animate beings. He developed this radical idealism partly to defend commonsense notions of knowledge against both science and skepticism, and partly to justify the existence of God, who becomes the source of all sense perceptions. Berkeley is English empiricism stood on its head.

• **George Berkeley**
BERKELEY'S PHILOSOPHICAL WRITINGS
Edited by David M. Armstrong
0–02–064170–2 Macmillan pb $6.95

PRINCIPLES OF HUMAN KNOWLEDGE: Three Dialogues
Edited by Roger Woolhouse
0–14–043293–0 Penguin pb $5.95

• **Jonathan Bennett**
LOCKE, BERKELEY, HUME: Central Themes
Treats the essential themes of 18th-century British empiricism
0–19–875016–1 Oxford pb $15.95

• **J.O. Urmson**
BERKELEY
A short sympathetic account that views Berkeley's philosophy against a broad intellectual background
0–19–287546–9 Oxford pb $4.95

George Berkeley, John Locke & David Hume
THE EMPIRICISTS
Includes *Essay Concerning Human Understanding, Principles of Human Knowledge, Three Dialogues,* and *Enquiry Concerning Human Understanding*
0–385–09622–4 Doubleday pb $7.95

HUME

A cheerful, engaging Scot with a disconcertingly skeptical philosophy, David Hume found no basis for believing in causation, the self, or a benevolent God. He could set aside his doubts by turning to friends and backgammon, but his radical skepticism would awaken Kant from his "dogmatic slumber" and begin an Anglo-German dialogue that still dominates Western philosophy.

• **David Hume**
A TREATISE OF HUMAN NATURE
Edited by Ernest G. Mossner
0–14–043244–2 Penguin pb $6.95

ENQUIRIES CONCERNING HUMAN UNDERSTANDING AND CONCERNING THE PRINCIPLES OF MORALS
Edited by P.H. Nidditch
0–19–824536–X Oxford pb $12.95

DIALOGUE CONCERNING NATURAL RELIGION
0–317–30530–1 Free Press pb $5.95

HUME ON HUMAN NATURE AND THE UNDERSTANDING
Introduction by A. Flew
0–02–065830–3 Macmillan pb $5.95

MORAL AND POLITICAL PHILOSOPHY
0–317–30537–9 Free Press pb $11.95

• **A.J. Ayer**
HUME
A British analytical philosopher confronts an intellectual ancestor
0–19–287528–0 Oxford pb $4.95

• Tom L. Beauchamp & Alexander Rosenberg
HUME AND THE PROBLEM OF CAUSATION
"This is certainly the best available discussion of Hume and causality"—Donald Davidson
0–19–520236–8 Oxford $29.95

• Barry Stroud
HUME
A superb, accessible study that emphasizes Hume's relevance to contemporary philosophy
0–7100–0667–5 RC&H pb $14.95

> Where am I, or what? From what causes do I derive my existence, and to what condition shall I return? Whose favour shall I court, and whose anger must I dread? What beings surround me? and in whom have I any influence, or who have any influence on me? I am confounded with all these questions, and begin to fancy myself in the most deplorable condition imaginable, inviron'd with the deepest darkness, and utterly depriv'd of the use of every member and faculty. Most fortunately it happens, that since reason is incapable of dispelling these clouds, nature herself suffices to that purpose, and cures me of this philosophical melancholy and delirium, either by relaxing this bent of mind, or by some avocation ... I dine, I play a game of back-gammon, I converse and am merry with my friends, and when after three or four hour's amusement, I wou'd return to these speculations, they appear so cold, and strain'd, and ridiculous, that I cannot find it in my heart to enter into them any farther.
>
> David Hume
> **A TREATISE OF HUMAN NATURE**
> 0–14–043244–2 Penguin pb $6.95

ROUSSEAU

"Man is born free but is everywhere in chains." Jean-Jacques Rousseau made an eloquent case for the goodness of human nature and natural moral sentiment and for replacing a corrupt social order with one based on liberty and equality. His ideas played a major role in the French Revolution, the romantic movement, and every subsequent radical and utopian European movement through 1968.

• Jean-Jacques Rousseau
A DISCOURSE ON INEQUALITY
Translated by Maurice Cranston
0–14–044439–4 Penguin pb $3.95

THE ESSENTIAL ROUSSEAU
Translated by Lowell Bair
Introduction by Matthew Josephson
0–452–00674–0 NAL pb $3.95

FIRST AND SECOND DISCOURSE, TOGETHER WITH REPLIES TO THE CRITICS, & ESSAYS ON THE ORIGIN OF LANGUAGES
Translated by Victor Gourevitch
0–06–015538–8 Harper & Row $23.95
0–06–096029–9 Harper & Row pb $9.95

REVERIES OF THE SOLITARY WALKER
Translated by Peter France
0–14–044363–0 Penguin pb $4.95

ROUSSEAU SELECTIONS
Edited by Paul Edwards
0–02–325521–8 Macmillan pb $9.00

THE SOCIAL CONTRACT
Translated by Maurice Cranston
0–14–044201–4 Penguin pb $3.95

• Judith N. Shklar
MEN AND CITIZENS: A Study of Rousseau's Social Theory
Examines Rousseau's central concern: if modern civilization is intolerable and a return to the state of nature is impossible, how is man to arrange his existence in society?
0–521–31640–5 Cambridge pb $14.95

• Jean Starobinski
JEAN-JACQUES ROUSSEAU: Transparency and Obstruction
"A classic of modern literary criticism"—Robert Darnton
Translated by Arthur Goldhammer
0–226–77128–8 Chicago pb $19.95

KANT

Immanuel Kant took the whole of Western philosophy as his starting point, and his work would become the foundation for every subsequent philosophical movement. He remains important for both Anglo-American analytic philosophy and European metaphysics.

• Immanuel Kant
CRITIQUE OF PURE REASON
The major work of Kant's "critical philosophy," an intricate, profound, perennially challenging system of thought
Edited by Norman K. Smith
0–312–45010–9 St. Martin's pb $16.95

CRITIQUE OF JUDGEMENT
Kant's major work in aesthetics relates the beautiful and sublime to our capacities for understanding, and offers an analysis of teleological arguments applied to nature and theology
Translated by J.C. Meredith
0–19–824589–0 Oxford pb $12.95

CRITIQUE OF PRACTICAL REASON
In Kant's full treatment of ethics, morality is seen as unconditional, constituting acts done for their own sake, not for some ulterior end
Translated by Lewis W. Beck
0–02–307760–3 Bobbs-Merrill pb $6.50

GROUNDWORK OF THE METAPHYSICS OF MORALS
The short but monumental treatise in which Kant presents his famous "categorical imperative": act so that you can accept the principle of your action as a universal moral law
Translated by H.J. Paton
0–06–131159–6 Harper & Row pb $7.95

KANT'S POLITICAL WRITINGS
Kant as champion of liberalism
Edited by H. Reiss
0–521–29212–3 Cambridge pb $13.95

OBSERVATIONS ON THE FEELING OF THE BEAUTIFUL AND SUBLIME
An early treatise on the favorite distinction of 18th-century aesthetics
Edited by John T. Goldthwaite
0–520–04421–5 California $14.50

ON HISTORY
Edited & translated by Lewis W. Beck
0–02–307860–X Bobbs-Merrill pb $7.50

THE PHILOSOPHY OF KANT
Edited by Carl J. Friedrich
0–394–60465–2 Modern Library $8.95

• Hannah Arendt
LECTURES ON KANT'S POLITICAL PHILOSOPHY
Edited by Ronald Beiner
0–226–02594–2 Chicago $17.50

• Ernst Cassirer
KANT'S LIFE AND THOUGHT
A lucid intellectual biography by a neo-Kantian philosopher
Introduction by Stephan Korner
0–300–02982–9 Yale pb $14.95

• Karl Jaspers
KANT
An interpretation by a major 20th-century existentialist
Translated by Ralph Manheim
0–15–646685–6 HBJ pb $5.95

• P.F. Strawson
THE BOUNDS OF SENSE: An Essay on Kant's Critique of Pure Reason
A clear, scrupulous interpretation by a major British analytical philosopher
0–416–29100–7 RC&H pb $14.95

BENTHAM

Based on "the greatest happiness of the greatest number," Jeremy Bentham's utilitarianism had, as he wished, a major impact on English social, political, and legal reform. Although his moral psychology seems crude in light of the discoveries of modern psychology, his ideas still influence modern economic and political thought.

• Jeremy Bentham
AN INTRODUCTION TO THE PRINCIPLES OF MORALS AND LEGISLATION
0–317–30528–X Free Press pb $10.95

• Herbert L. Hart
ESSAYS ON BENTHAM: Studies in Jurisprudence and Political Theory
Corrects the widespread impression of Bentham as a chilly rationalist
0–19–825468–7 Oxford pb $13.95

• **John Stuart Mill**
MILL ON BENTHAM AND COLERIDGE
Mill's sympathetic account of two thinkers
at opposite poles: the doggedly
materialistic and utilitarian philosopher-
reformer, and the dreamy romantic poet
and idealist
Edited by F.R. Leavis
0–521–29917–9 Cambridge pb $9.95

HEGEL

Georg Wilhelm Friedrich Hegel viewed
history as a sort of ongoing cosmic
argument by which the Absolute Spirit becomes conscious of itself. His combination
of rationalism, idealism, and history proved
formidable, influencing Marxists, theologians, historians, and sociologists as well as
modern philosophers, who have either had
to assimilate Hegel or argue with him.

• **G.W.F. Hegel**
THE PHENOMENOLOGY OF MIND
Hegel's masterpiece, an account of
philosophy's emergence as absolute
knowledge
Translated by J.B. Baillie
0–06–131303–3 Harper & Row pb $13.95

**HEGEL'S LOGIC: Being Part One of the
Encyclopedia of Philosophical Sciences
(1830)**
The fundamentals of the dialectic
Foreword by John N. Findlay
0–19–824512–2 Oxford pb $12.95

THE PHILOSOPHY OF RIGHT
Hegel's philosophy of law and politics is
an argument for a disciplined
parliamentary liberalism
Translated by T.M. Knox
0–19–500276–8 Oxford pb $12.95

THE ESSENTIAL WRITINGS
Edited by Frederick G. Weiss
0–06–131831–0 Harper & Row pb $9.95

**HEGEL'S INTRODUCTION TO
AESTHETICS: Being the Introduction to
the Berlin Aesthetics Lectures of the 1820s**
The fusion of subjective and objective
spirit in art
Translated by Charles Karelis
Edited by T.M. Knox
0–19–824608–0 Oxford $19.95

**LECTURES ON THE PHILOSOPHY OF
WORLD HISTORY: Reason in History**
History as logical, purposeful progress
toward freedom
Edited by D. Forbes & H.B. Nisbet
0–521–28145–8 Cambridge pb $16.95

Illustration by Gustave Doré

**INTRODUCTION TO THE LECTURES
ON THE HISTORY OF PHILOSOPHY**
Demonstrates Hegel's profound grasp of
Plato and other Greek philosophers
Translated by T.M. Knox & A.V. Miller
0–19–824991–8 Oxford pb $17.95

Commentaries

• **Benedetto Croce**
**WHAT IS LIVING AND WHAT IS DEAD
OF THE PHILOSOPHY OF HEGEL**
One of Croce's more enduring works
Translated by Douglas Ainslie
Introduction by Pete A. Gunter
0–8191–4279–4 University Press pb $11.25

• **J.N. Findlay**
HEGEL: A Re-Examination
0–391–00893–5 Humanities $29.95

• **Jean Hyppolite**
**GENESIS AND STRUCTURE OF
HEGEL'S PHENOMENOLOGY OF
SPIRIT**
Hyppolite's students included Foucault,
Derrida, and Deleuze
Translated by Samuel Cherniak & John Heckman
0–8101–0447–4 Northwestern $43.95

• **Alexandre Kojeve**
**INTRODUCTION TO THE READING
OF HEGEL: Lectures on the
"Phenomenology of Spirit"**
Sartre, Camus, and Merleau-Ponty studied
with Kojeve
Edited by Allan Bloom
0–8014–9203–3 Cornell pb $12.95

• **Georg Lukács**
**THE YOUNG HEGEL: Studies in the
Relations Between Dialectics and Economics**
Translated by Rodney Livingstone
0–262–62033–2 MIT pb $13.50

• **Herbert Marcuse**
**REASON AND REVOLUTION: Hegel and
the Rise of Social Theory**
Hegel believed that reason could lead to
action; Marcuse, following Marx, argued
that revolution was an action dictated by
reason
0–391–02999–1 Humanities pb $17.50

• **Peter Singer**
HEGEL
A very good short introduction
0–19–287564–7 Oxford pb $4.95

• **Charles Taylor**
HEGEL
0–521–29199–2 Cambridge pb $19.95

SCHOPENHAUER

Defying the prevailing progressive rationalism of Hegel, Arthur Schopenhauer's
pessimistic philosophy described the world
in terms of pure, irrational will, a ceaseless
blind striving. Schopenhauer was the first
major Western philosopher to be influenced
by Buddhism, and despite his pessimism, he
was one of the most popular 19th-century
thinkers with the larger reading public.

• **Arthur Schopenhauer**
ESSAYS AND APHORISMS
Schopenhauer's essays (on fame, style,
genius, education) and incisive aphorisms
demonstrate his outstanding gifts
Translated by R.J. Hollingdale
0–14–044227–8 Penguin pb $4.95

ON THE FREEDOM OF THE WILL
Translated & edited by Konstantin Kolenda
0–631–14552–4 Blackwell pb $14.95

**THE WORLD AS WILL AND
REPRESENTATION**
His major philosophical work
Translated by E.F. Payne

Volume 1
0–486–21761–2 Dover pb $9.95

Volume 2
0–486–21762–0 Dover pb $8.95

• **Bryan Magee**
**THE PHILOSOPHY OF
SCHOPENHAUER**
The most comprehensive study in English,
with a biographical sketch and an
examination of Schopenhauer's influence
on artists and philosophers
0–19–824484–3 Oxford pb $16.95

• **Georg Simmel**
SCHOPENHAUER AND NIETZSCHE
0–87023–515–X Massachusetts $25.00

FEUERBACH

Ludwig Feuerbach is the overshadowed
link between Hegel and Marx. He rejected Hegel for concealing theology in his
rationalism and the empiricists for excluding
consciousness from their materialism. His
own rational humanism places human
thought in the material world and resolves
philosophy into the study of human society.

• **Ludwig Feuerbach**
THE ESSENCE OF CHRISTIANITY
In his most famous work, Feuerbach sees
religion as alienating humanity from itself
Introduction by Karl Barth
Foreword by Reinhold H. Niebuhr
0–06–130011–X Harper & Row pb $9.95

**THOUGHTS ON DEATH AND
IMMORTALITY: From the Pages of a
Thinker, Along with an Appendix of
Theological Satirical Epigrams, Edited by
One of His Friends**
A caustic critic of theology, Feuerbach was
an influence on the great 20th-century
theologian Karl Barth, as well as on
existentialists like Heidegger and Sartre
Translated by James A. Massey
0–520–04062–7 California pb $8.95

• **Karl Marx & Friedrich Engels**
**THE GERMAN IDEOLOGY: Part 1 &
Selections From Parts 2 & 3**
Edited by C.J. Arthur
0–7178–0301–5 International $6.95
0–7178–0302–3 International pb $4.25

• **Marx Wartofsky**
FEUERBACH
0–521–28929–7 Cambridge pb $16.95

MILL

John Stuart Mill's father exercised absolute dominion over his son's early development; the mature philosopher advanced a political theory that stressed the value of liberty.

- **John Stuart Mill**
  THE AUTOBIOGRAPHY OF JOHN STUART MILL
  Edited by Jack Stillinger
  0–395–05120–7 Houghton Mifflin pb $6.50

  ON LIBERTY
  The classic exposition of liberalism and tolerance
  0–14–043207–8 Penguin pb $3.95

  UTILITARIANISM
  Edited by Mary Warnock
  0–452–00598–1 NAL pb $6.95

  THREE ESSAYS: On Liberty, Representative Government, The Subjection of Women
  Mill's eloquent defense of women's rights, collected with two classics of political liberalism
  Introduction by Richard Wollheim
  0–19–283013–9 Oxford pb $8.95

  JOHN STUART MILL'S PHILOSOPHY OF SCIENTIFIC METHOD
  0–317–30541–7 Free Press pb $11.95

- **Bernard Semmel**
  JOHN STUART MILL AND THE PURSUIT OF VIRTUE
  0–300–03006–1 Yale $22.00

KIERKEGAARD

Choice is at the center of Søren Kierkegaard's philosophy. He hated any system that imposed a predetermined role on the individual, advocating risk and the confrontation of anxiety and dread. His own "leap of faith" led him to an austere Christianity, but the existentialist impulse in philosophy, which he was the first to formulate, has carried later thinkers to many different destinations.

- **Søren Kierkegaard** .
  THE CONCEPT OF ANXIETY
  Subtitled "A Simple Psychologically Orienting Deliberation on the Dogmatic Issue of Hereditary Sin"
  Translated by Reider Thomte
  Edited by Howard V. & Edna H. Hong
  0–691–02011–6 Princeton pb $8.95

  CONCLUDING UNSCIENTIFIC POSTSCRIPT
  Translated by D.F. Swenson & Walter Lowrie
  0–691–01960–6 Princeton pb $12.50

  EITHER/OR
  The choice between the aesthetic and the ethical ways of life, presented in a series of ironic essays including the famous "Diary of a Seducer" and a long commentary on Mozart's *Don Giovanni*
  Translated by Walter Lowrie

  Volume 1
  0–691–01976–2 Princeton pb $9.95

  Volume 2
  0–691–01977–0 Princeton pb $12.95

  FEAR AND TREMBLING
  The risk and anxiety of religious choice, as exemplified by the story of Abraham and Isaac
  Translated by Alastair Hannay
  0–14–044449–1 Penguin pb $4.95

  FEAR AND TREMBLING & REPETITION
  Translated and edited by Howard V. & Edna H. Hong
  0–691–02026–4 Princeton pb $8.95

  PHILOSOPHICAL FRAGMENTS: Or, A Fragment of Philosophy
  Translated by Howard V. & Edna H. Hong
  0–691–02036–1 Princeton pb $7.95

  THE SICKNESS UNTO DEATH
  Kierkegaard's most famous work is subtitled "A Christian Psychological Exposition for Upbuilding and Awakening"
  Translated by Howard V. & Edna H. Hong
  0–691–02028–0 Princeton pb $10.00

- **Patrick Gardiner**
  KIERKEGAARD
  0–19–287642–2 Oxford pb $5.95

- **Walter Lowrie**
  A SHORT LIFE OF KIERKEGAARD
  An intellectual biography
  0–691–01957–6 Princeton pb $12.50

PEIRCE

Charles S. Peirce was a secretive New England genius, who did important work in logic and developed a peculiarly American philosophical approach, pragmatism. His ideas were not generally appreciated until after World War I.

- **Charles S. Peirce**
  SELECTED WRITINGS
  Edited by Philip P. Wiener
  0–486–21634–9 Dover pb $7.95

  PHILOSOPHICAL WRITINGS OF PEIRCE
  Edited by Justus Buchler
  0–486–20217–8 Dover pb $7.50

- **A.J. Ayer**
  ORIGINS OF PRAGMATISM: Studies in the Philosophy of Charles Sanders Peirce and William James
  0–87735–501–0 Freeman, Cooper $12.50

- **Umberto Eco & Thomas A. Sebeok, editors**
  THE SIGN OF THREE: Dupin, Holmes, Peirce
  A semiotic analysis of the relation of Peirce's philosophy to some aspects of detective fiction
  0–253–20487–9 Indiana pb $10.95

- **Christopher Hookway**
  PEIRCE: Arguments of the Philosophers Series
  0–7100–9715–8 RC&H $55.00

> One need only shut oneself in a closet and begin to think of the fact of one's being there, of one's queer bodily shape in the darkness (a thing to make children scream at, as Stevenson says), of one's fantastic character and all, to have the wonder steal over the detail as much as over the general fact of being, and to see that it is only familiarity that blunts it. Not only that *anything* should be, but that *this* very thing should be, is mysterious! Philosophy stares, but brings no reasoned solution, for from nothing to being there is no logical bridge.
> from *Some Problems of Philosophy* in
> **William James**
> **WRITINGS, 1902–1910**
> 0–940450–38–0 Library of America $27.50

WILLIAM JAMES

William James, a robust and open-minded thinker, is a throwback to the 17th-century philosopher-polymath. He became the foremost champion of pragmatism, the theory that truth is simply that which works out in practice; and he also made a pioneering contribution to scientific psychology. His "neutral monism" was adopted by Russell, and pragmatic tendencies have turned up in postwar analytical philosophy as well.

- **William James**
  WRITINGS, 1902–1910
  Includes *The Varieties of Religious Experience, Pragmatism, A Pluralistic Universe, The Meaning of Truth, Some Problems of Philosophy,* and selected essays
  Edited by Bruce Kuklick
  0–940450–38–0 Library of America $27.50

  THE VARIETIES OF RELIGIOUS EXPERIENCE: A Study in Human Nature
  A classic in the philosophy and psychology of religion that stresses personal religious and mystical experience
  Edited by Martin Marty
  0–14–039034–0 Penguin pb $4.95

  PRAGMATISM & THE MEANING OF TRUTH
  Introduction by A.J. Ayer
  0–674–69737–5 Harvard pb $9.95

  ESSAYS IN PRAGMATISM
  0–317–30538–7 Free Press pb $6.95

- **A.J. Ayer**
  ORIGINS OF PRAGMATISM: Studies in the Philosophy of Charles Sanders Peirce and William James
  0–87735–501–0 Freeman, Cooper $12.50

- **Gerald E. Myers**
  WILLIAM JAMES: His Life and Thought
  A highly acclaimed recent study
  0–300–03417–2 Yale $45.00

☞ FOR ALL OTHER INQUIRIES, PLEASE CALL (212) 333-7900

NIETZSCHE

Friedrich Nietzsche regarded philosophical systems as instruments with which a philosopher deceives himself and others. His own philosophy was conveyed in swift, incisive, and deliberately provocative aphorisms, and many of his major ideas remain elusive. But the central problem he wished to diagnose is clear: nihilism. As the "death of God" penetrates modern culture, all ultimate values and truths must evaporate, and all that remains is an infinity of perspectives on a meaningless flux. To find values that can confront this nihilism, he examined the underlying motives of past and present cultures and moralities, calling for a "revaluation of values" that could say yes to life at its most terrible.

- Friedrich Nietzsche

  BEYOND GOOD AND EVIL: Prelude to a Philosophy of the Future
  Nietzsche's most complete presentation of his moral philosophy
  Translated by Walter Kaufmann
  0–394–70337–5 Random House pb $3.95

  THE BIRTH OF TRAGEDY
  Tragedy considered as a synthesis of the turbulent Dionysian and serene Apollonian elements in Greek culture, and Socrates as the embodiment of a perverse rationalism that killed it off
  Translated by Walter Kaufmann
  0–394–70369–3 Random House pb $4.95

  DAYBREAK: Thoughts on the Prejudices of Morality
  The aphoristic books of Nietzsche's skeptical, rationalistic middle period owe much of their spirit and tone to the classical maxims of La Rochefoucauld and Chamfort. Many readers prefer them to his more polemical and rhapsodic later works
  Translated by R.J. Hollingdale
  0–521–24396–3 Cambridge $22.95
  0–521–28662–X Cambridge pb $9.95

  ECCE HOMO
  A high-spirited, sometimes strident, often witty intellectual autobiography
  Translated by R.J. Hollingdale
  0–14–044393–2 Penguin pb $4.95

  THE GAY SCIENCE
  Brilliant aphorisms that introduce themes prominent in Nietzsche's later work, including the death of God and the eternal recurrence
  Translated by Walter Kaufmann
  0–394–71985–9 Random House pb $7.95

  HUMAN, ALL-TOO HUMAN: Including Assorted Opinions and Maxims & The Wanderer and His Shadow
  The first work of Nietzsche's skeptical, antiromantic middle period, full of shrewd and lucid aphorisms
  Translated by R.J. Hollingdale
  Introduction by Erich Heller
  0–521–26543–6 Cambridge $42.50
  0–521–31945–5 Cambridge pb $10.95

  ON THE GENEALOGY OF MORALS
  A speculative history of the conflict between a self-affirming "master" morality

and a vengeful, guilt-mongering "slave" morality
Translated by Walter Kaufmann
0–394–70401–0 Random House pb $6.50

THE PORTABLE NIETZSCHE
A selection from the whole range of Nietzsche's work, including *Zarathustra, Twilight of the Idols, The Anti-Christ,* and *Nietzsche Contra Wagner*
Edited by Walter Kaufmann
0–14–015062–5 Penguin pb $7.95

THUS SPOKE ZARATHUSTRA
A work cast in prophetic form, introducing, in mysterious and vivid imagery, the idea of the Superman (*Übermensch*)
Translated by R.J. Hollingdale
0–14–044118–2 Penguin pb $4.95

THUS SPOKE ZARATHUSTRA
Translated by Walter Kaufmann
0–14–004748–4 Penguin pb $4.95

THE TWILIGHT OF THE IDOLS & THE ANTI-CHRIST
Two polemical and incandescent late works: one a succinct summary of major themes; the other a serious attempt at a cultural psychology of Buddhism and Christianity
Translated by R.J. Hollingdale
0–14–044207–3 Penguin pb $3.95

UNTIMELY MEDITATIONS
Nietzsche's early critical assessment of his influences: Schopenhauer, Wagner, academic history and philology, and the rationalist biblical critic David Strauss
Translated by R.J. Hollingdale
0–521–28927–0 Cambridge pb $10.95

THE WILL TO POWER
Nietzsche's sister gathered passages from his notebooks and imposed an order and a title on them after he went mad. They are nevertheless illuminating fragments of his mature philosophy
Translated by Walter Kaufmann
0–394–70437–1 Random House pb $10.95

- Arthur C. Danto

  NIETZSCHE AS PHILOSOPHER
  Concentrates on aspects of Nietzsche's work that anticipate the epistemological and linguistic concerns of 20th-century analytical philosophy
  0–231–05053–4 Columbia pb $12.00

- Martin Heidegger

  NIETZSCHE
  Heidegger's examination of the philosopher who most influenced him

  Volume 1: The Will to Power As Art
  Translated by David Farrell Krell
  0–06–063847–8 Harper & Row $20.95

  Volume 2: The Eternal Recurrence of the Same
  Translated by David Farrell Krell
  0–06–063844–3 Harper & Row $21.95

  Volume 3: Will to Power As Knowledge and As Metaphysics
  Translated by Joan Stambaugh & Frank A. Capuzzi
  Edited by David Farrell Krell
  0–06–063843–5 Harper & Row $21.95

  Volume 4: Nihilism
  Translated by Frank A. Capuzzi
  Introduction by David Farrell Krell
  0–06–063857–5 Harper & Row $21.95

"Where has God gone?" he cried. "I shall tell you. *We have killed him*—you and I. We are all his murderers. But how have we done this? How were we able to drink up the sea? Who gave us the sponge to wipe away the entire horizon? What did we do when we unchained this earth from its sun? Whither is it moving now? Away from all suns? Are we not perpetually falling? Backward, sideward, forward, in all directions? Is there any up or down left? Are we not straying as through an infinite nothing? Do we not feel the breath of empty space? Has it not become colder? Is more and more night not coming on all the time? Must not lanterns be lit in the morning? Do we not hear anything yet of the noise of the gravediggers who are burying God? Do we not smell anything yet of God's decomposition?—gods too decompose. God is dead. God remains dead. And we have killed him. How shall we, the murderers of all murderers, console ourselves? ... Is not the greatness of this deed too great for us? Must not we ourselves become gods simply to seem worthy of it?"

"The Madman" in *The Gay Science* quoted in the introduction to *Thus Spoke Zarathustra*

Friedrich Nietzsche

THUS SPOKE ZARATHUSTRA: A Book For Everyone and No One
Translated with an introduction by R.J. Hollingdale
0–14–004748–4 Penguin pb $4.95

- R.J. Hollingdale

  NIETZSCHE
  Hollingdale has succeeded Walter Kaufmann as the principal English-language translator and editor of Nietzsche's works; his study is a good introduction to Nietzsche
  0–7448–0029–3 RC&H pb $8.95

- Karl Jaspers

  NIETZSCHE: An Introduction to the Understanding of His Philosophical Activity
  A critical study by an existentialist thinker
  0–8191–4544–0 University Press $18.75

- Walter Kaufmann

  NIETZSCHE: Philosopher, Psychologist, Antichrist
  Kaufmann catalogs Nietzsche's masks and disguises
  0–691–07207–8 Princeton pb $11.95

- Alexander Nehamas

  NIETZSCHE: Life As Literature
  Argues that Nietzsche regarded life as a text to be both created and interpreted
  0–674–62426–2 Harvard pb $9.95

- J.P. Stern

  A STUDY OF NIETZSCHE
  A study by a distinguished German-literature specialist
  0–521–28380–9 Cambridge pb $16.95

IF YOU CAN'T FIND IT, LOOK IN THE INDEX

BRADLEY

F.H. Bradley is the most important English-speaking philosopher to advance an idealist philosophy based on the work of Hegel. His influence on T.S. Eliot is as great as Dante's.

- F.H. Bradley
COLLECTED ESSAYS
0–19–824341–3 Oxford $52.00

THE PHILOSOPHY OF F.H. BRADLEY
Edited by Anthony Manser & Guy Stock
0–19–824972–1 Oxford pb $26.00

FREGE

Many philosophers of Gottlob Frege's time devised grand systems of thought and presented them aggressively. Most of these thinkers are now forgotten and unread. Frege, who did little to dramatize his contribution, is considered a founder of modern analytic philosophy.

- Gottlob Frege
TRANSLATIONS FROM THE PHILOSOPHICAL WRITINGS OF GOTTLOB FREGE
Edited by Peter Geach & Max Black
0–8476–6287–X Rowman & Littlefield pb $15.95

- Michael Dummett
FREGE: Philosophy of Language
0–674–31930–3 Harvard $50.00

THE INTERPRETATION OF FREGE'S PHILOSOPHY
0–674–45976–8 Harvard pb $18.50

DEWEY

John Dewey gave pragmatism a practical turn, applying it to educational reform and liberal politics. For Dewey ideas have meaning, truth, and value insofar as they are effective in solving the problems encountered in immediate human experience.

- John Dewey
DEMOCRACY AND EDUCATION: An Introduction to the Philosophy of Education
0–02–907370–7 Free Press pb $14.95

EXPERIENCE AND NATURE
0–486–20471–5 Dover pb $6.95

HUMAN NATURE AND CONDUCT
0–8093–1437–1 Southern Illinois pb $9.95

THE PHILOSOPHY OF JOHN DEWEY
Edited by John J. McDermott
0–226–14401–1 Chicago (2-volume set) pb $14.00

- Sidney Morgenbesser, editor
DEWEY AND HIS CRITICS
0–931206–01–4 Hackett pb $12.50

HUSSERL

The aim of Edmund Husserl's phenomenology is to examine the data of immediate experience with as few presuppositions as possible. In the essential intentionality of human consciousness Husserl hoped to find a way of bridging the mind-matter dualism that had troubled philosophers since Descartes.

- Edmund Husserl
IDEAS
0–02–065910–5 Macmillan pb $7.95

PHENOMENOLOGY AND THE CRISIS OF PHILOSOPHY
Translated by Quentin Lauer
0–06–131170–7 Harper & Row pb $6.95

- Jacques Derrida
SPEECH AND PHENOMENA & Other Essays on Husserl's Theory of Signs
The fashionable Derrida acknowledges his debt to the monkish professor
Translated by David B. Allison
0–8101–0590–X Northwestern pb $9.95

- Leszek Kolakowski
HUSSERL AND THE SEARCH FOR CERTITUDE
0–226–45036–8 Chicago pb $8.95

- Paul Ricoeur
HUSSERL: An Analysis of His Phenomenology
Translated by Edward G. Ballard & Lester Embree
0–8101–0530–6 Northwestern pb $11.95

BERGSON

Henri Bergson's vitalism might be described as life for life's sake. Reacting against the drab scientific materialism and determinism of the late 19th century, he made the *élan vital* (life force) a metaphysical principle that lifts humanity above the mechanical repetitions of matter and serves as the creative secret of evolution. His intuitive, antirational philosophy was very fashionable in France just before World War I.

- Henri Bergson
CREATIVE EVOLUTION
Translated by Arthur Mitchell
0–8191–3553–4 University Press pb $14.50

AN INTRODUCTION TO METAPHYSICS
Two sources of morality and religion
Translated by T.E. Hulme
0–023–58470–X Bobbs-Merrill pb $4.00

- Gilles Deleuze
BERGSONISM
Translated by Hugh Tomlinson & Barbara Habberjam
0–932299–06–X Zone pb $19.95

- Leszek Kolakowski
BERGSON
0–19–287645–7 Oxford pb $4.95

WHITEHEAD

Alfred North Whitehead's philosophical course diverged sharply from Russell's after their epochal collaboration on *Principia Mathematica*. While Russell tried to weld philosophy to physics, Whitehead warned against using physics to account for all reality. He developed a sometimes enthralling, sometimes abstruse metaphysics, in which the universe consists of aggregates of becomings and God is identified as the source of creative possibility.

- Alfred North Whitehead & Bertrand Russell
PRINCIPIA MATHEMATICA: To 56
0–521–09187–X Cambridge pb $37.50

PRINCIPIA MATHEMATICA
A three-volume set
0–521–06791–X Cambridge (set) $297.00

- Alfred North Whitehead
ADVENTURES OF IDEAS
The most accessible statement of his philosophy
0–02–935170–7 Free Press pb $12.95

THE CONCEPT OF NATURE
0–521–09245–0 Cambridge pb $14.95

PROCESS AND REALITY: Corrected Edition
Whitehead's central and most difficult work
0–02–934–570–7 Free Press pb $14.95

- Victor Lowe
ALFRED NORTH WHITEHEAD: The Man and His Work
Volume 1: 1861–1910
0–8018–2488–5 Johns Hopkins $34.50

UNDERSTANDING WHITEHEAD
Whitehead's student at Harvard draws on conversations with him and on Whitehead's correspondence with Russell
0–8018–0400–0 Johns Hopkins pb $9.95

SANTAYANA

Poet, novelist, essayist, and critic, George Santayana in his philosophy combined a firm naturalism with a serene sensibility informed by his Spanish Catholic background. In imperturbably lucid prose, Santayana set forth the realm of matter, established by our "animal faith," and the more compelling realm of essences, wherein our ideals, values, art, and ultimate interests lie.

- George Santayana
PERSONS AND PLACES: The Autobiography of George Santayana
Edited by William Holzberger & Herman Saatkamp, Jr.
0–262–69114–0 MIT pb $12.50

THE LIFE OF REASON
Volume 1: Reason in Science
0–486–24439–3 Dover pb $6.00

Volume 2: Reason in Art
0–486–24358–3 Dover pb $4.50

Volume 3: Reason in Religion
0–486–24253–6 Dover pb $5.95

Volume 4: Reason in Common Sense
0–486–23919–5 Dover pb $5.00

- Timothy Sprigge
SANTAYANA: An Examination of His Philosophy
0–7100–7721–1 RC&H $27.00

UNAMUNO

The greatest modern Spanish philosopher, and a passionate student of *Don Quixote,* Miguel de Unamuno argued for discarding all illusions and for resignation to "the tragic sense of life."

- Miguel De Unamuno
THE TRAGIC SENSE OF LIFE IN MEN AND NATIONS
Edited by Anthony Kerrigan
0–691–01820–0 Princeton pb $13.95

- Victor Ouimette
REASON AFLAME: Unamuno and the Heroic Will
0–300–01666–2 Yale $32.00

CROCE

Benedetto Croce is the most important Italian philosopher after Vico, from whom, along with Hegel, he learned to place history at the center of philosophy. He is best known for his *Aesthetic,* in which he conceives of art as both expression and a form of intuitive knowledge.

- Benedetto Croce
AESTHETIC
Croce's most famous and influential work
Translated by Douglas Ainslie
0–87923–255–2 Godine pb $10.95

HISTORY AS THE STORY OF LIBERTY
0–8191–3312–4 University Press pb $14.50

RUSSELL

Bertrand Russell is the principal figure in the evolution of English-language philosophy from speculation to analysis. Taking his cue from contemporary German work in logic, he rebuked the German-inspired idealism of F.H. Bradley, introducing a new leanness and precision to the discipline of philosophy.

- Bertrand Russell
THE AUTOBIOGRAPHY OF BERTRAND RUSSELL
An absorbing account, written with characteristic lucidity and candor
0–04–921022–X Unwin Hyman pb $14.95

AN INQUIRY INTO MEANING AND TRUTH
0–04–121019–0 Unwin Hyman pb $7.95

MY PHILOSOPHICAL DEVELOPMENT
0–04–192030–9 Unwin Hyman pb $7.95

OUR KNOWLEDGE OF THE EXTERNAL WORLD
0–04–121008–5 Humanities $39.95

PHILOSOPHICAL ESSAYS
0–671–50583–1 Simon & Schuster pb $5.95

PRINCIPLES OF MATHEMATICS
0–393–00249–7 Norton pb $12.95

THE PROBLEMS OF PHILOSOPHY
An early (1912) work summing up Russell's revolutionary work in epistemology and logic
0–19–500212–1 Oxford pb $5.95

▶ **For other works by Bertrand Russell, see 20th-Century British Essays and Other Prose**

- A.J. Ayer
BERTRAND RUSSELL AS A PHILOSOPHER
"The confrontation or conjunction of Ayer and Russell is a notable event and has produced a remarkable book"—*Nation*
0–85672–056–9 Longwood pb $5.50

- Ronald Clark
BERTRAND RUSSELL AND HIS WORLD
An illustrated biography
0–500–13070–1 Thames & Hudson $14.95

MOORE

G.E. Moore fired the first shot at the Hegelian idealism that dominated British philosophy at the turn of the century and then, with Russell, developed the analytical approach that replaced it. But Moore was less interested than Russell in mathematics, logic, and a logically purified philosophical language than in clarifying and defending a commonsense view of the world.

- G.E. Moore
PHILOSOPHICAL PAPERS
0–391–00810–2 Humanities $27.50

PRINCIPIA ETHICA
0–521–05753–1 Cambridge $32.95
0–521–09114–4 Cambridge pb $12.95

- A.J. Ayer
RUSSELL AND MOORE: The Analytical Heritage
By a major inheritor
0–674–78103–1 Harvard $15.00

- Paul A. Schilpp, editor
THE PHILOSOPHY OF G.E. MOORE
A 2-volume set
0–87548–136–1 Open Court (set) $29.95
0–87548–280–5 Open Court pb (set) $14.95

- J.O. Urmson
PHILOSOPHICAL ANALYSIS: Its Development Between the Two World Wars
0–19–824172–0 Oxford $29.95

COLLINGWOOD

Unsympathetic to the analytical trend of 20th-century British philosophy, Robin George Collingwood, an archaeologist as well as philosopher, is best known, like his mentor Croce, for his philosophy of history and art. His *Principles of Art* has been as much acclaimed by artists as by philosophers.

- R.G. Collingwood
THE IDEA OF HISTORY
0–19–500205–9 Oxford pb $9.95

THE PRINCIPLES OF ART
0–19–500209–1 Oxford pb $9.95

WITTGENSTEIN

Ludwig Wittgenstein produced two landmarks in 20th-century philosophy, the second repudiating the first. The *Tractatus Logico-Philosophicus* is the consummation of logical atomism, the attempt to reduce language and knowledge to its fundamental logical forms. *Philosophical Investigations* presents a philosophy that "leaves everything as it is," contending that most philosophical problems are confusions resulting from inattention to ordinary language. The elliptical and penetrating aphorisms of *Philosophical Investigations,* in which such influential concepts as "language games," "family resemblances," and "forms of life" are developed, have had a revolutionary effect on postwar analytical philosophy.

- Ludwig Wittgenstein
THE BLUE AND BROWN BOOKS: Preliminary Studies for the Philosophical Investigations
Notebooks from Wittgenstein's later period. "There could be no better introduction to Wittgenstein's thought than the *Blue Book,* whose simplicity and forthrightness must make an instant appeal. The progressive complications of the *Brown Book* make a natural bridge to the still more subtle, but often confusing, exposition of the *Investigations*"—Max Black
0–06–131211–8 Harper & Row pb $7.95

ON CERTAINTY
0–06–131686–5 Harper & Row pb $6.95

PHILOSOPHICAL INVESTIGATIONS
Translated by G.E.M. Auscombe
0–02–428800–4 Macmillan pb $28.95

TRACTATUS LOGICO-PHILOSOPHICUS
Translated by C.K. Ogden
0–7100–0962–3 RC&H pb $12.95

TRACTATUS LOGICO-PHILOSOPHICUS
Translated by D.F. Pears & B.F. McGuinness
Introduction by Bertrand Russell
0–391–00359–3 Humanities $17.50
0–7100–0962–3 RC&H pb $12.95

Ludwig Wittgenstein by David Levine

ZETTEL
A notebook from the 1930s
Translated by G.E.M. Anscombe
0–520–01635–1 California pb $8.95

> Philosophy may in no way interfere with
> the actual use of language; it can in the
> end only describe it.
>
> For it cannot give it any foundation
> either.
>
> It leaves everything as it is.
>
> Ludwig Wittgenstein
> **PHILOSOPHICAL
> INVESTIGATIONS**
> 0–02–428810–1 Macmillan pb $19.95

• G.E.M. Anscombe
**INTRODUCTION TO
WITTGENSTEIN'S TRACTATUS**
Foreword by H.J. Paton
0–8122–1019–0 Pennsylvania pb $10.95

• A.J. Ayer
WITTGENSTEIN
A careful, fair-minded, and frank critical
assessment by a major analytical
philosopher. Addressing Wittgenstein's
views on religion and psychology as well as
on language and knowledge, Ayer
concedes much to him while arguing that
certain positions were "mistakes"
0–226–03337–6 Chicago pb $8.95

• Robert J. Fogelin
WITTGENSTEIN
A thorough study of Wittgenstein's
Tractatus and later work emphasizing the
radical originality of his point of view.
"This is the best general introduction to
Wittgenstein's work that I have read"—
John R. Searle
0–7102–0975–4 RC&H $14.95

• Saul A. Kripke
**WITTGENSTEIN ON RULES AND
PRIVATE LANGUAGE**
Kripke makes public the influence of
Wittgenstein on his own thought
0–674–95401–7 Harvard pb $6.95

HEIDEGGER

Martin Heidegger's work is perhaps best
understood as the consummate philosophical expression of the German romantic
tradition. The search for an authentic way of
being; the brooding contemplation of the
solitary path that ends in death; the burden
of existence dominated by technology and
out of touch with being; the conception of
the poet as the guide back to being—all
these are familiar elements of that tradition, as are the unsavory nationalistic and
irrationalist overtones of the philosophy.
Yet Heidegger no less than Nietzsche succeeded in transforming this tradition into
something philosophically creative and provocative.

• Martin Heidegger
BASIC WRITINGS
Edited by David F. Krell
0–06–063845–1 Harper & Row pb $12.95

BEING AND TIME
Heidegger's magnum opus
0–06–063850–8 Harper & Row $25.95

POETRY, LANGUAGE, THOUGHT
Includes such essays as "The Origin of the
Work of Art," "What Are Poets For?" and
"The Thing." "As a whole this very
valuable collection deals with the later
Heidegger's highly aesthetic, highly poetic,
view of Being and of Dasein's relationship
to Being"—*Review of Metaphysics*
Translated by Albert Hofstadter
0–06–090430–5 Harper & Row pb $7.95

WHAT IS CALLED THINKING?
Translated by J. Glenn Gray & Fred D. Wieck
0–06–090528–X Harper & Row pb $7.95

• Michael Murray, editor
**HEIDEGGER AND MODERN
PHILOSOPHY**
Essays by Wittgenstein, Hannah Arendt, Paul Ricoeur,
and others
0–300–02236–0 Yale pb $12.95

• Thomas Sheehan, editor
HEIDEGGER: The Man and the Thinker
Argues that the thinker is more attractive
than the man
0–913750–16–6 Transaction $29.95

• George Steiner
MARTIN HEIDEGGER
"It would be hard to imagine a better
introduction to the work of Martin
Heidegger "—*New Republic*
0–226–77232–2 Chicago pb $10.95

LOGICAL POSITIVISM

Logical positivism limited meaningful
sentences to propositions that can be
verified scientifically, and dismissed most
traditional philosophy—notably metaphysics, ethics, and aesthetics—as nonsense. Its
most prominent exponents were Rudolf Carnap, Moritz Schlick, and Otto Neurath.

• Rudolf Carnap
**FOUNDATIONS OF LOGIC AND
MATHEMATICS**
0–226–57578–0 Chicago pb $4.50

**INTRODUCTION TO SYMBOLIC
LOGIC AND ITS APPLICATIONS**
0–486–60453–5 Dover pb $5.95

**THE LOGICAL STRUCTURE OF THE
WORLD AND PSEUDOPROBLEMS IN
PHILOSOPHY**
Translated by Rolf A. George
0–520–01417–0 California pb $12.95

**MEANING AND NECESSITY: A Study in
Semantics and Modal Logic**
0–226–09347–6 Chicago pb $12.95

• Oswald Hanfling
**ESSENTIAL READINGS IN LOGICAL
POSITIVISM**
Central writings of the Vienna Circle
group of logical positivists (including
Neurath, Carnap, Schlick, and
Reichenbach) as well as English
philosophers such as Moore and Ayer
0–631–12566–3 Basil Blackwell pb $11.95

• Hans Reichenbach
**THE RISE OF SCIENTIFIC
PHILOSOPHY**
0–520–01055–8 California pb $9.95

• Moritz Schlick
GENERAL THEORY OF KNOWLEDGE
0–87548–442–5 Open Court pb $12.95

Commentaries

• Oswald Hanfling
LOGICAL POSITIVISM
Debates of the Vienna Circle examined
and compared with classic empiricism and
the philosophy of Wittgenstein
0–231–05386–X Columbia $26.50

• Paul A. Schilpp, editor
**THE PHILOSOPHY OF RUDOLPH
CARNAP**
Twenty-six essays on his work and
Carnap's reply to them along with an
autobiographical essay
0–87548–130–2 Open Court $44.95

SARTRE

The most famous and influential French
philosopher of the century, Jean-Paul
Sartre began with a Heideggerian existentialism that combined an affirmation of
human freedom with an unflinching metaphysical pessimism. Stressing choice, commitment, and responsibility, he declared that

man makes himself—but he also asserted that life is ultimately meaningless. He later attempted to reconcile his existentialist faith in freedom with a commitment to Marxist historical determinism and to revolutionary violence.

- Jean-Paul Sartre
BEING AND NOTHINGNESS
Translated by Hazel E. Barnes
0–671–49606–9 Washington Square pb $6.95

ESSAYS IN EXISTENTIALISM
Introduction by S. Wahl
0–8065–0162–6 Lyle Stuart pb $7.95

SEARCH FOR A METHOD
Translated by Hazel E. Barnes
0–394–70464–9 Random House pb $4.95

▶ For other works by Jean-Paul Sartre, see Modern French Literature & Modern European Drama

- Peter Caws
SARTRE
A systematic reading of the entire corpus of Sartre's philosophical writings, with special attention to the concept of freedom
0–7102–0233–4 RC&H pb $10.95

- David G. Cooper & R.D. Laing
REASON AND VIOLENCE
Laing and Cooper enter the jungle of Sartre's *Critique of Dialectical Reason* and report what they find
0–394–71582–9 Random House pb $5.95

- Iris Murdoch
SARTRE: Romantic Rationalist
The novelist who teaches philosophy, on a philosopher who wrote novels
0–670–81726–0 Viking $14.95

- Paul A. Schilpp, editor
THE PHILOSOPHY OF JEAN-PAUL SARTRE
0–87548–354–2 Open Court $29.95

- Mary Warnock
EXISTENTIALISM
0–19–888052–9 Oxford pb $5.95

MERLEAU-PONTY

Often regarded as a disciple of Sartre, Maurice Merleau-Ponty was a more rigorous and persistent exponent of phenomenology, paying close attention to problems of perception. Like Sartre, he attempted to fuse his early thought with orthodox Marxism, and like Sartre, he ended up quarreling with orthodox Marxists.

- Maurice Merleau-Ponty
PHENOMENOLOGY OF PERCEPTION
Translated by Colin Smith
0–391–02551–1 Humanities pb $22.50

STRUCTURE OF BEHAVIOR
Translated by Alden Fisher
0–8207–0163–7 Duquesne pb $12.50

ADVENTURES OF THE DIALECTIC
Translated by Joseph J. Bien
0–8101–0596–9 Northwestern pb $12.95

- John O'Neill
PERCEPTION, EXPRESSION, AND HISTORY: The Social Phenomenology of Maurice Merleau-Ponty
0–8101–0299–4 Northwestern $12.95

IMPORTANT PHILOSOPHERS OF THE PAST 50 YEARS

Theodor Adorno

The leading figure of the postwar German Frankfurt school of philosophy and social theory, Theodor Adorno combined Marxism and Freudianism in an attempt to vindicate an ideal of enlightened human freedom. A gifted musicologist and a composer, he made several notable contributions to aesthetics.

- Theodor Adorno
AESTHETIC THEORY
0–7102–0990–8 RC&H pb $16.95

PRISMS
Translated by Samuel & Sherry Weber
0–262–51025–1 MIT pb $7.95

NEGATIVE DIALECTICS
0–8264–0132–5 Continuum pb $19.95

J.L. Austin

J.L. Austin modestly preached and practiced the careful examination of the distinctions and usages of ordinary language and is the purest representative of this strain of postwar British analytical philosophy.

- J.L. Austin
HOW TO DO THINGS WITH WORDS
Edited by J.O. Urmson and Marina Sbisa
0–674–41152–8 Harvard pb $5.95

SENSE AND SENSIBILIA
Edited by Geoffrey J. Warnock
0–19–500307–1 Oxford pb $8.95

A.J. Ayer

One of the most eminent and productive British analytical philosophers, A.J. Ayer wrote with clarity and something of the trenchant wit of his mentor Bertrand Russell.

- A.J. Ayer
THE PROBLEM OF KNOWLEDGE
0–14–020377–X Penguin pb $6.95

LANGUAGE, TRUTH AND LOGIC
0–486–20010–8 Dover pb $2.95

Brand Blanshard

A tenacious critic of analytical philosophy, existentialism, and other 20th-century tendencies, Brand Blanshard is the most eminent champion of rational idealism in recent philosophy, giving it a less religious, more rigorous form than his 19th-century prede-

cessors. He has forcefully upheld the rational basis of ethics against the prevalent emotive and relativistic theories.

- Brand Blanshard
THE NATURE OF THOUGHT
0–391–00923–0 Humanities (2-volume set) $50.00

REASON AND ANALYSIS
0–87548–104–3 Open Court $11.95

Donald Davidson

The most important American analytic philosopher since Quine, Donald Davidson has brought a fresh, subtle, and uncommonly rigorous approach to the questions of meaning and truth. He rejects not only pluralistic theories of interpretation but also atomistic theories of meaning in favor of a holistic theory of truth based on the coherence of entire sentences with one another.

- Donald Davidson
ESSAYS ON ACTIONS AND EVENTS
0–19–824637–4 Oxford pb $13.95

INQUIRIES INTO TRUTH AND INTERPRETATION
0–19–875046–3 Oxford pb $13.95

- Bruce Vermazen & Merrill B. Hintikka, editors
ESSAYS ON DAVIDSON: Actions and Events
0–19–824963–2 Oxford pb $15.95

Nelson Goodman

Nelson Goodman is noted for his stress on the frames of reference through which we approach and construct the world.

- Nelson Goodman
OF MIND AND OTHER MATTERS
0–674–63125–0 Harvard $18.50
0–674–63126–9 Harvard pb $8.95

FACT, FICTION AND FORECAST
0–674–29070–4 Harvard $13.50
0–674–29071–2 Harvard pb $6.95

WAYS OF WORLDMAKING
0–915144–51–4 Hackett pb $5.95

THE LANGUAGES OF ART
0–915144–35–2 Hackett $19.50
0–915144–34–4 Hackett pb $9.95

Herbert Marcuse

Herbert Marcuse, another member of the Frankfurt school, became a chief intellectual sponsor of the New Left and the 1960s counterculture through his insistence that erotic liberation must accompany radical political and economic change.

- Herbert Marcuse
EROS AND CIVILIZATION: A Philosophical Inquiry into Freud
Reducing the discontents of civilization by reintegrating eros
0–8070–1555–5 Beacon pb $10.95

ONE DIMENSIONAL MAN
A scathing criticism of consumer capitalism
0–8070–1575–X Beacon pb $8.95

Karl Popper

The most important contemporary philosopher of science, Karl Popper argues that a hypothesis is scientific only if it can specify the results that would show it to be false. This allowed him to dismiss Marxism and similarly circular theories as pseudoscience, and to formulate an influential attack on totalitarian ideology.

● Karl Popper
POPPER SELECTIONS
Edited by David Miller
0–691–07287–6 Princeton pb $34.50

OBJECTIVE KNOWLEDGE: An Evolutionary Approach
0–19–875024–2 Oxford pb $12.95

THE OPEN SOCIETY AND ITS ENEMIES
Volume 1: The Spell of Plato
0–691–01968–1 Princeton pb $10.95

Volume 2: The High Tide of Prophecy: Hegel, Marx and the Aftermath
0–691–01972–X Princeton pb $10.50

THE LOGIC OF SCIENTIFIC DISCOVERY
0–06–130576–6 Harper & Row pb $10.95

● Anthony O'Hear
KARL POPPER
Illustrates the nature of Popper's thought and examines his views on knowledge, science, probability, society, evolution, and the self
0–7100–9334–9 RC&H pb $13.95

● Paul A. Schilpp, editor
THE PHILOSOPHY OF KARL POPPER
0–87548–353–4 Open Court $39.95

W.V. Quine

W.V. Quine, an acute and original logician, is the most important American philosopher to work in the analytic tradition. Through his influence the center of philosophical activity has shifted to the United States.

● W.V. Quine
QUIDDITIES: An Intermittently Philosophical Dictionary
0–674–74351–2 Harvard $20.00

THE WAYS OF PARADOX AND OTHER ESSAYS
0–674–94835–1 Harvard $18.50
0–674–94837–8 Harvard pb $9.95

WORD AND OBJECT
0–262–67001–1 MIT pb $10.95

● Lewis Hahn & Paul A. Schilpp, editors
THE PHILOSOPHY OF W.V. QUINE
0–8126–9010–9 Open Court $49.95
0–8126–9012–5 Open Court pb $24.95

John Rawls

Rawls's *Theory of Justice* is the most important book in ethical philosophy to appear in English since G.E. Moore's *Principia Ethica* of 1903.

● John Rawls
THEORY OF JUSTICE
0–874–88010–2 Harvard $27.00
0–674–88014–5 Harvard pb $11.95

Gilbert Ryle

Gilbert Ryle, with his behavioristic account of mental phenomena, is the last philosopher to have made an important contribution to psychology.

● Gilbert Ryle
THE CONCEPT OF MIND
0–226–73295–9 Chicago pb $10.95

● William Lyons
GILBERT RYLE: An Introduction to His Philosophy
0–391–01800–0 Humanities $45.00

P.F. Strawson

Beginning as an exponent of ordinary-language analytical philosophy, P.F. Strawson developed a related position he called "descriptive metaphysics," the attempt to uncover and describe the actual, unchanging structures of human thought.

● P.F. Strawson
SKEPTICISM AND NATURALISM: Some Varieties
0–231–05916–7 Columbia $19.50
0–231–05917–5 Columbia pb $10.00

INDIVIDUALS: An Essay in Descriptive Metaphysics
0–416–68310–X RC&H pb $16.95

Jacques Derrida

Jacques Derrida's philosophy has brought the influence of Nietzsche and Heidegger to bear on questions of semiotics and literary language. He has been the chief philosophical exponent of deconstructionism, which has had a pervasive influence on contemporary literary theory and confines itself to unmasking hidden assumptions and the prejudices of language.

● Jacques Derrida
DISSEMINATION
Translated by Barbara Johnson
0–226–14334–1 Chicago pb $13.95

MARGINS OF PHILOSOPHY
Translated by Alan Bass
0–226–14325–2 Chicago $25.00
0–226–14326–0 Chicago pb $12.95

OF GRAMMATOLOGY
Translated by Gayatri C. Spivak
0–8018–1879–6 Johns Hopkins pb $9.95

WRITING AND DIFFERENCE
Translated by Alan Bass
0–226–14329–5 Chicago pb $12.00

Jürgen Habermas

Jürgen Habermas has inherited the critical theory of the Frankfurt school, with its Marxist emphasis on social, cultural, and historical analysis, but he has assimilated to it the concern with language and meaning found in Wittgenstein and the ordinary-language school of British analytical philosophy. His most important work is found in his theories of communication and its social basis.

● Jürgen Habermas
THE PHILOSOPHICAL DISCOURSE OF MODERNITY
A series of twelve lectures
Translated by Frederick G. Lawrence
0–262–08163–6 MIT $27.50

THEORY AND PRACTICE
Translated by John Viertel
0–8070–1526–1 Beacon pb $10.95

THE THEORY OF COMMUNICATIVE ACTION
Generally regarded as Habermas' chief work
Translated by Thomas McCarthy

Volume 1: Reason and the Rationalization of Society
0–8070–1507–5 Beacon pb $15.95

Volume 2: Lifeword and System: A Critique of Functional Reason
0–8070–1400–1 Beacon $37.50

IMPORTANT RECENT WORK

● D.M. Armstrong
UNIVERSALS AND SCIENTIFIC REALISM
Volume 1
0–521–28033–8 Cambridge pb $10.95
Volume 2
0–521–28032–X Cambridge pb $10.95

● Arthur C. Danto
NARRATION AND KNOWLEDGE
An analytical approach to the philosophy of history
0–231–06117–X Columbia pb $14.50

● Ronald Dworkin
Dworkin is among the most eminent of contemporary legal philosophers, notable for finding a theoretical basis for liberal social policy.
LAW'S EMPIRE
0–674–51836–5 Harvard pb $11.95

A MATTER OF PRINCIPLE
0–674–55461–2 Harvard pb $9.95

TAKING RIGHTS SERIOUSLY
0–674–86711–4 Harvard pb $10.95

● Paul K. Feyerabend
PHILOSOPHICAL PAPERS
A critical and historical discussion of scientific theory by an iconoclastic philosopher of science
Volume 1: Realism, Rationalism and Scientific Method
0–521–31642–1 Cambridge pb $15.95

★ **FOR COMPLETE ORDERING INFORMATION, SEE PAGE 1**

Volume 2: Problems of Empiricism
0–521–31641–3 Cambridge pb $14.95

AGAINST METHOD
0–86091–222–1 RC&H $50.00
0–86091–934–X RC&H pb $14.95

• Stuart Hampshire
FREEDOM OF THE INDIVIDUAL
An analysis of the problems surrounding the concept of intentional actions, by an important contemporary analytical philosopher
0–691–07208–6 Princeton $18.00
0–691–01984–3 Princeton pb $7.95

• Norwood R. Hanson
PATTERNS OF DISCOVERY: An Enquiry into the Conceptual Foundations of Science
0–521–09261–2 Cambridge pb $15.95

• Saul A. Kripke
NAMING AND NECESSITY
Kripke's work runs against the tide of recent analytic philosophy by championing a rigorous theory of meaning and truth reminiscent of Russell and Frege
0–674–59845–8 Harvard $15.00
0–674–59846–6 Harvard pb $6.95

• Thomas S. Kuhn
THE STRUCTURE OF SCIENTIFIC REVOLUTIONS
Kuhn caused a revolution in the history of science with his groundbreaking theory of paradigms and their role in the development of scientific knowledge
0–226–45804–0 Chicago pb $6.95

• Ernest Nagel
THE STRUCTURE OF SCIENCE
0–915–144–71–9 Hackett pb $16.50

• Robert Nozick
ANARCHY, STATE AND UTOPIA
A brilliant and provocative work that offers a libertarian alternative to John Rawls's *Theory of Justice*
0–465–00270–6 Basic Books $21.95
0–465–09720–0 Basic Books pb $11.95

PHILOSOPHICAL EXPLANATIONS
"His arguments link his explanations to what he is rightly confident of . . . his vision of a persistent role for philosophy in common life"—*New Republic*
0–674–66479–5 Harvard pb $10.95

• Derek Parfit
REASONS AND PERSONS
"Parfit's book, besides contributing, as it certainly does, intellectual illumination and delight, may possibly do more: it may point the way to the emergence of a satisfactory theory of rational beneficence, and this might, in the long run, be capable of influencing political behavior"—P.F. Strawson, *NY Review of Books*
0–19–824908–X Oxford pb $14.95

• Hilary Putnam
REASON, TRUTH, AND HISTORY
0–521–29776–1 Cambridge pb $12.95

• Richard Rorty
PHILOSOPHY AND THE MIRROR OF NATURE
Argues from a pragmatist perspective against philosophy's post-Cartesian epistemological obsession
0–691–02016–7 Princeton pb $9.95

• John R. Searle
INTENTIONALITY: An Essay in the Philosophy of Mind
0–521–27302–1 Cambridge pb $14.95

• Bernard Williams
ETHICS AND THE LIMITS OF PHILOSOPHY
"To read this book is to be taken through one of the most sophisticated discussions available of such questions by an engaging, skeptical, often wryly witty and extraordinarily subtle professional"—*NY Times Book Review*
0–674–26858–X Harvard pb $8.95

MORALITY: An Introduction to Ethics
0–06–131632–6 Harper & Row pb $5.95

• Richard Wollheim
ART AND ITS OBJECTS
A major work of contemporary aesthetics
0–521–29706–0 Cambridge pb $14.95

ON ART AND THE MIND
According to Wollheim the interest of art lies in its capacity to reflect inner states, and the workings of the mind are inaccessible unless we take account of their inherent creativity
0–674–63406–3 Harvard pb $10.95

READINGS IN PHILOSOPHY

• Edwin A. Burtt, editor
THE ENGLISH PHILOSOPHERS FROM BACON TO MILL
0–394–60411–3 Modern Library $13.95

• Monroe C. Beardsley, editor
THE EUROPEAN PHILOSOPHERS FROM DESCARTES TO NIETZSCHE
0–394–60412–1 Modern Library $11.95

• Philippa Foot, editor
THEORIES OF ETHICS
0–19–875005–6 Oxford pb $12.95

• J.C. Glover, editor
THE PHILOSOPHY OF MIND
0–19–875038–2 Oxford pb $11.95

• A. Philips Griffiths, editor
KNOWLEDGE AND BELIEF
0–19–875003–X Oxford pb $10.95

• Ian Hacking
SCIENTIFIC REVOLUTIONS
0–19–875051–X Oxford pb $11.95

• Rom Harre
THE PHILOSOPHIES OF SCIENCE: An Introductory Survey
0–19–289201–0 Oxford pb $9.95

• Albert Hofstadter & Richard Kuhns, editors
PHILOSOPHIES OF ART AND BEAUTY: Selected Readings in Aesthetics from Plato to Heidegger
0–226–34812–1 Chicago pb $15.95

• Hilary Putnam
PHILOSOPHY OF MATHEMATICS: Selected Readings
Edited by Hilary Benacerraf
0–521–29648–X Cambridge pb $20.95

• Anthony Quinton, editor
POLITICAL PHILOSOPHY
0–19–875002–1 Oxford pb $9.95

• J.R. Searle, editor
THE PHILOSOPHY OF LANGUAGE
0–19–875015–3 Oxford pb $8.95

• P.F. Strawson, editor
PHILOSOPHICAL LOGIC
0–19–875004–8 Oxford pb $8.95

• Gary Watson
FREE WILL
0–19–875054–4 Oxford pb $11.95

• Alan R. White, editor
THE PHILOSOPHY OF ACTION
0–19–875006–4 Oxford pb $11.95

➤ **FOR OVERSEAS ORDERING INFORMATION, SEE PAGE 1**

PART 12

SOCIAL STUDIES

Anthropology

In some respects, the field of anthropology has existed as long as people have encountered other cultures. Modern anthropology sometimes recognizes this by tracing its genealogy back to Herodotus, Montaigne, and Marco Polo. But anthropology as a professional discipline began in the United States at Columbia University with Franz Boas and his students, among them Ruth Benedict and Margaret Mead. Since the 1960s, the scientific aspiration toward an objective, "value-free" ethnographic method represented by cognitive anthropology and the structuralism of Claude Lévi-Strauss has been challenged by new interpretive methods, influenced by such poststructuralist thinkers as Barthes, Foucault, Lacan, and Derrida.

GENERAL ANTHROPOLOGICAL STUDIES

- Gregory Bateson
MIND AND NATURE
An attempt to integrate cultural experience into a comprehensive, general system or cybernetic theory of life processes
0–553–34575–3 Bantam pb $9.95

- Franz Boas
ANTHROPOLOGY AND MODERN LIFE
First published in 1928
0–486–25245–0 Dover pb $5.95

- Michael Carrithers & others, editors
THE CATEGORY OF THE PERSON
The concept "person" considered cross-culturally
0–521–27757–4 Cambridge pb $14.95

- Dan Sperber
ON ANTHROPOLOGICAL KNOWLEDGE
Critical questions about what anthropologists know and how they come to know it
0–521–31851–3 Cambridge pb $10.95

- Roy W. Wagner
THE INVENTION OF CULTURE
A kind of "poetics of culture" that attempts to pass beyond the defining of culture as an object, insisting that it can be seen instead as a process of constant modification, creativity, and innovation
0–226–86934–2 Chicago pb $5.95

- Leslie A. White
THE CONCEPT OF CULTURAL SYSTEMS: A Key to Understanding Tribes and Nations
0–231–03961–1 Columbia $27.00

- Eric R. Wolf
ANTHROPOLOGY
A brief, comprehensive overview
0–393–09290–9 Norton pb $2.95

Classics

The following are of historical interest as founding texts that have influenced several generations of anthropologists.

- Ruth Benedict
PATTERNS OF CULTURE
0–395–50088–5 Houghton Mifflin pb $8.95

- Emile Durkheim & Marcel Mauss
PRIMITIVE CLASSIFICATION
Translated by Rodney Needham
0–226–17334–8 Chicago pb $7.00

- James G. Frazer
THE GOLDEN BOUGH
A one-volume abridgment of Frazer's pioneering work of comparative mythology
0–02–095570–7 Macmillan pb $11.95

- Maurice Leenhardt
DO KAMO: Person and Myth in the Melanesian World
A superb selection, well translated
Translated by Basia M. Gulati
0–226–47039–3 Chicago $18.00

- Claude Lévi-Strauss
INTRODUCTION TO THE WORK OF MARCEL MAUSS
Mauss, a major figure in the development of anthropology who taught at the University of Paris, founded the Institute of Ethnology there in 1925
0–7100–9066–8 RC&H pb $12.95

- Marcel Mauss
THE GIFT: Forms and Functions of Exchange in Archaic Societies
Mauss's work provided the basis for subsequent work on reciprocity and exchange
0–393–00378–7 Norton pb $5.95

- Arnold Van Gennep
RITES OF PASSAGE
Translated by Monika Vizedon & Gabrielle Caffee
0–226–84849–3 Chicago pb $6.95

Research and Methodology

The following works address various aspects of "doing anthropology"—from methodological theory to memoirs of experience in the field.

- Franz Boas
RACE, LANGUAGE, AND CULTURE
A wide-ranging collection presenting the major themes of Boas' work
0–226–06242–2 Chicago pb $23.95

- Jean-Paul Dumont
THE HEADMAN AND I: Ambiguity and Ambivalence in the Fieldworking Experience
An examination of the assumptions and methods of fieldwork
0–292–73007–1 Texas pb $14.95

- Hussein M. Fahim, editor
INDIGENOUS ANTHROPOLOGY IN NON-WESTERN COUNTRIES
0–89089–198–2 Carolina pb $12.95

- Paul Rabinow
REFLECTIONS ON FIELDWORK IN MOROCCO
A work that takes anthropological field research itself as a subject of study
0–520–03450–3 California $19.50
0–520–03529–1 California pb $9.95

- Kenneth E. Read
THE HIGH VALLEY
A narrative of fieldwork in New Guinea
0–684–15134–0 Scribners $20.00
0–231–05035–6 Columbia pb $13.00

- Edith Turner
THE SPIRIT AND THE DRUM: A Memoir of Africa
0–8165–1009–1 Arizona $18.95

- Victor Turner
ON THE EDGE OF THE BUSH: Anthropology As Experience
A book that conveys the complexity of encountering "foreignness" or the Other and depicts "anthropology as experience" rather than merely as an academic exercise
Edited by Edith Turner
0–8165–0949–2 Arizona $29.95

History

The recent appearance of outstanding histories of anthropology is a welcome and exciting development.

- Marvin Harris
THE RISE OF ANTHROPOLOGICAL THEORY: A History of Theories of Culture
0–690–70322–8 Harper & Row $40.50

- Curtis M. Hinsley, Jr.
SAVAGES AND SCIENTISTS: The Smithsonian Institution and the Development of American Anthropology, 1846-1910
0–87474–518–7 Smithsonian $24.95

- Margaret T. Hodgen
EARLY ANTHROPOLOGY IN THE SIXTEENTH AND SEVENTEENTH CENTURIES
A fascinating study of anthropology before anthropologists
0–8122–1014–X Pennsylvania pb $15.95

- George W. Stocking, Jr.
OBJECTS AND OTHERS: Essays on Museums and Material Culture
Stocking's essays constitute important contributions to anthropological self-knowledge
0–299–10320–X Wisconsin $25.00

OBSERVERS OBSERVED: Essays on Ethnographic Fieldwork
0–299–09454–5 Wisconsin pb $12.95

Biographies of Anthropologists

- Robert Ackerman
J.G. FRAZER: His Life and Work
0–521–34093–4 Cambridge $39.50

- Catherine Bateson
  WITH A DAUGHTER'S EYE
  A memoir by the daughter of Margaret Mead and Gregory Bateson
  0–671–55424–7 Pocket pb $4.95

- Nicole Belmont
  ARNOLD VAN GENNEP: The Creator of French Ethnography
  Translated by Derek Coltman
  0–226–04216–2 Chicago $17.00

- Margaret Caffrey
  RUTH BENEDICT: Stranger in This Land
  A new biography of the author of *Patterns of Culture*
  0–292–74655–5 Texas $24.95

- Derek Freeman
  MARGARET MEAD AND SAMOA: The Making and Unmaking of an Anthropological Myth
  This harshly critical account of Mead's work has stirred much controversy
  0–674–54830–2 Harvard $25.00

- Theodora Kroeber
  ALFRED KROEBER: A Personal Configuration
  About one of Boas' best students; by his wife
  0–520–03720–0 California pb $6.95

- Margaret Mead
  BLACKBERRY WINTER
  A memoir rich in anecdotes and instructive details about Mead's work
  0–671–54307–5 Washington Square pb $5.95

  RUTH BENEDICT
  A lucid, sympathetic overview of her work
  0–231–03520–9 Columbia pb $14.00

- Rhoda Metraux, editor
  MARGARET MEAD: Some Personal Views
  Edited by an intimate of Mead
  0–8027–0626–6 Walker pb $9.95

ANTHROPOLOGISTS FROM NEW GUINEA.

An Australian newspaper notes the arrival of Gregory Bateson, Margaret Mead, and Reo Fortune, from With a Daughter's Eye *by Catherine Bateson (Morrow)*

- Carl Resek
  LEWIS HENRY MORGAN, AMERICAN SCHOLAR
  Morgan, working among the Iroquois in the 19th century, pioneered the study of tribal organization
  0–226–71012–2 Chicago pb $8.00

CLASSIC ETHNOGRAPHIES

Different anthropologists would no doubt come up with vastly different lists of the five or ten most important descriptive classics in the field. But anyone with a serious interest in anthropology would be familiar with, for instance, the Nuer of Evans-Pritchard and with Firth's Tikopia. Some peoples made famous by anthropologists are known less for their culture *per se* than for the way the ethnographer wrote about them.

- Gregory Bateson
  NAVEN
  An influential 1936 study of the rituals and culture of a New Guinea people
  0–8047–0520–8 Stanford pb $10.95

- E.E. Evans-Pritchard
  THE NUER: A Description of the Modes of Livelihood and Political Institutions of a Nilotic People
  Published in 1940, this was the first in a celebrated series of ethnographies of a people apparently without government
  0–19–500322–5 Oxford pb $11.95

- Raymond Firth
  WE, THE TIKOPIA: A Sociological Study of Kinship in Primitive Polynesia
  Firth's study of a Solomon Islands people first appeared in 1936
  Preface by Bronislaw Malinowski
  0–8047–1202–6 Stanford pb $11.95

- R.F. Fortune
  SORCERERS OF DOBU: The Social Anthropology of the Dobu Islanders of the Western Pacific
  0–8495–1736–2 Arden $34.50

- Clifford Geertz
  THE RELIGION OF JAVA
  A readable account, rich in details of ritual life
  0–226–28510–3 Chicago pb $14.00

- Clifford & Hildred Geertz & L. Rosen
  MEANING AND ORDER IN MOROCCAN SOCIETY
  0–521–22175–7 Cambridge $59.50

- Pierre-Jakez Hélias
  THE HORSE OF PRIDE: Life in a Breton Village
  Translated by June Guicharnaud
  0–300–02036–8 Yale $35.00
  0–300–02599–8 Yale pb $10.95

- Edmund R. Leach
  POLITICAL SYSTEMS OF HIGHLANDS BURMA: A Study of Kachin Social Structure
  Leach became the foremost English exponent of structuralist anthropology
  0–485–19644–1 Humanities pb $25.00

- Godfrey Lienhardt
  DIVINITY AND EXPERIENCE: The Religion of the Dinka
  0–19–823405–8 Oxford pb $19.95

- Robert H. Lowie
  THE CROW INDIANS
  This 1935 study resulted from many years of field work under the auspices of the American Museum of Natural History
  0–8032–7909–4 Nebraska pb $8.95

- Margaret Mead
  COMING OF AGE IN SAMOA
  A controversial account of female adolescence, published in 1928
  0–688–30974–7 Morrow pb $9.95

  GROWING UP IN NEW GUINEA
  0–688–0789–X Morrow pb $5.95

- Nancy D. Munn
  WALBIRI ICONOGRAPHY: Graphic Representation and Cultural Symbolism in a Central Australian Society
  0–226–55110–5 Chicago pb $11.95

- Alfonso Ortiz
  THE TEWA WORLD: Space, Time, Being and Becoming in a Pueblo Society
  0–226–63307–1 Chicago pb $9.00

- Roy A. Rappaport
  PIGS FOR THE ANCESTORS: Ritual in the Ecology of a New Guinea People
  0–300–03205–6 Yale pb $12.95

ESSAYS IN ANTHROPOLOGY

- James Clifford
  THE PREDICAMENT OF CULTURE: Twentieth-Century Ethnography, Literature, and Art
  A particularly lucid and stimulating recent collection
  0–674–69843–6 Harvard pb $15.95

- Louis Dumont
  ESSAYS ON INDIVIDUALISM: Modern Ideology in Anthropological Perspective
  Challenging, erudite essays on individualism as the dominant cultural orientation of the West
  0–226–16956–1 Chicago $27.50

- Charles O. Frake
  LANGUAGE AND CULTURAL DESCRIPTION: Essays by Charles O. Frake
  Edited by Anwar S. Dil
  0–8047–1074–0 Stanford $37.50

Clifford Geertz
THE INTERPRETATION OF CULTURES
One of the most influential figures of recent decades, Geertz is also noted for the elegance of his literary style
0–465–09719–7 Basic Books pb $12.95

LOCAL KNOWLEDGE: Further Essays in Interpretive Anthropology
Very readable and thought-provoking. "By displaying the tools with which an interpretive anthropologist works, he excites us over what is happening"— *NY Times*
0–465–04162–0 Basic Books pb $9.95

WORKS AND LIVES: The Anthropologist as Author
0–8047–1428–2 Stanford $19.95

● **Ernest Gellner**
THE CONCEPT OF KINSHIP & Other Essays on Anthropological Method and Explanation
0–631–15287–3 Blackwell pb $16.95

● **Edward T. Hall**
BEYOND CULTURE
0–385–12474–0 Doubleday pb $6.95

THE DANCE OF LIFE: The Other Dimension of Time
0–385–19248–7 Doubleday pb $6.95

THE HIDDEN DIMENSION
0–385–08476–5 Doubleday pb $5.95

THE SILENT LANGUAGE
0–385–05549–8 Doubleday pb $5.95

● **Marvin Harris**
CANNIBALS AND KINGS: The Origins of Cultures
0–394–72700–2 Random House pb $5.95

COWS, PIGS, WARS, AND WITCHES: The Riddles of Culture
0–394–71372–9 Random House pb $5.95

THE SACRED COW AND THE ABOMINABLE PIG: Riddles of Food and Culture
0–671–63308–2 Simon & Schuster pb $7.95

WHY THINGS DON'T WORK: The Anthropology of Daily Life
0–671–63577–8 Simon & Schuster pb $9.95

● **A.M. Hocart**
KINGS AND COUNCILLORS: An Essay in the Comparative Anatomy of Human Society
Edited by Rodney Needham
Foreword by E.E. Evans-Pritchard
0–226–34568–8 Chicago pb $3.95

● **Edmund R. Leach**
RETHINKING ANTHROPOLOGY
Incisive essays on a variety of topics including Leach's famous essays on the symbolic representation of time
0–485–19622–0 Humanities pb $18.50

● **Rodney Needham**
CIRCUMSTANTIAL DELIVERIES
0–520–04389–8 California $25.00

COUNTERPOINTS
0–520–05835–6 California $30.00

● **Rodney Needham**, editor
STRUCTURE AND SENTIMENT: A Test Case in Social Anthropology
0–226–56989–6 Chicago pb $9.95

● **A.R. Radcliffe-Brown**
STRUCTURE AND FUNCTION IN PRIMITIVE SOCIETY
Essays, mostly on kinship and social organization in Africa, making a strong case for social anthropology
0–02–925630–5 Free Press $19.95
0–02–925620–8 Free Press pb $14.95

● **Roy A. Rappaport**
ECOLOGY, MEANING, AND RELIGION
0–913028–65–7 North Atlantic $19.95
0–938190–27–X North Atlantic pb $12.95

● **Marshall Sahlins**
ISLANDS OF HISTORY
Engaging, often humorous essays on the early history of Hawaii
0–226–73358–0 Chicago pb $8.95

Victor Turner
THE FOREST OF SYMBOLS: Aspects of Ndembu Ritual
A classic work, published in 1967, containing detailed studies of the Ndembu of central Africa that have become prototypes for the interpretation of ritual symbolism
0–8014–9101–0 Cornell pb $12.95

The concept of person is...an excellent vehicle by means of which to examine this whole question of how to go about poking into another people's turn of mind. In the first place, some sort of concept of this kind, one feels reasonably safe in saying, exists in recognizable form among all social groups. The notion of what persons are may be, from our point of view, sometimes more than a little odd. They may be conceived to dart about nervously at night shaped like fireflies. Essential elements of their psyches, like hatred, may be thought to be lodged in granular black bodies within their livers, discoverable upon autopsy. They may share their fates with *doppelgänger* beasts, so that when the beast sickens or dies they sicken or die too. But at least some conception of what a human individual is, as opposed to a rock, an animal, a rainstorm, or a god, is, so far as I can see, universal.

Clifford Geertz
LOCAL KNOWLEDGE: Further Essays in Interpretive Anthropology
0–465–04162–0 Basic Books pb $9.95

CLAUDE LEVI-STRAUSS

While the structuralism of Lévi-Strauss appears to be passing out of fashion, his work remains a monument to anthropological expertise and sophistication.

Claude Lévi-Strauss by David Levine

● **Claude Lévi-Strauss**
ANTHROPOLOGY AND MYTH: Lectures, 1957-1982
0–631–14474–9 Blackwell $29.95

INTRODUCTION TO A SCIENCE OF MYTHOLOGY
An astounding structural comparison of hundreds of myths of the peoples of the Americas

Volume 1: The Raw and the Cooked
Translated by John & Doreen Weightman
0–226–47487–9 Chicago pb $14.95

Volume 2: From Honey to Ashes
Translated by John & Doreen Weightman
0–226–47489–5 Chicago pb $13.00

THE JEALOUS POTTER
Translated by Bénédicte Chorier
0–226–47480–1 Chicago $19.95

MYTH AND MEANING
An accessible and intriguing introduction to his thought, originally written in English
0–8052–0622–1 Schocken pb $5.95

THE SAVAGE MIND
A best-seller in the 1960s, important both for its analyses of myth, ritual, and social organization and for its controversial attack on Jean-Paul Sartre
0–226–47484–4 Chicago pb $10.95

STRUCTURAL ANTHROPOLOGY
Contains his best-known essay, "The Structural Study of Myth," a fundamental text of structural analysis, in which he discusses the myth of Oedipus
Translated by Monique Layton

Volume 1
0–465–09516–X Basic Books pb $13.95

Volume 2
0–226–47491–7 Chicago pb $14.00

TRISTES TROPIQUES
Lévi-Strauss' experiences in Brazil provide the point of departure for this meditative masterpiece, the most accessible of his writings
Translated by John & Doreen Weightman
0–689–70122–5 Atheneum pb $10.95

THE VIEW FROM AFAR
Translated by Joachim Neugroschel & Phoebe Hoss
0–465–09026–5 Basic Books pb $10.95

IF YOU CAN'T FIND IT, LOOK IN THE INDEX

SPECIALIZED STUDIES

Art

- Franz Boas
PRIMITIVE ART
Examines art of the native population of the Pacific Northwest and uncovers an artistic "language"
0–8446–1695–8 Peter Smith $15.50
0–486–20025–6 Dover pb $6.95

- John M. Chernoff
AFRICAN RHYTHM AND AFRICAN SENSIBILITY: Aesthetics and Social Action in African Musical Idioms
0–226–10345–5 Chicago pb $12.95

- Douglas Cole
CAPTURED HERITAGE: The Scramble for the Northwest Coast Artifacts
0–295–96215–1 Washington $20.00

- Nelson H. Graburn, editor
ETHNIC AND TOURIST ARTS: Cultural Expressions from the Fourth World
0–520–03842–8 California pb $12.95

- Bennetta Jules-Rosette
THE MESSAGES OF TOURIST ART: An African Semiotic System in Comparative Perspective
0–306–41598–4 Plenum $35.00

- Jacques Maquet
THE AESTHETIC EXPERIENCE: An Anthropologist Looks at the Visual Arts
0–300–04134–9 Yale pb $17.95

- Richard & Sally Price
AFRO-AMERICAN ARTS OF THE SURINAME RAIN FOREST
0–520–04412–6 California pb $15.95

- Gary Witherspoon
LANGUAGE AND ART IN THE NAVAJO UNIVERSE
Contains excellent ethnographic material
Foreword by Clifford Geertz
0–472–08965–X Michigan $24.95
0–472–08966–8 Michigan pb $15.95

Kinship

It used to be said that if an anthropologist did not publish work on kinship, his professional credentials would never be fully accepted. Although this is no longer assumed to be the case, the study of kinship is still viewed by many anthropologists as one of the few exclusive domains of their discipline.

- E.E. Evans-Pritchard
KINSHIP AND MARRIAGE AMONG THE NUER
0–19–823104–0 Oxford $35.00

- Robin Fox
KINSHIP AND MARRIAGE: An Anthropological Perspective
An introduction to the more technical literature of kinship
0–521–26073–6 Cambridge $34.50
0–521–27823–6 Cambridge pb $9.95

- Clifford & Hildred Geertz
KINSHIP IN BALI
0–226–28516–2 Chicago pb $3.95

- Francis Korn
ELEMENTARY STRUCTURES RECONSIDERED: Lévi-Strauss on Kinship
0–520–02476–1 California $30.00

- Claude Lévi-Strauss
ELEMENTARY STRUCTURES OF KINSHIP
0–8070–4669–8 Beacon pb $14.95

- Lewis Henry Morgan
ANCIENT SOCIETY
This work by the pioneering American ethnologist was first published in 1877
0–8165–0924–7 Arizona pb $14.95

- David M. Schneider
AMERICAN KINSHIP: A Cultural Account
Not only offers a powerful model of the culture of kinship in America but also imparts much wisdom regarding cultural analysis
0–226–73930–9 Chicago pb $7.95

Life Histories

Vincent Crapanzano
TUHAMI: Portrait of a Moroccan
A disturbing and puzzling story of the author's encounter with a far-from-typical Moroccan man
0–226–11870–3 Chicago $17.50
0–226–11871–1 Chicago pb $8.95

Oscar Lewis
THE CHILDREN OF SANCHEZ
In this classic on the culture of poverty, published in 1961, Lewis constructs a narrative from the direct testimony of a Mexican family
0–394–70280–8 Random House pb $10.95

FIVE FAMILIES: Mexican Case Studies in the Culture of Poverty
Foreword by Oliver LaFarge
0–465–09705–7 Basic Books pb $10.95

Henry Munson, Jr.
THE HOUSE OF SI ABD ALLAH: The Oral History of a Moroccan Family
0–300–03084–3 Yale $22.50

James D. Sexton
CAMPESINO: The Diary of a Guatemalan Indian
0–8165–0814–3 Arizona $29.95

Marjorie Shostak
NISA: The Life and Words of a !Kung Woman
0–674–62485–8 Harvard $27.00
0–394–71126–2 Random House pb $8.50

Leo W. Simmons, editor
SUN CHIEF: The Autobiography of a Hopi Indian
Foreword by Robert V. Hine
0–300–00227–0 Yale pb $11.95

Medicine

Medical anthropology explores the cross-cultural variations in the forms of medical knowledge and practice.

- George M. Foster & Barbara G. Anderson
MEDICAL ANTHROPOLOGY
A readable introductory textbook
0–394–34403–0 Random House $38.95

- John M. Janzen
THE QUEST FOR THERAPY IN LOWER ZAIRE
0–520–03295–0 California $42.50
0–520–04633–1 California pb $7.95

- Arthur Kleinman
PATIENTS AND HEALERS IN THE CONTEXT OF CULTURE: An Exploration of the Borderland Between Anthropology, Medicine, and Psychiatry
0–520–04511–4 California pb $12.95

Psychology

Psychological anthropology investigates the relationship of personality to culture through a cross-cultural understanding of socialization, identity and identity formation, personal cultures, cultural creativity, life histories, psychopathology, and psychoanalysis.

- Vincent Crapanzano
THE HAMADSHA: A Study in Moroccan Ethnopsychiatry
A striking interpretation of a "ritual" system for coping with stress and illness in Morocco which has religious overtones but which also carries on a Mediterranean tradition of ecstatic cults going back to Dionysus
0–520–04510–6 California pb $11.95

- George Devereux
BASIC PROBLEMS OF ETHNOPSYCHIATRY
Translated by Basia M. Gulati
0–226–14355–4 Chicago $31.00

- Sue E. Estroff
MAKING IT CRAZY: An Ethnography of Psychiatric Clients in an American Community
Foreword by H. Richard Lamb
0–520–03963–7 California $30.00
0–520–05451–2 California pb $11.95

- Arthur Kleinman
SOCIAL ORIGINS OF DISTRESS AND DISEASE: Depression, Neurasthenia, and Pain in Modern China
0–300–03541–1 Yale $30.00
0–300–04133–0 Yale pb $14.95

- Robert A. Paul
THE TIBETAN SYMBOLIC WORLD: Psychoanalytic Explorations
A psychoanalytic approach to ethnographic analysis
0–226–64987–3 Chicago pb $14.00

- Peggy R. Sanday
DIVINE HUNGER: Cannibalism As a Cultural System
0–521–31114–4 Cambridge pb $13.95

- Nancy Scheper-Hughes
SAINTS, SCHOLARS AND SCHIZOPHRENICS: Mental Illness in Rural Ireland
A study of Ireland that makes an important contribution to the understanding of mental illness
0–520–04786–9 California pb $11.95

- Melford Spiro
OEDIPUS IN THE TROBRIANDS
0–226–76988–7 Chicago $26.00
0–226–76989–5 Chicago pb $8.00

- Melford & Audrey G. Spiro
CHILDREN OF THE KIBBUTZ: A Study in Child Training and Personality
A reconsideration of Freudian concepts in a cross-cultural context
0–674–11606–2 Harvard pb $9.95

- Geoffrey M. White & John Kirkpatrick
PERSON, SELF AND EXPERIENCE: Exploring Pacific Ethnopsychologies
0–520–06038–5 California pb $11.95

Women and Sexuality

The literature on these topics has expanded dramatically over the last two decades. Topics of primary interest have included cultural variations in male and female roles and male-female dynamics, women's power, homosexuality in society, and the role of women in relation to social and cultural change.

▶ **See also Women's Studies**

- Lila Abu-Lughod
VEILED SENTIMENTS: Honor and Poetry in a Bedouin Society
0–520–05483–0 California $37.50

- Soraya Altorki
WOMEN IN SAUDI ARABIA
0–231–06182–X Columbia $34.50

- Pat Caplan, editor
THE CULTURAL CONSTRUCTION OF SEXUALITY
0–422–60880–7 RC&H pb $16.95

- Susan Dorsky
WOMEN OF AMRAN: A Middle Eastern Ethnographic Study
0–87480–250–4 Utah $22.50

- Thomas Gregor
ANXIOUS PLEASURES: The Sexual Lives of an Amazonian People
0–226–30742–5 Chicago $19.95
0–226–30743–3 Chicago pb $10.95

- Gilbert H. Herdt, editor
RITUALIZED HOMOSEXUALITY IN MELANESIA
0–520–05037–1 California $30.00

- Carol MacCormack & Marilyn Strathern, editors
NATURE, CULTURE AND GENDER
0–521–28001–X Cambridge pb $12.95

- Bronislaw Malinowski
THE SEXUAL LIFE OF SAVAGES
An early classic based on Malinowski's long observation of Trobriand Islands life
Preface by Havelock Ellis
0–8070–4607–8 Beacon $14.95

- Fatima Mernissi
BEYOND THE VEIL: Male-Female Dynamics in Modern Muslim Society
A feminist perspective
0–253–31162–4 Indiana $25.00
0–253–20423–2 Indiana pb $7.95

- Denise O'Brien & Sharon W. Tiffany, editors
RETHINKING WOMEN'S ROLES: Perspectives from the Pacific
0–520–05142–4 California $37.50

- Sherry Ortner & Harriet Whitehead, editors
SEXUAL MEANINGS: The Cultural Construction of Gender and Sexuality
Detailed, ethnographic studies
0–521–28375–2 Cambridge pb $17.95

- Michelle Z. Rosaldo & Louise Lamphere, editors
WOMAN, CULTURE, AND SOCIETY
A well-chosen collection
0–8047–0851–7 Stanford pb $9.95

- Walter L. Williams
THE SPIRIT AND THE FLESH: Sexual Diversity in American Indian Culture
"A valuable sourcebook, bringing together a wealth of information on the status of gender-variant men in a wide variety of Native American societies"—*San Francisco Chronicle*
0–8070–4611–6 Beacon pb $9.95

Power and Politics

- Louis Dumont
HOMO HIERARCHICUS: The Caste System and its Implications
An important study of Indian social structure
Translated by Basia Gulati
0–226–16963–4 Chicago pb $17.00

- Michel Foucault
Foucault's work on the nature of power has had an incalculable influence on anthropology in recent decades.
DISCIPLINE AND PUNISH: The Birth of the Prison
Translated by Alan Sheridan
0–394–72767–3 Random House pb $8.95
MADNESS AND CIVILIZATION: A History of Insanity in the Age of Reason
0–679–72110–X Random House pb $7.95
POWER-KNOWLEDGE: Selected Interviews & Other Writings, 1972-1977
0–394–73954–X Pantheon pb $8.95

- Clifford Geertz
NEGARA: Theatre-State in 19th-Century Bali
0–691–05316–2 Princeton $33.50
0–691–00778–0 Princeton pb $11.95

- Sidney W. Mintz
SWEETNESS AND POWER: The Place of Sugar in Modern History
0–14–009233–1 Penguin pb $7.95

Colonialism

Anthropology has been called a child of European colonialism, since so much ethnography was done under the umbrella of colonial administration. It would be an oversimplification, however, to regard all previous anthropology as a manifestation of "colonial discourse"; anthropologists have questioned both colonialism and its influence upon ethnographic practice.

- Talal Asad, editor
ANTHROPOLOGY AND THE COLONIAL ENCOUNTER
0–391–00391–7 Humanities pb $15.00

- T.O. Beidelman
COLONIAL EVANGELISM: A Socio-Historical Study of an East African Mission at the Grassroots
0–253–31386–4 Indiana $29.95
0–253–20278–7 Indiana pb $12.50

- Johannes Fabian
LANGUAGE AND COLONIAL POWER: The Appropriation of Swahili In the Former Belgian Congo, 1880-1938
0–521–30870–4 Cambridge $42.50

- Michael Taussig
SHAMANISM, COLONIALISM AND THE WILDMAN: A Study in Terror and Healing
0–226–79012–6 Chicago $29.95

Language

Anthropologists regard language in its broadest sense: not just as vocabulary and syntax, but as a cultural phenomenon.

- Ray L. Birdwhistell
KINESICS AND CONTEXT: Essays on Body Motion Communication
0–8122–1012–3 Pennsylvania $17.95

• Alan Dundes
THE STUDY OF FOLKLORE
0–13–858944–5 Prentice-Hall $20.95

• Joseph H. Greenberg
LANGUAGE, CULTURE, AND COMMUNICATION: Essays by Joseph H. Greenberg
Edited by Anwar S. Dil
0–8047–0781–2 Stanford $38.50

• Dell H. Hymes
ESSAYS IN THE HISTORY OF LINGUISTIC ANTHROPOLOGY
90–272–4507–X John Benjamins $54.00

• David J. Sapir & Christopher J. Crocker, editors
THE SOCIAL USE OF METAPHOR: Essays on the Anthropology of Rhetoric
0–8122–7725–2 Pennsylvania $21.95

Religion

Anthropologists are not concerned with the truth or falsity of religious systems, rituals, theologies, and symbolic representations. Their objective is to place religion in a social and cultural context that makes the behavior of believers intelligible.

• Jacob Bronowski
MAGIC, SCIENCE, AND CIVILIZATION
0–231–04484–4 Columbia $22.00
0–231–04485–2 Columbia pb $11.00

• Walter Burkert
HOMO NECANS: The Anthropology of Ancient Greek Sacrificial Ritual and Myth
Translated by Peter Bing
0–520–03650–6 California $35.00
0–520–05875–5 California pb $10.95

• E.E. Evans-Pritchard
THEORIES OF PRIMITIVE RELIGION
A lucid survey of the social anthropology of religious phenomena
0–19–823131–8 Oxford pb $12.95

E.E. Evans-Pritchard among the Azande

• James W. Fernandez
BWITI: An Ethnography of the Religious Imagination in Africa
An ethnographic study rich in texture and detail
0–691–10122–1 Princeton pb $29.50

• Clifford Geertz
ISLAM OBSERVED: Religious Development in Morocco and Indonesia
A brief yet comprehensive introduction to Islam as practiced from Morocco to Indonesia
0–226–28511–1 Chicago pb $6.00

• Marcel Griaule
CONVERSATIONS WITH OGOTEMMELI: An Introduction to Dogon Religious Ideas
An illuminating presentation of the complex cosmology underlying the Dogon culture of West Africa
Introduction by Germaine Dieterlen
0–19–519821–2 Oxford pb $9.95

• Michel Izard & Pierre Smith, editors
BETWEEN BELIEF AND TRANSGRESSION: Structuralist Essays in Religion, History and Myth
Translated by John Leavitt
0–226–38861–1 Chicago pb $20.00

• Joseph G. Jorgensen
THE SUN DANCE RELIGION: Power for the Powerless
A study of one of the most striking aspects of North American Plains Indian culture
0–226–41086–2 Chicago pb $14.95

• John Middleton
LUGBARA RELIGION: Ritual and Authority among an East African People
Foreword by Ivan Karp
0–87474–667–1 Smithsonian pb $14.95

• Gananath Obeyesekere
THE CULT OF THE GODDESS PATTINI
A vividly detailed study of religion in Sri Lanka
0–226–61602–9 Chicago $42.50

• Paul Stoller & Cheryl Olkes
IN SORCERY'S SHADOW: A Memoir of Apprenticeship Among the Songhay of Niger
0–226–77542–9 Chicago $19.95

• Stanley J. Tambiah
THE BUDDHIST SAINTS OF THE FOREST AND THE CULT OF AMULETS: A Study in Charisma, Hagiography, Sectarianism and Millennial Buddhism
0–521–27787–6 Cambridge pb $21.95

• Victor Turner
REVELATION AND DIVINATION IN NDEMBU RITUAL
Required reading for those interested in religious rituals, as well as rituals of everyday life which have no religious underpinnings
0–8014–9158–4 Cornell pb $10.95

RITUAL PROCESS: Structure and Anti-Structure
0–202–01043–0 Gruyter $29.95
0–801–9163–0 Cornell pb $8.95

• Victor & Edith Turner
IMAGE AND PILGRIMAGE IN CHRISTIAN CULTURE
0–231–04286–8 Columbia $28.00

Cargo Cults

Peter Lawrence
ROAD BELONG CARGO: A Study of the Cargo Movement in the Southern Madang District of New Guinea
Foreword by J.K. McCarthy
0–7190–0457–8 Humanities pb $12.50

Peter Worsley
THE TRUMPET SHALL SOUND: A Study of Cargo Cults in Melanesia
0–8052–0156–4 Schocken pb $8.95

Symbols and Semiotics

The current generation of "symbolic anthropologists" has taken much of its inspiration from the work of David Schneider and Clifford Geertz; many have also profited from reading Roland Barthes and Claude Lévi-Strauss. The move toward applying symbolic interpretation to the secular and to the political arenas of modern life as well as to small-scale societies has broadened the scope of anthropology.

• Arjun Appadurai
THE SOCIAL LIFE OF THINGS: Commodities in Cultural Perspective
0–521–35726–8 Cambridge pb $14.95

• Marc Auge
THE ANTHROPOLOGICAL CIRCLE: Symbol, Function, History
Translated by Martin Thom
0–521–23236–8 Cambridge $29.95
0–521–28548–8 Cambridge pb $12.95

• Mary Douglas
NATURAL SYMBOLS: Explorations in Cosmology
Two studies by a leading exponent of symbolic anthropology
0–394–71105–X Pantheon pb $7.95

PURITY AND DANGER: An Analysis of the Concepts of Pollution and Taboo
0–7448–0011–0 RC&H pb $8.95

• James W. Fernandez
PERSUASIONS AND PERFORMANCES: The Play of Tropes in Culture
Essays in symbolic anthropology with a traditional functional orientation
0–253–20374–0 Indiana pb $14.50

• Sally Falk Moore & Barbara G. Myerhoff, editors
SYMBOL AND POLITICS IN COMMUNAL IDEOLOGY: Cases and Questions
0–8014–9157–6 Cornell pb $8.95

• James L. Peacock
RITES OF MODERNIZATION: Symbolic and Social Aspects of Indonesian Proletarian Drama
Foreword by Dell Hymes
0–226–65131–2 Chicago pb $15.95

• Dan Sperber
RETHINKING SYMBOLISM
Critical reflections
Translated by A.L. Morton
0–521–09967–6 Cambridge pb $12.95

• Victor Turner
DRAMAS, FIELDS AND METAPHORS: Symbolic Action in Human Society
A collection of essays
0–8014–9151–7 Cornell pb $10.95

• Roy Wagner
THE INVENTION OF CULTURE
0–226–86934–2 Chicago pb $5.95

LETHAL SPEECH: Daribi Myth As Symbolic Obviation
Myth in New Guinea
0–8014–1193–9 Cornell $27.50

CRITICAL ANTHROPOLOGY

• Stanley Diamond
IN SEARCH OF THE PRIMITIVE: A Critique of Civilization
Discusses the constraints imposed on anthropology by the western domination of other cultures
Foreword by Eric R. Wolf
0–87855–582–X Transaction pb $19.95

• Marvin Harris
CULTURAL MATERIALISM: The Struggle for a Science of Culture
0–394–74426–8 Random House pb $8.95

• George E. Marcus & Michael M. Fischer
ANTHROPOLOGY AS CULTURAL CRITIQUE: An Experimental Moment in the Human Sciences
Provides an overview of the social and cultural grounds of anthropology and offers speculation about its future
0–226–50449–2 Chicago pb $9.95

Rethinking Anthropology

The books grouped here are recent works that have been instrumental in furthering a reassessment from within of the history and practice of anthropology.

• James A. Boon
OTHER TRIBES, OTHER SCRIBES: Symbolic Anthropology in the Comparative Study of Cultures, Histories, Religions, and Texts
0–521–27197–5 Cambridge pb $10.95

• Phyllis P. Chock & June R. Wyman
DISCOURSE AND THE SOCIAL LIFE OF MEANING
0–87474–308–7 Smithsonian $25.00

Romare Bearden's "Prevalence of Ritual" (Hirshhorn Museum), *from* Writers on Artists *edited by Daniel Halpern* (North Point)

• James Clifford & George E. Marcus, editors
WRITING CULTURE: The Poetics and Politics of Ethnography
0–520–05729–5 California pb $11.95

• Johannes Fabian
TIME AND THE OTHER
0–231–05591–9 Columbia pb $17.00

• Jay Ruby, editor
A CRACK IN THE MIRROR: Reflexive Perspectives in Anthropology
Anthropologists question their profession
0–8122–7815–1 Pennsylvania $26.95

• Marshall Sahlins
CULTURE AND PRACTICAL REASON
0–226–73361–0 Chicago pb $8.95

New Ethnographies

• Kevin Dwyer
MOROCCAN DIALOGUES: Anthropology in Question
0–8018–2759–0 Johns Hopkins $34.50

• Stephen William Foster
THE PAST IS ANOTHER COUNTRY: Representation, Historical Consciousness and Resistance in the Blue Ridge
0–520–06251–5 California $25.00

• June Nash
WE EAT THE MINES AND THE MINES EAT US: Dependency and Exploitation in Bolivian Tin Mines
0–231–04710–X Columbia $34.00
0–231–04711–8 Columbia pb $17.50

• Michael Z. Rosaldo
KNOWLEDGE AND PASSION
0–521–29562–9 Cambridge pb $13.95

• Renato Rosaldo
ILONGOT HEADHUNTING, 1883-1974: A Study in Society and History
0–8047–1046–5 Stanford $25.00
0–8047–1284–0 Stanford pb $8.95

Psychology

HISTORIES AND INTRODUCTIONS

William James
THE PRINCIPLES OF PSYCHOLOGY
A classic which remains unsurpassed for its range of allusion to philosophy, the arts, and actual experience; although published in 1890, it is still a valuable introduction to such topics as the stream of consciousness, self-consciousness, perception, memory, emotion, instinct, and will

Volume 1
0–486–20381–6 Dover pb $9.95
Volume 2
0–486–20382–4 Dover pb $9.95

• Edwin G. Boring
A HISTORY OF EXPERIMENTAL PSYCHOLOGY
A comprehensive history from 1690 to 1940
0–13–390039–8 Prentice-Hall $54.00

William James

• **Henri F. Ellenberger**
THE DISCOVERY OF THE UNCONSCIOUS: The History and Evolution of Dynamic Psychiatry
An excellent history of the exploration of the unconscious mind, from exorcists and hypnotists to Freud, Jung, and Adler
0–465–01673–1 Basic Books pb $24.95

• **Robert I. Watson, editor**
BASIC WRITINGS IN THE HISTORY OF PSYCHOLOGY
Excerpts from Bacon, Hume, Kant, Helmholtz, Darwin, James, Freud, Jung, Skinner, and many others. Illustrated
0–19–502444–3 Oxford pb $17.95

FREUD

Freud's theories can no longer be considered the rigorous scientific explanations he hoped he had achieved. Yet there is no doubt about their revolutionary impact, not only on psychology, but on almost every field of modern culture—anthropology, social and political theory, art, literature, criticism, philosophy, religion. His works have been called the "third blow" to Western anthropocentrism, after Copernicus and Darwin.

• **Sigmund Freud**
THE STANDARD EDITION OF THE COMPLETE PSYCHOLOGICAL WORKS OF SIGMUND FREUD
A 24-volume set. Freud's fundamental ideas about the importance of unconscious motivation and of infantile experience and development retain their force and continue to inspire new hypotheses and research. His books and papers, the work of a highly cultivated mind which ranged freely through literature, art, and history, have the further advantage of being brilliantly and gracefully written
Edited by James Strachey
0–393–01128–3 Norton (set) $795.00

BEYOND THE PLEASURE PRINCIPLE
An essay on the notion of a death instinct
0–393–00769–3 Norton pb $3.95

CHARACTER AND CULTURE
A collection of papers on the influence of neurotic symptoms in shaping art, religion, and philosophy
0–02–076200–3 Macmillan pb $5.95

CIVILIZATION AND ITS DISCONTENTS
A pessimistic assessment of the instinctual cost of civilization
0–393–30158–3 Norton pb $4.95

DORA: An Analysis of a Case of Hysteria
0–02–076250–X Macmillan pb $5.95

EARLY PSYCHOANALYTIC WRITINGS
Freud's first studies of obsessions, phobias, anxieties, hysterias, and other symptoms of neuroses
0–02–076300–X Macmillan pb $4.95

THE EGO AND THE ID
0–393–00142–3 Norton pb $3.95

THE FUTURE OF AN ILLUSION
Psychoanalysis as the most decisive argument against the consolations of religion
0–393–00831–2 Norton pb $3.95

GENERAL PSYCHOLOGICAL THEORY
0–02–076350–6 Macmillan pb $5.95

INHIBITIONS, SYMPTOMS AND ANXIETY
0–393–01166–6 Norton $6.95
0–393–00874–6 Norton pb $4.95

THE INTERPRETATION OF DREAMS
First published in 1900, this pioneering work introduced Freud's concept of the "Oedipus complex" and laid the foundation for many of his subsequent discoveries
0–380–01000–3 Avon pb $4.95

INTRODUCTORY LECTURES ON PSYCHOANALYSIS: A General Introduction to Psychoanalysis
Includes one section on "Parapraxes," a second on "Dreams" and a third on the "General Theory of the Neuroses"
0–87140–118–5 Liveright pb $6.95

JOKES AND THEIR RELATION TO THE UNCONSCIOUS
Written in response to Fliess's comment that *The Interpretation of Dreams* was too full of jokes
0–393–00145–8 Norton pb $4.95

LEONARDO DA VINCI & A MEMORY OF HIS CHILDHOOD
0–393–00149–0 Norton pb $4.95

MOSES AND MONOTHEISM
A provocative speculation on religion which argues, among other things, that Moses was an Egyptian
0–394–70014–7 Random House pb $4.95

NEW INTRODUCTORY LECTURES ON PSYCHOANALYSIS
A supplement to the original, published in 1933
0–393–00743–X Norton pb $4.95

ON DREAMS
0–393–00144–X Norton pb $3.95

AN OUTLINE OF PSYCHOANALYSIS
0–393–00151–2 Norton pb $2.95

THE PSYCHOPATHOLOGY OF EVERYDAY LIFE
Includes "Forgetting," "Slips of the Tongue," "Bungled Actions," and "Superstitions and Errors"
0–393–00611–5 Norton pb $6.95

THE QUESTION OF LAY ANALYSIS
0–393–00503–8 Norton pb $3.95

SEXUAL ENLIGHTENMENT IN CHILDREN
The sexual awareness and preoccupation of children, and how the frustration of such feelings results in adult neuroses
0–02–076500–2 Macmillan pb $5.95

STUDIES IN PARAPSYCHOLOGY
0–02–076550–9 Macmillan pb $4.95

THERAPY AND TECHNIQUE
The closest thing to a systematic treatise of his therapeutic techniques, including hypnosis, dream interpretation and free association
0–02–076600–9 Macmillan pb $5.95

THREE CASE HISTORIES
Includes the "Wolf Man," the "Rat Man" and the case of the psychotic Dr. Schreber who believed he was not only a woman but the wife of God
0–02–076650–5 Macmillan pb $5.95

THREE ESSAYS ON THE THEORY OF SEXUALITY
0–465–08606–3 Basic Books pb $8.95

TOTEM AND TABOO
Four essays first published as "Some Points of Agreement between the Mental Lives of Savages and Neurotics," one of his original efforts to extend analysis of the individual psyche to culture and society
0–394–70124–0 Random House pb $3.95

• **Sigmund Freud & Josef Breuer**
STUDIES IN HYSTERIA
0–465–08274–2 Basic Books $17.00

Sigmund Freud and his daughter Anna vacationing in the Dolomites in 1913, from Freud: A Life for Our Time *by Peter Gay (Doubleday)*

★ **FOR COMPLETE ORDERING INFORMATION, SEE PAGE 1**

- **William McGuire, editor**
THE FREUD/JUNG LETTERS
"Both as it bears upon the personal lives of the men between whom the letters passed and upon the intellectual history of our epoch, it is a document of inestimable importance"—Lionel Trilling
Translated by Ralph Manheim & R.F.C. Hull
0–674–32330–0 Harvard pb $15.95

- **Jeffrey Moussaieff Masson, editor**
THE COMPLETE LETTERS OF SIGMUND FREUD TO WILHELM FLIESS, 1887-1904
0–674–15421–5 Harvard pb $9.95

About Freud

- **J.A.C. Brown**
FREUD AND THE POST-FREUDIANS
The relation of Freud to Adler, Jung, Rank, and Stekel, and later developments in orthodox Freudian theory, especially in the US and Britain
0–14–020522–5 Penguin pb $7.95

- **Seymour Fisher & Roger P. Greenberg**
THE SCIENTIFIC CREDIBILITY OF FREUD'S THEORIES AND THERAPY
A survey of attempts to verify Freud's theories in empirical research
0–231–06215–X Columbia pb $16.00

- **Lucy Freeman & Herbert S. Strean**
FREUD AND WOMEN
How Freud's conflicted attitude toward women—a combination of idealization and fear—limited his contribution to the understanding of women's emotions and sexuality
0–8264–0385–9 Continuum pb $10.95

- **Peter Gay**
FREUD: A Life for Our Time
A new biography by an eminent historian of modern European culture
0–393–02517–9 Norton $24.50
0–385–26256–6 Doubleday pb $14.95

- **Adolf Grunbaum**
THE FOUNDATIONS OF PSYCHOANALYSIS: A Philosophical Critique
A thoroughgoing attack on Freud's scientific pretensions
0–520–05017–7 California pb $11.95

- **Ernest Jones**
THE LIFE AND WORK OF SIGMUND FREUD
An epic, largely admiring biography by a friend and associate
0–465–04015–2 Basic Books (set) $80.00

Volume 1: The Formative Years and the Great Discoveries, 1856-1900
0–465–04016–0 Basic Books $27.50

Volume 2: Years of Maturity, 1901-1919
0–465–04017–9 Basic Books $27.50

Volume 3: The Last Phase, 1919-1939
0–465–04018–7 Basic Books $27.50

- **Steven Marcus**
FREUD AND THE CULTURE OF PSYCHOANALYSIS
Essays on Freud's cases and their cultural context
0–393–30410–8 Norton pb $7.95

- **Jeffrey Moussaieff Masson**
THE ASSAULT ON TRUTH: Freud's Suppression of the Seduction Theory
This controversial work charges that Freud suppressed his original hypothesis about the seduction of children in favor of a less radical theory attributing seduction memories to fantasy
0–140–07658–1 Penguin pb $7.95

Philip Rieff
FREUD: The Mind of the Moralist
0–226–71639–2 Chicago pb $13.95

LATER FREUDIANISM

- **Morris N. Eagle**
RECENT DEVELOPMENTS IN PSYCHOANALYSIS
"The best survey of the current status of psychoanalytical theory that I have seen—clearly reasoned, incisive, balanced and fair in its judgments"—Robert R. Holt, New York University
0–674–75080–2 Harvard pb $9.95

- **Otto Fenichel**
THE PSYCHOANALYTIC THEORY OF NEUROSIS
0–393–01019–8 Norton $29.95

- **Anna Freud**
THE EGO AND THE MECHANISMS OF DEFENSE
A survey of the neurotic symptoms—such as obsessive-compulsive traits—that are used by the ego to ward off threatening thoughts and impulses
0–8236–6871–1 Intl Universities $27.50
0–8236–8035–5 Intl Universities pb $19.95

- **Otto F. Kernberg**
BORDERLINE CONDITIONS AND PATHOLOGICAL NARCISSISM
Kernberg's work assimilates into Freudianism the study of conditions formerly thought to be beyond psychoanalytic treatment
0–87668–762–1 Jason Aronson $35.00

INTERNAL WORLD AND EXTERNAL REALITY
0–87668–758–3 Jason Aronson $35.00

SEVERE PERSONALITY DISORDERS: Psychotherapeutic Strategies
0–300–03273–0 Yale $40.00

- **Heinz Kohut**
HOW DOES ANALYSIS CURE?: Contributions to the Psychology of the Self
Edited by Arnold Goldberg & Paul Stepansky
0–226–45034–1 Chicago $27.50

THE RESTORATION OF THE SELF
The most original and influential of recent theorists in the psychoanalytic tradition, Kohut stressed the child's need for "empathetically resonant self-objects," that

is, parents who reinforce the child's secure sense of self
0–8236–5810–4 Intl Universities $40.00

Jacques Lacan

Jacques Lacan
ECRITS: A Selection
Lacan's controversial and sometimes impenetrable reinterpretations of Freud have had a major impact on French thought and American literary theory
0–393–30047–1 Norton pb $10.95

THE FOUR FUNDAMENTAL CONCEPTS OF PSYCHOANALYSIS
The structure of psychoanalysis and language, and their relation to religion
0–393–00079–6 Norton pb $9.95

Anika Lemaire
JACQUES LACAN
A clear introduction to Lacan's thought
0–7100–8264–9 RC&H pb $13.95

Stuart Schneiderman
JACQUES LACAN
A history of Lacan's work and of Freudianism in France by Lacan's leading American disciple
0–674–47116–4 Harvard pb $7.95

Stuart Schneiderman, editor
RETURNING TO FREUD
An interview with a patient conducted by Lacan, and 15 case studies by his followers
0–300–03932–8 Yale pb $10.95

JANET MALCOLM:
Favorite Reading

Henry James
THE GOLDEN BOWL

Anton Chekhov
THE TALES OF CHEKHOV

George Eliot
MIDDLEMARCH

Marcel Proust
REMEMBRANCE OF THINGS PAST

Charles Dickens
OUR MUTUAL FRIEND

Ivan Turgenev
THE TORRENTS OF SPRING

Vladimir Nabokov
PALE FIRE

Truman Capote
IN COLD BLOOD

Leo Tolstoy
ANNA KARENINA

Fyodor Dostoevsky
CRIME AND PUNISHMENT

➤ **FOR OVERSEAS ORDERING INFORMATION, SEE PAGE 1**

- Joyce McDougall
THEATERS OF THE MIND: Illusion and Truth on the Psychoanalytic Stage
0–465–08418–4 Basic Books $24.95

- Janet Malcolm
PSYCHOANALYSIS: The Impossible Profession
A candid and controversial portrait of a practicing psychoanalyst in Manhattan
0–394–71034–7 Random House pb $6.95

- David Shapiro
AUTONOMY AND RIGID CHARACTER
A study of rigidity of character and loss of autonomy as revealed in sado-masochistic, obsessive-compulsive, and paranoid conditions
0–465–00408–3 Basic Books pb $7.95

NEUROTIC STYLES
An acclaimed work of character analysis focusing on paranoid, hysterical, impulsive, and obsessive-compulsive neurotic styles
0–465–09502–X Basic Books pb $9.95

JUNG

Jung's ideas have had a more gradual impact than those of Freud. His psychological theories, with their somewhat esoteric overtones of idealist philosophy and mystical religion, their flirtation with gnosticism, alchemy, Tantric Buddhism, and the occult, for a long time influenced mainly those who had come into contact with Jung himself or who had mastered his finely written but unsystematic works. More recently, however, the work of Joseph Campbell, Mircea Eliade, and others inspired by his synoptic view of mythology has awakened a much broader interest in his theories. His reputation has been enhanced by a general revival, during the last 20 years, of concern with spiritual values, Eastern and unorthodox forms of religious expression, and mythology.

- C.G. Jung
THE COLLECTED WORKS OF C.G. JUNG
Today such Jungian notions as *archetype* and *collective unconscious* are nearly as familiar as *introvert*, *extrovert*, and other aspects of Jung's influential theory of character types. Jung's own writings, less rigorous but more suggestive than Freud's, present the reader with a remarkable range of ideas and a fund of religious and historical allusions
Edited & translated by Gerhard Adler & R.F.C. Hull

Volume 1: Psychiatric Studies
0–691–09768–2 Princeton $45.00
0–691–01855–3 Princeton pb $9.50

Volume 2: Experimental Researches
Includes nine studies on word association with two lectures on the association method
0–691–09764–X Princeton $49.50
0–691–01840–5 Princeton pb $13.50

Volume 3: Psychogenesis of Mental Disease
0–691–09769–0 Princeton $39.50
0–691–01859–6 Princeton pb $10.50

Volume 4: Freud and Psychoanalysis
0–691–09765–8 Princeton $39.00
0–691–01864–2 Princeton pb $10.50

Volume 5: Symbols of Transformation
Jung's groundbreaking early work on symbolism and myth
0–691–09775–5 Princeton $52.50
0–691–01815–4 Princeton pb $13.95

Volume 6: Psychological Types
Jung's single most influential work, introducing opposed pairs of character types (introvert/extrovert, intuitive/sensing, thinking/feeling, and judging/perceiving) and relating them to masculine and feminine psychology
0–691–09770–4 Princeton $62.50
0–691–01813–8 Princeton pb $13.95

Volume 7: Two Essays on Analytical Psychology
Includes "The Relationship Between the Ego and the Unconscious" and "On the Psychology of the Unconscious"
0–691–09776–3 Princeton $45.00
0–691–01782–4 Princeton pb $9.50

Volume 8: Structure and the Dynamics of the Psyche
0–691–09774–7 Princeton $52.50

Volume 9 (Part 1): Archetypes and the Collective Unconscious
"His idea of archetypes involves profound attitudes towards man's existence and intimates values through which many people have found a new significance"—*Virginia Quarterly*
0–691–09761–5 Princeton $47.50
0–691–01833–2 Princeton pb $15.95

Volume 9 (Part 2): Aon: Researches into the Phenomenology of the Self
0–691–09759–3 Princeton $35.00
0–691–01826–X Princeton pb $10.50

Volume 10: Civilization in Transition
0–691–09762–3 Princeton $55.00

Volume 11: Psychology and Religion: West and East
Includes "A Psychological Approach to the Dogma of the Trinity" and "Transformation Symbolism in the Mass," among many others
0–691–09772–0 Princeton $52.50

Volume 12: Psychology and Alchemy
Jung's major application of alchemical symbolism to depth psychology; profusely illustrated
0–691–09771–2 Princeton $55.00
0–691–01831–6 Princeton pb $12.95

Volume 13: Alchemical Studies
0–691–09760–7 Princeton $39.50
0–691–01849–9 Princeton pb $16.95

Volume 14: Mysterium Coniunctionis
A detailed study of the alchemical symbol of the "sacred wedding"
0–691–09766–6 Princeton $55.00
0–691–01816–2 Princeton pb $14.95

Volume 15: The Spirit in Man, Art, and Literature
Essays on Paracelsus, Freud, Picasso, and James Joyce's *Ulysses* examining the qualities of personality that enable the creative spirit to introduce radical innovations
0–691–09773–9 Princeton $25.00
0–691–01775–1 Princeton pb $8.95

C.G. Jung

Volume 16: Practice of Psychotherapy
Essays on the "Psychology of the Transference" and other subjects
0–691–09767–4 Princeton $39.50
0–691–01870–7 Princeton pb $12.95

Volume 17: Development of Personality
Papers on child psychology, education, and related subjects
0–691–09763–1 Princeton $29.50
0–691–01838–3 Princeton pb $7.95

Volume 18: The Symbolic Life: Miscellaneous Writings
0–691–09892–1 Princeton $65.00

Volume 19: General Bibliography
0–691–09893–X Princeton $42.50

Volume 20: General Index
0–691–09867–0 Princeton $60.00

ANALYTICAL PSYCHOLOGY: Its Theory and Practice
Five lectures on psychological types, the personal and collective unconscious, archetypes, and dream analysis. "This, surely, is the most lucid, simple and orderly introduction to the basic principles and methods of the Jungian science of the psyche that has yet been offered to the public"—Joseph Campbell
0–394–70862–8 Random House pb $4.95

ANSWER TO JOB
A consideration of evil which reflects on its interdependence with good
0–691–01785–9 Princeton pb $6.50

ASPECTS OF THE FEMININE
On marriage, Eros, the mother, the maiden, and the anima/animus concept
0–691–01845–6 Princeton pb $7.95

C.G. JUNG SPEAKING: Interviews and Encounters
0–691–01871–5 Princeton pb $14.95

DREAMS
0–691–01792–1 Princeton pb $9.95

FOUR ARCHETYPES: Mother/Rebirth/ Spirit/Trickster
0–691–01766–2 Princeton pb $7.50

MANDALA SYMBOLISM
0–691–01781–6 Princeton pb $8.95

MEMORIES, DREAMS AND REFLECTIONS
An autobiography with emphasis on his religious ideas, recorded and edited by Aniela Jaffé
0–394–70268–9 Random House pb $8.95

MODERN MAN IN SEARCH OF A SOUL
A basic introduction to Jung's thought on dream analysis, the primitive unconscious and the relation between psychology and religion. Also includes "Freud and Jung: Contrasts"
0–15–661206–2 HBJ pb $4.95

ON THE NATURE OF THE PSYCHE
0–691–01751–4 Princeton pb $9.95

PSYCHE AND SYMBOL
Selections from Jung's writings on the archetypal origins and integrating function of symbols
Edited by Violet S. de Laszlo
0–385–09349–7 Doubleday pb $7.95

PSYCHOANALYTIC YEARS
0–691–01799–9 Princeton pb $7.95

PSYCHOLOGICAL REFLECTIONS: A New Anthology of His Writings
Aphoristic selections from Jung's works
0–691–01786–7 Princeton pb $9.95

PSYCHOLOGY AND THE EAST
0–691–01806–5 Princeton pb $9.95

PSYCHOLOGY AND THE OCCULT
0–691–01791–3 Princeton pb $9.95

PSYCHOLOGY AND RELIGION
Drawing on ancient and medieval gnostic, alchemistic and occultistic literature, Jung discusses the religious symbolism and continuity of the unconscious processes
0–300–00137–1 Yale pb $6.95

PSYCHOLOGY AND WESTERN RELIGION
0–691–01862–6 Princeton pb $9.95

THE PSYCHOLOGY OF TRANSFERENCE
0–691–01752–2 Princeton pb $8.95

SYNCHRONICITY
The psychological significance of meaningful coincidences
0–691–01794–8 Princeton pb $7.95

THE UNDISCOVERED SELF
How the bureaucratic character of modern society stands in the way of full self-realization
0–451–62650–8 Mentor pb $3.95

● C.G. Jung & Karl Kerenyi
ESSAYS ON A SCIENCE OF MYTHOLOGY
0–691–01756–5 Princeton pb $7.50

● Anthony Storr, editor
THE ESSENTIAL JUNG
0–691–02455–3 Princeton pb $9.95

Introductions to Jung

● Edward F. Edinger
EGO AND ARCHETYPE
A lucid synthesis of Jung's major ideas, taking in art, mythology, and religion, and emphasizing the human need for super-personal meaning that expresses itself in the convergence of ego and archetype
0–14–02172–8–2 Penguin pb $8.95

● Frieda Fordman
AN INTRODUCTION TO JUNG'S PSYCHOLOGY
A brief, clear introduction with a foreword by Jung
0–14–020273–0 Penguin pb $5.95

● Robert Hopcke
A GUIDED TOUR OF THE COLLECTED WORKS OF C.G. JUNG
0–87773–470–4 Shambhala $18.50

● June Singer
BOUNDARIES OF THE SOUL: The Practice of Jung's Psychology
"Certainly the very best introduction to Jung around . . . a beautifully conceived and constructed book with a personal quality that is warm and lovely and rich"—Joseph Campbell
0–385–06900–6 Doubleday pb $7.95

● Murray Stein, editor
JUNGIAN ANALYSIS
Introduction by June Singer
0–394–72333–3 Shambhala pb $17.95

Jungian Studies

● Marie-Louise von Franz
INDIVIDUATION IN FAIRY TALES
0–88214–112–0 Spring pb $13.50

AN INTRODUCTION TO THE INTERPRETATION OF FAIRY TALES
0–88214–101–5 Spring pb $12.50

ON DREAMS AND DEATH: A Jungian Interpretation
0–394–55249–0 Random House $17.50

PUER AETERNUS
A brilliant study of the psychology of the "eternal boy" and his fear of making commitments in love and work
0–938434–03–9 Sigo $32.00
0–938434–01–2 Sigo pb $16.95

● Marie-Louise von Franz & Emma Jung
THE GRAIL LEGEND
0–938434–07–1 Sigo $45.00
0–938434–08–X Sigo pb $16.95

● M. Esther Harding
THE "I" AND THE "NOT-I": A Study in the Development of Consciousness
0–691–01796–4 Princeton pb $9.95

PSYCHIC ENERGY: Its Source and Transformation
0–691–01790–5 Princeton pb $9.95

THE WAY OF ALL WOMEN
0–06–090399–6 Harper & Row pb $7.95

● James Hillman
ANIMA: The Anatomy of a Personified Notion
0–88214–316–6 Spring pb $15.00

THE DREAM AND THE UNDERWORLD
0–06–090682–0 Harper & Row pb $7.95

HEALING FICTION
0–930794–55–9 Station Hill $16.00
0–930794–56–7 Station Hill pb $9.95

INSEARCH: Psychology and Religion
0–88214–501–0 Spring pb $12.00

REVISIONING PSYCHOLOGY
An allusive philosophical and historical meditation on psychology and myth
0–06–090563–8 Harper & Row pb $8.95

● Erich Neumann
ART AND THE CREATIVE UNCONSCIOUS
The best application of Jungian ideas to aesthetics
0–691–01773–5 Princeton pb $9.95

AMOR AND THE PSYCHE: The Psychic Development of the Feminine
0–691–01772–7 Princeton pb $7.95

CREATIVE MAN
Essays on Freud, Jung, Trakl, Kafka, Chagall
0–691–01848–0 Princeton pb $8.50

THE GREAT MOTHER: An Analysis of an Archetype
0–691–01780–8 Princeton pb $14.95

THE ORIGINS AND HISTORY OF CONSCIOUSNESS
A study arguing that the individual and the human race as a whole pass through the same stages of archetypal development
0–691–01761–1 Princeton pb $9.95

● Carol Pearson
THE HERO WITHIN: Six Archetypes We Live By
0–86683–527–X Harper & Row pb $8.95

● Anthony Stevens
ARCHETYPES: A Natural History of the Self
A challenging attempt to find confirmation of Jung's theory of archetypes in ethology and sociobiology
0–688–01976–5 Morrow pb $10.50

● Ann & Barry Ulanov
THE WITCH AND THE CLOWN: Two Archetypes of Human Sexuality
A richly detailed cultural and psychological study of the witch as a figure of female power and the clown as a masculine figure lacking power
0–933029–07–1 Chiron pb $14.95

POST-FREUDIAN THEORISTS

Alfred Adler

● Alfred Adler
THE INDIVIDUAL PSYCHOLOGY OF ALFRED ADLER: A Systematic Presentation in Selections from His Writings
An excellent, well-organized introduction. Adler's concept of the inferiority and superiority complexes, and his

understanding of human motivation in terms of self-image and goals instead of drives, produced a more humanistic and social emphasis
Edited by Heinz & Rouena Ansbacher
0–06–131154–5 Harper & Row pb $11.95

Erik H. Erikson

• Erik H. Erikson
ADULTHOOD: Essays
0–393–09086–8 Norton pb $11.95

CHILDHOOD AND SOCIETY
Erikson's first book is a classic work in developmental psychology, comparable only to the work of Piaget
0–393–02295–1 Norton $22.00
0–393–30288–1 Norton pb $7.95

GANDHI'S TRUTH: On The Origins of Militant Nonviolence
0–393–00170–9 Norton pb $5.95

IDENTITY AND THE LIFE CYCLE
Erikson's theory of eight stages in the human life cycle had a revolutionary impact on developmental psychology; his conception of an "identity crisis" in adolescence is perhaps the best-known aspect of this approach
0–393–00949–1 Norton pb $4.95

IDENTITY: Youth and Crisis
0–393–09786–2 Norton pb $5.95

INSIGHT AND RESPONSIBILITY
0–393–99451–1 Norton pb $8.95

A WAY OF LOOKING AT THINGS: Selected Papers of Erik H. Erikson, 1930-1980
Edited by Stephen P. Schlein
0–393–02267–6 Norton $29.95

YOUNG MAN LUTHER
0–393–00741–3 Norton pb $5.95

• Robert Coles
ERIK ERIKSON: The Growth of His Work
0–306–80291–0 Da Capo pb $12.95

Erich Fromm

• Erich Fromm
THE ART OF LOVING
A famous work in which Fromm argues that the root of neurosis is an inability to love either oneself or others
0–06–080291–X Harper & Row pb $7.95

BEYOND THE CHAINS OF ILLUSION
0–317–16272–1 Simon & Schuster pb $7.95

ESCAPE FROM FREEDOM
0–380–01167–0 Avon pb $4.95

THE SANE SOCIETY
The alienation of modern man in a society dominated by purely economic imperatives
0–449–30028–5 Fawcett pb $3.95

TO HAVE OR TO BE?
A psychological and ethical argument against materialism
0–553–27485–6 Bantam pb $4.95

Karen Horney

• Karen Horney
NEUROSIS AND HUMAN GROWTH
A brilliant study of aggressive, compliant, and withdrawing forms of neurotic alienation
0–393–00135–0 Norton pb $4.95

THE NEUROTIC PERSONALITY OF OUR TIME
Under Adler's influence, Horney abandoned her earlier Freudianism and developed her theory of neurotic pride which protects the fantasy-bound ideal self from reality
0–393–00742–1 Norton pb $4.95

SELF-ANALYSIS
0–393–00134–2 Norton pb $5.95

• Susan Quinn
A MIND OF HER OWN: The Life of Karen Horney
A thorough and sympathetic biography of one of the first female psychoanalysts
0–201–15573–7 Addison-Wesley pb $14.95

Melanie Klein

• Melanie Klein
THE WRITINGS OF MELANIE KLEIN
Klein is celebrated for her contributions to child psychology and her development of object-relations theory
0–02–918460–4 Free Press (4-volume set) $98.00

Volume 1: Love, Guilt and Reparation & Other Works
0–02–918420–7 Free Press $30.00

Volume 2: The Psychoanalysis of Children
0–02–918430–4 Free Press $25.00

Volume 3: Envy and Gratitude & Other Works, 1946-1963
0–02–918440–1 Free Press $26.00

Volume 4: Narrative of Child Analysis
0–02–918450–9 Free Press $37.50

• Phyllis Grosskurth
MELANIE KLEIN: Her World and Her Work
0–674–56470–7 Harvard pb $12.50

• Juliet Mitchell, editor
THE SELECTED MELANIE KLEIN: The Essential Writings
0–02–921482–3 Free Press $19.95
0–02–921481–5 Free Press pb $8.95

Karl Menninger

• Karl Menninger
LOVE AGAINST HATE
0–15–653892–X HBJ pb $7.95

MAN AGAINST HIMSELF
A classic work on self-destruction, understood as a turning inward of instinctual aggression
0–15–656514–5 HBJ pb $7.95

Otto Rank

• Otto Rank
BEYOND PSYCHOLOGY
A broad view of culture, examining masculinity and femininity, love, sex, marriage, kinship, and religion, from the perspective of Rank's psychological theories
0–486–20485–5 Dover pb $5.95

TRUTH AND REALITY
0–393–00899–1 Norton pb $6.95

WILL THERAPY
A full statement of Rank's theories, which emphasize creativity and the constructive use of the patient's will in therapy
0–393–00898–3 Norton pb $8.95

Wilhelm Reich

• Wilhelm Reich
CHARACTER ANALYSIS
The most radical and controversial post-Freudian thinker, Reich believed that neurosis could not be cured until complete sexual gratification was attained
0–374–50269–2 Farrar, Straus & Giroux $16.95

CHILDREN OF THE FUTURE
A collection of his writings on children which includes "The Sexual Rights of Youth"
0–374–51846–7 Farrar, Straus & Giroux pb $8.95

THE FUNCTION OF THE ORGASM: Self-Economic Problems of Biologic Energy
"I maintain that every person who has succeeded in preserving a certain amount of naturalness knows this: those who are psychically ill need but one thing—complete and repeated genital gratification"—Wilhelm Reich
0–374–50204–8 Farrar, Straus & Giroux pb $10.95

THE SEXUAL REVOLUTION: Toward a Self-Regulating Character Structure
0–374–50209–2 Farrar, Straus & Giroux pb $9.95

Other Important Post-Freudian Theorists

• Gordon W. Allport
BECOMING: Basic Considerations for a Psychology of Personality
An antibehaviorist, antireductionist psychology that focuses on human freedom
0–300–00002–2 Yale pb $5.95

THE NATURE OF PREJUDICE
A classic study of discrimination
0–201–00179–9 Addison-Wesley pb $9.95

• Sandor Ferenczi & Otto Rank
THE DEVELOPMENT OF PSYCHOANALYSIS
0–8236–1197–3 Intl Universities $25.00

• Lucy Freeman
FIGHT AGAINST FEARS
0–8264–0413–8 Harper & Row pb $10.95

• Robert Lindner
THE FIFTY-MINUTE HOUR
0–385–29518–9 Doubleday pb $7.95

• Theodor Reik
LISTENING WITH THE THIRD EAR: The Inner Experience of a Psychoanalyst
0–374–51800–9 Farrar, Straus & Giroux pb $11.95

• Geza Roheim

THE ETERNAL ONES OF THE DREAM: Myth and Ritual, Dreams and Fantasies— Their Role in the Lives of Primitive Man
An application of Freudian theory to Australian aboriginal culture
0–8236–8044–4 Intl Universities pb $19.95

GATES OF THE DREAM
0–8236–8060–6 Intl Universities pb $19.95

THE RIDDLE OF THE SPHINX
0–8446–5238–5 Peter Smith $10.75

• Herbert S. Strean & Lucy Freeman

BEHIND THE COUCH: Revelations of a Psychoanalyst
0–471–85956–7 John Wiley $16.50

• Harry Stack Sullivan

CONCEPTIONS OF MODERN PSYCHIATRY
Sullivan's central ideas on the role of interpersonal relations in personality formation
0–393–00740–5 Norton pb $10.95

THE INTERPERSONAL THEORY OF PSYCHIATRY
A systematic presentation of Sullivan's theories, which shifted the emphasis from personal, internal factors to social factors in explaining mental health and illness
0–393–00138–5 Norton pb $4.95

EXISTENTIAL PSYCHOLOGY

• Viktor E. Frankl

MAN'S SEARCH FOR MEANING
The central statement of the theory of a human need for meaning in life that Frankl developed from his experience in a Nazi concentration camp
0–671–66736–X Washington Square pb $4.95

PSYCHOTHERAPY AND EXISTENTIALISM
0–671–54729–1 Washington Square pb $3.95

THE UNCONSCIOUS GOD
The case for a spiritual unconscious and a tacit universal belief in God
0–671–54728–3 Washington Square pb $3.50

THE WILL TO MEANING: Foundations and Applications of Logotherapy
0–452–00946–4 Meridian pb $7.95

• R.D. Laing

THE DIVIDED SELF
A famous and controversial existential analysis of schizophrenia
0–14–020734–1 Penguin pb $4.95

THE POLITICS OF EXPERIENCE
This iconoclastic assault on conventional morality was a rallying point of the '60s counterculture
0–394–71475–X Random House pb $4.95

THE POLITICS OF THE FAMILY
The family as a system of complicated, interlocking and interdependent relationships. "The basis of Laing's argument is that the concept of 'family' itself lies in the mutual collusion of those who believe themselves to be its members"—*London Times Educational Supplement*
0–394–71809–7 Random House pb $5.95

SELF AND OTHERS
Laing sees schizophrenia as rooted in "ontological insecurity"
0–14–021376–7 Penguin pb $5.95

• Rollo May

THE COURAGE TO CREATE
0–553–26361–7 Bantam pb $4.50

THE DISCOVERY OF BEING: Writings in Existential Psychology
A good short introduction to the major tenets of May's existential-humanist psychology
0–393–30315–2 Norton pb $5.95

LOVE AND WILL
0–393–01080–5 Norton $14.95

THE MEANING OF ANXIETY
0–671–60385–X Washington Square pb $5.95

• Jean-Paul Sartre

EXISTENTIAL PSYCHOANALYSIS
A spirited attack on Freudian determinism
0–89526–940–6 Regnery pb $8.95

HUMAN POTENTIAL PSYCHOLOGY

• Robert Assagioli

THE ACT OF WILL
The role of will in self-fulfillment, with exercises for strengthening it
0–14–003866–3 Penguin pb $7.95

PSYCHOSYNTHESIS
Argues that psychoanalysis is incomplete and that psychology must embrace the soul as well as the libido, the imagination as well as the complexes
0–14–004263–6 Penguin pb $6.95

• Abraham H. Maslow

RELIGIONS, VALUES, AND PEAK EXPERIENCES
The most influential advocate of a psychology of self-realization, Maslow finds religious experience at the heart of the "peak experiences" reached by healthy, fully functioning individuals
0–14–004262–8 Penguin pb $4.95

TOWARD A PSYCHOLOGY OF BEING
Maslow introduced a new spirit into psychology by studying healthy, self-fulfilled individuals and deriving principles of self-realization that can be used by those who feel unfulfilled
0–442–03805–4 Van Nostrand Reinhold pb $12.95

• Frank G. Goble

THE THIRD FORCE: The Psychology of Abraham Maslow
0–671–50983–7 Washington Square pb $3.95

• Carl R. Rogers

ON BECOMING A PERSON
A popular classic of the human potential movement
0–395–08409–1 Houghton Mifflin pb $8.95

A WAY OF BEING
Rogers presents a humanistic psychotherapy based on self-acceptance and the full assimilation of the individual's experience
0–395–30067–3 Houghton Mifflin pb $8.95

BEHAVIORISM

• Ivan P. Pavlov

CONDITIONED REFLEXES: An Investigation of the Physiological Activity of the Cerebral Cortex
The pioneering work presenting the stimulus-response theory of conditioned reflexes on which behaviorist psychology is based
0–486–60614–7 Dover pb $9.95

• B.F. Skinner

ABOUT BEHAVIORISM
Skinner assesses his life's work
0–394–71618–3 Random House pb $4.95

BEYOND FREEDOM AND DIGNITY
In this controversial 1971 work, Skinner argues that traditional notions of human freedom and dignity are wishful thinking and must be discarded if contemporary social disintegration is to give way to a harmonious society
0–394–42555–3 Knopf $17.95
0–553–25404–9 Bantam pb $4.95

A MATTER OF CONSEQUENCES
The concluding volume of the autobiography
0–8147–7845–3 NYU pb $11.95

PARTICULARS OF MY LIFE
The first of three volumes of Skinner's autobiography
0–8147–7843–7 NYU pb $11.95

SCIENCE AND HUMAN BEHAVIOR
The main statement of Skinner's behaviorist theory
0–02–929040–6 Free Press pb $11.95

THE SHAPING OF A BEHAVIORIST
The second volume of the autobiography
0–8147–7844–5 NYU pb $11.95

WALDEN TWO
Skinner's famous didactic novel, published in 1948, presents a utopian egalitarian community based on the positive reinforcement of behaviorist psychology; it actually inspired a small experimental community in Virginia
0–02–411490–1 Macmillan $6.95
0–02–411510–X Macmillan pb $3.95

  IF YOU CAN'T FIND IT, LOOK IN THE INDEX

• John B. Watson
BEHAVIORISM
A clear exposition of the behaviorist approach to psychology written in 1925 by the American psychologist who first developed it
0–393–00524–0 Norton pb $7.95

THE COGNITIVE REVOLUTION

▶ See also The Computer Revolution and Artificial Intelligence

• Gregory Bateson
STEPS TO AN ECOLOGY OF MIND
A multidisciplinary thinker who gained a wide and fervent readership, Bateson in this classic work gives a highly original account of the relation of mind and environment
0–345–33291–1 Ballantine pb $4.95

• Jerome S. Bruner
ACTUAL MINDS, POSSIBLE WORLDS
A cognitive approach to imaginative experience. "A splendid book, one which should contribute to the important reorientation that is taking place between psychology and the literary arts"—Howard Gardner
0–674–00366–7 Harvard pb $7.95

BEYOND THE INFORMATION GIVEN: Studies in the Psychology of Knowing
A classic which initiated the "cognitive revolution" against behaviorist-dominated psychology by stressing the mediation of cognitive processes in perception and behavior
Edited by Jeremy M. Angler
0–393–01095–3 Norton $13.95
0–393–09363–8 Norton pb $10.95

• Howard Gardner
THE MIND'S NEW SCIENCE: A History of Cognitive Revolution
A comprehensive and sophisticated history not only of the cognitive revolution itself but the historical background of cognitive science in Descartes, Kant, Wittgenstein, and other philosophers; covers Gestalt psychology, Piaget, cybernetics, and linguistics
0–465–04635–5 Basic Books pb $12.95

• P.N. Johnson-Laird
THE COMPUTER AND THE MIND: An Introduction to Cognitive Science
0–674–15615–3 Harvard $29.50

The Human Mind and Artificial Intelligence

• John R. Anderson
THE ARCHITECTURE OF COGNITION
A framework for a unified cognitive theory of the human mind
0–674–04426–6 Harvard pb $10.95

• Margaret Boden
ARTIFICIAL INTELLIGENCE AND NATURAL MAN
0–465–00456–3 Basic Books pb $14.95

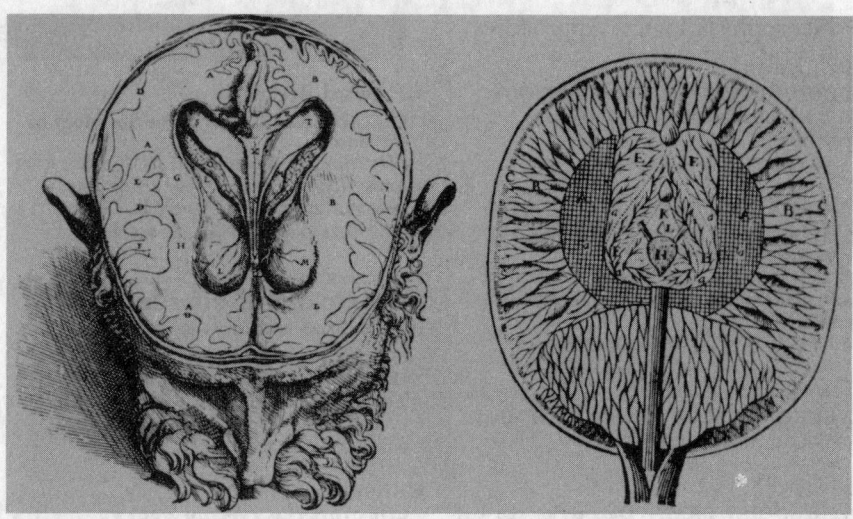
Drawings of the brain by Vesalius and Descartes

COMPUTER MODELS OF THE MIND
0–521–27033–2 Cambridge pb $15.95

• Daniel C. Dennett
BRAINSTORMS: Philosophical Essays on Mind and Psychology
0–262–54037–1 MIT pb $12.50

• Jerry A. Fodor
REPRESENTATIONS: Philosophical Essays on the Foundations of Cognitive Science
0–262–56027–5 MIT pb $10.95

• Andrew Hodges
ALAN TURING: The Enigma
A biography of the brilliant British mathematician-philosopher who did pioneering work in computer theory, helped break the Nazi code during World War II, and committed suicide in 1954 at the age of 41
0–671–49207–1 Simon & Schuster $24.95
0–671–52809–2 Simon & Schuster pb $10.95

Douglas R. Hofstadter
GODEL, ESCHER, BACH: An Eternal Golden Braid
A consistently engaging and challenging meditation on puzzles and paradoxes of logic, mathematics, physics, art, and philosophy, presented in a series of essays and dialogues. "A wondrous book that unites and explains, in a very entertaining way, many of the important ideas of recent intellectual history"—*Commonweal*
0–465–02685–0 Basic Books $34.50
0–394–74502–7 Random House pb $14.95

METAMAGICAL THEMAS: Questing for the Essence of Mind and Pattern
A wide-ranging, fascinating collection of essays on science, mathematics, and language, taken from a column in *Scientific American*
0–553–34683–0 Bantam pb $15.95

• Douglas R. Hofstadter & Daniel C. Dennett, editors
THE MIND'S I: Fantasies and Reflections of Self and Soul
A collection of diverse and entertaining essays, stories, and dialogues on mind, self, free will, computers, and God
0–553–34584–2 Bantam pb $13.95

• Marvin Minsky
THE SOCIETY OF MIND
0–671–60740–5 Simon & Schuster $22.50
0–671–65713–5 Simon & Schuster pb $19.95

• Seymour Papert
MINDSTORMS: Children, Computers, and Powerful Ideas
0–465–04627–4 Basic Books $15.95
0–465–04629–0 Basic Books pb $8.95

• Roger Schank & Robert Abelson
SCRIPTS, PLANS, GOALS, AND UNDERSTANDING: An Inquiry into Human Knowledge Structures
0–89859–138–4 Erlbaum pb $16.50

• John Searle
MINDS, BRAINS AND SCIENCE
A collection of lectures by a leading contemporary philosopher of language and mind
0–674–57633–0 Harvard pb $5.95

• Robert J. Sternberg, editor
HANDBOOK OF HUMAN INTELLIGENCE
Authoritative articles on all aspects of human intelligence, from genetics to social and cultural factors, including theories of development and methods of measurement
0–521–29687–0 Cambridge pb $34.50

• Norbert Wiener
CYBERNETICS: Control and Communication in the Animal and the Machine
Wiener invented the term *cybernetics* and suggested the possibility that the mathematical principles of communication and control that apply to machines also have broad implications in fields such as biology
0–262–73009–X MIT pb $9.95

☐ **TO ORDER BY FAX, SEE PAGE 1**

Neurophysiological Approaches

- **C.J. Adcock**
  FUNDAMENTALS OF PSYCHOLOGY
  A brief introduction to neurological
  psychology
  0–14–020664–7 Penguin pb $6.95

- **Nancy C. Andreasen**
  **THE BROKEN BRAIN: The Biological
  Revolution in Psychology**
  A clear account of the biological basis of
  schizophrenia, depression, and other
  conditions
  0–06–091272–3 Harper & Row pb $9.95

- **Jean-Pierre Changeuz**
  NEURONAL MAN: The Biology of Mind
  0–19–504226–3 Oxford pb $9.95

- **Michael S. Gazzaniga**
  **THE SOCIAL BRAIN: Discovering the
  Networks of the Mind**
  How the structure of the brain determines
  the way in which we interpret experience,
  form opinions, and act socially
  0–465–07851–6 Basic Books pb $8.95

- **A.R. Luria**
  **THE WORKING BRAIN: An Introduction
  to Neuropsychology**
  Foreword by Jerome S. Bruner
  0–465–09208–X Basic Books pb $12.95

- **Paul H. Wender & Donald F. Klein**
  **MIND, MOOD AND MEDICINE: A Guide
  to the New Biopsychology**
  Information and case histories concerning
  the biological origins and treatment of
  mental illnesses
  0–452–00878–6 Meridian pb $12.95

- **John Z. Young**
  A MODEL OF THE BRAIN
  0–19–857333–2 Oxford $35.00

GESTALT PSYCHOLOGY

- **Wolfgang Köhler**
  THE MENTALITY OF APES
  0–87140–108–8 Liveright pb $3.95

  **SELECTED PAPERS OF WOLFGANG
  KÖHLER**
  Edited by Solomon E. Asch & Mary Henle
  0–87140–505–9 Liveright $15.95
  0–87140–253–X Liveright pb $4.95

  THE TASK OF GESTALT PSYCHOLOGY
  Köhler's last work, an assessment of the
  development and future of Gestalt theory
  0–691–08614–1 Princeton $25.00
  0–691–02452–9 Princeton pb $8.50

- **Max Wertheimer**
  PRODUCTIVE THINKING
  One of the founders (with Köhler and
  Koffka) of Gestalt psychology, Wertheimer
  ranges beyond Gestalt theories of
  psychology to ethical and political
  questions
  0–226–89376–6 Chicago pb $8.95

SOCIAL PSYCHOLOGY

- **Howard Becker**
  **OUTSIDERS: Studies in the Sociology of
  Deviance**
  "The most instructive and most interesting
  introduction to the subject of deviant
  behavior available"—Albert K. Cohen
  0–02–902140–5 Free Press pb $10.95

- **Eric Berne**
  BEYOND GAMES AND SCRIPTS
  0–345–30053–X Ballantine pb $3.50

  **GAMES PEOPLE PLAY: The Basic
  Handbook of Transactional Analysis**
  The popular account of role-playing in
  everyday life
  0–345–32719–5 Ballantine pb $3.95

- **Bruno Bettelheim**
  SURVIVING & OTHER ESSAYS
  On Anne Frank, the sexual revolution,
  Portnoy's Complaint, and the psychological
  effects and implications of concentration
  camps
  0–394–74264–8 Random House pb $9.95

- **Norman O. Brown**
  **LIFE AGAINST DEATH: The
  Psychoanalytical Meaning of History**
  A book that had a major impact in the
  1960s, calling for a liberated,
  nonhierarchical, playful sexuality, or
  "polymorphous perversity," that would free
  humanity from the reality principle
  0–8195–5148–1 Wesleyan $30.00
  0–8195–6144–4 Wesleyan pb $9.95

- **Roger Brown**
  SOCIAL PSYCHOLOGY
  A collection of essays on recent research
  0–02–908300–1 Free Press $27.95

- **Erving Goffman**
  FORMS OF TALK
  Five papers on various forms of speech,
  including dialogues, lectures, and radio
  announcements
  0–8122–7790–2 Pennsylvania $35.95
  0–8122–1112–X Pennsylvania pb $13.95

  **INTERACTION RITUAL: Essays in Face-
  to-Face Behavior**
  0–394–70631–5 Pantheon pb $6.50

  RELATIONS IN PUBLIC
  Six papers on the structure of public
  transactions between individuals
  0–06–131957–0 Harper & Row pb $9.95

- **E. Maccoby**
  SOCIAL DEVELOPMENT
  A good introduction, stressing the parent-
  child relationship
  0–15–581422–2 HBJ pb $21.50

- **Herbert Marcuse**
  **EROS AND CIVILIZATION: A
  Philosophical Inquiry into Freud**
  Rejecting Freud's theory that civilization
  demands instinctual repression, Marcuse
  calls for a society in which sexual liberation
  will accompany political and economic
  liberation
  0–8070–1555–5 Beacon pb $10.95

- **George H. Mead**
  **MIND, SELF, AND SOCIETY: From the
  Standpoint of a Social Behaviorist**
  0–226–51668–7 Chicago pb $8.95

Stanley Milgram
OBEDIENCE TO AUTHORITY
An important study summing up recent
research on why people submit to
authority
0–06–131983–X Harper & Row pb $8.95

- **Philip Rieff**
  **TRIUMPH OF THE THERAPEUTIC:
  Uses of Faith after Freud**
  The cultural implications of the therapeutic
  model of human behavior
  0–226–71646–5 Chicago pb $11.95

CHILD PSYCHOLOGY

- **Bruno Bettelheim**
  **THE EMPTY FORTRESS: Infantile
  Autism and the Birth of the Self**
  A study of autistic children drawn from
  Bettelheim's experiences at the Sonia
  Shankman Orthogenic School at the
  University of Chicago. "Inspiring because
  it is evidence that the informed heart is
  possible and that the alienations of our age
  . . . need not be accepted as the permanent
  condition of man"—Eliot Fremont-Smith,
  NY Times
  0–02–903140–0 Free Press pb $17.95

  **A GOOD ENOUGH PARENT: A Book on
  Child Rearing**
  0–394–47148–2 Knopf $18.95

  LOVE IS NOT ENOUGH
  Bettelheim's account of his observations
  and methods at the Sonia Shankman
  School and the implications for child
  psychology in general
  0–02–903280–6 Free Press $22.95

  **TRUANTS FROM LIFE: The
  Rehabilitation of Emotionally Disturbed
  Children**
  Four case histories of severely disturbed
  children and the therapeutic teaching
  methods that Bettelheim used to guide
  them to normal lives; a widely influential
  work
  0–02–903440–X Free Press $21.95
  0–02–903450–7 Free Press pb $13.95

  **THE USES OF ENCHANTMENT: The
  Meaning and Importance of Fairy Tales**
  A psychoanalytic defense of traditional
  fairy tales and how they liberate the
  emotions of children. "A charming book
  about enchantment, a profound book
  about fairy tales"—John Updike. Winner
  of the National Book Award
  0–394–49771–6 Knopf $21.50
  0–679–72393–5 Random House pb $8.95

- **Bruno Bettelheim & Karen Zelan**
  **ON LEARNING TO READ: The Child's
  Fascination with Meaning**
  "Bettelheim and Zelan reaffirm one terribly
  important point: what we do with reading
  between kindergarten and third grade may
  be the single most important activity for
  our psychological health and future as
  individuals, our intelligence as a people

TO ORDER BOOKS AS GIFTS, SEE PAGE 1

and our strength as a nation"—George Keller, *Baltimore Sun*
0–394–51592–7 Knopf $13.95
0–394–71194–7 Random House pb $9.95

• Dorothy Bloch
"SO THE WITCH WON'T EAT ME":
Fantasy and the Child's Fear of Infanticide
"A daring look inside the human mind to reveal the human fears we all experience as children out of the desperate need to believe our mothers and fathers love us, as we turn anger inward, sometimes destroying ourselves"—Lucy Freeman
0–394–62104–2 Grove pb $7.95

• John Bowlby
SEPARATION: Anxiety and Anger
0–465–09716–2 Basic Books pb $13.95

• Robert Coles
THE MORAL LIFE OF CHILDREN
How children struggle with moral choice in the US and elsewhere. "There is no one who is more interested in what children say, sing, don't say or don't sing—and why—than Robert Coles. He is to the stories that children have to tell what Homer was to the tale of the Trojan War"—Neil Postman, *NY Times Book Review*
0–395–43153–0 Houghton Mifflin pb $10.95

THE POLITICAL LIFE OF CHILDREN
How children all over the world discover their political loyalties through language, nationalities, race, religion, exile, martyrdom, class and revolution. "A major contribution to our understanding of how children become socialized"—*NY Times Book Review*
0–87113–035–1 Little, Brown $19.95
0–395–43152–2 Houghton Mifflin pb $10.95

• Margaret Donaldson
CHILDREN'S MINDS
"One of the most powerful, most wisely balanced and best informed books on the development of the child's mind to have appeared in twenty years. Its implications for education are enormous"—Jerome S. Bruner
0–393–95101–4 Norton pb $6.95

• Judy Dunn & Carol Kendrick
SIBLINGS: Love, Envy, and Understanding
0–674–80735–9 Harvard $22.95

• Jerome Kagan
THE NATURE OF THE CHILD
0–465–04850–1 Basic Books $22.00
0–465–04851–X Basic Books pb $11.95

• Kenneth Kaye
THE MENTAL AND SOCIAL LIFE OF BABIES: How Parents Create Persons
0–226–42847–8 Chicago $22.50
0–226–42848–6 Chicago pb $11.00

• Melanie Klein
THE PSYCHOANALYSIS OF CHILDREN
Klein's influential work on child psychology stresses play and the child's relation to its mother
0–02–918430–4 Free Press $25.00

• Abraham H. Maslow, editor
MOTIVATION AND PERSONALITY
0–06–041987–3 Harper & Row pb $22.95

• Alice Miller
THE DRAMA OF THE GIFTED CHILD
A lucid, compassionate study of narcissism and the child's inability to feel because he has adapted too well to his parents' needs and neglected his own feelings. Published in hardcover as *Prisoners of Childhood*
0–465–06347–0 Basic Books $13.50
0–465–09735–9 Basic Books pb $6.95

FOR YOUR OWN GOOD: Hidden Cruelty in Child-Rearing and the Roots of Violence
With a riveting chapter on Adolf Hitler's upbringing
Translated by Hildegarde & Hunter Hannum
0–374–51859–9 Farrar, Straus & Giroux pb $8.95

THOU SHALT NOT BE AWARE!:
Society's Betrayal of the Child
"Long before child molestation became an appalling staple of the nightly news, Dr. Alice Miller formulated revolutionary psychological theories that might have prepared us for the grim actuality"—*LA Times Book Review*
0–374–27646–3 Farrar, Straus & Giroux $16.50
0–452–00929–4 NAL pb $9.95

• Patricia H. Miller
THEORIES OF DEVELOPMENTAL PSYCHOLOGY
0–7167–2002–7 Freeman pb $16.95

• Paul H. Mussen & others
CHILD DEVELOPMENT AND PERSONALITY
0–06–044694–3 Harper & Row $37.50
0–06–045148–3 Harper & Row pb $9.50

• Valerie P. Suransky
THE EROSION OF CHILDHOOD
Foreword by Paulo Freire
0–226–78007–4 Chicago pb $8.95

• Lorna Wing, editor
EARLY CHILDHOOD AUTISM
0–08–017177–X Pergamon $39.00
0–08–017178–8 Pergamon pb $22.00

Jean Piaget

• Jean Piaget
THE CHILD'S CONCEPTION OF MOVEMENT AND SPEED
0–345–32800–0 Ballantine pb $4.95

THE CONSTRUCTION OF REALITY IN THE CHILD
How the child's discovery of an independent physical reality affects the development of spatial and logical thinking
0–345–32803–5 Ballantine pb $4.95

THE LANGUAGE AND THOUGHT OF THE CHILD
Piaget's first work, originally published in 1923, set the foundation of his theory of child psychology
0–452–00722–4 NAL pb $7.95

THE ORIGINS OF INTELLIGENCE IN THE CHILD
An early and influential work on the relation of infantile sensory-motor experiences to cognitive development
0–8236–3900–2 Intl Universities $45.00

PLAY, DREAMS AND IMITATION IN CHILDHOOD
Piaget's theories of the role of play in children's cognitive development have been borne out in studies throughout the world
0–393–00171–7 Norton pb $8.95

• Jean Piaget & others
THE MORAL JUDGMENT OF THE CHILD
Focusing on a game of marbles, Piaget and his associates analyze children's attitudes toward lying, cheating, adult authority, punishments and responsibilities. "In a sense, child morality throws light on adult morality. If we want to form men and women, nothing will fit so well for the task as to study the laws that govern formation"—Jean Piaget
0–02–925240–7 Free Press pb $14.95

• Howard E. Gruber & J. Jacques Voneche, editors
THE ESSENTIAL PIAGET
Selections from all his major works, covering biology, developmental psychology, philosophy, structuralism, and education
Foreword by Jean Piaget
0–465–02064–X Basic Books pb $22.95

Object-Relations Theory

• John Bowlby
LOSS: Sadness and Depression
Bowlby demonstrated that attachment of the infant to the mother is of overwhelming importance in determining the individual's later security and success in forming relations with others, and that separation from or loss of the mother can have a devastating effect
0–465–04238–4 Basic Books pb $13.95

• Otto F. Kernberg
OBJECT RELATIONS THEORY AND CLINICAL PSYCHOANALYSIS
0–87668–870–9 Jason Aronson $25.00

• Melanie Klein
NARRATIVE OF A CHILD ANALYSIS
Through her work in child psychology, Klein developed the original hypothesis of object-relations theory
0–02–918450–9 Free Press $37.50

• Melanie Klein & Joan Riviere, editors
LOVE, HATE AND REPARATION
0–393–00260–8 Norton pb $5.95

• D.W. Winnicott
THE MATURATIONAL PROCESSES AND THE FACILITATING ENVIRONMENT: Studies in the Theory of Emotional Development
Winnicott examines the tendency of those who lacked a secure sense of attachment in infancy to develop a "false self" based on compliance with the wishes of others
0–8236–3200–8 Intl Universities $37.50

PLAYING AND REALITY
0–422–78310–2 Methuen pb $10.95

PSYCHOLOGY OF GENDER

• Ronald Bayer
HOMOSEXUALITY AND AMERICAN PSYCHIATRY: The Politics of Diagnosis
"A lucid, succinct and eminently fair-minded account of the controversy which resulted in the removal of homosexuality from the [American Psychiatric] Association's *Diagnostic and Statistical Manual of Psychiatric Disorders*"—Paul Robinson, *New Republic*
0–691–02837–0 Princeton pb $9.95

• Mary Field Belenky & others
WOMEN'S WAYS OF KNOWING: The Development of Self, Voice, and Mind
0–465–09212–8 Basic Books $19.95

• Jessica Benjamin
THE BONDS OF LOVE: Psychoanalysis, Feminism and the Problem of Domination
0–394–75730–0 Pantheon pb $12.95

• Martin Bergmann
THE ANATOMY OF LOVING: The Story of Man's Quest to Know What Love Is
"Contains some of the most original and scientific writing on the psychoanalytic study of love . . . a major contribution to the field"—Otto Kernberg
0–231–06487–X Columbia pb $14.50

• Nancy Chodorow
THE REPRODUCTION OF MOTHERING: Psychoanalysis and the Sociology of Gender
On the creation of sex differences through cultural and social processes
0–520–03892–4 California pb $9.95

• Arthur & Libby Coleman
THE FATHER: Mythology and Changing Roles
Examines the relatively neglected role of the father, in terms of the modern family and in terms of a man's evolving self-image
0–933029–35–7 Chiron pb $12.95

• Helene Deutsch
THE PSYCHOLOGY OF WOMEN
Volume 1: Girlhood
0–8089–0115–X Grune & Stratton $68.00
Volume 2: Motherhood
0–8089–0116–8 Grune & Stratton $60.00

• Anne Fausto-Sterling
MYTHS OF GENDER: Biological Theories about Women and Men
0–465–04791–2 Basic Books pb $9.95

• Carol Gilligan
IN A DIFFERENT VOICE: Psychological Theory and Women's Development
An important study of the relationship between personal and moral development and the self-images of women
0–674–44543–0 Harvard $20.00
0–674–44544–9 Harvard pb $6.95

• Robert W. Goy & Bruce S. McEwen, editors
SEXUAL DIFFERENTIATION OF THE BRAIN
0–262–07077–4 MIT $30.00

• Karen Horney
FEMININE PSYCHOLOGY
Horney rejects the feminine stereotypes embedded in orthodox Freudian psychology
Edited by Harold Kelman
0–393–00686–7 Norton pb $4.95

• Evelyn Fox Keller
REFLECTIONS ON GENDER AND SCIENCE
0–300–03636–1 Yale pb $8.95

• Hilary M. Lips & Nina L. Colwill
THE PSYCHOLOGY OF SEX DIFFERENCES
0–13–736561–6 Prentice-Hall $13.95

• Eleanor E. Maccoby & Carol N. Jacklin
THE PSYCHOLOGY OF SEX DIFFERENCES
Volume 1
0–8047–0974–2 Stanford pb $11.95
Volume 2
0–8047–0975–0 Stanford pb $7.95

• Jean B. Miller
TOWARD A NEW PSYCHOLOGY OF WOMEN
An attempt to develop a new psychology out of the actual life experiences of women, with many anecdotal case histories
0–8070–2910–6 Beacon $17.50
0–8070–2909–2 Beacon pb $7.95

• Mary R. Walsh
THE PSYCHOLOGY OF WOMEN: Ongoing Debates
A collection of essays on such questions as women's alleged proneness to masochism, the relevance of psychoanalytic theory to the psychology of women, androgyny, lesbianism, abortion, and pornography
0–300–03965–4 Yale $40.00
0–300–03966–2 Yale pb $12.95

DISORDERS AND TREATMENT

• Gordon Claridge
ORIGINS OF MENTAL ILLNESS
Argues that even severe mental disorders have their origins in common psychological and biological qualities
0–631–14198–7 Blackwell $45.00
0–631–14473–0 Blackwell pb $16.95

• Michel Foucault
MADNESS AND CIVILIZATION: A History of Insanity in the Age of Reason
Foucault asserts that the Enlightenment produced a "Great Confinement" in which the haphazard, relatively tolerant medieval treatment of the insane was replaced by a systematic attempt to isolate them from society and to deny them their humanity
0–679–72110–X Random House pb $7.95

• Jan Goldstein
CONSOLE AND CLASSIFY: The French Psychiatric Profession in the Nineteenth Century
0–521–32279–0 Cambridge pb $49.50

• Arthur Kleinman
THE SOCIAL ORIGINS OF DISTRESS AND DISEASE: Depression, Neurasthenia, and Pain in Modern China
0–300–03541–1 Yale $30.00

• Roy Porter
A SOCIAL HISTORY OF MADNESS
A history of madness from the 18th to the 20th century from the point of view of those confined to asylums, using their diaries, letters, and other writings; fascinating both for the deftly told individual stories and for their larger social and moral implications
1–555–84185–6 Weidenfeld & Nicolson $18.95

• Roy Porter & others, editors
THE ANATOMY OF MADNESS
Essays on Samuel Johnson's melancholy, Darwin's view of madness, the idea of holy madness in Christianity, 18th-century and Victorian approaches to madness, and other topics
Volume 1: People and Ideas
0–422–79430–9 Methuen $47.50
Volume 2: Institutions and Society
0–422–79440–6 Methuen $47.50

• Solomon H. Snyder
BIOLOGICAL ASPECTS OF MENTAL DISORDER
0–19–502888–0 Oxford pb $12.95

• Thomas Szasz
INSANITY: The Idea and Its Consequences
0–471–84708–9 John Wiley $17.95

• Elliot S. Valenstein
GREAT AND DESPERATE CURES: The Rise and Decline of Psychosurgery and Other Radical Treatments for Mental Illness
0–465–02710–5 Basic Books $19.95
0–465–02711–3 Basic Books pb $10.95

• Paul L. Wachtel
PSYCHOANALYSIS AND BEHAVIOR THERAPY: Toward an Integration
0–465–06562–7 Basic Books $21.95

Depression

• Robert Burton
THE ANATOMY OF MELANCHOLY
A classic of English literature, this eccentric, allusive, beautifully written 17th-century compendium of legend and lore on melancholy is also a psychologically acute

account of depression, as caused by everything from love to religion
Edited by Joan R. Peters
0–8044–6069–8 Ungar pb $6.95

- Paul Gilbert
DEPRESSION: From Psychology to Brain State
0–86377–007–X Erlbaum $29.95
0–86377–008–8 Erlbaum pb $17.50

- Gerald Klerman & others
INTERPERSONAL PSYCHOTHERAPY OF DEPRESSION
0–465–03396–2 Basic Books $22.95

- Peter Lewisohn & others
CONTROL YOUR DEPRESSION
0–13–171893–2 Prentice-Hall pb $9.95

- Alexander Lowen
DEPRESSION AND THE BODY: The Biological Basis of Faith and Reality
An analysis of depression as a dissociation from reality and the body and a prescription for overcoming it by exercises that enhance bodily awareness
0–14–021780–0 Penguin pb $6.95

Lovesickness, hypochondria, madness, and superstition, from the title page of Robert Burton's Anatomy of Melancholy

Schizophrenia

- Silvano Arieti
INTERPRETATION OF SCHIZOPHRENIA
A major work from a leading authority, winner of the National Book Award for Science
0–465–03429–2 Basic Books $41.95

UNDERSTANDING AND HELPING THE SCHIZOPHRENIC: A Guide for Family and Friends
A clear, practical guide, including advice on how to recognize the first signs of the illness which afflicts over three million Americans
0–671–41252–3 Simon & Schuster pb $7.95

- Kayla F. Bernheim & Richard R.J. Lewine
SCHIZOPHRENIA: Symptoms, Causes, Treatments
0–393–09017–5 Norton pb $9.95

- John Cutting & M. Shepherd, editors
THE CLINICAL ROOTS OF THE SCHIZOPHRENIA CONCEPT: Translations of Seminal European Contributions on Schizophrenia
0–521–26635–1 Cambridge $59.50

- Irving I. Gottesman & James Shields
SCHIZOPHRENIA: The Epigenetic Puzzle
A genetic and environmental explanation of schizophrenia
0–521–29559–9 Cambridge pb $15.95

- Robert G. Kvarnes & Gloria H. Parloff, editors
A HARRY STACK SULLIVAN CASE SEMINAR: Treatment of a Young Male Schizophrenic
0–393–01130–5 Norton $12.95

- R.D. Laing & A. Esterson
SANITY, MADNESS AND THE FAMILY
Laing and Esterson contend that schizophrenia is caused by the family rather than individual psychic development
0–14–021157–8 Penguin pb $6.95

Susan Sheehan
IS THERE NO PLACE ON EARTH FOR ME?
A Pulitzer Prize-winning account of a young woman's 17-year struggle with schizophrenia
Foreword by Robert Coles
0–394–71378–8 Random House pb $8.95

- Harry Stack Sullivan
SCHIZOPHRENIA AS A HUMAN PROCESS
Introduction by H.S. Perry
0–393–00721–9 Norton pb $10.95

- Thomas Szasz
SCHIZOPHRENIA: The Sacred Symbol of Psychiatry
Argues that schizophrenia is not a genuine disease, but has been invented by psychiatrists as a way of locking up the nonconforming against their will
0–8156–0224–3 Syracuse pb $12.95

- E. Fuller Torrey
SURVIVING SCHIZOPHRENIA: A Family Manual
A guide to the nature, causes, symptoms, pathology, and treatment of the illness, from both the patient's and the family's perspective
0–06–096249–6 Harper & Row pb $9.95

- Ming T. Tsuang
SCHIZOPHRENIA: The Facts
0–19–261336–7 Oxford $16.50

- Maryellen Walsh
SCHIZOPHRENIA
0–446–34160–6 Warner pb $4.95

- John Kenneth Wing
SCHIZOPHRENIA: Towards a New Synthesis
0–8089–1140–6 Grune & Stratton $36.50

Other Problems

- Donald W. Goodman
ANXIETY
Theories, literary accounts, and case studies of phobias
0–345–34082–5 Ballantine pb $8.95

- Alexander Lowen
BIOENERGETICS
Depression, fatigue, apathy, and their treatment through body training
0–14–004322–5 Penguin pb $7.95

NARCISSISM: Denial of the True Self
An analysis of narcissism as emotional numbness and how it can be treated by restoring the ability to feel
0–02–077290–4 Macmillan pb $5.95

- Stanton Peele
LOVE AND ADDICTION
The problem of addiction to love
0–451–15538–6 Signet pb $4.95

- Judith L. Rapoport
THE BOY WHO COULDN'T STOP WASHING: The Experience and Treatment of Obsessive-Compulsive Disorder
0–525–24708–4 Dutton $18.95

- Robert S. Weiss, editor
LONELINESS: The Experience of Emotional and Social Isolation
Foreword by David Riesman
0–262–73041–3 MIT pb $9.95

Case Histories

- Muriel Gardner, editor
THE WOLF-MAN: With the Cure of the Wolf-Man by Sigmund Freud
0–465–09196–2 Basic Books pb $8.95

- A.R. Luria
THE MAN WITH A SHATTERED WORLD: The History of a Brain Wound
Foreword by Jerome S. Bruner
0–674–54625–3 Harvard pb $7.95

THE MIND OF A MNEMONIST: A Little Book about a Vast Memory
0–317–59999–2 Harvard pb $7.95

Melancholy

• Oliver Sacks
A LEG TO STAND ON
A superbly written, often gripping account of Sacks's experiences after breaking a leg while climbing a mountain in Norway
0–671–46780–8 Summit $14.95
0–06–097082–0 Harper & Row pb $8.95

THE MAN WHO MISTOOK HIS WIFE FOR A HAT & OTHER CLINICAL TALES
Fascinating essays drawn from Sacks's experiences as a neurologist
0–06–097079–0 Harper & Row pb $8.95

Cognitive Therapy

• Aaron T. Beck
COGNITIVE THERAPY AND THE EMOTIONAL DISORDERS
An introduction to cognitive therapy, demonstrating the role of irrational and unrealistic "automatic thoughts" in depression and phobias and describing techniques for overcoming them
0–452–00928–6 Meridian pb $8.95

DEPRESSION: Causes and Treatment
0–8122–1032–8 Pennsylvania pb $14.95

• David D. Burns
FEELING GOOD: The New Mood Therapy
How to control the distorted thoughts that lead to low self-esteem, depression, and lethargy
0–451–15887–3 Signet pb $4.95

• Gary Emery
GETTING UNDEPRESSED: How a Woman Can Change Her Life Through Cognitive Therapy
A drug-free, three-step program to break through clinical depression, a disease that affects over 20 million American women
0–671–65891–3 Simon & Schuster pb $7.95

Rational and Reality Therapy

• Albert Ellis
ANGER: How to Live With and Without It
0–8065–0937–6 Lyle Stuart pb $7.95

HUMANISTIC PSYCHOTHERAPY
An approach to therapy that stresses rationality and responsibility
0–07–019237–5 McGraw-Hill pb $6.95

REASON AND EMOTION IN PSYCHOTHERAPY
Ellis proposes a vigorously active and directive, unpampering approach to emotional problems
0–8065–0909–0 Lyle Stuart pb $9.95

• William Glasser
CONTROL THERAPY: A New Explanation of How We Control Our Lives
The connection between mental images and problems such as addiction
0–06–091292–8 Harper & Row pb $8.95

POSITIVE ADDICTION
The importance of positive-reinforcing activities
0–06–091249–9 Harper & Row pb $7.95

REALITY THERAPY
Rejecting Freud and the concept of "mental illness," Glasser contends that the "mentally ill" are those who are unable to satisfy their needs realistically because they deny the reality of the world around them
0–06–090414–3 Harper & Row pb $7.95

• Thomas S. Szasz
THE ETHICS OF PSYCHOANALYSIS
0–8156–0229–4 Syracuse pb $13.95

THE MANUFACTURE OF MADNESS
0–06–131984–8 Harper & Row pb $10.95

THE MYTH OF MENTAL ILLNESS: Foundations of a Theory of Personal Conduct
This famous and provocative attack on the psychiatric profession rejects the medical pretenses of psychotherapy and advocates an approach that grants the individual full autonomy
0–06–091151–4 Harper & Row pb $7.95

THE MYTH OF PSYCHOTHERAPY: Mental Healing as Religion, Rhetoric and Repression
0–8156–0223–5 Syracuse pb $12.95

PSYCHIATRIC JUSTICE
How psychiatric encroachments into the legal process violate the constitutional right to a fair and speedy trial
0–8156–0231–6 Syracuse pb $13.95

THE THEOLOGY OF MEDICINE
0–8156–0225–1 Syracuse pb $10.95

• Garth Wood
THE MYTH OF NEUROSIS: Overcoming the Illness Excuse
Contending that "neurosis" is a bogus classification, Wood argues for a therapy based on moral responsibility and common sense
0–06–091386–X Harper & Row pb $7.95

Gestalt Therapy

• Frederick S. Perls
EGO, HUNGER AND AGGRESSION: The Beginning of Gestalt Therapy
An introduction by the founder of Gestalt as a form of psychotherapy
0–394–70558–0 Random House pb $4.95

• Irving & Miriam Polster
GESTALT THERAPY INTEGRATED: Contours of Theory and Practice
0–394–71006–1 Random House pb $6.95

• Joseph Zinker
CREATIVE PROCESS IN GESTALT THERAPY
0–394–72567–0 Random House pb $8.95

Family Therapy

• Nathan W. Ackerman
THE PSYCHODYNAMICS OF FAMILY LIFE
The classic study by a founder of family therapy
0–465–09503–8 Basic Books pb $12.95

TREATING THE TROUBLED FAMILY
0–465–09522–4 Basic Books pb $10.95

• Jay Haley & Lynn Hoffman
TECHNIQUES OF FAMILY THERAPY
Conversations with family therapists
0–465–09512–7 Basic Books pb $10.95

• Augustus Y. Napier & Carl Whitaker
THE FAMILY CRUCIBLE: The Intense Experience of Family Therapy
0–06–091489–0 Harper & Row pb $8.95

Child Therapy

• Virginia M. Axline
PLAY THERAPY
0–345–30335–0 Ballantine pb $3.95

• Stanley I. & Nancy T. Greenspan
THE ESSENTIAL PARTNERSHIP: How Parents and Children Can Meet the Challenges of Childhood
0–670–81279–X Viking $18.95

• Stanley K. Turecki & Leslie Tonner
THE DIFFICULT CHILD
A guide for parents
0–553–05349–3 Bantam $17.95

• D.W. Winnicott
BABIES AND THEIR MOTHERS
From the object-relations perspective
Introduction by Dr. Benjamin Spock
0–201–16516–3 Addison-Wesley $14.50
0–201–07677–2 Addison-Wesley pb $8.75

THE PIGGLE
A detailed description of a single child therapy case
0–8236–4137–6 Intl Universities $26.00

➤ **FOR OVERSEAS ORDERING INFORMATION, SEE PAGE 1**

Sleep and Dreams

- Alexander Borbély
SECRETS OF SLEEP
The latest word on sleep, dreams, and
sleep disorders by one of the world's
leading sleep researchers
0–465–07593–2 Basic Books pb $8.95

- Robert Bosnak
A LITTLE COURSE IN DREAMS
This "basic handbook in Jungian
dreamwork" offers a short, lucid
introduction to remembering and
recording dreams, analyzing a written
dream text and studying a series of dreams
for underlying themes
Foreword by Denise Levertov
0–87773–451–8 Shambhala pb $8.95

- Stephen Brook, editor
THE OXFORD BOOK OF DREAMS
A selection of dream accounts drawn from
literature (Coleridge, Yeats, Kafka,
Tolstoy) and psychiatric case histories
0–19–282014–1 Oxford pb $7.95

- Ernest Hartmann
**THE NIGHTMARE: The Psychology and
Biology of Terrifying Dreams**
Who has nightmares, why, and what they
mean
0–465–05110–3 Basic Books pb $7.95

- James Hillman
THE DREAM AND THE UNDERWORLD
The relation between dreams and myths of
the underworld, from a Jungian
perspective
0–06–090682–0 Harper & Row pb $7.95

Goya's "The Sleep of Reason Produces Monsters," from Writers on Artists edited by Daniel Halpern (North Point)

Creativity

- Silvano Arieti
CREATIVITY: The Magic Synthesis
"The most important work on creativity
and its 'magic synthesis' that the world has
yet had"—Leon Edel
0–465–01443–7 Basic Books $19.95
0–465–01442–9 Basic Books pb $12.95

- Betty Edwards
**DRAWING ON THE RIGHT SIDE OF
THE BRAIN: A Course in Enhancing
Creativity and Artistic Confidence**
0–87477–088–2 St. Martin's pb $10.95

- Howard Gardner
**ART, MIND AND BRAIN: A Cognitive
Approach to Creativity**
An impressive synthesis, drawing on
Piaget, Chomsky, and Gombrich; contains
discussions of Mozart and children's art,
the effects of television on children, and
the separate functions of the two halves of
the brain
0–465–00445–8 Basic Books pb $13.95

- Willis Harman & Howard Rheingold
**HIGHER CREATIVITY: Liberating the
Unconscious for Breakthrough Insights**
0–874–77335–0 St. Martin's pb $8.95

- Anthony Storr
THE DYNAMICS OF CREATION
A consistently intelligent and sensible
discussion of the psychology of creativity;
examples discussed range from Einstein
and Newton to Chopin and Kafka
0–689–10455–3 Atheneum pb $7.95

SOLITUDE: A Return to the Self
How psychologists underestimated the
creative potential of solitude and the
possibilities it offers for self-fulfillment
0–02–931620–0 Free Press $17.95

> The creative person is constantly seeking
> to discover himself, to remodel his own
> identity, and to find meaning in the uni-
> verse by means of what he creates. He
> finds this to be a valuable integrating
> process which, like meditation or prayer,
> has little to do with other people, but
> which has its own separate validity. His
> most significant moments are those in
> which he attains some new insight, or
> makes some new discovery; and these
> moments are chiefly, if not invariably,
> those in which he is alone.
>
> Anthony Storr
> **SOLITUDE: A Return to the Self**
> 0–02–931620–0 Free Press $17.95

Art and Perception

- Rudolf Arnheim
**ART AND VISUAL PERCEPTION: A
Psychology of the Creative Eye**
Influenced by Gestalt psychology, Arnheim
finds the relation of artistic form and
perception in the operation of an ordering
intelligence
0–520–02613–6 California pb $12.95

Descartes' model of perception

VISUAL THINKING
To see is to think; why the act of
perception is as complex and cognitive as
any other mental act
0–520–01871–0 California pb $12.95

- E.H. Gombrich
**ART AND ILLUSION: A Study in the
Psychology of Pictorial Presentation**
A classic, groundbreaking examination of
the ideal of representation in western art
and the means used to achieve it; profusely
and brilliantly illustrated
0–691–09785–2 Princeton $70.00
0–691–01750–6 Princeton $14.50

- Herman L. Helmholtz
ON THE SENSATIONS OF TONE
0–486–60753–4 Dover pb $11.95

- D. Marr
VISION
Marr's work on perception is the most
important contribution to the field in the
last 50 years
0–7167–1567–8 Freeman pb $25.95

- Irvin Rock
PERCEPTION
0–7167–5001–5 Freeman $32.95

Language

▶ **See also Linguistics**

- Roger Brown
A FIRST LANGUAGE: The Early Stages
0–674–30325–3 Harvard $25.00
0–674–30326–1 Harvard pb $10.95

- Jerome S. Bruner
**CHILD'S TALK: Learning to Use
Language**
0–393–95345–9 Norton pb $4.95

- Noam Chomsky
REFLECTIONS ON LANGUAGE
An accessible work of the most important
contemporary theorist of linguistics
0–394–73123–9 Pantheon pb $8.95

• Kornei Chukovsky
FROM TWO TO FIVE
Edited and translated by Miriam Morton
0–520–00238–5 California pb $8.95

• Lev S. Vygotsky
MIND IN SOCIETY: The Development of Higher Psychological Processes
Edited by Michael Cole & others
0–674–57628–4 Harvard $17.00
0–674–57629–2 Harvard pb $7.95

THOUGHT AND LANGUAGE
Edited by Alexey Kozulin
0–262–72010–8 MIT pb $9.95

Memory

• Donald A. Norman
MEMORY AND ATTENTION: An Introduction to Human Information Processing
0–471–65137–0 John Wiley pb $27.95

• Israel Rosenfield
THE INVENTION OF MEMORY: A New View of the Brain
0–465–03592–2 Basic Books $18.95

• Oliver Sacks
AWAKENINGS
0–671–64834–9 Summit $18.95
0–525–48350–0 Dutton pb $8.95

Noncognitive Perspectives on the Mind

• Julian Jaynes
THE ORIGIN OF CONSCIOUSNESS IN THE BREAKDOWN OF THE BICAMERAL MIND
"When Julian Jaynes . . . speculates that until late in the second millennium BC men had no consciousness but were automatically obeying the voices of the gods, we are astounded but compelled to follow this remarkable thesis through all the corroborative evidence"—John Updike
0–395–32440–8 Houghton Mifflin pb $10.95

• Gordon Rattray Taylor
THE NATURAL HISTORY OF THE MIND
Rejecting the reductive view of the mind offered by neuropsychology, Taylor examines such phenomena as déjà vu, out-of-body experiences, psychosomatic illness, euphoria, dreams, telepathy, and mysticism
0–14–005703–X Penguin pb $7.95

Miscellaneous

• Ernest Becker
THE DENIAL OF DEATH
Pulitzer Prize-winning book which argues that the repression of the knowledge of our own mortality is the source of much of our behavior and the root of anxiety and mental illness
0–02–902380–7 Free Press pb $9.95

ESCAPE FROM EVIL
Becker's last work argues that man seeks victims and scapegoats to bolster his own fragile sense of mortality. "A profoundly nourishing book which is absolutely

essential to the understanding of our troubled times"—Anaïs Nin
0–02–902300–9 Free Press $14.95
0–02–902450–1 Free Press pb $10.95

• Philip Goldberg
THE INTUITIVE EDGE: Understanding Intuition and Applying It in Everyday Life
0–87477–344–X St. Martin's pb $8.95

• Daniel Goleman
VITAL LIES, SIMPLE TRUTHS: The Psychology of Self-Deception
How our lives are affected by our denial of painful insights and memories
0–671–62815–1 Simon & Schuster pb $9.95

• Robert Ornstein
THE PSYCHOLOGY OF CONSCIOUSNESS
A classic study of intuition, reason, and the improvement of mental functioning
0–14–022621–4 Penguin pb $7.95

• Carol Tavris
ANGER: The Misunderstood Emotion
"Beautifully clarifies the difference between moral, useful anger and mere incivility or self-gratifying bad temper"—Morton Hunt
0–671–49533–X Simon & Schuster pb $10.95

REFERENCE

• J.P. Chaplin
DICTIONARY OF PSYCHOLOGY
0–440–31925–0 Dell pb $5.95

• Otto & Miriam Ehrenberg
THE PSYCHOTHERAPY MAZE: A Consumer's Guide
A guide for those seeking therapy
0–671–62287–0 Simon & Schuster pb $6.95

• R.L. Gregory, editor
THE OXFORD COMPANION TO THE MIND
A fascinating reference work encompassing philosophical and psychological approaches to everything concerning the human mind, from perception to art to religion
0–19–866124–X Oxford $49.95

• Rom Harré & Roger Lamb
THE ENCYCLOPEDIC DICTIONARY OF PSYCHOLOGY
Scholarly articles on major concepts, approaches, and figures in all areas of psychology, with a particular stress on cognitive psychology, psycholinguistics, and neuropsychology
0–262–08135–0 MIT $95.00
0–87967–608–6 Dushkin pb $10.95

• Richie Herink, editor
THE PSYCHOTHERAPY HANDBOOK
A guide to 250 varieties of psychotherapy, written by authorities in each field
0–452–00832–8 Meridian pb $14.95

• Joel Kovel
A COMPLETE GUIDE TO THERAPY: From Psychoanalysis to Behavior Modification
"Can be recommended to everyone—from people looking for help with emotional problems to those with serious questions

about the entire business of emotional help"—*NY Times*
0–394–73336–3 Pantheon pb $7.95

• Armand M. Nicholi, editor
THE NEW HARVARD GUIDE TO PSYCHIATRY
0–674–61540–9 Harvard $45.00

• Arthur S. Reber, editor
THE PENGUIN DICTIONARY OF PSYCHOLOGY
A concisely written, comprehensive guide to important terms, concepts, and theories
0–14–051079–6 Penguin pb $8.95

• Benjamin B. Wolman
DICTIONARY OF BEHAVIORAL SCIENCE
A guide to concepts and major figures in all areas of psychology and related fields such as psychiatry, biochemistry, psychopharmacology, and neurology
0–12–762455–4 Academic $39.95

Sociology

▶ **See also Topics in American History**

CLASSICAL EUROPEAN SOCIOLOGY

While different historians trace the roots of sociological thought to the classical Greek tradition, the French Enlightenment, or the Scottish moralists of the 18th century, most see the early 19th century as the birth date of modern sociology. The discipline arose at a time when industrialism, urbanization, and modern capitalism required novel explanations. Its first major figures were Auguste Comte, the French thinker who gave the field its name, and the widely influential English writer Herbert Spencer. Founders of modern European sociology include the French scholar Emile Durkheim and the German social scientists Max Weber and Georg Simmel. Karl Marx did not see himself as a sociologist, since his works were not merely studies but contained a call to socialist action; however, his legacy has proved inspirational to generations of later scholars.

• Auguste Comte
AUGUST COMTE AND POSITIVISM: The Essential Writings
Edited by Gertrude Lenzer
0–226–47217–5 Chicago pb $20.00

• Emile Durkheim
Although Comte set the theoretical foundation for the discipline of sociology, it was Durkheim who carried out the first systematic studies on a wide range of social phenomena, notably religion and class.
SELECTED WRITINGS
Edited by Anthony Giddens
0–521–09712–6 Cambridge pb $14.95

Max Weber by David Levine

THE DIVISION OF LABOR IN SOCIETY
Translated by W.D. Hall
0–02–907950–0 Free Press $29.95
0–02–907960–8 Free Press pb $9.95

THE ELEMENTARY FORMS OF RELIGIOUS LIFE
Translated by Joseph W. Swain
0–02–908010–X Free Press pb $16.95

THE RULES OF SOCIOLOGICAL METHOD & Selected Texts on Sociology and Its Method
Translated by W.D. Halls
Edited by Steven Lukes
0–02–907930–6 Free Press $22.95
0–02–908490–3 Free Press pb $14.95

SUICIDE: A Study in Sociology
0–02–908650–7 Free Press $24.95
0–02–908660–4 Free Press pb $11.95

• Georg Simmel
Simmel's highly original work on money and on social groups, which influenced Weber and other German contemporaries, has been taken up in recent years by American social and economic theorists.

CONFLICT AND THE WEB OF GROUP AFFILIATIONS
0–02–928830–4 Free Press $18.95

GEORG SIMMEL ON INDIVIDUALITY AND SOCIAL FORMS
Edited by Donald N. Levine
0–226–75776–5 Chicago pb $15.00

THE SOCIOLOGY OF GEORG SIMMEL
0–02–928920–3 Free Press pb $12.95

• Herbert Spencer
HERBERT SPENCER ON SOCIAL EVOLUTION
Edited by J.D. Peel
0–226–76893–7 Chicago pb $15.00

• Max Weber
Weber saw culture and cultural values as determining forces in history, and his studies of the development of such modern social institutions as bureaucracy and capitalism were groundbreaking works of historical interpretation as well as of social theory.

FROM MAX WEBER: Essays in Sociology
Translated & edited by H.H. Gerth & C. Wright Mills
0–19–500462–0 Oxford pb $11.95

THE AGRARIAN SOCIOLOGY OF ANCIENT CIVILIZATIONS
Introduction by Richard Frank
0–86091–938–2 RC&H pb $18.95

ECONOMY AND SOCIETY
A 2-volume set
Edited by Guenther Roth & Claus Wittich
0–520–02824–4 California (set) $72.50
0–520–03500–3 California pb (set) $29.95

THE PROTESTANT ETHIC AND THE SPIRIT OF CAPITALISM
0–02–424860–6 Macmillan pb $15.50

THE RELIGION OF CHINA
0–02–934440–9 Free Press $19.95
0–02–934450–6 Free Press pb $16.95

THE THEORY OF SOCIAL AND ECONOMIC ORGANIZATION
Translated by Talcott Parsons
0–02–934930–3 Free Press pb $16.95

Histories, Commentaries, and Biographies

• Jeffrey C. Alexander
DURKHEIMIAN SOCIOLOGY: Cultural Studies
0–521–34622–3 Cambridge $39.50

NEOFUNCTIONALISM
0–8039–2496–8 Sage $29.95
0–8039–2497–6 Sage pb $14.95

THEORETICAL LOGIC IN SOCIOLOGY

Volume 1: Positivism, Presuppositions and Current Controversies
0–520–04480–0 California $32.00
0–520–05612–4 California pb $10.95

Volume 2: The Antinomies of Classical Thought—Marx and Durkheim
0–520–04481–9 California $45.00
0–520–05613–2 California pb $12.95

Volume 3: The Classical Attempt at Theoretical Synthesis—Max Weber
0–520–04482–7 California $35.00
0–520–05614–0 California pb $11.95

SOCIOLOGICAL THEORY SINCE WORLD WAR II: Twenty Lectures
0–231–06210–9 Columbia $35.00

• Anthony Giddens
THE CLASS STRUCTURE OF THE ADVANCED SOCIETIES
0–06–131845–0 Harper & Row pb $6.95

• Dirk Käsler
MAX WEBER: An Introduction to His Life and Work
0–226–42560–6 Chicago pb $14.95

• Steven Lukes
EMILE DURKHEIM: His Life and Work— A Historical and Critical Study
0–8047–1282–4 Stanford $55.00
0–8047–1283–2 Stanford pb $14.95

• Arthur Mitzman
THE IRON CAGE: A Historical Interpretation of Max Weber
0–87855–984–1 Transaction pb $15.95

SOCIOLOGY AND ESTRANGEMENT: Three Sociologists of Imperial Germany
0–88738–605–9 Transaction pb $17.95

SOCIOLOGY AFTER WEBER

Marxism and the Frankfurt School

A product of Weimar Germany, the Frankfurt School attempted to develop a flexible Marxist theory of the role of ideas and culture in modern societies. Influenced by Freud, Simmel, and other "bourgeois" thinkers, it gradually lost faith in the redeeming role of the working class and assumed a more despairing stance toward the modern world. Alluding to their grand bourgeois life style, Georg Lukács once remarked of the school's adherents that they were rather comfortably installed in the "Hotel Abyss." The members of the Frankfurt School produced their major work in exile in America and in postwar Germany.

► For other works on Marxism, see also Modern Political Thought & Economics

• Theodor Adorno
MINIMA MORALIA
A trenchant criticism of contemporary life, considered his most brilliant stylistic achievement
0–8446–6135–X Peter Smith pb $15.50

NEGATIVE DIALECTICS
Detailed critiques of Heidegger's *Being and Time*, Kant's *Critique of Practical Reason*, and Hegel's *Philosophy of Right*
0–8264–0132–5 Harper & Row pb $19.95

THE PHILOSOPHY OF MODERN MUSIC
Praises Arnold Schoenberg's music and gives a negative assessment of Igor Stravinsky's
0–8264–0138–4 Harper & Row pb $10.95

• Theodor Adorno & Max Horkheimer
THE DIALECTIC OF ENLIGHTENMENT
Translated by John Cumming
0–8264–0093–0 Harper & Row pb $16.95

• Theodor Adorno & others
THE AUTHORITARIAN PERSONALITY
0–393–30042–0 Norton pb $12.95

• Max Horkheimer
CRITICAL THEORY: Selected Essays
Translated by Matthew J. O'Connell
0–8164–9272–7 Harper & Row pb $12.95

THE ECLIPSE OF REASON
0–8264–0009–4 Harper & Row pb $11.95

• Leo Lowenthal
LITERATURE, POPULAR CULTURE, AND SOCIETY
0–87015–166–5 Pacific Books pb $6.95

- Herbert Marcuse
  EROS AND CIVILIZATION: A Philosophical Inquiry into Freud
  0–8070–1555–5 Harper & Row pb $10.95

  REASON AND REVOLUTION: Hegel and the Rise of Social Theory
  0–391–02999–1 Humanities pb $17.50

- Jay Martin
  THE DIALECTICAL IMAGINATION: A History of the Frankfurt School and the Institute for Social Research
  0–316–45830–9 Little, Brown pb $11.95

German Social Thought

After the Weimar period German thought laid particular stress on the sociology of knowledge. Following the lead of such predecessors as Karl Marx and Max Scheler, Karl Mannheim developed his distinctive approach to the study of ideas and intellectuals. Mannheim's work has been a focal point for scholars concerned with the relations between knowledge and society.

- Ralf Dahrendorf
  Dahrendorf is an outstanding conflict theorist associated with the London School of Economics.
  CLASS AND CONFLICT IN INDUSTRIAL SOCIETY
  0–8047–0560–7 Stanford $35.00
  0–8047–0561–5 Stanford pb $11.95

  ESSAYS IN THE THEORY OF SOCIETY
  0–8047–0286–1 Stanford $30.00
  0–8047–0288–8 Stanford pb $10.95

- Jürgen Habermas
  Habermas' special interest is a theory of social communication built upon the work of his teachers at the Frankfurt School. He is now recognized as a major figure in normative and analytical theory.
  KNOWLEDGE AND HUMAN INTERESTS
  Translated by Jeremy J. Shapiro
  0–8070–1541–5 Harper & Row pb $10.95

  LEGITIMATION CRISIS
  Translated by Thomas McCarthy
  0–8070–1521–0 Harper & Row pb $8.95

  THEORY AND PRACTICE
  Translated by John Viertel
  0–8070–1526–1 Harper & Row $35.00
  0–8070–1527–X Harper & Row pb $10.95

  THE THEORY OF COMMUNICATIVE ACTION

  Volume 1: Reason and the Rationalization of Society
  0–8070–1506–7 Harper & Row $40.00
  0–8070–1507–5 Harper & Row pb $14.95

  Volume 2: Lifeword and System—A Critique of Functional Reason
  Translated by Thomas McCarthy
  0–8070–1400–1 Harper & Row $37.50

- Niklas Luhmann
  Luhmann attempts to extend and develop the theoretical system of the American Talcott Parsons by stressing the need to look at organizational structure as the key to reducing modern complexity.

  THE DIFFERENTIATION OF SOCIETY
  Translated by Stephen Holmes & Charles Larmore
  0–231–04996–X Columbia $45.00

  A SOCIOLOGICAL THEORY OF LAW
  Translated by Elizabeth King-Utz & Martin Albrow
  0–7100–9747–6 RC&H $59.95

- Karl Mannheim
  CONSERVATISM: A Contribution to the Sociology of Knowledge
  Edited by David Kettler & others
  Translated by Elizabeth King
  0–7102–0338–1 RC&H $49.95

  IDEOLOGY AND UTOPIA: An Introduction to the Sociology of Knowledge
  Mannheim's major work
  0–15–643955–7 HBJ pb $9.95

Postwar French and British Thought

- Raymond Boudon
  THE UNINTENDED CONSEQUENCES OF SOCIAL ACTION
  0–312–83303–2 St. Martin's $27.50

- Pierre Bourdieu
  DISTINCTION: A Social Critique of the Judgement of Taste
  Translated by Richard Nice
  0–674–21280–0 Harvard $29.50
  0–674–21277–0 Harvard pb $12.95

  HOMO ACADEMICUS
  Translated by Peter Collier
  0–8047–1466–5 Stanford $29.50

- Pierre Bourdieu & Jean-Claude Passeron
  THE INHERITORS: French Students and Their Relation to Culture
  Translated by Richard Nice
  0–226–06739–4 Chicago $15.00

- Anthony Giddens
  CENTRAL PROBLEMS IN SOCIAL THEORY: Action, Structure and Contradiction in Social Analysis
  0–520–03972–6 California $42.50
  0–520–03975–0 California pb $12.95

  THE CONSTITUTION OF SOCIETY: Outline of the Theory of Structuration
  0–520–05292–7 California $45.00
  0–520–05728–7 California pb $12.95

  THE NATION-STATE AND VIOLENCE: A Contemporary Critique of Historical Materialism
  0–520–05635–3 California $42.50
  0–520–06039–3 California pb $12.95

- A.H. Halsey & Jerome Karabel, editors
  POWER AND IDEOLOGY IN EDUCATION
  0–19–502139–8 Oxford pb $18.95

- Charles Lemert, editor
  FRENCH SOCIOLOGY: Rupture and Renewal Since 1968
  0–231–04698–7 Columbia $45.00
  0–231–04699–5 Columbia pb $19.00

- Steven Lukes
  ESSAYS IN SOCIAL THEORY
  0–231–04450–X Columbia $30.00

From The City *by Franz Masereel (Schocken)*

AMERICAN SOCIOLOGICAL THEORY

Before 1900, American sociological theory remained largely dependent on European trends. But around the turn of the century more independent theorizing began to appear. Particularly noteworthy was the interactionist social psychology developed by the pragmatist philosopher and social psychologist George Herbert Mead and his close companion Charles Horton Cooley. The hallmark of their theory was a rejection of the Cartesian split between the ego and the surrounding world. Self and society, Cooley and Mead argued, are interdependent and develop simultaneously.

Early Founders

- Charles Horton Cooley
  HUMAN NATURE AND THE SOCIAL ORDER
  0–87855–918–3 Transaction $21.95

  SOCIAL ORGANIZATION: A Study of the Larger Mind
  0–87855–824–1 Transaction $23.95

- George Herbert Mead
  MIND, SELF, AND SOCIETY: From the Standpoint of a Social Behavorist
  Edited by Charles W. Morris
  0–226–51668–7 Chicago pb $8.95

- Thorstein Veblen
  ABSENTEE OWNERSHIP
  0–678–00048–4 Augustus Kelley $17.50

  IMPERIAL GERMANY AND THE INDUSTRIAL REVOLUTION
  Introduction by J. Dorfman
  0–678–00050–6 Augustus Kelley $35.00

  AN INQUIRY INTO THE NATURE OF PEACE
  0–678–00052–2 Augustus Kelley $29.50

🍎 IF YOU CAN'T FIND IT, LOOK IN THE INDEX

THE INSTINCT OF WORKMANSHIP
Introduction by J. Dorfman
0–678–00051–4 Augustus Kelley $35.00

THE THEORY OF THE LEISURE CLASS
Veblen's classic social critique was first published in 1899
0–678–00057–3 Augustus Kelley $37.50
0–14–005363–8 Penguin pb $4.95

Postwar American Theory

Well into the 1960s, American sociological theory was dominated by what is known as structural functionalism, or functional theory. First developed by Durkheim and elaborated by the anthropologists Malinowski and Radcliffe-Brown, its chief American proponent was Talcott Parsons. The theory stresses analogies of the biological body with the social body. More recent theories take a variety of approaches, from the phenomenology of Alfred Schutz to the independent stances of Peter Blau, Edward Shils, and Arthur Stinchcombe.

• Bernard Barber
THE LOGIC AND LIMITS OF TRUST
0–8135–0958–0 Rutgers $30.00
0–8135–1002–3 Rutgers pb $11.00

• Peter M. Blau
INEQUALITY AND HETEROGENEITY: A Primitive Theory of Social Structure
0–02–903660–7 Free Press $22.95

• William J. Goode
THE CELEBRATION OF HEROES: Prestige as a Social Control System
0–520–03602–6 California $40.00
0–520–03811–8 California pb $11.95

• Robert K. Merton
SOCIAL THEORY AND SOCIAL STRUCTURE
0–02–921130–1 Free Press $29.95

THE SOCIOLOGY OF SCIENCE: Theoretical and Empirical Investigations
Edited by Norman Storer
0–226–52092–7 Chicago pb $15.95

Talcott Parsons
TALCOTT PARSONS ON INSTITUTIONS AND SOCIAL EVOLUTION: Selected Writings
Edited by Leon H. Mayhew
0–226–64747–1 Chicago $30.00
0–226–64749–8 Chicago pb $12.50

ESSAYS ON SOCIOLOGICAL THEORY PURE AND APPLIED
0–02–924030–1 Free Press $16.95

THE SOCIAL SYSTEM
0–02–924190–1 Free Press pb $21.95

THE STRUCTURE OF SOCIAL ACTION
The book that introduced the great European sociologists—Durkheim, Weber, Pareto—to American readers

Volume 1
0–02–924240–1 Free Press pb $13.95

Volume 2
0–02–924250–9 Free Press pb $16.95

• Alfred Schutz
ALFRED SCHUTZ ON PHENOMENOLOGY AND SOCIAL RELATIONS: Selected Writings
Edited by Helmut R. Wagner
0–226–74153–2 Chicago pb $9.00

PHENOMENOLOGY OF THE SOCIAL WORLD
Translated by George Walsh & Frederick Lehnert
0–8101–0227–7 Northwestern $26.95
0–8101–0390–7 Northwestern pb $13.95

• Edward Shils
THE CALLING OF SOCIOLOGY & Other Essays on the Pursuit of Learning
0–226–75323–9 Chicago $27.50

• Arthur L. Stinchcombe
ECONOMIC SOCIOLOGY
0–12–671380–4 Academic $22.00
0–12–671382–0 Academic pb $17.95

STRATIFICATION AND ORGANIZATION: Selected Papers
0–521–32588–9 Cambridge $47.50

TOPICS IN MODERN SOCIOLOGY

▶ **See also American Labor and Radical Movements**

Microsociology

Georg Simmel initiated the study of microsociology through his fascinating analyses of the differences between dyads and triads, and between small and large groups. As he himself put it, he was attempting to develop a geometry of social life. Although Simmel had few disciples in his native Germany, American sociologists have taken up his challenge.

The late Erving Goffman was one of the rare authentic geniuses of American sociology. Although often impressionistic and loosely structured, his work has illuminated many aspects of interactive life: the dramatic nature of social interaction, role-playing in everyday life, and the management of the social self.

• Peter M. Blau
EXCHANGE AND POWER IN SOCIAL LIFE
0–88738–628–8 Transaction pb $18.95

• Harold Garfinkel
STUDIES IN ETHNOMETHODOLOGY
0–13–858381–1 Prentice-Hall $40.95
0–7456–0005–0 Blackwell pb $12.95

Erving Goffman
ASYLUMS: Essays on the Social Situation of Mental Patients and Other Inmates
0–385–00016–2 Doubleday pb $7.95

ENCOUNTERS: Two Studies in the Sociology of Interaction
0–02–344560–2 Macmillan pb $12.50

FRAME ANALYSIS: An Essay on the Organization of Experience
0–674–31656–8 Harvard $27.00
0–06–131961–9 Harper & Row pb $7.95

INTERACTION RITUAL: Essays on Face-to-Face Behavior
0–394–70631–5 Pantheon pb $6.50

THE PRESENTATION OF SELF IN EVERYDAY LIFE
0–87951–014–5 Viking $25.00
0–385–09402–7 Doubleday pb $5.95

RELATIONS IN PUBLIC
0–06–131957–0 Harper & Row pb $9.95

• George Homans
THE HUMAN GROUP
0–15–540375–3 HBJ $32.00

• David Sudnow
STUDIES IN SOCIAL INTERACTION
0–02–932360–6 Free Press $23.95

Historical Sociology

• Reinhard Bendix
KINGS OR PEOPLE: Power and the Mandate to Rule
0–520–04090–2 California pb $12.95

• Craig Calhoun
THE QUESTION OF CLASS STRUGGLE: The Social Foundation of Popular Radicalism During the Industrial Revolution
0–226–09090–6 Chicago $25.00
0–226–09091–4 Chicago pb $11.00

Barrington Moore, Jr.
INJUSTICE: The Social Basis of Obedience and Revolt
0–87332–114–6 Sharpe $24.50
0–87332–145–6 Sharpe pb $10.95

PRIVACY: Studies in Social and Cultural History
0–87332–266–5 Sharpe $29.95
0–87332–269–X Sharpe pb $12.95

THE SOCIAL ORIGINS OF DICTATORSHIP AND DEMOCRACY
0–8070–5075–X Harper & Row pb $12.95

• Theda Skocpol
STATES AND SOCIAL REVOLUTIONS
0–521–29499–1 Cambridge pb $13.95

• Theda Skocpol, editor
VISION AND METHOD IN HISTORICAL SOCIOLOGY
0–521–22928–6 Cambridge $44.50
0–521–29724–9 Cambridge pb $14.95

• Charles Tilly
THE CONTENTIOUS FRENCH: Four Centuries of Popular Struggle
0–674–16695–7 Harvard $25.00

FROM MOBILIZATION TO REVOLUTION
0–394–34941–5 Random House pb $22.50

• Charles Tilly & others
THE REBELLIOUS CENTURY: 1830-1930
0–674–74956–1 Harvard pb $10.95

• David Zaret
THE HEAVENLY CONTRACT: Ideology and Organization in Pre-Revolutionary Puritanism
0–226–97882–6 Chicago $22.50

Modern Political Sociology

▶ **See also Modern Political Thought & American Politics and Foreign Policy**

• Reinhard Bendix
NATION-BUILDING AND CITIZENSHIP: Studies of Our Changing Social Order
0–520–02761–2 California pb $12.95

WORK AND AUTHORITY IN INDUSTRY: Ideologies of Management in the Course of Industrialization
0–520–02628–4 California pb $12.95

• Angus Campbell & others
THE AMERICAN VOTER
0–226–09254–2 Chicago pb $27.00

• William Gamson & others
ENCOUNTERS WITH UNJUST AUTHORITY
0–256–02746–3 Dorsey pb $16.00

• Seymour Martin Lipset
CONSENSUS AND CONFLICT: Essays in Political Sociology
0–88738–051–4 Transaction $29.00
0–88738–608–3 Transaction pb $16.95

THE FIRST NEW NATION: The United States in Historical and Comparative Perspective
0–393–00911–4 Norton pb $8.95

POLITICAL MAN: The Social Bases of Politics
0–8018–2522–9 Johns Hopkins pb $12.95

• Seymour Martin Lipset & others
UNION DEMOCRACY: The Internal Politics of the International Typographical Union
0–02–919210–1 Free Press pb $15.95

• Steven Lukes
POLITICAL PARTIES: A Sociological Study of the Oligarchical Tendencies of Modern Democracy
0–8446–2582–5 Peter Smith $13.25

POWER
0–8147–5030–3 Columbia $30.00
0–8147–5031–1 Columbia pb $15.00

Class Structure

Class and class structure remained taboo subjects in American sociology until the 1930s. Since then, however, they have attracted many of the best sociologists in the country. Because Marxist and Neo-Marxist students of class are listed elsewhere, only non-Marxist work is listed here.

▶ **See also American People and Places**

• Peter Blau & Otis D. Duncan
THE AMERICAN OCCUPATIONAL STRUCTURE
0–02–903670–4 Free Press pb $14.95

• Paul Blumberg
INEQUALITY IN AN AGE OF DECLINE
0–19–502967–4 Oxford pb $9.95

C. Wright Mills (photo by Yaroslava Mills), from Democracy Is in the Streets *by James E. Miller (Simon & Schuster)*

• Richard F. Hamilton & James Wright
THE STATE OF THE MASSES
0–202–30324–1 Gruyter $42.95
0–202–30325–X Gruyter pb $19.95

• Ira Katznelson
CITY TRENCHES: Urban Politics and the Patterning of Class in the United States
0–226–42673–4 Chicago pb $12.00

• Melvin Kohn
CLASS AND CONFORMITY: A Study in Values
0–226–45030–9 Chicago pb $11.00

• Melvin Kohn & Carmi Schooler
WORK AND PERSONALITY: An Inquiry into the Impact of Social Stratification
0–89391–121–6 Ablex $45.00
0–89391–199–2 Ablex pb $27.50

• George Konrad & Ivan Szelenyi
THE INTELLECTUALS ON THE ROAD TO CLASS POWER: A Sociological Study of the Role of the Intelligentsia in Socialism
Translated by Andrew Arato & Richard E. Allen
0–15–177860–4 HBJ pb $10.00

• Gerhard Lenski
POWER AND PRIVILEGE: A Theory of Social Stratification
0–8078–4119–6 North Carolina pb $10.95

Critical Commentary on American Culture

In the immediate postwar years America bathed in warm feelings of self-satisfaction; but from the 1950s on, critical voices—radical, liberal, and conservative—were increasingly audible.

• Daniel Bell
THE COMING OF POST-INDUSTRIAL SOCIETY: A Venture in Social Forecasting
0–465–09713–8 Harper & Row $14.95

THE CULTURAL CONTRADICTIONS OF CAPITALISM
0–465–09727–8 Harper & Row $11.95

THE END OF IDEOLOGY
This influential book appeared in 1960
0–674–25229–2 Harvard $25.00
0–674–25230–6 Harvard pb $10.95

THE WINDING PASSAGE: Essays and Sociological Journeys, 1960-1980
0–8191–4142–9 University Press $36.00

• Robert N. Bellah & others
HABITS OF THE HEART: Individualism and Commitment in American Life
0–520–05388–5 California $22.50
0–06–097027–8 Harper & Row pb $8.95

• Alvin Gouldner
THE COMING CRISIS OF WESTERN SOCIOLOGY
0–380–01109–3 Avon pb $5.95

C. Wright Mills
Mills was a preeminent voice of radical dissent in the 1950s.
THE POWER ELITE
0–19–500020–X Oxford $39.95
0–19–500680–1 Oxford pb $9.95

THE SOCIOLOGICAL IMAGINATION
0–19–500751–4 Oxford pb $7.95

WHITE COLLAR: The American Middle Classes
0–19–500024–2 Oxford $27.95
0–19–500677–1 Oxford pb $10.95

• David Riesman
THE LONELY CROWD: A Study of the Changing American Character
Published in 1950, this famous book became a bestseller, popularizing the phrases "inner-directed" and "other-directed"
0–300–00193–2 Yale pb $12.95

Modernization and Developing Nations

In the first two decades after World War II, studies of modernization and the Third World tended to be written in an optimistic spirit, generally assuming that the newly independent countries would overcome their difficulties, catch up with the West, and participate in a worldwide tendency toward progress and development.

Since the mid-1960s, however, this approach has come under increasing attack. Neo-Marxists and other theorists hold that the Third World's progress is compromised by its post-colonial dependence. Such critics also stress that conservative forces in Third World nations are likely to remain major obstacles to future development.

• Samir Amin
UNEQUAL DEVELOPMENT: An Essay on the Social Formation of Peripheral Capitalism
Translated by Brian Pearce
0–85345–433–7 Monthly Review pb $8.50

• S.N. Eisenstadt
TRADITION, CHANGE AND MODERNITY
0–89874–642–6 Krieger $33.50

• Peter Evans
DEPENDENT DEVELOPMENT: The Alliance of Multinational, State, and Local Capital in Brazil
0–691–07606–5 Princeton $38.00
0–691–02185–6 Princeton pb $9.95

• André Gunder Frank
CAPITALISM AND UNDERDEVELOPMENT IN LATIN AMERICA
0–85345–093–5 Monthly Review pb $10.00

DEPENDENT ACCUMULATION AND UNDERDEVELOPMENT
0–85345–468–X Monthly Review $15.00
0–85345–492–2 Monthly Review pb $7.95

• Alex Inkeles
EXPLORING INDIVIDUAL MODERNITY
0–231–05442–4 Columbia $32.50
0–231–05443–2 Columbia pb $17.00

• Alex Inkeles & David Smith
BECOMING MODERN: Individual Change in Six Developing Countries
0–674–06376–7 Harvard pb $10.95

• Lloyd & Susanne Rudolph
THE MODERNITY OF TRADITION: Political Development in India
0–226–73137–5 Chicago pb $16.00

Ethnicity and Race Relations

▶ **See also African-American Studies & American People and Places**

• Molefi K. Asante
THE AFROCENTRIC IDEA
0–87722–483–8 Temple $24.95

• Harold Cruse
PLURAL BUT EQUAL: Blacks and Minorities in America's Plural Society
0–688–04486–7 Morrow $22.95

• Nathan Glazer & Daniel P. Moynihan
BEYOND THE MELTING POT: The Negroes, Puerto Ricans, Jews, Italians, and Irish of New York City
0–262–57022–X MIT pb $10.95

• Stanley Lieberson
A PIECE OF THE PIE: Black and White Immigrants Since 1880
0–520–04362–6 California pb $14.95

• Ivan H. Light
ETHNIC ENTERPRISE IN AMERICA: Business and Welfare among Chinese, Japanese, and Blacks
0–520–01738–2 California $33.00
0–520–02485–0 California pb $9.95

• Aldon D. Morris
THE ORIGINS OF THE CIVIL RIGHTS MOVEMENT: Black Communities Organizing for Change
0–02–922120–X Free Press $24.95
0–02–922130–7 Free Press pb $9.95

• Orlando Patterson
SLAVERY AND SOCIAL DEATH: A Comparative Study
0–674–81082–1 Harvard $34.50
0–674–81083–X Harvard pb $11.95

• Jonathan Rieder
CANARSIE: The Jews and Italians of Brooklyn Against Liberalism
Photographs by Laurence Levin
0–674–09360–7 Harvard $25.00
0–674–09361–5 Harvard pb $8.95

• Howard Schuman & others
RACIAL ATTITUDES IN AMERICA: Trends and Interpretations
0–674–74574–4 Harvard $25.00

• Bruce M. Wright
BLACK ROBES, WHITE JUSTICE
0–8184–0422–1 Lyle Stuart $15.95

Urban Sociology

This popular field of inquiry was largely developed at the University of Chicago in the first half of this century. The major impetus came from Robert Park (1864-1944), who wrote many articles and introductions to his students' work but no full-scale book. Louis Wirth's *The Ghetto* (1928), an exemplary study of the Jewish ghetto, was largely inspired by Park's principles. The study of urban phenomena, somewhat neglected in the postwar years, has recently undergone a vigorous revival.

• Claude S. Fischer
TO DWELL AMONG FRIENDS: Personal Networks in Town and City
0–226–25137–3 Chicago $35.00
0–226–25138–1 Chicago pb $15.95

THE URBAN EXPERIENCE
0–15–593498–8 HBJ pb $17.50

• Herbert J. Gans
THE LEVITTOWNERS: Ways of Life and Politics in a New Suburban Community
0–231–05570–6 Columbia $42.00
0–231–05571–4 Columbia pb $15.00

THE URBAN VILLAGERS
0–02–911250–8 Free Press $19.95
0–02–911240–0 Free Press pb $10.95

• J. Anthony Lukas
COMMON GROUND: A Turbulent Decade in the Lives of Three American Families
0–394–41150–1 Knopf $19.95
0–394–74616–3 Random House pb $9.95

Robert S. & Helen M. Lynd
MIDDLETOWN
0–15–659550–8 HBJ pb $10.95

MIDDLETOWN IN TRANSITION: A Study in Cultural Conflicts
0–15–659551–6 HBJ pb $9.95

• Murray Melbin
NIGHT AS FRONTIER: Colonizing the World After Dark
0–317–58085–X Free Press pb $9.95

• Robert E. Park & others
THE CITY
0–226–64611–4 Chicago pb $12.00

• Gideon Sjoberg
PREINDUSTRIAL CITY: Past and Present
0–02–928980–7 Free Press pb $12.95

• Gerald Suttles
THE SOCIAL CONSTRUCTION OF COMMUNITIES
0–226–78189–5 Chicago pb $8.00

THE SOCIAL ORDER OF THE SLUM
0–226–78192–5 Chicago pb $9.00

• Ferdinand Tönnies
FERDINAND TONNIES ON SOCIOLOGY: Pure, Applied and Empirical Selected Writings
Tönnies' classic *Community and Society* appeared in 1887, and he remained at the forefront of German sociology until the Nazis dismissed him from his teaching post in 1933
0–226–80608–1 Chicago pb $3.95

• Arthur J. Vidich & Joseph Bensman
SMALL TOWN IN MASS SOCIETY: Class, Power and Religion in a Rural Community
0–691–02807–9 Princeton pb $14.95

• William F. Whyte
STREET CORNER SOCIETY: The Social Structure of an Italian Slum
0–226–89542–4 Chicago $23.00
0–226–89543–2 Chicago pb $9.00

The city as depicted in F.W. Murnau's film "Sunrise" (1927), from The Parade's Gone By . . . *by Kevin Brownlow (California)*

- Louis Wirth
THE GHETTO
0–226–90252–8 Chicago pb $14.95

- Michael Young & Peter Willmott
FAMILY AND KINSHIP IN EAST LONDON
0–14–055216–2 Penguin pb $4.95

- Harvey Zorbaugh
THE GOLD COAST AND THE SLUM: A Sociological Study of Chicago's Near Northside
0–226–98945–3 Chicago pb $16.00

Crime, Delinquency, and Deviance

- Howard S. Becker
OUTSIDERS: Studies in the Sociology of Deviance
0–02–902200–2 Free Press $14.95
0–02–902140–5 Free Press pb $10.95

- Donald Black
THE BEHAVIOR OF LAW
0–12–102650–7 Academic $25.00
0–12–102652–3 Academic pb $19.50

- A.K. Cohen
DELINQUENT BOYS: The Culture of the Gang
0–02–905760–4 Free Press $19.95
0–02–905770–1 Free Press pb $10.95

- Kai T. Erikson
WAYWARD PURITANS: A Study in the Sociology of Deviance
0–02–332200–4 Macmillan pb $22.00

- Travis Hirschi
CAUSES OF DELINQUENCY
0–520–01901–6 California pb $11.95

- Robert K. Merton & Robert Nisbet, editors
CONTEMPORARY SOCIAL PROBLEMS
0–15–513793–X HBJ $32.00

- Charles Silberman
CRIMINAL VIOLENCE—CRIMINAL JUSTICE: Criminals, Police, Courts and Prisons in America
0–394–74147–1 Random House pb $7.95

- Edwin Sutherland
ON ANALYZING CRIME
Edited by Karl Schuessler
0–226–78056–2 Chicago pb $2.95

WHITE COLLAR CRIME: The Uncut Version
Edited with an introduction by Gilbert Geis & Colin Goff
0–300–02921–7 Yale $35.00
0–300–03318–4 Yale pb $11.95

- Gresham Sykes
CRIMINOLOGY
0–15–516120–2 HBJ $34.95

- James Q. Wilson
THINKING ABOUT CRIME
0–394–72917–X Random House pb $7.95

- James Q. Wilson & Richard J. Herrnstein
CRIME AND HUMAN NATURE
0–671–62810–0 Simon & Schuster pb $13.95

- Nicholas Abercrombie & others
THE PENGUIN DICTIONARY OF SOCIOLOGY
0–14–051184–9 Penguin pb $7.95

- Tom Bottomore & Robert Nisbet
A HISTORY OF SOCIOLOGICAL ANALYSIS
0–465–03024–6 Basic Books pb $11.95

- Lewis A. Coser
INTRODUCTION TO SOCIOLOGY
0–15–545914–7 HBJ pb $20.00

- Dushkin Publishing Group
ENCYCLOPEDIC DICTIONARY OF SOCIOLOGY
0–87967–607–8 Dushkin pb $16.95

- Louis Filler
DICTIONARY OF AMERICAN SOCIAL CHANGE
0–89874–242–0 Robert Krieger $19.50
0–89874–564–0 Robert Krieger pb $11.50

- Robert A. Nisbet
THE SOCIOLOGICAL TRADITION
0–465–07952–0 Harper & Row pb $8.95

- Max Weber
BASIC CONCEPTS IN SOCIOLOGY
Translated by H.P. Secher
0–8065–0304–1 Lyle Stuart pb $3.95

Economics

Economics is the only social science comparable to the natural sciences in rigor and explanatory method. Like the phenomena treated by physics or chemistry, the data of economic life are pervasive and seemingly explainable by common-sense procedures. But the explanations of economic data, like those of physical states, go deeper than the connecting of observable events and may involve sophisticated mathematics. Economists explain the magnitude of prices and incomes by seeking out forces that exceed the wills, and even the comprehension, of most retailers and employers.

Economists must be sensitive to the historical nature of their discipline. The laws of economics may be true everywhere at the present, but they have not always been true. Economic analysis has emerged under the particular conditions of capitalism, and its history is mainly a record of corrections imposed on pure theory by changes in economic life. Economists are thus forced to make an assumption that no physicist would accept: they assume that the laws of their science are subject to change by human action and can be useful in guiding that action. The potential for application that characterizes the best work in economics would also seem to be a timely requirement, as Americans enter the 1990s uncertain whether they are experiencing unprecedented prosperity or the early stages of decline and pauperization.

GENERAL WORKS AND HISTORIES OF ECONOMIC THOUGHT

- Christine & Dean S. Ammer
DICTIONARY OF BUSINESS AND ECONOMICS
Valuable for its emphasis on the application of economic ideas
0–02–900790–9 Free Press $34.95
0–02–901480–8 Free Press pb $18.95

- Mark Blaug
ECONOMIC THEORY IN RETROSPECT
Excellent history by a neoclassical economist, for advanced students. Illustrated
0–521–31644–8 Cambridge pb $21.95

- Phyllis Deane
THE EVOLUTION OF ECONOMIC IDEAS
A streamlined history of difficult concepts by an authority on the industrial revolution in Britain
0–521–29315–4 Cambridge pb $17.95

- Maurice Dobb
THEORIES OF VALUE AND DISTRIBUTION SINCE ADAM SMITH
Theories of value and price determination by a leading English Marxist
0–521–09936–6 Cambridge pb $18.95

- John Eatwell, Murray Milgate & Peter Newman, editors
THE NEW PALGRAVE: A Dictionary of Economics
The finest dictionary of economics and probably the best of all social-science reference works; available in a 4-volume set
0–935859–10–1 Stockton (set) $650.00

- John Kenneth Galbraith
ECONOMICS IN PERSPECTIVE: A Critical History
The author is characteristically opinionated and irreverent in this survey of economic doctrines
0–395–35572–9 Houghton Mifflin $19.95

Robert L. Heilbroner
BEHIND THE VEIL OF ECONOMICS: Essays in the Worldly Philosophy
0–393–02542–X Norton $17.95

THE WORLDLY PHILOSOPHERS: The Lives, Times and Ideas of the Great Economic Thinkers
A charming blend of biography and intellectual history that sets forth the major ideas without mathematical interference
0–671–63318–X Simon & Schuster pb $9.95

- Frank H. Knight
ON THE HISTORY AND METHOD OF ECONOMICS
0–226–44689–1 Chicago pb $2.95

- David W. Pearce, editor
THE MIT DICTIONARY OF MODERN ECONOMICS
0–262–16104–4 MIT $40.00
0–262–66059–8 MIT pb $12.50

- Paul Samuelson & William Nordhaus
ECONOMICS
The standard college text, written from the neoclassical standpoint but open to other approaches
0–07–054786–6 McGraw-Hill $39.95

- Joseph A. Schumpeter
A HISTORY OF ECONOMIC ANALYSIS
A history of economic thought that stands as a classic in its own right
0–19–504185–2 Oxford pb $24.95

- Harold S. Sloan & Arnold J. Zurcher
DICTIONARY OF ECONOMICS
0–06–463266–0 Harper & Row pb $7.95

- George Stigler
ESSAYS IN THE HISTORY OF ECONOMIC DOCTRINES
0–226–77434–1 Chicago pb $20.00

GREAT ECONOMISTS

Adam Smith

Adam Smith (1723-1790) was the father of economics. He originated the idea that the unrestricted operations of a free market have the status of natural law; he was the first to note the importance of the division of labor and to hypothesize that the value of a commodity corresponds to its labor input.

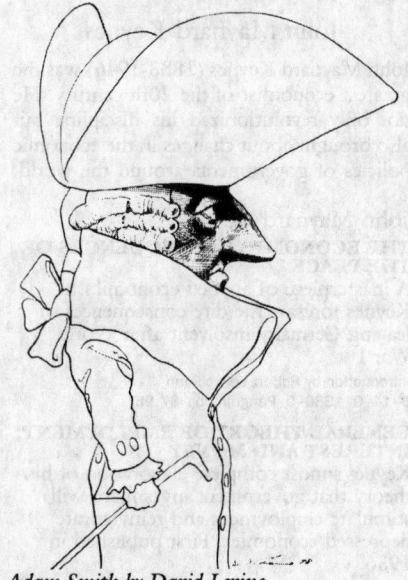

Adam Smith by David Levine

- Adam Smith
THE WEALTH OF NATIONS
First published in 1776
Edited by Andrew Skinner
0–14–043208–6 Penguin pb $4.95

- D.D. Raphael
ADAM SMITH
0–19–287558–2 Oxford pb $4.95

Thomas Malthus

Thomas Malthus (1766-1834) was an economic pessimist who argued that increases in population would nullify gains in productivity and lead to widespread impoverishment.

- Thomas Malthus
AN ESSAY ON THE PRINCIPLE OF POPULATION
Edited by Philip Appleman
0–393–04419–X Norton $10.00
0–393–09202–X Norton pb $7.95

David Ricardo

David Ricardo (1772-1823) deepened Smith's economic vision by emphasizing conditions of production, thus clearing the way for Marx.

- David Ricardo
WORKS AND CORRESPONDENCE OF DAVID RICARDO: Principles of Political Economy
Edited by Piero Sraffa
0–521–28505–4 Cambridge pb $19.95

John Stuart Mill

In *Principles of Political Economy* John Stuart Mill (1806-1873) offered a great synthesis of the major doctrines of classical political economy. He also introduced a supply-and-demand explanation of prices and an account of industrial growth that accommodated trade unionism.

- John Stuart Mill
PRINCIPLES OF POLITICAL ECONOMY
Edited by Donald Winch
0–14–043260–4 Penguin pb $6.95

Karl Marx

- Karl Marx
CAPITAL: A Critique of Political Economy
Marx (1818-1883) wrote his beautiful and uncompromising masterpiece over a period of 20 years while living in England. Its major arguments have been widely challenged but it remains the most influential single work in the social sciences, and is unmatched for its blending of data (drawn from the English society of its day) with pure theory

Volume 1
0–394–72657–X Random House pb $14.95

Volume 2
0–7178–0622–7 International pb $8.95

Volume 3
0–7178–0623–5 International pb $8.95

CONTRIBUTION TO THE CRITIQUE OF POLITICAL ECONOMY
0–8285–0021–5 Imported Publications pb $5.95

EARLY WRITINGS
Marx's mature economic doctrines were built upon his earlier philosophical preoccupations. This excellent selection includes the major writings of his youth
Translated by Rodney Livingston & Gregor Benton
Edited by Quintin Hoare
0–394–72005–9 Random House pb $8.95

THEORIES OF SURPLUS VALUE
Marx's review of the theories of his predecessors and contemporaries in the field of political economy; a 3-volume set
0–8464–0920–8 Beekman (set) $39.00

VALUE, PRICE AND PROFIT
Translated by Edward Aveling
Edited by Eleanor M. Aveling
0–88286–033–X Charles H. Kerr pb $2.50

● Paul A. Baran & Paul M. Sweezy
MONOPOLY CAPITAL: An Essay on the American Economic and Social Order
An influential updating and reapplication of Marxist theory
0–85345–073–0 Monthly Review pb $8.50

● Isaiah Berlin
KARL MARX: His Life and Environment
0–19–520052–7 Oxford pb $8.95

● G.A. Cohen
KARL MARX'S THEORY OF HISTORY: A Defence
Arguably the most important work on Marxian social philosophy published in English in the last 50 years
0–691–02008–6 Princeton pb $10.95

● Jon Elster
MAKING SENSE OF MARX
Attempts to clarify Marx's strong arguments and dismiss his weak ones
0–521–22896–4 Cambridge $57.50
0–521–29705–2 Cambridge pb $16.95

● Duncan K. Foley
UNDERSTANDING "CAPITAL"
A helpful guide to a forbidding work
0–674–92087–2 Harvard $21.00
0–674–92088–0 Harvard pb $9.50

● Robert L. Heilbroner
MARXISM: For and Against
A balanced appraisal of the economics of Marx and of his various disciples
0–393–95166–9 Norton pb $6.95

● Ronald L. Meek
STUDIES IN THE LABOR THEORY OF VALUE
Valuable for its historical discussion of the sources of Marx's theories
0–85345–428–0 Monthly Review pb $6.50

● Ernest Mandel
MARXIST ECONOMIC THEORY
A 2-volume set
Translated by Brian Pearce
0–85345–166–4 Monthly Review pb (set) $13.00

● I.I. Rubin
ESSAYS ON MARX'S THEORY OF VALUE
An outstanding explication of the labor theory of value, by an early Soviet economist
Translated by Milos Samardzija & Fredy Perlman
0–919618–11–1 Toronto $19.95
0–919618–18–9 Toronto pb $9.95

● Paul M. Sweezy
THE THEORY OF CAPITALIST DEVELOPMENT
A setting forth of Marxian concepts by the leading American Marxist economist of his time
0–85345–079–X Monthly Review pb $10.00

Alfred Marshall

Alfred Marshall (1842-1924) was the principal architect of neoclassical economics and the developer of the modern theory of marginal utility.

● Alfred Marshall
PRINCIPLES OF ECONOMICS
0–87991–051–8 Porcupine Press pb $19.95

Friedrich von Hayek

Friedrich von Hayek (1899-) offers the strongest modern argument for the political benefits of unregulated economic activity.

● Friedrich von Hayek
INDIVIDUALISM AND ECONOMIC ORDER
0–226–32089–8 Chicago pb $17.00

THE PURE THEORY OF CAPITAL
0–226–32081–2 Chicago pb $27.00

THE ROAD TO SERFDOM
An influential book first published in 1944
0–226–32077–4 Chicago $12.50
0–226–32078–2 Chicago pb $8.95

John Maynard Keynes

John Maynard Keynes (1883-1946) was the greatest economist of the 20th century. He not only revolutionized his discipline but also brought about changes in the economic policies of governments around the world.

● John Maynard Keynes
THE ECONOMIC CONSEQUENCES OF THE PEACE
A masterpiece of applied economics. Keynes foresaw the dire consequences of leaving Germany insolvent after World War I
Introduction by Robert Lekachman
0–14–011380–0 Penguin pb $7.95

GENERAL THEORY OF EMPLOYMENT, INTEREST AND MONEY
Keynes's most complete elaboration of his theory that government investment will stimulate employment and reinvigorate depressed economies. First published in 1936
0–15–634711–3 HBJ pb $7.95

John Maynard Keynes by David Low, from The Oxford Illustrated History of Britain *edited by Kenneth O. Morgan*

● Alvin H. Hansen
GUIDE TO KEYNES
Very helpful for beginners
0–07–026046–X McGraw-Hill pb $4.95

● Richard F. Kahn
THE MAKING OF KEYNES'S GENERAL THEORY
An exciting narrative of the stages by which Keynes developed his theory of government investment
0–521–25373–X Cambridge $34.50

● Milo Keynes, editor
ESSAYS ON JOHN MAYNARD KEYNES
0–521–29696–X Cambridge pb $15.95

● G.L. Shackle
THE YEARS OF HIGH THEORY: Invention and Tradition in Economic Thought, 1926-1939
A lively intellectual history of a rich period in the history of economics that began with the first serious assaults on Marshall's theory of competition and ended with the deification of Keynes
0–521–27478–8 Cambridge pb $17.95

● Robert Skidelsky
JOHN MAYNARD KEYNES: Hopes Betrayed, 1883-1920
A recent, well-received biography
0–670–40810–7 Viking $24.95

CONTEMPORARY ECONOMISTS

● Kenneth J. Arrow
Arrow's work in decision theory and in general equilibrium (a sophisticated upgrading of neoclassical value theory) has greatly influenced not only economics but also moral philosophy, political science, and sociology. His writings assume familiarity with logical symbolism and higher mathematics.

➤ **FOR OVERSEAS ORDERING INFORMATION, SEE PAGE 1**

COLLECTED PAPERS OF KENNETH J. ARROW

Volume 1: Social Choice and Justice
0–674–13760–4 Harvard $21.95

Volume 2: General Equilibrium
0–674–13761–2 Harvard $27.00

Volume 3: Individual Choice under Certainty and Uncertainty
0–674–13762–0 Harvard $27.00

Volume 4: The Economics of Information
0–674–13763–9 Harvard $25.00

Volume 5: Production and Capital
0–674–13777–9 Harvard $32.95

Volume 6: Applied Economics
0–674–13778–7 Harvard $25.00

● Gerard Debreu
THEORY OF VALUE: An Axiomatic Analysis of Economic Equilibrium
Debreu has developed, in partnership with Kenneth Arrow, the theory of general equilibrium; heavily mathematical
0–300–01559–3 Yale pb $7.95

● John Kenneth Galbraith
Galbraith has more in common with free-ranging social thinkers like Thorstein Veblen and C. Wright Mills than with most economists. *The Affluent Society* and *The New Industrial State* are influential works of social criticism.
THE AFFLUENT SOCIETY
0–395–36613–5 Houghton Mifflin $18.95
0–451–62394–0 NAL pb $4.95

BALANCING ACTS: Technology, Finance and the American Future
0–465–00584–5 Basic Books $21.95

ECONOMICS AND THE PUBLIC PURPOSE
0–452–00959–6 Penguin pb $4.95

THE NEW INDUSTRIAL STATE
0–395–38991–7 Houghton Mifflin $19.95
0–451–62511–0 NAL pb $4.95

● John Hicks
VALUE AND CAPITAL
In the 1930s Hicks developed ideas on equilibrium that today dominate economics; advanced mathematics
0–19–828269–9 Oxford $13.95

● Paul Samuelson
Samuelson is probably the most influential living American economist.
COLLECTED SCIENTIFIC PAPERS

Volume 1
0–262–19021–4 MIT $70.00

Volume 2
0–262–19022–2 MIT $65.00

Volume 3
0–262–19080–X MIT $65.00

Volume 4
0–262–19167–9 MIT $65.00

Volume 5
0–262–19251–9 MIT $65.00

ECONOMICS FROM THE HEART: A Samuelson Sampler
Edited by Maryann O. Keating
0–15–627551–1 HBJ pb $4.95

FOUNDATIONS OF ECONOMIC ANALYSIS
An important book, although heavily mathematical
0–674–31301–1 Harvard $30.00
0–674–31303–8 Harvard pb $9.95

● Robert M. Solow
GROWTH THEORY: An Exposition
Mathematical
0–19–505609–4 Oxford pb $10.95

● Piero Sraffa
PRODUCTION OF COMMODITIES BY MEANS OF COMMODITIES
One of the most important works in economic theory after Keynes's *General Theory*. Sraffa resurrects Ricardo's theory of value, adjusts it to meet current requirements for explanations of value and price, and reaches conclusions that are similar to the tenets of general equilibrium developed by Arrow and Debreu from a completely different tradition; moderately advanced mathematics
0–521–09969–2 Cambridge pb $16.95

● James Tobin
ASSET ACCUMULATION AND ECONOMIC ACTIVITY
0–262–80502–6 Chicago pb 5.95

ESSAYS IN ECONOMICS

Volume 1: Macroeconomics
0–226–20062–7 MIT $60.00

Volume 2: Consumption and Economics
0–262–20064–3 MIT $60.00

Volume 3: Theory and Policy
0–262–20042–2 MIT $60.00

POLICIES FOR PROSPERITY: Essays in Keynesian Mode
Edited by Peter Jackson
0–262–20066–X MIT $35.00

Milton Friedman and Monetarism

● Milton Friedman
CAPITALISM AND FREEDOM
Friedman is the principal exponent of monetarism, the view that the quantity of money is the determining factor in economic life
0–226–26401–7 Chicago pb $7.95

ESSAYS IN POSITIVE ECONOMICS
0–226–26403–3 Chicago pb $9.00

● Milton & Rose Friedman
FREE TO CHOOSE: A Personal Statement
The bestselling polemic for a free-market society, from the conservative economist and his wife
0–380–52548–8 Avon pb $4.95

● Nicholas Kaldor
THE SCOURGE OF MONETARISM
0–19–877248–3 Oxford pb $8.95

● Thomas Mayer
THE STRUCTURE OF MONETARISM
0–393–09045–0 Norton $11.95

● Wlodzimierz Brus
SOCIALIST OWNERSHIP AND POLITICAL SYSTEMS UNDER SOCIALISM
0–7100–8247–9 Methuen $26.95

● Maurice Dobb
WELFARE ECONOMICS AND THE ELEMENTS OF SOCIALISM
0–521–07462–2 Cambridge $49.50
0–521–09937–4 Cambridge pb $17.95

● Michael Ellman
SOCIALIST PLANNING
0–521–35866–3 Cambridge pb $19.95

● Michael Kalecki
SELECTED ESSAYS ON THE ECONOMIC GROWTH OF THE SOCIALIST AND MIXED ECONOMY
Kalecki independently developed ideas on government spending that were virtually identical with Keynes's
0–521–08447–4 Cambridge pb $12.50

● David Lane
THE END OF SOCIAL INEQUALITY: Class, Status and Power Under State Socialism
0–04–323024–5 Unwin Hyman $27.95
0–04–323025–3 Unwin Hyman pb $9.95

● Alec Nove
THE ECONOMICS OF FEASIBLE SOCIALISM
0–04–335048–8 Unwin Hyman $34.95

● Joseph A. Schumpeter
CAPITALISM, SOCIALISM AND DEMOCRACY
In this famous book, first published in 1942, Schumpeter predicts that capitalism will be crippled by its own achievements and will naturally evolve into socialism
0–8446–6027–2 Peter Smith $17.95

● Paul M. Sweezy
POST-REVOLUTIONARY SOCIETY: Essays
0–85345–550–3 Monthly Review $12.50
0–85345–551–1 Monthly Review pb $5.95

● Kenneth E. Boulding & Tapan Mukerjee, editors
ECONOMIC IMPERIALISM: A Book of Readings
0–472–16830–4 Michigan pb $10.00

● J.A. Hobson
IMPERIALISM
Hobson's book, published in 1902, was the first attempt to define imperialism in economic instead of political terms, and it greatly influenced Lenin
0–472–06103–8 Michigan pb $11.95

● V.G. Kiernan
MARXISM AND IMPERIALISM
0–312–51835–8 St. Martin's $25.00

- V.I. Lenin
IMPERIALISM: The Highest Stage of Capitalism
Although schematic and outdated, it remains interesting for its application of the concept of monopoly to Marxian economics
0–7178–0098–9 International pb $2.95

- Harry Magdoff
THE AGE OF IMPERIALISM
0–85345–101–X Monthly Review pb $7.50

- Wolfgang J. Mommsen
THEORIES OF IMPERIALISM
Translated by P.S. Falla
0–226–53396–4 Chicago pb $8.95

- Robert I. Rhodes, editor
IMPERIALISM AND UNDERDEVELOPMENT: A Reader
0–85345–155–9 Monthly Review pb $7.95

- Joseph A. Schumpeter
IMPERIALISM AND SOCIAL CLASSES
Translated by Heinz Norden
Edited with an introduction by Paul M. Sweezy
0–87991–256–1 Porcupine pb $19.95

ECONOMIC DEVELOPMENT AND INTERNATIONAL TRADE

- Jagdish Bhagwati
PROTECTIONISM
0–262–02282–6 MIT $16.95

- Richard E. Caves
MULTINATIONAL ENTERPRISE AND ECONOMIC GROWTH
0–521–27115–0 Cambridge pb $14.95

- W.M. Corden
INFLATION, EXCHANGE RATES, AND THE WORLD ECONOMY: Lectures on International Monetary Economics
0–226–11580–1 Chicago $22.50
0–226–11582–8 Chicago pb $12.95

- Edwin Denison
WHY GROWTH RATES DIFFER: Experience in Nine Western Countries
0–8157–1805–5 Brookings pb $17.95

- André G. Frank
DEPENDENT ACCUMULATION AND UNDERDEVELOPMENT
0–85345–492–2 Monthly Review pb $7.95

- Alexander Gerschenkron
ECONOMIC BACKWARDNESS IN HISTORICAL PERSPECTIVE: A Book of Essays
0–674–22600–3 Harvard $32.00

- Albert O. Hirschman
THE PASSIONS AND THE INTERESTS: Political Arguments for Capitalism Before Its Triumph
0–691–00357–2 Princeton pb $8.95

- Simon Kuznets
ECONOMIC GROWTH OF NATIONS
0–674–22780–8 Harvard $25.00

GROWTH, POPULATION AND INCOME DISTRIBUTION
0–393–95061–1 Norton $19.95

- W. Arthur Lewis
THE THEORY OF ECONOMIC GROWTH: An Introduction
Advances a controversial thesis on rates of development in backward economies
0–312–79775–3 St. Martin's $30.00

- Staffan B. Linder
THE PACIFIC CENTURY: Economic and Political Consequences of Asian-Pacific Dynamism
0–8047–1294–8 Stanford $22.95
0–8047–1305–7 Stanford pb $7.95

- Ian M. Little
ECONOMIC DEVELOPMENT: Theory, Policy, and International Relations
0–465–01793–2 Basic Books pb $14.95

- Gerald M. Meier & Dudley Seers, editors
PIONEERS IN DEVELOPMENT
0–19–520479–4 Oxford pb $12.95

- Mancur Olson
THE RISE AND DECLINE OF NATIONS
0–300–02307–3 Yale $30.00
0–300–03079–7 Yale pb $10.95

- A.K. Sen
EMPLOYMENT, TECHNOLOGY, AND DEVELOPMENT
0–19–877053–7 Oxford pb $12.95

POVERTY AND FAMILIES: An Essay on Entitlement and Deprivation
0–19–828463–2 Oxford pb $12.95

RESOURCES, VALUES, AND DEVELOPMENT
0–674–76525–7 Harvard $32.50

THE STANDARD OF LIVING
0–521–32101–8 Cambridge $29.95

- Robert Triffin
GOLD AND THE DOLLAR CRISIS
0–8240–5258–7 Garland $29.00

POLITICS AND THE INTERNATIONAL ECONOMY

- Benjamin J. Cohen
IN WHOSE INTEREST?: International Banking and American Foreign Policy
0–300–03614–0 Yale $27.50

- Alfred E. Eckes, Jr.
A SEARCH FOR SOLVENCY: Bretton Woods and the International Monetary System, 1941-1971
0–292–70712–6 Texas $20.00

- Charles Kindleberger
ECONOMIC RESPONSE: Comparative Studies in Trade, Finance, and Growth
0–674–23025–6 Harvard $24.50

MANIAS, PANICS AND CRASHES: A History of Financial Crises
0–8446–6209–7 Peter Smith $17.00
0–465–04402–6 Basic Books pb $9.95

POWER AND MONEY: The Politics of International Economics and the Economics of International Politics
0–465–06135–4 Basic Books pb $4.95

- Anthony Sampson
THE MONEY LENDERS: The People and Politics of International Banking
0–14–006485–0 Penguin pb $8.95

- W.M. Scammell
THE INTERNATIONAL ECONOMY SINCE 1945
0–312–42192–3 St. Martin's $27.50
0–312–42193–1 St. Martin's pb $12.95

- Robert Solomon
THE INTERNATIONAL MONETARY SYSTEM
0–06–015004–1 Harper & Row $26.00

- Herman Van der Wee
PROSPERITY AND UPHEAVAL: The World Economy, 1945-1980
0–520–05709–0 California $40.00

THE AMERICAN ECONOMY TODAY

- Barry Bluestone & Bennett Harrison
THE DEINDUSTRIALIZATION OF AMERICA
0–465–01590–5 Basic Books $19.95
0–465–01592–1 Basic Books pb $10.95

- Stanley Collender
THE GUIDE TO THE FEDERAL BUDGET, FISCAL 1989
By the director of Federal Budget Policy for Touche Ross & Co.
0–87766–416–1 Urban Institute Press pb $12.95

- Lloyd Jeffry Dumas
THE OVERBURDENED ECONOMY
"Lloyd Dumas has challenged one of the implicit assumptions of the Keynesian Revolution and the national income statistics that embodied it: the assumption that all activity which is paid for must be productive"—Kenneth Boulding, former president of the American Economics Association
0–520–06169–1 California pb $8.95

- Robert Eisner
HOW REAL IS THE FEDERAL DEFICIT?
Eisner argues that fear of the deficit is exaggerated
0–02–909430–5 Free Press $18.95

- Martin Feldstein, editor
THE AMERICAN ECONOMY IN TRANSITION
Twenty-nine contributors interpret the era of inflation and low productivity that followed the postwar boom; contributors include Richard Freeman, John T. Dunlop, Alan S. Blinder, Irving Kristol, James R. Schlesinger, and Paul Samuelson
0–226–24082–7 Chicago pb $17.95

Benjamin Friedman
DAY OF RECKONING
The best account of America's new
status as a debtor nation
0–394–56553–3 Random House $19.95

• Victor R. Fuchs
**HOW WE LIVE: An Economic Perspective
on Americans from Birth to Death**
Explores the intersection of economic
conditions with stages in the life cycle
0–674–41226–5 Harvard pb $7.95

• Norman J. Glickman & Douglas P.
Woodward
**THE NEW COMPETITORS: How Foreign
Investment is Changing the U.S. Economy**
0–465–05005–0 Basic Books $19.95

• Joel Kurtzman
**THE DECLINE AND CRASH OF THE
AMERICAN ECONOMY**
Argues that the loss of export markets, the
nation's deep debt, and other factors signal
an impending collapse
0–393–02523–3 Norton $18.95

• Robert Z. Lawrence
CAN AMERICA COMPETE?
0–8157–5176–1 Brookings $26.95
0–8157–5175–3 Brookings pb $9.95

• Harold Lever & Christopher Huhne
**DEBT AND DANGER: The World
Financial Crisis**
0–87113–067–X Atlantic Monthly $16.95

• George C. Lodge
THE AMERICAN DISEASE
0–394–52903–0 Knopf $18.95

• Ira C. Magaziner & Mark Patinkin
**THE SILENT WAR: America's Struggle
for World Markets**
0–394–56979–2 Random House $19.95

• Ira C. Magaziner & Robert B. Reich
**MINDING AMERICA'S BUSINESS: The
Decline and Rise of the American Economy**
0–394–71538–1 Random House pb $5.95

• John H. Makin
**THE GLOBAL DEBT CRISIS: America's
Growing Involvement**
0–465–02682–6 Basic Books pb $9.95

• Alfred L. Malabre, Jr.
**BEYOND OUR MEANS: How America's
Long Years of Debt, Deficits and Reckless
Borrowing Now Threaten to Overwhelm Us**
The *Wall Street Journal* economics editor
on the consequences of over-consumption
0–394–54345–9 Random House $17.95

**UNDERSTANDING THE NEW
ECONOMY**
1–55623–117–2 Dow Jones-Irwin $19.95

• Lawrence Malkin
THE NATIONAL DEBT
0–8050–0382–7 Henry Holt $17.95

• Hyman P. Minsky
**STABILIZING AN UNSTABLE
ECONOMY**
0–300–03386–9 Yale $35.00
0–300–04000–8 Yale pb $14.95

• William A. Niskanen
**REAGANOMICS: An Insider's Account of
the Policies and the People**
By a former member of the Council of
Economic Advisers
0–19–505394–X Oxford $22.95

• David Obey & Paul Sarbanes, editors
**THE CHANGING AMERICAN
ECONOMY**
Essays from James Tobin, Felix Rohatyn,
Robert Kuttner, Lester Thurow, Kevin
Phillips, and others
0–631–15395–0 Blackwell pb $12.95

• Adam Smith
THE ROARING '80s
0–671–44788–2 Simon & Schuster $18.95

• Lester C. Thurow
**THE ZERO-SUM SOCIETY: Distribution
and the Possibilities for Economic Change**
Examines the effect of economic stagnation
on the distribution of shares
0–465–09384–1 Basic Books $14.50
0–14–005807–9 Penguin pb $6.95

**THE ZERO-SUM SOLUTION: Building a
World Class American Economy**
0–671–55232–5 Simon & Schuster $18.95
0–671–62814–3 Simon & Schuster pb $9.95

• Howard M. Watchel
**THE MONEY MANDARINS: The Making
of a New Supranational Economic Order**
0–394–54299–1 Random House pb $8.95

• Murray Weidenbaum
**RENDEZVOUS WITH REALITY: The
American Economy After Reagan**
0–465–06914–2 Basic Books $19.95

Military Spending

• Mary Kaldor
THE BAROQUE ARSENAL
0–8090–1501–3 Hill & Wang pb $7.25

• Wassily Leontief & Faye Duchin
**MILITARY SPENDING: Facts and
Figures, Worldwide Implications, and
Future Outlook**
0–19–503191–1 Oxford $35.00

• Seymour Melman
THE PERMANENT WAR ECONOMY
0–671–60643–3 Simon & Schuster pb $9.95

PROFITS WITHOUT PRODUCTION
0–394–51895–0 Knopf $24.95
0–8122–1258–4 Pennsylvania pb $16.95

SPECIAL TOPICS

Microeconomics

• William J. Baumol & Alan S. Blinder
MICROECONOMICS
0–15–518854–2 HBJ pb $26.95

• Edward H. Chamberlin
**THEORY OF MONOPOLISTIC
COMPETITION: A Re-Orientation of the
Theory of Value**
0–674–88125–7 Harvard $27.50

• Joan Robinson
**ECONOMICS OF IMPERFECT
COMPETITION**
0–312–23345–0 St. Martin's pb $12.00

Discrimination, Education, and Income

• Gary S. Becker
**THE ECONOMICS OF
DISCRIMINATION**
0–226–04116–6 Chicago pb $6.00

• Barbara R. Bergmann
**THE ECONOMIC EMERGENCE OF
WOMEN**
0–465–01796–7 Basic Books $19.95
0–465–01797–5 Basic Books pb $10.95

• Alan S. Blinder
**HARD HEADS, SOFT HEARTS: Tough-
Minded Economics for a Just Society**
0–201–115011–2 Addison-Wesley $17.95

• Christopher Jencks
**INEQUALITY: A Reassessment of the
Effect of Family and Schooling in America**
0–06–131960–0 Harper & Row pb $5.95

• Jacob Mincer
**SCHOOLING, EXPERIENCE, AND
EARNINGS**
0–87014–265–8 Columbia $10.00

• Gunnar Myrdal
AN AMERICAN DILEMMA
A classic diagnosis of the condition of
black Americans

Volume 1
0–394–73042–9 Pantheon pb $5.95

Volume 2
0–394–73043–7 Pantheon pb $5.95

• Michael Reich
**RACIAL INEQUALITY: A Political-
Economic Analysis**
0–691–04227–6 Princeton $30.50

• Theodore W. Schultz
**INVESTING IN PEOPLE: The Economics
of Population Quality**
Foreword by John M. Letiche
0–520–04437–1 California $16.50
0–520–04787–7 California pb $6.95

- Thomas Sowell
THE ECONOMICS AND POLITICS OF RACE: An International Perspective
Sowell is America's leading black conservative thinker
0–688–01891–2 Morrow $15.95
0–688–04832–3 Morrow pb $6.95

MARKETS AND MINORITIES
0–465–04399–2 Basic Books pb $9.95

- Lester C. Thurow
GENERATING INEQUALITY: Mechanisms of Distribution in the U.S. Economy
0–465–02670–2 Basic Books $15.95
0–465–02668–0 Basic Books pb $8.95

Urban Economics

- David M. Gordon
PROBLEMS IN POLITICAL ECONOMY: An Urban Perspective
0–669–92841–0 Heath pb $20.95

- James Heilbrun
URBAN ECONOMICS AND PUBLIC POLICY
0–312–83442–X St. Martin's pb $34.95

Jane Jacobs
CITIES AND THE WEALTH OF NATIONS: Principles of Economic Life
Jacobs' fullest and most recent statement of her view that cities are the primary engine of economic development
0–394–72911–0 Random House pb $4.95

THE DEATH AND LIFE OF GREAT AMERICAN CITIES
Jacobs' classic account of the assault on city neighborhoods by urban renewal
0–394–70241–7 Random House pb $6.95

THE ECONOMY OF CITIES
An earlier and widely influential argument that economic life begins in cities
0–394–70584–X Random House pb $5.95

- William K. Tabb
THE LONG DEFAULT: New York City and the Urban Fiscal Crisis
0–85345–571–6 Monthly Review $16.00
0–85345–572–4 Monthly Review pb $6.95

The Economics of Energy and the Environment

- Cyrus Bina
THE ECONOMICS OF OIL CRISIS: Theories of Oil Crisis, Oil Rent and Internationalization of Capital in the Oil Industry
0–312–23661–1 St. Martin's $29.95

- Fred Hirsch
SOCIAL LIMITS TO GROWTH
0–674–81365–0 Harvard $16.00
0–674–81366–9 Harvard pb $7.95

- Edwin S. Mills & Philip E. Graves
THE ECONOMICS OF ENVIRONMENTAL QUALITY
0–393–95270–3 Norton $19.95

Social Choice and Game Theory

- Kenneth J. Arrow
SOCIAL CHOICE AND INDIVIDUAL VALUES
A classic by the American Nobel laureate
0–300–01364–7 Yale pb $7.95

- Robert Axelrod
THE EVOLUTION OF COOPERATION
0–465–02122–0 Basic Books $17.95
0–465–02121–2 Basic Books pb $8.95

- James Buchanan & Gordon Tullock
THE CALCULUS OF CONSENT
0–472–06100–3 Michigan pb $12.95

- Robert H. Frank
PASSIONS WITHIN REASON
0–393–02604–3 Norton $19.95

- Oslxan Morgenstern & John Von Neumann
GAME THEORY AND ECONOMIC BEHAVIOR
Heavily mathematical
0–691–00362–9 Princeton pb $22.50

- Mancur Olson
THE LOGIC OF COLLECTIVE ACTION: Public Goods and the Theory of Groups
0–674–03751–0 Harvard pb $6.95

- Thomas C. Schelling
STRATEGY OF CONFLICT
0–674–84031–3 Harvard pb $8.95

- A.K. Sen
COLLECTIVE CHOICE AND SOCIAL WELFARE
0–444–85127–5 Elsevier $45.00

Business, Industry, and Finance

The twin economic challenges of the 1980s—global competition and rapid technological change—have forced painful restructuring in companies across the United States. But our deep-seated economic problems have given rise to at least one growth industry: business books. What follows is not an exhaustive catalog of management fads and fixes to have appeared on bookshelves over the last ten years. Rather, the titles have been selected for their enduring value, originality, or wide popularity.

▶ **See also Topics in American Studies**

▶ See also Topics in American Studies

MANAGEMENT: Theory and Practice

- Kenneth R. Andrews
THE CONCEPT OF CORPORATE STRATEGY
A thoughtful overview of the responsibilities of top executives and the factors that shape competitive success. Required reading at most business schools
0–87094–983–7 Dow Jones-Irwin $25.00
0–256–03629–2 Irwin pb $15.95

- Kenneth Blanchard & Spencer Johnson
THE ONE MINUTE MANAGER
Business advice by parable
0–688–02632–X Morrow $15.00
0–425–07757–8 Berkley pb $7.95

- Alfred D. Chandler, Jr.
THE VISIBLE HAND: The Managerial Revolution in American Business
A Pulitzer prize-winning history of American business
0–674–94051–2 Harvard $32.00
0–674–94052–0 Harvard pb $12.95

- Peter F. Drucker
THE CONCEPT OF THE CORPORATION
Drucker's classic study of the management structure of General Motors, and the relevance of GM's organization for other large companies
0–451–62197–2 NAL pb $3.95

INNOVATION AND ENTREPRENEURSHIP: Practice and Principles
The world's leading student of big business turns his attention to the new entrepreneurial forces fueling economic growth
0–06–015428–4 Harper & Row $19.95
0–06–091360–6 Harper & Row pb $9.95

MANAGEMENT: Tasks, Responsibilities, Practices
A long book full of concise, engaging essays that address the question, "What does the manager have to know, or at least have to understand, to be equal to his task?"
0–06–011092–9 Harper & Row $24.50
0–06–091207–3 Harper & Row pb $11.95

- Richard N. Foster
INNOVATION—THE ATTACKER'S ADVANTAGE
A leading international consultant focuses on technology as a competitive weapon and offers lessons on managing production innovation
0–671–62250–1 Summit $19.95
0–671–64224–3 Summit pb $8.95

- Theodore Levitt
THE MARKETING IMAGINATION
A collection of influential essays by the most highly acclaimed marketing scholar of the last 30 years
0–02–92980–7 Free Press $22.95
0–02–91980–8 Free Press pb $8.95

The Parisian Stock Exchange (1856), from Daumier *edited by Charles F. Ramus (Dover)*

Tom Peters & Robert Waterman
IN SEARCH OF EXCELLENCE: Lessons from America's Best-Run Companies
The book that triggered the boom in management advice. It remains without peer for its seriousness of purpose, extensive research, and common-sense wisdom
0–317–17653–6 Macmillan pb $19.95

Tom Peters & Nancy Austin
A PASSION FOR EXCELLENCE: The Leadership Difference
More lessons for corporate success, this time with a focus on individual management champions
0–394–54484–6 Random House $19.95
0–446–38348–1 Warner pb $10.95

- Tom Peters
THRIVING ON CHAOS: Handbook for A Management Revolution
The co-author of *In Search of Excellence* reconsiders and declares, "There are no excellent companies." Still, the classic Peters formula—valuable insights and advice packaged in easy-to-digest lists
0–394–56784–6 Knopf $19.95
0–06–097184–3 Harper & Row pb $10.95

- Michael E. Porter
COMPETITIVE STRATEGY: Techniques for Analyzing Industries and Competitors
The bible of corporate strategy. Porter explains how to use his "five forces" model to understand competition within industries
0–02–925360–8 Free Press $25.95

COMPETITIVE ADVANTAGE: Creating and Sustaining Superior Performance
The celebrated Harvard Business School professor follows up his book on industry analysis with a study of the "value chain" and how companies build competitive strength
0–02–925090–0 Free Press $27.95

- Robert Townsend
FURTHER UP THE ORGANIZATION
Irreverent insights on life in the executive suite from a former CEO. Townsend describes management consultants as "people who borrow your watch to tell you what time it is and then walk off with it"
0–394–53578–2 Knopf $19.95
0–06–097136–3 Harper & Row pb $7.95

- Robert Waterman
THE RENEWAL FACTOR: How the Best Companies Get and Keep the Competitive Edge
The "other" co-author of *In Search of Excellence* describes eight strategies for maintaining a company's competitive vigor
0–553–05226–8 Bantam $19.95
0–553–27304–3 Bantam pb $4.95

- Shoshana Zuboff
IN THE AGE OF THE SMART MACHINE: The Future of Work and Power
A dense but pioneering analysis of how information technology changes the structure of companies and the relationship between management and labor
0–465–03212–5 Basic Books $19.95

CORPORATE LEADERSHIP AND CEO BIOGRAPHY

- Ken Auletta
THE ART OF CORPORATE SUCCESS
A lavish, sometimes slavish, portrait of French industrialist-statesman Jean Riboud and the global company he ran
0–399–12930–8 Putnam $15.95
0–14–007950–5 Penguin pb $7.95

- Henry Ford
TODAY AND TOMORROW
Henry Ford's vision of manufacturing, politics, and society. First published in 1926, the book still holds lessons for managers struggling to understand Japanese production efficiency
0–915299–36–4 Productivity $24.95

- Harold Geneen with Alvin Moscow
MANAGING
The retired chairman of ITT preaches the management gospel that made him famous—and feared
0–380–69986–9 Avon pb $4.95

- Armand Hammer with Neil Lydon
HAMMER
One of America's most famous executives takes us to Washington, Moscow, and Beijing to meet his many friends in high places
0–399–13275–9 Putnam $22.95
0–399–51441–4 Putnam pb $9.95

Lee Iacocca with William Novak
IACOCCA: An Autobiography
The CEO saga that started it all. Candid, sassy, funny, insightful—qualities lacking in so many of the executive biographies it inspired
0–553–05102–4 Bantam $19.95
0–553–25147–3 Bantam pb $4.95

Lee Iacocca with N.R. Kleinfield
TALKING STRAIGHT
Pointed reflections on Washington, trade with Japan, Wall Street, and other issues on the Chrysler chairman's mind
0–553–05270–5 Bantam $21.95

- Victor Kiam
GOING FOR IT!: How to Succeed as an Entrepreneur
Business advice from the man who liked the Remington shaver so much he bought the company
0–688–06060–9 Morrow $16.95
0–451–14851–7 NAL pb $4.95

- Sonny Kleinfield
STAYING AT THE TOP: The Life of a CEO
A tour of the high-pressure world of Avon CEO Hicks Waldron
0–453–00521–7 NAL $17.95
0–451–14977–7 NAL pb $4.50

- Albert Lee

CALL ME ROGER: The Story of How Roger Smith, Chairman of General Motors, Transformed the Industry Leader Into a Fallen Giant
A GM speechwriter's kiss-and-tell indictment of the personal and managerial shortcomings of Roger Smith. Light on analysis, but full of intriguing stories and anecdotes
0–8092–4630–9 Contemporary $19.95
0–55525–167–6 Nightingale-Conant pb $8.95

- Harry Levinson & Stuart Rosenthal

CEO: Corporate Leadership in Action
Polite but interesting profiles of six corporate titans, including Reginald Jones of General Electric, Walter Wriston of Citicorp, and IBM's Thomas Watson, Jr.
0–465–00790–2 Basic Books $19.95
0–465–00791–0 Basic Books pb $9.95

- Akio Morita with Edwin M. Reingold & Mitsuko Shimomura

MADE IN JAPAN: Akio Morita and the Sony Corporation
One of Japan's most creative business leaders tells his company's story and reflects on technology, world trade, and differences between his country and the US
0–525–24465–4 Dutton $18.95
0–452–25987–8 NAL pb $9.95

- Ralph Nader & William Taylor

THE BIG BOYS: Power and Position in American Business
Profiles of nine leading executives that explore different "styles of power" in corporate America
0–394–72111–X Pantheon pb $8.95

- T. Boone Pickens, Jr.

BOONE
How the corporate gunslinger from Amarillo, Texas, took on Big Oil and the Business Roundtable—and made millions in the process
0–395–41433–4 Houghton Mifflin $18.95
0–395–47811–1 Houghton Mifflin pb $4.95

- Cary Reich

FINANCIER: The Biography of André Meyer
The definitive account of the life and times of the man who built Lazard Frères into one of Wall Street's most prominent investment houses
0–688–01551–4 Morrow $15.95
0–688–04828–5 Morrow pb $9.95

- John Sculley with John A. Byrne

ODYSSEY: Pepsi to Apple
An uptight New York executive finds inner happiness in Silicon Valley—and saves a well-known computer company in the process
0–06–015780–1 Harper & Row $21.50
0–06–091527–7 Harper & Row pb $10.95

- Alfred P. Sloan

MY YEARS WITH GENERAL MOTORS
Management insights from one of the true giants of American business
0–385–04235–3 Doubleday pb $7.95

- Jeffrey Sonnenfeld

THE HERO'S FAREWELL: What Happens When CEOs Retire
An analysis of one of the least understood aspects of executive life. Sonnenfeld draws on dozens of case histories to identify four "styles" of how CEOs give up (often reluctantly) the power and privilege to which they are accustomed
0–19–505091–6 Oxford $22.95

- Noel Tichy & Maryann Devanna

THE TRANSFORMATIONAL LEADER: Molding Tomorrow's Corporate Winners
Upbeat tales of Big Business executives who are turning their companies from bureaucratic also-rans into world-class competitors
0–471–82259–0 John Wiley $22.95

- Donald Trump with Tony Schwartz

TRUMP: The Art of the Deal
"I like thinking big. I always have. To me, it's very simple; if you're going to be thinking anyway, you might as well think big"
0–394–55528–7 Random House $19.95
0–446–35325–6 Warner pb $5.95

- Richard F. Vancil

PASSING THE BATON: Managing the Process of CEO Succession
CEOs, former CEOs, heirs apparent, and outside directors describe how chief executive officers transfer power to their successors
0–87584–182–1 Harvard Business School $24.95

- Dr. An Wang with Eugene Linden

LESSONS: An Autobiography
Dr. Wang's flight from China, the birth of the company that made him famous, his competitive encounters with IBM, and reflections on the future of American business
0–201–09400–2 Addison-Wesley $17.95
0–201–07408–7 Addison-Wesley pb $9.95

- Peter C. Wensberg

LAND'S POLAROID
An unauthorized, comprehensive account of photographic innovator Edwin Land and the company he built
0–395–42114–4 Houghton Mifflin $18.95

COMPANIES AND INDUSTRIES

- Isadore Barmash

MACY'S FOR SALE: The Leveraged Buyout of the World's Largest Store
A veteran *New York Times* business reporter casts a critical eye on one of the biggest retailing deals of all time
1–55584–139–2 Weidenfeld & Nicolson $19.95

- John Byrne

THE HEADHUNTERS
An absorbing account of the rise of "executive search firms"—an industry devoted to persuading top-notch executives to leave their current jobs in pursuit of greener pastures—and their impact on corporate loyalty and management stability
0–02–51795–0 Macmillan $19.95

- Steve Coll

THE DEAL OF THE CENTURY: The Breakup of AT&T
A fast-paced chronicle of the ten-year battle for control of the world's largest corporation, which produced the most sweeping antitrust settlement in history
0–689–11757–4 Atheneum $19.95
0–671–64592–7 Simon & Schuster pb $8.95

- Roger Enrico & Jesse Kornbluth

THE OTHER GUY BLINKED & Other Dispatches from the Cola Wars
Behind the "Pepsi challenge," Michael Jackson, and other weapons in the never-ending battle for the hearts and minds of America's soft drinkers
0–553–05177–6 Bantam $17.95
0–553–26632–2 Bantam pb $4.95

- Peter Z. Grossman

AMERICAN EXPRESS: An Unauthorized History
The only book-length treatment of the rise of one of America's best-run and most powerful service companies
0–517–56238–3 Crown $19.95

- David Halberstam

THE RECKONING
Halberstam compares the humbling of Ford Motor Company with the rise of Japan's Nissan
0–688–04838–2 Morrow $19.95
0–380–70447–1 Avon pb $5.50

- Gary Hector

BREAKING THE BANK: The Decline of BankAmerica
How shoddy management and imprudent lending nearly destroyed what was once the world's largest bank
0–316–35392–2 Little, Brown $18.95

- John Hillkirk & Gary Jacobson

XEROX, AMERICAN SAMURAI: The Behind-the-Scenes Story of How a Corporate Giant Beat the Japanese at Their Own Game
A well-reported account of how Xerox almost lost its position as world leader in the industry it invented, and how it launched a successful comeback
0–02–551600–0 Macmillan $18.95
0–02–033830–9 Macmillan pb $9.95

- John P. Hoerr

AND THE WOLF FINALLY CAME: The Decline of the American Steel Industry
A sensitive and sophisticated analysis of labor-management relations, with a focus on US Steel's operations in the Monongahela Valley outside Pittsburgh
0–8229–3572–4 Pittsburgh $39.95
0–8229–5398–6 Pittsburgh pb $14.95

- Larry Kahaner

ON THE LINE: The Men of MCI—Who Took on AT&T, Risked Everything, And Won!
A fast-paced, entertaining history of how upstart MCI introduced competition to the long-distance telephone industry—and helped destroy the Bell System in the process
0–446–51313–X Warner $18.95
0–446–38550–6 Warner pb $9.95

• Donald Katz

THE BIG STORE: Inside the Crisis and Revolution at Sears
Business history as sociology: the story of CEO Edward Telling's struggle to breathe new life into a troubled American institution
0–670–80512–2 Viking $22.95
0–14–011525–0 Penguin pb $9.95

Tracy Kidder

THE SOUL OF A NEW MACHINE
A book that defined a new genre of business writing. Kidder sketches a tale of heartache and exhilaration as a group of Data General engineers design a computer whose success may determine the fate of their company
0–316–49170–5 Atlantic Monthly $16.95
0–380–59931–7 Avon pb $4.50

• John Love

McDONALD'S: Behind the Arches
A serious history of one of America's most dynamic and efficient companies
0–553–05127–X Bantam $19.95

• Laton McCartney

FRIENDS IN HIGH PLACES: The Bechtel Story
A hard-nosed investigative report on one of the world's most secretive corporations, whose executive alumni include Caspar Weinberger and George Schultz
0–671–47415–4 Simon & Schuster $19.95

• John Newhouse

THE SPORTY GAME
The gifted *New Yorker* writer explores the high-stakes world of building and selling jumbo jets
0–394–51447–5 Knopf $22.50

• Peter Prichard

THE MAKING OF McPAPER: The Inside Story of USA Today
An authorized, but still revealing, account of the struggle to launch "the nation's newspaper." A fascinating case study of the technology, money, and determined management behind *USA Today*
0–8362–7939–5 Andrews & McMeel $19.95

• Andrew Tobias

THE INVISIBLE BANKERS
A clever, often hilarious, explanation of how the insurance industry really works
0–671–61700–1 Washington Square pb $4.95

• Brock Yates

THE DECLINE AND FALL OF THE AMERICAN AUTO INDUSTRY
One of Detroit's most gifted auto writers explains how the industry lost its way
0–394–72252–3 Random House pb $6.95

THE JAPANESE CHALLENGE AND AMERICA'S ECONOMIC FUTURE

▶ See also Japan

• James Abegglen & George Stalk, Jr.

KAISHA, THE JAPANESE CORPORATION: How Marketing, Money, and Manpower Strategy, Not Management Style, Make the Japanese World Pace-Setters
One of the most perceptive books published on how Japanese manufacturers surpass their US rivals
0–465–03711–9 Basic Books $23.95
0–465–03712–7 Basic Books pb $12.95

• Daniel Burstein

YEN!: Japan's New Financial Empire and its Threat to America
A disturbing and thoroughly persuasive account of Japan's emergence as the world's leading financial power and what it means for US economic independence
0–671–64763–6 Simon & Schuster $19.95

• Robert Christopher

SECOND TO NONE: American Companies in Japan
A study of American companies (IBM, Coca-Cola, McDonald's, and others) that have cracked the Japan market and what other companies can learn from their experiences
0–517–56286–3 Crown $16.95
0–449–90273–0 Fawcett pb $8.95

• Stephen S. Cohen & John Zysman

MANUFACTURING MATTERS: The Myth of the Post-Industrial Economy
A tightly argued polemic against pundits who claim the United States can flourish as a "service society"
0–465–04384–4 Basic Books $19.95
0–465–04385–2 Basic Books pb $9.95

• Norman J. Glickman & Douglas P. Woodward

THE NEW COMPETITORS: How Foreign Investors are Changing the U.S. Economy
Two academic economists explore why more and more foreign companies are buying into the United States, what industries they are concentrating in, what the long-term effects will be, and how we can control the selling of America
0–465–05005–0 Basic Books $19.95

• Robert H. Hayes, Steven C. Wheelwright & Kim B. Clark

DYNAMIC MANUFACTURING: Creating the Learning Organization
Three of this country's most respected experts on manufacturing, all of them professors at the Harvard Business School, offer detailed prescriptions for the rebirth of US competitiveness
0–02–914211–3 Free Press $24.95

From Japan Inc. *by Shotaro Ishinomori (California)*

• Chalmers Johnson

MITI AND THE JAPANESE MIRACLE: The Growth of Industrial Policy, 1925-1975
Still the best analysis of the government planning agency that steers the Japanese economy
0–8047–1128–3 Stanford $30.00
0–8047–1206–9 Stanford pb $11.95

• James Lardner

FAST FORWARD: Hollywood, the Japanese, and the Onslaught of the VCR
Why is it that American companies invented the videocassette recorder but Japanese companies build virtually all of them? A fascinating case study in business, politics, and society
0–393–02389–3 Norton $18.95
0–451–62626–5 NAL pb $4.95

• Ira C. Magaziner & Robert B. Reich

MINDING AMERICA'S BUSINESS: The Decline and Rise of the American Economy
Two leading proponents of industrial policy make the case for government planning
0–394–71538–1 Random House pb $5.95

• John Naisbitt

MEGATRENDS: 10 New Directions Transforming Our Lives
A futuristic account of the forces moving America from an industrial economy rooted in the Northeast to a decentralized, high-tech, information society
0–446–51251–6 Warner $17.00
0–446–90991–2 Warner pb $4.50

• William Ouchi

THEORY Z: How American Business Can Meet the Japanese Challenge
One of the earliest, and still one of the best, explanations of quality circles, worker participation, and the other human dimensions of the Japanese management style
0–380–59451–X Avon pb $4.50

• Michael J. Piore & Charles F. Sabel
THE SECOND INDUSTRIAL DIVIDE: Possibilities for Prosperity
Two MIT economists explain the decline of American manufacturing and offer prescriptions for renewal
0-465-07562-2 Basic Books $21.95
0-465-07563-0 Basic Books pb $9.95

• Clyde V. Prestowitz, Jr.
TRADING PLACES: How We Allowed Japan to Take the Lead
A former high-ranking Commerce Department official makes a convincing case for get-tough trade policies with Japan
0-465-08680-2 Basic Books $19.95

• Martin & Susan Tolchin
BUYING INTO AMERICA: How Foreign Money is Changing the Face of Our Nation
An even-handed examination of the acceleration of foreign (mainly Japanese) investment in the US and its political, economic, and social consequences
0-8129-1667-0 Times Books $19.95

• Ezra Vogel
JAPAN AS NUMBER ONE: Lessons for America
How Japan's political, social, and economic institutions contribute to its global economic dominance
0-674-47215-2 Harvard $17.50
0-06-132055-2 Harper & Row pb $8.95

WALL STREET AND CORPORATE FINANCE

Ken Auletta
GREED AND GLORY ON WALL STREET: The Fall of the House of Lehman
An intimate account of the bitter internal clashes over money and power that eventually forced the sale of one of Wall Street's most respected investment houses
0-394-54410-2 Random House $19.95
0-446-38406-2 Warner pb $9.95

• John Brooks
THE TAKEOVER GAME
The author of *The Go-Go Years*, the definitive account of Wall Street excess in the 1960s, chronicles Wall Street excess in the 1980s
0-525-48440-X Dutton pb $9.95

• Connie Bruck
THE PREDATORS' BALL: The Junk Bond Raiders and the Man Who Staked Them
A glimpse inside Michael Milken's securities empire and the giant deals he engineered. Intelligent analysis and entertaining stories, including feared raider Carl Icahn playing Monopoly with real money
0-671-61780-X Simon & Schuster $19.95
0-14-012090-4 Penguin pb $8.95

• Timothy Carrington
THE YEAR THEY SOLD WALL STREET: The Inside Story of the Shearson-American Express Merger, and How It Changed Wall Street Forever
Behind the scenes of a deal that set the stage for even bigger deals
0-395-34394-1 Houghton Mifflin $17.95
0-14-009794-5 Penguin pb $6.95

• Steve Coll
THE TAKING OF GETTY OIL
Inside the titanic struggle between Texaco and Pennzoil for control of Getty Oil—a struggle that led to the largest bankruptcy in history
0-689-11860-0 Atheneum $19.95

• Dwight Crane & Robert Eccles
DOING DEALS: Investment Banks at Work
Wall Street anthropology: a unique analysis of investment bankers' customs, values, and work habits
0-87584-199-6 Harvard Business School $29.95

• Douglas Frantz
LEVINE AND CO.: The Story of Wall Street's Insider Trading Scandal
How Dennis Levine turned $40,000 into $12.6 million through an extensive Wall Street insider trading scheme
0-8050-0457-2 Henry Holt $19.95

• Institutional Investor
THE WAY IT WAS: An Oral History of Finance, 1967-1987
Conversations with the richest and most powerful figures on Wall Street and other centers of international finance
0-688-08005-7 Morrow $24.95

• Moira Johnson
TAKEOVER: The New Wall Street Warriors—The Men, the Money, the Impact
Blow-by-blow accounts of major takeovers engineered by the likes of Sir James Goldsmith, Carl Icahn, and T. Boone Pickens
0-87795-784-3 Arbor House $19.95
0-14-010505-0 Penguin pb $7.95

• Louis Lowenstein
WHAT'S WRONG WITH WALL STREET: Short-Term Gain and the Absentee Shareholder
Criticisms of the misguided practices and priorities of the investment world and their debilitating effects on the corporate heartland
0-201-17169-4 Addison-Wesley $17.95

• Thomas J. Petzinger, Jr.
OIL AND HONOR: Inside the $11 Billion Battle for Getty Oil
Texaco v. Pennzoil revisited. Petzinger's masterful narrative reads like a novel
0-399-13276-7 Putnam $19.95
0-425-11172-5 Berkley pb $4.95

• John Taylor
STORMING THE MAGIC KINGDOM: Wall Street, the Raiders, and the Battle for Disney
A conference-call-by-conference-call account of the hostile raid on the bastion

of American values, Walt Disney Productions, and the furious battle that ensued
0-394-54640-7 Knopf $18.95
0-345-35407-9 Ballantine pb $9.95

• R. Foster Winans
TRADING SECRETS: Seduction and Scandal at the Wall Street Journal
A dramatic and intimate account by the former Wall Street Journal reporter of his side of the story in the insider trading scheme that ended his career
0-312-90728-1 St. Martin's pb $4.95

BUSINESS AND SOCIETY

• Walter Adams & James W. Brock
THE BIGNESS COMPLEX: Industry, Labor, and Government in the American Economy
How big business and the "labor-industrial complex" sap US economic vitality and violate consumer rights
0-394-54721-7 Pantheon $22.95

• Paul Brodeur
OUTRAGEOUS MISCONDUCT: The Asbestos Industry on Trial
The definitive account of one of the great corporate crimes of the century—the asbestos industry's failure to disclose the toxic effects of its products
0-394-53320-8 Pantheon pb $9.95

• Council on Economic Priorities
RATING AMERICA'S CORPORATE CONSCIENCE
A buyer's guide to socially-conscious shopping that grades hundreds of companies by their environmental, equal employment, and health and safety records
0-201-15886-8 Addison-Wesley $21.95
0-201-15879-5 Addison-Wesley pb $14.95

• Morton Mintz
AT ANY COST: Corporate Greed, Women, and the Dalkon Shield
The veteran *Washington Post* investigative reporter tells the story of how A.H. Robins concealed the dangers of the Dalkon Shield—a decision that caused grief to thousands of women and led Robins to file for bankruptcy
0-394-54846-9 Pantheon pb $8.95

• Russel Mokhiber
CORPORATE CRIME AND VIOLENCE: Big Business Power and the Abuse of the Public Trust
A no-holds-barred review of what Mokhiber considers the worst episodes of corporate misconduct—from the Thalidomide tragedy to overseas bribery by price-fixing by General Electric
0-87156-723-7 Sierra Club $25.00

• Milton Moskowitz & others
EVERYBODY'S BUSINESS ALMANAC
Offbeat histories of companies and industries that emphasize their impact on society
0-06-250628-5 Harper & Row $16.95

• Martin & Susan Tolchin
DISMANTLING AMERICA: The Rush to Deregulate
A critical account of how the Reagan administration's promise "to get government off the backs" of business affected the health and safety of American workers and consumers
0–19–503577–1 Oxford pb $8.95

• David Vogel
FLUCTUATING FORTUNES: The Political Power of Business in America
An analysis of the power of the anti-business consumer movement during the late 1960s and 1970s and Big Business's political comeback in the 1980s
0–465–02470–X Basic Books $20.95

• Paul Weaver
THE SUICIDAL CORPORATION: How Big Business Has Failed America
Bitter confessions of a neoconservative magazine writer who joined Ford Motor Company to fight for capitalism, only to discover that Ford was less interested in capitalism than in profits—and in getting along with the political powers-that-be
0–671–52378–3 Simon & Schuster $18.95

Modern Political Thought

▶ See also Western Philosophy

CLASSICS
(in chronological order)

• Niccolò Machiavelli
The radical innovation of Machiavelli was to base political theory on experience rather than edifying ideals, and he drew on history (in his *Discourses*) as well as his own career as a Florentine diplomat. His ambiguous legacy includes both modern empirical political science and the *Realpolitik* of the nation state as a law unto itself.
THE PORTABLE MACHIAVELLI
Translated by Peter Bondanella & Mark Musa
0–14–015092–7 Penguin pb $8.95

THE DISCOURSES
A commentary on Livy's history of Rome
Edited by Bernard Crick
0–14–044428–9 Penguin pb $4.95

FLORENTINE HISTORIES
Translated by Laura Banfield & Harvey Mansfield
0–691–05521–1 Princeton $35.00

HISTORY OF FLORENCE AND OF THE AFFAIRS OF ITALY
0–8446–2503–5 Peter Smith $17.95

THE PRINCE
Translated by George Bull
0–14–044107–7 Penguin pb $2.25

So it should be noted that when he seizes a state the new ruler must determine all the injuries that he will need to inflict. He must inflict them once for all, and not have to renew them every day, and in that way he will be able to set men's minds at rest and win them over to him when he confers benefits ... Violence must be inflicted once for all; people will then forget what it tastes like and so be less resentful. Benefits must be conferred gradually; and in that way they will taste better.

Niccolò Machiavelli
THE PRINCE
Translated by George Bull
0–14–044107–7 Penguin pb $2.25

• Thomas Hobbes
Perhaps influenced by the unsettled times in which he lived, Hobbes took a dim view of human nature: in a state of nature the life of man was "solitary, poor, nasty, brutish and short." Thus the main motive of political life is security, to be achieved by establishing a commonwealth through a social contract and setting up over it an absolute, undivided authority who will prevent it from dissolving into factionalism and civil war.
LEVIATHAN
This great work, published in 1651 and subjected to a parliamentary investigation for atheism, heavily influenced much subsequent British political theory
Edited by C.B. Macpherson
0–14–043195–0 Penguin pb $5.95

• John Locke
Like Hobbes, Locke relied in his political theory on the notions of a state of nature and a social contract, but he maintained that the commonwealth's purpose is to provide liberty as well as security, and that citizens have a right to overthrow the government and replace it with a better one when it fails to provide either.
TWO TREATISES OF GOVERNMENT
First published anonymously in 1690; this edition is part of the new Cambridge Texts in the History of Political Thought series
Edited by Peter Laslett
0–521–35448–X Cambridge $39.50
0–521–35730–6 Cambridge pb $7.95

• Charles de Montesquieu
Montesquieu's theory of the separation of powers, though based on a somewhat mistaken view of the English constitution, became the inspiration for the United States constitution of 1789.
THE PERSIAN LETTERS
A satirical description of the condition of France, published in 1721
0–14–044281–2 Penguin pb $6.95

THE SPIRIT OF THE LAWS: A Compendium of the First English Edition Together with an English Translation of An Essay on Causes Affecting Mind and Characters
In his greatest work, published in 1748, Montesquieu argues that a separation of

government functions will ensure individual liberty
Edited by David W. Carrithers
0–520–02566–0 California $48.50
0–520–03455–4 California pb $12.95

• Jean-Jacques Rousseau
Some of the profound contradictions in Rousseau's life found their way into his political philosophy, which is meant to show the way to freedom and equality but finds true freedom in the submission of the individual to the "general will." Rousseau has been seen as both the champion of revolution and individual liberty and the harbinger of 20th-century totalitarianism.
POLITICAL WRITINGS
Contains the widely praised translation of *The Social Contract* (1762), the late and important *Government of Poland*, and the only published English translation of the fragment *Constitutional Project for Corsica*
Edited by Frederick Watkins
0–299–11904–X Wisconsin pb $14.50

THE SOCIAL CONTRACT
Translated by Maurice Cranston
0–14–044201–4 Penguin pb $3.95

It is now sixteen or seventeen years since I saw the queen of France, then the dauphiness, at Versailles; and surely never lighted on this orb, which she hardly seemed to touch, a more delightful vision ... Oh! What a revolution! and what an heart must I have, to contemplate without emotion that elevation and that fall! ... I thought ten thousand swords must have leaped from their scabbards to avenge even a look that threatened her with insult.—But the age of chivalry is gone.—That of sophisters, oeconomists, and calculators, has succeeded; and the glory of Europe is extinguished for ever. Never, never more, shall we behold that generous loyalty to rank and sex, that proud submission, that dignified obedience, that subordination of the heart, which kept alive, even in servitude itself, the spirit of an exalted freedom.

Edmund Burke
REFLECTIONS ON THE REVOLUTION IN FRANCE
0–14–043204–3 Penguin pb $5.95

• Edmund Burke
Burke, who had supported the American Revolution as a vindication of traditional English liberties, produced in *Reflections on the Revolution in France* (1790) the most influential arguments against the French Revolution and in the process invented conservatism as a distinct political philosophy. He favored gradual reform based on experience and local tradition, which distinguishes his conservatism from the more iron-handed and pessimistic variety developed on the Continent by De Maistre and others.
REFLECTIONS ON THE REVOLUTION IN FRANCE
0–14–043204–3 Penguin pb $5.95

• Edmund Burke & Thomas Paine
REFLECTIONS ON THE REVOLUTION IN FRANCE & THE RIGHTS OF MAN
0–385–08190–1 Doubleday pb $8.95

• Thomas Paine
After failed jobs and marriages in England, Paine came to America and found his vocation as a radical political pamphleteer. His *Common Sense* (1776) sold half a million copies and did more than any other work to inspire the demand for independence, but in 1809 he ended his days in poverty on a farm donated to him by New York State.
THE THOMAS PAINE READER
Includes *Common Sense*, and excerpts from *The Rights of Man*, *The American Crisis*, and *The Age of Reason*
Edited by Michael Foot & Isaac Kramnick
0–14–044496–3 Penguin pb $7.95

COMMON SENSE
0–14–039016–2 Penguin pb $2.95

THE RIGHTS OF MAN
0–14–039015–4 Penguin pb $2.95

• Thomas Jefferson
Jefferson envisioned a nation of prosperous farmers, who he thought were far more likely than city-dwellers to cultivate the virtues of self-reliance, hard work, moderation, and common sense on which a free society depends.
WRITINGS
A comprehensive survey of Jefferson's works, including *Notes on the State of Virginia*, *Autobiography*, public papers, addresses, and a large selection of letters
Edited by Merrill D. Peterson
0–940450–16–X Library of America $30.00

• James Madison, Alexander Hamilton & John Jay
THE FEDERALIST PAPERS
First appearing in New York newspapers in support of New York State's ratification of the Constitution, the *Federalist* became the most famous and complete exposition of the intentions of the founding fathers with respect to the federal system of divided powers and constitutional checks and balances
Edited by Isaac Kramnick
0–14–044495–5 Penguin pb $7.95

• William Godwin
AN ENQUIRY CONCERNING POLITICAL JUSTICE
Godwin was the most extreme of early English radicals. More anarchist than socialist, he believed that humanity could achieve perfection through political reform and saw the future in terms of small independent communities in which the individual would be allowed a maximum of personal freedom. His *Enquiry* appeared in 1793
Edited by Isaac Kramnick
0–14–040030–3 Penguin pb $7.95

• Mary Wollstonecraft
A VINDICATION OF THE RIGHTS OF WOMAN
Wollstonecraft, a friend of Blake and Paine and the wife of Godwin (their daughter Mary became Shelley's wife), produced the first theoretical exposition of women's liberation in *A Vindication of the Rights of Woman* (1792), in which she advocated the education of women as the foundation for their attainment of full political and legal rights
Edited by Miriam Kramnick
0–14–043199–3 Penguin pb $4.95

• G.W.F. Hegel
PHILOSOPHY OF RIGHT
Hegel's political philosophy was conservative, though liberal in the context of contemporary Prussia. He favored constitutional monarchy based on family and guild in which liberty was balanced with public order
Translated by T.M. Knox
0–19–824128–3 Oxford $45.00
0–19–500276–8 Oxford pb $12.95

• Alexis de Tocqueville
Tocqueville's stock as a political thinker has never been higher, for he is unsurpassed as a skeptical analyst and realistic defender of liberal democracy.
DEMOCRACY IN AMERICA
An aristocrat in frail health, Tocqueville visited the United States just once, in 1831-1832. The resulting account was acclaimed throughout Europe and seems more acute and prescient each year
Edited by Phillips Bradley

Alexis de Tocqueville by David Levine

Volume 1
0–394–70110–0 Random House pb $6.95

Volume 2
0–394–70111–9 Random House pb $4.95

THE OLD REGIME AND THE FRENCH REVOLUTION
Edited by J.P. Mayer & A.P. Kerr
0–385–09260–1 Doubleday pb $5.95

SELECTED LETTERS ON POLITICS AND SOCIETY
Translated by James Toupin
Edited by Roger Boesche
0–520–05047–9 California $27.50
0–520–05751–1 California pb $11.95

• John Stuart Mill
ON LIBERTY
On Liberty (1859) is the most famous argument ever made for the liberal, tolerant, pluralistic, democratic point of view. After a nervous breakdown in his early twenties, Mill opened himself to Coleridge and the romantics and tried to base his political philosophy on a broader view of human nature
0–14–043207–8 Penguin pb $3.95

Cambridge Texts in the History of Political Thought

This new series offers up-to-date editions of major texts. Volumes available so far include:

• Aristotle
THE POLITICS
Edited by Stephen Everson
0–521–35449–8 Cambridge $29.95
0–521–35731–4 Cambridge pb $6.95

• Jeremy Bentham
A FRAGMENT ON GOVERNMENT
Introduction by Ross Harrison
0–521–35054–9 Cambridge $29.95
0–521–35929–5 Cambridge pb $6.95

• Benjamin Constant
POLITICAL WRITINGS
Translated and edited by Biancamaria Fontana
0–521–30336–2 Cambridge $39.50
0–521–31632–4 Cambridge pb $12.95

• Gottfried Wilhelm Leibniz
POLITICAL WRITINGS
Translated and edited by Patrick Riley
0–521–35380–7 Cambridge $39.50
0–521–35899–X Cambridge pb $12.95

• Niccolò Machiavelli
THE PRINCE
Edited by Quentin Skinner & Russell Price
0–521–34240–6 Cambridge $29.50
0–521–34993–1 Cambridge pb $6.95

> But, indeed, the dictum that truth always triumphs over persecution is one of those pleasant falsehoods which men repeat after one another till they pass into commonplaces, but which all experience refutes. History teems with instances of truth put down by persecution. If not suppressed forever, it may be thrown back for centuries. To speak only of religious opinions: the Reformation broke out at least twenty times before Luther, and was put down. Arnold of Brescia was put down. Fra Dolcino was put down. Savonarola was put down. The Albigeois were put down. The Vaudois were put down. The Lollards were put down. The Hussites were put down . . . It is a piece of idle sentimentality that truth, merely as truth, has any inherent power denied to error of prevailing against the dungeon and the stake.
>
> John Stuart Mill
> **ON LIBERTY**
> 0–14–043207–8 Penguin pb $3.95

Utopias and Dystopias

Plato
THE REPUBLIC
Plato's ideally rational city-state—in which a trained elite of philosophers rules, everyone has an assigned role, and poets and others who might stir up passions are expelled—looks like utopia to some and dystopia to others
Translated by H.D. Lee
0–14–044048–8 Penguin pb $3.95

Thomas More
UTOPIA
More invented the word *utopia* (from the Greek for "no place" and a pun on the Greek for "good place"), and with it imagined a rational and tolerant communistic society that reflected his humanist sympathies and was very remote from the 16th-century England of Henry VIII that eventually had him beheaded
Translated by Paul Turner
0–14–044165–4 Penguin pb $2.95

Charles Fourier
THE UTOPIAN VISION OF CHARLES FOURIER: Selected Texts on Work, Love and Passionate Attraction
The utopia of Fourier, conceived as a cooperative, egalitarian agricultural community, inspired Brook Farm, the transcendentalist experiment in Massachusetts, and other American cooperative settlements
Translated and edited by Jonathan Beecher & Richard Bienvenu
0–8262–0426–0 Missouri $37.50
0–8262–0413–9 Missouri pb $14.50

William Morris
NEWS FROM NOWHERE
An 1891 novel describing an ideal rural socialist community by the medievalizing utopian socialist poet
0–7100–6756–9 RC&H pb $9.95

Aldous Huxley
BRAVE NEW WORLD
Written in 1932, this satirical vision of a psychologically manipulated and drugged humanity of the future is, along with *1984*, one of the two great anti-utopias of the century
0–06–083095–6 Harper & Row pb $4.95

George Orwell
ANIMAL FARM
The famous satire on Soviet communism depicted as a revolutionized barnyard in which "some animals are more equal than others"
0–452–26277–1 NAL pb $4.95

1984
Orwell's bleak 1948 vision of a totalitarian England under Big Brother
0–452–25426–4 NAL pb $5.95

MARXISM

▶ See also Economics & 19th-Century Europe

Marx

• **Karl Marx**
EARLY WRITINGS
The early "humanist" writings which many contemporary Marxists find more compelling than Marx's later, "scientific" phase
Translated by Rodney Livingston & Gregor Benton
Edited by Quintin Hoare
0–394–72005–9 Random House pb $8.95

THE EIGHTEENTH BRUMAIRE OF LOUIS BONAPARTE
"History repeats itself, the first time as tragedy, the second time as farce": Marx's analysis of Louis Bonaparte's conservative authoritarian state and his coup d'état of 1852
0–7178–0056–3 International pb $4.25

• **Karl Marx & Friedrich Engels**
THE MARX-ENGELS READER
Edited by Robert C. Tucker
0–393–09040–X Norton pb $10.95

THE GERMAN IDEOLOGY
Marx's account of German philosophy and its relation to religion and social alienation. Includes Part 1 and selections from Parts 2 and 3
Edited by C.J. Arthur
0–7178–0302–3 International pb $4.25

Marxism After Marx

• **Antonio Gramsci**
AN ANTONIO GRAMSCI READER: Selected Writings, 1916-1935
Gramsci wrote his major works during the eleven years he spent in fascist prisons, but his Marxism discards Marx's determinism and replaces it with a humanistic emphasis on the individual as a free agent acting in history
Edited with an introduction by David Gorgacs
0–8052–4059–4 Schocken $22.95
0–8052–0924–7 Schocken pb $12.95

LETTERS FROM PRISON
Translated with an introduction by Lynne Lawner
0–374–52182–4 Farrar, Straus & Giroux pb $8.95

PRISON NOTEBOOKS: Selections
Translated by Quintin Hoare & Geoffrey N. Smith
0–7178–0397–X International pb $7.50

• **Leszek Kolakowski**
MAIN CURRENTS OF MARXISM: Its Rise, Growth, and Dissolution
A classic history by a Polish philosopher who fled the communist regime for England
Translated by P.S. Falla

Volume 1: The Founders
0–19–285107–1 Oxford pb $15.95

Volume 2: The Golden Age
0–19–824569–6 Oxford $36.00
0–19–285108–X Oxford pb $15.95

Volume 3: The Breakdown
0–19–824570–X Oxford $36.00
0–19–285109–8 Oxford pb $14.95

• **Karl Korsch**
Korsch, a German Marxist who advocated a democratic socialism based on workers' control, was critical of both Leninist and Stalinist state socialism as well as of social democratic reform, and was an early analyst of the revolutionary potential of the Third World.
MARXISM AND PHILOSOPHY
Essays from the 1920s on the relation of Marxism to philosophy and on the Marxism of the First International
0–85345–189–3 Monthly Review pb $5.50

• **V.I. Lenin**
THE LENIN ANTHOLOGY
Lenin's revolutionary writings present what Lukács called a "revolutionary *Realpolitik*" sharply distinct from classical Marxist theory and totalitarian Stalinist practice
Edited by Robert C. Tucker
0–393–09236–4 Norton pb $14.95

WHAT IS TO BE DONE?
Lenin's main contribution to Marxist theory is his insistence on the role of a tightly disciplined revolutionary vanguard organization in bringing the working class into a revolutionary consciousness
0–14–044499–8 Penguin pb $7.95

• **Georg Lukács**
HISTORY AND CLASS CONSCIOUSNESS
Written between 1919 and 1922, these essays anticipate the 1960s revival of interest in the young, humanist Marx; they reject determinism and "reification" in scientific Marxism and focus on the concept of alienation in Marx's criticism of capitalist society
Translated by Rodney Livingstone
0–262–62020–0 MIT pb $8.95

• **Rosa Luxemburg**
Born in late 19th-century Russian Poland to assimilated middle-class Jewish parents, Luxemburg became the most uncompromising advocate of revolution in the German Social Democratic Party, a position that alienated moderates in the party and landed her in jail for most of World War I. She became a martyr to the cause when she was killed by paramilitary forces during a 1919 uprising in Berlin.
THE NATIONAL QUESTION: Selected Writings by Rosa Luxemburg
Edited by Horace B. Davis
0–85345–355–1 Monthly Review $16.50
0–85345–577–5 Monthly Review pb $7.00

REFORM OR REVOLUTION
0–87348–303–0 Pathfinder pb $2.95

THE RUSSIAN REVOLUTION & LENINISM OR MARXISM?
Although a firm supporter of the Bolshevik revolution, Luxemburg was critical of the repressive features of the Soviet regime
Introduction by Bertram D. Wolfe
0–472–06057–0 Michigan pb $6.95

• **Herbert Marcuse**
An exponent of the Marxist Frankfurt School of critical philosophy, Marcuse became a major influence on the New Left through *One Dimensional Man* (1964), which sees late capitalist society as

enslaving individuals through advertising and consumerism rather than overt force.

ESSAY ON LIBERATION
On the "repressive tolerance" of capitalist democracy
0–8070–0595–9 Beacon pb $6.95

ONE DIMENSIONAL MAN
0–8070–1575–X Beacon pb $8.95

• Leon Trotsky
It was Stalin's idea of socialism in one country, Trotsky believed, that led to the bureaucratic travesty of socialism known as Stalinism.

THE NEW COURSE & THE STRUGGLE FOR THE NEW COURSE
0–472–06099–6 Michigan pb $4.95

Trotsky

THE RUSSIAN REVOLUTION: The Overthrow of Tsarism and the Triumph of the Soviets
0–385–09398–5 Doubleday pb $7.95

REVOLUTIONARIES

• Amilcar Cabral
UNITY AND STRUGGLE: Speeches and Writings
A leader of the struggle to free Guinea-Bissau from Portuguese rule, Cabral was an important theorist of Third World revolution. He was assassinated in 1973
0–85345–510–4 Monthly Review $16.50
0–85345–625–9 Monthly Review pb $10.00

• Frantz Fanon
BLACK SKIN, WHITE MASKS
Fanon's first book analyzes the psychological costs, for both blacks and whites, of racism and colonialism
Translated by Charles L. Markmann
0–8021–5084–5 Grove pb $8.95

A DYING COLONIALISM
An account of the Algerian war, in which Fanon took part as a member of the Algerian liberation movement (FLN)
Translated by Haakon Chevalier
0–8021–5027–6 Grove pb $12.50

TOWARD THE AFRICAN REVOLUTION
A collection of essays on the prospects for a successful revolutionary liberation of Africa
Translated by Haakon Chevalier
0–8021–3090–9 Grove pb $7.95

THE WRETCHED OF THE EARTH
On the need for national liberation movements to release themselves from European models and to develop programs that will apply to all of the world's oppressed. A widely influential book, first published in 1961
Translated by Constance Farrington
Preface by Jean-Paul Sartre
0–8021–5083–7 Grove pb $7.95

• Che Guevara
GUERRILLA WARFARE
In contrast with orthodox Marxist theory, Guevara's revolutionary writings stressed individual will, feeling, and action, which, along with his death in Bolivia at the hands of the Bolivian army, accounted for his immense popularity in the New Left
Edited by Brian Loveman & Thomas M. Davies
0–8032–2116–9 Nebraska $25.95
0–8032–7010–0 Nebraska pb $10.95

• Malcolm X with Alex Haley
THE AUTOBIOGRAPHY OF MALCOLM X
The scathing work that made Malcolm X the most influential champion of black nationalism in the 1960s
0–345–35068–5 Ballantine pb $4.95

• Mao Tse-tung
MAO TSE-TUNG ON REVOLUTION AND WAR
Mao took Marx to the countryside with his theory of a peasant revolution; often platitudinous, his theoretical writings nevertheless became a blueprint for the agrarian guerrilla-based revolutions in poor countries since 1949
Edited by M. Rejai
0–8446–5275–X Peter Smith $15.25

• Kwame Nkrumah
NEO-COLONIALISM: The Last Stage of Imperialism
The 1965 work in which Nkrumah charts a fundamental link between economic dependence and the political independence of post-colonial Africa
0–7178–0140–3 International pb $4.95

Anarchism

Paul Avrich
ANARCHIST PORTRAITS
The lives and personalities of noted anarchists across the globe, from Bakunin and Kropotkin to Proudhon, C.W. Mowbray, and the persecution of Sacco and Vanzetti; divided into three sections, on Russia, America, and Europe and the World
0–691–04753–7 Princeton $27.50

Mikhail Bakunin
GOD AND THE STATE
As an opponent of socialist authoritarianism and dogma, Bakunin became the chief alternative to Marx on the revolutionary left
Introduction by Paul Avrich
0–486–22483–X Dover pb $3.50

Emma Goldman
LIVING MY LIFE
Goldman's extraordinary autobiography, first published in 1931
Volume 1
0–486–22543–7 Dover pb $8.95
Volume 2
0–486–22544–5 Dover pb $8.95

Peter Kropotkin
MEMOIRS OF A REVOLUTIONIST
0–486–25745–2 Dover pb $11.95

Georges Sorel
REFLECTIONS ON VIOLENCE
Sorel's irrationalism and belief in revolutionary spontaneity and direct action were derived more from Nietzsche and Bergson than from Marx; he became a major influence on both anarcho-syndicalism and Italian fascism, and eventually on the New Left of the 1960s. *Reflections on Violence* was published in 1908
0–8446–1416–5 Peter Smith $17.25

NON-MARXIST SOCIALISM

• Eduard Bernstein
EVOLUTIONARY SOCIALISM: A Criticism and Affirmation
Bernstein was the apostle of social democracy and pacifism in Germany; although a close friend of Engels, he rejected the Marxist belief in violent revolution and class warfare, favoring a reformist approach that made socialism an extension of liberalism
Introduction by Sidney Hook
0–8052–0011–8 Schocken pb $5.95

• Nikolai Chernyshevsky
WHAT IS TO BE DONE?
Chernyshevsky's call for political and social reform in this 1863 novel, written while he was in prison for spreading subversive ideas, became the most famous and influential radical tract in 19th-century Russia
Translated & edited by K. Feuer
0–87501–017–2 Ardis pb $6.95

• Alexander Herzen
CHILDHOOD, YOUTH AND EXILE
The first two parts of Herzen's memoir *My Past Thoughts*
Translated by J.D. Duff
Introduction by Isaiah Berlin
0–19–281505–9 Oxford pb $6.95

ENDS AND BEGINNINGS
Selections from the later sections of Herzen's autobiography
Translated by Constance Garnett
Selected and edited by Aileen Kelly
0–19–281604–7 Oxford pb $7.95

FROM THE OTHER SHORE & THE RUSSIAN PEOPLE AND SOCIALISM
From the Other Shore replaces Hegel's belief in an ineluctable logic of history with a

stress on accident, chance, and the free improvisation of the individual
Translated by Moura Budberg
Introduction by Isaiah Berlin
0–19–281268–8 Oxford pb $6.95

• David McLellan, editor
THE ESSENTIAL LEFT: Five Classic Texts on the Principles of Socialism
0–04–335056–9 Unwin Hyman pb $9.95

• George Orwell
Orwell became the most influential spokesman in English for the anti-totalitarian left; his socialism was based on a populist faith in the ordinary man and traditional working-class culture, and a corresponding distrust of intellectuals, theories, and modern industrial development.
COLLECTED ESSAYS, JOURNALISM AND LETTERS
Edited by Sonia Orwell & Ian Angus

Volume 1: An Age Like This, 1920-1940
0–15–118546–8 HBJ $17.95
0–15–618620–9 HBJ pb $8.95

Volume 2: My Country Right or Left, 1940-1943
0–15–118547–6 HBJ $15.95
0–15–618621–7 HBJ pb $6.95

Volume 3: As I Please, 1943-1945
0–15–118548–4 HBJ $15.95
0–15–618622–5 HBJ pb $6.95

Volume 4: In Front of Your Nose, 1945-1950
0–15–118549–2 HBJ $17.95
0–15–618623–3 HBJ pb $8.95

A COLLECTION OF ESSAYS
0–15–618600–4 HBJ pb $4.95

• George Bernard Shaw
THE INTELLIGENT WOMAN'S GUIDE TO SOCIALISM, CAPITALISM, SOVIETISM AND FASCISM
Shaw's famous introduction to Fabian Socialism, first published in 1928 and expanded in the 1930s to include fascism and Soviet communism
0–14–020001–0 Penguin pb $6.95

NON-VIOLENT POLITICS

• Mohandas K. Gandhi
GANDHI ON NON-VIOLENCE: Selected Texts from Gandhi's Non-Violence in Peace and War
Gandhi's philosophy of non-violent resistance became a tremendous political force, inspiring the campaign for Indian independence as well as anti-colonial movements throughout the world and the civil rights movement in the United States
Edited by Thomas Merton
0–8112–0097–3 New Directions pb $4.95

NON-VIOLENT RESISTANCE
Edited by Bharatan Kumarappa
0–8052–0017–7 Schocken pb $9.50

• Martin Luther King, Jr.
Influenced by Gandhi, King adapted the idea of a mass movement based on non-violent resistance to the conditions of American blacks and became the most eloquent spokesman for the full integration of blacks into American society.

Mahatma Gandhi, from The Humanist Tradition in the West *by Alan Bullock (Norton)*

STRENGTH TO LOVE
Introduction by Coretta Scott King
0–8027–2472–8 Walker pb $11.95

STRIDE TOWARD FREEDOM: The Montgomery Story
0–06–250490–8 Harper & Row pb $8.95

WHERE DO WE GO FROM HERE?: Chaos or Community
0–06–012394–X Harper & Row $12.50
0–8070–0571–1 Beacon pb $9.95

WHY WE CAN'T WAIT
0–451–62675–3 NAL pb $3.50

• Leo Tolstoy
HOW MUCH LAND DOES A MAN NEED?
Didactic fiction expressing Tolstoy's ideal of peasant anarchism
0–19–421765–5 Oxford pb $1.50

THE KINGDOM OF GOD IS WITHIN YOU
After a spiritual crisis, Tolstoy turned from novel-writing to espousing Christian anarchism, of which this book is his most complete account; it is an eloquent attack on war, militarism, and state power
Translated by Constance Garnett
Foreword by Martin Green
0–8032–4411–8 Nebraska $29.95
0–8032–9404–2 Nebraska pb $8.50

THE LAW OF VIOLENCE AND THE LAW OF LOVE
0–88695–016–3 Grove pb $8.75

REALISTS AND SKEPTICS

• Isaiah Berlin
AGAINST THE CURRENT: Essays in the History of Ideas
Outstanding essays on nationalism, Disraeli and Marx, Sorel, Machiavelli, Herder, and Montesquieu by a civilized critic of political dogmatism
0–670–10944–4 Viking pb $16.95

FOUR ESSAYS ON LIBERTY
An exploration of the meaning of liberty in the context of modern ideologies,

defending it as an ideal against theories of historical inevitability and monistic conceptions of political truth
0–19–500272–5 Oxford pb $8.95

• Richard M. Crossman, editor
THE GOD THAT FAILED
Arthur Koestler, Richard Wright, and others record their disillusionment with communism
0–89526–867–1 Regnery pb $8.95

• Milovan Djilas
Djilas played leading roles in the prewar Yugoslav Communist Party and the resistance and held several high positions in Tito's government, making his scathing study of the new privileged ruling class that had developed in communist societies all the more devastating (it earned him years of confinement in Tito's prisons).
THE NEW CLASS: An Analysis of the Communist System
0–15–665489–X HBJ pb $6.95

THE UNPERFECT SOCIETY: Beyond the New Class
Translated by Dorian Cooke
0–15–693125–7 HBJ pb $5.95

• Czeslaw Milosz
THE CAPTIVE MIND
0–374–95733–9 Hippocrene $18.50
0–394–74724–0 Random House pb $6.95

• Reinhold Niebuhr
MORAL MAN AND IMMORAL SOCIETY: A Study in Ethics and Politics
Published in 1932, Niebuhr's most famous book is a classic of political realism that appeared when many people were looking for utopia. It stressed the inevitable selfishness of political entities and the perilous path of progress through inherent human limitations
0–684–71857–X Scribners pb $10.95

• Karl Popper
THE OPEN SOCIETY AND ITS ENEMIES
Popper argues that the systematic, totalistic philosophies of Plato, Hegel, and Marx provided the intellectual foundations of the totalitarian states of the 20th century; he advocates a democratic "piecemeal" approach to politics

Volume 1: The Spell of Plato
0–691–01968–1 Princeton pb $10.95

Volume 2: The High Tide of Prophecy—Hegel, Marx and the Aftermath
0–691–01972–X Princeton pb $10.95

CONSERVATISM

• Friedrich von Hayek
The laissez-faire theory that the Austrian-British economist Hayek introduced into Anglo-American political discourse was different from the traditional British versions; he saw economic development as a process of experiment and evolution too complex to be fully understood or managed. State intervention and planning can only impede the process. Hayek's influence on British prime minister

Margaret Thatcher and on American conservatives made him a formative influence on policy in the 1980s.

THE CONSTITUTION OF LIBERTY
0–226–32084–7 Chicago $15.00

INDIVIDUALISM AND ECONOMIC ORDER
0–226–32089–8 Chicago pb $17.00

THE ROAD TO SERFDOM
Hayek's best-known book was a 1944 bestseller
0–226–32078–2 Chicago pb $8.95

● Willmoore Kendall
THE CONSERVATIVE AFFIRMATION
An attempt to delineate American conservatism in relation to other conservatisms, liberalism, and pacifism
0–89526–811–6 Regnery pb $8.95

Russell Kirk, editor
THE PORTABLE CONSERVATIVE READER
A highly diverse collection of readings including Burke, John Adams, Hamilton, Calhoun, Tocqueville, Henry Adams, Santayana, T.S. Eliot, C.S. Lewis, Michael Oakeshott, and fiction by Conrad and Kipling
0–14015–095–1 Penguin pb $8.95

● Irving Kristol
REFLECTIONS OF A NEOCONSERVATIVE: Looking Back, Looking Ahead
Essays about the author's Trotskyite phase, leftist intellectuals, pornography, Machiavelli, the decline of socialism, and the future of US foreign policy
0–465–67872–3 Basic Books $19.95
0–465–06873–1 Basic Books pb $9.95

● José Ortega y Gasset
THE REVOLT OF THE MASSES
A famous and incisive study of the effects of bureaucracy, specialization, mass production, and cultural mediocrity on the European spirit
0–393–09637–8 Norton pb $3.95

● Andrew Dobson
AN INTRODUCTION TO THE POLITICAL PHILOSOPHY OF JOSE ORTEGA Y GASSET
0–521–36068–4 Cambridge $39.50

● Thomas Sowell
COMPASSION VS. GUILT & OTHER ESSAYS
0–688–07114–7 Morrow pb $15.95

A CONFLICT OF VISIONS
How two radically opposed visions of human nature have manifested themselves in the political controversies of the past two centuries, including such contemporary issues as welfare reform, social justice, and crime
0–688–07951–2 Morrow pb $7.95

THE ECONOMICS AND POLITICS OF RACE: An International Perspective
Myths and realities about the varying fortunes of ethnic and racial groups in the United States and in the Third World
0–688–04832–3 Morrow pb $6.95

MARKETS AND MINORITIES
0–465–04399–2 Basic pb $9.95

MARXISM: Philosophy and Economics
A critical analysis by the leading American black conservative thinker
0–688–06426–4 Morrow pb $8.95

● Leo Strauss
Strauss, a refugee from Hitler, saw as the chief threat to democracy the mass culture fostered by democracy itself.

THE CITY AND MAN
0–226–77701–4 Chicago pb $11.95

NATURAL RIGHT AND HISTORY
0–226–77694–8 Chicago pb $10.95

ON TYRANNY
0–8014–9073–1 Cornell pb $9.95

THOUGHTS ON MACHIAVELLI
0–226–77704–9 Chicago pb $16.00

WHAT IS POLITICAL PHILOSOPHY?
0–226–77713–8 Chicago pb $12.95

● Eric Voegelin
FROM ENLIGHTENMENT TO REVOLUTION
The spiritual crisis of modern times seen in the attempts to create a new humanity in Marxism, Nietzscheanism, and Nazism
Edited by John Hallowell
0–8223–0478–3 Duke pb $11.95

SCIENCE, POLITICS AND GNOSTICISM
A short study linking the alienated pessimism of the ancient Gnostic heresy with modern theories of alienation and revolutionary deliverance in Hegel, Marx, Nietzsche, and German national socialism
0–89526–964–3 Regnery pb $6.50

● Richard Weaver
IDEAS HAVE CONSEQUENCES
A Platonic-Christian perspective on the modern fragmentation of humanity as revealed in philosophy, literature, psychology, and politics
0–226–87680–2 Chicago pb $7.95

FASCISM AND TOTALITARIANISM

● Adolf Hitler
MEIN KAMPF
Hitler's vituperative autobiography, written while he was in prison for his beer-hall *putsch*, gives his theories of Aryan superiority, Jewish conspiracy, and democratic degeneracy and provides a blueprint of his totalitarian regime and war aims
Translated by Ralph Manheim
0–395–07801–6 Houghton Mifflin $17.95
0–395–08362–1 Houghton Mifflin pb $9.95

Commentaries on Fascism

● T.W. Adorno, Else Frenkel-Brunswik & Daniel J. Levinson
THE AUTHORITARIAN PERSONALITY
A psychoanalytic attempt to isolate personality traits that would predispose an individual to fascism
0–393–30042–0 Norton pb $12.95

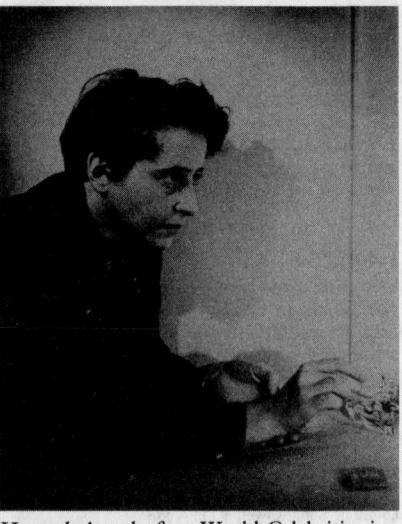

Hannah Arendt, from World Celebrities in Ninety Photographic Portraits *by Fred Stein (Dover)*

● Hannah Arendt
A student of Heidegger, Arendt fled Germany in 1933 and eventually settled in New York where she wrote *The Origins of Totalitarianism* and other works analyzing the political crises and disintegration of modern western civilization.

THE ORIGINS OF TOTALITARIANISM
0–15–670153–7 HBJ pb $10.95

ON REVOLUTION
0–14–021681–2 Penguin pb $7.95

ON VIOLENCE
0–15–669500–6 HBJ pb $3.95

IMPORTANT RECENT WORK

▶ **See also American Politics and Foreign Policy**

● Kenneth J. Arrow
SOCIAL CHOICE AND INDIVIDUAL VALUES
An important work on democratic decision-making by the influential Nobel-prize-winning American economist
0–300–01364–7 Yale pb $7.95

● James M. Buchanan
THE LIMITS OF LIBERTY: Between Anarchy and Leviathan
A leading economist's examination of questions of freedom and authority within the framework of rights and rules established by a social contract theory of democracy
0–226–07820–5 Chicago pb $10.95

● Bernard Crick
IN DEFENSE OF POLITICS
0–226–12064–3 Chicago pb $15.00

● Robert A. Dahl
DILEMMAS OF PLURALIST DEMOCRACY
On the possibility of a decentralized, worker-controlled socialist economy
0–300–03076–2 Yale pb $9.95

● **IF YOU CAN'T FIND IT, LOOK IN THE INDEX**

A PREFACE TO DEMOCRATIC THEORY
The case for a new theoretical model of democracy to replace the traditional alternatives, Madisonian and populist, which, Dahl argues, no longer apply
0–226–13426–1 Chicago pb $6.00

• John Dunn
MODERN REVOLUTIONS: An Introduction to the Analysis of a Political Phenomenon
A study of revolutions and their ideologies in Russia, China, Mexico, Vietnam, Algeria, Turkey, Cuba, and Yugoslavia
0–521–09698–7 Cambridge pb $14.95

RETHINKING MODERN POLITICAL THEORY: Essays 1979-1983
Incisive essays on Locke, revolution, political philosophy, and the future of liberalism by an advocate of a prudential, anti-utopian political theory and practice
0–521–31695–2 Cambridge pb $15.95

• Michael Harrington
THE NEXT LEFT: The History of the Future
On the approaching economic crisis and opportunities for democratic socialism
0–8050–0104–2 Henry Holt $17.95
0–8050–0792–X Henry Holt pb $8.95

THE TWILIGHT OF CAPITALISM
A largely economic study of the inevitability of crisis in welfare-state capitalism and the limited ability of Marxist theory to predict it precisely
0–671–22759–9 Simon & Schuster pb $10.95

• Morris Janowitz
SOCIAL CONTROL OF THE WELFARE STATE
On the dilemmas of welfare state programs in the U.S. and the need to increase democratic participation in them to reverse the drift toward coercion
0–226–39308–9 Chicago pb $3.95

• Steven Lukes
MARXISM AND MORALITY
According to Lukes, the inability of Marxism to give an adequate account of human rights, justice, and the relation of ends and means has left it no resources with which to resist the crimes committed in its name; a cogent, closely argued case for a new Marxist moral theory that examines the moral and philosophical arguments of Trotsky, Sartre, Camus, Merleau-Ponty, Brecht, Koestler, and others
0–19–876101–5 Oxford $24.95

• David McLellan
IDEOLOGY
A brief account of the history of the concept from the Enlightenment, through Marx, to Weber, Mannheim, Gramsci, and Habermas
0–8166–1523–3 Minnesota pb $9.95

• Bertell Ollman
ALIENATION: Marx's Conception of Man in Capitalist Society
Marx's theory of internal relations as the conceptual foundation of his views of alienation and ideology
0–521–29083–X Cambridge pb $15.95

SOCIAL AND SEXUAL REVOLUTION: Essays on Marx and Reich
0–89608–080–3 South End pb $7.50

• Roberto Unger
KNOWLEDGE AND POLITICS
0–02–932840–3 Free Press pb $14.95

LAW IN MODERN SOCIETY: Toward a Criticism of Social Theory
The development of law and legal theory in the West and the increasing irrelevance of traditional concepts of legality due to social and cultural changes that demand a new integration of law with social theory
0–02–932880–2 Free Press pb $14.95

• Michael Walzer
THE COMPANY OF CRITICS: Social Criticism and Political Commitment in the Twentieth Century
0–465–01331–7 Basic Books $19.95

THE SPHERE OF JUSTICE: A Defense of Pluralism and Equality
An ambitious, comprehensive study of the relation of social institutions to equality and justice, taking in such questions as citizenship, group membership, work, money, leisure, education, marriage and family, welfare, and religion, and comparing a wide range of societies and historical periods
0–465–08190–8 Basic Books $19.95
0–465–08189–4 Basic Books pb $11.95

International Relations and Strategic Studies

The study of relations and conflicts among states has few obvious parameters. Theorists of the international system must have a solid grounding in the history of war, diplomacy, economics, law, and philosophy, all of which have their own canons of discourse. Most scholars also take a keen interest in contemporary political affairs; whether explicitly or implicitly, the truths inherent in past events have relevance to the concerns of the present day. In a world that lives daily with the specter of nuclear armageddon and financial catastrophe, questions about the nature of war are as urgent as ever.

▶ **Many topics that might fall within this listing are treated elsewhere, notably in European and American history.**

THEORIES OF INTERNATIONAL RELATIONS

Historians explain particular events; political scientists classify, synthesize, generalize. The following works include samples of both approaches, with emphasis on the latter. The causes of war, the nature of international change, the operation of the balance of power, and the institutions of

international society are among the topics examined in these works, many of which are classics in the field of political writing.

• Bernard Brodie
WAR AND POLITICS
The distilled wisdom of the dean of American strategic studies, who died in 1978
0–02–315020–3 Macmillan $24.50

• Seyom Brown
CAUSES AND PREVENTION OF WAR
An examination of "the central survival question facing our species: How can we reduce the role of large-scale violence in world society?"
0–312–00473–7 St Martin's $32.50
0–312–12532–1 St Martin's pb $13.95

• Hedley Bull
THE ANARCHICAL SOCIETY: A Study of Order in World Politics
Argues that the state system is not an obstacle to world order but its essential foundation
0–231–04132–2 Columbia $37.50
0–231–04133–0 Columbia pb $15.00

• E.H. Carr
THE TWENTY YEARS' CRISIS, 1919-1939: An Introduction to the Study of International Relations
"The characteristic vice of the utopian," Carr held, "is naiveté; of the realist, sterility." First published on the eve of the Second World War, this is a classic analysis of realism and utopianism in world politics
0–06–131122–7 Harper & Row pb $6.95

• Robert Gilpin
WAR AND CHANGE IN WORLD POLITICS
An ambitious attempt to formulate a theory of international political change. "An intelligent and intellectually stimulating, if speculative, study of major issues in world politics"—*Times Higher Education Supplement*
0–521–27376–5 Cambridge pb $13.95

• Stanley Hoffmann
JANUS AND MINERVA: Essays in the Theory and Practice of International Politics
An impressive collection of writings on international politics over the years, which shows Hoffmann to be equally adept at theoretical and practical analysis
0–8133–0390–7 Westview $43.50

• Hans J. Morgenthau
POLITICS AMONG NATIONS
Morgenthau's 1948 work was a point of departure for a generation of scholars. Now in its sixth edition, it remains worthy of serious study
Edited by Kenneth W. Thompson
0–394–33564–3 Knopf $23.00

• Richard E. Neustadt & Ernest R. May
THINKING IN TIME: The Uses of History for Decision Makers
A Harvard political scientist and a Harvard historian offer rules that decision-makers

Pitt and Napoleon carving out their respective spheres of influence, from The Satirical Etchings *of James Gillray edited by Draper Hill (Dover)*

can follow to use history more widely and effectively
0–02–922790–9 Free Press $22.95
0–02–922791–7 Free Press pb $9.95

• Hugh Tinker
RACE, CONFLICT AND THE INTERNATIONAL ORDER: From Empire to United Nations
Published in 1977
0–312–66130–4 St. Martin's $22.50

• Stephen M. Walt
THE ORIGINS OF ALLIANCES
The author tests a variety of theories regarding the formation of alliances and concludes that states are more likely to "balance" rather than "bandwagon" when faced with would-be hegemons
0–8014–2054–7 Cornell $32.50

• Kenneth N. Waltz
MAN, THE STATE AND WAR: A Theoretical Analysis
The causes of war in the light of three approaches to interstate rivalry: as an expression of human nature, as a reflection of the internal character of the state, and as a consequence of the anarchical character of the state system
0–231–08564–8 Columbia pb $14.00

THEORY OF INTERNATIONAL POLITICS
A major treatise on international politics. This work is of great value for advanced students, but not recommended for beginners
0–07–55485–2 McGraw-Hill $20.95

• Martin Wight
POWER POLITICS
A neglected masterpiece, this book deserves a wide readership among students of international relations
Edited by Hedley Bull
0–8419–0344–1 Holmes & Meier $35.00

THE INTERNATIONAL SYSTEM TO 1900

• Gordon A. Craig & George L. Alexander
FORCE AND STATECRAFT: Diplomatic Problems of Our Time
0–19–503115–6 Oxford $22.50
0–19–503116–4 Oxford pb $12.95

• Michael W. Doyle
EMPIRES
A wide-ranging account of the birth, life, and death of empires
0–8014–1756–2 Cornell $43.50
0–8014–9334–X Cornell pb $14.95

• Murray G. Forsyth
UNIONS OF STATES: Theory and Practice of Confederation
0–8419–0691–2 Holmes & Meier $35.00
0–8419–0729–3 Holmes & Meier pb $19.50

• Edward V. Gulick
EUROPE'S CLASSICAL BALANCE OF POWER
Gulick's case history is the Congress of Vienna. The first part of the work identifies the assumptions, aims, and applications of balance of power theory in the 18th century
0–393–00413–9 Norton pb $8.95

• Francis H. Hinsley
POWER AND THE PURSUIT OF PEACE
Surveys the growth of internationalist thought from the end of the middle ages to the 20th century, and analyzes the evolution of the modern state system from the 18th century to the present day. Excellent, though difficult for the beginning reader
0–521–09448–8 Cambridge pb $17.95

• George F. Kennan
THE DECLINE OF BISMARCK'S EUROPEAN ORDER: Franco-Russian Relations, 1875-1890
The causes of World War I, by a distinguished American diplomat
0–691–05282–4 Princeton $44.50
0–691–00784–5 Princeton pb $14.50

THE FATEFUL ALLIANCE: France, Russia and the Coming of the First World War
0–394–72231–0 Pantheon pb $8.95

• Paul Kennedy
THE RISE AND FALL OF THE GREAT POWERS: Economic Change and Military Conflict from 1500 to 2000
A work of extraordinary breadth and learning, this national best seller examines cases of "imperial overstretch" in the past and concludes with a somber warning for the contemporary prospects of preserving the Pax Americana
0–394–54674–1 Random House $24.95
0–679–72019–7 Random House pb $12.95

• Henry A. Kissinger
A WORLD RESTORED: Metternich, Castlereagh and the Problems of Peace, 1812-1822
A stimulating work on the reconstruction of Europe after the Napoleonic Wars
0–395–17229–2 Houghton Mifflin pb $11.95

• Evan Luard
WAR IN INTERNATIONAL SOCIETY
0–300–04016–4 Yale $32.50

• Garrett Mattingly
RENAISSANCE DIPLOMACY
The classic study of the age of Machiavelli
0–486–25570–0 Dover pb $7.95

• William H. McNeill
THE PURSUIT OF POWER: Technology, Armed Force, and Society Since A.D. 1000
Society's conflicts and dilemmas from the cross-bow to the nuclear missile, and the arms race as the engine of change
0–226–56157–7 Chicago $20.00
0–226–56158–5 Chicago pb $11.95

• Ronald Robinson & John Gallagher
AFRICA AND THE VICTORIANS: The Official Mind of Imperialism
A superb history. Robinson and Gallagher invert the traditional explanation of imperialism by seeing it as a response to a series of profound upheavals
0–333–05552–7 Humanities pb $19.95

• Robert W. Tucker & David C. Hendrickson
THE FALL OF THE FIRST BRITISH EMPIRE: Origins of the War of American Independence
Another study of the rise and fall of an empire
0–8018–2780–9 Johns Hopkins $39.50

THE 20TH-CENTURY WORLD

• Geoffrey Barraclough
AN INTRODUCTION TO CONTEMPORARY HISTORY
First published in the early 1960s, this work remains a valuable introduction to the transformation of the international system in the 20th century
0–14–020827–5 Penguin pb $5.95

• David Calleo
THE GERMAN PROBLEM RECONSIDERED
An original essay on the central diplomatic question of the century from 1848 to 1948
0–521–22309–1 Cambridge $29.95
0–521–29966–7 Cambridge pb $11.95

• Peter Calvocoressi
WORLD POLITICS SINCE 1945
Accurate and concise, this work contains a wealth of detail on every region of the world and is a handy reference guide to the world history of the post-World War II era
0–582–29713–3 Longman pb $19.95

• Gordon A. Craig
GERMANY, 1866-1945
A superbly written book which traces the rise and fall of German power from Bismarck's victory over Austria in 1866 to Hitler's last days in the bunker
0–19–822113–4 Oxford $39.95
0–19–502724–8 Oxford pb $16.95

• Geoffrey F. Hudson
THE FAR EAST IN WORLD POLITICS
First published in 1937, this book remains an excellent introduction to the subject
0–374–94029–0 Hippocrene $19.50

• Paul Kennedy
STRATEGY AND DIPLOMACY: 1870-1945
A collection of eight essays concentrating on Britain's attempts to come to terms with decline
0–04–902007–2 Unwin Hyman $29.95
0–04–902008–0 Unwin Hyman pb $9.95

• William R. Keylor
THE TWENTIETH-CENTURY WORLD: An International History
0–19–503370–1 Oxford pb $13.95

• George Lenczowski
THE MIDDLE EAST IN WORLD AFFAIRS
A comprehensive work on the history, government, and politics of the Middle East to 1980
0–8014–1273–0 Cornell $45.00
0–8014–9872–4 Cornell pb $21.95

• Evan Luard
A HISTORY OF THE UNITED NATIONS, 1945-1955
0–312–38654–0 St. Martin's $27.50

• R.K. Ramazani
REVOLUTIONARY IRAN: Challenge and Response in the Middle East
Published in 1987
0–8018–3377–9 Johns Hopkins $27.50
0–8018–3610–7 Johns Hopkins pb $10.95

• Nadav Safran
ISRAEL: The Embattled Ally
The second part of this excellent work contains a clear and readable examination of the Arab-Israeli conflict. Published in 1978
0–674–46881–3 Harvard $32.00
0–674–46882–1 Harvard pb $12.50

• D.C. Watt
SUCCEEDING JOHN BULL: America in Britain's Place, 1900-1975
An Englishman reviews the transition with a begrudging but always intelligent eye
0–521–25022–6 Cambridge $39.50

The Third World

Graham Hancock
LORDS OF POVERTY: The Power, Prestige, and Corruption of the International Aid Business
An unflattering portrait of the business and politics of foreign aid
0–87113–253–2 Atlantic Monthly $17.95

Nigel Harris
THE END OF THE THIRD WORLD
0–14–022563–3 Penguin pb $6.95

Hernando De Soto
THE OTHER PATH: The Invisible Revolution in the Third World
A revolutionary analysis of the economies and political alliances of the Third World, based on a case study of Lima
Preface by Mario Vargas Llosa
0–06–016020–9 Harper & Row $22.95

L.S. Stavrianos
GLOBAL RIFT: The Third World Comes of Age
0–688–00657–4 Morrow pb $17.00

THE COLD WAR: Soviet-American Relations

▶ See also Russian and Soviet Studies

• Seweryn Bialer
THE SOVIET PARADOX: External Expansion, Internal Decline
A leading Kremlinologist at Columbia University examines the prospects for Russia under Gorbachev. Published in 1987
0–394–54095–6 Knopf $22.95
0–394–75288–0 Random House pb $9.95

• Seweryn Bialer & Michael Mandelbaum
THE GLOBAL RIVALS
The companion to the PBS series
0–394–57194–0 Knopf $18.95

• Noam Chomsky
TOWARDS A NEW COLD WAR: Essays on the Current Crisis and How We Got There
Published in 1982
0–394–74944–8 Pantheon pb $11.95

• Richard Crockatt & Steve Smith, editors
THE COLD WAR: Past and Present
Essays from American and European scholars on such topics as "Detente: A United States View," "SDI and the New Cold War," and "Eastern Europe and the New Cold War"
0–04–27102–2 Unwin Hyman pb $14.95

The Big Four of 1919: Lloyd George, Orlando, Clemenceau, and Wilson, from The American Century *by Walter LaFeber and others (Knopf)*

The Big Three of 1945: Churchill, Roosevelt, and Stalin at Yalta, from Europe In the Twentieth Century *by Robert Paxton (HBJ)*

• Anton W. DePorte

EUROPE BETWEEN THE SUPERPOWERS: The Enduring Balance
A clear-headed account of the origins of the Cold War, seeing it as a solution to the German problem
0–300–04081–4 Yale $35.00
0–300–03758–9 Yale pb $10.95

• John L. Gaddis

THE LONG PEACE: Inquiries into the History of the Cold War
A collection of essays notable for their mastery of historical sources and for an attempt to identify the elements of stability within the Soviet-American competition
0–19–504336–7 Oxford $24.95

• Gregg Herken

THE WINNING WEAPON: The Atomic Bomb in the Cold War, 1945-1950
"A major contribution to our understanding of American nuclear policy in the years after Hiroshima"—McGeorge Bundy
0–691–02286–0 Princeton pb $12.50
0–394–75160–4 Random House pb $7.95

Seymour M. Hersh
"THE TARGET IS DESTROYED":
What Really Happened to Flight 007 and What America Knew About It
"A sordid, nasty story"—William Hines, *Chicago Sun-Times*
0–394–75527–8 Random House pb' $4.95

R.W. Johnson
SHOOTDOWN: Flight 007 and the American Connection
0–14–009474–1 Penguin pb $4.50

• William G. Hyland

MORTAL RIVALS: Understanding the Hidden Pattern of Soviet-American Relations
By the editor of *Foreign Affairs*, who was a deputy to Henry Kissinger and participated in four summit meetings. Published in 1988
0–671–66871–4 Simon & Schuster pb $8.95

• Walter LaFeber

AMERICA, RUSSIA AND THE COLD WAR, 1945-1984
The fifth edition of a classic work
0–394–34391–3 Random House pb $13.50

• Joseph S. Nye, Jr., editor

THE MAKING OF AMERICA'S SOVIET POLICY
Contributors include Nye, Richard K. Betts, Ernest R. May, Stanley Hoffmann, and others
0–300–03416–4 Yale pb $14.95

• Adam B. Ulam

THE RIVALS: America and Russia Since World War II
0–14–004309–8 Penguin pb $8.95

THE DEBATE OVER NATO

• David P. Calleo

BEYOND AMERICAN HEGEMONY: The Future of the Western Alliance
A political scientist at Johns Hopkins calls for a devolution of responsibility; published in 1987
0–465–00655–8 Basic Books $20.95

• Don Cook

FORGING THE ALLIANCE: The Birth of the NATO Treaty and the Dramatic Transformation of U.S. Foreign Policy Between 1945 and 1950
The actors in this drama include Churchill, Truman, Bevin, Acheson, Eisenhower, De Gaulle, Kennan, Monnet, Adenauer, and Marshall
1–557–10043–8 Morrow $21.95

• Jonathan Dean

WATERSHED IN EUROPE: Dismantling the East-West Military Confrontation
The prospects for arms control negotiations in Europe; published in 1986
0–669–11120–1 Lexington $29.00
0–669–11121–X Lexington pb $9.95

• Alfred Grosser

THE WESTERN ALLIANCE: European-American Relations since 1945
An excellent introduction to the history of the Alliance, by the distinguished French historian
Foreword by Stanley Hoffmann
0–8264–0004–3 Continuum $19.50
0–394–70815–6 Random House pb $8.50

• Josef Joffe

THE LIMITED PARTNERSHIP: Europe, the United States, and the Burdens of Alliance
A brilliant examination of the Atlantic Alliance from a European perspective; published in 1987
0–88730–216–5 Ballinger $29.95

• Lawrence S. Kaplan

NATO AND THE UNITED STATES: The Enduring Alliance
The founding of NATO and the impact of such major events as the Korean War, the launching of Sputnik, and De Gaulle's decision to pull France out in 1966
0–8057–9200–7 Twayne pb $10.95

• Melvyn Krauss

HOW NATO WEAKENS THE WEST
A "neo-conservative" attack on the Atlantic Alliance; published in 1987
0–671–54455–1 Simon & Schuster $18.95

• Paul H. Nitze & others

SECURING THE SEAS: The Soviet Naval Challenge and Western Alliance Options
Published in 1979
0–89158–360–2 Westview pb $19.95

• Robert W. Tucker & Linda Wrigley, editors

THE ATLANTIC ALLIANCE AND ITS CRITICS
Excellent essays from Pierre Hassner, A.W. DePorte, Theodore Draper, Pierre Lelouche, Simon Serfaty, and Robert W. Tucker
0–275–91094–6 Praeger $29.95
0–275–91592–1 Praeger pb $13.95

TERRORISM AND COUNTER-TERRORISM

• Richard Falk

REVOLUTIONARIES AND FUNCTIONARIES: The Dual Face of Terrorism
Points the finger at recognized governments as well as at underground organizations
0–525–24604–5 Dutton $17.95

• Che Guevara

GUERRILLA WARFARE
Guevara's works and the application of his theories to guerrilla campaigns in Central and South America
Introduction & case studies by Brian Loveman & Thomas M. Davies, Jr.
0–8032–7010–0 Nebraska pb $10.95

• Michael T. Klare & Peter Kornbluh
LOW INTENSITY WARFARE: Counter Insurgency, Proinsurgency, and Antiterrorism in the '80s
0–394–74653–8 Pantheon pb $8.95

• Michael King
DEATH OF THE RAINBOW WARRIOR
Full investigation into the French secret service bombing that sank the Greenpeace vessel and killed one of the crew
0–14–009738–4 Penguin pb $5.95

Walter Laqueur
THE AGE OF TERRORISM
Based on Laqueur's indispensable classic, *Terrorism*, which first appeared in 1977, this study traces the history of political terror from its roots in 19th-century Europe, through the anarchists of the 1880s and 1890s (responsible for the assassinations of a czar and a US president), to the multinational operations of our own time and the crucial role of the media
0–316–51478–0 Little, Brown $19.95
0–316–51479–9 Little, Brown pb $10.95

• Robin Morgan
THE DEMON LOVER: On the Sexuality of Terrorism
"By taking us to the sexual place where violence begins, *The Demon Lover* gives us a new belief that it can never be justified and is never inevitable"—Gloria Steinem
0–393–02642–6 Norton $18.95

• Conor Cruise O'Brien
PASSION AND CUNNING: Essays on Nationalism, Terrorism, and Revolution
The wide range covers the Sandinistas, Bobby Sands, Chaim Weizmann and David Ben-Gurion, and Archbishop Tutu
0–671–66724–6 Simon & Schuster $18.95

• David C. Rapaport, editor
INSIDE TERRORIST ORGANIZATIONS
Published in 1988
0–231–06721–6 Columbia pb $14.50

• Richard E. Rubenstein
ALCHEMISTS OF REVOLUTION: Terrorism in the Modern World
Reports on the Shining Path, the Quebec Liberation Front, the PLO, and Gush Emunim, as well as general essays on the nature of terrorism
0–465–00094–0 Basic Books pb $8.95

• Theodore Shackley
THE THIRD OPTION: An American View of Counterinsurgency Operations
A 1988 study suggesting the unused possibilities of counterinsurgency through intelligence agencies
0–440–20219–1 Dell pb $3.95

INTERNATIONAL POLITICAL ECONOMY

• David A. Baldwin
ECONOMIC STATECRAFT
Examines not only the utility of economic statecraft but also its morality and legality, and its role in the history of international thought
0–691–10175–2 Princeton pb $12.50

• Robert Gilpin
THE POLITICAL ECONOMY OF INTERNATIONAL RELATIONS
Excellent study of the political and economic forces affecting money, trade, development, finance, and the multinational corporation; likely to become the standard text on the subject
0–691–07732–0 Princeton $45.00
0–691–02262–3 Princeton pb $9.95

• Marshall I. Goldman
GORBACHEV'S CHALLENGE: Economic Reform in the Age of High Technology
The prospects for perestroika
0–393–02454–7 Norton $16.95

• Mikhail Gorbachev
PERESTROIKA: New Thinking for Our Country and the World
The glasnost czar's own blueprint for domestic and world reform
0–060–39085–9 Harper & Row $19.95

• Roger D. Hansen
BEYOND THE NORTH-SOUTH STALEMATE
0–07–026048–6 McGraw-Hill $23.95
0–07–026049–4 McGraw-Hill pb $5.95

• Robert O. Keohane
AFTER HEGEMONY: Cooperation and Discord in the World Political Economy
Keohane disputes the argument that the decline of American hegemony makes cooperation among the advanced capitalist nations impossible
0–691–07676–6 Princeton $31.50
0–691–02228–3 Princeton pb $8.95

• Charles Kindleberger
MANIAS, PANICS, AND CRASHES: A History of Financial Crises
The author, a professor emeritus at MIT, shows how financial institutions decompose and recommends the seeking out of a "lender of the last resort."
Published in 1980
0–465–04402–6 Basic Books pb $9.95

• Stephen D. Krasner
STRUCTURAL CONFLICT: The Third World Against Global Liberalism
Argues that many analysts have mistakenly emphasized economics at the expense of politics in their analyses of relations between developed and developing states.
Published in 1985
0–520–05400–8 California $30.00
0–520–05478–4 California pb $11.95

• Charles Lipson
STANDING GUARD: Protecting Foreign Capital in the Nineteenth and Twentieth Centuries
0–520–03468–6 California $37.00
0–520–05327–3 California pb $11.95

• Gerald M. Meier
EMERGING FROM POVERTY: The Economics that Really Matters
An overview of the state of the economics of development; published in 1984
0–19–503714–6 Oxford pb $11.95

• Peter R. Odell
OIL AND WORLD POWER
The best introduction to the energy problem and a model work in political economy
0–14–022731–8 Penguin pb $6.95

• Richard Rosecrance
THE RISE OF THE TRADING STATE: Commerce and Conquest in the Modern World
Argues that a new "trading world" in international relations offers the possibility of escaping the "vicious cycle" of endemic warfare and of finding new patterns of cooperation among nation-states
0–465–07035–3 Basic Books $19.95
0–465–07036–1 Basic Books pb $9.95

LAW, MORALITY, AND JUSTICE

• Michael Akehurst
A MODERN INTRODUCTION TO INTERNATIONAL LAW
An up-to-date (1987) examination of the state of international law
0–04–341037–5 Unwin Hyman pb $14.95

• Charles R. Beitz
POLITICAL THEORY AND INTERNATIONAL RELATIONS
Sets forth a case for a global redistribution of resources. Published in 1979
0–691–07614–6 Princeton $26.50
0–691–02192–9 Princeton pb $9.50

• Sissela Bok
A STRATEGY FOR PEACE: Human Values and the Threat of War
Postscript by Erik Erikson
0–394–55670–4 Pantheon $17.95

• Ken Booth
LAW, FORCE AND DIPLOMACY AT SEA
Published in 1985
0–04–341028–6 Unwin Hyman pb $13.95

• Thomas M. Franck
NATION AGAINST NATION: What Happened to the U.N. Dream and What the U.S. Can Do About It
An examination of the United Nations by a law professor and former employee of the organization
0–19–503587–9 Oxford $22.95

- James T. Johnson
CAN MODERN WAR BE JUST?
A distinguished historian of the "just war"
examines a range of issues
0–300–03165–3 Yale $25.00
0–300–03626–4 Yale pb $10.95

- Steven Kull
**MINDS AT WAR: Nuclear Reality and the
Inner Conflicts of Defense Policymakers**
Published in 1988
0–465–04610–X Basic Books $19.95

- Terry Nardin
**LAW, MORALITY, AND THE
RELATIONS OF STATES**
This ambitious work defends a "practical"
conception of international association, in
which international law is understood to
regulate the relations of states with
differing and even incompatible goals
0–691–07663–4 Princeton $41.00
0–691–10155–8 Princeton pb $15.50

Michael Walzer
JUST AND UNJUST WARS
An excellent work notable not only for
its conclusions but for its historical and
analogical method of discourse.
Recommended for beginning and
advanced students alike
0–465–03705–4 Basic Books pb $9.95

STRATEGIC STUDIES

Strategy, as Sir Basil Liddell-Hart once
put it, is "the art of distributing and
applying military means to fulfill the ends of
policy." The following books take up a range
of historical and contemporary problems in
strategic studies, largely from an American
perspective.

- Lawrence Freedman
**THE EVOLUTION OF NUCLEAR
STRATEGY**
Published in 1983
0–312–27269–3 St Martin's $35.00
0–312–27270–7 St Martin's pb $11.95

- Michael Howard
WAR IN EUROPEAN HISTORY
A short and authoritative study of warfare
as it has developed in Western Europe
from the middle ages to the present day
0–19–289095–6 Oxford pb $9.95

- John Keegan
THE FACE OF BATTLE
A brilliant work on the predicament of
individual soldiers in battle
0–14–004897–9 Penguin pb $8.95

THE MASK OF COMMAND
A comprehensive analysis of generalship
0–670–45988–7 Viking $18.95

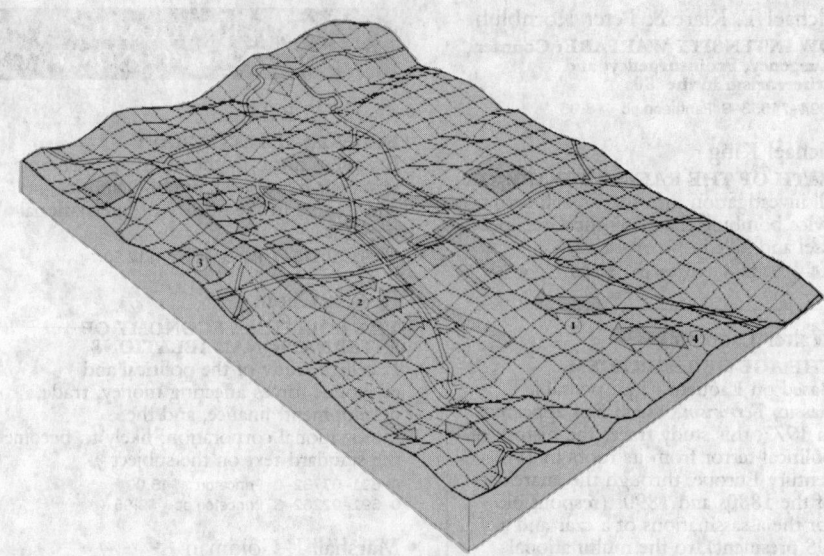

A computer recreation of the terrain at Waterloo, from Great Battlefields of the World *by John MacDonald (Macmillan)*

- Edward N. Luttwak
**THE MEANING OF VICTORY: Essays on
Strategy**
Topics include the arms race, Pentagon
spending and US-Soviet competition;
published in 1987
0–671–63317–1 Simon & Schuster pb $9.95

STRATEGY: The Logic of War and Peace
Sets forth a general theory of the
"paradoxical logic" of strategy
0–674–83995–1 Harvard $20.00

Carl von Clausewitz
ON WAR
Clausewitz's study of war, first
published in 1832, is generally
acknowledged to be the great
theoretical treatment of the subject.
This edition contains valuable
introductory essays by Paret, Howard,
and Bernard Brodie that explain the
genesis, influence, and continuing
relevance of *On War*, as well as an
entertaining and instructive
commentary on the text by Brodie
Edited by Peter Paret & Michael Howard
0–691–05657–9 Princeton $33.00
0–14–044427–0 Penguin pb $5.95

Raymond Aron
CLAUSEWITZ: Philosopher of War
An English translation of Aron's last
great work, *Penser la Guerre, Clausewitz*
0–671–62826–7 Simon & Schuster pb $9.95

Michael Howard
CLAUSEWITZ
An excellent short essay on the master
of strategic thought. Highly
recommended
0–19–287607–4 Oxford pb $4.95

- John J. Mearsheimer
CONVENTIONAL DETERRENCE
How nations faced with the prospect of
large-scale conventional war choose
offensive or defensive strategies
0–8014–1569–1 Cornell $34.95
0–8014–9346–3 Cornell pb $12.95

- Steven Miller, editor
**MILITARY STRATEGY AND THE
ORIGINS OF THE FIRST WORLD WAR:
An International Security Reader**
Essays on the relationship between military
doctrine and the outbreak of the First
World War
0–691–02232–1 Princeton pb $7.50

- John Mueller
**RETREAT FROM DOOMSDAY: The
Obsolescence of Major War**
Why a major war among the developed
nations of the world has become
increasingly unlikely
0–465–06939–8 Basic Books $20.95

- Peter Paret, Gordon A. Craig & Felix
Gilbert, editors
**MAKERS OF MODERN STRATEGY:
From Machiavelli to the Nuclear Age**
An excellent compendium of essays from
many of the leading historians of strategic
thought
0–691–09235–4 Princeton $47.50
0–691–02764–1 Princeton pb $12.95

- Theodore Ropp
WAR IN THE MODERN WORLD
A good introduction to the history of war
since 1415
0–02–036390–7 Macmillan pb $8.95

- Paul Seabury & Angelo Codevilla
WAR: Ends and Means
A new study on the meaning and uses of
war. "An elegant and learned essay with
historical examples in the style of
Machiavelli"—Samuel P. Huntington
0–465–09067–2 Basic Books $19.95

• Harry G. Summers, Jr.
ON STRATEGY: A Critical Analysis of the Vietnam War
An American colonel explains his ideas on strategy and tells how the US could have won the war
0–89141–156–9 Presidio $14.95

• Martin Van Creveld
COMMAND IN WAR
The development of the nature of command from "the stone age" to Vietnam
0–674–14440–6 Harvard $22.50
0–674–14441–4 Harvard pb $10.95

• Russell F. Weigley
THE AMERICAN WAY OF WAR: A History of U.S. Military Strategy and Policy
The best introduction to American military thought. Published in 1973
0–253–28029–X Indiana pb $12.95

NUCLEAR WEAPONS AND ARMS CONTROL

The Nuclear Test Ban Debate

Howard Ball
JUSTICE DOWNWIND: America's Atomic Testing Program in the 1950s
The astonishing story of how the US exploded atomic weapons on its own soil between 1951 and 1963 as part of a postwar military nuclear testing program. "A praiseworthy job of exploring one of the great scandals of the atomic age"—*Chicago Sun-Times*
0–19–503672–7 Oxford $21.95
0–19–505357–7 Oxford pb $8.95

Robert A. Divine
BLOWING ON THE WIND: The Nuclear Test Ban Debate, 1954-1960
Using contemporary sources and formerly inaccessible Eisenhower papers, Divine traces the development of the H-bomb by the US and USSR
0–19–502390–0 Oxford $24.95

Glenn T. Seaborg & Benjamin S. Loeb
KENNEDY, KHRUSHCHEV, AND THE TEST BAN
0–520–04332–4 California $23.00
0–520–04961–6 California pb $8.95

Nuclear Strategy

• Bruce D. Berkowitz
CALCULATED RISKS
A provocative analysis of arms control published in 1987
0–671–60087–7 Simon & Schuster $18.95

• Bruce G. Blair
STRATEGIC COMMAND AND CONTROL: Redefining the Nuclear Threat
An original study (1985) of the command and control of strategic weapons
0–8157–0982–X Brookings $32.95
0–8157–0981–1 Brookings pb $12.95

• McGeorge Bundy
DANGER AND SURVIVAL: Choices About the Bomb in the First Fifty Years
The most comprehensive political history of the nuclear bomb ever written
0–394–52278–8 Random House $24.95

• David DeWitt, editor
NUCLEAR NON-PROLIFERATION AND GLOBAL SECURITY
Published in 1987
0–312–00367–6 St. Martin's $37.50

• James F. Dunnigan
HOW TO MAKE WAR: A Comprehensive Guide to Modern Warfare
"Why the most modern weapons will not work as expected and there's not much anyone can do about it"
0–688–07979–2 Morrow pb $14.95

• Colin S. Gray
NUCLEAR STRATEGY AND NATIONAL STYLE
A 1986 study
0–8191–5334–6 University Press pb $18.95

• Peter Hayes & others
AMERICAN LAKE: Nuclear Peril in the Pacific
Why World War III is more likely to begin in the Pacific than in the Middle East or Europe
0–14–009396–6 Penguin pb $6.95

• Charles W. Kegley, Jr. & Eugene R. Wittkopf, editors
THE NUCLEAR READER: Strategy, Weapons, War
Published in 1985
0–312–57982–9 St. Martin's $27.50
0–312–57979–9 St. Martin's pb $14.00

• Henry A. Kissinger
NUCLEAR WEAPONS AND FOREIGN POLICY
0–393–00494–5 Norton pb $8.95

• Steven Kull
MINDS AT WAR: Nuclear Reality and the Inner Conflicts of Defense Policymakers
0–465–04610–X Basic Books $19.95

• Robert McNamara
BLUNDERING INTO DISASTER: Surviving the First Century of the Nuclear Age
The Secretary of Defense under John Kennedy and Lyndon Johnson analyzes the nuclear dilemma
0–394–55850–2 Pantheon $14.95
0–394–74987–1 Pantheon pb $5.95

• Michael Mandelbaum
THE NUCLEAR FUTURE
A clear introduction published in 1983
0–8014–9254–8 Cornell pb $6.95

THE NUCLEAR REVOLUTION: International Politics Before and After Hiroshima
0–521–28239–X Cambridge pb $10.95

• Charles R. Morris
IRON DESTINIES, LOST OPPORTUNITIES: The Arms Race Between the USA and the USSR, 1945-1987
0–06–039082–4 Harper & Row $22.95
0–88184–474–8 Carroll & Graf pb $13.95

• John Newhouse
WAR AND PEACE IN THE NUCLEAR AGE
A comprehensive survey of its subject and companion volume to the 1989 PBS series
0–394–56217–8 Knopf $22.95

• Eric Semler, James Benjamin & Adam Gross
THE LANGUAGE OF NUCLEAR WAR: An Intelligent Citizen's Dictionary
0–06–096123–6 Harper & Row pb $9.95

• Michael Sheehan
ARMS CONTROL: Theory and Practice
An introduction
0–631–16059–0 Blackwell pb $17.95

• Alan B. Sherr
THE OTHER SIDE OF ARMS CONTROL: Soviet Objectives in the Gorbachev Era
Analysis of how circumstances within and outside the Soviet Union make progress on arms control crucial to Soviet political and economic goals
0–04–445063–X Unwin Hyman pb $19.95

Strobe Talbott
DEADLY GAMBITS: The Reagan Administration and the Stalemate in Nuclear Arms Control
A history of the bureaucratic infighting, ideological conflicts, and personal antagonisms that hindered arms talks during the first Reagan administration
0–394–74009–2 Random House pb $7.95

THE MASTER OF THE GAME: Paul Nitze and the Nuclear Peace
0–394–56881–8 Knopf $19.95

• Robert W. Tucker
THE NUCLEAR DEBATE: Deterrence and the Lapse of Faith
A 1985 study
0–8419–1038–3 Holmes & Meier $24.50
0–8419–1039–1 Holmes & Meier pb $9.95

• Alvin M. Weinberg & Jack N. Barkenbus, editors
STRATEGIC DEFENSES AND ARMS CONTROL
Argues that a defense-dominated world may be safer than the current world situation
0–88702–219–7 Paragon pb $12.95

Nuclear Ethics and the Case Against the Bomb

• Nigel Calder
NUCLEAR NIGHTMARES
0–14–005867–2 Penguin pb $6.95

• Freeman Dyson
WEAPONS AND HOPE
A layman's guide to the problems and concepts of nuclear deterrence by one of America's leading physicists
0–06–039039–5 Harper & Row pb $6.95

⇨ **TO ORDER ANY BOOK IN THIS CATALOG, ASK YOUR BOOKSELLER OR CALL 1-800-882-8770**

• John Finnis & others
NUCLEAR DETERRENCE, MORALITY AND REALISM
A call for unilateral disarmament
0–19–824791–5 Oxford pb $19.95

• Owen Greene, Ian Percival & Irene Ridge
NUCLEAR WINTER: The Evidence and the Risks
0–7456–0177–4 Blackwell pb $9.95

• Lester Grinspoon, editor
THE LONG DARKNESS: Psychological and Moral Perspectives on Nuclear Winter
0–300–03663–9 Yale $27.50
0–300–03664–7 Yale pb $8.95

• Mark A. Harwell
NUCLEAR WINTER
0–387–96093–7 Springer-Verlag $25.00

• Robert J. Lifton & Richard Falk
INDEFENSIBLE WEAPONS: The Political and Psychological Case Against Nuclearism
"Nuclearism is defined as the psychological, political and military dependence on nuclear weapons, the embrace of the weapons as a solution to the wide variety of human dilemmas, most ironically, that of 'security' "—*Foreign Affairs*
0–465–03236–2 Basic Books $15.50
0–465–03237–0 Basic Books pb $8.95

• Joseph S. Nye, Jr.
NUCLEAR ETHICS
A Harvard political scientist examines the ethical dilemmas raised by nuclear weapons
0–02–922460–8 Free Press $14.95
0–02–923091–8 Free Press pb $8.95

• Joseph S. Nye, Jr., editor
FATEFUL VISIONS: Avoiding Nuclear Catastrophe
0–88730–272–6 Ballinger $19.95

• Jonathan Schell
THE ABOLITION
0–394–53818–8 Knopf $11.95
0–380–69912–5 Avon pb $3.95

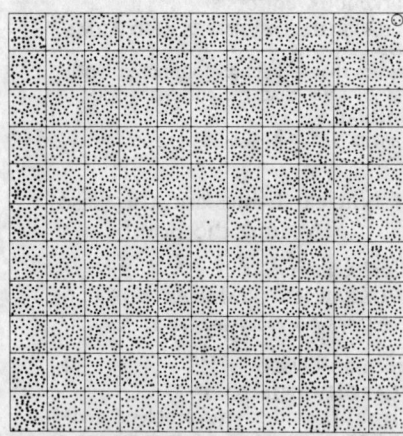

"The dot in the center represents all the firepower of World War II. The other dots represent the firepower of existing nuclear weapons. The top right circle represents the weapons on one Poseidon submarine. It is equal to the firepower of three world wars." From Nuclear War Atlas *by William Bunge (Blackwell)*

THE FATE OF THE EARTH
0–380–61325–5 Avon pb $4.50

• Fredric Solomon & Robert Q. Marston, editors
THE MEDICAL IMPLICATIONS OF NUCLEAR WAR
Foreword by Lewis Thomas
0–309–03636–4 National Academy pb $33.50

• Spencer R. Weart
NUCLEAR FEAR: A History of Images
0–674–62835–7 Harvard $29.50
0–674–62836–5 Harvard pb $14.95

• Solly Zuckerman
THE DAY AFTER WORLD WAR III
0–380–69954–0 Avon pb $5.95

NUCLEAR ILLUSION AND REALITY
0–394–71363–X Random House pb $2.95

War in Space

• Philip M. Boffey, William J. Broad & others
CLAIMING THE HEAVENS: The New York Times Guide to the Star Wars Debate
Expanded version of the 1986 Times series on SDI
0–8129–1647–6 Times Books $17.95

• B. Bruce-Briggs
THE SHIELD OF FAITH: A Chronicle of Strategy
A history of the political, military and technological effort to guard against enemy attacks from the sky, from the response to the zeppelins of World War I to the Star Wars debate
0–671–61086–4 Simon & Schuster $22.95

• James Chace & Caleb Carr
AMERICA INVULNERABLE: The Quest for Absolute Security from 1812 to Star Wars
0–671–61778–8 Summit $19.95

• Angelo Coderilla
WHILE OTHERS BUILD: A Commonsense Approach to the Strategic Defense Initiative
Published in 1988
0–02–905671–3 Free Press $22.50

• H. Bruce Franklin
WAR STARS: The Superweapon and the American Imagination
A history of the American belief that miraculous new weapons will somehow end war and ensure global triumph of American ideals
0–19–505295–1 Oxford $22.95

• Franklin A. Long & others, editors
WEAPONS IN SPACE
Essays on space weapons originally published in *Daedalus*
0–393–01989–6 Norton $16.95
0–393–95527–3 Norton pb $9.95

• Paul B. Stares
THE MILITARIZATION OF SPACE: U.S. Policy, 1945-1984
0–8014–9471–0 Cornell pb $10.95

• John Tirman, editor
THE FALLACY OF STAR WARS
0–394–72894–7 Random House pb $4.95

• Robert W. Tucker & others
SDI AND U.S. FOREIGN POLICY
0–8133–0468–7 Westview pb $21.00

• Solly Zuckerman
STAR WARS IN A NUCLEAR WORLD
0–394–75445–X Random House pb $5.95

AMERICAN DEFENSE POLICY

• Ray Bonds
THE MODERN U.S. WAR MACHINE
The best introduction to weapons systems and the organization of the US armed services
0–517–56097–6 Crown pb $14.95

• Zbigniew Brzezinski
GAME PLAN: How to Conduct the US-Soviet Contest
Advice from the former National Security Advisor on how to conduct military competition with the Soviet Union. "A hard-headed analysis of the forces moving the real world"—Richard M. Nixon
0–87113–164–1 Atlantic Monthly pb $8.95

THE GRAND FAILURE: The Birth and Death of Communism in the 20th Century
Published in 1989
0–684–19034–6 Scribners $19.95

• John L. Gaddis
STRATEGIES OF CONTAINMENT: A Critical Appraisal of Postwar American National Security Policy
This reassessment, based on declassified documents, compares and evaluates the assumptions that shaped policy; published in 1982
0–19–502944–5 Oxford $29.95
0–19–503097–4 Oxford pb $10.95

• Norman A. Graebner, editor
THE NATIONAL SECURITY: Its Theory and Practice in the United States, 1945-1960
Essays exploring policies of the Truman and Eisenhower administrations
0–19–503986–6 Oxford $34.00
0–19–503987–4 Oxford pb $8.95

• David C. Hendrickson
THE FUTURE OF AMERICAN STRATEGY
Argues for the introduction of a new defense strategy in the early 1990s, one that responds to budgetary pressures and that is more sensitive than the Reagan programs to foreign politics
0–8419–1104–5 Holmes & Meier $34.95
0–8419–1105–3 Holmes & Meier pb $16.95

• Saul Landau
THE DANGEROUS DOCTRINE: National Security and U.S. Foreign Policy
Published in 1988 by the Policy Alternatives for the Caribbean and Central America
0–8133–7508–8 Westview pb $12.95

- Carnes Lord

THE PRESIDENCY AND THE MANAGEMENT OF NATIONAL SECURITY
A history of the National Security Council by a former member. Traces the NSC's transformation from an organization conceived as a constraint on presidential power into an instrument allowing the president greater control of the policy-making process
0–02–919341–9 Free Press $22.50

- Steven E. Miller, editor

CONVENTIONAL FORCES AND AMERICAN DEFENSE POLICY: An International Security Reader
Published in 1986
0–691–07700–2 Princeton $36.50
0–691–02246–1 Princeton pb $9.95

NAVAL STRATEGY AND NATIONAL SECURITY: An International Security Reader
Published in 1988
0–691–02272–0 Princeton pb $12.95

- Jeffrey Record

REVISING U.S. MILITARY STRATEGY: Tailoring Means to Ends
Combines a historical overview of postwar American strategy with recommendations for the future; published in 1984
0–08–031619–0 Pergamon $18.95
0–08–031618–2 Pergamon pb $10.95

Military Reform and Civil-Military Relations

- James Coates & Michael Kilian

HEAVY LOSSES: The Dangerous Decline of American Defense
Two Washington journalists demonstrate how America's huge defense budget is mismanaged. Published in 1986
0–14–006858–9 Penguin pb $8.95

- Eliot A. Cohen

CITIZENS AND SOLDIERS: The Dilemmas of Military Service
0–8014–1581–0 Cornell $25.00

- Asa A. Clark, Peter W. Chiarelli & others, editors

THE DEFENSE REFORM DEBATE: Issues and Analysis
0–8018–3205–5 Johns Hopkins $37.50
0–8018–3206–3 Johns Hopkins pb $12.95

James Fallows

NATIONAL DEFENSE
A well-written explication of the thought of "military reformers"
0–394–51824–1 Random House $12.95
0–394–75306–2 Random House pb $5.95

- A. Ernest Fitzgerald

THE PENTAGONISTS: An Insider's View of Waste, Mismanagement, and Fraud in Defense Spending
The original "Defense Department whistle blower" tells of his fight for honest procurement practices, better equipment, and the defense of the taxpayers' interest
0–395–36245–8 Houghton Mifflin $19.95

- Tom Gervasi

THE MYTH OF SOVIET MILITARY SUPREMACY
A 1987 analysis. "Clearly and sharply points up the intellectual, political and statistical inconsistencies which have plagued our presentation of the US-Soviet strategic balance"—Gerard C. Smith
0–06–091378–9 Harper & Row pb $10.95

- Arthur T. Hadley

THE STRAW GIANT: America's Armed Forces—Triumphs and Failures
0–394–55181–8 Random House $19.95
0–380–70391–2 Avon pb $10.95

- Richard Halloran

TO ARM A NATION: Rebuilding America's Endangered Defenses
A military correspondent for the *New York Times* analyzes the defects of the current system and "challenges our military structure to a sweeping overhaul."
Published in 1986
0–02–547540–1 Macmillan $21.95

- Gary Hart & William S. Lind

AMERICA CAN WIN: The Case for Military Reform
0–917561–10–4 Adler & Adler $17.95

- David C. Hendrickson

REFORMING DEFENSE: An Inquiry into the State of American Civil-Military Relations
The military reform movements of the 1980s, studied in the light of the dilemmas of civil-military relations
0–8018–3550–X Johns Hopkins $24.50

- Samuel P. Huntington

THE SOLDIER AND THE STATE: The Theory and Politics of Civil-Military Relations
The classic study of American civil-military relations
0–674–81736–2 Harvard pb $12.50

- Nick Kotz

WILD BLUE YONDER: Money, Politics, and the B-1 Bomber
0–394–55700–X Pantheon $19.95

- Edward N. Luttwak

THE PENTAGON AND THE ART OF WAR
"Why our military power is so costly in peacetime and continues to fail in combat despite the abundant talent and patriotism in our forces." Published in 1986
0–671–61770–2 Simon & Schuster pb $8.95

Law

LEGAL THEORY

▶ **See also Western Philosophy**

- Benjamin N. Cardozo

THE NATURE OF THE JUDICIAL PROCESS
The classic 1921 work describing the process by which a judge decides a case
0–300–00033–2 Yale pb $7.95

- Ronald Dworkin

LAW'S EMPIRE
Morality and law discussed by "America's leading legal philosopher"(*Journal of Philosophy*)
0–674–51835–7 Harvard $25.00
0–674–51836–5 Harvard pb $11.95

A MATTER OF PRINCIPLE
0–674–55460–4 Harvard $27.00
0–674–55461–2 Harvard pb $12.50

TAKING RIGHTS SERIOUSLY
"The most significant book on the philosophy of law in this decade"—*Ethics*
0–674–86710–6 Harvard $21.00
0–674–86711–4 Harvard pb $10.95

- George Fletcher

RETHINKING CRIMINAL LAW
A re-examination of the theory underlying criminal law doctrine from the standpoint of moral philosophy
0–316–28592–7 Little, Brown $28.00

- Grant Gilmore

THE DEATH OF CONTRACT
0–8142–0267–5 Ohio State pb $6.95

- Herbert L. Hart

THE CONCEPT OF LAW
0–19–876072–8 Oxford pb $12.95

ESSAYS ON BENTHAM: Studies in Jurisprudence and Political Theory
0–19–825348–6 Oxford $34.00
0–19–825468–7 Oxford pb $13.95

- Oliver Wendell Holmes

THE COMMON LAW
Edited by Mark DeWolfe Howe
0–316–37131–9 Little, Brown $25.00
0–316–37132–7 Little, Brown pb $10.95

- Leo Katz

BAD ACTS AND GUILTY MINDS: Conundrums of the Criminal Law
The paradoxes of criminal law theory; aimed at the lay reader
0–226–42592–4 Chicago pb $14.95

- Richard A. Posner

THE ECONOMICS OF JUSTICE
Justice and government intervention discussed by a leader of the "law and economics" school
0–674–23525–8 Harvard $27.95
0–674–23526–6 Harvard pb $9.95

LAW AND LITERATURE: A Misunderstood Relation
"An outstanding work, as stimulating as it is intellectually distinguished"—John Gross, *NY Times*
0–674–51468–8 Harvard $25.00

• Roscoe Pound
AN INTRODUCTION TO THE PHILOSOPHY OF LAW
"The recognized American classic"—*American Bar Association Journal*
0–300–00188–6 Yale pb $8.95

• John Rawls
A THEORY OF JUSTICE
A broad and important work of philosophy, elaborating the idea of "justice as fairness"
0–674–88010–2 Harvard $27.00
0–674–88014–5 Harvard pb $11.95

• Kim Lane Scheppele
LEGAL SECRETS: Equality and Efficiency in the Common Law
Explores the broad issues of legal secrecy to challenge the economic theory of law and develop a new view of legal interpretation and legal morality. "Powerful and original"—James S. Coleman, University of Chicago
0–226–73779–9 Chicago pb $17.95

• Roberto Mangabeira Unger
THE CRITICAL LEGAL STUDIES MOVEMENT
0–674–17735–5 Harvard $18.95
0–674–17736–3 Harvard pb $7.95

LEGAL HISTORY

• Harold J. Berman
LAW AND REVOLUTION: The Formation of the Western Legal Tradition
0–674–51776–8 Harvard pb $14.95

• Lawrence M. Friedman
A HISTORY OF AMERICAN LAW
"The best single, coherent history of American law that now exists . . . a stupendous achievement"—*NY Times Book Review*
0–671–81591–1 Simon & Schuster $29.95
0–671–52807–6 Simon & Schuster pb $18.95

• Leonard W. Levy
ORIGINS OF THE FIFTH AMENDMENT
A 1969 Pulitzer Prize winner
0–02–919570–5 Macmillan $24.95
0–02–919580–2 Macmillan pb $14.95

• Michael C. Tigar & Madeleine R. Levy
LAW AND THE RISE OF CAPITALISM
Law and social change from a Marxist perspective
0–85345–477–9 Monthly Review pb $12.50

The Supreme Court

• Henry J. Abraham
JUSTICES AND PRESIDENTS: A Political History of Appointments to the Supreme Court
0–19–503479–1 Oxford $34.00
0–19–503480–5 Oxford pb $13.95

• Robert S. Alley
THE SUPREME COURT ON CHURCH AND STATE
0–19–505028–2 Oxford $45.00
0–19–505029–0 Oxford pb $15.95

• Archibald Cox
THE COURT AND THE CONSTITUTION
A history of the Supreme Court by the first Watergate Special Prosecutor and current head of Common Cause
0–395–37933–4 Houghton Mifflin $19.95

• Peter Irons
THE COURAGE OF THEIR CONVICTIONS: Sixteen Americans Who Fought their Way to the Supreme Court
0–02–915670–X Free Press $22.95

• Joel D. Joseph
BLACK MONDAYS: Worst Moments of the Supreme Court
Foreword by Thurgood Marshall
0–915765–44–6 National Press $17.95

• Robert C. McCloskey
THE AMERICAN SUPREME COURT
0–226–55675–1 Chicago pb $9.00

• William H. Rehnquist
THE SUPREME COURT: How It Was, How It Is
Personal and general insights into the history and operation of the Court, from its current Chief Justice
0–688–05714–4 Morrow $18.95

• Bernard Schwartz
UNPUBLISHED OPINIONS OF THE BURGER COURT
0–19–505317–6 Oxford $34.50

• Herman Schwartz, editor
THE BURGER YEARS: Rights and Wrongs in the Supreme Court, 1969-1986
0–670–81270–6 Viking $22.95
0–14–010818–1 Penguin pb $8.95

• Lawrence H. Tribe
GOD SAVE THIS HONORABLE COURT: How the Choice of Supreme Court Justices Shapes Our History
0–394–54842–6 Random House $17.95
0–451–62527–7 NAL pb $4.50

• Bob Woodward & Scott Armstrong
THE BRETHREN
A portrait of the Supreme Court at work
0–380–52183–0 Avon pb $5.95

Landmark Decisions

Marian Faux
ROE V. WADE: The Untold Story of the Landmark Court Decision That Made Abortion Legal
0–02–537151–7 Macmillan $22.50

Richard Kluger
SIMPLE JUSTICE
The history of *Brown v. Board of Education* and black America's struggle for equality under law
0–394–47289–6 Knopf $34.50
0–394–72255–8 Random House pb $16.95

Anthony Lewis
GIDEON'S TRUMPET
Best-selling account of the prisoner who took his case to the Supreme Court and forever changed the American criminal justice system
0–679–72312–9 Random House pb $6.95

The genesis of the American judicial tradition was the transformation of the office of appellate judge under John Marshall. This tradition has, since its origins, contained certain core elements: a measure of true independence and autonomy for the appellate judiciary from the other two branches of government; the extension, within limits, of judicial authority to questions of politics in addition to technical questions of law; and the presence of a set of internalized constraints upon the office of judge that circumscribe judicial freedom of choice and give the office an identity discrete from the personalities of the individuals who occupy it at any specific time. Since Marshall the appellate judiciary in America has been consciously aloof from direct participation in politics and an active and weighty political force; at once the least regulated and the most constrained branch of American government. Marshall was the primary creator of this unique institutional role.

G. Edward White
THE AMERICAN JUDICIAL TRADITION: Profiles of Leading American Judges
0–19–505685–X Oxford pb $14.95

Lawyers and Judges

• G. Edward White
THE AMERICAN JUDICIAL TRADITION: Profiles of Leading American Judges
The most famous appellate judges in American history, from John Marshall to Warren Burger; updated edition includes two new chapters, on William O. Douglas and the Burger Court
0–19–505685–X Oxford pb $14.95

• Leonard Baker
BRANDEIS AND FRANKFURTER: A Dual Biography
0–8147–1086–7 NYU pb $15.00

• Philippa Strum
LOUIS D. BRANDEIS: Justice for the People
A new biography of the noted Supreme Court Justice, Zionist, and presidential adviser
0–8052–0884–4 Schocken pb $14.95

IF YOU CAN'T FIND IT, LOOK IN THE INDEX

Thurgood Marshall (center) and other lawyers for the Brown case entering the Supreme Court, from Eyes on the Prize: America's Civil Rights Years, 1954-1965 *by Juan Williams (Viking)*

Roy Cohn & Sidney Zion
THE AUTOBIOGRAPHY OF ROY COHN
0–8184–0471–X Lyle Stuart $18.95

Nicholas von Hoffman
CITIZEN COHN
0–385–23690–5 Doubleday $19.95

• Arthur & Lila Weinberg
CLARENCE DARROW: A Sentimental Rebel
0–689–70717–7 Atheneum pb $14.95

• Arthur Weinberg, editor
ATTORNEY FOR THE DAMNED: Clarence Darrow in the Courtroom
Darrow's work presented through a collection of his court summations and lectures. "Nothing gives quite the full flavor of the man as do these addresses"—William O. Douglas
Foreword by William O. Douglas
0–226–13649–3 Chicago pb $13.95

• Melvin I. Urofsky, editor
THE DOUGLAS LETTERS: Selections from the Private Papers of Justice William O. Douglas
0–917561–46–5 Adler & Adler $24.95

• Bruce Allen Murphy
FORTAS: The Rise and Ruin of a Supreme Court Justice
The life of a young star of the New Deal and member of the Warren Court who was forced to resign in 1968
0–688–05357–2 Morrow $25.00

• Sheldon M. Novick
HONORABLE JUSTICE: The Life of Oliver Wendell Holmes
The first biography of an often paradoxical figure and one of the greatest American legal thinkers
0–316–61325–8 Little, Brown $24.95

• Mario Merola
BIG CITY D.A.
0–394–55263–6 Random House $17.95

• Sue Davis
JUSTICE REHNQUIST AND THE CONSTITUTION
"Represents a remarkably comprehensive survey of Justice Rehnquist's constitutional positions and correctly identifies the major patterns in those positions"—Rogers M. Smith, Yale University
0–691–07800–9 Princeton $19.95

• G. Edward White
EARL WARREN: A Public Life
0–19–503121–0 Oxford $35.00
0–19–504936–5 Oxford pb $9.95

THE CONSTITUTION

▶ **See also US History to the Civil War**

• Mortimer J. Adler
WE HOLD THESE TRUTHS: Understanding the Ideas and the Ideals of the Constitution
0–02–064130–3 Macmillan pb $6.95

• Paul C. Bartholomew & Joseph F. Menez
SUMMARIES OF THE LEADING CASES ON THE CONSTITUTION
0–8226–0364–0 Rowman pb $14.95

• Jerry Fresia
TOWARD AN AMERICAN REVOLUTION: Exposing the Constitution and Other Illusions
Argues that the true intent of the Founding Fathers was to protect property and ensure that the poorer majority would have no real voice in political affairs
0–89608–297–0 South End pb $10.00

• John A. Garraty, editor
QUARRELS THAT HAVE SHAPED THE CONSTITUTION
Twenty leading historians describe landmark cases that have altered the Constitution
0–06–055062–7 Harper & Row $22.95

• Angela Roddey Holder
THE MEANING OF THE CONSTITUTION
The Constitution explained, phrase by phrase
Foreword by Henry Steele Commager
0–8120–3847–9 Barron's pb $7.95

• Leonard W. Levy
ORIGINAL INTENT AND THE FRAMERS' CONSTITUTION
0–02–918791–5 Macmillan $19.95

• Saul K. Padover & Jacob W. Landynski
THE LIVING U.S. CONSTITUTION
Bicentennial edition
0–451–62174–3 NAL pb $4.95

• Page Smith
THE CONSTITUTION: A Documentary and Narrative History
From the Magna Carta to Watergate
0–688–08349–8 Morrow pb $15.95

• Jerold S. Auerbach
JUSTICE WITHOUT LAW?: Resolving Disputes Without Lawyers
Examines why Americans are the most litigious people in the world and looks through American history for alternatives to litigation in dispute settlement
0–19–503175–X Oxford $19.95
0–19–503447–3 Oxford pb $8.95

UNEQUAL JUSTICE: Lawyers and Social Change in Modern America
"Stands as a powerful and well-documented indictment of the elite bar's failure to live up to the trust that has been bestowed upon it by our system of justice"—*NY Times*
0–19–502170–3 Oxford pb $11.95

• Raoul Berger
GOVERNMENT BY JUDICIARY: The Transformation of the Fourteenth Amendment
"The most devastating book on the abuse of power by the Supreme Court written in our time"—*Boston Globe*
0–674–35795–7 Harvard $25.00
0–674–35796–5 Harvard pb $9.95

• Lee C. Bollinger
THE TOLERANT SOCIETY
Free speech in American society
0–19–504000–7 Oxford $24.95
0–19–505430–X Oxford pb $9.95

• Norman Dorsen, editor
OUR ENDANGERED RIGHTS: The ACLU Report on Civil Liberties Today
0–394–72229–9 Pantheon pb $11.95

• Billie Wright Dziech & Judge Charles B. Schudson
ON TRIAL: Sexually Abused Children in America's Courts
0–8070–0408–1 Beacon $24.95

• Herbert Jacob
SILENT REVOLUTION: The Transformation of Divorce Law in the United States
"Well written, carefully researched, and persuasively argued"—Barbara J. Nelson, University of Minnesota
0–226–38951–0 Chicago $19.95

• James B. Jacobs
DRUNK DRIVING: An American Dilemma
An interdisciplinary study both of the social problem of drunk driving and of government policies and jurisprudence
Foreword by Franklin E. Zimring
0–226–38979–0 Chicago pb $12.95

• David Kairys, editor
THE POLITICS OF LAW: A Progressive Critique
Essays that challenge the assumptions and myths of American law
0–394–51981–7 Pantheon $22.50
0–394–71110–6 Pantheon pb $11.50

• Rita Kramer
AT A TENDER AGE: Violent Youth and Juvenile Justice
0–8050–0419–X Henry Holt $18.95

• Jethro H. Lieberman
THE LITIGIOUS SOCIETY
The pros and cons of America's growing urge to sue
0–465–04133–7 Basic Books pb $8.95

• Jeremy Rabkin
JUDICIAL COMPULSIONS: How Public Law Distorts Public Policy
0–465–03687–2 Basic Books $19.95

• Gerry Spence
WITH JUSTICE FOR NONE: Destroying an American Myth
0–8129–1696–4 Times Books $18.95

• Scott Turow
ONE L: An Inside Account of Life in the First Year of Harvard Law School
From the author of the best-selling *Presumed Innocent*, memoirs of an initiation by fire. "It should be read by anyone who has ever contemplated going to law school. Or anyone who has ever worried about being human"—Christopher Lehmann-Haupt, *NY Times*
0–14–004913–4 Penguin pb $6.95

• Arlene Violet & Suda J. Prohaska
CONVICTIONS: My Journey from the Convent to the Courtroom
A nun who left her order after 23 years to become the Attorney General for Rhode Island
0–394–55182–6 Random House $17.95

• Joseph A. Wapner
A VIEW FROM THE BENCH
The Solomon of TV's *People's Court* recalls his 20 years as a California judge
0–671–63873–4 Simon & Schuster $17.95

Criminal Law and the Death Penalty

• David L. Bazelon
QUESTIONING AUTHORITY: Justice and Criminal Law
Examinations of controversies surrounding crime and law, based on 37 years on the D.C. Court of Appeals
0–394–55304–7 Knopf $19.95

• Hugo Adam Bedau, editor
THE DEATH PENALTY IN AMERICA
0–19–502986–0 Oxford $24.95
0–19–502987–9 Oxford pb $11.95

• Elizabeth F. Loftus
EYEWITNESS TESTIMONY
Examines the fallibility of the eyewitness
0–674–28776–2 Harvard pb $8.95

• James B. Stewart
THE PROSECUTORS: Inside the Offices of Government's Most Powerful Lawyers
The prosecution of six cases, from insider trading at Morgan Stanley to the investigation of Edwin Meese
0–671–49747–2 Simon & Schuster $19.95

• H. Richard Uviller
TEMPERED ZEAL: A Columbia Law Professor's Year On the Streets with the New York City Police
0–8092–4607–4 Contemporary $19.95

• Seymour Wishman
ANATOMY OF A JURY: The Inside Story of How Twelve Ordinary People Decide the Fate of an Accused Murderer
0–8129–1260–8 Times $17.95
0–14–009851–8 Penguin pb $6.95

CONFESSIONS OF A CRIMINAL LAWYER
"A candid, often shocking picture of what passes for criminal justice in America by a criminal lawyer whose experiences in the courtroom left him sadder, wiser—and angry"—*NY Times*
0–14–006360–9 Penguin pb $7.95

• Renata Adler
RECKLESS DISREGARD
The *Westmoreland v. CBS* and *Sharon v. Time* cases. "What *Reckless Disregard* most visibly dramatizes is the contest of a single reasonable mind against the brute forces of institutional behavior"—*NY Times*
0–394–52751–8 Knopf $16.95
0–394–75525–1 Random House pb $6.95

• F. Lee Bailey & Harvey Aronson
THE DEFENSE NEVER RESTS
The famous defense lawyer recounts his greatest trials
0–451–12640–8 NAL pb $3.95

• Sara C. Charles & Eugene Kennedy
DEFENDANT: A Psychiatrist on Trial for Medical Malpractice
A psychiatrist sued for malpractice by her suicidal patient describes her trial and reflects on the effects of the malpractice epidemic. "Absolutely hair-raising"—John Gregory Dunne
0–02–905910–0 Free Press $17.95
0–394–74663–5 Random House pb $7.95

• Alan M. Dershowitz
THE BEST DEFENSE
Courtroom adventures of Claus von Bülow's lawyer. "Has the feel of a vintage Coney Island roller coaster ride"—*Village Voice*
0–394–71380–X Random House pb $6.95

TAKING LIBERTIES
The Harvard professor, defense lawyer and syndicated columnist tackles the legal issues of the last ten years
0–8092–4616–3 Contemporary $19.95

• George P. Fletcher
A CRIME OF SELF-DEFENSE: Bernhard Goetz and the Law on Trial
0–02–910311–8 Free Press $19.95

• Martin Garbus
READY FOR THE DEFENSE
The lawyer discusses five of his cases, including his defenses of Lenny Bruce and Timothy Leary
0–88184–373–3 Carroll & Graf pb $4.95

Michael Gilbert, editor
THE OXFORD BOOK OF LEGAL ANECDOTES
0–19–214112–0 Oxford $19.95

• Barbara Goldsmith
JOHNSON V. JOHNSON
J. Seward Johnson's $500 million will and the court battle and tangled family history surrounding it
0–394–56043–4 Knopf $18.95
0–440–20041–5 Dell pb $4.95

• Peter Hay
THE BOOK OF LEGAL ANECDOTES
0–8160–1523–6 Facts On File $24.95

• Rodney R. Jones & others, editors
DISORDERLY CONDUCT: Verbatim Excerpts from Actual Court Cases
Intentionally and unintentionally humorous dialogue from actual transcripts
0–393–02456–3 Norton $12.95

• Arthur Kinoy
RIGHTS ON TRIAL: The Odyssey of a People's Lawyer
The stories of Watergate, the Rosenbergs, the Montgomery bus boycott, and the Chicago Seven, all told by a lawyer who was there
0–674–77013–7 Harvard $24.50
0–674–77014–5 Harvard pb $8.95

• Ronald Markman & Dominick Bosco
ALONE WITH THE DEVIL: Famous Cases of a Courtroom Psychiatrist
0–385–24427–4 Doubleday $18.95

• John Mortimer, editor
FAMOUS TRIALS
The most sensational trials in British history, selected by the creator of *Rumpole of the Bailey*
0–88029–080–3 Hippocrene $16.95
0–14–006924–0 Penguin pb $7.95

• Steven Phillips
NO HEROES, NO VILLAINS: The Story of a Murder Trial
First-hand account of a 1972 murder trial. "The finest and simplest explanation of the process of criminal law and its practice that I have ever read"—*NY Times*
0–394–72531–X Random House pb $5.95

• Charles Rembar
THE END OF OBSCENITY: The Trials of Lady Chatterley, Tropic of Cancer and Fanny Hill By the Lawyer Who Defended Them
0–06–097061–8 Harper & Row pb $10.95

• Richard H. Rovere
HOWE AND HUMMELL: Their True and Scandalous History
The story of the most notorious law office in post-Civil War New York City, defenders of John L. Sullivan, P.T. Barnum, and countless underworld figures. Illustrated by Reginald Marsh and originally published in *The New Yorker*
Introduction by Calvin Trillin
0–374–17336–2 Farrar, Straus & Giroux $16.95

• Peter H. Schuck
AGENT ORANGE ON TRIAL: Mass Toxic Disasters in the Courts
"A Dickensian drama of personality clashes, misguided idealism, power struggles, greed, immeasurable suffering and bitter disillusionment"—*USA Today*
0–674–01026–4 Harvard pb $12.95

• James Shannon
TEXACO AND THE $100 BILLION JURY
The story of the Pennzoil v. Texaco trial, told by a member of the jury that awarded Pennzoil $10.5 billion, the largest settlement in US history
0–13–911959–0 Prentice-Hall $19.95

• A.W. Brian Simpson
CANNIBALISM AND THE COMMON LAW: The Story of the Tragic Last Voyage of the Mignonette and the Strange Legal Proceedings to Which It Gave Rise
"Should such an awful subject be fun?"—Walter Clemons, *Newsweek*
0–226–75942–3 Chicago $25.00
0–226–75943–1 Chicago pb $12.95

• Gerald M. Stern
THE BUFFALO CREEK DISASTER: How the Survivors of One of the Worst Disasters in Coal-Mining History Brought Suit Against the Coal Company—and Won
0–394–72343–0 Random House pb $6.95

• Herbert J. Stern
JUDGMENT IN BERLIN
An escape from behind the Iron Curtain and the subsequent trial of the escapees in the west, and recently a movie. "Equal to any fictional thriller"—*San Francisco Chronicle*
0–87663–441–2 Universe $18.95
0–451–15566–1 NAL pb $4.50

• Ann & John Tusa
THE NUREMBERG TRIAL
Judging the unjudgeable in the aftermath of the Holocaust
0–689–11496–6 Atheneum $22.95
0–07–065511–1 McGraw-Hill pb $9.95

REFERENCE AND PRACTICAL GUIDES

• Henry C. Black
BLACK'S LAW DICTIONARY
0–8299–2041–2 West $25.95
0–314–77135–2 West (abridged edition) pb $15.95

• Consumer Law Foundation
THE COMPLETE LEGAL KIT
Includes more than 150 legal forms for home, family, and business use
0–89471–613–1 Running Press pb $17.95

• Ronald L. Goldfarb & Gail E. Ross
THE WRITER'S LAWYER: Essential Legal Advice for Writers and Editors in All Media
A handbook on libel law (including libel in fiction), copyrights, confidentiality, prior restraint, and other legal issues facing writers and journalists
0–8129–1744–8 Times Books $18.95

• Tom Goldstein & Jethro K. Leiberman
THE LAWYER'S GUIDE TO WRITING WELL
0–70–023803–0 McGraw-Hill $19.95

• Reader's Digest
THE LEGAL QUESTION AND ANSWER BOOK: A Lifetime of Legal Questions Answered in One Book
0–89577–291–4 Reader's Digest $28.95

Lawyers on the staircase of the Palais de Justice, by Daumier

Education

Every few years Americans seem to discover that their schools are in crisis. And each crisis produces its own set of critics, polemicists, and antagonists. In recent years, the subject has once again aroused controversy and concern, emerging from academic circles into the political spotlight, and in the process generating best-sellers, television documentaries, front-page news, and campaign slogans. Yet for all its urgency, the fundamental issue of the debate remains the same: What should be the purpose of education in a democracy? Whatever those goals are, is our education system living up to them?

THE STATE OF THE SCHOOLS

For the past half-century, a series of reform movements have battled to influence the philosophy and practices in America's schools. Traditionalists and progressives have waged verbal war with regularity. Their debate has ranged from practical disagreements over the most successful methods of conveying skills and knowledge, to deep divisions over the very essence of public education. Do children learn better in a tightly structured environment, or in a free system in which they learn to make decisions for themselves? Is a liberal education the birthright of all children in a democracy, or are some better served by technical and vocational training?

The reform literature of the 1980s is in some ways a reaction against the progressivism of the 1960s. It is characterized by concern for academic standards, for reducing non-academic electives, and for bringing nearly all students into an academic curriculum.

● Mortimer J. Adler
THE PAIDEIA PROPOSAL: An Educational Manifesto
A committee of leading educators proposes a democratic restructuring of basic schooling to overcome inherent elitism
0–02–064100–1 Macmillan pb $4.95

REFORMING EDUCATION: The Opening of the American Mind
0–02–500551–0 Macmillan $19.95

● Arthur Bestor
EDUCATIONAL WASTELANDS: The Retreat from Learning in Our Public Schools
A critique of progressivism in the 1950s
Contributions by Clarence J. Karier & Foster McMurray
0–252–01226–7 Illinois $24.95

● Ernest L. Boyer
HIGH SCHOOL: A Report of the Carnegie Foundation for the Advancement of Teaching
One of the key documents that provoked the current wave of school reform. "Offers a comprehensive plan for school improvement that is exceptional in its breadth and creativity. It adds significantly to the national debate"—Terrel H. Bell
0–06–015193–5 Harper & Row $16.95

● John H. Bunzel, editor
CHALLENGE TO AMERICAN SCHOOLS: The Case for Standards and Values
Eleven essays on the current state of the classroom
0–19–503556–9 Oxford $24.95

● J.I. Goodlad
A PLACE CALLED SCHOOL
A statistically rich landmark study, with proposals for reform of secondary education
0–07–023626–7 McGraw-Hill $26.50
0–07–023627–5 McGraw-Hill pb $12.00

● Gerald Grant
THE WORLD WE CREATED AT HAMILTON HIGH
An in-depth look at a real (but disguised) American high school. "Gerald Grant moves the discourse of the debate on school renewal far beyond the slogans. He forces the reader to consider the school in larger context"—Ernest L. Boyer
0–674–96200–1 Harvard $24.95

● Beatrice & Ronald Gross, editors
THE GREAT SCHOOL DEBATE: Which Way for American Education?
A primer on the current debate, featuring excerpts from most of the major works, along with a useful who's who and bibliography
0–671–53010–0 Simon & Schuster $17.95
0–671–54136–6 Simon & Schuster pb $12.95

● Michael W. Kirst
WHO CONTROLS OUR SCHOOLS?: American Values in Conflict
0–7167–1719–0 Freeman $20.95
0–7167–1720–4 Freeman pb $13.95

● Herbert Kohl
THIRTY-SIX CHILDREN
Behind the scenes at a Harlem public school. "All of this is by now a scandalously old story, but it still hurts"—NY Times
0–452–26155–4 NAL pb $7.95

Jonathan Kozol
DEATH AT AN EARLY AGE
An indictment of public education, from the front lines in 1964 Boston. "A very disturbing book. He is writing of the Boston Public School system, but he could be writing of the system in almost any city in the country"—Christian Science Monitor
0–452–25769–7 NAL pb $6.95

● Michael Leahy
PRIVILEGED CLASS: Senior Year at Beverly Hills High
The author follows six American teenagers through a school where drugs, privilege, and casual sex are as much a part of the landscape as the honor roll and academic achievement
0–316–51815–8 Little, Brown $17.95

● Sara L. Lightfoot
THE GOOD HIGH SCHOOL: Portraits of Character and Culture
Six high schools in different types of communities, all with a reputation for excellence. "An antidote to despair and a road map to better education"—Fred M. Hechinger, NY Times
0–465–02696–6 Basic Books pb $12.95

● Eleanor W. Orr
TWICE AS LESS: Black English and the Performance of Black Students in Mathematics and Science
0–393–02392–3 Norton $15.95

● Arthur G. Powell & others
THE SHOPPING MALL HIGH SCHOOL: Winners and Losers in the Educational Marketplace
0–395–37904–0 Houghton Mifflin $16.95
0–395–42638–3 Houghton Mifflin pb $9.95

● Diane Ravitch
THE SCHOOLS WE DESERVE: Reflections on the Educational Crisis of Our Time
Essays offering a re-evaluation of contemporary educational issues, from a historical perspective
0–465–07235–6 Basic Books pb $8.95

● Michael Rutter & others
FIFTEEN THOUSAND HOURS: Secondary Schools and Their Effects on Children
0–674–30025–4 Harvard $17.50
0–674–30026–2 Harvard pb $7.95

● Gilbert T. Sewall
NECESSARY LESSONS: Decline and Renewal in American Schools
0–02–929030–9 Free Press $19.95

Monument to Rousseau as the reformer of children's education, from The Humanist Tradition in the West *by Alan Bullock* (Norton)

● Theodore R. Sizer
HORACE'S COMPROMISE: The Dilemma of the American High School
An unflattering portrait, with proposals for reform
0–395–34423–9 Houghton Mifflin $16.95
0–395–37753–6 Houghton Mifflin pb $8.95

Radical Critics

Since the 1960s, radical critics have subjected education to a searching examination, arguing that the flaws in the system are so deep and pervasive that the educational system itself is corrupt and beyond the help of gradual change.

Another source of radical criticism, however, comes from conservatives who assail John Dewey and progressive education as the philosophical source of irremediable error.

● Michael W. Apple
EDUCATION AND POWER: Reproduction and Contradiction in Education
0–7100–0977–1 Methuen $26.95
0–7448–0030–7 RC&H pb $10.95

IDEOLOGY AND CURRICULUM
0–7100–0686–1 Methuen pb $12.95

● Samuel L. Blumenfeld
IS PUBLIC EDUCATION NECESSARY?
A critique of American education, from the right
0–8159–5829–3 Devin–Adair pb $10.95

● Samuel Bowles & Herbert Gintis
SCHOOLING IN CAPITALIST AMERICA: Educational Reform and the Contradictions of Economic Life
A neo-Marxist critique of American education, from its historical origins. "A genuinely creative attempt to develop a Marxist point of view about the interaction between schooling and the labor market"—Mark Blaug, Challenge
0–465–09718–9 Basic Books pb $11.95

- Paulo Freire
PEDAGOGY OF THE OPPRESSED
On the ties between education and liberation, particularly in the Third World
Translated by Myra B. Ramos
Foreword by Richard Shaull
0-8264-0047-7 Continuum pb $9.95

- Paul Goodman
GROWING UP ABSURD
0-394-70032-5 Random House pb $4.95

- John Holt
FREEDOM AND BEYOND
0-913677-01-9 Pinchpenny pb $4.50

HOW CHILDREN LEARN
Revised edition of a classic
0-440-55051-3 Delacorte pb $9.95

TEACH YOUR OWN: A Hopeful Path for Education
A practical manual from a leader of the home schooling movement
0-385-29006-3 Delacorte pb $11.95

- Ivan Illich
DESCHOOLING SOCIETY
"Illich goes miles beyond everybody else and renders almost every other writer obsolete. *Deschooling Society* is a very dangerous book"—Jonathan Kozol
0-06-132086-2 Harper & Row pb $7.95

- A.S. Neill
SUMMERHILL: A Radical Approach to Child Rearing
The legendary "free" school in England, by its founder
0-671-81302-1 Wallaby pb $4.95

- Neil Postman
TEACHING AS A CONSERVING ACTIVITY
The need to use schools in the fight against what Postman sees as the dangerous cultural bombardment of children by the instant gratification of mass media. "A technocracy such as ours, which is prone to alienate the individual from himself, needs a counter-argument if our young people are to function as thinking humanists. Such a counter-argument is offered, most compellingly, in the present study"—*Best Sellers*
0-440-38486-9 Dell pb $4.95

- Neil Postman & Charles Weingartner
TEACHING AS A SUBVERSIVE ACTIVITY
"The authors describe the students who emerge from a 'subversive education' as 'crap detectors.' All educators, parents, and students could use some lessons in 'crap detecting.' This book offers the best short course around"—*Library Journal*
0-440-38485-0 Dell pb $4.95

READING AND LITERACY

- Bruno Bettelheim & Karen Zelan
ON LEARNING TO READ: The Child's Fascination with Meaning
"Above all, Bettelheim and Zelan reaffirm one terribly important point: What we do with reading between kindergarten and third grade may be the single most important activity for our psychological health and future as individuals, our intelligence as a people and our strength as a nation"—George Keller, *Baltimore Sun*
0-394-71194-7 Random House pb $9.95

- Jeanne S. Chall
LEARNING TO READ: The Great Debate
0-07-010391-7 McGraw-Hill pb $4.95

- Rudolf Flesch
WHY JOHNNY CAN'T READ: And What You Can Do about It
A promotion of the use of phonics, instead of the popular "look-and-say" method, to teach reading
0-06-091340-1 Harper & Row pb $7.95

WHY JOHNNY STILL CAN'T READ: A New Look at the Scandal of Our Schools
"I hope this book reaches a wide audience, because Flesch is right about phonics. Children want to learn to read; English is, for the most part, a phonetic language; once children learn the alphabetic code, they become readers. It is as simple as that"—John Merrow, *New Republic*
0-06-014842-X Harper & Row $12.95
0-06-091031-3 Harper & Row pb $5.95

- E.D. Hirsch, Jr.
CULTURAL LITERACY: What Every American Needs to Know
A call for a new emphasis on information—as opposed to skills—in education, including an exhaustive, 63-page appendix of names, dates and terms that educated people should know. "Because it so powerfully demonstrates that reading—like thinking—is not a skill that can be separated from substance and content, I can think of no other book of recent years more important for the formulation of curriculum policy than this one"—Albert Shanker
0-395-43095-X Houghton Mifflin $16.95
0-394-75843-9 Random House pb $6.95

- E.D. Hirsch, Jr., Joseph Kett & James Trefil
THE DICTIONARY OF CULTURAL LITERACY: What Every American Needs to Know
0-395-43748-2 Houghton Mifflin $19.95

- Carman Hunter & David Harman
ADULT ILLITERACY IN THE UNITED STATES: A Report to the Ford Foundation
0-07-031369-5 McGraw-Hill pb $8.95

- Ivan Illich & Barry Sanders
ABC: The Alphabetization of the Popular Mind
"A highly literate challenge to many of the fundamental assumptions about literacy"—Les Adler, *San Francisco Chronicle*
0-679-72192-4 Random House pb $10.95

- Jonathan Kozol
ILLITERATE AMERICA
Kozol's argument that one-third of all Americans are functionally illiterate sparked a national debate and helped bring the topic into the media limelight. "A stunning sequel to *Death at an Early Age*. Kozol, with passion and eloquence, reveals a devastating truth: Domestic illiteracy, en masse, is a graver threat than foreign weaponry"—Studs Terkel
0-452-26203-8 NAL pb $8.95

- John Paulos
INNUMERACY: Mathematical Illiteracy and Its Consequences
0-8090-7447-8 Hill & Wang $18.95

- Arlene Silberman
GROWING UP WRITING: Why Johnny and Janie Can't Write, and What We Can Do About It
The author describes methods of overcoming a system in which "our schools begin to curb a student's enthusiasm for writing during the first few months of first grade—and continue to suppress it for the next twelve years"
0-8129-1823-1 Times Books $18.95

TEACHING

- Jacques Barzun
TEACHER IN AMERICA
A critical look at what's wrong with the way America's teachers are trained
0-8191-5447-4 University Press pb $11.00
0-913966-79-7 Liberty Fund pb $4.00

- Joe Clark with Joe Picard
LAYING DOWN THE LAW: Joe Clark's Strategy for Saving Our Schools
Notes from the controversial New Jersey high school principal whose work inspired the film *Lean on Me*
0-89526-763-2 Regnery pb $17.95

- Robert Coles
THE CALL OF STORIES: Teaching and the Moral Imagination
The noted child psychologist on the importance of stories and literature in teaching children
0-395-42935-8 Houghton Mifflin $18.95

- Marva Collins & Civia Tamarkin
MARVA COLLINS' WAY
The Chicago teacher who fought the status quo and founded her own school
0-87477-310-5 Tarcher pb $6.95

- James Herndon
NOTES FROM A SCHOOL TEACHER
0-671-62816-X Simon & Schuster pb $7.95

- Gilbert Highet
THE ART OF TEACHING
A classic on the principles of teaching
0-679-72314-5 Random House pb $6.95

- William James
TALKS TO TEACHERS ON PSYCHOLOGY AND TO STUDENTS ON SOME OF LIFE'S IDEALS
Introduction by P. Woodring
0-393-00165-2 Norton pb $7.95

- Kenneth Koch
ROSE, WHERE DO YOU GET THAT RED: Teaching Great Poetry to Children
A poet and veteran teacher's iconoclastic method. "A handbook, anthology, and instructor's guide combined, Koch's work will instantly endear itself to writers and

teachers of every age and competence"—
Library Journal
0–394–71885–2 Random House pb $5.95

• Dan C. Lortie
SCHOOLTEACHER: A Sociological Study
Classic study on the state of the profession,
using interviews and surveys
0–226–49354–7 Chicago pb $10.00

• Jay Mathews
ESCALANTE: The Best Teacher in America
The story of the barrio high school teacher
in East Los Angeles, whose life was the
basis for the film *Stand and Deliver*
0–8050–0450–5 Henry Holt $19.95

• Joe Nathan
FREE TO TEACH: Achieving Equity and
Excellence in Schools
0–86683–859–7 Harper & Row pb $7.95

• Lucille G. Natkins
OUR LAST TERM: A Teacher's Diary
0–8191–4965–9 University Press $27.25
0–8191–4966–7 University Press pb $9.25

• Donald A. Schon
THE REFLECTIVE PRACTITIONER:
How Professionals Think in Action
0–465–06874–X Basic Books $19.95
0–465–06878–2 Basic Books pb $12.95

• Kenneth A. Strike & Jonas Soltis
THE ETHICS OF TEACHING
0–8077–2709–1 Teachers College pb $8.95

• Patrick Welsh
TALES OUT OF SCHOOL: A Teacher's
Candid Account from the Front Lines of
the American High School Today
0–140–09442–3 Viking pb $6.95

SEGREGATION, INTEGRATION, AND EQUAL OPPORTUNITY

• Derrick Bell, editor
SHADES OF BROWN: New Perspectives
on School Desegregation
0–8077–2595–1 Teachers College $13.95

• Paul R. Dimond
BEYOND BUSING: Inside the Challenge
to Urban Segregation
0–472–10062–9 Michigan $32.50

• David Kirp
JUST SCHOOLS: The Idea of Racial
Equality in American Education
0–520–04575–0 California $25.00
0–520–05084–3 California pb $10.95

• Richard Kluger
SIMPLE JUSTICE: The History of Brown
v. Board of Education and Black America's
Struggle for Equality
A journalist's magnificent weaving of the
tale that led to the landmark Supreme
Court decision
0–394–47289–6 Knopf $35.00
0–394–72255–8 Random House pb $16.95

• Gary Orfield
MUST WE BUS?: Segregated Schools and
National Policy
0–8157–6638–6 Brookings $31.95
0–8157–6637–8 Brookings pb $12.95

Richard Rodriguez
HUNGER OF MEMORY: The
Education of Richard Rodriguez, An
Autobiography
An eloquent memoir from a Mexican-
American intellectual. "Shows more
insight and understanding into the
familiar problems of contemporary
American education than a roomful of
studies and reports by social
scientists"—Diane Ravitch
0–87923–418–0 Godine $14.95
0–553–27293–4 Bantam pb $4.50

• J. Harvie Wilkinson
FROM BROWN TO BAKKE: The
Supreme Court and School Integration,
1954–1978
0–19–502567–9 Oxford $27.50
0–19–502897–X Oxford pb $9.95

• Arthur E. Wise
RICH SCHOOLS, POOR SCHOOLS: The
Promise of Equal Educational Opportunity
0–226–90299–4 Chicago $19.00
0–226–90300–1 Chicago pb $2.25

• Raymond Wolters
THE BURDEN OF BROWN: Thirty Years
of School Desegregation
"A thoroughly researched and well-written
description of the history of race relations
since 1954 in the five school districts
involved in the famous Brown decision"—
L.E. Noble, Jr., *Choice*
0–87049–423–6 Tennessee $27.95

Public and Private Education

• James S. Coleman & others
HIGH SCHOOL ACHIEVEMENT:
Public, Catholic, and Private Schools
Compared
0–465–02956–6 Basic Books $21.95

• Thomas James & Henry M. Levin,
editors
PUBLIC DOLLARS FOR PRIVATE
SCHOOLS: The Case of Tuition Tax
Credits
0–87722–316–5 Temple $29.95
0–87722–386–6 Temple pb $12.95

THEORY AND PHILOSOPHY

From Rousseau to Dewey and beyond, a
handful of thinkers have had a major
influence on the development of educational
thinking. For much of the past century,
philosophy of education in the United States
may be seen as an extended commentary
on—or debate with—the ideas of John
Dewey (1859-1952). Even today, admirers
invoke his name and words and critics assail
his influence; his presence is inescapable.

Classics

▶ See also Western Philosophy

• Lawrence A. Cremin, editor
THE REPUBLIC AND THE SCHOOL:
Horace Mann on the Education of Free Men
0–8077–1206–X Teachers College pb $5.00

• John Dewey
THE CHILD AND THE CURRICULUM
& THE SCHOOL AND SOCIETY
0–226–14392–9 Chicago pb $6.95

DEMOCRACY AND EDUCATION: An
Introduction to the Philosophy of
Education
0–02–907370–7 Free Press pb $14.95

EXPERIENCE AND EDUCATION
Dewey's concise statement on education,
written more than two decades after
Democracy and Education, and taking into
account critics and his own experiences
with progressive schools
0–02–013660–9 Macmillan pb $4.50

• Howard M. Jones, editor
EMERSON ON EDUCATION: Selections
0–8077–1584–0 Teachers College pb $6.00

• Jean-Jacques Rousseau
EMILE, OR ON EDUCATION
Translated by Allan Bloom
0–465–01931–5 Basic Books pb $14.95

• Robert Ulich, editor
THREE THOUSAND YEARS OF
EDUCATIONAL WISDOM: Selections
from Great Documents
0–674–89072–8 Harvard pb $16.00

• Alfred North Whitehead
THE AIMS OF EDUCATION
0–02–935180–4 Free Press pb $12.95

"You will conjugate . . . " by Félix Vallotton

➤ FOR OVERSEAS ORDERING INFORMATION, SEE PAGE 1

Recent Philosophy

● **Stephen Arons**
COMPELLING BELIEF: The Culture of American Schooling
A critique of the ideology of public education
0–07–002326–3 McGraw-Hill $19.95
0–87023–524–9 Massachusetts pb $9.95

● **Eva T.H. Brann**
PARADOXES OF EDUCATION IN A REPUBLIC
0–226–07135–9 Chicago $12.95

● **Jerome S. Bruner**
THE PROCESS OF EDUCATION
The classic argument for the "spiral curriculum," in which basic concepts of science and the humanities are taught at an early age
0–674–71001–0 Harvard pb $4.95

● **Steven M. Cahn**
EDUCATION AND THE DEMOCRATIC IDEAL
The case for a liberal education
0–88229–589–6 Nelson-Hall $19.95
0–88229–661–2 Nelson-Hall pb $10.95

● **John W. Gardner**
EXCELLENCE
Reflections on the importance of excellence in an egalitarian society. "A balanced, informed, and positive statement of democratic belief by a man who in temperament, experience and performance has shown himself to be a gifted educator"—Harold Taylor, *Saturday Review*
0–393–01848–2 Norton $12.95
0–393–30377–2 Norton pb $6.95

● **Henry A. Giroux**
SCHOOLING AND THE STRUGGLE FOR PUBLIC LIFE: Critical Pedagogy in the Modern Age
The author urges a theory and practice that link schooling to the quest for a concrete form of democracy
0–8166–1706–6 Minnesota pb $14.95

● **Maxine Greene**
LANDSCAPES OF LEARNING
Essays from a noted theorist on such topics as emancipatory education, social issues, and predicaments of women in American education
0–8077–2534–X Teachers College pb $14.95

● **Amy Gutmann**
DEMOCRATIC EDUCATION
"The book is free from technical jargon and other academic quirks, and non-professionals should find it both interesting and accessible"—William H. Nelson, University of Houston
0–691–07736–3 Princeton $19.95

● **Paul H. Hirst**
KNOWLEDGE AND THE CURRICULUM: A Collection of Philosophical Papers
0–7100–7930–3 Methuen pb $9.95

● **Richard Hofstadter**
ANTI-INTELLECTUALISM IN AMERICAN LIFE
0–394–41535–3 Knopf $13.95
0–394–70317–0 Random House pb $8.95

● **Jacques Maritain**
EDUCATION AT THE CROSSROADS
The Catholic philosopher's notes on Christian values and education
0–300–00163–0 Yale pb $6.95

● **Jane R. Martin**
RECLAIMING A CONVERSATION: The Ideal of the Educated Woman
"Conversations" with Plato, Rousseau, Wollstonecraft, Beecher, and Gilman on how women should be educated in an ideal society
0–300–03324–9 Yale $25.00

● **Israel Scheffler**
THE LANGUAGE OF EDUCATION
0–398–01656–9 Charles Thomas $16.25

● **Douglas Sloan**
EDUCATION AND VALUES
Twelve theorists ponder the relationship between knowledge and moral values
0–8077–2574–9 Teachers College pb $11.95

● **Jonas F. Soltis**
PHILOSOPHY OF EDUCATION SINCE MID-CENTURY
0–8077–2651–6 Teachers College pb $9.95

Maria Montessori

Maria Montessori
THE ABSORBENT MIND
Montessori's analysis of children's physical and psychological growth in their first six years
0–385–28012–2 Delacorte pb $9.95

THE DISCOVERY OF THE CHILD
9–999–46439–4 Ballantine pb $3.95

Elizabeth Hamstock, editor
THE ESSENTIAL MONTESSORI
0–452–26090–6 NAL pb $9.95

E. M. Standing
MARIA MONTESSORI: Her Life and Work
0–452–25624–0 NAL pb $8.95

HISTORY OF EDUCATION

Overviews

● **James Bowen**
A HISTORY OF WESTERN EDUCATION

Volume 1: Civilization of Europe, Sixth to Sixteenth Century
0–312–38745–8 St. Martin's $30.00

Volume 2: The Modern West, Europe and the New World
0–312–38780–6 St. Martin's $35.00
0–312–38781–4 St. Martin's pb $14.95

● **Lawrence A. Cremin**
Cremin's history of American education is an exhaustive, first-rate work of synthesis that sets the standard for the field.

AMERICAN EDUCATION: The Colonial Experience, 1607-1783
0–06–131670-9 Harper & Row pb $12.95

AMERICAN EDUCATION: The National Experience, 1783-1876
0–06–010912–2 Harper & Row $30.50

THE TRANSFORMATION OF THE SCHOOL: Progressivism in American Education, 1876-1957
"Easily the best-balanced book on 20th-century education...an admirable history of the ideas, personalities, organizations, and pressure groups in American education"—Harvey Wish, *Cleveland Plain Dealer*
0–394–70519–X Random House pb $6.50

AMERICAN EDUCATION: The Metropolitan Experience, 1876-1980
"A major work of synthesis and analysis...a necessary starting point for all subsequent studies"—Jack P. Greene, *Reviews in American History*
0–06–015804–2 Harper & Row $35.00

● **H.I. Marrou**
HISTORY OF EDUCATION IN ANTIQUITY
A landmark in the history of education, first published in France in 1948. "A rare combination of good writing and masses of information"—*Manchester Guardian*
0–299–08814–6 Wisconsin pb $12.95

● **R.R. Palmer**
THE IMPROVEMENT OF HUMANITY: Education and the French Revolution
By the co-author of *A History of the Modern World*
0–691–05434–7 Princeton $33.50

● **Diane Ravitch**
THE TROUBLED CRUSADE: American Education, 1945-1980
0–465–08756–6 Basic Books $19.95
0–465–08757–4 Basic Books pb $12.95

● **David B. Tyack**
THE ONE BEST SYSTEM: A History of American Urban Education
0–674–63780–1 Harvard $24.50

History of American Education

● **Paul Avrich**
THE MODERN SCHOOL MOVEMENT: Anarchism and Education in the United States
0–691–04669–7 Princeton $49.50
0–691–10094–2 Princeton pb $17.95

● **Bernard Bailyn**
EDUCATION IN THE FORMING OF AMERICAN SOCIETY: Needs and Opportunities for Study
0–8078–0797–4 North Carolina $15.00
0–393–00643–3 Norton pb $6.95

● **Joan N. Burstyn**
VICTORIAN EDUCATION AND THE IDEAL OF WOMANHOOD
0–8135–1031–7 Rutgers pb $12.00

• Lawrence A. Cremin
TRADITIONS OF AMERICAN EDUCATION
0–465–08684–5 Basic Books pb $8.95

• Merle Curti
THE SOCIAL IDEAS OF AMERICAN EDUCATORS
0–8226–0105–2 Littlefield, Adams pb $12.95

• Hugh D. Graham
THE UNCERTAIN TRIUMPH: Federal Education Policy in the Kennedy and Johnson Years
0–8078–1599–3 North Carolina $22.00

• Robert L. Hampel
THE LAST LITTLE CITADEL: American High Schools since 1940
Foreword by Theodore R. Sizer
0–395–44201–X Houghton Mifflin pb $8.95

• Carl F. Kaestle
PILLARS OF THE REPUBLIC: Common Schools and American Society, 1780-1860
Edited by Eric Foner
0–8090–0154–3 Hill & Wang pb $7.95

• Bruce Kimball
ORATORS AND PHILOSOPHERS: A History of the Idea of Liberal Education
0–8077–2790–3 Teachers College $19.95

• Ellen C. Lagemann
A GENERATION OF WOMEN: Education in the Lives of Progressive Reformers
0–674–34471–5 Harvard $16.00

• Robert C. Morris
READING, RITING AND RECONSTRUCTION: The Education of Freedmen in the South, 1861-1870
0–226–53928–8 Chicago $28.00

• Henry J. Perkinson
IMPERFECT PANACEA: American Faith in Education, 1865-1968
0–394–31216–3 Random House pb $10.50

• Paul E. Peterson
THE POLITICS OF SCHOOL REFORM, 1870-1940
0–226–66295–0 Chicago pb $11.95

• Diane Ravitch
THE GREAT SCHOOL WARS: A History of the New York City Public Schools
0–465–02702–4 Basic Books $20.00
0–465–02704–0 Basic Books pb $14.95

• David Tyack & Elisabeth Hansot
MANAGERS OF VIRTUE: Public School Leadership in America, 1820–1980
0–465–04376–3 Basic Books $17.95

• David Tyack & others
PUBLIC SCHOOLS IN HARD TIMES: The Great Depression and Recent Years
0–674–73800–4 Harvard $20.00

• Rush Welter
POPULAR EDUCATION AND DEMOCRATIC THOUGHT IN AMERICA
0–231–02560–2 Columbia $49.50

An Arizona Little League team, from In America *by Eve Arnold* (*Knopf*)

INTERNATIONAL EDUCATION

• Urie Bronfenbrenner
TWO WORLDS OF CHILDHOOD: US and USSR
0–671–21238–9 Pocket pb $9.95

• John Chandos
BOYS TOGETHER: English Public Schools, 1800-1864
0–300–03215–3 Yale $35.00

• Theodore Hsi-en Chen
CHINESE EDUCATION SINCE THE REVOLUTION: Development, Modernization or Revolutionary Communism?
0–08–023861–0 Pergamon $32.00

• Burton R. Clark, editor
THE SCHOOL AND THE UNIVERSITY: An International Perspective
0–520–05423–7 California pb $40.00

• Philip H. Coombs
THE WORLD CRISIS IN EDUCATION: A View from the Eighties
0–19–503502–X Oxford $24.95
0–19–503503–8 Oxford pb $12.95

• Danny Danziger
ETON VOICES
Interviews with more than 40 graduates of the famous "public school" probe the realities of privileged schooling in Britain
0–670–81630–2 Viking $19.95

• Torstein Husen
THE SCHOOL IN QUESTION: A Comparative Study of School and Its Future in Western Societies
0–19–874085–9 Oxford $34.00
0–19–874086–7 Oxford pb $13.95

• John Simmons
THE EDUCATION DILEMMA
0–08–024304–5 Pergamon $51.00
0–08–024303–7 Pergamon pb $24.00

The Japanese Advantage

William K. Cummings
EDUCATION AND EQUALITY IN JAPAN
0–691–10088–8 Princeton $17.50

Benjamin Duke
THE JAPANESE SCHOOL: Lessons for Industrial America
Foreword by Clark Kerr & James M. Hestor
0–275–92003–8 Praeger pb $14.95

Thomas P. Rohlen
JAPAN'S HIGH SCHOOLS
0–520–04863–6 California pb $11.95

Merry White
THE JAPANESE EDUCATIONAL CHALLENGE: A Commitment to Children
0–02–933800–X Free Press $18.95
0–02–933801–8 Free Press pb $9.95

HIGHER EDUCATION

• Alexander W. Astin
FOUR CRITICAL YEARS: Effects of College on Beliefs, Attitudes, and Knowledge
0–87589–346–5 Jossey-Bass $23.95

• Burton J. Bledstein
THE CULTURE OF PROFESSIONALISM: The Middle Class and the Development of Higher Education in America
0–393–05574–4 Norton $12.95
0–393–00891–6 Norton pb $9.95

• Allan Bloom
THE CLOSING OF THE AMERICAN MIND: Education and the Crisis of Reason
Introduction by Saul Bellow
0–671–47990–3 Simon & Schuster $18.95
0–671–65715–1 Simon & Schuster pb $8.95

• **Derek C. Bok**
BEYOND THE IVORY TOWER: Social Responsibilities of the Modern University
0–674–06899–8 Harvard $21.00
0–674–06898–X Harvard pb $8.95

HIGHER LEARNING
Wide-ranging thoughts on the purposes and practices of American higher education today, from the president of Harvard
0–674–39175–6 Harvard $16.50 .

• **Pierre Bourdieu**
HOMO ACADEMICUS
A brilliant, best-selling self-analysis of the French academic world by its leading sociologist
Translated by Peter Collier
0–8047–1466–5 Stanford $29.50

• **Ernest L. Boyer**
COLLEGE: The Undergradute Experience in America
A Carnegie Foundation study, based on visits to 30 public and private college campuses. "The most comprehensive, perceptive, and constructive report in recent years on the undergraduate experience"—David Pierpont Gardner, President, University of California
0–06–091458–0 Harper & Row pb $9.95

• **Steven M. Cahn**
SAINTS AND SCAMPS: Ethics in Academia
Ethical guidelines for teaching, scholarship, and personnel decisions in higher education. "A unique, stimulating and useful guide"—Israel Scheffler
0–8476–7517–3 Rowman $15.95
0–8476–7518–1 Rowman pb $8.50

• **Michael D. Cohen & James G. March**
LEADERSHIP AND AMBIGUITY
0–87584–174–0 Harvard Business $24.95
0–87584–131–7 Harvard Business pb $9.95

• **A. Bartlett Giamatti**
A FREE AND ORDERED SPACE: The Real World of the University
0–393–02622–1 Norton $19.95

• **Gerald Grant & David Riesman**
THE PERPETUAL DREAM: Reform and Experiment in the American College
0–226–30606–2 Chicago pb $6.95

Helen Lefkowitz Horowitz
CAMPUS LIFE: Undergraduate Cultures from the End of the 18th Century to the Present
0–226–35373–7 Chicago pb $13.95

• **Christopher Jencks & David Riesman**
THE ACADEMIC REVOLUTION
The rise of faculty domination in the college and university world
0–226–39628–2 Chicago pb $7.95

• **Clark Kerr**
THE USES OF THE UNIVERSITY
0–674–93171–8 Harvard pb $9.95

• **Kenneth M. Ludmerer**
LEARNING TO HEAL: The Development of American Medical Education
0–465–03881–6 Basic Books pb $12.95

• **Walter P. Metzger**
ACADEMIC FREEDOM IN THE AGE OF THE UNIVERSITY
0–231–08512–5 Columbia pb $13.00

• **Samuel Eliot Morison**
THREE CENTURIES OF HARVARD
0–674–88890–1 Harvard $25.00
0–674–88891–X Harvard pb $10.95

• **Mabel Newcomer**
A CENTURY OF HIGHER EDUCATION FOR AMERICAN WOMEN
0–89201–002–9 Zenger $19.95

• **David Riesman**
ON HIGHER EDUCATION: The Academic Enterprise in an Era of Rising Student Consumerism
How higher education has become increasingly student-oriented since the 1960s. "This shift from academic merit to student consumerism is one of the two greatest reversals of direction in all the history of American higher education; the other being the replacement of the classical college by the modern university a century ago"—Clark Kerr
0–87589–484–4 Jossey-Bass $27.95

• **Ellen W. Schrecker**
NO IVORY TOWER: McCarthyism and the Universities
0–19–505663–9 Oxford $20.95

• **Barbara M. Solomon**
IN THE COMPANY OF EDUCATED WOMEN: A History of Women and Higher Education in America
0–300–03639–6 Yale pb $13.95

• **Robert Stevens**
LAW SCHOOL: Legal Education in America from the 1850s to the 1980s
0–8078–1537–3 North Carolina $22.50
0–8078–4175–7 North Carolina pb $12.95

TECHNOLOGY AND EDUCATION

President James A. Garfield is said to have remarked that the ideal college was Mark Hopkins on one end of a log and a student on the other. For years, that saying was reiterated, usually to reaffirm the importance of the relationship between the teacher and the student.

Since at least mid-century, however, technology has loomed large as the answer to those who have longed for a "teacher-proof" method of education. With each scientific advance, the promise of technology has seemed brighter. But amid the euphoria there are also warnings that the electronic cure for education's ills may be more dangerous than the disease itself.

Whether the computer, the videodisc, or some other version of the blinking screen will take Mark Hopkins' place remains to be seen.

• **M. Cetron & others**
SCHOOLS OF THE FUTURE: Education into the 21st Century
0–07–010350–X McGraw-Hill $12.95

• **Larry Cuban**
TEACHERS AND MACHINES: The Classroom Use of Technology Since 1920
0–8077–2792–X Teachers College pb $10.95

• **W.P. Dizard**
THE COMING INFORMATION AGE: An Overview of Technology, Economics, and Politics
0–801–30305–2 Longman pb $18.50

• **Christopher Evans**
THE MICRO MILLENNIUM
0–671–46212–1 Washington Square pb $3.95

• **Patricia Greenfield**
MIND AND MEDIA: The Effects of Television, Video Games, and Computers
0–674–57620–9 Harvard $13.50
0–674–57621–7 Harvard pb $4.95

• **Seymour Papert**
MINDSTORMS: Children, Computers, and Powerful Ideas
0–465–04627–4 Basic Books $15.95
0–465–04629–0 Basic Books pb $8.95

• **Neil Postman**
AMUSING OURSELVES TO DEATH: Public Discourse in the Age of Show Business
0–14–009438–5 Penguin pb $6.95

• **Theodore Roszak**
THE CULT OF INFORMATION: The Folklore of Computers and the True Art of Thinking
0–394–54622–9 Pantheon $17.95
0–394–75175–2 Pantheon pb $7.95

• **Douglas Sloan, editor**
THE COMPUTER IN EDUCATION: A Critical Perspective
0–8077–2782–2 Teachers College pb $11.95

• **Tom Snyder & Jane Palmer**
IN SEARCH OF THE MOST AMAZING THING: Children, Education and Computers
0–201–16437–X Addison-Wesley pb $10.95

• **Robert Taylor, editor**
THE COMPUTER IN THE SCHOOL: Tutor, Tutee, Tool
0–8077–2611–7 Teachers College pb $15.95

• **Sherry Turkle**
SECOND SELF: Computers and the Human Spirit
0–671–60602–6 Simon & Schuster pb $8.95

• **Marie Winn**
THE PLUG-IN DRUG: Television, Children and the Family
0–14–007698–0 Penguin pb $6.95

The Nuclear Age

• Berger Gould & others
GROWING UP SCARED?: The Psychological Effect of the Nuclear Threat on Children
0–931416–04–3 Open Books pb $10.00

• David S. Greenwald & Steven J. Zeitlin
NO REASON TO TALK ABOUT IT: Families Confront the Nuclear Taboo
0–393–70021–6 Norton $22.95

• Phyllis La Farge
THE STRANGELOVE LEGACY: Children, Parents and Teachers in the Nuclear Age
0–06–091469–6 Harper & Row pb $7.95

• Spencer R. Weart
NUCLEAR FEAR: A History of Images
0–674–62835–7 Harvard $29.50

PRACTICAL ADVICE

Guides for Parents

▶ See also Parents and Children

• Benjamin S. Bloom
ALL OUR CHILDREN LEARNING: A Primer for Parents, Teachers, and Other Educators
0–07–006121–1 McGraw-Hill pb $6.95

• Martha C. Brown
SCHOOLWISE: A Parent's Guide to Getting the Best Education for Your Child
0–87477–364–4 Tarcher pb $9.95

• Thomas Gordon
TEACHING CHILDREN SELF-DISCIPLINE AT HOME AND AT SCHOOL
0–8129–1780–4 Times Books $18.95

• Bill Honig
LAST CHANCE FOR OUR CHILDREN: How You Can Help Save Our Schools
Notes and suggestions from the longtime California superintendent of public instruction
0–395–43095–X Houghton Mifflin $16.95
0–201–12648–6 Addison-Wesley pb $8.95

• Herbert Kohl
LESSONS FOR LIFE: Guiding Our Kids to the Right Choices for the Post-High School Years
A parent's guide by the author of *Thirty-Six Children*
0–8129–1698–0 Times Books $17.95

• Tom & Harriet Sobol
YOUR CHILD IN SCHOOL: Kindergarten Through Second Grade
0–688–08247–5 Arbor House pb $8.95

YOUR CHILD IN SCHOOL: Grades Three Through Five
0–87795–924–2 Arbor House $18.95

Public and Private Schools

• Christopher J. Georges & James A. Messina, editors
THE HARVARD INDEPENDENT INSIDER'S GUIDE TO PREP SCHOOLS
0–452–25920–7 NAL pb $9.95

• Charles Harrison
PUBLIC SCHOOLS USA: A Comparative Guide to School Districts
0–913589–36–5 Williamson pb $17.95

• Peterson's Guides
PETERSON'S GUIDE TO INDEPENDENT SECONDARY SCHOOLS, 1988-89
0–87866–690–7 Peterson's pb $18.95

College Guides

• Barron's Educational Series
BARRON'S GUIDE TO THE MOST PRESTIGIOUS COLLEGES
Includes listings for what Barron's ranks as "most competitive," "highly competitive," and "very competitive" colleges for "B" and better students
0–8120–3985–8 Barron's pb $9.95

BARRON'S PROFILES OF AMERICAN COLLEGES
Descriptions of 1500 American four-year colleges
0–8120–3979–3 Barron's pb $13.95

• Lisa Birnbach
LISA BIRNBACH'S COLLEGE BOOK
A hip, occasionally nasty guide by the author of *The Official Preppy Handbook*
0–345–30918–9 Ballantine pb $9.95

• James Cass & Max Birnbaum
COMPARATIVE GUIDE TO AMERICAN COLLEGES
0–06–463725–5 Harper & Row pb $15.95

• College Research Group
ARCO DOLLARWISE GUIDE TO AMERICAN COLLEGES
0–13–044827–3 Arco pb $12.95

THE RIGHT COLLEGE, 1989
Includes information about student life, admissions, prominent alumni, financial aid, and basic profiles of many colleges
0–13–781212–4 Arco pb $15.95

Edward Fiske
THE FISKE GUIDE TO COLLEGES, 1989
A newly renamed and revised edition of a first-rate guide by the *New York Times* education writer
0–8129–1732–4 Times Books pb $10.95

Edward Fiske & Joseph Michalak
THE BEST BUYS IN COLLEGE EDUCATION
Profiles of 260 colleges offering high-quality education at reasonable cost, arranged by state, with commentary by students at each school
0–8129–1701–4 Times Books pb $10.95

• Guidance Information Systems
THE GIS GUIDE TO FOUR-YEAR COLLEGES
Uses statistics from a database of educational information, and includes such information as student views of campus life, sports, residential life, and campus activities for each listing
0–395–47348–9 Houghton Mifflin pb $14.95

• Andrea E. Lehman, editor
PETERSON'S GUIDE TO FOUR-YEAR COLLEGES, 1989
A standard, very informative guide
0–87866–718–0 Peterson's pb $15.95

• Richard Moll
THE PUBLIC IVYS: A Guide to America's Best State Colleges and Universities
Detailed descriptions of the nation's best state-run colleges
0–14–009384–2 Penguin pb $7.95

• Peterson's Guides
PETERSON'S GUIDE TO TWO-YEAR COLLEGES, 1989
0–87866–719–9 Peterson's pb $12.95

• Charles J. Shields
THE COLLEGE GUIDE FOR PARENTS
0–87447–316–0 College Board pb $12.95

• Charles & Barbarasue Lovejoy Straughn
LOVEJOY'S COLLEGE GUIDE
A statistically rich volume
0–671–64759–8 Monarch pb $16.95

• Yale Daily News
THE INSIDER'S GUIDE TO THE COLLEGES
One of the best college guides around; offers accurate portraits of a wide range of schools
0–312–02223–9 St. Martin's pb $11.95

Graduate and Professional Schools

• Harold R. Doughty
GUIDE TO AMERICAN GRADUATE SCHOOLS
0–14–046725–4 Penguin pb $15.95

• Elliott M. Epstein & others
BARRON'S GUIDE TO LAW SCHOOLS
0–8120–3984–X Barron's pb $11.95

• Sally F. Goldfarb
INSIDE THE LAW SCHOOLS: A Guide by Students for Students
0–525–48201–6 Dutton pb $9.95

• Eugene Miller
BARRON'S GUIDE TO GRADUATE BUSINESS SCHOOLS
0–8120–3986–6 Barron's pb $12.95

• T.C. Moore, editor
PETERSON'S GUIDE TO GRADUATE AND PROFESSIONAL PROGRAMS, 1989
0–87866–743–1 Peterson's pb $19.95

• Saul Wischnitzer, editor
BARRON'S GUIDE TO MEDICAL AND DENTAL SCHOOLS
0–8120–3842–8 Barron's pb $9.95

A Venetian schoolroom of the late 15th century

Testing

• Samuel Brownstein & others
BARRON'S HOW TO PREPARE FOR THE SAT
The granddaddy of Scholastic Aptitude preparation manuals offers sample tests (with answers and explanations) for both the verbal and math exams and a self-evaluation section for improvement
0–8120–3844–4 Barron's pb $9.95

BASIC TIPS FOR THE SAT
0–8120–3713–8 Barron's pb $4.95

BASIC TIPS FOR THE GRADUATE RECORD EXAMINATION
0–8120–2414–1 Barron's pb $3.95

• Joan Davenport Carris & others
PETERSON'S SAT SUCCESS
0–87866–580–3 Peterson's pb $9.95

• Eugene D. Jaffe & Stephen Hilbert
BARRON'S HOW TO PREPARE FOR THE GMAT
A preparation manual for the Graduate Management Admissions Test
0–8120–3882–7 Barron's pb $9.95

• Thomas H. Martinson
SUPERCOURSE FOR THE ACT
Guide to the American College Testing exam
0–13–003170–4 Arco pb $12.95

SUPERCOURSE FOR THE SAT
0–13–788506–7 Arco pb $12.95

SUPERCOURSE FOR THE GRE
Guide to the Graduate Record Exam
0–13–363516–3 Arco pb $12.95

SUPERCOURSE FOR THE LSAT
How to prepare for the Law School Admissions Test
0–13–541145–9 Arco pb $12.95

• David Owen
NONE OF THE ABOVE: Behind the Myth of Scholastic Aptitude
Not a guide as much as an exposé of what's wrong with the much-vaunted test
0–395–41500–4 Houghton Mifflin pb $7.95

• Adam Robinson & John Katzman
PRINCETON REVIEW: Cracking the System—The SAT and PSAT
Based on a systematized coaching program for improving test scores through intelligent guessing and other test-taking methods
0–679–72135–5 Random House pb $9.95

CRACKING THE SYSTEM: The GRE
The Princeton Review meets the Graduate Record Exam
0–394–75684–3 Random House pb $9.95

• Murray Rockowitz & others
BARRON'S HOW TO PREPARE FOR THE GED
Preparation for the high school diploma equivalency test
0–8120–3888–6 Barron's pb $9.95

• Murray Shapiro, editor
BARRON'S HOW TO PREPARE FOR THE ACT
A standard guide for the American College Testing exam
0–8120–3891–6 Barron's pb $9.95

• Eve Steinberg
AMERICAN COLLEGE TESTING PROGRAM
Four complete model exams with their answers, and intensive reviews of English usage, social studies, math, and the natural sciences
0–130–24613–1 Simon & Schuster pb $10.95

College Admissions

• Edward B. Fiske
HOW TO GET INTO THE RIGHT COLLEGE: Secrets of College Admissions Officers
A useful guidebook by the author of *The Fiske Guide to Colleges*
0–8129–1686–7 Times Books pb $7.95

• Christopher & Gigi Georges
100 SUCCESSFUL COLLEGE APPLICATION ESSAYS
Using essays from applicants who were admitted to various colleges, offers advice and guidance on how to write an essay that can help win admission
0–452–26153–8 Plume pb $8.95

• Frank Leana
GETTING INTO COLLEGE
Interesting strategies and advice on all stages of the college admission process, from taking tests to being interviewed
0–8090–1393–2 Hill & Wang pb $7.95

• Paolo de Oliveira & Steve Cohen
GETTING IN!
Strategies on how to get into the college of your choice
0–89480–359–X Workman pb $5.95

• Harlow Unger
STUDENTS GUIDE TO COLLEGE ADMISSIONS: Everything Your Counselor Has No Time to Tell You
How to select a university, apply for admission, and pass the necessary entrance tests
0–8160–1418–3 Facts On File $19.95
0–8160–1542–2 Facts On File pb $8.95

• Fred Zuker & Karen C. Hegener
PETERSON'S GUIDE TO COLLEGE ADMISSIONS: How to Plan Your Admissions Strategy and Get into the College of Your Choice
0–87866–463–7 Peterson's pb $11.95

College Finance and Financial Aid

• Daniel J. Cassidy
THE GRADUATE SCHOLARSHIP BOOK
Lists many sources of graduate financial aid
0–13–362229–0 Prentice-Hall pb $19.95

• Daniel J. Cassidy & Michael J. Alves
THE SCHOLARSHIP BOOK
A comprehensive listing of sources for undergraduate financial aid
0–13–792417–8 Prentice-Hall pb $19.95

• College Scholarship Service
THE COLLEGE COST BOOK, 1988-89
0–87447–315–2 College Board pb $12.95

• James P. Duffy
CUTTING COLLEGE COSTS
0–06–463728–X Harper & Row pb $8.95

• Gerald Krefetz
HOW TO PAY FOR YOUR CHILDREN'S COLLEGE EDUCATION
0–87447–248–2 College Board pb $12.95

• Andrea E. Lehman & Eric A. Suber
PETERSON'S COLLEGE MONEY HANDBOOK: The Only Complete Guide to Scholarships, College Costs, and Financial Aid
0–87866–702–4 Peterson's pb $17.95

• Robert Leider
LOVEJOY'S GUIDE TO FINANCIAL AID
Revised by Anna Leider
0–671–64716–4 Monarch pb $10.95

Linguistics

INTRODUCTIONS TO LANGUAGE

• Roland Barthes
THE RUSTLE OF LANGUAGE
Witty and informed essays on how language affects our lives and literature
Translated by Richard Howard
0–8090–8344–2 Hill & Wang $25.00
0–8090–1527–7 Hill & Wang pb $9.95

• Roger Brown
WORDS AND THINGS
0–02–904800–1 Free Press $19.95
0–02–904810–9 Free Press pb $10.95

• Victoria Fromkins & Robert Rodman
AN INTRODUCTION TO LANGUAGE
0–03–006532–1 HR&W pb $26.50

• Kenneth Katzner
LANGUAGES OF THE WORLD
0–7102–0861–8 RC&H pb $13.95

• Winfred P. Lehmann
LANGUAGE: An Introduction
0–07–554251–X McGraw-Hill pb $18.50

☐ **TO ORDER BY FAX, SEE PAGE 1**

• James MacKillop & Donna W. Cross
SPEAKING OF WORDS: A Language Reader
0–03–003953–3 HR&W pb $18.95

LANGUAGE THEORY

• Jean Aitchison
TEACH YOURSELF LINGUISTICS
This is an excellent, clearly presented introduction to the field, with many helpful diagrams
0–679–10258–2 Hodder & Stoughton pb $8.95

• Jeremy Campbell
GRAMMATICAL MAN: Information, Entropy, Language and Life
"Synthesizes all the most interesting aspects of contemporary thinking, showing where linguistics meets physics"—Annie Dillard
0–671–44061–6 Simon & Schuster $16.95
0–671–44062–4 Simon & Schuster pb $10.95

• Philip S. Dale
LANGUAGE DEVELOPMENT: Structure and Function
0–03–089705–X Henry Holt pb $34.00

• Suzette H. Elgin
WHAT IS LINGUISTICS?
0–13–952333–2 Prentice-Hall pb $22.95

• Alison J. Elliot
CHILD LANGUAGE
A clear and concise survey of the field of language acquisition
0–521–29556–4 Cambridge pb $12.95

• C.A. Ferguson & Shirley Brice Heath, editors
LANGUAGE IN THE UNITED STATES OF AMERICA
Foreword by Dell H. Hymes
0–521–29834–2 Cambridge pb $19.95

• John Lyons
LANGUAGE AND LINGUISTICS
Lyons has moved from a syntactic orientation to a romantic one
0–521–29775–3 Cambridge pb $14.95

• Frederick J. Newmayer
THE POLITICS OF LINGUISTICS
Deals with 200 years of debate over whether language should be studied as an autonomous entity, or as part of the cultural and social fabric
0–226–57722–8 Chicago pb $9.95

• Frank Parker
LINGUISTICS FOR NON-LINGUISTS
0–316–69086–4 College-Hill pb $19.50

• Bruce L. Pearson
INTRODUCTION TO LINGUISTIC CONCEPTS
0–07–553627–7 McGraw-Hill pb $12.95

• Geoffrey Sampson
SCHOOLS OF LINGUISTICS
"A fresh, funny, clear, literate and scholarly survey of the prelude and cacophonous

Building the Tower of Babel: a 1490 Venetian woodcut

themes of recent linguistic theory in the English-speaking world"—*Choice*
0–8047–1125–9 Stanford pb $9.95

• John Searle
EXPRESSION AND MEANING: Studies in the Theory of Speech Acts
One of the most influential theories applied by one of its leading exponents to metaphor and fiction
0–521–31393–7 Cambridge pb $14.95

• Ronald Wardhaugh
INTRODUCTION TO LINGUISTICS
0–07–068152–X McGraw-Hill pb $34.95

PIONEERS IN LINGUISTICS

• J.L. Austin
HOW TO DO THINGS WITH WORDS
The short but extremely influential work by the founder of speech act theory
0–674–41152–8 Harvard pb $5.95

• Leonard Bloomfield
LANGUAGE
The early American behaviorist cleared the ground for later scientific methods of language study; this summation of his views was published in 1933
Foreword by Charles Hockett
0–226–06067–5 Chicago pb $15.95

A LEONARD BLOOMFIELD ANTHOLOGY
Edited by Charles Hockett
0–226–06071–3 Chicago pb $14.95

• Roman Jakobson
LANGUAGE IN LITERATURE
Highly influential literary theory based on linguistics, by the cofounder of the Prague School
Edited by Krystyna Pomorska & Stephen Rudy
0–674–51027–5 Harvard $30.00

VERBAL ART, VERBAL SIGN, VERBAL TIME
Carries Russian formalism into a study of Yeats, Mayakovsky, and the poetry that can emerge from psychological disturbance
Edited by Krystyna Pomorska & Stephen Rudy
0–8166–1358–3 Minnesota $29.50
0–8166–1361–3 Minnesota $13.95

• Roman Jakobson & Morris Halle
FUNDAMENTALS OF LANGUAGE
90–2793–074–0 Mouton de Gruyter pb $9.25

• Roman Jakobson & Krystyna Pomorska
DIALOGUES
Intimate and casual interviews between the linguist and his wife give their thought a charming accessibility
0–262–60016–1 MIT pb $9.95

• Edward Sapir
LANGUAGE: An Introduction to the Study of Speech
With Whorf, Sapir was one of the originators of the idea that "the real world is unconsciously built up on the language habits of the group"; this classic study appeared in 1921
0–15–648233–9 HBJ pb $6.95

SELECTED WRITINGS OF EDWARD SAPIR IN LANGUAGE, CULTURE, AND PERSONALITY
Edited by David G. Mandelbaum
0–520–05594–2 California pb $15.95

Ferdinand de Saussure
COURSE IN GENERAL LINGUISTICS
Published in 1916, this was the greatest single influence in detaching language study from the historical methods of the 19th century and approaching it as a system
Edited by Roy Harris
Translated by Wade Baskin
0–07–016524–6 McGraw-Hill pb $6.95

Jonathan Culler
FERDINAND DE SAUSSURE
A brief introduction to the founder of semiotics and modern linguistics, aimed at the general reader
0–14–004369–1 Penguin pb $4.95

• Wilhelm von Humboldt
ON LANGUAGE: The Diversity of Human Language-Structure and its Influence on the Mental Development of Mankind
A new translation of the milestone work by the early 19th century philologist acknowledged by Chomsky as an early "transformationalist"
Translated by Peter Heath
Introduction by Hans Aarsleff
0–521–31513–1 Cambridge pb $14.95

• Benjamin Lee Whorf
LANGUAGE, THOUGHT AND REALITY: Selected Writings
A classic statement of the influence of language on perception, based on the study of Hopi and native Mexican languages
0–262–73006–5 MIT pb $9.95

Noam Chomsky

Chomsky is the founder of the major revolution in linguistics at mid-century that used the idea of "deep structure" to explain how a language user can generate an infinite variety of sentences without learning their individual forms.

TO ORDER BOOKS AS GIFTS, SEE PAGE 1

- Noam Chomsky
KNOWLEDGE OF LANGUAGE: Its Nature, Origin, and Use
0–275–90025–8 Praeger $35.00
0–275–91761–4 Praeger pb $11.95

LANGUAGE AND MIND
0–15–549257–8 HBJ pb $14.95

LANGUAGE AND RESPONSIBILITY
0–394–73619–2 Pantheon pb $6.95

REFLECTIONS ON LANGUAGE
0–394–73123–9 Pantheon pb $8.95

RULES AND REPRESENTATIONS
0–231–04826–2 Columbia $34.00
0–231–04827–0 Columbia pb $16.00

- Gilbert Harman, editor
ON NOAM CHOMSKY: Critical Essays
0–87023–355–6 Massachusetts pb $11.95

- John Lyons
NOAM CHOMSKY
0–14–004370–5 Penguin pb $5.95

LANGUAGE AND SOCIETY

- J.L. Dillard
BLACK ENGLISH: Its History and Usage in the United States
Not merely a collection of errors but an alternative system, Black English has a history of its own and its rules can be regularized like those of any other language
0–394–71872–0 Random House pb $7.95

- John Edwards
LANGUAGE, SOCIETY AND IDENTITY
The rise of linguistic nationalism and the attempt to control individual identity through language legislation, language academies, and dictionaries
0–631–14233–9 Blackwell pb $19.95

- Roger Fowler
LANGUAGE AND CONTROL
How ideological social structures are expressed and reproduced through syntax as well as content
0–7100–0288–2 RC&H $29.95

- Michael Gregory & Susanne Carroll
LANGUAGE AND SITUATION: Language Varieties and Their Social Contexts
0–7100–8773–X RC&H pb $9.95

- Shirley Brice Heath
WAYS WITH WORDS: Language, Life and Work in Communities and Classrooms
Two neighboring blue-collar communities, white Roadville and black Trackton, provide a comparison of language use based on education, upbringing, and working conditions
0–521–27319–6 Cambridge pb $20.95

- Alette Olin Hill
MOTHER TONGUE, FATHER TIME: A Decade of Linguistic Revolt
Language and feminism
0–253–20389–9 Indiana pb $9.95

- Gunther Kress & Robert Hodge
SOCIAL SEMIOTICS
Analyzes communication processes in literary texts, television, advertising billboards, and daily social interactions
0–8104–9515–6 Cornell pb $14.95

- Robert K. Logan
THE ALPHABET EFFECT
This story of the evolution of writing systems from clay tablets to computers focuses on the phonetic alphabet
0–312–00993–3 St. Martin's pb $9.95

Robert McCrum & others
THE STORY OF ENGLISH
A companion volume to the television series. "The study of the language will never be the same again after the publication of this book. It travels at the speed of a bullet train to every corner of the globe where English is spoken. It also authentically describes the mysterious power of older dazzling forms of the language"—Robert Burchfield, Editor in Chief, The Oxford Dictionaries
0–670–80467–3 Viking $24.95
0–14–009435–0 Penguin pb $12.95

- Lawrence Paros
THE EROTIC TONGUE: A Sexual Lexicon
Obscenities, rich and colorful; arcane slang; euphemisms; quaint terms rescued from Standard English; and words of the four-letter variety
0–8050–0796–2 Henry Holt pb $8.95

- David Simpson
THE POLITICS OF AMERICAN ENGLISH, 1776-1850
The story of the fierce debate on both sides of the Atlantic over what American English was, what it might become, and what it ought to be
0–19–505643–4 Oxford pb $12.95

- Michael Stubbs
LANGUAGE AND LITERACY: The Sociolinguistics of Reading and Writing
"Ghoti," said Shaw, could spell "fish." Stubbs uses sociolinguistics to investigate this and other language problems
0–7100–0499–0 RC&H pb $13.95

- David Sutcliffe & Ansel Wang
THE LANGUAGE OF THE BLACK EXPERIENCE
An exciting study of the connections between the cultural and social forms of British Caribbean dialect speakers in the Islands and in London
0–631–14816–7 Blackwell pb $12.95

LANGUAGE AND LITERATURE

- Marshall Edelson
LANGUAGE AND INTERPRETATION IN PSYCHOANALYSIS
Attempts to link Chomsky and Freud, and offers interpretations of a Bach prelude and Wallace Stevens' "Snow Man"
0–226–18433–1 Chicago pb $9.00

- Roger Fowler
LINGUISTIC CRITICISM
A leading British theorist looks at literature through the linguistic lens
0–19–289111–1 Oxford pb $9.95

- Barbara Herrnstein Smith
ON THE MARGINS OF DISCOURSE: The Relation of Literature to Language
0–226–76453–2 Chicago pb $7.50

- Elizabeth C. Traugott & Mary L. Pratt
LINGUISTICS FOR STUDENTS OF LITERATURE
0–15–551030–4 HBJ pb $18.95

REFERENCE

- David Crystal
THE CAMBRIDGE ENCYCLOPEDIA OF LANGUAGE
The exhaustive entries, along with the delightful diagrams and illustrations, make this book a pleasure for browsers as well as for serious readers
0–521–26438–3 Cambridge $39.50

- Oswald Ducrot & Tzvetan Todorov
ENCYCLOPEDIC DICTIONARY OF THE SCIENCES OF LANGUAGE
Excellent up-to-date collection of short articles that cover the major movements from transformational grammar to grammatology
Translated by Catherine Porter
0–8018–2857–0 Johns Hopkins pb $15.95

- H.L. Mencken
THE AMERICAN LANGUAGE
The classic work on the development of a specifically American vernacular that is also a history of the growth of the professions and the effect of immigration
0–394–73315–0 Knopf pb $15.95

Volume 1
0–394–40075–5 Knopf $30.00

Volume 2: Supplement One
0–394–40076–3 Knopf $30.00

Volume 3: Supplement Two
0–394–40077–1 Knopf $34.50

Women's Studies

A diverse and rapidly growing body of literature addresses the central questions of women's studies: What are the sources—and consequences—of the differences between men and women? What are the implications of viewing gender as a social construct rather than as a biological mandate? How has the history of women differed from that of men? How are differences among women determined by race, class, and ethnicity?

FEMINIST THEORY

• Simone de Beauvoir
THE SECOND SEX
A classic of feminist theory
Translated by H.M. Parshley
0–394–44415–9 Knopf $25.00
0–394–71227–7 Random House pb $5.95

Simone de Beauvoir (courtesy of Pantheon)

• Susan Brownmiller
FEMININITY
A historical and personal look at the accoutrements of femininity from 16th-century corsets to 20th-century cosmetics
0–449–90142–4 Ballantine pb $7.95

• Charlotte Bunch
PASSIONATE POLITICS: Essays, 1968-1986, Feminist Theory in Action
A noted feminist's collection of essays on a wide range of issues, including the ERA, Geraldine Ferraro, women's publishing, lesbianism, and the 1985 U.N. world conference on women
0–312–01804–5 St. Martin's pb $8.95

• Mary Daly
BEYOND GOD THE FATHER: Toward a Philosophy of Women's Liberation
"What other feminists have revealed by analyzing patriarchal society's political, economic, social and sexual institutions, Daly does for the spiritual instititution . . . Not for the timid, this brilliant book calls for nothing short of the overthrow of patriarchy"—*Village Voice*
0–8070–1503–2 Beacon pb $9.95

• Angela Davis
WOMEN, RACE AND CLASS
0–394–71351–6 Random House pb $5.95

• Barbara S. Deckard
THE WOMEN'S MOVEMENT: Political, Socioeconomic, and Psychological Issues
0–06–041615–7 Harper & Row pb $18.95

• Marilyn French
BEYOND POWER: On Women, Men and Morals
"French does believe that, by and large, men and women live by different moralities, and that a woman's morality is better. Her book is . . . a plea for the world to adopt a feminine morality"—*Newsday*
0–671–49959–9 Summit $19.95
0–345–33405–1 Ballantine pb $11.95

• Betty Friedan
THE FEMININE MYSTIQUE
This 1963 book had a wide impact
0–393–01775–3 Norton $17.50
0–440–32497–1 Dell pb $4.95

THE SECOND STAGE
Friedan's controversial update on the failures and future of feminism
0–671–45951–1 Summit pb $5.95

• Margaret Fuller
WOMAN IN THE NINETEENTH CENTURY
Fuller stresses in this 1845 work that men and women have a duty to fulfill their potential for the spiritual good of both sexes
0–393–00615–8 Norton pb $7.95

• Emma Goldman
THE TRAFFIC IN WOMEN & OTHER ESSAYS ON FEMINISM
Three key 1917 essays from the great anarchist
Edited by Alix Kates Shulman
0–87810–001–6 Times Change pb $3.00

• Vivian Gornick & Barbara K. Moran, editors
WOMAN IN SEXIST SOCIETY: Studies in Power and Powerlessness
Writings by Nancy Chodorow, Phyllis Chesler, and others on love, marriage, work, and social issues
0–451–62459–9 NAL pb $5.95

• Sylvia Ann Hewlett
A LESSER LIFE: The Myth of Women's Liberation in America
Statistics and case studies documenting how American women have been stripped of traditional support systems and thrust into the harsh realities of economic life
0–446–38511–5 Warner pb $10.95

• Gloria T. Hull & others, editors
ALL THE WOMEN ARE WHITE, ALL THE BLACKS ARE MEN, BUT SOME OF US ARE BRAVE: Black Women's Studies
A collection for the general reader covering such topics as political theory, major writers, and racism in higher education, plus annotated bibliographies on a wide range of subjects
0–912670–95–9 Feminist Press pb $12.95

• Alison M. Jaggar & Paula Rothenberg Strahl, editors
FEMINIST FRAMEWORKS: Alternative Theoretical Accounts of the Relations Between Men and Women
0–07–032251–1 McGraw-Hill $24.95

• Eleanor B. Leacock
MYTHS OF MALE DOMINANCE: Collected Articles
0–85345–537–6 Monthly Review $17.50
0–85345–538–4 Monthly Review pb $11.00

• Audre Lorde
SISTER OUTSIDER
Collection of her essays on women, racism, and self-acceptance
0–89594–141–4 Crossing pb $8.95

• Catherine A. MacKinnon
FEMINISM UNMODIFIED: Discourses on Life and Law
Rape, abortion, athletics, sexual harassment, pornography, and other topics, developed from speeches by a noted feminist and legal scholar. "Fundamental to [MacKinnon's] radical feminism is the claim that gender is a system of dominance rather than of difference"—Alison M. Jaggar, *NY Times*
0–674–29873–X Harvard $25.00
0–674–29874–8 Harvard pb $9.95

SEXUAL HARASSMENT OF WORKING WOMEN: A Case of Sex Discrimination
0–300–02299–9 Yale pb $11.95

• Elaine Marks & Isabelle De Courtivron, editors
NEW FRENCH FEMINISMS: An Anthology
0–8052–0681–7 Schocken pb $9.95

• Kate Millett
SEXUAL POLITICS
A classic feminist work in which Millett writes that sexual dominion is "perhaps the most pervasive ideology of our culture and provides its most fundamental concept of power"
0–345–29270–7 Ballantine pb $4.95

• Juliet Mitchell & Ann Oakley, editors
WHAT IS FEMINISM?: A Re-Examination by Nancy Cott, Linda Gordon, Judith Stacey, Juliet Mitchell, Ann Oakley, and Six Other Major Feminist Thinkers
Essays on motherhood, the ERA, social welfare, and other major topics affecting women
0–394–72261–2 Pantheon pb $9.95

• Toril Moi
FRENCH FEMINIST THOUGHT: A Reader
Writings by Julia Kristeva, Simone de Beauvoir, Anne Tristan, and others
0–631–14973–2 Blackwell $14.95

• Robin Morgan, editor
SISTERHOOD IS POWERFUL: An Anthology of Writings from the Women's Liberation Movement
Articles, poems, photographs, manifestos, and personal accounts
0–394–70539–4 Random House pb $9.95

• Evelyn Reed
WOMAN'S EVOLUTION: From Matriarchal Clan to Patriarchal Family
Reed hypothesizes that women played the leading role in prehistoric societies
0–87348–422–3 Pathfinder pb $11.95

• Lillian Robinson
SEX, CLASS AND CULTURE
A recent Marxist-feminist approach to high and pop culture
0–416–01241–8 RC&H pb $12.95

• Rosalind Rosenberg
BEYOND SEPARATE SPHERES: Intellectual Roots of Modern Feminism
The stories of the women who launched theories on sex differences, including personality development and sex roles
0–300–03092–4 Yale pb $11.95

• Anne W. Schaef
WOMEN'S REALITY: An Emerging Female System in the White Male Society
Explores the psycho-social differences between men and women
0–86683–753–1 Harper & Row pb $8.95

• Gloria Steinem
OUTRAGEOUS ACTS AND EVERYDAY REBELLIONS
A collection of writings, from notes on being a Playboy Bunny, to profiles of women, to satires like "If Men Could Menstruate"
0–451–15500–9 NAL pb $4.95

• Alice Walker
IN SEARCH OF OUR MOTHER'S GARDENS
0–15–644544–1 HBJ pb $6.95

LIVING BY THE WORD: Selected Writings, 1973-1987
0–15–152900–0 HBJ $15.95

Mary Wollstonecraft
A VINDICATION OF THE RIGHTS OF WOMAN
A founding statement of feminism, first published in 1792, applying the egalitarian principles of the times to women
Edited by Miriam Kramnick
0–14–043199–3 Penguin pb $4.95

Economics

• Barbara R. Bergmann
THE ECONOMIC EMERGENCE OF WOMEN
The transformation of women from homemakers to wage earners
0–465–01797–5 Basic Books pb $10.95

Charlotte Perkins Gilman (courtesy of Pantheon)

• Zillah R. Eisenstein, editor
CAPITALIST PATRIARCHY AND THE CASE FOR SOCIALIST FEMINISM
0–85345–476–0 Monthly Review pb $9.00

• Charlotte Perkins Gilman
WOMEN AND ECONOMICS: The Economic Factor Between Men and Women As a Factor in Social Evolution
"Gilman became the leading intellectual in the women's movement during the first two decades of the twentieth century . . . she challenged the Victorian assumption that men and women were so different that their social activities ought not and could not overlap"—Carl Degler
Edited by Carl Degler
0–06–133073–6 Harper & Row pb $10.95

• Cynthia B. Lloyd & Beth T. Niemi
THE ECONOMICS OF SEX DIFFERENTIALS
0–231–04038–5 Columbia pb $37.00

• John Stuart Mill
THE SUBJECTION OF WOMEN
First published in 1869, Mill's tract attacks the inequality manifested in marriage contracts, property rights, and women's responsibilities for family and marriage
0–87975–335–8 Prometheus pb $3.95

Politics, Law, and the ERA

• Barbara A. Babcock & others
SEX DISCRIMINATION AND THE LAW (1975): Causes and Remedies
Materials for a history of women's legal status
0–316–07421–7 Little, Brown pb $7.95

• Mary Frances Berry
WHY ERA FAILED: Politics, Women's Rights, and the Amending Process of the Constitution
The noted historian and lawyer examines the systemic problems of politics and the amending process as they relate to the Equal Rights Amendment. "Berry has placed the rise and fall of the ERA into constitutional, political, and ideological contexts"—Blanche Wiesen Cook
0–253–36537–6 Indiana $22.50

• Cynthia Fuchs Epstein
WOMEN IN LAW
0–465–09205–5 Basic Books $18.50

• Joan Hoff-Wilson, editor
RIGHTS OF PASSAGE: The Past and Future of the ERA
Foreword by Arthur S. Link
0–253–35013–1 Indiana $22.50
0–253–20368–6 Indiana pb $6.95

• Alison M. Jaggar
FEMINIST POLITICS AND HUMAN NATURE
Analysis of liberal feminism, traditional Marxism, radical feminism and socialist feminism
0–8476–7254–9 Rowman $29.95
0–8476–7181–X Rowman pb $14.95

• Ethel Klein
GENDER POLITICS
A study of why women have become politically active and how that affects public policy
0–674–34197–X Harvard pb $7.95

• Karen B. Morello
THE INVISIBLE BAR: The Woman Lawyer in America, 1638 to the Present
A social history with lively and amusing anecdotes about these pioneering women and the obstacles they confronted
0–394–52964–2 Random House $19.95

Crime

• Angela Browne
WHEN BATTERED WOMEN KILL
Drawing upon interviews with 250 battered women, 42 of whom killed their abusers, Browne examines the psychological and legal plight of battered women
0–92–903880–4 Free Press $19.95

• Clarice Feinman
WOMEN IN THE CRIMINAL JUSTICE SYSTEM
0–275–90045–2 Praeger $26.95
0–275–91462–3 Praeger pb $13.95

• Ann Jones
WOMEN WHO KILL
Histories and punishments of battered and abused women who kill in self-defense
0–449–90058–4 Fawcett pb $2.98

SCIENCE, SEXUALITY AND HEALTH

Science has traditionally viewed itself as "objective," and therefore exempt from questions of gender. Feminist inquiry in the 1980s challenged this assumption, and refuted the idea of a biological basis for women's "inferiority."

Science and Gender

- Ruth Bleier
SCIENCE AND GENDER
A critique of biology and its theories of women
0-08-030971-2 Pergamon $34.00
0-08-030972-0 Pergamon pb $15.95

- Ruth Bleier, editor
FEMINIST APPROACHES TO SCIENCE
0-08-032787-7 Pergamon $27.50

- Irene Elia
THE FEMALE ANIMAL
A biological anthropologist's study of the sexual lives and behavioral traits of females in a wide range of species
Introduction by Ashley Montagu
0-8050-0702-4 Henry Holt $21.95

- Anne Fausto-Sterling
MYTHS OF GENDER: Biological Theories about Women and Men
A readable study of social bias in sociobiological and sex difference research, by a Brown University biologist. "A temperate, judiciously argued book that makes its complicated subjects accessible in clear and uncomplicated prose"—Daniel J. Kevles, NY Times
0-465-04790-4 Basic Books $18.95
0-465-04791-2 Basic Books pb $9.95

- Sarah Blaffer Hrdy
THE WOMAN THAT NEVER EVOLVED
New hypotheses on the evolution of women. "Provides the layperson with a fascinating account of the selective pressures that have shaped the behavior of males and females"—Science
0-674-95540-4 Harvard pb $6.95

- Evelyn Fox Keller
REFLECTIONS ON GENDER AND SCIENCE
A widely-read work that ponders why objectivity has been cast as "male" and subjectivity as "female"
0-300-03291-9 Yale $25.00
0-300-03636-1 Yale pb $7.95

- Carol MacCormack & Marilyn Strathern, editors
NATURE, CULTURE AND GENDER
0-521-28001-X Cambridge pb $12.95

- Ashley Montagu
THE NATURAL SUPERIORITY OF WOMEN
An anthropologist and social biologist, Montagu argues that women are biologically superior to men with examples showing that women have overall higher IQ scores, are less susceptible to alcoholism and suicide, and are emotionally and constitutionally stronger
0-02-096080-8 Macmillan pb $5.95

- Margaret W. Rossiter
WOMEN SCIENTISTS IN AMERICA: Struggles and Strategies to 1940
"A record of hopes squelched, strategies thwarted, and uncomfortable compromises easily made"—Ruth Schwartz Cowan, Journal of American History
0-8018-2443-5 Johns Hopkins $40.00
0-8018-2509-1 Johns Hopkins pb $10.95

Sexuality

- Andrea Dworkin
INTERCOURSE
A controversial work on how sexual intercourse enslaves women
0-02-907970-5 Free Press $19.95

PORNOGRAPHY: Men Possessing Women
0-399-50532-6 Putnam pb $8.95

- Barbara Ehrenreich
THE HEARTS OF MEN
Why men flee intimacy
0-385-17615-5 Doubleday pb $7.95

- Barbara Ehrenreich & others
RE-MAKING LOVE: The Feminization of Sex
"It destroys the myth that only men had a sexual revolution and reclaims the power and pleasure inherent in sex for all of us"—Shere Hite
0-385-18499-9 Doubleday pb $8.95

- Lillian Faderman
SURPASSING THE LOVE OF MEN: Love Between Women from the Renaissance to the Present
Edited by Maria D. Guarnaschelli
0-688-00396-6 Morrow $18.95
0-688-03733-X Morrow pb $12.95

- Shere Hite
WOMEN AND LOVE: A Cultural Revolution in Progress
Hite's much-contested work is an analysis of the stages of falling in love, having a relationship, and getting married
0-394-53052-7 Knopf $24.95

- Sheila Jeffreys
THE SPINSTER AND HER ENEMIES: Feminism and Sexuality, 1880–1930
0-86358-050-5 RC&H pb $10.95

- Janice G. Raymond
A PASSION FOR FRIENDS: Toward a Philosophy of Female Affection
0-8070-6724-5 Beacon $22.95
0-8070-6739-3 Beacon pb $10.95

- Catherine Stimpson & Ethel S. Person, editors
WOMEN: Sex and Sexuality
0-226-77476-7 Chicago $20.00

- Carole Vance, editor
PLEASURE AND DANGER: Exploring Female Sexuality
A diverse collection of essays on the nature of sexuality from a Barnard scholar and the Feminist IX conference
0-7102-0248-2 RC&H pb $11.95

Rape, Incest, and Battered Women

▶ See also Crisis

- Susan Brownmiller
AGAINST OUR WILL: Men, Women, and Rape
"A history of rape in all its overt and subtle manifestations. It's a consciousness-raising session that should force both men and women to agonize over their assumptions"—NY Times
0-553-34516-8 Bantam pb $5.95

- Susan Estrich
REAL RAPE
An important book by the Harvard law professor
0-674-74944-X Harvard $15.95
0-674-74944-8 Harvard pb $7.95

- Judith Herman
FATHER-DAUGHTER INCEST
An academic study of women as victims within families
0-674-29506-4 Harvard pb $9.95

- Lenore E. Walker
THE BATTERED WOMAN
"In addition to carefully written but inevitably disturbing case studies, Professor Walker's book includes sections on preventative remedies, including safe-houses, and a careful discussion of psychotherapy"—NY Times
0-06-090742-8 Harper & Row pb $8.95

- Robin Warshaw
I NEVER CALLED IT RAPE
The Ms. magazine report on recognizing, fighting, and surviving date and acquaintance rape
0-06-096276-3 Harper & Row pb $7.95

Health

The Boston Women's Health Book Collective
THE NEW OUR BODIES, OURSELVES
The new version of the classic feminist health guide updates its coverage and adds chapters on such topics as psychotherapy and new reproductive technologies
0-671-46088-9 Simon & Schuster pb $15.95

Paula Brown Doress & others
OURSELVES, GROWING OLDER
An Our Bodies, Ourselves for the special needs of women over 35, delving into such topics as childbearing at midlife, menopause, hysterectomy, osteoporosis, cancer, and many other subjects
0-671-64424-6 Simon & Schuster pb $15.95

- Gena Corea
THE HIDDEN MALPRACTICE: How American Medicine Mistreats Women
Women's exclusion as patients and professionals
0-06-091215-4 Harper & Row pb $7.95

➤ FOR OVERSEAS ORDERING INFORMATION, SEE PAGE 1

• Barbara Ehrenreich & Deirdre English
FOR HER OWN GOOD: 150 Years of Experts' Advice to Women
The history of American women's dealings with the medical and psychological professions
0–385–12651–4 Doubleday pb $5.95

Reproduction and Birth Control

• Suzanne Arms
IMMACULATE DECEPTION: A New Look at Women and Childbirth
Birth intervention versus midwifery
Foreword by Frederick Leboyer
0–89789–060–4 Bergin & Garvey $29.95

• Gena Corea
THE MOTHER MACHINE: Reproductive Technologies from Artificial Insemination to Artificial Wombs
The politics of reproductive technologies
0–06–091325–8 Harper & Row pb $7.95

• Linda Gordon
WOMAN'S BODY, WOMAN'S RIGHT: Birth Control in America
In this historical analysis, Gordon argues that birth control has relied on political and social acceptability and not medicine. She stresses that women must continue to assert their right to safe and effective birth control
0–14–004683–6 Penguin pb $8.95

The Abortion Debate

• Marshall Cohen & others, editors
RIGHTS AND WRONGS OF ABORTION: A Philosophy and Public Affairs Reader
0–691–01979–7 Princeton pb $8.50

• Paige C. Cunningham & others, editors
ABORTION AND THE CONSTITUTION: Reversing Roe v. Wade Through the Courts
This collection of essays points to the legal errors of the Roe v. Wade decision and suggests a course of litigation for its reversal
0–87840–446–5 Georgetown $22.95
0–87840–447–3 Georgetown pb $12.95

• Marian Faux
ROE V. WADE: The Untold Story of the Landmark Decision that Made Abortion Legal
0–02–537151–7 Macmillan $22.50

• Faye Ginsburg
CONTESTED LIVES: The Abortion Debate in an American Community
"Ginsburg demonstrates a fine sympathy for all of the protagonists and a profound historical understanding of the structural forces and the cultural traditions at work in the abortion controversy"—Judith Walkowitz
0–520–06492–5 California $25.00

Margaret Sanger in 1920

• Robert D. Goldstein
MOTHER-LOVE AND ABORTION: A Legal Interpretation
A defense of Roe v. Wade
0–520–06084–9 California $19.95

• Beverly Harrison
OUR RIGHT TO CHOOSE: Toward a New Ethic of Abortion
0–8070–1509–1 Beacon pb $10.95

• Thomas Hilgers & others, editors
NEW PERSPECTIVES ON HUMAN ABORTION
Medical, legal, and social issues from a pro-life perspective
0–313–27080–5 Greenwood pb $17.95

• Kristin Luker
ABORTION AND THE POLITICS OF MOTHERHOOD
A balanced analysis of the abortion debate. "Like all good science, her book tries to enlighten rather than to persuade"—*Boston Globe*
0–520–04314–6 California $27.50
0–520–05597–7 California pb $10.95

• L.W. Sumner
ABORTION AND MORAL THEORY
0–691–02017–5 Princeton pb $9.95

Motherhood

• Barbara Berg
THE CRISIS OF THE WORKING MOTHER: Resolving the Conflict Between Family and Work
A readable study on guilt and work
0–671–49956–4 Simon & Schuster $16.95

• Phyllis Chesler
MOTHERS ON TRIAL: The Battle for Children and Custody
A controversial work re-examines the legal position of mothers in the 1980s
0–07–010701–7 McGraw-Hill $22.95
0–931188–46–6 Seal Press-Feminist pb $11.95

SACRED BOND: The Legacy of Baby M
0–8129–1745–6 Times Books $16.95
0–679–72226–2 Random House pb $7.95

• Ann Dally
INVENTING MOTHERHOOD: The Consequences of an Ideal
Suggests that the ideal of mom-in-the-house was largely a construction of post-World War II ideology
0–8052–3830–1 Schocken $19.95
0–8052–0765–1 Schocken pb $9.95

• Louis Genevie & Eva Margolies
THE MOTHERHOOD REPORT: How Women Feel about Being Mothers
A report based on interviews with more than 1,000 women on subjects from why mothers play favorites to how they feel about their spouses as fathers
0–02–542970–1 Macmillan $19.95

• Kathleen Gerson
HARD CHOICES: How Women Decide about Work, Career, and Motherhood
An academic study
0–520–05174–2 California $22.50
0–520–05745–7 California pb $9.95

• Julius Held & Anita Shreve
REMAKING MOTHERHOOD: How Working Mothers Are Shaping Our Children's Future
The positive effects of mothers working outside the home
0–670–80722–2 Viking $18.95
0–449–90300–1 Fawcett pb $7.95

• Sandra Pollack & Jeanne Vaughn, editors
POLITICS OF THE HEART: A Lesbian Parenting Anthology
0–932379–36–2 Firebrand $24.95
0–932379–35–4 Firebrand pb $11.95

• Adrienne Rich
OF WOMAN BORN: Motherhood As Experience and Institution
0–393–02379–6 Norton $17.95
0–393–30386–1 Norton pb $7.95

• Sirgay Sanger & Joan Kelly
THE WOMAN WHO WORKS, THE PARENT WHO CARES: A Revolutionary Program for Raising Your Child
0–316–77049–3 Little, Brown $17.95
0–06–97159–2 Harper & Row pb $7.95

• Isabel V. Sawhill & Heather L. Ross
TIME OF TRANSITION: The Growth of Families Headed by Women
0–87766–148–0 Urban Institute pb $8.50

• Ursula Sharma
WOMEN'S WORK, CLASS AND THE URBAN HOUSEHOLD
0–422–79330–2 RC&H pb $15.95

• Ruth Sidel
WOMEN AND CHILDREN LAST: The Plight of Poor Women in Affluent America
0–14–010013–X Penguin pb $6.95

• Barbara Levy Simpson
NEVER MARRIED WOMEN
Fifty never-married women born before 1919 talk about day-to-day life, adaptations, and stigmas
0–87722–497–8 Temple $24.95

PSYCHOLOGY

● Mary Field Belenky & others
WOMEN'S WAYS OF KNOWING: The Development of Self, Voice, and Mind
Interviews with 135 women of differing backgrounds, probing the question of why so many women are reluctant to speak out
0–465–09212–8 Basic Books $19.95
0–465–09213–6 Basic Books pb $10.95

● Jessica Benjamin
THE BONDS OF LOVE: Psychoanalysis, Feminism, and the Problem of Domination
Analysis of the acceptance and perpetuation of relationships of domination and submission, from a leading theorist and psychoanalyst
0–394–55133–8 Pantheon $22.95
0–394–75730–0 Pantheon pb $12.95

● Jean Shinoda Bolen
GODDESSES IN EVERY WOMAN: A New Psychology of Women
A psychoanalyst's popular theory of women's seven personality types—or archetypal "goddesses"
Foreword by Gloria Steinem
0–06–091291–X Perennial pb $8.95

● Paula J. Caplan
THE MYTH OF WOMEN'S MASOCHISM
Challenges Freud's theory that women are masochistic by showing that they often remain in bad situations because their choices are limited
0–525–24361–5 Dutton $16.95
0–451–14738–3 NAL pb $3.95

● Nancy Chodorow
THE REPRODUCTION OF MOTHERING: Psychoanalysis and the Sociology of Gender
Why women in almost all societies are responsible for parenting. "Provides careful psychoanalytic grounding for the radical position that both sexes can and should parent equally, and—an additional boon—its style is not too academic"—*Ms.*
0–520–03892–4 California pb $9.95

Photograph by Laura McPhee, from Mothers & Daughters *edited by Nan Richardson (*Aperture*)*

● Dorothy Dinnerstein
THE MERMAID AND THE MINOTAUR: Sexual Arrangements and Human Malaise
Examines why we continue to submit to traditional old sexual arrangements and argues that men must be involved in child care
0–06–090587–5 Harper & Row pb $8.95

● Jane Gallop
THE DAUGHTER'S SEDUCTION: Feminism and Psychoanalysis
The relationship between feminism and the work of the controversial French psychoanalyst Jacques Lacan
0–8014–1493–8 Cornell $24.95
0–8014–9235–1 Cornell pb $9.95

● Carol Gilligan
IN A DIFFERENT VOICE: Psychological Theory and Women's Development
Gilligan, a Harvard professor, argues that psychological development theories have been based on the experiences of men and suggests we reshape our understanding of human development to include women's voices
0–674–44543–0 Harvard $20.00
0–674–44544–9 Harvard pb $6.95

● Miriam Greenspan
A NEW APPROACH TO WOMEN AND THERAPY
"Offers a devastating insider's look into conventional therapies—from Freudian psychiatry to the human potential movement—and goes beyond them to outline a truly egalitarian and compassionate approach to therapy"—Barbara Ehrenreich
0–07–024349–2 McGraw-Hill $16.95

● Karen Horney
FEMININE PSYCHOLOGY
Edited by Harold Kelman
0–393–00686–7 Norton pb $4.95

● Doris Howard
A GUIDE TO THE DYNAMICS OF FEMINIST THERAPY
Essays on the practice of feminist psychotherapy
0–918393–37–X Harrington Park pb $14.95

● Eleanor E. Maccoby & Carol N. Jacklin
THE PSYCHOLOGY OF SEX DIFFERENCES
Volume 1
0–8047–0974–2 Stanford pb $11.95
Volume 2
0–8047–0975–0 Stanford pb $7.95

● Jean B. Miller
TOWARD A NEW PSYCHOLOGY OF WOMEN
A psychiatrist's view of women's day-to-day mental and emotional lives
0–8070–2910–6 Beacon $17.50
0–8070–2909–2 Beacon pb $7.95

● Juliet Mitchell
PSYCHOANALYSIS AND FEMINISM
"Mitchell's attack on Reich, Laing, and the neofeminists is inspired by unflinching loyalty to the original psychoanalytic concepts, difficult, uncompromising and

seemingly unflattering to women as these concepts are"—Christopher Lasch, *NY Review of Books*
0–394–71442–3 Random House pb $6.95

● Mary R. Walsh
THE PSYCHOLOGY OF WOMEN
0–300–03965–4 Yale $40.00
0–300–03966–2 Yale pb $12.95

● DeMaris S. Wehr
JUNG AND FEMINISM: Liberating Archetypes
Wehr suggests that Jung's theories and therapeutic ideas may be beneficial for women
0–8070–6734–2 Beacon $17.95

ANTHROPOLOGY AND CROSS-CULTURAL STUDIES

● Jessie Bernard
THE FEMALE WORLD FROM A GLOBAL PERSPECTIVE
0–253–32167–0 Indiana $35.00
0–253–20431–3 Indiana pb $10.95

● Robin Morgan, editor
SISTERHOOD IS GLOBAL
This International Women's Movement anthology features original articles by leading feminists from around the world, each preceded by statistics on the status of women in the author's country
0–385–17797–6 Doubleday $14.95

● Sherry Ortner & Harriet Whitehead, editors
SEXUAL MEANINGS: The Cultural Construction of Gender and Sexuality
0–521–28375–2 Cambridge pb $17.95

● Rayna R. Reiter, editor
TOWARD AN ANTHROPOLOGY OF WOMEN
A collection of papers on family and women's roles in different countries, including China, Nigeria, and Italy
0–85345–372–1 Monthly Review $16.50
0–85345–399–3 Monthly Review pb $8.00

● Michelle Z. Rosaldo & Louise Lamphere, editors
WOMAN, CULTURE, AND SOCIETY
Sixteen anthropologists examine women's roles in different societies as well as society's and anthropology's attitudes towards women
0–8047–0851–7 Stanford pb $9.95

● Alice Schlegel, editor
SEXUAL STRATIFICATION: A Cross-Cultural View
0–231–04214–0 Columbia $32.00

● Filomina Steady, editor
THE BLACK WOMAN CROSS-CULTURALLY
Essays on black women in Africa, South America, the Caribbean and America
0–87073–345–1 Schenkman $34.50

• Wellesley Editorial Committee
WOMEN AND NATIONAL DEVELOPMENT: The Complexities of Change
0–226–89315–4 Chicago pb $8.95

WORLD HISTORY

History is one of the most richly developed fields in women's studies. New historical works document the role of women and correct the distortions of traditional accounts.

• Marilyn J. Boxer & Jean H. Quataert, editors
CONNECTING SPHERES: Women in the Western World, 1500 to the Present
Overviews of major periods along with writings on specific aspects of women's lives
Foreword by Joan W. Scott
0–19–504123–2 Oxford $29.95
0–19–504133–X Oxford pb $10.95

• R.J. Evans
THE FEMINISTS: Women's Emancipation Movements in Europe, America and Australasia, 1840–1920
0–06–492044–5 Barnes & Noble pb $15.95

• Gerda Lerner
THE CREATION OF PATRIARCHY
"Dramatically reopens a chapter of women's history that historians had thought was forever closed to them—the origins of the collective dominance of women by men"—Katherine Kish Sklar, UCLA
0–19–505185–8 Oxford pb $8.95

THE MAJORITY FINDS ITS PAST: Placing Women in History
Twelve essays dealing with a range of feminist issues, focusing on women's role in history
0–19–502597–0 Oxford $21.95
0–19–502899–6 Oxford pb $8.95

• Rosalind Miles
THE WOMEN'S HISTORY OF THE WORLD
A sociologist traces the female from Neanderthal times to the present
0–88162–348–2 Salem House $18.95

AMERICAN HISTORY

Overviews

• Margaret Hope Bacon
MOTHERS OF FEMINISM: The Story of Quaker Women in America
A survey of the influence of Quaker women on American history and feminism
0–06–250046–5 Harper & Row pb $8.95

• William Henry Chafe
THE AMERICAN WOMAN: Her Changing Social, Economic and Political Roles, 1920–1970
A history of public perceptions of women's "place," and the impact of major events

such as war and the Depression on the nature of women's lives
0–19–501785–4 Oxford pb $9.95

WOMEN AND EQUALITY: Changing Patterns in American Culture
A provocative analysis of how sex roles have changed—and how serious the remaining obstacles are to full equality
0–19–502365–X Oxford pb $8.95

• Nancy F. Cott & Elizabeth H. Pleck
A HERITAGE OF HER OWN: Toward a New Social History of American Women
0–671–25069–8 Simon & Schuster pb $16.95

• Carl N. Degler
AT ODDS: Women and the Family in America from the Revolution to the Present
A major work on the history of women and the family
0–19–502934–8 Oxford pb $12.95

• Ann Douglas
THE FEMINIZATION OF AMERICAN CULTURE
Traces values in today's culture back to their Victorian roots
0–385–24241–7 Doubleday pb $10.95

• Sara M. Evans
BORN FOR LIBERTY: A History of Women in America
0–02–902990—2 Free Press $24.95

Sojourner Truth

• Peter G. Filene
HIM-HER-SELF: Sex Roles in Modern America
0–8018–2893–7 Johns Hopkins $32.50
0–8018–2895–3 Johns Hopkins pb $10.95

• Judith Friedlander & others
WOMEN IN CULTURE AND POLITICS: A Century of Change
0–253–31328–7 Indiana $39.50
0–253–20375–9 Indiana pb $12.95

• Paula Giddings
WHEN AND WHERE I ENTER: The Impact of Black Women on Race and Sex in America
Portraits of such historical figures as Mary McLeod Bethune and Fannie Lou Hamer and their struggles
0–688–01943–9 Morrow $17.95
0–553–34225–8 Bantam pb $8.95

• Jacqueline Jones
LABOR OF LOVE, LABOR OF SORROW: Black Women, Work and the Family, from Slavery to the Present
"Exorcises several malignant stereotypes and stubborn myths"— Toni Morrison, *NY Times*
0–465–03756–9 Basic Books $25.95

• Linda Kerber & Jane De Hart Mathews, editors
WOMEN'S AMERICA: Refocusing the Past
A collection of articles and documents tracing women's history from colonial times to the present, covering a wide range of subjects from obstetric practices in the 17th century to an analysis of contemporary feminism
0–19–504202–6 Oxford $32.50
0–19–504203–4 Oxford pb $16.95

• Judith W. Leavitt
BROUGHT TO BED: Childbearing in America, 1750-1950
Birthing, obstetrics, and medicine, and the influence of women on the history of childbearing
0–19–505690–9 Oxford pb $9.95

• Gerda Lerner, editor
BLACK WOMEN IN WHITE AMERICA: A Documentary History
0–394–71880–1 Random House pb $9.95

• Sheila M. Rothman
WOMAN'S PROPER PLACE: A History of Changing Ideals and Practices, 1870 to the Present
0–465–09204–7 Basic Books pb $11.95

Colonial America

• Linda Kerber
WOMEN OF THE REPUBLIC: Intellect and Ideology in Revolutionary America
0–393–30345–4 Norton pb $8.95

• Laurel Thatcher Ulrich
GOOD WIVES: Image and Reality in the Lives of Women in Northern New England, 1650 to 1750
The women of the period participated more vitally in the community and led more complex lives than has generally been supposed
0–394–51940–X Knopf $22.50
0–19–503360–4 Oxford pb $9.95

The 19th Century and the Industrial Revolution

• Barbara J. Berg
THE REMEMBERED GATE: Origins of American Feminism—The Woman and the City, 1800-1860
The roots of feminism in a key period: as industrialization grew in antebellum America, upper- and middle-class women were freed from manual labor, and the first all-women benevolent societies were established
0–19–502704–3 Oxford pb $7.95

• Nancy F. Cott
**THE BONDS OF WOMANHOOD:
"Woman's Sphere" in New England, 1780-
1835**
Emphasizes the virtues of women's
activities which are usually denigrated
0–300–02289–1 Yale pb $9.95

• Thomas Dublin
**WOMEN AT WORK: The Transformation
of Work and Community in Lowell,
Massachusetts, 1826-1860**
0–231–04166–7 Columbia $29.50
0–231–04167–5 Columbia pb $13.00

• Barbara L. Epstein
**THE POLITICS OF DOMESTICITY:
Women, Evangelism, and Temperance in
Nineteenth-Century America**
0–8195–6184–3 Wesleyan pb $12.95

• Elizabeth Fox-Genovese
**WITHIN THE PLANTATION
HOUSEHOLD: Black and White Women
in the Old South**
Argues that class and race did affect
women's experiences and that slaves and
slaveholders were never linked in
sisterhood
0–8078–4232–X North Carolina pb $12.95

• Angela John
**COALMINING WOMEN: Victorian Lives
and Campaigns**
0–521–27872–4 Cambridge pb $4.95

• Suzanne Lebsock
**THE FREE WOMEN OF PETERSBURG:
Status and Culture in a Southern Town,
1784-1860**
Using Petersburg, Virginia, as an example,
Lebsock attempts to show that women
were able to form an alternative value
system in a society committed to slavery,
male dominance, and materialism
0–393–01738–9 Norton $24.95
0–393–95264–9 Norton pb $7.95

• Kathy Peiss
**CHEAP AMUSEMENTS: Working
Women and Leisure in Turn-of-the-
Century New York**
A vivid survey of dance styles, silent
movies, amusement parks, and other
diversions for working women
0–87722–389–0 Temple $29.95

• Carroll Smith-Rosenberg
**DISORDERLY CONDUCT: Visions of
Gender in Victorian America**
Argues that the sexual and social spheres
are intertwined. How and why male-female
relations, families, sex, and social custom
changed as America embarked on
industrialization
0–394–53545–6 Knopf $19.95
0–19–504039–2 Oxford pb $9.95

• Christine Stansell
**CITY OF WOMEN: Sex and Class in New
York, 1789-1860**
A first-rate work of history focusing on
economic and personal aspects of working-
class women
0–394–51534–X Knopf $30.00
0–252–01481–2 Illinois pb $9.95

Voices from the Industrial Revolution

Rebecca Harding Davis
**LIFE IN THE IRON MILLS &
OTHER STORIES**
Reprinted after 124 years, "Life in the
Iron Mills" is a classic account of
difficult working conditions
Edited by Tillie Olsen
0–935312–39–0 Feminist Press pb $7.95

Benita Eisler, editor
**THE LOWELL OFFERING: Writings
by New England Mill Women, 1840-
1845**
0–06–131996–1 Harper & Row pb $5.95

Lucy Larcom
A NEW ENGLAND GIRLHOOD
An 1889 account of life in the Lowell
factories
0–87928–078–6 Corner House $18.95

Suffrage, Liberation and Beyond

• D'Ann Campbell
**WOMEN AT WAR WITH AMERICA:
Private Lives in a Patriotic Era**
0–674–95475–0 Harvard $21.00

• Ellen Cantarow & others
**MOVING THE MOUNTAIN: Women
Working for Social Change**
Oral histories of the lives of three political
activists: Florence Luscomb, a suffrage
campaigner; Ella Baker, a civil rights and
black liberation organizer; and Jessie
Lopez De La Cruz, a farmworker
organizer
0–912670–61–4 Feminist Press pb $9.95

1915 poster from Make Way! 200 Years of
American Women in Cartoons *by Monika
Franzen and Nancy Ethiel (Chicago Review
Press)*

Marcia Cohen
**THE SISTERHOOD: The True Story
of the Women Who Changed the World**
An intimate history of the women's
movement, focusing on Betty Friedan,
Gloria Steinem, Germaine Greer, and
Kate Millett
0–671–49553–4 Simon & Schuster $19.95

• Ellen C. DuBois
**FEMINISM AND SUFFRAGE: The
Emergence of an Independent Women's
Movement in America, 1848-1869**
0–8014–1043–6 Cornell $29.95
0–8014–9182–7 Cornell pb $7.95

• Sara Evans
**PERSONAL POLITICS: The Roots of
Women's Liberation in the Civil Rights
Movement and the New Left**
0–394–74228–1 Random House pb $6.95

• Eleanor Flexner
**CENTURY OF STRUGGLE: The Woman's
Rights Movement in the United States**
0–674–10652–0 Harvard pb $8.95

• Margaret Forster
**SIGNIFICANT SISTERS: The Grassroots
of Active Feminism, 1839-1939**
Portraits of eight women's rights activists:
Caroline Norton, Elizabeth Blackwell,
Florence Nightingale, Emily Davies,
Josephine Butler, Elizabeth Cady Stanton,
Margaret Sanger, and Emma Goldman
0–394–54153–7 Knopf $17.95
0–19–504014–7 Oxford pb $9.95

• Aileen S. Kraditor
**THE IDEAS OF THE WOMAN
SUFFRAGE MOVEMENT, 1880-1920**
0–393–01449–5 Norton $18.95
0–393–00039–7 Norton pb $8.95

• Winifred D. Wandersee
**ON THE MOVE: American Women in the
1970s**
An analysis of the major events in the
1970s that brought new prominence to
women's roles, including the ERA, NOW,
and an increased number of women in the
workplace
0–8057–9909–5 Twayne $19.95
0–8057–9910–9 Twayne pb $9.95

• Susan Ware
**BEYOND SUFFRAGE: Women in the New
Deal**
The impact and attitudes of women in
positions of national leadership in the
1930s
0–674–06921–8 Harvard $21.00
0–674–06922–6 Harvard pb $8.95

America's Working Women

• Rosalyn Baxandall
**AMERICA'S WORKING WOMEN: A
Documentary History, 1600 to the Present**
0–394–72208–6 Random House pb $12.95

IF YOU CAN'T FIND IT, LOOK IN THE INDEX

• **Ruth S. Cowan**
MORE WORK FOR MOTHER: The Ironies of Household Technology from the Open Hearth to the Microwave
An entertaining survey of 300 years of housework, including photographs
0–465–04731–9 Basic Books $17.95
0–465–04732–7 Basic Books pb $9.95

• **Margery W. Davies**
WOMAN'S PLACE IS AT THE TYPEWRITER: Office Work and Office Workers, 1870-1930
0–87722–291–6 Temple $29.95
0–87722–368–8 Temple pb $12.95

• **Philip S. Foner**
WOMEN AND THE AMERICAN LABOR MOVEMENT: From Colonial Times to the Eve of World War I
0–02–910370–3 Free Press $34.95

• **Penina Glazer & Miriam Slater**
UNEQUAL COLLEAGUES: The Entrance of Women into the Professions, 1890-1940
0–8135–1186–0 Rutgers $30.00
0–8135–1187–9 Rutgers pb $9.95

• **Sherna Berger Gluck**
ROSIE THE RIVETER REVISITED: Women, the War and Social Change
An oral history of the women who went to work to help with the war effort during World War II and the lives they led after the war was over
0–452–00911–1 NAL pb $8.95

• **David M. Katzman**
SEVEN DAYS A WEEK: Women and Domestic Service in Industrializing America
The lives of domestics examined through their writings and interviews
0–19–502368–4 Oxford $27.95
0–252–00882–0 Illinois pb $10.95

• **Susan E. Kennedy**
IF ALL WE DID WAS TO WEEP AT HOME: A History of White Working-Class Women in America
0–253–19154–8 Indiana $20.00
0–253–20267–1 Indiana pb $7.95

• **Alice Kessler-Harris**
OUT TO WORK: A History of Wage-Earning Women in the United States
0–19–503024–9 Oxford $27.95
0–19–503353–1 Oxford pb $10.95

• **Ruth Milkman, editor**
WOMEN, WORK AND PROTEST: A Century of U.S. Women's Labor History
0–7100–9940–1 RC&H pb $14.95

• **Judith Rollins**
BETWEEN WOMEN: Domestics and Their Employers
This history of domestic work brings up the issue of women using other women to enhance their status
0–87722–383–1 Temple $29.95
0–87722–491–9 Temple pb $14.95

• **Susan Strasser**
NEVER DONE: A History of American Housework
0–394–70841–5 Pantheon pb $12.95

• **Leslie Woodcock Tentler**
WAGE-EARNING WOMEN: Industrial Work and Family Life in the United States, 1900-1930
The author reconstructs day-to-day realities of working women—on the job, in the home, and in the industrial neighborhoods of major cities
0–19–503211–X Oxford pb $9.95

• **Winifred D. Wandersee**
WOMEN'S WORK AND FAMILY VALUES, 1920-1940
0–674–95535–8 Harvard $21.00

• **Barbara M. Wertheimer**
WE WERE THERE: The Story of Working Women in America
A narrative history from pre-colonial times to the present
0–394–73257–X Pantheon pb $10.50

Historical Biography

• **Allen F. Davis**
AMERICAN HEROINE: The Life and Legend of Jane Addams
0–19–501897–4 Oxford pb $9.95

• **Kathleen L. Barry**
SUSAN B. ANTHONY: A Biography of a Singular Feminist
The life of the charismatic feminist, 1820-1906
0–8147–1105–7 NYU $27.95

• **Jeanne Boydston & others**
THE LIMITS OF SISTERHOOD: The Beecher Sisters on Women's Rights and Women's Sphere
Catherine, a writer and educator, Harriet, an author of novels, and Isabella, a political activist, were all committed to women's rights, but with different opinions on how this should be achieved
0–8078–4207–9 North Carolina pb $12.95

• **Kathryn Kish Sklar**
CATHARINE BEECHER: A Study in American Domesticity
0–300–01580–1 Yale $37.00
0–393–00812–6 Norton pb $8.95

• **Bell G. Chevigny, editor**
THE WOMAN AND THE MYTH: Margaret Fuller's Life and Writings
Fuller (1810-1850), was a member of Emerson's circle, editor of *The Dial*, and a reporter for the *NY Tribune*
0–912670–43–6 Feminist Press pb $8.95

• **Joyce Antler**
LUCY SPRAGUE MITCHELL: The Making of a Modern Woman
0–300–03665–5 Yale $32.50

• **Joan Hoff-Wilson & Marjorie Lightman, editors**
WITHOUT PRECEDENT: The Life and Career of Eleanor Roosevelt
Foreword by Joseph P. Lash
0–253–19100–9 Indiana $17.50
0–253–20327–9 Indiana pb $8.95

• **Elisabeth Griffith**
IN HER OWN RIGHT: The Life of Elizabeth Cady Stanton
The definitive biography of a pioneer feminist
0–19–503440–6 Oxford $21.95
0–19–503729–4 Oxford pb $9.95

• **Ruth Bordin**
FRANCES WILLARD: A Biography
0–8078–1697–3 North Carolina $25.00

EUROPEAN HISTORY

• **Bonnie S. Anderson & Judith Zinsser**
A HISTORY OF THEIR OWN: Women in Europe, From Prehistory to the Present
Both volumes are organized according to women's societal roles. The first volume covers the history of women to the Renaissance, the second from the 17th century to the present
Volume 1
0–06–015850–6 Harper & Row $27.50
0–06–091452–1 Harper & Row pb $12.95
Volume 2
0–06–015899–9 Harper & Row $27.50

• **Susan G. Bell, editor**
WOMEN: From the Greeks to the French Revolution
0–8047–1094–5 Stanford $32.00
0–8047–1082–1 Stanford pb $10.95

• **Renate Bridenthal & others, editors**
BECOMING VISIBLE: Women in European History
0–395–41950–6 Houghton Mifflin pb $22.00

• **Julia O'Faolain & Lauro Martines, editors**
NOT IN GOD'S IMAGE: A History of Women in Europe from the Greeks to the Nineteenth Century
Includes first-hand accounts by women
0–06–131677–6 Harper & Row pb $9.95

• **Louise Tilly & Joan Scott**
WOMEN, WORK AND FAMILY
0–416–01681–2 Methuen pb $11.95

Medieval History

• **Frances & Joseph Gies**
WOMEN IN THE MIDDLE AGES
An overview plus an in-depth study of the lives of seven women from different classes, countries and centuries
0–06–464037–X Harper & Row pb $4.95

• **Margaret W. Labarge**
A SMALL SOUND OF THE TRUMPET: Women in Medieval Life
From queens to prostitutes, the daily lives and character sketches of various women
0–8070–5626–X Beacon $21.95
0–8070–5627–8 Beacon pb $12.95

• **Christine de Pizan**
THE BOOK OF THE CITY OF LADIES
Translated by Earl J. Richards
0–89255–066–X Persea pb $13.95

Modern European History

- Bram Dijkstra
IDOLS OF PERVERSITY: Fantasies of Feminine Evil in Fin-de-Siècle Culture
An exploration of pervasive turn-of-the-century misogyny in the work of hundreds of artists and writers
0–19–505652–3 Oxford $14.95

- Antonia Fraser
THE WEAKER VESSEL
"An almost encyclopedic chronicle of women in 17th-century England . . . wives, warriors, heiresses, preachers . . . alive with anecdote after anecdote"—*NY Times*
0–394–73251–0 Random House pb $9.95

- Erna Olafson Hellerstein & others, editors
VICTORIAN WOMEN: A Documentary Account of Women's Lives in Nineteenth-Century England, France, and the United States
Diaries, letters, poems, wills, autobiographies, and other documents from women of all classes
0–8047–1096–1 Stanford pb $16.95

- Bridget Hill
EIGHTEENTH CENTURY WOMEN: An Anthology
0–04–909013–5 Unwin Hyman $34.95
0–04–909014–3 Unwin Hyman pb $12.95

- Claudia Koonz
MOTHERS IN THE FATHERLAND: Women, Family Life and Nazi Ideology, 1919-1945
How the Nazis mobilized women in their support
0–312–54933–4 St. Martin's $25.00

- Midge Mackenzie
SHOULDER TO SHOULDER
A documentary history of the militant suffragists in turn-of-the-century England, including photographs, memoirs, speeches, and newspaper articles on individual women and their struggle to win the vote
0–679–72131–2 Random House pb $15.95

- James F. McMillan
HOUSEWIFE OR HARLOT: The Place of Women in French Society, 1870-1940
0–312–39348–2 St. Martin's pb $11.95

- Eleanor S. Riener & John C. Font, editors
EUROPEAN WOMEN: A Documentary History, 1789-1945
Writings by Russian, French, Swedish, Italian, and other European women on health, abortion, work, and marriage
0–8052–3737–2 Schocken $17.50
0–8052–0644–2 Schocken pb $8.95

- Samia I. Spencer, editor
FRENCH WOMEN AND THE AGE OF ENLIGHTENMENT
Preface by Germaine Bree
Introduction by Elizabeth Fox-Genovese
0–253–32481–5 Indiana $35.00

- Martha Vicinus, editor
SUFFER AND BE STILL: Women in the Victorian Age
0–253–35572–9 Indiana $18.50
0–253–20168–3 Indiana pb $9.95

Man, are you capable of being just? It is a woman who poses the question; you will not deprive her of that right at least. Tell me, what gives you sovereign empire to oppress my sex? Your strength? Your talents? Observe the Creator in his wisdom; survey in all her grandeur that nature with whom you seem to want to be in harmony, and give me, if you dare, an example of this tyrannical empire. Go back to animals, consult the elements, study plants, finally glance at all the modifications of organic matter, and surrender to the evidence when I offer you the means; search, probe, and distinguish, if you can, the sexes in the administration of nature. Everywhere you will find them mingled; everywhere they cooperate in harmonious togetherness in this immortal masterpiece.

from Marie-Olympe de Gouges, *The Rights of Woman*

John W. Boyer & Julius Kirshner, general editors
READINGS IN WESTERN CIVILIZATION, Volume 7: The Old Regime and the French Revolution
0–226–06950–8 Chicago pb $11.95

ARTS AND LETTERS

- Elaine Hedges & Ingrid Wendt, editors
IN HER OWN IMAGE: Women Working in the Arts
A collection of fiction, poetry, autobiography, essays, journals, and photography
0–912670–62–2 Feminist Press pb $9.95

Art and Photography

- Norma Broude & Mary D. Garrard, editors
FEMINISM AND ART HISTORY: Questioning the Litany
Chronologically arranged essays on Egyptian to contemporary art show how art has been distorted by sexual bias
0–06–430117–6 Harper & Row pb $18.95

- Ann Sutherland Harris & Linda Nochlin
WOMEN ARTISTS, 1550-1950
0–394–73326–6 Knopf pb $19.95

- Thomas B. Hess & Elizabeth C. Baker
ART AND SEXUAL POLITICS
A collection of essays by artists and art historians on subjects such as "Why Have There Been No Great Women Artists" and "Artists Transgress All Boundaries"
0–02–003940–9 Macmillan pb $6.95

"Self-Portrait as the Allegory of Painting" (1630), *from* Artemisia Gentileschi *by Mary D. Garrard (Princeton)*

- Lucy R. Lippard
FROM THE CENTER: Feminist Essays on Women's Art
Essays on artists and the current status of women's art
0–525–47427–7 Dutton pb $13.95

- Jeanne Moutoussamy-Ashe
VIEWFINDERS: Black Women Photographers, 1839-1985
0–396–08609–8 Dodd, Mead $19.95
0–396–08611–X Dodd, Mead pb $12.95

- Eleanor Munro
ORIGINALS: American Women Artists
In addition to analyses of the women and their work, Munro offers a look into the mind of the artist: what it takes to be an artist and how it feels. Includes black-and-white and color reprints of artists' works
0–671–42812–8 Simon & Schuster pb $15.95

- Rozsica Parker & Griselda Pollack
OLD MISTRESSES: Women, Art, and Ideology
0–394–52430–6 Pantheon $19.50
0–394–70814–8 Pantheon pb $11.50

- Karen Petersen & J.J. Wilson
WOMEN ARTISTS: Recognition and Reappraisal From the Early Middle Ages to the Twentieth Century
An illustrated history of women's art
0–06–090387–2 Harper & Row pb $11.50

- Charlotte S. Rubenstein
AMERICAN WOMEN ARTISTS
The individual stories of hundreds of women artists since the birth of America
0–380–61101–5 Avon pb $15.95

Architecture

- Doris Cole
FROM TIPI TO SKYSCRAPER: A History of Women in Architecture
0–262–53033–3 MIT pb $6.95

TO ORDER BOOKS AS GIFTS, SEE PAGE 1

• Dolores Hayden
THE GRAND DOMESTIC REVOLUTION: A History of Feminist Designs for American Homes, Neighborhoods, and Cities
0–262–08108–3 MIT $30.00
0–262–58055–1 MIT pb $11.95

Film

• Teresa De Lauretis
ALICE DOESN'T: Feminism, Semiotics, Cinema
0–253–30467–9 Indiana $22.50
0–253–20316–3 Indiana pb $10.95

• Molly Haskell
FROM REVERENCE TO RAPE: The Treatment of Women in the Movies
An excellent study of how film has reflected and reshaped images of women
0–226–31884–2 Chicago $39.95
0–226–31885–0 Chicago pb $14.95

• E. Ann Kaplan
WOMEN IN FILM NOIR
Argues that film noir is the exception to women's subordination in film, since in this genre strong female characters emerged, often challenging patriarchy
0–85170–105–1 Illinois pb $9.95

• Constance Penley, editor
FEMINISM AND FILM THEORY
This collection of essays reconsiders basic ideas about genre, narrative, image, and the audience
0–415–90108–1 RC&H pb $13.95

Music

• Jane Bowers & Judith Tick, editors
WOMEN MAKING MUSIC: The Western Art Tradition, 1150-1950
Biographies of performers and composers with musical examples, from medieval chants to 20th-century compositions
0–252–01470–7 Illinois pb $14.95

• Carol Neuls-Bates, editor
WOMEN IN MUSIC: An Anthology of Source Readings from the Middle Ages to the Present
0–06–014992–2 Harper & Row $18.50

Theater

• Kathleen Betsko & Rachel Koenig, editors
INTERVIEWS WITH CONTEMPORARY WOMEN PLAYWRIGHTS
0–688–07033–7 Morrow pb $12.95

• Karen Malpede
WOMEN IN THEATRE: Compassion and Hope
Diary excerpts from Martha Graham and Katherine Dunham, critical pieces by Lorraine Hansberry and Rosamand Gilder, and reminiscences by actress Ellen Terry and others
0–89676–054–5 Drama pb $10.00

• Victoria Sullivan & James Hatch, editors
PLAYS BY AND ABOUT WOMEN
0–394–71896–8 Random House pb $6.95

• Margaret B. Wilkerson, editor
NINE PLAYS BY BLACK WOMEN
0–451–62506–4 NAL pb $4.95

ANTHOLOGIES OF WOMEN'S WRITING

• Carol Ascher & others, editors
BETWEEN WOMEN: Biographers, Novelists, Critics, Teachers and Artists Write About Their Work on Women
Twenty-five writers, including Alice Walker and Michelle Cliff, write about women who inspired them and their work
0–8070–6713–X Beacon pb $12.95

• Helen Barolini, editor
THE DREAM BOOK: An Anthology of Writings by Italian-American Women
Fiction, poetry, drama, essays, and memoirs
0–8052–0832–1 Schocken pb $10.95

• Margo Culley, editor
A DAY AT A TIME: The Diary Literature of American Women from 1764 to the Present
An anthology collected from 29 diaries, covering such experiences as the daily life of an 18th-century New England family to the politics of the 1970s; with an extensive bibliography
0–935312–50–1 Feminist Press $29.95
0–935312–51–X Feminist Press pb $12.95

• Bernard A. Drew, editor
HARD-BOILED DAMES: Stories Featuring Women Detectives, Reporters, Adventurers and Criminals from the Pulp Fiction Magazines of the 1930s
Preface by Marcia Muller
0–312–36188–2 St. Martin's $16.95

• Moira Ferguson, editor
FIRST FEMINISTS: British Women Writers, 1578-1799
0–253–32213–8 Indiana $25.00
0–253–28120–2 Indiana pb $12.95

• Judith Fetterley, editor
PROVISIONS: A Reader from Nineteenth-Century American Women
0–253–17040–0 Indiana $35.00
0–253–20349–X Indiana pb $12.95

From The Delights of Reading *by Otto Bettmann (Godine)*

• Nancy Hoffman & Florence Howe, editors
WOMEN WORKING: An Anthology of Stories and Poems
Thirty-four selections by such writers as Willa Cather, Zora Neale Hurston, Tillie Olsen, Alice Walker, and Sarah Orne Jewett
Illustrated by Ann Toulmin-Roth
0–912670–57–6 Feminist Press pb $9.95

• Susan Koppelman, editor
BETWEEN MOTHERS AND DAUGHTERS: Stories Across a Generation
Eighteen stories dating from the 1840s to the 1980s
0–935312–26–9 Feminist Press pb $9.95
THE OTHER WOMAN: Stories of Two Women and A Man
Eighteen more stories
0–935312–25–0 Feminist Press pb $9.95

• Alberto Manguel, editor
OTHER FIRES: Short Fiction by Latin American Women
Stories by Brazilian, Argentinian, Colombian, Mexican, Cuban and Uruguayan writers
0–517–55870–X Crown pb $9.95

• Cherrie Moraga & Gloria Anzaldua, editors
THIS BRIDGE CALLED MY BACK: Writings by Radical Women of Color
Poetry, prose and narrative by African-American, Asian-American, Latin American and Native American women
Illustrated by Johnetta Tinker
Foreword by Toni Cade Bambara
0–913175–15–3 Kitchen Table $18.95
0–913175–03–X Kitchen Table pb $9.95

• Charlotte Nekola & Paula Rabinowitz, editors
WRITING RED: An Anthology of American Women Writers, 1930-1940
Poetry and prose by revolutionary women who were both class-conscious and feminist, covering fiction, poetry, reportage, and critical theory
0–935312–77–3 Feminist Press $29.95
0–935312–76–5 Feminist Press pb $12.95

• Nancy Newhouse, editor
HERS: Through Women's Eyes
Essays from the weekly "Hers" column of the *New York Times*
0–06–097028–6 Harper & Row pb $7.95

• Ursula Owen, editor
FATHERS: Reflections by Daughters
Women writers' personal accounts of
relationships with their fathers; includes
entries from Doris Lessing, Alice Walker,
and Adrienne Rich
0–394–72572–7 Pantheon pb $7.95

• Ethel J. Phelps
**THE MAID OF THE NORTH: Feminist
Folk Tales from Around the World**
"Here the fables are turned: women rescue
men, outwit demons and fight like
Cossacks"—*Time*
Illustrated by Lloyd Bloom
0–0306–2374–X Henry Holt pb $6.95

• Vicki Piekarski, editor
**WESTWARD THE WOMEN: An
Anthology of Western Stories by Women**
0–8263–1063–X New Mexico pb $10.95

• Pamela Sargent, editor
**MORE WOMEN OF WONDER: Science
Fiction Novelettes by Women about Women**
0–394–71041–X Random House pb $4.95

• Jean Reith Schroedel
**ALONE IN A CROWD: Women in the
Trades Tell Their Stories**
Twenty-five women with nontraditional
blue-collar jobs talk about their experiences
0–87722–378–5 Temple $29.95
0–87722–397–1 Temple pb $14.95

• Barbara Smith, editor
**HOME GIRLS: A Black Feminist
Anthology**
Writings by Audre Lorde, Alice Walker,
Gloria T. Hull, and others
0–913175–14–5 Kitchen Table $20.95
0–913175–02–1 Kitchen Table pb $11.95

• Mary Helen Washington, editor
**BLACK-EYED SUSANS: Classic Stories by
and about Black Women**
Includes, "If You're Light and Have Long
Hair" by Gwendolyn Brooks and "A
Sudden Trip Home in the Spring" by
Alice Walker
0–385–09043–9 Doubleday pb $4.95

Poetry Anthologies

• Fleur Adcock, editor
**THE FABER BOOK OF TWENTIETH
CENTURY WOMEN'S POETRY**
Includes Stevie Smith, Edna St. Vincent
Millay, Gwendolyn Brooks, and Denise
Levertov
0–571–13693–1 Faber pb $8.95

• Aliki & Willis Barnstone
**A BOOK OF WOMEN POETS: From
Antiquity to Now**
Among the 300 poets included are Anne
Bradstreet, Anne Sexton, and Margaret
Atwood
0–8052–0680–9 Schocken pb $15.95

Biographies, Autobiographies, and Letters

• Simone de Beauvoir
MEMOIRS OF A DUTIFUL DAUGHTER
An autobiographical view of the
intellectual and emotional growth of the
author of *The Second Sex*
0–06–090351–1 Harper & Row pb $8.95

• Shari Benstock
WOMEN OF THE LEFT BANK
The lives and work of American, English
and French women in Paris, 1900-1940,
including Gertrude Stein, Edith Wharton
and Jean Rhys
0–292–79040–6 Texas pb $12.95

• Dorothy Day
**THE LONG LONELINESS: An
Autobiography**
The radical Catholic leader noted for her
social programs
Introduction by Daniel Berrigan
0–06–061751–9 Harper & Row pb $9.95

• Janet Flanner
DARLINGHISSIMA: Letters to a Friend
Janet Flanner wrote about France for the
New Yorker for 50 years under the pen
name Genêt. This collection includes her
correspondence with her close friend
Natalia D. Murray, written in a style far
different from that of her magazine writing
Edited by Natalia D. Murray
0–15–623937–X HBJ pb $10.95

• Vivian Gornick
FIERCE ATTACHMENTS: A Memoir
"Gornick takes readers deep into that
primitive no-man's-land where mothers
and daughters struggle, separate, reconcile,
try to talk, and sometimes devour one
another alive"—*Boston Globe*
0–374–15485–6 Farrar, Straus & Giroux $15.95
0–671–66234–1 Simon & Schuster pb $6.95

• Kathy Kahn
HILLBILLY WOMEN
A collection of interviews with
Appalachian women
0–380–00171–3 Avon pb $2.75

• Evelyn Fox Keller
**A FEELING FOR THE ORGANISM: The
Life and Work of Barbara McClintock**
A portrait of one of this century's
pioneering geneticists
0–7167–1504–X Freeman pb $10.95

• Rita Levi-Montalcini
IN PRAISE OF IMPERFECTION
An autobiography by the winner of the
1986 Nobel Prize in medicine
0–465–03217–6 Basic Books $18.95

• Linda Lovelace
OUT OF BONDAGE
0–425–10650–0 Berkley pb $3.95

• Beryl Markham
WEST WITH THE NIGHT
The aviator who became the first person to
fly alone east to west across the Atlantic.
"With the skill of someone who has filled
long nights with stories, Markham
recounts her adventures—discoveries,
rescues, and narrow escapes, the glint of an
airplane abandoned in the desert, the look
of a lion about to pounce"—*Nation*
0–86547–304–8 North Point $19.95
0–86547–118–5 North Point pb $12.50

• Susan Quinn
**A MIND OF HER OWN: The Life of
Karen Horney**
Psychoanalyst who took issue with Freud's
views on women
0–201–15573–7 Addison-Wesley $14.95

• Ruth Rosen & Sue Davidson, editors
THE MAIMIE PAPERS
Correspondence between prostitute and
socialite
0–253–23600–2 Indiana pb $10.95

• Huda Shaarawi
**HAREM YEARS: The Memoirs of an
Egyptian Feminist, 1879-1924**
A first-hand account of the private world
of a Cairo harem at the turn of the century
by the founder of the Egyptian Feminist
Union who publicly removed her veil in a
Cairo railroad station in 1923
Translated and edited by Margot Badran
0–935312–71–4 Feminist Press $33.00
0–935312–70–6 Feminist Press pb $9.95

LANGUAGE

• Deborah Cameron
FEMINISM AND LINGUISTIC THEORY
0–312–00984–4 St. Martin's pb $14.95

• Jennifer Coates
WOMEN, MEN AND LANGUAGE
0–582–29133–X Longman pb $12.95

• Alette Olin Hill
**MOTHER TONGUE, FATHER TIME: A
Decade of Linguistic Revolt**
0–253–33879–4 Indiana $29.50
0–253–20389–9 Indiana pb $9.95

• Robin Lakoff
LANGUAGE AND WOMAN'S PLACE
0–06–090389–9 Harper & Row pb $6.95

- Sally McConnell-Ginet & others, editors
WOMEN AND LANGUAGE IN LITERATURE AND SOCIETY
0–275–90520–9 Praeger $38.95
0–275–91498–4 Praeger pb $17.95

- Casey Miller & Kate Swift
THE HANDBOOK OF NONSEXIST WRITING: For Writers, Editors and Speakers
The standard guide for avoiding gender bias in writing
0–06–181602–7 Harper & Row $15.95
0–06–096238–0 Harper & Row pb $6.95

- Dale Spender
MAN MADE LANGUAGE
Suggests that the subordination of women is reinforced through language
0–7102–0605–4 RC&H $27.95
0–7102–0315–2 RC&H pb $13.95

- Valerie Walkerdine & others
LANGUAGE, GENDER AND CHILDHOOD
The use of language in socialization and education from the 19th century to the present
0–7100–9977–0 RC&H pb $18.95

I myself have never been able to find out precisely what feminism is: I only know that people call me a feminist whenever I express sentiments that differentiate me from a doormat.

Rebecca West, 1913, in *The Clarion*

Cheris Kramarae & Paula A. Treichler
A FEMINIST DICTIONARY
0–86358–060–2 Unwin Hyman $33.00
0–86358–015–7 Unwin Hyman pb $12.95

- Judith Freeman Clark
ALMANAC OF AMERICAN WOMEN IN THE TWENTIETH CENTURY
An illustrated compendium
0–13–022641–6 Prentice-Hall pb $15.95

- Edward T. & Janet W. James, editors
NOTABLE AMERICAN WOMEN, 1607-1950: A Biographical Dictionary
A 3-volume set
0–674–62734–2 Harvard pb (set) $40.00

- Barbara Sicherman & Carold Hurd Green, editors
NOTABLE AMERICAN WOMEN: The Modern Period
0–674–62732–6 Harvard $47.00
0–674–62733–4 Harvard pb $12.95

- Cheris Kramarae & Paula A. Treichler
A FEMINIST DICTIONARY
From "Alice in Wonderland" to "Zeitgeist," a reference book that focuses on women
0–86358–060–2 Unwin Hyman $33.00
0–86358–015–7 Unwin Hyman pb $12.95

- Elaine Partnow, editor
THE QUOTABLE WOMEN

Volume 1: Eve to 1799
0–87196–307–8 Facts On File $29.95
0–8160–1385–3 Facts On File pb $14.95

Volume 2: 1800-1981
0–87196–580–1 Facts On File $29.95

- Jennifer S. Uglow, editor
THE INTERNATIONAL DICTIONARY OF WOMEN'S BIOGRAPHY
Quick reference on the lives of 1,500 women
0–8264–0192–9 Continuum $34.50
0–8264–0358–1 Continuum pb $17.95

- Ethlie Ann Vare & Greg Ptacek
MOTHERS OF INVENTION: From the Bra to the Bomb, Forgotten Women and Their Unforgettable Ideas
Two journalists remind the world that women invented such things as drip coffee, solar heating, nuclear fission, the ice cream cone, and the Barbie doll
0–688–06464–7 Morrow $17.95

- Barbara Walker
THE WOMEN'S ENCYCLOPEDIA OF MYTHS AND SECRETS
Stories behind legends, customs, and superstitions; information on magic, witchcraft, fairies, goddesses, and gods; and ancient and contemporary attitudes towards sex, rape, death, and sin
0–06–250925–X Harper & Row pb $22.95

Gay Studies

Twenty years ago the field of "gay studies" did not exist. Books on the subject of homosexuality were mostly sociological or academic, starting from the premise that homosexuality was an illness or a depravity, and justifying that premise with scientific arguments or psychological observations.

The modern gay rights movement began in 1969, when a police raid on the Stonewall Inn in New York's Greenwich Village caused irate patrons to resist and riot. The ensuing gay movement has ignited an explosion in publishing, with major publishers regularly adding gay titles to their lists, while small gay-oriented presses thrive. Far from viewing homosexuality as an illness or an ignoble condition, the current literature is more

often a celebration of gay life, or at least an objective, unbiased examination of it.

Until recently, many gay men and lesbians shared no sense of a common history, for their past was hidden in shame and secrecy. Even if historians had wanted to tackle the subject, few publishers would have accepted a work focusing on gay history. Today, however, books on all aspects of that history—traditions in classical Greece, the persecution of homosexuals by the Nazis, the recent liberation movement—are readily available.

- John Boswell
CHRISTIANITY, SOCIAL TOLERANCE, AND HOMOSEXUALITY: Gay People in Western Europe from the Beginning of the Christian Era to the Fourteenth Century
An acclaimed study of the church's attitude toward homosexuality from the first century onward
0–226–06711–4 Chicago pb $12.95

- Judith C. Brown
IMMODEST ACTS: The Life of a Lesbian Nun in Renaissance Italy
The story of an abbess who had an affair with a nun, reconstructed from the archives of a church investigation
0–19–504225–5 Oxford pb $7.95

- B.R. Burg
SODOMY AND THE PIRATE TRADITION: English Sea Rovers in the Seventeenth-Century Caribbean
The sexual mores and practices of English buccaneers in the 17th century
0–8147–1073–5 NYU pb $12.50

- Thomas Cowan
GAY MEN AND WOMEN WHO ENRICHED THE WORLD
Concise portraits of famous gay figures, including Herman Melville, Virginia Woolf, John Maynard Keynes, Charles Laughton, and James Baldwin
0–934791–16–3 William Mulvey $17.95

- Louis Crompton
BYRON AND GREEK LOVE: Homophobia in Nineteenth-Century England
Historical account of Regency attitudes towards homosexuality
0–520–05172–6 California $35.00
0–520–05732–5 California pb $12.95

- John D'Emilio
SEXUAL POLITICS, SEXUAL COMMUNITIES: The Making of a Homosexual Minority in the United States, 1940-1970
The rise of gay consciousness, from a historical perspective. "An intelligent, trustworthy, and welcome addition to our understanding of minority history"—Peter G. Filene, *Journal of American History*
0–226–14266–3 Chicago pb $9.95

• Kent Gerard & Gert Hekma, editors
THE PURSUIT OF SODOMY: Male Homosexuality in Renaissance and Enlightenment Europe
A collection of writings by noted historians from around the world
0–918393–49–3 Harrington Park pb $22.95

• Heinz Heger
THE MEN WITH THE PINK TRIANGLE
A first-hand account of gay men in Nazi concentration camps
Translated by David Fernbach
0–932870–06–6 Alyson pb $5.95

• Salvatore Licata & Robert Peterson, editors
THE GAY PAST: A Collection of Historical Essays
Prominent academics' descriptions of attitudes towards homosexuality in earlier times
0–918393–11–6 Harrington Park pb $11.95

• Richard Plant
THE PINK TRIANGLE: The Nazi War Against Homosexuals
History of discrimination against gays in World War II Europe
0–8050–0059–3 Henry Holt $19.95
0–8050–0600–1 Henry Holt pb $9.95

• A.L. Rowse
HOMOSEXUALS IN HISTORY: A Study of Ambivalence in Society, Literature and the Arts
Famous gay men of the past
0–88184–060–2 Carroll & Graf pb $9.95

• Michael Ruse
HOMOSEXUALITY: A Philosophical Inquiry
The history of homosexuality and the evolution of society's attitude toward it
0–631–15275–X Blackwell $19.95

• Bernard Sergent
HOMOSEXUALITY IN GREEK MYTH
A survey that offers an overview of homosexuality in ancient Greece
Translated by Arthur Goldhammer
0–8070–5700–2 Beacon $24.95

• Andrea Weiss & Greta Schiller
BEFORE STONEWALL: The Making of a Gay and Lesbian Community
An illustrated guide to the Emmy-winning documentary
0–941483–20–7 Naiad pb $7.95

GAY LIFE AND SEXUALITY

The titles listed here include books about coming out, anthologies of writings by various minority groups within the gay community, political analyses of the relationships between the gay and straight worlds, and sociological commentaries on gay coupling—as well as some books on sexuality without the politics.

• Marcy Adelman, editor
LONG TIME PASSING: Lives of Older Lesbians
Interviews
0–932870–74–0 Alyson pb $7.95

• Ronald Bayer
HOMOSEXUALITY AND AMERICAN PSYCHIATRY: The Politics of Diagnosis
A classic account of the fight to have homosexuality removed from the American Psychiatric Association's catalog of mental disorders
0–691–02837–0 Princeton pb $9.95

• Evelyn T. Beck, editor
NICE JEWISH GIRLS: A Lesbian Anthology
True stories about being lesbian and Jewish
0–89594–138–4 Crossing $23.95
0–89594–137–6 Crossing pb $10.95

• Betty Berzon
PERMANENT PARTNERS: Building Gay and Lesbian Relationships That Last
A manual for gay and lesbian couples, written by a lesbian psychotherapist specializing in the counseling of same-sex couples
0–525–24698–3 Dutton $18.95

• Warren J. Blumenfeld & Diane Raymond
LOOKING AT GAY AND LESBIAN LIFE
A well-documented and up-to-date look at issues central to the gay and lesbian experience, written by two leading activist scholars
0–8022–2551–9 Philosophical Library $25.00

Cover art for Immodest Acts: The Life of a Lesbian Nun in Renaissance Italy *by Judith Brown (Oxford)*

• Anne Bolin
IN SEARCH OF EVE: Transsexual Rites of Passage
The stages in the transition from one sex to another
0–89789–082–5 Bergin & Garvey $44.95
0–89789–115–5 Bergin & Garvey pb $12.95

• Howard Brown
FAMILIAR FACES, HIDDEN LIVES: The Story of Homosexual Men in America Today
Accounts of contemporary gay men, written by a former New York City official
0–15–630120–2 HBJ pb $5.95

• John D. Cecco, editor
GAY RELATIONSHIPS
A series of essays addressing gay coupling from a variety of perspectives
0–86656–637–6 Haworth $27.95
0–918393–33–7 Harrington Park pb $14.95

• Margaret L. Cruikshank, editor
THE LESBIAN PATH
Collection of accounts of lesbian experiences
0–912516–96–8 Grey Fox pb $8.95

• Trudy Darty & Sandra Potter
WOMEN-IDENTIFIED WOMEN
Essays by and about women
0–87484–573–4 Mayfield $13.95

• Frances FitzGerald
CITIES ON A HILL
A study of four American communities, including San Francisco's Castro Street district
0–671–55209–0 Simon & Schuster $19.95
0–671–64561–7 Simon & Schuster pb $9.95

• Richard Green
THE SISSY BOY SYNDROME AND THE DEVELOPMENT OF HOMOSEXUALITY
A study of the early life development of male homosexual behavior
0–300–03696–5 Yale $40.00
0–300–04239–6 Yale pb $15.95

• David F. Greenberg
THE CONSTRUCTION OF HOMOSEXUALITY
An exhaustive cross-cultural and historical account of homosexuality in its societal organization
0–226–30627–5 Chicago $29.95

• Ann Heron, editor
ONE TEENAGER IN TEN: Testimony by Gay and Lesbian Youth
Introduction by Rita Mae Brown
0–446–32653–4 Warner pb $3.95

• Gary Kinsman
THE REGULATION OF DESIRE: Sexuality in Canada
A sociologist studies the relationships among government regulation, social mores, and gay life in Canada
0–920057–79–9 Toronto $36.95

• Seymour Kleinberg
ALIENATED AFFECTIONS: Being Gay in America
Kleinberg investigates his own life in order to understand what it means to be gay in America, and discusses the "gay

➤ **FOR OVERSEAS ORDERING INFORMATION, SEE PAGE 1**

sensibility," passing as straight, the new masculinity of gay men, and aging
0–312–02158–5 St. Martin's pb $8.95

● JoAnn Loulan
LESBIAN PASSION
A ground-breaking work on lesbian life, incorporating research from a study of 1600 women
0–933216–29–7 Spinsters/Aunt Lute pb $10.95

● William H. Masters & Virginia E. Johnson
HOMOSEXUALITY IN PERSPECTIVE
The celebrated sex researchers on homosexuality
0–316–54984–3 Little, Brown $27.00

● David P. McWhirter & Andrew M. Mattison
THE MALE COUPLE: How Relationships Develop
Sociological study of gay relationships
0–13–547563–5 Prentice-Hall pb $7.95

● Cherrie Moraga & Gloria Anzaldua, editors
THIS BRIDGE CALLED MY BACK: Writings by Radical Women of Color
Poetry, stories and essays by black, Latina, Native American, and Asian-American women
Foreword by Toni Cade Bambara
0–913175–15–3 Kitchen Table $18.95
0–913175–03–X Kitchen Table pb $9.95

● Len Richmond & Gary Noguera, editors
THE NEW GAY LIBERATION BOOK
Reflections on gay liberation in a series of essays
0–87867–070–X Ramparts $14.00
0–87867–071–8 Ramparts pb $5.95

● Eric Rofes
GAY LIFE: Leisure, Love and Living for the Contemporary Gay Male
An anthology of 40 essays
0–385–19386–6 Doubleday pb $12.95

● Charles Silverstein
MAN TO MAN: Gay Couples in America
0–688–00803–8 Morrow pb $8.95

● Emily L. Sisley & Bertha Harris
THE JOY OF LESBIAN SEX
Sexual techniques for lesbians; illustrated
0–671–63133–0 Simon & Schuster pb $14.95

● Donald Vining
HOW CAN YOU COME OUT OF IT IF YOU'VE NEVER BEEN IN!: Essays on Gay Life and Relationships
Reflections and advice on coping with coming out
0–89594–188–0 Crossing $20.95
0–89594–187–2 Crossing pb $6.95

● Edmund White
STATES OF DESIRE: Travels in Gay America
A study of contemporary gay American life, written by the prominent novelist
0–525–48068–4 Dutton pb $9.95

AIDS AND HEALTH

▶ See also Health & The AIDS Crisis

AIDS is the biggest crisis faced by the gay community since the beginning of the gay liberation movement. The many AIDS-related books include histories of the disease, health or safer sex manuals, and spiritual or meditative essays on coping with the tragedy.

● Martin Delaney & Peter Goldblum
STRATEGIES FOR SURVIVAL: A Gay Men's Health Manual for the Age of AIDS
A comprehensive guide covering gay health
0–312–00558–X St. Martin's pb $10.95

● Larry Kramer
REPORTS FROM THE HOLOCAUST: The Making of An AIDS Activist
A collection of essays on AIDS from 1978 to the present, written by a leading gay activist and playwright, author of *The Normal Heart*
0–312–02634–X St. Martin's $18.95

● The Names Project
THE QUILT: Stories from The Names Project
An illustrated look at San Francisco's Names Project and its quilt, in which nearly 2000 panels celebrate the lives of people who have died from AIDS
0–671–66597–9 Pocket $22.95

● Barbara Peabody
THE SCREAMING ROOM: A Mother's Journal of Her Son's Struggle with AIDS
A moving account by the mother of a young man with AIDS
0–86679–030–6 Oak Tree $15.95
0–380–70345–9 Avon pb $3.95

● Michael Shernoff & William A. Scott, editors
THE SOURCEBOOK ON LESBIAN/GAY HEALTH CARE
An exhaustive look at the many health issues that affect the gay and lesbian community: physical and mental health, substance abuse, AIDS, and more
0–9621128–0–1 Lesbian & Gay Health $20.00

Randy Shilts
AND THE BAND PLAYED ON: Politics, People, and the AIDS Epidemic
A controversial best-seller that chronicles the history of the disease and the government's failure to react quickly to control it
0–312–00994–1 St. Martin's $24.95
0–14–011369–X Penguin pb $12.95

● Edmund White & Adam Mars-Jones
THE DARKER PROOF: Stories From a Crisis
Seven short stories about AIDS, written by two outstanding gay writers
0–452–26070–1 NAL pb $7.95

FAMILIES AND FRIENDS

Fearing rejection, many gay men and lesbians find it difficult to tell their families and friends of their sexual orientation. A growing number of books have been written to help these loved ones understand and accept the situation. At the same time, gay men and women are addressing the issue of being parents themselves.

● Bev & Martin Arthur
MAMA'S BOY
A mother and her gay son discuss their relationship
0–89407–054–1 Strawberry Hill pb $9.95

● Frederick W. Bozett, editor
GAY AND LESBIAN PARENTS
Psychological, sociological, and legal aspects of gay parenting
0–275–92541–2 Praeger $38.95
0–275–92370–3 Praeger pb $14.95

● Don Clark
THE NEW LOVING SOMEONE GAY
Updated version of a sympathetic guide for families and friends of gay men and women
0–89087–505–7 Celestial Arts pb $7.95

● Andre Corley
THE LAST CLOSET: A Gay Parent's Guide for Coming Out to Your Children
Advice for gays with children
0–682–40343–1 Exposition $12.50

● Betty Fairchild & Nancy Hayward
NOW THAT YOU KNOW: What Every Parent Should Know About Homosexuality
Advice for the parents of gays, written by two mothers with gay children
0–15–667702–4 HBJ pb $6.95

● Ivan Hill, editor
THE BISEXUAL SPOUSE
Interviews with bisexuals and their spouses
0–937525–01–4 Barlina Books $16.95

● Laura Z. Hobson
CONSENTING ADULT
A pioneering novel
0–446–32780–8 Warner pb $3.50

● Ann Muller
PARENTS MATTER: Parents' Relationships with Lesbian Daughters and Gay Sons
Sons and daughters describe their relationships with their families
0–930044–91–6 Naiad pb $9.95

● Sandra Pollack & Jeanne Vaughn, editors
POLITICS OF THE HEART: A Lesbian Parenting Anthology
First-person accounts by lesbians with children
0–932379–36–2 Firebrand $24.95
0–932379–35–4 Firebrand pb $11.95

- Charles Silverstein
A FAMILY MATTER: A Parent's Guide to Homosexuality
Practical advice for parents
0–07–057452–9 McGraw-Hill pb $6.95

- Marian & Arthur Wirth & Carolyn Griffin
BEYOND ACCEPTANCE: Parents of Lesbians and Gays Talk About Their Experiences
First-hand accounts by parents with gay children
Foreword by Adele Starr
0–13–075938–4 Prentice-Hall $16.95

BIOGRAPHY

- Michael Baker
OUR THREE SELVES: The Life of Radclyffe Hall
A biography of the author of the classic lesbian novel *The Well of Loneliness*
0–688–06673–9 William Morrow pb $8.95

- Gerald Clarke
CAPOTE: A Biography
A frank biography of the late writer, with accounts of his many affairs
0–671–22811–0 Simon & Schuster $22.95

- Quentin Crisp
THE NAKED CIVIL SERVANT
The autobiography of the English civil servant who chose to flaunt his homosexuality in conventional 1930s London
0–452–25413–2 NAL pb $6.95

HOW TO BECOME A VIRGIN
More reflections from Quentin Crisp
0–312–39544–2 St. Martin's pb $6.95

- Albert J. Devlin
CONVERSATIONS WITH TENNESSEE WILLIAMS
Interviews with the playwright
0–87805–262–3 Mississippi $25.95
0–87805–263–1 Mississippi pb $14.95

- Jack Dunphy
DEAR GENIUS: A Memoir of My Life with Truman Capote
An account spanning 35 years, written by Capote's lover
0–07–018317–1 McGraw-Hill $17.95

- Richard Ellman
OSCAR WILDE
Definitive biography of the great Irish writer, who was persecuted and imprisoned because of his homosexuality
0–394–55484–1 Knopf $24.95

- Aaron Fricke
REFLECTIONS OF A ROCK LOBSTER: A Story About Growing Up Gay
The story of the teenager whose right to take a same-sex date to his high school prom was upheld in a court case
0–932870–09–0 Alyson pb $5.95

- Boze Hadleigh
CONVERSATIONS WITH MY ELDERS
Six famous gays (Sal Mineo, Luchino Visconti, Cecil Beaton, Rainer Werner Fassbinder, George Cukor, and Rock Hudson) talk frankly about their lives
Introduction by Quentin Crisp
0–312–00115–0 St. Martin's $14.95
0–312–01404–X St. Martin's pb $7.95

- Barbara Haskell
CHARLES DEMUTH
The life and work of the pioneering modernist, with more than 100 color illustrations
0–8109–1135–3 Abrams $40.00

- Andrew Hodges
ALAN TURING: The Enigma
An excellent biography of the brilliant British mathematician instrumental in cracking German codes during World War II
0–671–49207–1 Simon & Schuster $24.95
0–671–52809–2 Simon & Schuster pb $10.95

- Rock Hudson & Sara Davidson
ROCK HUDSON: His Own Story
0–688–06472–8 Morrow $16.95
0–380–70292–4 Avon pb $4.50

- Christopher Isherwood
CHRISTOPHER AND HIS KIND
The writer's life from 1929 to 1939
0–374–12330–6 Farrar, Straus & Giroux $18.95
0–374–52036–4 Farrar, Straus & Giroux pb $8.95

- Justin Kaplan
WALT WHITMAN: A Life
A definitive biography that offers a frank discussion of the poet's homosexuality
0–671–62257–9 Simon & Schuster pb $12.95

From Gay Comics edited by Robert Triptow (Plume)

- David Kopay & Perry Deane Young
THE DAVID KOPAY STORY
The autobiography of the football running back, the first professional athlete publicly to reveal his homosexuality. "A dazzling and wonderful book"—Merle Miller
Foreword by Dick Schaap
1–55611–080–4 Donald Fine pb $8.95

- Robert LaGuardia
MONTY: A Biography of Montgomery Clift
A comprehensive, in-depth look at the late film star, including accounts of his homosexual relationships
1–55611–110–X Donald Fine pb $8.95

- John Lahr
PRICK UP YOUR EARS: The Biography of Joe Orton
0–394–75305–4 Random House pb $4.95

- Martina Navratilova with George Vecsey
MARTINA
Autobiography of the tennis star
0–449–20982–2 Fawcett pb $3.95

- Joe Orton
THE ORTON DIARIES
Excerpts from the playwright's personal diary
Edited by John Lahr
0–06–015743–7 Harper & Row $19.95
0–06–091498–X Harper & Row pb $8.95

- Dotson Rader
TENNESSEE: Cry of the Heart
A personal memoir of Tennessee Williams
0–452–25801–4 NAL pb $8.95

- Vita Sackville-West
THE LETTERS OF VITA SACKVILLE-WEST TO VIRGINIA WOOLF
Correspondence between these two prominent women, who were lovers in England in the 1920s
Edited by Louise DeSalvo & Mitchell A. Leaska
0–688–06271–7 William Morrow pb $8.95

- May Sarton
AT SEVENTY: A Journal
Memoirs of the poet and novelist
0–393–30434–5 Norton pb $7.95

- Randy Shilts
THE MAYOR OF CASTRO STREET: The Life and Times of Harvey Milk
A biography of Harvey Milk, San Francisco's first openly gay elected official who was assassinated in 1978
0–312–01900–9 St. Martin's pb $10.95

- Donald Spoto
THE KINDNESS OF STRANGERS: The Life of Tennessee Williams
The playwright as seen by a celebrated biographer
0–316–80781–8 Little, Brown $19.95
0–345–32618–0 Ballantine pb $4.95

• John Addington Symonds

THE MEMOIRS OF JOHN ADDINGTON SYMONDS: The Secret Homosexual Life of a Leading Nineteenth-Century Man of Letters
Autobiography of the writer and critic, in which he details his closeted life in Victorian England
Edited with an introduction by Phyllis Grosskurth
0–226–78783–4 Chicago pb $11.95

• W.J. Weatherby

JAMES BALDWIN: Artist on Fire
A portrait of the late writer and civil rights activist
1–55611–126–6 Donald Fine $19.95

ARTS AND LITERATURE

• Emmanuel Cooper

THE SEXUAL PERSPECTIVE: Homosexuality and Art in the Last 100 Years in the West
A critical and sociological study of prominent gays in the arts
0–7102–0902–9 Unwin Hyman pb $18.95

• Colin Wilson

THE MISFITS: A Study of Sexual Outsiders
An examination of prominent literary figures for whom unorthodox sexuality was an expression of creativity
0–88184–420–9 Carroll & Graf $19.95

Theater and Film

Although those working in theater and film have always been aware of the contributions of gay men and lesbians, these contributions were usually invisible to members of the audience. Gay writers are now illuminating the prominence of gays in the history of these arts. At the same time, openly gay characters are becoming increasingly common in plays and films.

• Kaier Curtin

WE CAN ALWAYS CALL THEM BULGARIANS: The Emergence of Lesbians and Gay Men on the American Stage
A fascinating historical study
0–932870–36–8 Alyson $18.95

• Rainer Werner Fassbinder

QUERELLE: The Film Book
Background on Fassbinder's filming of Genet's novel
0–394–62477–7 Grove pb $16.95

• Terry Helbing, editor

GAY THEATRE ALLIANCE DIRECTORY OF GAY PLAYS
0–935672–00–1 JH pb $5.95

• Vito Russo

THE CELLULOID CLOSET: Homosexuality in the Movies
A groundbreaking, provocative study
0–06–096132–5 Harper & Row pb $8.95

Marchers protesting Anita Bryant's campaign against the Dade County, Florida, gay rights ordinance, 1977, from Intimate Matters *by Estelle B. Freedman and John D'Emilio (Harper & Row/photo by Cathy Cade)*

• Michelene Wandor

CARRY ON, UNDERSTUDIES: Theatre and Sexual Politics
Gay politics in the theater
0–7102–0937–1 RC&H pb $10.95

Plays

• Jane Chambers

LAST SUMMER AT BLUEFISH COVE
The best-known play by the late lesbian playwright
0–935672–05–2 JH pb $6.95

• Jill Davis, editor

LESBIAN PLAYS
A collection of noteworthy plays by or about lesbians
0–413–15310–X Methuen $13.95

• Rainer Werner Fassbinder

PLAYS
Stage work by the great German film director and writer
Translated by Denis Calandra
0–933826–81–8 Performing Arts $21.95
0–933826–82–6 Performing Arts pb $8.95

Harvey Fierstein
SAFE SEX
Three one-act plays about living with AIDS
0–689–11953–4 Atheneum $15.95

TORCH SONG TRILOGY
The Tony-award winning play
0–451–15130–5 NAL pb $3.95

• William H. Hoffman, editor

GAY PLAYS: The First Collection
Eight plays on gay and lesbian life, written by Joe Orton, Lanford Wilson, Jane Chambers, and others
0–380–42788–5 Bard pb $4.95

• William M. Hoffman

AS IS
Highly acclaimed play dealing with AIDS
0–394–74286–9 Random House pb $3.95

• Larry Kramer

THE NORMAL HEART
A polemical but powerful play, a semi-autobiographical account of the early years of the AIDS epidemic
0–452–25798–0 NAL pb $6.95

• Robert Patrick

UNTOLD DECADES
Seven plays on gay themes by a leading off-Broadway playwright
Introduction by Harvey Fierstein
0–312–02307–3 St. Martin's $16.95

• Don Shewey, editor

OUT FRONT: Contemporary Gay and Lesbian Plays
Contains work by Harvey Fierstein, Terrence McNally, Robert Chesley, Doric Wilson, William M. Hoffman, and others
0–8021–1041–X Grove $24.95
0–8021–3025–9 Grove pb $14.95

• Michael Wilcox, editor

GAY PLAYS
Collections of plays with gay themes and characters

Volume 1
0–413–52330–6 RC&H pb $6.95

Volume 2
0–413–59510–2 RC&H pb $8.95

Volume 3
0–413–14740–1 RC&H pb $11.95

• Doric Wilson

A PERFECT RELATIONSHIP
A comedy with gay characters and themes
0–933322–12–7 Sea Horse pb $5.95

Literature and Poetry

• Stephen Coote, editor

THE PENGUIN BOOK OF HOMOSEXUAL VERSE
0–14–058551–6 Penguin pb $6.95

• Adam Mars-Jones, editor
MAE WEST IS DEAD: Recent Lesbian and Gay Fiction
A collection of short stories
0–571–14898–0 Faber & Faber pb $8.95

• Carl Morse & Joan Larkin, editors
GAY AND LESBIAN POETRY IN OUR TIME
Some 200 poems by 94 writers. Contributions by W.H. Auden, James Baldwin, Judy Grahn, Susan Griffin, James Merrill, Adrienne Rich, and others
0–312–02213–1 St. Martin's $29.95

• Gregory Woods
ARTICULATE FLESH: Male Homoeroticism and Modern Poetry
A critical study of gay influences on modern poetry
0–300–03872–0 Yale $28.50

EDMUND WHITE:
Some Favorite Works of Gay Literature

Colette
THE PURE AND THE IMPURE
Out of print

Robert Ferro
THE FAMILY OF MAX DESIR
0–452–26015–9 NAL pb $7.95

Ronald Firbank
CONCERNING THE ECCENTRICITIES OF CARDINAL PIRELLI
In *Five Novels*
0–8112–0799–4 New Directions pb $8.95

Andrew Holleran
DANCER FROM THE DANCE
0–452–25883–9 NAL pb $6.95

Alan Hollinghurst
THE SWIMMING POOL LIBRARY
0–394–57025–1 Random House $16.95

Christopher Isherwood
A SINGLE MAN
0–374–52038–0 FS&G pb $6.95

Thomas Mann
DEATH IN VENICE
0–679–72206–8 Random House pb $7.95

Marcel Proust
CITIES OF THE PLAIN
Included in *Remembrance of Things Past*
Translated by C.K. Scott-Moncrieff & Terence Kilmartin
0–394–70597–1 Random House pb $4.95

Denton Welch
A VOICE THROUGH A CLOUD
Out of print

Virginia Woolf
ORLANDO: A Biography
0–15–670160–X HBJ pb $7.95

• Ian Young, editor
THE MALE MUSE: A Gay Poetry Anthology
Includes work by Robert Duncan, Allen Ginsberg, Paul Goodman, and others
0–912278–34–X Crossing pb $7.95

RELIGION AND SPIRITUALITY

Most established religions express disapproval or condemnation of homosexuality. In recent years, however, gay clergymen, laymen, and historians of religion have been challenging such teachings. By reexamining and refuting the assumptions underlying this prejudice, they have sought to establish a foundation for acceptance of gay men and women within various religious traditions, and to affirm the validity of their spiritual aspirations.

• Malcolm Boyd
GAY PRIEST: An Inner Journey
An Episcopalian minister comes out and challenges some teachings of the church
Introduction by Rev. Paul Moore, Jr.
0–312–01031–1 St. Martin's pb $7.95

• Rosemary Curb & Nancy Manahan, editors
LESBIAN NUNS: Breaking Silence
Much-discussed study of a hidden aspect of Catholic life
0–930044–62–2 Naiad pb $9.95
0–446–32659–3 Warner pb $3.95

• Tom Horner
JONATHAN LOVED DAVID: Homosexuality in Biblical Times
A discussion of homosexuality in the Bible
0–664–24185–9 Westminster pb $8.95

• Sonia Johnson
GOING OUT OF OUR MINDS: The Metaphysics of Liberation
Philosophy from a former Mormon housewife
0–89594–239–9 Crossing $26.95
0–89594–240–2 Crossing pb $10.95

• John J. McNeill
THE CHURCH AND THE HOMOSEXUAL
A sensitive discussion of the relationship between the Catholic church and gay men and women by a Jesuit priest and vocal church critic
0–8070–7901–4 Beacon pb $9.95

• Robin Scroggs
THE NEW TESTAMENT AND HOMOSEXUALITY
Examines the cultural context of anti-gay attitudes in the New Testament
0–8006–1854–8 Fortress pb $8.95

• Mark Thompson
GAY SPIRIT: Myth and Meaning
A collection of essays exploring the unique possibilities for gay people in human culture
0–312–00600–4 St. Martin's $18.95

• Larry Uhrig
SEX POSITIVE: A Gay Contribution to Sexual and Spiritual Union
A gay pastor argues that Biblical teachings support gay fulfillment and tolerance
0–932870–82–1 Alyson pb $6.95

ANTHROPOLOGY

Along with gay liberation has come a realization that different societies vary widely in their attitudes toward homosexuality.

• Evelyn Blackwood, editor
THE MANY FACES OF HOMOSEXUALITY: Anthropological Approaches to Homosexual Behavior
Homosexuality in different historical periods and cultures
Preface by John De Cecco
Foreword by Joseph Carrier
0–918393–20–5 Harrington Park pb $11.95

• Gilbert H. Herdt
GUARDIANS OF THE FLUTES: Idioms of Masculinity
Study of a New Guinea tribe where young boys are encouraged to practice homosexuality at an early age
0–07–028315–X McGraw-Hill $31.95
0–231–06631–7 Columbia pb $14.00

• Frederick L. Whitman & Robin M. Mathy
MALE HOMOSEXUALITY IN FOUR SOCIETIES: Brazil, Guatemala, the Philippines, and the United States
Results of a 10-year research study
0–275–90037–1 Praeger $39.95

• Walter L. Williams
THE SPIRIT AND THE FLESH: Sexual Diversity in American Indian Culture
Includes an in-depth look at the berdeche, American Indian males who conform to female roles and behavior
0–8070–4602–7 Beacon $21.95

HUMOR

• Alison Bechdel
DYKES TO WATCH OUT FOR
Cartoons from a noted lesbian humorist
0–932379–18–4 Firebrand $14.95
0–932379–17–6 Firebrand pb $6.95

• Howard Cruse
DANCIN' NEKKID WITH THE ANGELS
Comic strips from the creator of Wendel
0–312–01104–0 St. Martin's pb $9.95

• Gerard Donelan
DRAWING ON THE GAY EXPERIENCE
Cartoons from *The Advocate*
0–917076–07–9 Liberation pb $5.95

• Kevin Michaels
THE GAY BOOK OF ETIQUETTE
Satirical insider's look at gay males
0–939020–76–9 MLP pb $11.95

IF YOU CAN'T FIND IT, LOOK IN THE INDEX

- Gail Sausser
LESBIAN ETIQUETTE: Humorous Essays
A collection of essays satirizing
contemporary lesbian life
0-89594-197-X Crossing $19.95
0-89594-196-1 Crossing pb $6.95

- Robert Triptow, editor
GAY COMICS
0-452-26229-1 Plume pb $7.95

ANTHOLOGIES AND REFERENCE

- Denis Clifford & Hayden Curry
**A LEGAL GUIDE FOR LESBIAN AND
GAY COUPLES**
Practical book covering all legal aspects of
couples living together
0-87337-077-X Nolo Press pb $17.95

- Michael Denneny, editor
THE CHRISTOPHER STREET READER
Selections from the gay magazine
0-399-50812-0 Putnam pb $10.95

- Wayne R. Dynes
HOMOSEXUALITY: A Research Guide
Exhaustive reference book with 5000
listings on gay history, health, legal issues,
and other topics
0-8240-8692-9 Garland $49.00

- Fag Rag
**FAG RAG TWELFTH ANNIVERSARY
ISSUE**
Commemorative work containing
highlights from the radical gay newspaper
0-914852-13-2 Fag Rag pb $9.95

- Judy Grahn
**ANOTHER MOTHER TONGUE: Gay
Words, Gay Worlds**
The derivations of gay and lesbian words,
by an outstanding contemporary poet
0-8070-6717-2 Beacon pb $10.95

- Martin Greif
THE GAY BOOK OF DAYS
A coffee-table book with pictures of
history's famous gays
0-8184-0332-2 Lyle Stuart $17.95
0-8184-0384-5 Lyle Stuart pb $12.95

- Marny Hall
**THE LAVENDER COUCH: A Consumer's
Guide to Psychotherapy for Lesbians and
Gay Men**
0-932870-41-4 Alyson pb $7.95

- Margaret R. Rodway & Brian L.
Wingrove
THE HEALTHY HOMOSEXUAL
A psychological and sociological study
0-87212-180-1 Libra pb $9.95

- Leigh W. Rutledge
THE GAY BOOK OF LISTS
Gay trivia and minutiae
1-55583-120-6 Alyson pb $6.95

Travel

Specifically written for the gay traveler, these
guidebooks provide information about
guesthouses, bars, restaurants, and other establishments around the country and the
world.

- Joseph H. Bain
ODYSSEUS '88
Information on accommodations in the
United States and, to a lesser degree,
around the world
0-9614266-4-0 Odysseus $14.95

- Bob Damron
BOB DAMRON'S ADDRESSBOOK, 1989
0-929435-01-X Damron pb $12.00

ROAD ATLAS, Volume 1
Highlights gay meccas of over 70 cities
with "real" maps done by the in-house
cartographer
0-929435-02-8 Damron pb $10.00

WOMEN'S TRAVELLER
0-929435-03-6 Damron pb $8.00

People with Disabilities

▶ See also Health

- Edward D. Berkowitz
**DISABLED POLICY: America's Programs
for the Handicapped**
0-521-34014-4 Cambridge $24.95

- Susan E. Browne & Nanci Stern,
editors
**WITH THE POWER OF EACH
BREATH: A Disabled Women's Anthology**
0-939416-06-9 Cleis pb $9.95

- Jock A. Carlisle
**TANGLED TONGUE: Living with a
Stutter**
0-201-11243-4 Addison-Wesley pb $9.95

- Walter P. Christian & others, editors
**PROGRAMMING EFFECTIVE HUMAN
SERVICES: Strategies for Institutional
Change and Client Transition**
0-306-41526-7 Plenum $49.50

- Norman Cousins
**ANATOMY OF AN ILLNESS: As
Perceived by the Patient**
0-393-01252-2 Norton $14.95
0-553-34365-3 Bantam pb $6.95

- Michelle Fine & Adrienne Asch,
editors
**WOMEN WITH DISABILITIES: Essays in
Psychology, Culture and Politics**
A collection of essays examining the
difficulties disabled women confront in
work, sex, and reproduction
0-87722-474-9 Temple $34.95

- Foundation for Children with
Learning Disabilities
**THE FCLD RESOURCE GUIDE: A State-
by-State Directory of Programs and Services**
0-8147-2579-1 NYU $40.00

- Alan Gartner & Tom Joe
**IMAGES OF THE DISABLED—
DISABLING IMAGES**
0-275-92178-6 Praeger $35.95

- Lori A. Goldfarb & others
**MEETING THE CHALLENGE OF
DISABILITY OR CHRONIC ILLNESS: A
Family Guide**
Describes a decision-making process that
develops the skills and resources necessary
to confront the daily challenges of life for
families with a member who is disabled
0-933716-55-9 Brookes pb $16.00

- Matthew P. Janicki & Henryk M.
Wisniewski, editors
**AGING AND DEVELOPMENTAL
DISABILITIES: Developmental Issues and
Approaches**
For the professional
0-933716-46-X Brookes $36.95

- Lauri Klobas
**DISABILITY DRAMA IN TELEVISION
AND FILM**
Over 400 chronological entries with
critiques of television programs and films
noting stereotypical or positive depictions
of disabilities
0-89950-309-8 McFarland $39.95

- Harlan Lane
**WHEN THE MIND HEARS: A History of
the Deaf**
0-394-50878-5 Random House pb $27.95

THE WILD BOY OF AVEYRON
0-674-95282-0 Harvard $24.50
0-674-95300-2 Harvard pb $10.95

- Chalda Maloff & Susan M. Wood
**BUSINESS AND SOCIAL ETIQUETTE
WITH DISABLED PEOPLE: A Guide to
Getting Along with Persons Who Have
Impairments of Mobility, Vision, Hearing
or Speech**
Foreword by Mel Tillis
0-398-05463-0 Charles Thomas $30.25

• Christopher Nolan
UNDER THE EYE OF THE CLOCK: The Life Story of Christopher Nolan
0–312–01266–7 St. Martin's $16.95
0–440–55028–9 Dell pb $7.95

• Carol Padden
DEAF IN AMERICA: Voices from a Culture
0–674–19423–3 Harvard $17.95

• Thomas H. Powell & Peggy A. Ogle
BROTHERS AND SISTERS: A Special Part of Exceptional Families
Provides successful strategies for helping siblings of the disabled cope with and benefit from their unique role in the exceptional family
0–933716–45–1 Brookes pb $18.00

• William Roth
THE HANDICAPPED SPEAK
0–89950–022–6 McFarland $18.95

• Oliver Sacks
SEEING VOICES: A Journey into the World of the Deaf
0–520–06083–0 California $15.95

• Marsha Saxton & Florence Howe, editors
WITH WINGS: An Anthology of Literature By and About Women with Disabilities
Personal accounts, fiction, and poetry about the physical and emotional effects of disability
0–935312–61–7 Feminist Press $29.95
0–935312–62–5 Feminist Press pb $12.95

• Jean Ann Summers
THE RIGHT TO GROW UP: An Introduction to Adults with Developmental Disabilities
For family members and professionals; describes government programs and policy issues relative to adults with disabilities as well as a good overview of the adult life cycle
0–933716–47–8 Brookes pb $21.95

• H. Rutherford Turnbull & others
DISABILITY AND THE FAMILY: A Guide to Decisions for Adulthood
1–557–66004–2 Brookes pb $29.00

Blindness and Visual Impairment

• John H. Dobree & Eric Boulter
BLINDNESS AND VISUAL HANDICAP: The Facts
0–19–261328–6 Oxford $13.95

• Helen Keller
THE STORY OF MY LIFE
0–385–04453–4 Doubleday $15.95
0–451–52245–1 NAL pb $2.95

• Berthold Lowenfeld
BERTHOLD LOWENFELD ON BLINDNESS AND BLIND PEOPLE
0–89128–101–0 Am Fdn for the Blind pb $9.00

• Ved Mehta
THE STOLEN LIGHT
0–393–02632–9 Norton $19.95

• Dean W. Tuttle
SELF-ESTEEM AND ADJUSTING WITH BLINDNESS: The Process of Responding to Life's Demands
0–398–04887–8 Charles Thomas $36.25

From Gallaudet University

"Deaf people can do anything—except hear."—I. King Jordan, President, Gallaudet University

Evelyn Cherow
HEARING IMPAIRED CHILDREN AND YOUTH WITH DEVELOPMENTAL DISABILITIES: An Interdisciplinary Foundation for Service
0–913580–97–X Gallaudet $29.95

Jack R. Gannon
THE WEEK THE WORLD HEARD GALLAUDET
0–930323–54–8 Gallaudet $29.95
0–930323–50–5 Gallaudet pb $19.95

Leonard G. Lane
THE GALLAUDET SURVIVAL GUIDE TO SIGNING
A pocket-size dictionary of more than 500 words in American Sign Language
0–930323–34–3 Gallaudet pb $3.50

Jerome D. Schein
AT HOME AMONG STRANGERS
Views the unique culture of deaf people, their families, and organizations
0–930323–51–3 Gallaudet $19.95

John Van Cleve & Barry Crouch
A PLACE OF THEIR OWN: Creating a Deaf Community in America
0–930323–49–1 Gallaudet pb $14.95

Environments

• Michael J. Bednar
BARRIER-FREE ENVIRONMENTS
0–87933–277–8 Van Nostrand Reinhold $39.95

• Robert H. Bruininks
LIVING AND LEARNING IN THE LEAST RESTRICTIVE ENVIRONMENT
0–933716–42–7 Brookes pb $26.00

• Bettyann B. Raschko
HOUSING INTERIORS FOR THE DISABLED AND ELDERLY
0–442–22001–4 Van Nostrand Reinhold $47.95

Employment

• Bertram J. Black
WORK AND MENTAL ILLNESS: Transitions to Employment
0–8018–3565–8 Johns Hopkins $35.00

• Caven S. McLoughlin & others
GETTING EMPLOYED, STAYING EMPLOYED: Job Development and Training for Persons with Severe Handicaps
An exhaustive manual for both the job seeker and the professional vocational counselor
0–933716–70–2 Brookes pb $22.95

Health, Exercise, and Therapy

• Donna B. Bernhardt, editor
RECREATION FOR THE DISABLED CHILD
For both the professional and parents
0–86656–263–X Haworth $29.95

• David D. Burns
FEELING GOOD: The New Mood Therapy
See especially chapters "Depression and Inventory Scale," and "Dysfunctional Attitudes Scale"
0–688–03633–3 Morrow $19.95
0–451–15887–3 NAL pb $4.95

• Gerald G. May
CARE OF MIND, CARE OF SPIRIT: Psychiatric Dimensions of Spiritual Direction
0–06–065533–X Harper & Row $15.50

• Thomas O. Mooney & others
SEXUAL OPTIONS FOR PARAPLEGICS AND QUADRIPLEGICS
0–316–57937–8 Little, Brown pb $15.00

• Richard Simmons
RICHARD SIMMONS' REACH FOR FITNESS: A Special Book of Exercise for the Physically Challenged
0–446–51302–4 Warner $17.95

• Frances Taira
HOME NURSING: Basic Rehabilitation Care of Adults
0–87762–422–4 Technomic pb $25.00

• Jules C. Weiss, editor
EXPRESSIVE THERAPY WITH ELDERS AND THE DISABLED: Touching the Heart of Life
This therapy works through the difficulties of finding a new and positive lifestyle
0–86656–266–4 Haworth $29.95
0–86656–372–5 Haworth pb $19.95

✉ **TO ORDER BOOKS AS GIFTS, SEE PAGE 1**

PART 13

SCIENCE

Mathematics

The exponential growth of science and technology during the past 300 years could not have occurred without a corresponding increase in mathematical knowledge. Higher math today is fundamental not only in relativity theory and quantum mechanics; in the biological and medical fields a firm grasp of probability and statistics is essential. Businessmen can perhaps get along without advanced math, but not economists. Not long ago Europeans who considered themselves educated were able to read and write Latin, a language replaced by mathematics, the new universal language of science and technology. Without some knowledge of its lower levels, a layman can no more comprehend modern science than he can understand the *Iliad* without knowing Homeric Greek.

Even though there are translations of Homer, "translations" by science writers presuppose some insight into mathematics. This is surely one reason for the growing demand for popularly written books about math. In surveying these works, keep in mind that no sharp line separates technical from non-technical. At one end of the spectrum are those books which only the professional mathematicians can read. At the other are books written for children. Occasionally, a book published for the general reader will be harder to understand than a college textbook.

INTRODUCTIONS TO MATHEMATICS

Classics

Godfrey Hardy
A MATHEMATICIAN'S APOLOGY
Hardy's famous essay, with an introduction by C.P. Snow, is must reading
0–521–09577–8 Cambridge pb $10.95

Lancelot Hogben
MATHEMATICS FOR THE MILLION
Probably the most successful book ever intended as an introduction to elementary mathematics. "It makes alive the contents of the elements of mathematics"—Albert Einstein
0–393–06361–5 Norton $22.50
0–393–30035–8 Norton pb $10.95

Alfred North Whitehead
AN INTRODUCTION TO MATHEMATICS
This small book has long been a classic
0–19–500211–3 Oxford pb $8.95

General Introductions

• Eric Temple Bell
MATHEMATICS: Queen and Servant of Science
1–55615–173–X Tempus pb $11.95

• Bela Bollobas
LITTLEWOOD'S MISCELLANY
0–521–33702–X Cambridge pb $13.95

• William Chinn & Philip Davies
3.1416 AND ALL THAT
0–8176–3304–9 Birkhauser pb $16.95

• Tobias Dantzig
NUMBER, THE LANGUAGE OF SCIENCE
0–02–906990–4 Free Press pb $14.95

• Michael Guillen
BRIDGES TO INFINITY
0–87477–233–8 Jeremy Tarcher $12.95
0–87477–345–8 Jeremy Tarcher pb $6.95

• Morris Kline
MATHEMATICS AND THE PHYSICAL WORLD
The growth of mathematics, from arithmetic to calculus and the non-Euclidian geometries
0–486–24104–1 Dover pb $7.95

• Dan Pedoe
THE GENTLE ART OF MATHEMATICS
0–486–22949–1 Dover pb $4.95

• George Polya
HOW TO SOLVE IT
0–691–02356–5 Princeton pb $7.95

• Rudy Rucker
INFINITY AND THE MIND: The Science and Philosophy of the Infinite
0–8176–3034–1 Birkhauser $19.95

MIND TOOLS: The Five Levels of Mathematical Reality
"An original and fascinating look at various aspects of mathematics that is sure to fascinate the non-mathematician"—Isaac Asimov
0–395–46810–8 Houghton Mifflin pb $9.95

• W.W. Sawyer
PRELUDE TO MATHEMATICS
A noted mathematician's account, with emphasis on novel aspects
0–486–24401–6 Dover pb $4.50

• Jagjit Singh
GREAT IDEAS OF MODERN MATHEMATICS
0–486–20587–8 Dover pb $6.50

• Sheila Tobias
OVERCOMING MATH ANXIETY
Strategies for changing one's approach to math
0–393–06439–5 Norton $16.95
0–395–29088–0 Houghton Mifflin pb $8.95

• Leo Zippin
USES OF INFINITY
0–88385–607–7 Mathematical Assoc pb $10.00

Advanced Mathematical Studies

• Richard Courant & Herbert Robbins
WHAT IS MATHEMATICS?: An Elementary Approach to Ideas and Methods
Justly admired for its wide range, clear exposition, and inclusion of actual proofs not often found in a book of this type
0–19–502517–2 Oxford pb $15.95

• Philip Davis & Reuben Hersh
THE MATHEMATICAL EXPERIENCE
An exciting view of the development of mathematics; for the general reader. Winner of an American Book Award
0–8176–3018–X Birkhauser $27.95

DESCARTES' DREAM: The World According to Mathematics
"A passionate plea against the use of formal mathematical reasoning as a method for solving mankind's problems"—*NY Times*
0–15–125260–2 HBJ $24.95
0–395–43154–9 Houghton Mifflin pb $12.95

• Heinrich Dorrie
ONE HUNDRED GREAT PROBLEMS OF ELEMENTARY MATHEMATICS: Their History and Solution
Problems that beset the great mathematicians
0–486–61348–8 Dover pb $6.95

• Paul Hoffman
ARCHIMEDES' REVENGE: The Challenge of the Unknown
An engaging, anecdotal history of the problems that continue to puzzle mathematicians
0–393–02522–5 Norton $17.95

• George Polya
MATHEMATICS AND PLAUSIBLE REASONING
Volumes are *Induction and Analogy in Mathematics* and *Patterns of Plausible Inference*
0–685–23091–0 Princeton (2-volume set) $51.00

• H. Rademacher
HIGHER MATHEMATICS FROM AN ELEMENTARY POINT OF VIEW
0–8176–3064–3 Birkhauser $32.95

• Lynn Steen
MATHEMATICS TOMORROW
An anthology of nontechnical articles (intermediate level)
0–387–90564–2 Springer-Verlag $29.80

• Sherman K. Stein
MATHEMATICS, THE MAN-MADE UNIVERSE: An Introduction to the Spirit of Mathematics
0–7167–0465–X W. H. Freeman $28.95

Reference

• W. Gellert, editor
VNR CONCISE ENCYCLOPEDIA OF MATHEMATICS
A more advanced level
0–442–22646–2 Van Nostrand Reinhold $28.95

☏ **TO ORDER ANY BOOK IN THIS CATALOG, ASK YOUR BOOKSELLER OR CALL 1-800-882-8770**

M.C. Escher's "Möbius Strip I," from Gödel, Escher, Bach *by Douglas Hofstadter* (*Vintage*)

- **Kiyoshi Ito, editor**
  ENCYCLOPEDIC DICTIONARY OF MATHEMATICS
  The highest level of difficulty
  0–262–09026–0 MIT $350.00

- **William & T. Alaric Middleton**
  DICTIONARY OF MATHEMATICS
  An advanced-level work
  0–06–463311–X Barnes & Noble pb $6.95

- **Max Shapiro, editor**
  MATHEMATICS ENCYCLOPEDIA
  A popular-level dictionary
  0–385–12427–9 Doubleday pb $6.95

- **N.J. Sloane**
  A HANDBOOK OF INTEGER SEQUENCES
  A marvelous reference that includes lists of more than 2000 integers and rules for generating them
  0–12–648550–X Academic $39.50

HISTORY OF MATHEMATICS

Early Histories

- **W.W. Ball**
  A SHORT ACCOUNT OF THE HISTORY OF MATHEMATICS
  Although written before 1900, still an excellent elementary account
  0–486–20630–0 Dover pb $9.95

- **Florian Cajori**
  A HISTORY OF MATHEMATICS
  A pre-1950 classic
  0–8284–1303–7 Chelsea $22.50

- **David E. Smith**
  A HISTORY OF MATHEMATICS
  A reliable early work distinguished by hundreds of illustrations. Volume 1 is a chronological survey, Volume 2 is organized by topic

  Volume 1: General Survey of the History of Elementary Mathematics
  0–486–20429–4 Dover pb $10.95

  Volume 2: Special Topics of Elementary Math
  0–486–20430–8 Dover pb $10.95

Modern Histories

- **Carl B. Boyer**
  A HISTORY OF MATHEMATICS
  Especially recommended
  0–471–09763–2 John Wiley $49.00
  0–691–02391–3 Princeton pb $14.95

- **Howard Eves**
  GREAT MOMENTS IN MATHEMATICS
  A 2-volume work that focuses on historic turning points
  0–88385–312–4 Mathematical Assoc pb $28.00

- **K.O. Friedrichs**
  FROM PYTHAGORAS TO EINSTEIN
  0–88385–616–6 Mathematical Assoc pb $9.50

- **Morris Kline**
  MATHEMATICAL THOUGHT FROM ANCIENT TO MODERN TIMES
  The most comprehensive history in English
  0–19–501496–0 Oxford $75.00

  MATHEMATICS IN WESTERN CULTURE
  Stresses the influence of math on science and the humanities
  0–19–500714–X Oxford pb $12.95

- **Dirk Struik**
  A CONCISE HISTORY OF MATHEMATICS
  A good brief history
  0–486–60255–9 Dover pb $7.95

Histories of Ancient Mathematics

- **Richard Gillings**
  MATHEMATICS IN THE TIME OF THE PHARAOHS
  A fascinating, notable work
  0–486–24315–X Dover pb $6.95

- **Thomas Heath**
  A HISTORY OF GREEK MATHEMATICS
  Outstanding for its authoritative coverage

  Volume 1
  0–486–24073–8 Dover pb $10.95

  Volume 2
  0–486–24074–6 Dover pb $10.95

Biography

- **Donald Albers & G.L. Alexanderson, editors**
  MATHEMATICAL PEOPLE: Profiles and Interviews
  A lively account of contemporary mathematicians
  0–8176–3191–7 Birkhauser $24.95
  0–8092–4976–6 Contemporary pb $12.95

- **E.T. Bell**
  MEN OF MATHEMATICS
  An outstanding early work. "Any [one] engaged in learning mathematics will profit by reading him, since he humanizes the subject and helps to a realization of the historic environment"—Bertrand Russell
  0–671–62818–6 Simon & Schuster pb $12.95

- **W.K. Buehler**
  GAUSS: A Biographical Study
  A fine biography of the great German mathematician
  0–387–10662–6 Springer-Verlag $28.00

- **Auguste Dick**
  EMMY NOETHER
  The dramatic story of Emmy Noether, considered one of the greatest woman mathematicians of all time, who came to the U.S. from Germany in 1933 and taught at the Institute of Advanced Study
  0–8176–3019–8 Birkhauser pb $15.95

- **Ann Koblitz**
  A CONVERGENCE OF LIVES
  A splendid biography of Sofia Kovalevskaia, "the greatest woman mathematician prior to the 20th century" (*Dictionary of Scientific Biography*)
  0–8176–3162–3 Birkhauser $40.50

- **Lynn M. Osen**
  WOMEN IN MATHEMATICS
  From Hypatia of 5th-century Alexandria, murdered by a fanatic mob, down to modern times
  0–262–65009–6 MIT pb $6.95

- **C. Reid**
  HILBERT-COURANT
  Outstanding biographies of David Hilbert and Richard Courant
  0–387–96256–5 Springer-Verlag pb $32.00

- **Herbert Turnbull**
  THE GREAT MATHEMATICIANS
  Another outstanding early work
  0–8147–0419–0 New York $15.00

Archimedes, Newton, and Gauss, these three, are in a class by themselves among the great mathematicians, and it is not for ordinary mortals to attempt to range them in order of merit. All three started tidal waves in both pure and applied mathematics: Archimedes esteemed his pure mathematics more highly than its applications; Newton appears to have found the chief justification for his mathematical inventions in the scientific uses to which he put them, while Gauss declared that it was all one to him whether he worked on the pure or the applied side.

E.T. Bell
MEN OF MATHEMATICS
0–671–62818–6 Simon & Schuster pb $12.95

Autobiographies

Few mathematicians have written autobiographies, but in the late 1970s and early '80s several top mathematicians undertook the task.

- **P.R. Halmos**
  I WANT TO BE A MATHEMATICIAN
  Crammed with anecdotes about famous friends, and pervaded with the subtle humor for which Halmos is known
  0–387–96078–3 Springer-Verlag $46.00

☞ **FOR ALL OTHER INQUIRIES, PLEASE CALL (212) 333-7900**

• Mark Kac
ENIGMAS OF CHANCE: An Autobiography
0–06–015433–0 Harper & Row $18.95

• Willard van Orman Quine
THE TIME OF MY LIFE: An Autobiography
Best known as a philosopher, he made enormous contributions to set theory and logic
0–262–17003–5 MIT $25.00

• S.M. Ulam
ADVENTURES OF A MATHEMATICIAN
Entertaining account of the Polish mathematician who, with Edward Teller, invented the hydrogen bomb
0–684–15064–6 Scribner's pb $7.95

PHILOSOPHY OF MATHEMATICS

Philosophers are more interested in the philosophical foundations of mathematics than working mathematicians, but many books on the topic can be understood by outsiders.

• Robert J. Baum, editor
PHILOSOPHY AND MATHEMATICS: From Plato to the Present
A comprehensive history
0–87735–514–2 Cooper Freeman pb $12.00

• Jacques Hadamard
PSYCHOLOGY OF INVENTION IN THE MATHEMATICAL FIELD
Emphasizes mathematical creativity and offers insight into Einstein's thought processes
0–486–20107–4 Dover pb $3.50

• Stephan Korner
THE PHILOSOPHY OF MATHEMATICS: An Introductory Essay
An excellent introduction
0–486–25048–2 Dover pb $5.95

• Hilary Putnam
PHILOSOPHY OF MATHEMATICS: Selected Readings
An anthology of papers
0–521–22796–8 Cambridge $62.50
0–521–29648–X Cambridge pb $20.95

• Bertrand Russell
INTRODUCTION TO MATHEMATICAL PHILOSOPHY
A classic
0–671–20927–2 Simon & Schuster pb $9.95

Cultural Interpretations

Most mathematicians believe that mathematical structure is "out there," independent of the human mind, and that theorems are discovered, not created. However, some hold more subjective views, stressing mathematics as a cultural construct—like art, music, ethics, and even traffic regulations.

• Morris Kline
MATHEMATICS: The Loss of Certainty
0–19–502754–X Oxford $25.00
0–19–503085–0 Oxford pb $9.95

MATHEMATICS AND THE SEARCH FOR KNOWLEDGE
0–19–503533–X Oxford $24.95
0–19–504230–1 Oxford pb $8.95

• John Allen Paulos
INNUMERACY: Mathematical Illiteracy and Its Consequences
A best-selling book, which argues that our inability to deal rationally with very large numbers results in misinformed governmental policies, confused personal decisions, and an increased susceptibility to pseudo-sciences. A quantitative way of looking at the world, filled with astonishing facts
0–8090–7447–8 Hill & Wang $18.95

• Paul Watzlawick, editor
THE INVENTED REALITY: How Do We Know What We Believe We Know?
0–393–01731–1 Norton $19.95

• Raymond Wilder
MATHEMATICS AS A CULTURAL SYSTEM
0–08–025796–8 Pergamon $31.00

NUMBER THEORY

• Georges Ifrah
FROM ONE TO ZERO: A Universal History of Numbers
The history of systems of numeration in a profusely illustrated translation
0–14–009919–0 Penguin pb $14.95

• Oystein Ore
INVITATION TO NUMBER THEORY
0–88385–620–4 Mathematical Assoc pb $9.90

NUMBER THEORY AND ITS HISTORY
0–486–65620–9 Dover pb $8.95

• Andre Weil
NUMBER THEORY FOR BEGINNERS
0–387–90381–X Springer-Verlag pb $24.00

Elementary Number Theory

• Isaac Asimov
THE REALM OF NUMBERS
0–449–24399–0 Fawcett pb $2.50

• Tobias Dantzig
NUMBER: The Language of Science
0–02–906990–4 Free Press $14.95

• Philip Davis
THE LORE OF LARGE NUMBERS
0–88385–606–9 Mathematical Assoc pb $10.00

• Keith Ellis
NUMBER POWER
0–312–57989–6 St Martin's pb $4.95

• Ivan Niven
IRRATIONAL NUMBERS
0–88385–011–7 Mathematical Assoc $21.00

The Menger sponge, from Benoit Mandelbrot's "The Fractal Geometry of Nature," reproduced in Mind Tools *by Rudy Rucker (Houghton Mifflin)*

• Ivan Niven & Herbert Zuckerman
AN INTRODUCTION TO THE THEORY OF NUMBERS
0–471–02851–7 John Wiley $53.50

ALGEBRA AND COMBINATRICS

There is a dearth of popularly written books on algebra (there are, of course, hundreds of textbooks).

• Garrett Birkhoff & Saunders MacLane
A SURVEY OF MODERN ALGEBRA
The undisputed classic on an advanced level
0–02–310070–2 Macmillan $45.95

• W.W. Sawyer
A CONCRETE APPROACH TO ABSTRACT ALGEBRA
A good introduction to such structures as groups, rings, fields, matrices, and so on
0–486–63647–X Dover pb $5.95

Combinatrics

Combinatrics is one of the fastest-growing areas of mathematics.

• Chung Liu
INTRODUCTION TO APPLIED COMBINATORIAL MATHEMATICS
0–07–038124–0 McGraw-Hill $56.95

• Ivan Niven
THE MATHEMATICS OF CHOICE
0–88385–615–8 Mathematical Assoc pb $11.00

• John Riordan
AN INTRODUCTION TO COMBINATORIAL ANALYSIS
One of the best and most widely used books on combinatrics; advanced level
0–691–08262–6 Princeton $29.50
0–691–02365–4 Princeton pb $15.50

• Herbert Ryser
COMBINATORIAL MATHEMATICS
A good introduction and clear presentation of a difficult subject
0–88385–014–1 Mathematical Assoc $19.00

🐾 **IF YOU CAN'T FIND IT, LOOK IN THE INDEX**

PROBABILITY AND STATISTICS

- **Richard Brook & others**
THE FASCINATION OF STATISTICS
0–8247–7329–2 Marcel Dekker $27.75

- **Stephen Campbell**
FLAWS AND FALLACIES IN STATISTICAL THINKING
0–13–322214–4 Prentice-Hall pb $21.00

- **Florence David**
GAMES, GODS AND GAMBLING: The Origins and History of Probability and Statistical Ideas from the Earliest Times to the Newtonian Era
A readable history
0–1952–0566–9 Oxford $21.50

- **Richard Epstein**
THE THEORY OF GAMBLING AND STATISTICAL LOGIC
0–12–240760–1 Academic $39.50

- **Richard Hooke**
HOW TO TELL THE LIARS FROM THE STATISTICIANS
0–8247–1817–8 Marcel Dekker $22.75

- **Darrel Huff & Irving Geis**
HOW TO TAKE A CHANCE
An amusing illustrated introduction on a lower level
0–393–00263–2 Norton pb $6.95

HOW TO LIE WITH STATISTICS
Companion volume, covering a loosely related topic
0–393–09426–X Norton pb $3.95

- **Frederick Mosteller**
FIFTY CHALLENGING PROBLEMS IN PROBABILITY
0–486–65355–2 Dover pb $3.95

- **E.W. Packel**
THE MATHEMATICS OF GAMES AND GAMBLING
A good survey; how mathematics can be used to analyze games of chance and skill
0–88385–628–X Mathematical Assoc pb $11.00

- **Theodore Porter**
THE RISE OF STATISTICAL THINKING, 1820-1900
A nontechnical history that stresses the role of statistics in the natural and social sciences
0–691–08416–5 Princeton $42.00
0–691–02409–X Princeton pb $12.50

- **Stephen Stigler**
THE HISTORY OF STATISTICS
Recommended history, up to 1900
0–674–40340–1 Harvard $27.00

- **Edward Thorp**
BEAT THE DEALER: A Winning Strategy for the Game of Twenty-One
Edward Thorp startled the gambling world by writing the first general trade book on how to win the game of Black Jack. This created a wave of "counters" who still are able to win until the casino asks them to leave
0–394–70310–3 Random House pb $4.95

- **W. Allen Wallis & Harry Roberts**
NATURE OF STATISTICS
0–02–933730–5 Macmillan $14.95

- **Warren Weaver**
LADY LUCK: The Theory of Probability
The best popularly written introduction to probability theory
0–486–24342–7 Dover pb $6.95

> The relevance of no branch of mathematics to one or other aspect of the contemporary world's work is more wide open to dispute than is the theory of so-called probability. On the other hand, its unsavoury origin is on record. The first impetus came from a situation in which the dissolute nobility of France were competing in a race to ruin at the gaming tables. An algebraic calculus of probability takes its origin from a correspondence between Pascal and Fermat (about 1654) over the fortunes and misfortunes of the Chevalier de Mere, a great gambler and by that token "très bon esprit," but alas (wrote Pascal) "il n'est pas géomètre." Alas indeed. The Chevalier had made his pile by always betting small favorable odds on getting at least one six in 4 tosses of a die, and had then lost it by always betting small odds on getting at least one double six in 24 double tosses . . . The problem out of which the calculus took shape was . . . how to adjust the stakes in a game of chance in accordance with a rule which ensures success if applied consistently regardless of the fortunes of the session.
>
> Lancelot Hogben
> **MATHEMATICS FOR THE MILLION**
> 0–393–06361–5 Norton $22.50
> 0–393–30035–8 Norton pb $10.95

GAME AND DECISION THEORY

Introductory

- **Morton Davis**
THE ART OF DECISION-MAKING
Emphasizes the paradoxical aspects
0–387–96228–X Springer-Verlag $24.00

GAME THEORY: A Non-Technical Introduction
An excellent elementary introduction
0–465–02627–3 Basic $20.00
0–465–02628–1 Basic pb $10.95

- **J.D. Williams**
THE COMPLEAT STRATEGYST: Being a Primer on the Theory of Games of Strategy
Another fine elementary introduction
0–486–25101–2 Dover pb $5.95

Higher-Level

- **Richard Jeffrey**
THE LOGIC OF DECISION
0–226–39581–2 Chicago $22.00

- **Howard Raiffa**
DECISION ANALYSIS: Introductory Lectures on Choices Under Uncertainty
0–394–35019–7 Random House pb $24.00

Steven Brams
Steven Brams has applied game and decision theory to politics in the following books:
PARADOXES IN POLITICS: An Introduction to the Non-Obvious in Political Science
0–02–904590–8 Free Press pb $12.95

GAME THEORY AND POLITICS
0–02–904550–9 Free Press pb $16.95

THE PRESIDENTIAL ELECTION GAME
0–300–02254–9 Yale $30.00
0–300–02296–4 Yale pb $7.95

SUPERPOWER GAMES: Applying Game Theory to Superpower Conflict
0–300–03323–0 Yale $25.00
0–300–03364–8 Yale pb $9.95

Surprising applications to theology are discussed in two other Brams books:
BIBLICAL GAMES: A Strategic Analysis of Stories in the Old Testament
0–262–52074–5 MIT pb $7.95

SUPERIOR BEINGS: If They Exist How Would We Know?
0–387–91223–1 Springer-Verlag $29.80
0–387–90877–3 Springer-Verlag pb $18.00

GEOMETRY

- **H.S.M. Coxeter**
INTRODUCTION TO GEOMETRY
Deserves special mention among the numerous geometry books because its central theme, symmetry, now plays such a major role in physics
0–471–18283–4 Wiley $59.00

- **Henry Cundy & A.P. Rollett**
MATHEMATICAL MODELS
An outstanding work on building models of geometric objects
0–19–832504–5 Oxford $24.95

- **David Hilbert & Stephan Cohn-Vossen**
GEOMETRY AND THE IMAGINATION
A famous general work on geometry
0–8284–0087–3 Chelsea $18.95

- **Dan Pedoe**
GEOMETRY AND THE VISUAL ARTS
The crucial importance of geometry in the development of Western aesthetics
0–486–24458–X Dover pb $6.95

Symmetry

- **Hermann Weyl**
SYMMETRY
0–691–02374–3 Princeton pb $7.95

- Robert Williams
THE GEOMETRIC FOUNDATION OF NATURAL STRUCTURE: A Source Book of Design
0–486–23729–X Dover pb $9.95

The Golden Ratio

The Golden Ratio plays a whimsical role in aesthetics and plant growth.

Theodore Cook
THE CURVES OF LIFE
0–486–23701–X Dover pb $8.95

H.E. Huntley
DIVINE PROPORTION: A Study in Mathematical Beauty
A bridge between science and art
0–486–22254–3 Dover pb $4.50

Fractals

Fractals are finding increasing applications in the study of nature's random processes such as the formation of mountains, coastlines, clouds, and a thousand other shapes and in a fledgling branch of mathematics called chaos theory, with its "strange attractors" and gorgeous patterns on computer screens. Science-fiction films are also using fractal theory to generate exotic computer landscapes.

- James Gleick
CHAOS: Making a New Science
"The questions *Chaos* instills in the reader do not arise from lack of understanding or clarity; rather, they spring from the revolutionary nature of the material—can I believe what I just read? Can this really be true?"—*NY Times*
0–670–81178–5 Viking $19.95
0–14–009250–1 Penguin pb $8.95

- Benoit Mandelbrot
THE FRACTAL GEOMETRY OF NATURE
A work of unusual elegance and timely interest. Mandelbrot invented the term "fractals" to describe a class of highly irregular shapes, and he discusses various ways of calculating and measuring their dimension, with hundreds of illustrations
0–7167–1186–9 W.W. Freeman $34.95

- H.O. Peitgen & P.H. Richter
THE BEAUTY OF FRACTALS
On a popular level, with many color pictures
0–387–15851–0 Springer-Verlag $39.00

Topology

Topology is a branch of modern geometry concerned with properties that remain the same regardless of how an object is continuously distorted. It has endless applications and has spawned hundreds of advanced books; those listed here are popularly written introductions.

Now that science is looking, chaos seems to be everywhere. A rising column of cigarette smoke breaks into wild swirls. A flag snaps back and forth in the wind. A dripping faucet goes from a steady pattern to a random one. Chaos appears in the behavior of the weather, the behavior of cars clustering on an expressway, the behavior of oil flowing in underground pipes. No matter what the medium, the behavior obeys the same newly discovered laws. The realization has begun to change the way business executives make decisions about insurance, the way astronomers look at the solar system, the way political theorists talk about the stresses leading to armed conflict.

James Gleick
CHAOS: Making a New Science
0–670–81178–5 Viking $19.95
0–14–009250–1 Penguin pb $8.95

- Stephen Barr
EXPERIMENTS IN TOPOLOGY
0–690–27862–4 Harper & Row $11.75

- W.G. Chinn & N.E. Steenrod
FIRST CONCEPTS OF TOPOLOGY
0–88385–618–2 Mathematical Assoc pb $10.00

Graph Theory

A branch of topology that is rapidly finding applications in the social sciences as well as in many areas of mathematics is graph theory, which studies sets of points connected by lines.

- Norman Biggs & others
GRAPH THEORY: 1736-1936
A pioneering history
0–19–853916–9 Oxford pb $26.95

- Gary Chartrand
INTRODUCTORY GRAPH THEORY
A nontechnical introduction
0–486–24775–9 Dover pb $6.95

- Israel Grossman & Wilhelm Magnus
GROUPS AND THEIR GRAPHS
Popularly written introduction
0–88385–614–X Mathematical Assoc pb $11.00

- Frank Harary
GRAPH THEORY
The standard introductory book
0–201–02787–9 Addison-Wesley $39.75

- Oystein Ore
GRAPHS AND THEIR USE
0–88385–610–7 Mathematical Assoc pb $9.90

- Richard Trudeau
DOTS AND LINES
An introductory work
0–87338–223–4 Kent State $15.00
0–87338–224–2 Kent State pb $9.95

Four-Color Theorem

The famous four-color map theorem of graph theory (which states that every planar map can be colored with as few as four colors) was finally solved with computer help in 1977.

- Edwin Abbott
FLATLAND
An imaginary society of intelligent two-dimensional creatures is the basis of this book, combining geometry with social satire
0–14–007615–8 Penguin pb $3.95

- A. K. Dewdney
THE PLANIVERSE: Computer Contact with a Two-Dimensional World
Destined to become a similar classic
0–671–46362–4 Poseiden $16.95
0–671–46363–2 Pocket $9.95

- Paul Kainen
THE FOUR-COLOR PROBLEM: Assaults and Conquests
An account of the combinatorial problem, its history and solution
0–486–65092–8 Dover pb $6.00

Advanced Geometry

- Branko Grunbaum & G.C. Shephard
TILINGS AND PATTERNS
The first attempt to bring together the newest development in tiling theory, including the famous Penrose tiles, which have had surprising applications to quasicrystals
0–7167–1193–1 W.W. Freeman $59.95

- Rudy Rucker
THE FOURTH DIMENSION: Toward a Geometry of Higher Reality
A good introduction, combining math, philosophy, and fantasy, including dozens of puzzles and problems
0–395–39388–4 Houghton Mifflin pb $8.95

GEOMETRY, RELATIVITY AND THE FOURTH DIMENSION
Another good introduction
0–486–23400–2 Dover pb $3.95

Calculus

- Carl Boyer
HISTORY OF THE CALCULUS AND ITS CONCEPTUAL DEVELOPMENT
The definitive modern history
0–486–60509–4 Dover pb $6.95

- Ivan Niven
MAXIMA AND MINIMA WITHOUT CALCULUS
Many problems that seem to require calculus can be solved by more elementary means
0–88385–306–X Mathematical Assoc $31.50

- W.W. Sawyer
WHAT IS CALCULUS ABOUT?
The best introduction for a beginner
0–88385–602–6 Mathematical Assoc pb $9.90

- Silvanus Thompson
CALCULUS MADE EASY
0–312–11410–9 St Martin's pb $6.95

TO ORDER BOOKS AS GIFTS, SEE PAGE 1

LOGIC AND SET THEORY

Formal logic, once the domain of philosophy departments, is now considered part of mathematics, closely related to set theory. Although there are many excellent college-level textbooks on both logic and set theory, there are few popularly written books on either topic.

- Nagel Muzzio & James Newman
GODEL'S PROOF
The best introduction to Gödel's theorem for non-specialists
0–8147–0325–9 New York pb $6.50

- Raymond Smullyan
Smullyan's books not only contain brilliant, unusual puzzles of his own invention, but also lead painlessly into modern logic and set theory, including Kurt Gödel's famous undecidability theorem.
ALICE IN PUZZLELAND: A Carrollian Tale for Children
0–1400–7056–7 Penguin pb $6.95

FOREVER UNDECIDED: A Puzzle Guide to Gödel
0–317–59956–9 Knopf $17.95

THE LADY OR THE TIGER? & Other Logic Puzzles
0–394–51466–1 Knopf $15.95

TO MOCK A MOCKINGBIRD
0–394–53491–3 Knopf $14.95

THIS BOOK NEEDS NO TITLE: A Budget of Living Paradoxes
0–671–62831–3 Simon & Schuster pb $6.95

- Clarence Wylie
101 PUZZLES IN THOUGHT AND LOGIC
A typical book on logic puzzles
0–486–20367–0 Dover pb $2.50

RECREATIONAL MATHEMATICS

- W.W. Rouse Ball & H.S.M. Coxeter
MATHEMATICAL RECREATIONS AND ESSAYS
The classic work in English
0–486–25357–0 Dover pb $8.95

- Ross Honsberger
Honsberger has written five splendid books about recreational problems
INGENUITY IN MATHEMATICS
Ingenious approaches to such topics as number theory, geometry, combinatrics, logic, and probability
0–88385–623–9 Mathematical Assoc pb $11.00

MATHEMATICAL GEMS
These three books contain dozens of mathematical vignettes from elementary combinatrics, number theory, and geometry
0–88385–301–9 Mathematical Assoc $21.00

MATHEMATICAL GEMS II
0–88385–302–7 Mathematical Assoc $21.00

MATHEMATICAL GEMS III
0–88385–313–2 Mathematical Assoc $28.00

MATHEMATICAL MORSELS
Solutions to problems from algebra, arithmetic, number theory, probability, and geometry
0–88385–303–5 Mathematical Assoc $26.50

- J.A. Hunter & Joseph Madachy
MATHEMATICAL DIVERSIONS
0–486–23110–0 Dover pb $3.95

- Maurice Kraitchik
MATHEMATICAL RECREATIONS
Another basic reference
0–486–20163–5 Dover pb $6.95

- Joseph Madachy
MADACHY'S MATHEMATICAL RECREATIONS
0–486–23762–1 Dover pb $4.95

- T.H. O'Beirne
PUZZLES AND PARADOXES: Fascinating Excursions in Recreational Mathematics
0–486–24613–2 Dover pb $4.95

- Isaac Schoenberg
MATHEMATICAL TIME EXPOSURES
0–88385–438–4 Mathematical Assoc pb $21.00

- Fred Schuh
THE MASTER BOOK OF MATHEMATICAL PUZZLES AND RECREATIONS
0–486–22134–2 Dover pb $6.95

- Benjamin Schwartz, editor
MATHEMATICAL SOLITAIRES AND GAMES
0–89503–017–9 Baywood pb $6.00

- Hugo Steinhaus
MATHEMATICAL SNAPSHOTS
Steinhaus's books are good reference works
0–19–500117–6 Oxford $17.95

ONE HUNDRED PROBLEMS IN ELEMENTARY MATHEMATICS
0–486–23875–X Dover pb $3.95

Martin Gardner's Recreational Math

"In Gardner's writing, numbers break out of their gray procession toward infinity and take on personalities: the measured march of the square numbers; the primes in their unfathomable progression; the irrationals always a decimal place away from being captured; the imaginaries occupying the nonexistent gaps between the reals . . . Alone with his typewriter, he can find more excitement in the square root of 2 than most men could find in Faye Dunaway's whole telephone number."—*Newsweek*

Martin Gardner
AHA! GOTCHA: Paradoxes to Puzzle and Delight
0–7167–1361–6 W.H. Freeman pb $10.95

AHA! INSIGHT
0–7167–1017–X W.H. Freeman pb $10.95

ENTERTAINING MATHEMATICAL PUZZLES
0–486–25211–6 Dover pb $2.95

KNOTTED DOUGHNUTS & OTHER MATHEMATICAL AMUSEMENTS
0–7167–1794–8 W.H. Freeman $16.95
0–7167–1799–9 W.H. Freeman pb $12.95

THE MAGIC NUMBERS OF DR. MATRIX
0–87975–281–5 Prometheus $20.95
0–87975–282–3 Prometheus pb $14.95

MATHEMATICS, MAGIC, AND MYSTERY
0–486–20335–2 Dover pb $3.95

TIME TRAVEL & OTHER MATHEMATICAL BEWILDERMENTS
0–7167–1924–X W.H. Freeman $17.95
0–7167–1925–8 W.H. Freeman pb $12.95

THE UNEXPECTED HANGING & Other Mathematical Diversions
0–671–62819–4 Simon & Schuster pb $7.95

WHEELS, LIFE AND OTHER MATHEMATICAL AMUSEMENTS
0–7167–1589–9 W.H. Freeman pb $12.95

THE SCIENTIFIC AMERICAN BOOK OF MATHEMATICAL PUZZLES AND DIVERSIONS
0–671–24559–7 Simon & Schuster pb $6.95

THE SECOND SCIENTIFIC AMERICAN BOOK OF MATHEMATICAL PUZZLES & DIVERSIONS
0–226–28253–8 Chicago pb $10.95
0–671–63653–7 Simon & Schuster pb $6.95

MARTIN GARDNER'S SIXTH BOOK OF MATHEMATICAL DIVERSIONS FROM SCIENTIFIC AMERICAN
0–226–28250–3 Chicago pb $7.95

MARTIN GARDNER'S NEW MATHEMATICAL DIVERSIONS FROM SCIENTIFIC AMERICAN
0–226–28247–3 Chicago pb $7.95

MATHEMATICAL CARNIVAL: A New Round-up of Tantalizers and Puzzles from Scientific American
0–394–49406–7 Random House $12.95

Special Topics

- Albert Beiler
RECREATIONS IN THE THEORY OF NUMBERS
The best reference on recreations involving numbers
0–486–21096–0 Dover pb $6.95

- Elwyn Berlekamp & others
WINNING WAYS
A modern classic about competitive games of all varieties

Volume 1: Games in General
0–12–091150–7 Academic $72.00

Volume 2: Games in Particular
0–12–091102–7 Academic pb $42.00

- Maxey Brooke
  150 PUZZLES IN CRYPT-ARITHMETIC
  The best collection of a type of number
  puzzle similar to a cryptogram
  0–486–21039–1 Dover pb $2.95

- John Conway
  ON NUMBERS AND GAMES
  Deals with an application to games of a
  strange new class of numbers invented by
  Conway. The numbers are explained in a
  curious novel by Donald Knuth, *Surreal
  Numbers*
  0–12–186350–6 Academic $44.00

- Donald E. Knuth
  SURREAL NUMBERS
  0–201–03812–9 Addison-Wesley $24.75

- Stephen Richards
  A NUMBER FOR YOUR THOUGHTS
  Two excellent books by Richards (a
  pseudonym for Malcolm Lines, a
  mathematician at Bell Laboratories)
  0–9608224–0–2 S.P. Richards pb $8.95

  NUMBERS AT WORK AND AT PLAY
  0–9608224–2–9 S.P. Richards pb $8.95

- David Wells
  **THE PENGUIN DICTIONARY OF
  CURIOUS AND INTERESTING
  NUMBERS**
  0–14–008029–5 Penguin pb $6.95

Puzzle Collections

- Stephen Barr
  **MATHEMATICAL BRAIN BENDERS:
  Second Miscellany of Puzzles**
  0–486–24260–9 Dover pb $4.95

- Pierre Berloquin
  **THE GARDEN OF THE SPHINX: 150
  Challenging and Instructive Puzzles**
  0–684–18342–0 Scribners $13.95

- Lewis Carroll
  **PILLOW PROBLEMS & A TANGLED
  TALE**
  0–486–20493–6 Dover pb $4.95

- Crypton
  **DR. CRYPTON AND HIS PROBLEMS:
  Mind Benders from Science Digest**
  "The mysterious Dr. Crypton (presumably
  a friend of Superman except that he has a
  superbrain instead of a superbody) has
  assembled a super collection of puzzles and
  curiosities involving mathematics, words,
  and anything at all that lends to logical
  and creative thinking. A delightful book to
  read and ponder"—Martin Gardner
  0–312–21477–4 St. Martin's pb $4.95

  **TIMID VIRGINS MAKE DULL
  COMPANY & OTHER PUZZLES,
  PITFALLS AND PARADOXES**
  0–14–008043–0 Penguin pb $6.95

- Angela Dunn
  MATHEMATICAL BAFFLERS
  0–486–23961–6 Dover pb $4.50

  **SECOND BOOK OF MATHEMATICAL
  BAFFLERS**
  0–486–24352–4 Dover pb $3.95

- Martin Gardner
  **PUZZLES FROM OTHER WORLDS:
  Fantastical Brainteasers from Isaac Asimov's
  Science Fiction Magazine**
  0–394–72140–3 Random House pb $5.95

- Lloyd Graham
  **INGENIOUS MATHEMATICAL
  PROBLEMS AND METHODS**
  0–486–20545–2 Dover pb $4.95

  **SURPRISE ATTACK IN
  MATHEMATICAL PROBLEMS**
  0–486–21846–5 Dover pb $4.50

- J.A. Hunter
  **CHALLENGING MATHEMATICAL
  TEASERS**
  0–486–23852–0 Dover pb $3.50

  **ENTERTAINING MATHEMATICAL
  TEASERS AND HOW TO SOLVE THEM**
  0–486–24500–4 Dover pb $3.50

  FUN WITH FIGURES
  0–486–21364–1 Dover pb $3.95

  MATHEMATICAL BRAIN-TEASERS
  0–486–23347–2 Dover pb $2.95

  MORE FUN WITH FIGURES
  0–486–21670–5 Dover pb $3.50

- Scot Morris
  OMNI GAMES
  0–03–060297–1 Henry Holt pb $12.95

- Ronnie Shushan, editor
  **THE GAMES MAGAZINE BIG BOOK OF
  GAMES**
  0–89480–806–0 Workman pb $10.95

- Charles Trigg
  **MATHEMATICAL QUICKIES: 270
  Stimulating Problems with Solutions**
  0–486–24949–2 Dover pb $4.95

Mechanical Puzzles

- John Beasley
  **THE INS AND OUTS OF PEG
  SOLITAIRE**
  A special type of mechanical puzzle
  0–19–853203–2 Oxford $19.95

- Henry Dudeney
  AMUSEMENTS IN MATHEMATICS
  England's greatest puzzle inventor
  0–486–20473–1 Dover pb $5.95

  **536 PUZZLES AND CURIOUS
  PROBLEMS**
  Two of Dudeney's books gathered in a
  single volume, edited by Martin Gardner
  0–684–71755–7 Scribner's pb $12.95

- Edward Hordern
  SLIDING PIECE PUZZLES
  Another type of mechanical puzzle
  0–19–853204–0 Oxford $27.50

- Sam Loyd
  **BEST MATHEMATICAL PUZZLES OF
  SAM LOYD**
  America's greatest puzzle inventor
  0–486–20498–7 Dover pb $3.95

  EIGHTH BOOK OF TAN: 700 Tangrams
  The ancient Oriental puzzle of tangrams
  0–486–22011–7 Dover pb $3.95

- Ronald Read
  TANGRAMS: 330 Puzzles
  0–486–21483–4 Dover pb $3.50

- Pieter Van Delft & Jack Botermans
  CREATIVE PUZZLES OF THE WORLD
  Another glossy picture book
  0–8109–0765–8 Abrams $19.95

Magic Squares

- William Benson & Oswald Jacoby
  MAGIC CUBES: New Recreations
  0–486–24140–8 Dover pb $4.95

  **NEW RECREATIONS WITH MAGIC
  SQUARES**
  0–486–23236–0 Dover pb $4.95

Rapid Calculation

- Gerard Kelly
  SHORT-CUT MATH
  A good book on arithmetic shortcuts
  0–486–24611–6 Dover pb $2.95

- Steven Smith
  **THE GREAT MENTAL CALCULATORS:
  The Psychology, Methods, and Lives of
  Calculating Prodigies Past and Present**
  An admirable history of lightning
  calculators—human ones, that is
  0–231–05640–0 Columbia $37.00
  0–231–05641–9 Columbia pb $17.00

- Henry Sticker
  HOW TO CALCULATE QUICKLY
  Includes shortcuts to solving more than
  8000 problems
  0–486–20295–X Dover pb $2.95

Humor

- John Paulos
  **I THINK, THEREFORE I LAUGH: An
  Alternative Approach to Philosophy**
  0–231–06030–0 Columbia $26.00
  0–231–06031–9 Columbia pb $13.00

  MATHEMATICS AND HUMOR
  0–226–65025–1 Chicago pb $10.95

Science and Technology

Most American adults don't know that electrons are smaller than atoms and more than a quarter of all Americans 18 or older are unaware that the earth revolves around the sun; almost one in five thinks sound travels faster than light. The extent of such basic ignorance was revealed in a recent survey, which concluded that perhaps no more than five percent of America's adults are "scientifically literate."

But at least one phenomenon suggests that we are not all turning into a nation of technical dunces: an unprecedented number of popular science books are being bought and read by an apparently growing audience.

Most science books were formerly written for adults who also happened to be scientists—books like *Microbial Degradation of Xenobiotics and Recalcitrant Compounds*. But popular science is now flourishing in works on such arcane topics as quantum physics, plate tectonics, and genetic engineering. Even books on cosmology and the mathematics of chaos now find their way to bestseller lists.

• Isaac Asimov
ASIMOV'S NEW GUIDE TO SCIENCE
0–465–00473–3 Basic Books $29.95

ISAAC ASIMOV'S WONDERFUL WORLDWIDE SCIENCE BAZAAR: 72 Up-to-Date Reports on the State of Everything from Inside the Atom to Outside the Universe
0–395–41554–3 Houghton Mifflin $16.95

• Isaac Asimov & Jason Shulman, editors
ASIMOV'S BOOK OF SCIENCE AND NATURE QUESTIONS
1–55584–111–2 Weidenfeld & Nicolson $19.95

• Charles Cazeau
SCIENCE TRIVIA: From Anteaters to Zeppelins
0–306–42353–7 Plenum $17.95

• Joseph Corn
IMAGINING TOMORROW: History, Technology, and the American Future
0–262–03115–9 MIT $20.00

• Will Curtis
THE NATURE OF THINGS: How and Why Things Work in the Natural World
0–88001–207–2 Ecco pb $10.95

• Dennis Flanagan
FLANAGAN'S VERSION: A Spectator's Guide to Science on the Eve of the 21st Century
Essays by the former editor of *Scientific American*
0–394–55547–3 Knopf $18.95

• Ira Flatow
WHY RAINBOWS? & Other Wonders of the Natural World Explained
An entertaining look at the science behind everyday things
0–688–06705–0 Morrow $15.95

• Martin Gardner
SCIENCE: Good, Bad and Bogus
0–87975–144–4 Prometheus $23.95

• Martin Gardner, editor
THE SACRED BEETLE & OTHER GREAT ESSAYS IN SCIENCE
A collection of popular writing about science, primarily from the 19th century
0–87975–257–2 Prometheus $24.95
0–452–00804–2 NAL pb $10.95

David Macaulay
THE WAY THINGS WORK
A whimsical demystification of the principles and workings of common devices, with many four-color illustrations
0–395–42857–2 Houghton Mifflin $24.95

• Holcomb B. Noble
NEXT: The Coming Era in Science
Essays from the science and health editor of the *New York Times*
0–316–61133–6 Little, Brown pb $9.95

• Max Perutz
IS SCIENCE NECESSARY?: Essays on Science and Scientists
0–525–24673–8 Dutton $18.95

• Howard Rheingold & Howard Levine
TALKING TECH: A Conversational Guide to Science and Technology
0–688–01603–0 Morrow pb $6.95

• Martin Sherwood & Christine Sutton, editors
THE PHYSICAL WORLD
A nontechnical, nonmathematical tour of physical phenomena, with nearly 500 illustrations, most in color
0–19–520632–0 Oxford $35.00

• James Trefil
MEDITATIONS AT 10,000 FEET: A Scientist in the Mountains
"Trefil is one of that small group of scientists who can convey to the general reader both the facts about science and the pleasure of it"—*LA Times*
0–02–025890–9 Macmillan pb $8.95

A magnified view of the zipper, from The Way Things Work (*copyright 1988 by David Macaulay, reprinted by permission of Houghton Mifflin*)

The can opener in action, from The Way Things Work (*copyright 1988 by David Macaulay, reprinted by permission of Houghton Mifflin*)

A SCIENTIST AT THE SEASHORE
"So easy to understand yet so dense with knowledge that you'll never look at waves on a beach the same way again"—*San Francisco Chronicle*
0–02–025920–4 Macmillan pb $8.95

THE UNEXPECTED VISTA: A Physicist's View of Nature
0–684–17869–9 Scribners $14.95
0–02–096780–2 Macmillan pb $7.95

• Alfred North Whitehead
SCIENCE AND THE MODERN WORLD
Whitehead's approach, at once philosophical and scientific, yields many unique insights; physics, for example, was originally an anti-intellectual activity
0–02–935190–1 Free Press pb $13.95

• Robert Wright
THREE SCIENTISTS AND THEIR GODS: A Search for Meaning in an Age of Information
0–8129–1328–0 Times Books $18.95

HISTORY OF SCIENCE AND TECHNOLOGY

• Anthony Alioto
A HISTORY OF WESTERN SCIENCE
0–13–392390–8 Prentice-Hall pb $25.00

• Daniel Boorstin
THE DISCOVERERS: A History of Man's Search to Know His World and Himself
0–394–7265–1 Random House pb $9.95

• Leonard Bruno
THE TRADITION OF SCIENCE
The history of science from the Greeks to the present; with 200 illustrations, including historical woodcuts and drawings
0–8076–1196–4 Braziller pb $25.00

• Facts On File
THE HISTORY OF SCIENCE AND TECHNOLOGY: A Narrative Chronology
From prehistoric times to the mid-20th century; a two-volume set
0–87196–477–5 Facts On File (set) $160.00

• Jack Meadows
THE GREAT SCIENTISTS
Science through the lives of Aristotle,
Galileo, Harvey, Newton, Lavoisier,
Humboldt, Faraday, Darwin, Pasteur,
Curie, Freud, and Einstein
0–19–520620–7 Oxford $35.00
0–19–520815–3 Oxford pb $18.95

• Joseph Needham
SCIENCE IN TRADITIONAL CHINA
By the author of the respected
multivolume *Science and Civilization in
China*
0–674–79439–7 Harvard pb $6.95

• Roy Porter, editor
**MAN MASTERS NATURE: 25 Centuries
of Science**
0–8076–1193–X Braziller $19.95

• Colin Ronan
**SCIENCE: Its History and Development
Among the World's Cultures**
0–87196–745–6 Facts On File $29.95
0–8160–1165–6 Facts On File pb $16.95

• Cecil Schneer
**THE EVOLUTION OF PHYSICAL
SCIENCE: Major Ideas from Earliest
Times to the Present**
0–8191–3790–1 University Press pb $14.50

• Steven Shapin & Simon Schaffer
**LEVIATHAN AND THE AIR-PUMP:
Hobbes, Boyle, and the Experimental Life**
0–691–08393–2 Princeton $60.00
0–691–02432–4 Princeton pb $16.95

• Charles Singer & Trevor Williams,
editors
A HISTORY OF TECHNOLOGY

**Volume 1: From Early Times to the Fall of
Ancient Empires**
0–19–858105–X Oxford $98.00

**Volume 2: The Mediterranean Civilizations
and the Middle Ages, c. 700 B.C. to c. A.D.
1500**
0–19–858106–8 Oxford $98.00

**Volume 3: From the Renaissance to the
Industrial Revolution, c. 1500 to c. 1750**
0–19–858107–6 Oxford $98.00

**Volume 4: The Industrial Revolution,
c. 1750 to c. 1850**
0–19–858108–4 Oxford $98.00

**Volume 5: The Late Nineteenth Century,
c. 1850 to c. 1900**
0–19–858109–2 Oxford $98.00

**Volume 6: The Twentieth Century, c. 1900
to c. 1950, Part 1**
0–19–858151–3 Oxford $98.00

**Volume 7: The Twentieth Century, c. 1900
to c. 1950, Part 2**
0–19–858155–6 Oxford $98.00

Volume 8: Consolidated Indexes
0–19–822905–4 Oxford $45.00

• R.S. Westfall
**THE CONSTRUCTION OF MODERN
SCIENCE**
0–521–21863–2 Cambridge $34.50
0–521–29295–6 Cambridge pb $11.95

• L. Pearce Williams & Henry Steffens
**THE HISTORY OF SCIENCE IN
WESTERN CIVILIZATION**

Volume 1: Antiquity and the Middle Ages
0–8191–0191–5 University Press pb $13.75

Volume 2: The Scientific Revolution
0–8191–0327–6 University Press pb $13.75

Volume 3: Modern Science, 1700-1900
0–8191–0333–0 University Press pb $17.50

• Trevor Williams
**THE HISTORY OF INVENTION: From
Stone Axes to Silicon Chips**
0–8160–1788–3 Facts On File $35.00

Ancient and Medieval Science

• Thomas Goldstein
**THE DAWN OF MODERN SCIENCE:
From the Arabs to Leonardo da Vinci**
0–395–26298–4 Houghton Mifflin $12.95
0–395–48924–5 Houghton Mifflin pb $9.95

• Richard Olson
**SCIENCE DEIFIED AND SCIENCE
DEFIED: The Historical Significance of
Science in Western Culture from the
Bronze Age to the Beginnings of the
Modern Era, c. 3500 B.C. to c. A.D. 1640**
0–520–04621–8 California $40.00
0–520–04716–8 California pb $12.95

• S. Sambursky
**THE PHYSICAL WORLD OF LATE
ANTIQUITY**
0–691–08476–9 Princeton $21.00
0–691–02410–3 Princeton pb $8.95

The Scientific Revolution

▶ **See also Early Modern Europe**

• Marie Boas
SCIENTIFIC RENAISSANCE, 1450-1630
0–06–130583–9 Harper & Row pb $9.95

• Amos Funkenstein
**THEOLOGY AND THE SCIENTIFIC
IMAGINATION FROM THE MIDDLE
AGES TO THE SEVENTEENTH
CENTURY**
0–691–08408–4 Princeton $47.50

A portable bridge, 1472, from Prints and
People *by A. Hyatt Mayor* (Princeton)

• Thomas Hankins
SCIENCE AND THE ENLIGHTENMENT
0–521–28619–0 Cambridge pb $10.95

• Margaret Jacob
**THE CULTURAL MEANING OF THE
SCIENTIFIC REVOLUTION**
The road from the scientific to the
industrial revolution
0–87722–536–2 Temple $34.95
0–394–32799–3 Knopf pb $10.50

• Robert Mandrou
**FROM HUMANISM TO SCIENCE,
1480-1700**
Intellectual developments and their social
context, from Erasmus to Newton. "The
story is skillfully told and many themes—
literary, theological, philosophical, social
and economic—are woven together into a
convincing narrative"—*Classical Review*
0–14–022079–8 Penguin pb $6.95

Modern Science

• Stephen Bush
**HISTORY OF MODERN SCIENCE: A
Guide to the Second Scientific Revolution,
1800-1950**
0–8138–0883–9 Iowa State $34.95

• Elisabeth Crawford
**THE BEGINNINGS OF THE NOBEL
INSTITUTION: The Science Prizes,
1901-1950**
0–674–05273–0 Cambridge $30.00

• Thomas F. Glick
**THE COMPARATIVE RECEPTION OF
DARWINISM**
The worldwide reaction to Darwin's
Origin of Species
0–226–29977–5 Chicago pb $17.95

• David Knight
THE AGE OF SCIENCE
An excellent introduction to 19th-century
science
0–631–16176–7 Blackwell pb $14.95

• Wolfgang Schivelbusch
**DISENCHANTED NIGHT: The
Industrialization of Light in the Nineteenth
Century**
How electric light changed the nature of
the home and the individual's relation to
society, by a cultural historian of
technology
Translated by Angela Davies
0–520–05903–4 California $22.50

• Trevor Williams
**A SHORT HISTORY OF TWENTIETH-
CENTURY TECHNOLOGY, 1900-1950**
0–19–858159–9 Oxford $29.95

History of Science in America

▶ **See also Topics in American Studies**

• Robert Bruce
**THE LAUNCHING OF AMERICAN
SCIENCE, 1846-1876**
"Spellbinding . . . A tour de force"—*LA
Times*
0–394–55394–2 Knopf $30.00
0–8014–9496–6 Cornell pb $12.95

➤ **FOR OVERSEAS ORDERING INFORMATION, SEE PAGE 1**

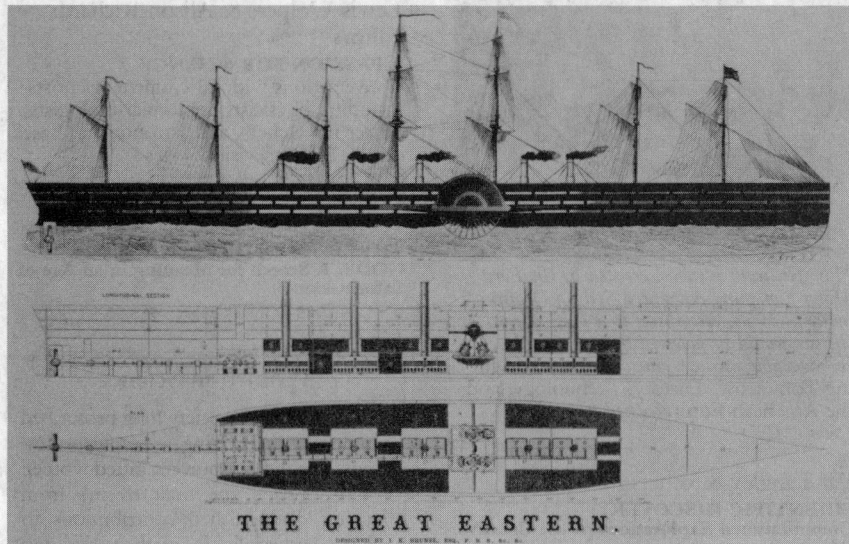

The "Great Eastern" steamship, which laid the first Atlantic telegraph cable, from Prints and People *by A. Hyatt Mayor (Princeton)*

- John Greene
AMERICAN SCIENCE IN THE AGE OF JEFFERSON
0–8138–0102–8 Iowa State pb $15.95

- David Freeman Hawke
NUTS AND BOLTS OF THE PAST: A History of American Technology, 1776-1860
0–06–015901–4 Harper & Row $18.95

- Brooke Hindle & Steven Lubar
ENGINES OF CHANGE: The American Industrial Revolution, 1790-1860
With 200 black-and-white illustrations
0–87474–540–3 Smithsonian $29.95
0–87474–539–X Smithsonian pb $14.95

- Peter Kuznick
BEYOND THE LABORATORY: Scientists as Political Activists in 1930s America
0–226–46583–7 Chicago $29.95

- Carroll W. Purcell, Jr.
TECHNOLOGY IN AMERICA: A History of Individuals and Ideas
0–262–66049–0 MIT pb $9.95

- Nathan & Ida Reingold
SCIENCE IN AMERICA: A Documentary History
0–226–70946–9 Chicago $37.50

Science in Today's Society

- Stewart Brand
THE MEDIA LAB: Inventing the Future at M.I.T.
0–14–009701–5 Penguin pb $10.00

- William Broad & Nicholas Wade
BETRAYERS OF THE TRUTH: Fraud and Deceit in the Halls of Science
0–671–49549–6 Simon & Schuster pb $8.95

- David Dickson
THE NEW POLITICS OF SCIENCE
0–226–14763–0 Chicago pb $14.95

- Alexander Kohn
FALSE PROPHETS: Fraud and Error in Science and Medicine
0–631–16237–2 Blackwell pb $12.95

- Arno Penzias
IDEAS AND INFORMATION: Managing in a High-Tech World
A Nobel Prize-winning physicist ruminates on a wide variety of topics, from the differences between human and machine intelligence and the prospects for artificial intelligence, to microchip technology and the promise of superconducting ceramics
0–393–02649–3 Norton $17.95

- Simon Ramo
THE BUSINESS OF SCIENCE: Winning and Losing in the High-Tech Age
"Demonstrates the degree to which U.S. political and business leaders are today scientifically illiterate. And he points to the actions we as a nation should initiate to overcome what will become an increasingly serious barrier to our economic and social advance"—Robert S. McNamara
0–809032–55–4 Hill & Wang $19.95

Superconductivity

Tom Forester, editor
THE MATERIALS REVOLUTION: Superconductors, New Materials, and the Japanese Challenge
0–262–56043–7 MIT pb $16.95

Robert Hazen
THE BREAKTHROUGH: The Race for the Superconductor
The development of a material that becomes superconducting at the relatively tropical temperature of −297 degrees Fahrenheit, by a member of the scientific team that did it
0–671–65829–8 Summit $18.95

Jonathan Mayo
SUPERCONDUCTIVITY: The Threshold of a New Technology
An introduction to the concept of superconductivity and an overview of recent developments; for the general reader
0–8306–9322–X TAB pb $12.95

Bruce Schechter
THE PATH OF NO RESISTANCE: The Story of the Revolution in Superconductivity
A history of research in superconductivity and a portrait of the people now competing to advance its frontiers
0–671–65785–2 Simon & Schuster $19.95

SCIENTIFIC THOUGHT AND DISCOVERY

Philosophers' efforts to describe the scientific process often reveal as much about the thinker as the thought. In the words of the British astronomer and physicist Arthur Eddington: "We have found a strange footprint on the shores of the unknown. We have devised profound theories, one after another, to account for its origin. At last we have succeeded in reconstructing the creature that made the footprint. And lo! it is our own."

- George Basalla
THE EVOLUTION OF TECHNOLOGY
Argues that Darwin's theory can be applied to the development of human creativity and inventions
0–521–22855–7 Cambridge $32.50
0–521–29681–1 Cambridge pb $10.95

- I. Bernard Cohen
REVOLUTION IN SCIENCE
A thorough historical analysis of revolution as a mechanism for explaining change in scientific theories
0–674–76777–2 Harvard $29.95

- Philip Davis & David Park
NO WAY: The Nature of the Impossible
Explores the challenges, limits, and illusions at the frontiers of scientific discovery
0–7167–1966–5 Freeman pb $10.95

- James Gorman
THE MAN WITH NO ENDORPHINS & Other Reflections on Science
0–14–010359–7 Penguin pb $6.95

- Rom Harre
GREAT SCIENTIFIC EXPERIMENTS: Twenty Experiments That Changed Our View of the World
With well-illustrated summaries for a general audience
0–19–520436–0 Oxford $19.95
0–19–286036–4 Oxford pb $9.95

● Gerald Holton
INTRODUCTION TO CONCEPTS AND THEORIES IN PHYSICAL SCIENCE
0–691–08384–3 Princeton pb $19.95

THE SCIENTIFIC IMAGINATION: Case Studies
0–521–29237–9 Cambridge pb $16.95

THEMATIC ORIGINS OF SCIENTIFIC THOUGHT: Kepler to Einstein
0–674–87747–0 Harvard $25.00
0–674–87746–2 Harvard pb $12.95

● David Hull
SCIENCE AS A PROCESS: An Evolutionary Account of the Social and Conceptual Development of Science
0–226–36050–4 Chicago $39.95

● Thomas Kuhn
BLACK-BODY THEORY AND THE QUANTUM DISCONTINUITY, 1894-1912
0–19–502383–8 Oxford $26.50
0–226–45800–8 Chicago pb $18.95

THE COPERNICAN REVOLUTION: Planetary Astronomy in the Development of Western Thought
0–674–17103–9 Harvard pb $9.95

THE STRUCTURE OF SCIENTIFIC REVOLUTIONS
The classic study of the development and displacement of scientific "paradigms"
0–226–45803–2 Chicago $19.95
0–226–45804–0 Chicago pb $7.95

Examining the record of past research from the vantage of contemporary historiography, the historian of science may be tempted to exclaim that when paradigms change, the world itself changes with them. Led by a new paradigm, scientists adopt new instruments and look in new places. Even more important, during revolutions scientists see new and different things when looking with familiar instruments in places they have looked before. It is rather as if the professional community had been suddenly transported to another planet where familiar objects are seen in a different light and are joined by unfamiliar ones as well. Of course, nothing of quite that sort does occur: there is no geographical transplantation; outside the laboratory everyday affairs usually continue as before. Nevertheless, paradigm changes do cause scientists to see the world of their research-engagement differently. In so far as their only recourse to that world is through what they see and do, we may want to say that after a revolution scientists are responding to a different world.

Thomas Kuhn
THE STRUCTURE OF SCIENTIFIC REVOLUTIONS
0–226–45803–2 Chicago $19.95
0–226–45804–0 Chicago pb $7.95

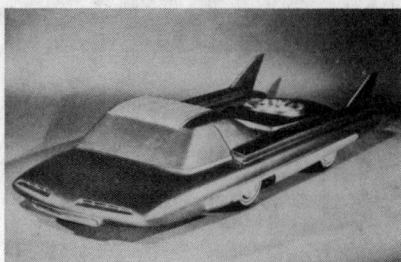

"The Nucleon, a model created by the Ford Motor Company Advanced Styling Department in 1958. According to a press release, the car would be powered by a replaceable, rechargeable nuclear reactor." From Imagining Tomorrow: History, Technology, and the American Future *edited by Joseph J. Corn (MIT)*

● Pat Langley & others
SCIENTIFIC DISCOVERY: Computational Explorations of the Creative Processes
A fascinating study that shows how the discovery process can be described and modeled
0–262–12116–6 MIT $27.50
0–262–62052–9 MIT pb $9.95

● Richard Morris
DISMANTLING THE UNIVERSE: The Nature of Scientific Discovery
0–671–45239–8 Simon & Schuster $14.95
0–671–52818–1 Simon & Schuster pb $6.95

● Philip & Phyllis Morrison
THE RING OF TRUTH: An Inquiry into How We Know What We Know
Companion volume to the public television series, and a richly illustrated guide to the experimental method. "The Morrisons . . . actually do experiments on the foundations of science, and sweep the reader up into an exhilarating adventure"—Carl Sagan
0–394–55663–1 Random House $24.95

● Karl R. Popper
THE LOGIC OF SCIENTIFIC DISCOVERY
A classic work on the philosophy of science
0–06–130576–6 Harper & Row pb $10.95

● Boyce Rensberger
HOW THE WORLD WORKS: A Guide to Science's Greatest Discoveries
0–688–05398–X Morrow $18.95

● Roger Schank
THE CREATIVE ATTITUDE: Learning to Ask and Answer the Right Questions
Thoughts on how creative people think, with recommendations for better problem-solving
0–02–607170–3 Macmillan $22.50

● Renée Weber
DIALOGUES WITH SCIENTISTS AND SAGES: The Search for Unity in Science and Mysticism
Views from America, Europe, India, and Nepal on space, time, matter, energy, life, consciousness, creation, and our place in the scheme of things
0–7102–0655–0 RC&H pb $14.95

● Lewis Wolpert & Alison Richards, editors
A PASSION FOR SCIENCE
Conversations with 13 eminent scientists—including physicists, molecular biologists, cancer researchers, and astronomers. Based on the BBC television series
0–19–854213–5 Oxford $21.95

● Robert Wright
THREE SCIENTISTS AND THEIR GODS: A Search for Meaning in an Age of Information
0–8129–1328–0 Times Books $18.95

Women in Science

Though Western society long proscribed women from entering scientific professions, this did not prevent gifted women (often outside the mainstream) from making distinguished contributions to science, especially in mathematics and astronomy.

Margaret Alic
HYPATIA'S HERITAGE: A History of Women in Science from Antiquity through the Nineteenth Century
0–8070–6731–8 Beacon pb $9.95

Emily Hahn
EVE AND THE APES
Profiles of women other than Goodall and Fossey who have devoted themselves to the study of primates
1–55584–172–4 W&N $17.95

Marilyn Ogilvie
WOMEN IN SCIENCE: Antiquity through the Nineteenth Century—A Biographical Dictionary
0–262–15031–X MIT $27.50

Margaret Rossiter
WOMEN SCIENTISTS IN AMERICA: Struggles and Strategies to 1940
How women scientists coped with social barriers to obtaining a scientific education and participating in science
0–8018–2509–1 Johns Hopkins pb $10.95

REFERENCE

● Robert Bernhardt
THE HOUGHTON MIFFLIN DICTIONARY OF SCIENCE
0–395–48367–0 Houghton Mifflin $19.95

● William Bynum & others, editors
DICTIONARY OF THE HISTORY OF SCIENCE
0–691–02384–0 Princeton pb $14.50

● Bernard Dixon & others
THE ENCYCLOPEDIC DICTIONARY OF SCIENCE
Explains 7,000 terms and concepts
0–8160–2021–3 Facts On File $29.95

- Cesare Emiliani
DICTIONARY OF PHYSICAL SCIENCES
Terms, formulas, and data in physics, chemistry, geology, and cosmology
0–19–503651–4 Oxford $35.00
0–19–503652–2 Oxford pb $19.95

- Harry Judge & others, editors
CONCISE SCIENCE DICTIONARY
0–19–211593–6 Oxford $24.95
0–19–286068–2 Oxford pb $9.95

OXFORD ILLUSTRATED ENCYCLOPEDIA: The Physical World
0–19–869129–7 Oxford $39.95

- McGraw-Hill
McGRAW-HILL CONCISE ENCYCLOPEDIA OF SCIENCE AND TECHNOLOGY
Contains 7300 alphabetically arranged articles, 1600 illustrations, and a 30,000-entry index. An excellent reference book
0–07–045512–0 McGraw-Hill $110.00

McGRAW-HILL DICTIONARY OF SCIENTIFIC AND TECHNICAL TERMS
A 2200-page reference book comprising 100,100 terms and over 117,500 definitions, and over 3000 illustrations
0–07–045270–9 McGraw-Hill $95.00

McGRAW-HILL ENCYCLOPEDIA OF SCIENCE AND TECHNOLOGY
This sixth edition in 20 volumes includes 7700 articles, 2000 of them new or completely revised, covering 77 major subject areas; 15,000 illustrations. "A first-class tool without substitute"—*Scientific American*
0–07–079292–5 McGraw-Hill $1,600.00

- Kenneth Jon Rose
QUICK SCIENTIFIC TERMINOLOGY: A Self-Teaching Guide
0–471–85763–7 John Wiley pb $12.95

- E.B. Uvaroy & Alan Isaacs
FACTS ON FILE DICTIONARY OF SCIENCE
0–8160–1386–1 Facts On File $24.95

- Peter Walker, editor
CHAMBERS SCIENCE AND TECHNOLOGY DICTIONARY: New Edition
1–85296–150–3 Chambers $39.50

Physics

The revolution in physics that began in the 1960s is based upon the discovery that "elementary particles" of matter are not really fundamental constituents after all, but are made up of even more basic particles. Physicists have used these findings to formulate a theory of nuclear forces, and are also making progress toward formulating a supertheory that would explain the four known forces of nature: gravity, electromagnetism, and the strong and weak nuclear forces. Such a unifying theory could not only ex-

plain all the properties of matter, but would also offer astonishing insights into the origin, structure, and evolution of the universe.

Highly technical books intended for professional scientists are not listed here; semi-technical books are identified as such. Most titles can be read by persons with no scientific or technical background. In fact, many readers may be surprised at how much they do understand; scientific popularizers are often skilled and entertaining authors, adept at explaining abstruse ideas.

GENERAL WORKS

- John Barrow
THE WORLD WITHIN THE WORLD
A look at some of the philosophical problems raised by modern physics, by the co-author of *The Anthropic Cosmological Principle*
0–19–851979–6 Oxford $24.95

- K.C. Cole
SYMPATHETIC VIBRATIONS: Reflections on Physics As a Way of Life
Foreword by Frank Oppenheimer
0–553–34234–7 Bantam pb $9.95

- Nick Herbert
FASTER THAN LIGHT: Superluminal Loopholes in Physics
A quantum physicist explains how to take quantum leaps through space—and around Dr. Einstein's theory of relativity
0–453–00604–3 NAL $18.95

- James Jeans
SCIENCE AND MUSIC
0–486–61964–8 Dover pb $5.50

- Russell McCormmach
NIGHT THOUGHTS OF A CLASSICAL PHYSICIST
An absorbing novel set in early 20th-century Europe, concerning a physicist who has trouble coming to terms with new ideas
0–380–56283–9 Avon pb $5.95

- Erwin Schrödinger
WHAT IS LIFE?
Schrödinger was one of the discoverers of quantum mechanics, and this is something of a classic, although much of it relates only marginally to physics. This edition also includes *Mind and Matter*
0–521–09397–X Cambridge pb $12.95

- Frank Wilczek & Betsy Devine
LONGING FOR THE HARMONIES: Themes and Variations for Modern Physics
For scientists and laymen alike. "The explanations have an originality and a simplicity that come about through the deepest knowledge"—*New Yorker*
0–393–02482–2 Norton $19.95

Asimov on Physics

Asimov's books are non-technical accounts of such phenomena as light, sound, heat, electricity, magnetism, motion, and energy.

Isaac Asimov
ASIMOV ON PHYSICS
Asimov's mastery of scientific popularization is equally evident in a collection of essays and articles
0–380–41848–7 Avon pb $4.50

COUNTING THE EONS
0–380–67090–9 Avon pb $3.95

THE ROAD TO INFINITY
0–380–54155–6 Avon pb $2.75

THE SUN SHINES BRIGHT
0–380–61390–5 Avon pb $2.95

UNDERSTANDING PHYSICS
A useful reference work surveying the elements of physics

Volume 1: Light, Magnetism and Electricity
0–451–62304–5 NAL pb $3.95

Volume 2: Motion, Sound and Heat
0–451–62662–1 NAL pb $4.95

Volume 3: The Electron, Proton and Neutron
0–451–62634–6 NAL pb $5.95

VIEW FROM A HEIGHT
0–380–00356–2 Avon pb $2.25

Essays

Physicists turned essayists are often quite entertaining and the following collections are especially recommended:

- Jeremy Bernstein
SCIENCE OBSERVED: Essays Out of My Mind
0–465–07340–9 Basic Books $16.95

- Freeman Dyson
INFINITE IN ALL DIRECTIONS
The world-class mathematician, physicist, biologist, and nuclear arms expert writes on the origins of life, space exploration, Darwin's theory of natural selection, the future of humanity, and much more with a unifying theme: diversity
0–06–039081–6 Harper & Row $19.95
0–06–091569–2 Perennial pb $8.95

- Gerald Feinberg
SOLID CLUES: Quantum Physics, Molecular Biology, and the Future of Science
0–671–62252–8 Simon & Schuster pb $8.95

I do not know what the word "materialism" means. Speaking as a physicist, I judge matter to be an imprecise and rather old-fashioned concept. Roughly speaking, matter is the way particles behave when a large number of them are lumped together. When we examine matter in the finest detail in the experiments of particle physics, we see it behaving as an active agent rather than as an inert substance. Its actions are in the strict sense unpredictable. It makes what appear to be arbitrary choices between alternative possibilities. Between matter as we observe it in the laboratory and mind as we observe it in our own consciousness, there seems to be only a difference in degree but not in kind. If God exists and is accessible to us, then his mind and ours may likewise differ from each other only in degree and not in kind. We stand, in a manner of speaking, midway between the unpredictability of matter and the unpredictability of God.

Freeman Dyson
INFINITE IN ALL DIRECTIONS
0–06–039081–6 Harper & Row $19.95
0–06–091569–2 Perennial pb $8.95

Reference

- John Daintith, editor
DICTIONARY OF PHYSICS
0–06–463560–0 Harper & Row pb $6.95

- Cesare Emiliani
PHYSICAL SCIENCES DICTIONARY
0–19–503651–4 Oxford $35.00
0–19–503652–2 Oxford pb $19.95

- Facts On File
THE FACTS ON FILE DICTIONARY OF PHYSICS: Revised and Expanded
"The most important and the most commonly used terms in the ever-expanding field of physics are explained. Line drawings enhance the text"—*Science News*
0–816018–68–5 Facts On File $19.95

- McGraw-Hill
DICTIONARY OF PHYSICS
Terms drawn from the *McGraw-Hill Dictionary of Scientific and Technical Terms*
0–07–04518–3 McGraw-Hill pb $21.95

M.C. Escher's "Rippled Surface," from Gödel, Escher, Bach *by Douglas Hofstadter* (*Vintage*)

McGRAW-HILL ENCYCLOPEDIA OF PHYSICS
A 1350-page reference containing 763 detailed articles spanning all of classic physics, modern physics, and related areas in mathematics
0–07–045253–9 McGraw-Hill $76.00

- A.M. Prokhorov
ENCYCLOPEDIA OF PHYSICS
Compiled by a Nobel Prize winner in physics. Three thousand entries, 1000 figures, tables and diagrams, covering the latest advances in such areas as superconductivity and superconductors
0–89116–422–7 Hemisphere $140.00

THE PHILOSOPHY OF PHYSICS

Many physicists like to speculate on the metaphysical implications of their theories, and they sometimes do so in a less rigorous manner than in their scientific work. Philosophers—who tend nowadays to be sceptical about metaphysical speculation—more often concern themselves with the logical structure of physical law.

- David Bohm
WHOLENESS AND THE IMPLICATE ORDER
0–7448–0000–5 Methuen pb $11.95

- Herbert Butterfield
THE ORIGINS OF MODERN SCIENCE
0–02–905070–7 Free Press pb $14.95

- Fritjof Capra
THE TAO OF PHYSICS
This book has received so much attention that it can hardly be ignored, but most physicists are skeptical of a connection between physics and Eastern mysticism
0–553–26379–X Bantam pb $4.95

- Nancy Cartwright
HOW THE LAWS OF PHYSICS LIE
Argues that the regularities described by explanatory laws do not actually exist in nature
0–19–824704–4 Oxford pb $12.95

- Paul Davies
GOD AND THE NEW PHYSICS
0–671–47688–2 Simon & Schuster $17.95
0–671–52806–8 Simon & Schuster pb $8.95

- Richard Feynman
THE CHARACTER OF PHYSICAL LAW
0–262–56003–8 MIT pb $6.95

- Richard Gregory
MIND IN SCIENCE: A History of Explanations in Psychology and Physics
0–521–24307–6 Cambridge $42.50

- Werner Heisenberg
PHYSICS AND BEYOND
0–06–131622–9 Harper & Row pb $8.95

PHYSICS AND PHILOSOPHY: The Revolution in Modern Science
0–06–130549–9 Harper & Row pb $8.95

- Henry Margenau
THE NATURE OF PHYSICAL REALITY: A Philosophy of Modern Physics
0–918024–02–1 Ox Bow $26.00
0–918024–03–X Ox Bow pb $14.00

SPACE AND TIME

On close examination, space and time are neither simple nor basic. There is much, in particular, about the nature of time that scientists have yet to understand.

- P.C. Davies
SPACE AND TIME IN THE MODERN UNIVERSE
A bit more difficult than most of the books listed
0–521–29151–8 Cambridge pb $15.95

THE NATURE OF TIME
Like the above title it occupies a kind of no-man's-land between the popular and the semi-technical
0–631–14807–8 Blackwell $19.95

- Stephen Hawking
A BRIEF HISTORY OF TIME: From the Big Bang to Black Holes
"The basic ideas about the origin and fate of the universe can be stated without mathematics in a form that people without scientific education can understand. This is what I have attempted to do in this book"—Stephen Hawking
Introduction by Carl Sagan
0–553–05340–X Bantam $18.95

- Stephen Hawking & G.F.R. Ellis
THE LARGE-SCALE STRUCTURE OF SPACE-TIME
An early work by Hawking published in 1973
0–521–20016–4 Cambridge $82.50
0–521–09906–4 Cambridge pb $29.95

- Richard Morris
TIME'S ARROWS: Scientific Attitudes Toward Time in Western Culture
"Questions of time—and the cosmology that suggests that time was created with the Big Bang—are lucidly explained"—*New Yorker*
0–671–50158–5 Simon & Schuster $18.95
0–671–61766–4 Simon & Schuster pb $8.95

- David Park
THE IMAGE OF ETERNITY: Roots of Time in the Physical World
0–452–00551–5 NAL pb $5.95

- Hans Reichenbach
THE PHILOSOPHY OF SPACE AND TIME
0–486–60443–8 Dover pb $5.95

- G.J. Whitrow
THE NATURAL PHILOSOPHY OF TIME
A comprehensive but sometimes quite technical treatment, covering the role of time in the different sciences
0–19–858215–3 Oxford pb $26.50

The Milky Way Galaxy, with a side view of its rotating disk, from Darkness At Night: A Riddle of the Universe *by Edward Harrison (Harvard)*

RELATIVITY

Most of the following titles will be accessible to the lay reader.

- **Max Born**
EINSTEIN'S THEORY OF RELATIVITY
Probably the most easily understandable of these books
0–486–60769–0 Dover pb $6.00

- **Nigel Calder**
EINSTEIN'S UNIVERSE
A brief but cogent summary
0–670–29076–9 Viking $15.95
0–14–005499–5 Penguin pb $6.95

- **Eric Chaisson**
RELATIVELY SPEAKING: Relativity, Black Holes, and the Fate of the Universe
0–393–02536–5 Norton $18.95

- **Albert Einstein**
THE COLLECTED PAPERS OF ALBERT EINSTEIN: The Early Years, 1879-1902
The first of approximately 40 projected volumes containing over 14,000 documents drawn from the Einstein archives
Edited by John Stachel
0–691–08407–6 Princeton $52.50

THE COLLECTED PAPERS OF ALBERT EINSTEIN: Volume 2
0–691–08526–9 Princeton $85.00

THE PRINCIPLE OF RELATIVITY
0–486–60081–5 Dover pb $4.50

- **Martin Gardner**
THE RELATIVITY EXPLOSION: A Lucid Account of Why Quasars, Pulsars, Black Holes and the New Atomic Clocks Are Vindicating Einstein's Revolutionary Theory
0–394–72104–7 Random House pb $6.95

- **Robert Geroch**
GENERAL RELATIVITY FROM A TO B
Somewhat difficult
0–226–28864–1 Chicago pb $7.95

- **Stanley Goldberg**
RELATIVITY AND COSMOLOGY
0–06–043572–0 Harper & Row pb $13.50

UNDERSTANDING RELATIVITY: Origin and Impact of a Scientific Revolution
0–8176–3150–X Birkhauser $27.50

- **Delo Mook & Thomas Vargish**
INSIDE REALITY
Special and general relativity skillfully explained by a physicist and a professor of literature
0–691–08472–6 Princeton $30.00

- **Jayant Narlikar**
THE LIGHTER SIDE OF GRAVITY
0–7167–1343–8 W.H. Freeman $20.95
0–7167–1344–6 W.H. Freeman pb $12.95

- **Bertrand Russell**
THE ABC OF RELATIVITY
Still one of the best popularizations
0–451–62381–9 NAL pb $4.50

- **Julian Schwinger**
EINSTEIN'S LEGACY
"It is particularly gratifying that the subject's intricacies, including glimpses of non-Euclidian and Riemannian geometries, and the theory's early successes . . . are so well conveyed here in simple language. Altogether, this well printed and pleasingly illustrated book is an ideal gift for the curious non-expert"—*Nature*
0–7167–5011–2 W.H. Freeman $32.95

- **Clifford Will**
WAS EINSTEIN RIGHT?: Putting General Relativity to the Test
"Of course Einstein was right! But this book tells you why. This is the best popular book describing the experimental basis for general relativity"—Heinz Pagels
0–465–09088–5 Basic Books $18.95
0–465–09087–7 Basic Books pb $8.95

- **Anthony Zee**
AN OLD MAN'S TOY: Gravity at Work and Play in Einstein's Universe
A look at gravity, using as a point of departure the simple toy constructed from a heavy ball, spring, and a broomstick that was given to Einstein on his last birthday
0–02–633440–2 Macmillan $19.95

Perspectives on Einstein

The centennial of Einstein's birth in 1979 gave rise to symposia on his life and work whose proceedings were published in book form. Of these, the following can be recommended to the general reader:

A.P. French, editor
EINSTEIN: A Centenary Volume
0–674–24230–0 Harvard $25.00
0–674–24231–9 Harvard pb $12.95

Gerald Holton & Yehuda Elkana, editors
ALBERT EINSTEIN, HISTORICAL AND CULTURAL PERSPECTIVES: The Centennial Symposium in Jerusalem
0–691–08299–5 Princeton $47.00
0–691–02383–2 Princeton pb $13.50

QUANTUM MECHANICS

Physicists are still arguing about the interpretation and philosophical implications of the theory of subatomic phenomena. No matter what interpretation one accepts, it seems impossible to avoid certain abiding questions about the nature of physical reality and the role of the observer.

- **Barbara Cline**
THE GHOST IN THE ATOM: A Discussion of the Mysteries of Quantum Physics
Slightly more difficult than the others listed here. "A useful introduction to a variety of ideas and approaches about understanding quantum mechanics"—*Nature*
0–521–30790–2 Cambridge $32.50
0–521–31316–3 Cambridge pb $12.95

THE MEN WHO MADE A NEW PHYSICS: Physicists and the Quantum Theory
A very readable history of the discovery of quantum mechanics
0–226–11027–3 Chicago pb $11.95

- **Richard Feynman**
QED: The Strange Theory of Light and Matter
0–691–08388–6 Princeton $25.00

- **Arthur Fine**
THE SHAKY GAME: Einstein, Realism, and the Quantum Theory
A comprehensive account of Einstein's realism and his opposition to quantum theory, also examines the realism-

---

antirealism debate in philosophy of science, and proposes a bold and original solution to the "natural ontological attitude" and its emphasis on the actual practice of the sciences
0-226-24947-6 Chicago pb $10.95

● Henry Folse, Jr.
THE PHILOSOPHY OF NIELS BOHR: Framework of Complementarity
The most widely accepted approach to quantum mechanics was developed by Bohr and his colleagues at the Institute for Theoretical Physics in Copenhagen
0-444-86914-X North-Holland $46.50
0-444-86938-7 Elsevier pb $19.50

● A.P. French & P.J. Kennedy, editors
NIELS BOHR: A Centenary Volume
0-674-62415-7 Harvard $29.50
0-674-62416-5 Harvard pb $14.95

● George Gamow
THIRTY YEARS THAT SHOOK PHYSICS: The Story of Quantum Theory
Another excellent historical survey
0-486-24895-X Dover pb $4.95

● John Gribbin
IN SEARCH OF THE BIG BANG: Quantum Physics and Cosmology
0-553-34617-2 Bantam pb $10.95

IN SEARCH OF SCHRODINGER'S CAT: Quantum Physics and Reality
0-553-34253-3 Bantam pb $9.95

● Nick Herbert
QUANTUM REALITY
"Takes up the question of reality in the puzzling light of quantum theory and Bell's theorem. Be prepared for a roller-coaster ride that will stretch your mind and leave you gasping"—Isaac Asimov
0-385-23569-0 Anchor pb $9.95

Niels Bohr (photo by Erik Petersen, Politikens Presse Foto), from Niels Bohr: The Man, His Science, and the World They Changed *by Ruth Moore (MIT)*

● Anthony Hey & Patrick Walters
THE QUANTUM UNIVERSE
A colorfully illustrated explanation of quantized properties
0-521-26744-7 Cambridge $47.50
0-521-31845-9 Cambridge pb $16.95

● Max Jammer
THE PHILOSOPHY OF QUANTUM MECHANICS: The Interpretations of Quantum Mechanics in Historical Perspective
Although highly technical at times, this is the most comprehensive survey
0-471-43958-4 John Wiley $54.95

● Heinz Pagels
THE COSMIC CODE: Quantum Physics As the Law of Nature
"A reliable guide for the non-mathematical reader across the higher ridges of physical theory"—Philip Morrison
0-671-24802-2 Simon & Schuster $17.50
0-553-24625-9 Bantam pb $4.95

● Eugene Wigner
SYMMETRIES AND REFLECTIONS
A collection of essays, some more technical than others, that includes Wigner's celebrated writings on quantum mechanics and consciousness
0-918024-16-1 Ox Bow pb $10.00

● Anthony Zee
FEARFUL SYMMETRY: The Search for Beauty in Modern Physics
"A masterpiece of popular science exposition that should not be missed . . . It is the best popular book on the role of symmetry in quantum physics"—Heinz Pagels
0-02-633430-5 Macmillan $25.00
0-02-040911-7 Collier pb $9.95

PARTICLE PHYSICS, COSMOLOGY, AND THE "NEW" PHYSICS

Theoretical research in cosmology and particle physics are intertwined. Particle physicists speculate about something that they have never observed, but whose existence is required by accepted theories. Energy of the magnitude necessary to create such particles existed in the Big Bang, the explosion that took place shortly after the creation of the universe. Similarly, the cosmologist—who cannot expect to see his theories confirmed in the laboratory—attempts to understand their consequences in relation to what is known about subnuclear particles. Of the books dealing with this combined field, the following place more emphasis on particle physics:

● Nigel Calder
THE KEY TO THE UNIVERSE
0-14-005065-5 Penguin pb $8.95

● Richard E. Carrigan, Jr. & W. Peter Trower, editors
PARTICLE PHYSICS IN THE COSMOS: Readings from Scientific American
0-7167-1919-3 W.H. Freeman pb $9.95

● Frank Close & others
THE PARTICLE EXPLOSION
Interesting for its descriptions of numerous experiments, unlike most popular science books which emphasize theory. "A pictorial feast"—*Nature*
0-19-851965-6 Oxford $35.00

● P.C.W. Davies, editor
THE NEW PHYSICS
An accessible collection with contributions from 18 leading international physicists
0-521-30420-2 Cambridge $39.50

● Sheldon Glashow & Ben Bova
INTERACTIONS: A Journey Through the Mind of a Particle Physicist and the Matter of the World
0-446-51315-6 Random House $19.95

● Andrew Pickering
CONSTRUCTING QUARKS: A Sociological History of Particle Physics
Though somewhat technical, long sections can be read by someone with no mathematical background. Pickering is interesting for his heretical view that quarks (the theoretical constituents of protons and neutrons) were "invented" rather than "discovered"
0-226-66798-7 Chicago $37.50
0-226-66799-5 Chicago pb $19.95

● Michael Riordan
THE HUNTING OF THE QUARK
The 20-year search for the quark, in a lively recounting by a participant
0-671-50466-5 Simon & Schuster $21.95
0-671-64884-5 Simon & Schuster pb $9.95

● Christine Sutton
THE PARTICLE CONNECTION: The Most Exciting Scientific Chase since DNA and the Double Helix
0-671-49659-X Simon & Schuster $16.95

● Gary Taubes
NOBLE DREAMS: Power, Deceit and the Ultimate Experiment
Searching for the W and Z particles with Carlo Rubbia at the European Center for Nuclear Research
0-394-54503-6 Random House $19.95

● Sharon Traweek
BEAMTIMES AND LIFETIMES: The World of High Energy Physics
A cultural anthropologist looks at contemporary experimental physics and its practitioners
0-674-06347-3 Harvard $20.00

● James Trefil
FROM ATOMS TO QUARKS: The Strange World of Particle Physics
0-684-16484-1 Scribners $12.95
0-684-17460-X Scribners pb $8.95

TO ORDER BOOKS AS GIFTS, SEE PAGE 1

- Peter Watkins
THE STORY OF THE W AND Z
A firsthand account of the experiments that proved the existence of the W and Z bosons
0–521–31875–0 Cambridge pb $13.95

- Steven Weinberg
THE DISCOVERY OF SUBATOMIC PARTICLES
0–7167–1488–4 W.H. Freeman $32.95

The Search for a "Supertheory"

The following books range somewhat more widely over both cosmology and particle physics, discussing their interconnections as well as the search for a "supertheory" that would explain the four known forces of nature.

- Paul Davies
SUPERFORCE: The Search for a Grand Unified Theory of Nature
0–671–47685–8 Simon & Schuster $17.95

- P.C.W. Davies & J. Brown, editors
SUPERSTRINGS: A Theory of Everything?
Superstring theory explained—followed by the pro and con views of leading theorists and critics
0–521–35741–1 Cambridge pb $10.95

> Everything in the natural world is a little bit fuzzy because of Heisenberg's uncertainty principle and the basic ideas of quantum mechanics. If you've got some extra dimensions but they are so tiny that the fuzziness of everyday life blurs everything out on a size which is bigger than the size of the extra dimensions, then you would only notice the extra dimensions with extraordinary efforts. The idea is that if the extra dimensions are so tiny, then you just don't notice them.
>
> I might say that the idea of extra dimensions might sound a little bit strange to anyone who hasn't studied physics. Anyone who has gone into physics professionally, will know that there are many things that are a lot stranger than extra dimensions. General relativity is strange, quantum mechanics is strange, antimatter is strange. All these things are strange but true. Compared to a lot of things that have come true in physics in the past, extra dimensions are not such a radical departure.
>
> Edward Witten in
>
> **P.C.W. Davies & J. Brown, editors**
> **SUPERSTRINGS: A Theory of Everything?**
> 0–521–35741–1 Cambridge pb $10.95

- A.J. Leggett
THE PROBLEMS OF PHYSICS
Is the universe infinite? Do we live in the only possible universe? What is it made of? Why does it have one time and three space dimensions—or does it?
0–19–219205–1 Oxford $17.95
0–19–289186–3 Oxford pb $10.95

- Richard Morris
THE NATURE OF REALITY: The Universe After Einstein
The new physics: its history, theories, experimental basis, and impact on scientists
0–07–043278–3 McGraw-Hill $17.95
0–374–52124–7 Noonday pb $8.95

- Barry Parker
THE SEARCH FOR A SUPERTHEORY: From Atoms to Superstrings
"This story is, indeed, physics for poets"—*NY Times*
0–306–42702–8 Plenum $21.95

- Fred Alan Wolf
PARALLEL UNIVERSES: Worlds Within Our Present Senses
How recent advances in theoretical physics predict the existence of universes that are similar to—and perhaps even duplicates of—our own. "A remarkable bridge between the scientific intelligence and the creative imagination"—Norman Cousins
0–671–66091–8 Simon & Schuster $19.95

HISTORY OF PHYSICS

- Isaac Asimov
THE HISTORY OF PHYSICS
0–8027–0751–3 Walker $29.95

- Jeremy Bernstein
THE TENTH DIMENSION: An Informal History of High Energy Physics
0–07–005017–1 McGraw-Hill pb $9.95

- I. Bernard Cohen
THE BIRTH OF A NEW PHYSICS
The "new" physics of Galileo, Kepler, and Newton—not the 1980s
0–393–01944–2 Norton $17.95
0–393–30045–5 Norton pb $7.95

- Robert Crease & Charles Mann
THE SECOND CREATION: Makers of the Revolution in Twentieth-Century Physics
"A magnificent history of modern physics"—*San Francisco Examiner*
0–02–084550–2 Macmillan pb $11.95

- Albert Einstein & Leopold Infeld
THE EVOLUTION OF PHYSICS
0–671–20156–5 Simon & Schuster pb $10.95

- Rupert Hall
FROM GALILEO TO NEWTON
0–486–24227–7 Dover pb $7.95

- P.M. Harman
ENERGY, FORCE AND MATTER: The Conceptual Development of Nineteenth-Century Physics
A history of 19th-century "classical" physics
0–521–28812–6 Cambridge pb $13.95

- Stephen Hawking & W. Israel, editors
THREE HUNDRED YEARS OF GRAVITATION
Eleven papers by world-class cosmologists and physicists to commemorate the 300th anniversary of the publication of Newton's *Principia*
0–521–34312–7 Cambridge $69.50

- Alex Keller
THE INFANCY OF ATOMIC PHYSICS: Hercules in His Cradle
Early developments culminating in the discovery of X-rays, uranic rays and radioactivity, radium, and inert gases
0–19–853904–5 Oxford $29.95

- Daniel Kevles
THE PHYSICISTS
Less a history of physics than of the physics community in the 20th century. Issues such as funding and politics are explored. "The vivid descriptions of the personalities involved make it a living tapestry celebrating the great record of intellectual achievement"—I.I. Rabi
0–394–46631–4 Knopf $15.95

- Arthur I. Miller
IMAGERY IN SCIENTIFIC THOUGHT: Creating Twentieth-Century Physics
0–8176–3196–8 Birkhauser $27.50
0–262–63104–0 MIT pb $10.95

- Abraham Pais
INWARD BOUND: Of Matter and Forces in the Physical World
A history of the physics of the very small: the atom, the nucleus, the constituent particles. Mathematically sophisticated but also anecdotal and readable
0–19–851971–0 Oxford $35.00
0–19–851997–4 Oxford pb $17.95

- Ed Regis
WHO GOT EINSTEIN'S OFFICE: Eccentricity and Genius at the Institute for Advanced Study
"I cannot praise this extraordinary book too highly. It signals the sudden entrance of Regis into the first rank of today's science writers"—Martin Gardner
0–201–12065–8 Addison-Wesley $17.95
0–201–12278–2 Addison-Wesley pb $10.95

- Emilio Segre
FROM FALLING BODIES TO RADIO WAVES: Classical Physicists and Their Discoveries
0–7167–1482–5 W.H. Freeman pb $13.95

FROM X-RAYS TO QUARKS: Modern Physicists and Their Discoveries
0–7167–1147–8 W.H. Freeman pb $14.95

• C.P. Snow
THE PHYSICISTS
Introduction by W. Cooper
0–316–80221–2 Little, Brown $15.95

• Nathan Spielberg & Bryon Anderson
SEVEN IDEAS THAT SHOOK THE UNIVERSE
A non-mathematical introduction to such basic ideas as entropy, relativity, and quantum theory
0–471–85974–5 John Wiley $24.95

• Stephen Toulmin & June Goodfield
THE ARCHITECTURE OF MATTER
0–226–80840–8 Chicago pb $14.00

The following historically significant texts have been included because of their accessibility to the lay reader.

• Aristotle
ARISTOTLE'S PHYSICS
Translated by Richard Hope
0–8032–5093–2 Nebraska pb $6.25
ARISTOTLE'S PHYSICS
Volume 1: Books 1 & 2
Translated by W. Charleton
0–19–872026–2 Oxford pb $16.95
Volume 2: Books 3 & 4
Translated by Edward Hussey
0–19–872069–6 Oxford pb $15.95

• Galileo Galilei
DIALOGUES CONCERNING TWO NEW CHIEF WORLD SYSTEMS, PTOLEMAIC AND COPERNICAN
0–520–00450–7 California pb $12.95

• Isaac Newton
OPTICKS
Foreword by Albert Einstein
0–486–60205–2 Dover pb $8.95

• Jefferson Weaver
THE WORLD OF PHYSICS: A Small Library of the Literature of Physics from Antiquity to the Present
A three-volume collection covering virtually all fields of physics
0–671–64216–2 Simon & Schuster (set) $90.00
Volume 1
0–671–49926–2 Simon & Schuster $29.95
Volume 2
0–671–49930–0 Simon & Schuster $29.95
Volume 3
0–671–49931–9 Simon & Schuster $29.95

BIOGRAPHIES AND AUTOBIOGRAPHIES

• Luis Alvarez
ALVAREZ: Adventures of a Physicist
Diary of a Nobel laureate frequently in the scientific spotlight
0–465–00115–7 Basic Books $19.95

• Jeremy Bernstein
THE LIFE IT BRINGS: One Physicist's Beginnings
"An ironic, penetrating, and anecdotally vivid look at the early years of an American physicist and of modern American physics. Even readers who, like me, know less than nothing about the subject, should be fascinated"—Alison Lurie
0–89919–470–2 Ticknor & Fields $16.95

• A.P. French & P.J. Kennedy, editors
NIELS BOHR: A Centenary Volume
The creative work, ideals, and life of the man who cracked the quantum code, as remembered by his students
0–674–62415–7 Harvard $29.50
0–674–62416–5 Harvard pb $14.95

• Freeman Dyson
DISTURBING THE UNIVERSE: A Life in Science
0–06–090771–1 Harper & Row pb $8.95

• Jeremy Bernstein
EINSTEIN
0–14–004317–9 Penguin pb $5.95

• Ronald Clark
EINSTEIN: The Life and Times
0–380–01159–X Avon pb $5.95

• Albert Einstein
ALBERT EINSTEIN: Philosopher-Scientist
Contains Einstein's own autobiographical notes, the only memoir he ever wrote, among other writings on his work
Edited by Paul A. Schilpp
0–87548–133–7 Open Court $35.95
0–87548–286–4 Open Court pb $17.95

• Banesh Hoffmann & Helen Dukas
ALBERT EINSTEIN, CREATOR AND REBEL
0–452–25703–4 NAL pb $6.95

• Abraham Pais
SUBTLE IS THE LORD: The Science and Life of Albert Einstein
Fills many gaps, including Einstein's interest in philosophy, his concern with Jewish destiny, and his opinions of great figures from Newton to Freud
0–19–853907–X Oxford $35.00
0–19–520438–7 Oxford pb $14.95

Albert Einstein and J. Robert Oppenheimer (photo courtesy Niels Bohr Library), from Looking the Tiger in the Eye: Confronting the Nuclear Threat *by Ronald Bee and Carl Feldbaum (Harper & Row)*

• L. Pearce Williams
MICHAEL FARADAY
0–306–80299–6 Da Capo pb $13.95

• Richard Feynman with Ralph Leighton
SURELY YOU'RE JOKING, MR. FEYNMAN!: Adventures of a Curious Character
Autobiographical musings by the late world-famous physicist who was probably the only Nobel Prize winner ever judged mentally deficient by the US Army. "Anyone who can read it without laughing is bad crazy"—LA Times
0–393–01921–7 Norton $18.95
0–553–34668–7 Bantam pb $8.95
WHAT DO YOU CARE WHAT OTHER PEOPLE THINK?: Further Adventures of a Curious Character
0–393–02659–0 Norton $17.95

• Stillman Drake
GALILEO
A short biography that raises questions about the history of science and its relation to religion and philosophy
0–19–287526–4 Oxford pb $5.95
GALILEO AT WORK: His Scientific Biography
0–226–16227–3 Chicago pb $9.95

• Maurice A. Finocchiaro, translator & editor
THE GALILEO AFFAIR: A Documentary History
0–520–06662–6 California pb $12.95

• Pietro Redondi
GALILEO: Heretic
"Redondi places before us not just Galileo but the entire milieu that surrounded the dispute of the 'new science' during a crucial twenty-year period of the 17th century"—Italo Calvino
Translated by Raymond Rosenthal
0–691–08451–3 Princeton $9.95

• Gale Christianson
IN THE PRESENCE OF THE CREATOR: Isaac Newton and His Times
0–02–905190–8 Free Press $19.95

• Richard Westfall
NEVER AT REST: A Biography of Isaac Newton
A masterful rendering, from his absorption with Christian chronology to his tenure as master of the British Mint
0–521–27435–4 Cambridge pb $24.95

• Peter Goodchild
ROBERT OPPENHEIMER: Shatterer of Worlds
0–88064–021–9 Fromm pb $10.95

• Rudolf Peierls
BIRD OF PASSAGE: Recollections of a Physicist
"Anybody with some interest in the way scientists live, feel and think, should read this book. They will be richly rewarded and entertained"—Times Higher Education Supplement
0–691–08390–8 Princeton $42.50
0–691–02416–2 Princeton pb $12.50

- John Rigden
RABI: Scientist and Citizen
"This excellent work is the first full biography of Professor Rabi, the scientist who epitomizes the passing of the torch of physics from Europe to the U.S. almost half a century ago"—*Rosalyn Yalow*
0–465–06792–1 Basic Books $21.95

- David Wilson
RUTHERFORD: Simple Genius
0–262–23115–8 MIT $37.50

Astronomy

- Phillippe de la Cotardière & others
ASTRONOMY
A beautifully illustrated introduction
0–8160–1219–9 Facts On File $24.95

- Meir Degani
ASTRONOMY MADE SIMPLE
0–385–08854–X Doubleday pb $5.95

- David DeVorkin
PRACTICAL ASTRONOMY: Lectures on Time, Place, and Space
0–87474–359–1 Smithsonian pb $12.95

- Martin Harwit
COSMIC DISCOVERY: The Search, Scope and Heritage of Astronomy
0–465–01426–3 Basic Books $26.50
0–262–58068–3 MIT pb $10.95

- Nigel Henbest & Michael Marten
THE NEW ASTRONOMY
"Easy reading . . . some of the best color photographs of the heavens I have ever seen"—*Forbes*
0–521–25683–6 Cambridge $39.50
0–521–31057–1 Cambridge pb $14.95

- William Liller & Ben Mayer
THE CAMBRIDGE ASTRONOMY GUIDE: An Introduction to Practical Astronomy
For amateur photographers and astronomists
0–521–25778–6 Cambridge $24.95

- Bernard Lovell & F. Graham Smith
THE GUIDE TO MODERN ASTRONOMY
A rich introduction with 70 black-and-white photos and 100 line drawings
0–521–32004–6 Cambridge $34.50

- Patrick Moore
1989 YEARBOOK OF ASTRONOMY
An annual summary of findings and a schedule of what the next year will bring to astronomers, with monthly star charts for both hemispheres. This is the 27th edition of a "must" for amateur and professional astronomers alike
0–393–02633–7 Norton $19.95

Voyager I photo of the far side of Saturn

- Carl Sagan
COSMOS
Based on the TV series; with 250 color illustrations
0–345–33135–4 Ballantine pb $4.95

THE SOLAR SYSTEM

- John Brandt & Robert Chapman
INTRODUCTION TO COMETS
0–521–27218–1 Cambridge pb $17.95

- Eric Burgess
URANUS AND NEPTUNE: The Distant Giants
These two planets—plus Pluto—and their satellites described, with 58 line drawings and 42 photos
0–231–06492–6 Columbia $29.95

- Peter Cadogan
THE MOON: Our Sister Planet
0–521–23684–3 Cambridge $80.00
0–521–28152–0 Cambridge pb $32.50

- Clark Chapman
PLANETS OF ROCK AND ICE: From Mercury to the Moons of Saturn
0–684–17484–7 Scribners $13.95

- Joel Davis
FLYBY: The Interplanetary Odyssey of Voyager 2
Introduction by Isaac Asimov
0–689–11657–8 Atheneum $19.95

- Robert Dodd
THUNDERSTORMS AND SHOOTING STARS
"An excellent, up-to-date discussion of the nature and origin of meteorites"—*New Scientist*
0–674–89138–4 Harvard pb $11.95

- James Elliot & Richard Kerr
RINGS: Discoveries from Galileo to Voyager
0–262–05031–5 MIT $22.50
0–262–55013–X MIT pb $8.95

- Kathleen Mark
METEORITE CRATERS
A nontechnical history of how scientists came to recognize craters as the result of meteoritic impact
0–8165–0902–6 Arizona $24.95

- Harry Y. McSween, Jr.
METEORITES AND THEIR PARENT PLANETS
A comprehensive and readable introduction
0–521–32431–9 Cambridge $19.95

- Brian O'Leary & J. Kelley Beatty, editors
THE NEW SOLAR SYSTEM
Introduction by Carl Sagan
0–933346–26–3 Sky $22.95

- Carl Sagan
COMET
0–394–54908–2 Random House $27.00

- David Seargent
COMETS: Vagabonds of Space
0–385–17869–7 Doubleday $15.95

- Roman Smoluchowski
THE SOLAR SYSTEM
0–7167–1492–2 W.H. Freeman $29.95

- Jonathan Weiner
PLANET EARTH
0–553–05096–6 Bantam $24.95
0–553–34358–0 Bantam pb $14.95

- Fred Whipple
THE MYSTERY OF COMETS
0–87474–968–9 Smithsonian $24.95
0–87474–971–9 Smithsonian pb $12.50

ORBITING THE SUN: Planets and Satellites of the Solar System
0–674–64126–4 Harvard pb $7.95

- Laurel Wilkening
COMETS
0–8165–0769–4 Arizona $29.95

STARS

- Isaac Asimov
THE EXPLODING SUNS: The Secrets of the Supernovas
0–525–24323–2 Dutton $18.45
0–451–62481–5 NAL pb $4.50

QUASAR, QUASAR, BURNING BRIGHT
0–380–44610–3 Avon pb $2.25

- Robert Burnham
THE STAR BOOK
"An exceedingly practical, durable, and inexpensive tool which newcomers to observational astronomy will find useful. Experienced users will also praise its utility"—*Journal of the Association of Lunar and Planetary Observers*
0–521–25833–2 Cambridge pb $9.95

- David Clark
THE QUEST FOR SS433
0–670–80388–X Viking $15.95
0–14–008996–9 Penguin pb $6.95

- Martin Cohen
IN DARKNESS BORN: The Story of Star Formation
0–521–26270–4 Cambridge $19.95

- Donald A. Cooke
THE LIFE AND DEATH OF STARS
0–517–55268–X Crown $29.95

- Edward Harrison
DARKNESS AT NIGHT: A Riddle of the Universe
Why don't the billions of stars out there make the night sky bright as day? "It is refreshing to consider that so grand a matter as the boundaries of the universe can be investigated with only the unaided human eye"—Timothy Ferris
0–674–19270–2 Harvard $25.00

- Rudolf Kippenhahn
ONE HUNDRED BILLION SUNS: The Birth, Life, and Death of the Stars
Translated by Jean Steinberg
0–465–05263–0 Basic Books $25.00
0–465–05262–2 Basic Books pb $12.95

- Laurence Marschall
THE SUPERNOVA STORY
All about 1987A and earlier supernovas. "Everything you want to know about supernovas is here"—Heinz Pagels
0–306–42955–1 Plenum $22.95

- Simon Mitten
DAYTIME STAR: The Story of Our Sun
0–684–16840–5 Scribners $14.95
0–684–17829–X Scribners pb $6.95

- Walter Sullivan
BLACK HOLES
0–446–32288–1 Warner pb $4.50

In the twentieth century we have grown accustomed to the idea that our vision slices through space and time. When we gaze at the night sky, looking far out in space, we are fully aware that we see the apparitions of long ago. We find it difficult to understand why Descartes and other philosophers once viewed with alarm the prospect of splicing space and time together. Yet even to us, accustomed to the idea of looking out in space and back in time, the thought that at the horizon of the visible universe lies the creation, unveiled and open to inspection, comes as a shock.

Edward Harrison
DARKNESS AT NIGHT: A Riddle of the Universe
0–674–19270–2 Harvard $25.00

GALAXIES

- Richard Berendzen
MAN DISCOVERS THE GALAXIES
0–231–05826–8 Columbia $34.00
0–231–05827–6 Columbia pb $14.50

- Bart & Priscilla Bok
THE MILKY WAY
0–674–57503–2 Harvard $25.00

- Timothy Ferris
GALAXIES
A beautifully illustrated account
0–941434–01–X ST&C $27.50
0–941434–02–8 ST&C pb $18.95

- Paul Hodge
GALAXIES
0–674–34065–5 Harvard $22.50

- Paul Hodge, editor
UNIVERSE OF GALAXIES
Readings from *Scientific American*
0–7167–1675–5 W.H. Freeman $20.95
0–7167–1676–3 W.H. Freeman pb $10.95

- Roman Smoluchowski & others, editors
THE GALAXY AND THE SOLAR SYSTEM
0–8165–0982–4 Arizona $29.95

- R. Brent Tully
NEARBY GALAXIES CATALOG
A companion to the *Atlas of Nearby Galaxies*, providing information on the 2367 galaxies mapped in the atlas, including positions, morphological descriptions, sizes, luminosities, red shifts, and characteristics of each galaxy's environment
0–521–35299–1 Cambridge $49.00

- R. Brent Tully & Richard J. Fisher
ATLAS OF NEARBY GALAXIES
0–521–30136–X Cambridge $59.50

- James Wray
COLOR ATLAS OF GALAXIES
0–521–32236–7 Cambridge $79.50

THE UNIVERSE AND COSMOLOGY

"The most incomprehensible thing about the Universe is that it is comprehensible."—Albert Einstein

- John Barrow & Joseph Silk
THE LEFT HAND OF CREATION: The Origin and Evolution of the Expanding Universe
0–465–03895–6 Basic Books $17.95
0–465–03897–2 Basic Books pb $7.95

- John Barrow & Frank Tipler
THE ANTHROPIC COSMOLOGICAL PRINCIPLE
Does the fundamental structure of the universe depend on the existence of intelligent observers? "The erudition displayed here is simply awesome"—*Physics Today*
0–19–851949–4 Oxford $29.95
0–19–282147–4 Oxford pb $15.95

- Marcia Bartusiak
THURSDAY'S UNIVERSE: A Report from the Frontier on the Origin, Nature, and Density of the Universe
"Bartusiak entered the universe of research at the frontiers of astronomy and cosmology and returned with a gem of a book. I recommend it"—Heinz Pagels
0–8129–1202–0 Times Books $19.95
1–55615–153–5 Tempus pb $8.95

- John Boslough
STEPHEN HAWKING'S UNIVERSE: An Introduction to the Most Remarkable Scientist of Our Time
0–688–03530–2 Morrow $12.95
0–688–06270–9 Morrow pb $7.95

- William Calvin
THE RIVER THAT FLOWS UPHILL: A Journey from the Big Bang to the Big Brain
The log of an expedition down the Colorado River through the Grand Canyon
0–87156–719–9 Sierra Club pb $12.95

- Eric Chaisson
COSMIC DAWN: The Origins of Matter and Life
0–316–13590–9 Little, Brown $18.95

- Nathan Cohen
GRAVITY'S LENS: Views of the New Cosmology
Features 100 black-and-white photos and two four-page color inserts. An imaginative history of astronomy, methods of observing the universe, and the universe's future
0–471–63282–1 John Wiley $19.95

- James Cornell, editor
BUBBLES, VOIDS AND BUMPS IN TIME: The New Cosmology
A "state of the universe" report from six leading cosmologists
0–521–35297–5 Cambridge $22.50

- P.C. Davies
THE ACCIDENTAL UNIVERSE
0–521–24212–6 Cambridge $24.95
0–521–28692–1 Cambridge pb $12.95

➤ **FOR OVERSEAS ORDERING INFORMATION, SEE PAGE 1**

• Paul Davies
THE EDGE OF INFINITY
The origin and ultimate end of the
universe. "Science at its abstract,
speculative best"—Jeremy Bernstein
0–671–46062–5 Simon & Schuster pb $7.95

• P.C.W. Davies & J. Brown, editors
SUPERSTRINGS: A Theory of Everything?
The Superstring theory explained, through
the pro and con views of leading theorists
and critics
0–521–35741–1 Cambridge pb $9.95

• Timothy Ferris
COMING OF AGE IN THE MILKY WAY
"An exhilarating, wide-ranging journey
that takes us from the shores of the
Mediterranean, where the second-century
astronomer Claudius Ptolemy fashioned his
creaky celestial spheres, to modern-day
research institutes, where theorists
contemplate this and other universes
bubbling out of a quantum vacuum"—*NY
Times*
0–688–05889–2 Morrow $19.95
0–385–26326–0 Doubleday pb $9.95

**THE RED LIMIT: The Search for the Edge
of the Universe**
Introduction by Carl Sagan
0–688–01836–X Morrow pb $12.95

• Harald Fritzsch
**THE CREATION OF MATTER: The
Universe from Beginning to End**
A history of the universe and modern
cosmology for the general reader. "One of
the clearest explanations of the equivalence
of matter and energy I've encountered"—
Timothy Ferris
0–465–01447–X Basic Books pb $9.95

• G.W. Gibbons & others, editors
THE VERY EARLY UNIVERSE
0–521–31677–4 Cambridge $24.95

• George Greenstein
**THE SYMBIOTIC UNIVERSE: An
Unorthodox Look at the Origin of the
Cosmos and the Development of Life**
"Essentially, Greenstein has condensed the
massive work of John Barrow and Frank
Tipler on the anthropic principle to a more
manageable, popular format"—*New
Scientist*
0–688–07604–1 Morrow $18.95

• John Gribbin
**IN SEARCH OF THE BIG BANG:
Quantum Physics and Cosmology**
0–553–34258–4 Bantam pb $9.95

**THE OMEGA POINT: The Search for the
Missing Mass and Ultimate Fate of the
Universe**
If there's as much stuff out there as today's
astronomers think there is, where is it?
And is there enough of whatever it is
(wherever it happens to be) to cause the
cosmos to do an about turn and collapse
back onto itself?
0–553–34515–X Bantam pb $8.95

• Edward Harrison
MASKS OF THE UNIVERSE
A history of cosmology, from ancient
myths to the present
0–07–026839–8 McGraw-Hill $19.95
0–02–020980–0 Macmillan pb $9.95

• Jean Heidmann
**THE COSMIC BLUEPRINT: New
Discoveries in Nature's Creative Ability to
Order the Universe**
Is there scientific evidence for a higher
intelligence at work in the cosmos?
0–671–67561–3 Simon & Schuster pb $8.95

COSMIC ODYSSEY
About the universe: past, present, and
future
Translated by Simon Mitton
0–521–34377–1 Cambridge $18.95

• Michio Kaku & Jennifer Trainer
**BEYOND EINSTEIN: The Cosmic Quest
for the Theory of the Universe**
0–553–34349–1 Bantam pb $9.95

• Neil McAleer
THE MIND-BOGGLING UNIVERSE
0–385–23040–0 Doubleday $16.95
0–385–23039–7 Doubleday pb $8.95

• Paolo Maffei
THE UNIVERSE IN TIME
A trip through time, from the fireball of
the Big Bang 15 million years ago,
through the present, to several conceivable
futures, observing the life cycle of the stars
and planetary systems and geological and
biological evolution on earth along the
way
0–262–13236–2 MIT $25.00

• Patrick Moore
THE UNFOLDING UNIVERSE
From the longtime editor of the *Yearbook
of Astronomy*
0–517–54836–4 Crown $17.95

• Patrick Moore & Iain Nicolson,
editors
THE UNIVERSE
0–02–922110–2 Macmillan $50.00

• Jayant Narlikar
THE PRIMEVAL UNIVERSE
Speculation, based on the latest
information, about the universe in its
earliest history
0–19–219229–9 Oxford $29.95

• Heinz Pagels
**PERFECT SYMMETRY: The Search for
the Beginning of Time**
0–671–46548–1 Simon & Schuster $18.95
0–553–24000–5 Bantam pb $4.95

• Barry Parker
**CREATION: The Story of the Origin and
Evolution of the Universe**
"A detailed look at the universe in all its
mind-boggling aspects as well as personal
glimpses of some of the people who have
built our understanding"—Arno Penzias
0–306–42952–7 Plenum $22.95

**EINSTEIN'S DREAM: The Search for a
Unified Theory of the Universe**
0–306–42343–X Plenum $18.95

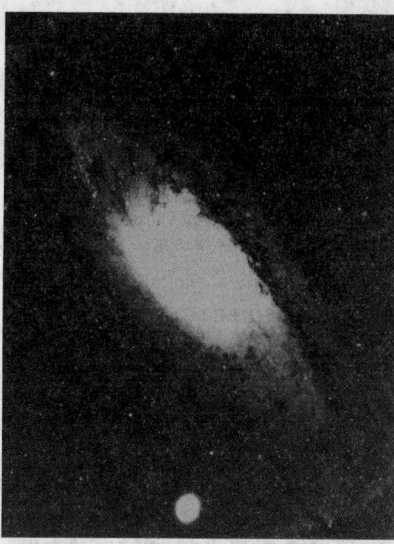

*The Andromeda Nebula, a large spiral galaxy
similar to our own, two million light-years
away, from* Darkness at Night: A Riddle of
the Universe *by Edward Harrison (Harvard/
photo courtesy of Kitt Peak National
Observatory)*

• Byron Preiss, editor
THE UNIVERSE
0–553–05227–6 Bantam $29.95

• Richard Preston
**FIRST LIGHT: The Search for the Edge of
the Universe**
"A remarkably readable and illuminating
account of researchers at southern
California's Mount Palomar Observatory
. . . [where] they seek quasars, believed to
be the most luminous and most distant
objects in the universe"—*NY Times*
0–87113–200–1 Atlantic Monthly $18.95
0–452–26170–8 NAL pb $8.95

• Hubert Reeves
**ATOMS OF SILENCE: An Exploration of
Cosmic Evolution**
Introduction by Victor F. Weisskopf
0–262–18112–6 MIT $22.50
0–262–68049–1 MIT pb $8.95

• Joseph Silk
**THE BIG BANG: The Creation and
Evolution of the Universe**
0–7167–1084–6 W.H. Freeman $19.95
0–7167–1085–4 W.H. Freeman pb $13.95

• James Trefil
**THE DARK SIDE OF THE UNIVERSE:
Searching for the Outer Limits of the
Cosmos**
An account of efforts to find the dark
matter that many scientists think makes up
at least 90 percent of the universe
0–684–18795–7 Scribners $12.95
0–385–26212–4 Doubleday pb $9.95

**THE MOMENT OF CREATION: Big
Bang Physics from Before the First
Millisecond to the Present Universe**
0–02–096770–5 Collier pb $6.95

• Wallace & Karen Tucker
THE DARK MATTER: Contemporary Science's Quest for the Mass Hidden in Our Universe
"The scientific reporting is sound, and the ongoing enigma of the dark matter, with its haunting implication that we have scarcely begun to comprehend how the cosmos is put together, comes shining (or darkening) through"—*NY Times*
0–688–06112–5 Morrow $16.95

• Steven Weinberg
THE FIRST THREE MINUTES: A Modern View of the Origin of the Universe
"One comes away from his book feeling not only that the idea of an original cosmic explosion is not crazy but that any other theory appears scientifically irrational"—Jeremy Bernstein
0–465–02435–1 Basic Books $14.95
0–465–02436–X Basic Books pb $7.95

ASTRONOMICAL OBSERVATION

• Martin Cohen
IN QUEST OF TELESCOPES
0–521–24989–9 Cambridge $13.95

• James Cornell & John Carr, editors
INFINITE VISTAS: New Tools for Astronomy
0–684–18287–4 Scribners $18.95

• Nigel Henbect, editor
OBSERVING THE UNIVERSE
A *New Scientist* magazine guide
0–85520–727–2 Blackwell $24.95
0–85520–726–4 Blackwell pb $9.95

• Richard Hirsh
GLIMPSING AN INVISIBLE UNIVERSE: The Emergence of X-Ray Astronomy
0–521–25121–4 Cambridge $44.50
0–521–31232–9 Cambridge pb $17.95

• K. Krisciunas
ASTRONOMICAL CENTERS OF THE WORLD
Observatories ancient and recent, their major accomplishments, and the astronomers who made them famous
0–521–30278–1 Cambridge $24.95

• W.T. Sullivan, editor
THE EARLY YEARS OF RADIO ASTRONOMY: Reflections Fifty Years After Jansky's Discovery
Reports—some specialized, some informal—of the highlights of radio astronomy
0–521–25485–X Cambridge $42.50

• Wallace Tucker & Riccardo Giacconi
THE X-RAY UNIVERSE
0–674–96285–0 Harvard $20.00
0–674–96286–9 Harvard pb $7.95

• Wallace & Karen Tucker
THE COSMIC INQUIRERS: Modern Telescopes and Their Makers
0–674–17435–6 Harvard $20.00
0–674–96286–9 Harvard pb $7.95

• G.L. Verschuur
THE INVISIBLE UNIVERSE—REVEALED
0–387–96280–8 Springer $19.95

Amateur Astronomy

• Richard Berry
DISCOVERING THE STARS: Star Watching Using the Naked Eye, Binoculars, or a Telescope
0–517–56529–3 Harmony pb $9.95

• Michael Covington
ASTROPHOTOGRAPHY FOR THE AMATEUR
"An up-to-date book for the budding astrophotographer, and a reference book that should be in your library"—*The Reflector*
0–521–25391–8 Cambridge $27.95

• Peter Duffet-Smith
PRACTICAL ASTRONOMY WITH YOUR CALCULATOR
0–521–35629–6 Cambridge $44.95
0–521–35699–7 Cambridge pb $19.95

• David J. Eicher & others
THE UNIVERSE FROM YOUR BACKYARD: A Guide to Deep-Sky Objects from Astronomy Magazine
Over 150 color and black-and-white photos and 116 telescopic sketches accompany the text
0–521–36299–7 Cambridge $24.95

• Terry Holt
THE UNIVERSE NEXT DOOR: A Complete Guide to Exploring the Skies and Understanding What You See
0–684–18358–7 Scribners $24.95

• Will Kyselka & Ray Lanternman
NORTH STAR TO SOUTHERN CROSS
0–8248–0411–2 Hawaii $10.00
0–8248–0419–8 Hawaii pb $4.95

• Svend Laustsen & others
EXPLORING THE SOUTHERN SKY: A Pictorial Atlas from the European Southern Observatory
Ninety color and 147 black-and-white photos of the southern sky, including pictures of Supernova 1987A and Halley's Comet and a four-foot panoramic poster of the Milky Way
0–387–17735–3 Springer $39.00

• J.M. Levitt & Roy K. Marshall
STAR MAPS FOR BEGINNERS
0–671–63676–6 Simon & Schuster pb $7.95

• David Levy
VARIABLE STAR OBSERVING
Includes a seasonal guide to observing the night sky in all latitudes
0–521–32113–1 Cambridge $19.95

• Patrick Moore
EXPLORING THE NIGHT SKY WITH BINOCULARS
0–521–30756–2 Cambridge $19.95

• Lloyd Motz & Carol Nathanson
THE CONSTELLATIONS: An Enthusiast's Guide to the Night Sky
Ideal for beginners, with 150 photographs
Introduction by Isaac Asimov
0–385–17600–7 Doubleday $24.95

• James Muirden
THE AMATEUR ASTRONOMER'S HANDBOOK
0–06–181622–1 Harper & Row $19.45
ASTRONOMY WITH A SMALL TELESCOPE
0–13–049941–2 Prentice-Hall $18.95
HOW TO USE AN ASTRONOMICAL TELESCOPE
0–671–47744–7 Linden $21.95

• Jack Newton & Philip Teece
THE CAMBRIDGE DEEP SKY ALBUM
0–521–25668–2 Cambridge $24.95
THE GUIDE TO AMATEUR ASTRONOMY
All about observing with binoculars, telescopes, and cameras
0–521–34028–4 Cambridge $24.95

• Jay Pasachoff
A FIELD GUIDE TO THE STARS AND PLANETS
0–395–34641–X Houghton Mifflin $17.95
0–395–34835–8 Houghton Mifflin pb $12.95

• Leslie Peltier
LESLIE PELTIER'S GUIDE TO THE STARS: Exploring the Sky with Binoculars
A handbook for beginners, with star charts, maps, and drawings. "Does the job simply and well"—*Sky & Telescope*
0–521–33595–7 Cambridge pb $12.95

• Fred W. Price
THE MOON OBSERVER'S HANDBOOK
What to look for, how to make observations, and how to record them
0–521–33500–0 Cambridge $27.50

• I. Ridpath & W. Tirion
THE MONTHLY SKY GUIDE
Help for beginning gazers in finding their way around the night sky
0–521–33921–9 Cambridge pb $7.95

• Brad Wallis & Robert Provin
A MANUAL OF ADVANCED CELESTIAL PHOTOGRAPHY
This technical handbook for the serious astro-photographer includes detailed discussions of photographic optics, instrument design, techniques at the telescope, films and developers, advanced darkroom methods, sensitometry and film hyper-sensitization, and more
0–521–25553–8 Cambridge $39.00

• Charles Whitney
WHITNEY'S STARFINDER
A slightly larger than pocket-size handbook that comes with a removable disk (locator wheel) showing every prominent star in the sky
0–394–72717–7 Knopf pb $12.95

SPACE EXPLORATION

▶ See also Topics in American Studies

• David Baker
CONQUEST: A History of Space Achievements from Science Fiction to the Shuttle
0–947703–00–4 Salem House pb $12.95

• Peter Bond
HEROES IN SPACE: From Gagarin to Challenger
The first book to cover the entire era of manned space flight
0–631–15349–7 Blackwell $24.95

• Ben Bova
WELCOME TO MOON BASE
0–345–32859–0 Ballantine pb $9.95

• Michael Collins
LIFTOFF: The Story of America's Adventure in Space
0–8021–3188–3 Grove pb $10.95

• Henry S. Cooper, Jr.
BEFORE LIFT-OFF: The Making of a Space Shuttle Crew
0–8018–3524–0 Johns Hopkins $18.95

• Ben Finney & Eric Jones, editors
INTERSTELLAR MIGRATION AND THE HUMAN EXPERIENCE
Twenty-five scholars examine the technical and human side of our future beyond Earth. "New and important in bringing together for the first time the points of view of astronomers, space scientists, anthropologists, and humanists"—Freeman J. Dyson
0–520–05898–4 California pb $9.95

• Louis Friedman
STARSAILING: Solar Sails and Interstellar Travel
The history and physics of solar sailing, a fuel-free form of space travel, from the director of the solar sailing project at the Jet Propulsion Laboratory
0–471–62593–0 John Wiley pb $9.95

• Harry Hurt III
FOR ALL MANKIND: Twenty-four Men Went to the Moon, This Is Their Story
Based on interviews with Apollo astronauts
0–87113–170–6 Atlantic Monthly $22.95

• Kevin Kelley, editor
THE HOME PLANET
One hundred and fifty color photographs of Earth taken from space, selected from Soviet and American archives, with text by astronauts from 18 countries, adapted from interviews and air-to-ground transmissions
0–201–15197–9 Addison-Wesley $39.95

• Richard Lewis
CHALLENGER: The Final Voyage
"A riveting account—not only of what happened to Challenger and why, but how the story was told"—LA Times
0–231–06490–X Columbia $29.95

• Thomas McDonough
SPACE: The Next 25 Years
0–471–85671–1 John Wiley $17.95

• Walter McDougall
THE HEAVENS AND THE EARTH: A Political History of the Space Program
0–465–02888–8 Basic Books pb $11.95

• National Commission on Space
PIONEERING THE SPACE FRONTIER: The Report of the National Commission on Space
0–553–34314–9 Bantam pb $14.95

• Robert Powers
MARS: Our Future on the Red Planet
0–395–35371–8 Houghton Mifflin $17.95

• Ron Schick & Julia Van Haaften
THE VIEW FROM SPACE: American Astronaut Photography, 1962-1972
More than 120 images from Projects Mercury, Gemini, and Apollo—along with reminiscences from the astronauts who took them
0–517–56082–8 Crown $30.00

• Harry L. Shipman
HUMANS IN SPACE: 21st Century Frontiers
Prospects for the future
0–306–43171–8 Plenum $22.95

• Joseph Trento, Jr.
PRESCRIPTION FOR DISASTER: From the Glory of Apollo to the Betrayal of the Shuttle
0–517–56415–7 Crown $18.95

• Werner von Braun & others
SPACE TRAVEL: A History
Revised in 1985
0–06–181898–4 Harper & Row $29.95

EXTRATERRESTRIAL LIFE

• Joseph Angelo
THE EXTRATERRESTRIAL ENCYCLOPEDIA: Our Search for Life in Outer Space
Four hundred entries cover recent information on such subjects as astrobiology, black holes, interstellar travel, robotics in space, and Voyagers I and II
0–87196–764–2 Facts On File $29.95

• Joseph Baugher
ON CIVILIZED STARS: The Search for Intelligent Life in Outer Space
0–13–634411–9 Prentice-Hall pb $9.95

• John Billingham & others
LIFE IN THE UNIVERSE
0–262–52062–1 MIT pb $15.00

• Ronald N. Bracewell
THE GALACTIC CLUB: Life in Outer Space
0–393–95022–0 Norton pb $3.95

• Henry S. Cooper, Jr.
THE SEARCH FOR LIFE ON MARS
0–03–046166–9 Henry Holt $10.95
0–03–059818–4 Henry Holt pb $6.95

A 17th-century illustration showing distant galaxies covering the whole sky, from Thomas Wright's "An Original Theory or New Hypothesis of the Universe," in Darkness at Night: A Riddle of the Universe *by Edward Harrison (Harvard)*

• Michael Crowe
THE EXTRATERRESTRIAL LIFE DEBATE, 1750 to 1900: The Idea of a Plurality of Worlds
0–521–26305–0 Cambridge $59.50

• Thomas McDonough
THE SEARCH FOR EXTRATERRESTRIAL INTELLIGENCE: Listening for Life in the Cosmos
"There simply is no better book on the subject"—Frederick Pohl
0–471–85671–1 John Wiley $17.95

• Edward Regis, editor
EXTRATERRESTRIALS: Science and Alien Intelligence
Fourteen essays—pro and con. "In terms of dazzling ideas per square inch, almost every page has something worth quoting"—Byte
0–521–34852–8 Cambridge pb $12.95

HISTORY OF ASTRONOMY

• Anthony Aveni
SKYWATCHERS OF ANCIENT MEXICO
0–292–77557–1 Texas $30.00
0–292–77578–4 Texas pb $17.50

• Anthony Aveni, editor
ARCHAEOASTRONOMY IN THE NEW WORLD: American Primitive Astronomy
0–521–24731–4 Cambridge $37.50

• Kenneth Brecher & Michael Fiertag, editors
ASTRONOMY OF THE ANCIENTS
Introduction by Philip Morrison
0–262–52070–2 MIT pb $9.95

☞ **FOR ALL OTHER INQUIRIES, PLEASE CALL (212) 333-7900**

- James Cornell
THE FIRST STARGAZERS: An Introduction to the Origins of Astronomy
0–684–16799–9 Scribners $15.95

- Evan Hadingham
EARLY MAN AND THE COSMOS
0–8027–0745–9 Walker $22.50
0–8061–1919–5 Oklahoma pb $12.95

- D.B. Herrmann
THE HISTORY OF ASTRONOMY FROM HERSCHEL TO HERTZSPRUNG
0–521–25733–6 Cambridge $24.00

- E.C. Krupp
ECHOES OF THE ANCIENT SKIES: The Astronomy of Lost Civilizations
0–06–015101–3 Harper & Row $19.45
0–452–00679–1 NAL pb $8.95

Thomas Kuhn
THE COPERNICAN REVOLUTION: Planetary Astronomy in the Development of Western Thought
An outstanding account of the impact of the revolution in astronomy by the author of *The Structure of Scientific Revolutions*
0–674–17100–4 Harvard $20.00
0–674–17103–9 Harvard pb $7.95

- Bartel Van Der Waerden
SCIENCE AWAKENING 2: The Birth of Astronomy
A beautiful work covering the Egyptian, Babylonian, and Greek periods
0–19–519753–4 Oxford $45.00

- Albert Van Helden
MEASURING THE UNIVERSE: Cosmic Dimensions from Aristarchus to Halley
0–226–84881–7 Chicago $30.00
0–226–84882–5 Chicago pb $8.95

Biography

- Joseph Ashbrook
THE ASTRONOMICAL SCRAPBOOK: Skywatchers, Pioneers, and Seekers in Astronomy
0–521–30045–2 Cambridge $22.95

- John Banville
KEPLER
0–87923–438–5 Godine $14.95
0–87923–527–6 Godine pb $8.95

- Gale E. Christiansen
THIS WILD ABYSS: The Story of the Men Who Made Modern Astronomy
0–02–905660–8 Free Press pb $9.95

- Arthur Koestler
THE WATERSHED: A Biography of Johannes Kepler
Foreword by John Durston
0–8191–4339–1 University Press pb $13.00

REFERENCE

- Joseph A. Angelo, Jr.
FACTS ON FILE DICTIONARY OF SPACE TECHNOLOGY
Explains more than 1500 terms
0–87196–583–6 Facts On File $24.95

- Jean Audouze & Guy Israel
THE CAMBRIDGE ATLAS OF ASTRONOMY
Updated to include the 1986 appearance of Halley's Comet, Voyager's encounter in the same year with Uranus, 1987A Supernova, and more. Over 1100 photos and illustrations
0–521–36360–8 Cambridge $90.00

- Geoffrey Briggs & Frederic Taylor
THE CAMBRIDGE PHOTOGRAPHIC ATLAS OF THE PLANETS
"The text, written for the layman, is a delight"—*Philadephia Inquirer*
0–521–31058–X Cambridge $15.95

- John Cox & Richard Monkhouse
3-D STAR MAPS: A View of the Universe in Three Dimensions
Includes 20 full-color photos and drawings, 27 3-D maps, 27 black-and-white maps, and 2 sets of 3-D glasses
0–06–016131–0 Harper & Row $15.95

- Valerie Illingworth, editor
FACTS ON FILE DICTIONARY OF ASTRONOMY
A clear, complete, and well-organized dictionary
0–8160–1357–8 Facts On File $19.95
0–8160–1892–8 Facts On File pb $12.95

- McGraw-Hill
THE McGRAW-HILL ENCYCLOPEDIA OF ASTRONOMY
Over 200 alphabetically arranged articles covering the latest advances, discoveries, models, and theories, and topics ranging from astronomical spectroscopy and the Big Bang theory to planetary physics, space probes, and stellar evolution
0–07–045251–2 McGraw-Hill $76.00

- Patrick Moore
PATRICK MOORE'S A-Z OF ASTRONOMY
0–393–30505–8 Norton pb $13.50

- Patrick Moore, editor
THE INTERNATIONAL ENCYCLOPEDIA OF ASTRONOMY
0–517–56179–4 Crown $40.00

- Adrian Room
DICTIONARY OF ASTRONOMICAL NAMES
The stories behind the names of stars, major features of the moon and other celestial bodies, the largest of the asteroids, and a number of nicknamed nebulae and star clusters
0–415–01298–8 RC&H $22.50

CARL SAGAN: Recommended Books on Astronomy

George Abelle & Barry Singer, editors
SCIENCE AND THE PARANORMAL
0–684–16655–0 Scribners $17.95
0–684–17820–6 Scribners pb $12.95

Timothy Ferris
THE RED LIMIT: The Search for the Edge of the Universe
0–688–01836–X Morrow pb $12.95

Edward Harrison
COSMOLOGY: The Science of the Universe
0–521–22981–2 Cambridge $37.50

Stephen Hawking
A BRIEF HISTORY OF TIME: From the Big Bang to Black Holes
0–553–05340–X Bantam $18.95

Robert Jastrow
RED GIANTS AND WHITE DWARFS
0–393–85002–1 Norton $14.95
0–446–32193–1 Warner pb $3.95

William Kaufmann
BLACK HOLES AND WARPED SPACETIME
0–7167–1153–2 Freeman pb $12.95

Byron Preiss, editor
THE UNIVERSE
0–553–05227–6 Bantam $27.95

Carl Sagan
COSMOS
0–345–33135–4 Ballantine pb $4.95

Carl Sagan & Ann Druyan
COMET
0–394–54908–2 Random House $27.00
0–671–61917–9 Pocket pb $14.95

James Trefil
SPACE, TIME, INFINITY: The Smithsonian Views of the Universe
0–394–54843–4 Pantheon $16.45

Chemistry

There are few books on chemistry for the general reader. That situation, of course, could change—chaos theory on the best-seller lists today, perhaps quantum chemistry tomorrow. Biochemistry, on the other hand, is a popular topic; for books in this area see Life Sciences.

- P.W. Atkins
MOLECULES
A *Scientific American* book
0–7167–5019–8 W.H. Freeman $32.95

- Jim Berger
CLEAR AND SIMPLE CHEMISTRY
0–317–37777–9 Simon & Schuster pb $6.95

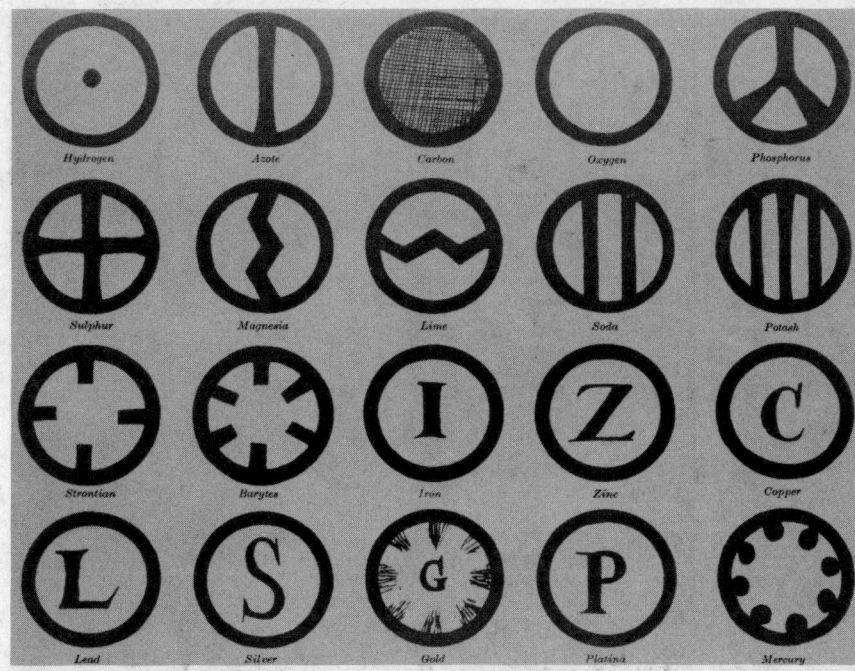

Dalton's symbols of the elements

- Richard Graham
  THE PROBLEMS OF CHEMISTRY
  0–19–219191–8 Oxford $24.95
  0–19–289172–3 Oxford pb $8.95

- A.O. Hall
  CHEMISTRY FOR BEGINNERS
  0–435–64310–X Heinemann pb $7.50

- Fred C. Hess
  CHEMISTRY MADE SIMPLE
  Revised by Arthur L. Thomas
  0–385–18850–1 Doubleday pb $6.95

Textbooks

- Raymond Chang
  GENERAL CHEMISTRY
  0–394–34122–8 Random House $41.95

- John W. Hill
  CHEMISTRY FOR CHANGING TIMES
  0–02–355010–4 Macmillan $41.50

- Karen Timberlake
  CHEMISTRY, Fourth Edition
  0–06–163409–3 Harper & Row $24.50

Reference

- John Daintith
  THE FACTS ON FILE DICTIONARY OF CHEMISTRY
  0–816018–66–9 Facts On File $19.95

- Arthur Godman
  THE LONGMAN ILLUSTRATED DICTIONARY OF CHEMISTRY
  0–582–55550–7 Longman $8.95

- McGraw-Hill
  McGRAW-HILL DICTIONARY OF CHEMISTRY
  Derived from *The McGraw-Hill Dictionary of Scientific and Mechnical Terms*
  0–07–045420–5 McGraw-Hill $42.00

  McGRAW-HILL ENCYCLOPEDIA OF CHEMISTRY
  Includes 790 articles and 800 illustrations
  0–07–045484–1 McGraw-Hill $76.00

History of Chemistry

- Frederic L. Holmes
  LAVOISIER AND THE CHEMISTRY OF LIFE: An Exploration of Scientific Creativity
  0–299–09980–6 Wisconsin $38.50
  0–299–09984–^ Wisconsin pb $15.95

- Aaron Ihde
  THE DEVELOPMENT OF MODERN CHEMISTRY
  A comprehensive history by an eminent authority
  0–486–64235–6 Dover pb $15.95

- Bernard Jaffee
  CRUCIBLES: The Story of Chemistry from Ancient Alchemy to Nuclear Fission
  Fourth, revised edition. Brief biographies, primarily of physical chemists
  0–486–23342–1 Dover pb $6.95

The Life Sciences

Until the 19th century most biologists tallied and described plants and animals, turning to philosophy and religion to explain almost everything they observed. The modern trend, by contrast, has been toward the experimental and analytical, not only in biology but in anatomy, natural history, and other fields as well.

A major landmark of modern biology was the discovery that living things are composed of large molecules. This led to the discovery of cellular respiration, energy metabolism, the functions of DNA and RNA, and the factors that promote cell growth and cancer. At the same time, geneticists created a formal explanation of how characteristics are transmitted from one generation to the next, how mutations occur, and how evolution might proceed. Neurobiologists located those regions of the brain and nervous system which are responsible for carrying out the tasks of motion, sensation, and cognition.

Many of these discoveries were made possible by the invention of new techniques. Whatever the object of study, the development of antibiotics, histological stains, the electron microscope, and X-ray crystallography permitted new and deeper observations and provided new answers to old questions.

Virology, cell biology, neurochemistry, and oncology are all younger than the century. Unfortunately, many descriptions of these disciplines are highly technical and unsuitable for the nonspecialist. Readers interested in immunology, cell biology, or embryology, for instance, are perhaps better off reading accounts of scientists who worked in those fields. The essays of such biologists as Peter Medawar, Lewis Thomas, and Stephen Jay Gould can also be highly recommended.

GENERAL WORKS

- Renato Dulbecco
  THE DESIGN OF LIFE
  The state of the biological sciences, from a Nobel laureate and professor at the Salk Institute
  0–300–03791–0 Yale $39.50

- Patty Kreikemeier-Gaffney & Charles Wert
  CLEAR AND SIMPLE BIOLOGY
  0–671–54786–0 Simon & Schuster pb $6.95

- Alexander Rosenberg
  THE STRUCTURE OF BIOLOGICAL SCIENCE
  0–521–25566–X Cambridge $39.50
  0–521–27561–X Cambridge pb $14.95

- Lewis Thomas
  Thomas' brief essays on biology are unfailingly accessible and entertaining.

THE LIVES OF A CELL: Notes of a Biology Watcher
0–14–004743–3 Penguin pb $5.95

THE MEDUSA AND THE SNAIL: More Notes of a Biology Watcher
0–553–25913–X Bantam pb $3.95

Textbooks

- Karen Arms & Pamela Camp
  BIOLOGY
  0–03–003644–5 Saunders $46.75

- Jeffrey Baker & Garland E. Allen
  THE STUDY OF BIOLOGY
  0–201–10180–7 Addison-Wesley $47.50

- William Keeton & James Gould
  BIOLOGICAL SCIENCE
  0–393–95385–8 Norton $44.95

- John Kimball
  BIOLOGY
  0–201–10245–5 Addison-Wesley $47.50

Reference

- Adrian Friday & David Ingram, editors
  THE CAMBRIDGE ENCYCLOPEDIA OF LIFE SCIENCES
  Includes illustrations, photographs, and diagrams
  0–521–25696–8 Cambridge $52.50

- D. Lapedes
  McGRAW-HILL DICTIONARY OF THE LIFE SCIENCES
  0–07–045262–8 McGraw-Hill $42.00

- Oxford University Press
  DICTIONARY OF BIOLOGY
  0–446–38150–0 Warner pb $7.95

  CONCISE DICTIONARY OF BIOLOGY
  0–19–866144–4 Oxford $17.95

- Elizabeth Toothill, editor
  THE FACTS ON FILE DICTIONARY OF BIOLOGY
  Short and simple definitions for 31,000 common terms
  0–87196–510–0 Facts On File $19.95
  0–87196–637–9 Facts On File $5.95

THE ORIGINS OF LIFE

One of the most intriguing questions suggested by the theory of evolution is when the first living organisms arose. Although Pasteur's experiments with fermentation toppled the doctrine of spontaneous generation, that idea has returned in a subtle form in the Soviet scientist Oparin's suggestion that organic chemicals in earth's early seas may have formed a proto-organism by "happy chance." Other theories for the advent of life are almost as varied as life itself.

- Isaac Asimov
  BEGINNINGS: The Story of Origins—of Mankind, Life, the Earth, the Universe
  0–8027–1003–4 Walker $19.95

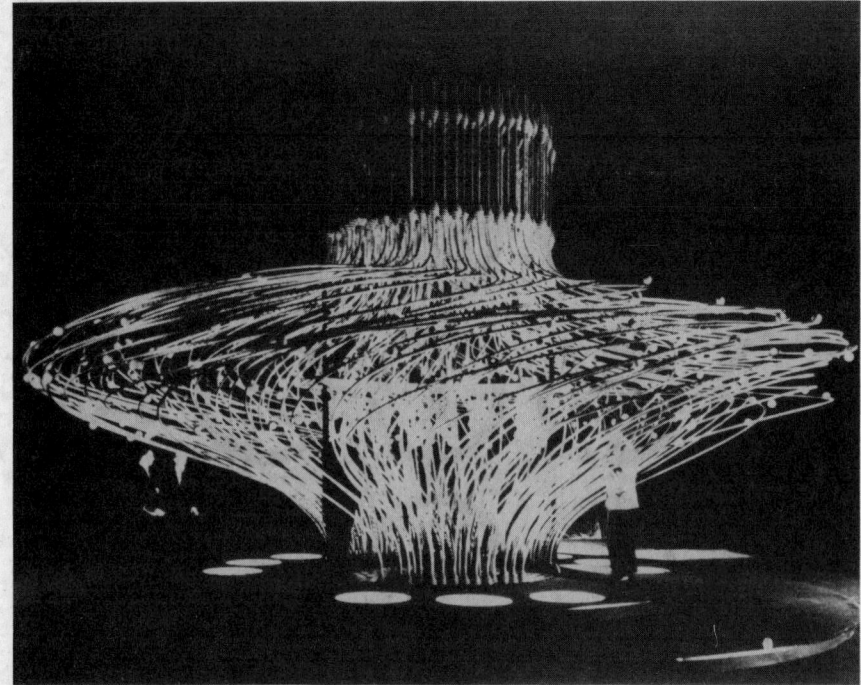

Model of a gene enlarged over 250,000 times, from Medicine: An Illustrated History *by Albert S. Lyons, M.D., and R. Joseph Pertrucelli II, M.D. (Abradale Press)*

- A.G. Cairns-Smith
  GENETIC TAKEOVER AND THE MINERAL ORIGINS OF LIFE
  Proposes that life and the genetic code might have first originated in the lattices of crystals
  0–521–23312–7 Cambridge $42.50

  SEVEN CLUES TO THE ORIGIN OF LIFE: A Scientific Detective Story
  An entertaining overview of the dominant theories
  0–521–33793–3 Cambridge pb $8.95

- A.G. Cairns-Smith & H. Hartman, editors
  CLAY MINERALS AND THE ORIGIN OF LIFE
  The continuation of a fascinating argument
  0–521–32408–4 Cambridge $34.50

- Francis Crick
  LIFE ITSELF: Its Origin and Nature
  Controversial ideas from the Nobel laureate and codiscoverer of the structure of DNA
  0–671–25563–0 Simon & Schuster pb $7.95

- William Day
  GENESIS ON PLANET EARTH: The Search for Life's Beginnings
  0–300–02954–3 Yale $40.00
  0–300–03202–1 Yale pb $13.95

- Sidney Fox
  THE EMERGENCE OF LIFE: Darwinian Evolution from the Inside
  Molecular evolution and the origin of life, from a leading researcher
  0–465–01925–0 Basic $17.95

- George Greenstein
  THE SYMBIOTIC UNIVERSE: An Unorthodox Look at the Origin of the Cosmos and the Development of Life
  0–688–07604–1 Morrow $18.95

- H. Hartman & others, editors
  THE SEARCH FOR THE UNIVERSAL ANCESTORS: The Origins of Life
  0–86542–328–8 Blackwell pb $17.95

- Lynn Margulis
  EARLY LIFE
  0–86720–005–7 Jones & Bartlett pb $15.00

  SYMBIOSIS IN CELL EVOLUTION: Life and Its Environment on the Early Earth
  A controversial theory
  0–7167–1255–5 W.H. Freeman $32.95
  0–7167–1256–3 W.H. Freeman pb $18.95

- Andrew Scott
  THE CREATION OF LIFE: Past, Future, Alien
  Where life came from, what our newfound ability to alter it might lead to, and what life elsewhere might be like. "An introduction for the non-scientist who is intrigued by the puzzles surrounding the origins of life"—*Nature*
  0–631–16336–0 Blackwell pb $12.95

- Robert Shapiro
  ORIGINS: A Skeptic's Guide to the Creation of Life on Earth
  A general book on various creation theories
  0–671–45939–2 Simon & Schuster $17.95
  0–553–34355–6 Bantam pb $9.95

TO ORDER BOOKS AS GIFTS, SEE PAGE 1

EVOLUTION

The orthodox conception of divine creation persisted in the 19th century but was increasingly challenged by conflicting evidence: the discovery of fossils of both extinct and living creatures, of strata overlaid with distinct flora, of disruptive breaks in the geological record, and of signs pointing to the earth's immense age. Darwin's *Origin of Species*, published in 1859, enriched these observations with insight into nature's evolutionary changes. Natural selection—the struggle among organisms for existence, and their adaptation to the environment—was the mechanism for evolution.

Charles Darwin

• Charles Darwin
THE NYU PRESS EDITION OF THE WORKS OF CHARLES DARWIN
The first 20 volumes in the first complete edition of Darwin's published books (Volumes 21 to 29 are to be published soon). As many of these books have been out of print for years, this is an invaluable reference
Edited by Peter Gautrey

Volume 1: Diary of the Voyage of the H.M.S. Beagle
0-8147-1796-9 NYU $95.00

Volume 2: Journal of Researches into the Geology and Natural History of the Various Countries Visited by H.M.S Beagle, Part 1
0-8147-1787-X NYU $95.00

Volume 3: Journal of Researches into the Geology and Natural History of the Various Countries Visited by H.M.S Beagle, Part 2
0-8147-1788-8 NYU $95.00

Volume 4: The Zoology of the Voyage of H.M.S. Beagle, Under the Command of Captain Fitzroy, During the Years 1832-1836—Fossil Mammalia, Mammalia
0-8147-1789-6 NYU $95.00

Volume 5: The Zoology of the Voyage of H.M.S. Beagle, Under the Command of Captain Fitzroy, During the Years 1832-1836—Birds
0-8147-1790-X NYU $95.00

Volume 6: The Zoology of the Voyage of H.M.S. Beagle, Under the Command of Captain Fitzroy, During the Years 1832-1836—Fish, Reptiles
0-8147-1791-8 NYU $95.00

Volume 7: The Structure and Distribution of Coral Reefs
0-8147-1792-6 NYU $95.00

Volume 8: Geological Observations on the Volcanic Island Visited During the Voyage of H.M.S. Beagle
0-8147-1793-4 NYU $95.00

Volume 9: Geological Observations on South America
0-8147-1794-2 NYU $95.00

Volume 10: The Foundations of the Origin of the Species
0-8147-1795-0 NYU $95.00

Volume 11: A Monograph on the Subclass Cirripedia, Part 1
0-8147-1800-0 NYU $95.00

Volume 12: A Monograph on the Subclass Cirripedia, Part 2
0-8147-1801-9 NYU $95.00

Volume 13: A Monograph on the Subclass Cirripedia, Part 3
0-8147-1802-7 NYU $95.00

Volume 14: A Monograph on the Fossil Lepadidae
0-8147-1803-5 NYU $95.00

Volume 15: On the Origin of Species
The first edition, written in 1859
0-8147-1804-3 NYU $95.00

Volume 16: On the Origin of Species
The sixth edition, written in 1876
0-8147-1805-1 NYU $95.00

Volume 17: The Various Contrivances by which Orchides are Fertilized by Insects
0-8147-1806-X NYU $95.00

Volume 18: The Movements and Habits of Climbing Plants
0-8147-1807-8 NYU $95.00

Volume 19: The Variation of Animals and Plants Under Domestication, Part 1
0-8147-1808-6 NYU $95.00

Volume 20: The Variation of Animals and Plants Under Domestication, Part 2
0-8147-1809-4 NYU $95.00

AUTOBIOGRAPHY OF CHARLES DARWIN
0-393-00487-2 Norton pb $6.95

CHARLES DARWIN'S BEAGLE DIARY
A fresh transcript of Darwin's diary, about half of which, together with material from his scientific notes, was used as the basis for his famous account of the *Beagle* voyage published in 1839
Edited by R. D. Keynes
0-521-23503-0 Cambridge $59.50

Darwin's finches, arranged to show their evolutionary development, from The Voyage of the Beagle *by Charles Darwin (Anchor Press)*

THE DESCENT OF MAN & SELECTION IN RELATION TO SEX
A facsimile of the first edition (1871)
0-691-08278-2 Princeton $52.50
0-691-02369-7 Princeton pb $14.50

THE ORIGIN OF SPECIES
0-14-043205-1 Penguin pb $3.95

THE VOYAGE OF THE BEAGLE
0-385-02767-2 Doubleday pb $6.95

• Frederick Burkhardt & Sydney Smith, editors
THE CORRESPONDENCE OF CHARLES DARWIN
"In all, they have provided admirably self-contained volumes, which one need not be a Darwin scholar to read with profit"—*New Yorker*

Volume 1: 1821-1836
0-521-25587-2 Cambridge $37.50

Volume 2: 1837-1843
0-521-25588-0 Cambridge $37.50

Volume 3: 1844-1846
0-521-25589-9 Cambridge $37.50

Volume 4: 1847-1850
0-521-25590-2 Cambridge $37.50

• H.S. Gruber
DARWIN ON MAN: A Psychological Study of Scientific Creativity
0-226-31008-8 Chicago $25.00
0-226-31007-8 Chicago pb $7.95

• David Kohn, editor
THE DARWINIAN HERITAGE
This major collection of essays includes the proceedings of the Charles Darwin Centenary Conference held in 1982 in Florence
0-691-02414-6 Princeton pb $25.00

• Mark Ridley, editor
THE DARWIN READER
"Ridley's artful selections . . . and entertaining introductions leave us in no doubt that Darwin's lesser achievements are all of a piece with his major discovery . . . Darwin is shown to be one of the 19th century's greatest geologists and biologists"—Richard Dawkins
0-393-02476-8 Norton $19.95
0-393-95673-3 Norton pb $8.95

• Michael Ruse
DARWINISM DEFENDED: Guide to the Evolution Controversy
0-201-06273-9 Addison-Wesley pb $26.95

TAKING DARWIN SERIOUSLY: A Naturalist Approach to Philosophy
0-631-13543-X Blackwell $24.95
0-631-15478-7 Blackwell pb $15.95

The natural history of these islands is eminently curious, and well deserves attention. Most of the organic productions are aboriginal creations, found nowhere else; there is even a difference between the inhabitants of the different islands; yet all show a marked relationship with those of America, though separated from that continent by an open space of ocean, between 500 and 600 miles in width. The archipelago is a little world within itself, or rather a satellite attached to America, whence it has derived a few stray colonists, and has received the general character of its indigenous productions. Considering the small size of these islands, we feel the more astonished at the number of their aboriginal beings, and at their confined range. Seeing every height crowned with its crater, and the boundaries of most of the lava-streams still distinct, we are led to believe that within a period, geologically recent, the unbroken ocean was here spread out. Hence, both in space and time, we seem to be brought somewhat near to that great fact—that mystery of mysteries—the first appearance of new beings on this earth.

Charles Darwin
THE VOYAGE OF THE BEAGLE
0–451–62620–6 NAL pb $4.95

The Theory of Evolution

• Doug Boucher, editor
THE BIOLOGY OF MUTUALISM:
Ecology and Evolution
Population biologists discuss the ecological strategies and evolutionary constraints that govern the maintenance of mutualistic relationships. "Required reading for everyone interested in species interactions"—*Ecology*
0–19–505392–3 Oxford $24.95

• Peter Bowler
EVOLUTION: The History of an Idea
From the 17th century to the present
0–520–04890–3 California pb $12.95

• R.W. Burkhardt
THE SPIRIT OF SYSTEM: Lamarck and Evolutionary Biology
A discussion of the origins of evolutionary theory
0–674–83317–1 Harvard $18.00

• Richard Dawkins
THE BLIND WATCHMAKER: Why the Evidence of Evolution Reveals a Universe Without Design
A popular defense of Darwinian theory. Includes a computer model of how minute changes, such as those that occur in evolution, can lead to vastly divergent results
0–393–30448–5 Norton pb $7.95

THE SELFISH GENE
A controversial, entertaining discussion of what is "selected" during evolution
0–19 520000–4 Oxford pb $6.95

THE EXTENDED PHENOTYPE: The Gene as the Unit of Selection
A more technical sequel to *The Selfish Gene*
0–7167–1358–6 W.H. Freeman $26.95
0–19–857609–9 Oxford pb $9.95

• Gerald M. Edelman
NEURAL DARWINISM: The Theory of Neuronal Group Selection
0–465–04934–6 Basic Books $29.95

TOPOBIOLOGY: An Introduction to Molecular Embryology
0–465–08634–9 Basic Books $21.95

• Maitland Edey & Donald Johanson
BLUEPRINTS: Solving the Mystery of Evolution
A history of the evidence of evolution by the authors of *Lucy: The Beginnings of Humankind*. "This book should be welcomed by anyone with a love of truth in a dark time"—Richard Dawkins, *NY Times Book Review*
0–316–21076–5 Little, Brown $19.95

• Niles Eldridge
TIME FRAMES: The Rethinking of Darwinian Evolution and the Theory of Punctuated Equilibria
0–671–62245–5 Simon & Schuster pb $8.95

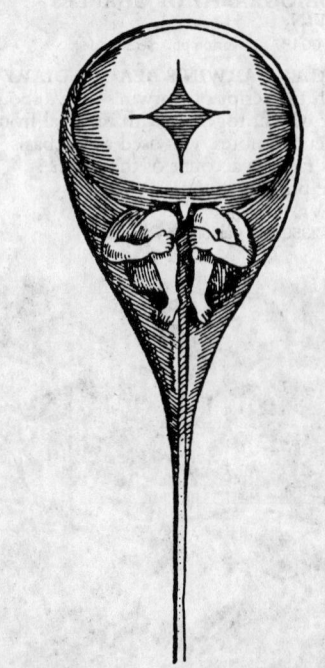

Depiction of a human spermatozoon by Niklaas Hartsoeker (1656-1725)

UNFINISHED SYNTHESIS: Biological Hierarchies and Modern Evolutionary Thought
0–19–503633–6 Oxford $29.95
0–19–505574–8 Oxford pb $14.95

• Niles Eldridge, editor
THE NATURAL HISTORY READER IN EVOLUTION
A collection of 27 articles from *Natural History* magazine
0–231–06156–0 Columbia $25.00

• Niles Eldridge & Ian Tattersall
THE MYTHS OF HUMAN EVOLUTION
0–231–05145–X Columbia pb $14.00

Stephen Jay Gould
Gould's provocative and witty columns in *Natural History* demonstrate the subtleties of evolution through concrete examples of the extraordinary.
EVER SINCE DARWIN: Reflections in Natural History
0–393–06425–5 Norton $19.95
0–393–00917–3 Norton pb $5.95

THE FLAMINGO'S SMILE: Reflections in Natural History
0–393–02228–5 Norton $17.95
0–393–30375–6 Norton pb $8.95

HEN'S TEETH AND HORSE'S TOES: Further Reflections in Natural History
0–393–01716–8 Norton $15.50
0–393–30200–8 Norton pb $6.95

THE MISMEASURE OF MAN
A discussion of ideas about human intelligence in history
0–393–01489–4 Norton $17.95
0–393–30056–0 Norton pb $7.95

ONTOGENY AND PHYLOGENY
A classic on the relationship between individual development and the evolution of species and lineages
0–674–63940–5 Harvard $29.50
0–674–63941–3 Harvard pb $9.95

THE PANDA'S THUMB: More Reflections in Natural History
0–393–01380–4 Norton $15.95
0–393–30023–4 Norton pb $5.95

AN URCHIN IN THE STORM: Essays about Books and Ideas
Biological determinism, "cardboard Darwinism," evolutionary theory, and other subjects
0–393–02492–X Norton $18.95
0–393–30537–6 Norton pb $7.95

• François Jacob
THE LOGIC OF LIFE: A History of Heredity
The Nobel Prize winner demonstrates the inappropriate application in earlier periods of nonbiological principles to heredity
0–394–71007–X Random House pb $7.95

THE POSSIBLE AND THE ACTUAL
0–394–70671–4 Random House pb $5.25

• Richard Lewontin
THE GENETIC BASIS OF EVOLUTION AND CHANGE
An extremely important study of the importance of environmental factors on evolution
0–231–08318–1 Columbia pb $19.00

HUMAN DIVERSITY
The larger implications of evolutionary theory in terms of human values
0–7167–1469–8 W.H. Freeman $27.95

- Vincent Maglio & H.B. Cooke, editors
THE EVOLUTION OF AFRICAN MAMMALS
One of the best continental overviews of mammalian evolution; not for the novice
0–674–27075–4 Harvard $75.00

- Lynn Margulis & Dorion Sagan
MICROCOSMOS: Four Billion Years of Microbial Evolution
0–671–44169–8 Simon & Schuster $17.95

THE ORIGINS OF SEX: Three Billion Years of Genetic Recombination
0–300–03340–0 Yale $37.50

- Ernst Mayr
THE GROWTH OF BIOLOGICAL THOUGHT: Evolution and the Diversity of Life
One of the finest discussions of the evolutionary ideas that have given rise to modern biology
0–674–27104–1 Harvard $37.00
0–674–36446–5 Harvard pb $14.95

SYSTEMATICS AND THE ORIGIN OF SPECIES
0–231–05449–1 Columbia pb $18.50

TOWARD A NEW PHILOSOPHY OF BIOLOGY: Observations of an Evolutionist
Reflections on evolutionary theory by the Harvard zoology professor
0–674–89665–3 Harvard $36.50

- H.M. Morris, editor
SCIENTIFIC CREATIONISM
The official statement of the defenders of creationism
0–89051–003–2 Master Books $8.95

- E.S. Russell
FORM AND FUNCTION: A Contribution to the History of Animal Morphology
A brilliant early history
0–226–73173–1 Chicago pb $12.00

- J. Maynard Smith
EVOLUTION AND THE THEORY OF GAMES
The importance of strategies in evolution
0–521–28884–3 Cambridge pb $14.95

THE EVOLUTION OF SEX
0–521–29302–2 Cambridge pb $14.95

- Elliot Sober, editor
CONCEPTUAL ISSUES IN EVOLUTIONARY BIOLOGY: An Anthology
0–262–69084–5 MIT pb $21.95

- Steven Stanley
THE NEW EVOLUTIONARY TIMETABLE: Fossils, Genes, and the Origin of Species
A contentious reinterpretation of the fossil record, written for a general audience
0–465–05014–X Basic Books pb $8.95

- George Williams
SEX AND EVOLUTION
0–691–08147–6 Princeton $32.00
0–691–08152–2 Princeton pb $13.95

- Edward O. Wilson
ON HUMAN NATURE
A popular discussion of sociobiology, one of the more controversial results of evolutionary theory
0–674–63441–1 Harvard $15.00
0–674–63442–X Harvard pb $8.95

NATURAL HISTORY

Biological Diversity

- Bryan Norton
WHY PRESERVE NATURAL VARIETY?
A comprehensive rationale for preserving wild species and ecosystems
0–691–07762–2 Princeton $30.00

- Bryan Norton, editor
THE PRESERVATION OF SPECIES: The Value of Biological Diversity
An important collection, resulting from a conference on the preservation of biological diversity held at the University of Maryland
0–691–08389–4 Princeton $37.50
0–691–02415–4 Princeton pb $16.95

- Edward Wilson
BIODIVERSITY
"The most comprehensive book, by the most distinguished group of scholars, ever published on one of the most important subjects of our (and all) time"—Stephen Jay Gould
0–309–03739–5 National Academy pb $19.50

Classification of Organisms

"At least three million and perhaps ten million species of living organisms are now alive . . . The effort to discern order in this incredible variety has given rise to systematics, the classification of the living world . . . This conceptual hierarchy grew gradually, in the course of about a century, from a solid base established by the Swede Carolus Linnaeus (1707-1778), who began the modern practice of binomial nomenclature. Every known organism is given a unique two-part name, Latin in form."—Lynn Margulis & Karlene Schwartz, *Five Kingdoms: An Illustrated Guide to the Phyla of Life on Earth*

- Sandra Holmes
OUTLINE OF PLANT CLASSIFICATION
0–582–44650–3 Longman pb $10.95

- C. Jeffrey
AN INTRODUCTION TO PLANT TAXONOMY
0–521–28775–8 Cambridge pb $14.95

- Lynn Margulis & Karlene Schwartz
FIVE KINGDOMS: An Illustrated Guide to the Phyla of Life on Earth
0–7167–1885–5 W.H. Freeman $35.95
0–7167–1912–6 W.H. Freeman pb $24.95

- Sybil Parker, editor
SYNOPSIS AND CLASSIFICATION OF LIVING ORGANISMS
An award-winning two-volume work, containing 8200 illustrated articles, describing the taxa of all living organisms
0–07–079031–0 McGraw-Hill $265.00

- Cedric Porter
TAXONOMY OF FLOWERING PLANTS
0–7167–0709–8 W.H. Freeman $34.95

- Albert Radford
FUNDAMENTALS OF PLANT SYSTEMATICS
0–06–045305–2 Harper & Row $41.95

Zoology

- Dougal Dixon
AFTER MAN: A Zoology of the Future
0–312–01162–8 St. Martin's pb $10.95

- Lawrence Elson
THE ZOOLOGY COLORING BOOK
For young readers
0–06–460301–6 Harper & Row pb $10.95

- Jean-Baptiste Lamarck
ZOOLOGICAL PHILOSOPHY: An Exposition with Regard to the Natural History of Animals
The 1809 classic by the great French naturalist, zoologist, and coiner of the term "biology"
0–226–46809–7 Chicago $30.00
0–226–46810–0 Chicago pb $15.00

Botany

- E.J. Corner
THE LIFE OF PLANTS
0–226–11586–0 Chicago pb $10.95

- François Delaporte
NATURE'S SECOND KINGDOM
0–262–54040–1 MIT pb $8.95

- A. Fahn
PLANT ANATOMY
0–08–028030–7 Pergamon $87.00
0–08–028029–3 Pergamon pb $35.00

- D.G. Frodin
A GUIDE TO STANDARD FLORAS OF THE WORLD
0–521–23688–6 Cambridge $182.50

- Janice Glimn-Lacy & Peter Kaufman
BOTANY ILLUSTRATED
0–442–22969–0 Van Nostrand pb $23.95

- Edward Greene
LANDMARKS IN BOTANICAL HISTORY
A 2-volume work
0–8047–1075–9 Stanford $100.00

- Anthony Huxley
PLANT AND PLANET
0–14–007946–7 Penguin pb $6.95

• A.G. Morton
HISTORY OF BOTANICAL SCIENCE:
An Account of the Development of Botany
from the Ancient Time to the Present
0–12–508380–7 Academic $67.00
0–12–508382–3 Academic pb $35.00

• Anthony Robards, editor
BOTANICAL MICROSCOPY
0–19–854587–8 Oxford $32.50

• Doris Stone
THE LIVES OF PLANTS: Exploring the
Wonders of Botany
0–684–17907–5 Scribners $15.95

Tree roots crack rock by imperceptible expansion. More spectacular results can be observed with fast-growing plants, the most remarkable I have seen being the lifting of a large concrete paving slab by a horse mushroom. Here the expansion is due to hydraulic pressure, for it is the result of preformed cells expanding rapidly as they take up water. But why the flimsy mushroom is not brought to a halt, or its base is not forced into the soil by the weight on top of the expanding cap, can only be a source of amazement. Shoots too can sometimes penetrate apparently impossible substances. I have records, for instance, of daffodils emerging through 8 cm of Tarmac and flowering successfully, and of suckering shoots of *Rosa hispida* coming through 20 cm of rubble foundations and top layers of gravel and Tarmac. At the other extreme of plant life the germinating spores of single-cell marine algae have been shown to burrow into and under the paint on ships' hulls, cracking it and exposing the metal to corrosion.

Anthony Huxley
PLANT AND PLANET
0–14–007946–7 Penguin pb $6.95

• Elizabeth Toothill & Stephen Blackmore, editors
THE FACTS ON FILE DICTIONARY OF
BOTANY
Covers terms in taxonomy, anatomy, biochemistry, cell biology, plant pathology,

genetics, ecology, horticulture, and microbiology
0–87196–861–4 Facts On File $21.95

• Tyler Whittle
THE PLANT HUNTERS
The story of the botanists who accompanied Captain Cook, Sir Walter Raleigh and other explorers, and other early plant scientists who went far afield to advance botany and horticulture
1–55554–037–6 PAJ pb $13.95

MICROBIOLOGY

The 16th-century Italian scholar Fracastorius first combined historical reports with his own observations to define the process of contagion, which transmits invisible "seeds" of disease from person to person. In the 17th century, the haberdasher Leeuwenhoek was astounded to discover such "beasts" in a drop of water by means of the newly invented microscope. However, it was not until the experiments of Pasteur and Koch that "germs" were identified as the microscopic causes of disease.

• Austin & Priest
MODERN BACTERIAL TAXONOMY
0–442–31736–0 Van Nostrand Reinhold pb $23.95

• J.I. Cooper & F.O. MacCallum
VIRUSES AND THE ENVIRONMENT
0–412–22870–X Methuen $35.00
0–412–22880–7 Methuen pb $17.95

• Johanna Laybourn-Perry
A FUNCTIONAL BIOLOGY OF FREE-
LIVING PROTOZOA
0–520–05339–7 California $35.00
0–520–05340–0 California pb $19.95

• Michael Madigan & Thomas Brock
THE BIOLOGY OF MICROORGANISMS
A popular textbook
0–13–076829–4 Prentice-Hall $57.00

• John Postgate
MICROBES AND MAN
The revised edition of a classic
0–14–022666–4 Penguin pb $6.95

• Dorian Sagan & Lynn Margulis
A GARDEN OF MICROBIAL
DELIGHTS: A Practical Guide to the
Subvisible World
"With photographs, illustrations, or diagrams on almost every page, the authors present the beauty and complexity of these tiny creatures that perform important jobs like transferring DNA and RNA, cleaning the air, and fertilizing the soil"—*American Scientist*
0–15–134290–3 HBJ $24.95

• Andrew Scott
PIRATES OF THE CELL: The Story of
Viruses from Molecule to Microbe
0–631–15637–2 Blackwell pb $12.95

• R. Stainer & others
THE MICROBIAL WORLD
0–13–581042–6 Prentice-Hall $55.00

• A. P. Waterson & L. Wilkinson
AN INTRODUCTION TO THE
HISTORY OF VIROLOGY
The conceptual, experimental, and personal steps that elucidated the nature of virus particles
0–521–21917–5 Cambridge $49.50

GENETICS

• Daniel Kevles
IN THE NAME OF EUGENICS: Genetics
and the Uses of Human Heredity
"It stands as a powerful warning against anyone today who would use the fruits of legitimate science to bolster arguments and policies that echo the social and racial prejudices of the past"—*Washington Post*
0–394–50702–9 Knopf $22.95
0–520–05763–5 California pb $10.95

• Robert King & William Stansfield
DICTIONARY OF GENETICS
0–19–503494–5 Oxford $32.50
0–19–503495–3 Oxford pb $18.95

• Benjamin Lewin
GENES
A popular textbook
0–471–83278–2 Wiley $54.25

• Robert Olby
THE ORIGINS OF MENDELISM
0–226–62591–5 Chicago $38.00
0–226–62592–3 Chicago pb $14.95

• Norman Rothwell
UNDERSTANDING GENETICS
A good textbook
0–19–505108–4 Oxford $39.95

• Scientific American
GENETICS: Readings from Scientific
American
A useful collection of elementary articles
0–7167–1201–6 W.H. Freeman pb $14.95

Genetic Engineering and Biotechnology

• Elizabeth Antebi & David Fishlock
BIOTECHNOLOGY: Strategies for Life
A lavishly illustrated coffee-table book
0–262–01089–5 MIT $45.00

• William Bains
GENETIC ENGINEERING FOR
ALMOST EVERYBODY
The technology's past, present, and potential problems
0–14–022740–7 Penguin pb $6.95

• Jeremy Cherfas
MAN-MADE LIFE: An Overview of the
Science, Technology, and Commerce of
Genetic Engineering
0–394–52926–X Random House $15.95

⇒ **FOR OVERSEAS ORDERING INFORMATION, SEE PAGE 1**

● James Coombs, editor
DICTIONARY OF BIOTECHNOLOGY
0–444–01070–X Elsevier pb $27.50

● O.J. Crocomo, editor
BIOTECHNOLOGY OF PLANTS AND MICROORGANISMS
0–8142–0375–2 Ohio State $60.00

● Karl Drlica
UNDERSTANDING DNA AND GENE CLONING: A Guide for the Curious
Genetic engineering made easier
0–471–87942–8 Wiley pb $19.95

● John Elkington
THE GENE FACTORY: The Science and Business of Biotechnology
0–88184–293–1 Carroll & Graf pb $8.95

● Howard & Margery Facklam
FROM CELL TO CLONE: The Story of Genetic Engineering
0–15–230262–X HBJ $9.95

● Stephen Hall
INVISIBLE FRONTIERS: The Race to Synthesize a Human Gene
A fast-paced account of the high-stakes race to genetically engineer human insulin; for the general reader
0–87113–147–1 Atlantic Monthly $19.95
1–55615–172–1 Tempus pb $8.95

● Jean Marx, editor
A REVOLUTION IN BIOTECHNOLOGY
A survey by 26 eminent scientists of the major developments in the biotechnology revolution, sponsored by the International Council of Scientific Unions
0–521–32749–0 Cambridge $39.50

● R.W. Old & S.B. Primrose
PRINCIPLES OF GENE MANIPULATION
0–632–01318–4 Blackwell pb $27.50

● S.G. Oliver & J.M. Ward
A DICTIONARY OF GENETIC ENGINEERING
0–521–26080–9 Cambridge $24.95

● Scientific American editors
INDUSTRIAL MICROBIOLOGY AND THE ADVENT OF GENETIC ENGINEERING
0–7167–1386–1 W.H. Freeman pb $12.95

● John Smith
BIOTECHNOLOGY
A comprehensive introduction to the field. "A very readable and highly stimulating account"—*Nature*
0–7131–2960–3 Edward Arnold pb $13.95

● Edward Sylvester & Lynn Klotz
THE GENE AGE: Genetic Engineering and the Next Industrial Revolution
0–684–18819–8 Scribners pb $12.95

● P.R. Wheale & Ruth McNally
GENETIC ENGINEERING: Catastrophe or Utopia?
0–312–00479–6 St. Martin's $29.95

● Raymond Zilinkas & Burke Zimmerman
THE GENE SPLICING WARS: Reflections on the Recombinant DNA Controversy
0–07–072875–5 McGraw Hill $27.95

MOLECULAR BIOLOGY

Even smaller than microbes are the larger biological molecules, proteins, and nucleic acids, which constitute the heritage of all living things. Watson and Crick's dramatic discovery of the double helix of DNA advanced the idea that a molecule's structure and function were intertwined. DNA's helical strands allow genetic information to be duplicated and passed on to the next generation.

● H. Baltimore, editor
NOBEL LECTURES IN MOLECULAR BIOLOGY: 1933 to 1975
0–444–00236–7 Elsevier $38.00

● Herrick Baltscheffsky & others, editors
THE MOLECULAR EVOLUTION OF LIFE
0–521–33642–2 Cambridge $69.50

● Erwin Chargaff
HERACLITEAN FIRE: Sketches from a Life Before Nature
The discovery of the DNA structure
0–87470–029–9 Rockefeller $14.50

● Ernest Fischer & Carol Lipson
THINKING ABOUT SCIENCE: Max Delbruck and the Origins of Molecular Biology
0–393–02508–X Norton $19.95

● Gerald Feinberg
SOLID CLUES: Quantum Physics, Molecular Biology, and the Future of Science
0–671–62252–8 Simon & Schuster pb $8.95

● Horace Judson
THE EIGHTH DAY OF CREATION: The Makers of the Revolution in Biology
A highly journalistic book on the discoveries and the discoverers in molecular biology
0–671–25410–3 Simon & Schuster pb $15.95

● Maclyn McCarty
THE TRANSFORMING PRINCIPLE: Discovering That Genes Are Made of DNA
The beginning of the story of the discovery of DNA. "The most interesting and portentous biological experiment of the 20th century authoritatively described by one of the three principal executants"— Peter Medawar
0–393–30450–7 Norton pb $5.95

● Peter Medawar
MEMOIR OF A THINKING RADISH: An Autobiography
Reflections on his role in the development of the new biology. "Has all the wonderful informality, immediacy and odd digressiveness that make this genre such a pleasure to read"—*NY Times*
0–19–217737–0 Oxford $17.95

● Anne Sayre
ROSALIND FRANKLIN AND DNA
A version of the events surrounding the famous discovery of the DNA structure
0–393–00868–1 Norton pb $7.95

● Andrew Scott
VITAL PRINCIPLES: The Molecular Mechanisms of Life
What living things are made of and the vital principles for every activity of life
0–631–15398–5 Blackwell $19.95

● Lubert Stryer
BIOCHEMISTRY
An excellent textbook for details of the new technology
0–7167–1843–X Freeman $47.95

● James Watson
THE DOUBLE HELIX
A personal, candid memoir of the discovery of the structure of DNA. A good introduction
0–451–62594–3 NAL pb $4.50

THE MOLECULAR BIOLOGY OF THE GENE
Explanation of the new technology
0–8053–9614–4 Addison-Wesley $59.25

● James Watson & John Tooze
THE DNA STORY: A Documentary History of Gene Cloning
Includes a number of interesting documents on the bioengineering debate
0–7167–1292–X W.H. Freeman $32.95

RECOMBINANT DNA: A Short Course
A good short introduction that goes beyond standard popularizations
0–7167–1484–1 W.H. Freeman pb $17.95

Philosophical and Social Implications

● J.B. Haldane
THE PHILOSOPHICAL BASIS OF BIOLOGY
A classic written in the 1930s
0–8274–4213–0 Richard West $25.00

• Richard Lewontin, Steven Rose & Leon Kamin
NOT IN OUR GENES: Biology, Ideology, and Human Nature
An attack on the simplistic view that genes determine character, intelligence, and other traits
0–394–72888–2 Random House pb $8.95

• Peter & J.S. Medawar
ARISTOTLE TO ZEUS: A Philosophical Dictionary of Biology
0–674–04535–1 Harvard $20.00
0–674–04537–8 Harvard pb $7.95

• Derek de Solla Price
LITTLE SCIENCE, BIG SCIENCE AND BEYOND
0–2310–4957–9 Columbia pb $14.95

• Steven Rose & Lisa Appignanesi, editors
SCIENCE AND BEYOND
Essays on the implications of the industrialization of the new biology
0–631–14483–8 Blackwell $34.95

• Erwin Schrödinger
WHAT IS LIFE AND MIND & MATTER
Classic writings by a Nobel prize-winning German physicist
0–521–09397–X Cambridge pb $12.95

• J. Maynard Smith
THE PROBLEMS OF BIOLOGY
The philosophical implications
0–19–289198–7 Oxford pb $7.95

HUMAN BEHAVIOR

Sociobiology

Edward O. Wilson and his fellow sociobiologists believe that genes influence behavior and that the theory of evolution applies not only to physical and structural characteristics but to social behavior as well. If a particular behavioral pattern contributes to an organism's reproductive success, they argue, the genes responsible for that behavior will be selected and transmitted to succeeding generations. Many critics disagree, especially when sociobiological thinking is applied to human behavior.

• David Barash
THE HARE AND THE TORTOISE: Culture, Biology, and Human Nature
Most of humanity's problems are due to a conflict between our slow-moving biology (the Tortoise) and our fast-moving culture (the Hare)
0–14–008748–6 Penguin pb $8.95

• John & Mary Gribbin
THE ONE PERCENT ADVANTAGE: The Sociobiology of Being Human
"One percent" is the amount of DNA that separates humans from chimps. "The Gribbins explain the basis and paradox of sociobiology in language that can be understood by all"—Edward O. Wilson
0–631–16004–3 Blackwell $19.95

• Philip Kitcher
VAULTING AMBITION: Sociobiology and the Quest for Human Nature
"The best dissection ever published on the logic and illogic (mostly the latter) of sociobiology"—Stephen Jay Gould
0–262–11109–8 MIT pb $27.50

• Ashley Montagu
SOCIOBIOLOGY EXAMINED
A critical look
0–19–502711–6 Oxford $24.95
0–19–502712–4 Oxford pb $8.95

• Edward O. Wilson
BIOPHILIA
Proposes that our natural affinity for life (biophilia) is the essence of our humanity and binds us to all other species. "Erudite, elegant, and poetic"—*Natural History*
0–674–07441–6 Harvard $15.00
0–674–07442–4 Harvard pb $7.95
ON HUMAN NATURE
Winner of the 1979 Pulitzer Prize in general nonfiction
0–674–63441–1 Harvard $15.00
SOCIOBIOLOGY: The New Synthesis
0–674–81621–8 Harvard $40.50
SOCIOBIOLOGY: The New Synthesis
Abridged edition
0–674–81623–4 Harvard $20.50
0–674–81624–2 Harvard pb $14.95

Biological Rhythms

Life is adjusted like clockwork according to internal self-sustaining mechanisms that control a range of cyclic, biological rhythms. Certain brain activities occur several times a second; circannual rhythms occur yearly with the regularity of the seasons.

• Jeremy Campbell
WINSTON CHURCHILL'S AFTERNOON NAP: A Wide-Awake Inquiry into the Human Nature of Time
0–671–65717–8 Simon & Schuster pb $9.95

• Richard Coleman
WIDE AWAKE AT 3:00 AM: By Choice or By Chance?
0–7167–1795–6 W.H. Freeman $21.95
0–7167–1796–4 W.H. Freeman pb $12.95

• J.A. Michon & J.L. Jackson
TIME, MIND, AND BEHAVIOR
0–387–15444–2 Springer-Verlag $55.00

• Kenneth Rose
THE BODY IN TIME
0–317–70059–6 Wiley $19.95

• Arthur Winfree
THE TIMING OF BIOLOGICAL CLOCKS
A vivid account of the internal cycles that govern the processes of life. "Winfree stands unique in the science of biological time-keeping by visiting all fields, from population dynamics . . . to biochemistry"—*Nature*
0–7167–5018–X W.H. Freeman $32.95

• Michael Young
THE METRONOMIC SOCIETY: Natural Rhythms and Human Timetables
0–674–57195–9 Harvard $25.00

THE NEUROSCIENCES

▶ **See also Psychology**

Much of the philosophical and scientific discussion of brain function is based on clinical observations and research.

• M. Critchley
THE DIVINE BANQUET OF THE BRAIN AND OTHER ESSAYS
An entertaining and unorthodox collection by an eminent clinician
0–89004–348–5 Raven $23.00

• Michael Gazzaniga & others
THE INTEGRATED MIND
Uses clinical examples to explain brain function
0–306–31085–6 Plenum $27.50

• A.R. Luria
THE MAN WITH A SHATTERED WORLD
0–674–54625–3 Harvard pb $7.95
THE MIND OF THE MNEMONIST
0–317–59999–2 Harvard pb $7.95
THE WORKING BRAIN: An Introduction to Neuropsychology
Somewhat technical but filled with fascinating observations
0–465–09208–X Harper & Row pb $12.95

• Oliver Sacks
"In his books . . . Dr. Oliver Sacks has been acclaimed for his extraordinary compassion in the treatment of patients afflicted with profound neurological disorders"—*Washington Post*
AWAKENINGS
A classic study
0–671–64834–9 Simon & Schuster $18.45
0–525–48350–0 Dutton pb $8.95
A LEG TO STAND ON
"A neurologist in the great tradition . . . Sacks has written a book about a leg; but it is a story about the nature of selfhood— a narrative comparable to Conrad's *The Secret Sharer*"—*NY Review of Books*
0–06–097082–0 Harper & Row pb $8.95
THE MAN WHO MISTOOK HIS WIFE FOR A HAT & Other Clinical Tales
"Dr. Sacks's most absorbing book . . . His tales are so compelling that many of them serve as eerie metaphors not only for the condition of modern medicine but of modern man"—*New York*
0–06–097079–0 Harper & Row pb $8.95
MIGRAINE
A wealth of clinical examples explain this troubling disorder
0–520–05199–8 California $27.50
0–520–05889–5 California pb $9.95

I tried one final test. It was still a cold day, in early spring, and I had thrown my coat and gloves on the sofa.

"What is this?" I asked, holding up a glove.

"May I examine it?" he asked, and, taking it from me, he proceeded to examine it as he had examined the geometrical shapes.

"A continuous surface," he announced at last, "infolded on itself. It appears to have"—he hesitated—"five outpouchings, if this is the word."

"Yes," I said cautiously. "You have given me a description. Now tell me what it is."

"A container of some sort?"

"Yes," I said, "and what would it contain?"

"It would contain its contents!" said Dr. P., with a laugh. "There are many possibilities. It could be a change purse, for example, for coins of five sizes. It could . . ."

I interrupted the barmy flow. "Does it not look familiar? Do you think it might contain, might fit, a part of your body?"

No light of recognition dawned on his face.

Oliver Sacks
THE MAN WHO MISTOOK HIS WIFE FOR A HAT & Other Clinical Tales
0–06–097079–0 Harper & Row pb $8.95

- John Spillane
THE DOCTRINE OF THE NERVES: Chapters in the History of Neurology
An excellent history, by a practicing neurologist, that uses extensive source material from Galen to the 19th century
0–19–261135–6 Oxford $70.00

- Eliot Valenstein
GREAT AND DESPERATE CURES
An excellent history of the use of prefrontal lobotomies
0–465–02710–5 Harper & Row $19.50
0–465–02711–3 Harper & Row pb $10.95

The Brain

- Colin Blakemore & Susan Greenfield, editors
MINDWAVES: Thoughts on Intelligence, Identity, and Consciousness
Essays on the mind-body "problem" by noted researchers
0–631–14622–9 Blackwell $24.00

- Edmund Blair Bolles
REMEMBERING AND FORGETTING: An Inquiry into the Nature of Memory
0–8027–1004–2 Walker $22.95

- Michael Gazzaniga
MIND MATTERS: How the Mind and Brain Interact to Create Our Conscious Lives
Cognitive neuroscience in an accessible survey
0–395–42159–4 Houghton Mifflin $17.95

- Richard Gregory, editor
THE OXFORD COMPANION TO THE MIND
Nine hundred entries—accompanied by over 160 illustrations—on the physiology, psychology, and philosophy of the mind, contributed by R.D. Laing, B.F. Skinner, Noam Chomsky, Oliver Sacks, and others
0–19–866124–X Oxford $49.95

- J. Allan Hobson
THE DREAMING BRAIN
0–465–01703–7 Basic Books $22.95

- David Hubel
EYE, BRAIN, AND VISION
0–7167–5020–1 Freeman $32.95

- Israel Rosenfield
THE INVENTION OF MEMORY: A New View of the Brain
"A remarkable synthesis of the most important developments in neurobiology today"—Oliver Sacks
0–465–03592–2 Basic $18.95

Eminent Scientists on the Brain

- Jean-Pierre Changeux
NEURONAL MAN: The Biology of Mind
0–19–504226–3 Oxford pb $9.95

- Max Delbruck
MIND FROM MATTER: An Essay on Evolutionary Epistemology
0–86542–311–3 Blackwell pb $16.95

- J. Eccles
THE HUMAN MYSTERY
0–387–09016–9 Springer-Verlag $25.00

- J. Eccles & Karl Popper
THE SELF AND ITS BRAIN
0–7100–9584–8 RC&H pb $14.95

- L.R. Squire
MEMORY AND BRAIN
0–19–504207–7 Oxford $29.95
0–19–504208–5 Oxford pb $15.95

- J.Z. Young
MODEL OF THE BRAIN
0–19–857333–2 Oxford $35.00
0–19–286019–4 Oxford pb $9.95

PROGRAMS OF THE BRAIN
0–19–857545–9 Oxford $29.95

Popular Works on the Brain

- Colin Blakemore
MECHANICS OF THE MIND
0–521–21559–5 Cambridge $54.50
0–521–29185–2 Cambridge pb $15.95

- Diagram Group
THE BRAIN: A User's Manual
0–399–51379–5 Putnam pb $11.95
0–425–06053–5 Berkley pb $5.50

- R. Ornstein & R.F. Thompson
THE AMAZING BRAIN
0–395–35486–2 Houghton Mifflin $16.95
0–395–40800–8 Houghton Mifflin pb $8.75

- M. Reiser
MIND, BRAIN, BODY: Toward a Convergence of Psychoanalysis and Neurobiology
0–465–04603–7 Harper & Row $22.95

- Richard Restak
THE MIND
An illustrated companion to the PBS television series
0–553–05314–0 Bantam $29.95

- Carl Sagan
BROCA'S BRAIN
0–394–50169–1 Random House $14.95
0–345–33689–5 Ballantine pb $4.50

- J. Winson
BRAIN AND PSYCHE: The Biology of the Unconcious
0–394–74148–X Doubleday pb $9.95

HISTORY OF BIOLOGY

- William Coleman
BIOLOGY IN THE NINETEENTH CENTURY
0–521–29293–X Cambridge pb $12.95

- Lois Magner
A HISTORY OF THE LIFE SCIENCES
Excellent summaries of each branch of modern biology
0–8247–8071–8 Dekker $39.75

Biography

- Francis Crick
WHAT MAD PURSUIT: A Personal View of Scientific Discovery
"Crick . . . recounts his failures as well as his successes . . . But then the failures of a scientist of Crick's calibre are nearly as instructive as the successes"—New Yorker
0–465–09137–7 Basic Books $16.95

- A. Hunter Dupree
ASA GRAY: American Botanist, Friend of Darwin
"Among the very finest scientific biographies I have read. The balance between the person and the career in science is unprecedented"—Thomas S. Kuhn
0–8018–3741–3 Johns Hopkins pb $14.95

- François Jacob
THE STATUE WITHIN: An Autobiography
Nobel Prize-winning French microbiologist
0–465–08223–8 Basic $22.95

- John Janovy, Jr.
ON BECOMING A BIOLOGIST
0–06–015467–5 Harper & Row $15.95

- Evelyn Fox Keller
A FEELING FOR THE ORGANISM: The Life and Work of Barbara McClintock
The Nobel Prize-winning geneticist who upset conventional wisdom by demonstrating that genes can spontaneously rearrange themselves
0–7167–1504–X W.H. Freeman pb $10.95

Chimpanzees, from The Emergence of Humankind *by John E. Pfeiffer (Harper & Row)*

• Rita Levi-Montalcini

IN PRAISE OF IMPERFECTION: My Life and Work
Memoirs of the Nobel Prize winner, who discovered nerve growth factor
0–465–03217–6 Basic Books $18.95

• Edward Lurie

LOUIS AGASSIZ: A Life in Science
"By far the best work on this central figure in the history of American biology"—Stephen Jay Gould
0–8018–3743–X Johns Hopkins pb $14.95

• Kenneth Manning

BLACK APOLLO OF SCIENCE: The Life of Ernest Everett Just
The engrossing story of a prominent marine biologist
0–19–503498–8 Oxford pb $10.95

Medicine

▶ See also Health

HISTORY OF MEDICINE

• Erwin Ackerknecht

A SHORT HISTORY OF MEDICINE
0–8018–2726–4 Johns Hopkins pb $9.95

• Mark Caldwell

THE LAST CRUSADE: The War on Consumption, 1872-1954
An entertaining and often surprising social and cultural history of tuberculosis, ranging from its role as an idealized, spiritualized affliction bestowed on sensitive fictional characters to the sanatorium subculture of Saranac Lake, New York
0–689–11810–4 Atheneum $22.50

• Kenneth J. Carpenter

A HISTORY OF SCURVY AND VITAMIN C
0–521–34773–4 Cambridge pb $12.95

• Ludwig Edelstein

ANCIENT MEDICINE
0–8018–3491–0 Johns Hopkins pb $14.95

• Ted Kaptchuk & Michael Croucher

THE HEALING ARTS: Exploring the Medical Ways of the World
0–671–64389–4 Simon & Schuster $17.95
0–671–64506–4 Simon & Schuster pb $7.95

• Lester King

MEDICAL THINKING: A Historical Preface
The logic traditionally used to identify an illness, considered as a way of evaluating present medical practices
0–691–02385–9 Princeton pb $13.95

• Judith Walzer Leavitt & Ronald Numbers, editors

SICKNESS AND HEALTH IN AMERICA: Readings in the History of Medicine and Public Health
0–299–10274–2 Wisconsin pb $14.95

• Albert Lyons & R. Joseph Petrucelli

MEDICINE: An Illustrated History
With over 1000 illustrations
0–8109–8080–0 Abrams $39.95

• Roderick McGrew

ENCYCLOPEDIA OF MEDICAL HISTORY
0–07–045087–0 McGraw-Hill $38.75

• Sherwin Nuland

DOCTORS: The Biography of Medicine
By a Yale professor. "The heroes of [this] story (and there is even one heroine) are the great doctors . . . whose hunger to know carried the business of discovery forward"—*NY Times*
0–394–55130–3 Knopf $24.95

• Ronald Numbers

MEDICINE IN THE NEW WORLD: New Spain, New France, and New England
0–87049–517–8 Tennessee $18.95

• William B. Ober

BOSWELL'S CLAP & OTHER ESSAYS: Medical Analyses of Literary Men's Afflictions
Witty, learned, digressive, and gossipy essays by a doctor investigating the literary evidence for the medical and psychological problems of writers such as Lawrence, Swinburne, Johnson, and Rochester
0–06–097187–8 Harper & Row pb $8.95

• Martin Pernick

A CALCULUS OF SUFFERING: Pain, Professionalism, and Anesthesia in 19th-Century America
0–231–05187–5 Columbia pb $14.50

Charles Rosenberg

THE CARE OF STRANGERS: The Rise of America's Hospital System
"The most ambitious historical work on the hospital and on American medicine generally"—*NY Times*
0–465–00877–1 Basic Books $22.45
0–465–00878–X Basic Books pb $12.95

• Edward Shorter

BEDSIDE MANNERS: The Troubled History of Doctors and Patients
0–671–63309–0 Simon & Schuster pb $9.95

• Paul Starr

THE SOCIAL TRANSFORMATION OF AMERICAN MEDICINE
0–465–07935–0 Basic Books pb $13.95

• Rosemary Stevens

IN SICKNESS AND IN WEALTH: American Hospitals in the 20th Century
The modern American hospital: part business, part social welfare organization, and part high-tech laboratory
0–465–03223–0 Harper & Row $24.95

• Morris Vogel

THE INVENTION OF THE MODERN HOSPITAL: Boston, 1870 to 1930
0–226–86241–0 Chicago pb $6.95

• Allen Weisse

CONVERSATIONS IN MEDICINE: The Story of 20th-Century American Medicine in the Words of Those Who Created It
0–8147–9200–6 Columbia $35.00
0–8147–9214–6 Columbia pb $15.00

Doctor and patient, late 15th century, in An Introduction to a History of Woodcut *by Arthur M. Hind (Dover)*

    IF YOU CAN'T FIND IT, LOOK IN THE INDEX

• Gerald Weissmann
THEY ALL LAUGHED AT CHRISTOPHER COLUMBUS: Tales of Medicine and the Art of Discovery
Essays on medicine, medical research, and society by the author of *The Woods Hole Cantata*
0–8129–1618–2 Times Books $17.95

• Guy Williams
THE AGE OF AGONY: The Art of Healing, c. 1700-1800
A popular account
0–89733–202–4 Academy Chicago $16.95
0–89733–203–2 Academy Chicago pb $8.95

THE AGE OF MIRACLES: Medicine and Surgery in the 19th Century
0–89733–286–5 Academy Chicago $16.95
0–89733–285–7 Academy Chicago pb $8.95

DISEASE AND RESEARCH

• Natalie Angier
NATURAL OBSESSIONS: The Search for the Oncogene
The search for the genes that give rise to cancer provides a demonstration of how biomedical science is done
Foreword by Lewis Thomas
0–395–45370–4 Houghton Mifflin $19.95

• Joel Davis
DEFENDING THE BODY: Unraveling the Mysteries of Immunology
The immune system and the latest research, explained for the general reader
0–689–11946–1 Atheneum $16.95

• Robert S. Desowitz
NEW GUINEA TAPEWORMS AND JEWISH GRANDMOTHERS: Tales of Parasites and People
0–393–34026–4 Norton pb $6.95

THE THORN IN THE STARFISH: The Immune System and How It Works
0–393–30556–2 Norton pb $6.95

• Sander Gilman
DISEASE AND REPRESENTATION: Images of Illness from Madness to AIDS
A pioneer in the study of stereotypes examines the images of disease and its victims that society creates
0–8014–2119–5 Cornell $37.50
0–8014–9476–1 Cornell pb $13.95

• Jeff Goldberg
ANATOMY OF A SCIENTIFIC DISCOVERY
The discovery of endorphins, natural opiates produced in the brain, and the international race to break their genetic codes and find a nonaddictive pain killer
0–553–05261–6 Bantam $17.95

• John Last, editor
A DICTIONARY OF EPIDEMIOLOGY
The standard reference. "Consider this an essential companion to serious reading of the medical literature"—*Yale Journal of Biology and Medicine*
0–19–505480–6 Oxford $24.95
0–19–505481–4 Oxford pb $12.95

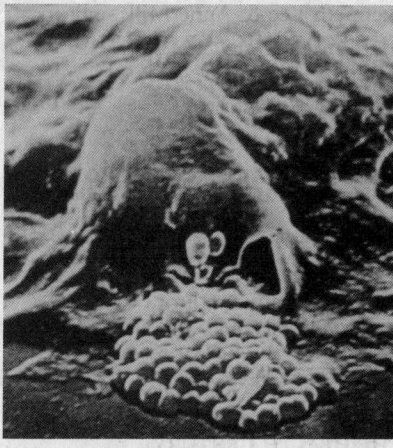

An electromicrograph of defense cells migrating toward a bacterial colony, from Medicine: An Illustrated History *by Albert S. Lyons, M.D., and R. Joseph Pertrucelli II, M.D. (Abradale)*

• Thomas McKeown
THE ORIGINS OF HUMAN DISEASE
A history drawing on archaeological, historical, and demographic evidence and on the author's own work in the history of infection
0–631–15505–8 Blackwell $34.95

• Lennart Nilsson
THE BODY VICTORIOUS
More than 300 photos of the immune system at work
0–385–29507–3 Delacorte $25.00

• William Sargent
THE YEAR OF THE CRAB: Marine Animals in Modern Medicine
How medical researchers have transformed such unlikely creatures as the horseshoe crab into benefactors of humanity
0–393–02403–2 Norton $14.95

• Lewis Thomas
THE YOUNGEST SCIENCE: Notes of a Medicine Watcher
An informal, nostalgic autobiography reflecting the vast changes in medicine since the early part of the century
0–553–34066–2 Bantam pb $6.95

Future Medicine

Laurence Foss & Kenneth Rothenberg
THE SECOND MEDICAL REVOLUTION: From Biomedicine to Infomedicine
Psychoneuro-immunology and other next-tech medical marvels
0–87773–394–5 Shambala $29.45

Marshall Goldberg
CELL WARS: The Immune System's Newest Weapons Against Cancer
Monoclonal antibodies—how they were developed and how they are likely to affect cancer therapy
0–374–12010–2 FS&G $17.95

Eve Nichols
HUMAN GENE THERAPY
An examination of the potentials and pitfalls of an exciting and controversial new medical treatment
0–674–41470–5 Harvard $22.95

Holcomb B. Noble, editor
NEXT: The Coming Era in Medicine
Essays on recent advances in such areas as cancer therapy, brain chemistry, organ transplants, and bioengineering
0–316–61132–8 Little, Brown $17.95
0–316–61133–6 Little, Brown pb $9.70

MEDICAL CARE AND HEALTH POLICY

• Arthur Barsky
WORRIED SICK: Our Troubled Quest for Wellness
A psychiatrist on hypochondria and the influence of medication on health care
0–316–08255–4 Little, Brown $17.95

• Robert Blank
RATIONING MEDICINE
Who is to benefit from new medical technologies?
0–231–06536–1 Columbia $25.00

• Joseph Califano
AMERICA'S HEALTH CARE REVOLUTION: Who Lives? Who Dies? Who Pays?
From the former Health, Education and Welfare Secretary
0–394–54291–6 Random House $17.95

• Daniel Callahan
SETTING LIMITS: Medical Goals in an Aging Society
A highly controversial book about medical priorities, by the director and co-founder of the Hastings Institute
0–671–22477–8 Simon & Schuster $18.95

• Jean De Kervasdoue & others, editors
THE END OF AN ILLUSION: The Future of Health Policy in Western Industrialized Nations
Comparative studies of health systems and medical care
0–520–04726–5 California $35.00

• Charles Dougherty
AMERICAN HEALTH CARE: Realities, Rights, and Reforms
A critical analysis, with arguments for creating a national health care system and health insurance
0–19–505271–4 Oxford $29.95
0–19–505272–2 Oxford pb $14.95

• Daniel Fox
HEALTH POLICIES, HEALTH POLITICS: The British and American Experience, 1911-1965
0–691–04733–2 Princeton $25.00

- **Ivan Illich**
  MEDICAL NEMESIS: The Expropriation of Health
  A polemic on the limitations inherent in our traditional concepts of health and medical care
  0–394–71245–5 Random House pb $8.95

- **Charles Inlander & others**
  MEDICINE ON TRIAL: Medical Mistakes and Incompetence in the Practice of Medicine Today
  An exposé with suggestions for change
  0–13–573544–0 Prentice-Hall $18.50

- **National Academy of Sciences**
  THE FUTURE OF PUBLIC HEALTH
  0–309–03831–6 National Academy $29.95
  0–309–03830–8 National Academy pb $19.95

- **Sandra Panem**
  THE AIDS BUREAUCRACY
  0–674–01270–4 Harvard $22.50
  0–674–01271–2 Harvard pb $9.95

- **Lynn Payer**
  MEDICINE AND CULTURE: Varieties of Treatment
  A thought-provoking comparison of medical practice in the United States, West Germany, Britain, and France. "Deserves an audience beyond the medical community"—*NY Times*
  0–8050–0443–2 Henry Holt $18.95

- **Edmund Pellegrino & David Thomas**
  FOR THE PATIENT'S GOOD: The Restoration of Beneficence in Health Care
  Acting in the patient's best interest, examined in the context of current medical trends
  0–19–504319–7 Oxford $29.95

- **Mary Dale Scheller**
  THE POWER OF THREE: A New Model for Hospital and Nursing Home Care
  An attack on de-personalized health care, from a pioneer of "care partnership"
  0–933071–22–1 Saybrook pb $7.70

MEDICAL ECONOMICS

- **David Blumenthal & others**
  RENEWING THE PROMISE: Medicare and Its Reform
  Its history, current problems, and future
  0–19–504304–9 Oxford $29.95

- **Victor Fuchs**
  THE HEALTH ECONOMY
  Economics applied to health care in America
  0–674–38341–9 Harvard pb $12.95

- **Bryan Jennett**
  HIGH TECHNOLOGY MEDICINE: Benefits and Burdens
  0–19–261588–2 Oxford pb $14.95

- **Rochelle Jones**
  THE SUPERMEDS: How Private For-Profit Medical Conglomerates Are Controlling Our Health Care and What We Can Do About It
  0–684–18695–0 Scribners $19.95

- **Kenneth Lee & Anne Mills, editors**
  THE ECONOMICS OF HEALTH IN DEVELOPING COUNTRIES
  0–19–261385–5 Oxford $32.50
  0–19–261549–1 Oxford pb $13.95

- **Paul Menzel**
  MEDICAL COSTS, MORAL CHOICES: A Philosophy of Health Care Economics in America
  0–300–02960–8 Yale $35.00
  0–300–03476–8 Yale pb $9.95

- **Carl J. Schramm, editor**
  HEALTH CARE AND ITS COSTS
  0–393–02437–7 Norton $18.95
  0–393–95671–7 Norton pb $8.25

- **Edward Shorter**
  THE HEALTH CENTURY
  Companion volume to the PBS television series
  0–385–24236–0 Doubleday $21.95

- **Anne Stoline & Jonathan Weiner**
  THE NEW MEDICAL MARKETPLACE: A Physician's Guide to the Health Care Revolution
  A guide for physicians to balancing medical care and medical costs
  0–8018–3644–1 Johns Hopkins $26.50
  0–8018–3645–X Johns Hopkins pb $12.95

MEDICAL ETHICS

- **Jonathan Austyn, editor**
  NEW PROSPECTS FOR MEDICINE
  The practical and ethical implications of new techniques and advances in clinical medicine
  0–19–261647–1 Oxford $24.95

- **Elsie & Bertram Bandman, editors**
  BIOETHICS AND HUMAN RIGHTS: A Reader for Health Professionals
  0–8191–5257–9 University Press pb $19.95

- **Tom Beauchamp & James Childress**
  PRINCIPLES OF BIOMEDICAL ETHICS
  0–19–503285–3 Oxford $29.95
  0–19–503286–1 Oxford pb $17.95

- **Marshall Cohen, & others, editors**
  MEDICINE AND MORAL PHILOSOPHY
  0–691–07268–X Princeton $29.50

- **John Dawson & Melanie Phillips**
  DOCTORS' DILEMMAS: Medical Ethics and Contemporary Science
  0–416–01121–7 Methuen pb $10.95

- **Diane Dutton**
  WORSE THAN THE DISEASE: Pitfalls of Medical Progress
  An assessment of the ethical and economic price we are paying—and will be paying—for medical progress
  0–521–34023–3 Cambridge $29.95

- **Abraham Edel & others**
  MORALITY, PHILOSOPHY, AND PRACTICE
  0–394–32814–0 Random House $22.00

- **Joseph Fletcher**
  MORALS AND MEDICINE: The Moral Problems of the Patient's Right to Know the Truth
  0–691–07234–5 Princeton $30.00
  0–691–02004–3 Princeton pb $9.50

- **Samuel Gorovitz**
  DOCTORS' DILEMMAS: Moral Conflict and Medical Care
  0–19–503695–6 Oxford pb $8.95

- **John Harris**
  THE VALUE OF LIFE: An Introduction to Medical Ethics
  0–7100–9895–2 RC&H $35.00
  0–7102–0437–X RC&H pb $12.95

- **Howard Levine**
  LIFE CHOICES: Confronting the Life and Death Decisions Created by Modern Medicine
  0–671–55385–2 Simon & Schuster $17.95

- **Robert Levine**
  ETHICS AND REGULATION OF CLINICAL RESEARCH
  A review of federal regulations, ethical analyses, and case studies
  0–300–04288–4 Yale pb $16.95

- **Michael Lockwood**
  MORAL DILEMMAS IN MODERN MEDICINE
  0–19–286056–9 Oxford pb $10.50

- **Ruth Macklin**
  MORTAL CHOICES: Ethical Dilemmas in Modern Medicine
  "A thoughtful and lively examination"—Sissela Bok
  0–395–46847–7 Houghton Mifflin pb $8.70

- **Kenneth Vaux, editor**
  POWERS THAT MAKE US HUMAN: The Foundations of Medical Ethics
  0–252–01187–2 Illinois $16.95

- **Robert Veatch**
  DEATH, DYING, AND THE BIOLOGICAL REVOLUTION: Our Last Quest for Responsibility
  "One of the most comprehensive and useful examples of the literature born of [the] new interest in dying"—*Washington Post*
  0–300–04364–3 Yale $40.00
  0–300–04365–1 Yale pb $14.95

- **Ronald Yezzi**
  MEDICAL ETHICS
  0–03–053256–6 Henry Holt pb $32.75

THE MEDICAL PROFESSION

- **Lawrence K. Altman**
  WHO GOES FIRST?: The Story of Self-Experimentation in Medicine
  The *New York Times* medicine reporter looks at doctors as guinea pigs
  0–394–50382–1 Random House $22.00

TO ORDER BOOKS AS GIFTS, SEE PAGE 1

• Bruce Dan, editor
A PIECE OF MY MIND: Doctors Share the Experiences That Have Moved Them, Inspired Them, Angered Them, Saddened Them, and Brought Them Joy
From the "Piece of My Mind" column in the *Journal of the American Medical Association*
Foreword by Art Ulene
0–394–57715–9 Random House $18.95

• Janet Kraegel & Mary Kachoyeanos
"JUST A NURSE"
Two nurses use interviews with nurses from every area of the profession—burn units, cancer wards, AIDS wards, children's hospices, delivery rooms—to discuss the experiences and problems of nurses today and to dispose of myths and stereotypes
0–525–24760–2 Dutton $18.95

• Robert Mendelsohn
CONFESSIONS OF A MEDICAL HERETIC
0–8092–7726–3 Contemporary $9.95
0–446–30627–4 Warner pb $3.95

• Marcia Millman
THE UNKINDEST CUT: Life in the Backrooms of Medicine
A not too kind behind-the-scenes account of surgeons and hospital personnel
0–688–03120–X Morrow $8.95
0–688–08120–7 Morrow pb $5.95

• Regina Morantz-Sanchez
SYMPATHY AND SCIENCE: Women Physicians in American Medicine
0–19–503627–1 Oxford $24.95

• Shirley Moskow, editor
HUNAN HAND AND OTHER AILMENTS: Letters to the New England Journal of Medicine
Shocking, irreverent or undignified, these letters reflect doctors smiling at life's absurdities
0–316–58533–5 Little, Brown $15.95

• John Pekkanen, editor
M.D.: Doctors Talk About Themselves
A medical journalist's foray into the physician's private world. "There is not a false note in *M.D.* I alternately winced at and took pride in my profession"—Dr. Richard Selzer
0–440–50028–1 Doubleday $18.95

• Edward Rosenbaum
A TASTE OF MY OWN MEDICINE: When the Doctor Is the Patient
0–394–56282–8 Random House $16.95

• Richard Selzer
CONFESSIONS OF A KNIFE
Candid essays by a surgeon about his life and work
0–688–06491–4 Morrow pb $6.95

LETTERS TO A YOUNG DOCTOR
0–671–44299–6 Simon & Schuster pb $7.95

MORTAL LESSONS: Notes on the Art of Surgery
0–671–64102–6 Simon & Schuster pb $7.95

RITUALS OF SURGERY
0–688–06490–6 Morrow pb $6.95

TAKING THE WORLD IN FOR REPAIRS
0–14–010305–8 Penguin pb $7.95

• Milton Slocum
MANHATTAN COUNTRY DOCTOR
The adventures of a Hell's Kitchen doctor
0–345–35659–4 Ballantine pb $7.95

• John Stoeckle & George Abbot White
PLAIN PICTURES OF PLAIN DOCTORING: Vernacular Expression in New Deal Medicine and Photography
0–262–19236–5 MIT $25.00

• Richard Weeder
SURGEON: The View from Behind the Mask
Inside the operating room—and inside the mind of a surgeon
0–8092–4606–6 Contemporary $17.95

I am scheduled to remove an Indian woman's gallbladder at 8:00 a.m. All night my own abdominal griping has spiraled to truly marvelous heights, my bowels vibrating like a harp. An operation performed under such intestinal duress is likely to become a photo-finish race. How I envy the antibodies of the roomful of Peruvian doctors and students who have gathered to assist and observe. And how I curse my insipid Connecticut colon. In the room where I work no one speaks English. We shall see.

Richard Selzer
TAKING THE WORLD IN FOR REPAIRS
0–14–010305–8 Penguin pb $7.95

Medical Education

• Stephen Hoffman
UNDER THE ETHER DOME: One Doctor's Apprenticeship at Massachusetts General Hospital
0–684–18580–6 Scribners $18.95

• Perri Klass
A NOT ENTIRELY BENIGN PROCEDURE: Four Years as a Medical Student
0–399–13223–6 Putnam $18.95
0–451–15358–8 NAL pb $4.50

• Robert Klitzman
A YEAR-LONG NIGHT: Tales of a Medical Intern
0–670–81777–5 Viking $17.95

• Melvin Konner
BECOMING A DOCTOR: A Journey of Initiation in Medical School
An anthropologist's career change
0–14–011116–6 Penguin pb $7.95

• Kenneth Ludmerer
LEARNING TO HEAL: The Development of American Medical Education
0–465–03881–6 Basic Books pb $12.95

The AIDS Crisis

"The Human Immunodeficiency Virus (HIV) epidemic will be a challenging factor in American life for years to come and should be a concern to all Americans. Recent estimates suggest that almost 500,000 Americans will have died or progressed to the later stages of the disease by 1992.

Even this incredible number, however, does not reflect the current gravity of the problem. One to 1.5 million Americans are believed to be infected with the human immunodeficiency virus but are not yet ill enough to realize it . . . .

Knowledge is a critical weapon against HIV—knowledge about the virus and how it is transmitted, knowledge of how to maintain one's health, knowledge of one's own infection status. It is critical too, that knowledge lead towards responsibility towards oneself and others. It is the responsibility of all Americans to become educated about HIV. It is the responsibility of those infected not to infect others. It is the responsibility of all citizens to treat those infected with HIV with respect and compassion. All individuals should be responsible for their actions and the consequences of those actions."—*Report of the Presidential Commission on the Human Immunodeficiency Virus Epidemic*, June 1988

• Dennis Altman
AIDS IN THE MIND OF AMERICA: The Social, Political, and Psychological Impact of a New Epidemic
0–385–19524–9 Doubleday pb $8.95

• Douglas Crimp, editor
AIDS: Cultural Analysis, Cultural Activism
Essays on the cultural images that have emerged in the AIDS crisis and how they have affected public and private response
0–262–03140–X MIT $20.00
0–262–53079–1 MIT pb $10.95

• Elizabeth Fee & Daniel Fox, editors
AIDS: The Burdens of History
Essays on how approaches to history affect attitudes toward AIDS, and on past parallels to issues of quarantine, privacy and public health
0–520–06395–3 California $25.00
0–520–06396–1 California pb $11.95

• Dr. Joseph Feldschuh with Doron Weber
SAFE BLOOD: Purifying the Nation's Blood Supply in the Age of AIDS
Reveals the unreported risks of the average transfusion and assails the unsafe practices of some of America's leading blood services
0–02–910065–8 Free Press $19.95

• Michael Koch
AIDS: From Molecule to Pandemic
0–19–261779–6 Oxford $35.00

- Larry Kramer
**REPORTS FROM THE HOLOCAUST:
The Making of An AIDS Activist**
A collection of essays on AIDS from 1978
to the present, written by a leading gay
activist and playwright, author of *The
Normal Heart*
0–312–02634–X St. Martin's $18.95

- William H. Masters, Virginia E.
Johnson & Robert C. Kolodny
**CRISIS: Heterosexual Behavior in the Age
of AIDS**
Controversial work in which the authors
claim that the AIDS virus is more
widespread in the non-drug-using
heterosexual community than is commonly
assumed
0–8021–1049–5 Grove $15.95

- The Names Project
**THE QUILT: Stories from The Names
Project**
An illustrated look at San Francisco's
Names Project and its quilt, in which
nearly 2000 panels celebrate the lives of
people who have died from AIDS
0–671–66597–9 Pocket $22.95

- National Academy of Sciences
**MOBILIZING AGAINST AIDS: The
Unfinished Story of a Virus**
0–674–57761–2 Harvard pb $7.95

- Scientific American
**THE SCIENCE OF AIDS: Readings from
Scientific American**
0–7167–2036–1 W.H. Freeman pb $9.95

- Susan Sontag
AIDS AND ITS METAPHORS
0–374–10257–0 Farrar, Straus & Giroux $14.95

Government and Health Policy

- Ronald Bayer
**PRIVATE ACTS, SOCIAL
CONSEQUENCES: AIDS and the Politics
of Public Health**
A critical examination of the health
establishment's response to the AIDS
epidemic
0–02–901961–3 Free Press $22.95

- Leon McCusick, editor
**WHAT TO DO ABOUT AIDS: Physicians
and Mental Health Professionals Discuss the
Issues**
A collection, first published in 1986,
focusing on the effects of AIDS in San
Francisco
0–520–05936–0 California pb $10.95

- Padraig O'Malley, editor
**THE AIDS EPIDEMIC: Private Rights and
the Public Interest**
A handbook of articles on various aspects
of the AIDS epidemic
0–8070–0600–9 Beacon $25.00
0–8070–0601–7 Beacon pb $12.95

- Sandra Panem
THE AIDS BUREAUCRACY
An investigation into the efficacy of
government efforts to deal with AIDS,
focusing in particular on the US Public
Health Service
0–674–01270–4 Harvard $22.50
0–674–01271–2 Harvard pb $9.95

- Randy Shilts
**AND THE BAND PLAYED ON: Politics,
People, and the AIDS Epidemic**
Widely-acclaimed best-seller that chronicles
the history of the epidemic and the
government's failure to react quickly to
contain it
0–312–00994–1 St. Martin's $24.95
0–14–011369–X Penguin pb $12.95

Women and AIDS

- Diane Richardson
WOMEN AND AIDS
0–416–01741–X RC&H $29.95
0–416–01751–7 RC&H pb $9.95

- Ines Rieder & Patricia Ruppelt,
editors
AIDS: The Women
An anthology of writings by women with
AIDS as well as by women whose lives
have been affected by the disease
0–939416–21–2 Cleis pb $9.95

- Helen Singer Kaplan
**THE REAL TRUTH ABOUT WOMEN
AND AIDS: How to Eliminate the Risks
Without Giving up Love and Sex**
Advice from the Director of the Human
Sexuality Program at New York Hospital-
Cornell Medical Center
0–671–65743–7 Simon & Schuster pb $5.95

- Bonnie Lester
**WOMEN AND AIDS: A Practical Guide for
Those Who Help Others**
0–8264–0501–0 Continuum $15.95

PRACTICAL GUIDES

- Consumer Reports
AIDS: Trading Fears for Facts
A guide for teenagers
0–89043–269–4 Consumer Reports pb $3.50

- Harlan Dalton & others
**AIDS AND THE LAW: A Guide for the
Public**
0–300–04078–4 Yale pb $7.95

- Martin Delaney & Peter Goldblum
**STRATEGIES FOR SURVIVAL: A Gay
Man's Health Manual for the Age of AIDS**
A comprehensive guide covering gay
health
0–312–00558–X St. Martin's pb $10.95

- Paul H. Douglas & Laura Pinsky
**THE ESSENTIAL AIDS FACT BOOK:
What You Need to Know to Protect
Yourself, Your Family, All Your Loved
Ones**
0–671–64772–5 Pocket pb $3.95

- Lyn Frumkin & John Leonard
QUESTIONS AND ANSWERS ON AIDS
0–380–75467–3 Avon pb $3.95

- Elisabeth Kübler-Ross & Mal
Warshaw
AIDS: The Ultimate Challenge
An expert on working with the terminally
ill offers compassionate advice to those
confronting AIDS
0–02–567170–7 Macmillan $17.95

- John Langone
AIDS: The Facts
Scientific consensus used to trace the
progress of the epidemic and to examine
its enigmas
0–316–51413–6 Little, Brown $17.95
0–316–51412–8 Little, Brown pb $8.95

- Leonard J. Martelli & others
**WHEN SOMEONE YOU KNOW HAS
AIDS: A Practical Guide**
Information and advice for the family,
friends, and loved ones of people with
AIDS
Foreword by Joyce I. Wallace
0–517–56556–0 Crown pb $9.95

- Bettyclare Moffatt
**WHEN SOMEONE YOU LOVE HAS
AIDS: A Book of Hope for Family and
Friends**
0–452–25945–2 NAL pb $8.95

- Tom O'Connor
LIVING WITH AIDS: Reaching Out
How those with AIDS or ARC can bolster
their immune systems
0–938569–00–7 Corwin pb $18.95

- Michael Shernoff & William A. Scott,
editors
**THE SOURCEBOOK ON LESBIAN/GAY
HEALTH CARE**
An exhaustive look at the many health
issues that affect the gay and lesbian
community: physical and mental health,
substance abuse, AIDS, and more
0–9621128–0–1 Lesbian & Gay Health $17.95

- James Slaff & John Brubaker
**THE AIDS EPIDEMIC: How You Can
Protect Yourself and Your Family, Why
You Must**
0–446–30143–4 Warner pb $3.95

- Art Ulene
SAFE SEX IN A DANGEROUS WORLD
0–394–75625–8 Random House pb $3.95

- Oralee Wachter
SEX, DRUGS AND AIDS
0–553–34454–4 Bantam pb $3.95

MEMOIRS AND LIFE STORIES

- Emmanuel Dreuilhe
MORTAL EMBRACE: Living With AIDS
Translated by Linda Coverdale
0–8090–7019–7 Hill & Wang $15.95

- Susan Kuklin
FIGHTING BACK
A look at several people with AIDS and at
the volunteers who offer them support
0–399–21621–9 Putnam $13.95

- Barbara Peabody
**THE SCREAMING ROOM: A Mother's
Journal of Her Son's Struggle with AIDS**
A moving account by the mother of a
young man with AIDS
0–86679–030–6 Oak Tree $15.95
0–380–70345–9 Avon pb $3.95

- George Whitmore
**SOMEONE WAS HERE: Problems in the
AIDS Epidemic**
0–453–00601–9 NAL $17.95

William M. Hoffman
AS IS
Highly acclaimed play dealing with
AIDS
0–394–74286–9 Random House pb $3.95

Michael Klein, editor
**POETS FOR LIFE: 76 Poets Respond
to AIDS**
Features the work of James Merrill,
Adrienne Rich, Allen Ginsberg, Jean
Valentine, June Jordan, Paul Monette,
Robert Creeley, and many others
0–517–52742–7 Crown $18.95

Paul Monette
**LOVE ALONE: Eighteen Elegies for
Rog**
"This is real poetry of real love, real
death in real life, as it is being
experienced by the generation of gay
men caught in the war called AIDS"—
Judy Grahn
0–312–02602–1 St. Martin's pb $7.95

Edmund White & Adam Mars-
Jones
**THE DARKER PROOF: Stories From a
Crisis**
Seven short stories about AIDS,
written by two outstanding gay writers
0–452–26070–1 NAL pb $7.95

Earth Sciences

Geology has historically been hampered by conflicts between physical evidence and theological constraints. Leonardo da Vinci kept private his correct explanation of the fossilized seashells found on Italian mountain peaks; a century later a Vatican cataloger described them as having been created "as is" by God, simultaneously with everything else. The great boulders perched oddly across the European landscape, far from the original outcrop, were widely believed to have been displaced by Noah's flood until Louis Agassiz's theory that during the Ice Age glaciers had moved across the continents, dragging rocks along. Even the fashionable theory of continental drift (plate tectonics is the latest formulation) was ignored for decades after its initial publication early in this century.

HISTORY

- Claude Albritton, Jr.
**THE ABYSS OF TIME: Changing
Conceptions of the Earth's Antiquity After
the Sixteenth Century**
0–87477–389–X Tarcher pb $9.95

- Henry & Carol Faul
**IT BEGAN WITH A STONE: A History of
Geology from the Stone Age to the Age of
Plate Tectonics**
0–471–89735–3 John Wiley $46.95
0–471–89605–5 John Wiley pb $22.95

- Stephen Jay Gould
**TIME'S ARROW, TIME'S CYCLE: Myth
and Metaphor in the Discovery of
Geological Time**
A most engaging account of geology's
discovery of "deep time"
0–674–89198–8 Harvard $17.50
0–674–89199–6 Harvard pb $8.95

- Mott Greene
**GEOLOGY IN THE NINETEENTH
CENTURY: Changing Views in a Changing
World**
0–8014–1467–9 Cornell $34.50
0–8014–9295–5 Cornell pb $12.95

- Rachael Laudan
**FROM MINERALOGY TO GEOLOGY:
The Foundations of a Science, 1650-1830**
0–226–46950–6 Chicago $27.50

- Martin Rudwick
**THE GREAT DEVONIAN
CONTROVERSY: The Shaping of
Scientific Knowledge Among Gentlemanly
Specialists**
Recounts the scientific debate of the 1830s and 1840s about the dating of puzzling rock strata and fossils. "[It] could become one of our century's key documents in understanding science and its history"—Stephen Jay Gould
0–226–73102–2 Chicago pb $19.95

Earth History

- Preston Cloud
**OASIS IN SPACE: Earth History from the
Beginning**
0–393–01952–7 Norton $29.95

- David Fisher
**THE BIRTH OF THE EARTH: A
Wanderlied Through Space, Time, and the
Human Imagination**
"A well-written, important, and novel history"—*New Scientist*
0–231–06042–4 Columbia $24.95
0–231–06043–2 Columbia pb $14.95

- W.B. Harland
A GEOLOGIC TIME SCALE
0–521–28919–X Cambridge pb $12.95

- John & Katherine Imbrie
ICE AGES: Solving the Mystery
0–674–44075–7 Harvard pb $8.95

GEOLOGY

- David Lambert
THE FIELD GUIDE TO GEOLOGY
Includes 500 illustrations, diagrams, charts, and maps
0–8160–1697–6 Facts On File $22.95

- John McPhee
"McPhee has demonstrated that he is our best and liveliest writer about the earth and earth sciences. He overspreads his territory like an ice sheet, and yet his touch is light: he can distribute silt and sand as deftly as he wears down mountains."—Wallace Steger, *LA Times*
BASIN AND RANGE
0–374–10914–1 Farrar, Straus & Giroux $10.95
0–374–51690–1 Farrar, Straus & Giroux pb $7.95
IN SUSPECT TERRAIN
0–374–17650–7 Farrar, Straus & Giroux $12.95
0–374–51794–0 Farrar, Straus & Giroux pb $7.95
RISING FROM THE PLAINS
0–374–25082–0 Farrar, Straus & Giroux $15.95

On the geologic time scale, a human lifetime is reduced to a brevity that is too inhibiting to think about. The mind blocks the information. Geologists, dealing always with deep time, find that it seeps into their beings and affects them in various ways. They see the unbelievable swiftness with which one evolving species on the earth has learned to reach into the dirt of some tropical island and fling 747s into the sky. They see the thin band in which are the all but indiscernible stratifications of Cro-Magnon, Moses, Leonardo, and now. Seeing a race unaware of its own instantaneousness in time, they can reel off all the species that have come and gone, with emphasis on those that have specialized themselves to death.

John McPhee
BASIN AND RANGE
0–374–10914–1 FS&G $10.95
0–374–51690–1 FS&G pb $7.95

- Ronald Parker
THE TENTH MUSE: The Pursuit of Earth Science
0–684–18608–X Scribners $15.95

- F.J. Pettijohn
MEMOIRS OF AN UNREPENTANT FIELD GEOLOGIST: A Candid Profile of Some Geologists and Their Science
0–226–66403–1 Chicago $25.00
0–226–66405–8 Chicago pb $10.95

PLATE TECTONICS

- Claude Allegre
THE BEHAVIOR OF THE EARTH: Continental and Seafloor Mobility
"Required reading for anyone interested in how science works and in the significance and benefits of its major breakthroughs"— Donald Turcotte
0–674–06457–7 Harvard $35.00

- Edwin Colbert
WANDERING LANDS AND ANIMALS: The Story of Continental Drift and Animal Populations
0–486–24918–2 Dover pb $7.95

- H.E. LeGrand
DRIFTING CONTINENTS AND SHIFTING THEORIES: The Modern Revolution in Geology and Scientific Change
0–521–32210–3 Cambridge $45.00
0–521–31105–5 Cambridge pb $19.95

- Chet Raymo
THE CRUST OF OUR EARTH: An Armchair Traveler's Guide to the New Geology
0–13–195099–1 Prentice-Hall pb $12.95

- Tjeerd H. Van Andel
NEW VIEWS OF AN OLD PLANET: Continental Drift and the History of the Earth
0–521–30084–3 Cambridge $22.95

EARTHQUAKES AND VOLCANOES

- James Gere & Haresh Shah
TERRA NON FIRMA: Understanding and Preparing for Earthquakes
0–7167–1497–3 W.H. Freeman pb $12.95

- T.A. Heppenheimer
THE COMING QUAKE: Science and Trembling on the California Earthquake Frontier
0–8129–1616–6 Times Books $17.95

- Cliff Ollier
VOLCANOES
The mechanism of volcanic activity, the products of eruption, and the landform produced by volcanoes
0–631–15664–X Blackwell $55.00
0–631–15977–0 Blackwell pb $24.95

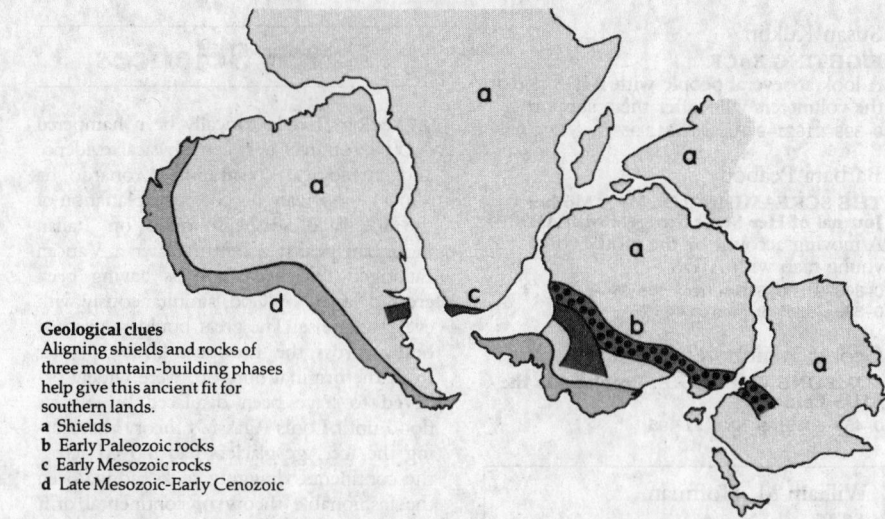

Geological clues
Aligning shields and rocks of three mountain-building phases help give this ancient fit for southern lands.
a Shields
b Early Paleozoic rocks
c Early Mesozoic rocks
d Late Mesozoic-Early Cenozoic

The geographical evidence for continental drift, from The Field Guide to Geology *by David Lambert and The Diagram Group* (Facts On File)

- David Ritchie
SUPERQUAKE: Why Earthquakes Occur and When the Big One Will Hit Southern California
0–517–56699–0 Crown $18.95

- Scientific American
VOLCANOES AND THE EARTH'S INTERIOR: Readings from Scientific American
0–7167–1384–5 W.H. Freeman pb $12.95

- Robert Wenkam
THE EDGE OF FIRE: Volcano and Earthquake Country in Western North America and Hawaii
The history, lore, and latest information on earthquakes and volcanoes, with more than 100 color photos
0–87156–714–8 Sierra Club $35.00

The San Andreas Fault, from Earthquakes *by Bruce A. Bolt (Freeman/photo courtesy Robert E. Wallace, USGS)*

- Robert Wood
EARTHQUAKES AND VOLCANOES
1–55584–083–3 Weidenfeld & Nicolson $12.95

METEOROLOGY

- M.I. Budyko & A.B. Ronov
A HISTORY OF THE EARTH'S ATMOSPHERE
0–387–17235–1 Springer pb $42.00

- John Gribbin
THE BREATHING PLANET
0–631–14289–4 Blackwell pb $12.95

- McGraw-Hill
THE METEOROLOGY SOURCE BOOK
Over 100 articles from the *Encyclopedia of Science and Technology* covering weather systems and meteorological phenomena, and the methods for studying, forecasting, and predicting weather
0–07–045511–2 McGraw-Hill $40.00

- William Reifsnyder
WEATHERING THE WILDERNESS: The Sierra Club Guide to Practical Meteorology
0–87156–266–9 Sierra Club pb $8.95

- Charles E. Roth
THE SKY OBSERVER'S GUIDEBOOK
0–13–812793–X Prentice-Hall $17.95
0–13–812785–9 Prentice-Hall pb $10.95

- Vincent Schaefer & John Day
A FIELD GUIDE TO THE ATMOSPHERE
A Peterson Field Guide
0–395–24080–8 Houghton Mifflin $17.95
0–395–33033–5 Houghton Mifflin pb $12.95

- Scientific American
LIGHT FROM THE SKY: Readings from Scientific American
0–7167–1222–9 W.H. Freeman pb $9.95

➤ **FOR OVERSEAS ORDERING INFORMATION, SEE PAGE 1**

- James Trefil
MEDITATIONS AT SUNSET: A Scientist Looks at the Sky
Puzzles of the atmosphere
0–684–18787–6 Scribners $16.95

OCEANOGRAPHY

- Willard Bascom
THE CREST OF THE WAVE: Adventures in Oceanography
Memoirs of a noted oceanographer
0–06–015927–8 Harper & Row $19.95

WAVES AND BEACHES: The Dynamics of the Ocean Surface
0–385–14844–5 Doubleday pb $9.95

- William Fox
AT THE SEA'S EDGE: An Introduction to Coastal Oceanography for the Amateur Naturalist
0–13–049775–4 Prentice-Hall pb $12.95

- Nixon Griffis, editor
THE MARINER'S GUIDE TO OCEANOGRAPHY
0–688–03976–6 Morrow pb $8.00

- Henry Parker
EXPLORING THE OCEANS: An Introduction for the Traveler and Amateur Naturalist
0–13–297706–0 Prentice-Hall pb $15.95

Glaciers

Robert Sharp
LIVING ICE: Understanding Glaciers and Glaciation
0–521–33009–2 Cambridge $29.95

REFERENCE

- American Geological Institute
DICTIONARY OF GEOLOGICAL TERMS
0–385–18101–9 Anchor pb $8.95

- Andrew Goudie & others, editors
THE ENCYCLOPEDIC DICTIONARY OF PHYSICAL GEOGRAPHY
0–631–15581–3 Blackwell pb $22.50

- Dorothy Lapidus & Donald Coates
THE FACTS ON FILE DICTIONARY OF GEOLOGY AND GEOPHYSICS
0–87196–703–0 Facts On File $24.95

- McGraw-Hill
McGRAW-HILL DICTIONARY OF EARTH SCIENCES
More than 15,000 terms
0–07–045252–0 McGraw-Hill $42.00

McGRAW-HILL ENCYCLOPEDIA OF GEOLOGICAL SCIENCES
0–07–045500–7 McGraw-Hill $85.00

Allan Eckert
EARTH TREASURES: Where to Collect Minerals, Rocks, and Fossils in the United States
Each volume contains over 300 maps, over 1000 numbered sites, and information on where to search; which minerals, rocks, or fossils are likely to be found; methods of searching; preparing for trips; local collecting regulations, and more

Volume 1: The Northeastern Quadrant
0–06–096101–5 Harper & Row pb $14.95

Volume 2: The Southeastern Quadrant
0–06–096131–7 Harper & Row pb $14.95

Volume 3: The Northwestern Quadrant
0–06–096177–5 Harper & Row pb $16.95

Volume 4: The Southwestern Quadrant
0–06–096178–3 Harper & Row pb $16.95

Paleontology

Life has existed on earth for at least 3.5 billion years, leaving behind an abundant fossil record as the visible trace of its grand procession. Paleontology seeks to re-create the progressive passage of life, and its practical endeavors concern the discovery of fossils and the study of the fossil record.

Paleontology embraces several disciplines, ranging from paleozoogeography to biostratigraphy, and contributes data to biomechanics, systematics, and geology. Thus, a balanced understanding of paleontology requires an overview of its principles, practices, and assumptions. Books dealing with the histories of specific fossil groups are enhanced by prior familiarity with a general text.

- David Lambert
A FIELD GUIDE TO PREHISTORIC LIFE
An excellent introductory book which includes over 500 illustrations, maps, and charts
0–8160–1125–7 Facts On File $21.95
0–8160–1389–6 Facts On File pb $14.95

- E.W. Nield & V.C. Tucker
PALAEONTOLOGY: An Introduction
0–08–023854–8 Pergamon $29.00
0–08–023853–X Pergamon pb $14.75

- David Raup & Steven Stanley
PRINCIPLES OF PALEONTOLOGY
0–7167–0022–0 W.H. Freeman $33.95

- B. Ziegler
INTRODUCTION TO PALEOBIOLOGY: General Paleontology
0–470–20067–7 Halsted pb $29.95

FOSSILS

Perhaps the most satisfying reading in paleontology involves works that deal with fossils and with the lost ages in which magnificent creatures—now standing silent in a museum hall—once lived.

- Audubon Society
THE AUDUBON SOCIETY FIELD GUIDE TO NORTH AMERICAN FOSSILS
0–394–52412–8 Knopf $14.95

- Gerard Case
A PICTORIAL GUIDE TO FOSSILS
0–442–22651–9 Van Nostrand Reinhold $34.95

- Niles Eldridge
LIFE PULSE: Episodes from the Story of the Fossil Record
The fossil record, explained by a noted paleontologist and curator at the American Museum of Natural History
0–8160–1151–6 Facts On File $21.95

Life was shaken up rather abruptly at what we now recognize as the Permo-Triassic boundary—the same line of demarcation that serves as the great divide between Paleozoic ("Ancient Life") and Mesozoic ("Middle Life"). I have already remarked that extinction events are real, and perhaps the very best evidence of extinction was the tendency of pre-Darwinian, creation-minded geologists to divide up geologic time according to natural divisions of life as seen arranged vertically in the rocks: phenomena we now know to be relatively sudden extinctions followed by equally large-scale proliferations. Some extinctions were greater than others, involving more different kinds of organisms over large regions of the Earth's surface. The extinction that wreaked such ecological havoc at the end of the Paleozoic was probably the most devastating to have hit life so far. Paleontologist David Raup of the University of Chicago estimates that over 90 percent (perhaps as much as 96 percent) of *all species* became extinct in the relatively brief span of roughly a million years.

Niles Eldridge
LIFE PULSE: Episodes from the Story of the Fossil Record
0–8160–1151–6 Facts On File $21.95

- Carroll & Mildred Fenton
THE FOSSIL BOOK
A record of prehistoric life with over 1500 illustrations
0–385–19327–0 Doubleday $40.00

- George Simpson
FOSSILS AND THE HISTORY OF LIFE
Essential for understanding the significance of fossils in the study of evolution
0–7167–1564–3 W.H. Freeman $32.95

Practical Guides

Bjorn Kurten
HOW TO DEEP-FREEZE A MAMMOTH
0–231–05978–7 Columbia $17.00

Richard Moody
FOSSILS: How to Find and Identify Over 300 Genera
A how-to guide for the amateur
0–02–063370–X Collier pb $8.95

E.W. Nield
DRAWING AND UNDERSTANDING FOSSILS: A Theoretical and Practical Guide for Beginners, with Self-Assessment
0–08–033941–7 Pergamon $33.00
0–08–033940–9 Pergamon pb $17.95

Paleobotany

Some of the best evidence of paleo-climatic change comes from fossil wood, seeds, and pollen. The great Sahara desert once held lush tropical rainforests, as fossil wood from sites in Libya and Egypt testifies. Pollen carried into marine sedimentary basins can often be traced to land origins, making it possible to re-create an earlier ecological scenario. The development of flowers, complex pollination strategies, growth mechanisms, and water retention schemes are other clues to the mystery of our planet's past.

• Henry Andrews
THE FOSSIL HUNTERS: In Search of Ancient Plants
0–8014–1248–X Cornell $42.50

• Frank Knowlton
PLANTS OF THE PAST: A Popular Account of Fossil Plants
0–404–03735–6 AMS $19.50

• Wilson Stewart
PALEOBOTANY AND THE EVOLUTION OF PLANTS
0–521–23315–1 Cambridge $37.50

• Thomas Taylor
PALEOBOTANY: An Introduction to Fossil Plant Biology
0–07–062954–4 McGraw-Hill $54.95

Paleoanthropology

Unlike dinosaurs, early hominids have left only isolated traces in a fragmentary record of broken skeletons and scattered cultural remains. The history of their discovery is filled with eccentric characters and contested theories. The meagerness of the human fossil record, particularly at crucial evolutionary "jumps," and the scarcity of good diagnostic material, have led to a lack of consensus on virtually every theoretical and interpretive issue.

• Michael Day
GUIDE TO FOSSIL MAN
Includes more than 140 illustrations
0–226–13889–5 Chicago $45.00

• Eric Delson
ANCESTORS: The Hard Evidence
An examination of the human fossil record
0–8451–0249–4 A.R. Liss $49.50

• Niles Eldredge & Ian Tattersall
THE MYTHS OF HUMAN EVOLUTION
0–231–05144–1 Columbia $26.00
0–231–05145–X Columbia pb $14.00

• David Lambert
THE FIELD GUIDE TO EARLY MAN
Traces man's growth from primitive primates to modern man, with 500 illustrations, diagrams, maps, and charts
0–8160–1517–1 Facts On File $21.95
0–8160–1801–4 Facts On File pb $10.95

• Mary Leaky
DISCLOSING THE PAST
Another member of the noted family on the search for man's ancestors
0–07–036837–6 McGraw-Hill pb $9.95

• Richard Leaky & Roger Lewin
ORIGINS: What New Discoveries Reveal About the Emergence of Our Species and Its Possible Future
A well-illustrated account from Australopithecines to their tool-making *Homo Sapiens* descendants
0–525–48246–6 Dutton pb $8.95

• Roger Lewin
BONES OF CONTENTION: Controversies in the Search for Human Origins
0–671–52688–X Simon & Schuster $19.95
0–671–66837–4 Simon & Schuster pb $9.95

• John Pfeiffer
THE EMERGENCE OF HUMANKIND
A good introduction, reaching back at least four million years, with observations on the troubled history of paleoanthropology
0–06–045201–3 Harper & Row pb $27.50

• John Reader
MISSING LINKS: The Hunt for Earliest Man
0–14–022800–X Pelican pb $7.95

• Jeffrey Schwartz
THE RED APE: Orang-utans and Human Origins
Proposes that the Asian apes, not the African, may be our closest evolutionary cousins
0–395–38017–0 Houghton Mifflin $18.95

• Robert Wenke
PATTERNS IN PREHISTORY: Humankind's First Three Million Years
0–19–503442–2 Oxford $18.95

HISTORY OF PALEONTOLOGY

• Url Lanham
THE BONE HUNTERS
The history of paleontology in the 1800s and early 1900s, riddled with the intense rivalries and bitter "bone wars," and the interesting lifestyles of the participants
0–231–03152–1 Columbia $36.00

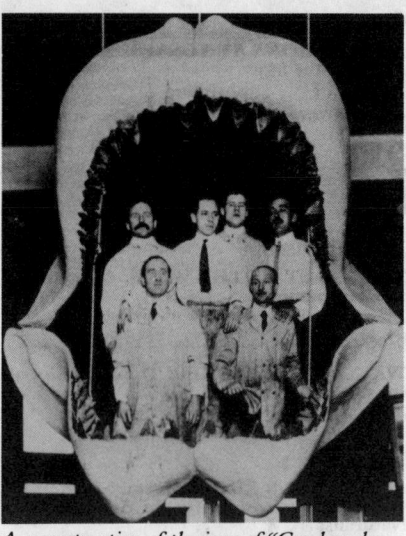

A reconstruction of the jaws of "Carcharodon megalodon," a larger Miocene relative of today's Great White Shark, from Life Pulse: Episodes from the Story of the Fossil Record *by Niles Eldredge (Facts On File)*

• Martin Rudwick
THE MEANING OF FOSSILS: Episodes in the History of Paleontology
0–226–73103–0 Chicago pb $11.95

• George Simpson
DISCOVERERS OF THE LOST WORLD
The search for evidence of long-lost South American mammals
0–300–03188–2 Yale $30.00

• Frank Spencer, editor
A HISTORY OF AMERICAN PHYSICAL ANTHROPOLOGY
0–12–656660–7 Academic $24.95

DINOSAURS AND OTHER EXTINCT ANIMALS

Dinosaurs ruled the earth for well over one hundred million years, only to vanish mysteriously in an event of spectacular magnitude. Possessing an array of spikes, horns, claws, and plated armor, these reptiles of the Mesozoic Era evoke images of monumental predatory battles and of true giants lumbering through primeval swamps and forests.

• R. McNeill Alexander
THE DYNAMICS OF DINOSAURS AND OTHER EXTINCT GIANTS
How did the biggest pterosaurs, the famous flying reptiles, take off and stay in the air? How fast could the biggest dinosaurs run? Could giant marine dinosaurs leap out of the water like today's dolphins? A biomechanics expert draws on mechanical engineering, aerodynamics, and heat-exchange theory for the answers and brings dinosaurs and extinct giant mammals back to life
0–231–06666–X Columbia $30.00

- Robert Bakker
THE DINOSAUR HERESIES
Unconventional ideas about dinosaurs
0–688–04287–2 Morrow $19.95

- Alan Charig
A NEW LOOK AT THE DINOSAURS
Examines long-held ideas and offers
startling alternatives
0–87196–139–3 Facts On File $18.95
0–8160–1167–2 Facts On File pb $12.95

- Edwin Colbert
DINOSAURS: An Illustrated History
0–8437–3332–2 Hammond $30.00

**THE GREAT DINOSAUR HUNTERS
AND THEIR DISCOVERIES**
0–486–24701–5 Dover pb $6.95

- Dougal Dixon, editor
**THE MACMILLAN ILLUSTRATED
ENCYCLOPEDIA OF DINOSAURS AND
PREHISTORIC ANIMALS**
A visual who's who of prehistoric life—
with full-color paintings based on the latest
paleontological discoveries
0–02–580191–0 Macmillan $39.95

- Donald Glut
THE NEW DINOSAUR DICTIONARY
0–8065–0782–9 Lyle Stuart $19.95
0–8065–0918–X Lyle Stuart pb $14.95

- Kevin Padian, editor
**THE BEGINNINGS OF THE AGE OF
DINOSAURS: Faunal Change Across the
Triassic-Jurassic Boundary**
0–521–30328–1 Cambridge $75.00

- David Raup
**THE NEMESIS AFFAIR: A Story of the
Death of Dinosaurs and the Ways of Science**
Does the sun have a companion star that
passed close enough around 65 million
years ago to rain a shower of lethal comets
on the earth that ended the reign of the
dinosaurs?
0–393–30409–4 Norton pb $6.95

Animals of the Ice Age

Flourishing during the great ice age that
lasted some two and a half million years were
such extinct beasts as the giant ground sloth
and giant bear, the heavily insulated wooly
mammoth and wooly rhinoceros, and the
spectacular saber-toothed cats.

- Bjorn Kurten
BEFORE THE INDIANS
A look at more than three million years of
vertebrate animal life in the New World
before the humans arrived at the end of
the ice age
0–231–06582–5 Columbia $29.95

- Antony Sutcliff
**ON THE TRACK OF ICE AGE
MAMMALS**
"The clear, concise text is densely packed
with useful information, while the
numerous, carefully selected photographs,
drawings, charts, graphs, and paintings are
easily worth their weight in words"—
Natural History
0–674–63778–4 Harvard pb $12.95

Natural History

Natural history impinges on nearly every province of knowledge, inevitably creating something of a classification problem. The works listed here touch on aspects of literature, philosophy, biology, and anthropology, as well as more absolute sciences. In *Nature's Diary*, Mikhail Prishvin writes that "most plants and animals are closely connected with the life of man ... but up to now science has done little to study this relationship, and that is where art comes in." There is a large part of art, as of science, in nearly every work here.

To understand the difficulty of selecting works of natural history, one need only consider the case of *Moby Dick*, probably the finest work of 19th-century cetology, or Virgil's *Eclogues*, a superb example of early agrarian poetry. The boundaries we have chosen exclude both works, as well as others that belong more to American literature or the classics than to natural history. We have placed heavy emphasis on North America and have generally stopped short of highly technical works, choosing instead to include those of broadest appeal and greatest practicality.

▶ See also The Outdoors & The Life Sciences

GENERAL WORKS

- David Attenborough
LIFE ON EARTH
The basis of the PBS series
0–316–05747–9 Little, Brown $19.95

- Harry Judge & others, editors
**THE OXFORD ILLUSTRATED
ENCYCLOPEDIA: The Natural World**
0–19–869134–3 Oxford $39.95

- R.J. Lincoln & G.A. Boxshall
**THE CAMBRIDGE ILLUSTRATED
DICTIONARY OF NATURAL HISTORY**
0–521–30551–9 Cambridge $24.95

- National Geographic Society
**OUR CONTINENT: A Natural History of
North America**
0–87044–153–1 National Geographic $14.95

- National Park Foundation
**THE COMPLETE GUIDE TO
AMERICA'S NATIONAL PARKS**
0–1315981–5–5 Simon & Schuster pb $9.95

- Reader's Digest
**THE JOY OF NATURE: How to Observe
and Appreciate the Great Outdoors**
0–89577–036–9 Reader's Digest $22.00

- Freeman Tilden
THE NATIONAL PARKS
A guide to and basic history of America's
national parks
0–394–53976–1 Knopf $25.00
0–394–74294–X Knopf pb $16.95

Essays and Meditations

- Edward Abbey
America's most famous former park ranger
was an excellent writer and passionate
conservationist.
ABBEY'S ROAD: Take the Other
On the road in Australia, Mexico, and the
United States
0–525–48233–4 Dutton pb $8.95

DOWN THE RIVER
Among other things, Abbey on the Green
River, contemplating Thoreau
0–525–48408–6 Dutton pb $9.95

- Edward Abbey & Philip Hyde
SLICKROCK
An oversize collection of excerpts from
Abbey's work and Philip Hyde's
photographs
0–87905–269–4 Peregrine Smith pb $24.95

- Marston Bates
**JUNGLE IN THE HOUSE: Essays in
Natural and Unnatural History**
0–8027–0159–0 Walker pb $7.50

- Wendell Berry
Berry's essays primarily concern land use
and ecology; they are humane, poetic, and
pragmatic all at once.
**A CONTINUOUS HARMONY: Essays
Cultural and Agricultural**
0–15–622575–1 HBJ pb $5.95

HOME ECONOMICS
0–86547–274–2 North Point $20.00
0–86547–275–0 North Point pb $9.95

RECOLLECTED ESSAYS, 1965-1980
0–86547–025–1 North Point $18.00

- Hugh Brody
MAPS AND DREAMS
0–394–74871–9 Pantheon pb $8.95

- Harvey Broome
FACES OF THE WILDERNESS
Visits to various American wildernesses in
the 1950s and '60s
0–87842–027–4 Mountain pb $7.95

- Erik Brown
SEAT IN A WILD PLACE
A retired businessman looks at life by a
New Hampshire pond
0–87233–059–1 Bauhan pb $8.95

- Catherine Caufield
**IN THE RAINFOREST: Report from a
Strange, Beautiful, Imperiled World**
0–394–52701–1 Knopf $16.95
0–226–09786–2 Chicago pb $11.95

Annie Dillard
Dillard's essays are masterpieces of terse
observation.
PILGRIM AT TINKER CREEK
0–06–121980–0 Harper & Row $11.95
0–06–09154–5 Harper & Row pb $7.95

**TEACHING A STONE TO TALK:
Expeditions and Encounters**
0–06–015030–0 Harper & Row $12.95
0–06–091541–2 Harper & Row pb $8.95

- **Loren Eiseley**
Ranging from the history of science to anthropology, Eiseley's meditations include some famous essays in natural history.
THE IMMENSE JOURNEY
0–394–70157–7 Random House pb $4.95

THE NIGHT COUNTRY
0–684–18908–9 Scribners pb $9.95

THE STAR THROWER
Introduction by W.H. Auden
0–15–684909–7 HBJ pb $6.95

THE UNEXPECTED UNIVERSE
0–15–692850–7 HBJ pb $4.95

- **John Fowles**
THE TREE
0–88001–033–9 Ecco $13.50
0–88001–040–1 Ecco pb $7.95

- **John Haines**
LIVING OFF THE COUNTRY: Essays on Poetry and Place
Meditations by a poet living in Alaska
0–472–06333–2 Michigan pb $8.95

- **Donald Hall**
STRING TOO SHORT TO BE SAVED: Recollections of Summers on a New England Farm
Country pieces by a superb poet and essayist
0–87923–282–X Godine pb $7.95

- **Jacquetta Hawkes**
NOTHING BUT OR SOMETHING MORE
A collection of essays and lectures by a distinguished British archaeologist
0–295–95231–8 Washington $10.00

- **John Hay**
Hay is an ardent, almost spiritual naturalist whose works, though centered in New England, are wide-ranging.
THE IMMORTAL WILDERNESS
0–393–02385–0 Norton $14.95

THE RUN
0–393–01269–7 Norton $9.95
0–393–00946–7 Norton pb $3.95

THE UNDISCOVERED COUNTRY
A collection of Hay's essays on nature
0–393–01571–8 Norton $12.95
0–393–30015–3 Norton pb $4.95

- **Bernd Heinrich**
IN A PATCH OF FIREWEED
0–674–44548–1 Harvard $18.50

- **Edward Hoagland**
Hoagland's nature essays are among the best in recent decades.
THE COURAGE OF TURTLES
0–86547–196–7 North Point pb $9.50

RED WOLVES AND BLACK BEARS
0–394–40091–7 Random House pb $8.95

- **Paul Horgan**
OF AMERICA EAST AND WEST: Selections from the Writings of Paul Horgan
Introduction by Henry Steele Commager
0–374–22428–5 Farrar, Straus & Giroux $25.50
0–374–51896–3 Farrar, Straus & Giroux pb $12.50

- **Sue Hubbell**
A COUNTRY YEAR: Living the Questions
A beekeeper in Missouri writes elegant, plain prose about country life
0–06–097086–3 Harper & Row pb $7.95

- **Anthony Huxley**
PLANT AND PLANET
The great-grandson of T.H. Huxley writes on plants and gardening
0–14–007946–7 Penguin pb $6.95

- **Maxine Kumin**
IN DEEP: Country Essays
Essays by a poet
0–670–81431–8 Viking $16.95
0–8070–6323–1 Beacon pb $8.95

- **Aldo Leopold**
Leopold was a pioneering, highly influential conservationist who wrote evocatively of flora, fauna, and seasonal changes in the Wisconsin countryside.
ROUND RIVER: From the Journals of Aldo Leopold
0–19–501563–0 Oxford pb $3.95

A SAND COUNTY ALMANAC & SKETCHES HERE AND THERE
0–19–505305–2 Oxford $17.95

- **Barry Lopez**
CROSSING OPEN GROUND
A new collection of essays by the author of *Arctic Dreams*
0–684–18817–1 Scribners $17.95

OF WOLVES AND MEN
Winner of the Burroughs Medal
0–684–15624–5 Scribners $14.95
0–684–16909–6 Scribners pb $5.95

- **Jonathan Maslow**
BIRD OF LIFE, BIRD OF DEATH: A Naturalist's Journey Through a Land of Political Turmoil
A journalist goes birding through Central America
0–671–52738–X Simon & Schuster $17.95
0–440–50708–1 Dell pb $6.95

- **Peter Matthiessen**
THE CLOUD FOREST: A Chronicle of the South American Wilderness
One of the most important American writers on wilderness
0–14–009549–7 Penguin pb $8.95

UNDER THE MOUNTAIN WALL
A year in New Guinea
0–14–009548–9 Penguin pb $8.95

- **James McConkey**
TO A DISTANT ISLAND
0–525–48256–3 Dutton pb $8.95

- **Thomas McNamee**
NATURE FIRST: Keeping Our Wild Places and Wild Creatures Wild
A brief meditation on the meaning and preservation of nature
0–911797–33–5 Rinehart, Roberts pb $12.50

- **Jake Page**
PASTORAL: A Natural History of Sorts
0–393–01903–9 Norton pb $13.95

"Snow Goose" by John James Audubon (courtesy of The New-York Historical Society)

- **Noel Perrin**
FIRST PERSON RURAL: Essays of a Sometime Farmer
Country essays, set in Vermont, by a farming English professor
0–14–005561–4 Penguin pb $6.95

- **Rutherford Platt**
THIS GREEN WORLD
Winner of the Burroughs Medal 1945
0–396–09188–1 Dodd, Mead $18.95
0–396–09189–X Dodd, Mead pb $12.95

- **David Quammen**
THE FLIGHT OF THE IGUANA: A Sidelong View of Science and Nature
0–385–29592–8 Delacorte $17.95

NATURAL ACTS
Essays collected from Quammen's column in *Outside* magazine; quirky, learned, amusing
0–8052–3967–7 Schocken $16.95
0–440–55696–1 Dell pb $6.95

- **Franklin Russell**
WATCHERS AT THE POND
Born and educated in New Zealand, Russell is the author of numerous nature books, of which this is the best
0–87923–390–7 Godine pb $7.95

- **Ernest Thompson Seton**
WILD ANIMALS I HAVE KNOWN
Among other things, Seton founded the Boy Scouts of America
0–14–017005–7 Penguin pb $7.95

- **Kim Stafford**
HAVING EVERYTHING RIGHT: Essays of Place
Nature essays by a medievalist in Oregon
0–917652–60–6 Confluence $14.95
0–14–010254–X Penguin pb $6.95

- **Wallace Stegner**
ALL THE LITTLE LIVE THINGS
Stegner's novels have won the Pulitzer Prize and the National Book Award; his natural history writings are no less distinguished
0–8032–4110–0 Nebraska $25.95
0–8032–9109–4 Nebraska pb $7.50

Edwin Way Teale
Teale's seasonal tetralogy comprises the following titles:
AUTUMN ACROSS AMERICA
0–396–07958–X Dodd, Mead pb $8.95

🍎 **IF YOU CAN'T FIND IT, LOOK IN THE INDEX**

WANDERING THROUGH WINTER
Winner of the Pulitzer Prize 1966
0–396–07959–8 Dodd, Mead pb $8.95

NORTH WITH THE SPRING
0–396–07956–3 Dodd, Mead pb $8.95

JOURNEY INTO SUMMER
0–396–07957–1 Dodd, Mead pb $8.95

• Lewis Thomas
Thomas' essays on biology, language, medicine, and other subjects, are plain and direct in style.
LATE NIGHT THOUGHTS ON LISTENING TO MAHLER'S NINTH
0–553–34533–8 Bantam pb $7.95

THE LIVES OF A CELL: Notes of a Biology Watcher
0–14–004743–3 Penguin pb $5.95

THE MEDUSA AND THE SNAIL
0–553–25913–X Bantam pb $3.95

• James Trefil
An engaging writer and skilled popularizer of science, Trefil brings alive the world around us.
MEDITATIONS AT SUNSET: A Scientist in the Atmosphere
0–684–18787–6 Scribners $16.95
0–02–025760–0 Macmillan pb $8.95

MEDITATIONS AT 10,000 FEET: A Scientist in the Mountains
0–02–025890–9 Macmillan pb $8.95

A SCIENTIST AT THE SEASHORE
0–02–025920–4 Macmillan pb $8.95

• David Rains Wallace
THE DARK RANGE: A Naturalist's Night Notebook
0–87156–212–X Sierra Club $15.00
0–87156–251–0 Sierra Club pb $8.95

THE UNTAMED GARDEN & OTHER PERSONAL ESSAYS
0–8142–0423–6 Ohio State $15.95

• Alfred North Whitehead
THE CONCEPT OF NATURE
0–521–09245–0 Cambridge pb $14.95

• Edward O. Wilson
BIOPHILIA
Essays in environmental philosophy by a sociobiologist and the Pulitzer Prize-winning author of *On Human Nature*
0–674–07441–6 Harvard $15.00
0–674–07442–4 Harvard pb $7.95

Early Classics

• John James Audubon
AUDUBON READER: The Best Writings of John James Audubon
A good selection of writings by America's best-known ornithologist
Edited by Scott Russell Sanders
0–253–31081–4 Indiana $29.95
0–253–20384–8 Indiana pb $9.95

• William Bartram
TRAVELS
The American south in the late 18th century described by a brilliantly eccentric prose stylist
Introduction by James Dickey
0–14–017008–1 Penguin pb $7.95

• William Beebe
THE ARCTURUS ADVENTURE: An Account of the New York Zoological Society's First Oceanographic Expedition
0–8482–0138–8 Norwood $27.50
0–06–090846–7 Harper & Row pb $5.95

THE LOG OF THE SUN: A Chronicle of Nature's Year
0–89760–087–8 Telegraph $25.00

• John Bradbury
TRAVELS IN THE INTERIOR OF AMERICA IN THE YEARS 1809, 1810 AND 1811
0–8032–6076–8 Nebraska pb $7.95

• John Burroughs
IN THE CATSKILLS, 1910
0–945677–04–9 Riverby pb $12.50

A RIVER VIEW & OTHER HUDSON VALLEY ESSAYS
0–88427–049–1 North River $15.00

A SHARP LOOKOUT: Selected Nature Essays of John Burroughs
0–87474–270–6 Smithsonian $39.95
0–87474–271–4 Smithsonian pb $19.95

• John Burroughs & John Muir
ALASKA: The Harriman Expedition, 1899
0–486–25109–8 Dover pb $11.95

• John Clare
THE NATURAL HISTORY PROSE WRITINGS OF JOHN CLARE
Close observations of rural life by an early 19th-century English poet
0–19–818517–0 Oxford $79.00

• Charles Darwin
THE VOYAGE OF THE BEAGLE
The classic account of Darwin's voyage to South America and the Galapagos
0–385–02767–2 Natural History pb $6.95

• Richard Jefferies
LANDSCAPE WITH FIGURES: An Anthology of Richard Jefferies' Prose
A little-known English writer portrays the agricultural world of 19th-century England
0–14–043146–2 Penguin pb $4.95

• Meriwether Lewis & William Clark
THE JOURNALS OF LEWIS AND CLARK
The classic first glimpse of the Louisiana Purchase
Edited with an introduction by Frank Bergon
0–14–017006–5 Penguin pb $8.95

• John Muir
Muir (1838-1914) is among the most romantic and sublime of American nature writers.
MY FIRST SUMMER IN THE SIERRA
0–14–017001–4 Penguin pb $6.95

THE MOUNTAINS OF CALIFORNIA
0–87156–663–X Sierra Club pb $9.95

A THOUSAND-MILE WALK TO THE GULF
0–395–31542–5 Houghton Mifflin pb $8.95

TRAVELS IN ALASKA
0–87156–783–0 Sierra Club pb $9.95

WILDERNESS ESSAYS
0–87905–072–1 Peregrine Smith pb $4.95

THE YOSEMITE
0–87156–782–2 Sierra Club pb $9.95

• John Wesley Powell
THE EXPLORATION OF THE COLORADO RIVER AND ITS CANYONS
Powell's great journey through the West in 1869
Introduction by Wallace Stegner
0–14–017000–6 Penguin pb $6.95

• Mikhail Prishvin
NATURE'S DIARY
Russian natural history in the early 20th century
Introduction by John Updike
0–14–017003–0 Penguin pb $6.95

• Theodore Roosevelt
THEODORE ROOSEVELT: Wilderness Writings
0–87905–219–8 Peregrine Smith pb $5.95

• John Steinbeck
THE LOG FROM THE SEA OF CORTEZ
0–14–004261–X Penguin pb $4.95

• Henry David Thoreau
Thoreau's works represent the heart of 19th-century American nature writing.
THE JOURNAL OF HENRY DAVID THOREAU

Volume 1
0–486–20312–3 Dover $40.00

Volume 2
0–486–20313–1 Dover $40.00

A WRITER'S JOURNAL
0–486–20678–5 Dover pb $5.00

A WEEK ON THE CONCORD AND MERRIMACK RIVERS, WALDEN, THE MAINE WOODS & CAPE COD
0–940450–27–5 Library of America $27.50

• Gilbert White
THE NATURAL HISTORY OF SELBORNE
An informal masterpiece of natural observation, first published in 1788
0–14–043112–8 Penguin pb $6.95

Arriving on the summit of this dividing crest, one of the most exciting pieces of pure wilderness was disclosed that I ever discovered in all my mountaineering. There, immediately in front, loomed the majestic mass of Mount Ritter, with a glacier swooping down its face nearly to my feet, then curving westward and pouring its frozen flood into a dark blue lake, whose shores were bound with precipices of crystalline snow; while a deep chasm drawn between the divide and the glacier separated the massive picture from everything else. I could see only the one sublime mountain, the one glacier, the one lake; the whole veiled with one blue shadow—rock, ice, and water close together without a single leaf or sign of life.

from "A Near View of the High Sierra"

John Muir
THE MOUNTAINS OF CALIFORNIA
0–87156–663–X Sierra Club pb $9.95

Anthologies

- **Robert Baron & Elizabeth Junkin,** editors
  OF DISCOVERY AND DESTINY: An Anthology of American Writers and the American Land
  1-55591-004-1 Fulcrum $17.95

- **William Beebe,** editor
  THE BOOK OF NATURALISTS: An Anthology of the Best Natural History
  0-691-02408-1 Princeton pb $12.50

- **Frank Bergon,** editor
  THE WILDERNESS READER
  0-451-62589-7 NAL pb $4.95

- **Daniel Halpern,** editor
  ON NATURE
  A superb collection of literary essays, with an invaluable bibliography
  0-86547-283-1 North Point $22.50
  0-86547-284-X North Point pb $9.95

- **Thomas J. Lyon,** editor
  THIS INCOMPERABLE LANDE: A Book of American Nature Writing
  "An unusually vigorous, comprehensive compilation of nature thought"—Edward Hoagland
  0-395-48312-3 Houghton Mifflin $29.95

- **Ann Ronald,** editor
  WORDS FOR THE WILD: The Sierra Club Trailside Reader
  0-87156-709-1 Sierra Club pb $10.95

- **Stephen Trimble,** editor
  WORDS FROM THE LAND: Encounters with Natural History Writing
  A good new collection
  0-87905-242-2 Peregrine Smith $17.95

REGIONAL WORKS

Coastal

- **Rachel Carson**
  THE SEA AROUND US
  A highly influential work which inspired a new consciousness of ocean ecology
  0-19-500500-7 Oxford $19.95
  0-451-62483-1 NAL pb $4.95

  THE EDGE OF THE SEA
  0-395-28519-4 Houghton Mifflin pb $9.95

- **Deborah Coulombe**
  THE SEASIDE NATURALIST: A Guide to Nature at the Seashore
  0-13-797242-3 Prentice-Hall pb $12.95

- **John Crompton**
  THE SEA
  A rediscovered classic by an English naturalist
  0-941130-83-5 Nick Lyons pb $8.95

- **Jan DeBlieu**
  HATTERAS JOURNAL: Paradox of a Fragile Land
  1-55591-010-6 Fulcrum $15.95

- **Kenneth Gosner**
  A FIELD GUIDE TO THE ATLANTIC SEASHORE
  0-395-31828-9 Houghton Mifflin pb $12.95

- **John Hay**
  THE GREAT BEACH
  A walking trip along the Outer Beach of Cape Cod; winner of the John Burroughs Medal (1984)
  0-393-00983-1 Norton pb $3.95

  SANDY SHORE
  0-85699-006-X Chatham $8.95

- **John Hay & Peter Farb**
  THE ATLANTIC SHORE
  0-940160-14-5 Parnassus pb $7.95

- **Michael Hoel**
  LAND'S EDGE: A Natural History of Barrier Beaches from Maine to North Carolina
  0-9616080-0-5 Globe Pequot pb $6.95

- **George Reiger**
  WANDERER ON MY NATIVE SHORE
  Tidewater essays by an ardent conservationist
  0-671-25423-5 Simon & Schuster $14.95
  0-671-25424-3 Simon & Schuster pb $7.95

- **William Warner**
  BEAUTIFUL SWIMMERS: Watermen, Crabs, and the Chesapeake Bay
  A fine book on the crabmen of the Chesapeake Bay
  Introduction by John Barth
  0-316-92326-5 Little, Brown $22.50
  0-14-017004-9 Penguin pb $6.95

The East

- **Henry Beston**
  THE OUTERMOST HOUSE
  Cape Cod in the 1920s
  0-140-17012-X Penguin pb $6.95

- **Alf Evers**
  THE CATSKILLS: From Wilderness to Woodstock
  A massive natural and social history
  0-87951-162-1 Overlook $37.50

- **Nathan Farb**
  THE ADIRONDACKS
  0-8478-0583-2 Rizzoli $40.00
  0-8478-0584-0 Rizzoli pb $25.00

Robert Finch
COMMON GROUND: A Naturalist's Cape Cod
0-87923-383-4 Godine $14.95
0-87923-427-X Godine pb $8.95

OUTLANDS: Journeys to the Outer Edges of Cape Cod
0-87923-619-1 Godine $15.95

THE PRIMAL PLACE
Essays grounded largely in Brewster, Massachusetts
0-393-01623-4 Norton $15.00
0-393-30228-8 Norton pb $5.95

- **Jean Gardner**
  URBAN WILDERNESS: Nature in New York City
  A dramatic photographic survey of New York City's 50,000 acres of parklands and wilderness
  Photographs by Joel Greenberg
  Foreword by Bill Moyers
  0-9621060-3-3 Earth Environmental Group $40.00

- **Paul Jamieson,** editor
  THE ADIRONDACK READER
  0-935272-21-6 Adirondack $29.50
  0-935272-22-4 Adirondack pb $18.50

- **John Kieran**
  A NATURAL HISTORY OF NEW YORK CITY
  A Burroughs Medal winner
  0-8232-1086-3 Fordham pb $9.95

- **John McPhee**
  THE PINE BARRENS
  An early McPhee book about a major natural area and New Jersey aquifer
  0-374-23362-4 Farrar Straus & Giroux $25.00
  0-374-51442-9 Farrar Straus & Giroux pb $5.95

- **Donald Stokes**
  A GUIDE TO NATURE IN WINTER: Northeast and North Central North America
  0-316-81720-1 Little, Brown $18.95
  0-316-81723-6 Little, Brown pb $9.95

- **Ann & Myron Sutton**
  EASTERN FORESTS
  0-394-73126-3 Knopf pb $15.95

- **W.D. Wetherell**
  VERMONT RIVER
  An angler's appreciation
  0-317-62720-1 Nick Lyons $13.95
  0-671-67344-0 Simon & Schuster pb $8.95

- **William White**
  ADIRONDACK COUNTRY
  An excellent natural portrait
  0-394-41855-7 Knopf $16.95
  0-8156-0193-X Syracuse pb $9.95

- **Ann Zwinger & Edwin Way Teale**
  A CONSCIOUS STILLNESS: Two Naturalists on Thoreau's Rivers
  The Concord and Merrimack rivers (the subjects of Thoreau's first book) revisited
  0-87023-452-8 Massachusetts pb $10.95

The South

- **William Niering**
  WETLANDS
  0-394-73147-6 Knopf pb $15.95

- **Franklin Russell**
  WINGS ON THE SOUTHWIND: Birds and Creatures of the Southern Wetlands
  Introduction by Roger Tory Peterson
  0-8487-0546-7 Oxmoor $29.95

- **John & Mildred Teal**
  PORTRAIT OF AN ISLAND
  0-8203-0581-2 Georgia pb $7.50

• John Terres
FROM LAUREL HILL TO SILER'S BOG:
The Walking Adventures of a Naturalist
Observations in North Carolina wildlife
preserves; winner of the Burroughs Medal
1971
0–912697–26–1 Algonquin pb $12.95

The Great Plains

• Roy Bedichek
ADVENTURES WITH A TEXAS
NATURALIST
0–292–70311–2 Texas pb $9.95

KARANKAWAY COUNTRY
0–292–74304–1 Texas pb $10.95

• Sally Carrighar
ONE DAY AT TETON MARSH
A piercing look at the life of marsh animals
0–8032–6302–3 Nebraska pb $7.95

• Terry Evans
PRAIRIE: Images of Ground and Sky
Indelible photographic images of the plains
0–7006–0287–9 Kansas $19.95

• John Graves
Graves is a funny, observant, and down-
to-earth writer whose subject is rural
Texas.
FROM A LIMESTONE LEDGE
0–394–51238–3 Knopf $13.95
0–932012–77–9 Texas Monthly pb $7.95

GOODBYE TO A RIVER
0–394–42690–8 Knopf $12.95
0–932012–75–2 Texas Monthly pb $7.95

HARD SCRABBLE
0–394–48386–3 Knopf $13.50
0–932012–76–0 Texas Monthly pb $7.95

• John Janovy, Jr.
BACK IN KEITH COUNTY
Nebraska natural history by a parasitologist
0–8032–7560–9 Nebraska pb $5.95

KEITH COUNTY JOURNAL
0–312–45124–5 St. Martin's pb $4.95

• Josephine Johnson
THE INLAND ISLAND
Johnson won the Pulitzer Prize in 1934
for her first novel, *Now in November*. This
is a collection of nature essays
0–8142–0450–3 Ohio State pb $8.95

• Verlyn Klinkenborg
MAKING HAY
A warmly personal account of agricultural
life in Minnesota, Iowa, and Montana
0–941130–18–5 Nick Lyons $14.95
0–394–75599–5 Random House pb $5.95

• John Madson
UP ON THE RIVER: An Upper Mississippi
Chronicle
A superb book
0–8052–3966–9 Schocken $17.95
0–14–008746–X Penguin pb $7.95

WHERE THE SKY BEGAN: Land of the
Tallgrass Prairie
0–87156–836–5 Sierra Club pb $8.95

• William Seno, editor
UP COUNTRY: Voices from the
Midwestern Wilderness
Illustrations by Frederic Remington & George Catlin
0–933437–00–5 Round River pb $9.95

• David Rains Wallace
IDLE WEEDS: The Life of an Ohio
Sandstone Ridge
Winner of the Ohioana Book Award for
Science 1981
0–8142–0409–0 Ohio State pb $7.95

The North Woods

• Helen Hoover
GIFT OF THE DEER
Wilderness life in the Minnesota woods
0–394–41803–4 Knopf $16.95

PLACE IN THE WOODS
0–394–44065–X Knopf $18.95

YEARS OF THE FOREST
0–394–47538–0 Knopf $15.95

• Anne LaBastille
BEYOND BLACK BEAR LAKE: Life at the
Edge of the Wilderness
LaBastille is a biologist and ecologist
0–393–02388–5 Norton $15.95
0–393–30539–2 Norton pb $7.95

WOODSWOMAN
LaBastille's account of her life in the
Adirondacks, where she has lived since
1954
0–525–48367–5 Dutton pb $8.95

• Edward Lueders
THE CLAM LAKE PAPERS: A Winter in
the North Woods
0–687–08580–2 Abingdon pb $3.25

• Sigurd Olson
Olson is an extremely popular writer on
the Minnesota wilderness.
LISTENING POINT
0–394–43358–0 Knopf $14.95

LONELY LAND
0–394–43383–1 Knopf $14.95

RUNES OF THE NORTH
0–394–44348–9 Knopf $16.95

THE SINGING WILDERNESS
0–394–44560–0 Knopf $17.95

• William O. Pruitt, Jr.
WILD HARMONY
1–55821–008–3 Nick Lyons pb $9.95

• John Rowlands
CACHE LAKE COUNTRY: Life in the
North Woods
A charming book by a Canadian timber
scout; beautifully illustrated
0–393–08468–X Norton $12.95
0–393–00908–4 Norton pb $5.95

The Southwest and the Desert

• Edward Abbey
DESERT SOLITAIRE: A Season in the
Wilderness
0–8165–1057–1 Arizona $24.95
0–345–32649–0 Ballantine pb $3.95

THE JOURNEY HOME: Some Words in
Defense of the American West
0–525–03700–4 Dutton pb $7.95

• Mary Austin
THE LAND OF LITTLE RAIN
Stories of the western desert, published in
1903
Introduction by Edward Abbey
0–14–017009–X Penguin pb $6.95

• Janice Bowers
SEASONS OF THE WIND: A Naturalist's
Look at the Plant Life of Southwestern
Sand Dunes
0–87358–393–0 Northland pb $10.95

• Philip Hyde
DRYLANDS: The Deserts of North
America
0–15–126590–9 HBJ $75.00

• Joseph Wood Krutch
THE DESERT YEAR
0–8165–0923–9 Arizona pb $9.95

THE FORGOTTEN PENINSULA: A
Naturalist in Baja California
0–8165–0987–5 Arizona pb $9.95

THE VOICE OF THE DESERT: A
Naturalist's Interpretation
0–688–07715–3 Morrow pb $8.95

• Barry Lopez
DESERT NOTES: Reflections in the Eye of
the Raven
0–8362–0661–4 Andrews & McMeel pb $6.95

Gary Nabhan
Nabhan is an important ethnobotanist
and naturalist of the southwestern
desert.
THE DESERT SMELLS LIKE RAIN:
A Naturalist in Papago Indian Country
Nabhan traces the relationship of the
Papagos to their Sonora desert
environment
0–86547–050–2 North Point pb $8.95

GATHERING THE DESERT
0–8165–1014–8 Arizona pb $14.95

SAGUARO: A Naturalist Looks at
Saguaro National Monument and the
Tucson Basin
0–911408–69–X SW Parks pb $6.95

• Paul Schullery, editor
THE GRAND CANYON: Early
Impressions
0–87081–086–3 Colorado Associated $15.00

• Virginia Simmons
SAN LUIS VALLEY: The Land of the Six-
Armed Cross
0–87108–688–3 Pruett pb $14.95

• John Van Dyke
THE DESERT
0–8274–2166–4 Richard West $60.00
0–87905–073–X Peregrine Smith pb $4.95

• Ann Woodin
HOME IS THE DESERT
0–8165–0857–7 Arizona pb $8.95

- **Ann Zwinger**
  DESERT COUNTRY NEAR THE SEA: A Natural History of the Cape Region of Baja California
  0–06–015208–7 Harper & Row $24.45
  0–8165–0988–3 Arizona pb $12.95

  LIGHTFALL AND TIME: Fifteen Southwestern National Parks
  0–87358–425–2 Northland pb $14.95

  WIND IN THE ROCK: A Naturalist Explores the Canyon Country of the Southwest
  0–06–014209–X Harper & Row $16.95
  0–8165–0985–9 Arizona pb $9.50

The Mountain West

- **Mary Back**
  SEVEN HALF-MILES FROM HOME
  Detailed natural observations from short walks in Wyoming's Wind River region
  0–933472–90–0 Johnson pb $9.95

- **Sally Carrighar**
  ONE DAY ON BEETLE ROCK
  Beetle Rock is in Sequoia National Park in California
  0–8032–6301–5 Nebraska pb $6.95

- **Gretel Ehrlich**
  THE SOLACE OF OPEN SPACES
  Sparse, affecting prose about the sheep plains of Wyoming
  0–670–80678–1 Viking $14.95
  0–14–008113–5 Penguin pb $5.95

- **Steven Meyers, editor**
  TRAILS AMONG THE COLUMBINE, 1985: A Colorado High Country Anthology
  0–913582–37–9 Sundance $35.00
  0–913582–38–7 Sundance pb $22.00

- **Paul Schullery**
  MOUNTAIN TIME: Man Meets Wilderness in Yellowstone
  Personal essays from Yellowstone Park
  0–8052–3932–4 Schocken $17.95
  0–671–65953–7 Simon & Schuster pb $6.95

- **Wallace Stegner**
  THE SOUND OF MOUNTAIN WATER
  Natural history by a well-respected novelist
  0–8032–9158–2 Nebraska pb $7.95

  THIS IS DINOSAUR: Echo Park Country and Its Magic Rivers
  0–911797–11–4 Roberts, Rinehart $24.95
  0–911797–12–2 Roberts, Rinehart pb $8.95

- **David Wallace**
  THE KLAMATH KNOT
  California's Trinity Alps; winner of the Burroughs Medal (1984)
  0–87156–316–9 Sierra Club $14.95
  0–87156–817–9 Sierra Club pb $8.95

- **Gleaves Whitney**
  COLORADO FRONT RANGE: A Landscape Divided
  0–933472–71–4 Johnson pb $8.95

- **Ann Zwinger**
  BEYOND THE ASPEN GROVE
  0–8165–1054–7 Arizona pb $14.95

RUN, RIVER, RUN: A Naturalist's Journey Down One of the Great Rivers of the West
Winner of the Burroughs Medal (1976)
0–06–014824–1 Harper & Row $15.75

- **Ann Zwinger & Beatrice Willard**
  LAND ABOVE THE TREES: A Guide to American Alpine Tundra
  0–06–014823–3 Harper & Row $19.95

The Northwest and Alaska

- **David Cooper**
  BROOKS RANGE PASSAGE
  0–89886–061–X Mountaineers $14.95

- **Sam Keith & Richard Proenneke**
  ONE MAN'S WILDERNESS: An Alaskan Odyssey
  0–88240–013–4 Alaska Northwest pb $9.95

- **Rockwell Kent**
  WILDERNESS: A Journal of Quiet Adventure in Alaska
  0–918172–12–8 Leete's Island pb $8.95

- **Robert Marshall**
  ALASKA WILDERNESS: Exploring the Central Brooks Range
  0–520–01711–0 California pb $12.95

- **John McPhee**
  COMING INTO THE COUNTRY
  About Alaska; perhaps McPhee's finest book
  0–374–12645–3 Farrar Straus & Giroux $19.95
  0–553–25527–4 Bantam pb $4.95

- **Richard Nelson**
  HUNTERS OF THE NORTHERN FOREST: Designs for Survival Among the Alaskan Kutchin
  0–226–57181–5 Chicago pb $12.95

"Monolith, The Face of Half Dome," Yosemite National Park, 1927 (copyright Ansel Adams Publishing Rights Trust), from Ansel Adams: Letters and Images 1916-1984 *(New York Graphic Society/Little, Brown)*

HUNTERS OF THE NORTHERN ICE
0–226–57176–9 Chicago pb $12.95

MAKE PRAYERS TO THE RAVEN: A Koyukon View of the Northern Forest
0–226–57162–9 Chicago $25.00
0–226–57163–7 Chicago pb $13.95

• Robert Pyle
WINTERGREEN
Winner of the John Burroughs Medal; set in the state of Washington
0–684–18321–8 Scribners $19.95
0–395–46559–1 Houghton Mifflin pb $8.95

• Galen Rowell & John McPhee
ALASKA: Images of the Country
Photos by Rowell, a well-known mountaineer, and text by McPhee, from *Coming into the Country*
0–87156–290–1 Sierra Club $37.50

Digging in the soil, picking away the rock, uprooting stumps, I became in time a grower of things sufficient to feed myself and another. Slowly finding my way into the skills of hunter and trapper, I understood what blood and bone, hide and muscle, marrow and sinew really are; not as things read about, but as things touched and handled until they became as familiar to me as my own skin. Land itself came alive for me as it never had before, more alive sometimes than the people who moved about on it. I learned that it is land, *place*, that makes people, provides for them the possibilities they will have of becoming something more than mere lumps of sucking matter.

from "The Writer as Alaskan"

John Haines
LIVING OFF THE COUNTRY: Essays on Poetry and Place
0–472–06333–2 Michigan pb $8.95

The Arctic and Antarctica

• Rockwell Kent
GREENLAND JOURNAL
0–8392–1042–6 Astor-Honor $20.00

N BY E
A trip to the coast of Greenland recorded in a beautifully produced book
0–8195–5018–3 Wesleyan $25.00

Barry Lopez
ARCTIC DREAMS: Imagination and Desire in a Northern Landscape
This poetic treatise on the Arctic is a masterpiece
0–684–18578–4 Scribners $22.95
0–317–56856–6 Bantam pb $4.95

• Sanford Moss
NATURAL HISTORY OF THE ANTARCTIC PENINSULA
By the author of *Sharks: An Introduction for the Amateur Naturalist*
0–231–06268–0 Columbia $27.50

Robert Scott's ship "The Terra Nova," photographed from an ice cave during his 1910 expedition to the Antarctic, from The War, the West, and the Wilderness *by Kevin Brownlow (Knopf) photo courtesy Paul Popper, Ltd.)*

• Stephen Pyne
THE ICE: A Journey to Antarctica
A trip to Antarctica by the historian of forest fires
0–87745–152–4 Iowa $37.50

ANIMAL LIFE

Mammals

• David Brown
THE GRIZZLY IN THE SOUTHWEST: Documentary of an Extinction
0–8061–1930–6 Oklahoma $21.95

• Douglas Chadwick
A BEAST THE COLOR OF WINTER: The Mountain Goat Observed
0–87156–805–5 Sierra Club $15.95

• Frank C. Craighead, Jr.
TRACK OF THE GRIZZLY
0–87156–322–3 Sierra Club pb $10.95

• J. David Henry
RED FOX: The Catlike Canine
0–87474–520–9 Smithsonian $22.50

• Peter Matthiessen
THE SNOW LEOPARD
Matthiessen in the Himalayas in search of an endangered cat; winner of the National Book Award
0–14–010266–3 Penguin pb $7.95

• Gavin Maxwell
RING OF BRIGHT WATER
Maxwell among otters in the Scottish Highlands
0–14–003923–6 Penguin pb $6.95

• Thomas McNamee
THE GRIZZLY BEAR
A beautifully written account of the grizzly's predicament and natural history
0–394–52998–7 Knopf $19.95
0–07–045668–2 McGraw-Hill pb $8.95

● Adolph Murie
THE GRIZZLIES OF MOUNT McKINLEY
0–295–96204–6 Washington pb $9.95

MAMMALS OF DENALI
0–9602876–6–3 Alaska Nat. Hist. Assoc. pb $4.50

THE WOLVES OF MOUNT McKINLEY
0–295–96203–8 Washington pb $9.95

● Olaus Murie
ELK OF NORTH AMERICA
0–933160–02–X Teton Bookshop $15.95

● Ronald Nowak & John Paradiso, editors
WALKER'S MAMMALS OF THE WORLD
A comprehensive 2-volume encyclopedia
0–8018–2525–3 Johns Hopkins $75.00

● Jeff Rennicke
THE BEARS OF ALASKA IN LIFE AND LEGEND
0–911797–29–7 Roberts, Rinehart pb $10.95

● Leonard Rue
DEER OF NORTH AMERICA
0–517–53630–7 Crown $14.95

● George Schaller
Schaller is a highly regarded zoologist and extremely capable writer.
THE DEER AND THE TIGER: A Study of Wildlife in India
0–226–73631–8 Chicago pb $19.95

THE MOUNTAIN GORILLA: Ecology and Behavior
0–226–73649–0 Chicago pb $19.95

THE SERENGETI LION: A Study of Predator-Prey Relations
Winner of the National Book Award 1973
0–226–73640–7 Chicago pb $16.95

YEAR OF THE GORILLA
0–226–73648–2 Chicago pb $12.95

● George Schaller & others
THE GIANT PANDAS OF WOLONG
0–226–73643–1 Chicago $25.00

● Paul Schullery
THE BEARS OF YELLOWSTONE
0–911797–20–3 Roberts, Rinehart $29.95
0–911797–21–1 Roberts, Rinehart pb $10.95

● Paul Shepard & Barry Sanders
THE SACRED PAW: The Bear in Nature, Myth and Literature
0–670–15133–5 Viking $17.95

● Shirley Strum
ALMOST HUMAN: A Journey into the World of Baboons
0–394–54724–1 Random House $22.00

Birds

● John Baker
THE PEREGRINE
0–89301–115–0 Idaho pb $10.95

● Andrew Berger
BIRD STUDY
0–486–22699–9 Dover pb $7.95

● Chuck Bernstein
THE JOY OF BIRDING: A Guide to Better Bird Watching
A "collection of anecdotes, love and knowledge"
Introduction by Roger Tory Peterson
0–88496–220–2 Capra pb $8.95

● Stephen Bodio
A RAGE FOR FALCONS
By a columnist and editor of *Gray's Sporting Journal*
0–8052–3931–6 Nick Lyons $16.50

● John Burroughs
THE BIRDS OF JOHN BURROUGHS
Eleven of Burroughs' classic essays
0–879–51301–2 Overlook $18.95

● Jack Connor
THE COMPLETE BIRDER: A Guide to Better Birding
Designed to upgrade your field skills
Introduction by Roger Tory Peterson
0–317–67000–X Houghton Mifflin $17.95
0–317–67001–8 Houghton Mifflin pb $8.95

● John & Frank Craighead
HAWKS, OWLS AND WILDLIFE
0–486–22123–7 Dover pb $8.95

● David Darlington
IN CONDOR COUNTRY
0–395–40798–2 Houghton Mifflin $15.95

● Paul Eriksson & Joseph Wood Krutch, editors
SONGBIRDS IN YOUR GARDEN
Introduction by Roger Tory Peterson
0–06–091377–0 Harper & Row pb $10.95

TREASURY OF NORTH AMERICAN BIRDLORE
0–8397–8372–8 Eriksson $24.95

● Jon Gerrard & Gary Bortolotti
THE BALD EAGLE: Haunts and Habits of a Wilderness Monarch
0–87474–450–4 Smithsonian $24.95
0–87474–451–2 Smithsonian pb $12.95

● Louis Halle
THE STORM PETREL AND THE OWL OF ATHENA
Halle won the Burroughs Medal in 1941 for *Birds Against Men*
0–691–09349–0 Princeton $30.50

● Frances Hamerstrom
HARRIER, HAWK OF THE MARSHES: The Hawk That is Ruled by a Mouse
Foreword by Roger Tory Peterson
0–87474–538–1 Smithsonian $24.95
0–87474–537–3 Smithsonian pb $11.95

● Bernd Heinrich
ONE MAN'S OWL
Life with a great horned owl, by a zoologist at the University of Vermont
0–691–08470–X Princeton $19.50

● Joseph Kastner
A WORLD OF WATCHERS: An Informal History of the American Passion for Birds
"Traces bird watching and the personalities affecting it from the early watchers—explorers and military men and

governors—to its current vast appeal"—
NY Times
0–87156–784–9 Sierra Club pb $10.95

● Lawrence Kilham
ON WATCHING BIRDS
0–930031–14–8 Chelsea Green $17.95

● Donald Knowler
THE FALCONER OF CENTRAL PARK
The "natural world at the heart of a great city"
0–943828–62–7 Karz-Cohl $14.95
0–553–34205–3 Bantam pb $8.95

● Robert Nero
THE GREAT GRAY OWL: Phantom of the Northern Forest
0–87474–672–8 Smithsonian $19.95
0–317–60387–6 Smithsonian pb $12.95

● Roger Tory Peterson & Edward Chalif
REDWINGS
0–87474–677–9 Smithsonian pb $12.95

● Donald & Lillian Stokes
A GUIDE TO BIRD BEHAVIOR: In the Wild and at Your Feeder
0–316–81726–0 Little, Brown $16.95
0–316–81729–5 Little, Brown pb $9.95

A GUIDE TO THE BEHAVIOR OF COMMON BIRDS
0–316–81722–8 Little, Brown $16.95
0–316–81725–2 Little, Brown pb $9.95

● John Terres
THE AUDUBON SOCIETY ENCYCLOPEDIA OF NORTH AMERICAN BIRDS
A comprehensive reference; highly recommended
0–394–46651–9 Knopf $75.00

HOW BIRDS FLY
0–06–097099–5 Harper & Row pb $7.95

The variegated foliage of the woods indicates that the latter days of October have arrived ... and as the observer of nature stands watching the appearances and events of this season of change, he hears from on high the notes of the swiftly travelling but unseen Whooping Crane. Suddenly the turbid atmosphere clears, and now he can perceive the passing birds. Gradually they descend, dress their extended lines, and prepare to alight on the earth. With necks outstretched, and long bony legs extended behind, they proceed supported by wings white as the snow but tipped with jet, until arriving over the great savannah they wheel their circling flight, and slowly approach the ground, on which with half-closed wings, and outstretched feet they alight, running along for a few steps to break the force of their descent.

John James Audubon
AUDUBON READER: The Best Writings of John James Audubon
Edited by Scott Russell Sanders
0–253–20384–8 Indiana pb $9.95

➤ **FOR OVERSEAS ORDERING INFORMATION, SEE PAGE 1**

- Richard Wood
  WOOD NOTES: A Companion and Guide for Birdwatchers
  0–13–962580–1 Prentice-Hall $15.95
  0–13–962572–0 Prentice-Hall pb $6.95

Aquatic Life

- Richard Ellis
  Excellent oversize books, amply illustrated
  THE BOOK OF WHALES
  0–394–73371–1 Random House pb $24.95

  DOLPHINS AND PORPOISES
  0–394–51800–4 Random House pb $24.95

- Paul Horsman
  SEA WATCH
  A captivating book
  0–8160–1191–5 Facts On File $22.95

- Erich Hoyt
  THE WHALE-WATCHER'S HANDBOOK
  0–385–19036–0 Doubleday pb $12.95

- Joan McIntyre
  THE DELICATE ART OF WHALE WATCHING
  0–87156–323–1 Sierra Club $12.50

- John Varley & others
  FRESH WATER WILDERNESS: Yellowstone Fishes and Their World
  0–934948–06–2 Yellowstone $19.95
  0–934948–04–6 Yellowstone pb $12.95

Reptiles and Amphibians

- John Crompton
  THE SNAKE
  Crompton is a recently rediscovered British naturalist
  0–941130–28–2 Nick Lyons pb $8.95

- Hobart Smith & Edmund Brodie
  REPTILES OF NORTH AMERICA
  0–307–13666–3 Western pb $9.95

Insects

- Marston Bates
  THE NATURAL HISTORY OF MOSQUITOS
  0–8446–0480–1 Peter Smith $11.75

John Crompton
These remarkable books—along with *The Snake* and *The Sea*—are attracting new readers to this amateur British naturalist.

A HIVE OF BEES
Introduction by Verlyn Klinkenborg
0–941130–50–9 Nick Lyons pb $8.95

THE HUNTING WASP
Introduction by Stephen Bodio
0–941130–49–5 Nick Lyons pb $8.95

THE SPIDER
Introduction by David Quammen
0–941130–29–0 Nick Lyons pb $8.95

A 30-ton, 50-foot humpback whale, from LIFE: The First Fifty Years *edited by Philip B. Kunhardt, Jr. (Little, Brown)*

- Howard Evans
  LIFE ON A LITTLE-KNOWN PLANET
  The little-known planet is Earth
  0–226–22258–6 Chicago pb $11.95

  THE PLEASURES OF ENTOMOLOGY: Portraits of Insects and the People Who Study Them
  0–87474–421–0 Smithsonian pb $14.95

- Bernd Heinrich
  BUMBLEBEE ECONOMICS
  0–674–08580–9 Harvard $21.00
  0–674–08581–7 Harvard pb $8.95

- Donald Stokes
  A GUIDE TO OBSERVING INSECT LIVES
  0–316–81724–4 Little, Brown $17.95
  0–316–81727–9 Little, Brown pb $9.95

- Edward O. Wilson
  INSECT SOCIETIES
  By the Pulitzer prize-winning sociobiologist
  0–674–45495–2 Harvard pb $20.00

ANIMAL BEHAVIOR

- Frans de Waal
  CHIMPANZEE POLITICS: Power and Sex Among Apes
  0–8018–3833–9 Johns Hopkins pb $12.95

- Michael Ghiglieri
  EAST OF THE MOUNTAINS OF THE MOON: Chimpanzee Society in the African Jungle
  0–02–911580–9 Free Press $22.50

- Jane Goodall
  THE CHIMPANZEES OF GOMBE
  A comprehensive account of Goodall's lifework
  0–674–11649–6 Harvard $37.95

- Donald Griffin
  ANIMAL THINKING
  An important work on the "mental experiences" of animals
  0–674–03713–8 Harvard pb $7.95

  BIRD MIGRATION
  0–486–20529–0 Dover pb $4.95

- Vicki Hearne
  ADAM'S TASK: Calling Animals by Name
  A philosophical work on the language shared by humans and animals
  0–394–54214–2 Knopf $17.95
  0–394–75530–8 Random House pb $8.95

- Eugene Linden
  SILENT PARTNERS: The Legacy of Ape Language Experiments
  0–345–34234–8 Ballantine pb $3.95

- Konrad Lorenz
  KING SOLOMON'S RING
  A seminal work by the founder of modern ethology
  Foreword by Julian Huxley
  0–06–131976–7 Harper & Row pb $6.95

Baby chimp

ON AGGRESSION
A controversial theory of human violence
and territoriality
0–15–668741–0 HBJ pb $8.95

• David McFarland, editor
**THE OXFORD COMPANION TO
ANIMAL BEHAVIOR**
0–19–866120–7 Oxford $49.95
0–19–281990–9 Oxford pb $19.95

• Desmond Morris
THE NAKED APE
0–440–36266–0 Dell pb $4.50

• Nikolaas Tinbergen
HERRING GULL'S WORLD
Tinbergen shared the 1973 Nobel Prize in
Physiology or Medicine with Konrad
Lorenz and Karl von Frisch
Introduction by Konrad Lorenz
0–06–131594–X Harper & Row pb $3.95

TREES, PLANTS, AND FUNGI

• Jerry Franklin
**FAMILIAR TREES OF NORTH
AMERICA, WESTERN REGION**
0–317–56714–4 Knopf pb $4.95

• Sara Ann Friedman
**CELEBRATING THE WILD
MUSHROOM**
0–396–08755–8 Dodd, Mead $18.95
0–396–08845–7 Dodd, Mead pb $10.95

• Ronald Lanner
**THE PINON PINE: A Natural and
Cultural History**
0–87417–065–6 Nevada $16.95
0–87417–066–4 Nevada pb $9.95

**TREES OF THE GREAT BASIN: A
Natural History**
0–87417–081–8 Nevada $22.95
0–87417–082–6 Nevada pb $16.95

• Donald Peattie
**A NATURAL HISTORY OF WESTERN
TREES**
0–8032–8701–1 Nebraska pb $14.95

• Charles Roth
**THE PLANT OBSERVER'S
GUIDEBOOK: A Field Botany Manual for
the Amateur Naturalist**
0–13–680745–3 Prentice-Hall pb $9.95

• Jane Scott
**BOTANY IN THE FIELD: An
Introduction to Plant Communities for the
Amateur Naturalist**
0–13–080292–1 Prentice-Hall pb $8.95

• Donald & Lillian Stokes
**A GUIDE TO ENJOYING
WILDFLOWERS**
0–316–81728–7 Little, Brown $18.95
0–316–81731–7 Little, Brown pb $10.95

HISTORY OF NATURAL HISTORY

• Paul Brooks
**SPEAKING FOR NATURE: How Our
Literary Naturalists Have Shaped America**
0–87156–332–0 Sierra Club pb $8.95

• Arthur A. Ekirch, Jr.
MAN AND NATURE IN AMERICA
0–8032–5785–6 Nebraska pb $4.75

• Antonello Gerbi
**NATURE IN THE NEW WORLD: From
Christopher Columbus to Gonzalo
Fernandez de Oviedo**
An account of the natural history of the
New World as written by Columbus, Peter
Martyr, and Oviedo
0–8229–3516–3 Pittsburgh $39.95

• Joseph Kastner & Miriam Gross,
editors
THE BIRD ILLUSTRATED, 1550 to 1900
Introduction by Roger Tory Peterson
0–8109–0746–1 Abrams $29.95

• Peter Matthiessen
WILDLIFE IN AMERICA
0–670–81906–9 Viking $29.95

• Lee Clark Mitchell
**WITNESSES TO A VANISHING
AMERICA: The Nineteenth-Century
Response**
0–691–06461–X Princeton $29.50
0–691–10223–6 Princeton pb $14.95

• Roderick Nash
**THE AMERICAN ENVIRONMENT:
Readings in the History of Conservation**
0–394–37398–7 Knopf pb $9.75

• Peter Wild
**PIONEER CONSERVATIONISTS OF
EARLY AMERICA**
0–87842–126–2 Mountain $14.95

**PIONEER CONSERVATIONISTS OF
EASTERN AMERICA**
0–87842–126–2 Mountain $14.95

Agriculture

"I have often thought that if heaven had
given me a choice of my position and
calling, it should have been on a rich spot of
earth, well watered, and near a good market
for the products of the garden. No occupation is so delightful to me as the culture of
the earth."—Thomas Jefferson

• Wendell Berry
**THE UNSETTLING OF AMERICA:
Culture and Agriculture**
A collection of essays
0–87156–772–5 Sierra Club pb $7.95

**THE GIFT OF GOOD LAND: Further
Essays Cultural and Agricultural**
0–86547–051–0 North Point $18.00
0–86547–052–9 North Point pb $9.50

• Jack Doyle
**ALTERED HARVEST: Agriculture,
Genetics, and the Fate of the World's Food
Supply**
0–670–11524–X Viking $25.00
0–14–009696–5 Penguin pb $8.95

• Wes Jackson
ALTARS OF UNHEWN STONE
Essays on sustainable agriculture and
related topics
0–86547–272–6 North Point $19.95
0–86547–287–4 North Point pb $9.95

NEW ROOTS FOR AGRICULTURE
0–8032–7562–5 Nebraska pb $6.95

• Wes Jackson, Wendell Berry, & Bruce
Coleman, editors
**MEETING THE EXPECTATIONS OF
THE LAND: Essays in Sustainable
Agriculture and Stewardship**
0–86547–172–X North Point pb $12.50

• Mark Kramer
**THREE FARMS: Making Milk, Meat, and
Money from the American Soil**
A small independent dairy farm in
Massachusetts, a subsidized hog farm in
Iowa, and a huge corporate farmerless
farm in California. A classic study
0–674–88936–3 Harvard pb $8.95

• Gary Paul Nabhan
ENDURING SEEDS: Cultivating Wildness
A criticism of the loss of diversity and
wildness resulting from mainstream
agricultural practices
0–86547–343–9 North Point $17.95

• Nancy Paddock & others
SOIL AND SURVIVAL
Scientific, philosophical, theological,
cultural, and ethical arguments in response
to the threatened loss of the nation's
farmlands
0–87156–766–0 Sierra Club $19.95

• John Rosenblum, editor
**AGRICULTURE IN THE TWENTY-
FIRST CENTURY**
0–471–88538–X John Wiley $37.50

• Terry Silber
A SMALL FARM IN MAINE
A city couple makes the move from the
fast lane to the country lane
0–395–37911–3 Houghton Mifflin $17.95

Global Agriculture

• Kenneth Dahlberg, editor
**BEYOND THE GREEN REVOLUTION:
The Ecology and Politics of Global
Agricultural Development**
0–306–40120–7 Plenum $25.00

**NEW DIRECTIONS FOR
AGRICULTURE AND AGRICULTURAL
RESEARCH: The Ecology and Politics of
Global Agricultural Development**
0–8476–7417–7 Rowman $45.00

• J. Sholto Douglas & Robert Hart
**FOREST FARMING: Towards a Solution
to Problems of World Hunger and
Conservation**
0–8133–0331–1 Westview pb $21.00

- Carl Eicher & John Staatz
AGRICULTURAL DEVELOPMENT IN THE THIRD WORLD
0–8018–3015–X Johns Hopkins pb $17.50

Agriculture and the Environment

- Miguel Altieri
AGROECOLOGY: The Scientific Basis of Alternative Agriculture
0–8133–7284–4 Westview pb $22.50

- William Lockertz
ENVIRONMENTALLY SOUND AGRICULTURE
0–27–591401–1 Praeger $44.95

- R.W. Widdowson
TOWARDS HOLISTIC AGRICULTURE: A Scientific Approach
0–08–034211–6 Pergamon $24.95

FARM ECONOMICS AND MANAGEMENT

- M. Buckett
INTRODUCTION TO FARM ORGANIZATION AND MANAGEMENT
How to run a farm by the book
0–08–024433–5 Pergamon $60.00
0–08–024432–7 Pergamon pb $27.50

- Gary Comstock, editor
IS THERE A MORAL OBLIGATION TO SAVE THE FAMILY FARM?
Essays by farmers, journalists, politicians, economists, lawyers, academics, and religious leaders
0–8138–0999–1 Iowa State $34.95
0–8138–1000–0 Iowa State pb $12.95

- Larry Connor & others
MANAGING THE FARM BUSINESS
0–13–550376–0 Prentice-Hall $37.00

- Duane Erickson & others
MICROCOMPUTERS ON THE FARM: Getting Started
0–8138–1156–2 Iowa State pb $7.95

- Alistair Fraser & Katie Thear, editors
THE SMALL FARMER'S GUIDE TO RAISING LIVESTOCK AND POULTRY
0–668–04687–2 Arco pb $14.95

- New Farm Magazine
PROFITABLE FARMING NOW
0–913107–01–8 Rodale pb $17.95

- Deter Tomkins & Christopher Bird
SECRETS OF THE SOIL: A Fascinating Account of Recent Breakthroughs— Scientific and Spiritual—That Can Save Your Garden or Farm
0–06–015817–4 Harper & Row $22.50

HISTORY OF AGRICULTURE

- Mark Cohen
THE FOOD CRISIS IN PREHISTORY: Overpopulation and the Origins of Agriculture
0–300–02351–0 Yale pb $13.95

- Mark Friedberger
FARM FAMILIES AND CHANGE IN TWENTIETH-CENTURY AMERICA
0–8131–1636–8 Kentucky $28.00

- Howard Russell
A LONG, DEEP FURROW: Three Centuries of Farming in New England
0–87451–214–X University Press pb $15.95

- Hubert G. Schmidt
AGRICULTURE IN NEW JERSEY: A 300-Year History
0–8135–0756–1 Rutgers $30.00

The Environment

ENVIRONMENTAL HISTORY

- Thomas Allen
GUARDIAN OF THE WILD: The Story of the National Wildlife Federation, 1936-1986
0–253–32605–2 Indiana $18.95

- Christopher Bosso
PESTICIDES AND POLITICS: The Life Cycle of a Public Issue
Traces the battle over control of pesticides through 40 years of technological and political changes
0–8229–3547–3 Pittsburgh $29.95

- Anna Bramwell
ECOLOGY IN THE 20TH CENTURY: A History
0–300–04521–2 Yale pb $16.95

- Clarence Glacken
TRACES OF THE RHODIAN SHORE: Nature and Culture in Western Thought from Ancient Times to the End of the 18th Century
0–520–03216–0 California $22.00

- Samuel Hays
CONSERVATION AND THE GOSPEL OF EFFICIENCY: The Progressive Conservation Movement, 1890-1920
0–674–16501–2 Harvard pb $7.95

- J. Donald Hughes
AMERICAN INDIAN ECOLOGY
0–87404–070–1 Texas Western $20.00

- Hans Huth
NATURE AND THE AMERICAN: Three Centuries of Changing Attitudes
0–8032–0926–6 Nebraska $25.50
0–8032–5761–9 Nebraska pb $7.50

- Geoffrey & Susan Jellicoe
LANDSCAPE OF MAN: Shaping the Environment from Prehistory to the Present Day
0–500–27431–2 Thames & Hudson pb $22.50

- Martin Melosi
GARBAGE IN THE CITIES: Refuse, Reform, and the Environment, 1880-1980
0–89096–119–0 Texas A&M $21.50

- Lee Clark Mitchell
WITNESS TO A VANISHING AMERICA: The 19th-Century Response
The last century's reaction to the rapid alteration of America's natural environment
0–691–06461–X Princeton $29.50
0–691–10223–6 Princeton pb $14.95

- Roderick Nash
WILDERNESS AND THE AMERICAN MIND
0–300–02905–5 Yale $40.00
0–300–02910–1 Yale pb $12.95

- Stephen Pyne
FIRE IN AMERICA: A Cultural History of Wildland and Rural Fire
0–691–08300–2 Princeton $44.50

- Keith Thomas
MAN AND THE NATURAL WORLD: A History of the Modern Sensibility
0–394–72712–6 Pantheon pb $10.95

- Peter Wild
PIONEER CONSERVATIONISTS OF EARLY AMERICA
0–87842–187–4 Mountain Press $14.95
PIONEER CONSERVATIONISTS OF EASTERN AMERICA
0–87842–126–2 Mountain Press $14.95

- Donald Worster
NATURE'S ECONOMY: A History of Ecological Ideas
0–521–26792–7 Cambridge $37.50
0–521–31870–X Cambridge pb $10.95

- Donald Worster, editor
THE END OF THE EARTH: Perspectives on Modern Environmental History
0–521–34846–3 Cambridge pb $12.95

Environmental Classics

Rachel Carson
SILENT SPRING
Carson's attack on pesticides, published in 1962, helped launch the environmentalist movement
0–395–45390–9 Houghton Mifflin pb $7.95

Aldo Leopold
A SAND COUNTY ALMANAC: And Sketches Here and There
Essays on changes in the Wisconsin countryside and other observations by this pioneering conservationist. Awarded the John Burroughs Medal of the American Museum of Natural History (1978)
0–19–500777–8 Oxford $17.95

George Marsh
MAN AND NATURE: Or Physical Geography as Modified by Human Action
This 1869 book by an American statesman, scholar, and diplomat aroused great contemporary interest in conservation
0–674–54400–5 Harvard pb $17.50

THE ENVIRONMENTAL MOVEMENT

• John H. Adams & others
AN ENVIRONMENTAL AGENDA FOR THE FUTURE
Essays by the heads of Sierra Club, National Audubon Society, World Wildlife Fund, and the Conservation Foundation assess key issues of the past and future. "Environmentalists and their opponents alike will find this preview of ecological battles-to-come a useful blueprint for strategy"—*Washington Post*
0–933280–29–7 Island pb $9.95

• Walter Truett Anderson
TO GOVERN EVOLUTION: Further Adventures of a Political Animal
The complex ethical and political issues connected with artificial insemination, in vitro fertilization, embryo transplant, and birth control, with attention to the political movements emerging around animal rights, global environmentalism, biotechnology, and population control
0–15–190483–9 HBJ $22.95

• Ian Barbour
TECHNOLOGY, ENVIRONMENT, AND HUMAN VALUES
0–03–055886–7 Praeger $34.95
0–27–590448–2 Praeger pb $17.95

• Peter Borrelli, editor
CROSSROADS: Environmental Priorities for the Future
Barry Commoner, Stewart Udall, and others evaluate the movement's successes and failures
0–933280–68–8 Island $29.95
0–933280–67–X Island pb $17.95

• Lester Brown & others
STATE OF THE WORLD 1989: A Worldwatch Institute Report on Progress Toward a Sustainable Society
0–393–02788–0 Norton $18.95
0–393–30614–3 Norton pb $9.95

• Anne & Paul Ehrlich
EARTH
Two noted biologists assess our impact on the planet
0–531–15036–4 Watts $19.95

• Bentley Glass
PROGRESS OR CATASTROPHE: The Nature of Biological Science and Its Impact on Human Society
0–275–90107–6 Praeger $29.95
0–275–91806–8 Praeger pb $9.95

• Lester Milbrath
ENVIRONMENTALISTS: Vanguard of a New Society
0–87395–887–X SUNY $44.50
0–87395–888–8 SUNY pb $16.95

• Joseph Petulla
AMERICAN ENVIRONMENTALISM: Values, Tactics, Priorities
0–89096–087–9 Texas A&M $22.50

ENVIRONMENTAL PROTECTION IN THE UNITED STATES
0–936434–21–X SF Study Center $22.50
0–936434–22–8 SF Study Center pb $14.50

• Tom Regan
EARTHBOUND: New Introductory Essays in Environmental Ethics
0–87722–351–3 Temple $34.95

NATURAL RESOURCES AT RISK

• William Burch & Donald DeLuca
MEASURING THE SOCIAL IMPACT OF NATURAL RESOURCE POLICIES
0–8263–0690–X New Mexico $29.95

• Council on Environmental Quality
THE GLOBAL 2000 REPORT TO THE PRESIDENT: Entering the 21st Century
0–14–022441–6 Penguin pb $12.95

• J. Sholto Douglas & Robert Hart
FOREST FARMING: Towards a Solution to Problems of World Hunger and Conservation
0–8133–0331–1 Westview pb $19.50

• Mary Douglas & Aaron Wildavsky
RISK AND CULTURE: An Essay on the Selection of Technological and Environmental Dangers
0–520–05063–0 California pb $8.95

• Julius Fabos
LAND-USE PLANNING: From Global to Local Challenge
0–412–25210–4 Methuen pb $18.95

• International Institute for Environment and Development & The World Resource Institute
WORLD RESOURCES, 1988-1989: An Assessment of the Resource Base that Supports the Global Economy
0–465–09240–3 Basic Books $32.95
0–465–09241–1 Basic Books pb $16.95

From This Incomperable Lande: A Book of American Nature Writing *edited by Thomas J. Lyon (Houghton Mifflin/illustration by Paul Landacre)*

• Simon Julian & Herman Kahn
THE RESOURCEFUL EARTH: A Response to Global 2000
0–631–13467–0 Blackwell $39.95

• William Ramsay
BIOENERGY AND ECONOMIC DEVELOPMENT: Planning for Biomass Energy Programs in the Third World
0–8133–7037–X Westview pb $33.00

Air Pollution, Acid Rain, and the Greenhouse Effect

• Dean E. Abrahamson, editor
THE CHALLENGE OF GLOBAL WARMING
An up-to-date, nontechnical compendium of research by scientists and policymakers on causes, effects, policies, and solutions
Introduction by Senator Timothy E. Wirth
0–933280–87–4 Island $34.95
0–933280–86–6 Island pb $19.95

• Bert Bolin & Bo Doos
THE GREENHOUSE EFFECT, CLIMATE CHANGE, AND ECOSYSTEMS
0–471–91012–0 John Wiley $142.00

• Donald Carr
THE SKY IS STILL FALLING
0–393–01508–4 Norton $14.95

• Mark Douglas
OZONE LAYER PERIL
0–941287–00–9 Pye pb $6.95

• John Gribbin
THE BREATHING PLANET
0–631–14289–4 Blackwell pb $12.95

• John Luoma
THE AIR AROUND US: An Air Pollution Primer
0–935577–10–6 Acid Rain Foundation pb $8.95

• Robert A. Mello
LAST STAND OF THE RED SPRUCE
Written as a detective story, Mello's nontechnical assessment of the effects of acid rain on our forests and the role of the federal government is compelling
Introduction by Senator Patrick J. Leahy
0–933280–37–8 Island pb $14.95

• Alan Miller & Irving Mintzer
THE SKY IS THE LIMIT: Strategies for Protecting the Ozone Layer
0–915825–17–1 World Resource Inst pb $10.00

• National Academy of Sciences
AIR POLLUTION, THE AUTOMOBILE, AND THE PUBLIC HEALTH
0–309–03726–3 National Academy pb $60.00

• Sandra Postel
AIR POLLUTION, ACID RAIN, AND THE FUTURE OF FORESTS
0–916468–57–7 Worldwatch Institute pb $3.00

Industrial Hazards and Solid Wastes

- **James Bellini**
  HIGH TECH HOLOCAUST
  How airborne pollution, nuclear waste, acid rain, pesticides, and other products of technology are threatening the planet
  0–87156–686–9 Sierra Club pb $10.95

- **Louis Blumberg & Robert Gottlieb**
  WAR ON WASTE: Can America Win Its Battle With Garbage?
  0–933280–92–0 Island $34.95
  0–933280–91–2 Island pb $19.95

- **Michael Edelstein**
  CONTAMINATED COMMUNITIES: The Social and Psychological Impacts of Residential Toxic Exposure
  Love Canal and other toxic communities, and the physical and psychological effects of contamination
  0–8133–7447–2 Westview $29.95

- **Lois M. Gibbs**
  LOVE CANAL: My Story
  0–87395–587–0 SUNY $14.95

- **Floyd Hasselriis**
  REFUSE-DERIVED FUEL PROCESSING
  Extracting recyclable materials from municipal solid waste in order to produce fuel
  0–250–40314–5 Butterworth $42.95

- **Dan Kurzman**
  KILLING WIND: Inside the Bhopal Catastrophe
  0–07–035687–4 McGraw-Hill $19.95

- **John Withers**
  MAJOR INDUSTRIAL HAZARDS: Their Appraisal and Control
  Using disasters such as Bhopal and Seveso, Withers shows how hazards are analyzed and examines their impact on the local population
  0–470–21067–2 John Wiley $57.95

Nuclear Reactors

- **Luther J. Carter**
  NUCLEAR IMPERATIVES AND PUBLIC TRUST: Dealing with Radioactive Waste
  0–915707–47–0 RFF pb $14.95

- **Robert Peter Gale & Thomas Hauser**
  FINAL WARNING: The Legacy of Chernobyl
  0–446–51409–8 Warner $18.95

- **Anna Gyorgy**
  NO NUKES: Everyone's Guide to Nuclear Power
  0–89608–007–2 South End $20.00
  0–89608–006–4 South End pb $10.00

- **Michio Kaku & Jennifer Trainer, editors**
  NUCLEAR POWER: Both Sides (The Best Arguments For and Against the Most Controversial Technology)
  "A clear and balanced representation of the complex issue of nuclear power"—William Simon
  0–393–30128–1 Norton pb $8.95

- **The Observer**
  CHERNOBYL: The End of the Nuclear Dream
  0–394–75107–8 Random House pb $4.95

- **Marilynne Robinson**
  MOTHER COUNTRY
  The author of *Housekeeping* charts her anger over learning "that the largest commercial producer of plutonium in the world, and the largest source, by far, of radioactive contamination of the world's environment, is Great Britain"
  0–374–21361–5 Farrar, Straus & Giroux $16.95

Water Use and Pollution

- **Robert Gottlieb**
  A LIFE OF ITS OWN: The Politics and Power of Water
  Struggles over water supply as a factor in American history, and growing concerns over contamination
  0–15–195190–X HBJ $20.95

- **Barbara Graves, editor**
  RADON, RADIUM, AND OTHER RADIOACTIVITY IN GROUND WATER: Hydrogeologic Impact and Application to Indoor Airborne Contamination
  A compilation of conference papers presented by the EPA and Association of Ground Water Scientists and Engineers, with numerous case studies
  0–87371–117–3 Lewis $44.95

- **Jon A. Kusler**
  OUR NATIONAL WETLAND HERITAGE: A Protection Guidebook
  A comprehensive discussion of preservation, combined with a literature review, examination of statutes and cases, and a survey of protection programs; for both the professional and layperson
  0–911937–11–0 Environmental Law pb $14.00

- **Ed Marston, editor**
  WESTERN WATER MADE SIMPLE
  By focusing on the Colorado, the Columbia, and the Missouri rivers, this series of articles illustrates the most important issues affecting the conservation and management of our western water. George Polk Award for Environmental Reporting (1986)
  0–933280–39–4 Island pb $15.95

Practical Advice

- **Edward Bergin & Ronald Grandon**
  THE AMERICAN SURVIVAL GUIDE: How to Survive in Your Toxic Environment
  How to avoid, deal with, and seek compensation for exposure to environmental toxins
  0–380–87460–1 Avon pb $11.95

- **Debra Dadd**
  NONTOXIC HOME: Protecting Yourself and Your Family from Everyday Toxics and Health Hazards
  How to avoid toxins in cleaning products, food, tap water, and other dangers
  0–87477–401–2 Tarcher pb $9.95

- **Mike LaFavore**
  RADON: The Quiet Killer
  0–87857–712–2 Rodale pb $12.95

- **Allan Savory**
  HOLISTIC RESOURCE MANAGEMENT
  A comprehensive planning model for integrating environment and people in farming, ranching, and livestock management. "Savory's special genius is combining high-minded idealism with thorough-going practicality, and he has a nose for generating profit in the process"—Gretel Ehrlich, *Time*
  0–933280–62–9 Island $39.95
  0–933280–61–0 Island pb $24.95

- **Sierra Club Legal Defense Fund**
  THE POISONED WELL: New Strategies for Groundwater Protection
  A useful guide for determining the existence of pollutants, protection against contamination, explanation of federal regulations, and legal strategies
  0–933280–56–4 Island $31.95
  0–933280–55–6 Island pb $19.95

FORESTRY AND LAND CONSERVATION

You don't have to be a professional forester to recognize bad forestry ... If logging looks bad, it is bad. If a forest appears to be mismanaged, it is mismanaged. But a certain level of expertise is needed if you are going to be effective in doing something about it.

Gordon Robinson
THE FOREST AND THE TREES: A Guide to Excellent Forestry
0–933280–41–6 Island $34.95
0–933280–40–8 Island pb $19.95

- **Russell L. Brenneman & Sarah M. Bates, editors**
  LAND-SAVING ACTION: A Written Symposium by Twenty-Nine Experts on Private Land Conservation in the 1980s
  0–933280–23–8 Island $39.95
  0–933280–22–X Island pb $24.95

- **Mark Francis & others**
  COMMUNITY OPEN SPACES: Green Neighborhoods Through Community Action and Land Conservation
  0–933280–27–0 Island $24.95

- **Nancy P. Pittman, editor**
  FROM "THE LAND": Articles Compiled from The Land, 1941-1954
  Humor, science, short stories, and poetry; over 40 authors, including E.B. White and Aldo Leopold, on the subject of conservation
  0–933280–66–1 Island $34.95
  0–933280–65–3 Island pb $19.95

- **Ray Raphael**
  TREE TALK: The People and Politics of Timber
  The forest industry as seen by loggers, woodsmen, and environmentalists
  0–933280–10–6 Island pb $14.95

A modern Yanomami Indian, from People of the Tropical Rain Forest *edited by Julie S. Denslow and Christine Padoch (California/photo: Victor Englebert photo researchers)*

• Paul B. Sears
DESERTS ON THE MARCH
Written in 1935, this book is a timely reminder of how mankind continues to unbalance nature
0–933280–46–7 Island $29.95
0–933280–90–4 Island pb $14.95

• David J. Simon, editor
OUR COMMON LANDS: Defending the National Parks
Eighteen legal and environmental scholars discuss key environmental legislation. "This superb book contains all of the elements of a battle plan to preserve the national parks"—Stewart Udall
0–933280–58–0 Island $45.00
0–933280–57–2 Island pb $24.95

Tropical Forests

• Catherine Caufield
IN THE RAINFOREST: Report from a Strange, Beautiful, Imperiled World
0–394–52701–1 Knopf $16.95
0–226–09786–2 Chicago pb $11.95

• Julie S. Denslow & Christine Padoch, editors
PEOPLE OF THE TROPICAL RAIN FOREST
0–520–06295–7 California $39.50
0–520–06351–1 California pb $19.95

• Philip Fearnside
THE HUMAN CARRYING CAPACITY OF THE BRAZILIAN RAINFORESTS
0–231–06104–8 Columbia $39.00

• Adrian Forsyth & Ken Miyata
TROPICAL NATURE: Life and Death in the Rain Forests of Central and South America
0–684–18710–8 Scribners pb $7.95

• International Commission on International Humanitarian Issues
THE VANISHING FOREST: The Human Consequences of Deforestation
0–86232–631–1 Humanities $18.50
0–86232–632–X Humanities pb $6.95

• Marius Jacobs & R.A.A. Oldeman
THE TROPICAL RAIN FOREST: A First Encounter
"An outstanding 'first encounter' with tropical rain forests, and a compelling plea—a *cri de coeur*—for conservation of large tracts of them"—*Nature*
0–387–17996–8 Springer pb $39.95

• C.F. Jordan
AMAZONIAN RAINFORESTS
0–387–96397–9 Springer $45.00

• Kenneth Longman
THE TROPICAL RAINFOREST AND ITS ENVIRONMENT
0–470–20742–6 John Wiley $52.50

• D.J. Maberlev
TROPICAL RAIN FOREST ECOLOGY
0–412–00431–3 Methuen $49.50
0–412–00441–0 Methuen pb $19.95

• Andrew Mitchell
THE ENCHANTED CANOPY
A journey to the rainforest roof
0–02–585420–8 Macmillan $29.95

• Donald Perry
LIFE ABOVE THE JUNGLE FLOOR
A biologist explores a strange and hidden world: the rainforest canopy, inhabited by two-thirds of the forest's wildlife
0–671–54454–3 Simon & Schuster $16.95
0–671–64426–2 Fireside pb $8.95

• Douglas Shane
HOOFPRINTS ON THE FOREST: Cattle Ranching and the Destruction of Latin America's Tropical Forests
0–89727–054–1 Human Resources $27.50

BIOLOGICAL DIVERSITY

• Michael Soule
CONSERVATION BIOLOGY: The Science of Scarcity and Diversity
0–87893–795–1 Sinaur $28.95

• Colin Tudge, editor
THE ENVIRONMENT OF LIFE
Examines the setting shared by all flora and fauna—and the impact of one species on it
0–19–520621–5 Oxford $35.00

• Langdon Winner
THE WHALE AND THE REACTOR: A Search for Limits in an Age of High Technology
0–226–90211–0 Chicago pb $8.95

Human beings are the most adaptable creatures that have ever lived on Earth. Reason and insight, the chief human talents, have given us the power to forge a world increasingly fit for our own comfort. We feed voraciously on all manner of life, from whale to lily. We have no significant predators save a diminishing roster of infectious diseases. Of course, there is the odd shark, crocodile, or lion, but they are disappearing even faster than the diseases. We carve the planet's surface into fields and streets, shopping malls and parking lots, with little regard to what was there before, because what we replace it with offers a more immediate, short-term benefit. Never before in Earth's history has such an abundant, aggressive, industrious omnivore at the peak of the energy pyramid comprised such a large portion of the living biomass. The prognosis is clear for the five to ten million other kinds of living things that share the Earth. They are in big trouble.

Les Kaufman & Kenneth Mallory, editors
THE LAST EXTINCTION
0–262–11115–2 MIT $18.95
0–262–61053–1 MIT pb $7.95

ENDANGERED SPECIES

• David Day
THE WHALE WARS
Whalers versus Save the Whales
0–87156–778–4 Sierra Club pb $9.95

• Thomas Dunlap
SAVING AMERICA'S WILDLIFE
Illustrates the shift in American attitudes toward preserving wildlife as we are faced with losing it
0–691–04750–2 Princeton $24.95

• Paul & Anne Ehrlich
EXTINCTION: The Causes and Consequences of the Disappearing Species
0–394–51312–6 Random House $16.95
0–345–33094–3 Ballantine pb $4.95

• Errol Fuller
EXTINCT BIRDS
More than 135 illustrations
0–8160–1833–2 Facts On File $35.00

TO ORDER BOOKS AS GIFTS, SEE PAGE 1

- International Union for the Conservation of Nature & Natural Resources Conservation Monitoring Center
1988 IUCN RED LIST OF THREATENED ANIMALS
2–88032–935–3 Pinter pb $10.00

- Les Kaufman & Kenneth Mallory, editors
THE LAST EXTINCTION
An important collection of essays intended to educate the public about the threat of mass extinction of species
0–262–11115–2 MIT $18.95
0–262–61053–1 MIT pb $7.95

- Harold Koopowitz & Hilary Kaye
PLANT EXTINCTION: A Global Crisis
0–913276–44–8 Stone Wall $18.95

- Jon Luoma
A CROWDED ARK: The Role of Zoos in Wildlife Conservation
0–395–40879–2 Houghton Mifflin $17.95

- Norman Myers
THE SINKING ARK: A New Look at the Problem of Disappearing Species
0–08–024501–3 Pergamon $25.00

A WEALTH OF WILD SPECIES: Storehouse for Human Welfare
0–86531–132–3 Westview $42.50
0–86531–133–1 Westview pb $19.95

- Malcolm Penny
RHINOS: Endangered Species
0–8160–1882–0 Facts On File $19.95

- Steven Stanley
EXTINCTION
0–7167–5014–7 W.H. Freeman $32.95

ANIMAL RIGHTS

- Michael Fox
THE CASE FOR ANIMAL EXPERIMENTATION: An Evolutionary and Ethical Perspective
Argues that it is permissible for humans to experiment on animals, but only within carefully qualified ethical guidelines
0–520–05501–2 California $27.50

- Tom Regan
ALL THAT DWELL THEREIN: Animal Rights and Environmental Ethics
0–520–04571–8 California $27.50

ANIMAL SACRIFICES: Religious Perspectives on the Use of Animals in Science
0–87722–411–0 Temple $29.95

THE CASE FOR ANIMAL RIGHTS
"Makes any objections to the inclusion of animals in the moral community sound exactly like the feeble tenets that have supported racism, sexism, or antisemitism"—*Spectator*
0–520–04904–7 California $29.95
0–520–05460–1 California pb $11.95

- Peter Singer
ANIMAL LIBERATION
The first closely argued philosophical case for animal rights, Singer's 1975 book was a major inspiration for the animal rights movement
0–380–01782–2 Avon pb $4.95

IN DEFENCE OF ANIMALS
0–06–097044–8 Harper & Row pb $6.95

- Susan Sperling
ANIMAL LIBERATORS: Research and Morality
A critical study of activists in the animal rights movement
0–520–06198–5 California $19.95

BIOGRAPHIES

- Lewis Gould
LADY BIRD JOHNSON AND THE ENVIRONMENT
0–7006–0336–0 Kansas $29.95

- Curt Meine
ALDO LEOPOLD: His Life and Work
Forester, scientist, sportsman, philosopher, writer, and conservation activist, Leopold advocated a "land ethic" to guide industrial man through the natural world. This biography offers an excellent personal view of the American conservation movement
0–299–11490–2 Wisconsin $29.50

- Michael Cohen
THE PATHLESS WAY: John Muir and American Wilderness
0–299–09720–X Wisconsin $26.50

- Linnie Marsh Wolfe
SON OF THE WILDERNESS: The Life of John Muir
0–299–07730–6 Wisconsin $29.50
0–299–07734–9 Wisconsin pb $10.95

The Computer Revolution and Artificial Intelligence

THE COMPUTER REVOLUTION

The computer revolution, still in its infancy, has generated thousands of books, most of them about the latest hardware, the latest computer languages, how to write programs, and how to design faster, smaller, and more powerful machines. The following books are broad in scope: they discuss what the revolution is all about, its history, its philosophical implications, and how it is likely to affect our lives.

- Michael Crichton
ELECTRONIC LIFE: How to Think About Computers
0–345–31739–4 Ballantine pb $3.95

- Tom Forester, editor
COMPUTERS IN THE HUMAN CONTEXT: Information Technology, Productivity, and People
0–262–06124–4 MIT $37.50
0–262–56050–X MIT pb $16.95

A Kuikuru village, surrounded by old fields, fallows, and forest, from People of the Tropical Rain Forest *edited by Julie S. Denslow and Christine Padoch (California/photo by Loren McIntyre)*

- James Jesperson & Jane
Fitz-Randolph
RAMS, ROMS, AND ROBOTS
Aimed at young adult readers
0–689–31063–3 Macmillan $13.95

- Tracy Kidder
THE SOUL OF A NEW MACHINE
0–380–59931–7 Avon pb $4.95

- Donald Sanders
COMPUTERS IN SOCIETY
0–07–054672–X McGraw-Hill $36.95

- Nancy & Robert Stern
COMPUTERS IN SOCIETY
0–13–165282–6 Prentice-Hall pb $34.00

- Norbert Wiener
**THE HUMAN USE OF HUMAN
BEINGS: Cybernetics and Society**
0–306–80320–8 Da Capo pb $9.95

Mechanical and Electronic Calculators

- Charles & Ray Eames
A COMPUTER PERSPECTIVE
0–674–15625–0 Harvard $15.00

- Martin Gardner
LOGIC MACHINES AND DIAGRAMS
0–226–28244–9 Chicago pb $5.95

- Herman Goldstine
**THE COMPUTER FROM PASCAL TO
VON NEUMANN**
0–691–08104–2 Princeton $43.50
0–691–02367–0 Princeton pb $12.95

- Anthony Hyman
**CHARLES BABBAGE: Pioneer of the
Computer**
0–691–02377–8 Princeton pb $14.50

- Brian Randell, editor
**THE ORIGINS OF DIGITAL
COMPUTERS**
0–387–11319–3 Springer $40.00

- Joel Shurkin
**ENGINES OF THE MIND: A History of
the Computer**
0–393–01804–0 Norton $17.00

- Michael Williams
**A HISTORY OF COMPUTING
TECHNOLOGY**
0–13–389917–9 Prentice-Hall $32.00

Biographies

Ada Lovelace, Lord Byron's beautiful daughter who wrote with such prophetic insight about the work of her mentor Charles Babbage (his Analytical Engine was the mechanical ancestor of modern calculators), has been the subject of several biographies. The Defense Department recently named its supercomputer language ADA in honor of her writings.

- Joan Baum
**THE CALCULATING PASSION OF ADA
BYRON**
0–208–02119–1 Shoe String $21.50

- Dorothy Stein
ADA: A Life and Legacy
0–262–69116–7 MIT pb $9.95

Andrew Hodges
ALAN TURING: The Enigma
The sad life of Alan Turing, the British computer scientist who killed himself at age 41, has been the topic of two recent books and a Broadway play. Turing invented the Turing Machine, an abstract design of enormous significance in computer theory, and the famous "Turing Game," proposed as a way to decide if and when computers can be said to "think" like humans
0–671–52809–2 Simon & Schuster pb $10.95

ARTIFICIAL INTELLIGENCE

Artificial intelligence is the attempt to build electronic machines that calculate and behave like humans. Its theory is closely linked to theories of how the brain works, and how humans go about solving problems.

- Igor Aleksander & Piers Burnett
**THINKING MACHINES: The Search for
Artificial Intelligence**
0–394–74459–4 Knopf pb $17.95

- Margaret Boden
**ARTIFICIAL INTELLIGENCE AND THE
NATURAL MAN**
0–465–00456–3 Harper & Row pb $14.95

- Jeremy Campbell
**GRAMMATICAL MAN: Information,
Entropy, Language, and Life**
A discussion of information theory that ranges over many fields, from cosmology to computers
0–671–44062–4 Simon & Schuster pb $10.95

Daniel Dennett & Douglas
Hofstadter, editors
**THE MIND'S I: Fantasies and
Reflections of Self and Soul**
Artificial intelligence is central to this anthology
0–465–04624–X Harper & Row $16.95
0–553–34343–2 Bantam pb $13.95

Douglas Hofstadter
**GODEL, ESCHER, BACH: An Eternal
Golden Braid**
This best-selling book ranges far beyond artificial intelligence
0–394–74502–7 Random House pb $13.95

- Philip Jackson
**AN INTRODUCTION TO ARTIFICIAL
INTELLIGENCE**
0–486–24864–X Dover pb $8.95

- George Johnson
**MACHINERY OF THE MIND: Inside the
New Science of Artificial Intelligence**
"An ideal presentation . . . Lively and provocative, peppered with wit, a delight to read"—Douglas Hofstadter
1–55615–010–5 Tempus pb $9.95

- Pamela McCorduck
MACHINES WHO THINK
0–7167–1135–4 W.H. Freeman pb $14.95

- Bertram Raphael
**THE THINKING COMPUTER: Mind
Inside Matter**
0–7167–0723–3 W.H. Freeman pb $16.95

- Mitchell Waldrop
**MAN-MADE MINDS: The Promise of
Artificial Intelligence**
0–8027–7297–8 Walker pb $14.95

- Patrick Winston
ARTIFICIAL INTELLIGENCE
0–201–08259–4 Addison-Wesley $45.25

This technique of slowing down maturity, retaining into grown-up life the juvenile traits of ancestral species, is called neoteny, a word coined in 1883. It means, literally, "holding youth." . . . Neoteny slows down the rate of bodily development in humans, giving them a longer childhood than their primate ancestors and a brain which grows in early life as fast as it grew in the womb. This was a revolutionary change, resulting in a unique openness to new information at a time when the child is fully dependent on its parents, who spend much time on its care and mental enrichment. The plasticity of the child's brain, its flexibility and redundancy, enabling it to shift and reorganize its resources to meet the needs of various modes of life, make the human species the least narrowly specialized of all animals. The brain comes provided with a generous number of possible patterns of organization in early childhood. Which patterns are actually developed may depend on the experiences of each child, his or her capacities, tastes, drives, and the mental stimulation given in the critical period. The large, slowly maturing brain helped to provide an escape from the trap of overspecialization which blocks the avenue to further evolutionary advance. No single evolutionary event has had such a transforming effect on the life of the planet; neoteny is the biological principle which made civilization possible.

Jeremy Campbell
**GRAMMATICAL MAN: Information,
Entropy, Language, and Life**
0–671–44062–4 Simon & Schuster pb $10.95

Robotics

Robotics, a term coined by Isaac Asimov, is a branch of artificial intelligence that concerns the design of machines to replace physical labor at home or in industry. The following are nontechnical books on the subject.

- James Albus
BRAINS, BEHAVIOR, AND ROBOTICS
0–07–000975–9 McGraw-Hill $29.95

- Arthur Critchlow
INTRODUCTION TO ROBOTICS
0–02–325590–0 Macmillan $47.00

- Daniel Hunt
SMART ROBOTS: A Handbook of Intelligent Robotic Systems
0–412–00531–X Routledge $44.50

- Tom Logsdon
ROBOT REVOLUTION
0–671–46705–0 Simon & Schuster pb $17.95

Do Computers Think?

Efforts by artificial intelligence researchers to simulate human thinking have given rise to strong controversy, not only among computer scientists but also among philosophers. Is one justified in saying that computers "think" (or soon will think), or should the term be restricted to what organic brains do? Most artificial intelligence workers believe, in the words of Marvin Minsky, that the brain is simply a computer made of meat—that it does nothing that cannot eventually be done just as well (though not necessarily in the same way) by a machine. Airplanes don't flap their wings, nevertheless they "fly" faster than a bird. Computer scientists outside the artificial intelligence field tend to be more skeptical.

- Alan Anderson, editor
MINDS AND MACHINES
0–13–583393–0 Prentice-Hall pb $16.00

- Margaret Boden
ARTIFICIAL INTELLIGENCE AND NATURAL MAN
0–465–00456–3 Harper & Row pb $14.95

- Daniel Dennett
BRAINSTORMS: Philosophical Essays on Mind and Psychology
0–262–54037–1 MIT pb $12.50

- Pamela McCorduck
THE UNIVERSAL MACHINE: Confessions of a Technological Optimist
0–07–044882–5 McGraw-Hill $16.95
0–15–692873–6 HBJ pb $7.95

- Geoff Simons
ARE COMPUTERS ALIVE?: Evolution and New Life Forms
0–8176–3144–5 Birkhauser pb $17.50

- Joseph Weizenbaum
COMPUTER POWER AND HUMAN REASON: From Judgment to Calculation
0–7167–0463–3 W.H. Freeman pb $13.95

Critiques of Computers and Artificial Intelligence

- David Burnham
THE RISE OF THE COMPUTER STATE
Potential dangers in government use of computers
0–394–72375–9 Random House pb $6.95

- Theodore Roszak
THE CULT OF INFORMATION: The Folklore of Computers and the True Art of Thinking
A recent critique of computer enthusiasm
0–394–75175–2 Pantheon pb $7.95

- John Searle
MINDS, BRAINS, AND SCIENCE
A leading philosopher gives us a restrained attack on artificial intelligence
0–674–57633–0 Harvard pb $5.95

Computer Games

Martin Gardner
WHEELS, LIFE, AND OTHER MATHEMATICAL AMUSEMENTS
One recreation stands above all others in the time consumed by computer buffs in debating its implications. Invented by Cambridge mathematician John Conway, who named it *Life*, the game is closely related to a growing branch of mathematics called "cellular automata theory." This book devotes three chapters to the game
0–7167–1589–9 W.H. Freeman pb $12.95

REFERENCE

Computers have made it necessary to invent thousands of new terms. Although this terminology changes rapidly, it has stabilized enough to permit dozens of dictionaries and encyclopedias.

- William Birnes, editor
McGRAW-HILL PERSONAL COMPUTER PROGRAMMING ENCYCLOPEDIA: Languages and Operating Systems
0–07–005389–8 McGraw-Hill $95.00

- Philip Burton
A DICTIONARY OF MINICOMPUTING AND MICROCOMPUTING
0–8240–7286–3 Garland pb $17.95

- Douglas Downing
DICTIONARY OF COMPUTER TERMS
0–8120–2905–4 Barron's pb $8.95

- Harry Helms, editor
THE McGRAW-HILL COMPUTER HANDBOOK
0–07–027972–1 McGraw-Hill $89.95

Computer Manuals

In the early 1900s, divers dredged up a puzzling clocklike mechanism from the hull of an ancient ship which had sunk near the Greek island of Antikythera. Certain calibrated elements showed it to be a measuring device of some kind, but it was years before archaeologists figured out that the Antikythera Device, dated at around 100 BC, had been used to perform astronomical calculations *automatically*.

The modern term "computer" refers to high-speed electronic equipment capable of reading and writing data, executing various series of instructions (programs) to process such data and, finally, storing the results. At the end of the 17th century new kinds of calculating machines began to be invented as nascent capitalism demanded an accelerated rate of exchange. But it was Charles P. Babbage's visionary "Difference Engine" and "Analytical Engine" which definitively prefigured the modern computer. Both of his designs could have worked, except that the 19th century was incapable of making parts for them. Not until 1930 did anything comparable to Babbage's inventions appear. Over the next decades there appeared a "differential analyzer" built by the US military for plotting artillery trajectories; the Mark I, the first fully automatic computer; and the first electronic computer, the ENIAC, produced by the University of Pennsylvania in 1946.

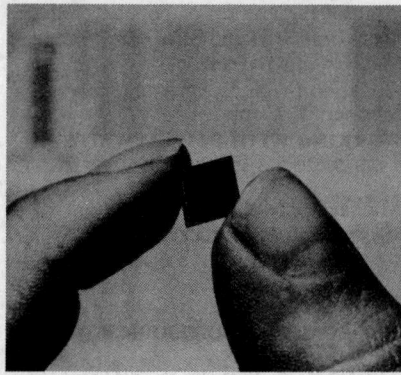

Microchip, from The American Century *by Walter LaFeber and others (Knopf)*

By today's standards the ENIAC was a hulking colossus which weighed over 30 tons. Its vacuum tubes threw off tremendous heat and required an elaborate cooling system. All that changed with the development of solid-state technology in the mid 1960s. Transistorized circuitry miniaturized the computer, eliminated the heat problem, and greatly reduced production costs as well. Subsequently the silicon microprocessor "chip" or integrated circuit has permitted even smaller and cheaper designs, making possible today's "home" or "personal" computer, the PC.

★ **FOR COMPLETE ORDERING INFORMATION, SEE PAGE 1**

When the PC first began to work its way into the everyday life of the American consumer, the need for information geared to the nonspecialist spawned a new field of publishing. Many of the books which meet this demand are instruction manuals written to augment or replace the often insufficient manuals of hardware and software vendors. Others are intended to improve the user's skills and techniques. Because most of these publications are linked to a rapidly changing technology, they offer fast-paced information open to continued revision. Accordingly, the following list is a broad survey of the field as a whole, not an exhaustive bibliography. It highlights major equipment and programs. But given the multiple functions of these, some overlapping between categories is inevitable.

WORD PROCESSING

Word processing first became popular in the early 1970s with specialized, hardwired machines which enabled secretaries to correct and process text instead of having to type revised manuscripts from scratch. Today, powerful word processing programs have made earlier systems like Exxon's Vydec totally obsolete; accordingly, the PC has become a standard writer's tool.

DisplayWrite

IBM's DisplayWrite 4 has made a niche for itself in the corporate world. While lacking many of the features of popular programs like WordPerfect and Microsoft Word, it is relatively easy to learn.

- Stephen T. Cobb
WORKING WITH DISPLAYWRITE 4
0–673–38020–3 Scott, Foresman pb $21.95

- Michael E. McCarthy
MASTERING DISPLAYWRITE 4
0–89588–510–7 Sybex pb $22.95

- Gail Todd
THE COMPLETE REFERENCE TO DISPLAYWRITE 4
0–07–881344–1 McGraw-Hill pb $24.95

DISPLAYWRITE 4 MADE EASY
0–07–881270–4 McGraw-Hill pb $19.95

Microsoft Word

Microsoft Word, one of the most popular word processing packages, is the dominant program in the Macintosh environment and WordPerfect's closest rival in the IBM world. It was one of the first word processing programs to offer desktop publishing features.

- Eric Alderman
MICROSOFT WORD: The Complete Reference
0–07–881335–2 McGraw-Hill pb $24.95

- Michael A. Fischer
MICROSOFT WORD FOR THE MACINTOSH: The Complete Reference
0–07–881331–X McGraw-Hill pb $26.95

- John V. Hedtke
MICROSOFT WORD: Power User's Guide
0–07–881357–3 McGraw-Hill pb $22.95

- Paul Hoffman
MICROSOFT WORD MADE EASY
0–07–881483–9 McGraw-Hill pb $19.95

MICROSOFT WORD MADE EASY FOR THE MACINTOSH
0–07–881478–2 McGraw-Hill pb $19.95

- Matthew Holtz
MASTERING MICROSOFT WORD
0–89588–524–7 Sybex pb $21.95

- Steve Lambert & Marsha L. Miliman
USING MICROSOFT WORD: Macintosh Version
0–88022–333–2 Que pb $19.95

- Rhyder McClure & John Dickinson
FAST ACCESS/MICROSOFT WORD
0–13–307539–7 Prentice-Hall pb $14.95

WordPerfect

WordPerfect is far and away the best-selling word processing package on the market. The new 5.0 version adds desktop publishing features and enhanced printer support to an already impressive program.

- Vincent Alfieri
THE BEST BOOK OF WORDPERFECT: Version 5.0
0–672–48423–4 Hayden $21.95

- Janet Crider
WORDPERFECT POWER: 5.0
0–13–964198–X Prentice-Hall pb $24.95

- Ruth Halpern
WORDPERFECT: Power User's Guide
0–07–881364–6 McGraw-Hill pb $22.95

- Susan Baake Kelly
MASTERING WORDPERFECT 5
0–89588–500–X Sybex pb $21.95

- Milia Mincberg
WORDPERFECT 5: Secrets, Solutions, Shortcuts
0–07–881359–X McGraw-Hill pb $21.95

- Donna M. Mosich
WORDPERFECT 5.0: New Features and Advanced Techniques For Upgraders
0–8306–9384–X TAB pb $19.95

- Alan Neibauer
THE ABC'S OF WORDPERFECT 5
0–89588–504–2 Sybex pb $17.95

- Kay Yarborough Nelson
MASTERING WORDPERFECT ON THE MACINTOSH
0–89588–515–8 Sybex pb $21.95

- Beverly & S. Scott Zimmerman
WORKING WITH WORDPERFECT ON THE APPLE IIC, IIE, AND IIGS
0–317–66974–5 Scott, Foresman pb $17.95

Wordstar

Once the marvel of the word processing world, Wordstar has been overtaken by more fully featured programs like Microsoft Word and WordPerfect. Nonetheless, it still has many loyal adherents.

- David Bary & Rob Krumm
USING WORDSTAR 2000 AND 2000 PLUS
0–89303–925–X Prentice-Hall pb $17.95

- Steve Ditlea
USING WORDSTAR: Professional Release 5
0–88022–361–8 Que pb $21.95

- Greg Harvey
MASTERING WORDSTAR RELEASE 5
0–89588–491–7 Sybex pb $19.95

- Carole Boggs Matthews
USING WORDSTAR PROFESSIONAL: Series 5
0–07–881466–9 McGraw-Hill pb $21.95

- Carole Boggs Matthews & Martin S. Matthews
WORDSTAR PROFESSIONAL: The Complete Reference
0–07–881332–8 McGraw-Hill pb $24.95

- Greg Perry
WORDSTAR 2000 HANDBOOK
0–07–881334–4 McGraw-Hill pb $21.95

DATA BASE MANAGEMENT

A data base can consist of subscription lists, inventories, personnel files, or any other data produced within a given system. Data base software allows the user to organize and recombine this information in a variety of ways.

dBASE

Long the industry standard, dBASE is to data base software what WordPerfect is to word processing and Lotus 1-2-3 to spreadsheets.

- Robert Byers & Cary Prague
EVERYMAN'S DATA BASE PRIMER FEATURING dBASE IV
0–13–292798–5 Prentice-Hall pb $19.95

- George T. Chou
dBASE IV HANDBOOK
0–88022–380–4 Que pb $23.95

- Robert Cowart
THE ABC'S OF dBASE IV
0–89588–531–X Sybex pb $18.95

- Russel DeMaria & George Fontaine
WORKING WITH dBASE MAC: Pushing Productivity to the Limit
0–13–939760–4 Prentice-Hall pb $24.95

- Howard Dickler & Cathy Ledbetter
dBASE IV FOR THE FIRST-TIME USER
0–13–198748–8 Prentice-Hall pb $21.95

- Dan Shafer & Don Huntington
THE COMPLETE GUIDE TO dBASE MAC
0–673–18732–2 Scott, Foresman pb $21.95

- Carol Townsend
MASTERING dBASE IV
0–89588–540–9 Sybex pb $22.95

Other Data Base Programs

- Mary Campbell
USING AGENDA
0–07–881409–X McGraw-Hill pb $21.95

- John R. Ottensmann & Jan Nevenschwander
WORKING WITH LOTUS AGENDA
0–8306–3161–5 TAB pb $24.95

- James T. Perry & Joseph G. Lateer
UNDERSTANDING ORACLE
0–89588–534–4 Sybex pb $24.95

- George T. Chou
USING PARADOX
0–88022–362–6 Que pb $22.95

- Douglas Cobb & others
PARADOX COMPANION
0–553–34361–0 Bantam pb $24.95

- Edward Jones
PARADOX MADE EASY
0–07–881413–8 McGraw-Hill pb $19.95

- James Keogh
PARADOX: The Complete Reference
0–07–881390–5 McGraw-Hill pb $26.95

- Alan Simpson
MASTERING PARADOX
0–89588–490–9 Sybex pb $21.95

- Alan Simpson & Karen Watterson
UNDERSTANDING R:BASE
0–89588–503–4 Sybex pb $21.95

- Stephen Cobb
USING REFLEX: The Database Manager
0–07–881287–9 McGraw-Hill pb $21.95

- William B. Sanders
THE POWER OF REFLEX PLUS
0–673–38593–0 Scott, Foresman pb $19.95

SPREADSHEETS

Spreadsheet programs are the digital replacement for the traditional forecaster's columns, pad, and calculator. They are an invaluable tool for financial planners, ac-countants, statisticians, engineers, and scientists.

Lotus 1-2-3

Lotus 1-2-3 was the first widely popular software package for the IBM PC. The fact that Lotus chose to develop the program for the IBM PC was instrumental in making it, rather than Apple, the standard computer in the business world. Despite the fact that programs like Excel outperform it, 1-2-3 remains the most popular spreadsheet program as well as one of the best-selling computer programs in any category.

- Mary Campbell
1-2-3: The Complete Reference
0–07–881318–2 McGraw-Hill pb $24.95

1-2-3 MADE EASY
0–07–881293–3 McGraw-Hill pb $18.95

- Chris Gilbert & Laurie Williams
THE ABC'S OF 1-2-3 RELEASE 3
0–89588–355–4 Sybex pb $17.95

- Carolyn Jorgensen
MASTERING 1-2-3 RELEASE 3
0–89588–517–4 Sybex pb $22.95

- Ira Krakow
LOTUS 1-2-3 SELF TAUGHT
0–13–540667–6 Prentice-Hall pb $19.95

- Peter G. Randall
TOTAL 1-2-3
0–13–925728–4 Prentice-Hall $24.95

- Roger James Seymour
UNLEASHING THE POWER OF LOTUS
0–13–510181–6 Prentice-Hall pb $21.95

- Gene Weisskopf
LOTUS 1-2-3 TIPS AND TRICKS
0–89588–454–2 Sybex pb $21.95

Excel

- Mary Campbell
USING EXCEL: Macintosh Version
0–88022–209–3 Que pb $21.95

- Danny Goodman & Gordon McComb
HANDS ON EXCEL!
0–673–38479–9 Scott, Foresman pb $22.95

HANDS ON IBM EXCEL
0–673–38480–2 Scott, Foresman pb $22.95

- Amanda Hixson
ADVANCED EXCEL FOR THE PC
0–07–881273–9 McGraw-Hill pb $21.95

- Edward Jones
USING EXCEL FOR THE PC
0–07–881281–X McGraw-Hill pb $21.95

- Robert Krumm
UNDERSTANDING AND USING MICROSOFT EXCEL
0–13–942103–3 Prentice-Hall pb $29.95

- Carl Townsend
MASTERING EXCEL ON THE MACINTOSH
0–89588–439–9 Sybex pb $24.95

Other Spreadsheet Titles

- Lisa Biow
QUATTRO MADE SIMPLE
0–07–881347–6 McGraw-Hill pb $19.95

- Stephen Cobb
QUATTRO: Power User's Guide
0–07–881367–0 McGraw-Hill pb $22.95

- Yvonne McCoy
QUATTRO: The Complete Reference
0–07–881337–9 McGraw-Hill pb $24.95

- John R. Ottensmann
QUATTRO SIMPLIFIED
0–8306–9111–1 TAB $27.95
0–8306–3111–9 TAB pb $17.95

- Elna Tymes & Charles Prael
QUATTRO FOR THE PROFESSIONAL
0–8306–1078–2 TAB $28.95
0–8306–9378–5 TAB pb $17.95

- Greg Harvey
MASTERING SUPERCALC4
0–89588–419–4 Sybex pb $21.95

- James T. Perry & Joseph G. Lateer
USING SUPERCALC4
0–88022–276–X Que pb $21.95

DESKTOP PUBLISHING

The development of low-cost laser printers and sophisticated page layout programs has radically affected the way that newsletters, magazines, newspapers, and business presentations are produced. The relative cheapness of electronic typography and graphics places them well within reach of small businesses and private individuals.

PageMaker

- Diane Burns & S. Venit
USING PAGEMAKER ON THE IBM
0–88022–285–9 Que pb $24.95

- Antonia Stacy Jolles
MASTERING PAGEMAKER ON THE IBM PC
0–89588–521–2 Sybex pb $22.95

- Douglas Kramer & Roger Parker
USING ALDUS PAGEMAKER 3.0
0–553–34624–5 Bantam pb $22.95

- Martin S. Matthews & Carole Boggs Matthews
USING PAGEMAKER FOR THE PC
0–07–881264–X McGraw-Hill pb $22.95

USING PAGEMAKER FOR THE PC: Version 3
0–07–881422–7 McGraw-Hill pb $22.95

- Kevin Strehlo
PAGEMAKER: Desktop Publishing on the Macintosh
0–673–18764–0 Scott, Foresman pb $21.95

Ventura Publisher

- Diane Burns & S. Venit
USING VENTURA PUBLISHER
0–88022–406–1 Que pb $24.95

- James Cavuoto & Jesse Berst
INSIDE XEROX VENTURA PUBLISHER
0–934035–13–X New Riders pb $19.95

- Matthew Holtz
MASTERING VENTURA
0–89588–427–5 Sybex pb $24.95

- Martha Lubow & Jesse Berst
PUBLISHING POWER WITH VENTURA
0–934035–19–9 New Riders pb $24.95

- Ted Nace
VENTURA TIPS AND TRICKS
0–938151–03–7 Peachpit pb $22.95

Other Desktop Publishing Titles

- Tony Bove, Cheryl Rhodes & Wes Thomas
THE ART OF DESKTOP PUBLISHING
0–553–34565–6 Bantam pb $21.95

- Diane Burns & S. Venit
THE ELECTRONIC PUBLISHER
0–13–251877–5 Prentice-Hall pb $24.95

- Tim Ericson
DESKTOP PUBLISHING WITH MICROSOFT WORD ON THE MACINTOSH
0–89588–447–X Sybex pb $22.95

- David Kater
MASTERING READY, SET, GO!
0–89588–536–0 Sybex pb $22.95

- Tom Lichty
DESIGN PRINCIPLES FOR DESKTOP PUBLISHING
0–673–38162–5 Scott, Foresman pb $19.95

- Roger C. Parker
DESKTOP PUBLISHING WITH WORDPERFECT
0–940087–15–4 Ventana pb $21.95

GRAPHICS

The computer is becoming as much an artist's tool as the T-square. An ever-growing selection of impressive programs lets commercial artists prepare slides, color separations, graphs, and illustrations with greater speed and flexibility than with traditional methods.

- Michael Gosney & Linnea Dayton
MAKING ART WITH THE MACINTOSH II
0–673–38159–5 Scott, Foresman pb $22.95

- David A. Holzgang
MASTERING ADOBE ILLUSTRATOR
0–89588–463–1 Sybex pb $22.95

- Gordon McComb
MASTERING MACDRAW
0–87455–102–1 Compute! pb $18.95

- David Miller
MASTERING APPLESOFT GRAPHICS
0–673–38148–X Scott, Foresman pb $18.95

- Gia L. Rozells & W. Ryan Ennis
SUPERPAINT SECRETS
0–673–38190–0 Scott, Foresman pb $22.95

- Susan Schmeiman
MACPAINT: Drawing, Drafting, Design
0–89303–648–X Prentice-Hall pb $15.95

INTEGRATED SOFTWARE PROGRAMS

Integrated software programs combine spreadsheet, database, word processing, graphics, and communications features in one package.

- Elna Tynes
MASTERING APPLEWORKS
0–89588–398–8 Sybex pb $21.95

- Christopher Van Buren & Steve High
APPLEWORKS MASTERY: An Advanced Guide to AppleWorks 2.0
0–673–18833–7 Scott, Foresman pb $19.95

- Keith D. Bishop
MASTERING ENABLE
0–89588–440–2 Sybex pb $22.95

- Walter Bruce
USING ENABLE 3
0–88022–400–2 Que pb $23.95

- Charles Spezzano
USING ENABLE
0–88022–329–4 Que pb $22.95

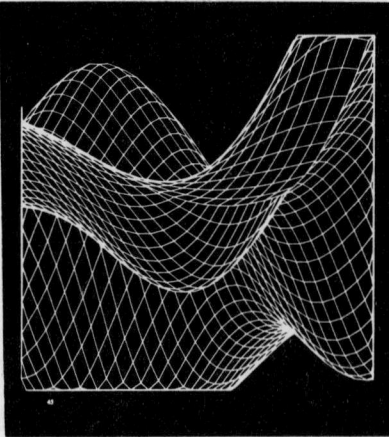

A computer graphic of a mathematical equation

- Bill Harrison
FRAMEWORK III: An Introduction
0–13–330150–8 Prentice-Hall pb $24.95

- Douglas Hergert & Jonathan Kamin
MASTERING FRAMEWORK III
0–89588–513–1 Sybex pb $24.95

- Cary N. Prague & Lawrence S. Kasevich
FRAMEWORK III
0–8306–9386–6 TAB pb $24.95

- Robert Cowart
MICROSOFT WORKS FOR THE PC
0–07–881272–0 McGraw-Hill pb $19.95

- Ronald Mansfield
USING MICROSOFT WORKS
0–88022–296–4 Que pb $19.95

- Donald J. Scellato
THE ADVANCED GUIDE TO MICROSOFT WORKS
0–07–881240–2 McGraw-Hill pb $18.95

- Edward M. Baras
THE SYMPHONY BOOK
0–07–881160–0 McGraw-Hill pb $19.95

- David Bolocan
MASTERING SYMPHONY
0–8306–9368–8 TAB pb $17.95

COMPUTER-AIDED DESIGN

A few years ago CAD programs cost $100,000 or more. Today there are a number of superb programs that put the drafting and design power of CAD in the hands of architects, urban planners, and designers for less than $1000.

AutoCAD

- Brenda L. Fouch
USING AUTOCAD
0–88022–288–3 Que pb $29.95

- Gerald E. Jones
AUTOCAD APPLICATIONS
0–673–38038–6 Scott, Foresman pb $24.95

- Alan R. Miller
THE ABC'S OF AUTOCAD
0–89588–498–4 Sybex pb $22.95

HYPERCARD

HyperCard is a hard-to-define program that has potentially revolutionary uses. It can be seen as a sophisticated relational database that lets users develop their own applications without having to program them in the traditional sense.

- Danny Goodman
THE COMPLETE HYPERCARD HANDBOOK
0–553–34577–X Bantam pb $29.95

- Greg Harvey
UNDERSTANDING HYPERCARD
0–89588–506–9 Sybex pb $24.95

- William B. Sanders
HYPERCARD MADE EASY
0–673–38577–9 Scott, Foresman pb $19.95

- W. Tay Vaughan III
USING HYPERCARD: From Home to HyperTalk
0–88022–340–5 Que pb $24.95

MICROSOFT WINDOWS

Windows is Microsoft's attempt to introduce a Macintosh-like graphic interface to the IBM environment.

- Nancy Andrews & Graig Stinson
RUNNING WINDOWS: The Microsoft Guide to Windows
1–556–15047–4 Microsoft pb $19.95

- Lana K. Bryan & Robert E. Whitsitt
ILLUSTRATED MICROSOFT WINDOWS 2.0
1–556–22069–3 Wordware pb $19.95

- Katherine Stuart Ewing
UNDERSTANDING MICROSOFT WINDOWS
0–672–27279–2 Howard Sams pb $17.95

- Ron Persons
USING MICROSOFT WINDOWS
0–88022–336–7 Que pb $19.95

TELECOMMUNICATIONS

Telecommunications is the electronic transfer of data from one place to another via telephone lines. "Going online" allows users to access and transmit a wealth of information.

- Tom Anderson
CONNECTING WITH CROSSTALK MK.4
0–673–38093–9 Scott, Foresman pb $19.95

- Michael A. Banks
THE MODEM REFERENCE
0–13–586646–4 Prentice-Hall pb $21.95

- Charles Bowen & David Peyton
HOW TO GET THE MOST OUT OF COMPUSERVE
0–553–34476–5 Bantam pb $19.95

HOW TO GET THE MOST OUT OF DOW JONES NEWS/RETRIEVAL
0–553–34327–0 Bantam pb $19.95

- Alfred Glossbrenner
MASTER GUIDE TO COMPUSERVE
0–13–159302–1 Prentice-Hall pb $19.95

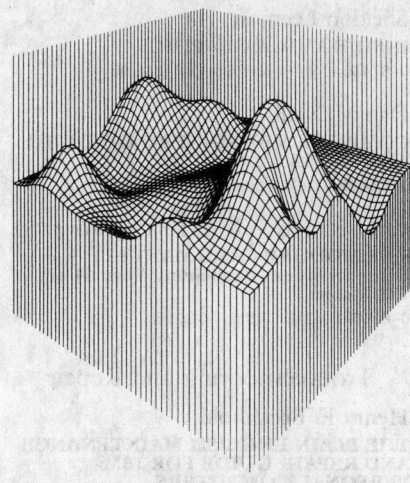

- Patrick Kincaid & Merlin Ouverson
THROUGH THE MICROMAZE: A Visual Guide to Telecommunications
0–13–920539–X Prentice-Hall pb $9.95

- Stephen Manes
THE COMPLETE MCI MAIL HANDBOOK
0–553–34587–7 Bantam pb $22.95

- Clifford A. Schaffer
COMMUNICATING WITH CROSSTALK XVI AND CROSSTALK MK.4
0–8306–9020–4 TAB pb $16.95

- Lisa B. Stahr & the Editors of PC World
COMMUNICATIONS FOR IBM PERSONAL COMPUTERS AND COMPATIBLES
0–671–49280–2 Prentice-Hall pb $16.95

MONEY MANAGEMENT

- John Hannah
USING DOLLARS AND SENSE
0–88022–164–X Que pb $19.95

- Gia L. Rozells & James V. Bartino
MAKING DOLLARS AND CENTS WITH DOLLARS AND SENSE
0–87455–101–3 Compute! pb $19.95

- Mark Weinberg
USING MANAGING YOUR MONEY
0–88022–277–8 Que pb $19.95

OPERATING SYSTEMS

DOS

Originally released in 1981, DOS has become the standard operating system for the IBM PC and compatibles. Put simply, DOS provides an interface between the user and the computer. The operating system manages system resources such as printers, disk drives, modems, and other peripheral devices while allowing the execution of all other programs that run on the PC.

- David D. Busch
PC-DOS 4.0 FOR HARD DISK USERS
0–553–34600–8 Bantam pb $22.95

- Chris DeVoney
MS-DOS USER'S GUIDE
0–88022–349–9 Que pb $22.95

- Kris Jamsa
USING DOS 4
0–07–881470–7 McGraw-Hill pb $22.95

USING MS-DOS
0–07–881442–1 McGraw-Hill pb $22.95

- Alan R. Miller
THE ABC'S OF MS-DOS
0–89588–493–3 Sybex pb $18.95

- Peter Norton
PETER NORTON'S DOS GUIDE
0–13–662073–6 Prentice-Hall pb $19.95

- Herbert Schildt
DOS 4 MADE EASY
0–07–881448–0 McGraw-Hill pb $19.95

- Van Wolverton
RUNNING MS-DOS
1–556–15193–4 Microsoft $39.95
1–556–15186–1 Microsoft pb $22.95

OS/2

OS/2, billed as DOS's successor, is designed to exploit the 32-bit 80386 microprocessor, which will enable users to run large, powerful programs simultaneously. Whether OS/2 will succeed in replacing DOS is still debatable; at present there is little software written for it.

- Ted Crooks
COMPUTE!'S QUICK AND EASY GUIDE TO OS/2
0–87455–137–4 Compute! pb $12.95

- Kris Jamsa
OS/2: The Complete Reference
Volume 1
0–07–881398–0 McGraw-Hill pb $24.95
Volume 2
0–07–881399–9 McGraw-Hill pb $24.95
USING OS/2
0–07–881306–9 McGraw-Hill pb $19.95

- Robert LaFore & Peter Norton
PETER NORTON'S INSIDE OS/2
0–13–467895–8 Prentice-Hall pb $24.95

HARD DISK MANAGEMENT

- Don Berliner
MANAGING YOUR HARD DISK
0–88022–348–0 Que pb $22.95

- Stephen Fisher & Lynn Frantz
HARD DISK MANAGEMENT
0–87455–116–1 Compute! pb $19.95

• Jonathan Kamin
UNDERSTANDING HARD DISK MANAGEMENT
0–89588–561–1 Sybex pb $22.95

• Peter Norton & Robert Jourdain
THE HARD DISK COMPANION
0–13–383761–0 Prentice-Hall pb $21.95

• Thomas Wrona
HOW TO RUN A HARD DISK PC
0–673–38057–2 Scott, Foresman pb $19.95

COMPUTER SYSTEMS AND HARDWARE

• Apple Computer, Inc.
THE APPLE MACINTOSH FAMILY HARDWARE REFERENCE
0–201–19255–1 Addison-Wesley $25.95

• Paul Freiberger & Dan McNeill
THE APPLE IIC: Your First Computer
0–87455–001–7 Compute! pb $9.95

• Cary Lu
THE APPLE MACINTOSH BOOK
1–556–15110–1 Microsoft pb $21.95

• Arthur Naiman, editor
THE MACINTOSH BIBLE
0–940235–01–3 Goldstein & Blair pb $28.00

• Mark D. Veljkov
THE MACINTOSH II REFERENCE GUIDE
0–673–38227–3 Scott, Foresman pb $21.95

• David O. Arnold & the Editors of PC World
GETTING STARTED WITH PCs AND COMPATIBLES
0–671–66285–6 Prentice-Hall pb $19.95

• Joan Lasselle & Carol Ramsey
THE ABC'S OF THE IBM PC
0–89588–370–8 Sybex pb $16.95

• Robert Wolenik
COMPUTE!'S BUYER'S GUIDE TO IBM PCs, COMPATIBLES, AND PORTABLES
0–87455–123–4 Compute! pb $12.95

• Sheldon Leemon
INSIDE AMIGA GRAPHICS
0–87455–040–8 Compute! pb $18.95

• Dan McNeill
COMPUTE!'S BEGINNER'S GUIDE TO THE AMIGA
0–87455–025–4 Compute! pb $16.95

• Chris Morrison & Teresa S. Stover
COMMODORE CARE MANUAL: Diagnosing and Maintaining Your 64 or 128 System
0–8306–3141–0 TAB pb $16.95

Troubleshooting and Repair

• Henry F. Beechhold
THE PLAIN ENGLISH MAINTENANCE AND REPAIR GUIDE FOR IBM PERSONAL COMPUTERS
0–671–52864–5 Prentice-Hall pb $14.95

• Hoyt Hilsman
MICRO DOCTOR: Care, Troubleshooting, and Simple Repair for Your Apple Computer
0–673–39100–0 Scott, Foresman pb $16.95

• Art Margolis
TROUBLESHOOTING AND REPAIRING YOUR COMMODORE 128
0–8306–9099–9 TAB $27.95
0–8306–9399–8 TAB pb $18.95

• Scott Mueller
UPGRADING AND REPAIRING PCS
0–88022–395–2 Que pb $24.95

PROGRAMMING LANGUAGES

A programming language is a set of rules through which instructions are coded for the computer. "Machine language" refers to binary code, the most basic level at which data can be represented in memory. Assembly language is a low-level language which converts the numeric code of machine language into mnemonic code. Ordinarily, users employ more convenient, problem-oriented languages which serve as specialized, shorthand versions of assembly language. The American National Standard Institute (ANSI) insures the consistency of these high-level languages.

• Robert L. Albrecht, LeRoy Finkel & Jerald R. Brown
BASIC FOR HOME COMPUTERS: A Self-Teaching Guide
0–471–03204–2 John Wiley pb $10.95

• Jeff Dunteman
COMPLETE TURBO PASCAL
0–673–38355–5 Scott, Foresman pb $22.95

• Werner Feibel
USING QUICK C
0–07–881487–1 McGraw-Hill pb $21.95

• Kris Jamsa & Steven Nameroff
TURBO PASCAL PROGRAMMER'S LIBRARY VERSION 4
0–07–881368–9 McGraw-Hill pb $22.95

• Peter Norton
PETER NORTON'S ASSEMBLY LANGUAGE PRIMER FOR THE IBM PC, XT AND AT
0–13–661901–0 Brady pb $21.95

• Jack Purdum
C PROGRAMMING GUIDE
0–88022–356–1 Que pb $24.95

• Leo J. Scanlon
ASSEMBLY LANGUAGE SUBROUTINES FOR MS-DOS COMPUTERS
0–8306–0867–2 TAB $27.95
0–8306–2767–7 TAB pb $19.95

• Namir C. Shammas
THE NEW BASICS
0–934375–37–2 M&T pb $24.95
0–934375–43–7 M&T pb (with disk) $39.95

PART 14

PRACTICAL
ADVICE

Courtship, Love, Sex, and Marriage

Most of the quotations in this chapter are taken from the following books:

W.H. Auden & Louis Kronenberger
THE VIKING BOOK OF APHORISMS: A Personal Selection
0–88029–056–0 Dorset $16.95
0–14–005966–0 Penguin pb $8.95

John Gross, editor
THE OXFORD BOOK OF APHORISMS
0–19–214111–2 Oxford $18.95
0–19–282015–X Oxford pb $7.95

FINDING A PARTNER

"Love looks not with the eyes, but with the mind,
And therefore is winged Cupid painted blind."
—William Shakespeare, *A Midsummer Night's Dream*

• Tracy Cabot
MAN POWER: How to Win the Woman You Want
0–312–01787–1 St. Martin's $16.95

• Margaret Kent
HOW TO MARRY THE MAN OF YOUR CHOICE
How to find a man and transform him into a husband
0–446–51387–3 Warner $14.95

• Anne Price & Nancy Dana
HOW TO FIND ROMANCE IN THE PERSONALS
An often humorous and practical guide to advertising in the personal columns
0–88166–103–1 Simon & Schuster pb $4.95

• Judith Sills
HOW TO STOP LOOKING FOR SOMEONE PERFECT AND FIND SOMEONE TO LOVE
Quit looking for the partner your mother would choose, and find someone to please you
0–345–32597–4 Ballantine pb $3.50

• Nita Tucker
BEYOND CINDERELLA
A positive guide to finding and marrying the man you want—no more difficult than looking for a car, a job, or an apartment
0–312–91161–0 St. Martin's pb $3.95

COURTSHIP AND DATING

"Women deprived of the company of men pine, men deprived of the company of women become stupid."—Anton Chekhov

Beth Bailey
FROM FRONT PORCH TO BACK SEAT: Courtship in 20th-Century America
0–8018–3609–3 Johns Hopkins $18.95

• Roger Fisher & Scott Brown
GETTING TOGETHER: Building a Relationship That Gets to Yes
How to deal with the emotional challenges in relationships
0–395–47099–4 Houghton Mifflin $17.95

• Herb Goldberg
THE NEW MALE-FEMALE RELATIONSHIP
The new male-female relationship, based on an unselfconscious, playful, and accepting sexuality
0–451–14840–1 NAL pb $4.95

• Dan Greenburg & Suzanne O'Malley
HOW TO AVOID LOVE AND MARRIAGE: Guaranteed to Ruin Any Deep Romantic Relationship or Your Money Back
0–89471–373–6 Running Press $12.95
0–89471–372–8 Running Press pb $4.95

• Cynthia Heimel
SEX TIPS FOR GIRLS
A New York City humor columnist gives advice on "The Great Boyfriend Crunch," "Lingerie Do's and Don't's," and "How to Cure a Broken Heart"
0–671–47725–0 Simon & Schuster pb $7.95

• Jenny Newman
THE FABER BOOK OF SEDUCTIONS
The most famous seduction scenes in English literature, including passages from Andrew Marvell, Graham Greene, Jane Austen, and Oscar Wilde
0–571–15110–8 Faber & Faber $19.95

LOVE AND ROMANCE

"If intelligence were taken out of my life, it would only be more or less reduced. If I had no one to love, it would be ruined."—Henry de Montherlant

• Joseph Barry
FRENCH LOVERS: From Heloise and Abelard to Beauvoir and Sartre
0–87795–844–0 Arbor House $19.95

• Roland Barthes
A LOVER'S DISCOURSE: Fragments
A series of laments and reflections on the words, gestures, and acts of the many moods of love
Translated by Richard Howard
0–8090–1388–6 Hill & Wang pb $8.95

• Barbara Cartland
BARBARA CARTLAND'S ETIQUETTE FOR LOVE AND ROMANCE
Advice from the queen of romance novels
0–671–50905–5 Books pb $6.95

• Anne De Courcy
THE ENGLISH IN LOVE: Passion Among the Elite
0–88162–267–2 Salem House pb $9.95

• Denis de Rougemont
LOVE IN THE WESTERN WORLD
A famous study of the origins of the concept of romantic love
0–691–06515–2 Princeton $37.00
0–691–01393–4 Princeton pb $11.95

• Erich Fromm
THE ART OF LOVING: An Enquiry into the Nature of Love
Advice on developing the ability to love fearlessly
0–06–011375–8 Harper & Row $14.95
0–06–080291–X Harper & Row pb $4.95

• Willard Gaylin & Ethel Person
PASSIONATE ATTACHMENTS: Thinking About Love
0–02–911430–6 Free Press $22.95

Woodcut of Florentine lovers from Prints and People *by A. Hyatt Mayor (Princeton)*

• Ethel Person
DREAMS OF LOVE AND FATEFUL ENCOUNTERS: The Power of Romantic Passion
"Charts a new topography in which romantic love is seen as a healthy, creative process, an imaginative journey, a powerful agent for change"—Jean Strouse
0–393–02527–6 Norton $18.95

• Jane Seymour
JANE SEYMOUR'S GUIDE TO ROMANTIC LIVING
The English actress offers suggestions for keeping fairy-tale romance in your life
0–689–11786–8 Atheneum $22.95

• Robert Solomon
ABOUT LOVE: Reinventing Romance for Our Times
A study of romantic love, and its possibilities in modern times
0–671–67557–5 Simon & Schuster pb $8.95

John Betjeman & Geoffrey Taylor, editors
ENGLISH LOVE POEMS
Classic poems that "crystallize . . . those thoughts and emotions that love provokes"
0–571–07065–5 Faber & Faber pb $6.95

Geoffrey Grigson, editor
THE FABER BOOK OF LOVE POEMS
Shakespeare, Dickinson, Lawrence and others on love, from early expectations to final renunciation
0–571–13118–2 Faber & Faber pb $7.95

Jon Stallworthy, editor
A BOOK OF LOVE POETRY
A thematically-arranged anthology, from Chaucer to e.e. cummings
0–19–519774–7 Oxford $24.95

RELATIONSHIPS

"Men always want to be a woman's first love, women like to be a man's last romance."—Oscar Wilde

• Steven Carter & Julia Sokol
MEN WHO CAN'T LOVE: When a Man's Fear Makes Him Run from Commitment (and What a Smart Woman Can Do About It)
Commitment Phobia, written for a popular audience with useful advice for female self-protection
0–87131–517–3 Little, Brown $15.95

• Connie Church & Stephen Gullo
LOVESHOCK: How to Survive a Broken Heart and Love Again
0–671–64958–2 Simon & Schuster $17.95

• Connell Cowan & Melvyn Kinder
SMART WOMEN, FOOLISH CHOICES
The complex negative issues surrounding women's choices of a love partner, and the unsatisfying unions that result
0–451–15257–3 NAL pb $4.95

WOMEN MEN LOVE—WOMEN MEN LEAVE: Why Men Are Drawn to Women—What Makes Them Want to Stay
Difficulties men have forming lasting relationships
0–517–56248–0 Crown $18.95
0–451–15306–5 NAL pb $4.95

• Colette Dowling
THE CINDERELLA COMPLEX: Woman's Hidden Fear of Independence
Why women often await a fairy godmother or handsome prince—an external force—to change their lives
0–671–40052–5 Summit $15.95
0–671–64075–5 Pocket pb $4.95

• Susan Forward & Joan Torres
MEN WHO HATE WOMEN AND THE WOMEN WHO LOVE THEM
Men's fear of women, and the propensity of certain women to involve themselves in destructive relationships
0–553–05135–0 Bantam $16.95
0–553–26507–5 Bantam pb $4.50

• Nancy Friday
JEALOUSY
From childhood to adult manifestations, with insight into healthier perspectives
0–688–04321–6 Morrow $19.95
0–553–26165–7 Bantam pb $4.50

• Philip Golabuk
RECOVERING FROM A BROKEN HEART
Comfort and advice for those who have been abandoned by someone they love
0–06–015935–9 Harper & Row $15.95

• Nancy Good
HOW TO LOVE A DIFFICULT MAN
How compromise and sensitivity can help women overcome the problem of loving difficult men
0–312–00134–7 St. Martin's $14.95
0–312–90963–2 St. Martin's pb $3.95

• Barbara Gordon
JENNIFER FEVER: Older Men, Younger Women
0–06–015936–7 Harper & Row $17.95

• Jody Hayes & Maureen Redl
SMART LOVE: Changing Painful Patterns, Choosing Satisfying Relationships
0–87477–472–1 Jeremy Tarcher pb $9.95

• Rosanna Hertz
MORE EQUAL THAN OTHERS: Women and Men in Dual-Career Marriages
0–520–05804–6 California $19.95

"Surely, once the name of jealousy has been applied to an unjust, perverse and unfounded suspicion, that other jealousy which is a just and natural feeling, founded on reason and experience, deserves another name."—La Bruyère

• Victoria Houston
LOVING A YOUNGER MAN: How Women Are Finding and Enjoying a Better Relationship
0–8092–4730–5 Contemporary $17.95

• Dan Kiley
THE PETER PAN SYNDROME: Men Who Have Never Grown Up
A Peter Pan type avoids responsibility and emotional demands. Suggestions for helping him let go
0–396–08218–1 Dodd, Mead $15.95
0–380–68890–5 Avon pb $4.50

THE WENDY DILEMMA: When Women Stop Mothering Their Men
Advice for Wendy personalities—women who want to protect and pamper their men to the point of obsession—to help them achieve emotional independence
0–380–69973–7 Avon pb $3.95

WHAT TO DO WHEN HE WON'T CHANGE: Getting What You Need from the Man You Love
Techniques for couples who fight, such as "loving confrontations" and sharing in the household chores
0–399–13324–0 Putnam $16.95

• Cheryl Merser
GROWN UPS: A Generation in Search of Adulthood
Adults who have trouble growing up and forming productive relations with others
0–399–13233–2 Putnam $17.95
0–452–26165–1 NAL pb $8.95

• Lisa Marsoli & Mel Green
SMART WOMEN, STUPID BOOKS: Stop Reading and Learn to Love Losers
A spoof of the current self-help books
0–8431–4706–7 Price Stern Sloan pb $4.95

• Robin Norwood
WOMEN WHO LOVE TOO MUCH: When You Keep Wishing and Hoping He'll Change
Involvement in a destructive relationship may be a manifestation of unconscious psychological needs
0–87477–355–5 Jeremy Tarcher $14.95
0–671–64541–2 Pocket pb $4.95

• Stanton Peele & Archie Brodsky
LOVE AND ADDICTION
An analysis of the obsession with being in love, often with the wrong person
0–451–14860–6 NAL pb $4.50

• Ayala Pines
KEEPING THE SPARK ALIVE: Preventing Burnout in Love and Marriage
Love burnout affects women more than men. How to handle pressure, prevent boredom, and avoid false expectations in relationships
0–312–01453–8 St. Martin's $17.95

• Karen Shanor
HOW TO STAY TOGETHER WHEN YOU HAVE TO BE APART
How to cope with long-distance relationships, working in different cities, separations
0–446–38418–6 Warner pb $9.95

• Peter Trachtenberg
THE CASANOVA COMPLEX: Compulsive Lovers and Their Women
Written by a recovered Casanova, a hard look at men (Byron, James Bond, and Gary Hart, among others) who live lives of compulsive sexuality
0–671–62048–7 Pocket $17.95

• David Viscott
I LOVE YOU, LET'S WORK IT OUT
Communication technique and advice for coping with jealousy, infidelity, and separation
0–671–62531–4 Simon & Schuster $17.95

• Eric Weber & Steven Simring
HOW TO WIN BACK THE ONE YOU LOVE
Ways of rekindling a romance through communication and sexual enthusiasm, plus advice on coping with affairs and when to go for professional help
0–02–624700–3 Macmillan $11.50
0–553–24350–0 Bantam pb $3.95

• Daniel Wile
AFTER THE HONEYMOON: Turning Conflict into Understanding
Learn how to argue and not flee from discord
0–471–85347–X John Wiley pb $14.95

SEX

● Lonnie Barbach
FOR EACH OTHER: Sharing Sexual Intimacy
A recommended work on female sexuality and desires
0–451–13989–5 NAL pb $4.95

FOR YOURSELF: Fulfillment of Female Sexuality
From anatomy to erotic pleasure and sexual response
0–451–14975–0 NAL pb $3.95

● Whit Barry
MAKING LOVE: A Man's Guide
The author's view of what women really want
0–451–14684–0 NAL pb $3.95

● Alex Comfort
THE JOY OF SEX: A Gourmet Guide to Lovemaking
A relaxed guide to sexual pleasure, both erotic and instructive, updated for the 1980s
0–517–56403–3 Crown $17.95
0–671–64876–4 Pocket pb $14.95

MORE JOY OF SEX: A Lovemaking Companion to The Joy of Sex
Instruction in developing deeper relations through an understanding of the body
0–517–56690–7 Crown $17.95

● Judith Davis
MAKING LOVE: A Woman's Guide
0–451–15539–4 NAL pb $4.50

● John D'Emilio & Estelle Freedman
INTIMATE MATTERS: A History of Sexuality in America
A serious and provocative scholarly study
0–06–015855–7 Harper & Row $24.95

● The Diagram Group
SEX: A User's Manual
A book intended to end fears and dispel myths about sex, written by a group of editors, researchers, and artists with the help of physicians
0–399–51353–1 Putnam pb $10.95
0–425–08972–X Berkley pb $4.95

● Nancy Friday
MEN IN LOVE, MALE SEXUAL FANTASIES: The Triumph of Love over Rage
Men from the ages of 14 to 60 discuss their sexual fantasies. The author's intent is to encourage awareness and acceptance of erotic pleasures
0–440–15903–2 Dell pb $5.50

MY SECRET GARDEN
Female sexual fantasies
0–671–61757–5 Pocket pb $4.95

FORBIDDEN FLOWERS
More female sexual fantasies
0–671–62225–0 Pocket pb $4.50

● Shere Hite
THE HITE REPORT
An exploration of female sexuality, from fantasy to practical experience
0–440–13690–3 Dell pb $5.95

● Linda Levine & Lonnie Barbach
THE INTIMATE MALE: Candid Discussions About Women, Sex, and Relationships
Conversations with over 100 American men on their current relationships, desires, and sexual fantasies
0–451–13662–4 NAL pb $4.95

● William Masters & Virginia Johnson
MASTERS AND JOHNSON ON SEX AND HUMAN LOVING
A survey of current findings on the biological, psychological, and social issues of sexuality. This updated study includes chapters on sexual abuse, contraception, and AIDS
0–316–54998–3 Little, Brown $24.95
0–316–50160–3 Little, Brown pb $12.95

HUMAN SEXUAL INADEQUACY
How to understand each other better and eliminate sexual problems
0–553–26317–X Bantam pb $6.95

● Graham Masterton
HOW TO DRIVE YOUR MAN WILD IN BED
0–451–14331–0 NAL pb $4.95

● Barry McCarthy
MALE SEXUAL AWARENESS: Increasing Sexual Pleasure
Advice for men on such matters as contraception, pregnancy, and homosexuality
0–88184–348–2 Carroll & Graf pb $9.95

● Joseph Nowinski
A LIFELONG LOVE AFFAIR: Keeping Sexual Desire Alive in Your Relationship
Sex can and should improve with time, and result in greater intimacy
0–396–09106–7 Dodd, Mead $17.95

● Alexandra Penney
GREAT SEX
0–399–13031–4 Putnam pb $5.00

HOW TO MAKE LOVE TO EACH OTHER
0–425–09913–X Berkley pb $3.95

HOW TO MAKE LOVE TO A MAN
Practical advice presented in an attractive, nonclinical way
0–440–13529–X Dell pb $3.95

● Alan Rusbridger
A CONCISE HISTORY OF THE SEX MANUAL: 1886–1986
A comic look at marital and sexual advice
Illustrated by Posy Simmonds
0–517–14547–7 Faber & Faber pb $7.95

● Ruth Westheimer
DR. RUTH'S GUIDE TO GOOD SEX
Sexual straight talk from the television personality, which dispels myth and clarifies facts and techniques
0–446–51260–5 Warner $15.00
0–446–34529–6 Warner pb $4.95

● Maurice Yaffe & Elizabeth Fenwick
SEXUAL HAPPINESS: A Practical Approach
A self-help guide for sex therapy
0–8050–0691–5 Henry Holt $24.95

WEDDINGS

"If it were not for the presents, an elopement would be preferable."—George Ade

● Bride's Magazine Editors
BRIDE'S BOOK OF ETIQUETTE: Golden Anniversary Edition
Practical advice from the editors of the bridal magazine: planning events from the engagement to the wedding reception, and organizing the details of wedding cakes and honeymoons
0–399–51496–1 Bantam pb $8.95

● John Loring
THE TIFFANY WEDDING
A compendium of elegant ideas that include suggestions from the finest decorators, dress designers, caterers, and florists, as well as etiquette. Lavish illustrations
0–385–24101–1 Doubleday $50.00

● Elizabeth Post
EMILY POST'S WEDDING PLANNER
0–06–090935–8 Harper & Row pb $4.95

● Christina Probert
BRIDES IN VOGUE SINCE 1910
Wedding fashions as shown in *Vogue* magazine
0–89659–500–5 Abbeville pb $12.95

● Nicole Rubel
GETTING MARRIED: A Guide for the Bride-to-Be
A cartoon spoof on planning weddings
0–312–01766–5 St. Martin's pb $5.95

Martha Stewart & Elizabeth Hawes
WEDDINGS
A beautiful book with color photographs, and suggestions for wedding settings and menus
0–517–55675–8 Crown $50.00

● Erica Wilson
ERICA WILSON'S BRIDE'S BOOK: All the Special Things to Make for Your Engagement, Your Wedding, and Your First Year of Marriage
A romantic selection of handworked items from the needlecraft expert, illustrated with instructions
0–316–94481–5 Little, Brown $24.95

MARRIAGE

"The particular charm of marriage is the duologue, the permanent conversation between two people who talk over everything and everyone till death breaks the record. It is this back-chat which, in the long run, makes a reciprocal equality more intoxicating than any form of servitude or domination."—Cyril Connolly

- Dave Barry
  DAVE BARRY'S GUIDE TO MARRIAGE AND/OR SEX
  Humor on topics like "How to find somebody to go on dates with and eventually marry who is not a total jerk" and "How to argue like a veteran couple"
  0–87857–725–4 Rodale pb $5.95

- Carol Botwin
  IS THERE SEX AFTER MARRIAGE?
  How to keep sex and love alive, and maintain a successful marriage
  0–671–60778–2 Pocket pb $3.95

- Joyce Brothers
  WHAT EVERY WOMAN OUGHT TO KNOW ABOUT LOVE AND MARRIAGE
  Advice from the popular columnist
  0–345–32113–8 Ballantine pb $3.95

- Marilyn Funt
  GROUNDS FOR MARRIAGE: Interviews with 136 Couples Who Are Making Marriage Work—Their Way
  The expectations, fantasies, and problems of marriage; without simplistic solutions
  0–396–09086–9 Dodd, Mead $18.95

- Francine Klagsbrun
  MARRIED PEOPLE: Staying Together in the Age of Divorce
  0–553–05080–X Bantam $16.95

- Susan Kohl & Alice Bregman
  HAVE A LOVE AFFAIR WITH YOUR HUSBAND: Before Someone Else Does
  Keeping excitement alive in marriage
  0–312–00606–3 St. Martin's $13.95

- Marcia Lasswell & Norman Lobsenz
  NO-FAULT MARRIAGE
  Advice for couples dealing with conflict and change in marriage
  0–345–32420–X Ballantine pb $3.50

- Paul Mickey & William Proctor
  TOUGH MARRIAGE: How to Make a Difficult Relationship Work
  A survival guide: twelve steps to a better marriage
  0–553–26861–9 Bantam pb $3.95

- Augustus Napier
  THE FRAGILE BOND: In Search of an Equal, Intimate and Enduring Marriage
  The common crises of modern marriages, based on the author's experience and other case histories
  0–06–015984–7 Harper & Row $18.95

- Dagmar O'Connor
  HOW TO MAKE LOVE TO THE SAME PERSON FOR THE REST OF YOUR LIFE
  The possibility of enjoying emotional commitment and good sex with one person
  0–553–26099–5 Bantam pb $3.95

- Harvey Ruben
  SUPERMARRIAGE: Overcoming the Predictable Crises of Married Life
  The importance of compromise
  0–553–26135–5 Bantam pb $4.50

L'IRREPARABLE

Woodcut by Félix Vallotton

- Maggie Scarf
  INTIMATE PARTNERS: Patterns in Love and Marriage
  A study by the author of *Unfinished Business*
  0–394–55485–X Random House $18.95

- Ruth Westheimer
  DR. RUTH'S GUIDE FOR MARRIED LOVERS
  Adding vitality to romance and sex to keep love alive in marriage
  0–446–34562–8 Warner pb $3.95

> "A married couple are well suited when both partners usually feel the need for a quarrel at the same time."—Jean Rostand

Parents and Children

Today's parents face old dilemmas and new decisions, and an increasing number of works offer them help; these books reflect recent changes in American family life. New technologies can now combat infertility, alternative methods of childbirth have evolved, and the traditional "family unit" has changed irrevocably with the prevalence of divorce, working mothers, and fathers who are more than mere breadwinners.

CONCEPTION

Birth Control

- Rebecca Chalker
  THE COMPLETE CERVICAL CAP GUIDE
  0–06–096113–9 Harper & Row pb $6.95

- Howard Shapiro
  THE NEW BIRTH CONTROL BOOK
  0–13–611781–3 Prentice-Hall $17.95

- Sherman Silber
  HOW NOT TO GET PREGNANT: Your Guide to Simple, Reliable Contraception
  0–684–18519–9 Scribners $15.95

Getting Pregnant

- Robin Blatt
  PRENATAL TESTS: What They Are, Their Benefits and Risks, and How to Decide Whether to Have Them or Not
  0–394–75887–0 Random House pb $9.95

• Alan Guttmacher
PREGNANCY, BIRTH, AND FAMILY PLANNING
Includes a useful chapter on birth control methods
0–525–24420–4 Dutton $18.95
0–452–25827–8 NAL pb $9.95

• Elizabeth Noble
HAVING YOUR BABY BY DONOR INSEMINATION: A Complete Resource Guide
0–395–45395–X Houghton Mifflin pb $12.95

• Sherman Silber
HOW TO GET PREGNANT
A small book with basic information on fertility
0–446–38228 Warner pb $9.95

• Josleen Wilson
THE PRE-PREGNANCY PLANNER
Includes guidelines for diet, exercise, career decisions, genetic counseling, fertility, and child care alternatives for women considering pregnancy
0–385–23174–1 Doubleday pb $9.95

Infertility

• Lori Andrews
NEW CONCEPTIONS: A Consumer's Guide to the Newest Infertility Treatments
The new technologies and their legal aspects
0–312–56610–7 St. Martin's $14.95
0–345–32307–6 Ballantine pb $3.95

• Joan Liebmann-Smith
IN PURSUIT OF PREGNANCY: How Couples Discover, Cope With, and Resolve Their Fertility Problems
The experiences of three couples. "Honest and sensitive"—*Ms.* magazine
1–55704–039–7 Newmarket pb $8.95

• Barbara Menning
INFERTILITY: A Guide for the Childless Couple
A good book on the physical and psychological aspects of infertility; includes new information on surrogate mothers and in vitro fertilization
0–13–464330–5 Prentice-Hall pb $8.95

• Linda Salzer
INFERTILITY: How Couples Can Cope
Psychological advice
0–8161–8782–7 G.K. Hall pb $18.95

• Lynda Stephenson
GIVE US A CHILD: The Personal Crisis of Infertility
0–06–067591–8 Harper & Row $15.95

Surrogate Parenting

• Lori Andrews
BETWEEN STRANGERS: Surrogate Mothers, Expectant Fathers, and Brave New Babies
Examines surrogate parenting—through court cases and the lives of parents
0–06–016058–6 Harper & Row $18.95

• Amy Zuckerman Overvold
SURROGATE PARENTING
Personal, medical, and legal aspects of surrogates
0–886–87328–2 Pharos $16.95

PREGNANCY

• Arlene Eisenberg & others
WHAT TO EXPECT WHEN YOU'RE EXPECTING
Attractively designed month-by-month guide
0–89480–769–2 Workman pb $7.95

• Clark Gillespie
YOUR PREGNANCY MONTH BY MONTH
A valuable monthly guide, from conception to delivery
0–06–181310–9 Harper & Row $14.95

• Tracy Hotchner
PREGNANCY AND CHILDBIRTH: Complete Guide for a New Life
A thorough guide (over 700 pages) to all aspects of pregnancy and childbirth
0–380–43083–5 Avon pb $10.95

• Sheila Kitzinger
COMPLETE BOOK OF PREGNANCY AND CHILDBIRTH
A complete, modern book
0–19–261472–X Knopf $17.95

• Nicola McClure & Jovanka Bach
THE RODALE BOOK OF PREGNANCY AND BIRTH
0–87857–590–1 Rodale $14.95

• Jonathan Scher & Carole Dix
EVERYTHING YOU NEED TO KNOW ABOUT PREGNANCY IN THE 1980s
Answers questions about amniocentesis and other aspects of modern pregnancy and childbirth
0–385–27692–3 Doubleday pb $12.95

• Miriam Stoppard
DR. MIRIAM STOPPARD'S PREGNANCY AND BIRTH BOOK
By a well-known British doctor
0–345–31908–7 Ballantine pb $7.95

• Donald Tapley & others, editors
THE COLUMBIA UNIVERSITY COLLEGE OF PHYSICIANS AND SURGEONS COMPLETE HOME MEDICAL GUIDE TO PREGNANCY
A complete medical guide on every aspect of pregnancy
0–517–57030–0 Crown $24.95

Diet and Exercise During Pregnancy

• Gail & Tom Brewer
WHAT EVERY PREGNANT WOMAN SHOULD KNOW: The Truth About Diets and Drugs in Pregnancy
"May well be the most important book of our generation for the health of all mothers and children in this country"—Dr. Robert Mendelson
0–14–007974–2 Penguin pb $6.95

• Femmy Delyser
JANE FONDA'S WORKOUT BOOK FOR PREGNANCY, BIRTH, AND RECOVERY
Easy-to-follow, well-illustrated exercise routine
0–671–63658–8 Simon & Schuster pb $10.95

• Arlene Eisenberg & others
WHAT TO EAT WHEN YOU'RE EXPECTING
Includes recipes, diet guidelines, and information about how diet affects side effects of pregnancy, such as morning sickness and mood swings
0–89480–0159 Workman pb $7.95

• Christine Kelley-Buchanan
PEACE OF MIND DURING PREGNANCY: An A-to-Z Guide to the Substances That Could Affect Your Unborn Baby
Alphabetical listing of more than 350 known or suspected teratogens, substances that can cause fetal malformations
0–8160–1907–X Facts On File $24.95

• Elizabeth Noble
ESSENTIAL EXERCISES FOR THE CHILDBEARING YEARS: A Guide to Health and Comfort Before and After Your Baby Is Born
0–395–47781–6 Houghton Mifflin $19.95
0–395–47780–8 Houghton Mifflin pb $9.95

• Carol Rinzler
THE SAFE PREGNANCY BOOK
0–451–14888–6 NAL pb $4.50

• Cecilia Worth
HEALTH AND BEAUTY DURING PREGNANCY
0–07–071820–2 McGraw-Hill $14.95
0–07–071823–7 McGraw-Hill pb $7.95

CHILDBIRTH

• Diana Bert & others
HAVING A BABY
The personal accounts of seven friends
0–440–53491–7 Dell pb $9.95

• Sally Inch
BIRTHRIGHTS: What Every Parent Should Know About Childbirth in Hospitals
A guide to choice of birth procedures
0–394–53685–1 Pantheon $17.95
0–394–72568–9 Pantheon pb $8.95

• Fritzi Kallop & Julie Houston
FRITZI KALLOP'S BIRTH BOOK
The physical and emotional concerns of childbirth. "An excellent, comprehensive book, written by a true expert"—Dr. Lee Salk
0–394–75345–3 Random House $12.95

• Sheila Kitzinger
GIVING BIRTH: How It Really Feels
From a childbirth educator and mother of five who believes that giving birth "is not a performance to be enacted, or an examination that must be passed, but a profound and all enveloping experience"
0–374–16304–9 Noonday $17.95
0–374–52111–5 Noonday pb $6.95

■ TO ORDER BOOKS AS GIFTS, SEE PAGE 1

• Judith Walzer Leavitt
BROUGHT TO BED: Childbearing in America, 1750–1950
A history based on personal accounts by birthing women and their attendants
0–19–505690–6 Oxford pb $9.95

• Adrienne Lieberman
GIVING BIRTH
0–312–01032–X St. Martin's pb $12.95

Alfred Kolatch
THE DICTIONARY OF FIRST NAMES
A comprehensive list
0–399–50570–9 Putnam pb $9.95

TODAY'S BEST BABY NAMES
Two thousand favorite and contemporary names
0–399–51271–3 Putnam pb $6.95

Linda Rosenkrantz & Pamela Redmond Satran
BEYOND JENNIFER AND JASON: An Enlightened Guide to Naming Your Baby
0–312–01908–4 St. Martin's pb $8.95

Caesarean and Premature Births

• Bonnie Donovan
THE CAESAREAN BIRTH EXPERIENCE
Includes the possible prevention of Caesareans
0–8070–2701–4 Beacon pb $9.95

• Patricia Robertson & Peggy Berlin
PREMATURE LABOR HANDBOOK: Successfully Sustaining Your High-Risk Pregnancy
0–385–19923–6 Doubleday $16.95
0–385–19924–4 Doubleday pb $9.95

• Helen Harrison & Ann Kositsky
THE PREMATURE BABY BOOK: A Parents' Guide to Coping and Caring in the First Years
0–312–63648–2 St. Martin's $25.95
0–312–63649–0 St. Martin's pb $15.95

• W.H. Kitchen & others
PREMATURE BABIES: A Guide for Parents
0–87857–557–X Rodale pb $6.95

• Sherri Nance
PREMATURE BABIES: A Handbook for Parents by Parents
0–425–07256–8 Berkley pb $3.50

Home, Lamaze, and Other Birth Methods

• Janet Balaskas
ACTIVE BIRTH
Birth standing up, the active approach
Introduction by Sheila Kitzinger
0–07–003545–8 McGraw-Hill pb $6.95

• Nancy Berezin
THE GENTLE BIRTH BOOK: A Practical Guide to LeBoyer Family-Centered Delivery
Nonviolent birth via a family-centered approach
0–671–49703–0 Pocket pb $3.95

• Marjorie Karmel
THANK YOU, DR. LAMAZE
From a Lamaze mother and instructor; includes a revised guide for the 1980s
0–06–090996–X Harper & Row pb $5.95

• Sheila Kitzinger
BIRTH AT HOME
Strong support and information for home birth
0–14–005866–4 Penguin pb $5.95

• Beverly Savage & Diana Simkin
PREPARATION FOR BIRTH: The Complete Guide to the Lamaze Method
A clear guide for natural childbirth
0–345–31230–9 Ballantine pb $10.95

Pregnancy After 30

• Gail Sforza Brewer
THE PREGNANCY AFTER 30 WORKBOOK
How to maximize health at every stage
0–87857–215–5 Rodale pb $11.95

• Elizabeth Fuller
HAVING YOUR FIRST BABY AFTER THIRTY: A Personal Journey from Infertility to Childbirth
0–396–08154–1 Dodd, Mead pb $10.95

• Clark Gillespie
PRIMELIFE PREGNANCY: All You Need to Know About Pregnancy After 35
Written by an obstetrician who specializes in high-risk pregnancies
0–06–096207–0 Harper & Row pb $10.95

• Joan Lisante
WE DELIVER
From personal experience, an informative account for mothers having their first babies after 30
1–55611–079–0 Donald Fine pb $7.95

• Monica Morris
LAST CHANCE CHILDREN: Growing Up with Older Parents
How the children of older parents fare as adults
0–231–06694–5 Columbia $19.95

Miscarriage

• Susan Borg & Judith Lasker
WHEN PREGNANCY FAILS: Families Coping with Miscarriage, Ectopic Pregnancy, Stillbirth, and Infant Death
"A dynamic example of women caring for themselves, their kin, and others. A woman in crisis could turn to this book and be greatly helped"—Boston Women's Health Book Collective
0–553–34594–X Bantam pb $8.95

• Rochelle Friedman & Bonnie Gradstein
SURVIVING PREGNANCY LOSS
0–316–29349–0 Little, Brown pb $10.95

• G.C. Lachelin
MISCARRIAGE: The Facts
0–19–261472–X Oxford $16.50

• Claudia Panuthos & Catherine Romero
ENDED BEGINNINGS: Healing Childbearing Losses
A guide to emotional healing
0–446–32956–8 Warner pb $4.95

• Hank Pizer & Christine Palinski
COPING WITH A MISCARRIAGE
0–451–14121–0 NAL pb $3.95

Postnatal Care

• Katharina Dalton
DEPRESSION AFTER CHILDBIRTH: How to Recognize and Treat Postnatal Illness
0–19–286008–9 Oxford pb $8.95

• Marvin Eiger & Sally Olds
THE COMPLETE BOOK OF BREASTFEEDING
A clear, practical guide
0–553–26232–7 Bantam pb $4.50

• Janet Spencer King
TAKING THE BLUES OUT OF POSTPARTUM
0–394–75556–1 Random House pb $9.95

• Diane Lynch-Fraser
THE COMPLETE POSTPARTUM GUIDE: Everything You Know You Need to Know to Take Care of Yourself After You've Had a Baby
0–345–32355–6 Ballantine pb $6.95

• Paula Siegel
THE NEW MOTHER'S BODY: A Complete Postpartum Guide to the First Year
Lets new mothers know what to expect and how to hasten postpartum recovery
0–553–26899–6 Bantam pb $4.50

Adoption

Edmund Bolles
THE PENGUIN ADOPTION HANDBOOK: A Guide to Creating Your New Family
0–14–046548–0 Penguin pb $9.95

Charlene Canape
ADOPTION: Parenthood Without Pregnancy
0–03–001594–4 Henry Holt $18.95

Jan De Hartog
ADOPTED CHILDREN
An informal personal account
0–915361–65–5 Franklin Watts pb $13.95

Lois Gilman
THE ADOPTION RESOURCE BOOK: All the Things You Need To Need to Know and Ought to Know about Creating an Adoptive Family
Finding support and resources
0–06–055097–X Harper & Row $18.95

Lois Melina
RAISING ADOPTED CHILDREN: A Manual for Adoptive Parents
0–06–096039–6 Harper & Row pb $8.95

CHILD CARE

• **Louise Bates Ames**
THE GESELL INSTITUTE'S CHILD FROM ONE TO SIX: Evaluating the Behavior of the Pre-School Child
0–06–010087–7 Harper & Row $18.95

• **Barry Behrstock & Richard Trubo**
THE PARENTS' WHEN-NOT-TO-WORRY BOOK: Straight Talk About All Those Myths You've Learned from Your Parents, Friends, and Even Doctors
0–690–01972–6 Harper & Row $13.95

• **Selma Fraiberg**
THE MAGIC YEARS: Understanding and Handling the Problems of Early Childhood
An early psychoanalytic classic
0–684–71768–9 Scribners pb $8.95

• **Stanley & Nancy Greenspan**
FIRST FEELINGS: Milestones in the Emotional Development of Your Baby and Child from Birth to Age Four
Overview of early emotional development, by child psychiatrists
0–14–007723–5 Penguin pb $3.95

• **Grace Hechinger**
HOW TO RAISE A STREET-SMART CHILD: The Complete Parents' Guide to Safety on the Street and at Home
Interviews with school officials, police, and children
0–449–20841–9 Fawcett pb $3.95

• **Penelope Leach**
THE CHILD CARE ENCYCLOPEDIA: A Parents' Guide to the Physical and Emotional Well-Being of Children from Birth Through Adolescence
A clear, constructive book, with practical advice on how children feel physically and emotionally
0–394–52532–9 Knopf $24.95

YOUR GROWING CHILD: From Babyhood to Adolescence
0–394–71066–5 Knopf $14.95

• **Kevin Leman**
THE BIRTH ORDER BOOK
How birth order affects children's behavior
0–440–10559–5 Dell pb $3.95

• **Lottie Pogrebin**
GROWING UP FREE: Raising Your Kids in the '80s
How to raise children free of sex-stereotyping
0–07–050370–2 McGraw-Hill $15.95

"The Little Girls" by Félix Vallotton

• **Mark Rubinstein & others**
THE GROWING YEARS: The New York Hospital/Cornell Medical Center Guide to Children's Emotional Development from Birth to Adolescence
"The best guide available for that most difficult and rewarding job: parenting . . . it should be the number one home reference for new and veteran parents alike"—Dr. Howard Walsh
0–689–11914–3 Atheneum $22.95
0–671–67726–8 Simon & Schuster pb $12.95

• **Benjamin Spock & Michael Rothenberg**
DR. SPOCK'S BABY AND CHILD CARE
The classic, still indispensable book
0–671–55187–6 Pocket pb $4.95

RAISING CHILDREN IN A DIFFERENT TIME
How to raise children today, with changing family and social values
0–671–60156–3 Pocket pb $3.95

Child Sexuality

Ronald & Juliette Goldman
SHOW ME YOURS: Understanding Children's Sexuality
A delightful book, which examines what children know and don't know about sexuality, gender, and reproduction
0–14–010714–2 Penguin pb $7.95

Lynn Leight
THE PARENT'S GUIDE TO RAISING SEXUALLY HEALTHY CHILDREN
A sex educator covers touchy topics
0–89256–331–1 Rawson $17.95

Mary Calderone & James Ramey
TALKING WITH YOUR CHILD ABOUT SEX: Questions and Answers for Children from Birth to Puberty
0–345–31379–8 Ballantine pb $2.95

Pediatric Guides

• **Ralph Berberich & Ann Parker**
THE AVAILABLE PEDIATRICIAN: Every Parent's Guide to Common Childhood Illnesses
0–394–56298–4 Pantheon $16.95
0–394–75509–X Pantheon pb $8.95

• **Tso & Howry Bindler**
THE PARENT'S GUIDE TO PEDIATRIC DRUGS
Presciption and over-the-counter drugs
0–06–181097–5 Harper & Row $20.00
0–06–096073–6 Harper & Row pb $9.95

• **Martin Green**
A SIGH OF RELIEF: First-Aid Handbook for Childhood Emergencies
Simple, clear instructions for common childhood injuries and illnesses
0–553–34364–5 Bantam pb $14.95

• **Barton Schmitt**
YOUR CHILD'S HEALTH: A Pediatric Guide for Parents
"This terrific reference sets a new standard for child care books"—Dr. Daniel Broughton
0–353–34400–5 Bantam pb $12.95

• **Gil Simon & Marcia Cohen**
PARENTS' PEDIATRIC COMPANION
"If you have any tendency to worry about physical conditions in your baby or child, this is the encyclopedia to have"—Dr. Benjamin Spock
0–688–07524–X Morrow pb $7.95

Special Children

▶ **See also People with Disabilities**

• **Cliff Cunningham & Patricia Sloper**
HELPING YOUR EXCEPTIONAL BABY: Practical and Honest Approach to Raising a Mentally Handicapped Baby
0–394–73867–5 Pantheon pb $6.95

• **Irving Dickman & Sol Gordon**
ONE MIRACLE AT A TIME: How to Get Help for Your Disabled Child from the Experience of Other Parents
0–671–50292–1 Simon & Schuster $16.95

UNDERSTANDING YOUR DISABLED CHILD
0–671–63458–5 Simon & Schuster pb $8.95

• **Helen Featherstone**
A DIFFERENCE IN THE FAMILY: Living with a Disabled Child
Help for the family with a handicapped child
0–14–005941–5 Penguin pb $6.95

• Monica Jones
HOME CARE FOR THE CHRONICALLY ILL OR DISABLED CHILD
A clear, comprehensive manual for parents
0–06–181433–4 Harper & Row $25.00

• Margaret Mantle
SOME JUST CLAP THEIR HANDS: Raising a Handicapped Child
Personal accounts and interviews
0–915361–74–4 Watts $12.95

• Eunice McClurg
YOUR DOWN'S SYNDROME CHILD: Everything Today's Parents Need to Know about Raising Their Special Child
A well-organized book for home care
0–385–23023–0 Doubleday $15.95

• Diana Millard
DAILY LIVING WITH A HANDICAPPED CHILD
Various solutions to practical daily problems
0–7099–1701–5 Methuen pb $19.95

STAGES OF DEVELOPMENT

Infancy

• Louise Bates Ames & others
YOUR ONE-YEAR-OLD: The Fun-Loving, Fussy 12- to 24-Month-Old
0–385–29186–8 Delacorte $11.95
0–385–29206–6 Dell pb $7.95

YOUR TWO YEAR OLD: Terrible or Tender
0–385–29141–8 Dell pb $7.95

• Athina Aston
HOW TO PLAY WITH YOUR BABY
Light-hearted play for babies; suggestions for toys
0–914788–73–6 Globe Pequot pb $7.95

• T. Berry Brazelton
WHAT EVERY BABY KNOWS
Based on the successful television series of Dr. Brazelton, called "the pediatric guru of the '80s"
0–201–09262–X Addison-Wesley $14.95

INFANTS AND MOTHERS: Differences in Development
0–385–29209–0 Doubleday pb $13.95

TODDLERS AND PARENTS: A Declaration of Independence
0–385–29034–9 Doubleday pb $12.95

• Frank Caplan, editor
THE FIRST TWELVE MONTHS OF LIFE
0–553–24233–4 Bantam pb $4.95

THE SECOND TWELVE MONTHS OF LIFE
Month-by-month courses in baby development
0–553–26438–9 Bantam pb $5.95

Penelope Leach
BABYHOOD
How a baby thinks, feels, learns, and expresses needs
0–394–53092–6 Knopf $17.95
0–394–71436–9 Knopf pb $10.95

YOUR BABY AND CHILD: From Birth to Age Five
"Well researched, well written and sensitive to both parents and children's needs in the task of growing up together"—T. Bérry Brazelton
0–384–40755–6 Knopf $19.95
0–384–73509–9 Knopf pb $14.95

• Genevieve Painter
TEACH YOUR BABY
A guide to playing with infants
0–346–12558–8 Cornerstone pb $7.95

• William Sears
THE FUSSY BABY
Care for the difficult, demanding baby
0–452–26002–7 NAL pb $7.95

• Marilyn Segal & Don Adcock
YOUR CHILD AT PLAY: One to Two Years
An informal, anecdotal book: on sleeping, eating, and playing
0–937858–52–8 Newmarket $16.95
0–937858–53–6 Newmarket pb $9.95

• Evelyn Shukat & Angela Haines
WHY IS MY BABY CRYING?: A Practical Guide to What Bothers Babies and Worries Parents During the First Six Months of Life
0–394–74642–2 Random House pb $6.95

• D.W. Winnicott
BABIES AND THEIR MOTHERS
"Winnicott is a major influence on all who have tried to bring emotional and behavioral issues into pediatrics"—T. Berry Brazelton
Introduction by Dr. Benjamin Spock
0–201–07677–2 Addison-Wesley pb $8.95

Childhood

• Louise Bates Ames & Francis Ilg
YOUR THREE YEAR OLD: Friend or Enemy
0–385–29142–6 Dell pb $7.95

YOUR FOUR YEAR OLD: Wild and Wonderful
0–385–29143–4 Dell pb $7.95

• Louise Bates Ames
YOUR FIVE YEAR OLD: Sunny and Serene
0–385–29145–0 Dell pb $7.95

YOUR SIX YEAR OLD
0–385–29146–9 Dell pb $7.95

• Louise Bates Ames & Carol Haber
YOUR SEVEN YEAR OLD: Life in a Minor Key
0–385–29465–4 Dell pb $7.95

HE HIT ME FIRST: When Brothers and Sisters Fight
Readable combination of research and children's accounts; what to expect at different ages and with different combinations of ages
0–934878–34–X Dembner pb $8.95

• Adele Faber & Elaine Mazlish
SIBLINGS WITHOUT RIVALRY: How to Help Your Children Live Together So You Can Live Too
How to prevent jealousy and conflicts. "A very human book about one of the toughest problems parents have to handle"—Dr. Benjamin Spock
0–393–02441–5 Norton $14.95

• Richard Ferber
SOLVE YOUR CHILD'S SLEEP PROBLEMS
0–671–46027–7 Simon & Schuster $16.95
0–671–62099–1 Simon & Schuster pb $7.95

• Ellen Galinsky & Judy David
THE PRESCHOOL YEARS
0–8129–1216–0 Times Books $19.95

• Arnold Gesell & others
THE CHILD FROM FIVE TO TEN
The growth process: behavior at each age
0–06–011501–7 Harper & Row $23.95

• Alice Honig
PLAYTIME LEARNING GAMES FOR YOUNG CHILDREN
A guide to playing with children
0–8156–0178–6 Syracuse pb $9.95

• Allyssa McCabe
LANGUAGE GAMES TO PLAY WITH YOUR CHILD
Enjoyable and instructive games for children of all ages
0–449–90270–6 Fawcett pb $6.95

• Grace Mitchell
A VERY PRACTICAL GUIDE TO DISCIPLINE WITH YOUNG CHILDREN
A friendly book written by an educator, which takes into consideration the child's point of view and limitations
0–910287–00–7 Telshare pb $9.95

• Marilyn Segal & Don Adcock
YOUR CHILD AT PLAY: Two to Three Years
0–937858–54–4 Newmarket $16.95
0–937858–55–2 Newmarket pb $9.95

YOUR CHILD AT PLAY: Three to Five Years
0–937858–72–2 Newmarket $15.95
0–937858–73–0 Newmarket pb $9.95

• Muriel Silberstein-Storfer & Mablen Jones
DOING ART TOGETHER: The Remarkable Parent-Child
From a workshop of the Metropolitan Museum of Art. Clear instructions for art projects
0–671–43428–4 Simon & Schuster pb $13.95

Adolescence

• Ruth Bell & Leni Wildflower
TALKING WITH YOUR TEENAGER: A Book for Parents
0–394–71605–1 Random House pb $8.95

• Marlene Brusko
LIVING WITH YOUR TEENAGER
0–8041–0135–3 Ballantine pb $3.50

• David Elkind
ALL GROWN UP AND NO PLACE TO GO: Teenagers in Crisis
Social pressures on teens and parents who expect too much
0–201–11379–1 Addison-Wesley pb $8.95

• Sol Gordon
THE TEENAGE SURVIVAL BOOK
0–8129–0972–0 Times Books pb $12.95

• Martin Herbert
LIVING WITH TEENAGERS
By a clinical psychologist
0–631–15298–9 Blackwell pb $15.95

• Kathleen McCoy
COPING WITH TEENAGE DEPRESSION: A Parent's Guide
Support for parents and teens
0–453–00415–6 NAL $14.95
0–452–25791–3 NAL pb $8.95

• Douglas Powell
TEENAGERS: When to Worry and What to Do
0–385–19341–6 Doubleday pb $8.95

Teenage Health

• Ruth Bell
CHANGING BODIES, CHANGING LIVES
Teenage health problems
0–394–56499–5 Random House pb $12.95

• Joanne Ikeda
WINNING WEIGHT LOSS FOR TEENS
0–915950–84–7 Bull pb 7.95

• Irwin Lubowe & Barbara Huss
A TEEN-AGE GUIDE TO HEALTHY SKIN AND HAIR
0–525–21458–5 Dutton $7.95

• Nelson Novick
SKIN CARE FOR TEENS
0–531–10521–0 Franklin Watts $11.95

Teenage Pregnancy

• Leon Dash
WHEN CHILDREN WANT CHILDREN: The Urban Crisis of Teenage Childbearing
The problem of teenage pregnancy in a poor neighborhood of Washington
0–688–06907–6 Morrow $19.95

• Donna & Roger Ewy
TEEN PREGNANCY: The Challenges We Faced, the Choices We Made
0–451–13915–1 NAL pb $3.95

• Sheila Kitzinger
YOUR BABY, YOUR WAY: Making Pregnancy Decisions
A book for teenagers
0–394–54573–7 Pantheon $19.95

BEING A PARENT

• Polly Berends
WHOLE CHILD—WHOLE PARENT
The psychology of parenthood, with practical tips
0–06–091427–0 Harper & Row pb $10.95

• Bruno Bettelheim
A GOOD ENOUGH PARENT: A Book on Child Rearing
A guide to becoming a good enough—not a perfect—parent. "Bound to provide every reader with some nuggets of good sense and wisdom and young parents in particular with a challenge and an inspiration"—*Washington Post*
0–394–47148–2 Knopf $18.95

• Boston Women's Health Book Collective
OURSELVES AND OUR CHILDREN: A Book by and for Parents
A book on the different stages of parenthood, from the editors of *Our Bodies, Ourselves*
0–394–73304–5 Random House $15.95

• Diane Ehrensaft
PARENTING TOGETHER: Men and Women Sharing the Care of Their Children
0–02–909440–2 Free Press $19.95

• Ellen Galinsky
THE SIX STAGES OF PARENTHOOD
How parents grow: interviews and theories
0–201–10529–2 Addison-Wesley $10.95

• Murray Kappelman
RAISING THE ONLY CHILD
0–525–18810–X Dutton pb $7.95

• Jean Liedloff
THE CONTINUUM CONCEPT
Spiritual and philosophical approaches to the daily task of being parents
0–201–05071–4 Addison-Wesley pb $8.95

Mothers

• Bruno Bettelheim
DIALOGUES WITH MOTHERS
0–380–01138–7 Avon pb $2.50

• Frances Burck
MOTHERS TALKING: Sharing the Secret
0–312–01069–9 St. Martin's pb $7.95

• Cherie Burns
STEPMOTHERHOOD: How to Survive Without Feeling Frustrated, Left Out, or Wicked
For stepmothers and single parents
0–8129–1145–8 Times Books $14.95

• Lyn DelliQuadri & Kati Breckenridge
THE NEW MOTHER CARE: Helping Yourself Through the Emotional and Physical Transitions of Motherhood
How the modern mother can take care of herself and everyone else
0–87477–315–6 Jeremy Tarcher pb $6.95

• Roseann Hirsch
SUPER WORKING MOM'S HANDBOOK
Helpful lists and tips
0–446–38073–3 Warner pb $8.95

• Joyce Maynard
DOMESTIC AFFAIRS: Enduring the Pleasures of Motherhood and Family Life
Funny and touching glimpses of family life
0–07–041092–5 McGraw Hill pb $7.95

• Pearl Ketover Prikik
STEP MOTHERING: Another Kind of Love
A sensible guide on what women who inherit step children can expect
0–936614–06–4 Forman $17.95

• Sirgay Sanger & John Kelly
THE WOMAN WHO WORKS, THE PARENT WHO CARES: A Revolutionary Program for Raising Your Child
"Addresses the critical issues that all working women who are concerned with family life must face—and it does so in the most innovative and reassuring program I have yet read"—Nancy Friday
0–316–77049–3 Little, Brown $17.95

Mothers and Daughters
Evelyn Bassoff
MOTHERS AND DAUGHTERS
From the mother's perspective; by a psychiatrist
0–453–00624–8 NAL $17.95

Lucy Rose Fischer
LINKED LIVES: Adult Daughters and Their Mothers
How relationships change as mothers and daughters age
0–06–091412–2 Harper & Row pb $7.95

Nancy Friday
MY MOTHER, MY SELF
Adult women's relationships with their mothers
0–385–29570–7 Delacorte $19.95
0–440–15664–5 Dell pb $4.95

Fathers

• Sam Bittman & Sue Zalk
EXPECTANT FATHERS
Preparing for the birth of a child
0–345–31763–7 Ballantine pb $7.95

• Bill Cosby
FATHERHOOD
The comedian's best-selling thoughts on family life
0–385–23410–4 Doubleday $14.95

• Bob Greene
GOOD MORNING, MERRY SUNSHINE: A Father's Personal Journey of His Child's First Year
Diary of a father's time with his new baby
0–689–11434–6 Atheneum $14.95
0–14–007948–3 Penguin pb $6.95

• Debra Klinman & Rhiana Kohl
FATHERHOOD U.S.A.: The First National Guide to Programs, Services, and Resources for and About Fathers
0–8240–9012–8 Garland pb $14.95

• George Newman
ONE HUNDRED AND ONE WAYS TO BE A LONG-DISTANCE SUPER-DAD
0–939894–00–9 Blossom Valley pb $6.95

• Thomas Oakland & Edwin Terry
DIVORCED FATHERS: Reconstructing a Quality Life
The personal adjustment of the father: his relationship with his children, the legal and financial aspects of divorce
0–89885–101–7 Human Sciences $24.95

• Kyle Pruett
THE NURTURING FATHER
Interviews with fathers who took care of their children
0–446–51269–9 Warner $18.95

• Mark Rosin
STEPFATHERING: Stepfathers' Advice on Creating a New Family
Guidelines from 50 stepfathers
0–671–54697–X Simon & Schuster $18.95

• S. Adams Sullivan
THE FATHERS' ALMANAC
An informal guide to the care of children
0–385–13626–9 Doubleday pb $14.95

Nontraditional Families

Contemporary variations on the traditional family include two-career couples, single parents, shared custody, stepfamilies, and living with a handicapped child.

• Stephen Atlas
PARENTS WITHOUT PARTNERS SOURCEBOOK
Practical solutions for single parents
0–89471–270–5 Running Press $19.95
0–89471–269–1 Running Press pb $8.95

• T. Berry Brazelton
WORKING AND CARING
Interviews, with commentary, on three working families with children
0–201–10629–9 Addison-Wesley pb $8.95

• Josephine Curto
HOW TO BECOME A SINGLE PARENT: A Guide for Single People Considering Adoption or Natural Parenthood Alone
0–13–396184–2 Prentice-Hall pb $6.95

• Fitzhugh Dodson
HOW TO SINGLE PARENT
Coping with the pressures of being a parent alone, from a well-known child psychologist
0–06–015492–6 Harper & Row $15.95

• Richard Gardner
THE PARENTS' BOOK ABOUT DIVORCE
0–553–26600–4 Bantam pb $4.95

• Claudia Jewett
HELPING CHILDREN COPE WITH SEPARATION AND LOSS
A mix of theory, examples, and advice
0–916782–27–1 Harvard Common $14.95
0–916782–53–0 Harvard Common pb $8.95

• Gayle Kimballe
FIFTY-FIFTY PARENTING: Sharing Family Rewards and Responsibilities
Includes chapters on stepfamilies and working parents
0–669–14866–0 Lexington $17.95

• Thomas Long & others
THE HANDBOOK FOR LATCHKEY CHILDREN AND THEIR PARENTS
0–425–07263–0 Berkley pb $3.95

• Kathleen McCoy
SOLO PARENTING: Your Essential Guide
0–452–25900–2 NAL $8.95
0–451–15137–0 NAL pb $4.50

• Erna Paris
STEPFAMILIES: Making Them Work
0–380–89670–2 Avon pb $2.95

• Doreen Virtue
MY KIDS DON'T LIVE WITH ME ANYMORE: Coping with the Custody Crisis
A guide for divorced parents
0–89638–157–9 CompCare pb $9.95

• Nancy Balaban
LEARNING TO SAY GOODBYE: Starting School and Other Childhood Separations
0–452–26003–5 NAL pb $7.95

• Bruno Bettelheim
THE USES OF ENCHANTMENT: The Meaning and Importance of Fairy Tales
The eminent child psychologist on how fairy tales educate, support, and liberate the emotions of children
0–394–49771–6 Random House $21.95

• Bruno Bettelheim & Karen Zelan
ON LEARNING TO READ: The Child's Fascination with Meaning
0–394–51592–7 Knopf $13.95

• Ann Boehm & Mary White
THE PARENTS' HANDBOOK ON SCHOOL TESTING
Preparing for aptitude and other tests
0–8077–2660–5 Columbia $14.95

• Martha Brown
SCHOOLWISE: A Parent's Guide to Getting the Best Education for Your Child
0–874–77364–4 Jeremy Tarcher pb $9.95

• Robert Coles
THE CALL OF STORIES: Teaching and the Moral Imagination
Harvard's well-known child psychiatrist shows how stories tell as much about life as they do about literature and can teach what teachers cannot
0–395–42935–8 Houghton Mifflin $17.95

• Thomas Gordon
TEACHING CHILDREN SELF-DISCIPLINE AT HOME AND AT SCHOOL
0–8129–1780–4 Times Books $17.95

• Sidney Ledson
RAISING BRIGHTER CHILDREN
0–8027–0924–9 Walker $17.95
0–8027–7299–4 Walker pb $9.95

• Joanne Miller & Susan Weissman
THE PARENTS' GUIDE TO DAY CARE
The selection of day care; for working parents
0–553–34295–9 Bantam pb $8.95

• Tom & Harriet Sobol
YOUR CHILD IN SCHOOL: Kindergarten Through Second Grade
A guide for parents on what to expect from school, how young children learn, the role of the teacher
0–688–08247–5 Arbor House pb $8.95

YOUR CHILD IN SCHOOL: Grades Three Through Five
0–87795–924–2 Arbor House $18.95

Gifted Children

• James Delisle
GIFTED CHILDREN SPEAK OUT
Accounts from gifted children, with discussion guides for parents
0–8027–0752–1 Walker $14.95

• James Delisle & Judy Galbraith
THE GIFTED KIDS SURVIVAL GUIDE II
For parents and teachers of gifted children, aged 11 to 18; educational and social issues
0-915793-09-1 Free Spirit pb $9.95

• David Elkind
MISEDUCATION: Preschoolers at Risk
Separating superkids from others in preschool
0-394-55256-3 Knopf $16.95
0-394-75634-7 Knopf pb $8.95

• Bill & Lori Granger
THE MAGIC FEATHER: The Truth About Special Education
Parents fight the mislabeling of their son as "gifted"
0-525-24451-4 Dutton $16.95

• Carol Takacs
ENJOY YOUR GIFTED CHILD
A readable book by an educational psychologist
0-8156-2357-7 Syracuse pb $12.95

Children with Learning Disabilities

• Sylvia Farnham-Diggory
LEARNING DISABILITIES: A Psychological Perspective
New advances in cognitive psychology
0-674-51922-1 Harvard pb $3.95

• Lawrence Greene
KIDS WHO UNDERACHIEVE: Strategies for Understanding and Parenting the Academically Troubled Child
0-671-55235-X Simon & Schuster $16.95
0-671-63962-5 Simon & Schuster pb $7.95

• Barbara Ingersoll
YOUR HYPERACTIVE CHILD
A parents' guide to coping with attention-deficit disorders
0-385-24069-4 Doubleday pb $8.95

• Sally Smith
NO EASY ANSWERS: The Learning Disabled Child
How parents can assist teachers at home
0-553-27095-8 Bantam pb $4.95

• Priscilla Vail
SMART KIDS WITH SCHOOL PROBLEMS
"Conundrum kids": brilliant in one subject but slow in another
0-525-24557-X Dutton $18.95
0-452-26154-6 NAL pb $8.95

Health

The books listed in this section include general reference books, useful in an emergency; drug guides, which detail the side effects of prescribed medicine; and books on medical insurance, hospitals, and home care for the chronically ill.

▶ **See also Medicine**

MEDICAL REFERENCES

• Robert Berkow, editor
THE MERCK MANUAL
Physicians have been relying on this text—which is now in its 15th edition—since 1899. It is an excellent all-around guide to illnesses and their treatments, with each entry summarizing the signs and symptoms of the disease, diagnostic procedures, alternative prognoses, and appropriate treatment

Volume 1: General Medicine
0-911910-07-7 Merck pb $12.50

Volume 2: Obstetrics, Gynecology, Pediatrics, Genetics
0-911910-08-5 Merck pb $6.95

• A.W.H. Black, editor
BLACK'S MEDICAL DICTIONARY
Detailed entries
0-389-20745-4 Barnes & Noble $36.95

• Mosby
MOSBY'S MEDICAL DICTIONARY
Includes a 44-page color atlas of the human body
0-452-25977-0 NAL pb $12.95

MOSBY'S MEDICAL ENCYCLOPEDIA
20,000 entries
0-452-25977-0 NAL pb $12.95

• Nancy Roper, editor
NEW AMERICAN POCKET MEDICAL DICTIONARY
The 14th edition of a popular portable medical reference, with more than 1000 new entries
0-684-19031-1 Scribners pb $12.95

• Merriam-Webster
WEBSTER'S MEDICAL DESK DICTIONARY
A popular reference arranged in alphabetical order
0-87779-025-6 Merriam-Webster $12.95

WEBSTER'S NEW WORLD/STEADMAN'S CONCISE MEDICAL DICTIONARY
An abridged version of Steadman's Dictionary, the 24th edition, with 35,000 entries; for a popular audience
0-13-948142-7 Prentice-Hall $18.95

HOME HEALTH AND FIRST-AID GUIDES

• American Medical Association
THE AMERICAN MEDICAL ASSOCIATION FAMILY MEDICAL GUIDE
Divided into four parts: the healthy body, symptoms and self-diagnosis, explanation of the most common physical and mental illnesses, and caring for the sick at home
0-394-55582-1 Random House $29.95

THE AMERICAN MEDICAL ASSOCIATION HOME MEDICAL ADVISER
Hundreds of clear and colorful illustrations accompany the text of this thorough self-help guide to symptoms, diseases, and medical emergencies
0-394-5623-1 Random House $24.95

• William Bennett & others
YOUR GOOD HEALTH: How to Stay Well, and What to Do When You're Not
Advice from Harvard Medical School doctors
0-674-96631-7 Harvard $24.95

• Jane Brody
THE NEW YORK TIMES GUIDE TO PERSONAL HEALTH
This useful reference covers enormous ground and includes brief sections on nutrition, exercise, emotional health, reproduction, addiction, dental and eye care, the environment, common illnesses, and pesky problems
0-380-64121-6 Avon pb $12.95

• Deltakron Institute
EMERGENCY MEDICAL PROCEDURES FOR THE HOME, AUTO, AND WORKPLACE
0-13-274408-2 Prentice-Hall pb $6.95

• Lawrence Galton
1001 HEALTH TIPS
Alphabetically arranged tips on common problems
0-671-47689-0 Simon & Schuster $17.95
0-671-50935-7 Simon & Schuster pb $7.95

• Good Housekeeping
THE NEW GOOD HOUSEKEEPING FAMILY HEALTH AND MEDICAL GUIDE
Written for the layperson, with 16 pages of full-color anatomical charts and over 200 helpful illustrations
0-688-06164-8 Hearst $24.95

• Lawrence Horowitz
TAKING CHARGE OF YOUR MEDICAL FATE
Argues that where you live and the doctor, hospital, lab, or treatment facility you

choose may affect the outcome of an illness than the medical facts themselves
0–394–56336–0 Random House $18.95

• Ellen Michaud & Lila Anastas
LISTEN TO YOUR BODY: A Head-to-Toe Guide to More than 400 Common Symptoms, Their Causes, and Best Treatments
Written with *Prevention* Magazine editors
0–87857–728–9 Rodale $27.95

• Cathy & Edward Pickney
THE PATIENT'S GUIDE TO MEDICAL TESTS
Covers hospital and outpatient procedures
0–8160–1292–X Facts On File $21.95
0–8160–1593–7 Facts On File pb $12.95

• Isadore Rosenfeld
MODERN PREVENTION: The New Medicine
Current ideas on how to prevent common illnesses
0–671–50735–4 Simon & Schuster $18.95
0–553–34460–9 Bantam pb $10.95

• Jack Stern & David Carroll
THE HOME MEDICAL GUIDE
The latest treatments, tests, and technologies in the field of home health care, with advice on prevention, diagnosis, and treatment of common ailments
0–688–06073–0 Morrow $17.95

• Donald Tapley & others, editors
THE COLUMBIA UNIVERSITY COLLEGE OF PHYSICIANS AND SURGEONS COMPLETE HOME MEDICAL GUIDE
The joint effort of 56 doctors from one of America's oldest and most distinguished medical institutions
0–517–55842–4 Crown $39.95

• Donald Vickery & James Fries
TAKE CARE OF YOURSELF: The Consumer's Guide to Medicine
A best-seller, now in its third edition
0–201–08091–X Addison-Wesley pb $14.50

DRUG GUIDES

• American Association of Retired Persons
THE AARP PHARMACY SERVICE PRESCRIPTION DRUG HANDBOOK
Organized by diseases
0–673–24842–9 AARP pb $13.95

• American Medical Association
THE AMERICAN MEDICAL ASSOCIATION GUIDE TO PRESCRIPTION AND OVER-THE-COUNTER DRUGS
Hundreds of clear illustrations, information on brand-name and generic drugs, vitamins, minerals, and food additives
0–394–56949–0 Random House $25.00

• American Society of Hospital Pharmacists
THE NEW CONSUMER DRUG DIGEST
0–8160–1254–5 Facts On File $21.95
0–8160–1255–5 Facts On File pb $10.95

• Ed Barnhart, editor
PHYSICIAN'S DESK REFERENCE
The 42nd edition of the drug guide on every doctor's desk
0–87489–844–7 Medical Economics $39.95

PHYSICIAN'S DESK REFERENCE CONSUMER'S GUIDE TO NONPRESCRIPTION DRUGS
0–87489–847–1 Medical Economics pb $9.95

• James Long
THE ESSENTIAL GUIDE TO PRESCRIPTION DRUGS: Everything You Need to Know for Safe Drug Use
Includes expected minor side effects and more serious effects which require immediate medical attention
0–06–181553–5 Harper & Row $27.50
0–06–096233–X Harper & Row pb $12.95

• Sidney Wolfe
WORST PILLS, BEST PILLS: The Older Adult's Guide to Avoiding Drug-Induced Death or Illness
Information on nearly 300 of the most commonly prescribed medications
0–937–18851–4 Pantheon pb $12.00

• David Zimmerman
THE ESSENTIAL GUIDE TO NONPRESCRIPTION DRUGS
0–06–014915–9 Harper & Row $27.00

HOSPITAL AND MEDICAL CARE

• Lila Anastas
HOW TO STAY OUT OF THE HOSPITAL: A Practical Guide to Healthy Options and Alternatives
Outpatient options, plus how to avoid or cope with hospitalization
0–87857–609–6 Rodale $16.95

• Richard Dawood
HOW TO STAY HEALTHY ABROAD
0–14–010692–8 Penguin pb $8.95

• Geri Harrington
THE HEALTH INSURANCE FACT AND ANSWER BOOK
Tips on how to read a policy, what insurance generally does not cover, group and individual plans, Health Maintenance Organizations, Medigap policies and Blue Cross/Blue Shield
0–06–091258–8 Harper & Row pb $6.95

• Kathleen Hogue & others
THE COMPLETE GUIDE TO HEALTH INSURANCE: How to Beat the High Cost of Being Sick
0–0827–1024–7 Walker $24.95

• Charles Inlander & others
HOW TO EVALUATE AND SELECT A NURSING HOME
0–201–07263–7 Addison-Wesley pb $7.95

• Robert Keet & Mary Nelson
THE SHOPPER'S GUIDE TO THE MEDICAL MARKETPLACE
How to get the best care while cutting costs
0–915166–52–6 Impact pb $11.95

• Judith Nierenberg & Florence Janovic
THE HOSPITAL EXPERIENCE: A Guide for Patients and Their Families
A friendly guidebook on what to expect in the hospital: including drugs, postoperative care, and therapy
0–425–07750–0 Berkley pb $3.95

• Ira Schneider & Ezra Huber
FINANCIAL PLANNING FOR LONG TERM CARE: A Guide for Lawyers, Caregivers, and Consumers
An explanation of Medicare and Medicaid
0–89885–417–2 Human Sciences $24.95

• Linda Sunshine & John Wright
THE BEST HOSPITALS IN AMERICA
Lists the hospitals with the best nursing staffs and top specialists; based on recommendations from physicians and government
0–8050–0583–8 Henry Holt $22.95

SPECIFIC HEALTH PROBLEMS

AIDS

▶ See also The AIDS Crisis

• Harlan Dalton & others
AIDS AND THE LAW: A Guide for the Public
0–300–04078–4 Yale pb $7.95

• Martin Delaney & Peter Goldblum
STRATEGIES FOR SURVIVAL: A Gay Man's Health Manual for the Age of AIDS
0–312–00558–X St. Martin's pb $10.95

• Elisabeth Kübler-Ross
AIDS: The Ultimate Challenge
The AIDS crisis from the viewpoint of a psychiatrist and authority on death and dying
0–02–567170–7 Macmillan $17.95

• Helen Singer Kaplan
THE REAL TRUTH ABOUT WOMEN AND AIDS: How to Eliminate the Risks Without Giving up Love and Sex
Advice from the Director of the Human Sexuality Program at New York Hospital-Cornell Medical Center
0–671–65743–7 Simon & Schuster pb $4.95

• John Langone
AIDS: The Facts
0–316–51413–6 Little, Brown $17.95
0–316–51412–8 Little, Brown pb $8.95

• Bonnie Lester
WOMEN AND AIDS: A Practical Guide for Those Who Help Others
0–8264–0501–0 Continuum $15.95

• Leonard Martelli & others
WHEN SOMEONE YOU KNOW HAS AIDS: A Practical Guide
Advice from professional therapists
0–517–56556–0 Crown pb $9.95

• National Academy of Sciences
MOBILIZING AGAINST AIDS: The Unfinished Story of a Virus
0–674–57761–2 Harvard pb $7.95

• Chris Norwood
ADVICE FOR LIFE: A Woman's Guide to AIDS Risks and Prevention
0–394–75428–X Pantheon pb $5.95

Allergies

• Natalie Golos & others
COPING WITH YOUR ALLERGIES
How to identify food and other substances in your home which can cause allergies, and to find safe alternatives
0–671–24078–1 Simon & Schuster $18.95
0–671–60199–7 Simon & Schuster pb $8.95

• Prevention Magazine Editors
THE ALLERGY SELF-HELP BOOK: A Complete Guide to Detection and Natural Treatment of Allergies
This book covers diet, cleaning one's environment, and other alternatives to drugs
0–87857–458–1 Rodale $19.95

• Harry Swartz
NEW ALLERGY GUIDE BOOK
A systematic approach that involves a healthy diet and home environment. With information for infants and children, how to cope with climate changes, travel, and dentists
0–8264–0388–3 Continuum pb $9.95

Alzheimer's Disease

• Alzheimer's Disease & Related Disorders Association
UNDERSTANDING ALZHEIMER'S DISEASE: What It Is, How to Treat It, How to Cope with It, Future Directions
0–684–18475–3 Scribners $15.95

• David Carroll
WHEN YOUR LOVED ONE HAS ALZHEIMER'S DISEASE: A Caregiver's Guide
Offers guidance on recognizing symptoms; finding doctors, hospitals and nursing homes; home health care; financial and legal problems; dealing with patient violence, guilt, anger, and more
0–06–015887–5 Harper & Row $17.95

• Donna Cohen & Carl Eisdorfer
THE LOSS OF SELF: A Family Resource for the Care of Alzheimer's Disease and Related Disorders
0–393–02263–3 Norton $18.95
0–452–25946–0 NAL pb $9.95

• Nancy Mace & Peter Rabins
THE 36-HOUR DAY: A Family Guide to Caring for Persons with Alzheimer's Disease, Related Dementing Illnesses, and Memory Loss in Later Life
0–446–32201–60 Warner pb $3.95

• Rose Oliver & Frances Bock
COPING WITH ALZHEIMER'S: A Caregiver's Emotional Survival Guide
Sound, practical advice on providing maximum care for the person with Alzheimer's while inflicting minimum emotional strain on oneself, written by two psychiatrists
0–396–08954–2 Dodd, Mead pb $9.95

• Judah Ronch
ALZHEIMER'S DISEASE: A Practical Guide for Those Who Help Others
A resource for family members, friends, nurses, physicians, counselors, and other caregivers
0–8264–0500–2 Continuum $15.95

• Jitka Zgola
DOING THINGS: A Guide to Programming Activities for Persons with Alzheimer's Disease and Related Disorders
Intended for professional caregivers but also a useful guide for patients' families
0–8018–3467–8 Johns Hopkins pb $8.95

Arthritic Diseases

• The Arthritis Foundation
UNDERSTANDING ARTHRITIS: What It Is, How It's Treated, How to Cope with It
The traditional viewpoint, including a critical look at nonmedical treatments
0–684–18199–1 Scribners $18.95
0–684–18736–1 Scribners pb $10.95

• Thomas Brown & Henry Scammell
RHEUMATOID ARTHRITIS: Its Cause and Its Treatment
0–87131–543–2 M. Evans $15.95

• James Fries
ARTHRITIS: A Comprehensive Guide to Understanding Your Arthritis
0–201–05408–6 Addison-Wesley pb $9.95

• Kate Loring & James Fries
THE ARTHRITIS HELP BOOK: A Tested Self-Management Program for Coping with Your Arthritis
Recommended by The Arthritis Foundation for use in its classes
0–201–05468–X Addison-Wesley pb $9.95

• Prevention Magazine Editors
NATURAL RELIEF FOR ARTHRITIS
The ten most common forms of arthritis, and natural ways to help relieve the pain
0–87857–686–X Rodale pb $15.95

• J.T. Scott
ARTHRITIS AND RHEUMATISM: The Facts
0–19–261168–2 Oxford $17.95
0–19–520278–3 Oxford pb $6.95

Asthma

• Eric Gershwin & E.L. Klingelhofer
ASTHMA: Stop Suffering, Start Living
New strategies for controlling asthma which include diet, medication, and exercise
0–201–11581–6 Addison-Wesley pb $10.95

• Donald Lane & Anthony Storr
ASTHMA: The Facts
0–19–261677–3 Oxford $18.95

• Allan Weinstein
ASTHMA: The Complete Guide for Patients and Their Families
0–07–069058–8 McGraw-Hill $17.95

Back Problems

• Edward Abraham
FREEDOM FROM BACK PAIN: An Orthopedist's Self-Help Guide
How to prevent acute and chronic back pain
0–87857–657–6 Rodale $18.95
0–87857–658–4 Rodale pb $10.95

• Arthur Klein & Dana Sobel
BACKACHE RELIEF
A book based on a survey of back pain sufferers; includes nonmedical therapies
0–451–14432–5 NAL pb $4.95

Cancer

• Oliver Alabaster
THE POWER OF PREVENTION: Reduce Your Risk of Cancer Through Diet and Nutrition
0–671–62798–8 Simon & Schuster pb $7.95

• Stewart Alsop
STAY OF EXECUTION: A Sort of Memoir
The journalist's moving account of his bout with leukemia
0–397–00897–X Harper & Row $12.95

• Marvin Barrett
SPARE DAYS
A cancer patient's journal. "As spare and beautiful as mortal bone"—Peter Matthiessen
1–55710–006–3 Arbor House $16.95

• Jeanne Munn Bracken
CHILDREN WITH CANCER: A Comprehensive Reference Guide for Parents
From practical tips to sophisticated medical facts, written by a librarian whose son survived cancer. "A remarkable job . . . The technical information is clearly stated, up-

to-date and accurate . . . But, most of all, this is a human book"—*LA Times*
0–19–505659–0 Oxford pb $9.95

- Nancy Bruning
COPING WITH CHEMOTHERAPY
0–345–33090–0 Ballantine pb $3.95

- Henry Dreher
YOUR DEFENSE AGAINST CANCER: The Complete Guide to Cancer Prevention
"I am sure that every person by following [Henry Dreher's] recommendations would be able to prepare himself or herself against cancer to a significant extent"—Linus Pauling
0–06–015740–2 Harper & Row $18.95

- Judith Glassman
THE CANCER SURVIVORS: And How They Did It
Personal accounts of metastasized cancer cured by unorthodox as well as conventional treatments
0–385–27673–7 Doubleday $19.95

- Jill Ireland
LIFE WISH
How the glamourous movie actress (and wife of Charles Bronson) coped with breast cancer
0–316–10926–6 Little, Brown $19.95

- Edward & Richard Larschan
THE DIAGNOSIS IS CANCER: A Psychological and Legal Resource Handbook for Cancer Patients, Their Families, and Helping Professionals
0–915950–78–2 Bull $17.95
0–915950–77–4 Bull pb $9.95

- John Laszlo
UNDERSTANDING CANCER: A Leading Expert Tells You What He Wishes Everyone Knew
An explanation of the disease and its treatments
0–06–015754–2 Harper & Row $17.95
0–06–091491–2 Harper & Row pb $8.95

- Albert Marchetti
BEATING THE ODDS: Alternative Treatments That Have Worked Miracles Against Cancer
0–8092–4769–0 Contemporary $17.95

- Marion Morra & Eve Potts
CHOICES: Realistic Alternatives in Cancer Treatment.
A handbook of down-to-earth questions and answers about every kind of cancer treatment
0–380–75308–1 Avon pb $10.95

- Ralph Moss
THE CANCER SYNDROME
The politics of cancer treatment, particularly the unorthodox methods
0–394–17655–3 Grove pb $4.95

- Prevention Magazine Editors
THE COMPLETE BOOK OF CANCER PREVENTION: Foods, Lifestyle, and Medical Care to Keep You Healthy
0–87857–740–8 Rodale $27.95

- Betty Rollin
FIRST YOU CRY
Inspiring personal account of breast cancer and its consequences
0–451–14427–9 NAL pb $3.50

- Anthony Sattilaro & Tom Monte
RECALLED BY LIFE: The Story of My Recovery from Cancer
The story of a physician who successfully overcame cancer of the prostate with a macrobiotic diet
0–395–32524–2 Houghton Mifflin pb $12.95

- Carl Simonton & others
GETTING WELL AGAIN: A Step-by-Step Self-Help Guide to Overcoming Cancer for Patients and Their Families
A psychological approach to treatment and pain control
0–87477–070–X Jeremy Tarcher $13.95

- Susan Sontag
ILLNESS AS METAPHOR
0–374–52073–9 Farrar, Straus & Giroux pb $7.95

Colds

- Michael Castleman
COLD CURES
Guide to a variety of prevention methods and treatments of the common cold and the flu
0–449–90225–0 Fawcett pb $5.95

Cosmetic Surgery

- American Academy of Facial Plastic and Reconstructive Surgery
THE FACE BOOK: The Pros and Cons of Facial Plastic Surgery
0–87491–914–2 Acropolis $19.95

- Elizabeth Morgan
THE COMPLETE BOOK OF COSMETIC SURGERY: A Candid Guide for Men, Women, and Teens
Well-illustrated, detailed book by a plastic surgeon
0–446–51370–9 Warner $19.95

- Paula Moynahan
DR. PAULA MOYNAHAN'S COSMETIC SURGERY FOR WOMEN: A Revolutionary Approach to Image Enhancement
0–517–56429–7 Crown $17.95

Dental Care

- Jerry & Mary Taintor
THE ORAL REPORT: The Consumer's Common Sense Guide to Better Dental Care
0–8160–1392–6 Facts On File $18.95

Diabetes

▶ See also Diet and Nutrition

- The American Diabetes Association
DIABETES IN THE FAMILY
A guide to a healthy lifestyle, with meal plans
0–13–208653–0 Prentice-Hall pb $9.95

- Richard Bernstein
DIABETES: The Glucograf Method for Normalizing Blood Sugar
A technique for minimizing the physical complications of diabetes, written by a diabetic doctor in collaboration with the Diabetes Research Center at Montefiore Hospital
0–87477–314 Jeremy Tarcher pb $9.95

- Jerry Edelwich & Archie Brodsky
DIABETES: Caring for Your Emotions As Well As Your Health
0–201–10608–6 Addison-Wesley pb $10.95

- Charles Peterson & Lois Jovanovic
THE DIABETES SELF-CARE METHOD
0–671–49189–X Simon & Schuster pb $7.95

- Julian Whitaker
REVERSING DIABETES
A lifestyle plan, from a Pritikin Longevity Center doctor, which promises to reduce or even eliminate dependence on insulin or oral drugs
0–446–51304–0 Warner $19.95

Eating Disorders: Anorexia and Bulimia

- Hilda Bruch
CONVERSATIONS WITH ANOREXICS
Written by a psychiatry professor, a leading authority on the emotional aspects of anorexia
0–465–01421–6 Basic Books $18.95
EATING DISORDERS: Obesity, Anorexia Nervosa, and the Person Within
0–465–01782–7 Basic Books pb $11.95

- Joan Jacobs Brumberg
FASTING GIRLS: The Emergence of Anorexia Nervosa as a Modern Disease
An excellent history, by a Cornell professor
0–674–29501–3 Harvard $25.00

- Katherine Byrne
A PARENT'S GUIDE TO ANOREXIA AND BULIMIA: Understanding and Helping Self-Starvers and Binge-Purgers; Including a List of Organizations, Resources, and Services
0–8052–4032–2 Schocken $14.95

- Janice Cauwels
BULIMIA: The Binge-Purge Compulsion
0–385–18377–1 Doubleday $15.95

- Kim Chernin
THE HUNGRY SELF: Women, Eating, and Identity
The connection between female identity and eating disorders
0–06–09726–X Harper & Row pb $8.95
THE OBSESSION: Reflections on the Tyranny of Slenderness
"Eloquently written, passionate in its rhetoric and consistently absorbing"—*NY Times*
0–06–090967–6 Harper & Row pb $6.95

- Ira Sacker & Marc Zimmer
DYING TO BE THIN
0–446–38417–8 Warner pb $12.95

• Michele Siegel & others
**SURVIVING AN EATING DISORDER:
Strategies for Family and Friends**
"A lucid and comprehensive book that I
am certain will be helpful to those whose
lives have been affected"—Craig Johnson
0–06–015859–X Harper & Row $15.95
0–06–091553–6 Harper & Row pb $8.95

Eye Care

• William Bates
**THE BATES METHOD FOR BETTER
EYESIGHT WITHOUT GLASSES**
Daily eye exercises as an alternative to
eyeglasses
003–058012–9 Henry Holt pb $5.95

• Helen Neal
**LOW VISION: What You Can Do to
Preserve, and Even Enhance Your Usable
Sight**
0–671–52379–1 Simon & Schuster $16.95

• Walter Zinn & Herbert Solomon
**THE COMPLETE GUIDE TO EYE
CARE, EYEGLASSES, AND CONTACT
LENSES**
0–8119–0687–6 Frederick Fell $15.95
0–8119–0642–6 Frederick Fell pb $9.95

Feet and Knees

• Glenn Copeland
**THE FOOT DOCTOR: Lifetime Relief for
Your Aching Feet**
Relief from foot problems, from calluses to
bone injuries, proper footwear, and home
remedies
0–87857–663–0 Rodale $12.95

• James Fox & Rick McGuire
SAVE YOUR KNEES
0–440–50011–7 Dell pb $7.95

• Myles Schneider & Mark Sussman
**HOW TO DOCTOR YOUR FEET
WITHOUT A DOCTOR**
0–87491–751–4 Acropolis pb $11.95

Headaches and Migraines

• James Lance
**MIGRAINE AND OTHER HEADACHES:
A Renowned Physician's Guide to Diagnosis
and Effective Treatment**
0–684–18654–3 Scribners pb $7.95

• Rodolfo Low
**MIGRAINE: The Breakthrough Study That
Explains What Causes It and How It Can
be Prevented Through Diet**
0–8050–0140–9 Henry Holt $16.95

• Oliver Sacks
MIGRAINE
"His commentary is so erudite, so
gracefully written that even those people
fortunate enough never to have had a
migraine in their lives should find it
compelling"—*NY Times*
0–520–05199–8 California pb $8.95

• Joel Saper & Kenneth Magge
FREEDOM FROM HEADACHES
0–671–25404–9 Simon & Schuster pb $7.95

Heart Disease

▶ **See also Diet and Nutrition**

• American Medical Association
GUIDE TO HEART CARE
0–394–73545–5 Random House pb $8.95

• Cleaves Bennett & Charles Cameron
**CONTROL YOUR HIGH BLOOD
PRESSURE—WITHOUT DRUGS!**
0–385–23579–8 Doubleday pb $9.95

• Timothy Caris
**A CLINICAL GUIDE TO
HYPERTENSION**
0–446–34079–0 Warner pb $3.95

• Keith Cohn & Darby Duke
**COMING BACK: A Guide to Recovering
from Heart Attack**
0–201–05498–1 Addison-Wesley pb $9.95

• Norman Cousins
**THE HEALING HEART: Antidotes to
Panic and Helplessness**
The importance of a patient's role in
recovering from a massive heart attack
0–393–01816–4 Norton $13.95

• Jonathan Halperin & Richard Levine
**BYPASS: A Cardiologist Reveals What
Every Patient Needs to Know**
0–8129–1157–1 Times Books $16.95

• Nancy Hoffman
**CHANGE OF HEART: The Bypass
Experience**
Twenty personal accounts of bypass
surgery
0–06–097071–5 Harper & Row pb $7.95

• Norman & Ilana Hollenberg
**THE HEART FACTS: What You Can Do
to Keep a Healthy Heart**
Addresses such lifestyle concerns as diet,
exercise, smoking, drinking, and stress, and
explains why tests are performed, how they
are done, what they feel like, and the risks
involved
0–673–24887–7 AARP pb $12.95

• M. Gabriel Khan
**HEART ATTACKS, HYPERTENSION,
AND HEART DRUGS: The Complete, Up-
to-Date, Commonsense Guide to a Healthy
Heart**
An explanation of the options for heart
care
0–87857–710–6 Rodale pb $12.95

• Larry King
**MR. KING, YOU'RE HAVING A HEART
ATTACK**
Heart attack, bypass surgery, and recovery
from the radio and television personality
0–940–50039–7 Delacorte $16.95

• Norman Richards
**HEART TO HEART: The Cleveland Clinic
Guide to Understanding Heart Disease and
Open Heart Surgery**
0–689–11854–6 Atheneum $14.95

• David Sonnenburg & others
UNDERSTANDING PACEMAKERS
0–935576–05–3 Scribners $12.95
0–671–55674–6 Scribners pb $4.50

• Art Ulene
**COUNT DOWN ON CHOLESTEROL:
How to Lower Your Blood Cholesterol
Level 30 Percent in Only 30 Days**
0–394–57716–7 Random House $18.95

Kidney Disorder

• Stewart Cameron
KIDNEY DISEASE: The Facts
0–19–261594–7 Oxford pb $18.95

Lupus

• Henrietta Aladjem
**UNDERSTANDING LUPUS: What It Is,
How to Treat It, How to Cope with It**
0–684–18348–X Scribners $15.95
0–684–18349–8 Scribners pb $9.95

**IN SEARCH OF THE SUN: A Woman's
Courageous Victory over Lupus**
0–684–18759–0 Scribners $19.95

• Laura Chester
LUPUS NOVICE: Toward Self-Healing
A poet stricken with lupus writes of her
journey to healing
0–88268–037–4 Station Hill $16.95

Multiple Sclerosis

• Elizabeth Forsythe
LIVING WITH MULTIPLE SCLEROSIS
An informed and reassuring book, written
by a doctor, herself a victim of MS
0–571–11293–5 Faber & Faber $11.95
0–571–11294–3 Faber & Faber pb $6.95

**MULTIPLE SCLEROSIS: Exploring
Sickness and Healing**
A discussion of the disease, current
theories about its causes, periods of
remission, and the search for a cure
0–571–13979–5 Faber & Faber pb $8.95

• Judy Graham
**MULTIPLE SCLEROSIS: A Self-Help
Guide to Its Management**
0–7225–0804–2 Thorsons pb $7.95

• Robert Shuman & Janice Schwartz
**UNDERSTANDING MULTIPLE
SCLEROSIS: A Guidebook for Families**
Written by two psychologists, one of
whom has MS, and endorsed by the
National Multiple Sclerosis Society of
America
0–684–18998–5 Scribners $17.95

Osteoporosis

• Kenneth Cooper
PREVENTING OSTEOPOROSIS
The causes and symptoms of osteoporosis,
the latest in estrogen replacement, drug
and hormone therapy, helpful exercises,
and proper nutrition, including Cooper's
special "Tough Bone Diet"
0–553–05335–3 Bantam $18.95

• David Fardon
**OSTEOPOROSIS: Your Head Start to the
Prevention of Fractures**
0–02–537120–7 Macmillan $15.95

◼ **TO ORDER BOOKS AS GIFTS, SEE PAGE 1**

• William Peck & Louis Avioli
OSTEOPOROSIS: The Silent Thief
Two researchers and physicians from The National Osteoporosis Foundation describe the pros and cons of estrogen replacement therapy, the effects of a calcium-rich diet and exercise, and new avenues of research
0–673–24837–2 AARP pb $9.95

Pain

• Ben Benjamin & Gail Border
LISTEN TO YOUR PAIN: The Active Person's Guide to Understanding
Organized by symptoms
0–14–006687–X Penguin pb $10.95

• David Bresler & Richard Trubo
FREE YOURSELF FROM PAIN
A range of conventional and nontraditional approaches
0–671–62334–6 Simon & Schuster pb $10.95

• Richard Linchitz
LIFE WITHOUT PAIN
Includes practical descriptions of pain control exercises, diet information, and relaxation techniques
0–201–11900–5 Addison-Wesley $14.95

• Ronald Melzack & Patrick Wall
THE CHALLENGE OF PAIN
A study by a leading theorist
0–465–00906–9 Basic Books $20.95
0–465–00907–7 Basic Books pb $10.95

Sexually Transmitted Diseases

• Henry Balfour & Ralph Heussner
HERPES DISEASES AND YOUR HEALTH
The facts on cold sores, chicken pox, shingles, mononucleosis, and genital herpes
0–8166–1432–6 Minnesota pb $8.95

• Frank Freudberg & Stephen Emmanuel
HERPES: A Complete Guide to Relief and Reassurance
0–89471–188–1 Running Press pb $6.95

• Stephen Zinner
HOW TO PROTECT YOURSELF FROM STDs
0–671–62876–3 Summit pb $6.95

Skin Care and Disorders

• Howard Donsky
BEAUTY IS SKIN DEEP: A Doctor's Guide to Healthy, Younger-Looking Skin
0–87857–645–2 Rodale pb $13.95

• William Dovine
A DERMATOLOGIST'S GUIDE TO HOME SKIN TREATMENT
0–684–17875–3 Scribners $12.95
0–684–18206–8 Scribners pb $6.95

• Kenneth Flandermeyer
CLEAR SKIN: A Step-by-Step Program to Stop Pimples, Blackheads, Acne
0–316–28545–5 Little, Brown $14.95
0–316–28546–3 Little, Brown pb $6.95

• James Fulton & Elizabeth Black
DR. FULTON'S STEP-BY-STEP PROGRAM FOR CLEARING ACNE
A detailed, practical regimen for getting rid of acne
0–06–038020–9 Harper & Row $14.50

• Thomas Goodman & Stephanie Young
SMART FACE: A Dermatologist's Guide to Cosmetics and Skin Care
0–13–814377–3 Prentice-Hall pb $9.95

• Nelson Novick
SUPER SKIN: A Leading Dermatologist's Guide to Head-to-Toe Skin Care
0–517–57035–1 Crown $18.95

• Linda Schoen
THE AMA BOOK OF SKIN AND HAIR CARE
0–397–01158–X Lippincott pb $4.95

Sleep Disorders

• Alexander Borbely
SECRETS OF SLEEP
The latest on sleep, dreams and sleep disorders
0–465–07593–2 Basic Books pb $8.95

• Consumer Reports
SLEEP: Problems and Solutions
0–89043–065–9 Consumer Reports $20.00
0–89043–055–1 Consumer Reports pb $14.95

• Shirley Linde & Louis Savary
THE JOY OF SLEEP: Facts, Fantasy, and Folklore
0–06–250515–7 Harper & Row pb $4.95

Stress

• American Health Magazine
THE RELAXED BODY BOOK: A High-Energy Anti-Tension Program
0–385–19983–X Doubleday $19.95
0–385–19984–8 Doubleday pb $12.95

• Rosalind Barnett & others
GENDER AND STRESS
An investigation of the cause of stress, and how men and women experience it differently
0–02–901380–1 Free Press $30.00

• Herbert Benson & William Proctor
BEYOND THE RELAXATION RESPONSE
Meditation as a means of alleviating stress and easing physical ills
0–425–08183–4 Berkley pb $3.50

• Joan Borysenko
MINDING THE BODY, MENDING THE MIND
A Harvard Medical School instructor presents the scientific rationale behind her acclaimed stress reduction program and shares the experiences of her patients
0–201–10707–4 Addison-Wesley $14.95
0–533–34556–7 Bantam pb $8.95

• Alix Krista
THE BOOK OF STRESS SURVIVAL: Identifying and Reducing the Stress in Your Life
A colorful illustrated guide
0–671–63026–1 Simon & Schuster pb $10.95

• Hans Seyle
THE STRESS OF LIFE
A classic work by the founder of the International Institute of Stress; includes new research
0–07–056212–1 McGraw-Hill pb $7.95

STRESS WITHOUT DISTRESS
How to use stress as a positive force
0–451–15268–9 Signet pb $3.95

Stroke

• John Lavin
STROKE: From Crisis to Victory—A Family Guide
0–531–09787–0 Franklin Watts $16.95

• Ellen Paullin
TED'S STROKE: The Caregiver's Story
"Ellen Paullin has written with sensitivity about a painful experience. Her courage, humor, and resourcefulness are enormously impressive"—Norman Cousins
0–932020–54–2 Seven Locks $14.95

WOMEN'S HEALTH

• The Boston Women's Health Book Collective
THE NEW OUR BODIES, OURSELVES
An overall book on how a woman's body functions, and the particular concerns of female health
0–671–46087–0 Simon & Schuster $19.95
0–671–46088–9 Simon & Schuster pb $14.95

• Mary Ballweg & Susan Deutsch
OVERCOMING ENDOMETRIOSIS: New Help from the Endometriosis Association
0–86553–190–0 Congdon & Weed pb $9.95

• Paula Brown Doress & others
OURSELVES, GROWING OLDER
An *Our Bodies, Ourselves* for the special needs of women over 35. Delves into such topics as childbearing at midlife, menopause, hysterectomy, osteoporosis, and cancer
0–671–64424–6 Simon & Schuster pb $15.95

• Larrian Gillespie
YOU DON'T HAVE TO LIVE WITH CYSTITIS: A Woman Urologist Tells How to Avoid It—And What to Do about It
Alternatives to the standard medical treatments for cystitis
0–89256–302–8 Rawson $18.95
0–380–70511–7 Avon pb $7.95

• Ada Kahn & Linda Hughey Holt
MIDLIFE HEALTH: Every Woman's Guide to Feeling Good
0–8160–1345–4 Facts On File pb $18.95

- Kerry McGinn
  KEEPING ABREAST: Breast Changes That Are Not Cancer
  0–915950–82–0 Bull pb $7.95

- Lynn Payer
  HOW TO AVOID A HYSTERECTOMY: An Indispensable Guide to Exploring All Your Options
  0–394–55511–2 Pantheon $17.95
  0–679–72142–8 Pantheon pb $6.95

- Jane Porcino
  GROWING OLDER, GETTING BETTER: A Handbook for Women in the Second Half of Life
  0–201–05592–9 Addison-Wesley pb $12.95

- Felicia Stewart & others
  UNDERSTANDING YOUR BODY: Every Woman's Guide to a Lifetime of Health
  0–553–34451–X Bantam $14.95

- Susan Trien
  CHANGE OF LIFE: The Menopause Handbook
  A comprehensive guide
  0–345–90188–6 Fawcett pb $7.95

- Kate Weinstein
  LIVING WITH ENDOMETRIOSIS: How to Cope with the Physical and Emotional Challenges
  0–201–19810–X Addison-Wesley pb $10.95

- Stella Weller
  PAIN-FREE PERIODS: Natural Ways to Overcome Menstrual Problems
  0–7225–1195–7 Thorsons pb $6.95

MEN'S HEALTH

- Monroe Greenberger & Mary Ellen Siegel
  WHAT EVERY MAN SHOULD KNOW ABOUT HIS PROSTATE
  0–8027–1023–9 Walker $21.95
  0–8027–0725–4 Walker pb $13.95

- Maureen Mylander
  THE HEALTHY MALE: A Guide to Longer Living for Men
  0–316–59368–0 Little, Brown pb $14.95

- Stephen Rous
  THE PROSTATE BOOK: Sound Advice on Symptoms and Treatment
  An expert discusses in nontechnical language the causes, symptoms, and surgical and nonsurgical treatment of the most common prostate problems
  0–393–02592–6 Norton $18.95

- Edward Wallerstein
  CIRCUMCISION: An American Health Fallacy
  An examination of routine circumcision for infants
  0–8261–3241–3 Springer pb $18.95

HEALTH CARE FOR THE AGING

- Robert Butler & Myrna Lewis
  AGING AND MENTAL HEALTH
  Robert Butler is the former director of the National Institute on Aging, and Myrna Lewis is a psychologist and gerontologist
  0–8016–1002–8 NAL pb $8.95
  LOVE AND SEX AFTER FORTY
  0–06–015491–8 Harper & Row pb $15.95

- Rene Cailliet & Leonard Gross
  REJUVENATION STRATEGY: A Medically Approved Fitness Program to Remove the Effects of Aging
  0–385–19714–4 Doubleday $16.95

- Jean Crichton
  THE AGE CARE SOURCEBOOK: A Resource Guide for the Aging and Their Families
  Options in care for the aging and their cost
  0–671–61148–8 Simon & Schuster pb $10.95

- Joe & Teresa Graedon
  50 PLUS: The Graedon's People's Pharmacy for Older Adults
  0–553–05245–4 Bantam $24.95
  0–553–34485–4 Bantam pb $13.95

- Thomas Hager & Lauren Kessler
  STAYING YOUNG: The Whole Truth About Aging, and What You Can Do to Slow Its Progress
  Explores how various parts of the body are affected by the aging process and offers advice on how such effects can be minimized
  0–8160–1303–9 Facts On File pb $17.95

- Robin Marantz
  THE MYTH OF SENILITY: The Truth About the Brain and Aging
  Why 95% of people over 65 are not senile
  0–673–24892–5 AARP $14.95

- Robert Weiss & Genell Subsk-Sharpe
  THE COLUMBIA UNIVERSITY SCHOOL OF PUBLIC HEALTH COMPLETE GUIDE TO HEALTH AND WELL-BEING AFTER 50
  0–8129–1325–6 Times Books $24.95

- Richard Wyatt
  AFTER MIDDLE AGE: A Physician's Guide to Growing Old and Staying Healthy
  0–07–072135–1 McGraw-Hill $21.95

CARE OF THE DISABLED AND CHRONICALLY ILL

▶ See also People with Disabilities

- Dana Nordrick
  CARING FOR YOUR OWN: Nursing the Ill at Home
  0–471–63702–5 John Wiley pb $12.95

- Sefra Pitzele
  WE ARE NOT ALONE: Learning to Live with Chronic Illness
  Useful, supportive information for the everyday problems of the chronically ill
  0–89480–139–2 Workman pb $8.95

- Cheri Register
  LIVING WITH CHRONIC ILLNESS: Days of Patience and Passion
  Emotions surrounding chronic illness, with anecdotes from real life
  0–02–925730–1 Free Press $19.95

- Tieneke Van Bentheim & Saskia Bos
  CARING FOR THE SICK AT HOME
  Nonclinical aspects of caring for the sick and the elderly, including psychological insight
  0–88010–254–3 Anthroposophic pb $11.95

- Florence Weiner
  NO APOLOGIES: A Survival Guide and Handbook for the Disabled Written by the Real Authorities—People with Disabilities and Their Families
  Personal stories with some practical advice
  0–312–57523–8 St. Martin's pb $13.95

ALTERNATIVE MEDICINE

The story of Norman Cousins' recovery from an incurable illness using laughter and high doses of vitamin C, published first in the *New England Journal of Medicine* and then as the best-seller *Anatomy of an Illness*, did much to introduce mainstream medicine to the efficacy of alternative therapies. Nonmedical forms of healing, such as homeopathy, chiropractice, and naturopathy are included here.

▶ See also New Age

Natural Health

- Norman Cousins
  ANATOMY OF AN ILLNESS: As Perceived by the Patient
  Natural healing and the importance of the patient's attitude, based on the author's own recovery from a crippling disease
  0–553–34365–3 Bantam pb $6.95

- Rina Nissim
  NATURAL HEALING IN GYNECOLOGY: A Manual for Women
  0–86358–069–6 RC&H pb $9.95

- Andrew Stanway
  ALTERNATIVE MEDICINE: A Guide to Natural Therapies
  0–14–008561–0 Penguin pb $6.95

- Andrew Stanway & Richard Grossman
  NATURAL FAMILY DOCTOR
  0–671–61974–8 Simon & Schuster $19.95
  0–671–61966–7 Simon & Schuster pb $12.95

- Andrew Weil
  HEALTH AND HEALING: Understanding Conventional and Alternative Medicine
  0–395–34430–1 Houghton Mifflin $13.95
  0–395–37764–1 Houghton Mifflin pb $7.95

Alternative Therapies

- Larry Dossey
  SPACE, TIME, AND MEDICINE
  Holistic medicine, by a noted Dallas doctor
  0–87773–224–8 Shambhala pb $14.95

- Ted Kaptchuk
  THE WEB THAT HAS NO WEAVER: Understanding Chinese Medicine
  0–312–92932–3 Congdon & Weed $19.95
  0–312–92933–1 Congdon & Weed pb $11.95

- Dolores Krieger
  THE THERAPEUTIC TOUCH: How to Use Your Hands to Help or to Heal
  0–13–914820–5 Prentice-Hall $14.95
  0–13–914812–4 Prentice-Hall pb $7.95

- Ruth Lever
  ACUPUNCTURE FOR EVERYONE
  0–14–008834–2 Penguin pb $5.95

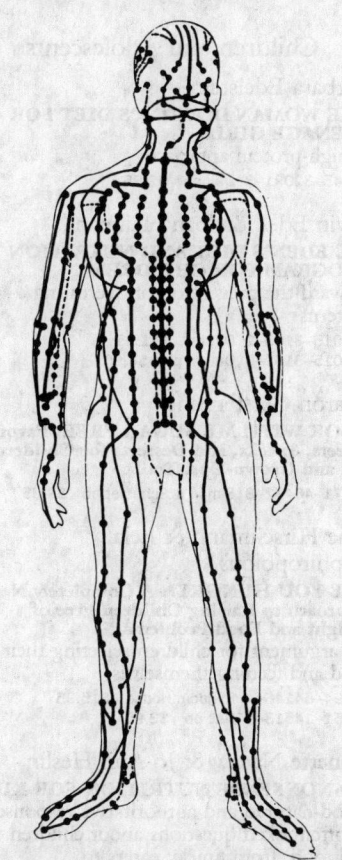

Acupuncturist's map of the body from The New Good Housekeeping Family Health and Medical Guide *(Hearst)*

- Yoshio Manaka & Ian Urquhart
  THE LAYMAN'S GUIDE TO ACUPUNCTURE
  Introduction by James Reston
  0–8348–0072–1 Weatherhill $12.50
  0–8348–0107–8 Weatherhill pb $7.50

- Jeanne Rose
  JEANNE ROSE'S MODERN HERBAL
  0–399–51394–9 Putnam pb $9.95

- George Vithoulkas
  THE SCIENCE OF HOMEOPATHY
  The principles of homeopathy in practical application
  0–394–17560–3 Grove pb $9.50

Mind-Body Healing

- Steven Locke & Douglas Colligan
  THE HEALER WITHIN: The New Medicine of Mind and Body
  The mind and immunity
  0–525–24283–X Dutton $22.50
  0–451–62554–4 NAL pb $4.95

- Carl Lowe & Jim Nechas
  WHOLE BODY HEALING
  0–87857–441–7 Rodale $12.95

- Emrika Padus
  THE COMPLETE GUIDE TO YOUR EMOTIONS AND YOUR HEALTH: New Dimensions in Mind-Body Healing
  Written with the staff of *Prevention* magazine
  0–87857–589–8 Rodale $12.95

- Ernest Lawrence Rossi
  THE PSYCHOBIOLOGY OF MIND-BODY HEALING: New Concepts of Therapeutic Hypnosis
  "Supplies the missing link between the theory that the mind can make a significant difference in dealing with disease and the clinical observations of physicians that the theory works in enough cases to be taken seriously"—Norman Cousins
  0–393–30554–6 Norton pb $9.95

- Bernard Siegel
  LOVE, MEDICINE, AND MIRACLES
  A surgeon stresses the importance of the patient's mind and emotions and offers a nonmedical means of overcoming illness; a best-seller
  0–06–015496–9 Harper & Row $17.95

Diet and Nutrition

Americans have been increasingly concerned with diet and nutrition as key factors in the prevention of disease. New eating styles recognize this link and, together with exercise, are seen as vital prescriptions for the health and well-being of the human animal. These books address a range of nutritional issues, such as vitamins and health foods and the special needs of heart patients, hypertensives, and diabetics.

▶ **See also Health**

- Eleanore Brenner
  GOURMET COOKING WITHOUT SALT
  0–385–24351–0 Doubleday pb $9.95

- Jane Brody
  JANE BRODY'S GOOD FOOD BOOK: Living the High-Carbohydrate Way
  A guide to changing and maintaining eating habits for health and slimness which includes a low-fat, high-carbohydrate plan with 350 easy-to-prepare recipes
  0–393–02210–2 Norton $22.95
  0–553–34346–7 Bantam pb $12.95

  JANE BRODY'S NUTRITION BOOK: A Lifetime Guide to Good Eating for Better Health and Weight Control
  All aspects of the current nutrition issues: health foods, vitamins, drinking water, athletics diets, and recipes
  0–393–01429–0 Norton $22.95
  0–553–34421–8 Bantam pb $12.95

- Jean Carper
  JEAN CARPER'S TOTAL NUTRITION GUIDE: The Complete Official Report on Healthful Eating
  0–553–34350–5 Bantam pb $12.95

- Craig Claiborne & Pierre Franey
  CRAIG CLAIBORNE'S GOURMET DIET
  Delicious, innovative, low-sodium, modified-fat, modified-cholesterol recipes from the *New York Times* chef
  0–8129–0914–3 Times Books $16.95
  0–345–33635–6 Ballantine pb $3.95

- Sonja & William Connor
  THE NEW AMERICAN DIET: The Lifetime Family Eating Plan for Good Health
  A lifetime diet and health plan (high-carbohydrate, low-fat) aimed at health and disease prevention; includes almost 350 recipes
  0–671–54324–5 Simon & Schuster $18.95
  0–671–66375–5 Simon & Schuster pb $10.95

- Cheryl Corbin
  NUTRITION
  A step-by-step plan for choosing and adapting to the changes in diet
  0–03–048276–3 Henry Holt pb $8.95

- Rose Dosti & others
  LIGHT STYLE: The New American Cuisine, the Low-Calorie, Low-Salt, Low-Fat Way to Good Food and Good Health
  0–06–250487–8 Harper & Row pb $10.95

• Anne Fletcher
EAT FISH, LIVE LONGER: How to Put More Fish into Your Diet for a Longer, Healthier Life
Advice from the former editor of the 300,000-circulation *Tufts University Diet and Nutrition Letter*
0–06–015833–6 Harper & Row $18.95

• Barbara Gibbons
THE INTERNATIONAL SLIM GOURMET COOKBOOK
International cuisine for weight loss and maintenance without dieting
0–06–011507–6 Harper & Row $16.95

• Nikki & David Goldbeck
THE GOLDBECKS' GUIDE TO GOOD FOOD
0–453–00566–7 NAL $19.95

• Barbara Griggs
THE FOOD FACTOR: Why We Are What We Eat
An account of the "nutrition revolution" and resistance to it
0–670–80201–8 Viking $19.95

• Karen MacNeil
THE BOOK OF WHOLE FOODS: Nutrition and Cuisine
An encyclopedic guide to natural foods
0–394–74012–2 Random House pb $8.95

• Linus Pauling
HOW TO LIVE LONGER AND FEEL BETTER
Vitamins and health, by the famous pioneer in the field
0–380–70289–4 Avon pb $4.95

• Paul Saltman & others
THE CALIFORNIA NUTRITION BOOK: Food for the '90s from University of California Faculty and American Health Magazine
An explanation of myths and trends in nutrition, vitamins, minerals, food, diets, disease
0–316–76964–9 Little, Brown $17.95

• Joan Stillman
FAST AND LOW: Easy Recipes for Low-Fat Cuisine
International cuisine; many recipes call for a food processor
0–316–81613–2 Little, Brown pb $9.95

• Time-Life
EATING RIGHT: Recipes for Health
Over 100 vegetable, grain, fruit, legume, seafood, meat, poultry, and dairy recipes preceded by a detailed chapter on nutrition
0–8094–6163–3 Time-Life $14.95

• Jack Yetic
POPULAR NUTRITIONAL PRACTICES
Diet and nutritional fads from the point of view of a physician and pharmacologist
0–440–20046–6 Dell pb $4.95

SPECIAL DIETS

Low Cholesterol

• American Heart Association, editors
THE AMERICAN HEART ASSOCIATION COOKBOOK
Popular and useful, with fat-cholesterol charts
0–345–32819–1 Ballantine $10.95
0–345–32278–4 Ballantine pb $3.95

• Hans Fisher & Eugene Boe
THE RUTGERS GUIDE TO LOWERING YOUR CHOLESTEROL: A Common Sense Approach
0–8135–1135–6 Rutgers $16.95
0–446–32657–7 Warner pb $3.95

• Ron & Nancy Goor
EATER'S CHOICE: A Food Lover's Guide to Lower Cholesterol
Includes recipes
0–395–42181–0 Houghton Mifflin $17.95
0–395–43075–5 Houghton Mifflin pb $11.95

• Robert Kowalski
THE EIGHT-WEEK CHOLESTEROL CURE: How to Lower Your Blood Cholesterol by up to 40 Percent Without Drugs or Deprivation
0–06–015613–9 Harper & Row $15.95

• Joseph Piscatella
CHOICES FOR A HEALTHY HEART
Prescriptive measures and recipes
0–89480–138–4 Workman pb $14.95

Diets for Special Health Problems

• American Diabetes Association
THE AMERICAN DIABETES ASSOCIATION FAMILY COOKBOOK
Several hundred recipes, with nutrient calculations and food exchange values

Volume 1
0–13–003915–2 Prentice-Hall pb $16.95

Volume 2
0–13–003955–1 Prentice-Hall pb $16.95

Volume 3
Includes microwave recipes
0–13–004145–9 Prentice-Hall pb $16.95

• Cleaves Bennett & Christine Newport
THE CONTROL YOUR HIGH BLOOD PRESSURE COOKBOOK
For those with hypertension, based on American Heart Association guidelines; over 200 varied recipes
0–385–19919–8 Doubleday $16.95
0–385–23579–8 Doubleday pb $9.95

• Helene & Ben Feingold
THE FEINGOLD COOKBOOK FOR HYPERACTIVE CHILDREN AND OTHERS WITH PROBLEMS ASSOCIATED WITH FOOD ADDITIVES AND SALICYLATES
Based on the Feingolds' work with diet and hyperactive children, focusing on food additives
0–394–41232–X Random House $10.95
0–394–73664–8 Random House pb $6.95

• Claude Frazier
COPING WITH FOOD ALLERGY: Symptoms and Treatment
A guide, including recipes and lists of suppliers for special foods
0–8129–1149–0 Times Books pb $8.95

• Euell & Joe Gibbons
FEAST ON A DIABETIC DIET
0–449–23853–9 Fawcett pb $2.95

• Marjorie Jones
THE ALLERGY SELF-HELP COOKBOOK
Over 325 natural foods recipes, free from wheat, milk, eggs, corn, yeast, sugar, and other common food-allergy substances
0–87857–505–7 Rodale $16.95

• Katherine Middleton & Mary Hess
THE ART OF COOKING FOR THE DIABETIC
0–8092–8270–4 Contemporary $15.95
0–451–12205–4 NAL pb $3.95

• Arlene Monk & Marion Franz
CONVENIENCE FOOD FACTS: Help for the Healthy Meal Planner
Dietary help for the diabetic
0–937721–20–4 Diabetes Center pb $8.95

• Diane Reader
PASS THE PEPPER PLEASE!: Healthy Meal Planning for People on Sodium-Restricted Diets
0–937721–17–4 Diabetes Center pb $3.95

Children and Adolescents

• Barbara Edelstein
THE WOMAN DOCTOR'S DIET FOR TEENAGE GIRLS
A high-protein approach
0–345–32091–3 Dell pb $2.95

• Alvin Eden & Joan Heilman
DR. EDEN'S DIET AND NUTRITION PROGRAM FOR CHILDREN
Toward the prevention of overeating patterns
0–8015–3180–2 Dutton $11.95
0–8015–3181–0 Dutton pb $6.95

• Sharon Gerstenzang
COOK WITH ME SUGAR FREE: Favorite Sweets, Snacks, and Desserts for Children . . . and Grown-Ups, Too!
0–671–46472–8 Simon & Schuster pb $9.95

• Jane Hirschmann & Lela Zaphiropolous
ARE YOU HUNGRY?: A Completely New Approach to Raising Children Free of Weight and Food Problems
An argument for children selecting their food and feeding themselves
0–394–54146–4 Random House $15.95
0–451–14513–5 NAL pb $3.95

• Annette Natow & Jo-Ann Heslin
NO-NONSENSE NUTRITION FOR KIDS
Good-natured and authoritative responses to often-asked questions about children and food, from finicky eaters to lunchboxes; how to balance the often bizarre tastes of children and teenagers
0–671–60779–0 Pocket pb $3.95

➤ FOR OVERSEAS ORDERING INFORMATION, SEE PAGE 1

- Lendon Smith
DR. LENDON SMITH'S DIET PLAN FOR TEENAGERS
A 21-day diet plan and recipes
0–07–058700–0 McGraw-Hill $16.95
0–07–058706–X McGraw-Hill pb $4.95

- John Taylor & Sharon Latta
SPECIAL DIETS AND KIDS: How to Keep Your Child on Any Prescribed Diet
Children with dietary restrictions
0–396–08762–0 Dodd, Mead $16.95

Middle and Later Years

- Elaine Feldman
NUTRITION IN THE MIDDLE AND LATER YEARS
For changing needs of those over 45
0–446–34081–2 Warner pb $3.95

- Annette Natow & Jo-Ann Heslin
NUTRITION FOR THE PRIME OF YOUR LIFE
By the "Dear Abby" and "Ann Landers" of nutrition: questions and answers about food, vitamins, and health, with recipes
0–07–028414–8 McGraw-Hill $17.95

Diets for Women

- Patricia Long
THE NUTRITIONAL AGES OF WOMEN: A Lifetime Guide to Eating Right for Health, Beauty, and Well-Being
0–02–574760–6 Macmillan $18.95
0–553–26472–9 Bantam pb $4.50

- Jean Perry Spodnik & Barbara Gibbons
THE 35 PLUS DIET FOR WOMEN: Kaiser Permanent Clinic's Breakthrough Metabolism Diet
For the changing metabolism of the over-35 woman: high protein, low carbohydrate, low fat, no sugar
0–06–015718–6 Harper & Row $15.45

Sports Nutrition

- Robert Haas
EAT TO WIN: The Sports Nutrition Bible
From a sports nutritionist: high-carbohydrate, low-cholesterol eating for a moderate to active sports life
0–451–13394–3 NAL pb $4.50

EAT TO SUCCEED: The Haas Maximum Performance Program
High-carbohydrate performance plans
0–89256–293–5 Rawson $15.95
0–451–40024–0 NAL pb $4.50

- Stephen Wooton
NUTRITION FOR SPORT: Eating to Improve Performance
Written by an MD and nutrition writer for *Running* magazine
0–8160–1470–1 Facts On File pb $17.95

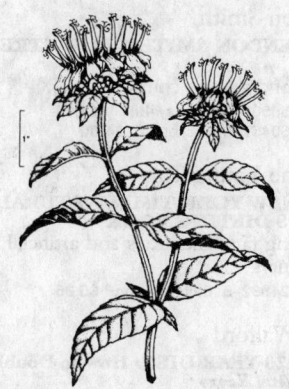

Wild bergamot, a member of the mint family, from A Garden of Wildflowers *by Henry Art, illustrated by Hyla M. Skudder (Garden Way)*

WEIGHT-LOSS DIETS

The following books offer alternative weight loss diets to the "New Eating" plans. Some focus on one central idea, such as the use of dietary fiber; others propose a high-protein, low-carbohydrate plan.

Psychological Approaches

- Jane Hirschmann & Carol Munter
OVERCOMING OVEREATING: Living Free in a World of Food
A program for ending the compulsive eater's addictive relationship to food
0–201–12219–7 Addison-Wesley $15.95

- Eda LeShan
WINNING THE LOSING BATTLE: Why I Will Never Be Fat Again
An informal personal account
0–690–01845–2 Crowell pb $8.95

- Gabe Mirkin
GETTING THIN: All About Fat—How You Lose It, How You Keep It Off for Good
0–316–57437–6 Little, Brown $18.95
0–316–57439–2 Little, Brown pb $8.95

- Susie Orbach
FAT IS A FEMINIST ISSUE: The Anti-Diet Guide to Permanent Weight Loss
Fatness as a response: how to change this response into thinness
0–425–10351–X Berkley pb $3.95

- Richard Stuart
ACT THIN, STAY THIN: New Ways to Lose Weight and Keep It Off
A psychological approach to keeping weight off
Foreword by Jean Nidetch
0–393–08805–7 Norton $12.95
0–515–08724–6 Berkley pb $3.95

Diet Plans

- Robert Atkins
DR. ATKINS' DIET REVOLUTION
A high-protein diet
0–553–25996–2 Bantam pb $4.50

- Stuart Berger
DR. BERGER'S IMMUNE POWER DIET
A diet aimed at improving the immune system
0–453–00483–0 NAL $14.95
0–451–14111–3 NAL pb $4.95

- Theodore Berland
THE DIETER'S ALMANAC
Comparison of over 50 diets, from Pritikin to grapefruits to macrobiotic
0–345–31628–2 Ballantine pb $7.95

- Consumer Guide, editors
RATING THE DIETS
0–451–14291–8 NAL pb $3.95

- Harvey & Marilyn Diamond
FIT FOR LIFE
A highly controversial natural body cycle, permanent weight-loss plan whose cardinal rule is only fruit before noon
0–446–51322–9 Warner $17.50
0–446–30015–2 Warner pb $4.95

- Audrey Eyton
THE F-PLUS DIET
A fiber diet
0–517–55738–X Crown $13.95
0–553–25301–8 Bantam pb $3.95

- Julius Fast
THE OMEGA-3 BREAKTHROUGH: The Revolutionary, Medically-Proven Fish Oil Diet
Fish oils for disease prevention
0–89586–625–0 HP $15.95

- Robert Gold & Kerry Rose-Gold
THE GOOD FAT DIET: Reduce Cholesterol and Lose Weight Fast with Omega-3
Omega-3 oil from seafood, for lower cholesterol
0–553–05186–5 Bantam $14.95
0–553–26642–X Bantam pb $4.50

- Martin Katahn
THE ROTATION DIET
A best-selling 21-day plan; weight loss through increased metabolism
0–553–26395–1 Bantam pb $4.50

THE ROTATION DIET COOKBOOK: A Lifetime of Good Eating and Staying Slim
0–393–02457–1 Norton $18.95

THE 200-CALORIE SOLUTION: A Lifetime Program of Weight Control Without Dieting
A weight-reducing plan for raising metabolism through activity without cutting calories
0–393–01530–0 Norton $13.95
0–425–10623–3 Berkley pb $3.95

- Karen Kreps & Richard Smith
THE 60-DAY DIET DIARY
A cheerful diet account
0–440–57946–5 Dell pb $3.95

- Michael & Kathryn Mahoney
PERMANENT WEIGHT CONTROL
0–393–30245–8 Norton pb $5.95

- Marshall & Fran Mandell
THE MANDELLS' IT'S NOT YOUR FAULT YOU'RE FAT DIET
Food allergies can explain why some gain weight
0–06–015114–5 Harper & Row $13.95
0–452–25607–0 NAL pb $6.95

- Joyce Nash
MAXIMIZE YOUR BODY POTENTIAL: 16 Weeks to a Lifetime of Weight Management
0–915950–68–5 Bull $24.95
0–915950–69–3 Bull pb $14.95

Jean Nidetch
THE WEIGHT WATCHERS NEW PROGRAM COOKBOOK
From the established diet organization: a three-stage plan to reduce and maintain weight
0–953–01003–2 NAL pb $9.95

WEIGHT WATCHERS FAST AND FABULOUS COOKBOOK
0–453–01008–3 NAL $15.50
0–452–25727–1 NAL pb $8.95

WEIGHT WATCHERS FOOD PLAN DIET COOKBOOK
0–453–01007–5 NAL $13.95

WEIGHT WATCHERS INTERNATIONAL COOKBOOK
0–453–01004–0 NAL $11.95
0–452–25780–8 NAL pb $7.95

WEIGHT WATCHERS 365-DAY MENU COOKBOOK
A year's worth of imaginative recipes
0–453–01009–1 NAL $15.95
0–452–25958–4 NAL pb $9.95

- Durk Pearson & Sandy Shaw
THE LIFE EXTENSION WEIGHT LOSS PROGRAM
A best-selling book for those who hate to diet and exercise: a nutritional program to make you feel like eating less
0–385–24109–7 Doubleday pb $8.95

- Ruth Fairchild Pomeroy, editor
REDBOOK'S WISE WOMAN'S DIET COOKBOOK
A 1200-calorie diet, endorsed by nutritionists
0–453–00436–9 NAL $14.95
0–452–25532–5 NAL pb $5.95

- Nathan & Ilene Pritikin
THE OFFICIAL PRITIKIN GUIDE TO RESTAURANT EATING
0–672–52773–1 Bobbs-Merrill $11.95
0–425–07667–9 Berkley pb $6.95

- Nathan Pritikin & Patrick McGrady
THE PRITIKIN PROGRAM FOR DIET AND EXERCISE
The best-selling weight-loss and longevity plan
0–553–25608–4 Bantam pb $4.95

- Richard Simmons
RICHARD SIMMONS' NEVER-SAY-DIET COOKBOOK
A slower but permanent approach to diet and exercise
0–446–51243–5 Warner $15.95
0–446–97041–7 Warner pb $7.95

- Lendon Smith
DR. LENDON SMITH'S LOW-STRESS DIET
Stress and weight control
0–07–058500–8 McGraw-Hill $14.95
0–671–60457–0 Pocket pb $4.50

- Yvonne Young Tarr
THE NEW YORK TIMES NATURAL FOODS DIETING BOOK
Avoiding fats, chemicals and artificial sweeteners
0–345–24832–5 Ballantine pb $5.95

- Roy Walford
THE 120-YEAR DIET: How to Double Your Vital Years
Longevity through high-nutrient, low-caloric eating
0–671–46677–1 Simon & Schuster $18.95
0–671–64904–3 Archway pb $4.95

- Betty Wason
SOUP-TO-DESSERT HIGH FIBER COOKBOOK
Fiber for every meal
0–451–09991–5 NAL pb $2.50

- Judith Wurtman
THE CARBOHYDRATE CRAVER'S DIET
For those who go off diets because of starch and sugar cravings
0–345–31493–X Ballantine pb $2.95

VEGETARIANISM AND NATURAL FOODS

▶ **See also Food**

- Helen Brassel
THE NATURAL FOODS RECIPE BOOK: 800 Low-Calorie Dishes to Help You Lose Weight
A lifelong plan for healthful eating and weight control; with a broad range of recipes, from tofu to haute cuisine
0–668–05626–6 Simon & Schuster $16.95
0–668–05631–2 Simon & Schuster pb $9.95

- Jean Hewitt
THE NEW YORK TIMES NEW NATURAL FOODS COOKBOOK
Not strictly vegetarian, but a solid source on a variety of natural foods
0–8129–1009–5 Times Books $17.95
0–380–62687–X Avon pb $7.95

- Frances Lappé
DIET FOR A SMALL PLANET
Classic vegetarian text, including information on combining grains, legumes, and dairy for complete protein; with recipes
0–345–00621–6 Ballantine pb $3.95

- Kenneth Lo
CHINESE VEGETARIAN COOKING
Chinese cooking without meat or fish
0–394–70639–0 Pantheon pb $6.95

- Paulette Mitchell
THE NEW AMERICAN VEGETARIAN MENU COOKBOOK: From Everyday Dining to Elegant Entertaining
Imaginative ideas
0–87857–501–4 Rodale $13.95
0–87857–494–8 Rodale pb $9.95

- Gary Null
THE NEW VEGETARIAN COOKBOOK
0–02–590890–1 Macmillan $15.95
0–02–010040–X Macmillan pb $11.95

- Laurel Robertson & others
THE NEW LAUREL'S KITCHEN
A new age classic: cookbook and guide
0–89815–167–8 Ten Speed $24.95
0–89815–166–X Ten Speed pb $15.95

- Shanta Sacharoff
THE ETHNIC VEGETARIAN KITCHEN
0–89286–238–6 One Hundred & One pb $7.95

- Anthony Sattilaro & Tom Monte
LIVING WELL NATURALLY
Grains and vegetable diet from a doctor who recovered from cancer
0–395–34422–0 Houghton Mifflin $13.95
0–395–39389–2 Houghton Mifflin pb $6.95

- Vic Sussman
A VEGETARIAN ALTERNATIVE
Thoughtful essays on the background, ethics, and practice of vegetarianism
0–87857–227–9 Rodale pb $8.95

From The Vegetarian Epicure *by Anna Thomas, illustrated by Julie Maas (Vintage)*

- Anna Thomas
THE VEGETARIAN EPICURE
A vegetarian classic for both beginning and experienced cooks
0–394–47606–9 Knopf $16.95
0–394–71784–8 Random House pb $9.95

- Lisa Tracy
THE GRADUAL VEGETARIAN
0–440–53124–1 Dell pb $7.95

VITAMINS AND DIETARY SUPPLEMENTS

- Consumer Guide editors
THE VITAMIN BOOK
0–671–24819–7 Simon & Schuster pb $5.95

- H. Winter Griffith
COMPLETE GUIDE TO VITAMINS, MINERALS, AND SUPPLEMENTS
1–55561–006–4 Fisher pb $9.95

● Patricia Hausman
THE CALCIUM BIBLE: How to Have Better Bones All Your Life
0-89256-284-6 Rawson $13.95

THE RIGHT DOSE: How to Take Vitamins and Minerals Safely
0-87857-678-9 Rodale $24.95

● Sheldon Saul Hendler
THE COMPLETE GUIDE TO ANTI-AGING NUTRIENTS
Views on the merits of different vitamins, minerals, and other nutrients for health and longevity
0-671-50615-3 Simon & Schuster $16.95

● Joseph Levy & Paul Bach-y-Rita
VITAMINS: Their Use and Abuse
0-87140-616-0 Liveright pb $8.95

● Patrick Quillin
HEALING NUTRIENTS
0-8092-4796-8 Contemporary $18.95

REFERENCE BOOKS AND NUTRIENT COUNTERS

● Jean Carper
THE ALL-IN-ONE CALORIE COUNTER
Calorie counts for 8800 food items including junk, health, and restaurant food
0-553-26326-9 Bantam pb $4.50

JEAN CARPER'S TOTAL NUTRITION GUIDE: The Complete Official Report on Healthful Eating
Questions on the sources and quality of nutrients in everyday foods
0-553-34350-5 Bantam pb $12.95

● Jean Carper & Patricia Krause
THE ALL-IN-ONE CARBOHYDRATE GRAM COUNTER
Includes 7500 entries for brand-name and fast foods
0-553-26405-2 Bantam pb $4.50

● Thomas Dale Cowan & Randi Aaron
THE CALCIUM AND CALORIE COUNTER
0-425-08780-8 Berkley pb $2.95

● Brian Ford
THE FOOD BOOK
A comprehensive guide to the contents of brand-name foods, plus overall recommendations in nutritional value of the products
0-241-11834-4 David & Charles pb $22.95

● Jo-Ann Heslin & Annette Natow
THE POCKET ENCYCLOPEDIA OF NUTRITION
0-671-61278-6 Pocket pb $5.95

● Michael Jacobson
COMPLETE EATER'S DIGEST AND NUTRITION SCOREBOARD
0-385-18245-7 Doubleday pb $9.95

● Michael Jacobson & others
SALT: The Brand-Name Guide to Sodium Content
Five thousand supermarket foods, fast foods, and natural foods, plus recipes
0-446-32847-2 Warner pb $4.50

● Barbara Kraus
CALORIES AND CARBOHYDRATES
A dictionary listing of over 8000 brand names and basic foods with their caloric and carbohydrate counts
0-452-26176-7 NAL pb $7.95

● John Kirschmann & Lavon Dunne
NUTRITION ALMANAC
Guide to how nutrients work, sources of calories, food composition, diet and health
0-07-034906-1 McGraw-Hill $19.95
0-07-034905-3 McGraw-Hill pb $10.95

● Leah Wallach
These books contain values for more than 8000 foods, including brand-name products, fast foods, prepared foods, fresh foods, health foods, and beverages.
FOOD VALUES: Calcium
0-06-096221-6 Harper & Row pb $4.95

FOOD VALUES: Carbohydrates
0-06-096220-8 Harper & Row pb $4.95

FOOD VALUES: Cholesterol and Fats
0-06-096219-4 Harper & Row pb $4.95

● Myron Winick, editor
THE COLUMBIA ENCYCLOPEDIA OF NUTRITION
0-399-13298-8 Putnam $22.95

Crisis

Public demand for information and advice on coping with such serious problems as rape, drug abuse, and suicide has increased dramatically in recent years. Most of the books that address these subjects are written by professionals and are directed to the victims and their families.

● Nina Donnelly
I NEVER KNOW WHAT TO SAY
Thoughtful advice for helping family and friends cope with tragedy
0-345-33942-8 Ballantine $14.95

● Eugene Kennedy
CRISIS COUNSELING: The Essential Guide for Non-Professional Counselors
Covers such topics as rape, drug abuse, and life changes
0-8264-0038-8 Continuum $16.95
0-8264-0244-5 Continuum pb $9.95

● Ann Kliman
CRISIS: Psychological First Aid for Recovery and Growth
The first general guide to deal with such crises as death, divorce, rape, and illness from a psychological and emotional

perspective. The author, a clinical psychologist, includes case histories
0-87668-929-2 Jason Aronson $17.50

● Reader's Digest
EMERGENCY: What to Do in an Emergency
How to avoid a crisis: first aid, emergency repair, and safety tips. A well-organized book
0-88850-157-9 Reader's Digest $24.95

● Judy Tatelbaum
YOU DON'T HAVE TO SUFFER: A Handbook for Moving Beyond Life's Crises
A provocative and reassuring book on overcoming pain, and learning to enjoy life
0-06-016028-4 Harper & Row $15.95

ADDICTION

● Melody Beattie
CODEPENDENT NO MORE: How to Stop Controlling Others and Start Caring for Yourself
A popular, helpful guide
0-06-255446-8 Harper & Row pb $8.95

● Mary Bratton
A GUIDE TO FAMILY INTERVENTION
A step-by-step approach for dealing with drug or alcohol dependency, written by a family therapist and directed to both therapists and the families of addicts
0-932194-52-4 Health Communications pb $6.95

● Bernard Green
GETTING OVER GETTING HIGH
From caffeine to cocaine—how to recognize addiction
0-688-03948-0 Morrow $15.95
0-688-03949-9 Morrow pb $6.95

● Katherine Ketcham & Ginny Lyford Gustafson
LIVING ON THE EDGE: A Guide to Intervention for Families of Alcohol and Drug Abusers
Covers the nature of addiction, "co-dependence" of family members, resources offered by Alcoholics Anonymous, treatment options, preparation for intervention, and the possible outcome
0-553-34606-7 Bantam pb $8.95

● Martha Morrison
WHITE RABBIT: A Doctor's Story of Her Addiction and Recovery
A moving and brave account of addiction to drugs and alcohol, recovery, and rehabilitation
0-517-56806-0 Crown $16.95

● Janice Phelps & Alan Nourse
THE HIDDEN ADDICTION
Addictions, from sugar to narcotics
0-316-70471-7 Little, Brown pb $9.95

● Linda Sunshine & John Wright
THE HUNDRED BEST TREATMENT CENTERS FOR ALCOHOLISM AND DRUG ABUSE
0-380-7589-4 Avon pb $10.95

Alcohol Abuse

• **Alcoholics Anonymous**
ALCOHOLICS ANONYMOUS
The text for the A.A. program. At 575 pages, it is known as "the Big Book"
0–916856–00–3 AAWS pb $3.60

• **Al-Anon**
AL-ANON FACES ALCOHOLISM
An explanation of the organization that helps families of alcoholics
0–910034–55–9 Al-Anon pb $6.00

• **Tom Dardis**
THE THIRSTY MUSE: Alcohol and the American Writer
The effect of drinking on Faulkner, Fitzgerald, Hemingway, and others
0–89919–376–5 Ticknor & Fields $18.95

• **Herbert Fingarette**
HEAVY DRINKING: The Myth of Alcoholism as a Disease
A UCLA professor's critical look at the efficacy of various alcoholic treatment programs
0–520–06290–6 California $16.95

• **Betty Ford**
THE TIMES OF MY LIFE
The former first lady tells of her addiction to alcohol and tranquilizers, and of her family's successful intervention
0–06–011298–0 Harper & Row $14.95
0–345–34826–5 Ballantine pb $3.95

• **Jean Kinney & Gwen Leaton**
UNDERSTANDING ALCOHOL
A guide to alcohol problems and their treatment
0–452–25338–1 NAL pb $8.95

• **Arnold Ludwig**
UNDERSTANDING THE ALCOHOLIC'S MIND: The Nature of Craving and How to Control It
0–19–504878–4 Oxford $16.95

• **M.A. Maxwell**
THE ALCOHOLICS ANONYMOUS EXPERIENCE
0–07–040996–X McGraw-Hill pb $11.50

• **M. David Meagher**
BEGINNING OF A MIRACLE
A detailed look at intervention; includes a checklist to help determine when to act
0–932194–47–8 Health Communications pb $6.95

• **Jack Mumey**
LOVING AN ALCOHOLIC: Help and Hope for Significant Others
0–8092–5182–5 Contemporary $13.95

• **Donald Newlove**
THOSE DRINKING DAYS: Myself and Other Writers
0–07–046416–2 McGraw-Hill pb $6.95

• **Nan Robertson**
GETTING BETTER: Inside Alcoholics Anonymous
An insider's look at the successful peer-support organization by the *New York Times* writer
0–688–06869–3 Morrow $17.95

• **Rachel V.**
A WOMAN LIKE YOU: Life Stories of Women Recovering from Alcoholism and Addiction
0–06–250701–X Harper & Row $15.95
0–06–250703–6 Harper & Row pb $9.95

• **George Valliant**
THE NATURAL HISTORY OF ALCOHOLISM
An excellent, somewhat technical book
0–674–60376–1 Harvard pb $9.95

• **Clark Vaughan**
ADDICTIVE DRINKING: The Road to Recovery for Problem Drinkers and Those Who Love Them
The medical and emotional effects of alcoholism, primarily directed to the abuser
0–14–006969–0 Penguin pb $9.95

• **Sharon Wegsheider**
ANOTHER CHANCE: Hope and Health for Alcoholic Families
Explores the patterns of families of alcoholics, offering suggestions for intervention and recovery
0–8314–0059–5 Science & Behavior $14.95

Tom Alibrandi
YOUNG ALCOHOLICS
Directed at young alcoholics and their parents
0–89638–014–9 CompCare pb $7.95

Wayne Coffey
STRAIGHT TALK ABOUT DRINKING: Teenagers Speak Out About Alcohol
0–452–26061–2 NAL pb $7.95

Gary Forrest
HOW TO COPE WITH A TEENAGE DRINKER: New Alternatives and Hope for Parents and Families
Specific advice on recovery strategies for alcoholic children
0–689–11346–3 Atheneum $10.95
0–449–20535–5 Fawcett pb $2.95

Jack Mumey
YOUNG ALCOHOLICS: A Book for Parents
0–8092–4852–2 Contemporary pb $8.95

Families of Alcoholics

• **Robert Ackerman**
CHILDREN OF ALCOHOLICS: A Guidebook for Parents, Educators, and Therapists
How to identify the children of alcoholics, and strategies to help those living in an alcoholic family. Includes a list of resource organizations
0–671–64527–7 Simon & Schuster pb $7.95

GROWING IN THE SHADOW: Children of Alcoholics
0–932194–32–X Health Communications pb $9.95

• **Timmen Cermak**
A TIME TO HEAL: The Road to Recovery for Adult Children of Alcoholics
0–87477–454–3 Jeremy Tarcher $15.95

• **Amy Dean**
ONCE UPON A TIME: Stories of Hope from Adult Children
The experiences of 20 adult children of alcoholics
0–06–255472–7 Harper & Row pb $7.95

• **Herbert Gravitz & Julie Bowden**
RECOVERY: A Guide for Adult Children of Alcoholics
Questions and answers on topics ranging from the definition of alcoholism to successful intervention
0–671–64528–5 Simon & Schuster pb $6.95

• **Edith Hornik-Beer**
A TEENAGER'S GUIDE TO LIVING WITH AN ALCOHOLIC PARENT
Questions and answers for children of alcoholics
0–89486–239–1 Hazelden Foundation pb $4.95

• **Suzanne Somers**
KEEPING SECRETS: An Autobiography
The television actress' childhood, growing up with an alcoholic father
0–446–35180–6 Warner pb $4.95

• **Rachel V.**
FAMILY SECRETS: Life Stories of Adult Children of Alcoholics
15 case histories
0–06–250702–8 Harper & Row pb $10.95

• **Dennis Wholey**
BECOMING YOUR OWN PARENT: The Solution for Adult Children of Alcoholic and Other Dysfunctional Families
0–385–24591–2 Doubleday $17.95

• **Barbara Wood**
CHILDREN OF ALCOHOLISM: The Struggle for Self and Intimacy in Adult Life
Strategies for intervention and step-by-step principles for therapists on how best to create an environment to help patients
0–8147–9222–7 NYU pb $12.50

Drug Abuse

• **Robert DuPont, Jr.**
GETTING TOUGH ON GATEWAY DRUGS: A Guide for the Family
Includes case histories, research, and practical advice for dealing with drug abuse
0–88048–046–7 American Psychiatric pb $9.95

• **Dan Ellis**
GROWING UP STONED
A serious exploration of the family's role in drug addiction, treatments, and therapies
0–932194–35–4 Health Communications pb $8.95

• **Mark Gold**
800-COCAINE
Questions and answers for both the user and families, by founder of national hotline for cocaine addicts
0–553–34388–2 Bantam pb $3.50

• **Barbara Gordon**
I'M DANCING AS FAST AS I CAN
The true story of a television executive who overcame an addiction to tranquilizers
0–06–011499–1 Harper & Row $13.95
0–553–23226–6 Bantam pb $3.95

- Ira Mothner & A. Weitz
  HOW TO GET OFF DRUGS
  A comprehensive, well-organized book for drug users and those who wish to help them. The chapters are organized by specific drugs and include a useful discussion of treatments and referral services
  0–671–49208–X Simon & Schuster $16.95
  0–671–46676–3 Simon & Schuster pb $7.95

- Roger Weiss & Steven Mirin
  COCAINE
  Includes sections on intervention by family and coworkers, treatment programs, and a list of treatment facilities
  0–88048–216–8 American Psychiatric $15.95
  0–345–35135–5 Ballantine pb $6.95

Ken Barun & Philip Bashe
HOW TO KEEP THE CHILDREN YOU LOVE OFF DRUGS
A step-by-step guide to prevention and intervention from a drug counselor credited with coining the slogan "Just Say No"
0–87113–180–3 Atlantic Monthly $12.95

Bob Meehan & Stephen Meyer
BEYOND THE YELLOW BRICK ROAD: Our Children and Drugs
Strategies for parents, written by a well-known figure in the prevention of teen drug abuse
0–8092–4981–2 Contemporary pb $9.95

William Perkins & Nancy McMurtrie-Perkins
RAISING DRUG-FREE KIDS IN A DRUG-FILLED WORLD
A brief self-help book for parents
0–89486–316–9 Harper & Row pb $5.95

BATTERED WOMEN

- Lee Bowker
  ENDING THE VIOLENCE: A Guidebook Based on the Experiences of One Thousand Battered Wives
  This book of interviews examines the resources available to the victims: police, courts, doctors, agencies, counselors
  0–918452–86–4 Learning Pub pb $12.95

- Edward Gondolf
  MEN WHO BATTER: An Integrated Approach for Stopping Wife Abuse
  Advice for the abusive male
  0–918452–79–1 Learning Pub pb $19.95

- Del Martin
  BATTERED WIVES
  History of the subject and specific guidance for victims. Includes a guide to shelters
  0–671–64197–2 Pocket pb $4.95

- Alan McEvoy & Jeff Brookings
  HELPING BATTERED WOMEN: A Volunteer's Handbook for Assisting Victims of Marital Violence
  Practical guide for volunteers and professionals: shelters, telephone counseling, helping the children of battered women
  0–918452–33–3 Learning $11.50

- Ginny NiCarthy
  GETTING FREE: A Handbook for Women in Abusive Relationships
  A comprehensive look at how to get emergency help from the police, the law, and doctors
  0–931188–37–7 Seal pb $10.95

- Linda Rouse
  YOU ARE NOT ALONE: A Guide for Battered Women
  Patterns of abusive relationships, the causes of battering, and information on shelter, medical, and legal services
  0–918452–73–2 Learning Pub pb $11.95

- Maria Roy, editor
  BATTERED WOMEN: A Psychosociological Study of Domestic Violence
  A scholarly study
  0–442–25645–0 Van Nostrand Reinhold pb $16.95

- Lydia Savina
  HELP FOR THE BATTERED WOMAN: One Woman's True Story with Complete Resource Sections for Those Who Are Abused or Abusive or Know Someone Who Is
  0–88270–606–3 Bridge pb $9.95

- Lenore Walker
  THE BATTERED WOMAN SYNDROME
  0–8261–4320–2 Springer $24.95

  THE BATTERED WOMAN
  0–06–090742–8 Harper & Row pb $8.95

CHILD ABUSE

Physical and Emotional Abuse

- Richard D'Ambrosio
  NO LANGUAGE BUT A CRY
  An immensely moving case history of an abused child
  0–440–36457–4 Dell pb $4.50

- Vincent Fontana
  SOMEWHERE A CHILD IS CRYING: Maltreatment—Causes and Prevention
  A book filled with shocking case histories and a directory of child-abuse programs
  0–451–62429–7 NAL pb $4.50

- Eliana Gil
  OUTGROWING THE PAIN
  A self-help book that uses cartoons effectively
  0–440–50006–0 Dell pb $5.95

- Ray Helfer & Henry Kempe, editors
  CHILD ABUSE AND NEGLECT: The Family and the Community
  A book primarily for professionals, dealing with prevention, family therapy, and the legal aspects of child abuse
  0–88410–240–8 Harper & Row pb $16.95

- Christine Herbruck
  BREAKING THE CYCLE OF CHILD ABUSE
  A comprehensive report on child abuse; includes many case histories
  0–03–045691–6 Harper & Row pb $5.95

- Ruth & Henry Kempe
  CHILD ABUSE
  A discussion of abuse and treatment, the results of the authors' work with abused children and their parents
  0–674–11425–6 Harvard $12.00
  0–674–11426–4 Harvard pb $4.95

- William Stacey & Anson Shupe
  THE FAMILY SECRET: Domestic Violence in America
  0–8070–4144–0 Harper & Row $18.95
  0–8070–4145–9 Harper & Row pb $9.95

Sexual Abuse

- Ellen Bass & Louise Thornton, editors
  I NEVER TOLD ANYONE: Writing by Women Survivors of Child Sexual Abuse
  A collection of personal accounts
  0–06–091050–X Harper & Row pb $7.95

- John Crewdson
  BY SILENCE BETRAYED: Sexual Abuse of Children in America
  "Mr. Crewdson's eloquent book allows all the complications and psychological nuances to emerge, but he does not allow them to obscure the terrible facts of the case"—*NY Times*
  0–06–097203–3 Perennial pb $8.95

- Edsel Erickson & Alan McEvoy
  TEENAGERS AT RISK
  A look at why some teenagers are sexually abused
  1–55691–010–X Learning pb $9.95

- Margaret Cronin Fisk
  INNOCENT VICTIMS: Child Sexual Abuse and Exploitation in America—and How You Can Protect Your Child
  Case histories, interviews with parents, children, molesters, and investigators, and advice on how to keep children from becoming victims
  0–689–11550–4 Atheneum $19.95

- Susan Forward & Craig Buck
BETRAYAL OF INNOCENCE: Incest and Its Devastation
Includes case histories and chapters devoted to each type of incest
0–14–005264–X Penguin pb $7.95

- Sylvia Fraser
MY FATHER'S HOUSE: A Memoir of Incest and Healing
Beautifully written account by a woman who had been sexually abused by her father
0–89919–779–5 Ticknor & Fields $17.95

- Judith Herman
FATHER-DAUGHTER INCEST
A clinical study of 40 incest victims; discusses prevention, recovery, legal recourse
0–674–29506–4 Harvard pb $9.95

- Henry & Ruth Kempe
THE COMMON SECRET: Sexual Abuse of Children and Adolescents
Treatment from a professional and sociological perspective, of interest to the general public
0–7167–1625–9 Freeman pb $12.95

- Carol Poston & Karen Lison
RECLAIMING OUR LIVES: Adult Survivors of Incest
Aimed at helping women survivors come to terms with their pasts and heal their emotional scars
0–316–71472–0 Little, Brown $17.95

- Diana Russell
SECRET TRAUMA: Incest in the Lives of Girls and Women
A landmark study
0–465–07595–9 Basic Books $24.95

- Linda Sanford
THE SILENT CHILDREN: A Parents' Guide to the Prevention of Child Sexual Abuse
0–07–054662–2 McGraw-Hill pb $7.95

- Elizabeth Ward
FATHER-DAUGHTER RAPE
A feminist study that includes many case histories and theories on the causes of abuse
0–394–54632–6 Grove $17.50
0–394–62032–1 Grove pb $7.95

CRIME VICTIMS

- David Austern
THE CRIME VICTIM'S HANDBOOK
Information on victims' legal rights, how to deal with crime, and an exhaustive list of rape crisis and domestic violence shelters
0–670–80475–4 Viking $17.95
0–14–046801–3 Penguin pb $6.95

- James Morris
VICTIM AFTERSHOCK: How to Get Results from the Criminal Justice System
This step-by-step guide to coping with specific crimes includes case histories and a discussion of the criminal justice system
0–531–09891–5 Franklin Watts $13.95

DEATH AND MOURNING

- Marguerite Bouvard & Evelyn Glado
THE PATH THROUGH GRIEF: A Practical Guide
Real-life stories of sibling loss and loss through suicide and homicide, as well as practical advice on coping with grief and rebuilding a life
0–932576–66–4 Breitenbush pb $9.95

- D.J. Enright
THE OXFORD BOOK OF DEATH
A wide-ranging anthology of literary and philosophical commentary on death
0–19–214129–5 Oxford $22.95
0–19–282013–3 Oxford pb $8.95

- Earl Grollman
CONCERNING DEATH: A Practical Guide for the Living
0–8070–2765–0 Harper & Row pb $10.95

- Robert Kavanaugh
FACING DEATH
Psychological observations on death, grief, mourning, and the fear of death
0–14–003812–4 Penguin pb $7.95

- Elisabeth Kübler-Ross
QUESTIONS AND ANSWERS ON DEATH AND DYING
From the respected doctor who has specialized in the terminally ill
0–02–089150–4 Macmillan pb $5.95

LIVING WITH DEATH AND DYING
An essential book for patients and their families
0–02–086490–6 Macmillan pb $5.95

WORKING IT THROUGH
Describes the author's experience running innovative workshops on dying
0–02–567160–X Macmillan $15.95
0–02–022000–6 Macmillan pb $5.95

- Robert Jay Lifton
THE BROKEN CONNECTION: On Death and the Continuity of Life
A scholarly book that explores the effect of death on the survivors
0–465–00776–7 Harper & Row pb $12.95

- Ernest Morgan
DEALING CREATIVELY WITH DEATH: A Manual of Death Education and Simple Burial
Discusses funerals, grief, and bereavement in a frank, straightforward way
Preface by Jessica Mitford
0–914064–19–3 Celo pb $9.00

- Harriet Schiff
LIVING THROUGH MOURNING: Finding Comfort and Hope When a Loved One Has Died
A analysis of the feelings of those left behind
0–670–80028–7 Viking $16.95

- Carol Staudacher
BEYOND GRIEF: A Guide for Recovering from the Death of a Loved One
0–934986–44–4 New Harbinger $19.95
0–934986–43–6 New Harbinger pb $10.95

- Judy Tatelbaum
THE COURAGE TO GRIEVE: Creative Living, Recovery, and Growth Through Grief
0–06–091185–9 Harper & Row pb $7.95

- Roberta Temes
LIVING WITH AN EMPTY CHAIR: A Guide Through Grief
Includes useful bibliographies at the end of each chapter
0–88282–012–8 New Horizons $13.95

- Savine Weizman & Phyllis Kamm
ABOUT MOURNING: Support and Guidance for the Bereaved
A thorough exploration of the mourning process
0–89885–136–X Human Sciences $29.95
0–89885–309–5 Human Sciences pb $16.95

Death of a Spouse

- E. Brockman
WIDOWER
The author's experience with grief and loneliness
0–553–26908–9 Bantam pb $4.50

- Lynn Caine & Eleanor Friede
BEING A WIDOW
A candid guide to the problems of widowhood, from the initial shock of death and the first timid steps toward a new life
0–87795–966–8 Morrow $18.95

- Scott Campbell & Phyllis Silverman
WIDOWER
Case histories
0–13–959503–1 Prentice-Hall $17.95

- Robert DiGiulio
BEYOND WIDOWHOOD: From Bereavement to Emergence and Hope
A sympathetic study that includes personal accounts and lists of support groups
0–02–907882–2 Free Press $19.95

- Genevieve Ginsburg
TO LIVE AGAIN: Rebuilding Your Life After You've Become a Widow
Written by a widowed therapist; includes chapters on widowers and young widows
0–87477–426–8 Jeremy Tarcher $14.95

TO ORDER BOOKS AS GIFTS, SEE PAGE 1

- Earl Goethals
WHAT HELPED ME WHEN MY LOVED ONE DIED
0-8070-32299-8 Bantam pb $7.95

- Ruth Loewinsohn
SURVIVAL HANDBOOK FOR WIDOWS: And for Relatives and Friends Who Want to Understand
Covers such practical issues as finances and wills, as well as the emotional aspects of grief
0-673-24820-8 Little, Brown pb $5.95

Death of a Parent

- Marc Angel
THE ORPHANED ADULT: Confronting the Death of a Parent
Religious and philosophical insights from a rabbi
0-89885-334-6 Human Sciences $19.95

- Katherine Donnelly
RECOVERING FROM THE LOSS OF A PARENT: Adult Sons and Daughters Reveal How They Overcame Their Grief
Fascinating accounts of dealing with grief
0-396-08858-9 Dodd, Mead $16.95
0-396-08874-0 Dodd, Mead pb $8.95

- Eda Le Shan
LEARNING TO SAY GOOD-BYE
A well-written book for adults who have lost parents
0-380-40105-3 Avon pb $6.95

- Edward Myers
WHEN PARENTS DIE: A Guide for Adults
A practical guide with resources for the bereaved
0-670-80771-0 Viking $13.95
0-14-009211-0 Penguin pb $6.95

Death of a Child

- Ronald Knapp
BEYOND ENDURANCE: When a Child Dies
Based on interviews with 55 families who have lost children
0-8052-3994-4 Schocken $21.95
0-8052-0823-2 Schocken pb $10.95

- Elisabeth Kübler-Ross
ON CHILDREN AND DEATH
Advice for parents on confronting the illness and death of a child
0-02-076670-X Macmillan pb $5.95

- Rana Limbo & Sara Wheeler
WHEN A BABY DIES: A Handbook for Healing and Helping
A simple, clear book that offers sensible advice
0-9612310-3-3 Harsand pb $8.95

- Harriet Schiff
THE BEREAVED PARENT
Includes a section on the effect of the loss on siblings and the parents' marriage
0-14-005043-4 Penguin pb $6.95

- John Tittensor
YEAR ONE: A Lesson of Hope from Personal Tragedy
0-14-007299-3 Penguin pb $4.95

Suicide

- Edward Donne & John McIntosh
SUICIDE AND ITS AFTERMATH: Research and Treatment
Addressed especially to caregivers, this book includes therapies written by different specialists and personal accounts from suicide survivors
0-393-70039-9 Norton $32.95

- Peter Giovacchini
THE URGE TO DIE
An excellent guide for recognizing and dealing with suicidal behavior in the young, based on the author's belief that most suicides can be prevented
0-14-006314-5 Penguin pb $6.95

- Sol Gordon
WHEN LIVING HURTS
Practical advice for helping those who are severely depressed and contemplating suicide
0-8074-0310-5 UAHC pb $8.95

- Earl Grollman
SUICIDE: Prevention, Intervention, Postvention
Offers prevention strategies and help for the victim's family
0-8070-2775-8 Harper & Row pb $8.95

- Herbert Hendin
SUICIDE IN AMERICA
A psychological approach
0-393-01517-3 Norton $16.95
0-393-30163-X Norton pb $9.95

- Polly Joan
PREVENTING TEENAGE SUICIDE: The Living Alternative Handbook
A how-to book for parents and guidance counselors
0-89885-247-1 Human Sciences $19.95
0-89885-349-4 Human Sciences pb $12.95

- Francine Klagsbrun
TOO YOUNG TO DIE: Youth and Suicide
Based on interviews of attempted suicides
0-395-24752-7 Houghton Mifflin $14.95
0-671-60405-8 Pocket pb $3.50

- Paul Quinnett
SUICIDE—THE FOREVER DECISION: A Book for Those Thinking About Suicide, and for Those Who Know, Love, or Counsel Them
A clearly written, straightforward book to deter people from suicide; includes case studies
0-8264-0395-6 Continuum $18.95
0-8264-0391-3 Continuum pb $7.95

- Susan White-Bowden
EVERYTHING TO LIVE FOR
A mother's story of her teenaged son's suicide
0-671-63587-5 Pocket pb $3.95

- Harriet Braiker
GETTING UP WHEN YOU'RE FEELING DOWN: A Woman's Guide to Overcoming and Preventing Depression
0-399-13383-6 Putnam $17.95

- Mark Gold & Lois Morris
THE GOOD NEWS ABOUT DEPRESSION
0-553-34511-7 Bantam pb $9.95

- John Greist & James Jefferson
DEPRESSION AND ITS TREATMENT
0-446-32718-2 Warner pb $3.95

- Kathleen McCoy
COPING WITH TEENAGE DEPRESSION: A Parent's Guide
0-452-25791-3 NAL pb $8.95

- Donald McKnew, Jr. & others
WHY ISN'T JOHNNY CRYING: Coping with Depression in Children
0-393-01724-9 Norton $15.50
0-393-30240-7 Norton pb $4.95

- Demitri & Janice Papolos
OVERCOMING DEPRESSION
0-06-015756-9 Harper & Row $18.95

- Maggie Scarf
UNFINISHED BUSINESS
An interesting analysis of the causes of depression in women
0-345-34248-8 Ballantine pb $4.95

- Melvin Belli & Mel Krantzler
DIVORCING
Advice from the well-known divorce lawyer
0-312-01760-X St. Martin's $22.95

- Richard Gardner
THE PARENTS' BOOK ABOUT DIVORCE
0-553-26600-4 Bantam pb $4.95

- Norma Harwood
A WOMAN'S LEGAL GUIDE TO SEPARATION AND DIVORCE IN ALL 50 STATES
0-684-18146-0 Scribners pb $11.95

- Mel Krantzler
CREATIVE DIVORCE
A discussion of the emotions brought on by a divorce: loneliness, anger, and a sense of failure
0-451-15444-4 NAL pb $4.95

- Catherine Napolitane & Victoria Pelligrino
LIVING AND LOVING AFTER DIVORCE
The importance of relearning independence and the ability to trust
0-451-14988-2 NAL pb $4.95

• Christina Robertson
A WOMAN'S GUIDE TO DIVORCE AND DECISION MAKING: A Supportive Workbook for Women Facing the Process of Divorce
0–671–67009–3 Simon & Schuster pb $11.95

• Harvey Rosenstock & others
JOURNEY THROUGH DIVORCE: Five Stages Toward Recovery
Based on clinical studies and personal experience; the predictable stages of divorce
0–89885–403–2 Human Sciences $19.95

• Elliot Samuelson
THE DIVORCE LAW HANDBOOK: A Comprehensive Guide to Matrimonial Law
Clear information from a matrimonial attorney
0–89885–411–3 Human Sciences pb $16.95

• Diane Vaughan
UNCOUPLING
The patterns that move couples apart, with one person initiating the separation
0–394–75539–1 Random House pb $4.95

• Judith Wallerstein & Sandra Blakeslee
SECOND CHANCES: Men, Women and Children a Decade After Divorce
0–89919–648–9 Ticknor & Fields $19.95

• Judith Wallerstein & Joan Kelly
SURVIVING THE BREAKUP: How Children and Parents Cope with Divorce
0–465–08339–0 Harper & Row pb $11.95

• Robert Weiss
MARITAL SEPARATION: Managing After a Marriage Ends
How to contend with the end of a marriage and the difficult transition to single life
0–465–09723–5 Harper & Row pb $11.95

RAPE

▶ **See also Women's Studies**

• Pauline Bart & Patricia O'Brien
STOPPING RAPE: Successful Survival Strategies
0–08–032814–8 Pergamon $29.50
0–08–032813–X Pergamon pb $12.95

• Helen Benedict
RECOVERY: How to Survive Sexual Assault for Women, Men, Teenagers, Their Friends and Families
0–385–19206–1 Doubleday $15.95

• Dianna Booher
RAPE: What Would You Do If . . . ?
0–671–49485–6 Julian Messner pb $4.95

• Rachel Gross & Others
SURVIVING SEXUAL ASSAULT
A comprehensive guide for rape victims, their friends, and families. Includes advice on prevention, how to care for the victim after the assault, and a listing of national crisis centers
Foreword by Patty Duke Astin
0–86553–093–9 Congdon & Weed pb $4.95

• Kathryn Johnson
IF YOU ARE RAPED: What Every Woman Needs to Know
Written for victims and counselors, with a focus on recovery
0–918452–72–4 Learning pb $12.95

• Linda Ledray
RECOVERING FROM RAPE
0–03–064002–4 Henry Holt $16.95
0–03–064001–6 Henry Holt pb $9.95

• Alan McEvoy & Jeff Brookings
IF SHE IS RAPED: A Book for Husbands, Fathers, and Male Friends
Includes case studies and community service
0–918452–71–6 Learning Pub pb $11.95

• Cheryl Reimold
THE WOMAN'S GUIDE TO STAYING SAFE
0–671–55620–7 Simon & Schuster pb $6.95

• William Sanders
RAPE AND WOMAN'S IDENTITY
0–8039–1449–0 Sage $35.00
0–8039–1450–4 Sage pb $12.50

David Finkelhor & Kersti Yllo
LICENSE TO RAPE: Sexual Abuse of Wives
An examination of the history and theory of rape in marriage, with testimony from victims
0–02–910401–7 Free Press pb $9.95

Diana Russell
RAPE IN MARRIAGE
Introduction by Susan Brownmiller
0–02–606190–2 Macmillan $16.95
0–02–096370–X Macmillan pb $8.95

Investing, Taxes, and Business Advice

▶ **See also Business, Industry, and Finance**

INVESTMENT ADVICE

• Janet Bamford & others
COMPLETE GUIDE TO MANAGING YOUR MONEY
Advice on investments, banking, taxes, insurance, budgeting, and other aspects of finance
0–89043–205–8 Consumer Reports $30.00
0–89043–069–1 Consumer Reports pb $20.00

• Richard Band
CONTRARY INVESTING: The Insider's Guide to Buying Low and Selling High
0–07–003604–7 McGraw-Hill $16.95
0–14–008862–8 Penguin pb $7.95

• Helen Breunig
NEST EGG INVESTING: How to Build a Secure Financial Foundation
The TV talk show host writes in simple terms about financial alternatives
0–87094–773–7 Dow Jones-Irwin $19.95

• Consumer Guide
ONE HUNDRED BEST-RATED STOCKS
An alphabetical guide with history, ratings, and future projections
0–451–15174–7 NAL pb $3.50

• Madelon DeVoe Talley
THE PASSIONATE INVESTORS: Winning on Wall Street Year After Year in Every Kind of Market
0–517–56563–3 Crown $18.95

• John Downes & Jordan Goodman
BARRON'S FINANCE AND INVESTMENT HANDBOOK
A dictionary of tax laws, mutual funds, investment newsletters, financial institutions, and analyses of investment alternatives
0–8120–5729–5 Barron's $21.95

• Nancy Dunnan
DUN AND BRADSTREET'S GUIDE TO YOUR INVESTMENT DOLLAR
0–06–055109–7 Harper & Row $19.95
0–06–096239–9 Harper & Row pb $10.95

• Harold Gourges
TOTAL FINANCIAL PLANNING: A Guide for Financial Advisors and Serious Investors
0–317–66804–8 Prentice-Hall $27.50

• Sandra Hildreth
THE A TO Z OF WALL STREET: 2500 Terms for the Street-Smart Investor
Dictionary of Wall Street terms, from boiler room to Q-tip trust. For example: a "Goldbug" is an analyst who recommends gold as a haven for investors concerned about possible disaster in the world economy
0–88462–711–X Longman pb $13.95

• Mark Johnson
THE RANDOM WALK AND BEYOND: An Inside Guide to the Stock Market
Filled with complex formulas for calculating stock market risk
0–471–63223–6 Wiley $22.95

• Marshall Loeb
MARSHALL LOEB'S MONEY GUIDE: 1989
Advice on investing, saving, spending, and earning, from the publisher and editor of *Fortune* magazine
0–316–53066–2 Little, Brown $24.95
0–316–53067–0 Little, Brown pb $12.95

• G. Michael & Eva Moebs
PRICING FINANCIAL SERVICES
An explanation of value, competition, and cost-plus analysis for pricing financial services
0–87094–594–7 Dow Jones-Irwin $40.00

• Sylvia Porter
SYLVIA PORTER'S YOUR OWN MONEY
The columnist gives specific advice on a variety of personal business questions:

financing a college education, buying a used car, and filing taxes
0–380–83527–4 Avon $12.95

• **Martin Pring**
HOW TO FORECAST INTEREST RATES: A Guide to Profits for Consumers, Managers, and Investors
Shows how to predict interest rate fluctuations based on the cycles of supply and demand for money
0–07–050865–8 McGraw-Hill $24.95
0–07–050917–4 McGraw-Hill pb $10.95

• **Andrew Rich & Jill Arowesty**
THE EXPERT'S GUIDE TO MANAGING AND MARKETING A SUCCESSFUL FINANCIAL PLANNING PRACTICE
Financial planners' tips on joining their profession
0–13–295155–X Prentice-Hall $50.00

• **David Scott**
EVERY INVESTOR'S GUIDE TO FINANCIAL TERMS
Over 3600 terms in brokerage, options and future trading, investment banking, and other business concerns; along with tips from experts and case histories
0–395–46777–2 Houghton Mifflin pb $9.95

• **Andrew Tobias**
THE ONLY OTHER INVESTMENT GUIDE YOU'LL EVER NEED
0–671–64166–2 Simon & Schuster $17.95
0–553–27705–7 Bantam pb $4.95

• **John Tracy**
HOW TO READ A FINANCIAL REPORT: Wringing Cash Flow and Other Vital Signs Out of the Numbers
This clear and concise book explains the basics of cash flow analysis and how to use financial ratios to evaluate a company's performance
0–471–88859–1 Wiley $24.95
0–471–83446–7 Wiley pb $9.95

• **John Train**
THE MONEY MASTERS: Nine Great Investors—Their Winning Strategies and How You Can Apply Them
0–06–091405–X Harper & Row pb $8.95
PRESERVING CAPITAL AND MAKING IT GROW
0–14–007215–2 Penguin pb $8.95

Commodities and Futures Trading

• **George Angell**
WINNING IN THE FUTURES MARKET
The Chicago floor trader writes about the futures market in simple, step-by-step terms
0–385–19949–X Doubleday $19.95

• **Robert Fink & Robert Feduniak**
FUTURES TRADING: Concepts and Strategies
The techniques for investing in futures, including trading, hedging, speculating, and spreads. Also includes explanations of the markets in cocoa, sugar, coffee, metals, and energy futures
0–318–22785–1 NY Finance $35.00

• **Anthony Herbst**
COMMODITIES FUTURES: Markets, Methods of Analysis, and Management of Risk
0–471–09769–1 Wiley $39.95

Gold

• **Robert Beale**
TRADING IN GOLD FUTURES
0–89397–219–3 Nichols $28.50

• **Timothy Green**
THE PROSPECT FOR GOLD
A short but comprehensive look at the history of the precious metal: its discovery, its use, its role in the global economy, and its value as an investment in the current market
0–8027–1002–6 Walker $29.95

• **Jeffrey Nichols**
THE COMPLETE BOOK OF GOLD INVESTING
0–87094–755–9 Dow Jones-Irwin $30.00

Options

• **George Angell**
AGRICULTURAL OPTIONS: Trading Puts and Calls in the New Grain and Livestock Futures Market
One of the first books to be written on the new, speculative options
0–8144–5822–X AMACOM $21.95

• **Jeffrey Little & Lucien Rhodes**
STOCK OPTIONS
1–55546–628–1 Chelsea House $9.95
0–89709–009–8 TAB pb $2.95

• **Courtney Smith**
OPTIONS STRATEGIES: Using Stock Index, Stock, and Commodity Options
0–471–84367–9 Wiley $24.95

• **James Yates**
THE OPTIONS STRATEGY SPECTRUM
0–87094–961–6 Dow Jones-Irwin $35.00

Mutual Funds and Money Market Funds

• **American Association of Individual Investors**
INDIVIDUAL INVESTOR'S GUIDE TO NO-LOAD MUTUAL FUNDS
0–942641–05–1 International Pub pb $19.95

• **William Donoghue**
DONOGHUE'S MUTUAL FUNDS ALMANAC
0–06–096246–1 Harper & Row pb $19.95

• **William Donoghue & Thomas Tilling**
WILLIAM DONOGHUE'S NO-LOAD MUTUAL FUND GUIDE: How to Take Advantage of the Investment Opportunity of the '80s
0–06–015096–3 Harper & Row $13.95
0–553–26068–5 Bantam pb $4.50

• **Richard Dorf**
THE NEW MUTUAL FUND INVESTMENT ADVISOR: A Guide for the Serious Investor
0–917253–13–2 Probus $22.50
0–917253–19–1 Probus pb $17.95

• **Werner Renberg & Jeremiah Blitzer**
MAKING MONEY WITH MUTUAL FUNDS: Investment Strategies to Beat the Market
0–471–85555–3 Wiley $19.95

• **Donald Rugg**
THE DOW JONES-IRWIN GUIDE TO MUTUAL FUNDS
0–87094–756–7 Dow Jones-Irwin $25.00

• **Bernard Seligman**
MONEY MARKET FUNDS
0–275–91728–2 Praeger $29.95

Bonds

• **Edward Altman & Scott Nammacher**
INVESTMENT IN JUNK BONDS: Inside the High-Yield Debt Market
An explanation in simple terms
0–471–84886–7 Wiley $24.95

• **David Darst**
THE COMPLETE BOND BOOK: A Guide to All Types of Fixed-Income Securities
The technical aspects of bonds, from government and corporate to tax-exempt
0–07–017390–7 McGraw-Hill $44.95

• **Sylvan Feldstein & Frank Fabozzi**
THE DOW JONES-IRWIN GUIDE TO MUNICIPAL BONDS
Discusses risk, maturities, and return, and includes information on the 1986 Tax Reform Act
0–87094–542–4 Dow Jones-Irwin $29.95

• **Jane Howe**
JUNK BONDS: Analysis and Portfolio Strategies
0–917253–72–8 Probus $29.50

IRAs

• **Peter Heerwagen**
SELF-DIRECTED IRAS FOR THE ACTIVE INVESTOR: Taking Charge of Building Your Nest Egg
0–917253–32–9 Probus $17.95

Foreign Markets

• **A.K. Chrystal & Robert Sedgwick, editors**
EXCHANGE RATES AND THE OPEN ECONOMY
0–312–01583–6 St. Martin's $39.95

• **Anthony Rowley**
ASIAN STOCK MARKETS: The Inside Story
A history and current risk assessment of the markets in Japan, South Korea, Taiwan, Hong Kong, Singapore, Thailand, and India
0–87094–987–X Dow Jones-Irwin $35.00

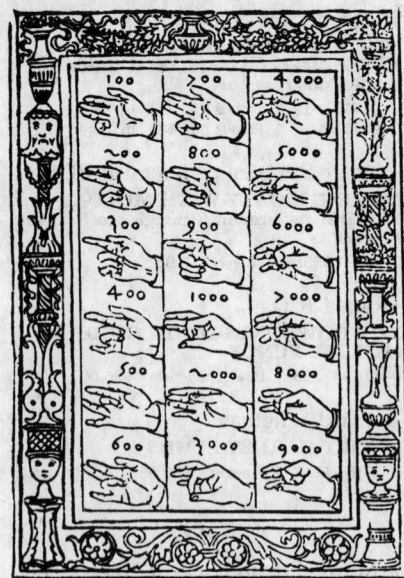

Auction hand signals from the first illustrated arithmetic, in Prints and People *by A. Hyatt Mayor (Princeton)*

- Paul Smith
  COMPARATIVE FINANCIAL SYSTEMS
  0–275–90905–0 Praeger $31.95

- Aron Viner
  THE EMERGING POWER OF JAPANESE MONEY
  1–55623–071–0 Dow Jones-Irwin $22.50

  INSIDE JAPANESE FINANCIAL MARKETS
  1–55623–020–6 Dow Jones-Irwin $39.95

TAX PREPARATION

- H&R Block Staff
  H&R BLOCK INCOME TAX GUIDE AND WORKBOOK, 1989
  0–02–041711–X Macmillan pb $8.95

- Andrew Ciaramataro
  BEAT THE IRS (LEGALLY)
  0–425–10777–9 Berkley pb $6.95

- Warren Esanu & others
  CONSUMER REPORTS GUIDE TO INCOME TAX PREPARATION 1989
  0–89043–252–X Consumer Reports pb $9.95

- Sandor Frankel & Robert Fink
  HOW TO DEFEND YOURSELF AGAINST THE IRS
  The government's right to audit taxpayers, and ways for taxpayers to shield themselves
  0–671–55513–8 Simon & Schuster $16.95
  0–671–63509–3 Simon & Schuster pb $8.95

- J.K. Lasser
  J.K. LASSER'S YOUR INCOME TAX, 1989
  0–13–510751–2 Prentice-Hall pb $10.95

- Price Waterhouse Staff
  THE PRICE WATERHOUSE PERSONAL TAX ADVISOR
  0–553–27203–9 Bantam pb $3.95

- Michael Savage
  GOOD NEWS, BAD NEWS
  0–89480–294–1 Workman pb $4.95

- Jeff Schnepper
  HOW TO PAY ZERO TAXES: 1989
  Deductions, shelters, investments, and other strategies
  0–201–07778–7 Addison-Wesley pb $9.95

- Robert Schriebman
  PROTECTING YOUR BUSINESS FROM THE IRS
  How the IRS and the tax code work, and how to work with them, in straightforward language
  0–87094–905–5 Dow Jones-Irwin $27.50

- Arthur Young Staff
  THE ARTHUR YOUNG TAX GUIDE 1989
  0–345–35678–0 Ballantine pb $10.95

BUSINESS ADVICE

Entrepreneurship

- Ray Bard & Sheila Henderson
  OWN YOUR OWN FRANCHISE: Everything You Need to Know about the 160 Best Opportunities in America
  A well-organized guide
  0–201–11439–9 Addison-Wesley $14.95

- Arnold Goldstein
  STARTING YOUR SUBCHAPTER "S" CORPORATION: How to Build a Business the Right Way
  A technical and legal guide, with examples
  0–471–60602–2 Wiley pb $14.95

From Taming the Paper Tiger *by Barbara Hemphill, illustrated by Sasha Georgevitch (Dodd, Mead)*

- Mortimer Levitt
  HOW TO START YOUR OWN BUSINESS WITHOUT LOSING YOUR SHIRT: Secrets of the Artful Entrepreneur
  Pragmatic instructions from the founder of the Custom Shirt Shops
  0–689–11950–5 Atheneum $16.95

- Judith McQuown
  INCORPORATE YOURSELF: How to Profit by Setting Up Your Own Corporation
  0–02–583750–8 Macmillan $18.95

Venture Capital

- David Gladstone
  VENTURE CAPITAL INVESTING: The Complete Handbook for Investing in Small Private Businesses for Outstanding Profits
  0–13–941428–2 Prentice-Hall $39.95

- Clinton Richardson
  THE VENTURE MAGAZINE COMPLETE GUIDE TO VENTURE CAPITAL
  0–452–25918–5 NAL pb $12.95

REAL ESTATE

▶ See also The Home

- Frank Cappiello & Karel McClellan
  FROM MAIN STREET TO WALL STREET: Making Money in Real Estate
  The strength of this book lies in its model portfolios, which illustrate real estate strategies
  0–471–60067–9 Wiley $19.95

- Daniel De Benedictis
  THE COMPLETE REAL ESTATE ADVISOR
  Written by a real estate lawyer, this excellent step-by-step guide contains savvy warnings to both buyer and seller
  0–671–62203–X Pocket pb $4.50

- Joseph Howell
  REAL ESTATE DEVELOPMENT SYNDICATION
  0–275–91010–5 Praeger $29.95
  0–275–91774–6 Praeger pb $14.95

- Carol Janek & Ruth Rejnis
  ALL AMERICA'S REAL ESTATE BOOK: An Extraordinary Guide for Ordinary People
  0–670–80510–6 Viking $29.95
  0–14–009416–4 Penguin pb $14.95

- Marvin Levin & Barbara Nichols
  HOW TO PROFIT ON THE REAL ESTATE ROLLER COASTER: An Investor's Guide to Avoiding Big Mistakes
  0–13–766320–X Prentice-Hall $17.95
  0–13–364936–9 Prentice-Hall pb $9.95

- Hollis Norton
  THE NEW REAL ESTATE GAME: Building Wealth Under the New Tax Laws
  0–8092–4577–9 Contemporary pb $8.95

- John Scavuzzo
  THE REAL ESTATE IRA
  0–396–08913–5 Dodd, Mead $19.95

- Martin Shenkman
  REAL ESTATE AFTER TAX REFORM: A Guide for Investors
  The effect of new laws on minimum taxes, limits on deductibility of passive losses, and itemized deductions
  0–471–85984–2 Wiley $19.95

- Eric Stevenson
  FINANCING INCOME-PRODUCING REAL ESTATE
  Concise outline format. Sponsored by the Mortgage Bankers Association of America
  0–07–061311–7 McGraw-Hill $49.95

➤ **FOR OVERSEAS ORDERING INFORMATION, SEE PAGE 1**

Buying a Home

● Robert Irwin
MAKING MORTGAGES WORK FOR YOU
Especially useful mortgage payment tables, classified for income, interest rates, and price
0–07–032129–9 McGraw-Hill $21.50

● Garth Marston & Hugh Kelleher
CREATIVE REAL ESTATE FINANCING: A Guide to Buying and Selling Homes in the 1980s
0–471–86678–4 Wiley $19.95

Careers

CAREER OPPORTUNITIES

● Dorothy Bestor
ASIDE FROM TEACHING, WHAT IN THE WORLD CAN YOU DO?: Career Strategies for Liberal Arts Graduates
Descriptions of fields from publishing to business and government, including a section for women
0–295–95903–7 Washington pb $10.95

● Steve Cohen & Paulo de Oliveira
GETTING TO THE RIGHT JOB
How to find a job to match one's interests, as well as advice on interviews and resumés and suggested salaries for entry-level positions
0–89480–040–X Workman pb $6.95

● Elizabeth Fowler
THE NEW YORK TIMES CAREER PLANNER: A Guide to Choosing the Perfect Job from the 101 Best Career Opportunities of Tomorrow
Directed at college graduates: career trends, corporate culture, and jobs in today's market
0–8129–1212–8 Times Books pb $9.95

● Dick Goldberg
CAREERS WITHOUT RESCHOOLING: A Survival Guide to the Job Hunt for Liberal Arts Graduates
Includes sections for returning homemakers and career changers
0–8264–0355–7 Continuum pb $9.95

● Les Krantz
THE JOBS RATED ALMANAC
250 jobs organized by income, job security, and future potential
0–886–8730–X Pharos pb $14.95

● Martha Leape & Susan Vacca
THE HARVARD GUIDE TO CAREERS
Introductions to various careers, trade associations, and sources for the job-hunter or the new graduate
0–674–37564–5 Harvard pb $8.95

● Robert Levering & others
THE ONE HUNDRED BEST COMPANIES TO WORK FOR IN AMERICA
Concise profiles of employers, with interviews and comments from insiders
0–451–14773–1 NAL pb $4.95

● William Lewis & Nancy Schuman
FAST-TRACK CAREERS: A Guide to the Highest Paying Jobs
Concentrates on careers in finance, advertising, media, real estate, and other high-powered areas
0–471–83801–2 Wiley pb $12.95

● Joseph & Amy Lombardo
THE JOB BELT: The 50 Best Places in America for High Quality Employment
0–14–008420–7 Penguin pb $10.95

● Al Sacharov
OFFBEAT CAREERS: The Directory of Unusual Work
Unusual jobs with useful and accurate information on obtaining them. Foreign Service Officer precedes Game Show Contestant in the alphabetical listings
089–815–240–2 Ten Speed pb $6.95

● Robert & Anne Snelling
JOBS: What They Are . . . Where They Are . . . What They Pay
0–671–66335–6 Simon & Schuster pb $11.95

● John Wright
THE AMERICAN ALMANAC OF JOBS AND SALARIES
A fact-filled almanac that includes standard jobs, as well as those in government, the arts, the sciences, and health care
0–380–75307–3 Avon pb $12.95

JOB SUCCESS

● Nancy Anderson
WORK WITH PASSION: How to Do What You Love for a Living
Advice on attaining career goals, with examples
0–88184–099–8 Carroll & Graf $15.95
0–88184–212–5 Carroll & Graf pb $8.95

● Sonya Hamlin
HOW TO TALK SO PEOPLE LISTEN: The Real Key to Job Success
0–06–0915373–0 Harper & Row pb $7.95

● Barbara Hemphill
TAMING THE PAPER TIGER: Organizing the Paper in Your Life
"A must read for anyone who spends more than five minutes a day shuffling paper"— Kenneth Blanchard
0–396–09198–9 Dodd, Mead pb $9.95

● Lester Korn
THE SUCCESS PROFILE: A Leading Headhunter Tells You How to Get to the Top
"Korn can tell you what big companies want when they look for high-level talent"—*Washington Post*
0–671–55263–5 Simon & Schuster $17.95

● Beverly Potter
MAVERICK CAREER STRATEGIES
Different ideas about career success and the corporate world
0–8144–7657–0 AMACOM pb $8.95

GETTING A JOB

● Patricia Birsner
JOB HUNTING FOR THE 40-PLUS EXECUTIVE
Specifically directed to managers and executives over 40 who have lost their jobs. Job searches, resumés, strategies, and moral encouragement for getting back into the job market
0–87196–634–4 Facts On File $19.95

● Tom Jackson
HOW TO GET THE JOB YOU WANT IN 28 DAYS
A plan for setting career goals, writing resumés, being interviewed, and making useful connections
0–8015–9202–X Dutton pb $12.95

GUERRILLA TACTICS IN THE JOB MARKET
Specific tactics for getting jobs, including interesting case histories
0–553–25777–3 Bantam pb $4.50

● Richard Lathrop
WHO'S HIRING WHO
Extensive practical advice on resumés, interviews, and job searches
0–913668–55–9 Ten Speed pb $7.95

● Kathryn & Ross Petras
THE ONLY JOB-HUNTING GUIDE YOU'LL EVER NEED
A step-by-step approach for job hunters and career switchers
0–671–67842–6 Simon & Schuster $21.95
0–671–63648–0 Simon & Schuster pb $8.95

Resumés

● Juvenal Angel
THE COMPLETE RESUME BOOK AND JOB GETTER'S GUIDE
Four hundred sample resumés for a variety of jobs
0–671–54638–4 Pocket pb $8.95

● Harold Dickhut
THE PROFESSIONAL RESUME AND JOB SEARCH GUIDE
Aimed at executives and managers; with a good list of national executive search firms
0–13–725705–8 Prentice-Hall pb $8.95

● Marian Faux
THE COMPLETE RESUME GUIDE
Two hundred job categories with sample resumés; includes sections for those over 40 and for the handicapped
0–671–18393–1 Monarch pb $6.95

Interviews

● Jeffrey Allen
HOW TO TURN AN INTERVIEW INTO A JOB
0–671–62134–3 Simon & Schuster pb $6.95

● Richard Beatty
THE FIVE-MINUTE INTERVIEW
Based on the theory that the first five minutes of an interview are the most crucial; sample questions and practice exercises
0–471–85889–7 John Wiley $19.95
0–471–84034–3 John Wiley pb $10.95

● Jack Biegeleisen
MAKE YOUR JOB INTERVIEW A SUCCESS: A Guide for the Career-Minded Job Seeker
Includes cardinal rules for interviews (such as punctuality), ways to muff an interview, and good advice for writing resumés and sample questions
0–13–545716–5 Arco pb $8.95

● John Marcus
THE COMPLETE JOB INTERVIEW HANDBOOK
Ways to obtain an interview, commonly asked questions and replies, suggestions for negotiating salaries
0–06–463727–1 Harper & Row pb $6.95

● Anthony Medley
SWEATY PALMS: The Neglected Art of Being Interviewed
A well-organized guide with cartoons
0–89815–139–2 Ten Speed pb $8.95

CAREER CHANGE

● Richard Bolles
WHAT COLOR IS YOUR PARACHUTE?
The classic work on job hunting and career change. Witty, with unusual graphics and amusing exercises for evaluating one's life and goals
0–89815–228–3 Ten Speed pb $8.95

● Juliet Brudney & Hilda Scott
FORCED OUT: What Veteran Employees Can Do When Driven from Their Careers
How to fight back, employment alternatives, and interviews with survivors
0–671–64422–X Simon & Schuster $16.95
0–671–64411–4 Simon & Schuster pb $7.95

● John Crystal & Richard Bolles
WHERE DO I GO FROM HERE WITH MY LIFE?
An intelligent book in an unusual design to help in making career decisions
0–89815–084–1 Ten Speed pb $9.95

● Howard Freedman
HOW TO GET A HEADHUNTER TO CALL
Advice for executives and managers
0–471–82844–0 John Wiley $19.95

● Gene Hawes
THE CAREER CHANGER'S SOURCEBOOK
Descriptions and entry requirements for jobs in the arts, medicine, business, sales, and other fields
0–87196–688–3 Facts On File $19.95
0–87196–793–6 Facts On File pb $10.95

● Bonnie Rubin
TIME OUT: How to Take a Year Off Without Jeopardizing Your Job, Your Family, or Your Bank Account
When to leave, and how to negotiate with the employer; includes a useful list of foundations and grants
0–393–02393–1 Norton $18.95
0–393–30510–4 Norton pb $12.95

● Kate Wendleton
THE FIVE O'CLOCK CLUB GUIDE TO CHANGING JOBS
A well-organized guide offering advice on using search firms and negotiating salaries
0–944054–05–6 Five O'Clock pb $14.95

CAREERS FOR WOMEN

● Mindy Bingham & Sandy Stryker
MORE CHOICES: A Strategic Planning Guide for Mixing Career and Family
Questionnaires to help women decide whether or how to mix a career with raising a family
0–911655–28–X Ingram pb $15.95

● Jill Fraser
THE BEST U.S. CITIES FOR WORKING WOMEN
Describes over 50 cities according to employment opportunities and lifestyles for women. Includes local lists of networking organizations
0–452–25813–8 NAL pb $9.95

● Joan Goldberg
HIGH-TECH CAREER STRATEGIES FOR WOMEN
Opportunities for women in such fields as engineering, systems analysis, and technical writing
0–02–544460–3 Macmillan $15.95

● Maureen Hanigan
SECRETS OF SUCCESSFUL SPEAKING
Emphasizes the importance of public speaking for the career woman. With useful exercises
0–02–012420–1 Macmillan pb $5.95

● Natasha Josefowitz
PATHS TO POWER: A Working Woman's Guide from First Job to Top Executive
For the managerial woman, specific problems women face in the corporate world
0–201–03486–7 Addison-Wesley pb $9.95

● Janice LaRouche & Regina Ryan
JANICE LAROUCHE'S STRATEGIES FOR WOMEN AT WORK
Women and the corporation
0–380–86744–3 Avon pb $8.95

● Nancy Lee
TARGETING THE TOP
Lucid advice on how women can achieve success in business. A good reference source
0–345–29643–5 Ballantine pb $2.95

● William Lewis & Nancy Schuman
BACK TO WORK: A Career Guide for the Returnee
Covers resumés, interviews, temporary work, and the automated office
0–8120–2703–5 Barron's pb $8.95

● Donald Lussier
THE HOMEMAKER'S COMPLETE GUIDE TO ENTERING THE JOB MARKET
A simple, practical guide
0–13–392910–8 Prentice-Hall $14.95
0–13–392902–7 Prentice-Hall pb $6.95

● Beatryce Nivens
THE BLACK WOMAN'S CAREER GUIDE
Job descriptions, salaries, current trends, and the qualifications and training required for over 50 career fields. Also included are profiles of successful black women, resumé and interview tips, and a reference list of support organizations
0–385–24160–7 Doubleday $24.95
0–385–24161–5 Doubleday pb $12.95

● Terry Ward
SMART WOMEN AT WORK: Twelve Steps to Career Breakthroughs
A challenge to the myths about women in the workplace, and specific strategies for success
0–8092–4681–3 Contemporary $15.95

● Joanne Wilkins
HER OWN BUSINESS: Success Secrets of Women Entrepreneurs
Research into what makes a successful woman, organized by case histories. Includes extensive resource lists for professional networking
0–07–050854–2 McGraw-Hill $16.95

● Baila Zeitz & Lorraine Dusky
THE BEST COMPANIES FOR WOMEN
Profiles of over 50 major US corporations, including insider opinions
0–671–60741–3 Simon & Schuster $19.95

Patricia McConnel
WOMEN'S WORK-AT-HOME HANDBOOK: Income and Independence
Ideas for working at home with a computer, setting up a business, and combining work and family life
0–553–34324–6 Bantam pb $9.95

Jeanette Scollard
THE SELF-EMPLOYED WOMAN: How to Start Your Own Business and Gain Control of Your Life
Discusses financing, partnerships, computers—all the aspects of running a small business
0–671–50084–8 Simon & Schuster $17.95

Demaris Smith
TEMPORARY EMPLOYMENT: The Flexible Alternative
For women reentering the job market, strategies for finding part-time work
0–932620–56–6 Betterway pb $9.95

BUSINESS CAREERS

• Lisa Birnbach
GOING TO WORK: A Unique Guided Tour Through Corporate America
0–394–75874–9 Random House pb $15.95

• James Clawson & David Ward
AN MBA'S GUIDE TO SELF-ASSESSMENT AND CAREER DEVELOPMENT
Sound information on jobs in different industries open to MBAs
0–13–566811–5 Prentice-Hall pb $15.95

• Jo Frohbieter-Mueller
STAY HOME AND MIND YOUR OWN BUSINESS: How to Manage Your Time, Space, Personal Obligations, Money, Business, and Yourself While Working at Home
0–932620–83–3 Betterway pb $9.95

• Betty Harragan
GAMES MOTHER NEVER TAUGHT YOU: Corporate Gamesmanship for Women
A common sense advice book for women just starting out in the corporate world
0–446–34400–1 Warner pb $4.95

• Bob Hisrich & Eugene Bronstein
THE MBA CAREER
How to choose the right job, with sample resumés, tips on interviewing, and job campaign tactics
0–8120–2485–0 Barron's pb $9.95

• Harvey Mackay
SWIM WITH THE SHARKS WITHOUT BEING EATEN ALIVE: Outsell, Outmanage, Outmotivate and Outnegotiate Your Competition
0–688–07473–1 Morrow $14.95

• Martin Salzman
WANTED: Liberal Arts Graduates
Lists company names, phone numbers, and addresses, with short descriptions of corporate culture
0–385–24008–2 Doubleday pb $9.95

• Stephen Stumpf & Celeste Rodgers
CHOOSING A CAREER IN BUSINESS
Methodical descriptions, from banking to accounting, sales, systems analysis, and securities consulting
0–671–53063–1 Simon & Schuster pb $8.95

• Ron Tepper
BECOME A TOP CONSULTANT: How the Experts Do It
How to determine the market, build a business, and set fees. Includes case histories
0–471–81706–6 John Wiley $19.95
0–471–85938–9 John Wiley pb $12.95

SECRETARIAL JOBS

• Diana Booher
THE NEW SECRETARY: How to Handle People As Well As You Handle Paper
0–8160–1160–5 Facts On File $21.95

• Mary De Vries
SECRETARY'S ALMANAC AND FACT BOOK
0–13–798307–7 Prentice-Hall $21.95

• Lillian Doris & Bessemoy Miller
COMPLETE SECRETARY'S HANDBOOK
0–13–163321–X Prentice-Hall $29.95

• Nicholas Mintzer
THE UNOFFICIAL SECRETARY'S HANDBOOK
A humorous book with chapters such as "20 Reasons to Call in Sick"
0–452–26156–2 NAL pb $6.95

• Jodie Morrow & Myrna Lebov
NOT JUST A SECRETARY: Using the Job to Get Ahead
Strategies for making a successful career as a secretary, especially in the high-tech, automated office of the future
0–471–87060–9 John Wiley pb $9.95

• Linda Morrow
THE SECRETARY'S BOOK OF HOPE
Practical strategies for a successful, satisfying career as a secretary
0–07–043200–7 McGraw-Hill $15.95

• Sarah Taintor & Kate Monro
THE SECRETARY'S HANDBOOK
0–02–610211–0 Macmillan $19.95

ADVERTISING

• Ed Caffrey, editor
SO YOU WANT TO BE IN ADVERTISING
Snappy prose offering useful information on advertising, from school courses to agency work
0–671–64590–0 Simon & Schuster pb $8.95

• Toron Douglas
THE COMPLETE GUIDE TO ADVERTISING
A good reference work
0–89009–784–4 Chartwell $15.95

• Jan Greenberg
ADVERTISING CAREERS: How Advertising Works and the People Who Make It Happen
Simple and direct, focusing on the types of agencies and how they are structured, how ads are created, and what it's like to work in the business
0–8050–0379–7 Henry Holt $17.95

• Judith Katz
THE AD GAME
Types of agencies, job descriptions, and profiles of people in the business
0–06–463576–7 Harper & Row pb $7.95

• David Laskin
GETTING INTO ADVERTISING
Informative, humorous, and anecdotal. Describes the industry through interviews with ad executives and includes lists of agencies with their major clients, headhunters, and professional associations
0–345–32598–2 Ballantine pb $8.95

• David Malickson & John Nason
ADVERTISING: How to Write the Kind That Works
Market research, planning a campaign, and copywriting
0–684–17632–7 Scribners pb $9.95

• David Ogilvy
CONFESSIONS OF AN ADVERTISING MAN
Words of wisdom from an industry legend; all aspects of the field from personal experience
0–689–70601–4 Atheneum pb $7.95

OGILVY ON ADVERTISING
Advice for beginners as well as experts
0–394–72903–X Random House pb $14.95

• Hank Seiden
ADVERTISING PURE AND SIMPLE
A classic: simply written and full of information, with discussions of famous ad campaigns
0–8144–7510–8 AMACOM pb $9.95

PUBLIC RELATIONS

• Paula Cohen
A PUBLIC RELATIONS PRIMER: Thinking and Writing in Context
0–13–738709–1 Prentice-Hall $22.00

• Ronald Fry, editor
PUBLIC RELATIONS CAREER DIRECTORY
Advice from the career experts, including entry-level job listings, internships, and training programs
0–934829–33–0 Career pb $26.95

• Herbert Schmertz & William Novak
GOODBYE TO THE LOW PROFILE: The Art of Creative Confrontation
The public relations executive for Mobil who inaugurated corporate sponsorship of the arts
0–316–77366–2 Little, Brown $16.95

• Robert J. Wood with Max Gunther
CONFESSIONS OF A PR MAN
Amusing and instructive anecdotes from a prominent public relations executive. "Must reading for anyone who wants to know how public relations really works and the impact it can have on American life"—Myron Kandel
0–453–00596–9 NAL $18.95

SALES

● Ron Fry, editor
MARKETING AND SALES CAREER DIRECTORY
Major company listings, with descriptions of agencies and kinds of jobs available
0–934829–34–9 Career pb $26.95

● Joe Girard & Stanley Brown
HOW TO SELL ANYTHING TO ANYBODY
Personal tips: brash, but interesting
0–446–35543–5 Warner pb $4.95

● Tom Hopkins
HOW TO MASTER THE ART OF SELLING
Best-seller by a millionaire salesman on everything from phone techniques to "power closes"
0–446–38063–6 Warner pb $8.95

● Chuck Lewis
YOU'RE GONNA LOVE IT
Witty, fast-paced observations on a career in sales
0–89815–138–4 Ten Speed pb $7.95

● Cheryl Merser & Markita Andrews
HOW TO SELL MORE COOKIES, CONDOS, CADILLACS, COMPUTERS . . . AND EVERYTHING ELSE
0–394–74307–5 Random House pb $5.95

WRITING AS A CAREER

● Leonard Bernstein
GETTING PUBLISHED: The Writer in the Combat Zone
0–688–06913–4 Morrow $14.95
0–688–06423–X Morrow pb $6.95

● Robert Bly
SECRETS OF A FREELANCE WRITER: How to Make $85,000 a Year
Advice for the serious freelance writer on how to set rates and market one's services; covers opportunities in public relations, direct mail, and advertising
0–396–09004–4 Dodd, Mead $18.95
0–396–09023–0 Dodd, Mead pb $9.95

● Sylvia Burack
THE WRITER'S HANDBOOK
A thorough, informative book on the different genres, from biographies to romance novels; with advice from prominent contemporary writers
0–87116–151–6 Writer $27.50

● Richard Curtis
HOW TO BE YOUR OWN LITERARY AGENT: The Business of Getting Your Book Published
Advice from a successful agent on negotiation and other business aspects of the literary world
0–395–36142–7 Houghton Mifflin pb $8.95

● Diane Gage & Marcia Coppess
GET PUBLISHED: Top Magazine Editors Tell You How
0–03–071836–8 Henry Holt $24.95
0–89586–639–0 Price Stern Sloan pb $12.95

● Dennis Hensley & Holly Miller
THE FREELANCE WRITER'S HANDBOOK: How to Succeed in a Competitive Business
0–06–055096–1 Harper & Row $15.95
0–06–096203–8 Harper & Row pb $6.95

● Jean Kent & Candace Shelton
THE ROMANCE WRITER'S PHRASE BOOK
Handy phrases organized by emotions, sex, parts of the body, physical characteristics, and more
0–399–51002–8 Putnam pb $7.95

● Scott Meredith
WRITING TO SELL
The classic guide by a prominent literary agent; covers markets, types of writing, and how to earn a living as a writer
0–06–015637–6 Harper & Row $15.95

● Glenda Neff, editor
WRITER'S MARKET '89: Where and How to Sell What You Write
An extremely useful reference
0–89879–330–0 Writer's Digest $22.95

● Kirk Polking
THE WRITER'S ENCYCLOPEDIA
A dictionary of literary terms, with sections on book contracts, copyrights, and other writing business
0–89879–265–7 Writer's Digest $16.95

PUBLISHING

● Marvin Arth & Helen Ashmore
THE NEWSLETTER EDITOR'S DESK BOOK
A well-organized manual, with concrete advice
0–938270–03–6 Parkway pb $11.50

● D.M. Brownstone & I.M. Franck
THE SELF-PUBLISHING HANDBOOK
How to estimate costs, find a printer, market, and distribute a publication
0–452–25685–2 NAL pb $7.95

● Dian Dincin Buchman & Seli Groves
WRITER'S DIGEST GUIDE TO MANUSCRIPT FORMATS
A simple and clear guide for all types of manuscript presentation
0–89879–253–2 Writer's Digest pb $16.95

● Gerald Gross
EDITORS ON EDITING
Advice on editing, from the practical to the theoretical
0–06–015381–4 Harper & Row $22.95
0–06–091120–4 Harper & Row pb $14.95

● Howard Hudson
PUBLISHING NEWSLETTERS
A recommended source, based on the author's experience as a successful newsletter publisher
0–684–17496–0 Scribners $19.95
0–684–18954–2 Scribners pb $12.95

● Marie Longyear, editor
MCGRAW-HILL STYLE MANUAL: Concise Guide for Writers and Editors
How to prepare a manuscript for publication
0–07–038676–5 McGraw-Hill $31.95

● Dan Poytner
THE SELF-PUBLISHING MANUAL
0–915516–87–3 Para $14.95

● Elizabeth Preston & others
PREPARING YOUR MANUSCRIPT
Punctuation, grammar, proofreading, and other important details
0–87116–144–3 Writer pb $8.95

● University of Chicago Press
THE CHICAGO MANUAL OF STYLE
0–226–10390–00 Chicago $37.50

● The Waite Group
THE DESKTOP PUBLISHING BIBLE
From software to graphics and layout
0–672–22524–7 Howard pb $24.95

MISCELLANEOUS JOBS

● Joan Anzalone, editor
GOOD WORKS: A Guide to Careers in Social Change
Job descriptions and interviews with social workers; with an informative national directory of social service agencies
Preface by Ralph Nader
0–934878–55–2 Dembner $25.00
0–934878–56–0 Dembner pb $16.50

● Ragnar Benson
ACTION CAREERS: Employment in the High-Risk Job Market
Describes unusual careers: from bodyguard to explosives handler, missionary, rodeo cowboy, and private eye
0–87364–408–5 Paladin $17.95
0–8065–1079–X Lyle Stuart pb $9.95

● Jane Blanksteen & Avi Odeni
TV: Careers Behind the Screen
Everything from production, writing, and engineering to editing and producing. Gives salary ranges and typical schedules and includes interviews with professionals
0–471–84815–8 John Wiley pb $12.95

● Curtis Casewit
MAKING A LIVING IN THE FINE ARTS: Advice from the Pros
Practical tips for succeeding as a fine artist: how to select an art school, where to market your work, dealing with art directors and dealers, and negotiating

contracts. Includes anecdotes about the careers of famous artists
0–02–522420–4 Macmillan $10.95
0–02–079330–8 Macmillan pb $5.95

• Lishka DeVoss
HOW TO BE A WAITRESS (OR WAITER): Everything You Need to Know to Get the Right Job, Make Good Money, and Stay Sane
Amusing and informative, with details on food, restaurant slang, and drinks
0–312–39537–X St. Martin's pb $7.95

• Shelly Field
CAREER OPPORTUNITIES IN THE MUSIC INDUSTRY
Short descriptions of 80 careers in music, from business management to conducting; includes lists of music publishers, agencies, and record companies
0–8160–1126–5 Facts On File $24.95
0–8160–1535–X Facts On File pb $12.95

• Deborah Hoover
SUPPORTING YOURSELF AS AN ARTIST: A Practical Guide
Sources of support, as well as information for media artists, visual artists, craft artists, poets, playwrights, composers, and choreographers
0–19–503669–7 Oxford $17.95
0–19–504215–8 Oxford pb $7.95

• Terry McAdam
DOING WELL BY DOING GOOD: The First Complete Guide to Careers in the Nonprofit Sector
Introduction by John Naisbitt
0–14–046820–X Penguin pb $6.95

• Melissa Sones
GETTING INTO FASHION: A Career Guide
An attractive and informative book of different jobs in the fashion industry, including interviews with top fashion designers and executives
0–345–30756–9 Ballantine pb $7.95

PUBLIC SPEAKING

• Steve Allen
HOW TO MAKE A SPEECH
0–07–001169–9 McGraw-Hill pb $7.95

• Lassor Blumenthal
THE ART OF ORAL AND WRITTEN PRESENTATIONS
The basic principles of good presentation
0–399–51330–2 Putnam pb $6.95

• Dale Carnegie
HOW TO DEVELOP SELF-CONFIDENCE AND INFLUENCE PEOPLE BY PUBLIC SPEAKING
0–671–64672–9 Pocket pb $4.50

• Charles Osgood
OSGOOD ON SPEAKING
The radio and television journalist gives his tips on effective speaking
0–688–06713–1 Morrow $14.95

• William Parkhurst
THE ELOQUENT EXECUTIVE: A Guide to High-Impact Speaking in Big Meetings, Small Meetings, and One-on-One
0–8129–1280–2 Times Books $14.95

• Dorothy Sarnoff & Gaylen Moore
NEVER BE NERVOUS AGAIN
Well-known specialist offers specific suggestions on all aspects of speaking in public and business life
0–517–56709–1 Crown $16.95

• Elayne Snyder
MACMILLAN'S 1001 PERFECT ANECDOTES AND QUOTES FOR THE PUBLIC SPEAKER
0–02–612260–X Macmillan $19.95
0–02–082010–0 Macmillan pb $9.95

• Jo Sprague & Douglas Stuart
THE SPEAKER'S HANDBOOK
0–15–583177–1 HBJ $13.95

Reference

ONE-VOLUME ENCYCLOPEDIAS

• Barron's
BARRON'S STUDENT'S CONCISE ENCYCLOPEDIA
0–8120–5937–9 Barron's $19.95

Columbia University Press
THE NEW COLUMBIA ENCYCLOPEDIA
0–231–03977–8 Columbia pb $135.00
THE CONCISE COLUMBIA ENCYCLOPEDIA
0–231–05678–8 Columbia $29.95
0–380–63396–5 Avon pb $14.95

• Random House
THE RANDOM HOUSE ENCYCLOPEDIA
Divided into 25,000 alphabetical listings and 11,000 color illustrations, arranged under The Earth, Life on Earth, Man, History and Culture, Man and Science, Man and Machines
0–394–40730–X Random House $79.95

GENERAL INFORMATION

Biographical Dictionaries

• Alan Bullock & R.B. Wooding, editors
20TH-CENTURY CULTURE: A Biographical Companion
0–06–015248–6 Harper & Row pb $34.50

• Cambridge University Press
CHAMBERS BIOGRAPHICAL DICTIONARY
0–550–18013–3 Cambridge $29.95

• Harper & Row
ENCYCLOPEDIA OF AMERICAN BIOGRAPHY
0–06–011438–X Harper & Row $25.00

• Macmillan
WHO'S WHO IN AMERICA
0–8379–0145–6 Macmillan $250.00
WHO'S WHO IN THE WORLD
0–8379–1108–7 Macmillan $199.00

• Merriam-Webster
WEBSTER'S NEW BIOGRAPHICAL DICTIONARY
0–87779–543–6 Merriam-Webster $21.95

• Charles Scribner's Sons
CONCISE DICTIONARY OF AMERICAN BIOGRAPHY
0–684–14654–1 Scribners $50.00

• Edward Vernoff & Rima Shore
INTERNATIONAL DICTIONARY OF 20TH CENTURY BIOGRAPHY
0–453–00529–2 NAL $34.95
0–452–00952–9 NAL pb $12.95

Almanacs and Books of Facts

• Tom and Nancy Biracree
ALMANAC OF THE AMERICAN PEOPLE
0–8160–1821–9 Facts On File $29.95

• Guinness Books
THE GUINNESS BOOK OF WORLD RECORDS
0–8069–6598–3 Sterling $15.95
0–553–27066–4 Bantam pb $4.95

• Houghton Mifflin
INFORMATION PLEASE ALMANAC
0–395–44610–4 Houghton Mifflin pb $5.95

• Reader's Digest
READER'S DIGEST BOOK OF FACTS
0–89577–256–6 Reader's Digest $24.95

• David Wallechinsky & Irving Wallace, editors
THE PEOPLE'S ALMANAC PRESENTS THE BOOK OF LISTS
0–553–25327–1 Bantam pb $4.95

• World Almanac
THE WORLD ALMANAC AND BOOK OF FACTS
0–345–34891–5 World Almanac pb $5.95

• Yankee Press
THE OLD FARMER'S ALMANAC
0–89909–193–8 Yankee pb $2.95

GEOGRAPHICAL INFORMATION

Geographical Dictionaries

- Cambridge University Press
CHAMBERS WORLD GAZETTEER
0–550–962003 Cambridge $34.50

- Merriam-Webster
WEBSTER'S NEW GEOGRAPHICAL DICTIONARY
0–87779–446–4 Merriam-Webster $19.95

- Reader's Digest
THE READER'S DIGEST GUIDE TO PLACES OF THE WORLD: A Geographical Dictionary of Countries, Cities, Natural and Man-made Wonders
0–276–39826–2 Reader's Digest $29.95

- Mauro Talocci, editor
GUIDE TO THE FLAGS OF THE WORLD
0–688–01103–9 Morrow $17.50
0–688–01141–1 Morrow pb $12.50

Atlases

- Hammond
AMBASSADOR WORLD ATLAS
0–8437–1244–9 Hammond $49.95

BARTHOLOMEW WORLD ATLAS
0–7028–0404–5 Hammond $35.00

GOLD MEDALLION WORLD ATLAS
0–8437–1247–3 Hammond $75.00

- National Geographic
NATIONAL GEOGRAPHIC ATLAS OF THE WORLD
0–87044–347–X National Geographic $44.95

- London Times
THE TIMES ATLAS OF THE WORLD
0–8129–1298–5 Times Books $149.95

- New York Times
THE NEW YORK TIMES ATLAS OF THE WORLD
0–8129–1626–3 Times Books $49.95

- Rand McNally
RAND McNALLY COSMOPOLITAN WORLD ATLAS
0–528–83284–0 Rand McNally $55.00

THE NEW INTERNATIONAL ATLAS
0–528–83214–X Rand McNally $150.00

RAND McNALLY CONCISE WORLD ATLAS
0–528–83285–9 Rand McNally $24.95

RAND McNALLY WORLD ATLAS OF NATIONS
0–528–83315–4 Rand McNally $34.95

RAND McNALLY ROAD ATLAS, 1989: United States, Canada, Mexico
0–528–89903–1 Rand McNally $9.95
0–528–89900–7 Rand McNally pb $6.95

- Reader's Digest
READER'S DIGEST ATLAS OF THE WORLD
0–528–83283–2 Rand McNally $34.95

Historical and Political Atlases

- Geoffrey Barraclough, editor
THE TIMES ATLAS OF WORLD HISTORY
0–8437–1129–9 Hammond $85.00

THE TIMES CONCISE ATLAS OF WORLD HISTORY
0–8437–1133–7 Hammond pb $24.95

- Gerard Chaliand & Jean-Pierre Rageau
STRATEGIC ATLAS: A Comparative Geopolitics of the World's Powers
0–06–091220–0 Harper & Row pb $16.95

- John Keegan & Andrew Wheatcroft
ZONES OF CONFLICT: An Atlas of Future Wars
0–671–62411–3 Simon & Schuster pb $10.95

- Michael Kidron & Dan Smith
THE STATE OF WAR ATLAS: Armed Conflict, Armed Peace
0–671–47253–4 Simon & Schuster pb $9.95

- Hermann Kinder & Werner Hilgemann
THE ANCHOR ATLAS OF WORLD HISTORY

Volume 1: From the Stone Age to the Eve of the French Revolution
0–385–06178–1 Doubleday pb $9.95

Volume 2: From the French Revolution to the American Bicentennial
0–385–13355–3 Doubleday pb $9.95

- Colin McEvedy
THE PENGUIN ATLAS OF AFRICAN HISTORY
0–14–051083–4 Penguin pb $8.95

THE PENGUIN ATLAS OF MODERN HISTORY TO 1815
0–14–051153–9 Penguin pb $6.95

THE PENGUIN ATLAS OF NORTH AMERICAN HISTORY TO 1870
0–14–051128–8 Penguin pb $6.95

THE PENGUIN ATLAS OF RECENT HISTORY
0–14–051154–7 Penguin pb $6.95

- R.I. Moore, general editor
ATLAS OF WORLD HISTORY
Well-written text accompanies 102 pages of color maps designed especially for this atlas
0–528–83288–3 Rand McNally pb $18.95

- Pierre Vidal-Naquet, editor
THE HARPER ATLAS OF THE WORLD
0–06–181884–4 Harper & Row $29.95

ENGLISH-LANGUAGE DICTIONARIES

- American Heritage Dictionary
THE AMERICAN HERITAGE DICTIONARY: 2nd College Edition
0–395–32944–2 Houghton Mifflin $19.95

THE AMERICAN HERITAGE DESK DICTIONARY
0–395–31256–6 Houghton Mifflin $11.95

- Cambridge University Press
CHAMBERS 20TH CENTURY DICTIONARY
0–550–10234–5 Cambridge $24.95

- Stuart Flexner, editor
THE RANDOM HOUSE COLLEGE DICTIONARY
0–394–05434–2 Random House $21.27

THE RANDOM HOUSE DICTIONARY OF THE ENGLISH LANGUAGE: Second Edition—Unabridged
The most recent American unabridged dictionary, which took over 20 years to compile and includes colloquialisms
0–394–50050–4 Random House $79.95

- Merriam-Webster
WEBSTER'S THIRD NEW INTERNATIONAL DICTIONARY
0–81779–201–1 Merriam-Webster $79.95

WEBSTER'S NEW WORLD DICTIONARY
With more than 170,000 entries, this reference is used by many newspapers
0–87779–505–6 Merriam-Webster $15.95

WEBSTER'S NINTH NEW COLLEGIATE DICTIONARY
The American dictionary used as a standard by editors and proofreaders
0–87779–508–8 Merriam-Webster $15.95

WEBSTER'S COMPACT DICTIONARY
0–87779–488–X Merriam-Webster pb $5.95

- Oxford University Press
THE OXFORD ENGLISH DICTIONARY: Second Edition
A new 20-volume edition
0–19–861–1862 Oxford $2,500.00

THE OXFORD ENGLISH DICTIONARY: The Compact Edition
An essential reference book in two volumes, boxed with a magnifying glass, and containing the complete text of the first edition multi-volume *Oxford English Dictionary* in smaller print
0–19–861117–X Oxford $175.00

THE COMPACT EDITION OF THE OXFORD ENGLISH DICTIONARY: Supplement to the Oxford English Dictionary, Volume 3
Words that have come into common usage in the English-speaking world since 1884
0–19–861211–7 Oxford $95.00

THE CONCISE OXFORD DICTIONARY OF CURRENT ENGLISH
0–19–861131–5 Oxford $22.50

SPECIALIZED DICTIONARIES

Etymological Dictionaries

- Cyril Leslie Beeching
A DICTIONARY OF EPONYMS
0–19–282156–3 Oxford pb $8.95

- E. Cobham Brewer
BREWER'S DICTIONARY OF PHRASE AND FABLE
The classic reference for the origin and meaning of words and expressions
0–06–014903–5 Harper & Row $35.00

TO ORDER BOOKS AS GIFTS, SEE PAGE 1

- William & Mary Morris
MORRIS DICTIONARY OF WORD AND PHRASE ORIGINS
Foreword by Isaac Asimov
0–06–015862–X Harper & Row $25.00

- Oxford University Press
OXFORD DICTIONARY OF ENGLISH ETYMOLOGY
0–19–861112–9 Oxford $45.95

THE CONCISE OXFORD DICTIONARY OF ENGLISH ETYMOLOGY
0–19–861182–X Oxford $24.95

- Eric Partridge
ORIGINS: A Short Etymological Dictionary of Modern English
0–02–594840–7 Macmillan $50.00

Pictorial Dictionaries

- David Fisher & Reginald Bragonier, Jr.
WHAT'S WHAT: A Visual Glossary of the Physical World
0–8437–3331–4 Hammond $19.95
0–345–30302–4 Ballantine pb $9.95

- Oxford University Press
THE OXFORD-DUDEN PICTORIAL ENGLISH DICTIONARY
Includes an alphabetical index
0–19–864155–9 Oxford pb $12.95

Rhyming Dictionaries and Poetic Handbooks

- Babette Deutsch
THE POETRY HANDBOOK: A Dictionary of Terms
0–06–463548–1 Harper & Row pb $8.95

- Willard Espy
WORDS TO RHYME WITH: A Rhyming Dictionary
0–8160–1239–7 Facts On File $40.00

- Rosalind Fergusson, editor
THE PENGUIN RHYMING DICTIONARY
0–14–051136–9 Penguin pb $6.95

- Burges Johnson
NEW RHYMING DICTIONARY AND POET'S HANDBOOK
0–06–012205–6 Harper & Row $17.95

- Lewis Turco
THE NEW BOOK OF FORMS: A Handbook of Poetics
0–87451–381–2 New England pb $10.95

- Jane Whitfield
WHITFIELD'S UNIVERSITY RHYMING DICTIONARY
0–06–463538–4 Harper & Row pb $5.95

Spelling Dictionaries

- New World Dictionary Editors
MISSPELLER'S DICTIONARY
0–671–46864–2 Simon & Schuster pb $3.95

- Harry Shaw
SPELL IT RIGHT
0–06–097048–0 Harper & Row pb $5.95

- Merriam-Webster
WEBSTER'S INSTANT WORD GUIDE
A dictionary without definitions
0–87779–273–9 Merriam-Webster pb $3.95

Slang Dictionaries

- Robert Chapman
NEW DICTIONARY OF AMERICAN SLANG
0–06–181157–2 Harper & Row $23.95

- Albert & Esther Lewin
THE THESAURUS OF SLANG
0–8160–1742–5 Facts On File $40.00

- Oxford University Press
OXFORD DICTIONARY OF CURRENT IDIOMATIC ENGLISH
0–19–431150–3 Oxford $18.00

- Eric Partridge
A DICTIONARY OF SLANG AND UNCONVENTIONAL ENGLISH
0–02–594980–2 Macmillan $75.00

- James Rogers
THE DICTIONARY OF CLICHES
0–8160–1010–2 Facts On File $18.95
0–345–33814–6 Ballantine pb $3.95

- Harold Wentworth & Stuart Flexner
DICTIONARY OF AMERICAN SLANG
0–690–00670–0 Crowell $16.95

Thesauruses

- American Heritage Dictionary
ROGET'S II: The New Thesaurus
0–395–29604–8 Houghton Mifflin $10.95

- Cambridge University Press
CHAMBERS 20TH CENTURY THESAURUS: A Comprehensive Word-Finding Dictionary
0–550–10559–X Cambridge $14.95

- S.I. Hayakawa
CHOOSE THE RIGHT WORD: A Modern Guide to Synonyms
0–06–0913393–2 Harper & Row pb $12.95

- Random House
THE RANDOM HOUSE THESAURUS: College Edition
0–394–52949–9 Random House $14.95

- J.I. Rodale
THE SYNONYM FINDER
0–446–37029–0 Warner pb $12.95

- Roget
ROGET'S INTERNATIONAL THESAURUS
0–06–091169–7 Harper & Row pb $9.95

- Webster
WEBSTER'S NEW WORLD THESAURUS
0–671–60738–3 Simon & Schuster $13.95

Quotations

- Bartlett
BARTLETT'S FAMILIAR QUOTATIONS
0–316–08275–9 Little, Brown $29.95

- James Charlton, editor
THE WRITER'S QUOTATION BOOK: A Literary Companion
0–14–008970–5 Penguin pb $4.95

- H.L. Mencken, editor
NEW DICTIONARY OF QUOTATIONS ON HISTORICAL PRINCIPLES FROM ANCIENT AND MODERN SOURCES
0–394–40079–8 Knopf $40.00

- Oxford University Press
THE OXFORD DICTIONARY OF QUOTATIONS
0–19–211560–X Oxford $39.95

THE CONCISE OXFORD DICTIONARY OF QUOTATIONS
0–19–281324–2 Oxford pb $8.95

- Alan Palmer, editor
QUOTATIONS IN HISTORY: A Dictionary of Historical Quotations, 800 AD to the Present
0–06–495368–8 Barnes & Noble $26.50

- Penguin
THE PENGUIN DICTIONARY OF QUOTATIONS
0–14–051016–8 Penguin pb $8.95

THE PENGUIN DICTIONARY OF MODERN QUOTATIONS
0–14–051038–9 Penguin pb $7.95

- James Simpson, editor
SIMPSON'S CONTEMPORARY QUOTATIONS: The Most Notable Quotes Since 1950
0–395–43085–2 Houghton Mifflin $19.95

- Jon Winoker, editor
THE PORTABLE CURMUDGEON
A small book of irreverent quotations, anecdotes, and interviews from an illustrious list of grouches
0–453–00565–9 NAL $15.95

> "A cult is a religion with no political power."—Tom Wolfe
>
> "Golf is a good walk spoiled."—Mark Twain
>
> Jon Winoker, editor
> **THE PORTABLE CURMUDGEON**
> 0–453–00565–9 NAL $15.95

Proverbs

- Macmillan
THE MACMILLAN BOOK OF PROVERBS, MAXIMS, AND FAMOUS PHRASES
0–02–614500–6 Macmillan $75.00

- Oxford University Press
  OXFORD DICTIONARY OF ENGLISH PROVERBS
  0–19–869118–1 Oxford $35.00

  THE CONCISE OXFORD DICTIONARY OF PROVERBS
  0–19–866131–2 Oxford $21.95
  0–19–281880–5 Oxford pb $6.95

- Penguin
  THE PENGUIN DICTIONARY OF PROVERBS
  0–14–051118–0 Penguin pb $7.95

- Prentice-Hall
  THE PRENTICE-HALL ENCYCLOPEDIA OF WORLD PROVERBS
  0–13–695586–X Prentice-Hall $39.95

Aphorisms

- W.H. Auden & Louis Kronenberger
  THE VIKING BOOK OF APHORISMS: A Personal Selection
  0–14–005966–0 Penguin pb $8.95

- Otto L. Bettmann
  THE DELIGHTS OF READING: Quotes, Notes and Anecdotes
  Fully illustrated
  Foreword by Daniel L. Boorstin
  0–87923–673–6 Godine $14.95

- John Gross, editor
  THE OXFORD BOOK OF APHORISMS
  0–19–214111–2 Oxford $18.95
  0–19–282015–X Oxford pb $7.95

WRITING GUIDES

Usage and Style Manuals

- Walter Achtert & Joseph Gibaldi
  MLA STYLE MANUAL
  The official style book of the Modern Language Association
  0–87352–136–6 MLA $18.95

- Jacques Barzun
  SIMPLE AND DIRECT: A Rhetoric for Writers
  0–06–015283–4 Harper & Row $14.50
  0–06–091122–0 Harper & Row pb $6.95

- Theodore Bernstein
  WATCH YOUR LANGUAGE
  0–689–70531–X Atheneum pb $7.95

  THE CAREFUL WRITER: A Modern Guide to English Usage
  0–689–70555–7 Atheneum pb $10.95

- John Bremner
  WORDS, WORDS, WORDS: A Dictionary for Writers and Others Who Care About Words
  0–231–04492–5 Columbia $36.00
  0–231–04493–3 Columbia pb $14.00

- Claire Cook
  LINE BY LINE: The MLA's Guide to Improving Your Writing
  0–395–38944–5 Houghton Mifflin $14.95
  0–395–39391–4 Houghton Mifflin pb $8.95

- Sidney Cox
  INDIRECTIONS: For Those Who Want to Write
  An inspirational book for writers, first published in 1947
  0–87923–389–3 Godine pb $6.95

- Frederick Crews
  THE RANDOM HOUSE HANDBOOK
  0–39–433944–4 Random House $17.00

- H.W. Fowler
  A DICTIONARY OF MODERN ENGLISH USAGE, Second Edition
  0–19–500154–0 Oxford $24.95
  0–19–281389–7 Oxford pb $9.95

- Lewis Jordan, editor
  THE NEW YORK TIMES MANUAL OF STYLE AND USAGE
  0–8129–0578–4 Times Books $15.95
  0–8129–6316–4 Times Books pb $5.95

- William & Mary Morris
  HARPER DICTIONARY OF CONTEMPORARY USAGE
  0–06–181606–X Harper & Row $22.50

- Eric Partridge
  USAGE AND ABUSAGE: A Guide to Good English
  0–14–051024–9 Penguin pb $7.95

- Harry Shaw
  ERRORS IN ENGLISH AND WAYS TO CORRECT THEM: The Practical Approach to Correct Word Usage, Sentence Structure, Spelling, Punctuation, and Grammar
  0–06–097047–2 Harper & Row pb $6.95

- William Strunk, Jr., & E.B. White
  THE ELEMENTS OF STYLE
  The classic manual of style
  0–02–418200–1 Macmillan pb $3.95

University of Chicago Press
THE CHICAGO MANUAL OF STYLE
The standard. For over 80 years, this reference has been used by American authors, editors, and proofreaders for its chapters on preparing and editing copy
0–226–10390–00 Chicago $37.50

- William Zinsser
  WRITING TO LEARN: How to Write and Think Clearly About Any Subject at All
  0–06–015884–0 Harper & Row $15.95
  0–06–047398–3 Harper & Row pb $10.95

  ON WRITING WELL: An Informal Guide to Writing Nonfiction
  0–06–047397–5 Harper & Row pb $12.95

  WRITING WITH A WORD PROCESSOR
  0–06–091060–7 Harper & Row pb $12.95

Grammar and Punctuation Guides

Karen Gordon
THE TRANSITIVE VAMPIRE: A Handbook of Grammar for the Innocent, the Eager, and the Doomed
0–8129–1101–6 Times Books pb $9.95

THE WELL-TEMPERED SENTENCE: A Punctuation Handbook for the Innocent, the Eager, and the Doomed
0–89919–170–3 Ticknor & Fields pb $7.95

- Philip Gucker
  ESSENTIAL ENGLISH GRAMMAR
  0–486–21649–7 Dover pb $3.50

- Margaret Schertzer
  THE ELEMENTS OF GRAMMAR
  0–02–015440–2 Macmillan pb $4.95

- Harry Shaw
  PUNCTUATE IT RIGHT!
  0–06–097049 Harper & Row pb $5.95

Research Guides

- Jacques Barzun & Henry Graff
  THE MODERN RESEARCHER
  Step-by-step help with composing research essays, articles, and books. Covers everything from fact finding and biased writing to the art of quoting and the rules of footnotes
  0–15–161479–2 HBJ $24.95
  0–15–562512–8 HBJ pb $13.95

- David Beasley
  HOW TO USE A RESEARCH LIBRARY
  A unique book, introducing cataloging systems, research methods, bibliographies, newspaper indexes
  0–19–504246–8 Oxford pb $8.95

- Bruce Felknor
  HOW TO LOOK THINGS UP AND FIND THINGS OUT
  0–688–06166–4 Morrow pb $9.95

- Joseph Gibaldi & Walter Achtert
  THE MLA HANDBOOK FOR WRITERS OF RESEARCH PAPERS
  0–87352–132–3 MLA pb $8.25

- Mona McCormick
  THE NEW YORK TIMES GUIDE TO REFERENCE MATERIALS
  0–451–14471–6 NAL pb $4.95

  THE FICTION WRITER'S RESEARCH HANDBOOK
  0–452–26157–0 NAL pb $8.95

Student Writing Guides

• Kate Turabian
A MANUAL FOR WRITERS OF TERM PAPERS, THESES, AND DISSERTATIONS
0–226–81625–7 Chicago pb $7.95

• University of Chicago Press
STUDENTS' GUIDE FOR WRITING COLLEGE PAPERS
0–226–81623–0 Chicago pb $6.95

• Sharon Sorenson
WEBSTER'S NEW WORLD STUDENT WRITING HANDBOOK
0–13–947789–6 Simon & Schuster pb $12.95

ABOUT LANGUAGE

• Mortimer Adler
SOME QUESTIONS ABOUT LANGUAGE
The humanist philosopher connects language to the way we live
0–87548–320–8 Open Court $19.95

• American Heritage Dictionary
WORD MYSTERIES AND HISTORIES: From Quiche to Humble Pie
0–395–40264–6 Houghton Mifflin pb $8.95

Tony Augarde
THE OXFORD GUIDE TO WORD GAMES
Anagrams, acrostics, palindromes, enigmas, lipograms and univocalics, chronograms, spoonerisms, puns, word squares, and more
0–19–214144–9 Oxford $14.95
0–19–282005–2 Oxford pb $6.95

• Theodore Bernstein
BERNSTEIN'S REVERSE DICTIONARY
Clue words to lead to the missing or forgotten word
0–8129–1593–3 Times Books $19.95

• Donald Chain Black
SPOONERISMS, SYCOPHANTS, AND SOPS: A Celebration of Fascinating Facts About Words
0–06–015886–7 Harper & Row $15.95

• Frederick Bodmer
THE LOOM OF LANGUAGE
Edited by Lancelot Hogben
0–393–30034–X Norton pb $9.95

• Peter Bowler
THE SUPERIOR PERSON'S BOOK OF WORDS
A small, witty book of unusual words
0–87923–556–X Godine $10.95

• Suzanne Brock
IDIOM'S DELIGHT: Curious Imagery in Everyday Language
0–8129–1722–7 Times Books $13.95

• Roger Brown
WORDS AND THINGS
0–02–904800–1 Free Press $18.95
0–02–904810–9 Free Press pb $8.95

• Stuart Chase
THE TYRANNY OF WORDS
How professions and disciplines impose their will through specialized vocabularies
0–15–692394–7 HBJ pb $7.95

• Robert Claiborne
LOOSE CANNONS AND RED HERRINGS: A Book of Lost Metaphors
0–393–02578–0 Norton $17.95

OUR MARVELOUS NATIVE TONGUE: The Life and Times of the English Language
0–8129–1635–2 Times Books pb $9.95

• David Crystal
THE CAMBRIDGE ENCYCLOPEDIA OF LANGUAGE
0–521–26438–3 Cambridge $39.50

• Mark & Diane Kender Dittrick
MISNOMERS
Dubious designations, inapt appellations, and misleading labels
0–02–013670–6 Macmillan pb $5.95

NO UNCERTAIN TERMS: The Word Book That Tells You (In No Uncertain Terms) Why a Meteroid Is Not a Meteor or a Meteorite, a Swamp Is Not a Bog, and an Elk Is Sometimes a Moose
0–87196–217–9 Facts On File pb $6.95

• David Feldman
WHO PUT THE BUTTER IN BUTTERFLY? & Other Fearless Investigations into Our Illogical Language
0–06–016072–1 Harper & Row $15.95

• Stuart Flexner
LISTENING TO AMERICA: An Illustrated History of Words and Phrases from our Lively and Splendid Past
0–671–52798–3 Simon & Schuster pb $13.95

• Charles Funk
HOG ON ICE & OTHER CURIOUS EXPRESSIONS
0–06–001770–8 Harper & Row $12.95
0–06–091259–6 Harper & Row pb $5.95

THEREBY HANGS A TALE: Stories of Curious Word Origins
0–06–001800–3 Harper & Row $10.95
0–06–091260–X Harper & Row pb $5.95

• Charles Funk & Charles Funk, Jr.
HORSEFEATHERS AND OTHER CURIOUS WORDS
0–06–001830–5 Harper & Row $10.95
0–06–091352–5 Harper & Row pb $5.95

• Karen Gordon
INTIMATE APPEAL: A Dictionary of the Senses from Absinthe to Zipper
0–8129–1222–5 Times Books $14.95

• David Grambs
DIMBOXES, EPOTS, AND OTHER QUIDAMS: Words to Describe Life's Indescribable People
0–89480–155–4 Workman pb $5.95

• Geoffrey Hughes
WORDS IN TIME: The Social History of English Vocabulary
0–631–15832–4 Oxford $24.95

• Charlton Laird
THE WORD: A Fresh and Engaging Look at How Words Enter and Leave Our Language
0–671–42185–9 Simon & Schuster $14.95

• Winfred P. Lehmann
LANGUAGE: An Introduction
0–07–554251–X McGraw-Hill $18.50

• James Lipton
AN EXALTATION OF LARKS
Definitions and origins of collective nouns, some familiar (a pride of lions) and some less so (a murder of crows)
0–670–30044–6 Viking $15.95
0–14–004536–8 Penguin pb $8.95

• Robert McCann, William Gray & Robert MacNeil
THE STORY OF ENGLISH
A lively anecdotal account based on the TV series
0–14–009435–0 Penguin pb $12.95

• Lawrence McNamee & Kent Biffle
A FEW WORDS: A Cornucopia of Questions and Answers Concerning Language, Literature, and Life
0–87833–615–X Taylor pb $9.95

• Leonard Michaels & Christopher Ricks
THE STATE OF THE LANGUAGE
A collection of essays, with contributions from M.F.K. Fisher, Anthony Burgess, Angela Carter, and Ishmael Reed, among others
0–520–04400–2 California pb $14.95

• Edwin Newman
STRICTLY SPEAKING
0–446–34218–1 Warner pb $3.95

I MUST SAY: Edwin Newman on English, the News, and Other Matters
0–446–51423–3 Warner $18.95
0–380–70049–2 Avon pb $10.95

• Mario Pei
THE STORY OF LANGUAGE
Foreword by Stuart B. Flexner
0–452–00870–0 NAL pb $12.95

• Simeon Potter
OUR LANGUAGE
A brief but thorough and entertaining outline of the history of English
0–14–020227–7 Penguin pb $6.95

• Hugh Rawson
A DICTIONARY OF EUPHEMISMS AND OTHER DOUBLETALK: Being a Compilation of Linguistic Fig Leaves and Verbal Flourishes for Artful Users of the English Language
0–517–55710–X Crown pb $8.95

• Howard Rheingold
THEY HAVE A WORD FOR IT: A Lighthearted Lexicon of Untranslatable Words and Phrases
0–87477–464–0 Jeremy Tarcher pb $7.95

• William Safire
ON LANGUAGE
0–380–56457–2 Avon pb $6.95

★ **FOR COMPLETE ORDERING INFORMATION, SEE PAGE 1**

TAKE MY WORD FOR IT
0–8129–1323–X Times Books $22.50
0–8050–0606–0 Henry Holt pb $9.95

YOU COULD LOOK IT UP: More on Language
0–8129–1324–8 Times Books $22.50

I STAND CORRECTED: More on Language
0–8129–1097–4 Times Books $17.95

WHAT'S THE GOOD WORD?
0–8129–1006–0 Times Books $15.95
0–380–64550–5 Avon pb $5.95

● Susan Kelz Sperling
POPLOLLIES AND BELLIBONES: A Celebration of Lost Words
0–517–53079–1 Clarkson Potter pb $7.95

● Tad Tuleja
NAMESAKES: An Entertaining Guide to the Origins of More Than 300 Words Named for People
0–07–065436–0 McGraw-Hill pb $7.95

THE CAT'S PAJAMAS: A Fabulous Fictionary of Familiar Phrases
Whimsical and imagined origins of more than 300 figures of speech, from "Ants in His Pants" to "Catching Some Z's"
0–449–90242–0 Fawcett pb $7.95

● Fred West
THE WAY OF LANGUAGE: An Introduction
0–15–595130–0 HBJ pb $11.95

FOREIGN-LANGUAGE DICTIONARIES

● International Book Centre
ARABIC-ENGLISH MODERN DICTIONARY
0–86685–287–5 International Book Centre $25.00

● Oxford University Press
OXFORD ENGLISH-ARABIC DICTIONARY OF CURRENT USAGE
0–19–864312–8 Oxford $49.50

● Spoken Language Services
ARABIC-ENGLISH DICTIONARY
0–87950–001–8 Spoken Language pb $15.00

● A.H. Yacobian
ENGLISH-ARMENIAN, ARMENIAN-ENGLISH DICTIONARY
0–87559–004–7 Shalom $35.00

● Beijing Foreign Language Institute
PINYIN CHINESE-ENGLISH DICTIONARY
0–471–27557–3 Wiley $89.95
0–471–86796–9 Wiley pb $25.95

● Cheng & Tsui
POCKET ENGLISH-CHINESE (PINYIN) DICTIONARY
0–88727–023–9 Cheng & Tsui pb $5.95

● Shi-Chiu Liang, editor
NEW PRACTICAL CHINESE-ENGLISH DICTIONARY
0–917056–52–3 Cheng & Tsui $45.00

NEW PRACTICAL ENGLISH-CHINESE DICTIONARY
0–686–92368–5 French & European $45.00

● Robert Matthews, editor
CHINESE-ENGLISH DICTIONARY
0–674–12350–6 Harvard $35.00

● Nina Trnka
CZECH-ENGLISH, ENGLISH-CZECH CONCISE DICTIONARY
0–87052–586–7 Hippocrene pb $6.95

● Cassell
CASSELL'S FRENCH DICTIONARY: French and English
0–02–522620–7 Macmillan $23.95
0–02–522670–3 Macmillan pb $9.95

● Harrap
HARRAP'S STANDARD FRENCH-ENGLISH DICTIONARY
Volume 1
0–245–50972–0 Harrap $65.00
Volume 2
0–245–50973–9 Harrap $125.00
Volume 3
0–245–51859–2 Harrap $125.00

● Collins-Robert
COLLINS-ROBERT FRENCH DICTIONARY
0–671–64189–1 Prentice-Hall $23.95

● Larousse
LAROUSSE FRANCAIS-ANGLAIS, ANGLAIS-FRANCAIS DE POCHE
0–317–45658–X Larousse pb $8.95

● Cassell
CASSELL'S GERMAN DICTIONARY: German-English, English-German
0–02–522930–3 Macmillan $23.95
0–02–522650–9 Macmillan pb $9.95

● Langenscheidt
LANGENSCHEIDT GERMAN STANDARD DICTIONARY
0–88729–044–2 Langenscheidt $14.95

● Oxford University Press
GREEK-ENGLISH LEXICON
0–19–864214–8 Oxford $89.00

THE OXFORD DICTIONARY OF MODERN GREEK: Greek-English, English-Greek
0–19–864137–0 Oxford $21.00
0–19–864148–6 Oxford pb $9.95

● Megiddo
MEGIDDO MODERN DICTIONARY: English-Hebrew, Hebrew-English
9–65010–080–6 Hippocrene (2-volume set) $75.00

THE NEW BANTAM-MEGIDDO HEBREW DICTIONARY
0–8052–3666–X Schocken $24.95
0–553–26387–0 Bantam pb $4.95

● Cambridge University Press
CHAMBERS ENGLISH-HINDI DICTIONARY
0–8364–1474–8 South Asia $16.00

● South Asia
A PRACTICAL HINDI-ENGLISH DICTIONARY
0–88386–380–4 South Asia $16.00

● Magay Tamas & others
HUNGARIAN-ENGLISH, ENGLISH-HUNGARIAN DICTIONARY
0–88254–986–3 Hippocrene pb $6.95

● Cambridge University
THE CONCISE CAMBRIDGE ITALIAN DICTIONARY
0–521–07273–5 Cambridge $44.50
0–14–051064–8 Penguin pb $9.95

● Sansoni Harrap
SANSONI HARRAP ENGLISH-ITALIAN DICTIONARY
Volume 1
0–245–59635–6 Harrap $175.00
Volume 2
0–245–59636–4 Harrap $175.00

● Kodansha
KODANSHA ENGLISH-JAPANESE DICTIONARY
0–87011–420–4 Kodansha $24.95
0–87011–672–X Kodansha pb $14.95

KODANSHA JAPANESE-ENGLISH DICTIONARY
0–87011–421–2 Kodansha $24.95
0–87011–671–1 Kodansha pb $14.95

● Andrew Nelson
MODERN READER'S JAPANESE-ENGLISH CHARACTER DICTIONARY
0–8048–0408–7 Tuttle $47.50

● Charles Tuttle
CONCISE ENGLISH-KOREAN DICTIONARY ROMANIZED
0–8048–0118–5 Tuttle pb $4.25

● Yale University Press
KOREAN-ENGLISH DICTIONARY
0–300–00753–1 Yale $92.00

● Oxford University Press
OXFORD LATIN DICTIONARY
0–19–864224–5 Oxford $175.00

● E.D. Gabrielsen
NORWEGIAN-ENGLISH, ENGLISH-NORWEGIAN POCKET DICTIONARY
0–88254–584–1 Hippocrene pb $7.95

● Abbas & Manoochehr Aryanpur-Kashani
THE COMBINED NEW PERSIAN-ENGLISH AND ENGLISH-PERSIAN DICTIONARY
0–939214–29–6 Mazda $36.00

● Routledge, Chapman & Hall
A COMPREHENSIVE PERSIAN-ENGLISH DICTIONARY: Including the Arabic Words and Phrases to be Met with in Persian Literature
0–7100–2152–6 RC&H $65.00

- Iwo C. Pogonowski
**PRACTICAL POLISH-ENGLISH,
ENGLISH-POLISH DICTIONARY**
0–87052–064–4 Hippocrene pb $7.95

- Collins
**COLLINS POCKET PORTUGUESE-
ENGLISH DICTIONARY**
0–671–64855–1 Prentice-Hall pb $7.95

- David McKay
**MCKAY'S MODERN PORTUGUESE-
ENGLISH AND ENGLISH-
PORTUGUESE DICTIONARY**
0–679–10077–6 David McKay $12.95

- Stanford University
PORTUGUESE-ENGLISH DICTIONARY
0–8047–0480–5 Stanford $32.50

- M.A. O'Brien, editor
**NEW RUSSIAN-ENGLISH AND
ENGLISH-RUSSIAN DICTIONARY**
0–486–20208–9 Dover pb $7.95

- Oxford University Press
**THE OXFORD ENGLISH-RUSSIAN
DICTIONARY**
0–19–864117–6 Oxford $65.00
**THE OXFORD RUSSIAN-ENGLISH
DICTIONARY**
0–19–864154–0 Oxford $65.00

- Oxford University Press
**PRACTICAL SANSKRIT DICTIONARY:
With Transliteration, Accentuation, and
Etymological Analysis Throughout**
0–19–864303–9 Oxford $39.95

- South Asia
SANSKRIT-ENGLISH DICTIONARY
81–208–0065–6 South Asia $36.00

- Monier Williams
ENGLISH-SANSKRIT DICTIONARY
0–89744–966–5 Auromere $52.00

- Branislav Grujic
**SERBO-CROATIAN/ENGLISH,
ENGLISH/SERBO-CROATIAN
DICTIONARY**
0–87052–139–X Hippocrene $19.95

- American Heritage
**THE AMERICAN HERITAGE
LAROUSSE SPANISH DICTIONARY**
0–395–32429–7 Houghton Mifflin $19.95
0–317–65694–5 Houghton Mifflin pb $3.95

- Cassell
**CASSELL'S SPANISH DICTIONARY:
Spanish-English, English-Spanish**
0–02–522910–9 Macmillan $21.95
0–02–522660–6 Macmillan pb $9.95

- Collins
**COLLINS POCKET SPANISH
DICTIONARY**
0–671–49221–7 Simon & Schuster pb $7.95

- Simon & Schuster
**SIMON & SCHUSTER
INTERNATIONAL DICTIONARY:
English-Spanish, Spanish-English**
0–671–21267–2 Simon & Schuster $45.00

- University of Chicago Press
**THE UNIVERSITY OF CHICAGO
SPANISH DICTIONARY**
0–226–10400–1 Chicago $19.95
0–226–10402–8 Chicago pb $6.95

- Oxford University Press
**STANDARD SWAHILI-ENGLISH
DICTIONARY**
0–19–864403–5 Oxford $37.00

- Prisma
**PRISMA'S MODERN SWEDISH-
ENGLISH AND ENGLISH-SWEDISH
DICTIONARY**
0–8166–1734–1 Minnesota $65.00
Volume 1: English-Swedish
0–8166–1733–5 Minnesota pb $19.95
Volume 2: Swedish-English
0–8166–1732–5 Minnesota pb $19.95

- Hippocrene
**TURKISH-ENGLISH, ENGLISH-
TURKISH CONCISE DICTIONARY**
0–87052–241–8 Hippocrene pb $5.95

- Alexander Harkavy
**YIDDISH-ENGLISH-HEBREW
DICTIONARY**
0–8052–4027–6 Schocken $29.95

- Schocken Press
**MODERN ENGLISH-YIDDISH,
YIDDISH-ENGLISH DICTIONARY**
0–8052–0576–6 Schocken $24.95

New Age

In recent years the term "New Age" has become a catchword to describe a broad range of phenomena linked by a common interest in metaphysical, spiritual, holistic, and other alternative approaches to age-old questions and concerns. New Age covers everything from herbal healing, channeling, and tarot reading to macrobiotic cooking, crystals, and UFOs.

Over the years, other terms—such as "occult" or "paranormal"—have been used to describe these interests. Yet many prefer "New Age" precisely because it is generic enough to include just about anything, while at the same time suggesting a forward-looking perspective and the dawning of a heightened consciousness and spiritual awareness.

GENERAL BOOKS

- Marcia Ingenito, editor
**NATIONAL NEW AGE YELLOW PAGES:
A United States Guide to Consciousness-
Raising Services, Products, and
Organizations**
0–943083–00–1 New Age Yellow Pages pb $14.95

- Psychic Guide Magazine
NEW AGE CATALOG
Information about New Age newsletters, magazines, workshops, and societies
0–385–24383–9 Doubleday pb $14.95

ANCIENT ROOTS AND TRADITIONS

Witchcraft and Magic

Prehistoric cave drawings offer some rudimentary proof that in their infancy, humans were preoccupied with efforts at magic or witchcraft—the use of rituals to influence events or to alter or affect their environment. Throughout history many societies have designated certain individuals—whether called "shamans," "medicine men," or "witch doctors"—as spiritual leaders who could heal the wounded, foretell the future, and manifest other supernatural or paranormal abilities. Sometimes, however, the effort to influence events through means not sanctioned by a community's religious system has been viewed as a mark of evil.

Those who identify themselves as witches today are far more likely to emphasize a spiritual communion with the earth and the forces of nature than an interest in casting spells and potions.

- Margot Adler
**DRAWING DOWN THE MOON: Witches,
Druids, Goddess-Worshippers, and Other
Pagans in America Today**
0–8070–3253–0 Beacon pb $14.95

- Grillot de Givry
**WITCHCRAFT, MAGIC, AND
ALCHEMY**
0–486–22493–7 Dover pb $9.95

- Mircea Eliade
**SHAMANISM: Archaic Techniques of
Ecstasy**
0–691–01779–4 Princeton pb $11.95

Alchemy

The effort to transform base metals into silver or gold had its roots in ancient China, India, and Greece. When interest in the art was revived in the Middle Ages, it was given the Latin name "alchemy." By the Renaissance, leading scientists were starting to doubt the possibility of transmuting one metal into another. That possibility was not irrefutably disproved until the 19th century. Nonetheless, the ancient and medieval alchemists, in the process of developing their theories, offered valuable contributions to the world of science: the techniques and equipment they used helped lay the foundation for modern-day chemistry.

- Frater Albertus
ALCHEMIST'S HANDBOOK
A working manual
0–87728–655–8 Samuel Weiser pb $10.95

- Stanislas Klossowski De Rola
ALCHEMY: The Secret Art
0–500–81003–6 Thames & Hudson pb $10.95

- H. Stanley Redgrove
ALCHEMY, ANCIENT AND MODERN
0–89005–344–8 Ares $20.00

Astrology

Astrology—the interpretation of how the movements of stars and planets affect events on earth—originated in ancient Mesopotamia, and flourished during the Hellenistic period, when the zodiac was established. The geocentric world view that astrology reflected remained widespread until the Copernican revolution in the 16th century.

The force of the idea, however, is powerful enough to make astrology one of the most popular strands of the resurgence of interest in New Age traditions. Hundreds of books explain how to create and read astrological charts, but the following are among the clearest.

- Jeanne Avery
ASTROLOGICAL ASPECTS: Your Inner Dialogues
0–385–18857–9 Doubleday pb $10.95

- Demetra George & Douglas Bloch
ASTROLOGY FOR YOURSELF: How to Understand and Interpret Your Own Horoscope
0–914728–61–X Wingbow pb $14.95

- Linda Goodman
LINDA GOODMAN'S LOVE SIGNS: A New Approach to the Human Heart
0–06–011550–5 Harper & Row $16.50

- Rose Lineman & Jan Popelka
COMPENDIUM OF ASTROLOGY
0–914918–43–5 Schiffer pb $14.95

- Dane Rudhyar
THE ASTROLOGICAL HOUSES: The Spectrum of Individual Experience
0–916360–24–5 CRCS pb $8.95

- Frances Sakoian & Louis Acker
THE ASTROLOGER'S HANDBOOK
A popular guide to interpreting and creating natal charts
0–06–091495–5 Harper & Row pb $9.95

- Suzanne White
THE NEW ASTROLOGY
0–312–01797–9 St. Martin's pb $12.95

Tarot

The origins of tarot—the deck of cards widely used for fortune-telling and other divination purposes—are hotly disputed. Many believe that the method was created in ancient Egypt, reaching Europe by Gypsy migrations; indeed, Gypsies around the world today remain among the foremost practitioners of the art of reading tarot cards.

There is still great variety in methods of interpretation and in the decks used by the different tarot traditions, although they may have some of the same symbolic cards, such as the juggler, high priestess, and hanged man. Among the more famous decks is that designed by 20th-century magician Aleister Crowley.

- Angeles Arrien
THE TAROT HANDBOOK: Practical Applications of Ancient Visual Symbols
0–916955–02–8 Arcus pb $25.00

- Eileen Connolly
THE TAROT: A New Handbook for the Apprentice
0–87877–045–3 Newcastle pb $9.95

- Aleister Crowley
THE BOOK OF THOTH
0–87728–268–4 Samuel Weiser pb $9.95

- Alfred Douglas
TAROT: The Origins, Meaning and Uses of the Cards
The historical, mystical, and psychological significance of tarot cards; with instructions on how to read them
0–14–003737–3 Penguin pb $6.95

- Jean Freer
THE NEW FEMINIST TAROT
0–85030–563–2 Sterling pb $8.95

The Four of Cups from The Tarot *by Alfred Douglas, illustrated by David Sheridan (Penguin)*

Other Systems of Divination

The I Ching is an ancient Chinese tradition using geometric diagrams; palmistry is the art of reading the lines in a person's palm; graphology involves examining handwriting to analyze an individual's personality; and runes are ancient characters and letters used for prognostication.

- Nathaniel Altman
THE PALMISTRY WORKBOOK
0–85030–352–4 Sterling pb $12.95

- Ralph Blum, editor
THE NEW BOOK OF RUNES: A Handbook for the the Use of an Ancient Oracle—The Viking Runes
0–312–00729–9 St. Martin's pb $24.95

- Mary Ruiz & Karen Amend
HANDWRITING ANALYSIS
0–89370–650–7 Borgo $24.95
0–87877–050–X Newcastle pb $9.95

- Richard Wilhelm & C.F. Baynes, translators
I CHING OR THE BOOK OF CHANGES
0–691–09750–X Princeton $17.50

Reincarnation

Reincarnation—also called "transmigration of the soul"—is the belief that after the death of the body, the soul passes into another body, whether animal or human. Although many ancient societies believed in some form of reincarnation, the doctrine reached its most developed form in India. An individual was reborn lower or higher up on the scale of possible rebirths depending upon "karma"—the sum total of a person's good and bad deeds.

Experiments in hypnotic regression have enhanced its popularity in recent decades; one particularly famous example, in the 1950s, was the account of a Colorado housewife who was purportedly an Irish girl—Bridey Murphy—in a prior life.

- Gina Cerminara
MANY MANSIONS: The Edgar Cayce Story of Reincarnation
0–451–15218–2 NAL pb $3.95

- Jonathan Cott
THE SEARCH FOR OMM SETY: A Story of Eternal Love
Reliving an affair with an Egyptian pharaoh
0–385–23746–4 Doubleday $17.95

- Joseph Head & S. L. Cranston, editors
REINCARNATION: An East–West Anthology
0–8356–0035–1 Quest pb $5.50

REINCARNATION: The Phoenix Fire Mystery
How renowned historical figures have viewed reincarnation
0–517–56101–8 Crown pb $12.95

- Shirley MacLaine
IT'S ALL IN THE PLAYING
0–553–05267–5 Bantam $18.95
0–553–27299–3 Bantam pb $4.95

OUT ON A LIMB
0–553–05035–4 Bantam $15.95
0–553–26352–8 Bantam pb $4.50

- Roger Woolger
OTHER LIVES, OTHER SELVES: A Jungian Psychotherapist Discovers Past Lives
0–385–23716–2 Doubleday $18.95

Meditation

Meditation is a practice in which intense concentration upon an object or sound leads to a higher state of consciousness, understanding, or awareness. Recent scientific studies have indicated that meditative techniques actually have an effect on brain waves, pulse, and respiratory rates, and can help alleviate stress-related conditions.

- Simon Court
MEDITATOR'S MANUAL: A Practical Introduction to the Art of Meditation
0–85030–410–5 Sterling pb $12.95

- Willard Johnson
RIDING THE OX HOME: A History of Meditation from Shamanism to Science
0–8070–1305–6 Beacon pb $9.95

- Yogi Mahesh Marharishi
TRANSCENDENTAL MEDITATION
0–451–15386–3 NAL pb $4.95

- Rammurti Mishra
THE TEXTBOOK OF YOGA PSYCHOLOGY
0–517–56434–3 Crown pb $10.95

- D.T. Suzuki
MANUAL OF ZEN BUDDHISM
0–802–13065–8 Grove pb $10.95

Eastern Traditions

A fascination with all things Eastern has spurred many writers and thinkers to find ways of adapting ancient teachings to make them accessible to modern audiences. The result, as these titles indicate, is often a curious blend of classic Eastern mysticism and Western pragmatism and materialism.

- Nik Douglas & Penny Slinger
SEXUAL SECRETS, THE ALCHEMY OF ECSTASY
0–89281–010–6 Destiny $24.95
0–89281–011–4 Inner Traditions pb $14.95

- John Heider
THE TAO OF LEADERSHIP: Lao Tzu's Tao Te Ching Adapted for a New Age
Adaptation of a Chinese classic
0–89334–079–0 Humanics pb $10.95

- Huang Chung-lian
EMBRACE TIGER, RETURN TO MOUNTAIN: The Essence of Tai Ji
0–89087–504–9 Celestial Arts pb $8.95

Fu Hsi inventing the eight diagrams of the I Ching, from Outlines of Chinese Symbolism and Art Motives *by C.A.S. Williams (Dover)*

- A.C. Prabhupada
DIALECTIC SPIRITUALISM: A Vedic View of Western Philosophy
A dialogue between Eastern and Western philosophic traditions
0–932215–10–6 Palace $14.95
0–932215–02–5 Palace pb $7.95

- Lati Rinbochay & Jeffrey Hopkins
DEATH, INTERMEDIATE STATE, AND REBIRTH IN TIBETAN BUDDHISM
Tibetan-Buddhist philosophy of death and dying
0–937938–00–9 Snow Lion pb $6.95

- Idries Shah
THE WAY OF THE SUFI
Sufi traditions and stories
0–525–47261–4 Dutton pb $8.95

Holistic and Herbal Healing

Long before the advent of modern medicine, societies placed a strong emphasis on the healing powers of spiritual leaders, sacred locations, and particular herbs and potions. The current era is witnessing a return to reliance on alternative methods of healing among many people, along with a parallel emphasis on the power of individuals to heal themselves.

▶ **See also Health**

- Shepherd Bliss, editor
THE NEW HOLISTIC HEALTH HANDBOOK: Living Well in a New Age
0–8289–0561–4 Stephen Greene pb $14.95

- Mark Bricklin
THE PRACTICAL ENCYCLOPEDIA OF NATURAL HEALING
0–87857–480–8 Rodale $21.95

- Yeshi Donden
HEALTH THROUGH BALANCE: An Introduction to Tibetan Medicine
0–937938–25–4 Snow Lion pb $10.95

- Vasant Lad & David Frawley
THE YOGA OF HERBS: An Ayurvedic Guide to Herbal Medicine
0–941524–24–8 Lotus Light pb $11.95

- S.G. Ouseley
COLOUR MEDITATIONS
0–85243–062–0 Ariel pb $3.50

- Erika Cheetham, editor
THE PROPHECIES OF NOSTRADAMUS: The Man Who Saw Tomorrow
Nostradamus was renowned in the 16th century for his predictions. Though they can be hard to decipher, since they are expressed in complex symbolism and anagrams, some are remarkably accurate, with uncanny descriptions of, for example, the French Revolution; some can be interpreted as predicting World War II and, around the year 2000, the end of the world
0–425–08757–3 Berkley pb $4.95
0–399–50345–5 Putnam pb $7.95

- Jean-Charles de Fontbrune
NOSTRADAMUS: Countdown to Apocalypse
0–03–064177–2 Henry Holt $18.95

- Emanuel Swedenborg
DIVINE LOVE AND WISDOM
The 18th-century scientist, inventor, philosopher, and visionary helped point the way for man to be reunited with God. His descriptions of the spiritual world influenced William Blake, the most mystical of the Romantic poets, as well as the spiritualists of the 19th-century revival
0–87785–129–8 Swedenborg Foundation pb $6.95

HEAVEN AND HELL
0–87785–167–0 Swedenborg Foundation pb $5.95

The 19th-Century Spiritualist Revival

The late 19th century witnessed a revival of interest in spiritualism and other occult sciences. Darwin's theory of evolution shook the foundations of traditional religious beliefs, and people began to look in other directions for answers: even some of the most respectable homes held seances and boasted Ouija boards. A number of noted spiritualists rode the crest of this revival, and such groups as the Hermetic Order of the Golden Dawn and the Theosophical Society served to focus public attention on the occult sciences and those who practiced them.

- Helena Blavatsky
THE SECRET DOCTRINE
Madame Blavatsky, co-founder with Henry Steel Olcott of the Theosophical Society, claimed that she had been chosen by superhuman mahatmas to reveal ancient knowledge to the world and perform miracles. This is a 2-volume abridged version of her masterpiece
0–911500–00–6 Theosophical $20.00
0–911500–01–4 Theosophical pb $17.00

- Aleister Crowley
BOOK OF THE LAW
Perhaps the most renowned magician of the last hundred years, Crowley's flamboyant life style and sexual escapades—purportedly required to expand

---

his magical capabilities—caused considerable controversy and scandal
0–87728–334–6 Samuel Weiser pb $4.50

THE BOOK OF LIES
A collection of paradoxes
0–87728–516–0 Samuel Weiser pb $8.95

• R.A. Gilbert
THE GOLDEN DAWN: Twilight of the Magicians
The Hermetic Order of the Golden Dawn claimed to be "the only repository of magical knowledge" in the West during the modern era. It was founded after the discovery in a London bookstore of a coded manuscript outlining magic rituals and practices
0–8095–7003–3 Borgo $19.95

• W. Somerset Maugham
THE MAGICIAN
This novel's central character was modeled on Aleister Crowley
0–14–002668–1 Penguin pb $4.95

• Robert McDermott, editor
THE ESSENTIAL RUDOLF STEINER
Steiner believed that man's attachment to material possessions had crippled his innate ability to participate in spiritual processes, and that only extensive training of the consciousness could help recapture that ability. His philosophy was the basis for the Waldorf School movement
0–06–065345–0 Harper & Row pb $13.95

• Israel Regardie
THE GOLDEN DAWN: An Account of the Teachings, Rites, and Ceremonies of the Order of the Golden Dawn
Account of the occult group that counted the poet W.B. Yeats among its well-known members
0–87542–663–8 Llewellyn pb $19.95

• Rudolf Steiner
THEOSOPHY: An Introduction to Supersensible Knowledge of the World and the Destination of Man
0–910142–65–3 Anthroposophic $14.00
0–910142–39–4 Anthroposophic pb $6.95

THE 20TH CENTURY: The New Age

As the millennium approaches, interest in the occult sciences seems to have flourished. In addition, a host of events with catastrophic implications for the world have inspired many individuals to search for alternative answers in all facets of their lives. Together, these alternative answers comprise what has been called the "New Age."

• Marilyn Ferguson
THE AQUARIAN CONSPIRACY: Personal and Social Transformation in the 1980s
0–87477–458–6 Jeremy Tarcher pb $10.95

20th-Century Gurus

Throughout this century, a number of individuals have attracted significant followings through their teachings, writings, and activities.

• Meher Baba
DISCOURSES
0–913078–57–3 Sheriar $19.95
0–913078–58–1 Sheriar pb $9.00

• Carlos Castaneda
THE TEACHINGS OF DON JUAN: A Yaqui Way of Knowledge
Castaneda's accounts of his mystical experiences with Don Juan, a Yaqui Indian, became best-sellers
0–520–00217–2 California $25.00
0–520–02258–0 California pb $9.95

• Gina Cerminara
EDGAR CAYCE REVISITED & OTHER CANDID COMMENTARIES
Revisionist thoughts on the teachings of Cayce, a healer and clairvoyant
0–89865–324–X Donning pb $5.95

• G.I. Gurdjieff
MEETINGS WITH REMARKABLE MEN
The writings of an Armenian mystic and founder of a quasireligious movement
0–525–47242–8 Dutton pb $6.95

• Jiddu Krishnamurti
An Indian philosopher and spiritual guide.
THE FIRST AND LAST FREEDOM
Introduction by Aldous Huxley
0–06–064831–7 Harper & Row pb $8.95

TRUTH AND ACTUALITY: Conversations on Science and Consciousness
0–06–064875–9 Harper & Row pb $8.95

TALKS AND DIALOGUES OF J. KRISHNAMURTI
0–380–01573–0 Avon pb $4.95

• C.S. Nott
TEACHINGS OF GURDJIEFF: The Journal of a Pupil
Account by a disciple
0–87728–395–8 Samuel Weiser pb $8.95

• Thomas Sugrue
THERE IS A RIVER: The Story of Edgar Cayce
A biography of Cayce
0–87604–151–9 ARE pb $4.50

• James Webb
THE HARMONIOUS CIRCLE: The Lives and Work of G.I. Gurdjieff, P.D. Ouspensky, and Their Followers
0–87773–427–5 Shambhala $19.95

ESP

• J.B. Rhine
EXTRA-SENSORY PERCEPTION
Rhine coined the term ESP; when his book received a positive review in the *New York Times*, it fostered widespread interest among the public that has continued to the present
0–8283–1464–0 Branden pb $9.00

Crystals

Among the strongest of the current New Age trends is an interest in the healing power of gems and other stones. Each crystal is said to have different properties, and can help foster spiritual growth and self-transformation.

• Randall & Vicki Baer
THE CRYSTAL CONNECTION: A Guidebook for Personal and Planetary Ascension
0–06–250033–3 Harper & Row pb $16.95

• Katrina Raphaell
CRYSTAL HEALING: The Therapeutic Application of Crystals and Stones
0–943358–30–2 Aurora pb $14.95

Channeling

This technique involves opening oneself up to superhuman entities known as "spirit guides," who impart wisdom through the voice and body of the channeler.

• William Kautz & Melanie Branon
CHANNELING: The Intuitive Connection
0–06–250451–7 Harper & Row $14.95

• Ramtha & Douglas Mahr
VOYAGE TO THE NEW WORLD: An Adventure into Unlimitedness
Communications from Ramtha
0–317–61697–8 Masterworks $9.95
0–449–13185–8 Fawcett pb $3.95

• Jane Roberts
SETH, DREAMS, AND PROJECTION OF CONSCIOUSNESS
Teachings from the spirit named Seth
0–913299–25–1 NAL $15.95
0–913299–42–1 NAL pb $9.95

Diet

Concern about the effects of pollution in the food chain and a diet heavy in meat has revitalized an interest in other healthful options. As an alternative strategy, vegetarianism, macrobiotics, and other Eastern-inspired food traditions fall within the New Age category.

• Yamuna Devi
LORD KRISHNA'S CUISINE: The Art of Indian Vegetarian Cooking
0–525–24564–2 Dutton $29.95

• East West Journal Editors
THE SHOPPER'S GUIDE TO NATURAL FOODS
0–89529–233–5 Avery pb $12.95

• Vegetarian Times Editors
VEGETARIAN TIMES' GUIDE TO NATURAL FOOD RESTAURANTS IN THE U.S. AND CANADA
0–89529–375–7 Avery pb $8.95

Personal and Psychic Development

Much of the emphasis in the current New Age vogue is on self-improvement, spiritual development, and personal growth. These books are designed to help people achieve those goals through diverse means.

- **Hal Bennett**
  THE LENS OF PERCEPTION
  Self-empowerment through guided imagery
  0–89087–492–1 Celestial Arts pb $6.95

- **Rick Fields & others**
  CHOP WOOD, CARRY WATER: A Guide to Finding Spiritual Fulfillment in Everyday Life
  0–87477–209–5 Jeremy Tarcher pb $11.95

- **Shakti Gawain**
  CREATIVE VISUALIZATION
  0–931432–02–2 Whatever $7.95
  0–553–24147–8 Bantam pb $4.50

- **H. Spencer Lewis**
  MENTAL POISONING
  How to resist negative mental energies
  0–912057–49–1 AMORC pb $6.95

- **Pat Rodegast & Judith Stanton, editors**
  EMMANUEL'S BOOK: A Manual for Living Comfortably in the Cosmos
  Advice from a spirit named Emmanuel
  0–553–34387–4 Bantam pb $9.95

- **Chögyam Trungpa**
  CUTTING THROUGH SPIRITUAL MATERIALISM
  0–87773–050–4 Shambhala pb $12.95

Science Crossover

Spiritual or paranormal phenomena are often dismissed by many critics as nonsense or fraud. Yet some writers and scientists, including those below, have sought to explore the relationship between such experiences and the rigorous demands of the natural sciences.

- **David Bohm & F. David Peat**
  SCIENCE, ORDER, CREATIVITY
  The nature of creativity
  0–553–34449–8 Bantam pb $8.95

- **John Brockman, editor**
  THE REALITY CLUB
  Essays by philosophers, anthropologists, and social critics on speculative theories about the mind
  1–55802–192–2 Lynx pb $9.95

- **Fritjof Capra**
  THE TAO OF PHYSICS
  Parallels between physics and Eastern philosophy
  0–87773–246–9 Shambhala $12.95
  0–553–26379–X Bantam pb $4.95

- **Joseph Pearce**
  THE CRACK IN THE COSMIC EGG: Challenging Constructs of Mind and Reality
  0–517–56661–3 Crown pb $8.95

- **Lyall Watson**
  BEYOND SUPERNATURE: A New Natural History of the Supernatural
  The degree to which science can and cannot explain natural phenomena
  0–553–34456–0 Bantam pb $8.95

UFOs

Unidentified Flying Objects have been hotly debated for much of this century. Thousands of sightings over the years have convinced many people that UFOs have, indeed, come from outer space; some individuals actually claim to have not only seen UFOs but to have been abducted by aliens.

- **George Andrews**
  EXTRA-TERRESTRIALS AMONG US
  Evidence that alien beings are living on earth
  0–87542–010–9 Llewellyn pb $9.95

- **Norman Briazack & Simon Mennick**
  THE UFO GUIDEBOOK
  Encyclopedia of UFO-related topics
  0–8065–0763–2 Lyle Stuart pb $4.95

- **D. Scott Rogo, editor**
  ALIEN ABDUCTIONS
  0–451–15210–7 Penguin pb $3.95

- **Robert Temple**
  THE SIRIUS MYSTERY
  Evidence of visits by beings from Sirius
  0–89281–163–3 Inner Traditions pb $12.95

Women's Spirituality

Some New Age thinkers have explored issues of spirituality with a feminist consciousness. This approach dovetails with a belief among many New Agers that early societies may have been organized matriarchally, with women deriving authority from the perceived identification of their procreative powers with the earth and its annual life cycle.

- **Lynn Andrews**
  CRYSTAL WOMAN: The Sisters of the Dreamtime
  True story of the author's spiritual search in the Australian outback
  0–446–51391–1 Warner $16.95

  STAR WOMAN
  Continuation of the saga
  0–446–38566–2 Warner pb $9.95

- **Lindsay River & Sally Gillespie**
  THE KNOT OF TIME: Astrology and the Female Experience
  Astrology from a feminist perspective
  0–06–015864–6 Harper & Row $17.95

- **Diane Stein**
  THE WOMEN'S SPIRITUALITY BOOK
  A "herstory" of civilization
  0–87542–761–8 Llewellyn pb $9.95

- **Barbara Walker**
  THE WOMAN'S ENCYCLOPEDIA OF MYTHS AND SECRETS
  0–06–250926–8 Harper & Row $29.95
  0–06–250925–X Harper & Row pb $22.95

MISCELLANEOUS

Because the term New Age is so broad, many of the books that fall within its scope avoid easy categorization. The following is a smattering of what's available.

- **José Argüelles**
  THE MAYAN FACTOR: Path Beyond Technology
  The Maya mysteries and their relevance for the New Age
  0–939680–38–6 Bear pb $12.95

- **Richard Bucke**
  COSMIC CONSCIOUSNESS
  A classic text examining man's mystical nature
  0–525–48278–4 Dutton pb $9.95

- **Ram Dass & Stephen Levine**
  GRIST FOR THE MILL
  0–89087–499–9 Celestial Arts pb $8.95

- **Barbara Foster**
  FORBIDDEN JOURNEY: The Life of Alexandra David-Neel
  Biography of the first European woman to visit Lhasa, Tibet
  Foreword by Lawrence Durrell
  0–06–250345–6 Harper & Row $21.95

- **John Lilly**
  THE CENTER OF THE CYCLONE: An Autobiography of Inner Space
  Autobiography of the noted researcher and expert on expanded states of consciousness
  0–517–52760–X Crown $14.95
  0–517–55614–6 Crown pb $7.95

- Ruth Montgomery with Joanne Garland
  RUTH MONTGOMERY: Herald of the New Age
  Spiritual autobiography of the psychic
  0-449-21252-1 Fawcett pb $3.50

- Raymond A. Moody, Jr.
  ELVIS AFTER LIFE
  Stories of people who see Elvis Presley during near-death experiences
  0-553-27345-0 Bantam pb $3.95
  LIFE AFTER LIFE
  Near-death experiences
  0-89176-037-7 Mockingbird $10.95

- Max Toth & Greg Nielson
  PYRAMID POWER
  0-89281-106-4 Inner Traditions pb $4.95

- Dhyani Ywahoo
  VOICES OF OUR ANCESTORS: Cherokee Teachings from the Wisdom Fire
  0-87773-410-0 Random House pb $9.95

Self-Help

- Walter Anderson
  COURAGE IS A THREE-LETTER WORD
  0-394-54656-3 Random House $17.95
  0-449-20902-4 Fawcett pb $3.95
  THE GREATEST RISK OF ALL: Why Some People Take Chances that Change Their Lives—and Why You Can Too
  0-395-46516-8 Houghton Mifflin $17.95

- Lucy Beale & Rich Fields
  THE WIN WIN WAY: The Ultimate Strategy for Personal and Professional Success
  0-15-197280-X HBJ $14.95
  0-15-696795-2 HBJ pb $6.95

- Joyce Brothers
  HOW TO GET WHATEVER YOU WANT OUT OF LIFE
  0-671-60515-1 Simon & Schuster $7.95
  0-345-34747-1 Ballantine pb $3.95

- Adelaide Bry
  HOW TO GET ANGRY WITHOUT FEELING GUILTY
  0-451-15862-8 NAL pb $3.95

- Leo Buscaglia
  LIVING, LOVING AND LEARNING
  0-449-90181-5 Fawcett pb $7.95
  PERSONHOOD
  0-449-90199-8 Fawcett pb $6.95

- Dale Carnegie
  HOW TO STOP WORRYING AND START LIVING
  0-671-50619-6 Simon & Schuster $15.95
  HOW TO WIN FRIENDS AND INFLUENCE PEOPLE
  0-671-42517-X Simon & Schuster $17.95

- Jimmy & Rosalynn Carter
  EVERYTHING TO GAIN: Making the Most of the Rest of Your Life
  0-394-55858-8 Random House $16.95
  0-449-14538-7 Fawcett pb $4.95

- Edward Charlesworth & Ronald Nathan
  STRESS MANAGEMENT: A Comprehensive Guide to Wellness
  0-345-32734-9 Ballantine pb $4.95

- Sara Kay Cohen
  WHOEVER SAID LIFE IS FAIR?: A Guide to Growing Through Life's Injustices
  0-425-10888-0 Berkley pb $3.95

- Richard Corriere & Patrick McGray
  LIFE ZONES: How to Win in the Game of Life
  0-345-30796-8 Ballantine pb $3.95

- Gary Emery
  OWN YOUR OWN LIFE: How the New Cognitive Therapy Can Make You Feel Wonderful
  0-451-14846-0 Signet pb $4.95

- Leonard Felder
  A FRESH START: How to Let Go of Emotional Baggage and Enjoy Your Life Again
  0-451-15759-1 Signet pb $4.50

- Lucy Freeman & Herbert Stream
  GUILT: Letting Go
  0-471-83636-2 Wiley $14.95
  0-471-61679-6 Wiley pb $9.95

- Robert Fulghum
  ALL I REALLY NEED TO KNOW I LEARNED IN KINDERGARTEN
  0-394-57102-9 Random House $16.95

- Celia Halas & Roberta Matteson
  I'VE DONE SO WELL—WHY DO I FEEL SO BAD?
  0-345-34532-0 Ballantine pb $3.95

- Carole Hyatt & Linda Gottlieb
  WHEN SMART PEOPLE FAIL: Rebuilding Yourself for Success
  0-671-61941-1 Simon & Schuster $16.95
  0-14-010727-4 Penguin pb $7.95

- Gerald Jampolsky
  GOODBYE TO GUILT: Releasing Fear Through Forgiveness
  0-553-34574-5 Bantam pb $9.95

- Susan Jeffers
  FEEL THE FEAR . . . AND DO IT ANYWAY
  0-15-130559-5 HBJ $14.95
  0-449-90292-7 Fawcett pb $6.95

- Harold Kushner
  WHEN BAD THINGS HAPPEN TO GOOD PEOPLE
  0-8052-3773-9 Schocken $19.95
  0-380-67033-X Avon pb $6.95

- Cheryl Merser
  GROWN UPS: In Search of Adulthood
  0-452-26165-1 NAL pb $8.95

- Mildred Newman & Bernard Berkowitz
  HOW TO BE YOUR OWN BEST FRIEND
  0-345-34239-9 Ballantine pb $2.95
  HOW TO TAKE CHARGE OF YOUR LIFE
  0-553-25590-8 Bantam pb $3.95

- Norman Vincent Peale
  THE POWER OF POSITIVE THINKING
  0-13-686402-3 Prentice-Hall pb $9.95
  THE TRUE JOY OF POSITIVE LIVING
  0-449-20833-8 Fawcett pb $3.95
  WHY SOME POSITIVE THINKERS GET POWERFUL RESULTS
  0-449-21359-5 Fawcett pb $3.95
  YOU CAN GET IT IF YOU WANT
  0-671-66072-1 Simon & Schuster pb $8.95

- Norman Vincent Peale & Smiley Banto
  THE ART OF REAL HAPPINESS
  0-13-048547-0 Prentice-Hall pb $7.95

- Paul Pearsall
  SUPER JOY: In Love with Living
  0-385-24459-2 Doubleday $18.95

- Anthony Robbins
  UNLIMITED POWER: The New Science of Personal Achievement
  0-671-61088-0 Simon & Schuster $17.95
  0-449-90280-3 Fawcett pb $9.95

- David Schwartz
  THE MAGIC OF GETTING WHAT YOU WANT
  0-425-10391-9 Berkley pb $5.95

- David Seabury
  THE ART OF SELFISHNESS: Fill Your Life With Confidence and Success
  0-671-64222-7 Simon & Schuster pb $5.95

- Gail Sheehy
  PASSAGES
  0-553-27106-7 Bantam pb $5.50
  PATHFINDERS
  0-553-27084-2 Bantam pb $5.50

- Sidney Simon
  GETTING UNSTUCK: Breaking Through the Barriers to Change
  0-446-51463-2 Warner $17.95

- Manuel Smith
  WHEN I SAY NO, I FEEL GUILTY
  0-553-26390-0 Bantam pb $4.95

- Judith Viorst
  NECESSARY LOSSES
  0-671-45655-5 Simon & Schuster $18.95

- Dennis Waitley
  THE PSYCHOLOGY OF WINNING
  0-425-09999-7 Berkley pb $3.50

- George Weinberg & Dianne Rowe
  THE PROJECTION PRINCIPLE
  0-312-00057-X St. Martin's $16.95

TO ORDER BOOKS AS GIFTS, SEE PAGE 1

LEISURE

Food

"Of all the books produced since the remote ages by human talents and industry those only that treat of cooking are, from a moral point of view, above suspicion. The intention of every other piece of prose may be discussed and even mistrusted, but the purpose of a cookery book is one and unmistakable. Its object can conceivably be no other than to increase the happiness of mankind."—Joseph Conrad

THE BASICS

• Jean Anderson & Elaine Hanna
THE NEW DOUBLEDAY COOKBOOK
Sensible basic recipes and techniques, and advice on nutritional values
0–385–19577–X Doubleday $16.95

• James Beard & others
CREATIVE COOKING
A superb collection of basic recipes with variations, clear instructions, and many useful illustrations
0–89577–037–7 Reader's Digest $16.50

• Marion Cunningham, editor
THE FANNIE FARMER COOKBOOK
Recently revised, this book exudes the same good sense and no-nonsense tone that made the original version famous. An American institution, with wonderful recipes, from butterscotch brownies to Spanish rice
0–394–40650–8 Knopf $18.95
0–553–25915–6 Bantam pb $6.95

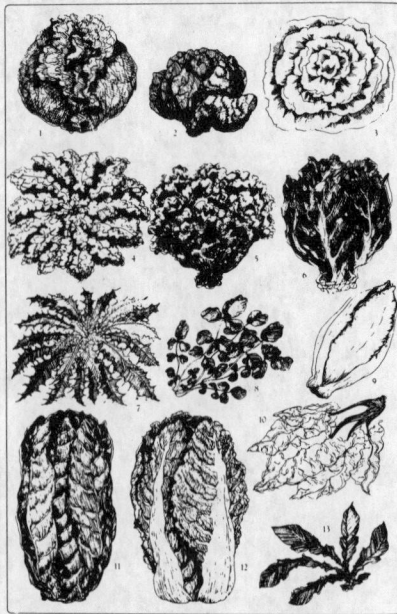

Drawing by Lauren Jarrett, from The Fannie Farmer Cookbook, *revised by Marion Cunningham (Knopf)*

• Pierre Franey
THE 60-MINUTE GOURMET
The former chef of Le Pavillon in New York City collects his columns from the *New York Times* for cooking by the clock. The recipes are superb, from cheese soufflé to pork chops with orange, and they can actually be prepared in an hour
0–449–90194–7 Fawcett pb $15.90

MORE 60-MINUTE GOURMET
A follow-up to the 1980 title. Don't miss the terrific chili recipe. A must for the busy household
Introduction by Craig Claiborne
0–449–90038–X Fawcett pb $7.95

• Pierre Franey & Bryan Miller
CUISINE RAPIDE
The companion volume to Franey's PBS television series
0–8129–1746–4 Times Books $22.50

• Gourmet Magazine
THE BEST OF GOURMET
A compilation of recipes from the magazine, divided into easy-to-use chapters. The magazine's famous food photos constitute Part One of each of these books

Volume 1
0–394–55258–X Random House $24.95

Volume 2
0–394–56039–6 Random House $24.95

Volume 3
0–394–56955–5 Random House $24.95

Volume 4
0–394–57529–6 Random House $24.50

• Jacques Pépin
LA TECHNIQUE: An Illustrated Guide to the Fundamental Techniques of Cooking
A master chef demonstrates the classic techniques in hundreds of step-by-step photos. Indispensable for the serious cook
0–8129–0610–1 Times Books $25.00

LA MÉTHODE: An Illustrated Guide to the Fundamental Methods of Cooking
More instructions and detailed photos. For the dedicated amateur as well as the professional
0–8129–0836–8 Times Books $25.00

THE ART OF COOKING
Much more ambitious than *La Technique* and *La Méthode,* and an extraordinary achievement in its own right. Here the emphasis is on the recipes: over 1300 color photographs show the step-by-step preparation of each dish. Comprehensive and complex, not for the beginner

Volume 1
0–394–54658–X Knopf $35.00

Volume 2
0–394–54659–8 Knopf $39.95

• Irma Rombauer & Marion Becker
THE JOY OF COOKING
From meat loaf to a definition of the mangosteen, this all-purpose volume, originally published in 1931 and since revised and enlarged many times, becomes a member of the family in most kitchens. "An invaluable reference work where techniques, cooking procedures, solid information about measurements, temperatures and even proper table settings are concerned"—Craig Claiborne
0–02–604570–2 Macmillan $16.95
0–452–25665–8 NAL pb $11.95

AMERICAN COOKERY

The History of American Food

• Harper & Row Editors
THE SETTLEMENT COOK BOOK 1903: A Facsimile Edition
0–671–22087–X Harper & Row $17.95

CRAIG CLAIBORNE: Important Cookbooks

Jenifer Harvey Lang, editor
LAROUSSE GASTRONOMIQUE: The New American Edition
This is, unarguably, the finest reference work on French cooking, classic and regional, ever published in English. Praising the book is tantamount to saying a few nice words about the finest wines of Burgundy, Bordeaux, and Champagne

Irma Rombauer & Marion Becker
THE JOY OF COOKING
This was the first cookbook I ever owned and it remains today one of the great treasures of American cooking

A.J. McClane
THE ENCYCLOPEDIA OF FISH COOKERY
This is the finest encyclopedia, both visually and verbally, relating to the looks, history, and evaluation of fish, ever printed in the English language. Great fish lore, scores of useful and interesting recipes

M.F.K. Fisher
THE ART OF EATING
To my mind, this is the best collection of essays about food written thus far in the 20th century. The book is serious but not pedantic, much of it relating to her early years of living in Provence

Jacques Pépin
THE ART OF COOKING: 2 Volumes
These are two of the most instructive and desirable books on French cooking ever printed. Each volume is magnificently illustrated in color with step-by-step photographs on how to prepare many of the most glorious dishes ever created in established French kitchens. This book should achieve the prestige once accorded the works of Auguste Escoffier in an earlier, less enlightened generation.

To my regret, many of the books I admire the most are out of print. These are listed in my autobiography:

Craig Claiborne
A FEAST MADE FOR LAUGHTER

- **Waverley Root & Richard De Rochemont**
  EATING IN AMERICA
  Not a cookbook but all about the fascinating reasons why we eat as we do. For the serious student of cookery
  0–912946–88–1 Ecco pb $9.95

- **Laura Shapiro**
  PERFECTION SALAD: Women and Cooking at the Turn of the Century
  0–374–23075–7 Farrar, Straus & Giroux $16.95
  0–8050–0228–6 Henry Holt pb $8.95

- **Amelia Simmons**
  THE FIRST AMERICAN COOKBOOK
  A facsimile of *American Cookery* (1796)
  0–486–24710–4 Dover pb $3.50

- **Jane & Michael Stern**
  REAL AMERICAN FOOD: From Yankee Red Flannel Hash and the Ultimate Navajo Taco to Beautiful Swimmer Pie and General Store Fudge Pie
  0–394–53953–2 Knopf $19.95

  SQUARE MEALS
  The recipes we all grew up on, collected from old cookbooks. Amusing, interesting, and practical
  0–394–74162–5 Knopf pb $8.95

  ROADFOOD AND GOODFOOD: A Restaurant Guidebook
  Not a cookbook, but two volumes in one—a cross-country tour of the Sterns' favorite highway restaurants. A diary of regional treats
  0–394–74396–2 Knopf pb $12.95

Famous American Chefs and Restaurants

- **Christopher Idone**
  GLORIOUS FOOD
  The first book from the renowned New York caterer, and still lovely in its 9 × 12 inch format, with many splendid color photographs
  0–941434–22–2 Stewart Tabori & Chang $20.00

- **Ellen Brown**
  COOKING WITH THE NEW AMERICAN CHEFS
  Young chefs share their techniques and combinations. Recipes by Paul Prudhomme, Wolfgang Puck, Jeremiah Tower, and Barbara Tropp; from the PBS television series
  0–06–015373–3 Harper & Row $22.95

- **John Clancy**
  JOHN CLANCY'S FAVORITE RECIPES: A Personal Cookbook
  The pastry chef and New York City restaurant owner collects his favorite recipes, including hot shrimp salad and chocolate roulade
  0–689–11710–8 Atheneum $21.95

- **Henry Haller & Virginia Aronson**
  THE WHITE HOUSE FAMILY COOKBOOK
  Presidential family favorites from Johnson to Reagan, by the former White House chef
  Foreword by Betty Ford
  0–394–55657–7 Random House $19.95

- **Tom Margittai & Paul Kovi**
  THE FOUR SEASONS COOKBOOK
  Favorite recipes from New York's great restaurant
  0–671–62796–1 Simon & Schuster pb $12.95

- **Wolfgang Puck**
  THE WOLFGANG PUCK COOKBOOK
  Recipes from Los Angeles' Spago and Chinois restaurants by their inspired creator. Don't miss the watercress salad with barbecued chicken breast or the lobster with sweet ginger and fried baby spinach leaves or Puck's famous grilled chicken with garlic and parsley. Not for the beginner but essential for any serious cook
  0–394–53366–6 Random House $19.95

- **Seppi Renggli**
  THE FOUR SEASONS SPA CUISINE
  The superb chef of The Four Seasons restaurant turns to lighter recipes
  0–671–54440–3 Simon & Schuster $17.95

- **Anne Rosenzweig**
  THE ARCADIA SEASONAL MURAL AND COOKBOOK
  Recipes by the founder of New York's Arcadia restaurant
  0–8109–1843–9 Abrams $14.95

- **Julee Rosso & others**
  THE SILVER PALATE COOKBOOK
  A great best-seller, filled with timely recipes that work: creamy pasta sauce with herbs, raspberry chicken, and many more
  0–89480–203–8 Workman $22.50
  0–89480–204–6 Workman pb $11.95

- **Jill St. John**
  THE JILL ST. JOHN COOKBOOK
  Easy-to-make gourmet dishes by the actress who also writes the food column for *USA Today*
  0–394–56132–5 Random House $24.95

- **Jeremiah Tower**
  JEREMIAH TOWER'S NEW AMERICAN CLASSICS
  The former chef at Chez Panisse and now owner of his own San Francisco restaurant, Tower is known for his stylish recipes using fresh American ingredients: for example, a warm salad of crayfish with cucumbers and dill, soft-shell crabs with tomato and basil, and black bean soup. Experience is necessary for many of these combinations
  0–06–181878–X Harper & Row $25.00

- **Alice Waters**
  THE CHEZ PANISSE MENU COOKBOOK
  One of the most influential American cookbooks, this classic has profoundly changed the way Americans cook and eat. The superb recipes, mingling the flavors and techniques of Provence and California, have inspired countless cooks, both professional and amateur. Not for beginners but essential for amateurs and professionals
  0–394–51787–3 Random House $19.95

- **Paul Bertolli & Alice Waters**
  CHEZ PANISSE COOKING: New Tastes and Techniques
  The first book of Chez Panisse main course recipes since the original *Chez Panisse Menu Cookbook*
  0–394–56970–9 Random House $24.95

American Food Writers

- **James Beard**
  JAMES BEARD'S AMERICAN COOKERY
  Probably the most inspiring American food writer and chef of the 20th century. Into his 80s, he taught and wrote and shared his unwavering enthusiasm for food, leaving an indelible mark on American cuisine
  0–316–08564–2 Little, Brown $29.95
  0–316–08566–9 Little, Brown pb $14.95

  THE JAMES BEARD COOKBOOK
  0–440–54188–3 Dell pb $12.95

  DELIGHTS AND PREJUDICES
  0–689–70605–7 Atheneum pb $7.95

  THE NEW JAMES BEARD
  Lighter recipes but just as delicious, including an all-time great marinade
  0-394–41154–4 Knopf $16.95

  JAMES BEARD'S THEORY AND PRACTICE OF GOOD COOKING
  0–394–48493–2 Knopf $18.95

  THE FIRESIDE COOKBOOK
  0–671–44774–2 Simon & Schuster pb $9.95

- **Julia Child**
  FROM JULIA CHILD'S KITCHEN
  Julia Child introduced classical French cuisine to the American kitchen and changed our lives forever. Her books are amusing, intelligent, and energetic
  0–394–71027–4 Knopf pb $14.95

  JULIA CHILD AND COMPANY
  A splendid and instructive cookbook based on her television series. Don't miss her green bean salad with watercress and tomatoes
  0–394–50200–0 Knopf $17.95

  JULIA CHILD AND MORE COMPANY
  Thirteen more menus. The spice cookies with molasses and peanuts are addictive
  0–394–50710–X Knopf $17.95
  0–394–73806–3 Knopf pb $12.95

- **Craig Claiborne**
  CRAIG CLAIBORNE'S NEW NEW YORK TIMES COOKBOOK
  A basic but imaginative collection of recipes by the former food writer for the *New York Times*. The pasta with ginger and garlic sauce is memorable
  0–8129–0835–X Times Books $24.95

  A FEAST MADE FOR LAUGHTER
  A very personal memoir, with a splendid final section of the books he would collect for a cookbook library
  0–03–064007–5 Henry Holt pb $7.95

- **Helen Corbitt**
  THE HELEN CORBITT COLLECTION
  0–395–31295–7 Houghton Mifflin $27.95

  HELEN CORBITT'S COOKBOOK
  More easy-to-prepare, accessible recipes
  0–395–07577–7 Houghton Mifflin $14.95

HELEN CORBITT'S GREENHOUSE COOKBOOK
0–395–25729–8 Houghton Mifflin $14.95

• Betty Crocker
BETTY CROCKER'S COOKBOOK
0–307–09801–X Western $19.95
0–553–26660–8 Bantam pb $5.95

BETTY CROCKER'S INTERNATIONAL COOKBOOK
0–394–50453–4 Random House $14.95

M.F.K. Fisher
A CORDIALL WATER: A Garland of Odd and Old Receipts to Assuage the Ills of Man and Beast
One of America's favorite writers on food and wine, called by W.H. Auden "the best prose writer in America." This is a charming mixed bag of restoratives and fortifiers
0–86547–036–7 North Point pb $6.95

THE ART OF EATING
"Two of the most delectable and humourous entries are titled 'How to Seduce' and 'How to Unseduce,' with accompanying menus"—Craig Claiborne
0–394–71399–0 Random House pb $11.95

SERVE IT FORTH
Her first book, published in 1937
0–86547–369–2 North Point pb $10.95

WITH BOLD KNIFE AND FORK
Essays on culinary matters such as "The Trouble with Tripe" and "One Way to Stay Young (Salads)"
0–399–50397–8 Putnam pb $8.95

M.F.K. Fisher (photo by Annie Leibowitz), author of As They Were (*Knopf*)

• Alice B. Toklas
THE ALICE B. TOKLAS COOKBOOK
Gertrude Stein's lifelong companion was a wonderful cook. Her famous cookbook

supplies an insight into the lives of Stein and Toklas and their friends
Introduction by M.F.K. Fisher
0–06–181876–3 Harper & Row $14.95
0–06–091327–4 Harper & Row pb $6.95

• James Villas
VILLAS AT TABLE: A Passion for Food and Drink
"In this selection of journalism and recipes, he details his passion for ocean liners, *crême brulée,* Parisian bistros and the Manhattan, arguing their merits with literate coherence and acerbic wit"—Florence Fabricant
0–06–015995–2 Harper & Row $19.95

JAMES VILLAS' COUNTRY COOKING
Hearty and basic recipes for informal meals
0–316–90302–7 Little, Brown $19.95

• Paula Wolfert
PAULA WOLFERT'S WORLD OF FOOD: A Collection of Recipes from her Kitchen, Travels and Friends
"A distinguished American cooking writer shares her experiences, insight and intelligent cooking sense"—*NY Times*
0–06–015995–3 Harper & Row $25.00

Reynaldo Alejandro, editor
CLASSIC MENUS
Fascinating menus from the collections of the New York Public Library
0–86636–064–6 PBC $55.00

Linda Wolfe, editor
THE LITERARY GOURMET: Menus from Masterpieces
Menus recreated from dining scenes in works by such authors as Shakespeare, Flaubert, Tolstoy, and Virginia Woolf. All the dishes have been tested at The Four Seasons restaurant by food critic Mimi Sheraton
0–671–67353–X Simon & Schuster $10.95

New England and the Atlantic Seaboard

• Judith & Evan Jones
THE L.L. BEAN BOOK OF NEW NEW ENGLAND COOKERY
The basic source for New England recipes, including traditional dishes and ethnic innovations: shepherd's pie, chicken with dumplings, and codfish cakes, as well as Portuguese salt cod—among hundreds of splendid, practical dishes for both amateur and professional
0–394–54456–0 Random House $22.50

• Clarissa Silitch, editor
YANKEE CHURCH SUPPER COOKBOOK
The kinds of homemade recipes we all love from *Yankee Magazine*
0–911658–14–9 Yankee pb $12.95

• Caroline Sloat, editor
OLD STURBRIDGE VILLAGE COOKBOOK: Authentic Early American Recipes for the Modern Kitchen
One hundred authentic recipes from the museum that recreates early 19th-century

New England life. Fricassees and poached fish and a "most delicious salad sauce"
0–87106–941–5 Globe Pequot pb $9.95

• Mrs. B.C. Howard
FIFTY YEARS IN A MARYLAND KITCHEN: 430 Authentic Regional Recipes
Evocative recipes, revised and updated, from a 19th-century kitchen
0–486–25220–5 Dover pb $5.95

The South

• Marcelle Bienvenu
THE PICAYUNE'S CREOLE COOK BOOK
Regional recipes with many variations. A basic source
0–394–576527 Random House $24.95
0–486–22678–6 Dover pb $8.50

• Ella & Dick Brennan
THE COMMANDER'S PALACE NEW ORLEANS COOKBOOK
The recipes that made this New Orleans landmark famous
0–517–55049–0 Crown $17.95

• Nathaniel Burton & Rudy Lombard
CREOLE FEAST: 15 Master Chefs of New Orleans Reveal Their Secrets
A perennial favorite
0–394–41328–8 Random House $19.95

• Craig Claiborne
CRAIG CLAIBORNE'S SOUTHERN COOKING
The basic source for Southern cooking by a Mississippi native and longtime food writer for the *New York Times:* smothered chicken, barbecued duck, and several cornbreads
0–8129–1599–2 Times Books $19.95

• Nathalie Dupree
NEW SOUTHERN COOKING
Traditional recipes brought up to date by the former food editor of *Atlanta Magazine.* Marvelous desserts, including a wonderful peanut butter cake
0–394–54494–3 Knopf $19.95

• John Egerton
SOUTHERN FOOD: At Home, On the Road, In History
A lively, handsomely illustrated celebration; a history, restaurant guide, and recipe book all in one
0–394–54494–3 Knopf $24.95

• Camille Glenn
THE HERITAGE OF SOUTHERN COOKING
A recipe tour of Southern cuisine from one of the South's foremost cooking teachers. Try the Kentucky-style ham in cream or Baltimore barbecue chicken
0–89480–132–5 Workman $22.95
0–89480–117–1 Workman pb $14.95

• Gene Hovis & Sylvia Rosenthal
GENE HOVIS' UPTOWN DOWN HOME COOKBOOK
0–316–37443–1 Little, Brown $17.95

- Junior League of Baton Rouge
RIVER ROAD RECIPES
0–9613026–0–7 Jr. League of Baton Rouge pb $9.00

- Edna Lewis
THE TASTE OF COUNTRY COOKING
The recipes and reminiscences of a brilliant cook from Virginia. The chicken with dumplings is unforgettable, as is her fresh peach cobbler with nutmeg sauce
0–394–73215–4 Knopf pb $12.95

- Sally Morrison
CROSS CREEK KITCHENS: Seasonal Recipes and Reflections
0–937404–50–0 Triad $19.95
0–937404–06–3 Triad pb $8.95

- Alex Patout
PATOUT'S CAJUN HOME COOKING
The best Cajun cookery book, by a renowned specialist
0–394–54725–X Random House $19.95

- Paul Prudhomme
CHEF PAUL PRUDHOMME'S LOUISIANA KITCHEN
The owner and chef of K-Paul's restaurant in New Orleans shares the recipes he has made famous, among them blackened redfish, deep-fried crayfish (also called Cajun popcorn), and coffee cookies
0–688–02847–0 Morrow $19.95

THE PRUDHOMME FAMILY COOKBOOK: Old-Time Louisiana Recipes
0–688–07549–5 Morrow $19.95

The Southwest

- Ellen Brown
SOUTHWEST TASTES: From the PBS Television Series "Great Chefs of the West"
Forty-four chefs contribute recipes from five western states, including *enchiladas verdes,* barbecued pork with tequila casserole, and caramel custard flavored with orange
0–89586–578–5 HP $19.95

- Jane Butel
FIESTA!: Southwestern Entertaining with Jane Butel
Recipes and advice on how to entertain southwestern-style. Thirty menus for brunch, lunch, supper, dinner, as well as a picnic of London broil with green chili stew topping and whole-wheat tortilla rolls
0–06–015690–2 Harper & Row $15.95

- Huntley Dent
THE FEAST OF SANTA FE: Cooking of the American Southwest
An informative, intelligent guide to the history and practice of Santa Fe cookery
0–671–47686–6 Simon & Schuster $18.95

- Anne Lindsay Greer
CUISINE OF THE AMERICAN SOUTHWEST
The flavors of the region abound: try the savory beef and tortilla casserole and caramel custard flavored with orange
0–06–181320–6 Harper & Row $22.50

American Home Cooking

- Nika Hazelton
AMERICAN HOME COOKING
These recipes are as good as they are simple. Note the barbecued spareribs and sour cream potato salad
0–345–31261–9 Ballantine pb $3.50

- Ronald Johnson
THE AMERICAN TABLE
Tempting regional recipes such as upside-down apple pie
0–671–60238–1 Pocket pb $7.95

- Marilyn Kluger
COUNTRY KITCHENS REMEMBERED: A Memoir with Favorite Family Recipes
A cookbook and memoir from a writer who grew up on an Indiana farm. Family recipes include grandma's light bread and coffee kuchen, and scalloped potatoes with ham and cheese
0–396–08760–4 Dodd, Mead $17.95

- Amy Bess Miller & Persis Wellington Fuller, editors
THE BEST OF SHAKER COOKING
Shaker cookery at its simplest and most authentic
0–02–584980–8 Macmillan $19.95

- Jeff Smith
THE FRUGAL GOURMET
A giant best-seller by the television chef
0–345–33523–6 Ballantine pb $4.95

THE FRUGAL GOURMET COOKS AMERICAN
Recipes using indigenous American produce and products
0–688–06347–0 Morrow $17.95

- Raymond Sokolov
FADING FEAST: A Compendium of Disappearing American Regional Foods
0–374–15213–6 Farrar, Straus & Giroux $17.95
0–525–48030–7 Dutton pb $6.95

- Miriam Ungerer
COUNTRY FOOD: A Seasonal Journal
Practical American recipes for the fresh provender that each season provides. Note the wild mushroom meat loaf and double peach sherbet
0–394–72906–4 Random House pb $8.95

Junior League Cookbooks

The recipes in these straightforward compilations are usually family favorites that are easy-to-prepare and eminently pleasing.

Junior League of Baltimore
HUNT TO HARBOR: An Epicurean Tour
An appealing collection of favorite tried-and-true recipes. Excellent dessert selection
0–9615011–0–3 Jr. L. of Baltimore $14.95

Junior League of Kansas City
BEYOND PARSLEY
Exceptional color photographs illustrate more than 400 combinations, like the

---

intriguing checkerboard chocolate chestnut pâté shortbreads
0–9607076–1–1 Jr. L. of Kansas City $24.50

Junior League of Pasadena
CALIFORNIA HERITAGE CONTINUES: A Cookbook
A handsome book of tempting recipes such as roast duckling with black peppercorn sauce and shoestring yams. Beautiful color photographs
0–385–19873–6 Doubleday pb $22.50

Junior League of San Francisco
SAN FRANCISCO A LA CARTE
A collection of recipes so successful that it generated the sequel *San Francisco Encore*
0–385–13545–9 Doubleday pb $22.50

SAN FRANCISCO ENCORE
A treasury of regional recipes, including Union Street salad—chicken, spinach, and pea pods with zesty curry dressing
0–385–19237–1 Doubleday pb $22.50

Anne Seranne, editor
THE WESTERN JUNIOR LEAGUE COOKBOOK
Thirty-three Junior Leagues, including one in Mexico City, have contributed their favorite recipes
0–679–51454–6 McKay $12.95

FRENCH COOKERY

- Julia Child
MASTERING THE ART OF FRENCH COOKING

Volume 1
The classic preparations, including clear instructions, drawings, and superb recipes. The French basics adapted to the American kitchen
0–394–53399–2 Knopf $29.95
0–394–72178–0 Knopf pb $16.95

Volume 2
An extraordinary book, particularly the chapters on pastry. Recommended for the accomplished cook
0–394–40152–2 Knopf $29.95
0–394–72177–2 Knopf pb $16.95

- Julia Child, Simone Beck & Louisette Bertholle
FRENCH CHEF COOKBOOK
Child's first book and still in print. A must
0–394–40135–2 Knopf $15.50
0–553–26434–6 Bantam pb $5.95

- Elizabeth David
FRENCH PROVINCIAL COOKING
A classic by the much-respected British authority whose taste and style have influenced two generations of cooks. This belongs in every collection
0–14–046099–3 Penguin pb $9.95

- Robert Freson
THE TASTE OF FRANCE
A picture book with recipes, capturing the quintessence of France and its cuisine. Exceptional photos
0–941434–36–2 Stewart, Tabori & Chang $45.00

- Mireille Johnston
THE CUISINE OF THE SUN: Classical French Cooking from Nice and Provence
From a cook who was born there and later lived in the United States
0–394–72824–6 Random House pb $8.95

- Richard Olney
THE FRENCH MENU COOKBOOK: A Revised and Updated Edition of a Culinary Classic
Subtle and splendid
0–87923–579–9 Godine pb $12.95

SIMPLE FRENCH FOOD
Another Olney classic
Preface by James Beard
0–689–70546–8 Atheneum pb $10.95

- Waverley Root
THE FOOD OF FRANCE
Not a cookbook but an essential background to French gastronomy
0–394–72428–3 Random House pb $10.95

- Paula Wolfert
THE COOKING OF SOUTH-WEST FRANCE: A Collection of Traditional and New Recipes
An authoritative and indispensable source for the cooking of Gascony—the land of foie gras, confits, and Armagnac
0–06–097195–9 Harper & Row pb $10.95

Classic French Cuisine

- Auguste Escoffier
THE ESCOFFIER COOK BOOK
The classic guide to French haute cuisine
0–517–50662–9 Crown $10.95

- Jenifer Harvey Lang, editor
LAROUSSE GASTRONOMIQUE: The New American Edition
The essential encyclopedia of classic French cuisine with techniques, definitions, and over 8500 recipes
0–517–57032–7 Crown $50.00

- Henri Paul Pellaprat
MODERN FRENCH CULINARY ART
From the former chief instructor of the Cordon Bleu cooking school
0–00–435143–6 Van Nostrand Reinhold $118.95

- André Simon
A CONCISE ENCYCLOPEDIA OF GASTRONOMY
A reprint of a famous and amusing reference book
0–87951–180–X Overlook pb $14.95

Famous French Chefs

- Georges Blanc
THE NATURAL CUISINE OF GEORGES BLANC
A stunning picture book with recipes, among them wild mushrooms with sea

scallops and vanilla crisps with apples and cider
1–55670–008–3 Stewart, Tabori & Chang $45.00

- Paul Bocuse
PAUL BOCUSE'S FRENCH COOKING
Recipes from Bocuse's famous restaurant. For the experienced cook
0–394–75545–6 Pantheon pb $16.95

- Andre Daguin & Anne de Ravel
FOIE GRAS, MAGRET, AND OTHER GOOD FOOD FROM GASCONY
0–394–57027–8 Random House $19.95

- Anton Moismann
CUISINE NATURELLE: Elegant Food for a Healthy Life
Nutritious food based on fresh ingredients
0–689–11587–3 Atheneum $29.95

- Albert & Michel Roux
THE ROUX BROTHERS ON PATISSERIE: Pastries and Desserts from Three-Star Master Chefs
An instructive step-by-step work with photographs. If your kitchen is large and your hands are cool, undertake the fine art of pulling sugar
0–13–783382–2 Prentice-Hall $24.95

- Alain & Eventhia Senderens
THE THREE-STAR RECIPES OF ALAIN SENDERENS
Fine fish and shellfish recipes, among many others, from the master chef of the renowned Parisian restaurants L'Archestrate and Lucas Carton. Try the roast lobster with vanilla butter sauce and the mixed fried dinner with garlic mayonnaise. Not for the beginner
0–688–00728–7 Morrow $22.50
0–688–06668–2 Morrow pb $9.95

French Cooking Lessons

- Madeleine Kamman
IN MADELEINE'S KITCHEN
Recipes from a gifted and opinionated professional with unwavering standards
Introduction by James Beard
0–689–11485–0 Atheneum $22.95

MADELEINE COOKS
From her television series; very French, with straightforward, basic recipes
0–688–06203–2 Morrow $17.95

WHEN FRENCH WOMEN COOK: A Gastronomic Memoir
A collection of interesting recipes by French women
0–689–70620–0 Atheneum pb $14.95

- Jacques Pépin
EVERYDAY COOKING WITH JACQUES PEPIN
Recipes from the chef and expert cooking teacher
0–06–014994–9 Harper & Row $19.95

JACQUES PEPIN: A French Chef Cooks at Home
0–671–25397–2 Simon & Schuster pb $8.95

ITALIAN COOKERY

- Ada Boni
THE TALISMAN ITALIAN COOK BOOK
A standard work
0–517–52040–0 Crown $9.95

- Giuliano Bugialli
THE FINE ART OF ITALIAN COOKING
Note the chapter on risotto, notably the recipe with garlic sauce
0–8129–0640–3 Times Books $19.95

GIULIANO BUGIALLI'S CLASSIC TECHNIQUES OF ITALIAN COOKING
A well-researched and fascinating collection of recipes
0–671–25218–6 Simon & Schuster $24.95

GIULIANO BUGIALLI'S FOODS OF ITALY
The splendor of Italian cooking, with striking color photographs. Expensive but worth it for the many original and well presented recipes
0–941434–52–4 Stewart, Tabori & Chang $45.00

- Elizabeth David
ITALIAN FOOD
This handsome volume, with remarkable color plates, celebrates Italy and Italian cooking. Reading the text is almost like going on the journey itself
0–06–015842–5 Harper & Row $27.00

- Virginie & George Elbert
DOLCI: The Fabulous Desserts of Italy
0–317–64604–4 Simon & Schuster $17.95

- Edward Giobbi
ITALIAN FAMILY COOKING
Introduction by Craig Claiborne
0–394–72564–6 Random House pb $9.95

- Edward Giobbi & Richard Wolff
EAT RIGHT, EAT WELL: The Italian Way
A creative home cook teams up with a physician to present Italian food low in calories and fat. Charts on the components in each recipe
0–394–53071–3 Knopf $19.95

Freshly made scamorze cheeses, from Giuliano Bugialli's Foods of Italy, *photo by John Dominis (Stewart, Tabori, and Chang)*

✉ **TO ORDER BOOKS AS GIFTS, SEE PAGE 1**

Marcella Hazan
THE CLASSIC ITALIAN COOK BOOK
A definitive work, the first of three wonderful books by the illustrious teacher of Italian cooking
0–394–40510–2 Knopf $22.50

MORE CLASSIC ITALIAN COOKING
More superb recipes by Hazan, such as drunk roast pork, and pasta with sardines, Palermo style
0–394–49855–0 Knopf $22.95
0–345–31403–4 Ballantine pb $4.95

MARCELLA'S ITALIAN KITCHEN
"Of all Marcella Hazan's marvelous books, this may be the best—personal, elegant, inventive, flavorful"—Barbara Kafka
0–394–50980–3 Knopf $19.95

• Nika Hazelton
THE REGIONAL ITALIAN KITCHEN
An authority on many cuisines of the world collects regional favorites for the beginner and more accomplished cook
0–87131–252–2 Little, Brown $14.95

• Angela Hederman & Barbara Raves
A TUSCAN IN THE KITCHEN: Recipes and Tales from My Home
0–517–56916–7 Crown $22.95

ALICE WATERS:
Inspiring Cookbooks

James Beard
DELIGHTS AND PREJUDICES

Giuliano Bugialli
THE FINE ART OF ITALIAN COOKING

Elizabeth David
FRENCH PROVINCIAL COOKING

Roy de Groot
THE AUBERGE OF THE FLOWERING HEARTH

M.F.K. Fisher
THE ART OF EATING

Diana Kennedy
THE CUISINES OF MEXICO

Richard Olney
THE FRENCH MENU COOKBOOK: A Revised and Updated Edition of a Culinary Classic

Angelo M. Pellegrini
THE UNPREJUDICED PALATE

Waverley Root
THE FOOD OF FRANCE

Alice B. Toklas
THE ALICE B. TOKLAS COOKBOOK

• Waverley Root
THE FOOD OF ITALY
A cultural history of Italian cooking that remains unequaled
0–394–72429–1 Random House pb $10.95

• Alfredo Viazzi
ALFREDO VIAZZI'S ITALIAN COOKING: More Than 150 Inspired Interpretations of Great Italian Cuisine
Recipes from the New York restauranteur who introduced Americans to the cuisine of northern Italy
0–394–50167–5 Random House $12.95
0–394–71747–3 Random House pb $6.95

BRITISH AND IRISH COOKERY

• Myrtle Allen
THE BALLYMALOE COOKBOOK
Distinctive recipes from this much-respected cooking school in Ireland. Try the brown bread recipe and any of the marvelous ice creams
0–7171–1339–6 Irish Books and Media pb $13.95

• Alison Armstrong
THE JOYCE OF COOKING
"This is a joyous book celebrating the best of Irish cooking. Food's an essential part of [James] Joyce's writing, which has enabled Armstrong to write a strong new cookbook, with humor and intelligence, using quotes from his work"—Shirley King
0–930794–85–0 Station Hill $18.95

• Elizabeth David
AN OMELETTE AND A GLASS OF WINE
David's recipes are deceptively simple but reveal the exact essence of the dish and its preparation. Read her as much for her wisdom as for exceptional knowledge of the world's cuisines
0–670–80769–9 Viking $19.95
0–14–046721–1 Penguin pb $8.95

• Jane Garmey
GREAT NEW BRITISH COOKING
Recipes with a lighter touch
0–671–53258–8 Simon & Schuster $16.95

• Jane Grigson
JANE GRIGSON'S BRITISH COOKERY
0–689–11524–5 Atheneum $24.95

• Diana Kennedy
NOTHING FANCY: Recipes and Recollections of Soul-Satisfying Food
Recipes from her English childhood and travels in Europe and Mexico. "Diana's passion, creativity, and sense of adventure created an outstanding and original cookbook, written with humor, provocation and perception"—Paula Wolfert
0–8654–374–9 North Point pb $12.95

• Hilary Walden
HARROD'S BOOK OF TRADITIONAL ENGLISH COOKERY
Recipes from London's famous department store
0–87795–839–4 Morrow $13.00

MEDITERRANEAN AND MIDDLE EASTERN COOKERY

• Robert Carrier
A TASTE OF MOROCCO: A Culinary Journey with Recipes
Magnificent color volume from a cook who knows his way in Morocco; recipes are only a part of this book, which provides a culinary tour of the region
0–517–56559–5 Crown $30.00

• Alan Davidson
MEDITERRANEAN SEAFOOD
Part 1 discusses the fish; Part 2 tells how to cook them. By a captivating and curious writer
0–8071–0972–X LSU $19.95
0–8071–0973–8 LSU pb $9.95

• Patience Gray
HONEY FROM A WEED: Fasting and Feasting in Tuscany, Catalonia, the Cyclades and Apulia
A 1987 award-winning autobiographical celebration of life near the Mediterranean as well as cooking and conserving that area's staple foods. Scholarly
0–06–181322–2 Harper & Row $25.00

Claudia Roden
MEDITERRANEAN COOKERY
Beautifully photographed, with over 250 tempting recipes, including Moroccan pigeon pie and orange and almond cake
0–394–54434–X Knopf $24.95

A BOOK OF MIDDLE EASTERN FOOD
0–394–47181–4 Knopf $19.45
0–394–71948–4 Knopf pb $11.95

• Paula Wolfert
COUSCOUS AND OTHER GOOD FOOD FROM MOROCCO
Don't miss the lamb tagine with raisins, almonds, and honey
0–06–014721–0 Harper & Row $18.95
0–06–091396–7 Harper & Row pb $10.95

MEDITERRANEAN COOKING
An authoritative source
0–88001–075–4 Ecco $18.50

OTHER EUROPEAN COOKERY

• Jean Anderson
THE FOOD OF PORTUGAL
The author has spent a lifetime learning about Portugal; this is the definitive work
0–688–04363–1 Morrow $24.95

• Penelope Casas
FOODS AND WINES OF SPAIN
A fascinating cookbook by an expert cook and scholar. Note the white gazpacho recipe and chicken in chorizo and red wine sauce
0–394–51348–7 Knopf $22.50

TAPAS: The Little Dishes of Spain
The small finger foods of Spain
0–394–54086–7 Knopf $24.95
0–394–74235–4 Knopf pb $12.95

• Vilma Liacouras Chantiles
THE FOOD OF GREECE
Recipes and anecdotes from the mainland
and islands
0–396–08613–6 Dodd, Mead pb $10.95

• Peter Grunauer & Andreas Kisler
VIENNESE CUISINE: The New Approach
Restaurant owner and chef present the
new lighter approach to Austrian cooking
0–385–27999–X Doubleday $24.95

• Nika Hazelton
THE BELGIAN COOKBOOK
An exceptional cookbook author presents
the authentic recipes of this sophisticated
cuisine
0–689–70545–X Atheneum pb $7.95

CLASSIC SCANDINAVIAN COOKING
0–684–18636–5 Scribners $18.95

THE SWISS COOKBOOK
0–689–70363–5 Atheneum pb $9.95

• George Lang
THE CUISINE OF HUNGARY
0–689–70621–9 Atheneum pb $11.95

• Mimi Sheraton
GERMAN COOKBOOK
The basic book for German cuisine
0–394–40138–7 Random House $24.95

• Anne Volokh & Mavis Manus
THE ART OF RUSSIAN CUISINE
From pirogi to baking powder and
buckwheat blini. The standard work,
comprehensive and exciting
0–02–622090–3 Macmillan $24.95

ASIAN COOKERY

• Jennifer Brennan
THE CUISINES OF ASIA
A very useful introduction to the cuisines
of China, India, Indonesia, Japan, Korea,
Malaysia and Singapore, the Philippines,
Thailand, and Vietnam
0–312–17841–7 St. Martin's $19.95

• Linda Burum
ASIAN PASTA
Devoted to the pastas of Japan, China,
Korea, Vietnam, and other Asian
countries. Instructive and not too detailed
0–201108–33–X Aris pb $12.95

• Bruce Cost
**BRUCE COST'S ASIAN INGREDIENTS:
Buying and Cooking the Staple Foods of
China, Japan, and Southeast Asia**
0–688–05877–9 Morrow $22.95

China

• Ken Hom
KEN HOM'S CHINESE COOKERY
Excellent recipes from a respected and
sensible writer and teacher
0–06–096059–0 Harper & Row pb $14.95

**KEN HOM'S EAST MEETS WEST
CUISINE: An American Chef Redefines the
Foodstyles of Two Cultures**
Chinese cooking sometimes with American
ingredients; American cooking sometimes
with Chinese ingredients: very clever, with
superb results
0–671–47086–8 Simon & Schuster $19.95

• Ken Hom & Harvey Steiman
CHINESE TECHNIQUE
Recipes, with many photographs
illustrating all aspects of Chinese technique
0–671–25348–4 Pocket pb $12.95

• Florence Lin
**FLORENCE LIN'S COMPLETE BOOK
OF CHINESE NOODLES, DUMPLINGS,
AND BREADS**
This great teacher's recipes include
crabmeat salad with fried rice noodles and
boiled dumplings Beijing style with three
fillings and two sauces. "Complete" is the
word
0–688–03796–8 Morrow $19.95

• Eileen Yin-Fei Lo
**THE DIM SUM BOOK: Art of the Chinese
Teahouse**
Buns and dumplings and breads and so on
0–517–54581–0 Crown $14.95

• Kenneth Lo
**NEW CHINESE VEGETARIAN
COOKING**
An instructive book from a well-respected
author
0–394–75005–5 Pantheon pb $7.95

• Ellen & John Schecker
**MRS. CHIANG'S SZECHWAN
COOKBOOK**
The spicy cuisine of Szechwan province
0–06–015828–X Harper & Row $18.95

• Nina Simonds
CLASSIC CHINESE CUISINE
Splendid recipes, not for the beginner,
from a young but accomplished American
student of Chinese cooking
0–395–36645–3 Houghton Mifflin pb $11.95

• Barbara Tropp
**THE MODERN ART OF CHINESE
COOKING**
The first-rate recipes and information on
substitutes, storing, and even wines make
this essential
0–688–00566–7 Morrow $24.95

Japan

• Elizabeth Andoh
AN AMERICAN TASTE OF JAPAN
Integrates Japanese ingredients and
culinary philosophy with American
foodstuffs and eating habits
0–688–04369–0 Morrow $24.95

• Shizuo Tsuji
JAPANESE COOKING: A Simple Art
An American shares her comprehensive
knowledge of Japanese cooking. For the
experienced cook
0–394–41219–2 Knopf $15.00

• Shizuo Tsuji
JAPANESE COOKING: A Simple Art
The intricacies of Japanese cooking with
detailed illustrations
Introduction by M.F.K. Fisher
0–87011–399–2 Kodansha $24.95

• Eri Yamaguchi
**THE WELL-FLAVORED VEGETABLE:
New and Traditional Japanese Methods of
Preparing Vegetables**
Ways to prepare vegetables without
cooking: pickling, marinating and so forth
0–87011–861–7 Kodansha $17.95

India

• Yamuna Devi
**LORD KRISHNA'S CUISINE: The Art of
Indian Vegetarian Cooking**
Superb recipes and personal anecdotes
0–525–24564–2 Dutton $29.95

• Madhur Jaffrey
INDIAN COOKERY
First published to accompany Jaffrey's
BBC series, these recipes, with color
photographs, are authentic and easy to
prepare
0–8120–2700–0 Barron's pb $11.95

**AN INVITATION TO INDIAN
COOKING**
One of the best guides to Indian cooking
0–394–48172–0 Knopf $14.95
0–394–71191–2 Random House pb $6.95

• Julie Sahni
CLASSIC INDIAN COOKING
A sensitive approach with particularly
clear text
0–688–03721–6 Morrow $22.95

**CLASSIC INDIAN VEGETARIAN AND
GRAIN COOKING**
Intelligent and expert. Try the stuffed
cauliflower with tart tomato-coriander
sauce, carrot salad with peanuts and
mustard seeds, and tandoor bread
0–688–04995–8 Morrow $22.00

Southeast Asia

• Reynaldo Alejandro
THE PHILIPPINE COOKBOOK
A useful book on this lesser-known cuisine.
Don't miss the ginger tea recipe
0–698–11174–5 Putnam $17.95
0–399–51144–X Putnam pb $10.95

• Charlie Amatykul
**THE ORIENTAL HOTEL'S THAI
COOKING SCHOOL COOKBOOK**
0–394–57518–0 Random House $24.95

• Copeland Marks & Aung Thein
THE BURMESE KITCHEN
0–87131–524–6 Evans $19.95

• Copeland Marks & Mintari Soeharjo
THE INDONESIAN KITCHEN
0–689–70667–7 Atheneum pb $9.95

• Puangkram Schmitz & Michael Worman
PRACTICAL THAI COOKING
0–87011–727–0 Kodansha $19.95

LATIN AMERICAN AND CARIBBEAN COOKERY

• Elisabeth Lambert Ortiz
THE BOOK OF LATIN AMERICAN COOKING
Includes Venezuelan steak with rice, black beans, and plantains
0–394–41226–5 Knopf $16.95
0–394–74514–0 Knopf $9.95

THE COMPLETE BOOK OF CARIBBEAN COOKING
Some simple recipes, some exotic—all easy to prepare
0–345–33256–3 Ballantine pb $4.95

Mexico

• Rick & Deanne Bayless
AUTHENTIC MEXICAN: Regional Cooking from the Heart of Mexico
A splendid compendium of information and recipes, such as cold chicken and avocado with chile chipotle, minced pork with almonds, raisins and sweet spices, and Mexican tomato-colored rice with vegetables
0–688–04394–1 Morrow $24.95

• Aida Gabiloldo
MEXICAN FAMILY COOKING
0–449–90162–9 Fawcett $19.95

• Diana Kennedy
THE CUISINES OF MEXICO
The definitive work
Foreword by Craig Claiborne
0–06–181481–4 Harper & Row $19.95

MEXICAN REGIONAL COOKING
An unsurpassable collection
0–06–091166–2 Harper & Row pb $10.95

BAKING

• Marion Cunningham
THE FANNIE FARMER BAKING BOOK
This companion volume to *The Fannie Farmer Cookbook* offers a remarkable variety of recipes with detailed instructions and text. If you could have only one book on baking, this would be it
0–394–53332–1 Knopf $16.95

• Jim Fobel
THE OLD-FASHIONED BAKING BOOK
The favorites as we remember them
0–345–34822–2 Ballantine $17.95

• Paula Peck
THE ART OF FINE BAKING
A classic by a disciple of James Beard
0–671–20611–7 Simon & Schuster pb $7.95

Breads

• James Beard
BEARD ON BREAD
One of the first books on the pleasures of baking bread, and still one of the best. Accessible, detailed recipes, with magnificent line drawings. The monkey bread recipe alone is worth the price
0–394–47345–0 Knopf $15.95

THE COMPLETE BOOK OF BREADS
For the more experienced baker
0–671–60222–5 Simon & Schuster $24.95

• Carol Field
THE ITALIAN BAKER
An award-winning book on a lesser-known subject. Recipes include a saltless Tuscan bread, an olive bread, and a sweet pepper loaf
0–06–181266–8 Harper & Row $24.95

• Mary Gubser
AMERICA'S BREAD BOOK: The Best Breads from Home Bakers All Across the Country
0–688–04176–0 Morrow $22.50

MARY'S BREAD BASKET AND SOUP KETTLE
A basic bread book plus soup combinations. An accessible text with nonthreatening recipes
0–688–05886–8 Morrow pb $8.95

• Judith & Evan Jones
THE BOOK OF BREAD
From basic white breads to popovers and stollen. Splendid illustrations, particularly on shaping loaves
0–06–091359–2 Harper & Row pb $10.95

• Marilyn Moore
THE WOODEN SPOON BREAD BOOK: The Secrets of Successful Baking
A friendly collection of simpler loaves, muffins, and doughnuts. Note the lovely and unusual sourdough doughnuts
0–87113–150–1 Atlantic Monthly $19.95

• Laurel Robertson & others
THE LAUREL'S KITCHEN BREAD BOOK: A Guide to Whole-Grain Breadmaking
Only whole grains. Try the buttermilk whole wheat and herb cottage loaf
0–394–72434–8 Random House $14.95

BARBECUE

• James Beard
BARBECUE WITH BEARD
A wonderful book from one of America's finest cooks
0–446–38546–8 Warner pb $9.95

• Jane Butel
FINGER LICKIN', RIB STICKIN', GREAT TASTIN' HOT AND SPICY BARBECUE
0–89480–208–9 Workman pb $4.95

• Philip Schulz
COOKING WITH FIRE AND SMOKE
0–671–55234–1 Simon & Schuster $17.95

• Jeanne Voltz
BARBECUED RIBS AND OTHER GREAT FEEDS
The last word on barbecue: ribs, steaks, chicken, and many other combinations; interesting and fun
0–394–73487–4 Knopf pb $11.95

BREAKFAST AND TEA FOOD

• Elizabeth Alston
BISCUITS AND SCONES: 72 Recipes—From Breakfast Biscuits to Homey Desserts
Homey, delicious items, including ham or smoked-turkey biscuits and zesty gingerbread scones
0–517–56345–2 Crown $8.95

MUFFINS: 60 Sweet and Savory Recipes from Old Favorites to New
A pretty, pocket-size collection of such treats as nutmeg and sticky pecan muffins and a wonderful blueberry muffin recipe
0–517–55587–5 Crown $8.95

• Marian Cunningham
THE BREAKFAST BOOK
Includes breads, fritters, eggs, and condiments, plus a recipe for orange marmalade, also known as orange squish. "Anyone who suffers under the false impression that breakfast is an unimportant, uninteresting meal will have a mouth-watering awakening while thumbing through *The Breakfast Book*"—James Villas
0–394–55529–5 Knopf $17.95

• Angela Hynes
THE PLEASURES OF AFTERNOON TEA
Over 150 traditional and regional English recipes with color photos
0–89586–579–3 HP Books $17.95

CHEESE

• Edward Edelman & Susan Grodnick
THE IDEAL CHEESE BOOK
From the famous New York City cheese store. A sound source of information
0–06–055073–2 Harper & Row $22.95
0–06–096116–3 Harper & Row pb $11.95

• Nika Hazelton
THE ART OF CHEESE COOKERY
A reliable writer selects some favorite, easy-to-prepare combinations
0–89496–003–2 Ross pb $6.95

• Vivienne Marquis & Patricia Haskell
THE CHEESE BOOK
0–671–53133–6 Simon & Schuster pb $8.95

DESSERTS

• Lee Bailey
LEE BAILEY'S COUNTRY DESSERTS: Cakes, Cookies, Ice Creams, Pies, Puddings and More
Filled with beautiful photographs and appealing recipes. Don't miss the fresh peach cake, tangerine mousse, and pear-

raspberry cobbler; and fruit combinations are only part of the selection. The cookie chapter is good, too
0–517–56515–3 Crown $19.95

• Gourmet Magazine
GOURMET'S BEST DESSERTS
The best from 25 years of *Gourmet* recipes—including some easy ones. Try the chocolate mousse cake with ganache icing or the white chocolate mousse with dark chocolate sauce
0–394–56422–7 Random House $29.95

• Maida Heatter
MAIDA HEATTER'S BOOK OF GREAT DESSERTS
Invaluable for dessert lovers
0–394–49111–4 Knopf $22.50
0–446–30710–6 Warner pb $4.95

MAIDA HEATTER'S NEW BOOK OF GREAT DESSERTS
There can never be enough Heatter desserts, and her "best damn lemon cake" is just that
0–394–51960–4 Knopf $17.50

• Gaston Lenôtre
LENOTRE'S DESSERTS AND PASTRIES
Classic French, very tempting and complicated but worth the effort
0–8120–5137–8 Barron's $21.95

• Lindsey Shere
CHEZ PANISSE DESSERTS
Dessert recipes from the great California restaurant. Some combinations are difficult, but the theme is simplicity of line, color, and texture based on the purest ingredients. Fruits and ice creams are put to marvelous use
Preface by Alice Waters
0–394–53860–9 Random House $17.95

Cookies

• American Farm Journal
FARM JOURNAL'S HOMEMADE COOKIES
A must for anyone who loves to bake
0–345–34784–6 Ballantine pb $2.95

• Maida Heatter
MAIDA HEATTER'S BOOK OF GREAT COOKIES
A great favorite. The chapter on bar cookies—hermit bars, brittle peanut bars, Dutch chocolate bars, to name just a few—is unsurpassed
0–394–41021–1 Knopf $15.95

• Sharon Tyler Herbst
THE JOY OF COOKIES
Foreword by Bert Greene
0–8120–5839–9 Barron's $15.95

• Susan Mahnke Peery
THE WELLESLEY COOKIE EXCHANGE COOKBOOK
The most-loved recipes, and for good reason
0–396–08832–5 Dodd, Mead $17.95

Pears stuffed with cream and chocolate, from Giuliano Bugialli's Foods of Italy, *photo by John Dominis (Stewart, Tabori, and Chang)*

• Richard Sax
THE COOKIE LOVER'S COOKIE BOOK
A writer, chef, and book reviewer contributes sound, irresistible recipes for cookie fans
0–06–096108–2 Harper & Row pb $7.95

• Helen Witty
MRS. WITTY'S MONSTER COOKIES
From a first-rate cook and baker, a glorious collection of cookies large and small
0–89480–609–2 Workman pb $5.95

Chocolate

• American Farm Journal
FARM JOURNAL'S CHOICE CHOCOLATE RECIPES
Good brownie recipes abound
0–345–30184–6 Ballantine pb $2.50

• Maida Heatter
MAIDA HEATTER'S BOOK OF GREAT CHOCOLATE DESSERTS
Temptations from this best-selling expert on desserts. The Palm Beach brownies are notoriously well liked
0–394–50391–0 Knopf $17.95

• Faye Levy
FAYE LEVY'S CHOCOLATE SENSATIONS
If you love chocolate, you will want this book
0–89586–411–8 HP Books $25.00

• Judith Olney
THE JOY OF CHOCOLATE
0–8120–5435–0 Barron's $15.95

Ice Cream

• Ben Cohen & others
BEN AND JERRY'S HOMEMADE ICE CREAM AND DESSERT BOOK
0–89480–312–3 Workman pb $7.95

• Anna Creery
THE DONVIER ICE CREAM DESSERT BOOK
The Donvier ice cream maker makes it easy and, with these recipes, delicious
0–89865–627–3 Donning pb $7.95

• Gaston Lenôtre
GASTON LENOTRE'S ICE CREAM AND CANDIES
From the great French pastry chef
0–8120–5334–6 Barron's $21.95

Pastry

• Bernard Clayton, Jr.
THE COMPLETE BOOK OF PASTRY: Sweet and Savory
0–671–24276–8 Simon & Schuster $17.95
0–671–53074–7 Simon & Schuster pb $9.95

• Jim Dodge & Elaine Ratner
THE AMERICAN BAKER: Exquisite Desserts from the Pastry Chef of the Stanford Court
Recipes from the renowned San Francisco hotel
0–671–61158–5 Simon & Schuster $22.95

Pies, Tarts, and Cakes

• American Farm Journal
FARM JOURNAL'S COMPLETE PIE BOOK
Pies, pies, and more delicious pies
0–345–29782–2 Ballantine pb $2.50

• Martha Stewart
MARTHA STEWART'S PIES AND TARTS
Appealing photos and recipes, such as chocolate pecan lattice tart, almost too pretty to eat
0–517–55751–7 Crown $18.95

➤ **FOR OVERSEAS ORDERING INFORMATION, SEE PAGE 1**

- Rose Levy Beranbaum
THE CAKE BIBLE
"One of the very few books that . . . would serve as textbook and inspiration for a generation of dessert makers"—*NY Times*
0–688–04402–6 Morrow $25.00

- Jeremy Iggers & Dana Bovbjerg
THE JOY OF CHEESECAKE
0–8120–5350–8 Barron's $15.95

Fruit

Jane Grigson
JANE GRIGSON'S FRUIT BOOK
0–689–11305–6 Atheneum $19.95

GAME

- Angus Cameron & Judith Jones
THE L.L. BEAN GAME AND FISH COOKBOOK
The classic, with over 800 recipes, ranging from trout and moose to grouse and pheasant. A compendium of information about all aspects of game and fish with hundreds of provocative and useful recipes
0–394–51191–3 Random House $21.95

- Rebecca Gray & Cintra Reeve
GRAY'S WILD GAME COOKBOOK: A Menu Cookbook
Note the menu for smoked-goose salad with sun-dried tomato bread that ends with chocolate cake. Not for the faint-hearted
0–9609842–1–6 GSJ $25.00

- Barbara Hargreaves
THE SPORTING WIFE: A Guide to Game and Fish Cooking
A classic English guide, with traditional and modern recipes and detailed instructions
0–85493–121–X David & Charles pb $15.95

- Paul Southey
THE EXPERT CARVER: How to Carve Meat, Poultry, and Game
A discussion of the common American, French, and English cuts of meat with step-by-step carving instructions; well illustrated
0–7126–1766–3 David & Charles $15.95

PASTA AND PIZZA

- James Beard
BEARD ON PASTA
0–394–52291–5 Knopf $15.95

- Giuliano Bugialli
BUGIALLI ON PASTA
"I was hooked by the very first chapter, on dishes combining pasta and beans, a toothsome pairing"—Florence Fabricant
0–671–62024–X Simon & Schuster $24.95

- Valentine Harris
PERFECT PASTA
0–688–03929–4 Morrow $14.95

- Linda Merinoff
THE GLORIOUS NOODLE: A Culinary Tour Around the World
The complete noodle cookbook: includes fettuccine with four cheeses, pasta with bacon and onion sauce, and goat cheese ravioli
0–671–52355–4 Pocket Books $16.95

- Fred Plotkin
THE AUTHENTIC PASTA BOOK
0–671–50909–8 Simon & Schuster $16.95

- Elizabeth Romer
ITALIAN PIZZAS AND SAVORY BREADS
An intelligent work on the history of Italian pizza and flatbreads
0–517–56693–1 Crown $15.95

- Jack & Maria Scott
THE NEW COMPLETE BOOK OF PASTA: An Italian Cookbook
A revised edition of the 1968 classic, now even more useful
0–688–04312–7 Morrow $24.95

- Evelyne Slomon
THE PIZZA BOOK: Everything There Is to Know About the World's Greatest Pie
This young chef makes pizza-making easy and fun. Calzone recipes include hearty eggplant and sausage; shrimp and pesto; and savory goat cheese and onion
0–8129–1113–X Times Books $14.95

- Alice Waters & Patricia Curtan
CHEZ PANISSE PASTA, PIZZA AND CALZONE
Innovative recipes from one of America's great restaurants: fettuccine with wild mushrooms and prosciutto, and pizza with caramelized onions, gorgonzola, and rosemary. For the sophisticated cook, but worth the effort
0–394–53094–2 Random House $17.95

SEAFOOD

- James Beard
JAMES BEARD'S NEW FISH COOKERY
A revised and updated version of the 1954 classic
0–446–38152–7 Warner pb $10.95

- Jerome Brody
THE GRAND CENTRAL OYSTER BAR AND RESTAURANT SEAFOOD COOKBOOK: Compiled and Edited from 64 Years of Recipes and Recollections
The recipes that have made this glorious New York City restaurant legendary
0–517–52829–0 Crown $12.95

- Isaac Cronin & others
THE CALIFORNIA SEAFOOD COOKBOOK: A Cook's Guide to the Fish and Shellfish of California, the Pacific Coast and Beyond
0–201–11708–8 Addison-Wesley pb $13.95

- Joan & Joe Foley
THE CHESAPEAKE BAY FISH AND FOWL COOKBOOK
A superb regional cookbook; the chapter on crabs is especially good
0–517–66802–5 Crown $25.00

- Pierre Franey & Bryan Miller
THE SEAFOOD COOKBOOK
Fine recipes by two writers for the *New York Times*
0–8129–1604–2 Times Books $22.50

- Rebecca Gray & Cintra Reeve
GRAY'S FISH COOKBOOK: A Menu Cookbook
A nice effort, particularly the salmon combinations
0–9609842–6–7 GSJ $25.00

- Barbara Grunes & Phyllis Magida
FISH ON THE GRILL
Over 70 recipes
0–8092–5033–0 Contemporary pb $7.95

- Shirley King
SAUCING THE FISH: A Chef's Collection of Recipes for Stylish Fish Dishes
An intelligent collection, including some good fish soufflés, pies, and salads
0–671–54076–9 Simon & Schuster $16.95

- A.J. McClane
THE ENCYCLOPEDIA OF FISH COOKERY
An indispensable reference. "Teaches the reader such basics as how to shuck a clam, how to split a lobster and how to use the roe of sea urchins, one of the most delectable of foods, abundant in some American waters but little known in this country"—Craig Claiborne
0–03–015431–6 Henry Holt $50.00

MCCLANE'S NORTH AMERICAN FISH COOKERY
Plain-speaking information about fish. Note the tilefish fillets with orange sauce, clam fritters, and the "hangtown" fry
0–03–043746–6 Henry Holt $22.95

- Anton Mosimann & Holger Hofmann
SHELLFISH
Beautifully illustrated, with intriguing recipes from the chef of London's Dorchester Hotel
0–688–06630–5 Hearst $30.00

- Margaret Deeds Murphy
A CAPE COD SEAFOOD COOKBOOK
Simple recipes for the kinds of chowder remembered fondly by those who have spent time on Cape Cod
0–940160–30–7 Parnassus $14.95

- Jean Reardon & Ruth Ebling
OYSTERS: A Culinary Celebration
All you need to know, and well worth the price
0–940160–26–9 Parnassus $25.00

- Christopher Reaske
THE COMPLEAT CLAMMER
0–941130–15–0 Nick Lyons $16.95
0–941130–11–8 Nick Lyons pb $9.95

- Ruth Spear
COOKING FISH AND SHELLFISH
0–345–31694–0 Ballantine pb $4.95

- Yvonne Young Tarr
THE GREAT EAST COAST SEAFOOD BOOK
Four hundred classic and regional recipes, plus information on boning, catching, and filleting. Instructive on lesser-known varieties of fish
0–394–75325–9 Random House pb $12.95

- Time-Life Editors
SHELLFISH
0–8094–2933–0 Time-Life $14.95

SAUCES AND SEASONINGS

- Raymond Sokolov
THE SAUCIER'S APPRENTICE: A Modern Guide to Classic French Sauces for the Home
An intelligent writer on a complex subject
0–394–48920–9 Knopf $19.95

- Craig Claiborne
COOKING WITH HERBS AND SPICES
A bestseller and a standard work
0–06–015251–6 Harper & Row $18.95

- Bruce Cost
GINGER EAST TO WEST: A Cook's Tour with Recipes, Techniques and Lore
The history of ginger from Asia to the Americas, with 90 notable recipes
0–943186–13–7 Aris $17.95
0–201–17344–1 Addison-Wesley pb $10.95

- Sal Gilbertie
KITCHEN HERBS
The noted Connecticut herb grower shares his enormous knowledge of the cultivation and use of culinary herbs and tells how to grow your own
0–553–05265–9 Bantam $24.95

- Maggie Klein
THE FEAST OF THE OLIVE: Cooking with Olives and Olive Oil
Over 75 recipes; note the recipe for chicken with leeks and olives
0–201–12226–X Addison-Wesley $16.95
0–201–12558–7 Addison-Wesley pb $10.95

- Abbie Zabar
THE POTTED HERB
1–55670–018–0 Stewart, Tabori & Chang $14.95

SOUPS

- Jane Butel
CHILI MADNESS
Chili and more chili. Good, lively recipes
0–89480–135–X Workman $7.95
0–89480–134–1 Workman pb $5.95

- Bernard Clayton, Jr.
THE COMPLETE BOOK OF SOUPS AND STEWS
A wonderful collection, from bouillabaisse provençale to minestrone to chicken and sausage gumbo
0–671–43863–8 Simon & Schuster $18.95
0–671–43864–6 Simon & Schuster pb $9.95

- Karen Lee & Alexandra Branyon
SOUP, SALAD, AND PASTA INNOVATIONS
A teacher and New York City caterer, Lee collects easy-to-do recipes with lots of flair
0–385–19864–7 Doubleday pb $10.95

- Julia Older & Steve Sherman
MENUS A TROIS: The Soup, Bread, and Salad Cookbook
0–8289–0599–1 Stephen Greene $16.95

VEGETABLES AND SALADS

- Bert Greene
GREENE ON GREENS
Vegetables arranged A to Z, with appealing recipes. Fun and informative
0–89480–758–7 Workman $19.95
0–89480–659–9 Workman pb $14.95

- Nika Hazelton
NIKA HAZELTON'S WAY WITH VEGETABLES: The Unabridged Vegetable Cookbook
A guide to fresh vegetables and over 250 recipes all in one
0–87131–490–8 Evans pb $8.95

- Christopher Idone
SALAD DAYS
Salads for all seasons, including a very tempting one for salmon and crab cakes with exotic greens and fruit. Sophisticated recipes and tone. All of Idone's books are known for their magnificent design and color photographs
0–394–56584–3 Random House $22.50

- Faye Levy
FRESH FROM FRANCE: Vegetable Creations
Remarkable and varied use of vegetables from a most talented young cook
0–525–24533–2 Dutton $21.95

- Marian Morash
THE VICTORY GARDEN COOKBOOK
A vegetable encyclopedia for gardeners who cook and for cooks who wish to garden
0–394–50897–1 Knopf $29.95
0–394–70780–X Knopf pb $22.95

- Richard Sax
FROM THE FARMER'S MARKET
How to use produce as it is available—an appealing approach with some outstanding recipes. Try the applesauce brownies
0–06–055005–8 Harper & Row $22.95

- Elizabeth Schneider
UNCOMMON FRUITS AND VEGETABLES
0–06–015420–9 Harper & Row $25.95

PARTY FOOD

▶ See also The Home

- Lee Bailey
LEE BAILEY'S CITY FOOD: Recipes for Good Food and Easy Living
Sophisticated, snappy, easy-to-prepare menus, such as the one for smoked salmon, new potatoes, snow peas, and meringues with berries and cream
Foreword by Geraldine Stutz
0–517–55154–3 Crown $19.95
LEE BAILEY'S COUNTRY WEEKENDS
Great taste and style, excellent menus
0–517–54880–1 Crown $19.95
LEE BAILEY'S GOOD PARTIES: Favorite Food, Tableware, Kitchen Equipment, and More to Make Entertaining a Breeze
Entertaining, right down to the chinaware to use. Imaginative, too; his "small birthday party" stars chicken pot pie and a glorious coconut cake
0–517–55934–X Crown $19.95

- James Beard
MENUS FOR ENTERTAINING
0–440–15569–X Dell pb $2.50

- Sarah Leah Chase
THE OPEN-HOUSE COOKBOOK
The owner of a Nantucket gourmet shop offers up many wonderful recipes. The tone is breezy and the recipes appetizing—as in steak, mushroom, and hearts of palm salad with Béarnaise mayonnaise, deep-dish broccoli pizza, and white chocolate brownies
0–89480–476–6 Workman $19.95
0–89480–465–0 Workman pb $11.95

- Florence Fabricant
THE PLEASURES OF THE TABLE
Innovative menus with 185 recipes for entertaining from this very knowledgeable food writer for the *New York Times*
0–8109–1488–3 Abrams $24.95

- Movia Hodgson
KEEPING COMPANY: Contemporary Menus for Delicious Food and Relaxed Entertaining
Imaginative ideas, practical advice
0–13–046814–2 Prentice-Hall $29.95

- Julee Rosso & others
THE SILVER PALATE GOOD TIMES COOKBOOK
Winning menus for special occasions. Note their swordfish marinated with lime and coriander and blueberry pie with cinnamon lattice crust
0–89480–832–X Workman $22.50
0–89480–831–1 Workman pb $12.95

- Martha Stewart
MARTHA STEWART'S HORS D'OEUVRES: The Creation and Presentation of Fabulous Finger Food
Party hors d'oeuvres by theme. Note the outdoor barbecue, for one: cocktail ribs, with a sauce spiced with pepper flakes, barbecued chicken wings, and grilled sausages, with piña coladas and daiquiris to wash it all down. Attractive and helpful photos
0–517–55455–0 Crown $19.95

ENTERTAINING
Extremely handsome, loaded with photographs and with ideas and recipes for many a festive occasion. There are omelette parties, kitchen parties, buffets, dinner parties, holiday parties, including a marvelous farmhouse Thanksgiving menu for eight, featuring roast turkey with herbed corn bread dressing, pumpkin soup in the pumpkin shell, buttermilk chive biscuits, applesauce spice cake, and lemon curd tartlets
0-517-54419-9 Crown $35.00

- Roger Vergé
ENTERTAINING IN THE FRENCH STYLE
0-941-434-90-7 Stewart, Tabori & Chang $45.00

- Susan Wyler
COOKING FOR A CROWD: Menus, Recipes and Step-by-Step Strategies for Entertaining 10 to 50
0-517-56833-0 Crown $24.95

Children's Cookbooks

- Rena Coyle
MY FIRST COOKBOOK
Written by a mother, with her three-year-old by her side. Fun and reliable
0-89480-846-X Workman pb $8.95

MY FIRST BAKING BOOK
More sensible material
0-317-66708-4 Workman pb $8.95

- Jill Krementz
THE FUN OF COOKING
0-394-54808-6 Knopf $18.95

PRESERVING AND CANNING

- Judith Choate
GOURMET PRESERVES: Sweet or Savory, Spread, Sauce, or Condiment, A Complete Guide to Delicious and Unique Preserving
For novices and experts
1-55584-316-6 Weidenfeld & Nicolson pb $7.95

- Janet Greene & others
PUTTING FOOD BY
The classic guide to pickling, preserving, canning, freezing, and storing; with recipes
0-8289-0644-0 Stephen Greene $22.95
0-8289-0645-9 Stephen Greene pb $9.95

- Helen Witty & Elizabeth Colchie
BETTER THAN STORE-BOUGHT: A Cookbook of Foods That Most People Never Knew They Could Make at Home
From pancake mix to candies, pickles, and relishes
0-06-014693-1 Harper & Row $14.95
0-06-091287-1 Harper & Row pb $8.95

FANCY PANTRY
The jaunty text includes recipes for "uncommon fruit and mushroom ketchups," herbal relishes, jams, conserves, fruit honeys, breads for spreads, crisps, rusks, and oatcakes. Witty shares her knowledge with a joy that makes you want to run into the kitchen and start cooking
0-89480-094-9 Workman $19.95
0-89480-037-X Workman pb $11.95

PAUL BERTOLLI:
A Small List of Books I Have Found Particularly Useful

W.J. Fance
THE STUDENTS' TECHNOLOGY OF BREADMAKING AND FLOUR CONFECTIONARY
The most complete and authoritative text on bread, cake, and pastry making; a detailed, indispensable reference book for professional bakers
0-7100-9046-3 RC&H pb $22.00

A.J. McClane, editor
THE ENCYCLOPEDIA OF FISH COOKERY
Information, both historical and anecdotal, by an author with a passion for fishing and eating fish. Exceptional photography; recipes limited to standard and classic preparation, many of which are borrowed from restaurants from around the world
0-03-015431-6 Henry Holt $50.00

Richard Olney
SIMPLE FRENCH FOOD
Brilliant, concise recipes full of common sense and true taste; firmly rooted in the traditions of the south of France, and animated by Olney's lively prose
Preface by James Beard
0-689-70546-8 Atheneum pb $10.95

THE FRENCH MENU COOKBOOK
An excellent introduction on menu making and the pairing of food and wine. Many fine examples of tasteful menus
0-87923-579-9 Godine $12.95

H. Escoffier
LE GUIDE CULINAIRE
A fundamental textbook to be reckoned with by any serious cook. Discursive recipes assume a thorough grounding in the basics
0-8317-5478-8 Van Nostrand Reinhold $49.95

Janet Greene & others
PUTTING FOOD BY
A thorough guide for those interested in the safe canning and preserving of food
0-8289-0644-0 Stephen Greene $21.95
0-8289-0645-9 Stephen Greene pb $8.95

Ada Boni
TALISMAN ITALIAN COOK BOOK
A vast resource for understanding the spirit of Italian cooking
0-517-52040-0 Crown $9.95

M.F.K. Fisher
THE ART OF EATING
No one before or since has written with as much wit, spirit, or imagination about the pleasures of the table. An inspiration to those who seriously mind their stomach and who enjoy reading about culinary matters
0-394-71399-0 Random House pb $10.95

SPECIAL DIETS

▶ **See also Diet and Nutrition**

Vegetarian

- Edward Espe Brown
THE TASSAJARA BREAD BOOK
Revised and updated and still very good
0-394-74196-X Shambhala pb $8.95

THE TASSAJARA RECIPE BOOK: Favorites of the Guest Season
0-394-73520-X Shambhala pb $8.95

- Annemarie Colbin
THE BOOK OF WHOLE MEALS: A Seasonal Guide to Assembling Balanced Vegetarian Breakfasts, Lunches and Dinners
Macrobiotic cooking
0-345-33274-1 Ballantine pb $8.95

- Mollie Katzen
THE MOOSEWOOD COOKBOOK
Charming, with hand-lettered recipes from the Moosewood Restaurant in Ithaca, New York
0-913668-69-9 Ten Speed $12.95
0-913668-68-0 Ten Speed pb $9.95

THE ENCHANTED BROCCOLI FOREST & Other Timeless Delicacies
More recipes from the Moosewood cook
0-89815-079-5 Ten Speed $16.95
0-89815-078-7 Ten Speed pb $14.95

NEW RECIPES FROM MOOSEWOOD RESTAURANT
Two hundred recipes, this time with some potions for fish
0-89815-209-7 Ten Speed $19.95
0-89815-208-9 Ten Speed pb $12.95

- Jeanne Lemlin
VEGETARIAN PLEASURES: A Menu Cookbook
"The recipes are light, flavorful, varied, and drawn from many international cuisines. I was especially happy to see desserts that no dessert lover could resist. . . . You don't have to be a vegetarian to love this food"—Richard Sax
0-394-54117-0 Knopf $22.95
0-394-74302-4 Knopf pb $13.95

Drawing by Julie Maas, from The Vegetarian Epicure *by Anna Thomas* (Vintage)

• Deborah Madison & Edward Espe Brown
THE GREENS COOKBOOK:
Extraordinary Vegetarian Cuisine from the
Celebrated Restaurant
Cooking from the renowned vegetarian restaurant in San Francisco. Note the mushroom lasagna, goat cheese and sun-dried tomato toasts, and the cherry apricot crumble
0–553–05195–4 Bantam $19.95

• Laurel Robertson & others
THE NEW LAUREL'S KITCHEN
0–89815–167–8 Ten Speed $24.95
0–89815–166–X Ten Speed pb $16.95

• Anna Thomas
THE VEGETARIAN EPICURE
A friendly informal tone and some splendid recipes, including a sensational cornbread, have made this a perennial best seller
0–394–71784–8 Random House pb $9.95

THE VEGETARIAN EPICURE: Book 2
0–394–41363–6 Knopf $12.50
0–394–73415–7 Knopf pb $12.95

Kosher

• Betty Goldberg
CHINESE KOSHER COOKING
0–8246–0292–7 Jonathan David $14.95

INTERNATIONAL COOKING FOR THE
KOSHER HOME
0–8246–0323–0 Jonathan David $16.95

• Gloria Greene
THE JEWISH HOLIDAY COOKBOOK:
An International Collection of Recipes and
Customs
0–8129–1224–1 Times Books $19.95

• Ruth & Bob Grossman
THE NEW KOSHER COOKBOOK
TRILOGY
Recipes for French, Chinese, and Italian kosher cooking
0–8397–6310–7 Paul Eriksson pb $10.95

• Anne London & Bertha Kahn Bishor
THE COMPLETE AMERICAN JEWISH
COOKBOOK
Over 3500 tested kosher recipes, with chapters on holiday and modern Jewish cooking
0–06–091590–0 Harper & Row pb $12.95

• Helen Nash
HELEN NASH'S KOSHER KITCHEN
An up-to-date approach, with variations on traditional dishes
0–394–57026–X Random House $18.95

KOSHER CUISINE
A serious, informative book for the kosher gourmet
0–394–52788–7 Random House $17.95

• Joan Nathan
THE JEWISH HOLIDAY KITCHEN
Almost 200 recipes from the US, Israel, and elsewhere for the Sabbath, holidays, weddings, and other special occasions
0–8052–3712–7 Schocken $16.95
0–8052–0724–4 Schocken pb $12.95

• Judy Zeidler
THE GOURMET JEWISH COOK
A wide range of recipes from around the world, with special attention to Jewish holidays and celebrations
0–688–06981–9 Morrow $22.95

COOKING WITH MODERN APPLIANCES

• Jean Anderson
JEAN ANDERSON'S NEW PROCESSOR
COOKING
One of the best books on how to put the food processor to maximum use. Note the soups chapter, in particular
0–688–02254–5 Morrow $17.50

• Barbara Kafka
MICROWAVE GOURMET
Nearly 600 recipes
0–688–06843–X Morrow $19.95

• Abby Mandel
ABBY MANDEL'S CUISINART
CLASSROOM
0–06–091182–4 Harper & Row pb $16.95

FAST AND FLAVORFUL: New Food
Processor Recipes
0–936662–09–3 Cuisinart Cooking $25.00

• The Microwave Cooking Institute
THE JOY OF MICROWAVING: A
Complete Guide
Step-by-step instructions and photo sequences
0–13–511551–5 Prentice-Hall $25.95

Wines and Spirits

GENERAL BOOKS ON WINE

• Leon Adams
THE COMMONSENSE BOOK OF WINE
A revised and updated edition of the standard work that helped to demystify the world of wine
0–07–000324–6 McGraw-Hill pb $7.95

• Alexis Bespaloff
THE NEW SIGNET BOOK OF WINE
A complete introduction to the wines of the world, with chapters on tasting, service, and storage. "As good an introduction to the subject as any book available today"—*NY Times*
0–451–14401–5 NAL pb $4.50

• Michael Broadbent
THE GREAT VINTAGE WINE BOOK
0–394–51099–2 Knopf $27.50

• Robert Finigan
THE ESSENTIALS OF WINE
A guide to the world's most pleasing wines that covers Europe, the United States, and

other countries, with a section on food and wine
0–394–51591–9 Knopf $19.95

• Frank Henriques
THE SIGNET ENCYCLOPEDIA OF
WINE
A complete guide to brand names, vineyards, vintages, and varieties, covering some 20,000 wines
0–451–13211–4 NAL pb $4.95

• Hugh Johnson
HUGH JOHNSON'S MODERN
ENCYCLOPEDIA OF WINE
"One of the most useful and attractive wine books ever published"—*NY Times*
0–671–64052–6 Simon & Schuster $29.95

HUGH JOHNSON'S POCKET
ENCYCLOPEDIA OF WINE, 1989
A quick reference guide that discusses modern wines, winemakers, and wine enjoyment
0–671–66786–6 Simon & Schuster pb $9.95

THE WORLD ATLAS OF WINE
A country-by-country, region-by-region format offers the first complete mapping of the world's great wine areas
0–671–50893–8 Simon & Schuster $45.00

• Alexis Lichine
ALEXIS LICHINE'S NEW
ENCYCLOPEDIA OF WINES AND
SPIRITS
A 750-page classic from *abboccato* to zymotechnology
0–394–51781–4 Knopf $45.00

• Robert M. Parker, Jr.
PARKER'S WINE BUYER'S GUIDE:
1989–1990
Ratings of more than 4000 wines from three continents. "He has risen to international preeminence as a wine writer by being of all things a hard-headed American"—*Esquire*
0–671–67648–2 Simon & Schuster $25.95
0–671–67649–0 Simon & Schuster pb $15.95

• Jancis Robinson
VINES, GRAPES AND WINES
A study by an esteemed British wine expert, generously illustrated with maps, facts, and figures
0–394–55598–8 Knopf $29.95

• Frank Schoonmaker
THE NEW FRANK SCHOONMAKER
ENCYCLOPEDIA OF WINE
A classic reference work, revised in 1988—concise, easy-to-use, and up-to-date. "The finest quick reference work in the literature of wine"—*NY Times*
Completely revised by Alexis Bespaloff
0–688–05749–7 Morrow $22.95

• André Simon
ANDRE SIMON'S WINES OF THE
WORLD
0–07–057423–5 McGraw-Hill $18.00

• Tom Stevenson
SOTHEBY'S WORLD WINE
ENCYCLOPEDIA: A Comprehensive
Reference Guide to the Wines of the World
0–8212–1690–2 NY Graphic Society $40.00

- Serena Sutcliffe
THE WINE HANDBOOK
An introduction from grape to glass and price to palate by an enthusiastic Master of Wine
0–671–63516–6 Simon & Schuster pb $10.95

COMMENTARIES

Burgundy
At Pommard and Volnay I observed [laborers] eating good wheat bread; at Mersault, rye. I asked the reason of this difference. They told me that the white wines fail in quality much more often than the red and remain on hand. The farmer therefore cannot afford to feed his laborer so well. At Meursault only white wines are made because there is too much stone for the red. On such slight circumstances depends the condition of man!

Thomas Jefferson
THOMAS JEFFERSON'S EUROPEAN TRAVEL DIARIES
0–9615964–3–0 Stephanus pb $7.95

- Gerald Asher
ON WINE
Informative and entertaining essays based on Asher's columns for *Gourmet* magazine
Introduction by Elizabeth David
0–394–74328–8 Random House pb $8.95

- Christine Atkinson
SECRET VINEYARDS OF FRANCE
0–87052–585–9 Hippocrene $24.95

- Leonard Bernstein
THE OFFICIAL GUIDE TO WINE SNOBBERY
A seriocomic reference book
0–688–01605–7 Morrow pb $6.95

- Clifton Fadiman, introduction
A TOAST TO WINES AND SPIRITS: Posters from the Collection of Nicolas Bailly
Posters from the effervescent 1890s through the roaring '20s up to 1940
0–8109–2404–8 Abrams pb $16.95

- Thomas Jefferson
THOMAS JEFFERSON'S EUROPEAN TRAVEL DIARIES
The record of a delightful backroads odyssey in 1787 and 1788 through the major wine regions of France, northern Italy, and Germany
Edited by James Morris & Persephone Weene
0–9615964–3–0 Stephanus pb $7.95

- Simon Loftus
ANATOMY OF THE WINE TRADE: Abe's Sardines and Other Stories
Amusing profiles of wine people in Britain, France, California, and elsewhere
0–06–015785–2 Harper & Row $15.95

- Kermit Lynch
ADVENTURES ON THE WINE ROUTE: A Wine Buyer's Tour of France
"Colorful portraits of some idiosyncratic vintners and commentaries on their wines make for some of the finest reading since Joseph Wechsberg ate and drank his way through France"—Robert Parker
0–374–10092–6 Farrar, Straus & Giroux $19.95

- Patrick Matthews, editor
CHRISTIE'S WINE COMPANION
For both serious imbibers and those who appreciate the occasional glass: 20 essays by experts, ranging from Russia to resin, Corsica to Oregon
Introduction by Michael Broadbent
0–88162–274–5 Salem House $24.95

- E.M. Quinlan & others
WINE TRIVIA
0–9611268–9–2 Quinlan pb $7.95

- Bernard Watney & Homer Babbidge
CORKSCREWS FOR COLLECTORS
Whimsical and sophisticated designs for corkscrews
0–85667–113–4 Sotheby $29.95

FRANCE

More books have been written about French wine than any other. It is worth remembering that the entire French wine industry came close to extinction in the late 19th century thanks to an indefatigable sap-eating aphid, the grape phylloxera, which was accidentally introduced to France from North America. Europe's vineyards were saved by the wide-scale grafting of vulnerable vines onto resistant North American root stocks. To this day, in many areas of France, each new vine planted is still grafted in this way.

- Hugh Johnson & Hubrecht Duijker
THE WINE ATLAS OF FRANCE & TRAVELER'S GUIDE TO THE VINEYARDS
Two experts merge their encyclopedic knowledge to open up France to those *à la recherche du bon vin*. This large-format atlas offers many detailed maps and good touring information
0–671–64232–4 Simon & Schuster $35.00

- Alexis Lichine
ALEXIS LICHINE'S GUIDE TO THE WINES AND VINEYARDS OF FRANCE
An invaluable companion for anyone embarking on this journey, be it in armchair or automobile. This discursive guide provides information and anecdotes about the wines as well as descriptions of hotels and restaurants
0–394–55335–7 Knopf $25.00
0–679–72285–8 Knopf pb $18.95

- Steven Spurrier
ACADEMIE DU VIN GUIDE TO FRENCH WINES
A comprehensive work ranging from the Grand Crus Classés of impeccable pedigree

to more modest country wines, well illustrated and with maps
0–88162–260–5 Salem House $19.95

Bordeaux

- John Baxevanis
THE WINES OF BORDEAUX AND WESTERN FRANCE
Explicit and helpful diagrams and photographs guide the reader through not only Bordeaux, but also the Loire, Bergerac, Cahors, Gaillac, and Béarn
0–8476–7490–8 Rowman & Littlefield $32.95

- Yves Durand
THE CONNOISSEUR'S GUIDE TO BORDEAUX WINES
A keen and finely illustrated look at 55 outstanding châteaux
0–8069–6556–8 Sterling $16.95

- Nicholas Faith
THE WINEMASTERS: The Story Behind the Glory and the Scandal of Bordeaux
0–06–011264–6 Harper & Row $12.95

CHATEAU MARGAUX
A visit to the Médoc château, with production details, menus, and recipes
0–86565–106–X Rizzoli $45.00

- Robert M. Parker, Jr.
BORDEAUX: The Definitive Guide for the Wines Produced Since 1961
Overall impressions and detailed tasting notes for almost all the châteaux one is likely to encounter, from the respected American wine authority
0–671–55509–X Simon & Schuster $21.95

- David Peppercorn
BORDEAUX
A rare combination of a professional's experience, a true wineman's passion, and a historian's eye
0–571–11758–9 Faber & Faber $15.95

POCKET GUIDE TO THE WINES OF BORDEAUX
0–671–63675–8 Simon & Schuster pb $7.95

Burgundy and Beaujolais

- Eunice Fried
BURGUNDY: The Country, The Wines, The People
"For Americans who love good Burgundy and are intrigued by the individuals who live and breathe good wine every working day, this is a book of revelations"—Hugh Johnson
0–06–039049–2 Harper & Row $17.95

- Anthony Hanson
BURGUNDY
An enthusiast leads us through the intricacies of viticulture, adding a good glossary and detailed information about individual producers
0–571–11798–8 Faber & Faber pb $13.95

1829 still life, from Women's Worlds: The Art and Life of Mary Ellen Best *by Caroline Davidson (Crown)*

• **Guy Jacquemont & Paul Mereaud**
BEAUJOLAIS: The Complete Guide
An inviting look at the history, cellars, and châteaux of the insufficiently known Beaujolais region
Introduction by Paul Bocuse
0–316–45598–9 Little, Brown $29.95

• **Serena Sutcliffe**
POCKET GUIDE TO THE WINES OF BURGUNDY
A handy book brimming with data on grapes, growers, merchants, and the local regions. The most practical quick-reference guide to the region
0–671–61695–1 Simon & Schuster pb $7.95

Champagne and Alsace

• **Jane MacQuitty**
POCKET GUIDE TO CHAMPAGNE AND SPARKLING WINES
Covers every region and country from Champagne to California to the USSR
0–671–62860–7 Simon & Schuster pb $7.95

• **Pamela Vandyke Price & Christopher Fielden**
ALSACE WINES AND SPIRITS
An exploration of the region ranging from Roman times to a current who's who of major wine firms
0–85667–183–5 Sotheby $29.95

• **Serena Sutcliffe**
CHAMPAGNE: The History and Character of the World's Most Celebrated Wine
"A well-known London wine broker and Master of Wine, Ms. Sutcliffe proves that the coffee table wine book is alive and well"—*NY Times*
0–671–66672–X Simon & Schuster $29.95

The Rhône and Other Regions

• **Robert M. Parker, Jr.**
THE WINES OF THE RHONE VALLEY AND PROVENCE
This definitive guide to the region evaluates all the leading producers, with extensive tasting notes
0–671–63379–1 Simon & Schuster $22.95

• **Roger Voss**
THE SIMON & SCHUSTER POCKET GUIDE TO FRENCH REGIONAL WINES
Covers the wines of Alsace, the Loire Valley, Provence, the Midi and the Southwest, and the Rhône
0–671–64233–2 Simon & Schuster pb $8.95

Cognac

• **Nicholas Faith**
COGNAC
Anyone can make brandy, it is said, but only the Cognacais can make Cognac: this study delves into its mysteries and secrets
0–87923–654–X Godine $30.00

THE POCKET GUIDE TO COGNAC AND OTHER BRANDIES
The noted expert offers ratings, best buys, and advice on proper uses for various types of cognac and brandy
0–671–64231–6 Simon & Schuster pb $9.95

GERMANY

• **Ian Jamieson**
THE POCKET GUIDE TO GERMAN WINES
In a convenient size and format, and brimming with practical information, this is an ideal companion
0–671–65247–8 Simon & Schuster pb $8.95

• **Hugh Johnson & Ian Jamieson**
THE ATLAS OF GERMAN WINE
A detailed tour guide to your journeys along the Rhine and the Moselle, the Main and the Neckar. This large-format atlas has detailed maps and profiles of all the leading producers, as well as touring information
0–671–61102–X Simon & Schuster $29.95

• **Frank Schoonmaker**
THE WINES OF GERMANY
First published in the United States and now recognized as a classic on the subject: concise, complete, and authoritative. Revised in 1986
0–571–18076–0 Faber & Faber $22.95
0–571–13056–9 Faber & Faber pb $11.95

ITALY

• **Burton Anderson**
THE SIMON & SCHUSTER POCKET GUIDE TO ITALIAN WINES
An indispensable pocket guide, as comprehensive as it is concise
Foreword by Hugh Johnson
0–671–63843–2 Simon & Schuster pb $8.95

VINO: The Wine and Winemakers of Italy
A far north to far south study by a Minnesotan now living in Tuscany
0–316–03948–9 Little, Brown $29.95

• **Philip Dallas**
ITALIAN WINES
A bright look at the civilization that has imbibed wine for 4000 years and made it for 2500, with assessments of today's major producers
0–571–11994–8 Faber & Faber pb $13.95

• **Raymond Flower**
CHIANTI: The Land, The People, and The Wine
0–7470–1011–0 David & Charles pb $17.95

SPAIN AND PORTUGAL

Though Spain is the world's third largest wine producer, it has been a rare subject of books, except for sherries. In recent years, the spreading popularity of the good Rioja wines of northern Spain have managed to enhance the country's standing in the wine league.

Portugal's wine renown is founded primarily on the port wines, but the country also produces tasty white *vinho verde* and sturdy new red wines.

• **Jan Read**
WINES OF SPAIN
"None can rival the author's detailed knowledge of the country's wines"—*Financial Times*
0–571–14621–X Faber & Faber pb $13.95

THE POCKET GUIDE TO SPANISH WINES
An essential reference book with advice on quality, variety, value, and reliability
0–671–66787–4 Simon & Schuster pb $9.95

WINES OF THE RIOJA
By the leading British authority on the wines of Spain and Portugal
0–85667–186–X Sotheby $29.95

TO ORDER BOOKS AS GIFTS, SEE PAGE 1

THE WINES OF PORTUGAL
"Mr. Read is completely at home on this territory and the information is not available elsewhere"—*Guardian*
0–571–15003–9 Faber & Faber pb $11.95

SHERRY, PORT, MADEIRA, SWEET, AND DESSERT WINES

• Jeffrey Benson & Alastair Mackenzie
SAUTERNES: A Study of the Great Sweet Wines of Bordeaux
A specialized look at the history, gastronomy, and vintages, with tasting notes and a glossary
0–85667–062–6 Sotheby $26.00

• Stephen Brook
LIQUID GOLD: Sweet Wines of the World
Assesses Sauternes and other famous French types, as well as the sweet wines of Germany, Austria, Hungary, and California
0–688–07461–8 Morrow $18.95

• Barnaby Conrad
ABSINTHE: History in a Bottle
An illustrated history and lore of absinthe focusing on the artists and writers who used and abused it to create their *fin de siècle* trance
0–87701–566–X Chronicle $25.00
0–87701–486–8 Chronicle pb $16.95

• Noël Cossart
MADEIRA: The Island Vineyard
A learned and comprehensive introduction to the island's famous product
0–903432–33–1 Christie's Wine $24.00

• Julian Jeffs
SHERRY
An examination by a true aficionado with plenty of colorful early history, ranging from Chaucer's tipple to modern export statistics
0–571–18047–7 Faber & Faber $17.95
0–571–11799–6 Faber & Faber pb $9.95

• Richard Olney
YQUEM
A complete history of the renowned white wine, by an American now settled in southern France
Preface by Michael Broadbent
0–87923–644–2 Godine $45.00

• George Robertson
PORT
"Heightened by a genuine feeling for the subject, his historic introduction is sound: but when he turns to the practical business of making wine and to the pleasures of drinking it, he is in his element"—*Financial Times*
0–571–14847–6 Faber & Faber $19.95
0–571–14848–4 Faber & Faber pb $7.95

NORTH AMERICA

A number of books on American wines consist of tasting notes on current releases and are therefore soon out of date; others are local touring guides. Nine-tenths of the wine production of the United States originates in California, ranging from mass-produced gallons to high-quality Cabernets and Chardonnays.

• Leon Adams
THE WINES OF AMERICA
A comprehensive description of every American wine region and its wineries
0–07–000331–9 McGraw-Hill $15.95
0–07–000324–6 McGraw-Hill pb $7.95

• Anthony Dias Blue
AMERICAN WINE
"A voluminous, courageous undertaking. A most informative and interesting reference work for everyone's vinous bookshelf"—Alexis Lichine
0–06–015914–6 Harper & Row $37.95

BUYER'S GUIDE TO AMERICAN WINES
Quality ratings for more than 5000 currently available wines
0–06–096274–7 Harper & Row pb $8.95

• Corbet Clark
AMERICAN WINES OF THE NORTHWEST: A Guide to the Wines of Washington, Oregon, and Idaho
0–688–07556–8 Morrow $19.95

• Barbara Ensrud
AMERICAN VINEYARDS
A generously illustrated picture book, with an engaging text
1–55670–010–5 Stewart, Tabori & Chang $35.00

• James Morris
WINERIES OF THE NORTHEAST: A Comprehensive Guide to Touring and Tasting Across New York and New England
0–9615964–7–3 Stephanus pb $9.95

• Doris Muscatine & others, editors
UNIVERSITY OF CALIFORNIA SOTHEBY BOOK OF CALIFORNIA WINE
More than 50 essays by authorities on the origins and science of viticulture, winemaking styles, and reflections on grapes
0–520–05085–1 California $77.50

• Jon Palmer
WINERIES OF THE MID-ATLANTIC
"Should be useful to East Coast wine fans who can't make it to the Napa Valley or the Finger Lakes"—Frank Prial
0–8135–1346–4 Rutgers $30.00
0–8135–1351–0 Rutgers pb $12.95

• Cyril Ray
ROBERT MONDAVI OF THE NAPA VALLEY
A warm portrait of a master Californian vintner—and character
0–89141–233–6 Presidio $14.95
0–446–38322–8 Warner pb $12.95

• Marvin Shanken
THE WINE SPECTATOR WINE MAPS, 1986: The Complete Guide to Wineries, Restaurants and Lodging in California Wine Country
Maps and addresses
0–918076–39–0 M. Shanken pb $4.95

• Bob Thompson
NOTES ON A CALIFORNIA CELLARBOOK: Reflections on Memorable Wines
"Mr. Thompson has been writing uncompromisingly about wine for 30 years and his knowledge is vast"—Frank Prial
0–688–07007–8 Morrow $19.95

THE POCKET ENCYCLOPEDIA OF CALIFORNIA WINES
"Nobody understands California's wines better"—Hugh Johnson
0–671–52324–4 Simon & Schuster pb $8.95

THE SOUTHERN HEMISPHERE

• Harm De Blij
WINE REGIONS OF THE SOUTHERN HEMISPHERE
0–8476–7390–1 Rowman & Littlefield $32.95

• Oliver Mayo
WINES OF AUSTRALIA
An agronomist and vineyard owner's history of the development of the country's wine trade, with a survey of all current wine regions
0–571–13868–3 Faber & Faber $25.00
0–571–13869–1 Faber & Faber pb $13.95

• Jan Read
CHILEAN WINES
A well-illustrated overview of vineyards and vinification, spirits and fortified wines, with a chapter on cuisine
Introduction and tasting notes by Hugh Johnson
0–85667–343–9 Wine Guild $39.95

TECHNICAL BOOKS

• Jeff Cox
FROM VINES TO WINES: The Complete Guide to Growing Grapes and Making Your Own Wine
0–88266–528–6 Garden Way pb $10.95

• Emile Peynaud
KNOWING AND MAKING WINE
A complete and informative guide to oenology for professionals and curious amateurs alike by the noted researcher and teacher
0–471–88149–X John Wiley $37.95

• Steven Spurrier
THE WINE CELLAR BOOK: A Practical Guide to Creating and Maintaining Your Own Personal Cellar
0–88162–197–8 Salem House $19.95

• Philip Wagner
GRAPES INTO WINE: The Art of Winemaking in America
A popular handbook for winemakers
0–394–73172–7 Knopf pb $10.95

Wine Tasting

• Michael Broadbent
COMPLETE GUIDE TO WINE TASTING AND WINE CELLARS
An acknowledged classic. An excellent introduction, practical and informative
0–671–50889–X Simon & Schuster pb $12.95

• Emile Peynaud
THE TASTE OF WINE: The Art and Science of Wine Appreciation
Recently translated, this volume is matchless on the subject
Introduction by Michael Broadbent
0–356–14911–0 Trans-Atlantic $27.50

WHISKEY AND OTHER SPIRITS

• Gerald Carson
THE SOCIAL HISTORY OF BOURBON: An Unhurried Account of Our Star-Spangled American Drink
0–8131–1509–4 Kentucky $22.00

• Michael Jackson
THE WORLD GUIDE TO WHISKY: A Comprehensive Taste-Guide to Single Malts and the World's Best-Known Blends
In this handsome volume, the "water of life" is assessed from Scotland and Ireland to the United States, Canada, and Japan
0–88162–284–2 Salem House $24.95

Cocktails

• David Embury
THE FINE ART OF MIXING DRINKS
0–385–09683–6 Doubleday pb $4.95

• Mr. Boston
THE MR. BOSTON OFFICIAL BARTENDER'S GUIDE: 50th Anniversary Edition
0–446–38714–2 Warner pb $7.95

• Tommy Murphy
ELEGANT WINE COCKTAILS: 111 Recipes for Delicious Wine Drinks
0–446–38313–9 Warner pb $6.95

• Fred Powell, editor
BARTENDER'S STANDARD MANUAL
0–06–465029–4 Harper & Row pb $3.95

• Charles Schumann
SCHUMANN'S TROPICAL BAR BOOK
More than 150 recipes, including Daiquiri, Black Widow, Jamaica Fever, and nonalcoholic drinks, along with passages from Hemingway, Naipaul, and Lowry describing life in the hotels and bars of the tropics
1–55670–065–2 Stewart, Tabori & Chang $25.00

ALES AND BEERS

• Will Anderson
FROM BEER TO ETERNITY: Everything You Always Wanted to Know About Beer
0–8289–0555–X Stephen Greene pb $14.95

• Christopher Finch
BEER: A Connoisseur's Guide to the World's Best
A lavishly illustrated history of beer, and a guide to the different brews
0–89659–913–2 Abbeville $29.95

• Michael Jackson
THE NEW WORLD GUIDE TO BEER
A beer drinker's world tour
0–89471–649–2 Running Press $29.95

THE POCKET GUIDE TO BEER
The connoisseur's comparative guide to more than 1000 beers from all over the world
0–671–66225–2 Simon & Schuster $7.95

Home Brewing

• William Mares
MAKING BEER
0–394–72328–7 Knopf pb $9.95

Illustration by Jeff Danziger, from Making Beer *by William Mares* (Knopf)

• Dave Miller
THE COMPLETE HANDBOOK OF HOME BREWING
0–88266–517–0 Storey pb $9.95

• Vrest Orton
THE HOMEMADE BEER BOOK
0–8048–1086–9 Tuttle pb $4.95

• Derek Watkins
WINE AND BEER MAKING
0–7153–7503–2 David & Charles pb $9.95

Travel Literature

ANTHOLOGIES

• Kevin Crossley-Holland, editor
THE OXFORD BOOK OF TRAVEL VERSE
Surprises with the new and comforts with the familiar
0–19–214156–2 Oxford $21.95

• Paul Fussell
ABROAD: British Literary Traveling Between the Wars
An excellent survey of the flowering of travel books between the wars
0–19–503068–0 Oxford pb $8.95

• Eric Newby, editor
A BOOK OF TRAVELLERS' TALES
A wide, intelligent selection
0–14–009567–5 Penguin pb $10.95

• John Julius Norwich
A TASTE FOR TRAVEL: An Anthology
"Norwich has managed to compress 1000 years of prodigious, intricate, sometimes unbelievable events"—Luigi Barzini
0–394–55855–3 Knopf $22.95

• Peter Yapp, editor
TRAVELLERS' DICTIONARY OF QUOTATIONS: Who Said What, About Where
An apt remark for almost every destination and situation
0–415–02760–8 RC&H pb $25.00

TRAVEL ESSAYS

• Lawrence Durrell
THE SPIRIT OF PLACE: Letters and Essays on Travel
A master of atmospheric description writes about Corfu, the Midi, and other places
0–918172–17–9 Leete's Island pb $8.95

• Jan Morris
JOURNEYS
"A mystery tour" whose stops range from Santa Fe, New Mexico, to Cetinje, Yugoslavia
0–19–503452–X Oxford pb $18.95

DESTINATIONS
More essays on travel, reprinted from *Rolling Stone*
0–19–503069–9 Oxford pb $8.95

• V.S. Pritchett
AT HOME AND ABROAD: Travel Essays
A dazzling array of portraits of both country and character from the eminent literary critic
0–86547–385–4 North Point $19.95

• Freya Stark
JOURNEY'S ECHO
Extracts from the great traveler's many books, ranging from the *Letters from Syria* (1927–28) to *Riding to the Tigris* (1958)
0–88001–218–8 Ecco pb $8.95

Illustration by Alison Seiffer, from E.B. White's Here is New York *(Warner)*

A PEAK IN DARIEN
Essays philosophical and autobiographical
0–7195–3291–4 Transatlantic Arts $12.00

• Angus Wilson
REFLECTIONS IN A WRITER'S EYE
Essays arguing that "if you like travelling, nowhere is provincial." To prove his point, Wilson takes on Brighton, Tokyo, South Africa, the Channel Islands, India, Martinique, Sri Lanka, and Arizona
0–670–81316–8 Viking $15.95
0–14–009580–2 Penguin pb $6.95

GREAT BRITAIN AND IRELAND

Though the selection is disappointingly small, the available accounts present widely diverging views of one small country; compare, for instance, J.B. Priestley's travels in the 1930s with those of Beryl Bainbridge 50 years later along the same route.

• Beryl Bainbridge
ENGLISH JOURNEY: Or, the Road to Milton Keynes
Dogging Priestley's footsteps of a half-century earlier, a contemporary Briton discovers that England "stretched no further than a day's drive" but that "North and South are separate countries"
0–8076–1101–8 Braziller $12.95

• George Borrow
WILD WALES: Its People, Language, and Scenery
A classic "open road" book by a 19th-century journeyer who set out to portray "a country in which Nature displays herself in her wildest, boldest, and occasionally loveliest forms"
0–7126–0448–0 David & Charles pb $11.95

• John Hillaby
JOURNEY THROUGH BRITAIN
A much-loved author who travels the world on foot takes on his own country
0–586–08019–8 Academy Chicago pb $5.95

• Henry James
ENGLISH HOURS
An excursion through Victorian England, illustrated with works by contemporary painters (Monet, Constable, Sisley, and others)
1–55584–375–1 Weidenfeld & Nicolson $24.95

• Carl Philip Moritz
JOURNEYS OF A GERMAN IN ENGLAND
A walking tour taken in 1782
0–907871–50–X Hippocrene pb $8.95

• Jan Morris
OXFORD
Written in the early 1960s, this book (with *The World of Venice*) established Jan Morris as a distinguished travel writer
0–19–282065–6 Oxford pb $9.95

WALES
0–19–214118–X Oxford $14.95

• J.B.S. Morritt
A GRAND TOUR: Letters and Journals 1794–1796
An enthusiastic and typical young Grand Tourist travels through Europe as far as Constantinople
0–7126–0993–8 David & Charles pb $11.95

• H.V. Morton
IN SEARCH OF ENGLAND
This popular writer of the late '20s and '30s still charms with his enthusiasm and eye for detail
0–396–08378–1 Dodd, Mead pb $9.95

IN SEARCH OF SCOTLAND
0–396–08377–3 Dodd, Mead pb $9.95

• J.B. Priestley
ENGLISH JOURNEY
London to the Tyne and back again in 1933, in search of "little England" and "that inner glowing tradition of the English spirit"
0–226–68212–9 Chicago $24.95

• Jonathan Raban
COASTING: A Private Journey
A writer sails around Britain, revisiting and glorying in the places associated with his own and his country's past
0–671–45480–3 Simon & Schuster $17.95
0–14–010657–X Penguin pb $7.95

• Paul Theroux
THE KINGDOM BY THE SEA
Theroux's encounters with the working classes and the seedier side of British life leave him thoroughly cynical about the state of Britain today
0–395–34645–2 Houghton Mifflin pb $4.00

Ireland

• H.V. Morton
IN SEARCH OF IRELAND
A picture of Ireland in the 1920s
0–396–08344–7 Dodd, Mead pb $9.95

• Dervla Murphy
A PLACE APART
An Irishwoman visits Northern Ireland in an attempt to understand the passions that separate the two countries
0–8159–6516–8 Devin-Adair $15.00

• Eric Newby
ROUND IRELAND IN LOW GEAR
The charms of rustic Ireland, as seen from a bicycle
0–670–82244–2 Viking $18.95

• Arthur Young
A TOUR IN IRELAND: With General Observations on the Present State of that Kingdom Made in the Years 1776, 1777 and 1778
A shrewd account of 18th-century Ireland
0–85640–303–2 Longwood $14.95

EUROPE

Travelers have long been drawn to Italy as a repository of classical civilization, and youthful British aristocrats commonly rounded out their education by gaining first-hand knowledge of France and Greece as well. In the 19th century, the advent of the railroad and a growing appreciation of the beauties of the Natural Sublime enabled voyagers to wander farther afield.

American visitors joined the British and European contingents when steamships began plying the New York-Liverpool route in 1819. Thus, two closely linked worlds began to record and examine myths and realities.

• Hans Christian Andersen
A POET'S BAZAAR: A Journey to Greece, Turkey, and Up the Danube
The renowned storyteller takes to the road
0–935576–23–1 Michael Kesend $21.95

• Kevin Andrews
THE FLIGHT OF IKAROS: Travels in Greece During a Civil War
Travels in the late 1940s through war-torn Greece
0–14–009531–4 Penguin pb $6.95

• Hilaire Belloc
THE PATH TO ROME
A witty account of the author's discovery that on the road from Toul to Rome one finds "more mountains than mole-hills"
0–14–009530–6 Penguin pb $6.95

• George Borrow
THE BIBLE IN SPAIN
Traversing the country in the 1830s to distribute bibles, Borrow also gathered material for a classic account of Gypsy life
0–7126–1039–1 David & Charles pb $15.95

• Gerald Brenan
SOUTH FROM GRANADA
A description of life in the poor village where the author lived between the World Wars, first published in 1957
0–521–28029–X Cambridge pb $12.95

- Samuel Butler
ALPS AND SANCTUARIES
The Italian Piedmont and the Swiss canton
of Ticino in the late 19th century
0–87052–315–5 Hippocrene pb $11.95

- Robert Byron
THE STATION: Athos: Treasures and Men
A visit to 20 monasteries in the region of
Mount Athos in 1926
0–7126–0339–5 David & Charles pb $11.95

- Charles Dickens
PICTURES FROM ITALY
Dickens didn't leave his social conscience
behind when he traveled abroad; in Italy
he found the effects of years of political
turmoil at odds with "the beauties, natural
and artificial, of which it is full to
overflowing"
0–88001–164–5 Ecco pb $7.50

- Edith Durham
HIGH ALBANIA
A woman travels alone among the tribes of
northern Albania in the first decade of this
century
0–8070–7035–1 Beacon pb $10.95

- Amelia Edwards
**UNTRODDEN PEAKS AND
UNFREQUENTED VALLEYS**
Italy's Dolomite Mountains, summer of
1872
0–8070–7037–8 Beacon pb $10.95

- Negley Farson
SAILING ACROSS EUROPE
The foreign correspondent of the *Chicago
Daily News,* waterborne in 1925
0–7126–0802–8 Hippocrene pb $11.95

- Ford Madox Ford
**PROVENCE: From Minstrels to the
Machine**
"Travel and moralizing" in the writer's
delightfully idiosyncratic style
0–912946–63–6 Ecco pb $8.50

- Johann Wolfgang von Goethe
ITALIAN JOURNEY: 1786–1788
The product of a great northern culture
encounters a great southern one
0–86547–076–6 North Point pb $16.50

- Barbara Grizzuti Harrison
ITALIAN DAYS
A mixture of history, politics, folklore,
food, and the arts—with local anecdotes
and personal reflection
1–55584–311–5 Weidenfeld & Nicolson $19.95

- Henry James
HENRY JAMES ON ITALY
1–55584–238–0 Weidenfeld & Nicolson $24.95

A LITTLE TOUR IN FRANCE
1–55584–129–5 Weidenfeld & Nicolson $24.95
0–374–51807–6 Farrar, Straus & Giroux pb $9.95

- D.H. Lawrence
D.H. LAWRENCE AND ITALY
Three books in one volume: *Twilight in
Italy, Sea and Sardinia,* and *Etruscan Places,*
all published between 1916 and 1932
0–14–009520–9 Penguin pb $7.95

Photo from Italy Observed *edited by Charles Traub and Luigi Ballerini* (Rizzoli)

- Henry Miller
THE COLOSSUS OF MAROUSSI
Miller's idiosyncratic account of his first
visit to Greece in the late 1930s captures
the essence of people and place like almost
no other writer
0–81120109–0 New Directions pb $6.95

- H.V. Morton
A TRAVELLER IN SOUTHERN ITALY
A sympathetic and serious account of Italy
between the wars
0–396–08926–7 Dodd, Mead $14.95

- Mark Twain
THE INNOCENTS ABROAD
Shrewd observation and typical Twain
humor in this familiar book about the
New World encountering the Old on a
trip to Europe and the Holy Land
0–451–51753–9 NAL pb $3.95

A TRAMP ABROAD
Details of a walking tour of the Alps and
the Black Forest in 1880, written to
counter the flood of paeans to Europe then
flooding America
0–06–014428–9 Harper & Row $12.50

Europe since 1945

- Gerald Brenan
THE FACE OF SPAIN
A member of the Bloomsbury Group
travels through Franco's Spain and
describes depressing conditions in the
aftermath of the Civil War
0–374–90977–6 Hippocrene $24.50

- Lawrence Durrell
THE GREEK ISLANDS
A novelist turns his pen to a part of the
world where he spent much of his
childhood
0–14–005661–0 Penguin pb $14.95

Patrick Leigh Fermor
**BETWEEN THE WOODS AND THE
WATER: From the Middle Danube to
the Iron Gates**
Conclusion of the trip begun in *A Time
of Gifts*
0–14–009430–X Penguin pb $6.95

**MANI: Travels in the Southern
Peloponnese**
A seldom-visited region of Greece
explored in a quest to seek out the
relationship between the Greeks, their
history, and the land
0–14–009503–9 Penguin pb $6.95

ROUMELI: Travels in Northern Greece
Wanderings in the "contracting
wilderness" of central Greece, with its
remote monasteries and local legends of
Lord Byron
0–14–009504–7 Penguin pb $6.95

**A TIME OF GIFTS: On Foot to
Constantinople from the Hook of
Holland**
A young traveler tries his luck on the
open road
0–14–004947–9 Penguin pb $7.95

- M.F.K. Fisher
TWO TOWNS IN PROVENCE
Includes *Map of Another Town* and *A
Considerable Town*
0–394–71631–0 Random House pb $9.95

- Robert Gibbings
COMING DOWN THE SEINE
From source to sea, touching on the
historical events that took place along the
river's banks
0–87052–300–7 Hippocrene pb $11.95

- Brian Hall
**STEALING FROM A DEEP PLACE:
Travels in Southeastern Europe**
A bicycle trip across Romania, Bulgaria,
and Hungary provides fascinating glimpses
of rural life amid often bleak landscapes
0–8090–8835–5 Hill & Wang $18.95

- Christina Hardyment
HEIDI'S ALP
An English family seeks out the locales of
their favorite fairy stories across the
Continent, often with humorous and
instructive results
0–87113–178–1 Atlantic Monthly pb $7.95

➢ **FOR OVERSEAS ORDERING INFORMATION, SEE PAGE 1**

- **John Hillaby**
  JOURNEY THROUGH EUROPE
  An ambitious recent walking tour
  0–586–08141–0 Academy Chicago pb $5.95

- **Rose Macaulay**
  FABLED SHORE: From Pyrenees to Portugal
  A vivid journey undertaken by a renowned British novelist
  0–19–281483–4 Oxford pb $9.95

- **Mary McCarthy**
  THE STONES OF FLORENCE
  A perceptive look into the spirit of one of Italy's greatest cities
  0–15–185079–8 HBJ pb $49.95
  0–15–685081–8 HBJ pb $19.95

  VENICE OBSERVED
  A companion to her book *The Stones of Florence*, both published in the 1950s
  0–15–693521–X HBJ pb $4.95

- **Jan Morris**
  THE WORLD OF VENICE
  0–15–698356–7 HBJ pb $8.95

- **Mary Taylor Simeti**
  ON PERSEPHONE'S ISLAND: A Sicilian Journal
  An evocative, knowledgeable guide to the changing landscape, seasons, and festivals of rural and urban Sicily, by an American who has lived there for 20 years
  0–394–54988–0 Knopf $18.95

- **Evelyn Waugh**
  LABELS: A Mediterranean Journal
  A comically xenophobic account of the satirist's journeys, including a visit to Mount Etna, of which Waugh wrote, "Nothing I have ever seen in Art or Nature was quite so revolting"
  0–7156–0859–2 Longwood pb $8.95

- **Rebecca West**
  BLACK LAMB AND GREY FALCON
  One of the great travel books of the century, an extraordinary account of a journey through Yugoslavia in 1937
  0–14–006355–2 Penguin pb $14.95

- **Freda White**
  THREE RIVERS OF FRANCE: Dordogne, Lot, Tarn
  This classic guide, published in 1952, remains a great piece of travel writing
  0–571–13386–X Faber & Faber pb $9.95

The Soviet Union

There have been few published accounts of travel in Russia, and as a result it remains in the minds of many Westerners a land of myth and rumor. The writers who have penetrated the layers of mystery and red tape are worth a read by anyone planning to essay the journey.

- **Stan Grossfeld**
  THE WHISPER OF STARS: A Siberian Journey
  Text and beautiful photographs document one man's winter travels
  0–87106–679–3 Globe Pequot $24.95

- **Laurence Kelly, editor**
  ST. PETERSBURG: A Traveller's Companion
  Historical selections grouped topographically, so that travelers can follow past visitors' wanderings
  0–689–70645–6 Atheneum pb $10.95

  MOSCOW: A Traveller's Companion
  0–689–70672–3 Atheneum pb $10.95

- **Andrea Lee**
  RUSSIAN JOURNAL
  Everyday events and lives as experienced by a young American student based at Moscow and Leningrad universities in 1978–79
  0–394–71127–0 Random House pb $5.95

- **Eric Newby**
  THE BIG RED TRAIN RIDE
  Often hilarious hardships aboard the Trans-Siberian Express from Moscow to Vladivostock
  0–14–009540–3 Penguin pb $7.95

- **Henry Seebohm**
  THE BIRDS OF SIBERIA: To the Petchora Valley
  A turn-of-the-century naturalist visits Russia in search of native birds
  0–86299–259–1 Hippocrene pb $5.95

  THE BIRDS OF SIBERIA: The Yenesei
  More natural adventures in old Russia
  0–86299–260–5 Hippocrene pb $5.95

- **Colin Thubron**
  WHERE NIGHTS ARE LONGEST: Travels by Car Through Western Russia
  An articulate, sometimes lyrical account of Thubron's 10,000-mile automobile journey that took him from the Baltic to the Caucasus in 1980
  0–87113–167–6 Atlantic Monthly pb $7.95

- **Laurens Van Der Post**
  JOURNEY INTO RUSSIA
  0–933280–25–4 Island pb $14.95

ASIA

The Near and Middle East

When Wilfred Thesiger set off, in the 1950s, to cross the Empty Quarter of Arabia because he "craved for adventure in savage lands," he was conscious of being the latest in a long line of British explorers who had found the savagery and beauty of the desert irresistible. The books of these British Arabists present a powerful and seductive picture of desert life before the discovery and exploitation of oil rendered it ever more precarious.

The Arabian desert may have been magnetic, but the British had been turning their attention eastward even before Napoleon's 1798 expedition to Egypt. The most notable early traveler, Alexander Kinglake, made a typical, relatively unadventurous journey to the eastern Mediterranean and the Near East in 1835. *Eothen,* his impressionistic account of the voyage, is written in a self-depre-

cating, ironic style that echoes in his literary heirs today.

- **Gertrude Bell**
  THE DESERT AND THE SOWN
  Bell, part of the long tradition of Englishwomen traveling abroad alone, went to Syria early in this century, when it was still under Turkish rule
  0–8070–7031–9 Beacon pb $9.95

- **Lady Anne Blunt**
  A PILGRIMAGE TO NEJD
  Lady Anne traveled in the 1880s with her husband, the poet Wilfrid Scawen Blunt, (who sometimes lived as an Arab sheikh near Cairo) to Jebel Shammur, "the metropolis of Bedouin life"
  0–7126–0989–X Hippocrene pb $15.95

- **Richard Burton**
  PERSONAL NARRATIVE OF A PILGRIMAGE TO AL-MADINAH AND MECCAH
  The preeminent Victorian Orientalist, fluent in Arabic, disguised himself in 1853 to become the first Englishman to visit the sacred cities of Mecca and Medina

  Volume 1
  0–486–21217–3 Dover pb $8.95

  Volume 2
  0–486–21218–1 Dover pb $8.95

- **Robert Byron**
  THE ROAD TO OXIANA
  Persia and Afghanistan in the early 1930s, described in a rich mixture of scholarship and adventure narrative
  0–19–503067–2 Oxford pb $8.95

- **Sir John Chardin**
  TRAVELS IN PERSIA, 1673–1677
  0–486–25636–7 Dover pb $7.95

- **Robert Curzon**
  VISIT TO MONASTERIES IN THE LEVANT
  A scholar goes in search of manuscripts in the 1930s
  0–317–61236–0 David & Charles $15.95

- **C.M. Doughty**
  PASSAGES FROM ARABIA DESERTA
  An edited version of an influential Victorian classic
  0–14–009508–X Penguin pb $7.95

- **E.M. Forster**
  ALEXANDRIA: A History and A Guide
  An outstanding essay on the city at the mouth of the Nile in all its eras
  0–19–504066–X Oxford pb $7.95

- **A.W. Kinglake**
  EOTHEN
  0–89987–734–6 Darby $27.00

- **V.S. Naipaul**
  AMONG THE BELIEVERS: An Islamic Journey
  The Islamic revolution from Iran to Indonesia, written in an attempt to come to terms with fundamentalist Muslim zeal
  0–394–50969–2 Knopf $14.50

- Jonathan Raban
ARABIA: A Journey Through the Labyrinth
Three months in the Persian Gulf region.
Each country is described through
vignettes of encounters with residents and
other travelers
0–671–25057–4 Simon & Schuster pb $7.95

- Harry St. John Philby
ARABIA OF THE WAHHABIS
A British civil servant recalls Arabia in
1917–18, poised on the brink of
modernization
0–7146–3073–X Biblio $32.50

- Christopher Pick, editor
**EMBASSY TO CONSTANTINOPLE: The
Travels of Lady Mary Wortley Montagu**
Letters full of keen observations from a
prominent British traveler in 18th-century
Turkey
0–941533–41–7 New Amsterdam $30.00

- Freya Stark
**ALEXANDER'S PATH: From Caria to
Cilicia**
Retracing in the 1950s the route of
Alexander the Great along the west and
south coasts of Turkey
0–7195–1332–4 Transatlantic Arts $28.50

HOME ON THE EUPHRATES
0–7195–1335–9 Transatlantic Arts $28.50

**THE SOUTHERN GATES OF ARABIA: A
Journey to the Hadhramaut**
In search of old trade routes and feuding
tribes in southern Arabia
0–87477–265–6 Tarcher pb $9.95

THE VALLEY OF THE ASSASSINS
Buried treasure and the haunts of the old
Assassins sect in Persia, seen in 1931
0–87477–261–3 Tarcher pb $9.95

- Wilfred Thesiger
ARABIAN SANDS
Travels made from 1945 to 1950 among
the Bedu of the Empty Quarter—a way of
life "doomed" in Thesiger's eyes by
encroaching technology
0–14–009514–4 Penguin pb $6.95

- Colin Thubron
JERUSALEM
Insights into Jerusalem past and present,
by a masterly observer and writer
0–7126–1492–3 David & Charles pb $13.95

MIRROR TO DAMASCUS
0–7126–9456–0 David & Charles pb $11.95

- Dale Walker
FOOL'S PARADISE
A sometimes disgruntled, thoroughly
deromanticized tale of today's Saudi Arabia
0–394–75818–8 Random House pb $7.95

Central Asia

Marco Polo's tale of his 20-year travels in the
service of Kublai Khan in the late 13th
century revealed an exotic world of which
the West had little inkling. Some of his
destinations—parts of Burma, for instance—
were not visited again by Europeans for
another 600 years.

Travelers still encounter strenuous difficulties in that remote area known as the
Roof of the World, where the very act of
traveling is often more important than arrival
at a destination.

- Fred Burnaby
**A RIDE TO KHIVA: Travels and
Adventures in Central Asia**
A captain in the Royal Horse Guards
investigates a perceived Russian threat in
Turkestan to the British Empire's Indian
borders
0–7126–0093–0 Hippocrene pb $11.95

**ON HORSEBACK THROUGH ASIA
MINOR**
Northern Turkey in the winter of
1876–77, and the Russian threat again.
Back home, the book solidified Burnaby's
status as a popular hero
0–87052–211–6 Hippocrene pb $5.95

- David Hatcher Childress
**LOST CITIES OF CHINA, CENTRAL
ASIA AND INDIA**
0–932813–07–0 Adventures Unlimited $12.95

- Nick Danzinger
**DANZINGER'S TRAVELS: Beyond
Forbidden Frontiers**
A young British traveler retraces the
ancient Silk Road
0–675–73994–7 McKay pb $8.95

- Alexandra David-Neel
MAGIC AND MYSTERY IN TIBET
Spiritual life and practices among the lamas
in the early 20th century, as described by a
Frenchwoman who became fluent in
Tibetan and lived as a Buddhist for many
years
0–486–22682–4 Dover pb $6.95

MY JOURNEY TO LHASA
A gripping account of the successful
attempt to become the first white woman
(and one of the first whites) to enter Lhasa
(in disguise) in 1923
0–8070–5901–3 Beacon pb $10.95

- Peter Fleming
BAYONETS TO LHASA
One of the great British 20th-century
adventurers
0–19–583862–9 Oxford pb $8.95

NEWS FROM TARTARY
A special correspondent for *The Times*
(London), Fleming journeyed through
war-torn Sinkiang province in 1935
0–87477–234–6 Tarcher pb $9.95

- André Guibart
TIBETAN VENTURE
0–19–584214–6 Oxford pb $7.95

- Heinrich Harrer
SEVEN YEARS IN TIBET
A German journalist escapes to Tibet from
a British POW camp in India and serves as
the Dalai Lama's private tutor until
China's 1950 invasion
0–87477–217–6 Tarcher pb $8.95

RETURN TO TIBET
Harrer returns to Tibet in 1980
0–8052–3947–2 Schocken $17.95

- Peregrine Hodson
**UNDER A SICKLE MOON: A Journey
Through Afghanistan**
0–87113–161–7 Atlantic Monthly pb $7.95

- Peter Hopkirk
FOREIGN DEVILS ON THE SILK ROAD
The lost cities and treasures of Chinese
Central Asia
0–87023–435–8 Massachusetts pb $13.95

- Pico Iyer
**VIDEO NIGHT IN KATHMANDU AND
OTHER REPORTS FROM THE NOT-
SO-FAR EAST**
A *Time* correspondent attempts to unravel
what happens when East meets West in
Asia in a witty and perceptive look at
"tourist culture" and beyond
0–394–55027–7 Knopf $19.95

- Evariste-Regis Huc & Joseph Gabet
**TRAVELS IN TARTARY, TIBET AND
CHINA, 1844–1846**
A French missionary's travels, marked by
good narrative style and an eye for
anthropological detail
0–486–25438–0 Dover pb $14.95

- Ella Maillart
TURKESTAN SOLO
On the track of Marco Polo at a time of
bloody civil war in Chinese Sinkiang
0–7126–0439–1 David & Charles pb $11.95

- Peter Matthiessen
THE SNOW LEOPARD
A nature diary and travelogue of the search
in the Himalayas for the shy snow leopard,
as well as for a deeper understanding of
Buddhism
0–14–010266–3 Penguin pb $7.95

- Geoffrey Moorhouse
TO THE FRONTIER
A modern traveler's extreme experiences in
this 1983 journey in Pakistan, across the
Punjab to the northwest frontier
0–15–690697–X HBJ pb $5.95

- Dervla Murphy
**FULL TILT: Ireland to India with a
Bicycle**
In fulfillment of a childhood dream,
Murphy pedaled through some of the
world's wildest terrain
0–87941–236–9 Overlook pb $17.95
0–87951–248–2 Overlook pb $9.95

WHERE THE INDUS IS YOUNG
In 1974, Murphy took her 6-year-old
daughter with her to "Little Tibet"—
Baltistan in Kashmir—through the Indus
Gorge in winter
0–7195–334–X Transatlantic Arts $19.95

- Eric Newby
A SHORT WALK IN THE HINDU KUSH
A strenuous expedition in 1958 recounted
as though it were a walk in the Cotswolds,
combining travel humor with scenic
description
0–14–009575–6 Penguin pb $6.95

SLOWLY DOWN THE GANGES
A funny account of a long trip down the
holy river
0–14–009572–1 Penguin pb $7.95

• Brad Newsham
ALL THE RIGHT PLACES: Traveling Light Through China, Japan, and Russia
A newly divorced man on a journey by bike and foot. Alternately humorous and moving
0–394–57410–9 Random House $16.95

• Vikram Seth
FROM HEAVEN LAKE: Travels Through Sinkiang and Tibet
Hitchhiking home from Nanjing to Delhi via Tibet and Nepal
0–394–75218–X Random House pb $5.95

• Stuart Stevens
NIGHT TRAIN TO TURKESTAN
A 1986 trip with friends along China's ancient Silk Road, following Peter Fleming's itinerary of 50 years before
0–87113–190–0 Atlantic Monthly pb $7.95

• Paul Theroux
THE GREAT RAILWAY BAZAAR
An entertaining, classic journey from Victoria Station, London, to Tokyo and back via the Trans-Siberian Railway
0–395–20708–8 Houghton Mifflin $18.95
0–345–30110–2 Ballantine pb $2.95

India

• J.R. Ackerley
HINDOO HOLIDAY: An Indian Journal
The hilarious account of a young Englishman's appointment as tutor to the son of a maharajah
0–14–009507–1 Penguin pb $6.95

• Michael Alexander
DELHI AND AGRA: A Traveller's Companion
Descriptions of two of India's most important destinations, ranging from mid-14th-century accounts to the present, linked with a historical essay
0–689–70725–8 Atheneum pb $10.95

• Jim Corbett
JIM CORBETT'S INDIA
Sketches of village life, customs, and people, by a lifelong resident of the city of Mokameh Ghat on the Ganges; Corbett served the crown early in this century
0–19–282042–7 Oxford pb $9.95

• Andrew Harvey
A JOURNEY IN LADAKH
A young English poet's pilgrimage to Ladakh in northern India in 1981, to see "one of the last places on earth . . . where a Tibetan Buddhist society can be experienced"
0–395–3667–0–4 Houghton Mifflin pb $7.95

• H.K. Kaul
TRAVELLERS' INDIA: An Anthology
An exhaustive selection of accounts from ancient times to the present
0–19–560654–X Oxford $34.95

• V.S. Naipaul
AN AREA OF DARKNESS: An Experience of India
0–394–74673–2 Random House pb $5.95

Photo of the Golden Temple of the Sikhs, Amritsar, by Alistair Shearer, from his book The Traveler's Key to Northern India *(Knopf)*

INDIA: A Wounded Civilisation
India in the mid-1970s
0–394–72463–1 Random House pb $4.95

• Lady Wilson
LETTERS FROM INDIA
Letters covering a stay from 1889–1909
0–317–14665–3 Hippocrene pb $11.95

China

• David Bonavia
THE CHINESE
Contemporary life by a resident journalist
0–690–01996–3 Harper & Row $14.95
0–14–010100–4 Penguin pb $6.95

• Mildred Cable & Francesca French
THE GOBI DESERT
The extraordinary nomadic life of three missionaries in the 1920s in one of the most inhospitable parts of the world
0–8070–7033–5 Beacon pb $10.95

• Christina Dodwell
A TRAVELLER IN CHINA
From Kashmir to the Yangtse River
0–8253–0371–0 Beaufort pb $2.00

• Robert Easton
CHINA CARAVANS: An American Adventure in Old China
Easton vividly recreates the travels of Fred Meyer Schroder in China, Mongolia, and Tibet between 1912 and 1920
0–88496–179–6 Capra pb $8.95

• Emily Hahn
CHINA TO ME
0–306–70695–4 Da Capo $45.00
0–8070–7101–3 Beacon pb $9.95

• Peter Jenkins
ACROSS CHINA
His adventurous trip across Tibet, China, and Mongolia
0–688–04223–6 Morrow $18.95
0–449–21456–7 Fawcett pb $4.95

• Jan Morris
HONG KONG
The city soon to be returned to China, and its fascinating history
0–394–55097–8 Random House $19.50

• Lynn Pann
INTO CHINA'S HEART
A Chinese-born resident of the West explores the Yellow River, visiting many off-limit sites
0–8348–0205–8 Weatherhill $17.50

• Frances Parsons
I DIDN'T HEAR THE DRAGON ROAR
The adventures of a deaf art history lecturer traveling through China and Tibet
0–93023–41–6 Gallaudet $17.95

• Mark Salzman
IRON AND SILK
The unusual experiences of a martial arts student teaching English in China
0–394–55156–7 Random House $16.95
0–394–75511–1 Random House pb $5.95

• Helen Foster Snow
MY CHINA YEARS: A Memoir
The author was a close observer of many events of the 1930s that led to revolution
0–688–00786–4 Morrow pb $9.95

• Paul Theroux
RIDING THE IRON ROOSTER: By Train Through China
0–399–13309–7 Putnam $21.95

• Colin Thubron
BEHIND THE WALL: A Journey Through China
"The narrative of a 10,000-mile trip across China by railway, boat, bicycle, and on foot, by an Englishman who makes travel writing an art"—*New Yorker*
0–87113–242–7 Atlantic Monthly $18.95

• Patrick & Maggie Whitehouse
CHINA BY RAIL
0–86565–090–X Vendome $45.00

Japan

- Isabella Bird
UNBEATEN TRACKS IN JAPAN
Letters describing journeys into Japan's interior circa 1878, mentioning many places never previously visited by foreigners
0–8070–7015–7 Beacon pb $9.95

- Alan Booth
THE ROADS TO SATA
Booth walked the 2000 miles from the northernmost point of Japan (Cape Soya) to the southernmost (Cape Sata)
0–670–80776–1 Viking $16.95
0–14–009566–7 Penguin pb $6.95

- Lafcadio Hearn
GLIMPSES OF UNFAMILIAR JAPAN
Hearn was an acute observer and vivid describer of late 19th-century Japan
0–8048–1145–8 Tuttle pb $10.95

WRITINGS FROM JAPAN
0–14–009532–2 Penguin pb $7.95

- Donald Richie
THE INLAND SEA
A film historian long resident in Japan writes sensitively and knowledgeably about its great interior waterways
0–7126–9575–3 David & Charles pb $13.95

- Oliver Statler
JAPANESE PILGRIMAGE
A Western scholar participates in the annual Buddhist pilgrimages on the island of Shikoku
0–688–01890–4 Morrow pb $5.00

Korea and Southeast Asia

- Isabella Bird
KOREA AND HER NEIGHBORS
Bird made four visits to Korea in the last decade of the 19th century, and her account touches on contemporary politics (especially the Sino-Japanese War) as well as on customs and daily life
0–7103–0135–X Oxford pb $8.95

- Geoffrey Gorer
BALI AND ANGKOR
Siam and Malaysia, among others, as seen on a 1935 trip to look at art and religious life
0–19–582692–2 Oxford pb $9.95

- Eric Hansen
STRANGER IN THE FOREST: On Foot Across Borneo
0–395–44093–9 Houghton Mifflin $17.50

- Norman Lewis
A DRAGON APPARENT: Travels in Indo-China
A thoughtful, erudite account of a 1951 trip to a doomed region
0–907871–00–3 Hippocrene pb $10.95

GOLDEN EARTH: Travels in Burma
A "literary sightseer" goes in search (in 1951) of "the traditional Burma, with its archaic and charming way of life"
0–907871–65–8 Hippocrene pb $9.95

- Peter Matthiessen
UNDER THE MOUNTAIN WALL
Two seasons experienced by the Stone Age tribesmen of New Guinea
0–14–009548–0 Penguin pb $8.95

- Colin McPhee
A HOUSE IN BALI
Fascinated by Balinese gamelan music, McPhee "wanted to hear every gamelan in the countryside." This enchanting account tells how he did just that in the 1930s and made the island his home
0–19–580448–1 Oxford pb $12.95

- Redmond O'Hanlon
INTO THE HEART OF BORNEO
Adventuring into a true wilderness
0–394–75540–5 Random House pb $6.95

- Hickman Powell
THE LAST PARADISE: An American's Discovery of Bali in the 1920s
Even 60 years ago, Westerners thought that Bali was the Last Eden, soon to be despoiled by tourism and civilization
0–19–582537–3 Oxford pb $9.95

AFRICA

- Bartle Bull
SAFARI: A Chronicle of Adventure
An illustrated history
0–670–81880–1 Penguin $40.00

- David Ewing Duncan
FROM THE CAPE TO CAIRO: One Man's Trek Across Africa
A young man's arduous journey through Africa by bicycle, foot, and train
1–55584–045–0 Weidenfeld & Nicolson $19.95

North Africa

- Ralph Bagnold
LIBYAN SANDS: Travel in a Dead World
Exploration in the 1930s
0–87052–384–8 Hippocrene pb $11.95

- Paul Bowles
THEIR HEADS ARE GREEN AND THEIR HANDS ARE BLUE
Morocco observed by a longtime resident
0–88001–043–6 Ecco pb $8.50

- Edward Cecil
LEISURE OF AN EGYPTIAN OFFICIAL
0–317–61175–5 David & Charles pb $11.95

- Amelia Edwards
A THOUSAND MILES UP THE NILE
Egypt in 1873, "in search of fine weather" and a look at antiquities
0–87477–271–0 Tarcher pb $11.95

- André Gide
AMYNTAS: North African Journals
Mystery and poetry in North Africa
0–88001–166–1 Ecco pb $7.50

- William Golding
AN EGYPTIAN JOURNAL
The novelist takes a trip down the Nile
0–571–12547–6 Faber & Faber pb $9.95

- Walter Harris
MOROCCO THAT WAS
0–8371–3460–9 Greenwood $27.50

- Wyndham Lewis
JOURNEY INTO BARBARY
Morocco in 1931: the writer and painter's escape from "dying European society" into a search for "the mirages of the great electric desert"
0–87685–518–4 Black Sparrow pb $12.50

- Peter Mayne
A YEAR IN MARRAKESH
0–907871–30–5 Hippocrene pb $9.95

- Edith Wharton
IN MOROCCO
Morocco during World War I
0–317–61173–9 David & Charles pb $13.95

Sub-Saharan Africa

- Isak Dinesen
OUT OF AFRICA & SHADOWS ON THE GRASS
"I had a farm in Africa," begins Dinesen, recalling her attempts to grow coffee in East Africa in these elegant autobiographies
0–517–56509–9 Crown $24.95
0–394–74211–7 Random House pb $4.95

- André Gide
TRAVELS IN THE CONGO
Gide dedicated this journey from Brazzaville to Lake Chad and back to Joseph Conrad
0–14–009555–1 Penguin pb $7.95

- Graham Greene
JOURNEY WITHOUT MAPS
Across Liberia in 1935
0–14–003280–0 Penguin pb $4.95

- Christopher Hibbert
AFRICA EXPLORED: Europeans in the Dark Continent
A well-told account of legendary 18th- and 19th-century explorers including Mungo Park, Richard Burton, and David Livingstone
0–393–01760–5 Norton $17.00

- John Hillaby
JOURNEY TO THE JADE SEA
Diary of an 1100-mile walk across Kenya in 1964
0–586–08140–2 Academy Chicago pb $5.95

- Edward Hoagland
AFRICAN CALLIOPE: A Journey to the Sudan
0–14–009543–8 Penguin pb $7.95

IF YOU CAN'T FIND IT, LOOK IN THE INDEX

- Mary Kingsley
TRAVELS IN WEST AFRICA
A Victorian lady proves that one didn't have to be a "heroic male" to explore successfully
0–8070–7105–6 Beacon pb $12.95

- Beryl Markham
WEST WITH THE NIGHT
A memoir of East Africa by an adventuresome aviator
0–86547–304–8 North Point $19.95
0–96547–118–5 North Point pb $12.95

- Shiva Naipaul
NORTH OF SOUTH: An African Journey
V.S. Naipaul's younger brother travels through Kenya, Tanzania, and Zambia, observing the relations between Europe and Africa
0–14–004894–4 Penguin pb $7.95

- George Packer
THE VILLAGE OF WAITING
Life in a Togo village
0–394–75754–8 Random House pb $8.95

- Frederic Selous
TRAVEL AND ADVENTURES IN SOUTH-EAST AFRICA
Eleven years exploring the Zambesi River and its tributaries
0–7126–0445–6 Hippocrene pb $13.95

- Alex Shoumatoff
IN SOUTHERN LIGHT: Trekking through Zaire and the Amazon
Two journeys by water to explore the natural, human, and mythical histories of tropical rain forests
0–671–49441–1 Simon & Schuster $17.50

- Patrick Synge
MOUNTAINS OF THE MOON
The 1934–35 British Museum Expedition to East Africa studied flora and fauna of the equatorial mountains and recorded the life of the Ethiopians, Kenyans, and Ugandans
0–94772–40–4 Hippocrene pb $11.95

- Anthony Trollope
SOUTH AFRICA
Probably the most important Victorian book on the subject. Trollope went to South Africa just after the Transvaal had been annexed by Britain and came back in 1877 raising questions that still go unanswered
Volume 1
0–87052–434–8 Hippocrene pb $5.95
Volume 2
0–87052–391–0 Hippocrene pb $5.95

- Laurens Van Der Post
THE LOST WORLD OF THE KALAHARI
"A journey in a great wasteland [the Kalahari Desert in southern Africa] and a search for some pure remnant of the unique and almost vanished First People of my native land, the Bushmen of Africa," writes Van Der Post
0–15–653706–0 HBJ pb $8.95

A VENTURE TO THE INTERIOR
A 1949 expedition to South Central Africa
0–15–693429–5 HBJ pb $7.95

- Evelyn Waugh
A TOURIST IN AFRICA
Looking to avoid another English February, Waugh set out in 1958 for Kenya, Rhodesia, and Tanganyika
0–316–92650–7 Little, Brown pb $7.95

NORTH AMERICA

- Jack Newcombe, editor
TRAVELS IN THE AMERICAS
From Florida to Alaska, travel writings by Charles Dickens, Henry James, Jack Kerouac, and Jonathan Raban, among others
1–55584–330–1 Weidenfeld & Nicolson $24.95

19th-Century Travelers

- Isabella Bird
THE ENGLISHWOMAN IN AMERICA
A young Victorian's honest though sometimes prejudiced impression of Canada and America in the 1850s
0–299–03524–7 Wisconsin pb $10.95
A LADY'S LIFE IN THE ROCKY MOUNTAINS
Bird returned 20 years after her first visit to journey by horseback through the Rockies, producing an excellent portrait of outdoor life in the American West
0–89174–025–2 Comstock pb $3.50

- Charles Dickens
AMERICAN NOTES
Dickens, though fond of America, offended many Americans with this strongly abolitionist account of manners and morals in 1842
0–14–043077–6 Penguin pb $5.95

- Henry James
THE AMERICAN SCENE
After a 20-year expatriation, James returned at the turn of the century to find his native country corrupted by its love of "the crudity of wealth," and "the shallowness of the American grab-bag"
0–312–00409–5 St. Martin's $16.95
0–253–20110–1 Indiana pb $8.95

- Anthony Trollope
NORTH AMERICA
A sympathetic, balanced account of mid-19th-century America
Volume 1
0–87052–389–9 Hippocrene pb $5.95
Volume 2
0–87052–436–4 Hippocrene pb $5.95

- Frances Trollope
DOMESTIC MANNERS OF THE AMERICANS
The novelist's mother ventured to America in 1827 and produced such a scathing report that her book allegedly set back US-British relations a generation
0–7126–0934–2 Hippocrene pb $11.95

Recent Writers

- Mark Abley
BEYOND FORGET
Rediscovering the Canadian prairies, from Hudson Bay to Edmonton and south to the US border
0–87156–669–9 Sierra Club pb $9.95

- Peter S. Beagle
I SEE BY MY OUTFIT
A trip across America by motorcycle
0–14–009553–5 Penguin pb $6.95

- Stephen Brock
MAPLE LEAF RAG
Humorous, good-natured account of a cross-Canada trek
0–394–75833–1 Random House pb $7.95

- Ted Conover
COYOTES: A Journey through the Secret World of America's Illegal Aliens
A revealing look at the underground railway between Mexico and the United States
0–394–75518–9 Random House pb $6.95
ROLLING NOWHERE
Traveling on freight trains and living with railroad hoboes, over thousands of miles and 15 states
0–14–009550–0 Penguin pb $7.95

- Dayton Duncan
OUT WEST
On the trail of the Lewis and Clark Expedition
0–14–008362–6 Penguin pb $7.95

- William Least Heat Moon
BLUE HIGHWAYS: A Journey Into America
0–316–35395–7 Little, Brown $18.95
0–449–21109–6 Fawcett pb $4.50

- John McPhee
THE SURVIVAL OF THE BARK CANOE
McPhee takes a traditional bark canoe through the backcountry of Maine
0–374–27207–7 Farrar, Straus & Giroux $13.95
0–374–51693–6 Farrar, Straus & Giroux pb $7.95

- V.S. Naipaul
A TURN IN THE SOUTH
Naipaul's picture of the American South
0–394–56477–4 Knopf $18.95

- Tim Palmer
THE SIERRA NEVADA: A Mountain Journey
A journey through the Lake Tahoe casinos and Yosemite campgrounds and into the mountains
0–933280–54–8 Island $31.95
0–933280–53–X Island pb $19.95

- William Sullivan
LISTENING FOR COYOTE: A Walk Across Oregon's Wilderness
A search for a "new Oregon Trail" and the adventures, mishaps, and people along the way
0–688–07880–X Morrow $17.95

Central Park skaters in 1890 with the Dakota apartment building in the background (photo courtesy of The New-York Historical Society)

• John Steinbeck
TRAVELS WITH CHARLEY IN SEARCH OF AMERICA
A poodle, a novelist, and a van named Rocinante in search of America in 1961
0–14–005320–4 Penguin pb $4.95

THE CARIBBEAN AND CENTRAL AMERICA

The Caribbean

• Michael Anthony
ALL THAT GLITTERS
0–233–97369–9 David & Charles $18.95

• Mary Bond
FAR AFIELD IN THE CARIBBEAN
A naturalist's wife does some exploring on her own
0–915180–13–8 Harrowood pb $4.95

• V.S. Naipaul
THE MIDDLE PASSAGE: Impressions of Five Societies
The Trinidad-born novelist examines British, Dutch, and French societies in the West Indies
0–394–74674–0 Random House pb $4.95

Mexico

• Frances Calderón de la Barca
LIFE IN MEXICO DURING A RESIDENCE OF TWO YEARS
Letters from the Scottish wife of the first Spanish envoy to the independent country, 1838–40
0–520–04661–7 California $35.00
0–520–04662–5 California pb $10.95

• Charles Macomb Flandrau
VIVA MEXICO!
Life in 1908, on the eve of the Mexican Revolution
0–907871–20–8 Hippocrene pb $8.95

• John Lincoln
ONE MAN'S MEXICO
Mexico since independence, as of 1967
0–317–61229–8 David & Charles pb $11.95

• Ronald Wright
TIME AMONG THE MAYA: Travels in Belize, Guatemala, and Mexico
"Wright is an acute and indefatigable observer, bound to be compared to Peter Matthiessen and Paul Theroux"—*LA Times*
1–55584–291–7 Weidenfeld & Nicolson $19.95

Central America

• Patrick Marnham
SO FAR FROM GOD: A Journey in Central America
Fascinating narrative of a journey through Guatemala, Nicaragua, El Salvador, and Costa Rica at a time of upheaval
0–14–008556–4 Penguin pb $5.95

• Salman Rushdie
THE JAGUAR SMILE: A Nicaraguan Journey
Rushdie went to Nicaragua in 1986 and produced what he termed "a portrait of a moment, no more, in that beautiful, volcanic country." His book is a mixture of information, anecdote, and impressions
0–14–010926–9 Penguin pb $6.95

SOUTH AMERICA

• Bruce Chatwin
IN PATAGONIA
A modern masterpiece of travel writing
0–671–40045–2 Summit $9.95
0–671–44857–9 Summit pb $7.95

• Peter Fleming
BRAZILIAN ADVENTURE
An advertisement in the London *Times* in 1932, calling for men to help trace a lost adventurer, led to Fleming's journey
0–87477–246–X Tarcher pb $10.95

• W.H. Hudson
FAR AWAY AND LONG AGO: A Childhood in Argentina
An idyllic childhood for a young naturalist allowed to wander at will on his pony
0–7126–1038–3 David & Charles $11.95

• Joe Kane
RUNNING THE AMAZON
The story of the first people to run the entire Amazon, encountering everything from deadly rapids to Maoist guerrillas
0–394–55331–4 Knopf $27.50

• Gordon MacGreagh
WHITE WATER AND BLACK
A hilarious account of a 1923 scientific expedition that set out to explore, and collect biological specimens in the upper tributaries of the Amazon, in Bolivia, Brazil, and Colombia
0–226–50016–0 Chicago pb $11.95

• Peter Matthiessen
THE CLOUD FOREST: A Chronicle of the South American Wilderness
A journey through the wild terrain from the Amazon rain forest to Tierra del Fuego
0–14–009549–7 Penguin pb $8.95

• Roger Stone
DREAMS OF AMAZONIA
The problems and history of the Amazonian rain forests
0–670–11533–9 Viking $17.95
0–14–009573–X Penguin pb $6.95

• Paul Theroux
THE OLD PATAGONIAN EXPRESS
By train from Boston to Patagonia, as described by an expert on rail travel
0–671–64849–7 Pocket pb $5.95

• A.F. Tschiffely
SOUTHERN CROSS TO POLE STAR
A classic 1920s adventure on horseback, from Argentina to Washington, D.C.
0–87477–282–6 Tarcher pb $9.95

• Charles Waterton
WANDERINGS IN SOUTH AMERICA
"It was the first and last time I ever was on a cayman's back. Should it be asked how I managed to keep my seat, I would answer—I hunted some years with Lord Darlington's foxhounds"
0–7126–0340–9 David & Charles pb $13.95

• Evelyn Waugh
92 DAYS
A journey in Guyana and Brazil in 1932
0–7156–0960–2 Longwood $19.50

• Ronald Wright
CUT STONES AND CROSSROADS: A Journey in the Two Worlds of Peru
An entertaining exploration of Peruvian history and archeology
0–14–009565–9 Penguin pb $7.95

AUSTRALIA, NEW ZEALAND, AND THE SOUTH PACIFIC

• Lady Mary Anne Barker
STATION LIFE IN NEW ZEALAND
An 1870 account of ranching life
0–8070–7029–7 Beacon pb $9.95

• Captain James Cook
EXPLORATIONS OF CAPTAIN JAMES COOK IN THE PACIFIC, AS TOLD BY SELECTIONS OF HIS OWN JOURNALS, 1768–1779
0–486–22766–9 Dover pb $6.50

• Bruce Chatwin
THE SONGLINES
Chatwin explores the nature of nomadism as he learns about the Australian Aborigines' "Songlines," the invisible melodic pathways that cross the Australian landscape and allow it to be continually resung into being
0–670–80605–6 Viking $18.95
0–14–009429–6 Penguin pb $7.95

• Linda Christmas
THE RIBBON AND THE RAGGED SQUARE: An Australian Journey
All over Down Under, from cities to outback: a picture of an "exuberant" society
0–14–006633–0 Penguin pb $6.95

• Robyn Davidson
TRACKS
The extraordinary journey of a young woman and four camels across 1700 miles of Australian outback
0–394–51473–4 Pantheon pb $5.95

• Robert Louis Stevenson
IN THE SOUTH SEAS: The Marquesas, Paumotu and the Gilbert Islands
An account of Polynesia at a time of rapid change
0–7103–0140–5 RC&H pb $12.95

• Anthony Trollope
AUSTRALIA
Volume 1
0–87052–390–2 Hippocrene pb $5.95
Volume 2
0–87052–435–6 Hippocrene pb $5.95
Volume 3
0–87052–391–0 Hippocrene pb $5.95

• Ronald Wright
ON FIJI ISLANDS
0–14–009551–9 Penguin pb $7.95

SEA TRAVELS

• Christopher Buckley
STEAMING TO BAMBOOLA: The World of a Tramp Freighter
On board the freighter *Columbiana*
0–14–009922–0 Penguin pb $6.95

• Thurston Clarke
EQUATOR: A Journey
0–688–06901–0 Morrow $20.95

• Eric Newby
THE LAST GRAIN RACE
The author served as apprentice seaman on a four-masted sailing vessel in the Australian grain trade
0–14–009571–3 Penguin pb $7.95

• Arthur Ransome
RACUNDRA'S FIRST CRUISE
A journalist describes the building of the *Racundra* in 1921–22 and its maiden voyage with a crew of three around the Baltic
0–7126–0446–4 David & Charles pb $11.95

• Tim Severin
THE JASON VOYAGE: The Quest of the Golden Fleece
The voyage of a 20-oared galley, a replica of the *Argo* of Greek mythology, from Greece to Soviet Georgia
0–671–49813–4 Simon & Schuster $18.50

• Joshua Slocum
SAILING ALONE AROUND THE WORLD
The account of the first man to sail around the world in the *Spray*; he left Boston in 1895 and returned to Newport in 1898
0–7126–0338–7 David & Charles pb $13.95

G. HEYWOOD HILL: Classic Travel Books

G. Heywood Hill is a well-known London bookshop, one of whose specialties is travel literature.

Sybille Bedford
A VISIT TO DON OTAVIO: A Mexican Journey

George Borrow
THE BIBLE IN SPAIN

Robert Byron
THE ROAD TO OXIANA

Edward Cecil
LEISURE OF AN EGYPTIAN OFFICIAL

Bruce Chatwin
IN PATAGONIA

Isak Dinesen
OUT OF AFRICA

Peter Fleming
BRAZILIAN ADVENTURE

Patrick Leigh Fermor
A TIME OF GIFTS

Walter Harris
MOROCCO THAT WAS

A.W. Kinglake
EOTHEN

Eric Newby
A SHORT WALK IN THE HINDU KUSH

• Gavin Young
SLOW BOATS TO CHINA
From Athens to Hong Kong, on the principle that one should "take a series of ships of many sizes and kinds; go where they lead for a few months; see what happens"
0–394–52114–5 Random House $16.00

Travel Photography

▶ See also Photography

• Robert Schiffer
THE EXPLODING CITY
A photographic essay of nine cities: New York, Rome, Moscow, Cairo, Tokyo, Mexico City, Shanghai, Bombay, and Lagos
Photographs by Jerry Cooke
0–312–02361–8 St. Martin's $35.00

AFRICA

• Tim Beddow
EAST AFRICA
0–500–24131–7 Thames & Hudson $34.50

• Basil Davidson
GHANA: An African Portrait
Photographs by Paul Strand
0–89381–009–6 Aperture pb $10.00

• Angela Fischer
AFRICA ADORNED
0–8109–1823–4 Abrams $60.00

• Tepilitole Saitoiti
MAASAI
Photographs by Carol Beckwith
0–8109–1303–8 Abrams $49.50

• Marian Van Ofelen
NOMADS OF NIGER
Photographs by Carol Beckwith
0–8109–0734–8 Abrams $49.50

ASIA AND THE PACIFIC

China

• Eve Arnold
IN CHINA
0–394–50901–3 Knopf $40.00

• William J.F. Jenner
CHINA: A Photohistory, 1937–1987
0–394–57281–5 Pantheon $34.95

• Kevin Sinclair
THE YELLOW RIVER: A 5,000 Year Journey Through China
0–89535–192–7 Knapp $35.00

- Weng Wan-go & Yang Boda
  PALACE MUSEUM, PEKING: Treasures of the Forbidden City
  0–8109–1477–8 Abrams $65.00

- Yu Zhuo-yun
  PALACES OF THE FORBIDDEN CITY
  0–670–53721–7 Viking $75.00

Japan

- David Cohen & Rick Smolan
  A DAY IN THE LIFE OF JAPAN
  0–00–217580–0 Collins $45.95

- Diane Durston
  KYOTO
  0–87011–857–9 Kodansha pb $9.95

1880s photo of a geisha by Kusakabe Kimbei, from Japan: Photographs 1854–1905 *edited by Clark Worswick (Knopf)*

- Mildred Friedman, editor
  TOKYO: Form and Spirit
  0–8109–1690–8 Abrams $40.00

- Donald Richie
  INTRODUCING JAPAN
  0–87011–308–9 Kodansha $22.95

- Clark Worswick, editor
  JAPAN: Photographs, 1854–1905
  0–394–50836–X Knopf $25.00

India and Nepal

- Anita Desai
  IN PURSUIT OF INDIA
  Photographs by Mitch Epstein
  0–89381–214–5 Aperture $30.00

- V. Carrol Durham
  HIDDEN HIMALAYAS
  Photographs by Thomas Kelly
  0–89659–758–X Abbeville $45.00

- Kyuya Fukada
  HIMALAYAS
  Photographs by Yoshikazu Shirakaura
  0–8109–8065–7 Abrams $39.95

- Raghu & Usha Rai
  TAJ MAHAL
  Photographs by Raghu Rai
  0–86565–078–0 Vendome $65.00

- Marilyn Silverstone
  OCEAN OF LIFE: Visions of India and the Himalayan Kingdoms
  0–89381–195–5 Aperture $25.00
  0–89381–200–5 Aperture pb $9.00

- Raghubir Singh
  BANARAS: The Sacred City of India
  0–317–65505–1 Thames & Hudson $40.00

- Eric Valli & Diane Summers
  HONEY HUNTERS OF NEPAL
  0–8109–2408–0 Abrams pb $29.95

Other Asian Countries

- Roland & Sabrina Michaud
  AFGHANISTAN: Paradise Lost
  0–86565–009–8 Vendome $45.00

- Leonard Lueras
  BALI: The Ultimate Island
  Photographs by R. Ian Loyd
  0–312–00863–5 St. Martin's $35.00

- Paul Zach
  INDONESIA: Paradise on the Equator
  Photographs by Kal Muller
  0–312–01902–5 St. Martin's $35.00

- Chong-Sik Lee
  KOREA: Land of Morning Calm
  Photographs by Mike Langford
  0–87663–693–8 Universe $34.95

- William Warren
  THAILAND: Seven Years in the Kingdom
  Foreword by Gore Vidal
  0–920691–37–4 CU Press $45.00

- David Bonavia & Magnus Bartlett
  TIBET
  0–86565–021–7 Vendome $50.00

Australia

- Longman
  AUSTRALIA: The Photographer's View, from the 1850s to the Bicentenary
  Photographs by Robert Cape
  0–582–66357–1 Longman $19.95

- Brian Morris
  AUSTRALIA TAKE A BOW: A Photographic Salute to Australia on the Occasion of Its Bicentennial
  0–312–02071–6 St. Martin's $35.00

Britain and Ireland

- Robert Cameron & Alistair Cooke
  ABOVE LONDON
  0–918684–10–2 Cameron $24.95

- Gareth Davies
  VANISHING ENGLAND
  Introduction by John LeCarré
  0–88162–247–8 Salem House $29.95

- Michael Jenner
  LONDON'S HERITAGE: The Changing Style of a City
  0–7181–2903–2 Penguin $24.95

- Brendan Kennelly
  REAL IRELAND
  Photographs by Liam Blake
  0–87701–507–4 Chronicle pb $12.95

- Jan Morris & Paul Wakefield
  SCOTLAND: The Place of Journeys
  0–517–56260–X Clarkson Potter $27.50

- Edna O'Brien & Richard Fitzgerald
  VANISHING IRELAND
  0–517–56508–0 Crown $22.50

- Ben Weinreb & Christopher Hibbert, editors
  THE LONDON ENCYCLOPAEDIA
  0–917561–07–4 Adler & Adler $44.95

France

- Robert Cameron & Pierre Salinger
  ABOVE PARIS
  0–918684–19–6 Cameron $24.95

- Hervé Champollion
  PARIS
  0–86565–091–8 Vendome $60.00

- Philip Conisbee
  PROVENCE MEMORIES
  Photographs by Dennis Stock
  0–8212–1715–1 NY Graphic Society $50.00

- John Russell
  PARIS
  Foreword by Rosamond Bernier
  0–8109–1457–3 Abrams $45.00

- Irwin Shaw
  PARIS-MAGNUM: Photographs, 1935–1981
  Introduction by Inge Morath
  0–89381–085–1 Aperture $30.00

- A.N. Wilson
  LANDSCAPE IN FRANCE
  Photographs by Charlie Waite
  0–312–02093–7 St. Martin's $29.95

Italy

- Susanna Agnelli
  ITALY: Seasons of Light
  Photographs by Michael Ruetz
  0–8212–1618–X NY Graphic Society $60.00

☞ **TO ORDER NEW BOOKS NOT YET LISTED, ASK YOUR BOOKSELLER OR CALL 1-800-882-8770**

- Olivier Bernier
  VENICE II
  Photographs by Fulvio Roiter
  0–86565–056–X Vendome $45.00

- Cesare Colombo & Susan Sontag
  ITALY: One Hundred Years of Photography
  0–8478–5516–3 Rizzoli $50.00
  0–8478–5517–1 Rizzoli pb $29.95

- Dominique Fernandez
  ROME: Mirror of the Centuries
  Photographs by Paolo Marton
  0–86565–049–7 Vendome $50.00

- Peter Lauritzen
  ISLANDS AND LAGOONS OF VENICE
  Photographs by Fulvio Roiter
  0–86565–001–2 Vendome $50.00

- Dennis Smith, editor
  SICILY
  0–8478–0958–7 Rizzoli $60.00

- Charles Taub & Luigi Ballerini
  ITALY OBSERVED: In Photography and Literature
  Preface by Umberto Eco
  0–8478–0996–X Rizzoli $50.00

- Gore Vidal
  VIDAL IN VENICE
  Photographs by Tore Gill
  0–671–64536–6 Simon & Schuster pb $14.95

Spain

- David Cohen & Rick Smolan
  A DAY IN THE LIFE OF SPAIN
  0–002–17967–9 Collins $45.00

- Nicholas Luard
  LANDSCAPE IN SPAIN
  0–8212–1706–2 NY Graphic Society $24.95

- Jan Morris
  SPAIN
  0–13–824152–X Prentice-Hall $24.95

The Soviet Union

- David Cohen & Rick Smolan
  A DAY IN THE LIFE OF THE SOVIET UNION
  0–00–217969–5 Collins $45.00

- Serge Faucherau & Stanislas Zadora, editors
  MOSCOW, 1900–1930
  0–8478–0981–1 Rizzoli $65.00

- Fitzroy Maclean
  PORTRAIT OF THE SOVIET UNION
  0–8050–0891–8 Henry Holt $23.45

THE MIDDLE EAST

- Fouad Ajami
  BEIRUT: The Fragmented City
  Photographs by Eli Reed
  0–393–30507–4 Norton $34.95
  0–393–02490–3 Norton pb $19.70

- Frederic Brenner & A.B. Yehoshua
  ISRAEL
  0–06–015959–6 Harper & Row $39.50

- Neil Folberg
  IN A DESERT LAND: Photos of Israel, Egypt and Jordan
  0–89659–759–8 Abbeville $60.00

- Leon Uris
  JERUSALEM
  Photographs by Jill Uris
  0–385–14863–1 Doubleday $19.95

NORTH AMERICA

- Eve Arnold
  IN AMERICA
  0–394–52235–4 Knopf $34.50

- Bruce Brown
  THE NORTHWEST: Pacific Coast and Cascades
  Photographs by Gary Braasch
  0–8478–0915–3 Rizzoli $40.00
  0–8478–0914–5 Rizzoli pb $25.00

- David Cohen & Rick Smolan
  A DAY IN THE LIFE OF AMERICA
  0–00–217705–6 Collins $45.00

  A DAY IN THE LIFE OF CANADA
  0–00–217380–8 Collins $45.95

- Eliot Porter
  MAINE
  0–8212–1630–9 NY Graphic Society $49.95

  THE WEST
  0–8212–1711–9 NY Graphic Society $60.00

- Lawrence Clark Powell
  PHOTOGRAPHS OF THE SOUTHWEST
  Photographs by Ansel Adams
  0–8212–0699–0 NY Graphic Society $44.00
  0–316–70261–7 Little, Brown pb $24.50

- Emil Shulthess
  ETERNAL LANDSCAPE: Utah, Arizona, Colorado, New Mexico
  0–394–57144–4 Knopf $60.00

- T.H. Watkins
  AMERICAN LANDSCAPE
  Photographs by David Muench
  0–932575–30–7 Graphic Arts $36.50

American Cities

▶ See also American People and Places

- Thomas Bolyston Adams
  BOSTON
  Photographs by Santi Visalli
  0–8478–0997–8 Rizzoli $45.00

- Robert Llewellyn
  BOSTON
  0–89909–046–X Foremost $30.00

- Bill Kurtis
  CHICAGO
  Photographs by Santi Visalli
  0–8478–0842–4 Rizzoli $45.00

- David Lowe
  LOST CHICAGO
  0–517–46888–3 Crown $13.00

- Edmund Swinglehurst
  LOS ANGELES: A City of Many Dreams
  0–517–43640–X Crescent $17.95

- Charles Dufour, editor
  NEW ORLEANS
  Photographs by Bernard Hermann
  0–8071–0799–9 LSU $24.95

- Robert Cameron
  ABOVE NEW YORK
  0–918684–42–0 Cameron $29.95

- Barbaralee Diamonstein
  THE LANDMARKS OF NEW YORK
  0–8109–1270–8 Abrams $45.00

- Michael George
  NEW YORK TODAY
  0–8109–1377–1 Abrams $29.95

- Jake Rajs
  MANHATTAN: An Island in Focus
  0–8478–0670–7 Rizzoli $49.95

- Lloyd Ultan
  THE BEAUTIFUL BRONX: 1920–1950
  0–517–54800–3 Crown $19.95

  THE BRONX IN THE INNOCENT YEARS: 1890–1925
  0–06–015419–5 Harper & Row $19.95

- Leonard Wallock, editor
  NEW YORK: Cultural Capital of the World, 1940–1965
  0–8478–0990–0 Rizzoli $65.00

- William Younger
  OLD BROOKLYN IN EARLY PHOTOGRAPHS, 1865–1929
  0–486–23587–4 Dover pb $8.95

- Robert Llewellyn
  PHILADELPHIA
  0–89909–097–4 Yankee $30.00

- Robert Bernhardi
  GREAT BUILDINGS OF SAN FRANCISCO
  0–486–23839–3 Dover pb $6.95

- Herb Caen & others
  SAN FRANCISCO
  Photographs by Morton Beebe
  0–8109–1608–8 Abrams $49.50

- Robert Cameron
  ABOVE SAN FRANCISCO
  Text by Herb Caen
  0–918684–28–5 Cameron $24.95

- Bill Harris
  SAN FRANCISCO: From the Air
  Photographs by Neil Sutherland
  0–517–49053–6 Crescent pb $10.00

- Robert Cameron
  ABOVE WASHINGTON
  Introduction by Alistair Cooke
  0–918684–08–0 Cameron $24.95

"Never Summer Range," Colorado, 1942, from Ansel Adams: Letters and Images 1916–1984 (*New York Graphic Society/Photo copyright The Ansel Adams Publishing Rights Trust*)

• Bill Harris
WASHINGTON, D.C.
Photographs by J.C. Suares
0–517–43179–3 Crescent $24.95

• Charles Kelly
WASHINGTON, D.C., THEN AND NOW: 69 Sites Photographed in the Past & Present
0–486–24586–1 Dover pb $8.95

MEXICO AND SOUTH AMERICA

• Kevin Kling
ECUADOR: Island of the Andes
0–500–01440–X Thames & Hudson $39.50

• Walter F. Morris, Jr.
LIVING MAYA
Photographs by Jeffrey Jay Fox
0–8109–1298–8 Abrams $40.00

Vinicius De Moraes
THE JOY OF RIO
Photographs by Bernard Hermann
0–86565–005–5 Vendome $19.95

Bruce Weber
O RIO DE JANEIRO
0–394–55–938–X Knopf $60.00

Travel Guides

The following series are included in this section. The glossary below highlights each guidebook's special features. Phrasebooks are listed in alphabetical order by language at the end of the section.

Access: City guides that list museums, shops, parks, restaurants, and other interesting spots. The guides are color-coded so that information on specific topics is easily spotted.

Baedeker: This series for independent travelers includes A–Z listings of sights, as well as museum floor plans and pullout maps. City and region guides are pocket-size.

Birnbaum: A series for moderate to upper-price range travel. Sights, driving tours and activities, as well as hotels and restaurants, are included.

Blue Guide: The intellectual's guidebook. In-depth, well-researched information on the arts and history. Includes maps, floor plans, and detailed itineraries.

Born to Shop: Where to shop and what to buy, including bargains.

Companion: Much more historical and anecdotal information than most guidebooks, with less emphasis on places to stay and eat.

Crown Insider: Overall guides with money-saving tips, itineraries, and a "perils and pitfalls" section.

Economist Business Traveller: Provides both tourist specifics and information on local business practices and etiquette.

Fodor: This series covers more countries and areas than any other. Each guidebook includes listings in a variety of price ranges for hotels, restaurants, shops, and sights, as well as background information on history and culture. Includes the "Fodor's Budget" and "Fodor's Fun In" guides, the latter tending to be livelier than the main Fodors, with more evaluation of hotels and restaurants.

Gault & Millau: A French series, with witty and opinionated reviews of restaurants, hotels, and sites, especially useful for France.

Hildebrand: Pocket-size guides with essays on the area, historical and cultural information, and some hotel listings. No restaurant listings.

The Independent Traveller: For those looking to get off the beaten track, save money, and plan their own itinerary.

Insight: Emphasizes history, people, and sites; illustrated with color photographs.

Karen Brown's Country Inns: Listings of country inns, chalets, and castles as well as itineraries and sightseeing tips.

Knopf Traveler's Guide to Art: A critical guide to masterpieces and little-known art treasures, with maps, museum plans, and photographs.

Let's Go: By the Harvard Student Agencies, these guides are popular with students and low-budget travelers; includes places to stay, restaurants, sightseeing, and where to get student discounts.

Lonely Planet: Includes "Travel Survival Kit" and "On a Shoestring" titles. The Asian and South Pacific series are the most popular of these guides. Used primarily by independent budget-minded travelers who want more than a list of places to stay, the guides include sightseeing information as well as essential practical information.

Michelin: These classic French guidebooks come in two series: the Red Guides list selected hotels and restaurants with an international rating system; the Green Guides provide historical, cultural, and sightseeing information with a star rating system. Each guide includes several good maps.

Moon Handbooks: Geared to the young and independent who generally rely on public transportation and moderate budgets; includes a very thorough background on history and culture for each region.

Nagel: The encyclopedia of travel books. Details on art, architecture, theaters, and museums, as well as historic and geographic information on each country. The *New York Times* has called the series "the Cadillac of cultural guide books."

Penguin: A general but selective series that includes all but the low-price range.

Rough Guide: A British series with practical and cultural information, and money- and time-saving tips. Though oriented toward the low-budget traveler, it also offers useful information to those on larger budgets.

Smithsonian Guides to Historic America: Beautifully illustrated guides devoted to particular regions with maps, descriptions of the important sites and landmarks, and background history.

Traveller's: Overview guides providing general information. A short list of hotels

---

➤ **FOR OVERSEAS ORDERING INFORMATION, SEE PAGE 1**

Drawing by William Steig, from The Decline and Fall of Practically Everybody *by Will Cuppy (Godine)*

and restaurants is included. Useful for areas not included in other guides.

Travels In: A British series offering individual tours through various European regions with mapped itineraries, hotel and restaurant guides, food samplings, and recipes; illustrated with line drawings.

Visitor's: General British guides locating less-visited spots; strong on sightseeing and useful for motorists.

Walking Through: Routes for rural walks, with maps.

Zagat: A respected guide to rated restaurants by food lovers. Their new hotel guides are compiled in the same manner.

GENERAL TRAVEL

- Deborah Burns & Sarah May Clarkson
TIPS FOR THE SAVVY TRAVELER
Helps you plan your trip and provides tips on traveling alone and with children
0–88266–464–6 Storey pb $4.95

- Miranda Davies & others, editors
HALF THE EARTH: Women's Experiences of Travel Worldwide
More than 50 women write about traveling in 70 countries. Includes listings of women's resources in various countries
0–86358–092–0 RC&H pb $10.95

- Greg Hayes & Joan Wright
GOING PLACES: The Guide to Travel Guides
A great source for thorough, in-depth information on choosing the right book for almost any destination
1–55832–007–5 Harvard Common $26.95
1–55832–007–5 Harvard Common pb $17.95

- Charles & Babette Jacobs
GREAT RAILTRIPS OF THE WORLD
0–912640–44–8 Travel Digests pb $11.95

- Sanford & Joan Portnoy
HOW TO TAKE GREAT TRIPS WITH YOUR KIDS
0–916782–51–4 Harvard Common pb $8.95

- Specialty Travel
THE ADVENTURE VACATION CATALOG
For those looking for more than a quiet beach
0–671–50770–2 Simon & Schuster pb $15.95

- Louise Weiss
ACCESS TO THE WORLD
Travel information for the disabled
Introduction by Lord Snowdon
0–87196–787–1 Facts On File $16.95

EUROPE

- APA Productions
INSIGHT GUIDES: Continental Europe
0–13–171422–8 Prentice-Hall pb $16.95

- Baedeker
BAEDEKER'S RAIL GUIDE TO EUROPE
0–13–055971–7 Prentice-Hall pb $15.95

- Birnbaum
BIRNBAUM'S EUROPE
0–395–48171–6 Houghton Mifflin pb $13.95

EUROPE FOR BUSINESS TRAVELERS
0–395–48166–X Houghton Mifflin pb $8.95

- Karen Brown
KAREN BROWN'S EUROPEAN COUNTRY INNS
0–446–38820–3 Warner pb $14.95

- Fodor
FODOR'S EUROPE
0–679–01620–1 Random House pb $15.95

- Harper & Row
EUROPE BY TRAIN: A Comprehensive, Economy-Minded Guide to Train Travel in 26 Countries
0–06–096322–0 Harper & Row pb $12.95

- Harvard Student Agencies
LET'S GO: Europe
0–312–02232–8 St. Martin's pb $12.95

- Michelin
MICHELIN RED GUIDE: Europe, Main Cities
2–06–007088–0 Michelin $16.95

AUSTRIA

- Blue Guide
BLUE GUIDE: Austria
0–393–30364–0 Norton pb $18.95

- Karen Brown
KAREN BROWN'S AUSTRIAN COUNTRY INNS AND CASTLES
0–446–38812–2 Warner pb $12.95

- Fodor
FODOR'S AUSTRIA
0–679–01599–X Random House pb $13.95

FODOR'S VIENNA
0–679–01711–9 Random House pb $6.95

- Michelin
MICHELIN GREEN GUIDE: Austria
2–06–015122–8 Michelin pb $10.95

- Phaidon
AUSTRIA: A Phaidon Cultural Guide
0–13–053836–1 Prentice-Hall $17.95

BENELUX

- Baedeker
BAEDEKER'S NETHERLANDS, BELGIUM, AND LUXEMBOURG
0–13–056028–6 Prentice-Hall pb $14.95

- Michelin
MICHELIN RED GUIDE: Benelux
2–06–006088–5 Michelin $16.95

BAEDEKER'S BRUSSELS
0–13–368788–0 Prentice-Hall pb $10.95

- Blue Guide
BLUE GUIDE: Belgium and Luxembourg
0–393–30063–3 Norton pb $15.95

- Fodor
FODOR'S BELGIUM AND LUXEMBOURG
0–679–01602–3 Random House pb $13.95

- Blue Guide
BLUE GUIDE: Holland
0–393–30373–X Norton pb $19.95

- Fodor
FODOR'S HOLLAND
0–679–01657–0 Random House pb $13.95

EASTERN EUROPE

- Fodor
FODOR'S EASTERN EUROPE
0–679–01618–X Random House pb $16.95

- Nagel
NAGEL'S ENCYCLOPEDIA GUIDE: Bulgaria
0–8442–9729–1 National Textbook $39.95

NAGEL'S ENCYCLOPEDIA GUIDE: Czechoslovakia
0–8442–9737–2 National Textbook $39.95

NAGEL'S ENCYCLOPEDIA GUIDE: German Democratic Republic
0–8442–9801–8 National Textbook $34.95

- Fodor
FODOR'S HUNGARY
0–679–01371–7 Random House pb $8.95

- Nagel
NAGEL'S ENCYCLOPEDIA GUIDE: Poland
0–8442–9774–7 National Textbook $39.95

NAGEL'S ENCYCLOPEDIA GUIDE: Rumania
0–8442–9777–1 National Textbook $29.95

- Fodor
FODOR'S YUGOSLAVIA
0–679–01715–1 Random House pb $14.95

FRANCE

- APA Productions
INSIGHT GUIDES: France
0–13–330856–1 Simon & Schuster pb $6.95

- Blue Guide
BLUE GUIDE: France
0–393–30366–7 Norton pb $19.95

- Karen Brown
KAREN BROWN'S FRENCH COUNTRY INNS AND CHATEAUX
0–446–38814–9 Warner pb $12.95

- The Economist
THE ECONOMIST BUSINESS TRAVELLER'S GUIDE: France
0–13–227521–X Prentice-Hall $17.95

- Fodor
FODOR'S FRANCE
0–679–01624–4 Random House pb $14.95

- Henri Gault & Christian Millau
THE BEST OF FRANCE
0–13–074022–5 Prentice-Hall pb $15.95

- Suzy Gershman & Judith Thomas
BORN TO SHOP: France
0–553–34371–8 Bantam pb $8.95

- Harvard Student Agencies
LET'S GO: France
0–312–02233–6 St. Martin's pb $11.95

- Knopf
THE KNOPF TRAVELER'S GUIDES TO ART: France
0–394–72324–4 Knopf pb $14.95

- Michelin
MICHELIN RED GUIDE: France
2–06–006488–0 Michelin $17.95

- Penguin
THE PENGUIN GUIDE TO FRANCE
0–14–019902–0 Penguin pb $14.95

Paris

Access
PARIS ACCESS
0–671–62577–2 Access pb $14.95

Mary Ellen Jordan Haight
WALKS IN GERTRUDE STEIN'S PARIS
Five walking tours for the literary traveller
0–87905–268–6 Peregrine Smith pb $11.95

Michelin
MICHELIN GREEN GUIDE: Paris
2–06–013543–5 Michelin pb $10.95

MICHELIN RED GUIDE: Paris and Environs
2–06–006888–6 Michelin pb $3.95

Photograph by Brassaï from his book Paris by Night *(Pantheon)*

The Provinces

- Geoffrey Barlow
TRAVELS IN THE LOIRE VALLEY
1–85391–039–2 David & Charles pb $13.95

- James Bentley
A GUIDE TO THE DORDOGNE
0–14–046629–0 Penguin pb $7.95

- Mary Elsy & Jill Norman
TRAVELS IN ALSACE-LORRAINE
1–85391–040–6 David & Charles pb $13.95

- Fiona Fennell
TRAVELS IN THE DORDOGNE
0–9465–7678–5 David & Charles pb $13.95

- Michelin
MICHELIN GREEN GUIDE: Brittany
2–06–013141–3 Michelin pb $9.95

MICHELIN GREEN GUIDE: Châteaux of the Loire
0–686–56395–6 Michelin pb $9.95

MICHELIN GREEN GUIDE: Dordogne
2–06–013231–2 Michelin pb $9.95

MICHELIN GREEN GUIDE: French Riviera
2–06–013302–5 Michelin pb $9.95

MICHELIN GREEN GUIDE: Normandy
2–06–014481–1 Michelin pb $9.95

MICHELIN GREEN GUIDE: Provence
2–06–013642–3 Michelin pb $9.95

GREECE

- Blue Guide
BLUE GUIDE: Greece
0–393–30372–1 Norton pb $19.95

- Fodor
FODOR'S GREECE
0–679–01641–4 Random House pb $13.95

- Harvard Student Agencies
LET'S GO: Greece
0–312–02234–4 St. Martin's pb $11.95

- Michelin
MICHELIN GREEN GUIDE: Greece
2–06–015201–1 Michelin pb $10.95

- Rough Guide
ROUGH GUIDE TO GREECE
0–7102–0311–X RC&H pb $7.95

ITALY

- Access
ROME ACCESS
0–671–62578–0 Access pb $14.95

- APA Productions
INSIGHT GUIDES: Italy
0–13–506544–5 Prentice-Hall pb $16.95

- James Bentley
  A GUIDE TO TUSCANY
  0–14–046683–5 Penguin pb $9.95

- Birnbaum
  BIRNBAUM'S ITALY
  0–395–48262–3 Houghton Mifflin pb $12.95

- Blue Guide
  BLUE GUIDE: Florence
  0–393–30479–5 Norton pb $15.95

- Fiona & Innes Fennell
  TRAVELS IN TUSCANY
  1–85391–004–X David & Charles pb $13.95

- Fodor
  FODOR'S ITALY
  0–679–01663–5 Random House pb $14.95

  FODOR'S ROME
  0–679–01689–9 Random House pb $9.95

- Henri Gault & Christian Millau
  THE BEST OF ITALY
  0–13–074030–6 Prentice-Hall pb $16.95

- Suzy Gershman & Judith Thomas
  BORN TO SHOP: Italy
  0–553–34370–X Bantam pb $8.95

- Harvard Student Agencies
  LET'S GO: Italy
  0–312–02236–0 St. Martin's pb $11.95

- Knopf
  THE KNOPF TRAVELER'S GUIDES TO ART: Italy
  0–394–72323–6 Knopf pb $14.95

- Michelin
  MICHELIN GREEN GUIDE: Italy
  2–06–015341–7 Michelin pb $10.95

  MICHELIN GREEN GUIDE: Rome
  2–06–015591–6 Michelin pb $10.95

- Penguin
  THE PENGUIN GUIDE TO ITALY
  0–14–019903–9 Penguin pb $14.95

- Kate Simon
  ITALY: The Places In Between
  0–06–091131–X Harper & Row pb $10.95

SCANDINAVIA

- Fodor
  FODOR'S SCANDINAVIA
  0–679–01692–9 Random House pb $15.95

  FODOR'S COPENHAGEN, STOCKHOLM, OSLO, HELSINKI, REYKJAVIK
  0–679–01702–X Random House pb $6.95

- Baedeker
  BAEDEKER'S DENMARK
  0–13–058124–0 Prentice-Hall pb $14.95

- Nagel
  NAGEL'S ENCYCLOPEDIA GUIDE: Finland
  0–8442–9741–0 National Textbook $34.95

- **NAGEL'S ENCYCLOPEDIA GUIDE: Iceland**
  0–8442–9753–4 National Textbook $29.95

- Hunter Publishing
  VISITOR'S GUIDE: Norway
  0–935161–15–5 Hunter pb $9.95

- Fodor
  FODOR'S SWEDEN
  0–679–01703–8 Random House pb $6.95

SOVIET UNION

- Blue Guide
  BLUE GUIDE: Moscow and Leningrad
  0–393–01545–9 Norton $24.95
  0–393–00098–2 Norton pb $18.95

- Fodor
  FODOR'S SOVIET UNION
  0–679–01700–3 Random House pb $16.95

- Nagel
  NAGEL'S ENCYCLOPEDIA GUIDE: U.S.S.R.
  0–8442–9788–7 National Textbook $49.95

SPAIN AND PORTUGAL

Spain

- Baedeker
  BAEDEKER'S MADRID
  0–13–058033–3 Prentice-Hall pb $10.95

- Blue Guide
  BLUE GUIDE: Spain—The Mainland
  0–393–01554–8 Norton pb $16.95

- Alastair Boyd
  THE COMPANION GUIDE TO MADRID AND CENTRAL SPAIN
  0–13–154717–8 Prentice-Hall pb $12.95

- Karen Brown
  KAREN BROWN'S SPANISH COUNTRY INNS AND PARADORS
  0–446–38813–0 Warner pb $12.95

- Fodor
  FODOR'S SPAIN
  0–679–01701–1 Random House pb $13.95

- Harvard Student Agencies
  LET'S GO: Spain, Portugal and Morocco
  0–312–02239–5 St. Martin's pb $11.95

- Michelin
  MICHELIN GREEN GUIDE: Spain
  2–06–015213–5 Michelin pb $10.95

Portugal

- Blue Guide
  BLUE GUIDE: Portugal
  0–393–30477–9 Norton pb $18.95

- Fodor
  FODOR'S PORTUGAL
  0–679–01687–2 Random House pb $13.95

- Michelin
  MICHELIN GREEN GUIDE: Portugal
  2–06–015572–X Michelin pb $10.95

- Rough Guide
  ROUGH GUIDE TO PORTUGAL
  0–7102–0967–3 RC&H pb $11.95

SWITZERLAND

- Baedeker
  BAEDEKER'S SWITZERLAND
  0–13–056044–8 Prentice-Hall pb $14.95

- Fodor
  FODOR'S SWITZERLAND
  0–679–01704–6 Random House pb $13.95

- Michelin
  MICHELIN GREEN GUIDE: Switzerland
  2–06–015631–9 Michelin pb $10.95

- Ira Spring & Harvey Edwards
  100 HIKES IN THE ALPS
  0–916890–72–4 Mountaineers pb $10.95

GREAT BRITAIN AND IRELAND

- APA Productions
  INSIGHT GUIDES: Great Britain
  0–13–363763–8 Prentice-Hall pb $15.95

- Birnbaum
  BIRNBAUM'S GREAT BRITAIN
  0–395–48170–8 Houghton Mifflin pb $12.95

- Blue Guide
  BLUE GUIDE: Literary Britain and Ireland
  0–393–30077–3 Norton pb $14.95

- Karen Brown
  KAREN BROWN'S ENGLISH, WELSH AND SCOTTISH COUNTRY INNS
  0–446–38817–3 Warner pb $12.95

- The Economist
  THE ECONOMIST BUSINESS TRAVELLER'S GUIDES: Britain
  0–13–234873–X Prentice-Hall $17.95

- Fodor
  FODOR'S GREAT BRITAIN
  0–679–01640–6 Random House pb $14.95

- Harvard Student Agencies
  LET'S GO: Britain and Ireland
  0–312–02230–1 St. Martin's pb $11.95

- Knopf
  THE KNOPF TRAVELER'S GUIDE TO ART: Great Britain and Ireland
  0–394–72426–7 Knopf pb $14.95

- Michelin
  MICHELIN RED GUIDE: Great Britain and Ireland
  2–06–006588–7 Michelin $16.95

• Penguin
THE PENGUIN GUIDE TO ENGLAND AND WALES
0–14–019901–2 Penguin pb $12.95

• Egon Ronay
EGON RONAY'S CELLNET GUIDE TO HOTELS, RESTAURANTS, AND INNS IN GREAT BRITAIN AND IRELAND
0–86145–404–9 Salem House pb $19.95

EGON RONAY'S GUINNESS PUB GUIDE TO FOOD AND ACCOMMODATION IN GREAT BRITAIN
0–312–04818–2 St. Martin's pb $6.95

England, Wales, and the Channel Islands

• Blue Guide
BLUE GUIDE: The Channel Islands
0–393–30371–3 Norton pb $16.95

BLUE GUIDE: England
0–393–00090–7 Norton pb $14.95

BLUE GUIDE: Wales and the Marches
0–393–30008–0 Norton pb $16.95

• Heather Clemenson
ENGLISH COUNTRY HOUSES AND LANDED ESTATES
0–312–25414–8 St. Martin's $30.00

• Michelin
MICHELIN GREEN GUIDE: England—The West Country
2–06–015621–1 Michelin pb $10.95

London

Blue Guide
BLUE GUIDE: London
0–393–30482–5 Norton pb $17.95

Fodor
FODOR'S LONDON
0–679–01670–8 Random House pb $9.95

Michelin
MICHELIN GREEN GUIDE: London
2–06–015433–2 Michelin pb $10.95

MICHELIN RED GUIDE: Greater London
2–06–006688–3 Michelin pb $4.95

Ian Nairn
NAIRN'S LONDON
0–14–099264–1 Penguin pb $12.95

Susan Gershman & Judy Thomas
BORN TO SHOP: London
0–553–34604–0 Bantam pb $8.95

Scotland

• Blue Guide
BLUE GUIDE: Scotland
0–393–30370–5 Norton pb $19.95

• Fodor
FODOR'S SCOTLAND
0–679–01693–7 Random House pb $12.95

• Michelin
MICHELIN GREEN GUIDE: Scotland
2–06–015751–X Michelin pb $10.95

Ireland

• APA Productions
INSIGHT GUIDES: Ireland
0–13–505728–0 Prentice-Hall pb $16.95

INSIGHT CITY GUIDES: Dublin
0–13–468091–X Prentice-Hall pb $14.95

• Blue Guide
BLUE GUIDE: Ireland
0–393–30367–5 Norton pb $17.95

• Karen Brown
KAREN BROWN'S IRISH COUNTRY INNS
0–446–38808–4 Warner pb $12.95

• Fodor
FODOR'S IRELAND
0–679–01661–9 Random House pb $13.95

• Don Fullington
THE CONNOISSEUR'S GUIDE TO IRELAND: A Select Compendium for the Discriminating Traveler
0–8050–0632–X Henry Holt pb $12.95

• Penguin
THE PENGUIN GUIDE TO IRELAND
0–14–019904–7 Penguin pb $10.95

WEST GERMANY

• APA Productions
INSIGHT GUIDES: Germany
0–13–354127–4 Prentice-Hall pb $16.95

• Baedeker
BAEDEKER'S GERMANY
0–13–055830–3 Prentice-Hall pb $15.95

BAEDEKER'S BERLIN
0–13–367996–9 Prentice-Hall pb $10.95

BAEDEKER'S RHINE
0–13–056466–4 Prentice-Hall pb $9.95

• Karen Brown
KAREN BROWN'S GERMAN COUNTRY INNS AND CASTLES
0–446–38815–7 Warner pb $12.95

• The Economist
THE ECONOMIST BUSINESS TRAVELLER'S GUIDE: West Germany
0–13–234956–6 Prentice-Hall $17.95

• Fodor
FODOR'S GERMANY
0–679–01639–2 Random House pb $14.95

FODOR'S MUNICH
0–679–01540–X Random House pb $6.95

• Michelin
MICHELIN GREEN GUIDE: Germany
2–06–015033–7 Michelin pb $10.95

SUB-SAHARAN AFRICA

• Hilary Bradt
BACKPACKER'S AFRICA
0–9505797–9–3 Hunter pb $12.95

• Fielding
FIELDING'S AFRICAN SAFARIS
0–688–05072–7 Morrow pb $17.95

• Lonely Planet
AFRICA ON A SHOESTRING
0–908086–89–X Lonely Planet pb $14.95

• Kim Naylor
AFRICA: The Nile Route
0–903–90922–2 Lascelles pb $12.95

• Nina Casimati
GUIDE TO EAST AFRICA: Kenya, Tanzania, The Seychelles
0–87052–246–9 Hippocrene pb $11.95

• Lonely Planet
EAST AFRICA: A Travel Survival Kit
0–86442–005–6 Lonely Planet pb $9.95

• APA Productions
INSIGHT GUIDES: Kenya
0–13–514563–5 Prentice-Hall pb $16.95

• Fodor
FODOR'S KENYA
0–679–01378–4 Random House pb $11.95

• Hunter Publishing
TRAVELLER'S GUIDE TO CENTRAL AND SOUTHERN AFRICA
0–905268–48–2 Hunter pb $12.95

• Michael Haag
GUIDE TO WEST AFRICA
0–87052–244–2 Hippocrene pb $11.95

• Lonely Planet
WEST AFRICA: A Travel Survival Kit
A budget guide for independent travelers
0–86442–028–5 Lonely Planet pb $12.95

• Richard Trillo
THE ROUGH GUIDE TO KENYA
0–7102–0616–X RC&H pb $12.95

THE MIDDLE EAST AND NORTH AFRICA

The Middle East

• Berlitz
BERLITZ: Saudi Arabia Travel Guide
2–83150–266–7 Macmillan pb $6.95

• The Economist
THE ECONOMIST BUSINESS TRAVELLER'S GUIDES: The Arabian Peninsula
0–13–234915–9 Prentice-Hall $17.95

• Fodor
FODOR'S JORDAN AND THE HOLY LAND
0–679–01303–2 Random House pb $12.95

- Lonely Planet
  JORDAN AND SYRIA: A Travel Survival Kit
  0–86442–016–1 Lonely Planet pb $8.95

  YEMEN: A Travel Survival Kit
  0–86442–006–4 Lonely Planet pb $8.95

- Nagel
  NAGEL'S ENCYCLOPEDIA GUIDE: Gulf Emirates
  0–8442–9749–6 National Textbook $38.00

  NAGEL'S ENCYCLOPEDIA GUIDE: Iran
  0–8442–9756–9 National Textbook $39.95

Egypt

- APA Productions
  INSIGHT GUIDES: Egypt
  0–13–246596–5 Prentice-Hall pb $16.95

- Fodor
  FODOR'S EGYPT
  0–679–01619–8 Random House pb $12.95

- Lonely Planet
  EGYPT AND THE SUDAN: A Travel Survival Kit
  0–86442–001–3 Lonely Planet pb $9.95

- Nagel
  NAGEL'S ENCYCLOPEDIA GUIDE: Egypt
  0–8442–9739–9 National Textbook $49.95

Israel

- APA Productions
  INSIGHT GUIDES: Israel
  0–13–506296–9 Prentice-Hall pb $16.95

- Baedeker
  BAEDEKER'S JERUSALEM
  0–13–058017–1 Prentice-Hall pb $10.95

- Bazak
  BAZAK GUIDE TO ISRAEL, 1989–90
  0–06–096317–4 Harper & Row pb $14.95

- Fodor
  FODOR'S ISRAEL
  0–679–01662–7 Random House pb $13.95

- Harvard Student Agencies
  LET'S GO: Israel and Egypt
  0–312–02235–2 St. Martin's pb $11.95

- Lonely Planet
  ISRAEL: A Travel Survival Kit
  0–86442–015–3 Lonely Planet pb $12.95

- Penguin
  THE ISRAEL ROAD AND TOURING GUIDE
  0–8289–0697–1 Penguin pb $10.95

North Africa

- Fodor
  FODOR'S NORTH AFRICA: Algeria, Morocco and Tunisia
  0–679–01682–1 Random House pb $16.95

- Peter Morris
  ROUGH GUIDE TO TUNISIA
  0–7102–0148–6 RC&H pb $7.95

Turkey and Cyprus

- Blue Guide
  BLUE GUIDE: Istanbul
  0–393–30082–X Norton pb $18.95

- Fodor
  FODOR'S TURKEY
  0–679–01709–7 Random House pb $16.95

- Lonely Planet
  TREKKING IN TURKEY: A Travel Survival Kit
  0–86442–037–4 Lonely Planet pb $9.95

  TURKEY: A Travel Survival Kit
  For independent budget travelers
  0–86442–018–8 Lonely Planet pb $12.95

- Nagel
  NAGEL'S ENCYCLOPEDIA GUIDE: Turkey
  0–8442–9786–0 National Textbook $49.95

- Ian Robertson
  BLUE GUIDE: Cyprus
  0–393–30365–9 Norton pb $17.95

ASIA

- Lonely Planet
  NORTH-EAST ASIA ON A SHOESTRING
  A general budget guide, geared to the independent traveler
  0–908086–35–0 Lonely Planet pb $7.95

- Taylor & Francis
  ALL-ASIA GUIDE
  962–7010–25–1 Taylor & Francis pb $20.00

CHINA, TAIWAN, HONG KONG, AND TIBET

China

- The Economist
  THE ECONOMIST BUSINESS TRAVELLER'S GUIDE: China
  0–13–234949–3 Prentice-Hall $17.95

- Fodor
  FODOR'S PEOPLE'S REPUBLIC OF CHINA
  0–679–01685–6 Random House pb $16.95

- Fredric Kaplan & others
  THE CHINA GUIDEBOOK: 1989 Edition
  0–395–48679–3 Houghton Mifflin pb $16.95

- Lonely Planet
  CHINA: A Travel Survival Kit
  0–86442–003–X Lonely Planet pb $17.95

- Nagel
  NAGEL'S ENCYCLOPEDIA GUIDE: China
  0–8442–9735–6 National Textbook $49.95

Member of militia, Inner Mongolia, photographed by Eve Arnold, from her book In China *(Knopf)*

Taiwan

- APA Productions
  INSIGHT GUIDES: Taiwan
  0–13–882192–5 Prentice-Hall pb $16.95

- Lonely Planet
  TAIWAN: A Travel Survival Kit
  Oriented to the independent, low-budget traveler
  0–86442–014–5 Lonely Planet pb $8.95

Hong Kong

- APA Productions
  INSIGHT GUIDES: Hong Kong
  0–13–394635–5 Prentice-Hall pb $16.95

- Fodor
  FODOR'S '89 HONG KONG AND MACAU
  0–679–01658–9 Random House pb $10.95

- Suzy Gershman & Judith Thomas
  BORN TO SHOP: Hong Kong
  0–553–34484–6 Bantam pb $7.95

- Lonely Planet
  HONG KONG, MACAU AND CANTON: A Travel Survival Kit
  0–908086–74–1 Lonely Planet pb $7.95

Tibet

- Stephen Batchelor
  THE TIBET GUIDE
  Forward by the Dalai Lama
  0–86171–046–0 Wisdom pb $26.95

- Lonely Planet
  TIBET: A Travel Survival Kit
  0–908086–88–1 Lonely Planet pb $7.95

THE SUBCONTINENT AND THE HIMALAYAS

- **APA Productions**
  INSIGHT GUIDES: India
  0–13–456856–7 Prentice-Hall pb $16.95

  INSIGHT GUIDES: Nepal
  0–13–611038–X Prentice-Hall pb $16.95

  INSIGHT GUIDES: Sri Lanka
  0–13–839944–1 Prentice-Hall pb $16.95

- **Fodor**
  FODOR'S INDIA, NEPAL AND SRI LANKA
  0–679–01525–6 Random House pb $16.95

- **Lonely Planet**
  BANGLADESH: A Travel Survival Kit
  0–908086–60–1 Lonely Planet pb $7.95

  INDIA: A Travel Survival Kit
  0–908086–93–8 Lonely Planet pb $17.95

  KATHMANDU AND THE KINGDOM OF NEPAL: A Travel Survival Kit
  0–86442–024–2 Lonely Planet pb $8.95

  PAKISTAN: A Travel Survival Kit
  0–86442–013–7 Lonely Planet pb $8.95

  SRI LANKA: A Travel Survival Kit
  0–86442–000–5 Lonely Planet pb $8.95

  TREKKING IN THE INDIAN HIMALAYA
  0–908086–61–X Lonely Planet pb $7.95

  TREKKING IN THE NEPAL HIMALAYA
  0–908086–66–0 Lonely Planet pb $7.95

- **Nagel**
  NAGEL'S ENCYCLOPEDIA GUIDE: India and Nepal
  0–8442–9754–2 National Textbook $49.95

- **Alistair Shearer**
  THE TRAVELER'S KEY TO NORTHERN INDIA: A Guide to the Sacred Places of Northern India
  0–394–51652–4 Knopf pb $18.95

JAPAN

- **Baedeker**
  BAEDEKER'S JAPAN
  0–13–056382–X Prentice-Hall pb $15.95

- **Judith Connor & Mayumi Yoshida**
  OLD KYOTO: A Guide to Traditional Shops, Restaurants, and Inns
  0–87011–757–2 Kodansha pb $11.95

- **The Economist**
  THE ECONOMIST BUSINESS TRAVELLER'S GUIDE: Japan
  0–13–234907–8 Prentice-Hall $17.95

- **Fodor**
  FODOR'S JAPAN
  0–679–01664–3 Random House pb $15.95

  FODOR'S TOKYO
  0–679–01707–0 Random House pb $10.95

- **Paul Hunt**
  HIKING IN JAPAN: An Adventurer's Guide to the Mountain Trails
  0–87011–893–5 Kodansha pb $12.95

- **Richard Kennedy**
  GOOD TOKYO RESTAURANTS
  0–87011–702–5 Kodansha pb $7.95

- **Lonely Planet**
  JAPAN: A Travel Survival Kit
  0–908086–70–9 Lonely Planet pb $12.95

- **Kimiko Nagasawa & Camy Condon**
  EATING CHEAP IN JAPAN: The Gaijin Gourmet's Guide to Ordering in Non-Tourist Restaurants
  4–07–971548–X Tuttle pb $9.95

- **Suzy Gershman & Judith Thomas**
  BORN TO SHOP: Tokyo
  0–553–34353–X Bantam pb $9.95

KOREA

- **APA Productions**
  INSIGHT GUIDES: Korea
  0–13–516641–1 Prentice-Hall pb $16.95

- **Fodor**
  FODOR'S '89 KOREA
  0–679–01667–8 Random House pb $11.95

- **Lonely Planet**
  KOREA: A Travel Survival Kit
  A budget guide for independent travelers
  0–86442–021–8 Lonely Planet pb $8.95

SOUTHEAST ASIA

- **The Economist**
  THE ECONOMIST BUSINESS TRAVELLER'S GUIDE: Southeast Asia
  0–13–227513–9 Prentice-Hall $17.95

- **Fodor**
  FODOR'S SOUTHEAST ASIA
  0–679–01699–6 Random House pb $15.95

- **Lonely Planet**
  SOUTHEAST ASIA ON A SHOESTRING
  0–86442–056–0 Lonely Planet pb $14.95

Burma and Thailand

- **APA Productions**
  INSIGHT GUIDES: Burma
  0–13–090902–5 Prentice-Hall pb $16.95

- **Lonely Planet**
  BURMA: A Travel Survival Kit
  0–86442–017–X Lonely Planet pb $8.95

- **APA Productions**
  INSIGHT GUIDES: Thailand
  0–13–912600–7 Prentice-Hall pb $16.95

- **Lonely Planet**
  THAILAND: A Travel Survival Kit
  0–908086–95–4 Lonely Planet pb $8.95

- **Nagel**
  NAGEL'S ENCYCLOPEDIA GUIDE: Thailand
  0–8442–9785–2 National Textbook $39.95

- **Baedeker**
  BAEDEKER'S BANGKOK
  0–13–057985–8 Prentice-Hall pb $10.95

Indonesia, Malaysia, and Singapore

- **APA Productions**
  INSIGHT GUIDES: Bali
  0–13–056200–9 Prentice-Hall pb $16.95

  INSIGHT GUIDES: Indonesia
  0–13–457391–9 Prentice-Hall pb $16.95

- **Bill Dalton**
  INDONESIA HANDBOOK
  0–918373–12–3 Moon pb $17.95

- **Lonely Planet**
  INDONESIA: A Travel Survival Kit
  0–908086–81–4 Lonely Planet pb $14.95

- **APA Productions**
  INSIGHT GUIDES: Malaysia
  0–13–547992–4 Prentice-Hall pb $15.95

  INSIGHT GUIDES: Singapore
  0–13–810713–0 Prentice-Hall pb $16.95

- **Lonely Planet**
  MALAYSIA, SINGAPORE AND BRUNEI: A Travel Survival Kit
  0–86442–022–6 Lonely Planet pb $9.95

- **Fodor**
  FODOR'S '89 SINGAPORE
  0–679–01694–5 Random House pb $7.95

The Philippines

- **APA Productions**
  INSIGHT GUIDES: The Philippines
  0–13–662197–X Prentice-Hall pb $16.95

- **Lonely Planet**
  THE PHILIPPINES: A Travel Survival Kit
  0–908086–92–X Lonely Planet pb $8.95

- **Nagel**
  NAGEL'S ENCYCLOPEDIA GUIDE: The Philippines
  0–8442–9773–9 National Textbook $39.95

AUSTRALIA, NEW ZEALAND, AND THE SOUTH PACIFIC

Australia and New Zealand

- **APA Productions**
  INSIGHT GUIDES: Australia
  0–13–053828–0 Prentice-Hall pb $16.95

  INSIGHT GUIDES: New Zealand
  0–13–621111–9 Prentice-Hall pb $16.95

- **Fodor**
  FODOR'S AUSTRALIA, NEW ZEALAND AND THE SOUTH PACIFIC
  0–679–01598–1 Random House pb $15.95

● Lonely Planet
AUSTRALIA: A Travel Survival Kit
0-908086-73-3 Lonely Planet pb $14.95

NEW ZEALAND: A Travel Survival Kit
0-86442-020-X Lonely Planet pb $8.95

● Penguin
THE PENGUIN GUIDE TO AUSTRALIA
0-14-019905-5 Penguin pb $11.95

The South Pacific

● Fodor
FODOR'S SOUTH PACIFIC
0-679-01698-8 Random House pb $8.95

● Lonely Planet
FIJI: A Travel Survival Kit
0-908086-87-3 Lonely Planet pb $7.95

MICRONESIA: A Travel Survival Kit
0-86442-019-6 Lonely Planet pb $8.95

PAPUA NEW GUINEA: A Travel Survival Kit
0-86442-048-X Lonely Planet pb $11.95

TAHITI AND FRENCH POLYNESIA: A Travel Survival Kit
0-86442-049-8 Lonely Planet pb $9.95

● Vicki Poggioli
TAHITI: A Complete Travel Guide to All of the Islands
For Tahiti, Bora Bora, Moorea, and other islands
0-87052-363-5 Hippocrene pb $9.95

● David Stanley
MICRONESIA HANDBOOK
0-918373-06-9 Moon pb $8.95

SOUTH PACIFIC HANDBOOK
0-918373-05-0 Moon pb $13.95

MEXICO, THE CARIBBEAN, AND LATIN AMERICA

Mexico

● APA Productions
INSIGHT GUIDES: Mexico
0-13-579524-9 Prentice-Hall pb $15.95

● Birnbaum
BIRNBAUM'S MEXICO
0-395-48162-7 Houghton Mifflin pb $12.95

● Rebecca Bruns
HIDDEN MEXICO: An Adventurer's Guide to the Beaches and Coasts
0-915233-05-3 Ulysses pb $12.95

● Bob Burleson & David Riskind
BACKCOUNTRY MEXICO: A Traveler's Guide and Phrasebook
0-292-70760-6 Texas $24.95
0-292-70755-X Texas pb $12.95

● Fodor
FODOR'S MEXICO
0-679-01673-2 Random House pb $13.95

● E.J. Guarino
THE OTHER MEXICO: A Guide to Ancient Wonders and Modern Pleasures in Mexico
0-914846-36-1 Golden West pb $9.00

● Harvard Student Agencies
LET'S GO: Mexico
0-312-02237-9 St. Martin's pb $11.95

● Lonely Planet
MEXICO: A Travel Survival Kit
0-86442-047-1 Lonely Planet pb $17.95

● Nagel
NAGEL'S ENCYCLOPEDIA GUIDE: Mexico
0-8442-9765-8 National Textbook $39.95

The Caribbean

● APA Productions
INSIGHT GUIDES: Cruising the Caribbean
0-13-194887-3 Prentice-Hall pb $16.95

● Birnbaum
BIRNBAUM'S CARIBBEAN: Bermuda and the Bahamas
0-395-48163-5 Houghton Mifflin pb $12.95

● Fodor
FODOR'S CARIBBEAN
0-679-01612-0 Random House pb $13.95

● Penguin
THE PENGUIN GUIDE TO THE CARIBBEAN
0-14-019900-4 Penguin pb $9.95

● APA Productions
INSIGHT GUIDE: Bahamas
0-13-056276-9 Prentice-Hall pb $16.95

● Fodor
FODOR'S BAHAMAS
0-679-01600-7 Random House pb $8.95

● APA Productions
INSIGHT GUIDES: Barbados
0-13-056995-X Prentice-Hall pb $16.95

● Fodor
FODOR'S BERMUDA
0-679-01603-1 Random House pb $8.95

● APA Productions
INSIGHT GUIDES: Jamaica
0-13-509000-8 Prentice-Hall pb $16.95

INSIGHT GUIDES: Puerto Rico
0-13-740168-X Prentice-Hall pb $16.95

● Fodor
FODOR'S SAINT MARTIN
0-679-01636-8 Random House pb $6.95

● APA Productions
INSIGHT GUIDES: Trinidad and Tobago
0-13-930868-7 Prentice-Hall pb $16.95

● Fodor
FODOR'S VIRGIN ISLANDS
0-679-01712-7 Random House pb $8.95

Latin America

● Birnbaum
BIRNBAUM'S SOUTH AMERICA
0-395-48263-1 Houghton Mifflin pb $12.95

● John Brooks, editor
THE SOUTH AMERICAN HANDBOOK: Including Caribbean, Mexico, and Central America
0-13-823717-4 Rand McNally $28.95

● Fodor
FODOR'S SOUTH AMERICA
0-679-01697-X Random House pb $14.95

FODOR'S CENTRAL AMERICA
0-679-01613-9 Random House pb $15.95

● Lonely Planet
SOUTH AMERICA ON A SHOESTRING
0-908086-75-X Lonely Planet pb $14.95

● Nagel
NAGEL'S ENCYCLOPEDIA GUIDE: Central America
0-8442-9731-3 National Textbook $39.95

NAGEL'S ENCYCLOPEDIA GUIDE: Bolivia
0-8442-9727-5 National Textbook $39.95

● Fodor
FODOR'S BRAZIL
0-679-01605-8 Random House pb $8.95

● Nagel
NAGEL'S ENCYCLOPEDIA GUIDE: Brazil
0-8442-9728-3 National Textbook $39.95

● Suzy Gershman & Judith Thomas
BORN TO SHOP: Rio
0-553-34469-2 Bantam pb $8.95

● Lonely Planet
CHILE AND EASTER ISLAND: A Travel Survival Kit
0-908086-99-7 Lonely Planet pb $8.95

COLOMBIA: A Travel Survival Kit
0-86442-002-1 Lonely Planet pb $11.95

● Paul Glassman
COSTA RICA GUIDE
0-930016-09-2 Passport pb $12.95

GUATEMALA GUIDE
0-930016-08-4 Passport pb $16.95

● Lonely Planet
ECUADOR AND THE GALAPAGOS ISLANDS: A Travel Survival Kit
0-908086-79-2 Lonely Planet pb $7.95

● Nagel
NAGEL'S ENCYCLOPEDIA GUIDE: Peru
0-8442-9772-0 National Textbook $39.95

CANADA

● APA Productions
INSIGHT GUIDES: Canada
0-13-113721-2 Prentice-Hall pb $15.95

- Birnbaum
BIRNBAUM'S CANADA
0–395–48168–6 Houghton Mifflin pb $12.95

- Fodor
FODOR'S CANADA
0–679–01608–2 Random House pb $14.95

FODOR'S SKI RESORTS OF NORTH AMERICA
0–679–01695–3 Random House pb $14.95

- Pamela Lanier
THE COMPLETE GUIDE TO BED AND BREAKFASTS, INNS AND GUESTHOUSES IN THE U.S. AND CANADA
0–912528–82–6 John Muir pb $13.95

- Lonely Planet
CANADA: A Travel Survival Kit
0–86442–042–0 Lonely Planet pb $10.95

- Michelin
MICHELIN GREEN GUIDE: Canada
2–06–015172–4 Michelin pb $10.95

- Nagel
NAGEL'S ENCYCLOPEDIA GUIDE: Canada
0–8442–9730–5 National Textbook $39.95

- Penguin
THE PENGUIN GUIDE TO CANADA
0–14–019906–3 Penguin pb $12.95

THE UNITED STATES

- APA Productions
INSIGHT GUIDES: Crossing the U.S.A.
0–13–194713–3 Prentice-Hall pb $15.95

- Birnbaum
BIRNBAUM'S UNITED STATES
0–395–48169–4 Houghton Mifflin pb $12.95

- Sue Browder
THE AMERICAN BIKING ATLAS AND TOURING GUIDE
0–911104–36–4 Workman pb $7.95

- Devereux Butcher
EXPLORING OUR NATIONAL PARKS AND MONUMENTS
0–87645–122–9 Harvard Common pb $14.95

- The Economist
THE ECONOMIST BUSINESS TRAVELLER'S GUIDE: United States
0–13–234881–0 Prentice-Hall $17.95

- Fodor
FODOR'S UNITED STATES OF AMERICA
0–679–01710–0 Random House pb $15.95

FODOR'S AMERICAN CITIES
0–679–01642–2 Random House pb $13.95

FODOR'S BUDGET TRAVEL IN AMERICA
0–679–01097–1 Random House pb $11.95

- Harvard Student Agencies
LET'S GO: The USA
0–312–01464–3 St. Martin's pb $12.95

- Rand McNally
RAND MCNALLY GREAT NATIONAL PARK VACATIONS
0–137–50712–7 Rand McNally $12.95

- Jane & Michael Stern
ROAD FOOD AND GOOD FOOD
0–394–74396–2 Knopf pb $12.95

New England and the Mid-Atlantic States

- Brenda Chapin
GUIDE TO THE RECOMMENDED COUNTRY INNS OF THE MID-ATLANTIC STATES & CHESAPEAKE REGION
0–87106–818–4 Globe Pequot pb $10.95

- Fodor
FODOR'S NEW ENGLAND
0–679–01676–7 Random House pb $13.95

- Henri Gault & Christian Millau
THE BEST OF NEW ENGLAND
0–13–072851–9 Prentice-Hall pb $15.95

- Michelin
MICHELIN GREEN GUIDE: New England
2–06–015693–9 Michelin pb $10.95

- Elizabeth Squier
GUIDE TO THE RECOMMENDED COUNTRY INNS OF NEW ENGLAND
0–87106–819–2 Globe Pequot pb $10.95

Michael Durham
THE SMITHSONIAN GUIDE TO HISTORIC AMERICA: The Mid-Atlantic States
1–55670–060–1 ST&C $24.95
1–55670–050–4 ST&C pb $17.95

Vance Muse
THE SMITHSONIAN GUIDE TO HISTORIC AMERICA: Northern New England
1–55670–049–0 ST&C $24.95
1–55670–066–6 ST&C pb $17.95

Henry Wiencek
THE SMITHSONIAN GUIDE TO HISTORIC AMERICA: Southern New England
1–55670–059–8 ST&C $24.95
1–55670–052–2 ST&C pb $17.95

Boston

- Blue Guide
BLUE GUIDE: Boston and Cambridge
0–393–01560–2 Norton $29.95
0–393–30012–9 Norton pb $15.95

- Fodor
FODOR'S BOSTON
0–679–01604–X Random House pb $7.95

- Eugene & Nina Zagat
ZAGAT BOSTON RESTAURANT SURVEY
0–943421–03–9 Zagat Survey pb $8.95

New York City

- Bubbles Fisher
THE CANDY APPLE: New York for Kids
0–13–114224–0 Simon & Schuster pb $11.95

- Fodor
FODOR'S NEW YORK CITY
0–679–01679–1 Random House pb $9.95

FODOR'S FUN IN NEW YORK CITY
0–679–01633–3 Random House pb $6.95

- Henri Gault & Christian Millau
THE BEST OF NEW YORK
0–13–076076–5 Prentice-Hall pb $14.95

- Suzy Gershman & Judith Thomas
BORN TO SHOP: New York
0–553–34383–1 Bantam pb $9.95

- Michelin
MICHELIN GREEN GUIDE: New York City
2–06–015513–4 Michelin pb $10.95

- Bryan Miller
THE NEW YORK TIMES GUIDE TO RESTAURANTS IN NEW YORK CITY
0–8129–1735–9 Times Books pb $12.95

- Mary Peacock, editor
VILLAGE VOICE GUIDE TO SHOPPING: A Guide to Manhattan's Hottest Shopping Spots
0–449–90206–4 Ballantine pb $10.95

- Mimi Sheraton
MIMI SHERATON'S FAVORITE NEW YORK RESTAURANTS
0–671–53202–2 Simon & Schuster pb $9.95

- Eugene & Nina Zagat
ZAGAT NEW YORK CITY RESTAURANT SURVEY
0–943421–09–8 Zagat Survey pb $9.95

The Brooklyn Bridge photographed in 1898 by George P. Hall & Sons, from the collection of The New-York Historical Society

Washington, D.C.

- Fodor
FODOR'S WASHINGTON, D.C.
0–679–01714–3 Random House pb $7.95

- Henri Gault & Christian Millau
THE BEST OF WASHINGTON, D.C.
0–13–076183–4 Prentice-Hall pb $14.95

- Betty Ross
A MUSEUM GUIDE TO WASHINGTON, D.C.
0–9616144–0–4 Americana pb $12.95

- Henry Wiencek
THE SMITHSONIAN GUIDE TO HISTORIC AMERICA: Virginia and the Capital Region
1–55670–058–X Stewart, Tabori & Chang $24.95
1–55670–048–2 Stewart, Tabori & Chang pb $17.95

- Eugene & Nina Zagat
ZAGAT WASHINGTON, D.C. RESTAURANT SURVEY
0–943421–01–2 Zagat Survey pb $8.95

The South

- Fodor
FODOR'S THE AMERICAN SOUTH
0–679–01696–1 Random House pb $12.95

FODOR'S THE CAROLINAS AND THE GEORGIA COAST
0–679–01493–4 Random House pb $8.95

FODOR'S FLORIDA
0–679–01623–6 Random House pb $10.95

FODOR'S NEW ORLEANS
0–679–01678–3 Random House pb $8.95

- William Logan & Vance Muse
THE SMITHSONIAN GUIDE TO HISTORIC AMERICA: The Deep South
1–55670–069–5 Stewart, Tabori & Chang $24.95
1–55670–068–7 Stewart, Tabori & Chang pb $17.95

- Corinne Ross
THE SOUTHERN BED AND BREAKFAST BOOK
0–88742–062–1 Globe Pequot pb $8.95

- Eugene & Nina Zagat
ZAGAT NEW ORLEANS RESTAURANT SURVEY
0–943421–04–7 Zagat Survey pb $8.95

The Midwest

- Fodor
FODOR'S '89 CHICAGO
0–679–01615–5 Random House pb $7.95

- Henri Gault & Christian Millau
THE BEST OF CHICAGO
0–13–072836–5 Prentice-Hall pb $15.95

- Anthony Hitchcock & Jean Lindgren, editors
COUNTRY INNS, LODGES AND HISTORIC HOTELS: The Midwest and the Rocky Mountain States
0–89102–376–3 Burt Franklin pb $8.95

Sid Grauman impressing John Barrymore's profile into cement in the forecourt of Grauman's Chinese Theater in Hollywood, 1940, from Los Angeles: An Illustrated History *by Bruce Henstell (Knopf)*

- Suzanne Winckler
THE SMITHSONIAN GUIDE TO HISTORIC AMERICA: The Great Lake States
1–55670–072–5 Stewart, Tabori & Chang $24.95
1–55670–071–7 Stewart, Tabori & Chang pb $17.95

The West

- Access
LAS VEGAS ACCESS
0–671–60335–3 Prentice-Hall pb $9.95

- John Annerino
HIKING THE GRAND CANYON
0–87156–755–5 Sierra Club pb $10.95

- APA Productions
INSIGHT GUIDES: American Southwest
0–13–029521–3 Prentice-Hall pb $15.95

INSIGHT GUIDES: The Rockies
0–13–782277–4 Prentice-Hall pb $15.95

- Fodor
FODOR'S ARIZONA
0–679–01596–5 Random House pb $8.95

FODOR'S COLORADO
0–679–01616–3 Random House pb $8.95

FODOR'S THE FAR WEST
0–679–01621–X Random House pb $13.95

FODOR'S LAS VEGAS
0–679–01628–7 Random House pb $6.95

FODOR'S NEW MEXICO
0–679–01542–6 Random House pb $7.95

FODOR'S THE ROCKIES: U.S. and Canada
0–679–01553–1 Random House pb $8.95

FODOR'S TEXAS
0–679–01706–2 Random House pb $8.95

- John Perry & Jane Greverus Perry
THE SIERRA CLUB GUIDE TO THE NATURAL AREAS OF IDAHO, MONTANA, AND WYOMING
0–87156–781–4 Sierra Club pb $12.95

- Sierra Club
THE SIERRA CLUB GUIDE TO THE NATURAL AREAS OF NEW MEXICO, ARIZONA AND NEVADA
0–87156–753–9 Sierra pb $10.95

- Bill Weir
UTAH HANDBOOK
0–918373–05–0 Moon pb $10.95

California

- Access
SAN FRANCISCO ACCESS
0–13–001836–8 Access pb $11.95

- APA Productions
INSIGHT GUIDES: Northern California
0–13–623562–X Prentice-Hall pb $15.95

- Fodor
FODOR'S CALIFORNIA
0–679–01607–4 Random House pb $12.95

FODOR'S LOS ANGELES, ORANGE COUNTY, PALM SPRINGS
0–679–01671–6 Random House pb $8.95

- Henri Gault & Christian Millau
THE BEST OF LOS ANGELES
0–13–076068–4 Prentice-Hall pb $14.95

THE BEST OF SAN FRANCISCO
0–13–076084–6 Prentice-Hall pb $14.95

- Suzy Gershman & Judith Thomas
BORN TO SHOP: Los Angeles
0–553–34517–6 Bantam pb $7.95

- Harvard Student Agencies
LET'S GO: California and Hawaii
0–312–02231–X St. Martin's pb $11.95

- Eugene & Nina Zagat
ZAGAT LOS ANGELES RESTAURANT SURVEY
0–943421–07–1 Zagat Survey pb $9.95

The Pacific Northwest, Alaska, and Hawaii

- Access
  HAWAII ACCESS
  0–13–001157–6 Prentice-Hall pb $12.95

- APA Productions
  INSIGHT GUIDES: Alaska
  0–13–021395–0 Prentice-Hall pb $15.95

  INSIGHT GUIDES: Pacific Northwest
  0–932575–22–6 Graphics Arts Center pb $16.95

- Fodor
  FODOR'S HAWAII
  0–679–01656–2 Random House pb $11.95

- Harvard Student Agencies
  LET'S GO: Pacific Northwest, Western Canada, and Alaska
  0–312–02238–7 St. Martin's pb $11.95

- Lonely Planet
  ALASKA: A Travel Survival Kit
  0–908086–77–6 Lonely Planet pb $8.95

PHRASEBOOKS

Berlitz Phrasebooks

- Berlitz
  BERLITZ ARABIC FOR TRAVELLERS
  0–02–964180–2 Macmillan pb $4.95

  BERLITZ CHINESE FOR TRAVELLERS
  0–686–93010–X Macmillan pb $4.95

  BERLITZ DANISH FOR TRAVELLERS
  0–317–12089–1 Macmillan pb $4.95

  BERLITZ DUTCH FOR TRAVELLERS
  0–02–963900–X Macmillan pb $4.95

  BERLITZ FINNISH FOR TRAVELLERS
  0–02–963910–7 Macmillan pb $4.95

  BERLITZ FRENCH FOR TRAVELLERS
  0–02–963840–2 Macmillan pb $4.95

  BERLITZ GERMAN FOR TRAVELLERS
  0–02–963860–7 Macmillan pb $4.95

  BERLITZ GREEK FOR TRAVELLERS
  0–317–12091–3 Macmillan pb $4.95

  BERLITZ HEBREW FOR TRAVELLERS
  0–02–964050–4 Macmillan pb $4.95

  BERLITZ HUNGARIAN FOR TRAVELLERS
  0–02–964270–1 Macmillan pb $4.95

  BERLITZ ITALIAN FOR TRAVELLERS
  0–02–963870–4 Macmillan pb $4.95

  BERLITZ JAPANESE FOR TRAVELLERS
  0–02–964070–9 Macmillan pb $4.95

  BERLITZ NORWEGIAN FOR TRAVELLERS
  0–02–963950–6 Macmillan pb $4.95

  BERLITZ POLISH FOR TRAVELLERS
  0–02–964160–8 Macmillan pb $4.95

  BERLITZ PORTUGUESE FOR TRAVELLERS
  0–02–963960–3 Macmillan pb $4.95

  BERLITZ RUSSIAN FOR TRAVELLERS
  0–02–964090–3 Macmillan pb $4.95

  BERLITZ SERBO-CROATIAN FOR TRAVELLERS
  0–02–964150–0 Macmillan pb $4.95

  BERLITZ SPANISH FOR TRAVELLERS
  0–02–963850–X Macmillan pb $4.95

  BERLITZ LATIN-AMERICAN SPANISH FOR TRAVELLERS
  0–02–963830–5 Macmillan pb $4.95

  BERLITZ SWAHILI FOR TRAVELLERS
  0–02–964220–5 Macmillan pb $4.95

  BERLITZ SWEDISH FOR TRAVELLERS
  2–8315–0743–X Macmillan pb $4.95

  BERLITZ TURKISH FOR TRAVELLERS
  0–02–964230–2 Macmillan pb $4.95

Lonely Planet Phrasebooks

- Lonely Planet
  BURMESE PHRASEBOOK
  0–86442–026–9 Lonely Planet pb $2.95

  CHINA PHRASEBOOK
  0–908086–82–2 Lonely Planet pb $2.95

  INDONESIA PHRASEBOOK
  0–908086–55–5 Lonely Planet pb $2.95

  KOREAN PHRASEBOOK
  0–86442–060–9 Lonely Planet pb $2.95

  NEPAL PHRASEBOOK
  0–908086–56–3 Lonely Planet pb $2.95

  PAPUA NEW GUINEA PHRASEBOOK
  0–908086–90–3 Lonely Planet pb $2.95

  PHILIPINO PHRASEBOOK
  0–86442–064–1 Lonely Planet pb $2.95

  SRI LANKA PHRASEBOOK
  0–908086–94–6 Lonely Planet pb $2.95

  SWAHILI PHRASEBOOK
  0–86442–025–0 Lonely Planet pb $2.95

  THAILAND PHRASEBOOK
  0–908086–57–1 Lonely Planet pb $3.95

  TIBET PHRASEBOOK
  0–86442–012–9 Lonely Planet pb $2.95

Boats, Cars, Planes, and Trains

▶ See also Military Affairs

BOATS

- Kevin Desmond
  POWER BOAT: The Quest for Speed over Water
  0–517–56821–7 Crown $35.00

- Julie Fitzpatrick
  ON THE WATER
  0–382–09058–6 Silver, Burdett & Ginn pb $10.00

- Francis Holland
  AMERICA'S LIGHTHOUSES: An Illustrated History
  0–486–25576–X Dover pb $10.95

- Robb Huff & Michael Farley
  SEA SURVIVAL: The Boatman's Emergency Manual
  0–8306–9377–7 TAB pb $14.95

- Benjamin Mendlowitz
  WOOD, WATER, AND LIGHT: A Celebration of Classic Wooden Boats
  0–393–03327–9 Norton $45.00

- Peter Neill, editor
  MARITIME AMERICA: Art and Artifacts from America's Great Nautical Collections
  0–8109–1527–8 Abrams $45.00

- Dag Pike
  INTRODUCTION TO POWERBOAT CRUISING
  0–688–08913–5 Morrow $18.95

Ocean Liners and Yachts

- John Brinnin
  BEAU VOYAGE: Life Aboard the Last Great Ships
  0–88029–140–0 Dorset $39.95

- Jill Bobrow & Dana Jinkins
  THE WORLD'S MOST EXTRAORDINARY YACHTS
  0–393–03314–7 Norton $50.00

  CLASSIC YACHT INTERIORS
  0–393–03274–4 Norton $45.00

- Frank Braynard & William Miller
  FIFTY FAMOUS LINERS

  Volume 1
  0–393–01611–0 Norton $29.95

  Volume 2
  0–393–01947–0 Norton $29.95

  Volume 3
  0–393–02551–9 Norton $29.95

- John Brinnin & Kenneth Gaulin
  GRAND LUXE: The Transatlantic Style
  0–8050–0899–3 Henry Holt $84.50

- Jonathan Eastland
GREAT YACHTS AND THEIR DESIGNERS
0–8478–0828–9 Rizzoli $45.00

- Bob Fisher
THE NEW OCEAN THOROUGHBREDS
Photographed by Beken of Cowes
0–525–24510–3 Dutton $45.00

- William Flayhart & Ronald Warwick
QE II
Foreword by Prince Philip
0–393–01885–7 Norton $19.95

- B. Foucart
NORMANDIE: Queen of the Seas
0–86565–057–8 Rizzoli $50.00

- William Miller
BRITISH OCEAN LINERS
0–393–02336–2 Norton $24.95

THE FIRST GREAT OCEAN LINERS IN PHOTOGRAPHS: 180 Views, 1897–1927
0–486–24574–8 Dover pb $9.95

- Ranulf Rayner
THE STORY OF YACHTING
0–393–02652–3 Norton $50.00

- John Rousmaniere
THE GOLDEN PASTIME: A New History of Yachting
0–393–03317–1 Norton $65.00

- Donald Street
THE OCEAN SAILING YACHT
Volume 1
0–393–03168–3 Norton $38.95
Volume 2
0–393–03209–4 Norton $27.95

- C.W. Winter
QUEEN MARY: Her Early Years Recalled
0–393–02351–6 Norton $24.95

Sailboats

- Jan Adkins
THE CRAFT OF SAIL: A Primer of Sailing
0–8027–0401–8 Walker $11.95
0–8027–7214–5 Walker pb $4.95

- Howard Chapelle
AMERICAN SMALL SAILING CRAFT
0–393–03143–8 Norton $32.50

- John Dyson
SPIRIT OF SAIL: On Board the World's Great Sailing Ships
0–8050–0566–8 Henry Holt $35.00

- Kenneth Giggal
CLASSIC SAILING SHIPS
0–393–03328–7 Norton $35.00

- Jeremy Howard-Williams
SAILS
0–8286–0093–7 TAB $22.50

- David MacGregor
FAST SAILING SHIPS, 1775–1875
0–87021–895–6 Naval Institute $29.95

The "Britannia," built in 1893 for Edward VII, then Prince of Wales, from The Handbook of Sailing *by Bob Bond (Knopf)*

- Ferenc Mate
THE WORLD'S BEST SAILBOATS
0–317–58092–2 Norton $39.95

- Joseph Novitski
WINDSTAR: The Building of a Sailship
0–02–590830–8 Macmillan $19.95

- Stanley Rosenfeld
A CENTURY UNDER SAIL
0–201–07963–1 Addison-Wesley pb $29.95

- John Rousmaniere
THE ANNAPOLIS BOOK OF SEAMANSHIP
0–671–67447–1 Simon & Schuster $29.95

- Joshua Slocum
SAILING ALONE AROUND THE WORLD
0–87021–582–5 Naval Institute $21.95
0–7126–0338–7 David & Charles pb $13.95

Ships

- George Bass, editor
SHIPS AND SHIPWRECKS OF THE AMERICAS: A History Based on Underwater Archaeology
0–500–05049–X Thames & Hudson $40.00

- Norman Brouwer
INTERNATIONAL REGISTER OF HISTORIC SHIPS
0–87021–306–7 Naval Institute $28.95

- Howard Chapelle
THE AMERICAN FISHING SCHOONERS: 1825–1935
0–393–03123–3 Norton $32.95

- Beken of Cowes
TALL SHIPS ON THE HIGH SEAS
Foreword by the Prince of Wales
0–525–24439–5 Dutton $35.00

- Charles Davis
AMERICAN SAILING SHIPS: Their Plans and History
0–486–24658–2 Dover pb $5.95

- George Dow
WHALE SHIPS AND WHALING: A Pictorial History
0–486–24808–9 Dover pb $8.95

- John Shaum & William Flayhart
MAJESTY AT SEA: The Four-Stackers
0–393–01527–0 Norton $29.95

- Basil Greenhill
THE MERCHANT SCHOONERS
0–87021–427–6 Naval Institute $29.95

- Octavius Howe & Frederick Matthews
AMERICAN CLIPPER SHIPS, 1833–1858
Volume 1
0–486–25115–2 Dover pb $8.95
Volume 2
0–486–25116–0 Dover pb $8.95

- Cy Liberman & Pat Liberman
THE MYSTIQUE OF TALL SHIPS
0–912608–28–5 Middle Atlantic $29.95

- F. Alexander Magoun
THE FRIGATE CONSTITUTION AND OTHER HISTORIC SHIPS
0–486–25524–7 Dover pb $9.95

- David Oliver
FLYING BOATS AND AMPHIBIANS SINCE 1945
0–87021–898–0 Naval Institute $19.95

Adventures at Sea

Christopher Buckley
STEAMING TO BAMBOOLA: The World of a Tramp Freighter
0–14–009922–0 Penguin pb $6.95

John Caldwell
DESPERATE VOYAGE
0–246–12708–2 Sheridan House pb $12.95

Francis Chichester
GYPSY MOTH CIRCLES THE WORLD
0–340–40667–4 David & Charles pb $22.95

Joseph Conrad
THE MIRROR OF THE SEA
0–317–65712–7 Marlboro pb $8.95

Thor Heyerdahl
KON-TIKI: Across the Pacific by Raft
0–671–63789–4 Washington Square pb $3.95

Eric Hiscock
SOU'WEST IN WANDERER IV
0–19–217528–9 Oxford $22.50
0–911378–60–X Sheridan House pb $12.95

J. Marriott
DISASTER AT SEA
0–87052–450–X Hippocrene $25.00

CARS

● Walter Boyne
POWER BEHIND THE WHEEL: Creativity and the Evolution of the Automobile
1–55670–042–3 Stewart, Tabori & Chang $35.00

● James Flink
THE AUTOMOBILE AGE
0–262–06111–2 MIT $25.00

● Alan Henry
FIFTY FAMOUS MOTOR RACES
0–85059–937–7 Sterling $29.95

● Jay Hirsch
GREAT AMERICAN DREAM MACHINES: Classic Cars of the '50s and '60s
0–679–72160–6 Random House pb $19.95

● Edward Janicki
CARS NEVER BUILT: American Experimental Cars 1938–1988
1–55562–088–4 Main Street $30.00

● David Lewis & Laurence Goldstein, editors
THE AUTOMOBILE AND AMERICAN CULTURE
0–472–08044–X Michigan pb $13.95

● Tom Swallow & Arthur Pill
FLYWHEEL: Memories of the Open Road
0–86350–151–6 Penguin pb $17.95

● Jean-Paul Thevenet & Peter Vann
CABRIOLETS
0–87938–225–2 Motorbooks International $17.98

Specific Car Models

● Automobile Quarterly Staff
CORVETTE: A Piece of the Action
0–915038–44–7 Motorbooks International $14.95

● Michael Cotton
PORSCHE PROGRESS: Stuttgart's Modern Development Story
0–85059–928–8 Sterling $24.95

● W.W. Fitzgerald & others
FERRARI: The Sports and Gran Turismo Cars
0–393–01276–X Norton $39.95

● Chris Harvey
ASTON MARTIN AND LAGONDA
0–902280–68–6 Haynes $29.95

E TYPE: End of an Era
0–946609–16–0 Haynes $34.95
0–312–22452–4 St. Martin's $29.95

THE LAMBORGHINIS: A Collector's Guide
0–900549–69–6 Motorbooks International $22.95

THE PORSCHE 911
0–902280–78–3 Motorbooks International $29.95

TR FOR TRIUMPH
0–902280–94–5 Haynes $29.95

● Michael Lamm
THE FABULOUS FIREBIRD
0–932128–01–7 Motorbooks International $19.95

● Karl Ludvigsen
PORSCHE: Excellence Was Expected—The Complete History of Porsche Sports and Racing Cars
0–915038–09–9 Automobile Quarterly $54.95

● Simon Moore
THE IMMORTAL 2.9: Alfa Romeo 8C 2900 A&B
0–9617266–0–1 Parkside $35.00

● Philip Porter
JAGUAR: History of a Classic Marque
0–517–56792–X Crown $40.00

● Antoine Prunet
THE FERRARI LEGEND: The Road Cars
0–393–01475–4 Norton $45.00

● Roy Query
CORVETTE: An American Legend
0–915038–51–X Automobile Quarterly $39.95

● David Scott-Moncrieff
THREE-POINTED STAR: The Story of the Mercedes-Benz
0–85614–058–9 Motorbooks International $18.95

● Louis Steinwedel & J. Herbert Newport
THE DUESENBERG
0–393–01589–0 Norton $15.95

Car Care

Larry Carley
DO-IT-YOURSELF CAR CARE
0–8306–2143–1 TAB pb $11.95

Chilton's Automotives
CHILTON'S EASY CAR CARE
0–8019–7553–0 Chilton pb $14.95

Jack Gillis & Tom Kelly
THE ARMCHAIR MECHANIC
0–06–096250–X Harper & Row pb $8.95

Paul Weissler
WEEKEND MECHANIC'S HANDBOOK: Complete Auto Repairs You Can Make
0–13–948100–1 Prentice-Hall pb $15.95

MOTORCYCLES

● David Ansell
MILITARY MOTOR CYCLES
0–7134–3837–1 David & Charles $34.95

● Roy Bacon
BRITISH MOTORCYCLES OF THE SIXTIES
0–85045–785–8 Motorbooks International $34.95

● Mike Clay
CAFE RACERS
0–85045–677–0 Motorbooks International $29.95

● Keith Code
THE SOFT SCIENCE OF ROAD RACING MOTORCYCLES
0–918226–11–2 Acrobat pb $16.95

A TWIST OF THE WRIST: The Motorcycle Road Racers Handbook
0–918226–08–2 Acrobat pb $14.95

● Susan Coman & Sharon Mason, editors
MOTORSPORTS
0–318–19006–0 Coman pb $19.50

● William Crouse & Donald Anglin
MOTORCYCLE MECHANICS
0–07–014781–7 McGraw-Hill pb $29.95

● A. Girdler
HARLEY RACERS: Machines and Men from Flat Track, Hillclimb, Speedway, Motocross and Road Racing
0–87938–260–0 Motorbooks International pb $21.95

● Jerry Hatfield
AMERICAN RACING MOTORCYCLES
0–85429–291–8 Motorbooks International $22.95

● Bruce Johns & David Edmundson
MOTORCYCLES: Fundamentals, Service, Repair
0–87006–654–4 Goodheart-Willcox $22.00

● Don Morley
CLASSIC BRITISH TWO-STROKE TRAILS BIKES
0–85045–745–9 Motorbooks International $24.95

● Lynn Mosher & George Lear
MOTORCYCLE MECHANICS
0–13–604090–X Prentice-Hall $32.00

● Victor Page
HANDBOOK OF EARLY MOTORCYCLES: Construction, Operation, Service
0–911160–62–0 Post-Era Books pb $21.95

● David Wright
THE HARLEY-DAVIDSON MOTOR COMPANY: An Official Eighty-Year History
0–87938–245–7 Motorbooks International $24.95

● Patricia Zonker
MURDERCYCLES
0–88229–553–5 Nelson-Hall $20.95

AIRPLANES

● Richard Allen
REVOLUTION IN THE SKY: The Lockheeds of Aviation's Golden Age
0–517–56678–8 Crown $24.95

● Roger Bilstein
FLIGHT IN AMERICA, 1900–1983, From the Wrights to the Astronauts
0–8018–2973–9 Johns Hopkins $39.50
0–8018–3561–5 Johns Hopkins pb $12.95

● Walter Boyne
THE LEADING EDGE
0–941434–93–1 Stewart, Tabori & Chang $29.95
1–55670–016–4 Stewart, Tabori & Chang pb $16.95

SMITHSONIAN BOOK OF FLIGHT
0–517–56614–1 Crown $35.00

- C.D. Bryan
THE NATIONAL AIR AND SPACE MUSEUM
0–8109–1380–1 Abrams $65.00

- Charles Coombs
SOARING: Where Hawks and Eagles Fly
0–8050–0496–3 Henry Holt $13.95

- Rene Francillon
LOCKHEED AIRCRAFT SINCE 1913
0–87021–897–2 Naval Institute $29.95

- M.J. Hardy
SEA, SKY AND STARS: An Illustrated History of Grumman Aircraft
0–85368–832–X Sterling $29.95

- Clive Hart
THE PREHISTORY OF FLIGHT
0–520–05213–7 California $45.00

- Fred Howard
WILBUR AND ORVILLE: A Biography of the Wright Brothers
0–394–54269–X Knopf $24.95
0–345–35393–5 Ballantine pb $12.95

- Gay Maher
THE JOY OF LEARNING TO FLY
0–02–579320–9 Macmillan $17.95

- Richard Rashke
STORMY GENIUS: The Life of Aviation's Maverick, Bill Lear
0–395–35372–6 Houghton Mifflin $19.95

- George Vecsey & George Dade
GETTING OFF THE GROUND: The Pioneers of Aviation Speak for Themselves
0–525–11333–9 Dutton $12.95

BALLOONS

- D. Botting
THE GIANT AIRSHIPS
0–8094–3270–6 Time-Life $18.95

- Tom Crouch
THE EAGLE ALOFT: Two Centuries of the Balloon in America
0–87474–346–X Smithsonian $49.50

- A. Hildebrant
BALLOONS AND AIRSHIPS
0–85409–879–8 Charles River $21.00

- Edwin Kirschner
AEROSPACE BALLOONS: From Montgolfiere to Space
0–8168–0951–8 TAB pb $12.95

- Wolfgang Langewiesche
STICK AND RUDDER: An Explanation of the Art of Flying
0–07–036240–8 McGraw-Hill $16.95

- Brian Lawler
WITH A LIGHT HEART: A Decade of Ballooning Adventures
Foreword by Malcolm Forbes
0–918303–10–9 Blake $49.95

- Time-Life Books
THE GIANT AIRSHIPS
0–8094–3270–6 Time-Life $14.95

Adventures in the Air

- Richard Bach
STRANGER TO THE GROUND
0–02–504520–2 Macmillan $16.95

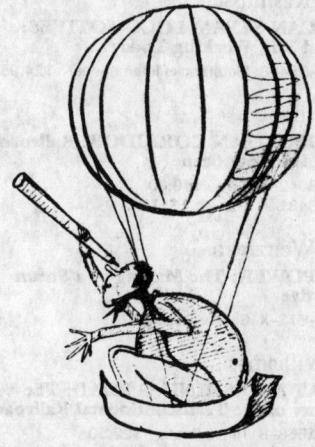

"There was an old man of the Hague/whose ideas were excessively vague./He bought a balloon, to examine the moon-/This distracted old man of the Hague"—Edward Lear

- Amelia Earhart
THE FUN OF IT
0–915864–55–X Academy Chicago pb $7.95
LAST FLIGHT
0–517–56794–6 Crown pb $9.95

- Beryl Markham
WEST WITH THE NIGHT
0–86547–304–8 North Point $19.95
0–86547–118–5 North Point pb $12.50

- Antoine de Saint-Exupéry
AIRMAN'S ODYSSEY
Translated by Stuart Gilbert & Lewis Galantière
0–15–603733–5 HBJ pb $6.95
FLIGHT TO ARRAS
Translated by Lewis Galantière
0–15–631880–6 HBJ pb $4.95
NIGHT FLIGHT
Translated by Stuart Gilbert
0–15–665605–1 HBJ pb $4.95
WIND, SAND AND STARS
0–15–697090–2 HBJ pb $3.95

TRAINS

- Abrams Editors
STEAM, STEEL AND STARS: America's Last Steam Railroad
0–8109–1645–2 Abrams $35.00

- Don Ball
AMERICA'S RAILROADS: The Second Generation
0–393–01416–9 Norton $49.95
RAILROADS
0–393–02236–6 Norton $37.50
RAILS
0–393–01480–0 Norton $24.95

- E.H. Cookridge
THE ORIENT EXPRESS: The Life and Times of the World's Most Famous Train
0–06–090770–3 Harper & Row pb $6.95

- Raymond Loewy
LOCOMOTIVE
0–87663–676–8 St. Martin's $22.50

Amelia Earhart (photo Bettmann Archive), from The Smithsonian Book of Flight *by Walter J. Boyne (Crown)*

☛ **FOR ALL OTHER INQUIRIES, PLEASE CALL (212) 333-7900**

- Henry Rasmussen
AMERICAN STEAM LOCOMOTIVES:
Alive and Still Working Today
0–87938–284–8 Motorbooks International $24.95

- John Stilgoe
METROPOLITAN CORRIDOR: Railroads
and the American Scene
0–300–03042–8 Yale $40.00
0–300–03481–4 Yale pb $17.95

- David Weitzman
SUPERPOWER: The Making of a Steam
Locomotive
0–87923–671–X Godine $19.95

- John Williams
A GREAT AND SHINING ROAD: The
Epic Story of the Transcontinental Railroad
0–8129–1668–9 Times Books $22.50

Geoffrey Moorhouse & Brian
Hollingsworth
RAIL ACROSS INDIA: A Photographic
Journey
0–89659–652–4 Abbeville $85.00

Eric Newby
THE BIG RED TRAIN RIDE
0–14–009540–3 Penguin pb $7.95

Paul Theroux
THE GREAT RAILWAY BAZAAR
0–671–55211–2 Washington Square pb $7.95

THE OLD PATAGONIAN EXPRESS:
By Train Through the Americas
0–395–27788–4 Houghton Mifflin $11.95
0–671–64849–7 Pocket pb $5.95

RIDING THE IRON ROOSTER: By
Train Through China
0–399–13309–7 Putnam $21.95

Sports

- Arthur Ashe
A HARD ROAD TO GLORY: A History of
the Afro-American Athlete
"This work is more than a history. It is a
cry of protest in which ancient sins are
revealed. Mr. Ashe is not merely a
historian, he is a witness as well"—David
Halberstam

Volume 1: 1619–1918
0–446–71006–7 Warner $29.95

Volume 2: 1919–1945
0–446–71007–5 Warner $39.95

Volume 3: Since 1946
0–446–71008–3 Warner $39.95

- Frank Deford
SPORTS PEOPLE
A gallery of photographs, with portraits of
such personalities as Wilt Chamberlain,
Martina Navratilova, Pete Rose, and
Arnold Palmer
Photographs by Walter Iooss, Jr.
0–8109–1520–0 Abrams $35.00

*Jackie Joyner-Kersee in 1986 (photo courtesy of
All Sport), from* A Hard Road to Glory:
Volume 3 *by Arthur Ashe (Warner)*

- Allen Guttmann
A WHOLE NEW BALL GAME: An
Interpretation of American Sports
A history and analysis of the place of
sports in American culture
0–8078–4220–6 North Carolina pb $10.95

- Phillip M. Hoose
NECESSITIES: Racial Barriers in
American Sports
An indictment of racism throughout
American sports
0–394–56944–X Random House $15.95

- James Michener
SPORTS IN AMERICA
A solid analysis of the crisis in American
sports
0–449–21450–8 Fawcett pb $4.95

- David Randall
GREAT SPORTING ECCENTRICS
The athletic quirks of the famous and the
obscure, including Albert Camus, the
goalkeeper for the Oran Football Club of
Algiers; and Netherton United, the
impoverished footballers who appealed to
the International Monetary Fund for relief
0–931933–69–2 Lyle Stuart pb $10.95

- Eric Schrier & William Allman,
editors
NEWTON AT THE BAT: The Science in
Sports
From the aerodynamics of the curve and
the knuckleball to an estimate of the limits
of human performance
0–684–18820–1 Scribners pb $7.95

- Peter Schwed
OVERTIME: A 20th-Century Sports
Odyssey
Essays from around the sports world by a
longtime writer on sports
0–8253–0438–5 Beaufort $15.95

- Chuck Wielgus & Alexander Wolff
FROM A-TRAIN TO YOGI: The Fan's
Book of Sports Nicknames
0–06–096163–5 Harper & Row pb $7.95

IF YOU CAN'T FIND IT, LOOK IN THE INDEX

- Edwin Pope
THE EDWIN POPE COLLECTION
Introduction by James Michener
0–87833–609–5 Taylor $14.95

- Blackie Sherrod
THE BLACKIE SHERROD COLLECTION
Introduction by Dan Jenkins
0–87833–606–0 Taylor $14.95

- Red Smith
THE RED SMITH READER
Foreword by Terence Smith
0–394–71750–3 Random House pb $6.95

TO ABSENT FRIENDS
Introduction by Dave Anderson
0–451–14387–6 NAL pb $4.95

- George Vecsey
A YEAR IN THE SUN: The Life and Times of a Sports Columnist
Revealing anecdotes of major sports personalities from Steinbrenner to Stengel, Dr. J to Joe Paterno
0–8129–1678–6 Times Books $19.95

- Bob Verdi
THE BOB VERDI COLLECTION
Introduction by Mike Royko
0–87833–608–7 Taylor $14.95

BASEBALL

Baseball is a consuming passion, a commitment of six months or more, from the first February workout to the last pitch of the World Series in October. In its greatest books, baseball emerges as not just a daily obsession, but as a metaphor for life—our yearning for our lost youth, our pastoral beginnings.

- Roger Angell
THE SUMMER GAME
Angell's baseball books are matched in artistic quality by few others. This collection includes his *New Yorker* essays from 1962 to 1971
0–345–34192–9 Ballantine pb $3.95

FIVE SEASONS
Essays from 1972 to 1976
0–671–65692–9 Simon & Schuster pb $8.95

LATE INNINGS: A Baseball Companion
From 1977 through the 1981 strike
0–345–30936–7 Ballantine pb $3.95

SEASON TICKET: A Baseball Companion
From 1982 through the classic World Series of 1986
0–395–38165–7 Houghton Mifflin $18.95

- Thomas Boswell
THE HEART OF THE ORDER
The most recent collection from the *Washington Post*'s great beat reporter
0–385–19967–8 Doubleday $18.95

HOW LIFE IMITATES THE WORLD SERIES
0–14–006469–9 Penguin pb $6.95

WHY TIME BEGINS ON OPENING DAY
0–14–007661–1 Penguin pb $6.95

- Jimmy Breslin
CAN'T ANYBODY HERE PLAY THIS GAME?
The 1962 Mets, fabled losers of 120 games
0–14–006217–3 Penguin pb $5.95

- Charles Einstein, editor
THE FIRESIDE BOOK OF BASEBALL
Introduction by Reggie Jackson
0–671–63812–2 Simon & Schuster pb $10.95

- Peter Gammons
BEYOND THE SIXTH GAME
The *Boston Globe* and *Sports Illustrated* baseball writer looks at the game as a sport and a business since the 1975 World Series. Written with a lot of energy and enthusiasm
0–395–35345–9 Houghton Mifflin $15.95
0–8289–0591–6 Stephen Greene pb $6.95

- Donald Hall
FATHERS PLAYING CATCH WITH SONS: Essays on Sport (Mostly Baseball)
"Half of my poet friends think I am insane to waste my time writing about sports and to loiter in the company of professional athletes. The other half would murder to take my place"
0–86547–168–1 North Point pb $13.50

- George V. Higgins
THE PROGRESS OF SEASONS: Forty Years of Baseball in Our Town
The author tells of his and his family's love affair with Fenway Park and the Red Sox
0–8050–0913–2 Henry Holt $18.95

- Christopher Lehmann-Haupt
ME AND DIMAGGIO
A *New York Times* editor pursues a dream by following the Yankees for a season
0–440–20073–3 Dell pb $3.95

- Bruce Nash & Allan Zullo
BASEBALL CONFIDENTIAL
A tabloid look at the grand old game
0–671–65832–8 Simon & Schuster pb $6.95

- Daniel Okrent
NINE INNINGS
Describes in close detail one midseason game
0–07–047757–4 McGraw-Hill pb $4.95

THE ULTIMATE BASEBALL BOOK
0–395–36145–1 Houghton Mifflin pb $15.95

- Daniel Okrent & Steve Wulf
BASEBALL ANECDOTES
A history of baseball, featuring stories of the great players, the great plays, and Yogi's wit
0–19–504396–0 Oxford $18.95

- Martin Quigley
THE CROOKED PITCH
The story of the curveball, told by the men who threw it
0–912697–82–2 Algonquin pb $9.95

- Sporting News
SPORTING NEWS SELECTS BASEBALL'S 50 GREATEST GAMES
0–89204–224–9 Sporting News $19.95

- John Thorn, editor
THE ARMCHAIR BOOK OF BASEBALL
More collected essays; fiction and nonfiction
0–684–18482–6 Scribners $19.95

THE ARMCHAIR BOOK OF BASEBALL II
Includes writings from Walt Whitman, Bill James, Garrison Keillor, George Will, Philip Roth, Tim McCarver, and others
0–684–18772–8 Scribners $19.95

- John Thorn & John Holway
THE PITCHER
0–13–676990–X Prentice-Hall pb $12.95

Baseball Statistics

Until recently, the notion that baseball fans had a limited appetite for statistics was widespread among book publishers. The market is now flooded with books offering statistics in raw form and books that analyze the reams of information now available.

- Sporting News
SPORTING NEWS OFFICIAL BASEBALL GUIDE, 1989
Includes complete major and minor league statistics and plenty of features on the highlights of the previous season
0–89204–293–1 Sporting News pb $10.95

OFFICIAL BASEBALL REGISTER, 1989
Like having the back of every active player's baseball card in one book: career batting, pitching, fielding, and personal statistics in both the minors and the majors
0–89204–293–1 Sporting News pb $10.95

- Bill James
THE 1989 BILL JAMES BASEBALL ABSTRACT
An opinionated and amusing annual that popularized "sabermetrics"—the scientific study of baseball. Entertaining even if you're not addicted to statistics
0–345–35171–1 Ballantine pb $8.95

THE BILL JAMES HISTORICAL ABSTRACT
Not nearly as statistically oriented as the annual. A fresh decade-by-decade look at baseball history from the knowledgeable fan's perspective
0–394–75805–6 Random House pb $15.95

- David Neft & Richard Cohen, editors
THE SPORTS ENCYCLOPEDIA: Baseball 1989
Less expensive and less exhaustive than *The Baseball Encyclopedia;* full player and team statistics since 1901 are organized by season
0–312–02644–7 St. Martin's pb $15.95

- Joseph Reichler, editor
THE BASEBALL ENCYCLOPEDIA
The final word on baseball statistics; updated every three years
0–02–579030–7 Macmillan $45.00

- Luke Salisbury
THE ANSWER IS BASEBALL: A Book of Questions that Illuminate the Great Game
0–8129–1601–8 Times Books $15.95

• Seymour Siwoff, Steve Hirdt & Peter Hirdt
THE 1989 ELIAS BASEBALL ANALYST
It has replaced the *Bill James Abstract* as the largest source of hard-to-find stats, but while it's long on bulk, it's short on insight
0–02–028711–9 Macmillan pb $12.95

Baseball Instruction

Statistics are largely irrelevant to these instructional books, for the game's great thinkers and great athletes inhabit two separate worlds. As a great hitter and sage of the diamond once said, "Who can hit and think at the same time?"

• Walter Alston & others
THE COMPLETE BASEBALL HANDBOOK: Strategies and Techniques for Winning
A large book by the former Dodgers manager
0–697–06819–6 William Brown $19.95

• Joe Brinkman & Charlie Euchner
THE UMPIRE'S HANDBOOK
Instruction for the most unpopular men on the diamond
0–8289–0628–9 Stephen Greene pb $9.95

• Steve Garvey with Bob Gluck
STEVE GARVEY'S HITTING SYSTEM: Raise Your Batting Average
The focus is on Little League and high school baseball; well illustrated
0–8092–4788–7 Contemporary pb $10.95

• Walt Hriniak with Henry Horenstein
WALT HRINIAK'S HITTING CLINIC
More advanced than Steve Garvey's book; from the guru of today's hitting coaches
0–06–096226–7 Harper & Row pb $10.95

• Pat Jordan
SPORTS ILLUSTRATED PITCHING: The Keys to Excellence
A very good book for younger players
0–452–26101–5 NAL pb $9.95

• Charley Lau with Alfred Glossbrenner
THE ART OF HITTING .300
The architect of George Brett's swing writes for players at the high school or college level
0–525–48219–9 Dutton pb $10.95

• Pete Rose with Bob Hertzel
PETE ROSE'S WINNING BASEBALL
Pete Rose doesn't know more about baseball than the average fan; he just applies the common wisdom with greater spirit and determination
0–8092–8102–3 Contemporary pb $6.95

• Earl Weaver with Terry Pluto
WEAVER ON STRATEGY
The former Oriole manager proselytizes about platooning and three-run homers; more anecdotal than instructive
0–02–029630–4 Macmillan pb $7.95

• Ted Williams with John Underwood
THE SCIENCE OF HITTING
Unquestionably the most authoritative book on hitting, written by the master; a must-read
0–671–62103–3 Simon & Schuster pb $9.95

Baseball Biographies

Baseball biographies are a mixed bag: some cover a retired star's entire life and attempt to put his achievements in meaningful perspective; others merely reflect on one season (usually a winning one), offering a brilliant chapter from an entire career. The biographies listed here focus on the greats of the past.

• Yogi Berra with Thomas Horton
IT AIN'T OVER
An autobiography
0–70–096947–7 McGraw-Hill $18.95

• Phil Pepe
THE WIT AND WISDOM OF YOGI
A biography of the most famous dugout philosopher
0–88736–000–0 Meckler $16.00

• Charles Alexander
TY COBB
0–19–503598–4 Oxford pb $8.95

• Jack Moore
JOE DIMAGGIO: Yankee Clipper
0–272–92712–1 Praeger pb $9.95

• Hank Greenberg
THE STORY OF MY LIFE
Greenberg was stricken with cancer and was unable to finish his memoirs, which were completed by *New York Times* sports columnist Ira Berkow
0–8129–1741–3 Times Books $19.95

• Whitey Herzog with Kevin Horrigan
WHITE RAT: A Life in Baseball
When the St. Louis Cardinal manager retires, it will be time for the definitive biography, but in the meantime, this is the best one
0–06–080910–8 Harper & Row pb $3.95

• Bowie Kuhn
HARDBALL: The Education of a Baseball Commissioner
Functions well as a history of a stormy era in baseball, from free agency to expansion, from Finley to Steinbrenner
0–8129–1278–0 Times Books $19.95

• Mickey Mantle with Herb Gluck
THE MICK
0–515–08599–5 Berkley pb $3.95

• Willie Mays with Lou Sahadi
SAY HEY: The Autobiography of Willie Mays
0–671–63292–2 Simon & Schuster $17.95

• Frank Robinson with Barry Stainback
EXTRA INNINGS
The life of baseball's fourth leading all-time home run hitter and its first black manager, with a sharp indictment of racism in baseball throughout his career and in the post-Campanis era
0–07–053183–8 McGraw-Hill $16.95

• Maury Allen
JACKIE ROBINSON: A Life Remembered
A true biography, not simply a remembrance of Robinson's place in baseball history
0–531–15042–9 Franklin Watts $16.95

• Robert Creamer
BABE: The Legend Comes to Life
A thoughtful, well-researched, well-written biography of baseball's greatest player
0–14–006859–7 Penguin pb $7.95

• Lawrence Ritter & Mark Rucker
THE BABE: A Life in Pictures
0–89919–768–X Ticknor & Fields $39.95

• Duke Snider with Bill Gilbert
THE DUKE OF FLATBUSH
His days in center field
0–8217–2469–X Zebra $17.95

• Robert Creamer
STENGEL: His Life and Times
0–440–57829–9 Dell pb $8.95

• Ted Williams with John Underwood
MY TURN AT BAT: The Story of My Life
0–671–63423–2 Simon & Schuster pb $7.95

• Dave Winfield with Tom Palmer
WINFIELD: A Player's Life
Less sensational than the tabloids made it seem
0–393–02467–9 Norton $16.95

Babe Ruth by Leo Hershfield (courtesy National Baseball Hall of Fame and Museum), from Images of America in Caricature and Cartoon *by Ron Tyler (Amon Carter Museum)*

TO ORDER BOOKS AS GIFTS, SEE PAGE 1

Group Biographies

• **Eliot Asinof**
EIGHT MEN OUT: The Black Sox and the 1919 World Series
An account of the most notorious "fix" in the history of professional sports. The source for the John Sayles movie
0–8050–0346–0 Henry Holt pb $9.95

• **Mike Bryan**
BASEBALL LIVES: Men and Women of the Game Talk About Their Jobs, Their Lives and the National Pastime
0–679–69638–5 Pantheon $19.95

• **Harvey Frommer**
NEW YORK CITY BASEBALL: The Last Golden Age, 1947–1957
Until the next golden age, that is
0–689–70684–7 Atheneum pb $9.95

• **Peter Golenbock**
DYNASTY: The New York Yankees, 1949–1964
With the exceptions of 1954 and 1959, the Yankees participated in every World Series during this era
0–425–07652–0 Berkley pb $4.50

• **David Halberstam**
THE SUMMER OF 'FORTY-NINE
0–688–06678–X Morrow $21.95

• **Ralph Houk & Robert Creamer**
SEASON OF GLORY
The story of the Yankees' brilliant 1961 season, alternating between manager Houk's recollections and Creamer's history
0–399–13260–0 Putnam $18.95

• **Roger Kahn**
THE BOYS OF SUMMER
The story of the 1950s Brooklyn Dodgers, carried to the present
0–06–091416–5 Harper & Row pb $8.95

• **Tim McCarver with Bob Levenson**
OH BABY, I LOVE IT!
McCarver will make it to Cooperstown, as an announcer if not as a player
0–394–55691–7 Random House $16.95

• **Lawrence Ritter & Donald Honig**
THE ONE HUNDRED GREATEST BASEBALL PLAYERS OF ALL TIME
0–517–56181–6 Crown $16.95

Donn Rogosin
INVISIBLE MEN: Life in Baseball's Negro Leagues
Ernie Banks is always quoted as saying "Let's play two"; these guys sometimes played four a day
0–689–11363–3 Atheneum $14.95

Picture Books

• **Peter Gordon, editor**
DIAMONDS ARE FOREVER: Artists and Writers on Baseball
A book of genuine literary value, well produced
0–87701–468–X Chronicle pb $18.95

• **Donald Honig**
BASEBALL IN THE '30s: A Decade of Survival
Contains 500 pictures
0–517–57250–8 Crown $24.95

THE AMERICAN LEAGUE: An Illustrated History
0–517–56685–0 Crown $22.50

THE NATIONAL LEAGUE: An Illustrated History
0–517–56684–2 Crown $22.50

• **Scott Mlyn & Louis D. Rubin, Jr.**
BEFORE THE GAME
A beautifully produced and reasonably priced picture book
0–87833–605–2 Taylor pb $13.95

• **Lawrence Ritter & Donald Honig**
THE IMAGE OF THEIR GREATNESS
0–517–55422–4 Crown $19.95

• **John Thorn**
THE GAME FOR ALL AMERICA
0–89204–279–6 Sporting News $35.00

Insider Accounts

Beginning in the early 1960s, several players who had hardly left their stamp on the game—at least, not on the playing field—made a splash with memoirs recalling often sordid (but always fascinating) details of life in the big leagues.

• **Jim Brosnan**
THE LONG SEASON
Brosnan was a well-traveled relief pitcher with a wry sense of humor and a taste for martinis. This excellent book was the first to treat baseball players as adults who carry adult baggage
0–14–006754–X Penguin pb $6.95

• **Jay Johnstone with Rick Talley**
OVER THE EDGE
Tales from the former journeyman outfielder and clubhouse cutup
0–8092–4975–8 Contemporary $16.95
0–553–27285–3 Bantam pb $3.95

• **Pat Jordan**
A FALSE SPRING
A beautifully written book about a failed bonus baby looking back at his use and abuse at baseball's lowest levels
0–671–65994–4 Simon & Schuster pb $7.95

• **Bill Lee with Dick Lally**
THE WRONG STUFF
Baseball's biggest flake and only presidential candidate
0–14–007941–6 Penguin pb $4.95

• **Ron Luciano with David Fisher**
THE UMPIRE STRIKES BACK
A humorous book from an unusual perspective; the first, and best, of his three books
0–553–24846–4 Bantam pb $3.95

THE FALL OF THE ROMAN UMPIRE
Second in the series
0–553–26133–9 Bantam pb $3.95

REMEMBRANCE OF SWINGS PAST
The most recent book from the witty umpire
0–553–05262–4 Bantam $17.95
0–553–27793–6 Bantam pb $3.95

• **Bob Uecker with Mickey Herskowitz**
CATCHER IN THE WRY
From the former backup backstop and current light beer pitchman and sitcom star
0–515–09029–8 Berkley pb $3.95

Baseball Fiction

Baseball has attracted the wild mythmakers more than the gritty realists.

• **Robert Coover**
THE UNIVERSAL BASEBALL ASSOCIATION, INC.
In this tale of fate and imagination, a bachelor accountant brings a baseball league of his own creation to life every night on his kitchen table
0–452–26030–2 NAL pb $7.95

• **Mark Harris**
THE SOUTHPAW
The first of the Henry Wiggen novels. Henry hurls his way to the MVP and the pennant and all that
0–8032–7220–0 Nebraska pb $8.95

BANG THE DRUM SLOWLY
Later a Robert DeNiro movie. Henry becomes attached to a dying catcher
0–8032–7221–9 Nebraska pb $6.50

A TICKET FOR A SEAMSTITCH
0–8032–7224–3 Nebraska pb $5.95

• **W.P. Kinsella**
THE FURTHER ADVENTURES OF SLUGGER McBAT
Collected baseball stories
0–395–47593–7 Houghton Mifflin pb $7.95

THE IOWA BASEBALL CONFEDERACY
The 1908 Chicago Cubs make a road trip to Iowa and play a game of over 2000 innings that has been forgotten by the record books
0–395–38952–6 Houghton Mifflin $16.95
0–345–34256–9 Ballantine pb $3.95

SHOELESS JOE
Based on the career of the player who was thrown out of the major leagues for his involvement in the 1919 Black Sox scandal; source of the movie *Field of Dreams*
0–345–34256–9 Ballantine pb $3.95

• **Ring Lardner**
HAIRCUT & OTHER STORIES
Only one baseball story in this collection, but it's the classic "Alibi Ike"
Introduction by Wilfrid Sheed
0–394–72610–3 Random House pb $6.95

YOU KNOW ME AL: A Busher's Letters
"The best prose that has come our way.... He lets Jack Keefe the baseball player cut out his own outline, fill in his own depths, until the figure of the foolish, boastful, innocent athlete lives before us"— Virginia Woolf
Introduction by Wilfrid Sheed
0–394–72634–0 Random House pb $7.95

- Bernard Malamud
THE NATURAL
Roy Hobbs and his bat Wonderboy
0–374–21960–5 Farrar, Straus & Giroux $13.95
0–374–50200–5 Farrar, Straus & Giroux pb $8.95

- Philip Roth
THE GREAT AMERICAN NOVEL
A ride through the mythical Patriot League, featuring unbeatable rookie hurler Gil Gamesh and iron-willed umpire Mike the Mouth Masterson
0–14–007678–6 Penguin pb $5.95

- John Tunis
THE KID FROM TOMKINSVILLE
The first in a series of recently reprinted novels from the 1940s, following Roy Tucker and the Brooklyn Dodgers without all the mythmaking. Written for a younger age group, but a cut above the usual kid's fare
0–15–200500–5 HBJ pb $4.95
KEYSTONE KIDS
0–15–200495–5 HBJ pb $4.95
ROOKIE OF THE YEAR
0–15–200570–6 HBJ pb $4.95
WORLD SERIES
0–15–200651–6 HBJ pb $4.95

- Ernest Thayer
CASEY AT THE BAT: A Centennial Edition
Possibly the best-known American poem
0–87923–722–8 David Godine $12.95

Softball

- Michael Ivankovich
THE STRATEGY OF PITCHING SLOW-PITCH SOFTBALL
0–9615843–4–3 Diamond Press pb $7.95

- Connie Johnson & Margie Wright
THE WOMAN'S SOFTBALL BOOK
0–88011–209–3 Leisure pb $11.95

- Gladys Meyer
SOFTBALL FOR GIRLS AND WOMEN
0–684–18140–1 Scribners pb $9.95

- Robert Meyer
THE COMPLETE BOOK OF SOFTBALL: The Loonies' Guide to Playing and Enjoying the Game
0–88011–212–3 Leisure pb $10.95

BASKETBALL

Despite its relative youth as a big-time sport, basketball boasts an impressive body of literature. Not only have such major writers as John McPhee and David Halberstam written splendid books, but players themselves, such as Kareem Abdul-Jabbar, have proven surprisingly frank and introspective in print.

- Charles Salzberg
FROM SET SHOT TO SLAM DUNK: The Glory Days of Basketball in the Words of Those Who Played It
0–525–24555–3 Dutton $17.95

- Chuck Wielgus & Alexander Wolff
THE IN-YOUR-FACE BASKETBALL BOOK
A sly appreciation of the world of pick-up basketball, from its best players to its best playgrounds
Introduction by Al McGuire
0–89696–067–6 Dodd, Mead $11.95
0–89696–081–1 Dodd, Mead pb $8.95

THE BACK-IN-YOUR-FACE GUIDE TO PICK-UP BASKETBALL
A listing of the best recreational courts from coast to coast, rating the level of competition, the condition of the rims, even the courtside music
0–396–08894–5 Dodd, Mead $19.95
0–396–08709–4 Dodd, Mead pb $11.95

Professional Basketball

- Kareem Abdul-Jabbar with Peter Knobler
GIANT STEPS
After years of seeming aloof and imperious, Abdul-Jabbar used this candid autobiography to reveal himself as sensitive, vulnerable, and likeable
0–553–27147–4 Bantam pb $4.95

- Red Auerbach with Joe Fitzgerald
ON AND OFF THE COURT
The brains behind the cigar and basketball's most successful franchise, the Boston Celtics
0–02–504390–0 Macmillan $14.95

- Darryl Dawkins with George Wirt
CHOCOLATE THUNDER: The In-Your-Face, All-Over-the-Place, Death-Defyin', Mesmerizin', Slam-Jam Adventures of Double D
The story of the high school phenomenon who moved directly to professional basketball and whose erratic talents have been overshadowed by his backboard-shattering dunks and his claims to be a visitor from the planet Lovetron
0–8092–4886–7 Contemporary $15.95

- Walt Frazier with Neil Offen
WALT FRAZIER: One Magic Season and a Basketball Life
The dapper guard of the New York Knicks in their glory days recalls the excitement of the 1969–1970 championship season and critiques players past and present
0–8129–1736–7 Times Books $17.95

- David Halberstam
THE BREAKS OF THE GAME
A splendid account of a year in the life of the Portland Trailblazers and of the varied personalities who make up a professional basketball team
0–394–51309–6 Knopf $15.00

- Gary Hoenig & Dan Shaughnessy
COURTSIDE: The Fan's Guide to Pro Basketball
0–916815–00–5 Contemporary $14.95

- Red Holzman with Harvey Frommer
RED ON RED
A memoir by the man who coached the New York Knicks when they played basketball the way it ought to be played
Introduction by Bill Bradley
0–553–05225–X Bantam $17.95

- Dan Issel & Buddy Martin
PARTING SHOTS
0–8092–5070–5 Contemporary pb $6.95

- Earvin Johnson with Richard Levin
MAGIC
The cheerful Laker playmaker. Not as introspective a book as his teammate Kareem's
0–670–44805–2 Viking $13.50

- Meadowlark Lemon with Jerry Jenkins
MEADOWLARK
The laughing man of the Harlem Globetrotters
0–8407–4220–7 Thomas Nelson $15.95

- Lee Daniel Levine
BIRD: The Making of an American Sports Hero
The story of Larry Bird of the Boston Celtics, considered by many the best player ever
0–07–037477–5 McGraw-Hill $17.95

- Scott Ostler & Steve Springer
WINNIN' TIMES: The Magical Journey of the Los Angeles Lakers
A snapshot of a dynasty. An entertaining, inside-the-locker-room look at the Lakers' 1986–1987 championship season
0–02–029591–X Collier pb $8.95

- Pat Riley
SHOW TIME: Inside the Lakers' Breakthrough Season
The Lakers' dapper strategist narrates the first of his back-to-back championship years. A far better than average account of how a coach's mind works
0–446–51427–6 Warner $17.95

- Bob Ryan & Terry Pluto
48 MINUTES: A Night in the Life of the N.B.A.
Two of the best pro basketball writers in the business use a seemingly inconsequential game—Boston vs. Cleveland—to examine every aspect of the world they cover
0–02–597770–9 Macmillan $16.95

- Spud Webb with Reid Slaughter
SPUD WEBB: Flying High
The little man in the land of the giants
0–06–015820–4 Harper & Row $14.95

College Basketball

- John Feinstein
A SEASON ON THE BRINK: A Year with Bobby Knight and the Indiana Hoosiers
A surprise best-seller that deserved its lofty status, this is a no-holds-barred look at the

profane and abusive, yet brilliant, generalissimo of Indiana basketball
Introduction by Al McGuire
0–02–537230–0 Macmillan $16.95
0–671–64656–7 Simon & Schuster pb $4.50

• Richard Harp & Joseph McCullough
TARKANIAN: Countdown of a Rebel
The Las Vegas coach who has built a highly successful and controversial program
0–88011–229–8 Leisure pb $11.95

• Phillip Hoose
HOOSIERS: The Fabulous Basketball Life of Indiana
0–317–53632–X Random House pb $7.95

John McPhee
A SENSE OF WHERE YOU ARE: A Profile of Bill Bradley at Princeton
A look at the New York Knick star and New Jersey senator in his days as a collegiate perfectionist, written by one of *The New Yorker*'s master stylists
0–374–51485–2 FS&G pb $7.95

• Ray Meyer with Ray Sons
COACH
Thirty-seven seasons at DePaul University with Meyer, the man who turned tangle-footed George Mikan into basketball's first dominant big man
0–8092–4803–4 Contemporary $17.95

• Bert Nelli
THE WINNING TRADITION: A History of Kentucky Wildcat Basketball
0–8131–1519–1 Kentucky $20.00

• Billy Packer
FIFTY YEARS OF THE FINAL FOUR: Golden Moments of the NCAA Tournament
By the insightful, impassioned TV commentator
0–87833–592–7 Taylor $19.95

• Billy Packer with Roland Lazenby
HOOPS!: Confessions of a College Basketball Analyst
0–8092–5304–6 Contemporary pb $7.95

Women's Basketball

• Maryalyce Jeremiah
BASKETBALL: The Woman's Game
0–87670–069–5 Athletic Institute pb $7.95

• Nancy Lieberman with Harvey Frommer
BASKETBALL MY WAY
The queen of the women's game
0–684–17012–4 Scribners $12.95
0–684–18203–3 Scribners pb $6.95

Basketball Instruction

• Larry Bird with John Bischoff
BIRD ON BASKETBALL: How-to Strategies From the Great Celtics Champion
0–201–14209–0 Addison-Wesley pb $9.95

LARRY BIRD'S BASKETBALL BIRDWISE
0–910109–00–1 Phoenix Projects pb $9.95

• William Dunn & others
STRENGTH TRAINING AND CONDITIONING FOR BASKETBALL: Featuring Ralph Sampson's Training Program
0–8092–5375–5 Contemporary pb $9.95

• Bill Foster
CONDITIONING FOR BASKETBALL: A Guide For Coaches and Athletes
0–918438–79–9 Leisure pb $11.00

• Howard Garfinkel
FIVE STAR BASKETBALL DRILLS
The paces through which Garf and his well-known counselors put the nation's best high school players at his famed summer camp
0–940279–22–3 Masters pb $12.95

• Roland Lazenby
CHAMPIONSHIP BASKETBALL: Top Coaches Present Their Winning Strategies and Techniques for Players and Coaches
0–8092–4874–3 Contemporary pb $9.95

• Michael Taraban & Robin Tolleson
ONE-ON-ONE HANDBOOK
0–943084–61–X Turnbull & Willoughby pb $5.95

• John Wooden
PRACTICAL MODERN BASKETBALL
By the coaching genius who guided UCLA to ten national titles and molded Bill Walton and Kareem Abdul-Jabbar
0–02–429470–5 Macmillan $33.00

BOXING AND WRESTLING

• E.A. Carmean, Jr.
BELLOWS: The Boxing Pictures
Bellows was a leading American painter in the first quarter of this century, and his work captured boxing's brutal beauty
0–295–96320–4 Washington pb $9.95

• Don Dunphy
DON DUNPHY AT RINGSIDE
The voice of the Friday Night Fights
0–8050–0530–7 Henry Holt $18.95

Muhammad Ali (photo by Howard L. Bingham)

• Nat Fleisher & others
A PICTORIAL HISTORY OF BOXING FROM THE BARE-KNUCKLE DAYS TO THE PRESENT
The resident geniuses of the original *Ring* magazine take a step up in class with this copious photographic salute
0–8065–1048–X Lyle Stuart $19.95

• Leonard Gardner
FAT CITY
A classic novel about the underbelly of small-time boxing
0–394–74316–4 Random House pb $6.95

• Elliott Gorn
THE MANLY ART: Bare-Knuckle Prize Fighting in America
0–8014–1920–4 Cornell $24.95

• A.J. Liebling
THE SWEET SCIENCE
One of the best books ever written about boxing, this is a collection of fighters' portraits that Liebling composed for *The New Yorker*. Includes his famous pieces on young Marciano and the venerable Mongoose, Archie Moore
0–941372–06–5 Holtzman $18.95
0–14–006191–6 Penguin pb $6.95

• Chris Mead
CHAMPION: Joe Louis, Black Hero in White America
A historical evaluation of perhaps the greatest heavyweight champion ever
0–684–18462–1 Scribners $18.95
0–14–009285–4 Penguin pb $6.95

• Ian Morrison
BOXING: Records, Facts and Champions
An updated reference of boxing records and personal profiles
0–85112–345–7 Sterling pb $14.95

• Joyce Carol Oates
ON BOXING
0–385–23890–8 Doubleday $14.95

• Joyce Carol Oates & Daniel Halpern, editors
READING THE FIGHTS
A compendium of some of the best short pieces on boxing by Norman Mailer, Gay Talese, John Schulian, Pete Hamill, and A.J. Liebling, among others
0–8050–0510–2 Henry Holt $17.95

• William Plummer
BUTTERCUPS AND STRONG BOYS: A Sojourn at the Golden Gloves
A vivid report on the world's most famous amateur boxing event
0–670–80321–9 Viking $17.95

• Sam Toperoff
SUGAR RAY LEONARD AND OTHER NOBLE WARRIORS
0–07–065003–9 McGraw-Hill $15.95

Boxing Instruction

• Chuck Bodak with Neil Milbert
BOXING BASICS
Bodak helped coach the young Ali
0–8092–7210–5 Contemporary pb $7.95

- Larry Holmes with Roy Nelson
LARRY HOLMES' BOXING TACTICS AND TECHNIQUES
0–8092–5325–9 Contemporary pb $8.95

Wrestling

- Ray Carson, editor
CHAMPIONSHIP WRESTLING: An Anthology
0–686–09318–6 Carson $14.95

- Steve Combs & Chuck Frank
WINNING WRESTLING
0–8092–7086–2 Contemporary pb $8.95

- Russ Hellickson & Andrew Baggot
AN INSTRUCTIONAL GUIDE TO AMATEUR WRESTLING
Illustrated guide to maneuvers and holds
0–399–51269–1 Putnam pb $10.95

- Mark Mysnyk
WRESTLING FUNDAMENTALS AND TECHNIQUES: The Iowa Hawkeyes Way
A product of college wrestling's dynastic program at the University of Iowa
0–918438–98–5 Leisure pb $13.95

- Larry Sciacchetano & Jack McCallum
SPORTS ILLUSTRATED WRESTLING
0–397–01275–6 Harper & Row pb $5.95

- Sharon Stark
A WRESTLING SEASON
0–688–06755–7 Morrow $17.95

FOOTBALL

Football books have been streaming out of American publishing houses ever since *McMahon!*, *Snake* and John Madden's *Hey, Wait a Minute! (I Wrote a Book!)* took control of the *New York Times* best-seller list. College fans will also find virtually every Top Ten powerhouse celebrated between hard covers.

Professional Football

- Jim Benagh
FOOTBALL: Startling Stories Behind the Records
0–8069–6858–3 Sterling pb $4.95

- Roy Blount, Jr.
ABOUT THREE BRICKS SHY OF A LOAD
The humorist's account of good times and bad with Mean Joe Greene and Terry Bradshaw on the cusp of their dynastic years with the Pittsburgh Steelers
0–345–34106–6 Ballantine pb $3.50

- Art Holst
SUNDAY ZEBRAS
The referees of the NFL
Introduction by Frank Gifford
0–9605118–0–6 Forest $12.95

- Jerry Kramer with Dick Schaap
INSTANT REPLAY
Kramer played for the Green Bay Packers in the Lombardi years and his diary of the '67 season offers an insightful, intimate look at one of history's greatest teams
0–451–14630–1 NAL pb $3.95
DISTANT REPLAY
The '67 Packers, then and now
0–399–13106–X Putnam $16.95
0–515–09015–8 Berkley pb $3.95

- John Madden
JOHN MADDEN'S PRO FOOTBALL ANNUAL, 1989
The ultimate yearly guide to the NFL
0–679–72169–X Random House pb $10.95

- Richard Raihall
THE WINNER'S EDGE: The Inside Guide to Betting Pro Football
0–915643–09–X Santa Barbara pb $9.95

- Dick Whittingham
SUNDAY MAYHEM: A Celebration of Pro Football in America
0–87833–548–X Taylor pb $13.95

- Paul Zimmerman
THE NEW THINKING MAN'S GUIDE TO PRO FOOTBALL
Sports Illustrated's irrepressible Doctor Z probes the psyches and strategies of a game that lesser minds would describe as fat men leaning on each other
0–671–60276–4 Simon & Schuster pb $9.95

Biographies

- Harry Carson with Jim Smith
POINT OF ATTACK: The Defense Strikes Back
Carson was the quiet leader of the NY Giants' defense throughout the '70s and '80s. His book is one of several published following the championship season of 1986, the first Giants title in almost 30 years
0–07–010231–7 McGraw-Hill pb $4.95

- Eric Dickerson with Steve Delsohn
ON THE RUN
0–8092–4973–1 Contemporary pb $7.95

- Mike Ditka with Don Pierson
DITKA: An Autobiography
Once the Bears' bone-cracking tight end, now their bone-cracking coach
Foreword by Tom Landry
0–933893–38–8 Bonus pb $7.95

- Art Donovan with Bob Drury
FATSO: The Football Follies of Artie Donovan
The reminiscences of the former Baltimore Colt defensive tackle, teammate of Raymond Berry and John Unitas, a Brooklyn lad who grew up to appreciate beer, crabcakes, and falling on runners half his size. One of the funniest books ever written about football
0–688–07340–9 Morrow $15.95

- David Kopay with Perry Young
THE DAVID KOPAY STORY
Kopay used this autobiography to go public with his homosexuality after finishing his career with the Washington Redskins
1–55611–080–4 Donald Fine pb $8.95

- Bill McCrane
BUD: The Other Side of the Glacier
Bud Grant and the Minnesota Vikings
0–06–015583–3 Harper & Row $15.95

- Jim McMahon with Bob Verdi
McMAHON!: The Bare Truth about Chicago's Brashest Bear
Finally, amid the hype and hoopla of modern American sports, a voice of reason, moderation, and dignity
0–446–34772–8 Warner pb $3.95

- John Madden with Dave Anderson
HEY, WAIT A MINUTE! (I Wrote a Book!)
The reminiscences and ramblings of the colorful ex-Raider coach and CBS commentator. The best-seller that started it all
0–345–32507–9 Ballantine pb $3.95
ONE KNEE EQUALS TWO FEET (And Everything Else You Need to Know About Football)
More reminiscences and ramblings
0–394–55328–4 Random House $16.95
0–515–09193–6 Berkley pb $3.95

- Dan Marino with Steve Delsohn
MARINO!
0–8092–4980–4 Contemporary pb $5.95

- John Matuszak with Steve Delsohn
CRUISIN' WITH THE TOOZ
What you'd expect from a defensive end who decorated his apartment with women's underwear and was once arrested carrying a machete and a .357 magnum
0–531–15055–0 Franklin Watts $16.95
0–317–67791–8 Berkley pb $3.95

- Joe Montana with Bob Raissman
AUDIBLES: My Life in Football
0–688–06298–9 Morrow $16.95

- Bill Parcells with Mike Lupica
PARCELLS: Autobiography of the Biggest Giant of Them All
The Giants coach
0–933893–40–X Bonus $17.95

- Phil Simms & Phil McConkey with Dick Schaap
SIMMS TO McCONKEY: Blood, Sweat and Gatorade
The Giant quarterback and his favorite receiver
0–517–56703–2 Crown $18.95

- Bubba Smith with Hal Dewindt
KILL, BUBBA, KILL!
Baltimore's all-world defensive end
0–671–47647–5 Pocket pb $8.95

• Ken Stabler with Berry Stainback
SNAKE: The Candid Autobiography of Football's Most Outrageous Renegade
The brilliant quarterback who played under Bear Bryant at Alabama, then starred for the Oakland Raiders and New Orleans Saints. The quarterback as honky-tonk hero
0–385–23450–3 Doubleday $15.95
0–441–77194–7 Berkley pb $3.95

• Lawrence Taylor with David Falkner
LT: Living on the Edge
The headline-making autobiography of one of the most devastating linebackers ever to play the game. It chronicles Taylor's drug abuse, recklessness, and near self-destruction
0–8129–1703–0 Times Books $16.95

The Business of Football

• Gene Klein with David Fisher
FIRST DOWN AND A BILLION
Klein, the former owner of the San Diego Chargers, provides an extraordinary, behind-the-scenes account of pro football's power brokers
0–688–06894–4 Morrow $17.95
0–312–90929–2 St. Martin's pb $3.95

• Ed Linn & Mel Durslag
THE ONE HUNDRED MILLION DOLLAR GAME
How pro football, aided and abetted by television and commercial sponsors, became the most lucrative of all big-time sports
0–671–47054–X Simon & Schuster $16.95

• Mike Trope & Steve Delsohn
NECESSARY ROUGHNESS
0–8092–4816–6 Contemporary $18.95

College Football

• Thomas Bergin & Will Cloney, editors
THE GAME: The Harvard-Yale Football Rivalry, 1875–1983
"Nearest and dearest foes" through 100 games, from the early glory of Walter Camp to the obscurity of Division 1-AA
0–300–03267–6 Yale $25.00

• Joseph Doye
FIGHTING IRISH: A Century of Notre Dame Football
Includes a fascinating selection of archival photos
0–943231–01–9 Howell $35.00

• Mickey Herskowitz
THE LEGEND OF BEAR BRYANT
The great Alabama coach, mentor to Joe Namath and Ken Stabler
0–07–028399–0 McGraw-Hill pb $6.95

• James Kirby
FUMBLE: Bear Bryant, Wally Butts and the Great College Football Scandal
The story of how the *Saturday Evening Post* got burned when it accused two major coaches of fixing a game
0–15–134143–5 HBJ $16.95

• Bill McIntyre
GRAMBLING: Cradle of the Pros
Eddie Robinson, college football's winningest coach, and the stars he molded at this small black college in Alabama
0–86518–015–6 Moran $12.50

• Richard Pennington
BREAKING THE ICE: The Racial Integration of Southwest Conference Football
Three black players who finally paved the way in the late '60s
0–89950–295–4 McFarland $19.95

Photography

• Angus G. Garber III
END ZONE: A Photographic Celebration of Football
0–8050–0556–0 Henry Holt $15.95

• Beau Riffenburgh & David Ross
RUNNING WILD: A Photographic Tribute to the NFL's Greatest Runners
0–452–26022–1 NAL pb $14.95

• Walter Iooss, Jr.
FOOTBALL
One of the premier sports photographers in the country focuses on the 100-yard war. Contribution by Dan Jenkins, Iooss' colleague at *Sports Illustrated* and the author of *Semi-Tough*
0–8109–0938–3 Abrams $29.95

Encyclopedias and Reference Books

• Bill Mazer & Stan Fischler
THE AMAZIN' BILL MAZER'S FOOTBALL TRIVIA BOOK
0–446–90785–5 Warner pb $2.50

• Bruce Nash & Allan Zullo
THE FOOTBALL HALL OF SHAME
0–671–61114–3 Pocket pb $6.95

• National Football League
THE OFFICIAL 1989 NFL RECORD AND FACT BOOK
0–89480–349–2 Workman pb $12.95

• David Neft & others
THE SPORTS ENCYCLOPEDIA: Pro Football, 6th Edition
0–312–02289–1 St. Martin's pb $15.95

• Mark Sabljak & Martin Greenberg
WHO'S WHO IN THE SUPER BOWL: The Performance of Every Player in Super Bowls I to XX
0–934878–80–3 Dembner $22.50
0–934878–81–1 Dembner pb $14.95

Jack Clary
TOPPS FOOTBALL CARDS: The Complete Picture Collection, A History 1956–1986
Introduction by Sy Berger, the reigning king of bubblegum cards
Foreword by Roger Staubach
0–446–51336–9 Warner $30.00

Football Instruction

• George Allen with Mickey Herskowitz
MOTIVATION: George Allen Style
0–07–001079–X McGraw-Hill $16.95

• Ken Anderson with Jack Clay
THE ART OF QUARTERBACKING
By the former Bengal All-Pro quarterback
0–671–50724–9 Simon & Schuster pb $10.95

• Raymond Berry with C.H. Gilbert, Jr.
RAYMOND BERRY'S COMPLETE GUIDE TO COACHING PASS RECEIVERS
By the Patriot coach and Hall of Fame receiver
0–13–753210–5 Prentice-Hall $19.95

• Paul Bryant
BEAR BRYANT ON WINNING FOOTBALL
0–13–071266–3 Prentice-Hall pb $7.95

• Dave Jennings, Rick Danmeier & Chris Bahr
THE ART OF PLACE-KICKING AND PUNTING
0–671–55721–1 Simon & Schuster pb $11.95

• Joe Namath
FOOTBALL FOR YOUNG PLAYERS AND PARENTS
0–671–63953–6 Simon & Schuster pb $10.95

• Bill Walsh & others, editors
THE ILLUSTRATED NFL PLAYBOOK
0–89480–210–0 Workman pb $8.95

• Bud Wilkinson
SPORTS ILLUSTRATED FOOTBALL WINNING OFFENSE
From Oklahoma's coach in the glory years of the 1950s
0–452–26035–3 NAL pb $9.95

SPORTS ILLUSTRATED FOOTBALL: Defense
0–452–26036–1 NAL pb $9.95

GOLF

Thomas Boswell
STROKES OF GENIUS
A great writer on the greatest shots ever made
0–385–19968–6 Doubleday $19.95

• Mike Bryan
DOGLEG MADNESS
A notable new novel; takes on the history and sociology of golf
0–87113–176–5 Atlantic Monthly $17.95

• Stephen Goodwin
THE GREATEST MASTERS: The 1986 Masters and Golf's Elite
An incredibly rich book, considering that all the action takes place in a four-day span
0–06–015874–3 Harper & Row $17.95

• Bobby Jones
BOBBY JONES ON GOLF
A broad look at the game of golf
0–914178–88–1 Golf Digest $9.95

• Bobby Jones & O.B. Keeler
DOWN THE FAIRWAY
Possibly the best golf book ever written
0–940889–00–5 Classics of Golf $17.95

• R.R. Knudson
BABE DIDRIKSON: Athlete of the Century
0–670–80550–5 Viking $10.95
0–14–032095–4 Penguin pb $3.50

• Tony Lema & G.S. Brown
GOLFER'S GOLD
An amusing look at the pro tour
0–940889–17–X Classics of Golf $17.95

• Charles MacDonald
SCOTLAND'S GIFT—GOLF
0–940889–07–2 Classics of Golf $17.95

• Mark McCormack
THE WORLD OF PROFESSIONAL GOLF
The business of golf
0–688–07029–9 Morrow $22.50

• Michael Murphy
GOLF IN THE KINGDOM
Murphy has been called the Carlos
Casteneda of golf writers; a fictional
account of a golfer finding enlightenment
0–440–53092–X Doubleday pb $9.95

• Greg Norman with George Peper
SHARK ATTACK!
The Great White Shark tells all
0–671–64316–9 Simon & Schuster $19.95

• George Peper, editor
GOLF IN AMERICA: The First 100 Years
Golf heroes, major championships, and
players of the decade; superbly illustrated
0–8109–1032–2 Abrams $39.95

• Gene Sarazen with Herbert Warren
Wind
30 YEARS OF CHAMPIONSHIP GOLF
0–940889–113–7 Classics of Golf $17.95

• Lee Trevino with Sam Blair
**THE SNAKE IN THE SANDTRAP (AND
OTHER MISADVENTURES ON THE
GOLF TOUR)**
A quick read by a prolific tipster
0–8050–0368–1 Henry Holt pb $5.95

• US Golf Association
GOLF RULES IN PICTURES
An illustrated rule book
0–399–50984–4 Putnam pb $6.95

• US Golf Association & St. Andrews
Golf Club
DECISION ON THE RULES OF GOLF
Tips for every conceivable links disaster—
and they all really happened
0–318–03115–9 US Golf Association $25.00

• Tom Watson & Frank Hannigan
**THE NEW RULES OF GOLF: The
1988–1991 Edition**
0–394–56271–2 Random House $14.95

**THE RULES OF GOLF ILLUSTRATED
AND EXPLAINED**
0–686–30837–9 US Golf Association pb $7.95

• Herbert Warren Wind
THE STORY OF AMERICAN GOLF
A comprehensive examination of American
golf since its inception
0–936557–02–8 Old Golf Shop $34.95

Golf Instruction

• Tommy Armour
**HOW TO PLAY YOUR BEST GOLF ALL
THE TIME**
Tips from the Silver Scot
0–671–21150–1 Simon & Schuster pb $6.95

• Seve Ballesteros & John Andrisani
NATURAL GOLF
An extensively illustrated manual
0–689–11846–5 Macmillan $29.95

• Percy Boomer
ON LEARNING GOLF
The underground classic; noted for its
famous description of the swing through
"feel"
0–394–41008–4 Knopf $18.95

• Ben Hogan
MODERN FUNDAMENTALS OF GOLF
Hogan's landmark book from 1957
0–671–61297–2 Simon & Schuster pb $6.95

BEN HOGAN'S POWER GOLF
An expert practitioner of the perfect swing
0–671–60258–6 Pocket pb $3.95

• John Jacobs & Ken Bowden
PRACTICAL GOLF
Easy to read, well-illustrated
0–689–70634–0 Atheneum pb $13.95

• Ernest Jones
SWING THE CLUBHEAD
Jones uses simplified imagery to expound
his particular theories of the swing
0–914178–91–1 Golf Digest $9.95

• Nancy Lopez with Don Wade
NANCY LOPEZ'S COMPLETE GOLFER
One of the few books written by and for
women golfers
0–8092–4712–7 Contemporary $19.95

• Richard Metz
THE GRADUATED SWING METHOD
A small but intriguing book
0–684–18365–X Scribners pb $9.95

• Jack Nicklaus
GOLF MY WAY
An overall examination of his techniques
0–671–22278–3 Simon & Schuster pb $10.95

**MY 55 WAYS TO LOWER YOUR GOLF
SCORE**
A series of tips rather than a detailed study
0–671–55395–X Simon & Schuster pb $8.95

• Arnold Palmer
MY GAME AND YOURS
0–671–47195–3 Simon & Schuster pb $9.95

• Arnold Palmer with Peter Dobereiner
**ARNOLD PALMER'S COMPLETE BOOK
OF PUTTING**
0–689–11624–1 Atheneum $24.95

• Arnold Palmer with Kenneth van
Kampen
**PLAY GREAT GOLF: Mastering the
Fundamentals of the Game**
0–385–24301–4 Doubleday $24.95

• Sam Snead
GOLF BEGINS AT 40
Advice for the older golfer; a how-to for
maintaining, rather than improving, one's
game
0–385–27642–7 Doubleday pb $12.95

• Ken Venturi with Al Barkow
THE VENTURI ANALYSIS
Studies the swings of the best modern
players
0–940889–08–0 Classics of Golf $17.95

• Tom Watson
GETTING UP AND DOWN
Technique and tricks of the short game
0–394–75300–3 Random House pb $9.95

Golf Courses

• Golf Digest
**THE 100 GREATEST GOLF COURSES
AND THEN SOME**
Broken down by region, and includes
lesser-known courses
0–394–56197–X Golf Digest $29.95

• F.W. Hawtree
**THE GOLF COURSE: Planning, Design,
Construction and Management**
A primer on creating resort, club, and
public courses
0–419–12250–8 Methuen $45.00

• Tom Hepburn & Selwyn Jacobson
**THE WORLD'S TOUGHEST GOLF
HOLES**
0–8431–1062–7 Price Stern Sloan $19.95

• George Peper
GOLF COURSES OF THE PGA TOUR
A beautifully illustrated book from *Golf*
magazine
0–8109–0994–4 Abrams $39.95

• Pat Ward-Thomas & others
THE WORLD ATLAS OF GOLF
Reputable British writers on golf
Foreword by Alistair Cooke
0–8317–9501–8 W.H. Smith $18.00

Golf Humor

• Bob Hope
**BOB HOPE'S CONFESSIONS OF A
HOOKER: My Lifelong Affair with Golf**
0–385–18896–X Doubleday pb $9.95

● Dan Jenkins
DEAD SOLID PERFECT
The life and times of a mythical golf pro
0–8431–1568–8 Price Stern Sloan pb $8.95

THE DOGGED VICTIMS OF INEXORABLE FATE
A collection of clever pieces written for *Sports Illustrated*
0–940889–03–X Classics of Golf $19.95

● Rex Lardner
DOWNHILL LIES AND OTHER FALSEHOODS: Or How to Play Dirty Golf
One of the funniest books of the genre
0–8015–2198–X Dutton pb $5.95

● P.G. Wodehouse
FORE!: The Best of P.G. Wodehouse on Golf
0–89919–358–7 Ticknor & Fields pb $7.95

Nina Garfinkel & Maria Reidelbach
MINIATURE GOLF
A celebration of America's roadside pastime, complete with a shaggy astroturf cover
0–89659–684–2 Abbeville $19.95

ICE HOCKEY

● Bruce Cooper & Gene Hart
THE HOCKEY TRIVIA BOOK
0–88011–233–6 Leisure pb $10.95

● Dan Diamond
HOCKEY: The Years Since Expansion, 1967–1987
0–385–25120–3 Doubleday pb $16.95

● Stan Fischler & Shirley Fischler
EVERYBODY'S HOCKEY BOOK
For the novice
0–684–18022–7 Scribners $22.50
0–684–18507–5 Scribners pb $12.95

● Zander Hollander & Hal Bock, editors
THE COMPLETE ENCYCLOPEDIA OF HOCKEY
Foreword by John Ziegler
0–453–00449–0 NAL $25.50

● Frank Polnaszek
505 HOCKEY QUESTIONS YOUR FRIENDS CAN'T ANSWER
0–8027–0669–X Walker $9.95
0–8027–7167–X Walker pb $3.95

● Gary Ronberg
THE ILLUSTRATED HOCKEY ENCYCLOPEDIA
0–917439–03–1 Balsam $24.95

THE SPORTING NEWS HOCKEY GUIDE, 1988–1989
0–89204–290–7 Sporting News pb $10.95

THE SPORTING NEWS HOCKEY REGISTER, 1988–1989
0–89204–291–5 Sporting News pb $10.95

Hockey Players

Ken Dryden
THE GAME
Probably the best book on hockey now available. Dryden was the Montreal Canadiens' premier goalie until he quit to study law. Contemplative, candid, and funny, it is unique among books of this kind in that Dryden really wrote it himself
0–14–007412–0 Penguin pb $6.95

● Stan Fischler
HOCKEY'S ONE HUNDRED: A Personal Ranking of the Best Players in Hockey History
Hull, Howe, Mikita, Orr, and others
0–8253–0245–5 Beaufort pb $9.95

● George Plimpton
OPEN NET
Plimpton's brief and bruising sojourn with the Boston Bruins, under the tutelage of Jerry Cheevers
0–14–009709–0 Penguin pb $6.95

● Vladisla Tretyak with V. Snegirev
THE HOCKEY I LOVE
By the great Soviet goalie (in the nets in 1980 when the Americans won) and one of the most formidable hockey talents who ever lived
0–88208–080–6 Lawrence Hill pb $7.50

Hockey Instruction

● Jack Falla
SPORTS ILLUSTRATED HOCKEY: Learn to Play the Modern Way
Probably the best of the instructional books
0–452–26042–6 NAL pb $9.95

HOCKEY RULES IN PICTURES
From the National Hockey League
0–399–51480–5 Putnam pb $6.95

● Roy Nelson
BOBBY HULL'S HOCKEY MADE EASY
For juniors
0–8253–0226–9 Beaufort pb $9.95

● Guy Palmer
HOCKEY DRILL BOOK
0–918438–76–4 Leisure pb $14.95

HOCKEY COACHING
By the staff of the US Amateur Hockey Coaching Association
0–684–17457–X Scribners $29.95

● Denis Potvin with Stan Fischler
POWER ON ICE
The techniques that made Potvin one of the best defensemen ever. For younger players
0–06–013387–2 Harper & Row $12.95

HORSE RACING

● Bill Barich
LAUGHING AT THE HILLS
A personal description of a racetrack in California
0–14–005832–X Penguin pb $6.95

● Dick Francis
A JOCKEY'S LIFE: The Biography of Lester Piggot
The detective writer and former jockey tries his hand at biography and it comes off very well. The life of Britain's best-known jockey
0–449–21330–7 Fawcett pb $4.95

THE SPORT OF QUEENS: The Autobiography of Dick Francis
0–445–40331–7 Mysterious pb $4.95

● Barry Gifford
A DAY AT THE RACES
In the style of Studs Terkel's *Working*, the characters that the track life attracts tell their stories
0–87113–195–1 Atlantic Monthly $17.95

● Joe Hirsch & Jim Bolus
KENTUCKY DERBY
A well-illustrated coffee table book of the peak event of the racing calendar
0–07–029069–5 McGraw-Hill $39.95

● Henry Hornstein & Brendan Boyd
RACING DAYS
There is very little to say about racing that this pictorial doesn't cover. The best picture book of a very graphic sport
0–670–81873–9 Viking $30.00

● William Nack
SECRETARIAT: The Making of a Champion
The horse whose records at Churchill Downs, Pimlico and Belmont still stand. "This book is supposed to be about a horse and racing. It misses the mark entirely and ends up, I think, as major reading"—Jimmy Breslin
0–306–80317–8 Da Capo pb $10.95

● Willie Shoemaker with Barney Nagler
SHOEMAKER: America's Greatest Jockey
0–385–23945–9 Doubleday $17.95

● Woody Stephens with James Brough
GUESS I'M LUCKY
The feisty trainer who saddled five straight Belmont Stakes winners tells his own story
0–14–010277–9 Penguin pb $3.95

● Guy St. John Williams & Francis Hyland
THE IRISH DERBY: 1866–1979
Another beautifully illustrated volume. The top winners may not have much to say, but they do make for a pretty picture
0–85131–358–2 Sporting Book Center $29.95

Handicapping

- **Tom Ainslie**
  TOM AINSLIE'S COMPLETE GUIDE TO THOROUGHBRED RACING
  The most important book on the subject. Clearly explains everything one needs to handicap a race, without burdening the reader with "foolproof" methods
  0–671–65655–4 Simon & Schuster pb $9.95

  AINSLIE'S ENCYCLOPEDIA OF THOROUGHBRED HANDICAPPING
  0–688–00446–0 Morrow pb $14.95

  TOM AINSLIE'S NEW COMPLETE GUIDE TO HARNESS RACING
  The only book worth reading on harness racing. It does for trotters what his other books do for thoroughbreds
  0–671–63036–9 Simon & Schuster pb $10.95

- **Andrew Beyer**
  PICKING WINNERS: A Horseplayer's Guide to Handicapping
  A good how-to for gamblers who would rather have been statisticians, by the guru of speed handicappers
  0–395–39379–5 Houghton Mifflin pb $7.95

  THE WINNING HORSEPLAYER: A Revolutionary Approach to Thoroughbred Handicapping and Betting
  A pleasant and amusing introduction to thoroughbred racing and to the handicapping methods of this Harvard dropout and *Washington Post* racing writer. Interesting even if you never buy the *Daily Racing Form*
  0–395–37761–7 Houghton Mifflin pb $8.95

- **James Quinn**
  THE BEST OF THOROUGHBRED HANDICAPPING: Advice on Handicapping from the Experts
  0–688–07012–4 Morrow $16.95

SAILING

- **Henry Beard & Roy McKie**
  SAILING
  0–89480–158–9 Workman $8.95
  0–89480–144–9 Workman pb $5.95

- **Bob Bond**
  THE HANDBOOK OF SAILING
  0–394–50838–6 Knopf $24.95

- **Bob Bond & Steve Sleight**
  SMALL BOAT SAILING: A Basic Guide
  0–394–52446–2 Knopf $15.95

- **Alan Dear**
  THE POCKET OXFORD GUIDE TO SAILING TERMS
  0–19–211663–0 Oxford $26.00
  0–19–282012–5 Oxford pb $10.95

- **Halsey Herreshoff, editor**
  THE SAILOR'S HANDBOOK
  0–316–54693–3 Little, Brown $14.95

- **Gary Jobson & Mike Toppa**
  SPEED SAILING
  0–688–03974–X Morrow $19.95

- **Elbert S. Maloney, editor**
  CHAPMAN PILOTING, SEAMANSHIP, AND SMALL BOAT HANDLING
  0–688–07246–1 Morrow $25.00

- **Tony Meisel**
  SINGLEHANDING: A Sailor's Guide
  0–02–583930–6 Macmillan $16.95

- **Larry & Lin Pardey**
  THE SELF-SUFFICIENT SAILOR
  0–393–03269–8 Norton $19.95

- **Wallace Ross**
  SAIL POWER: The Complete Guide to Sails and Sail Handling
  0–394–72715–0 Knopf pb $19.95

Sailboat Racing

- **Dennis Conner with Bruce Stannard**
  COMEBACK: My Race for the America's Cup
  Foreword by Walter Cronkite
  0–312–01749–9 St. Martin's pb $7.95

- **Stephen Falk**
  FUNDAMENTALS OF SAILBOAT RACING: A Complete Guide to Getting the Most from Your Boat and from Yourself
  0–312–31151–6 St. Martin's pb $6.95

- **Buddy Melges & Charles Mason**
  SAILING SMART: Winning Techniques, Tactics, and Strategies
  0–03–058579–1 Henry Holt $16.95

- **Jeff Toghill**
  YACHT RACING FOR BEGINNERS
  0–393–30297–0 Norton pb $6.95

- **Cornelius Van Rietschoten & Barry Pickthall**
  BLUE WATER RACING
  0–396–08754–X Dodd, Mead $24.95

- **Stuart Walker**
  ADVANCED RACING TACTICS
  0–393–30333–0 Norton pb $14.95

  TACTICS OF SMALL BOAT RACING
  0–393–03132–2 Norton $18.95

  WIND AND STRATEGY
  0–393–03136–5 Norton $20.00

SKIING

- **Steve Barnett**
  THE BEST SKI TOURING IN AMERICA
  Describes 31 classic ski tours of the best wilderness skiing in the United States, Canada, and Mexico
  0–87156–722–9 Sierra Club pb $10.95

- **John Caldwell**
  THE NEW CROSS-COUNTRY SKI BOOK
  "The Bible of the sport"—*Boston Globe*
  0–8289–0611–4 Stephen Greene pb $10.95

- **Karl Gamma**
  THE HANDBOOK OF SKIING
  0–394–51827–6 Knopf $24.95

- **Ned Gillette & John Dostal**
  CROSS-COUNTRY SKIING
  A complete guide to the sport that experts believe is the near-perfect form of exercise. More than 200 sequence photos, and the latest techniques and equipment
  0–89886–171–3 Mountaineers pb $10.95

- **William Hall**
  CROSS-COUNTRY SKIING RIGHT
  Equipment, technique, touring, and training
  0–06–250170–4 Harper & Row $17.95

- **Gordan Hardy & Jay Carroll**
  THE TELEMARK SKI BOOK: An Introduction to Cross Country Downhill
  0–8289–0545–2 Stephen Greene pb $7.95

- **Mark Heller**
  SKIING SCHOOL: An Illustrated Course in Downhill and Cross-Country Skiing
  0–8120–5836–4 Barron's $19.95

- **Brian Jackman & others**
  WE LEARNED TO SKI
  "Far and away the best book yet written on skiing"—*The Skier*
  0–312–85859–0 St. Martin's pb $10.95

- **Bob Jonas & Seth Masia**
  SKI MAGAZINE'S TOTAL SKIING
  An illustrated guide to every skiing style and terrain
  0–399–13171–X Putnam $19.95

- **Billy Kidd with Bill Grout**
  BILLY KIDD'S SKI RACING BOOK
  0–8092–5412–3 Contemporary pb $11.95

- **Richard Needlam**
  SKI: 50 Years in North America
  An informative and glamorous look at the sport
  0–8109–1504–9 Abrams $39.95

- **Paul Parker**
  FREE HEEL-SKIING: The Secrets of Telemark and Parallel Techniques
  For beginners and intermediate skiers
  0–930031–18–0 Chelsea Green pb $19.95

- **Lito Tejada-Flores**
  BREAKTHROUGH ON SKIS: How to Get Out of the Intermediate Rut
  "A rarity: a book by a ski instructor who can really write"—*Skiing Magazine*
  0–394–74703–8 Random House pb $8.95

SOCCER

- **Kurt Ascherman & Jim San Marco**
  COACHING KIDS TO PLAY SOCCER
  A complete guide to youth coaching, for both the experienced coach and the clueless parent who has just been drafted to take charge of a team
  0–671–63936–6 Simon & Schuster pb $7.95

- **Eric Batty**
  COACHING MODERN SOCCER: Defence
  0–571–11773–2 Faber & Faber pb $9.95

  COACHING MODERN SOCCER: Attack
  0–571–11605–1 Faber & Faber pb $9.95

- Stanley Lover
SOCCER MATCH CONTROL
0-7207-1655-1 Penguin pb $12.95

- Larry Maisner
PRACTICAL SOCCER TACTICS
For the player and coach, as well as the novice spectator who wants to be able to follow more than the ball
0-02-028790-9 Macmillan pb $7.95

- Bobby Moffat
THE BASIC SOCCER GUIDE
A very basic guide from the former NASL star
0-02-028780-1 Macmillan pb $7.95

THE INTERMEDIATE SOCCER GUIDE
0-24-99280-1 Macmillan pb $12.95

- Bryan Robson
BRYAN ROBSON'S SOCCER SKILLS
From England's top player, skills and training tips with color photos and diagrams
0-8069-6654-8 Sterling pb $9.95

- Alan Tomlinson & Garry Whannell, editors
OFF THE BALL: The 1986 Football World Cup
0-7453-0122-3 Longwood pb $6.95

TENNIS

- Rex Bellamy
GAME, SET AND DEADLINE: A Tennis Odyssey
0-434-98090-0 David & Charles $29.95

- John McPhee
LEVELS OF THE GAME
A narrative of a US Open semifinal between Arthur Ashe and Clark Graebner, with an eye for the contrasting styles and backgrounds of the players. A masterful account
0-374-51526-3 Farrar, Straus & Giroux pb $6.95

- Ilie Nastase
BREAK POINT
One of tennis's premier bad boys tries his hand at fiction in this story of murder and intrigue on the international circuit
0-312-90327-8 St. Martin's pb $4.50

- Fred Stolle with Kenneth Wydro
TENNIS DOWN UNDER
Tennis in Australia
Foreword by John Newcombe
0-915765-18-7 National Press $12.95
0-915765-07-1 National Press pb $5.95

- Tony Trabert with Gerald Couzens
TRABERT ON TENNIS: The View from Center Court
The current state of the game, from the CBS analyst and former Wimbledon champ
0-8092-4664-3 Contemporary $17.95

Photograph by Walter Iooss, Sports Illustrated, from Hitting Hot: Ivan Lendl's 14-Day Tennis Clinic *(Random House)*

Tennis Biographies

- Larry Englemann
THE GODDESS AND THE AMERICAN GIRL: Suzanne Lenglen and Helen Wills
Two stars of the golden age of sports in the 1920s, whose fame and fortune equaled that of Babe Ruth, Bobby Jones, and Jack Dempsey
0-19-504363-4 Oxford $21.95

- Martina Navratilova with George Vecsey
MARTINA
Even with eight Wimbledon titles under her belt, she remains one of the most misunderstood figures in sports. Here she writes candidly of her youth in Czechoslavakia, her emigration to the West, her bisexuality, and her well-known entourage of friends
0-449-20982-2 Fawcett pb $3.95

- Pam Shriver with Susan Adams & Frank Deford
PAM SHRIVER: A Season on Tour
A thoughtful and entertaining diary of nomadic life on the women's pro circuit, by a frequent doubles champion and singles bridesmaid
0-07-057177-5 McGraw-Hill $16.95

Tennis Instruction

- Vic Braden with Bill Bruns
VIC BRADEN'S QUICK FIXES: Expert Cures for Common Tennis Problems
The latest book by the most visible teaching pro in America
0-316-10514-7 Little, Brown $17.95

VIC BRADEN'S TENNIS FOR THE FUTURE
A mix of one-liners and tennis pointers and theory has made this book the classic of tennis instruction
0-316-10511-2 Little, Brown pb $14.95

- Lewis Brewer, editor
PROFESSIONAL TENNIS DRILLS
Seventy-five drills from US Tennis Association professionals, covering strokes and footwork, conditioning, and game strategy
0-684-18298-X Scribners pb $9.95

- Jimmy Connors with Robert LaMarche
HOW TO PLAY TOUGHER TENNIS
0-394-56195-3 Random House $18.95

- W. Timothy Gallwey
THE INNER GAME OF TENNIS
A bestseller on winning the mind game
0-553-27372-8 Bantam pb $4.50

- Ivan Lendl with Eugene Scott
IVAN LENDL'S TENNIS TECHNIQUE BOOK
0-686-44921-5 Simon & Schuster pb $8.95

- Martina Navratilova with Mary Carillo
TENNIS MY WAY: A Complete Guide to Training and Playing
0-14-007183-0 Penguin pb $6.95

- Dennis Ralston with Steve Flink & Bud Freeman
DENNIS RALSTON'S TENNIS WORKBOOK
By the Hall of Fame player and coach of Chris Evert, among others. Covers the strokes and the strategy, and includes checklists and performance charts to keep track of your development
0-13-198615-5 Prentice-Hall $19.95
0-13-198607-4 Prentice-Hall pb $12.95

- William Talbert & Bruce Old
TENNIS TACTICS: Singles and Doubles
0-06-091090-9 Harper & Row pb $8.95

OTHER TEAM SPORTS

Cricket

- Keith Andrew
THE SKILLS OF CRICKET
0-946284-93-8 Longwood pb $6.50

- Michael & Simon Davie, editors
THE FABER BOOK OF CRICKET
0-571-14777-1 Faber & Faber $15.95

- Hugh Formhals
THE JOLLIEST GAME UNDER THE SUN: A Beginner's Guide to Cricket
0-911265-04-X Western Mountain pb $10.95

- C.L.R. James
BEYOND A BOUNDARY
A Trinidadian historian writes of his life in cricket and of the place of sport in colonialism
0-394-72283-3 Pantheon pb $8.95

Field Hockey

- Donna Fong
**THE COACHES' COLLECTION OF
FIELD HOCKEY DRILLS**
0–88011–040–6 Leisure pb $9.95

- Jenny John
FIELD HOCKEY HANDBOOK
0–88839–043–2 Hancock House pb $8.95

Lacrosse

Lacrosse is a truly American sport, slowly breaking out of its Northeast prep school stronghold.

- Bob Scott
LACROSSE: Technique and Tradition
Instructional overview of the sport by the former coach of the Hopkins powerhouse, with an emphasis on strategy
0–8018–2060–X Johns Hopkins pb $10.95

- David Urick
**SPORTS ILLUSTRATED LACROSSE:
Fundamentals and Strategies for Winning**
0–452–26102–3 NAL pb $9.95

Volleyball

- Bob Bertucci, editor
**THE AVCA VOLLEYBALL MANUAL
HANDBOOK: The Official Handbook of
the American Volleyball Coaches'
Association**
0–940279–11–8 Masters pb $14.95

- Jeff Lucas
PASS, SET, CRUSH: Volleyball Illustrated
A shot-by-shot guide with detailed illustrations
0–9615088–3–3 Euclid Northwest pb $12.95

- Joe Pedersen & Victor Loggins
**BUMP, SET, SPIKE: Everybody's
Volleyball Book**
A lively handbook to all the incarnations of the game, from the beach to the college arena
0–8092–5075–6 Contemporary pb $9.95

- Arie Selenger
**ARIE SELENGER'S POWER
VOLLEYBALL**
A big book of technique and strategy from the coach of the 1984 US Women's Olympic team
0–312–04916–1 St. Martin's pb $27.95

RACKET SPORTS

Racquetball and Badminton

- James Breen & Donald Paup
**WINNING BADMINTON: A Coaching
and Playing Guide**
0–87670–067–9 Athletic Institute pb $7.95

- Marty Hogan with Ken Wong
HIGH-PERFORMANCE RACQUETBALL
The man who revolutionized the sport tells you how to play it his way
Foreword by Steve Garvey
0–89586–356–1 HP pb $8.95

- Marty Hogan with Ed Turner
**SKILLS AND STRATEGIES FOR
WINNING RACQUETBALL**
More technical than *High-Performance Racquetball*. Includes a section on advanced play
0–88011–289–1 Leisure pb $12.95

- Jack Kramer
BEGINNER'S RACQUETBALL
0–02–028250–8 Macmillan pb $6.95

- Dave Peck with Jerry Day & Armen Keteyian
**DAVE PECK'S WORLD
CHAMPIONSHIP RACQUETBALL:
Learning to Play by the Numbers**
Features a situation-by-situation shot guide, along with general information about equipment, training, and rules
0–671–49434–1 Simon & Schuster pb $8.95

- Victor Spear
**SPORTS ILLUSTRATED
RACQUETBALL**
0–452–26043–4 NAL pb $9.95

Squash

- Alan Colburn
SQUASH: The Ambitious Player's Guide
0–571–13361–4 Faber & Faber pb $9.95

- Jahangir Khan with Ramat Khan & Richard Eaton
WINNING SQUASH
A guide to the game from the world champion star of squash's Khan dynasty, interspersed with accounts of Khan's greatest matches
0–13–961103–7 Prentice-Hall pb $8.95

- Crawford Lindsey
**THE BOOK OF SQUASH: A Total
Approach to the Game**
0–87833–547–1 Taylor $18.95
0–87833–574–9 Taylor pb $12.95

- John O. Truby, Jr.
**THE SCIENCE AND STRATEGY OF
SQUASH**
0–684–14260–0 Scribners pb $12.50

- John O. Truby, Jr. & John O. Truby
**THE SECRET OF SQUASH: How to Win
Using the 4-CRO System**
An advanced system of shot-making and strategy
0–316–85353–4 Little, Brown pb $8.95

Table Tennis

- Dick Miles
**SPORTS ILLUSTRATED TABLE
TENNIS**
0–397–01036–2 Harper & Row pb $2.95

WINTER SPORTS

Curling

- E. Lukowich & others
CURLING TO WIN
0–07–549–442–6 McGraw-Hill pb $11.95

Figure Skating

- Carlo Fassi
FIGURE SKATING WITH CARLO FASSI
From the fabled coach of Olympic champions Peggy Fleming and Dorothy Hamill
0–684–16314–4 Scribners $17.95
0–684–17644–0 Scribners pb $12.95

- Ricky Harris
**CHOREOGRAPHY AND STYLE FOR
ICE SKATERS**
0–312–13388–X St. Martin's $11.95

- John Hennessy
TORVILL AND DEAN
The champion ice dancers
0–312–80937–9 St. Martin's pb $6.95

- Thomas Lynch
SKATING WITH HEATHER GRACE
0–394–55480–9 Knopf $14.95
0–394–74756–9 Knopf pb $9.95

- John Petkevich
THE SKATER'S HANDBOOK
Foreword by Scott Hamilton
0–684–18016–2 Scribners $15.95

**SPORTS ILLUSTRATED FIGURE
SKATING: Championship Techniques**
0–452–26209–7 NAL pb $9.95

- Michael Steere
SCOTT HAMILTON
Biography of the popular figure skater
0–312–70449–6 St. Martin's $17.95

> Julia Whedon
> **THE FINE ART OF ICE SKATING:
> An Illustrated History and Portfolio of
> Stars**
> A lavishly illustrated account of skating, its history and performers. A romantic as well as practical look at the sport
> 0–8109–1127–2 Abrams $35.00

WATER SPORTS

Canoeing and Kayaking

- Jock Bearse
**COMPLETE CANOE CAMPER AND
TRIPPER**
0–8289–0575–4 Stephen Greene $10.95

- Raymond Bridge
THE COMPLETE CANOEIST'S GUIDE
0–684–17176–7 Scribners pb $3.95

**THE COMPLETE GUIDE TO
KAYAKING**
0–684–15040–9 Scribners pb $4.95

Debbie Thomas in a photo by Margaret Williamson from The Art of Ice Skating *(Abrams)*

- James Davidson & John Rugge
THE COMPLETE WILDERNESS PADDLER
0–394–71153–X Random House pb $8.95

- Eliot DuBois
AN INNOCENT ON THE MIDDLE FORK: A Whitewater Adventure in Idaho's Wilderness
0–89886–125–X Mountaineers pb $9.95

- Jay Evans
THE KAYAKING BOOK
0–8289–0663–7 Stephen Greene pb $13.95

- Cliff Jacobson
THE NEW WILDERNESS CANOEING AND CAMPING
A practical introduction to canoe tripping
Illustrated by Cliff Moen
0–934802–29–7 ICS pb $14.95

- John McPhee
THE SURVIVAL OF THE BARK CANOE
0–374–27207–7 Farrar, Straus & Giroux $13.95
0–374–51693–6 Farrar, Straus & Giroux pb $7.95

- Carl & Marge Shepardson
THE FAMILY CANOE TRIP
0–934802–15–7 ICS pb $14.95

Diving

- Sammy Lee with Steve Lehrman
DIVING
By the coach of the Olympic gold-medalist, Greg Louganis
0–689–10815–X Atheneum pb $7.95

Rowing

- Bruce Brown
LONG STROKES
Gets you started in long-distance rowing, with tales of races that make you want to outfit your boat and start sculling
0–87742–950–2 International Marine $14.95

- David Churbuck
THE BOOK OF ROWING
0–87951–292–X Overlook $25.00

- David Halberstam
THE AMATEURS
0–688–04948–6 Morrow $14.95
0–14–008934–9 Penguin pb $6.95

- Benjamin Ivry
REGATTA: A Celebration of Oarsmanship
0–671–64711–3 Simon & Schuster $29.95

- Stephen Kiesling
THE SHELL GAME: Reflections on Rowing
0–688–00958–1 Morrow $10.50
0–8092–5570–7 Contemporary pb $8.95

- Susan Lezotte
ROWING: Power and Endurance
0–8092–4729–1 Contemporary pb $6.95

- Gordon Newell
READY ALL: George Yeoman Pocock and Crew Racing
0–295–96473–1 Washington $19.95

Skin and Scuba Diving

- Hank Kotels & Jack McDowell
SPORTS ILLUSTRATED SCUBA DIVING: Underwater Adventuring
0–452–26108–2 NAL pb $9.95

- Robert Smith, editor
THE NEW SCIENCE OF SKIN AND SCUBA DIVING
The standard work for the recreational diver, now in its sixth edition
0–8329–0399–X New Century pb $10.95

Surfing

- Leonard Lueras
SURFING: The Ultimate Pleasure
0–89480–708–0 Workman pb $16.95

- Nat Young
THE HISTORY OF SURFING
A big picture book of a very photogenic sport
0–89586–637–4 Price Stern Sloan pb $18.95

SURFING FUNDAMENTALS: How to Ride a Modern Short Board, the Art of Riding a Malibu, Kneeboard, Wave-Ski and Boogie Board
0–89586–688–9 Price Stern Sloan pb $10.95

Water Skiing and Windsurfing

- Jeremy Evans
COMPLETE GUIDE TO WINDSURFING
0–8160–1527–9 Facts On File $17.95

- Bruce Kistler
HIT IT!: Your Guide to Waterskiing Fun
Foreword by Bruce Jenner
0–88011–313–8 Leisure pb $9.95

- Glenn Taylor
WINDSURFING: The Complete Guide
0–07–063158–1 McGraw-Hill pb $9.95

EQUESTRIAN SPORTS

▶ See also Pets

Polo

- Steven Price & Charles Kauffman
THE POLO PRIMER: A Guide for Players and Spectators
0–8289–0707–2 Viking $16.95

- W.G. Vickers
PRACTICAL POLO
Preface by Lord Cowdray
0–85131–186–5 Sydney Smith pb $10.00

Riding

- Judy Bradwell
EVENTING: Preparation, Training and Competition
0–87605–877–2 Howell $19.95

- Anthony Crossley
DRESSAGE: The Seat, Aids and Exercises
Techniques for achieving correct posture
0–7207–1777–9 Viking $15.95

- Mary Drummond
  LONG DISTANCE RIDING
  0–87605–861–6 Howell $16.95

- Elwyn Hartley-Edwards
  THE HOWELL BOOK OF SADDLERY AND TACK
  0–87605–873–X Howell $19.95

- Sheila Wall Hundt
  INVITATION TO RIDING
  Covers the range of riding events and techniques as well as the purchase and care of a horse
  0–671–54197–8 Simon & Schuster pb $10.95

- Jennie Loriston-Clarke
  THE COMPLETE GUIDE TO DRESSAGE
  0–89471–562–3 Running Press $19.95

- Jennie Loriston-Clarke & Carol Wicken
  AN ILLUSTRATED GUIDE TO DRESSAGE
  A guide for all levels, with sequence photos of the paces and movements of riding
  0–8289–0662–9 Stephen Greene $17.95

- Mark Phillips
  CAPTAIN MARK PHILLIPS ON RIDING: A Complete Guide for Beginners
  An introduction to horsemanship from an Olympic gold medalist and riding teacher married to fellow Olympic rider Princess Anne
  0–13–114521–5 Prentice-Hall $19.95

- Sarah Pilliner
  THE PERFORMANCE HORSE: Management, Care and Training
  0–87605–867–5 Howell $14.95

- John Smart
  SHOWJUMPING: Preparation Training and Competition
  0–87605–868–3 Howell $16.95

OLYMPIC SPORTS

- Steve Barr & John Poppy
  THE FLAME
  Story of the Olympic torch traveling across the country
  0–688–06557–0 Morrow $16.95

- Lewis Carlson & John Fogarty
  TALES OF GOLD: An Oral History of the Summer Olympic Games Told by America's Gold Medal Winners
  0–8092–5067–5 Contemporary $25.00

- Bill Toomey with Barry King
  THE OLYMPIC CHALLENGE 1988
  The players, the pageant, the spectacle, by the 1968 decathlon gold medalist
  0–937359–35–1 HDL pb $14.95

- David Wallechinsky
  THE COMPLETE BOOK OF THE OLYMPICS
  "The ultimate Olympic sourcebook . . . Humanity in all its pride and wonder"—*Times*
  0–14–010771–1 Penguin pb $12.95

Gymnastics

- Peter Aykroyd
  MODERN GYMNASTICS: Skills and Techniques
  Covers the four women's events with plenty of diagrams and photos of the world's best gymnasts
  0–668–06458–7 Arco $12.95
  0–668–06462–5 Arco pb $8.95

- John Goodbody
  THE ILLUSTRATED HISTORY OF GYMNASTICS
  0–09–143350–9 Beaufort $14.95

- Bill Sands & Mike Conklin
  EVERYBODY'S GYMNASTICS BOOK
  0–684–18091–X Scribners $19.95

- Don Tonry
  SPORTS ILLUSTRATED WOMEN'S GYMNASTICS: The Floor Exercise Event
  0–690–01909–2 Crowell $8.95

  SPORTS ILLUSTRATED WOMEN'S GYMNASTICS: The Vaulting, Balance Beam, and Uneven Parallel Bars Events
  0–690–01908–4 Crowell $8.95
  0–690–01906–8 Crowell pb $5.95

Track and Field

- William Baker
  JESSE OWENS: An American Life
  Dispels the myth of Owens as superman. "A remarkable biography"—*NY Times*
  0–02–901780–7 Free Press $19.95
  0–02–901760–2 Free Press pb $9.95

- Roger Bannister
  THE FOUR-MINUTE MILE
  0–396–07946–6 Dodd, Mead pb $5.95

- Peter Matthews
  TRACK AND FIELD ATHLETICS: The Records
  Part of the Guinness records series
  0–85112–463–1 Sterling pb $12.95

- John Randolph, editor
  CHAMPIONSHIP TRACK AND FIELD BY THE EXPERTS
  Volume 1: Track Events
  0–918438–14–4 Leisure pb $9.95
  Volume 2: Field Events
  0–918438–15–2 Leisure pb $9.95

- Myron Tassin
  BOB MATHIAS: The Life of the Olympic Champion
  Foreword by Bruce Jenner
  0–312–08730–6 St. Martin's $13.95

RECREATIONAL AND OTHER SPORTS

Archery

- Fred Bear
  THE ARCHER'S BIBLE
  0–385–15155–1 Doubleday pb $7.95

- John Williams
  ARCHERY FOR BEGINNERS
  An introductory guide to the equipment and technique from an Olympic gold medalist and the 1984 US Olympic coach
  0–8092–5256–2 Contemporary pb $8.95

Auto Racing

- Bob Bondurant with John Blakemore
  BOB BONDURANT ON HIGH PERFORMANCE DRIVING
  0–87938–256–2 Motorbooks International pb $12.95

- Allan Brown
  THE HISTORY OF THE AMERICAN SPEEDWAY
  0–931105–03–X Slideways $14.95
  0–931105–04–8 Slideways pb $8.95

- Tom Carnegie
  INDY 500: More Than a Race
  A big picture book of photos and anecdotes of the "Greatest Spectacle in Racing," by the track announcer for the Indianapolis Speedway
  0–07–050604–3 McGraw-Hill $34.95

- A.J. Foyt with William Neeley
  A.J.: My Life as America's Greatest Race Car Driver
  0–446–32418–3 Warner pb $3.50

- Robin MacGowan & Graham Watson
  KINGS OF THE ROAD: A Portrait of Racers and Racing
  0–88011–297–2 Leisure $22.95

- Ian Morrison
  MOTOR RACING: The Records
  The history and results of international racing; part of the Guinness series
  0–85112–890–4 Sterling pb $14.95

- Richard Petty with William Neely
  KING RICHARD I: The Autobiography of America's Greatest Auto Racer
  A career of racing with and beating the good old boys of the stock car circuit, from a man who has brought home the checkered flag over 200 times
  0–02–595910–7 Macmillan $17.95
  0–7701–0649–8 Paper Jacks pb $3.50

Bowling

- Earl Anthony with Dawson Taylor
  EARL ANTHONY'S CHAMPIONSHIP BOWLING
  0–8092–5490–5 Contemporary pb $9.95

• Marshall Holman with Roy Nelson
MARSHALL HOLMAN'S BOWLING TIPS AND TECHNIQUES
An advanced guide, including advice for would-be touring pros, from one of the PBA's most flamboyant and successful bowlers
0–8092–5324–0 Contemporary pb $8.95

• Chuck Pezzano
PROFESSIONAL BOWLERS ASSOCIATION GUIDE TO BETTER BOWLING: 25th Anniversary Edition
Tips from bowling's professionals with statistics and biographies from the history of the PBA
0–671–47244–5 Simon & Schuster pb $8.95

• Carmen Salvino with Frederick Klein
FAST LANES
After turning pro at age 17, he was a part of bowling's rise to television success and became a member of its Hall of Fame
0–933893–46–9 Bonus pb $9.95

• H. Thomas Steele
BOWL-O-RAMA: The Visual Arts of Bowling
0–89659–607–9 Abbeville $19.95

Bullfighting

• Barnaby Conrad
MATADOR
By a practiced American fan
0–88496–286–5 Capra $18.95

• Ernest Hemingway
DEATH IN THE AFTERNOON
0–684–71796–4 Scribners pb $14.95

• P. Hofer, editor
TAUROMAQUIA AND THE BULLS OF BORDEAUX
Bullfighting paintings by Goya
0–486–22342–6 Dover pb $7.95

• Garry Marvin
BULLFIGHT
An explanation of this singular sport and an anthropological examination of its place in Spanish culture
0–631–15471–X Blackwell $19.95

Croquet

• James Charlton & others
CROQUET: Its History, Strategy, Rules and Records
0–8289–0666–1 Stephen Greene pb $11.95

• Christopher Reaske
CROQUET: The Gentle but Wicket Game
A conversational, pun-laden guide to the game and its joys. "The next best thing to being out there on the cricket 'sward itself"—George Plimpton
0–525–48385–3 Dutton pb $11.95

• Donald Charles Richardson
CROQUET: The Art and Elegance of Playing the Game
Along with the history and techniques of the game, a menu for tea and a list of addresses where the fashions and accessories can be ordered
0–517–56826–8 Crown $19.95

Darts

• Keith Turner
DARTS: The Complete Book of the Game
0–06–097006–5 Harper & Row pb $4.95

Fencing

• Michel Alaux
MODERN FENCING
Foil, épée, and sabre, covered by the US Olympic coach
0–684–16945–2 Scribners pb $12.95

• Istvan Lukovich
FENCING
0–317–56214–2 Newbury $20.00

Frisbee

• Judy Horowitz & Billy Bloom
FRISBEE: More Than a Game of Catch
0–88011–105–4 Scribners pb $9.95

• Irv Kalb & Tom Kennedy
ULTIMATE: Fundamentals of the Sport
0–942156–00–5 Revolution pb $7.95

Handball

• John Reznik, editor
CHAMPIONSHIP HANDBALL BY THE EXPERTS
0–918438–04–7 Leisure pb $11.00

• Pete Tyson & James Turman, editors
THE HANDBALL BOOK
An exhaustive survey of the literature of the game. Every angle is covered by top players and coaches, and a bibliography is provided of those articles that didn't make this already thick volume
0–88011–065–1 Leisure pb $14.95

New Games

• Andrew Fluegelman, editor
THE NEW GAMES BOOK
Plenty of traditional and invented games, with a maximum of action and cooperation and a minimum of violence and overcompetition
0–385–12516–X Doubleday pb $9.95

MORE NEW GAMES AND PLAYFUL IDEAS
More new games, and a guide for inventing your own
0–385–17514–0 Doubleday pb $9.95

Pool and Billiards

• Robert Byrne
BYRNE'S STANDARD BOOK OF POOL AND BILLIARDS
0–15–614972–9 HBJ $12.95

BYRNE'S TREASURY OF TRICK SHOTS IN POOL AND BILLIARDS
0–15–115224–1 HBJ $19.95
0–15–614973–7 HBJ pb $14.95

• Ray Martin & Rosser Reeves
THE 99 CRITICAL SHOTS IN POOL
0–8129–6313–X Times Books pb $9.95

• Steve Mizerak
JUST SHOWIN' OFF
Trick shots and match strategy from the Miller Lite pitchman and billiards champion
0–8092–4602–3 Contemporary pb $7.95

Rodeo

• David Brown
GOLD BUCKLE DREAMS: The Rodeo Life of Chris LeDoux
0–933341–71–7 Quinlan $16.95

• Kristine Fredriksson
AMERICAN RODEO: From Buffalo Bill to Big Business
0–89096–181–6 Texas A&M $21.50

• Ben Maddow
RODEO: Photographs
0–942642–20–1 Twelve Trees $30.00

• Larry Pointer
RODEO CHAMPIONS: Eight Memorable Moments in Riding, Wrestling, and Roping
The action and the personalities of contemporary championship rodeo
0–8263–0798–1 New Mexico pb $9.95

• Ron Tyler
THE RODEO OF JOHN A. STRYKER
0–88426–050–X Encino $15.00

• Clifford Westermeier
MAN, BEAST, DUST: The Story of Rodeo
A classic immersion in the sport and its culture, recently reprinted after 40 years
0–8032–9715–7 Nebraska pb $10.95

Roller Skating

• Randy Dayney & Joel Cohen
WINNING ROLLER SKATING: Figure and Freestyle
0–8092–8153–8 Contemporary pb $5.95

• Hal Straus & Marilou Sturges
ROLLER SKATING GUIDE
0–89037–203–9 Anderson World pb $6.95

Shooting

• Art Blatt
GUN DIGEST BOOK OF TRAP AND SKEET SHOOTING
0–910676–66–6 DBI pb $14.95

• John Marchington
SHOOTING: A Complete Guide for Beginners
0–571–11932–8 Faber & Faber pb $7.95

• Claire Rees
BE AN EXPERT SHOT: With Rifle, Handgun, or Shotgun
0–8329–0358–2 New Century $19.95

Skateboarding

- Albert Cassorla
  THE ULTIMATE SKATEBOARD BOOK
  0–89471–565–8 Running Press $20.00
  0–89471–564–X Running Press pb $8.95

- Tom Culbertson
  ANYBODY'S SKATEBOARD BOOK
  0–913668–57–5 Ten Speed pb $3.00

Fitness

AEROBICS AND GENERAL FITNESS

- Bob Anderson
  STRETCHING FOR EVERYBODY
  0–394–73874–8 Shelter pb $9.95

- Kenneth Cooper
  THE AEROBICS PROGRAM FOR TOTAL WELL-BEING
  The man who started America running now brings you the ultimate fitness program
  0–553–34422–6 Bantam pb $11.95

- Michael Creedman
  THE NFL ALL-PRO WORKOUT: A Complete Conditioning Program for People of All Ages, Shapes, and Fitness Levels from NFL Trainers, Coaches, and Players
  0–312–01071–0 St. Martin's pb $12.95

- Ellington Darden
  THE NAUTILUS BOOK
  0–8092–4609–0 Contemporary pb $10.95

- Jane Fonda
  JANE FONDA'S WORKOUT BOOK
  Guarantees the reader a lifetime of health and energy
  0–671–50896–2 Simon & Schuster pb $10.95

- Jane Fonda & Mignon McCarthy
  WOMEN COMING OF AGE
  Words of wisdom on diet, exercise, sexuality, and self-image for women from age 35 to 65
  0–671–62102–5 Fireside pb $10.95

- Robert Haas
  EAT TO WIN: The Sports Nutrition Bible
  "A winning recipe for energy, strength, speed and endurance!"—*NY Times*
  Foreword by Martina Navratilova
  0–451–15509–2 NAL pb $4.95

- Richard Mangi & others
  SPORTS FITNESS AND TRAINING
  "Jam-packed with solid, accessible information, including exercises for individual injuries and sources of training equipment"—*Publisher's Weekly*
  0–679–72207–6 Pantheon pb $17.95

- Dan Millman
  THE WARRIOR ATHLETE: Mind, Body, and Spirit
  "An innovative approach to fitness that applies Eastern philosophies to the Western concepts of physical well-being"—*Publisher's Weekly*
  0–913299–22–7 Stillpoint pb $9.95

- George Sheehan
  DOCTOR SHEEHAN ON FITNESS
  Insight, information, and motivation for any athlete
  0–671–53020–8 Simon & Schuster pb $7.95

BICYCLING

- Dennis Coello
  THE ROADSIDE GUIDE TO BIKE REPAIR
  Pocket-size and easy to follow; as essential as your air pump
  0–446–34820–1 Warner pb $3.95

- David Duncan
  PEDALING THE ENDS OF THE EARTH
  A bicycling adventure covering 14,000 miles through 19 countries on four continents
  0–671–49289–6 Simon & Schuster $17.95

- Bernard Hinault with Claude Genzling
  ROAD RACING: Technique and Training
  The first book in English to bring you the training methods of the five-time winner of the Tour de France
  0–941950–13–1 Velo-news pb $16.95

- Greg LeMond with Kent Gordis
  GREG LEMOND'S COMPLETE BOOK OF BICYCLING
  One of the best cycling books by the American winner of the 1986 Tour de France
  0–399–51439–2 Putnam pb $9.95

- James McCullagh
  THE COMPLETE BICYCLE FITNESS BOOK
  0–446–38363–5 Warner pb $9.95

- Peter Nye
  HEART OF LIONS: The History of American Bicycle Racing
  Stories of the good old days when American cyclists were equals to Jack Dempsey and Ty Cobb
  Foreward by Eric Heiden
  0–393–02543–8 Norton $19.95

- Michael Shermer
  SPORT CYCLING: A Guide to Training, Racing and Endurance
  0–8092–5244–9 Contemporary pb $8.95

BODYBUILDING

- Charles Gaines & George Butler
  PUMPING IRON: The Art and Sport of Bodybuilding
  0–671–41737–1 Simon & Schuster $19.95
  0–671–42688–5 Simon & Schuster pb $10.95

- **PUMPING IRON II: The Unprecedented Woman**
  0–671–44105–1 Simon & Schuster pb $9.95

- Tom Kubistant
  MIND PUMP: The Psychology of Bodybuilding
  A systematic mental training approach for bodybuilders
  0–88011–296–4 Leisure pb $12.95

- Lynne Pirie & Bill Reynolds
  GETTING BUILT
  Written by a physician and surgeon and one of the world's top competitive bodybuilders
  0–446–38289–2 Warner pb $12.50

- Arnold Schwarzenegger & Bill Dobbins
  ARNOLD SCHWARZENEGGER ENCYCLOPEDIA OF MODERN BODYBUILDING
  Complete information on training principles, competition strategy, and nutrition
  0–671–63381–3 Fireside $18.95

MARTIAL ARTS

The martial arts are ancient systems of self-defense devised in China by monks and peasants as a means of protection against bandits and soldiers. Handed down from generation to generation, these slowly evolving disciplines are taught throughout the world and help the practitioner develop confidence, discipline, and strength. Though it's difficult (if not impossible) to become proficient from reading a book, we've included some of the best how-to guides to show the reader the particulars of the most common martial arts (karate, judo, t'ai chi, aikido), as well as to help students refine techniques with which they may already be familiar. Also, you'll find some inspirational biographies of the great masters and interesting accounts by westerners who traveled east to learn the ways of the warrior.

- Black Belt Magazine
  THE LEGENDARY BRUCE LEE
  Explores Lee's spartan training regime, the principles of *jeet kune do,* as well as the reality behind the man
  0–89750–106–3 Ohara pb $6.95

- Paul Crompton
  T'AI CHI FOR TWO: The Practice of Push Hands
  0–87773–468–2 Random House $14.95

- Deng Ming-Dao
  SEVEN BAMBOO TABLETS OF THE CLOUDY SATCHEL
  Part Chinese history, part biography, part Taoist thought
  0–06–250229–8 Harper & Row pb $7.95

- Michael Finn
  MARTIAL ARTS: A Complete History
  0–87951–335–7 Overlook $29.95

• Gichin Funakoshi
KARATE-DO: My Way of Life
The autobiography of the great karate master, filled with the incidents of a long and dedicated life
0–87011–463–8 Kodansha pb $4.95

• E.J. Harrison
THE FIGHTING SPIRIT OF JAPAN
An in-depth study of judo, karate, aikido, and jujitsu, written by an English journalist who spent 20 years in Japan
0–87951–154–0 Overlook pb $8.95

• Eugen Herrigel
ZEN IN THE ART OF ARCHERY
This remarkable book discusses how the practice of archery helps toward an understanding of Zen
0–394–71663–9 Random House pb $4.95

• Joe Hyams
ZEN IN THE MARTIAL ARTS
The author recounts his more than 25 years of experience in the martial arts under such masters as Ed Parker and Bruce Lee, and reveals how the application of Zen principles develops physical expertise and mental discipline
0–553–27559–3 Bantam pb $3.95

• Isao Inokuma & Nobuyuki Sato
BEST JUDO
Joint effort by two of Japan's foremost judo instructors
0–87011–786–6 Harper & Row pb $14.95

• Herman Kauz
TAI CHI HANDBOOK: Exercise, Meditation and Self Defense
0–385–09370–5 Doubleday pb $10.95

• Bruce Klickstein
LIVING AIKIDO
0–938190–85–7 North Atlantic pb $16.95

• Yagyu Munenori
THE SWORD AND THE MIND
A translation of the classic treatise on swordsmanship with commentary
Translated by Hiroaki Sato
0–87951–209–1 Overlook $16.95
0–87951–256–3 Overlook pb $8.95

• Miyamoto Musashi
A BOOK OF FIVE RINGS
Attributed to a legendary swordsman
0–553–27096–6 Bantam pb $3.95

• C.W. Nicol
MOVING ZEN: Karate As a Way to Gentleness
An extraordinary memoir, revealing the rites and disciplines of karate
0–688–01181–0 Morrow pb $7.95

• Howard Reid & Michael Croucher
THE WAY OF THE WARRIOR
Interviews with eight masters of the martial arts, studying the origins, evolution, and legends of the fighting arts
0–671–64674–5 Simon & Schuster pb $12.95

• Susan Ribner & Richard Chin
THE MARTIAL ARTS
0–06–440139–1 pb $4.95

Praying mantis style of kung fu, from The Martial Arts *by Susan Ribner and Richard Chin, illustrated by Melanie Gaines Arwin (Harper & Row)*

• Mark Salzman
IRON AND SILK
The adventures of a young martial arts master in China
0–394–55156–7 Random House $16.95
0–394–75511–1 Random House pb $5.95

MARK SALZMAN:
Favorite Books on Asian Martial Arts

Although martial arts have been practiced and written about in Asia for thousands of years, they have been popular in the West only since the early 1970s. A great number of martial arts books have been published in English since then. Unfortunately, most of these books cater to an audience with very low expectations. Only a few are both well written and successful in conveying something of the spirit or flavor of authentic martial arts.

Eugen Herrigel
ZEN IN THE ART OF ARCHERY
Eugen Herrigel spent a five-year apprenticeship in Japanese archery that resulted in his deep understanding of Zen and this wonderful book, written long before martial arts became a fad. Although not specifically about martial arts, it captures the philosophy of training that distinguishes Asian martial arts from western fencing or boxing
0–394–71663–9 Random House pb $4.95

Gichin Funakoshi
KARATE-DO: My Way of Life
In this brief, simple autobiography, Funakoshi, known in Japan as "the father of modern karate," tells us about his lifetime of studying, practicing, and teaching karate. He describes the austere beauty and discipline of martial arts without romanticizing the skills he developed
0–87011–241–4 Kodansha $14.95
0–87011–463–8 Kodansha pb $4.95

Donn Draeger & Robert Smith
COMPREHENSIVE ASIAN FIGHTING ARTS
An illustrated encyclopedia of martial arts, covering most of the major schools, their historical and mythical backgrounds, and commonly used terms. It is the most useful and complete reference of its kind
0–87011–436–0 Kodansha pb $19.95

• Bill Sosa & Bryan Robbins
THE ESSENCE OF AIKIDO
Guide to one of the youngest of the martial arts
0–86568–097–3 Unique pb $8.95

• John Stevens
ABUNDANT PEACE: The Biography of Morihei Ueshiba, Founder of Aikido
Considered by many to be the greatest martial artist of the 20th century
0–87773–350–3 Shambhala pb $12.95

• Taisen Deshimaru
THE ZEN WAY TO THE MARTIAL ARTS
A Japanese master reveals the secrets of the samurai that provide wisdom to students of the martial arts or any reader interested in Zen
0–525–48360–8 Dutton pb $6.95

RUNNING AND WALKING

The books on this list explain how many miles to run and how fast, which shoes to wear, and what to eat—in short, everything the runner needs to reach his or her potential. Others deal with the psychological and philosophical side of the sport, while the rest are yarns to motivate the mind when the body says no. There are also several fine books on sportwalking that tell you how fast, how far, and how long you need to go to get the most out of your mile.

• George Dintiman & Robert Ward
SPORT SPEED: The #1 Speed Improvement Program for All Athletes
0–88011–325–1 Leisure pb $11.95

• Richard Elliot
THE COMPETITIVE EDGE: Mental Preparation for Distance Running
Filled with techniques and strategies that help lower your times by gaining control over the psychological factors that influence performance
0–13–154980–4 Prentice-Hall pb $7.95

• James Fixx
THE COMPLETE BOOK OF RUNNING
A virtual encyclopedia that covers every aspect of the sport
0–394–41159–5 Random House $16.95

- Ardy Friedberg
HOW TO RUN YOUR FIRST MARATHON
Contains progress charts, tables, and a 20-week training calendar, plus a list of the top 80 marathons around the world
0–671–44206–6 Simon & Schuster pb $7.95

- Jeff Galloway
GALLOWAY'S BOOK ON RUNNING
"If there were a literary Olympics, Galloway's book would take gold in the distance events"—*Sports Fitness*
0–394–72709–6 Random House pb $9.95

- Bob Glover & Pete Schuder
THE NEW COMPETITIVE RUNNERS HANDBOOK
A complete training program, with strategies for the 10K and marathon
0–14–046837–4 Penguin pb $9.95

- Joe Henderson
RUNNING A TO Z: An Encyclopedia for the Thoughtful Runner
Down-to-earth approach to running, for those who wish to run as a way of life
0–8289–0504–5 Stephen Greene pb $2.00

- Don Kardong
THIRTY PHONE BOOTHS TO BOSTON: Tales of a Wayward Runner
Amusing, perceptive essays about running by the fourth-place finisher in the 1976 Olympic Marathon
0–8289–0627–0 Viking pb $7.95

- Allan Lawrence & Mark Scheid
THE SELF-COACHED RUNNER
A running book that teaches you to coach yourself
0–316–51672–4 Little, Brown $17.95

- Nathan Pritikin
DIET FOR RUNNERS
0–671–55623–1 Simon & Schuster pb $7.95

- George Sheehan
RUNNING AND BEING: The Total Experience
Philosophy laced with practical advice
0–446–97090–5 Warner pb $7.95

- Joan Ullyot
THE NEW WOMEN'S RUNNING BOOK
Drawing on her experience as the authority on sports medicine for women, Dr. Ullyot offers advice for all levels of runners
0–8289–0536–3 Stephen Greene pb $7.95

Walking

- Smoke Blanchard
WALKING UP AND DOWN IN THE WORLD: Memories of a Mountain Rambler
"The life and motivation of an unusual and devoted mountain man"—Sir Edmund Hillary
0–87156–827–6 Sierra Club $15.95

- Colin Fletcher
THE COMPLETE WALKER III
A complete revision of the famous book *Field & Stream* called "The Thinker's Bible"
0–394–51962–0 Knopf $22.95

- Gary Yanker
GARY YANKER'S SPORTWALKING
The complete handbook for today's fitness walker by America's leading authority
0–8092–4966–9 Contemporary pb $9.95

SWIMMING

- Marianne Brems
THE FIT SWIMMER: 120 Workout and Training Tips
Stop counting laps and learn how to create your own fitness program
0–8092–5454–9 Contemporary pb $7.95

- John Jerome
STAYING WITH IT: On Becoming an Athlete
A personal account of Jerome's quest, starting with laps in a pool and ending with fulfillment
0–14–008270–0 Penguin pb $6.95

- Jane Katz & Nancy Bruning
SWIMMING FOR TOTAL FITNESS: A Progressive Aerobic Program
Contains over 80 workouts gradually increasing from 100 yards to two miles
0–385–15932–3 Doubleday pb $14.95

- Joseph McEvoy
FITNESS SWIMMING: Lifetime Programs
The women's swimming coach at the University of Georgia details 124 workouts
0–916622–34–7 Princeton Book pb $14.95

- Bill Reed & Murray Rose
WATER WORKOUT: 120 Water Exercises for Swimmers and Nonswimmers
Step-by-step instructions geared toward pregnant women, arthritis sufferers, and people recovering from sports injuries
0–517–56183–2 Crown pb $9.95

- Katherine Vaz & Chip Zempel
SWIM, SWIM: A Complete Handbook for Fitness Swimmers
Information on everything from basic-stroke technique to advanced interval training and masters competition
0–8092–5134–5 Contemporary pb $7.95

- Harvey Wiener
TOTAL SWIMMING: How The Perfect Exercise Can Offer Rewards Both to the Body and to the Inner Self
0–671–42807–1 Simon & Schuster pb $9.95

TRIATHLONS

- Sally Edwards
TRIATHLON: A Triple Fitness Sport
Profiles and training tips by one of America's most accomplished endurance athletes
0–8092–5555–3 Contemporary $10.95

- Albert Gross
ENDURANCE: The Events, the Athletes, the Attitude
Discusses many of the mind-boggling multisport competitions
0–396–08888–0 Dodd, Mead pb $8.95

- Katherine Katz
CROSS TRAINING: The Complete Book of the Triathlon
0–380–87957–3 Avon pb $9.95

- Mike Plant
IRON WILL: The Heart and Soul of the Triathlon's Ultimate Challenge
Brings to life the mystique of the Ironman race, the king of all triathlons
0–8092–4823–9 Contemporary $17.95

- Kay Porter
THE MENTAL ATHLETE
A complete guide to inner training for peak performance for running, swimming, biking, and other sports
0–345–34174–0 Ballantine pb $3.95

- Dave Scott
DAVE SCOTT'S TRIATHLON TRAINING
From the five-time Ironman winner
0–671–60473–2 Simon & Schuster pb $9.95

YOGA

- Birram Choudong & Bonnie Reynolds
BIRRAM'S BEGINNING YOGA CLASS
0–87477–082–3 Tarcher pb $10.95

- Alice Christensen
THE AMERICAN YOGA ASSOCIATION BEGINNER'S MANUAL
Three easy 10-week programs of exercise, breathing, and meditation
0–671–61935–7 Simon & Schuster pb $10.95

- James Hewitt
THE COMPLETE YOGA BOOK: Yoga of Breathing, Yoga of Posture and Yoga of Meditation
0–8052–0592–6 Schocken pb $13.95

- Lucy Lidell & others
THE SIVANANDA COMPANION TO YOGA
A comprehensive guide to the postures, breathing exercises, diet, relaxation, and meditation techniques
0–671–47088–4 Simon & Schuster pb $11.95

- Ramamurti Mishra
FUNDAMENTALS OF YOGA: A Handbook of Theory, Practice and Application
0–517–56422–X Crown pb $12.95

- Swami Vishnudervananda
THE COMPLETE ILLUSTRATED BOOK OF YOGA
0–517–57095–5 Crown $20.00
0–671–60220–9 Simon & Schuster pb $3.95

The Outdoors

Recent literature on the outdoors ranges from philosophical and meditative treatises, memoirs of adventure, and studies in ecology, to field guides, camping tips, hunting and fishing manuals, and cookbooks.

▶ See also Natural History

- Vin Sparano
  THE COMPLETE OUTDOORS ENCYCLOPEDIA
  1–5565–4026–4 Outdoor Life $39.95

ESSAYS

- Edward Abbey
  DESERT SOLITAIRE
  0–8165–1057–1 Arizona $24.95
  0–345–32649–0 Ballantine pb $3.95

- Stephen Bodio
  A RAGE FOR FALCONS
  0–8052–3931–6 Schocken $16.50

- Vance Bourjaily
  THE UNNATURAL ENEMY
  A novelist's essays on bird hunting
  0–8165–0884–4 Arizona pb $6.95

- Alston Chase
  PLAYING GOD IN YELLOWSTONE: The Destruction of America's First National Park
  The most iconoclastic book on conservation policy in decades, with implications that go far beyond Yellowstone
  0–87113–025–4 Little, Brown $24.95
  0–15–672036–1 HBJ pb $12.95

- David Duncan
  THE RIVER WHY
  A comic novel, whimsical yet serious, on man and nature as seen through the eyes of a fly-fishing fanatic
  0–87156–321–5 Sierra Club $12.95
  0–553–34486–2 Bantam pb $7.95

- Bill Gilbert
  OUR NATURE
  0–8032–2123–1 Nebraska $23.95
  0–8032–7023–2 Nebraska pb $7.50

- William Humphrey
  OPEN SEASON: Sporting Adventures
  Contains, among other gems, the full text of two outstanding books on fishing
  0–385–29513–8 Delacorte $18.95

- Ted Kerasote
  NAVIGATIONS: One Man Explores the Americas and Discovers Himself
  A reflective, highly personal book on travel and wilderness
  0–8117–1013–0 Stackpole $16.95

Photo of Ernest Hemingway and friends, from Mary Hemingway's memoir How It Was *(Knopf)*

- Aldo Leopold
  A SAND COUNTY ALMANAC: With Other Essays on Conservation from Round River
  Seminal essays on "the land ethic"
  0–19–505305–2 Oxford $17.95
  0–19–500777–8 Oxford pb $7.95

- Norman Maclean
  A RIVER RUNS THROUGH IT & OTHER STORIES
  One of the finest "books with trees in it" ever written
  0–226–50055–1 Chicago $15.00
  0–226–50057–8 Chicago pb $7.95

- Thomas McGuane
  AN OUTSIDE CHANCE: Essays on Sport
  Broad-based essays by a master prose stylist
  0–374–10472–7 Farrar, Straus & Giroux $10.95
  0–14–006067–7 Penguin pb $6.95

- Roderick Nash
  WILDERNESS AND THE AMERICAN MIND
  0–300–02905–5 Yale $40.00
  0–300–02910–1 Yale pb $12.95

- José Ortega y Gasset
  MEDITATIONS ON HUNTING
  A philosophical defense of hunting by a modern Spanish thinker
  0–684–18630–6 Scribners pb $7.95

- Grace Seton-Thompson
  A WOMAN TENDERFOOT
  Reprint of a remarkably modern book first published in 1900
  0–941130–47–9 Nick Lyons pb $9.95

- David Seybold, editor
  SEASONS OF THE ANGLER: A Fisherman's Anthology
  Literary works by Thomas McGuane, Jim Harrison, P.J. O'Rourke, and others
  1–55584–091–4 Weidenfeld & Nicolson $19.95

- James Vickery
  WILDERNESS VISIONARIES
  Biographies of Muir, Olson, Thoreau, and others
  0–934802–27–0 ICS $19.95
  0–934802–28–9 ICS pb $9.95

- Ted Williams
  DON'T BLAME THE INDIANS: Native Americans and the Mechanized Destruction of Fish and Wildlife
  An outspoken view of the Indian rights controversy
  0–9609842–5–9 GSJ pb $12.95

GUIDES

Sierra Club Guides

The Sierra Club Naturalist's Guides are skillfully written, well-printed, and beautifully illustrated. They also include species identification.

- Michael & Deborah Berrill
  A SIERRA CLUB NATURALIST'S GUIDE TO THE NORTH ATLANTIC COAST: Cape Cod to Newfoundland
  0–87156–243–X Sierra Club pb $12.95

- Glena Daniel & Jerry Sullivan
  A SIERRA CLUB NATURALIST'S GUIDE TO THE NORTH WOODS OF MICHIGAN, WISCONSIN, MINNESOTA AND SOUTHERN ONTARIO
  0–87156–248–0 Sierra Club $24.95
  0–87156–277–4 Sierra Club pb $12.95

- Michael Godfrey
  A SIERRA CLUB NATURALIST'S GUIDE TO THE PIEDMONT OF EASTERN NORTH AMERICA
  0–87156–268–5 Sierra Club $20.45
  0–87156–269–3 Sierra Club pb $9.95

- Neil Jorgensen
  A SIERRA CLUB NATURALIST'S GUIDE TO SOUTHERN NEW ENGLAND
  0–87156–190–5 Sierra Club $25.00
  0–87156–183–2 Sierra Club pb $14.95

- Dean Krakel II
  DOWNRIVER: A Yellowstone Journey
  0–87156–708–3 Sierra Club $16.95

- Peggy & Lane Larson
  A SIERRA CLUB NATURALIST'S GUIDE TO THE DESERTS OF THE SOUTHWEST
  0–87156–186–7 Sierra Club pb $9.95

- Bill Perry
  A SIERRA CLUB NATURALIST'S GUIDE TO THE MIDDLE ATLANTIC COAST: Cape Hatteras to Cape Cod
  0–87156–810–1 Sierra Club $25.00
  0–87156–816–0 Sierra Club pb $12.95

- John & Jane Perry
  THE SIERRA CLUB GUIDE TO THE NATURAL AREAS OF COLORADO AND UTAH
  0–87156–832–2 Sierra Club pb $9.95

  THE SIERRA CLUB GUIDE TO THE NATURAL AREAS OF IDAHO, MONTANA AND WYOMING
  0–87156–781–4 Sierra Club pb $12.95

**THE SIERRA CLUB GUIDE TO THE
NATURAL AREAS OF NEW MEXICO,
ARIZONA, AND NEVADA**
0–87156–753–9 Sierra Club pb $10.95

• Stephen Whitney
**A SIERRA CLUB NATURALIST'S
GUIDE TO THE SIERRA NEVADA**
0–87156–215–4 Sierra Club $24.95
0–87156–216–2 Sierra Club pb $14.95

Audubon Nature Guides

• William & Stephen Amos
ATLANTIC AND GULF COASTS
0–394–73109–3 Knopf pb $14.95

• Lauren Brown
GRASSLANDS
0–394–73121–2 Knopf pb $14.95

• Susannah Lawrence & Barbara Gross
MID-ATLANTIC STATES: Coastal
0–394–72279–5 Knopf pb $11.95

MID-ATLANTIC STATES: Inland
0–394–72280–9 Knopf pb $11.95

• Bayard & Evelyn McConnaughey
PACIFIC COAST
0–394–73130–1 Knopf pb $15.95

• James McMahon
DESERTS
0–394–73139–5 Knopf pb $14.95

• William Niering
WETLANDS
0–394–73147–6 Knopf pb $15.95

• Ann & Myron Sutton
EASTERN FORESTS
0–394–73126–3 Knopf pb $15.95

• Stephen Whitney
WESTERN FORESTS
0–394–73127–1 Knopf pb $14.95

Mammals

• Sydney Anderson, editor
**THE SIMON & SCHUSTER GUIDE TO
MAMMALS**
0–671–43727–5 Simon & Schuster $30.95
0–671–42805–5 Simon & Schuster pb $11.95

• William Burt
A FIELD GUIDE TO THE MAMMALS
0–395–24082–4 Houghton Mifflin $17.95
0–395–24084–0 Houghton Mifflin pb $12.95

• John O. Whitaker, Jr.
**THE AUDUBON FIELD GUIDE TO
NORTH AMERICAN MAMMALS**
0–394–50762–2 Knopf $14.95

Birds

• John Bull & John Farrand
**THE AUDUBON SOCIETY GUIDES TO
NORTH AMERICAN BIRDS: Eastern
Region**
0–394–41405–5 Knopf $14.95

• William Clark & Brian Wheeler
A FIELD GUIDE TO HAWKS
0–395–36001–3 Houghton Mifflin $19.95
0–395–44112–9 Houghton Mifflin pb $13.95

• John Farrand, Jr., editor
**THE AUDUBON SOCIETY MASTER
GUIDE TO BIRDING**
An indispensable three-volume guide
0–394–54121–9 Knopf $41.85

• Hal Harrison
**A FIELD GUIDE TO WESTERN BIRDS'
NESTS**
0–395–27629–2 Houghton Mifflin $17.95

• Peter Harrison
**A FIELD GUIDE TO BIRDS' NESTS
FOUND EAST OF THE MISSISSIPPI
RIVER**
0–395–20434–8 Houghton Mifflin $17.95

SEABIRDS: An Identification Guide
Foreword by Roger Tory Peterson
0–395–33253–2 Houghton Mifflin $34.00

• Les Line & Franklin Russell
**THE AUDUBON SOCIETY BOOK OF
WILD BIRDS**
0–8109–0661–9 Abrams $35.00

• Steven Magde
**WATERFOWL: An Identification Guide to
the Ducks, Geese and Swans of the World**
Introduction by Roger Tory Peterson
0–395–46727–6 Houghton Mifflin $35.00

• John Marchant & Tony Prater
SHOREBIRD: An Identification Guide
Foreword by Roger Tory Peterson
0–395–37903–2 Houghton Mifflin $35.00

• Roger Tory Peterson
**A FIELD GUIDE TO THE BIRDS EAST
OF THE ROCKIES**
0–395–26619–X Houghton Mifflin pb $12.95

• Roger Tory Peterson & Edward
Chalif
A FIELD GUIDE TO MEXICAN BIRDS
0–395–17129–6 Houghton Mifflin $18.95

**A FIELD GUIDE TO THE BIRDS OF
TEXAS AND ADJACENT STATES**
0–395–08087–8 Houghton Mifflin $17.95
0–395–26252–6 Houghton Mifflin pb $12.95

• M.D. Udvardy
**AUDUBON SOCIETY GUIDE TO
NORTH AMERICAN BIRDS: Western
Region**
0–394–41410–1 Knopf $14.95

Sea Creatures

• Herbert Boschung & others, editors
**THE AUDUBON SOCIETY FIELD
GUIDE TO NORTH AMERICAN
FISHES, WHALES, AND DOLPHINS**
0–394–53405–0 Knopf $14.95

• Harold Feinberg
**THE SIMON & SCHUSTER GUIDE TO
SHELLS**
0–671–25320–4 Simon & Schuster pb $12.95

• Eugene Kaplan
**A FIELD GUIDE TO CORAL REEFS OF
THE CARIBBEAN AND FLORIDA**
0–395–31321–X Houghton Mifflin $22.95

• Stephen Leatherwood & Randall
Reeves
**THE SIERRA CLUB HANDBOOK OF
WHALES AND DOLPHINS**
0–87156–341–X Sierra Club $25.00
0–87156–340–1 Sierra Club pb $14.95

• Norman Meinkoth
**THE AUDUBON SOCIETY FIELD
GUIDE TO NORTH AMERICAN
SEASHORE CREATURES**
0–394–51993–0 Knopf $14.95

• Percy Morris
**A FIELD GUIDE TO PACIFIC COAST
SHELLS**
0–395–08029–0 Houghton Mifflin $17.95
0–395–18322–7 Houghton Mifflin pb $12.95

• Harrold Rehder
**THE AUDUBON SOCIETY FIELD
GUIDE TO NORTH AMERICAN
SEASHELLS**
0–394–51913–2 Knopf $14.95

Reptiles and Amphibians

• Roger Conant
**A FIELD GUIDE TO REPTILES AND
AMPHIBIANS OF EASTERN AND
CENTRAL NORTH AMERICA**
0–395–19979–4 Houghton Mifflin $17.95
0–395–19977–8 Houghton Mifflin pb $12.95

From The Audubon Society Field Guide to
North American Reptiles and Amphibians
(*Knopf*)

- F. Wayne King & John Behler
THE AUDUBON SOCIETY FIELD GUIDE TO NORTH AMERICAN REPTILES AND AMPHIBIANS
0–394–50824–6 Knopf $14.95

Insects

- R. Arnett & R. Jacques, Jr.
THE SIMON & SCHUSTER GUIDE TO INSECTS
0–671–25014–0 Simon & Schuster pb $12.95

- Donald Borror & Richard White
A FIELD GUIDE TO THE INSECTS OF AMERICA NORTH OF MEXICO
0–395–18523–8 Houghton Mifflin pb $12.95

- Charles V. Covell, Jr.
A FIELD GUIDE TO THE MOTHS OF EASTERN NORTH AMERICA
0–395–26056–6 Houghton Mifflin $18.95
0–395–36100–1 Houghton Mifflin pb $13.95

- Alexander Klots
A FIELD GUIDE TO THE BUTTERFLIES OF NORTH AMERICA, EAST OF THE GREAT PLAINS
0–395–07865–2 Houghton Mifflin $17.95
0–395–25859–6 Houghton Mifflin pb $12.95

- Les Line, Lorus & Margery Milne
THE AUDUBON SOCIETY BOOK OF INSECTS
0–8109–1806–4 Abrams $35.00

- Lorus & Margery Milne
THE AUDUBON SOCIETY FIELD GUIDE TO NORTH AMERICAN INSECTS AND SPIDERS
0–394–50763–0 Knopf $14.95

Trees, Plants, and Fungi

- Lauren Brown
GRASSES: An Identification Guide
0–395–27624–1 Houghton Mifflin $14.95

- Boughton Cobb
A FIELD GUIDE TO FERNS AND THEIR RELATED FAMILIES
0–395–07560–2 Houghton Mifflin $17.95
0–395–19431–8 Houghton Mifflin pb $12.95

- John Craighead
A FIELD GUIDE TO ROCKY MOUNTAIN WILDFLOWERS
0–395–07578–5 Houghton Mifflin $17.95
0–395–18324–3 Houghton Mifflin pb $12.95

- Gary Lincoff
THE AUDUBON SOCIETY FIELD GUIDE TO NORTH AMERICAN MUSHROOMS
0–394–51992–2 Knopf $14.95

- Elbert L. Little, Jr.
AUDUBON FIELD GUIDE TO NORTH AMERICAN TREES: Eastern Edition
0–394–50760–6 Knopf $14.95

From The Audubon Society Field Guide to North American Wildflowers (*Knopf*)

- Kent & Vera McKnight
A FIELD GUIDE TO MUSHROOMS
0–395–42101–2 Houghton Mifflin $19.95
0–395–42102–0 Houghton Mifflin pb $13.95

- Theodore Niehaus
A FIELD GUIDE TO PACIFIC STATES WILDFLOWERS
Foreword by Roger Tory Peterson
0–395–21624–9 Houghton Mifflin $16.95
0–395–31662–6 Houghton Mifflin pb $12.95

- William Niering & Nancy Olmstead
THE AUDUBON SOCIETY FIELD GUIDE TO NORTH AMERICAN WILDFLOWERS: Eastern Region
0–394–50432–1 Knopf $14.95

- Lee Peterson
A FIELD GUIDE TO EASTERN EDIBLE WILD PLANTS
0–395–20445–3 Houghton Mifflin $17.95
0–395–31870–X Houghton Mifflin pb $12.95

- Roger Tory Peterson & Margaret McKenny
A FIELD GUIDE TO WILDFLOWERS OF NORTHEASTERN AND NORTH-CENTRAL NORTH AMERICA
0–395–08086–X Houghton Mifflin $17.95
0–395–18325–1 Houghton Mifflin pb $12.95

- Stanley Schuler, editor
THE SIMON & SCHUSTER GUIDE TO TREES
0–671–24125–7 Simon & Schuster pb $10.95

- Richard Spellenberg
THE AUDUBON SOCIETY FIELD GUIDE TO NORTH AMERICAN WILDFLOWERS: Western Region
0–394–50431–3 Knopf $14.95

CAMPING AND MOUNTAINEERING

- Nessmuk
WOODCRAFT AND CAMPING
0–486–21145–2 Dover pb $3.50

- William Riviere
THE L.L. BEAN GUIDE TO THE OUTDOORS
0–394–51928–0 Random House $15.50

- Ernest Thompson Seton
TWO LITTLE SAVAGES
0–486–20985–7 Dover pb $5.95

Hiking and Backpacking

- Colin Fletcher
THE COMPLETE WALKER
Still indispensable
0–394–51962–0 Knopf $22.95
0–394–72264–7 Knopf pb $14.95

- David Ganci
DESERT HIKING
0–89997–036–2 Wilderness pb $9.95

- John Hart
WALKING SOFTLY IN THE WILDERNESS: The Sierra Club Guide to Backpacking
0–87156–813–6 Sierra Club pb $9.95

- Noelle Liebrenz & Penny Hargrove
BACKPACKERS' SOURCEBOOK
0–89997–062–1 Wilderness pb $6.95

- Jim Ottman
HUNTING ON HORSEBACK
0–87364–427–1 Paladin $16.95

- Calvin Rutstrum
HIKING
0–934802–20–3 ICS pb $8.95

Mountaineering

- Richard G. Mitchell, Jr.
MOUNTAIN EXPERIENCE: The Psychology and Sociology of Adventure
0–226–53224–0 Chicago $25.00
0–226–53225–9 Chicago pb $10.95

- Ed Peters, editor
MOUNTAINEERING: The Freedom of the Hills
0–89886–001–6 Mountaineers $17.00

Survival

- Bradford Angier
SURVIVAL WITH STYLE
0–394–71982–4 Random House pb $5.95

• E. Russel Kodet & Bradford Angier
BEING YOUR OWN WILDERNESS DOCTOR
0–8117–2044–6 Stackpole pb $8.95

• James Wilkerson, editor
MEDICINE FOR MOUNTAINEERING
0–89886–086–5 Mountaineers pb $11.95

Bird Watching

Bird watching has become one of the largest outdoor sports in America, with an estimated eight million enthusiasts.

> John Farrand, Jr.
> Farrand's books are indispensable sources.
> **EASTERN BIRDS**
> 0–07–019976–0 McGraw-Hill $13.50
> **HOW TO IDENTIFY BIRDS**
> 0–07–019975–2 McGraw-Hill $13.50
> **WESTERN BIRDS**
> 0–07–019977–9 McGraw-Hill $13.50

• George Harrison
BACKYARD BIRD WATCHER
0–671–22664–9 Simon & Schuster $17.45

• Eliot Howard
TERRITORY IN BIRD LIFE
Psychology and behavior of birds
0–689–70100–4 Atheneum pb $1.75

• Konrad Lorenz
KING SOLOMON'S RING
A classic nature book with a brilliant chapter on jackdaws and avian communication
0–06–131976–7 Harper & Row pb $6.95

• Thomas McElroy, Jr.
THE HABITAT GUIDE TO BIRDING: A Guide to Birding East of the Rockies
0–941130–36–3 Nick Lyons pb $13.95

• Michael Scofield
THE COMPLETE OUTFITTING AND RESOURCE BOOK FOR BIRD WATCHING
Crammed with lists and sundry bits of information
0–03–045615–0 Henry Holt pb $6.95

HUNTING

• Robert Elman
THE HUNTER'S FIELD GUIDE TO THE GAME BIRDS AND ANIMALS OF NORTH AMERICA
0–394–71260–9 Knopf $15.95

• Gene Hill
HILL COUNTRY: Stories about Hunting and Fishing and Dogs and Guns and Such
0–87690–297–2 Dutton $15.95

Birds

• Bruce Bowlen
THE ORVIS WING SHOOTING HANDBOOK
0–941130–05–3 Nick Lyons pb $8.95

• Byron Dalrymple
BIRD HUNTING WITH DALRYMPLE: The Rewards of Shotgunning Across North America
Much on western birds
0–8117–0252–9 Stackpole $24.95

• Guy De la Valdene
MAKING GAME: An Essay on Woodcock
A literate book about woodcock
0–932558–26–7 Willow Creek $20.00

• Steve Grooms
MODERN PHEASANT HUNTING
0–8117–2208–2 Stackpole pb $10.95

• Bob Hinman
THE DUCK HUNTER'S HANDBOOK
0–8329–0404–X New Century $15.95
0–88317–071–X Stoeger pb $9.95

• Tom Huggler
QUAIL HUNTING IN AMERICA
Tactics for finding and taking Bobwhite, Valley, Gambel's Mountain, Scaled, and Mearn Quail by season and habitat
0–8117–1277–X Stackpole $19.95

• John McDaniel
SPRING TURKEY HUNTING: The Serious Hunter's Guide
0–8117–1688–0 Stackpole $21.95

• Steve Smith
PICKING YOUR SHOTS AND OTHER STORIES OF DOGS AND BIRDS AND GUNS AND DAYS AFIELD
0–8117–1241–9 Stackpole $16.95

• Burton Spiller
DRUMMER IN THE WOODS
0–8117–0528–5 Stackpole $19.95

• Dennis Walrod
HUNTER'S GUIDE: Solid Facts, Observations, and Insights on How to Hunt the Ruffed Grouse
0–8117–0772–5 Stackpole $16.95

• Charles Waterman
GUN DOGS AND BIRD GUNS: A Charley Waterman Reader
Thoughtful essays; not "how-to"
0–9609842–4–0 GSJ $25.00

• David Wesley & William Leitch, editors
FIRESIDE WATERFOWLER: Fundamentals of Duck and Goose Ecology
0–8117–0617–6 Stackpole $29.95

• Frank Woolner
GROUSE AND GROUSE HUNTING
0–941130–51–7 Nick Lyons $18.95

TIMBERDOODLE: A Guide to Woodcock
0–941130–52–5 Nick Lyons $18.95

Hare, Deer, and Big Game

• Stephen Bodio
GOOD GUNS
An extended essay for beginners and connoisseurs
0–941130–21–5 Nick Lyons $14.95

• Bob Brister
SHOTGUNNING: The Art and the Science
The best on the subject
0–8329–1840–7 New Century $17.95

• Peter Capstick
SAFARI—THE LAST ADVENTURE: How You Can Share in It
0–312–69657–4 St. Martin's $15.95

• Richard Grozik
GAME GUN
Fine shotguns and their making
0–932558–29–1 Willow Creek $39.00

• Norm Nelson
MULE DEER: How to Bring Home North America's Big Deer of the West
0–8117–0984–1 Stackpole $16.95

• Richard Smith
HUNTING RABBITS AND HARES: The Complete Guide to North America's Favorite Small Game
0–8117–2056–X Stackpole pb $12.95

• Jack Thomas & Dale Toweill, editors
ELK OF NORTH AMERICA: Ecology and Management
0–8117–0571–4 Stackpole $49.95

• Robert Wegner
DEER AND DEER HUNTING: The Serious Hunter's Guide
Volume 1
0–8117–0434–3 Stackpole $24.95
Volume 2
0–8117–0525–0 Stackpole $29.95

Gun Dogs and Dog Training

• Kenneth Roebuck
GUN-DOG TRAINING: Spaniels and Retrievers
0–8117–0778–4 Stackpole $14.95
GUN-DOG TRAINING: Pointing Dogs
0–8117–0714–8 Stackpole $14.95

• Richard Wolters
His innovative photo books on basic training are deservedly popular.
GAME DOG: The Hunter's Retriever
0–525–93299–2 Dutton $15.95
GUN DOG: Revolutionary Rapid Training Method
0–525–24549–9 Dutton $15.95
WATER DOG
0–525–24430–1 Dutton $15.95

Post-Hunt Guides

• James Churchhill
THE COMPLETE BOOK OF TANNING SKINS AND FURS
0–8117–1719–4 Stackpole $16.95

FIELD DRESSING SMALL GAME AND FOWL: The Illustrated Guide to Dressing 20 Birds and Mammals
0–8117–2154–X Stackpole pb $10.95

FISHING

• Harold Blaisdell
THE PHILOSOPHICAL FISHERMAN
0–941130–13–4 Nick Lyons pb $12.95

• Terry Brykczynski & David Reuther, editors
THE ARMCHAIR ANGLER
A fine anthology with some surprising contributors
0–684–18565–2 Scribners $22.50

• Stephen Downes
BRIGHT RIVERS: Celebrations of Rivers and Fly-fishing
0–671–65744–5 Simon & Schuster pb $6.95

THE NEW COMPLEAT ANGLER
Fantastic underwater paintings by Martin Knowelden, with a literate and scientific text
0–8117–1011–4 Stackpole $24.95

• John Gierach
TROUT BUM
0–671–64413–0 Simon & Schuster pb $7.95

THE VIEW FROM RAT LAKE
"Gierach writes with more knowledge and more humour about all the joys, vicissitudes, horrors, and hallelujahs of pursuing fish than almost anyone else laboring at the craft today"—John Nichols
0–87108–749–9 Pruett $18.95

• Arnold Gingrich
THE WELL-TEMPERED ANGLER
0–452–26008–6 NAL pb $8.95

• Grey Hackle
FISHLESS DAYS, ANGLING NIGHTS
A great storyteller's classic compendium of tall tales and humorous anecdotes. "A compound of sage judgment, warm memory, and dry wit"—Arnold Gingrich
0–671–66100–0 Simon & Schuster pb $7.95

• Jack Hemingway
MISADVENTURES OF A FLY FISHERMAN: My Life With and Without Papa
0–07–028063–0 McGraw-Hill pb $7.95

• Nick Lyons
THE SEASONED ANGLER: The Adventures and Misadventures of an Angling Addict
Nick Lyons is a dedicated literary angler tied to a city job, and he writes about it superbly
0–671–66328–3 Simon & Schuster pb $6.95

• Nick Lyons, editor
TROUT RIVER
Photographs by Larry Madison
0–8109–1697–5 Abrams $49.50

• Steve Richmond
THE YEAR OF THE ANGLER
A fishing expedition on Puget Sound
0–8329–0319–1 New Century $19.95
0–671–66174–4 Simon & Schuster pb $7.95

• Odell Shepard
THY ROD AND THY CREEL
0–317–62712–0 Nick Lyons pb $8.95

• Izaak Walton
THE COMPLEAT ANGLER
0–14–059007–2 Penguin pb $4.95

Trout, Fly-fishing, and Fly-tying

• Ray Bergman & Edward James
TROUT
"The only true American angling classic still read widely . . . It remains the best all-around basic text, managing to cover fundamentals of theory and practice in a smooth relaxed way"—*NY Times*
0–394–49957–3 Knopf $25.00
0–394–73144–1 Knopf pb $15.95

• John Buckland
THE SIMON & SCHUSTER POCKET GUIDE TO TROUT AND SALMON FLIES
0–671–64064–X Simon & Schuster pb $9.95

• Hugh Falkus
FIRST CAST: The Beginner's Guide to Fly-fishing
0–671–64564–1 Simon & Schuster pb $5.95

SALMON FISHING: A Practical Guide
0–85493–144–9 Greycliff $43.95

SEA TROUT FISHING
These books are encyclopedic, written by an Englishman, but useful for Americans
0–85493–115–5 Greycliff $43.95

Photo by Larry Madison from Trout River *by Nick Lyons (Abrams)*

• Les Hill & Graeme Marshall
STALKING TROUT: A Serious Fisherman's Guide
0–913276–51–0 Stone Wall $24.95

• Vincent Marinaro
IN THE RING OF THE RISE
0–941130–59–2 Nick Lyons $24.95

• Ron Moser
ANGLING ENTOMOLOGY: Basics for Fly Fishermen
0–941130–59–2 Nick Lyons pb $9.95

• Paul Schullery
AMERICAN FLY-FISHING
0–941130–32–0 Nick Lyons $29.95

• Helen Shaw
FLY TYING
0–941130–54–1 Nick Lyons $16.95

TROUT STRATEGIES
Techniques of fly-fishing
0–525–48052–8 Dutton pb $10.95

• Richard Talleur
MASTERING THE ART OF FLY-TYING
0–8117–0907–8 Stackpole $29.95

• Joan Wulff
JOAN WULFF'S FLY-CASTING TECHNIQUES
0–941130–38–X Nick Lyons $24.95

Bait, Bottom, and Saltwater Fishing

• Erwin Bauer
THE BASS FISHERMAN'S BIBLE
0–385–14993–X Doubleday pb $7.95

SALTWATER FISHERMAN'S BIBLE
0–385–17220–6 Doubleday pb $7.95

• Viad Evanoff
FRESH-WATER FISHERMAN'S BIBLE
0–385–14405–9 Doubleday pb $7.95

• John Hersey
BLUES
"*Blues* is, of course, about much more than the pleasures and techniques of fishing; it is . . . about interconnections—the ties between mankind and the natural world, among others"—*New Yorker*
0–394–55960–6 Knopf $16.95
0–394–75702–5 Random House pb $6.95

• Henry Lyman
BLUEFISHING
0–941130–57–6 Nick Lyons $16.95
0–941130–58–4 Nick Lyons pb $8.95

• John Weiss
ADVANCED BASS FISHING
0–88317–081–7 Stoeger pb $9.95

• Lou Whitman
THE COMPLETE BAIT ANGLER'S GUIDE
0–934802–32–7 ICS pb $9.95

Game and Fish Cookery

Angus Cameron & Judith Jones
THE L.L. BEAN GAME AND FISH COOKBOOK
0–394–51191–3 Random House $21.95

Louis De Gouy
THE DERRYDALE COOK BOOK OF FISH AND GAME
0–932558–41–0 Willow Creek $25.00

THE DERRYDALE FISH COOK BOOK
Volume 1
0–932558–41–0 Willow Creek $25.00
Volume 2
0–932558–39–9 Willow Creek $25.00

Rebecca Gray & Cintra Reeve
GRAY'S FISH COOKBOOK: A Menu Cookbook
0–9609842–6–7 GSJ $25.00

GRAY'S WILD GAME COOKBOOK: A Menu Cookbook
0–9609842–1–6 GSJ $25.00

Gardening

It is possible to be a very good gardener without opening a single book, but most lovers of plants and trees always want to know more. Appreciation of classic works on cultivation, design, and the history of gardens is increasing, and many titles can be enjoyed apart from their value as practical guides.

STARTING OUT

Some novice gardeners do not know quite where to begin. Confronted with an old, overgrown yard or a bald, rough-graded site around a new house, they often tend to do either too much or too little. The following titles provide practical help in a cheerful, competent way.

- Barbara Barton
GARDENING BY MAIL: A Source Book
An indispensable guide for finding plants, seeds, suppliers, and services
0–937633–02–X Tusker $16.00

- John Brookes
THE GARDEN BOOK
A complete guide to creating gardens by a leading English garden designer
0–517–55299–X Crown $27.50

- Hugh Johnson
THE PRINCIPLES OF GARDENING
A brilliant British book
0–671–50805–9 Simon & Schuster pb $17.95

- Phoebe Leighton & others
THE NEW AMERICAN LANDSCAPE GARDENER: A Guide to Beautiful Backyards and Sensational Surroundings
A plain and practical guide despite its fancy title
0–87857–672–X Rodale $21.95

- Patricia Thorpe
THE AMERICAN WEEKEND GARDEN
A fresh and realistic approach to planting easy-to-care-for gardens inspired by the American landscape
0–394–56025–6 Random House $24.95

- Donald Wyman
THE GARDENING ENCYCLOPEDIA
This can be compared to *The Joy of Cooking*. It is trenchant and truthful: a basic book
0–02–632070–3 Macmillan $50.00

The Taylor Guide Series

A first-rate series of handy, how-to guides, based on the authoritative Taylor's *Encyclopedia of Gardening*. Each guide is written by a team of experts and contains hundreds of color photographs illustrating species and varieties. Most guides in the series also contain climate zone maps, timetables, plant charts, a color key, and cultivation tips.

TAYLOR'S GUIDE TO ANNUALS
0–395–40447–9 Houghton Mifflin pb $14.95

TAYLOR'S GUIDE TO GARDEN DESIGN
0–395–46784–5 Houghton Mifflin pb $16.95

TAYLOR'S GUIDE TO GROUND COVERS, VINES, AND GRASSES
0–395–43094–1 Houghton Mifflin pb $14.95

TAYLOR'S GUIDE TO HOUSE-PLANTS
0–317–53568–4 Houghton Mifflin pb $14.95

TAYLOR'S GUIDE TO PERENNIALS
0–395–40448–7 Houghton Mifflin pb $14.95

TAYLOR'S GUIDE TO ROSES
0–395–40450–9 Houghton Mifflin pb $14.95

TAYLOR'S GUIDE TO SHRUBS
0–395–43093–3 Houghton Mifflin pb $14.95

TAYLOR'S GUIDE TO TREES
0–395–46783–7 Houghton Mifflin pb $14.95

TAYLOR'S GUIDE TO VEGETABLES AND HERBS
0–395–43092–5 Houghton Mifflin pb $14.95

PRACTICAL MATTERS FOR INTERMEDIATE GARDENERS

- Oliver Allen
GARDENING WITH THE NEW SMALL PLANTS: The Complete Guide to Growing Dwarf and Miniature Shrubs, Flowers, Trees, and Vegetables
0–317–56425–0 Ticknor & Fields $19.95
0–395–43288–X Houghton Mifflin pb $12.95

- Bonnie Lee Appleton
LANDSCAPE REJUVENATION: Remodeling the Home Landscape
Expert advice and encouragement on renovating a tired landscape
0–88266–495–6 Garden Way $19.95

- Caroline Boisset
VERTICAL GARDENING
An imaginative range of ideas for using climbers, hedges, window boxes, and others. Includes 200 plants especially appropriate for vertical gardens
1–55584–252–6 Weidenfeld & Nicolson $24.95

- Nancy Bubel
THE NEW SEED-STARTERS HANDBOOK
An encyclopedia of more than 200 plants to grow from seeds with details on planting and care
0–87857–747–5 Rodale $19.95

- Stefan Buczacki
GARDENERS' QUESTIONS ANSWERED
0–317–56609–1 Random House $19.95

- Anna Carr
RODALE'S COLOR HANDBOOK OF GARDEN INSECTS
A clear guide for the average gardener
0–87857–460–3 Rodale pb $12.95

- A.M. Clevely
TOPIARY: The Art of Clipped Trees and Ornamental Hedges
An inspiring guide to the history of topiary in Europe and America; includes detailed plant list and clipping techniques
0–88162–309–1 Salem House $29.95

- H. Lincoln Foster
ROCK GARDENING: A Guide to Growing Alpines and Other Wildflowers in the American Garden
0–917304–29–2 Timber pb $22.95

From Topiary *by A.M. Clevely (Salem House)*

- Barbara Gallup & Deborah Reich
THE COMPLETE BOOK OF TOPIARY
From modest windowsill projects to tree
tunnels; a lively book by the American
topiary specialists
0–89480–318–2 Workman pb $10.95

- Lewis Hill
**COLD-CLIMATE GARDENING: How to
Extend Your Growing Season by at Least 30
Days**
0–88266–449–2 Storey $18.95
0–88266–441–7 Storey pb $9.95

PRUNING SIMPLIFIED
0–88266–416–6 Storey $20.00
0–88266–417–4 Storey pb $12.95

**SECRETS OF PLANT PROPAGATION:
Starting Your Own Flowers, Vegetables,
Fruits, Berries, Shrubs, Trees, and
Houseplants**
0–88266–371–2 Storey $20.00
0–88266–370–4 Storey pb $12.95

- Lewis & Nancy Hill
**SUCCESSFUL PERENNIAL
GARDENING: A Practical Guide**
A comprehensive handbook on care and
cultivation; includes a descriptive catalog
of the best garden perennials
0–88266–472–7 Garden Way $16.95

- Harriet Morse
GARDENING IN THE SHADE
The revision of a standard work, with
gardens in all degrees of shade: light, half,
and full
0–917304–16–0 Timber pb $12.95

- Graham Rice
PLANTS FOR PROBLEM PLACES
Practical advice on more than a dozen
problems commonly faced by gardeners
0–88192–090–8 Timber $29.95

- Graham Rose
THE SMALL GARDEN PLANNER
A helpful British book
0–671–64709–1 Simon & Schuster $19.95

- George Schenk
THE COMPLETE SHADE GARDENER
A fine nurseryman shows how to make the
most of limited sunlight
0–395–35397–1 Houghton Mifflin $24.95
0–317–14693–9 Houghton Mifflin pb $14.95

- Anne Scott-James
PERFECT PLANT, PERFECT GARDEN
A noted English horticulturist presents a
large and distinctive assortment of bulbs,
perennials, shrubs, and climbers to enhance
the individual garden site
0–671–64531–5 Summit $24.95
0–671–64532–3 Summit pb $14.95

- Philip Swindells
BULBS FOR ALL SEASONS
0–88162–242–7 Salem House $14.95

FOR THE MORE EXPERT GARDENER

- John Diekelmann & Robert Schuster
**NATURAL LANDSCAPING: Designing
with Native Plant Communities**
0–07–016813–X McGraw-Hill $44.95

- Michael Dirr
**PHOTOGRAPHIC MANUAL FOR
WOODY LANDSCAPE PLANTS**
0–87563–156–8 Stipes $26.00
0–87563–153–3 Stipes pb $18.95

**MANUAL OF WOODY LANDSCAPE
PLANTS**
0–87563–231–9 Stipes $31.80
0–87563–226–2 Stipes pb $24.95

- Mabel Harkness
**THE BERNARD E. HARKNESS
SEEDLIST HANDBOOK**
0–88192–059–2 Timber $27.95

- Warren Johnson & H.H. Lyon
**INSECTS THAT FEED ON TREES AND
SHRUBS: An Illustrated Practical Guide**
0–8014–2108–X Cornell $49.95

- Baker Morrow
**A DICTIONARY OF LANDSCAPE
ARCHITECTURE**
0–8263–0943–7 New Mexico $35.00
0–8263–0944–5 New Mexico pb $19.95

- Pascal Pirone
**DISEASES AND PESTS OF
ORNAMENTAL PLANTS**
0–471–07249–4 Wiley $37.95

- William Robinson
THE ENGLISH FLOWER GARDEN
A reprint of the English 19th-century
classic, updated for contemporary
gardeners by Graham Stuart Thomas
0–317–65045–9 Sagapress $35.00

- John Simonds
EARTHSCAPE
0–442–28016–5 Van Nostrand Reinhold $34.95

**LANDSCAPE ARCHITECTURE: A
Manual of Site Planning and Design**
0–07–057448–0 McGraw-Hill $52.50

- Wayne Sinclair & others
DISEASES OF TREES AND SHRUBS
0–8014–1517–9 Cornell $49.95

- William Stearn
BOTANICAL LATIN
0–7153–8548–8 David & Charles $39.95

- Graham Thomas
PERENNIAL GARDEN PLANTS
One of Britain's great gardeners discusses
plants and the best way to grow them
0–460–04575–X Biblio $29.95

REFERENCE

- American Horticultural Society Staff
NORTH AMERICAN HORTICULTURE
Includes complete information on plant
societies, botanical gardens, garden centers,
and much more
0–684–17604–1 Scribners $50.00

- Liberty Bailey
**HORTUS THIRD: A Concise Dictionary of
Plants Cultivated in the United States and
Canada**
A comprehensive 4000-page compendium
of American gardening with thousands of
entries and the last word in nomenclature
and spelling
0–02–505470–8 Macmillan $135.00

- John Brookes & others
**THE GARDENER'S INDEX OF PLANTS
AND FLOWERS**
An ideal companion for garden planning at
home or for selecting plants at a nursery.
Includes detailed charts with essential
information
0–02–516690–5 Macmillan $24.95
0–02–049100–X Macmillan pb $14.95

- Ruth Rogers Clausen & Nicolas H.
Ekstrom
**PERENNIALS FOR AMERICAN
GARDENS**
More than 3000 species are included in
this comprehensive, stunningly illustrated
reference
0–394–55740–9 Random House $35.00

- Alan Coombes
DICTIONARY OF PLANT NAMES
A useful and surprisingly entertaining
garden reference book from a noted
botanist
0–88192–023–1 Timber pb $9.95

Thomas Everett
**THE NEW YORK BOTANICAL
GARDEN ILLUSTRATED ENCY-
CLOPEDIA OF HORTICULTURE**
A monumental work in ten volumes
with helpful cultural information and
many black-and-white photographs.
Expensive, but indispensable for the
serious gardener
0–686–82042–8 Garland $600.00

- Patrick Goode & Michael Lancaster,
editors
**THE OXFORD COMPANION TO
GARDENS**
A highly accurate and entertaining
reference book covering the history and
design of gardens all over the world
0–19–866123–1 Oxford $49.95

- Kenneth Lampe & Mary McCann
**THE AMA HANDBOOK OF POISONOUS
AND INJURIOUS PLANTS**
0–89970–183–3 AMA $35.00

- Organic Gardening & Farming
Magazine Editors
**ENCYCLOPEDIA OF ORGANIC
GARDENING**
0–87857–225–2 Rodale $24.95

- Mary Helen Ray & Robert P.
Nicholls, editors
**THE TRAVELER'S GUIDE TO
AMERICAN GARDENS**
More than 1000 varied public gardens,
organized by location
0–8078–4214–1 North Carolina pb $9.95

- Miranda Smith & Anna Carr
**RODALE'S GARDEN INSECT, DISEASE,
AND WEED IDENTIFICATION GUIDE**
In one handy volume, everything that can
go wrong in the garden; a comprehensive
guide to pest control
0–87857–758–0 Rodale $21.95

- Patrick Synge, editor
DICTIONARY OF GARDENING
This four-volume work plus supplement is
easy to use as all cultivars are listed
alphabetically. Excellent drawings
throughout
0–19–869116–5 Oxford $74.00

- Elizabeth Tootill & Stephen
Blackmore, editors
**THE FACTS ON FILE DICTIONARY OF
BOTANY**
Covers every aspect of plant science in
clear, succinct entries; includes line
drawings and charts for advanced and
expert gardeners
0–87196–861–4 Facts On File $21.95

- Donald Wyman
**WYMAN'S GARDENING
ENCYCLOPEDIA**
A new edition of the classic reference
book. An excellent, well-organized one-
volume work
0–02–632070–3 Macmillan $50.00

LANDSCAPE AND GARDEN DESIGN

▶ **See also Architecture**

- Rosemary Alexander & Anthony
Pasley
**THE ENGLISH GARDENING SCHOOL:
The Complete Master Course on Garden
Planning and Landscape Design for the
American Gardener**
1–55584–031–0 Weidenfeld & Nicolson $17.95

- Michael Balston
THE WELL-FURNISHED GARDEN
How to embellish a garden by adding
paths, steps, fences, a sundial, pergolas,
and more
0–671–63474–7 Simon & Schuster $24.95

- Thomas Church & others
GARDENS ARE FOR PEOPLE
Revised edition of a classic work by one of
the foremost 20th-century landscape
designers, which covers every aspect of
garden design
0–07–010844–7 McGraw-Hill $49.50

- Guy Cooper & Gordon Taylor
ENGLISH HERB GARDENS
0–8478–0689–8 Rizzoli $25.00

**FLOWERS FOR ALL SEASONS: A Guide
to Colorful Trees, Shrubs and Vines**
A discriminating selection of flowering
plants for year-round color
0–87857–726–2 Rodale $24.95

- Lys de Bray
**BORDERS: A Guide to Spring, Summer,
and Autumn Color**
The noted English garden writer shows
how to create the right border by using
planting plans, photographs, and paintings
0–7063–6522–4 David & Charles $34.95

- William Douglas & others
**GARDEN DESIGN: History, Principles,
Elements, Practice**
Beautifully photographed tours of the best
work of contemporary designers, along
with a thorough treatment of garden
design basics
0–671–47993–8 Simon & Schuster $35.00

- Karl Foerster
**ROCK GARDENS THROUGH THE
YEAR**
An updated, illustrated edition of a
gardening classic
0–8069–6530–4 Sterling $29.95

- Charlotte Frieze
**SOCIAL GARDENS: Outdoor Spaces for
Living and Entertaining**
A stunning array of American garden
rooms, which have been skillfully planned
as living spaces
1–55670–047–4 Stewart, Tabori & Chang $40.00

- Penelope Hobhouse
COLOR IN YOUR GARDEN
0–316–36748–6 Little, Brown $40.00

GARDEN STYLE
Portraits of more than 20 gardens around
the world
0–316–36750–8 Little, Brown $40.00

**THE NATIONAL TRUST BOOK OF
GARDENING: A Practical Guide**
A beautiful, practical guide for gardeners
who've mastered the basics
0–316–36749–4 Little, Brown $29.95

- Theodore James, Jr.
LANDSCAPING: A Five-Year Plan
A witty, opinionated text. James's five-year
plan establishes a comprehensive
framework within which to undertake
major landscaping projects; for new to
intermediate gardeners
0–02–558910–5 Macmillan $22.00

- Mary Keen
THE GARDEN BORDER BOOK
A British book, with original plans
0–913643–02–5 Capability's $27.50

- Christopher Lloyd
THE YEAR AT GREAT DIXTER
A British master's distillation of a lifetime
in the garden
0–670–80982–9 Viking $24.95

- Peter Loewer
AMERICAN GARDENS
A tour of 30 private gardens in the United
States, from one of the country's leading
garden writers; superb photographs
0–671–66267–8 Simon & Schuster $35.00

**THE ANNUAL GARDEN: Flowers,
Foliage, Fruits, and Grasses for one
Summer Season**
The well-known American garden writer
presents an illustrated guide to more than
350 annuals; includes comprehensive plans
for 14 gardens
0–87857–742–4 Rodale $19.95

- Elizabeth Murray & Derek Fell
**HOME LANDSCAPING: Ideas, Styles, and
Designs for Creative Outdoor Spaces**
An exciting guide to landscape design,
showing homeowners how to create
landscapes that are both beautiful and
functional
0–671–64710–5 Simon & Schuster $29.95

- Carole Ottesen
THE NEW AMERICAN GARDEN
Sophisticated and easy-to-maintain
American gardens with plantings
appropriate to local landscapes
0–02–594090–2 Macmillan $24.95

- Anthony Paul & Yvonne Rees
THE GARDEN DESIGN BOOK
A photographic survey of the work of
today's most talented garden designers
0–88162–273–7 Salem House $34.95

- Graham Rose
THE SMALL GARDEN PLANNER
The best of English design enhanced with
hardy American plants. Schemes may be
adapted to any site, climate, or budget
0–671–64709–1 Simon & Schuster $19.95

- Wilhelm Schacht
ROCK GARDENS
0–87663–525–7 Universe pb $14.95

- Jane Taylor
FRAGRANT GARDENS
The trees, shrubs, climbers, flowers, and
herbs that fill the garden with lovely and
appealing scents
0–88162–245–1 Salem House $14.95

- Patricia Thorpe
**THE AMERICAN WEEKEND
GARDENER**
For beginners and intermediate gardeners;
a guide to designing a flowery, countrylike
setting and maintaining it two days a week
0–394–56025–6 Random House $24.95

- Rosemary Verey
CLASSIC GARDEN DESIGN
A great English gardener shares her
knowledge
0–86553–128–5 Congdon & Weed $24.95

THE GARDEN IN WINTER
A superbly illustrated book of gardens in
England, Europe, and the United States
0–8212–1669–4 Little, Brown $40.00

➤ **FOR OVERSEAS ORDERING INFORMATION, SEE PAGE 1**

- John Williamson
PERENNIAL GARDENS: A Practical Guide to Home Landscaping
A book of plans for more than 40 different perennial gardens: Elizabethan knot, silver and gold, prairie, and others
0–06–015858–1 Harper & Row $27.95

Mild and Temperate Climates

- Emily Brown
LANDSCAPING WITH PERENNIALS
0–88192–063–0 Timber $34.95

- Beth Chatto
THE DAMP GARDEN
For the more advanced and adventurous gardener
0–460–04551–2 Biblio $19.95
0–460–02457–4 Biblio pb $12.95

THE DRY GARDEN
0–460–02222–9 Biblio pb $9.95

- Gordon Courtright
TREES AND SHRUBS FOR TEMPERATE CLIMATES
The standard reference for landscape plants in temperate zones. Includes hundreds of plants readily available in retail nurseries, with information on their requirements and growth; 800 color photographs
0–88192–097–5 Timber $45.00

TROPICALS
A visual dictionary of tropical trees, shrubs, and vines for those with gardens in California and the south; also of use to greenhouse owners
0–88192–098–3 Timber $35.95

- Mildred Mathias, editor
FLOWERING PLANTS IN THE LANDSCAPE
0–520–04350–2 California $25.00
0–520–05414–8 California pb $12.95

SPECIFIC PLANTS

Trees

- Alec Blombery & Tony Rodd
PALMS
0–207–14848–1 Salem House $24.95

- The Garden Club of America
PLANTS THAT MERIT ATTENTION: Trees
0–917304–75–6 Timber $44.95

- H.G. Hillier
HILLIER'S COLOUR DICTIONARY OF TREES AND SHRUBS
0–7153–8192–X David & Charles $29.95

- Joseph Hudak
TREES FOR EVERY PURPOSE
0–07–030841–1 McGraw-Hill $39.95

- Alan Mitchell
THE TREES OF NORTH AMERICA
0–8160–1806–5 Facts On File $24.95

- Roger Phillips
TREES OF NORTH AMERICA AND EUROPE
0–394–73541–2 Random House pb $17.95

- Dick van Gelderen
CONIFERS
With more than 1000 color photographs
0–88192–056–8 Timber $65.00

- J.D. Vertrees
JAPANESE MAPLES
0–88192–048–7 Timber $40.00

- Donald Wyman
TREES FOR AMERICAN GARDENS
0–02–632200–5 Macmillan $27.95

Flowering Plants

- Paul Aden, editor
THE HOSTA BOOK
A definitive sourcebook on one of the most versatile of perennials
0–88192–087–8 Timber $29.95

- John Fiala
LILACS: The Genus Syringa
The first comprehensive modern treatment with color and black-and-white photographs
0–88192–001–0 Timber $59.95

- Fred Galle
AZALEAS
An up-to-date and complete guide to the species
0–88192–091–6 Timber $65.00

- Harold Greer & Homer Salley
THE RHODODENDRON HYBRIDS
The parentage of nearly 5000 hybrids; an authoritative reference for both the amateur and the professional
0–88192–061–4 Timber $55.00

- Michael Jefferson-Brown
THE LILY: For Garden, Patio and Display
A complete review of the species including an evaluation of the latest hybrids
0–7153–9023–6 David & Charles $24.95

- Homer Salley & Harold Greer
RHODODENDRON HYBRIDS: A Guide to Their Origins
0–88192–061–4 Timber $55.00

Roses

- Peter Beales
CLASSIC ROSES: An Illustrated Encyclopedia of Old Roses, Shrub Roses and Climbers
0–03–006022–2 Henry Holt $49.50

- Stelvio Coggiatti
SIMON & SCHUSTER'S GUIDE TO ROSES
A pocket-size, well-illustrated, and informative guide which covers 27 species and over 200 varieties
0–671–63955–2 Simon & Schuster $22.95
0–671–63957–9 Simon & Schuster pb $11.95

- Eva Dierauff & Anny Jacob
OLD GARDEN ROSES AND SELECTED MODERN HYBRIDS
Eighty magnificent roses, concentrating on the popular old varieties
0–500–54138–8 Thames & Hudson $50.00

- John Fisher
THE COMPANION TO ROSES
Lively, wide-ranging, and a useful aid to growing roses. The alphabetical entries are splendidly illustrated
0–88162–230–3 Salem House $24.95

- Sean McCann
MINIATURE ROSES
0–668–06317–3 Simon & Schuster $19.95

- Roger Phillips & Martyn Rix
ROSES
Fourteen hundred varieties from around the world; includes a detailed description of origin and parentage, appearance, and growing conditions
0–394–75867–6 Random House pb $19.95

- Nancy Steen
THE CHARM OF OLD ROSES
0–941569–00–4 Milldale $24.95

Taylor Guides
TAYLOR'S GUIDE TO ROSES
The best book on this subject: a fine all-around guide to rose culture for the average gardener
0–395–40450–9 Houghton Mifflin pb $14.95

- Graham Thomas
THE OLD SHRUB ROSES
Foreword by Vita Sackville-West
0–460–04345–5 Biblio $17.50

SHRUB ROSES OF TODAY
0–460–04533–4 Biblio $22.50

Ferns, Cacti, and Carnivorous Plants

- F. Gordon Foster
FERNS TO KNOW AND GROW
0–917304–98–5 Timber $29.95

- David Jones
ENCYCLOPEDIA OF FERNS
0–88192–054–1 Timber $55.95

- James & Patricia Pietropaolo
THE CARNIVOROUS PLANTS OF THE WORLD
0–88192–066–5 Timber $29.95

- John Pilbeam
CACTI FOR THE CONNOISSEUR
0–88192–043–6 Timber $44.95

INDOOR GARDENING

- Kenneth Beckett
THE ROYAL HORTICULTURAL SOCIETY ENCYCLOPEDIA OF HOUSE PLANTS: Including Greenhouse Plants
0–88162–285–0 Salem House $34.95

- John Brookes
  THE INDOOR GARDEN BOOK
  0–517–56313–4 Crown $27.50

- David Du Puy & Phillip Cribb
  THE GENUS CYMBIDIUM
  A comprehensive study of one of the most
  popular orchids grown
  0–88192–119–X Timber $59.95

  J.N. Rentoul
  **GROWING ORCHIDS: The Specialist
  Orchid Grower**
  0–88192–085–1 Timber $34.95
  0–88192–086–X Timber pb $22.95

  **GROWING ORCHIDS I: Cymbidiums
  and Slippers**
  0–88192–009–6 Timber $34.95
  0–88192–010–X Timber pb $22.95

  **GROWING ORCHIDS II: The
  Cattleyas and Other Epiphytes**
  0–917304–20–9 Timber $34.95
  0–917304–28–4 Timber pb $22.95

  **GROWING ORCHIDS III: Vandas,
  Dendrobiums and Others**
  0–917304–22–5 Timber $34.95
  0–917304–32–2 Timber pb $22.95

  **GROWING ORCHIDS IV: The
  Australasian Families**
  0–88192–020–7 Timber $34.95
  0–88192–021–5 Timber pb $22.95

- Brian & Wilma Rittershausen
  ORCHID GROWING ILLUSTRATED
  0–7137–1365–8 Sterling $24.95

- George Seddon & others
  **THE ESSENTIAL GUIDE TO PERFECT
  HOUSEPLANTS**
  Choosing the right plants, keeping them
  healthy, and placing them in an
  imaginative way indoors
  0–671–55726–2 Summit $24.95
  0–671–55641–X Summit pb $14.95

- Ogden Tanner
  **GARDEN ROOMS: Greenhouses,
  Sunrooms and Solariums**
  0–671–60274–8 Simon & Schuster $24.95

  ### VEGETABLES AND FRUIT

- James Crockett
  CROCKETT'S VICTORY GARDEN
  0–316–16120–9 Little, Brown $29.95
  0–316–16121–7 Little, Brown pb $19.95

- Denys De Saulles
  HOME GROWN
  A complete guide to growing more than
  130 fruits, vegetables, and herbs including
  the new gourmet varieties and the best of
  the old favorites
  0–395–45686–X Houghton Mifflin $35.00

- Lewis Hill
  **FRUITS AND BERRIES FOR THE
  HOME GARDEN**
  0–88266–168–X Storey pb $8.95

- John Jeavons
  **HOW TO GROW MORE VEGETABLES
  THAN YOU EVER THOUGHT
  POSSIBLE ON LESS LAND THAN YOU
  CAN IMAGINE**
  The secrets of French intensive gardening
  0–89815–073–6 Ten Speed pb $10.95

- National Gardening Association
  **GARDENING: The Complete Guide to
  Growing America's Favorite Fruits and
  Vegetables**
  0–201–10855–0 Addison-Wesley pb $19.95

- Rebecca Rupp
  **BLUE CORN AND SQUARE
  TOMATOES: Unusual Facts About
  Common Garden Vegetables**
  The little-known history of 20 common
  vegetables by a former research biologist
  0–88266–504–9 Garden Way $19.95

  ## Herbs

- James Adams
  LANDSCAPING WITH HERBS
  Covers a range of garden designs, formal
  and informal, traditional and modern,
  fragrant and wild
  0–88192–073–8 Timber $29.95

- Jane Courtier
  HERBS
  A handsomely illustrated guide to growing
  herbs, which includes planning and
  planting, the uses of herbs, and a listing of
  popular names
  0–88162–207–9 Salem House $14.95

- Claire Kowalchik & William Hyeton,
  editors
  **RODALE'S ILLUSTRATED
  ENCYCLOPEDIA OF HERBS**
  Comprehensive information and
  illustrations on more than 140 herbs. A
  matchless source
  0–87857–699–1 Rodale $24.95

- Allen Patterson
  HERBS IN THE GARDEN
  A practical and informative book that
  discusses herbs in the formal garden, the
  mixed border, the kitchen garden, and the
  window box
  0–460–04520–2 Biblio $24.95

- Emelie Tolley & Chris Mead
  HERBS: Gardens, Decorations, and Recipes
  An elegant book on how to set up a
  simple but sophisticated herb garden, with
  ideas for gardeners in all climates
  0–517–55244–2 Crown $35.00

  ### WILD GARDENING

- Henry Art
  **A GARDEN OF WILDFLOWERS: 101
  Native Species and How to Grow Them**
  Excellent for beginners
  0–88266–404–2 Garden Way $22.50
  0–88266–405–0 Storey pb $12.95

- Richard Austin
  WILD GARDENING
  A general overview for the novice gardener
  with handy lists of sources
  0–671–60241–1 Simon & Schuster pb $12.95

- John Brookes
  THE COUNTRY GARDEN BOOK
  The most recent and beautifully illustrated
  British book on elegant but low-
  maintenance landscaping
  0–517–56704–0 Crown $30.00

- John Dennis
  THE WILDLIFE GARDENER
  How to create a well-designed garden that
  is also attractive to all manner of bees,
  birds, small mammals, and amphibians
  0–394–53582–0 Knopf $17.95

- Ruth Shaw Ernest
  THE NATURALIST'S GARDEN
  A guide to creating a garden that is a
  haven for wildlife and wildflowers, using
  natural methods
  0–87857–730–0 Rodale $19.95
  0–87857–731–9 Rodale pb 12.95

- Laura Martin
  **THE WILDFLOWER MEADOW BOOK:
  A Gardener's Guide**
  Step-by-step instructions on how to
  establish a garden of wildflowers and
  native grasses
  0–88742–073–7 Globe Pequot $18.95
  0–88742–065–6 Globe Pequot pb $12.95

- Harry Phillips
  **GROWING AND PROPAGATING WILD
  FLOWERS**
  0–8078–1648–5 North Carolina $24.95
  0–8078–4131–5 North Carolina pb $14.95

- William Robinson
  THE WILD GARDEN
  A British classic written in 1870 by an
  early advocate of this style of planting
  0–317–62655–8 David & Charles pb $13.95

- Edwin Steffek
  **THE NEW WILD FLOWERS AND HOW
  TO GROW THEM**
  0–917304–51–9 Timber pb $17.95

- Violet Stevenson
  THE WILD GARDEN
  How to grow the best of these plants in
  settings that enhance their natural beauty
  0–670–80566–1 Viking $27.50
  0–14–046710–6 Penguin pb $14.95

- James & Cheryl Young
  **COLLECTING, PROCESSING AND
  GERMINATING SEEDS OF WILDLAND
  PLANTS**
  Technical information on this delightful
  activity
  0–88192–057–6 Timber $24.95

GARDEN HISTORY

English Gardens

● Stefan Buczacki
CREATING A VICTORIAN FLOWER GARDEN
A practical guide to style and technique, with a vivid depiction of the Victorian garden in every season. Illustrated with recently discovered watercolors by Alice Drummond-Hay
1–55584–285–2 Weidenfeld & Nicolson $22.95

● John Feltwell
THE NATURALIST'S GARDEN: A History of the Natural Garden
The great naturalists, their contributions to garden design, and a history of the plants they introduced
0–88162–270–2 Salem House $24.95

● Geoffrey & Susan Jellicoe
THE LANDSCAPE OF MAN: Shaping the Environment from Prehistory to the Present Day
A brilliant and entertaining classic that ranges over philosophy, art, and literature as they pertain to landscape history
0–500–27431–2 Thames & Hudson pb $22.50

● Arabella Lennox-Boyd
TRADITIONAL ENGLISH GARDENS
National Trust gardens, from the enchantment of Hidcote Manor to the grandeur of Ham House
0–8478–0829–7 Rizzoli $25.00

● Charles Moore & others
THE POETICS OF GARDENS
A knowledgeable, instructive, and entertaining book on garden history and design; gardens from different cultures and parts of the world with over 500 illustrations
0–262–13231–1 MIT $35.00

● Christopher Thacker
THE HISTORY OF GARDENS
A fast-moving and clearly written scholarly text
0–520–03736–7 California $45.00
0–520–05629–9 California pb $18.95

● Celia Thaxter
AN ISLAND GARDEN
A facsimile edition; the creation of Celia Thaxter's beautiful garden on Appledore Island, off the coast of New Hampshire. With paintings by Childe Hassam
0–395–48591–6 Houghton Mifflin $19.95

American Gardens

● Diana Balmori & others
BEATRIX FARRAND'S AMERICAN LANDSCAPES: Her Gardens and Campuses
The great American landscape architect, creator of Dumbarton Oaks
0–89831–003–2 Sagapress pb $24.95

From Traditional English Gardens *by Arabella Lennox-Boyd and others* (Rizzoli)

● Ann Leighton
EARLY AMERICAN GARDENS: For Meate or Medicine
A vivid and carefully researched history of American gardens written by a practical and witty gardener
0–87023–530–3 Massachusetts pb $14.95

AMERICAN GARDENS IN THE 18TH CENTURY: For Use or for Delight
0–87023–531–1 Massachusetts pb $15.95

AMERICAN GARDENS OF THE 19TH CENTURY: For Comfort and Affluence
0–87023–532–X Massachusetts $35.00
0–87023–533–8 Massachusetts pb $15.95

● Rosemary Verey & Ellen Samuels
THE AMERICAN WOMAN'S GARDEN
Contemporary gardens across the country
0–3160–4369–9 Little, Brown $40.00

British and Irish Gardens

● Jane Brown
GARDENS OF A GOLDEN AFTERNOON
An account, complete with photographs, plans, and sketches, of the fruitful partnership of two great gardeners, Sir Edwin Lutyens and Gertrude Jekyll
0–14–008021–X Viking pb $12.95

● Jane Brown
VITA'S OTHER WORLD: A Gardening Biography of Vita Sackville-West
The creator of Sissinghurst, one of England's great gardens
0–670–80163–1 Viking $20.00
0–14–009354–0 Viking pb $12.95

LANNING ROPER & HIS GARDENS
0–8478–0787–8 Rizzoli $37.50

● Tom Carter
THE VICTORIAN GARDEN
0–317–54976–6 Apollo $19.95

● Thomas Hinde
CAPABILITY BROWN: The Story of a Master Gardener
0–393–02421–0 Norton $27.50

● Penelope Hobhouse
PRIVATE GARDENS OF ENGLAND
Beautifully maintained and seldom seen contemporary gardens with historical resonance
0–517–56267–7 Crown $40.00

● Gervase Jackson-Stops & James Pipkin
THE COUNTRY HOUSE GARDEN: A Grand Tour
0–8212–1668–6 Little, Brown $35.00

Gertrude Jekyll
COLOUR SCHEMES FOR THE FLOWER GARDEN: The Illustrated Gertrude Jekyll
A new, illustrated edition of a classic by one of the greatest English gardeners, containing new color photographs, hitherto unpublished designs, and new illustrations. Miss Jekyll's planting plans have also been redrawn and interpreted in color
0–316–30699–1 Little, Brown $29.95

THE GARDENER'S ESSENTIAL GERTRUDE JEKYLL
0–87923–599–3 Godine pb $8.95

● Alvilde Lees-Milne & Rosemary Verey, editors
THE ENGLISH GARDEN IN OUR TIME: From Gertrude Jekyll to Geoffrey Jellicoe
1–85149–012–4 Antique Collectors $49.50

THE NEW ENGLISHWOMAN'S GARDEN
0–88162–317–2 Salem House $29.95

French Gardens

● Marguerite Duval
THE KING'S GARDEN
An imaginative account of the French kings' botanical gardens and their search for exotic plants
0–8139–0916–3 Virginia $20.00

- **F. Hamilton Hazlehurst**
  GARDENS OF ILLUSION: The Genius of André Le Nostre
  0–8265–1209–7 Vanderbilt $47.50

- **Anita Pereire & Gabrielle van Zuylen**
  GARDENS OF FRANCE
  Private gardens in France today, superbly photographed, with a text by one of the leading French garden writers
  0–517–55125–X Crown $40.00

- **Michel Racine & others**
  THE GARDENS OF PROVENCE AND THE FRENCH RIVIERA
  This vivid portrayal of the Provençal and Côte d'Azur gardens includes garden plans, plant lists, and color photographs
  0–262–18128–2 MIT pb $50.00

- **Daniel Wildenstein & Gerald Van Der Kemp**
  THE GARDENS AT GIVERNY: A View of Monet's World
  A collection of splendid color photographs of Monet's famous garden and water-lily pond
  Introduction by John Rewald
  0–89381–113–0 Aperture $22.50
  0–89381–114–9 Aperture pb $13.00

- **Kenneth Woodbridge**
  PRINCELY GARDENS: The Origins and Development of the French Formal Style
  0–8478–0684–7 Rizzoli $45.00

Italian Gardens

- **Marella Agnelli & others**
  GARDENS OF THE ITALIAN VILLAS
  Privileged information with excellent color photos
  0–8478–0825–4 Rizzoli $50.00

- **John Hunt**
  GARDEN AND GROVE: The Italian Renaissance Garden in the English Imagination, 1600–1750
  0–691–04041–9 Princeton $32.50

- **Georgina Masson**
  ITALIAN GARDENS
  1–85149–027–2 Antique Collectors $69.50

Islamic Gardens

- **John Brookes**
  GARDENS OF PARADISE: The History and Design of the Great Islamic Gardens
  Lavishly illustrated; includes maps and plans
  0–941533–07–7 New Amsterdam $33.00

Chinese Gardens

- **David Engel**
  CREATING A CHINESE GARDEN
  Foreword by Sir Harold Acton
  0–88192–025–8 Timber $38.95

- **Maggie Keswick**
  THE CHINESE GARDEN
  0–312–13383–9 St. Martin's pb $24.95

- **Pierre & Susanne Rambach**
  GARDENS OF LONGEVITY IN CHINA AND JAPAN
  0–8478–0837–8 Rizzoli $85.00

Japanese Gardens

- **Teiji Itoh**
  THE GARDENS OF JAPAN
  0–87011–648–7 Kodansha $95.00

  SPACE AND ILLUSION IN THE JAPANESE GARDEN
  0–8348–1522–2 Weatherhill pb $14.95

- **Paul Lesniewicz**
  BONSAI: The Complete Guide to Art and Technique
  Covers all the essentials; with color photographs, drawings, and a convenient chart of Japanese terms
  0–7137–1362–3 Sterling $24.95

- **H. Ohasi**
  JAPANESE COURTYARD GARDENS
  The best of Japan's small private gardens in a collection of evocative photographs
  0–87040–766–X Kodansha $29.95

- **Kiyoshi Seike & others**
  A JAPANESE TOUCH FOR YOUR GARDEN
  0–87011–391–7 Kodansha $22.95

ESSAYS, MEMOIRS, AND REFLECTIONS

- **Geoffrey Charlesworth**
  THE OPINIONATED GARDENER: Random Offshoots from an Alpine Garden
  Essays on the pleasures and difficulties of gardening in the woods by a superb plantsman and incisive writer
  0–87923–672–8 Godine $15.95

- **Colette**
  FLOWERS AND FRUIT
  Brilliant portraits of subjects the writer celebrates with dazzling skill and intense love
  0–374–15683–2 Farrar, Straus & Giroux $14.95

- **Gertrude Jekyll**
  THE MAKING OF A GARDEN
  0–907462–52–9 Antique Collector's $39.00

- **Allen Lacy, editor**
  THE AMERICAN GARDENER
  An instructive sampler of American writing on gardening—from Jefferson's notes on growing oak trees to the best of the modern essayists
  0–374–10404–2 Farrar, Straus & Giroux $18.95

- **Ann Lovejoy**
  THE YEAR IN BLOOM: Gardening for All Seasons in the Pacific Northwest
  An enthusiastic and practical approach to gardening
  0–912365–11–0 Sasquatch pb $11.95

From A Redouté Treasury *by Frances and Peter Mallary* (*Vendome*)

- **Bonnie Marranca, editor**
  AMERICAN GARDEN WRITING: Gleanings from Garden Lives Then and Now
  Letters, journals, and essays by such diverse figures as George Washington, Henry David Thoreau, and Edith Wharton offer a unique view of American garden history
  1–55554–029–5 PAJ $23.95

- **Sara Stein**
  MY WEEDS: A Gardener's Botany
  A thoughtful and informative book, combining experience and technical knowledge
  0–06–015882–4 Harper & Row $19.95

- **Richardson Wright**
  THE GARDENER'S BED-BOOK
  Charming essays on garden history, travel, and the triumphs and disasters that can occur in the garden
  1–55554–028–7 PAJ $20.50

Contemporary American Writers

- **Florence Bellis**
  GARDENING AND BEYOND
  A down-to-earth book that discusses with charm and clarity such difficult topics as soil structure, and many other scientific subjects
  0–88192–015–0 Timber $19.95

- **Allen Lacy**
  FARTHER AFIELD: A Gardener's Excursions
  0–374–15355–8 Farrar, Straus & Giroux $17.95
  0–374–52063–1 Farrar, Straus & Giroux pb $8.95

  HOME GROUND: A Gardener's Miscellany
  0–374–17254–4 Farrar, Straus & Giroux $14.95

- **Henry Mitchell**
  THE ESSENTIAL EARTHMAN
  The *Washington Post* garden columnist's best work
  0–374–51765–7 Farrar, Straus & Giroux pb $8.95

IF YOU CAN'T FIND IT, LOOK IN THE INDEX

- Eleanor Perenyi
GREEN THOUGHTS: A Writer in the Garden
Clear, pithy, and practical. A classic
0–394–71714–7 Random House pb $6.95

- Katharine S. White
ONWARD AND UPWARD IN THE GARDEN
Timeless essays from the great *New Yorker* editor
Edited by E.B. White
0–374–51629–4 Farrar, Straus & Giroux pb $9.95

Contemporary British Writers

- Christopher Brickell & Fay Sharman
THE VANISHING GARDEN: A Conservation Guide to Garden Plants
0–88192–030–4 Timber $24.95

- Ursula Buchan, editor
A BOUQUET OF GARDEN WRITING: Selected from Five Grand Masters
The best introduction to the writing of the British 19th- and 20th-century master gardeners: Gertrude Jekyll, Vita Sackville-West, William Robinson, E.A. Bowles, and Reginald Farrer. Wittily presented by a passionate professional gardener
0–87923–658–2 Godine $25.00

- Robin Lane Fox
VARIATIONS ON A GARDEN
A treasure for the intelligent gardener
0–87923–657–4 Godine $17.50

- Russell Page
THE EDUCATION OF A GARDENER
A worldly and brilliant landscape designer writes about gardening for beginner and expert alike
0–394–72920–X Random House pb $8.95

ART BOOKS

- Mac Griswold
PLEASURES OF THE GARDEN: Images from the Metropolitan Museum of Art
An illuminating and intelligent survey
0–8109–0997–9 Abrams $29.95

- Judith Leet
FLOWERING TREES AND SHRUBS
Botanical paintings by Esther Heins that capture the diversity of the woody plants of the northeastern United States in gardens and wild landscapes. Includes historical and practical information on each plant
0–8109–0940–5 Abrams $29.95

- Richard Mabey
THE FRAMPTON FLORA
Victorian flower paintings, recently discovered in the attic of Frampton Court
0–671–62025–80 Prentice-Hall $25.00

- Frances & Peter Mallary
A REDOUTE TREASURY: 468 Watercolors from Les Liliacées
Considered to be among the most exact and beautiful botanical prints ever made
0–86565–067–5 Vendome pb $23.00

- Ruth Stiff
FLOWERS FROM THE ROYAL GARDENS OF KEW
Superb flower portraits from *Curtis's Botanical Magazine*
0–87451–464–9 New England pb $15.95

- Graham Thomas
THE COMPLETE FLOWER PAINTINGS AND DRAWINGS OF GRAHAM STUART THOMAS
His life's artistic work presented in a beautiful book
0–8109–1666–5 Sagapress $45.00

G. HEYWOOD HILL: The English Garden Tradition

G. Heywood Hill is a well-known London bookshop, one of whose specialties is gardening books.

William Robinson
THE WILD GARDEN
0–317–62655–8 David & Charles $13.95

Gertrude Jekyll
GERTRUDE JEKYLL ON GARDENING
Edited by Penelope Hobhouse
0–87923–496–2 Godine $20.00

Vita Sackville-West
SACKVILLE-WEST'S GARDEN BOOK
0–689–70647–2 Atheneum pb $10.95

Russell Page
THE EDUCATION OF A GARDENER
0–394–72920–X Random House pb $8.95

Roy Hay & Patrick Synge
THE COLOR DICTIONARY OF FLOWERS AND PLANTS FOR HOME AND GARDEN
0–517–52456–2 Crown pb $13.95

Christopher Lloyd
THE WELL-TEMPERED GARDEN
0–394–54053–0 Random House $24.95
0–14–046562–6 Penguin pb $14.95

Robin Lane Fox
BETTER GARDENING
0–87923–611–6 Godine $19.95

Reader's Digest Editors
READER'S DIGEST GUIDE TO CREATIVE GARDENING
0–276–35223–8 Reader's Digest $24.95

Penelope Hobhouse
GARDEN STYLE
0–316–36750–8 Little, Brown $40.00

Peter Beales
CLASSIC ROSES: An Illustrated Encyclopedia of Old Roses, Shrub Roses and Climbers
0–03–006022–2 Henry Holt $45.00

Rosemary Verey
CLASSIC GARDEN DESIGN
0–86553–128–5 Cogdon & Weed $24.95

Pets

The overwhelming majority of pet books focuses on particular species and favorite breeds. There is, however, a small but interesting body of literature that takes a more general view of pets and their role in human society.

- Leo Bustad
ANIMALS, AGING, AND THE AGED
A study of the positive roles animals play in the lives of the elderly
0–8166–0997–7 Minnesota $19.50

- Bruce Fogle
PETS AND THEIR PEOPLE
A lucid introduction, both practical and philosophical, to the bonds between humans and animals
0–14–007786–3 Penguin pb $6.95

- Joel Goldman
THE BOXER REBELLION & OTHER TALES
Memoirs of a dedicated veterinarian; warm tales of animals and their owners told with wit and insight
1–55611–105–3 Donald Fine $17.95

- Vicki Hearne
ADAM'S TASK: Calling Animals by Name
A critically acclaimed book on communication between humans and animals
0–394–54214–2 Knopf $17.95
0–394–75530–8 Random House pb $8.95

- James Herriot
ALL CREATURES GREAT AND SMALL
Best-selling memoirs of a Yorkshire country veterinarian with a genuine love of life and a natural storyteller's gift
0–553–26812–0 Bantam pb $4.95

- Harriet Ritvo
THE ANIMAL ESTATE: The English and Other Creatures in the Victorian Age
Seven case studies showing how animals have been made to embody human values and institutions
0–674–03706–5 Harvard $25.00

- Janet Ruckert
THE FOUR-FOOTED THERAPIST: How Your Pet Can Help You Solve Your Problems
The therapeutic value of companion animals
0–89815–185–6 Ten Speed pb $7.95

- Barbara Woodhouse
TALKING TO ANIMALS
"Woodhouse tells of her peculiar gift of making friends with everything from a hedgehog to the family cows . . . a delightful book"—*Chicago Tribune*
0–425–09788–9 Berkley pb $3.50

PET CARE AND PET LOSS

• Don Aslett
PET CLEAN UP MADE EASY
This book provides many useful tips, all illustrated with comical drawings
0–89879–262–2 Writer's Digest pb $8.95

• Warren & Fay Eckstein
UNDERSTANDING YOUR PET: The Eckstein Method of Pet Therapy and Behavior Training
How to deal with pet behavior problems by looking at the family's life
0–03–000699–6 Henry Holt $15.95

• Michael Fox
THE NEW ANIMAL DOCTOR'S ANSWER BOOK
A valuable reference, which answers more than 1000 questions about the care and behavior of cats, dogs, fish, birds, rabbits, hamsters, and other pets. Written by the author of the popular newspaper column "The Animal Doctor"
1–55704–034–6 Newmarket $24.95
1–55704–035–4 Newmarket pb $12.95

• Barbara Nicholas
THE PORTABLE PET: How to Travel Anywhere with Your Dog or Cat
0–916782–50–6 Harvard Common $12.95
0–916782–49–2 Harvard Common pb $5.95

• Herbert Nieburg & Arlene Fischer
PET LOSS: A Thoughtful Guide for Adults and Children
How to deal with grief at the death of a beloved pet
0–06–014947–7 Harper & Row $14.95

• Jamie Quackenbush & Denise Graveline
WHEN YOUR PET DIES: How to Cope With Your Feelings
0–671–66930–X Simon & Schuster pb $4.50

• Peter Roach
THE COMPLETE BOOK OF PET CARE
A practical, up-to-date household reference book by an Australian veterinarian; with sections on birds, cats, dogs, fish, guinea pigs, horses, mice, rabbits, and reptiles
0–7018–1617–1 Howell $19.95

Animals in Art

Norman Arlott
BIRD PAINTINGS
0–437–00630–1 David & Charles $28.00

John Audubon
THE BIRDS OF AMERICA
0–02–504450–8 Macmillan $38.50

T.H. Clark
THE RHINOCEROS FROM DURER TO STUBBS: An Aspect of the Exotic
0–85667–322–6 Sotheby $29.95

Elizabeth Foucart-Walter & Pierre Rosenberg
THE PAINTED CAT
0–8478–0995–1 Rizzoli $50.00

Philippe Grunchec
GERICAULT'S HORSES: Drawings and Watercolors
0–86565–047–0 Vendome $60.00

John O'Neill
METROPOLITAN CATS
0–8109–1337–2 Abrams $27.50

Constance-Anne Parker
MR. STUBBS: Horsepainter
0–85131–123–7 Sydney Smith $24.50

Robert Rosenblum
THE DOG IN ART FROM ROCOCO TO POST-MODERNISM
0–8109–1143–4 Abrams $27.50

DOGS

The dog, a domesticated wolf, is generally thought to have been mankind's first pet. Originally a hunting ally, by 7000 BC he was a domesticated friend as well. The superior quality and quantity of dog books attests to the abiding hold of canines on mankind's affection and imagination. Today it is estimated that 40 percent of all American households own a dog. Howell Book House is the outstanding publisher of dog literature, offering the most serious, comprehensive and up-to-date books. Denlingers, though smaller, also publishes quality dog books.

American Kennel Club Staff
THE COMPLETE DOG BOOK
The indispensable dog book: America's official guide to the purebred dog, a superb compendium dedicated to "acquainting the public with the appearance and qualification of each breed, and guiding owners in keeping their dogs healthy, happy and well-balanced"
0–87605–463–7 Howell $17.95

• Elizabeth M. Schuler, editor
SIMON AND SCHUSTER'S GUIDE TO DOGS
Identifying pictures and characteristics of over 300 breeds, including all those not recognized by the American Kennel Club
0–671–25527–4 Simon & Schuster pb $11.95

• Carrie Shook
WHAT TO NAME YOUR DOG
An entertaining book, with thousands of imaginative names
0–87605–807–1 Howell pb $9.95

• Chris Walkowicz & Bonnie Wilcox
THE COMPLETE QUESTION AND ANSWER BOOK ON DOGS
"Generously laced with common sense and good humor"—Betty White
0–525–48387–X Dutton pb $8.95

Dog Behavior and Psychology

• Myrna Milani
THE BODY LANGUAGE AND EMOTIONS OF DOGS
A practical guide to the physical behavior of dogs and their owners, and how to use them to create a lasting bond
0–688–06239–3 Morrow $17.95

THE INVISIBLE LEASH: A Better Way to Communicate with Your Dog
0–451–14613–1 NAL pb $3.95

• Desmond Morris
DOGWATCHING
Random observations and little-known facts by a celebrated author and zoologist
0–517–56519–6 Crown $10.95

• Clarence Pfaffenberger
NEW KNOWLEDGE OF DOG BEHAVIOR
A clear exposition of the four critical stages of development in a puppy's life
0–87605–704–0 Howell $14.95

• John Scott & John Fuller
DOG BEHAVIOR: The Genetic Basis
The major work on dog behavior
0–226–74338–1 Chicago pb $12.50

Dog Training

• Carol Benjamin
DOG PROBLEMS
How to control and correct undesirable behavior patterns
0–87605–514–5 Howell pb $12.95

MOTHER KNOWS BEST: The Natural Way to Train Your Dog
A thoughtful guide based on the natural way a mother dog trains her puppies
0–87605–666–4 Howell $16.95

• Job Michael Evans
THE EVANS GUIDE FOR CIVILIZED CANINES
How to choose the right dog for the city, how to care for it, and how to train it
0–87605–543–9 Howell $16.95

• William Koehler
KOEHLER METHOD OF DOG TRAINING
A standard text by the former Disney animal trainer
0–87605–657–5 Howell pb $12.95

• Margaret Pearsall
THE PEARSALL GUIDE TO SUCCESSFUL DOG TRAINING
Obedience from the dog's point of view: a gentler approach than Koehler's
0–87605–759–8 Howell $17.95

• Mordecai Siegal & Matthew Margolis
GOOD DOG, BAD DOG
Self-help reference for dog training. "It will be read and revered for many years to come"—Roger Caras
0–451–15521–1 NAL pb $4.95

✉ TO ORDER BOOKS AS GIFTS, SEE PAGE 1

- Barbara Woodhouse
NO BAD DOGS: Training Dogs the Woodhouse Way
The popular British TV personality shares her unique and successful methods
0–671–44962–1 Simon & Schuster $15.95
0–671–54185–4 Simon & Schuster pb $7.95

Health and Care

- Carol Lea Benjamin
SECOND-HAND DOG: How to Turn Yours into a First-Rate Pet
The special needs of dogs adopted from shelters or rescued from the streets
0–87605–735–0 Howell pb $4.95

- Delbert Carlson & James Giffin
DOG OWNER'S HOME VETERINARY HANDBOOK
The leader in the field of professional dog doctoring. Covers every health need your dog will face in its lifetime
0–87605–764–4 Howell $18.95

- William Kay & Elizabeth Randolph
THE COMPLETE BOOK OF DOG HEALTH: The Animal Medical Center
0–02–600930–7 Macmillan $19.95

- David Taylor
YOU AND YOUR DOG
0–394–72983–8 Knopf pb $9.95

- Leon & George Whitney
COMPLETE BOOK OF DOG CARE
A thorough, classic guide
0–385–15547–6 Doubleday pb $9.95

Grooming

- Charlotte Gold
GROOMING DOGS FOR PROFIT
A professional groomer covers all aspects of the grooming business
0–87605–618–4 Howell $16.95

- Shirlee Kalstone
THE KALSTONE GUIDE TO GROOMING ALL TOY DOGS
How to trim, groom, and condition a Toy dog
0–87605–323–1 Howell $17.95

- Ben Stone & Pearl Stone
THE STONE GUIDE TO DOG GROOMING FOR ALL BREEDS
A comprehensive guide with full grooming instructions and techniques for all AKC breeds
0–87605–403–3 Howell $22.95

Breeding and Showing

- Robert & Jane Forsyth
THE FORSYTH GUIDE TO SUCCESSFUL DOG SHOWING
A concise guide by two renowned handlers
0–87605–523–4 Howell $13.95

- Alvin Grossman
THE STANDARD BOOK OF DOG BREEDING
0–87714–054–5 Denlingers $16.95

- Anne Katherine Nicholas
THE NICHOLAS GUIDE TO DOG JUDGING
A new edition on what motivates the judges at dog shows
0–87605–690–7 Howell $19.95

- Mary Smith
THE JOY OF BREEDING YOUR OWN SHOW DOG
A serious introduction to a complex art
0–87605–413–0 Howell $16.95

- Chris Walkowicz & Bonnie Wilcox
SUCCESSFUL DOG BREEDING
Selected as Best Dog Book of the Year
0–668–06134–0 Arco $19.95

Popular Breeds

- Constance Miller & Edward Gilbert, Jr.
THE NEW COMPLETE AFGHAN HOUND
0–87605–001–1 Howell $17.95

- Joan Linderman & Virginia Funk
THE COMPLETE AKITA
0–87605–006–2 Howell $17.95

- Mercedes Braun
THE NEW COMPLETE BASSET HOUND
0–87605–021–6 Howell $17.95

- Robert Berndt
YOUR BEAGLE
0–87714–034–0 Denlingers $13.95

- Billie McFadden
THE NEW BOXER
0–87605–062–3 Howell $19.95

"Village Schoolteacher" by August Sander, from The Dog Observed: Photographs, 1844–1983 *edited by Ruth Silverman (Knopf)*

- John Remer, Jr., editor
THE NEW BULL TERRIER
0–87605–096–8 Howell $19.95

- L.J. Kip Kopatch
THE COMPLETE CHOW CHOW
0–87605–102–6 Howell $18.95

- Anna Nicholas
A COMPLETE INTRODUCTION TO COCKER SPANIELS
0–86622–364–9 TFH $9.95
0–86622–381–9 TFH pb $5.95

- Collie Club of America
THE NEW COLLIE
0–87605–130–1 Howell $17.95

- George Roos
COLLIE CONCEPT
0–931866–36–7 Alpine $24.95

- Mary Sargent & Deborah Harper
THE COMPLETE PEMBROKE WELSH CORGI
0–87605–224–3 Howell $17.95

- Lois Meistrell
THE NEW DACHSHUND
0–87605–107–7 Howell $17.95

- Alfred & Esmeralda Treen
THE DALMATIAN: Coach Dog— Firehouse Dog
0–87605–109–3 Howell $17.95

- Joanna Walker
THE NEW DOBERMAN PINSCHER
0–87605–113–1 Howell $17.95

- Jane Bennett
THE NEW COMPLETE GERMAN SHEPHERD DOG
0–87605–151–4 Howell $15.95

- Gertrude Fischer
THE NEW COMPLETE GOLDEN RETRIEVER
0–87605–185–9 Howell $17.95

- Evelyn Schneider
THE GOLDEN RETRIEVER
0–87714–122–3 Denlingers $29.95

THE NEW COMPLETE GREAT DANE
0–87605–161–1 Howell $16.95

- E. Irving Eldredge & Connie Vanacore
THE NEW COMPLETE IRISH SETTER
0–87605–166–2 Howell $18.95

- D. Brian Plummer
THE COMPLETE JACK RUSSELL TERRIER
0–85115–121–3 Howell $16.95

- Helen Warwick
THE NEW COMPLETE LABRADOR RETRIEVER
0–87605–230–8 Howell $17.95

- Anna Nicholas & Joan Brearley
THE BOOK OF THE PEKINGESE
0–87666–348–X TFH $29.95

- Mackey J. Irick, Jr.
THE NEW POODLE
0–87605–256–1 Howell $22.95

- Frank Sabella
YOUR POODLE: Standard, Miniature and Toy
0–87714–023–5 Denlingers $12.95

- Esther Wolf
YOUR PUG
0–87714–001–4 Denlingers $13.95

- Paul Strang & Eve Olsen
THE CHINESE SHAR-PEI
0–87714–072–3 Denlingers $29.95

- Sylvia Woods & Ray Owen
OLD ENGLISH SHEEPDOGS
0–571–11620–5 Faber & Faber $18.95

- Audrey Dadds
THE SHIH TZU
0–87605–309–6 Howell $17.95

- John Marvin
THE BOOK OF ALL TERRIERS
0–87605–316–9 Howell $15.95

THE NEW COMPLETE SCOTTISH TERRIER
0–87605–306–1 Howell $17.95

THE COMPLETE WEST HIGHLAND WHITE TERRIER
0–87605–355–X Howell $17.95

- Joan Gordon & Janet Bennett
THE COMPLETE YORKSHIRE TERRIER
0–87605–360–6 Howell $17.95

Dog Stories and Humor

- Roger Caras
ROGER CARAS' TREASURY OF GREAT DOG STORIES
Stories about dogs, from Jack London and Mark Twain to R.K. Narayan and Françoise Sagan. Essential for any dog lover
0–525–24399–2 Dutton $19.95

- John Donegan
DOG ALMIGHTY!
Satirical, good-natured cartoons
0–87605–466–1 Howell pb $7.95

- James Herriot
JAMES HERRIOT'S DOG STORIES
A collection of all the dog stories from the best-selling author
0–312–43968–7 St. Martin's $19.95
0–312–90143–7 St. Martin's pb $4.95

- Ilene Hochberg
CQ: CANINE QUARTERLY: A Parody of the World's Most Elegant Magazine for Men
1–55562–035–3 Main Street pb $8.95

DOGUE: A Parody of the World's Most Famous Fashion Magazine
1–55562–002–7 Main Street pb $9.95

- Volker Kriegel
THE TRUTH ABOUT DOGS
Cartoons, irresistible to dog lovers and haters
Introduction by Julian Barnes
0–06–016038–1 Harper & Row pb $7.95

- Louise Shattuck
FROM RICHES TO BITCHES (and a Cadillac for Your Vet): Being a Mirthful Recounting of the Carry-on Kennel Chronicles
0–87605–548–X Howell $12.95

- Garrett Simmons & Dorian Yeager
PUPPLE
A take-off of *People* magazine, with such celebrities as the Rolling Bones and Lee Iacocker
0–399–59549–X Bantam pb $4.95

- John Tickner
TICKNER'S DOGS
British humor, combined with the legendary British love for dogs
0–87605–950–7 Howell pb $9.95

Illustrated Dog Books

- Rien Poorvliet
DOGS
0–8109–0809–3 Abrams $29.95

- Priscilla Rattazzi
BEST FRIENDS
A splendid book of photographs of dogs with their owners, many of them famous
Introduction by Giovanni Agnelli
0–8478–1058–5 Rizzoli $25.00

- Robert Rosenblum
THE DOG IN ART FROM ROCOCO TO POST-MODERNISM
0–8109–1143–4 Abrams $27.50

- Ruth Silverman, editor
THE DOG OBSERVED: Photographs, 1844–1983
A wonderful book of photographs by some of the world's greatest photographers, such as Diane Arbus and Richard Avedon
0–394–53596–0 Knopf $25.00
0–87701–499–X Chronicle pb $14.95

Felicity Wigan & Victoria Mather
THE ENGLISH DOG AT HOME
English dogs as masters of the house in some of the grandest English country houses. Stylish and highly entertaining
0–88162–264–8 Salem House $27.50

CATS

Domesticated since prehistoric times, cats were once used as retrievers in hunting. The modern domestic and the Egyptian cat are both thought to derive from a type of North African wildcat. The personality of the cat, with its air of mystery and independence, has always been fascinating, and the literature on cats reflects this mystique.

- Muriel Beadle
THE CAT
"A natural history colored with affection, stuffed with anecdote, and as graceful as its subject"—*NY Times*
0–671–25190–2 Simon & Schuster pb $7.95

- Roger Caras
A CELEBRATION OF CATS
In praise of cats, for sheer pleasure and great joy
0–671–49287–X Simon & Schuster $16.95
0–671–64576–5 Simon & Schuster pb $7.95

Cat Breeds

Harper & Row
HARPER'S ILLUSTRATED HANDBOOK OF CATS: A Guide to Every Breed Recognized in America
A comprehensive and essential book on cats, as there is no single governing body (such as the American Kennel Club for dogs) that regulates breeds and standards for cats
0–06–091199–9 Harper & Row pb $9.95

Gino Pugnetti
SIMON AND SCHUSTER'S GUIDE TO CATS
0–671–49167–9 Simon & Schuster $23.95
0–671–49170–9 Simon & Schuster pb $9.95

- Joan Brearley
ALL ABOUT HIMALAYAN CATS
0–87666–756–6 TFH pb $9.95

- Kate Faler
THIS IS THE ABYSSINIAN CAT
0–87666–866–X TFH $16.95

- Gwen Jenkins
THE HOWELL BEGINNER'S GUIDE TO BURMESE CATS
0–87605–904–3 Howell pb $3.95

- Grace Pond
LONGHAIR CATS
0–8120–2923–2 Barron's pb $6.95

- Ingeborg Urcia
THIS IS THE RUSSIAN BLUE
0–87666–864–3 TFH $19.95

- Rod U'ren
THE HOWELL BEGINNER'S GUIDE TO PERSIAN CATS
0–87605–942–6 Howell pb $3.95

Health and Care

- Delbert Carlson & James Giffin
CAT OWNER'S HOME VETERINARY HANDBOOK
Like its canine counterpart, this is the most serious, most comprehensive health book for cats
0–87605–814–4 Howell $19.95

- Marna Fogarty
THE CAT YELLOW PAGES: The Cat Owner's Guide to Goods and Services
0–684–18094–4 Scribners $19.95
0–684–18158–4 Scribners pb $12.95

- Fredric Frye
  FIRST AID FOR YOUR CAT
  0–8120–5827–5 Barron's pb $9.95

- Stephen Kritsick
  DR. KRITSICK'S TENDER LOVING CAT CARE
  Short and to the point
  0–671–46725–5 Simon & Schuster $16.95
  0–671–64615–X Simon & Schuster pb $7.95

- Mordecai Siegal
  THE GOOD CAT BOOK
  Sensible, practical advice
  0–671–45623–7 Simon & Schuster pb $8.95

- David Taylor
  YOU AND YOUR CAT
  0–394–72984–6 Knopf pb $9.95

Psychology, Behavior, and Training

- Jo & Paul Loeb
  YOU CAN TRAIN YOUR CAT
  0–671–25147–3 Simon & Schuster pb $8.95

- Myrna Milani
  THE BODY LANGUAGE AND EMOTION OF CATS
  A behavioral approach to improving one's relations with cats
  0–688–06786–7 Morrow $17.95

- Desmond Morris
  CATWATCHING
  Observations and thoughts on the double life of cats, from a seasoned observer
  0–517–56518–8 Crown $10.95

- Debra Pirotin & Sherry Cohen
  NO NAUGHTY CATS: The First Guide to Intelligent Cat Training
  0–06–015438–1 Harper & Row pb $12.95

- Roz Riddle
  THE CITY CAT: How to Live Healthily and Happily with Your Indoor Pet
  0–684–18208–4 Scribners pb $12.95

- Carole Wilbourn
  CATS ON THE COUCH: The Complete Guide for Loving and Caring for Your Cat
  0–02–628460–X Macmillan pb $12.95

Legends, Stories, and Entertainments

- Cleveland Amory
  THE CAT WHO CAME FOR CHRISTMAS
  A humorous best-selling memoir of a strange feline friend
  0–316–03737–0 Little, Brown $15.95
  0–14–011342–8 Penguin pb $6.95

- Robert Byrne & Teresa Skelton
  CAT SCAN: All the Best from the Literature of Cats
  0–449–20640–8 Fawcett pb $2.95

- Louis Camuti
  ALL MY PATIENTS ARE UNDER THE BED
  The popular memoirs and anecdotes of a cat doctor
  0–671–55450–6 Simon & Schuster pb $6.95

- Roger Caras
  ROGER CARAS' TREASURY OF GREAT CAT STORIES
  Literary anthology includes stories by Poe, Twain, Kipling
  0–525–24398–4 Dutton $19.95

- Paul Gallico & Suzanne Szasz
  THE SILENT MIAOW: A Manual for Kittens, Strays, and Homeless Cats
  Fictional "guide" for cats on how to win their way into a household and take over the family
  0–517–55683–9 Crown pb $6.95

- Ilene Hochberg
  CATMOPOLITAN
  Hilarious spoof of *Cosmopolitan* magazine, featuring cats as the models
  0–671–64704–0 Pocket pb $9.95

- Alice Muncaster & Ellen Yanow
  THE CAT MADE ME BUY IT: A Collection of Cats Who Sold Yesterday's Products
  A delightful history of feline stars in the advertising world
  0–517–55338–4 Crown pb $8.95

- Shep Steneman & Jim Davis
  GARFIELD: The Complete Cat Book
  0–394–94893–9 Random House $7.95
  0–394–84893–4 Random House pb $5.95

Illustrated Cat Books

- B. Kliban
  CATCALENDAR CATS
  Sixty-five classic originals from Kliban's best-selling cat calendars
  0–89480–223–2 Workman pb $9.95

- John O'Neill
  METROPOLITAN CATS
  Fifty centuries of the cat through paintings, sculptures, prints, drawings, needlework, ceramics. A beautiful book from the Metropolitan Museum of Art
  0–8109–1337–2 Abrams $27.50

Woodcut by Félix Vallotton

- Wilbur Pippin & Marian Winters
  CATWISE
  0–394–73786–5 Knopf pb $5.95

HORSES

Recent years have seen an increase in the popularity of equestrian sports in the United States, and many new books cover the field.

- Joan Embery & Robert Vavra
  ON HORSES
  Well illustrated
  0–688–04070–5 Morrow $24.95

- Tamas Flandorffer & Jozsef Hajas
  THE HORSE AND HORSEMANSHIP
  A series of wash drawings on anatomy, riding techniques, tack, training, and health
  0–963–131643–2 Newbury $12.95

- Margaret Hodges
  IF YOU HAD A HORSE: Steeds of Myth and Legend
  0–684–18220–3 Macmillan $12.95

- Hans Isenbart & Emil Buhrer
  THE IMPERIAL HORSE: The Saga of the Lipizzaners
  The 4000-year history of the great white horse, with color illustrations
  0–394–549–65–1 Knopf $39.50

- Franz Mairinger
  HORSES ARE MADE TO BE HORSES
  A personal philosophy of horsemanship from the renowned Spanish Riding School instructor and Olympic trainer
  0–87605–855–1 Howell $14.95

- Bruce Mills & Barbara Carne
  A BASIC GUIDE TO HORSE CARE AND MANAGEMENT
  0–87605–871–3 Howell $17.95

- Steven Price & others, editors
  THE WHOLE HORSE CATALOG
  A complete up-to-date sensible handbook
  0–671–54196–X Simon & Schuster pb $12.95

- William Steinkraus & M.A. Stoneridge
  THE HORSE IN SPORT
  With a preface by the Duke of Edinburgh
  1–55670–014–8 Stewart, Tabori & Chang $35.00

- M.A. Stoneridge
  A HORSE OF YOUR OWN
  A complete guide for horse owners and riders
  0–385–14617–5 Doubleday $21.95

- Robert Vavra
  EQUUS: The Creation of a Horse
  A photographic essay, with a foreword by James Michener
  0–688–03958–8 Morrow pb $14.95

- Barbara Woodhouse
BARBARA'S WORLD OF HORSES AND PONIES
From the inimitable British TV personality
0–517–49181–8 Sisch pb $4.00

- James Young
A FIELD OF HORSES: The World of Marshall P. Hawkins
Scenes of foxhunting, racing, and hunting captured by the renowned photographer
0–87833–625–7 Taylor $35.00

Horse Breeds

There are over 150 registered breeds of horses. Unlike a thoroughbred dog, a thoroughbred horse is a specific breed that traces its ancestry to England in the 1660s. The thoroughbred line has produced the most valuable horses in the world, dominating flat and steeplechase racing as well as hunter/jumper horse shows and dressage competition. The graceful, fine-featured Arabian is one of the oldest breeds. The Quarter Horse, the classic "western" horse, is so named because of its ability to run one-quarter of a mile faster than any other breed.

- Anthony Amaral
MUSTANG: The Life and Legends of Nevada's Wild Horses
0–87417–046–X Nevada pb $9.95

- Robert Denhardt
THE QUARTER RUNNING HORSE: America's Oldest Breed
0–8061–1500–9 Oklahoma $32.50

- Karen Flanigan
THOSE MAGNIFICENT CLYDESDALES: The Gentle Giants
0–517–53426–6 Crown pb $6.95

- Glynn Haynes
THE AMERICAN PAINT HORSE
0–8061–2144–0 Oklahoma $12.95

- Lorna Howlett
THE COMPLETE BOOK OF PONIES
0–87605–856–X Howell $19.95

- Jeanne Mellin
THE MORGAN HORSE
0–8289–0590–8 Viking pb $19.95

- Miles Napier
THOROUGHBRED PEDIGREES SIMPLIFIED
0–85131–191–1 Sporting Book Center pb $7.95

- William Pereira, Jr.
THE MAJESTIC WORLD OF ARABIAN HORSES
0–8109–1846–3 Abrams $60.00

- Bill & Dana Richardson
THE APPALOOSA
0–87980–182–4 Wilshire pb $7.00

- Reginald Summerhays
THE ARABIAN HORSE
0–87980–183–2 Wilshire pb $5.00

A Lipizzaner stallion of the Spanish Riding School (photo copyright Janos Kalmar), from The Imperial Horse *by Hans Isenbart and Emil Buhrer (Knopf)*

Breeding

- M. Phyllis Lose
BLESSED ARE THE BROOD MARES
An essential book on breeding and foaling
0–02–575250–2 Macmillan $22.95

- Ron & Val Males
FOALING: Brood Mare and Foal Management
Veteran stud managers conduct the reader through a guided tour of the foaling paddock to witness a foaling first-hand; illustrated with color photos
0–87605–851–9 Howell $12.95

Health and Care

- Melvin Bradley
HORSES: A Practical and Scientific Approach
0–07–007065–2 McGraw-Hill $39.95

- Gaydell Collier
BASIC HORSE CARE
0–385–17229–X Doubleday $19.95

- James Giffin & Tom Gore
HORSE OWNER'S VETERINARY HANDBOOK
A thorough, well-organized health guide
0–87605–880–2 Howell $29.95

- Tim Hawcroft
THE COMPLETE BOOK OF HORSE CARE
Reliable information on many aspects of horse care, with color photos
0–7018–1518–3 Howell $19.95

- Horace Hayes
VETERINARY NOTES FOR HORSE OWNERS
The most thorough and professional book on the subject
0–13–941956–X Simon & Schuster $26.95

- Ann Hyland
FOAL TO FIVE YEARS
A popular and practical guide
0–668–04952–9 Simon & Schuster $16.95

- Jane Kidd
A YOUNG RIDER'S GUIDE TO HORSE AND PONY CARE
A handy reference for young equestrians
0–87605–870–5 Howell $12.95

- Bruce Mills & Barbara Carne
A BASIC GUIDE TO HORSE CARE AND MANAGEMENT
What to look for in terms of health and conformation
0–87605–871–3 Howell $17.95

Training

- Gaydell Collier
BASIC TRAINING FOR HORSES: English and Western
Specific instructions for safe, step-by-step training methods
0–385–03244–7 Doubleday $19.95

- Peter Jones
EDUCATING HORSES FROM BIRTH TO RIDING
Step-by-step on developing a well-trained horse
0–87605–854–3 Howell $14.95

- Bertalan de Nemethy
THE DE NEMETHY METHOD: Modern Techniques for Training the Show Jumper and Rider
By the coach of the US equestrian team
0–385–23620–4 Doubleday $24.95

- Alois Podhajsky
COMPLETE TRAINING OF HORSE AND RIDER IN THE PRINCIPLES OF CLASSICAL HORSEMANSHIP
A classic from the former director of the Spanish Riding School
0–385–07872–2 Doubleday $19.95
0–87980–235–9 Wilshire pb $7.00

Grooming and Showing

- Susan Harris
GROOMING TO WIN: How to Groom, Trim, Braid, and Prepare Your Horse for Show
0–684–14859–5 Scribners pb $16.95

- Elwyn Hartley-Edwards
THE HOWELL BOOK OF SADDLERY AND TACK
A lavish survey of the history of equestrian gear, modern equipment, and riders
0–87065–873–X Howell $24.95

- Elaine Knox-Thompson & Suzanne Dickens
GUIDE TO RIDING AND HORSE CARE
0–87605–852–7 Howell $16.95

➤ **FOR OVERSEAS ORDERING INFORMATION, SEE PAGE 1**

- Janet Macdonald
  THE RIGHT HORSE: An Owner's and Buyer's Guide
  0–668–06246–0 Simon & Schuster pb $9.95

Horsemanship

▶ See also Sports

- The British Horse Society
  RIDING CLASS
  An excellent manual on riding for young equestrians
  0–87605–860–8 Howell $16.95

- Marcy Drummond
  LONG-DISTANCE RIDING
  A good introduction with many photographs
  0–87605–861–6 Howell $16.95

- Vladimir Littauer
  COMMONSENSE HORSEMANSHIP
  A milestone in the development of a modern system of riding and schooling. Essential for all horse people
  0–668–05791–2 Simon & Schuster pb $9.95

- George Morris
  HUNTER SEAT EQUITATION
  From the successful instructor who gave us the "Morris method"
  0–385–15253–1 Doubleday $17.95

- Wilhelm Museler
  RIDING LOGIC
  First published in 1937 and now a classic on the art of riding and horsemanship
  0–668–06116–2 Simon & Schuster $12.95

- Mark Phillips
  CAPTAIN MARK PHILLIPS ON RIDING: A Complete Guide for Beginners
  From the British Olympic medalist
  0–13–114521–5 Prentice Hall $19.95

- Sally Swift
  CENTERED RIDING
  0–312–12734–0 David & Charles $15.95

Dressage and Show Jumping

- Jonathan Burton & Darlene Sordillo
  HOW TO RIDE A WINNING DRESSAGE TEST: The Judge's Guide to Step-by-Step Improvement
  Takes you through every official test used in dressage and combined competition
  0–395–38217–3 Houghton Mifflin pb $10.95

- Anthony Crossley
  DRESSAGE: The Seat, Aids and Exercises
  0–7207–1777–9 Viking $15.95

- R.L. Ffrench Blake
  DRESSAGE FOR BEGINNERS
  0–395–24399–8 Houghton Mifflin pb $7.95

- John Smart
  SHOWJUMPING: Preparation, Training and Competition
  From basic movements to advanced jumps
  0–87605–868–3 Howell $16.95

Today approximately 60 million Americans practice the hobby of aviculture, ranging from the canary owner to the breeder of exotic swans and pheasants.

- Ernest Choate
  THE DICTIONARY OF AMERICAN BIRD NAMES
  0–87645–121–0 Harvard Common $17.95

- Irene Christie
  BIRDS: A Guide to a Mixed Collection
  Descriptions and photos of 85 species, with pertinent chapters on every aspect of aviculture
  0–948075–00–7 Howell $13.95

- Jean Dorst
  THE LIFE OF BIRDS
  A good illustrated survey, published as a two-volume set
  0–231–03909–3 Columbia $99.50

- Alan Feduccia
  THE AGE OF BIRDS
  On the origin and evolution of birds. "Bird-watching on a cosmic scale"—Roger Caras
  0–674–00975–4 Harvard $27.00
  0–674–00976–2 Harvard pb $12.95

- Don Harper
  THE PRACTICAL ENCYCLOPEDIA OF PET BIRDS FOR HOME AND GARDEN: Featuring 200 Birds from Around the World
  0–517–56546–3 Crown $17.95

- W.B. Lockwood
  THE OXFORD BOOK OF BRITISH BIRD NAMES
  0–19–214155–4 Oxford $18.95

- Matthew Vriends
  SIMON AND SCHUSTER'S GUIDE TO PET BIRDS
  Includes information on 206 species of cage and aviary birds, illustrated in color
  0–671–50696–X Simon & Schuster pb $11.95

Bird Species

The most popular pet birds today in the United States are canaries, budgerigars, finches, and parrots. Cockatiels, cockatoos, lovebirds, macaws, and parakeets are all members of the parrot family.

- Karl Diefenbach
  THE WORLD OF COCKATOOS
  0–86622–034–8 TFH $24.95

- G.T. Dodwell
  THE COMPLETE BOOK OF CANARIES
  0–87605–824–1 Howell $19.95

- Arthur Freud
  ALL ABOUT THE PARROTS
  0–87605–815–2 Howell $17.95

- Derek Goodwin
  PIGEONS AND DOVES OF THE WORLD
  0–8014–1434–2 Cornell $48.50

- Jim Hayward
  LOVEBIRDS AND OTHER COLOUR MUTATIONS
  0–7137–1981–8 Sterling $19.95

- Paul Johnsgard
  THE PHEASANTS OF THE WORLD
  0–19–857185–2 Oxford $85.00

- Rosemary Low
  MYNAH BIRDS
  0–7028–1002–9 Avian pb $3.95
  PARROTS: Their Care and Breeding
  0–7137–1437–9 Sterling $90.00

- Matthew Vriends
  THE COMPLETE BUDGERIGAR
  0–87605–822–5 Howell $17.95
  THE COMPLETE COCKATIEL
  0–87605–817–9 Howell $15.95
  THE COMPLETE BOOK OF FINCHES
  0–87605–825–X Howell $17.95

Breeding, Health, and Care

- Gary Gallerstein
  THE BIRD OWNER'S HOME HEALTH AND CARE HANDBOOK
  Well organized and informative
  0–87605–820–9 Howell $17.95

- Sheldon Gerstenfeld
  THE BIRD CARE BOOK
  0–201–03909–5 Addison-Wesley pb $9.95

- Matthew Vriends
  BREEDING CAGE AND AVIARY BIRDS
  0–87605–821–7 Howell $15.95

Garden Birds

- John Dennis
  A COMPLETE GUIDE TO BIRD FEEDING
  0–394–47937–8 Knopf $18.95

- Walter Schutz
  HOW TO ATTRACT, HOUSE, AND FEED BIRDS: 48 Plans for Bird Feeders and Houses You Can Make
  With step-by-step drawings, photographs, and directions
  0–02–011910–0 Macmillan pb $8.95

- John Terres
  SONGBIRDS IN YOUR GARDEN
  0–06–091377–0 Harper & Row pb $10.95

In the United States today there are over five million hobbyists who maintain aquariums.
The newly formed Tetra Press publishes well-organized, informative books on fish. Tropical Fish Hobbyists also publishes some

useful literature; the subjects include tropical, cold-water, and marine species suitable for the home aquarium.

- **Herbert Axelrod**
  BREEDING AQUARIUM FISHES: A Complete Introduction
  0–86622–256–1 TFH $9.95
  0–86622–294–4 TFH pb $5.95

  EXOTIC TROPICAL FISHES
  How to care for these fish at home; tips on aquariums
  0–87666–543–1 TFH $39.95

- **Brian Curtis**
  LIFE STORY OF THE FISH
  0–486–20929–6 Dover pb $6.95

- **N.B. Marshall**
  EXPLORATIONS IN THE LIFE OF FISHES
  Fish behavior
  0–674–27951–4 Harvard $18.50

- **Bethen Penzes & Istvan Tolg**
  GOLDFISH AND ORNAMENTAL CARP
  0–8120–5634–5 Barron's $18.95

- **Simon & Schuster**
  SIMON & SCHUSTER'S GUIDE TO FRESHWATER AND MARINE AQUARIUM FISH
  0–671–22809–9 Simon & Schuster pb $11.95

- **Gunther Sterba, editor**
  THE AQUARIUM ENCYCLOPEDIA
  From a major pioneer in fish research
  0–262–19207–1 MIT $45.00

The Aquarium

- **Dick Mills**
  YOU AND YOUR AQUARIUM
  0–394–72985–4 Knopf pb $9.95

- **Joseph Stilton**
  THE HOWELL BEGINNER'S GUIDE TO AQUARIUM PLANTS AND DECORATION
  0–87605–901–9 Howell pb $3.95

REPTILES AND LIZARDS

- **Harald Jes**
  LIZARDS IN THE TERRARIUM
  0–8120–3925–4 Barron's pb $4.50

- **Christopher Mattison**
  THE CARE OF REPTILES AND AMPHIBIANS IN CAPTIVITY
  0–7137–1826–9 Sterling $24.95

- **Hobart Smith**
  SNAKES AS PETS
  0–87666–908–9 TFH $14.95

RABBITS, HAMSTERS, GERBILS, AND GUINEA PIGS

- **Will Bradford**
  THE HOWELL BEGINNER'S GUIDE TO RABBITS
  0–87605–943–4 Howell pb $3.95

- **Raymond Gudas**
  GERBILS
  0–8120–3725–1 Barron's pb $4.50

- **Pat Hutchinson**
  THE HOWELL BEGINNER'S GUIDE TO GUINEA PIGS
  0–87605–930–2 Howell pb $3.95

- **Leila Watts**
  THE HOWELL BEGINNER'S GUIDE TO HAMSTERS
  0–87605–933–7 Howell pb $3.95

EXOTIC PETS

- **Arthur Rosenblum**
  EXOTIC ANIMALS AS PETS
  0–671–63690–1 Simon & Schuster $21.95
  0–671–47654–8 Simon & Schuster pb $12.95

Games and Puzzles

- **R.C. Bell**
  BOARD AND TABLE GAMES FROM MANY CIVILIZATIONS
  A revised edition of this classic work, originally published in the 1960s, in which the rules and strategies for 182 games are explained
  0–486–23855–5 Dover pb $6.50

CHESS

- **Andras Adorjan & Jeno Dory**
  WINNING WITH THE GRUNFELD
  An analysis of the Grunfeld Defense, an aggressive defense ideal for the tournament player, written by two Hungarian champions
  0–02–016080–1 Macmillan pb $8.95

- **Alexander Alekhine**
  MY BEST GAMES OF CHESS, 1908–1937
  The triumphs of Alexander Alekhine, the world champion from 1927–1935 and again from 1937–1946
  0–486–24941–7 Dover pb $11.95

- **Y. Averbakh**
  CHESS TACTICS FOR ADVANCED PLAYERS
  An invaluable guide
  0–8285–3430–6 Imported Publications $19.95

- **Joseph Blackburne**
  BLACKBURNE'S CHESS GAMES
  Four hundred games selected and analyzed by the British chess expert
  0–486–23857–1 Dover pb $6.95

- **Mikhail Botvinnik & Yakov Estrin**
  THE GRUNFELD DEFENSE
  An essential book on this strategy
  0–89058–017–0 RHM pb $11.95

- **José Capablanca**
  MY CHESS CAREER
  One of the best chess biographies
  0–486–21548–2 Dover pb $4.50

  PRIMER OF CHESS
  A classic introduction by one of the game's great players
  0–15–673900–3 HBJ pb $5.95

- **Irving Chernev**
  CAPABLANCA'S BEST CHESS ENDINGS: 60 Complete Games
  0–486–24249–8 Dover pb $5.95

  COMBINATIONS: The Heart of Chess
  0–486–21744–2 Dover pb $4.95

  THE ONE THOUSAND BEST SHORT GAMES OF CHESS
  A classic collection of 1000 five-to-fifteen-move games
  0–671–53801–2 Simon & Schuster pb $9.95

- **Larry Evans & others**
  HOW TO OPEN A CHESS GAME
  Seven international grand masters analyze the principles and methods of a logical opening play
  0–89058–203–3 RHM $13.95

- **Reuben Fine, editor**
  BASIC CHESS ENDINGS
  "The definitive work on the end game which all serious students of the game have been waiting for"—NY Times
  0–679–14002–6 David McKay pb $13.95

  THE WORLD'S GREATEST CHESS GAMES
  The greatest games ever played, compiled and annotated by the renowned chess author and grand master
  0–486–24512–8 Tartan pb $7.95

- **Bobby Fischer**
  BOBBY FISCHER TEACHES CHESS
  An introduction to the game by the youngest international grand master in chess history
  0–553–26315–3 Bantam pb $4.95

- **W.R. Hartston**
  THE PENGUIN BOOK OF CHESS OPENINGS
  The various theories on the opening play
  0–14–046312–7 Penguin pb $4.95

- **David Hooper & Kenneth Whyld**
  THE OXFORD COMPANION TO CHESS
  A comprehensive chess encyclopedia, with a history of the game and an analysis of strategies and moves
  0–19–217540–8 Oxford $29.95
  0–19–281986–0 Oxford pb $13.95

- Israel Horowitz
CHESS OPENINGS: Theory and Practice
A collection of 2660 variations, with 439 illustrative games. "The greatest aid I have ever seen for preparing a tournament"—Samuel Reshevsky
0–671–20553–6 Simon & Schuster $16.95

- Israel Horowitz & Alexandra Mark
CHESS FOR BEGINNERS
An introduction to the game by the chess editor of the *New York Times* and former US Open champion
0–671–21184–6 Simon & Schuster pb $6.95

- Israel Horowitz & Fred Reinfeld
CHESS TRAPS
0–671–21041–6 Simon & Schuster pb $7.95

- Kenneth Howard
CLASSIC CHESS PROBLEMS
An essential book for all chess players
0–486–22522–4 Dover pb $3.50

- R.D. Keene
THE CHESS COMBINATION FROM PHILIDOR TO KARPOV
0–08–019758–2 Pergamon $16.95

- Walter Korn, editor
MODERN CHESS OPENINGS
The chess player's bible and the only chess book regularly kept up to date since it was first published more than 50 years ago
0–679–14106–5 David McKay pb $14.95

- Alexander Kotov
PLAY LIKE A GRANDMASTER
0–7134–1807–9 David & Charles pb $17.95
THINK LIKE A GRANDMASTER
0–7134–3160–1 David & Charles pb $17.95

- Edward Lasker
CHESS FOR FUN AND CHESS FOR BLOOD
0–486–20146–5 Dover pb $4.95
COMMON SENSE IN CHESS
0–486–21440–0 Dover pb $3.50
MODERN CHESS STRATEGY
A revision of the author's popular classic *Chess Strategies*
0–679–14022–0 David McKay pb $6.95

Illustration by Alison Seiffer, from E.B. White's Here Is New York *(Warner Books)*

- Emmanuel Lasker
COMMON SENSE IN CHESS
0–486–21440–0 Dover pb $3.50
LASKER'S MANUAL OF CHESS
One of the most thorough studies of chess by the great modern chess players
0–486–20640–8 Dover pb $6.50

- David Levy
KARPOV'S COLLECTED GAMES
Five hundred thirty games played by the Soviet champion Anatoly Karpov, Bobby Fischer's challenger in the 1974 World Chess Championship
0–89058–005–7 RHM pb $11.95

- Johann Lowenthal
MORPHY'S GAMES OF CHESS
0–7134–5057–6 David & Charles $39.95

- James Mason
ART OF CHESS
A recent revision of the famous general study of the game
0–486–20463–4 Dover pb $6.95

- Edmar Mednis
FROM THE MIDDLEGAME INTO THE ENDGAME
0–08–032037–6 Pergamon $32.00
0–08–032038–4 Pergamon pb $18.95

- Yakov Nieshtadt, editor
CATASTROPHE IN THE OPENING
0–08–023121–7 Pergamon $18.50
0–08–024097–6 Pergamon pb $14.95

- Ludek Pachman
DECISIVE GAMES IN CHESS HISTORY
Sixty-five games from important matches and tournaments played in the last 100 years
0–486–25323–6 Dover pb $6.95
MODERN CHESS STRATEGY
A classic study of chess strategy by the Czech grand master
0–486–20290–9 Dover pb $5.95

- Bruce Pandolfini
THE BEST OF CHESS LIFE AND REVIEW
A two-volume collection of writings from *Chess Review* and *Chess Life* magazines
Volume 1: 1933–1960
0–671–61986–1 Simon & Schuster $12.95
Volume 2: 1960–1988
0–671–66175–2 Simon & Schuster $12.95
KASPAROV'S WINNING CHESS TACTICS
0–671–61985–3 Simon & Schuster pb $6.95
RUSSIAN CHESS
A complete course in intermediate chess logic, based on six actual games played by the Kasparov generation of Soviet players
0–671–61984–5 Simon & Schuster pb $6.95

- Fred Reinfeld
THE COMPLETE BOOK OF CHESS STRATAGEMS
0–486–20690–4 Dover pb $4.50

- Samuel Reshevsky
THE ART OF POSITIONAL PLAY
0–679–14101–4 David McKay pb $9.95

- Richard Reti
MASTERS OF THE CHESSBOARD
The last and most important work of the well-known chess writer, this book contains 70 games by 23 chess masters
0–486–23384–7 Dover pb $7.95
MODERN IDEAS IN CHESS
A classic of chess literature, which includes a history of the evolution of the game
0–486–20638–6 Dover pb $3.75

- Philip Sergeant
MORPHY'S GAMES OF CHESS
Introduction by Fred Reinfeld
0–486–20386–7 Dover pb $6.95

- Leonid Shamkovich
THE MODERN CHESS SACRIFICE
A classification of sacrifices in opening and middle games, with examples from actual contemporary games
0–679–14103–0 David McKay pb $6.95

- Siegbert Tarrasch
THE GAME OF CHESS
A classic instruction book by a legendary grand master
0–486–25447–X Dover pb $8.95

- A. Tartakower & J. Du Mont
FIVE HUNDRED MASTER GAMES OF CHESS
One of the great collections of chess games in English
0–486–23208–5 Dover pb $10.95
U.S. CHESS FEDERATION'S OFFICIAL RULES OF CHESS
An essential volume for every serious player
0–679–14154–5 David McKay pb $7.95

- Fred Waitzkin
SEARCHING FOR BOBBY FISCHER: The World of Chess, Observed by the Father of a Child Prodigy
0–394–54455–2 Random House $17.95

- Ken Whyld
CHESS: The Records
The results of all the great matches, with cross tables for 120 tournaments
0–85112–455–0 Sterling pb $12.95

- Fred Wilson, editor
THE PICTURE HISTORY OF CHESS
The game's most illustrious players and moments, with 295 illustrations
0–486–23856–3 Dover pb $8.95

OTHER BOARD GAMES

Checkers

- Millard Hopper
WIN AT CHECKERS
Advice from the Unrestricted Checker Champion of the World
0–486–20363–8 Dover pb $3.50

- Fred Reinfeld
HOW TO WIN AT CHECKERS
More tips on improving your game
0–87980–068–2 Wilshire pb $3.00

Backgammon

• Tim Holland
BEGINNING BACKGAMMON
0–679–14038–7 David McKay pb $4.95

• Millard Hopper
WIN AT BACKGAMMON
The basics of the game, illustrated with
many diagrams and containing a
description of gambling conventions
0–486–22894–0 Dover pb $2.75

• Oswald Jacoby
BACKGAMMON BOOK
0–14–046260–0 Penguin pb $6.95

• Paul Magriel
BACKGAMMON
The most thorough guide to the game
0–8129–0615–2 Times Books $24.95

Dominoes

• Dominic Armanino
DOMINOES: Games, Rules and Strategies
0–671–63942–0 Simon & Schuster pb $5.95

Go

• Kaoru Iwamoto
GO FOR BEGINNERS
An introduction to the ancient Japanese
game of territory
0–394–73331–2 Random House pb $6.95

• Shigemi Kishikawa
STEPPINGSTONES TO GO
The basics of go, written for the Westerner
0–8048–0547–4 Tuttle pb $7.95

• O. Korschelt
THE THEORY AND PRACTICE OF GO
The classic treatise on go, first published in
1880 in a German magazine
0–8048–0572–5 Tuttle $10.95

• Edward Lasker
**GO AND GO-MOKU: The Oriental Board
Games**
"The importance of republishing Mr.
Smith's book is a real one, for although it
was first published in 1908 his classic work
on the subject has never been surpassed for
completeness, lucidity, and all-round
excellence"—*Mainichi Shimbun*
0–8048–0202–5 Tuttle pb $5.95

Mah-Jongg

• Marcia Hammer
LEARN TO PLAY MAH-JONGG
An introduction to the ancient Chinese
game, written by a Mah-Jongg expert and
tournament winner
0–679–14375–0 David McKay pb $5.95

• Shozo Kanai & Margaret Farrell
MAH-JONGG FOR BEGINNERS
A guide to the game, based on the rules
and regulations of the Mah-Jongg
Association of Japan
0–8048–0391–9 Tuttle pb $5.25

• Carol Rinzler & Joan Gelman
**HOW TO SET UP A MAH-JONGG GAME
& OTHER LOST ARTS**
0–671–55428–X Simon & Schuster $12.95

• Kitty Strauser & Lucille Evans
**MAH-JONGG ANYONE?: A Manual of
Modern Play**
0–8048–0390–0 Tuttle pb $7.50

• Eleanor Whitney
**MAH-JONGG HANDBOOK: How to Play,
Score and Win the Modern Game**
0–8048–0392–7 Tuttle pb $9.95

Monopoly

• Kaz Darzinskis
WINNING MONOPOLY
Tips on strategy for the player, based upon
an analysis of 187,000 games of Monopoly
0–06–096127–9 Harper & Row pb $6.95

CROSSWORD PUZZLES

It may seem that crossword-solving is a
very trivial pursuit, yet it has been
claimed that crosswords extend one's vocabulary, stimulate the mind, and even
encourage a healthy skepticism towards
accepting things at their face value. They
are predominantly a solitary pastime, although lone solvers are likely to find that
bystanders want to help, even if no help
is wanted.

Tony Augarde
**THE OXFORD GUIDE TO WORD
GAMES**
0–19–214144–9 Oxford $14.95

• Margaret Farrar
**MARGARET FARRAR'S SUPER
CROSSWORD**
From the former editor of the *New York
Times* puzzles
Volume 1
0–671–45690–3 Simon & Schuster pb $8.95
Volume 2
0–671–49436–8 Simon & Schuster pb $8.95

• Margaret Farrar & Eugene Maleska
**SIMON & SCHUSTER'S SUPER
CROSSWORD BOOK**
The most recent anthology compiled by
two former puzzle editors at the *New York
Times,* from the multivolume series
0–671–63302–3 Simon & Schuster pb $8.95

• John Grant
**THE EIGHTH PENGUIN BOOK OF
TIMES CROSSWORDS**
The most recent collection of puzzles from
the *Times* (London). Difficult
0–14–009688–4 Penguin pb $3.95

• Maura Jacobson
PUZZLES WITH A POINT
Each volume contains 40 crossword
puzzles with a theme, from *New York*
magazine. Medium difficulty

Volume 1: Flying Down to Rio
0–385–23851–7 Doubleday pb $3.95
Volume 2: Menagerie à Trois
0–385–23852–5 Doubleday pb $3.95
Volume 3: Shakespeare Plays Tennis
0–385–23850–9 Doubleday pb $3.95

• Tap Osborn
**THE PEN AND PENCIL CLUB
CROSSWORDS**
Volume 6
0–89471–505–4 Running Press pb $5.95
Volume 7
0–89471–545–3 Running Press pb $5.95
Volume 8
0–89471–595–X Running Press pb $5.95

• Charles Preston
**CROSSWORDS FOR THE
CONNOISSEUR OMNIBUS**
Each volume contains 100 puzzles
assembled from the popular series
Crosswords for the Connoisseur
Volume 2
0–317–45982–1 Putnam pb $6.95
Volume 3
0–399–52056–2 Putnam pb $7.95
Volume 4
0–399–52067–8 Putnam pb $7.95

• William Shortz
**GAMES MAGAZINE BOOK OF
CROSSWORD PUZZLES**
0–89480–840–0 Workman pb $5.95
**WORLD CLASS CHAMPIONSHIP
CROSSWORDS**
0–671–44319–4 Simon & Schuster pb $6.95

• Barry Tunick & Sylvia Bursztyn
**LOS ANGELES TIMES CROSSWORD
PUZZLE COLLECTION**
0–317–45981–3 Putnam pb $5.95

• Will Weng, editor
**THE NEW YORK TIMES CROSSWORD
PUZZLES OMNIBUS**
These are collections of the daily *New York
Times* puzzles (also published annually in
spiral-bound editions), which are among
the most popular and challenging
crosswords in the country. They are
shorter and less difficult than the Sunday
New York Times puzzles
Volume 1
0–8129–0733–7 Times Books pb $8.95
Volume 2
0–8129–1018–4 Times Books pb $8.95
Volume 3
0–8129–1066–4 Times Books pb $8.95
Volume 4
0–8129–1117–2 Times Books pb $8.95
Volume 5
0–8129–1708–1 Times Books pb $8.95
**THE NEW YORK TIMES SUNDAY
CROSSWORD PUZZLE OMNIBUS**
Volume 2
0–812–91791–X Times Books pb $8.95

🍎 **IF YOU CAN'T FIND IT, LOOK IN THE INDEX**

THE WILL WENG CROSSWORD PUZZLE OMNIBUS

Volume 1
0–8129–1300–0 Times Books pb $8.95

Volume 2
0–8129–1645–X Times Books pb $8.95

Reference Books

- John Griffiths, editor
CASSELL'S CROSSWORD FINISHER
Twenty-one thousand words and names of three to seven letters have been fed into a computer in order to provide the word combinations presented in this book
0–304–31127–8 Sterling pb $9.95

- Helene Hovanec
CREATIVE CRUCIVERBALISTS
Profiles of crossword puzzle creators, with an original puzzle by each one
0–688–06578–3 Morrow pb $10.95

- Eugene Maleska
SIMON & SCHUSTER'S CROSSWORD BOOK OF QUOTATIONS
0–671–44322–4 Simon & Schuster pb $5.95

- Merriam-Webster
WEBSTER'S OFFICIAL CROSSWORD PUZZLE DICTIONARY
Comprehensive and authoritative crossword puzzle dictionary, containing specialized lists to aid in the "answer word" search
0–87779–021–3 Merriam-Webster $13.95

- Tom Pulliam & Clare Grundman, editors
THE NEW YORK TIMES CROSSWORD PUZZLE DICTIONARY
Contains over 600,000 words as well as thousands of names of famous people and fictional characters. Especially useful when doing *New York Times* puzzles
0–8129–1131–8 Times Books $19.95
0–446–38250–7 Warner pb $12.50

- Andrew Swanfeldt
CROSSWORD PUZZLE DICTIONARY
More than 365,000 words covered in this popular dictionary
0–06–091313–4 Harper & Row pb $9.95

- Barry Tunick & Sylvia Bursztyn
CROSSWORD CROSSTALK: The Secrets of Puzzle Making and Solving
0–88496–281–4 Capra pb $8.95

WORD GAMES

- Tony Augarde
THE OXFORD GUIDE TO WORD GAMES
"Everything you want to know, and a little more, about man's ageless fascination with word play"—Will Weng
0–19–214144–9 Oxford $14.95

- A. Ross Eckler
WORD RECREATIONS: Games and Diversions from Word Ways
0–486–23854–7 Dover pb $4.95

- Herbert Kohl
A BOOK OF PUZZLEMENTS: Play and Invention with Language
0–8052–0797–X Schocken pb $11.95

- George McCallum
ONE HUNDRED AND ONE WORD GAMES
0–19–502742–6 Oxford pb $8.50

- Thomas Middleton
CROSTICS

Volume 95
0–671–62104–1 Simon & Schuster pb $6.95

Volume 96
0–671–63018–0 Simon & Schuster pb $6.95

NEW YORK TIMES ACROSTIC PUZZLES

Volume 1
0–8129–1064–8 Times Books pb $5.95

Volume 2
0–8129–1065–6 Times Books pb $5.95

- Tom Pulliam & Gorton Carruth
THE COMPLETE WORD GAME DICTIONARY
0–87196–112–1 Facts On File pb $6.00

- Wilbur Webster
WEBSTER'S DICTIONARY GAME
Over 5000 obscure words designed for the Dictionary Game, invented by the black sheep of the Webster family in the 1890s
0–671–64172–7 Simon & Schuster pb $5.95

SCRABBLE

- Gyles Brandreth & Darryl Francis
THE SCRABBLE COMPANION
A guidebook for the game, which includes its history and official rules
0–09–172698–0 David & Charles pb $17.95

- Drue Conklin
THE OFFICIAL SCRABBLE PLAYERS HANDBOOK
0–517–52547–X Crown pb $5.95

- Michael Lawrence & John Ozag
THE ULTIMATE GUIDE TO WINNING SCRABBLE BRAND CROSSWORD GAME
0–553–34306–8 Bantam pb $8.95

- G.C. Merriam
THE OFFICIAL SCRABBLE PLAYERS DICTIONARY
0–671–45936–8 Simon & Schuster pb $4.95

- Robert Schachner
THE OFFICIAL SCRABBLE WORD-FINDER
This book contains thousands of words arranged for easy access
0–02–029802–1 David & Charles pb $4.95

QUIZ BOOKS AND BRAINTEASERS

▶ See also Mathematics

- Franco Agostini & Nicola Alberto DeCarlo
INTELLIGENCE GAMES
Over 100 brainteasers, puzzles, and quizzes
0–671–63201–9 Simon & Schuster pb $12.95

- Philip Carter & Ken Russell
TAKE THE IQ CHALLENGE
Two volumes of IQ quizzes and brainteasers, designed by members of the MENSA group

Volume 1
0–7137–1736–X Javelin pb $4.95

Volume 2
0–7137–2000–X Javelin pb $4.95

- Ken Fisher
ISAAC ASIMOV PRESENTS SUPER QUIZ III
Questions and answers from the renowned science fiction writer
0–934878–862 Dembner pb $8.95

- Marvin Grosswirth & others
THE MENSA GENIUS QUIZ BOOK
Quizzes and puzzles that challenge readers to test their intelligence

Volume 1
0–201–05959–2 Addison-Wesley pb $6.95

Volume 2
0–201–05958–4 Addison-Wesley pb $6.95

- Rosalind Moore, editor
THE DELL BOOK OF LOGIC PROBLEMS
Each volume contains 75 brainteasers

Volume 1
0–440–51891–1 Dell pb $9.95

Volume 2
0–440–51875–X Dell pb $8.95

- Eugene Raudsepp
CREATIVE GROWTH GAMES
Contains challenging games designed to test the reader's imagination and creative power
0–399–50415–X Putnam pb $7.95

MORE CREATIVE GROWTH GAMES
0–399–50456–7 Putnam pb $6.95

- Marcia Rosen
TEST YOUR OWN IQ
A complete intelligence test, along with answers and a scoring table
0–399–51120–2 Putnam pb $5.95

- Abbie Salny
THE MENSA BOOK OF WORDS, WORD GAMES, PUZZLES AND ODDITIES
Lexicographical brainteasers, from the MENSA group
0–06–096208–9 Harper & Row pb $5.95

- Abbie Salny & Lewis Burke Frumkes
MENSA THINK-SMART BOOK
Quizzes and exercises designed to strengthen the mind
0–06–091255–3 Harper & Row pb $6.95

• Victor Serebriakoff
THE THINKING PERSON'S BOOK OF PUZZLES AND PROBLEMS
One hundred challenging brainteasers
0440–58749–2 Dell pb $7.95

CARD GAMES

• Tom Ainslie
AINSLIE'S COMPLETE HOYLE: Rules, Strategies, Scoring, Bidding, Betting Systems
Includes 1800 entries and all popular card games, with variations and strategies
0–671–24779–4 Simon & Schuster pb $11.95

• Walter Gibson
HOYLE'S MODERN ENCYCLOPEDIA OF CARD GAMES
A thorough guide to card games, with the basic rules and popular variations of each game
0–385–07680–0 Doubleday pb $9.95

• Oswald & James Jacoby
JACOBY ON CARD GAMES
0–345–00589–9 Ballantine pb $14.95

• Joseph Leeming
GAMES AND FUN WITH PLAYING CARDS
0–486–23977–2 Dover pb $3.95

• Albert Morehead, editor
THE COMPLETE BOOK OF SOLITAIRE AND PATIENCE GAMES
0–553–26240–8 Bantam pb $3.95

OFFICIAL RULES OF CARD GAMES
Up-to-date rules of over 300 card games, including the New International Laws of Contract Bridge
0–449–21381–1 Fawcett pb $3.50

Venus as Ace of Spades from an 1828 deck in the collection of The New-York Historical Society

• Albert Morehead & Geoffrey Mott-Smith, editors
HOYLE'S RULES OF GAMES
0–452–26049–3 NAL pb $7.95

• David Parlett
SOLITAIRE: Aces Up and 399 Other Card Games
0–394–73868–3 Random House pb $5.95

• John Scarne
SCARNE'S ENCYCLOPEDIA OF CARD GAMES
The histories and variations of the world's greatest card games
0–06–091052–6 Harper & Row $12.95

• Ed Taylor, editor
THE HISTORY OF PLAYING CARDS: With Anecdotes of Their Use in Conjuring, Fortune-Telling, and Card-Sharking
0–8048–1026–5 Tuttle pb $7.95

Bridge

• George Coffin
BRIDGE PLAY FROM A TO Z
A thorough and useful book for all players
0–486–23891–1 Dover pb $6.95

• Shelly de Satnick
BRIDGE FOR EVERYONE
A beginner's step-by-step guide to learning bridge, presented in 18 easy-to-follow lessons
0–380–81083–2 Avon pb $9.95

• Richard Frey
HOW TO WIN AT CONTRACT BRIDGE IN 10 EASY LESSONS
The author of *According to Hoyle* clearly explains winning contract bridge techniques
0–449–20995–4 Fawcett pb $3.95

• Charles Goren
CONTRACT BRIDGE FOR BEGINNERS
A beginner's book that introduces the novice player to the "point count" method of bidding
0–671–21052–1 Simon & Schuster pb $6.95

GOREN'S NEW BRIDGE COMPLETE
The revised edition of the classic bridge book
0–385–23324–8 Doubleday $20.95

• James Jacoby
JACOBY ON BRIDGE
A guide for all levels of bridge players, written by the first player to ever amass 1000 points in one year
0–88687–305–3 Pharos $14.95

• Oswald Jacoby
IMPROVE YOUR BRIDGE WITH OSWALD JACOBY: 125 Bridge Hands from the Master
0–07–032238–4 McGraw-Hill pb $4.95

• Edgar Kaplan
WINNING CONTRACT BRIDGE
A world-renowned expert explains techniques that helped him win many championships
0–486–24559–4 Dover pb $7.95

• Fred Karpin
BRIDGE STRATEGY AT TRICK ONE
An indispensable guide to playing winning bridge, concentrating on strategy at trick one, when many hands are decided
0–486–23296–4 Dover pb $5.95

• Norman Kay & others
THE COMPLETE BOOK OF DUPLICATE BRIDGE
A comprehensive guide to bidding, playing, and scoring in duplicate bridge
Foreword by Oswald Jacoby
0–06–463262–8 Barnes & Noble pb $8.95

• Terence Reese & Albert Dormer
THE COMPLETE BOOK OF BRIDGE
Includes modern techniques and an account of all the important systems
0–571–13528–5 Faber & Faber pb $9.95

• William Root
COMMONSENSE BIDDING
A renowned expert's guide to basic bidding
0–517–56129–8 Crown pb $10.95

• Alan Truscott
DOUBLES AND REDOUBLES
The latest volume in the *New York Times* bridge series, featuring the Lightner double and other plays and defenses
0–8129–1628–X Times Books pb $7.95

• Louis Watson
THE PLAY OF THE HAND AT BRIDGE
The classic guide to all aspects of playing strategy, written by one of the world's foremost authorities on contract bridge
0–06–463209–1 Harper & Row pb $6.95

Gin Rummy

• Sam Fry
GIN RUMMY: How to Play and Win
0–486–23630–7 Dover pb $2.75

• Oswald Jacoby
HOW TO WIN AT GIN RUMMY
0–03–042886–6 Henry Holt pb $4.95

Poker

• John Archer
AN EXPERT'S GUIDE TO WINNING AT POKER
0–87980–362–2 Wilshire pb $5.00

• David Hayano
POKER FACES: The Life and Work of Professional Card Players
"An intelligent study of a subculture that risks millions of dollars each year on the rank and color of five slips of pasteboard"—*Psychology Today*
0–520–05067–3 California pb $10.95

• Terence Reese & Anthony Watkins
HOW TO WIN AT POKER
0–87980–070–4 Wilshire pb $5.00

• Jeff Rubens
WIN AT POKER
A complete guide to poker, starting with the fundamentals and moving step-by-step to more complex areas of the game
0–486–24626–4 Dover pb $4.95

• John Scarne
SCARNE'S GUIDE TO MODERN POKER
The rules of all 117 forms of poker, presented by today's greatest gambling expert
0–671–53076–3 Simon & Schuster pb $9.95

• Norman Zadeh
WINNING POKER SYSTEMS
The "bible of poker," written by a professional with years of card-playing experience
0–87980–332–0 Wilshire pb $3.00

Blackjack

• Richard Canfield
BLACKJACK: Your Way to Riches
How to be a winning player
0–8184–0273–3 Lyle Stuart $12.00

• Lance Humble & Carl Cooper
THE WORLD'S GREATEST BLACKJACK BOOK
A comprehensive guide, updated to include the rules of play in Atlantic City
0–385–15382–1 Doubleday pb $9.95

• Jerry Patterson
BLACKJACK: A Winner's Handbook
"This vitamin-packed work might also be labeled 'Current Guide to 50 Blackjack Systems.' It could also be your very best guideline to selecting the system you wish to play—complex or simplified"—*Gambler's Book Club*
0–399–50617–9 Putnam pb $7.95

• Lawrence Revere
PLAYING BLACKJACK AS A BUSINESS
Accurate and up-to-date guide to blackjack, with strategies devised by Julian Braun of the IBM Corporation
0–8184–0064–1 Lyle Stuart $14.95

MAGIC TRICKS

• Harry Blackstone
BLACKSTONE'S TRICKS ANYONE CAN DO
One of the great magicians of the 20th century reveals the secrets of 200 magic tricks
0–8065–0862–0 Citadel pb $6.95

• J.C. Cannell
THE SECRETS OF HOUDINI
A rational explanation of Houdini's tricks, written by a personal friend of the magician's and published shortly after Houdini's death
0–486–22913–0 Dover pb $5.95

• Nelson Downs
THE ART OF MAGIC
A compilation of renowned magic tricks, along with transcriptions of appropriate patter to use while performing these tricks
0–486–24005–3 Dover pb $6.50

• Walter Gibson
THE NEW MAGICIAN'S MANUAL
Thirty-six tricks explained
0–486–23113–5 Dover pb $6.95

• Professor Hoffman
HOFFMAN'S MODERN MAGIC
A classic on magic tricks, first published over a century ago, in which several hundred tricks are explained
0–486–23623–4 Dover pb $6.95

• Johann Hofzinser
HOFZINSER'S CARD CONJURING
Thirty-one of the original card tricks of Johann N. Hofzinser (1806–1875)
0–486–25085–7 Dover pb $4.95

• Harry Houdini
HOUDINI ON MAGIC
Houdini's own account of some of his most famous feats, with instructions for performing 44 stage tricks
0–486–20384–0 Dover pb $4.95

• Jean Hugard, editor
ENCYCLOPEDIA OF CARD TRICKS
An explanation of over 600 professional card tricks
0–486–21252–1 Dover pb $6.95

• Jean Hugard & Frederick Brave
EXPERT CARD TECHNIQUES: Close-Up Table Magic
A definitive work on card tricks, with step-by-step instructions
0–486–21755–8 Dover pb $7.95

• Bernard Mason & Elmer Mitchell
PARTY GAMES
Hundreds of party games in a classic originally published in 1946
0–06–097050–2 Harper & Row pb $6.95

• Henning Nelms
MAGIC AND SHOWMANSHIP: A Handbook for Conjurers
An examination of the tricks and devices of conjuring, including the chat and misdirection used to deceive the audience
0–486–22337–X Dover pb $4.95

• T.A. Waters
THE ENCYCLOPEDIA OF MAGIC AND MAGICIANS
A compendium of magic knowledge using information gleaned from rare documents; written by a magician for magicians
0–8160–1349–7 Facts On File $35.00

LATE
ARRIVALS

The following titles were announced too late to be included in the main part of The Reader's Catalog; most are scheduled for publication in the fall of 1989. These late arrivals are not listed in the index. Please note that in a few cases there may be last-minute changes in title, price, or publication date.

LITERATURE OF EUROPE, AFRICA, AND ASIA

Literature of Egypt and the Ancient Near East

- Stephanie Dalley, editor
  MYTHS FROM MESOPOTAMIA
  0–19–814397–4 Oxford $55.00

- Raymond D. Faulkner, translator
  THE ANCIENT EGYPTIAN BOOK OF THE DEAD
  0–02–901470–0 Macmillan $19.95

Ancient Greek Literature

- Aeschylus
  PROMETHEUS BOUND
  Translated by James Scully & C. John Herington
  0–19–506165–9 Oxford pb $6.95

- Georgios Chortatsis
  PLAYS OF THE CRETAN RENAISSANCE
  Edited by Rosemary Bancroft-Marcus
  0–19–815808–4 Oxford $125.00

- Euripides
  ALCESTIS
  Translated by William Arrowsmith
  0–19–506166–7 Oxford pb $6.95

- B.P. Reardon, editor
  COLLECTED ANCIENT GREEK NOVELS
  0–520–04303–0 California $75.00

- D.A. Russell & M. Winterbottom
  CLASSICAL LITERARY CRITICISM
  0–19–281830–9 Oxford pb $6.95

- Sophocles
  ANTIGONE
  Translated by Richard Emil Braun
  0–19–506167–5 Oxford pb $6.95

Latin Literature

- Catullus
  THE POEMS OF CATULLUS
  Translated by Charles Martin
  0–8018–3925–4 Johns Hopkins $32.50
  0–8018–3926–2 Johns Hopkins pb $11.95

- Marcus Aurelius Antoninus
  THE MEDITATIONS OF MARCUS AURELIUS ANTONINUS & A SELECTION FROM THE LETTERS OF MARCUS AND FRONTO
  Edited by R.B. Rutherford
  0–19–814761–9 Oxford $29.95

- David Armstrong
  HORACE
  0–300–04579–4 Yale $27.50
  0–300–04573–5 Yale pb $9.95

The Loeb Classics

- Apuleius
  METAMORPHOSES
  Translated by J. Arthur Hanson

  Volume 1
  0–674–99049–8 Harvard $14.50

  Volume 2
  0–674–99498–1 Harvard $14.50

- David A. Campbell, translator
  GREEK LYRIC, Volume 2
  0–674–99158–3 Harvard $14.50

- Hippocrates
  HIPPOCRATES
  Translated by Paul Potter

  Volume 5
  0–674–99520–1 Harvard $14.50

  Volume 6
  0–674–99522–8 Harvard $14.50

French Literature

- Honoré de Balzac
  BEATRIX
  0–88184–532–9 Carroll & Graf pb $8.95

- Georges Bataille
  MY MOTHER, MADAME EDWARDA, THE DEAD MAN
  Translated by Austryn Wainhouse
  0–7145–2886–2 Marion Boyars $19.95

- Maurice Blanchot
  THE SPACE OF LITERATURE
  Translated with an introduction by Ann Smock
  0–8032–6092–X Nebraska pb $10.95

- Jean Cocteau
  THOMAS, THE IMPOSTOR
  0–374–52208–1 Farrar, Straus & Giroux pb $6.95

- Claudine Herrmann
  THE TONGUE SNATCHERS
  Translated with an introduction by Nancy Kline
  0–8032–2346–3 Nebraska $17.95

- Abdelkebir Khatibi
  LOVE IN TWO LANGUAGES
  Translated by Richard Howard
  0–8166–1780–5 Minnesota pb $9.95

- Marcel Proust
  MARCEL PROUST: Selected Letters, Volume 2: 1904-1909
  Translated by Terence Kilmartin
  0–19–505965–1 Oxford $29.95

- George Sand
  A WOMAN'S VERSION OF THE FAUST LEGEND: The Seven Strings of the Lyre
  Translated by George A. Kennedy
  0–8078–1856–9 North Carolina $34.95

- Victor Segalen
  RENE LEYS
  0–87951–350–0 Overlook $10.95

- Marguerite Yourcenar
  THAT MIGHTY SCULPTOR, TIME
  Translated by Walter Kaiser with the author
  0–374–27358–8 Farrar, Straus & Giroux $18.95

- Denis Hollier, editor
  A NEW HISTORY OF FRENCH LITERATURE
  0–674–61565–4 Harvard $49.95

- George D. Painter
  MARCEL PROUST: A Biography
  0–394–57669–1 Random House $39.95

- Helen Waddell
  THE WANDERING SCHOLARS
  0–472–06412–6 Michigan pb $13.95

Spanish Literature

- Pedro Calderón de la Barca
  THE PAINTER OF HIS DISHONOUR
  Edited by Alan K.G. Paterson
  0–85668–347–7 Humanities pb $18.50

- Miguel de Cervantes
  THE TRIALS OF PERSILES AND SIGISMUNDA
  Translated by Celia Richmond Weller & Clark A. Colahan
  0–520–06315–5 California $35.00

- Lope de Vega
  FUENTE OVEJUNA
  Edited by Victor Dixon
  0–85668–328–0 Humanities pb $18.50

  PERIBANEZ
  Edited by J.M. Loyd
  0–85668–439–2 Humanities pb $18.50

- Tirso de Molina
  TAMAR'S REVENGE
  Edited by J.E. Lyon
  0–85668–324–8 Humanities pb $18.50

- Francisco de Quevedo
  DREAMS AND DISCOURSES
  Edited by R.K. Britton
  0–85668–353–1 Humanities pb $18.50

- Ian Gibson
  FEDERICO GARCIA LORCA: A Life
  0–394–50964–1 Pantheon $29.95

Italian Literature

- Paola Drigo
  MARIA ZEF
  Translated with an introduction by Blossom Steinberg Kirschenbaum
  0–8032–1676–9 Nebraska $19.95
  0–8032–6577–8 Nebraska pb $9.95

- Umberto Eco
  FOUCAULT'S PENDULUM
  Translated by William Weaver
  0–15–132765–3 HBJ $22.95

- Primo Levi
  THE MIRROR MAKER: Stories and Essays
  Translated by Raymond Rosenthal
  0–8052–4076–4 Pantheon $16.95

• Eugenio Montale
MOTTETI: Poems of Love—The Motets of Eugenio Montale
1–55597–123–7 Graywolf $13.00

Dutch Literature

• Hella S. Haasse
IN A DARK WOOD WANDERING
Translated by Lewis Kaplan & Anita Miller
0–89733–336–5 Academy Chicago $22.95

German Literature

• Günter Grass
DOG YEARS
Translated by Ralph Manheim
0–15–626112–X HBJ pb $12.95

• Mark Anderson, editor
READING KAFKA: Prague, Politics, and the Fin-de-Siècle
0–8052–4050–0 Pantheon $22.95
0–8052–0945–X Pantheon pb $14.95

• Gregor von Rezzori
MEMOIRS OF AN ANTI-SEMITE: A Novel in Five Stories
0–8101–0858–5 Northwestern pb $12.95

Scandinavian Literature

• Jan Fridegård
LAND OF WOODEN GODS: Volume 1 in the Holme Trilogy
Translated by Robert E. Bjork
0–8032–6870–X Nebraska pb $8.95

• Pål Espolin Johnson
FOR LOVE OF NORWAY
Translated by Conrad Røyksund
0–8032–7571–4 Nebraska pb $11.95

• Pär Lagerkvist
BARABBAS
Translated by Alan Blair
0–679–72544–X Random House pb $7.95

• Elias Lönnrot
THE KALEVALA
Translated by Keith Bosley
0–19–281700–0 Oxford pb $12.95

THE KALEVALA: Epic of the Finnish People
Translated by Eino Friberg
Edited by Jan George C. Schoolfield
951–1–10137–4 Illinois $39.95

Eastern European Literature

• Jerzy Andrzejewski
ASHES AND DIAMONDS
0–8101–0856–9 Northwestern pb $9.95

• Luican Blaga
AT THE COURT OF YEARNING
Translated with an introduction by Andrei Codrescu
0–8142–0489–9 Ohio State $18.95

• Bohumil Hrabal
CLOSELY WATCHED TRAINS
0–8101–0857–7 Northwestern pb $8.95

• Danilo Kis
A TOMB FOR BORIS DAVIDOVICH
0–8101–0855–0 Northwestern pb $9.95

• Milorad Pavić
A DICTIONARY OF THE KHAZARS: A Lexicon Novel
Translated by Christina Pribićević-Zorić
0–679–72461–3 Random House pb $12.95

• Aleksander Wat
LUCIFER UNEMPLOYED
Translated by Lillian Vallee
0–8101–0840–2 Northwestern pb $8.95

• Alexander Fiut
THE ETERNAL MOMENT: The Poetry of Czeslaw Milosz
0–520–06689–8 California $25.00

Russian Literature

• Fyodor Dostoyevsky
UNCLE'S DREAM & OTHER STORIES
Translated with an introduction by David McDuff
0–14–044518–8 Penguin pb $6.95

• Velimir Khlebnikov
COLLECTED WORKS OF VELIMIR KHLEBNIKOV, Volume 2: Prose, Plays, and Supersagas
Translated by Paul Schmidt
Edited by Ronald Vroon
0–674–14046–X Harvard $39.50

• Vladimir Nabokov
INVITATION TO A BEHEADING
0–679–72531–8 Random House pb $7.95

• Irina Ratushinskaya
GREY IS THE COLOR OF HOPE
Translated by Alyona Kojevnikov
0–679–72447–8 Random House pb $8.95

PENCIL LETTER: Poems
0–679–72600–4 Knopf pb $9.95

• Mikhail Sholokov
AND QUIET FLOWS THE DON
0–679–72521–0 Random House pb $10.95

• Vladimir Voinovich
THE FUR HAT
0–15–139100–0 HBJ $17.95

• Elaine Feinstein
MARINA TSVETAYEVA
0–14–008733–8 Penguin pb $5.95

• Joseph Frank
THROUGH THE RUSSIAN PRISM: Essays on Literature and Culture
0–691–01456–6 Princeton pb $9.95

• Charles A. Moser, editor
THE CAMBRIDGE HISTORY OF RUSSIAN LITERATURE
0–521–30994–8 Cambridge $79.50

• V.S. Pritchett
CHEKHOV: A Spirit Set Free
0–679–72546–6 Random House pb $8.95

Modern European Drama

STRINDBERG'S THE FATHER & IBSEN'S HEDDA GABLER
Adapted by John Osborne
0–571–14066–1 Faber & Faber pb $10.95

Modern Hebrew Literature

• S.Y. Agnon
SHIRA
Translated by Zeva Shapiro
0–8052–4043–8 Pantheon $21.95

• Amos Oz
THE SLOPES OF LEBANON
Translated by Maurie Goldberg Bartura
0–15–183090–8 HBJ $18.95

• David Aberbach
BIALIK
0–8021–3146–8 Grove pb $6.95

African Literature

• Chinua Achebe
HOPES AND IMPEDIMENTS: Selected Essays
0–385–24730–3 Doubleday $16.95

• Stephen Gray, editor
THE PENGUIN BOOK OF SOUTHERN AFRICAN VERSE
0–14–058510–9 Penguin pb $8.95

• Mongane Serote
TO EVERY BIRTH ITS BLOOD
0–938410–70–9 Thunder's Mouth pb $10.95

• Wole Soyinka
AKE: The Years of Childhood
0–679–72540–7 Random House pb $9.95

ISARA: A Voyage Around Essay
0–394–54077–8 Random House $18.95

Arabic Literature

• Salma Khadra Jayyusi, editor
THE LITERATURE OF MODERN ARABIA
0–292–74662–8 Texas $24.95

• Naguib Mahfouz
THE BEGINNING AND THE END
0–385–26457–7 Doubleday $19.95
0–385–26458–5 Doubleday pb $8.95

THE THIEF AND THE DOGS
0–385–26461–5 Doubleday $16.95
0–385–26426–3 Doubleday pb $7.95

WEDDING SONG
0–385–26463–1 Doubleday $16.95
0–385–26464–X Doubleday pb $7.95

Literatures of India

• Attia Hosain
PHOENIX FLED
0–14–016192–9 Penguin pb $7.95

SUNLIGHT ON A BROKEN COLUMN
0–14–016191–0 Penguin pb $7.95

- Jayanta Mahapatra
SELECTED POEMS
0–19–562051–8 Oxford pb $4.95

- Bharati Mukherjee
JASMINE
0–8021–1032–0 Grove $17.95

- Satyajit Ray
THE ADVENTURES OF FELUDA
0–14–011221–9 Penguin pb $7.95

- Edward C. Dimock, Jr.
THE SOUND OF SILENT GUNS & OTHER ESSAYS
0–19–562308–8 Oxford $19.95

Chinese Literature

- Ding Ling
I MYSELF AM A WOMAN: Selected Writings of Ding Ling
0–8070–6736–9 Beacon $24.95

- Wang Anyi
BAOTOWN
Translated by Martha Avery
0–393–02711–2 Norton $17.95

- Wang Wei
POEMS
Translated with an introduction by G.W. Robinson
0–14–044296–0 Penguin pb $5.95

- Zhang Jie
HEAVY WINGS
Translated by Howard Goldblatt
0–8021–1039–8 Grove $22.50

- Marston Anderson
THE LIMITS OF REALISM: Chinese Fiction in the Revolutionary Period
0–520–06436–4 California $30.00

- Shelley Hsueh-lun Chang
HISTORY AND LEGEND: Ideas and Images in the Ming Historical Novels
0–472–10117–X Michigan $32.50

- Yoshikawa Kōjirō
FIVE HUNDRED YEARS OF CHINESE POETRY, 1150-1650: The Chin, Yuan, and Ming Dynasties
0–691–06768–6 Princeton $34.00

- James J. Y. Liu
LANGUAGE–PARADOX–POETICS: A Chinese View
Edited by Richard John Lynn
0–691–06741–4 Princeton $35.00

- David L. Rolston
HOW TO READ THE CHINESE NOVEL
0–691–06753–8 Princeton $55.00

Japanese Literature

- Kometani Foumiko
PASSOVER
Translated by the author
0–88184–509–4 Carroll & Graf $14.95

- Mishima Yukio
ACTS OF WORSHIP: Seven Stories by Yukio Mishima
Translated with an introduction by John Bester
0–87011–937–0 Kodansha $17.95

- Murakami Haruki
A WILD SHEEP CHASE
Translated by Alfred Birnbaum
0–87011–905–2 Kodansha $17.95

- Tanizaki Jun'ichiro
CHILDHOOD YEARS: A Memoir
Translated by Paul McCarthy
0–87011–924–9 Kodansha pb $6.95

- Kenneth Yasuda, translator
MASTERWORKS OF THE NO THEATER
0–253–36805–7 Indiana $57.50

- Heinz Horioka & Miyoko Sasaki
RAKUGO: The Popular Narrative Art of Japan
0–674–74725–9 Harvard $30.00

- Edwin McClellan
WOMAN IN THE CRESTED KIMONO: The Life of Shibue Io and Her Family Drawn from Mori Ogai's Shibue Chūsai
0–300–04618–9 Yale pb $10.95

- Ivan Morris, translator
AS I CROSSED A BRIDGE OF DREAMS: Recollections of a Woman in Eleventh-Century Japan
0–14–044282–0 Penguin pb $5.95

Other Asian Literature

- O Sukkwon
A KOREAN STORYTELLER'S MISCELLANY: The P'aegwan Chapki of O Sukkwon
Translated by Peter H. Lee
0–691–06771–6 Princeton $38.00

- Alice M. Terada, editor
UNDER THE STARFRUIT TREE: Folktales from Vietnam
0–8248–1252–2 Hawaii $15.95

Australian Literature

- Thomas Keneally
TO ASMARA: A Novel of Africa
0–446–51542–6 Warner $18.95

Literary Criticism and Theory

- Jean Baudrillard
AMERICA
0–86091–978–1 RC&H pb $13.95

- Peter Bishop
THE MYTH OF SHANGRI-LA: Tibet, Travel Writing and the Western Creation of Sacred Landscape
0–520–06686–3 California $29.95

- John B. Gabel & Charles B. Wheeler
THE BIBLE AS LITERATURE
0–19–505932–8 Oxford $32.50
0–19–505933–6 Oxford pb $12.95

- Frank Kermode
AN APPETITE FOR POETRY
0–674–04093–7 Harvard $22.50

- Julia Kristeva
BLACK SUN: Depression and Melancholia
0–231–06706–2 Columbia $29.00

- David Perkins
A HISTORY OF MODERN POETRY: Modernism and After
0–674–39947–1 Harvard pb $14.95

- Marjorie Perloff
CONTRA-DICTIONS: Essays in Modern and Postmodern Poetics
0–8101–0844–5 Northwestern pb $12.95

- F.D. Reeve
THE WHITE MONK: An Essay on Dostoevsky and Melville
0–8265–1234–8 Illinois $17.95

- M.L. Rosenthal
ESSAYS OF FOUR DECADES
0–89255–149–6 Persea $27.50

- Jean Starobinski
THE LIVING EYE
0–674–53664–9 Harvard $29.50

- Helen Vendler
THE MUSIC OF WHAT HAPPENS: Poems, Poets, Critics
0–674–59153–4 Harvard pb $12.95

World Literature: Surveys and Anthologies

- William Theodore deBary & Irene Bloom, editors
APPROACHES TO ASIAN CLASSICS
0–231–07004–7 Columbia $32.50

- Scott Walker, editor
THE GRAYWOLF ANNUAL SIX: Stories from the Rest of the World
1–55597–122–9 Graywolf pb $8.50

LITERATURE OF THE BRITISH ISLES

Pre-20th Century

- Robert Burns
THE ESSENTIAL BURNS
Edited by Robert Creeley
0–88001–194–7 Ecco pb $6.00

- Daniel Defoe
COLONEL JACK
Edited by Samuel Holt Monk
0–19–282224–1 Oxford pb $8.95

- Edward Lear
A NEW NONSENSE ALPHABET
Edited by Susan Hyman
0–7475–0320–6 David & Charles $19.95

- Charlotte Lennox
THE FEMALE QUIXOTE
0–19–281765–5 Oxford pb $9.95

IF YOU CAN'T FIND IT, LOOK IN THE INDEX

- Philip Sidney
  THE OXFORD AUTHORS: Sir Philip Sidney
  Edited by Katherine Duncan-Jones
  0–19–254197–8 Oxford $55.00
  0–19–282024–9 Oxford pb $16.95

- Anthony Trollope
  THE MACDERMOTS OF BALLYCLORAN
  0–19–282181–4 Oxford pb $8.95
  THE THREE CLERKS
  0–19–281829–5 Oxford pb $8.95

- Betty Travitsky, editor
  THE PARADISE OF WOMEN: Writings by Englishwomen of the Renaissance
  0–231–06885–9 Columbia $16.00

- Roger Lonsdale, editor
  EIGHTEENTH-CENTURY WOMEN POETS
  0–19–811769–8 Oxford $35.00

20th-Century Fiction

- Peter Ackroyd
  FIRST LIGHT
  0–8021–1161–0 Grove $19.95

- Julian Barnes
  A HISTORY OF THE WORLD IN 10½ CHAPTERS
  0–394–58061–3 Knopf $18.95

- Arnold Bennett
  CLAYHANGER
  0–14–018269–1 Penguin pb $7.95

- Anthony Burgess
  THE DEVIL'S MODE
  0–394–57670–5 Random House $18.95

- Bruce Chatwin
  UTZ
  0–14–011576–5 Penguin pb $7.95

- Margaret Drabble
  A NATURAL CURIOSITY
  0–670–82837–8 Viking $19.95

- E.M. Forster
  A ROOM WITH A VIEW
  0–679–72476–1 Random House pb $7.95

- Graham Greene
  THE CAPTAIN AND THE ENEMY
  0–14–012418–7 Penguin pb $7.95

- Aldous Huxley
  ANTIC HAY
  0–88184–535–X Carroll & Graf pb $10.95

- Molly Keane
  QUEEN LEAR
  0–525–24799–8 Dutton $17.95

- Kazuo Ishiguro
  AN ARTIST OF THE FLOATING WORLD
  0–679–72266–1 Random House pb $8.95
  THE REMAINS OF THE DAY
  0–394–57343–9 Knopf $18.95

- Penelope Lively
  JUDGEMENT DAY
  0–06–097198–3 Harper & Row pb $7.95
  MOON TIGER
  0–06–097200–9 Harper & Row pb $7.95
  PASSING ON
  0–8021–1155–6 Grove $16.95

- David Lodge
  NICE WORK
  0–670–82806–8 Viking $18.95

- Ian McEwan
  IN BETWEEN THE SHEETS
  0–14–011281–2 Penguin pb $6.95

- John Mortimer
  THE NARROWING STREAM
  0–670–81930–1 Viking $17.95

- Dennis Potter
  TICKET TO RIDE
  0–679–72353–6 Random House pb $6.95

- V.S. Pritchett
  A CARELESS WIDOW
  0–394–57612–8 Random House $16.95

- Angela Thirkell
  WILD STRAWBERRIES
  0–88184–555–8 Carroll & Graf pb $4.95

- Jeanette Winterson
  THE PASSION
  0–679–72437–0 Random House pb $7.95

20th-Century Poetry

- Tony Harrison
  V. & OTHER POEMS
  0–374–28206–4 Farrar, Straus & Giroux $14.95

- Michael Hofmann
  K.S. IN LAKELAND: New and Selected Poems
  0–88001–197–1 Ecco $17.95

- Thomas Kinsella, editor
  THE NEW OXFORD BOOK OF IRISH VERSE
  0–19–211868–4 Oxford pb $9.95

- Stevie Smith
  SOME ARE MORE HUMAN THAN OTHERS
  0–8112–1110–X New Directions pb $7.95

- Charles Tomlinson
  ANNUNCIATIONS
  0–19–282680–8 Oxford pb $9.95

20th-Century Essays and Other Prose

- W.H. Auden
  THE DYER'S HAND
  0–679–72484–2 Random House pb $12.95
  FOREWORDS AND AFTERWORDS
  0–679–72485–0 Random House pb $12.95

- Bruce Chatwin
  WHAT AM I DOING HERE?
  0–670–82508–5 Viking $19.95

- Jan Morris
  PLEASURES OF A TANGLED LIFE
  0–394–57649–7 Random House $18.95

- Philip O'Connor
  MEMOIRS OF A PUBLIC BABY
  Introduction by Stephen Spender
  0–393–02763–5 Norton $18.95

- Jonathan Raban
  FOR LOVE AND MONEY: A Writing Life
  0–06–016166–3 Harper & Row $22.50

- Leonard Woolf
  THE AUTOBIOGRAPHY OF LEONARD WOOLF
  Volume 1: Sowing, 1880-1904
  0–15–683945–8 HBJ pb $8.95
  Volume 2: Growing, 1904-1911
  0–15–637215–0 HBJ pb $8.95
  Volume 3: Beginning Again, 1911-1918
  0–15–611680–4 HBJ pb $8.95
  Volume 4: Downhill All the Way, 1919-1939
  0–15–626145–6 HBJ pb $8.95
  Volume 5: The Journey Not the Arrival Matters, 1939-1969
  0–15–646523–X HBJ pb $8.95
  THE LETTERS OF LEONARD WOOLF
  Edited by Frederic Spotts
  0–15–150915–8 HBJ $32.95

- Virginia Woolf
  THE ESSAYS OF VIRGINIA WOOLF, Volume 1
  Edited by Andrew McNeillie
  0–15–629054–5 HBJ $12.95

Critical Studies

- Daniel Danielson, editor
  THE CAMBRIDGE COMPANION TO MILTON
  0–521–33402–0 Cambridge $42.50
  0–521–36885–5 Cambridge pb $12.95

- Paula Backscheider
  DANIEL DEFOE: His Life
  0–8018–3785–5 Johns Hopkins $29.95

- Don Gifford
  ULYSSES ANNOTATED
  0–520–06745–2 California pb $17.95

- John Hollander
  RHYME'S REASON: A Guide to English Verse
  0–300–04307–3 Yale pb $7.95

- Michael Holroyd
  BERNARD SHAW, Volume 2: In Pursuit of Power, 1898-1918
  0–394–57553–9 Random House $24.95

- A. Norman Jeffares
  W.B. YEATS: A New Biography
  0–374–28588–8 Farrar, Straus & Giroux $25.00

- Frank Kersnowski, editor
CONVERSATIONS WITH ROBERT GRAVES
0–87805–414–6 Mississippi pb $14.95

- Christopher Ricks
TENNYSON
0–520–06784–3 California $25.00

- David Riggs
BEN JONSON: A Life
0–674–06626–X Harvard pb $14.95

- James Anderson Winn
JOHN DRYDEN AND HIS WORLD
0–300–04591–3 Yale pb $19.95

LITERATURE OF THE AMERICAS

Canadian Literature

- Marie-Claire Blais
DEAF TO THE CITY
0–87951–296–2 Penguin pb $10.95

American Literature to 1900

- William L. Andrews, introduction
SIX WOMEN'S SLAVE NARRATIVES
0–19–506083–0 Oxford pb $9.95

- James Fenimore Cooper
THE AMERICAN DEMOCRAT
Edited by George Dekker & Larry Johnston
0–14–039068–5 Penguin pb $6.95

- Charlotte L. Forten Grimké
THE JOURNALS OF CHARLOTTE FORTEN GRIMKE
Edited by Brenda Stevenson
0–19–506086–5 Oxford pb $10.95

- Elizabeth Keckley
BEHIND THE SCENES: Or, Thirty Years a Slave, and Four Years in the White House
0–19–506084–9 Oxford pb $9.95

- Mark Twain
HUCK FINN AND TOM SAWYER AMONG THE INDIANS & Other Unfinished Stories
0–520–05090–7 California $25.00
0–520–05110–6 California pb $8.95

- Phillis Wheatley
THE COLLECTED WORKS OF PHILLIS WHEATLEY
0–19–505241–2 Oxford pb $9.95

20th-Century Fiction

- Edward Abbey
HAYDUKE LIVES!
0–316–00411–1 Little, Brown $17.95

- Alice Adams
AFTER YOU'VE GONE
0–394–57926–7 Knopf $18.95

- Margaret Atwood with Shannon Ravenel, editors
THE BEST AMERICAN SHORT STORIES 1989
0–395–47097–8 Houghton Mifflin $17.95
0–395–47098–6 Houghton Mifflin pb $8.95

- Russell Banks
AFFLICTION
0–06–016142–6 Harper & Row $18.95

- Ann Beattie
PICTURING WILL
0–394–56987–3 Random House $18.95

- Saul Bellow
THE BELLAROSA CONNECTION
0–14–012686–4 Penguin pb $6.95

- Thomas Berger
CHANGING THE PAST
0–316–09149–9 Little, Brown $22.95
THE FEUD
0–316–11600–0 Little, Brown pb $8.95
REINHART'S WOMEN
0–316–11601–7 Little, Brown pb $8.95

- Harold Brodkey
STORIES IN AN ALMOST CLASSICAL MODE
0–679–72431–1 Random House pb $12.95

- Frank Bergon
SHOSHONE MIKE
0–14–009876–3 Penguin pb $7.95

- George Cain
BLUESCHILD BABY
0–88001–133–5 Ecco pb $7.50

- Hortense Calisher
AGE
1–55584–371–9 Weidenfeld & Nicolson pb $6.95

- Susan Cheever
ELIZABETH COLE
0–374–14657–8 Farrar, Straus & Giroux $18.95

- Rick DeMarinis
THE YEAR OF THE ZINC PENNY
0–393–02758–9 Norton $17.95

- Melvin Dixon
TROUBLE THE WATER
0–932511–23–6 Fiction Collective $18.95
0–932511–24–4 Fiction Collective pb $8.95

- Gretel Ehrlich
HEART MOUNTAIN
0–14–008113–5 Penguin pb $8.95

- Leslie Epstein
KING OF THE JEWS
0–671–69003–5 Simon & Schuster pb $8.95

- Jessie Redmon Fauset
THERE IS CONFUSION
1–55553–066–4 Northeastern pb $12.95

- F. Scott Fitzgerald
THE SHORT STORIES OF F. SCOTT FITZGERALD
0–684–19160–1 Scribners $29.95

- Kaye Gibbons
ELLEN FOSTER
0–912697–52–0 Algonquin $11.95
A VIRTUOUS WOMAN
0–945575–09–2 Algonquin $13.95

- Ellen Gilchrist
LIGHT CAN BE BOTH WAVE AND PARTICLE
0–316–31318–1 Little, Brown $17.95

- Ellen Glasgow
VIRGINIA
0–14–039072–3 Penguin pb $4.95

- Mitchell Goodman
THE END OF IT
0–374–52191–3 Farrar, Straus & Giroux pb $8.95

- Mary Gordon
THE OTHER SIDE
0–670–82566–2 Viking $19.95

- Robert Gover
ONE HUNDRED DOLLAR MISUNDERSTANDING
0–8021–3181–6 Grove pb $8.95

- Elizabeth Hardwick
THE GHOSTLY LOVER
0–88001–240–4 Ecco pb $8.95

- Oscar Hijuelos
THE MAMBO KINGS PLAY SONGS OF LOVE
0–374–20125–0 Farrar, Straus & Giroux $18.95

- Warren Kiefer
OUTLAW
1–55611–148–7 Donald Fine $19.95

- William Kotzwinkle
THE HOT JAZZ TRIO
0–395–50096–6 Houghton Mifflin $17.95

- Armistead Maupin
SURE OF YOU
0–06–016164–7 Harper & Row $19.95

- Julian Mayfield
THE HIT & THE LONG NIGHT
1–55553–065–6 Northeastern pb $14.95

- Joseph McElroy
THE LETTER LEFT TO ME
0–88184–536–1 Carroll & Graf pb $6.95

- Thomas McGuane
KEEP THE CHANGE
0–395–48887–7 Houghton Mifflin $17.95

- Larry McMurtry
SOME CAN WHISTLE
0–671–64267–7 Simon & Schuster $19.95

- James A. Michener
CARIBBEAN
0–394–56561–4 Random House $22.95

- N. Scott Momaday
THE ANCIENT CHILD
0–385–27972–8 Doubleday $17.95

- Vladimir Nabokov
TRANSPARENT THINGS
Edited by Dmitri Nabokov & Matthew J. Bruccoli
0–679–72541–5 Random House pb $6.95

- Charles Nordhoff & James Norman Hall
MEN AGAINST THE SEA
0–316–61163–8 Little, Brown pb $8.95

PITCAIRN'S ISLAND
0–316–61169–7 Little, Brown pb $8.95

- Cynthia Ozick
THE SHAWL
0–394–58199–7 Knopf $12.95

- Richard Powers
PRISONER'S DILEMMA
0–02–036055–X Macmillan pb $8.95

- Thomas Pynchon
VINELAND
0–316–72444–0 Little, Brown $19.95

- Ishmael Reed
FLIGHT TO CANADA
0–689–70733–9 Macmillan pb $8.95

SHROVETIDE IN OLD NEW ORLEANS
0–689–70729–0 Macmillan pb $9.95

- Mary Robison
BELIEVE THEM
0–02–036380–X Macmillan pb $7.95

- Philip Roth
THE FACTS: A Novelist's Autobiography
0–14–011405–X Penguin pb $7.95

- Richard Russo
THE RISK POOL
0–679–72334–X Random House pb $8.95

- Thomas Sanchez
MILE ZERO
0–394–57859–7 Knopf $19.95

- William Saroyan
MADNESS IN THE FAMILY
0–8112–1064–2 New Directions $16.95

THE MAN WITH THE HEART IN THE HIGHLANDS & OTHER EARLY STORIES
0–8112–1115–0 New Directions $15.95

- Budd Schulberg
WHAT MAKES SAMMY RUN?
0–394–47618–7 Random House $19.95

- George Samuel Schuyler
BLACK NO MORE
1–55553–063–X Northeastern pb $10.95

- Lynne Sharon Schwartz
BALANCING ACTS
0–14–011944–2 Penguin pb $6.95

- Mary Lee Settle
CHARLEY BLAND
0–374–12078–1 Farrar, Straus & Giroux $18.95

- Jane Smiley
ORDINARY LOVE & GOOD WILL
0–394–57772–8 Knopf $17.95

- Booth Tarkington
THE MAGNIFICENT AMBERSONS
0–253–35875–2 Indiana $17.50
0–253–20546–8 Indiana pb $9.95

- William T. Vollmann
THE RAINBOW STORIES
0–689–11961–5 Atheneum $19.95

- Paul West
THE PLACE IN FLOWERS WHERE POLLEN RESTS
0–02–038260–X Collier pb $9.95

LORD BYRON'S DOCTOR
0–385–26129–2 Doubleday $19.95

- Larry Woiwode
BEYOND THE BEDROOM WALL
0–14–012186–2 Penguin pb $8.95

BORN BROTHERS
0–14–012185–4 Penguin pb $8.95

20th-Century Poetry

- Bruce Andrews
I DON'T HAVE ANY PAPER SO SHUT UP (OR, SOCIAL ROMANTICISM)
1–55713–077–9 Sun & Moon pb $11.95

- John Ashbery
THREE POEMS
0–88001–227–7 Ecco pb $8.95

- April Bernard
BLACKBIRD BYEBYE
0–394–57536–9 Random House $16.95

- Charles Bernstein
ROUGH TRADES
1–55713–080–9 Sun & Moon pb $10.95

- David Bromige
AN AMERICAN TESTAMENT
1–55713–089–2 Sun & Moon pb $10.95

- Hayden Carruth
TELL ME AGAIN HOW THE WHITE HERON RISES AND FLIES ACROSS THE NACREOUS RIVER AT TWILIGHT TOWARD THE DISTANT ISLANDS
0–8112–0681–5 New Directions $15.00

- Gregory Corso
MINDFIELD: New and Selected Poems
Prefaces by William Burroughs & Allen Ginsberg
0–938410–85–7 Thunder's Mouth $24.95
0–938410–86–5 Thunder's Mouth pb $12.95

- e.e. cummings
E.E. CUMMINGS: Complete Poems, 1904-1962
Edited by George J. Firmage
0–87140–145–2 Norton $45.00

- Alan Dugan
POEMS 6
0–88001–199–8 Ecco $17.95

- Henry Dumas
KNEES OF A NATURAL MAN
Edited with a foreword by Eugene B. Redmond
0–938410–75–X Thunder's Mouth $19.95
0–938410–74–1 Thunder's Mouth pb $9.95

- Randall Jarrell
SELECTED POEMS
0–374–25867–8 Farrar, Straus & Giroux $17.95

- June Jordan
NAMING OUR DESTINY: New and Selected Poems
0–938410–84–9 Thunder's Mouth pb $12.95

- Maxine Kumin
NURTURE
0–14–058619–9 Penguin pb $8.95

- Sandra McPherson
STREAMERS
0–88001–214–5 Ecco pb $7.95

- Joyce Carol Oates
THE TIME TRAVELER: Poems 1983-1989
0–525–24802–1 Dutton $18.95
0–525–48505–8 Dutton pb $9.95

- Jena Osman
TWELVE PARTS OF HER
0–930901–63–0 Burning Deck pb $4.00

- Ishmael Reed
NEW AND COLLECTED POEMS
0–689–12004–4 Macmillan pb $9.95

- Jerome Rothenberg
KHURBN & OTHER POEMS
0–8112–1109–6 New Directions pb $9.95

- Jimmy Santiago Baca
BLACK MESA POEMS
0–8112–1102–9 New Directions pb $8.95

- David Shapiro
HOUSE (BLOWN APART)
0–87951–331–4 Overlook pb $9.95

- Anne Waldman
BLUE MOSQUE
0–935992–07–9 United States pb $6.00

- Richard Wilbur
NEW AND COLLECTED POEMS
0–15–665491–1 HBJ pb $12.95

- C.K. Williams
POEMS, 1963-1983
0–374–52204–9 Farrar, Straus & Giroux $10.95

- Donald Hall, editor
THE BEST AMERICAN POETRY, 1989
0–02–044182–7 Macmillan pb $9.95

- Maureen Honey, editor
WOMEN'S POETRY OF THE HARLEM RENAISSANCE
0–8135–1419–3 Rutgers $35.00

20th-Century Drama

- Richard Greenberg
EASTERN STANDARD
0–8021–3174–3 Grove pb $9.95

- Eugene O'Neill
LONG DAY'S JOURNEY INTO NIGHT
0–300–04600–6 Yale $18.50
0–300–04601–4 Yale pb $5.95

• Kathy A. Perkins, editor
BLACK FEMALE PLAYWRIGHTS: An Anthology of Plays Before 1950
0–253–34358–5 Indiana $35.00

20th-Century Essays and Journalism

• Annie Dillard
THE WRITING LIFE
0–06–016156–6 Harper & Row $15.95

• Michiko Kakutani
THE POET AT THE PIANO: Portraits of Writers, Filmmakers, and Performers at Work
0–87226–210–3 Bedrick pb $8.95

• Jack London
JOHN BARLEYCORN
Edited by John Sutherland
0–19–281804–X Oxford pb $8.95

• Alice Walker
LIVING BY THE WORD: Selected Writings, 1973-1987
0–15–652865–7 HBJ pb $8.95

• Geoffrey Wolff & Robert Atwan, editors
THE BEST AMERICAN ESSAYS
0–89919–891–0 Ticknor & Fields $17.95
0–89919–892–9 Ticknor & Fields pb $8.95

Critical Studies

• Jonathan Arac
COMMISSIONED SPIRITS: The Shaping of Social Motion in Dickens, Carlyle, Melville, Hawthorne
0–231–07117–5 California pb $14.00

• Charles Bernstein, editor
THE POLITICS OF POETIC FORM: Poetry and Public Policy
0–937804–35–5 Roof pb $12.95

• John Cheever
THE LETTERS OF JOHN CHEEVER
Edited by Benjamin Cheever
0–671–68744–1 Simon & Schuster pb $10.95

• Michael Davidson
THE SAN FRANCISCO RENAISSANCE: Poetics and Community at Mid-Century
0–521–25880–4 Cambridge $34.50

• Bettina Drew
NELSON ALGREN: A Life on the Wild Side
0–399–13422–0 Putnam $24.95

• Thomas Fensch, editor
CONVERSATIONS WITH JAMES THURBER
0–87805–410–3 Mississippi pb $14.95

• Henry Louis Gates, Jr.
FIGURES IN BLACK: Words, Signs, and the "Racial" Self
0–19–506074–1 Oxford pb $10.95

THE SIGNIFYING MONKEY: A Theory of African-American Literary Criticism
0–19–506075–X Oxford pb $10.95

• George Hartley
TEXTUAL POLITICS AND THE LANGUAGE POETS
0–253–32716–4 Indiana $20.00

• Karen & Barbara Hinckley
AMERICAN BEST SELLERS: A Reader's Guide to Popular Fiction
0–253–32728–8 Indiana $27.50

• Myra Jehlen
AMERICAN INCARNATION: The Individual, the Nation, and the Continent
0–674–02427–3 Harvard pb $12.95

• Leo Marx
THE PILOT AND THE PASSENGER: Essays on Literature, Technology, and Culture in the United States
0–19–500738–7 Oxford pb $9.95

• Lee Milazzo, editor
CONVERSATIONS WITH JOYCE CAROL OATES
0–87805–412–X Mississippi pb $14.95

• Vladimir Nabokov
VLADIMIR NABOKOV: Selected Letters, 1940-1977
0–15–164190–0 HBJ $29.95

• Lyall H. Powers, editor
HENRY JAMES AND EDITH WHARTON: Letters, 1900-1915
0–684–19146–6 Macmillan $29.95

• William H. Pritchard
RANDALL JARRELL: A Literary Life
0–374–24677–7 Farrar, Straus & Giroux $25.00

• Arnold Rampersad
THE LIFE OF LANGSTON HUGHES, Volume 2: 1941-1967: I Dream a World
0–19–504426–1 Oxford pb $11.95

• David S. Reynolds
BENEATH THE AMERICAN RENAISSANCE: The Subversive Imagination in the Age of Emerson and Melville
0–674–06565–4 Harvard pb $14.95

• Ernest Samuels
HENRY ADAMS
0–674–38735–X Harvard $25.00

• Edith Wharton
THE LETTERS OF EDITH WHARTON
Edited by R.W.B. & Nancy Lewis
0–02–034400–7 Macmillan pb $12.95

• Rosalind Baker Wilson
NEAR THE MAGICIAN: A Memoir of My Father, Edmund Wilson
1–55584–342–5 Weidenfeld & Nicolson $18.95

• Hugh Witemeyer, editor
WILLIAM CARLOS WILLIAMS AND JAMES LAUGHLIN: Selected Letters
0–393–02682–5 Norton $27.50

Caribbean Literature

• Derek Walcott
OMEROS
0–374–22591–5 Farrar, Straus & Giroux $20.00

Latin American Literature

• Alejo Carpentier
THE CHASE
Translated by Alfred MacAdam
0–374–12083–8 Farrar, Straus & Giroux $15.95

EXPLOSION IN A CATHEDRAL
Translated by John Sturrock
0–374–52198–0 Farrar, Straus & Giroux pb $9.95

THE LOST STEPS
Translated by Harriet de Onís
0–374–52199–9 Farrar, Straus & Giroux pb $8.95

THE KINGDOM OF THIS WORLD
Translated by Harriet de Onís
0–374–52197–2 Farrar, Straus & Giroux pb $7.95

• Julio Cortázar
NICARAGUAN SKETCHES
Translated by Kathleen Weaver
0–393–02764–3 Norton $15.95
0–393–30642–9 Norton pb $7.95

• José Donoso
CURFEW
Translated by Alfred MacAdam
1–55584–448–0 Weidenfeld & Nicolson pb $9.95

• Ariel Dorfman
MASCARA
0–14–011253–7 Penguin pb $7.95

• Mario Vargas Llosa
THE REAL LIFE OF ALEJANDRO MAYTA
Translated by Alfred MacAdam
0–679–72478–8 Random House pb $8.95

THE STORYTELLER
Translated by Helen Lane
0–374–27086–4 Farrar, Straus & Giroux $17.95

POPULAR READING

Crime and Spy Fiction

• Raymond Chandler & Robert B. Parker
POODLE SPRINGS
0–399–13482–4 Putnam $18.95

• Len Deighton
SPY LINE
0–394–55179–6 Knopf $18.95

• Peter Dickinson
SKELETON IN WAITING
0–394–58002–8 Pantheon $16.95

• Dick Francis
STRAIGHT
0–399–13470–0 Putnam $18.95

• Erle Stanley Gardner
THE ADVENTURES OF PAUL PRY
0–89296–976–8 Mysterious pb $9.95

• Stephen Greenleaf
IMPACT
0–688–07668–8 Morrow $18.95

• Martha Grimes
THE OLD SILENT
0–316–32318–7 Little, Brown $18.95

- Joseph Hansen
BOHANNON'S BOOK
0–14–012053–X Penguin pb $3.95

- Patricia Highsmith
FOUND IN THE STREET
0–87113–326–1 Atlantic Monthly pb $8.95

- C.H.B. Kitchin
THE DEATH OF MY AUNT
0–88184–549–3 Carroll & Graf pb $3.50

- Arthur Lyons
OTHER PEOPLE'S MONEY
0–89296–218–6 Mysterious $17.95

- Ed McBain
DOWNTOWN
0–688–08736–1 Morrow $18.95

- J.D. Reed & Christine Reed
EXPOSURE
0–8041–0222–8 Ballantine pb $3.50

- Ruth Rendell
THE BRIDESMAID
0–89296–388–3 Mysterious $17.95

- Mickey Spillane
THE KILLING MAN: A Mike Hammer Novel
0–525–24827–7 Dutton $17.95

- Charles Willeford
THE WOMAN CHASER
0–88184–556–6 Carroll & Graf pb $3.95

- Thomas Godfrey, editor
ENGLISH COUNTRY HOUSE MURDERS
0–89296–355–7 Mysterious $18.95

- Susan Oleksiw
A READER'S GUIDE TO THE CLASSIC BRITISH MYSTERY
0–89296–968–7 Mysterious $15.95

- Charles Viney
SHERLOCK HOLMES IN LONDON: A Photographic Record of Conan Doyle's Stories
0–395–51530–0 Houghton Mifflin $24.95

Science Fiction and Fantasy

- Brian W. Aldiss
MAN IN HIS TIME
0–689–12052–4 Macmillan $19.95

- J.G. Ballard
RUNNING WILD
0–374–25288–2 Farrar, Straus & Giroux $12.95

- Philip K. Dick
EYE IN THE SKY
0–02–031590–2 Macmillan pb $4.50

THE ZAP GUN
0–88184–553–1 Carroll & Graf pb $3.95

- Jack Finney
INVASION OF THE BODY SNATCHERS
0–671–68211–3 Simon & Schuster pb $8.95

- Stephen King
THE DARK HALF
0–670–82982–X Viking $21.95

- Stanislaw Lem
EDEN
Translated by Marc E. Heine
0–15–127580–7 HBJ $19.95

- Anthony Boucher
THE COMPLEAT WEREWOLF & Other Tales of Fantasy and Science Fiction
0–88184–557–4 Carroll & Graf pb $4.50

- Michael Cox & R.A. Gilbert, editors
THE OXFORD BOOK OF ENGLISH GHOST STORIES
0–19–282666–2 Oxford pb $9.95

- Robert Phillips, editor
THE TRIUMPH OF NIGHT: 20th-Century Ghost Stories
0–88184–517–5 Carroll & Graf $18.95

- Alan Ryan, editor
THE PENGUIN BOOK OF VAMPIRE STORIES
0–14–012445–4 Penguin pb $8.95

Westerns

- Brian Garfield
MANIFEST DESTINY
0–89296–382–4 Mysterious $18.95

Comics and Popular Graphics

- Ernie Bushmiller
NANCY EATS FOOD
0–87816–060–4 Kitchen Sink pb $7.95

- Milton Caniff
IN FORMOSA'S DIRE STRAITS: A Steve Canyon Adventure
0–87816–044–2 Kitchen Sink pb $11.95

- Jules Feiffer
FEIFFER: The Collected Works, Volume 1
0–930193–40–7 Fantagraphic pb $9.95

- Matt Groening
AKBAR AND JEFF'S GUIDE TO LIFE
0–679–72680–2 Pantheon pb $6.95

- M. Thomas Inge
COMICS AS CULTURE
0–87805–408–1 Mississippi pb $14.95

- Edward Koren
WHAT ABOUT ME?
0–679–72636–5 Pantheon pb $9.95

- Richard Marschall
AMERICA'S GREAT COMIC-STRIP ARTISTS
0–89659–917–5 Abbeville $55.00

- Joseph Witek
COMIC BOOKS AS HISTORY: The Narrative Art of Jack Jackson, Art Spiegelman, and Harvey Pekar
0–87805–406–5 Mississippi pb $14.95

Historical and Romantic Fiction

- C.S. Forester
ADMIRAL HORNBLOWER IN THE WEST INDIES
0–316–28941–8 Little, Brown pb $7.95

LORD HORNBLOWER
0–316–28943–4 Little, Brown pb $7.95

Humor

- Art Buchwald
WHOSE ROSE GARDEN IS IT ANYWAY?
0–399–13480–8 Putnam $18.95

- Marvin Kitman
THE MAKING OF THE PRESIDENT, 1789
0–06–015981–2 Harper & Row $19.95

- James Thurber
COLLECTING HIMSELF: James Thurber on Writing and Writers, Humor and Himself
0–06–016135–3 Harper & Row $19.95

- Calvin Trillin
TRAVELS WITH ALICE
0–89919–910–0 Ticknor & Fields $18.95

BOOKS FOR YOUNG READERS

Books for Children Under Five

- Byron Barton
DINOSAURS, DINOSAURS
0–694–00269–0 Crowell $7.95

- Margaret Wise Brown
BIG RED BARN
0–06–020748–5 Harper & Row $11.95

- Amy Ehrlich
THE STORY OF HANUKKAH
Illustrations by Ori Sherman
0–8037–0615–4 Dial $14.95

- Eric Hill
SPOT'S BABY SISTER
0–399–21640–5 Putnam $10.95

- Tana Hoban
OF COLORS AND THINGS
0–688–07534–7 Greenwillow $12.95

- James Marshall
THE THREE LITTLE PIGS
0–8037–0591–3 Dial $11.95

- Michael Rosen
WE'RE GOING ON A BEAR HUNT
Illustrations by Helen Oxenbury
0–689–50476–4 Macmillan $14.95

- Lynne Sharon Schwartz
THE FOUR QUESTIONS
Illustrations by Ori Sherman
0–8037–0600–6 Dial $15.95

- Wendy Watson
WENDY WATSON'S MOTHER GOOSE
0–688–05708–X Lothrop, Lee & Sheperd $19.95

Books for Ages Five, Six, and Seven

● Ann Durell, editor
THE DIANE GOODE BOOK OF AMERICAN FOLK TALES AND SONGS
Illustrations by Diane Goode
0–525–44458–0 Dutton $14.95

● Eleanor Estes
THE HUNDRED DRESSES
0–15–642350–2 HBJ pb $4.95

● Margot Fonteyn
SWAN LAKE
Illustrated by Trina Schart Hyman
0–15–224435–2 HBJ $13.95

● Rosmarie Hausherr
CHILDREN AND THE AIDS VIRUS
0–395–51167–4 Ticknor & Fields pb $5.95

● Alice Low, editor
THE FAMILY READ-ALOUD CHRISTMAS TREASURY
Illustrations by Marc Brown
0–316–53371–8 Little, Brown $17.95

● Diane Siebert
HEARTLAND
Illustrations by Wendell Minor
0–690–04732–0 Crowell $13.95

● Virginia Driving Hawk Sneve, editor
DANCING TEEPEES: Poems of American Indian Youth
Illustrations by Stephen Gammell
0–8234–0724–1 Holiday House $14.95

Books for Eights, Nines, and Up

● Nancy Ekholm Burkert
VALENTINE AND ORSON
0–374–38078–3 Farrar, Straus & Giroux $16.95

● Mark Helprin
SWAN LAKE
Illustrated by Chris Van Allburg
0–395–49858–9 Houghton Mifflin $19.95

● Judith Levey, editor
MACMILLAN DICTIONARY FOR CHILDREN
0–02–761561–8 Macmillan $14.95

● Janet Taylor Lisle
AFTERNOON OF THE ELVES
0–531–53371–8 Orchard $12.95

● Bill Peet
BILL PEET: An Autobiography
0–395–50932–7 Houghton Mifflin $14.95

Young Adult Fiction and Nonfiction

● Jean Fritz
THE GREAT LITTLE MANSION
0–399–21768–1 Putnam $15.95

● Cynthia Voigt
SEVENTEEN AGAINST THE DEALER
0–689–31497–3 Atheneum $13.95

ART HISTORY

Art History: General Studies

● Rudolf Arnheim
PARABLES OF SUN LIGHT: Observations on Psychology, the Arts, and the Rest
0–520–06516–6 California $27.50

● John Ashbery
REPORTED SIGHTINGS: Art Chronicles, 1957-1987
Edited by David Bergman
0–394–57387–0 Knopf $35.00

● Bruce Cole & Adelheid Gealt
ART OF THE WESTERN WORLD: From Ancient Greece to Post-Modernism
0–671–67007–7 Summit $35.00

● Pierre Skira
STILL LIFE: A History
0–8478–1111–5 Rizzoli $85.00

● Calvin Tomkins
MERCHANTS AND MASTERPIECES: The Story of the Metropolitan Museum of Art
0–8050–1034–3 Henry Holt $22.95

● John Updike
JUST LOOKING: Essays on Art
0–394–57904–6 Knopf $35.00

Art of Egypt and the Ancient Near East

● Edna R. Russman & David Finn
EGYPTIAN SCULPTURE: Cairo and Luxor
0–292–76498–7 Texas $39.95

● Christine el Mahdy
MUMMIES, MYTH AND MAGIC: In Ancient Egypt
0–500–05055–4 Thames & Hudson $19.95

European Art: Medieval and Renaissance

● Glenn Andres & others
THE ART OF FLORENCE
0–89659–402–5 Abbeville $385.00

● Colin Eisler
THE GENIUS OF JACOPO BELLINI: The Complete Paintings and Drawings
0–8109–0727–5 Abrams $195.00

● Alain Erlande-Brandenburg
GOTHIC ART
0–8109–0631–7 Abrams $135.00

● Walter S. Gibson
MIRROR OF THE EARTH: The World Landscape in Sixteenth-Century Flemish Painting
0–691–04054–0 Princeton $55.00

● Rona Goffen
GIOVANNI BELLINI
0–300–04334–1 Yale $60.00

● Ronald Lightbown
SANDRO BOTTICELLI: Life and Work
0–89659–931–0 Abbeville $85.00

● James Marrow & others
THE GOLDEN AGE OF DUTCH MANUSCRIPT PAINTING
0–8076–1227–8 Braziller $65.00

● Christopher Wilson
THE GOTHIC CATHEDRAL
0–500–34105–2 Thames & Hudson $39.95

European Art: From the Renaissance to the 20th Century

● Colin B. Bailey & others
MASTERPIECES OF IMPRESSIONISM AND POST-IMPRESSIONISM: The Annenberg Collection
0–8109–1546–6 Abrams $49.50

● Gabriella Belli
GUSTAV KLIMT MASTERPIECES
0–8212–1762–3 Bulfinch $50.00

● Alicia Craig Faxon
DANTE GABRIEL ROSSETTI
0–89659–928–0 Abbeville $85.00

● Pierre Gassier
GOYA
0–8478–1108–5 Rizzoli $25.00

● J.G. Links & Katharine Baetjer
CANALETTO
0–8109–3155–9 Abrams $60.00

● Pierre Rosenberg & Jacques Thuillier
LAURENT DE LA HYRE
0–8478–5530–9 Rizzoli $75.00

● Daniel J. Sherman
WORTHY MONUMENTS: Art Museums and the Politics of Culture in Nineteenth-Century France
0–674–96230–3 Harvard $30.00

● Paul Hayes Tucker
MONET IN THE '90s
0–300–04659–6 Yale $45.00

● J.N.P. Watson
MILLAIS: Three Generations in Nature, Art and Sport
0–948253–28–2 David & Charles $39.95

American Art to 1900

● William Innes Homer & Lloyd Goodrich
ALBERT PINKHAM RYDER: Painter of Dreams
0–8109–1599–5 Abrams $45.00

● Marc Simpson, Sally Mills & Jennifer Saville
THE AMERICAN CANVAS: Paintings from the Collection of The Fine Arts Museums of San Francisco
1–55595–025–6 Hudson Hills $50.00

● Robin Spencer, editor
WHISTLER: A Retrospective
0–88363–689–1 Macmillan $75.00

➤ **FOR OVERSEAS ORDERING INFORMATION, SEE PAGE 1**

20th-Century Art

- Dawn Ades, editor
ART IN LATIN AMERICA
0–300–04556–5 Yale $50.00

- John Arthur
SPIRIT OF PLACE: Contemporary Landscape Painting and the American Tradition
0–8122–1707–0 Little, Brown $60.00

- David Bourdon
WARHOL
0–8109–1761–0 Abrams $49.50

- David Britt
MODERN ART: Impressionism to Post-Modernism
0–8212–1764–X Bulfinch $35.00

- Marc Dachy
THE DADA MOVEMENT
0–8478–1110–7 Rizzoli $85.00

- John Elderfield
THE DRAWINGS OF RICHARD DIEBENKORN
0–87070–304–8 MOMA pb $30.00

- Howard Fox & others
ROBERT LONGO
0–8478–1104–2 Rizzoli $45.00
0–8478–1105–0 Rizzoli pb $29.95

- Robert Frankel, editor
JACK LEVINE
0–8478–0977–3 Rizzoli $45.00

- John Golding
CUBISM: A History and an Analysis, 1907-1914
0–674–17930–7 Harvard $19.95

- Lloyd Goodrich
EDWARD HOPPER
0–8109–0187–0 Abrams $67.50

- Lawrence Gowing & Sam Hunter
FRANCIS BACON
0–500–09200–1 Thames & Hudson $50.00

- Robert Hobbs
MILTON AVERY
0–933920–95–4 Hudson Hills $75.00

- Sam Hunter
LARRY RIVERS
0–8478–1094–1 Rizzoli $75.00

- Aleksandr Kamensky
CHAGALL: The Russian Years, 1907-1922
0–8478–1080–1 Rizzoli $100.00

- Ellen G. Landau
JACKSON POLLOCK
0–8109–3702–6 Abrams $67.50

- Roger Manley
SIGNS AND WONDERS: Outsider Art Inside North Carolina
0–88259–957–7 North Carolina pb $14.95

- John Manship
PAUL MANSHIP
1–55859–002–1 Abbeville $95.00

- Roxana Robinson
GEORGIA O'KEEFE: A Life
0–06–015965–0 Harper & Row $25.00

- William Rubin
PICASSO AND BRAQUE: Pioneering Cubism
0–87070–675–6 MOMA $60.00
0–87070–676–4 MOMA $30.00

- Peter Webb
PORTRAIT OF DAVID HOCKNEY
0–525–24826–9 Dutton $29.95

Arts of Africa

- Marshall W. Mount
AFRICAN ART: The Years Since 1920
0–306–80373–9 Da Capo $16.95

Islamic Arts

- Nurhan Atasoy & Julian Raby
IZNIK: The Pottery of Ottoman Turkey
0–500–97374–1 Thames & Hudson $150.00

- R.W. Ferrier
THE ARTS OF PERSIA
0–300–03987–5 Yale $60.00

East Asian Art

- Ronald G. Knapp
CHINA'S VERNACULAR ARCHITECTURE: House Form and Culture
0–8248–1204–2 Hawaii $38.00

- Itō Jakuchū
ON A RIVER BOATING JOURNEY
0–8076–1229–4 Braziller $45.00

- Richard Lane
HOKUSAI: Life and Work
0–525–24455–7 Dutton $50.00

- Laurence Liu
CHINESE ARCHITECTURE
0–8478–1082–8 Rizzoli $75.00

- Peter Morse
HOKUSAI: 100 Poets
0–8076–1213–8 Braziller $80.00

- Pratapaditya Pal & others
THE ROMANCE OF THE TAJ MAHAL
0–500–23556–2 Thames & Hudson $45.00

- Paul Varley & Kumakura Isao, editors
TEA IN JAPAN: Essays on the History of Chanoyu
0–8248–1218–2 Hawaii $25.00

Native American Arts

- Eduardo Matos Moctezuma
THE AZTECS
0–8478–1091–7 Rizzoli $75.00

Illustration and Popular Graphics

- Leonard de Vries
A TREASURY OF ILLUSTRATED CHILDREN'S BOOKS: Early Nineteenth-Century Classics from the Osborne Collection
0–89659–939–6 Abbeville $75.00

- Erté
ERTE: My Life/My Art
0–525–24808–0 Dutton $65.00

- Mildred Friedman & others
GRAPHIC DESIGN IN AMERICA: A Visual Language History
0–8109–1036–5 Abrams $49.50

- The New Yorker
THE COMPLETE BOOK OF COVERS FROM THE NEW YORKER, 1925-1989
Introduction by John Updike
0–394–57841–4 Knopf $75.00

- Nicholas Fox Weber
THE ART OF BABAR: The Work of Jean and Laurent de Brunhoff
0–8109–1893–5 Abrams $39.95

Photography

- Eve Arnold
ALL IN A DAY'S WORK
0–553–05721–9 Bantam $35.00

- William Betsch
THE HAKIMA: Love and Death in Fez (A Photographic Novel)
Introduction by Paul Bowles
0–89381–287–0 Aperture $35.00

- Robert Frank
THE LINES OF MY HAND
0–394–55255–5 Pantheon $60.00

- William Manchester
IN OUR TIME: The World as Seen by Magnum Photographers
0–393–02767–8 Norton $59.95

- Robert Mapplethorpe
SOME WOMEN
Introduction by Joan Didion
0–8212–1716–X Little, Brown $50.00

- Lorraine Monk
PHOTOGRAPHS THAT CHANGED THE WORLD
Introduction by Walter Cronkite
0–385–26195–0 Doubleday $30.00

- Gilles Mora
WALKER EVANS: Havana, 1933
0–394–57493–1 Pantheon $35.00

- Naomi Rosenblum
A WORLD HISTORY OF PHOTOGRAPHY
1–55859–054–4 Abbeville $49.95

- Bruce Weber
BRUCE WEBER
0–394–57246–7 Knopf $69.50

ARCHITECTURE AND DESIGN

European Architecture to 1900

- Cleo Baldon & Ib Melchior
STEPS AND STAIRWAYS
Photographs by Julius Shulman & others
0–8478–1075–5 Rizzoli $45.00

- Anthony Blunt
BORROMINI
0–674–07926–4 Harvard $12.95

- Franco Borsi
LEON BATTISTA ALBERTI: The Complete Works
0–8478–1149–2 Rizzoli pb $29.95

- Denis Hollier, editor
AGAINST ARCHITECTURE: The Writings of Georges Bataille
0–262–08186–5 MIT $19.95

- Stephen Murray
BEAUVAIS CATHEDRAL: Architecture of Transcendence
0–691–04236–5 Princeton $55.00

- Lionello Puppi
ANDREA PALLADIO: The Complete Works
0–8478–1150–6 Rizzoli $29.95

American Architecture to 1900

- Roger G. Kennedy
GREEK REVIVAL AMERICA
Photographs by John Hall & others
1–55670–094–6 Stewart, Tabori & Chang $85.00

- Mills Lane
ARCHITECTURE OF THE OLD SOUTH: Mississippi and Alabama
1–55859–008–0 Abbeville $55.00

ARCHITECTURE OF THE OLD SOUTH: South Carolina
1–55859–004–8 Abbeville $55.00

ARCHITECTURE OF THE OLD SOUTH: Virginia
0–89659–970–1 Abbeville $55.00

20th-Century Architecture

- Peter Haiko, editor
ARCHITECTURE OF THE EARLY TWENTIETH CENTURY
0–8478–1083–6 Rizzoli $75.00

- Heinrich Klotz, editor
NEW YORK ARCHITECTURE: 1970-1990
0–8478–1138–7 Rizzoli $75.00

- Jean-François Pinchon, editor
ROB MALLET-STEVENS: Architecture, Furniture, Interior Design
0–262–16116–8 MIT $30.00

Interior Decoration

- Paul Atterbury, editor
BRITISH INTERIOR DESIGN
Introduction by Mario Buatta
1–55859–052–8 Abbeville $49.95

- John Cornforth
THE SEARCH FOR A STYLE: Country Life and Architecture, 1897-1935
0–393–02703–1 Norton $39.95

- Florence de Dampierre
THE DECORATOR
0–8478–1118–2 Rizzoli $45.00

- Linda Dannenberg & others
PIERRE DEUX'S BRITTANY: A French Country Style and Source Book
Photographs by Guy Bouchet
0–517–57376–8 Crown $37.50

- Mary Emmerling, editor
MARY EMMERLING'S AMERICAN COUNTRY SOUTH
Text by Carol Sama Sheehan
Photographs by Langdon Clay
0–517–56175–1 Crown $40.00

- Charlotte Gere
NINETEENTH-CENTURY DECORATION: The Art of the Interior
0–8109–1382–8 Abrams $95.00

- Robin Guild
THE VICTORIAN HOUSE BOOK
0–8478–1095–X Rizzoli $45.00

- Gerd Hatje & Herbert Weisskamp
ROOMS BY DESIGN
0–8109–1598–7 Abrams $39.95

- Elizabeth Heyert
METROPOLITAN PLACES: Interiors from New York, Barcelona, Milan, Mexico City, Paris, West Berlin, London, and Los Angeles
0–670–81743–0 Viking $40.00

- Chester Jones
COLEFAX AND FOWLER: The Best in English Interior Decoration
0–8212–1746–1 Bulfinch $35.00

- Hugh Lander
ENGLISH COTTAGE INTERIORS
Photographs by Peter Rauter
0–8478–1113–1 Rizzoli $27.50

- Pauline C. Metcalf, editor
OGDEN CODMAN AND THE DECORATION OF HOUSES
0–87923–777–5 Godine $40.00

- Pat Ross
FORMAL COUNTRY
Photographs by David Phelps
0–670–82574–3 Viking $35.00

- Tim Street-Porter
CASA MEXICANA: The Architecture, Design, and Style of Mexico
1–55670–097–0 Stewart, Tabori & Chang $45.00

The Decorative Arts

- Nicholas Barnard
LIVING WITH DECORATIVE TEXTILES: Tribal Art from Africa, Asia, and the Americas
0–385–26537–9 Doubleday $45.00

- Lawrence Branyan & others
WORCESTER BLUE AND WHITE PORCELAIN: 1751-1790
0–7126–2090–7 David & Charles $100.00

- Josette Brédit
PRINTED FRENCH FABRICS: Toile de Jouy
0–8478–1135–2 Rizzoli $60.00

- Garth Clark & others
THE MAD POTTER OF BILOXI: The Art and Life of George E. Ohr
Photographs by John White
0–89659–927–2 Abbeville $65.00

- Michael Collins & Andreas Papadakis
POST-MODERN DESIGN
0–8478–1136–0 Rizzoli $65.00

- Alastair Duncan & others
MASTERWORKS OF LOUIS COMFORT TIFFANY
0–8109–1537–5 Abrams $39.95

- Stephen Guernsey Cook Ensko
AMERICAN SILVERSMITHS AND THEIR MARKS
Compiled by Dorothea Ensko Wyle
0–87923–778–3 Godine $65.00

- Geoffrey A. Godden
ENGLISH CHINA
0–09–158300–4 David & Charles $65.00

- Cara Greenberg
MID-CENTURY MODERN: Furniture of the 1950s
Photographs by Tim Street-Porter
0–517–55667–7 Crown pb $20.00

- Gerard Hill & others, editors
FABERGE AND THE RUSSIAN MASTER GOLDSMITHS
0–88363–889–4 Levin $75.00

- Marilyn G. Karmason with Joan B. Stacke
MAJOLICA: A Complete History and Illustrated Survey
0–8109–1534–0 Abrams $75.00

- Annelies Krekel-Aalberse
ART NOUVEAU AND ART DECO SILVER
0–8109–1892–7 Abrams $65.00

- Gillian Naylor & others
THE ENCYCLOPEDIA OF ARTS AND CRAFTS: The International Arts Movement, 1850-1920
0–525–24804–8 Dutton $39.95

- Bruce Newman & Alastair Duncan
FANTASY FURNITURE
0–8478–1119–0 Rizzoli $50.00

- Christopher Payne, editor
SOTHEBY'S CONCISE ENCYCLOPEDIA OF FURNITURE
0–06–016141–8 Harper & Row $49.95

- Mary Schoeser & Celia Rufey
ENGLISH AND AMERICAN TEXTILES: 1790-1990
0–500–01473–6 Thames & Hudson $49.95

- Leonard Whiter
  SPODE: A History of the Family, Factory and Wares From 1733 to 1833
  0–7126–2175–X David & Charles $100.00

The Home

- Letitia Baldrige
  LETITIA BALDRIGE'S COMPLETE GUIDE TO THE NEW MANNERS: Plus the Time-Honored Ones That Everyone Needs to Know
  0–89256–320–6 Rawson $24.95

- Dorothy Gates & others
  THE COMPLETE BOOK OF SOFT FURNISHINGS: Upholstery, Curtains and Blinds, Cushions and Covers
  0–7063–6697–2 David & Charles $29.95

- Kay Johnson & others
  CHAIR SEATING: Techniques in Cane, Rush, Willow and Cords
  0–8521–9736–5 David & Charles $34.95

- Jack Lenor Larsen
  JACK LENOR LARSEN'S GUIDE TO MATERIAL WEALTH
  1–55859–007–2 Abbeville $55.00

- Mary Kerney Levenstein & Cordelia Frances Biddle
  CARING FOR YOUR CHERISHED POSSESSIONS
  0–517–57087–4 Crown $14.95

- Barbara Milo Ohrbach
  ANTIQUES AT HOME: Cherchez's Book of Collecting and Decorating with Antiques
  Photographs by John Hall
  0–517–56986–8 Crown $22.95

- Sue Peverill
  THE FABRIC DECORATOR: Painting, Printing, and Dyeing Fabrics for the Home
  0–316–70390–7 Little, Brown $29.95

- Pierre Ramond
  MARQUETRY
  0–942391–19–5 Dembner $59.95

- Kenneth Turner
  KENNETH TURNER'S FLOWER STYLE: The Art of Floral Design and Decoration
  1–55584–247–X Weidenfeld & Nicolson $35.00

Crafts

- Noel Dyrenforth
  THE TECHNIQUE OF BATIK
  0–7134–0407–8 David & Charles $39.95

- Jean Fraser
  TRADITIONAL SCOTTISH DYES AND HOW TO MAKE THEM
  0–86241–108–4 David & Charles pb $11.95

- Felice Hodges
  PERIOD PASTIMES: A Practical Guide to Four Centuries of Decorative Crafts
  1–55584–395–6 Weidenfeld & Nicolson $29.95

- Albert Jackson & David Day
  THE COMPLETE MANUAL OF WOODWORKING
  0–394–56488–X Knopf $40.00

- Richard Kollath & Tim Frew
  BASKETS: Design Ideas, Techniques and Materials, Step-by-Step Projects
  1–55584–305–0 Weidenfeld & Nicolson $18.95

- Vogue Knitting Magazine
  VOGUE KNITTING: The Ultimate Knitting Book
  0–394–58157–1 Pantheon $34.95

Collectibles

- James Challenger
  TOBACCO TINS ENCYCLOPEDIA
  0–88740–179–1 Schiffer $69.95

- Teruhisa Kitahara, editor
  YESTERDAY'S TOYS
  Photographs by Masashi Kudo
  Volume 1: Celluloid Dolls, Clowns, and Animals
  0–87701–615–1 Chronicle pb $14.95
  Volume 2: Planes, Trains, Boats, and Cars
  0–87701–621–6 Chronicle pb $14.95
  Volume 3: Robots, Spaceships, Astronauts, and Monsters
  0–87701–630–5 Chronicle pb $14.95

- John Marion with Christopher Andersen
  THE UNIVERSAL PASSION: An Insider's Indispensable Advice on Collecting Everything from Oil Paintings and Furniture to Autographs and Automobiles
  0–671–66783–1 Simon & Schuster $19.95

- Derek Roberts
  CONTINENTAL AND AMERICAN SKELETON CLOCKS
  0–88740–182–1 Schiffer $79.95

- Lynn Wenzel & Carol J. Binkowski
  I HEAR AMERICA SINGING: The Story of American Popular Sheet Music
  0–517–56967–1 Crown $29.95

Fashion and Costume

- Elizabeth Ann Coleman
  THE OPULENT ERA: Fashions of Worth, Doucet and Pingat
  0–500–01476–0 Thames & Hudson $45.00

- Stephen de Pietri & others
  NEW LOOK TO NOW: French Haute Couture, 1947-1987
  0–8478–1139–5 Rizzoli $22.50

- Alfred Fornay
  FORNAY'S GUIDE TO SKIN CARE AND MAKEUP FOR WOMEN OF COLOR
  0–671–66900–1 Simon & Schuster $12.95

- Sandy Summers Head
  SIZING UP: Fashion, Fitness, and Self-Esteem for Full-Figured Women
  0–671–67572–9 Simon & Schuster $16.95

- Marie-Andrée Jouve & Jacqueline Demornex
  BALENCIAGA
  0–8478–1079–8 Rizzoli $110.00

- Jill Liddell
  THE STORY OF THE KIMONO
  0–525–24574–X Dutton $60.00

- Colin McDowell
  SHOES: Fashion and Fantasy
  0–8478–1112–3 Rizzoli $50.00

- Arthur Marwick
  BEAUTY IN HISTORY: Society, Politics and Personal Appearance, c. 1500 to the Present
  0–500–25101–0 Thames & Hudson $19.95

- Caroline Rennolds Milbank
  NEW YORK FASHION: The Evolution of American Style
  0–8109–1388–7 Abrams $49.50

- Shirley Miles O'Donnoll
  AMERICAN COSTUME, 1915-1970: A Source Book for the Stage Costume
  0–253–20543–3 Indiana pb $15.00

- Pam Martin Sarnoff
  THE ULTIMATE SPA BOOK
  0–446–51520–5 Warner $24.95

- Pamela Redmond Satran
  DRESSING SMART: The Complete Guide for Women Who Are Beyond Dressing for Success
  0–385–24525–4 Doubleday $17.95

- Skrebneski
  SKREBNESKI: Black-and-White and Color Photographs, 1949-1989
  0–8212–1748–8 Bulfinch $50.00

- Mary Trasko
  HEAVENLY SOLES: Extraordinary Twentieth-Century Shoes
  1–55859–046–3 Abbeville $29.95

PERFORMING ARTS AND MEDIA

Western Classical Music

- Gerald Abraham, editor
  THE NEW OXFORD HISTORY OF MUSIC, Volume 9: Romanticism, 1830-1890
  0–19–316309–8 Oxford $96.00

- Carl Bamberger, editor
  THE CONDUCTOR'S ART
  0–231–07129–9 Columbia pb $15.00

- Volkmar Braunbehrens
  MOZART IN VIENNA: 1781-1791
  0–8021–1009–6 Grove $25.00

- Ernst Burger
  FRANZ LISZT: A Chronicle of His Life in Pictures and Documents
  0–691–09133–1 Princeton $75.00

- Aaron Copland & Vivian Perlis
  COPLAND: Since 1943
  0–312–01149–0 St. Martin's pb $29.95

- Richard Crocker & David Hiley, editors
  THE NEW OXFORD HISTORY OF MUSIC, Volume 2: The Early Middle Ages to 1300
  0–19–316329–2 Oxford $95.00

- David Dubal
  THE ART OF THE PIANO: Its Performers, Literature, and Recordings
  0–671–49238–1 Summit $40.00

- Richard Dufallo
  TRACKINGS: Composers Speak with Richard Dufallo
  0–19–505816–X Oxford $35.00

- Laelia Goehr & John Amis
  MUSICIANS IN CAMERA: A Private View of the World's Greatest Composers, Conductors and Performers
  0–7475–0042–8 David & Charles $34.95

- Karl Haas
  INSIDE MUSIC
  0–385–18536–7 Doubleday $22.50

- The Earl of Harewood
  KOBBE'S ILLUSTRATED OPERA BOOK: 26 of the World's Best-Loved Operas
  0–399–13475–1 Putnam $34.95

- H. Wiley Hitchcock
  MARC-ANTOINE CHARPENTIER
  0–19–316411–6 Oxford $32.50
  0–19–316410–8 Oxford pb $13.95

- D. Kern Holoman
  BERLIOZ
  0–674–06778–9 Harvard $30.00

- Leos Janacek
  JANACEK'S UNCOLLECTED ESSAYS ON MUSIC
  0–7145–2857–9 Marion Boyars $35.00

- H.C. Robbins Landon
  MOZART: The Golden Years
  0–02–872025–3 Schirmer $29.95

- Arbie Orenstein
  A RAVEL READER: Correspondence, Articles, Interviews
  0–231–04962–5 Columbia $49.00

- Henry Pleasants
  OPERA IN CRISIS: Tradition, Present, Future
  0–500–01468–X Thames & Hudson $19.95

- Andrew Porter
  MUSICAL EVENTS: A Chronicle, 1983-1986
  0–671–63537–9 Simon & Schuster $29.95

- Francis Poulenc
  DIARY OF MY SONGS: Journal de Mes Mélodies
  0–575–04473–X David & Charles pb $17.95

- Ronald Ratcliffe
  STEINWAY
  0–87701–592–9 Chronicle $40.00

- Felix Salzer & Carl Schachter
  COUNTERPOINT IN COMPOSITION
  0–231–07039–X Columbia pb $25.00

- Michael Scott
  THE GREAT CARUSO
  1–55553–061–3 Northeastern pb $14.95

- Virgil Thomson
  MUSIC WITH WORDS: A Composer's View
  0–300–04505–0 Yale $19.95

  SELECTED LETTERS OF VIRGIL THOMSON
  Edited by Tim Page & Vanessa Weeks Page
  0–671–68869–3 Simon & Schuster pb $14.95

- Derek Watson
  LISZT
  0–02–872705–3 Macmillan $24.95

Jazz

- Whitney Balliett
  BRADLEY, BARNEY, AND MAX: Sixteen Portraits in Jazz
  0–19–506124–1 Oxford $19.95

- James Lincoln Collier
  BENNY GOODMAN AND THE SWING ERA
  0–19–505278–1 Oxford $21.95

- Miles Davis with Quincy Troupe
  MILES: The Autobiography
  0–671–63504–2 Simon & Schuster $22.45

- Andy Kirk
  TWENTY YEARS ON WHEELS: As Told to Amy Lee
  0–472–10134–X Michigan $19.95

- Paul Oliver, editor
  THE BLACKWELL GUIDE TO BLUES RECORDS
  0–631–16516–9 Blackwell $19.95

- Phyllis Rose
  JAZZ CLEOPATRA: Josephine Baker in Her Time
  0–385–24891–1 Doubleday $19.95

- Arnold Shaw
  THE JAZZ AGE: Popular Music in the 1920s
  0–19–506082–2 Oxford $9.95

Rock

- Patti Jean Birosik
  THE NEW AGE MUSIC GUIDE: Profiles and Recordings of 500 Top New Age Musicians
  0–02–041640–7 Macmillan pb $12.95

- Robin Denselow
  WHEN THE MUSIC'S OVER: The Story of Political Pop
  0–571–15380–1 Faber & Faber $19.95

- Marc Eliot
  DEATH OF A REBEL: A Biography of Phil Ochs
  0–531–15111–5 Franklin Watts $18.95

- Simon Frith & Andrew Goodwin, editors
  ON RECORD: Rock, Pop, and the Written Word
  0–394–56475–8 Pantheon $24.95
  0–679–72288–2 Pantheon pb $14.95

- Timothy W. Ryback
  ROCK AROUND THE BLOC: A History of Rock Music in Eastern Europe and the Soviet Union
  0–19–505633–7 Oxford $21.95

- Otis Williams with Patricia Romanowski
  TEMPTATIONS
  0–671–68415–9 Simon & Schuster pb $8.95

- Gareth L. Pawlowski
  HOW THEY BECAME THE BEATLES: The Definitive History of the Early Years, 1960-1964
  0–525–24823–4 Dutton $24.95

Dance

- Harvey Edwards
  THE ART OF DANCE
  0–8212–1734–8 Bulfinch $35.00

- Lynn Garafola
  DIAGHILEV'S BALLETS RUSSES
  0–19–505701–5 Oxford $29.95

- Deborah Jowitt
  TIME AND THE DANCING IMAGE
  0–520–06627–8 California pb $15.95

Theater

- Andrew Gurr with John Orrell
  REBUILDING SHAKESPEARE'S GLOBE
  0–87830–156–9 RC&H $25.00

- Peter Hay
  THEATRICAL ANECDOTES
  0–19–506078–4 Oxford pb $8.95

- Anthony Holden
  LAURENCE OLIVIER: A Biography
  0–02–033285–8 Macmillan pb $14.95

- Shauneille Perry
  IN THE SHADOW OF THE GREAT WHITE WAY: Images from the Black Theatre
  Photographs by Bert Andrews
  0–938410–81–4 Thunder's Mouth $38.50

- Robert W. Snyder
  THE VOICE OF THE CITY: Vaudeville and Popular Culture in New York
  0–19–505285–4 Oxford $19.95

Film

- Michael Barson, editor
  BORN TO BE BAD: Postcards from the Great Trash Films, Volume 2
  0–679–72555–5 Pantheon pb $8.95

- Ingmar Bergman
  THE MAGIC LANTERN: An Autobiography
  0–14–010469–0 Penguin pb $10.95

- Donald Bogle
  BLACKS IN AMERICAN FILMS AND TELEVISION
  0–671–67538–9 Simon & Schuster $19.95

- Herb Bridges & Terryl C. Boodman
  GONE WITH THE WIND: The Definitive Illustrated History of the Book, the Movie, and the Legend
  0–671–68451–5 Simon & Schuster $29.95
  0–671–68387–X Simon & Schuster pb $14.95

- Leo Braudy
  JEAN RENOIR: The World of His Films
  0–231–07101–9 Columbia pb $17.50

- Nick Browne, editor
  CAHIERS DU CINEMA, 1969–1972: The Politics of Representation
  0–674–09063–2 Harvard $30.00

- Vincent Curcio
  SUICIDE BLONDE: The Life of Gloria Grahame
  0–688–06718–2 Morrow $19.95

- David King Dunaway
  HUXLEY IN HOLLYWOOD
  0–06–039095–6 Harper & Row $24.95

- Sergei Eisentein
  IVAN THE TERRIBLE: Parts 1, 2, 3
  0–571–12586–7 Faber & Faber pb $14.95

- John Fricke & others
  THE WIZARD OF OZ: The Official 50th Anniversary Pictorial History
  0–446–51446–2 Warner $29.95

- Neal Gabler
  AN EMPIRE OF THEIR OWN: How the Jews Invented Hollywood
  0–385–26557–3 Doubleday pb $12.95

- Michael Goodwin & Naomi Wise
  ON THE EDGE: The Life and Times of Francis Coppola
  0–688–04767–X Morrow $22.95

- Lasse Hallström
  MY LIFE AS A DOG
  0–571–15479–4 Faber & Faber pb $8.95

- Annette Insdorf
  FRANCOIS TRUFFAUT
  0–671–67166–9 Simon & Schuster pb $9.95

- Chuck Jones
  CHUCK AMOK: The Life and Times of an Animated Cartoonist
  0–374–12348–9 Farrar, Straus & Giroux $24.95

- Chen Kaige & Tony Rayns
  KING OF THE CHILDREN AND THE NEW CHINESE CINEMA
  0–571–15448–4 Faber & Faber pb $10.95

- Mary Pat Kelly
  MARTIN SCORSESE: A Journey
  0–938410–79–2 Thunder's Mouth $24.95

- Al LaValley, editor
  INVASION OF THE BODY SNATCHERS
  0–8135–1461–4 Rutgers pb $13.00

- Barbara Leaming
  IF THIS WAS HAPPENING: A Biography of Rita Hayworth
  0–670–81978–6 Viking $21.95
  ORSON WELLES: A Biography
  0–14–012762–3 Penguin pb $10.95

- Leonard J. Leff & Jerold L. Simmons
  THE DAME IN THE KIMONO: Hollywood, Censorship, and the Production Code, from the 1920s to the 1960s
  1–55584–224–0 Weidenfeld & Nicolson $22.50

- Ethan Mordden
  THE HOLLYWOOD STUDIOS
  0–671–68046–3 Simon & Schuster pb $12.95

- Barry Paris
  LOUISE BROOKS
  0–394–55923–1 Knopf $30.00

- Yvonne Rainer & others
  THE FILMS OF YVONNE RAINER
  0–253–20542–5 Indiana pb $12.50

- Satyajit Ray
  THE CHESS PLAYERS & OTHER SCREENPLAYS
  0–571–14074–2 Faber & Faber pb $13.95

- Helen Taylor
  SCARLETT'S WOMEN: Gone With the Wind and Its Female Fans
  0–8135–1496–7 Rutgers pb $12.95

- Martin Scorsese
  SCORSESE ON SCORSESE
  Edited by David Thompson & Ian Christie
  0–571–14103–X Faber & Faber $17.95

- Robert Towne
  CHINATOWN, THE LAST DETAIL, SHAMPOO: Screenplays
  0–87113–316–4 Atlantic Monthly $24.95
  0–87113–213–3 Atlantic Monthly pb $12.95

- François Truffaut & Claude de Givray
  LA PETITE VOLEUSE
  0–571–14175–7 Faber & Faber $9.95

- Andrew Tudor
  MONSTERS AND MAD SCIENTISTS: A Cultural History of the Horror Movie
  0–631–16992–X Blackwell pb $14.95

- Erich von Stroheim
  GREED
  0–571–12581–6 Faber & Faber pb $12.95

- Alexander Walker
  VIVIEN: The Life of Vivien Leigh
  1–55584–296–8 Weidenfeld & Nicolson pb $9.95

- Wim Wenders
  EMOTION PICTURES: Reflections on Cinema
  0–571–15271–6 Faber & Faber $17.95

- Michael Wood
  AMERICA IN THE MOVIES
  0–231–07099–3 Columbia pb $14.50

- Robin Wood
  HITCHCOCK'S FILMS REVISITED
  0–231–06550–7 Columbia $35.00

Journalism

- Alistair Cooke
  AMERICA OBSERVED: From the 1940s to the 1980s
  0–02–031151–6 Macmillan pb $8.95

- Hedley Donovan
  RIGHT PLACES, RIGHT TIMES: Forty Years in Journalism Not Counting My Paper Route
  0–8050–0564–1 Holt $24.95

- Ellen Goodman
  MAKING SENSE
  0–87113–281–8 Atlantic Monthly $17.95

- Philip B. Kunhardt, Jr.
  LIFE LAUGHS LAST
  0–671–68797–2 Simon & Schuster pb $10.95

- Marshall McLuhan & Quentin Fiore
  THE MEDIUM IS THE MASSAGE
  0–671–68997–5 Simon & Schuster pb $8.95

- Brigitte Lebens Nacos
  THE PRESS, PRESIDENTS, AND CRISES
  0–231–07064–0 Columbia $35.00

- Chalmers M. Roberts
  IN THE SHADOW OF POWER: The Story of the Washington Post
  0–932020–71–2 Seven Locks pb $16.95

- John Taylor
  CIRCUS OF AMBITION: The Culture of Wealth and Power in the '80s
  0–446–71005–9 Warner $19.95

- Jerome Tuccille
  RUPERT MURDOCH
  1–55611–154–1 Donald Fine $19.95

- Kendall J. Wills, editor
  THE PULITZER PRIZES, 1989
  0–671–68748–4 Simon & Schuster $24.95
  0–671–68749–2 Simon & Schuster pb $12.95

- Brenda Wineapple
  GENET: The Life of Janet Flanner
  0–89919–442–7 Ticknor & Fields $24.95

Radio and Television

- Laurie Harper
  DON SHERWOOD: The Life and Times of "The World's Greatest Disc Jockey"
  1–55958–001–1 St. Martin's $19.95

- Tamar Liebes & Elihu Katz
  THE EXPORT OF MEANING: Cross Cultural Readings of "Dallas"
  0–19–505487–3 Oxford $22.95

- Donna McCrohan
  PRIME TIME, OUR TIME: What Lucy, Archie, J.R., Dr. Huxtable—and 40 Years of Top-Rated TV Shows—Tell Us About Ourselves
  1–55958–005–4 St. Martin's $18.95

- Marshall McLuhan & Quentin Fiore
  WAR AND PEACE IN THE GLOBAL VILLAGE
  0–671–68996–7 Simon & Schuster pb $8.95

• Monty Python
MONTY PYTHON'S FLYING CIRCUS: The Complete Television Scripts
0–679–72702–7 Pantheon pb (set) $26.00
Volume 1
0–679–72647–0 Pantheon pb $12.95
Volume 2
0–679–72648–9 Pantheon pb $12.95

• Ella Taylor
PRIME-TIME FAMILIES: Television Culture in Post-War America
0–520–05867–4 California $20.00

• Huntington Williams
BEYOND CONTROL: ABC and the Fate of the Networks
0–689–11818–X Atheneum $21.95

WORLD HISTORY

General Historical Studies

• Colin Campbell
THE ROMANTIC ETHIC AND THE SPIRIT OF MODERN CONSUMERISM
0–631–16941–5 Blackwell pb $16.95

• Mark Nathan Cohen
HEALTH AND THE RISE OF CIVILIZATION
0–300–04006–7 Yale $29.95

• V.G. Kiernan
THE DUEL IN EUROPEAN HISTORY: Honour and the Reign of Aristocracy
0–19–285128–4 Oxford pb $14.95

• Alan MacFarlane
THE CULTURE OF CAPITALISM
0–631–16557–6 Blackwell pb $16.95

• Julián Marías
UNDERSTANDING SPAIN
0–472–10143–9 Michigan $32.50

• Fred Singleton
A SHORT HISTORY OF FINLAND
0–521–32275–8 Cambridge $39.95
0–521–31136–5 Cambridge pb $12.95

• Adam Westoby
THE EVOLUTION OF COMMUNISM
0–02–934545–6 Macmillan $22.95

• G.J. Whitrow
TIME IN HISTORY: Views of Time from Prehistory to the Present Day
0–19–285211–6 Oxford pb $8.95

Ancient Greece and Rome

• Peter Brown
SOCIETY AND THE HOLY IN LATE ANTIQUITY
0–520–06800–9 California pb $10.95

• Walter Burkert
ANCIENT MYSTERY CULTS
0–674–03387–6 Harvard pb $8.95

• K.J. Dover
GREEK HOMOSEXUALITY
0–674–36270–5 Harvard pb $12.95

• Michael Grant
THE CLASSICAL GREEKS
0–684–19126–1 Macmillan $27.50

Europe to the French Revolution

• Richard Barber & Juliet Barker
TOURNAMENTS: Jousting, Chivalry and Pageants in the Middle Ages
1–55584–400–6 Weidenfeld & Nicolson $29.95

• Alain Boureau & others
THE CULTURE OF PRINT: Power and the Uses of Print in Early Modern Europe
0–691–05580–7 Princeton $45.00

• Felipe Fernández-Armesto
THE SPANISH ARMADA: The Experience of War in 1588
0–19–285196–9 Oxford pb $12.95

• Robert M. Isherwood
FARCE AND FANTASY: Popular Entertainment in Eighteenth-Century Paris
0–19–506159–4 Oxford pb $12.95

• David Herlihy & Christiane Klapisch-Zuber
TUSCANS AND THEIR FAMILIES: A Study of the Florentine Catasto of 1427
0–300–04611–1 Yale pb $16.95

• John Lynch
BOURBON SPAIN, 1700-1808
0–631–14576–1 Blackwell $39.95

• Geoffrey Parker
THE DUTCH REVOLT
0–14–055233–2 Penguin pb $8.95

The French Revolution and Napoleon

• Duchesse d'Abrantès
AT THE COURT OF NAPOLEON: Memoirs of the Duchesse d'Abrantès
Edited with an introduction by Olivier Bernier
0–385–26639–1 Doubleday $19.95

• Robert Darnton
THE KISS OF LAMOURETTE: Reflections in Cultural History
0–393–02753–8 Norton $19.95

• François Furet & Mona Ozouf, editors
A CRITICAL DICTIONARY OF THE FRENCH REVOLUTION
0–674–17728–2 Harvard $69.95

• Georges Lefebvre
THE GREAT FEAR OF 1789: Rural Panic in Revolutionary France
0–8052–0939–5 Schocken pb $9.95

• Jacques Solé
QUESTIONS OF THE FRENCH REVOLUTION: A Historical Overview
0–394–58001–X Pantheon $29.95

Europe from Napoleon to the Second World War

• Philip D. Curtin
DEATH BY MIGRATION: Europe's Encounter with the Tropical World in the Nineteenth Century
0–521–37162–7 Cambridge $44.50
0–521–38922–4 Cambridge pb $12.95

• István Deák
BEYOND NATIONALISM: A Social and Political History of the Habsburg Officer Corps
0–19–504505–X Oxford $39.95

• Alexander De Grand
ITALIAN FASCISM: Its Origins and Development
0–8032–6578–6 Nebraska pb $9.95

• François Delaporte
DISEASE AND CIVILIZATION: The Cholera in Paris, 1832
0–262–54055–X MIT pb $9.95

• Frederic Morton
THUNDER AT TWILIGHT: Vienna, 1913-1914
0–684–19143–1 Macmillan $22.50

• Peter Paret
THE BERLIN SECESSION: Modernism and Its Enemies in Imperial Germany
0–674–06774–6 Harvard pb $12.95

• James J. Sheehan
GERMANY, 1770-1866
0–19–822120–7 Oxford $39.95

The Second World War

• John Baynes
FORGOTTEN VICTOR: The Life of General Sir Richard O'Connor
0–08–036269–9 Macmillan $24.95

• John Campbell, editor
THE EXPERIENCE OF WORLD WAR II
0–19–520792–X Oxford $29.95

• Winston Churchill
BLOOD, TOIL, TEARS AND SWEAT: The Speeches of Winston Churchill
Edited with an introduction by David Cannadine
0–395–51744–3 Ticknor & Fields $18.95

• Norman Gelb
DUNKIRK: The Complete Story of the First Step in the Defeat of Hitler
0–688–07793–5 Morrow $22.95

• Martin Gilbert
THE SECOND WORLD WAR: A Complete History
0–8050–0534–X HR&W $29.95

• John Hersey
INTO THE VALLEY: A Skirmish of the Marines
0–8052–4078–0 Schocken $15.95

• Edwin P. Hoyt
MACARTHUR'S NAVY: The Seventh Fleet and the Battle for the Philippines
0–517–56769–5 Crown $18.95

TO ORDER BOOKS AS GIFTS, SEE PAGE 1

- Philip Kaplan & Richard Collier
THEIR FINEST HOUR: The Battle of Britain Remembered
1-55859-047-1 Abbeville $49.95

- John Keegan, editor
THE TIMES ATLAS OF THE SECOND WORLD WAR
0-06-016178-7 Harper & Row $45.00

- Charles Messenger
THE CHRONOLOGICAL ATLAS OF WORLD WAR II
0-02-584391-5 Macmillan $32.50

- Samuel Eliot Morison
THE TWO-OCEAN WAR: A Short History of the United States Navy in the Second World War
0-316-58352-9 Little, Brown pb $15.95

- Marcel Ophuls
HOTEL TERMINUS: The Life and Times of Klaus Barbie
0-671-68703-4 Simon & Schuster $18.95

- Gilles Perrault & Pierre Azema
PARIS UNDER THE OCCUPATION
0-86565-111-6 Rizzoli $37.50

- Barrie & Frances Pitt
THE MONTH BY MONTH CHRONOLOGICAL ATLAS OF WORLD WAR II
0-671-68880-4 Simon & Schuster $35.00

- Christine Zamoyska-Panek with Fred Benton Holmberg
HAVE YOU FORGOTTEN?: A Memoir of Poland, 1939-1945
0-385-24688-9 Doubleday $19.95

- Alfred M. de Zayas
THE WEHRMACHT WAR CRIMES BUREAU, 1939-1945
Foreword by Howard S. Levie
0-8032-9908-7 Nebraska $15.95

The Holocaust

- Jacques Adler
THE JEWS OF PARIS AND THE FINAL SOLUTION: Communal Response and Internal Conflicts, 1940-1944
0-19-504306-5 Oxford pb $12.95

- Dan Bar-On
LEGACY OF SILENCE: Encounters with Children of the Third Reich
0-674-52185-4 Harvard $25.00

- David Fisher & Anthony Read
KRISTALLNACHT: The Tragedy of the Nazi Night of Terror
0-8129-1723-5 Times Books $19.95

- Jeremy Josephs
SWASTIKA OVER PARIS: The Story of the French Jews Under the Nazi Occupation
1-55970-036-X Little, Brown $19.95

- Yehuda Nir
THE LOST CHILDHOOD
0-15-158862-7 HBJ $19.95

- Robert N. Proctor
RACIAL HYGIENE: Medicine Under the Nazis
0-674-74578-7 Harvard pb $14.95

- Anne Roiphe
A SEASON FOR HEALING: Reflections on the Holocaust
0-671-68879-0 Simon & Schuster pb $8.95

- David Rosenberg, editor
TESTIMONY: Contemporary Writers Make the Holocaust Personal
0-8129-1817-7 Times Books $24.95

Postwar Europe and Current Affairs

- Dennis L. Bark & David R. Gress
A HISTORY OF WEST GERMANY

Volume 1: From Shadow to Substance, 1945-1963
0-631-16924-5 Blackwell $34.95

Volume 2: Democracy and Its Discontents, 1963-1988
0-631-16788-9 Blackwell $34.95

- Jürgen Habermas
THE NEW CONSERVATISM: Cultural Criticism and the Historians' Debate
0-262-08188-1 MIT $19.95

- Karel Kaplan
REPORT ON THE MURDER OF THE GENERAL SECRETARY
0-8142-0477-5 Ohio State $39.95

- Edwina Moreton, editor
GERMANY BETWEEN EAST AND WEST
0-521-37891-5 Cambridge pb $14.95

- Jean-Pierre Rioux
THE FOURTH REPUBLIC, 1944-1958
0-521-38916-X Cambridge pb $18.95

Great Britain and Ireland

- Kenneth Baker, editor
THE FABER BOOK OF ENGLISH HISTORY IN VERSE
0-571-13807-1 Faber & Faber pb $10.95

- Christopher Bayley, editor
ATLAS OF THE BRITISH EMPIRE
0-8160-1995-9 Facts On File $40.00

- David Eltis
ECONOMIC GROWTH AND THE ENDING OF THE TRANSATLANTIC SLAVE TRADE
0-19-504563-7 Oxford pb $13.95

- Aaron L. Friedberg
THE WEARY TITAN: Britain and the Experience of Relative Decline, 1895-1905
0-691-00844-2 Princeton pb $14.95

- Elizabeth Hallam, editor
THE PLANTAGENET ENCYCLOPEDIA
1-55584-260-7 Weidenfeld & Nicolson $32.95

- Peter Hennessy
WHITEHALL
0-02-914441-8 Free Press $35.00

- Alistair Horne
HAROLD MACMILLAN, Volume 2: 1957-1986
0-670-82980-3 Viking $24.95

- Kenneth Hudson & Ann Nicholls
THE CAMBRIDGE GUIDE TO THE HISTORIC PLACES OF BRITAIN AND IRELAND
0-521-36077-3 Cambridge $24.95

- Peter Jenkins
MRS. THATCHER'S REVOLUTION: The Ending of the Socialist Era
0-674-58833-9 Harvard pb $12.95

- Paul Johnson, editor
THE OXFORD BOOK OF BRITISH POLITICAL ANECDOTES
0-19-282110-5 Oxford pb $8.95

- Robert Kee
THE GREEN FLAG

Volume 1: The Most Distressful Country
0-14-011104-2 Penguin pb $7.95

Volume 2: The Bold Fenian Men
0-14-011103-4 Penguin pb $7.95

Volume 3: Ourselves Alone
0-14-011106-9 Penguin pb $7.95

- David Lagomarsino & Charles T. Woods, editors
THE TRIAL OF CHARLES I: A Documentary History
0-87451-499-1 New England pb $10.00

- J.J. Lee
IRELAND, 1912-1985: Politics and Society
0-521-37741-2 Cambridge pb $24.95

- William Roger Louis & Hedley Bull, editors
THE "SPECIAL RELATIONSHIP": Anglo-American Relations Since 1945
0-19-820183-4 Oxford pb $19.95

- F.S.L. Lyons
CULTURE AND ANARCHY IN IRELAND, 1890-1939
0-19-285121-7 Oxford pb $10.95

- John Manley
ATLAS OF PREHISTORIC BRITAIN
0-19-520807-2 Oxford $39.95

- Harold Perkin
THE RISE OF PROFESSIONAL SOCIETY: England Since 1880
0-415-00890-5 RC&H $49.95

- Retha M. Warnicke
THE RISE AND FALL OF ANNE BOLEYN
0-521-37000-0 Cambridge $29.95

- Hugo Young
THE IRON LADY: A Biography of Margaret Thatcher
0-374-22651-2 Farrar, Strauss & Giroux $25.00

Russian and Soviet Studies

• John T. Alexander
CATHERINE THE GREAT: Life and Legend
0–19–506162–4 Oxford pb $9.95

• Stephen F. Cohen & Katrina van den Heuvel
VOICES OF GLASNOST: Conversations with Gorbachev's Reformers
0–393–02625–6 Norton $19.95

• Nadezhda Durova
THE CAVALRY MAIDEN: Journals of a Russian Officer in the Napoleonic Wars
Translated with an introduction by Mary Fleming Zirin
0–253–20549–2 Indiana pb $11.95

• George F. Kennan
SOVIET-AMERICAN RELATIONS, 1917-1920
0–691–00847–7 Princeton pb (set) $26.95
Volume 1: Russia Leaves the War
0–691–00841–8 Princeton pb $14.95
Volume 2: The Decision to Intervene
0–691–00842–6 Princeton pb $14.95

• Philip Pomper
LENIN, TROTSKY, AND STALIN: The Intelligentsia and Power
0–231–06906–5 Columbia $35.00

• Vladimir Pozner with Brian J. Kahn
PARTING WITH ILLUSIONS
0–87113–287–7 Atlantic Monthly $19.95

• Amin Saikal & William Maley, editors
THE SOVIET WITHDRAWAL FROM AFGHANISTAN
0–521–37577–0 Cambridge $34.50
0–521–37588–6 Cambridge pb $8.95

• Nikolai Shmelev & Vladimir Popov
THE TURNING POINT: Revitalizing the Soviet Economy
0–385–24654–4 Doubleday $21.95

Jewish History

• Glenda Abramson, editor
THE BLACKWELL COMPANION TO JEWISH CULTURE: From the Eighteenth Century to the Present
0–631–15111–7 Blackwell $50.00

• Judith Ramsey Ehrlich & Barry Rehfeld
THE NEW CROWD: The Changing of the Jewish Guard on Wall Street
0–316–22285–2 Little, Brown $19.95

• Eli N. Evans
JUDAH P. BENJAMIN: The Jewish Confederate
0–02–909911–0 Free Press pb $12.95

• David Leviatin
FOLLOWERS OF THE TRAIL: Jewish Working-Class Radicals in America
0–300–04354–6 Yale $29.95

• Sergio I. Minerbi
THE VATICAN AND ZIONISM: Conflict in the Holy Land, 1895-1925
0–19–505892–5 Oxford $24.95

• Pinhas Sadeh
JEWISH FOLKTALES
0–385–19573–7 Doubleday $24.95

• Gershom Scholem
ON JEWS AND JUDAISM IN CRISIS: Selected Essays
0–8052–0954–9 Schocken pb $11.95

The Middle East

• Akbar S. Ahmed
DISCOVERING ISLAM: Making Sense of Muslim History and Society
0–415–03930–4 RC&H pb $14.95

• Said Amir Arjomand
THE TURBAN FOR THE CROWN: The Islamic Revolution in Iran
0–19–504258–1 Oxford pb $9.95

• Gerald Blake & others
THE CAMBRIDGE ATLAS OF THE MIDDLE EAST AND NORTH AFRICA
0–521–37598–3 Cambridge pb $29.95

• Amos Elon
JERUSALEM: City of Mirrors
0–316–23388–9 Little, Brown $18.95

• Philip S. Khoury
SYRIA AND THE FRENCH MANDATE: The Politics of Arab Nationalism, 1920-1945
0–691–00843–4 Princeton pb $22.50

• William Roger Louis & Roger Owen, editors
SUEZ 1956: The Crisis and Its Consequences
0–19–820141–9 Oxford $45.00

• Moshe Ma'oz
ASAD: The Sphinx of Damascus
1–55584–433–2 Weidenfeld & Nicolson pb $9.95

• Henry Munson, Jr.
ISLAM AND REVOLUTION IN THE MIDDLE EAST
0–300–04127–6 Yale $22.50
0–300–04604–9 Yale pb $8.95

• Daniel Pipes
GREATER SYRIA: The History of an Ambition
0–19–506021–0 Oxford $29.95

• Laila Said
MIDDLE EAST JOURNAL: A Woman's Journey into the Heart of the Arab World
0–684–19136–9 Scribners $21.95

• William Shawcross
THE SHAH'S LAST RIDE
0–671–68745–X Simon & Schuster pb $10.95

• Aaron Wolf
A PURITY OF ARMS: An American in the Israeli Army
0–385–26039–9 Doubleday $17.95

Africa

• Cheryl Bentsen
MAASAI DAYS
0–671–66035–7 Simon & Schuster $19.95

• Axel-Ivar Berglund
ZULU THOUGHT: Patterns and Symbolism
0–253–21205–7 Indiana pb $17.50

• Alexander De Waal
FAMINE THAT KILLS: Darfur, Sudan, 1984-1985
0–19–827349–5 Oxford $36.00
0–19–827749–0 Oxford pb $12.95

• Robert B. Edgerton
MAU MAU: An African Chronicle
0–02–908920–4 Free Press $22.95

• Christopher Hope
WHITE BOY RUNNING
0–385–26329–5 Anchor pb $8.95

The Indian Subcontinent

• Brigid Keenan
TRAVELS IN KASHMIR: A Popular History of Its People, Places and Crafts
0–19–562236–7 Oxford $14.95

• B.R. Nanda
MAHATMA GANDHI: A Biography
0–19–561357–0 Oxford $24.95

• Francis Robinson, editor
THE CAMBRIDGE ENCYCLOPEDIA OF INDIA, PAKISTAN, BANGLADESH, SRI LANKA, NEPAL, BHUTAN AND THE MALDIVES
0–521–33451–9 Cambridge $49.50

China

• Sechin Jagchid & Van Jay Symons
PEACE, WAR, AND TRADE ALONG THE GREAT WALL: Nomadic-Chinese Interaction Through Two Millennia
0–253–33187–0 Indiana $29.95

• Owen Lattimore
INNER ASIAN FRONTIERS OF CHINA
0–19–582781–3 Oxford $29.95

• Morris Rossabi
KHUBILAI KHAN: His Life and Times
0–520–06740–1 California pb $12.95

• Orville Schell
DISCOS AND DEMOCRACY: China in the Throes of Reform
0–385–26187–X Anchor pb $9.95

• John S. Service, editor
GOLDEN INCHES: The China Memoir of Grace Service
0–520–06656–1 California $19.95

• Jonathan D. Spence
THE QUESTION OF HU
0–679–72580–6 Random House pb $8.95

• Ezra F. Vogel
ONE STEP AHEAD IN CHINA: Guangdong Under Reform
0–674–63901–3 Harvard $29.95

☞ **TO ORDER NEW BOOKS NOT YET LISTED, ASK YOUR BOOKSELLER OR CALL 1-800-882-8770**

Japan

• Edward Behr
HIROHITO: Behind the Myth
0-394-58072-9 Villard $22.50

• Yoichi Harashima
MEIJI JAPAN THROUGH WOODBLOCK PRINTS
0-86008-450-7 Columbia $250.00

• Masao Maruyama
STUDIES IN THE INTELLECTUAL HISTORY OF TOKUGAWA JAPAN
Translated by Mikiso Hane
0-691-00832-9 Princeton pb $19.95

• Chie Nakane, editor
TOKUGAWA JAPAN
0-86008-447-7 Columbia $42.50

• Edwin O. Reischauer
THE JAPANESE TODAY: Change and Continuity
0-674-47182-2 Harvard pb $11.95

Southeast Asia and the Philippines

• S. Baring-Gould & C.A. Bampfylde
A HISTORY OF SARAWAK UNDER ITS TWO WHITE RAJAHS, 1839-1908
0-19-588926-6 Oxford $24.95

• Joan D. Criddle & Teeda Butt Mam
TO DESTROY YOU IS NO LOSS: The Odyssey of a Cambodian Family
0-385-26628-6 Anchor pb $9.95

• Karl D. Jackson, editor
CAMBODIA, 1975-1978: Rendezvous with Death
0-691-07807-6 Princeton $35.50

• Richard J. Kessler
REBELLION AND REPRESSION IN THE PHILIPPINES
0-300-04406-2 Yale $25.00

• F.M. Schnitger
FORGOTTEN KINGDOMS IN SUMATRA
0-19-588905-3 Oxford pb $13.95

Australia, New Zealand, and Polynesia

• S.L. Goldberg & F.B. Smith, editors
AUSTRALIAN CULTURAL HISTORY
0-521-37758-7 Cambridge pb $14.95

• Jan Kociumbras, editor
THE OXFORD HISTORY OF AUSTRALIA, Volume 2: Colonial Australia, 1770-1860
0-19-554610-5 Oxford $39.95

• David Money
AUSTRALIA TODAY
0-521-36962-2 Cambridge pb $7.95

Military Affairs

• Rick Atkinson
THE LONG GRAY LINE: West Point and the American Journey, 1962-1987
0-395-48008-6 Houghton Mifflin $22.95

• Manuel De Landa
WAR IN THE AGE OF INTELLIGENT MACHINES
0-942299-76-0 MIT $24.50
0-942299-75-2 MIT pb $11.95

• John Ellis
EYE-DEEP IN HELL: Trench Warfare in World War I
0-8018-3947-5 Johns Hopkins pb $12.95

• Noble Frankland, editor
ENCYCLOPEDIA OF TWENTIETH CENTURY WARFARE
0-517-56770-9 Crown $40.00

• J.F.C. Fuller
THE GENERALSHIP OF ALEXANDER THE GREAT
0-306-80371-3 Da Capo pb $13.95

• Richard Holmes
ACTS OF WAR: The Behavior of Men in Battle
0-02-914851-0 Free Press $12.95

• Archer Jones
THE ART OF WAR IN THE WESTERN WORLD
0-19-506241-8 Oxford $15.95

• Anthony Livesey
GREAT BATTLES OF WORLD WAR I
0-02-583131-3 Macmillan $39.95

• Geoffrey Parker
THE MILITARY REVOLUTION: Military Innovation and the Rise of the West, 1500-1800
0-521-37680-7 Cambridge pb $14.95

• Justin Wintle
THE DICTIONARY OF WAR QUOTATIONS
0-02-935411-0 Free Press $29.95

Historiography

• Carlo Ginzburg
CLUES, MYTHS, AND THE HISTORICAL METHOD
Translated by John & Anne C. Tedeschi
0-8018-3458-9 Johns Hopkins $24.95

• C. Vann Woodward
THE FUTURE OF THE PAST: Historical Writings
0-19-505704-9 Oxford $24.95

HISTORY OF THE AMERICAS

Native American Cultures

• George Catlin
NORTH AMERICAN INDIANS
0-14-017014-6 Penguin pb $9.95

• Jesse J. Cornplanter
LEGENDS OF THE LONGHOUSE
0-8032-6335-X Nebraska pb $7.50

• John Ehle
TRAIL OF TEARS: The Rise and Fall of the Cherokee Nation
0-385-23954-8 Doubleday pb $9.95

• Peter R. Gerber & Maximilien Bruggman
INDIANS OF THE NORTHWEST COAST
0-8160-2028-0 Facts On File $45.00

• Weston La Barre
THE PEYOTE CULT
0-8061-2214-5 Oklahoma pb $14.95

• Roberta H. & Peter T. Markman
MASKS OF THE SPIRIT: Image and Metaphor in Mesoamerica
0-520-06418-6 California $55.00

• James R. Murie
CEREMONIES OF THE PAWNEE
Edited by Douglas R. Parks
0-8032-8162-5 Nebraska pb $19.95

• Arthur C. Parker
SENECA MYTHS AND FOLK TALES
0-8032-8723-2 Nebraska pb $11.95

• James R. Walker
LAKOTA MYTH
0-8032-9706-8 Nebraska pb $13.50

US History to the Civil War

• John R. Alden
A HISTORY OF THE AMERICAN REVOLUTION
0-306-80366-6 Da Capo $15.95

• Richard E. Ellis
THE UNION AT RISK: Jacksonian Democracy, States' Rights and the Nullification Crisis
0-19-506187-X Oxford pb $10.95

• Donald R. Hickey
THE WAR OF 1812: A Forgotten Conflict
0-252-01613-0 Illinois $32.50

• John F. Sears
SACRED PLACES: American Tourist Attractions in the Nineteenth Century
0-19-505350-8 Oxford $24.95

• Ivan Van Sertima
THEY CAME BEFORE COLUMBUS: The African Presence in Ancient America
0-679-72530-X Random House pb $14.95

The Civil War and Reconstruction

• Bern Anderson
BY SEA AND BY RIVER: A Naval History of the Civil War
0-306-80367-4 Da Capo $13.95

• Iver Bernstein
THE NEW YORK CITY DRAFT RIOTS: Their Significance for American Society and Politics in the Age of the Civil War
0-19-505006-1 Oxford $29.95

• Robert V. Bruce
LINCOLN AND THE TOOLS OF WAR
0–252–06090–3 Illinois pb $11.95

• Richard Nelson Current
THOSE TERRIBLE CARPETBAGGERS: A Reinterpretation
0–19–504873–3 Oxford pb $12.95

• Burke Davis
THE LONG SURRENDER: The Collapse of the Confederacy and the Flight of Jefferson Davis
0–679–72409–5 Random House pb $9.95

• Russell Freedman
LINCOLN: A Photobiography
0–395–51848–2 Houghton Mifflin pb $7.95

• Joseph T. Glatthaar
FORGED IN BATTLE: The Civil War Alliance of Black Soldiers and White Officers
0–02–911815–8 Free Press $24.95

• Robert Selph Henry
THE STORY OF THE CONFEDERACY
0–306–80370–4 Da Capo $14.95

• Reid Mitchell
CIVIL WAR SOLDIERS: Their Expectations and Their Experiences
0–671–68641–0 Simon & Schuster pb $8.95

• Allan Pinkerton
THE SPY OF THE REBELLION
0–8032–8722–4 Nebraska pb $14.50

• Stephen W. Sears
GEORGE B. McCLELLAN: The Young Napoleon
0–89919–914–3 Houghton Mifflin pb $10.95

• Annette Tapert
THE BROTHERS' WAR: Civil War Letters to Their Loved Ones from the Blue and Gray
0–679–72211–4 Random House pb $8.95

• Noah Andre Trudeau
BLOODY ROADS SOUTH: The Wilderness to Cold Harbor, May-June 1864
0–316–85326–7 Little, Brown $19.95

US History since 1877

• Stephen E. Ambrose
NIXON, Volume 2: The Triumph of a Politician, 1962-1972
0–671–52837–8 Simon & Schuster $24.95

• Eliot Asinof
1919: America's Loss of Innocence
1–55611–150–9 Donald Fine $19.95

• Ken Babbs
ON THE BUS: The Legendary Trip of Ken Kesey and the Merry Pranksters
0–938410–91–1 Thunder's Mouth pb $19.95

• Howard Blum
WANTED!: The Search for Nazis in America
0–671–67607–5 Simon & Schuster pb $8.95

• Taylor Branch
PARTING THE WATERS: America in the King Years, 1954-1963
0–671–68742–5 Simon & Schuster pb $14.95

• Senators William S. Cohen & George J. Mitchell
MEN OF ZEAL: A Candid Inside Story of the Iran-Contra Hearings
0–14–011089–5 Penguin pb $9.95

• Richard M. Fried
NIGHTMARE IN RED: The McCarthy Era in Perspective
0–19–504360–X Oxford $22.95

• Dorothy Gallagher
ALL THE RIGHT ENEMIES: The Life and Murder of Carlo Tresca
0–14–012400–4 Penguin pb $8.95

• Martin Green
NEW YORK 1913: The Armory Show and the Paterson Strike Pageant
0–02–032790–0 Macmillan pb $12.95

• Tom Hayden
REUNION: A Memoir
0–02–033105–3 Macmillan pb $12.95

• Abbie Hoffman
THE BEST OF ABBIE HOFFMAN: Selections from Revolution for the Hell of It, Woodstock Nation, and Steal This Book
0–941423–27–1 4 Walls 8 Windows $21.95

• Mary Ann Johnson, editor
THE MANY FACES OF HULL HOUSE: The Photographs of Wallace Kirkland
0–252–06108–X Illinois pb $19.95

• Richard M. Ketchum
THE BORROWED YEARS: America on the Way to War, 1938-1941
0–394–56011–6 Random House $29.95

• Philip B. Kunhardt, Jr., editor
LIFE IN CAMELOT: The Kennedy Years
0–316–50602–8 Little, Brown pb $19.95

• Lewis H. Lapham
IMPERIAL MASQUERADE
1–55584–449–9 Weidenfeld & Nicholson $21.95

• Doris C. O'Neil, editor
LIFE: The '60s
0–8212–1752–6 Little, Brown $35.00

• Herbert S. Parmet
RICHARD NIXON AND HIS AMERICA
0–316–69232–8 Little, Brown $24.95

• Ronald Reagan
SPEAKING MY MIND: Selected Speeches
0–671–68857–X Simon & Schuster $24.95

• William L. Shirer
20TH-CENTURY JOURNEY: Return of a Native, 1945-1987—A Memoir of A Life and the Times
0–316–78713–2 Little, Brown $24.95

• Christopher Simpson
BLOWBACK: The First Full Account of America's Recruitment of Nazis, and Its Disastrous Effect on Our Domestic and Foreign Policy
0–02–044995–X Macmillan pb $10.95

• Paul Slansky
THE CLOTHES HAVE NO EMPEROR: A Chronicle of the American Eighties
0–671–67339–4 Simon & Schuster pb $12.95

• I.F. Stone
A NONCONFORMIST HISTORY OF OUR TIMES: Polemics and Prophecies, 1967-1970
0–316–81763–5 Little, Brown $19.95
0–316–61747–3 Little, Brown pb $9.95

• Harry S. Truman
WHERE THE BUCK STOPS: The Personal and Private Writings of Harry S. Truman
Edited by Margaret Truman
0–446–51494–2 Warner $22.95

American Regional History

• Carol Bleser, editor
SECRET AND SACRED: The Diaries of James Henry Hammond, a Southern Slaveholder
0–19–506163–2 Oxford pb $8.95

• John R. Borchert
AMERICA'S NORTHERN HEARTLAND
0–8166–1499–7 Minnesota pb $19.50

• David King Gleason
VIRGINIA PLANTATION HOMES
0–8071–1570–3 LSU $39.95

• James N. Gregory
AMERICAN EXODUS: The Dust Bowl Migration and Okie Culture in California
0–19–504423–1 Oxford $24.95

• David G. McComb
TEXAS: A Modern History
0–292–73048–9 Texas $24.95
0–292–74665–2 Texas pb $12.95

• Michael P. Malone & Richard W. Etulain
THE AMERICAN WEST: A Twentieth-Century History
0–8032–3093–1 Nebraska $31.50
0–8032–8167–6 Nebraska pb $11.95

• Daniel Okrent
THE WAY WE WERE: New England Then, New England Now
1–55584–358–1 Weidenfeld & Nicolson $35.00

• Robert M. Utley
BILLY THE KID: A Short and Violent Life
0–8032–4553–X Nebraska $22.95

• Charles Reagan Wilson & William Ferris, editors
ENCYCLOPEDIA OF SOUTHERN CULTURE
Foreword by Alex Haley
0–8078–1823–2 North Carolina $49.95

American People and Places

• Elaine S. Abelson
WHEN LADIES GO A-THIEVING:
Middle-Class Shoplifters in the Victorian
Department Store
0–19–505125–4 Oxford $24.95

• Rick Beard, editor
ON BEING HOMELESS: Historical
Perspectives
0–910961–01–X Rutgers pb $16.95

• Lawrence DiStasi
DREAM STREETS: A Celebration of
Italian-American Culture
0–06–016030–6 Harper & Row $27.95

• Angus Kress Gillespie & Michael
Aaron Rockland
LOOKING FOR AMERICA ON THE
NEW JERSEY TURNPIKE
0–8135–1466–5 Rutgers $18.95

• William D. Griffin
THE IRISH-AMERICAN ALMANAC
0–8129–1264–1 Times Books pb $12.95

• Katherine S. Newman
FALLING FROM GRACE: The Experience
of Downward Mobility in the American
Middle Class
0–679–72397–8 Random House pb $9.95

African-American Studies

• Ralph David Abernathy
AND THE WALLS CAME TUMBLING
DOWN: An Autobiography
0–06–016192–2 Harper & Row $25.00

• W.E.B. DuBois
THE QUEST OF THE SILVER FLEECE
1–55553–064–8 Northeastern pb $14.95

• Linda Goss & Marian E. Barnes,
editors
TALK THAT TALK: An Anthology of
African-American Storytelling
0–671–67167–7 Simon & Schuster $22.95
0–671–67168–5 Simon & Schuster pb $10.95

• Jonathan Greenberg
STAKING A CLAIM: The Simmons Family
and the Making of an African-American Oil
Dynasty
0–689–11791–4 Atheneum $19.95

• Darlene Clark Hine
THE STATE OF AFRO-AMERICAN
HISTORY: Past, Present, and Future
0–8071–1581–9 LSU pb $9.95

• Blyden Jackson
A HISTORY OF AFRO-AMERICAN
LITERATURE, Volume 1: The Long
Beginning, 1746-1895
0–8071–1511–8 LSU $29.95

• Bernard C. Nalty
STRENGTH FOR THE FIGHT: A History
of Black Americans in the Military
0–02–922411–X Free Press $12.95

• Robert Weisbrot
FREEDOM BOUND: A History of
America's Civil Rights Movement
0–393–02704–X Norton $21.95

American Politics and Foreign Policy

• James A. Bill
THE EAGLE AND THE LION: The
Tragedy of American-Iranian Relations
0–300–04412–7 Yale pb $13.95

• James Chace & Caleb Carr
AMERICA INVULNERABLE: The Quest
for Absolute Security from 1812 to Star
Wars
0–671–68876–6 Simon & Schuster pb $12.95

• Robert Dallek
THE AMERICAN STYLE OF FOREIGN
POLICY: Cultural Politics and Foreign
Affairs
0–19–506205–1 Oxford pb $8.95

• William A. DeGregorio
THE COMPLETE BOOK OF U.S.
PRESIDENTS
0–942637–17–8 Dembner $29.95

• Morris P. Fiorina
CONGRESS: Keystone of the Washington
Establishment
0–300–04640–5 Yale pb $8.95

• Peter Goldman & Tom Mathews
THE QUEST FOR THE PRESIDENCY,
1988
0–671–69079–5 Simon & Schuster $19.95
0–671–69080–9 Simon & Schuster pb $8.95

• Fred I. Greenstein, editor
LEADERSHIP IN THE MODERN
PRESIDENCY
0–674–51855–1 Harvard pb $14.95

• Jerome L. Himmelstein
TO THE RIGHT: The Transformation of
American Conservatism
0–520–06649–9 California $25.00

• Walter L. Hixson
GEORGE F. KENNAN: Cold War
Iconoclast
0–231–06894–8 Columbia $32.00

• Walter LaFeber
THE PANAMA CANAL: The Crisis in
Historical Perspective, Updated Edition
0–19–505930–1 Oxford $27.95

• Constantine C. Menges
INSIDE THE NATIONAL SECURITY
COUNCIL: The True Story of the Making
and Unmaking of Reagan's Foreign Policy
0–671–68734–4 Simon & Schuster pb $9.95

• Paul H. Nitze
FROM HIROSHIMA TO GLASNOST: A
Memoir of Five Perilous Decades
1–55584–110–4 Weidenfeld & Nicolson $25.00

• Robert A. Pastor & Jorge G.
Castañeda
LIMITS TO FRIENDSHIP: The United
States and Mexico
0–679–72543–1 Random House pb $10.95

• Robert B. Reich
THE FEARLESS LIBERAL'S GUIDE
THROUGH PERILOUS TIMES
0–8129–1833–9 Times Books $18.95

• Robert D. Schulzinger
HENRY KISSINGER: Doctor of
Diplomacy
0–231–06952–9 Columbia $27.95

• Abigail M. Thernstrom
WHOSE VOTES COUNT?: Affirmative
Action and Minority Voting Rights
0–674–95196–4 Harvard pb $10.95

Topics in American Studies

• R. David Arkush & Leo O. Lee,
editors
LAND WITHOUT GHOSTS: Chinese
Impressions of America from the Mid-
Nineteenth Century to the Present
0–520–05265–6 California $25.00

• Bruce Brown
THE LONE TREE TRAGEDY: A True
Story of Murder in America's Heartland
0–517–56987–6 Crown $17.95

• Howard P. Chudacoff
HOW OLD ARE YOU?: Age Consciousness
in American Culture
0–691–04768–5 Princeton $19.95

• Herbert Croly
THE PROMISE OF AMERICAN LIFE
Foreword by Michael E. McGerr
1–55553–062–1 Northeastern pb $14.95

• Gerald Early
TUXEDO JUNCTION: Essays on American
Culture
0–88001–232–3 Ecco $19.95

• Nathan O. Hatch
THE DEMOCRATIZATION OF
AMERICAN CHRISTIANITY
0–300–04470–4 Yale $25.00

• Mary S. Lovell
THE SOUND OF WINGS: The Biography
of Amelia Earhart
0–312–03431–8 St. Martin's $22.95

• David W. Noble
THE END OF AMERICAN HISTORY:
Democracy, Capitalism, and the Metaphor
of Two Worlds in Anglo-American
Historical Writing
0–8166–1416–4 Minnesota pb $14.95

• Jerry E. Patterson
THE VANDERBILTS
0–8109–1748–3 Abrams $45.00

• A.H. Saxon
P.T. BARNUM: The Legend and the Man
0–231–05686–9 Columbia $32.95

• Herbert I. Schiller
CULTURE, INC.: The Corporate Takeover
of Public Expression
0–19–505005–3 Oxford $22.50

- Rick Simonson & Scott Walker, editors
MULTI-CULTURAL LITERACY: Opening the American Mind
1-55597-114-8 Graywolf pb $8.50

- William L. Vance
AMERICA'S ROME
Volume 1
0-300-03670-1 Yale $30.00
Volume 2
0-300-04453-4 Yale $30.00

- Richard W. & Dorothy C. Wertz
LYING-IN: A History of Childbirth in America
0-300-04088-1 Yale $35.00
0-300-04087-3 Yale pb $15.95

The Vietnam War

- R.D. Camp with Eric Hammel
LIMA-6: A Marine Company Commander in Vietnam
0-689-12045-1 Macmillan $19.95

- Jeffrey Ethell & Alfred Price
ONE DAY IN A LONG WAR: May 10, 1972, Air War, North Vietnam
0-394-57622-5 Random House $18.95

- Bill McCloud
WHAT SHOULD WE TELL OUR CHILDREN ABOUT VIETNAM?
0-8061-2229-3 Oklahoma $17.95

Canada

- Jack McLeod, editor
THE OXFORD BOOK OF CANADIAN POLITICAL ANECDOTES
0-19-540667-2 Oxford $29.95

- Victor Suthren, editor
THE OXFORD BOOK OF CANADIAN MILITARY ANECDOTES
0-19-540711-3 Oxford $29.95

- George Woodcock
THE CENTURY THAT MADE US: Canada, 1814-1914
0-19-540703-2 Oxford pb $19.95

Latin America and the Caribbean

- Leslie Bethell, editor
THE CAMBRIDGE HISTORY OF LATIN AMERICA, Volume 7: Latin America Since 1930
0-521-24518-4 Cambridge $69.50

- Arturo Cruz, Jr.
MEMOIRS OF A COUNTERREVOLU-TIONARY: Life with the Contras, the Sandinistas, and the CIA
0-385-24879-2 Doubleday $18.95

- John Mason Hart
REVOLUTIONARY MEXICO: The Coming and Process of the Mexican Revolution
0-520-06744-4 California pb $12.95

- Nicola Miller
SOVIET RELATIONS WITH LATIN AMERICA, 1959-1987
0-521-35979-1 Cambridge pb $12.95

- Sidney Mintz
CARIBBEAN TRANSFORMATIONS
0-231-07115-9 Columbia pb $16.50

- Hector Pérez-Brignoli
A BRIEF HISTORY OF CENTRAL AMERICA
0-520-06832-7 California pb $9.95

- Alan Riding
DISTANT NEIGHBORS: Portrait of the Mexicans
0-679-72441-9 Random House pb $8.95

- Alain Rouquié
THE MILITARY AND THE STATE IN LATIN AMERICA
0-520-06664-2 California pb $12.95

- Sidney Weintraub
A MARRIAGE OF CONVENIENCE: Relations Between Mexico and the United States—A Twentieth Century Fund Report
0-19-506125-X Oxford $24.95

RELIGION AND PHILOSOPHY

Mythology and Folklore

- Iona Opie & Moira Tatem, editors
A DICTIONARY OF SUPERSTITION
0-19-211597-9 Oxford $30.00

- Henri Pourrat
FRENCH FOLKTALES: From the Collection of Henri Pourrat
0-394-54451-X Pantheon $21.95

- Jack Zipes
THE BROTHERS GRIMM: From Enchanted Forests to the Modern World
0-415-90209-6 RC&H pb $13.95

Asian Religion and Philosophy

- Bodhidharma
THE ZEN TEACHING OF BODHIDHARMA
Translated with introduction by Red Pine
0-86547-398-6 North Point $19.95
0-86547-399-4 North Point pb $7.95

- Arthur Braverman, translator
MUD AND WATER: A Collection of Talks by the Zen Master Bassui
0-86547-400-1 North Point $19.95
0-86547-401-X North Point pb $8.95

- Wing-tsit Chan
CHU HSI: New Studies
0-8248-1201-8 Hawaii $40.00

- Heinrich Dumoulin
ZEN BUDDHISM: A History, Volume 2: Japan
0-02-908240-4 Macmillan pb $14.95

- Ishikawa Jun
THE BODHISATTVA
0-231-06962-6 Columbia $35.00

- Royall Tyler
THE MIRACLES OF THE KASUGA DEITY
0-231-06958-8 Columbia $45.00

- Wladimir Zwalf
BUDDHISM: Art and Faith
0-02-934500-6 Macmillan $19.95

Judaism

- Roselyn Bell, editor
THE HADASSAH MAGAZINE JEWISH PARENTING BOOK
0-02-913460-9 Free Press $19.95

- Freema Gottlieb
THE LAMP OF GOD: A Jewish Book of Light
0-87668-898-9 Jason Aronson $35.00

- Adin Steinsaltz
THE TALMUD: The Steinsaltz Edition, Volume 1
0-394-57666-7 Random House $40.00
THE TALMUD: The Steinsaltz Edition: A Reference Guide
0-394-57665-9 Random House $40.00

- Geoffrey Wigoder, editor
THE ENCYCLOPEDIA OF JUDAISM
0-02-628410-3 Macmillan $69.95

Christianity

- Linda Brandi Cateura
CATHOLICS USA: Makers of a Modern Church
0-688-07911-3 Morrow $19.95

- Marcello Craveri
THE LIFE OF JESUS
0-88001-238-2 Ecco pb $14.95

- John Farrow
DAMIEN THE LEPER
0-385-26512-3 Doubleday pb $7.95

- C.L. Franklin
GIVE ME THIS MOUNTAIN: Life History and Selected Sermons
Foreword by Jesse L. Jackson
0-252-01018-3 Illinois $29.95
0-252-06087-3 Illinois pb $12.95

- George A. Kelly
INSIDE MY FATHER'S HOUSE
0-385-26227-2 Doubleday $19.95

- J.N.D. Kelly
THE OXFORD DICTIONARY OF POPES
0-19-282085-0 Oxford pb $8.95

- Elizabeth A. Livingstone, editor
THE CONCISE OXFORD DICTIONARY OF THE CHRISTIAN CHURCH
0-19-283014-7 Oxford pb $9.95

• Cathy Luchetti
UNDER GOD'S SPELL: Frontier Evangelists, 1793-1915
0-15-192799-5 HBJ $26.95

• The Metropolitan Museum of Art
THE LIFE OF CHRIST: Images from The Metropolitan Museum of Art
0-684-19142-3 Scribners $22.50

• John Henry Cardinal Newman
APOLOGIA PRO VITA SUA
0-385-12646-8 Doubleday $8.95

• Heiko A. Oberman
LUTHER: Man Between God and the Devil
0-300-03794-5 Yale $29.95

• Elaine Pagels
ADAM, EVE, AND THE SERPENT
0-679-72232-7 Random House pb $8.95

• The Revised English Bible
THE REVISED ENGLISH BIBLE
0-521-15136-8 Cambridge $19.95

THE REVISED ENGLISH BIBLE (APOCRYPHA)
0-521-15137-6 Cambridge $21.95

• Douglas F. Tobler & Nelson B. Wadsworth
THE HISTORY OF THE MORMONS: In Photographs and Text, 1830 to the Present
0-312-03359-1 St. Martin's $39.95

• William Tyndale, translator
THE NEW TESTAMENT
Edited and introduced by David Daniell
0-300-04419-4 Yale $29.95

• Paul L. Williams & George A. Kelly
EVERYTHING YOU ALWAYS WANTED TO KNOW ABOUT THE CATHOLIC CHURCH BUT WERE AFRAID TO ASK
0-385-24882-2 Doubleday $17.95

Western Philosophy

• T.S. Eliot
KNOWLEDGE AND EXPERIENCE IN THE PHILOSOPHY OF F.H. BRADLEY
0-231-07151-5 Columbia pb $14.00

• Stuart Hampshire
INNOCENCE AND EXPERIENCE
0-674-45448-0 Harvard $20.00

• Søren Kierkegaard
PARABLES OF KIERKEGAARD
Edited by Thomas C. Oden
0-691-02053-1 Princeton pb $9.95

• Herbert Marcuse
HEGEL'S ONTOLOGY AND THE THEORY OF HISTORICITY
0-262-63125-3 MIT $14.95

• Robert Nozick
THE EXAMINED LIFE: Philosophical Meditations
0-671-47218-6 Simon & Schuster $21.95

• Plato
THE SYMPOSIUM OF PLATO
Translated by Tom Griffith
0-520-06694-4 California $25.00

• Richard Rorty
CONTINGENCY, IRONY, AND SOLIDARITY
0-521-36781-6 Cambridge pb $10.95

• Jean-Jacques Rousseau
THE COLLECTED WRITINGS OF JEAN-JACQUES ROUSSEAU, Volume 1: Rousseau, Judge of Jean-Jacques: Dialogues
Edited by Roger D. Masters & Christopher Kelly
0-87451-495-9 New England $40.00

SOCIAL STUDIES

Anthropology

• Phyllis Grosskurth
MARGARET MEAD
0-14-008760-5 Penguin pb $4.95

• Marvin Harris
OUR KIND: Who We Are, Where We Came From, Where We Are Going
0-06-015776-3 Harper & Row $22.95

Psychology

• Uta Frith
AUTISM: Explaining the Enigma
0-631-15833-2 Blackwell $19.95

• Peter Gay
A GODLESS JEW: Freud, Atheism, and the Making of Psychoanalysis
0-300-04608-1 Yale pb $9.95

• C.G. Jung
ANALYTICAL PSYCHOLOGY: Notes of the Seminar Given in 1925
Edited by William McGuire
0-691-09897-2 Princeton $35.00

• Edith Kurzweil
THE FREUDIANS: A Comparative Perspective
0-300-04009-1 Yale $35.00

• Robert Ornstein
MULTIMIND: A New Way of Looking at Human Behavior
0-385-26446-1 Anchor pb $9.95

• Robert J. Sternberg & Michael L. Barnes, editors
THE PSYCHOLOGY OF LOVE
0-300-03950-6 Yale $35.00
0-300-04589-1 Yale pb $17.95

• Richard Wollheim
SIGMUND FREUD
0-521-28385-X Cambridge pb $10.95

• Elisabeth Young-Bruehl
ANNA FREUD: A Biography
0-671-68751-4 Simon & Schuster pb $12.95

Sociology

• Hans Haferkamp & Neil J. Smelser, editors
SOCIAL CHANGE AND MODERNITY
0-520-06828-9 California pb $17.95

• Robert J. Holton & Bryan S. Turner
TALCOTT PARSONS ON ECONOMY AND SOCIETY
0-415-03292-3 RC&H pb $14.95

• Bruce Mazlish
A NEW SCIENCE: The Breakdown of Connections and the Birth of Sociology
0-19-505846-1 Oxford $29.95

• Robert Wuthnow
COMMUNITIES OF DISCOURSE: Ideology and Social Structure in the Reformation, the Enlightenment, and European Socialism
0-674-15164-X Harvard $49.50

Economics

• Benjamin Friedman
DAY OF RECKONING: The Consequences of American Economic Policy
0-679-72569-5 Random House pb $8.95

• Paul L. Knox & John A. Agnew
THE GEOGRAPHY OF THE WORLD-ECONOMY
0-7131-6517-0 RC&H pb $21.95

• Jürg Niehans
A HISTORY OF ECONOMIC THEORY: Classic Contributions, 1720-1980
0-8018-3834-7 Johns Hopkins $59.95

• John O'Shaughnessy
WHY PEOPLE BUY
0-19-504087-2 Oxford pb $10.95

• Charles E. Staley
A HISTORY OF ECONOMIC THOUGHT FROM ARISTOTLE TO ARROW
1-55786-031-9 Blackwell $32.50

• Alice Teichova & others
MULTINATIONAL ENTERPRISE IN HISTORICAL PERSPECTIVE
0-521-38914-3 Cambridge pb $22.95

Business, Industry, and Finance

• Walter Adams & James Brock
DANGEROUS PURSUITS: Mergers and Acquisitions in the Age of Wall Street
0-394-57967-4 Pantheon $18.95

• Ron Chernow
THE HOUSE OF MORGAN: An American Banking Dynasty and the Rise of the Modern Financial World
0-87113-338-5 Atlantic Monthly $24.95

• Edwin Green
BANKING: An Illustrated History
0-8478-1072-0 Rizzoli $40.00

• Robert Jackall
MORAL MAZES: The World of Corporate Managers
0-19-506080-6 Oxford pb $9.95

• Maryann Keller
RUDE AWAKENING: The Rise, Fall and Struggle for Recovery of General Motors
0–688–07527–4 Morrow $19.95

• Michael M. Lewis
LIAR'S POKER: Rising Through the Wreckage of Salomon Brothers
0–393–02750–3 Norton $19.95

• Paul Zane Pilzer with Robert Deitz
OTHER PEOPLE'S MONEY: The Inside Story of the S&L Mess
0–671–68101–X Simon & Schuster $19.95

• Steve Weinberg
ARMAND HAMMER: The Untold Story
0–316–92839–9 Little, Brown $22.95

Modern Political Thought

• Eric Hobsbawm
POLITICS FOR A RATIONAL LEFT: Political Writing, 1977-1988
0–86091–958–7 RC&H pb $15.95

• Thomas Paine
POLITICAL WRITINGS
Edited by Bruce Kuklick
0–521–36665–8 Cambridge $29.95
0–521–36678–X Cambridge pb $6.95

• Peter Wollen & others
ON THE PASSAGE OF A FEW PEOPLE THROUGH A RATHER BRIEF MOMENT IN TIME: Situationists, 1957-1972
0–262–23146–8 MIT $25.00

International Relations and Strategic Studies

• Kenneth L. Adelman
THE GREAT UNIVERSAL EMBRACE: Arms Summitry—A Skeptic's Account
0–671–67206–1 Simon & Schuster $19.95

• Seweryn Bialer & Michael Mandelbaum
THE GLOBAL RIVALS
0–679–72649–7 Random House pb $9.95

• Fred Halliday
FROM KABUL TO MANAGUA: Superpower Politics in the Bush-Gorbachev Era
0–394–57310–2 Pantheon $22.95
0–679–72667–5 Pantheon pb $11.95

• International Institute for Strategic Studies
STRATEGIC SURVEY, 1988-1989
0–08–037556–1 Macmillan pb $21.00

• Conor Cruise O'Brien
PASSION AND CUNNING: Essays on Nationalism, Terrorism and Revolution
0–671–68746–8 Simon & Schuster pb $9.95

• Thomas G. Paterson
MEETING THE COMMUNIST THREAT: Truman to Reagan
0–19–504532–7 Oxford pb $9.95

• Strobe Talbott
THE MASTER OF THE GAME: Paul Nitze and the Nuclear Peace
0–679–72165–7 Random House pb $9.95

Law

• Robert H. Bork
THE TEMPTING OF AMERICA: The Political Seduction of the Law
0–02–903761–1 Free Press $22.50

• Steven Brill, editor
TRIAL BY JURY: The American Way of Justice—Today
0–671–67132–4 Simon & Schuster $24.95
0–671–67133–2 Simon & Schuster pb $12.95

• Ethan Bronner
BATTLE FOR JUSTICE: How the Bork Nomination Shook America
0–393–02690–6 Norton $22.50

• Kim Isaac Eisler
FINAL ARGUMENTS: Greed, Politics, and the Collapse of Finley, Kumble, America's Second-Largest Law Firm
0–312–03340–0 St. Martin's $18.95

• Anne Hobson Freeman
THE STYLE OF A LAW FIRM: Eight Gentlemen from Virginia
0–945575–25–4 Algonquin $24.95

• Michael Gilbert, editor
THE OXFORD BOOK OF LEGAL ANECDOTES
0–19–282112–1 Oxford pb $9.95

• Mary Ann Glendon
ABORTION AND DIVORCE IN WESTERN LAW
0–674–00161–3 Harvard pb $10.95

• Deborah L. Rhode
JUSTICE AND GENDER
0–674–49100–9 Harvard $39.50

• James F. Simon
THE ANTAGONISTS: Hugo Black, Felix Frankfurter and Civil Liberties in Modern America
0–671–47797–8 Simon & Schuster $19.95

• Sol Stein
A FEAST FOR LAWYERS
0–87131–589–0 Little, Brown $18.95

• Irving Stone
CLARENCE DARROW FOR THE DEFENSE
0–385–26689–8 Doubleday $21.95

• Samuel Walker
IN DEFENSE OF AMERICAN LIBERTIES: A History of the ACLU
0–19–504539–4 Oxford $24.95

Education

• Harry S. Ashmore
UNSEASONABLE TRUTHS: The Life of Robert Maynard Hutchins
0–316–05396–1 Little, Brown $27.50

• William J. Bennett
OUR CHILDREN AND OUR COUNTRY: Improving America's Schools and Affirming the Common Culture
0–671–68735–2 Simon & Schuster pb $9.95

• Paula S. Fass
OUTSIDE IN: Minorities and the Transformation of American Education
0–19–503790–1 Oxford $24.95

• Paul Gagnon & others
THE FUTURE OF OUR PAST: The Plight of History in American Education
0–02–542111–5 Macmillan $22.50

• Gerald Grant
THE WORLD WE CREATED AT HAMILTON HIGH
0–674–96201–X Harvard pb $9.95

• Mary V. Jackson
ENGINES OF INSTRUCTION, MISCHIEF, AND MAGIC: Children's Literature in England from Its Beginnings to 1839
0–8032–7570–6 Nebraska pb $16.50

• Sharon L. Kagan & Edward F. Zigler, editors
EARLY SCHOOLING: The National Debate
0–300–03995–6 Yale pb $10.95

• Tracy Kidder
AMONG SCHOOLCHILDREN
0–395–47591–0 Houghton Mifflin $18.95

• Edward J. Larson
TRIAL AND ERROR: The American Controversy Over Creation and Evolution
0–19–506143–8 Oxford pb $8.95

Linguistics

• John DeFrancis
VISIBLE SPEECH: The Diverse Oneness of Writing Systems
0–8248–1207–7 Hawaii $27.50

• Christopher Ricks & Leonard Michaels, editors
THE STATE OF THE LANGUAGE: 1990 Edition
0–520–05906–9 California $25.00

• Wayne M. Senner, editor
THE ORIGINS OF WRITING
0–8032–4202–6 Nebraska $35.00

Women's Studies

• Frances Bartkowski
FEMINIST UTOPIAS
0–8032–1205–4 Nebraska $17.95

• Laura Chester, editor
CRADLE AND ALL: Women Writers on Pregnancy and Birth
0–571–12989–7 Faber & Faber pb $12.95

• Nancy J. Chodorow
FEMINISM AND PSYCHOANALYTIC THEORY
0–300–04417–8 Yale $25.00

IF YOU CAN'T FIND IT, LOOK IN THE INDEX

- Alice Echols
DARING TO BE BAD: Radical Feminism in America, 1967-1975
0–8166–1787–2 Minnesota pb $14.95

- Gloria K. Fiero & others, translators & editors
THREE MEDIEVAL VIEWS OF WOMEN: La Contenance des Fames, Le Bien des Fames, Le Blasme des Fames
0–300–04442–9 Yale pb $8.95

- Lorraine Gamman & Margaret Marshment, editors
THE FEMALE GAZE: Women as Viewers of Popular Culture
0–941104–41–9 Real Comet pb $12.95

- Norma Lorre Goodrich
PRIESTESSES
0–531–15113–1 Franklin Watts $24.95

- Catharine A. MacKinnon
TOWARD A FEMINIST THEORY OF THE STATE
0–674–89645–9 Harvard $27.95

Gay Studies

- Harold Brown, M.D.
FAMILIAR FACES, HIDDEN LIVES: The Story of Homosexual Men in America Today
0–15–630120–2 HBJ pb $8.95

- Hall Carpenter Archives Lesbian Oral History Project
INVENTING OURSELVES: Lesbian Life Stories
0–415–02959–7 RC&H pb $12.95

People With Disabilities

- Edward D. Berkowitz
DISABLED POLICY: America's Programs for the Handicapped
0–521–38930–5 Cambridge pb $14.95

SCIENCE AND MATHEMATICS

Mathematics

- Morris Kline
MATHEMATICAL THOUGHT FROM ANCIENT TO MODERN TIMES
Volume 1
0–19–506135–7 Oxford pb $12.95
Volume 2
0–19–506136–5 Oxford pb $12.95
Volume 3
0–19–506137–3 Oxford pb $12.95

Science and Technology

- Malcolm Abrams & Harriet Bernstein
FUTURE STUFF: More than 250 Useful, Time-Saving, Delicious, Stimulating, Silly, and Energy-Saving Products That Will Be Available by the Year 2000
0–14–012639–2 Penguin pb $8.95

- Silvio A. Bedini
THOMAS JEFFERSON: Statesman of Science
0–02–897041–1 Macmillan $29.95

- Richard Golub & Eric Brus, editors
ALMANAC OF SCIENCE AND TECHNOLOGY: What's New and What's Known
0–15–105050–3 HBJ $59.95
0–15–600050–4 HBJ pb $34.95

- Helge Kragh
AN INTRODUCTION TO THE HISTORIOGRAPHY OF SCIENCE
0–521–38921–6 Cambridge pb $14.95

- Robert Scott Root-Bernstein
DISCOVERING
0–674–21175–8 Harvard $35.00

- Lewis Wolpert & Alison Richards, editors
A PASSION FOR SCIENCE
0–19–854212–7 Oxford pb $8.95

Physics

- Robert K. Adair
THE GREAT DESIGN: Particles, Fields and Creation
0–19–506069–5 Oxford pb $12.95

- Rosalynd Pflaum
GRAND OBSESSION: Madame Curie and Her World
0–385–26135–7 Doubleday $22.50

- Fritz Rohrlich
FROM PARADOX TO REALITY: Basic Concepts of the Physical World
0–521–37605–X Cambridge pb $14.95

Astronomy

- Patrick Moore
ASTRONOMERS' STARS
0–393–02663–9 Norton $17.95

- John Noble Wilford
MARS: The Red Planet Beckons
0–8129–1597–6 Times Books $19.95

Earth Sciences and Paleontology

- Stephen Jay Gould
WONDERFUL LIFE: The Burgess Shale and the Nature of History
0–393–02705–8 Norton $19.95

- Donald Johanson & James Shreeve
LUCY'S CHILD: The Search for Our Beginnings
0–688–06492–2 Morrow $22.95

The Life Sciences

- David Attenborough & others
THE ATLAS OF THE LIVING WORLD
0–395–49481–8 Houghton Mifflin $40.00

- John F. Avedon
WINGS FOR THE MAD FLIGHT: In Pursuit of Understanding the Brain
0–385–24060–0 Doubleday $18.95

- Kenneth Klivington
THE SCIENCE OF MIND
0–262–11141–1 MIT $39.95

Medicine

- Eliot Freidson
MEDICAL WORK IN AMERICA
0–300–04517–8 Yale $30.00
0–300–04518–6 Yale pb $15.95

- Patricia Illingworth
AIDS AND THE GOOD SOCIETY
0–415–00024–6 RC&H pb $12.95

- Monroe E. Price
SHATTERED MIRRORS: Our Search for Identity and Community in the AIDS Era
0–674–80590–9 Harvard $19.95

- James T. Patterson
THE DREAD DISEASE: Cancer and Modern American Culture
0–674–21626–1 Harvard pb $14.95

- Lynn Payer
MEDICINE AND CULTURE
0–14–012404–7 Penguin pb $8.95

Natural History, Agriculture, and Environmental Studies

- Pierre Berton
THE ARCTIC GRAIL: The Quest for the North West Passage and the North Pole, 1818-1909
0–14–011680–X Penguin pb $12.95

- Paul Brooks
THE HOUSE OF LIFE: Rachel Carson at Work
0–395–51742–7 Houghton Mifflin pb $9.95

- John Haines
THE STARS, THE SNOW, THE FIRE
1–55597–117–2 Graywolf $16.00

- Susan Hecht & Alexander Cockburn
THE FATE OF THE FOREST: Developers, Destroyers and Defenders of the Amazon
0–86091–261–2 RC&H $24.95

- Clarence King
MOUNTAINEERING IN THE SIERRA NEVADA
Introduction by William Howarth
0–14–017015–4 Penguin pb $8.95

- Chris Maser
FOREST PRIMEVAL: The Natural History of an Ancient Forest
0–87156–683–4 Sierra Club $25.00

- John May
THE GREENPEACE BOOK OF ANTARCTICA: A New View of the Seventh Continent
0–385–26280–9 Doubleday $24.95

- Roger Tory Peterson & others
SAVE THE BIRDS
0–395–51172–0 Houghton Mifflin $40.00

- **Richard Rhodes**
  FARM: A Year in the Life of an American
  Farmer
  0–671–63647–2 Simon & Schuster $19.95

- **Stephen H. Schneider**
  GLOBAL WARMING
  0–87156–693–1 Sierra Club $18.95

- **Marty Strange**
  FAMILY FARMING: A New Economic
  Vision
  0–8032–4156–9 Nebraska $18.95
  0–8032–9194–9 Nebraska pb $7.50

- **John Terborgh**
  WHERE HAVE ALL THE BIRDS GONE?
  0–691–02428–6 Princeton pb $14.95

- **Jack Westoby**
  INTRODUCTION TO WORLD
  FORESTRY
  0–631–16134–1 Blackwell pb $19.95

Computers and Artificial Intelligence

- **Jeremy Campbell**
  THE IMPROBABLE MACHINE: What the
  New Upheaval in Artificial Intelligence
  Research Reveals About How the Mind
  Really Works
  0–671–65711–9 Simon & Schuster $19.95

- **Barbara Garson**
  THE ELECTRONIC SWEATSHOP: How
  Computers Are Transforming the Office of
  the Future into the Factory of the Past
  0–14–012145–5 Penguin pb $7.95

- **W. Eric L. Grimson & Ramesh S. Patil, editors**
  AI IN THE 1980s AND BEYOND: An MIT
  Survey
  0–262–57077–7 MIT pb $11.95

- **Roger Penrose**
  THE EMPEROR'S NEW MIND: On
  Computers, Minds, and the Laws of Physics
  0–19–851973–7 Oxford $24.95

PRACTICAL ADVICE

Courtship, Love, Sex, and Marriage

- **Antonia Fraser**
  LOVE LETTERS: An Illustrated Anthology
  0–8092–4314–8 Contemporary $19.95

- **Karen Lystra**
  SEARCHING THE HEART: Women,
  Men, and Romantic Love in Nineteenth-
  Century America
  0–19–505817–3 Oxford $24.95

Parents and Children

- **Gary S. Berger, Marc Goldstein, & Mark Fuerst**
  THE COUPLE'S GUIDE TO FERTILITY:
  How New Medical Advances Can Help You
  Have a Baby
  0–385–24546–7 Doubleday $18.95
  0–385–26390–2 Doubleday pb $8.95

- **Femmy DeLyser**
  JANE FONDA'S NEW PREGNANCY
  WORKOUT AND TOTAL BIRTH
  PROGRAM
  0–671–66763–7 Simon & Schuster $24.95

- **Sheila Kitzinger**
  BREASTFEEDING YOUR BABY
  0–679–72433–8 Knopf pb $14.95

  THE COMPLETE BOOK OF
  PREGNANCY AND CHILDBIRTH
  0–394–58011–7 Knopf $18.95

- **Penelope Leach**
  YOUR BABY AND CHILD: From Birth to
  Age Five
  0–394–57951–8 Knopf $29.95
  0–679–72425–7 Knopf pb $16.95

- **Judith Schaffer & Christina Lindstrom**
  HOW TO RAISE AN ADOPTED CHILD
  0–394–57303–2 Random House $18.95

- **Benjamin Spock & Mary Morgan**
  SPOCK ON SPOCK
  0–394–57813–9 Pantheon $19.95

Health and Nutrition

- **Norman Cousins**
  HEAD FIRST: The Biology of Hope
  0–525–24805–6 Dutton $18.95

- **Donald F. Tapeley & others, editors**
  THE COLUMBIA UNIVERSITY
  COLLEGE OF PHYSICIANS AND
  SURGEONS COMPLETE HOME
  MEDICAL GUIDE
  0–517–57216–8 Crown $39.95

- **Myron Winick, editor**
  THE COLUMBIA ENCYCLOPEDIA OF
  NUTRITION
  0–399–51573–9 Putnam pb $12.95

Crisis

- **Joseph Beasley**
  HOW TO DEFEAT ALCOHOL: A Guide
  to Understanding Your Disease, Fighting
  Back, and Getting Well
  0–8128–1807–X Times Books $16.95

- **Miriam Galper Cohen**
  LONG DISTANCE PARENTING: A
  Guide for Divorced Parents
  0–453–00698–1 NAL $17.95

- **Craig Frazer & Deirdre Sullivan**
  BURNT: A Teenage Addict's Road to
  Recovery
  0–453–00696–5 NAL $18.95

Careers

- **Forest Bowman**
  THE COMPLETE RETIREMENT
  HANDBOOK
  0–8131–1710–0 Kentucky $25.00
  0–8131–0192–1 Kentucky pb $15.00

Investing, Taxes, and Business Advice

- **Norman F. Dacey**
  HOW TO AVOID PROBATE
  0–02–008181–2 Macmillan $24.95

- **Marshall Loeb**
  MARSHALL LOEB'S 1990 MONEY
  GUIDE
  0–316–53064–6 Little, Brown pb $12.95

- **John Train**
  THE NEW MONEY MASTERS: Ten Great
  Investors of the '80s—Their Winning
  Strategies and How You Can Apply Them
  0–06–015966–9 Harper & Row $22.50

Reference

- **Columbia Encyclopedia**
  THE CONCISE COLUMBIA
  ENCYCLOPEDIA
  0–231–06938–3 Columbia $39.95

- **John Small & Michael Witherick**
  A MODERN DICTIONARY OF
  GEOGRAPHY
  0–340–49317–8 RC&H $45.00
  0–340–49318–6 RC&H pb $16.95

- **Avraham Zilkha**
  MODERN HEBREW-ENGLISH
  DICTIONARY
  0–300–04647–2 Yale $25.00
  0–300–04648–0 Yale pb $8.95

LEISURE

Food and Wine

- **Maurice & Jean-Jacques Bernachon**
  A PASSION FOR CHOCOLATE
  Translated by Rose Levy Beranbaum
  0–688–07554–1 Morrow $19.95

- **Antoine Bouterin & Ruth Gardner**
  ANTOINE BOUTERIN'S DESSERTS
  FROM LE PERIGORD
  0–399–13468–9 Putnam $24.95

- **Giuliano Bugialli**
  THE FINE ART OF ITALIAN COOKING
  0–8129–1838–X Times Books $22.50

- **Julia Child**
  THE WAY TO COOK
  0–394–53264–3 Knopf $50.00

- **Curnonsky**
  LAROUSSE TRADITIONAL FRENCH
  COOKING
  0–385–26532–8 Doubleday $45.00

● Alan Davidson
SEAFOOD: A Connoisseur's Guide and Cookbook
0–671–67011–5 Simon & Schuster $29.95

● Sheila Ferguson
SOUL FOOD: Classic Cuisine from the Deep South
1–55584–420–0 Weidenfeld & Nicolson $18.95

● Mary Goodbody
GLORIOUS CHOCOLATE: The Ultimate Chocolate Cookbook
0–671–67289–4 Simon & Schuster $29.95

● Ken Hom
FRAGRANT HARBOR TASTE: The New Chinese Cooking of Hong Kong
0–671–64469–6 Simon & Schuster $24.95

● Hugh Johnson
VINTAGE: The Story of Wine
0–671–68702–6 Simon & Schuster $39.95

HUGH JOHNSON'S POCKET ENCYCLOPEDIA OF WINE 1990
0–671–68701–8 Simon & Schuster pb $9.95

● Diana Kennedy
THE ART OF MEXICAN COOKING
Photographs by Michael Calderwood
0–553–05706–5 Bantam $22.50

● Nicole Routhier
THE FOODS OF VIETNAM
Photographs by Martin Jacobs
1–55670–095–4 Stewart, Tabori & Chang $35.00

● Horst Scharfenberg
THE CUISINES OF GERMANY: Regional Specialties and Traditional Home Cooking
0–671–63197–7 Simon & Schuster $24.95

● Mary Taylor Simeti
POMP AND SUSTENANCE: Twenty-Five Centuries of Sicilian Food
0–394–56850–8 Knopf $25.00

● Raymond Sokolov
THE JEWISH-AMERICAN KITCHEN
Recipes by Susan R. Friedland
1–55670–096–2 Stewart, Tabori & Chang $30.00

● Kathy Starr
THE SOUL OF SOUTHERN COOKING
0–87805–421–9 Mississippi $29.95
0–87805–415–4 Mississippi pb $14.95

● Anne Willan
LA VARENNE PRATIQUE: The Complete Illustrated Guide to the Techniques, Tools, and Ingredients of Classic Modern Cooking
0–517–57383–0 Crown $60.00

Travel

● Paul Blanchard
BLUE GUIDE: Yugoslavia
0–393–30485–X Norton pb $18.95

● George Borrow
WILD WALES: The People, Language and Scenery
0–7126–0448–0 David & Charles pb $11.95

● John O. Coote, editor
THE NORTON BOOK OF THE SEA
Introduction by Hammond Innes
0–393–02778–3 Norton $22.50

● J.P. Donleavy
IRELAND: A Singular Country
Photographs by Patrick Prendergast
0–393–02760–0 Norton $40.00

● Aldous Huxley
ALONG THE ROAD: Notes and Essays of a Tourist
0–88001–230–7 Ecco pb $8.95

● Robin Magowan
FABLED CITIES OF CENTRAL ASIA: Samarkand, Bukhara, Khiva
Photographs by Vadim Gippenreiter
0–89659–964–7 Abbeville $49.95

● Bernard McDonagh
BLUE GUIDE: Turkey, from Bursa to Hatay
0–393–30489–2 Norton pb $19.95

● Sir Ernest Shackleton
SOUTH: The Story of Shackleton's Last Expedition, 1914-1917
0–7126–3414–2 David & Charles pb $11.95

Boats, Cars, Planes, and Trains

● Ron Holland
SPLENDOUR UNDER SAIL: The New Generation of Superyachts
0–393–03336–8 Norton $39.95

● Cynthia Kaul
HARBORS OF ENCHANTMENT: A Yachtmen's Anthology
0–393–02761–9 Norton $45.00

● National Auto Museum of France
THE SCHLUMPF AUTOMOBILE COLLECTION
0–88740–192–9 Schiffer pb $19.95

● Joel White
WOOD, WATER AND LIGHT: Classic Wooden Boats
Photographs by Benjamin Mendlowitz
0–393–03327–9 Norton $50.00

Sports

● Al Barkow
THE HISTORY OF THE PGA TOUR
Introduction by Ben Crenshaw
0–385–26145–4 Doubleday $24.95

● Larry Bird with Bob Ryan
DRIVE: The Story of My Life
0–385–24921–7 Doubleday $17.95

● Tony Dorsett with Harvey Frommer
RUNNING TOUGH: Memoirs of a Football Maverick
0–385–26248–5 Doubleday $17.95

● John Feinstein
FOREVER'S TEAM: The Story of the 1977-1978 Duke University Basketball Team
0–394–56892–3 Villard $18.95

A SEASON INSIDE: One Year in College Basketball
0–671–68882–0 Simon & Schuster pb $9.95

A SEASON ON THE BRINK: A Year with Bob Knight and the Indiana Hoosiers
0–671–68877–4 Simon & Schuster pb $8.95

● Benny Green
A HISTORY OF CRICKET
0–7126–2080–X David & Charles $35.00

● Richard Harris
MARATHON: A Story of Endurance and Friendship
0–393–02765–1 Norton $18.95

● Martin Heckelman
THE NEW GUIDE TO SKIING
0–393–30609–7 Norton pb $12.95

● Donald Honig
BASEBALL: The Illustrated History of America's Game
0–517–57295–8 Crown $45.00

● Dan Jenkins
YOU CALL IT SPORTS, BUT I SAY IT'S A JUNGLE OUT THERE
0–671–69021–3 Simon & Schuster $19.95

● Peter Johnson
THE SAIL MAGAZINE BOOK OF SAILING
0–394–57457–5 Knopf $40.00

● David Levine
LIFE ON THE RIM: A Year in the Continental Basketball Association
0–02–570381–1 Macmillan $17.95

● Elbert S. Maloney
CHAPMAN PILOTING, SEAMANSHIP AND SMALL BOAT HANDLING
0–688–09127–X Morrow $29.95

● National Basketball Association
THE OFFICIAL NBA BASKETBALL ENCYCLOPEDIA: The Complete History and Statistics of Professional Basketball
Foreword by Julius Erving
0–394–58039–7 Villard $29.95

● David S. Neft & Richard M. Cohen
THE SPORTS ENCYCLOPEDIA: Pro Basketball
0–312–03432–6 St. Martin's pb $16.95

THE SPORTS ENCYCLOPEDIA: Pro Football, the Modern Era 1960-1989
0–312–03433–4 St. Martin's pb $16.95

● Joe Paterno with Bernard Asbell
PATERNO: By the Book
0–394–56501–0 Random House $18.95

● Randy Roberts & James Olson
WINNING IS THE ONLY THING: Sports in America since 1945
0–8018–3830–4 Johns Hopkins $18.95

● Bo Schembechler with Mitch Albom
BO
0–446–51536–1 Warner $17.95

● John Slaughter & Richard Lapchick
THE RULES OF THE GAME: Ethics in College Sports
0–02–897401–8 Macmillan $19.95

- Mike Sowell
  THE PITCH THAT KILLED: The Tragic Death of Ray Chapman in the Pennant Race of 1920
  0–02–612410–6 Macmillan $17.95

- Isaiah Thomas & Matt Dobek
  IGNITION: An Inside Look at the Detroit Pistons' 1988-1989 Season
  0–940279–10–X Little, Brown $19.95

- David Whitford
  A PAYROLL TO MEET: A Story of Greed, Corruption, and Football at SMU
  0–02–627191–5 Macmillan $18.95

- Joel Zoss & John Bownman
  DIAMONDS IN THE ROUGH: The Untold Story of Baseball
  0–02–633590–5 Macmillan $29.95

The Outdoors

- Jeremy Bernstein
  ASCENT: The Invention of Mountain Climbing and Its Practice
  0–671–68275–X Simon & Schuster pb $9.95

  MOUNTAIN PASSAGES
  0–671–68276–8 Simon & Schuster pb $10.95

  IN THE HIMALAYAS: Journey Through Nepal, Tibet, and Bhutan
  0–671–68223–7 Simon & Schuster pb $10.95

- Nick Lyons
  FISHING WIDOWS
  0–671–66359–3 Simon & Schuster pb $7.95

Gardening

- Allessandro Albrizzi & Jane Pool
  THE GARDENS OF VENICE
  Photographs by Allessandro Albrizzi
  0–8478–1089–5 Rizzoli $85.00

- Basilius Besler
  THE BESLER FLORILEGIUM: Plants of the Four Seasons
  0–8109–1174–4 Abrams $150.00

- Christopher Brickell, editor
  AMERICAN HORTICULTURAL SOCIETY ENCYCLOPEDIA OF GARDEN PLANTS
  0–02–557902–7 Macmillan $45.00

- Madison Cox & Marianne McEvoy
  PRIVATE GARDENS OF PARIS
  Photographs by Philippe Perdereau
  0–517–57336–9 Crown $40.00

- Bonnie Marranca
  AMERICAN GARDEN WRITING
  0–14–012331–8 Penguin pb $10.95

- Bernard McTigue
  NATURE ILLUSTRATED: Flowers, Plants, and Trees, 1550-1900, From the Collection of the New York Public Library
  0–8109–1176–0 Abrams $39.95

- Nippon Bonsai Association
  CLASSIC BONSAI OF JAPAN
  0–87011–933–8 Kodansha $85.00

- Reader's Digest
  READER'S DIGEST ILLUSTRATED GUIDE TO GARDENING
  0–89577–046–6 Reader's Digest $26.95

- Graham Rose
  THE CLASSIC GARDEN
  0–671–68840–5 Simon & Schuster $29.95

- Caroline Seebohm & Christopher Simon Sykes
  PRIVATE LANDSCAPES
  0–517–57261–3 Crown $40.00

Pets

- E. Ruth Terry
  THE NEW CHIHUAHA
  0–87605–125–5 Howell $19.95

- Shirley Thomas
  THE NEW PUG
  0–87605–264–2 Howell $19.95

- Mordecai Siegal
  THE CORNELL BOOK OF CATS: A Comprehensive Medical Reference for Every Cat and Kitten
  0–394–56787–0 Villard $24.95

- Colin Vogel
  HOW TO KEEP YOUR HORSE HEALTHY
  0–87605–881–0 Howell $19.95

Games and Puzzles

- Bobby Fischer
  MY 60 MEMORABLE GAMES
  0–571–09987–4 Faber & Faber pb $9.95

- Alan Truscott & Phillip Alder
  ON BIDDING
  0–671–66463–8 Simon & Schuster pb $10.95

- Fred Waitzkin
  SEARCHING FOR BOBBY FISCHER: The Father of a Prodigy Observes the World of Chess
  0–14–012657–0 Penguin pb $7.95

THE READER'S CATALOG

STAFF

Geoffrey O'Brien (EDITOR) is the author of *Hardboiled America*, *Dream Time: Chapters from the Sixties*, and *A Book of Maps*. He contributes frequently to *The Village Voice* and *The New York Review of Books* and was the recipient of a 1988 Whiting Foundation Award.

Stephen Wasserstein (EDITORIAL DIRECTOR) has worked in publishing in New York since 1978. He is the maker of two short narrative films—the award-winning *Le Plan américain* and *Double Dealing*.

Helen S.K. Morris (ASSOCIATE EDITOR) is editorial consultant on *Bookmark*, the PBS book program. She studied Chinese Literature at Columbia and the University of London, and previously worked at The Asia Society and the New York Public Library.

Ellen Livingston (SENIOR EDITOR) is a New York-based writer and editor. She studied history at Princeton and is a former staff writer for *The Miami Herald* and editorial staff member of *Esquire*.

Tracy A. Smith (OFFICE ADMINISTRATOR) is a freelance writer and editor. She studied medieval history at the University of Washington and has been a contributor to many reference publications. She is currently writing a teleplay for children.

Mark Caldwell (CONTRIBUTING EDITOR) is Professor of English at Fordham University. He is the author of *The Last Crusade* and is a frequent contributor to *The Village Voice*, *The Philadelphia Inquirer*, and *7 Days*.

Peter Cosgrove (CONTRIBUTING EDITOR) teaches English Literature at Dartmouth. He has published in *Eightenth-Century Studies* and is a contributor to the forthcoming collection *Annotation and Its Texts*. He is currently working on a book about Edward Gibbon.

Barbara Epstein (CONTRIBUTING EDITOR) is editor of *The New York Review of Books*.

Judith Hendra (CONTRIBUTING EDITOR) has been an editor, freelance writer, and anthologist. She is

currently working on a study of 20th century storytellers.

Joel Honig (CONTRIBUTING EDITOR) is a freelance editor with an interest in history, biography, literature, the arts, and New York City history and architecture.

Lawrence Klepp (CONTRIBUTING EDITOR) is an editor and writer with a particular interest in philosophy and religion. He has contributed to *The Washington Post*, *The Village Voice*, and other publications.

Simon Pleasance (CONTRIBUTING EDITOR) has translated numerous books from Italian and French. He received his M.A. from Oxford University.

Robert B. Silvers (CONTRIBUTING EDITOR) is editor of *The New York Review of Books*.

Bob Tashman (CONTRIBUTING EDITOR) is assistant editor of *The New York Review of Books*.

Doron Weber (CONTRIBUTING EDITOR) is working on a novel entitled *Yored*. He is the coauthor of *Safe Blood: Purifying the Nation's Blood Supply in the Age of AIDS*.

Beth Tondreau (ART DIRECTOR) is the principal of Beth Tondreau Design. She has been the designer and art director for books which have been included in the American Institute of Graphic Arts book shows and the New York Book Show.

Derek Ungless (DESIGNER), creative director of Angle Design Office, is the art director for *Vogue*.

R.D. Scudellari (COVER DESIGNER) is vice-president of graphic arts at Random House. He designed the book jackets of the Library of America and is currently working on the Literary Classics series. He has won three American Book Awards for design.

Valerie Humes (PICTURE EDITOR) is a freelance picture researcher and documentary filmmaker.

Ellen L. Vanook (PRODUCTION CONSULTANT) is Production Manager, Special Projects, at Random House.

Anthony W. Toogood (PROGRAMMING CONSULTANT) is president of Organized Solutions Ltd., a computer consulting company. He has designed and implemented computer systems for major American corporations.

Laurence Vétu-Kane (ASSOCIATE DESIGNER) is a freelance designer, currently working on *The New York Times Magazine*. She previously was design director at *Vogue*.

Noël Claro (ASSOCIATE DESIGNER) is designer at *Vogue* and was previously junior designer at Angle Design Office.

Gabrielle Hamberg (ASSISTANT ART DIRECTOR) is a designer who works at Beth Tondreau Design.

Jane Treuhaft (ASSISTANT ART DIRECTOR) is a designer who works at Beth Tondreau Design.

Marguerite Jones is a journalist and writer.

Jacquelin McCarthy is a freelance writer with an interest in dance and art history.

Thomas Nissley is a recent graduate of the University of Pennsylvania, where he studied English and economics.

Marpessa Dawn Outlaw is a freelance writer, specializing in the arts.

Freya A. Read is a freelance photographer and world traveler.

Jasjiv Sahney is a recent graduate of Columbia, where he studied literature. He now lives in Bombay.

Sal Terillo is a software consultant, specializing in desktop publishing applications.

Fronza Woods is a writer and award-winning filmmaker.

Peter Zabelskis is a writer and a founder of Slate Press, New York. He is the author of *LOOP: 50 Ideas for Pictures*.

Jason Epstein (PUBLISHER) is editorial director of Random House.

Blynn Garnett (SECRETARY-TREASURER) is circulation manager of *The New York Review of Books* and general manager of The Readers' Subscription and The Garden Book Club.

CONSULTANTS

Mindy Aloff writes frequently on dance for *The Village Voice* and *The Threepenny Review*.

Hilary Ainger is an anthropologist, avid reader, and traveler who teaches at the United Nations International School.

Laurie Baum is a former staff editor at *Business Week* and a former marketing columnist at *The Miami Herald*.

Paolo Berdini is a Ph.D. candidate in art history at Columbia University. His publications include *Walter Gropius*.

Russell A. Berman is Professor of German Studies and Comparative Literature at Stanford University. His recent publications include *The Rise of the Modern German Novel* and *Modern Culture and Critical Theory: Art, Politics, and the Legacy of the Frankfurt School*.

Paul Bernabeo is senior editor in the Trade and Reference Division of Houghton Mifflin Company and formerly served as associate project editor of *The Encyclopedia of Religion*.

John Bierhorst is the author of *The Mythology of North America*, *The Mythology of South America*, *A Nahuatl-*

English Dictionary, and the forthcoming *Mythology of Mexico and Central America*.

Stephen Bodio is an associate editor of *Gray's Sporting Journal* and *Game Country*. His memoir *Querencia* will be published this fall.

James Boylan is Professor of Journalism at the University of Massachusetts, Amherst. He was founding editor of *The Columbia Journalism Review*.

Janet Byrne is at work on a biography of Frieda Lawrence.

Mary Cargill is a reference librarian in the History and Humanities Division of Columbia University. Previously she was the performing arts reference specialist at the Library of Congress.

Elizabeth Cavicchi is a physics instructor at the University of Lowell (MA) and a consultant in the history of science. Recently she conducted research for the public television series *The Ring of Truth* and *The Painter's World*.

Andrew Cockburn is the author of *The Threat: Inside the Soviet Military Machine*.

Andrew Cohen is a regular contributor to the sports sections of *The Village Voice* and *7 Days*. His work has also appeared in *The New York Times*, *Essence*, and *Golf Illustrated*.

Joel Colton is Professor of History at Duke University. He is the author of *Léon Blum: Humanist in Politics*, and coauthor, with R.R. Palmer, of *A History of the Modern World*, now in its sixth edition.

Lewis Coser is Distinguished Professor of Sociology at State University of New York, Stony Brook. Among his many books are *Introduction to Sociology*, *The Pleasures of Sociology*, and *Masters of Sociological Thought*.

David Cronin is the manager of the Public Education Program at the New York Public Library.

Mark D. Cummings trained in Buddhist studies at Yale University and served as staff editor for Asian religions for *The Encyclopedia of Religion*. He is the coeditor, with Joseph M. Kitagawa, of *Buddhism and Asian History*.

Diane Kender Dittrick is a contributing editor of *The Random House Dictionary of the English Language: Second Edition—Unabridged*, life science editor of *The McGraw-Hill Encyclopedia of Science and Technology* and *The McGraw-Hill Dictionary of Scientific and Technical Terms*, and coauthor of *No Uncertain Terms* and *Misnomers*.

Mark Dittrick is a contributing editor of *The Random House Dictionary of the English Language: Second Edition—Unabridged*, a senior editor of *The Funk & Wagnalls New Encyclopedia*, and coauthor of *No Uncertain Terms* and *Misnomers*.

Peggy Dye is a freelance writer who has covered strikes in America and abroad and wars in the Third World and written political profiles for the labor press, the American Bar Association, *Newsday*, and *The Christian Science Monitor*.

Sue Elwyn is writing a doctoral dissertation in ancient history at the University of Pennsylvania, on Hellenistic treaties of kinship. She also has extensive knowledge of military history, particularly World War II.

Tony Eprile has taught writing at Brown University, the Kennedy School of Government, and the University of San Diego, where he also guest-lectured on African literature. He is the author of *Temporary Sojourner and Other South African Stories*.

Helen Epstein is a biologist in Cambridge, England.

Jacob Epstein was executive story editor on *Hill Street Blues* and *L.A. Law*.

Mary Anne Evans is a travel writer, journalist, and publisher of the monthly newsletter *Letter from London*. She is currently editing an anthology of travel writers and travel literature.

James Fallows has reported from Asia for *The Atlantic* for the past three years. He is the author of the recently published *More Like Us: An American Plan for American Recovery* and *National Defense*.

Martin Filler is an architecture and design critic and an editor of *House & Garden* magazine.

Ronald E. Findlay is Ragnar Nurkse Professor of Economics at Columbia University. He is the author of *International Trade and Development Theory*.

Henry Flesh is an editor at Western Publishing Company.

Stephen William Foster is an anthropologist and associate director of psychiatric nursing at San Francisco General Hospital. His most recent publication is *The Past Is Another Country: Representation, Historical Consciousness and Resistance in the Blue Ridge*.

Edward Fox is a staff writer in the public relations department of the Saudi Arabian Oil Company (Saudi Aramco) in Dhahran, Saudi Arabia. He has an MA in Middle Eastern Languages and Cultures from Columbia University, New York.

Martin Gardner is a science writer who for 25 years wrote the "Mathematical Games" column for *Scientific American*. The most recent of his many books is *Penrose Tiles to Trapdoor Ciphers*.

Cyril Glassé is a graduate student at Columbia University in Middle Eastern Studies. He is the author of *The Concise Encyclopedia of Islam* and *The Berlitz Guide to Saudi Arabia*.

Joe Glickman's articles have appeared in *The Village Voice*, *The New York Times*, *Newsday*, *The Daily News*, *Outside*, and *Condé Nast's Traveler*, among others.

Arthur S. Goldwag is editor of the The Readers' Subscription book club.

Marilyn Greco is a writer and designer of curriculum, specializing in reading and the language arts for Early Childhood Through High School Educational Product.

David Guss is a Visiting Assistant Professor of Anthropology at Vassar College. His most recent publications include *To Weave and Sing: Art, Symbol, and Narrative in the South American Rain Forest*, and *The Language of the Birds: Tales, Texts, and Poems of Interspecies Communication*.

Ellen Handy is a doctoral candidate in the history of photography at Princeton University, and writes regularly on contemporary art.

Peter Hay has taught drama at several universities, most recently at UCLA. He is a dramaturg and author of six books, including *Theatrical Anecdotes* and *Broadway Anecdotes*.

David C. Hendrickson is Associate Professor of Political Science at Colorado College. His books include *The Future of American Strategy* and *Reforming Defense: The State of American Civil-Military Relations*.

David Herlihy is Mary Critchfield and Barnaby Keeney Professor of History at Brown University. His special interest is the social and economic history of the Middle Ages. He is currently president of the American Historical Association.

Rabbi Arthur Hertzberg is Professor of Religion at Dartmouth College and Adjunct Professor of History at Columbia University. His books include *The Zionist Idea*, *The French Enlightenment and the Jews*, and most recently, *Jews in America*.

Jennifer Howard is on the staff of *The New York Review of Books*.

Ewa Jankowska-Lategano is a librarian at the General Research Library, a branch of the New York Public Library, where she is Polish Selection Officer.

Kathrine Jason is a poet and translator whose work has appeared in *The New Yorker* and other magazines. She is the editor and translator of *Words in Commotion and Other Stories* by Tommaso Landolfi, and of a forthcoming anthology of contemporary Italian fiction.

Karyn Kay was the screenwriter and co-producer of the film *Call Me*. She is the author of two books, *Women and the Cinema* and *Myrna Loy*.

Verlyn Klinkenborg is the Briggs-Copeland Lecturer in Nonfiction at Harvard University. His most recent book is *Making Hay*.

Heidi Knecht is a doctoral candidate in the Department of Anthropology at New York University. Her present research concerns technological innovation and design during the Ice Age in Europe.

Bernard Knox is Director Emeritus of the Center for Hellenistic Studies in Washington, D.C. His most recent publications include *Word and Action* and *Essays Ancient and Modern*.

Robert Lamberton is Assistant Professor of Classics at Princeton University. His most recent books include *Hesiod* and *Homer the Theologian*.

Paul Landau is a doctoral candidate in history at the University of Wisconsin. He is currently conducting field research on Christianity and social change in central Botswana.

Ira M. Lapidus is Professor of History and Chairman of the Center for Middle Eastern Studies at the University of California at Berkeley. His most recent publications are *Contemporary Islamic Movements in Historical Perspective*, *A History of Islamic Societies*, and *Islam, Politics, and Social Movements* with Edmund Burke.

Sherman E. Lee, retired director of the Cleveland Museum of Art, is now Adjunct Professor of Far Eastern Art at the University of North Carolina, Chapel Hill, and at Duke University. He is author of *A History of Far Eastern Art*.

Jonathan Lieberson was contributing editor of *The New York Review of Books* and the author of *Varieties*. He died in 1989.

Pam Lord, a landscape designer, is editorial director of The Garden Book Club.

Richard John Lynn is currently director of Corporate Asian Language Training in Palo Alto, California. His publications include *Guide to Chinese Poetry and Drama* and *Tradition and Creativity: Theory and Practice in Later Chinese Poetry*. He is also the editor of James J.Y. Liu's *Language-Paradox-Poetics: A Chinese View*.

Michael McGerr is Associate Professor of History at Indiana University. The author of *The Decline of Popular Politics*, he is presently writing *The Gospel of Wealth, 1900-1933*, a volume in the Oxford History of the United States.

David Mermelstein is Professor of Economics at Polytechnic University. His most recent publications include *The Anti-Apartheid Reader* and *El Salvador: Central America in the New Cold War*.

John Miller is currently a visiting artist at California Institute of the Arts. He is also a contributing editor for the British magazine *Artscribe International*.

Richard Morris is the author of numerous books on physics and cosmology, including *Time's Arrows* and the forthcoming *The Edges of Science*.

Barbara Probst Morrow is a freelance editor and copy editor.

Michael Moskowitz is Adjunct Associate Professor of Clinical Psychology at the City University of New York (CUNY).

Deborah Nadler, currently director of international public relations for Revlon, has served in the same capacity for Sotheby's, the New York Public Library, and the New-York Historical Society.

Maryann Napoli is associate director of the Center for Medical Consumers in New York City and the editor of *Healthfacts*, the Center's monthly newsletter. Her articles on health and medicine have appeared in *The New York Times Health Supplement*, *The New Republic*, *Ms.*, *Family Circle*, and *Working Mother*.

Charlotte Nekola is Assistant Professor of English at William Paterson College. Her poetry has appeared in *New Letters*, *Massachusetts Review*, *Calyx*, and other publications, and she is coeditor, with Paula Rabinowitz, of *Writing Red: An Anthology of American Women Writers, 1930-1940*.

Craig Osbern works as a freelance copy editor and is currently working on a novel entitled *Deception*.

Jena Osman's most recent publications include *twelve parts of her*, as well as poetry appearing in *O-blēk*, *Tyuonyi*, *Central Park*, and *Notus*.

Samuel M. Paley is Associate Professor and Chairman of the Department of Classics at the State University of New York at Buffalo, specializing in the ancient Near East and Judaic studies. His most recent publication is a collaboration with Richard P. Sobolewski, *The Reconstruction of the Relief-Representations and Their Positions in the Northwest Palace of Kalhu (Nimrud), Part II*.

Jerry E. Patterson, formerly a senior vice-president of Sotheby's, is the author of many books and articles on the art market and collecting, including *Autographs: A Collector's Guide*, *Antiques of Sport*, and *The Vanderbilts*.

Tom Piazza is a short story writer who has written about jazz for *The New Republic*, *The New York Times Book Review*, and *The Village Voice*, among other publications. His critical study of jazz recordings is forthcoming.

Darryl Pinckney, a frequent contributor to *The New York Review of Books*, is currently at work on a novel.

David Potenziani is vice-president of Symetrix, a software development company.

George Preston is Professor of Art History at City College of New York and the author of *Sets, Series, and Ensembles in African Art*.

Missy Prowell, winner of two Clio Awards, is former creative director of Publicis New York. She previously held creative positions at Peter Rogers Associates and Grey Advertising.

Diane Ravitch is Adjunct Professor of History and Education at Teachers College, Columbia University. She has written five books, including *The Troubled Crusade: American Education, 1945-1980* and *The Great School Wars: New York City, 1805-1973*.

Evie Righter is editor of Gourmet Books and a cofounder of The Chelsea Baking Company, a wholesale bakery in New York City. She edited and wrote the text for *Gourmet's Menus for Contemporary Living* and *Gourmet's Best Desserts*.

Diane Roback is children's book editor of *Publishers Weekly*, and currently serves as New York chapter president of the Woman's National Book Association.

Bruce Robbins teaches English at Rutgers University and is an editor of *Social Text*. His most recent publication is *The Grounding of Intellectuals*.

Patricia Romanowski is a writer and editor who specializes in popular culture and rock and roll.

Israel Rosenfield is Professor of History at the City University of New York. His most recent book is *The Invention of Memory: A New View of the Brain*.

Edward Rothstein is the music critic for *The New Republic*. He is currently working on a book about music and mathematics to be published by Knopf. He is a fellow of the New York Institute for the Humanities at New York University.

Josh Rubins won the National Book Critics Circle's Citation (1987) for excellence in book reviewing. He is a frequent contributor to *The New York Review of Books* and *The New York Times Book Review*.

William J. Sanders is a research associate in the Museum of Paleontology at the University of Michigan. He is currently studying the origins of bipedalism in early humans and the functional morphology of ancient whales.

Luc Sante is film critic for *Interview* and a frequent contributor to *The New York Review of Books*. His book *Slum Culture* will be published in 1990.

Hiroaki Sato is an author, translator, columnist, and poet. His many books include *From the Country of Eight Islands*, *One Hundred Frogs*, and the recently published *A Future of Ice: Poems and Stories of a Japanese Buddhist*, a volume of translations from Miyazawa Kenji.

Robert Schirmer is a freelance writer, book editor, and translator. He has been a contributing movie reviewer for *Video Review*.

John Schulian is executive story editor of the CBS-TV series *Wiseguy*. A former sports columnist for *The Chicago Sun-Times* and *The Philadelphia Daily News*, he is the author of *Writer's Fighters and Other Sweet Scientists*.

Barry Schwabsky is editor of *Arts Magazine*. His poems have been published in two chapbooks, *The New Lessons* and *Fate/Seen in the Dark*.

Baird Searles is the former owner of The Science Fiction Shop in New York City and is currently a consulting editor at Warner Books. He contributes a regular column to *Isaac Asimov's Science Fiction Magazine* and recently published *Films of Science Fiction and Fantasy*.

Mark Selden teaches sociology and history at State University of New York at Binghamton. His recent books include *The Political Economy of Chinese Socialism* and *After the Bomb: Voices from Hiroshima and Nagasaki*.

Vijay Seshadri is a graduate student in Middle Eastern Languages and Cultures at Columbia University, where he studies the Islamic literatures of the Indian subcontinent.

Nancy Spector is assistant curator for Research at the Guggenheim Museum. She is a frequent contributor to *Artscribe* and *Contemporanea*.

William R. Spiegelberger is a Ph.D. candidate in Russian Literature at Columbia University.

Gloria Steinem is a writer, editor, and feminist organizer who cofounded the magazines *New York* and *Ms.*. Her recent books include *Outrageous Acts and Everyday Rebellions* and *Marilyn: Norma Jeane*.

Irwin Stern is lecturer in Portuguese and Brazilian Literatures at Columbia University. He is the editor of *The Dictionary of Brazilian Literature* and coeditor of *Modern Spanish and Portuguese Literatures*.

Bhob Stewart, designer of humor products (*Wacky Packages*), books, magazines, and software, has scripted comics (*Heavy Metal*) and contributed to books (*Bare Bones*) and magazines (*TV Guide, Publishers Weekly, The Comics Journal*).

Claudia Swan is a Ph.D. candidate in the history of art at Columbia University, and the translator of several books from Dutch.

William Taylor is associate editor of *Harvard Business Review*, and coauthor, with Ralph Nader, of *The Big Boys: Power and Position in American Business*.

Diane Tong is a New York City-based independent scholar and photographer specializing in Gypsy studies. Her most recent publication is *Gypsy Folktales*.

Jessica Teich is a frequent contributor to *The Los Angeles Times*, *American Theatre*, and other publications. She is a graduate of Yale and Oxford, and a Rhodes Scholar.

David Tuller is a reporter at the *San Francisco Chronicle*.

Alice K. Turner is the fiction editor of *Playboy*.

Stephen J. Vogel is a translator of French literature. His translations include plays by Daniel Besnehard (France), Kateb Yacine (Algeria), and Abdou Anta Ka (Senegal).

Priscilla Wald is Assistant Professor of American Literature at Columbia University.

Carl Waldman is a freelance writer and researcher whose books include *Atlas of the North American Indian*, *Encyclopedia of Native American Tribes*, and *Who Was Who in Native American History*.

Mark Wasserman is Associate Professor of History at Rutgers University. He is the author of *Capitalists, Caciques, and Revolution: The Native Elite and Foreign Enterprise in Chihuahua, 1854-1911* and coauthor, with Benjamin Keen, of *A History of Latin America*.

David Wheeler is a freelance writer specializing in music literature. He is the cofounder of The Archive of Contemporary Music and editor of *No, But I Saw the Movie*.

Arnold Wilson is Assistant Professor in the Graduate Faculty of the New School for Social Research Psychology Department. He has published extensively on a variety of psychoanalytic topics.

Michael Zeilik is Professor of Astronomy at the University of New Mexico and director of the Center for Graduate Studies at Los Alamos. His most recent book is *Astronomy: The Evolving Universe*.

INDEX

Blank, Robert, 1101
Blankert, Albert, 479
Blanksteen, Jane, 1164
Blanshard, Brand, 978
Blanshard, Paul, 935
Blaser, Werner, 552
Blasier, Cole, 929
Blasio, Maria de, 712
Blasis, Carlo, 616
Blass, Bill, 580
Blassingame, John W., 840, 878, 879, 886
Blatt, Art, 1235
Blatt, Robin, 1135
Blau, Herbert, 627
Blau, Peter M., 1005, 1006
Blaug, Mark, 1009
Blaukoph, Kurt, 589
Blauner, Robert, 899
Blavatsky, Helena, 1173
Blaylock, James P., 378
Blecher, Marc, 782
Bledstein, Burton J., 874, 1042
Bleich, J. David, 952
Bleier, Ruth, 1050
Bleiler, Everett F., 381
Bleser, Carol, 868
Blesh, Rudi, 602, 604
Bligh, William, 808
Blight, James G., 856
Blij, Harm De, 1193
Blik, Tyler, 523
Blinder, Alan, 1013
Blinderman, Charles, 658
Blindness, 1066
Blinkin, Meir, 107
Bliss, Anne, 574
Bliss, Shepherd, 1173
Blitzer, Jeremiah, 1159
Blitzer, Wolf, 372
Bloch, Dorothy, 997
Bloch, Douglas, 1172
Bloch, Marc, 675, 679, 713, 819
Bloch, Michael, 743
Bloch, Sonny, 565
Block, Fred, 875
Block, Lawrence, 360, 363
Blocksman, Dewey, 426
Blocksman, Mary, 426
Blok, Alexander, 90
Blokker, Roy, 589
Blombery, Alec, 1247
Blomfield, Reginald, 540
Blonsky, Marshall, 154
Bloody Mary. See Mary Tudor
Bloom, Alexander, 158, 906
Bloom, Allan, 1042
Bloom, Benjamin S., 1044
Bloom, Billy, 1235
Bloom, Harold, 155, 181, 228, 335
Bloom, Marc, 452
Bloomer, Kent, 553
Bloomfield, Leonard, 1046
Bloore, Carolyn, 525
Blossfeldt, Karl, 526
Blotkamp, Carel, 497
Blotner, Joseph, 332
Blount, Roy, Jr., 404, 1226
Blue, Anthony Dias, 1193
Bluegrass, 600
Blues music, 602
Bluestone, Barry, 1012
Blum, Daniel, 629
Blum, David, 595
Blum, Howard, 372
Blum, John Morton, 711, 831
Blum, Leon, 706

Blum, Ralph, 1172
Blum, Stella, 579
Blumberg, Louis, 1121
Blumberg, Paul, 1006
Blumberg, Rhoda, 448
Blume, Friedrich, 587
Blume, Judy, 391, 429, 433, 434, 437, 451, 455
Blumenfeld, Samuel L., 1038
Blumenfeld, Warren J., 1060
Blumenson, Martin, 719
Blumenthal, David, 1102
Blumenthal, Eileen, 624
Blumenthal, Howard, 650
Blumenthal, Lassor, 1165
Blumenthal, Ralph, 370
Blumenthal, Sidney, 860, 892
Blunden, Caroline, 512, 783
Blunden, Edmund, 210
Blunden, Godfrey, 483
Blunden, Maria, 483
Blunt, Anthony, 372, 472, 478, 538
Blunt, Lady Anne, 1197
Bly, Robert, 161, 301, 329, 1164
Blythe, Ronald, 729
Boahen, A. Adu, 770
Boardman, John, 467, 535, 663, 666, 668
Boas, Franz, 824, 982, 985
Boas, Marie, 692, 1076
Boase, T.S.R., 473
Boatner, Mark M., III, 843
Boats, 1216-1217
  adventures at sea, 1217
  English, 730
  military, 815
  ocean liners and yachts, 1216-1217
  sailboats, 1217, 1230
  World War II, 717, 815
Bobo, Lawrence, 881
Bobrick, Benson, 745
Bobrow, Jill, 1216
Bobrowski, Johannes, 77
Boccaccio, Giovanni, 31, 61, 68
Bock, Audie, 631
Bock, Carl, 805
Bock, Frances, 1144
Bock, Hal, 1229
Bockus, William, 522
Bocuse, Paul, 1182
Bodak, Chuck, 1225
Boden, Margaret, 995, 1124, 1125
Bodio, Stephen, 1116, 1239, 1242
Bodmer, Frederick, 1169
Bodmer, Karl, 492
Bodnar, John, 869
Bodybuilding, 1236
Boe, Eugene, 1150
Boehm, Ann, 1141
Boehm, David A., 452
Boehme, Sarah, 492
Boesche, Robert, 696
Boessenecker, John, 865
Boethius, 21, 28, 968
Boethius, Axel, 535, 668
Boettcher, Thomas D., 911
Boff, Leonardo, 961
Boffey, Philip M., 1032
Bofill, Ricardo, 552
Bogan, Louise, 293
Bogard, Travis, 334
Bogart, Humphrey, 635
Bogel, Cynthea, 516
Boger, Louise, 558
Boggs, Jean Sutherland, 484
Bogle, Donald, 633, 883

Bogosian, Eric, 316
Bohm, David, 1080, 1175
Bohr, Neils, 1084
Boiardo, Matteo Mario, 62
Boime, Albert, 481, 482
Boisset, Caroline, 1244
Boissiere, Ralph de, 338
Bojcun, Marko, 750
Bok, Bart, 1086
Bok, Derek C., 1043
Bok, Priscilla, 1086
Bok, Sissela, 1029
Bokenkotter, Thomas, 957
Boland, Bridget, 167
Bolcom, William, 608
Boldt, Menno, 826
Bolen, Jean Shinoda, 1052
Boleslavsky, Richard, 628
Boleyn, Anne, 732
Bolgar, R.R., 17
Bolger, Daniel P., 810
Bolin, Anne, 1060
Bolin, Bert, 1120
Bolingbroke, Lord, 817
Bolivia, 924
Bolivian literature, 341
Boll, Heinrich, 77
Boller, Paul F., Jr., 632, 654, 889, 890
Boller, Richard, 567
Bolles, Edmund Blair, 1099, 1138
Bolles, Richard, 1162
Bollinger, Lee C., 1036
Bollobas, Bela, 1068
Bolocan, David, 1128
Bolshevik Revolution. See Soviet Union, Revolution
Bolt, Robert, 217
Bolton, Geoffrey, 807
Bolton, Guy, 625
Bolton, W.F., 228
Bolus, Jim, 1229
Bombal, Maria Luisa, 342
Bona, Damien, 633
Bonafoux, Pascal, 462, 480, 483
Bonando, Wanda, 573
Bonaparte, Louis, 699, 700, 1021
Bonavia, David, 1199, 1204
Bond, Bob, 1230
Bond, Christopher, 317
Bond, Edward, 217
Bond, Mary, 1202
Bond, Michael, 433
Bond, Nancy, 455
Bond, Peter, 1089
Bondanella, Peter, 631
Bonds, 1159
Bonds, Ray, 819, 1032
Bondurant, Bob, 1234
Bonham, Frank, 455
Bonheur, Rosa, 482
Bonhoeffer, Dietrich, 960, 961
Boni, Ada, 1182, 1189
Bonk, Ecke, 498
Bonnard, Pierre, 485, 495
Bonnefoy, Yves, 42, 53
Bonnell, Victoria E., 745, 746
Bonner, Elena, 751
Bonner, Raymond, 804, 894
Bonnie Prince Charlie, 735
Bontemps, Arna, 311, 884
Bonventure, Peter, 1220
Bony, Jean, 535
Booher, Dianna, 1158, 1163
Bookbinding, 574-575
Books, Bruce, 455
Books, rare, 577
Boomer, Percy, 1228

Boon, James A., 988
Boone, Elizabeth Hill, 518
Boorman, John, 634
Boorstin, Daniel J., 645, 652, 831, 832, 838, 888, 904, 1075
Booth, Alan, 1029
Booth, Connie, 648
Booth, John A., 928
Booth, Ken, 1029
Booth, Martin, 229
Booth, Philip, 301
Booth, Stanley, 612
Booth, Wayne C., 153
Booth-Clibborn, Edward, 520
Borbely, Alexander, 1001, 1147
Borchgrave, Arnaud De, 392
Borcoman, James, 526
Borden, Lizzie, 369
Border, Gail, 1147
Bordin, Ruth, 1055
Bordman, Gerald, 624, 629
Bordwell, David, 630, 632, 634, 635, 639
Borg, Susan, 1137
Borges, Jorge Luis, 149, 340, 348
Borgia, Lucrezia, 681
Borgia family, 682
Boring, Edwin G., 988
Borisova, Elena, 557
Boritt, Gabor, 844
Born, Max, 1081
Borns, Betsy, 449
Borodin, Aleksandr, 589
Boroff, Marie, 165
Borofsky, Jonathan, 505
Borowitz, Eugene B., 953
Borowski, Tadeusz, 84
Borrelli, Peter, 1120
Borromini, Francesco, 538
Borror, Donald, 1241
Borrow, George, 182, 189, 1195
Borsi, Franco, 538, 547
Borsook, Eve, 471
Bortolotti, Gary, 1116
Borysenko, Joan, 1147
Bos, Saskia, 1148
Bosch, Hieronymous, 476
Boshung, Herbert, 1240
Bosker, Gideon, 581
Bosco, Dominick, 1037
Bosher, J.F., 695
Bosker, Gideon, 578
Boskin, Joseph, 881
Bosley, Keith, 161
Boslough, John, 1086
Bosnak, Robert, 1001
Bosso, Christopher, 1119
Bossy, John, 686
Boston, Jonathan, 808
Boston (Mass.), 1214
Boswell, James, 175-176, 230, 735
Boswell, John, 675, 1059
Boswell, Thomas, 1221, 1227
Bosworth, C.E., 762
Bosworth, Patricia, 526
Botany, 1095-1096
Botermans, Jack, 451, 1074
Botero, Fernando, 499
Bothwell, Robert, 917
Botta, Mario, 552
Botticelli, Sandro, 474
Botting, Douglas, 726, 1219
Bottingheimer, Karl, 729
Bottles, Scott L., 877
Bottomore, Tom, 1008
Bottoms, David, 270
Botvinnik, Mikhail, 1258
Botwin, Carol, 1135

Griffin, Peter, 333
Griffin, Susan, 160
Griffis, Nixon, 1107
Griffith, Bill, 398
Griffith, Elisabeth, 1055
Griffith, H. Winter, 1152
Griffith, Helen, 554
Griffith, Paddy, 811
Griffith, Robert, 856
Griffith, Sally Foreman, 641
Griffith, Samuel B., II, 716
Griffiths, A. Philips, 980
Griffiths, John, 1261
Griffiths, Paul, 590, 592, 595, 598
Griffiths, Ralph, 743
Griffiths, Trevor, 219
Griggs, Barbara, 1150
Griggs, John, 636
Grigson, Geoffrey, 161, 211, 227, 1133
Grigson, Jane, 1183, 1187
Grilli, Peter, 792
Grim, Kenan, 662
Grimal, Pierre, 939
Grimes, Martha, 361
Grimke, Charlotte L. Forten, 245
Grimm Brothers, 71, 79, 424, 441, 941
Grimmelshausen, Hans Jakob von, 69
Grimson, Todd, 278
Grimstone, A.V., 948, 949
Grinnell, George B., 823
Grinspoon, Lester, 1032
Gris, Juan, 494
Grisewood, John, 447
Grist, Everett, 578
Griswold, Mac, 1251
Griswold, Ralph, 546
Griswold, Robert L., 909
Gritsch, Eric W., 908
Groce, George, 489
Grodecki, Louis, 470, 535
Grodnick, Susan, 1185
Groening, Matt, 398
Grohmann, Will, 496
Grollenberg, Luc, 662
Grollman, Earl, 1156, 1157
Grooms, Red, 503
Grooms, Steve, 1242
Groot, Georg Van Der, 480
Groover, Jan, 528
Gropius, Walter, 549
Gropper, Rena, 752
Grose, Peter, 757, 766
Gross, Adam, 1031
Gross, Albert, 1238
Gross, Barbara, 1240
Gross, Beatrice, 1038
Gross, David C., 753, 954
Gross, Gerald, 1164
Gross, John, 1132, 1168
Gross, Leonard, 722, 1148
Gross, Miriam, 1118
Gross, Rachel, 1158
Gross, Ronald, 1038
Gross, Susan H., 671
Gross, Theodore L., 326
Grossberg, Kenneth A., 792
Grosberg, Michael, 909
Grosser, Alfred, 1028
Grossfeld, Stan, 1197
Grosshans, Henry, 707
Grosskurth, Phyliss, 993
Grossman, Allen, 307
Grossman, Alvin, 1253
Grossman, Bob, 1190
Grossman, David, 103, 767

Grossman, Israel, 1072
Grossman, Peter Z., 1016
Grossman, Richard, 1149
Grossman, Ruth, 1190
Grossman, Vasily, 93, 722
Grosswirth, Marvin, 1261
Grosz, George, 496
Groth, Gary, 399
Grotz, George, 567
Grousset, Rene, 782, 791
Grout, Bill, 1230
Grout, Donald, 586, 596
Grove, George, 587
Grover, Lee, 560
Grover, Ray, 560
Groves, Alan, 607
Groves, Seli, 1164
Grow, Lawrence, 565
Grozik, Richard, 1242
Gruber, Frank, 381
Gruber, Gary R., 454
Gruber, H.S., 1093
Gruber, Howard E., 997
Gruber, Ruth, 774
Grujic, Branislav, 1171
Grun, Bernard, 652
Grunauer, Peter, 1184
Grunbaum, Adolf, 990
Grunbaum, Branko, 1072
Grunchec, Philippe, 482, 1252
Grundman, Clare, 1261
Grunelbaum, Gabriele, 575
Grunes, Barbara, 1187
Grunfeld, A.T., 791
Grunfeld, Frederic, 486
Grusa, Jiri, 82
Grushkin, Paul, 519, 613
Gruson, Lindsey, 370
Guardi, Francesco, 478
Guare, John, 315
Guarini, Guarino, 538
Guarino, E.J., 1213
Guatemala, 927
Guatemalan literature, 343, 347
Guattari, Felix, 157
Gubar, Susan, 159, 160, 1057
Gubaryev, Vladimir, 101
Gubser, Mary, 1185
Gucker, Philip, 1168
Gudas, Raymond, 1258
Guderian, Heinz, 719
Gudiol i Ricart, Jose, 481
Guenther, Herbert V., 945, 949
Guernsey, Otis, 623, 625
Guest, Barbara, 307
Guest, Ivor, 616, 619
Guevara, Che, 925, 1022, 1028
Gugliotta, Guy, 370, 911
Guha, Ranajit, 779
Guibaut, Andre, 791, 1198
Guicciardini, Francesco, 681, 682, 817
Guilbaut, Serge, 501
Guild, Thelma S., 864
Guillaud, Jacqueline, 471, 474, 476, 480, 495
Guillaud, Maurice, 471, 474, 476, 480, 495
Guillaume, Alfred, 760, 963
Guillen, Jorge, 56-57
Guillen, Michael, 1068
Guillen, Nicolas, 346-347
Guillevic, Eugene, 43
Guilmartin, John, 914
Guimard, Hector, 549
Guinness, Alec, 625
Guinther, John, 871
Guisewite, Cathy, 398

Guiton, Jacques, 549
Gulbadan, Princess, 779
Gulick, Edward V., 1026
Gullo, Stephen, 1133
Gumerman, George J., 658
Gundersheimer, W.L., 477
Gunderson, Gerald, 901
Gunn, Edward M., 132, 133
Gunn, Thom, 211, 222
Gunnarsson, Gunnar, 81
Gunther, Max, 1163
Gupte, Pranay, 781, 782
Gura, Philip F., 834
Guralnick, Peter, 609
Gurdjieff, G.I., 1174
Gurney, A.R., 315
Gurney, Ivor, 211
Guse, Ernst-Gerhard, 504
Gusman, Don Gaspar de, 689
Guss, David M., 830
Gustafson, Ginny Lyford, 1153
Gustafson, Richard F., 95
Gustafsson, Lars, 81
Guston, Philip, 506
Gutcheon, Beth, 574
Gutenberg, Johann, 686-687
Guthrie, A.B., Jr., 262, 381
Guthrie, John, 616
Guthrie, Ramon, 302
Guthrie, Tyrone, 625
Guthrie, W.K., 965
Guthrie, Woody, 600-601, 861
Gutierrez, Felix, 645
Gutman, David, 611
Gutman, Herbert G., 883, 896
Gutman, Roy, 894
Gutman, Yisrael, 722
Gutmann, Amy, 1041
Gutmann, Joseph, 760
Guttmacher, Alan, 1136
Guttmann, Allen, 907, 1220
Guttmann, Julius, 953
Guttridge, Len, 607
Guy, John, 732
Guy, Rosa, 438, 456
Guy, Willy, 752
Guyanan literature, 336
Guyette, Barbara, 580
Guzman, Martin L., 349
Gwaltney, John L., 885
Gwathmey, Charles, 552
Gyatso, Geshe K., 949
Gymnastics, 1234
Gyorgy, Anna, 1121
Gypsies, 752
Gysin, Brion, 203

H

Haacke, Hans, 504
Haag, Michael, 1210
Haagsma, Ids, 548
Haak, Bob, 479, 480
Haan, Hilde de, 548
Haas, Ernst, 528
Haas, Robert, 1151, 1236
Habachi, Labib, 661
Haber, Carol, 1139
Habermas, Jurgen, 979, 1004
Habib, Irfan, 778, 779
Habiby, Emile, 119
Habsburg, Geza von, 561
Habsburg Empire, 685, 701-702
Hacker, Marilyn, 307
Hackett, John, 391
Hackett, Pat, 503
Hacking, Ian, 980

Hackle, Grey, 1243
Hackman, Gene, 636
Hackwell, W. John, 449, 657
Hadamard, Jacques, 1070
Hadas, Moses, 17, 21-22, 664, 755, 951
Hadas, Rachel, 307
Hadda, Janet, 110
Hadden, Jeffrey, 908
Hadden, Tom, 743
Hadingham, Evan, 659, 1090
Hadleigh, Boze, 1062
Hadley, Arthur T., 1033
Hadlock, Richard, 603
Hadrian, 670
Haestrup, Jorgen, 712
Hafetz Hayyim, 953
Haffner, Sebastian, 707, 708
Hafiz, 121
Hafkin, Nancy, 773
Hagan, Chet, 600
Hagedorn, Jessica, 307
Hagen, Charles, 524
Hagen, Uta, 625, 628
Hager, Steven, 610
Hager, Thomas, 1148
Hagerfors, Lennart, 82
Hagerman, Edward, 849
Haggard, H. Rider, 185, 378
Hagiwara, Sakutaro, 138
Hagstrom, Jerry, 831
Hague, Michael, 441
Hahn, Emily, 1078, 1199
Hahn, Harold, 815
Hahn, Lewis, 979
Hahn, Oscar, 346
Hahn, Steven, 868, 901
Haig, Axel, 540
Haigh, Christopher, 730
Haight, Gordon S., 232
Haight, Mary Ellen Jordan, 1208
Haiko, Peter, 550
Hailey, Arthur, 390, 391, 393
Haines, Angela, 1139
Haines, John, 302, 329, 1110
Hair, care of, 583-584
Hair, William I., 882
Haiti, 926
Haitian literature, 336
Haitor, Nikolai, 82
Hajas, Jozsef, 1255
Hake, Theodore, 577
Hakeda, Yoshita S., 948
Hakim, Tawfiq al-, 120
Hakluyt, Richard, 167
Halabi, Rafik, 768
Halas, Celia, 1176
Halberstadt, Hans, 814
Halberstam, David, 641, 797, 912, 1016, 1223, 1224, 1233
Halbfass, Wilhelm, 778
Halbreich, Kathy, 506
Haldane, J.B., 1097
Haldeman, Joe, 377
Hale, J.R., 472, 682, 683
Hale, Oron J., 705
Haley, Alex, 391, 885, 886, 1022
Haley, Gail E., 424
Haley, Jay, 1000
Halford, Aubrey S., 142
Halford, Giovanna M., 142
Hall, A.O., 1091
Hall, Adam, 368
Hall, Brian, 1196
Hall, Caroline, 581
Hall, Daniel G., 801
Hall, Dennis, 232

Kung Shang-jen, 130, 784
Kunhardt, Dorothy, 408
Kunhardt, Edith, 444
Kunhardt, Philip B., 857
Kunio, Komparu, 141
Kunitz, Stanley, 296
Kunstadt, Leonard, 605
Kunze, Michael, 687
Kuper, Peter, 401
Kupersmith, Judith, 621
Kureishi, Hanif, 639
Kurelek, William, 425
Kurokawa, Kisho, 553
Kurosawa, Akira, 635, 639
Kurten, Bjorn, 1108, 1109
Kurth, Peter, 745
Kurth, Willi, 476
Kurtis, Bill, 1205
Kurtz, Henry, 578
Kurtz, Katherine, 379
Kurtz, Michael L., 857
Kurtz, Paul, 935
Kurtzman, Harvey, 396, 401
Kurtzman, Joel, 1013
Kurzman, Dan, 1121
Kurzweil, Arthur, 954
Kurzweil, Edith, 154
Kushner, Harold, 955, 1176
Kuskin, Karla, 425
Kusler, Jon A., 1121
Kuspit, Donald, 505, 506
Kutler, Stanley I., 856
Kuttner, Henry, 374
Kuttner, Robert, 888
Kuzmin, Mikhail, 91
Kuznets, Simon, 1012
Kuznick, Peter, 1077
Kuzwayo, Ellen, 116
Kvarnes, Robert G., 999
Kwitny, Jonathan, 855, 893, 895
Kwock, C.H., 127
Kwong, Peter, 871
Kyasht, Lydia, 618
Kyd, Thomas, 168
Kyselka, Will, 1088

L

Labaree, Benjamin Woods, 834, 836
Labarge, Margaret W., 1055
LaBarre, George, 578
LaBastille, Anne, 1113
Labbe, Francoise, 553
Laber, Jeri, 751, 781
Labiche, Eugene, 39
Labor
  American biographies, 900
  in Europe, 702-703
  in Japan, 797
  twentieth-century histories and studies, 898-899
  Wobblies, 898
  women, 1054-1055
LaBranche, Carol, 574
Labrousse, Elisabeth, 820
Lacan, Jacques, 157, 990
LaCapra, Dominick, 653, 819
Lacey, Robert, 743, 769, 902
Lachaise, Gaston, 499
Lachelin, G.C., 1137
Lackner, Stephen, 496
Laclos, Choderlos de, 35
Laclotte, Michel, 481
LaCouture, Jean, 727
Lacrosse, 1232
Lacy, Allen, 1250

Lacy, Norris J., 32
Lad, Vasant, 1173
Ladd, James, 816
Laddis, Andrew, 471
Lader, Melvin, 500
Ladurie, Emmanuel Le Roy, 654, 677, 690, 820
La Farge, Phyllis, 1044
LaFavore, Mike, 1121
Lafaye, Jacques, 923
La Fayette, Madame de, 34
LaFeber, Walter, 850, 852, 856, 893, 894, 1028
Laferriere, Dany, 336
Lafferty, Sarah, 503
Laffin, John, 809
La Fontaine, Jean de, 34
LaFore, Robert, 1129
Laforgue, Jules, 39, 41
Lagemann, Ellen C., 1042
Lagerkvist, Par, 82
LaGuardia, Robert, 636, 1062
Laguerre, Enrique A., 345
La Guma, Alex, 116
Lahr, John, 233, 626, 1062
Lai, T.C., 513
Laing, R.D., 978, 994, 999
Laird, Charlton, 1169
Laird, Peter, 402
Lajolo, Davide, 68
Lake, Anthony, 894, 927
Laker, Rosalind, 386
Lakoff, Robin, 1058
Lal, P., 123
Lalla, Barbara, 339
Lally, Dick, 1223
Lamadrid, Enrique R., 350
Lamar, Howard R., 862
LaMarche, Robert, 1231
Lamarck, Jean-Baptiste, 1095
Lamaze method, 1137
Lamb, Charles, 179
Lamb, David, 764, 770
Lamb, Mary, 179
Lamb, Roger, 1002
Lamb, Wendy, 448
Lambert, David, 450, 1105, 1107, 1108
Lambert, Jean-Clarence, 504
Lambert, Malcolm, 959
Lambert, Royston, 670
Lambert, Steve, 1126
Lambert, Wilfred, 12
Lamberton, Robert, 18
Lamis, Alexander P., 869, 888
Lamm, Maurice, 955
Lamm, Michael, 1218
Lamming, George, 336
Lamorisse, Albert, 422
L'Amour, Louis, 382, 393
Lampe, Kenneth, 1245
Lampedusa, Giuseppe Tomasi di, 64, 390
Lamphere, Louise, 986, 1052
Lamps, 560
Lampton, Christopher, 451
Lampugnani, Vittorio, 548
Lamsa, George M., 956
Lancaster, Clay, 542, 543
Lancaster, Michael, 1245
Lance, James, 1146
Lancher, Carolyn, 496
Land, Edwin, 1016
Landau, Elaine, 452
Landau, Saul, 1032
Land conservation, 1121-1122
Landes, David S., 699
Landis, Joseph, 110

Landolfi, Tommaso, 64
Landon, H.C., 588
Landon, H. Robbins, 588
Landor, Walter Savage, 179
Landow, George, 232
Landry, Bart, 881
Landscape architecture, 537, 540-541, 543, 1246-1247, 1249-1250
Landynski, Jacob W., 1035
Lane, Barbara, 476, 549
Lane, David, 1011
Lane, Donald, 1144
Lane, Frederic C., 682
Lane, Harlan, 1065
Lane, John, 499
Lane, Leonard G., 1066
Lane, Maggie, 571, 574
Lane, Peter, 560
Lanes, Selma, 521
Lang, Andrew, 441
Lang, Bernhard, 654, 960
Lang, Donna, 568
Lang, Fritz, 635
Lang, George, 1184
Lang, Jenifer Harvey, 1178, 1182
Lang, Paul, 588, 596
Langdon, Philip, 554
Lange, Dorothea, 443, 528
Langenbach, Randolph, 899
Langer, Paul, 803
Langewiesche, Wolfgang, 1219
Langguth, A.J., 837
Langland, William, 165
Langley, Lester D., 872, 924
Langley, Noel, 639
Langley, Pat, 1078
Langone, John, 452, 1104, 1144
Langton, Jane, 362
Language
  and anthropology, 986-987
  and archaeology, 657
  linguistics, 1045-1047
  Native American, 827
  and psychology, 1001-1002
  travel phrasebooks, 1215-1216
  and women, 1058-1059
Lanham, Url, 1108
Lanier, Pamela, 1214
Lanier, Sterling E., 377
Lanner, Ronald, 1118
Lannoy, Richard, 126
Lansdale, Edward, 895
Lanternman, Ray, 1088
Lanzmann, Claude, 639, 724
Lao She, 132, 133
Lao Tzu, 947
Lapedes, D., 1092
Lapham, Lewis H., 647, 873
Lapidge, Michael, 677
Lapidus, Dorothy, 1107
Lapidus, Gail W., 748
Lapidus, Ira M., 761, 763, 764
LaPierre, Dominique, 393, 766, 780
Lapine, James, 317
Laporte, Dominique, 504
Lappe, Frances Moore, 893, 1152
Lapping, Brian, 742
Laqueur, Walter, 707, 708, 724, 727, 747, 756, 764, 1029
Laraque, Paul, 336
Larcom, Lucy, 1054
Lardner, James, 1017
Lardner, Rex, 1229
Lardner, Ring, 254, 333, 1223
Lardy, Nicholas, 789
Larimar, Tamela, 457

Larison, C.W., 246
Larkin, David, 520, 554
Larkin, Joan, 1064
Larkin, Maurice, 727
Larkin, Philip, 203, 212, 214, 223, 604
Larner, John, 682
La Rochefoucauld, Francois de, 34
LaRouche, Janice, 1162
Larouche, Lyndon, 871
Larrabee, Eric, 720
Larreta, Antonio, 345
Larschan, Edward, 1145
Larschan, Richard, 1145
Larsen, Ellouise, 564
Larsen, Jens, 588
Larsen, Lawrence H., 869
Larsen, Nella, 246, 254
Larsen, Susan, 499
Larson, Donald R., 59
Larson, Gary, 398
Larson, Judy, 520
Larson, Lane, 1239
Larson, Peggy, 1239
Lasch, Christopher, 905, 909
Lasdun, Denys, 554
Lash, Joseph P., 854, 861
Lasker, Edward, 1259, 1260
Lasker, Emmanuel, 1259
Lasker, Joe, 443
Lasker, Judith, 1137
Lasker-Schuler, Else, 73
Laski, Harold J., 889
Laski, Marghanita, 231, 232
Laskin, David, 1163
Lasky, Kathryn, 457
Laslett, John H.M., 900
Laslett, Peter, 729
Lasselle, Joan, 1130
Lasser, J.K., 1160
Lasson, Kenneth, 451
Lasswell, Marcia, 1135
Last, John, 1101
Laszlo, John, 1145
Lateer, Joseph G., 1127
Latham, Caroline, 649, 902
Latham, Sid, 519
Lathen, Emma, 362
Lathrop, Richard, 1161
Latimer, Hugh, 167
Latimer, Jonathan, 357
Latimer, Margery, 254
Latin America
  archaeology, 658-659
  art, 499
  cooking, 1185
  economy, 928
  history, 918-929
  international relations and finance, 929
  travel, 1202, 1206, 1213
  See also specific nations
Latin American literature, 339-350
  See also Caribbean literature; specific types, e.g., Argentinian literature
Latin literature, 19-22
  critical studies, 21-22
  early period, 19
  Golden Age, 20-21
  late writers, 21
  Loeb classics, 28-31
  Silver Age, 21
Latner, Helen, 954
Latourette, Kenneth S., 957
Latta, Sharon, 1151
Lattimore, David, 127
Lattimore, Richmond, 14, 956
Lau, Charley, 1222